Stanley Gibbons SIMPLIFIED CATALOGUE

Stamps of the World

2006 Edition

IN COLOUR

An illustrated and priced five-volume guide to the postage stamps of the whole world, excluding changes of paper, perforation, shade and watermark

VOLUME 2

COUNTRIES D–H

STANLEY GIBBONS LTD
London and Ringwood

By Appointment to
Her Majesty the Queen
Stanley Gibbons Limited
London
Philatelists

71st Edition

Published in Great Britain by
Stanley Gibbons Ltd
Publications Editorial, Sales Offices and Distribution Centre
Parkside, Christchurch Road,
Ringwood, Hampshire BH24 3SH
Telephone 01425 472363

ISBN: 085259-604-9

Published as Stanley Gibbons Simplified Stamp Catalogue from 1934 to 1970, renamed Stamps of the World in 1971, and produced in two (1982-88), three (1989-2001), four (2002-2005) or five (from 2006) volumes as Stanley Gibbons Simplified Catalogue of Stamps of the World.
This volume published October 2005

S.G. Item No. 2882 (06)

Printed in Great Britain by CPI Bath Press, Somerset

Stanley Gibbons
SIMPLIFIED CATALOGUE

Stamps of the World

This popular catalogue is a straightforward listing of the stamps that have been issued everywhere in the world since the very first–Great Britain's famous Penny Black in 1840.

This edition, in which both the text and the illustrations have been captured electronically, is arranged completely alphabetically in a five-volume format. Volume 1 (Countries A–C), Volume 2 (Countries D–H), Volume 3 (Countries I–M), Volume 4 (Countries N–R) and Volume 5 (Countries S-Z).

Readers are reminded that the Catalogue Supplements, published in each issue of **Gibbons Stamp Monthly**, can be used to update the listings in **Stamps of the World** as well as our 22-part standard catalogue. To make the supplement even more useful the Type numbers given to the illustrations are the same in the Stamps of the World as in the standard catalogues. The first Catalogue Supplement to this Volume appeared in the September 2005 issue of **Gibbons Stamp Monthly**.

Gibbons Stamp Monthly can be obtained through newsagents or on postal subscription from Stanley Gibbons Publications, Parkside, Christchurch Road, Ringwood, Hants BH24 3SH.

The catalogue has many important features:

- The vast majority of illustrations are now in full colour to aid stamp identification.
- All Commonwealth and all Europe and Asia miniature sheets are now included.
- As an indication of current values virtually every stamp is priced. Thousands of alterations have been made since the last edition.
- By being set out on a simplified basis that excludes changes of paper, perforation, shade, watermark, gum or printer's and date imprints it is particularly easy to use. (For its exact scope see "Information for users" pages following.)
- The thousands of colour illustrations and helpful descriptions of stamp designs make it of maximum appeal to collectors with thematic interests.
- Its catalogue numbers are the world-recognised Stanley Gibbons numbers throughout.
- Helpful introductory notes for the collector are included, backed by much historical, geographical and currency information.
- A very detailed index gives instant location of countries in this volume, and a cross-reference to those included in the other volumes.

Over 2,485 stamps and miniature sheets and 950 new illustrations have been added to the listings in this volume.

The listings in this edition are based on the standard catalogues: Part 1, Commonwealth & British Empire Stamps 1840–1952, Part 2 (Austria & Hungary) (6th edition), Part 3 (Balkans) (4th edition), Part 4 (Benelux) (5th edition), Part 5 (Czechoslovakia & Poland) (6th edition), Part 6 (France) (5th edition), Part 7 (Germany) (6th edition), Part 8 (Italy & Switzerland) (6th edition), Part 9 (Portugal & Spain) (5th edition), Part 10 (Russia) (5th edition), Part 11 (Scandinavia) (5th edition), Part 12 (Africa since Independence A-E) (2nd edition), Part 13 (Africa since Independence F-M) (1st edition), Part 14 (Africa since Independence N-Z) (1st edition), Part 15 (Central America) (2nd edition), Part 16 (Central Asia) (3rd edition), Part 17 (China) (6th edition), Part 18 (Japan & Korea) (4th edition), Part 19 (Middle East) (6th edition), Part 20 (South America) (3rd edition), Part 21 (South-East Asia) (4th edition) and Part 22 (United States) (5th edition).

This edition includes major repricing for some Europe countries in addition to the changes for Germany Part 7, Portugal and Spain Part 9 and Middle East Part 19.

Acknowledgements

A wide-ranging revision of prices for European countries has been undertaken for this edition with the intention that the catalogue should be more accurate to reflect the market for foreign issues.

Many dealers in both Great Britain and overseas have participated in this scheme by supplying copies of their retail price lists on which the research has been based.

We would like to acknowledge the assistance of the following for this edition:

ALMAZ CO
of Brooklyn, U.S.A.

AMATEUR COLLECTOR LTD, THE
of London, England

AVION THEMATICS
of Nottingham, England

J BAREFOOT LTD
of York, England

Sir CHARLES BLOMEFIELD
of Chipping Camden, England

T. BRAY
of Shipley, West Yorks, England

CENTRAL PHILATELIQUE
of Brussels, Belgium

EUROPEAN & FOREIGN STAMPS
of Pontypridd, Wales

FILATELIA LLACH SL
of Barcelona, Spain

FILATELIA RIVA RENO
of Bologna, Italy

FILATELIA TORI
of Barcelona, Spain

FORMOSA STAMP COMPANY, THE
of Koahsiung, Taiwan

HOLMGREN STAMPS
of Bollnas, Sweden

INDIGO
of Orewa, New Zealand

ALEC JACQUES
of Selby, England

M. JANKOWSKI
of Warsaw, Poland

D.J.M. KERR
of Earlston, England

LEO BARESCH LTD
of Hassocks, England

LORIEN STAMPS
of Chesterfield, England

MANDARIN TRADING CO
of Alhambra, U.S.A.

MICHAEL ROGERS INC
of Winter Park, U.S.A.

NORAYR AGOPIAN
of Lymassol, Cyprus

PHIL-INDEX
of Eastbourne, England

PHILTRADE A/S
of Copenhagen, Denmark

PITTERI SA
of Chiasso, Switzerland

KEVIN RIGLER
of Shifnal, England

ROLF GUMMESSON AB
of Stockholm, Sweden

R. D. TOLSON
of Undercliffe, England

R. SCHNEIDER
of Belleville, U.S.A.

ROBSTINE STAMPS
of Hampshire, England

ROWAN S BAKER
of London, England

REX WHITE
of Winchester, England

Where foreign countries have been repriced this year in Stamps of the World and where there is no up-to-date specialised foreign volume in a country these will be the new Stanley Gibbons prices.

It is hoped that this improved pricing scheme will be extended to other foreign countries and thematic issues as information is consolidated.

Information for users

Aim

The aim of this catalogue is to provide a straightforward illustrated and priced guide to the postage stamps of the whole world to help you to enjoy the greatest hobby of the present day.

Arrangement

The catalogue lists countries in alphabetical order and there is a complete index at the end of each volume. For ease of reference country names are also printed at the head of each page.

Within each country, postage stamps are listed first. They are followed by separate sections for such other categories as postage due stamps, parcel post stamps, express stamps, official stamps, etc.

All catalogue lists are set out according to dates of issue of the stamps, starting from the earliest and working through to the most recent.

Scope of the Catalogue

The *Simplified Catalogue of Stamps of the World* contains listings of postage stamps only. Apart from the ordinary definitive, commemorative and airmail stamps of each country – which appear first in each list – there are sections for the following where appropriate:

postage due stamps
parcel post stamps
official stamps
express and special delivery stamps
charity and compulsory tax stamps
newspaper and journal stamps
printed matter stamps
registration stamps
acknowledgement of receipt stamps
late fee and too late stamps
military post stamps
recorded message stamps
personal delivery stamps

We receive numerous enquiries from collectors about other items which do not fall within the categories set out above and which consequently do not appear in the catalogue lists. It may be helpful, therefore, to summarise the other kinds of stamp that exist but which we deliberately exclude from this postage stamp catalogue.

We do *not* list the following:

Fiscal or revenue stamps: stamps used solely in collecting taxes or fees for non-postal purposes. Examples would be stamps which pay a tax on a receipt, represent the stamp duty on a contract or frank a customs document. Common inscriptions found include: Documentary, Proprietary, Inter. Revenue, Contract Note.

Local stamps: postage stamps whose validity and use are limited in area, say to a single town or city, though in some cases they provided, with official sanction, services in parts of countries not covered by the respective government.

Local carriage labels and Private local issues: many labels exist ostensibly to cover the cost of ferrying mail from one of Great Britain's offshore islands to the nearest mainland post office. They are not recognised as valid for national or international mail. Examples: Calf of Man, Davaar, Herm, Lundy, Pabay, Stroma. Items from some other places have only the status of tourist souvenir labels.

Telegraph stamps: stamps intended solely for the prepayment of telegraphic communication.

Bogus or "phantom" stamps: labels from mythical places or non-existent administrations. Examples in the classical period were Sedang, Counani, Clipperton Island and in modern times Thomond and Monte Bello Islands. Numerous labels have also appeared since the War from dissident groups as propaganda for their claims and without authority from the home governments. Common examples are labels for "Free Albania", "Free Rumania" and "Free Croatia" and numerous issues for Nagaland, Indonesia and the South Moluccas ("Republik Maluku Selatan").

Railway letter fee stamps: special stamps issued by railway companies for the conveyance of letters by rail. Example: Talyllyn Railway. Similar services are now offered by some bus companies and the labels they issue likewise do not qualify for inclusion in the catalogue.

Perfins ("perforated initials"): numerous postage stamps may be found with initial letters or designs punctured through them by tiny holes. These are applied by private and public concerns as a precaution against theft and do not qualify for separate mention.

Information for users

Labels: innumerable items exist resembling stamps but – as they do not prepay postage – they are classified as labels. The commonest categories are:

- propaganda and publicity labels: designed to further a cause or campaign;
- exhibition labels: particularly souvenirs from philatelic events;
- testing labels: stamp-size labels used in testing stamp-vending machines;
- Post Office training school stamps: British stamps overprinted with two thick vertical bars or SCHOOL SPECIMEN are produced by the Post Office for training purposes;
- seals and stickers: numerous charities produce stamp-like labels, particularly at Christmas and Easter, as a means of raising funds and these have no postal validity.

Cut-outs: items of postal stationery, such as envelopes, cards and wrappers, often have stamps impressed or imprinted on them. They may usually be cut out and affixed to envelopes, etc., for postal use if desired, but such items are not listed in this catalogue.

Collectors wanting further information about exact definitions are referred to *Philatelic Terms Illustrated,* published by Stanley Gibbons and containing many illustrations in colour.

There is also a priced listing of the postal fiscals of Great Britain in our *Commonwealth & British Empire Stamps 1840–1952* Catalogue and in Volume 1 of the *Great Britain Specialised* Catalogue (5th and later editions).

Catalogue Numbers

Stanley Gibbons catalogue numbers are recognised universally and any individual stamp can be identified by quoting the catalogue number (the one at the left of the column) prefixed by the name of the country and the letters "S.G.". Do not confuse the catalogue number with the type numbers which refer to illustrations.

Prices

Prices in the left-hand column are for unused stamps and those in the right-hand column for used. Prices are given in pence and pounds:

100 pence (p) 1 pound (£1).

Prices are shown as follows:

10 means 10p (10 pence);
1.50 means £1.50 (1 pound and 50 pence);
For £100 and above, prices are in whole pounds.

Our prices are for stamps in fine condition, and in issues where condition varies we may ask more for the superb and less for the sub-standard.

The minimum catalogue price quoted is 10p. For individual stamps prices between 10p and 45p are provided as a guide for catalogue users. The lowest price charged for individual stamps purchased from Stanley Gibbons is £1.00.

The prices quoted are generally for the cheapest variety of stamps but it is worth noting that differences of watermark, perforation, or other details, outside the scope of this catalogue, may often increase the value of the stamp.

Prices quoted for mint issues are for single examples. Those in se-tenant pairs, strips, blocks or sheets may be worth more.

Where prices are not given in either column it is either because the stamps are not known to exist in that particular condition, or, more usually, because there is no reliable information as to value.

All prices are subject to change without prior notice and we give no guarantee to supply all stamps priced. Prices quoted for albums, publications, etc. advertised in this catalogue are also subject to change without prior notice.

Due to different production methods it is sometimes possible for new editions of Parts 2 to 22 to appear showing revised prices which are not included in that year's *Stamps of the World.*

Unused Stamps

In the case of stamps from *Great Britain* and the *Commonwealth,* prices for unused stamps of Queen Victoria to King George V are for lightly hinged examples; unused prices of King Edward VIII to Queen Elizabeth II issues are for unmounted mint. The prices of unused Foreign stamps are for lightly hinged examples for those issued before 1946, thereafter for examples unmounted mint.

Used Stamps

Prices for used stamps generally refer to fine postally used examples, though for certain issues they are for cancelled-to-order.

Information for users

Guarantee

All stamps supplied by us are guaranteed originals in the following terms:

If not as described, and returned by the purchaser, we undertake to refund the price paid to us in the original transaction. If any stamp is certified as genuine by the Expert Committee of the Royal Philatelic Society, London, or by B.P.A. Expertising Ltd., the purchaser shall not be entitled to make any claim against us for any error, omission or mistake in such certificate.

Consumers' statutory rights are not affected by the above guarantee.

Currency

At the beginning of each country brief details give the currencies in which the values of the stamps are expressed. The dates, where given, are those of the earliest stamp issues in the particular currency. Where the currency is obvious, e.g. where the colony has the same currency as the mother country, no details are given.

Illustrations

Illustrations of any surcharges and overprints which are shown and not described are actual size; stamp illustrations are reduced to $\frac{3}{4}$ linear, *unless otherwise stated.*

"Key-Types"

A number of standard designs occur so frequently in the stamps of the French, German, Portuguese and Spanish colonies that it would be a waste of space to repeat them. Instead these are all illustrated on page xiv together with the descriptive names and letters by which they are referred to in the lists.

Type Numbers

These are the bold figures found below each illustration. References to "Type **6**", for example, in the lists of a country should therefore be understood to refer to the illustration below which the number **"6"** appears. These type numbers are also given in the second column of figures alongside each list of stamps, thus indicating clearly the design of each stamp. In the case of Key-Types – see above – letters take the place of the type numbers.

Where an issue comprises stamps of similar design, represented in this catalogue by one illustration, the corresponding type numbers should be taken as indicating this general design.

Where there are blanks in the type number column it means that the type of the corresponding stamps is that shown by the last number above in the type column of the same issue.

A dash (–) in the type column means that no illustration of the stamp is shown.

Where type numbers refer to stamps of another country, e.g. where stamps of one country are overprinted for use in another, this is always made clear in the text.

Stamp Designs

Brief descriptions of the subjects of the stamp designs are given either below or beside the illustrations, at the foot of the list of the issue concerned, or in the actual lists. Where a particular subject, e.g. the portrait of a well-known monarch, recurs frequently the description is not repeated, nor are obvious designs described.

Generally, the unillustrated designs are in the same shape and size as the one illustrated, except where otherwise indicated.

Surcharges and Overprints

Surcharges and overprints are usually described in the headings to the issues concerned. Where the actual wording of a surcharge or overprint is given it is shown in bold type.

Some stamps are described as being "Surcharged in words", e.g. **TWO CENTS**, and others "Surcharged in figures and words", e.g. **20 CENTS**, although of course many surcharges are in foreign languages and combinations of words and figures are numerous. There are often bars, etc., obliterating old values or inscriptions but in general these are only mentioned where it is necessary to avoid confusion.

No attention is paid in this catalogue to colours of overprints and surcharges so that stamps with the same overprints in different colours are not listed separately.

Numbers in brackets after the descriptions of overprinted or surcharged stamps are the catalogue numbers of the unoverprinted stamps.

Note – the words "inscribed" or "inscription" always refer to wording incorporated in the design of a stamp and not surcharges or overprints.

Coloured Papers

Where stamps are printed on coloured paper the description is given as e.g. "4 c. black on blue" – a stamp printed in black on blue paper. No attention is paid in this catalogue to difference in the texture of paper, e.g. laid, wove.

Information for users

Watermarks

Stamps having different watermarks, but otherwise the same, are not listed separately. No reference is therefore made to watermarks in this volume.

Stamp Colours

Colour names are only required for the identification of stamps, therefore they have been made as simple as possible. Thus "scarlet", "vermilion", "carmine" are all usually called red. Qualifying colour names have been introduced only where necessary for the sake of clearness.

Where stamps are printed in two or more colours the central portion of the design is in the first colour given, unless otherwise stated.

Perforations

All stamps are perforated unless otherwise stated. No distinction is made between the various gauges of perforation but early stamp issues which exist both imperforate and perforated are usually listed separately.

Where a heading states "Imperf. or perf". or "Perf. or rouletted" this does not necessarily mean that all values of the issue are found in both conditions.

Dates of Issue

The date given at the head of each issue is that of the appearance of the earliest stamp in the series. As stamps of the same design or issue are usually grouped together a list of King George VI stamps, for example, headed "1938" may include stamps issued from 1938 to the end of the reign.

Se-tenant Pairs

Many modern issues are printed in sheets containing different designs or face values. Such pairs, blocks, strips or sheets are described as being "se-tenant" and they are outside the scope of this catalogue, although reference to them may occur in instances where they form a composite design.

Miniature Sheets

As an increasing number of stamps are now only found in miniature sheets, Stamps of the World will, in future, list these items. This edition lists all Commonwealth, European and Asian countries' miniature sheets, plus those of all other countries which have appeared in the catalogue supplement during the past three years. Earlier miniature sheets of non-Commonwealth countries will be listed in future editions.

"Appendix" Countries

We regret that, since 1968, it has been necessary to establish an Appendix (at the end of each country as appropriate) to which numerous stamps have had to be consigned. Several countries imagine that by issuing huge quantities of unnecessary stamps they will have a ready source of income from stamp collectors – and particularly from the less-experienced ones. Stanley Gibbons refuse to encourage this exploitation of the hobby and we do not stock the stamps concerned.

Two kinds of stamp are therefore given the briefest of mentions in the Appendix, purely for the sake of record. Administrations issuing stamps greatly in excess of true postal needs have the offending issues placed there. Likewise it contains stamps which have not fulfilled all the normal conditions for full catalogue listing.

These conditions are that the stamps must be issued by a legitimate postal authority, recognised by the government concerned, and are adhesives, valid for proper postal use in the class of service for which they are inscribed. Stamps, with the exception of such categories as postage dues and officials, must be available to the general public at face value with no artificial restrictions being imposed on their distribution.

The publishers of this catalogue have observed, with concern, the proliferation of 'artificial' stamp-issuing territories. On several occasions this has resulted in separately inscribed issues for various component parts of otherwise united states or territories.

Stanley Gibbons Publications have decided that where such circumstances occur, they will not, in the future, list these items in the SG catalogue without first satisfying themselves that the stamps represent a genuine political, historical or postal division within the country concerned. Any such issues which do not fulfil this stipulation will be recorded in the Catalogue Appendix only.

Stamps in the Appendix are kept under review in the light of any newly acquired information about them. If we are satisfied that a stamp qualifies for proper listing in the body of the catalogue it is moved there.

Information for users

"Undesirable Issues"

The rules governing many competitive exhibitions are set by the Federation Internationale de Philatelie and stipulate a downgrading of marks for stamps classed as "undesirable issues".

This catalogue can be taken as a guide to status. All stamps in the main listings and Addenda are acceptable. Stamps in the Appendix should not be entered for competition as these are the "undesirable issues".

Particular care is advised with Aden Protectorate States, Ajman, Bhutan, Chad, Fujeira, Khor Fakkan, Manama, Ras al Khaima, Sharjah, Umm al Qiwain and Yemen. Totally bogus stamps exist (as explained in Appendix notes) and these are to be avoided also for competition. As distinct from "undesirable stamps" certain categories are not covered in this catalogue purely by reason of its scope (see page viii). Consult the particular competition rules to see if such are admissable even though not listed by us.

Where to Look for More Detailed Listings

The present work deliberately omits details of paper, perforation, shade and watermark. But as you become more absorbed in stamp collecting and wish to get greater enjoyment from the hobby you may well want to study these matters.

All the information you require about any particular postage stamp will be found in the main Stanley Gibbons Catalogues.

Commonwealth countries before 1952 are covered by the Commonwealth & British Empire Stamps 1840–1952 published annually.

For foreign countries you can easily find which catalogue to consult by looking at the country headings in the present book.

To the right of each country name are code letters specifying which volume of our main catalogues contains that country's listing.

The code letters are as follows:

Pt. 2 Part 2

Pt. 3 Part 3 etc.

(See page xiii for complete list of Parts.)

So, for example, if you want to know more about Chinese stamps than is contained in the *Simplified Catalogue of Stamps of the World* the reference to

CHINA Pt. 17

guides you to the Gibbons Part 17 *(China)* Catalogue listing for the details you require.

New editions of Parts 2 to 22 appear at irregular intervals.

Correspondence

Whilst we welcome information and suggestions we must ask correspondents to include the cost of postage for the return of any stamps submitted plus registration where appropriate. Letters should be addressed to The Catalogue Editor at Ringwood.

Where information is solicited purely for the benefit of the enquirer we regret we cannot undertake to reply.

Identification of Stamps

We regret we do not give opinions as to the genuineness of stamps, nor do we identify stamps or number them by our Catalogue.

Users of this catalogue are referred to our companion booklet entitled *Stamp Collecting – How to Identify Stamps.* It explains how to look up stamps in this catalogue, contains a full checklist of stamp inscriptions and gives help in dealing with unfamiliar scripts.

Stanley Gibbons would like to complement your collection

At Stanley Gibbons we offer a range of services which are designed to complement your collection.

Our modern stamp shop, the largest in Europe, together with our rare stamp department has one of the most comprehensive stocks of Great Britain in the world, so whether you are a beginner or an experienced philatelist you are certain to find something to suit your special requirements.

Alternatively, through our Mail Order services you can control the growth of your collection from the comfort of your own home. Our Postal Sales Department regularly sends out mailings of Special Offers. We can also help with your wants list—so why not ask us for those elusive items?

Why not take advantage of the many services we have to offer? Visit our premises in the Strand or, for more information, write to the appropriate address on page x.

The Stanley Gibbons Group Addresses

Stanley Gibbons Limited,
Stanley Gibbons Auctions

339 Strand, London WC2R 0LX
Telephone 020 7836 8444, Fax 020 7836 7342,
E-mail: enquiries@stanleygibbons.co.uk
Website: www.stanleygibbons.com for all departments.

Auction Room and Specialist Stamp Departments. Open Monday–Friday 9.30 a.m. to 5 p.m.

Shop. Open Monday–Friday 9 a.m. to 5.30 p.m. and Saturday 9.30 a.m. to 5.30 p.m.

Fraser's Autographs, photographs, letters, documents

399 Strand, London WC2R 0LX
Autographs, photographs, letters and documents

Telephone 020 7836 8444, Fax 020 7836 7342,
E-mail: info@frasersautographs.co.uk
Website: www.frasersautographs.com

Monday–Friday 9 a.m. to 5.30 p.m. and Saturday 10 a.m. to 4 p.m.

Stanley Gibbons Publications

Parkside, Christchurch Road, Ringwood, Hants BH24 3SH.
Telephone 01425 472363 (24 hour answer phone service), Fax 01425 470247,
E-mail: info@stanleygibbons.co.uk
Website: www.stanleygibbons.com

Publications Mail Order. FREEPHONE 0800 611622
Monday–Friday 8.30 a.m. to 5 p.m.

Stanley Gibbons Publications Overseas Representation

Stanley Gibbons Publications are represented overseas by the following sole distributors (*), distributors (**) or licensees (***).

Australia
Lighthouse Philatelic (Aust.) Pty. Ltd.*
Locked Bag 5900 Botany DC, New South Wales, 2019 Australia.

Stanley Gibbons (Australia) Pty. Ltd.***
Level 6, 36 Clarence Street, Sydney, New South Wales 2000, Australia.

Belgium and Luxembourg**
Davo c/o Philac, Rue du Midi 48, Bruxelles, 1000 Belgium.

Canada*
Lighthouse Publications (Canada) Ltd., 255 Duke Street, Montreal Quebec, Canada H3C 2M2.

Denmark**
Samlerforum/Davo, Ostergade 3, DK 7470 Karup, Denmark.

Finland**
Davo c/o Kapylan Merkkiky Pohjolankatu 1 00610 Helsinki, Finland.

France*
Davo France (Casteilla), 10, Rue Leon Foucault, 78184 St. Quentin Yvelines Cesex, France.

Hong Kong**
Po-on Stamp Service, GPO Box 2498, Hong Kong.

Israel**
Capital Stamps, P.O. Box 3769, Jerusalem 91036, Israel.

Italy*
Ernesto Marini Srl, Via Struppa 300, I-16165, Genova GE, Italy.

Japan**
Japan Philatelic Co. Ltd., P.O. Box 2, Suginami-Minami, Tokyo, Japan.

Netherlands*
Davo Publications, P.O. Box 411, 7400 AK Deventer, Netherlands.

New Zealand***
Mowbray Collectables.
P.O. Box 80, Wellington, New Zealand.

Norway**
Davo Norge A/S, P.O. Box 738 Sentrum, N-0105, Oslo, Norway.

Singapore**
Stamp Inc Collectibles Pte Ltd., 10 Ubi Cresent, #01-43 Ubi Tech Park, Singapore 408564.

Sweden*
Chr Winther Soerensen AB, Box 43, S-310 Knaered, Sweden.

Abbreviations

Anniv.	denotes	Anniversary
Assn.	,,	Association
Bis.	,,	Bistre
Bl.	,,	Blue
Bldg.	,,	Building
Blk.	,,	Black
Br.	,,	British or Bridge
Brn.	,,	Brown
B.W.I.	,,	British West Indies
C.A.R.I.F.T.A.	,,	Caribbean Free Trade Area
Cent.	,,	Centenary
Chest.	,,	Chestnut
Choc.	,,	Chocolate
Clar.	,,	Claret
Coll.	,,	College
Commem.	,,	Commemoration
Conf.	,,	Conference
Diag.	,,	Diagonally
E.C.A.F.E.	,,	Economic Commission for Asia and Far East
Emer.	,,	Emerald
E.P.T. Conference	,,	European Postal and Telecommunications Conference
Exn.	,,	Exhibition
F.A.O.	,,	Food and Agriculture Organization
Fig.	,,	Figure
G.A.T.T.	,,	General Agreement on Tariffs and Trade
G.B.	,,	Great Britain
Gen.	,,	General
Govt.	,,	Government
Grn.	,,	Green
Horiz.	,,	Horizontal
H.Q.	,,	Headquarters
Imperf.	,,	Imperforate
Inaug.	,,	Inauguration
Ind.	,,	Indigo
Inscr.	,,	Inscribed or inscription
Int.	,,	International
I.A.T.A.	,,	International Air Transport Association
I.C.A.O.	,,	International Civil Aviation Organization
I.C.Y.	,,	International Co-operation Year
I.G.Y.	,,	International Geophysical Year
I.L.O.	,,	International Labour Office (or later, Organization)
I.M.C.O.	,,	Inter-Governmental Maritime Consultative Organization
I.T.U.	,,	International Telecommunication Union
Is.	,,	Islands
Lav.	,,	Lavender
Mar.	,,	Maroon
mm.	,,	Millimetres
Mult.	,,	Multicoloured
Mve.	denotes	Mauve
Nat.	,,	National
N.A.T.O.	,,	North Atlantic Treaty Organization
O.D.E.C.A.	,,	Organization of Central American States
Ol.	,,	Olive
Optd.	,,	Overprinted
Orge. or oran.	,,	Orange
P.A.T.A.	,,	Pacific Area Travel Association
Perf.	,,	Perforated
Post.	,,	Postage
Pres.	,,	President
P.U.	,,	Postal Union
Pur.	,,	Purple
R.	,,	River
R.S.A.	,,	Republic of South Africa
Roul.	,,	Rouletted
Sep.	,,	Sepia
S.E.A.T.O.	,,	South East Asia Treaty Organization
Surch.	,,	Surcharged
T.	,,	Type
T.U.C.	,,	Trades Union Congress
Turq.	,,	Turquoise
Ultram.	,,	Ultramarine
U.N.E.S.C.O.	,,	United Nations Educational, Scientific Cultural Organization
U.N.I.C.E.F.	,,	United Nations Children's Fund
U.N.O.	,,	United Nations Organization
U.N.R.W.A.	,,	United Nations Relief and Works Agency for Palestine Refugees in the Near East
U.N.T.E.A.	,,	United Nations Temporary Executive Authority
U.N.R.R.A.	,,	United Nations Relief and Rehabilitation Administration
U.P.U.	,,	Universal Postal Union
Verm.	,,	Vermilion
Vert.	,,	Vertical
Vio.	,,	Violet
W.F.T.U.	,,	World Federation of Trade Unions
W.H.O.	,,	World Health Organization
Yell.	,,	Yellow

Arabic Numerals

As in the case of European figures, the details of the Arabic numerals vary in different stamp designs, but they should be readily recognised with the aid of this illustration:

٠	١	٢	٣	٤
0	1	2	3	4
٥	٦	٧	٨	٩
5	6	7	8	9

Stanley Gibbons Stamp Catalogue
Complete List of Parts

1 Commonwealth & British Empire Stamps 1840–1952 (Annual)

Foreign Countries

2 Austria & Hungary (6th edition, 2002)
Austria · U.N. (Vienna) · Hungary

3 Balkans (4th edition, 1998)
Albania · Bosnia & Herzegovina · Bulgaria · Croatia · Greece & Islands · Macedonia · Rumania · Slovenia · Yugoslavia

4 Benelux (5th edition, 2003)
Belgium & Colonies · Luxembourg · Netherlands & Colonies

5 Czechoslovakia & Poland (6th edition, 2002)
Czechoslovakia · Czech Republic · Slovakia · Poland

6 France (5th edition, 2001)
France · Colonies · Post Offices · Andorra · Monaco

7 Germany (6th edition, 2002)
Germany · States · Colonies · Post Offices

8 Italy & Switzerland (6th edition, 2003)
Italy & Colonies · Liechtenstein · San Marino · Switzerland · U.N. (Geneva) · Vatican City

9 Portugal & Spain (5th edition, 2004)
Andorra · Portugal & Colonies · Spain & Colonies

10 Russia (5th edition, 1999)
Russia · Armenia · Azerbaijan · Belarus · Estonia · Georgia · Kazakhstan · Kyrgyzstan · Latvia · Lithuania · Moldova · Tajikistan · Turkmenistan · Ukraine · Uzbekistan · Mongolia

11 Scandinavia (5th edition, 2001)
Aland Islands · Denmark · Faroe Islands · Finland · Greenland · Iceland · Norway · Sweden

12 Africa since Independence A-E (2nd edition, 1983)
Algeria · Angola · Benin · Burundi · Cameroun · Cape Verdi · Central African Republic · Chad · Comoro Islands · Congo · Djibouti · Equatorial Guinea · Ethiopia

13 Africa since Independence F-M (1st edition, 1981)
Gabon · Guinea · Guinea-Bissau · Ivory Coast · Liberia · Libya · Malagasy Republic · Mali · Mauritania · Morocco · Mozambique

14 Africa since Independence N-Z (1st edition, 1981)
Niger Republic · Rwanda · St. Thomas & Prince · Senegal · Somalia · Sudan · Togo · Tunisia · Upper Volta · Zaire

15 Central America (2nd edition, 1984)
Costa Rica · Cuba · Dominican Republic · El Salvador · Guatemala · Haiti · Honduras · Mexico · Nicaragua · Panama

16 Central Asia (3rd edition, 1992)
Afghanistan · Iran · Turkey

17 China (6th edition,1998)
China · Taiwan · Tibet · Foreign P.O.s · Hong Kong · Macao

18 Japan & Korea (4th edition, 1997)
Japan · Korean Empire · South Korea · North Korea

19 Middle East (6th edition, 2005)
Bahrain · Egypt · Iraq · Israel · Jordan · Kuwait · Lebanon · Oman · Qatar · Saudi Arabia · Syria · U.A.E. · Yemen

20 South America (3rd edition, 1989)
Argentina · Bolivia · Brazil · Chile · Colombia · Ecuador · Paraguay · Peru · Surinam · Uruguay · Venezuela

21 South-East Asia (4th edition, 2004)
Bhutan · Burma · Indonesia · Kampuchea · Laos · Nepal · Philippines · Thailand · Vietnam

22 United States (5th edition, 2000)
U.S. & Possessions · Marshall Islands · Micronesia · Palau · U.N. (New York, Geneva, Vienna)

Thematic Catalogues

Stanley Gibbons Catalogues for use with **Stamps of the World.**
Collect Aircraft on Stamps (out of print)
Collect Birds on Stamps (5th edition, 2003)
Collect Chess on Stamps (2nd edition, 1999)
Collect Fish on Stamps (1st edition, 1999)
Collect Fungi on Stamps (2nd edition, 1997)
Collect Motor Vehicles on Stamps (1st edition, 2004)
Collect Railways on Stamps (3rd edition, 1999)
Collect Shells on Stamps (1st edition, 1995)
Collect Ships on Stamps (3rd edition, 2001)

Key-Types

(see note on page vii)

French Group

A. "Blanc."

B. "Mouchon."

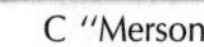

C "Merson."

D. "Tablet."

E.

F.

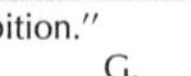

G.

H.

"International Colonial Exhibition."

I. "Faidherbe."

J. "Palms."

K. "Balay."

L. "Natives."

M. "Figure."

German Group

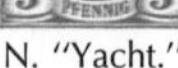

N. "Yacht."

O. "Yacht."

Spanish Group

X. "Alfonso XII."

Y. "Baby."

Z. "Curly Head"

Portuguese Group

P. "Crown."

Q. "Embossed."

R. "Figures."

S. "Carlos."

T. "Manoel."

U. "Ceres."

V. "Newspaper."

W. "Due."

STANLEY GIBBONS SIMPLIFIED CATALOGUE OF STAMPS OF THE WORLD—VOLUME 2 COUNTRIES D–H

DAHOMEY Pt. 6; Pt. 12

A French colony on the W. Coast of Africa, incorporated in French West Africa in 1944. In 1958 it became an autonomous republic within the French Community, and in 1960 was proclaimed fully independent. The area used the issues of French West Africa from 1944 until 1960.

100 centimes = 1 franc.

1899. "Tablet" key-type inscr "DAHOMEY ET DEPENDANCES".

1 D 1c. black and red on blue 85 90
2 2c. brown & blue on buff 60 70
3 4c. brown & blue on grey 1·40 1·50
4 5c. green and red 2·75 1·10
5 10c. red and blue 3·25 2·50
6 15c. grey and red 4·00 1·75
7 20c. red & blue on green 9·00 14·50
8 25c. black & red on pink 6·75 3·50
9 25c. blue and red 6·75 11·50
10 30c. brown & bl on drab 13·50 17·00
11 40c. red & blue on yellow 9·00 8·75
12 50c. brown & red on blue 10·00 21·00
13 50c. brown & blue on blue 32·00 17·00
14 75c. brown & red on orge 65·00 50·00
15 1f. green and red 32·00 32·00
16 2f. violet and red on pink 80·00 85·00
17 5f. mauve & blue on blue 85·00 90·00

1906. "Faidherbe", "Palms" and "Balay" key-types inscr "DAHOMEY".

18 I 1c. grey and red 1·40 85
19 2c. brown and red 1·40 65
20 4c. brown & red on blue 1·90 1·25
21 5c. green and red 4·75 50
22 10c. pink and blue 19·00 55
23 J 20c. black & red on blue 9·50 9·00
24 25c. blue and red 6·00 6·25
25 30c. brown & red on pink 12·50 13·00
26 35c. black & red on yellow 45·00 5·00
27 45c. brown & red on green 16·00 17·00
28 50c. violet and red 11·50 16·00
29 75c. green & red on orange 16·00 19·00
30 K 1f. black and red on blue 23·00 32·00
31 2f. blue and red on pink 90·00 85·00
32 5f. red & blue on yellow £100 £110

1912. Surch in figures.

33 05 on 2c. brown & blue on buff 85 1·25
34 05 on 4c. brown & blue on grey 95 1·40
35 05 on 15c. grey and red 1·10 2·00
36 05 on 20c. red & blue on green 80 2·25
37 05 on 25c. blue and red 1·25 3·00
38 05 on 30c. brown & bl on drab 95 1·75
39 10c. on 40c. red & bl on yellow 85 1·00
40 10c. on 50c. brn & bl on blue 1·10 2·75
40a 10c. on 50c. brn & red on blue £850 £900
41 10c. on 75c. brown and red on orange 4·50 8·00

6 Native Climbing Palm

11 Rene Caillie

1913.

42 6 1c. black and violet 10 15
43 2c. pink and brown 10 20
44 4c. brown and black 10 45
45 5c. green and light green 1·40 70
60 5c. violet and purple 15 45
46 10c. pink and red 1·75 55
61 10c. green and lt green 75 1·25
75 10c. green and red 10 10
47 15c. purple and brown 20 25
48 20c. brown and grey 60 1·10
76 20c. green 15 1·40
77 20c. black and mauve 15 60
49 25c. blue & ultramarine 2·50 1·60
62 25c. orange and purple 20 20
50 30c. violet and brown 3·00 4·00
63 30c. carmine and red 95 4·00
78 30c. violet and yellow 60 50
79 30c. green and olive 50 75
51 35c. black and brown 1·10 1·75
80 35c. green and turquoise 85 3·25
52 40c. orange and black 65 70
53 45c. blue and grey 70 2·50
54 50c. brown & chocolate 4·50 6·50
64 50c. blue & ultramarine 20 2·25
81 50c. blue and red 20 20
82 55c. brown and green 50 2·50
83 60c. violet on pink 1·75 2·75
84 65c. green and brown 25 95
55 75c. violet and blue 35 55
85 80c. blue and brown 50 3·00
86 85c. pink and blue 50 2·75
87 90c. red and carmine 75 1·90
87a 90c. red and brown 1·40 3·25
56 1f. black and green 65 1·00
88 1f. light blue and blue 1·25 1·00
89 1f. red and brown 50 45
90 1f. red and light red 2·00 2·75
91 1f.10 brown and violet 3·25 4·50
92 1f.25 brown and blue 17·00 18·00
93 1f.50 light blue and blue 2·50 2·00
94 1f.75 orange and brown 3·75 3·50
94a 1f.75 ultramarine & blue 60 2·00
57 2f. brown and yellow 1·00 65
95 3f. mauve on pink 3·00 3·00
58 5f. blue and violet 2·50 3·50

1915. Surch **5c** and red cross.

59 6 10c.+5c. pink and red 45 2·00

1922. Surch in figures and bars.

65 6 25c. on 2f. brown & yellow 1·40 3·00
66 60 on 75c. violet on pink 25 2·75
67 65 on 15c. purple & brown 1·60 3·75
68 85 on 15c. purple & brown 1·75 3·75
69 90c. on 75c. red and carmine 2·00 3·50
70 1f.25 on 1f. lt blue & blue 45 3·00
71 1f.50 on 1f. lt blue & blue 1·40 1·90
72 3f. on 5f. red and green 6·50 10·00
73 10f. on 5f. brown & blue 4·25 7·00
74 20f. on 5f. green and red 2·50 8·00

1931. "Colonial Exhibition" key-types inscr "DAHOMEY".

96 E 40c. green 5·00 7·50
97 F 50c. mauve 5·25 7·25
98 G 90c. red 5·50 6·75
99 H 1f.50 blue 5·50 7·00

1937. Paris Int Exn. As T **58a** of Guadeloupe.

100 20c. violet 1·25 3·25
101 30c. green 1·00 3·00
102 40c. red 65 3·25
103 50c. brown 1·00 2·00
104 90c. red 70 2·25
105 1f.50 blue 60 1·60
MS105a 120 × 100 mm. 3f. blue and agate (as T **16**). Imperf 5·75 13·00

1938. Int Anti-cancer Fund. As T **58b** of Guadeloupe.

106 1f.75+50c. blue 5·00 15·00

1939. Death Centenary of R. Caillie (explorer).

107 11 90c. orange 40 2·00
108 2f. violet 95 3·25
109 2f.25 blue 1·25 3·50

1939. New York World's Fair. As T **58c** of Guadeloupe.

110 1f.25 red 1·90 3·00
111 2f.25 blue 2·00 2·25

1939. 150th Anniv of French Revolution. As T **58d** of Guadeloupe.

112 45c.+25c. green 4·25 11·00
113 70c.+30c. brown 5·25 11·00
114 90c.+35c. orange 4·50 11·00
115 1f.25+1f. red 4·50 11·00
116 2f.25+2f. blue 4·25 11·00

12 African Landscape

13 Native Poling Canoe

1940. Air.

117 12 1f.90 blue 1·25 2·50
118 2f.90 red 1·25 3·00
119 4f.50 green 1·40 2·75
120 4f.90 olive 1·10 2·75
121 6f.90 orange 90 3·25

1941.

122 13 2c. red 15 1·25
123 3c. blue 15 2·50
124 5c. violet 95 2·75
125 10c. green 25 2·50
126 15c. black 15 2·25
127 – 20c. brown 1·10 2·75
128 – 30c. violet 45 2·75
129 – 40c. red 55 2·75
130 – 50c. green 95 2·75
131 – 60c. black 65 2·75
132 – 70c. mauve 1·75 3·25
133 – 80c. black 1·10 2·75
134 – 1f. violet 30 35
135 – 1f.30 violet 1·00 3·25
136 – 1f.40 green 1·75 3·25
137 – 1f.50 red 1·25 3·00
138 – 2f. orange 95 3·50
139 – 2f.50 blue 1·90 3·25
140 – 3f. red 55 2·75
141 – 5f. green 60 2·25
142 – 10f. brown 70 4·00
143 – 20f. black 1·00 4·50

DESIGNS—HORIZ: 20c. to 70c. Village on piles. VERT: 80c. to 2f. Sailing pirogue on Lake Nokoue; 2f.50 to 20f. Dahomey warrior.

1941. National Defence Fund. Surch **SECOURS NATIONAL** and value.

143a 6 +1f. on 50c. blue & red 3·75 5·50
143b +2f. on 80c. blue & brn 4·50 6·25
143c +2f. on 1f.50 lt blue & bl 6·00 9·25
143d +3f. on 2f. brown & yell 6·00 8·25

14b Village on Piles and Marshal Petain

1942. Marshal Petain Issue.

143e 14b 1f. green 40 2·75
143f 2f.50 blue 25 3·00

14c Maternity Hospital, Dakar

1942. Air. Colonial Child Welfare Fund.

143g 14c 1f.50+3f.50 green 20 2·50
143h – 2f.+6f. brown 20 2·50
143i – 3f.+9f. red 90 2·50

DESIGNS: 2f. Dispensary, Mopti. (48½ × 27 mm): 3f. "Child welfare".

14d "Vocation"

1942. Air. "Imperial Fortnight".

143j 14d 1f.20+1f.80 blue & red 1·10 2·50

14e Camel Caravan

1942. Air.

143k 14e 50f. blue and green 3·75 4·75

15 Ganvie Village

1960.

144 15 25f. brn, red & bl (postage) 75 25
145 – 100f. brown, ochre & bl (air) 3·25 2·25
146 – 500f. red, bistre & green 12·00 4·25

DESIGNS: 100f. Somba fort; 500f. Royal Court, Abomey.

15a CCTA Emblem

1960. 10th Anniv of African Technical Co-operation Commission.

147 15a 5f. blue and purple 1·60 2·00

16 Conseil de l'Entente Emblem

17 Prime Minister Maga

1960. 1st Anniv of Conseil de l'Entente.

148 16 25f. multicoloured 1·75 1·90

1960. Independence Proclamation.

149 17 85f. purple and sepia 90 55

18 Weaver

1961. Artisans.

150 18 1f. purple and orange 10 10
151 – 2f. chocolate and brown 10 10
152 – 3f. orange and green 10 10
153 – 4f. lake and bistre 15 15
154 18 6f. red and lilac 15 15
155 – 10f. myrtle and blue 25 20
156 – 15f. violet and purple 35 25
157 – 20f. turquoise and blue 45 30

DESIGNS—VERT: 2f., 10f. Wood-carver. HORIZ: 3f., 15f. Fisherman casting net; 4f., 20f. Potter.

1961. 1st Anniv of Independence. No. 149 surch **100 F President de la Republique**.

158 17 100f. on 85f. pur & sepia 1·50 1·50

20 Doves and U.N. Emblem

22 Wrecked Car and Fort

20a European, African and Airliners

1961. 1st Anniv of Admission into U.N.O.
159 **20** 5f. multicoloured (postage) 25 20
160 60f. multicoloured 75 60
161 200f. multicoloured (air) 2·50 1·90

1961. Abidjan Games. Optd **JEUX SPORTIFS D'ABIDJAN 24 AU 31 DECEMBRE 1961**.
162 **15** 25f. brown, red and blue 45 30

1962. Air. Foundation of "Air Afrique" Airline.
163 **20a** 25f. blue, brown & black 45 35

1962. Malaria Eradication. As T **55a** of French Somali Coast.
164 25f.+5f. brown 45 45

1962. 1st Anniv of Portuguese Evacuation from Fort Ouidah.
165 **22** 30f. multicoloured 45 25
166 60f. multicoloured 70 40

1962. 1st Anniv of Union of African and Malagasy States. As T **38** of Gabon.
167 **72** 30f. multicoloured 50 35

23 Map, Nurses and Patients

1962. Red Cross.
168 **23** 5f. red, blue and purple . . 15 15
169 20f. red, blue and green . . 30 25
170 25f. red, blue and sepia . . 40 30
171 30f. red, blue and brown 45 40

24 Peuhl Herd-boy **25** Boxing

1963. Dahomey Tribes.
172 A 2f. violet and blue 10 10
173 B 3f. black and blue 10 10
174 **24** 5f. green, brown & black 15 10
175 C 15f. brown, chest & turq 25 15
176 D 20f. black, red & green . . 40 20
177 E 25f. turquiose, brown & bl 40 15
178 D 30f. brown, mauve & red 45 30
179 E 40f. blue, brown, & green 55 25
180 C 50f. brown, black & green 65 30
181 **24** 60f. orange, red & purple 70 45
182 B 65f. brown and red 90 50
183 A 85f. brown and blue . . . 1·50 75
DESIGNS—VERT: A, Ganvie girl in pirogue; B, Bariba chief of Nikki; C, Ouidah witch-doctor and python; D, Nessoukoue witch-doctors of Abomey. HORIZ: E, Dahomey girl.

1963. Freedom from Hunger. As T **41** of Gabon.
184 25f.+5f. red, brown & green 50 50

1963. Dakar Games.
185 **25** 50c. black and green . . . 10 10
186 – 1f. black, bistre & brown 10 10
187 – 2f. brown, blue & bronze 10 10
188 – 5f. black, red & brown . . 15 10
189 **25** 15f. purple and violet . . . 25 20
190 – 20f. black, green & red . . 40 30
DESIGNS—HORIZ: 1f., 20f. Football. VERT: 2f., 5f. Running.

27 U.A.M. Palace

1963. Air. Meeting of Heads of State of African and Malagasy Union.
191 **27** 250f. multicoloured . . . . 3·00 1·75

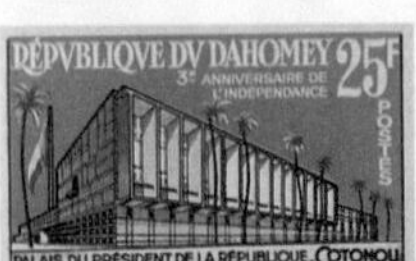

28 Presidential Palace, Cotonou

1963. 3rd Anniv of Independence.
192 **28** 25f. multicoloured 35 25

1963. Air. African and Malagasy Posts and Telecommunications Union. As T **44** of Gabon.
193 25f. red, buff, brown & blue 40 25

29 Boeing 707 Airliner

1963. Air.
194 **29** 100f. bistre, green & violet 1·75 60
195 – 200f. violet, brown & grn 3·00 1·60
196 – 300f. purple, grn and blue 4·25 2·25
197 – 500f. purple, brown & blue 7·75 3·25
DESIGNS: 200f. Aerial views of Boeing 707; 300f. Cotonou Airport; 500f. Boeing 707 in flight.

30 Toussaint L'Ouverture **31** Flame on U.N. Emblem

1963. 150th Death Anniv of Toussaint L'Ouverture (Haitian statesman).
198 **30** 25f. multicoloured 35 20
199 30f. multicoloured 40 25
200 100f. multicoloured . . . . 1·10 65

1963. 15th Anniv of Declaration of Human Rights. Multicoloured. Background colours given.
201 **31** 4f. blue 10 10
202 6f. brown 15 15
203 25f. green 35 25

32 Sacred Boat of Isis, Philae

1964. Air. Nubian Monuments Preservation.
204 **32** 25f. brown and violet . . . 80 50

33 Somba Dance (Taneka Coco)

1964. Native Dances.
205 **33** 2f. black, red and green . . 10 10
206 – 3f. red, green and blue . . 10 10
207 – 10f. black, red & violet . . 20 15
208 – 15f. sepia, lake & green . . 25 15
209 – 25f. blue, brown and orge 40 25
210 – 30f. red, orange & brown 45 30
DANCES—HORIZ: 3f. Nago (Pobe-Ketou). 15f. Nago (Ouidah). 30f. Nessou houessi (Abomey). VERT: 10f. Baton (Paysbariba). 25f. Sakpatassi (Abomey).

34 Running

1964. Olympic Games, Tokyo.
211 **34** 60f. green and brown . . . 65 50
212 – 85f. purple and blue . . . 1·25 75
DESIGN: 85f. Cycling.

1964. French, African and Malagasy Co-operation. As T **58** of Gabon.
213 25f. brown, violet & orange 40 25

35 Mother and Child **36** Satellite and Sun

1964. 18th Anniv of UNICEF.
214 **35** 20f. black, green & red . . 35 25
215 – 25f. black, blue & red . . . 40 25
DESIGN: 25f. Mother and child (different).

1964. International Quiet Sun Year.
216 **36** 25f. green and yellow . . . 45 20
217 – 100f. yellow and purple . . 1·25 65
DESIGN: 100f. Another satellite and Sun.

37 "Weather"

1965. Air. World Meteorological Day.
218 **37** 50f. multicoloured 65 45

38 Rug Pattern

1965. Abomey Rug-weaving. Multicoloured.
219 20f. Bull, tree, etc. (vert) . . 30 25
220 25f. Witch-doctor, etc. (vert) 45 30
221 50f. Type **38** 70 35
222 85f. Ship, tree, etc . . . . . 1·25 70

39 Baudot's Telegraph and Ader's Telephone **40** Sir Winston Churchill

1965. Centenary of I.T.U.
223 **39** 100f. black, purple & orge 1·40 1·00

1965. Air. Churchill Commemoration.
224 **40** 100f. multicoloured . . . . 1·40 1·10

41 Heads of Three Races within I.C.Y. Emblem

1965. Air. International Co-operation Year.
225 **41** 25f. lake, green & violet . . 35 20
226 85f. lake, green & blue . . 80 55

42 Lincoln

1965. Air. Death Centenary of Abraham Lincoln.
227 **42** 100f. multicoloured . . . . 1·25 95

43 Cotonou Port

1965. Inaug of Cotonou Port. Multicoloured.
228 25f. Type **43** 65 25
229 100f. Cotonou Port . . . . . 1·60 85
The two stamps joined together form a complete design and were issued se-tenant in the sheets.

44 Spanish Mackerel **45** Independence Monument

1965. Fishes.
230 **44** 10f. black, turquoise & bl 40 25
231 – 25f. orange, grey & blue 55 40
232 – 30f. blue and turquoise . . 1·00 50
233 – 50f. grey, orange & blue 1·40 80
FISHES: 25f. Sama seabream. 30f. Sailfish. 50f. Tripletail.

1965. 2nd Anniv of 28th October Revolution.
234 **45** 25f. red, grey and black . . 35 20
235 30f. red, blue and black . . 40 25

1965. No. 177 surch **1f.**
236 1f. on 25f. turq, brn & bl . . 15 10

47 Arms and Pres. Kennedy

1965. Air. 2nd Death Anniv of Pres. Kennedy.
237 **47** 100f. brown and green . . 1·50 1·00

48 Dr. Schweitzer and Hospital Scene

1966. Air. Schweitzer Commemoration.
238 **48** 100f. multicoloured . . . . 1·50 90

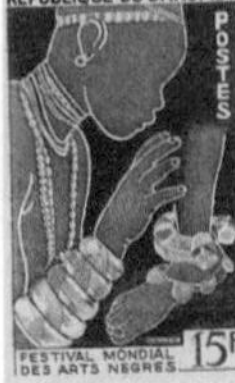

49 Porto-Novo Cathedral **50** Beads, Bangles and Anklets

1966. Dahomey Cathedrals.
239 **49** 30f. purple, blue & green 30 20
240 – 50f. brown, blue & purple 50 30
241 – 70f. purple, blue & green 80 50
DESIGNS—VERT: 50f. Ouidah Church (old Pro-Cathedral). HORIZ: 70f. Cotonou Cathedral.

1966. World Festival of Negro Arts, Dakar.
242 **50** 15f. purple and black . . . 25 15
243 – 30f. red, purple & blue . . 35 25
244 – 50f. blue and brown . . . 60 40
245 – 70f. lake and black . . . . 1·10 65
DESIGNS: 30f. Building construction; 50f. Craftsman; 70f. Religious carvings.

1966. 5th Anniv of France–Dahomey Treaty. Nos. 228/9 surch **ACCORD DE COOPERATION FRANCE - DAHOMEY 5e Anniversaire - 24 Avril 1966.**
246 **43** 15f. on 25f. mult 35 25
247 – 15f. on 100f. mult 35 25

52 W.H.O. Building and Emblem

1966. Inaug of W.H.O. Headquarters, Geneva.
248 **52** 30f. multicoloured (post) 40 30

249 – 100f. multicoloured (air) 1·40 1·00
DESIGN (48×27 mm): 100f. W.H.O. building (different view) and emblem.

53 African Pygmy Goose
54 Industrial Emblems

1966. Air. Birds. Multicoloured.
250 50f. Type **53** . . . . 2·50 95
251 100f. Fiery-breasted bush shrike . . . . 3·50 1·40
252 500f. Iris glossy starling . . . 17·00 9·25
See also Nos. 271/2.

1966. Air. "Europafrique".
253 **54** 100f. multicoloured . . . . 1·50 85

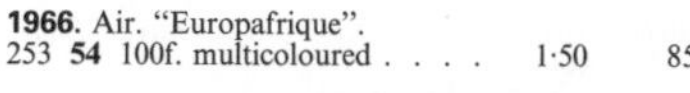

55 Pope Paul and St. Peter's

1966. Air. Pope Paul's Visit to U.N.
254 **55** 50f. red, brown & green . . 55 35
255 – 70f. red, green and blue . . 85 45
256 – 100f. purple and blue . . . 1·25 85
DESIGNS—HORIZ: 70f. Pope Paul and New York. VERT: (36×48 mm); 100f. Pope Paul and U.N. General Assembly.

1966. Air. Inauguration of DC-8F Air Services. As T **84** of Gabon.
258 30f. grey, black and purple 50 30

56 Scout signalling with flags

1966. Scouting.
259 **56** 5f. red, ochre and brown 10 10
260 – 10f. mauve, green & black 15 10
261 – 30f. orange, red & violet 35 25
262 – 50f. brown, green & blue 70 40
DESIGNS—VERT: 10f. Tent-pole and banners; 30f. Scouts, camp-fire and map. HORIZ: 50f. Constructing bridge.

57 Scientific Emblem

1966. Air. 20th Anniv of UNESCO.
264 **57** 30f. plum, blue & purple 35 25
265 – 45f. lake and green 50 40
266 – 100f. blue, lake & black . . 1·25 80
DESIGNS—VERT: 45f. Cultural Emblem; HORIZ: 100f. Educational emblem.

58 "The Nativity" (15th-cent. Beaune Tapestry)

1966. Air. Christmas. Multicoloured.
268 50f. Type **58** . . . . 10·25 3·00
269 100f. "The Adoration of the Shepherds" (after Jose Ribera) . . . . 10·25 4·50
270 200f. "Madonna and Child" (after A. Baldovinetti) . . 19·00 6·75
See also Nos. 311/14, 348/51, 384/7 and 423/6.

59 African Broad-billed Roller
60 "Clappertonia ficifolia"

1967. Air. Birds. Multicoloured.
271 200f. Type **59** . . . . 9·50 3·75
272 250f. African Emerald cuckoo 12·50 5·25

1967. Flowers. Multicoloured.
273 1f. Type **60** 10 10
274 3f. "Hewittia sublobata" . . 15 10
275 5f. "Clitoria ternatea" . . . 20 15
276 10f. "Nymphaea micrantha" 35 15
277 5f. "Commelina forskalaei" 35 25
278 30f. "Eremomastax speciosa" 75 35

1967. Nos. 182/3 surch.
279 30f. on 65f. brown & red . . 40 30
280 30f. on 85f. brown & blue . . 40 30

62 Bird bearing Lions Emblem
63 "Ingres" (self-portrait)

1967. 50th Anniv of Lions International.
281 **62** 100f. blue, green & violet 1·50 80

1967. Air. Death Centenary of Ingres (painter). Multicoloured.
282 100f. Type **63** . . . . 2·10 1·25
283 100f. "Oedipus and the Sphinx" (after Ingres) . . . 2·10 1·25
See also Nos. 388/90, 429/30, 431/2 and 486/7.

64 "Suzanne" (barque)

1967. Air. French Sailing ships. Multicoloured.
284 30f. Type **64** 90 35
285 45f. "Esmeralda" (schooner) (vert) . . . . 1·25 55
286 80f. "Marie Alice" (schooner) (vert) . . . . 2·10 75
287 100f. "Antonin" (barque) . . 2·50 1·10

1967. Air. 50th Birth Anniv of Pres. Kennedy. Nos. 227 and 237 surch **29 MAI 1967 50e Anniversaire de la naissance de John F. Kennedy**.
288 **42** 125f. on 100f. mult . . . . 1·75 90
289 **47** 125f. on 100f. brn & grn 1·75 90

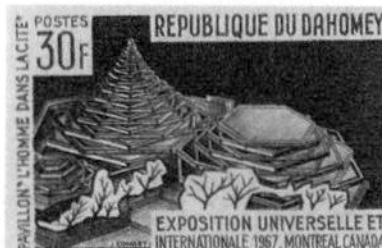

66 "Man in the City" Pavilion

1967. World Fair, Montreal.
290 **66** 30f. brn & grn (postage) 40 20
291 – 70f. red and green 90 50

292 – 100f. blue & brown (air) 1·10 65
DESIGNS—HORIZ: 70f. "New Africa" pavilions. VERT: (27×48 mm): 100f. "Man Examines the Universe".

67 Dr. Konrad Adenauer (from painting by O. Kokoschka)
68 "Economic Association"

1967. Air. Dr. Adenauer Commemoration.
294 **67** 70f. multicoloured . . . . 1·10 90

1967. Europafrique.
296 **68** 30f. multicoloured 35 25
297 – 45f. multicoloured 50 25

69 Scouts Climbing

1967. World Scout Jamboree, Idaho.
298 **69** 30f. ind, brn & bl (postage) 35 15
299 – 70f. purple, green & blue 90 55

300 – 100f. pur, grn & bl (air) . . 1·10 65
DESIGNS—HORIZ: 70f. Scouts with canoe. VERT: (27×48 mm): 100f. Jamboree emblem, rope and map.

1967. Air. Riccione Stamp Exhibition. No. 270 surch **RICCIONE 12-29 Aout 1967** and value.
302 150f. on 200f. mult . . . . . 2·10 1·50

71 Rhone at Grenoble

1967. Winter Olympic Games, Grenoble.
303 **71** 30f. blue, brown & green 40 25
304 – 45f. blue, green & brown 60 40
305 – 100f. purple, green & blue 1·40 90
DESIGNS—VERT: 45f. View of Grenoble. HORIZ: 100f. Rhone Bridge, Grenoble, and Pierre de Coubertin.

1967. Air. 5th Anniv of U.A.M.P.T. As T **104** of Gabon.
307 100f. green, red & purple . . 1·10 90

72 Currency Tokens
73 Pres. de Gaulle

1967. 5th Anniv of West African Monetary Union.
308 **72** 30f. black, red & green . . 40 30

1967. Air. "Homage to General de Gaulle". President Soglo of Dahomey's visit to Paris.
309 **73** 100f. multicoloured . . . . 2·10 1·40

74 "The Adoration (Master of St. Sebastian)

1967. Air. Christmas. Religious paintings. Mult.
311 30f. "Virgin and Child" (M. Grunewald) (vert) . . 40 35
312 50f. Type **74** 80 45
313 100f. "The Adoration of the Magi" (Ulrich Apt the Elder) (vert) . . . . 1·40 90
314 200f. "The Annunciation" (M. Grunewald) (vert) . . 3·00 1·40

75 Venus de Milo and "Mariner 5"
76 African Buffalo

1968. Air. "Exploration of the Planet Venus". Multicoloured.
315 70f. Type **75** . . . . 1·00 55
316 70f. Venus de Milo and "Venus 4" . . . . 1·00 55

1968. Fauna (1st series). Multicoloured.
318 15f. Type **76** 25 15
319 30f. Lion 45 25
320 45f. Kob 80 40
321 70f. Crocodile . . . . 1·25 45
322 100f. Hippopotamus . . . . 2·25 1·10
See also Nos. 353/7.

77 W.H.O. Emblem

1968. 20th Anniv of W.H.O.
323 **77** 30f. brown, blue & ultram 40 30
324 70f. multicoloured . . . . 3·75 1·25

78 Gutenberg Memorial, Strasbourg
79 Dr. Martin Luther King

1968. Air. 500th Death Anniv of Johann Gutenberg.
325 **78** 45f. green and orange . . . 60 35
326 – 100f. deep blue & blue . . 1·40 85
DESIGNS: 100f. Gutenberg statue, Mainz, and printing-press.

1968. Air. Martin Luther King Commemoration.
328 – 30f. black, brown & yellow 50 30
329 – 55f. multicoloured 80 45
330 **79** 100f. multicoloured . . . . 1·25 80
DESIGNS: 55f. Dr. King receiving Nobel Peace Prize. LARGER (25×46 mm): 30f. Inscription "We must meet hate with creative love" (also in French and German).

80 Schuman

1968. Air. 5th Anniv of Europafrique.
332 **80** 30f. multicoloured 40 25
333 – 45f. purple, olive & orge 55 35
334 – 70f. multicoloured 90 40
DESIGNS: 45f. De Gasperi; 70f. Dr. Adenauer.

81 "Battle of Montebello" (Philippoteaux)

1968. Air. Red Cross. Paintings. Multicoloured.
335 30f. Type **81** 50 35
336 45f. "2nd Zouaves at Magenta" (Riballier) . . . 65 45
337 70f. "Battle of Magenta" (Charpentier) . . . . . . 1·25 80
338 100f. "Battle of Solferino" (Charpentier) . . . . . . 1·75 1·00

82 Mail Van

1968. Air. Rural Mail Service. Multicoloured.
339 30f. Type **82** 35 25
340 45f. Rural Post Office and mail van 45 30
341 55f. Collecting mail at river-side 60 35
342 70f. Loading mail on train 3·75 1·25

83 Aztec Stadium

1968. Air. Olympic Games, Mexico.
343 **83** 30f. green and purple . . . 40 25
344 – 45f. lake and blue 65 35
345 – 70f. brown and green . . . 1·00 55
346 – 150f. brown and red . . . 1·90 1·10
DESIGNS—VERT: 45f. "Pelota-player" (Aztec figure); 70f. "Uxpanapan wrestler" (Aztec figure). HORIZ: 150f. Olympic Stadium.

1968. Air. Christmas. Paintings by Foujita. As T **74**. Multicoloured.
348 30f. "The Nativity" (horiz) 55 40
349 70f. "The Visitation" . . . . 1·10 55
350 100f. "Virgin and Child" . . 1·40 95
351 200f. "Baptism of Christ" . . 2·75 1·90

1968. Air. "Philexafrique" Stamp Exhibition, Abidjan (Ivory Coast, 1969). As T **125** of Gabon. Multicoloured.
352 100f. "Diderot" (L. M. Vanloo) . . . . 1·75 1·75

84 Warthog

1969. Fauna (2nd series). Multicoloured.
353 5f. Type **84** 15 10
354 30f. Leopard 50 25
355 60f. Spotted hyena . . . . . 1·00 45
356 75f. Olive baboon . . . . . 1·40 55
357 90f. Hartebeest . . . . . . 2·00 90

1969. Air. "Philexafrique" Stamp Exn, Abidjan, Ivory Coast (2nd issue). As T **127** of Gabon.
358 50f. violet, sepia and blue . . 1·10 1·10
DESIGN: 50f. Cotonou harbour and stamp of 1941.

85 Heads and Globe

1969. 50th Anniv of I.L.O.
359 **85** 30f. multicoloured 40 25
360 70f. multicoloured 95 55

86 "The Virgin of the Scales" (C. da Sesto-Da Vinci School)

1969. Air. Leonardo da Vinci Commem. Mult.
361 100f. Type **86** . . . . 1·40 75
362 100f. "The Virgin of the Rocks" (Da Vinci) . . . . 1·40 75

87 "General Bonaparte" (J. L. David)

1969. Air. Birth Bicentenary of Napoleon Bonaparte. Multicoloured.
363 30f. Type **87** . . . . 1·10 1·00
364 60f. "Napoleon I in 1809" (Lefevre) . . . . 2·00 1·25
365 75f. "Napoleon at the Battle of Eylau" (Gros) (horiz) 2·50 1·75
366 200f. "General Bonaparte at Arcola" (Gros) . . . . . 5·50 3·25

88 Arms of Dahomey

1969.
367 **88** 5f. multicoloured (postage) 15 15
368 30f. multicoloured 45 30
369 50f. multicoloured (air) . . 45 25

89 "Apollo 8" over Moon

1969. Air. Moon flight of "Apollo 8". Embossed on gold foil.
370 **89** 1,000f. gold . . . . 15·00

1969. Air. 1st Man on the Moon (1st issue). Nos. 315/6 surch **ALUNISSAGE APOLLO XI JUILLET 1969**, lunar module and value.
371 **75** 125f. on 70f. (No. 315) . . 1·75 1·40
372 – 125f. on 70f. (No. 316) . . 1·75 1·40

91 Bank Emblem and Cornucopia

93 Dahomey Rotary Emblem

92 Kenaf Plant and Mill, Bohicon

1969. 5th Anniv of African Development Bank.
373 **91** 30f. multicoloured 50 40

1969. "Europafrique". Multicoloured.
374 30f. Type **92** (postage) . . . 40 25
375 45f. Cotton plant & mill, Parakou 50 30
376 100f. Coconut and palm-oil plant, Cotonou (air) . . . 1·10 70

1969. Air. Rotary International Organization.
378 **93** 50f. multicoloured 65 40

1969. Air. No. 250 surch.
379 **53** 10f. on 50f. multicoloured 50 20

95 Sakpata Dance

96 F. D. Roosevelt

1969. Dahomey Dances. Multicoloured.
380 10f. Type **95** (postage) . . . 30 25
381 30f. Guelede dance 40 30
382 45f. Sato dance 50 35
383 70f. Teke dance (air) 80 45

1969. Air. Christmas. Paintings. As T **58**. Mult.
384 30f. "The Annunciation" (Van der Stockt) 40 30
385 45f. "The Nativity" (15th-cent. Swabian School) 60 40
386 110f. "Virgin and Child" (Masters of the Gold Brocade) . . . . 1·60 1·00
387 200f. "The Adoration of the Magi" (Antwerp School, c. 1530) . . . . . 2·50 1·90

1969. Air. Old Masters. As T **63**. Multicoloured.
388 100f. "The Painter's Studio" (G. Courbet) . . . . . . 1·40 90
389 100f. "Self-portrait with Gold Chain" (Rembrandt) . . . 1·40 90
390 150f. "Hendrickje Stoffels" (Rembrandt) . . . . . . 2·10 1·25

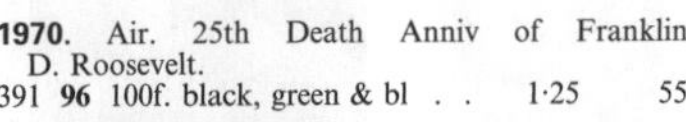

1970. Air. 25th Death Anniv of Franklin D. Roosevelt.
391 **96** 100f. black, green & bl . . 1·25 55

97 Rocket and Men on Moon

98 "U.N. in War and Peace"

1970. Air. 1st Man on Moon (2nd issue).
392 **97** 30f. multicoloured 40 25
The 50, 70, 110f. values were only issued in miniature sheet form.

1970. 25th Anniv of U.N.
394 **98** 30f. indigo, blue & red . . 40 25
395 40f. green, blue & brown 50 30

99 Walt Whitman and African Village

1970. Air. 150th Birth Anniv of Walt Whitman (American poet).
396 **99** 100f. brown, blue & grn . . 1·25 50

1970. Air. Space Flight of "Apollo 13". No. 392 surch **40F APOLLO 13 SOLIDARITE SPATIALE INTERNATIONALE**.
397 **97** 40f. on 30f. multicoloured 75 75

101 Footballers and Globe

1970. Air. World Cup Football Championship, Mexico. Multicoloured.
398 40f. Type **101** 50 40
399 50f. Goalkeeper saving goal 60 45
400 200f. Player kicking ball . . 2·50 1·10

1970. 10th Anniv (1969) of Aerial Navigation Security Agency for Africa and Madagascar (A.S.E.C.N.A.). As T **147** of Gabon.
401 40f. red and purple 60 25

103 Mt. Fuji and "EXPO" Emblem

104 "La Justice" and "La Concorde" (French warships)

1970. World Fair "EXPO 70", Osaka, Japan. Multicoloured.
402 5f. Type **103** (postage) . . . 45 20
403 70f. Dahomey Pavilion (air) 70 45
404 120f. Mt. Fuji and temple . . 1·25 65

1970. 300th Anniv of Ardres Embassy to Louis XIV of France.
405 **104** 40f. brown, blue & green 1·00 35
406 – 50f. red, brown & green 60 35
407 – 70f. brown, slate & brown 90 50
408 – 200f. brown, blue & red 2·50 1·10
DESIGNS: 50f. Matheo Lopes; 70f. King Alkemy of Ardres; 200f. Louis XIV of France.

1970. Air. Brazil's Victory in World Cup Football Championship. No. 400 surch **BRESIL–ITALIE 4 – 1** and value.
409 100f. on 200f. multicoloured 1·40 70

106 Mercury

107 Order of Independence

1970. Air. Europafrique.
410 **106** 40f. multicoloured 50 35
411 70f. multicoloured 80 45

1970. 10th Anniv of Independence.
412 **107** 30f. multicoloured 25 15
413 40f. multicoloured 40 20

108 Bariba Horseman

109 Beethoven

1970. Bariba Horsemen. Multicoloured.
414 1f. Type **108** 10 10
415 2f. Two horsemen 10 10
416 10f. Horseman facing left . . 25 20
417 40f. Type **108** 50 30
418 50f. As 2f. 70 35
419 70f. As 10f. 95 60

1970. Air. Birth Bicentenary of Beethoven.
420 **109** 90f. violet and blue . . . 90 40
421 110f. brown and green . . 1·00 55

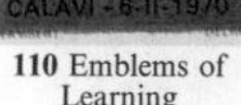

110 Emblems of Learning

112 De Gaulle and Arc de Triomphe

111 "The Annunciation"

1970. Air. Laying of Foundation Stone, Calavi University.
422 **110** 100f. multicoloured . . . 1·00 50

1970. Air. Christmas. Miniatures of the Rhenish School c. 1340. Multicoloured.
423 40f. Type **111** 40 25
424 70f. "The Nativity" 70 45
425 110f. "The Adoration of the Magi" . . . . 1·60 90
426 200f. "The Presentation in the Temple" . . . . 2·50 1·60

1971. Air. 1st Death Anniv of Gen. Charles de Gaulle. Multicoloured.
427 40f. Type **112** 55 45
428 500f. De Gaulle and Notre Dame, Paris . . . . 5·00 2·50

1971. Air. 250th Death Anniv of Watteau. Paintings. As T **63**. Multicoloured.
429 100f. "The Dandy" . . . . . 1·75 1·10
430 100f. "Girl with Lute" . . . 1·75 1·10

1971. Air. 500th Birth Anniv of Durer. As T **63**. Multicoloured.
431 100f. Self-portrait, 1498 . . . 1·40 90
432 200f. Self-portrait, 1500 . . . 2·75 1·60

113 Hands supporting Heart

114 "The Twins" (wood-carving) and Lottery Ticket

1971. Racial Equality Year.
433 **113** 40f. red, brn & green . . 40 25
434 – 100f. red, blue & green . . 95 50
DESIGN—HORIZ: 100f. "Heart" on Globe.

1971. 4th Anniv of National Lottery.
435 **114** 35f. multicoloured 35 15
436 40f. multicoloured 40 25

115 Kepler, Earth and Planets

1971. Air. 400th Birth Anniv of Johannes Kepler (astronomer).
437 **115** 40f. black, pur and blue 55 40
438 – 200f. green, red & blue . . 2·25 1·25
DESIGN: 200f. Kepler, globe, satellite and rocket.

116 Boeing 747 Airliner linking Europe and Africa

1971. Air. Europafrique.
439 **116** 50f. orge, blue & black . . 75 45
440 – 100f. multicoloured . . . 2·25 80
DESIGN: 100f. "General Mangin" (liner) and maps of Europe and Africa.

117 Cockerel and Drum (King Ganyehoussou)

1971. Emblems of Dahomey Kings. Multicoloured.
441 25f. Leg, saw and hatchet (Agoliagbo) 25 15
442 35f. Type **117** 40 25
443 40f. Fish and egg (Behanzin) (vert) 40 25
444 100f. Cow, tree and birds (Guezo) (vert) . . . . . . 1·00 45
445 135f. Fish and hoe (Ouegbadja) . . . . 1·75 90
446 140f. Lion and sickle (Glele) 1·60 90

1971. Air. 10th Anniv of U.A.M.P.T. As T **166** of Gabon. Multicoloured.
447 100f. U.A.M.P.T. H.Q., Brazzaville and Arms of Dahomey . . . . 1·00 50

119 "Adoration of the Shepherds" (Master of the Hausbuch)

1971. Air. Christmas. Paintings. Multicoloured.
448 40f. Type **119** 60 35
449 70f. "Adoration of the Magi" (Holbein) 95 45
450 100f. "Flight into Egypt" (Van Dyck) (horiz) . . . . 1·25 60
451 200f. "Birth of Christ" (Durer) (horiz) . . . . . . 2·50 1·40

120 "Prince Balthazar" (Velazquez)

1971. Air. 25th Anniv of UNICEF. Paintings of Children. Multicoloured.
452 40f. Type **120** 65 40
453 100f. "The Maids of Honour" (detail, Velazquez) . . . . 1·40 65

1972. No. 395 surch in figures.
454 **98** 35f. on 40f. green, bl & brn 40 25

122 Cross-country Skiing

123 Scout taking Oath

1972. Winter Olympic Games, Sapporo, Japan.
455 **122** 35f. purple, brown and green (postage) 50 30
456 – 150f. purple, blue and brown (air) . . . . . . 1·75 90
DESIGN: 150f. Ski-jumping.

1972. Air. International Scout Seminar, Cotonou. Multicoloured.
457 35f. Type **123** 25 20
458 40f. Scout playing "xylophone" 40 25
459 100f. Scouts working on the land (26 × 47 mm) . . . . 1·00 55

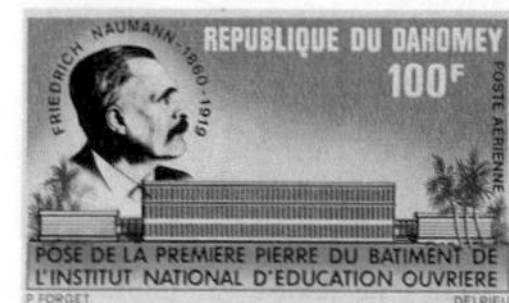

124 Friedrich Naumann and Institute Building

1972. Air. Laying of Foundation Stone for National Workers Education Institute. Multicoloured.
461 100f. Type **124** 90 50
462 250f. Pres. Heuss of West Germany and Institute . . 25 1·10

125 Stork with Serpent

1972. Air. UNESCO. "Save Venice" Campaign. Mosaics in St. Mark's Basilica. Multicoloured.
463 35f. Type **125** 55 35
464 40f. Cockerels carrying fox 65 45
465 65f. Noah releasing dove . . 1·10 80

126 Exhibition Emblem and Dancers

1972. Air. 12th International Philatelic Exhibition, Naples.
466 **126** 100f. multicoloured . . . 95 50

127 Running

129 Brahms, and Clara Schumann at Piano

128 Louis Bleriot and Bleriot XI

1972. Air. Olympic Games, Munich.
467 **127** 20f. brown, grn & blue . . 30 20
468 – 85f. brown, blue & green 85 45
469 – 150f. brown, blue & grn 1·75 80
DESIGNS: 85f. High-jumping; 150f. Putting the shot.

1972. Air. Birth Centenary of Louis Bleriot (pioneer airman).
471 **128** 100f. blue, violet & red 1·75 90

1972. 75th Death Anniv of Johannes Brahms (composer).
472 – 30f. black, brn & violet 40 25
473 **129** 65f. black, violet & lake 70 45
DESIGN—VERT: Brahms and opening bars of "Soir d'Ete".

130 "The Hare and the Tortoise"

1972. Fables of Jean de La Fontaine.
474 **130** 10f. grey, blue & lake . . 25 15
475 – 35f. blue, lake & purple 40 25
476 – 40f. indigo, blue & purple 55 35
DESIGNS—VERT: 35f. "The Fox and the Stork". HORIZ: 40f. "The Cat, the Weasel and the Little Rabbit".

131 "Adam" (Cranach)

1972. Air. 500th Birth Anniv of Lucas Cranach (painter). Multicoloured.
477 150f. Type **131** . . . . . . 1·75 1·00
478 200f. "Eve" (Cranach) . . . 2·50 1·40

132 Africans and 500f. Coin

1972. 10th Anniv of West African Monetary Union.
479 **132** 40f. brown, grey & yell 65 20

133 "Pauline Borghese" (Canova)

1972. Air. 150th Death Anniv of Antonio Canova.
480 **133** 250f. multicoloured . . . 2·75 1·40

1972. Air. Olympic Medal Winners. Nos. 467/9 optd as listed below.
481 **127** 20f. brown, blue & grn . . 30 20
482 – 85f. brown, blue & green 85 40
483 – 150f. brown, blue & grn 1·75 85
OVERPRINTS: 20f. **5.000m. – 10.000m. VIREN 2 MEDAILLES D'OR**. 85f. **HAUTEUR DAMES MEYFARTH MEDAILLE D'OR**. 150f. **POIDS KOMAR MEDAILLE D'OR**.

135 Pasteur and Apparatus

1972. Air. 150th Birth Anniv of Louis Pasteur (scientist).
485 **135** 100f. pur, violet & grn . . 1·00 50

1972. Air. Paintings by G. de la Tour. As T **63**. Multicoloured.
486 35f. "Hurdy-gurdy Player" (vert) 40 30
487 150f. "The New-born Child" 1·75 1·10

136 "The Annunciation" (School of Agnolo Gaddi)

1972. Air. Christmas. Religious Paintings. Mult.
488 35f. Type **136** 35 20
489 125f. "The Nativity" (Simone dei Crociffissi) . . . . . . 1·00 50
490 140f. "The Adoration of the Shepherds" (P. di Giovanni) . . . . 1·50 80
491 250f. "Adoration of the Magi" (Giotto) . . . . . 2·25 1·25

137 Dr. Hansen, Microscope and Bacillus

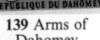

139 Arms of Dahomey

138 Statue and Basilica, Lisieux

1973. Centenary of Identification of Leprosy Bacillus by Hansen.
492 **137** 35f. brown, purple & blue 30 25
493 – 85f. brown, orange & grn 65 50
DESIGN: 85f. Dr. Gerhard Armauer Hansen.

1973. Air. Birth Centenary of St. Theresa of Lisieux. Multicoloured.
494 40f. Type **138** 45 30
495 100f. St. Theresa of Lisieux (vert) . . . . 1·20 65

1973.
496 **139** 5f. multicoloured 10 10
497 35f. multicoloured 25 15
498 40f. multicoloured 30 15

140 Scouts in Pirogue

1973. Air. 24th World Scouting Congress, Nairobi, Kenya.
499 **140** 15f. purple, green & blue 35 15
500 – 20f. blue and brown . . . 25 20
501 – 40f. blue, green & brown 40 25
DESIGNS—VERT: 20f. Lord Baden-Powell. HORIZ: 40f. Bridge-building.

141 Interpol Badge and "Communications"

142 "Education in Nutrition"

1973. 50th Anniv of International Criminal Police Organization (Interpol).
503 – 35f. brown, green & red 30 20
504 **141** 50f. green, brown & red 45 30
DESIGN—HORIZ: 35f. Interpol emblem and web.

1973. 25th Anniv of World Health Organization. Multicoloured.
505 35f. Type **142** 30 20
506 100f. Pre-natal examination 80 45

1973. Pan-African Drought Relief. No. 321 surch **SECHERESSE SOLIDARITE AFRICAINE** and value.
507 100f. on 70f. multicoloured 1·00 55

144 Copernicus, "Venera" and "Mariner" Probes and Plane of Solar System

1973. Air. 500th Birth Anniv of Copernicus.
508 **144** 65f. black, purple & yell 85 45
509 – 125f. green, blue & purple 1·40 70
DESIGN—VERT: 125f. Copernicus.

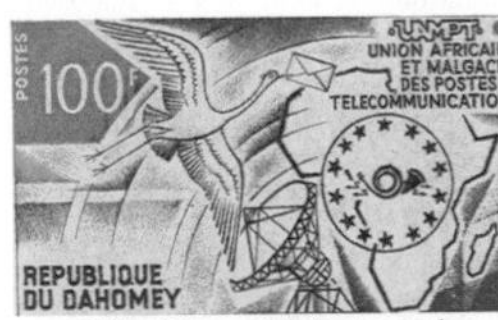

144a Crane with Letter and Telecommunications Emblem

1973. U.A.M.P.T.
510 **144a** 100f. violet, red & black 80 40

1973. Air. African Fortnight, Brussels. As No. 696 of Cameroun.
511 100f. black, green & blue . . 70 40

145 White Grouper

1973. Fishes.
512 **145** 5f. dp blue and blue . . . 25 20
513 – 15f. black and blue . . . 40 20
514 – 35f. lt brn, brn & grn . . 90 40
DESIGNS: 15f. African spadefish; 35f. Blue-pointed porgy.

148 W.M.O. Emblem and World Weather Map

1973. Air. Centenary of I.M.O./W.M.O.
515 **148** 100f. brown and green . . 95 10

149 "Europafrique"

1973. Air. Europafrique.
516 **149** 35f. blue, green & yell . . 35 20
517 – 40f. brown, ultram & bl 40 25
DESIGN: 40f. Europafrique, plant and cogwheels.

150 President John F. Kennedy

152 Chameleon

151 Footballers

1973. Air. 10th Death Anniv of President Kennedy.
518 **150** 200f. grn, violet & grn . . 1·90 1·40

1973. Air. World Football Championship Cup.
520 **151** 35f. green, brn & bistre 35 20
521 – 40f. brown, blue & orange 40 25
522 – 100f. green, brown & blue 65 45
DESIGNS: 40f., 100f. Football scenes similar to Type **151**.

1973. 1st Anniv of 26th October Revolution. Multicoloured.
523 35f. Type **152** 35 20
524 40f. Arms of Dahomey (vert) 35 25

153 "The Annunciation" (Dirk Bouts)

155 "The Elephant, the Chicken and the Dog"

1973. Air. Christmas. Multicoloured.
525 35f. Type **153** 40 30
526 100f. "The Nativity" (Giotto) 70 50
527 150f. "The Adoration of the Magi" (Botticelli) . . . . 1·40 80
528 200f. "The Adoration of the Shepherds" (Bassano) (horiz) . . . . 1·75 1·25

1974. Air. "Skylab". No. 515 surch **OPERATION SKYLAB 1973-1974** and value.
529 **148** 200f. on 100f. brn & grn 1·50 95

1974. Dahomey Folk Tales. Multicoloured.
530 5f. Type **155** 15 10
531 10f. "The Sparrowhawk and the Dog" 20 10
532 25f. "The Windy Tree" (horiz) 30 20
533 40f. "The Eagle, the Snake and the Chicken" (horiz) 40 20

156 Snow Crystal and Skiers

1974. Air. 50th Anniv of Winter Olympic Games.
534 **156** 100f. blue, brn and vio . . 95 65

157 Alsatian

1974. Breeds of Dogs. Multicoloured.
535 40f. Type **157** 35 25
536 50f. Boxer 40 25
537 100f. Saluki 80 50

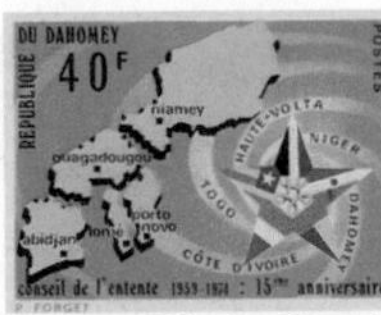

158 Map of Member Countries

1974. 15th Anniv of Council of Accord.
538 **158** 40f. multicoloured 35 15

159 Lenin (50th Death Anniv)

1974. Air. Celebrities' Anniversaries.
539 **159** 50f. purple and red . . . 50 30
540 – 125f. brn & green . . . . 1·10 65
541 – 150f. blue & purple . . . 1·60 1·10
DESIGNS AND ANNIVERSARIES: 125f. Marie Curie (40th death anniv); 150f. Sir Winston Churchill (birth cent).

160 18th-century Persian Bishop

161 Beethoven and opening bars of the "Moonlight" Sonata

1974. Air. 21st Chess Olympiad, Nice. Mult.
542 50f. Type **160** 55 35
543 200f. 19th-century Siamese queen . . . . 1·75 1·10

1974. Air. Famous Composers.
544 **161** 150f. red and black . . . 1·25 80
545 – 150f. red and black . . . 1·25 80
DESIGN: No. 545, Chopin.

162 Earth seen through Astronaut's Legs

1974. Air. 5th Anniv of 1st Manned Moon Landing.
546 **162** 150f. brn, blue & red . . 1·40 85

Sets commemorating the World Cup, U.P.U. Centenary, Treaty of Berne, Space Exploration and West Germany's World Cup Victory appeared in 1974. Their status is uncertain.

1974. Air. 11th Pan-Arab Scout Jamboree, Batroun, Lebanon. Nos. 499/500 surch **XIe JAMBOREE PANARABE DE BATROUN – LIBAN** and value.
547 **140** 100f. on 15f. purple, green and blue 65 45
548 – 140f. on 20f. bl & brn . . 1·25 65

1974. Air. West Germany's Victory in World Cup Football Championships. Nos. 521/2 surch **R F A 2 HOLLANDE 1** and value.
549 100f. on 40f. brn, bl & orge 65 45
550 150f. on 100f. grn, brn & bl 1·00 80

165 U.P.U. Emblem and Globe

1974. Air. Centenary of U.P.U.
551 **165** 35f. violet and red 35 30
552 – 65f. blue and red . . . . 1·25 60
553 – 125f. green, blue & lt bl 2·75 1·00
554 – 200f. blue, yellow & brn 1·75 1·25
DESIGNS: 65f. Concorde in flight over African village; 125f. French mobile post office, circa 1860; 200f. Drummer and mail van.

166 "Lion of Belfort"

1974. Air. 70th Death Anniv of F. Bartholdi (sculptor).
555 **166** 100f. brown . . . . . . 1·25 65

1974. Air. 30th Death Anniv of Philippe de Champaigne (painter). As T **153**. Mult.
556 250f. "Young Girl with Falcon" . . . . 2·25 1·40

167 Locomotive No. 3.1102, 1911, France

1974. Steam Locomotives.
557 **167** 35f. multicoloured 80 35
558 – 40f. grey, black & red . . 1·00 45
559 – 100f. multicoloured . . . 2·50 85
560 – 200f. multicoloured . . . 4·25 1·90
DESIGNS: 40f. Goods locomotive, 1877; 100f. Crampton Type 210 locomotive, 1849; 200f. Stephenson locomotive "Aigle", 1846, France.

168 Rhamphorhynchus

1974. Air. Prehistoric Animals. Multicoloured.
561 35f. Type **168** 35 20
562 150f. Stegosaurus . . . . . 1·00 70
563 200f. Tyrannosaurus . . . . 1·50 95

169 Globe, Notes and Savings Bank

1974. World Savings Day.
564 **169** 35f. brown, myrtle & grn 35 25

170 Europafrique Emblem on Globe

1974. Air. Europafrique.
565 **170** 250f. multicoloured . . . 1·90 1·40

1974. Air. Christmas. Paintings by Old Masters. As T **153**. Multicoloured.
566 35f. "The Annunciation" (Schongauer) 30 20
567 40f. "The Nativity" (Schongauer) 35 25
568 100f. "The Virgin of the Rose Bush" (Schongauer) . . . 80 45
569 250f. "The Virgin, Infant Jesus and St. John the Baptist" (Botticelli) . . . . 2·25 1·40

171 "Apollo" and "Soyuz" Spacecraft

1975. Air. "Apollo–Soyuz" Space Link. Mult.
570 35f. Type **171** 35 25
571 200f. Rocket launch and flags of Russia and U.S.A. . . . 1·60 90
572 500f. "Apollo" and "Soyuz" docked together . . . . . 3·50 2·25

172 Dompago Dance, Hissi

173 Flags on Map of Africa

1975. Dahomey Dances and Folklore. Mult.
573 10f. Type **172** 20 15
574 25f. Fetish dance, Vaudou-Tchinan 30 15
575 40f. Bamboo dance, Agbehoun 40 30
576 100f. Somba dance, Sandoua (horiz) 75 50

1975. "Close Co-operation with Nigeria". Multicoloured.
577 65f. Type **173** 40 30
578 100f. Arrows linking maps of Dahomey and Nigeria (horiz) 65 40

174 Community Emblem and Pylons

1975. Benin Electricity Community. Mult.
579 40f. Type **174** 35 25
580 150f. Emblem and pylon (vert) . . . . 1·10 65
C.E.B. = "Communaute Electrique du Benin".

175 Head of Ceres

1975. Air. "Arphila 75" International Stamp Exhibition, Paris.
581 **175** 100f. purple, ind & blue 90 55

176 Rays of Light and Map

178 Dr. Schweitzer

1975. "New Dahomey Society".
582 **176** 35f. multicoloured 30 20

1975. Air. "Apollo–Soyuz" Space Test Project. Nos. 570/1 surch **RENCONTRE APOLLO-SOYOUZ 17 Juil. 1975** and value.
583 **171** 100f. on 35f. mult 65 45
584 – 300f. on 200f. mult . . . 2·00 1·10

1975. Birth Centenary of Dr. Albert Schweitzer.
585 **178** 200f. olive, brown & green . . . . 1·75 90

179 "The Holy Family" (Michelangelo)

180 Woman and I.W.Y. Emblem

1975. Air. Europafrique.
586 **179** 300f. multicoloured . . . 1·90 1·25

1975. International Women's Year.
587 **180** 50f. blue and violet . . . 35 25
588 – 150f. orange, brn & grn 1·10 65
DESIGN: 150f. I.W.Y. emblem within ring of bangles.

181 Continental Infantry

183 "Allamanda cathartica"

182 Diving

1975. Air. Bicent of American Revolution.
589 **181** 75f. lilac, red & green . . 55 35
590 – 135f. brown, pur & bl . . 95 70
591 – 300f. brown, red & blue 2·00 1·40
592 – 500f. brown, red & grn 3·50 1·75
DESIGNS: 135f. "Spirit of 76"; 300f. Artillery battery; 500f. Cavalry.

1975. Air. Olympic Games, Montreal.
593 **182** 40f. brown, bl and vio . . 35 25
594 – 250f. brown, grn & red 1·60 1·10
DESIGN: 250f. Football.

1975. Flowers. Multicoloured.
595 10f. Type **183** 15 10
596 35f. "Ixora coccinea" 30 15
597 45f. "Hibiscus rosa-sinensis" 45 30
598 60f. "Phaemeria magnifica" 55 40

184 "The Nativity" (Van Leyden)

1975. Air. Christmas. Multicoloured.
599 40f. Type **184** 35 25
600 85f. "Adoration of the Magi" (Rubens) (vert) 55 45
601 140f. "Adoration of the Shepherds" (Le Brun) . . . 1·00 65
602 300f. "The Virgin of the Blue Diadem" (Raphael) (vert) 2·00 1·50

For later issues see **BENIN**.

PARCEL POST STAMPS

1967. Surch **COLIS POSTAUX** and value.
P271 **18** 5f. on 1f. (postage) . . . 10 10
P272 – 10f. on 2f. (No. 151) . . 25 25
P273 **18** 20f. on 6f. 30 30
P274 – 25f. on 3f. (No. 152) . . 40 40
P275 – 30f. on 4f. (No. 153) . . 45 45
P276 – 50f. on 10f. (No. 155) . . 70 70
P277 – 100f. on 20f. (No. 157) 1·50 1·50
P278 – 200f. on 200f. (No. 195) (air) . . . . 3·00 2·25
P279 **29** 300f. on 100f. . . . . . 3·50 3·00
P280 – 500f. on 300f. (No. 196) 6·50 4·50
P281 – 1000f. on 500f. (No. 197) 14·00 11·00
P282 – 5000f. on 100f. (No. 145) 55·00 55·00

POSTAGE DUE STAMPS

1906. "Natives" key-type inscr "DAHOMEY" in blue (10, 30c.) or red (others).
D33 L 5c. green . . . . 1·75 1·50
D34 10c. red . . . . 3·00 2·75
D35 15c. blue on blue . . . . 4·00 3·00
D36 20c. black on yellow . . . 3·00 7·00
D37 30c. red on cream . . . . 3·25 8·00
D38 50c. violet . . . . 8·50 25·00
D39 60c. black on buff . . . . 6·50 21·00
D40 1f. black on pink . . . . . 30·00 55·00

1914. "Figure" key-type inscr "DAHOMEY".
D59 M 5c. green . . . . 10 2·25
D60 10c. red . . . . 15 2·00
D61 15c. grey . . . . 40 2·00
D62 20c. brown . . . . 40 2·75
D63 30c. blue . . . . 1·00 3·00
D64 50c. black . . . . 75 3·75
D65 60c. orange . . . . 1·25 2·25
D66 1f. violet . . . . 1·75 3·25

1927. Surch in figures.
D96 M 2f. on 1f. mauve . . . . . 1·75 1·75
D97 3f. on 1f. brown . . . . . 2·50 4·50

D 14 Native Head

D 26 Panther attacking African

1941.
D143 **D 14** 5c. black . . . . . . 1·10 2·75
D144 10c. red . . . . . . 20 2·75
D145 15c. blue . . . . . . 10 2·00
D146 20c. green . . . . . . 35 2·75
D147 30c. orange . . . . . 1·25 3·00
D148 50c. brown . . . . . 1·90 3·25
D149 60c. green . . . . . . 1·90 3·50
D150 1f. red . . . . 2·25 3·50
D151 2f. yellow . . . . . . 2·75 3·25
D152 3f. purple . . . . . . 2·75 4·25

1963.
D191 **D 26** 1f. red and green . . . 10 10
D192 2f. green & brown . . 10 10
D193 5f. blue and orange . . 10 10
D194 10f. black and purple 25 25
D195 20f. orange & blue . . 30 30

D 72 Pirogue

1967.
D308 **D 72** 1f. plum, blue & brn 10 10
D309 A 1f. brown, bl & plum 10 10
D310 B 3f. green, orge & brn 10 10
D311 C 3f. brown, orge & grn 10 10
D312 D 5f. purple, blue & brn 15 15
D313 E 5f. brown, blue & pur 35 20
D314 F 10f. green, vio & brn 30 30
D315 G 10f. brown, grn & vio 30 30
D316 H 30f. violet, red & bl 50 50
D317 I 30f. blue, red & vio . . 50 50
DESIGNS: A, Heliograph; B, Old morse receiver; C, Postman on cycle; D, Old telephone; E, Renault ABH diesel railcar; F, Citroen "2-CV" mail van; G, Radio station; H, Douglas DC-8-10/50CF airliner; I, "Early Bird" satellite.

DANISH WEST INDIES Pt. 11

A group of islands in the West Indies formerly belonging to Denmark and purchased in 1917 by the United States, whose stamps they now use. Now known as the United States Virgin Islands.

1855. 100 cents = 1 dollar.
1905. 100 bit = 1 franc.

1

2

5

1855. Imperf.
4 **1** 3c. red . . . . 29·00 48·00

1872. Perf.
6 **1** 3c. red . . . . 60·00 £150
7 4c. blue £150 £300

1873.
31 **2** 1c. red and green . . . . . 8·75 13·00
32 3c. red and blue . . . . . . 7·25 9·50
33 4c. blue and brown . . . . . 8·00 7·50
19 5c. brown and green . . . . 19·00 12·00
21 7c. yellow and purple . . . . 21·00 70·00
25 10c. brown and blue . . . . 19·00 22·00
27 12c. green and purple . . . . 29·00 £100

28 14c. green and lilac £450 £800
29 50c. lilac £100 £180

1887. Handstamped **1 CENT**.
37 **2** 1c. on 7c. yellow & purple . . 45·00 £140

1895. Surch **10 CENTS 1895**.
38 **2** 10c. on 50c. lilac . . . . . . 26·00 48·00

1900.
39 **5** 1c. green . . . . 2·40 2·40
40 2c. red . . . . 6·25 18·00
41 5c. blue . . . . 12·50 18·00
42 8c. brown . . . . 22·00 40·00

1902. Surch **2** (or **8**) **CENTS 1902**.
43 **2** 2c. on 3c. red and blue . . . 6·50 17·00
47 8c. on 10c. brown & blue . . 8·00 8·25

1905. Surch **5 BIT 1905**.
48 **2** 5b. on 4c. blue & brown . . 12·00 38·00
49 **5** 5b. on 5c. blue . . . . . . 10·00 29·00
50 5b. on 8c. brown . . . . . . 10·00 30·00

10 King Christian IX

11 Charlotte Amalie Harbour and Training ship "Ingolf"

1905.
51 **10** 5b. green . . . . 3·75 3·00
52 10b. red . . . . 3·75 3·00
53 20b. blue and green . . . . 7·50 6·50
54 25b. blue . . . . 7·50 7·50
55 40b. grey and red . . . . . 7·50 6·00
56 50b. grey and yellow . . . . 7·50 8·25
57 **11** 1f. blue and green . . . . . 16·00 26·00
58 2f. brown and red . . . . . 26·00 38·00
59 5f. brown and yellow . . . 55·00 £180

14 King Frederik VIII

15 King Christian X

1907.
60 **14** 5b. green . . . . 2·25 1·10
61 10b. red . . . . 2·25 1·00
62 15b. brown and violet . . . 3·75 3·75
63 20b. blue and green . . . . 22·00 18·00
64 25b. blue . . . . 2·25 1·90
65 30b. black and red . . . . 40·00 38·00
66 40b. grey and red . . . . . 5·50 4·50
67 50b. brown and yellow . . . 5·25 7·00

1915.
68 **15** 5b. green . . . . 4·25 4·00
69 10b. red . . . . 4·25 42·00
70 15b. brown and lilac . . . . 4·25 42·00
71 20b. blue and green . . . . 4·25 42·00
72 25b. blue . . . . 4·25 10·00
73 30b. black and red . . . . 4·25 55·00
74 40b. grey and red . . . . . 4·25 55·00
75 50b. brown and yellow . . . 4·25 55·00

POSTAGE DUE STAMPS

D 6

D 12

1902.
D43 **D 6** 1c. blue . . . . 4·75 13·50
D44 4c. blue . . . . 9·00 19·00
D45 6c. blue . . . . 17·00 40·00
D46 10c. blue . . . . 16·00 45·00

1905.
D60 **D 12** 5b. grey and red . . . 4·00 5·00
D61 20b. grey and red . . . 5·75 12·00
D62 30b. grey and red . . . 5·25 12·00
D63 50b. grey and red . . . 5·00 26·00

DANZIG Pt. 7

A Baltic seaport, from 1920–1939 (with the surrounding district) a free state under the protection of the League of Nations. Later incorporated in Germany. Now part of Poland.

1920. 100 pfennige = 1 mark.
1923. 100 pfennige = 1 Danzig gulden.

Stamps of Germany inscr "DEUTSCHES REICH" optd or surch.

1920. Optd **Danzig** horiz.
1 **10** 5pf. green 20 20
2 10pf. red 25 20
3 **24** 15pf. brown 25 20
4 **10** 20pf. blue . . . . 25 1·10
5 30pf. black & orge on buff 25 20
6 40pf. red 25 20
7 50pf. black & pur on buff 25 20
8 **12** 1m. red 45 65
9 1m.25 green 45 65
10 1m.50 brown 90 90
11 **13** 2m. blue . . . . 2·40 5·00
12 2m.50 red . . . . 1·80 4·00
13 **14** 3m. black . . . . 6·75 11·00
14 **10** 4m. red and black . . . 4·50 7·50
15a **15** 5m. red and black . . . 2·00 2·75

1920. Surch **Danzig** horiz and large figures of value.
16 **10** 5 on 30pf. black and orange on buff 20 25
17 10 on 20pf. blue 20 25
18 25 on 30pf. black and orange on buff 20 25
19 60 on 30pf. black and orange on buff . . . . . 65 1·10
20 80 on 30pf. black and orange on buff . . . . . 65 1·10

1920. Optd **Danzig** diagonally and bar.
21 **24** 2pf. grey £110 £225
22 2½pf. grey £160 £300
23 **10** 3pf. brown . . . . 8·75 18·00
24 5pf. green 45 65
25 **24** 7½pf. orange . . . . 40·00 55·00
26 **10** 10pf. red . . . . 3·00 7·50
27 **24** 15pf. violet 60 65
28 **10** 20pf. blue 60 65
29 25pf. blk & red on yell . . 60 65
30 30pf. blk & orge on buff 49·00 90·00
31 40pf. black and red . . . . 1·80 2·75
32 50pf. blk & pur on buff . . £180 £325
32a 60pf. mauve £1100 £3000
33 75pf. black and green . . . 60 65
34 80pf. blk & red on pink . . 2·40 5·00
34a **12** 1m. red £1100 £3000

1920. Optd **DANZIG** three times in semicircle.
34b **13** 2m. blue £1100 £3000

1920. No. 5 of Danzig surch **MARK 1 MARK** and Types of Germany with burelage added surch with new value and **DANZIG** (36/37), **Danzig** (38, 40f) or **DANZIG** and flag (40e).
35 A **10** 1m. on 30pf. black and orange on buff . . . . 90 1·60
36 A 1¼m. on 3pf. brown . . 90 1·60
37 A **24** 2m. on 35pf. brown . . 90 1·60
38 A 3m. on 7½pf. orange . . 90 1·60
39 A 5m. on 2pf. grey . . . . 90 1·60
40AF 10m. on 7½pf. orange . . 1·10 2·20

1920. Air. No. 6 of Danzig surch with airplane or wings and value.
41 **10** 40 on 40pf. red . . . . . . 1·30 3·25
42 60 on 40pf. red . . . . . . 1·30 3·25
43 1m. on 40pf. red . . . . . 1·30 3·25

13 Hanse Kogge

1921. Constitution of 1920.
44 **13** 5pf. purple and brown . . . 20 25
45 10pf. violet and orange . . 20 25
46 25pf. red and green 55 65
55 40pf. red . . . . 65 1·30
48 80pf. blue 45 65
49 – 1m. grey and red . . . . 1·60 2·00
50 – 2m. green and blue . . . 5·75 5·50
51 – 3m. green and black . . . 2·00 2·40
52 – 5m. red and grey . . . . 2·00 2·40
53 – 10m. brown and green . . . 2·75 5·25
The mark values are as Type **13**, but larger.

15

16 Sabaltnig PIII over Danzig

1921. Air.
57 **15** 40pf. green 25 65
58 60pf. purple 25 65
59 1m. red 25 65
60 2m. brown 25 65
116 **16** 5m. violet 45 90
117 10m. green 45 90
118 20m. brown 45 90
119 **15** 25m. blue 40 65
120 **16** 50m. orange 40 65
121 100m. red 40 65
122 250m. brown 40 65
123 500m. red 40 65
Nos. 120 to 123 are similar to Type **16**, but larger.

1921. No. 33 of Danzig surch **60** and bars.
63 **10** 60 on 75pf. black & green 65 1·00

18

19

1921.
64 **18** 5pf. orange 20 20
65 10pf. brown 20 20
66 15pf. green 20 20
67 20pf. grey 20 20
68 25pf. green 20 20
69 30pf. red and blue 25 25
70 40pf. red and green 20 20
71 50pf. red and green 20 20
72 60pf. red 35 45
73 75pf. purple 20 25
74 80pf. red and black 25 45
75 80pf. green 20 25
76 1m. red and orange 20 45
77 1.20m. blue . . . . 1·30 1·30
78 1.25m. red and purple . . 20 25
79 1.50m. grey 20 45
80 2m. red and grey . . . . . 3·00 4·50
81 2m. red 20 25
82 2.40m. red and brown . . 1·00 2·00
83 3m. red and purple . . . . 10·00 11·00
84 3m. red 20 45
106 4m. blue 30 50
86 5m. green 20 45
87 6m. red 35 50
88 8m. blue . . . . 35 1·10
89 10m. orange 20 45
90 20m. brown 20 45
110 40m. blue 30 45
111 80m. red 30 45

1921. Rouletted.
91 **19** 5m. green, black and red 1·40 3·00
91b 9m. orange and red . . . 3·00 10·50
92 10m. blue, black and red 1·40 3·00
93 20m. black and red . . . . 1·40 3·00

20

21

1921. Tuberculosis Week.
93a **20** 30pf.(+30pf.) grn & orge 1·40 3·00
93b 60pf.(+60pf.) red & yell . . 1·30 1·30
93c 1.20m.(+1.20m.) bl & orge (25 × 29½ mm) . . . . . . 2·40 2·20

1922.
94b **21** 50m. red and gold . . . . 1·80 3·75
95a 100m. red and green . . . 3·00 5·50

1922. Surch in figures.
96 **18** 6 on 3m. red 25 65
97 8 on 4m. blue 20 90
98 20 on 8m. blue 25 65

25

26

1923.
99 **25** 50m. red and blue 30 50
136 50m. blue 25 55
100 100m. red and green . . . 30 50
137 100m. green 25 55
101 150m. red and purple . . . 30 50
138 200m. orange 25 55
102 **26** 250m. red and purple . . . 40 50
103 500m. red and grey 40 50
104 1000m. pink and brown . . 40 50
105 5000m. pink and silver . . 1·60 5·50
139 10000m. red and orange . . 45 55
140 20000m. red and blue . . . 45 1·00
141 50000m. red and green . . 45 1·00

28

1923. Poor People's Fund.
123b **28** 50+20m. red 25 60
123c 100+30m. purple 25 60

29

35 Etrich/Rumpler Taube

1923.
124 **29** 250m. red and purple . . . 20 90
125 300m. red and green . . . 20 25
126 500m. red and grey 20 90
127 1000m. brown 20 45
128 1000m. red and brown . . 20 90
129 3000m. red and violet . . 20 90
130 5000m. pink 20 45
131 20000m. blue 20 90
132 50000m. green 20 45
133 100000m. blue 20 45
134 250000m. purple 20 45
135 500000m. grey 20 45

1923. Surch with figure of value and **Tausend** (T) or **Million** or **Millionen** (M).
142 **25** 40T. on 200m. orange . . 90 2·40
143 100T. on 200m. orange . . 90 2·40
144 250T. on 200m. orange . . 8·00 16·00
145 400T. on 100m. green . . . 25 45
146 **29** 500T. on 50000m. green . . 25 45
147 1M. on 10000m. orange . . 4·00 7·50
148 1M. on 10000m. red . . . 20 45
149 2M. on 10000m. red . . . 20 45
150 3M. on 10000m. red . . . 20 45
151 5M. on 10000m. red . . . 20 45
152 10M. on 10000m. lavender 35 65
158 **26** 10M. on 1000000m. orge 45 1·30
153 **29** 20M. on 10000m. lavender 35 65
154 25M. on 10000m. lavender 25 65
155 40M. on 10000m. lavender 25 65
156 50M. on 10000m. lavender 25 65
159 100M. on 10000m. lav . . 25 65
160 300M. on 10000m. lav . . 25 65
161 500M. on 10000m. lav . . 25 65

1923. Surch **100000** and bar.
157 **26** 100000 on 20000m. red and blue . . . . 1·20 6·75

1923. Air.
162a **35** 250,000m. red . . . . . 40 1·00
163a 500,000m. red . . . . . 35 1·00

1923. Surch in **Millionen**.
164a **35** 2m. on 100,000m. red . . 35 1·30
165a 5m. on 50,000m. red . . . 35 1·30

1923. Surch with new currency, **Pfennige** or **Gulden**.
166 **25** 5pf. on 50m. red 45 45
167 10pf. on 50m. red 45 45
168 20pf. on 100m. red 45 45
169 25pf. on 50m. red . . . . 4·00 8·75
170 30pf. on 50m. red . . . . 3·50 2·20
171 40pf. on 100m. red . . . . 2·40 2·40
172 50pf. on 100m. red . . . . 2·40 3·25
173 75pf. on 100m. red . . . . 7·50 18·00
174 **26** 1g. on 1000000m. red . . . 5·00 7·00
175 2g. on 1000000m. red . . . 13·50 18·00
176 3g. on 1000000m. red . . . 27·00 75·00
177 5g. on 1000000m. red . . . 31·00 80·00

39

40 Etrich/Rumpler Taube

1924.
177a **39** 3pf. brown . . . . 1·30 1·60
268 5pf. orange . . . . 90 1·80
178e 7pf. green . . . . 1·20 2·10
178f 8pf. green . . . . 1·70 4·50
270 10pf. green . . . . 90 1·80
180 15pf. grey . . . . 4·00 65
180b 15pf. red . . . . 1·80 1·10
181 20pf. red and carmine . . 10·50 80
182 20pf. grey . . . . 1·70 1·70
183 25pf. red and grey . . . . 18·00 3·50
272 25pf. red . . . . 2·20 8·75
185 30pf. red and green . . . 8·75 80
186 30pf. purple . . . . 1·70 4·00
186a 35pf. blue . . . . 2·30 1·60
187 40pf. blue and indigo . . 8·25 1·00
188 40pf. red and brown . . . 4·75 10·00
189 40pf. blue . . . . 1·90 4·00
274 50pf. red and blue . . . . 2·75 10·00
190b 55pf. red and purple . . . 4·50 12·50
191 60pf. red and green . . . 4·50 13·50
192 70pf. red and green . . . 2·10 4·50
193 75pf. red and purple . . . 8·50 8·50
194 80pf. red and brown . . . 2·30 5·75

1924. Air.
195 **40** 10pf. red . . . . 27·00 5·25
196 20pf. mauve . . . . 2·20 1·60
197 40pf. brown . . . . 3·25 2·00
198 1g. green . . . . 3·25 2·00
199 – 2½g. purple (22 × 40 mm) 20·00 40·00

42 Oliva

44 Fountain of Neptune

1924.
200 **42** 1g. black and green . . . . 24·00 49·00
275 1g. black and orange . . . 5·75 18·00
201 – 2g. black and purple . . . 55·00 £120
206 – 2g. black and red . . . . 4·50 9·75
202 – 3g. black and blue . . . . 4·50 5·25
203 – 5g. black and lake . . . . 4·50 8·75
204 – 10g. black and brown . . . 27·00 £110

DESIGNS—HORIZ: 2g. Krantor and River Mottlau; 3g. Zoppot. VERT: 5g. St. Mary's Church; 10g. Town Hall and Langemarkt.

1929. Int Philatelic Exhibition. Various frames.

207	**44**	10pf.(+10pf.) blk & grn	2·75	3·50
208		15pf.(+15pf.) blk & red	2·75	3·50
209		25pf.(+25pf.) blk & bl	10·50	11·00

1930. 10th Anniv of Constitution of Free City of Danzig. Optd **1920 15. November 1930.**

210	**39**	5pf. orange	2·20	3·25
211		10pf. green	3·00	4·25
212		15pf. red	5·25	10·50
213		20pf. red and carmine	2·75	5·25
214		25pf. red and grey	5·00	10·50
215		30pf. red and green	8·75	27·00
216		35pf. blue	38·00	£100
217		40pf. blue and indigo	11·00	35·00
218		50pf. red and blue	38·00	80·00
219		75pf. red and purple	38·00	80·00
220	**42**	1g. black and orange	38·00	80·00

1932. Danzig Int Air Post Exn ("Luposta"). Nos. 200/4 surch **Luftpost-Ausstellung 1932** and value.

221	**42**	10pf.+10pf. on 1g. black and green	10·00	25·00
222	–	15pf.+15pf. on 2g. black and purple	10·00	25·00
223	–	20pf.+20pf. on 3g. black and blue	10·00	25·00
224	–	25pf.+25pf. on 5g. black and lake	10·00	25·00
225	–	30pf.+30pf. on 10g. black and brown	10·00	25·00

1934. "Winter Relief Work" Charity. Surch **5 W.H.W.** in Gothic characters.

226	**39**	5pf.+5pf. orange	5·75	15·00
227		10pf.+5pf. green	18·00	37·00
228		15pf.+5pf. red	11·50	26·00

1934. Surch.

229	**39**	6pf. on 7pf. green	90	1·60
230a		8pf. on 7pf. green	1·30	2·20
231		30pf. on 35pf. blue	13·50	20·00

50 Junkers F-13 **51**

1935. Air.

233	**50**	10pf. red	1·80	90
234		15pf. yellow	1·80	1·60
235		25pf. green	1·80	2·00
236		50pf. blue	8·75	11·00
237	**51**	1g. purple	6·75	16·00

52 Stockturm, 1346 **54** Brosen War Memorial

1935. Winter Relief Fund.

238	**52**	5pf.+5pf. orange	65	1·30
239	–	10pf.+5pf. green	1·10	2·20
240	–	15pf.+10pf. red	2·00	3·50

DESIGNS—HORIZ: 10pf. Lege Tor. VERT: 15pf. Georgshalle, 1487.

1936. 125th Anniv of Brosen. Inscr "125 JAHRE OSTEEBAD BROSEN".

241	–	10pf. green	90	90
242	–	25pf. red	1·10	2·40
243	**54**	40pf. blue	2·00	5·25

DESIGNS—HORIZ: 10pf. Brosen Beach; 25pf. Zoppot end of Brosen Beach.

55 Frauentor and Observatory **56** D(anziger) L(uftschutz) B(und) **57a** Danziger Dorf, Magdeburg

57 Marienkriche, Danzig

1936. Winter Relief Fund.

244	–	10pf.+5pf. blue	1·80	4·00
245	**55**	15pf.+5pf. green	1·80	5·25
246	–	25pf.+10pf. red	2·75	7·50
247	–	40pf.+20pf. brn & red	3·50	12·50
248	–	50pf.+20pf. blue	5·25	20·00

DESIGNS—VERT: 10pf. Milchkannenturm; 25pf. Krantor. HORIZ: 40pf. Langgartertor; 50pf. Hohestor.

1937. Air Defence League.

249	**56**	10pf. blue	45	1·30
250		15pf. purple	1·80	2·40

1937. 1st National Philatelic Exhibition, Danzig. Sheets 147 × 104 mm.

MS251 **57**	50pf. blue-green/toned (postage)	1·80	8·75
MS252 **57**	50pf. blue/toned (air)	1·80	8·75

1937. Foundation of Danzig Community. Magdeburg.

253	**57a**	25pf. (+25pf.) red	3·00	6·25
254	–	40pf. (+40pf.) red & bl	3·00	6·25

DESIGN—HORIZ: 40pf. Village and Arms of Danzig and Magdeburg.

1937. Danzig Productivity Show. Sheet 146 × 105 mm.

MS254a Nos. 253/4 (sold for 1g.50)	55·00	£100

58 Madonna and Child **59** Schopenhauer

1937. Winter Relief Fund. Statues.

255	**58**	5pf.+5pf. violet	2·75	6·25
256	–	10pf.+5pf. brown	2·75	6·25
257	–	15pf.+5pf. orange & blue	2·75	8·50
258	–	25pf.+10pf. green & blue	4·00	8·75
259	–	40pf.+25pf. blue & red	7·50	19·00

DESIGNS: 10pf. Mercury; 15pf. The "Golden Knight"; 25pf. Fountain of Neptune; 40pf. St. George and Dragon.

1938. 150th Birth Anniv of Schopenhauer (philosopher). Portraits inscr as in T **59**.

260	–	15pf. blue (as old man)	1·30	2·20
261	–	25pf. brown (as youth)	3·25	8·50
262	**59**	40pf. red	1·30	4·00

60 Yacht "Peter von Danzig" (1936) **61** Teutonic Knights

1938. Winter Relief Fund. Ships.

276	**60**	5pf.+5pf. green	1·10	2·20
277	–	10pf.+5pf. brown	1·60	3·25
278	–	15pf.+10pf. olive	1·80	3·25
279	–	25pf.+10pf. blue	2·50	5·00
280	–	40pf.+15pf. purple	3·50	8·75

DESIGNS: 10pf. Dredger "Fu Shing"; 15pf. Liner "Columbus"; 25pf. Liner "Hansestadt Danzig"; 40pf. Sailing ship "Peter von Danzig" (1472).

1939. 125th Anniv of Prussian Annexation. Historical designs.

281	**61**	5pf. green	55	2·40
282	–	10pf. brown	90	2·75
283	–	15pf. blue	1·10	3·25
284	–	25pf. purple	1·60	4·50

DESIGNS: 10pf. Danzig–Swedish treaty of neutrality, 1630; 15pf. Danzig united to Prussia, 2.1.1814; 25pf. Stephen Batori's defeat at Weichselmunde, 1577.

62 Gregor Mendel

1939. Anti-cancer Campaign.

285	**62**	10pf. brown	45	90
286	–	15pf. black (Koch)	65	2·00
287	–	25pf. green (Rontgen)	90	3·00

OFFICIAL STAMPS

1921. Stamps of Danzig optd **D M.**

O 94	**18**	5f. orange	20	20
O 95		10pf. brown	20	20
O 96		15pf. green	20	20
O 97		20pf. grey	20	20
O 98		25pf. green	20	20
O 99		30pf. red and blue	60	65
O100		40pf. red and green	20	20
O101		50pf. red and green	20	20
O102		60pf. red	20	20
O103		75pf. purple	20	45
O104		80pf. red and black	90	1·10
O105		80pf. green	20	3·00
O106		1m. orange	20	20
O107		1m.20 blue	1·30	1·30
O108		1m.25 red and purple	20	45
O109		1m.50 grey	20	45
O110		2m. red and grey	17·00	13·00
O111		2m. red	20	45
O112		2m.40 red and brown	1·30	3·00
O113		3m. red and purple	11·00	13·00
O114		3m. red	20	45
O122		4m. blue	25	65
O116		5m. green	20	45
O117		6m. red	20	45
O118		10m. orange	20	45
O119		20m. brown	20	45

1922. Stamps of Danzig optd **D M.**

O120a	**19**	5m. green, black and red (No. 91)	3·75	7·00
O126a	**25**	50m. red and blue	20	30
O142		50m. blue	20	65
O127a		100m. red and green	20	30
O143		100m. green	20	65
O144		200m. orange	20	65
O145	**29**	300m. red and green	25	65
O146		500m. red and grey	20	65
O147		1000m. red and brown	20	65

1922. No. 96 optd **D M.**

O121	**18**	6 on 3m. red	25	65

1924. Optd **Dienst-marke.**

O195	**39**	5pf. orange	2·20	2·20
O196		10pf. green	2·20	2·20
O197		15pf. grey	2·20	2·20
O198		15pf. red	22·00	11·00
O199		20pf. red and carmine	2·20	1·80
O200		25pf. red and black	22·00	29·00
O201		30pf. red and green	3·00	3·00
O202		35f. blue	44·00	55·00
O203		40pf. blue and indigo	7·00	8·75
O204		50pf. red and blue	22·00	35·00
O205		75pf. red and purple	40·00	£120

POSTAGE DUE STAMPS

D 20 D 39

1921. Value in "pfennig" (figures only).

D 94	**D 20**	10pf. purple	25	45
D 95		20pf. purple	25	45
D 96		40pf. purple	25	45
D 97		60pf. purple	25	45
D 98		75pf. purple	25	45
D 99		80pf. purple	25	45
D112		100pf. purple	65	90
D100		120pf. purple	25	45
D101		200pf. purple	1·10	1·30
D102		240pf. purple	1·00	1·30
D114		300pf. purple	65	90
D115		400pf. purple	65	90
D116		500pf. purple	65	1·10
D117		800pf. purple	1·80	4·50

Value in "marks" ("M" after figure).

D118a	**D 20**	10m. purple	65	1·10
D119a		20m. purple	65	90
D120a		50m. purple	65	90
D121		100m. purple	65	1·10
D122		500m. purple	65	1·10

1923. Surch with figures and bar.

D162	**D 20**	1000 on 100m. pur	£160	£325
D163		5000 on 50m. purple	45	1·10
D164		10000 on 20m. pur	45	1·10
D165		50000 on 500m. pur	45	1·10
D166		100000 on 20m. pur	90	1·80

1924.

D178	**D 39**	5pf. blue and black	65	90
D179		10pf. blue and black	45	90
D180		15pf. blue and black	1·10	1·30
D181		20pf. blue and black	1·10	2·20
D182		30pf. blue and black	8·75	2·20
D183		40pf. blue and black	2·20	3·50
D184		50pf. blue and black	2·20	2·75
D185		60pf. blue and black	13·50	22·00
D186		100pf. blue and black	18·00	11·00
D187		3g. blue and red	8·75	55·00

1932. Surch in figures over bar.

D226	**D 39**	5 on 40pf. blue & blk	2·20	8·75
D227		10 on 60pf. bl & blk	38·00	11·00
D228		20 on 100pf. bl & blk	2·20	8·75

DEDEAGATZ Pt. 6

Former French Post Office, closed in August 1914. Dedeagatz was part of Turkey to 1913, then a Bulgarian town.

25 centimes = 1 piastre.

1893. Stamps of France optd **Dedeagh** or surch also in figures and words.

59	**10**	5c. green	8·50	11·00
60		10c. black on lilac	18·00	17·00
62a		15c. blue	23·00	24·00
63		1pi. on 25c. black on red	29·00	25·00
64		2pi. on 50c. red	55·00	45·00
65		4pi. on 1f. olive	60·00	55·00
66		8pi. on 2f. brn on blue	80·00	70·00

1902. "Blanc", "Mouchon" and "Merson" key-types inscr "DEDEAGH". Some surch in figures and words.

67a	A	5c. green	1·90	2·25
68	B	10c. red	1·25	1·50
70		15c. orange	2·50	2·40
71		1pi. on 25c. blue	2·75	3·00
72	C	2pi. on 50c. brown & lav	6·00	8·00
73		4pi. on 1f. red and green	12·50	11·50
74		8pi. on 2f. lilac & yellow	19·00	19·00

DENMARK Pt. 11

A kingdom in N. Europe, on a peninsula between the Baltic and the North Sea.

1851. 96 rigsbank skilling = 1 rigsdaler.
1875. 100 ore = 1 krone.

1 2 4

1851. Imperf.

3	**1**	2r.b.s. blue	£2750	£850
4	**2**	4r.b.s. brown	£750	22·00

1854. Dotted background. Brown burelage. Imperf.

8	**4**	2sk. blue	50·00	38·00
9b		4sk. orange	£700	5·00
12		8sk. green	£275	44·00
13		16sk. lilac	£425	£100

5 7 8

1858. Background of wavy lines. Brown burelage. Imperf.

15	**5**	4sk. brown	65·00	4·00
18		8sk. green	£500	60·00

1863. Brown burelage. Roul

20	**5**	4sk. brown	75·00	10·00
21	**4**	16sk. mauve	£1200	£400

1864. Perf.

22	**7**	2sk. blue	55·00	25·00
25		3sk. mauve	70·00	44·00
28		4sk. red	35·00	5·25
29		8sk. bistre	£275	75·00
30a		16sk. green	£400	75·00

1870. Value in "skilling".

39	**8**	2sk. blue and grey	42·00	17·00
42		3sk. purple and grey	80·00	55·00
44		4sk. red and grey	42·00	6·00
46		8sk. brown and grey	£160	42·00
48		16sk. green and grey	£200	£100
37		48sk. lilac and brown	£375	£130

1875. As T **8**, but value in "ore".

80	**8**	3ore grey and blue	5·00	2·20
81		4ore blue and grey	4·75	30
56		5ore blue and red	45·00	41·00
82		8ore red and grey	4·75	30
83		12ore purple and grey	6·00	1·70
84		16ore brown and grey	13·50	2·10
72		20ore grey and red	£120	13·00
85		25ore green and grey	8·75	2·30
86		50ore purple and brown	23·00	10·50
87		100ore orange and grey	27·00	7·25

10 **14** King Christian IX **15**

1882.

96	**10**	1ore orange	50	40
97		5ore green	4·50	15
98		10ore red	3·50	15
99		15ore mauve	14·50	45

100 20ore blue . . . . 17·00 1·70
101 24ore brown . . . . 12·00 2·30

1904. No. 82 and 101 surch.
102 **8** 4ore on 8ore red & grey 1·80 2·30
103 **10** 15ore on 24ore brown . . 2·30 3·25

1904.
119 **14** 5ore green . . . . 4·75 15
104 10ore red . . . . 2·20 15
105 20ore blue . . . . 9·75 55
106 25ore brown . . . . 21·00 2·00
107 50ore lilac . . . . 50·00 35·00
108 100ore brown . . . . . . 9·25 20·00

1905. Solid background.
173 **15** 1ore orange 35 25
174 2ore red . . . . 2·75 30
175 3ore grey . . . . 6·75 30
176 4ore blue . . . . 7·50 30
177 5ore brown 90 20
178 5ore green . . . . 1·30 25
179 7ore green . . . . 3·25 1·50
180 7ore violet . . . . 16·00 2·75
181 8ore grey . . . . 5·50 1·60
114 10ore pink . . . . 7·50 15
182 10ore green . . . . 1·10 20
183 10ore brown . . . . 2·75 25
184 12ore lilac . . . . 24·00 4·25
115 15ore mauve . . . . . . 13·50 65
116 20ore blue . . . . 43·00 2·10
For stamps with lined background but without hearts, see Nos. 265/76k.

17 King Frederik VIII **20** G.P.O., Copenhagen

1907.
121 **17** 5ore green 90 10
122 10ore red . . . . 1·70 10
124 20ore blue . . . . 9·00 45
125 25ore brown . . . . 19·00 35
127 35ore orange . . . . . . 3·50 2·20
128 50ore purple . . . . 20·00 2·20
130 100ore brown . . . . . . 70·00 1·50

1912. (a) Nos. 84 and 72 surch **35 ORE**.
131 **8** 35ore on 16ore brn & grey 9·00 21·00
132 35ore on 20ore grey and red 15·00 26·00
(b) No. O98 surch **35 ORE FRIMAERKE**.
133 **O 9** 35ore on 32ore green . . 15·00 36·00

1912.
134 **20** 5k. red . . . . £150 65·00

21 King Christian X **22**

1913.
135 **21** 5ore green 55 10
136 7ore orange . . . . . . 2·00 55
137 8ore grey . . . . 5·25 3·00
138 10ore red . . . . 1·20 10
139 12ore grey . . . . 2·75 4·50
141a 15ore mauve . . . . . . 1·30 10
142 20ore blue . . . . 7·50 25
143 20ore brown 55 15
144 20ore red 80 10
145 25ore brown . . . . . . 17·00 20
146 25ore black and brown 85·00 2·10
147 25ore red . . . . 2·50 30
148 25ore green . . . . . . 1·60 20
149 27ore black and red . . 20·00 22·00
150 30ore black and green . . 20·00 1·00
151 30ore orange . . . . . . 1·50 75
152 30ore blue 85 30
153 35ore yellow . . . . . . 13·00 1·90
154 35ore black and yellow 4·00 2·50
155 40ore black and violet . . 11·00 1·60
156 40ore blue . . . . 2·30 55
157 40ore yellow . . . . . . 1·00 60
158 50ore purple . . . . . . 24·00 1·60
159 50ore black and purple 33·00 65
160a 50ore grey . . . . 5·25 20
161 60ore blue and brown . . 35·00 2·10
162 60ore blue . . . . 6·75 50
163 70ore green and brown 16·00 1·40
164 80ore green . . . . . . 30·00 7·75
165 90ore red and brown . . 9·00 1·70
166 **22** 1k. brown . . . . 65·00 50
167 **21** 1k. blue and brown . . . 22·00 95
168 **22** 2k. black . . . . 85·00 3·25
169 **21** 2k. purple and grey . . . 31·00 6·75
170 **22** 5k. violet . . . . 7·50 4·75
171 **21** 5k. brown and mauve . . 3·75 3·50
172 10k. green and red . . . £150 19·00

1915. (a) No. O94 surch **DANMARK 80 ORE POSTFRIM.**
186 **O 9** 80ore on 8ore red . . . . 15·00 55·00
(b) No. 83 surch **80 ORE**.
187 **8** 80ore on 12ore pur & grey 13·00 50·00

1918. Newspaper stamps surch **POSTFRIM. ORE 27 ORE DANMARK.**
197 **N 18** 27ore on 1ore green . . 1·90 5·75
198 27ore on 5ore blue . . . 3·75 12·50
199 27ore on 7ore red . . . 2·00 4·50
200 27ore on 8ore green . . 2·50 7·25
201 27ore on 10ore lilac . . 1·90 5·00
202 27ore on 20ore green . . 2·40 7·00
203 27ore on 29ore orge . . 2·10 5·00
204 27ore on 38ore orge . . 10·50 39·00
205 27ore on 41ore brn . . 5·00 20·00
194 27ore on 68ore brn . . 2·75 14·50
206 27ore on 1k. pur & grn 1·80 3·75
195 27ore on 5k. grn & pk 3·25 7·50
196 27ore on 10k. bl & stone 3·25 11·00

1919. No. 135 surch **2 ORE**.
207 **21** 2ore on 5ore green £900 £250

27 Castle of Kronborg, Elsinore **29** Roskilde Cathedral

1920. Recovery of Northern Schleswig.
208 **27** 10ore red . . . . 2·00 15
209 10ore green . . . . 10·50 25
210 – 20ore slate . . . . 2·00 25
211 **29** 40ore brown . . . . 5·25 2·50
212 40ore blue . . . . 29·00 4·75
DESIGN—HORIZ: 20ore Sonderborg Castle.

1921. Nos. 136 and 139 surch **8 8**.
217 **21** 8 on 7ore orange . . . . . 1·50 1·80
213 8 on 12ore green . . . . . 1·70 4·00

1921. Red Cross. Nos. 209/10 surch with figure of value between red crosses.
214 **27** 10ore+5ore green . . . . 9·00 21·00
215 – 20ore+10ore grey . . . . 11·50 26·00

1921. No. 175 surch **8**.
216 **15** 8 on 3ore grey . . . . . . 1·80 1·70

33 King Christian IV **34** King Christian X **35**

1924. 300th Anniv of Danish Post. A. Head facing to left.
218A **33** 10ore green . . . . . . 2·40 1·80
221A **34** 10ore green . . . . . . 2·40 1·80
219A **33** 15ore mauve . . . . . . 2·40 1·80
222A **34** 15ore mauve . . . . . . 2·40 1·80
220A **33** 20ore brown . . . . . . 2·40 1·80
223A **34** 20ore brown . . . . . . 2·40 1·80
B. Head facing to right.
218B **33** 10ore green . . . . . . 2·40 1·80
221B **34** 10ore green . . . . . . 2·40 1·80
219B **33** 15ore mauve . . . . . . 2·40 1·80
222B **34** 15ore mauve . . . . . . 2·40 1·80
220B **33** 20ore brown . . . . . . 2·40 1·80
223B **34** 20ore brown . . . . . . 2·40 1·80

1925. Air.
224 **35** 10ore green . . . . 13·00 18·00
225 15ore lilac . . . . 29·00 37·00
226 25ore red . . . . 18·00 27·00
227 50ore grey . . . . 55·00 95·00
228 1k. brown . . . . 55·00 95·00

1926. Surch **20 20**.
229 **21** 20 on 30ore orange . . . . 2·10 5·75
230 20 on 40ore blue . . . . 2·40 6·75

38 **39** **40** Caravel

1926. 75th Anniv of First Danish stamps.
231 **38** 10ore olive 60 10
232 **39** 20ore red 90 10
233 30ore blue . . . . 3·50 55

1926. Various stamps surch.
234 **15** 7 on 8ore grey . . . . . . 95 2·00
235 **21** 7 on 20ore red 40 65
236 7 on 27ore black & red . . 2·00 6·25
237 12 on 15ore lilac . . . . . 1·20 2·50

1926. Official stamps surch **DANMARK 7 ORE POSTFRIM.**
238 **O 9** 7ore on 1ore orange . . . 1·20 5·75
239 7ore on 3ore grey . . . . 8·50 13·00
240 7ore on 4ore blue . . . . 2·10 5·25
241 7ore on 5ore green . . . 29·00 41·00
242 7ore on 10ore green . . . 1·40 5·25
243 7ore on 15ore lilac . . . 2·10 4·75
244 7ore on 20ore blue . . . 6·75 34·00

1927. Solid background.
246 **40** 15ore red . . . . 2·75 10
247 20ore grey . . . . 5·75 55
248 25ore blue 45 10
249 30ore yellow 60 10
250 35ore red . . . . 12·00 50
251 40ore green . . . . 10·50 10

For stamps with lined background see Nos. 277b, etc.

41 **42** King Christian X **43** Numeral

1929. Danish Cancer Research Fund.
252 **41** 10ore (+5ore) green . . . 2·50 3·75
253 15ore (+5ore) red . . . . 4·25 6·00
254 25ore (+5ore) blue . . . . 14·50 24·00

1930. 60th Birthday of King Christian X.
255 **42** 5ore green 85 20
256 7ore violet . . . . 4·00 1·80
257 8ore grey . . . . 12·50 12·50
258 10ore brown . . . . 1·60 10
259 15ore red . . . . 6·75 10
260 20ore grey . . . . 11·50 3·75
261 25ore blue . . . . 4·00 40
262 30ore yellow . . . . . . 4·00 1·10
263 35ore red . . . . 6·25 1·30
264 40ore green . . . . 5·75 60

1933. Lined background.
265 **43** 1ore green 10 25
266 2ore red 10 15
267 4ore blue 35 20
268 5ore green 70 25
268c 5ore purple 15 10
268d 5ore orange 20 10
268e 6ore orange 10 10
269 7ore violet 95 15
269a 7ore green 95 45
269b 7ore brown 20 20
270 8ore grey 35 25
270a 8ore green 20 15
271 10ore orange . . . . . . 4·50 25
271b 10ore brown . . . . . . 4·75 20
271c 10ore violet 20 20
271d 10ore green 15 10
272 12ore green 25 10
272a 15ore green 25 10
272c 20ore blue 20 10
272e 25ore green 40 10
272f 25ore blue 25 10
273 30ore green 20 10
273a 30ore orange 25 10
273c 40ore orange 30 10
273d 40ore purple 20 10
274 50ore brown 20 10
274d 60ore green . . . . . . 1·20 35
274e 60ore grey 60 40
275 70ore red 70 10
275a 70ore green 30 20
275d 80ore green 40 10
275e 80ore brown 50 30
276 100ore green 45 10
276a 100ore blue 45 10
276b 125ore brown 60 20
276c 150ore green 60 30
276ca 150ore violet 55 35
276d 200ore green 70 10
276e 230ore green 95 30
276f 250ore green 95 30
276g 270ore green 95 40
276h 300ore green . . . . . . 1·10 30
276i 325ore green . . . . . . 1·10 35
276j 350ore green . . . . . . 1·10 40
276k 375ore green . . . . . . 1·20 50
276l 400ore green 75 45

45 King Christian X **47** Fokker FVIIa over Copenhagen **49** Hans Andersen

1933. T **40** with lined background.
277b **40** 15ore red . . . . 2·00 20
277de 15ore green . . . . . . 2·50 20
278a 20ore grey . . . . 3·25 15
278b 20ore red 35 10
279 25ore blue . . . . 36·00 13·00
279b 25ore brown 40 20
280a 30ore orange 50 15
280b 30ore blue 65 20
281 35ore violet 35 25
282 40ore green . . . . . . 2·50 10
282b 40ore blue 90 10
283 **45** 50ore grey 90 10
283a 60ore green . . . . . . 2·20 20
283b 75ore blue 50 25
284 1k. brown . . . . 3·25 10
284a 2k. red . . . . 5·00 40
284b 5k. violet . . . . 7·75 1·90

1934. Nos. 279 and 280a surch.
285 **40** 4 on 25ore blue 25 25
286 10 on 30ore orange . . . . 2·10 1·70

1934. Air.
287 **47** 10ore orange . . . . . . 85 1·10
288 15ore red . . . . 2·40 3·50
289 20ore green . . . . 2·40 3·75
290 50ore green . . . . 2·50 3·75
291 1k. brown . . . . 8·00 11·50

1935. Centenary of Hans Andersen's Fairy Tales.
292 – 5ore green . . . . 3·75 15
293 **49** 7ore violet . . . . 2·20 1·20
294 – 10ore orange . . . . . . 4·25 10
295 **49** 15ore red . . . . 10·50 15
296 20ore grey . . . . 8·75 65
297 30ore blue . . . . 2·10 25
DESIGNS: 5ore "The Ugly Duckling"; 10ore "The Little Mermaid".

51 St. Nicholas's Church, Copenhagen **52** Hans Tausen

53 Ribe Cathedral **54** Dybbol Mill

1936. 400th Anniv of Reformation.
298 **51** 5ore green . . . . 1·10 20
299 7ore mauve . . . . 1·20 1·60
300 **52** 10ore brown . . . . 1·60 10
301 15ore red . . . . 2·30 10
302 **53** 30ore blue . . . . 10·00 60

1937. H. P. Hanssen (North Schleswig patriot) Memorial Fund.
303 **54** 5ore+5ore green 40 75
304 10ore+5ore brown . . . . 1·80 4·75
305 15ore+5ore red . . . . . 1·80 4·75

56 King Christian X

1937. Silver Jubilee of King Christian X.
306 – 5ore green . . . . 1·30 15
307 **56** 10ore brown . . . . 1·10 20
308 – 15ore red . . . . 1·00 10
309 **56** 30ore blue . . . . 11·00 1·30
DESIGNS—HORIZ: 5ore Marselisborg Castle and "Rita" (King's yacht); 15ore Amalienborg Castle.

1937. Copenhagen Philatelic Club's 50th Anniv Stamp Exhibition. No. 271b optd **K.P.K. 17.-26. SEPT. 19 37** (="Kobenhavns Philatelist Klub").
310 **43** 10ore brown . . . . 95 1·20

58 Emancipation Monument **59** B. Thorvaldsen **61** Queen Alexandrine

1938. 150th Anniv of Abolition of Villeinage.
311 **58** 15ore red 50 20

1938. Centenary of Return of Sculptor Thorvaldsen to Denmark.
312 **59** 5ore purple 25 10
313 – 10ore violet 35 10
314 **59** 30ore blue . . . . 1·50 40
DESIGN: 10ore Statue of Jason.

1939. Red Cross Charity. Cross in red.
314a **61** 5ore+3ore purple 25 25
315 10ore+5ore violet 25 20
316 15ore+5ore red 35 40

1940. Stamps of 1933 (lined background) surch.
317 **43** 6 on 7ore green 15 25
318 6 on 8ore grey 15 30
319a **40** 15 on 40ore green 50 80
320 20 on 15ore red . . . . . 1·00 15
321 40 on 30ore blue 50 20

65 Queen Ingrid (when Princess) and Princess Margrethe

66 Bering's Ship "Sv. Pyotr"

1941. Child Welfare.
322 **65** 10ore+5ore violet 25 25
323 20ore+5ore red 25 25

1941. Death Bicent of Vitus Bering (explorer).
324 **66** 10ore violet 30 15
325 20ore brown 65 15
326 40ore blue 50 35

67 King Christian X

68 Round Tower of Trinity Church

1942.
327 **67** 10ore violet 15 10
328 15ore green 25 10
329 20ore red 30 10
330 25ore brown 40 15
331 30ore orange 35 10
332 35ore purple 30 30
333 40ore blue 35 10
333a 45ore olive 50 20
334 50ore grey 75 10
335 60ore green 50 10
335a 75ore blue 65 15

1942. Tercentenary of the Round Tower.
336 **68** 10ore violet 15 10

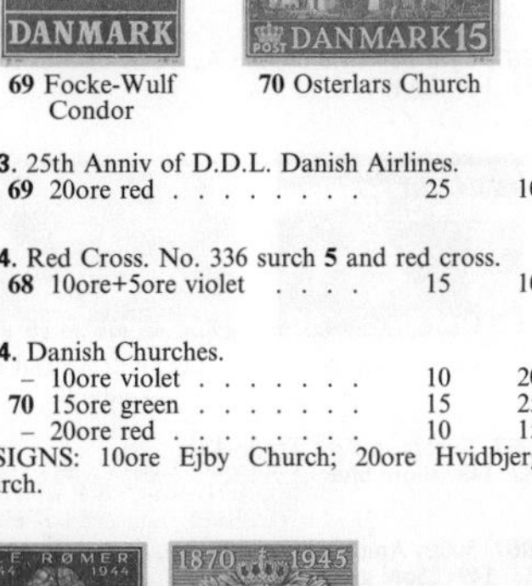

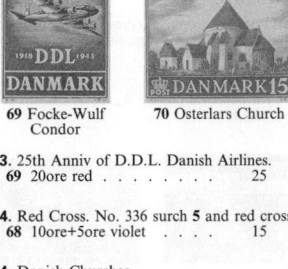

69 Focke-Wulf Condor

70 Osterlars Church

1943. 25th Anniv of D.D.L. Danish Airlines.
337 **69** 20ore red 25 10

1944. Red Cross. No. 336 surch **5** and red cross.
338 **68** 10ore+5ore violet 15 10

1944. Danish Churches.
339 – 10ore violet 10 20
340 **70** 15ore green 15 25
341 – 20ore red 10 15
DESIGNS: 10ore Ejby Church; 20ore Hvidbjerg Church.

71 Ole Romer

72 King Christian X

73 Arms

1944. Birth Tercent of Romer (astronomer).
342 **71** 20ore brown 20 10

1945. King Christian's 75th Birthday.
343 **72** 10ore mauve 20 15
344 20ore red 25 15
345 40ore blue 50 25

1946.
346 **73** 1k. brown 65 10
346a 1k.10 purple . . . . . 2·40 95
346b 1k.20 grey . . . . . 1·10 10
346c 1k.20 blue . . . . . 1·10 30
346d 1k.25 orange . . . . . 1·80 20
346e 1k.30 green . . . . . 2·75 95
346f 1k.50 purple 90 20
346g 2k. red . . . . . . 1·30 10
347 2k.20 orange . . . . . 1·60 10
347a 2k.50 orange . . . . . 1·00 10
347b 2k.80 grey . . . . . 1·60 20
347c 2k.80 green 85 55
347d 2k.80 green 85 40
347e 2k.90 purple . . . . . 2·75 10
347f 3k. green 85 10
347g 3k.10 purple . . . . . 3·25 30
347h 3k.30 red 95 50
347i 3k.50 purple . . . . . 1·10 10
347j 3k.50 blue . . . . . 1·50 95
347k 4k. grey . . . . . . 1·00 10
347l 4k.10 brown . . . . . 3·50 30
347m 4k.30 brown . . . . . 1·80 2·20
347n 4k.30 green . . . . . 2·40 1·60
347o 4k.50 brown . . . . . 3·25 25
347p 4k.60 grey . . . . . 1·80 1·90
347q 4k.70 purple . . . . . 2·10 1·40
348 5k. blue . . . . . . 2·75 10
348a 5k.50 blue . . . . . 2·50 40
348b 6k. black . . . . . . 1·40 10
348c 6k.50 green . . . . . 1·70 40
348d 6k.60 green . . . . . 2·00 1·40
348e 7k. mauve . . . . . . 1·70 10
348f 7k.10 purple . . . . . 1·60 80
348g 7k.30 green . . . . . 2·00 1·80
348h 7k.50 green . . . . . 2·00 1·80
348i 7k.70 purple . . . . . 2·10 65
348j 8k. orange . . . . . . 1·80 30
348k 9k. brown . . . . . . 2·00 10
348l 10k. yellow . . . . . . 2·00 10
348la 10k.50 blue . . . . . 2·20 2·20
348m 11k. brown . . . . . . 2·50 1·70
348ma 11k.50 blue . . . . . 3·00 1·60
348n 12k. brown . . . . . . 3·00 40
348o 14k. brown . . . . . . 3·50 40
348p 16k. red . . . . . . 4·00 45
348pa 16k.50 brown . . . . . 4·00 55
348q 17k. red . . . . . . 4·50 55
348r 18k. brown . . . . . . 4·75 60
348s 20k. blue . . . . . . 4·50 45
348t 22k. red . . . . . . 5·00 65
348ta 22k. maroon . . . . . 5·00 65
348u 23k. green . . . . . . 5·25 1·00
348v 24k. green . . . . . . 5·25 75
348w 25k. green . . . . . . 5·50 30
348x 26k. green . . . . . . 6·00 85
348z 50k. red . . . . . . 11·50 1·20

74 Tycho Brahe

75 Symbols of Freedom

1946. 400th Birth Anniv of Tycho Brahe (astronomer).
349 **74** 20ore red 35 20

1947. Liberation Fund.
350 **75** 15ore+5ore green 15 20
351 – 20ore+5ore red (Bombed railways) 90 45
352 – 40ore+5ore blue (Flag) . . 65 50

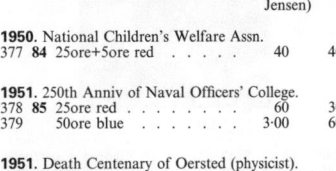

77 Class H Steam Goods Train

79 I. C. Jacobsen

1947. Centenary of Danish Railways.
353 – 15ore green 55 15
354 **77** 20ore red 70 10
355 – 40ore blue . . . . 3·00 1·00
DESIGNS—HORIZ: 15ore First Danish locomotive "Odin"; 40ore Diesel-electric train "Lyntog" and train ferry "Fyn".

1947. 60th Death Anniv of Jacobsen and Centenary of Carlsberg Foundation for Promotion of Scientific Research.
356 **79** 20ore red 20 10

80 King Frederick IX

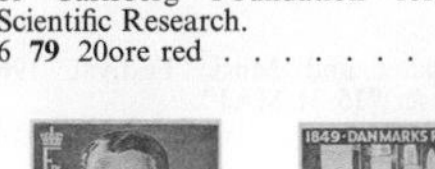

81 "The Constituent Assembly of the Kingdom" (after Constantin Hansen)

1948.
357a **80** 15ore green 80 25
358 15ore violet 50 10
359a 20ore red 45 10
360 20ore brown 20 10
361 25ore brown 85 25
362 25ore red . . . . . . 2·50 10
362a 25ore blue 50 20
362b 25ore violet 20 10
363 30ore orange . . . . . . 8·25 35
363b 30ore red 35 20
364 35ore green 20 20
365 40ore blue . . . . . . 3·00 40
366 40ore grey 75 10
367 45ore bistre . . . . . . 1·00 10
368 50ore grey . . . . . . 1·20 25
369 50ore blue . . . . . . 1·90 10
369a 50ore green 20 10
370 55ore brown . . . . . . 17·00 1·10
371a 60ore blue 45 10
371b 65ore grey 45 20
372 70ore green . . . . . . 1·10 10
373 75ore purple . . . . . . 1·30 10
373a 80ore orange 70 10
373b 90ore bistre . . . . . . 1·70 10
373c 95ore orange 55 25

1949. Centenary of Danish Constitution.
374 **81** 20ore brown 35 10

82 Globe

83 Kalundborg Transmitter

1949. 75th Anniv of U.P.U.
375 **82** 40ore blue 55 40

1950. 25th Anniv of State Broadcasting.
376 **83** 20ore brown 35 20

84 Princess Anne-Marie

85 "Fredericus Quartus" (warship)

86 H. C. Oersted (after C. A. Jensen)

1950. National Children's Welfare Assn.
377 **84** 25ore+5ore red 40 40

1951. 250th Anniv of Naval Officers' College.
378 **85** 25ore red 60 30
379 50ore blue . . . . 3·00 60

1951. Death Centenary of Oersted (physicist).
380 **86** 50ore blue . . . . 1·00 40

87 Mail Coach

88 Hospital Ship "Jutlandia"

1951. Danish Stamp Centenary.
381 **87** 15ore violet 50 10
382 25ore red 50 10

1951. Danish Red Cross Fund.
383 **88** 25ore +5ore red 55 60

89 "Life-Saving" (relief, H. Solomon)

91 Memorial Stone, Skamlings-banken

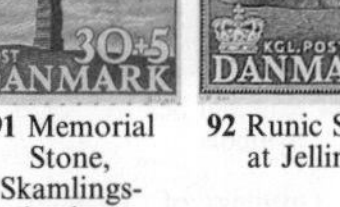

92 Runic Stone at Jelling

1952. Centenary of Danish Life-Saving Service.
384 **89** 25ore red 35 20

1953. Netherlands Flood Relief Fund. Surch **NL+10.**
385 **80** 30ore+10ore red . . . . . 1·00 85

1953. Danish Border Union Fund.
386 **91** 30ore+5ore red . . . . . 1·00 85

1953. 1,000 years of Danish Kingdom. Inscr "KONGERIGE i 1000 AR". (a) 1st series.
387 **92** 10ore green 20 20
388 – 15ore lilac 20 20
389 – 20ore brown 20 20
390 – 30ore red 40 20
391 – 60ore blue 55 20
DESIGNS: 15ore Vikings' camp, Trelleborg; 20ore Kalundborg Church; 30ore Nyborg Castle; 60ore Goose Tower, Vordinborg.

(b) 2nd series.
392 – 10ore green 20 15
393 – 15ore lilac 20 15
394 – 20ore brown 20 15
395 – 30ore red 30 15
396 – 60ore blue 75 15
DESIGNS: 10ore Spottrup Castle; 15ore Hammershus Castle; 20ore Copenhagen Stock Exchange; 30ore King Frederik V statue; 60ore Soldier's Statue (H. V. Bissen).

93 Telegraph Table, 1854

94 Head of Statue of King Frederik V at Amalienborg

1954. Telecommunications Centenary.
397 **93** 30ore brown 35 20

1954. Bicent of Royal Academy of Fine Arts.
398 **94** 30ore red 50 20

1955. Liberty Fund. Nos. 350/1 surch.
399 **75** 20+5 on 15ore +5ore grn 1·00 80
400 – 30+5 on 20ore +5ore red 1·00 80

1955. Nos. 268e, 269b, 359a and 362 surch.
401 **43** 5ore on 6ore orange . . . 15 10
402 5ore on 7ore brown . . . 15 10
403 **80** 30ore on 20ore red 30 20
404 30ore on 25ore red 45 20

98 S. Kierkegaard (philosopher)

99 Ellehammer's Aircraft

1955. Death Centenary of Kierkegaard.
405 **98** 30ore red 35 10

1956. 50th Anniv of 1st Flight by J. C. H. Ellehammer.
406 **99** 30ore red 45 10

100 Whooper Swans

102 National Museum

1956. Northern Countries' Day.
407 **100** 30ore red . . . . 1·20 15
408 60ore blue 85 45

1957. Danish Red Cross Hungarian Relief Fund. No. 373c surch **Ungarns-hjaelpen 30 + 5.**
409 **80** 30ore+5ore on 95ore orange 50 40

1957. 150th Anniv of National Museum.
410 **102** 30ore red 45 15
411 – 60ore blue 60 55
DESIGN: 50ore "Sun-God's Chariot" (bronze age model).

103 Harvester

105 King Frederik IX

106 Margrethe Schanne in "La Sylphide"

1958. Centenary of Danish Royal Veterinary and Agricultural College.
412 **103** 30ore red 20 10

1959. Greenland Fund. No. 363b surch **Gronlands-fonden + 10.**
413 **80** 30ore+10ore red 75 60
The Greenland Fund was devoted to the relatives of the crew and passengers of the "Hans Hedtoft", the Greenland vessel lost at sea on 30 January 1959.

1959. 60th Birthday of King Frederik IX.
414 **105** 30ore red 25 10
415 35ore purple 30 25
416 60ore blue 30 20

1959. Danish Ballet and Music Festival, 1959.
417 **106** 35ore purple 20 10
See also Nos. 445 and 467.

107

109 Sowing Machine

1959. Centenary of Red Cross.
418 **107** 30ore+5ore red 30 30
419 60ore+5ore red & blue . . 55 55

1960. World Refugee Year. Surch 30 **Verdensflygtninge-aret 1959-60** and uprooted tree.
420 **80** 30ore on 15ore violet . . . 20 10

1960. 1st Danish Food Fair.
421 **109** 12ore green 20 10
422 – 30ore red 25 15
423 – 60ore blue 50 25
DESIGNS: 30ore Combine-harvester; 60ore Plough.

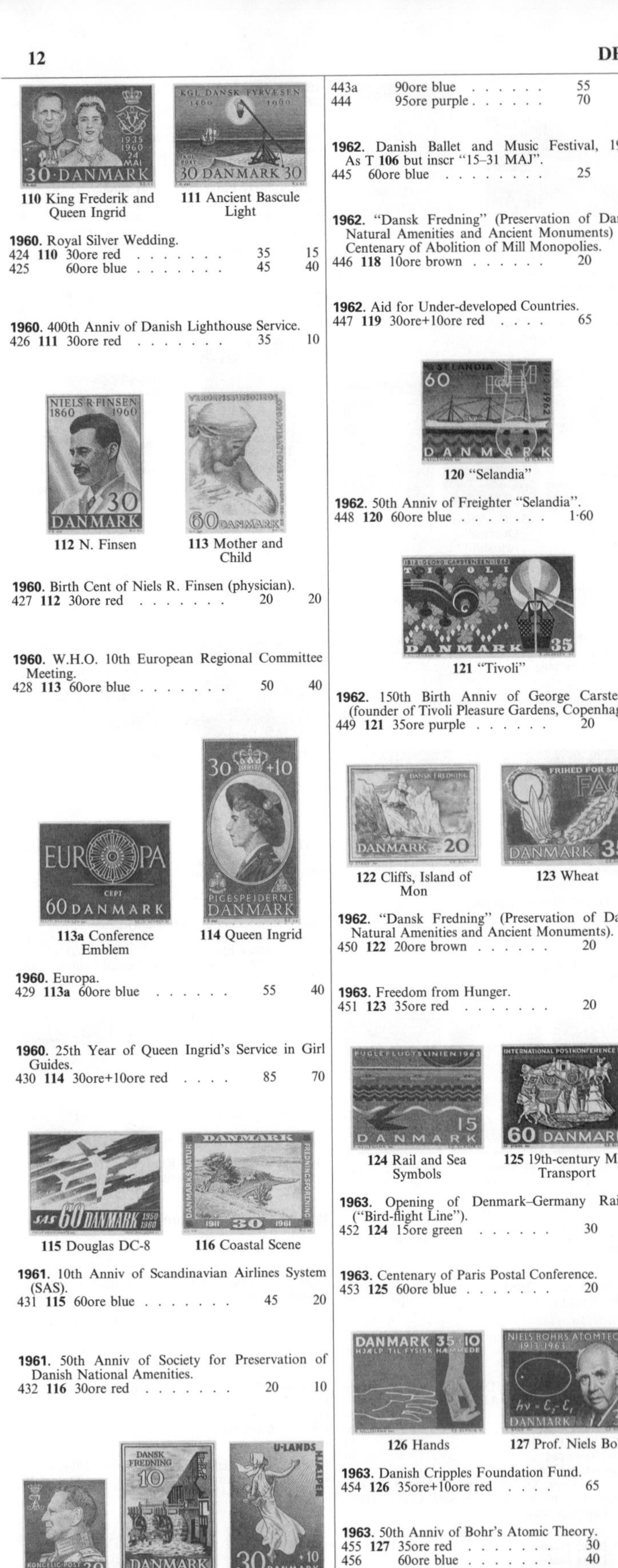

110 King Frederik and Queen Ingrid **111** Ancient Bascule Light

1960. Royal Silver Wedding.
424 **110** 30ore red 35 15
425 60ore blue 45 40

1960. 400th Anniv of Danish Lighthouse Service.
426 **111** 30ore red 35 10

112 N. Finsen **113** Mother and Child

1960. Birth Cent of Niels R. Finsen (physician).
427 **112** 30ore red 20 20

1960. W.H.O. 10th European Regional Committee Meeting.
428 **113** 60ore blue 50 40

113a Conference Emblem **114** Queen Ingrid

1960. Europa.
429 **113a** 60ore blue 55 40

1960. 25th Year of Queen Ingrid's Service in Girl Guides.
430 **114** 30ore+10ore red 85 70

115 Douglas DC-8 **116** Coastal Scene

1961. 10th Anniv of Scandinavian Airlines System (SAS).
431 **115** 60ore blue 45 20

1961. 50th Anniv of Society for Preservation of Danish National Amenities.
432 **116** 30ore red 20 10

117 King Frederik IX **118** Borkop Watermill **119** African Mother and Child

1961.
433 **117** 20ore brown 20 10
434 25ore brown 20 10
435 30ore red 20 10
436 35ore green 50 40
437 35ore red 20 10
438 40ore grey 65 10
438a 40ore brown 20 10
439 50ore turquoise 35 10
439a 50ore red 35 10
439b 50ore brown 35 10
440 60ore blue 45 10
440a 60ore red 50 15
441 70ore green 70 20
442 80ore orange 90 10
442a 80ore blue 95 10
442b 80ore green 45 10
443 90ore olive . . . . . . 2·50 35
443a 90ore blue 55 15
444 95ore purple 70 40

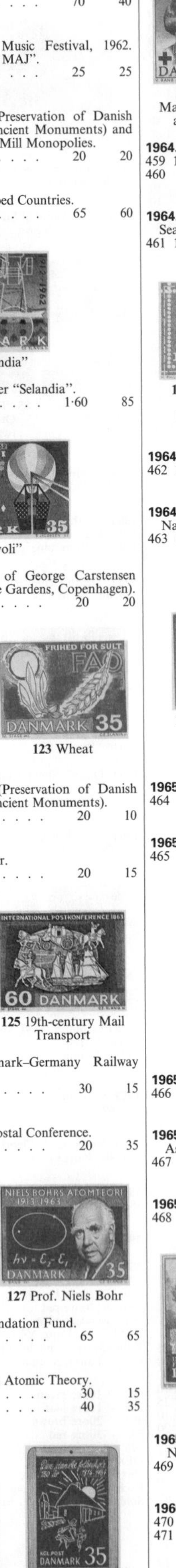

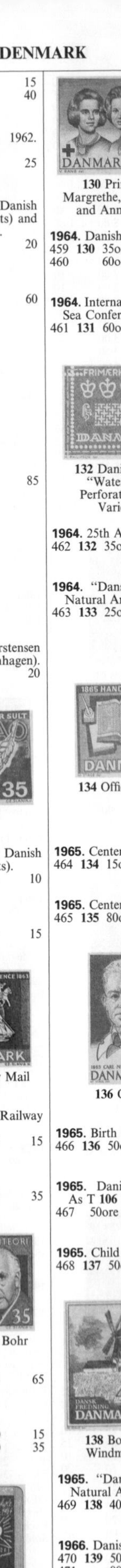

1962. Danish Ballet and Music Festival, 1962. As T **106** but inscr "15–31 MAJ".
445 60ore blue 25 25

1962. "Dansk Fredning" (Preservation of Danish Natural Amenities and Ancient Monuments) and Centenary of Abolition of Mill Monopolies.
446 **118** 10ore brown 20 20

1962. Aid for Under-developed Countries.
447 **119** 30ore+10ore red 65 60

120 "Selandia"

1962. 50th Anniv of Freighter "Selandia".
448 **120** 60ore blue . . . . 1·60 85

121 "Tivoli"

1962. 150th Birth Anniv of George Carstensen (founder of Tivoli Pleasure Gardens, Copenhagen).
449 **121** 35ore purple 20 20

122 Cliffs, Island of Mon **123** Wheat

1962. "Dansk Fredning" (Preservation of Danish Natural Amenities and Ancient Monuments).
450 **122** 20ore brown 20 10

1963. Freedom from Hunger.
451 **123** 35ore red 20 15

124 Rail and Sea Symbols **125** 19th-century Mail Transport

1963. Opening of Denmark–Germany Railway ("Bird-flight Line").
452 **124** 15ore green 30 15

1963. Centenary of Paris Postal Conference.
453 **125** 60ore blue 20 35

126 Hands **127** Prof. Niels Bohr

1963. Danish Cripples Foundation Fund.
454 **126** 35ore+10ore red 65 65

1963. 50th Anniv of Bohr's Atomic Theory.
455 **127** 35ore red 30 15
456 60ore blue 40 35

128 Ancient Bridge, Immervad **129** "Going to School" (child's slate)

1964. Danish Border Union Fund.
457 **128** 35ore+10ore red 45 50

1964. 150th Anniv of Institution of Primary Schools.
458 **129** 35ore brown 20 10

130 Princesses Margrethe, Benedikte and Anne-Marie **131** "Exploration of the Sea"

1964. Danish Red Cross Fund.
459 **130** 35ore+10ore red 40 40
460 60ore+10ore blue & red 60 60

1964. International Council for the Exploration of the Sea Conference, Copenhagen.
461 **131** 60ore blue 25 20

132 Danish Stamp "Watermarks, Perforations and Varieties" **133** Landscape, R. Karup

1964. 25th Anniv of Stamp Day.
462 **132** 35ore pink 20 10

1964. "Dansk Fredning" (Preservation of Danish Natural Amenities and Ancient Monuments).
463 **133** 25ore brown 20 20

134 Office Equipment **135** Morse Key, Teleprinter Tape and I.T.U. Emblem

1965. Centenary of 1st Commercial School.
464 **134** 15ore green 20 20

1965. Centenary of I.T.U.
465 **135** 80ore blue 40 15

136 C. Nielsen **137** Child in Meadow

1965. Birth Centenary of Carl Nielsen (composer).
466 **136** 50ore red 20 15

1965. Danish Ballet and Music Festival, 1965. As T **106** but inscr "15-31 MAJ".
467 50ore red 20 10

1965. Child Welfare.
468 **137** 50ore+10ore red 45 40

138 Bogo Windmill **139** Titles of International Red Cross Organizations

1965. "Dansk Fredning" (Preservation of Danish Natural Amenities and Ancient Monuments).
469 **138** 40ore brown 20 10

1966. Danish Red Cross Fund.
470 **139** 50ore+10ore red 40 40
471 80ore+10ore bl & red . . 55 60

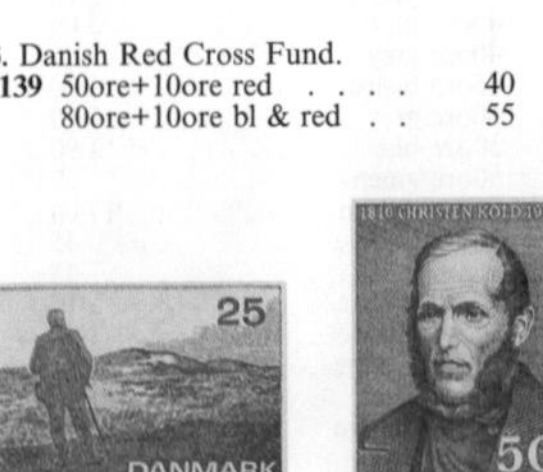

140 Heathland **141** C. Kold

1966. Centenary of Danish Heath Society.
472 **140** 25ore green 20 20

1966. 150th Birth Anniv of Christen Kold (educationist).
473 **141** 50ore red 20 10

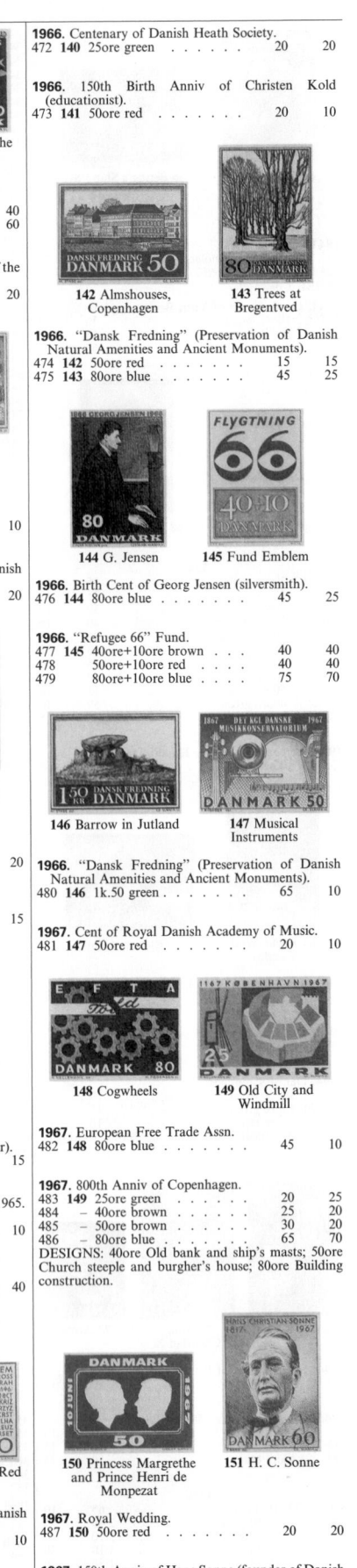

142 Almshouses, Copenhagen **143** Trees at Bregentved

1966. "Dansk Fredning" (Preservation of Danish Natural Amenities and Ancient Monuments).
474 **142** 50ore red 15 15
475 **143** 80ore blue 45 25

144 G. Jensen **145** Fund Emblem

1966. Birth Cent of Georg Jensen (silversmith).
476 **144** 80ore blue 45 25

1966. "Refugee 66" Fund.
477 **145** 40ore+10ore brown . . . 40 40
478 50ore+10ore red 40 40
479 80ore+10ore blue 75 70

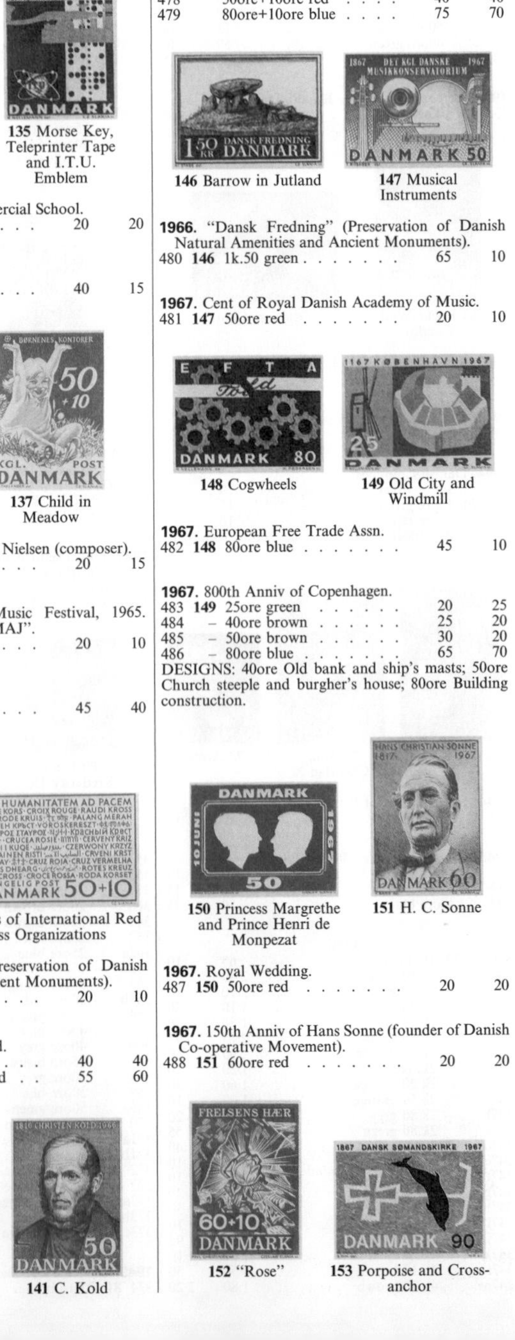

146 Barrow in Jutland **147** Musical Instruments

1966. "Dansk Fredning" (Preservation of Danish Natural Amenities and Ancient Monuments).
480 **146** 1k.50 green 65 10

1967. Cent of Royal Danish Academy of Music.
481 **147** 50ore red 20 10

148 Cogwheels **149** Old City and Windmill

1967. European Free Trade Assn.
482 **148** 80ore blue 45 10

1967. 800th Anniv of Copenhagen.
483 **149** 25ore green 20 25
484 – 40ore brown 25 20
485 – 50ore brown 30 20
486 – 80ore blue 65 70

DESIGNS: 40ore Old bank and ship's masts; 50ore Church steeple and burgher's house; 80ore Building construction.

150 Princess Margrethe and Prince Henri de Monpezat **151** H. C. Sonne

1967. Royal Wedding.
487 **150** 50ore red 20 20

1967. 150th Anniv of Hans Sonne (founder of Danish Co-operative Movement).
488 **151** 60ore red 20 20

152 "Rose" **153** Porpoise and Cross-anchor

1967. The Salvation Army.
489 **152** 60ore+10ore red 45 40

1967. Centenary of Danish Seamen's Church in Foreign Ports.
490 **153** 90ore blue 45 25

154 Esbjerg Harbour **155** Koldinghus Castle

1968. Cent of Esbjerg Harbour Construction Act.
491 **154** 30ore green 20 10

1968. 700th Anniv of Koldinghus Castle.
492 **155** 60ore red 20 10

156 "The Children in the Round Tower" (Greenlandic legend) **157** Shipbuilding

1968. Greenlandic Child Welfare.
493 **156** 60ore+10ore red 45 50

1968. Danish Industries.
494 **157** 30ore green 20 15
495 – 50ore brown 20 15
496 – 60ore red 20 15
497 – 90ore blue 80 80
INDUSTRIES: 50ore Chemicals, 60ore Electric power, 90ore Engineering.

158 "The Sower" **159** Viking Ships (from old Swedish coin)

1969. Bicentenary of Danish Royal Agricultural Society.
498 **158** 30ore green 20 10

1969. 50th Anniv of Northern Countries' Union.
499 **159** 60ore red 45 10
500 90ore blue . . . . 85 1·00

160 King Frederik IX **161** Colonnade

1969. King Frederik's 70th Birthday.
501 **160** 50ore brown 25 25
502 60ore red 25 25

1969. Europa.
503 **161** 90ore blue 70 50

162 Kronborg Castle **163** Fall of Danish Flag

1969. 50th Anniv of "Danes Living Abroad" Association.
504 **162** 50ore brown 20 10

1969. 750th Anniv of "Danish Flag Falling from Heaven".
505 **163** 60ore red, blue & black 20 15

164 M. A. Nexo **165** Niels Stensen (geologist)

1969. Birth Cent of Martin Andersen Nexo (poet).
506 **164** 80ore green 45 10

1969. 300th Anniv of Stensen's "On Solid Bodies".
507 **165** 1k. sepia 45 10

166 "Abstract" **167** Symbolic "P"

1969. "Non-figurative" stamp.
508 **166** 60ore red, rose and blue 20 10

1969. Birth Cent of Valdemar Poulsen (inventor).
509 **167** 30ore green 20 10

168 Princess Margrethe, Prince Henri and Prince Frederik (baby) **169** "Postgiro"

1969. Danish Red Cross.
510 **168** 50ore+10ore brn & red 45 40
511 60ore+10ore brn & red 45 40

1970. 50th Anniv of Danish Postal Giro Service.
512 **169** 60ore and orange 20 10

170 School Safety Patrol **171** Child appealing for Help

1970. Road Safety.
513 **170** 50ore brown 20 10

1970. 25th Anniv of Save the Children Fund.
514 **171** 60ore+10ore red 45 50

172 Candle in Window **173** Red Deer in Park

1970. 25th Anniv of Liberation.
515 **172** 50ore black, yellow & bl 30 10

1970. 300th Anniv of Jaegersborg Deer Park.
516 **173** 60ore brown, red & grn 20 10

174 Ship's Figurehead ("Elephanten") **175** "The Reunion"

1970. 300th Anniv of "Royal Majesty's Model Chamber" (Danish Naval Museum).
517 **174** 30ore multicoloured . . . 20 10

1970. 50th Anniv of North Schleswig's Reunion with Denmark.
518 **175** 60ore violet, yellow & grn 20 10

176 Electromagnetic Apparatus

1970. 150th Anniv of Oersted's Discovery of Electromagnetism.
519 **176** 80ore green 45 10

177 Bronze-age Ship (from engraving on razor)

1970. Danish Shipping.
520 **177** 30ore purple and brown 25 10
521 – 50ore brn and purple . . 25 10
522 – 60ore brown and green 35 10
523 – 90ore blue and green . . 65 55
DESIGNS: 50ore Viking shipbuilders (Bayeux Tapestry); 60ore "Emanuel" (schooner); 90ore "A. P. Moller" (tanker).

178 Strands of Rope **179** B. Thorvaldsen from self-portrait

1970. 25th Anniv of United Nations.
524 **178** 90ore red, green & blue 65 60

1970. Birth Bicentenary of Bertel Thorvaldsen (sculptor).
525 **179** 2k. blue 65 40

180 Mathilde Fibiger (suffragette) **181** Refugees

1971. Centenary of Danish Women's Association ("Kvindesamfund").
526 **180** 80ore green 45 10

1971. Aid for Refugees.
527 **181** 50ore brown 40 20
528 60ore red 40 20

182 Danish Child **183** Hans Egede

1971. National Children's Welfare Association.
529 **182** 60ore+10ore red 45 50

1971. 25th Anniv of Hans Egede's Arrival in Greenland.
530 **183** 1k. brown 45 15

184 Swimming **185** Georg Brandes

1971. Sports.
531 **184** 30ore green and blue . . 25 25
532 – 50ore dp brown & brown 25 15
533 – 60ore yellow, blue & grey 45 15
534 – 90ore violet, green & bl 75 65
DESIGNS: 50ore Hurdling; 60ore Football; 90ore Yachting.

1971. Centenary of First Lectures by Georg Brandes (writer).
535 **185** 90ore blue 45 30

186 Beet Harvester

1972. Centenary of Danish Sugar Production.
536 **186** 80ore green 45 25

187 Meteorological Symbols

1972. Cent of Danish Meteorological Office.
537 **187** 1k.20 brown, blue & pur 60 40

188 King Frederik IX **189** "N. F. S. Grundtvig" (pencil sketch, P. Skovgaard)

1972. King Frederik IX-In Memoriam.
538 **188** 60ore red 20 10

1972. Death Centenary of N. F. S. Grundtvig (poet and clergyman).
539 **189** 1k. brown 45 25

190 Locomotive "Odin", Ship and Passengers **191** Rebild Hills

1972. 125th Anniv of Danish State Railways.
540 **190** 70ore red 35 10

1972. Nature Protection.
541 **191** 1k. green, brown & blue 45 15

192 Marsh Marigold **193** "The Tinker" (from Holberg's satire)

1972. Centenary of "Vanforehjemmet" (Home for the Disabled).
542 **192** 70ore+10ore yellow & bl 55 45

1972. 250th Anniv of Theatre in Denmark and of Holberg's Comedies.
543 **193** 70ore red 20 10

194 W.H.O. Building, Copenhagen **195** Little Belt Bridge

1972. Inauguration of World Health Organization Building, Copenhagen.
544 **194** 2k. black, blue and red 65 45

1972. Danish Construction Projects.
545 **195** 40ore green 20 20
546 – 60ore brown 30 20
547 – 70ore red 30 15
548 – 90ore green 45 35
DESIGNS: 60ore Hanstholm port; 70ore Limfjord Tunnel; 90ore Knudshoved port.

196 House, Aeroskobing **197** Johannes Jensen

1972. Danish Architecture.
549 **196** 40ore black, brown & red . . . 20 15
550 – 60ore blue, green & brn . . . 20 15
551 – 70ore brown, red & verm . . . 25 15
552 – 1k.20 grn, brn & dp brn . . . 85 65
DESIGNS—28 × 21 mm: 60ore Farmhouse, East Bornholm; 37 × 21 mm: 1k.20, Farmhouse, Hvide Sande; 21 × 37 mm: 70ore House, Christanshavn.

1973. Birth Cent of Johannes Jensen (writer).
553 **197** 90ore green 45 10

198 Cogwheels and Guardrails **199** P. C. Abildgaard (founder)

1973. Centenary of 1st Danish Factory Act.
554 **198** 50ore brown 20 10

1973. Bicentenary of Royal Veterinary College, Christianshavn.
555 **199** 1k. blue 45 30

200 "Rhododendron impeditum" **201** Nordic House, Reykjavik

1973. Cent of Jutland Horticultural Society.
556 **200** 60ore violet, green & brn . . . 40 20
557 – 70ore pink, green & red . . . 40 20
DESIGN: 70ore "Queen of Denmark" rose.

1973. Nordic Countries' Postal Co-operation.
558 **201** 70ore multicoloured . . . 25 15
559 1k. multicoloured 85 70

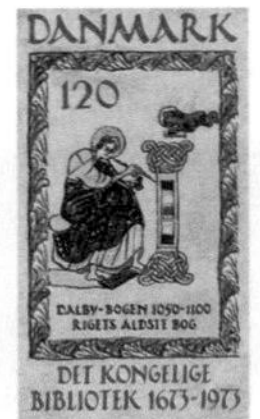

202 Stella Nova and Sextant **203** "St. Mark the Evangelist" (Book of Dalby)

1973. 400th Anniv of Tycho Brahe's "De Nove Stella" (book on astronomy).
560 **202** 2k. blue 65 25

1973. 300th Anniv of Royal Library.
561 **203** 1k.20 multicoloured . . . 45 45

204 Heimaey Eruption **205** "Devil and Scandalmongers" (Fanefjord Church)

1973. Aid for Victims of Heimaey Eruption, Iceland.
562 **204** 70ore+20ore red and blue 60 45

1973. Church Frescoes. Each red, turquoise and yellow on cream.
563 70ore Type **205** . . . . . . 1·00 30
564 70ore "Queen Esther and King Xerxes" (Tirsted Church) . . . . 1·00 30
565 70ore "The Harvest Miracle" (Jetsmark Church) . . . . 1·00 30
566 70ore "The Crowning with Thorns" (Biersted Church) 1·00 30
567 70ore "Creation of Eve" (Fanefjord Church) . . . . 1·00 30

206 Drop of Blood and Donors **207** Queen Margrethe

1974. Blood Donors Campaign.
568 **206** 90ore red and violet . . . 35 10

1974.
569 **207** 60ore brown 30 30
570 60ore orange 30 25
571 70ore red 20 10
572 70ore brown 20 20
573 80ore green 45 25
574 80ore brown 30 15
575 90ore purple 45 10
576 90ore red 45 15
577 90ore olive 45 20
577a 90ore grey . . . . . 1·30 35
578 100ore blue 45 20
579 100ore grey 45 15
580 100ore red 45 20
580a 100ore brown 40 10
580b 110ore orange 55 30
580c 110ore brown 45 25
581 120ore grey 45 30
581b 120ore red 45 15
582 130ore blue 90 65
582a 130ore red 45 10
582b 130ore brown 45 30
582c 140ore orange . . . . . 1·00 1·10
582d 150ore blue 60 50
582e 150ore red 60 40
582f 160ore blue 80 55
582g 160ore red 55 15
582h 180ore green 55 20
582i 180ore blue 80 60
582j 200ore blue 70 60
582k 210ore grey . . . . . 1·10 95
582l 230ore green 80 30
582m 250ore green 85 45

208 Theatre Facade **209** Hverringe

1974. Centenary of Tivoli Pantomime Theatre, Copenhagen.
583 **208** 100ore blue 45 15

1974. Provincial Series.
584 **209** 50ore multicoloured . . . 35 30
585 – 60ore grn, dp grn & mve . . . 50 40
586 – 70ore multicoloured . . . 45 45
587 – 90ore multicoloured . . . 35 15
588 – 120ore grn, red & orge . . . 45 45
DESIGNS—HORIZ: 60ore Carl Nielsen's birthplace, Norre Lyndelse; 70ore Hans Christian Andersen's birthplace, Odense; 1k.20, Hindsholm. VERT: 90ore Hessselagergaard.

210 Orienteering **211** "Iris spuria"

1974. World Orienteering Championships.
589 **210** 70ore brown and blue . . 55 40
590 – 80ore blue and brown . . 25 15
DESIGN: 80ore Compass.

1974. Cent of Botanical Gardens, Copenhagen.
591 **211** 90ore blue, green & brn 30 15
592 – 120ore red, green and blue 50 40
DESIGN: 120ore "Dactylorhiza purpurella" (orchid).

212 Mail-carriers of 1624 and 1780 **213** Pigeon with Letter

1974. 350th Anniv of Danish Post Office.
593 **212** 70ore bistre and purple . . 35 30
594 – 90ore green and purple . . 45 10
DESIGN: 90ore Johan Colding's postal balloon (1808) H.M.S. "Edgar" and H.M.S. "Dictator".

1974. Centenary of U.P.U.
595 **213** 120ore blue 45 15

214 Stamp Essay (Arms)

1975. "Hafnia 76" Stamp Exhibition (1st issue). Sheet 67 × 93 mm containing T **214** and similar vert designs.
MS596 70ore grey and green; 80ore grey and green; 90ore brown and green; 100ore brown and green (sold at 5k.) . . . . 6·75 6·75
DESIGNS: 80ore King Frederik VII; 90ore King Frederik VII (different); 100ore Mercury.
See also Nos. **MS**617 and 629/**MS**630.

215 Radio Equipment of 1925 **216** Queen Margrethe and I.W.Y. Emblem

1975. 50th Anniv of Danish Broadcasting.
597 **215** 90ore pink 45 15

1975. International Women's Year.
598 **216** 90ore+20ore red 55 50

217 Floral Decorated Plate **218** Moravian Brethren Church Christiansfeld

1975. Danish Porcelain.
599 **217** 50ore green 20 10
600 – 90ore red 40 10
601 – 130ore blue 70 85
DESIGNS: 90ore Floral decorated tureen; 130ore Floral decorated vase and tea-caddy.

1975. European Architectural Heritage Year.
602 **218** 70ore brown 40 35
603 – 120ore green 45 35
604 – 150ore blue 35 25
DESIGNS—HORIZ: 120ore Farmhouse, Lejre. VERT: 150ore Anna Queenstraede (street), Helsingore.

219 "Numskull Jack" (V. Pedersen) **220** Watchman's Square, Aabenraa

1975. 170th Birth Anniv of Hans Christian Andersen.
605 **219** 70ore grey and brown . . 50 45
606 – 90ore brown and red . . 60 10
607 – 130ore brown and blue 1·00 75
DESIGNS: 90ore Hans Andersen (from photograph by G. E. Hansen); 130ore "The Marshking's Daughter" (L. Frolich).

1975. Provincial series. South Jutland.
608 **220** 70ore multicoloured . . . 40 30
609 – 90ore brown, red & blue 40 15
610 – 100ore multicoloured . . 45 30
611 – 120ore blue, black & grn 60 30
DESIGNS—VERT: 90ore, Haderslev Cathedral. HORIZ: 100ore, Mogeltonder Polder; 120ore, Estuary of Vidaaen at Hojer floodgates.

221 River Kingfisher

1975. Danish Endangered Animals.
612 **221** 50ore blue 50 30
613 – 70ore brown 40 30
614 – 90ore brown 40 10
615 – 130ore blue . . . . . . 1·10 75
616 – 200ore black 55 10
DESIGNS: 70ore West European hedgehog; 90ore Cats; 130ore Pied avocets; 200ore European otter.

The 90ore also commemorates the centenary of the Danish Society for the Prevention of Cruelty to Animals.

1975. "Hafnia 76" Stamp Exhibition (2nd issue). Sheet 69 × 93 mm containing vert designs similar to T **214** showing early Danish stamps.
MS617 50ore brown and buff; 70ore blue, brown and buff; 90ore blue, brown and buff; 130ore brown, olive and buff (sold at 5k.) . . 2·75 2·75
DESIGNS: 50ore 1851 4 R.B.S. stamp; 70ore 1851 2 R.B.S. stamp; 90ore 1864 2sk. stamp; 130ore 1870 8sk. stamp with inverted frame.

222 Viking Longship

1976. Bicentenary of American Revolution.
618 **222** 70ore+20ore brown . . . 55 50
619 – 90ore+20ore red 55 50
620 – 100ore+20ore green . . . 55 50
621 – 130ore+20ore blue . . . 55 50
DESIGNS: 90ore Freighter "Thingvalla"; 100ore Liner "Frederik VIII"; 130ore Cadet full-rigged ship "Danmark".

223 "Humanity" **224** Old Copenhagen

1976. Centenary of Danish Red Cross.
622 **223** 100ore+20ore black and red 30 25
623 130ore+20ore black, red and blue 50 30

1976. Provincial Series. Copenhagen.
624 **224** 60ore multicoloured . . . 25 35
625 – 80ore multicoloured . . . 25 25
626 – 100ore red & vermilion 40 10
627 – 130ore grn, dp brn & brn 95 1·00
DESIGNS—VERT: 80ore View from the Round Tower; 100ore Interior of the Central Railway Station. HORIZ: 130ore Harbour buildings.

225 Handicapped Person in Wheelchair **226** Mail Coach Driver (detail from "A String of Horses outside an Inn" (O. Bache))

1976. Danish Foundation for the Disabled.
628 **225** 100ore+20ore black and red 45 40

1976. "Hafnia 76" Stamp Exhibition.
629 **226** 130ore multicoloured . . 60 65
MS630 103 × 82 mm. **226** 130ore multicoloured . . . . 8·75 8·75

227 Prof. Emil Hansen **228** Moulding Glass

1976. Centenary of Carlsberg Foundation.
631 **227** 100ore red 40 15

1976. Danish Glass Industry.
632 **228** 60ore green 30 25
633 – 80ore brown 35 15
634 – 130ore blue 70 65
635 – 150ore red 45 15
DESIGNS: 80ore Removing glass from pipe; 130ore Cutting glass; 150ore Blowing glass.

229 Five Water Lilies 230 "Give Way"

1977. Northern Countries Co-operation in Nature Conservation and Environment Protection.
636 **229** 100ore multicoloured . . 30 20
637 130ore multicoloured . . 75 80

1977. Road Safety.
638 **230** 100ore brown 55 10

231 Mother and Child 232 Allinge

1977. 25th Anniv of Danish Society for the Mentally Handicapped.
639 **231** 100ore+20ore green, blue and brown 50 50

1977. Europa.
640 **232** 1k. brown 45 15
641 – 1k.30 blue . . . . 2·50 1·90
DESIGN: 1k.30, Farm near Ringsted.

233 Kongeaen 234 Hammers and Horseshoes

1977. Provincial Series. South Jutland.
642 **233** 60ore green and blue . . 1·10 75
643 – 90ore multicoloured . . . 60 40
644 – 150ore multicoloured . . 60 40
645 – 200ore grn, pur & emer 60 25
DESIGNS: 90ore Skallingen; 150ore Torskind; 200ore Jelling.

1977. Danish Crafts.
646 **234** 80ore brown 40 15
647 – 1k. red 40 15
648 – 1k.30 blue 85 40
DESIGNS: 1k. Chisel, square and plane; 1k.30, Trowel, ceiling brush and folding rule.

235 Globe Flower 236 Handball Player and Emblem

1977. Endangered Flora.
649 **235** 1k. green, yellow & brn 35 15
650 – 1k.50 green, ol & brn . . 90 50
DESIGN: 1k.50, "Cnidium dubium".

1978. Men's Handball World Championship.
651 **236** 1k.20 red 50 15

237 Christian IV on Horseback 238 Jens Bang's House, Aalborg

1978. Centenary of National History Museum, Frederiksborg.
652 **237** 1k.20 brown 55 15
653 – 1k.80 black 70 25
DESIGN: 1k.80, North-west aspect of Frederiksborg Castle.

1978. Europa.
654 **238** 1k.20 brown 35 15
655 – 1k.50 blue and dp blue 1·00 65
DESIGN: 1k.50, Plan and front elevation of Frederiksborg Castle, Copenhagen.

239 Kongenshus Memorial Park 240 Boats in Harbour

1978. Provincial Series. Central Jutland.
656 **239** 70ore multicoloured . . . 55 25
657 – 1k.20 multicoloured . . . 65 15
658 – 1k.50 multicoloured . . . 1·30 65
659 – 1k.80 blue, brn & grn . . 85 40
DESIGNS: 1k.20, Post office, Aarhus Old Town; 1k.50, Lignite fields, Soby; 1k.80, Church wall, Stadil Church.

1978. Fishing Industry.
660 **240** 70ore green 60 25
661 – 1k. brown 60 15
662 – 1k.80 black 90 25
663 – 2k.50 brown . . . . . . 1·30 25
DESIGNS: 1k. Eel traps; 1k.80, Fishing boats on the slipway; 2k.50, Drying ground.

241 Campaign Emblem

1978. 50th Anniv of Danish Cancer Campaign.
664 **241** 120ore+20ore red 80 50

242 Common Morel 243 Early and Modern Telephones

1978. Mushrooms.
665 **242** 1k. brown 80 40
666 – 1k.20 red 80 15
DESIGN: 1k.20, Satan's mushroom.

1979. Centenary of Danish Telephone System.
667 **243** 1k.20 red 80 15

244 Child 245 University Seal

1979. International Year of the Child.
668 **244** 1k.20+20ore red & brn . . 50 50

1979. 500th Anniv of Copenhagen University.
669 **245** 1k.30 red 40 15
670 – 1k.60 black 60 40
DESIGN: 1k.60, Pentagram representing the five faculties.

246 Letter Mail Cariole 247 Pendant

1979. Europa.
671 **246** 1k.30 red 90 15
672 – 1k.60 blue . . . . 1·20 65
DESIGN: 1k.60, Morse key and sounder.

1979. Viking "Gripping Beast" Decorations.
673 **247** 1k.10 brown 35 15
674 – 2k. green 90 25
DESIGN: 2k. Key.

248 Mols Bjerge 249 Silhouette of Oehlenschlager

1979. Provincial Series. North Jutland.
675 **248** 80ore green, ultram & brown 55 25
676 – 90ore multicoloured . . . 1·60 1·00
677 – 200ore grn, orge & red . . 90 15
678 – 280ore slate, sepia & brn 1·10 65
DESIGNS. 90ore Orslev Kloster; 200ore Trans; 280ore Bovbjerg.

1979. Birth Bicentenary of Adam Oehlenschlager (poet).
679 **249** 1k.30 red 50 15

250 Music, Violin and Dancers (birth cent of Jacob Gade (composer)) 251 Royal Mail Guards' Office, Copenhagen (drawing, Peter Klaestrup)

1979. Anniversaries.
680 **250** 1k.10 brown 40 25
681 – 1k.60 blue 65 40
DESIGN: 1k.60, Dancer at bar (death centenary of August Bournonville (ballet master)).

1980. Bicentenary of National Postal Service.
682 **251** 1k.30 red 50 15

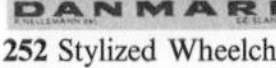

252 Stylized Wheelchair 253 Karen Blixen (writer)

1980. 25th Anniv of Foundation for the Disabled.
683 **252** 130ore+20ore red 80 40

1980. Europa.
684 **253** 1k.30 red 45 15
685 – 1k.60 blue 85 40
DESIGN: 1k.60, August Krogh (physiologist).

254 Symbols of Employment, Health and Education 255 Lindholme Hoje

1980. U.N. Decade for Women World Conference.
686 **254** 1k.60 blue 80 25

1980. Provincial Series. Jutland North of Limfjorden. Multicoloured.
687 80ore Type **255** 45 25
688 110ore Skagen lighthouse (vert) 70 25
689 200ore Borglum 80 15
690 280ore Fishing boats at Vorupor . . . . 1·60 75

256 Silver Pitcher, c. 1641

1980. Nordic Countries Postal Co-operation.
691 **256** 1k.30 black and red . . . 50 15
692 – 1k.80 blue & dp blue . . 1·20 65
DESIGN: 1k.80, Bishop's bowl.

257 Earliest Danish Coin, Hedeby (c. 800)

1980. Coins from the Royal Collection.
693 **257** 1k.30 red and brown . . 55 25
694 – 1k.40 olive and green . . 1·00 65
695 – 1k.80 blue and grey . . . 1·00 65
DESIGNS: 1k.40, Silver coin of Valdemar the Great and Bishop Absalon (1152–82); 1k.80, Christian VII gold current ducat (1781).

258 Lace Pattern 259 Children Playing in Yard

1980. Lace Patterns. Various designs showing lace.
696 **258** 1k.10 brown 55 25
697 – 1k.30 red 55 15
698 – 2k. green 80 15

1981. National Children's Welfare Association.
699 **259** 1k.60+20ore red 80 50

260 Original Houses, 1631 261 Tilting at a Barrel (Shrovetide custom)

1981. 350th Anniv of Nyboder (Naval Barracks), Copenhagen.
700 **260** 1k.30 red and yellow . . 70 50
701 – 1k.60 red and yellow . . 55 15
DESIGN: 1k.60, 18th-century terraced houses.

1981. Europa.
702 **261** 1k.60 red 70 25
703 – 2k. blue . . . . 1·10 25
DESIGN: 2k. Midsummer bonfire.

262 Soro 263 Rigensgade District, Copenhagen

1981. Provincial Series. Zealand and Surrounding Islands.
704 **262** 100ore blue and brown 45 25
705 – 150ore black and green 60 40
706 – 160ore brown and green 60 15
707 – 200ore multicoloured . . 80 40
708 – 230ore blue and brown 90 40
DESIGNS: 150ore N. F. S. Grundtvig's childhood home, Udby; 160ore Kaj Munk's childhood home, Opager; 200ore Gronsund; 230ore Bornholm.

1981. European Urban Renaissance Year.
709 **263** 1k.60 red 50 15

264 Decaying Tree 265 Ellehammer at Lindholm, 1906

1981. International Year for Disabled Persons.
710 **264** 2k.+20ore blue . . . . . 1·00 70

1981. History of Aviation.
711 **265** 1k. green and black . . . 55 40
712 – 1k.30 brown & dp brn . . 80 40
713 – 1k.60 vermilion & red . . 55 15
714 – 2k.30 blue & dp blue . . 80 40
DESIGNS: 1k.30, A. T. Botved's Fokker biplane "R-1" (Copenhagen–Tokyo, 1926); 1k.60, Hojriis Hillig's Bellanca Special "Liberty" (U.S.A.–Denmark, 1931); 2k.30. Douglas DC-7C "Seven Seas" (first Polar flight, 1957).

266 Queen Margrethe II 267 Revenue Cutter "Argus"

1982.
715 **266** 1k.60 red 50 15
716 1k.60 green . . . . . . 2·50 1·90
717 1k.80 brown 80 40
718 2k. red 80 15
719 2k.20 green . . . . . . 2·10 65
720 2k.30 violet 80 65
721 2k.50 red 80 15
722 2k.70 blue . . . . 1·00 40
723 2k.70 red . . . . 1·00 15
724 2k.80 red . . . . 1·00 20
725 3k. violet . . . . 1·00 25
726 3k. red . . . . 1·00 15
727 3k.20 violet . . . . . . 1·00 40
727a 3k.20 red . . . . 1·20 15
728 3k.30 black . . . . . . 1·20 50
729 3k.40 green . . . . . . 2·30 1·60
730 3k.50 blue . . . . 1·20 25
730a 3k.50 purple . . . . . . 1·20 40
730b 3k.50 red . . . . 1·20 15
731 3k.70 blue . . . . 1·20 40
732 3k.75 green . . . . . . 1·60 65
733 3k.80 blue . . . . 1·20 40
734 3k.80 purple . . . . . . 1·60 1·30
735 4k.10 blue . . . . 1·60 25
736 4k.20 violet . . . . . . 2·30 90
737 4k.40 blue . . . . 1·60 40

738 4k.50 purple . . . . . . 1·80 1·30
739 4k.75 blue . . . . . . 1·80 25

1982. 350th Anniv Customs Service.
740 **267** 1k.60 red 50 15

268 Skater

269 Villein (Abolition of adscription, 1788)

1982. World Figure Skating Championships, Copenhagen.
741 **268** 2k. blue 80 25

1982. Europa.
742 **269** 2k. brown . . . . 1·00 15
743 – 2k.70 blue . . . . 1·40 65
DESIGN: 2k.70, Procession of women (Enfranchisement of women, 1915).

270 Distorted Plant

271 Dairy Farm at Hjedding and Butter Churn

1982. 25th Anniv of Danish Multiple Sclerosis Society.
744 **270** 2k.+40ore red . . . . . 1·60 90

1982. Centenary of Co-operative Dairy Farming.
745 **271** 1k.80 brown 80 40

272 Hand holding Quill Pen

273 Blicher (after J. V. Gertner)

1982. 400th Anniv of Record Office.
746 **272** 2k.70 green . . . . 1·00 25

1982. Birth Bicent of Steen Steensen Blicher (poet).
747 **273** 2k. red 80 15

274 Odense Printing Press, 1482

275 Petersen and the Number Men

1982. 500th Anniv of Printing in Denmark.
748 **274** 1k.80 brown 80 40

1982. Birth Centenary of Robert Storm Petersen (cartoonist).
749 **275** 1k.50 red and blue . . . 50 25
750 – 2k. green and red 80 25
DESIGN—HORIZ: 2k. Peter and Ping with dog.

276 Library Seal

1982. 500th Anniv University Library.
751 **276** 2k.70 brown and black . . 1·00 25

277 "Interglobal Communications"

278 Nurse tending Patient

1983. World Communications Year.
752 **277** 2k. orange, red & blue . . 1·60 25

1983. Red Cross.
753 **278** 2k.+40ore blue & red . . 1·00 90

279 Clown and Girl with Balloon

280 Lene Koppen

1983. 400th Anniv of Dyrehavsbakken Amusement Park.
754 **279** 2k. multicoloured 80 15

1983. World Badminton Championships.
755 **280** 2k.70 blue . . . . 1·00 25

281 Burin and Engraving of lore Numeral Stamp

282 Egeskov Castle

1983. 50th Anniv of Danish Recess-printed Stamps.
756 **281** 2k.50 red 80 15

1983. Nordic Countries Postal Co-operation. "Visit the North".
757 **282** 2k.50 dp brown & brn . . 70 20
758 – 3k.50 dp blue & blue . . 90 65
DESIGN: 3k.50, Troldkirken long barrow, North Jutland.

283 Kildeskovshallen Recreation Centre, Copenhagen

284 Weights and Measures

1983. Europa.
759 **283** 2k.50 red and brown . . 1·20 15
760 – 3k.50 dp blue & blue . . 1·40 40
DESIGN: 3k.50, Sallingsund Bridge.

1983. 300th Anniv of Weights and Measures Ordinance.
761 **284** 2k.50 red 80 10

285 Title Page of Law

286 Crashed Car and Hand with Eye (Police)

1983. 300th Anniv of King Christian V's Danish Law (code of laws for Norway).
762 **285** 5k. dp brown & brown 1·80 50

1983. Life-saving Services.
763 **286** 1k. brown 50 25
764 – 2k.50 red 90 25
765 – 3k.50 blue . . . . 1·60 40
DESIGNS: 2k.50 Ladder, stretcher and fire-hose (ambulance and fire services); 3k.50 Lifebelt and lifeboat (sea-rescue services).

287 Family Group

288 Grundtvig (after Constantin Hansen)

1983. The Elderly in Society.
766 **287** 2k. green 70 40
767 – 2k.50 red 90 15
DESIGN: 2k.50 Elderly people in train.

1983. Birth Bicentenary of Nicolai Frederik Severin Grundtvig (writer).
768 **288** 2k.50 brown 80 25

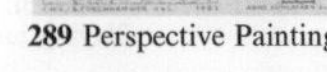
289 Perspective Painting

1983. Birth Bicentenary of Christoffer Wilhelm Eckersberg (painter).
769 **289** 2k.50 red 80 25

290 Spade and Sapling

291 Billiards

1984. Plant a Tree Campaign.
770 **290** 2k.70 yellow, red and green . . . . 1·00 25

1984. World Billiards Championships.
771 **291** 3k.70 green . . . . 1·20 25

292 Athletes

293 Compass Rose

1984. Olympic Games, Los Angeles.
772 **292** 2k.70+40ore mult . . . . 1·80 1·00

1984. Bicentenary of Hydrographic Department (2k.30) and 300th Anniv of Pilotage Service (2k.70).
773 **293** 2k.30 green 90 50
774 – 2k.70 red . . . . 1·00 15
DESIGN: 2k.70, Pilot boat.

294 Parliament Emblem

295 Girl Guides

1984. 2nd Direct Elections to European Parliament.
775 **294** 2k.70 yellow and blue . . 1·00 25

1984. Scout Movement.
776 **295** 2k.70 multicoloured . . . 1·00 15

296 Bridge

297 Anchor (memorial to Danish Sailors)

1984. Europa. 25th Anniv of European Post and Telecommunications Conference.
777 **296** 2k.70 red . . . . 1·20 15
778 3k.70 blue . . . . 1·20 90

1984. 40th Anniv of Normandy Invasion.
779 **297** 2k.70 purple . . . . . . 1·70 15

298 Prince Henrik

299 Old Danish Inn

1984. 50th Birthday of Prince Henrik.
780 **298** 2k.70 brown . . . . . . 1·00 15

1984.
781 **299** 3k. multicoloured . . . . 1·20 65

300 Shoal of Fish (research)

1984. Danish Fisheries and Shipping.
782 **300** 2k.30 blue and green . . 1·40 75
783 – 2k.70 blue and red . . . 1·00 15
784 – 3k.30 blue and violet . . 1·40 75
785 – 3k.70 blue & ultramarine 1·60 75
DESIGNS: 2k.70, Ships (sea transport); 3k.30, "Bettina" (deep sea fishing boat); 3k.70, Deck of trawler "Jonna Tornby".

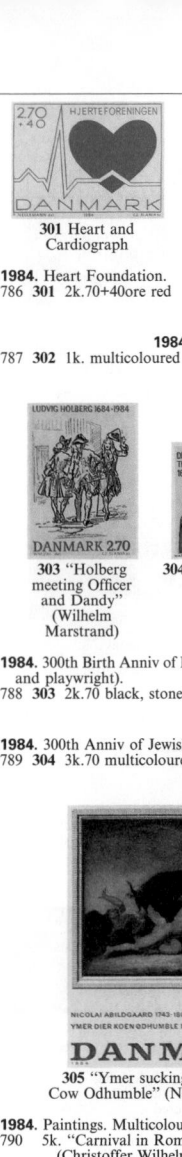

301 Heart and Cardiograph

302 Bird with Letter

1984. Heart Foundation.
786 **301** 2k.70+40ore red . . . . 1·80 1·00

1984.
787 **302** 1k. multicoloured 50 15

303 "Holberg meeting Officer and Dandy" (Wilhelm Marstrand)

304 Woman and Sabbath Candles

1984. 300th Birth Anniv of Ludvig Holberg (historian and playwright).
788 **303** 2k.70 black, stone & red 1·00 15

1984. 300th Anniv of Jewish Community.
789 **304** 3k.70 multicoloured . . . 1·20 65

305 "Ymer sucking Milk from the Cow Odhumble" (Nicolai Abildgaard)

1984. Paintings. Multicoloured.
790 5k. "Carnival in Rome" (Christoffer Wilhelm Eckersberg) (horiz) . . . . 2·50 1·80
791 10k. Type **305** . . . . . . 4·25 2·50

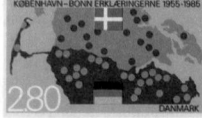

306 Gothersgade Reformed Church, Copenhagen

1985. 300th Anniv of French and German Reformed Church in Denmark.
792 **306** 2k.80 red . . . . 1·00 15

307 Flags and Border

1985. 30th Anniv of Copenhagen–Bonn Declarations.
793 **307** 2k.80 multicoloured . . . 1·20 15

308 Flag, Girl and Boy

1985. International Youth Year.
794 **308** 3k.80 multicoloured . . . 1·20 40

309 Statue on Postmen

310 Music Score

1985. "Hafnia 87" International Stamp Exhibition, Copenhagen (1st issue). Sheet 70×95 mm containing T **309** and similar vert designs, each black, ochre and red.

MS795 200ore Type **309**; 250ore 1711 mandate on disinfection of letters; 280ore 1775 decree granting postal monopoly to Danish Post Office; 380ore 1851 title page of *Law on Postal Mail* (sold at 15k.) . . . . 4·50 4·50

See also Nos. **MS**817, **MS**836 and 851/**MS**852.

1985. Europa. Music Year.

796 **310** 2k.80 yell, red & verm . . 1·10 40

797 – 3k.80 black, bl & grn . . 1·80 1·10

DESIGN: 3k.80, Music score (different).

311 Flames and Houses

312 Queen Ingrid and "Chrysanthemum frutescens" "Sofieri"

1985. 40th Anniv of Liberation.

798 **311** 2k.80+50ore mult . . . . 1·80 1·00

The surtax was for the benefit of Resistance veterans.

1985. 50th Anniv of Queen Ingrid's Arrival in Denmark.

799 **312** 2k.80 multicoloured . . . 1·00 25

313 Faro Bridges

314 St. Canute and Lund Cathedral

1985. Inauguration of Faro Bridges.

800 **313** 2k.80 multicoloured . . . 1·00 15

1985. 900th Anniv of St. Canute's Deed of Gift to Lund.

801 **314** 2k.80 black and red . . . 80 15

802 – 3k. black and red . . . . 1·70 1·00

DESIGN: 3k. St. Canute and Helsingborg.

315 Gymnastics

316 Woman Cyclist

1985. Sports. Multicoloured.

803 2k.80 Type **315** . . . . . . 1·10 15

804 3k.80 Canoeing . . . . . . 1·40 50

805 6k. Cycling . . . . 2·20 75

1985. United Nations Women's Decade.

806 **316** 3k.80 multicoloured . . . 1·20 50

317 Kronborg Castle

318 Dove and U.N. Emblem

1985. 400th Anniv of Kronborg Castle, Elsinore.

807 **317** 2k.80 multicoloured . . . 1·00 15

1985. 40th Anniv of U.N.O.

808 **318** 3k.80 multicoloured . . . 1·20 65

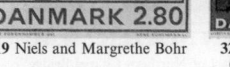

319 Niels and Margrethe Bohr

320 Tapestry (detail) by Caroline Ebbesen

1985. Birth Centenary of Niels Bohr (nuclear physicist).

809 **319** 2k.80 multicoloured . . . 1·20 90

1985. 25th Anniv of National Society for Welfare of the Mentally Ill.

810 **320** 2k.80+40ore mult . . . . 1·60 1·00

321 "D" in Sign Language

322 Stern of Boat

1985. 50th Anniv of Danish Association of the Deaf.

811 **321** 2k.80 brown & black . . 1·10 25

1985.

812 **322** 2k.80 multicoloured . . . 1·00 25

323 "Head"

1985.

813 **323** 3k.80 multicoloured . . . 2·50 1·60

324 Leaves and Barbed Wire

1986. 25th Anniv of Amnesty International.

814 **324** 2k.80 multicoloured . . . 1·00 15

325 Girl with Bird

326 Reichhardt as Papageno in "The Magic Flute"

1986.

815 **325** 2k.80 multicoloured . . . 1·00 65

1986. 1st Death Anniv of Poul Reichhardt (actor).

816 **326** 2k.80+50ore mult . . . . 1·20 90

327 Holstein Carriage, 1840

1986. "Hafnia 87" International Stamp Exhibition, Copenhagen (2nd issue). Sheet 70×94 mm containing T **327** and similar vert designs. Multicoloured.

MS817 100ore Type **327** 250ore Ice boat, 1880; 280ore Mail van, 1908; 380ore First regular mail plane, 1919 (sold at 15k.) . . . . . . 6·75 6·75

328 Hands reading Braille

329 Bands of Colour

1986. 75th Anniv of Danish Society for the Blind.

818 **328** 2k.80+50ore red, brown and black . . . . . . 1·60 75

1986. 50th Anniv of Danish Arthritis Association.

819 **329** 2k.80+50ore mult . . . . 1·60 75

330 Changing the Guard at Barracks

1986. Bicentenary of Royal Danish Life Guards Barracks, Rosenborg.

820 **330** 2k.80 multicoloured . . . 1·00 25

331 Academy and Arms

332 Hands reaching out

1986. 400th Anniv of Soro Academy.

821 **331** 2k.80 multicoloured . . . 1·00 15

1986. International Peace Year.

822 **332** 3k.80 multicoloured . . . 1·20 40

333 Prince Frederik

334 Station

1986. 18th Birthday of Crown Prince Frederik.

823 **333** 2k.80 black and red . . . 1·20 15

1986. Inaug of Hoje Tastrup Railway Station.

824 **334** 2k.80 black, bl & red . . 1·00 15

335 Aalborg

336 Common Raven

1986. Nordic Countries Postal Co-operation. Twinned Towns.

825 **335** 2k.80 black . . . . 1·10 15

826 – 3k.80 blue and red . . . 1·20 40

DESIGN: 3k.80, Thisted.

1986. Birds. Multicoloured.

827 2k.80 Type **336** . . . . . . 1·60 40

828 2k.80 Common starling ("Sturnus vulgaris") . . . 1·60 40

829 2k.80 Mute swan ("Cygnus olor") . . . . 1·60 40

830 2k.80 Northern lapwing ("Vanellus vanellus") . . . 1·60 40

831 2k.80 Eurasian skylark ("Alauda arvensis") . . . 1·60 40

337 Post Box, Wires and Telephone

338 Sports Pictograms

1986. 19th International Postal Telegraph and Telephone Congress, Copenhagen.

832 **337** 2k.80 multicoloured . . . 1·00 15

1986. 125th Anniv of Danish Rifle, Gymnastics and Sports Clubs.

833 **338** 2k.80 multicoloured . . . 1·00 15

339 Roadsweeper

340 Stagecoach, 1840

1986. Europa.

834 **339** 2k.80 red . . . . 1·30 15

835 – 3k.80 blue . . . . 1·60 65

DESIGN: 3k.80, Refuse truck.

1986. "Hafnia 87" International Stamp Exhibition, Copenhagen (3rd issue). Sheet 70×94 mm containing T **340** and similar vert design. Multicoloured.

MS836 100ore Type **340**; 250ore Postmaster, 1840; 280ore Postman, 1851; 380ore Rural Postman, 1893 (sold at 15k.) 6·75 6·75

341 Man fleeing

1986. Aid for Refugees.

837 **341** 2k.80 blue, brown & blk 1·00 25

342 Cupid

343 Lutheran Communion Service in Thorslunde Church

1986. Bicentenary of First Performance of "The Whims of Cupid and the Ballet Master" by V. Galeotti and J. Lolle.

838 **342** 3k.80 multicoloured . . . 1·20 50

1986. 450th Anniv of Reformation.

839 **343** 6k.50 multicoloured . . . 2·50 75

344 Graph of Danish Economic Growth and Unemployment Rate

345 Abstract

1986. 25th Anniv of Organization of Economic Co-operation and Development.

840 **344** 3k.80 multicoloured . . . 1·80 75

1987.

841 **345** 2k.80 multicoloured . . . 1·00 15

346 Price Label through Magnifying Glass

347 Fresco

1987. 40th Anniv of Danish Consumer Council.

842 **346** 2k.80 black and red . . . 1·00 15

1987. Ribe Cathedral. Multicoloured.

843 3k. Type **347** . . . . 1·00 40

844 3k.80 Stained glass window (detail) . . . . 1·60 75

845 6k.50 Mosaic (detail) . . . . 2·50 1·30

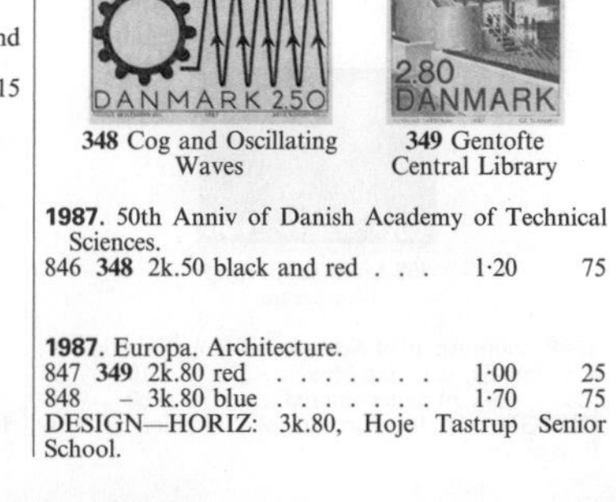

348 Cog and Oscillating Waves

349 Gentofte Central Library

1987. 50th Anniv of Danish Academy of Technical Sciences.

846 **348** 2k.50 black and red . . . 1·20 75

1987. Europa. Architecture.

847 **349** 2k.80 red . . . . 1·00 25

848 – 3k.80 blue . . . . 1·70 75

DESIGN—HORIZ: 3k.80, Hoje Tastrup Senior School.

350 Ball and Ribbons

351 Pigs

1987. 8th Gymnaestrada (World Gymnastics Show), Herning.
849 **350** 2k.80 multicoloured . . . 1·00 15

1987. Centenary of First Co-operative Bacon Factory, Horsens.
850 **351** 3k.80 multicoloured . . . 1·20 50

352 1912 5k. Stamp, Steam Locomotive and Mail Wagon

1987. "Hafnia 87" International Stamp Exhibition, Copenhagen.
851 **352** 280ore multicoloured . . 1·60 1·20
MS852 70 × 95 mm. No. 851 (sold at 45k.) . . . . 22·00 22·00

353 Single Scull

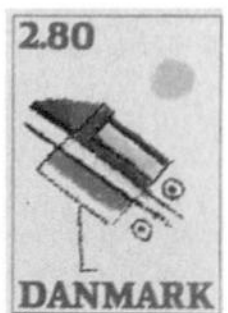
354 Abstract

1987. World Rowing Championships, Bagsvaerd Lake.
853 **353** 3k.80 indigo and blue . . 1·20 40

1987.
854 **354** 2k.80 multicoloured . . . 1·00 15

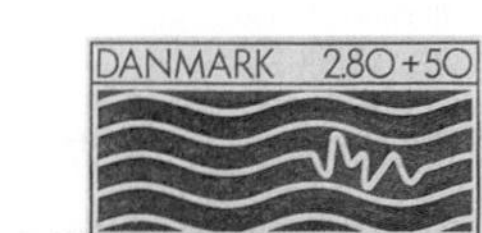
355 Waves

1987. 25th Anniv of Danish Epileptics Association.
855 **355** 2k.80+50ore blue, red and green . . . . 1·80 90

356 Rask

357 Association Badge

1987. Birth Bicentenary of Rasmus Kristjan Rask (philologist).
856 **356** 2k.80 red and brown . . 1·00 15

1987. 125th Anniv of Clerical Association for Home Mission in Denmark.
857 **357** 3k. brown . . . . 1·00 15

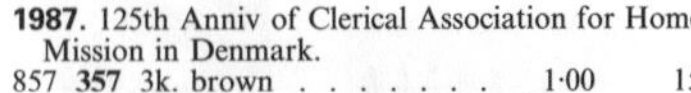

358 Lions supporting Monogram

1988. 400th Anniv of Accession of King Christian IV.
858 **358** 3k. gold and blue . . . . 1·10 15
859 – 4k.10 multicoloured . . . . 1·60 40
DESIGN: 4k.10, Portrait of Christian IV by P. Isaacsz.

359 Worm and Artefacts

360 St. Canute's Church

1988. 400th Birth Anniv of Ole Worm (antiquarian).
860 **359** 7k.10 brown . . . . 2·30 1·30

1988. Millenary of Odense.
861 **360** 3k. brown, black & green 1·00 15

361 African Mother and Child

362 Sirens, Workers and Emblem

1988. Danish Church Aid.
862 **361** 3k.+50ore mult . . . . . 1·80 75

1988. 50th Anniv of Civil Defence Administration.
863 **362** 2k.70 blue and orange . . 80 50

363 Blood Circulation of Heart

364 Postwoman on Bicycle

1988. 40th Anniv of W.H.O.
864 **363** 4k.10 red, blue and black 1·20 50

1988. Europa. Transport and Communications. Multicoloured.
865 3k. Type **364** 80 15
866 4k.10 Mobile telephone . . . 1·80 50

365 "King Christian VII riding past Liberty Monument" (C. W. Eckersberg)

366 "Men of Industry" (detail, P. S. Kroyer)

1988. Bicentenary of Abolition of Villeinage.
867 **365** 3k.20 multicoloured . . . 1·20 65

1988. 150th Anniv of Federation of Danish Industries.
868 **366** 3k. multicoloured . . . . 1·00 25

367 Speedway Riders

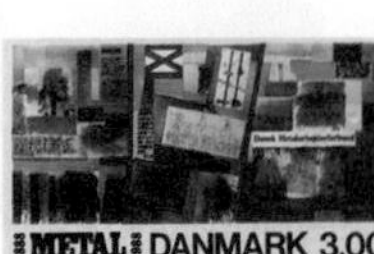
368 Glass Mosaic (Niels Winkel)

1988. World Speedway Championships.
869 **367** 4k.10 multicoloured . . . 1·20 40

1988. Centenary of Danish Metalworkers' Union.
870 **368** 3k. multicoloured . . . . 1·00 15

369 College

1988. Bicent of Tonder Teacher Training College.
871 **369** 3k. brown . . . . 1·00 15

370 "Tribute to Leon Degand" (Robert Jacobsen)

1988. Franco-Danish Cultural Co-operation.
872 **370** 4k.10 red and black . . . 2·50 1·30

371 Emblem

372 Lumby Windmill

1988. 5th Anniv of National Council for the Unmarried Mother and Her Child.
873 **371** 3k.+50ore red . . . . . 1·80 75

1988. Mills.
874 **372** 3k. black, red & orange 1·00 15
875 – 7k.10 black, ultramarine and blue . . . . 3·00 1·30
DESIGN: 7k.10, Veistrup water mill.

373 "Bathing Boys 1902" (Peter Hansen)

1988. Paintings. Multicoloured.
876 4k.10 Type **373** . . . . . . 2·30 1·60
877 10k. "Hill at Overkoerby. Winter 1917" (Fritz Syberg) . . . . 5·25 3·25

374 "The Little Mermaid" (statue, Edvard Eriksen), Copenhagen

375 Army Members in Public House

1989. Centenary of Danish Tourist Association.
878 **374** 3k.20 green . . . . 1·20 15

1989. 102nd Anniv of Salvation Army in Denmark.
879 **375** 3k.20+50ore mult . . . . 2·10 75

376 Footballer

377 Emblem

1989. Centenary of Danish Football Association.
880 **376** 3k.20 red, blk & lt red . . 1·20 15

1989. 40th Anniv of N.A.T.O.
881 **377** 4k.40 bl, cobalt & gold 1·60 50

378 "Valby Woman"

379 "Parliament Flag

1989. Nordic Countries' Postal Co-operation. Traditional Costumes. Engravings by Christoffer Wilhelm Eckersberg. Multicoloured.
882 3k.20 Type **378** . . . . . . 1·00 15
883 4k.40 "Pork Butcher" . . . 2·00 65

1989. 3rd Direct Elections to European Parliament.
884 **379** 3k. blue and yellow . . . 1·20 65

380 Lego Bricks

381 Tractor, 1917

1989. Europa. Children's Toys. Multicoloured.
885 3k.20 Type **380** . . . . . . 1·00 15
886 4k.40 Wooden guardsmen by Kay Bojesen . . . . 2·00 65

1989. Centenary of Danish Agricultural Museum.
887 **381** 3k.20 red . . . . 1·20 15

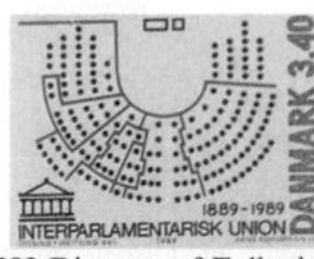
382 Diagram of Folketing (Parliament) Chamber

1989. Centenary of Interparliamentary Union.
888 **382** 3k.40 red and black . . . 2·30 90

383 Chart and Boat Identity Number

1989. Centenary of Danish Fishery and Marine Research Institute.
889 **383** 3k.20 multicoloured . . . 1·20 15

384 "Ingemann" (after J. V. Gertner)

385 Scene from "They Caught the Ferry" (50th anniv of Danish Government Film Office)

1989. Birth Bicentenary of Bernhard Severin Ingemann (poet).
890 **384** 7k.70 green . . . . 2·50 90

1989. Danish Film Industry.
891 **385** 3k. blue, black & orge . . 1·20 40
892 – 3k.20 pink, blk & orge . . 1·00 15
893 – 4k.40 brown, blk & orge 1·70 50
DESIGNS: 3k.20, Scene from "The Golden Smile" (birth cent of Bodil Ipsen, actress); 4k.40, Carl Th. Dreyer (director, birth cent).

386 Stamps

1989. 50th Stamp Day.
894 **386** 3k.20 salmon, orge & brn 1·20 15

387 "Part of Northern Citadel Bridge" (Christen Kobke)

1989. Paintings. Multicoloured.
895 4k.40 Type **387** . . . . . . 2·10 1·50
896 10k. "A Little Girl, Elise Kobke, with Cup" (Constantin Hansen) . . . 3·25 2·75

388 Silver Coffee Pot (Axel Johannes Kroyer, 1726)

389 Andrew Mitchell's Steam Engine

1990. Centenary of Museum of Decorative Art, Copenhagen.
897 **388** 3k.50 black and blue . . 1·20 25

1990. Bicent of Denmark's First Steam Engine.
898 **389** 8k.25 brown . . . . . . 2·75 1·10

390 Queen Margrethe II

391 Royal Monogram over Door of Haderslev Post Office

1990.
910 **390** 3k.50 red . . . . 1·20 15
911 3k.75 green . . . . 2·10 1·50
912 3k.75 red . . . . 1·20 15
913 4k. brown . . . . 1·20 50
914 4k.50 violet . . . . . . 1·60 65
915 4k.75 blue . . . . 1·60 40
916 4k.75 violet . . . . . . 1·60 75
917 5k. blue . . . . 1·60 40
918 5k.25 black . . . . 1·80 75
919 5k.50 green . . . . 1·80 1·60

1990. Europa. Post Office Buildings.
930 **391** 3k.50 yellow, red & blk 1·00 15
931 – 4k.75 multicoloured . . . 1·30 50
DESIGN: 4k.75, Odense Post Office.

392 Main Guardhouse, Rigging Crane and Ships (after C. O. Willars)

1990. 300th Anniv of Nyholm.
932 **392** 4k.75 black . . . . 1·60 40

393 Covered Ice Dish

394 Marsh Mallow

1990. Bicentenary of Flora Danica Banquet Service. Multicoloured.
933 3k.50 Type **393** . . . . . . 1·60 65
934 3k.50 Sauce boat . . . . . . 1·60 65
935 3k.50 Lidded ice pot . . . . 1·60 65
936 3k.50 Serving dish . . . . . 1·60 65

1990. Endangered Flowers. Multicoloured.
937 3k.25 Type **394** . . . . . . 1·20 50
938 3k.50 Red helleborine . . . . 1·90 15
939 3k.75 Purple orchis . . . . . 1·60 75
940 4k.75 Lady's slipper . . . . 1·90 50

395 Insulin Crystals

396 Gjellerup Church

1990. 50th Anniv of Danish Diabetes Association.
941 **395** 3k.50+50ore mult . . . . 2·00 1·60

1990. Jutland Churches. Each brown.
942 3k.50 Type **396** . . . . . . 1·20 15
943 4k.75 Veng Church . . . . . 1·70 40
944 8k.25 Bredsten Church (vert) 3·00 90

397 Slogan and Braille

1990. Fredericia: "Town for Everybody" (access for the handicapped project).
945 **397** 3k.50 red and black . . . 1·20 25

398 "Tordenskiold and Karlsten's Commandant" (Otto Bache)

399 Bicycle (Bicycle stealing)

1990. 300th Birth Anniv of Admiral Tordenskiold (Peter Wessel).
946 **398** 3k.50 multicoloured . . . 1·20 25

1990. Campaigns.
947 **399** 3k.25 multicoloured . . . 1·20 65
948 – 3k.50 black, bl & mve . . 1·40 25
DESIGN: 3k.50, Glass and car (Drunken driving).

400 IC3 Diesel Passenger Train, 1990

1991. Railway Locomotives.
949 **400** 3k.25 blue, red & green 1·40 90
950 – 3k.50 black and red . . . 1·30 25
951 – 3k.75 brown & dp brn . . 1·30 65
952 – 4k.75 black and red . . . 1·60 40
DESIGNS: 3k.50, Class A steam locomotive, 1882; 3k.75, Class MY diesel-electric locomotive, 1954; 4k.75, Class P steam locomotive, 1907.

401 Satellite Picture of Denmark's Water Temperatures

402 First Page of 1280s Manuscript

1991. Europa. Europe in Space. Mult.
953 3k.50 Type **401** . . . . . . 1·10 25
954 4k.75 Denmark's land temperatures . . . . . . 1·80 50

1991. 750th Anniv of Jutland Law.
955 **402** 8k.25 multicoloured . . . 2·75 1·10

403 Fano

404 Child using Emergency Helpline

1991. Nordic Countries' Postal Co-operation. Tourism. Multicoloured.
956 3k.50 Type **403** . . . . . . 1·60 25
957 4k.75 Christianso . . . . . 1·60 50

1991. 15th Anniv of Living Conditions of Children (child welfare organization).
958 **404** 3k.50+50ore blue . . . . 1·70 1·30

405 Stoneware Vessels (Christian Poulsen)

406 Man cleaning up after Dog

1991. Danish Design. Multicoloured.
959 3k.25 Type **405** . . . . . . 1·20 40
960 3k.50 Chair, 1949 (Hans Wegner) (vert) . . . . . . 1·20 25
961 4k.75 Silver cutlery, 1938 (Kay Bojesen) (vert) . . . 1·70 50
962 8k.25 "PH5" lamp, 1958 (Poul Henningsen) . . . . 2·75 1·60

1991. "Keep Denmark Clean".
963 **406** 3k.50 red . . . . 1·10 25
964 – 4k.75 blue . . . . 1·80 75
DESIGN: 4k.75, Woman putting litter into bin.

407 Nordic Advertising Congress 1947 (Arne Ungermann)

1991. Posters. Multicoloured.
965 3k.50 Type **407** . . . . . . 1·30 25
966 4k.50 Poster Exhibition, Copenhagen Zoo, 1907 (Valdemar Andersen) . . . 2·10 1·50
967 4k.75 D.D.L. (Danish Airlines, 1945) (Ib Andersen) . . . . 1·80 65
968 12k. Casino's "The Sinner", 1925 (Sven Brasch) . . . . 3·50 2·50

408 "Lady at Her Toilet" (Harald Giersing)

409 Skarpsalling Earthenware Bowl

1991. Paintings. Multicoloured.
969 4k.75 Type **408** . . . . . . 2·20 1·50
970 14k. "Road through Wood" (Edvard Weie) . . . . . . 3·75 3·75

1992. Re-opening of National Museum, Copenhagen. Exhibits from Prehistoric Denmark Collection.
971 **409** 3k.50 brown and lilac . . 1·10 25
972 – 4k.50 green and blue . . 1·80 65
973 – 4k.75 black & brown . . 1·70 50
974 – 8k.25 purple & green . . 2·75 1·50
DESIGNS: 4k.50, Grevensvaenge bronze figure of dancer; 4k.75, Bottom plate of Gundestrup Cauldron; 8k.25, Hindsgavl flint knife.

410 Aspects of Engineering

411 Queen Margaret I (detail, Vastra Sallerup Church fresco)

1992. Centenary of Danish Society of Chemical, Civil, Electrical and Mechanical Engineers.
975 **410** 3k.50 red . . . . 1·20 25

1992. "Nordia 94" International Stamp Exhibition, Arhus. Sheet 70×94 mm containing T **411** and similar vert design, each brown, slate and red.
MS976 3k.50, Type **411**; 4k.75 Alabaster bust of Queen Margaret I (attr. Johannes Junge) (sold at 12k.) . . . . 4·50 4·50

412 Potato Plant

1992. Europa. 500th Anniv of Discovery of America by Columbus.
977 **412** 3k.50 green & brown . . 1·20 25
978 – 4k.75 green & yellow . . 1·80 1·00
DESIGN: 4k.75, Head of maize.

413 Royal Couple in 1992 and in Official Wedding Photograph

1992. Silver Wedding of Queen Margrethe and Prince Henrik.
979 **413** 3k.75 multicoloured . . . 1·60 65

414 Hare, Eurasian Sky Lark and Cars

1992. Environmental Protection. Multicoloured.
980 3k.75 Type **414** . . . . . . 1·20 25
981 5k. Atlantic herrings and sea pollution . . . . 1·60 50
982 8k.75 Felled trees and saplings (vert) . . . . . . 2·50 1·30

415 Celebrating Crowd

416 Danish Pavilion

1992. Denmark, European Football Champion.
983 **415** 3k.75 multicoloured . . . 1·60 25

1992. "Expo '92" World's Fair, Seville.
984 **416** 3k.75 blue . . . . 1·20 25

417 "Word"

418 "A Hug"

1992. 50th Anniv of Danish Dyslexia Association.
985 **417** 3k.75+50ore mult . . . . 2·00 1·30

1992. Danish Cartoon Characters.
986 **418** 3k.50 purple, red & gold 1·40 40
987 – 3k.75 violet and red . . . 1·20 25
988 – 4k.75 black and red . . . 1·80 1·30
989 – 5k. blue and red . . . . 1·60 40
DESIGNS: 3k.75, "Love Letter"; 4k.75, "Domestic Triangle"; 5k. "The Poet and his Little Wife".

419 Abstract

420 "Jacob's Fight with the Angel" (bible illustration by Bodil Kaalund)

1992. European Single Market.
990 **419** 3k.75 blue and yellow . . 1·20 25

1992. Publication of New Danish Bible.
991 **420** 3k.75 multicoloured . . . 1·20 25

421 "Landscape from Vejby, 1843" (Johan Thomas Lundbye)

1992. Paintings. Multicoloured.
992 5k. Type **421** . . . . 1·90 1·10
993 10k. "Motif from Halleby Brook, 1847" (Peter Christian Skovgaard) . . . 3·25 2·50

422 Funen Guldgubber **423** Small Tortoiseshell

1993. Danish Treasure Trove. Guldgubber (anthropomorphic gold foil figures). Mult.
994 3k.75 Type **422** . . . . . . 1·20 25
995 5k. Bornholm guldgubber (vert) . . . . 1·70 40

1993. Butterflies. Multicoloured.
996 3k.75 Type **423** . . . . . . 1·60 25
997 5k. Large blue . . . . 1·80 40
998 8k.75 Marsh fritillary . . . . 3·25 1·60
999 12k. Red admiral . . . . . 3·75 2·50

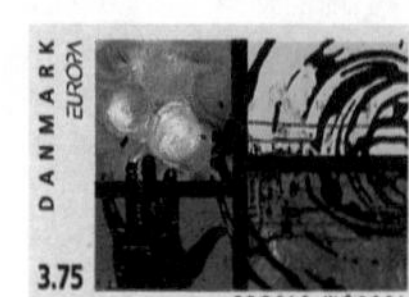

424 Untitled Painting (Troels Worsel)

1993. Europa. Contemporary Art. Mult.
1000 3k.75 Type **424** . . . . . 1·20 25
1001 5k. "The 7 Corners of the Earth" (Stig Brogger) (vert) . . . . 2·10 65

425 "Pierrot" (Thor Bogelund, 1947) **426** "Danmark"

1993. Nordic Countries' Postal Co-operation. Tourism. Publicity posters for Tivoli Gardens, Copenhagen. Multicoloured.
1002 3k.75 Type **425** . . . . . 1·20 25
1003 5k. Child holding balloons (Wilhelm Freddie, 1987) (vert) . . . . 2·10 40

1993. Training Ships. Multicoloured.
1004 3k.75 Type **426** . . . . . 1·40 35
1005 4k.75 "Jens Krogh" (25 × 30 mm) . . . . . . 2·20 1·90
1006 5k. "Georg Stage" . . . . 1·90 80
1007 9k.50 "Marilyn Anne" (36 × 26 mm) . . . . . . 2·75 3·50

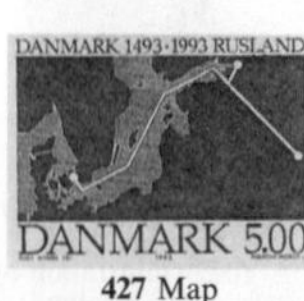

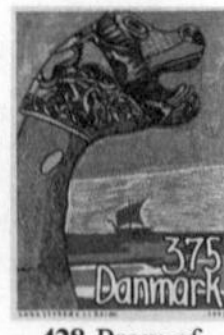

427 Map **428** Prow of Viking Ship

1993. Inauguration of Denmark–Russia Submarine Cable and 500th Anniv of Friendship Treaty.
1008 **427** 5k. green . . . . 2·00 40

1993. Children's Stamp Design Competition.
1009 **428** 3k.75 multicoloured . . 1·20 25

429 Emblem **430** "If you want a Letter...Write one Yourself"

1993. 75th Anniv of Social Work of Young Men's Christian Association.
1010 **429** 3k.75+50ore green, red and black . . . . . . 2·00 1·00

1993. Letter-writing Campaign.
1011 **430** 5k. ultram, bl & blk . . 1·80 40

431 Silver Brooch and Chain, North Falster

1993. Traditional Jewellery. Multicoloured.
1012 3k.50 Type **431** . . . . . 1·40 65
1013 3k.75 Gilt-silver brooch with owner's monogram, Amager . . . . 1·60 25
1014 5k. Silver buttons and brooches, Laeso . . . . . 2·10 40
1015 8k.75 Silver buttons, Romo 2·75 1·50

432 "Assemblage" (Vilhelm Lundstrom) **433** Duck

1993. Paintings. Multicoloured.
1016 5k. Type **432** . . . . . . 2·10 1·40
1017 15k. "Composition" (Franciska Clausen) . . . 4·50 3·25

1994. Save Water and Energy Campaign.
1018 **433** 3k.75 multicoloured . . 1·30 25
1019 – 5k. green, red & black 1·70 40
DESIGN: 5k. Spade (in Danish "spar" = save) and "CO2".

434 Marselisborg Castle, Aarhus

1994. Royal Residences.
1020 **434** 3k.50 dp brn, grn & brn 1·40 65
1021 – 3k.75 multicoloured . . 1·40 25
1022 – 5k. grn, dp brn & brn 2·00 50
1023 – 8k.75 dp brn, grn & brn 3·25 1·60
DESIGNS: 3k.75, Amalienborg Castle, Copenhagen; 5k. Fredensborg Castle, North Zealand; 8k.75, Graasten Castle, South Jutland.

435 "Danmark" and Wegener's Weather Balloon, Danmarkshavn **436** Copenhagen Tram No. 2, 1911

1994. Europa. Discoveries. "Danmark" Expedition to North-East Greenland, 1906–08.
1024 **435** 3k.75 purple . . . . . . 1·40 25
1025 – 5k. black . . . . 1·80 50
DESIGN: 5k. Johan Peter Koch and theodolite.

1994. Trams. Multicoloured.
1026 3k.75 Type **436** . . . . . 1·10 25
1027 4k.75 Aarhus tram, 1928 . . 1·70 1·30
1028 5k. Odense tram, 1911 (vert) 1·70 65
1029 12k. Copenhagen horse tram "Honen", 1880 (37 × 21 mm) . . . . . . 3·50 3·25

437 Prince Henrik **438** Kite

1994. Danish Red Cross Fund. 60th Birthday of Prince Henrik, the Prince Consort.
1030 **437** 3k.75+50ore mult . . . 1·40 1·10

1994. Children's Stamp Design Competition.
1031 **438** 3k.75 multicoloured . . 1·20 65

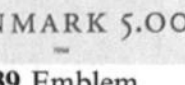

439 Emblem **440** House Sparrows

1994. 75th Anniv of I.L.O.
1032 **439** 5k. multicoloured . . . 1·60 40

1994. Protected Animals. Multicoloured.
1033 3k.75 Type **440** . . . . . 1·00 25
1034 4k.75 Badger . . . . 1·80 1·10
1035 5k. Red squirrel (vert) . . . 1·60 50
1036 9k.50 Pair of black grouse 2·75 2·30
1037 12k. Black grass snake (36 × 26 mm) . . . . . . 3·50 3·25

441 Teacher

1994. 150th Anniv of Folk High Schools.
1038 **441** 3k.75 multicoloured . . 1·20 25

442 Study for "Italian Woman with Sleeping Child" (Wilhelm Marstrand)

1994. Paintings. Multicoloured.
1039 5k. Type **442** . . . . . . 1·80 1·30
1040 15k. "Interior from Amaliegade with the Artist's Brothers" (Wilhelm Bendz) . . . . 4·00 3·75

443 The Red Building (architect's drawing, Hack Kampmann) **444** Anniversary Emblem

1995. 800th Anniv of Aarhus Cathedral School.
1041 **443** 3k.75 multicoloured . . 1·20 25

1995. 50th Anniv of United Nations Organization. U.N. World Summit for Social Development, Copenhagen.
1042 **444** 5k. multicoloured . . . 1·60 50

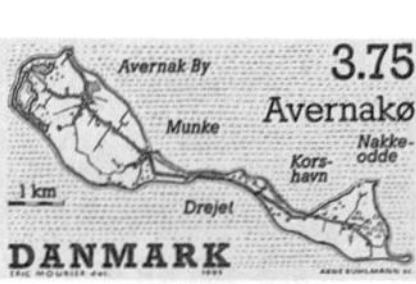

445 Avernako **446** Field-Marshal Montgomery and Copenhagen Town Hall

1995. Danish Islands. Each brown, blue and red.
1043 3k.75 Type **445** . . . . . 1·30 25
1044 4k.75 Fejo . . . . 2·00 1·30
1045 5k. Fur . . . . 2·00 50
1046 9k.50 Endelave . . . . . . 3·25 1·90

1995. Europa. Peace and Freedom. Mult.
1047 3k.75 Type **446** . . . . . 1·20 25
1048 5k. White coaches (repatriation of Danes from German concentration camps) (horiz) . . . . 1·60 50
1049 8k.75 Dropping of supplies from Allied aircraft (horiz) . . . . 2·75 1·50
1050 12k. Jews escaping by boat to Sweden (horiz) . . . . 3·75 2·50

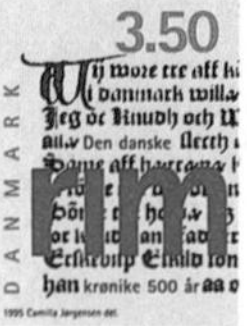

447 Detail of Page **448** Stage

1995. 500th Anniv of "The Rhymed Chronicle" by Friar Niels (first book printed in Danish).
1051 **447** 3k.50 multicoloured . . 1·20 50

1995. Nordic Countries' Postal Co-operation. Music Festivals. Multicoloured.
1052 3k.75 Type **448** (25th anniv of Roskilde Festival) . . . 1·20 25
1053 5k. Violinist (21st anniv of Tonder Festival) (20 × 38 mm) . . . . . . 1·70 40

449 Broken Feather

1995. 50th Anniv of National Society of Polio and Accident Victims.
1054 **449** 3k.75+50ore red . . . . 1·60 1·10

450 "Midsummer Eve" (Jens Sondergaard)

1995. Paintings. Multicoloured.
1055 10k. Type **450** . . . . . . 2·75 1·90
1056 15k. "Landscape at Gudhjem" (Niels Lergaard) . . . . 4·50 3·75

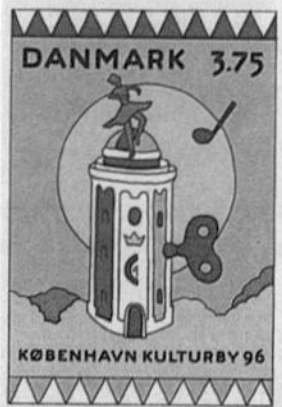

451 Sextant **453** The Round Tower

452 TEKNO Model Vehicles

1995. 450th Birth Anniv of Tycho Brahe (astronomer). Multicoloured.
1057 3k.75 Uraniborg (Palace Observatory) . . . . . . 1·20 25
1058 5k.50 Type **451** . . . . . 1·80 1·10

1995. Danish Toys. Multicoloured.
1059 3k.75 Type **452** . . . . . 1·60 25
1060 5k. Edna (celluloid doll), Kirstine (china doll) and Holstebro teddy bear . . 1·60 50
1061 8k.75 Toy bin-plate locomotives and rolling stock . . . . 3·00 1·80
1062 12k. Glud & Marstrand horse-drawn fire engine and carriage . . . . . . 3·50 2·50

1996. Copenhagen, European Cultural Capital. Multicoloured.
1063 3k.75 Type **453** . . . . . 1·20 25
1064 5k. Christiansborg . . . . . 1·80 40
1065 8k.75 Dome of Marble Church as hot-air balloon 3·00 1·90
1066 12k. "The Little Mermaid" on stage . . . . 3·50 3·25

454 Disabled Basketball Player 455 Businessmen

1996. Sport. Multicoloured.
1067 3k.75 Type **454** . . . . . 1·10 25
1068 4k.75 Swimming . . . . . 1·80 1·00
1069 5k. Yachting . . . . 1·80 50
1070 9k.50 Cycling . . . . 3·00 2·30

1996. Cent of Danish Employers' Confederation.
1071 **455** 3k.75 multicoloured . . 1·20 25

456 Asta Nielsen (actress) 457 Roskilde Fjord Boat

1996. Europa. Famous Women.
1072 – 3k.75 brown & dp brn 1·20 25
1073 **456** 5k. grey and blue . . . 1·70 50
DESIGN: 3k.75, Karin Blixen (writer).

1996. Wooden Sailing Boats.
1074 **457** 3k.50 brn, bl & red . . . 1·40 90
1075 – 3k.75 lilac, grn & red . . 1·20 25
1076 – 12k.25 blk, brn & red . . 3·75 3·00
DESIGNS—As T **457**: 12k.25, South Funen Archipelago smack; 20 × 38 mm: 3k.75, Limfjorden skiff.

458 Fornaes 459 Ribbons forming Hearts within Star

1996. Lighthouses. Multicoloured.
1077 3k.75 Type **458** . . . . . 1·40 25
1078 5k. Blavandshuk . . . . . 2·00 40
1079 5k.25 Bovbjerg . . . . . 2·10 1·30
1080 8k.75 Mon . . . . 2·75 1·30

1996. AIDS Foundation.
1081 **459** 3k.75+50ore red & blk 1·40 1·10

460 Vase

1996. 150th Birth Anniv of Thorvald Bindesboll (ceramic artist). Multicoloured.
1082 3k.75 Type **460** . . . . . 1·10 25
1083 4k. Portfolio cover . . . . 1·40 1·00

461 "At Lunch" (Peder Kroyer)

1996. Paintings. Multicoloured.
1084 10k. Type **461** . . . . . . 3·00 2·50
1085 15k. "Girl with Sunflowers" (Michael Ancher) . . . . 4·00 3·75

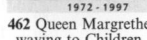

462 Queen Margrethe waving to Children 463 Queen Margrethe

1997. Silver Jubilee of Queen Margrethe. Mult.
1086 3k.50 Queen Margrethe and Prince Henrik 90 65
1087 3k.75 Queen Margrethe and Crown Prince Frederik . . 1·40 25
1088 4k. Queen Margrethe at desk . . . . 1·30 1·00
1089 5k.25 Type **462** . . . . . 1·60 1·30

1997.
1092 **463** 3k.75 red . . . . 1·20 15
1093 4k. green . . . . 1·20 65
1094 4k. red . . . . 1·20 15
1095 4k.25 brown . . . . . 1·60 1·10
1096 4k.50 blue . . . . . . 1·60 90
1097 4k.75 brown . . . . . 1·60 1·40
1098 5k. violet . . . . . . 1·60 40
1099 5k.25 blue . . . . . . 1·80 50
1100 5k.50 red . . . . . . 1·60 1·10
1101 5k.75 blue . . . . . . 1·70 40
1104 6k.75 green . . . . . . 1·80 1·50

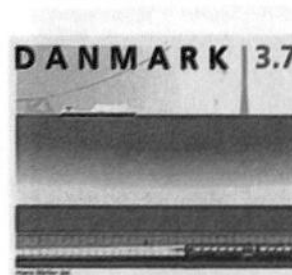

464 Karlstrup Post Mill, Zealand 465 The East Tunnel

1997. Centenary of Open Air Museum, Lyngby. Construction Drawings by B. Ehrhardt.
1111 **464** 3k.50 brown & purple 1·20 65
1112 – 3k.75 lilac and green . . 1·40 25
1113 – 5k. green and lilac . . . 1·70 25
1114 – 8k.75 green & brown . . 3·00 1·30
DESIGNS: 3k.75, Ellested water mill, Funen; 5k. Fjellerup Manor Barn, Djursland; 8k.75, Toftum farm, Romo.

1997. Inauguration of Railway Section of the Great Belt Link. Multicoloured.
1115 3k.75 Type **465** . . . . . 1·10 25
1116 4k.75 The West Bridge . . . 1·60 1·10

466 Sneezing 468 King Erik and Queen Margrete I

467 Electric Trains under New Carlsberg Bridge

1997. Asthma Allergy Association.
1117 **466** 3k.75+50ore mult . . . 1·60 1·10

1997. 150th Anniv of Copenhagen–Roskilde Railway. Multicoloured.
1118 3k.75 Type **467** . . . . . 1·20 25
1119 8k.75 Steam train under original Carlsberg bridge (after H. Holm) . . . . . 2·50 1·30

1997. 600th Anniv of Kalmar Union (of Denmark, Norway and Sweden). Multicoloured.
1120 4k. Type **468** . . . . . . 1·30 1·00
1121 4k. The Three Graces . . . 1·30 1·00
Nos. 1120/1 were issued, se-tenant, forming a composite design of a painting by an unknown artist.

469 Post Office Cars on Great Belt Ferry

1997. Closure of Travelling Post Offices.
1122 **469** 5k. multicoloured . . . 1·60 50

470 "The Tinder-box"

1997. Europa. Tales and Legends by Hans Christian Andersen.
1123 **470** 3k.75 dp brn & brn . . 1·20 25
1124 – 5k.25 red, dp grn & grn 1·80 1·00
DESIGN: 5k.25, "Thumbelina".

471 "Dust dancing in the Sun" (Vilheim Hammershoi) 472 Faaborg Chair (Kaare Klint)

1997. Paintings. Multicoloured.
1125 9k.75 Type **471** . . . . . 2·75 2·50
1126 13k. "Woman Mountaineer" (Jens Willumsen) . . . . 3·50 3·25

1997. Danish Design. Multicoloured.
1127 3k.75 Type **472** . . . . . 1·40 25
1128 4k. Margrethe bowls (Sigvard Bernadotte and Acton Bjorn) . . . . . . 1·60 1·00
1129 5k. The Ant chairs (Arne Jacobsen) (horiz) . . . . 1·80 40
1130 12k.25 Silver bowl (Georg Jensen) . . . . 3·50 3·25

473 Workers 474 Roskilde Cathedral and Viking Longship

1998. Centenary of Danish Confederation of Trade Unions. Multicoloured.
1131 3k.50 Type **473** (General Workers' Union in Denmark) . . . . 1·10 75
1132 3k.75 Crowd at meeting (Danish Confederation of Trade Unions) . . . . . 1·30 25
1133 4k.75 Nurse (Danish Nurses' Organization) . . . . . . 1·70 1·10
1134 5k. Woman using telephone (Union of Commercial and Clerical Employees in Denmark) . . . . 1·80 25

1998. Millenary of Roskilde.
1135 **474** 3k.75 multicoloured . . 1·20 25

475 Seven-spotted Ladybird 476 Postman, 1922

1998. Environmental Issues. Gardening Without Chemicals.
1136 **475** 5k. red and black . . . 1·40 25

1998. Post and Tele Museum, Copenhagen. Mult.
1137 3k.75 Type **476** . . . . . 1·60 25
1138 4k.50 Morse operator, 1910 1·80 1·00
1139 5k.50 Telephonist, 1910 . . 1·90 1·30
1140 8k.75 Postman, 1998 . . . . 3·00 2·00

477 The West Bridge

1998. Inauguration of Road Section of the Great Belt Link. Each blue, black and red.
1141 5k. Type **477** . . . . . . 2·50 65
1142 5k. The East Bridge . . . . 2·50 65

478 Harbour Master 479 Horse (Agriculture Show)

1998. Nordic Countries' Postal Co-operation. Shipping. Multicoloured.
1143 6k.50 Type **478** . . . . . 1·80 1·50
1144 6k.50 Sextant and radar image of Copenhagen harbour . . . . 1·80 1·50
MS1145 106 × 75 mm. Nos. 1143/4 4·50 4·50
Nos. 1143/4 were issued together, se-tenant, forming a composite design.

1998. Europa. National Festivals. Mult.
1146 3k.75 Type **479** . . . . . 1·20 25
1147 4k.50 Aarhus Festival Week 1·30 1·00

480 Reaching Hand

1998. Anti-cancer Campaign.
1148 **480** 3k.75+50ore red, orange and black . . . . . . 1·20 1·00

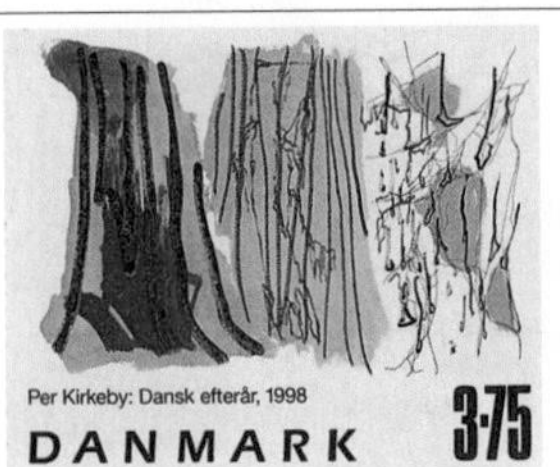

481 "Danish Autumn" (Per Kirkeby)

1998. Philatelic Creations. Multicoloured.
1149 3k.75 Type **481** . . . . . 1·40 1·00
1150 5k. "Alpha" (Mogens Andersen) (vert) . . . . 2·00 1·10
1151 8k.75 "Imagery" (Ejler Bille) (vert) . . . . 3·00 2·00
1152 19k. "Celestial Horse" (Carl-Henning Pedersen) 5·75 4·50

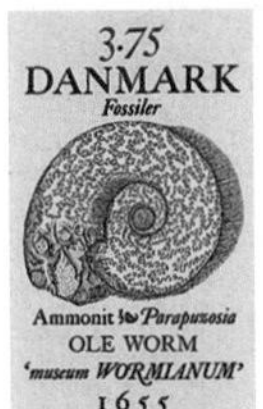

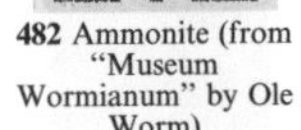

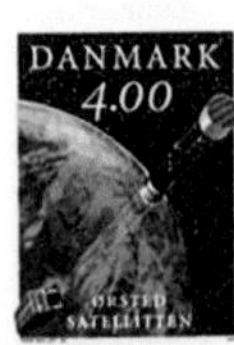

482 Ammonite (from "Museum Wormianum" by Ole Worm) **483** Satellite and Earth

1998. Fossils. Designs reproducing engravings from geological works. Each black and red on cream.
1153 3k.75 Type **482** . . . . . 1·10 25
1154 4k.50 Shark's teeth (from "De Solido" by Niels Stensen) . . . . 1·20 1·00
1155 5k.50 Sea urchin (from "Stevens Klint" by Soren Abildgaard) . . . . . . 1·80 1·30
1156 15k. Pleurotomariida (from "Den Danske Atlas" by Erich Pontoppidan) . . . 4·00 3·75
MS1157 114×142 mm. Nos. 1153/6 6·75 6·75

1999. Launch of "Orsted" Satellite (Danish research satellite).
1158 **483** 4k. multicoloured . . . 1·20 25

484 Beech

1999. Deciduous Trees. Multicoloured.
1159 4k. Type **484** . . . . . . 1·40 25
1160 5k. Ash (vert) . . . . . . 1·70 1·10
1161 5k.25 Small-leaved lime (vert) . . . . 1·80 65
1162 9k.25 Pendunculate oak . . 2·75 1·70

485 Home Guard

1999. 50th Anniv of Home Guard.
1163 **485** 3k.75 multicoloured . . 1·40 1·10

486 Northern Lapwing and Eggs

1999. Harbingers of Spring. Multicoloured.
1164 4k. Type **486** . . . . . . 1·00 25
1165 5k.25 Greylag goose with chicks . . . . 1·60 50
MS1166 99×82 mm. Nos. 1164/5 2·10 2·10

487 Emblem and Jet Fighters **488** Vejlerne

1999. 50th Anniv of North Atlantic Treaty Organization.
1167 **487** 4k.25 multicoloured . . 1·20 1·10

1999. Europa. Parks and Gardens. Multicoloured.
1168 4k.50 Type **488** . . . . . 1·10 1·00
1169 5k.50 Langli Island . . . . 1·60 1·30

489 Anniversary Emblem **490** "g" and Paragraph Sign

1999. 50th Anniv of Council of Europe.
1170 **489** 9k.75 blue . . . . 2·50 1·90

1999. 150th Anniv of Danish Constitution.
1171 **490** 4k. red and black . . . 1·10 25

491 Kjeld Petersen and Dirch Passer

1999. 150th Anniv of Danish Revue.
1172 **491** 4k. red . . . . 1·20 35
1173 – 4k.50 black . . . . . . 1·40 1·30
1174 – 5k.25 blue . . . . 1·70 1·20
1175 – 6k.75 mauve . . . . . . 1·60 1·90
DESIGNS: 4k.50, Osvald Helmuth; 5k.25, Preben Kaas and Jorgen Ryg; 6k.75, Liva Weel.

492 Emblem **493** The "Black Diamond"

1999. Alzheimer's Disease Association.
1176 **492** 4k.+50ore. red and blue 1·20 1·10

1999. Inauguration of Royal Library Extension, Copenhagen.
1177 **493** 8k.75 black . . . . . . 2·30 2·00

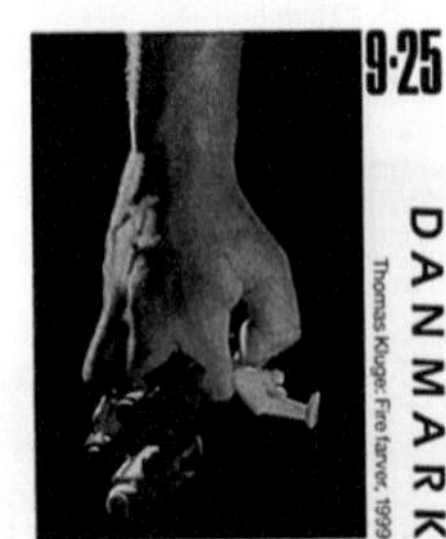

494 "Four Colours" (Thomas Kluge)

1999. Paintings. Multicoloured.
1178 9k.25 Type **494** . . . . . 2·30 1·90
1179 16k. "Boy" (Lise Malinovsky) . . . . . . 4·00 3·75

495 Barn Swallows **496** Hearts

1999. Migratory Birds. Multicoloured.
1180 4k. Type **495** . . . . . . 1·20 25
1181 5k.25 Greylag geese with goslings . . . . 1·70 65
1182 5k.50 Eiders . . . . 1·80 1·30
1183 12k.25 Arctic tern feeding chick . . . . 3·25 2·50
MS1184 Two sheets, each 116×72 mm. (a) Nos. 1180/1. (b) Nos. 1182/3 . . . . 6·25 6·25

1999. New Millennium. Multicoloured.
1185 4k. Type **496** . . . . . . 1·10 25
1186 4k. Horizontal wavy lines 1·10 25

497 Johan Henrik Deuntzer (Prime Minister) on Front Page of *Aftenposten* (newspaper) **498** Queen Margrethe II (Pia Schutzmann)

2000. The Twentieth Century (1st series).
1187 **497** 4k. black and cream . . 1·00 25
1188 – 4k.50 multicoloured . . 1·20 1·00
1189 – 5k.25 multicoloured . . 1·40 50
1190 – 5k.75 multicoloured . . 1·80 65
DESIGNS—4k. Type **497** (Venstre (workers') party victory in election, 1901); 4k.50, Caricature of Frederik Borgbjerg (party member, Alfred Schmidt) (first Social Democrat Lord Mayor in Denmark, 1903); 5k.25, Asta Nielson and Poul Reumert (actors) in scene from *The Abyss* (film), 1910; 5k.75, Telephone advertising poster, 1914.
See also Nos. 1207/10, 1212/15 and 1221/4.

2000. 60th Birthday of Queen Margrethe II.
1191 **498** 4k. black and red . . . 1·00 25
1192 5k.25 black and blue . . 1·30 50
MS1193 63×60 mm. Nos. 1191/2 2·20 2·20

499 Queen Margrethe II

2000.
1194 **499** 4k. red . . . . 1·10 15
1195 4k.25 blue . . . . . 1·20 1·00
1195a 4k.25 red 80 50
1196 4k.50 red . . . . . 1·20 1·00
1196b 4k.75 brown . . . . 1·20 1·00
1197 5k. green . . . . . 1·30 1·00
1198 5k.25 blue . . . . . 1·40 50
1199 5k.50 violet . . . . 1·40 50
1200 5k.75 green . . . . 1·60 65
1201 6k. brown . . . . . 1·60 95
1201a 6k.25 green . . . . 1·20 75
1201b 6k.50 green . . . . 1·20 75
1202 6k.75 red . . . . . 1·70 1·50
1203 7k. purple . . . . . 1·80 1·70
1203a 7k.50 ultramarine . . . 1·80 1·70
1204 8k.50 blue . . . . . 1·80 1·10

500 Map of Oresund Region

2000. Inauguration of Oresund Link (Denmark–Sweden road and rail system).
1205 **500** 4k.50 blue, white & blk 1·20 1·00
1206 – 4k.50 blue, green & blk 1·20 1·00
DESIGN: No. 1206, Oresund Bridge.

501 Suffragette on Front Page of *Politiken* (newspaper) **502** "Building Europe"

2000. The Twentieth Century (2nd series).
1207 **501** 4k. red, blk & cream . . 1·00 55
1208 – 5k. multicoloured . . . 1·30 1·10
1209 – 5k.50 multicoloured . . 1·40 1·10
1210 – 6k.75 multicoloured . . 2·10 1·70
DESIGNS—4k. Type **501** (women's suffrage, 1915); 5k. Caricature of Thorvald Stauning (Prime Minister 1924–26 and 1929–42) (Herluf Jensenius) (The Kanslergade Agreement (economic and social reforms)), 1933; 5k.50, Poster for *The Wheel of Fortune* (film), 1927; 6k.75, Front page of *Radio Weekly Review* (magazine), 1925.

2000. Europa.
1211 **502** 9k.75 multicoloured . . 2·30 2·10

503 Front Page of *Kristeligt Dagblad* (newspaper), 5 May 1945 **504** Linked Hands

2000. The Twentieth Century (3rd series).
1212 **503** 4k. black and cream . . 1·00 25
1213 – 5k.75 multicoloured . . 1·60 65
1214 – 6k.75 multicoloured . . 1·80 1·50
1215 – 12k.25 multicoloured . . 3·00 2·50
DESIGNS—4k. Type **503** (Liberation of Denmark); 5k.75, Caricature of Princess Margrethe (Herlif Jenserius) (adoption of new constitution, 1953); 6k.75, Ib Schonberg and Hvid Moller (actors) in a scene from *Cafe Paradise* (film), 1950; 12k.25, Front cover of brochure for Danish Arena televisions, 1957.

2000. Cerebral Palsy Association.
1216 **504** 4k.+50ore blue and red 1·20 1·10

505 Lockheed C-130 Hercules Transport Plane

2000. 50th Anniv of Royal Danish Air Force.
1217 **505** 9k.75 black and red . . 2·50 2·00
MS1218 116×60 mm. No. 1217 2·20 2·20

506 "Pegasus" (Kurt Trampedach)

2000. Paintings. Multicoloured.
1219 4k. Type **506** . . . . . . 1·00 95
1220 5k.25 "Untitled" (Nina Sten-Knudsen) . . . . . 1·40 1·20

507 Front Page of *Berlingske Tidende* (newspaper), 3 October 1972

2000. The Twentieth Century (4th series).
1221 **507** 4k. red, blk & cream . . 1·00 40
1222 – 4k.50 multicoloured . . 1·20 1·00
1223 – 5k.25 blk, red & cream . 1·40 75
1224 – 5k.50 multicoloured . . 1·60 75
DESIGNS: 4k. Type **507** (referendum on entry to European Economic Community); 4k.50, Caricature from *Blaeksprutten* (magazine), 1969 (The Youth Revolt); 5k.25, Poster for *The Olsen Gang* (film, 1968); 5k.50, Web page (development of the internet).

508 Kite

2001. 40th Anniv of Amnesty International.
1225 **508** 4k.+50 ore blk & red . . 1·10 1·00

509 Palm House

2001. 400th Anniv of Copenhagen University Botanical Gardens. Multicoloured.
1226 4k. Type **509** 90 45
1227 6k. Lake (28 × 21 mm) . . . 1·30 85
1228 12k.25 Giant lily-pad (28 × 21 mm) . . . . . . 2·75 3·00

510 "a", Text and Flowers

2001. Reading. Danish Children's Book "ABC" (first reader) by Halfdan Rasmussen. Multicoloured.
1229 4k. Type **510** 90 45
1230 7k. "Z" and text . . . . . 1·60 1·40

511 Martinus William Ferslew (designer and engraver)

512 Hands catching Water

2001. 150th Anniv of First Danish Stamp. Each black, red and brown.
1231 4k. Type **511** . . . . . . 1·00 45
1232 5k.50 Andreas Thiele (printer) . . . . 1·30 1·00
1233 6k. Frantz Christopher von Jessen (Copenhagen postmaster) . . . . 1·40 1·30
1234 10k.25 Magrius Otto Sophus (Postmaster-General) . . 2·50 2·50

2001. Europa. Water Resources. Multicoloured.
1235 4k.50 Type **512** . . . . . 1·10 80
1236 9k.75 Woman in shower . . 2·30 2·30

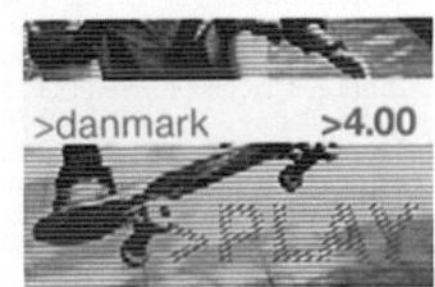

513 Skateboarder

2001. Youth Culture. Multicoloured.
1237 4k. Type **513** . . . . . . 1·00 35
1238 5k.50 Couple kissing . . . . 1·30 1·20
1239 6k. Mixing records . . . . 1·40 1·30
1240 10k.25 Pierced tongue . . . 2·10 2·40
MS1241 121 × 70 mm. Nos. 1237/40 6·25 6·25

514 "Missus" (Jorn Larsen)

2001. Paintings.
1242 **514** 18k. black and red . . . 4·00 3·75
1243 – 22k. multicoloured . . . 5·25 5·00
DESIGN: 22k. "Postbillede" (Henning Damgaard-Sorensen).

515 Queen Margrethe II with 1984 Prince Henrik and 1994 Marselisborg Castle Stamps

517 Rasmus Klump (Vilhelm Hansen)

516 *Bukken-Bruse*

2001. "HAFNIA '01" International Stamp Exhibition, Copenhagen. Multicoloured.
1244 4k. Type **515** . . . . 1·00 65
1245 4k.50 King Frederik IX with 1985 Queen Ingrid and 1994 Graasten Castle stamps . . . . 1·00 75
1246 5k.50 King Christian X with 1994 Amalienborg Castle and 1939 Queen Alexandrine stamps . . . 1·20 1·40
1247 7k. King Christian IX with 1994 Fredensborg Castle and 1907 King Frederick VIII stamps . . 1·60 1·80
MS1248 90 × 100 mm. Nos. 1244/7 6·25 6·25

2001. Ferries.
1249 **516** 3k.75 black, green and emerald 85 60
1250 – 4k. black, brown and green 90 70
1251 – 4k.25 black, green and blue . . . . 1·00 80
1252 – 6k. grey, black and red 1·30 1·30
DESIGNS: 4k. *Ouro*; 4k.25, *Hjarno*; 6k. *Barsofargen*.

2002. Danish Cartoons. Multicoloured.
1253 4k. Type **517** 90 35
1254 5k.50 Valhalla (Peter Madsen) . . . . 1·20 1·30
1255 6k.50 Jungo and Rita (Flemming Quist Moller) 1·40 1·50
1256 10k.50 Cirkleen (Hanne and Jannik Hastrup) . . . . 2·25 2·40
MS1257 142 × 80 mm. Nos. 1253/6 5·25 5·25

518 Back View

2002. Nordic Countries' Postal Co-operation. Modern Art. Showing "The Girls in the Airport" (sculpture, Hanne Varming). Each black, bronze on cream.
1258 4k. Type **518** 90 55
1259 5k. Front view . . . . 1·10 1·10

519 Face

2002. L.E.V. National Association (mental health foundation).
1260 **519** 4k. +50ore brown, agate on cream . . . . . . 1·00 95

520 Clown (Luna Ostergard)

521 Jon's Chapel, Bornholm

2002. Europa. Circus. Winning Entries in Stamp Design Competition. Multicoloured.
1261 4k. Type **520** 90 95
1262 5k. Clown (different) (Camille Wagner Larsen) 1·10 95

2002. Landscape Photographs by Kirsten Klein.
1263 **521** 4k. black and brown . . 90 55
1264 – 6k. black . . . . 1·30 1·30
1265 – 6k.50 deep green and green . . . . 1·60 1·40
1266 – 12k.50 black and blue 2·50 2·75
DESIGNS: 6k. Trees, Vestervig; 6k.50, Woods, Karskov, Langeland; 12k.50, Cliffs and beach, Stenbjerg, West Jutland.

522 1953 Nimbus Motorcycle and Sidecar

2002. Postal Vehicles. Multicoloured.
1267 4k. Type **522** 90 55
1268 5k.50 1962 Bedford CA van 1·20 1·20
1269 10k. 1984 Renault 4 van . . 2·20 2·20
1270 19k. 1998 Volvo FH12 lorry 4·00 4·25

523 *Dana* (marine research ship) and Atlantic Cod

2002. Centenary of International Council for the Exploration of the Sea. Multicoloured.
1271 4k. Type **523** . . . . 1·00 55
1272 10k. Hirtshals lighthouse and atlantic cod . . . . . 2·20 2·20
MS1273 186 × 61 mm. 4k. Type **523**; 10k.50 Lighthouse and atlantic cod . . . . 3·25 3·25
Stamps of a similar design were issued by Faroe Islands and Greenland.

524 "Children's Corner" (Jens Birkemose)

2002. Paintings.
1274 **524** 5k. red and blue . . . . 1·10 1·10
1275 – 6k.50 multicoloured . . 1·40 1·40
DESIGN: 6k.50 "Maleren og modellen" (Frans Kannik).

525 Underground Train

2002. Inauguration of Copenhagen Metro.
1276 **525** 5k.50 black, green and brown on cream . . . 1·20 1·20

526 Dianas Have, Horsholm (Vandkunsten Design Studio)

2002. Domestic Architecture (1st series). Multicoloured.
1277 4k. Type **526** 75 40
1278 4k.25 Bapistry, Long House and Gate (Poul Ingemann) Blangstedgard, Odense . . . . 80 1·00
1279 5k.50 Dansk Folkeferie, Karrebaecksminde (Stephan Kappel) . . . . 1·00 1·30
1280 6k.50 Terrasser, Fredensborg (Jorn Utzon) 1·20 1·50
1281 9k. Soholm, Klampenborg (Arne Jacobsen) . . . . . 1·70 2·00
See also Nos. 1296/1300, 1369/73 and 1398/1402.

527 Football

529 Expedition Members

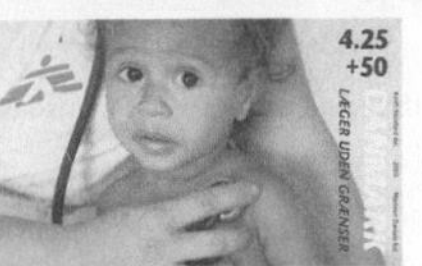

528 Child and Doctor

2003. Youth Sports. Multicoloured.
1282 4k.25 Type **527** 80 50
1283 5k.50 Swimming . . . . . 1·00 60
1284 8k.50 Gymnastics . . . . . 1·60 95
1285 11k.50 Basketball . . . . . 2·10 1·25

2003. Medicins sans Frontieres (medical charity).
1286 **528** 4k.25+50ore multicoloured 90 90

2003. Centenary of the Danish Literary Expedition to Greenland.
1287 **529** 4k.25 blue 80 50
1288 – 7k. brown, green and blue (60 × 22 mm) . . 1·30 75
MS1289 167 × 61 mm. Nos. 1287/81 2·20 1·30
DESIGN: 7k. Tents and mountains.
Stamps of a similar design were issued by Greenland.

530 Mayfly (*Ephemera danica*)

531 "Fools" Festival Poster' (Ole Flick)

2003. Insects. Multicoloured.
1290 4k.25 Type **530** 80 50
1291 6k.50 Water beetle (*Dysticus latissimus*) . . . . 1·20 70
1292 12k. Dragonfly (*Cordulegaster boltoni*) (20 × 39 mm) . . . . . . 2·20 1·30
MS1293 80 × 76 mm. Nos. 1290/2 4·25 2·50

2003. Europa. Poster Art.
1294 **531** 4k.25 multicoloured . . 80 50
1295 – 5k.50 black . . . . . . 1·00 60
DESIGN: 5k.50, "Thorvaldsen's Museum" (Ole Woldbye).

2003. Domestic Architecture (2nd series). As T **526**. Multicoloured.
1296 4k. Bellahoj, Copenhagen (Tage Nielsen and Mogens Irming) 75 45
1297 4k.25 Anchersvej Christiansholm Fort, Klampenborg (Mogens Lasen) 80 50
1298 5k.25 Gerthasminde, Odense (Anton Rosen) . . . . . 1·00 60
1299 9k. Solvang, Vallekilde (Anton Bentsen) . . . . 1·70 1·00
1300 15k. Stenbrogard, Brorup (Peder Holden Hansen) 2·75 1·60

532 "Baering" (Sys Hindsbo)

2003. Paintings. Multicoloured.
1301 5k.50 Type **532** . . . . . . 1·00 60
1302 19k. "The Forgotten Land" (Poul Anker Bech) . . . 3·50 2·10

533 Thyra's Stone

534 "Towards the Light" (statue, Rudolph Tegner)

2003. UNESCO World Heritage Site. Royal Jelling Open Air Museum.
1303 **533** 4k.25 black, sepia and brown 80 50
1304 – 5k.50 black, brown and sepia . . . . 1·00 60
1305 – 8k.50 black and bistre 1·60 95
1306 – 11k.50 black and deep olive . . . . 2·10 1·25
DESIGNS: Type **533**; 5k.50, Gorm's cup; 8k.50, Harald's stone; 11k.50, Jelling church.

2003. Centenary of Niels Finsen's Nobel Prize for Physiology and Medicine.
1307 **534** 6k.50 indigo . . . . . . 1·20 70

2004. Arms. As T **73**.
1308 **73** 12k.50 indigo . . . . . . 2·20 1·30
1309 13k. orange . . . . . . 2·40 1·40
1310 15k. blue . . . . 2·75 1·60

535 Butterfly and Caterpillar

536 Heimdal carrying Gjallar Horn on Bifrost Bridge

2004. Centenary of Children's Aid Day (fund raising charity).
1368 **535** 4k.25+50ore multicoloured 90 60

2004. Domestic Architecture (3rd series). As T **526**. Multicoloured.
1369 4k.50 Spurveskjul, Virum Copenhagen (Nicolai Abildgaard) 85 55
1370 6k. Liselund, Møn (Andreas Kirkerup) . . . . 1·20 65
1371 7k. Kampmann's Yard, Varde (Hans Ollgaard) . . 1·30 75
1372 12k.50 Harsdorff's House, Copenhagen (Caspar Harsdorff) . . . . 2·20 1·30
1373 15k. Nyso, Praesto (Jens Lauridsen) . . . . 2·75 1·60

2004. Nordic Mythology. Each sepia, blue and black.
1374 4k.50 Type **536** 85 55
1375 6k. Gefion ploughing Sealand out of Sweden . . 1·20 65
MS1376 105 × 71 mm. Nos. 1374/5 2·00 2·00
Stamps of a similar theme were issued by Aland Islands, Faroe Islands, Finland, Greenland, Iceland, Norway and Sweden.

537 Artist's Wooden Figure and Academy Seal

2004. 250th Anniv of Academy of Fine Arts, Copenhagen.
1377 **537** 5k.50 multicoloured . . 1·00 60

538 Fountain viewed through Doorway

539 Prince Frederik and Mary Donaldson

2004. 300th Anniv of Frederiksberg Palace. Multicoloured.
1378 4k.25 Type **538** 80 50
1379 4k.50 Courtyard viewed through arch 85 50
1380 6k.50 Aerial view of palace (57 × 33 mm) . . . . . . 1·20 70
MS1381 125 × 78 mm. Nos. 1378/80 2·75 2·75

2004. Marriage of Crown Prince Frederik and Mary Elizabeth Donaldson. Multicoloured.
1382 4k.50 Type **539** 85 50
1383 4k.50 As No. 1382 but with design reversed 85 50
MS1384 130 × 65 mm. Nos. 1382/3 1·70 1·00
Stamps of same design were issued by Faroe Islands and Greenland.

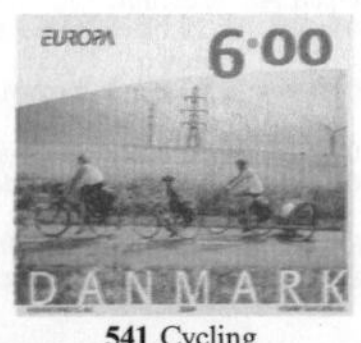

540 Prince Henrik

541 Cycling

2004. 70th Birthday of Prince Henrik.
1385 **540** 4k.50 multicoloured . . 85 50

2004. Europa. Holidays. Multicoloured.
1386 6k. Type **541** . . . . 1·10 65
1387 9k. Sailing . . . . 1·70 1·00

542 Trial Sailing of Skuldelev Reconstruction

2004. Viking Ship Museum, Roskilde. Multicoloured.
1388 4k.50 Type **542** 85 50
1389 5k.50 Reconstructed hull . . 1·00 60
1390 6k.50 Exhibition . . . . . 1·20 70
1391 12k.50 Excavation . . . . . 2·40 1·40

543 "Senses the Body Landscape" (Lars Ravn)

2004. Paintings. Multicoloured.
1392 13k. Type **543** . . . . . . 2·50 1·50
1393 21k. "The Dog Bites" (Lars Norgard) . . . . 4·00 2·40

544 Kestrel (*Falco tinnunculus*)

2004. Birds of Prey. Multicoloured.
1394 4k.50 Type **544** 85 50
1395 5k.50 Northern sparrow hawk (*Accipter nisus*) . . 1·00 60
1396 6k. Common buzzard (*Buteo buteo*) . . . . 1·10 65
1397 7k. Western marsh harrier (*Circus aeruginosus*) . . . 1·30 75

2005. Domestic Architecture (4th series). As T **526**. Multicoloured.
1398 4k.25 Hjarup Manse, Vamdrup 80 50
1399 4k.50 Ejdersted Farm, South-West Schleswig (Adriaen Alberts Hauwert) 85 50
1400 7k.50 Provstegade, Randers 1·40 85
1401 9k.50 Smith's Yard, Kirkestræde, Koge . . . 1·80 1·00
1402 16k.50 Carmelite Monastery, Elsinore . . . . 3·00 1·80

545 Boys

2005. SOS Children's Villages.
1403 **545** 4k.50 +50 ore multicoloured 90 90

546 Hans Christian Andersen

2005. Birth Bicentenary of Hans Christian Andersen (writer).
1404 **546** 4k.50 black 85 50
1405 – 5k.50 multicoloured (23 × 38 mm) . . . . 1·00 60
1406 – 6k.50 multicoloured (23 × 38 mm) . . . . 1·20 70
1407 – 7k.50 multicoloured (23 × 38 mm) . . . . 1·40 85
DESIGNS: 5k.50 Paper cut-out; 6k.50 Duckling, script, quill and ink pot; 7k.50 Boots.

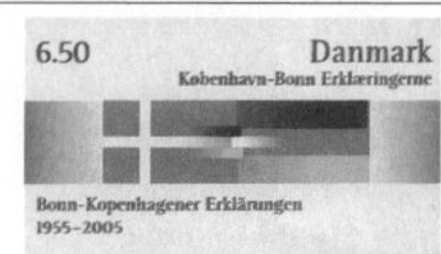

547 Danish and German Flags

2005. 50th Anniv of Copenhagen—Bonn Declarations (tolerance for minorities).
1408 **547** 6k.50 multicoloured . . 1·20 70

MILITARY FRANK STAMPS

1917. Nos. 135 and 138 optd **S F** (= "Soldater Frimaerke").
M188 **21** 5ore green . . . . . . 11·50 20·00
M189 10ore red . . . . 11·50 19·00

NEWSPAPER STAMPS

N 18

1901.
N185 **N 18** 1ore green . . . . . 11·00 75
N186 5ore blue . . . . . . 27·00 6·25
N133 7ore red . . . . . . 13·50 55
N188 8ore green . . . . . 28·00 1·00
N189 10ore lilac . . . . . 27·00 1·80
N135 20ore green . . . . . 23·00 75
N191 29ore orange . . . . 40·00 2·30
N136 38ore orange . . . . 32·00 80
N193 41ore brown . . . . 45·00 2·20
N137 68ore brown . . . . . 80·00 15·00
N138 1k. purple & green . . 23·00 1·20
N139 5k. green and pink . . £140 19·00
N140 10k. blue and stone . . £150 25·00

OFFICIAL STAMPS

O 9

1871. Value in "skilling".
O51a **O 9** 2sk. blue . . . . £110 60·00
O52 4sk. red . . . . 40·00 9·25
O53 16sk. green £375 £130

1875. Value in "ore".
O185 **O 9** 1ore orange 70 75
O100 3ore lilac 70 65
O186 3ore grey . . . . 2·30 4·50
O101 4ore blue . . . . . . 1·10 95
O188 5ore green 50 25
O189 5ore brown . . . . . . 1·40 14·00
O 94 8ore red . . . . 7·25 1·30
O104 10ore red . . . . . . 1·00 95
O191 10ore green . . . . . 2·30 1·50
O192 20ore lilac . . . . . 16·00 20·00
O193 20ore blue . . . . . 12·50 8·00
O 98 32ore green . . . . . 17·00 15·00

PARCEL POST STAMPS

1919. Various types optd **POSTFAERGE**.
P208 **21** 10ore red . . . . 27·00 44·00
P209 **15** 10ore green . . . . . . 9·50 8·75
P210 10ore brown . . . . . . 11·00 5·75
P211 **21** 15ore lilac . . . . . . 16·00 19·00
P212 30ore orange . . . . . 12·50 18·00
P213 30ore blue . . . . . . 1·90 3·25
P214 50ore black & purple . . £160 £150
P215a 50ore grey . . . . . . 18·00 8·75
P216 **22** 1k. brown . . . . . . 80·00 £110
P217 **21** 1k. blue and brown . . 40·00 19·00
P218 5k. brown & mauve . . 90 1·40
P219 10k. green and red . . . 35·00 60·00

1927. Stamps of 1927 (solid background) optd **POSTFAERGE**.
P252 **40** 15ore red . . . . 13·00 7·50
P253 30ore yellow . . . . . . 13·00 8·75
P254 40ore green . . . . . . 16·00 8·25

1936. Stamps of 1933 (lined background) optd **POSTFAERGE**.
P491 **43** 5ore purple 25 25
P299 10ore orange . . . . . 14·50 12·50
P300 10ore brown . . . . . 90 1·10
P301 10ore violet 25 30
P302 10ore green 35 25
P303a **40** 15ore red 30 90
P304 30ore blue . . . . . . 3·75 2·75
P305 30ore orange 25 75
P306 40ore green . . . . . 2·40 2·75
P307 40ore blue 25 75
P308 **45** 50ore grey 45 90
P309 1k. brown . . . . . . 1·00 65

1945. Stamps of 1942 optd **POSTFAERGE**.
P346 **67** 30ore orange . . . . . . 1·30 1·00
P347 40ore blue 60 90
P348 50ore grey 70 90

1949. Stamps of 1946 and 1948 optd **POSTFAERGE**.
P376 **80** 30ore orange . . . . . . 2·30 1·10
P377 30ore red . . . . 90 1·00
P378 40ore blue . . . . 1·80 1·10
P379 40ore grey . . . . 90 1·00
P380 50ore grey . . . . 9·25 2·30
P381 50ore green . . . . . . 75 1·00
P382 70ore green . . . . . . 75 1·00
P383 **73** 1k. brown . . . . . . 1·00 75
P384 1k.25 orange . . . . . . 3·75 5·00
P495 2k. red . . . . 2·50 1·80
P496 5k. blue . . . . 5·25 3·75

1967. Optd **POSTFAERGE**.
P488 **117** 40ore brown 70 50
P492 50ore brown 80 40
P489 80ore blue 85 50
P493 90ore blue . . . . . . 1·60 75

1975. Optd **POSTFAERGE**.
P597 **207** 100ore blue . . . . . . 1·60 1·00

POSTAGE DUE STAMPS

1921. Stamps of 1905 and 1913 optd **PORTO**.
D214 **15** 1ore orange . . . . . . 1·40 1·20
D215 **21** 5ore green . . . . 3·50 1·50
D216 7ore orange . . . . . . 2·50 1·40
D217 10ore red . . . . 14·00 5·75
D218 20ore blue . . . . 10·50 4·75
D219 25ore black and brown 17·00 1·50
D220 50ore black & purple . . 5·75 2·10

D 32

1921. Solid background.
D221 **D 32** 1ore orange 40 55
D222 4ore blue . . . . . . 1·60 1·90
D223 5ore brown . . . . . 1·90 50
D224 5ore green . . . . . 1·40 40
D225 7ore green . . . . . 9·00 12·50
D226 7ore violet . . . . . 20·00 25·00
D227 10ore green . . . . . 2·00 35
D228 10ore brown . . . . . 1·50 25
D229 20ore blue 90 40
D230 20ore grey . . . . . 1·90 1·00
D231 25ore red . . . . . . 3·25 75
D232 25ore lilac . . . . . 2·50 1·10
D233 25ore blue . . . . . 3·25 3·25
D234 1k. blue . . . . 39·00 4·75
D235 1k. blue and brown . . 7·25 3·25
D236 5k. violet . . . . . . 9·50 5·75
For stamps with lined background see Nos. D285/97.

1921. Military Frank stamp optd **PORTO**.
D237 **21** 10ore red (No. M189) . . 6·75 5·00

1934. Lined background.
D285 **D 32** 1ore green 15 15
D286 2ore red 15 15
D287 5ore green 15 15
D288 6ore green 25 15
D289 8ore mauve . . . . . 1·80 1·50
D290 10ore orange 15 10
D291 12ore blue 35 25
D292 15ore violet 35 25
D293 20ore grey 15 10
D294 25ore blue 35 20
D295 30ore green 35 25
D296 40ore purple 60 40
D297 1k. brown 60 15

1934. Surch **PORTO 15**.
D298 **15** 15 on 12ore lilac . . . . 2·50 2·20

SPECIAL FEE STAMPS

1923. No. D227 optd **GEBYR GEBYR**.
S218 **D 32** 10ore green . . . . . 9·25 1·50

S 36

1926. Solid background.
S229 **S 36** 10ore green . . . . . . 4·25 55
S230 10ore brown . . . . . . 5·25 50

1934. Lined background.
S285 **S 36** 5ore green 15 15
S286 10ore orange 15 15

DHAR Pt. 1

A state of Central India. Now uses Indian stamps.

4 pice = 1 anna.

1

2

1897. Imperf.
1 **1** ½pice black on red . . . . . 2·75 3·00
3 ¼a. black on orange . . . . . 2·75 3·25
4 ½a. black on mauve . . . . . 4·25 5·00
5 1a. black on green . . . . . 8·50 14·00
6 2a. black on yellow . . . . . 28·00 45·00

1898. Perf.
7b **2** ½a. red . . . . 3·50 6·00
8 1a. purple . . . . 3·75 7·50
10 2a. green . . . . 7·00 23·00

DIEGO-SUAREZ Pt. 6

A port in N. Madagascar. A separate colony till 1896, when it was incorporated with Madagascar.

100 centimes = 1 franc.

1890. Stamps of French Colonies (Type J Commerce), surch **15** sideways.
1 J 15 on 1c. black on blue . . . £170 70·00
2 15 on 5c. green . . . . . . £450 70·00
3 15 on 10c. black on lilac . . . £180 55·00
4 15 on 20c. red on green . . . £450 70·00
5 15 on 25c. black on red . . . 85·00 21·00

2

3

1890. Various designs.
6 **2** 1c. black . . . . £350 85·00
7 5c. black . . . . £325 75·00
8 15c. black . . . . 85·00 32·00
9 25c. black . . . . £110 35·00

1891.
10 **3** 5c. black . . . . £120 70·00

1891. Stamps of French Colonies. (Type J Commerce) surch **1891 DIEGO-SUAREZ 5 c.**
13 J 5c. on 10c. black on lilac . . £160 80·00
14 5c. on 20c. red on green . . . £140 65·00

1892. Stamps of French Colonies (Type J Commerce) optd **DIEGO-SUAREZ**.
15 J 1c. black on blue . . . . . 24·00 12·50
16 2c. brown on buff . . . . . 28·00 13·50
17 4c. brown on grey . . . . . 28·00 22·00
18 5c. green on green . . . . . 85·00 55·00
19 10c. black on lilac . . . . . 23·00 23·00
20 15c. blue on blue . . . . . . 18·00 12·50
21 20c. red on green . . . . . . 26·00 21·00
22 25c. black on pink . . . . . 16·00 13·50
23 30c. brown on drab £850 £600
24 35c. black on orange £850 £600
25 75c. red on pink . . . . . . 65·00 26·00
26 1f. green . . . . 60·00 40·00

1892. "Tablet" key-type inscr "DIEGO-SUAREZ ET DEPENDANCES".
38 D 1c. black on blue . . . . . 1·75 3·75
39 2c. brown on buff . . . . . 2·25 1·25
40 4c. brown on grey . . . . . 85 4·00
41 5c. green on green . . . . . 1·60 4·75
42 10c. black on lilac . . . . . 5·75 6·50
43 15c. blue . . . . 4·25 11·00
44 20c. red on green . . . . . 8·75 10·00
45 25c. black on pink . . . . . 6·50 8·75
46 30c. brown on drab . . . . 9·00 22·00
47 40c. red on yellow . . . . . 15·00 13·50
48 50c. red on pink . . . . . . 19·00 13·00
49 75c. brown on yellow . . . . 42·00 26·00
50 1f. green . . . . 60·00 35·00

1894. "Tablet" key-type inscr "DIEGO-SUAREZ".
51 D 1c. black on blue . . . . . 50 2·75
52 2c. brown on buff . . . . . 1·25 3·50
53 4c. brown on grey . . . . . 1·75 3·50
54 5c. green on green . . . . . 2·25 5·25
55 10c. black on lilac . . . . . 5·75 6·25
56 15c. blue . . . . 3·50 5·50
57 20c. red on green . . . . . 8·00 14·50
58 25c. black on pink . . . . . 4·25 4·00
59 30c. brown on drab . . . . 9·00 6·25
60 40c. red on yellow . . . . . 7·75 5·00
61 50c. red on pink . . . . . . 6·00 8·00
62 75c. brown on yellow . . . . 2·75 6·00
63 1f. green . . . . 8·25 12·00

POSTAGE DUE STAMPS

D 4

1891.
D11 **D 4** 5c. violet . . . . 65·00 24·00
D12 50c. black on yellow . . 65·00 35·00

1892. Postage Due stamps of French Colonies overprinted **DIEGO-SUAREZ**.
D27 **D 4** 1c. black . . . . £100 50·00
D28 2c. black . . . . £110 45·00
D29 3c. black . . . . £110 50·00
D30 4c. black . . . . £100 60·00
D31 5c. black . . . . £110 60·00
D32 10c. black . . . . 27·00 25·00
D33 15c. black . . . . 27·00 27·00
D34 20c. black £160 £110
D35 30c. black . . . . 90·00 60·00
D36 60c. black £850 £600
D37 1f. brown £1600 £850

DJIBOUTI Pt. 6

A port in French Somaliland S. of the Red Sea, later capital of French Territory of the Afars and the Issas.

100 centimes = 1 franc.

1893. "Tablet" key-type stamp of Obock optd **DJ**.
83 D 5c. green & red on green . . £110 £120

1894. Same type surch in figures and **DJIBOUTI**.
85 D 25 on 2c. brn & bl on buff £275 £180
86 50 on 1c. blk & red on blue £325 £225

1894. Triangular stamp of Obock optd **DJIBOUTI** or surch **1** also.
87 **5** 1f. on 5f. red £600 £400
88 5f. red £1400 £1100

12 Djibouti (The apparent perforation is part of the design.)

13 "Pingouin" (French gunboat)

14 Crossing the Desert

1894. Imperf.
89 **12** 1c. red and black . . . . 1·10 1·25
90 2c. black and red 45 45
91 4c. blue and brown . . . 3·00 1·90
92 5c. red and green . . . . 2·25 1·60
93 5c. green . . . . 2·50 3·50
94 – 10c. green and brown . . . 3·75 1·00
95 – 15c. green and lilac . . . 3·25 1·75
96 – 25c. blue and red . . . . 5·00 2·00
97 – 30c. red and brown . . . 3·75 3·75
98 – 40c. blue and yellow . . . 55·00 48·00
99 – 50c. red and blue . . . . 18·00 12·00
100 – 75c. orange and mauve . . . 35·00 29·00
101 – 1f. black and olive . . . 21·00 21·00
102 – 2f. red and brown . . . . 85·00 70·00
103 **13** 5f. blue and red £190 £120
104 **14** 25f. blue and red £850 £850
105 50f. red and blue £650 £650
DESIGNS— As Type **12**: 10 to 75c. Different views of Djibouti; 1, 2f. Port of Djibouti.

1899. As last, surch.
108 – 0.05 on 75c. orge & mve 55·00 32·00
109 – 0.10 on 1f. blk & olive . . 70·00 60·00
106 **12** 0.40 on 4c. blue & brown £2750 19·00
110 – 0.40 on 2f. red & brown £550 £350
111 **13** 0.75 on 5f. blue and red . . £450 £375

1902. Rectangular stamp of Obock surch **0.05**.
107 **6** 0.05 on 75c. lilac & orange £1200 £900

1902. Triangular stamps of Obock surch.
112 **7** 5c. on 25f. blue and brown 55·00 60·00
113 10c. on 50f. green & red . . 75·00 60·00

1902. Nos. 98/9 surch.
114 5c. on 40c. blue and yellow 2·25 2·00
115 10c. on 50c. red and blue . . 15·00 20·00

1902. Stamps of Obock surch **DJIBOUTI** and value.
120 **6** 5c. on 30c. yellow & grn . . 5·50 12·50
116 10c. on 25c. black & blue 4·50 7·75
118 **7** 10c. on 2f. orange & lilac 35·00 50·00
119 10c. on 10f. lake and red . . 30·00 30·00

For later issues see **FRENCH SOMALI COAST**, **FRENCH TERRITORY OF THE AFARS AND THE ISSAS** and **DJIBOUTI REPUBLIC**.

DJIBOUTI REPUBLIC Pt. 12

Formerly French Territory of the Afars and the Issas.

112 Map and Flag

116 Ostrich

115 Head Rest

1977. Independence. Multicoloured.
685 45f. Type **112** . . . . 1·50 80
686 65f. Map of Djibouti (horiz) 2·25 95

1977. Various stamps of the French Territory of the Afars and the Issas optd **REPUBLIQUE DE DJIBOUTI** or surch also. (a) Sea Shells.
687 **81** 1f. on 4f. mult 20 20
688 – 2f. on 5f. brown, mauve and violet (629) 20 20
689 – 20f. brown & grn (633) . . 55 55
690 – 30f. brn, pur & grn (634) 65 65
691 – 40f. brown & grn (635) . . 90 90
692 – 45f. brn, grn & bl (636) . . 1·00 1·00
693 – 60f. black & brn (638) . . 1·40 1·40
694 – 70f. brn, bl & blk (639) . . 1·90 1·90

(b) Flora and Fauna.
695 **103** 5f. on 20f. multicoloured 20 20
696 **106** 45f. multicoloured 90 90
697 – 50f. multicoloured (675) 1·40 1·40
698 **107** 70f. multicoloured . . . . 1·60 1·60
699 – 100f. multicoloured (653) 2·50 2·50
700 – 150f. multicoloured (676) 3·00 3·00
701 – 300f. multicoloured (654) 7·50 7·50

(c) Buildings.
702 **99** 8f. grey, red & bl (postage) 30 30
703 **109** 500f. mult (air) . . . . . 9·75 8·25

(d) Celebrities.
704 **111** 55f. red, grey & grn (air) 1·40 1·10
705 – 75f. red, brn & grn (682) 2·50 2·50
706 **104** 200f. blue, green and orange (postage) . . . 3·75 3·75

(e) Sport.
707 **108** 200f. multicoloured . . . 4·50 4·50

1977. Local Art. Multicoloured.
708 10f. Type **115** 20 10
709 20f. Water cask (vert) 45 15
710 25f. Washing jar (vert) . . . 65 20

1977. Birds. Multicoloured.
711 90f. Type **116** . . . . 2·75 1·00
712 100f. Vitelline masked weaver 3·75 1·75

117 "Glossodoris"

1977. Sea Life. Multicoloured.
713 45f. Type **117** . . . . 1·00 90
714 70f. Turtle . . . . 1·10 45
715 80f. Catalufa . . . . 1·60 65

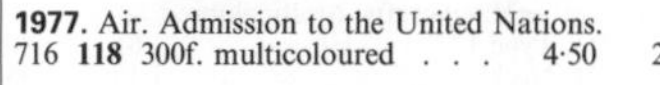
118 Map, Dove and U.N. Emblem

1977. Air. Admission to the United Nations.
716 **118** 300f. multicoloured . . . 4·50 2·75

119 Crabs "Uca lactea"

1977. Fauna. Multicoloured.
717 15f. Type **119** 45 15
718 50f. Klipspringer . . . . . . 1·25 40
719 150f. Dolphin (fish) . . . . . 3·25 2·00

120 President Hassan Gouled Aptidon and Flag

1978.
720 **120** 65f. multicoloured 90 45

121 Marcel Brochet MB 101

1978. Air. Djibouti Aero Club. Multicoloured.
721 60f. Type **121** 95 60
722 85f. De Havilland Tiger Moth . . . . 1·25 80
723 200f. Morane Saulnier Rallye Commodore . . . . 2·75 1·60

122 "Charaxes hansali"

123 "Head of an Old Man"

1978. Butterflies. Multicoloured.
724 5f. Type **122** 10 10
725 20f. "Colias electo" 55 20
726 25f. "Acraea chilo" 80 40
727 150f. "Junonia hierta" . . . 3·00 1·50

1978. Air. 400th Birth Anniv of Rubens. Mult.
728 50f. Type **123** 85 35
729 500f. "The Hippopotamus Hunt" (detail) . . . . . . 8·00 3·25

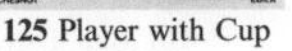

124 Necklace **125** Player with Cup

1978. Native Handicrafts. Multicoloured.
730 45f. Type **124** 85 40
731 55f. Necklace . . . . 1·10 45

1978. Air. World Cup Football Championship, Argentina. Multicoloured.
732 100f. Type **125** . . . . . . 1·40 45
733 300f. World Cup, footballer and map of Argentina . . 4·25 1·25

126 "Bougainvillea glabra"

1978. Flowers. Multicoloured.
734 15f. Type **126** 40 10
735 35f. "Hibiscus schizopetalus" 70 20
736 250f. "Caesalpinia pulcherrima" . . . . . . 4·50 85

1978. Air. Argentina's Victory in World Cup Football Championship. Nos. 722/3 optd.
737 100f. Type **125** . . . . . . 1·60 45
738 300f. World Cup, footballer and map of Argentina . . 4·50 1·50
OVERPRINTS: 100f. **ARGENTINE CHAMPION 1978**; 300f. **ARGENTINE HOLLANDE 3–1.**

128 "The Hare" (Albrecht Durer)

1978. Air. Paintings. Multicoloured.
739 100f. "Tahitian Women" (Paul Gauguin) (horiz) . . 1·90 55
740 250f. Type **128** . . . . . . 4·75 1·90

129 Knobbed Triton

1978. Sea Shells. Multicoloured.
741 10f. Type **129** 75 35
742 80f. Trumpet triton . . . . . 2·50 90

130 Copper-banded Butterflyfish **131** Dove and U.P.U. Emblem

1978. Fishes. Multicoloured.
743 8f. Type **130** 40 15
744 30f. Yellow tang 85 25
745 40f. Harlequin sweetlips . . . 1·60 45

1978. Air. "Philexafrique" Exhibition, Libreville, Gabon (1st issue) and Int. Stamp Fair, Essen, W. Germany. As T **262** of Gabon. Multicoloured.
746 90f. Jay and Brunswick 1852 3sqr. stamp . . . . 1·90 1·40
747 90f. African spoonbill and Djibouti 1977 optd 300f. stamp . . . . 1·90 1·40

1978. Air. Centenary of Paris U.P.U. Congress.
748 **131** 200f. green, brn & turq 2·75 1·40

132 Alsthom BB 1201 Diesel Locomotive

1979. Djibouti–Addis Ababa Railway. Mult.
749 40f. Type **132** 90 40
750 55f. Pacific locomotive No. 231 . . . . 80 30
751 60f. Steam locomotive No. 130 . . . . 1·00 35
752 75f. Alsthom CC 2001 diesel-electric locomotive . . . . 1·40 60

133 Children learning to Count

1979. International Year of the Child. Multicoloured.
753 20f. Type **133** 35 10
754 200f. Mother and child . . . 3·00 1·25

134 De Havilland Twin Otter over Crater

1979. Ardoukoba Volcano. Multicoloured.
755 30f. Sud Aviation Alouette II helicopter over crater . . . 65 40
756 90f. Type **134** . . . . 1·90 70

135 Sir Rowland Hill and 300f. Stamp, 1977

1979. Death Centenary of Sir Rowland Hill. Multicoloured.
757 25f. Type **135** 35 10
758 100f. Letters with 1894 50f. and 1977 45f. stamps . . . 2·25 60
759 150f. Loading mail on ship 2·25 80

136 Junkers Ju 52/3m and Dewoitine D-338 Trimotor

1979. Air. 75th Anniv of Powered Flight. Multicoloured.
760 140f. Type **136** . . . . . . 2·25 95
761 250f. Potez 63-11 bomber and Supermarine Spitfire Mk. VII . . . . 3·25 1·90
762 500f. Concorde and Sikorsky S-40 flying boat "American Clipper" . . . . 7·25 3·25

137 Djibouti, Local Woman and Namaqua Dove

1979. "Philexafrique 2" Exhibition, Gabon (2nd issue). Multicoloured.
763 55f. Type **137** . . . . 2·25 1·40
764 80f. U.P.U. emblem, map, Douglas DC-8-60 "Super Sixty", Alsthom diesel-electric train and postal runner . . . . 2·75 1·25

138 "Opuntia"

1979. Flowers. Multicoloured.
765 2f. Type **138** 10 10
766 8f. "Solanacea" (horiz) . . . 20 10
767 15f. "Trichodesma" (horiz) 35 10
768 45f. "Acacia etbaica" (horiz) 65 15
769 50f. "Thunbergia alata" . . . 90 15

139 "The Washerwoman"

1979. Air. Death Centenary of Honore Daumier (painter).
770 **139** 500f. multicoloured . . . 8·25 2·75

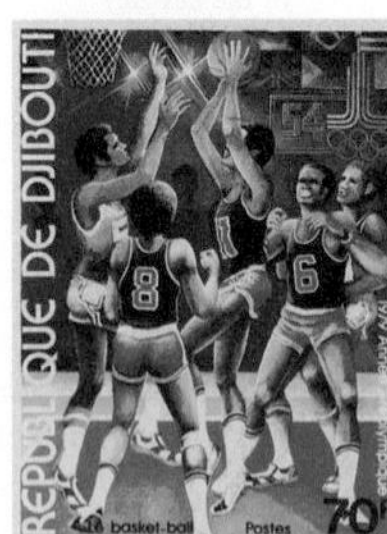

140 Basketball

1979. Pre-Olympic Year. Multicoloured.
771 70f. Type **140** . . . . 1·10 30
772 120f. Running . . . . 1·60 55
773 300f. Football . . . . 2·75 85

141 Bull-mouth Helmet

1979. Shells. Multicoloured.
774 10f. Type **141** 20 15
775 40f. Arthritic spider conch . . 1·00 20
776 300f. Ventral harp . . . . . 5·50 1·60

142 Winter Sports Equipment and Mosque

1980. Air. Winter Olympic Games, Lake Placid.
777 **142** 150f. multicoloured . . . 2·25 65

143 Lions Club Banner and Steam Locomotive

1980. Djibouti Clubs. Multicoloured.
778 90f. Rotary Club banner and Morane Saulnier MS 892 (75th anniv of Rotary International) . . . . . . 1·75 70
779 100f. Type **143** . . . . . . 2·50 50

144 "Colotis danae" **147** Basketball

145 Boeing 737

1980. Butterflies. Multicoloured.
780 5f. Type **144** 20 20
781 55f. "Danaus chrysippus" . . 1·00 65

1980. Air. Foundation of "Air Djibouti".
782 **145** 400f. multicoloured . . . 6·00 2·25

1980. Air. Winter Olympic Games. No. 777 surch with names of Medal Winners.
783 **142** 80f. on 150f. . . . . . . 1·10 45
784 200f. on 150f. . . . . . 2·75 1·25
OVERPRINTS: 80f. **A.M. MOSER-PROEL AUTRICHE DESCENT DAMES MEDAILLE D'OR.** 200f. **HEIDEN USA 5 MEDAILLES D'OR PATINAGE DE VITESSE.**

1980. Olympic Games, Moscow. Multicoloured.
785 60f. Type **147** 90 20
786 120f. Football . . . . 1·60 45
787 250f. Running . . . . 3·00 1·00

148 "Apollo XI" Moon Landing

1980. Air. Conquest of Space. Multicoloured.
788 200f. Type **148** . . . . . . 2·75 65
789 300f. "Apollo-Soyuz" link-up 4·50 1·00

149 Samisch v Romanovsky Game, Moscow, 1925

1980. Founding of International Chess Federation, 1924. Multicoloured.
790 20f. Type **149** 70 15
791 75f. "Royal Chess Party" (15th-century Italian book illustration) . . . . 1·90 40

150 Satellite and Earth Station

1980. Air. Inauguration of Satellite Earth Station.
792 **150** 500f. multicoloured . . . 7·25 1·90

151 Sieve Cowrie

1980. Shells. Multicoloured.
793 15f. Type **151** 50 20
794 85f. Chambered nautilus . . 1·90 65

152 Sir Alexander Fleming and Penicillin

1980. Anniversaries. Multicoloured.
795 20f. Type **152** 50 20
796 130f. Jules Verne and space capsules . . . . 2·25 65
ANNIVERSARIES: 20f. Discovery of penicillin, 25th anniv. 130f. Jules Verne, 75th death anniv.

153 "Graf Zeppelin" and Sphinx

1980. Air. 80th Anniv of First Zeppelin Flight. Multicoloured.
797 100f. Type **153** . . . . . . 2·00 60
798 150f. Ferdinand von Zeppelin 2·50 90

154 Capt. Cook and H.M.S. "Endeavour"

1980. Death Bicentenary (1979) of Captain James Cook. Multicoloured.
799 55f. Type **154** 90 80
800 90f. Cook's ships and map of voyages . . . . 1·60 1·10

155 "Voyager" and Saturn

1980. Air. Space Exploration.
801 **155** 250f. multicoloured . . . 4·00 1·10

156 Saving a Goal

1981. Air. World Cup Football Eliminators. Multicoloured.
802 80f. Type **156** . . . . 1·10 35
803 200f. Tackle . . . . 2·75 80

157 Transport 158 Yuri Gagarin and "Vostok 1"

1981. Air European–African Economic Convention.
804 **157** 100f. multicoloured . . . 3·00 90

1981. Air. Space Anniversaries and Events. Multicoloured.
805 75f. Type **158** (20th anniv of first man in space) . . . . 1·10 35
806 120f. "Viking" exploration of Mars (horiz) . . . . 1·60 50
807 150f. Alan Shepard and "Freedom 7" (20th anniv of first American in space) 2·25 65

159 Arabian Angelfish

1981. Djibouti Tropical Aquarium. Mult.
808 25f. Type **159** 60 15
809 55f. Moorish idol . . . . . 1·40 35
810 70f. Golden trevally . . . . 1·60 90

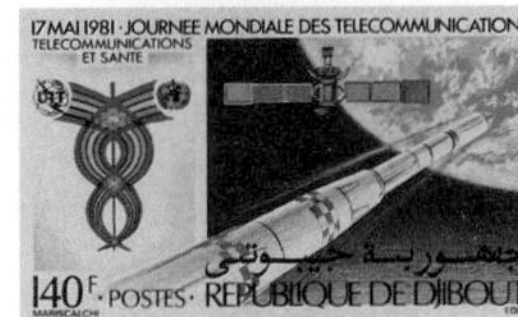

160 Caduceus, Satellite and Rocket

1981. World Telecommunications Day.
811 **160** 140f. multicoloured . . . 1·90 55

161 German 231 and American RC4 Diesel Locomotives

1981. Locomotives. Multicoloured.
812 40f. Type **161** 85 30
813 55f. George Stephenson, "Rocket" (1829) and Djibouti locomotive . . . 1·25 40
814 65f. French TGV and Japanese "Hikari" high speed trains . . . . 1·75 40

162 Antenna on Globe and Morse Key

1981. Djibouti Amateur Radio Club.
815 **162** 250f. multicoloured . . . 3·50 1·10

163 Prince Charles and Lady Diana Spencer

1981. Royal Wedding. Multicoloured.
816 180f. Type **163** . . . . . . 2·75 85
817 200f. Prince Charles and Lady Diana in wedding dress . . . . 3·00 1·10

164 Admiral Nelson and H.M.S. "Victory"

1981. Admiral Nelson Commemoration. Mult.
818 100f. Type **164** . . . . . . 1·60 1·00
819 175f. Nelson and stern view of H.M.S. "Victory" . . . 2·75 1·50

165 Tree Hyrax and Scout tending Camp-fire

1981. 28th World Scouting Congress, Dakar, and Fourth Panafrican Scouting Conference, Abidjan. Multicoloured.
820 60f. Type **165** . . . . 1·25 40
821 105f. Scouts saluting, map reading and greater kudu 1·60 50

166 "Football Players" (Picasso)

1981. Air. Paintings. Multicoloured.
822 300f. Type **166** . . . . . . 5·00 1·40
823 400f. "Portrait of a Man in a Turban" (Rembrandt) . . 5·50 1·90

167 Launch 168 19th-century Chinese Pawn and Knight

1981. Air. Space Shuttle. Multicoloured.
824 90f. Type **167** . . . . 1·40 45
825 120f. Space Shuttle landing 1·75 65

1981. Chess Pieces. Multicoloured.
826 50f. 13th-century Swedish pawn and queen (horiz) . . 1·10 35
827 130f. Type **168** . . . . . . 2·25 80

169 Aerial View

1981. Inauguration of Djibouti Sheraton Hotel.
828 **169** 75f. multicoloured . . . . 1·10 40

1981. 2nd Flight of Space Shuttle "Columbia". Nos. 824/5 optd.
829 90f. Type **167** . . . . 1·40 55
830 120f. Space Shuttle landing 1·75 85
OPTS: 90f. **COLUMBIA 2eme VOL SPATIAL 12 NOVEMBRE 1981**. 120f. **JOE ENGLE et RICHARD TRULY 2eme VOL SPATIAL—12 Nov. 1981**.

171 "Clitoria ternatea"

1981. Flowers. Multicoloured.
831 10f. Type **171** 20 10
832 30f. "Acacia mellifera" (horiz) 45 15
833 35f. "Punica granatum" (horiz) 70 20
834 45f. Malvacee 85 20

1981. World Chess Championship, Merano (1st issue). Nos. 826/7 optd.
835 50f. multicoloured 95 35
836 130f. multicoloured . . . . . 2·25 80
OPTS: 50f. **Octobre-Novembre 1981 ANATOLI KARPOV VICTOR KORTCHNOI MERANO (ITALIE)**. 130f. **ANATOLI KARPOV Champion du Monde 1981**.
See also Nos. 843/4.

173 Saving Goal

1982. Air. World Cup Football Championship, Spain. Multicoloured.
837 110f. Type **173** . . . . . . 1·60 55
838 220f. Footballers . . . . . . 3·25 1·10

174 John H. Glenn 176 14th-century German Bishop and 18th-century Marie de Medici Bishop

175 Dr. Robert Koch, Bacillus and Microscope

1982. Air. Space Anniversaries. Mult.
839 40f. "Luna 9" (15th anniv of first unmanned moon landing) 55 20
840 60f. Type **174** (20th anniv of flight) 90 35
841 180f. "Viking 1" (5th anniv of first Mars landing) (horiz) . . . . 2·40 85

1982. Centenary of Robert Koch's Discovery of Tubercle Bacillus.
842 **175** 305f. multicoloured . . . 4·75 1·60

1982. World Chess Championship, Merano (2nd issue). Multicoloured.
843 125f. Type **176** . . . . . . 2·50 75
844 175f. Late 19th-century queen and pawn from Nuremberg 3·00 95

177 Princess of Wales

1982. Air. 21st Birthday of Princess of Wales. Multicoloured.
845 120f. Type **177** . . . . . . 1·60 85
846 180f. Princess of Wales (different) . . . . 2·50 1·00

178 I.Y.C. Stamp, Collector, Greater Flamingoes and Emblems

1982. "Philexfrance" International Stamp Exhibition, Paris. Multicoloured.
847 80f. Type **178** . . . . 2·50 1·25
848 140f. Rowland Hill stamp Exhibition Centre and U.P.U. emblem . . . . . 2·25 95

179 Microwave Antenna **180** Mosque, Medina

1982. World Telecommunications Day.
849 **179** 150f. multicoloured . . . 2·25 90

1982. Air. 1350th Death Anniv of Mohammed.
850 **180** 500f. multicoloured . . . 6·75 2·50

181 Lord Baden-Powell

1982. Air. 125th Birth Anniv of Lord Baden-Powell. Multicoloured.
851 95f. Type **181** . . . . 1·25 55
852 200f. Saluting Scout and camp . . . . 2·75 1·10

182 Bus and Jeep

1982. Transport. Multicoloured.
853 20f. Type **182** 35 15
854 25f. Ferry and dhow 65 35
855 55f. Boeing 727-100 airliner and Alsthom Series BB 500 diesel locomotive and train 3·75 55

1982. Air. World Cup Football Championship winners. Nos. 837/8 optd.
856 110f. Type **173** . . . . . . 1·60 65
857 220f. Footballers . . . . . . 3·00 1·40
OPTS: 110f. **ITALIE RFA 3-1 POLOGNE FRANCE 3-2**. 220f. **ITALIE RFA 3-1 2 RFA 3 POLOGNE.**

1982. Air. Birth of Prince William of Wales. Nos. 845/6 optd.
858 120f. Type **177** . . . . . . 1·60 85
859 180f. Princess of Wales (different) . . . . 2·50 1·10

OPTS: 120f. **21 JUIN 1982 WILLIAM-ARTHUR-PHILIPPE-LOUIS PRINCE DES GALLES**. 180f. **21ST JUNE 1982 WILLIAM-ARTHUR-PHILIP-LOUIS PRINCE OF WALES.**

185 Satellite, Dish Aerial and Conference

1982. Air. Second U.N. Conference on the Exploration and Peaceful Uses of Outer Space, Vienna.
860 **185** 350f. multicoloured . . . 5·00 1·60

186 Franklin D. Roosevelt

1982. Air. 250th Birth Anniv of George Washington and Birth Centenary of Franklin D. Roosevelt. Multicoloured.
861 115f. Type **186** . . . . . . 1·60 55
862 250f. George Washington . . 3·25 1·10

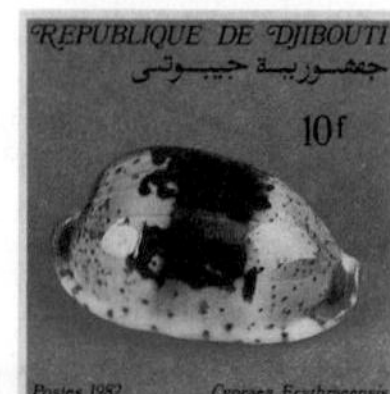

187 Red Sea Cowrie

1982. Shells. Multicoloured.
863 10f. Type **187** 25 15
864 15f. Sumatran cone 40 20
865 25f. Lovely cowrie 55 25
866 30f. Engraved cone 75 40
867 70f. Heavy bonnet . . . . . 1·75 75
868 150f. Burnt cowrie . . . . . 3·50 1·25

188 Dove perched on Gun **189** Montgolfier's Balloon, 1783

1982. Palestinian Solidarity Day.
869 **188** 40f. multicoloured 55 25

1983. Air. Bicentenary of Manned Flight. Mult.
870 35f. Type **189** 60 25
871 45f. Henri Giffard's balloon "Le Grand Ballon Captif", 1878 . . . . 90 45
872 120f. Balloon "Double Eagle II", 1978 . . . . 2·25 1·10

190 Volleyball **192** Martin Luther King

191 Bloch 220 Gascogne

1983. Air. Olympic Games, Los Angeles (1984). Multicoloured.
873 75f. Type **190** . . . . 1·10 45
874 125f. Wind-surfing . . . . . 2·25 1·25

1983. Air. 50th Anniv of Air France. Mult.
875 25f. Type **191** 40 25
876 100f. Douglas DC-4 . . . . 1·40 1·00
877 175f. Boeing 747-200 . . . . 2·50 1·25

1983. Flowers. As T **171**. Multicoloured.
878 5f. Ipomoea 10 10
879 50f. Moringa (horiz) 85 35
880 55f. Cotton flower . . . . . 1·00 40

1983. Air. Celebrities. Multicoloured.
881 180f. Type **192** (15th death anniv) . . . . 2·25 90
882 250f. Alfred Nobel (150th birth anniv) . . . . 3·25 1·40

193 W.C.Y. Emblem

1983. World Communications Year.
883 **193** 500f. multicoloured . . . 6·75 2·75

194 Yacht and Rotary Club Emblem

1983. Air. International Club Meetings. Mult.
884 90f. Type **194** . . . . 2·00 1·50
885 150f. Minaret and Lions Club emblem . . . . 2·00 90

195 Renault, 1904

1983. Air. Early Motor Cars. Multicoloured.
886 60f. Type **195** . . . . 1·25 40
887 80f. Mercedes Knight, 1910 (vert) . . . . 1·90 50
888 100f. Lorraine-Dietrich, 1912 2·25 80

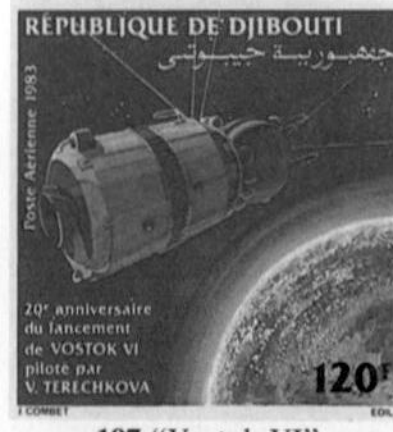

197 "Vostok VI"

1983. Air. Conquest of Space. Multicoloured.
890 120f. Type **197** . . . . . 1·60 65
891 200f. "Explorer I" . . . . . 2·75 1·10

198 Development Projects

1983. Donors Conference.
892 **198** 75f. multicoloured . . . . 1·10 55

199 Red Sea Marginella

1983. Shells. Multicoloured.
893 15f. Type **199** 40 15
894 30f. Jickeli's cone 85 25
895 55f. MacAndrew's cowrie . . 1·40 60
896 80f. Cuvier's cone . . . . . 1·90 75
897 100f. Tapestry turban . . . . 2·10 1·00

200 "Colotis chrysonome"

1984. Butterflies.
898 5f. Type **200** 10 10
899 20f. "Colias erate" 25 20
900 30f. "Junonia orithyia" . . . 45 30
901 75f. "Acraea doubledayi" . . 1·40 90
902 110f. "Byblia ilithya" . . . . 1·75 1·40

201 Speed Skating

1984. Air. Winter Olympic Games, Sarajevo. Mult.
903 70f. Type **201** . . . . 1·10 40
904 130f. Ice dancing . . . . . . 1·90 70

203 Microlight

1984. Air. Microlight Aircraft. Multicoloured.
906 65f. Type **203** . . . . 1·00 80
907 85f. Powered hang-glider "Jules" . . . . 1·25 1·00
908 100f. Microlight (different) 1·50 1·25

1984. Air. Winter Olympic Games Medal Winners. Nos. 903/4 optd.
909 70f. **1000 METRES HOMMES OR: BOUCHER (CANADA) ARGENT: KHLEBNIKOV (URSS) BRONZE: ENGELSTADT (NORV.)** 1·10 55
910 130f. **DANSE OR: TORVILL-DEAN (G.B.) ARGENT: BESTEMIANOVA-BUKIN (URSS) BRONZE: KLIMOVA-PONOMARENKO (URSS)** . . . . 1·90 85

205 "Marguerite Matisse with Cat"

1984. Air. 30th Death Anniv of Matisse and Birth Centenary of Modigliani. Multicoloured.

911 150f. Type **205** . . . . . . 2·50 90
912 200f. "Mario Varvogli" (Modigliani) . . . . 3·50 1·40

206 Randa

1984. Landscapes. Multicoloured.

913 2f. Type **206** 10 10
914 8f. Ali Sabieh 10 10
915 10f. Lake Assal 15 10
916 15f. Tadjoura 20 10
917 40f. Alaili Dada (vert) . . . 55 20
918 45f. Lake Abbe 60 25
919 55f. Obock . . . . 1·50 85
920 125f. Presidential Palace . . . 3·00 1·60

207 Marathon

1984. Air. Olympic Games, Los Angeles. Mult.

921 50f. Type **207** 65 30
922 60f. High jump 85 35
923 80f. Swimming . . . . 1·10 45

208 Battle of Solferino

1984. Air. 125th Anniv of Battle of Solferino and 120th Anniv of Red Cross.

924 **208** 300f. multicoloured . . . 4·50 1·60

209 Bleriot and Diagram of Bleriot XI

1984. Air. 75th Anniv of Louis Bleriot's Cross-Channel Flight. Multicoloured.

925 40f. Type **209** 65 50
926 75f. Bleriot and Bleriot XI and Britten Norman Islander aircraft . . . . . 1·10 90
927 90f. Bleriot and Boeing 727 airliner . . . . 1·25 1·10

210 Marathon

212 Men on Moon, Telescope and Planets

211 U.S.A. Attack-pumper Fire Engine

1984. Membership of International Olympic Committee.

928 **210** 45f. multicoloured 65 30

1984. Fire Fighting. Multicoloured.

929 25f. Type **211** 70 20
930 95f. French P.P.M. rescue crane . . . . 2·10 65
931 100f. Canadair CL-215 fire-fighting amphibian . . . . 2·25 1·25

1984. Air. 375th Anniv of Galileo's Telescope. Multicoloured.

932 120f. Type **212** . . . . . . 1·60 65
933 180f. Galileo, telescope and planets . . . . 2·50 1·00

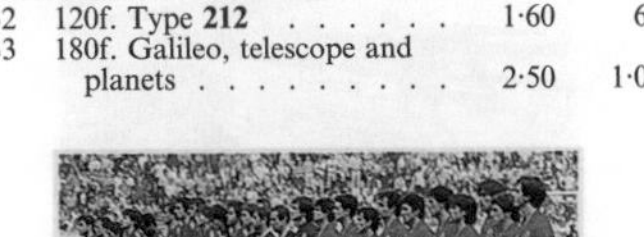

213 Football Teams (Europa Cup)

1984. Air. European Football Championship and Olympic Games, Los Angeles. Multicoloured.

934 80f. Type **213** . . . . 1·25 55
935 80f. Football teams (Olympic Games) . . . . 1·25 55

214 Motor Carriage, 1886

1984. 150th Birth Anniv of Gottlieb Daimler (automobile designer). Multicoloured.

936 35f. Type **214** 55 20
937 65f. Cannstatt-Daimler cabriolet, 1896 . . . . . . 1·00 35
938 90f. Daimler "Phoenix", 1900 1·50 55

215 Pierre Curie

1985. Pierre and Marie Curie (physicists). Mult.

939 150f. Type **215** (150th birth anniv) . . . . 2·25 85
940 150f. Marie Curie (50th death anniv) . . . . 2·25 85

216 White-throated Bee Eater

1985. Birth Bicentenary of John J. Audubon. Multicoloured.

941 5f. Type **216** 25 15
942 15f. Chestnut-bellied sand-grouse . . . . 1·10 45
943 20f. Yellow-breasted barbet 1·25 50
944 25f. European roller . . . . 1·50 55

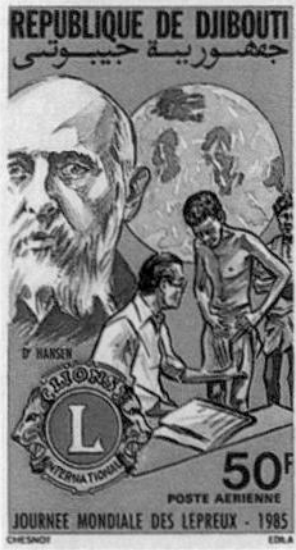

217 Dr. Hansen, Bacilli, Lepers and Lions Emblem

218 Globe and Pictograms

1985. Air. International Organizations. Mult.

946 50f. Type **217** (World Leprosy Day) 80 40
947 60f. Rotary International emblem and pieces on chessboard . . . . 1·40 65

1985. International Youth Year.

948 **218** 10f. multicoloured 80 25
949 30f. multicoloured . . . . 2·25 50
950 40f. multicoloured . . . . 3·00 90

219 Steam Locomotive No. 29, Addis Ababa–Djibouti Railway

1985. Railway Locomotives. Multicoloured.

951 55f. Type **219** . . . . . . 1·50 65
952 75f. "Adler", 1835 (150th anniv of German railways) 2·25 85

220 Planting Sapling

221 Victor Hugo (novelist)

1985. Foundation of Djibouti Scouting Association. Multicoloured.

953 35f. Type **220** 65 30
954 65f. Childcare . . . . 1·40 45

1985. Writers. Multicoloured.

955 80f. Type **221** . . . . 1·10 50
956 100f. Arthur Rimbaud (poet) 1·40 60

222 Dish Aerials, Off-shore Oil Rigs and Building

1985. Air. "Philexafrique" Stamp Exhibition, Lome (1st issue). Multicoloured.

957 80f. Type **222** . . . . 2·25 1·50
958 80f. Carpenter, girl at microscope and man at visual display unit . . . . 1·60 1·10

See also Nos. 969/70.

1985. Shells. As T **199**. Multicoloured.

959 10f. Twin-blotch cowrie . . . 25 15
960 15f. Thrush cowrie 35 20
961 30f. Vice-Admiral cowrie . . 95 25
962 40f. Giraffe cone . . . . . . 1·10 55
963 55f. Terebra cone . . . . . 1·75 75

223 Team Winners on Rostrum

1985. 1st Marathon World Cup, Hiroshima. Multicoloured.

964 75f. Type **223** . . . . 1·00 45
965 100f. Finishing line and officials . . . . 1·50 65

224 Launch of "Ariane"

1985. Air. Telecommunications Development. Mult.

966 50f. International Transmission Centre . . . 65 30
967 90f. Type **224** . . . . 1·25 50
968 120f. "Arabsat" satellite . . . 1·60 65

225 Windsurfing and Tennis

1985. Air. "Philexafrique" Stamp Exhibition, Lome, Togo (2nd issue). Multicoloured.

969 100f. Type **225** . . . . . . 2·00 1·25
970 100f. Construction of Tadjoura road . . . . . . 1·60 1·10

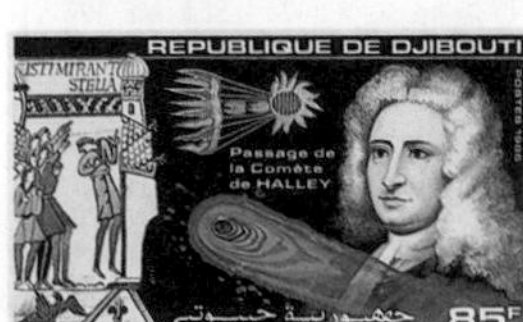

226 Edmond Halley, Bayeux Tapestry and Comet

1986. Appearance of Halley's Comet. Multicoloured.

971 85f. Type **226** . . . . 1·10 45
972 90f. Solar system, comet trajectory and space probes "Giotto" and "Vega 1" . . 1·40 55

227 Footballers

1986. Air. World Cup Football Championship, Mexico. Multicoloured.

973 75f. Type **227** . . . . 1·00 45
974 100f. Players and stadium . . 1·40 65

228 Runners on Shore

1986. "ISERST" Solar Energy Project. Mult.

975 50f. Type **228** 65 30
976 150f. "ISERST" building . . 2·00 85

229 "Santa Maria"

1986. Historic Ships of Columbus, 1492. Multicoloured.
977 60f. Type **229** . . . . 1·90 1·25
978 90f. "Nina" and "Pinta" . . 2·50 2·00

230 Statue of Liberty, Eiffel Tower and French and U.S. Flags

1986. Air. Centenary of Statue of Liberty.
979 **230** 250f. multicoloured . . . 3·25 1·40

231 Rainbow Runner

1986. Red Sea Fish. Multicoloured.
980 20f. Type **231** 80 50
981 25f. Sehel's grey mullet . . . 1·00 50
982 55f. Blubber-lipped snapper 2·40 1·25

232 People's Palace

1986. Public Buildings. Multicoloured.
983 105f. Type **232** . . . . . . 1·40 55
984 115f. Ministry of the Interior, Posts and Telecommunications . . . 1·60 65

233 Transmission Building and Keyboard

1986. Inauguration of Sea-Me-We Submarine Communications Cable.
985 **233** 100f. multicoloured . . . 1·40 65

1986. Air. World Cup Football Championship Winners. Nos. 973/4 optd. Multicoloured.
987 75f. **FRANCE-BELGIQUE 4–2** . . . . 1·00 65
988 100f. **3–2 ARGENTINA-RFA** 1·40 90

235 Javanese Bishop, Knight and Queen

1986. Air. World Chess Championship, London and Leningrad. Multicoloured.
989 80f. Type **235** . . . . 1·40 65
990 120f. German rook, pawn and king . . . . 2·25 1·00

1986. 5th Anniv of Inaug of Djibouti Sheraton Hotel. No. 828 surch **5e ANNIVERSAIRE**.
991 **169** 55f. on 75f. mult 90 55

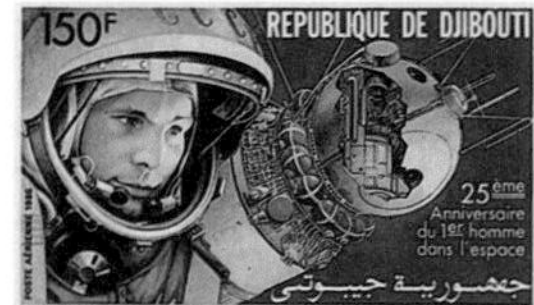

237 Gagarin and Space Capsule

1986. Air. 25th Anniv of First Man in Space and 20th Anniv of "Gemini 8"–"Agena" Link-up. Multicoloured.
992 150f. Type **237** . . . . . . 2·25 65
993 200f. "Gemini 8" and "Agena" craft over Earth 3·00 1·00

238 Amiot 370

1987. Air. Flight Anniversaries and Events. Multicoloured.
994 55f. Type **238** (45th anniv of first Istres-Djibouti flight) 90 60
995 80f. "Spirit of St Louis" and Charles Lindbergh (60th anniv of first solo flight across North Atlantic) . . 1·10 95
996 120f. Dick Rutan, Jeana Yeager and "Voyager" (first non-stop flight around the world) . . . . 1·75 1·25

239 Louis Pasteur and Vaccination Session

1987. Centenary of Pasteur Institute. National Vaccination Campaign in Djibouti.
997 **239** 220f. multicoloured . . . 3·25 1·10

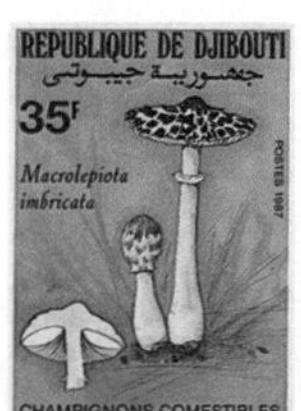

241 "Macrolepiota imbricata"

1987. Fungi. Multicoloured.
999 35f. Type **241** . . . . . . 1·25 65
1000 50f. "Lentinus squarrosulus" 2·00 95
1001 95f. "Terfezia boudieri" . . 3·50 1·50

242 Hare

1987. Wild Animals. Multicoloured.
1002 5f. Type **242** 10 10
1003 30f. Young dromedary with mother 45 20
1004 140f. Cheetah . . . . 2·25 80

243 President Hassan Gouled Aptidon, Map, Flag and Crest

1987. Air. 10th Anniv of Independence.
1005 **243** 250f. multicoloured . . . 3·25 1·40

244 Pierre de Coubertin (founder of modern Games) and Athlete lighting Flame

1987. Olympic Games, Calgary and Seoul (1st issue) (1988). Multicoloured.
1006 85f. Type **244** . . . . . . 1·10 45
1007 135f. Ski-jumper . . . . . 1·60 65
1008 140f. Runners and spectators . . . . 1·90 80
See also No. 1021.

245 "Telstar" Satellite

1987. Air. Telecommunications Anniversaries. Multicoloured.
1009 190f. Type **245** (25th anniv) 2·50 90
1010 250f. Samuel Morse and morse key (150th anniv of morse telegraph) . . . . 3·25 1·40

246 Djibouti Creek and Quay, 1887

1987. Air. Centenary of Djibouti City.
1011 **246** 100f. agate and stone . . 2·00 1·40
1012 – 150f. multicoloured . . . 2·25 80
DESIGN: 150f. Aerial view of Djibouti, 1987.

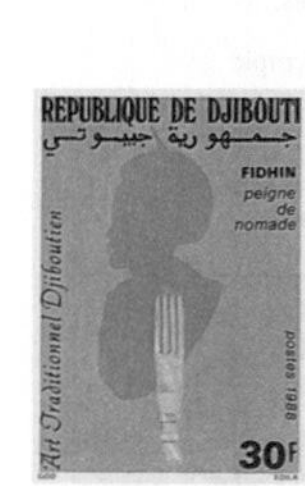

247 Comb **249** Anniversary Emblem

1988. Traditional Djibouti Art. Multicoloured.
1014 30f. Type **247** 45 20
1015 70f. Water pitcher 95 45

1988. Air. 125th Anniv of Red Cross.
1017 **249** 300f. multicoloured . . . 4·25 1·60

250 Rabat and Footballers

1988. 16th African Nations Cup Football Championship, Morocco.
1018 **250** 55f. multicoloured . . . 85 35

251 Ski Jumping **252** Doctor examining Child

1988. Winter Olympic Games, Calgary.
1019 **251** 45f. multicoloured . . . 65 30

1988. UNICEF. "Universal Vaccinations by 1990" Campaign.
1020 **252** 125f. multicoloured . . . 1·75 65

253 Runners and Stadium

1988. Air. Olympic Games, Seoul (2nd issue).
1021 **253** 105f. multicoloured . . . 1·40 55

1988. Air. Paris–Djibouti–St. Denis (Reunion) Roland Garros Air Race. No. 994 surch **PARIS-DJIBOUTI-ST DENIS LA REUNION RALLYE ROLAND GARROS 70 F**.
1022 **238** 70f. on 55f. mult . . . . 1·25 65

255 Animals at Water Trough

1988. Anti-drought Campaign.
1023 **255** 50f. multicoloured . . . 85 35

256 Djibouti Post Offices of 1890 and 1977

1988. Air. World Post Day.
1024 **256** 1000f. multicoloured . . 13·50 4·00

257 Combine Harvester, Tractor and Ploughman with Camel

1988. 10th Anniv of International Agricultural Development Fund.
1025 **257** 135f. multicoloured . . . 1·75 65

258 De Havilland Tiger Moth, 1948, and Socata Tobago, 1988

1988. 40th Anniv of Michel Lafoux Air Club.
1026 **258** 145f. multicoloured . . . 2·00 95

1988. 1st Djibouti Olympic Medal Winner. No. 1021 optd **AHMED SALAH 1re MEDAILLE OLYMPIQUE**.
1027 **253** 105f. multicoloured . . . 1·40 90

260 "Lobophyllia costata"

1989. Underwater Animals. Multicoloured.
1028 90f. Type **260** . . . . . . 1·40 35
1029 160f. Giant spider conch . . 3·25 1·40

261 "Colotis protomedia"

1989.
1030 **261** 70f. multicoloured . . . 90 60

1989. Nos. 849 and 913 surch **70f.**
1031 **206** 70f. on 2f. mult 95 45
1032 **179** 70f. on 150f. mult . . . 95 45

263 Dancers

264 Pale-bellied Francolin ("Francolin de Djibouti")

1989. Folklore. Multicoloured.
1033 30f. Type **263** 40 20
1034 70f. Dancers with parasol 1·00 45

1989.
1035 **264** 35f. multicoloured . . . 75 35

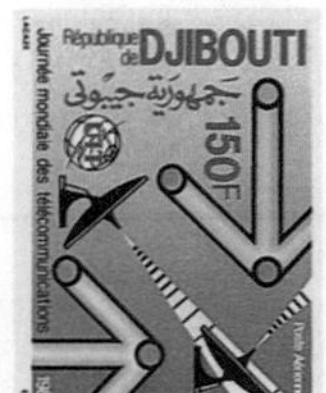

265 Arrows and Dish Aerials

1989. Air. World Telecommunications Day.
1036 **265** 150f. multicoloured . . . 1·90 65

266 "Calotropis procera"

1989.
1037 **266** 25f. multicoloured . . . 35 15

267 Emblem, Declaration and People

1989. Air. "Philexfrance 89" International Stamp Exhibition, Paris, and Bicentenary of Declaration of Rights of Man.
1038 **267** 120f. multicoloured . . . 1·60 65

268 Emblem and State Arms

270 Child going to School

269 Collecting Salt

1989. Cent of Interparliamentary Union.
1039 **268** 70f. multicoloured . . . 95 35

1989. Air. Lake Assal.
1040 **269** 300f. multicoloured . . . 4·00 1·10

1989. International Literacy Year.
1041 **270** 145f. multicoloured . . . 1·90 65

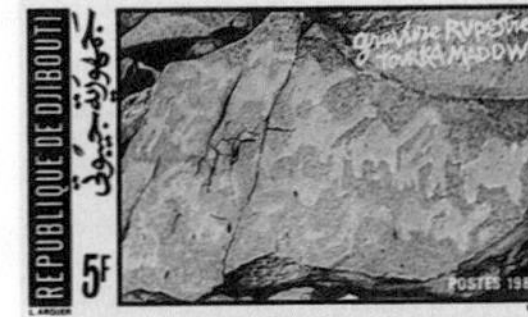

271 Tourka Maddw Cave Painting

1989.
1042 **271** 5f. multicoloured 10 10

272 Traditional Ornaments

1989.
1043 **272** 55f. multicoloured . . . 80 35

1990. Nos. 914 and 916/17 surch.
1044 30f. on 8f. multicoloured . . 40 15
1045 50f. on 40f. mult 65 30
1046 120f. on 15f. mult . . . . . 1·60 45

274 Water-storage Drums and Arid Landscape

1990. Anti-drought Campaign.
1047 **274** 120f. multicoloured . . . 1·60 55

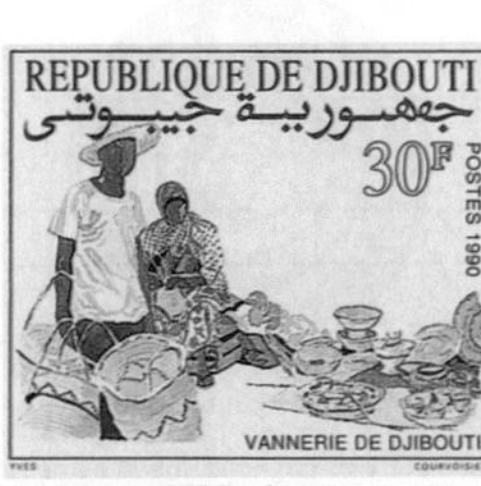

275 Basketry

1990. Traditional Crafts. Multicoloured.
1048 30f. Type **275** 40 20
1049 70f. Jewellery (vert) 95 35

275a Blue-spotted Stingray

277 Footballers

276 "Commiphora sp."

1990. Multicoloured, colour of face-value box given.
1049b **275a** 70f. yellow . . . . .
1049c 100f. green . . . . .

1990.
1050 **276** 30f. multicoloured . . . 45 30

1990. World Cup Football Championship, Italy.
1051 **277** 100f. multicoloured . . . 1·40 55

278 Athlete

279 Queue of Patients

1990. Djibouti 20 km Race.
1052 **278** 55f. multicoloured . . . 80 35

1990. Vaccination Campaign.
1053 **279** 300f. multicoloured . . . 3·25 1·40

280 De Gaulle

281 Technology in Developed Countries

1990. Birth Centenary of Charles de Gaulle (French statesman).
1054 **280** 200f. multicoloured . . . 2·50 1·25

1990. United Nations Conference on Less Developed Countries.
1055 **281** 45f. multicoloured . . . 60 35

282 Mammoth and Fossilized Remains

283 Hamadryas Baboon

1990.
1056 **282** 90f. multicoloured . . . 1·40 65

1990.
1057 **283** 50f. multicoloured . . . 65 35

284 Emblem and Map

285 "Acropora"

1991. African Tourism Year.
1058 **284** 115f. multicoloured . . . 1·50 85

1991. Corals. Multicoloured.
1059 40f. Type **285** 55 35
1060 45f. "Seriatopora hytrise" 65 35

286 Pink-backed Pelican

1991. Birds. Multicoloured.
1061 10f. Type **286** 35 15
1062 15f. Western reef heron . . 50 25
1063 20f. Goliath heron (horiz) 75 30
1064 25f. White spoonbill (horiz) 90 40

287 Osprey

1991.
1065 **287** 200f. multicoloured . . . 4·00 2·50

288 Traditional Game

1991.
1066 **288** 250f. multicoloured . . . 3·25 1·40

289 Diesel Locomotive

1991. Djibouti–Ethiopia Railway (1st issue).
1067 **289** 85f. multicoloured . . . 2·25 75
See also No. 1076.

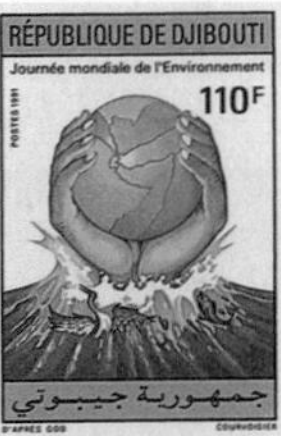

290 Hands holding Earth above Polluted Sea

1991. World Environment Day.
1068 **290** 110f. multicoloured . . . 1·50 55

291 Windsurfers and Islets

1991. "Philexafrique" Stamp Exhibition.
1069 **291** 120f. multicoloured . . . 90 45

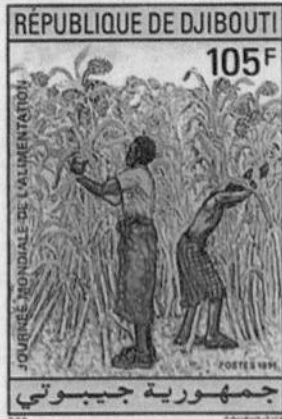

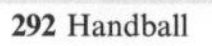

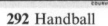

292 Handball **293** Harvesting Crops

1991. Olympic Games, Barcelona (1992) (1st issue).
1070 **292** 175f. multicoloured . . . 1·40 70
See also No. 1079.

1991. World Food Day.
1071 **293** 105f. multicoloured . . . 80 40

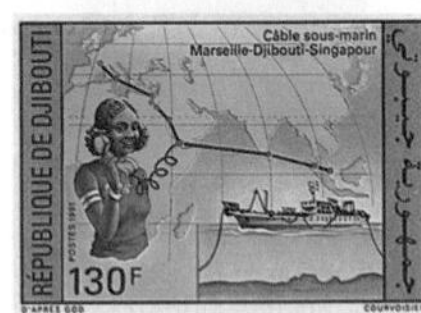

294 Route-map, Woman using Telephone and Cable-laying Ship

1991. Inauguration of Marseilles–Djibouti–Singapore Submarine Cable.
1072 **294** 130f. multicoloured . . . 1·50 70

295 Columbus and Ships

1991. 500th Anniv (1992) of Discovery of America by Columbus (1st issue).
1073 **295** 145f. multicoloured . . . 1·60 80
See also No. 1080.

296 Rimbaud, Ship and Serpent

1991. Death Centenary of Arthur Rimbaud (poet). Multicoloured.
1074 90f. Type **296** . . . . . . 1·10 50
1075 150f. Rimbaud, camel train and map . . . . 1·10 55

297 Camel Driver and Diesel Train

1992. Djibouti–Ethiopia Railway (2nd issue).
1076 **297** 70f. multicoloured . . . 1·50 45

298 Boys Playing Game

1992. Traditional Games.
1078 **298** 100f. multicoloured . . . 80 40

299 Athlete and Globe **301** Crushing Grain

300 Caravel crossing Atlantic

1992. Olympic Games, Barcelona (2nd issue).
1079 **299** 80f. multicoloured . . . 60 30

1992. 500th Anniv of Discovery of America by Columbus (2nd issue).
1080 **300** 125f. multicoloured . . . 1·40 65

1992. Traditional Methods of Preparing Food. Multicoloured.
1081 30f. Type **301** 25 10
1082 70f. Winnowing 55 25

302 Players, Map of Africa and Final Result **303** "Ariane" Rocket and Satellite

1992. 18th African Nations Cup Football Championship, Senegal.
1083 **302** 15f. multicoloured . . . 10 10

1992. International Space Year. Multicoloured.
1084 120f. Type **303** 90 45
1085 135f. Satellite and astronaut (horiz) . . . . 1·00 50

304 Salt's Dik-dik

1992.
1086 **304** 5f. multicoloured 10 10

305 Loggerhead Turtle

1992.
1087 **305** 200f. multicoloured . . . 1·50 75

306 Preparing Mofo

1992. Mofo. Multicoloured.
1088 45f. Type **306** . . . . . .
1089 75f. Cooking mofo . . . .

307 Nomadic Girl

1993. Traditional Costumes. Multicoloured.
1090 70f. Type **307** 55 25
1091 120f. Nomadic girl with headband 90 45

308 White-eyed Gull ("Geoland a Iris Blanc")

1993.
1092 **308** 300f. multicoloured . . . 3·50 1·40

309 Amin Salman Mosque

1993.
1093 **309** 500f. multicoloured . . .

310 Headrest

1993. Crafts. Multicoloured.
1094 100f. Type **310** . . . . . .
1095 125f. Flask . . . .

311 Savanna Monkey

1993.
1096 **311** 150f. multicoloured . . .

312 Flags of Member Countries

1993. 30th Anniv of Organization of African Unity.
1097 **312** 200f. multicoloured . . .

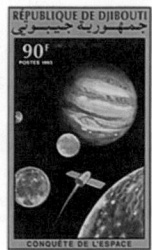

313 Woman carrying Water on Back **314** Plants and Spacecraft

1993. Water Carriers. Multicoloured.
1098 30f. Type **313** . . . . . .
1099 50f. Man carrying water on yoke . . . .

1993. Space.
1100 **314** 90f. multicoloured . . .

315 Water Jar **316** Pipes

1993. Utensils. Multicoloured.
1101 15f. Type **315** 10 10
1102 20f. Hangol (agricultural tool) 15 10
1103 25f. Comb 20 10
1104 30f. Water-skin 25 10

1993. Musical Instruments. Multicoloured.
1105 5f. Type **316** 10 10
1106 10f. Hand-held drum and lines of women 10 10

318 Runners and Route Map **319** Mother with Children

1994. Djibouti 20 km Race.
1108 **318** 50f. multicoloured . . . 40 20

1994. UNICEF. Breast-feeding Campaign. Multicoloured.
1109 40f. Type **319** 30 15
1110 45f. Woman breast-feeding baby 35 15

320 Stadium

1994. Hassan Gouled Aptidon Stadium.
1111 **320** 70f. multicoloured . . . 55 25

321 Spinner Dolphins

1994.
1112 **321** 120f. multicoloured . . .

322 Houses encircling Globe

1994. World Housing Day.
1113 **322** 30f. multicoloured . . .

323 White-bellied Bustards

1994.
1114 **323** 10f. multicoloured . . .

324 Trophy, Globe and Players

1994. World Cup Football Championship, U.S.A.
1115 **324** 200f. multicoloured . . .

325 Nomadic Man

1994. Traditional Costumes. Multicoloured.
1116 100f. Type **325** . . . . . .
1117 150f. Town dress . . . . .

326 Golden Jackals

1994.
1118 **326** 400f. multicoloured . . .

327 Walkers

1994. World Walking Day.
1119 **327** 75f. multicoloured . . .

328 Book Rests

329 Traditional Dancers

1994. Traditional Crafts.
1120 **328** 55f. multicoloured . . .

1994. Folklore.
1121 **329** 35f. multicoloured . . .

330 Camel, Ostrich and Net

331 U.N. Flag tied around Cracked Globe

1995. Centenary of Volleyball.
1122 **330** 70f. multicoloured . . .

1995. 50th Anniv of U.N.O.
1123 **331** 120f. multicoloured . . .

332 Drawing Water from Well

1995. Drought Relief Campaign.
1124 **332** 100f. multicoloured . . .

333 Greater Flamingo

1995. Birds. Multicoloured.
1125 30f. Type **333** . . . . . .
1126 50f. Sacred ibis . . . . . .

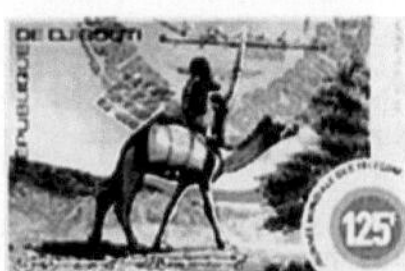

334 Camel Rider

1995. Telecommunications Day.
1127 **334** 125f. multicoloured . . .

335 Spotted Hyena

1995.
1128 **335** 200f. multicoloured . . .

336 Council held under Tree

337 Nomads

1995.
1129 **336** 150f. multicoloured . . .

1995. Nomadic Life.
1130 **337** 45f. multicoloured . . .

338 Palm Tree, Map and Emblem

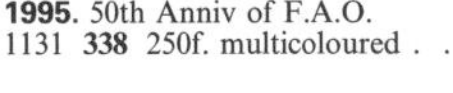

1995. 50th Anniv of F.A.O.
1131 **338** 250f. multicoloured . . .

339 Development Project and Emblem

340 Traditional Costume

1995. 30th Anniv of African Development Bank.
1132 **339** 300f. multicoloured . . .

1995.
1133 **340** 90f. multicoloured . . .

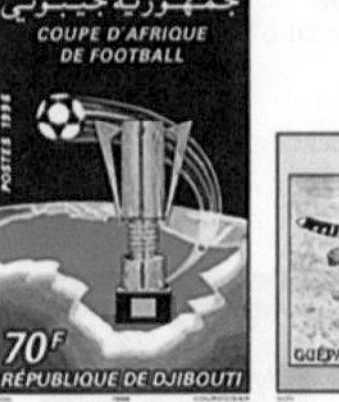

341 Trophy on Map and Football

342 Leopard

1996. Africa Cup Football Championship.
1134 **341** 70f. multicoloured . . .

1996. Wildlife. Multicoloured.
1135 70f. Type **342** . . . . .
1136 120f. Ostrich (vert) . . . .

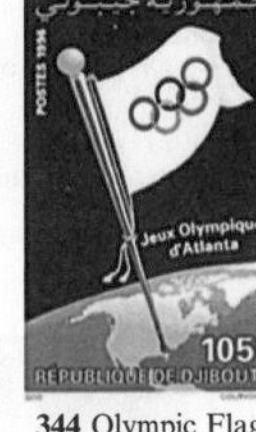

343 Woman wearing Amber Necklace

344 Olympic Flag

1996. Traditional Crafts.
1137 **343** 30f. multicoloured . . .

1996. Olympic Games, Atlanta.
1138 **344** 105f. multicoloured . . .

345 "Commicarpus grandiflorus"

346 Women's Rite

1996.
1139 **345** 350f. multicoloured . . .

1996. Folklore.
1140 **346** 95f. multicoloured . . .

347 The Lion and the Three Bullocks

1996. Stories and Legends.
1141 **347** 95f. multicoloured . . .

348 Children with Flags

1996. National Children's Day.
1142 **348** 130f. multicoloured . . .

349 Fox and Tortoise

350 Mother and Child

1997. Stories and Legends. The Tortoise and the Fox. Multicoloured.
1143 60f. Type **349** . . . . . .
1144 60f. Fox running away from tortoise . . . .
1145 60f. Tortoise winning race

1997. 50th Anniv of UNICEF. Multicoloured.
1146 80f. Type **350** . . . . . .
1147 90f. Arms cradling globe of children . . . .

351 Dancers

352 Using Necklace as Pendulum

1997. Folklore.
1148 **351** 70f. multicoloured . . .

1997. Local Fortune Telling. Multicoloured.
1149 200f. Type **352** . . . . . .
1150 300f. Using pebbles . . . .

353 Woman weaving Basket

355 Arta Post Office

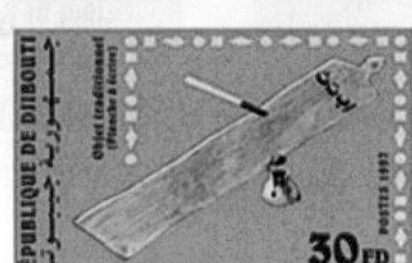

354 Writing Board

1997. Women's Day.
1151 **353** 250f. multicoloured . . .

1997. Traditional Implements. Multicoloured.
1152 30f. Type **354** . . . . . .
1153 400f. Bowl and spoon (vert)

1997. 20th Anniv of Independence. Multicoloured.
1154 30f. Type **355** . . . . . .
1155 100f. Telecommunications station . . . .
1156 120f. Undersea cable, route map and cable ship (horiz) . . . .

356 Goats in Tree

1997.
1157 **356** 120f. multicoloured . . .

357 Diana, Princess of Wales

1998. Diana, Princess of Wales Commemoration.
1158 **357** 125f. multicoloured . . . 95 45
1159 130f. multicoloured . . . 1·00 50
1160 150f. multicoloured . . . 1·25 60

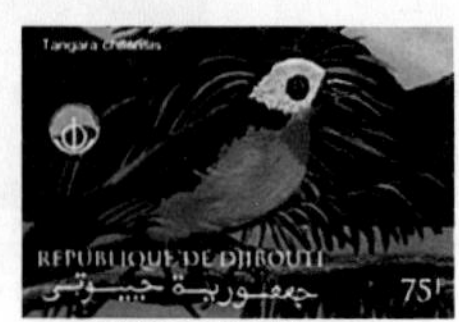

358 Paradise Tanager

1998. International Year of the Ocean. Mult.
1161 75c. Type **358** . . . . . .
1162 75c. Red-eyed tree frog ("Agalychnis callidryas")
1163 75c. Common dolphin ("Delphinus delphis") and humpback whale ("Megaptera novaeangliae") . . . . .
1164 75c. Savanna monkey ("Cercopithecus aethiops") . . . .
1165 75c. Great hammerhead ("Sphyrna mokarran") and yellow-lipped sea snakes ("Laticaudia colubrina") . . . .
1166 75c. Long-horned cowfish ("Lactoria cornuta") and common dolphin ("Delphinus delphis") . .
1167 75c. Common dolphins ("Delphinus delphis") . .
1168 75c. Striped mimic blenny ("Aspidontus taeniatus") and foxface ("Lovulpinus") . . . . .
1169 75c. Big-fin reef squid ("Sepioteuthis lessoniana)
1170 75c. Ornate butterflyfish ("Chaetodon ornatissimus) and blue shark ("Prionace glauca")
1171 75c. Hermit crab ("Eupagurus bernherdus")
1172 75c. Common octopus ("Octopus vulgaris") . . .

Nos. 1161/72 were issued together, se-tenant, forming a composite design.

359 Gandhi

360 Vase

1998. 50th Death Anniv of Mahatma Gandhi (Indian patriot).
1173 **359** 250f. multicoloured . . .

1998. Traditional Art.
1174 **360** 30f. multicoloured . . .

361 Woman carrying Basket on Back and Road-crossing Officer

1998. Women's Rights and International Peace.
1175 **361** 70f. multicoloured . . .

362 Water Pump and Donkey carrying Water Containers

1998. World Water Day.
1176 **362** 45f. multicoloured . . .

363 Football, Trophy and Eiffel Tower

364 Octopus

1998. World Cup Football Championship, France.
1177 **363** 200f. multicoloured . . .

1998. Marine Life. Multicoloured.
1178 20f. Type **364** . . . . . .
1179 25f. Shark (horiz) . . . . .

365 Catmint and Cats

366 Globe using Mobile Phone and Computer

1998.
1180 **365** 120f. multicoloured . . .

1998. World Telecommunications Day.
1181 **366** 150f. multicoloured . . .

367 National Bank

368 Flags of Member States and Emblem

1998. Public Buildings.
1182 **367** 100f. multicoloured . . .

1998. Inter-Governmental Authority on Development.
1183 **368** 85f. multicoloured . . .

369 Boys playing Goos

1998. Traditional Games.
1184 **369** 110f. multicoloured . . .

370 Fishing Harbour

1998. Public Buildings.
1185 **370** 100f. multicoloured . . .

371 Gulls sp. and Maskali Island

1998. Tourist Sites.
1186 **371** 500f. multicoloured . . .

372 Mother Teresa

1998. Mother Teresa (founder of Missionaries of Charity) Commemoration.
1187 **372** 130f. multicoloured . . . 90 45

POSTAGE DUE STAMP

D 248 Milking Bowl

1988. Traditional Djibouti Art.
D1016 **D 248** 60f. multicoloured 90 65

DODECANESE ISLANDS Pt. 8

A group of islands off the coast of Asia Minor occupied by Italy in May 1912 and ceded to her by Turkey in 1920. The islands concerned are now known as Kalimnos, Kasos, Kos, Khalki, Leros, Lipsoi, Nisiros, Patmos, Tilos (Piskopi), Rhodes (Rodos), Karpathos, Simi and Astipalaia. Castelrosso came under the same administration in 1921.

In 1944 the Dodecanese Islands were occupied by British forces (see **BRITISH OCCUPATION OF ITALIAN COLONIES**). In 1947 they were transferred to Greek administration, since when Greek stamps have been used.

A. ITALIAN OCCUPATION

100 centesimi = 1 lira.

1912. Stamps of Italy optd **EGEO.**
1 **39** 25c. blue . . . . 30·00 17·00
2 – 50c. violet . . . . 30·00 17·00

1912. Stamps of Italy optd, or surch also, for the individual islands (all in capitals on Nos. 6 and 10, in upper and lower case on others). A. Calimno
3A **31** 2c. brown . . . . . . 4·50 4·25
4A **37** 5c. green . . . . . . 1·40 4·25
5A 10c. red . . . . . . 40 4·25
6A **41** 15c. grey . . . . . . 19·00 8·25
7A **37** 15c. grey . . . . . . 2·75 25·00
8A **41** 20c. on 15c. grey . . . . 10·00 17·00
10A 20c. orange . . . . . . 2·75 25·00
11A **39** 25c. blue . . . . . . 4·00 4·25
12A 40c. brown . . . . . . 40 4·25
13A 50c. violet . . . . . . 40 4·25

B. Caso
3B **31** 2c. brown . . . . . . 4·75 4·25
4B **37** 5c. green . . . . . . 1·60 4·25
5B 10c. red . . . . . . 40 4·25
6B **41** 15c. grey . . . . . . 22·00 8·25
7B **37** 15c. grey . . . . . . 2·75 25·00
8B **41** 20c. on 15c. grey . . . . 65 12·00
10B 20c. orange . . . . . . 2·10 20·00
11B **39** 25c. blue . . . . . . 40 4·25
12B 40c. brown . . . . . . 40 4·25
13B 50c. violet . . . . . . 40 7·50

C. Cos
3C **31** 2c. brown . . . . . . 4·75 4·25
4C **37** 5c. green . . . . . . 45·00 4·25
5C 10c. red . . . . . . 2·25 4·25
6C **41** 15c. grey . . . . . . 22·00 8·25
7C **37** 15c. grey . . . . . . 2·75 35·00
8C **41** 20c. on 15c. grey . . . . 10·00 21·00
10C 20c. orange . . . . . . 2·10 21·00
11C **39** 25c. blue . . . . . . 19·00 4·25
12C 40c. brown . . . . . . 40 4·25
13C 50c. violet . . . . . . 40 7·50

D. Karki
3D **31** 2c. brown . . . . . . 4·75 4·25
4D **37** 5c. green . . . . . . 1·60 4·25
5D 10c. red . . . . . . 1·60 4·25
6D **41** 15c. grey . . . . . . 22·00 8·25
7D **37** 15c. grey . . . . . . 2·75 26·00
8D **41** 20c. on 15c. grey . . . . 1·25 15·00
10D 20c. orange . . . . . . 2·75 24·00
11D **39** 25c. blue . . . . . . 40 4·25
12D 40c. brown . . . . . . 40 4·25
13D 50c. violet . . . . . . 40 7·50

E. Leros
3E **31** 2c. brown . . . . . . 4·75 4·25
4E **37** 5c. green . . . . . . 3·50 4·25
5E 10c. red . . . . . . 70 4·25
6E **41** 15c. grey . . . . . . 35·00 8·25
7E **37** 15c. grey . . . . . . 2·75 22·00
8E **41** 20c. on 15c. grey . . . . 10·00 16·50
9E 20c. orange . . . . . . 27·00 85·00
11E **39** 25c. blue . . . . . . 21·00 4·25
12E 40c. brown . . . . . . 2·75 4·25
13E 50c. violet . . . . . . 40 7·50

F. Lipso
3F **31** 2c. brown . . . . . . 4·75 4·25
4F **37** 5c. green . . . . . . 1·90 4·25
5F 10c. red . . . . . . 85 4·25
6F **41** 15c. grey . . . . . . 21·00 8·25
7F **37** 15c. grey . . . . . . 2·75 22·00
8F **41** 20c. on 15c. grey . . . . 80 15·00
10F 20c. orange . . . . . . 2·75 25·00
11F **39** 25c. blue . . . . . . 40 4·25
12F 40c. brown . . . . . . 1·25 4·25
13F 50c. violet . . . . . . 40 7·50

G. Nisiros
3G **31** 2c. brown . . . . . . 4·75 4·25
4G **37** 5c. green . . . . . . 1·60 4·25
5G 10c. red . . . . . . 40 4·25
6G **41** 15c. grey . . . . . . 19·00 8·25
7G **37** 15c. grey . . . . . . 13·50 23·00
8G **41** 20c. on 15c. grey . . . . 80 15·00
10G 20c. orange . . . . . . 55·00 65·00
11G **39** 25c. blue . . . . . . 1·40 4·25
12G 40c. brown . . . . . . 40 4·25
13G 50c. violet . . . . . . 2·75 7·50

H. Patmos
3H **31** 2c. brown . . . . . . 4·75 4·25
4H **37** 5c. green . . . . . . 1·60 4·25
5H 10c. red . . . . . . 1·40 4·25
6H **41** 15c. grey . . . . . . 19·00 8·25
7H **37** 15c. grey . . . . . . 2·75 25·00
8H **41** 20c. on 15c. grey . . . . 10·00 20·00
9H 20c. orange . . . . . . 45·00 85·00
11H **39** 25c. blue . . . . . . 55 4·25
12H 40c. brown . . . . . . 2·50 4·25
13H 50c. violet . . . . . . 40 7·50

I. Piscopi
3I **31** 2c. brown . . . . . . 4·75 4·25
4I **37** 5c. green . . . . . . 1·50 4·25
5I 10c. red . . . . . . 40 4·25
6I **41** 15c. grey . . . . . . 22·00 8·25
7I **37** 15c. grey . . . . . . 10·00 25·00
8I **41** 20c. on 15c. grey . . . . 80 15·00
10I 20c. orange . . . . . . 27·00 38·00
11I **39** 25c. blue . . . . . . 40 4·25
12I 40c. brown . . . . . . 40 4·25
13I 50c. violet . . . . . . 40 7·50

J. Rodi
3J **31** 2c. brown . . . . . . 40 4·25
4J **37** 5c. green . . . . . . 1·40 4·25
5J 10c. red . . . . . . 40 4·25
6J **41** 15c. grey . . . . . . 23·00 8·25
7J **37** 15c. grey . . . . . . 85·00 38·00
8J **41** 20c. on 15c. grey . . . . 75·00 80·00
10J 20c. orange . . . . . . 4·25 10·00
11J **39** 25c. blue . . . . . . 1·40 4·25
12J 40c. brown . . . . . . 2·25 4·25
13J 50c. violet . . . . . . 40 7·50

K. Scarpanto
3K **31** 2c. brown . . . . . . 4·75 4·25
4K **37** 5c. green . . . . . . 1·40 4·25
5K 10c. red . . . . . . 40 4·25
6K **41** 15c. grey . . . . . . 17·00 8·25
7K **37** 15c. grey . . . . . . 10·00 19·00
8K **41** 20c. on 15c. grey . . . . 80 17·00
10K 20c. orange . . . . . . 27·00 27·00
11K **39** 25c. blue . . . . . . 4·50 4·25
12K 40c. brown . . . . . . 40 4·25
13K 50c. violet . . . . . . 1·40 7·50

L. Simi
3L **31** 2c. brown . . . . . . 4·75 4·25
4L **37** 5c. green . . . . . . 14·50 4·25
5L 10c. red . . . . . . 40 4·25
6L **41** 15c. grey . . . . . . 28·00 28·00
7L **37** 15c. grey . . . . . . 75·00 75·00
8L **41** 20c. on 15c. grey . . . . 5·75 5·75
10L 20c. orange . . . . . . 38·00 38·00
11L **39** 25c. blue . . . . . . 1·90 4·25
12L 40c. brown . . . . . . 40 4·25
13L 50c. violet . . . . . . 40 7·50

M. Stampalia
3M **31** 2c. brown . . . . . . 4·75 4·25
4M **37** 5c. green . . . . . . 40 4·25
5M 10c. red . . . . . . 40 4·25
6M **41** 15c. grey . . . . . . 21·00 8·25
7M **37** 15c. grey . . . . . . 6·75 19·00
8M **41** 20c. on 15c. grey . . . . 65 12·00
10M 20c. orange . . . . . . 25·00 27·00
11M **39** 25c. blue . . . . . . 55 4·25
12M 40c. brown . . . . . . 2·25 4·25
13M 50c. violet . . . . . . 40 7·50

1916. Optd **Rodi**.
14 **33** 20c. orange . . . . 2·00 4·25
15 **39** 85c. brown . . . . 40·00 60·00
16 **34** 1l. brown & green . . . . . 2·00

1 Rhodian Windmill

2 Knight kneeling before the Holy City

1929. King of Italy's Visit.
17 **1** 5c. purple 85 20
18 – 10c. brown 85 20
19 – 20c. red 85 20
20 – 25c. green 85 20
21 **2** 30c. blue 85 20
22 – 50c. brown 85 20
23 – 1l.25 blue . . . . 85 1·00
24 **2** 5l. purple . . . . 85 1·25
25 10l. green . . . . 1·75 2·75

DESIGNS—As Type **1**: 10c. Galley of Knights of St. John; 20c., 25c. Knight defending Christianity; 50c., 1l.25, Knight's tomb.

1930. 21st Hydrological Congress. Nos. 17/25 optd **XXI Congresso Idrologico.**
26 5c. purple . . . . 13·50 11·50
27 10c. brown . . . . 15·00 11·50
28 20c. red . . . . 23·00 10·00
29 25c. green . . . . 30·00 10·00
30 30c. blue . . . . 15·00 12·00
31 50c. brown . . . . £375 30·00
32 1l.25 blue . . . . £300 50·00
33 5l. purple £160 £250
34 10l. green £160 £275

1930. Ferrucci issue of Italy (colours changed) optd for each individual island, in capitals. A. CALINO; B. CASO; C. COO; D. CALCHI; E. LERO; F. LISSO; G. NISIRO; H. PATMO; I. PISCOPI; J. RODI; K. SCARPANTO; L. SIMI; M. STAMPALIA.
35 **114** 20c. violet . . . . 1·90 3·00
36 – 25c. green . . . . 1·90 3·00
37 – 50c. black . . . . 1·90 5·75
38 – 1l.25 blue . . . . 1·90 5·75
39 – 5l.+2l. red . . . . 2·75 10·00

Same prices for each of the 13 islands.

1930. Air. Ferrucci air stamps of Italy (colours changed) optd **ISOLE ITALIANE DELL'EGEO.**
40 **117** 50c. purple . . . . 5·75 11·50
41 1l. blue . . . . 5·75 11·50
42 5l.+2l. red . . . . 12·00 32·00

1930. Virgil stamps of Italy optd **ISOLE ITALIANE DELL'EGEO.**
43 – 15c. violet (postage) . . . 1·00 5·75
44 – 20c. brown . . . . 1·00 5·75
45 – 25c. green . . . . 1·00 2·50
46 – 30c. brown . . . . 1·00 2·50
47 – 50c. purple . . . . 1·00 2·50
48 – 75c. red . . . . 1·00 5·75
49 – 1l.25 blue . . . . 1·00 8·25
50 – 5l+1l.50 purple . . . . . 2·40 17·00
51 – 10l.+2l.50 brown . . . . . 2·40 17·00
52 **119** 50c. green (air) . . . . . 1·40 12·00
53 1l. red . . . . 1·40 13·50
54 7l.70+1l.30 brown . . . . 3·00 24·00
55 9l.+2l. grey . . . . 3·00 25·00

1931. Italian Eucharistic Congress. Nos. 17/25 optd **1931 CONGRESSO EUCARISTICO ITALIANO.**
56 5c. red . . . . 4·00 5·75
57 10c. brown . . . . 4·00 5·75
58 20c. red . . . . 4·00 10·00
59 25c. green . . . . 4·00 10·00
60 30c. blue . . . . 4·00 10·00
61 50c. brown . . . . 30·00 24·00
62 1l.25 blue . . . . 23·00 42·00

1932. St. Antony of Padua stamps of Italy optd **ISOLE ITALIANE DELL'EGEO.**
63 **121** 20c. purple . . . . 15·00 9·00
64 – 25c. green . . . . 15·00 9·00
65 – 30c. brown . . . . 15·00 11·00
66 – 50c. purple . . . . 15·00 7·50
67 – 75c. red . . . . 15·00 12·50
68 – 1l.25 blue . . . . 15·00 14·50
69 – 5l.+2l.50 orange . . . . . 15·00 55·00

1932. Dante stamps of Italy optd **ISOLE ITALIANE DELL'EGEO.**
70 – 10c. green (postage) . . . 95 2·40
71 – 15c. violet . . . . 95 2·40
72 – 20c. brown . . . . 95 2·40
73 – 25c. green . . . . 95 2·40
74 – 30c. red . . . . 95 2·40
75 – 50c. purple . . . . 95 1·00
76 – 75c. red . . . . 95 3·00
77 – 1l.25 blue . . . . 95 2·40
78 – 1l.75 sepia . . . . 1·10 3·00
79 – 2l.75 red . . . . 1·10 3·00
80 – 5l.+2l. violet . . . . . . 1·40 9·25
81 **124** 10l.+2l.50 brown . . . . . 1·40 13·50
82 **125** 50c. red (air) . . . . . . 1·00 2·40
83 – 1l. green . . . . 1·00 2·40
84 – 3l. purple . . . . 1·00 2·75
85 – 5l. red . . . . 1·00 2·75
86 **125** 7l.70+2l. sepia . . . . . 1·40 6·75
87 – 10l.+2l.50 blue . . . . . . 1·40 12·00
88 **127** 100l. olive and blue . . . . 15·00 70·00
No. 88 is inscribed instead of optd.

1932. Garibaldi issue of Italy (colours changed) optd for each individual island in capital letters. A. CALINO; B. CASO; C. COO; D. CARCHI; E. LERO; F. LIBO; G. NISIRO; H. PATMO; I. PISCOPI; J. RODI; K. SCARPANTO; L. SIMI; M. STAMPALIA.
89 – 10c. sepia . . . . 8·00 12·00
90 **128** 20c. brown . . . . 8·00 12·00
91 – 25c. green . . . . 8·00 12·00
92 **128** 30c. black . . . . 8·00 12·00
93 – 50c. lilac . . . . 8·00 12·00
94 – 75c. red . . . . 8·00 12·00
95 – 1l.25 blue . . . . 8·00 12·00
96 – 1l.75+25c. sepia . . . . . 8·00 12·00
97 – 2l.55+50c. red . . . . . . 8·00 12·00
98 – 5l.+1l. violet . . . . . . 8·00 12·00
Same prices for each of the 13 islands.

1932. Air. Garibaldi air stamps of Italy optd **ISOLE ITALIANE DELL'EGEO.**
99 **130** 50c. green . . . . 30·00 55·00
100 – 80c. red . . . . 30·00 55·00
101 **130** 1l.+25c. blue . . . . . . 30·00 55·00
102 – 2l.+50c. brown . . . . . . 30·00 55·00
103 – 5l.+1l. black . . . . . . 30·00 55·00

8

1932. 20th Anniv of Italian Occupation of Dodecanese Islands.
106 **8** 5c. red, black and green . . 5·00 8·25
107 10c. red, black and blue . . 5·00 5·00
108 20c. red, black and yellow 5·00 5·00
109 25c. red, black and violet . . 5·00 5·00
110 30c. red, black and red . . . 5·00 5·00
111 – 50c. red, black and blue . . 5·00 5·00
112 – 1l.25 red, purple & blue . . 5·00 12·00
113 – 5l. red and blue . . . . . . 15·00 35·00
114 – 10l. red, green and blue . . 42·00 55·00
115 – 25l. red, brown and blue . . £275 £600
DESIGN—VERT: 50c. to 25l. Arms on map of Rhodes.

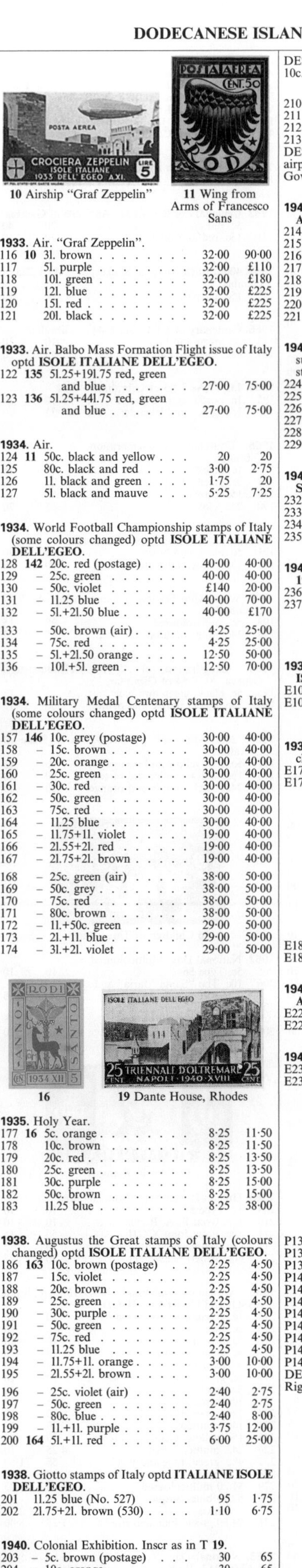

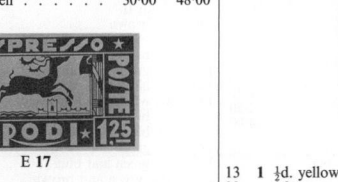

10 Airship "Graf Zeppelin"

11 Wing from Arms of Francesco Sans

1933. Air. "Graf Zeppelin".
116 **10** 3l. brown . . . . 32·00 90·00
117 5l. purple . . . . 32·00 £110
118 10l. green . . . . 32·00 £180
119 12l. blue . . . . 32·00 £225
120 15l. red . . . . 32·00 £225
121 20l. black . . . . 32·00 £225

1933. Air. Balbo Mass Formation Flight issue of Italy optd **ISOLE ITALIANE DELL'EGEO.**
122 **135** 5l.25+19l.75 red, green and blue . . . . 27·00 75·00
123 **136** 5l.25+44l.75 red, green and blue . . . . 27·00 75·00

1934. Air.
124 **11** 50c. black and yellow . . . 20 20
125 80c. black and red . . . . 3·00 2·75
126 1l. black and green . . . . 1·75 20
127 5l. black and mauve . . . 5·25 7·25

1934. World Football Championship stamps of Italy (some colours changed) optd **ISOLE ITALIANE DELL'EGEO.**
128 **142** 20c. red (postage) . . . . 40·00 40·00
129 – 25c. green . . . . 40·00 40·00
130 – 50c. violet . . . . £140 20·00
131 – 1l.25 blue . . . . 40·00 70·00
132 – 5l.+2l.50 blue . . . . . . 40·00 £170
133 – 50c. brown (air) . . . . . 4·25 25·00
134 – 75c. red . . . . 4·25 25·00
135 – 5l.+2l.50 orange . . . . . 12·50 50·00
136 – 10l.+5l. green . . . . . . 12·50 70·00

1934. Military Medal Centenary stamps of Italy (some colours changed) optd **ISOLE ITALIANE DELL'EGEO.**
157 **146** 10c. grey (postage) . . . 30·00 40·00
158 – 15c. brown . . . . 30·00 40·00
159 – 20c. orange . . . . 30·00 40·00
160 – 25c. green . . . . 30·00 40·00
161 – 30c. red . . . . 30·00 40·00
162 – 50c. green . . . . 30·00 40·00
163 – 75c. red . . . . 30·00 40·00
164 – 1l.25 blue . . . . 30·00 40·00
165 – 1l.75+1l. violet . . . . . 19·00 40·00
166 – 2l.55+2l. red . . . . . . 19·00 40·00
167 – 2l.75+2l. brown . . . . . 19·00 40·00
168 – 25c. green (air) . . . . . 38·00 50·00
169 – 50c. grey . . . . 38·00 50·00
170 – 75c. red . . . . 38·00 50·00
171 – 80c. brown . . . . 38·00 50·00
172 – 1l.+50c. green . . . . . . 29·00 50·00
173 – 2l.+1l. blue . . . . 29·00 50·00
174 – 3l.+2l. violet . . . . . . 29·00 50·00

16

19 Dante House, Rhodes

1935. Holy Year.
177 **16** 5c. orange . . . . 8·25 11·50
178 10c. brown . . . . 8·25 11·50
179 20c. red . . . . 8·25 13·50
180 25c. green . . . . 8·25 13·50
181 30c. purple . . . . 8·25 15·00
182 50c. brown . . . . 8·25 15·00
183 1l.25 blue . . . . 8·25 38·00

1938. Augustus the Great stamps of Italy (colours changed) optd **ISOLE ITALIANE DELL'EGEO.**
186 **163** 10c. brown (postage) . . 2·25 4·50
187 – 15c. violet . . . . 2·25 4·50
188 – 20c. brown . . . . 2·25 4·50
189 – 25c. green . . . . 2·25 4·50
190 – 30c. purple . . . . 2·25 4·50
191 – 50c. green . . . . 2·25 4·50
192 – 75c. red . . . . 2·25 4·50
193 – 1l.25 blue . . . . 2·25 4·50
194 – 1l.75+1l. orange . . . . . 3·00 10·00
195 – 2l.55+2l. brown . . . . . 3·00 10·00
196 – 25c. violet (air) . . . . . 2·40 2·75
197 – 50c. green . . . . 2·40 2·75
198 – 80c. blue . . . . 2·40 8·00
199 – 1l.+1l. purple . . . . . . 3·75 12·00
200 **164** 5l.+1l. red . . . . 6·00 25·00

1938. Giotto stamps of Italy optd **ITALIANE ISOLE DELL'EGEO.**
201 1l.25 blue (No. 527) . . . . 95 1·75
202 2l.75+2l. brown (530) . . . . 1·10 6·75

1940. Colonial Exhibition. Inscr as in T **19**.
203 – 5c. brown (postage) . . . 30 65
204 – 10c. orange 30 65
205 **19** 25c. green . . . . 65 1·25
206 – 50c. violet . . . . 65 1·25
207 – 75c. red . . . . 65 1·60
208 **19** 1l.25 blue . . . . 65 1·90
209 – 2l.+75c. red . . . . 65 10·00

DESIGNS—VERT: 5c., 50c. Roman Wolf statue; 10c., 75c., 2l. Crown and Maltese Cross.

210 50c. brown (air) . . . . . . 85 1·90
211 1l. violet . . . . 85 1·90
212 2l.+75c. blue . . . . 85 3·75
213 5l.+2l.50 brown . . . . . . 85 6·00
DESIGNS—HORIZ: Savoia Marchetti S.M.75 airplane over: 50c., 2l. statues, Rhodes Harbour; 1, 5l. Government House, Rhodes.

1943. Aegean Relief Fund. Nos. 17/25 surch **PRO ASSISTENZA EGEO** and value.
214 **1** 5c.+5c. purple 70 70
215 – 10c.+10c. brown 70 70
216 – 20c.+20c. red 70 70
217 – 25c.+25c. green 70 70
218 **2** 30c.+30c. blue . . . . . . 1·40 1·10
219 – 50c.+50c. brown . . . . . 1·40 1·40
220 – 1l.25+1l.25 blue . . . . . 1·75 1·75
221 **2** 5l.+5l. purple . . . . . . 70·00 70·00

1944. War Victims' Relief. Nos. 17/20 and 22/23 surch **PRO SINISTRATI DI GUERRA**, value and stag symbol.
224 **1** 5c.+3l. purple . . . . . . 1·40 2·40
225 – 10c.+3l. brown . . . . . . 1·40 2·40
226 – 20c.+3l. red . . . . 1·40 2·40
227 – 25c.+3l. green . . . . . . 1·40 2·40
228 – 50c.+3l. brown . . . . . . 1·40 2·40
229 – 1l.25+5l. blue . . . . . . 21·00 25·00

1944. Air. War Victims Relief. Surch **PRO SINISTRATI DI GUERRA** and value.
232 **11** 50c.+2l. blk & yellow . . . 6·75 2·50
233 80c.+2l. black and red . . 8·25 5·00
234 1l.+2l. black & green . . . 10·00 5·75
235 5l.+2l. black & mauve . . 50·00 55·00

1945. Red Cross Fund. Nos. 24/5 surch **FEBBRAIO 1945 + 10** and Cross.
236 +10l. on 5l. purple . . . . . 6·75 10·00
237 +10l. on 10l. green . . . . . 6·75 10·00

EXPRESS STAMPS

1932. Air. Garibaldi Air Express stamps of Italy optd **ISOLE ITALIANE DELL'EGEO.**
E104 **E 3** 2l.25+1l. red & blue . . 38·00 70·00
E105 4l.50+1l.50 grey and yellow . . . . 38·00 70·00

1934. Air. As Nos. E442/3 of Italy, but colours changed, optd **ISOLE ITALIANE DELL'EGEO.**
E175 2l.+1l.25 blue . . . . . . 30·00 48·00
E176 4l.50+2l. green . . . . . . 30·00 48·00

E 17

1935.
E184 **E 17** 1l.25 green . . . . . . 1·75 1·40
E185 2l.50 orange . . . . . 2·50 3·00

1943. Aegean Relief Fund. Surch **PRO ASSISTENZA EGEO** and value.
E222 **E 17** 1l.25+1l.25 green . . . 35·00 20·00
E223 2l.50+2l.50 orge . . . 40·00 27·00

1944. Nos. 19/20 surch **ESPRESSO** and value.
E230 1l.25 on 25c. green . . . . 40 1·25
E231 2l.50 on 50c. red . . . . . 40 1·25

PARCEL POST STAMPS

P 12

1934.
P137 **P 12** 5c. orange . . . . . . 1·75 1·75
P138 10c. red . . . . 1·75 1·75
P139 20c. green . . . . . . 1·75 1·75
P140 25c. violet . . . . . . 1·75 1·75
P141 50c. blue . . . . 1·75 1·75
P142 60c. black . . . . . . 1·75 1·75
P143 – 1l. orange . . . . . . 1·75 1·75
P144 – 2l. red . . . . 1·75 1·75
P145 – 3l. green . . . . 1·75 1·75
P146 – 4l. violet . . . . . . 1·75 1·75
P147 – 10l. blue . . . . 1·75 1·75
DESIGN: 1l. to 10l. Left half: Stag as in Type **E 17**; Right half: Castle.

POSTAGE DUE STAMPS

D 14 Badge of the Knights of St. John

D 15 Immortelle

1934.
D148 **D 14** 5c. orange . . . . . . 1·10 1·40
D149 10c. red . . . . 1·10 1·40
D150 20c. green . . . . . . 1·10 70
D151 30c. violet . . . . . . 1·10 1·00
D152 40c. blue . . . . . . 1·10 2·40
D153 **D 15** 50c. orange . . . . . 1·10 70
D154 60c. red . . . . 1·10 3·75
D155 1l. green . . . . 1·10 3·75
D156 2l. violet . . . . . . 1·10 2·40

B. GREEK MILITARY ADMINISTRATION

100 lepta = 1 drachma.

1947. Stamps of Greece optd with characters as in Type **G 1**.
G1 – 10d. on 2000d. blue (No. 623) 55 55
G3 **89** 50d. on 1d. grn (No. 642) 1·10 1·10
G4 250d. on 3d. brn (No. 643) 1·10 1·10

(G 1)

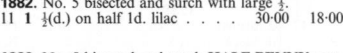

1947. Stamps of Greece surch as Type **G 1**.
G 5 – 20d. on 500d. brown (No. 582) 55 55
G 6 – 30d. on 5d. green (No. 574) 55 55
G 7 **106** 50d. on 2d. brown . . . 70 70
G 8 – 250d. on 10d. brown (No. 510) . . . . . . 1·10 1·10
G 9 – 400d. on 15d. green (No. 511) . . . . . . 1·60 1·60
G10 – 1000d. on 200d. blue (No. 581) . . . . . . 1·10 1·10

DOMINICA Pt. 1

Until 31 December 1939 one of the Leeward Islands, but then transferred to the Windward Islands. Used Leeward Island stamps concurrently with Dominican issues from 1903 to above date.

1874. 12 pence = 1 shilling;
20 shillings = 1 pound.
1949. 100 cents = 1 West Indian dollar.

1

1874.
13 **1** ½d. yellow . . . . 3·50 10·00
20 ½d. green . . . . 1·75 5·50
5 1d. lilac . . . . 6·50 2·00
22a 1d. red . . . . 3·00 7·00
15 2½d. brown . . . . £140 2·00
23 2½d. blue . . . . 3·75 5·00
7 4d. blue . . . . £110 2·75
24 4d. grey . . . . 3·75 5·50
8 6d. green . . . . £150 20·00
25 6d. orange . . . . 10·00 50·00
9 1s. mauve . . . . £120 50·00

1882. No. 5 bisected and surch with a small ½.
10 **1** ½(d.) on half 1d. lilac . . . . £180 45·00

1882. No. 5 bisected and surch with large ½.
11 **1** ½(d.) on half 1d. lilac . . . . 30·00 18·00

1883. No. 5 bisected and surch **HALF PENNY** vert.
12 **1** ½d. on half 1d. lilac . . . . 65·00 21·00

1886. Nos. 8 and 9 surch in words and bar.
17 **1** ½d. on 6d. green . . . . . . 4·50 4·00
18 1d. on 6d. green £22000 £10000
19 1d. on 1s. mauve . . . . . . 15·00 18·00

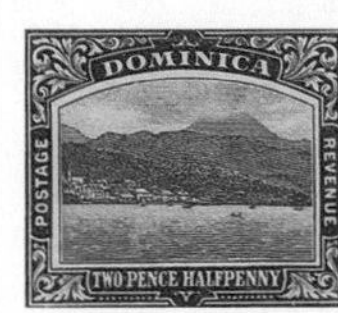

9 "Roseau from the Sea" (Lt. Caddy)

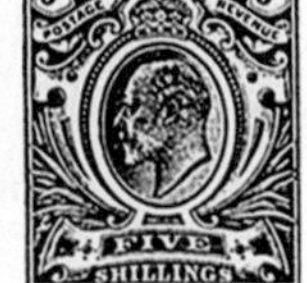

10

1903.
37 **9** ½d. green . . . . 3·50 3·25
38 1d. grey and red . . . . . 2·00 40
29 2d. green and brown . . . . 2·50 4·50
30 2½d. grey and blue . . . . 5·00 4·00
31 3d. purple and black . . . . 8·00 3·25
32 6d. grey and brown . . . . 4·75 18·00
43 1s. mauve and green . . . . 3·75 55·00
34 2s. black and purple . . . . 26·00 29·00
45 2s.6d. green and orange . . 22·00 60·00
46 **10** 5s. black and brown . . . . 60·00 60·00

1908.
48bw **9** 1d. red . . . . 1·00 50
64 1½d. orange . . . . 3·00 12·00
65 2d. grey . . . . 2·75 3·25

66 2½d. blue 2·00 8·50
51 3d. purple on yellow 3·00 4·25
52a 6d. purple 3·50 18·00
53 1s. black on green 3·00 2·75
53b 2s. purple and blue on blue 25·00 85·00
70 2s.6d. black and red on blue 32·00 95·00

1914. As T **10**, but portrait of King George V.
54 5s. red and green on yellow 55·00 80·00

1916. No. 37 surch **WAR TAX ONE HALFPENNY.**
55 **9** ½d. on ½d. green 1·00 75

1918. Optd **WAR TAX.**
57 **9** ½d. green 15 50
58 3d. purple on yellow 1·75 4·00

1919. Surch **WAR TAX 1½D.**
59 **9** 1½d. on 2½d. orange 15 55

1920. Surch **1½D.**
60 **9** 1½d. on 2½d. orange 3·00 4·50

16

1923.
71 **16** ½d. black and green 1·75 60
72 1d. black and violet 2·50 1·75
73 1d. black and red 10·00 1·00
74 1½d. black and red 3·25 65
75 1½d. black and brown 10·00 70
76 2d. black and grey 2·00 50
77 2½d. black and yellow 1·75 9·00
78 2½d. black and blue 4·50 2·00
79 3d. black and blue 1·75 12·00
80 3d. black and red on yellow 1·50 1·00
81 4d. black and brown 2·75 5·50
82 6d. black and mauve 3·50 7·00
83 1s. black on green 2·25 2·75
84 2s. black and blue on blue 10·00 20·00
85 2s.6d. black and red on blue 18·00 20·00
86 3s. black and purple on yellow 3·25 12·00
87 4s. black and red on green 11·00 22·00
90 5s. black and green on yellow 9·00 50·00
91 £1 black and purple on red £225 £350

1935. Silver Jubilee. As T **10a** of Gambia.
92 1d. blue and red 75 20
93 1½d. blue and grey 1·75 1·25
94 2½d. brown and blue 1·75 2·50
95 1s. grey and purple 1·75 4·00

1937. Coronation. As T **10b** of Gambia.
96 1d. red 40 10
97 1½d. brown 40 10
98 2½d. blue 60 1·75

17 Fresh Water Lake

21 King George VI

1938.
99 **17** ½d. brown and green 10 15
100 – 1d. black and red 20 20
101 – 1½d. green and purple 30 70
102 – 2d. red and black 50 1·25
103a – 2½d. purple and blue 20 1·25
104 – 3d. olive and brown 30 50
104a – 3½d. blue and mauve 2·00 2·00
105 **17** 6d. green and violet 1·75 1·50
105a 7d. green and brown 2·00 1·50
106 – 1s. violet and olive 3·50 1·50
106a – 2s. grey and purple 6·00 8·00
107 **17** 2s.6d. black and red 12·00 4·75
108 – 5s. blue and brown 7·50 8·00
108a – 10s. black and orange 13·00 15·00
DESIGNS—As Type **17**: 1d., 3d., 2s., 5s. Layou River; 1½d., 2½d., 3½d. Picking Limes; 2d., 1s., 10s. Boiling Lake.

1940.
109a **21** ½d. brown 10 10

1946. Victory. As T **11a** of Gambia.
110 1d. red 20 10
111 3½d. blue 20 10

1948. Silver Wedding. As T **11b/c** of Gambia.
112 1d. red 15 10
113 10s. brown 12·00 23·00

1949. U.P.U. As T **11d/c** of Gambia.
114 5c. blue 20 15
115 6c. brown 1·25 2·50
116 12c. purple 45 1·50
117 24c. olive 30 30

1951. Inauguration of B.W.I. University College. As T **23a/b** of Grenada.
118 3c. green and violet 50 1·25
119 12c. green and red 75 40

23 Drying Cocoa

1951. New Currency.
120 – ½c. brown 10 30
121 **23** 1c. black and red 10 30
122 – 2c. brown and green 10 30
123 – 3c. green and purple 15 2·00
124 – 4c. orange and sepia 70 2·00
125 – 5c. black and red 85 30
126 – 6c. olive and brown 90 30
127 – 8c. green and blue 90 70
128 – 12c. black and green 60 1·25
129 – 14c. blue and purple 95 2·00
130 – 24c. purple and red 75 30
131 – 48c. green and orange 3·75 8·50
132 – 60c. red and black 3·75 6·50
133 – $1.20 green and black 4·50 6·50
134 – $2.40 orange and black 23·00 40·00
DESIGNS: ½c. As Type **21**, but with portrait as Type **23**. HORIZ (as Type **23**): 2c., 60c. Carib baskets; 3c., 48c. Lime plantation; 4c. Picking oranges; 5c. Bananas; 6c. Botanical Gardens; 8c. Drying vanilla beans; 12c., $1.20, Fresh Water Lake; 14c. Layou River, 24c. Boiling Lake. VERT: $2.40, Picking oranges.

1951. New Constitution. Stamps of 1951 optd **NEW CONSTITUTION 1951.**
135 3c. green and violet 15 70
136 5c. black and red 15 1·25
137 8c. green and blue 15 15
138 14c. blue and violet 90 20

1953. Coronation. As T **11h** of Gambia.
139 2c. black and green 20 10

1954. As Nos 120/34 but with portrait of Queen Elizabeth II.
140 ½c. brown 10 30
141 1c. black and red 10 10
142 2c. brown and green 55 2·00
143 3c. green and purple 1·50 30
144 3c. black and red 3·25 2·25
145 4c. orange and brown 20 10
146 5c. black and red 2·00 50
147 5c. blue and brown 10·00 1·00
148 6c. green and brown 40 10
149 8c. green and blue 1·00 10
150 10c. green and brown 5·00 2·75
151 12c. black and green 50 10
152 14c. blue and purple 50 10
153 24c. purple and red 50 10
154 48c. green and orange 2·00 9·50
155 48c. brown and violet 1·25 80
156 60c. red and black 1·25 1·00
157 $1.20 green and black 17·00 7·00
158 $2.40 orange and black 17·00 14·00
DESIGNS (New)—HORIZ: Nos. 144, 155, Mat making; 147, Canoe making; 150, Bananas.

1958. British Caribbean Federation. As T **47a** of Grenada.
159 3c. green 40 10
160 6c. blue 60 1·25
161 12c. red 70 15

40 Seashore at Rosalie

1963.
162 **40** 1c. green, blue and sepia 10 85
163 – 2c. blue 30 30
164 – 3c. brown and blue 1·75 1·25
165 – 4c. green, sepia and violet 10 10
166 – 5c. mauve 30 30
167 – 6c. green, bistre and violet 10 80
168 – 8c. green, sepia and black 30 20
169 – 10c. sepia and pink 10 20
170 – 12c. green, blue and sepia 1·00 10
171 – 14c. multicoloured 70 10
204 – 15c. yellow, green and brown 70 10
173 – 24c. multicoloured 9·00 20
174 – 48c. green, blue and black 75 1·00
175 – 60c. orange, green and black 1·00 70
176 – $1.20 multicoloured 6·50 1·00
177 – $2.40 blue, turq & brn 3·25 2·50
178 – $4.80 green, blue and brown 9·50 20·00
DESIGNS—VERT: 2c., 5c. Queen Elizabeth II (after Annigoni); 14c. Traditional costume; 24c. Imperial amazon ("Sisserou Parrot"); $2.40, Trafalgar Falls; $4.80, Coconut palm. HORIZ: 3c. Sailing canoe; 4c. Sulphur springs; 6c. Road making; 8c. Dug-out canoe; 10c. Crapaud (frog); 12c. Scott's Head; 15c. Bananas; 48c. Goodwill; 60c. Cocoa tree; $1.20, Coat of Arms.

1963. Freedom from Hunger. As T **20a** of Gambia.
179 15c. violet 15 10

1963. Centenary of Red Cross. As T **20b** of Gambia.
180 5c. red and black 20 40
181 15c. red and blue 40 60

1964. 400th Birth Anniv of Shakespeare. As T **22a** of Gambia.
182 15c. purple 20 10

1965. Centenary of I.T.U. As T **44** of Gibraltar.
183 2c. green and blue 10 10
184 48c. turquoise and grey 45 20

1965. I.C.Y. As T **45** of Gibraltar.
185 1c. purple and turquoise 10 20
186 15c. green and lavender 35 10

1966. Churchill Commemoration. As T **46** of Gibraltar.
187 1c. blue 10 75
188 5c. green 25 10
189 15c. brown 50 10
190 24c. violet 65 20

1966. Royal Visit. As T **49** of Grenada.
191 5c. black and blue 75 30
192 15c. black and mauve 1·00 30

1966. World Cup Football Championship. As T **47** of Gibraltar.
193 5c. multicoloured 25 15
194 24c. multicoloured 85 15

1966. Inauguration of W.H.O. Headquarters, Geneva. As T **54** of Gibraltar.
195 5c. black, green and blue 15 15
196 24c. black, purple and ochre 30 15

1966. 20th Anniv of UNESCO. As T **55a/c** of Gibraltar.
197 5c. red, yellow and orange 20 15
198 15c. yellow, violet and olive 50 10
199 24c. black, purple and orange 60 15

56 Children of Three Races

1967. National Day. Multicoloured.
205 5c. Type **56** 10 10
206 10c. The "Santa Maria" and motto 40 15
207 15c. Hands holding motto ribbon 15 15
208 24c. Belaire dancing 15 20

57 John F. Kennedy

1968. Human Rights Year. Multicoloured.
209 1c. Type **57** 10 10
210 10c. Cecil E. A. Rawle 10 10
211 12c. Pope John XXIII 50 15
212 48c. Florence Nightingale 20 25
213 60c. Albert Schweitzer 20 25

1968. Associated Statehood. Nos. 162 etc, optd **ASSOCIATED STATEHOOD.**
214 1c. green, blue and sepia 10 10
215 2c. blue 10 10
216 3c. brown and blue 10 10
217 4c. green, sepia and violet 10 10
218 5c. mauve 10 10
219 6c. green, bistre and violet 10 10
220 8c. green, sepia and black 10 10
221 10c. sepia and pink 55 10
222 12c. green, blue and brown 10 10
224 14c. multicoloured 10 10
225 15c. yellow, green and brown 10 10
226 24c. multicoloured 4·25 10
227 48c. green, blue and black 55 1·50
228 60c. orange, green and black 90 1·00
229 $1.20 multicoloured 1·00 3·25
230 $2.40 blue, turquoise and brown 1·00 2·50
231 $4.80 green, blue and brown 1·25 8·00

1968. National Day. Nos. 162/4, 171 and 176 optd **NATIONAL DAY 3 NOVEMBER 1968.**
232 1c. green, blue and sepia 10 10
233 2c. blue 10 10
234 3c. brown and blue 10 10
235 14c. multicoloured 10 10
236 $1.20 multicoloured 55 40

60 Forward shooting at Goal

1968. Olympic Games, Mexico. Multicoloured.
237 1c. Type **60** 10 10
238 1c. Goalkeeper attempting to save ball 10 10
239 5c. Swimmers preparing to dive 10 10
240 5c. Swimmers diving 10 10
241 48c. Javelin-throwing 15 15
242 48c. Hurdling 15 15
243 60c. Basketball 90 25
244 60c. Basketball players 90 25

61 "The Small Cowper Madonna" (Raphael)

62 "Venus and Adonis" (Rubens)

1968. Christmas.
245 **61** 5c. multicoloured 10 10

1969. 20th Anniv of World Health Organization.
246 **62** 5c. multicoloured 20 10
247 – 15c. multicoloured 30 10
248 – 24c. multicoloured 30 10
249 – 50c. multicoloured 50 40
DESIGNS: 15c. "The Death of Socrates" (J.-L. David); 24c. "Christ and the Pilgrims of Emmaus" (Velasquez); 50c. "Pilate washing his Hands" (Rembrandt).

66 Picking Oranges

71 "Spinning" (J. Millet)

67 "Strength in Unity" Emblem and Fruit Trees

1969. Tourism. Multicoloured.
250 10c. Type **66** 15 10
251 10c. Woman, child and ocean scene 15 10
252 12c. Fort Yeoung Hotel 50 10
253 12c. Red-necked amazon 50 10
254 24c. Calypso band 30 10
255 24c. Women dancing 30 15
256 48c. Underwater life 30 25
257 48c. Skin-diver and turtle 30 25

1969. 1st Anniv of C.A.R.I.F.T.A. (Caribbean Free Trade Area). Multicoloured.
258 5c. Type **67** 10 10
259 8c. Hawker Siddeley H.S.748 aircraft, emblem and island 30 20
260 12c. Chart of Caribbean Sea and emblem 30 25
261 24c. Steamship unloading, tug and emblem 40 25

1969. 50th Anniv of International Labour Organization. Multicoloured.
262 15c. Type **71** 10 10
263 30c. "Threshing" (J. Millet) 15 15
264 38c. "Flax-pulling" (J. Millet) 15 15

72 Mahatma Gandhi weaving and Clock Tower, Westminster

1969. Birth Cent of Mahatma Gandhi. Mult.
265 6c. Type **72** 25 10
266 38c. Gandhi, Nehru and Mausoleum 40 15
267 $1.20 Gandhi and Taj Mahal 45 1·50
All stamps are incorrectly inscribed "Ghandi".

75 "Saint Joseph"

1969. National Day. Multicoloured.
268 6c. Type **75** 10 10
269 8c. "Saint John" 10 10
270 12c. "Saint Peter" 10 10
271 60c. "Saint Paul" 30 50

79 Queen Elizabeth II

99 "Virgin and Child with St. John" (Perugino)

80 Purple-throated Carib ("Humming Bird") and Flower

1969. Centres multicoloured; colours of "D" given.
272a **79** ½c. black and silver 30 1·75
273 **80** 1c. black and yellow . . . 1·00 2·25
274 – 2c. black and yellow . . . 15 10
275a – 3c. black and yellow . . . 2·75 1·50
276a – 4c. black and yellow . . . 2·75 1·50
277a – 5c. black and yellow . . . 2·75 1·75
278a – 6c. black and brown . . . 2·75 2·75
279 – 8c. black and brown . . . 20 10
280 – 10c. black and yellow . . 20 10
281 – 12c. black and yellow . . 20 10
282 – 15c. black and blue . . 20 10
283 – 25c. black and red . . . 30 10
284a – 30c. black and olive . . . 1·50 70
285 – 38c. black and purple . . 8·00 1·75
286 – 50c. black and brown . . 50 45
287 – 60c. black and yellow . . 55 1·50
288 – $1.20 black and yellow . 1·00 1·75
289 – $2.40 black and gold . . 1·00 4·00
290 – $4.80 black and gold . . 1·25 7·00
DESIGNS—HORIZ (As Type **80**): 2c. Poinsettia; 3c. Redneck pigeon ("Ramier"); 4c. Imperial amazon ("Sisserou"); 5c. "Battus polydamas" (butterfly); 6c. "Dryas julia" (butterfly); 8c. Shipping bananas; 10c. Portsmouth Harbour; 12c. Copra processing plant; 15c. Straw workers; 25c. Timber plant; 30c. Pumice mine; 38c. Grammar school and playing fields; 50c. Roseau Cathedral. (38 × 26½ mm): 60c. Government Headquarters. (40 × 27 mm): $1.20, Melville Hall airport. (39½ × 26 mm): $2.40, Coat of arms. VERT: (26 × 39 mm): $4.80, As Type **79**, but larger.

1969. Christmas. Paintings. Multicoloured.
291 6c. "Virgin and Child with St. John" (Lippi) 10 10
292 10c. "Holy Family with Lamb" (Raphael) 10 10
293 15c. Type **99** 10 10
294 $1.20 "Madonna of the Rose Hedge" (Botticelli) 35 40
MS295 89 × 76 mm. Nos. 293/4. Imperf . . . . 75 1·00

101 Astronaut's First Step onto the Moon

1970. Moon Landing. Multicoloured.
296 ½c. Type **101** 10 10
297 5c. Scientific experiment on the Moon and flag 15 10
298 8c. Astronauts collecting rocks 15 10
299 30c. Module over Moon . . 30 15
300 50c. Moon plague 40 25
301 60c. Astronauts 40 30
MS302 116 × 112 mm. Nos. 298/301. Imperf . . . . 2·00 2·00

107 Giant Green Turtle

1970. Flora and Fauna. Multicoloured.
303 6c. Type **107** 30 20
304 24c. Atlantic flyingfish . . . 40 45
305 38c. Anthurium lily 50 65
306 60c. Imperial and red-necked amazons . . . . 2·75 5·50
MS307 160 × 111 mm. Nos. 303/6 5·50 6·50

108 18th-century National Costume

1970. National Day. Multicoloured.
308 5c. Type **108** 10 10
309 8c. Carib basketry 10 10
310 $1 Flag and chart of Dominica 30 40
MS311 150 × 85 mm. Nos. 308/10 50 1·75

109 Scrooge and Marley's Ghost

1970. Christmas and Death Centenary of Charles Dickens. Scenes from "A Christmas Carol". Multicoloured.
312 2c. Type **109** 10 10
313 15c. Fezziwig's Ball 20 10
314 24c. Scrooge and his Nephew's Party 20 10
315 $1.20 Scrooge and the Ghost of Christmas Present . . . 65 90
MS316 142 × 87 mm. Nos. 312/15 1·00 3·75

110 "The Doctor" (Sir Luke Fildes)

1970. Centenary of British Red Cross. Multicoloured.
317 8c. Type **110** 10 10
318 10c. Hands and Red Cross 10 10
319 15c. Flag of Dominica and Red Cross emblem 15 10
320 50c. "The Sick Child" (E. Munch) 50 45
MS321 108 × 76 mm. Nos. 317/20 1·00 3·00

111 Marigot School

1971. International Education Year. Multicoloured.
322 5c. Type **111** 10 10
323 8c. Goodwill Junior High School 10 10
324 14c. University of West Indies (Jamaica) 10 10
325 $1 Trinity College, Cambridge 35 30
MS326 85 × 85 mm. Nos. 324/5 50 1·25

112 Waterfall

1971. Tourism. Multicoloured.
327 5c. Type **112** 15 10
328 10c. Boat-building 15 10
329 30c. Sailing 25 10
330 50c. Yacht and motor launch 40 30
MS331 130 × 86 mm. Nos. 327/30 85 1·00

113 UNICEF Symbol in "D"

1971. 25th Anniv of UNICEF.
332 **113** 5c. violet, black and gold 10 10
333 10c. yellow, blk & gold 10 10
334 38c. green, blk & gold . . 10 10
335 $1.20 orange, blk & gold 30 45
MS336 84 × 79 mm. Nos. 333 and 335 . . . . 50 1·75

114 German Boy Scout

1971. World Scout Jamboree, Asagiri, Japan. Various designs showing Boy Scouts from the nations listed. Multicoloured.
337 20c. Type **114** 15 20
338 24c. Great Britain 20 20
339 30c. Japan 25 25
340 $1 Dominica . . . . 50 2·25
MS341 114 × 102 mm. Nos. 339/40 1·00 2·25
Both No. 340 and the $1 value from the miniature sheet show the national flag of the Dominican Republic in error.
"Dominica" on the scout's shirt pocket is omitted on the $1 value from the miniature sheet.

115 Groine at Portsmouth

1971. National Day. Multicoloured.
342 8c. Type **115** 10 10
343 15c. Carnival scene 10 10
344 20c. Carifta Queen (vert) . . 10 10
345 50c. Rock of Atkinson (vert) 20 25
MS346 63 × 89 mm. $1.20, As 20c. 50 70

116 Eight Reals Piece, 1761

1972. Coins.
347 **116** 10c. black, silver and violet 10 10
348 – 30c. black, silver and green 15 15
349 – 35c. black, silver and blue 15 20
350 – 50c. black, silver and red 25 1·75
MS351 86 × 90 mm. Nos. 349/50 50 1·25
DESIGNS—HORIZ: 30c. Eleven and three bitt pieces, 1798. VERT: 35c. Two reals and two bitt pieces, 1770; 50c. Mocos, pieces-of-eight and eight reals-eleven bitts piece, 1798.

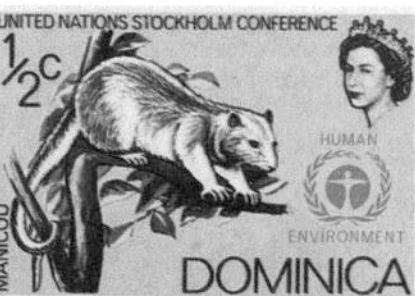
117 Common Opossum

1972. U.N. Conference on the Human Enviroment, Stockholm. Multicoloured.
352 ½c. Type **117** 10 10
353 35c. Brazilian agouti (rodent) 30 15
354 60c. Orchid . . . . 2·00 50
355 $1.20 Hibiscus . . . . 1·25 1·60
MS356 139 × 94 mm. Nos. 352/5 5·00 9·50

118 Sprinter

1972. Olympic Games, Munich. Multicoloured.
357 30c. Type **118** 10 10
358 35c. Hurdler 15 15
359 58c. Hammer-thrower (vert) 20 20
360 72c. Long-jumper (vert) . . . 40 40
MS361 98 × 96 mm. Nos. 359/60 75 1·00

119 General Post Office

1972. National Day. Multicoloured.
362 10c. Type **119** 10 10
363 20c. Morne Diablotin 10 10
364 30c. Rodney's Rock 15 15
MS365 83 × 96 mm. Nos. 363/4 50 70

1972. Royal Silver Wedding. As T **98** of Gibraltar, but with Bananas and Imperial Parrot in background.
366 5c. green 20 10
367 $1 green 60 40

121 "The Adoration of the Shepherds" (Caravaggio)

122 Launching of Weather Satellite

1972. Christmas. Multicoloured.
368 8c. Type **121** 10 10
369 14c. "The Myosotis Virgin" (Rubens) 10 10
370 30c. "Madonna and Child with St Francesca Romana" (Gentileschi) . . 15 10
371 $1 "Adoration of the Kings" (Mostaert) . . . . 50 1·75
MS372 102 × 79 mm. Nos. 370/1. Imperf 60 80

1973. Centenary of I.M.O./W.M.O. Multicoloured.
373 ½c. Type **122** 10 20
374 1c. Nimbus satellite 10 20
375 2c. Radiosonde balloon . . . 10 20
376 30c. Radarscope (horiz) . . . 15 15
377 35c. Diagram of pressure zones (horiz) 20 20
378 50c. Hurricane shown by satellite (horiz) 30 35
379 $1 Computer weather-map (horiz) 60 70
MS380 90 × 105 mm. Nos. 378/9 70 1·75

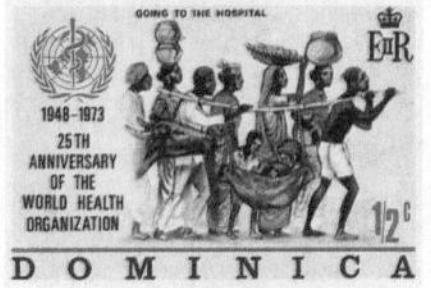
123 Going to Hospital

1973. 25th Anniv of W.H.O. Multicoloured.
381 ½c. Type **123** 10 10
382 1c. Maternity care 10 10
383 2c. Smallpox inoculation . . 10 10
384 30c. Emergency service . . . 30 15
385 35c. Waiting for the doctor 30 15

386 50c. Medical examination 30 25
387 $1 Travelling doctor 40 60
MS388 112 × 110 mm. Nos. 386/7 75 1·25

124 Cyrique Crab

1973. Flora and Fauna. Multicoloured.
389 ½c. Type **124** 10 10
390 22c. Blue land-crab 30 10
391 25c. Bread fruit 30 15
392 $1.20 Sunflower 55 2·00
MS393 91 × 127 mm. Nos. 389/2 1·00 4·00

125 Princess Anne and Captain Mark Phillips

1973. Royal Wedding.
394 **125** 25c. multicoloured 10 10
395 – $2 multicoloured 30 30
MS396 79 × 100 mm. 75c. as 25c. and $1.20 as $2 40 30
DESIGN: $2 As Type **125**, but with different frame.

126 "Adoration of the Kings" (Brueghel)

1973. Christmas. Religious Paintings. Multicoloured.
397 ½c. Type **126** 10 10
398 1c. "Adoration of the Magi" (Botticelli) 10 10
399 2c. "Adoration of the Magi" (Durer) 10 10
400 12c. "Mystic Nativity" (Botticelli) 20 10
401 22c. "Adoration of the Magi" (Rubens) 25 10
402 35c. "The Nativity" (Durer) 25 10
403 $1 "Adoration of the Shepherds" (Giorgione) 60 55
MS404 122 × 98 mm. Nos. 402/3 85 1·10

127 Carib Basket-weaving

1973. National Day. Multicoloured.
405 5c. Type **127** 10 10
406 10c. Staircase of the Snake 10 10
407 50c. Miss Caribbean Queen (vert) 15 15
408 60c. Miss Carifta Queen (vert) 15 15
409 $1 Dance group (vert) 25 30
MS410 95 × 127 mm. Nos. 405/6 and 409 40 65

128 University Centre, Dominica

1973. 25th Anniv of West Indies University. Multicoloured.
411 12c. Type **128** 10 10
412 30c. Graduation ceremony 10 10
413 $1 University coat of arms 25 35
MS414 97 × 131 mm. Nos. 411/13 30 55

129 Dominica 1d. Stamp of 1874 and Map

1974. Stamp Centenary. Multicoloured.
415 ½c. Type **129** 10 10
416 1c. 6d. stamp of 1874 and posthorn 10 10
417 2c. 1d. stamp of 1874 and arms 10 10
418 10c. Type **129** 20 10
419 50c. As 1c. 40 30
420 $1.20 As 2c. 50 70
MS421 105 × 121 mm. Nos. 418/20 1·00 1·50

130 Footballer and Flag of Brazil

1974. World Cup Football Championship, West Germany. Multicoloured.
422 ½c. Type **130** 10 10
423 1c. West Germany 10 10
424 2c. Italy 10 10
425 30c. Scotland 50 10
426 40c. Sweden 50 10
427 50c. Netherlands 55 35
428 $1 Yugoslavia 90 90
MS429 89 × 87 mm. Nos. 427/8 70 80

131 Indian Hole

1974. National Day. Multicoloured.
430 10c. Type **131** 10 10
431 40c. Teachers' Training College 10 10
432 $1 Bay Oil distillery plant, Petite Savanne 50 45
MS433 96 × 143 mm. Nos. 430/2 60 65

132 Churchill with "Colonist"

1974. Birth Centenary of Sir Winston Churchill. Multicoloured.
434 ½c. Type **132** 10 10
435 1c. Churchill and Eisenhower 10 10
436 2c. Churchill and Roosevelt 10 10
437 20c. Churchill and troops on assault-course 15 10
438 45c. Painting at Marrakesh 20 10
439 $2 Giving the "V" sign 50 1·00
MS440 126 × 100 mm. Nos. 438/9 70 1·50

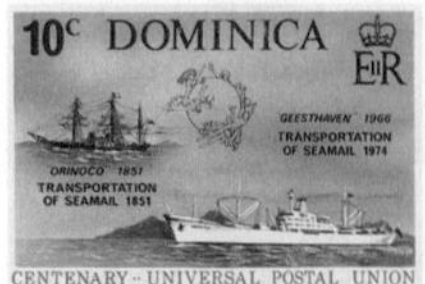

133 Mailboats "Orinoco" (1851) and "Geesthaven" (1974)

1974. Centenary of U.P.U. Multicoloured.
441 10c. Type **133** 20 10
442 $2 De Haviland D.H.4 (1918) and Boeing 747-100 (1974) 80 1·00
MS443 107 × 93 mm. $1.20 as 10c. and $2.40 as $2 1·00 1·40
Nos. 442 and **MS**443 are inscr "De Haviland".

134 "The Virgin and Child" (Tiso)

1974. Christmas. Multicoloured.
444 ½c. Type **134** 10 10
445 1c. "Madonna and Child with Saints" (Costa) 10 10
446 2c. "The Nativity" (school of Rimini, 14th-century) 10 10
447 10c. "The Rest on the Flight into Egypt" (Romanelli) 20 10
448 25c. "The Adoration of the Shepherds" (da Sermoneta) 35 10
449 45c. "The Nativity" (Guido Reni) 45 10
450 $1 "The Adoration of the Magi" (Caselli) 65 40
MS451 114 × 78 mm. Nos. 449/50 60 1·00

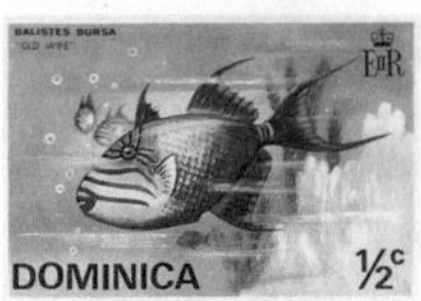

135 Queen Triggerfish

1975. Fishes. Multicoloured.
452 ½c. Type **135** 10 10
453 1c. Porkfish 10 10
454 2c. Sailfish 10 10
455 3c. Swordfish 10 10
456 20c. Great barracuda 50 50
457 $2 Nassau grouper 1·40 2·75
MS458 104 × 80 mm. No. 457 1·90 6·00

136 "Myscelia antholia"

1975. Dominican Butterflies. Multicoloured.
459 ½c. Type **136** 10 60
460 1c. "Lycorea ceres" 10 60
461 2c. "Anaea marthesia" ("Siderone nemesis") 15 60
462 6c. "Battus polydamas" 40 1·00
463 30c. "Anartia lytrea" 60 70
464 40c. "Morpho peleides" 60 75
465 $2 "Dryas julia" 1·00 6·50
MS466 108 × 80 mm. No. 465 1·25 4·75

137 "Yare" (cargo liner)

1975. "Ships tied to Dominica's History". Mult.
467 ½c. Type **137** 20 35
468 1c. "Thames II" (liner), 1890 20 35
469 2c. "Lady Nelson" (cargo liner) 20 35
470 20c. "Lady Rodney" (cargo liner) 40 35
471 45c. "Statesman" (freighter) 60 55
472 50c. "Geestcape" (freighter) 60 80
473 $2 "Geeststar" (freighter) 1·00 4·50
MS474 78 × 103 mm. Nos. 472/3 1·50 5·00

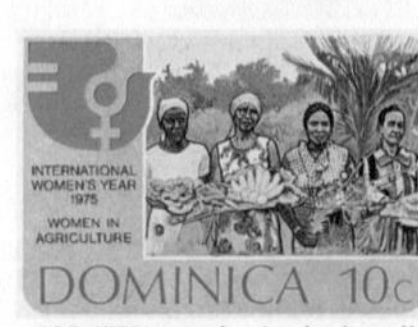

138 "Women in Agriculture"

1975. International Women's Year. Multicoloured.
475 10c. Type **138** 10 10
476 $2 "Women in Industry and Commerce" 40 60

139 Miss Caribbean Queen, 1975

140 "Virgin and Child" (Mantegna)

1975. National Day. Multicoloured.
477 5c. Type **139** 10 10
478 10c. Public library (horiz) 10 10
479 30c. Citrus factory (horiz) 10 10
480 $1 National Day Trophy 25 50
MS481 130 × 98 mm. Nos. 478/80. Imperf 50 1·40

1975. Christmas. "Virgin and Child" paintings by artists named. Multicoloured.
482 ½c. Type **140** 10 10
483 1c. Fra Filippo Lippi 10 10
484 2c. Bellini 10 10
485 10c. Botticelli 15 10
486 25c. Bellini 25 10
487 45c. Correggio 30 10
488 $1 Durer 55 50
MS489 139 × 85 mm. Nos. 487/88 1·00 1·50

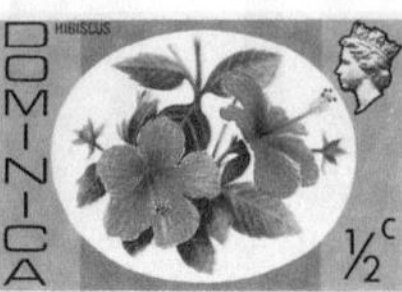

141 Hibiscus

1975. Multicoloured.
490 ½c. Type **141** 10 1·00
491 1c. African tulip 15 1·00
492 2c. Castor-oil tree 15 1·00
493 3c. White cedar flower 15 1·00
494 4c. Egg plant 15 1·00
495 5c. Needlefish ("Gare") 20 1·00
496 6c. Ochro 20 1·10
497 8c. Zenaida dove ("Mountain Dove") 3·00 1·10
498 10c. Screw pine 20 15
499 20c. Mango longue 30 15
500 25c. Crayfish 35 15
501 30c. Common opossum 90 80
502 40c. Bay leaf groves 90 80
503 50c. Tomatoes 40 50
504 $1 Lime factory 55 65
505 $2 Rum distillery 1·00 3·50
506 $5 Bay Oil distillery 1·00 5·00
507 $10 Queen Elizabeth II (vert) 1·40 15·00
Nos. 502/7 are larger, 28 × 44 mm ($10) or 44 × 28 (others).

142 American Infantry **143** Rowing

1976. Bicentenary of American Revolution. Mult.
508 ½c. Type **142** 10 10
509 1c. British three-decker, 1782 10 10
510 2c. George Washington 10 10
511 45c. British sailors 30 10
512 75c. British ensign 40 40
513 $2 Admiral Hood 60 1·25
MS514 105 × 92 mm. Nos. 512/13 1·00 3·00

1976. Olympic Games, Montreal. Multicoloured.
515 ½c. Type **143** 10 10
516 1c. Shot putting 10 10
517 2c. Swimming 10 10
518 40c. Relay 15 10
519 45c. Gymnastics 15 10
520 60c. Sailing 20 20
521 $2 Archery 55 80
MS522 90 × 140 mm. Nos. 520/1 85 75

144 Ringed Kingfisher

1976. Wild Birds. Multicoloured.
523 ½c. Type **144** 10 75
524 1c. Mourning dove 15 75
525 2c. Green-backed heron ("Green Heron") 15 75
526 15c. Blue-winged hawk (vert) 75 35

527 30c. Blue-headed hummingbird (vert) 80 55
528 45c. Bananaquit (vert) 85 60
529 $2 Imperial amazon ("Imperial Parrot") (vert) 1·75 12·00
MS530 133×101 mm. Nos. 527/9 2·75 14·00

1976. West Indian Victory in World Cricket Cup. As T **223a** of Grenada.
531 15c. Map of the Caribbean 75 1·25
532 25c. Prudential Cup 75 1·75

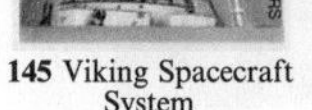

145 Viking Spacecraft System
146 "Virgin and Child with Saints Anthony of Padua and Roch" (Giorgione)

1976. Viking Space Mission. Multicoloured.
533 ½c. Type **145** 10 10
534 1c. Landing pad (horiz) 10 10
535 2c. Titan IIID and Centaur DII 10 10
536 3c. Orbiter and lander capsule 10 10
537 45c. Capsule, parachute unopened 15 15
538 75c. Capsule, parachute opened 20 70
539 $1 Lander descending (horiz) 25 75
540 $2 Space vehicle on Mars (horiz) 35 2·00
MS541 104×78 mm. Nos. 539/40 1·10 2·25

1976. Christmas. "Virgin and Child" paintings by artists named. Multicoloured.
542 ½c. Type **146** 10 10
543 1c. Bellini 10 10
544 2c. Mantegna 10 10
545 6c. Mantegna (different) 10 10
546 25c. Memling 15 10
547 45c. Correggio 20 10
548 $3 Raphael 1·00 1·00
MS549 104×85 mm. 50c. as No. 547 and $1 as No. 548 1·00 1·10

147 Island Craft Co-operative

1976. National Day. Multicoloured.
550 10c. Type **147** 10 10
551 50c. Harvesting bananas 15 10
552 $1 Boxing plant 30 35
MS553 96×122 mm. Nos. 550/2 50 1·00

148 American Giant Sundial
150 Joseph Haydn

149 The Queen Crowned and Enthroned

1976. Shells. Multicoloured.
554 ½c. Type **148** 10 10
555 1c. Flame helmet 10 10
556 2c. Mouse cone 10 10
557 20c. Caribbean vase 35 10
558 40c. West Indian fighting conch 55 25
559 50c. Short coral shell 55 25
560 $3 Apple murex 1·40 3·25
MS561 101×55 mm. $2 Long-spined star shell 1·10 1·40

1977. Silver Jubilee. Multicoloured.
562 ½c. Type **149** 10 10
563 1c. Imperial State Crown 10 10
564 45c. The Queen and Princess Anne 15 10
565 $2 Coronation Ring 25 30
566 $2.50 Ampulla and Spoon 30 40
MS567 104×97 mm. $5 Queen Elizabeth and Prince Philip 75 1·25

1977. 150th Death Anniv of Ludwig van Beethoven. Multicoloured.
568 ½c. Type **150** 10 10
569 1c. Scene from "Fidelio" 10 10
570 2c. Maria Casentini (dancer) 10 10
571 15c. Beethoven and pastoral scene 30 10
572 30c. "Wellington's Victory" 30 10
573 40c. Henriette Sontag (singer) 30 10
574 $2 The young Beethoven 75 2·00
MS575 138×93 mm. Nos. 572/4 1·10 3·25

151 Hiking

1977. Caribbean Scout Jamboree, Jamaica. Mult.
576 ½c. Type **151** 10 10
577 1c. First-aid 10 10
578 2c. Camping 10 10
579 45c. Rock climbing 25 15
580 50c. Canoeing 30 20
581 $3 Sailing 1·40 1·75
MS582 111×113 mm. 75c. Map-reading; $2 Campfire sing-song 1·00 1·25

152 Holy Family

1977. Christmas. Multicoloured.
583 ½c. Type **152** 10 10
584 1c. Angel and Shepherds 10 10
585 2c. Holy Baptism 10 10
586 6c. Flight into Egypt 15 10
587 15c. Three Kings with gifts 15 10
588 45c. Holy Family in the Temple 30 10
589 $3 Flight into Egypt (different) 80 1·10
MS590 113×85 mm. 50c. Virgin and Child; $2 Flight into Egypt (different) 60 75

1977. Royal Visit. Nos. 562/66 optd **ROYAL VISIT W.I. 1977.**
591 ½c. Type **149** 10 10
592 1c. Imperial State Crown 10 10
593 45c. The Queen and Princess Anne 15 10
594a $2 Coronation Ring 30 30
595a $2.50 Ampulla and Spoon 35 35
MS596 104×79 mm. $5 Queen Elizabeth and Prince Philip 1·00 1·50

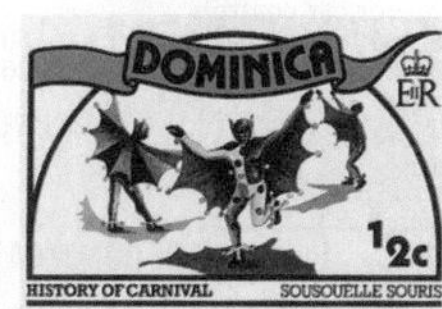

154 "Sousouelle Souris"

1978. "History of Carnival". Multicoloured.
597 ½c. Type **154** 10 10
598 1c. Sensay costume 10 10
599 2c. Street musicians 10 10
600 45c. Douiette band 15 10
601 50c. Pappy Show wedding 15 10
602 $2 Masquerade band 45 60
MS603 104×88 mm. $2.50, No. 602 60 65

155 Colonel Charles Lindbergh and "Spirit of St. Louis"

1978. Aviation Anniversaries. Multicoloured.
604 6c. Type **155** 20 60
605 10c. "Spirit of St. Louis", New York, 20 May, 1927 25 10
606 15c. Lindbergh and map of Atlantic 35 10
607 20c. Lindbergh reaches Paris, 21 May, 1927 45 10
608 40c. Airship LZ-1, Lake Constance, 1900 55 20
609 60c. Count F. von Zeppelin and Airship LZ-2, 1906 65 30
610 $3 Airship "Graf Zeppelin", 1928 1·40 2·25
MS611 139×108 mm. 50c. Ryan NYP Special "Spirit of St. Louis" in mid-Atlantic; $2 Airship LZ-127 "Graf Zeppelin", 1928 1·60 1·10

The 6, 10, 15, 20 and 50c. values commemorate the 50th anniversary of first solo transatlantic flight by Col. Charles Lindbergh; the other values commemorate anniversaries of various Zeppelin airships.

156 Queen receiving Homage
158 "Two Apostles"

157 Wright Flyer III

1978. 25th Anniv of Coronation. Multicoloured.
612 45c. Type **156** 15 10
613 $2 Balcony scene 30 30
614 $2.50 Queen and Prince Philip 40 40
MS615 76×107 mm. $5 Queen Elizabeth II 75 75

1978. 75th Anniv of First Powered Flight. Mult.
616 30c. Type **157** 15 15
617 40c. Wright Type A, 1908 20 20
618 60c. Wright Flyer I 25 30
619 $2 Wright Flyer I (different) 85 1·25
MS620 116×89 mm. $3 Wilbur and Orville Wright 1·00 1·00

1978. Christmas. Paintings by Rubens. Mult.
621 20c. Type **158** 10 10
622 45c. "Descent from the Cross" 15 10
623 50c. "St Ildefonso receiving the Chasuble" 15 10
624 $3 "Assumption of the Virgin" 35 80
MS625 113×83 mm. $2 "The Holy Family" (Sebastiano del Piombo*) 75 75
*This painting was incorrectly attributed to Rubens on the stamp.

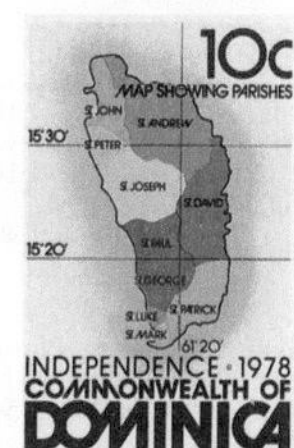

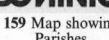

159 Map showing Parishes
161 Sir Rowland Hill

1978. Independence. Multicoloured.
626 10c. Type **159** 75 30
627 25c. "Sabinea carinalis" (national flower) 55 15
628 45c. New National flag 1·25 30
629 50c. Coat of arms 60 30
630 $2 Prime Minister Patrick John 70 2·75
MS631 113×90 mm. $2.50, Type **159** 1·00 1·25

1978. Nos. 490/507 optd **INDEPENDENCE 3rd NOVEMBER 1978.**
632 ½c. Type **57** 40 60
633 1c. African tulip 45 60
634 2c. Castor-oil tree 45 50
635 3c. White cedar flower 50 50
636 4c. Egg plant 50 50
637 5c. Needlefish ("Gare") 50 50
638 6c. Ochro 50 50
639 8c. Zenaida dove 3·50 60
640 10c. Screw pine 50 15
641 20c. Mango longue 60 40
642 25c. Crayfish 70 40
643 30c. Common opossum 70 40
644 40c. Bay leaf groves 70 25
645 50c. Tomatoes 80 30
646 $1 Lime factory 80 65
647 $2 Rum distillery 1·00 1·00
648 $5 Bay Oil distillery 1·00 2·25
649 $10 Queen Elizabeth II 1·50 4·50

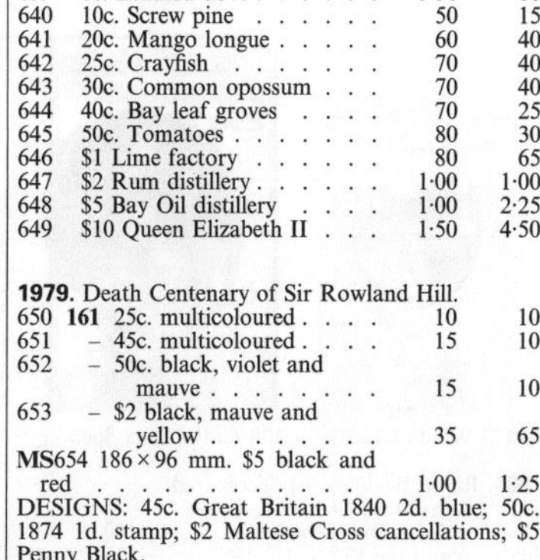

1979. Death Centenary of Sir Rowland Hill.
650 **161** 25c. multicoloured 10 10
651 – 45c. multicoloured 15 10
652 – 50c. black, violet and mauve 15 10
653 – $2 black, mauve and yellow 35 65
MS654 186×96 mm. $5 black and red 1·00 1·25
DESIGNS: 45c. Great Britain 1840 2d. blue; 50c. 1874 1d. stamp; $2 Maltese Cross cancellations; $5 Penny Black.

162 Children and Canoe

1979. International Year of the Child. Multicoloured.
655 30c. Type **162** 25 15
656 40c. Children with bananas 25 15
657 50c. Children playing cricket 1·25 80
658 $3 Child feeding rabbits 1·75 2·00
MS659 117×85 mm. $5 Child with catch of fish 1·00 1·50

163 Nassau Grouper

1979. Marine Wildlife. Multicoloured.
660 10c. Type **163** 40 15
661 30c. Striped dolphin 70 35
662 50c. White-tailed tropic-bird 2·25 65
663 60c. Brown pelican 2·25 1·50
664 $1 Long-finned pilot whale 2·50 1·75
665 $2 Brown booby 3·00 4·50
MS666 120×94 mm. $3 Elkhorn coral 1·25 1·40
No. 661 is inscr "SPOTTED DOLPHIN" in error.

164 H.M.S. "Endeavour"

1979. Death Bicent of Captain Cook. Mult.
667 10c. Type **164** 65 30
668 50c. H.M.S. "Resolution" (Second Voyage) 1·00 1·00
669 60c. H.M.S. "Discovery" (Third Voyage) 1·00 1·50
670 $2 Detail of Cook's chart of New Zealand, 1770 1·25 2·75
MS671 97×90 mm. Captain Cook and signature 1·25 2·00

165 Cooking at Campfire

1979. 50th Anniv of Girl Guide Movement in Dominica. Multicoloured.
672 10c. Type **165** 20 10
673 20c. Pitching emergency rain tent 25 10
674 50c. Raising Dominican flag 35 10
675 $2.50 Singing and dancing to accordion 90 80
MS676 110×86 mm. $3 Guides of different age-groups 75 1·25

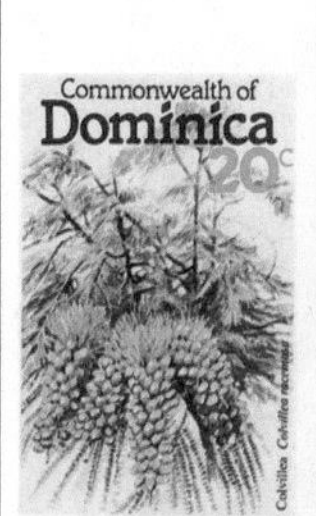

166 Colvillea
169 Mickey Mouse and Octopus playing Xylophone

167 Cathedral of the Assumption, Roseau

1979. Flowering Trees. Multicoloured.
677 20c. Type **166** 15 10
678 40c. "Lignum vitae" 20 15

679 60c. Dwarf poinciana 25 15
680 $2 Fern tree 50 75
MS681 114×89 mm. $3 Perfume tree . . . . 75 1·10

1979. Christmas. Cathedrals. Multicoloured.
682 6c. Type **167** 10 10
683 45c. St. Paul's, London (vert) 15 10
684 60c. St. Peter's, Rome . . . 15 10
685 $3 Notre Dame, Paris (vert) 55 60
MS686 113×85 mm. 40c. St. Patrick's, New York; $2 Cologne Cathedral (both vert) 50 80

1979. Hurricane Relief. Nos. 495, 502 and 506/7 optd **HURRICANE RELIEF.**
687 5c. Gare 10 10
688 40c. Bay leaf groves 10 10
689 $5 Bay Oil distillery . . . . 1·00 1·25
690 $10 Queen Elizabeth II . . . 1·25 1·75

1979. International Year of the Child. Walt Disney Cartoon Characters. Multicoloured.
691 ½c. Type **169** 10 10
692 1c. Goofy playing guitar on rocking-horse 10 10
693 2c. Mickey Mouse playing violin and Goofy on bagpipes 10 10
694 3c. Donald Duck playing drum with a pneumatic drill 10 10
695 4c. Minnie Mouse playing saxophone 10 10
696 5c. Goofy one-man band . . 10 10
697 10c. Horace Horsecollar blowing Dale from french horn 10 10
698 $2 Huey, Dewey and Louie playing bass . . . . 1·00 2·00
699 $2.50 Donald Duck at piano and Huey playing trumpet 1·00 2·25
MS700 127×102 mm. $3 Mickey Mouse playing piano . . . . . 2·50 3·00

170 Hospital Ward

1980. 75th Anniv of Rotary International. Mult.
701 10c. Type **170** 10 10
702 20c. Electro-cardiogram . . . 15 10
703 40c. Mental hospital site . . 20 15
704 $2.50 Paul Harris (founder) 55 90
MS705 128×113 mm. $3 Interlocking cogs of Rotary emblem and globe 60 80

1980. "London 1980" International Stamp Exhibition. Optd **LONDON 1980.**
706 **161** 25c. multicoloured 25 10
707 – 45c. multicoloured 30 15
708 – 50c. brown, blue and red 30 15
709 – $2 brown, red and yellow 80 60

171 Shot Putting

1980. Olympic Games, Moscow. Multicoloured.
710 30c. Type **171** 15 10
711 40c. Basketball 60 15
712 60c. Swimming 35 20
713 $2 Gymnastics 60 65
MS714 114×86 mm. $3 The marathon 70 90

172 "Supper at Emmaus" (Caravaggio)

1980. Famous Paintings. Multicoloured.
715 20c. Type **172** 20 10
716 25c. "Portrait of Charles I Hunting" (Van Dyck) (vert) 20 10
717 30c. "The Maids of Honour" (Velasquez) (vert) 25 10
718 45c. "The Rape of the Sabine Women" (Poussin) 25 10
719 $1 "Embarkation for Cythera" (Watteau) . . . 35 35
720 $5 "Girl before a Mirror" (Picasso) (vert) . . . . . . 1·00 1·50
MS721 114×111 mm. $3 "The Holy Family" (Rembrandt) (vert) . . 60 80

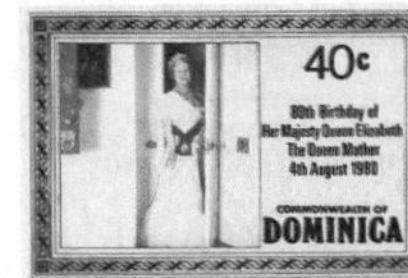

173 Scene from "Peter Pan"

1980. Christmas. Scenes from "Peter Pan". Multicoloured.
722 ½c. Type **173** (Tinker Bell) . . 10 10
723 1c. Wendy sewing back Peter's shadow 10 10
724 2c. Peter introduces the mermaids 10 10
725 3c. Wendy and Peter with lost boys 10 10
726 4c. Captain Hook, Pirate Smee and Tiger Lily . . . 10 10
727 5c. Peter with Tiger Lily and her father 10 10
728 10c. Captain Hook captures Peter and Wendy 10 10
729 $2 Peter fights Captain Hook 2·25 1·50
730 $2.50 Captain Hook in crocodile's jaws . . . . . 2·25 1·75
MS731 124×98 mm. $4 Peter Pan 4·25 3·50

174 Queen Elizabeth the Queen Mother in Doorway

1980. 80th Birthday of the Queen Mother.
732a **174** 40c. multicoloured . . . 15 15
733a $2.50 multicoloured . . 45 60
MS734 85×66 mm. $3 multicoloured . . . . 75 2·00

175 Douglas Bay

1981. "Dominica Safari". Multicoloured.
735 20c. Type **175** 10 10
736 30c. Valley of Desolation . . 10 10
737 40c. Emerald Pool (vert) . . 10 10
738 $3 Indian River (vert) . . . . 75 1·10
MS739 84×104 mm. $4 Trafalgar Falls (vert) . . . . 1·10 1·40

1981. Walt Disney's Cartoon Character, Pluto. As T **169**. Multicoloured.
740 $2 Pluto and Fifi . . . . . . 1·00 1·50
MS741 128×102 mm. $4 Pluto in scene from film "Pluto's Blue Note" . . . . 1·25 1·50

177 Windsor Castle **178** Lady Diana Spencer

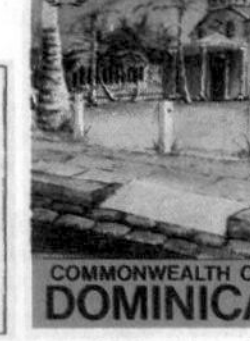

176 Forest Thrush

1981. Birds. Multicoloured.
742 20c. Type **176** 55 30
743 30c. Wied's crested flycatcher 65 35
744 40c. Blue-hooded euphonia 75 45
745 $5 Lesser Antillean pewee . . 3·50 4·75
MS746 121×95 mm. $3 Imperial Amazon . . . . 2·75 1·75

1981. Royal Wedding. Multicoloured.
747 40c. Prince Charles and Lady Diana Spencer . . . 10 10
748 60c. Type **177** 15 15
749a $4 Prince Charles flying helicopter 30 50
MS750 96×82 mm. $5 Westland HU Mk 5 Wessex helicopter of Queen's Flight . . . . 1·00 90

1981. Royal Wedding. Multicoloured.
751 25c. Type **178** 20 35
752 $2 Prince Charles . . . . . 50 1·00
753 $5 Prince Charles and Lady Diana Spencer . . . . . . 1·75 2·50

1981. Christmas. Scenes from Walt Disney's cartoon film "Santa's Workshop". As T **169**.
754 ½c. multicoloured 10 10
755 1c. multicoloured 10 10
756 2c. multicoloured 10 10
757 3c. multicoloured 10 10
758 4c. multicoloured 15 10
759 5c. multicoloured 15 10
760 10c. multicoloured 20 10
761 45c. multicoloured . . . . . 1·50 30
762 $5 multicoloured . . . . . . 4·25 5·50
MS763 129×103 mm. $4 multicoloured . . . . 4·00 3·50

179 Ixora **180** Curb Slope for Wheelchairs

1981. Plant Life. Multicoloured.
764A 1c. Type **179** 10 75
765A 2c. Flamboyant 10 80
766A 4c. Poinsettia 15 80
767A 5c. Bois caribe (national flower of Dominica) . . . 15 70
768A 8c. Annatto or roucou . . 20 1·00
769A 10c. Passion fruit 30 20
770A 15c. Breadfruit or yampain 55 20
771A 20c. Allamanda or buttercup 40 20
772A 25c. Cashew nut 40 20
773A 35c. Soursop or couassol 45 30
774A 40c. Bougainvillea 45 30
775A 45c. Anthurium 50 35
776A 60c. Cacao or cocoa . . . 1·25 70
777A 90c. Pawpaw tree or papay 70 1·50
778A $1 Coconut palm . . . . . 1·50 1·75
779A $2 Coffee tree or cafe . . . 1·00 3·50
780B $5 Heliconia or lobster claw 3·25 5·50
781A $10 Banana fig . . . . . . 2·25 12·00
Nos. 769, 770, 776, 778, 780 and 781 come with or without imprint date.

1981. International Year for Disabled People. Multicoloured.
782 45c. Type **180** 40 15
783 60c. Bus with invalid step . . 50 20
784 75c. Motor car controls adapted for handicapped 60 30
785 $4 Bus with wheelchair ramp 1·00 2·50
MS786 82×96 mm. $5 Specially designed elevator control panel 4·25 3·00

181 "Olga Picasso in an Armchair" **182** "Gone Fishing"

1981. Birth Centenary of Picasso. Multicoloured.
787 45c. Type **181** 35 15
788 60c. "Bathers" 40 15
789 75c. "Woman in Spanish Costume" 40 25
790 $4 "Detail of Dog and Cock" 1·00 2·25
MS791 140×115 mm. $5 "Sleeping Peasants" (detail) . . . . . . 2·50 3·50

1982. World Cup Football Championship, Spain. Walt Disney Cartoon Characters. As T **169**. Mult.
792 ½c. Goofy chasing ball with butterfly net 10 10
793 1c. Donald Duck with ball in beak 10 10
794 2c. Goofy as goalkeeper . . . 10 10
795 3c. Goofy looking for ball . . 10 10
796 4c. Goofy as park attendant puncturing ball with litter spike 10 10
797 5c. Pete and Donald Duck playing 10 10
798 10c. Donald Duck after kicking rock instead of ball 15 10
799 60c. Donald Duck feeling effects of a hard game and Daisy Duck dusting ball 1·50 1·25
800 $5 Goofy hiding ball under his jersey from Mickey Mouse . . . . 5·50 6·50
MS801 132×105 mm. $4 Dale making off with ball . . . . . 4·00 3·25

1982. Norman Rockwell (painter) Commemoration. Multicoloured.
802 10c. Type **182** 10 10
803 25c. "Breakfast" 20 10
804 45c. "The Marbles Champ" 30 30
805 $1 "Speeding Along" 55 65
No. 802 is inscribed "Golden Days" and No. 803 "The Morning News".

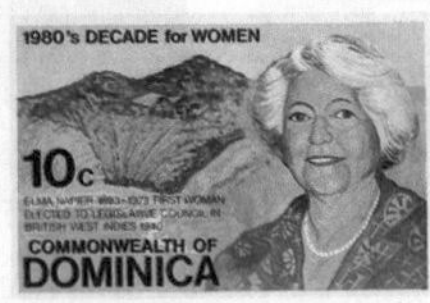

183 Elma Napier (first woman elected to B.W.I. Legislative Council)

1982. Decade for Women. Multicoloured.
806 10c. Type **183** 10 10
807 45c. Margaret Mead (anthropologist) 30 30
808 $1 Mabel (Cissy) Caudeiron (folk song composer and historian) 55 55
809 $4 Eleanor Roosevelt . . . . 2·25 2·25
MS810 92×83 mm. $3 Florence Nightingale . . . . 2·00 3·00

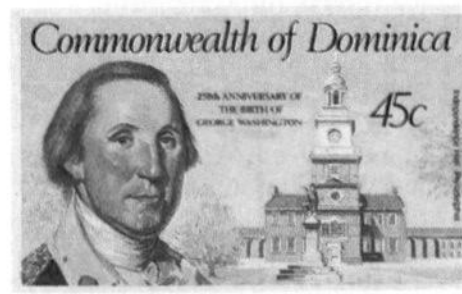

184 George Washington and Independence Hall, Philadelphia

1982. 250th Birth Anniv of George Washington and Birth Centenary of Franklin D. Roosevelt. Multicoloured.
811 45c. Type **184** 25 25
812 60c. Franklin D. Roosevelt and Capitol, Washington D.C. 30 35
813 90c. Washington at Yorktown (detail "The Surrender of Cornwallis" by Trumbull) 40 55
814 $2 Construction of dam (from W. Groppers' mural commemorating Roosevelt's) "New Deal" 70 1·60
MS815 115×90 mm. $5 Washington and Roosevelt with U.S.A. flags of 1777 and 1933 . . . . . . 2·00 3·25

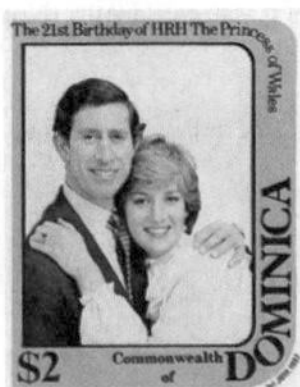

185 "Anaea dominicana" **186** Prince and Princess of Wales

1982. Butterflies. Multicoloured.
816 15c. Type **185** . . . . 1·50 35
817 45c. "Heliconius charithonia" 2·50 65
818 60c. "Hypolimnas misippus" 2·75 1·75
819 $3 "Biblis hyperia" . . . . . 5·50 6·00
MS820 77×105 mm. $5 "Marpesia petreus" . . . . 7·00 5·00

1982. 21st Birthday of Princess of Wales. Multicoloured.
821 45c. Buckingham Palace . . . 20 10
822 $2 Type **186** 50 70
823 $4 Princess of Wales . . . . 1·10 1·25
MS824 103×75 mm. $5 Princess Diana (different) . . . . 2·50 2·25

187 Scouts around Campfire

1982. 75th Anniv of Boy Scouts Movement. Mult.
825 45c. Type **187** . . . . 1·25 50
826 60c. Temperature study, Valley of Desolation . . . 1·75 1·25

827 75c. Learning about native birds 2·25 1·50
828 $3 Canoe trip along Indian River 4·25 5·50
MS829 99 × 70 mm. Dominican scouts saluting the flag (vert) 1·50 3·25

1982. Birth of Prince William of Wales. Nos. 821/3 optd **ROYAL BABY 21.6.82.**
830 45c. Buckingham Palace 30 30
831 $2 Type **186** 80 1·10
832 $4 Princess of Wales 1·40 1·90
MS833 103 × 75 mm. $5 Princess Diana (different) 2·00 2·75

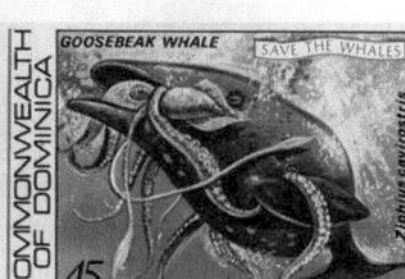

188 "Holy Family of Francis I" **189** Cuvier's Beaked Whale

1982. Christmas. Raphael Paintings. Multicoloured.
834 25c. Type **188** 15 10
835 30c. "Holy Family of the Pearl" 15 10
836 90c. "Canigiani Holy Family" 30 35
837 $4 "Holy Family of the Oak Tree" 1·25 1·50
MS838 95 × 125 mm. $5 "Holy Family of the Lamp" 1·25 2·00

1983. Save the Whales. Multicoloured.
839 45c. Type **189** 2·00 65
840 60c. Humpback whale 2·25 1·75
841 75c. Black right whale 2·25 2·25
842 $3 Melon-headed whale 4·50 6·50
MS843 99 × 72 mm. $5 Pygmy sperm whale 4·00 4·00

190 Banana Export

1983. Commonwealth Day. Multicoloured.
844 25c. Type **190** 15 15
845 30c. Road building 15 20
846 90c. Community nursing 30 45
847 $3 Tourism-handicrafts 75 1·50

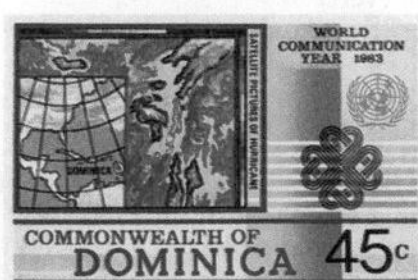

191 Map and Satellite Picture of Hurricane

1983. World Communications Year. Multicoloured.
848 45c. Type **191** 20 25
849 60c. Aircraft-to-ship transmission 25 35
850 90c. Satellite communications 30 45
851 $2 Shortwave radio 75 1·00
MS852 110 × 85 mm. $5 Communications satellite 1·25 2·75

192 Short-Mayo Composite

1983. Bicentenary of Manned Flight. Mult.
853 45c. Type **192** 50 30
854 60c. Macchi M.39 Schneider Trophy seaplane 60 65
855 90c. Fairey Swordfish torpedo bomber 70 1·50
856 $4 Airship LZ-3 1·25 4·75
MS857 105 × 79 mm. $5 "Double Eagle II" (balloon) 1·25 2·75

193 Duesenberg "SJ", 1935

1983. Classic Motor Cars. Multicoloured.
858 10c. Type **193** 25 15
859 45c. Studebaker "Avanti", 1962 35 25
860 60c. Cord "812" 40 35
861 75c. MG "TC", 1945 45 50
862 90c. Camaro "350 SS", 1967 50 60
863 $3 Porsch "356", 1948 1·00 1·60
MS864 110 × 75 mm. $5 Ferrari "312 T", 1975 1·50 2·75

194 "Charity"

1983. Christmas. 500th Birth Anniv of Raphael. Multicoloured.
865 45c. Type **194** 30 30
866 60c. "Hope" 30 30
867 90c. "Faith" 40 60
868 $4 "The Cardinal Virtues" 1·00 3·25
MS869 101 × 127 mm. $5 "Justice" 1·25 2·75

195 Plumbeous Warbler

1984. Birds. Multicoloured.
870 5c. Type **195** 2·50 1·10
871 45c. Imperial amazon ("Imperial Parrot") 5·00 75
872 60c. Blue-headed hummingbird 5·50 3·25
873 90c. Red-necked amazon ("Red-necked Parrot") 6·50 6·00
MS874 72 × 72 mm. $5 Greater flamingos 4·00 4·50

196 Donald Duck **197** Gymnastics

1984. Easter. Multicoloured.
875 ½c. Type **196** 10 10
876 1c. Mickey Mouse 10 10
877 2c. Tortoise and Hare 10 10
878 3c. Brer Rabbit and Brer Bear 10 10
879 4c. Donald Duck (different) 10 10
880 5c. White Rabbit 10 10
881 10c. Thumper 10 10
882 $2 Pluto 3·25 2·75
883 $4 Pluto (different) 4·50 4·00
MS884 126 × 100 mm. $5 Chip and Dale 3·50 4·00

1984. Olympic Games, Los Angeles. Multicoloured.
885 30c. Type **197** 20 25
886 45c. Javelin-throwing 30 35
887 60c. High diving 40 45
888 $4 Fencing 2·00 2·50
MS889 104 × 85 mm. $5 Equestrian event 3·25 3·25

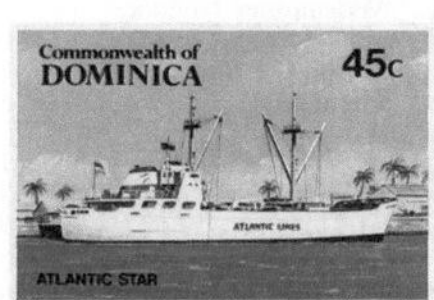

198 "Atlantic Star"

1984. Shipping. Multicoloured.
890 45c. Type **198** 1·75 75
891 60c. "Atlantic" (liner) 2·00 1·25
892 90c. Carib fishing boat 2·50 2·50
893 $4 "Norway" (liner) 6·00 9·00
MS894 106 × 79 mm. $5 "Santa Maria", 1492 3·25 5·50

1984. U.P.U. Congress, Hamburg. Nos. 769 and 780 optd **19th UPU CONGRESS HAMBURG**.
895 10c. Passion fruit 10 10
896 $5 Heliconia or lobster claw 2·75 4·00

200 "Guzmania lingulata" **201** "The Virgin and Child with Young St. John" (Correggio)

1984. "Ausipex" International Stamp Exhibition, Melbourne. Bromeliads. Multicoloured.
897 45c. Type **200** 30 35
898 60c. "Pitcairnia angustifolia" 40 55
899 75c. "Tillandsia fasciculata" 50 75
900 $3 "Aechmea smithiorum" 2·00 3·50
MS901 75 × 105 mm. $5 "Tillandsia utriculata" 2·25 4·25

1984. 450th Death Anniv of Correggio (painter). Multicoloured.
902 25c. Type **201** 30 20
903 60c. "Christ bids Farewell to the Virgin Mary" 40 40
904 90c. "Do not Touch Me" 50 80
905 $4 "The Mystical Marriage of St Catherine" 80 3·50
MS906 89 × 60 mm. $5 "The Adoration of the Magi" 1·75 3·50

202 "Before the Start" (Edgar Degas)

1984. 150th Birth Anniv of Edgar Degas (painter). Multicoloured.
907 30c. Type **202** 30 25
908 45c. "Race on the Racecourse" 35 35
909 $1 "Jockeys at the Flagpole" 55 1·25
910 $3 "Racehorses at Longchamp" 80 3·75
MS911 89 × 60 mm. $5 "Self-portrait" (vert) 2·00 3·75

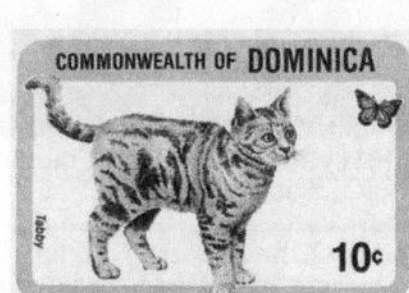

203 Tabby

1984. Cats. Multicoloured.
912 10c. Type **203** 20 15
913 15c. Calico shorthair 25 15
914 20c. Siamese 35 15
915 25c. Manx 40 20
916 45c. Abyssinian 65 30
917 60c. Tortoise-shell longhair 70 65
918 $1 Cornish rex 80 1·00
919 $2 Persian 1·00 3·00
920 $3 Himalayan 1·00 4·00
921 $5 Burmese 1·25 7·00
MS922 105 × 75 mm. $5 Grey Burmese, Persian and American shorthair 3·50 7·00

204 Hawker Siddeley H.S.748 **205** Donald Duck, Mickey Mouse and Goofy with Father Christmas

1984. 40th Anniv of International Civil Aviation Organisation. Multicoloured.
923 30c. Type **204** 1·00 50
924 60c. De Havilland Twin Otter 100 1·75 50
925 $1 Britten Norman Islander 2·00 1·60
926 $3 De Havilland Twin Otter 100 (different) 3·00 6·50
MS927 102 × 75 mm. $5 Boeing 747–200 2·50 3·50

1984. Christmas. Walt Disney Cartoon Characters. Multicoloured.
928 45c. Type **205** 1·25 30
929 60c. Donald Duck as Father Christmas with toy train 1·50 70
930 90c. Donald Duck as Father Christmas in sleigh 2·00 1·75
931 $2 Donald Duck and nephews in sledge 3·25 3·75
932 $4 Donald Duck in snow with Christmas tree 4·25 6·00
MS933 127 × 102 mm. $5 Donald Duck and nephews opening present 3·50 4·00

206 Mrs. M. Bascom presenting Trefoil to Chief Guide Lady Baden-Powell

1985. 75th Anniv of Girl Guide Movement. Mult.
934 35c. Type **206** 60 30
935 45c. Lady Baden-Powell inspecting Dominican brownies 80 35
936 60c. Lady Baden-Powell with Mrs. M. Bascom and Mrs. A. Robinson (guide leaders) 1·00 65
937 $3 Lord and Lady Baden-Powell (vert) 2·50 3·75
MS938 77 × 105 mm. $5 Flags of Dominica and Girl Guide Movement 3·50 4·00

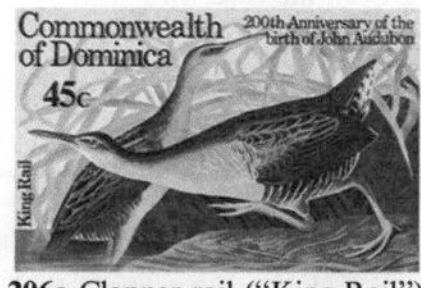

206a Clapper rail ("King Rail")

1985. Birth Bicentenary of John J Audubon (ornithologist) (1st issue). Multicoloured.
939 45c. Type **206a** 1·10 30
940 $1 Black and white warbler (vert) 2·00 1·50
941 $2 Broad-winged hawk (vert) 2·75 3·00
942 $3 Ring-necked duck 3·50 4·00
MS943 101 × 73 mm. $5 Reddish egret 3·50 3·75
See also Nos. 1013/**MS**17.

207 Student with Computer **208** The Queen Mother visiting Sadlers Wells Opera

1985. Duke of Edinburgh's Award Scheme. Multicoloured.
944 45c. Type **207** 50 30
945 60c. Assisting doctor in hospital 1·75 40
946 90c. Two youths hiking 1·90 80
947 $4 Family jogging 3·50 6·50
MS948 100 × 98 mm. $5 Duke of Edinburgh 2·75 3·00

1985. Life and Times of Queen Elizabeth the Queen Mother. Multicoloured.
949 60c. Type **208** 1·75 60
950 $1 Fishing in Scotland 1·75 70
951 $3 On her 84th birthday 2·25 3·25
MS952 56 × 85 mm. $5 Attending Garter ceremony, Windsor Castle 3·25 3·00

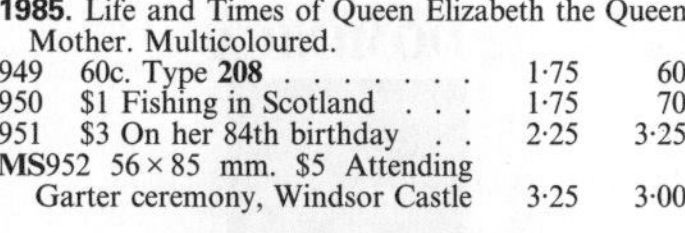
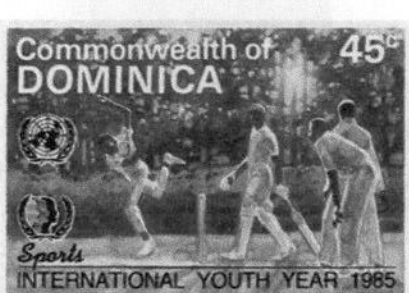

209 Cricket Match ("Sports")

1985. International Youth Year. Multicoloured.
953 45c. Type **209** 4·25 1·50
954 60c. Bird-watching ("Environmental Study") 4·25 2·25
955 $1 Stamp collecting ("Education") 4·25 3·50
956 $3 Boating ("Leisure") 5·50 8·00
MS957 96 × 65 mm. $5 Young people linking hands 2·75 4·00

1985. 300th Birth Anniv of Johann Sebastian Bach (composer). As T **309a** of Grenada. Antique musical instruments.
958 45c. multicoloured 1·50 40
959 60c. multicoloured 1·75 60
960 $1 multicoloured 2·25 1·00
961 $3 multicoloured 4·00 3·50
MS962 199 × 75 mm. $5 black 3·00 4·50

DESIGNS: 45c. Cornett; 60c. Coiled trumpet; $1 Piccolo; $3 Violoncello piccolo; $5 Johann Sebastian Bach.

1985. Royal Visit. As T **310** of Grenada. Mult.
963 60c. Flags of Great Britain and Dominica 75 50
964 $1 Queen Elizabeth II (vert) 75 1·25
965 $4 Royal Yacht "Britannia" 1·75 5·50
MS966 111 × 83 mm. $5 Map of Dominica 3·50 4·00

209a "The Glorious Whitewasher"

1985. 150th Birth Anniv of Mark Twain (author). Walt Disney cartoon characters in scenes from "Tom Sawyer". Multicoloured.
967 20c. Type **209a** 75 30
968 60c. "Aunt Polly's home dentistry" 1·50 75
969 $1 "Aunt Polly's pain killer" 2·00 1·25
970 $1.50 Mickey Mouse balancing on fence 2·50 3·00
971 $2 "Lost in the cave with Becky" 2·75 3·50
MS972 126 × 101 mm. $5 Mickey Mouse as pirate 5·50 7·00

209b Little Red Cap (Daisy Duck) meeting the Wolf

1985. Birth Bicentenaries of Grimm Brothers (folklorists). Walt Disney cartoon characters in scenes from "Little Red Cap". Multicoloured.
973 10c. Type **209b** 30 20
974 45c. The Wolf at the door 85 30
975 90c. The Wolf in Grandmother's bed 1·75 1·75
976 $1 The Wolf lunging at Little Red Cap 2·00 1·75
977 $3 The Woodsman (Donald Duck) chasing the Wolf 3·75 5·00
MS978 126 × 101 mm. $5 The Wolf falling into cooking pot 5·00 5·50

1985. 40th Anniv of United Nations Organization. Designs as T 311a of Grenada showing United Nations (New York) stamps. Multicoloured.
979 45c. Lord Baden-Powell and 1984 International Youth Year 35c. 70 50
980 $2 Maimonides (physician) and 1966 W.H.O. Building 11c. 1·50 3·25
981 $3 Sir Rowland Hill (postal reformer) and 1976 25th anniv of U.N. Postal Administration 13c. 1·50 3·50
MS982 110 × 85 mm. $5 "Apollo" spacecraft 2·75 3·25

210 Two Players competing for Ball

1986. World Cup Football Championship, Mexico. Multicoloured.
983 45c. Type **210** 1·75 40
984 60c. Player heading ball 2·00 1·50
985 $1 Two players competing for ball (different) 2·25 1·75
986 $3 Player with ball 4·50 6·00
MS987 114 × 84 mm. $5 Three players 8·00 10·00

211 Police in Rowing Boat pursuing River Pirates, 1890

1986. Centenary of Statue of Liberty. Mult.
988 15c. Type **211** 2·75 65
989 25c. Police patrol launch, 1986 2·75 85
990 45c. Hoboken Ferry Terminal c. 1890 2·50 85
991 $4 Holland Tunnel entrance and staff, 1986 5·00 7·50
MS992 104 × 76 mm. $5 Statue of Liberty (vert) 4·00 5·00

211a Nasir al Din al Tusi (Persian astronomer) and Jantal Mantar Observatory, Delhi

1986. Appearance of Halley's Comet (1st issue). Multicoloured.
993 5c. Type **211a** 40 50
994 10c. Bell XS-1 Rocket Plane breaking sound barrier for first time, 1947 45 50
995 45c. Halley's Comet of 1531 (from "Astronomicum Caesareum", 1540) 1·00 30
996 $4 Mark Twain and quotation, 1910 3·75 4·25
MS997 104 × 71 mm. $5 Halley's Comet over Dominica 3·00 3·50
See also Nos. 1032/6.

1986. 60th Birthday of Queen Elizabeth II. As T **151b** of Gambia.
998 2c. multicoloured 10 15
999 $1 multicoloured 70 80
1000 $4 multicoloured 2·00 3·00
MS1001 120 × 85 mm. $5 black and brown 4·00 4·25
DESIGNS: 2c. Wedding photograph, 1947; $1 Queen meeting Pope John Paul II, 1982; $4 Queen on royal visit, 1982; $5 Princess Elizabeth with corgis, 1936.

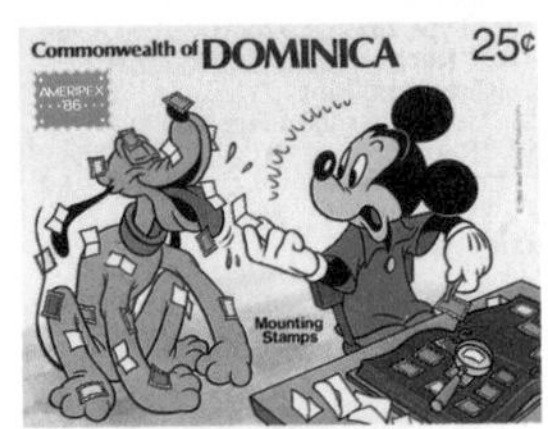

212 Mickey Mouse and Pluto mounting Stamps in Album

1986. "Ameripex" International Stamp Exhibition, Chicago. Showing Walt Disney cartoon characters. Multicoloured.
1002 25c. Type **212** 60 40
1003 45c. Donald Duck examining stamp under magnifying glass 80 65
1004 60c. Chip n' Dale soaking and drying stamps 1·10 1·50
1005 $4 Donald Duck as scoutmaster awarding merit badges to Nephews 3·50 6·00
MS1006 127 × 101 mm. $5 Uncle Scrooge conducting stamp auction 4·00 8·00

213 William I **214** "Virgin at Prayer"

1986. 500th Anniv (1985) of Succession of House of Tudor to English Throne. Multicoloured.
1007 10c. Type **213** 40 40
1008 40c. Richard II 80 80
1009 50c. Henry VIII 90 90
1010 $1 Charles II 1·00 1·75
1011 $2 Queen Anne 1·50 3·00
1012 $4 Queen Victoria 2·00 4·50

1986. Birth Bicentenary (1985) of John J. Audubon (ornithologist) (2nd issue). As T **312b** of Grenada showing original paintings. Multicoloured.
1013 25c. Black-throated diver 1·50 50
1014 60c. Great blue heron (vert) 2·00 1·50
1015 90c. Yellow-crowned night heron (vert) 2·00 2·25
1016 $4 Common shoveler ("Shoveler Duck") 4·50 6·50
MS1017 73 × 103 mm. $5 Canada goose ("Goose") 10·00 12·00

1986. Royal Wedding. As T **153b** of Grenada. Multicoloured.
1018 45c. Prince Andrew and Miss Sarah Ferguson 35 30
1019 50c. Prince Andrew 45 45
1020 $4 Prince Andrew climbing aboard aircraft 2·00 3·00
MS1021 88 × 88 mm. $5 Prince Andrew and Miss Sarah Ferguson (different) 4·25 4·75

1986. World Cup Football Championship Winners, Mexico. Nos. 983/6 optd **WINNERS Argentina 3 W. Germany 2**.
1022 45c. Type **210** 1·50 55
1023 60c. Player heading ball 1·75 1·50
1024 $1 Two players competing for ball 2·25 2·50
1025 $3 Player with ball 5·00 7·00
MS1026 114 × 84 mm. $5 Three players 8·50 11·00

1986. Christmas. Paintings by Durer. Multicoloured.
1027 45c. Type **214** 1·00 35
1028 60c. "Madonna and Child" 1·50 1·25
1029 $1 "Madonna of the Pear" 2·00 2·25
1030 $3 "Madonna and Child with St. Anne" 5·50 8·50
MS1031 76 × 102 mm. $5 "The Nativity" 8·00 11·00

214a

1986. Appearance of Halley's Comet (2nd issue). Nos. 993/6 optd as T **214a**.
1032 5c. Nasir al Din al Tusi (Persian astronomer) and Jantal Mantar Observatory, Delhi 15 15
1033 10c. Bell XS-1 Rocket Plane breaking sound barrier for first time, 1947 20 15
1034 45c. Halley's Comet of 1531 (from "Astronomicum Caesareum", 1540) 55 30
1035 $4 Mark Twain and quotation, 1910 2·50 3·50
MS1036 104 × 71 mm. $5 Halley's Comet over Dominica 3·25 3·50

215 Broad-winged Hawk **216** Poulsen's Triton

1987. Birds of Dominica. Multicoloured.
1037 1c. Type **215** 20 1·00
1038 2c. Ruddy quail dove 20 1·00
1039 5c. Red-necked pigeon 30 1·00
1040 10c. Green-backed heron ("Green Heron") 30 20
1041 15c. Moorhen ("Common Gallinule") 40 30
1042 20c. Ringed kingfisher 40 30
1043 25c. Brown pelican 40 20
1044 35c. White-tailed tropic bird 40 30
1045 45c. Red-legged thrush 50 30
1046 60c. Purple-throated carib 65 45
1047 90c. Magnificent frigate bird 70 70
1048 $1 Brown trembler ("Trembler") 80 80
1049 $2 Black-capped petrel 1·25 4·50
1050 $5 Barn owl 3·00 7·00
1051 $10 Imperial amazon ("Imperial Parrot") 5·00 12·00

1987. America's Cup Yachting Championships. As T **321b** of Grenada. Multicoloured.
1052 45c. "Reliance", 1903 60 30
1053 60c. "Freedom", 1980 70 55
1054 $1 "Mischief", 1881 80 90
1055 $3 "Australia", 1977 1·25 3·00
MS1056 113 × 83 mm. $5 "Courageous", 1977 (horiz) 3·00 3·50

1987. Birth Centenary of Marc Chagall (artist). As T **156** of Gambia. Multicoloured.
1057 25c. "Artist and His Model" 50 25
1058 35c. "Midsummer Night's Dream" 60 25
1059 45c. "Joseph the Shepherd" 70 25
1060 60c. "The Cellist" 80 30
1061 90c. "Woman with Pigs" 1·00 55
1062 $1 "The Blue Circus" 1·10 75
1063 $3 "For Vava" 1·75 2·00
1064 $4 "The Rider" 1·90 2·25
MS1065 Two sheets, each 110 × 95 mm. (a) $5 "Purim" (104 × 89 mm). (b) $5 "Firebird" (stage design) (104 × 89 mm) Set of 2 sheets 6·00 6·50

1987. Sea Shells.
1066 **216** 35c. multicoloured 20 20
1067 – 45c. violet, black and red 25 25
1068 – 60c. multicoloured 30 40
1069 – $5 multicoloured 2·40 4·25
MS1070 109 × 75 mm. $5 multicoloured 3·25 5·50
DESIGNS—VERT: 45c. Elongate janthina; 60c. Banded tulip; $5 Deltoid rock shell. HORIZ: $5 (**MS**1070) Junonia volute.
No. 1066 is inscribed "TIRITON" in error.

217 "Cantharellus cinnabarinus"

1987. "Capex '87" International Stamp Exhibition, Toronto. Mushrooms of Dominica. Multicoloured.
1071 45c. Type **217** 1·50 50
1072 60c. "Boletellus cubensis" 2·00 1·25
1073 $2 "Eccilia cystiophorus" 4·25 4·50
1074 $3 "Xerocomus guadelupae" 4·50 5·00
MS1075 85 × 85 mm. $5 "Gymnopilus chrysopellus" 10·00 11·00

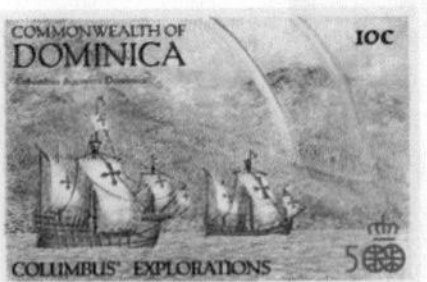

218 Discovery of Dominica, 1493

1987. 500th Anniv (1992) of Discovery of America by Columbus (1st issue). Multicoloured.
1076 10c. Type **218** 40 25
1077 15c. Caribs greeting Columbus's fleet 50 30
1078 45c. Claiming the New World for Spain 65 35
1079 60c. Wreck of "Santa Maria" 80 60
1080 90c. Fleet leaving Spain 1·00 1·00
1081 $1 Sighting the New World 1·10 1·25
1082 $3 Trading with Indians 2·25 3·00
1083 $5 Building settlement 3·25 4·00
MS1084 Two sheets, each 109 × 79 mm. (a) $5 Fleet off Dominica, 1493. (b) $5 Map showing Columbus's route, 1493 Set of 2 sheets 8·00 11·00
See also Nos. 1221/5, 1355/63, 1406/14, 1547/53 and 1612/13.

1987. Milestones of Transportation. As T **322a** of Gambia. Multicoloured.
1085 10c. H.M.S. "Warrior" (first ironclad warship, 1860) 50 50
1086 15c. "MAGLEV-MLU 001" (fastest train), 1979 60 60
1087 25c. "Flying Cloud" (fastest clipper passage New York–San Francisco) (vert) 70 70
1088 35c. First elevated railway, New York, 1868 (vert) 80 80
1089 45c. Peter Cooper's locomotive "Tom Thumb" (first U.S. passenger locomotive), 1829 80 80
1090 60c. "Spray" (Slocum's solo, circumnavigation), 1895–98 (vert) 90 90
1091 90c. "Sea-Land Commerce" (fastest Pacific passage), 1973 (vert) 1·25 1·25
1092 $1 First cable cars, San Francisco, 1873 1·40 1·40
1093 $3 "Orient Express", 1883 3·00 3·50
1094 $4 "Clermont" (first commercial paddle-steamer), 1807 3·25 3·75

219 "Virgin and Child with St. Anne" (Durer) **220** Three Little Pigs in People Mover, Walt Disney World

1987. Christmas. Religious Paintings. Mult.
1095 20c. Type **219** 30 15
1096 25c. "Virgin and Child" (Murillo) 30 15
1097 $2 "Madonna and Child" (Foppa) 1·50 2·25
1098 $4 "Madonna and Child" (Da Verona) 2·75 4·25
MS1099 100 × 78 mm. $5 "Angel of the Annunciation" (anon, Renaissance period) 2·50 3·75

1987. 60th Anniv of Mickey Mouse (Walt Disney cartoon character). Cartoon characters in trains. Multicoloured.
1100 20c. Type **220** 45 35
1101 25c. Goofy driving horse tram, Disneyland 45 35
1102 45c. Donald Duck in "Roger E. Broggie", Walt Disney World 75 65

1103 60c. Goofy, Mickey Mouse, Donald Duck and Chip 'n Dale aboard "Big Thunder Mountain" train, Disneyland 85 75
1104 90c. Mickey Mouse in "Walter E. Disney", Disneyland . . . . 1·40 1·25
1105 $1 Mickey and Minnie Mouse, Goofy, Donald and Daisy Duck in monorail, Walt Disney World . . . . 1·50 1·40
1106 $3 Dumbo flying over "Casey Jr" . . . . 3·25 3·75
1107 $4 Daisy Duck and Minnie Mouse in "Lilly Belle", Walt Disney World . . . 3·75 4·50
MS1108 Two sheets, each 127 × 101 mm. (a) $5 Seven Dwarfs in Rainbow Caverns Mine train, Disneyland (horiz). (b) $5 Donald Duck and Chip n'Dale on toy train (from film "Out of Scale") (horiz) Set of 2 sheets . . . . 5·50 7·00

1988. Royal Ruby Wedding. As T **330a** of Grenada.
1109 45c. multicoloured 70 30
1110 60c. brown, black and green 80 50
1111 $1 multicoloured . . . . . 1·00 1·00
1112 $3 multicoloured . . . . . 2·00 3·75
MS1113 102 × 76 mm. $5 multicoloured . . . . 3·00 3·75
DESIGNS: 45c. Wedding portrait with attendants, 1947; 60c. Princess Elizabeth with Prince Charles, c. 1950; $1 Princess Elizabeth and Prince Philip with Prince Charles and Princess Anne, 1950; $3 Queen Elizabeth; $5 Princess Elizabeth in wedding dress, 1947.

221 Kayak Canoeing

222 Carib Indian

1988. Olympic Games, Seoul. Multicoloured.
1114 45c. Type **221** 60 25
1115 60c. Taekwon-do 80 60
1116 $1 High diving . . . . . . 85 1·00
1117 $3 Gymnastics on bars . . . 1·75 3·75
MS1118 81 × 110 mm. $5 Football 2·50 3·50

1988. "Reunion '88" Tourism Programme. Mult.
1119 10c. Type **222** 10 10
1120 25c. Mountainous interior (horiz) 10 15
1121 35c. Indian River 10 15
1122 60c. Belaire dancer and tourists 15 30
1123 90c. Boiling Lake 20 60
1124 $3 Coral reef (horiz) . . . . 60 2·00
MS1125 112 × 82 mm. $5 Belaire dancer . . . . 1·75 4·50

1988. Stamp Exhibitions. Nos. 1092/3 optd.
1126 $1 First cable cars, San Francisco, 1873 (optd **FINLANDIA 88**, Helsinki) . . . . 1·00 75
1127 $3 "Orient Express", 1883 (optd **INDEPENDENCE 40**, Israel) . . . . 2·75 2·75
MS1128 Two sheets, each 109 × 79 mm. (a) $5 Fleet off Dominica, 1493 (optd **OLYMPHILEX '88, Seoul**). (b) $5 Map showing Columbus's route, 1493 (optd **Praga '88, Prague**) Set of 2 sheets . . . . . . 4·25 5·50

223 White-tailed Tropic Bird

225 Gary Cooper

224 Battery Hens

1988. Dominica Rain Forest Flora and Fauna. Multicoloured.
1129 45c. Type **223** 65 50
1130 45c. Blue-hooded euphonia ("Blue-throated Euphonia") 65 50
1131 45c. Smooth-billed ani . . . 65 50
1132 45c. Scaly-breasted thrasher 65 50
1133 45c. Purple-throated carib 65 50
1134 45c. "Marpesia petreus" and "Strymon maesites" (butterflies) 65 50
1135 45c. Brown trembler ("Trembler") 65 50
1136 45c. Imperial amazon ("Imperial Parrot") . . . 65 50
1137 45c. Mangrove cuckoo . . . 65 50
1138 45c. "Dynastes hercules" (beetle) 65 50
1139 45c. "Historis odius" (butterfly) 65 50
1140 45c. Red-necked amazon ("Red-necked Parrot") . . 65 50
1141 45c. Tillandsia (plant) . . . 65 50
1142 45c. Bananaquit and "Polystacha luteola" (plant) 65 50
1143 45c. False chameleon . . . 65 50
1144 45c. Iguana 65 50
1145 45c. "Hypolimnas misippus" (butterfly) 65 50
1146 45c. Green-throated carib 65 50
1147 45c. Heliconia (plant) . . . 65 50
1148 45c. Agouti 65 50
Nos. 1129/48 were printed together, se-tenant, forming a composite design.

1988. 10th Anniv of International Fund for Agricultural Development. Multicoloured.
1149 45c. Type **224** 50 30
1150 60c. Pig 70 65
1151 90c. Cattle . . . . 95 1·25
1152 $3 Black belly sheep . . . . 2·25 4·00
MS1153 95 × 68 mm. $5 Tropical fruits (vert) . . . . 2·25 3·75

1988. Entertainers. Multicoloured.
1154 10c. Type **225** 35 25
1155 35c. Josephine Baker . . . 40 25
1156 45c. Maurice Chevalier . . . 45 25
1157 60c. James Cagney 60 30
1158 $1 Clark Gable 80 50
1159 $2 Louis Armstrong . . . . 1·40 1·00
1160 $3 Liberace . . . . 1·60 1·75
1161 $4 Spencer Tracy . . . . . 2·00 2·25
MS1162 Two sheets, each 105 × 75 mm. (a) $5 Humphrey Bogart. (b) $5 Elvis Presley Set of 2 sheets . . . . 8·50 6·50

1988. Flowering Trees. As T **339** of Grenada. Multicoloured.
1163 15c. Sapodilla 10 10
1164 20c. Tangerine 10 10
1165 25c. Avocado pear 10 10
1166 45c. Amherstia 20 25
1167 90c. Lipstick tree 40 55
1168 $1 Cannonball tree 45 55
1169 $3 Saman . . . . 1·25 1·75
1170 $4 Pineapple . . . . 1·60 2·00
MS1171 Two sheets, each 96 × 66 mm. (a) $5 Lignum vitae. (b) $5 Sea grape Set of 2 sheets 4·50 6·50

1988. 500th Birth Anniv of Titian (artist). As T **168a** of Gambia. Multicoloured.
1172 25c. "Jacopo Strada" . . . 15 15
1173 35c. "Titian's Daughter Lavinia" 20 15
1174 45c. "Andrea Navagero" . . 20 15
1175 60c. "Judith with Head of Holoferenes" 25 15
1176 $1 "Emilia di Spilimbergo" 40 50
1177 $2 "Martyrdom of St. Lawrence" . . . . . 70 1·25
1178 $3 "Salome" . . . . 1·00 2·00
1179 $4 "St. John the Baptist" . . 1·25 2·25
MS1180 Two sheets, each 110 × 95 mm. (a) $5 "Self Portrait". (b) $5 "Sisyphus" Set of 2 sheets . . . . 6·00 7·00

226 Imperial Amazon

227 President and Mrs. Kennedy

1988. 10th Anniv of Independence. Multicoloured.
1181 20c. Type **226** . . . . . . 1·50 40
1182 45c. Dominica 1874 1d. stamp and landscape (horiz) 90 30
1183 $2 1978 Independence 10c. stamp and landscape (horiz) . . . . 1·50 2·75
1184 $3 Carib wood (national flower) . . . . 1·75 3·25
MS1185 116 × 85 mm. $5 Government Band (horiz) . . . 2·25 3·75

1988. 25th Death Anniv of John F. Kennedy (American statesman). Multicoloured.
1186 20c. Type **227** 10 10
1187 25c. Kennedy sailing 10 10
1188 $2 Outside Hyannis Port house . . . . 80 1·50
1189 $4 Speaking in Berlin (vert) 1·60 2·50
MS1190 100 × 71 mm. $5 President Kennedy (vert) . . . . . . 2·10 3·75

228 Donald Duck's Nephews decorating Christmas Tree

1988. Christmas. "Mickey's Christmas Mall". Walt Disney Cartoon Characters. Multicoloured.
1191 60c. Type **228** 55 65
1192 60c. Daisy Duck outside clothes shop 55 65
1193 60c. Winnie the Pooh in shop window 55 65
1194 60c. Goofy with parcels . . 55 65
1195 60c. Donald Duck as Father Christmas 55 65
1196 60c. Mickey Mouse contributing to collection 55 65
1197 60c. Minnie Mouse 55 65
1198 60c. Chip n' Dale with peanut 55 65
MS1199 Two sheets, each 127 × 102 mm. (a) $6 Mordie Mouse with Father Christmas. (b) $6 Mickey Mouse at West Indian market Set of 2 sheets . . . . 6·50 8·00
Nos. 1191/8 were printed together, se-tenant, forming a composite design.

229 Raoul Wallenberg (diplomat) and Swedish Flag

1988. 40th Anniv of Universal Declaration of Human Rights. Multicoloured.
1200 $3 Type **229** . . . . 2·00 2·50
MS1201 92 × 62 mm. $5 Human Rights Day logo (vert) . . . . 3·00 3·50

230 Greater Amberjack

1988. Game Fishes. Multicoloured.
1202 10c. Type **230** 20 15
1203 15c. Blue marlin 20 15
1204 35c. Cobia 35 30
1205 45c. Dolphin (fish) 45 30
1206 60c. Cero 60 55
1207 90c. Mahogany snapper . . 85 95
1208 $3 Yellow-finned tuna . . . 2·50 3·25
1209 $4 Rainbow parrotfish . . . 3·00 3·75
MS1210 Two sheets, each 104 × 74 mm. (a) $5 Manta. (b) $5 Tarpon Set of 2 sheets . . . . 11·00 11·00

231 Leatherback Turtle

1988. Insects and Reptiles. Multicoloured.
1211 10c. Type **231** 45 35
1212 25c. "Danaus plexippus" (butterfly) . . . . 1·25 75
1213 60c. Green anole (lizard) . . 1·60 1·25
1214 $3 "Mantis religiosa" (mantid) . . . . 4·00 6·50
MS1215 119 × 90 mm. $5 "Dynastes hercules" (beetle) . . . . . . 3·00 4·50

1989. Olympic Medal Winners, Seoul. Nos. 1114/17 optd.
1216 45c. Type **221** (optd **Men's C-1, 500m O. Heukrodt DDR**) 20 25
1217 60c. Taekwon-do (optd **Women's Flyweight N. Y. Choo S. Korea**) 25 35
1218 $1 High diving (optd **Women's Platform Y. Xu China**) 40 60
1219 $3 Gymnastics on bars (optd **V. Artemov USSR**) 1·25 2·25
MS1220 81 × 110 mm. $5 Football (optd **USSR defeated Brazil 3–2 on penalty kicks after a 1–1 tie**) 3·50 4·00

1989. 500th Anniv (1992) of Discovery of America by Columbus (2nd issue). Pre-Columbian Carib Society. As T **97a** of Grenadines of Grenada but horiz. Multicoloured.
1221 20c. Carib canoe 20 20
1222 35c. Hunting with bows and arrows 30 20
1223 $1 Dugout canoe making . . 70 90
1224 $3 Shield contest . . . . . 1·75 3·00
MS1225 87 × 71 mm. $6 Ceremonial dress . . . . 2·75 4·00

233 Map of Dominica, 1766

235 "Oncidium pusillum"

234 "Papilio homerus"

1989. "Philexfrance '89" International Stamp Exhibition, Paris. Multicoloured.
1226 10c. Type **233** . . . . . . 1·00 55
1227 35c. French coin of 1653 (horiz) . . . . 1·00 40
1228 $1 French warship, 1720 (horiz) . . . . 1·75 1·25
1229 $4 Coffee plant (horiz) . . . 2·25 3·50
MS1230 98 × 98 mm. $5 Exhibition inscription (horiz) (black, grey and yellow) . . . . 3·00 4·00

1989. Japanese Art. Paintings by Taikan. As T **177a** of Gambia, but vert. Multicoloured.
1231 10c. "Lao-tzu" (detail) . . . 10 10
1232 20c. "Red Maple Leaves" (panels 1 and 2) 10 10
1233 45c. "King Wen Hui learns a Lesson from his Cook" (detail) 20 25
1234 60c. "Red Maple Leaves" (panels 3 and 4) 25 35
1235 $1 "Wild Flowers" (detail) 45 50
1236 $2 "Red Maple Leaves" (panels 5 and 6) . . . . . 85 1·10
1237 $3 "Red Maple Leaves" (panels 7 and 8) . . . . . 1·00 1·60
1238 $4 "Indian Ceremony of Floating Lamps on the River" (detail) . . . . . 1·25 2·00
MS1239 Two sheets. (a) 78 × 102 mm. $5 "Innocence" (detail). (b) 101 × 77 mm. $5 "Red Maple Leaves" (detail) Set of 2 sheets . . . . 4·75 5·75

1989. Butterflies. Multicoloured.
1255 10c. Type **234** 40 30
1256 15c. "Morpho peleides" . . 45 30
1257 25c. "Dryas julia" 65 30
1258 35c. "Parides gundlachianus" 70 30
1259 60c. "Danaus plexippus" . . 1·00 75
1260 $1 "Agraulis vanillae" . . . 1·25 1·25
1261 $3 "Phoebis avellaneda" . . 2·75 3·25
1262 $5 "Papilio andraemon" . . 3·75 5·00
MS1263 Two sheets. (a) 105 × 74 mm. $6 "Adelpha cytherea". (b) 105 × 79 mm. $6 "Adelpha iphicala" Set of 2 sheets 8·00 9·00

1989. Orchids. Multicoloured.
1264 10c. Type **235** 35 30
1265 35c. "Epidendrum cochleata" 70 30
1266 45c. "Epidendrum ciliare" 75 40
1267 60c. "Cyrtopodium andersonii" . . . . 1·00 80
1268 $1 "Habenaria pauciflora" 1·25 1·25
1269 $2 "Maxillaria alba" . . . 2·00 2·25
1270 $3 "Selenipedium palmifolium" . . . . . . 2·50 2·75
1271 $4 "Brassavola cucullata" 3·25 3·75
MS1272 Two sheets, each 108 × 77 mm. (a) $5 "Oncidium lanceanum". (b) $5 "Comparettia falcata" Set of 2 sheets . . . . 8·00 9·00

236 "Apollo 11" Command Module in Lunar Orbit

1989. 20th Anniv of First Manned Landing on Moon. Multicoloured.
1273 10c. Type **236** 30 30
1274 60c. Neil Armstrong leaving lunar module 70 70
1275 $2 Edwin Aldrin at Sea of Tranquility . . . . 1·60 2·00
1276 $3 Astronauts Armstrong and Aldrin with U.S. flag 2·00 2·50
MS1277 62 × 77 mm. $6 Launch of "Apollo 11" (vert) . . . . . . 4·50 6·00

237 Brazil v Italy Final, 1970

1989. World Cup Football Championship, Italy (1st issue). Multicoloured.
1278 $1 Type **237** . . . . 2·00 2·25
1279 $1 England v West Germany, 1966 . . . . . 2·00 2·25
1280 $1 West Germany v Holland, 1974 . . . . . 2·00 2·25
1281 $1 Italy v West Germany, 1982 . . . . 2·00 2·25
MS1282 106 × 86 mm. $6 Two players competing for ball . . 4·00 4·75
Nos. 1278/81 were printed together, se-tenant, forming a composite central design of a football surrounded by flags of competing nations.
See also Nos. 1383/7.

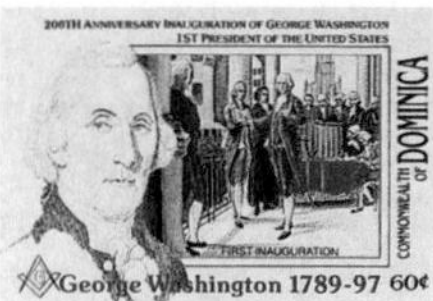

238 George Washington and Inauguration, 1789

1989. "World Stamp Expo '89" International Stamp Exhibition, Washington. Bicentenary of U.S. Presidency. Multicoloured.
1283 60c. Type **238** 90 80
1284 60c. John Adams and Presidential Mansion, 1800 . . . . 90 80
1285 60c. Thomas Jefferson, Graff House, Philadelphia and Declaration of Independence 90 80
1286 60c. James Madison and U.S.S. "Constitution" defeating H.M.S. "Guerriere", 1812 . . . . 90 80
1287 60c. James Monroe and freed slaves landing in Liberia 90 80
1288 60c. John Quincy Adams and barge on Erie Canal 90 80
1289 60c. Millard Fillmore and Perry's fleet off Japan . . 90 80
1290 60c. Franklin Pierce, Jefferson Davis and San Xavier Mission, Tucson 90 80
1291 60c. James Buchanan, "Buffalo Bill" Cody carrying mail and Wells Fargo Pony Express stamp 90 80
1292 60c. Abraham Lincoln and U.P.U. Monument, Berne 90 80
1293 60c. Andrew Johnson, polar bear and Mount McKinley, Alaska 90 80
1294 60c. Ulysses S. Grant and Golden Spike Ceremony, 1869 . . . . 90 80
1295 60c. Theodore Roosevelt and steam shovel excavating Panama Canal 90 80
1296 60c. William H. Taft and Admiral Peary at North Pole 90 80
1297 60c. Woodrow Wilson and Curtis "Jenny" on first scheduled airmail flight, 1918 . . . . 90 80
1298 60c. Warren G. Harding and airship U.S.S. "Shenandoah" at Lakehurst 90 80
1299 60c. Calvin Coolidge and Lindbergh's "Spirit of St Louis" on trans-Atlantic flight 90 80
1300 60c. Mount Rushmore National Monument . . . 90 80
1301 60c. Lyndon B. Johnson and Earth from Moon as seen by "Apollo 8" crew . . . 90 80
1302 60c. Richard Nixon and visit to Great Wall of China 90 80
1303 60c. Gerald Ford and "Gorch Fock" (German cadet barque) at Bicentenary of Revolution celebrations 90 80
1304 60c. Jimmy Carter and President Sadat of Egypt with Prime Minister Begin of Israel 90 80
1305 60c. Ronald Reagan and space shuttle "Columbia" 90 80
1306 60c. George Bush and Grumman TBF Avenger (fighter-bomber) 90 80

1989. "Expo '89" International Stamp Exhibition, Washington (2nd issue). Landmarks of Washington. Sheet 77 × 62 mm, containing horiz design as T **182** of Gambia. Multicoloured.
MS1307 $4 The Capitol . . . . 2·50 3·50

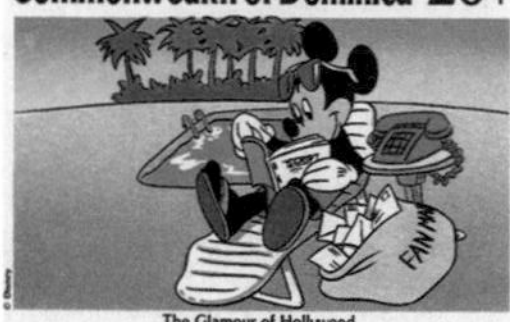

239 Mickey Mouse reading Script

1989. Mickey Mouse in Hollywood (Walt Disney cartoon character). Multicoloured.
1308 20c. Type **239** 40 40
1309 35c. Mickey Mouse giving interview 55 55
1310 45c. Mickey and Minnie Mouse with newspaper and magazines 65 65
1311 60c. Mickey Mouse signing autographs 75 75
1312 $1 Trapped in dressing room . . . . 1·25 1·25
1313 $2 Mickey and Minnie Mouse with Pluto in limousine . . . . 2·00 2·50
1314 $3 Arriving at Awards ceremony . . . . 2·25 2·75
1315 $4 Mickey Mouse accepting award . . . . 2·40 2·75
MS1316 Two sheets, each 127 × 102 mm. (a) $5 Mickey Mouse leaving footprints at cinema. (b) $5 Goofy interviewing Set of 2 sheets . . . . 7·50 9·00

1989. Christmas. Paintings by Botticelli. As T **352a** of Grenada. Multicoloured.
1317 20c. "Madonna in Glory with Seraphim" 40 30
1318 25c. "The Annunciation" . . 40 30
1319 35c. "Madonna of the Pomegranate" 55 40
1320 45c. "Madonna of the Rosegarden" 65 45
1321 60c. "Madonna of the Book" 80 60
1322 $1 "Madonna under a Baldachin" . . . . 1·00 90
1323 $4 "Madonna and Child with Angels" . . . . . . 3·00 4·50
1324 $5 "Bardi Madonna" . . . 3·50 4·75
MS1325 Two sheets, each 71 × 96 mm. (a) $5 "The Mystic Nativity". (b) $5 "The Adoration of the Magi" Set of 2 sheets . . 7·00 9·00

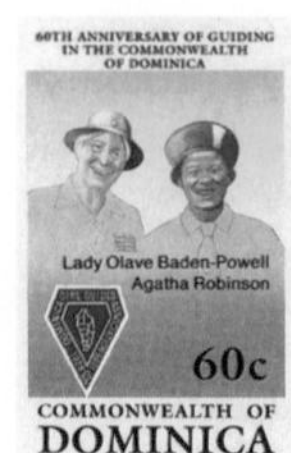

240 Lady Olave Baden-Powell and Agatha Robinson (Guide leaders)

60c
COMMONWEALTH OF
DOMINICA
241 Jawaharal Nehru

1989. 60th Anniv of Girl Guides in Dominica. Multicoloured.
1326 60c. Type **240** . . . . . . 1·00 1·00
MS1327 70 × 99 mm. $5 Doris Stockmann and Judith Pestaina (horiz) . . . . 3·50 4·00

1989. Birth Centenary of Jawaharal Nehru (Indian statesman). Multicoloured.
1328 60c. Type **241** . . . . . . 1·50 1·25
MS1329 101 × 72 mm. $5 Parliament House, New Delhi (horiz) . . . 3·50 4·00

242 Cocoa Damselfish

1990. Tropical Fishes. Multicoloured.
1330 45c. Type **242** 45 55
1331 45c. Stinging jellyfish . . . 45 55
1332 45c. Dolphin (fish) 45 55
1333 45c. Atlantic spadefish and queen angelfish 45 55
1334 45c. French angelfish . . . 45 55
1335 45c. Blue-striped grunt . . . 45 55
1336 45c. Porkfish 45 55
1337 45c. Great hammerhead . . . 45 55
1338 45c. Atlantic spadefish . . . 45 55
1339 45c. Great barracuda . . . 45 55
1340 45c. Southern stingray . . . 45 55
1341 45c. Black grunt 45 55
1342 45c. Spot-finned butterflyfish 45 55
1343 45c. Dog snapper 45 55
1344 45c. Band-tailed puffer . . . 45 55
1345 45c. Four-eyed butterflyfish 45 55
1346 45c. Lane snapper 45 55
1347 45c. Green moray 45 55
Nos. 1330/47 were printed together, se-tenant, forming a composite design.

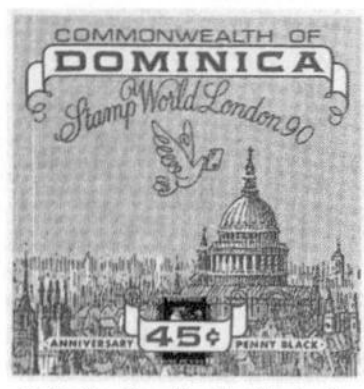

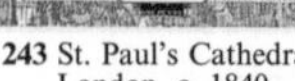

243 St. Paul's Cathedral, London, c. 1840

244 Blue-headed Hummingbird

1990. 150th Anniv of the Penny Black and "Stamp World London 90" International Stamp Exhibition.
1348 **243** 45c. green and black . . 55 25
1349 – 50c. blue and black . . . 75 35
1350 – 60c. blue and black . . . 75 45
1351 – 90c. green and black . . 1·40 85
1352 – $3 blue and black . . 3·50 3·50
1353 – $4 blue and black . . 3·50 3·50
MS1354 Two sheets. (a) 103 × 79 mm. $5 ochre and black. (b) 85 × 86 mm. $5 red and brown Set of 2 sheets . . . . . . 6·50 7·50
DESIGNS: 50c. British Post Office "accelerator" carriage, 1830; 60c. St. Paul's and City of London; 90c. Travelling post office, 1838; $3 "Hen and chickens" delivery cycle, 1883; $4 London skyline; $5 (a) Type **243**; (b) Motor mail van, 1899.

1990. 500th Anniv (1992) of Discovery of America by Columbus (3rd issue). New World Natural History—Seashells. As T **354a** of Grenada. Mult.
1355 10c. Reticulated cowrie-helmet 30 30
1356 20c. West Indian chank . . 40 40
1357 35c. West Indian fighting conch 50 35
1358 60c. True tulip 75 60
1359 $1 Sunrise tellin . . . . . . 1·00 1·00
1360 $2 Crown cone . . . . . . 1·75 2·75
1361 $3 Common dove shell . . . 2·50 3·50
1362 $4 Common or Atlantic fig shell . . . . 2·75 3·50
MS1363 Two sheets, each 103 × 70 mm. (a) $5 King helmet. (b) $6 Giant tun Set of 2 sheets 6·50 8·00

1990. Birds. Multicoloured.
1364 10c. Type **244** 35 35
1365 20c. Black-capped petrel . . 45 45
1366 45c. Red-necked amazon ("Red-necked Parrot") . . 65 40
1367 60c. Black swift 80 70
1368 $1 Troupial . . . . 1·25 1·25
1369 $2 Common noddy ("Brown Noddy") . . . . 2·00 2·50
1370 $4 Lesser Antillean pewee . 3·25 3·50
1371 $5 Little blue heron . . . . 3·75 4·25
MS1372 Two sheets, each 103 × 70 mm. (a) $6 Imperial amazon. (b) $6 House wren Set of 2 sheets . . . . 7·00 8·50

244a Queen Elizabeth the Queen Mother

1990. 90th Birthday of Queen Elizabeth the Queen Mother. As T **244a**.
1373 **244a** 20c. multicoloured . . . 20 15
1374 – 45c. multicoloured . . . 35 25
1375 – 60c. multicoloured . . . 60 60
1376 – $3 multicoloured . . . 2·25 3·00
MS1377 80 × 90 mm. $5 multicoloured . . . . 2·75 3·75
DESIGNS: 45c. to $5, Recent photographs of Queen Mother.

1990. Olympic Games, Barcelona (1992) (1st issue). As T **195a** of Gambia. Multicoloured.
1378 45c. Tennis . . . . 1·25 40
1379 60c. Fencing . . . . 1·25 50
1380 $2 Swimming . . . . 2·00 3·25
1381 $3 Yachting . . . . 2·50 3·75
MS1382 100 × 70 mm. $5 Boxing 4·25 6·00
See also Nos. 1603/11.

245 Barnes, England

1990. World Cup Football Championship, Italy (2nd issue). Multicoloured.
1383 15c. Type **245** 40 30
1384 45c. Romario, Brazil . . . 70 30
1385 60c. Franz Beckenbauer, West Germany manager 85 70
1386 $4 Lindenberger, Austria . . 3·25 5·00
MS1387 Two sheets, each 105 × 90 mm. (a) $6 McGrath, Ireland (vert). (b) $6 Litovchenko, Soviet Union (vert) Set of 2 sheets 7·50 10·00

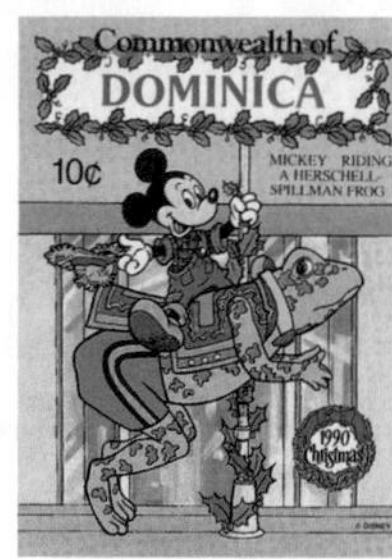

246 Mickey Mouse riding Herschell-Spillman Frog

1990. Christmas. Walt Disney cartoon characters and American carousel animals. Multicoloured.
1388 10c. Type **246** 40 20
1389 15c. Huey, Dewey and Louie on Allan Herschell elephant 50 25
1390 25c. Donald Duck on Allan Herschell polar bear . . . 60 30
1391 45c. Goofy on Dentzel goat 90 30
1392 $1 Donald Duck on Zalar giraffe . . . . 1·25 1·00
1393 $2 Daisy Duck on Herschell-Spillman stork 2·00 2·75
1394 $4 Goofy on Dentzel lion 3·25 4·50
1395 $5 Daisy Duck on Stein and Goldstein palomino stander . . . . 3·50 4·50
MS1396 Two sheets, each 127 × 101 mm. (a) $6 Mickey, Morty and Ferdie Mouse on Philadelphia Toboggan Company swan chariot (horiz). (b) $6 Mickey and Minnie Mouse with Goofy on Philadelphia Toboggan Company winged griffin chariot Set of 2 sheets . . . . 12·00 14·00

246a Steam locomotive, Glion-Roches De Naye Rack Railway, 1890

1991. Cog Railways.
1397 10c. Type **246a** 65 40
1398 35c. Electric railcar, Mt. Pilatus rack railway . . . 1·00 30
1399 45c. Schynige Platte rack railway train . . . . . . 1·10 30
1400 60c. Steam train on Bugnli Viaduct, Furka–Oberalp rack railway (vert) . . . . 1·40 55
1401 $1 Jungfrau rack railway train, 1910 . . . . 1·75 1·25
1402 $2 Testing Pike's Peak railcar, Switzerland, 1983 2·25 2·25

1403 $4 Brienz–Rothorn railway locomotive, 1991 . . . . 2·75 3·25
1404 $5 Steam locomotive, Arth-Rigi, 1890 . . . . 2·75 3·25
MS1405 Two sheets. (a) 100×70 mm. $6 Swiss Europa stamps of 1983 showing Riggenbach's locomotive of 1871 (50×37 mm). (b) 90×68 mm. $6 Brunig line train and Sherlock Holmes (50×37 mm) Set of 2 sheets . . . . 9·50 10·00

1991. 500th Anniv (1992) of Discovery of America by Columbus (4th issue). History of Exploration. As T **363a** of Grenada. Multicoloured.
1406 10c. Gil Eannes sailing south of Cape Bojador, 1433–34 . . . . 25 25
1407 25c. Alfonso Baldaya sailing south to Cape Blanc, 1436 35 35
1408 45c. Bartolomeu Dias in Table Bay, 1487 . . . . . 45 35
1409 60c. Vasco da Gama on voyage to India, 1497–99 55 50
1410 $1 Vallarte the Dane off African coast 75 90
1411 $2 Aloisio Cadamosto in Cape Verde Islands, 1456–58 . . . . 1·40 2·00
1412 $4 Diogo Gomes on River Gambia, 1457 . . . . . 2·75 3·75
1413 $5 Diogo Cao off African coast, 1482–85 . . . . . 3·25 4·00
MS1414 Two sheets, each 105×71 mm. (a) $6 Green-winged macaw and bow of "Santa Maria". (b) $6 Blue and yellow macaw and caravel Set of 2 sheets 7·50 8·50

1991. "Phila Nippon '91" International Stamp Exhibition, Tokyo. As T **198c** of Gambia. Mult.
1415 10c. Donald Duck as Shogun's guard (horiz) . . 60 20
1416 15c. Mickey Mouse as Kabuki actor (horiz) . . . 70 25
1417 25c. Minnie and Mickey Mouse as bride and groom (horiz) 85 25
1418 45c. Daisy Duck as geisha 1·00 25
1419 $1 Mickey Mouse in Sokutai court dress . . . 2·00 1·00
1420 $2 Goofy as Mino farmer 2·50 2·75
1421 $4 Pete as Shogun . . . . . 3·75 4·00
1422 $5 Donald Duck as Samurai (horiz) . . . . 3·75 4·25
MS1423 Two sheets, each 127×112 mm. (a) $6 Mickey Mouse as Noh actor. (b) $6 Goofy as Kabubei-jishi dancer Set of 2 sheets . . . . 14·00 14·00

247 "Craterellus cornucopioides"

248 Empire State Building, New York

1991. Fungi. Multicoloured.
1424 10c. Type **247** 25 25
1425 15c. "Coprinus comatus" . . 50 25
1426 45c. "Morchella esculenta" 50 25
1427 60c. "Cantharellus cibarius" 60 30
1428 $1 "Lepista nuda" 80 70
1429 $2 "Suillus luteus" . . . . 1·40 1·75
1430 $4 "Russula emetica" . . . 2·25 2·75
1431 $5 "Armillaria mellea" . . . 2·25 2·75
MS1432 Two sheets, each 100×70 mm. (a) $6 "Fistulina hepatica". (b) $6 "Lactarius volemus" Set of 2 sheets . . . 8·00 9·00

1991. 65th Birthday of Queen Elizabeth II. As T **198a** of Gambia. Multicoloured.
1433 10c. Queen and Prince William on Buckingham Palace Balcony, 1990 . . 80 35
1434 60c. The Queen at Westminster Abbey, 1988 1·50 50
1435 $2 The Queen and Prince Philip in Italy, 1990 . . . 2·25 2·50
1436 $5 The Queen at Ascot, 1986 . . . . 5·00 4·50
MS1437 68×90 mm. $5 Separate portraits of Queen and Prince Philip . . . . 5·00 5·50

1991. 10th Wedding Anniv of Prince and Princess of Wales. As T **198a** of Gambia. Multicoloured.
1438 15c. Prince and Princess of Wales in West Germany, 1987 . . . . 1·50 35
1439 40c. Separate photographs of Prince, Princess and sons . . . . 2·00 35
1440 $1 Separate photographs of Prince William and Prince Henry . . . . 2·00 1·25
1441 $4 Prince Charles at Caister and Princess Diana in Thailand . . . . 5·50 5·00
MS1442 68×90 mm. $5 Prince Charles, and Princess Diana with sons on holiday . . . . . . 5·00 5·00

1991. Death Centenary (1990) of Vincent van Gogh (artist). As T **200b** of Gambia. Multicoloured.
1443 10c. "Thatched Cottages" (horiz) 65 30
1444 25c. "The House of Pere Eloi" (horiz) 90 30
1445 45c. "The Midday Siesta" (horiz) . . . . 1·10 30
1446 60c. "Portrait of a Young Peasant" . . . . 1·40 35
1447 $1 "Still Life: Vase with Irises against Yellow Background" . . . . . . 2·00 1·10
1448 $2 "Still Life: Vase with Irises" (horiz) . . . . . 2·50 2·75
1449 $4 "Blossoming Almond Tree" (horiz) . . . . . 3·25 4·00
1450 $5 "Irises" (horiz) . . . . . 3·25 4·00
MS1451 Two sheets. (a) 77×102 mm. $6 "Doctor Gachet's Garden in Auvers". (b) 102×77 mm. $6 "A Meadow in the Mountains: Le Mas de Saint-Paul" (horiz). Imperf Set of 2 sheets . . . . 11·00 12·00

248a Ariel, Flounder and Sebastian (horiz)

1991. International Literacy Year (1990). Scenes from Disney cartoon film "The Little Mermaid" Multicoloured.
1452 10c. Type **248a** 30 25
1453 25c. King Triton (horiz) . . 45 30
1454 45c. Sebastian playing drums (horiz) 60 30
1455 60c. Flotsam and Jetsam taunting Ariel (horiz) . . 85 55
1456 $1 Scuttle, Flounder and Ariel with pipe (horiz) . . 1·25 1·00
1457 $2 Ariel and Flounder discovering book (horiz) 2·00 2·00
1458 $4 Prince Eric and crew (horiz) . . . . 3·25 3·50
1459 $5 Ursula the Sea Witch (horiz) . . . . 3·50 4·00
MS1460 Two sheets, each 127×102 mm. $6 Ariel without tail (horiz). (b) $6 Ariel and Prince Eric dancing Set of 2 sheets . . 8·50 10·00

1991. World Landmarks. Multicoloured.
1461 10c. Type **248** 40 30
1462 25c. Kremlin, Moscow (horiz) 40 30
1463 45c. Buckingham Palace, London (horiz) 70 30
1464 60c. Eiffel Tower, Paris . . 85 60
1465 $1 Taj Mahal, Agra (horiz) 3·75 1·75
1466 $2 Opera House, Sydney (horiz) . . . . 5·00 3·25
1467 $4 Colosseum, Rome (horiz) 3·75 4·25
1468 $5 Pyramids, Giza (horiz) 4·25 4·50
MS1469 Two sheets, each 100×68 mm. (a) $6 Galileo on Leaning Tower, Pisa (horiz). (b) $6 Emperor Shi Huang and Great Wall of China (horiz) Set of 2 sheets . . . . 14·00 14·00

249 Japanese Aircraft leaving Carrier "Akagi"

1991. 50th Anniv of Japanese Attack on Pearl Harbor. Multicoloured.
1470 10c. Type **249** 55 50
1471 15c. U.S.S. "Ward" (destroyer) and Consolidated Catalina flying boat attacking midget submarine 60 40
1472 45c. Second wave of Mitsubishi A6M Zero-Sen aircraft leaving carriers . . 85 35
1473 60c. Japanese Mitsubishi M6M Zero-Sen aircraft attacking Kaneche naval airfield . . . . 1·10 50
1474 $1 U.S.S. "Breeze", "Medusa" and "Curtiss" (destroyers) sinking midget submarine . . . . 1·25 90
1475 $2 U.S.S. "Nevada" (battleship) under attack 1·60 1·75
1476 $4 U.S.S. "Arizona" (battleship) sinking . . . 2·50 3·00
1477 $5 Mitsubishi A6M Zero-Sen aircraft . . . . 2·50 3·00
MS1478 Two sheets, each 118×78 mm. (a) $6 Mitsubishi A6M Zero-Sen over anchorage. (b) $6 Mitsubishi A6M Zero-Sen attacking Hickam airfield Set of 2 sheets . . . . 8·00 8·50

250 "Eurema venusta"

251 Symbolic Cheque

250a De Gaulle in Uniform

1991. Butterflies. Multicoloured.
1479 1c. Type **250** 40 80
1480 2c. "Agraulis vanillae" . . 40 80
1481 5c. "Danaus plexippus" . . 60 80
1482 10c. "Biblis hyperia" . . . 60 15
1483 15c. "Dryas julia" 70 15
1484 20c. "Phoebis agarithe" . . 70 20
1485 25c. "Junonia genoveva" . 70 20
1486 35c. "Battus polydamas" 80 30
1487 45c. "Leptotes cassius" . . 80 30
1487a 55c. "Ascia monuste" . . . 1·00 55
1488 60c. "Anaea dominicana" 80 35
1488a 65c. "Hemiargus hanno" 85 55
1489 90c. "Hypolimnas misippus" . . . . 1·00 55
1490 $1 "Urbanus proteus" . . 1·00 60
1490a $1.20 "Historis odius" . . 1·10 1·50
1491 $2 "Phoebis sennae" . . . 1·75 2·00
1492 $5 "Cynthia cardui" ("Vanessa cardui") . . . 2·75 4·50
1493 $10 "Marpesia petreus" . . 5·00 7·00
1494 $20 "Anartia jatrophae" 9·50 12·00

1991. Birth Centenary (1990) of Charles De Gaulle (French statesman).
1495 **250a** 45c. brown . . . . . . 1·75 75
MS1496 70×100 mm. $5 brown and blue . . . . 4·75 5·50
DESIGN: $5 De Gaulle in uniform.

1992. 40th Anniv of Credit Union Bank.
1497 **251** 10c. grey and black . . . 30 20
1498 – 60c. multicoloured . . . 1·25 80
DESIGN—HORIZ: 60c. Credit Union symbol.

252 "18th-Century Creole Dress" (detail) (Agostino Brunias)

254 Cricket Match

253 Island Beach

1991. Creole Week. Multicoloured.
1499 45c. Type **252** 80 25
1500 60c. Jing Ping band . . . . 1·00 60
1501 $1 Creole dancers . . . . . 1·40 1·90
MS1502 100×70 mm. $5 "18th-century Stick-fighting Match" (detail) (Agostino Brunias) (horiz) . . . . 4·25 6·00

1991. Year of Environment and Shelter. Mult.
1503 15c. Type **253** 25 15
1504 60c. Imperial amazon . . . 3·50 1·50
MS1505 Two sheets. (a) 100×70 mm. $5 River estuary. (b) 70×100 mm. $5 As 60c. Set of 2 sheets . . . . 14·00 14·00

1991. Christmas. Religious Paintings by Jan van Eyck. As T **200c** of Gambia. Multicoloured.
1506 10c. "Virgin Enthroned with Child" (detail) 70 30
1507 20c. "Madonna at the Fountain" 85 30
1508 35c. "Virgin in a Church" 1·00 30
1509 45c. "Madonna with Canon van der Paele" . . . . . 1·10 30
1510 60c. "Madonna with Canon van der Paele" (detail) . . 1·75 60
1511 $1 "Madonna in an Interior" . . . . 2·00 1·00
1512 $3 "The Annunciation" . . 3·25 4·50
1513 $5 "The Annunciation" (different) . . . . 4·50 7·00
MS1514 Two sheets, each 102×127 mm. (a) $5 "Virgin and Child with Saints and Donor". (b) $5 "Madonna with Chancellor Rolin" Set of 2 sheets . . . . 13·00 14·00

1992. 40th Anniv of Queen Elizabeth II's Accession. As T **202a** of Gambia. Multicoloured.
1515 10c. Coastline 10 10
1516 15c. Mountains overlooking small village 10 10
1517 $1 River estuary 70 70
1518 $5 Waterfall . . . . 3·75 3·75
MS1519 Two sheets, each 74×97 mm. (a) $6 Roseau. (b) $6 Mountain stream Set of 2 sheets 8·00 8·50

1992. Centenary (1991) of Botanical Gardens. Multicoloured.
1520 10c. Type **254** . . . . . . 1·75 70
1521 15c. Scenic entrance 40 20
1522 45c. Traveller's tree 40 25
1523 60c. Bamboo House 55 30
1524 $1 The Old Pavilion 80 70
1525 $2 "Ficus benjamina" . . . 1·40 2·00
1526 $4 Cricket match (different) 5·00 3·75
1527 $5 Thirty-five Steps . . . . 3·00 3·75
MS1528 Two sheets, each 104×71 mm. (a) $6 Past and present members of national cricket team. (b) $6 The Fountain Set of 2 sheets . . . . 8·00 9·00

1992. Easter. Religious Paintings. As T **204a** of Gambia. Multicoloured.
1529 10c. "The Supper at Emmaus" (Van Honthorst) 20 20
1530 15c. "Christ before Caiaphas" (Van Honthorst) (vert) 25 25
1531 45c. "The Taking of Christ" (De Boulogne) 40 30
1532 60c. "Pilate washing his Hands" (Preti) (vert) . . . 55 45
1533 $1 "The Last Supper" (detail) (Master of the Church of S. Francisco d'Evora) 75 75
1534 $2 "The Three Marys at the Tomb" (detail) (Bouguereau) (vert) . . . 1·50 2·00
1535 $3 "Denial of St. Peter" (Terbrugghen) . . . . . 1·75 2·50
1536 $5 "Doubting Thomas" (Strozzi) . . . . 2·75 3·75
MS1537 Two sheets, each 72×102 mm. (a) $6 "The Crucifixion" (detail) (Grünewald) (vert). (b) $6 "The Resurrection" (detail) (Caravaggio) (vert) Set of 2 sheets . . . . 7·50 8·50

1992. "Granada '92" International Stamp Exhibition, Spain. Art of Diego Rodriguez Velasquez. As T **481a** of Ghana. Mult.
1538 10c. "Pope Innocent X" (detail) 15 10
1539 15c. "The Forge of Vulcan" (detail) 20 10
1540 45c. "The Forge of Vulcan" (different detail) 40 25
1541 60c. "Queen Mariana of Austria" (detail) 50 30
1542 $1 "Pablo de Valladolid" . . 80 70
1543 $2 "Sebastian de Morra" . . 1·25 1·60
1544 $3 "King Felipe IV" (detail) 1·60 2·25
1545 $4 "King Felipe IV" . . . . 1·75 2·40
MS1546 Two sheets, each 120×95 mm. (a) $6 "The Drunkards" (110×81 mm). (b) $6 "Surrender of Breda" (110×81 mm). Imperf Set of 2 sheets . . . . 7·00 8·00

255 Columbus and "Dynastes hercules" (beetle)

1992. 500th Anniv of Discovery of America by Columbus (5th issue). World Columbian Stamp "Expo '92", Chicago. Multicoloured.

1547 10c. Type **255** 65 30
1548 25c. Columbus and "Leptodactylus fallax" (frog) . . . . 1·10 25
1549 75c. Columbus and red-necked amazon (bird) . . 3·00 1·00
1550 $2 Columbus and "Ameiva fuscata" (lizard) . . . . . 2·25 2·25
1551 $4 Columbus and royal gramma (fish) . . . . . . 2·50 3·25
1552 $5 Columbus and "Rosa sinensis" (flower) . . . . 2·50 3·25
MS1553 Two sheets, each 100 × 67 mm. (a) $6 Ships of Columbus (horiz). (b) $6 "Mastophyllum scabricolle" (katydid) (horiz) Set of 2 sheets 7·00 8·00

1992. "Genova '92" International Thematic Stamp Exhibition. Hummingbirds. As T **370** of Grenada. Multicoloured.

1554 10c. Female purple-throated carib 80 25
1555 15c. Female rufous-breasted hermit 80 25
1556 45c. Male Puerto Rican emerald . . . . 1·25 30
1557 60c. Female Antillean mango . . . . 1·50 45
1558 $1 Male green-throated carib . . . . 1·75 85
1559 $2 Male blue-headed hummingbird . . . . . . 2·25 2·25
1560 $4 Female eastern streamertail . . . . . . 3·00 3·25
1561 $5 Female Antillean crested hummingbird . . . . . . 3·00 3·25
MS1562 Two sheets, each 105 × 72 mm. (a) $6 Jamaican Mango ("Green Mango"). (b) $6 Vervain hummingbird Set of 2 sheets . . . . 10·00 11·00

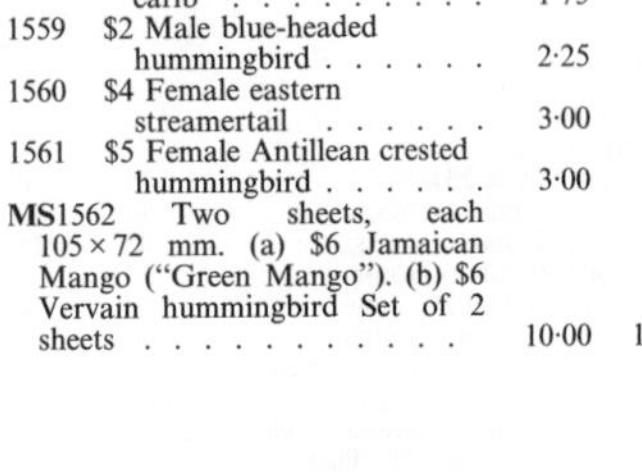

255a Head of Camptosaurus

1992. Prehistoric Animals. As T **290** of Antigua, but horiz. Multicoloured.

1563 10c. Type **255a** 80 30
1564 15c. Edmontosaurus 85 30
1565 25c. Corythosaurus 95 30
1566 60c. Stegosaurus . . . . . 1·60 40
1567 $1 Torosaurus . . . . . . 2·00 1·00
1568 $3 Euoplocephalus . . . . 2·50 3·00
1569 $4 Tyrannosaurus . . . . . 3·00 3·25
1570 $5 Parasaurolophus . . . . 3·00 3·25
MS1571 Two sheets, each 100 × 70 mm. (a) $6 As 25c. (b) $6 As $1 Set of 2 sheets . . . . . 7·50 8·50

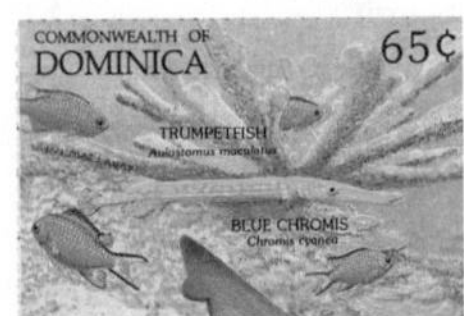

256 Trumpetfish and Blue Chromis

1992. Marine Life. Multicoloured.

1572/1601 65c. × 30. As Type **256** 14·00 15·00
MS1602 Two sheets, each 73 × 105 mm. (a) $6 multicoloured (Harlequin bass). (b) $6 multicoloured (Flamefish) Set of 2 sheets . . . . 9·50 11·00

1992. Olympic Games, Barcelona (2nd issue). As T **372** of Grenada. Multicoloured.

1603 10c. Archery 30 25
1604 15c. Two-man canoeing . . 35 25
1605 25c. Men's 110 m hurdles 40 25
1606 60c. Men's high jump . . . 70 30
1607 $1 Greco-Roman wrestling 1·00 65
1608 $2 Men's gymnastics—rings 1·50 2·00
1609 $4 Men's gymnastics—parallel bars . . . . . . 2·75 3·25
1610 $5 Equestrian dressage . . . 3·50 3·50
MS1611 Two sheets, each 100 × 70 mm. (a) $6 Women's platform diving. (b) $6 Men's hockey Set of 2 sheets . . . . 8·50 10·00

1992. 500th Anniv of Discovery of America by Columbus (6th issue). Organization of East Caribbean States. As Nos. 1670/1 of Antigua. Multicoloured.

1612 $1 Columbus meeting Amerindians 65 65
1613 $2 Ships approaching island 1·10 1·25

1992. Hummel Figurines. As T **501a** of Ghana. Multicoloured.

1614 20c. Angel playing violin . . 40 15
1615 25c. Angel playing recorder 40 15
1616 55c. Angel playing lute . . . 65 30
1617 65c. Seated angel playing trumpet 75 35
1618 90c. Angel on cloud with lantern . . . . 1·00 65
1619 $1 Angel with candle . . . 1·10 70
1620 $1.20 Flying angel with Christmas tree . . . . . 1·25 1·25
1621 $6 Angel on cloud with candle . . . . 3·75 6·00
MS1622 Two sheets, each 97 × 127 mm. (a) Nos. 1614/17. (b) Nos. 1618/21 Set of 2 sheets . . 8·00 9·00

257 Brass "Reno" Locomotive, Japan (1963)

1992. Toy Trains from Far Eastern Manufacturers. Multicoloured.

1623 15c. Type **257** 65 35
1624 25c. Union Pacific "Golden Classic" locomotive, China (1992) 75 35
1625 55c. L.M.S. third class brake carriage, Hong Kong (1970s) . . . . 1·25 40
1626 65c. Brass Wabash locomotive, Japan (1958) 1·40 50
1627 75c. Pennsylvania "Duplex" type locomotive, Korea (1991) . . . . 1·50 1·00
1628 $1 Streamlined locomotive, Japan (post 1945) . . . . 1·60 1·00
1629 $3 Japanese National Railways Class "C62" locomotive, Japan (1960) 2·50 3·00
1630 $5 Tinplate friction driven trains, Japan (1960s) . . . 3·00 3·75
MS1631 Two sheets, each 119 × 87 mm. (a) $6 "Rocket's" tender, Japan (1972) (multicoloured) (51½ × 40 mm). (b) $6 American model steam train presented to Emperor of Japan, 1854 (black, blackish olive and flesh) (40 × 51½ mm). Set of 2 sheets . . . . 10·00 10·00

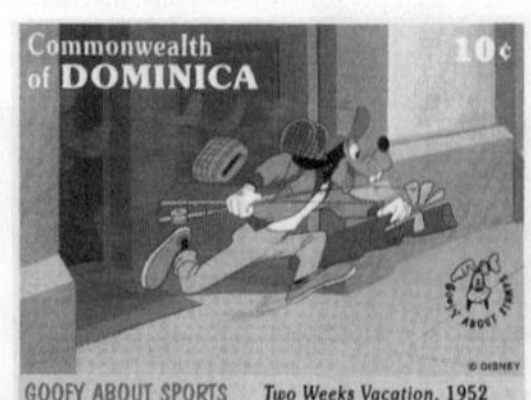

258 Goofy in "Two Weeks Vacation", 1952

1992. 60th Anniv of Goofy (Disney cartoon character). Designs showing sports from cartoon films. Multicoloured.

1632 10c. Type **258** 70 30
1633 15c. "Aquamania", 1961 . . 80 30
1634 25c. "Goofy Gymnastics", 1949 . . . . 95 20
1635 45c. "How to Ride a Horse", 1941 . . . . . 1·25 25
1636 $1 "Foul Hunting", 1947 . . 2·00 85
1637 $2 "For Whom the Bulls Toil", 1953 . . . . 2·75 3·00
1638 $4 "Tennis Racquet", 1949 3·50 4·00
1639 $5 "Double Dribble", 1946 3·50 4·00
MS1640 Two sheets, each 128 × 102 mm. (a) $6 "The Goofy Sports Story", 1956 (vert). (b) $6 "Aquamania", 1961 (different) (vert) Set of 2 sheets . . . . . 11·00 12·00

259 "Graf Zeppelin", 1929

260 Elvis Presley

1992. Anniversaries and Events. Multicoloured.

1641 25c. Type **259** 75 40
1642 45c. Elderly man on bike . . 1·25 45
1643 45c. Elderly man with seedling 40 30
1644 45c. Elderly man and young boy fishing 40 30
1645 90c. Space Shuttle "Atlantis" . . . . 1·00 60
1646 90c. Konrad Adenauer (German statesman) . . . 60 60
1647 $1.20 Sir Thomas Lipton and "Shamrock N" (yacht) . . . . 1·50 1·75
1648 $1.20 Snowy egret (bird) . . 2·50 1·75
1649 $1.20 Wolfgang Amadeus Mozart . . . . 3·00 1·75
1650 $2 Pulling fishing net ashore 2·00 2·50
1651 $3 Helen Keller (lecturer) . . 2·25 2·75
1652 $4 Eland (antelope) . . . . 3·50 4·00
1653 $4 Map of Allied Zones of Occupation, Germany, 1949 . . . . 4·00 4·00
1654 $4 Earth resources satellite 3·50 4·00
1655 $5 Count von Zeppelin . . 3·50 4·00
MS1656 Five sheets. (a) 100 × 70 mm. $6 Airship propeller. (b) 100 × 70 mm. $6 "Mir" Russian space station with "Soyuz". (c) 70 × 100 mm. $6 Cologne Cathedral. (d) 100 × 70 mm. $6 Rhinoceros hornbill (bird). (e) 100 × 70 mm. $6 Monostatos from "The Magic Flute" Set of 5 sheets . . . . 24·00 25·00

ANNIVERSARIES AND EVENTS: Nos. 1641, 1655, **MS**1656a, 75th death anniv of Count Ferdinand von Zeppelin; 1642/4, International Day of the Elderly; 1645, 1654, **MS**1656b, International Space Year; 1646, 1653, **MS**1656c, 25th death anniv of Konrad Adenauer; 1647, Americas Cup Yachting Championship; 1648, 1652, **MS**1656d, Earth Summit '92, Rio; 1649, **MS**1656e, Death bicent of Mozart; 1650, International Conference on Nutrition, Rome; 1651, 75th anniv of International Association of Lions Clubs.

No. **MS**1656b is inscribed "M.I.R." and No. **MS**1656d "Rhinocerus Hornbill", both in error.

1993. Bicentenary of the Louvre, Paris. As T **209b** of Gambia. Multicoloured.

1657 $1 "Madonna and Child with St. Catherine and a Rabbit" (left detail) (Titian) 70 70
1658 $1 "Madonna and Child with St. Catherine and a Rabbit" (right detail) (Titian) 70 70
1659 $1 "Woman at her Toilet" (Titian) 70 70
1660 $1 "The Supper at Emmaus" (left detail) (Titian) 70 70
1661 $1 "The Supper at Emmaus" (right detail) (Titian) 70 70
1662 $1 "The Pastoral Concert" (Titian) 70 70
1663 $1 "An Allegory, perhaps of Marriage" (detail) (Titian) 70 70
1664 $1 "An Allegory, perhaps of Marriage" (different detail) (Titian) 70 70
MS1665 70 × 100 mm. $6 "The Ship of Fools" (Bosch) (52 × 85 mm) 4·00 4·50

1993. 15th Death Anniv of Elvis Presley (singer). Multicoloured.

1666 $1 Type **260** . . . . 1·10 90
1667 $1 Elvis with guitar . . . . 1·10 90
1668 $1 Elvis with microphone 1·10 90

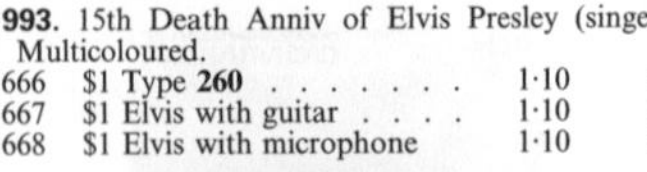

261 Plumbeous Warbler

1993. Birds. Multicoloured.

1669 90c. Type **261** . . . . . . 1·40 1·25
1670 90c. Black swift . . . . . . 1·40 1·25
1671 90c. Blue-hooded euphonia 1·40 1·25
1672 90c. Rufous-throated solitaire . . . . 1·40 1·25
1673 90c. Ringed kingfisher . . . 1·40 1·25
1674 90c. Blue-headed hummingbird . . . . . . 1·40 1·25
1675 90c. Bananaquit . . . . . . 1·40 1·25
1676 90c. Brown trembler ("Trembler") . . . . 1·40 1·25
1677 90c. Forest thrush . . . . . 1·40 1·25
1678 90c. Purple-throated carib 1·40 1·25
1679 90c. Ruddy quail dove . . . 1·40 1·25
1680 90c. Least bittern . . . . . 1·40 1·25
MS1681 Two sheets, each 100 × 70 mm. (a) $6 Imperial amazon. (b) $6 Red-necked amazon Set of 2 sheets . . . . 9·50 9·50

Nos. 1669/80 were printed together, se-tenant, forming a composite design.

262 School Crest

1993. Cent of Dominica Grammar School. Mult.

1682 25c. Type **262** 20 15
1683 30c. V. Archer (first West Indian headmaster) . . . 25 20
1684 65c. Hubert Charles (first Dominican headmaster) 45 50
1685 90c. Present school buildings 65 80

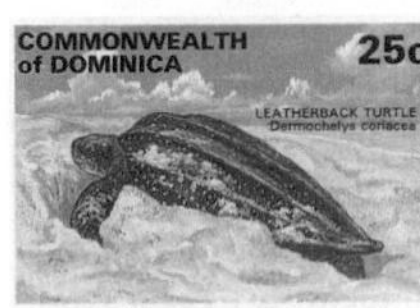

263 Leatherback Turtle on Beach

1993. Turtles. Multicoloured.

1686 25c. Type **263** 50 15
1687 55c. Hawksbill turtle swimming 70 40
1688 65c. Atlantic ridley turtle . . 80 50
1689 90c. Green turtle laying eggs 1·00 70
1690 $1 Green turtle swimming 1·00 70
1691 $2 Hawksbill turtle swimming (different) . . . 1·50 2·00
1692 $4 Loggerhead turtle . . . 2·25 3·00
1693 $5 Leatherback turtle swimming . . . . 2·25 3·00
MS1694 Two sheets, each 99 × 70 mm. (a) $6 Green turtle hatchling. (b) $6 Head of hawksbill turtle Set of 2 sheets 8·50 10·00

264 Ford "Model A", 1928

1993. Centenaries of Henry Ford's First Petrol Engine (90c., $5) and Karl Benz's First Four-wheeled Car (others). Multicoloured.

1695 90c. Type **264** 75 45
1696 $1.20 Mercedes Benz car winning Swiss Grand Prix, 1936 . . . . 1·00 55
1697 $4 Mercedes Benz car winning German Grand Prix, 1935 . . . . 2·50 3·25
1698 $5 Ford "Model T", 1915 2·50 3·25
MS1699 Two sheets, each 99 × 70 mm. (a) $3 Benz "Viktoria", 1893; $3 Mercedes Benz sports coupe, 1993. (b) $6 Ford "G.T.40", Le Mans, 1966 (57½ × 48 mm) Set of 2 sheets 7·50 8·50

1993. 40th Anniv of Coronation. As T **215a** of Gambia.

1700 20c. multicoloured . . . . . 80 1·00
1701 25c. brown and black . . . 80 1·00
1702 65c. multicoloured . . . . . 1·10 1·25
1703 $5 multicoloured . . . . . 4·25 4·50
MS1704 71 × 101 mm. $6 multicoloured . . . . 6·50 7·00

DESIGNS: 20c. Queen Elizabeth II at Coronation (photograph by Cecil Beaton); 25c. Queen wearing King Edward's Crown during Coronation ceremony; 65c. Coronation coach; $5 Queen and Queen Mother in carriage. (28½ × 42½ mm)—$6 "Queen Elizabeth II, 1969" (detail) (Norman Hutchinson).

265 New G.P.O. and Duke of Edinburgh

1993. Anniversaries and Events. Each brown, deep brown and black (Nos. 1707, 1717) or multicoloured (others).

1705 25c. Type **265** 45 40
1706 25c. "Bather with Beach Ball" (Picasso) (vert) . . . 45 40
1707 65c. Willy Brandt and Pres. Eisenhower, 1959 . . . . 55 40
1708 90c. As Type **265** but portrait of Queen Elizabeth II 85 60
1709 90c. "Portrait of Leo Stein" (Picasso) (vert) 85 60
1710 90c. Monika Holzner (Germany) (speed skating) (vert) 85 60
1711 90c. "Self-portrait" (Marian Szczyrbula) (vert) 85 60
1712 90c. Prince Naruhito and engagement photographs 85 60
1713 $1.20 16th-century telescope (vert) . . . . 1·50 1·25
1714 $3 "Bruno Jasienski" (Tytus Czyzewski) (vert) . . . . 2·00 2·50
1715 $3 Modern observatory (vert) . . . . 2·75 3·00
1716 $4 Ray Leblanc and Tim Sweeney (U.S.A.) (ice hockey) (vert) . . . . . . 3·50 3·75
1717 $5 "Wilhelm Unde" (Picasso) (vert) . . . . . 3·00 3·75
1718 $5 Willy Brandt and N. K. Winston at World's Fair, 1964 . . . . 3·00 3·75
1719 $5 Masako Owada and engagement photographs 3·00 3·75
1720 $5 Pres. Clinton and wife applauding . . . . 3·00 3·75
MS1721 Seven sheets, each 105×75 mm (a, c and f) or 75×105 mm (others). (a) $5 Copernicus (vert). (b) $6 "Man with Pipe" (detail) (Picasso) (vert). (c) $6 Willy Brandt, 1972. (d) $6 Toni Nieminen (FInland) (120 metre ski jump) (vert). (e) $6 "Miser" (detail) (Tadeusz Makowski) (vert). (f) $6 Masako Owada (vert). (g) $6 Pres. W. Clinton (vert) Set of 7 sheets 20·00 23·00

ANNIVERSARIES AND EVENTS: Nos. 1705, 1708, Opening of New General Post Office Building; 1706, 1709, 1717, **MS**1721b, 20th death anniv of Picasso (artist); 1707, 1718, **MS**1721c, 80th birth anniv of Willy Brandt (German politician); 1710, 1716, **MS**1721d, Winter Olympic Games '94, Lillehammer; 1711, 1714, **MS**1721e, "Polska '93" International Stamp Exhibition, Poznan; 1712, 1719, **MS**1721f, Marriage of Crown Prince Naruhito of Japan; 1713, 1715, **MS**1721a, 450th death anniv of Copernicus (astronomer); 1720, **MS**1721g, Inauguration of U.S. President William Clinton.

No. 1714 is inscribed "Tyrus" in error.

266 Hugo Eckener in New York Parade, 1928

1993. Aviation Anniversaries. Multicoloured.

1722 25c. Type **266** . . . . . . 1·00 40
1723 55c. English Electric Lightning F.2 (fighter) . . 2·00 50
1724 65c. Airship "Graf Zeppelin" over Egypt, 1929 . . . . 2·00 65
1725 $1 Boeing 314A (flying boat) on transatlantic mail flight . . . . 2·25 1·10
1726 $2 Astronaut carrying mail to the Moon . . . . . . 2·75 3·00
1727 $4 Airship "Viktoria Luise" over Kiel harbour, 1912 3·75 4·50
1728 $5 Supermarine Spitfire (vert) . . . . 3·75 4·50
MS1729 Three sheets, each 99×70 mm. (a) $6 Hugo Eckener (42½×57 mm). (b) $6 Royal Air Force crest (42½×57 mm). (c) $6 Jean-Pierre Blanchard's hot air balloon, 1793 (vert) Set of 3 sheets 13·00 13·00

ANNIVERSARIES: Nos. 1722, 1724, 1727, **MS**1729a, 125th birth anniv of Hugo Eckener (airship commander); 1723, 1728, **MS**1729b, 75th anniv of Royal Air Force; 1725/6, **MS**1729c, Bicentenary of first airmail flight.

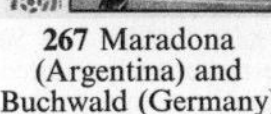

267 Maradona (Argentina) and Buchwald (Germany)

268 Ornate Chedi, Wat Phra Boromathat Chaiya

1993. World Cup Football Championship, U.S.A. (1994) (1st issue). Multicoloured.

1730 25c. Type **267** 80 20
1731 55c. Ruud Gullit (Netherlands) . . . . . . 1·10 40
1732 65c. Chavarria (Costa Rica) and Bliss (U.S.A.) . . . . 1·10 45
1733 90c. Diego Maradona (Argentina) . . . . 1·60 90
1734 90c. Leonel Alvares (Colombia) . . . . 1·60 90
1735 $1 Altobelli (Italy) and Yong-hwang (South Korea) . . . . 1·60 90
1736 $2 Stopyra (France) . . . . 2·75 2·75
1737 $5 Renquin (Belgium) and Yaremtchuk (Russia) . . 3·75 4·50
MS1738 Two sheets. (a) 73×103 mm. $6 Nestor Fabbri (Argentina). (b) 103×73 mm. $6 Andreas Brehme (Germany) Set of 2 sheets . . . . 7·50 8·50

See also Nos. 1849/56.

1993. Asian International Stamp Exhibitions. Multicoloured. (a) "Indopex '93", Surabaya, Indonesia.

1739 25c. Type **268** 30 30
1740 55c. Temple ruins, Sukhothai 50 30
1741 90c. Prasat Hin Phimai, Thailand 70 45
1742 $1.65 Arjuna and Prabu Gilling Wesi puppets . . 1·00 1·00
1743 $1.65 Loro Blonyo puppet 1·00 1·00
1744 $1.65 Yogyanese puppets . . 1·00 1·00
1745 $1.65 Wayang gedog puppet, Ng Setro . . . . 1·00 1·00
1746 $1.65 Wayang golek puppet 1·00 1·00
1747 $1.65 Wayang gedog puppet, Raden Damar Wulan . . . . 1·00 1·00
1748 $5 Main sanctuary, Prasat Phanom Rung, Thailand 2·25 2·50
MS1749 105×136 mm. $6 Sculpture of Majaphit noble, Pura Sada 3·25 3·75

(b) "Taipei '93", Taiwan.

1750 25c. Aw Boon Haw Gardens, Causeway Bay 30 30
1751 65c. Observation building, Kenting Park 50 30
1752 90c. Tzu-en pagoda on lakeshore, Taiwan 70 45
1753 $1.65 Chang E kite . . . . 1·00 1·00
1754 $1.65 Red Phoenix and Rising Sun kite . . . . . 1·00 1·00
1755 $1.65 Heavenly Judge kite 1·00 1·00
1756 $1.65 Monkey King kite . . 1·00 1·00
1757 $1.65 Goddess of Luo River kite . . . . 1·00 1·00
1758 $1.65 Heavenly Maiden kite 1·00 1·00
1759 $5 Villa, Lantau Island . . 2·25 2·50
MS1760 105×136 mm. $6 Jade sculpture of girl, Liao Dynasty 3·25 3·75

(c) "Bangkok '93", Thailand.

1761 25c. Tugu Monument, Java 30 30
1762 55c. Candi Cangkuang mon, West Java 50 30
1763 90c. Merus, Pura Taman Ayun, Mengwi 70 45
1764 $1.65 Hun Lek puppets of Rama and Sita . . . . . 1·00 1·00
1765 $1.65 Burmese puppet . . . 1·00 1·00
1766 $1.65 Burmese puppets . . . 1·00 1·00
1767 $1.65 Demon puppet at Wat Phra Kaew . . . . 1·00 1·00
1768 $1.65 Hun Lek puppet performing Khun Chang 1·00 1·00
1769 $1.65 Hun Lek puppets performing Ramakien . . 1·00 1·00
1770 $5 Stone mosaic, Ceto . . . 2·25 2·50
MS1771 105×136 mm. $6 Thai stone carving . . . . 3·25 3·75

No. 1753 is inscribed "Chang E Rising Up th the Moon" in error.

269 Willie

1993. "Willie the Operatic Whale". Scenes from Walt Disney's cartoon film. Multicoloured.

1772 $1 Type **269** . . . . 1·40 1·10
1773 $1 Willie's pelican friend . . 1·40 1·10
1774 $1 Willie singing to seals . . 1·40 1·10
1775 $1 Willie singing "Lucia" 1·40 1·10
1776 $1 Willie in "Pagliacci" . . 1·40 1·10
1777 $1 Willie as Mephistopheles 1·40 1·10
1778 $1 Tetti Tatti searching for Willie . . . . 1·40 1·10
1779 $1 Whalers listening to Willie . . . . 1·40 1·10
1780 $1 Tetti Tatti with harpoon gun . . . . 1·40 1·10
MS1781 Two sheets. (a) 130×102 mm. $6 Seals listening to Willie. (b) 97×118 mm. $6 Willie in Heaven (vert) Set of 2 sheets 7·00 8·00

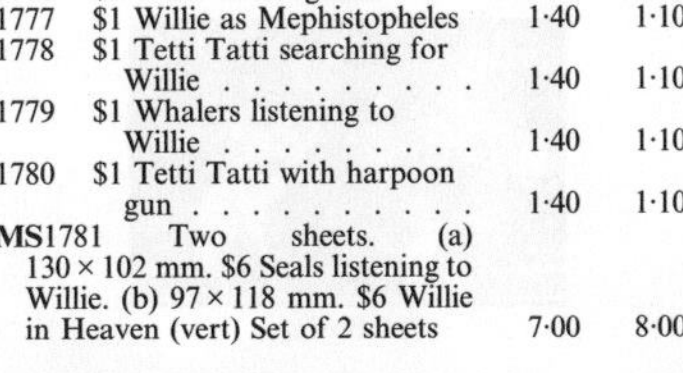

270 "Adoration of the Magi" (detail) (Durer)

1993. Christmas. Religious Paintings. Each black, yellow and red (Nos. 1782/5) or multicoloured (others).

1782 25c. Type **270** 35 20
1783 55c. "Adoration of the Magi" (different detail) (Durer) 55 30
1784 65c. "Adoration of the Magi" (different detail) (Durer) 65 35
1785 90c. "Adoration of the Magi" (different detail) (Durer) 80 75
1786 90c. "Madonna of Foligno" (detail) (Raphael) 80 75
1787 $1 "Madonna of Foligno" (different detail) (Raphael) 90 75
1788 $3 "Madonna of Foligno" (different detail) (Raphael) 2·00 3·25
1789 $5 "Madonna of Foligno" (different detail) (Raphael) 2·75 4·50
MS1790 Two sheets, each 105×130 mm. (a) $6 "Adoration of the Magi" (different detail) (Dürer) (horiz). (b) $6 "Madonna of Foligno" (different detail) (Raphael) Set of 2 sheets . . . 7·00 8·50

1994. "Hong Kong '94" International Stamp Exhibition (1st issue). As T **222a** of Gambia. Multicoloured.

1791 65c. Hong Kong 1988 Peak Tramway 50c. stamp and skyscrapers . . . . 1·00 1·10
1792 65c. Dominica 1991 Cog Railways $5 stamp and Hong Kong Peak tram . . 1·00 1·10

Nos. 1791/2 were printed together, se-tenant, forming a composite design.

See also Nos. 1793/8.

1994. "Hong Kong '94" International Stamp Exhibition (2nd issue). Tang Dynasty Jade. As T **222b** of Gambia, but vert. Multicoloured.

1793 65c. Horse 80 85
1794 65c. Cup with handle . . . 80 85
1795 65c. Vase with birthday peaches 80 85
1796 65c. Vase 80 85
1797 65c. Fu Dog with puppy . . 80 85
1798 65c. Drinking cup 80 85

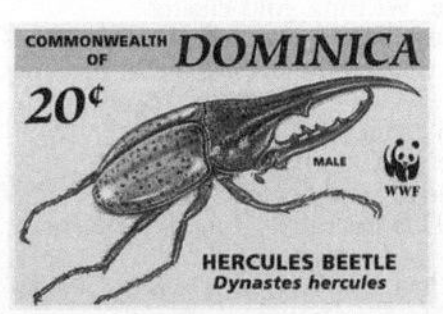

271 Male "Dynastes hercules" (beetle)

1994. Endangered Species. Birds and Insects. Multicoloured.

1799 20c. Type **271** 20 15
1800 25c. Male "Dynastes hercules" (different) . . . 20 15
1801 65c. Male "Dynastes hercules" (different) . . . 45 35
1802 90c. Female "Dynastes hercules" 60 55
1803 $1 Imperial Amazon ("Imperial Parrot") . . . 90 75
1804 $2 "Marpesia petreus" (butterfly) . . . . 1·50 2·00
1805 $3 "Hypolimnus misippus" (butterfly) . . . . 2·00 2·50
1806 $5 Purple-throated carib . . 2·75 3·50
MS1807 Two sheets, each 98×70 mm. (a) $6 Blue-headed hummingbird. (b) $6 "Libytheana fulvescens" (butterfly) Set of 2 sheets . . . . 8·00 9·00

Nos. 1803/7 do not carry the W.W.F. Panda emblem.

272 "Laelio-cattleya"

273 "Russula matoubensis"

1994. Orchids. Multicoloured.

1808 20c. Type **272** 35 15
1809 25c. "Sophrolaelio cattleya" 35 15
1810 65c. "Odontocidium" . . . 70 45
1811 90c. "Laelio-cattleya" (different) 90 75
1812 $1 "Cattleya" . . . . . . 1·00 75
1813 $2 "Odontocidium" (different) . . . . 1·50 2·00
1814 $3 "Epiphronitis" . . . . . 2·00 2·75
1815 $4 "Oncidium" . . . . . . 2·00 2·75
MS1816 Two sheets, each 100×70 mm. (a) $6 "Cattleya" (different). (b) $6 "Schombo cattleya" Set of 2 sheets . . . 7·50 8·50

1994. Fungi. Multicoloured.

1817 20c. Type **273** 40 25
1818 25c. "Leptonia caeruleocapitata" 40 25
1819 65c. "Inocybe littoralis" . . 60 35
1820 90c. "Russula hygrophytica" 70 55
1821 $1 "Pyrrhoglossum lilaceipes" 80 70
1822 $2 "Hygrocybe konradii" . . 1·25 1·75
1823 $3 "Inopilus magnificus" . . 1·75 2·25
1824 $5 "Boletellus cubensis" . . 2·25 2·75
MS1825 Two sheets, each 110×85 mm. (a) $6 "Lentinus strigosus". (b) $6 "Gerronema citrinum" Set of 2 sheets . . . 7·50 7·50

274 "Appias drusilla"

1994. Butterflies. Multicoloured.

1826 20c. Type **274** 35 15
1827 25c. "Didonis biblis" . . . 35 15
1828 55c. "Eurema daira" . . . 70 45
1829 65c. "Hypolimnas misippus" 75 45
1830 $1 "Phoebis agarithe" . . . 1·00 75
1831 $2 "Marpesia petreus" . . . 1·50 2·00
1832 $3 "Libytheana fulvescens" 1·75 2·75
1833 $5 "Precis evarete" . . . . 2·50 3·50
MS1834 Two sheets, each 100×70 mm. (a) $6 "Chlorostrymon maesites". (b) $6 "Vanessa cardui" Set of 2 sheets 9·00 9·50

275 Dachshund

1994. Chinese New Year ("Year of the Dog"). Multicoloured.

1835 20c. Type **275** 30 25
1836 25c. Beagle 30 25
1837 55c. Greyhound 50 30
1838 90c. Jack Russell terrier . . 70 55
1839 $1 Pekingese 80 70
1840 $2 Wire fox terrier . . . . 1·25 1·50
1841 $4 English toy spaniel . . . 2·25 2·75
1842 $5 Irish setter . . . . 2·25 2·75
MS1843 Two sheets, each 102×72 mm. (a) $6 Welsh corgi. (b) $6 Labrador retriever Set of 2 sheets . . . . 8·00 8·00

1994. Royal Visit. Nos. 1700/4 optd **ROYAL VISIT FEBRUARY 19, 1994.**

1844 20c. multicoloured . . . . 1·25 1·40
1845 25c. brown and black . . . 1·25 1·40
1846 65c. multicoloured . . . . 2·00 2·25
1847 $5 multicoloured . . . . . 3·75 4·25
MS1848 71×101 mm. $6 multicoloured . . . . 7·00 7·50

277 Des Armstrong (U.S.A.)

1994. World Cup Football Championship, U.S.A. (2nd issue). Multicoloured.

1849 25c. Jefferey Edmund (Dominica) 50 25
1850 $1 Type **277** 75 80
1851 $1 Dennis Bergkamp (Netherlands) 75 80
1852 $1 Roberto Baggio (Italy) 75 80
1853 $1 Rai (Brazil) 75 80
1854 $1 Cafu (Brazil) 75 80
1855 $1 Marco van Basten (Netherlands) 75 80
MS1856 Two sheets. (a) 70×100 mm. $6 Roberto Mancini (Italy). (b) 100×70 mm. $6 Player and Stanford Stadium, San Francisco Set of 2 sheets . . . 8·00 9·00

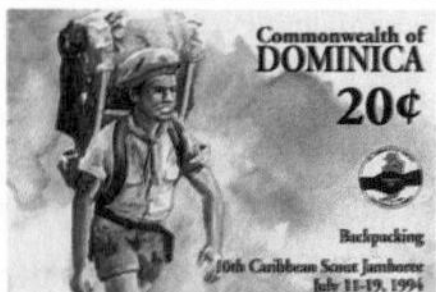

278 Scout Backpacking

1994. 10th Caribbean Scout Jamboree. Multicoloured.

1857 20c. Type **278** 35 15
1858 25c. Cooking over campfire 35 15
1859 55c. Erecting tent 60 30
1860 65c. Serving soup 70 45
1861 $1 Corps of drums . . . . 1·00 75
1862 $2 Planting tree . . . . . . 1·50 2·00
1863 $4 Sailing dinghy . . . . . 2·25 2·75
1864 $5 Saluting . . . . 2·25 2·75
MS1865 Two sheets, each 100 × 70 mm. (a) $6 Early scout troop. (b) $6 Pres. Crispin Sorhaindo (chief scout) (vert) Set of 2 sheets . . . . 8·50 9·00

278a Crew of "Apollo 14"

1994. 25th Anniv of First Manned Moon Landing. Multicoloured.

1866 $1 Type **278a** . . . . 1·25 1·00
1867 $1 "Apollo 14" mission logo 1·25 1·00
1868 $1 Lunar module "Antares" on Moon . . . . 1·25 1·00
1869 $1 Crew of "Apollo 15" . . 1·25 1·00
1870 $1 "Apollo 15" mission logo 1·25 1·00
1871 $1 Lunar crater on Mt. Hadley . . . . 1·25 1·00
MS1872 99 × 106 mm. $6 "Apollo 11" logo and surface of Moon . . . . 4·50 5·00

1994. Centenary of International Olympic Committee. Gold Medal Winners. As T **227d** of Gambia. Multicoloured.

1873 55c. Ulrike Meyfarth (Germany) (high jump), 1984 . . . . 75 40
1874 $1.45 Dieter Baumann (Germany) (5000 m), 1992 1·75 2·00
MS1875 106 × 76 mm. $6 Ji Hoon Chae (South Korea) (500 metres speed skating), 1994 . . . . . 3·50 4·00

1994. Centenary (1995) of First English Cricket Tour to the West Indies. As T **397a** of Grenada. Multicoloured.

1876 55c. David Gower (England) (vert) 40 30
1877 90c. Curtly Ambrose (West Indies) and Wisden Trophy 60 60
1878 $1 Graham Gooch (England) (vert) 70 80
MS1879 76 × 96 mm. $3 First English touring team, 1895 . . 3·75 3·25

1994. 50th Anniv of D-Day. As T **227c** of Gambia. Multicoloured.

1880 65c. American Waco gliders 85 45
1881 $2 British Horsa glider . . . 1·75 1·75
1882 $3 British glider and troops attacking Pegasus Bridge 2·00 2·25
MS1883 107 × 77 mm. $6 British Hadrian glider . . . . 3·25 3·75

279 Pink Bird and Red Flowers Screen Painting

280 Dippy Dawg

1994. "Philakorea '94" International Stamp Exhibition, Seoul. Multicoloured.

1884 55c. Type **279** 30 40
1885 55c. Bird with yellow, pink and red flowers 30 40
1886 55c. Pair of birds and yellow flowers 30 40
1887 55c. Chickens and flowers 30 40
1888 55c. Pair of birds and pink flowers 30 40
1889 55c. Ducks and flowers . . 30 40
1890 55c. Blue bird and red flowers 30 40
1891 55c. Common pheasant and flowers 30 40
1892 55c. Stork and flowers . . . 30 40
1893 55c. Deer and flowers . . . 30 40
1894 65c. P'alsang-jon Hall (38 × 24 mm) 40 40
1895 90c. Popchu-sa Temple (38 × 24 mm) 50 55
1896 $2 Uhwajong Pavillion (38 × 24 mm) . . . . . . 1·10 1·50
MS1897 100 × 70 mm. $4 Spirit Post Guardian (38 × 24 mm) . . . . 2·25 3·00

1994. 65th Anniv (1993) of Mickey Mouse. Walt Disney Cartoon Characters. Multicoloured.

1898 20c. Type **280** 60 25
1899 25c. Clarabelle Cow 60 25
1900 55c. Horace Horsecollar . . 90 35
1901 65c. Mortimer Mouse . . . 1·00 45
1902 $1 Joe Piper . . . . 1·50 85
1903 $3 Mr. Casey . . . . 2·75 3·00
1904 $4 Chief O'Hara . . . . . . 3·00 3·25
1905 $5 Mickey and The Blot . . 3·00 3·25
MS1906 Two sheets, each 127 × 102 mm. (a) $6 Minnie Mouse with Tanglefoot. (b) $6 Minnie and Pluto (horiz) Set of 2 sheets . . . . 10·00 11·00

281 Marilyn Monroe

284 Pig's Head facing

283 Wood Duck

1994. Entertainers. Multicoloured.

1907 20c. Sonia Lloyd (folk singer) 40 25
1908 25c. Ophelia Marie (singer) 40 25
1909 55c. Edney Francis (accordion player) 60 30
1910 65c. Norman Letang (saxophonist) 70 35
1911 90c. Edie Andre (steel-band player) 80 55
1912 90c. Type **281** . . . . . . 1·10 1·25
1913 90c. Marilyn Monroe wearing necklace . . . . 1·10 1·25
1914 90c. In yellow frilled dress 1·10 1·25
1915 90c. In purple dress . . . . 1·10 1·25
1916 90c. Looking over left shoulder . . . . 1·10 1·25
1917 90c. Laughing . . . . . . 1·10 1·25
1918 90c. In red dress . . . . . 1·10 1·25
1919 90c. Wearing gold cluster earrings . . . . 1·10 1·25
1920 90c. In yellow dress . . . . 1·10 1·25
MS1921 Two sheets, each 106 × 76 mm. (a) $6 Marilyn Monroe with top hat. (b) $6 With arms above head Set of 2 sheets 7·50 8·50

No. 1907 is inscribed "Llyod" in error.

1994. Christmas. Religious Paintings. As T **230** of Gambia. Multicoloured.

1922 20c. "Madonna and Child" (Luis de Morales) 30 10
1923 25c. "Madonna and Child with Yarn Winder" (De Morales) 30 10
1924 55c. "Our Lady of the Rosary" (detail) (Zurbaran) 50 30
1925 65c. "Dream of the Patrician" (detail) (Murillo) 65 55
1926 90c. "Madonna of Charity" (El Greco) 90 45
1927 $1 "The Annunciation" (Zurbaran) . . . . 1·00 60
1928 $2 "Mystical Marriage of St. Catherine" (Jusepe de Ribera) . . . . 1·50 2·25
1929 $3 "The Holy Family with St. Bruno and Other Saints" (detail) (De Ribera) . . . . 1·75 3·00
MS1930 Two sheets. (a) 136 × 97 mm. $6 "Adoration of the Shepherds" (detail) (Murillo). (b) 99 × 118 mm. $6 "Vision of the Virgin to St. Bernard" (detail) (Murillo) Set of 2 sheets . . . 7·50 8·50

1994. First Recipients of Order of the Caribbean Community. As **T 239a** of Gambia. Mult.

1931 25c. Sir Shridath Ramphal 20 10
1932 65c. William Demas 50 50
1933 90c. Derek Walcott . . . . 1·00 80

1995. 18th World Scout Jamboree, Netherlands. Nos. 1860 and 1863/4 optd **18th World Scout Jamboree Mondial, Holland, May 6, 1995.**

1934 65c. Serving soup 60 35
1935 $4 Sailing dinghy . . . . . 2·25 2·75
1936 $5 Saluting . . . . 2·25 2·75
MS1937 Two sheets, each 100 × 70 mm. (a) $6 Early scout troop. (b) $6 Pres. Crispin Sorhaindo (chief scout) (vert) Set of 2 sheets . . . . 7·50 8·50

1995. Water Birds. Multicoloured.

1938 25c. Type **283** . . . . . . 1·00 30
1939 55c. Mallard . . . . 1·10 40
1940 65c. Blue-winged teal . . . 1·10 55
1941 65c. Cattle egret (vert) . . . 1·10 1·10
1942 65c. Snow goose (vert) . . . 1·10 1·10
1943 65c. Peregrine falcon (vert) 1·10 1·10
1944 65c. Barn owl (vert) . . . . 1·10 1·10
1945 65c. Black-crowned night heron (vert) . . . . . . 1·10 1·10
1946 65c. Common grackle (vert) 1·10 1·10
1947 65c. Brown pelican (vert) . . 1·10 1·10
1948 65c. Great egret (vert) . . . 1·10 1·10
1949 65c. Ruby-throated hummingbird (vert) . . . 1·10 1·10
1950 65c. Laughing gull (vert) . . 1·10 1·10
1951 65c. Greater flamingo (vert) 1·10 1·10
1952 65c. Moorhen ("Common Morehen") (vert) . . . . 1·10 1·10
1953 $5 Red-eared conure ("Blood eared parakeet") 3·25 4·00
MS1954 Two sheets, each 105 × 75 mm. (a) $5 Trumpeter swan (vert). (b) $6 White-eyed vireo Set of 2 sheets . . . . . 8·00 9·00

Nos. 1941/5 were printed together, se-tenant, forming a composite design.

No. 1946 is inscribed "Common Gralkle" in error.

1995. Chinese New Year ("Year of the Pig"). Multicoloured.

1955 25c. Type **284** 40 40
1956 65c. Pig facing to the front 45 45
1957 $1 Pig facing left 50 50
MS1958 101 × 50 mm. Nos. 1955/7 1·25 1·50
MS1959 105 × 77 mm. Two pigs (horiz) . . . . 1·25 1·50

284a German Panther Tankin the Ardennes

1995. 50th Anniv of End of Second World War in Europe. Multicoloured.

1960 $2 Type **284a** . . . . . . 1·25 1·25
1961 $2 American fighter-bomber 1·25 1·25
1962 $2 American mechanized column crossing the Rhine 1·25 1·25
1963 $2 Messerschmitt Me 163B Komet and Allied bombers . . . . 1·25 1·25
1964 $2 V2 rocket on launcher 1·25 1·25
1965 $2 German U-boat surrendering . . . . . . 1·25 1·25
1966 $2 Heavy artillery in action 1·25 1·25
1967 $2 Soviet infantry in Berlin 1·25 1·25
MS1968 106 × 76 mm. $6 Statue and devastated Dresden (56½ × 42½ mm) . . . . 4·50 4·75

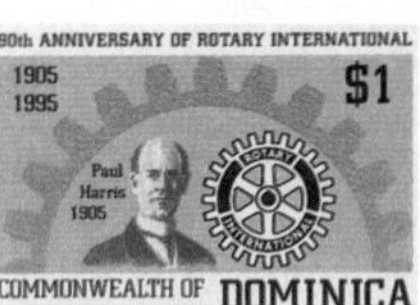

285 Paul Harris (founder) and Emblem

1995. 90th Anniv of Rotary International.

1969 **285** $1 brown, purple & blk 75 75
MS1970 70 × 100 mm. $6 red and black . . . . 2·75 3·25

DESIGN: $6 Rotary emblems.

1995. 50th Anniv of End of Second World War in the Pacific. As T **284a**. Multicoloured.

1971 $2 Mitsubishi A6M Zero-Sen torpedo-bomber . . . 1·25 1·25
1972 $2 Aichi D3A "Val" dive bomber . . . . 1·25 1·25
1973 $2 Nakajima B5N "Kate" bomber . . . . 1·25 1·25
1974 $2 "Zuikaku" (Japanese aircraft carrier) . . . . . 1·25 1·25
1975 $2 "Akagi" (Japanese aircraft carrier) . . . . . 1·25 1·25
1976 $2 "Ryuho" (Japanese aircraft carrier) . . . . . 1·25 1·25
MS1977 108 × 76 mm. $6 Japanese torpedo-bomber at Pearl Harbor 4·50 4·50

286 Boxing

1995. Olympic Games, Atlanta (1996). (1st Issue). Multicoloured.

1978 15c. Type **286** 40 25
1979 20c. Wrestling 45 25
1980 25c. Judo 55 25
1981 55c. Fencing 60 30
1982 65c. Swimming 70 35
1983 $1 Gymnastics (vert) 90 80
1984 $2 Cycling (vert) . . . . . 2·50 2·25
1985 $5 Volleyball . . . . 2·75 3·50
MS1986 Two sheets, each 104 × 74 mm. (a) $6 Show jumping. (b) $6 Football (vert) Set of 2 sheets . . . . 8·00 9·00

See also Nos. 2122/45 and 2213.

286a Signatures and U.S Delegate

1995. 50th Anniv of United Nations. Multicoloured.

1987 65c. Type **286a** 40 45
1988 $1 U.S. delegate 55 60
1989 $2 Governor Stassen (U.S. delegate) . . . . 85 1·25
MS1990 100 × 71 mm. $6 Winston Churchill . . . . 3·25 3·50

Nos. 1987/9 were printed together, se-tenant, forming a composite design.

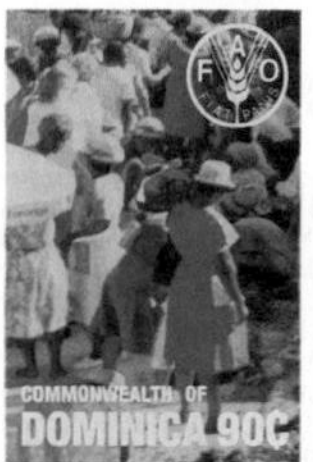

287 Market Customers

289 Oscar Sanchez (1987 Peace)

288 Monoclonius

1995. 50th Anniv of Food and Agriculture Organization. T **287** and similar multicoloured designs.

MS1991 110 × 74 mm. 90c., $1, $2 Panorama of Dominican market 1·60 1·90
MS1992 101 × 71 mm. $6 Women irrigating crops (horiz) . . . . 2·50 3·00

1995. 95th Birthday of Queen Elizabeth the Queen Mother. As T **239a** of Gambia.

1993 $1.65 brown, lt brown & blk 1·10 1·25
1994 $1.65 multicoloured . . . . 1·10 1·25
1995 $1.65 multicoloured . . . . 1·10 1·25
1996 $1.65 multicoloured . . . . 1·10 1·25
MS1997 103 × 126 mm. $6 multicoloured . . . . 4·50 4·75

DESIGNS: No. 1993, Queen Elizabeth the Queen Mother (pastel drawing); 1994, Holding bouquet of flowers; 1995, At desk (oil painting); 1996, Wearing blue dress; **MS**1997, Wearing ruby and diamond tiara and necklace.

1995. "Singapore '95" International Stamp Exhibition. Prehistoric Animals. Multicoloured.

1998 20c. Type **288** 50 30
1999 25c. Euoplocephalus 50 30
2000 55c. Head of coelophysis . . 60 30
2001 65c. Head of compsognathus 65 35
2002 90c. Dimorphodon 75 75
2003 90c. Ramphorynchus . . . 75 75
2004 90c. Head of giant alligator 75 75
2005 90c. Pentaceratops 75 75
2006 $1 Ceratosaurus (vert) . . . 75 75
2007 $1 Comptosaurus (vert) . . 75 75
2008 $1 Stegosaur (vert) 75 75
2009 $1 Camarasaurs (vert) . . . 75 75
2010 $1 Baronyx (vert) 75 75
2011 $1 Dilophosaurus (vert) . . 75 75
2012 $1 Dromaeosaurids (vert) 75 75
2013 $1 Deinonychus (vert) . . . 75 75
2014 $1 Dinichthys (terror fish) (vert) 75 75
2015 $1 Head of carcharodon (Giant-toothed shark) (vert) 75 75
2016 $1 Nautiloid (vert) 75 75
2017 $1 Trilobite (vert) 75 75
MS2018 Two sheets. (a) 95 × 65 mm. $5 Sauropelta. (b) 65 × 95 mm. $6 Triceratops (vert) Set of 2 sheets 7·50 8·50

Nos. 2002/5 and 2006/17 were respectively printed together, se-tenant, forming composite designs.

Nos. 2002/5 do not carry the "Singapore '95" exhibition logo.

1995. Centenary of Nobel Prize Trust Fund. Mult.
2019 $2 Type **289** . . . . 1·40 1·40
2020 $2 Ernst Chain (1945 Medicine) . . . . 1·40 1·40
2021 $2 Aage Bohr (1975 Physics) 1·40 1·40
2022 $2 Jaroslav Seifert (1984 Literature) . . . . 1·40 1·40
2023 $2 Joseph Murray (1990 Medicine) . . . . 1·40 1·40
2024 $2 Jaroslav Heyrovsky (1959 Chemistry) . . . . 1·40 1·40
2025 $2 Adolf von Baeyer (1905 Chemistry) . . . . 1·40 1·40
2026 $2 Eduard Buchner (1907 Chemistry) . . . . 1·40 1·40
2027 $2 Carl Bosch (1931 Chemistry) . . . . 1·40 1·40
2028 $2 Otto Hahn (1944 Chemistry) . . . . 1·40 1·40
2029 $2 Otto Diels (1950 Chemistry) . . . . 1·40 1·40
2030 $2 Kurt Alder (1950 Chemistry) . . . . 1·40 1·40
MS2031 76 × 106 mm. $2 Emil von Behring (1901 Medicine) . . . 1·40 1·60

1995. Christmas. Religious Paintings. As T **245a** of Gambia. Multicoloured.
2032 20c. "Madonna and Child with St. John" (Pontormo) 25 20
2033 25c. "The Immaculate Conception" (Murillo) . . 25 20
2034 55c. "The Adoration of the Magi" (Filippino Lippi) 45 30
2035 65c. "Rest on the Flight into Egypt" (Van Dyck) . . . 55 35
2036 90c. "The Holy Family" (Van Dyck) 75 50
2037 $5 "The Annunciation" (Van Eyck) . . . . 2·75 4·00
MS2038 Two sheets, each 102 × 127 mm. (a) $5 "Madonna and Child Reading" (detail) (Van Eyck). (b) $6 "The Holy Family" (detail) (Ribera) Set of 2 sheets 6·50 7·50

289a Florida Panther

1995. Centenary (1992) of Sierra Club (environmental protection society). Endangered Species. Multicoloured.
2039 $1 Type **289a** 60 60
2040 $1 Manatee 60 60
2041 $1 Sockeye salmon 60 60
2042 $1 Key deer facing left . . . 60 60
2043 $1 Key deer doe 60 60
2044 $1 Key deer stag 60 60
2045 $1 Wallaby with young in pouch 60 60
2046 $1 Wallaby feeding young 60 60
2047 $1 Wallaby and young feeding 60 60
2048 $1 Florida panther showing teeth (horiz) 60 60
2049 $1 Head of Florida panther (horiz) 60 60
2050 $1 Manatee (horiz) 60 60
2051 $1 Pair of manatees (horiz) 60 60
2052 $1 Pair of sockeye salmon (horiz) 60 60
2053 $1 Sockeye salmon spawning (horiz) 60 60
2054 $1 Pair of southern sea otters (horiz) 60 60
2055 $1 Southern sea otter with front paws together (horiz) 60 60
2056 $1 Southern sea otter with front paws apart (horiz) 60 60

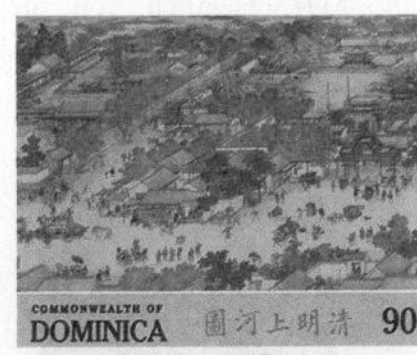

290 Street Scene

1995. "A City of Cathay" (Chinese scroll painting). Multicoloured.
2057 90c. Type **290** 60 70
2058 90c. Street scene and city wall 60 70
2059 90c. City gate and bridge . . 60 70
2060 90c. Landing stage and junk 60 70
2061 90c. River bridge 60 70
2062 90c. Moored junks 60 70
2063 90c. Two rafts on river . . 60 70
2064 90c. Two junks on river . . 60 70
2065 90c. Roadside tea house . . 60 70
2066 90c. Wedding party on the road 60 70
MS2067 Two sheets, each 106 × 77 mm. (a) $2 City street and sampan; $2 Footbridge. (b) $2 Stern of sampan (vert); $2 Bow of sampan (vert) Set of 2 sheets 4·25 4·75

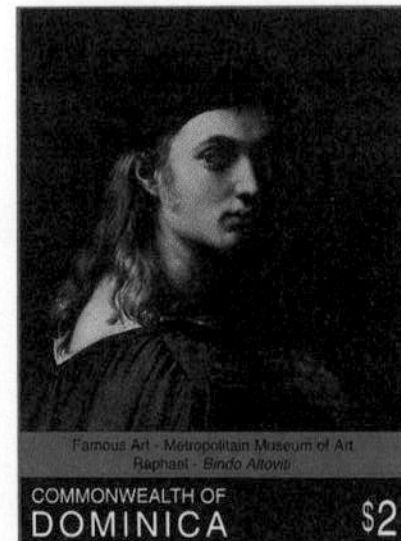

291 "Bindo Altoviti" (Raphael)

1995. Paintings by Raphael. Multicoloured.
2068 $2 Type **291** . . . . 1·75 1·75
2069 $2 "Pope Leo with Nephews" . . . . 1·75 1·75
2070 $2 "Agony in the Garden" 1·75 1·75
MS2071 110 × 80 mm. $6 "Pope Leo X with Cardinals Giulio de Medici and Luigi dei Rossi" (detail) 4·00 4·75

292 Rat

1996. Chinese New Year ("Year of the Rat").
2072 **292** 25c. black, violet and brown 35 40
2073 – 65c. black, red and green 60 70
2074 – $1 black, mauve and blue 70 80
MS2075 100 × 50 mm. Nos. 2072/4 1·25 1·50
MS2076 105 × 77 mm. $2 black, green and violet (two rats) . . 1·25 1·50
DESIGNS: 65c., $1, $2, Rats and Chinese symbols (different).

293 Mickey and Minnie Mouse (Year of the Rat)

1996. Chinese Lunar Calendar. Walt Disney Cartoon Characters. Multicoloured.
2077 55c. Type **293** 65 70
2078 55c. Casey Jones (Year of the Ox) 65 70
2079 55c. Tigger, Pooh and Piglet (Year of the Tiger) . . . 65 70
2080 55c. White Rabbit (Year of the Rabbit) 65 70
2081 55c. Dragon playing flute (Year of the Dragon) . . 65 70
2082 55c. Snake looking in mirror (Year of the Snake) . . 65 70
2083 55c. Horace Horsecollar and Clarabelle Cow (Year of the Horse) 65 70
2084 55c. Black Lamb and blue birds (Year of the Ram) 65 70
2085 55c. King Louis reading book (Year of the Monkey) 65 70
2086 55c. Cock playing lute (Year of the Cock) 65 70
2087 55c. Mickey and Pluto (Year of the Dog) 65 70
2088 55c. Pig building bridge (Year of the Pig) 65 70
MS2089 Two sheets. (a) 127 × 102 mm. $3 Basil the Great Mouse Detective (Year of the Rat). (b) 102 × 127 mm. $6 Emblems for 1996, 1997 and 2007 Set of 2 sheets . . . . 7·00 8·00

294 Steam Locomotive "Dragon", Hawaii

1996. Trains of the World. Multicoloured.
2090 $2 Type **294** . . . . 1·25 1·40
2091 $2 Class 685 steam locomotive "Regina", Italy . . . . 1·25 1·40
2092 $2 Class 745 steam locomotive, Calazo to Padua line, Italy . . . . 1·25 1·40
2093 $2 Mogul steam locomotive, Philippines . . . . 1·25 1·40
2094 $2 Class 23 and 24 steam locomotives, Germany . . 1·25 1·40
2095 $2 Class BB-15000 electric locomotive "Stanislaus", France . . . . 1·25 1·40
2096 $2 Class "Black Five" steam locomotive, Scotland . . 1·25 1·40
2097 $2 Diesel-electric locomotive, France . . . . 1·25 1·40
2098 $2 LNER class A4 steam locomotive "Sir Nigel Gresley", England . . . . 1·25 1·40
2099 $2 Class 9600 steam locomotive, Japan . . . . 1·25 1·40
2100 $2 "Peloponnese Express" train, Greece . . . . . . 1·25 1·40
2101 $2 Porter type steam locomotive, Hawaii . . . . . 1·25 1·40
2102 $2 Steam locomotive "Holand", Norway . . . 1·25 1·40
2103 $2 Class 220 diesel-hydraulic locomotive, Germany . . 1·25 1·40
2104 $2 Steam locomotive, India 1·25 1·40
2105 $2 East African Railways Class 29 steam locomotive 1·25 1·40
2106 $2 Electric trains, Russia . . 1·25 1·40
2107 $2 Steam locomotive, Austria . . . . 1·25 1·40
MS2108 Two sheets, each 103 × 73 mm. (a) $5 L.M.S. steam locomotive "Duchess of Hamilton", England. (b) $6 Diesel locomotives, China Set of 2 sheets 7·50 8·00

295 Horse-drawn Gig, 1965

1996. Traditional Island Transport. Multicoloured.
2109 65c. Type **295** . . . . . . 1·10 35
2110 90c. Early automobile, 1910 1·25 55
2111 $2 Lorry, 1950 . . . . . . 2·00 2·00
2112 $3 Bus, 1955 . . . . 2·50 3·00

296 Giant Panda

1996. "CHINA '96" 9th Asian International Stamp Exhibition, Peking. Giant Pandas. Multicoloured.
2113 55c. Type **296** 70 70
2114 55c. Panda on rock 70 70
2115 55c. Panda eating bamboo shoots 70 70
2116 55c. Panda on all fours . . 70 70
MS2117 Two sheets. (a) 90 × 125 mm. $2 Huangshan Mountain, China (50 × 75 mm). (b) 160 × 125 mm. $3 Panda sitting (50 × 37 mm) Set of 2 sheets . . 3·75 3·75

296a Queen Elizabeth II

1996. 70th Birthday of Queen Elizabeth II. Multicoloured.
2118 $2 Type **296a** . . . . 1·25 1·40
2119 $2 Queen in robes of Order of St. Michael and St. George . . . . 1·25 1·40
2120 $2 Queen in blue dress with floral brooch . . . . . . 1·25 1·40
MS2121 103 × 125 mm. $6 Queen at Trooping the Colour . . . . . 4·50 4·75

297 Moscow Stadium, 1980

1996. Olympic Games, Atlanta (2nd issue). Multicoloured.
2122 20c. Type **297** 35 25
2123 25c. Hermine Joseph (running) (vert) 35 25
2124 55c. Zimbabwe women's hockey team, 1980 . . . 1·00 40
2125 90c. Jerome Romain (long jump) (vert) 70 75
2126 90c. Sammy Lee (diving), 1948 and 1952 (vert) . . . 70 75
2127 90c. Bruce Jenner (decathalon), 1976 (vert) 70 75
2128 90c. Olga Korbut (gymnastics), 1972 (vert) 70 75
2129 90c. Steffi Graf (tennis), 1988 (vert) 70 75
2130 90c. Florence Griffith-Joyner (track and field), 1988 (vert) 70 75
2131 90c. Mark Spitz (swimming), 1968 and 1972 (vert) . . . 70 75
2132 90c. Li Ning (gymnastics), 1984 (vert) 70 75
2133 90c. Erika Salumae (cycling), 1988 (vert) . . . 70 75
2134 90c. Abebe Bikila (marathon), 1960 and 1964 (vert) 70 75
2135 90c. Ulrike Meyfarth (high jump), 1972 and 1984 (vert) 70 75
2136 90c. Pat McCormick (diving), 1952 and 1956 (vert) 70 75
2137 90c. Takeichi Nishi (equestrian), 1932 (vert) 70 75
2138 90c. Peter Farkas (Greco-Roman wrestling), 1992 (vert) 70 75
2139 90c. Carl Lewis (track and field), 1984, 1988 and 1992 (vert) 70 75
2140 90c. Agnes Keleti (gymnastics), 1952 and 1956 (vert) 70 75
2141 90c. Yasuhiro Yamashita (judo), 1984 (vert) 70 75
2142 90c. John Kelly (single sculls), 1920 (vert) 70 75
2143 90c. Naim Suleymanoglu (weightlifting), 1988 and 1992 (vert) 70 75
2144 $1 Polo (vert) 80 80
2145 $2 Greg Louganis (diving), 1976, 1984 and 1988 . . . 1·40 1·60
MS2146 Two sheets, each 105 × 75 mm. (a) $5 Joan Benoit (marathon), 1984 (vert). (b) $5 Milt Campbell (discus) Set of 2 sheets . . . . 6·00 7·50
Nos. 2126/34 and 2135/43 respectively were printed together, se-tenant, the backgrounds forming composite designs.

297a Child and Globe

1996. 50th Anniv of UNICEF. Multicoloured.
2147 20c. Type **297a** 25 15
2148 55c. Child with syringe and stethoscope 45 35
2149 $5 Doctor and child . . . . 2·75 3·50
MS2150 74 × 104 mm. $5 African child (vert) . . . . 2·75 3·50

297b Shrine of the Book, Israel Museum

1996. 3000th Anniv of Jerusalem. Multicoloured.
MS2151 114 × 95 mm. 90c. Type **297b**; $1 Church of All Nations; $2 The Great Synagogue 2·50 2·50
MS2152 104 × 74 mm. $5 Hebrew University, Mount Scopus . . 4·00 4·00

1996. Centenary of Radio. Entertainers. As T **259a** of Gambia. Multicoloured.
2153 90c. Artie Shaw 60 50
2154 $1 Benny Goodman 65 55

2155 $2 Duke Ellington . . . . . 1·25 1·40
2156 $4 Harry James . . . . . . 2·25 2·50
MS2157 70 × 99 mm. $6 Tommy and Jimmy Dorsey (horiz) . . . . 3·50 4·00

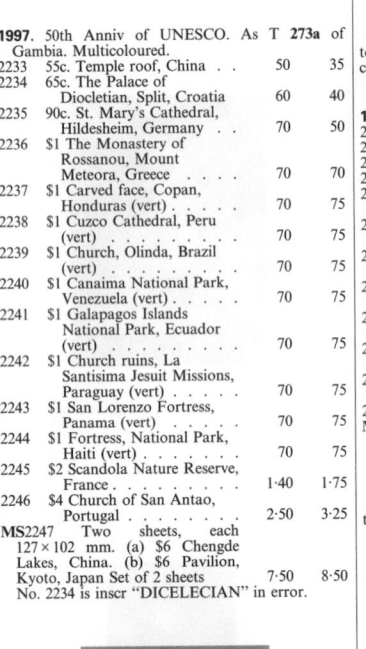

298 Irene Peltier in National Dress

1996. Local Entertainers. Multicoloured.
2158 25c. Type **298** 25 20
2159 55c. Rupert Bartley (steel-band player) 40 35
2160 65c. Rosemary Cools-Lartigue (pianist) 50 40
2161 90c. Celestine 'Orion' Theophile (singer) 65 65
2162 $1 Cecil Bellot (band master) 70 80

299 Humphrey Bogart as Sam Spade

1996. Centenary of Cinema. Screen Detectives. Multicoloured.
2163 $1 Type **299** 75 75
2164 $1 Sean Connery as James Bond 75 75
2165 $1 Warren Beatty as Dick Tracy 75 75
2166 $1 Basil Rathbone as Sherlock Holmes 75 75
2167 $1 William Powell as the Thin Man 75 75
2168 $1 Sidney Toler as Charlie Chan 75 75
2169 $1 Peter Sellers as Inspector Clouseau 75 75
2170 $1 Robert Mitchum as Philip Marlowe 75 75
2171 $1 Peter Ustinov as Hercule Poirot 75 75
MS2172 105 × 75 mm. $6 Margaret Rutherford as Miss Marple . . 4·00 4·50

300 Scribbled Filefish

301 Anthony Trollope and Postal Scenes

1996. Fishes. Multicoloured.
2173 1c. Type **300** 20 50
2174 2c. Lionfish 20 50
2175 5c. Porcupinefish 30 50
2176 10c. Powder-blue surgeon fish 40 50
2177 15c. Red hind 50 50
2178 20c. Golden butterflyfish . . 55 25
2179 25c. Copper-banded butterflyfish 55 25
2180 35c. Pennant coralfish . . . 60 30
2181 45c. Spotted drum 65 30
2182 55c. Blue-girdled angelfish 70 35
2183 60c. Scorpionfish 70 35
2184 65c. Harlequin sweetlips . . 70 40
2185 90c. Flame angelfish . . . . 1·00 60
2186 $1 Queen triggerfish . . . . 1·25 75
2187 $1.20 Spotlight parrotfish 1·50 1·25
2188 $1.45 Black durgon . . . . 1·75 2·00
2189 $2 Glass-eyed snapper . . . 2·25 2·50
2190 $5 Balloonfish . . . . . . 4·25 5·00
2191 $10 Creole wrasse . . . . . 7·50 8·50
2192 $20 Sea bass . . . . 12·00 14·00
For these designs size 24 × 21 mm, see Nos. 2374/91.

1996. World Post Day. Multicoloured.
2193 10c. Type **301** 25 15
2194 25c. Anthony Trollope and Dominican postmen . . . 30 20
2195 55c. "Yare" (mail streamer) 60 35
2196 65c. Rural post office . . . 60 40
2197 90c. Postmen carrying mail 90 50
2198 $1 Grumman Goose (seaplane) and 1958 Caribbean Federation 12c. stamp . . . . 1·00 80
2199 $2 Old and new post offices and 1978 Independence 10c. stamp . . . . 1·40 1·75
MS2200 74 × 104 mm. $5 18th-century naval officer . . . 3·75 4·00

302 "Enthroned Madonna and Child" (S. Veneziano)

303 "Herdboy playing the Flute" (Li Keran)

1996. Christmas. Religious Paintings. Mult.
2201 25c. Type **302** 30 20
2202 55c. "Noli Me Tangere" (Fra Angelico) 55 35
2203 65c. "Madonna and Child Enthroned" (Angelico) . . 65 40
2204 90c. "Madonna of Corneto Tarquinia" (F. Lippi) . . 80 50
2205 $2 "The Annunciation" and "The Adoration of the Magi" (School of Angelico) . . . . 1·50 1·75
2206 $5 "Madonna and Child of the Shade" (Angelico) . . 3·00 3·75
MS2207 Two sheets. (a) 76 × 106 mm. $6 "Coronation of the Virgin" (Angelico). (b) 106 × 76 mm. $6 "Holy Family with St. Barbara" (Veronese) (horiz) Set of 2 sheets . . . . 7·50 8·50

1997. Lunar New Year ("Year of the Ox"). Paintings by Li Keran. Multicoloured.
2208 90c. Type **303** 60 70
2209 90c. "Playing Cricket in the Autumn" 60 70
2210 90c. "Listening to the Summer Cicada" 60 70
2211 90c. "Grazing in the Spring" 60 70
MS2212 76 × 106 mm. $2 "Return in Wind and Rain" (34 × 51 mm). 1·00 1·25
MS2212a 135 × 80 mm. 55c. × 4. Designs as Nos. 2208/11 . . . 1·00 1·25

304 Lee Lai-shan (Gold Medal – Windsurfing, 1996)

1997. Olympic Games, Atlanta (3rd issue). Mult.
2213 $2 Type **304** . . . . 1·50 1·75
MS2214 97 × 67 mm. $5 Lee Lai-shan wearing Gold medal (37 × 50 mm) . . . . 3·00 3·50

305 "Meticella metis"

1997. Butterflies. Multicoloured.
2215 55c. Type **305** 50 55
2216 55c. "Coeliades forestan" 50 55
2217 55c. "Papilio dardanus" . . 50 55
2218 55c. "Mylothris chloris" . . 50 55
2219 55c. "Poecilmitis thysbe" . . 50 55
2220 55c. "Myrina silenus" . . . 50 55
2221 55c. "Bematistes aganice" 50 55
2222 55c. "Euphaedra neophron" 50 55
2223 55c. "Precis hierta" 50 55
2224 90c. "Coeliadas forestan" (vert) 60 65
2225 90c. "Spialia spio" (vert) . . 60 65
2226 90c. "Belenois aurota" (vert) 60 65
2227 90c. "Dingana bowkom" (vert) 60 65
2228 90c. "Charaxes jasius" (vert) 60 65
2229 90c. "Catacroptera cloanthe" (vert) 60 65
2230 90c. "Colias electo" (vert) 60 65
2231 90c. "Junonia archesia" (vert) 60 65
MS2232 Two sheets, each 102 × 71 mm. (a) $6 "Eurytela dryope". (b) "Acraea natalica" Set of 2 sheets . . . . 8·00 9·00
No. 2230 is inscribed "Collas electo" in error.

Nos. 2215/23 and 2224/31 respectively were printed together, se-tenant, with the backgrounds forming a composite design.

1997. 50th Anniv of UNESCO. As T **273a** of Gambia. Multicoloured.
2233 55c. Temple roof, China . . 50 35
2234 65c. The Palace of Diocletian, Split, Croatia 60 40
2235 90c. St. Mary's Cathedral, Hildesheim, Germany . . 70 50
2236 $1 The Monastery of Rossanou, Mount Meteora, Greece 70 70
2237 $1 Carved face, Copan, Honduras (vert) 70 75
2238 $1 Cuzco Cathedral, Peru (vert) 70 75
2239 $1 Church, Olinda, Brazil (vert) 70 75
2240 $1 Canaima National Park, Venezuela (vert) 70 75
2241 $1 Galapagos Islands National Park, Ecuador (vert) 70 75
2242 $1 Church ruins, La Santisima Jesuit Missions, Paraguay (vert) 70 75
2243 $1 San Lorenzo Fortress, Panama (vert) 70 75
2244 $1 Fortress, National Park, Haiti (vert) 70 75
2245 $2 Scandola Nature Reserve, France . . . . 1·40 1·75
2246 $4 Church of San Antao, Portugal . . . . 2·50 3·25
MS2247 Two sheets, each 127 × 102 mm. (a) $6 Chengde Lakes, China. (b) $6 Pavilion, Kyoto, Japan Set of 2 sheets 7·50 8·50
No. 2234 is inscr "DICELECIAN" in error.

306 Tanglefoot and Minnie

1997. Disney Sweethearts. Multicoloured.
2248 25c. Type **306** 45 20
2249 35c. Mickey and Minnie kissing on ship's wheel . . 55 20
2250 55c. Pluto and kitten . . . 70 30
2251 65c. Clarabelle Cow kissing Horace Horsecollar . . . 70 35
2252 90c. Elmer Elephant and tiger 85 55
2253 $1 Minnie kissing Mickey in period costume 95 70
2254 $2 Donald Duck and nephew . . . . 1·60 1·75
2255 $4 Dog kissing Pluto . . . 2·50 3·50
MS2256 Three sheets. (a) 126 × 100 mm. $5 Simba and Nala in "The Lion King". (b) 133 × 104 mm. $6 Mickey covered in lipstick and Minnie (horiz). (c) 104 × 124 mm. $6 Mickey and Pluto Set of 3 sheets . . . . . 9·50 10·00

307 Afghan Hound

308 "Oncidium altissimum"

1997. Cats and Dogs. Multicoloured.
2257 20c. Type **307** 45 25
2258 25c. Cream Burmese 45 25
2259 55c. Cocker spaniel 55 35
2260 65c. Smooth fox terrier . . 60 40
2261 90c. West highland white terrier 70 75
2262 90c. St. Bernard puppies . . 70 75
2263 90c. Boy with grand basset 70 75
2264 90c. Rough collie 70 75
2265 90c. Golden retriever . . . 70 75
2266 90c. Golden retriever, Tibetan spaniel and smooth fox terrier . . . 70 75
2267 90c. Smooth fox terrier . . 70 75
2268 $1 Snowshoe 75 75
2269 $2 Sorrell Abyssinian . . . 1·40 1·50
2270 $2 British bicolour shorthair 1·40 1·50
2271 $2 Maine coon and Somali kittens . . . . 1·40 1·50
2272 $2 Maine coon kitten . . . 1·40 1·50
2273 $2 Lynx point Siamese . . . 1·40 1·50
2274 $2 Blue Burmese kitten and white Persian . . . . . . 1·40 1·50
2275 $2 Persian kitten . . . . . 1·40 1·50
2276 $5 Torbie Persian . . . . . 3·25 3·75
MS2277 Two sheets, each 106 × 76 mm. (a) $6 Silver tabby. (b) $6 Shetland sheepdog Set of 2 sheets . . . . 8·00 9·00
Nos. 2262/7 and 2270/5 respectively were printed together, se-tenant, with the backgrounds forming composite designs.

1997. Orchids of the Caribbean. Multicoloured.
2278 20c. Type **308** 50 25
2279 25c. "Oncidium papilio" . . 50 25
2280 55c. "Epidendrum fragrans" 60 35
2281 65c. "Oncidium lanceanum" 70 40
2282 90c. "Campylocentrum micranthum' 90 50
2283 $1 "Brassavola cucculata" (horiz) . . . . 1·00 1·10
2284 $1 "Epidendrum ibaguense" (horiz) . . . . 1·00 1·10
2285 $1 "Ionopsis utricularioides" (horiz) . . . . 1·00 1·10
2286 $1 "Rodriguezia lanceolata" (horiz) . . . . 1·00 1·10
2287 $1 "Oncidium cebolleta" (horiz) . . . . 1·00 1·10
2288 $1 "Epidendrum ciliare" (horiz) . . . . 1·00 1·10
2289 $4 "Pogonia rosea" . . . . 2·75 3·00
MS2290 Two sheets, each 106 × 76 mm. (a) $5 "Oncidium ampliatum" (horiz). (b) $5 "Starhopea grandiflora" (horiz) Set of 2 sheets . . . . . . 7·00 7·50
Nos. 2283/8 were printed together, se-tenant, with the backgrounds forming a composite design.

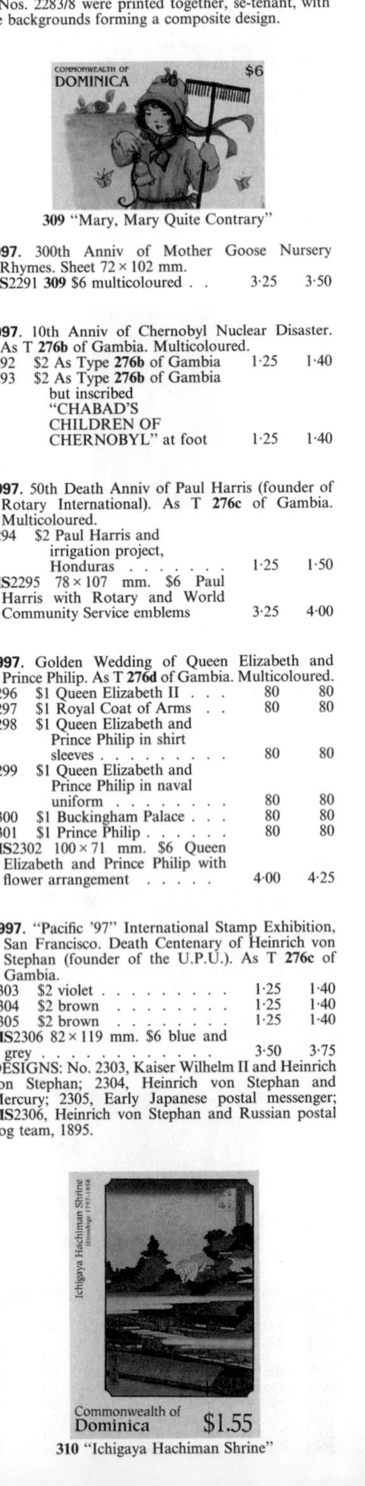

309 "Mary, Mary Quite Contrary"

1997. 300th Anniv of Mother Goose Nursery Rhymes. Sheet 72 × 102 mm.
MS2291 **309** $6 multicoloured . . 3·25 3·50

1997. 10th Anniv of Chernobyl Nuclear Disaster. As T **276b** of Gambia. Multicoloured.
2292 $2 As Type **276b** of Gambia 1·25 1·40
2293 $2 As Type **276b** of Gambia but inscribed "CHABAD'S CHILDREN OF CHERNOBYL" at foot 1·25 1·40

1997. 50th Death Anniv of Paul Harris (founder of Rotary International). As T **276c** of Gambia. Multicoloured.
2294 $2 Paul Harris and irrigation project, Honduras . . . . 1·25 1·50
MS2295 78 × 107 mm. $6 Paul Harris with Rotary and World Community Service emblems 3·25 4·00

1997. Golden Wedding of Queen Elizabeth and Prince Philip. As T **276d** of Gambia. Multicoloured.
2296 $1 Queen Elizabeth II . . . 80 80
2297 $1 Royal Coat of Arms . . 80 80
2298 $1 Queen Elizabeth and Prince Philip in shirt sleeves 80 80
2299 $1 Queen Elizabeth and Prince Philip in naval uniform 80 80
2300 $1 Buckingham Palace . . . 80 80
2301 $1 Prince Philip 80 80
MS2302 100 × 71 mm. $6 Queen Elizabeth and Prince Philip with flower arrangement . . . . . 4·00 4·25

1997. "Pacific '97" International Stamp Exhibition, San Francisco. Death Centenary of Heinrich von Stephan (founder of the U.P.U.). As T **276c** of Gambia.
2303 $2 violet . . . . 1·25 1·40
2304 $2 brown . . . . 1·25 1·40
2305 $2 brown . . . . 1·25 1·40
MS2306 82 × 119 mm. $6 blue and grey . . . . 3·50 3·75
DESIGNS: No. 2303, Kaiser Wilhelm II and Heinrich von Stephan; 2304, Heinrich von Stephan and Mercury; 2305, Early Japanese postal messenger; MS2306, Heinrich von Stephan and Russian postal dog team, 1895.

310 "Ichigaya Hachiman Shrine"

1997. Birth Centenary of Hiroshige (Japanese painter). "One Hundred Famous Views of Edo". Multicoloured.

2307 $1.55 Type **310** . . . . . . 1·40 1·40
2308 $1.55 "Blossoms on the Tama River Embankment" . . . . . 1·40 1·40
2309 $1.55 "Kumano Junisha Shrine, Tsunohazu" . . . 1·40 1·40
2310 $1.55 "Benkei Moat from Soto-Sakurada to Kojimachi" . . . . 1·40 1·40
2311 $1.55 "Kinokuni Hill and View of Akasak Tameike" 1·40 1·40
2312 $1.55 "Naito Shinjuku, Yotsuya" . . . . 1·40 1·40
MS2313 Two sheets, each 102 × 127 mm. (a) $6 "Sanno Festival Procession at Kojimachi I-chome". (b) $6 "Kasumigaseki" Set of 2 sheets . . . . 8·50 9·00

1997. 175th Anniv of Brothers Grimm's Third Collection of Fairy Tales. The Goose Girl. As T **380** of Gambia. Multicoloured.

2314 $2 Goose girl with horse . . 1·50 1·60
2315 $2 Geese in front of castle 1·50 1·60
2316 $2 Goose girl . . . . 1·50 1·60
MS2317 124 × 96 mm. $6 Goose girl (horiz) . . . . 4·00 4·25

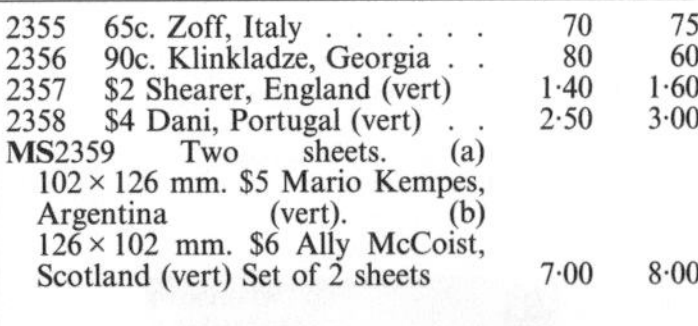

311 Hong Kong Skyline at Dusk

312 Yukto Kasaya (Japan) (ski jump), 1972

1997. Return of Hong Kong to China. Multicoloured.

2318 65c. Type **311** 60 70
2319 90c. Type **311** 70 80
2320 $1 Type **311** 75 85
2321 $1 Hong Kong at night . . 75 85
2322 $1.45 Hong Kong by day 1·00 1·25
2323 $2 Hong Kong at night (different) . . . . 1·25 1·75
2324 $3 Type **311** . . . . 1·50 2·00

1997. Winter Olympic Games, Nagano, Japan (1998). Multicoloured.

2325 20c. Type **312** 50 25
2326 25c. Jens Weissflog (Germany) (ski jump), 1994 . . . . 50 25
2327 55c. Anton Maier (Norway) (100 m men's speed skating), 1968 . . . . . 60 45
2328 55c. Ljubov Egorova (Russia) (women's 5 km cross-country skiing), 1994 60 45
2329 65c. Swedish ice hockey, 1994 . . . . 80 45
2330 90c. Bernhard Glass (Germany) (men's single luge), 1980 . . . . 85 60
2331 $1 Type **312** . . . . 90 1·00
2332 $1 As No. 2326 . . . . . . 90 1·00
2333 $1 As No. 2327 . . . . . . 90 1·00
2334 $1 Christa Rethenburger (Germany) (women's 100 m speed skating), 1988 . . . . 90 1·00
2335 $4 Frank-Peter Roetsch (Germany) (men's biathlon), 1988 . . . . . 2·50 3·00
MS2336 Two sheets, each 106 × 76 mm. (a) $5 Charles Jewtraw (U.S.A.) (men's 500 m speed skating), 1924. (b) $5 Jacob Tullin Thams (Norway) (ski jumping), 1924 Set of 2 sheets 6·00 7·00

1997. World Cup Football Championship, France (1998). As T **283a** of Gambia. Multicoloured (except Nos. 2343/4, 2348, 2350, 2353/4).

2337 20c. Klinsmann, Germany (vert) 50 25
2338 55c. Bergkamp, Holland (vert) 70 35
2339 65c. Ravanelli, Italy (vert) 70 75
2340 65c. Wembley Stadium, England 70 75
2341 65c. Bernabeu Stadium, Spain 70 75
2342 65c. Maracana Stadium, Brazil 70 75
2343 65c. Stadio Torino, Italy (black) 70 75
2344 65c. Centenary Stadium, Uruguay (black) 70 75
2345 65c. Olympiastadion, Germany 70 75
2346 65c. Rose Bowl, U.S.A. . . 70 75
2347 65c. Azteca Stadium, Mexico 70 75
2348 65c. Meazza, Italy (black) 70 75
2349 65c. Matthaus, Germany . . 70 75
2350 65c. Walter, West Germany (black) 70 75
2351 65c. Maradona, Argentina 70 75
2352 65c. Beckenbaur, Germany 70 75
2353 65c. Moore, England (black) 70 75
2354 65c. Dunga, Brazil (black) 70 75
2355 65c. Zoff, Italy 70 75
2356 90c. Klinkladze, Georgia . . 80 60
2357 $2 Shearer, England (vert) 1·40 1·60
2358 $4 Dani, Portugal (vert) . . 2·50 3·00
MS2359 Two sheets. (a) 102 × 126 mm. $5 Mario Kempes, Argentina (vert). (b) 126 × 102 mm. $6 Ally McCoist, Scotland (vert) Set of 2 sheets 7·00 8·00

313 Joffre Robinson (former Credit Union President)

314 Louis Pasteur

1997. 40th Anniv of Co-operative Credit Union League.

2360 **313** 25c. blue and black . . . 25 20
2361 – 55c. green and black . . 45 40
2362 – 65c. purple and black . . 55 55
2363 – 90c. multicoloured 65 70
MS2364 94 × 106 mm. $5 multicoloured . . . . 3·00 3·50

DESIGNS—As T **313**: 55c. Sister Alicia (founder); 65c. Lorrel Bruce (first Credit Union President). 30 × 60 mm: $5 Sister Alicia, Joffre Robinson and Lorrel Bruce.

1997. Medical Pioneers.

2365 **314** 20c. brown 50 25
2366 – 25c. pink and red . . . 50 25
2367 – 55c. violet 70 35
2368 – 65c. red and brown . . . 75 45
2369 – 90c. yellow and olive . . 85 55
2370 – $1 blue and ultramarine 1·00 80
2371 – $2 black . . . . 1·60 1·75
2372 – $3 red and brown . . . 1·90 2·25
MS2373 Two sheets, each 70 × 100 mm. (a) $5 multicoloured. (b) $6 multicoloured Set of 2 sheets . . . . 8·00 8·50

DESIGNS: 25c. Christiaan Barnard (first heart transplant); 55c. Sir Alexander Fleming (discovery of penicillin); 65c. Camillo Golgi (neurologist); 90c. Jonas Salk (discovery of polio vaccine); $1 Har Gobind Khorana (genetics); $2 Elizabeth Black (first woman doctor); $3 Sir Frank MacFarlane Burnet (immunologist); $5 (**MS**2373a), Sir Alexander Fleming (different); $6 (**MS**2373b), Louis Pasteur (different).

1997. Fishes. As Nos. 2175/92, but smaller, 24 × 21mm.

2374 5c. Porcupinefish 45 60
2375 10c. Powder-blue surgeonfish 45 60
2376 15c. Red hind 60 60
2377 20c. Golden butterflyfish . . 60 30
2378 25c. Copper-banded butterflyfish 60 30
2379 35c. Pennant coralfish . . . 70 35
2380 45c. Spotted drum 70 30
2381 55c. Blue-girdled angelfish 80 40
2382 60c. Scorpionfish 80 40
2383 65c. Harlequin sweetlips . . 80 40
2384 90c. Flame angelfish . . . . 1·00 60
2385 $1 Queen triggerfish . . . . 1·25 85
2386 $1.20 Spotlight parrotfish 1·50 1·50
2387 $1.45 Black durgon . . . . 1·75 2·00
2388 $2 Glass-eyed snapper . . . 2·50 3·50
2389 $5 Balloonfish . . . . . . 4·00 4·50
2390 $10 Creole wrasse . . . . . 4·00 4·25
2391 $20 Seabass . . . . 8·00 8·25

315 Diana, Princess of Wales

316 "Echo et Narcisse" (Toile)

1997. Diana, Princess of Wales Commemoration. Multicoloured.

2392 $2 Type **315** . . . . 1·25 1·40
2393 $2 Wearing diamond-drop earrings . . . . 1·25 1·40
2394 $2 Resting head on hand . . 1·25 1·40
2395 $2 Wearing tiara . . . . . 1·25 1·40
MS2396 76 × 106 mm. $5 Diana, Princess of Wales . . . . . . 3·50 3·50

1997. Christmas. Paintings.

2397 20c. Type **316** 35 15
2398 55c. "The Archangel Raphael leaving the Family of Tobias" (Rembrandt) 55 35
2399 65c. "Seated Nymphs with Flute" (Francois Boucher) 65 40
2400 90c. "Angel" (Rembrandt) 80 50
2401 $2 "Dispute" (Raphael) . . 1·50 1·75
2402 $4 "Holy Trinity" (Raphael) 2·50 3·25
MS2403 Two sheets, each 114 × 104 mm. (a) $6 "The Annunciation" (Botticelli) (horiz). (b) $6 "Christ on the Mount of Olives" (El Greco) (horiz) Set of 2 sheets . . . . 8·00 9·00

No. **MS**2403a is inscribed "Study (of the) Muse" in error.

317 "Tiger" (Gao Qifeng)

318 Akira Kurosawa

1998. Chinese New Year ("Year of the Tiger"). Multicoloured.

2404 55c. Type **317** 50 40
2405 65c. "Tiger" (Zhao Shao'ang) 60 45
2406 90c. "Tiger" (Gao Jianfu) 70 55
2407 $1.20 "Tiger" (different) (Gao Jianfu) . . . . . . 85 1·00
MS2408 95 × 65 mm. $3 "Spirit of Kingship" (Gao Jianfu) (48 × 40 mm) . . . . 1·75 2·00

1998. Millennium Series. Famous People of the Twentieth Century. Multicoloured (except Nos. 2411, 2414/15 and **MS**2417). (a) Japanese Cinema Stars.

2409 $1 Type **318** 80 85
2410 $1 "Rashomon" directed by Kursawa (56 × 42 mm) . . 80 85
2411 $1 Toshiro Mifune in "Seven Samurai" (black and grey) (56 × 42 mm) 80 85
2412 $1 Toshiro Mifune 80 85
2413 $1 Yasujiro Ozu 80 85
2414 $1 "Late Spring" directed by Ozu (black and grey) (56 × 42 mm) 80 85
2415 $1 Sessue Hayakawa in "Bridge on the River Kwai" (brown, deep brown and black) (56 × 42 mm) 80 85
2416 $1 Sessue Hayakawa 80 85
MS2417 110 × 80 mm. $6 Akira Kurosawa (brown, red and black) 4·25 4·50

(b) Sporting Record Holders. Multicoloured.

2418 $1 Jesse Owens (winner of four Olympic gold medals, Berlin, 1936) 80 85
2419 $1 Owens competing at Berlin (56 × 42 mm) . . . 80 85
2420 $1 Isaac Berger competing (56 × 42 mm) 80 85
2421 $1 Isaac Berger (weightlifter) 80 85
2422 $1 Boris Becker (Wimbledon champion) 80 85
2423 $1 Boris Becker on court (56 × 42 mm) 80 85
2424 $1 Ashe with Wimbledon trophy (56 × 42 mm) . . . 80 85
2425 $1 Arthur Ashe (1st African-American Wimbledon singles champion, 1975) 80 85
MS2426 $6 Franz Beckenbauer (captain of German football team) (horiz) . . . . 4·25 4·50

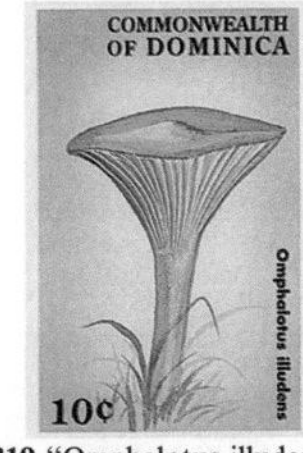

319 "Omphalotus illudens"

1998. Fungi of the World. Multicoloured.

2427 10c. Type **319** 40 50
2428 15c. "Inocybe fastigiata" . . 40 40
2429 20c. "Marasmius plicatulus" 40 40
2430 50c. "Mycena lilacifolia" . . 55 40
2431 55c. "Armillaria straminea" and "Calastrina argiolus" (butterfly) 55 40
2432 90c. "Tricholomopsis rutilans" and "Melitaea didyma" (butterfly) . . . 30 50
2433 $1 "Lepiota naucina" . . . 70 75
2434 $1 "Cortinarius violaceus" 70 75
2435 $1 "Boletus aereus" 70 75
2436 $1 "Tricholoma aurantium" 70 75
2437 $1 "Lepiota procera" . . . 70 75
2438 $1 "Clitocybe geotropa" . . 70 75
2439 $1 "Lepiota acutesquamosa" 70 75
2440 $1 "Tricholoma saponaceum" 70 75
2441 $1 "Lycoperdon gemmatum" 70 75
2442 $1 "Boletus ornatipes" . . . 70 75
2443 $1 "Russula xerampelina" 70 75
2444 $1 "Cortinarius collinitus" 70 75
2445 $1 "Agaricus meleagris" . . 70 75
2446 $1 "Coprinus comatus" . . 70 75
2447 $1 "Amanita caesarea" . . 70 75
2448 $1 "Amanita brunnescens" 70 75
2449 $1 "Amanita muscaria" . . 70 75
2450 $1 "Morchella esculenta" . . 70 75
MS2451 76 × 106 mm. $6 "Cortinarius violaceus" . . . . 4·00 4·25

Nos. 2433/41 and 2442/50 respectively were printed together, se-tenant, with the backgrounds forming composite designs.

320 Topsail Schooner

1998. History of Sailing Ships. Multicoloured.

2452 55c. Type **320** 50 50
2453 55c. "Golden Hind" (Drake) 50 50
2454 55c. "Moshulu" (barque) . . 50 50
2455 55c. "Bluenose" (schooner) 50 50
2456 55c. Roman merchant ship 50 50
2457 55c. "Gazela Primiero" (barquentine) 50 50
2458 65c. Greek war galley . . . 50 40
2459 90c. Egyptian felucca . . . 65 60
2460 $1 Viking longship 70 75
2461 $2 Chinese junk . . . . . . 1·25 1·50
MS2462 Two sheets, each 106 × 76 mm. (a) $5 "Pinta" (Columbus). (b) $5 Chesapeake Bay skipjack Set of 2 sheets . . 7·00 7·50

No. 2457 is inscribed "GAZELA PRIMERIRO", and both Nos. 2458/9 "EGYPTIAN FELUCCA", all in error.

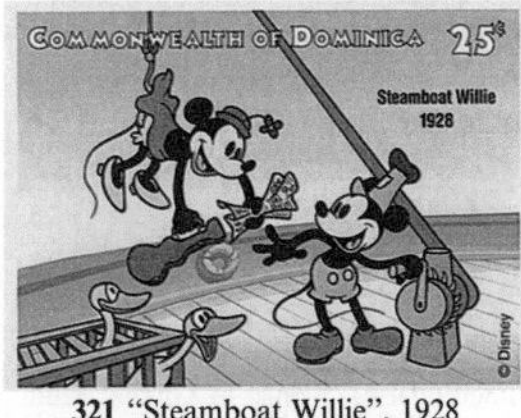

321 "Steamboat Willie", 1928

1998. 70th Anniv of Mickey and Minnie Mouse. Multicoloured.

2463 25c. Type **321** 80 85
2464 55c. "The Brave Little Tailor", 1938 . . . . . . 95 1·10
2465 65c. "Nifty Nineties", 1941 1·00 1·25
2466 90c. "Mickey Mouse Club", 1955 . . . . 1·25 1·40
2467 $1 Mickey and Minnie at opening of Walt Disney World, 1971 . . . . . . 1·25 1·40
2468 $1.45 "Mousercise Mickey and Minnie", 1980 . . . 1·40 1·60
2469 $5 "Runaway Brain", 1995 (97 × 110 mm) . . . . . 2·75 3·00
MS2470 Two sheets, each 130 × 104 mm. (a) $5 Walt Disney with Mickey and Minnie Mouse. (b) $5 Mickey and Minnie at 70th birthday party with Donald and Daisy Duck, Goofy and Pluto. Imperf Set of 2 sheets . . . . 9·00 9·50

322 Big-crested Penguin ("Erect Crested Penguin")

1998. Sea Birds. Multicoloured.

2471 25c. Type **322** 50 40
2472 65c. Humboldt penguin . . 65 40
2473 90c. Red knot 70 75
2474 90c. Greater crested tern . . 70 75
2475 90c. Franklin's gull 70 75
2476 90c. Australian pelican . . . 70 75
2477 90c. Fairy prion 70 75
2478 90c. Andean gull 70 75
2479 90c. Blue-eyed cormorant ("Imperial Shag") 70 75
2480 90c. Grey phalarope ("Red Phalarope") 70 75
2481 90c. Hooded grebe 70 75
2482 90c. Least aucklet 70 75
2483 90c. Little grebe 70 75
2484 90c. Pintado petrel ("Cape Petrel") 70 75

2485 90c. Slavonian grebe ("Horned Grebe") 70 75
2486 $1 Audubon's shearwater 70 70
MS2487 Two sheets, each 100×70 mm. (a) $5 Blue-footed booby. (b) $5 Fulmar Set of 2 sheets 7·50 8·00

Nos. 2474/85 were printed together, se-tenant, with the backgrounds forming a composite design.

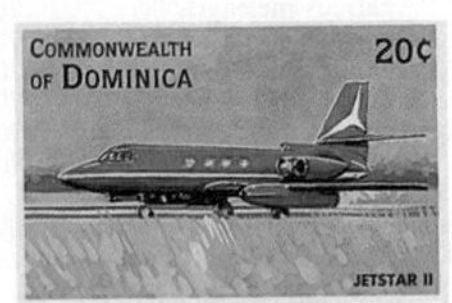

323 Jetstar II

1998. Modern Aircraft. Multicoloured.
2488 20c. Type **323** 50 50
2489 25c. AN 225 50 50
2490 55c. L.I.A.T. Dash-8 60 35
2491 65c. Cardinal Airlines, Beech-99 65 40
2492 90c. American Airlines Eagle 70 50
2493 $1 SR 71 "Blackbird" spy plane 70 75
2494 $1 Stealth Bomber 70 75
2495 $1 Northrop YF23 70 75
2496 $1 F-14A Tomcat 70 75
2497 $1 F-15 Eagle S 70 75
2498 $1 MiG 29 Fulcrum 70 75
2499 $1 Europa X5 70 75
2500 $1 Camion 70 75
2501 $1 E 400 70 75
2502 $1 CL-215 C-GKDN amphibian 70 75
2503 $1 Piper Jet 70 75
2504 $1 Beech Hawker 70 75
2505 $1 Lockheed YF22 70 75
2506 $1 Piper Seneca V 70 75
2507 $1 CL-215 amphibian 70 75
2508 $1 Vantase 70 75
2509 $2 Itansa HFB 320 1·25 1·40
MS2510 Two sheets. (a) 88×69 mm. $6 F1 Fighter. (b) 69×88 mm. $6 Sea Hopper seaplane Set of 2 sheets 8·50 9·00

1998. 50th Anniv of Organization of American States. As T **454b** of Grenada. Multicoloured.
2511 $1 Stylised Americas 75 75

1998. 25th Death Anniv of Pablo Picasso (painter). As T **291a** of Gambia. Multicoloured.
2512 90c. "The Painter and his Model" 60 50
2513 $1 "The Crucifixion" 70 70
2514 $2 "Nude with Raised Arms" (vert) 1·25 1·50
MS2515 122×102 mm. $6 "Cafe at Royan" 3·50 4·00

1998. Birth Centenary of Enzo Ferrari (car manufacturer). As T **564a** of Ghana. Mult.
2516 55c. 365 GT 2+2 80 40
2517 90c. Boano/Ellena 250 GT 1·10 85
2518 $1 375 MM coupe 1·25 1·40
MS2519 104×70 mm. $5 212 (91×34 mm) 4·00 4·25

1998. 19th World Scout Jamboree, Chile. As T **454c** of Grenada. Multicoloured.
2520 65c. Scout saluting 50 35
2521 $1 Scout handshake 70 70
2522 $2 International scout flag 1·50 1·50
MS2523 76×106 mm. $5 Lord Baden-Powell 3·50 3·75

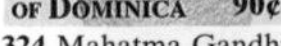

324 Mahatma Gandhi **327** Common Cardinal ("Northern Cardinal")

325 Fridman Fish

1998. 50th Death Anniv of Mahatma Gandhi. Multicoloured.
2524 90c. Type **324** 1·00 75
MS2525 106×75 mm. $6 Gandhi spinning thread 4·25 4·25

1998. 80th Anniv of Royal Air Force. As T **292a** of Gambia. Multicoloured.
2526 $2 H.S. 801 Nimrod MR2P (reconnaissance) 1·50 1·60
2527 $2 Lockheed C-130 Hercules (transport) 1·50 1·60
2528 $2 Panavia Tornado GR1 1·50 1·60
2529 $2 Lockheed C-130 Hercules landing 1·50 1·60
MS2530 Two sheets, each 90×68 mm. (a) $5 Bristol F2B fighter and Golden eagle (bird). (b) $6 Hawker Hart and EF-2000 Euro-fighter Set of 2 sheets 7·50 8·50

No. 2529 is inscribed "Panavia Tornado GR1" in error.

1998. International Year of the Ocean. Multicoloured.
2531 25c. Type **325** 45 35
2532 55c. Hydrocoral 55 35
2533 65c. Feather-star 60 35
2534 90c. Royal angelfish 70 50
2535 $1 Monk seal 70 75
2536 $1 Galapagos penguin 70 75
2537 $1 Manta ray 70 75
2538 $1 Hawksbill turtle 70 75
2539 $1 Moorish idols 70 75
2540 $1 Nautilius 70 75
2541 $1 Giant clam 70 75
2542 $1 Tubeworms 70 75
2543 $1 Nudibranch 70 75
2544 $1 Spotted dolphins 70 75
2545 $1 Atlantic sailfish 70 75
2546 $1 Sailfin flying fish 70 75
2547 $1 Fairy basslet 70 75
2548 $1 Atlantic spadefish 70 75
2549 $1 Leatherback turtle 70 75
2550 $1 Blue tang 70 75
2551 $1 Coral-banded shrimp 70 75
2552 $1 Rock beauty 70 75
MS2553 Two sheets, each 110×85 mm. (a) $5 Humpback whale and calf (56×41 mm). (b) $6 Leafy sea-dragon (56×41 mm) Set of 2 sheets 7·50 8·00

Nos. 2535/43 and 2544/52 respectively were printed together, se-tenant, with the backgrounds forming composite designs.

1998. Save the Turtles Campaign. Nos. 1686/7, 1689/90 and 1692 optd **Save the Turtles.**
2554 25c. Type **263** 35 30
2555 55c. Hawksbill turtle swimming 50 30
2556 90c. Green turtle laying eggs 65 45
2557 $1 Green turtle swimming 70 65
2558 $4 Loggerhead turtle 2·75 3·25

1998. Christmas. Birds. Multicoloured.
2559 25c. Type **327** 40 25
2560 55c. Eastern bluebird 50 25
2561 65c. Carolina wren 55 30
2562 90c. Blue jay 70 50
2563 $1 Evening grosbeak 80 75
2564 $2 Bohemian waxwing 1·50 1·75
MS2565 Two sheets, each 70×97 mm. (a) $5 Northern Parula. (b) $6 Painted bunting Set of 2 sheets 7·50 8·00

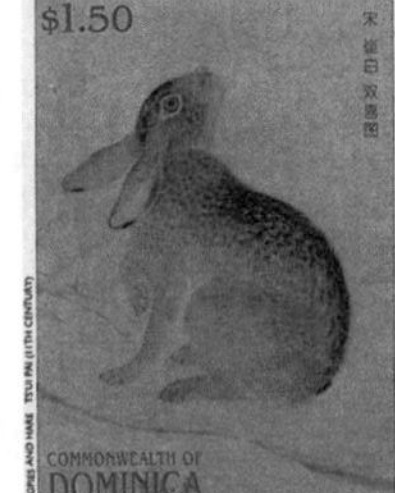

328 "Magpies and Hare" (Ts'ui Pai)

1999. Chinese New Year ("Year of the Rabbit").
2566 **328** $1.50 multicoloured 1·40 1·60

329 "Broughtonia sanguinea"

1999. Orchids of the Caribbean. Multicoloured.
2567 55c. Type **329** 50 35
2568 65c. "Cattleyonia Keith Roth" "Roma" 60 40
2569 90c. "Comparettia falcata" 70 50
2570 $1 "Dracula erythiochaete" 70 75
2571 $1 "Lycasle aromatica" 70 75
2572 $1 "Masdevallia marguerile" 70 75
2573 $1 "Encyclia marlae" 70 75
2574 $1 "Laelia gouldiana" 70 75
2575 $1 "Huntleya meleagris" 70 75
2576 $1 "Galeandria baueri" 70 75
2577 $1 "Lycale deppei" 70 75
2578 $1 "Anguloa clowesii" 70 75
2579 $1 "Lemboglossum cervantesii" 70 75
2580 $1 "Oncidium cebolleta" 70 75
2581 $1 "Millonia" 70 75
2582 $1 "Pescatorea lehmannll" 70 75
2583 $1 "Sophronitis coccinea" 70 75
2584 $1 "Pescatorea cerina" 70 75
2585 $1 "Encyclia vitellina" 70 75
2586 $2 "Cochleanthes discolor" 1·25 1·40
MS2587 Two sheets, each 76×89 mm. (a) $5 "Lepanthes ovalis". (b) $5 "Encyclia cochleata" Set of 2 sheets 7·00 8·00

330 County Donegal Petrol Rail Car No. 10, Ireland

1999. "Australia '99" International Stamp Exhibition, Melbourne. Diesel and Electric Trains. Multicoloured.
2588 $1 Type **330** 75 75
2589 $1 Canadian Pacific rail car, Canada 75 75
2590 $1 Class WDM locomotive, India 75 75
2591 $1 Bi-polar locomotive, No. E-2, U.S.A. 75 75
2592 $1 Class X locomotive, Australia 75 75
2593 $1 Class "Beijing" locomotive, China 75 75
2594 $1 Class E428 locomotive, Italy 75 75
2595 $1 Class 581 twelve-car train, Japan 75 75
2596 $1 Class 103.1 locomotive, West Germany 75 75
2597 $1 Class 24 Trans-Pennine train, Great Britain 75 75
2598 $1 Amtrak Class GG1, No. 902, U.S.A. 75 75
2599 $1 Class LRC train, Canada 75 75
2600 $1 Class EW train, New Zealand 75 75
2601 $1 Class SS1 Shao-Shani, China 75 75
2602 $1 Gulf, Mobile and Ohio train, U.S.A. 75 75
2603 $1 Class 9100 locomotive, France 75 75
MS2604 Two sheets, each 106×76 mm. (a) $5 X-2000 tilting express train, Sweden (vert). (b) $6 Class 87 locomotive, Great Britain (vert) Set of 2 sheets 7·00 8·00

No. 2589 is inscribed "USA - RDC Single Rail Car" in error.

331 Hypacrosaurus

1999. Prehistoric Animals. Multicoloured.
2605 25c. Tyrannosaurus (vert) 50 40
2606 65c. Type **331** 65 40
2607 90c. Sauropelta 70 50
2608 $1 Barosaurus 70 75
2609 $1 Rhamphorhynchus 70 75
2610 $1 Apatosaurus 70 75
2611 $1 Archaeopteryx 70 75
2612 $1 Diplodocus 70 75
2613 $1 Ceratosaurus 70 75
2614 $1 Stegosaurus 70 75
2615 $1 Elaphrosaurus 70 75
2616 $1 Vulcanodon 70 75
2617 $1 Psittacosaurus 70 75
2618 $1 Pteranodon 70 75
2619 $1 Ichythyornis 70 75
2620 $1 Spinosaurus 70 75
2621 $1 Parasaurolophus 70 75
2622 $1 Ornithomimus 70 75
2623 $1 Anatosaurus 70 75
2624 $1 Triceratops 70 75
2625 $1 Baryonx 70 75
2626 $2 Zalambdalestes 1·25 1·40
MS2627 Two sheets, each 106×80 mm. (a) $5 Yangchuanosaurus. (b) $6 Brachiosaurus (vert) Set of 2 sheets 7·50 8·00

Nos. 2608/16 and 2617/25 respectively were printed together, se-tenant, with the backgrounds forming composite designs.

332 Miss Sophie Rhys-Jones

1999. Royal Wedding.
2628 **332** $3 blue and black 1·75 2·00
2629 – $3 multicoloured 1·75 2·00
2630 – $3 blue and black 1·75 2·00
MS2631 78×108 mm. $6 multicoloured 3·50 4·00

DESIGNS: No. 2629 and **MS**2631, Miss Sophie Rhys-Jones and Prince Edward; 2630, Prince Edward.

1999. "iBRA '99" International Stamp Exhibition, Nuremberg. As T **299a** of Gambia. Multicoloured.
2632 65c. "Eendracht" (Dirk Hartog) with Cameroons Expeditionary Force 1915 2d. and 3d. surcharges 60 35
2633 90c. "Eendracht" with Kamerun 1900 10pf. and 25pf. stamps 70 50
2634 $1 Early German railway locomotive with Kamerun 1900 5m. stamp 80 75
2635 $2 Early German railway locomotive with Kamerun 1890 overprinted 50pf. stamp 1·50 1·75
MS2636 138×109 mm. $6 Exhibition emblem and Kamerun 5m. stamp postmarked 1913 3·50 4·00

1999. 150th Death Anniv of Katsushika Hokusai (Japanese artist). As T **299b** of Gambia. Multicoloured.
2637 $2 "Pilgrims at Kirifuri Waterfall" 1·25 1·40
2638 $2 "Kakura-Sato" (rats pulling on rope) 1·25 1·40
2639 $2 "Travellers on the Bridge by Ono Waterfall" 1·25 1·40
2640 $2 "Fast Cargo Boat battling the Waves" 1·25 1·40
2641 $2 "Kakura-Sato" (rats with barrels) 1·25 1·40
2642 $2 "Buufinfinh and Weeping Cherry" 1·25 1·40
2643 $2 "Cuckoo and Azalea" 1·25 1·40
2644 $2 "Soldiers" (with lamp) 1·25 1·40
2645 $2 "Lovers in the Snow" 1·25 1·40
2646 $2 "Ghost of Koheiji" 1·25 1·40
2647 $2 "Soldiers" (with hand on hip) 1·25 1·40
2648 $2 "Chinese Poet in Snow" 1·25 1·40
MS2649 Two sheets, each 101×72 mm. (a) $5 "Empress Jito". (b) $6 "One Hundred Poems by One Hundred Poets" Set of 2 sheets 6·50 7·00

1999. 10th Anniv of United Nations Rights of the Child Convention. As T **299c** of Gambia. Multicoloured.
2650 $3 Small girl (vert) 1·25 1·40
2651 $3 Small boy (vert) 1·25 1·40
2652 $3 Small boy and girl (vert) 1·25 1·40
MS2653 85×110 mm. $6 Peace dove 3·50 4·00

Nos. 2650/2 were printed together, se-tenant, forming a composite design which continues onto the sheet margins.

1999. "PhilexFrance '99" International Stamp Exhibition, Paris. Railway Locomotives. Two sheets, each containing horiz designs as T **299d** of Gambia. Multicoloured.
MS2654 Two sheets, each 106×81 mm. (a) $5 Steam locomotive "L'Aigle", 1855. (b) $6 Mainline diesel locomotive, 1963 Set of 2 sheets 7·00 7·00

1999. 250th Birth Anniv of Johann von Goethe (German writer). As T **299a** of Gambia.
2655 $2 multicoloured 1·25 1·25
2656 $2 blue, purple and black 1·25 1·25
2657 $2 multicoloured 1·25 1·25
MS2658 76×100 mm. $6 grey, black and brown 3·50 4·00

DESIGNS—HORIZ: No. 2655, Faust and astrological sign; 2656, Von Goethe and Von Schiller; 2657, Faust tempted by Mephistopheles. VERT: No. **MS**2658, Johann von Goethe.

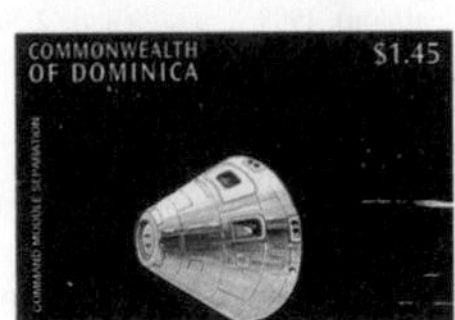

333 Command Module

1999. 30th Anniv of First Manned Landing on Moon. Multicoloured.
2659 $1.45 Type **333** 1·10 1·25
2660 $1.45 Service module 1·10 1·25
2661 $1.45 Booster separation 1·10 1·25
2662 $1.45 Lunar and command modules 1·10 1·25
2663 $1.45 Tracking telescope 1·10 1·25
2664 $1.45 Goldstone radio telescope 1·10 1·25
MS2665 106×76 mm. $6 "Apollo 11" after splashdown 3·50 4·00

1999. "Queen Elizabeth the Queen Mother's Century". As T **305a** of Gambia.
2666 $2 black and gold 1·40 1·40
2667 $2 black and gold 1·40 1·40
2668 $2 multicoloured 1·40 1·40
2669 $2 multicoloured 1·40 1·40
MS2670 153×157 mm. $6 multicoloured 4·00 4·25

DESIGNS: No. 2666, Queen Elizabeth, 1939; 2667, Queen Mother in Australia, 1958; 2668, Queen Mother in blue hat and coat, 1982; 2669, Queen Mother laughing, 1982. (37×50 mm)—No. **MS**2670, Queen Mother in 1953.

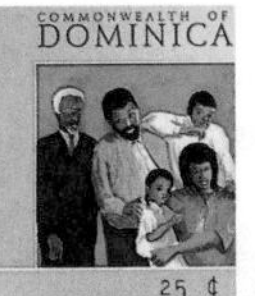

334 Female Dancer and "DOMFESTA" **335** Family

1999. 21st Anniv of Dominica Festivals Commission. Multicoloured.
2671 25c. Type **334** 40 25
2672 55c. "21st BIRTHDAY" logo 55 30
2673 65c. Carnival Development Committee emblem . . . 60 40
2674 90c. World Creole music emblem 70 55
MS2675 90 × 90 mm. $5 "21st BIRTHDAY" logo (different) (33 × 48 mm) . . . . 3·25 3·75

1999. International Year of the Elderly. Sheet 90 × 50 mm, containing T **335** and similar vert designs. Multicoloured.
MS2676 25c. Type **335**; 65c. Parents and grandparents; 90c. Family around elderly woman in chair 1·50 1·75

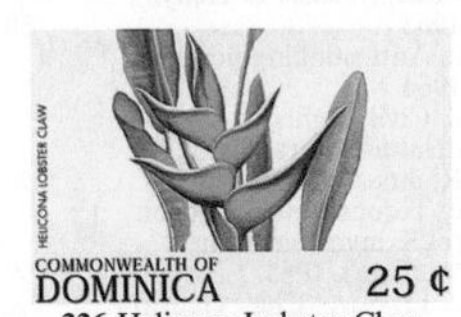

336 Helicona Lobster Claw

1999. Flora and Fauna. Multicoloured.
2677 25c. Type **336** 40 25
2678 65c. Broad-winged hawk . . 65 50
2679 90c. White-throated sparrow 70 70
2680 90c. Blue-winged teal . . . 70 70
2681 90c. Racoon 70 70
2682 90c. Alfalfa butterfly 70 70
2683 90c. Foot bridge 70 70
2684 90c. Whitetail deer 70 70
2685 90c. Grey squirrel 70 70
2686 90c. Banded-purple butterfly 70 70
2687 90c. Snowdrops 70 70
2688 90c. Bullfrog 70 70
2689 90c. Mushrooms 70 70
2690 90c. Large-blotched ensatina 70 70
2691 $1 Anthurium 70 70
2692 $1.55 Blue-headed hummingbird . . . . . . 1·10 1·10
2693 $2 Bananaquit . . . . . . 1·25 1·25
2694 $4 Agouti . . . . 2·25 2·50
MS2695 Two sheets, each 100 × 70 mm. (a) $5 Eastern chipmunk. (b) $6 Black-footed ferret Set of 2 sheets . . . . . 6·50 7·50
Nos. 2679/90 were printed together, se-tenant, with the backgrounds forming a composite design.

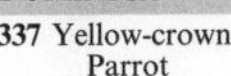

337 Yellow-crowned Parrot **337a** Leonardo Fibonacci (mathematician, 1202)

1999. Christmas. Birds. Multicoloured.
2696 25c. Type **337** 45 35
2697 55c. Red bishop 60 40
2698 65c. Troupial 70 40
2699 90c. Puerto Rican woodpecker . . . . . . 1·00 55
2700 $2 Mangrove cuckoo . . . 1·40 1·40
2701 $3 American robin . . . . 2·00 2·50
MS2702 76 × 98 mm. $6 "Mary with Child beside the Wall" (Dürer) (drab, black and cream) . . . 3·50 4·00
No. 2699 is inscribed "PUERTO RECAN WOODPECKER" and No. **MS**2702 "MARYWITH", both in error.

1999. New Millennium. People and Events of Thirteenth Century (1200–50). As T **445** of Antigua. Multicoloured.
2703 55c. Type **337a** 55 55
2704 55c. St. Francis of Assisi (founder of Franciscan Order, 1207) 55 55
2705 55c. Mongol horsemen (Conquest of China, 1211) 55 55
2706 55c. Children with banner (Children's Crusade, 1212) 55 55
2707 55c. King John signing Magna Carta, 1215 . . . 55 55
2708 55c. University class (foundation of Salamanca University, 1218) 55 55
2709 55c. Snorre Sturlusson (author of the "Edda", 1222) 55 55
2710 55c. Ma Yuan (Chinese painter) in garden (died 1224) 55 55
2711 55c. Genghis Khan (Mongol Emperor) (died 1227) . . 55 55
2712 55c. Student and Buddha (establishment of Zen Buddhism in Japan, 1227) 55 55
2713 55c. Galleys (The Sixth Crusade, 1228) 55 55
2714 55c. Seals (Lubeck–Hamburg Treaty, 1230) 55 55
2715 55c. Cardinal and angel (Holy Inquisition, 1231) 55 55
2716 55c. Palace interior (conquest of Cordoba, 1236) 55 55
2717 55c. San Marino (town founded, 1243) 55 55
2718 55c. Maimonides (Jewish philosopher) (died 1204) (59 × 39 mm) 55 55
2719 55c. Notre Dame Cathedral, Paris (completed 1250) . . 55 55

338 Bombing of Pearl Harbor, 1941

1999. New Millennium. People and Events of Twentieth Century (1940–49). Multicoloured.
2720 55c. Type **338** 40 40
2721 55c. Sir Winston Churchill (British Prime Minister, 1940) 40 40
2722 55c. Children in front of set (start of television broadcasting in U.S.A., 1940) 40 40
2723 55c. Anne Frank (Holocaust, 1942) 40 40
2724 55c. Troops wading ashore (D-Day, 1944) 40 40
2725 55c. Churchill, Roosevelt and Stalin (Yalta Conference, 1945) 40 40
2726 55c. U.N. Headquarters, New York (United Nations Organization, 1945) 40 40
2727 55c. American G.I. and concentration camp (Surrender of Germany, 1945) 40 40
2728 55c. Hoisting the Red Flag on the Reichstag (Fall of Berlin, 1945) 40 40
2729 55c. "Eniac" (first operational computer, 1946) 40 40
2730 55c. Indian with flag (Independence of India, 1947) 40 40
2731 55c. Early transistor, 1947 40 40
2732 55c. Mahatma Gandhi assassinated, 1948 . . . . 40 40
2733 55c. Israelis with flag (Establishment of Israel, 1948) 40 40
2734 55c. Aircraft and children (Berlin Airlift, 1948) . . . 40 40
2735 55c. Atomic bomb test, New Mexico, 1948 (59 × 39 mm) 40 40
2736 55c. Great Wall of China (People's Republic established, 1949) 40 40
No. 2732 is inscribed "Ghandi" in error.

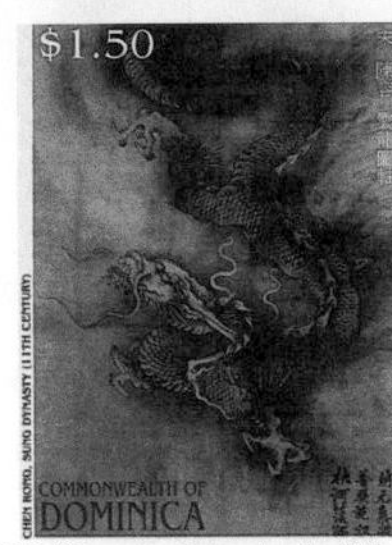

339 "Dragon flying in the Mist" (Chen Rong)

2000. Chinese New Year ("Year of the Dragon"). Multicoloured.
2737 $1.50 Type **339** . . . . . . 1·00 1·10
MS2738 80 × 60 mm. $4 Red dragon (horiz) . . . . 2·25 2·50

340 European Shorthair

2000. Cats and Dogs of the World. Multicoloured.
2739 $1 Type **340** 55 55
2740 $1 Devon rex 55 55
2741 $1 Chartreux 55 55
2742 $1 Bengal 55 55
2743 $1 American wirehair . . . 55 55
2744 $1 Siberian 55 55
2745 $1 Burmese 55 55
2746 $1 American shorthair . . . 55 55
2747 $1 Asian longhair 55 55
2748 $1 Burmilla 55 55
2749 $1 Snowshoe 55 55
2750 $1 Pekeface Persian 55 55
2751 $1 Himalayan Persian . . . 55 55
2752 $1 Japanese bobtail 55 55
2753 $1 Seychelles longhair . . . 55 55
2754 $1 Exotic shorthair 55 55
2755 $1 Jack Russell puppy (vert) 55 55
2756 $1 Shar pei puppies (vert) 55 55
2757 $1 Basset hound puppy (vert) 55 55
2758 $1 Boxer puppies (vert) . . 55 55
2759 $1 Wire-haired terrier (cross) puppy (vert) 55 55
2760 $1 Golden retriever puppies (vert) 55 55
MS2761 Three sheets, each 101 × 81 mm. (a) $6 Sleeping cat. (b) $6 Grey cat with yellow eyes. (c) $6 Beagle puppy (vert) Set of 3 sheets . . . . 9·00 10·00

341 Flowers forming Top of Head

2000. Faces of the Millennium: Diana, Princess of Wales. Designs showing collage of miniature flower photographs. Multicoloured.
2762 $1 Type **341** (face value at left) 65 70
2763 $1 Top of head (face value at right) 65 70
2764 $1 Ear (face value at left) 65 70
2765 $1 Eye and temple (face value at right) 65 70
2766 $1 Cheek (face value at left) 65 70
2767 $1 Cheek (face value at right) 65 70
2768 $1 Blue background (face value at left) 65 70
2769 $1 Chin (face value at right) 65 70
Nos. 2762/9 were printed together, se-tenant, in sheetlets of 8 with the stamps arranged in two vertical columns separated by a gutter also containing miniature photographs. When viewed as a whole, the sheetlet forms a portrait of Diana, Princess of Wales.

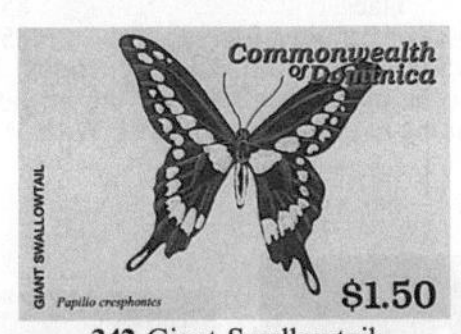

342 Giant Swallowtail

2000. Butterflies. Multicoloured.
2770 $1.50 Type **342** 85 90
2771 $1.50 Tiger pierid 85 90
2772 $1.50 Orange theope butterfly 85 90
2773 $1.50 White peacock 85 90
2774 $1.50 Blue tharops 85 90
2775 $1.50 Mosaic 85 90
2776 $1.50 Banded king shoemaker 85 90
2777 $1.50 Figure-of-eight butterfly 85 90
2778 $1.50 Grecian shoemaker . . 85 90
2779 $1.50 Blue night butterfly 85 90
2780 $1.50 Monarch 85 90
2781 $1.50 Common morpho . . 85 90
2782 $1.50 Orange-barred sulphur 85 90
2783 $1.50 Clorinde 85 90
2784 $1.50 Small flambeau . . . 85 90
2785 $1.50 Small lace-wing . . . 85 90
2786 $1.50 Polydamas swallowtail 85 90
2787 $1.50 The atala 85 90
MS2788 Three sheets, each 100 × 70 mm. (a) $6 Polydamas swallowtail (vert). (b) $6 Blue-green reflector (vert). (c) $6 Sloane's urania (vert) Set of 3 sheets . . . . 9·00 10·00

343 Passion Flower

2000. Flowers. Multicoloured. (a) Size 28 × 42 mm.
2789 65c. Type **343** 50 30
2790 90c. Spray orchid 70 60
2791 $1 Peach angels trumpet . . 70 65
2792 $4 Allamanda . . . . . . 2·25 2·25

(b) Size 32 × 48 mm.
2793 $1.65 Bird of paradise . . . 85 90
2794 $1.65 Lobster claw heliconia 85 90
2795 $1.65 Candle bush 85 90
2796 $1.65 Flor de San Miguel 85 90
2797 $1.65 Hibiscus 85 90
2798 $1.65 Oleander 85 90
2799 $1.65 Anthurium 85 90
2800 $1.65 Fire ginger 85 90
2801 $1.65 Shrimp plant 85 90
2802 $1.65 Sky vine thumbergia 85 90
2803 $1.65 Ceriman 85 90
2804 $1.65 Morning glory 85 90
MS2805 Two sheets, each 76 × 106 mm. (a) $6 Bird of Paradise and butterfly (38 × 50 mm). (b) $6 Hibiscus and hummingbird (38 × 50 mm) Set of 2 sheets . . . . 7·00 7·50
Nos. 2793/8 and 2799/804 were each printed together, se-tenant, with the backgrounds forming composite designs.

2000. 400th Birth Anniv of Sir Anthony Van Dyck (Flemish painter). As T **312a** of Gambia. Multicoloured.
2806 $1.65 "The Ages of Man" (horiz) 85 90
2807 $1.65 "Portrait of a Girl as Ermina accompanied by Cupid" (horiz) 85 90
2808 $1.65 "Cupid and Psyche" (horiz) 85 90
2809 $1.65 "Vertumnus and Pomona" (horiz) 85 90
2810 $1.65 "The Continence of Scipio" (horiz) 85 90
2811 $1.65 "Diana and Endymion surprised by a Satyr" (horiz) 85 90
2812 $1.65 "Ladies-in-Waiting" (horiz) 85 90
2813 $1.65 "Thomas Wentworth, Earl of Strafford, with Sir Philip Mainwaring" (horiz) 85 90
2814 $1.65 "Dorothy Rivers Savage, Viscountess Andover, and her sister Lady Elizabeth Thimbleby" (horiz) . . . 85 90
2815 $1.65 "Mountjoy Blount, Earl of Newport, and Lord George Goring with a Page" (horiz) 85 90
2816 $1.65 "Thomas Killigrew and an Unidentified Man" (horiz) 85 90
2817 $1.65 "Elizabeth Villiers, Lady Dalkeith, and Cecilia Killigrew" (horiz) 85 90
2818 $1.65 "Lady Jane Goodwin (Mrs. Arthur)" 85 90
2819 $1.65 "Philip Herbert, Earl of Pembroke" 85 90
2820 $1.65 "Philip, Lord Wharton" 85 90
2821 $1.65 "Sir Thomas Hammer" 85 90
2822 $1.65 "Olivia Porter" . . . 85 90
2823 $1.65 "Sir Thomas Chaloner" 85 90
MS2824 Three sheets, each 128 × 103 mm. (a) $5 "Archilles and the Daughters of Lycomedes" (vert). (b) $5 "Amaryllis and Mirtilo" (vert). (c) $6 "Aletheia, Countess of Arundel" (vert) Set of 3 sheets . . . . 8·00 9·00
No. 2813 is inscribed "Wenthworth" in error.

343a In Skiing Gear

2000. 18th Birthday of Prince William. Multicoloured.
2825 $1.65 Type **343a** 90 90
2826 $1.65 In red jumper 90 90
2827 $1.65 Holding order of service 90 90
2828 $1.65 Prince William laughing 90 90
MS2829 100 × 80 mm. $6 Prince William with Prince Harry (37 × 50 mm) . . . . 4·00 4·25

2000. "EXPO 2000" World Stamp Exhibition, Anaheim. Space Satellites. As T **582a** of Ghana. Multicoloured.
2830 $1.65 "Essa 8" 85 90
2831 $1.65 "Echo 1" 85 90
2832 $1.65 "Topex Poseidon" . . 85 90
2833 $1.65 "Diademe" 85 90
2834 $1.65 "Early Bird" 85 90
2835 $1.65 "Molyna" 85 90
2836 $1.65 "Explorer 14" 85 90
2837 $1.65 "Luna 16" 85 90
2838 $1.65 "Copernicus" 85 90
2839 $1.65 "Explorer 16" 85 90

2840 $1.65 "Luna 10" 85 90
2841 $1.65 "Arybhattan" 85 90
MS2842 Two sheets, each 106 × 76 mm. (a) $6 "Eole". (b) $6 "Hipparcos" . . . . 7·00 7·50

Nos. 2830/5 and 2836/41 were printed together, se-tenant, with the backgrounds forming composite designs.

2000. 25th Anniv of "Apollo–Soyuz" Joint Project. As T **582b** of Ghana. Multicoloured.

2843 $3 Saturn 1B ("Apollo" launch vehicle) . . . . . 1·75 1·90
2844 $3 "Apollo 18" command module . . . . 1·75 1·90
2845 $3 Donald Slayton ("Apollo 18" crew) . . . 1·75 1·90
MS2846 88 × 71 mm. $6 Spacecraft about to dock (horiz) . . . . 3·75 4·00

No. 2843 is inscribed "Vechicle" in error.

2000. 50th Anniv of Berlin Film Festival. As T **582** of Ghana. Multicoloured.

2847 $1.65 Satyajit Ray (director of *Ashani Sanket*) 85 90
2848 $1.65 *Mahanagar*, 1964 . . 85 90
2849 $1.65 *La Tulipe*, 1952 . . . 85 90
2850 $1.65 *Le Salaire de la Peur*, 1953 . . . . 85 90
2851 $1.65 *Les Cousins*, 1959 . . 85 90
2852 $1.65 *Hon Dansade en Sommar*, 1952 . . . . . 85 90
MS2853 97 × 103 mm. $6 *Buffalo Bill and the Indians*, 1976 . . . . . 3·75 4·00

2000. 175th Anniv of Stockton and Darlington Line (first public railway). As T **582d** of Ghana. Multicoloued.

2854 $3 George Stephenson and *Locomotion No. 1*, 1875 1·75 1·90
2855 $3 John B. Jervis's *Brother Jonathan*, 1832 . . . . . 1·75 1·90

No. 2855 is inscribed "Jonathon" in error.

2000. 250th Death Anniv of Johann Sebastian Bach (German composer). Sheet 77 × 88 mm, containing vert portrait as T **312c** of Gambia.

MS2856 $6 brown and black . . 4·00 4·25

2000. Election of Albert Einstein (mathematical physicist) as *Time Magazine* "Man of the Century". Sheet 117 × 91 mm, containing vert portrait as T **312d** of Gambia.

MS2857 $6 multicoloured . . . . 3·75 4·00

344 Count Ferdinand von Zeppelin

2000. Centenary of First Zeppelin Flight. Mult.

2858 $1.65 Type **344** 85 90
2859 $1.65 LZ-1 at Lake Constance, 1900 . . . . 85 90
2860 $1.65 LZ-10 *Schwaben*, over flock of sheep, 1911 . . . 85 90
2861 $1.65 LZ-6 and LZ-7 *Deutschland* in hangar, Friedrichshafen 85 90
2862 $1.65 LZ-4 at Luneville, 1913 . . . . 85 90
2863 $1.65 LZ-11 *Viktoria-Luise* over Kiel Harbour . . . 85 90
MS2864 93 × 115 mm. $6 As No. 2859 . . . . 4·00 4·25

No. 2861 is inscribed "Friedrichshrfed" in error.

2000. Olympic Games, Sydney. As T **582f** of Ghana. Multicoloured.

2865 $2 Jesse Owens (athletics), Berlin (1936) . . . . . . 1·10 1·25
2866 $2 Pole-vaulting . . . . . . 1·10 1·25
2867 $2 Lenin Stadium, Moscow (1980) and U.S.S.R. flag 1·10 1·25
2868 $2 Ancient Greek discus-thrower . . . . 1·10 1·25

2000. West Indies Cricket Tour and 100th Test Match at Lord's. As T **472a** of Grenada. Multicoloured.

2869 $4 Norbert Phillip . . . . . 2·25 2·40
MS2870 121 × 104 mm. $6 Lord's Cricket Ground (horiz) . . . . 4·00 4·25

No. 2869 is inscribed "Phillp" in error.

2000. 80th Birthday of Pope John Paul II. As T **341**, showing collage of miniature religious photographs. Multicoloured.

2871 $1 Top of head (face value at left) 75 75
2872 $1 Top of head (face value at right) 75 75
2873 $1 Ear (face value at left) 75 75
2874 $1 Forehead (face value at right) 75 75
2875 $1 Neck (face value at left) 75 75
2876 $1 Cheek (face value at right) 75 75
2877 $1 Shoulder (face value at left) 75 75
2878 $1 Hands (face value at right) 75 75

Nos. 2871/8 were printed together, se-tenant, in sheetlets of 8 with the stamps arranged in two vertical columns separated by a gutter also containing miniature photographs. When viewed as a whole, the sheetlet forms a portrait of Pope John Paul.

345 Roger the Shrubber

2000. *Monty Python and the Holy Grail* (comedy film). Multicoloured.

2879 90c. Type **345** 65 65
2880 90c. Three-headed giant . . . 65 65
2881 90c. Attacking the castle . . 65 65
2882 90c. King Arthur and knight 65 65
2883 90c. Headless knight 65 65
2884 90c. Limbless Black Knight 65 65

346 Member of The Crystals

347 Bob Hope singing

2000. Famous Girl Pop Groups. The Crystals. Mult.

2885 90c. Type **346** 65 65
2886 90c. Group member with long hair (blue background in top right corner) 65 65
2887 90c. Group member with long hair (yellow background in top right corner) 65 65
2888 90c. Group member with short hair 65 65

Nos. 2885/8 were printed together, se-tenant, forming a composite design.

2000. Bob Hope (American entertainer).

2889 **347** $1.65 black, blue and lilac 85 90
2890 – $1.65 multicoloured . . 85 90
2891 – $1.65 black, blue and lilac 85 90
2892 – $1.65 multicoloured . . 85 90
2893 – $1.65 black, blue and lilac 85 90
2894 – $1.65 multicoloured . . 85 90

DESIGNS: No. 2890, Entertaining troops; 2891, As English comic character; 2892, In 50th birthday cake; 2893, Making radio broadcast; 2894, With Man in the Moon.

348 David Copperfield

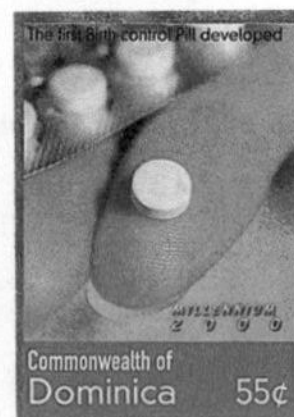

349 First Birth-control Pill, 1961

2000. David Copperfield (conjurer).

2895 **348** $2 multicoloured . . . . 1·25 1·25

2000. Monarchs of the Millennium. As T **314a** of Gambia.

2896 $1.65 multicoloured 85 90
2897 $1.65 black, stone and brown 85 90
2898 $1.65 multicoloured 85 90
2899 $1.65 black, stone and brown 85 90
2900 $1.65 multicoloured 85 90
2901 $1.65 black, stone and brown 85 90
MS2902 115 × 135 mm. $6 multicoloured . . . . 4·00 4·25

DESIGNS: No. 2896, King Edward IV of England; 2897, Tsar Peter the Great of Russia; 2898, King Henry VI of England; 2899, King Henry III of England; 2900, King Richard III of England; 2901, King Edward I of England; **MS**2902, King Henry VIII of England.

2000. Popes of the Millennium. As T **314b** of Gambia. Each black, yellow and green.

2903 $1.65 Clement X 90 90
2904 $1.65 Innocent X 90 90
2905 $1.65 Nicholas V 90 90
2906 $1.65 Martin V 90 90
2907 $1.65 Julius III 90 90
2908 $1.65 Innocent XII 90 90
MS2909 115 × 135 mm. $6 Clement XIV (brown, yellow and black) 4·00 4·25

2000. Christmas and Holy Year. As T **491** of Grenada. Multicoloured.

2910 25c. Angel in blue robe . . 25 15
2911 65c. Young angel 45 30
2912 90c. Angel with drapery . . 70 40
2913 $1.90 As 25c. . . . . 1·00 1·25
2914 $1.90 As 65c. . . . . 1·00 1·25
2915 $1.90 As 90c. . . . . 1·00 1·25
2916 $1.90 As $5 . . . . 1·00 1·25
2917 $5 Head and shoulders of angel . . . . 2·50 3·00
MS2918 110 × 120 mm. $6 Angel's face (as 25c.) . . . . 3·75 4·00

349a Couple with hawk (Minnesangers in Germany, 1350)

2000. New Millennium. People and Events of the Fourteenth Century (1350–1400). As T **445** of Antigua. Multicoloured.

2919 65c. Type **349a** 55 55
2920 65c. Acamapitzin, first King of the Aztecs, 1352 . . . 55 55
2921 65c. Rat (end of Black Death, 1353) 55 55
2922 65c. Giotto's *Campanile* (completed by Francesco Talenti, 1355) 55 55
2923 65c. First French franc, 1360 . . . . 55 55
2924 65c. Emperor Hung-wu (foundation of Ming Dynasty, 1360) 55 55
2925 65c. Tamerlane (foundation of Timurid Empire, 1369) 55 55
2926 65c. "Triumph of Death" (Francis Traini), 1370 . . 55 55
2927 65c. Robin Hood (first appearance in English legends, 1375) 55 55
2928 65c. "The Knight" (The Canterbury Tales by Geoffrey Chaucer, 1387) 55 55
2929 65c. Mounted samurai (disputed succession in Japan, 1392) 55 55
2930 65c. Refugees (Jews expelled from France, 1394) . . . 55 55
2931 65c. Temple of the Golden Pavilion, Kyoto (constructed, 1394) . . . 55 55
2932 65c. Carving, Strasbourg Cathedral (completed, 1399) 55 55
2933 65c. Alhambra Palace, Granada (completed, 1390) (60 × 40 mm) . . . 55 55
2934 65c. Ife Bronzes produced in Nigeria, 1400 . . . . . . 55 55

No. 2929 is inscribed "SUDDESSION" in error.

349b "Eight Prize Steeds" (Guiseppe Castiglione)

2000. New Millennium. Two Thousand Years of Chinese Paintings. Multicoloured.

2935 55c. Type **349b** 40 45
2936 55c. "Oleanders" (Wu Hsi Tsai) 40 45
2937 55c. "Mynah and Autumn Flowers" (Chang Hsiung) 40 45
2938 55c. "Hen and Chicks beneath Chrysanthemums," (Chu Ch'ao) 40 45
2939 55c. "Long Living Pine and Crane" (Xugu) 40 45
2940 55c. "Flowers and Fruits" (Chu Lien) 40 45
2941 55c. "Lotus and Willow" (Pu Hua) 40 45
2942 55c. "Kuan-Yin" (Ch'ien Hui-an) 40 45
2943 55c. "Human Figures" (Jen Hsun) 40 45
2944 55c. "Han-Shan and Shih-Te" (Ren Yi) 40 45
2945 55c. "Landscape and Human Figure" (Jen Yu) 40 45
2946 55c. "Poetic Thoughts while Walking with a Staff" (Wangchen) 40 45
2947 55c. "Peony" (Chen Heng-ko) 40 45
2948 55c. "Plum and Orchid" (Wu Chang-shih) 40 45
2949 55c. "Monkey" (Kao Chi-feng) 40 45
2950 55c. "Grapes and Locust" (Chi Pai-shih); and "Galloping Horse" (Xu Beihong) (60 × 40 mm) . . 40 45
2951 55c. "The Beauty" (Lin Fengmian) 40 45

No. 2937 is inscribed "YNAH" and No. 2948 "ORCHIS", both in error.

2000. New Millennium. People and Events of Twentieth Century (1960–69). Multicoloured.

2952 55c. Type **349** 50 50
2953 55c. Yuri Gagarin (first man in Space), 1961 . . . . . 50 50
2954 55c. Fans with The Beatles tickets, 1962 . . . . . . 50 50
2955 55c. Funeral of President John F. Kennedy, 1963 50 50
2956 55c. Martin Luther King's "I Have a Dream" speech, 1963 . . . . . . 50 50
2957 55c. Betty Friedan (author of *The Feminist Mystique*), 1963 . . . . 50 50
2958 55c. Duke of Edinburgh and Jomo Kenyatta (independence of Kenya), 1963 . . . . 50 50
2959 55c. Anti-smoking poster, 1964 . . . . 50 50
2960 55c. Civil Rights demonstrators (U.S. Civil Rights Act), 1964 . . . . 50 50
2961 55c. Troops outside Saigon (U.S. involvement in Vietnam), 1965 . . . . . 50 50
2962 55c. Ernesto "Che" Guevara (Cuban revolutionary) killed in Peru, 1965 . . . 50 50
2963 55c. Dr. Christiaan Barnard (first heart transplant operation), 1967 . . . . 50 50
2964 55c. General Moshe Dayan addressing Arabs ("Six-Day" War), 1967 . . . . 50 50
2965 55c. Death of Ho Chi Minh (North Vietnamese leader), 1969 . . . . . . 50 50
2966 55c. Neil Armstrong on the Moon, 1969 . . . . . . 50 50
2967 55c. Couple at Berlin Wall, 1961 (60 × 40 mm) 50 50
2968 55c. Woodstock Festival, 1969 . . . . 50 50

350 Ancient Star Signs

2000. New Millennium. Inventions. Multicoloured.

2969 55c. Type **350** 40 45
2970 55c. Precision tools 40 45
2971 55c. Astral chart 40 45
2972 55c. Growth of medicine . . 40 45
2973 55c. Exchange of medical information 40 45
2974 55c. Monastic chapterhouse 40 45
2975 55c. Water alarm clock . . 40 45
2976 55c. Weighted clock 40 45
2977 55c. Spring-loaded miniature clock movement 40 45
2978 55c. Glass blowing 40 45
2979 55c. Early screws 40 45
2980 55c. Wood lathe 40 45
2981 55c. Ship building 40 45
2982 55c. Interchangeable rifle parts 40 45
2983 55c. Study of movement . . 40 45
2984 55c. The Industrial Revolution (60 × 40 mm) 40 45
2985 55c. Concept of efficiency 40 45

351 "Snake in the Wilderness" (Hwa Yan)

2001. Chinese New Year. "Year of the Snake".

2986 **351** $1.20 multicoloured . . 70 75

352 Female Green-throated Carib

2001. Hummingbirds. Multicoloured.

2987 $1.25 Type **352** 80 80
2988 $1.25 Male bee hummingbird ("Mellisuga helenae") 80 80
2989 $1.25 Male bee hummingbird ("Russelia eqoisetiformis") 80 80
2990 $1.25 Female bahama woodstar 80 80
2991 $1.25 Antillean mango 80 80
2992 $1.25 Female blue-headed hummingbird 80 80
2993 $1.65 Male streamertail 90 90
2994 $1.65 Purple-throated carib 90 90
2995 $1.65 Vervain hummingbird 90 90
2996 $1.65 Bahama woodstar 90 90
2997 $1.65 Puerto Rican emerald 90 90
2998 $1.65 Antillean crested hummingbird 90 90
MS2999 Two sheets. (a) $5 Unidentified hummingbird. (b) $6 Hispaniolan emerald Set of 2 sheets 6·50 7·00

Nos. 2987/92 and 2993/8 were each printed together, se-tenant, with the backgrounds forming composite designs.

No. 2987 is inscribed "Fehale Greentriroated Carib", No. 2990 "Tenale", No. 2994 "Triroated", No. 2998 "Cresteo" and No. **MS**2999b "Hispaniolian", all in error.

No. 2989 carries the inscription "Russelia eqoisetiformis". This should read "Russelia equisetiformis", and refers to the plant (commonly known as a Firecracker Plant) at the bottom of the stamp, not the hummingbird.

353 Puerto Rican Crested Toad

2001. Caribbean and Latin-American Fauna. Mult.

3000 15c. Type **353** 25 15
3001 20c. Axolotl 25 15
3002 $1.45 St. Vincent amazon ("St. Vincent Parrot") 85 90
3003 $1.45 Indigo macaw 85 90
3004 $1.45 Guianian cock of the rock ("Cock of the Rock") 85 90
3005 $1.45 Cuban solenodon 85 90
3006 $1.45 Cuban hutia 85 90
3007 $1.45 Chinchilla 85 90
3008 $1.45 Chilian flamingo ("South American Flamingo") 85 90
3009 $1.45 Golden conure 85 90
3010 $1.45 Ocelot 85 90
3011 $1.45 Giant armadillo 85 90
3012 $1.45 Margay 85 90
3013 $1.45 Maned wolf 85 90
3014 $1.90 Panamanian golden frog 1·10 1·10
3015 $2.20 Manatee 1·25 1·25
MS3016 Two sheets, each 106 × 71 mm. (a) $6 Hawksbill turtle. (b) $6 Anteater Set of 2 sheets 7·00 8·00

Nos. 3002/7 and 3008/13 were each printed together, se-tenant, with the backgrounds forming composite designs.

2001. Characters from "Pokemon" (children's cartoon series). As T **332a** of Gambia. Multicoloured.

3017 $1.65 "Butterfree No. 12" 85 90
3018 $1.65 "Bulbasaur No. 01" 85 90
3019 $1.65 "Caterpie No. 10" 85 90
3020 $1.65 "Charmander No. 04" 85 90
3021 $1.65 "Squirtle No. 07" 85 90
3022 $1.65 "Pidgeotto No. 17" 85 90
MS3023 75 × 105 mm. $6 "Nidoking No. 34" 3·75 4·00

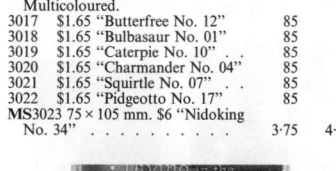

354 Large Blue and Green Fish

2001. Diving in the Caribbean. Depicting marine life. Multicoloured.

3024 15c. Type **354** 20 15
3025 65c. Ray 45 30
3026 90c. Octopus 60 40
3027 $2 Shark 1·10 1·25
3028 $2 Starfish 1·10 1·25
3029 $2 Seahorse 1·10 1·25
3030 $2 Pink anemonefish 1·10 1·25
3031 $2 Crab 1·10 1·25
3032 $2 Moray eel 1·10 1·25
3033 $3 Pink anemonefish 1·60 1·75
MS3034 78 × 57 mm. $5 Young turtle 3·25 3·50

355 Banded Sea-snake

2001. Caribbean Marine Life. Multicoloured.

3035 15c. Type **355** 20 15
3036 25c. Soldierfish 25 15
3037 55c. False moorish idol ("Banner Fish") 45 25
3038 90c. Crown of Thorns starfish 60 40
3039 $1.65 Red sponge and shoal of anthias 85 90
3040 $1.65 Undulate triggerfish ("Orange-Striped Trigger Fish") 85 90
3041 $1.65 Coral hind ("Coral Grouper") and soft tree coral 85 90
3042 $1.65 Peacock fan-worms and Gorgonian sea fan 85 90
3043 $1.65 Sweetlips and sea fan 85 90
3044 $1.65 Giant clam and golden cup coral 85 90
3045 $1.65 White-tipped reef shark, lionfish and sergeant majors 85 90
3046 $1.65 Blue-striped snappers 85 90
3047 $1.65 Great hammerhead shark, stovepipe sponge and pink vase sponge 85 90
3048 $1.65 Hawaiian monk seal and bluetube coral 85 90
3049 $1.65 False clown anemonefish ("Common Clown Fish"), chilka seahorse and red feather star coral 85 90
3050 $1.65 Bat starfish and brown octopus 85 90
MS3051 Two sheets, each 88 × 83 mm. (a) $5 Regal anglefish. (b) $5 Pink anenomefish Set of 2 sheets 6·00 6·50

Nos. 3039/44 and 3045/50 were each printed together, se-tenant, with the backgrounds forming composite designs.

No. 3045 is inscribed "Sargent" and 3049 "Cconn", both in error.

356 Prince Albert in Military Uniform

357 Mao Tse-tung in 1945

2001. Death Centenary of Queen Victoria. Multicoloured.

3052 $2 Type **356** 1·25 1·25
3053 $2 Young Queen Victoria wearing crown 1·25 1·25
3054 $2 Young Queen Victoria wearing tiara 1·25 1·25
3055 $2 Prince Albert in evening dress 1·25 1·25
MS3056 106 × 122 mm. $6 Queen Victoria in 1897 (38 × 50 mm) 3·75 4·00

2001. 25th Death Anniv of Mao Tse-tung (Chinese leader). Portraits. Multicoloured.

3057 $2 Type **357** 1·10 1·25
3058 $2 Mao in 1926 1·10 1·25
3059 $2 Mao in 1949 1·10 1·25
MS3060 135 × 110 mm. $3 Mao Tse-tung with farm workers in 1930 1·50 1·75

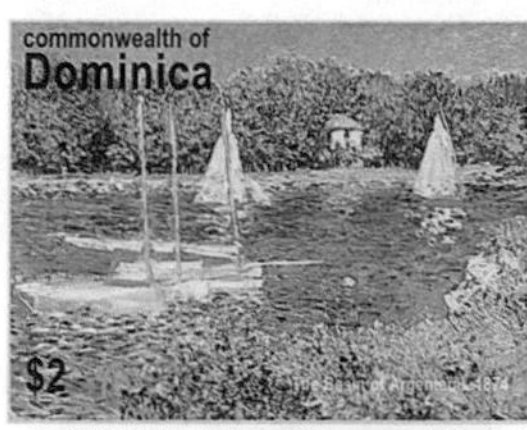

358 "The Lake at Argenteuil"

2001. 75th Death Anniv of Claude-Oscar Monet (French painter). Multicoloured.

3061 $2 Type **358** 1·25 1·40
3062 $2 "Bridge at Argenteuil" 1·25 1·40
3063 $2 "Railway bridge at Argenteuil" 1·25 1·40
3064 $2 "Seine bridge at Argenteuil" 1·25 1·40
MS3065 139 × 111 mm. $6 "Woman with Parasol – Madame Monet and her Son" (vert) 3·75 4·00

359 Queen Elizabeth at Coronation

360 Verdi as a Young Man

2001. 75th Birthday of Queen Elizabeth II. Multicoloured.

3066 $1.20 Type **359** 70 70
3067 $1.20 Queen Elizabeth wearing yellow hat 70 70
3068 $1.20 Bare-headed portrait after Annigoni 70 70
3069 $1.20 Queen Elizabeth wearing fur hat 70 70
3070 $1.20 With Prince Andrew as a baby 70 70
3071 $1.20 Wearing white hat and pearl necklace 70 70
MS3072 78 × 102 mm. $6 Queen Elizabeth in Guards uniform taking salute at Trooping the Colour 3·75 4·00

2001. Death Centenary of Giuseppe Verdi (Italian composer). Multicoloured.

3073 $2 Type **360** 1·25 1·40
3074 $2 "Lady Macbeth" 1·25 1·40
3075 $2 Orchestra 1·25 1·40
3076 $2 Score for Verdi's *Macbeth* (opera) 1·25 1·40
MS3077 76 × 105 mm. $6 Verdi as an old man 4·00 4·25

Nos. 3073/6 were printed together, se-tenant, with the backgrounds forming a composite design.

361 "Daruma" (Tsuji Kako)

363 *Cantharellus cibarius*

362 "Two Women Waltzing"

2001. "Philanippon '01" International Stamp Exhibition, Tokyo. Japanese Paintings. Multicoloured.

3078 25c. Type **361** 20 15
3079 55c. "Village by Bamboo Grove" (Takeuchi Seiho) 40 25
3080 65c. "Mountain Village in Spring" (Suzuki Hyakunen) 50 30
3081 90c. "Gentleman amusing Himself" (Domoto Insho) 65 40
3082 $1 "Calmness of Spring Light" (Takeuchi Seiho) 70 45
3083 $1.65 "Thatched Cottages in Willows" (Tsuji Kako) 85 90
3084 $1.65 "Joy in the Garden" (Tsuji Kako) 85 90
3085 $1.65 "Azalea and Butterfly" (Kikuchi Hobun) 85 90
3086 $1.65 "Pine Grove" (Tsuji Kako)
3087 $1.65 "Woodcutters talking in an Autumn Valley" (Kubota Beisen) 85 90
3088 $1.65 "Waterfowl in Snow" (Tsuji Kako) 85 90
3089 $1.65 "Heron and Willow" (Tsuji Kako) 85 90
3090 $1.65 "Crow and Cherry Blossoms" (Kikuchi Hobun) 85 90
3091 $1.65 "Chrysanthemum Immortal" (Yamamoto Shunkyo) 85 90
3092 $1.65 "Cranes of Immortality" (Tsuji Kako) 85 90
3093 $2 "Su's Embankment on a Spring Morning" (Tomioka Tessai) 1·10 1·25
MS3094 Three sheets. (a) 95 × 118 mm. $6 "Girl" (Suzuki Harunobu) (38 × 50 mm). (b) 105 × 90 mm. $6 "Kamo Riverbank in the Misty Rain" (Tsuji Kak) (38 × 50 mm). (c) 125 × 91 mm. $6 "Diamond Gate" (Tsuji Kak) (38 × 50 mm) Set of 3 sheets 8·50 9·50

No. **MS**3094c is inscribed "DIAMON GATE" in error.

2001. Death Centenary of Henri de Toulouse-Lautrec (French painter). Multicoloured.

3095 $2 Type **362** 1·10 1·25
3096 $2 "The Medical Inspection" 1·10 1·25
3097 $2 "Two Girlfriends" 1·10 1·25
3098 $2 "Woman pulling up her Stockings" 1·10 1·25
MS3099 66 × 86 mm. $6 "Self-portrait" 3·75 4·00

2001. Fungi of the World. Multicoloured.

3100 15c. Type **363** 20 15
3101 25c. *Hygrocybe pratensis* 25 15
3102 55c. *Leccinum aurantiacum* 40 25
3103 90c. *Caesar's amanita* (horiz) 65 70
3104 90c. *Agaricus augustus* (horiz) 65 70
3105 90c. *Clitocybe nuda* (horiz) 65 70
3106 90c. *Hygrocybe plavescens* (horiz) 65 70
3107 90c. *Stropharia kaufmanii* (horiz) 65 70
3108 90c. *Hygrophorus speciosus* (horiz) 65 70
3109 $2 *Marasmiellus candidus* 1·10 1·25
3110 $2 *Calostoma cinnabarina* 1·10 1·25
3111 $2 *Cantharellus infundibuliformis* 1·10 1·25
3112 $2 *Hygrocybe punicea* 1·10 1·25
3113 $2 *Dictyophora indusiata* 1·10 1·25
3114 $2 *Agrocybe praecox* 1·10 1·25
3115 $3 *Mycena haematopus* 1·50 1·60
MS3116 Two sheets. (a) 76 × 54 mm. $5 Gymnophilus spectabilis (horiz). (b) 54 × 76 mm. $5 Amanita muscaria (horiz) Set of 2 sheets 6·50 7·00

364 St. Vincent Amazon ("St. Vincent Parrot")

2001. Caribbean Fauna. Multicoloured.

3117 $1.45 Type **364** 85 90
3118 $1.45 Painted bunting 85 90
3119 $1.45 Jamaican giant anole 85 90
3120 $1.45 White-fronted capuchin monkey 85 90
3121 $1.45 Strand racerunner 1·10 1·25
3122 $1.45 Agouti 1·10 1·25
3123 $2 Cook's tree boa 1·10 1·25
3124 $2 Tamandua 1·10 1·25
3125 $2 Common iguana 1·10 1·25
3126 $2 Solenodon 80 85
MS3127 Four sheets. (a) 63 × 92 mm. $5 American purple gallinule. (b) 63 × 92 mm. $5 Rufous-tailed jaramar. (c) 92 × 63 mm. $5 Ruby-throated hummingbird (horiz). (d) 73 × 52 mm. $5 Bottlenose dolphins (horiz) Set of 4 sheets 10·00 11·00

365 Yellow Warbler

365a Baltimore ("Northern" Oriole)

2001. Birds. Multicoloured. (a) Design as T **365**.

3128 5c. Type **365** 15 15
3129 10c. Palm chat 20 15
3130 15c. Snowy cotinga 25 15
3131 20c. Blue-grey gnatcatcher 25 15
3132 25c. Belted kingfisher . . . 25 15
3133 55c. Red-legged thrush . . 35 25
3134 65c. Bananaquit 45 30
3135 90c. Yellow-bellied sapsucker 60 40
3136 $1 White-tailed tropicbird 70 55
3137 $1.45 Ruby-throated hummingbird 85 90
3138 $1.90 Painted bunting . . 1·00 1·10
3139 $2 Great frigate bird . . . 1·00 1·10
3140 $5 Brown trembler . . . . 2·40 2·75
3141 $10 Red-footed booby . . 4·50 5·00
3142 $20 Sooty tern . . . . . . 8·50 9·50
3142b 50c Design as T **365a** . . . 35 30

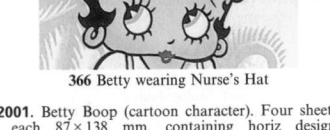

366 Betty wearing Nurse's Hat

2001. Betty Boop (cartoon character). Four sheets, each 87×138 mm, containing horiz designs as T **366**. Multicoloured.

MS3143 (a) $5 Type **366**. (b) $5 Betty as film star. (c) $5 Betty in front of foliage. (d) $5 Betty in front of roses. Set of 4 sheets 9·50 10·00

367 Larry, Moe and Curly in Overalls

2001. Scenes from *The Three Stooges* (American T.V. comedy series). Multicoloured.

3144 $1 Type **367** 60 65
3145 $1 Larry, Moe and Curly with woman in floral dress 60 65
3146 $1 Larry, Moe and Curly under table 60 65
3147 $1 Larry, Moe and Curly attacking singer in red dress 60 65
3148 $1 Larry, Moe and Curly with pony in cot 60 65
3149 $1 Larry in naval uniform, being arrested 60 65
3150 $1 Larry in evening dress (face value at top left) . . 60 65
3151 $1 Curly in green shirt . . . 60 65
3152 $1 Moe in evening dress (face value at top right) 60 65

MS3153 Two sheets. (a) 126×95 mm. $5 Larry with pony in cot. (b) 95×126 mm. $5 Moe and Larry in radio studio Set of 2 sheets . . . . 6·00 6·50

368 Queen Elizabeth II

369 United States Team, Brazil, 1950

2001. Golden Jubilee.

3154 $1 multicoloured 75 75

No. 3154 was printed in sheetlets of 8, containing two vertical rows of four, separated by a large illustrated central gutter. Both the stamp and the illustration on the central gutter are made up of a collage of miniature flower photographs.

2001. World Cup Football Championship, Japan and Korea (2002). Multicoloured.

3155 $2 Type **369** . . . . 1·10 1·25
3156 $2 Publicity poster, Switzerland, 1954 . . . . 1·10 1·25
3157 $2 Publicity poster, Sweden, 1958 . . . . 1·10 1·25
3158 $2 Zozimo (Brazil), Chile, 1962 . . . . 1·10 1·25
3159 $2 Gordon Banks (England), England, 1966 1·10 1·25
3160 $2 Pele (Brazil), Mexico, 1970 . . . . 1·10 1·25
3161 $2 Daniel Passarella (Argentina), Argentina, 1978 . . . . 1·10 1·25
3162 $2 Paolo Rossi (Italy), Spain, 1982 . . . . . . 1·10 1·25
3163 $2 Diego Maradona (Argentina), Mexico, 1986 1·10 1·25
3164 $2 Publicity poster, Italy, 1990 . . . . 1·10 1·25
3165 $2 Seo Jungulon (South Korea), U.S.A., 1994 . . 1·10 1·25
3166 $2 Jürgen Klinsmann (Germany), France, 1998 1·10 1·25

MS3167 Two sheets, each 88×75 mm. (a) $5 Detail of Jules Rimet Trophy, Uruguay, 1930. (b) $5 Detail of World Cup Trophy, Japan/Korea, 2002 Set of 2 sheets 6·00 6·50

370 "Madonna and Child" (Giovanni Bellini)

2001. Christmas. Paintings by Giovanni Bellini. Multicoloured.

3168 25c. Type **370** 25 15
3169 65c. "Madonna with Child" 45 30
3170 90c. "Baptism of Christ" . . 65 40
3171 $1.20 "Madonna with Child" (different) 80 85
3172 $4 "Madonna with Child" (different) . . . . 2·25 2·50

MS3173 136×76 mm. $6 "Madonna with Child and Sts. Catherine and Mary Magdalene" . . . . . . 3·75 4·00

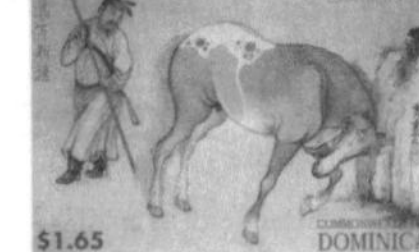

371 Horse and Groom

2001. Chinese New Year ("Year of the Horse"). Paintings by Lum Mei. Multicoloured.

3174 $1.65 Type **371** 85 90
3175 $1.65 Two horses grazing 85 90
3176 $1.65 Groom with sick horse 85 90
3177 $1.65 Two horses galloping 85 90

2002. Golden Jubilee (2nd issue). As T **507** of Grenada. Multicoloured.

3178 $2 Queen Elizabeth in blue hat and coat . . . . . . 1·25 1·25
3179 $2 Queen Elizabeth presenting Prince Philip with polo trophy . . . . 1·25 1·25
3180 $2 Queen Elizabeth in evening dress . . . . . . 1·25 1·25
3181 $2 Queen Elizabeth in pink hat and coat . . . . . . 1·25 1·25

MS3182 76×108 mm. $6 Princess Elizabeth and Duke of Edinburgh, 1948. . . . . 4·00 4·25

2002. "United We Stand". Support for Victims of 11 September 2001 Terrorist Attacks. As T **506** of Grenada.

3183 $2 U.S. Flag as Statue of Liberty and Dominica flag 1·25 1·40

2002. Shirley Temple in *Just Around the Corner*. As T **519** of Grenada showing film scenes. Mult.

3184 $1.90 With maid and dogs (horiz) . . . . 1·00 1·10
3185 $1.90 Penny (Shirley Temple) with father and Lola (horiz) . . . . . . 1·00 1·10
3186 $1.90 With father in study (horiz) . . . . 1·00 1·10
3187 $1.90 Carving turkey (horiz) 1·00 1·10
3188 $1.90 Talking to S. G. Henshaw (horiz) . . . . 1·00 1·10
3189 $1.90 Collecting money from crowd (horiz) . . . . . 1·00 1·10
3190 $2 Frowning at boy . . . . 1·10 1·25
3191 $2 Pretending to shoot with Gus the chauffeur . . . . 1·10 1·25
3192 $2 Penny wearing apron and talking to father . . . . 1·10 1·25
3193 $2 Cutting boy's hair . . . 1·10 1·25

MS3194 106×75 mm. $6 Dancing in the rain . . . . 3·50 3·75

372 "Courtesan Tsukioka" (Ichirakutei Eisui)

2002. Japanese Art. Multicoloured.

3195 $1.20 Type **372** 65 70
3196 $1.20 "Woman and Servant in the Snow" (Eishosai Choki) 65 70
3197 $1.20 "Courtesan Shiratsuyu" (Chokosai Eisho) 65 70
3198 $1.20 "Ohisa of the Takashima-Ya" (Utagawa Toyokuni) 65 70
3199 $1.20 "Woman and Cat" (Utagawa Kunimasa) . . 65 70
3200 $1.20 "Genre Scenes of Beauties" (detail) (Keisai Eisen) 65 70
3201 $1.65 "Women inside and outside a Mosquito Net" (Suzuki Harushige) . . . 85 90
3202 $1.65 "Komachi at Shimizu" (Suzuki Harushige) 85 90
3203 $1.65 "Women viewing Plum Blossoms" (Suzuki Harunobu) 85 90
3204 $1.65 "Women cooling themselves at Shijogawara in Kyoto" (Utagawa Toyohiro) 85 90
3205 $1.65 "Women reading a Letter" (Kitagawa Utamaro) 85 90
3206 $1.65 "Women dressed for Kashima Dance at Niwaka Festival" (Kitagawa UTamaro) . . 85 90
3207 $1.90 "Iwai Kiyotaro" (Kunimasa) . . . . 95 1·00
3208 $1.90 "Otani Hiriji III and Arashi Ryuzo" (Toshusai Sharaku) . . . . 95 1·00
3209 $1.90 "Ichikawa Komazo II" (Katsukawa Shunko) 95 1·00
3210 $1.90 "Ichikawa Yaozo III and Sakata Hangoro III" (Sharaku) . . . . 95 1·00
3211 $1.90 "Tanimura Torazo" (Sharaku) . . . . 95 1·00
3212 $1.90 "Iwai Kiyotaro as Oishi" (Toyokuni) . . . . 95 1·00

MS3213 Three sheets. (a) 85×125 mm. $5 "Iwai Hanshiro IV and Sawamura Sojuro III" (Torii Kyonaga) (horiz). (b) 85×110 mm. $5 "Actor Nakamura Riko" (Katsukawa Shunsho). (c) $6 "Daughter of the Motoyanagi-Ya" (Suzuki Harunobu) . . . . 8·50 9·00

372a Mount Everest

2002. International Year of Mountains. Multicoloured.

3214 $2 Type **372a** . . . . . . 1·25 1·25
3215 $2 Mount Kilimanjaro . . . 1·25 1·25
3216 $2 Mount McKinley . . . . 1·25 1·25

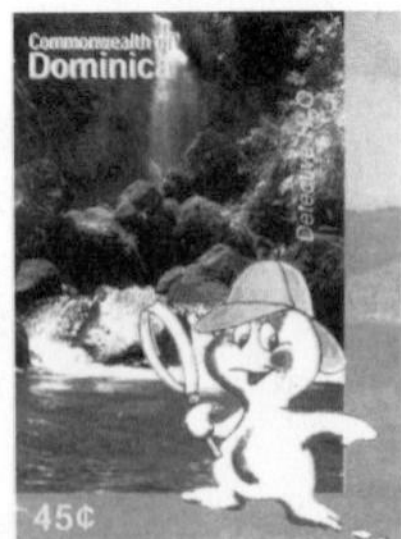

373 Waterfall and "Detective H2O"

2002. U.N. Year of Ecotourism. Each including a member of the Eco Squad (cartoon characters). Multicoloured.

3217 45c. Type **373** 30 25
3218 50c. Waterfall and "Factman" 35 25
3219 55c. River and "B.B." . . . 35 25
3220 60c. Sea cliffs and "Stanley the Starfish" 35 30
3221 90c. River and "Toxi" . . . 50 50
3222 $1.20 Forest and "Adopt" 65 70

MS3223 117× 96 mm. $6 Park and "Litterbit" . . . . 3·75 4·00

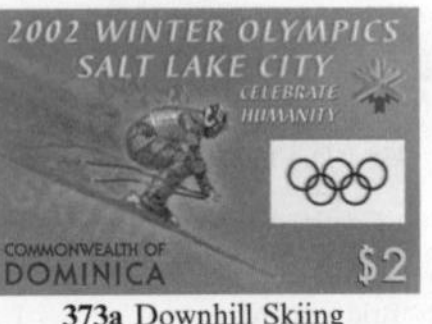

373a Downhill Skiing

2002. Winter Olympic Games, Salt Lake City. As T **482**. Multicoloured.

3224 $2 Type **373a** . . . . 1·25 1·40
3225 $2 Two man bobsleigh . . . 1·25 1·40

MS3226 84×114 mm. Nos. 3218/19 2·50 2·75

374 Colonel Baden-Powell in Military Uniform

374a *Charles Lindbergh and The Spirit of St. Louis* (aircraft)

2002. 20th World Scout Jamboree, Thailand. Mult.

3227 $3 Type **374** . . . . 1·60 1·75
3228 $3 Agnes Baden-Powell (founder of Girl Guides) 1·60 1·75
3229 $3 Maceo Johnson . . . . 1·60 1·75

MS3230 80×99 mm. $6 Lord Baden-Powell in Scout uniform 3·75 4·00

2002. 75th Anniv of First Solo Transatlantic Flight. Multicoloured.

3231 $3 . . . . 1·60 1·75
3232 $3 Charles and Anne Lindbergh in flying kit . . 1·60 1·75

MS3233 117×83 mm. $6 Charles Lindbergh and the *Spirit of St. Louis* . . . . 3·75 4·00

375 Olive Oyl in Rowing Boat

2002. "Popeye " (cartoon character) in New York. Multicoloured.

3234 $1 Type **375** 60 65
3235 $1 Brutus with oar 60 65
3236 $1 Sweet Pea 60 65
3237 $1 Wimpy 60 65
3238 $1 Jeep 60 65
3239 $1 Popeye with telescope . . 60 65
3240 $1.90 Popeye and Olive Oyl at Bronx Zoo . . . . . . 95 1·00
3241 $1.90 Popeye and Olive Oyl on ferry passing Statue of Liberty . . . . 95 1·00
3242 $1.90 Popeye and Olive Oyl by Empire State Building 95 1·00
3243 $1.90 Popeye skating at Rockefeller Centre . . . 95 1·00
3244 $1.90 Popeye pitching at baseball game . . . . . 95 1·00
3245 $1.90 Popeye holding hose 95 1·00

MS3246 Two sheets, each 83×114 mm. (a) $6 Popeye and Olive Oyl dancing (horiz). (b) $6 Popeye flexing muscles . . . . 6·50 7·00

No. 3243 is inscribed "ROCKERFELLER" in error

376 Brown Trembler

377 Willem Einthoven (Medicine, 1924)

2002. Fauna. Multicoloured designs.

3247 $1.50 Type **376** 80 85
3248 $1.50 Snowy cotinga 80 85
3249 $1.50 Bananaquit 80 85
3250 $1.50 Painted bunting . . . 80 85
3251 $1.50 Belted kingfisher . . . 80 85
3252 $1.50 Ruby-throated hummingbird 80 85
3253 $1.50 Field cricket 80 85

3254 $1.50 Migratory grasshopper 80 85
3255 $1.50 Honey bee 80 85
3256 $1.50 Hercules beetle . . . 80 85
3257 $1.50 Black ant 80 85
3258 $1.50 Cicada 80 85
3259 $1.50 Carolina sphinx . . . 80 85
3260 $1.50 White-lined sphinx . . 80 85
3261 $1.50 Orizaba silkmoth . . 80 85
3262 $1.50 Hieroglyphic moth . . 80 85
3263 $1.50 Hickory tussock moth 80 85
3264 $1.50 Diva moth 80 85
3265 $1.50 Sei whale 80 85
3266 $1.50 Killer whale 80 85
3267 $1.50 Blue whale 80 85
3268 $1.50 White whale 80 85
3269 $1.50 Pygmy whale 80 85
3270 $1.50 Sperm whale 80 85
MS3271 Four sheets, each 100 × 70 mm. (a) $6 Yellow-bellied sapsucker (horiz). (b) $6 Bumble bee (horiz). (c) $6 Ornate moth (horiz). (d) $6 Grey whale (horiz) 12·00 13·00

Nos. 3241/6 (birds), 3247/52 (insects), 3253/8 (moths) and 3259/64 (whales) were each printed together, se-tenant, with the backgrounds forming composite designs.

Nos. 3248 and 3259 are inscribed “Ctinga” or “Carilina”, both in error.

2002. “Amphilex ‘02”, International Stamp Exhibition, Amsterdam. (a) Dutch Nobel Prize Winners.
3272 **377** $1.50 black and green . . 80 85
3273 – $1.50 black and orange 80 85
3274 – $1.50 black and violet 80 85
3275 – $1.50 black and salmon 80 85
3276 – $1.50 black and sepia . . 80 85
3277 – $1.50 black and green . . 80 85

DESIGNS: No. 3273, Economics Prize medal; 3274, Peter Debye (Chemistry, 1935); 3275, Frits Zernike (Physics, 1953); 3276, Jan Tinbergen (Economics, 1969); 3277, Simon van de Meer (Physics, 1984).

(b) Dutch Lighthouses. Multicoloured.
3278 $1.50 Marken lighthouse . . 90 90
3279 $1.50 Harlingen lighthouse 90 90
3280 $1.50 Den Oever lighthouse 90 90
3281 $1.50 De Ven lighthouse . . 90 90
3282 $1.50 Urk lighthouse . . . 90 90
3283 $1.50 Oosterleek lighthouse 90 90

(c) Dutch Women’s Traditional Costumes. Multicoloured. Each 37 × 51 mm.
3284 $3 Lace cap from Zuid Holland . . . .
3285 $3 Winged headdress from Zeeland . . . . 1·75 1·75
3286 $3 Scarf and shawl from Limburg . . . . 1·75 1·75

377a Elvis Presley

2002. 25th Death Anniv of Elvis Presley (American entertainer).
3287 **377a** $1.50 black . . . . . . 1·00 1·00

378 Compass

2002. 550th Birth Anniv of Amerigo Vespucci (explorer). Multicoloured.
3288 $3 Type **378** . . . . 1·75 1·75
3289 $3 Studying chart . . . . . 1·75 1·75
3290 $3 Rolled chart . . . . . . 1·75 1·75
MS3291 98 × 78 mm. $5 Amerigo Vespucci and Spanish soldier (30 × 42mm) . . . . 2·50 2·75

379 Princess Diana

380 John F. Kennedy in Navy Uniform

2002. 5th Death Anniv of Diana, Princess of Wales. Multicoloured.
3292 $1.90 Type **379** . . . . . . 1·00 1·10
3293 $1.90 Princess Diana carrying rose spray . . . 1·00 1·10
3294 $1.90 Wearing white yoked dress . . . . 1·00 1·10
3295 $1.90 In lace top . . . . . 1·00 1·10
MS3296 98 × 66 mm. $5 Princess Diana wearing tiara fur coat 2·50 2·75

2002. Presidents John F. Kennedy and Ronald Reagan Commemoration. Multocoloured.
3297 $1.90 Type **380** . . . . . . 90 1·00
3298 $1.90 Wearing brown suit (face value in red) . . . . 90 1·00
3299 $1.90 Wearing brown suit (face value in blue) . . . 90 1·00
3300 $1.90 In fawn suit . . . . . 90 1·00
3301 $1.90 John F. Kennedy smiling . . . . 90 1·00
3302 $1.90 John F. Kennedy frowning . . . . 90 1·00
3303 $1.90 Looking up . . . . . 90 1·00
3304 $1.90 With hand on chin . . 90 1·00
3305 $1.90 Ronald Reagan in film role as deputy marshal . . 90 1·00
3306 $1.90 Wearing green T-shirt 90 1·00
3307 $1.90 In red pullover . . . 90 1·00
3308 $1.90 Wearing blue T-shirt 90 1·00
3309 $1.90 Nancy and Ronald Reagan (wearing blue shirt) (horiz) . . . . . . 90 1·00
3310 $1.90 Nancy Reagan (horiz) 90 1·00
3311 $1.90 Ronald Reagan (horiz) . . . . 90 1·00
3312 $1.90 Nancy and Ronald Reagan (wearing pink shirt) (horiz) . . . . . . 90 1·00

381 Rams

2003. Chinese New Year (“Year of the Ram”).
3313 **381** $1.65 multicoloured . . 85 90

382 Confucius (Chinese philosopher)

2003. Science Fiction. Six sheets, each 145 × 100 mm, containing T **382** and similar vert designs. Multicoloured.
MS3314 Six sheets. (a) $6 Type **382**. (b) $6 Nazca Lines, Peru. (c) $6 Atlas carrying Globe. (d) $6 Zoroaster. (e) $6 Mayan calendar. (f) $6 Presidents Franklin D. Roosevelt and John F. Kennedy (both deaths predicted by Edgar Casey) . . . . 16·00 18·00

No. **MS**3314(e) is inscribed “Calender” in error.

383 Elizabeth “Ma Pampo” Israel

384 Queen Elizabeth II in Pale Grey Dress

2003. 128th Birthday of Elizabeth “Ma Pampo” Israel (world’s oldest person).
3315 **383** 90c. multicoloured . . . 70 55

2003. 50th Anniv of Coronation. Multicoloured.
MS3316 155 × 93 mm. $3 Type **384**; $3 Queen in Garter robes; $3 Queen wearing tiara . . . . . 4·00 4·00
MS3317 75 × 105 mm. $6 Queen wearing tiara . . . . 4·00 4·25

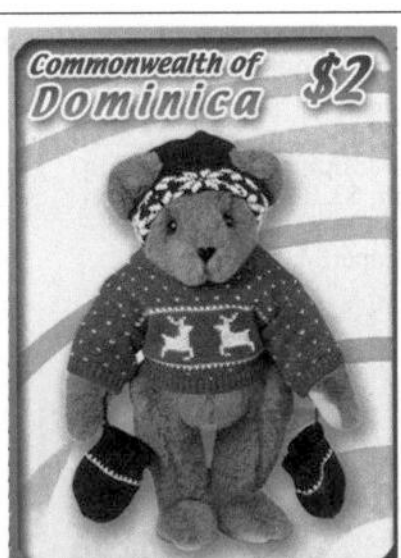

384a Teddy Bear wearing Black T–shirt and Blue Jeans

2003. Centenary of the Teddy Bear. Multicoloured.
MS3318 90 × 166 mm. $1.65 Type **384a**; $1.65 Wearing conical party hat and carrying streamers; $1.65 Carrying party blower; $1.65 Wearing black bowler hat, t-shirt and jeans; $1.65 Wearing mauve bowler hat, black t-shirt and green jeans; $1.65 Holding birthday cake (all 27 × 41 mm) . . . . 5·50 6·00
MS3319 165 × 127 mm. $2 × 2 Teddy bear wearing jumper, hat and mittens; $2 × 2 Father Christmas teddy bear . . . . 4·25 4·50

385 Bobby Moore

385a Prince William wearing Blue– collared Shirt

2003. World Cup Football Championship, Japan and Korea (2002). Multicoloured.
MS3320 165 × 84 mm. $1.45 Type **385**; $1.45 Roger Hunt; $1.45 Gordon Banks; $1.45 Bobby Charlton; $1.45 Alan Ball; $1.45 Geoff Hurst . . . . 3·75 4·00
MS3321 165 × 84 mm. $1.45 Danny Mills; $1.45 Paul Scholes; $1.45 Darius Vassell; $1.45 Michael Owen; $1.45 Emile Heskey; $1.45 Rio Ferdinand . . . . 3·75 4·00
MS3322 Five sheets, each 84 × 84 mm. (a) $3 Ashley Cole; $3 David Seaman. (b) $3 Franz Beckenbauer; $3 Oliver Kahn. (c) $3 Charlton, Ball, Hunt; $3 Nobby Stiles. (d) $3 Sven-Goran Eriksson; $3 Nikki Butt. (e) $3 Robbie Fowler; $3 Sol Campbell Set of 5 sheets . . . . 14·00 15·00

2003. 21st Birthday of Prince William of Wales. As T **509** of Antigua. Multicoloured.
MS3323 148 × 78 mm. $3 Type **385a**; $3 Wearing blue jacket and tie; $3 Playing polo . . . . 5·00 5·50
MS3324 68 × 98 mm. $6 In school uniform . . . . 3·75 4·00

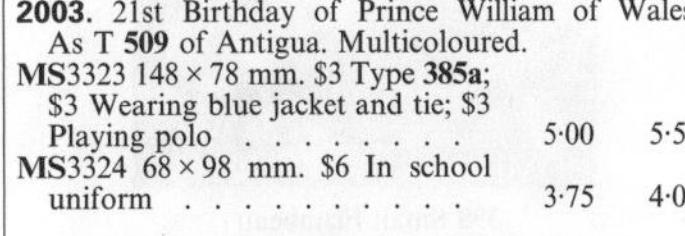

386 Model A Runabout (1903)

2003. Centenary of General Motors Cadillac. Multicoloured.
MS3325 120 × 170 mm. $2 Type **386**; $2 Model 30 (1912); $2 Type 57 Victoria Coupe (1918); $2 Lasalle Convertible Coupe (1927) . . . 4·25 4·50
MS3326 120 × 84 mm. $5 355-C V8 Sedan (1933) . . . . 2·50 2·75

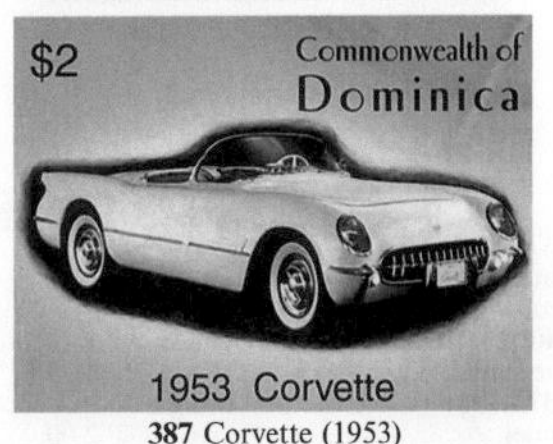

387 Corvette (1953)

2003. Centenary of General Motors Chevrolet Corvette. Multicoloured..
MS3327 120 × 170 mm. $2 Type **387**; $2 Corvette (1956); $2 Corvette (1957); $2 Corvette (1962) . . 4·25 4·50
MS3328 120 × 84 mm. $5 Corvette (1959) . . . . 2·50 2·75

388 “Sputnik I” (first orbiting satellite, 1957)

2003. Centenary of Powered Flight. Multicoloured.
MS3329 180 × 110 mm. $2 Type **388**; $2 Yuri Gagarin (first man in space, 1961); $2 Neil Armstrong (first man on the Moon, 1969); $2 “Skylab 1” (1973) . . . . . . 4·25 4·50
MS3330 104 × 74 mm. $6 Flight over Mount Everest (1933) . . . . 3·00 3·25

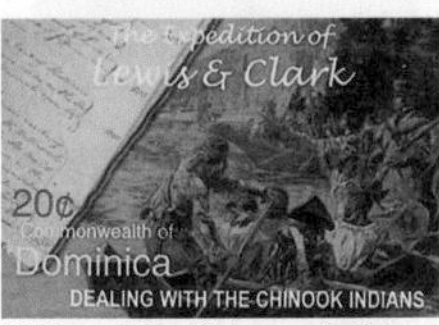

389 Expedition Canoe and Chinook Indians

2003. Bicentenary (2004) of Lewis and Clark’s Expedition to the American West and Pacific North West. Multicoloured.
3331 20c. Type **389** 25 20
3332 50c. Lewis and Clark and expedition compass . . . 40 25
3333 55c. Lewis and Clark with map and telescope 40 25
3334 65c. Medal presented to Indians (vert) 40 30
3335 90c. Expedition members and grizzly bear 55 50
3336 $1 Lewis and Clark with Sacagawea (Indian interpreter) 65 65
3337 $2 Captain Meriwether Lewis (vert) . . . . . . 1·25 1·40
3338 $4 Statue of Lewis and Clark (vert) . . . . . . 2·25 2·50
MS3339 Two sheets, each 80 × 115 mm. (a) $5 Captain Meriwether Lewis (vert). (b) $5 Lieutenant William Clark (vert) Set of 2 sheets . . . . 5·00 5·50

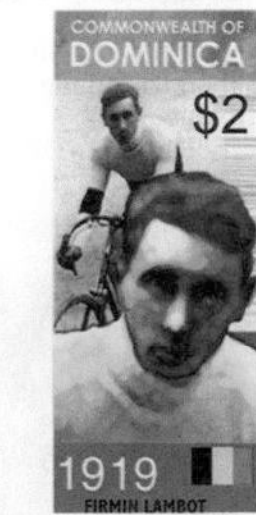

389a Firmin Lambot (1919)

2003. Centenary of Tour de France Cycle Race. Showing past winners. Multicoloured.
MS3340 160 × 100 mm. $2 Type **389a**; $2 Phillipe Thys (1920); $2 Leon Scieur (1921); $2 Firmin Lambot (1922) . . . . 4·50 4·50
MS3341 100 × 70 mm. $6 Francois Faber . . . . 3·25 3·50

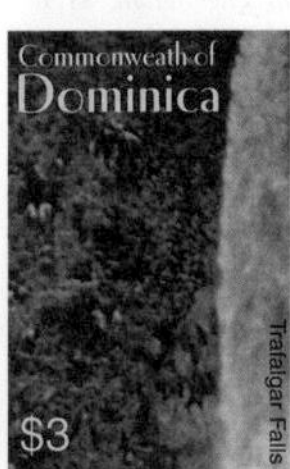

390 Trafalgar Falls, Dominica

2003. International Year of Freshwater. Multicoloured.
MS3342 96 × 146 mm. $3 Type **390**; $3 YS Falls, Jamaica; $3 Dunn’s River, Jamaica . . . . 4·25 4·50
MS3343 70 × 100 mm. $6 Annandale Falls, Grenada . . . . 3·25 3·50

391 Imperial Parrot and Emblem

2003. 30th Anniv of CARICOM.
3344 **391** $1 multicoloured 40 45

392 "Madonna and Child with the Young St. John" (detail) (Correggio)

2003. Christmas. Multicoloured.
3345 50c. Type **392** 20 25
3346 90c. "Madonna in Glory with the Christ Child and the Saints Frances and Alvise with the Donor" (detail) (Titian) 35 40
3347 $1.45 "Madonna and Child with Angels playing Musical Instruments" (detail) (Correggio) . . . 55 60
3348 $3 "Madonna of the Cherries" (detail) (Titian) 1·20 1·30
MS3349 75 × 97 mm. $6 "Holy Family with St. John the Baptist" (Andrea del Sarto) . . . . . . 1·20 1·30
No. **MS**3349 also commemorates the 300th anniversary of St. Petersburg.

393 Small Orange Marmoset

2004. Chinese New Year ("Year of the Monkey"). Sheet 143 × 116 mm containing T **393** and similar horiz designs. Multicoloured.
MS3350 $1.50 Type **393**; $1.50 Monkey; $1.50 Baboon drinking; $1.50 Baboon with blue face 2·40 2·50

394 *Epidendrum pseudepidendrum*

2004. Orchids. Multicoloured.
3351 25c. Type **394** 10 15
3352 55c. *Aspasia epidendroides* 20 25
3353 $1.50 *Cochleanthes discolor* 60 65
3354 $4 *Brassavola nodosa* . . . 1·60 1·70
MS3355 116 × 132 mm. $1.90 *Laelia anceps*; $1.90 *Caularthron bicornutum*; $1.90 *Cattleya velutina*; $1.90 *Cattleya warneri*; $1.90 *Oncidium splendidum*; $1.90 *Psychlis atropurpurea* . . . . . 4·50 4·60
MS3356 96 × 66 mm. $5 *Maxillaria cuculata* (vert) . . . . 2·00 2·10

395 Dwight D. Eisenhower

2004. 25th Death Anniv (2003) of Norman Rockwell (artist). Type **395** and similar vert designs. Multicoloured.
MS3357 160 × 186 mm. $2 Type **395**; $2 John F. Kennedy; $2 Lyndon B. Johnson; $2 Richard M. Nixon 3·25 3·50
MS3358 55 × 78 mm. $5 Abraham Lincoln. Imperf . . . . 2·00 2·10

396 "Portrait of Manuel Pallares , 1909"

2004. 30th Death Anniv (2003) of Pablo Picasso (artist). T **396** and similar multicoloured designs.
MS3359 171 × 142 mm. $1 Type **396**; $1 "Woman with Vase of Flowers, 1909"; $1 "Woman with a Fan (Fernande), 1908"; $1 "Portrait of Clovis Sagot, 1909" . . . . . 1·60 1·70
MS3360 95 × 74 mm. $5 "Brick Factory at Torosa (The Factory), 1909". Imperf . . . . 2·00 2·10

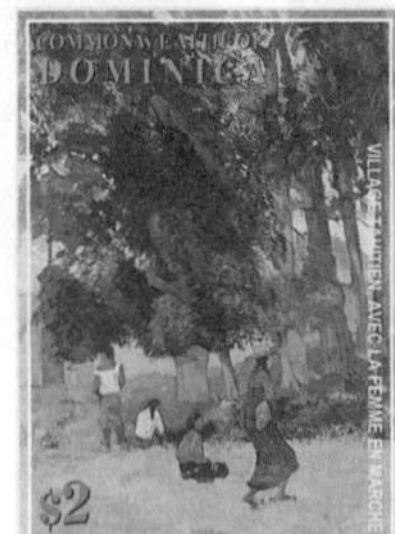

397 "Village Tahitien, Avec La Femme En Marche"

2004. Death Centenary of Paul Gauguin (artist). T **397** and similar vert designs. Multicoloured.
MS3361 165 × 116 mm. $2 Type **397**; $2 "La Barriere"; $2 "Bonjour, Monsieur Gauguin"; $2 "Vegetation Tropicale" . . . . 3·25 3·50
MS3362 60 × 78 mm. $5 "Petites Bretonnes Devant La Mer". Imperf . . . . 2·00 2·10

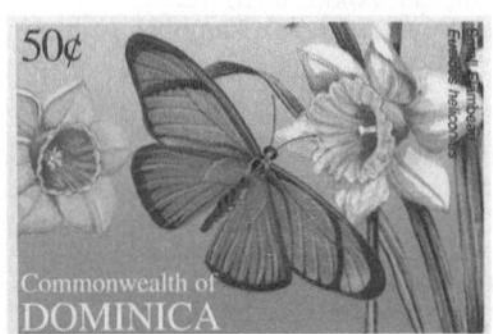

398 Small Flambeau

2004. Butterflies. Multicoloured.
3363 50c. Type **398** 20 25
3364 90c. Tiger pierid 35 40
3365 $1 White peacock 40 45
3366 $2 Cramer's mesene 80 85
MS3367 116 × 133 mm. $2 Figure-of-eight; $2 Orange theope; $2 Clorinde; $2 Grecian shoemaker; $2 Orange-barred sulphur; $2 Common Morpho . . . . . . 4·75 5·00
MS3368 66 × 96 mm. $5 Giant swallowtail (vert) . . . . . . 2·00 2·10

399 Banded Butterflyfish

2004. Tropical Fish. Multicoloured.
3369 20c. Type **399** 10 10
3370 25c. Queen angelfish 10 15
3371 55c. Porkfish 20 25
3372 $5 Redband parrotfish . . . 2·00 2·10
MS3373 116 × 133 mm. $2 Beaugregory; $2 Two porkfish; $2 Bicolor cherubfish; $2 Rock beauty; $2 Blackfin snapper; $2 Blue tang . . . . 4·75 5·00
MS3374 96 × 66 mm. $5 Indigo hamlet . . . . 2·00 2·10

400 "Symphony in White No. 3"

2004. Birth Bicentenary of James McNeill Whistler (artist). Multicoloured.
3375 50c. Type **400** 20 25
3376 $1 "The Artists Studio" (vert) 40 45
3377 $1.65 "The Thames in Ice" (vert) 65 70
3378 $2 "Arrangement in Black: Portrait of F.R. Leyland" (vert) 80 85
MS3379 168 × 122 mm. $2 "Arrangement in Brown and Black: Portrait of Miss Rosa Corder" (36 × 72 mm); $2 "Harmony in Red; Lamplight" (36 × 72 mm); $2 "Symphony in Flesh Color and Pink: Portrait of Mrs Frances Leyland" (36 × 72 mm); $2 "Arrangement in Yellow and Grey: Effie Deans" (36 × 72 mm) . . . . 3·25 3·50
MS3380 71 × 103 mm. $5 "Harmony in Grey and Green: Miss Cicely Alexander". Imperf . . . . . 2·00 2·10

401 *Siratus perelegans*

2004. Sea Shells. Multicoloured.
3381 20c. Type **401** 10 15
3382 90c. *Polystira albida* 35 40
3383 $1.45 *Cypraea cervus* . . . 55 60
3384 $2 *Strombus gallus* 80 85
MS3385 116 × 133 mm. $1.90*Strombus pugilis*; $1.90 *Cittarium pica*; $1.90 *Distorsio clathrata*; $1.90 *Melongeria morio*; $1.90 *Prunum labiata*; $1.90 *Chione paphia* . . . . 4·50 4·75
MS3386 96 × 66 mm. $5 *Strombus alatus* . . . . 2·00 2·10

402 E. Robinson (Amsterdam, 1928)

2004. Olympic Games, Athens. Multicoloured.
3387 20c. Type **402** 10 15
3388 25c. K. Takacs (London, 1948) 10 15
3389 55c. B. Beamon (Mexico, 1968) 20 25
3390 65c. M. Didrikson (Los Angeles, 1932) 25 30
3391 $1 V. Ritola (Paris, 1924) 40 45
3392 $1.65 A. Hajos (Guttman) (Athens, 1896) 65 70
3393 $2 P. Nurmi (Antwerp, 1920) 80 85
3394 $4 N. Nadi (Antwerp, 1920) 1·60 1·70

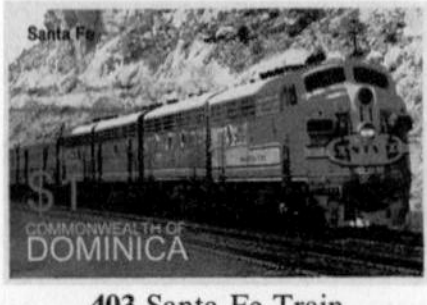

403 Santa Fe Train

2004. Bicentenary of Steam Trains. Multicoloured.
MS3395 Three sheets each 147 × 153 mm. (a) $1 Type **403**; $1 ViaRail Canada; $1 Conrail 6435; $1 Strasburg Rail Road 90; $1 Deltic diesel-electric engine; $1 *Brighton Belle*. (b) $1 Canadian Pacific freight train; $1 Queensland Rail IMU Railcar; $1 Shinkansen (green and white); $1 Amtrak; $1 Shinkansen (blue and white); $1 Passenger carriage. (c) $1 Three early steam engines; $1 Green locomotive; $1 Baldwin 2-D-D; $1 Southern Engine No. 20; $1 Electric locomotive; $1 Roaring Camp and Big Trees railroad Set of 3 sheets . . . . 7·00 7·25
MS3396 Three sheets each 98 × 68 mm. (a) $6 Shinkansen (blue, yellow and white). (b) $6 Southern Pacific steam locomotive. (c) $6 Golsdorf two-cylinder compound engine Set of 3 sheets . . . . 7·00 7·25

404 Eddie Hannath M.B.E. (7th Battalion, Hampshire Regiment)

2004. 60th Anniv of D-Day Landings.
3397 **404** $1 multicoloured 40 45
3398 – $4 multicoloured . . . . 1·60 1·70
MS3399 177 × 107 mm. $2 blue and black; $2 brown and black; $2 blue and black; $2 brown and black 3·25 3·25
MS4000 101 × 69 mm. $6 purple and black . . . . 2·40 2·50
DESIGNS: No. 3397 Type **403**; No. 3398 Franklin D. Roosevelt; No. **MS**3399 Rangers at the cliffs of Pointe du Hoc; Rangers climbing cliffs; British troops advancing towards Sword Beach; AVRE Petard tank on Sword Beach; No. **MS**4000 British troops on Sword Beach.

405 Marilyn Monroe

406 George Herman Ruth Jr.

2004. Marilyn Monroe Commemoration. Sheet 125 × 125 mm containing T **405** and similar vert designs. Each red and carmine.
MS4001 $2 Type **405**; $2 Wearing drop earrings and off the shoulder top; $2 Close up of face; $2 Wearing pearl necklace . . . . 3·25 3·50

2004. Centenary of Baseball World Series. Sheet 127 × 178 mm containing T **406** and similar vert designs showing George Herman Ruth Jr. ("Babe Ruth"). Multicoloured.
MS4022 $2 Type **406**; $2 Poised to hit ball; $2 Holding three bats; $2 With hands on hip and knee 3·25 3·50

407 Jode Luis Villalonga

2004. European Football Championship 2004, Portugal. Commemoration of Match between Spain and USSR (1964). Multicoloured designs as T **407**.
MS3403 148 × 86 mm. $2 Type **407**; $2 Lev Yashin; $2 Marcelino Martinez; $2 Santiago Bernabeu 2·40 2·50
MS3404 97 × 86 mm. $6 Spanish team, 1964 (51 × 38 mm) . . . 2·40 2·50

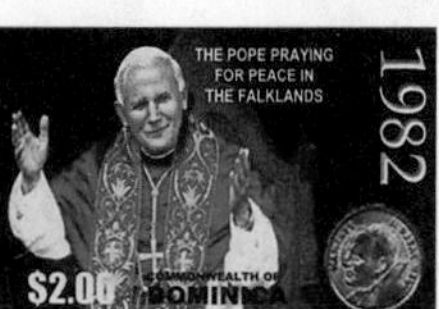

408 Pope Praying

2004. 25th Anniv of the Pontificate of Pope John Paul II. Sheet 166 × 154 mm containing horiz designs as T **408**. Multicoloured.
MS3405 $2 Type **408**; $2 Facing lines of people, Croatia; $2 With hands clasped; $2 With Franciscan monks; $2 Remembering the Holocaust . . . . 4·00 4·25

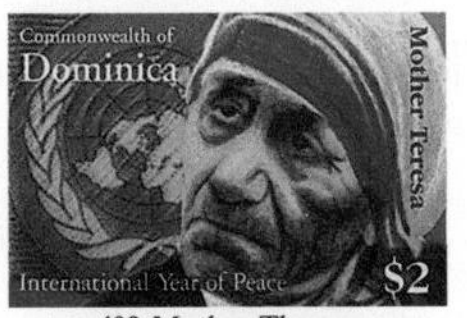

409 Mother Theresa

2004. United Nations International Year of Peace. Sheet 137 × 77 mm containing horiz designs as T **409**. Multicoloured.
MS3406 $2 Type **409**; $2 Mother Theresa with feeding utensils; $2 Peace dove carrying olive branch 2·40 2·50

410 Deng Xiaoping meeting with Chairman Mao

2004. Birth Centenary of Deng Xiaoping (Chinese politician). Sheet 96 × 67 mm.
MS3407 **410** $6 multicoloured . . 2·40 2·50

411 Princess Juliana, 1925

2004. Queen Juliana of the Netherlands Commemoration.
3408 **411** $2 multicoloured 80 85

412 Players

2004. National Football Team.
3409 **412** 90c. multicoloured . . . 35 40

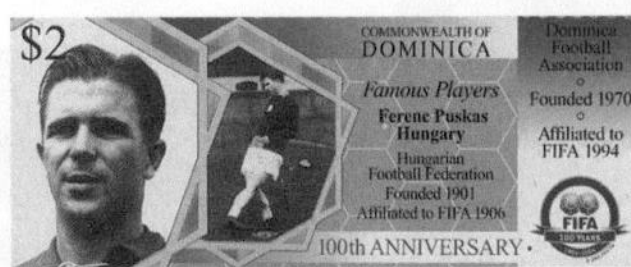

413 Ferenc Puskas

2004. Centenary of FIFA (Federation Internationale de Football Association). Multicoloured.
MS3410 192 × 97 mm. $2 Type **413**; $2 Rivaldo (Brazil); $2 Carsten Jancker (Germany); $2 Johan Cruyff (Holland) . . . . . . 3·25 3·50
MS3411 107 × 87 mm. $6 George Best (Ireland) . . . . 2·40 2·50

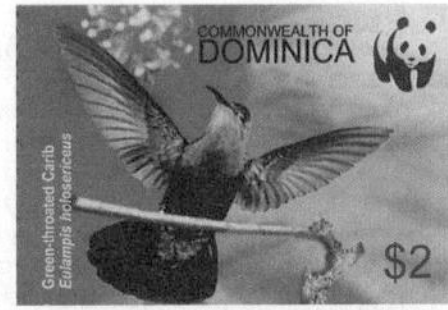

414 Green-throated Carib

2005. Endangered Species. Hummingbirds. Multicoloured.
3412 $2 Type **414** 80 85
3413 $2 Purple-throated carib on nest 80 85
3414 $2 Green-throated carib on nest 80 85
3415 $2 Purple-throated carib on branch 80 85
MS3416 205 × 130 mm. Nos. 3412/15, each × 2 . . . . 6·25 6·50

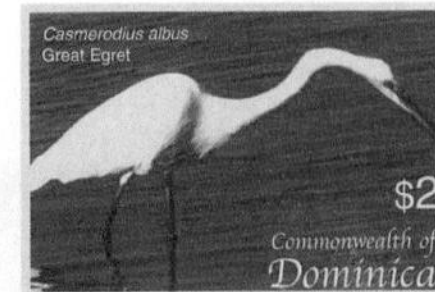

415 Great Egret

2005. Birds, Mushrooms and Flowers. Multicoloured.
3417 25c. Brown booby 10 15
3418 90c. Brown pelican 35 40
3419 $1 Red-billed tropic bird . . 40 45
3420 $4 Northern gannet . . . . 1·60 1·70
MS3421 135 × 105 mm. $2 Type **415**; $2 Black-necked grebe; $2 Turkey vulture; $2 Everglade kite ("Snail Kite") . . . . 3·25 3·40
MS3422 $2 *Cortinarius mucosus*; $2 *Cortinarius splendens*; $2 *Cortinarius rufo-olivaceus*; $2 *Inocybe erubescens* . . . . . . 3·25 3·50
MS3423 $2 Sweetshrub; $2 Pink turtleheads; $2 Flowering quince; $2 Water lily . . . .
MS3424 Three sheets. (a) 65 × 95 mm. $6 Red Knot. (b) 97 × 66 mm. $6 *Inocybe rimosa*. (c) 65 × 97 mm. $6 Glory-of-the-Snow (vert). Set of 3 sheets . . . . . 12·00 12·50

416 Mammuthus columbi

2005. Prehistoric Animals. Multicoloured.
MS3425 138 × 101 mm. $2 Type **416**; $2 Spinosaurus; $2 Ankylosaurus; $2 Mammuthus primigenius . . 3·25 3·50
MS3426 152 × 111 mm. $2 Pterodactylus; $2 Pteranodon; $2 Sordes; $2 Caudipteryx zoui . . 3·25 3·50
MS3427 138 × 101 mm. $2 Tyrannosaurus rex; $2 Velociraptor; $2 Stegosaurus; $2 Psittacosaurus . . . . 3·25 3·50
MS3428 Three sheets, each 100 × 70 mm. (a) $3 Compsongnathus. (b) $5 Archaeopteryx. (c) $6 Mammuthus primigenius. Set of 3 sheets . . . . 6·25 6·50

417 Rooster

2005. Chinese New Year ("Year of the Rooster"). Multicoloured.
MS3429 $1 Type **417** × 4 . . . . 1·60 1·70
MS3430 100 × 70 mm. $4 Three roosters (60 × 40 mm) . . . . 1·60 1·70

APPENDIX

The following stamps have either been issued in excess of postal needs, or have not been made available to the public in reasonable quantities at face value.

1978.

History of Aviation. $16 × 30, each embossed on gold foil.

DOMINICAN REPUBLIC Pt. 15

The Eastern portion of the island of Hispaniola in the W. Indies finally became independent of Spain in 1865.

1865. 8 reales = 1 peso.
1880. 100 centavos = 1 peso.
1883. 100 centimos = 1 franco.
1885. 100 centavos = 1 peso.

1

3

1865. Imperf.
1 **1** ½r. black on red £225 £200
3 ½r. black on green £350 £350
2 1r. black on green £600 £550
4 1r. black on yellow £1100 £950

1865. Imperf.
5 **3** ½r. black on buff £125 £100
7 ½r. black on red . . . . . . 40·00 40·00
12 ½r. black on grey £120 £120
18 ½r. black and blue on red . . 50·00 30·00
19 ½r. black on yellow . . . . . 25·00 25·00
20 1r. black on green . . . . . 50·00 50·00
9 1r. black on blue . . . . . . 35·00 35·00
15 1r. black on flesh £100 £100
21 1r. black on lilac £200 £200

4

5

15

1879. Perf.
22 **4** ½r. violet . . . . 1·50 1·50
24 1r. red . . . . 1·50 1·50

1880. Rouletted.
35 **5** 1c. green 60 60
36 2c. red 60 60
28 5c. blue 85 70
38 10c. pink 60 60
39 20c. bistre 70 70
40 25c. mauve . . . . 1·25 1·00
32 50c. orange . . . . 1·50 1·10
33 75c. blue . . . . 3·25 3·25
34 1p. gold . . . . 4·00 4·00

1883. Surch.
44 **5** 5c. on 1c. green . . . . . . 1·10 1·00
73 10c. on 2c. red . . . . 2·00 2·00
46 25c. on 5c. blue . . . . . . 4·00 3·50
47 50c. on 10c. pink . . . . . . 12·00 6·00
58 1f. on 20c. bistre . . . . . . 7·00 7·00
51 1f.25 on 25c. mauve . . . . 11·00 11·00
52 2f.50 on 50c. orange . . . . 14·00 14·00
53 3f.75 on 75c. blue . . . . . 16·00 16·00
64 5f. on 1p. gold . . . . 50·00 50·00

1885. Figures in lower corners only.
77 **15** 1c. green 30 15
78 2c. red 30 15
79 5c. blue 50 20
80 10c. orange 80 30
81 20c. brown 85 50
82 50c. violet . . . . 4·50 3·00
83 1p. red . . . . 10·00 10·00
84 2p. brown . . . . 12·00 10·00

1895. As T **15** but figures in four corners.
85 1c. green 60 30
86 2c. red 60 30
87 5c. blue 70 30
88 10c. orange 75 30

18 Voyage of Mendez from Jamaica to Santo Domingo

19 Sarcophagus of Columbus

1899. Columbus Mausoleum Fund.
98 **19** ½c. black . . . . 1·00 1·00
99 – ½c. black . . . . 1·00 1·00
89 **18** 1c. purple . . . . 4·50 3·50
90 1c. green . . . . 1·00 40
91 – 2c. red 50 50
92 **19** 5c. blue 75 55
93 – 10c. orange . . . . 2·00 1·00
94 – 20c. brown . . . . 4·00 4·00
95 – 50c. green . . . . 4·00 4·00
96 – 1p. black on blue . . . . . 12·00 10·00
97 – 2p. brown on cream . . . . 25·00 25·00
DESIGNS—AS TYPE **18**: ½c. (No. 99), 1p. Columbus at Salamanca Assembly; 2c. Enriquillo's Rebellion; 20c. Toscanelli replying to Columbus; 50c. Las Casas defending Indians. As Type **19**: 10c. Hispaniola guarding remains of Columbus; 2p. Columbus Mausoleum, Santo Domingo Cathedral.

20 Island of Hispaniola

21

1900.
100 **20** ¼c. blue 45 40
101 ½c. red 45 40
102 1c. olive 45 35
103 2c. green 45 35
104 5c. brown 45 35
105 10c. orange 35 35
106 20c. purple . . . . 1·50 1·50
107 50c. black . . . . 1·40 1·25
108 1p. brown . . . . 1·40 1·25

1901.
109 **21** ½c. lilac and red 25 25
110 1c. lilac and olive 35 20
111 2c. lilac and green 35 20
112 5c. lilac and brown 35 25
113 10c. lilac and orange . . . 75 30
114 20c. lilac and brown . . . 1·50 80
115 50c. lilac and black . . . . 4·50 2·50
116 1p. lilac and brown . . . . 9·50 7·00

24 Sanchez

25 Fortress of Santo Domingo

1902. 400th Anniv of Santo Domingo.
125 **24** 1c. black & green 25 25
126 2c. black & red (Duarte) 25 25
127 5c. blk & blue (Duarte) . . 25 25
128 10c. blk & orge (Sanchez) 25 25
129 12c. blk & violet (Mella) 25 25
130 20c. black & red (Mella) 25 25
131 **25** 50c. black and brown . . . 1·60 1·75

1904. Surch with new value.
132 **21** 2c. on 50c. lilac & black 5·50 4·25
133 2c. on 1p. lilac & brown 7·50 4·50
134 5c. on 50c. lilac & black 2·00 1·60
135 5c. on 1p. lilac and brown 3·00 2·40
136 10c. on 50c. lilac & black 4·75 4·00
137 10c. on 1p. lilac & brown 4·75 4·00

1904. Official stamps optd **16 de Agosto 1904** or surch **1 1** also.
138 O **23** 1c. on 20c. blk & yell . . 3·25 2·75
139 2c. black and red . . . 5·00 3·00
140 5c. black and blue . . . 3·00 2·25
141 10c. black and green . . 4·75 3·25

1904. Postage Due stamps optd **REPUBLICA DOMINICANA CENTAVOS CORREOS** or surch **1** also.
142 D **22** 1c. on 2c. sepia . . . . 1·75 85
143 1c. on 4c. sepia 70 50
145 2c. sepia 70 35

1905. Surch **1905** and new value.
146 **15** 2c. on 20c. brown . . . . 5·00 4·00
147 5c. on 20c. brown . . . . 2·25 1·40
148 10c. on 20c. brown . . . . 5·00 4·00

1905.
149 **21** ½c. orange and black . . . 1·00 55
150 1c. blue and black . . . . 1·25 50
151 2c. mauve and black . . . 1·25 40
152 5c. red and black . . . . 1·50 70
153 10c. green and black . . . 2·75 1·40
154 20c. olive and black . . . 8·50 4·75
155 50c. brown and black . . . 27·00 15·00
156 1p. grey and black £150 £150

1906. Postage Due stamps surch **REPUBLICA DOMINICANA.** and new value.
157 D **22** 1c. on 4c. sepia 70 40
158 1c. on 10c. sepia 85 40
159 2c. on 5c. sepia 85 40

1907.
168 **21** ½c. black and green 55 15
169 1c. black and red 55 15
170 2c. black and brown . . . 55 15
171 5c. black and blue 60 20
164 10c. black and purple . . . 85 35
165 20c. black and olive . . . 4·75 2·40
166 50c. black and brown . . . 4·75 4·00
167 1p. black and violet . . . 12·00 6·50

1911. No. O178 optd **HABILITADO. 1911.**
182 O **23** 2c. black and red . . . 1·00 50

34

35 Jaun Pablo Duarte

1911.
183 **34** ½c. black and orange . . . 25 15
184 1c. black and green 25 10

185 2c. black and red 25 10
186 5c. black and blue 50 15
187 10c. black and purple 1·00 40
188 20c. black and olive 5·50 3·25
189 50c. black and brown 2·40 2·00
190 1p. black and violet 4·00 2·40
For stamps in other colours see Nos. 235/8 and for stamps in similar type see No. 240/6.

1914. Birth Centenary of Duarte. Background in red, white and blue.
195 **35** ½c. black and orange 45 35
196 1c. black and green 45 35
197 2c. black and red 45 35
198 5c. black and grey 55 40
199 10c. black and mauve 85 50
200 20c. black and olive 2·00 1·40
201 50c. black and brown 2·75 2·40
202 1p. black and lilac 4·00 3·00

1915. Nos. O177/181 optd **Habilitado 1915** or surch **MEDIO CENTAVO** also.
203 O **23** ½c. on 20c. blk & yell 50 35
204 1c. black and green 70 25
205 2c. black and red 70 35
206 5c. black and blue 85 35
207 10c. black and green 2·00 1·60
208 20c. black and yellow 6·50 5·50

1915. Optd **1915**.
209 **34** ½c. black and mauve 55 15
210 1c. black and brown 55 10
211 2c. black and olive 2·00 25
213 5c. black and red 2·00 25
214 10c. black and blue 2·00 35
215 20c. black and red 5·50 1·25
216 50c. black and green 6·00 2·75
217 1p. black and orange 12·00 5·50

1916. Optd **1916**.
218 **34** ½c. black and mauve 70 10
219 1c. black and green 1·40 10

1917. Optd **1917**.
220 **34** ½c. black and mauve 1·00 25
221 1c. black and green 1·00 10
222 2c. black and olive 85 10
223 5c. black and red 7·50 70

1919. Optd **1919**.
224 **34** 2c. black and olive 4·00 10

1920. Optd **1920**.
225 **34** ½c. black and mauve 45 20
226 1c. black and green 45 10
227 2c. black and olive 45 10
228 5c. black and red 4·75 45
229 10c. black and blue 2·75 20
230 20c. black and red 4·75 45
231 50c. black and green 40·00 10·00

1921. Optd **1921**.
233 **34** 1c. black and green 1·25 25
234 2c. black and olive 2·40 30

1922.
235 **34** ½c. black and red 25 10
236 1c. green 70 10
237 2c. red 1·00 10
238 5c. blue 2·00 25

41 **43** Exhibition Pavilion

1924. Straight top to shield.
240 **41** 1c. green 40 10
241 2c. red 55 10
242 5c. blue 55 10
243 10c. black and blue 6·50 1·40
245 50c. black and green 35·00 2·00
246 1p. black and orange 12·00 8·50

1927. National and West Indian Exn, Santiago.
248 **43** 2c. red 70 45
249 5c. blue 85 45

45 Air Mail Routes

1928. Air.
256 **45** 10c. deep blue 5·75 3·00
280 10c. pale blue 1·90 75
271 10c. yellow 4·00 3·00
272 15c. red 7·75 4·00
281 15c. turquoise 4·00 1·10
273 20c. green 3·75 60
282 20c. brown 4·50 55
274 30c. violet 7·75 4·50
283 30c. brown 7·25 1·75

46 Ruins of Fortress of Columbus **47** Horacio Vasquez

1928.
258 **46** ½c. red 45 25
259 1c. green 40 10
260 2c. red 40 10
261 5c. blue 1·00 25
262 10c. blue 1·00 25
263 20c. red 1·50 40
264 50c. green 8·50 4·75
265 1p. yellow 15·00 10·00

1929. Frontier Agreement with Haiti.
266 **47** ½c. red 40 20
267 1c. green 40 15
268 2c. red 45 15
269 5c. blue 85 25
270 10c. blue 3·00 55

48 Jesuit Convent of San Ignacio de Loyola **49** After the Hurricane

1930.
275 **48** ½c. brown 50 40
276 1c. green 45 10
277 2c. red 45 10
278 5c. blue 1·25 35
279 10c. blue 2·40 85

1930. Hurricane Relief.
284 – 1c. green and red 15 35
285 – 2c. red 20 25
286 **49** 5c. blue and red 35 50
287 10c. yellow and red 40 70
DESIGN: 1c., 2c. Riverside.

1931. Air. Hurricane Relief. Surch with airplane, **HABILITADO PARA CORREO AEREO** and premium. Imperf or perf.
288 **49** 5c.+5c. blue and red 6·50 6·50
289 5c.+5c. black and red 15·00 15·00
290 10c.+10c. yellow & red 5·00 6·50
291 10c.+10c. black & red 15·00 15·00

52 Cathedral of Santo Domingo

1931.
294 **52** 1c. green 50 15
295 2c. red 50 15
296 3c. purple 55 10
297 7c. blue 1·40 20
298 8c. brown 2·40 70
299 10c. blue 3·00 85

53 Old Sun Dial, 1754

1931. Air.
300 **53** 10c. red 5·00 60
301 10c. blue 2·00 55
302 10c. green 8·00 2·75
303 15c. mauve 3·75 55
304 20c. blue 7·25 1·60
306 30c. green 3·25 40
307 50c. brown 8·00 80
308 1p. orange 13·00 2·75

54 Fort Ozama

1932.
309 **54** 1c. green 50 40
310 1c. green 25 10
311 3c. violet 35 10
No. 310 is inscribed "CORREOS".

1932. Red Cross stamps inscr "CRUZ ROJA DOMINICANA", with cross in red and optd **HABILITADO Dic. 20-1932 En. 5-1933 CORREOS** or surch also.
312 1c. green 20 15
313 3c. on 2c. violet 30 15
314 5c. blue 70 60
315 7c. on 10c. blue 1·10 85

56 F. A. de Merino **57** Cathedral of Santo Domingo

1933. Birth Centenary of F. A. de Merino.
316 – ½c. violet 25 15
317 **56** 1c. green 25 15
318 – 2c. red 70 55
319 **56** 3c. violet 35 15
320 – 5c. blue 45 20
321 – 7c. blue 90 35
322 – 8c. green 1·25 70
323 **56** 10c. orange 1·00 25
324 – 20c. red 2·25 1·40
325 **57** 50c. olive 9·00 5·50
326 1p. sepia 22·00 13·00
DESIGNS—VERT: ½c., 5c., 8c. Merino's Tomb; 2c., 7c., 20c. Merino in uniform.

1933. Portraits as T **56**.
327 1c. black and green 50 25
328 3c. black and violet 55 15
329 7c. black and blue 1·60 55
DESIGNS: 1c., 7c. Pres. Trujillo in uniform; 3c. Pres. Trujillo in evening dress.

1933. Air. Optd **CORREO AEREO INTERNO**.
330 **52** 2c. red 40 30

60 Fokker Super Universal over Fort Ozama

1933. Air.
331 **60** 10c. blue 3·50 50

61 San Rafael Suspension Bridge

1934.
332 **61** ½c. mauve 55 25
333 1c. green 80 15
334 3c. violet 1·25 10

62 Trujillo Bridge

1934. (a) Postage. As T **62** but without airplane and inscr "CORREOS".
335 – ½c. brown 50 15
336 – 1c. green 80 10
337 – 3c. violet 1·00 10

(b) Air.
338 **62** 10c. blue 3·25 50

64 National Palace

1935. For obligatory use on mail addressed to the President.
346 **64** 25c. orange 2·00 15

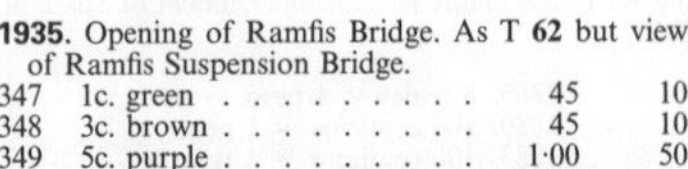

1935. Opening of Ramfis Bridge. As T **62** but view of Ramfis Suspension Bridge.
347 1c. green 45 10
348 3c. brown 45 10
349 5c. purple 1·00 50
350 10c. pink 2·00 1·00

66 Airplane and Carrier Pigeon

1935. Air.
351 **66** 10c. light blue and blue 2·50 45

67 President Trujillo

1935. Frontier Agreement.
352 **67** 3c. brown and yellow 30 15
353 – 5c. brown and orange 35 10
354 – 7c. brown and blue 55 10
355 – 10c. brown and purple 85 10
RECTANGULAR DESIGNS: Portrait as Type **67**. Red, white and blue ribbons in side panels on 7c. or diagonally across 5c. and 10c.

69 Post Office, Santiago de los Caballeros

1936.
356 **69** ½c. violet 30 20
357 1c. green 30 10

70

1936. Air.
358 **70** 10c. blue 2·75 45

71 George Washington Avenue, Ciudad Trujillo

1936. Dedication of George Washington Avenue.
359 **71** ½c. brown 35 25
360 2c. brown and red 60 20
361 3c. brown and yellow 60 15
362 7c. brown and blue 85 50

72 Gen. A. Duverge **74** "Flight"

1936. National Archives and Library Fund. Inscr "PRO ARCHIVO Y BIBLIOTECA NACIONALES".
363 – ½c. lilac 25 15
364 – 1c. green 20 10
365 – 2c. red 20 10
366 – 3c. violet 25 10
367 – 5c. blue 40 25
368 **72** 7c. blue 70 50
369 – 10c. orange 85 30
370 – 20c. olive 3·25 1·90
371 – 25c. purple 3·25 2·00
372 – 30c. red 5·00 2·75
373 – 50c. brown 6·00 2·75
374 – 1p. black 15·00 12·00
375 – 2p. brown 40·00 35·00
DESIGNS—As Type **72**: ½c. J. N. de Caceres; 1c. Gen. G. Luperon; 2c. E. Tejera; 3c. Pres. Trujillo; 5c. Jose Reyes; 10c. Felix M. Del Monte; 25c. F. J. Peynado; 30c. Salome Urena; 50c. Gen. Jose Ma. Cabral; 1p. Manuel Js. Galvan; 2p. Gaston F. Deligne. TRIANGULAR: 20c. National Library.

1936. Air.
376 **74** 10c. blue 2·10 35

75 Obelisk in Ciudad Trujillo

1937. 1st Anniv of Naming of Ciudad Trujillo (formerly Santo Domingo).
377 **75** 1c. green 20 10
378 3c. violet 40 10
379 7c. blue . . . . 1·25 60

76 Discus Thrower and National Flag

1937. 1st National Olympic Games, Ciudad Trujillo. Flag blue, white and red.
380 **76** 1c. green . . . . 6·50 70
381 3c. violet . . . . 8·50 50
382 7c. blue . . . . 15·00 2·75

77 "Peace, Labour and Progress"

1937. 8th Year of Trujillo Presidency.
383 **77** 3c. violet 35 10

78 San Pedro de Macoris Airport

1937. Air.
384 **78** 10c. green . . . . 1·25 10

79 Fleet of Columbus

1937. Air. Pan-American Goodwill Flight.
385 **79** 10c. red . . . . 3·75 1·25
386 A 15c. violet . . . . 1·75 70
387 B 20c. blue . . . . 1·75 70
388 A 25c. purple . . . . 2·50 85
389 B 30c. green . . . . 2·25 70
390 A 50c. brown . . . . 4·25 1·00
391 B 75c. olive . . . . 11·00 11·00
392 **79** 1p. red . . . . 12·00 2·75
DESIGNS—A, Junkers F-13 aircraft in Goodwill Flight; B, Junkers F-13 aircraft over Columbus Lighthouse.

83 Father Billini

1938. Birth Centenary of Father Billini.
396 **83** ½c. orange 15 10
397 5c. violet 45 15

1938. 150th Anniv of U.S. Constitution.
398 **84** 1c. green 30 10
399 3c. violet 45 10
400 10c. orange 85 20

85 Bastion, Trinitarian Oath and National Flag

1938. Centenary of Trinitarian Rebellion.
401 **85** 1c. green 40 20
402 3c. violet 50 15
403 10c. orange . . . . 1·00 45

86 Martin M-130 Flying Boat over Obelisk
87 Arms of University

1938. Air.
404 **86** 10c. green . . . . 1·40 15

1938. 400th Anniv of Santo Domingo University.
405 **87** ½c. orange 25 15
406 1c. green 35 10
407 3c. violet 40 10
408 7c. blue 85 40

89 N.Y. Fair Symbol, Lighthouse, Flag and Cornucopia

1939. New York World's Fair. (a) Postage. Flag in blue, white and red.
418 **89** ½c. orange 35 15
419 1c. green 40 15
420 3c. violet 40 15
421 10c. yellow . . . . 1·25 45

(b) Air. Flag, etc, replaced by airplane.
422 10c. green . . . . 1·50 55

90 Jose Trujillo Valdez
91

1939. 4th Death Anniv of Jose Trujillo Valdez. Black borders.
423 **90** ½c. grey 25 15
424 1c. green 35 10
425 3c. brown 40 10
426 7c. blue 85 50
427 10c. violet . . . . 1·50 40

1939. Air.
428 **91** 10c. green . . . . 1·40 20

92 Western Hemisphere and Union Flags
93 Sir Rowland Hill

1940. 50th Anniv of Pan-American Union. Flags in national colours.
429 **92** 1c. green 25 10
430 2c. red 35 15
431 3c. violet 55 10
432 10c. orange . . . . 1·10 20
433 1p. brown . . . . 15·00 10·00

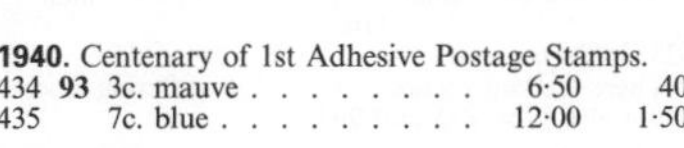
1940. Centenary of 1st Adhesive Postage Stamps.
434 **93** 3c. mauve . . . . 6·50 40
435 7c. blue . . . . 12·00 1·50

94 Julia Molina de Trujillo

1940. Mothers' Day.
436 **94** 1c. green 30 10
437 2c. red 40 10
438 3c. orange 50 10
439 7c. blue . . . . 1·25 45

95 Central America and Arms of Dominican Republic

1940. 2nd Caribbean Conference, Trujillo City.
440 **95** 3c. red 40 10
441 7c. blue 85 15
442 1p. green . . . . 8·50 4·25

96 Lighthouse, Aeroplane and Caravels

1940. Air. Discovery of America and Columbus Memorial Lighthouse. Inscr "PRO FARO DE COLON".
443 **96** 10c. blue . . . . 1·40 50
444 – 15c. brown 80 70
445 – 20c. red 80 70
446 – 25c. mauve 80 35
447 – 50c. green . . . . 4·00 1·60
DESIGNS: 15c. Columbus and lighthouse; 20c. Lighthouse; 25c. Columbus; 50c. Caravel and wings.

99 Marion Military Hospital
100 Post Office, San Cristobal

1940.
457 **99** ½c. brown 25 20

1941. Air.
458 **100** 10c. mauve 65 15

101 Trujillo Fortress

1941.
460 **101** 1c. green 15 10
461 – 2c. red 15 10
462 – 10c. brown 55 10
DESIGN—VERT: 2, 10c. Statue of Columbus, Ciudad Trujillo.

103 Sanchez, Duarte, Mella and Trujillo

1941. Trujillo-Hull Treaty.
463 **103** 3c. mauve 25 10
464 4c. red 30 10
465 13c. blue 70 20
466 15c. brown . . . . 2·00 85
467 17c. blue . . . . 2·00 90
468 1p. orange . . . . 7·50 3·25
469 2p. grey . . . . 15·00 7·50

104 Bastion of 27 February

1941.
470 **104** 5c. blue 55 20

105 Rural School, Torch of Knowledge and Pres. Trujillo

1941. Popular Education Campaign.
471 **105** ½c. brown 20 10
472 1c. green 25 10

106 Globe and Winged Envelope

1941. Air.
473 **106** 10c. brown 55 10
474 75c. orange . . . . 3·25 2·00

107 National Reserve Bank

1942.
475 **107** 5c. brown 40 10
476 17c. blue . . . . 1·00 40

108 Symbolic of Communications
109 Our Lady of Highest Grace

1942. 8th Anniv of Postal and Telegraph Services Day.
477 **108** 3c. multicoloured . . . . 4·00 1·00
478 15c. multicoloured . . . . 8·00 4·00

1942. 20th Anniv of Our Lady of Highest Grace.
479 **109** ½c. grey 85 10
480 1c. green . . . . 1·60 10
481 3c. mauve . . . . 7·50 10
482 5c. purple . . . . 2·40 10
483 10c. red . . . . 6·50 25
484 15c. blue . . . . 7·50 35

111 Banana Tree
112 Cows

1942.
494 **111** 3c. green and brown . . . 45 10
495 4c. black and red 50 20
496 **112** 5c. brown and blue . . . 45 10
497 15c. green and purple . . 85 35

113 Party Emblems and Votes

1943. Re-election of Gen. Trujillo to Presidency.
498 **113** 3c. orange 40 10
499 4c. red 50 15
500 13c. purple . . . . 1·10 20
501 1p. blue . . . . 5·00 1·90

114 Trujillo Market

1943.
502 **114** 2c. brown 15 10

115 Douglas DC-3

1943. Air.

503 **115** 10c. mauve 50 10
504 20c. blue 55 15
505 25c. olive . . . . 6·75 2·75

116 Bastion of 27 February

117 Monument and Dates

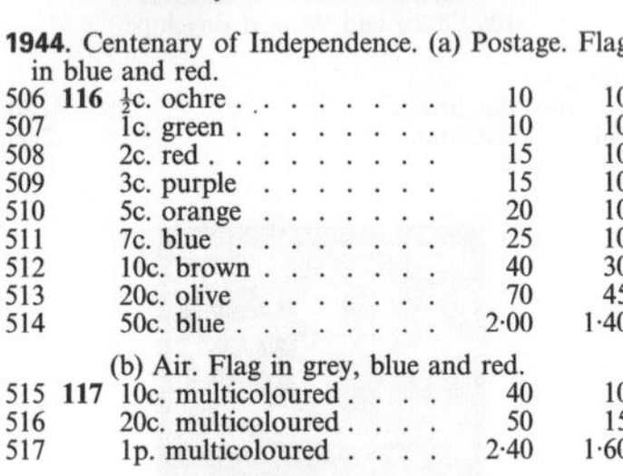

1944. Centenary of Independence. (a) Postage. Flag in blue and red.

506 **116** ½c. ochre 10 10
507 1c. green 10 10
508 2c. red 15 10
509 3c. purple 15 10
510 5c. orange 20 10
511 7c. blue 25 10
512 10c. brown 40 30
513 20c. olive 70 45
514 50c. blue . . . . 2·00 1·40

(b) Air. Flag in grey, blue and red.

515 **117** 10c. multicoloured 40 10
516 20c. multicoloured 50 15
517 1p. multicoloured . . . . 2·40 1·60

118 Dr. Martos Sanatorium

1944. Tuberculosis Relief Fund.

518 **118** 1c. blue and red 15 10

119 Nurse and Battlefield

1944. 80th Anniv of International Red Cross.

519 **119** 1c. green, red and yellow 15 10
520 2c. brown, red and yellow 35 10
521 3c. blue, red and yellow 35 10
522 10c. red and yellow . . . 70 15

120 Communications Building, Ciudad Trujillo

1944. Air.

523 **120** 9c. blue and green 25 10
524 13c. red and brown . . . 35 10
525 25c. red and orange . . . 50 10
526 30c. blue and black . . . 1·10 80

121 Municipal Building, San Cristobal

122 Emblem of Communications

1945. Centenary of 1st Constitution of Dominican Republic.

527 **121** ½c. blue 10 10
528 1c. green 10 10
529 2c. orange 10 10
530 3c. brown 15 10
531 10c. blue 45 15

1945. Centres in blue and red.

532 **122** 3c. orange (postage) . . . 15 10
533 20c. green 80 20
534 50c. blue . . . . 1·60 60
535 7c. green (air) 20 25
536 12c. orange 25 15
537 13c. blue 30 15
538 25c. brown 60 20

124 Flags and National Anthem

125 Law Courts, Ciudad Trujillo

1946. Air. National Anthem.

540 **124** 10c. red 45 40
541 15c. blue . . . . 1·00 70
542 20c. brown . . . . 1·25 70
543 35c. orange . . . . 1·40 70
544 – 1p. green . . . . 13·00 10·00

DESIGN: 1p. As Type **124**, but horiz.

1946.

545 **125** 3c. brown and buff . . . 20 10

126 Caribbean Air Routes

1946. 450th Anniv of Santo Domingo.

546 **126** 10c. mult (postage) . . . 40 15
547 10c. multicoloured (air) 35 15
548 13c. multicoloured 55 15

127 Jimenoa Waterfall

128 Nurse and Child

1947. Centres multicoloured, frame colours given.

549 **127** 1c. green (postage) . . . 15 10
550 2c. red 15 10
551 3c. blue 15 10
552 13c. purple 45 25
553 20c. brown . . . . 1·00 25
554 50c. yellow . . . . 1·90 1·00
555 18c. blue (air) 50 50
556 23c. red 70 55
557 50c. violet . . . . 1·00 45
558 75c. brown . . . . 1·40 1·00

1947. Obligatory Tax. Tuberculosis Relief Fund.

559 **128** 1c. blue and red 15 10

129 State Building, Ciudad Trujillo

1948.

560 **129** 1c. green (postage) . . . 10 10
561 3c. blue 15 10
562 37c. brown (air) . . . . . 1·00 70
563 1p. orange . . . . 2·75 1·60

130 Ruins of San Francisco Church, Ciudad Trujillo

131 El Santo Socorro Sanatorium

1949.

564 **130** 1c. green (postage) . . . 10 10
565 3c. blue 15 10
566 7c. olive (air) 15 10
567 10c. brown 15 10
568 15c. red 50 25
569 20c. green 70 45

1949. Tuberculosis Relief Fund.

570 **131** 1c. blue and red 15 10

132 General Pedro Santana

133 Monument

1949. Centenary of Battle of Las Carreras.

571 **132** 3c. blue (postage) 15 10
572 **133** 10c. red (air) 25 10

134 Bird and Globe

136 Hotel Jimani

135 Youth Holding Banner

138 Ruins of Church and Hospital of St. Nicholas of Bari

1949. 75th Anniv of U.P.U.

573 **134** 1c. brown and green . . . 15 10
574 2c. brown and yellow . . 15 10
575 5c. brown and blue . . . 20 10
576 7c. brown and blue . . . 45 15

1950. Tuberculosis Relief Fund.

584 **135** 1c. blue and red 20 10

1950. Various Hotels.

585 **136** ½c. brown (postage) . . . 10 10
586 – 1c. green (Hamaca) . . . 10 10
587 – 2c. orange (Hamaca) . . 10 10
588 – 5c. blue (Montana) . . . 20 10
589 – 15c. orge (San Cristobal) 45 10
590 – 20c. lilac (Maguana) . . . 85 15
591 **136** $1 yellow and brown . . 3·25 1·40
592 – 12c. bl (Montana) (air) . . 25 10
593 – 37c. red (San Cristobal) 1·90 1·50

1950. 13th Pan-American Sanitary Congress. Inscr as T **138**.

595 **138** 2c. brown & green (postage) 20 10
596 – 5c. brown and blue . . . 25 10
597 – 12c. orange & brn (air) 55 10

DESIGNS—VERT: 5c. Medical school; 12c. Map and aeroplane.

139 "Suffer Little Children to Come Unto Me"

148

148a

148b

1950. Child Welfare. (a) Child at left with light hair.

598 **139** 1c. blue 25 10

(b) Child at left with dark hair.

599 **139** 1c. blue 85 15

(c) Child at left with dark hair.

626 **148** 1c. blue 20 10

(d) Child at left with light hair.

627 **148a** 1c. blue 15 10

(e) Dark hair, smaller figures and square value tablet.

628 **148b** 1c. blue 15 10

There are two versions of No. 628, differing in size.
See also Nos. 835 and 907.

140 Isabella the Catholic

1951. 500th Birth Anniv of Isabella the Catholic.

600 **140** 5c. brown and blue . . . 25 10

141 Santiago Tuberculosis Sanatorium

1952. Tuberculosis Relief Fund.

601 **141** 1c. blue and red 15 10

142 Dr. S. B. Gautier Hospital

1952.

602 **142** 1c. green (postage) . . . 10 10
603 2c. red 15 10
604 5c. blue 25 10
605 23c. blue (air) 55 55
606 29c. red . . . . 1·40 1·00

143 Columbus Lighthouse and Flags

144

1953. 460th Anniv of Columbus's Discovery of Santo Domingo. (a) Postage.

607 **143** 2c. green 15 10
608 5c. blue 20 10
609 10c. red 35 20

(b) Air. Similar design inscr "S./S.A.S./XMY", etc.

610 12c. brown 35 15
611 14c. blue 35 20
612 20c. sepia 65 40
613 23c. purple 70 45
614 25c. blue 70 45
615 29c. green 90 45
616 1p. brown . . . . 3·25 2·00

DESIGN: Nos. 610/16, Douglas DC-6 airplane over Columbus Lighthouse.

1953. Anti-cancer Fund. No. 619 has "1 c" larger with line through "c" and no stop. No. 620 is as 619 but with smaller "c".

618 **144** 1c. red 20 10
619 1c. red 35 10
620 1c. red 15 10

See also Nos. 1029/30, 1066/7, 1171a, 1196a, 1237a, 1270a and 1338a.

145 T.B. Children's Dispensary

1953. Obligatory Tax. Tuberculosis Relief Fund.

621 **145** 1c. blue and red 15 10

There are two versions of this design.

146 Treasury

149 Jose Marti

150 Monument to Trujillo Peace

147 Rio Haina Sugar Factory

1953.

622 **146** ½c. brown 10 10
623 2c. blue 10 10
624 **147** 5c. brown and blue . . . 15 10
625 **146** 15c. orange 50 15

1953. Birth Cent of Marti (Cuban revolutionary).
629 **149** 10c. sepia and blue . . . 30 15

1954.

630 **150** 2c. green 10 10
631 7c. blue 15 10
632 20c. orange 55 10
There are two versions of No. 631.

151

152 Rotary Emblem

1954. Air. Marian Year.
633 **151** 8c. purple 15 10
634 11c. blue 25 10
635 33c. orange 70 45

1955. 50th Anniv of Rotary International.
636 **152** 7c. blue (postage) 30 10
637 11c. red (air) 25 15

153

154 Pres. R. Trujillo

1955. Obligatory Tax. Tuberculosis Relief Fund.
638 **153** 1c. black, red & yellow 15 10

1955. 25th Year of Trujillo Era.
639 **154** 2c. red (postage) 10 10
640 – 4c. green 15 10
641 – 7c. blue 15 10
642 – 10c. brown 35 15
643 – 11c. red, yell & bl (air) . . 30 10
644 – 25c. purple 45 25
645 – 33c. brown 70 40
DESIGNS: 4c. Pres. R. Trujillo in civilian clothes; 7c. Equestrian statue; 10c. Allegory of Prosperity; 11c. National flags; 25c. Gen. Hector B. Trujillo in evening clothes; 33c. Gen. Hector B. Trujillo in uniform.

156 Angelita Trujillo

1955. Child Welfare.
654 **156** 1c. violet 15 10

157 Angelita Trujillo

158 Gen. R. Trujillo

1955. Peace and Brotherhood Fair, Ciudad Trujillo.
656 **158** 7c. purple (postage) . . . 25 10
657 10c. green 35 15
655 **157** 10c. blue and ultramarine 35 15
658 **158** 11c. red (air) 25 10

159 "B.C.G." = "Bacillus" Calmette-Guerin

160 Punta Caucedo Airport

1956. Obligatory Tax. Tuberculosis Relief Fund.
659 **159** 1c. multicoloured 15 10

1956. 3rd Caribbean Region Aerial Navigation Conference.
660 **160** 1c. brown (postage) . . . 10 10
661 2c. orange 20 10
662 11c. blue (air) 35 10

161 Cedar Tree

162 Fanny Blankers-Koen and Dutch Flag

1956. Re-afforestation. Inscr "REPOBLACION FORESTAL".
664 **161** 5c. green, brown and red (postage) 20 10
665 – 6c. green and purple . . . 25 10
666 – 13c. green & orge (air) . . 35 10
DESIGNS: 6c. Pine tree; 13c. Mahogany tree.

1957. Olympic Games (1st issue). Famous Athletes. Flags in national colours.
667 **162** 1c. mult (postage) 10 10
668 – 2c. sepia, purple & blue 10 10
669 – 3c. purple and red 15 15
670 – 5c. orange, pur & blue . . 25 15
671 – 7c. green and purple . . . 35 25
673 – 11c. blue and red (air) . . 20 20
674 – 16c. red and green 30 30
675 – 17c. black and purple . . 40 40
DESIGNS—(each with national flag of athlete): 2c. Jesse Owens; 3c. Kee Chung Sohn; 5c. Lord Burghley; 7c. Bob Mathias; 11c. Paavo Nurmi; 16c. Ugo Frigerio; 17c. Mildred Didrickson.
See also Nos. 689/96, 713/21, 748/56 and 784/91.

163 Horse's Head and Globe

165

1957. 2nd Int Livestock Fair, Ciudad Trujillo.
677 **163** 7c. blue, brown & red . . 25 10

1957. Hungarian Refugees Fund. Nos. 667/75 surch with red cross in circle surrounded by **ASISTENCIA REFUGIADOS HUNGAROS 1957** and **+2c.**
678 **162** 1c.+2c. (postage) 10 10
679 – 2c.+2c. 10 10
680 – 3c.+2c. 10 10
681 – 5c.+2c. 15 15
682 – 7c.+2c. 25 25
684 – 11c.+2c. (air) 40 40
685 – 16c.+2c. 40 40
686 – 17c.+2c. . . . . 1·50 1·50

1957. Obligatory Tax. Tuberculosis Relief Fund.
688 **165** 1c. multicoloured 15 10

166 Chris Brasher and Union Jack (steeplechase)

1957. Olympic Games (2nd issue). Winning Athletes. Inscr "MELBOURNE 1956". Flags in national colours.
689 – 1c. brown & bl (postage) 10 10
690 – 2c. red and blue 10 10
691 – 3c. blue 10 10
692 – 5c. olive and blue 15 10
693 – 7c. red and blue 25 15
694 – 11c. green & blue (air) . . 20 20
695 **166** 16c. purple and blue . . . 25 25
696 – 17c. sepia and green . . . 30 30
DESIGNS—(each with national flag of athlete): 1c. Lars Hall (Sweden, pentathlon); 2c. Betty Cuthbert (Australia, 100 and 200 m); 3c. Egil Danielson (Norway, javelin-throwing); 5c. Alain Mimoum (France, marathon); 7c. Norman Read (New Zealand, 50 km walk); 11c. Robert Morrow (U.S.A.; 100 and 200 m); 17c. A. Ferreira da Silva (Brazil; hop, step and jump).

1957. 50th Anniv of Boy Scout Movement, and Birth Cent of Lord Baden-Powell. Nos 689/96 surch **CENTENARIO LORD BADEN-POWELL, 1857-1957 +2c.** surrounding Scout badge.
699 1c.+2c. brn & bl (postage) . . 15 15
700 2c.+2c. red and blue 20 15
701 3c.+2c. blue 25 25
702 5c.+2c. olive and blue . . . 35 25
703 7c.+2c. red and blue 40 30
704 11c.+2c. grn & blue (air) . . 40 35
705 16c.+2c. purple and blue . . 50 50
706 17c.+2c. sepia and green . . 55 55

168 Mahogany Flower

1957.

709 **168** 2c. red and green 10 10
710 4c. red and mauve 10 10
711 7c. green and blue 25 10
712 25c. orange and brown . . 55 25

169 Gerald Ouellette and Canadian Flag (rifle-shooting)

1957. Olympic Games (3rd issue). More winning athletes. Flags in national colours.
713 **169** 1c. brown (postage) . . . 10 10
714 – 2c. sepia 10 10
715 – 3c. violet 10 10
716 – 5c. orange 15 15
717 – 7c. slate 20 20
719 – 11c. blue (air) 20 15
720 – 16c. red 30 30
721 – 17c. purple 35 35
DESIGNS—(each with national flag of athlete): 2c. Ron Delaney (Ireland, 1500 m); 3c. Tenley Albright (U.S.A., figure-skating); 5c. J. Capilla (Mexico, high-diving); 7c. Ercole Baldini (Italy, cycle-racing); 11c. Hans Winkler (Germany, horse-jumping); 16c. Alfred Oerter (U.S.A., discus-throwing); 17c. Shirley Strickland (Australia, 80 m hurdles).
The designs of Nos. 714, 716 and 720 are arranged with the long side of the triangular format uppermost.

170

171 Cervantes, Open Book, Marker and Globe

1958. Tuberculosis Relief Fund.
723 **170** 1c. red and claret 10 10
See also No. 763.

1958. 4th Latin-American Book Fair.
724 **171** 4c. green 10 10
725 7c. mauve 15 10
726 10c. bistre 25 10

1958. U.N. Relief and Works Agency for Palestine Refugees. Nos. 713/21 surch. A. For Jewish Refugees. Star of David and **REFUGIADOS**.
727 1c.+2c. brown (postage) . . . 15 15
728 2c.+2c. brown 20 20
729 3c.+2c. violet 20 20
730 5c.+2c. orange 25 25
731 7c.+2c. blue 35 35
732 11c.+2c. blue (air) 25 25
733 16c.+2c. red 35 35
734 17c.+2c. purple 40 40

B. For Arab Refugees. Red Crescent and **REFUGIADOS**.
735 1c.+2c. brown (postage) . . . 15 15
736 2c.+2c. brown 20 20
737 3c.+2c. violet 20 20
738 5c.+2c. orange 25 25
739 7c.+2c. blue 35 35
740 11c.+2c. blue (air) 25 25
741 16c.+2c. red 35 35
742 17c.+2c. purple 40 40

172 Gen. R. Trujillo and Arms of Republic

1958. 25th Anniv of Gen Trujillo's designation as "Benefactor of the Country".
743 **172** 2c. mauve and yellow . . 10 10
744 4c. green and yellow . . . 10 10
745 7c. sepia and yellow . . . 15 10

173 "Rhadames" (freighter)

1958. Merchant Marine Day.
747 **173** 7c. blue . . . . 1·25 30

174 Gillian Sheen and Union Jack (fencing)

175

176 Dominican Republic Pavilion

1958. Olympic Games (4th issue). More winning athletes. Flags in national colours.
748 **174** 1c. slate, blue and red (postage) 10 10
749 – 2c. brown and blue . . . 10 10
750 – 3c. multicoloured 15 15
751 – 5c. multicoloured 20 20
752 – 7c. multicoloured 25 25
754 – 11c. sepia, olive and blue (air) 25 25
755 – 16c. blue, orge & grn . . 30 30
756 – 17c. blue, yell and red . . 1·00 50
DESIGNS (each with national flag of athlete)—VERT: 2c. Milton Campbell (U.S.A., decathlon). HORIZ: 3c. Shozo Sasahara (Japan, featherweight wrestling); 5c. Madeleine Berthod (Switzerland, skiing); 7c. Murray Rose (Australia, 400 m and 1,500 m free-style); 11c. Charles Jenkins and Thomas Courtney (U.S.A., 400 m and 800 m, and 1600 m relay); 16c. Indian team in play (India, hockey); 17c. Swedish dinghies (Sweden, sailing).

1958. Inauguration of UNESCO Headquarters Building, Paris.
758 **175** 7c. blue and red 15 10

1958. Brussels International Exhibition.
759 **176** 7c. green (postage) . . . 20 15
760 9c. grey (air) 20 15
761 25c. violet 50 30

1959. Obligatory Tax. Tuberculosis Relief Fund. As T **170** but inscr "1959".
763 **170** 1c. red and lake 15 10

1959. I.G.Y. Nos. 748/56 surch with globe and **ANO GEOFISICO INTERNACIONAL 1957-1958 +2c.**
764 1c.+2c. (postage) 25 25
765 2c.+2c. 30 30
766 3c.+2c. 35 35
767 5c.+2c. 40 40
768 7c.+2c. 45 45
770 11c.+2c. (air) 50 50

771 16c.+2c. 70 70
772 17c.+2c. . . . . 1·00 1·00

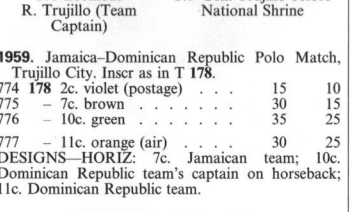

178 Leonidas R. Trujillo (Team Captain)

179 Gen. Trujillo before National Shrine

1959. Jamaica–Dominican Republic Polo Match, Trujillo City. Inscr as in T **178**.
774 **178** 2c. violet (postage) . . . 15 10
775 – 7c. brown 30 15
776 – 10c. green 35 25
777 – 11c. orange (air) 30 25
DESIGNS—HORIZ: 7c. Jamaican team; 10c. Dominican Republic team's captain on horseback; 11c. Dominican Republic team.

1959. 29th Year of Trujillo Era.
778 **179** 9c. multicoloured 20 10

180 Gen. Trujillo and Cornucopia

1959. National Census of 1960. Centres in black, red and blue. Frame colours given.
780 **180** 1c. pale blue 15 10
781 9c. green 30 15
782 13c. orange 35 25

181 Trujillo Stadium

1959. 3rd Pan-American Games, Chicago.
783 **181** 9c. black and green . . . 35 20

1959. 3rd Pan-American Games, Chicago. Nos. 667/71 and 673/5, surch **III JUEGOS DEPORTIVOS PANAMERICANOS + 2** and runner.
784 **162** 1c.+2c. mult (postage) . . 15 15
785 – 3c.+2c. multicoloured . . 15 15
786 – 3c.+2c. pur & red 15 15
787 – 5c.+2c. multicoloured . . 15 15
788 – 7c.+2c. multicoloured . . 20 20
789 – 11c.+2c. blue, red and orange (air) 20 20
790 – 16c.+2c. red, green and carmine 30 30
791 – 17c.+2c. multicoloured . . 30 30

182 Emperor Charles V

183 Rhadames Bridge

1959. 4th Death Centenary of Emperor Charles V.
792 **182** 5c. mauve 15 10
793 9c. blue 15 10

1959. Opening of Rhadames Bridge.
794 – 1c. black and green . . . 10 10
795 **183** 2c. black and blue 15 10
796 – 2c. black and red 15 10
797 **183** 5c. brown and bistre . . . 20 15
DESIGN—Nos. 794, 796, Close-up view of Rhadames Bridge.

184 Douglas DC-4 Airliner, "San Cristobal"

1960. Air. Dominican Civil Aviation.
798 **184** 13c. multicoloured 45 15

185

1960. Obligatory Tax. Tuberculosis Relief Fund.
779 **185** 1c. red, blue and cream 20 15

186 Sosua Refugee Colony

1960. World Refugee Year. Inscr "ANO MUNDIAL DE LOS REFUGIADOS". Centres in black.
800 **186** 5c. green & brn (postage) 10 10
801 9c. blue, purple & red . . 20 10
802 13c. green, brn & orge . . 25 15
803 – 10c. green, mauve and purple (air) 35 30
804 – 13c. green and grey . . . 45 35
DESIGN: Nos. 802/803, Refugee children.

1960. World Refugee Year Fund. Nos. 800/4 surch **+5** with **c** below.
805 **186** 5c.+5c. green and brown (postage) 15 15
806 9c.+5c. bl, pur & red . . 20 20
807 13c.+5c. green, brown and orange 40 40
808 – 10c.+5c. green, mauve and purple (air) 25 25
809 – 13c.+5c. green & grey . . 30 30

188 General Post Office, Ciudad Trujillo

1960.
811 **188** 2c. black and blue 10 10

189 Cattle in Street

1960. Agricultural and Industrial Fair, San Juan de la Maguana.
812 **189** 9c. black and red 25 15

190 Gholam Takhti (Iran, lightweight wrestling)

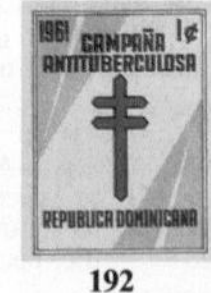

192

1960. Olympic Games, 1960. More Winning Athletes of Olympic Games, Melbourne, 1956. Flags in national colours.
813 **190** 1c. black, grn & red (postage) 10 10
814 – 2c. brown, turq & orge 10 10
815 – 3c. blue and red 10 10
816 – 5c. brown and blue . . . 15 15
817 – 7c. brn, blue & green . . 15 15
819 – 11c. brown, grey & bl (air) 20 20
820 – 16c. green, brown & red 25 25
821 – 17c. ochre, blue & black 30 30
DESIGNS (each with national flag of athlete): 2c. Mauru Furukawa (Japan, 200 m breast-stroke swimming); 3c. Mildred McDaniel (U.S.A., high jump); 5c. Terence Spinks (spelt "Terrence" on stamp) (Great Britain, featherweight boxing); 7c. Carlo Pavesi (Italy, fencing); 11c. Pat McCormick (U.S.A., high diving); 16c. Mithat Bayrack (Turkey, Greco-Roman welterweight wrestling); 17c. Ursula Happe (Germany, women's 200 m breaststroke swimming).

1961. Surch **HABILITADO PARA** and value.
823 – 2c. on 1c. black and green (No. 794) 15 10
824 **168** 9c. on 4c. red & mauve 45 10
825 9c. on 7c. green & blue 45 15
826 **146** 36c. on ½c. brown . . . . 1·50 70
827 **127** 1p. on 50c. yellow . . . . 3·25 1·90

1961. Obligatory Tax. Tuberculosis Relief Fund.
828 **192** 1c. red and blue 10 10
See also No. 876.

193 Madame Trujillo and Houses

1961. Welfare Fund.
829 **193** 1c. red 20 10

194

195 Coffee Plant and Cocoa Beans

1961.
830 **194** 1c. brown 10 10
831 2c. myrtle 10 10
832 4c. purple 40 35
833 5c. blue 25 10
834 9c. orange 30 20

1961. Obligatory Tax. Child Welfare. As Nos. 627/8 but with "ERA DE TRUJILLO" omitted. (a) Size 23½ × 32 mm.
835 **148a** 1c. blue 15 10

(b) Size 21¾ × 32 mm.
907 **148b** 1c. blue 15 10

1961.
836 **195** 1c. green (postage) . . . 10 10
837 2c. brown 10 10
838 4c. violet 10 10
839 5c. blue 10 10
840 9c. grey 25 10
841 13c. red (air) 25 25
842 33c. yellow 55 55

1961. 15th Anniv of UNESCO. Nos. 813/21 surch **XV ANIVERSARIO DE LA UNESCO +2c**.
843 1c.+2c. (postage) 10 10
844 2c.+2c. 10 10
845 3c.+2c. 10 10
846 5c.+2c. 15 15
847 7c.+2c. 15 15
849 11c.+2c. (air) 25 25
850 16c.+2c. 35 35
851 17c.+2c. 35 35

197 Mosquito and Dagger

198 Plantation

1962. Malaria Eradication.
853 **197** 10c. mauve (postage) . . 15 10
854 10c.+2c. mauve 20 15
855 20c. sepia 35 30
856 20c.+2c. sepia 35 25
857 25c. green 45 55
858 13c. red (air) 25 20
859 13c.+2c. red 25 25
860 33c. orange 50 50
861 33c.+2c. orange 60 60

1962. Farming and Industrial Development. Flag in red and blue.
863 **198** 1c. green and blue 10 10
864 2c. red and blue 10 10
865 3c. brown and blue . . . 10 10
866 5c. blue 15 10
867 15c. orange and blue . . 25 15

199 Laurel Sprig and Broken Link

1962. 1st Anniv of Assassination of Pres. Trujillo.
868 **199** 1c. mult (postage) 10 10
869 – 9c. red, blue and ochre . . 25 15
870 – 20c. red, blue & turq . . 45 25
871 – 1p. red, blue & violet . . 2·75 1·60
873 **199** 13c. multicoloured (air) 25 20
874 – 50c. red, blue & mauve 1·00 70
DESIGNS—VERT: 9c., 1p. "Justice" on map. HORIZ: 20c., 50c. Flag and flaming torch.

200 Map and Laurel

201 U.P.A.E. Emblem

1962. Martyrs of June 1959 Revolution.
875 **200** 1c. black 25 15

1962. Tuberculosis Relief Fund. As No. 828 but inscr "1962".
876 **192** 1c. red and blue 10 10

1962. 50th Anniv of Postal Union of the Americas and Spain.
877 **201** 2c. red (postage) 10 10
878 9c. orange 25 15
879 14c. turquoise 25 20
880 13c. blue (air) 35 20
881 22c. brown 45 40

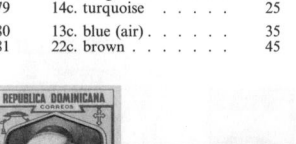

202 Archbishop Nouel

203 Globe, Riband and Campaign Emblem

1962. Birth Cent of Archbishop Adolfo Nouel.
882 **202** 2c. myrtle & green (postage) 10 10
883 9c. brown and orange . . 25 15
884 13c. purple and brown . . 30 20
885 – 12c. blue (air) 35 20
886 – 25c. violet 50 40
DESIGN: Air stamps as Type **202** but different frame.

1963. Freedom from Hunger. Riband in red and blue.
888 **203** 2c. green 10 10
891 2c.+1c. green 10 10
889 5c. mauve 15 10
892 5c.+2c. mauve 20 20
890 9c. orange 25 15
893 9c.+2c. orange 20 20

204 Duarte

1963. 120th Anniv of Separation from Haiti.
895 **204** 2c. blue (postage) 10 10
896 – 7c. green (Sanchez) . . . 15 15
897 – 9c. purple (Mella) 15 15
898 – 15c. salmon (air) 20 15
DESIGN—HORIZ: 15c. Sanchez, Duarte and Mella.

205 Espaillat, de Rojas and Bono

1963. "Centenary of the Restoration".
899 **205** 2c. green 10 10
900 – 4c. red 10 10
901 – 5c. brown 10 10
902 – 9c. blue 15 15
DESIGNS: 4c. Rodriguez, Cabrera and Moncion; 5c. Capotillo Monument; 9c. Polanco, Luperon and Salcedo.

206 Nurse tending Patient

207

1963. Centenary of Red Cross. Cross in red.
904 **206** 3c. grey (postage) 10 10
905 6c. green 15 10
906 – 10c. grey (air) 25 20
DESIGN—HORIZ: 10c. Map of continents bordering Atlantic.

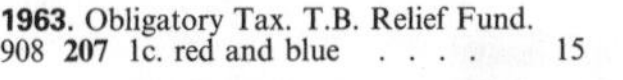

1963. Obligatory Tax. T.B. Relief Fund.
908 **207** 1c. red and blue 15 10

208 Scales of Justice and Globe

1963. 15th Anniv of Declaration of Human Rights.
911 **208** 6c. red (postage) 15 10
912 50c. green 80 55
913 7c. brown (air) 20 15
914 10c. blue 25 15

209 Rameses II in War Chariot, Abu Simbel

1964. Nubian Monuments Preservation. Designs as T **209**, also surch **2c** in circle.
915 **209** 3c. red (postage) 10 10
916 3c.+2c. red 15 15
917 – 6c. blue 15 10
918 – 6c.+2c. blue 15 15
919 **209** 9c. brown 20 15
920 9c.+2c. brown 25 25
921 – 10c. violet (air) 25 20
922 – 10c.+2c. violet 20 20
923 – 13c. yellow 25 20
924 – 13c.+2c. yellow 25 25
DESIGNS—HORIZ: 6c. Heads of Rameses II. VERT: 10c., 13c. As Type **209**.

211 M. Gomez (founder)

212 Palm Chat

1964. Bicentenary of Bani Foundation.
925 **211** 2c. blue & light blue . . . 10 10
926 6c. purple and brown . . 15 10

1964. Dominican Birds. Multicoloured.
927 1c. Narrow-billed tody (postage) . . . . 1·75 15
928 2c. Hispaniolan emerald . . . 1·75 15
929 3c. Type **212** . . . . 1·75 15
930 6c. Hispaniolan amazon . . . 2·10 15
931 6c. Hispaniolan trogons . . . 2·50 15
932 10c. Hispaniolan woodpecker (air) . . . . 3·75 20
The 1c., 2c. and 6c. (No. 931) are smaller (26 × 37½ mm); the 10c. is horiz (43½ × 27½ mm).

213 Rocket

1964. "Conquest of Space".
933 – 1c. blue (postage) 10 10
934 **213** 2c. green 10 10
935 – 3c. blue 15 10
936 **213** 6c. blue 25 15
937 **213** 7c. green (air) 25 25
938 – 10c. blue 35 70
DESIGNS—VERT: 1c. Rocket launching. HORIZ: 3c., 10c. Capsule in orbit.

214 Pres. Kennedy

1964. Air. Pres. Kennedy Commemoration.
940 **214** 10c. brown and buff . . . 35 25

215 U.P.U. Monument, Berne

1964. 15th U.P.U. Congress, Vienna.
941 **215** 1c. red (postage) 10 10
942 4c. green 15 10
943 5c. orange 15 10
944 7c. blue (air) 15 10

216 I.C.Y. Emblem

217 Hands and Lily

1965. International Co-operation Year.
945 **216** 2c. blue and light-blue (postage) 10 10
946 3c. green and emerald . . 10 10
947 6c. red and pink 15 10
948 10c. violet & lilac (air) . . 25 20

1965. 4th Mariological and 11th Int Marian Congresses. Multicoloured.
949 2c. Type **217** (postage) . . . 10 10
950 6c. Virgin of the Altagracia 35 25
951 10c. Douglas DC-8 airliner over Basilica of Virgin of Altagracia (39½ × 31½ mm) (air) 30 15

218 Flags Emblem

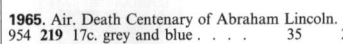

219 Lincoln

1965. 75th Anniv of Organization of American States.
952 **218** 2c. multicoloured 10 10
953 6c. multicoloured 15 10

1965. Air. Death Centenary of Abraham Lincoln.
954 **219** 17c. grey and blue 35 25

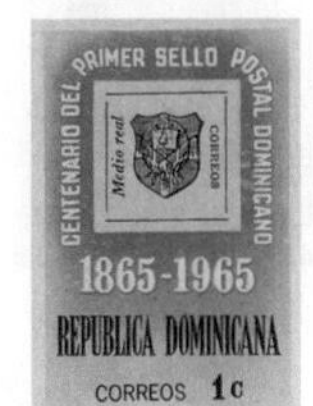

220 ½r. Stamp of 1865

221 Hibiscus

1965. Stamp Centenary.
955 **220** 1c. multicoloured (post) 10 10
956 2c. multicoloured 10 10
957 6c. multicoloured 15 10
958 – 7c. multicoloured (air) . . 25 20
959 – 10c. multicoloured 25 25
DESIGN: 7c., 10c. As Type **220**, but showing 1r. stamp of 1865.

1966. Obligatory Tax. Tuberculosis Relief Fund.
963 **221** 1c. red and green 15 10
999 – 1c. mauve, lilac & red 10 10
1015 – 1c. multicoloured 10 10
1016 – 1c. multicoloured 10 10
1017 – 1c. multicoloured 10 10
DESIGN (21½ × 30 mm): No. 999, Orchid. (20 × 28 mm): No. 1015, Dogbane; 1016, Violets; 1017, "Eeanthus capitatus".

222 I.T.U. Emblem and Symbols

223 W.H.O. Building

1966. Air. Centenary (1965) of I.T.U.
964 **222** 28c. red and pink 55 40
965 45c. green and emerald 55 70

1965. Inaug of W.H.O. Headquarters, Geneva.
966 **223** 6c. blue 15 10
967 10c. purple 20 15

224 Man supporting "Republic"

225 "Ascia monuste"

1966. General Elections.
968 **224** 2c. black and green . . . 10 10
969 6c. black and red 15 10

1966. Butterflies. Multicoloured.
970 1c. Type **225** (postage) . . . 10 10
971 2c. "Heliconius charitonius" 10 10
972 3c. "Phoebis sennae sennae" 15 15
973 6c. "Anteos clorinde clorinde" 25 25
974 8c. "Siderone hemesis" . . . 35 35
975 10c. "Eurema gundlachia" (air) 45 25
976 50c. "Clothilda panthérata pantherata" . . . . 2·10 1·00
977 75c. "Papilio androgeus epidaurus" . . . . 3·00 1·50
Nos. 975/7 are larger, 35 × 24½ mm.

1966. Hurricane Inez Relief. Nos. 970/77 surch **PRO DAMNIFICADOS CICLON INES** and value.
978 **225** 1c.+2c. mult (postage) . . 15 10
979 – 2c.+2c. multicoloured . . 15 10
980 – 3c.+2c. multicoloured . . 15 10
981 – 6c.+4c. multicoloured . . 30 25
982 – 8c.+4c. multicoloured . . 40 30
983 – 10c.+5c. mult (air) . . . 40 35
984 – 50c.+10c. mult . . . . . 1·40 1·40
985 – 75c.+10c. mult . . . . . 1·75 1·75

227 National Shrine

228 Emblem and Map

1967. (a) Postage.
986 **227** 1c. blue 10 10
987 2c. red 10 10
988 3c. green 10 10
989 4c. grey 10 10
990 5c. yellow 10 10
991 6c. orange 10 10
(b) Air. Size 20½ × 25 mm.
992 **227** 7c. olive 15 10
993 10c. lilac 15 15
994 20c. brown 30 25

1967. Development Year. Emblem and map in black and blue.
996 **228** 2c. orange and yellow . . 10 10
997 6c. orange 15 10
998 10c. green 25 15

229 Rook and Knight

230 Civil Defence Emblem

1967. 5th Central American Chess Championship, Santo Domingo.
1000 **229** 25c. mult (postage) . . . 55 40
1001 – 10c. black & grn (air) . . 35 25
DESIGN: 10c. Bishop and pawn.

1967. Obligatory Tax. Civil Defence Fund.
1003 **230** 1c. multicoloured 15 15

231 Alliance Emblem

232 Institute Emblem

1967. 6th Anniv of "Alliance for Progress".
1004 **231** 1c. green (postage) . . . 10 10
1005 8c. grey (air) 15 10
1006 10c. blue 20 15

1967. 25th Anniv of Inter-American Agricultural Institute.
1007 **232** 3c. green (postage) . . . 10 10
1008 6c. pink 15 10
1009 – 12c. mult (air) 20 15
DESIGN: 12c. Emblem and cornucopia.

233 Child and Children's Home

234 Hand Holding Invalid

1967. Obligatory Tax. Child Welfare.
1010 **233** 1c. red 25 10
1010a 1c. orange 15 10
1011 1c. violet 10 10
1011a 1c. brown 15 10
1037 1c. green 10 10
See also No. 1278a.

1968. Obligatory Tax. Rehabilitation of the Handicapped.
1012 **234** 1c. yellow and green . . 10 10
1013 1c. blue 10 10
1014 1c. bright purple 10 10
1015 1c. brown 10 10

236 W.M.O. Emblem

1968. World Meteorological Day.
1019 **236** 6c. mult (postage) . . . 20 15
1020 10c. multicoloured (air) 25 20
1021 15c. multicoloured . . . 35 25

237 Ortiz v. Cruz

238 "Lions" Emblem

1968. World Lightweight Boxing Championship. Designs showing similar scenes of the contest.
1024 **237** 6c. pur & red (postage) 15 15
1025 – 7c. green & yellow (air) 15 10
1026 – 10c. blue and brown 25 15

1968. Lions International.
1027 **238** 6c. mult (postage) 15 10
1028 10c. multicoloured (air) 25 15

1968. Obligatory Tax. Anti-cancer Fund.
1029 **144** 1c. green 10 10
1030 1c. orange 10 10

239 Wrestling

1968. Olympic Games, Mexico. Multicoloured.
1031 1c. Type **239** (postage) 10 10
1032 6c. Running 15 10
1033 25c. Boxing 70 35
1034 10c. Weightlifting (air) 25 25
1035 33c. Pistol-shooting 80 70

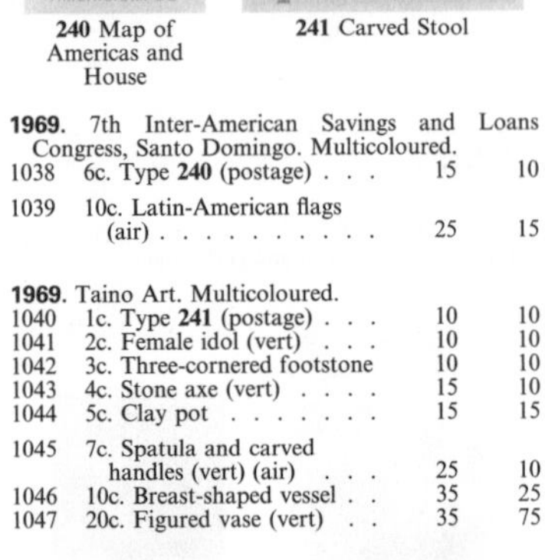

240 Map of Americas and House

241 Carved Stool

1969. 7th Inter-American Savings and Loans Congress, Santo Domingo. Multicoloured.
1038 6c. Type **240** (postage) 15 10
1039 10c. Latin-American flags (air) 25 15

1969. Taino Art. Multicoloured.
1040 1c. Type **241** (postage) 10 10
1041 2c. Female idol (vert) 10 10
1042 3c. Three-cornered footstone 10 10
1043 4c. Stone axe (vert) 15 10
1044 5c. Clay pot 15 15
1045 7c. Spatula and carved handles (vert) (air) 25 10
1046 10c. Breast-shaped vessel 35 25
1047 20c. Figured vase (vert) 35 75

242 School Playground and Torch

243 Community Emblem

1969. Obligatory Tax. Education Year.
1048 **242** 1c. blue 10 10

1969. Community Development Day.
1049 **243** 6c. gold and green 15 10

244 C.O.T.A.L. Emblem

245 I.L.O. Emblem

1969. 12th C.O.T.A.L. (Confederation of Latin American Tourist Organizations) Congress, Santo Domingo.
1050 **244** 1c. blue, red and light blue (postage) 10 10
1051 – 2c. lt green & green 10 10
1052 – 6c. red 15 10
1053 – 10c. brown (air) 30 10
DESIGNS—VERT: 2c. Boy with flags. HORIZ: (39 × 31 mm): 6c. C.O.T.A.L. Building and emblem; 10c. "Airport of the Americas", Santo Domingo.

1969. 50th Anniv of I.L.O.
1054 **245** 6c. blk & turq (postage) 25 10
1055 10c. black and red (air) 15 15

246 Taking a Catch

247 Las Damas Hydro-electric Scheme

1969. World Baseball Championships, Santo Domingo.
1056 **246** 1c. grey and green (postage) 10 10
1057 – 2c. green 10 10
1058 – 3c. brown and violet 10 10
1059 – 7c. orange and purple (air) 20 15
1060 – 10c. red 25 15
1061 – 1p. brown and blue 2·00 1·40
DESIGNS—VERT: 3c. Making for base; 10c. Player making strike. HORIZ: (43 × 30½ mm): 2c. Cibao Stadium; 7c. Tetelo Vargas Stadium; 1p. Quisqueya Stadium.

1969. National Electrification Plan.
1062 **247** 2c. mult (postage) 10 10
1063 – 3c. multicoloured 10 10
1064 – 6c. purple 15 10
1065 – 10c. red (air) 20 10
DESIGNS—HORIZ: 3c. Las Damas Dam; 6c. Arroyo Hondo substation; 10c. Haina River power station.

1969. Obligatory Tax. Anti-cancer Fund. T **144** re-drawn in larger format and inscriptions.
1066 **144** 1c. purple 10 10
1067 1c. green 15 10

248 Tavera Dam

1969. Completion of Dam Projects. Mult.
1068 6c. Type **248** (postage) 15 10
1069 10c. Valdesia Dam (air) 20 10

249 Juan Pablo Duarte

250 Outline Map, Arms of Census Office and Family

1970. Juan Pablo Duarte (patriot) Commem.
1070 **249** 1c. green (postage) 10 10
1071 2c. red 10 10
1072 3c. purple 10 10
1073 6c. blue 15 10
1074 10c. brown (air) 20 15

1970. National Census.
1075 **250** 5c. blk & grn (postage) 10 10
1076 – 6c. ultram and blue 15 10
1077 – 10c. multicoloured (air) 25 15
DESIGNS: 6c. Arms and quotation; 10c. Arms and buildings.

251 Open Book and Emblem

252 Abelardo Urdaneta

1970. Obligatory Tax. Int Education Year.
1078 **251** 1c. purple 10 10

1970. Birth Cent of A. R. Urdaneta (sculptor).
1079 **252** 3c. blue (postage) 10 10
1080 – 6c. green 15 10
1081 – 10c. blue (air) 20 15
DESIGNS—HORIZ: (39½ × 27 mm): 6c. "One of Many" (sculpture). VERT: (25 × 39 mm): 10c. Prisoner (statue).

253 Masonic Symbols

255 New U.P.U. Building

254 Telecommunications Satellite

1970. 8th Inter-American Masonic Conference, Santo Domingo.
1082 **253** 6c. green (postage) 15 10
1083 10c. brown (air) 20 10

1970. World Telecommunications Day.
1084 **254** 20c. grey & grn (postage) 50 30
1085 7c. grey and blue (air) 15 10

1970. New U.P.U. Headquarters Building, Berne.
1086 **255** 6c. brn & grey (postage) 15 10
1087 10c. brown & yell (air) 15 10

256 I.E.Y. Emblem

257 Pedro Alejandrino Pina

1970. International Education Year.
1088 **256** 4c. purple (postage) 10 10
1089 15c. mauve (air) 20 15

1970. 150th Birth Anniv and Death Centenary of Pedro A. Pina (writer).
1090 **257** 6c. black & brown 15 10

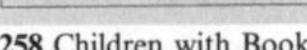

258 Children with Book

259 Emblem and Stamp Album

1970. 1st World Book Exhibition, and Cultural Festival, Santo Domingo.
1091 **258** 5c. green (postage) 10 10
1092 – 7c. multicoloured (air) 15 10
1093 – 10c. multicoloured 20 15
DESIGNS: 7c. Dancers; 10c. U.N. emblem within "wheel".

1970. Air. "EXFILICA 70" Inter-American Philatelic Exhibition, Caracas, Venezuela.
1094 **259** 10c. multicoloured 20 15

260 Communications Emblems

261 Virgin of Altagracia

1971. Obligatory Tax. Postal and Telecommunications School. (a) Size 18 × 20½ mm.
1095 **260** 1c. blue and red (white background) 15 10

(b) Size 19 × 22 mm.
1095a **260** 1c. blue and red (red background) 15 10
1095b 1c. blue, red and green 15 10
1095c 1c. blue, red and yellow 15 10
1095d 1c. blue, red and mauve 15 10
1095e 1c. blue, red and light blue 10 10
1096 1c. blue and red (blue background) 10 10

1971. Inauguration of Our Lady of Altagracia Basilica. Multicoloured.
1097 3c. Type **261** (postage) 10 10
1098 17c. Basilica (22½ × 36 mm) (air) 35 25

262 Parcel, Emblem and Map

263 Manuel Objio

1971. Air. 25th Anniv of C.A.R.E. (Cooperative for American Relief Everywhere).
1099 **262** 10c. green and blue 15 15

1971. Death Cent of Manuel Rodriguez Objio (poet).
1100 **263** 6c. blue 15 10

264 Boxing and Canoeing

265 Goat and Fruit

1971. 2nd National Games.
1101 **264** 2c. brown and orange (postage) 10 10
1102 – 5c. brown and green 15 10
1103 – 7c. purple & grey (air) 15 10
DESIGNS: 5c. Basketball; 7c. Volleyball.

1971. 6th National Agricultural Census. Mult.
1104 1c. Type **265** (postage) 10 10
1105 2c. Cow and goose 10 10
1106 3c. Cocoa pods and horse 10 10
1107 6c. Bananas, coffee beans and pig 15 10
1108 25c. Cockerel and grain (air) 40 30

266 Jose Nunez de Caceres

267 Shepherds and Star

1971. 150th Anniv of 1st Declaration of Independence.
1109 **266** 6c. blue, violet and light blue (postage) 15 10
1110 – 10c. bl, red & yell (air) 25 20
DESIGN: 10c. Flag of the Santo Domingo–Colombia Union.

1971. Christmas.
1111 **267** 6c. brn, yell & bl (post) 15 10
1112 – 10c. red, blk & yell (air) 15 15
DESIGN: 10c. Spanish bell of 1493.

268 Child on Beach

269 Book Year Emblem

1971. 25th Anniv of UNICEF.
1113 **268** 6c. mult (postage) 15 10
1114 15c. multicoloured (air) 25 20

1971. International Book Year.
1115 **269** 1c. green, red and blue (postage) 10 10
1116 2c. brown, red and blue 10 10
1117 12c. purple, red and blue (air) 20 15

270 Magnifier on Map 271 Orchid

1972. Air. "Exfilima 71" Inter American Philatelic Exhibition, Lima, Peru.
1118 **270** 10c. multicoloured . . . 25 15

1972. Obligatory Tax. Tuberculosis Relief Fund.
1119 **271** 1c. multicoloured 10 10

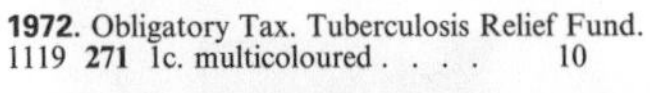

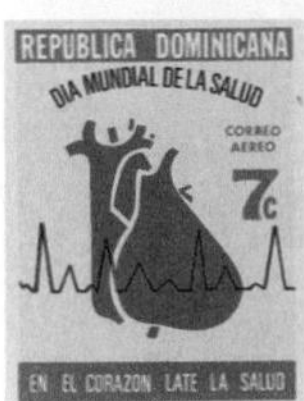

272 Heart Emblem 273 Mask

1972. Air. World Health Day.
1120 **272** 7c. multicoloured 15 10

1972. Taino Arts and Crafts. Multicoloured.
1121 2c. Type **273** (postage) . . . 10 10
1122 4c. Spoon and amulet . . . 10 10
1123 6c. Nasal aspirator (horiz) 10 10
1124 8c. Ritual vase (horiz) (air) 15 10
1125 10c. Atlantic trumpet triton (horiz) 30 10
1126 25c. Ritual spatulas 45 25

274 Globe

1972. World Telecommunications Day.
1127 **274** 6c. mult (postage) . . . 15 10
1128 21c. multicoloured (air) 35 20

275 Map and "Stamps"

1972. 1st National Stamp Exn, Santo Domingo.
1129 **275** 2c. mult (postage) . . . 10 10
1130 33c. mult (air) 60 35

276 Basketball

1972. Olympic Games, Munich. Mult.
1131 2c. Type **276** (postage) . . . 10 10
1132 33c. Running (air) 70 40

277 Club Badge

1972. 50th Anniv of Int Activo 20–30 Club.
1133 **277** 1c. mult (postage) . . . 10 10
1134 20c. mult (air) 35 20

278 Emilio Morel and Quotation

1972. Morel (poet and journalist). Commem.
1135 **278** 6c. mult (postage) . . . 15 10
1136 10c. mult (air) 15 10

279 Bank Building

1972. 25th Anniv of Central Bank. Mult.
1137 1c. Type **279** 10 10
1138 5c. One-peso banknote . . . 10 10
1139 25c. 1947 50c. coin and mint 40 25

280 Nativity Scene 281 Student and Letter-box

1972. Christmas. Multicoloured.
1140 2c. Type **280** (postage) . . . 10 10
1141 6c. Poinsettia (horiz) 15 10
1142 10c. "La Navidad" Fort, 1492 (horiz) (air) 15 10

1972. Publicity for Correspondence Schools.
1143 **281** 2c. red and pink 10 10
1144 6c. blue and light blue 15 10
1145 10c. green and yellow . . 20 10

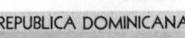

282 View of Dam 283 Invalid in Wheel-chair

1973. Inauguration of Tavera Dam.
1146 **282** 10c. multicoloured . . . 20 10

1973. Obligatory Tax. Rehabilitation of the Handicapped.
1147 **283** 1c. green 10 10

284 Long-jumping, Diving, Running, Cycling and Weightlifting 285 Hibiscus

1973. 12th Central American and Caribbean Games, Santo Domingo, Multicoloured.
1148 2c. Type **284** (postage) . . . 10 10
1149 2c. Boxing, football, wrestling and shooting . . 10 10
1150 2c. Fencing, tennis, high-jumping and sprinting . . 10 10
1151 2c. Putting the shot, throwing the javelin and show-jumping 10 10
1152 25c. Type **284** 55 25
1153 25c. As No. 1149 . . . . . 55 25
1154 25c. As No. 1150 . . . . . 55 25
1155 25c. As No. 1151 . . . . . 55 25
1156 8c. Type **284** (air) 15 10
1157 8c. As No. 1149 . . . . . 15 10
1158 8c. As No. 1150 . . . . . 15 10
1159 8c. As No. 1151 . . . . . 15 10
1160 10c. Type **284** 25 15
1161 10c. As No. 1149 . . . . . 25 15

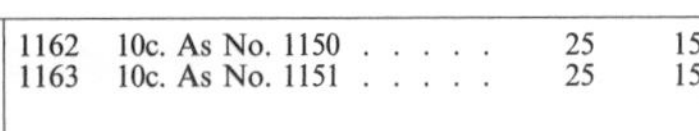

1162 10c. As No. 1150 . . . . . 25 15
1163 10c. As No. 1151 . . . . . 25 15

1973. Obligatory Tax. Tuberculosis Relief Fund.
1164 **285** 1c. multicoloured 10 10

286 Christ carrying the Cross 287 Global Emblem

1973. Easter. Multicoloured.
1165 2c. Type **286** (postage) . . . 10 10
1166 6c. Belfry, Church of Our Lady of Carmen (vert) . . 15 10
1167 10c. Belfry, Chapel of Our Lady of Succour (vert) (air) 20 10

1973. Air. 70th Anniv of Pan-American Health Organization.
1168 **287** 7c. multicoloured 15 10

288 Weather Zones

1973. Cent of World Meteorological Organization.
1169 **288** 6c. mult (postage) . . . 15 10
1170 7c. multicoloured (air) 15 10

289 Forensic Scientist

1973. Air. 50th Anniv of International Criminal Police Organization (Interpol).
1171 **289** 10c. blue, green and light blue 20 15

1973. Obligatory Tax. Anti-cancer Fund. As T **144** but dated "1973".
1171a **144** 1c. olive 15 10
See also Nos. 1270a and 1338a.

290 Maguey Drum

1973. Opening of Museum of Dominican Man, Santo Domingo. Multicoloured.
1172 1c. Type **290** (postage) . . . 10 10
1173 2c. Amber carvings 10 10
1174 4c. Cibao mask (vert) . . . 10 10
1175 6c. Pottery (vert) 15 10
1176 7c. Model ship in mosaic (vert) (air) 15 10
1177 10c. Maracas rattles 20 15

291 Nativity Scene

1973. Christmas. Multicoloured.
1178 2c. Type **291** (postage) . . . 10 10
1179 6c. "Prayer" (stained-glass window) (vert) 15 10
1180 10c. Angels beside crib (air) 20 15

292 Scout Badge

1973. 50th Anniv of Dominican Boy Scouts. Multicoloured.
1181 1c. Type **292** (postage) . . . 10 10
1182 5c. Scouts and flag 10 10
1183 21c. Scouts cooking, and Lord Baden Powell (air) 40 30
No. 1182 is smaller, size 26 × 36 mm.

293 Stadium and Basketball Players 294 Belfry, Santo Domingo Cathedral

1974. 12th Central American and Caribbean Games, Santo Domingo. Multicoloured.
1184 2c. Type **293** (postage) . . . 10 10
1185 6c. Arena and cyclist . . . 15 10
1186 10c. Swimming pool and diver (air) 20 15
1187 25c. Stadium, soccer players and discus-thrower . . . 50 35

1974. Obligatory Tax. Rehabilitation of the Handicapped. As T **283** but larger, 22 × 27 mm.
1187a **283** 1c. blue 15 15

1974. Holy Week.
1188 **294** 2c. mult (postage) . . . 10 10
1189 – 6c. purple, green & ol . . 15 10
1190 – 10c. multicoloured (air) 20 15
DESIGN—VERT: 6c. "Sorrowful Mother" (D. Bouts). HORIZ: 10c. "The Last Supper" (R. M. Budi).

295 Francisco del Rosario Sanchez Bridge

1974. Dominican Bridges. Multicoloured.
1191 6c. Type **295** (postage) . . . 15 10
1192 10c. Higuamo Bridge (air) 20 15

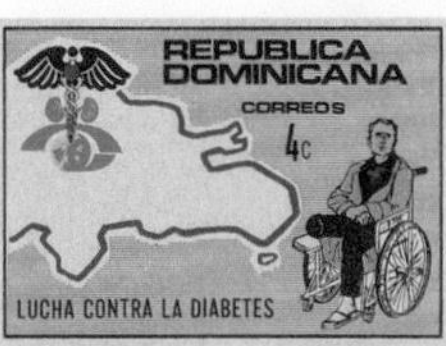

296 Emblem and Patient

1974. Anti-diabetes Campaign. Mult.
1193 4c. Type **296** (postage) . . . 10 10
1194 5c. Emblem and pancreas 10 10
1195 7c. Emblem and Kidney (air) 15 10
1196 33c. Emblem, eye and heart 70 45

1974. Obligatory Tax. Anti-cancer Fund. As T **144** but dated "1974".
1196a **144** 1c. orange 15 10

297 Steam Train

1974. Centenary of Universal Postal Union. Mult.
1197 2c. Type **297** (postage) . . . 45 55
1198 6c. Stage-coach 15 10
1199 7c. "Eider" mail steamer (air) 60 15
1200 33c. Boeing 727-200 of Dominicana Airways . . 95 30

298 Emblems of World Amateur Golf Council and of Dominican Golf Association

1974. World Amateur Golf Championships.
1202 **298** 2c. black and yellow (postage) 10 10
1203 – 6c. multicoloured 10 10
1204 – 10c. multicoloured (air) 25 15
1205 – 20c. multicoloured . . . 45 30
DESIGNS—VERT: 6c. Golfers teeing-off. HORIZ: 10c. Council emblem and golfers; 20c. Dominican Golf Association emblem, golfer and hand with ball and tee.

299 Christmas Decorations **301** Dr. Defillo

300 Tomatoes

1974. Christmas. Multicoloured.
1206 2c. Type **299** (postage) . . . 10 10
1207 6c. Virgin and Child 15 10
1208 10c. Hand holding dove (horiz) (air) 20 15

1974. 10th Anniv of World Food Programme. Multicoloured.
1209 2c. Type **300** (postage) . . . 10 10
1210 3c. Avocado pears 10 10
1211 5c. Coconuts 10 10
1212 10c. Bee, hive and cask of honey (air) 20 15

1975. Birth Centenary of Dr. Fernando Defillo (medical scientist).
1213 **301** 1c. brown 10 10
1214 6c. green 15 10

1975. Obligatory Tax. Rehabilitation of the Handicapped. As T **283** but dated "1975".
1214a **283** 1c. brown 15 10

302 "I am the Resurrection and the Life" **303** Spanish 6c. Stamp of 1850

1975. Holy Week. Multicoloured.
1215 2c. Type **302** (postage) . . . 10 10
1216 6c. Bell tower, Nuestra Senora del Rosario convent 15 10
1217 10c. Catholic emblems (air) 20 15

1975. Obligatory Tax. Tuberculosis Relief Fund. As T **221** but dated "1975".
1217a **221** 1c. multicoloured . . . 15 10
DESIGN: 1c. "Catteeyopsis rosea".

1975. Air. "Espana 75" International Stamp Exhibition, Madrid.
1218 **303** 12c. black, red & yell . . 25 15

304 Hands supporting "Agriculture" and Industry **305** Earth Station

1975. 16th Meeting of Industrial Development Bank Governors, Santo Domingo.
1219 **304** 6c. mult (postage) . . . 15 10
1220 10c. mult (air) 20 15

1975. Opening of Satellite Earth Station. Multicoloured.
1221 5c. Type **305** (postage) . . . 10 10
1222 15c. Hemispheres and satellites (horiz) (air) . . . 30 20

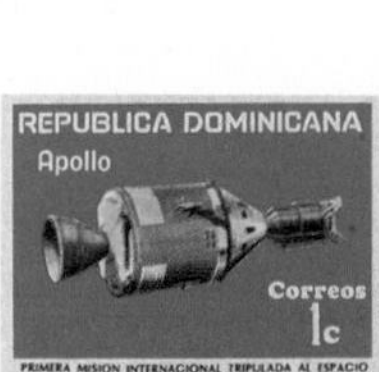

306 "Apollo" Spacecraft with Docking Tunnel **307** Father Castellanos

1975. "Apollo–Soyuz" Space Link. Mult.
1223 1c. Type **306** (postage) . . . 10 10
1224 4c. "Soyuz" spacecraft . . . 10 10
1225 2p. Docking manoeuvre (air) 3·25 2·00
The 2p. is larger, 42 × 28 mm.

1975. Birth Cent of Father Rafael C. Castellanos.
1226 **307** 6c. brown and buff . . . 15 10

308 Women encircling I.W.Y. Emblem

1975. International Women's Year.
1227 **308** 3c. multicoloured 10 10

309 Guacanagarix **310** Basketball

1975. Indian Chiefs. Multicoloured.
1228 1c. Type **309** (postage) . . . 10 10
1229 2c. Guarionex 10 10
1230 3c. Caonabo 10 10
1231 4c. Bohechio 10 10
1232 5c. Cayacoa 10 10
1233 6c. Anacaona 15 10
1234 9c. Hatuey 20 15
1235 7c. Mayobanex (air) 15 10
1236 8c. Cotubanama with Juan de Esquivel 15 10
1237 10c. Enriquillo and wife, Mencia 20 15

1975. Obligatory Tax. Anti-cancer Fund. As T **144** but dated "1975".
1237a **144** 1c. violet 15 10

1975. 7th Pan-American Games, Mexico City. Multicoloured.
1238 2c. Type **310** (postage) . . . 10 10
1239 6c. Baseball 15 10
1240 7c. Volleyball (horiz) (air) 15 15
1241 10c. Weightlifting (horiz) . . 25 15

311 Carol-singers

1975. Christmas. Multicoloured.
1242 2c. Type **311** (postage) . . . 10 10
1243 6c. "Dominican" Nativity 15 10
1244 10c. Dove and Peace message (air) 20 15

312 Pearl Sergeant Major ("Abudefdul marginatus")

1976. Fishes. Multicoloured.
1245 10c. Type **312** 35 25
1246 10c. Puddingwife ("Halichoeres radiata") 35 25
1247 10c. Squirrelfish ("Holocentrus ascensionis") 35 25
1248 10c. Queen angelfish ("Angelochthys ciliaris") 35 25
1249 10c. Aya snapper ("Lutianus aya") 35 25

313 Valdesia Dam

1976. Air. Inauguration of Valdesia Dam.
1250 **313** 10c. multicoloured . . . 15 15

1976. Obligatory Tax. Rehabilitation of the Disabled. As T **283** but dated "1976".
1250a **283** 1c. blue 15 10

314 Orchid

1976. Obligatory Tax. Tuberculosis Relief Fund.
1251 **314** 1c. multicoloured 10 10

315 "Magdalene" (E. Godoy) **316** Schooner "Separacion Dominicana"

1976. Holy Week. Multicoloured.
1252 2c. Type **315** (postage) . . . 10 10
1253 6c. "The Ascension" (V. Priego) 10 10
1254 10c. "Mount Calvary" (E. Castillo) (air) 20 15

1976. Navy Day.
1255 **316** 20c. multicoloured . . . 1·75 40

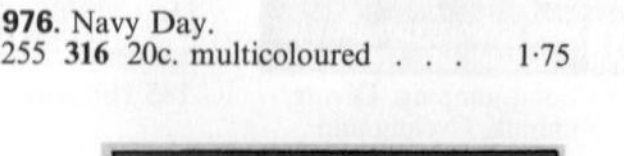

317 National Flower and Maps

1976. Bicentenary of American Revolution, and "Interphil '76" Int Stamp Exn, Philadelphia.
1256 **317** 6c. mult (postage) . . . 15 10
1257 – 9c. multicoloured 20 10
1258 – 10c. multicoloured (air) 50 15
1259 – 75c. black and orange 1·50 1·00
DESIGNS—HORIZ: 9c. Maps within cogwheels; 10c. Maps within hands. VERT: 75c. George Washington and Philadelphia buildings.

318 Flags of Spain and Dominican Republic

1976. Visit of King and Queen of Spain. Multicoloured.
1260 6c. Type **318** (postage) . . . 35 10
1261 21c. King Juan Carlos I and Queen Sophia (air) . . . 1·00 35

319 Various Telephones

1976. Telephone Centenary. Multicoloured.
1262 6c. Type **319** (postage) . . . 15 10
1263 10c. A. Graham Bell (horiz) (air) 20 15

320 "Duarte's Vision" (L. Desangles)

1976. Death Centenary of Juan Duarte (patriot). Multicoloured.
1264 2c. Type **320** (postage) . . . 10 10
1265 6c. "Juan Duarte" (R. Mejia) (vert) 15 10
1266 10c. Text of Duarte's Declaration (vert) (air) . . 20 15
1267 33c. "Duarte Sailing to Exile" (E. Godoy) 70 45

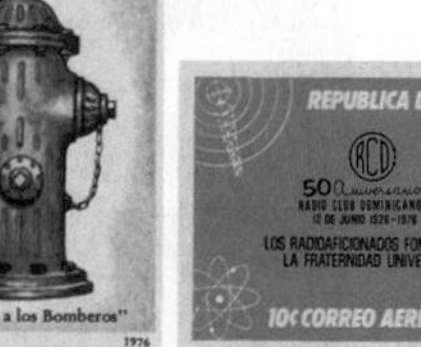

321 Fire Hydrant **322** Commemorative Text and Emblem

1976. Dominican Fire Service. Multicoloured.
1268 4c. Type **321** (postage) . . . 10 10
1269 6c. Fire Service emblem . . 15 10
1270 10c. Fire engine (horiz) (air) 20 15

1976. Obligatory Tax. Anti-cancer Fund. As T **144** but dated "1976".
1270a **144** 1c. green 15 10

1976. 50th Anniv of Dominican Radio Club.
1271 **322** 6c. black & red (postage) 15 10
1272 10c. black & blue (air) 20 15

323 Map and Caravel **325** Virgin and Child

324 Boxing

1976. "Hispanidad 1976". Multicoloured.
1273 6c. Type **323** (postage) . . . 60 15
1274 21c. Heads of Spaniard and Dominicans (air) 45 30

1976. Olympic Games, Montreal. Mult.
1275 2c. Type **324** (postage) . . . 10 10
1276 3c. Weightlifting 10 10
1277 10c. Running (air) 20 15
1278 25c. Basketball 50 35

1976. Obligatory Tax. Child Welfare. As T **233** but dated "1976".
1278a **233** 1c. mauve 15 10

1976. Christmas. Multicoloured.
1279 2c. Type **325** (postage) . . . 10 10
1280 6c. The Three Kings (22 × 32 mm) 15 10
1281 10c. Angel with bells (22 × 32 mm) (air) 20 15

326 Cable-car and Beach Scenes

1977. Tourism. Multicoloured.
1282 6c. Type **326** (postage) . . . 15 10
1283 10c. Tourist activities (air) 20 15
1284 12c. Fishing and hotel . . . 25 15
1285 25c. Horse-riding and waterfall 50 35
No. 1283 measures 36 × 36 mm, No. 1284 35 × 26 mm and No. 1285 26 × 35 mm.

327 Championships Emblem

1977. 10th Central American and Caribbean Children's Swimming Championships, Santo Domingo.
1286 **327** 3c. mult (postage) . . . 10 10
1287 5c. multicoloured 10 10
1288 10c. multicoloured (air) 20 15
1289 25c. multicoloured . . . 30 35

1977. Obligatory Tax. Rehabilitation of the Disabled. As T **283** but dated "1977".
1289a **283** 1c. blue 15 10

328 Allegory of Holy Week

329 "Oncidium variegatum" (orchid)

1977. Holy Week.
1290 **328** 2c. mult (postage) . . . 10 10
1291 – 6c. black and mauve . . 10 10
1292 – 10c. blk, red & bl (air) 20 10
DESIGNS: 6c. Christ crowned with thorns; 10c. Church and book.

1977. Obligatory Tax. Tuberculosis Relief Fund.
1293 **329** 1c. multicoloured 10 10

330 Gulls in Flight

1977. 12th Annual Lions Clubs Convention, Santo Domingo.
1294 **330** 2c. mult (postage) . . . 10 10
1295 6c. multicoloured 15 10
1296 7c. multicoloured (air) 15 10

331 "Battle of Tortuguero" (G. Fernandez)

1977. Navy Day.
1297 **331** 20c. multicoloured . . . 90 30

332 "Miss Universe" Emblem

333 "Nymphaea ampla" ("Nymphea" on stamp)

1977. Air. "Miss Universe" Competition.
1298 **332** 10c. multicoloured . . . 20 15

1977. Dominican Flora. Plants in the Dr. Rafael M. Moscoso National Botanical Gardens. Mult.
1299 2c. Type **333** (postage) . . . 10 10
1300 4c. "Broughtonia domingensis" 10 10
1301 6c. "Cordia sebestena" . . . 15 10
1302 7c. "Melocatus lemairei" (cactus) (air) 15 10
1303 33c. "Coccothrinax argentea" (tree) 70 45

334 Computers and Graph

1977. Seventh Inter-American Statistic Conference. Multicoloured.
1304 6c. Type **334** (postage) . . . 15 10
1305 28c. Factories and graph (27 × 37 mm) (air) 55 35

335 Haitian Solenodon

1977. 8th Inter-American Veterinary Congress. Multicoloured.
1306 6c. Type **335** (postage) . . . 15 10
1307 20c. Iguana 40 25
1308 10c. "Red Roman" stud bull (air) 20 15
1309 25c. Greater Flamingo (vert) 3·00 45

336 Main Gateway of Casa del Cordon

337 Tools and Crown of Thorns at Foot of Cross

1978. "Hispanidad 1977". Multicoloured.
1310 6c. Type **336** (postage) . . . 15 10
1311 21c. Gothic-style window, Casa del Tostado (28 × 41 mm) (air) 45 30

1978. Holy Week.
1312 **337** 2c. mult (postage) . . . 10 10
1313 – 6c. green 15 10
1314 – 7c. multicoloured (air) 15 10
1315 – 10c. multicoloured . . . 20 15
DESIGNS—(22 × 33 mm): 6c. Christ wearing Crown of Thorns. (27 × 37 mm): 7c. Facade of Santo Domingo Cathedral; 10c. Facade of Dominican Convent.

338 Schooner "Duarte"

339 Cardinal Octavio A. Beras Rojas

1978. Air. Navy Day.
1316 **338** 7c. multicoloured 75 15

1978. Consecration of First Cardinal from Dominican Republic.
1317 **339** 6c. mult (postage) . . . 15 10
1318 10c. multicoloured (air) 20 15

340 Microwave Antenna

1978. Air. 10th World Telecommunications Day.
1319 **340** 25c. multicoloured . . . 50 35

341 First Dominican Airmail Stamp and Map of First Airmail Service

342 Pres. Manuel de Troncoso

1978. Air. 50th Anniv of First Dominican Airmail Stamp.
1320 **341** 10c. multicoloured . . . 20 15

1978. Birth Centenary of President Troncoso.
1321 **342** 2c. brown, mauve & blk 10 10
1322 6c. brown, grey & black 15 10

343 Globe, Football and Emblem

344 Father Juan N. Zegri y Moreno (founder)

1978. Air. World Cup Football Championship, Argentina. Multicoloured.
1323 12c. Type **343** 25 15
1324 33c. Emblem and map on football pitch 75 45

1978. Centenary of Merciful Sisters of Charity. Multicoloured.
1325 6c. Type **344** (postage) . . . 15 10
1326 21c. Symbol of the Order (air) 40 30

345 Boxing

1978. 13th Central American and Caribbean Games, Medellin, Colombia. Multicoloured.
1327 2c. Type **345** (postage) . . . 10 10
1328 6c. Weightlifting 15 10
1329 7c. Baseball (vert) (air) . . . 15 10
1330 10c. Football (vert) 20 15

346 Douglas DC-6, Boeing 707 and Wright Flyer I

347 Sun over Landscape

1978. Air. 75th Anniv of First Powered Flight.
1331 **346** 7c. multicoloured 15 15
1332 – 10c. brown, yellow & red 35 15
1333 – 13c. blue & dp blue . . 45 20
1334 – 45c. multicoloured . . . 1·25 75
DESIGNS: 10c. Wright brothers and Wright Glider No. I; 13c. Diagram of airflow over wing; 45c. Wright Flyer I and world map.

1978. Tourism. Multicoloured.
1335 2c. Type **347** (postage) . . . 10 10
1336 6c. Sun over beach 15 10
1337 7c. Sun and musical instruments (air) 15 10
1338 10c. Sun over Santo Domingo 20 15

1978. Obligatory Tax. Anti-cancer Fund. As T **144** but dated "1977".
1338a **144** 1c. purple 15 10

348 Galleons

349 Flags of Dominican Republic and United Nations

1978. "Hispanidad 1978". Multicoloured.
1339 2c. Type **348** (postage) . . . 10 10
1340 21c. Figures holding hands in front of globe (air) . . 45 25

1978. Air. 33rd Anniv of United Nations.
1341 **349** 33c. multicoloured . . . 70 25

350 Mother and Child

351 Dove, Lamp and Poinsettia

1978. Obligatory Tax. Child Welfare.
1342 **350** 1c. green 10 10

1978. Christmas. Multicoloured.
1343 2c. Type **351** (postage) . . . 10 10
1344 6c. Dominican family and star 15 10
1345 10c. Statue of the Virgin (vert) (22 × 33 mm) (air) 20 15

352 Pope John Paul II

353 Map of Island, Iguana and Radio Transmitter

1979. Air. Visit of Pope John Paul II.
1346 **352** 10c. multicoloured . . . 70 20

1979. Air. 1st Expedition of Radio Amateurs to Beata Island.
1347 **353** 10c. multicoloured . . . 20 15

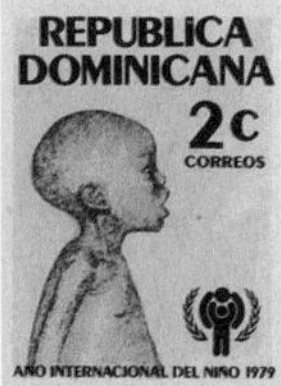

354 University Seal 355 Starving Child

1979. Obligatory Tax. 440th Anniv of Santo Domingo University.
1348 **354** 2c. blue 10 10

1979. International Year of the Child.
1349 **355** 2c. orge & blk (postage) 10 10
1350 – 7c. multicoloured (air) 15 10
1351 – 10c. multicoloured . . . 20 15
1352 – 33c. multicoloured . . . 70 45
DESIGNS: 7c. Children reading book; 10c. Head and protective hands; 33c. Hands and vases.

1979. Obligatory Tax. Rehabilitation of the Disabled. As T **283** but dated "1979".

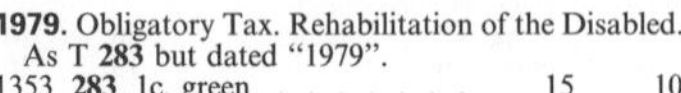

1353 **283** 1c. green 15 10

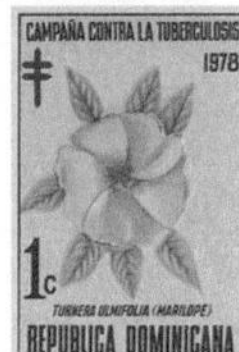

356 Crucifixion 357 "Turnera ulmifolia"

1979. Holy Week. Multicoloured.
1354 2c. Type **356** (postage) . . . 10 10
1355 3c. Christ carrying cross (horiz) 10 10
1356 10c. Pope John Paul II with Crucifix (air) 20 15

1978. Obligatory Tax. Tuberculosis Relief Fund. Dated "1978".
1357 **357** 1c. multicoloured 10 10

358 Admiral J. Cambiaso 359 Map, Stamp Album and Philatelic Equipment

1979. Air. 135th Anniv of Battle of Tortuguero.
1358 **358** 10c. multicoloured . . . 20 15

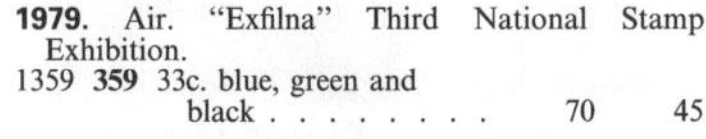

1979. Air. "Exfilna" Third National Stamp Exhibition.
1359 **359** 33c. blue, green and black 70 45

360 "Stigmaphyllon periplocifolium"

1979. Flowers from National Botanical Gardens.
1360 **360** 50c. grey, yellow and black (postage) . . . 1·00 70
1361 – 7c. multicoloured (air) 15 10
1362 – 10c. multicoloured . . . 20 15
1363 – 13c. blue, mauve & blk 25 15
DESIGNS: 7c. "Passiflora foetida"; 10c. "Isidorea pungens"; 13c. "Calotropis procera".

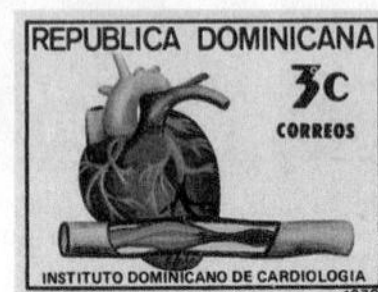

362 Heart and Section through Artery

1979. Dominican Cardiology Institute.
1364 **362** 3c. mult (postage) . . . 10 10
1365 – 1p. black, red & blue . . 2·00 1·40
1366 – 10c. multicoloured (air) 20 15
DESIGNS: VERT: 10c. Human figure showing blood circulation. HORIZ: 1p. Cardiology Institute and heart.

363 Baseball

1979. 8th Pan-American Games, Puerto Rico. Multicoloured.
1367 2c. Type **363** (postage) . . . 10 10
1368 3c. Cycling (vert) 10 10
1369 7c. Running (vert) (air) . . 15 10

364 Football 365 Sir Rowland Hill and First Dominican Republic Stamp

1979. 3rd National Games. Multicoloured.
1370 2c. Type **364** (postage) . . . 10 10
1371 25c. Swimming (horiz) . . . 55 35
1372 10c. Tennis (air) 20 15

1979. Air. Death Centenary of Sir Rowland Hill.
1373 **365** 2p. multicoloured . . . 4·25 1·10

366 Thomas Edison (inventor) 367 Hand removing Electric Plug

1979. Centenary of Electric Light-bulb. Mult.
1374 25c. Type **366** (postage) . . 55 30
1375 10c. "100" forming lightbulb (horiz) (air) 20 15

1979. "Save Energy". Multicoloured.
1376 2c. Type **367** 10 10
1377 6c. Car being refuelled . . . 15 10

368 Hispaniolan Conure 369 Lions Emblem

1979. Birds. Multicoloured.
1378 2c. Type **368** (postage) . . . 1·00 25
1379 6c. Hispaniolan trogon . . . 1·10 25
1380 7c. Black-crowned palm tanager (air) . . . . . . 1·60 35
1381 10c. Chat-tanager . . . . . 2·40 35
1382 45c. Black-cowled oriole . . 7·00 1·25

1979. 15th Anniv of Dominican Republic Lions Club. Multicoloured.
1383 20c. Type **369** (postage) . . 45 20
1384 10c. Melvin Jones (founder) (air) 20 10

371 Holy Family 372 Christ carrying Cross

1979. Christmas. Multicoloured.
1386 2c. Type **371** (postage) . . . 10 10
1387 10c. Three Kings (air) . . . 20 15

1980. Holy Week.
1388 **372** 3c. black, red and lilac (postage) 10 10
1389 – 7c. blk, red & yell (air) 15 10
1390 – 10c. black, red & bistre 20 15
DESIGNS: 7c. Crucifixion; 10c. Resurrection.

1980. Obligatory Tax. Rehabilitation of the Disabled. As T **283** but dated "1980".

1391 **283** 1c. olive and green . . . 10 10

374 Navy Crest 376 Cocoa Harvest

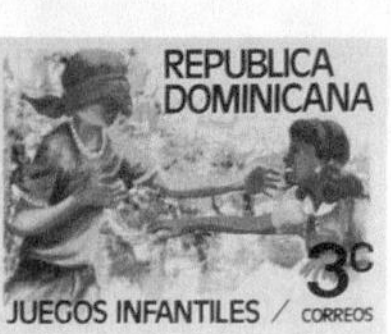

375 "Stamp"

1980. Air. Navy Day.
1392 **374** 21c. multicoloured . . . 45 30

1980. Air. 25th Anniv of Dominican Philatelic Society.
1393 **375** 10c. multicoloured . . . 20 15

1980. Agricultural Year. Multicoloured.
1394 1c. Type **376** 10 10
1395 2c. Coffee 10 10
1396 3c. Plantain 10 10
1397 4c. Sugar cane 10 10
1398 5c. Maize 10 10

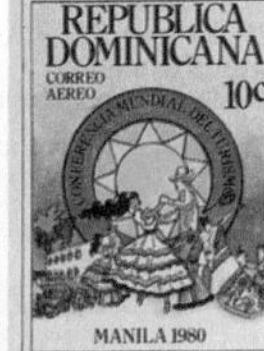

377 Cotuf Gold Mine, Pueblo Viejo 379 "Tourism"

378 Blind Man's Buff

1980. Nationalization of Gold Mines. Mult.
1399 6c. Type **377** (postage) . . . 15 10
1400 10c. Drag line mining (air) 20 15
1401 33c. General view of location of gold mines . . 70 45

1980. Children's Games. Multicoloured.
1402 3c. Type **378** 10 10
1403 4c. Marbles 10 10
1404 5c. Spinning top 10 10
1405 6c. Hopscotch 15 10

1980. Air. World Tourism Conference, Manila, Philippines. Multicoloured.
1406 10c. Type **379** 20 15
1407 33c. Conference emblem . . 70 45

REPUBLICA DOMINICANA

20c IGUANA DE RICORD/CYCLURA RICORDI FAUNA NACIONAL

380 Cuban Iguana

1980. Animals. Multicoloured.
1408 20c. Type **380** (postage) . . 45 30
1409 7c. American crocodile (air) 15 10
1410 10c. Hispaniolan hutia . . . 25 15
1411 25c. American manatee . . 65 35
1412 45c. Hawksbill turtle 95 60

381 "El Merengue" (Jaime Colson)

1980. Paintings. Multicoloured.
1413 3c. Type **381** (postage) . . . 10 10
1414 50c. "The Mirror" (G. H. Ortega) . . . . 1·10 70
1415 10c. "Genesis de un Ganga" (Paul Guidicelli) (air) . . 20 15
1416 17c. "The Countryman" (Yoryi Morel) 35 25

1980. Obligatory Tax. Anti-cancer Fund. As T **144** but dated "1980".
1417 **144** 1c. blue and violet . . . 10 10

383 Map of Catalina Island 384 Rotary Emblem on Globe

1980. Air. Visit of Radio Amateurs to Catalina Island.
1418 **383** 7c. green, blue & black 15 10

1980. Air. 75th Anniv of Rotary International. Multicoloured.
1419 10c. Type **384** 20 15
1420 33c. Rotary emblem in "75" 70 45

385 Carrier Pigeons with Letters

1980. Centenary of U.P.U. Membership. Mult.
1421 33c. Type **385** 70 45
1422 45c. Row of stylized pigeons and letter 95 60
1423 50c. Carrier pigeon with letter and letter . . . . . 1·10 70

1980. Obligatory tax. Child Welfare. As T **350** but dated "1980".
1425 **350** 1c. blue 10 10

386 The Three Kings 387 Arms of Salcedo

1980. Christmas. Multicoloured.
1426 3c. Type **386** (postage) . . . 10 10
1427 6c. Carol singers 15 10
1428 10c. The Holy Family (air) 20 15

1981. Centenary of Salcedo Province. Mult.
1429 6c. Type **387** (postage) . . . 15 10
1430 10c. Arms and map of Salcedo (air) 20 15

388 Juan Pablo Duarte 389 Industrial Symbols

1981. Juan Pablo Duarte (patriot). Commemoration.
1431 **388** 2c. brown and ochre . . 10 10

1981. Air. Chemical Engineering Seminar.
1432 **389** 10c. multicoloured . . . 20 15
1433 – 33c. gold and black . . . 70 45
DESIGN: 33c. Emblem of Dominican College of Engineering and Architecture (CODIA).

390 Gymnastics 391 Mother Mazzarello

1981. Fifth National Games (1st issue). Mult.
1434 1c. Type **390** (postage) . . . 10 10
1435 2c. Running 10 10
1436 3c. Pole-vaulting 10 10
1437 6c. Boxing 15 10
1438 10c. Baseball (air) 20 15
See also Nos. 1463/4.

1981. Death Centenary of Mother Mazarello (founder of Daughters of Mary).
1439 **391** 6c. brown and black . . 15 10

392 Admiral Juan Alejandro Acosta 393 Radio Waves

1981. Air. 137th Anniv of Battle of Tortuguero.
1440 **392** 10c. multicoloured . . . 20 15

1981. Obligatory Tax. Tuberculosis Relief Fund. Dated "1981".
1441 **357** 1c. multicoloured 10 10

1981. Air. World Telecommunications Day.
1442 **393** 10c. multicoloured . . . 15 15

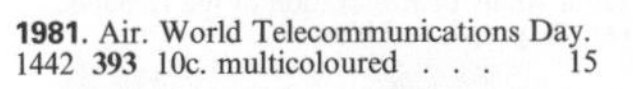

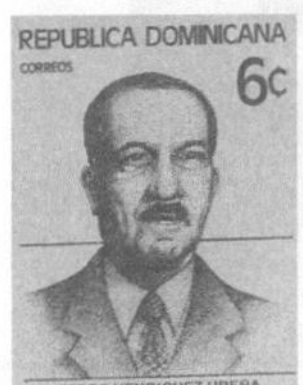

394 Pedro Henriquez Urena 395 Forest

1981. 35th Death Anniv of Pedro Henriquez Urena.
1443 **394** 6c. pale grey and grey 15 10

1981. Forest Conservation. Multicoloured.
1444 2c. Type **395** 10 10
1445 6c. Forest river 15 10

396 Heinrich von Stephan 397 "Disabled People"

1981. Air. 150th Birth Anniv of Heinrich von Stephan (founder of U.P.U.).
1446 **396** 33c. brown and yellow 70 45

1981. Air. International Year of Disabled Persons. Multicoloured.
1447 7c. Type **397** 15 10
1448 33c. Cobbler in wheelchair 70 45

398 Exhibition Emblem

1981. Air. "Expuridom '81" International Stamp Exhibition, Santo Domingo.
1149 **398** 7c. black, blue and red 15 10

399 Target

1981. Air. 2nd World Air Gun Shooting Championship. Multicoloured.
1450 10c. Type **399** 20 15
1451 15c. Stylized riflemen . . . 30 20
1452 25c. Stylized pistol shooters 55 55

400 Family and House

1981. National Census. Multicoloured.
1453 3c. Type **400** 10 10
1454 6c. Farmer with cow and agricultural produce . . . 15 10

1981. Obligatory Tax. Anti-cancer Fund. As T **144** but dated "1981".
1455 **144** 1c. blue and deep blue 10 10

401 Fruit

1981. Air. World Food Day. Multicoloured.
1456 10c. Type **401** 20 15
1457 50c. Fish, eggs and vegetables . . . . 1·10 70

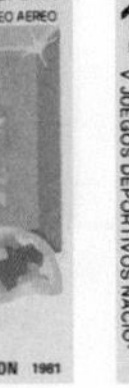

402 Gem Stones and Jewellery 403 Javelin-throwing

1981. Air. Exports. Multicoloured.
1458 7c. Type **402** 15 10
1459 10c. Handicrafts 20 15
1460 11c. Fruit 25 15
1461 17c. Cocoa, coffee, tobacco and sugar 35 25

1981. Obligatory Tax. Child Welfare. As T **350** but dated "1981".
1462 **350** 1c. green 10 10

1981. Air. 5th National Games, Barahona (2nd issue). Multicoloured.
1463 10c. Type **403** 20 15
1464 50c. Cycling . . . . 1·10 70

404 "Encyclia cochleata"

1981. Air. Orchids. Multicoloured.
1465 7c. Type **404** 10 15
1466 10c. "Broughtonia domingensis" 15 20
1467 25c. "Encyclia truncata" . . 55 35
1468 65c. "Elleanthus capitatus" 1·60 1·10

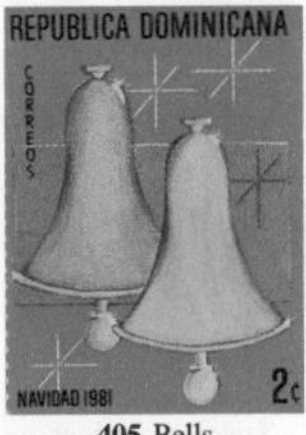

405 Bells 406 Juan Pablo Duarte

1981. Christmas. Multicoloured.
1469 2c. Type **405** (postage) . . . 10 10
1470 3c. Holly 10 10
1471 10c. Dove and moon (air) 20 15

1982. Juan Pablo Duarte (patriot) Commemoration.
1472 **406** 2c. light blue and blue 10 10

407 Citizens arriving at Polling Station

1982. National Elections. Multicoloured.
1473 2c. Type **407** 10 10
1474 3c. Entering polling booth (vert) 10 10
1475 6c. Casting vote 15 10

408 American Air Forces Co-operation Emblem

1982. Air. 22nd American Air Force's Commanders Conference, Buenos Aires.
1476 **408** 10c. multicoloured . . . 20 15

409 Naval Cadet Parade

1982. Air. Battle of Tortuguero Commem.
1477 **409** 10c. multicoloured . . . 20 15

410 Tackling 411 Lord Baden-Powell (statue)

1982. Air. World Cup Football Championship, Spain. Multicoloured.
1478 10c. Type **410** 20 15
1479 21c. Dribbling 45 30
1480 33c. Heading ball into goal 70 45

1982. Air. 75th Anniv of Boy Scout Movement. Multicoloured.
1481 10c. Type **411** 20 15
1482 15c. Scouting emblems (horiz) 30 20
1483 25c. Baden-Powell and scout at camp fire 55 35

412 "Study of Daylight" 413 Cathedral and House

1982. Energy Conservation. Multicoloured.
1484 1c. Type **412** 10 10
1485 2c. "Save rural electricity" 10 10
1486 3c. "Use wind power" . . . 10 10
1487 4c. "Switch off lights" . . . 10 10
1488 5c. "Conserve fuel" 15 10
1489 6c. "Use solar energy" . . . 15 10

1982. Air. 25th Congress of Latin-American Tourist Organizations Confederation, Santo Domingo. Multicoloured.
1490 7c. Congress emblem . . . 15 10
1491 10c. Type **413** 20 15
1492 33c. Dancers and beach scene 70 45

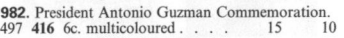

414 Exhibition Emblem

1982. Air. "Espamer '82" Stamp Exhibition, Puerto Rico. Multicoloured.
1493 7c. Stamp bearing map of Puerto Rico (horiz) . . . 15 10
1494 13c. Stylized postage stamps (horiz) 30 20
1495 50c. Type **414** . . . . . . 1·10 70

415 Emilio Prud'Homme and Score of Dominican National Anthem 416 President Guzman

1982. 50th Death Anniv of Emilio Prud'Homme (composer).
1496 **415** 6c. multicoloured 15 10

1982. President Antonio Guzman Commemoration.
1497 **416** 6c. multicoloured 15 10

417 Baseball

1982. Central American and Caribbean Games, Cuba. Multicoloured.
1498 3c. Type **417** (postage) . . . 10 10
1499 10c. Basketball (air) 20 15
1500 13c. Boxing 30 20
1501 25c. Gymnastics 55 30

418 "Harbour" (Alejandro Bonilla)

1982. Air. Paintings. Multicoloured.
1502 7c. Type **418** 15 10
1503 10c. "Portrait of a Woman" (Leopoldo Navarro) . . . 20 15
1504 45c. "Portrait of Amelia Francasci" (Luis Desangles) 95 65
1505 2p. "Portrait" (Abelardo Rodriguez Urdaneta) . . 4·25 2·75

419 Horse-drawn Carriage

1982. Centenary of San Pedro de Macoris Province. Multicoloured.
1506 1c. Type **419** (postage) . . . 10 10
1507 2c. Stained-glass window, San Pedro Apostle Church (25 × 34½ mm) . . 10 10

1508 5c. Centenary emblem . . . 15 10
1509 7c. View of San Pedro de Macoris City (air) 45 20

420 "Santa Maria" and Map of Voyage

1982. Air. 490th Anniv of Discovery of America by Columbus. Multicoloured.
1510 7c. Type **420** . . . . 1·00 30
1511 10c. "Santa Maria" . . . . 1·25 35
1512 21c. Statue of Columbus, Santo Domingo 45 30

421 Central Bank

1982. 35th Anniv of Central Bank.
1513 **421** 10c. multicoloured . . . 20 15

422 St. Theresa of Avila

423 Christmas Tree Decorations

1982. 400th Death Anniv of St. Theresa of Avila.
1514 **422** 6c. multicoloured 15 10

1982. Christmas. Multicoloured.
1515 6c. Type **423** (postage) . . . 10 10
1516 10c. Tree decorations (different) (air) 20 15

424 Hand holding Rural and Urban Environments

1982. Environmental Protection. Mult.
1517 2c. Type **424** 10 10
1518 3c. Hand holding river in the country 10 10
1519 6c. Hand holding forest . . 10 10
1520 20c. Hand holding swimming fish 35 25

425 Adults writing

1983. National Literacy Campaign. Mult.
1521 2c. Girl and boy writing on blackboard 10 10
1522 3c. Type **425** 10 10
1523 6c. Children, rainbow and pencil 10 10

426 Clasped Hands and Eiffel Tower

1983. Air. Centenary of French Alliance (French language-teaching association).
1524 **426** 33c. multicoloured . . . 50 30

427 Arms of Mao City Council

428 Frigate "Mella"

1983. Centenary of Mao City Council. Mult.
1525 1c. Type **427** 10 10
1526 5c. Centenary monument . . 10 10

1983. Air. Battle of Tortuguero. Commemoration.
1527 **428** 15c. multicoloured . . . 1·50 40

429 Antonio del Monte y Tejada

430 Red Cross

1983. Dominican Historians.
1528 **429** 2c. red & brn (postage) 10 10
1529 – 3c. pink and brown . . . 10 10
1530 – 5c. blue and brown . . . 15 10
1531 – 6c. lt brown & brown . . 15 10
1532 – 7c. pink & brown (air) 15 10
1533 – 10c. grey and brown . . 20 15
DESIGNS: 3c. Manuel Ubaldo Gomez; 5c. Emiliano Tejera; 6c. Bernardo Pichardo; 7c. Americo Lugo; 10c. Jose Gabriel Garcia.

1983. Obligatory Tax. Red Cross.
1534 **430** 1c. red, gold & black . . 10 10

431 Dish Aerial and W.C.Y. Emblem

432 "Simon Bolivar" (Plutarco Andujar)

1983. Air. World Communications Year.
1535 **431** 10c. light blue & blue . . 20 15

1983. Air. Birth Bicentenary of Simon Bolivar.
1536 **432** 9c. multicoloured 15 10

433 Pictogram of Rehabilitation

434 Basketball and Gymnastics

1983. Obligatory Tax. Rehabilitation of the Disabled.
1537 **433** 1c. blue 10 10

1983. Air. Pan-American Games, Venezuela. Multicoloured.
1538 7c. Type **434** 15 10
1539 10c. Boxing and pole vaulting 20 15
1540 15c. Baseball, weightlifting and cycling 25 15

435 Emilio Prud'Homme and Jose Reyes (composers)

1983. Cent of Dominican National Anthem.
1541 **435** 6c. multicoloured 10 10

1983. Obligatory Tax. Anti-cancer Fund. As T **144** but dated "1983".
1542 **144** 1c. turquoise & green . . 10 10

436 "Sotavento" (winner of 1982 regatta)

437 Arms

1983. Air. Christopher Columbus Regatta and 500th Anniv (1992) of Discovery of America by Columbus (1st issue).
1543 – 10c. stone, brn & blk . . 1·00 45
1544 – 21c. multicoloured . . . 1·25 60
1545 **436** 33c. multicoloured . . . 1·90 65
DESIGNS—HORIZ: 10c. Old map of Greater Antilles; 21c. Christopher Columbus Regatta trophy.
See also Nos. 1583/5, 1617/20, 1649/52, 1683/6, 1717/20, 1754/7, 1777/80, 1791/4 and 1805/8.

1983. 125th Anniv of Dominican Freemasons.
1547 **437** 4c. multicoloured 10 10

438 Our Lady of Regla Church

439 Clocktower

1983. 300th Anniv of Our Lady of Regla Church.
1548 **438** 3c. deep blue & blue . . 10 10
1549 – 6c. red and deep red . . 10 10
DESIGN: 6c. Statue of Our Lady of Regla.

1983. 450th Anniv of Monte Cristi Province.
1550 **439** 1c. green and black . . . 10 10
1551 – 2c. multicoloured 10 10
1552 – 5c. grey 10 10
1553 – 7c. grey and blue 15 10
DESIGNS—VERT: 2c. Provincial coat of arms. HORIZ: 5c. Wooden building in which independence of Cuba was signed; 7c. Men digging out salt crystals.

1983. Obligatory Tax. Child Welfare. As T **350** but dated "1983".
1554 **350** 1c. green 10 10

440 Commission Emblem

1983. Air. 10th Anniv of Latin American Civil Aviation Commission.
1555 **440** 10c. blue 15 10

441 Baseball, Boxing and Cycling

442 Bells and Christmas Tree Decorations

1983. 6th National Games, San Pedro de Macoris. Multicoloured.
1556 6c. Type **441** (postage) . . . 10 10
1557 10c. Weightlifting, running and swimming (air) . . . 15 10

1983. Air. Christmas.
1558 **442** 10c. multicoloured . . . 15 10

443 "Portrait of a Girl" (Adriana Billini)

1983. Air. Paintings. Multicoloured.
1559 10c. "The Litter" (Juan Bautista Gomez) (horiz) 15 10
1560 15c. "The Meeting between Maximo Gomez and Jose Marti at Guayubin" (Enrique Garcia Godoy) (horiz) 20 15
1561 21c. "St. Francis" (Angel Perdomo) 30 20
1562 33c. Type **443** 45 30

444 Monument to Heroes of Capotillo

1983. 120th Anniv of Restoration of the Republic.
1563 **444** 1c. purple and blue . . . 10 10

445 Man holding Dominican Flag and Rifle

1983. 67th Anniv of Battle of Barranquita.
1564 **445** 5c. multicoloured 10 10

446 Matias Ramon Mella and Dominican Flag

1984. 140th Anniv of Independence. Mult.
1565 6c. Type **446** 10 10
1566 25c. Puerta de la Misericordia and Mella's rifle 15 15

447 Dr. Heriberto Pieter

1984. Birth Centenary of Dr. Heriberto Pieter.
1567 **447** 3c. multicoloured 10 10

448 Jose Maria Imbert, Fernando Valerio, Cannon and National Flag

1984. 140th Anniv of Battle of Santiago.
1568 **448** 7c. multicoloured 10 10

449 Coastguard Patrol Boat

1984. 140th Anniv of Battle of Tortuguero.
1569 **449** 10c. multicoloured . . . 1·00 20

450 Monument to the Heroes of June 1959

1984. 25th Anniv of Expedition to Constanza, Maimon and Estero Hondo.
1570 **450** 6c. multicoloured 10 10

451 Salome Urena

1984. Birth Centenary of Pedro Henriquez Urena (poet).
1571 **451** 7c. pink and brown . . . 10 10
1572 – 10c. yellow and brown 10 10
1573 – 22c. yellow and brown 15 15
DESIGNS: 10c. Lines from poem "Mi Pedro"; 22c. Pedro H. Urena.

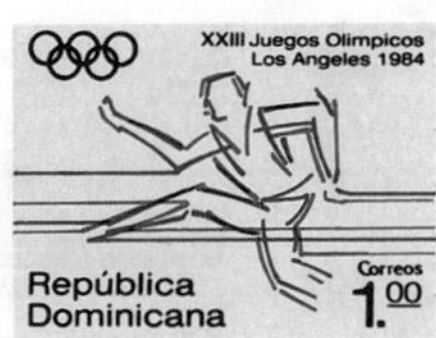

452 Running

1984. Olympic Games, Los Angeles. Each in blue, red and black.
1574 1p. Type **452** 55 50
1575 1p. Weightlifting 55 50
1576 1p. Boxing 55 50
1577 1p. Baseball 55 50

453 Stygian Owl **455** Pope John Paul II

454 Christopher Columbus landing in Hispaniola

1984. Protection of Wildlife. Multicoloured.
1578 10c. Type **453** . . . . . . 1·50 30
1579 15c. Greater flamingo . . . 2·00 40
1580 25c. White-lipped peccary 15 10
1581 35c. Haitian solenodon . . . 25 20

1984. 500th Anniv (1992) of Discovery of America by Columbus (2nd issue).
1582 **454** 10c. multicoloured . . . 10 10
1583 – 35c. multicoloured . . . 25 20
1584 – 65c. brown, yell & blk 40 35
1585 – 1p. multicoloured . . . 55 50
DESIGNS: 35c. Destruction of Fort La Navidad; 65c. First mass in America; 1p. Battle of Santo Cerro.

1984. Papal Visit to Santo Domingo. 500th Anniv of Christianity in the New World. Multicoloured.
1586 75c. Type **455** 45 40
1587 75c. Pope in priest's attire and map 45 40
1588 75c. Globe and Pope in ceremonial attire 45 40
1589 75c. Bishop's crosier 45 40

456 Gomez on Horseback

1984. 150th Birth Anniv (1986) of Maximo Gomez (leader of Cuban Revolution). Multicoloured.
1590 10c. Type **456** 10 10
1591 20c. Maximo Gomez . . . 15 10

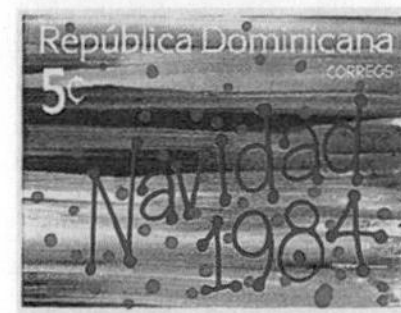

457 "Navidad 1984"

1984. Christmas.
1592 **457** 5c. mauve, blue and gold 10 10
1593 – 10c. blue, gold & mauve 10 10
DESIGN: 10c. "Navidad 1984" (different).

458 "The Sacrifice of the Kid" (Eligio Pichardo)

1984. Art. Multicoloured.
1594 5c. Type **458** 10 10
1595 10c. "Pumpkin Sellers" (statuette, Gaspar Mario Cruz) (vert) 10 10
1596 25c. "The Market" (Celeste Woss y Gil) 15 15
1597 50c. "Horses in a Storm" (Dario Suro) 30 25

459 Old Church, Higuey

1985. Our Lady of Altagracia's Day. Mult.
1598 5c. Type **459** 10 10
1599 10c. "Our Lady of Altagracia" (1514 painting) 15 10
1600 25c. Basilica of Our Lady of Altagracia, Higuey . . . 35 30

460 Sanchez, Durate and Mella

1985. 141st Anniv of Independence.
1601 **460** 5c. multicoloured 10 10
1602 10c. multicoloured . . . 15 10
1603 25c. multicoloured . . . 35 30

461 Gen. Antonia Duverge

1985. 141st Anniv of Azua Battle.
1604 **461** 10c. cream, red & brown 15 10

462 Santo Domingo Lighthouse, 1853

463 Flags and Emblem

1985. 141st Anniv of Battle of Tortuguero.
1605 **462** 25c. multicoloured . . . 35 30

1985. 25th Anniv of American Airforces Co-operation System.
1606 **463** 35c. multicoloured . . . 50 45

464 Carlos Maria Rojas (first Governor)

465 Table Tennis Player

1985. Centenary of Espaillat Province.
1607 **464** 10c. multicoloured . . . 10 10

1985. "MOCA 85" (Seventh National Games). Multicoloured.
1608 5c. Type **465** 10 10
1609 10c. Walking race 10 10

466 Young People of Different Races

1985. International Youth Year. Mult.
1610 5c. Type **466** 10 10
1611 25c. The Haitises 15 10
1612 35c. Mt. Duarte summit . . 20 15
1613 2p. Mt. Duarte 90 85

467 Evangelina Rodriguez (first Dominican woman doctor)

468 Emblem

1985. International Decade for Women.
1614 **467** 10c. multicoloured . . . 10 10

1985. 15th Central American and Caribbean Games, Santiago.
1615 **468** 5c. multicoloured 10 10
1616 25c. multicoloured . . . 15 10

469 Fourth Christopher Columbus Regatta

1985. 500th Anniv (1992) of Discovery of America by Columbus (3rd issue). Multicoloured.
1617 35c. Type **469** . . . . . . 1·00 30
1618 50c. Foundation of Santo Domingo, 1496 . . . . . 25 20
1619 65c. Chapel of Our Lady of the Rosary, 1496 . . . . 35 30
1620 1p. Christopher Columbus's arrival in New World . . 45 40

470 Bust of Enriquillo

471 Arturo de Merino

1985. 450th Death Anniv of Enriquillo (Indian chief). Multicoloured.
1621 5c. Enriquillo in Bahoruco mountains (mural) (46 × 32 mm) 10 10
1622 10c. Type **470** 10 10

1985. Centenary of Ordination of Fernando Arturo de Merino (former President).
1623 **471** 25c. multicoloured . . . 15 10

472 Fruit, Candle and Holly

1985. Christmas.
1624 **472** 10c. multicoloured . . . 15 10
1625 25c. multicoloured . . . 15 10

473 Haina Harbour

1985. 25th Anniv of Inter-American Development Bank. Multicoloured.
1626 10c. Type **473** 55 15
1627 25c. Map and ratio diagram of development activities 15 10
1628 1p. Tavera-Bao-Lopez hydro-electric complex . . 45 40

474 Mirabal Sisters

1985. 25th Death Anniv of Minerva, Patria and Maria Mirabal.
1629 **474** 10c. multicoloured . . . 10 10

475 Tomb of Duarte, Sanchez and Mella

1986. National Independence Day.
1630 **475** 5c. multicoloured 10 10
1631 10c. multicoloured . . . 10 10

476 St. Michael's Church **478** Voters, Ballot Box and Map

477 "Leonor" (schooner) and Dominican Navy Founders

1986. Holy Week. Santo Domingo Churches. Multicoloured.

1632 5c. Type **476** 10 10
1633 5c. St. Andrew's Church . . 10 10
1634 10c. St. Lazarus's Church 10 10
1635 10c. St. Charles's Church . . 10 10
1636 10c. St. Barbara's Church 10 10

1986. Navy Day.

1637 **477** 10c. multicoloured . . . 80 20

1986. National Elections. Multicoloured.

1638 5c. Type **478** 10 10
1639 10c. Hand dropping voting slip into ballot box . . . 30 10

479 Emblem **480** Weightlifting

1986. Creation of "Inposdom" (Dominican Postal Institute).

1640 **479** 10c. blue, red and gold 10 10
1641 25c. blue, red and silver 15 10
1642 50c. blue, red and black 25 20

1986. 15th Central American and Caribbean Games, Santiago. Multicoloured.

1643 10c. Type **480** 10 10
1644 25c. Gymnast on rings . . . 15 10
1645 35c. Diving 20 15
1646 50c. Show-jumping 25 20

481 Ercilia Pepin **482** Fifth Christopher Columbus Regatta

1986. Writers' Birth Centenaries. Each brown and silver.

1647 5c. Type **481** 10 10
1648 10c. Ramon Emilio Jiminez and Victor Garrido . . . 10 10

1986. 500th Anniv (1992) of Discovery of America by Columbus (4th issue). Multicoloured.

1649 25c. Type **482** 30 10
1650 50c. Foundation of Isabela city 25 20
1651 65c. Spanish soldiers 35 30
1652 1p. Columbus before King of Spain 45 40

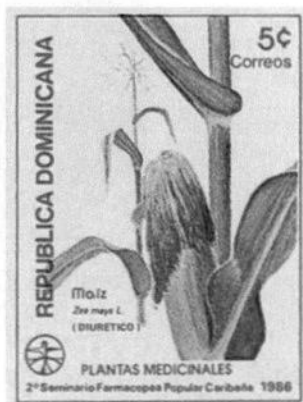

483 Goalkeeper saving Ball **484** Maize

1986. World Cup Football Championship, Mexico. Multicoloured.

1654 50c. Type **483** 25 20
1655 75c. Footballer and ball . . 40 35

1986. 2nd Caribbean Pharmacopoeia Seminar. Medicinal Plants. Multicoloured.

1656 5c. Type **484** 10 10
1657 10c. Arnotto 10 10
1658 25c. "Momordica charantia" 15 10
1659 50c. Custard-apple 25 20

485 Town with Christmas Tree

1986. Christmas. Multicoloured.

1660 5c. Type **485** 15 10
1661 25c. Village 15 10

486 Gomez on Horseback **488** Emblem

1986. 150th Birth Anniv of Maximo Gomez.

1662 **486** 10c. black and mauve . . 10 10
1663 – 25c. black and brown . . 15 10

DESIGN: 25c. Head of Gomez.

1987. 16th Pan-American Ophthalmology Congress, Santo Domingo.

1676 **488** 50c. red, blue & black 20 15

489 "Ascension of Jesus Christ" (stained glass window, St. John Bosco Church) **490** "Sorghum bicolor"

1987. Ascension Day.

1677 **489** 35c. multicoloured . . . 10 10

1987. Edible Plants. Multicoloured.

1678 5c. Type **490** 10 10
1679 25c. "Maranta arundinacea" 10 10
1680 65c. "Calathea allouia" . . 20 15
1681 1p. "Voandzeia subterranea" 35 30

491 Emblem and People on Map

1987. 25th Anniv of Club Activo 20–30 in Dominican Republic.

1682 **491** 35c. multicoloured . . . 10 10

492 Sixth Christopher Columbus Regatta

1987. 500th Anniv (1992) of Discovery of America by Columbus (5th issue). Multicoloured.

1683 50c. Type **492** 10 10
1684 75c. Columbus writing diary 15 10
1685 1p. Foundation of city of Santiago 20 15
1686 1p.50 Columbus and Bobadilla 30 25

493 Games Emblem **494** Jose Antonio Hungria

1987. 50th Anniv of La Vega Province Games.

1688 **493** 40c. multicoloured . . . 10 10

1987. Writers' Birth Anniversaries.

1689 **494** 10c. brown & lt brown 10 10
1690 – 25c. dp green & green 10 10

DESIGN: 25c. Joaquin Sergio Inchaustegui.

495 Baseball **496** Statue

1987. 8th National Games, San Cristobal. Multicoloured.

1691 5c. Type **495** 10 10
1692 10c. Boxing 10 10
1693 50c. Karate 10 10

1987. 150th Birth Anniv of Fr. Francisco Xavier Billini.

1694 **496** 10c. deep blue and blue 10 10
1695 – 25c. green and olive . . 10 10
1696 – 75c. brown and pink . . 15 10

DESIGNS: 25c. Fr. Billini; 75c. Ana Hernandez de Billini (mother).

497 Maj. Frank Feliz and Airplane

1987. 50th Anniv of Pan-American Flight for Columbus Lighthouse Fund.

1697 **497** 25c. multicoloured . . . 20 10

498 Spit-roasting Pig

1987. Christmas. Multicoloured.

1699 10c. Type **498** 10 10
1700 50c. Passengers disembarking from airplane 20 10

499 "Bromelia pinguin"

1988. Flowers. Multicoloured.

1701 50c. Type **499** 10 10
1702 50c. "Tillandsia compacta" (vert) 10 10
1703 50c. "Tillandsia fasciculata" 10 10
1704 50c. "Tillandsia hotteana" (vert) 10 10

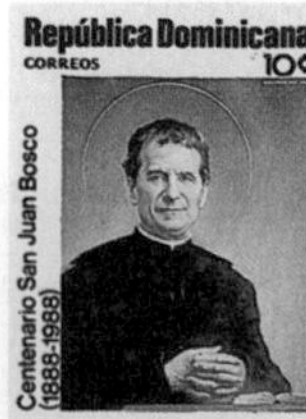

500 St. John Bosco

1988. Death Centenary of St. John Bosco (founder of Salesian Brothers). Multicoloured.

1705 10c. Type **500** 10 10
1706 70c. Stained glass window 15 10

501 Rainbow, Doves and Cloud

1988. 25th Anniv of Dominican Rehabilitation Association.

1707 **501** 20c. multicoloured . . . 10 10

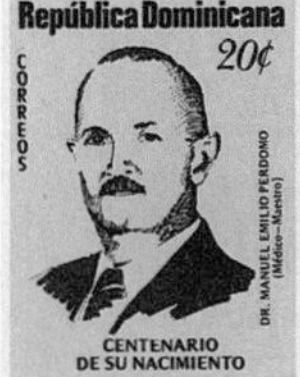

502 Perdomo **503** Emblem

1988. Birth Centenary of Dr. Manuel Emilio Perdomo.

1708 **502** 20c. brown and flesh . . 10 10

1988. 25th Anniv of Dominican College of Engineering and Architecture (CODIA).

1709 **503** 20c. multicoloured . . . 10 10

504 Church and Madonna and Child **505** Flags and Juan Pablo Duarte (Dominican patriot)

1988. Centenary of Parish Church of Our Lady of the Carmelites, Duverge.

1710 **504** 50c. multicoloured . . . 10 10

1988. Mexican Independence Day. Mult.

1711 50c. Type **505** 10 10
1712 50c. Flags and Miguel Hidalgo (Mexican patriot) 10 10

506 Athletics **507** Seventh Christopher Columbus Regatta

1988. Olympic Games, Seoul. Multicoloured.

1713 50c. Type **506** 10 10
1714 70c. Table tennis 15 10
1715 1p. Judo 20 15
1716 1p.50 "Ying Yang symbol and Balls" (Tete Marella) (horiz) 30 25

1988. 500th Anniv of Discovery of America by Columbus (6th issue). Multicoloured.

1717 50c. Type **507** 10 10
1718 70c. Building fort at La Vega Real, 1494 . . . . 15 10
1719 1p.50 Bonao Fort 30 25
1720 2p. Nicolas de Ovando (Governor of Hispaniola) 40 35

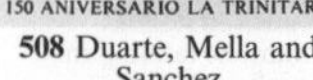

508 Duarte, Mella and Sanchez **509** Parchment, Knife and Pestle and Mortar

1988. 150th Anniv of Trinitarian Rebellion.

1722 **508** 10c. silver, red and blue 10 10
1723 – 1p. multicoloured . . . 20 15
1724 – 5p. multicoloured . . . 95 90

DESIGNS: 1p. Plaza La Trinitaria; 5p. Plaza de la Independencia.

1988. 13th Pan-American and 16th Central American Congresses of Pharmacy and Biochemistry.

1725 **509** 1p. multicoloured . . . 20 15

510 "Doni Tondo" (Michelangelo)   **511** Emblem

1988. Christmas. Multicoloured.
1726 10c. Type **510** 10 10
1727 20c. Stained glass window 10 10

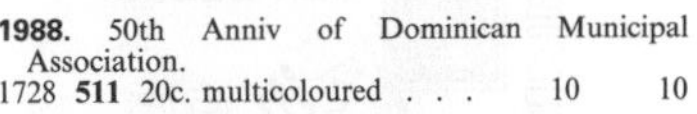

1988. 50th Anniv of Dominican Municipal Association.
1728 **511** 20c. multicoloured . . . 10 10

512 Ana Teresa Paradas

1988. 28th Death Anniv of Ana Teresa Paradas (lawyer).
1729 **512** 20c. red 10 10

513 Birds

1989. Bicentenary of French Revolution.
1730 **513** 3p. red, blue and black 30 25

516 Battle Scene

1989. 145th Anniv of Battle of Tortuguero.
1737 **516** 40c. multicoloured . . . 70 25

517 Drug Addict

1989. Anti-drugs Campaign.
1738 **517** 10c. multicoloured . . . 10 10
1739 20c. multicoloured . . . 10 10
1740 50c. multicoloured . . . 10 10
1741 70c. multicoloured . . . 10 10
1742 1p. multicoloured . . . 10 10
1743 1p.50 multicoloured . . 15 15
1744 2p. multicoloured . . . 20 15
1745 5p. multicoloured . . . 50 45
1746 10p. multicoloured . . . 1·00 95

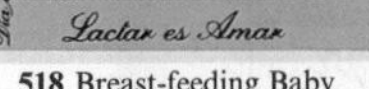

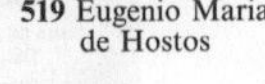

518 Breast-feeding Baby   **519** Eugenio Maria de Hostos

1989. Mothers' Day.
1747 **518** 20c. multicoloured . . . 10 10

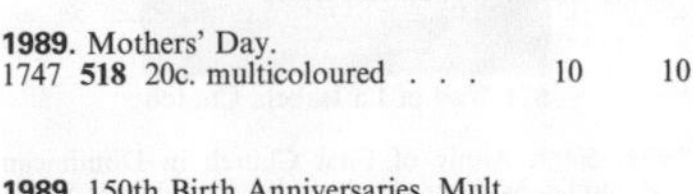

1989. 150th Birth Anniversaries. Mult.
1748 20c. Type **519** 10 10
1749 20c. Gen. Gregorio Luperon 10 10

520 Baseball

1989. 50th Anniv of Baseball Minor League.
1750 **520** 1p. multicoloured . . . 10 10

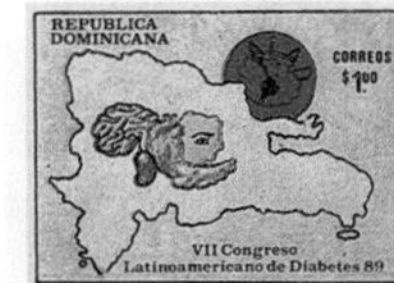

521 Map and Human Organs

1989. 7th Latin American Diabetes Association Congress.
1751 **521** 1p. multicoloured . . . 10 10

522 Cohoba Artefact and Ritual Dance

1989. America. Pre-Columbian Culture. Mult.
1752 20c. Type **522** 10 10
1753 1p. Taina vessel, pounding instrument and Indians preparing manioc cake . . 10 10

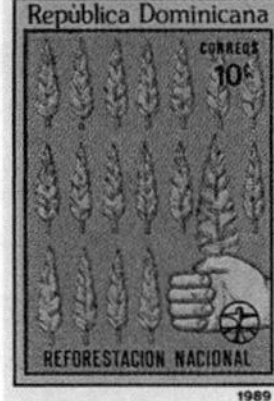

523 Eighth Christopher Columbus Regatta   **524** Dead and Living Leaves

1989. 500th Anniv (1992) of Discovery of America by Columbus (7th issue). Multicoloured.
1754 50c. Type **523** 10 10
1755 70c. Brother Pedro de Cordoba preaching to Indians (horiz) 10 10
1756 1p. Columbus dividing Indian lands (horiz) . . . 10 10
1757 3p. Brother Antonio Montesinos giving sermon (horiz) 30 25

1989. National Reafforestation Campaign. Mult.
1758 10c. Type **524** 10 10
1759 20c. Forest 10 10
1760 50c. Forest and lake 10 10
1761 1p. Living tree and avenue of dead trees 10 10

525 Map and Cyclist   **526** Mary and Body of Jesus

1990. 9th National Games, La Vega. Mult.
1762 10c. Type **525** 10 10
1763 20c. Map and runner . . . 10 10
1764 50c. Map and handball player 10 10

1990. Holy Week. Multicoloured.
1765 20c. Type **526** 10 10
1766 50c. Jesus carrying cross . . 10 10

527 Cogwheel and Workers

1990. International Labour Day.
1767 **527** 1p. multicoloured . . . 10 10

528 Avenida Mexico

1990. Urban Development. Multicoloured.
1768 10c. Type **528** 10 10
1769 20c. Avenida Nunez de Caceres road tunnel . . . 10 10
1770 50c. National Library . . . 10 10
1771 1p. V Centenario Motorway 10 10

529 Penny Black   **530** "Ruins of St. Nicholas's Church, Bari"

1990. 150th Anniv of the Penny Black. Mult.
1772 **529** 1p. multicoloured . . . 10 10

1990. Children's Drawings. Multicoloured.
1774 50c. Type **530** 10 10
1775 50c. "House, Tostado" . . . 10 10

531 Members' Flags   **532** Yachts (Ninth Christopher Columbus Regatta)

1990. Centenary of Organization of American States.
1776 **531** 2p. multicoloured . . . 20 15

1990. 500th Anniv (1992) of Discovery of America by Columbus (8th issue). Multicoloured.
1777 50c. Type **532** 40 10
1778 1p. Confrontation between natives and sailors (horiz) 10 10
1779 2p. Meeting of Columbus and Guacanagari (horiz) 20 15
1780 5p. Caonabo imprisoned by Columbus (horiz) 45 30

533 Amerindians in Canoe   **534** Perez Rancier

1990. America. Multicoloured.
1781 50c. Type **533** 30 10
1782 3p. Amerindian in hammock 25 15

1991. Birth Centenary of Dr. Tomas Eudoro Perez Rancier (physician).
1783 **534** 2p. black and yellow . . 20 10

535 First Official Mass in America   **536** Boxing

1991. Spanish America. Multicoloured.
1784 50c. Type **535** 10 10
1785 1p. Arms (first religious orders) 10 10
1786 3p. Map of Hispaniola (first European settlement) (horiz) 30 20
1787 4p. Christopher Columbus (first viceroy and governor) 45 30

1991. 11th Pan-American Games, Havana. Multicoloured.
1788 30c. Type **536** 10 10
1789 50c. Cycling 10 10
1790 1p. Putting the shot 10 10

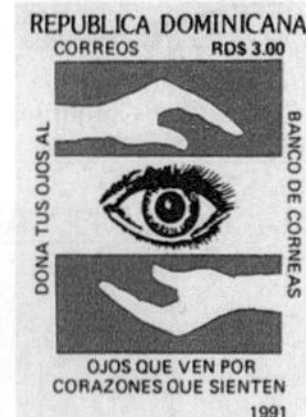

537 Yachts (10th Christopher Columbus Regatta)   **538** Eye and Hands

1991. 500th Anniv (1992) of Discovery of America by Columbus (9th issue). Multicoloured.
1791 30c. Type **537** 10 10
1792 50c. Meeting of three cultures (horiz) 10 10
1793 3p. Columbus and Doctor Alvarez Chanco (horiz) 30 20
1794 4p. Enriquillo's war (horiz) 45 30

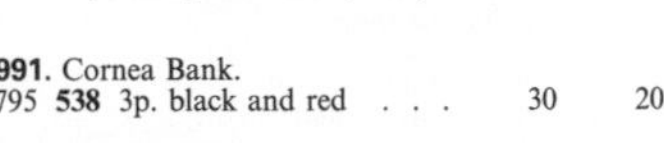

1991. Cornea Bank.
1795 **538** 3p. black and red . . . 30 20

539 "Santa Maria"   **540** Meeting Emblem

1991. America. Voyages of Discovery. Mult.
1796 1p. Type **539** 20 15
1797 3p. Columbus and fleet . . 40 25

1992. 33rd Annual Meeting of Governors of Inter-American Development Bank, Santo Domingo.
1798 **540** 1p. multicoloured . . . 10 10

541 Valentin Salinero (founder)   **542** Flags of Cuba, Dominican Republic and Puerto Rica, and Magnifying Glass

1992. Centenary (1991) of Order of the Apostles.
1799 **541** 1p. brown, black & blue 10 10

1992. "Espanola 92" Stamp Exhibition.
1800 **542** 3p. black, violet & red 30 20

543 First Monastery in Americas

1992. Ruins. Multicoloured.
1801 50c. Type **543** 10 10
1802 3p. First hospital in Americas 30 20

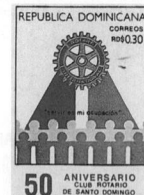

544 La Vega Cathedral and Pope

1992. Visit of Pope John Paul II. Mult.
1803 50c. Type **544** 10 10
1804 3p. Santo Domingo Cathedral and Pope . . . 30 20

545 Yacht (11th Christopher Columbus Regatta)

547 Convention Emblem

546 Columbus Lighthouse

1992. 500th Anniv of Discovery of America by Columbus (10th issue). Multicoloured.
1805 50c. Type **545** 10 10
1806 1p. Amerindian women preparing food and Columbus (horiz) 10 10
1807 2p. Amerindians demonstrating use of tobacco to Columbus (horiz) 20 10
1808 3p. Amerindian woman and Columbus by maize field (horiz) 30 20

1992.
1809 **546** 30c. multicoloured . . . 10 10
1810 1p. multicoloured . . . 10 10

1992. 23rd Pan-American Round Table Convention, Santo Domingo.
1812 **547** 1p. brown, cream & red 10 10

548 First Royal Palace in Americas, Santo Domingo

549 Torch Bearer

1992. America. Multicoloured.
1813 50c. Type **548** 10 10
1814 3p. First Vice-regal residence in Americas, Colon . . . 30 20

1992. 10th National Games, San Juan.
1815 **549** 30c. multicoloured . . . 10 10
1816 – 1p. multicoloured . . . 10 10
1817 – 4p. black and blue . . . 40 25
DESIGNS: 1p. Emblem of Secretary of State for Sports Education and Recreation; 4p. Judo.

550 Emblem

551 Ema Balaguer

1993. 7th Population and Housing Census.
1818 **550** 50c. blue, black & pink 10 10
1819 1p. blue, black & brown 10 10
1820 3p. blue, black & grey 30 20
1821 4p. blue, black & green 40 25

1993. Ema Balaguer (humanitarian worker) Commemoration.
1822 **551** 30c. multicoloured . . . 10 10
1823 50c. multicoloured . . . 10 10
1824 1p. multicoloured . . . 10 10

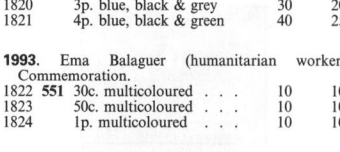

552 Emblem and Stylized Figures

1993. 50th Anniv of Santo Domingo Rotary Club. Multicoloured.
1825 30c. Type **552** 10 10
1826 1p. National flags and rotary emblem 10 10

553 Institute

1993. Inauguration of New Dominican Postal Institute Building.
1827 **553** 1p. multicoloured . . . 10 10
1828 3p. multicoloured . . . 30 20
1829 4p. multicoloured . . . 40 25
1830 5p. multicoloured . . . 50 30
1831 10p. multicoloured . . . 95 60

554 Palm Chat and Books

556 Chest (first university)

555 Racketball

1993. Ten Year Education Plan.
1833 **554** 1p.50 multicoloured . . 1·40 1·40

1993. 17th Central American and Caribbean Games, Ponce (Puerto Rico). Multicoloured.
1834 50c. Type **555** 10 10
1835 4p. Swimming 40 25

1993. American Firsts in Hispaniola (1st series). Multicoloured.
1836 50c. Type **556** 10 10
1837 3p. First arms conferred on American city 30 20
See also Nos. 1840 and 1882/3.

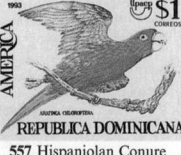

557 Hispaniolan Conure

1993. America. Endangered Animals. Mult.
1838 1p. Type **557** . . . . . . 1·25 95
1839 3p. Rhinoceros iguana . . . 30 20

558 Cross and Eucharist (500th anniv of first Mass)

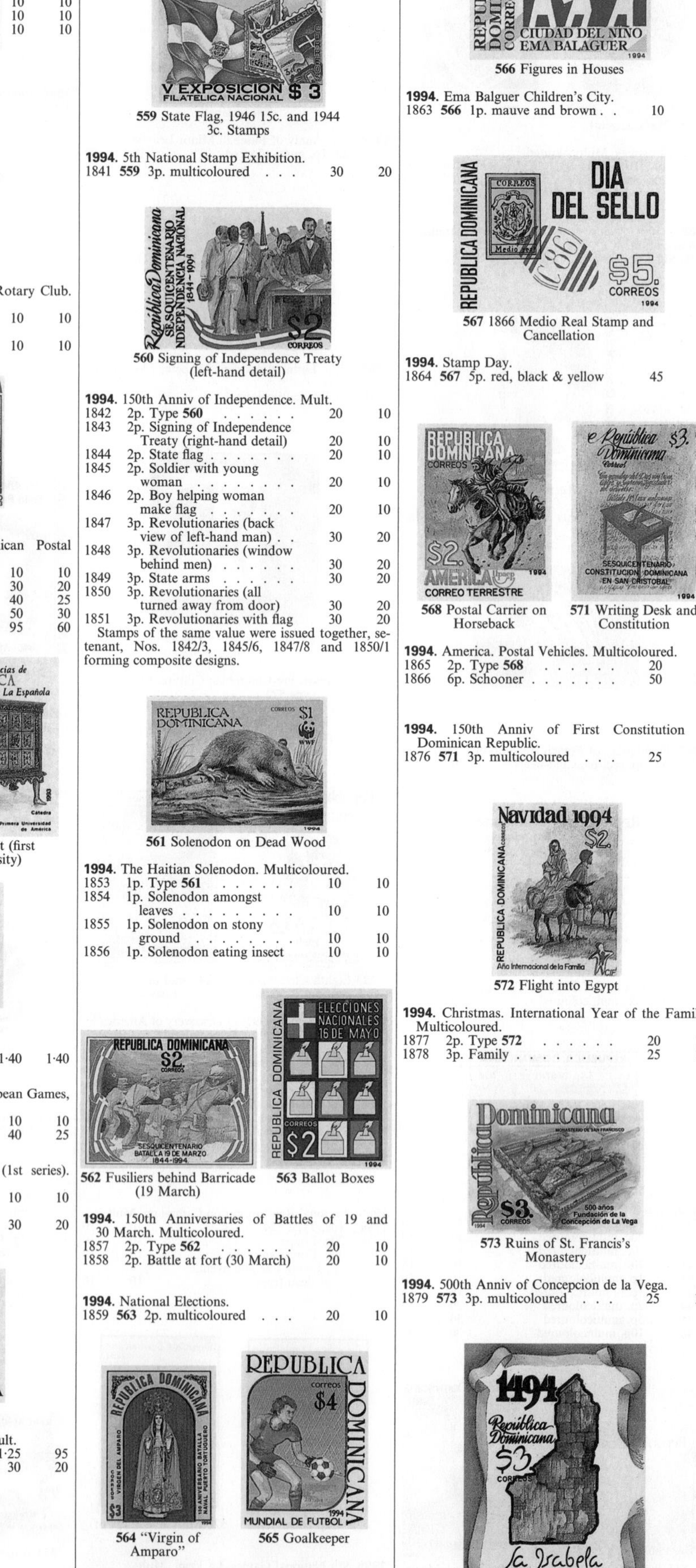

1994. American Firsts in Hispaniola (2nd series).
1840 **558** 2p. multicoloured . . . 20 10

559 State Flag, 1946 15c. and 1944 3c. Stamps

1994. 5th National Stamp Exhibition.
1841 **559** 3p. multicoloured . . . 30 20

560 Signing of Independence Treaty (left-hand detail)

1994. 150th Anniv of Independence. Mult.
1842 2p. Type **560** 20 10
1843 2p. Signing of Independence Treaty (right-hand detail) 20 10
1844 2p. State flag 20 10
1845 2p. Soldier with young woman 20 10
1846 2p. Boy helping woman make flag 20 10
1847 3p. Revolutionaries (back view of left-hand man) . . 30 20
1848 3p. Revolutionaries (window behind men) 30 20
1849 3p. State arms 30 20
1850 3p. Revolutionaries (all turned away from door) 30 20
1851 3p. Revolutionaries with flag 30 20
Stamps of the same value were issued together, se-tenant, Nos. 1842/3, 1845/6, 1847/8 and 1850/1 forming composite designs.

561 Solenodon on Dead Wood

1994. The Haitian Solenodon. Multicoloured.
1853 1p. Type **561** 10 10
1854 1p. Solenodon amongst leaves 10 10
1855 1p. Solenodon on stony ground 10 10
1856 1p. Solenodon eating insect 10 10

562 Fusiliers behind Barricade (19 March)

563 Ballot Boxes

1994. 150th Anniversaries of Battles of 19 and 30 March. Multicoloured.
1857 2p. Type **562** 20 10
1858 2p. Battle at fort (30 March) 20 10

1994. National Elections.
1859 **563** 2p. multicoloured . . . 20 10

564 "Virgin of Amparo"

565 Goalkeeper

1994. 150th Anniv of Naval Battle of Puerto Tortuguero.
1860 **564** 3p. multicoloured . . . 30 20

1994. World Cup Football Championship, U.S.A. Multicoloured.
1861 4p. Type **565** 40 25
1862 6p. Players contesting possession of ball 60 40

566 Figures in Houses

1994. Ema Balguer Children's City.
1863 **566** 1p. mauve and brown . . 10 10

567 1866 Medio Real Stamp and Cancellation

1994. Stamp Day.
1864 **567** 5p. red, black & yellow 45 30

568 Postal Carrier on Horseback

571 Writing Desk and Constitution

1994. America. Postal Vehicles. Multicoloured.
1865 2p. Type **568** 20 10
1866 6p. Schooner 50 35

1994. 150th Anniv of First Constitution of Dominican Republic.
1876 **571** 3p. multicoloured . . . 25 15

572 Flight into Egypt

1994. Christmas. International Year of the Family. Multicoloured.
1877 2p. Type **572** 20 10
1878 3p. Family 25 15

573 Ruins of St. Francis's Monastery

1994. 500th Anniv of Concepcion de la Vega.
1879 **573** 3p. multicoloured . . . 25 15

574 Wall of La Isabela Church

1994. 500th Anniv of First Church in Dominican Republic. Multicoloured.
1880 3p. Type **574** 25 15
1881 3p. Temple of the Americas 25 15

Nos. 1880/1 were issued together, se-tenant, forming a composite design.

1994. American Firsts in Hispaniola (3rd series). As T **556**. Multicoloured.
1882 2p. First coins, 1505 . . . . 20 10
1883 5p. Antonio Montesino (first plea for justice (in Advent sermon), 1511) 45 30

575 "Hypsirhynchus ferox"

1994. National Natural History Museum. Snakes. Multicoloured.
1884 2p. Type **575** 20 10
1885 2p. "Antillophis parvifrons" 20 10
1886 2p. "Uromacer catesbyi" . . 20 10
1887 2p. Bahama boa ("Epicrates striatus") 20 10
Nos. 1884/5 and 1886/7 respectively were issued together, se-tenant, each pair forming a composite design of a tree and the snakes.

576 Taekwondo

1995. Pan-American Games, Mar del Plata, Argentine Republic.
1888 **576** 4p. blue, red & black . . 35 20
1889 – 13p. green, black & yell 1·25 80
DESIGN: 13p. Tennis.

577 Allegory of Dominican Agriculture

1995. 50th Anniv of F.A.O.
1890 **577** 4p. multicoloured . . . 35 20

578 Jose Marti, Maximo Gomez and Monte Cristi Clock Tower

579 Emblem

1995. Centenaries.
1891 **578** 2p. brown, pink & black 20 10
1892 – 3p. pink, black & blue 25 15
1893 – 4p. black and pink . . . 35 20
DESIGNS: 3p. Jose Marti on Cuban national flag (death centenary); 4p. Gomez and Marti signing Monte Cristi manifesto.

1995. "Centrobasket" Basketball Championship, Santo Domingo.
1894 **579** 3p. blue, red & black . . 25 15

580 "Pimenta ozua"

581 San Souci Port

1995. Medicinal Plants. Multicoloured.
1895 2p. Type **580** 20 10
1896 2p. "Melocactus communis" 20 10
1897 3p. "Smilax sp." 25 15
1898 3p. "Zamia sp." 25 15

1995. Tourism. Multicoloured.
1899 4p. Type **581** 35 20
1900 5p. Barahona airport . . . 45 30
1901 6p. G. Luperon airport . . 55 35
1902 13p. Las Americas airport 1·25 80

582 Ruins of Jacagua Church

1995. 500th Anniv of Santiago de los Caballeros.
1903 **582** 3p. multicoloured . . . 25 15

583 Sei Whale ("Balaenoptera borealis")

1995. Natural History Museum. Whales. Mult.
1904 3p. Type **583** 25 15
1905 3p. Humpback whales ("Megaptera novaeangliae") 25 15
1906 3p. Sperm whales ("Physeter macrocephalus") 25 15
1907 3p. Cuvier's beaked whales ("Ziphius cavirostris") . . 25 15

584 Rafael Colon

585 Cancelled 1880 2c. Stamp

1995. Singers. Multicoloured.
1908 2p. Type **584** 20 10
1909 3p. Casandra Damiron . . . 25 15

1995. Stamp Day.
1910 **585** 4p. multicoloured . . . 35 20

586 Player

587 Anniversary Emblem

1995. Centenary of Volleyball.
1911 **586** 6p. multicoloured . . . 55 35

1995. 50th Anniv of U.N.O.
1913 **587** 2p. blue and gold . . . 20 10
1914 – 6p. multicoloured . . . 55 35
DESIGN—33 × 55 mm: 6p. Allegorical design.

588 Allegory

589 Columbus Lighthouse

1995. 4th World Conference on Women, Peking.
1915 **588** 2p. multicoloured . . . 20 10

1995.
1916 **589** 10p. ultram, blue & blk 90 60
1994 10p. green and silver . . 85 55
2025 10p. mauve and silver . . 75 50
2089 10p. yellow and black . . 75 50

590 Enriquillo Lake

591 Antonio Mesa (tenor)

1995. America. Environmental Protection. Mult.
1917 2p. Type **590** 20 10
1918 6p. Mangrove plantation . . 55 35

1995. Singers. Each red and brown.
1919 2p. Type **591** 20 10
1920 2p. Susano Polanco (tenor) 20 10
1921 2p. Julieta Otero (soprano) 20 10

592 Cathedral

1995. Centenary of Santiago Cathedral.
1922 **592** 3p. multicoloured . . . 25 15

593 Corsair Fighter

1995. 50th Anniv of Dominican Air Force (1st issue). Multicoloured.
1923 2p. Type **593** 20 10
1924 2p. Stearman Pt-17 Kaydett bomber 20 10
1925 2p. North American T-6 Texan trainer 20 10
1926 2p. Consolidated PBY-5A Catalina amphibian . . . 20 10
1927 2p. Bristol Beaufighter fighter 20 10
1928 2p. De Havilland Mosquito bomber 20 10
1929 2p. Lockheed P-38 Lightning fighter 20 10
1930 2p. North American P-51 Mustang fighter 20 10
1931 2p. Boeing B-17 Flying Fortress bomber 20 10
1932 2p. Republic P-47 Thunderbolt fighter . . . 20 10
1933 2p. De Havilland Vampire jet fighter 20 10
1934 2p. Curtiss C-46 Commander 20 10
1935 2p. Boeing B-26 Invader . . 20 10
1936 2p. Douglas C-47 Skytrain transport 20 10
1937 2p. T-28D Trojan 20 10
1938 2p. T-33A Silverstar 20 10
1939 2p. Cessna T-41D 20 10
1940 2p. T-34 Mentor 20 10
1941 2p. Cessna O-2A 20 10
1942 2p. Cessna A-37B Dragonfly fighter 20 10
See also Nos. 1958/63, 2026/31 and 2040/4.

594 Brito

596 Children

595 Yachts

1996. 50th Death Anniv of Eduardo Brito (singer).
1943 **594** 1p. multicoloured . . . 10 10
1944 – 2p. multicoloured . . . 20 10
1945 – 3p. black and pink . . . 25 15
DESIGNS—55 × 35 mm: 2p. Brito playing maracas. As T **594**: 3p. Brito (different).

1996. Hispaniola Cup Yachting Championship.
1946 **595** 5p. multicoloured . . . 45 30

1996. 50th Anniv of UNICEF.
1947 **596** 2p. black and green . . 20 10
1948 – 4p. black and green . . 35 20
DESIGN—4p. As T **596** but motif reversed.

597 Arturo Pallerano, Freddy Gaton and Rafael Herrera

1996. National Journalists' Day.
1949 **597** 5p. multicoloured . . . 45 30

598 Emblem, Astronaut and Biplane

1996. "Espamer" Spanish–Latin American and "Aviation and Space" Stamp Exhibitions, Seville, Spain.
1950 **598** 15p. multicoloured . . . 1·40 90

599 Judo

1996. Olympic Games, Atlanta. Each black, blue and red.
1951 5p. Type **599** 45 30
1952 15p. Torchbearer . . . . . 1·40 90

600 Greek 1896 2l. Olympic Stamp

1996. Centenary of Modern Olympic Games.
1953 **600** 6p. green, red & black 55 35
1954 – 15p. multicoloured . . . 1·40 90
DESIGN: 15p. Dominican Republic 1937 7c. Olympic stamp.

601 "Girl at Postbox"

1996. "The Post is your Friend". Winning Entries in Children's Stamp Design Competition. Mult.
1955 3p. Type **601** 20 10
1956 3p. Representations of world post 20 10
1957 3p. Postal carrier on horseback delivering letter (vert) 20 10

602 Sikorsky S-55

1996. 50th Anniv of Air Force (2nd issue). Helicopters. Multicoloured.
1958 3p. Type **602** 20 10
1959 3p. Sud Aviation Alouette II 20 10

1960 3p. Sud Aviation Alouette III 20 10
1961 3p. OH-6A Cayuse 20 10
1962 3p. Bell 205 A-1 . . . . . 20 10
1963 3p. Aerospatiale SA.365 Dauphin 2 . . . . 20 10

603 Workers and Children

604 Man

1996. United Nations Decade against Drug Trafficking.
1964 **603** 15p. multicoloured . . . 1·40 90

1996. America. Costumes. Multicoloured.
1965 2p. Type **604** 15 10
1966 6p. Woman 50 30

605 Stylized Dinghy

1996. 26th International "Sunfish" Dinghy Sailing Championships. Multicoloured.
1967 6p. Type **605** 50 30
1968 10p. Sailor in dinghy (horiz) 85 55

606 1905 1p. Stamp

1996. Stamp Day.
1969 **606** 5p. stone and black . . . 40 25

607 Ridgway's Hawk ("Buteo ridgwayi")

608 Mirabal Sisters

1996. Birds. Multicoloured.
1970 2p. Type **607** 15 10
1971 2p. Hispaniolan conure ("Aratinga chloroptera") 15 10
1972 2p. Hispaniolan amazon ("Amazona ventralis") . . 15 10
1973 2p. Rufous-breasted cuckoo ("Hyetornis rufigularis") 15 10
1974 2p. Hispaniolan lizard cuckoo ("Saurothera longirostris") 15 10
1975 2p. Least pauraque ("Siphonorhis brewsteri") 15 10
1976 2p. Hispaniolan emerald ("Chlorostilbon swainsonii") 15 10
1977 2p. Narrow-billed tody ("Todus angustirostris") 15 10
1978 2p. Broad-billed tody ("Todus subulatus") . . . 15 10
1979 2p. Hispaniolan trogon ("Temnotrogon roseigaster") 15 10
1980 2p. Antillean piculet ("Nesoctites micromegas") 15 10
1981 2p. Hispaniolan woodpecker ("Melanerpes striatus") 15 10
1982 2p. La Selle thrush ("Turdus swalesi") 15 10
1983 2p. Antillean siskin ("Carduelis dominicensis") 15 10
1984 2p. Palm chat ("Dulus dominicus") 15 10
1985 2p. Green-tailed ground warbler ("Microligea palustris") 15 10
1986 2p. Flat-billed vireo ("Vireo nanus") 15 10
1987 2p. White-winged ground warbler ("Xenoligea montana") 15 10
1988 2p. La Selle thrush ("Turdus swalesi dodae") 15 10
1989 2p. Chat-tanager ("Calyptophilus frugivorus tertius") . . . 15 10
1990 2p. White-necked crow ("Corvus leucognaphalus") 15 10
1991 2p. Chat-tanager ("Calyptophilus frugivorus neibae") . . . 15 10

1996. International Day of No Violence against Women.
1992 **608** 5p. multicoloured . . . 40 25
1993 10p. multicoloured . . . 85 55

609 Leatherback Turtles ("Dermochelys coriacea")

1996. Turtles. Multicoloured.
1995 5p. Type **609** 40 25
1996 5p. Loggerhead turtles ("Caretta caretta") . . . 40 25
1997 5p. Indian Ocean green turtles ("Chelonia mydas") 40 25
1998 5p. Hawksbill turtles ("Eretmochelys imbricata") 40 25
Nos. 1995/8 were issued together, se-tenant, forming a composite design.

610 Youths leaping for Sun

611 Flag and Lyrics by Emilio Prudhomne

1997. National Youth Day.
1999 **610** 3p. multicoloured . . . 25 15

1997. National Anthem. Each black, blue and red.
2000 2p. Type **611** 15 10
2001 3p. Flag and score by Jose Reyes 25 15

612 Salome Urena

613 Comet, Palm Tree and House

1997. Death Cent of Salome Urena (educationist).
2002 **612** 3p. multicoloured . . . 25 15

1997. Hale-Bopp Comet.
2003 **613** 5p. multicoloured . . . 40 25

614 Mascot with Torch and Emblem

1997. 11th National Games. Multicoloured.
2005 2p. Type **614** 15 10
2006 3p. Mascot with baseball bat (26 × 36 mm) 25 15
2007 5p. Athlete breasting tape (36 × 26 mm) 40 25

615 Von Stephan

616 Blood Vessel

1997. Death Centenary of Heinrich von Stephan (founder of U.P.U).
2008 **615** 10p. violet, blk & red . . 85 55

1997. 15th International Haemostasis and Thrombosis Congress.
2010 **616** 10p. multicoloured . . . 85 55

617 Helmet, Flowers and Epaulettes

618 Emblem

1997. Death Cent of General Gregorio Luperon.
2011 **617** 3p. multicoloured . . . 25 15

1997. 80th Anniv of Spanish House in Santo Domingo.
2012 **618** 5p. multicoloured . . . 40 25

619 First Minting

1997. Centenary of the Peso.
2013 **619** 2p. multicoloured . . . 15 10

620 Icon

1997. 75th Anniv of Coronation of "Our Lady of Altagracia" (icon). Multicoloured.
2014 3p. Type **620** 25 15
2015 5p. Icon and church 40 25

621 Dog attacking Postman on Motor Cycle

1997. America. The Postman. Multicoloured.
2016 2p. Type **621** 15 10
2017 6p. Dog attacking postman delivering letter ($35\frac{1}{2}$ × 37 mm) 45 30

622 Weeping Child, Mother Teresa and Man on Donkey

1997. Int Fight against Poverty Day.
2018 **622** 5p. multicoloured . . . 40 25

623 1936 and 1899 2p. Stamps

1997. Stamp Day.
2019 **623** 5p. brown and black . . 40 25

624 Buildings

1997. 50th Anniv of Central Bank.
2020 **624** 10p. multicoloured . . . 75 50

625 "Erophyllus bombifrons"

1997. Bats. Multicoloured.
2021 5p. Type **625** 40 25
2022 5p. Cuban fruit-eating bat ("Brachyphylla nana") . . 40 25
2023 5p. Kerr's mastiff bat ("Molossus molossus") . . 40 25
2024 5p. Red bat ("Lasiurus borealis") 40 25

626 Air Force Badge

1997. 50th Anniv of Air Force (3rd issue). Division Badges, Multicoloured.
2026 3p. Type **626** 25 15
2027 3p. Air Command North . . 25 15
2028 3p. Air Command 25 15
2029 3p. Rescue 25 15
2030 3p. Maintenance Command 25 15
2031 3p. Combat Squadron . . . 25 15

627 Facade

1997. 50th Anniv of National Palace.
2032 **627** 10p. multicoloured . . . 75 50

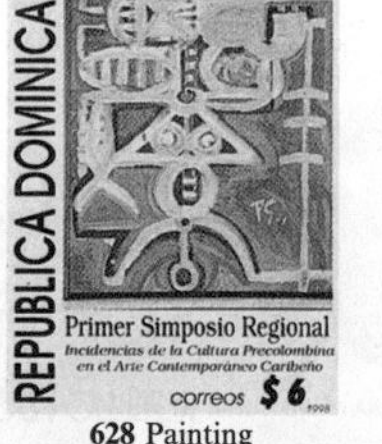

628 Painting

1998. 1st Regional Symposium on Influence of Pre-Columbian Culture on Contemporary Caribbean Art.
2033 **628** 6p. multicoloured . . . 45 30

629 Emblem 630 Open Book

1998. 75th Anniv of American Chamber of Commerce of Dominican Republic.
2034 **629** 10p. blue, red and gold . . . 75 50

1998. 25th Anniv of National Book Fair and First International Book Fair, Santo Domingo.
2035 **630** 3p. blue, red and black . . . 25 15
2036 – 5p. blue, red and black . . . 40 25
DESIGN—40 × 40 mm: 5p. Book Fair emblem.

631 Emblem

1998. 50th Anniv of Organization of American States. Multicoloured.
2037 5p. Type **631** 40 25
2038 5p. As Type **631** but inscr for the 50th anniv of signing of the Organization charter . . . 40 25

632 Olive Branches, Menorah and Star of David

1998. 50th Anniv of State of Israel.
2039 **632** 10p. ultram, bl & mve . . . 75 50

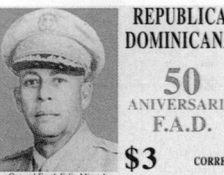

633 General Frank Felix Miranda

1998. 50th Anniv of Air Force (4th issue). Mult.
2040 3p. Type **633** 25 15
2041 3p. Curtiss-Wright R-19 . . 25 15
2042 3p. Coronel Ernesto Tejeda (portrait at right) 25 15
2043 3p. As No. 2042, but portrait at left 25 15
2044 3p. As Type **633**, but portrait at right 25 15

634 Sundial

1998. 500th Anniv of Santo Domingo. Mult.
2045 2p. Type **634** 15 10
2046 3p. St. Lazarus's Church and Hospital (horiz) . . . 25 15
2047 4p. First cathedral in the Americas (horiz) 30 20
2048 5p. Fortress (horiz) 40 25
2049 6p. Tower of Honour (horiz) 45 30
2050 10p. St. Nicholas of Bari's Church and Hospital . . 75 50

635 Theatre

1998. 25th Anniv of National Theatre.
2051 **635** 10p. multicoloured . . . 75 50

636 Latin Inscription

1998. 44th Anniv of Latin Union.
2052 **636** 10p. gold, grey & black . . . 75 50

637 Cocoa Beans and Route Map of First American–Europe Shipment, 1502

1998. 25th Anniv of Int Cocoa Organization.
2053 **637** 10p. multicoloured . . . 75 50

638 Nino Ferrua (stamp designer)

1998. Stamp Day.
2054 **638** 5p. multicoloured . . . 40 25

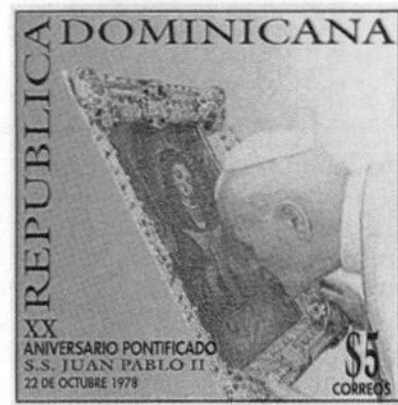

639 Pope John Paul II venerating Portrait of Virgin Mary

1998. 20th Anniv of Pontificate of Pope John Paul II. Multicoloured.
2055 5p. Type **639** 40 25
2056 10p. Pope John Paul II . . 75 50

640 Bay Rum

1998. Medicinal Plants. Multicoloured.
2057 3p. Type **640** 20 10
2058 3p. "Pimenta haitiensis" . . 20 10
2059 3p. "Cymbopogon citratus" . . 20 10
2060 3p. Seville orange ("Citrus aurantium") 20 10

641 Juana Saltitopa (Independence fighter)

1998. America. Famous Women. Multicoloured.
2061 2p. Type **641** 15 10
2062 6p. Anacaona (Indian chief) . . 45 30

642 Earth and Emblem 643 Statue of Columbus

1998. International Year of the Ocean.
2063 **642** 5p. multicoloured . . . 35 25

1998. "Expofila 98" Stamp Exhibition, Santo Domingo. 500th Anniv of Santo Domingo.
2064 **643** 5p. multicoloured . . . 35 25

644 Fernando Valerio

1998. Military Heroes. Each brown and green.
2065 3p. Type **644** 20 10
2066 3p. Benito Moncion 20 10
2067 3p. Jose Maria Cabral . . . 20 10
2068 3p. Antonio Duverge . . . 20 10
2069 3p. Gregorio Luperon . . . 20 10
2070 3p. Jose Salcedo 20 10
2071 3p. Fco. Salcedo 20 10
2072 3p. Gaspar Polanco 20 10
2073 3p. Santiago Rodriguez . . 20 10
2074 3p. Admiral Juan Cambiaso 20 10
2075 3p. Jose Puello 20 10
2076 3p. Jose Imbert 20 10
2077 3p. Admiral Juan Acosta . . 20 10
2078 3p. Marcos Adon 20 10
2079 3p. Matias Mella 20 10
2080 3p. Francisco Sanchez . . . 20 10
2081 3p. Juan Pablo Duarte . . . 20 10
2082 3p. Olegario Tenares . . . 20 10
2083 3p. General Pedro Santana 20 10
2084 3p. Juan Sanchez Ramirez 20 10

645 Banknotes

1998. 150th Anniv of Paper Money.
2085 **645** 10p. multicoloured . . . 75 50

646 Spit-roasting Pig

1998. Christmas. Multicoloured.
2086 2p. Type **646** 15 10
2087 5p. Three Wise Men on camels 35 25

647 Couple and Human Rights Emblem

1998. 50th Anniv of Universal Declaration of Human Rights.
2088 **647** 10p. multicoloured . . . 75 50

648 Vega's Lyria

1998. Shells. Multicoloured.
2090 5p. Type **648** 35 25
2091 5p. Queen conch ("Strombus gigas") . . . 35 25
2092 5p. West Indian top shell ("Cittarium pica") 35 25
2093 5p. Bleeding tooth ("Nerita peloronta") 35 25

649 Hernandez

1998. Birth Bicentenary of Gaspar Hernandez (priest and Independence fighter).
2094 **649** 3p. multicoloured . . . 20 10

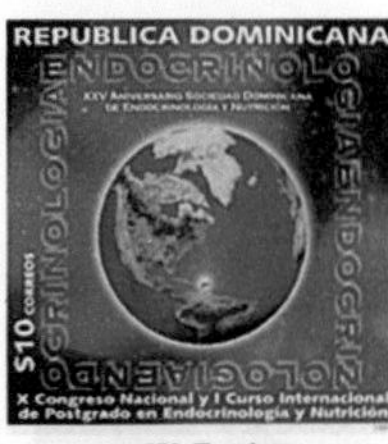

650 Earth

1999. 10th National Congress, First International Postgraduate Lectures and 25th Anniv of Dominican Society for Endocrinology and Nutrition.
2095 **650** 10p. multicoloured . . . 75 50

652 Cigar and Tobacco Leaf

1999. Exports. Multicoloured.
2097 6p. Type **652** 45 30
2098 10p. Woman sewing (textiles) (vert) 75 50

653 Magnifying Glass over Map of Dominican Republic

1999. 155th Anniv of Office of Comptroller-General.
2099 **653** 2p. multicoloured . . . 15 10

654 Bosch, "The Seagull" (poem) and Main Tower, Santo Domingo

1999. Contemporary Writers. 90th Birthday of Pres. Juan Bosch (poet). Multicoloured.
2100 2p. Type **654** 15 10
2101 10p. Portrait of Bosch (vert) 75 50

655 "Pseudophoenix ekmanii" 657 Baseball

656 Gen. Juan Pablo Duarte (revolutionary)

1999. Flowers and their Fruit. Multicoloured.
2102 5p. Type **655** 35 25
2103 5p. "Murtigia colabura" . . 35 25
2104 5p. "Pouteria dominguensis" 35 25
2105 5p. "Rubus dominguensis" 35 25

1999.
2106 **656** 3p. multicoloured . . . 20 15

1999. 13th Pan-American Games, Winnipeg, Canada. Multicoloured.
2107 5p. Type **657** 35 25
2108 6p. Weightlifting 45 30

658 Tomas Bobadilla y Briones

1999. Leaders of the Dominican Republic. Mult.
2109 3p. Type **658** 20 15
2110 3p. Pedro Santana (President, 1844–48, 1853–56 and 1859–61) 20 15
2111 3p. Manuel Jimenez (President, 1848–49) . . . 20 15
2112 3p. Buenaventura Baez (President, 1849–53, 1856–58, 1865–66, 1868–74 and 1876–78) 20 15
2113 3p. Manuel de Regla Motta (President, June–October 1856) 20 15
2114 3p. Jose Desiderio Valverde (President, 1858–59) . . . 20 15
2115 3p. Jose Antonio Salcedo . . 20 15
2116 3p. Gaspar Polanco 20 15

659 "St. Christopher"

1999. Jose Vela Zanetti (Spanish artist) Commemoration. Multicoloured.
2117 2p. Type **659** 15 10
2118 3p. "Bride and Groom" . . 20 15
2119 5p. "Burial of Christ" (horiz) 35 20
2120 6p. "Cock-fighting" 45 30
2121 10p. "Self-portrait" 75 50

660 "Strataegus quadrifoveatus"

1999. Insects. Multicoloured.
2122 5p. Type **660** 35 20
2123 5p. "Anetia jaegeri" (butterfly) 35 20
2124 5p. "Polyancistroydes tettigonidae" 35 20
2125 5p. Stick insect ("Phasmidae aploppus") 35 20

661 Emblem and Cross-section of Skin

1999. 50th Anniv of Dominican Dermatological Society.
2126 **661** 3p. multicoloured . . . 20 15

662 Maternity Clinic, Santo Domingo

1999. 900th Anniv of Sovereign Military Order of Malta. Multicoloured.
2127 2p. Type **662** 15 10
2128 10p. Maltese Cross and anniversary emblem ($36\frac{1}{2} \times 38$ mm) 75 50

663 Children 664 Man

1999. 50th Anniv of S.O.S. Children's Villages.
2129 **663** 10p. multicoloured . . . 85 55

1999. International Year of the Elderly.
2130 **664** 2p. black and blue . . . 20 10
2131 – 5p. black and red . . . 45 30
DESIGN: 5p. Woman.

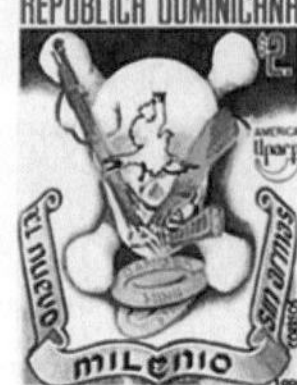

665 Teacher and Students 666 Dove, Skull and Crossbones, Gun, Emblem and Mines

1999. Teachers' Day.
2132 **665** 5p. multicoloured . . . 45 30

1999. America. A New Millennium without Arms. Multicoloured.
2133 2p. Type **666** 20 10
2134 6p. Atomic cloud and emblem 50 30

667 Luis F. Thomen (philatelist and author) 669 Map of Caribbean and Whale

668 Globe and Forests

1999. Stamp Day.
2135 **667** 5p. drab, black and green 45 30

1999. New Millennium. Multicoloured.
2136 3p. Type **668** 25 10
2137 5p. Astronaut, satellite, computer and man . . . 45 30

1999. 2nd Summit of African, Caribbean and Pacific Heads of State. Multicoloured.
2138 5p. Type **669** 45 30
2139 6p. Moai Statues, Easter Island 50 30
2140 10p. Map of Africa and lion 85 55

670 Means of Communication

1999. 125th Anniv of Universal Postal Union.
2141 **670** 6p. multicoloured . . . 50 30

671 Globe and "50"

1999. 50th Anniv of Union of Latin American Universities.
2143 **671** 6p. multicoloured . . . 50 30

1999. As No. 1916 but colours changed.
2144 **589** 10p. brown and silver . . 85 55

672 Juan Garcia (trumpeter)

1999. Classical Musicians.
2145 **672** 5p. blue and black . . . 45 30
2146 – 5p. mauve and black . . 45 30
2147 – 5p. green and black . . 45 30
DESIGNS: 2146, Manuel Simo (saxophonist); 2147, Jose Ravelo (clarinettist).

673 Santiago and Cotui Banknotes

1999. Centenary of Banknotes. Multicoloured.
2148 2p. Type **673** 20 10
2149 2p. San Francisco de Macoris and La Vega banknotes 20 10
2150 2p. San Cristobal and Samana banknotes . . . 20 10
2151 2p. Santo Domingo and San Pedro de Macoris banknotes (horiz) 20 10
2152 2p. Puerto Plata and Moca banknotes (horiz) 20 10

674 Emblem

1999. 75th Anniv of Spanish Chamber of Trade and Industry.
2154 **674** 10p. multicoloured . . . 85 55

675 Emblem

2000. 25th Anniv of Anti-Drugs Campaign.
2155 **675** 5p. multicoloured . . . 45 30

676 Institute Facade

2000. Duartiano Institute.
2156 **676** 2p. multicoloured . . . 20 10

677 Child's Head and Emblem

2000. Prevention of Child Abuse Programme.
2157 **677** 2p. multicoloured . . . 20 10

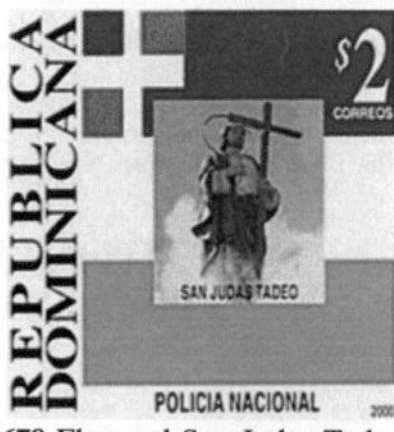

678 Flag and San Judas Tadeo (statue)

2000. National Police Force. Multicoloured.
2158 2p. Type **678** 20 10
2159 5p. Flag and Police emblem (37×28 mm) 45 30

679 Institute Building and Emblem

2000. 25th Anniv of Industry and Technology Institute.
2160 **679** 2p. multicoloured . . . 20 10

680 Emblem

2000. 50th Anniv of Independence.
2161 **680** 3p. multicoloured . . . 25 10

681 Baseball Glove and Ball

2000. 12th National Youth Games, La Romana. Multicoloured.

2162	2p. Type **681**	20	15
2163	3p. Boxing gloves	25	15
2164	5p. Emblem and mascot (35 × 36 mm)	45	30

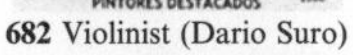

682 Violinist (Dario Suro) **683** Building, Scales of Justice and Hand posting Ballot Paper

2000. Art. Multicoloured.

2165	5p. Type **682**	45	30
2166	10p. Portrait of man (Theodore Chasseriau)	85	55

2000. Presidential Elections.

2167 **683**	2p. multicoloured	20	15

684 Enrique de Marchena Dujarric (pianist)

2000. Classical Musicians. Each black, orange and brown.

2168	5p. Type **684**	45	30
2169	5p. Julio Alberto Hernandez Camejo (pianist)	45	30
2170	5p. Ramon Diaz (flautist)	45	30

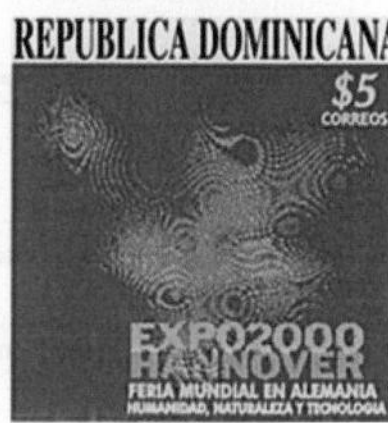

685 Emblem

2000. "EXPO 2000" World's Fair, Hanover. Multicoloured.

2171	5p. Type **685**	45	30
2172	10p. Emblem	85	55

686 Santo Cristo de Los Milagros Church, Bayaguana

2000. Holy Year. Multicoloured.

2173	2p. Type **686**	20	15
2174	5p. Cathedral, Santo Domingo (vert)	45	30
2175	10p. Senora de la Altagracia Basilica, Higuey (vert)	90	60

2000. Columbus Lighthouse. As T **589**.

2176 **589**	10p. ochre, deep brown and silver	90	60
2177	15p. blue, azure and silver	1·40	90
2178	15p. multicoloured	1·40	90

687 "Prince Arnau"

2000. 25th Death Anniv of Jaime Colson (artist). Multicoloured.

2186	2p. Type **687**	20	15
2187	3p. "Merengue" (dance)	30	25
2188	5p. "Guachupita Fiesta" (horiz)	45	30
2189	6p. "Castor and Pollux"	60	50
2190	10p. "Self-portrait"	90	60

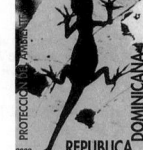

688 Flags and Chinese Dragon **689** Lizard on Leaf

2000. 60th Anniv of Dominican Republic—China Diplomatic Relations. Multicoloured. Self-adhesive gum.

2191	5p. Type **688**	45	30
2192	10p. Flags and wooden artefact	90	60

2000. Environmental Protection. Multicoloured. Self-adhesive gum.

2193	2p. Type **689**	20	15
2194	3p. Trees and hut	30	25
2195	5p. Rapids	45	30

690 Sick Child **691** Emblem and Rose

2000. America. AIDS Awareness Campaign. Multicoloured. Self-adhesive gum.

2196	2p. Type **690**	20	15
2197	6p. Sick child (38 × 38 mm)	60	50

2000. 50th Anniv of United Nations High Commissioner for Refugees. Self-adhesive gum.

2198 **691**	10p. multicoloured	90	60

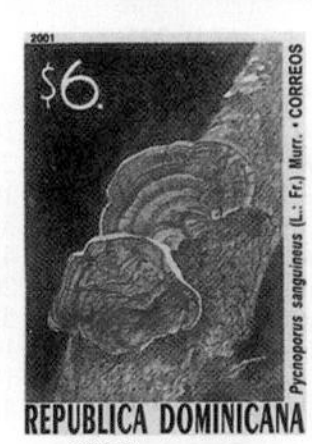

692 *Pycnoporus sanguineus* **693** *Isidorea pungens*

2001. Fungi. Multicoloured.

2199	6p. Type **692**	60	50
2200	6p. *Morchella elata*	60	50
2201	6p. *Mycena epipterygia*	60	50
2202	6p. *Coriolopsis polyzona*	60	50

2001. 25th Anniv of National Botanic Garden. Multicoloured.

2203	4p. Type **693**	40	30
2204	4p. *Pereskia quisqueyana*	40	30
2205	4p. *Goetzea ekmanii*	40	30
2206	4p. *Cubanola domingensis*	40	30

694 Jose Maria Cabral (president, 1866–68) **696** Dominican Republic 1914 1c. Stamp

695 San Felipe Fortress, Puerto Plata

2001. Leaders of the Dominican Republic. Sheet 129 × 170 mm containing T **694** and similar vert. Multicoloured.

MS2207 6p. × 8, Type **694**; Gregorio Luperon (president, 1879–80); Ignacio Gonzalez (president, 1874–76); Ulises Francisco Espaillet (president, 1876; 1887–99); Pedro Antonio Pimental (president, 1865); Federico de Garcia; Fernando de Merino (president, 1880–84); Ulises Heureaux (president, 1884–85) 3·50 3·50

No. **MS**2207 contains a central label showing the arms of the Dominican Republic.

2001. America. UNESCO World Heritage Sites. Each silver and black.

2208	4p. Type **695**	40	30
2209	15p. San Nicolás de Bari, Santo Domingo (39 × 39 mm)	1·40	90

2001. Stamp Day.

2210 **696**	5p. multicoloured	45	30

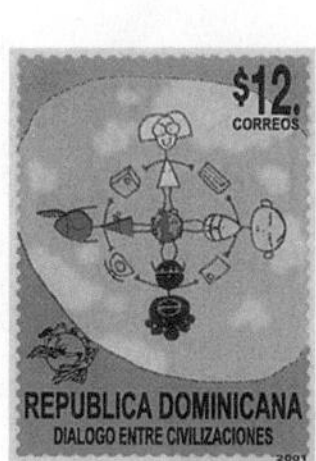

697 Children encircling Globe **698** Conception Bona

2001. United Nations International Year of Dialogue Among Civilizations.

2211 **697**	12p. multicoloured	1·10	75

2001. Death Centenary of Conception Bona (political campaigner).

2212 **698**	10p. multicoloured	90	60

699 Josemaria Escriva de Balaguer

2002. Birth Centenary of Josemaría Escrivá de Balaguer (founder of Opus Dei (religious organization)).

2213 **699**	10p. multicoloured	90	60

700 Building and Emblem **702** Adult and Child Hands Writing

701 Flags of Participating Countries surrounding Globe

2002. 50th Anniv of Polytechnic Institute, Loyola.

2214 **700**	6p. multicoloured	60	50

2002. 12th Spanish American Summit Conference.

2215 **701**	12p. multicoloured	1·10	75

2002. America. Education and Literacy Campaign. Multicoloured.

2216	4p. Type **702**	40	30
2217	15p. Child and blackboard	1·40	90

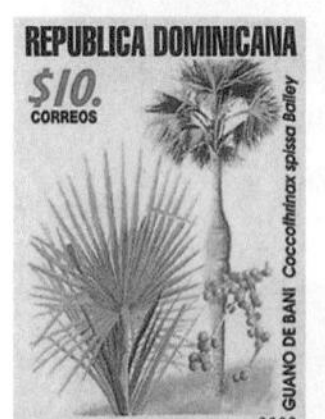

703 *Coccothrinax spissa* (palm) **704** Emblem

2002.

2218 **703**	10p. multicoloured	90	60

2003. 14th Pan American Games, Santo Domingo.

2219 **704**	4p. multicoloured	40	30
2220	6p. multicoloured	60	50
2221	12p. multicoloured	1·10	75

705 *Hymenaea courbaril*

2003. Medicinal Plants. Trees. Multicoloured.

2222	5p. Type **705**	35	20
2223	5p. *Spandias mombin*	35	20
2224	5p. *Genipa Americana*	35	20
2225	5p. *Guazuma ulmifonia*	35	20

Nos. 2222/3 and 2224/5, respectively, were issued together, se-tenant, forming a composite design.

706 Jose Marti with Cuban and Dominican Republic Flags

2003. 150th Birth Anniv of Jose Marti (Cuban writer).

2226 **706**	15p. multicoloured	1·00	60

707 Pope John Paul II **708** Jose Francisco Pena Gomez

2003. 25th Anniv of Pontificate of Pope John Paul II. Multicoloured.

2227	10p. Type **707**	60	35
2228	15p. Pope John Paul II addressing crowds (horiz)	1·00	60
MS2229	57 × 86 mm. As Nos. 2227/8. Imperf	1·60	1·60

2003. 5th Death Anniv of Jose Francisco Pena Gomez (politician).

2230 **708**	10p. multicoloured	60	35

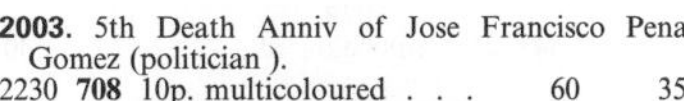

709 *Aristelliger* (inscr "Aristelliger lar")

2004. America. Flora and Fauna. Multicoloured.

2231		5p. Type **709**	35	
2232		15p. *Copernicia berteroana* (vert)	1·60	1·00

EXPRESS DELIVERY STAMPS

E **40** Biplane

1920.

E232	E **40**	10c. blue	5·50	1·00

E **42**

1925. Inscr "ENTREGA ESPECIAL".

E247	E **42**	10c. blue	10·00	2·00

1927. Inscr "EXPRESO".

E250	E **42**	10c. brown	5·00	1·00
E459		10c. green	2·00	70

E **123**

1945.

E539	E **123**	10c. blue, red & carm	45	20

E **137** Shield, Hand and Letter

1950.

E594	E **137**	10c. red, grn & blue	45	20

E **161**

1956.

E663	E **161**	25c. green	70	30

E **228** Pigeon and Letter

1967.

E995	E **228**	25c. blue	65	25

E **345** Globe, and Pigeon carrying Letter

E **370** Motorcycle Messenger and Airplane

1978.

E1330	E **345**	25c. multicoloured	55	30

1979.

E1385	E **370**	25c. ultram, bl & red	55	35

E **514** Motor Cyclist

1989. Special Delivery.

E1731	E **514**	1p. multicoloured	10	10

E **651** Postman

1999.

E2096	E **651**	8p. multicoloured	60	30

OFFICIAL STAMPS

O **23** Bastion of 27 Febuary

O **44** Columbus Lighthouse

1902.

O121	O **23**	2c. black and red	25	15
O122		5c. black and blue	40	15
O123		10c. black and green	45	20
O124		20c. black and yellow	55	35

1910. As Type O **23**, but inscr "27 DE FEBRERO 1844" and "10 DE AGOSTO 1865" at sides.

O177	O **23**	1c. black and green	15	15
O178		2c. black and red	15	15
O179		5c. black and blue	25	20
O180		10c. black and green	55	40
O181		20c. black and yellow	1·00	55

1928.

O251	O **44**	1c. green	10	10
O252		2c. red	10	10
O253		5c. blue	15	15
O254		10c. blue	25	25
O255		20c. yellow	35	35

1931. Air. Optd **CORREO AEREO**.

O292	O **44**	10c. blue	12·00	10·00
O293		20c. yellow	12·00	10·00

O **82** Columbus Lighthouse

1937. White letters and figures.

O393	O **82**	3c. violet	25	10
O394		7c. blue	35	25
O395		10c. yellow	45	35

O **88** Columbus Lighthouse

1939. Coloured letters and figures.

O409	O **88**	1c. green	10	10
O410		2c. red	10	10
O411		3c. violet	10	10
O412		5c. blue	25	15
O414		5c. blue	55	15
O415		10c. orange	40	15
O416		20c. brown	1·00	25
O577		50c. mauve	1·25	70
O417		50c. red	2·00	85

No. O417 has smaller figures of value than No. O577.

1950. Values inscr "CENTAVOS ORO".

O578	O **88**	5c. blue	15	10
O581		7c. blue	15	10
O579		10c. yellow	35	15
O582		20c. brown	35	25
O583		50c. purple	85	55

POSTAGE DUE STAMPS

D **22**

D **110**

1901.

D117	D **22**	2c. sepia	40	10
D118		4c. sepia	50	15
D119		5c. sepia	1·00	20
D175		6c. sepia	1·40	50
D120		10c. sepia	1·60	20

1913.

D239	D **22**	1c. olive	40	35
D191		2c. olive	35	20
D192		4c. olive	40	15
D193		6c. olive	50	15
D194		10c. olive	70	30

1942. Size $20\frac{1}{2} \times 25\frac{1}{2}$ mm.

D485	D **110**	1c. red	15	10
D486		2c. blue	15	10
D487		2c. blue	70	50
D488		4c. green	15	15
D489		6c. brown and buff	20	20
D490		8c. orange & yellow	25	20
D491		10c. mauve and pink	35	30

1966. Size $21 \times 25\frac{1}{2}$ mm. Inscr larger and in white.

D492	D **110**	1c. red	70	70
D493		2c. blue	70	70
D494		4c. green	1·75	1·75

REGISTRATION STAMPS

1935. De Merino stamps of 1933 surch **PRIMA VALORES DECLARADOS SERVICIO INTERIOR** and value in figures and words.

R339	–	8c. on ½c. (No. 316)	1·40	1·00
R340	–	8c. on 7c. blue	35	15
R342	**56**	15c. on 10c. orange	35	15
R343	–	30c. on 8c. green	1·40	50
R344	–	45c. on 20c. red	2·00	70
R345	**57**	70c. on 50c. olive	4·75	1·00

R **97** National Coat of Arms

R **98** National Coat of Arms

1940.

R448	R **97**	8c. black and red	45	20
R449		15c. black & orange	85	30
R450		30c. black and green	1·40	15
R451		70c. black & purple	3·25	1·00

1944. Redrawn. Larger figures of value and "c" as in Type R **98**.

R452	R **98**	45c. black and blue	1·60	35
R453		70c. black and green	2·00	30

1953.

R454	R **98**	8c. black and red	45	20
R455		10c. black and red	50	15
R456		15c. black & orange	9·50	2·40

R **155**

R **221**

1955. Redrawn. Arms and "c" smaller.

R646	R **155**	10c. black and red	35	10
R647		10c. black and lilac	70	25
R648		15c. black & orange	1·40	1·10
R649		20c. black & orange	60	35
R650		20c. black and red	70	45
R651		30c. black and green	90	20
R652a		40c. black and green	1·25	55
R653		45c. black and blue	2·50	1·10
R654		60c. black & yellow	1·60	1·10
R655		70c. black & brown	2·50	1·40

1963. Redrawn as Type R **97**.

R909		10c. black and orange	40	25
R910		20c. black and orange	55	45

1965.

R961	R **221**	10c. black & lilac	35	20
R962		40c. black & yellow	1·40	85

R **282a**

R **487**

1973.

R1335	R **282a**	10c. black & violet	35	15
R1148		20c. black & orge	70	55
R1149		40c. black & green	85	45
R1150		70c. black and blue	1·60	1·10

1986. Redrawn with figures of value and "c" smaller. Inscribed "PRIMA DE VALORES DECLARADOS". Arms in black.

R1664	R **487**	20c. mauve	10	10
R1665		60c. orange	20	15
R1666		1p. blue	35	30
R1667		1p.25 pink	40	35
R1668		1p.50 red	50	45
R1669		3p. green	1·00	95
R1670		3p.50 bistre	1·25	1·10
R1671		4p. yellow	1·40	1·25
R1672		4p.50 green	1·50	1·40
R1673		5p. brown	1·75	1·50
R1674		6p. grey	2·00	1·75
R1675		6p.50 blue	2·25	2·00

R **515**

1989. Inscr "PRIMA VALORES DECLARADOS". Arms in black.

R1732	R **515**	20c. purple	10	10
R1733		60c. orange	10	10
R1734		1p. blue	10	10
R1735		1p.25 pink	15	10
R1736		1p.50 red	15	15

R **569**

R **570**

1994. Arms in black.

R1867	R **569**	50c. mauve	10	10
R1868	R **570**	1p. blue	10	10
R1869		1p.50 red	15	10
R1870		2p. pink	20	10
R1871		3p. blue	25	15
R1872		5p. yellow	45	30
R1873		6p. green	55	35
R1874		8p. green	70	45
R1875		10p. silver	90	60

DUBAI — Pt. 19

One of the Trucial States in the Persian Gulf. Formerly used the stamps of Muscat. British control of the postal services ceased in 1963.

On 2 December 1971, Dubai and six other Gulf Sheikhdoms formed the State of the United Arab Emirates. U.A.E. issues commenced in 1973.

1963. 100 naye paise = 1 rupee.
1966. 100 dirhams = 1 riyal.

IMPERF STAMPS. Some of the following issues exist imperf from limited printings.

1 Hermit Crab

2 Shaikh Rashid bin Said

1963.

1	**1**	1n.p. red & blue (postage)	15	15
2	A	2n.p. brown and blue	15	15
3	B	3n.p. sepia and green	15	15
4	C	4n.p. orange and purple	15	15
5	D	5n.p. black and violet	25	15
6	E	10n.p. black and brown	25	25
7	**1**	15n.p. red and drab	35	25
8	A	20n.p. orange and red	50	35
9	B	25n.p. brown and green	50	35
10	C	30n.p. red and grey	50	40
11	D	35n.p. deep blue and lilac	65	40
12	E	50n.p. sepia and orange	1·10	60
13	F	1r. salmon and blue	2·20	1·00
14	G	2r. brown and bistre	5·00	2·20
15	H	3r. black and red	10·00	5·00
16	**1**	5r. brown and turquoise	17·00	8·50
17	**2**	10r. black, turq & purple	38·00	17·00
18	J	20n.p. blue & brown (air)	1·70	25
19	K	25n.p. purple and yellow	1·80	35
20	J	30n.p. black and red	2·20	40
21	K	40n.p. purple and brown	2·30	50
22	J	50n.p. red and green	2·75	60
23	K	60n.p. black and brown	3·25	60
24	J	75n.p. green and violet	5·00	65
25	K	1r. brown and yellow	6·25	85

DESIGNS (Postage)—HORIZ: A, Common cuttlefish; B, Edible snail; C, Crab; D, Turban sea urchin; E, Radish murex; F, Mosque; G, Buildings; H, Ancient wall and tower; I, Dubai view. (Air)—HORIZ: J, Peregrine falcon in flight over bridge. VERT: K, Peregrine falcon.

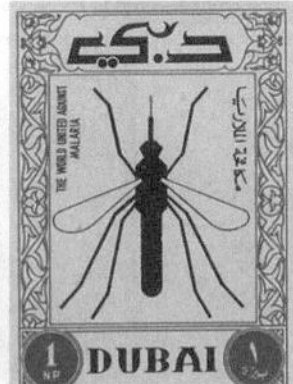

3 Dhows 4 Mosquito

1963. Centenary of Red Cross.
26 **3** 1n.p. bl, yell & red (postage) 40 35
27 – 2n.p. brown, yellow & red . . 40 35
28 – 3n.p. brown, orange & red 40 35
29 – 4n.p. brown, red & green . . 40 35

30 **3** 20n.p. brn, yell & red (air) 1·20 65
31 – 30n.p. blue, orange & red . . 1·20 65
32 – 40n.p. black, yellow & red . . 1·20 65
33 – 50n.p. violet, red & turq . . 2·75 1·40
MS33a Four sheets, each 119 × 99 mm. Block of four of each of Nos. 30/33 in new colour 50·00 50·00
DESIGNS: 2, 30n.p. First aid field post; 3, 40n.p. Camel train; 4, 50n.p. March moth.

1963. Malaria Eradication.
34 **4** 1n.p. brown & red (postage) 20 20
35 1n.p. brown and green . . . 20 20
36 1n.p. red and blue 20 20
37 – 2n.p. blue and red 20 20
38 – 2n.p. red and brown 20 20
39 – 3n.p. blue and brown 20 20

40 **4** 30n.p. green & purple (air) 35 25
41 – 40n.p. grey and red 50 35
42 – 70n.p. yellow and purple . . 1·00 65
MS42a Three sheets, each 100 × 120 mm. Block of four of each of Nos. 40/42 in new colours. Imperf . . . . 20·00 20·00
DESIGNS: 2, 40n.p. Mosquito and snake emblem; 3, 70n.p. Mosquitoes and swamp.

5 Ears of Wheat 7 Scout Gymnastics

6 U.S. Seal and Pres. Kennedy

1963. Air. Freedom from Hunger.
43 **5** 30n.p. brown and violet . . . 40 15
44 – 40n.p. olive and red 65 25
45 – 70n.p. orange and green . . . 1·30 1·30
46 – 1r. blue and brown . . . . . 1·80 1·30
MS46a Four sheets, each 100 × 120 mm. Block of four of each of Nos. 43/6 in new colours surch 5n.p. on 30n.p., 10n.p. on 40n.p., 15n.p. on 70n.p., 20n.p. on 1r. Imperf . . . . 24·00 22·00
DESIGNS: 40n.p. Palm and campaign emblem; 70n.p. Emblem within hands; 1r. Woman bearing basket of fruit.

1964. Air. Pres. Kennedy Memorial Issue.
47 **6** 75n.p. black & green on grn 85 60
48 1r. black & brown on buff 1·20 65
49 1½r. black & red on grey . . 1·40 90
MS49a 100 × 60 mm. No. 49 in black and brown. Imperf . . . . . . 5·00 5·00

1964. World Scout Jamboree, Marathon (1963).
50 **7** 1n.p. bistre & brown (postage) 15 15
51 – 2n.p. brown and red 15 15
52 – 3n.p. brown and blue 15 15
53 – 4n.p. blue and mauve 15 15
54 – 5n.p. turquoise and blue . . 35 15

55 **7** 20n.p. brown & green (air) 40 25
56 – 30n.p. brown and violet . . . 60 35
57 – 40n.p. green and blue 85 40
58 – 70n.p. grey and green . . . . 1·10 65
59 – 1r. red and blue . . . . . . 2·00 1·10
MS59a Five sheets each 100 × 120 mm. Block of four of each of Nos. 55/9 in new colours. Imperf . . . . 29·00 29·00
DESIGNS: 2, 30n.p. Bugler; 3, 40n.p. Wolf cubs; 4, 70n.p. Scouts on parade; 5n.p., 1r. Scouts with standard.

1964. Nos. 27/8 surch.
59b 20n.p. on 2n.p. brown, yellow and red . . . . 50·00
59c 30n.p. on 3n.p. brown, orange and red . . . . . 50·00

8 Spacecraft

1964. Air. "Honouring Astronauts". Multicoloured.
60 1n.p. "Atlas" rocket (vert) . . 15 15
61 2n.p. "Mercury" capsule (vert) 15 15
62 3n.p. Type **8** 15 15
63 4n.p. Two spacecraft 15 15
64 5n.p. As No. 60 . . . . 15 15
65 1r. As No. 61 . . . . 75 75
66 1½r. Type **8** . . . . 1·40 1·40
67 2r. As No. 63 . . . . 1·70 1·70
MS67a 90 × 65 mm. No. 67. Imperf . . . . 6·25 6·25

9 Globe, New York and Dubai Harbours

1964. New York World's Fair.
68 **9** 1n.p. red & blue (postage) . . 15 15
69 – 2n.p. blue, red and mauve . . 15 15
70 **9** 3n.p. green and brown . . . 15 15
71 – 4n.p. red, green & turquoise 15 15
72 **9** 5n.p. violet, olive & green . . 15 15
73 – 10n.p. black, brown & red . . 75 60

74 – 75n.p. black, grn & bl (air) 75 40
75 – 2r. ochre, turquoise & brn . . 1·30 90
76 – 3r. orange, turquoise & green 1·80 1·30
MS76a 110 × 90 mm. Nos. 75/6 in new colours. Imperf . . . . . 9·25 8·50
DESIGNS: 2, 4, 10n.p. New York skyline and Dubai hotel; 75n.p., 2, 3r. Statue of Liberty, New York, and "Rigorous" (tug), Dubai.

10 Flame of Freedom and Scales of Justice

1964. Air. 15th Anniv of Human Rights Declaration. Flame in red.
77 **10** 35n.p. brown and blue . . . 40 15
78 50n.p. green and blue . . . 65 40
79 1r. black and turquoise . . 1·40 65
80 3r. ultramarine and blue . . 3·75 1·80
MS80a 100 × 60 mm. No. 80 in green and ultramarine. Imperf . . . 7·25 7·25

11 Shaikh Rashid bin Said and View of Dubai

1964.
81 **11** 10n.p. olive, red & brown (postage) 35 15
82 A 20n.p. brown, red & green 40 15
83 **11** 30n.p. black, red & blue . . 50 25
84 A 40n.p. blue, red & cerise . . 65 35

85 B 1r. olive, red & brn (air) . . 1·40 65
86 C 2r. brown, red & green . . . 3·25 1·40
87 B 3r. black, red and blue . . . 5·00 2·50
88 C 5r. blue, red and cerise . . . 9·25 4·50
SCENES: A, Waterfront; B, Waterside buildings; C, Harbour.

1964. Air. Winter Olympic Games, Innsbruck. Nos. 55/9 optd with Olympic Rings, Games Emblem and **INNSBRUCK 1964**.
89 **7** 20n.p. brown and green . . . 85 40
90 – 30n.p. brown and violet . . . 1·20 60
91 – 40n.p. green and blue . . . . 1·70 1·00
92 – 70n.p. grey and green . . . . 2·75 1·60
93 – 1r. red and blue . . . . . . 4·25 2·00
MS93a Five sheets, each 100 × 120 mm. . . . . 55·00 55·00

1964. Air. 48th Birth Anniv of Pres. Kennedy. Optd **MAY 29** (late President's birthday).
94 **6** 75n.p. blk & grn on grn . . . 1·70 1·70
95 1r. black & brown on buff 2·10 2·10
96 1½r. black and red on grey 2·50 2·50
MS96a 100 × 60 mm. . . . . . . 7·25 7·25

1964. Air. Anti-T.B. Campaign. Optd **ANTI TUBERCULOSE** in English and Arabic, and Cross of Lorraine. Perf or roul.
101 **3** 20n.p. brown, yell & red . . 4·25 4·25
102 – 30n.p. blue, orange & red 4·25 4·25
103 – 40n.p. black, yellow & red 4·25 4·25
104 – 50n.p. violet, red & turq . . 4·25 4·25
MS104a Four sheets, each 119 × 99 mm. Imperf £130

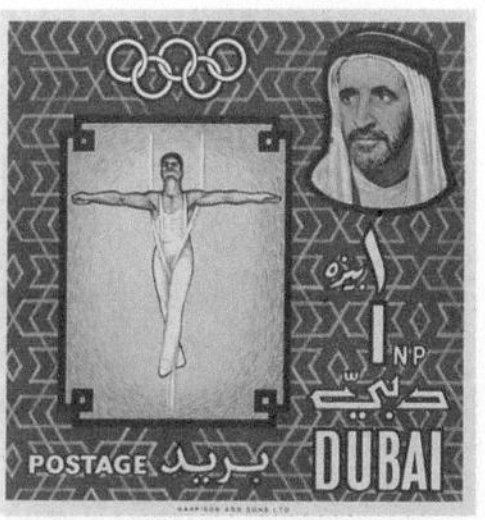

15 Gymnastics

1964. Olympic Games, Tokyo.
105 **15** 1n.p. brown and olive . . . 10 10
106 – 2n.p. sepia & turquoise . . 10 10
107 – 3n.p. blue and brown . . . 10 10
108 – 4n.p. violet and yellow . . . 10 10
109 – 5n.p. ochre and slate . . . 15 15
110 – 10n.p. blue and buff . . . 20 20
111 – 20n.p. olive and red . . . 35 35
112 – 30n.p. blue and yellow . . . 60 60
113 – 40n.p. green and buff . . . 1·30 85
114 – 1r. purple and blue . . . . 3·00 2·10
MS114a 102 × 102 mm. No. 114 (larger). Imperf . . . . 5·00 5·00
DESIGNS: 2n.p. to 1r. Various gymnastic exercises as Type **15**, each with portrait of Ruler.

1964. Air. 19th Anniv of U.N. Nos. 43/6 optd **UNO 19th ANNIVERSARY** in English and Arabic.
115 **5** 30n.p. brown and violet . . 1·10 65
116 – 40n.p. olive and red . . . . 1·70 1·30
117 – 70n.p. orange and green . . 2·75 2·50
118 – 1r. blue and brown . . . . 3·75 3·00

17 Shaikh Rashid and Shaikh Ahmad of Qatar

1964. "Educational Progress". Portraits in black; torch orange.
119 **17** 5n.p. purple (postage) . . . 15 15
120 10n.p. red 15 15
121 15n.p. blue 25 15
122 – 20n.p. olive 35 15

123 – 30n.p. red (air) . . . . . . 1·30 60
124 – 40n.p. brown . . . . 3·00 1·00
125 – 50n.p. blue . . . . 3·75 1·30
126 – 1r. green . . . . 5·50 2·10
MS126a 100 × 60 mm. No. 126. Imperf . . . . 10·00 8·50
DESIGNS: 20, 30, 40n.p. Shaikh Rashid and Shaikh Abdullah of Kuwait; 50n.p., 1r. Shaikh Rashid and Pres. Nasser of Egypt.

1964. Air. Outer Space Achievements, 1964. Optd (a) Also.65/7 optd in English and Arabic, **RANGER 7** and space capsule motif.
127 1r. multicoloured . . . . . 3·25 3·25
128 1½r. multicoloured . . . . . 3·25 3·25
129 2r. multicoloured . . . . . 3·25 3·25
MS129a 90 × 65 mm. . . . . . . 8·50 8·50
(b) Miniature sheet (No.**MS** 67a) optd as Nos. 65/7, but without space capsule and "Ranger 7" which appears larger in sheet margins instead.

19 Globe and Rockets

1964. Space Achievements. Unissued stamps surch as T **19**. Multicoloured.
130 10n.p. on 75n.p. "Man on Moon" (25 × 78 mm) . . . 2·50 2·50
131 20n.p. on 1r.50 Type **19** . . 3·00 3·00
132 30n.p. on 2r. "Universe" (25 × 78 mm) . . . . . . 3·00 3·00

1964. Air. 1st Death Anniv of Pres. J. Kennedy. As No. 47 with colours changed, optd **22 NOVEMBER.**
133 **6** 75n.p. black and green . . . 10·00 8·50

21 Telephone Handset

1966. Opening of Dubai Automatic Telephone Exchange.
134 **21** 10n.p. brn & grn (postage) 15 15
135 15n.p. red and plum . . . 25 15
136 25n.p. green and blue . . . 50 15

137 – 40n.p. blue & grn (air) . . . 50 25
138 – 60n.p. orange and sepia . . 1·20 50
139 – 75n.p. violet and black . . 1·30 85
140 – 2r. green and red . . . . . 4·50 3·00
MS141 102 × 60 mm. No. 14. Imperf . . . . 8·50 7·25
DESIGN: Nos. 137/40, As Type **21** but showing telephone dial.

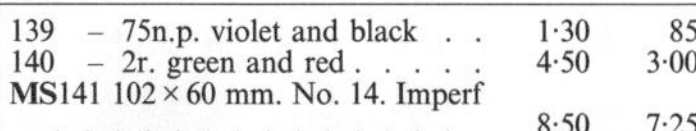

22 Sir Winston Churchill and Catafalque

1966. Churchill Commemoration. (a) Postage.
142 **22** 1r. black and violet 60 40
143 1r.50 black and olive . . . 1·00 65
144 3r. black and blue . . . . 2·20 1·70
145 4r. black and red . . . . . 3·75 2·75
MS146 134 × 90 mm. Nos. 141/44. Imperf . . . . 10·00 10·00

(b) Air. Nos. 142/5 optd **AIR MAIL** in English and Arabic and with black borders.
147 **22** 1r. black and violet 60 40
148 1r.50 black and olive . . . 1·00 65
149 3r. black and blue . . . . 2·20 1·70
150 4r. black and red . . . . . 3·75 2·75
MS151 134 × 90 mm. Nos. 147/9. Imperf . . . . 10·00 10·00

23 Ruler's Palace 24 Bridge

1966.
152 **23** 5n.p. brown and blue . . . 25 25
153 10n.p. black and orange . . 25 25
154 15n.p. blue and brown . . 35 25
155 A 20n.p. blue and brown . . 40 35
156 25n.p. red and blue 40 40
157 B 35n.p. violet and green . . 65 60
158 40n.p. turquoise & blue . . 1·00 60
159 **24** 60n.p. green and red . . . 1·20 1·10
160 1r. ultramarine and blue 2·20 1·70
161 C 1r.25 brown and black . . 2·75 2·20
162 D 1r.50 purple and green . . 4·50 2·30
163 3r. brown and violet . . . 9·25 4·50
164 E 5r. red . . . . 16·00 8·50
165 10r. blue . . . . 34·00 18·00
DESIGNS—HORIZ: (28 × 21 mm): A, Waterfront, Dubai; B, Bridge and dhow. As Type **24**: C, Minaret (Ruler's portrait on right); D, Fort Dubai. VERT: (32½ × 42½ mm): E, Shaikh Rashid bin Said.

25 Oil Rig 26 "Tasman" (oil rig)

1966. Air. Oil Exploration. (a) "Land" series as T **25**.
166 – 5n.p. black and lilac . . . 25 10
167 – 15n.p. black and bistre . . 50 25
168 – 25n.p. black and red . . . 75 40
169 – 35n.p. black and red . . . 1·00 50
170 – 50n.p. black and brown . . 1·40 65
171 **25** 70n.p. black and red . . . 3·25 1·60
MS172 Two sheets, each 60 × 100 mm. 70n.p. (No. 170) and 1r. black and green .Imperf . . 12·50 10·00
DESIGNS—HORIZ: 5n.p. Map of Dubai; 15n.p. Surveying; 25n.p. Dubai Petroleum Company building; 35n.p. Oil drilling. VERT: 50n.p. Surveying with level.

(b) "Sea" series as T **26**.
173 **26** 10n.p. purple and blue . . 25 10
174 – 20n.p. mauve and green . . 40 10
175 **26** 30n.p. brown and green . . 75 10
176 – 40n.p. lilac and agate . . . 75 15
177 **26** 50n.p. blue and olive . . . 1·30 25
178 – 60n.p. blue and violet . . . 1·40 50
179 **26** 75n.p. green and brown . . 2·20 65
180 – 1r. green and blue . . . . 2·50 1·00
MS181 100 × 120 mm. Nos. 179/80. Imperf . . . . 11·00 10·00
DESIGN: 20, 40, 60n.p. and 1r. Ocean well-head.

27 Rulers of Gulf Arab States (⅗-size illustration)

1966. Gulf Arab States Summit Conference.
182 **27** 35p. multicoloured . . . . 1·80 85
183 60p. multicoloured . . . . 5·00 2·10
184 150p. multicoloured . . . 10·00 5·50

28 Jules Rimet Cup

1966. World Cup Football Championship. Multicoloured.
185 40d. Type **28** 60 25
186 60d. Various football scenes 75 40
187 1r. Various football scenes . . 1·20 60
188 1r.25 Various football scenes 1·50 75
189 3r. Wembley Stadium, London . . . . 2·30 1·80
MS190 105 × 75 mm. 5r. Type **28** 8·50 8·50

1966. England's World Cup Victory. Nos. 185/9 optd **ENGLAND WINNERS.**
191 **28** 40d. multicoloured 60 25
192 – 60d. multicoloured 75 40
193 – 1r. multicoloured . . . . . 1·20 60
194 – 1r.25 multicoloured . . . . 1·50 75
195 – 3r. multicoloured . . . . . 2·30 1·80
MS196 105 × 75 mm. 5r. multicoloured . . . . 8·50 8·50

29 Rulers of Dubai and Kuwait, and I.C.Y. Emblem

1966. International Co-operation Year (1965). Currency expressed in rupees.
197 **29** 1r. brown and green . . . 1·70 85
198 A 1r. green and brown . . . 1·70 85
199 B 1r. blue and violet . . . . 1·70 85
200 C 1r. blue and violet . . . . 1·70 85
201 D 1r. turquoise and red . . . 1·70 85
202 E 1r. turquoise and red . . . 1·70 85
203 F 1r. violet and blue . . . . 1·70 85
204 G 1r. violet and blue . . . . 1·70 85
205 H 1r. red and turquoise . . . 1·70 85
206 I 1r. red and turquoise . . . 1·70 85
MS207 76 × 101 mm. Nos. 197/8 9·25 9·25
HEADS OF STATE and POLITICAL LEADERS (Ruler of Dubai and): A, Pres. John F. Kennedy. B, Prime Minister Harold Wilson; C, Pres. Helou of the Lebanon; D, Pres. De Gaulle; E, Pres. Nasser; F, Pope Paul VI; G, Ruler of Bahrain; H, Pres. Lyndon Johnson; I, Ruler of Qatar.

30 "Gemini" Capsules manoeuvring

1966. "Gemini" Space Rendezvous. Mult.
208 35d. Type **30** 50 25
209 40d. "Gemini" capsules linked 50 25
210 60d. "Gemini" capsules separating 60 35
211 1r. Schirra and Stafford in "Gemini 6" . . . . . . 1·10 50
212 1r.25 "Gemini" orbits . . . 1·50 85
213 3r. Borman and Lovell in "Gemini 7" . . . . 2·50 1·70
MS214 130 × 100 mm. 1r. As 60d. Imperf . . . . 7·25 5·00

1967. Nos. 197/206 surch **Riyal** in English and Arabic and bars.
215 **29** 1r. on 1r. . . . . 1·30 85
216 A 1r. on 1r. . . . . 1·30 85
217 B 1r. on 1r. . . . . 1·30 85
218 C 1r. on 1r. . . . . 1·30 85
219 D 1r. on 1r. . . . . 1·30 85
220 E 1r. on 1r. . . . . 1·30 85
221 F 1r. on 1r. . . . . 1·30 85
222 G 1r. on 1r. . . . . 1·30 85
223 H 1r. on 1r. . . . . 1·30 85
224 I 1r. on 1r. . . . . 1·30 85
MS225 76 × 101 mm. Nos. 215/16 8·50 7·25

1967. Gemini Flight Success. Nos. 208/13 optd **SUCCESSFUL END OF GEMINI FLIGHT.**
226 **30** 35d. multicoloured 50 20
227 – 40d. multicoloured 50 20
228 – 60d. multicoloured 60 35
229 – 1r. multicoloured . . . . . 1·10 50
230 – 1r.25 multicoloured . . . . 1·50 85
231 – 3r. multicoloured . . . . . 2·50 1·70
MS232 130 × 100 mm. 1r. multicoloured. Imperf . . . . 8·50 8·50

1967. Nos. 152/61, 163/5 with currency names changed by overprinting in English and Arabic (except Nos. 244/5 which have the currency name in Arabic only).
233 **23** 5d. on 5n.p. 25 15
234 10d. on 10n.p. 25 15
235 15d. on 15n.p. 40 25
236 A 20d. on 20n.p. 65 25
237 25d. on 25n.p. 65 25
238 B 35d. on 35n.p. 85 25
239 40d. on 40n.p. . . . . . 1·20 40
240 **24** 60d. on 60n.p. . . . . . 1·80 40
241 1r. on 1r. . . . . 2·75 65
242 C 1r.25 on 1r.25 . . . . . 5·00 1·30
243 D 3r. on 3r. . . . . 8·50 3·75
244 E 5r. on 5r. . . . . 16·00 7·25
245 10r. on 10r. . . . . 25·00 14·50

37 "The Moving Finger writes..."

1967. Rubaiyat of Omar Khayyam. Mult.
246 60d. Type **37** . . . . 1·70 35
247 60d. "Here with a Loaf of Bread..." . . . . 1·70 35
248 60d. "So, while the Vessels..." 1·70 35
249 60d. "Myself when young..." 1·70 35
250 60d. "One Moment in Annihilation's Waste..." . . 1·70 35
251 60d. "And strange to tell..." 1·70 35
MS252 100 × 80 mm. 60d. Omar Khayyam (smaller, 43 × 30 mm). Imperf . . . . 5·00 5·00

38 "The Straw Hat" (Rubens)

1967. Paintings. Multicoloured.
253 1r. Type **38** . . . . 2·10 40
254 1r. "Thomas, Earl of Arundel" (Rubens) . . . . 2·10 40
255 1r. "A peasant boy leaning on a sill" (Murillo) . . . . 2·10 40
MS256 105 × 177 mm. Nos. 253/6 in tete-beche pairs (2 × 3) . . . . 12·50 6·00
See also Nos. 273/5.

39 Ruler and Lanner Falcon

40 "Bayan" (dhow)

1967.
257 **39** 5d. red and orange . . . . 1·00 35
258 10d. sepia and green . . . 1·00 25
259 20d. purple and blue . . . 1·30 35
260 35d. turquoise & mauve . . 1·70 35
261 60d. blue and green . . . 3·50 65
262 1r. green and purple . . . 5·00 65
263 **40** 1r.25 purple and blue . . . 5·00 85
264 3r. purple and blue . . . . 5·75 2·50
265 5r. violet and green . . . . 11·50 5·00
266 10r. green and mauve . . . 17·00 9·25

41 Globe and Scout Badge

1967. World Scout Jamboree, Idaho. Mult.
267 10d. Type **41** 50 15
268 20d. Dubai scout and dromedaries . . . . 1·00 25
269 35d. Bugler . . . . 1·30 35
270 60d. Jamboree emblem and U.S. flags . . . . 2·20 40
271 1r. Lord Baden-Powell . . . 3·25 85
272 1r.25 Idaho on U.S. Map . . 4·50 1·80

1967. Goya's Paintings in National Gallery, London. As T **38**. Multicoloured.
273 1r. "Dr. Peral" . . . . . . 2·10 25
274 1r. "Dona Isabel Cobos de Porcel" . . . . 2·10 25
275 1r. "Duke of Wellington" . . 2·10 25
MS276 105 × 178 mm. Nos. 273/5 14·50 6·75

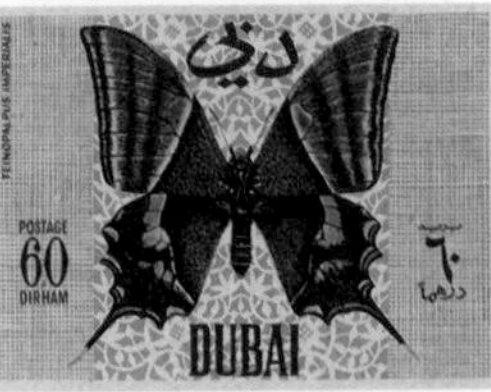

42 Kaiser-i-Hind ("Teinopalpus imperialis")

1968. Butterflies and Moths. Multicoloured.
277 60d. Type **42** . . . . . . 2·30 25
278 60d. "Erasmia pulchella" . . 2·30 25
279 60d. Gaudy baron ("Euthalia indica") . . . . 2·30 25
280 60d. Atlas moth ("Attacus atlas") . . . . 2·30 25
281 60d. "Dysphania militaris" . . 2·30 25
282 60d. "Neochera butleri" . . . 2·30 25
283 60d. African monarch ("Danaus chrysippus") . . 2·30 25
284 60d. Chestnut tiger ("Danaus tytia") . . . . 2·30 25

43 "Madonna and Child" (Ferruzi)

1968. Arab Mothers' Day. Multicoloured.
285 60d. "Games in the Park" (Zandomeneghi) 50 25
286 1r. Type **43** 85 40
287 1r.25 "Mrs Cockburn and Children" (Reynolds) (wrongly inscr "Cookburn") . . . . . . 1·00 50
288 3r. "Self-portrait with Daughter" (Vigee-Lebrun) 2·30 1·50

44 "Althea rosea"

1968. Flowers. Multicoloured.
289 60d. Type **44** . . . . 2·30 25
290 60d. "Geranium lancastriense" . . . . . . 2·30 25
291 60d. "Catharanthus roseus" 2·30 25
292 60d. "Convolvulus minor" . . 2·30 25
293 60d. "Opuntia" . . . . . . 2·30 25
294 60d. "Gaillardia aristata" . . 2·30 25
295 60d. "Heliopsis" . . . . . . 2·30 25
296 60d. "Centaurea moschata" 2·30 25

45 Running

1968. Olympic Games, Mexico. Multicoloured.
297 15d. Type **45** . . . . 1·00 10
298 20d. Swimming . . . . . . 1·10 10
299 25d. Boxing . . . . 1·80 15
300 35d. Water-polo . . . . . . 2·10 25
301 40d. High jump . . . . . . 2·50 25
302 60d. Gymnastics . . . . . . 3·75 40
303 1r. Football . . . . 5·00 60
304 1r.25 Fencing . . . . 7·25 65
MS305 70 × 90 mm. No. 303. Imprf 8·50 6·25

46 "Young Girl with Kitten" (Perronneau)

1968. Children's Day. Multicoloured.
306 60d. "Two Boys with Mastiff" (Goya) 50 15
307 1r. Type **46** 65 35
308 1r.25 "Soap Bubbles" (Manet) . . . . 1·00 35
309 3r. "The Fluyder Boys" (Lawrence) . . . . 2·50 1·00

47 Common Pheasant

1968. Arabian Gulf Birds. Multicoloured.
310 60d. Type **47** . . . . 2·50 25
311 60d. Red-collared dove ("Turtle Dove") . . . . . 2·50 25
312 60d. Western red-footed falcon ("Red-footed flaca") 2·50 25
313 60d. European bee eater ("Bee-eater") . . . . . . 2·50 25
314 60d. Hoopoe . . . . 2·50 25
315 60d. Great egret ("Common Egret") . . . . 2·50 25
316 60d. Little terns . . . . . . 2·50 25
317 60d. Lesser black-backed gulls . . . . 2·50 25

48 "Bamora" (freighter), 1914

1969. 60th Anniv of Dubai Postal Service. Multicoloured.
318 25d. Type **48** 25 25
319 35d. De Havilland D.H.66 Hercules airplane, 1930 . . 35 25
320 60d. "Sirdhana" (liner), 1947 65 25
321 1r. Armstrong Whitworth Atalanta airplane, 1938 . . 85 25
322 1r.25 "Chandpara" (freighter), 1949 . . . . . 1·10 25
323 3r. Short Sunderland flying boat, 1943 . . . . 1·80 40
MS324 117 × 80 mm. 1r.25 *Bombala* (freighter), 1961, and Vickers Super VC-10 airliner, 1969 . . 4·25 4·25

49 "Madonna and Child" (Bartolome Murillo)

1969. Arab Mothers' Day. Multicoloured.
325 60d. Type **49** 65 25
326 1r. "Madonna with Rose" (Francesco Mozzola (Parmigianino)) . . . . . 1·20 25
327 1r.25 "Mother and Children" (Peter Paul Rubens) . . . 1·40 25
328 3r. "Campori Madonna" (Antonio Correggio) . . . 3·25 50
No. 326 wrongly inscribed "Mazzuoli".

50 Porkfish

1969. Fishes. Multicoloured.
329 60d. Type **50** . . . . 1·70 25
330 60d. Greasy ("Spotted") grouper . . . . 1·70 25
331 60d. Diamond fingerfish ("Moonfish") . . . . . . 1·70 25
332 60d. Striped sweetlips . . . . 1·70 25
333 60d. Blue-ringed angelfish ("Blue angel") . . . . . . 1·70 25
334 60d. Roundel ("Texas") skate 1·70 25
335 60d. Black-backed ("Striped") butterflyfish . . . . 1·70 25
336 60d. Emperor ("Imperial") angelfish . . . . 1·70 25

51 Burton, Doughty, Burckhardt, Thesiger and Map

1969. Explorers of Arabia.
337 **51** 25d. brown and green . . . 1·00 25
338 60d. blue and brown . . . 1·80 50
339 1r. green and blue . . . . 3·50 65
340 1r.25 black and red . . . . 4·50 1·90

52 Underwater Storage Tank Construction

1969. Oil Industry. Multicoloured.
341 5d. Type **52** 25 15
342 20d. Floating-out storage tank 65 15
343 35d. Underwater tank in operation . . . . 1·30 15
344 60d. Ruler, oil rig and monument . . . . 2·75 15
345 1r. Fateh marine oilfield . . . 3·50 15

53 Astronauts on Moon

1969. 1st Man on the Moon. Multicoloured.
346 60d. Type **53** (postage) . . . 75 30
347 1r. Astronaut and ladder . . 90 30
348 1r.25 Astronauts planting U.S. flag on Moon (horiz) (62 × 38 mm) (air) . . . . 1·30 35

54 "Weather Reporter" launching Radio-Sonde and Handley Page Hastings Weather Reconnaissance Airplane

1970. World Meteorological Day. Mult.
349 60d. Type **54** 40 25
350 1r. Kew-type radio-sonde and dish aerial 85 25
351 1r.25 "Tiros" satellite and rocket . . . . 1·00 25
352 3r. "Ariel" satellite and rocket . . . . 1·90 40

55 New Headquarters Building

1970. New U.P.U. Headquarters Building, Berne. Multicoloured.
353 5d. Type **55** 40 10
354 60d. U.P.U. Monument, Berne . . . . 1·70 35

56 Charles Dickens

58 Shaikh Rashid

57 "The Graham Children" (Hogarth)

1970. Death Cent of Charles Dickens. Mult.
355 60d. Type **56** 50 25
356 1r. Signature, quill and London sky-line (horiz) . . 1·00 25
357 1r.25 Dickens and Victorian street . . . . 1·30 1·10
358 3r. Dickens and books (horiz) 2·50 65

1970. Children's Day. Multicoloured.
359 35d. Type **57** 50 25
360 60d. "Caroline Murat and Children" (Gerard) (vert) 1·20 25
361 1r. "Napoleon as Uncle" (Ducis) . . . . 2·10 25

1970. Multicoloured.
362 5d. Type **58** 15 15
363 10d. Dhow building (horiz) 35 10
364 20d. Al Maktum Bridge (horiz) 60 15
365 35d. Great Mosque 65 10
366 60d. Dubai National Bank (horiz) . . . . 1·10 15
367 1r. International airport (horiz) . . . . 1·80 35
368 1r.25 Harbour project (horiz) 3·25 90
369 3r. Hospital (horiz) . . . . . 4·50 1·80
370 5r. Trade school (horiz) . . . 6·75 3·75
371 10r. Television and "Intelsat 4" . . . . 11·50 6·75
The riyal values are larger, 40 × 25 or 25 × 40 mm.

59 Terminal Building and Control Tower

1971. Opening of Dubai International Airport. Multicoloured.
372 1r. Type **59** . . . . 3·00 1·70
373 1r.25 Airport entrance . . . 3·75 2·10

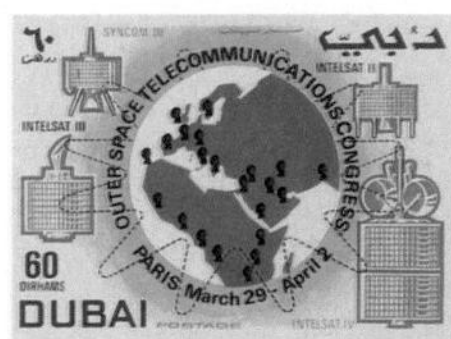
60 Telecommunications Map and Satellites

1971. Outer Space Telecommunications Congress, Paris. Multicoloured.
374 60d. Type **60** (postage) . . . 40 25
375 1r. Rocket and "Intelsat 4" (air) 60 40
376 5r. Eiffel Tower and Goonhilly aerial . . . . . 3·00 2·30

61 Scout Badge, Fan and Map

62 Albrecht Durer

1971. 13th World Scout Jamboree, Asagiri (Japan). Multicoloured.
377 60d. Type **61** 40 15
378 1r. Canoeing . . . . 1·00 40
379 1r.25 Rock-climbing . . . . 1·20 50
380 3r. Scouts around camp-fire (horiz) . . . . 2·75 1·00

1971. Famous People (1st issue). Mult.
381 60d. Type **62** (postage) . . . 65 25
382 1r. Sir Isaac Newton (air) . . 75 65
383 1r.25 Avicenna . . . . 1·00 85
384 3r. Voltaire . . . . 3·25 2·00
See also Nos. 388/91.

63 Boy in Meadow

1971. 25th Anniv of UNICEF. Mult.
385 60d. Type **63** (postage) . . . 40 25
386 5r. Children with toys (horiz) 3·75 2·00
387 1r. Mother and children (air) 85 35

1972. Famous People (2nd issue). As T **62**. Multicoloured.
388 10d. Leonardo da Vinci (postage) 25 25
389 35d. Beethoven 40 25
390 75d. Khalil Gibran (poet) (air) 75 35
391 5r. Charles de Gaulle . . . . 4·50 2·20

65 Nurse supervising children

1972. Air. World Health Day. Multicoloured.
392 75d. Type **65** . . . . 1·30 50
393 1r.25 Doctor treating baby (horiz) . . . . 2·10 1·20

67 Gymnastics

1972. Olympic Games, Munich. Multicoloured.
399 35d. Type **67** (postage) . . . 35 10
400 40d. Fencing 60 10
401 65d. Hockey 90 15
402 75d. Water-polo (air) . . . . 1·30 15
403 1r. Horse-jumping . . . . . 1·50 15
404 1r.25 Athletics . . . . 2·10 15

POSTAGE DUE STAMPS

1963. Designs as T **1** but inscr "DUE".
D26 L 1n.p. red and grey 50 35
D27 M 2n.p. blue and bistre . . . 65 40
D28 N 3n.p. green and red . . . 1·10 65
D29 L 4n.p. red and green . . . 1·40 1·00
D30 M 5n.p. black and red . . . 1·60 1·20
D31 N 10n.p. violet and olive . . . 2·10 1·60
D32 L 15n.p. red and blue . . . 3·00 2·00
D33 M 25n.p. green & brown . . 3·25 2·10
D34 N 35n.p. orange and blue . . 3·75 2·50
DESIGNS—HORIZ: L, Common European cockle; M, Common blue mussel; N, Portuguese oyster.

D **66** Shaikh Rashid

1972.
D394 D **66** 5d. grey, blue & brn 85 85
D395 10d. brn, ochre & bl 1·20 1·20
D396 20d. brn, red and blue 2·20 2·20
D397 30d. violet, lilac & blk 3·00 3·00
D398 50d. brn, ochre & pur 6·25 6·25

DUNGARPUR Pt. 1

A state of Rajasthan. Now uses Indian stamps.

12 pies = 1 anna; 16 annas = 1 rupee.

1 State Arms

2 Maharawal Lakshman Singh

1933.
1 **1** ½a. yellow . . . . — £180
2 ½a. red . . . . — £550
3 ½a. brown . . . . — £350
4 1a. blue . . . . — £150
5 1a. red . . . . — £1800
6 1a.3p. mauve . . . . — £225
7 2a. green . . . . — £325
8 4a. red . . . . — £550

1932. T **2** (various frames).
9 **2** ¼a. orange . . . . £900 75·00
10 ½a. red . . . . £275 55·00
11 1a. blue . . . . £275 50·00
12 1a.3p. mauve £900 £200
13 1½a. violet £950 £250
14 2a. green £1200 £400
15 4a. brown £900 £170

DUTTIA (DATIA) Pt. 1

A state of Central India. Now uses Indian stamps.

12 pies = 1 anna; 16 annas = 1 rupee.

2 (½a.) Ganesh

3 (4a.) Ganesh

1894?. Imperf.
1 **2** ½a. black on green £10000
2a 2a. blue on yellow £2750
Nos. 1/2a are as Type **2**, but have rosettes in lower corners.

1896. Imperf.
4 **3** ½a. black on orange £3250
5 ½a. black on green £5500
6 2a. black on yellow £2000
7 4a. black on red £1300
Stamps of Type **3** come with the circular handstamp as shown on Type **2**. Examples of Nos. 4/5 without handstamp are worth slightly less than the prices quoted.

1896. Imperf.
8b **2** ½a. black on green . . . . 21·00 £225
3 1a. red £2750 £3250
9 1a. black . . . . 85·00 £2750
10 2a. black on yellow . . . . 27·00 £250
11 4a. black on red . . . . . 23·00 £200

4 (½a.)

5 (½a.)

1897. Imperf.

No.	Type	Description	Unused	Used
12	**4**	½a. black on green	80·00	£475
13		1a. black	£150	
14		2a. black on yellow	95·00	
15		4a. black on red	90·00	

1899. Imperf, roul or perf.

No.	Type	Description	Unused	Used
16c	**5**	¼a. red	3·75	18·00
38		¼a. blue	2·75	12·00
37		¼a. black	4·75	22·00
17		½a. black on green	2·75	18·00
30		½a. green	5·50	24·00
35		½a. blue	3·50	16·00
39		½a. pink	3·25	16·00
18		1a. black	3·00	18·00
31		1a. purple	6·00	25·00
36		1a. pink	3·25	18·00
19b		2a. black on yellow	2·75	20·00
32		2a. brown	15·00	29·00
33		2a. lilac	5·50	27·00
20		4a. black on red	3·25	19·00
34		4a. brown	75·00	

EAST SILESIA Pt. 5

Special overprints were applied to Czechoslovakian and Polish stamps prior to a plebiscite. The plebiscite was never held, due to disorders, and the area was divided between Czechoslovakia and Poland in 1920.

100 haleru = 1 krone.
100 fenni = 1 korona.

1920. Stamps of Czechoslovakia optd **SO 1920**. Imperf or perf.

23 **3**	1h. brown	20	10
2 **2**	3h. mauve	15	10
24 **3**	5h. green	25	30
25	10h. green	25	30
26	15h. red	40	15
6 **2**	20h. green	20	10
27 **3**	20h. red	40	30
28	25h. purple	40	30
9 **2**	30h. olive	20	30
35 **3**	30h. mauve	40	30
10 **2**	40h. orange	25	30
11 **3**	50h. purple	55	45
12	50h. blue	1·50	1·25
36	60h. orange	45	45
14	75h. green	45	45
15	80h. olive	45	45
16 **2**	100h. brown	80	60
17 **3**	120h. black	1·40	1·25
18 **2**	200h. blue	1·40	1·25
19 **3**	300h. green	6·50	1·90
20 **2**	400h. violet	1·90	1·50
21 **3**	500h. brown	4·25	3·75
22	1000h. purple	13·00	7·50

1920. Stamps of Poland of 1919 optd **S. O. 1920.** Perf.

57 **15**	5f. green	10	10
58	10f. brown	10	10
59	15f. red	10	10
60 **16**	25f. olive	10	10
61	50f. green	10	10
62 **17**	1k. green	10	10
63	1k.50 brown	10	10
64	2k. blue	10	10
65 **18**	2k.50 purple	10	10
66 **19**	5k. blue	10	10

EXPRESS STAMPS FOR PRINTED MATTER

1920. Express stamps of Czechoslovakia optd **S O 1920**.

E39 E **4**	2h. purple on yellow	15	10
E40	5h. green on yellow	15	10

NEWSPAPER STAMPS

1920. Newspaper stamps of Czechoslovakia optd **SO 1920**. Imperf.

N41 N **4**	2h. green	20	30
N42	6h. red	20	10
N43	10h. lilac	35	30
N44	20h. blue	50	30
N45	30h. brown	50	30

POSTAGE DUE STAMPS

1920. Postage Due stamps of Czechoslovakia optd **SO 1920**. Imperf.

D46 D **4**	5h. olive	20	15
D47	10h. olive	20	10
D48	15h. olive	20	15
D49	20h. olive	30	30
D50	25h. olive	30	30
D51	30h. olive	30	30
D52	40h. olive	45	45
D53	50h. olive	2·10	45
D54	100h. brown	2·25	90
D55	500h. green	5·75	3·75
D56	1000h. violet	9·00	6·75

EASTERN ROUMELIA AND SOUTH BULGARIA Pt. 3

This area, part of the Turkish Empire, situated south of the Balkan Mts., became semi-autonomous after 1878. In 1885 the population revolted against the Turks, changing the district's name to South Bulgaria. Incorporation into Bulgaria followed in 1886.

40 paras = 1 piastre.

A. EASTERN ROUMELIA

1880. Stamps of Turkey optd **R.O**.

1 **2**	½pre. on 20pa. green (No. 78)	35·00	35·00
2 **9**	20pa. purple & green (No. 83)	38·00	38·00
3	2pi. black & orange (No. 85)	60·00	60·00
4	5pi. red and blue (No. 86)	£200	£200

1881. Stamp of Turkey optd **R.O** and **ROUMELIE ORIENTALE**.

5 **9**	10pa. black and mauve	45·00	45·00

1881. As T **9** of Turkey but inscr "ROUMELIE ORIENTALE" at left.

6 **9**	5pa. black and olive	1·50	50
11	5pa. lilac	25	25
7	10pa. black and green	4·00	50
12	10pa. green	10	25
8	20pa. black and red	40	50
9	1pi. black and blue	2·50	3·00
10	5pi. red and blue	25·00	45·00

B. SOUTH BULGARIA

1885. As T **9** of Turkey, but inscr "RO" at left and optd with lion.

13 **9**	5pa. black and olive	£225	£225
29	5pa. lilac	7·50	24·00
14	10pa. black and green	£550	£550
30	10pa. green	15·00	30·00
15	20pa. black and red	£225	
34	20pa. red	14·00	48·00
18	1pi. black and blue	45·00	90·00
26	5pi. red and blue	£375	

1885. As T **9** of Turkey, but inscr "ROUMELIE ORIENTALE" and optd with lion and inscription in frame.

43 **9**	5pa. black and olive	£250	£250
48a	5pa. lilac	9·00	15·00
44	10pa. black and green	£250	£250
49	10pa. green	12·00	18·00
45	20pa. black and red	60·00	75·00
50	20pa. red	12·00	18·00
46	1pi. black and blue	60·00	75·00
47	5pi. red and blue	20·00	25·00

ECUADOR Pt. 20

A Republic on the W. Coast of S. America. Independent since 1830.

1865. 8 reales = 1 peso.
1881. 100 centavos = 1 sucre.
2000. 100c. = 1 dollar (U.S.)

1 2

1865. Imperf.

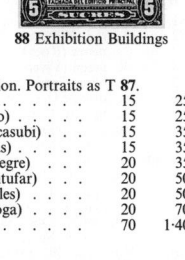

1b **1**	½r. blue	13·00	6·75
2d	1r. yellow	10·00	7·25
3	1r. green	£150	17·50
4 **2**	4r. red	£160	80·00

3 4 5

1872.

10 **3**	½r. blue	10·00	2·10
11 **4**	1r. orange	11·50	3·50
12a **3**	1p. red	2·10	7·00

1881. Various frames.

13 **5**	1c. brown	10	10
14	2c. lake	10	10
15	5c. blue	1·90	25
16	10c. orange	10	10
17	20c. violet	30	25
18	50c. green	40	1·50

1883. Surch **DIEZ CENTAVOS**.

19 **5**	10c. on 50c. green	15·00	11·50

13 — 19 Pres. Juan Flores — 20 Pres. Rocafuerte

1887. Various frames.

26 **13**	1c. green	10	10
27	2c. red	15	10
28	5c. blue	85	15
29	80c. olive	1·50	4·25

1892.

34 **19**	1c. orange	10	10
35	2c. brown	10	10
36	5c. red	10	10
37	10c. green	10	10
38	20c. brown	10	10
39	50c. red	10	20
40	1s. blue	10	75
41	5s. violet	25	75

1893. Surch **5 CENTAVOS**.

53 **19**	5c. on 50c. red	40	35
49	5c. on 1s. blue	65	55
50	5c. on 5s. violet	3·00	2·75

1894. Dated "1894".

57 **20**	1c. blue	10	10
58	2c. brown	10	10
59	5c. green	15	15
60	10c. red	30	15
61	20c. black	30	15
62	50c. orange	2·00	75
63	1s. red	3·75	1·50
64	5s. blue	4·75	2·25

1895. Dated "1895".

74 **20**	1c. blue	25	25
75	2c. brown	25	25
76	5c. green	20	20
77	10c. red	20	10
78	20c. black	30	30
79	50c. orange	1·40	75
80	1s. red	7·00	3·00
81	5s. blue	3·00	1·50

These two series were re-issued in 1897 optd "1897–1898".

22 — F 1

1896. Arms designs, inscr "U.P.U. 1896".

89 **22**	1c. green	30	10
90	2c. red	30	10
91	5c. blue	30	10
92	10c. brown	25	25
93	20c. orange	40	70
94	50c. blue	25	1·25
95	1s. brown	1·25	1·50
96	5s. lilac	5·50	2·10

This series was re-issued in 1897 optd "1897–1898".

1896. Dated "1887 1888". Surch.

112 F **1**	5c. on 10c. orange	75	15
113	10c. on 4c. brown	75	30

1896. As Type F 1, but dated "1891 1892".

114 F **1**	10c. on 4c. brown	6·50	5·25

1896. As Type F 1, but dated "1893 1894". Surch.

115 F **1**	1c. on 1c. red	40	15
116	2c. on 2c. blue	75	50
117	5c. on 10c. orange	2·10	1·90

34 V. Roca, D. Noboa and J. Olmedo — (40)

1896. Triumph of Liberal Party. Dated "1845–1895".

118 **34**	1c. red	40	40
119 –	2c. blue	40	40
120 **34**	5c. green	30	50
121 –	10c. yellow	30	50
122 **34**	20c. red	35	75
123 –	50c. lilac	50	1·25
124 **34**	1s. orange	95	1·50

DESIGN: 2c., 10c., 50c. Gen. Elizalde.
This series was re-issued in 1897 optd "1897–1898".

1896. Surch.

125 **22**	5c. on 20c. orange	13·50	13·50
126	10c. on 50c. blue	13·50	13·50

1897. 1896 Jubilee issue optd with T **40**.

167 **34**	1c. red	1·75	1·50
168 –	2c. blue (No. 119)	1·75	1·50
169 **34**	5c. green	1·75	1·50
170 –	10c. yellow (No. 121)	1·75	1·50

41 — 45 Louis Varags Torres

1897.

173 **41**	1c. green	10	10
174	2c. red	10	10
175	5c. lake	10	10
176	10c. brown	10	10
177	20c. yellow	15	25
178	50c. blue	15	40
179	1s. grey	20	50
180	5s. purple	60	75

1899. Surch.

191 **41**	1c. on 2c. red	1·25	50
192	5c. on 10c. brown	1·00	25

1899.

193 **45**	1c. black and grey	10	10
205	1c. black and red	10	10
194 –	2c. black and brown	10	10
206 –	2c. black and green	10	10
195 –	5c. black and red	10	10
207 –	5c. black and lilac	10	10
196 –	10c. black and lilac	10	10
208 –	10c. black and blue	10	10
197 –	20c. black and green	10	10
209 –	20c. black and grey	10	10
198 –	50c. black and red	60	30
210 –	50c. black and blue	35	30
199 –	1s. black and yellow	3·25	1·00
211 –	1s. black and brown	2·75	1·40
200 –	5s. black and lilac	6·25	3·00
212 –	5s. black and grey	4·50	2·25

PORTRAITS: 2c. A. Calderon. 5c. J. Montalvo. 10c. Mejia. 20c. Espejo. 50c. Carbo. 1s. J. J. Olmendo. 5s. Moncayo.

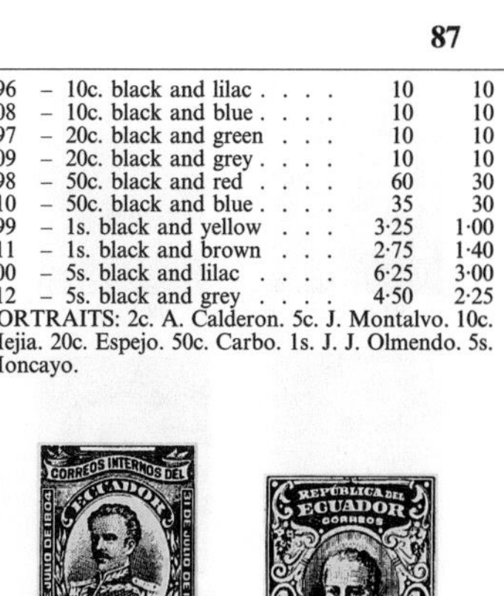

73 Capt. Abdon Calderon

76 President Roca

1904. Birth Centenary of Captain Calderon.

310 **73**	1c. black and red	25	20
311	2c. black and blue	25	20
312	5c. black and yellow	1·00	70
313	10c. black and red	1·75	70
314	20c. black and blue	4·50	1·60
315	50c. black and yellow	42·00	23·00

The 5c. and 50c. are larger (25 × 30 mm).

1907. Portraits in black.

323 **76**	1c. red (Roca)	20	10
324 –	2c. blue (Noboa)	40	10
325 –	3c. orange (Robles)	50	10
326 –	5c. purple (Urvina)	75	10
327 –	10c. blue (Garcia Moreno)	1·50	15
328 –	20c. green (Carrion)	2·25	20
329 –	50c. lilac (Espinoza)	4·50	50
330 –	1s. green (Borrero)	6·25	1·10

84 Baldwin Steam Locomotive

86 Mount Chimborazo

85 Garcia Moreno

1908. Opening of Guayaquil to Quito Railway.

331 **84**	1c. brown	65	50
332 **85**	2c. black and blue	90	70
333 –	5c. black and red	2·00	1·40
334 –	10c. black and yellow	1·50	85
335 –	20c. black and green	1·50	1·00
336 –	50c. black and grey	1·50	1·00
337 **86**	1s. black	3·00	2·00

PORTRAITS—As Type **85**: 5c. Gen E. Alfaro. 10c. A. Moncayo. 20c. A. Harman (engineer). 50c. Sivewright.

87 Jose Mejia Vallejo

88 Exhibition Buildings

1909. National Exhibition. Portraits as T **87**.

340 **87**	1c. green	15	25
341 –	2c. blue (Espejo)	15	25
342 –	3c. orange (Ascasubi)	15	35
343 –	5c. lake (Salinas)	15	35
344 –	10c. brown (Alegre)	20	35
345 –	20c. grey (Montufar)	20	50
346 –	50c. red (Morales)	20	50
347 –	1s. olive (Quiroga)	20	70
348 **88**	5s. violet	70	1·40

1909. Surch **CINCO CENTAVOS**.

349	5c. on 50c. red (No. 346)	60	50

90 Pres. Roca

91 Pres. Dr. Noboa

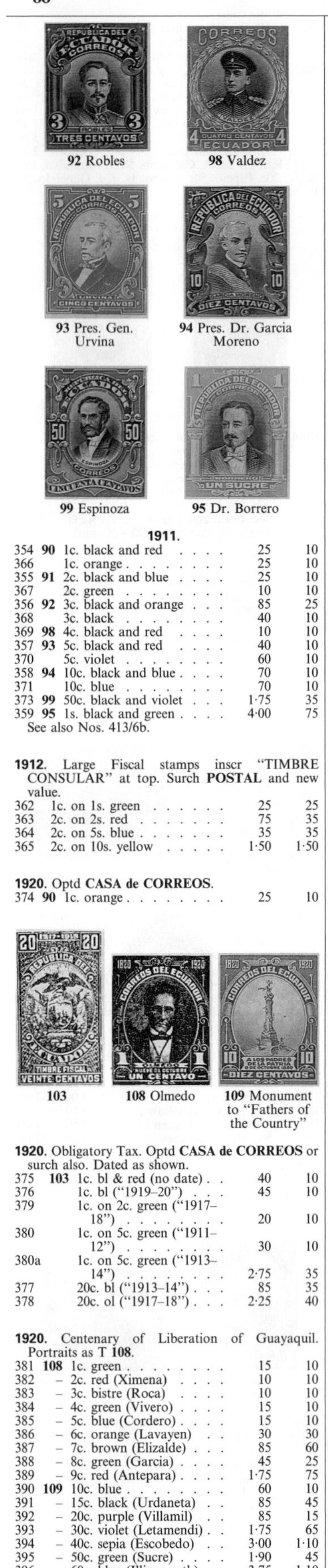

92 Robles — 98 Valdez — 93 Pres. Gen. Urvina — 94 Pres. Dr. Garcia Moreno — 99 Espinoza — 95 Dr. Borrero

1911.

354 **90** 1c. black and red 25 10
366 1c. orange 25 10
355 **91** 2c. black and blue 25 10
367 2c. green 10 10
356 **92** 3c. black and orange . . . 85 25
368 3c. black 40 10
369 **98** 4c. black and red 10 10
357 **93** 5c. black and red 40 10
370 5c. violet 60 10
358 **94** 10c. black and blue 70 10
371 10c. blue 70 10
373 **99** 50c. black and violet . . . 1·75 35
359 **95** 1s. black and green . . . . 4·00 75
See also Nos. 413/6b.

1912. Large Fiscal stamps inscr "TIMBRE CONSULAR" at top. Surch **POSTAL** and new value.
362 1c. on 1s. green 25 25
363 2c. on 2s. red 75 35
364 2c. on 5s. blue 35 35
365 2c. on 10s. yellow . . . . . 1·50 1·50

1920. Optd **CASA de CORREOS**.
374 **90** 1c. orange 25 10

103 — 108 Olmedo — 109 Monument to "Fathers of the Country"

1920. Obligatory Tax. Optd **CASA de CORREOS** or surch also. Dated as shown.
375 **103** 1c. bl & red (no date) . . 40 10
376 1c. bl ("1919–20") . . . 45 10
379 1c. on 2c. green ("1917–18") . . . 20 10
380 1c. on 5c. green ("1911–12") . . . 30 10
380a 1c. on 5c. green ("1913–14") . . . 2·75 35
377 20c. bl ("1913–14") . . . 85 35
378 20c. ol ("1917–18") . . . 2·25 40

1920. Centenary of Liberation of Guayaquil. Portraits as T **108**.
381 **108** 1c. green 15 10
382 – 2c. red (Ximena) 10 10
383 – 3c. bistre (Roca) 10 10
384 – 4c. green (Vivero) 15 10
385 – 5c. blue (Cordero) 15 10
386 – 6c. orange (Lavayen) . . 30 30
387 – 7c. brown (Elizalde) . . . 85 60
388 – 8c. green (Garcia) 45 25
389 – 9c. red (Antepara) . . . . 1·75 75
390 **109** 10c. blue 60 10
391 – 15c. black (Urdaneta) . . 85 45
392 – 20c. purple (Villamil) . . 85 15
393 – 30c. violet (Letamendi) . . 1·75 65
394 – 40c. sepia (Escobedo) . . 3·00 1·10
395 – 50c. green (Sucre) . . . . 1·90 45
396 – 60c. blue (Illingworth) . . 3·75 1·10
397 – 70c. grey (Roca) . . . . 6·25 2·50
398 – 80c. yellow (Rocafuerte) . 6·50 2·50
399 – 90c. green (Star and wreath) . . . . 7·00 2·50
400 – 1s. blue (Bolivar) . . . . 9·75 4·25

112 Post Office, Quito — 123 Post Office, Quito

1920. Obligatory Tax. G.P.O. Rebuilding Fund.
401 **112** 1c. olive 10 10
402 2c. green 15 10
403 20c. brown 50 10
404 2s. violet . . . . 3·00 2·25
405 5s. blue . . . . 5·50 3·75

1921. Obligatory Tax. Surch **Casa de Correos VEINTE CTS. 1921–1922.**
405a **103** 20c. on 1c. blue . . . . 19·00 2·25
405b 20c. on 2c. green . . . . 19·00 2·25

1924. Obligatory Tax. Surch **DOS CENTAVOS – 2 –**.
406 **112** 2c. on 20c. brown 10 10

1924. Oblong Tobacco Tax stamps optd **CASA-CORREOS**.
407 1c. red (Loco.) . . . . 4·50 75
408 2c. blue (Arms) 20 15

1924. Telegraph stamps as T **103**, but inscr "TELEGRAFOS DEL ECUADOR" optd **CASA-CORREOS**. (a) Inscr "TIMBRE FISCAL".
409 1c. yellow . . . . 1·50 50
410 2c. blue 25 10

(b) Inscr "REGION ORIENTAL".
411 1c. yellow 25 20
412 2c. blue 50 20

1925.
413 **90** 1c. blue 10 10
414 **91** 2c. violet 10 10
415 **93** 5c. red 15 10
415a 5c. brown 20 10
416 **94** 10c. green 15 10
416a 10c. black 50 10
416b **95** 1s. black and orange . . 2·75 20

1925. Optd **POSTAL** over ornament.
417 **112** 20c. brown . . . . 1·00 35

1926. Opening of Quito–Esmeraldas Railway. Optd **QUITO**, railway train and **ESMERALDAS 1926**.
418 **90** 1c. blue . . . . 11·00 5·00
419 **91** 2c. violet . . . . 11·00 5·00
420 **92** 3c. black . . . . 8·75 5·00
421 – 4c. green (No. 384) . . . 8·75 5·00
422 **93** 5c. red . . . . 16·00 5·00
423 **94** 10c. green . . . . 16·00 5·00

1927. Optd **POSTAL**.
424 **112** 1c. olive 10 10
425 2c. green 10 10
426 20c. brown 70 10

1927. Opening of New Post Office, Quito.
427 **123** 5c. orange 20 10
428 10c. green 15 10
429 20c. purple 35 10

1928. Opening of Quito-Cayambe Railway. Stamps of 1920 issue surch **Frril. Norte Julio 8 de 1928 Est. Cayambe** and value.
431 10c. on 30c. (No. 393) . . . 12·00 10·50
432 50c. on 70c. (No. 397) . . . 19·00 18·00
433 1s. on 80c. (No. 398) . . . . 22·00 21·00

1928. National Assembly. Stamps of 1920 surch **ASAMBLEA NCNAL. 1928** and value.
434 **108** 1c. on 1c. green (381) . . 6·25 5·25
435 – 1c. on 2c. red (382) . . . 15 15
436 – 2c. on 3c. bistre (383) . . 95 95
437 – 2c. on 4c. green (384) . . 50 50
438 – 2c. on 5c. (No. 385) . . . 25 25
440 – 5c. on 6c. (No. 386) . . . 15 10
441 – 10c. on 2c. on 7c. (387) . 15 10
442 – 10c. on 7c. (No. 387) . . 40 40
443 – 20c. on 8c. (No. 388) . . 15 10
444 **109** 40c. on 10c. (No. 390) . . 1·75 1·50
445 – 40c. on 15c. (No. 391) . . 35 35
446 – 50c. on 20c. (No. 392) . . 5·75 4·50
447 – 1s. on 40c. (No. 394) . . 1·40 1·40
448 – 5s. on 50c. (No. 395) . . 1·90 1·90
449 – 10s. on 60c. (No. 396) . . 7·00 4·50

1928. Opening of Railway at Otavalo. Consular Service stamps inscr "TIMBRE-CONSULAR" surch **Postal–Frril Norte Est. OTAVALO** and value.
450 5c. on 20c. lilac . . . . . . 3·50 1·60
451 10c. on 20c. lilac . . . . . 3·75 1·60
452 20c. on 1s. green . . . . . . 3·75 1·60
453 50c. on 1s. green . . . . . . 4·25 1·25
454 1s. on 1s. green . . . . . . 5·50 1·60
455 5s. on 2s. red . . . . 13·00 7·25
456 10s. on 2s. red . . . . 16·00 11·50

130 Ryan B-5 Brougham over the River Guayas — 133 Ploughing

1929. Air.
458 **130** 2c. black 10 10
459 5c. red 10 10
460 10c. brown 15 10
461 20c. purple 25 10
462 50c. green 60 25
463 1s. blue . . . . 1·75 95
467 1s. red . . . . 1·75 35
709 1s. green 40 10
464 5s. yellow . . . . 5·00 3·75
468 5s. olive . . . . 2·50 1·90
710 5s. violet 60 10
465 10s. red . . . . 25·00 20·00
469 10s. black . . . . 7·75 2·75
711 10s. blue . . . . 1·10 10

1929. As T **103**, but inscr "MOVILES" and optd **POSTAL**.
466 **103** 1c. blue 10 10

1930. Air. Official Air stamps of 1929 optd **MENDEZ BOGOTA–QUITO Junio 4 de 1930**.
470 **130** 1s. red . . . . 13·50 13·50
471 5s. olive . . . . 13·50 13·50
472 10s. black . . . . 13·50 13·50

1930. Independence Cent. Dated "1830 1930".
473 **133** 1c. red and yellow 10 10
474 – 2c. green and yellow . . . 10 10
475 – 5c. purple and green . . . 10 10
476 – 6c. red and yellow 20 10
477 – 10c. olive and orange . . 90 15
478 – 16c. green and red . . . . 2·50 40
479 – 20c. yellow and blue . . . 35 10
480 – 40c. sepia and yellow . . 40 10
481 – 50c. sepia and yellow . . 50 10
482 – 1s. black and green . . . 1·40 10
483 – 2s. black and deep blue . 2·50 35
484 – 5s. black and purple . . . 4·50 50
485 – 10s. black and red . . . . 12·50 3·00
DESIGNS—As Type **133**: 1c. Labourer and oxen, ploughing; 2c. Cocoa cultivation; 6c. Tobacco plantation; 10c. Exportation of fruit; 10s. Bolivar's monument (41 × 37½ mm). LARGER (27 × 42½ mm): 5c. Cocoa pod; 20c. Sugar plantation; 1s. Olmedo; 2s. Sucre; 5s. Bolivar. (41½ × 28 mm): 16c. Mountaineer, steam train and airplane; 40, 50c. Views of Quito.

1933. Optd **CORREOS**.
486 **103** 10c. brown 40 10

1933. Optd **CORREOS Emision Junio 1933 Dcto. No 200**.
487 **103** 10c. brown 15 10

1933. Nos. 476 and 478 surch.
488 5c. on 6c. red and yellow . . 20 10
489 10c. on 16c. green and red . . 90 20

1934. Obligatory Tax. Optd **CASA de Correos y Telegrafos de Guayaquil**. (a) Fiscal stamp as T **103**, but inscr "MOVILES" (instead of dates at top).
490 **103** 2c. green 10 10

(b) Centenary stamp of 1930 (No. 479).
491 20c. yellow and blue 15 10

(c) Telegraph stamp as T **103**, but inscr "TELEGRAFOS DEL ECUADOR" surch **2 ctvos.** also.
492 **103** 2c. on 10c. brown 25 10

143 Mount Chimborazo — 144 Mount Chimborazo

1934.
493 **143** 5c. mauve 10 10
494 5c. blue 15 10
495 5c. brown 15 10
495a 5c. grey 15 10
496 10c. red 15 10
497 10c. green 15 10
498 10c. orange 15 10
499 10c. brown 15 10
500 10c. olive 15 10
500a 10c. black 10 10
500b 10c. lilac 10 10

1934.
501 **144** 1s. red 75 40

1934. Optd **CASA de Correos y Teleg. de Guayaquil**.
502 **112** 2c. green (No. 425) . . . 10 10

146 Symbol of Telegraphy — 150 Map of Galapagos Islands

1934. G.P.O. Rebuilding Fund.
503 **146** 2c. green 10 10
504 – 20c. red 10 10
The symbolic design of the 20c. is 38 × 18½ mm.

1935. Unveiling of Bolivar Monument, Quito. Optd **INAUGURACION MONUMENTO A BOLIVAR QUITO, 24 DE JULIO DE 1935** or surch also. (a) Postage. On 1930 Independence Issue.
505 5c. on 6c. red and yellow . . 20 10
506 10c. on 6c. red and yellow . . 25 10
507 20c. yellow and blue 25 10
508 40c. sepia and yellow 35 20
509 50c. sepia and yellow 45 35
510 $1 on 5s. black and purple . 1·10 60
511 $2 on 5s. black and purple . 1·50 1·10
512 $5 on 10s. black and red . . 2·50 2·50

(b) Air. On Official stamps of 1929.
513 **130** 50c. green . . . . 3·25 3·25
514 50c. brown . . . . 3·25 3·25
515 $1 on 5s. olive . . . . . 3·25 3·25
516 $2 on 10s. black . . . . 3·25 3·25

1935. Fiscal stamp, but without dates and inscr "TELEGRAFOS DEL ECUADOR", optd **POSTAL**.
517 **103** 10c. brown 15 10

1935. Rural Workers Social Insurance Fund. No. 503 surch **Seguro Social del Campesino Quito, 16 de Otbre.-1935** and value.
518 **146** 3c. on 2c. green 10 10

1936. Centenary of Darwin's Visit to the Galapagos Islands.
519 **150** 2c. black 10 10
520 – 5c. olive 25 10
521 – 10c. brown 40 10
522 – 20c. purple . . . . 2·50 40
523 – 1s. red 85 35
524 – 2s. blue . . . . 1·10 70
DESIGNS—HORIZ: 10c. Galapagos tortoise. VERT: 5c. Giant lizard; 20c. Charles Darwin and H.M.S. "Beagle"; 1s. Columbus; 2s. View of Galapagos Islands.

1936. Oblong Tobacco Tax Stamps. (a) Charity. Surch **Seguro Social del Campesino 3 ctvs.**
525 – 3c. on 1c. red . . . . 1·90 55

(b) Charity. Surch **SEGURO SOCIAL DEL CAMPESINO 3 ctvs.**
526 – 3c. on 1c. red . . . . 1·90 55

(c) Optd **POSTAL**.
527 – 1c. red . . . . 1·90 55

1936. No. 479 optd **Casa de Correos y Telegrafos de Guayaquil**.
528 – 20c. yellow and blue 20 10

160 Ulloa, La Condamine and Juan — 162 Woodman

1936. Bicentenary of La Condamine Scientific Expedition. (a) Postage.
529 – 2c. blue 10 10
530 **160** 5c. green 10 10
531 – 10c. orange 10 10
532 **160** 20c. violet 20 10
533 – 50c. red 40 25

(b) Air. Nos. 531/3 optd **AEREO**.
534 – 10c. orange 20 10
535 **160** 20c. violet 20 10
536 – 50c. red 35 10

(c) Air. Inscr "CORREO AEREO".
537 – 70c. grey 55 25
DESIGNS: 2c., 10c., 50c. Godin. La Condamine and Bouguer; 70c. La Condamine, Arms and Maldonado.

1936. Building and National Defence Funds. Surch **5 Centavos Dect. Junio 13 de 1936**.
539 **162** 5c. on 3c. blue 10 10

1936. Social Insurance.
540 **162** 3c. blue 10 10

1936. Oblong Tobacco Tax stamp surch **TIMBRE PATRIOTICO DIEZ CENTAVOS**.
541 – 10c. on 1c. red . . . . . . 2·25 40

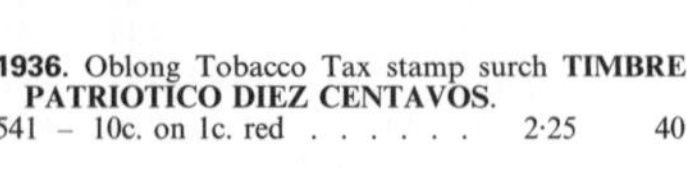

165 Independence Monument, Quito

166 Condor and Martin M-130 Flying Boat

1936. 1st International Philatelic Exn, Quito.
541a **165** 2c. green (postage) . . . 85 20
542 5c. purple 85 20
543 10c. red 85 25
543a 20c. black 85 60
544 50c. blue . . . . 1·50 1·00
545 1s. red . . . . 1·75 1·50
546 **166** 70c. brown (air) 90 50
547 1s. violet 90 70

1936. Air. Optd **AEREA**.
547a **165** 2c. red . . . . 3·25 3·25
547b 5c. orange . . . . 3·25 3·25
547c 10c. brown . . . . 3·25 3·25
547d 20c. blue . . . . 3·25 3·25
547e 50c. purple . . . . 3·25 3·25
547f 1s. green . . . . 3·25 3·25

167 Symbolical of Defence **169**

1937. Obligatory Tax. National Defence Fund. (a) Surch **POSTAL ADICIONAL** and value in figures.
548 **167** 5c. on 10c. blue 40 10

(b) Without surch.
549 **167** 10c. blue 10 10

1937. Fiscal stamps inscr "MOVILES" at top optd **POSTAL** or surch also.
550 **169** 5c. olive (I) 40 10
955a 5c. olive (II) 20 10
551 10c. blue 40 10
819 10c. orange 50 10
952 20c. on 30c. blue 20 10
953 30c. blue 20 10
954 40c. on 50c. purple . . . 10 10
955 50c. purple 30 10
Nos. 952/3 are smaller (19½ × 25½ mm). Nos. 550 (I) with imprint. 955a (II) without imprint.
See also No. 685.

171 Andean Landscape **172** Andean Condor over El Altar

1937. (a) Postage.
552 **171** 2c. green 10 10
553 – 5c. red 10 10
554 – 10c. blue 15 10
555 – 20c. red 40 10
556 – 1s. olive 55 25
DESIGNS—VERT: 5c. Atahualpa; 1s. Gold washer. HORIZ: 10c. Straw-hat makers; 20c. Salinas Beach.

(b) Air.
557 **172** 10c. brown 30 10
558 20c. olive 40 10
558a 40c. red 40 10
559 70c. brown 55 10
560 1s. slate 65 15
561 2s. violet 80 25

173

1937. Optd **TIMBRE PATRIOTICO**.
562 **173** 5c. brown 75 20

174 "Liberty" supporting Ecuadorian Flag between American Bald Eagle and Andean Condor

1938. 150th Anniv of U.S. Constitution. Flags in yellow, blue and red.
563 **174** 2c. blue (postage) 20 10
564 5c. violet 30 10
565 10c. black 30 10
566 20c. purple 45 15
567 50c. black 65 15
568 1s. olive . . . . 1·10 30
569 2s. brown . . . . 2·00 45

570 – 2c. olive (air) 15 10
571 – 5c. black 15 10
572 – 10c. brown 20 10
573 – 20c. blue 45 10
574 – 50c. purple 70 15
575 – 1s. black . . . . 1·25 15
576 – 2s. violet . . . . 2·50 65
DESIGN (air): Washington portrait, American bald eagle and flags.

176 Ecuador **178** "Road Transport"

1938. Obligatory Tax. Social Insurance Fund for Rural Workers and Guayaquil G.P.O. Rebuilding Funds.
577 **176** 5c. red 25 10

1938. Obligatory Tax. No. 537 surch **CASA DE CORREOS Y TELEGRAFOS DE GUAYAQUIL** and **20** in each corner.
578 – 20c. on 70c. grey 20 10

1938. National Progress Exn. Inscr "1830 – 1937".
579 **178** 10c. blue 10 10
580 – 50c. purple . . . . 1·00 15
581 – 1s. red . . . . 1·40 25
582 – 2s. green 50 10
DESIGNS—VERT: 50c. "Railways"; 1s. "Communication". HORIZ: 2s. "Building" (inscr "CONSTRUCCION").

1938. Air. Surch **AEREO SEDTA** and value.
582a **162** 65c. on 3c. blue 10 10

1938. Obligatory Tax. International Anti-cancer Fund. No. 476 surch **CAMPANA CONTRA EL CANCER 5 5**.
583 5c. on 6c. red and yellow . . 10 10

181 Running **182** Ryan B-5 Brougham over Mt. Chimborazo

1939. Ecuadorean Victories at South American Olympic Games, La Paz. Inscr "EN CONMEMORACION DE LA PRIMERA OLIMPIADA BOLIVARIANA DE 1938".
584 – 5c. red (postage) . . . . 1·60 35
585 **181** 10c. blue . . . . 2·25 40
586 – 50c. olive . . . . 3·75 50
587 – 1s. violet . . . . 6·50 50
588 – 2s. green . . . . 11·00 70
DESIGNS—HORIZ: 5c. Parade of athletes; 50c. Basketball. VERT: 1s. Wrestling; 2s. Diving.

589 – 5c. green (air) 40 10
590 – 10c. orange 55 15
591 – 50c. brown . . . . 3·50 15
592 – 1s. sepia . . . . 8·00 35
593 – 2s. red . . . . 12·00 70
DESIGNS—HORIZ: 5c. Riding; 1s. Boxing. VERT: 10c. Running; 50c. Tennis; 2s. Olympic flame.

1939. Air.
594 **182** 1s. brown 40 15
595 2s. purple 85 15
596 5s. black . . . . 1·25 15

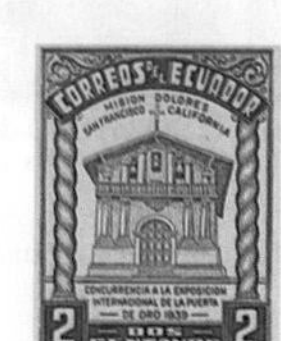

183 Dolores Mission, San Francisco **184** Golden Gate Bridge and Mountain

1939. San Francisco International Exhibition.
597 **183** 2c. green (postage) . . . 10 10
598 5c. red 10 10
599 10c. blue 10 10
600 50c. brown 25 10
601 1s. slate 45 10
602 2s. violet 80 15

603 **184** 2c. black (air) 10 10
604 5c. red 10 10
605 10c. blue 10 10
606 50c. purple 10 10
607 1s. brown 25 10
608 2s. brown 25 10
609 5s. green 55 10

185 Symbol of N.Y. World's Fair **186** Empire State Building and Mountain

1939. New York World's Fair.
610 **185** 2c. olive (postage) 10 10
611 5c. orange 10 10
612 10c. blue 10 10
613 50c. grey 40 10
614 1s. red 60 15
615 2s. brown 75 20

616 **186** 2c. brown (air) 10 10
617 5c. red 10 10
618 10c. blue 10 10
619 50c. olive 10 10
620 1s. orange 20 10
621 2s. mauve 35 15
622 5s. black 70 10

1939. Obligatory Tax. Social Insurance Fund for Rural Workers. Oblong Tobacco Tax stamps surch **POSTAL ADICIONAL CINCO CENTAVOS**.
623 5c. on 1c. pink . . . . 1·50 25

1940. Obligatory Tax. G.P.O. Rebuilding Fund. Oblong Tobacco Tax stamp surch **CASAS DE CORREOS Y TELEGRAFOS CINCO CENTAVOS**.
624 5c. on 1c. pink . . . . 1·25 20

1940. Obligatory Tax. Guyaquil G.P.O. Rebuilding Fund. No. 567 surch **CASA DE CORREOS y TELEGRAFOS DE GUAYAQUIL 20 20**.
625 **174** 20c. on 50c. multicoloured 40 15

1940. Obligatory Tax. National Defence Fund. Oblong Tobacco Tax stamps surch **TIMBRE PATRIOTICO VEINTE CENTAVOS**.
625b 20c. on 1c. pink . . . . . 16·00 3·50

191 Pan-American Union Flags **192** Allegory of Union

1940. 50th Anniv of Pan-American Union.
626 **191** 5c. black & red (postage) 10 10
627 10c. black and blue . . . 10 10
628 50c. black and green . . . 35 10
629 1s. black and violet . . . 50 20

630 **192** 10c. blue & orange (air) 15 10
631 70c. blue and purple . . . 25 10
632 1s. blue and brown . . . 35 10
633 10s. blue and black . . . 85 50

193 Ploughing **194** Symbolic of Communications

1940. Obligatory Tax. Social Insurance Fund for Rural Workers and Guayaquil G.P.O. Rebuilding Funds.
634 **193** 5c. red 15 10

1940. Obligatory Tax. G.P.O. Rebuilding Fund.
635 **194** 5c. brown 10 10
636 5c. green 10 10

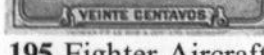

195 Fighter Aircraft **196** Dr. de Santa Cruz y Espejo

1941. Obligatory Tax. National Defence Fund.
637 **195** 20c. blue 40 10

1941. 1st National Periodical Exhibition.
638 **196** 30c. blue (postage) . . . 25 10
639 1s. orange . . . . 1·10 10

640 3s. red (air) 70 10
641 10s. orange . . . . 1·40 25

197 Francisco de Orellana **198** Early Map of S. America

1942. 400th Anniv of Discovery of R. Amazon.
642 **197** 10c. brown (postage) . . 25 10
643 – 40c. red 25 10
644 – 1s. violet 70 10
645 – 2s. blue 95 25

646 **198** 40c. bistre & black (air) 35 10
647 – 70c. olive 60 10
648 – 2s. green 70 25
649 – 5s. red 75 35
DESIGNS—VERT: 40c. (No. 643); 70c. Portraits of G. Pizarro and G. Diaz de Pineda; 2s. (No. 645) Quito; 5s. Expedition leaving Quito. HORIZ: 1s. Guayaquil; 2s. (No. 648) Relief map of R. Amazon.

199 R. Crespo Toral **201** Mt. Chimborazo

1942.
650 **199** 10c. green (postage) . . . 10 10
651 50c. brown 20 10

652 10c. violet (air) 25 10

1942. As T **199** but portrait of Pres. A. B. Moreno.
653 10c. green 10 10

1942.
654 **201** 30c. brown 20 10
654a 30c. blue 20 10
654b 30c. orange 10 10
654c 30c. green 20 10

202 "Defence" **203** Guayaquil Riverside

1942. Obligatory Tax. National Defence Fund.
655 **202** 20c. blue 40 10
655a 40c. brown 40 10

1942. Obligatory Tax. National Defence Fund. As T **173** surch.
655b **173** 20c. on 5c. pink . . . . — 5·00
655c 20c. on 1s. brown . . . — 5·00
655d 20c. on 2s. green . . . . — 5·00

1942. Obligatory Tax. Guayaquil G.P.O. Rebuilding Fund. No. 567 surch **CASA DE CORREOS Y TELEGRAFOS DE GUAYAQUIL VEINTE CENTAVOS**.
655e – 20c. on 50c. mult 60 25

1943.
656 **203** 20c. red . . . . 2·40 10
656a 20c. blue . . . . 2·40 10

1943. Guayaquil G.P.O. Rebuilding Fund. Surch **ADICIONAL CINCO CENTAVOS 5 Centavos CASA DE CORREOS DE GOQUIL. y.**
657 **162** 5c.+5c. on 3c. blue 20 10

1943. Surch **ADICIONAL CINCO CENTAVOS**.
658 **162** 5c. on 3c. blue 20 10

206 Gen. Alfaro **207** Alfaro's Birthplace

1943. Birth Centenary of Alfaro.
659 **206** 10c. black & red (postage) 10 10
660 – 20c. brown and olive . . 1·50 75
661 – 30c. green and olive . . . 45 45
662 **207** 1s. red and grey 75 75

663 **206** 70c. black and red (air) 40 20
664 – 1s. brown and olive . . . 2·50 90
665 – 3s. green and olive . . . 60 60
666 **207** 5s. red and grey 95 70
DESIGNS—HORIZ: 20c., 1s. Devil's Nose Zigzag, Guayaquil-Quito Rly; 30c., 3s. Alfaro Military College.

208 Labourers **213** Arms of Ecuador

1943. Obligatory Tax. Social Insurance Fund for Rural Workers and Guayaquil G.P.O. Rebuilding Funds.
667 **208** 5c. blue 30 10

1943. Welcome to Henry A. Wallace, Vice-President of U.S.A. Optd **BIENVENIDO – WALLACE Abril 15 – 1943.**
668 **174** 50c. mult (postage) . . . 75 60
669 1s. multicoloured . . . . 1·60 1·25
670 2s. multicoloured . . . . 2·50 1·90

671 – 50c. multicoloured (No. 574) (air) . . . . 2·00 70

672 – 1s. multicoloured (No. 575) . . . . . . 2·50 85
673 – 2s. multicoloured (No. 576) . . . . . . 3·00 1·25

1943. Obligatory Tax. National Defence Fund. Fiscal stamp optd **TIMBRE PATRIOTICO**.
674 20c. orange . . . . 23·00 1·10

1943. Air. Visits of Presidents of Bolivia, Paraguay and Venezuela to Ecuador. (a) Optd **AEREO LOOR A BOLIVIA JUNIO 11 – 1943**.
675 – 50c. purple (No. 580) . . . 1·75 1·10
676 – 1s. red (No. 581) . . . . . 2·50 1·50
677 – 2s. green (No. 582) 50 35

(b) Optd **AEREO LOOR AL PARAGUAY JULIO 5 – 1943**.
678 – 50c. purple (No. 580) . . . 1·75 1·10
679 – 1s. red (No. 581) . . . . . 2·50 1·50
680 – 2s. green (No. 582) 50 35

(c) Optd **AEREO LOOR A VENEZUELA JULIO 23 – 1943**.
681 – 50c. purple (No. 580) . . . 1·75 1·10
682 – 1s. red (No. 581) . . . . . 2·50 1·50
683 – 2s. green (No. 582) 50 35

1943. Obligatory Tax National Defence Fund. Fiscal stamp surch **TIMBRE PATRIOTICO VEINTE CENTAVOS.**
684 – 20c. on 10c. orange 75 20

1943. Fiscal stamp as T **169** surch **POSTAL 30 Centavos** with or without bars.
685 **169** 30c. on 50c. brown . . . 25 10

As No. 685 but surch **POSTAL 30 Ctvs**.
780 **169** 30c. on 50c. brown . . . 10 10

1943. Obligatory Tax. National Defence Fund.
686 **213** 20c. red 20 10

214 Arms of Ecuador and Map of Central America

215 Pres. Arroyo del Rio at Washington

1943. President's Visit to Washington.
687 **214** 10c. violet (postage) . . . 20 10
698 10c. green 10 10
688 20c. brown 20 10
699 20c. pink 15 10
689 30c. orange 15 15
700 30c. brown 20 15
690 50c. olive 35 20
701 50c. purple 35 25
691 1s. violet 40 20
702 1s. grey 40 35
692 10s. brown . . . . 2·50 2·40
703 10s. orange . . . . 2·50 2·50
693 **215** 50c. brown (air) 40 35
704 50c. purple 40 20
694 70c. red 50 50
705 70c. brown 40 35
695 3s. blue 40 50
706 3s. green 40 35
696 5s. green 85 60
707 5s. blue 70 55
697 10s. olive . . . . 3·50 3·00
708 10s. red 95 95

1944. Nos. 698/708 surch **Hospital Mendez** and new value.
711a **214** 10c.+10c. grn (postage) 35 25
711b 20c.+20c. pink 35 25
711c 30c.+20c. brown 35 35
711d 50c.+20c. purple 45 50
711e 1s.+50c. grey 75 85
711f 10s.+2s. orange . . . . 2·75 2·75
711g **215** 50c.+50c. pur (air) . . . 2·25 2·25
711h 70c.+30c. brown . . . . 2·25 2·25
711i 3s.+50c. green . . . . . 2·25 2·25
711j 5s.+1s. blue . . . . . . 2·25 2·25
711k 10s.+2s. red . . . . . . 2·25 2·25

1944. No. 600. Surch **30 Centavos**.
712 **183** 30c. on 50c. brown . . . 15 10

1944. Obligatory Tax. National Defence Fund. No. 686 surch **POSTAL 30 Centavos**.
713 **213** 30c. on 20c. red 25 10

1944. 606 and 619 Surch **POSTAL 30 Centavos**.
714 **184** 30c. on 50c. purple . . . 15 10
715 **186** 30c. on 50c. olive 15 10

218 F. Gonzales Suarez
219 Cathedral, Quito

1944. Birth Cent of F. G. Suarez (Archbishop).
716 **218** 10c. blue (postage) . . . 10 10
717 20c. green 10 10
718 30c. purple 20 15
719 1s. violet 40 10
720 **219** 70c. green (air) 50 25
721 1s. olive 50 25
722 3s. red 60 30
723 5s. red 75 35

1944. Surch **CINCO Centavos**.
724 **183** 5c. on 2c. green 10 10
725 **185** 5c. on 2c. green 10 10

221 Government Palace, Quito
222 Red Cross Symbol

1944.
726 **221** 10c. green (postage) . . 10 10
727 30c. blue 10 10
728 3s. orange (air) 25 10
729 5s. brown 40 10
730 10s. red 85 10
730a 10s. violet 85 10

1945. 80th Anniv of Int Red Cross. Cross in red.
731 **222** 30c. brown (postage) . . 50 10
732 1s. brown 35 20
733 5s. green 75 70
734 10s. red . . . . 2·10 1·25
735 2s. blue (air) 40 40
736 3s. green 70 40
737 5s. violet . . . . 1·10 70
738 10s. red . . . . 2·75 2·10

1945. Air. Surch **AEREO 40 Ctvs**.
739 **208** 40c. on 5c. blue 15 10

1945. Obligatory Tax. Air. No. 726 surch **FOMENTO-AERO-COMUNICACIONES 20 Ctvs.**
740 **221** 20c. on 10c. green 25 10

1945. Air. Victory. Optd **V SETIEMBRE 5 1945**.
742 **221** 3s. orange 50 50
743 5s. brown 40 40
744 10s. red . . . . 1·40 1·40

1945. Visit of Pres. Juan Antonio Rios of Chile. Optd **LOOR A CHILE OCTUBRE 2 1945** and five-pointed star. Flags in yellow, blue and red.
745 **174** 50c. black (postage) . . . 50 25
746 1s. olive 80 40
747 2s. brown . . . . 1·50 75
748 – 50c. pur (No. 574) (air) . . 1·10 75
749 – 1s. black (No. 575) . . . 1·25 85
750 – 2s. violet (No. 576) . . . 1·25 85

227 Marshal Sucre
230 Pan-American Highway

1945. 150th Birth Anniv of Marshal Sucre.
751 **227** 10c. green (postage) . . . 20 10
752 20c. brown 20 10
753 40c. grey 20 10
754 1s. green 20 20
755 2s. brown 45 25
756 – 30c. blue (air) 15 10
757 – 40c. red 25 10
758 – 1s. violet 50 25
759 – 3s. black 60 40
760 – 5s. purple 85 55
DESIGN—Air stamps: Liberty Monument.

1945. Surch **c VEINTE CENTAVOS**.
761 **221** 20c. on 10c. green 10 10

1946. Completion of Pan-American Highway.
762 **230** 20c. brown (postage) . . 10 10
763 30c. green 10 10
764 1s. blue 10 10
765 5s. purple 60 60
766 10s. red . . . . 1·10 85
767 1s. red (air) 35 20
768 2s. violet 45 30
769 3s. green 45 35
770 5s. orange 60 50
771 10s. blue 85 45

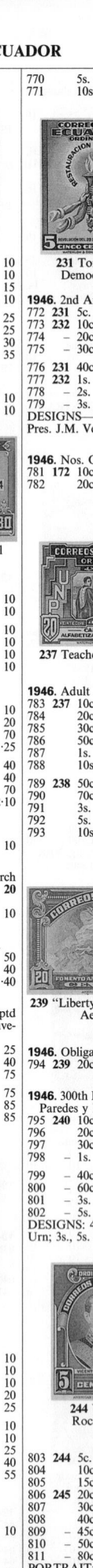

231 Torch of Democracy
232 Popular Suffrage

1946. 2nd Anniv of Revolution.
772 **231** 5c. blue (postage) 10 10
773 **232** 10c. green 10 10
774 – 20c. red 20 10
775 – 30c. brown 35 10
776 **231** 40c. red (air) 10 10
777 **232** 1s. brown 10 10
778 – 2s. blue 40 10
779 – 3s. green 55 30
DESIGNS—VERT: 20c., 2s. National flag; 30c., 3s. Pres. J.M. Velasco Ibarra.

1946. Nos. O567/8 optd **POSTAL**.
781 **172** 10c. brown 15 15
782 20c. olive 25 25

237 Teacher and Scholar
238 Seal of National Periodicals Union

1946. Adult Instruction.
783 **237** 10c. blue (postage) . . . 10 10
784 20c. brown 10 10
785 30c. green 15 10
786 50c. black 35 20
787 1s. red 50 15
788 10s. purple . . . . 2·10 50
789 **238** 50c. violet (air) 35 25
790 70c. green 40 25
791 3s. red 45 35
792 5s. blue 60 25
793 10s. brown . . . . 1·75 40

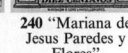

239 "Liberty", "Mercury" and Aeroplanes
240 "Mariana de Jesus Paredes y Flores"

1946. Obligatory Tax. Air. National Defence Fund.
794 **239** 20c. brown 15 10

1946. 300th Death Anniv of Blessed Mariana de Jesus Paredes y Flores.
795 **240** 10c. brown (postage) . . 15 10
796 20c. green 10 10
797 30c. violet 20 10
798 – 1s. brown 40 30
799 – 40c. brown (air) 25 10
800 – 60c. blue 30 30
801 – 3s. yellow 45 60
802 – 5s. green 85 75
DESIGNS: 40c., 60c. Mariana teaching children; 1s. Urn; 3s., 5s. Cross and lilies.

244 Vicente Rocafuerte
245 Jesuit Church, Quito

1947.
803 **244** 5c. brown (postage) . . . 10 10
804 10c. purple 10 10
805 15c. black 10 10
806 **245** 20c. lake 15 10
807 30c. mauve 15 10
808 40c. blue 25 10
809 – 45c. green 25 10
810 – 50c. grey 35 15
811 – 80c. red 40 10
PORTRAIT: 45c. to 80c. F. J. E. de Santa Cruz y Espejo.
812 – 60c. green (air) 10 10
813 – 70c. violet 10 10
814 – 1s. brown 10 10
815 – 1s.10 red 10 10
816 – 1s.30 blue 10 10

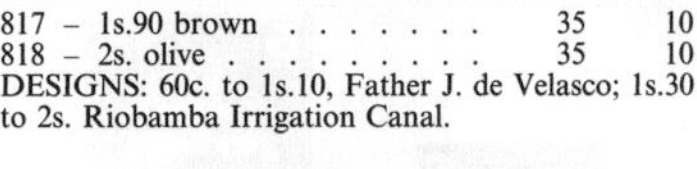
817 – 1s.90 brown 35 10
818 – 2s. olive 35 10
DESIGNS: 60c. to 1s.10, Father J. de Velasco; 1s.30 to 2s. Riobamba Irrigation Canal.

250 Andres Bello

1948. 83rd Death Anniv of Andres Bello (educationalist).
820 **250** 20c. blue (postage) . . . 15 10
821 30c. pink 25 10
822 40c. green 25 10
823 1s. black 50 15
824 60c. mauve (air) 20 10
825 1s.30 green 40 25
826 1s.90 red 35 25

1948. Economic Conference Optd **CONFERENCIA ECONOMICA GRANCOLOMBIANA MAYO 24 DE 1.948.**
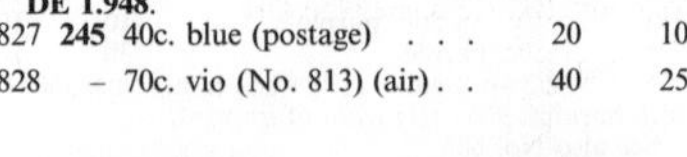
827 **245** 40c. blue (postage) . . . 20 10
828 – 70c. vio (No. 813) (air) . . 40 25

252 The "Santa Maria"

253 Christopher Columbus

1948. Completion of Columbus Memorial Lighthouse.
829 **252** 10c. green (postage) . . . 60 20
830 20c. brown . . . . 1·00 20
831 30c. violet . . . . 1·40 30
832 50c. red . . . . 1·75 30
833 1s. blue . . . . 2·50 30
834 5s. red . . . . 6·50 85
835 **253** 50c. green (air) 20 10
836 70c. red 20 10
837 3s. blue 40 30
838 5s. brown 70 25
839 10s. violet 95 35

1948. National Fair. Nos. 811 and 816 optd **Feria Nacional 1948 ECUADOR de hoy y del MANANA.**
840 80c. red (postage) 25 25
841 1s.30c. blue (air) 40 30

255 "Telegrafo I" on First Postal Flight

256 Elia Liut and "Telegrafo I"

1948. 25th Anniv of First Ecuadorian Postal Flight.
842 **255** 30c. orange (postage) . . 20 10
843 40c. mauve 20 10
844 60c. blue 25 10
845 1s. brown 35 10
846 3s. brown . . . . 1·00 20
847 5s. black 80 30
848 **256** 60c. red (air) 35 25
849 1s. green 45 25
850 1s.30 red 45 30
851 1s.90 violet 50 30
852 2s. brown 60 35
853 5s. blue 90 55

257 "Reading and Writing"

258 "Education For All"

1948. National Education Campaign.
854 **257** 10c. claret (postage) . . . 10 10
855 20c. brown 20 20
856 30c. green 10 30
857 50c. red 40 20
858 1s. violet 55 40
859 10s. blue . . . . 1·50 60
860 **258** 50c. violet (air) 35 20
861 70c. blue 35 20
862 3s. green 55 30
863 5s. red 70 25
864 10s. brown . . . . 1·40 45

259 "Freedom from Fear"

260 "Freedom of Religion"

261 "Freedom of Speech and Expression"

262 "Freedom from Want"

1948. Homage to Franklin D. Roosevelt.
865 **259** 10c. red & grey (postage) 15 10
866 20c. olive and blue 15 15
867 **260** 30c. olive and red 25 10
868 40c. purple and sepia 35 10
869 1s. brown and red 40 25

870 **261** 60c. green & brn (air) 10 10
871 1s. red and black 10 10
872 **262** 1s.50 green & brown 25 15
873 2s. red and black 50 15
874 5s. blue and black 75 20

263 Maldonado at Academy of Sciences, Paris

264 Riobamba Aqueduct

1948. Death Bicentenary of Maldonado (geographer and scientist).
875 **263** 5c. red & black (postage) 15 10
876 **264** 10c. black and red 20 10
877 – 30c. blue and brown 25 10
878 **264** 40c. violet and green 60 10
879 **263** 50c. red and green 40 10
880 – 1s. blue and brown 75 10

881 – 60c. red & orange (air) 25 10
882 – 90c. black and red 25 10
883 – 1s.30 orange & mauve 40 20
884 – 2s. green and blue 40 20
DESIGN—VERT: 30c., 60c., 1s.30, Maldonado making road to Esmeraldas; 90c., 1s., 2s. P. Vicente Maldonado.

266 Cervantes, Don Quixote and Windmill

267 Don Quixote and Sheep

1949. 400th Birth Anniv of Cervantes.
885 – 30c. blue & pur (postage) 10 10
886 **266** 60c. brown & purple 25 10
887 – 1s. red and green 75 15
888 **266** 2s. black and red 1·50 25
889 – 5s. green and brown 2·75 75

890 – 1s.30 brown & blue (air) 1·50 1·50
891 **267** 1s.90 red and green 40 25
892 – 3s. violet and red 40 25
893 **267** 5s. black and red 95 10
894 – 10s. purple and green 1·60 10
DESIGNS—HORIZ: 30c., 1s., 5s. (No. 889) Cervantes, Don Quixote and Sancho Panza; 1s.30, 3s., 10s. Don Juan Montalvo and Cervantes.

1949. 2nd Eucharistic Congress. Stamps of 1947 surch **II CONGRESO Junio 1949 Eucaristico Ncl.** and values. (a) Postage. No. 808 surch.
895 **245** 10c. on 40c. blue 15 10
896 20c. on 40c. blue 25 10
897 30c. on 40c. blue 25 15

(b) Air. No. 815 surch.
898 – 50c. on 1s.10 red 10 10
899 – 60c. on 1s.10 red 10 10
900 – 90c. on 1s.10 red 20 20

269 Equatorial Line Monument

274 Lake San Pablo

1949.
901 **269** 10c. purple 20 10

1949. 75th Anniv of U.P.U. Surch **75 ANIVERSARIO** (or **Aniversario** on air stamps) **U.P.U.** and value.
902 **274** 10c. on 50c. grn (postage) 10 10
903 20c. on 50c. green 15 10
904 30c. on 50c. green 25 10

905 **221** 60c. on 3s. orge (air) 40 35
906 90c. on 3s. orange 35 25
907 1s. on 3s. orange 40 35
908 2s. on 3s. orange 90 45
For unoverprinted stamp Type **274**, see No. 926.

272

272a

1949. Consular Service stamps optd or surch for postal use. I. On T **272**. A. Postage. (a) Vert surch **POSTAL** and value before **ct vs.**
908a **272** 5c. on 10c. red 10 10
909 20c. on 25c. brown 10 10
910 30c. on 50c. black 10 10

(b) Optd **CORREOS** diag.
927 **272** 10c. red 10 10

(c) Optd **POSTAL** diag.
929 **272** 10c. red 10 10

(d) Vert surch with figs. before and after **Ctvs.** (i) **CORREOS** upwards.
928 **272** 30c. on 50c. black 10 10

(ii) **POSTAL** upwards.
930 **272** 20c. on 25c. brown 10 10
931 30c. on 50c. black 20 10

(e) Surch **POSTAL centavos** with figs between.
969 **272** 10c. on 20s. blue 15 10
970 20c. on 10s. grey 15 10
971 20c. on 20s. blue 15 10
972 30c. on 10s. grey 15 10
973 30c. on 20s. blue 10 10

B. Air. Surch **AEREO** and value.
913 **272** 60c. on 50c. black 20 10
913a 60c. on 2s. brown 20 10
913b 1s. on 2s. brown (D.) 30 10
913c 1s. on 2s. brown (U.) 30 10
913d 2s. on 2s. brown 30 10
913e 3s. on 5s. violet 55 15
In No. 913b the surch reads down and in No. 913c it reads up.

II. On T **272a**. A. Postage. Surch **POSTAL** and value.
935 **272a** 30c. on 50c. red 15 10
934 40c. on 25c. blue 15 10
936 50c. on 25c. blue 15 10

B. Air. Surch **AEREO** and value.
913f **272a** 60c. on 1s. green 10 10
913g 60c. on 5s. sepia 15 10
913h 70c. on 5s. sepia 20 10
913i 90c. on 50c. red 30 10
913j 1s. on 1s. green 20 10

1950. Optd **POSTAL**.
911 **194** 5c. green 10 10
912 **208** 5c. blue 10 10

1950. Air. (a) Nos. 816/7 surch **90 ctvs. 90.**
914 90c. on 1s.30 blue 15 10
914a 90c. on 1s.90 brown 35 10

(b) No. 816 surch **90 CENTAVOS.**
914b 90c. on 1s.30 blue 10 10

1950. Literary Campaign. Optd **ALFABETIZACION.** Four values also surch with new values and No. 920 also optd **POSTAL.**
915 **269** 10c. purple (postage) 20 20
916 **264** 20c. on 40c. (878) 30 30
917 30c. on 40c. (878) 40 40
918 **263** 50c. red and green 60 60
919 – 1s. blue & brown (880) 70 70
920 **221** 10s. violet 1·90 95

921 – 50c. on 1s.10 (815) (air) 25 10
922 – 70c. on 1s.10 (815) 20 25
923 **221** 3s. orange 45 30
924 5s. brown 80 40
925 10s. violet 85 30

1950.
926 **274** 50c. green 20 10

1951. Air. Panagra Airlines' 20,000th Flight across Equator. Optd **20.000 Cruce Linea Ecuatorial PANAGRA 26-Julio-1951.**
932 **221** 3s. orange 50 50
933 5s. brown 90 70

1951. Adult Education. Surch **CAMPANA Alfabetizacion** and values. (a) Postage.
937 **272a** 20c. on 25c. blue 10 10
938 30c. on 25c. blue 15 10

(b) Air.
939 – 60c. on 1s.30 (890) 20 10
940 **267** 1s. on 1s.90 (891) 20 10

278 Reliquary and St. Peter's, Vatican City

279 St. Mariana de Jesus

1952. Canonization of St. Mariana de Jesus.
941 **278** 10c. green & lake (postage) 20 10
942 20c. blue and violet 10 10
943 30c. red and green 25 10

944 **279** 60c. red & turquoise (air) 35 10
945 90c. green and blue 40 10
946 1s. red and green 45 10
947 2s. blue and mauve 45 10

280 Presidents Plaza and Truman

1952. Visit of President of Ecuador to U.S.A.
948 **280** 1s. black & red (postage) 25 15
949 – 2s. sepia and blue 50 20

950 **280** 3s. green and lilac (air) 40 30
951 – 5s. olive and brown 80 65
DESIGN: 2s., 5s. Pres. Plaza addressing U.S. Congress.

1952. Consular Service stamps surch **TIMBRE ESCOLAR 20 ctvs. 20.**
957 **272** 20c. on 1s. red 10 10
958 20c. on 2s. brown 10 10
959 20c. on 5s. violet 10 10

282 Pres. Urvina, Slave and "Liberty"

284 Teacher and Scholars

1952. Centenary of Abolition of Slavery in Ecuador. Roul.
960 **282** 20c. green & red (postage) 10 10
961 30c. red and blue 20 10
962 50c. blue and red 35 20

963 – 60c. red and blue (air) 85 25
964 – 90c. lilac and red 85 30
965 – 1s. orange and green 85 10
966 – 2s. brown and blue 85 20
DESIGN—VERT: Nos. 963/6, Pres. Urvina, condor and freed slave.

1952. Obligatory Tax. Literacy Campaign.
967 **284** 20c. green 20 10

1952. Obligatory Tax. Public Health Fund. Fiscal stamp optd **PATRIOTICO y SANITARIO.**
968 **103** 40c. olive 40 10

286 Learning Alphabet

287 Flag-bearer and Health Emblem

1953. Literacy Campaign. Inscr "UNP LAE".
974 – 5c. blue (postage) 25 10
975 – 10c. red 15 10
976 – 20c. orange 25 10
977 – 30c. purple 30 10

978 – 1s. blue (air) 35 10
979 **286** 2s. red 60 10
DESIGNS—VERT: 5c. Teacher and pupils; 10c. Instructor and student; 1s. Hand and torch. HORIZ: 20c. Men and ballot-box; 30c. Teaching the alphabet.

1953. Obligatory Tax. Public Health Fund.
980 **287** 40c. blue 45 10

288

289 Equatorial Line Monument

1953. Air. Crossing of Equator by Pan-American Highway.
981 **288** 60c. yellow 25 20
982 90c. blue 35 20
983 3s. red 40 35

1953.
984 – 5c. blue and black 10 10
985 **289** 10c. green and black 10 10
986 – 20c. lilac and black 10 10
987 – 30c. brown and black 10 10
988 – 40c. orange and black 10 10
989 – 50c. red and black 25 10
DESIGNS: 5c. Cuicocha Lagoon; 20c. Quininde landscape; 30c. River Tomebamba; 40c. La Chilintosa rock; 50c. Iliniza Mountains.

290 Cardinal de la Torre

291 Cardinal de la Torre

1954. 1st Anniv of Elevation of De la Torre to Cardinal.
990 **290** 30c. blk & red (postage) 20 10
991 50c. black and purple 15 10

992 **291** 60c. black & pur (air) 15 10
993 90c. black and green 20 10
994 3s. black and orange 35 20

292 Isabella the Catholic

293 Isabella the Catholic

1954. 500th Birth Anniv of Isabella the Catholic.
995 **292** 30c. blk & bl (postage) 15 25
996 50c. black and yellow 15 10

997 **293** 60c. green (air) 10 20
998 90c. purple 10 10
999 1s. black and pink 25 20
1000 2s. black and blue 15 10
1001 5s. black and flesh 35 25

294 Guayaquil Post Office

1954. Air. Silver Jubilee of Panagra Air Lines. Unissued stamp surch as in T **294**.
1002 **294** 80c. on 20c. red 15 10
1003 1s. on 20c. red 20 10

1954. Obligatory Tax. Literacy Campaign. Telegraph stamp (18½ × 22½ mm) surch **ESCOLAR 20 Centavos.**
1004 20c. on 30c. brown 45 10

1954. Obligatory Tax. Literacy Campaign. Fiscal stamp as T **103** (19½ × 25½ mm) optd **ESCOLAR**.
1004a **103** 20c. olive 60 10

1954. Obligatory Tax. Tourist Promotion Fund.
(a) Telegraph stamp as No. 1004 but surch **Pro-Turismo 1954 10 ctvs. 10.**
1005 10c. on 30c. brown 60 10
(b) Judicial stamp as T **103** (19½ × 25½ mm) optd **PRO TURISMO 1954.**
1006 10c. red 25 10
(c) Fiscal stamp as T **103** (19½ × 25½ mm) surch **PRO TURISMO 1954 10 ctvs. Diez Centavos.**
1006a **103** 10c. on 50c. red 45 10
(d) Consular Service stamp surch **PRO TURISMO 1954 10 ctvs.**
1007 **272a** 10c. on 25c. blue . . . 45 10

1954. Consular Service stamp surch **0.20 0.20 ESCOLAR Veinte centavos.**
1007a **272** 20c. on 10s. grey . . . 60 10

299 "Chasqui" (Inca Message Carrier)
300 Airliner over Building

1954. Postal Employees' Day.
1008 **299** 30c. sepia (postage) . . . 20 10
1009 **300** 80c. blue (air) 20 10

301 Bananas
302 Douglas DC-4 over San Pablo Lake

1954.
1010 **301** 10c. orange (postage) . . 10 10
1011 20c. red 10 10
1012 30c. mauve 10 10
1013 40c. myrtle 20 10
1014 50c. brown 25 10
1015 **302** 60c. orange (air) 20 10
1016 70c. mauve 20 10
1017 90c. green 20 10
1018 1s. myrtle 25 10
1019 2s. blue 50 10
1020 3s. brown 50 10

302a
303 Death on Battlefield

1954. Obligatory Tax. Literacy Fund.
1020a **302a** 20c. red 25 10

1954. Air. 150th Death Anniv of Captain Calderon Garaicoa.
1021 **303** 80c. mauve 20 10
1022 – 90c. blue 20 10
PORTRAIT—VERT: 90c. Capt. Calderon.

304 El Cebollar College
305 "Transport"

1954. Air. Birth Centenary of F. F. Cordero.
1023 **304** 70c. myrtle 10 10
1024 – 80c. sepia 10 10
1025 – 90c. blue 10 10
1026 – 2s.50 slate 20 15
1027 – 3s. lilac 30 25
DESIGNS—VERT: 80c. Febres Cordero and boys; 90c. Febres Cordero; 2s.50, Tomb. HORIZ: 3s. Monument.

1954. Obligatory Tax. Tourist Promotion Fund.
1028 **305** 10c. mauve 25 10

306 Kissing the Flag
308 La Rotonda, Guayaquil

1955. Obligatory Tax. National Defence Fund.
1029 **306** 40c. blue 60 10

1955. Air. World Press Exhibition. No. 730a surch **E. M. P. 1955** and value.
1030 **221** 1s. on 10s. violet 20 10
1031 1s.70 on 10s. violet . . . 30 10
1032 4s.20 on 10s. violet . . . 50 35

1955. Air. 50th Anniv of Rotary International.
1033 **308** 80c. brown 30 20
1034 – 90c. green 30 25
DESIGN: 90c. Eugenio Espejo Hospital, Quito.

310 Castillo and "Telegrafo 1"

1955. Birth Centenary of Jose Abel Castillo (pioneer aviator).
1035 – 30c. bistre (postage) . . 10 10
1036 – 50c. black 10 10
1037 **310** 60c. brown (air) 45 10
1038 90c. green 45 10
1039 1s. mauve 45 10
1040 – 2s. red 45 15
1041 – 5s. blue 90 45
DESIGNS—VERT: 30c., 50c. Bust of Castillo. HORIZ: 2s., 5s. Castillo and map of Ecuador.

1955. Air. Surch **1 X SUCRE X** over ornamental bar.
1042 **130** 1s. on 5s. violet 20 15

312 Palm Trees
313 Vazquez in 1883

1955. Pictorial designs as T **312**.
1043 **312** 5c. green (postage) . . 10 10
1043a 5c. blue 10 10
1043b B 5c. green 10 10
1044 C 10c. blue 20 10
1044a 10c. brown 35 10
1044b B 10c. brown 10 10
1045 A 20c. brown 30 10
1045a 20c. pink 30 10
1045b 20c. green 35 10
1045c B 20c. plum 10 10
1046 D 30c. black 10 10
1046a 30c. red 10 10
1046b B 30c. blue 10 10
1046c E 40c. blue . . . . . . 1·25 25
1047 F 50c. green 30 10
1047a 50c. violet 35 10
1048 E 70c. olive . . . . . . 1·75 25
1049 G 80c. violet 60 10
1049a B 80c. red 10 10
1049b G 90c. blue 20 20
1050 H 1s. orange 20 10
1050a 1s. sepia 15 10
1050b I 1s. black 50 10
1051 J 2s. red 60 15
1051a 2s. brown 25 10
1052 K 50c. slate (air) 25 10
1052a 50c. green 20 10
1053 L 1s. blue 50 10
1053a 1s. orange 40 10
1054 M 1s.30 red 30 15
1055 N 1s.50 green 20 10
1056 O 1s.70 brown 20 10
1057 P 1s.90 olive 25 25
1058 Q 2s.40 red 30 15
1059 R 2s.50 violet 30 15
1060 S 4s.20 black 40 25
1061 T 4s.80 yellow 50 35
DESIGNS—POSTAGE: A, River Babahoyo; B, "The Virgin of Quito" (after L. y del Arco); C, Manta fisherman; D, Guayaquil; E, Cactus; F, River Pital; G, Orchids; H, Agucate Mission; I, San Pablo; J, Jibaro Indian. AIR: K, Rumichaca Grotto; L, San Pablo; M, "The Virgin of Quito"; N, Cotopaxi Volcano; O, Tungurahua Volcano; P, Guanaco; Q, Selling mats; R, Ingapirca ruins; S, El Carmen, Cuenca; T, Santo Domingo Church.

1956. Air. Birth Centenary of Vazquez.
1062 **313** 1s. green 10 10
1063 – 1s.50 red 20 10
1064 – 1s.70 blue 15 10
1065 – 1s.90 slate 20 10
PORTRAITS OF VAZQUEZ: 1s.50, 1905. 1s.70, 1910. 1s.90, 1931.

314 J. A. Schwarz
315 Title Page of First Book printed in Ecuador

1956. Bicentenary of Printing in Ecuador.
1066 **314** 5c. green (postage) . . . 10 10
1067 10c. red 10 10
1068 20c. violet 10 10
1069 30c. green 10 10
1070 40c. blue 10 10
1071 50c. blue 10 10
1072 70c. orange 15 10
1073 **315** 1s. black (air) 10 10
1074 1s.70 slate 15 10
1075 2s. sepia 25 20
1076 3s. brown 30 25

316 Hands reaching for U.N. Emblem

1956. Air. 10th Anniv of U.N.O.
1077 **316** 1s.70 red 40 20
For stamp as Type **316** see No. 1095.

317 Emblem and Girl with Ball

1956. Air. 6th S. American Women's Basketball Championships.
1078 **317** 1s. mauve 50 25
1079 – 1s.70 green 30 15
DESIGN: 1s.70, Map, flags and players.

318 Marquis of Canete
319 Cuenca Cathedral

1957. 400th Anniv of Cuenca.
1082 **318** 5c. blue on flesh (post) 10 10
1083 – 10c. bronze on green . . 10 10
1084 – 20c. brown on buff . . . 10 10
1085 – 50c. sep on cream (air) 10 10
1086 **319** 80c. red on blue 10 10
1087 – 1s. violet on yellow . . . 20 10
DESIGNS— HORIZ: 10c. Gil Ramirez Davalos and Cuenca landscape; 50c. Early plan of Cuenca; 1s. Municipal Palace. VERT: 20c. Father Vicente Solano.

320 Delegates to the 1838 Postal Congress
321 Gabriela Mistral (Chilean poet)

1957. 7th U.P.A.E. Postal Congress, 1955.
1088 **320** 40c. yellow 10 10
1089 50c. blue 10 10
1090 2s. red 40 10

1957. Air. Gabriela Mistral Commem.
1091 **321** 2s. grey, black & red . . 20 10

322 Arms of Espejo
323 Blue and Yellow Macaw

1957. Air. Carchi Cantonal Arms. Inscr "PROVINCIA DEL CARCHI". Arms mult.
1092 **322** 1s. red 15 10
1093 – 2s. black (Montufar) . . 20 10
1094 – 4s.20 blue (Tulcan) . . . 45 30
For other Arms as Type **322** see Nos 1124/7, 1147/51, 1155/9, 1197 and 1220/3.

1957. Air. United Nations Day. As T **316** but without dates.
1095 2s. blue 35 25

1958. Tropical Birds. Birds in natural colours.
(a) As T **323**.
1096 **323** 10c. brown 60 20
1097 – 20c. grey and buff . . . 60 25
1098 – 30c. green . . . . 1·60 30
1099 – 40c. orange . . . . . . 1·60 35
BIRDS: 20c. Red-breasted Toucan. 30c. Andean Condor. 40c. Sword-billed Hummingbird and Black-tailed Trainbearer.
(b) As T **323** but "ECUADOR" at top in black.
1120 – 20c. turquoise and red . . 1·00 20
1121 – 30c. blue and yellow . . . 1·10 30
1122 – 50c. orange and green . . 1·60 45
1123 – 60c. pink & turquoise . . . 1·90 45
BIRDS: 20c. Masked Crimson Tanager. 30c. Andean Cock of the Rock. 50c. Solitary Cacique. 60c. Red-fronted Conures.

324 The Virgin of Sorrows
325 Vice-Pres. Nixon and Flags of Ecuador and the U.S.A.

1958. Air. 50th Anniv of The Miracle of the Virgin of Sorrows of St. Gabriel College, Quito.
1100 **324** 30c. purple on purple . . 10 10
1101 – 30c. purple on purple . . 10 10
1102 – 1s. blue on blue 15 10
1103 **324** 1s.70 blue on blue . . . 15 15
DESIGN: Nos. 1101/2, Gateway of St. Gabriel College, Quito.

1958. Visit of Vice-Pres. of the United States. Flags in red, blue and yellow.
1104 **325** 2s. salmon and green . . 40 10

1958. Visit of Pres. Morales of Honduras. As T **325** but with portrait of Pres. Morales, flags of Ecuador and Honduras, and inscriptions changed. Flags in red, blue and yellow.
1105 2s. brown 40 10

326 Dr. C. Sanz de Santamaria

1958. Visit of Chancellor of Colombia.
1106 **326** 1s.80 multicoloured . . . 40 10

327 Dr. R. M. Arizaga
328 Gonzalo Icaza Cornejo Bridge

1958. Air. Birth Cent of Arizaga (diplomat).
1107 **327** 1s. multicoloured 10 10
See also Nos. 1135, 1142 and 1241.

1958. Air. Inauguration of Gonzalo Icaza Cornejo Bridge.
1108 **328** 1s.30 green 20 10

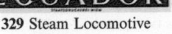

329 Steam Locomotive **330** Basketball Player

1958. 50th Anniv of Opening of Guayaquil–Quito Railway.
1109 **329** 30c. black . . . . 1·75 20
1110 – 50c. red . . . . 2·75 20
1111 – 5s. brown 95 25
DESIGNS—HORIZ: 50c. Diesel-electric train; DIAMOND, 5s. State presidents.

1958. Air. South American Basketball Champions' Tournament, Quito.
1112 **330** 1s.30 green & brown . . 40 30

331 J. C. de Macedo Soares **332** Monstrance and Doves

1958. Visit of Brazilian Chancellor.
1113 **331** 2s.20 multicoloured . . . 40 10

1958. Air. 3rd National Eucharistic Congress, Guayaquil. Inscr as in T **332**.
1114 **332** 10c. violet and yellow . . 10 10
1115 – 60c. violet and salmon 10 10
1116 **332** 1s. sepia and turquoise 15 10
DESIGN: 60c. Guayaquil Cathedral.

333 Stamps of 1865 and 1920

1958. Air. National Stamp Exn, Guayaquil.
1117 **333** 1s.30 red and green . . . 20 15
1118 – 2s. violet and blue . . . 35 20
1119 – 4s.20 sepia 45 45
DESIGNS: 2s. Stamps of 1920 and 1948; 4s.20, Guayaquil Municipal Library and Museum.

1958. Air. Imbabura Cantonal Arms. As T **322**. Inscr "PROVINCIA DE IMBABURA". Arms multicoloured.
1124 50c. red and black 10 10
1125 60c. blue, red and black . . 10 10
1126 80c. yellow and black . . . 10 10
1127 1s.10 red and black 15 10
ARMS: 50c. Cotacachi. 60c. Antonio Ante. 80c. Otavalo. 1s.10, Ibarra.

335 UNESCO Headquarters, Paris **336** Emperor Charles V (after Titian)

1958. Inauguration of UNESCO Headquarters Building, Paris.
1128 **335** 80c. brown 20 10

1958. Air. 400th Death Anniv of Emperor Charles V.
1129 **336** 2s. sepia and red 20 10
1130 4s.20 brown & black . . 40 35

337 Globe and Satellites **338** Paul Rivet (anthropologist)

1958. International Geophysical Year.
1131 **337** 1s.80 blue 60 35

1958. Air. Rivet Commemoration.
1132 **338** 1s. sepia 10 10
See also No. 1134.

339 Front page of "El Telegrafo"

1959. Air. 75th Anniv of "El Telegrafo" (newspaper).
1133 **339** 1s.30 black and green . . 15 10

1959. Air. Death Centenary of Alexander von Humboldt (naturalist). Portrait in design as T **338**.
1134 2s. grey 20 10

1959. Air. Birth Centenary of Dr. Jose L. Tamayo (statesman). Portrait in design as T **327**.
1135 1s.30 multicoloured 15 10

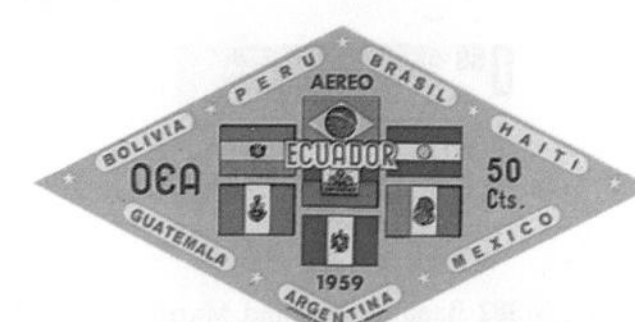

340 House of M. Canizares **341** Pope Pius XII

1959. Air. 150th Anniv of Independence.
1136 **340** 20c. brown and blue . . 10 10
1137 – 80c. brown and blue . . 10 10
1138 – 1s. myrtle and brown . . 10 10
1139 – 1s.30 orange and blue . . 25 10
1140 – 2s. brown and blue . . . 25 10
1141 – 4s.20 blue and red . . . 35 30
DESIGNS—HORIZ: 80c. St. Augustine's chapter-house; 1s. The Constitution. VERT: 1s.30, Condor with broken chains; 2s. Royal Palace; 4s.20, "Liberty" (statue).

1959. Air. Birth Centenary of Dr. A. B. Moreno (statesman). Portrait in design as T **327**.
1142 1s. multicoloured 10 10

1959. Air. Pope Pius XII Commem.
1143 **341** 1s.30 multicoloured . . . 25 20

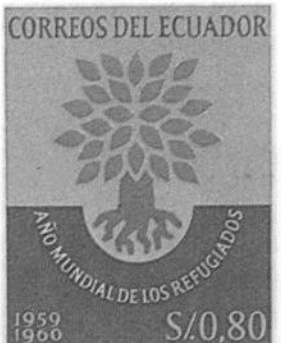

342 Flags of Argentina, Bolivia, Brazil, Guatemala, Haiti, Mexico and Peru

1959. Air. Organization of American States Commemoration. Flag design inscr "OEA".
1144 **342** 50c. multicoloured . . . 10 10
1145 – 80c. red, blue & yellow 15 10
1146 – 1s.30 multicoloured . . . 25 15
FLAGS: 80c. Chile, Costa Rica, Cuba, Dominican Republic, Panama, Paraguay and U.S.A. 1s.30. Colombia, Ecuador, Honduras, Nicaragua, El Salvador, Uruguay and Venezuela.

1959. Air. Pichincha Cantonal Arms. As T **322**. Inscr "PROVINCIA DE PICHINCHA". Arms multicoloured.
1147 10c. red and black 10 10
1148 40c. yellow and black . . . 10 10
1149 1s. brown and black . . . 10 10
1150 1s.30 green and black . . . 10 10
1151 4s.20 yellow and black . . . 40 25
ARMS: 10c. Ruminahui. 40c. Pedro Moncayo. 1s. Mejia. 1s.30, Cayambe. 4s.20, Quito.

343 Arms of Quito and Flags

1960. Air. 11th Inter-American Conference, Quito (1st issue). Centres multicoloured within red circle.
1152 **343** 1s.30 turquoise 10 10
1153 2s. sepia 20 15

344 "Uprooted Tree"

1960. World Refugee Year.
1154 **344** 80c. green and lake . . . 10 10

1960. Air. Cotopaxi Cantonal Arms. As T **322**. Inscr "PROVINCIA DE COTOPAXI". Arms multicoloured.
1155 40c. red and black 10 10
1156 60c. blue and black 15 10
1157 70c. turquoise and black . . 20 10
1158 1s. red and black 25 10
1159 1s.30 orange and black . . . 15 30
ARMS: 40c. Pangua. 60c. Pujili. 70c. Saquisili. 1s. Salcedo. 1s.30. Latacunga.

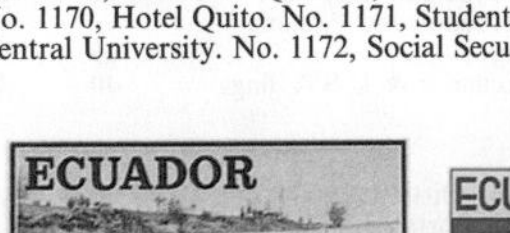

345 Giant Ant-eater

1960. 4th Cent of Baeza. Inscr as in T **345**.
1160 **345** 20c. black, orge & grn 10 10
1161 – 40c. brown, grn & turq 15 10
1162 – 80c. black, blue & brown 30 10
1163 – 1s. orange, blue & purple 50 20
DESIGNS: 40c. Mountain tapir; 80c. Spectacled bear; 1s. Puma.

346 Quito Airport

1960. 11th Inter-American Conference, Quito. (2nd issue). Views of Quito. Inscr as in T **346**.
1164 **346** 1s. blue and deep blue 20 10
1165 – 1s. violet and black . . . 15 10
1166 – 1s. red and violet 15 10
1167 – 1s. green and blue . . . 15 10
1168 – 1s. blue and violet . . . 15 10
1169 – 1s. brown and blue . . . 15 10
1170 – 1s. brown and violet . . 15 10
1171 – 1s. red and black 15 10
1172 – 1s. brown and black . . 15 10
VIEWS: No. 1165, Legislative Palace. No. 1166, Southern approach motorway and flyover. No. 1167, Government Palace. No. 1168, Foreign Ministry. No. 1169, Students' Quarters, Catholic University. No. 1170, Hotel Quito. No. 1171, Students' Quarters, Central University. No. 1172, Social Security Bank.

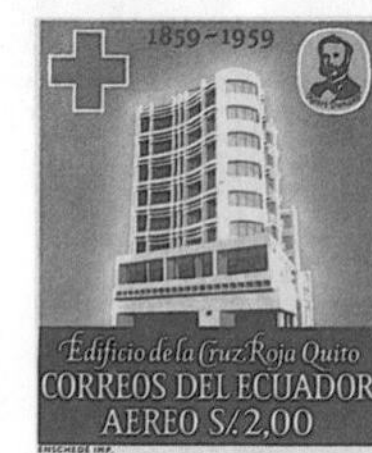

347 Ambato Railway Bridge **348** "Liberty of Expression"

1960. Air. New Bridges.
1173 – 1s.30 brown 20 10
1174 – 1s.30 green 20 10
1175 **347** 2s. brown . . . . 1·10 30
DESIGNS—No. 1173, Bridge of the Juntas; No. 1174, Saracay Bridge.

1960. Five Year Development Plan (1st issue).
(a) Postage.
1176 **348** 5c. blue 10 10
1177 – 10c. violet 10 10
1178 – 20c. orange 10 10
1179 – 30c. turquoise 10 10
1180 – 40c. brown and blue . . 15 15
DESIGNS—VERT: 10c. Mother voting; 20c. People at bus-stop; 30c. Coins. HORIZ: (37×22 mm): 40c. Irrigation project Manabi.

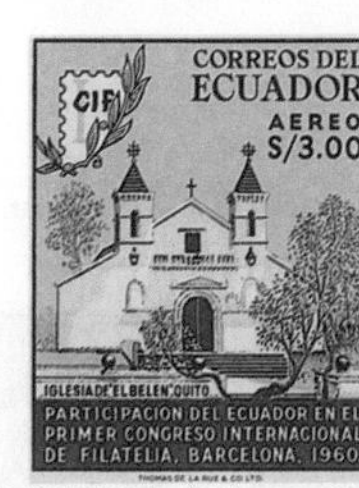

349 Road at Chone Bay

(b) Air.
1181 **349** 1s. 30 black and ochre 15 10
1182 – 4s. 20 lake and green . . 35 35
1183 – 5s. brown and lemon . . 70 40
1184 – 10s. indigo and blue . . 70 50
DESIGNS—As Type **349**: 4s.20, Ministry of Works and Communications, Cuenca; 5s. El Coca Airport; 10s. New port of Guayaquil under construction.
See also Nos. 1214/17.

350 Pres. Camilo Ponce Enriquez and Constitution

1960. Air. 5th Anniv of Constitution.
1185 **350** 2s. black and brown . . 1·10 30

351 H. Dunant and Red Cross Buildings, Quito

1960. Air. Red Cross Commem.
1186 **351** 2s. purple and red . . . 30 15

352 "El Belen" Church, Quito

1961. Air. 1st Int Philatelic Congress, Barcelona.
1187 **352** 3s. multicoloured 40 15

353 Map of River Amazon

1961. Air. "Amazon Week". Map in green.
1188 **353** 80c. purple and brown 20 10
1189 1s.30 blue and grey . . . 25 15
1190 2s. red and grey 30 20

354 J. Montalvo, J. L. Mera and J. B. Vela

1961. Air. Cent of Tungurahua Province.
1191 **354** 1s.30 black & salmon . . 20 10

355 1936 Philatelic Exhibition Air Stamp

1961. Air. 3rd International Philatelic Exn, Quito.
1192 **355** 80c. violet and orange 25 15
1193 – 1s.30 multicoloured . . . 35 20
1194 – 2s. black and red . . . 40 25
DESIGNS: 1s.30, San Lorenzo–Belem route map of S. America and 1r. stamp of 1865. (41×33½ mm); 2s., 10s. Independence stamp of 1930 postmarked "QUITO" (41×36 mm).

356 Statue of H. Ortiz Garces **357** Arms of Los Rios and Great Egret

1961. Air. H. Ortiz Garces (national hero). Commemoration. Multicoloured.
1195 1s.30 Type **356** 15 10
1196 1s.30 Portrait 15 10

1961. Air. Centenary of Los Rios Province.
1197 **357** 2s. multicoloured 60 30

358 "Graphium pausianus" **359** Collared Peccary

1961. Butterflies.
1198 **358** 20c. yellow, green, black and salmon . . 25 10
1198a 20c. yell, grey, blk & grn 15 10
1199 – 30c. yell, black & blue 35 10
1200 – 50c. black, grn & yell 45 10
1200a – 50c. blk, grn & salmon 25 10
1201 – 80c. pur, yell, blk & grn 70 20
1201a – 80c. turq, yell, blk & brn 40 15
BUTTERFLIES: 30c. "Papilio torquatus leptalea". 50c. "Graphium molops molops". 80c. "Battus lycidas".

1961. 4th Centenary of Tena.
1202 **359** 10c. blue, green & red 10 10
1203 – 20c. brown, violet & blue 10 10
1204 – 80c. orange, blk & bistre 30 10
1205 – 1s. brown, orge & green 20 15
ANIMALS: 20c. Kinkajou. 80c. Jaguar. 1s. Little coatimundi.

360 G. G. Moreno **362** R. Crespo Toral

1961. Air. Centenary of Re-establishment of "National Integrity".
1206 **360** 1s. brown, buff & blue 15 10

1961. Opening of Marine Biology Station on Galapagos Is. and 15th Anniv of UNESCO. Nos. 1/6 of Galapagos Is. optd with UNESCO emblem, obliterating crosses and **1961 Estacion de Biologia Maritima de Galapagos.**
1207 **1** 20c. brown (postage) . . . 15 10
1208 – 50c. violet 15 15
1209 – 1s. green 35 25
1210 – 1s. blue (air) 25 20
1211 – 1s.80 purple 35 20
1212 – 4s.20 black 55 30

1961. Air. Birth Centenary of Remigio Crespo Toral (writer).
1213 **362** 50c. multicoloured . . . 10 10

362a Soldier and Flag **363** Daniel Enrique Proana School, Quito

1961. Obligatory Tax. National Defence Fund.
1213a **362a** 40c. blue 10 10

1961. Five Year Development Plan.
1214 **363** 50c. black and blue . . . 10 10
1215 – 60c. black and green . . 10 10
1216 – 80c. black and red . . . 15 10
1217 – 1s. black and purple . . 20 10
DESIGNS—VERT: 60c. Loja-Zamora Highway. HORIZ: 80c. Aguirre Abad College, Guayaquil; 1s. Epiclachima Barracks, Quito.

364 Pres. C. Arosemena and Duke of Edinburgh

1962. Air. Visit of Duke of Edinburgh.
1218 **364** 1s.30 multicoloured . . . 20 10
1219 2s. multicoloured 20 10

1962. Air. Tungurahua Cantonal Arms. As T **322**. Inscr "PROVINCIA DE TUNGURAHUA". Arms multicoloured.
1220 50c. black (Pillaro) 10 10
1221 1s. black (Pelileo) 15 10
1222 1s.30 black (Banos) 20 10
1223 2s. black (Ambato) 25 15

365 Mountain and Spade in Field **366** Mosquito

1963. Air. Freedom from Hunger.
1224 **365** 30c. black, grn & yell . . 10 10
1225 3s. black, red & orange 40 20
1226 4s.20 black, blue & yell 50 35

1963. Air. Malaria Eradication.
1227 **366** 50c. black, yellow & red 10 10
1228 80c. black, green & red 10 10
1229 2s. black, pink & purple 20 20

367 Mail Coach and Boeing 707 **370** Pres. Arosemena and Flags of Ecuador

1963. Air. Centenary of Paris Postal Conf.
1230 **367** 2s. red and orange . . . 40 15
1231 4s.20 blue and purple . . 60 30

1963. Air. Unissued Galapagos Is. stamps in designs as Ecuador T **321** surch **ECUADOR** and value.
1232 **321** 5s. on 2s. mult 40 30
1233 10s. on 2s. mult 80 60

1963. Air. Red Cross Cent. Optd **1863–1963 Centenario de la Fundacion de la Cruz Roja Internacional.**
1234 **351** 2s. purple and red . . . 25 15

1963. Presidential Goodwill Tour. Mult.
1235 10c. Type **370** (postage) . . 10 10
1236 20c. Ecuador & Panama flags 10 10
1237 60c. Ecuador & U.S.A. flags 10 10
1238 70c. Type **370** (air) 10 10
1239 2s. Ecuador and Panama flags 25 10
1240 4s. Ecuador & U.S.A. flags 40 30

1963. 150th Birth Anniv of Dr. M. Cueva (statesman). Portrait in design as T **327**.
1241 2s. multicoloured 20 10

371 "Shield of Security" **372** Terminal Building

1963. 25th Anniv of Social Insurance Scheme. Multicoloured.
1242 10c. Type **371** (postage) . . 10 10
1243 10s. "Statue of Security" (air) . . . . 5·25 1·25

1963. Air. Inauguration of Simon Bolivar Airport, Guayaquil.
1244 **372** 60c. black 15 10
1245 70c. black and blue . . . 20 10
1246 5s. purple and black . . 75 25

373 Nurse and Child **380** "Commerce"

1963. Air. 7th Pan-American Pediatrics Congress, Quito.
1247 **373** 1s.30 blue, black and orange 20 15
1248 5s. lake, red and grey . . 45 30

1963. Postal Employees' Day. No. 1049a optd **1961 DIA DEL EMPLEADO POSTAL** and posthorn or surch also.
1249 B 10c. on 80c. red 10 10
1250 20c. on 80c. red 10 10
1251 50c. on 80c. red 10 10
1252 60c. on 80c. red 10 10
1253 80c. red 20 10

1964. Nos. 1164, etc, surch.
1254 10c. on 1s. blue and violet 10 10
1255 10c. on 1s. brown & violet 10 10
1256 20c. on 1s. green and blue 10 10
1257 20c. on 1s. brown and blue 10 10
1258 30c. on 1s. red and violet . . 10 10
1259 40c. on 1s. brown & black 10 10
1260 60c. on 1s. red and black . . 10 10
1261 80c. on 1s. blue & dp blue 30 10
1262 80c. on 1s. violet & black 20 10

1964. Optd **1961** and ornaments.
1263 **344** 80c. green and lake . . . 1·10 75

1964. Air. Optd **AEREO**. Honduras flag in red, blue and yellow.
1264 **326** 1s.80 violet 40 25
1265 – 2s. brown (No. 1105) . . 40 25
1266 **331** 2s.20 sepia and green . . 40 25

1964. "Columbus Lighthouse". (a) Optd **FARO DE COLON.**
1267 **337** 1s.80 blue (postage) . . 1·50 1·50
(b) Optd **FARO DE COLON AEREO.**
1268 **337** 1s.80 blue (air) . . . . . 1·90 1·25

1964. Air. Nos. 1144/6 optd **1961.**
1269 **342** 50c. multicoloured . . . 50 20
1270 – 80c. red, blue & yellow 50 20
1271 – 1s.30 multicoloured . . . 50 20

1964. O.E.A. Commemoration. Optd **OEA** with decorative frame across a block of four stamps.
1272 **344** 80c. green and lake . . . 1·50 25
The unused price is for the block of four.

1964. "Alliance for Progress".
1273 – 40c. bistre and violet . . 10 10
1274 – 50c. red and black . . . 15 10
1275 **380** 80c. blue and brown . . 10 10
DESIGNS: 40c. "Agriculture"; 50c. "Industry".

1964. Air. 15th Anniv of Declaration of Human Rights. Optd **DECLARATION DERECHOS HUMANOS 1964 XV-ANIV.**
1276 **316** 1s.70 red 30 15

382 Banana Tree and Map

1964. Banana Conference, Quito.
1277 **382** 50c. olive, brown and grey (postage) 10 10
1278 80c. olive, blk & orge . . 10 10
1279 4s.20 olive, black & ochre (air) 30 20
1280 10s. olive, blk & red . . 55 40

383 Pres. Kennedy and his Son

1964. Air. Pres. Kennedy Commem.
1281 **383** 4s.20 brn, red, bl & grn 70 55
1282 5s. brown, blue & violet 85 70
1283 10s. brown, blue & mve 85 75

384 Old Map of Ecuador and Philip II of Spain

1964. 400th Anniv of Royal High Court, Quito.
1284 **384** 10c. black, buff & red 10 10
1285 – 20c. black, buff & green 10 10
1286 – 30c. black, buff & blue 10 10
DESIGNS: As Type **384** but portrait of Juan de Salinas Loyola (20c.), Hernando de Santillan (30c.).

385 Pole vaulting

1964. Olympic Games, Tokyo. Mult.
1287 80c. Type **385** (postage) . . 10 10
1288 1s.30 Gymnastics (vert) (air) 20 10
1289 1s.80 Hurdling 20 15
1290 2s. Basketball 25 15

386 Two-toed Sloth and P. Fleming (missionary)

1965. Death of Missionaries in Ecuador's Eastern Forests. Multicoloured.
1291 20c. Nine-banded armadillo and J. Elliot 10 10
1292 30c. Eurasian red squirrel and E. McCully 10 10
1293 40c. Peruvian guemal and R. Youderian 10 10
1294 60c. Piper Vagabond airplane over Napo River, and N. Saint 30 10
1295 80c. Type **386** 40 20

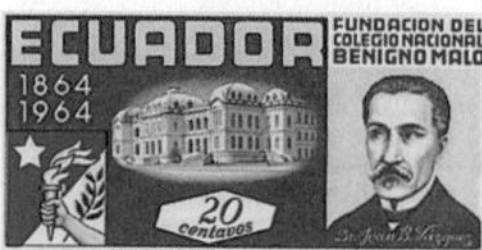

387 Dr. J. B. Vazquez (founder) and College Buildings

1965. Centenary of Benigno Malo College.
1296 **387** 20c. multicoloured . . . 10 10
1297 60c. multicoloured . . . 10 10
1298 80c. multicoloured . . . 10 10

388 J. L. Mera (wrongly inscr "MERAN"), A. Neumane and Part of Anthem

1965. Centenary of National Anthem.
1299 **388** 50c. black and red . . . 10 10
1300 80c. black and green . . 20 10
1301 5s. black and ochre . . . 40 30
1302 10s. black and blue . . . 80 60

389 "Olympic" Flame and Athletic Events

1965. 5th Bolivar Games, Quito. Flame in gold and black; athletes in black.
1303 **389** 40c. orange (postage) . . 15 10
1304 – 50c. red 15 10
1305 – 60c. blue 15 10
1306 **389** 80c. green 10 10
1307 – 1s. violet 25 10
1308 – 1s.50 mauve 40 25
1309 – 2s. blue (air) 15 10
1310 – 2s.50 orange 20 10
1311 – 3s. mauve 25 15
1312 – 3s.50 violet 25 20
1313 – 4s. green 30 20
1314 – 5s. red 35 25
DESIGNS: 50c., 1s. Running; 60c., 1s.50, Football; 2s., 3s. Diving, gymnastics, etc; 2s.50, 4s. Cycling; 3s.50, 5s. Pole-vaulting, long-jumping, etc.

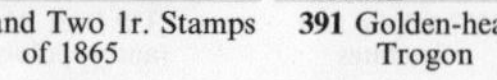
390 ½r. and Two 1r. Stamps of 1865 **391** Golden-headed Trogon

1965. Stamp Centenary.
1315 **390** 80c. multicoloured . . . 15 10
1316 1s.30 multicoloured . . . 20 10
1317 2s. multicoloured . . . 25 10
1318 4s. multicoloured 75 20

1966. Birds. Multicoloured.
1320 40c. Type **391** (postage) . . 1·40 15
1321 50c. Blue-crowned mot-mot 1·40 15
1322 60c. Paradise tanager . . . 1·40 15
1323 80c. Wire-tailed manakin . . 1·40 20
1324 1s. Yellow bellied grosbeak (air) . . . . 1·40 20
1325 1s.30 Black-headed caique 2·00 20
1326 1s.50 Scarlet tanager . . . . 2·00 20
1327 2s. Sapphire quail dove . . 2·10 20
1328 2s.50 Violet-tailed sylph . . 2·50 25
1329 3s. Lemon-throated barbet 3·00 30
1330 4s. Yellow-tailed oriole . . . 3·25 40
1331 10s. Collared puffbird . . . 6·25 1·00

1967. Various stamps surch. (a) Postage.
1332 30c. on 1s.10 (No. 1127) 15 15
1332a 40c. on 1s.70 (No. 1056) 15 15
1333 40c. on 3s.50 (No. 1312) 15 10
1334 80c. on 1s.50 (No. 1308) 10 10
1335 80c. on 2s.50 (No. 1328) 40 25
1336 1s. on 4s. (No. 1330) . . . 50 25
(b) Air.
1337 80c. on 1s.50 (No. 1326) . . 40 25
1338 80c. on 2s.50 (No. 1310) . . 15 10

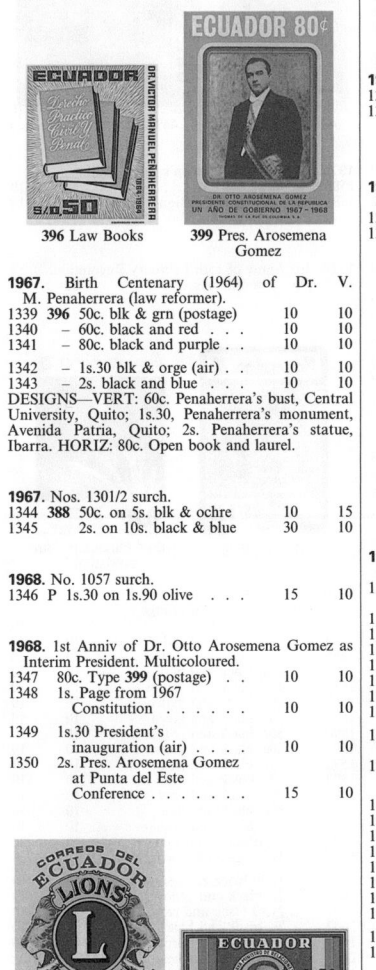

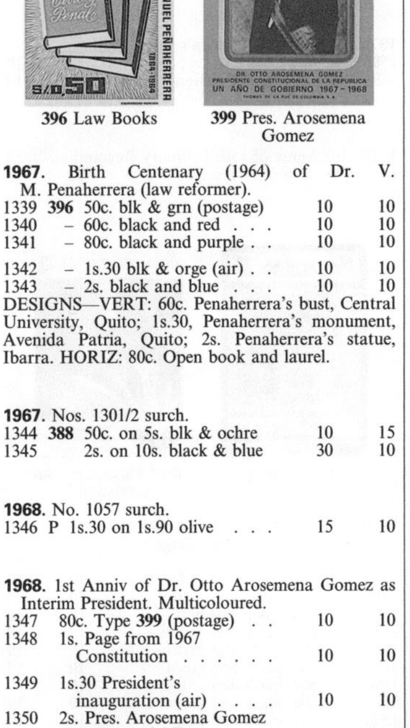
396 Law Books
399 Pres. Arosemena Gomez

1967. Birth Centenary (1964) of Dr. V. M. Penaherrera (law reformer).
1339 **396** 50c. blk & grn (postage) 10 10
1340 – 60c. black and red . . . 10 10
1341 – 80c. black and purple . . 10 10
1342 – 1s.30 blk & orge (air) . . 10 10
1343 – 2s. black and blue . . . 10 10
DESIGNS—VERT: 60c. Penaherrera's bust, Central University, Quito; 1s.30, Penaherrera's monument, Avenida Patria, Quito; 2s. Penaherrera's statue, Ibarra. HORIZ: 80c. Open book and laurel.

1967. Nos. 1301/2 surch.
1344 **388** 50c. on 5s. blk & ochre 10 15
1345 2s. on 10s. black & blue 30 10

1968. No. 1057 surch.
1346 P 1s.30 on 1s.90 olive . . . 15 10

1968. 1st Anniv of Dr. Otto Arosemena Gomez as Interim President. Multicoloured.
1347 80c. Type **399** (postage) . . 10 10
1348 1s. Page from 1967 Constitution 10 10
1349 1s.30 President's inauguration (air) 10 10
1350 2s. Pres. Arosemena Gomez at Punta del Este Conference 15 10

400 Lions Emblem
404 I.L. Arcaya, Foreign Minister of Venezuela

1968. 50th Anniv (1967) of Lions Int.
1351 **400** 80c. multicoloured . . . 15 15
1352 1s.30 multicoloured . . . 20 10
1353 2s. multicoloured 15 10

1969. Various stamps surch. (a) "AEREO" obliterated.
1355 **333** 40c. on 1s.30 . . . . . 20 20
1356 **330** 50c. on 1s.30 . . . . . 20 20
(b) Air. Inscr "AEREO".
1357 – 80c. on 10s. (No. 1331) . . 60 25
1358 – 1s. on 10s. (No. 1331) . . 60 25
1359 – 2s. on 10s. (No. 1331) . . 60 25

1969. Unissued stamp surch or optd only (No. 1363) **RESELLO**.
1360 **404** 50c. on 2s. mult 15 15
1361 80c. on 2s. mult 15 15
1362 1s. on 2s. mult 15 15
1363 2s. multicoloured 10 15

405 Map of Ecuador

1969. Revenue stamp surch.
1364 **405** 20c. on 30c. mult . . . 10 10
1365 40c. on 30c. mult . . . 10 10
1366 50c. on 30c. mult . . . 10 10
1367a 60c. on 30c. mult . . . 10 10
1368 80c. on 30c. mult . . . 10 10
1369 1s. on 30c. mult 10 10
1370 1s.30 on 30c. mult . . . 25 10
1371 1s.50 on 30c. mult . . . 15 25
1372 2s. on 30c. mult 25 15
1373 3s. on 30c. mult 35 25
1374 4s. on 30c. mult 25 15
1375 5s. on 30c. mult 25 20

406 John F. Kennedy, Robert Kennedy and Martin Luther King

407 Handshake Emblem

1969. "Apostles for Peace".
1376 **406** 4s. multicoloured 30 10
1377 4s. blk, green & blue . . 30 10

1969. Air. "Operation Friendship". Multicoloured. Emblem's background colour given.
1378 **407** 2s. blue 15 10
1379 2s. yellow 15 10

408 "Papilio zabreus" (inscr "zagreus" on stamp)

411 Arms of Zamora Chinchipe

1970. Butterflies. Multicoloured. (a) Coloured backgrounds.
1380 10c. "Thecla coronata" (postage) 10 25
1381 20c. Type **408** 10 25
1382 30c. "Heliconius erato" . . 15 25
1383 40c. "Eurytides pausanias" 15 10
1384 50c. "Pereute leucodrosime" 15 10
1385 60c. "Philaethiria dido" . . 15 10
1386 80c. "Morpho cypris" . . . 15 10
1387 1s. "Catagramma astarte" 35 10
1388 1s.30 "Morpho peleides" (air) 35 10
1389 1s.50 "Anartia amathea" . . 40 10
(b) White backgrounds. As Nos. 1380/9.
1390 – 10c. mult (postage) . . . 25 10
1391 **408** 20c. multicoloured . . . 10 25
1392 – 30c. multicoloured . . . 15 25
1393 – 40c. multicoloured . . . 15 10
1394 – 50c. multicoloured . . . 15 10
1395 – 60c. multicoloured . . . 15 10
1396 – 80c. multicoloured . . . 15 10
1397 – 1s. multicoloured 25 10
1398 – 1s.30 mult (air) 35 10
1399 – 1s.50 multicoloured . . . 40 10

1970. Air. No. 1104 surch **S/. 5 AEREO**.
1400 **325** 5s. on 2s. mult . . . . . 1·10 45

1970. Public Works Fiscal Stamps surch **POSTAL** and value.
1401 1s. on 1s. blue 10 10
1402 1s.30 on 1s. blue 15 10
1403 1s.50 on 1s. blue 15 20
1404 2s. on 1s. blue 20 15
1405 5s. on 1s. blue 40 15
1406 10s. on 1s. blue 85 35
The basic stamps are inscr "TIMBRE DE LA RECONSTRUCCION".

1970. Provincial Arms and Flags. Mult.
1407 50c. Type **411** (postage) . . 15 10
1408 1s. Esmeraldas 15 10
1409 1s.30 El Oro (air) 15 10
1410 2s. Loja 25 10
1411 3s. Manabi 15 10
1412 5s. Pichincha 30 20
1413 10s. Guayas 60 40

412

413 "Presentation of the Virgin"

1971. Revenue stamps surch for postal use.
1414 **412** 60c. on 1s. violet 10 10
1415 80c. on 1s. violet 10 10
1416 1s. on 1s. violet 10 10
1417 1s.10 on 1s. violet . . . 10 15
1418 1s.10 on 2s. green . . . 10 10
1419 1s.30 on 1s. violet . . . 10 10
1420 1s.30 on 2s. green . . . 15 10
1421 1s.50 on 1s. violet . . . 20 10
1422 1s.50 on 2s. green . . . 20 10
1423 2s. on 1s. violet 15 10
1424 2s. on 2s. green 15 10
1425 2s.20 on 1s. violet . . . 25 10
1426 3s. on 1s. violet 35 10
1427 3s. on 5s. blue 25 10
1428 3s.40 on 2s. green . . . 35 10
1429 5s. on 2s. green 50 15
1430 5s. on 5s. blue 50 20
1431 10s. on 2s. green 85 20
1432 10s. on 40s. orange . . . 70 40
1433 20s. on 2s. green . . . . 1·40 35
1434 50s. on 2s. green . . . . 3·00 1·50

1971. Air. Quito Religious Art. Mult.
1435 1s.30 Type **413** 10 10
1436 1s.50 "St. Anne" 15 10
1437 2s. "St. Teresa of Jesus" . . 25 10
1438 2s.50 Retable, Carmen altar (horiz) 25 10
1439 3s. "Descent from the Cross" 35 10
1440 4s. "Christ of St. Mariana" 50 20
1441 5s. St. Anthony Shrine . . . 50 25
1442 10s. Cross of San Diego . . 75 50

414 Flags of Chile and Ecuador

415 Emblem on Globe

1971. Visit of Pres. Allende of Chile. Mult.
1443 1s.30 Type **414** (postage) . . 10 10
1444 2s. Pres. Allende (horiz) (air) 10 10
1445 2s.10 Pres. Ibarra of Ecuador and Pres. Allende (horiz) 10 10

1971. Air. Opening of Postal Museum, Quito.
1446 **415** 5s. blue and black . . . 50 25
1447 5s.50 purple & black . . 50 30

416 Ismael Paz Pazmino (founder)

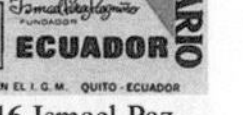
417 Punch-card and Map

1971. 50th Anniv of "El Universo" (newspaper).
1448 **416** 1s. mult (postage) . . . 10 10
1449 1s.50 multicoloured (air) 10 10
1450 2s.50 multicoloured . . . 10 10

1971. Air. Pan-American Road Conference.
1451 **417** 5s. multicoloured 50 30
1452 – 10s. black and orange . . 90 60
1453 – 20s. black, red & blue 1·25 65
1454 – 50s. black, lilac & blue 1·90 95
DESIGNS: 10s. Converging roads; 20s. Globe and equator; 50s. Mountain road.

418 C.A.R.E. Parcel

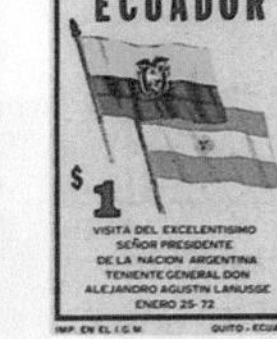
419 Flags of Ecuador and Argentine Republic

1972. 25th Anniv of C.A.R.E. Organization.
1455 **418** 30c. purple 10 10
1456 40c. green 10 10
1457 50c. blue 10 10
1458 60c. red 10 10
1459 80c. brown 10 10

1972. State Visit of President Lanusse of Argentine Republic. Multicoloured.
1460 1s. Type **419** (postage) . . . 10 10
1461 3s. Arms of Ecuador and Argentine Republic (horiz) (air) 20 15
1462 5s. Presidents Velasco Ibarra and Lanusse (horiz) . . . 35 20

420 "Jesus giving Keys to St. Peter" (M. de Santiago)

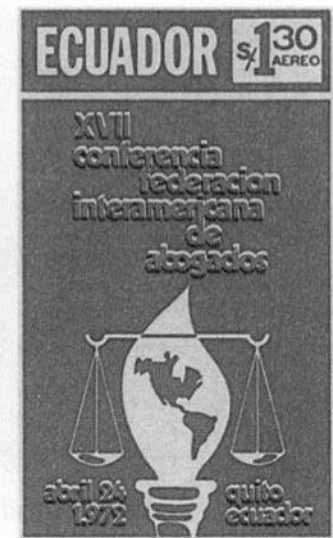
421 Map in Flame, and Scales of Justice

1972. Religious Paintings of 18th-century Quito School. Multicoloured.
1463 50c. Type **420** (postage) . . 10 10
1464 1s.10 "Virgin of Mercy" (Quito School) 20 20
1465 2s. "The Immaculate Conception" (M. Samaniego) 15 30
1466 3s. "Virgin of the Flowers" (M. de Santiago) (air) . . 20 20
1467 10s. "Virgin of the Rosary" (Quito School) 70 50

1972. Air. Inter-American Lawyers' Federation Congress, Quito.
1469 **421** 1s.30 blue and red . . . 10 10

422 "Our Lady of Sorrow" (Caspicara)

1972. 18th-century Ecuador Statues. Mult.
1470 50c. Type **422** (postage) . . 10 10
1471 1s.10 "Nativity" (Quito School) (horiz) 10 20
1472 2s. "Virgin of Quito" (anon.) 15 10
1473 3s. "St. Dominic" (Quito School) (air) 20 20
1474 10s. "St. Rosa of Lima" (B. de Legarda) 70 40

423 Juan Ignacio Pareja

424 Woman in Poncho

1972. 150th Anniv of Battle of Pichincha (1st issue). Multicoloured.
1476 30c. Type **423** (postage) . . 10 10
1477 40c. Juan Jose Flores . . . 10 10
1478 50c. Leon de Febres Cordero 10 10
1479 60c. Ignacio Torres 10 10
1480 70c. F. de Paula Santander 10 10
1481 1s. Jos M. Cordova 10 10
1482 1s.30 Jose M. Saenz (air) . . 10 15
1483 3s. Tomas Wright 20 15
1484 4s. Antonio Farfan 25 20
1485 5s. A. Jose de Sucre 35 25

1486 10s. Simon Bolivar 35 25
1487 20s. Arms of Ecuador . . . 2·00 2·10
See also Nos. 1508/19.

1972. Ecuador Handicrafts and Costumes. Mult.
1488 2s. Type **424** (postage) . . . 15 15
1489 3s. Girl in striped poncho 25 25
1490 5s. Girl in embroidered poncho 40 40
1491 10s. Copper urn 85 75
1492 2s. Woman in floral poncho (air) 15 10
1493 3s. Girl in banded poncho 20 15
1494 5s. Woman in rose poncho 35 25
1495 10s. "Sun" sculpture 70 75

425 Epidendrum orchid

1972. Air. Ecuador Flowers. Multicoloured.
1497 4s. Type **425** 75 45
1498 6s. Canna . . . . 1·00 60
1499 10s. Jimson weed . . . . . 1·75 1·00

426 Oil Rigs 427 Arms

1972. Air. Oil Industry.
1501 **426** 1s.30 multicoloured . . . 10 10

1972. Air. Civic and Armed Forces Day.
1502 **427** 2s. multicoloured 15 15
1503 3s. multicoloured 25 15
1504 4s. multicoloured 35 20
1505 4s.50 multicoloured . . . 35 25
1506 6s.30 multicoloured . . . 40 35
1507 6s.90 multicoloured . . . 40 40

428 Statue of Sucre, Santo Domingo 429 Dish Aerial

1972. 150th Anniv of Battle of Pichincha (2nd issue). Multicoloured.
1508 1s.20 Type **428** (postage) . . 10 10
1509 1s.80 San Augustin Monastery 15 10
1510 2s.30 Independence Square 20 10
1511 2s.50 Bolivar's statue, La Alameda 25 15
1512 4s.75 Carved chapel doors 40 20
1513 2s.40 Cloister, San Augustin Monastery (air) 15 10
1514 4s.50 La Merced Monastery 30 25
1515 5s.50 Chapel column . . . 40 30
1516 6s.30 Altar, San Augustin Monastery 45 35
1517 6s.90 Ceiling, San Augustin Monastery 45 35
1518 7s.40 Crucifixion, Cantuna Chapel 50 40
1519 7s.90 Ceiling detail, San Augustin Monastery . . . 55 45

1973. Inauguration (1972) of Satellite Earth Station, Chillotal.
1520 **429** 1s. multicoloured 20 10

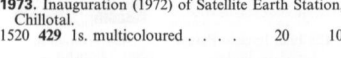

431 U.N. Emblem 432 O.E.A. Emblem

1973. Air. 25th Anniv of U.N. Economic Committee for Latin America (C.E.P.A.L.).
1521 **431** 1s.30 black and blue . . 15 10

1973. Air. "Day of the Americas".
1522 **432** 1s.50 multicoloured . . . 15 10

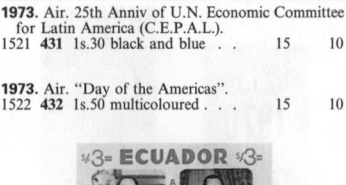

433 Presidents Rodriguez Lara and Caldera

1973. Air. Visit of Pres. Caldera of Venezuela.
1523 **433** 3s. multicoloured 30 15

434 Blue-footed Boobies

1973. Formation of Galapagos Islands Province. Multicoloured.
1524 30c. Type **434** (postage) . . 40 15
1525 40c. Blue-faced boobies . . 40 15
1526 50c. Oystercatcher 40 15
1527 60c. Basking Galapagos fur seals 50 10
1528 70c. Giant tortoise 50 10
1529 1s. Californian sealion . . . 50 10
1530 1s.30 Blue-footed boobies (different) (air) . . . . . 2·00 25
1531 3s. Brown pelican . . . . . 2·00 25

435 Silver Coin, 1934 436 Black-chinned Mountain Tanager

1973. Air. Coins. Multicoloured.
1532 5s. Type **435** 35 15
1533 10s. Reverse of silver coin, showing arms 70 30
1534 50s. Gold Coin, 1928 . . . 3·00 1·50

1973. Birds. Multicoloured.
1536 1s. Type **436** 55 25
1537 2s. Maniche oriole 90 40
1538 3s. Toucan barbet (vert) . . 90 50
1539 5s. Masked crimson tanager (vert) . . . . 2·25 90
1540 10s. Blue-necked tanager (vert) . . . . 4·75 1·60

437 OPEC Emblem

438 Dr. Marco Tulio Varea Quevedo (botanist)

1974. Air. OPEC (Oil exporters) Meeting, Quito.
1542 **437** 2s. multicoloured 15 10

1974. Ecuadorian Personalities (1st series).
1543 **438** 1s. blue 10 10
1544 – 1s. orange 10 10
1545 – 1s. green 10 10
1546 – 1s. brown 10 10
PERSONALITIES: No. 1544, Dr. J. M. Carbo Noboa (medical scientist). No. 1545, Dr. A. J. Valenzuela (physician). No. 1546, Capt. E. Chiriboga (national hero).
See also Nos. 1551/6 and 1565/9.

439 Flag of Ecuador and U.P.U. Emblem 440 Postman with Letter

1974. Air. Centenary of U.P.U.
1548 **439** 1s.30 multicoloured . . . 10 10

1974. Personalities (2nd series). As T **438**.
1551 60c. red (postage) 10 10
1552 70c. lilac 10 10
1553 1s.20 green 10 10
1554 1s.80 blue 20 10
1555 1s.30 blue and black (air) 10 10
1556 1s.50 grey on pale grey . . 10 10
PERSONALITIES: 60c. Dr. Pio Jaramillo Alvarado (sociologist). 70c. Prof. Luciano Andrade Marin (naturalist). 1s.20, Dr. Francisco Campos Ruiadaneira (entomologist). 1s.30, Teodore Wolf (geographer). 1s.50, Capt. Edmundo Chiriboga G. (national hero). 1s.80, Luis Vernaza Lazarte (philanthropist).

1974. Air. 8th Inter-American Postmasters' Congress, Auibo.
1557 **440** 5s. multicoloured 30 15

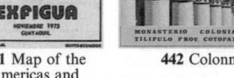

441 Map of the Americas and F.I.A.F. Emblem 442 Colonnade

1974. Air. "Exfigua" Stamp Exhibition and Inter-American Philatelic Federation 5th General Assembly, Guayaquil (1973).
1558 **441** 3s. multicoloured 20 10

1974. Colonial Monastery, Tilipulo, Cotopaxi Province. Multicoloured.
1559 20c. Type **442** 10 10
1560 30c. Entrance 10 10
1561 40c. Church 10 10
1562 50c. Archway (vert) 10 10
1563 60c. Chapel (vert) 10 10
1564 70c. Cemetery (vert) 15 10

1975. Personalities (3rd series). As T **438**.
1565 80c. blue (postage) 10 10
1566 80c. red and pink 10 10
1567 5s. red (air) 40 20
1568 5s. grey 40 20
1569 5s. violet 40 20
PORTRAITS: No. 1565, Dr. Angel Polibio Chaves (statesman). No. 1566, Emilio Estrada Ycaza (archaeologist). No. 1567, Manuel J. Calle (journalist). No. 1568, Leopoldo Benites Vinueza (statesman). No. 1569, Adolfo H. Simmonds G. (journalist).

443 President Rodriguez Lara

1975. Air. State Visits of President Rodriguez Lara to Algeria, Rumania and Venezuela.
1570 **443** 5s. black and red 40 20

444 Ministerial Greetings 445 "The Sacred Heart"

1975. Meeting of Public Works' Ministers of Ecuador and Colombia, Quito. Multicoloured.
1571 1s. Type **444** (postage) . . . 10 10
1572 1s.50 Ministers at opening ceremony (air) 15 10
1573 2s. Ministers signing treaty 15 10

1975. Air. 3rd Eucharistic Congress, Quito. Multicoloured.
1574 1s.30 Type **445** 10 10
1575 2s. Golden monstrance . . . 15 10
1576 3s. Quito Cathedral 20 10

446 President Martinez Mera 447 Jorge Delgado Panchana (swimming champion)

1975. Air. Birth Centenary of Juan de Dios Martinez Mera (President, 1932–33).
1577 **446** 5s. red and black 40 20

1975. Air. Jorge Delgado Panchana Commemoration. Multicoloured.
1578 1s.30 Type **447** 15 10
1579 3s. Delgado Panchana in water (horiz) 30 10

448 "Women of Peace" 449 "Armed Forces"

1975. International Women's Year. Mult.
1580 1s. Type **448** 10 10
1581 1s. "Women of Action" . . 10 10

1975. 3rd Anniv of 15th February Revolution.
1582 **449** 2s. multicoloured 80 20

450 Hurdling 451 "Phragmipedum candatum"

1975. 3rd Ecuadorian Games, Quito.
1583 **450** 20c. black and orange (postage) 10 10
1584 – 20c. black and yellow . . 10 10
1585 – 30c. black and mauve . . 10 10
1586 – 30c. black and buff . . . 10 10
1587 – 40c. black and yellow . . 10 10
1588 – 40c. black and mauve . . 10 10
1589 – 50c. black and green . . 10 10
1590 – 50c. black and red . . . 10 10
1591 – 60c. black and green . . 10 10
1592 – 60c. black and pink . . 10 10
1593 – 70c. black and drab . . 10 10
1594 – 70c. black and grey . . . 10 10
1595 – 80c. black and blue . . . 10 10
1596 – 80c. black and orange 10 10
1597 – 1s. black and olive . . . 10 10
1598 – 1s. black and brown . . 10 10
1599 1s.30 black & orge (air) 10 10
1600 – 2s. black and yellow . . 15 10
1601 – 2s.80 black and red . . . 20 10
1602 – 3s. black and blue . . . 25 10
1603 – 5s. black and purple . . 40 20
DESIGNS: No. 1584, Chess; No. 1585, Boxing; No. 1586, Basketball; No. 1587, Showjumping; No. 1588, Cycling; No. 1589, Football; No. 1590, Fencing; No. 1591, Golf; No. 1592, Gymnastics; No. 1593, Wrestling; No. 1594, Judo; No. 1595, Swimming; No. 1596, Weightlifting; No. 1597, Handball; No. 1598, Table tennis; No. 1599, Squash; No. 1600, Rifle shooting; No. 1601, Volleyball; No. 1602, Rafting; No. 1603, Inca mask.

1975. Flowers. Multicoloured.
1604 20c. Type **451** (postage) . . 10 10
1605 30c. "Genciana" (horiz) . . 10 10
1606 40c. "Bromeliaeae cactaceae" 10 10
1607 50c. "Cachlioda volcanica" (horiz) 10 10
1608 60c. "Odontoglossum hallii" (horiz) 10 10
1609 80c. "Cactaceae sp." (horiz) 10 10
1610 1s. "Odontoglossum sp." (horiz) 10 10
1611 1s.30 "Pitcairnia pungens" (horiz) (air) 15 10
1612 2s. "Salvia sp." (horiz) . . . 25 10
1613 3s. "Bomarea" (horiz) . . . 30 10
1614 4s. "Opuntia quitense" (horiz) 25 15
1615 5s. "Bomarea" (different) (horiz) 30 20

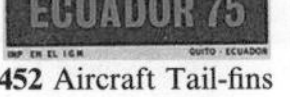

452 Aircraft Tail-fins — 453 Statue of Benalcazar

1976. Air. 23rd Anniv of TAME Airline. Mult.
1616 1s.30 Type **452** 10 10
1617 3s. Douglas DC-3 and Lockheed L.188 Electra encircling map 40 10

1976. Air. Sebastian de Benalcazar Commem.
1618 **453** 2s. multicoloured 20 10
1619 3s. multicoloured 30 10

454 "Venus" (Chorrera Culture) — 455 Strawberries

1976. Archaeological Discoveries. Mult.
1620 20c. Type **454** (postage) . . 10 10
1621 30c. "Venus" (Valdivia) . . 10 10
1622 40c. Seated monkey (Chorrera) 10 10
1623 50c. Man wearing poncho (Panzaleo Tardio) 10 10
1624 60c. Mythical figure (Cashaloma) 10 10
1625 80c. Musician (Tolita) . . . 10 10
1626 1s. Chief priest (censer-Mantema) 10 10
1627 1s. Female mask (Tolita) . . 10 10
1628 1s. Gold and platinum brooch (Tolita) 10 10
1629 1s. "Angry person" mask (Tolita) 10 10
1630 1s.30 Coconut-dealer (Carchi) (air) 15 15
1631 2s. Funerary urn (Tuncahuan) 15 10
1632 3s. Priest (Bahia de Caraquez) 25 10
1633 4s. Seashell (Cuasmal) . . . 35 10
1634 5s. Bowl supported by figurines (Guangala) . . . 40 20

1976. Flowers and Fruits Festival, Ambato. Multicoloured.
1635 1s. Type **455** (postage) . . . 10 10
1636 2s. Apples (air) 10 10
1637 5s. Rose 40 15

456 S. Cueva Celi — 457 Douglas DC-10 crossing "50" and Dornier Wal Flying Boat

1976. Musical Celebrities. Multicoloured.
1638 1s. Type **456** 10 10
1639 1s. C. Ojeda Davila 10 10
1640 1s. S. Maria Duran 10 10
1641 1s. C. Amable Ortiz 10 10
1642 1s. L. Alberto Valencia . . 10 10

1976. Air. 50th Anniv of Lufthansa Airline.
1643 **457** 10s. multicoloured . . . 1·25 50

458 Cerros del Carmen y Santa Ana

1976. Air. 441st Anniv of Guayaquil. Mult.
1644 1s.30 Type **458** 10 10
1645 1s.30 "Pregonero" (vert) . . 10 10
1646 1s.30 "Estibador" (vert) . . 10 10
1647 2s. Sebastian de Benalcazar (vert) 15 10
1648 2s. Francisco de Orellana (vert) 15 10
1649 2s. Guayas and Quil (vert) 15 10

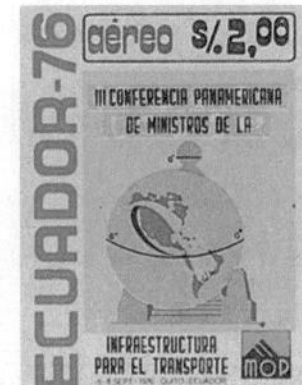

459 New Post Office Building — 461 The Americas on Globe

460 Emblem and Wreath

1976. Air. Post Office Building Project.
1650 **459** 5s. multicoloured 30 15

1976. Air. 50th Anniv of Bolivarian Society.
1651 **460** 1s.30 multicoloured . . . 10 10

1976. Air. 3rd Pan-American Ministers' Conference on Transport Infrastructure, Quito.
1652 **461** 2s. multicoloured 10 10

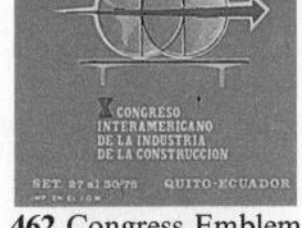

462 Congress Emblem — 463 George Washington

1976. Air. 10th Inter-American Construction Industry Congress, Quito.
1654 **462** 1s.30 multicoloured . . . 10 10
1655 3s. multicoloured 20 25

1976. Air. Bicentenary of American Revolution. Multicoloured.
1657 3s. Type **463** 45 25
1658 5s. Battle of Flamborough Head, 1779 (horiz) . . . 2·50 50

464 Dr. H. Noguchi — 465 Bolivar Memorial

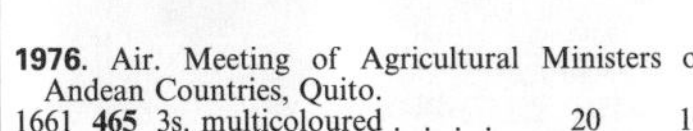

1976. Air. Birth Centenary of Dr. Hideyo Noguchi (bacteriologist).
1659 **464** 3c. multicoloured 25 10

1976. Air. Meeting of Agricultural Ministers of Andean Countries, Quito.
1661 **465** 3s. multicoloured 20 10

466 M. Febres Cordero — 467 Dr. Luis Cordero

1976. Air. Mariuxi Febres Cordero, South American Swimming Champion.
1663 **466** 3s. multicoloured 25 10

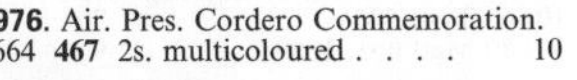

1976. Air. Pres. Cordero Commemoration.
1664 **467** 2s. multicoloured 10 10

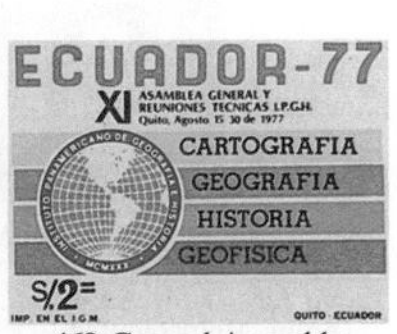

468 Sister Catalina de Jesus Herrera — 469 General Assembly Emblem

1977. Air. 260th Birth Anniv of Sister Catalina de Jesus Herrera (religious author).
1665 **468** 1s.30 pink and black . . 10 10

1977. 11th General Assembly of Technical Committees of the Pan-American Historical and Geographical Institute. Multicoloured.
1666 2s. Type **469** (postage) . . . 10 10
1667 5s. Congress Building, Quito (air) 30 15

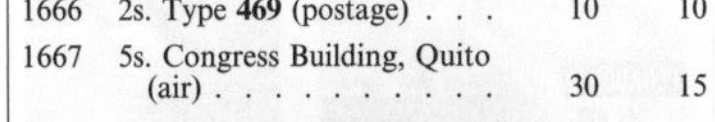

470 Mythological Figure ("La Tolita" ceramic)

1977. Air. 50th Anniv of Foundation of Central Bank of Ecuador. Multicoloured.
1669 7s. Type **470** 45 20
1670 9s. "The Holy Shepherdess Spinning" (B. de Legarda) 60 30
1671 11s. "The Fruitseller" (B. de Legarda) 75 60

471 Hands holding Rotary Emblem

1977. 50th Anniv of Guayaquil Rotary Club.
1673 **471** 1s. multicoloured 15 10
1674 2s. multicoloured 25 10

472 President Michelsen of Colombia

1977. Air. Meeting of the Presidents of Colombia and Ecuador. Multicoloured.
1676 2s.60 Type **472** 25 10
1677 5s. Ecuador junta 45 15
1678 7s. Ecuador junta (vert) . . 45 20
1679 9s. President Michelsen with Ecuador junta 75 40

473 Brother Miguel and St. Peter's, Rome — 474 Lungs

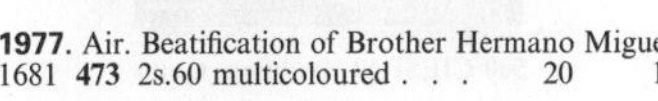

1977. Air. Beatification of Brother Hermano Miguel.
1681 **473** 2s.60 multicoloured . . . 20 10

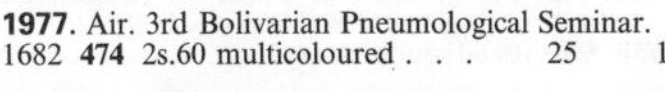

1977. Air. 3rd Bolivarian Pneumological Seminar.
1682 **474** 2s.60 multicoloured . . . 25 10

475 Jose Peralta — 476 Blue-faced Booby

1977. 40th Death Anniv of Jose Peralta (writer).
1683 **475** 1s.80 mult (postage) . . 10 10
1684 – 2s.40 multicoloured . . . 15 15
1685 – 2s.60 blk, red & yell (air) 15 10

DESIGNS: 2s.40, Statue of Peralta; 2s.60, Titles of Peralta's works, and his "ex libris".

1977. Birds of the Galapagos Islands. Mult.
1686 1s.20 Type **476** 60 10
1687 1s.80 Red-footed booby . . 80 10
1688 2s.40 Blue-footed boobies 90 15
1689 3s.40 Dusky gull . . . . . 1·40 15
1690 4s.40 Galapagos hawk . . . 1·75 30
1691 5s.40 Map of the islands and finches (vert) . . . . 2·25 35

477 Broadcast Tower — 478 Dr. Remigio Romero y Cordero

1977. Air. World Telecommunications Day.
1692 **477** 5s. multicoloured 30 15

1978. Air. 10th Death Anniv of Dr. Remigio Romero y Cordero (poet).
1693 **478** 3s. multicoloured 15 10
1694 10s.60 multicoloured . . 60 30

479 Children — 480 General San Martin

1978. Air. 50th Anniv of Social Insurance Institute. Multicoloured.
1696 7s. Type **479** 45 20
1697 9s. Insurance emblem . . . 40 30
1698 11s. Hands reaching for sun 70 35

1978. Air. Birth Bicent of General San Martin.
1700 **480** 10s.60 multicoloured . . 50 40

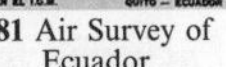

481 Air Survey of Ecuador — 482 Dr. Vicente Corral Moscoso Hospital

1978. 50th Anniv of Military Geographical Institute. Multicoloured.
1702 6s. Type **481** (postage) . . . 60 25
1703 7s.60 Air survey of mountains (air) 80 30

1978. Inauguration of Dr. Vicente Corral Moscoso Regional Hospital. Multicoloured.
1705 3s. Type **482** (postage) . . . 25 10
1706 7s.60 Dr. Moscoso (air) . . 60 30

483 Map of the Americas and Lions Emblem — 484 Anniversary Emblem

1978. 7th Meeting of Latin American Lions. Multicoloured.
1708 3s. Type **483** (postage) . . . 25 10
1709 4s.20 Type **483** 35 10
1710 5s. As Type **483** but smaller emblem (air) 40 20
1711 6s.20 As No. 1710 . . . . . 25 25

1978. 70th Anniv of Filanbanco (Philanthropic Bank). Multicoloured.
1713 4s.20 Type **484** (postage) . . 30 10
1714 5s. Bank emblem (air) . . . 35 15

485 Goal

1978. World Cup Football Championship, Argentina. Multicoloured.
1715 1s.20 Type **485** (postage) . . 10 10
1716 1s.80 Gauchito and emblem (vert) 15 10
1717 4s.40 Gauchito (vert) . . . 35 15
1718 2s.60 Gauchito, "78" and emblem (air) 20 10
1719 7s. Football 30 20
1720 9s. Emblem (vert) 40 35

486 Old Men of Vilcabamba

487 Bernardo O'Higgins

1978. Air. Vilcabamba (valley of longevity).
1722 **486** 5s. multicoloured 35 15

1978. Air. Birth Bicentenary of General Bernardo O'Higgins (national hero of Chile).
1723 **487** 10s.60 multicoloured . . 50 30

488 Hubert Humphrey (former U.S. Vice-President)

489 "Virgin and Child"

1978. Air. Hubert Humphrey Commem.
1725 **488** 5s. multicoloured 35 15

1978. Air. Christmas. Children's Paintings. Mult.
1726 2s.20 Type **489** 15 10
1727 4s.60 "Holy Family" . . . 25 15
1728 6s.20 "Candle and Children" 40 20

490 "Village" (Anibal Villacis)

491 Male and Female Symbols

1978. Air. Ecuadorian Painters. Mult.
1729 5s. Type **490** 35 20
1730 5s. "Mountain Village" (Gilberto Almeida) . . . 35 20
1731 5s. "Bay" (Roura Oxandaberro) 35 20
1732 5s. "Abstract" (Luis Molinari) 35 20
1733 5s. "Statue" (Oswaldo Viteri) 35 20
1734 5s. "Tools" (Enrique Tabara) 35 20

1979. 50th Anniv of Inter-American Women's Commission.
1735 **491** 3s.40 multicoloured . . . 20 10

492 House and Monument

1979. Air. 150th Anniv of Battle of Portete and Tarqui. Multicoloured.
1736 2s.40 Type **492** 15 10
1737 3s.40 Monument (vert) . . . 20 10

493 Bank Emblem

494 Deep Sea Trawler and Fish

1979. 16th Anniv of Ecuadorian Mortgage Bank.
1739 **493** 4s.40 multicoloured . . . 30 15
1740 5s.40 multicoloured . . . 35 15

1979. Air. 25th Anniv of Extension to 200-mile Offshore Limit. Multicoloured.
1741 5s. Type **494** 90 25
1742 7s. Map of Ecuador and territorial waters (horiz) 55 25
1743 9s. Map of South America 70 35

495 Street Scene

496 Coat of Arms

1979. Galapagos Islands. Multicoloured.
1744 3s.40 Type **495** (postage) . . 25 15
1745 10s.60 Church bells in tower (horiz) (air) 50 20
1746 13s.60 Aerial view of coast 55 20

1979. Air. 5th Anniv of Ecuador-American Chamber of Commerce.
1748 **496** 7s.60 multicoloured . . . 45 25
1749 10s.60 multicoloured . . 65 35

497 Young Girl

498 Games Emblem

1979. Air. International Year of the Child.
1751 **497** 10s. multicoloured . . . 50 40

1979. Air. 5th National Games.
1752 **498** 28s. multicoloured . . . 1·10 80

499 Rejoicing People with Flags

1979. Air. Restoration of Democracy. Mult.
1753 7s.60 Type **499** 55 30
1754 10s.60 President Jamie Roldos Aguilera 70 35

500 CIESPAL Building, Quito

1980. Air. Inauguration of CIESPAL (Ecuadorian Institute of Engineers) Building.
1755 **500** 10s.60 multicoloured . . 50 35

501 Jose Joaquin de Olmedo

502 Enriquillo (Dominican Republic)

1980. Birth Bicentenary of Jose Joaquin de Olmedo (physician).
1756 **501** 3s. multicoloured (postage) 25 10
1757 5s. multicoloured 40 20
1758 10s. multicoloured (air) 50 40

1980. Chiefs of the Indo-American Indian Tribes. Multicoloured.
1759 3s. Type **502** (postage) . . . 25 10
1760 3s.40 Guaycaypuro (Venezuela) 30 15
1761 5s. Abayuba (Uruguay) . . 40 20
1762 5s. Atlacati (El Salvador) . . 40 20
1763 7s.60 Cuantemoc (Mexico) (air) 60 30
1764 7s.60 Lempira (Honduras) 60 30
1765 7s.60 Nicaragua (Nicaragua) 60 30
1766 10s. Lambare (Paraguay) . . 50 40
1767 10s. Urraca (Panama) . . . 50 40
1768 10s.60 Anacaona (Haiti) . . 50 45
1769 10s.60 Caupolican (Chile) 50 45
1770 10s.60 Tecun-Uman (Guatemala) 50 45
1771 12s.80 Calarca (Colombia) 65 30
1772 12s.80 Garabito (Costa Rica) 65 30
1773 12s.80 Hatuey (Cuba) . . . 65 30
1774 13s.60 Camarao (Brazil) . . 65 30
1775 13s.60 Tehuelche (Argentina) 65 30
1776 13s.60 Tupaj Katari (Bolivia) 65 30
1777 17s.80 Sequoyah (U.S.A.) 75 40
1778 22s.80 Ruminahui (Ecuador) 1·10 55

503 King Juan Carlos and Queen Sophia of Spain

504 Provincial Administration Council Building, Pichincha

1980. Visit of King and Queen of Spain.
1779 **503** 3s.40 mult (postage) . . 30 15
1780 10s.60 mult (air) 50 40

1980. Air. Pichincha Provincial Council.
1781 **504** 10s.60 multicoloured . . 80 40

505 Cofan Indian (Napo Province)

506 U.P.U. Monument

1980. Equatorial Indians. Multicoloured.
1782 3s. Type **505** (postage) . . . 25 10
1783 3s.40 Zuleta woman (Imbabura) 30 15
1784 5s. Chota negro woman (Imbabura) 40 20
1785 7s.60 Salasaca boy (Tungurahua) (air) . . . 60 30
1786 10s. Girl from Amula (Chimborazo) 50 40
1787 10s.60 Girl from Canar (Canar) 50 45
1788 13s.60 Colorado Indian (Pichincha) 65 30

1980. Air. Cent of U.P.U. Membership. Mult.
1789 10s.60 Type **506** 70 35
1790 17s.80 Mail box, 1880 . . . 95 65

507 Our Lady of Mercy Basilica, Quito

508 Olympic Torch

1980. Virgin of Mercy, Patron Saint of Ecuadorian Armed Forces. Multicoloured.
1792 3s.40 Type **507** (postage) . . 30 15
1793 3s.40 Balcony 30 15
1794 3s.40 Tower and cupola . . 30 15
1795 7s.60 Cupola and cloisters (air) 60 30
1796 7s.60 Tower and view of Quito 60 30
1797 7s.60 Gold screen 60 30
1798 10s.60 Retable 60 45
1799 10s.60 Pulpit 60 45
1800 13s.60 Cupola 75 30
1801 13s.60 Statue of Virgin . . . 75 30

1980. Olympic Games, Moscow. Multicoloured.
1803 5s. Type **508** (postage) . . . 40 20
1804 7s.60 Type **508** 35 30
1805 10s.60 Moscow games emblem (air) 50 45
1806 13s.60 As No. 1805 . . . . 65 55

509 Rotary Anniversary Emblem

510 "Marshal Sucre" (after Marco Salas)

1980. Air. 75th Anniv of Rotary International.
1808 **509** 10s. multicoloured . . . 75 40

1980. Air. 150th Death Anniv of Marshal Antonio Jose de Sucre.
1809 **510** 10s.60 multicoloured . . 50 45

511 J. J. Olmeda, Father de Velasco, Government Building and Constitution

512 The Virgin of the Swans

1980. 150th Anniv of Constitutional Assembly of Riobamba. Multicoloured.
1810 3s.40 Type **511** (postage) . . 25 10
1811 5s. Type **511** 40 15
1812 7s.60 Monstrance, Riobamba Cathedral (vert) (air) 55 25
1813 10s.60 As No. 1812 . . . . 50 35

1980. 50th Anniv of Coronation of the Virgin of the Swans. Multicoloured.
1815 1s.20 Type **512** 10 10
1816 3s.40 The Virgin (different) 20 10

513 Young Indian

514 O.P.E.C. Emblem and Globe

1980. 1st Anniv of Return to Democracy. Multicoloured.
1817 1s.20 Type **513** (postage) . . 10 10
1818 3s.40 Type **513** 20 10
1819 7s.60 President Roldos with Indian (air) 55 25
1820 10s.60 As No. 1819 . . . . 50 35

1980. 20th Anniv of Organization of Petroleum Exporting Countries. Multicoloured.
1822 3s.40 Type **514** (postage) . . 30 10
1823 7s.60 Figures supporting O.P.E.C. emblem (air) . . 60 30

515 Dr. Isidro Ayora Cueva

516 Ornamental Hedge, Capitol Gardens

1980. Air. Birth Centenary of Dr. Isidro Ayora Cueva (President, 1926–31).
1824 **515** 18s.20 multicoloured . . 1·10 75

1980. Centenary of Carchi Province. Mult.
1825 3s. Type **516** (postage) . . . 20 10
1826 10s.60 Governor's palace (air) 70 35
1827 17s.80 Freedom statue, Zulcan 95 65

517 "Cattleya maxima"

1980. Orchids. Multicoloured.
1828 1s.20 Type **517** (postage) . . 10 10
1829 3s. "Comparettia speciosa" 25 10
1830 3s.40 "Cattleya iricolor" . . 30 15
1831 7s.60 "Anguloa uniflora" (air) 60 20
1832 10s.60 "Scuticaria salesiana" 80 35
1833 50s. "Helcia sanguinolenta" (vert) . . . . 1·10 85
1834 100s. "Anguloa virginalis" 1·50 1·50

518 Emblem and Radio Waves

519 Simon Bolivar (after Marco Salas)

1980. 50th Anniv of Radio Station HCJB.
1836 2s. Type **518** (postage) . . . 15 10
1837 7s.60 Emblem and radio waves (horiz) (air) 50 25
1838 10s.60 Anniversary emblem 65 35

1980. Air. 150th Death Anniv of Simon Bolivar.
1839 **519** 13s.60 multicoloured . . 1·10 55

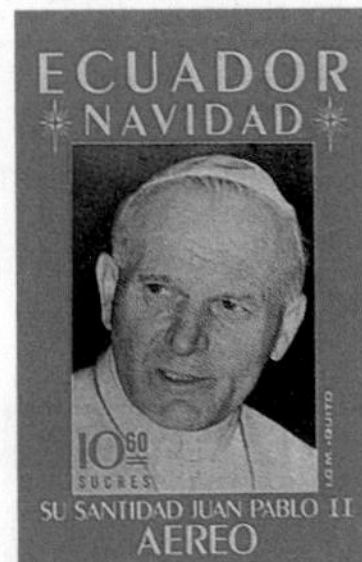

520 Pope John Paul II

1980. Christmas. Multicoloured.
1840 3s.40 Pope John Paul II with children (horiz) (postage) 30 15
1841 7s.60 Pope blessing crowd (air) 60 25
1842 10s.60 Type **520** 50 35

521 Carlos and Jorge Mantilla Ortega (editors)

1981. 75th Anniv of "El Comercio" (newspaper). Multicoloured.
1843 2s. Type **521** 15 10
1844 3s.40 Cesar and Carlos Mantilla Jacome 25 15

522 Oldest letter-box, Galapagos, 1793

1981. Air. Galapagos Islands.
1845 – 50s. yellow and black . . 3·00 2·25
1846 **522** 100s. multicoloured . . . 4·50 3·00
DESIGN—HORIZ: 50s. Turtle.

523 Flag, Map and Soldier

1981. National Defence. Multicoloured.
1847 3s.40 Type **523** 25 15
1848 3s.40 Flag, map and Pres. Roldos Aguilera 25 15

524 Theodore E. Gildred and "Ecuador 1"

525 Dr. Octavio Cordero Palacios

1981. 50th Anniv of Flight of "Ecuador 1" from San Diego to Quito.
1849 **524** 2s. black and blue . . . 30 15

1981. 50th Death Anniv (1980) of Dr. Octavio Cordero Palacios.
1850 **525** 2s. multicoloured 15 10

526 Miraculous Painting of the Virgin of Sorrows

527 Football Emblem

1981. 75th Anniv of Miracle of the Virgin blinking at San Gabriel College. Multicoloured.
1851 2s. Type **526** 15 10
1852 2s. San Gabriel College Church 15 10

1981. Air. World Cup Football Championship, Spain (1982). Multicoloured.
1853 7s.60 Type **527** 60 30
1854 10s.60 Footballer 90 45
1855 13s.60 World Cup trophy 1·10 55

528 Mendoza Aviles and Bridge

1981. Inauguration of Dr. Rafael Mendoza Aviles Bridge.
1857 **528** 2s. multicoloured 15 10

529 "Still-life"

1981. Air. Birth Centenary of Pablo Picasso (artist). Multicoloured.
1858 7s.60 Type **529** 35 30
1859 10s.60 "First Communion" (vert) 50 45
1860 13s.60 "Las Meninas" (vert) 60 55

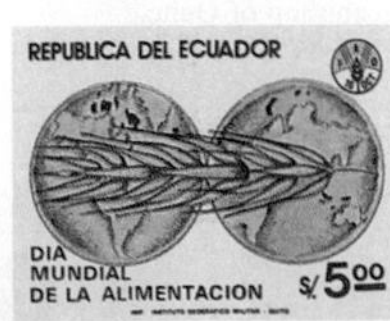

530 Ear of Wheat on World Map

1981. World Food Day. Multicoloured.
1862 5s. Type **530** (postage) . . . 40 20
1863 10s.60 Agricultural products and farmer sowing seed (air) 50 35

531 "Isla Salango" (freighter)

532 Person in Wheelchair

1982. 10th Anniv of Transnave Shipping Company.
1864 **531** 3s.50 multicoloured . . . 1·50 30

1982. International Year of Disabled Persons (1981).
1865 **532** 3s.40 brown, red and black (postage) . . . 30 15
1866 – 7s.60 silver, green and blue (air) 60 30
1867 – 10s.60 brn, blk and red 50 45
DESIGNS: 7s.60, I.Y.D.P. emblem; 10s.60, Man breaking crutch.

533 Gateway, Quito

534 Flags of Member Countries and Emblem

1982. "Quitex '82" National Stamp Exn.
1868 **533** 2s. yellow, brown & blk 15 10
1869 – 3s. yellow, brown & blk 20 10
DESIGN. 3s. Old houses, Quito.

1982. 22nd American Air Forces' Commanders Conference.
1871 **534** 5s. multicoloured 40 20

535 Juan Montalvo (after C. A. Villacres)

536 Swimming Pool

1982. 150th Birth Anniv of Juan Montalvo (writer).
1872 **535** 2s. pink, brown and black (postage) . . . 15 10
1873 – 3s. multicoloured 20 10
1874 – 5s. multicoloured (air) 35 20
DESIGNS—VERT: 3s. Mausoleum. HORIZ: 5s. Montalvo's villa.

1982. World Swimming Championships, Guayaquil. Multicoloured.
1875 1s.80 Type **536** (postage) . . 20 10
1876 3s.40 Water polo 30 10
1877 10s.20 Games emblem (vert) (air) 60 50
1878 14s.20 Diving (vert) 85 70

537 Juan Leon Mera (after Victor Mideros)

538 "The Ecstasy of St. Theresa" (detail of sculpture by Bernini)

1982. 150th Birth Anniv of Juan Leon Mera (author).
1879 **537** 5s.40 brn, blk & lt brn 30 15
1880 – 6s. multicoloured 40 15
DESIGN: 6s. Statue of Mera, Ambato.

1983. 400th Death Anniv of St. Theresa of Avila.
1881 **538** 2s. multicoloured 15 10

539 Pres. and Martha Roldos and Independence Monument

1983. Air. 2nd Death Anniv of President and Martha Roldos.
1882 **539** 13s.60 multicoloured . . 35 35

540 Californian Sealions

541 Statue of Rocafuerte in Guayaquil

1983. 150th Anniv of Ecuadorian Rule over Galapagos Islands and Death Centenary of Charles Darwin (evolutionary biologist). Multicoloured.
1883 3s. Type **540** 10 10
1884 5s. James's flamingoes and inset portrait of Darwin 1·50 30

1983. Birth Bicentenary of Vicente Rocafuerte Bejarano (President, 1835–39). Multicoloured.
1885 5s. Type **541** 20 10
1886 20s. Painting of Rocafuerte 45 35

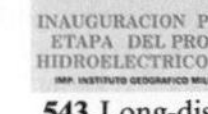

542 Bolivar (after Antonio Salguero)

543 Long-distance View of Daniel Palacios Dam

1983. Birth Bicentenary of Simon Bolivar.
1887 **542** 20s. multicoloured . . . 45 35

1983. Inauguration of First Stage of Paute Hydro-electric Project. Multicoloured.
1888 5s. Type **543** 20 10
1889 10s. Close-up of dam . . . 40 15

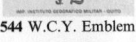

544 W.C.Y. Emblem

545 Bolivar and Bananas

1983. World Communications Year.
1891 **544** 2s. multicoloured 10 10

1983. Centenaries of Provinces of Bolivar and El Oro.
1892 **545** 3s. multicoloured 10 10

546 Atahualpa

547 "Holy Family"

1984. 450th Death Anniv (1983) of Atahualpa (last Inca emperor).

1893 **546** 15s. multicoloured . . . 20 10

1984. Christmas. Multicoloured.

1894 5s. Type **547** 10 10

1895 5s. Jesus and the lawyers . . 10 10

1896 5s. Marzipan kings 10 10

1897 6s. Marzipan preacher (vert) 10 10

548 Visit to Brazil

1984. President Hurtado's International Policies. Multicoloured.

1898 8s. Type **548** 10 10

1899 9s. Visit to China 15 10

1900 24s. Addressing U.N. General Assembly 15 10

1901 28s. Meeting President Reagan of U.S.A. 20 15

1902 29s. Visit to Caracas, Venezuela, for Bolivar's birth bicentenary 45 15

1903 37s. Opening Latin-American Economic Conference, Quito 60 20

549 Diaz and Scales

1984. Birth Centenary of Miguel Diaz Cueva (lawyer).

1904 **549** 10s. multicoloured . . . 25 10

550 Games Emblem

551 Montgolfier Balloon

1984. Winter Olympic Games, Sarajevo. Mult.

1905 2s. Type **550** 10 10

1906 4s. Ice skating 10 10

1907 6s. Ice skating (different) . . 15 10

1908 10s. Skiing 15 10

1984. Bicent of Manned Fight (1983). Mult.

1910 3s. Type **551** 10 10

1911 6s. Charles's hydrogen balloon 20 10

552 La Marimba (dance)

1984. "San Mateo '83" Provincial Stamp Exhibition, Esmeraldas.

1913 **552** 8s. multicoloured 10 10

553 Language Academy

554 Yerovi

1984. Canonization of Brother Miguel. Mult.

1915 9s. Type **553** 10 10

1916 24s. Pope, St. Miguel and St. Peter's, Rome (vert) 35 25

1984. 165th Birth Anniv of Jose Maria de Jesus Yerovi, Archbishop of Quito.

1918 **554** 5s. multicoloured 15 10

555 Pope's Arms

556 Mercedes de Jesus Molina

1985. Visit of Pope John Paul II. Mult.

1919 1s.60 Type **555** 10 10

1920 5s. Pope holding crucifix . . 10 10

1921 9s. Map of papal route . . 15 10

1922 28s. Pope waving 35 20

1923 29s. Pope 40 20

1985. Beatification of Mercedes de Jesus Molina. Multicoloured.

1925 1s.60 Type **556** 10 10

1926 5s. "Madonna of Czestochowa" (icon) . . . 10 10

1927 9s. "Our Lady of La Alborada" (statue) . . . 10 10

557 Hummingbird

558 Exhibition Emblem

1985. Samuel Valarezo Delgado (ornithologist and former Director of Posts).

1929 **557** 2s. red, green & brown 30 15

1930 – 3s. green, yellow and bl 10 10

1931 – 6s. black and brown . . 10 10

DESIGNS: 3s. Sailfish and tuna; 6s. Valarezo Delgado.

1985. "Espana 84" International Stamp Exhibition, Madrid.

1932 **558** 6s. brn & cinnamon . . 10 10

1933 – 10s. brn & cinnamon . . 15 10

DESIGN: 10s. Spanish royal family.

559 Dr. Pio Jaramallo Alvarado

560 Sugar Cane and Water Tower

1985. Death Centenary (1984) of Dr. Pio Jaramallo Alvarado (historian).

1935 **559** 6s. multicoloured 15 10

1985. Centenary of Valdez Sugar Refinery. Mult.

1936 50s. Type **560** 60 25

1937 100s. Rafael Valdez Cervantes (founder) . . . 1·25 50

561 Emblem

1985. 10th Anniv of Chamber of Commerce.

1939 **561** 24s. multicoloured . . . 30 20

1940 28s. multicoloured . . . 35 25

562 Emblem

1985. 50th Anniv of Ecuador Philatelic Association. Multicoloured.

1942 25s. Type **562** 30 15

1943 30s. Philatelic Exhibition 1s. stamp, 1936 (horiz) . . . 35 20

563 Fire Engine, 1882

564 Children and Tree

1985. 150th Anniv of Guayaquil Fire Station. Multicoloured.

1944 6s. Type **563** 10 10

1945 10s. Fire-engine, 1899 . . . 10 10

1946 20s. Fire service anniversary emblem 20 10

1985. Infant Survival Campaign.

1947 **564** 10s. multicoloured . . . 10 10

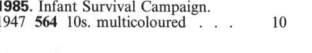

565 Israeli Aircraft Industry Kfir-C2

566 Boxer

1985. Armed Forces. Multicoloured.

1948 10s. Type **565** (65th anniv of Air Force) 30 10

1949 10s. Seaman and gunboat "Calderon" (centenary of Navy) . . . . 1·25 30

1950 10s. Insignia (30th anniv of Parachute Regiment) . . 40 25

1985. Bolivar Games, Cuenca. Each silver, blue and red.

1951 10s. Type **566** 15 10

1952 25s. Gymnast 30 20

1953 30s. Discus thrower 35 25

567 "Royal Audience Quarter, Quito" (J. M. Roura)

568 U.N. Emblem

1985. First National Philatelic Congress and "50th Anniv of Ecuador Philatelic Association" Stamp Exhibition, Quito.

1954 **567** 5s. black, yellow & orge 10 10

1955 – 10s. black, green & red 20 10

1956 – 15s. black, blue and red 20 10

1957 – 20s. black, red and lilac 30 15

DESIGNS—VERT: 10s. "Riobamba Cathedral" (O. Munoz). HORIZ: 15s. "House of a Hundred Windows, Guayaquil" (J.M. Roura); 20s. "Rural House, near Cuenca" (J.M. Roura).

1985. 40th Anniv of U.N.O. Multicoloured.

1959 10s. Type **568** 15 10

1960 20s. State flag 30 15

569 Child on Donkey

570 "Embotrium grandiforum"

1985. Christmas. Multicoloured.

1962 5s. Type **569** 10 10

1963 10s. Food display 15 10

1964 15s. Child seated upon display 20 10

1986. Flowers. Multicoloured.

1966 24s. Type **570** 35 15

1967 28s. Orchid ("Topobea" sp.) 35 15

1968 29s. "Befaria resinosa mutis" 35 15

571 Land Iguana

1986. Galapagos Islands. Multicoloured.

1970 10s. Type **571** 15 10

1971 20s. Californian sealion . . 25 15

1972 30s. Magnificent frigate birds . . . . 1·50 80

1973 40s. Galapagos penguins . . 1·75 1·10

1974 50s. Tortoise (25th anniv (1984) of Charles Darwin Foundation) 60 30

1975 100s. Charles Darwin (150th anniv (1985) of visit) . . 3·00 1·40

1976 200s. Bishop Tomas de Berlanga and map (450th anniv (1985) of Islands' discovery) . . . . 2·10 1·40

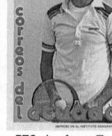

572 Antonio Ortiz Mena (President)

573 Andres Gomez Santos

1986. 25th Anniv (1985) of Inter-American Development Bank. Multicoloured.

1978 5s. Type **572** 10 10

1979 10s. Felipe Herrera (President, 1960–71) . . . 15 10

1980 50s. Emblem 75 30

1986. 75th Anniv (1985) of Guayaquil Tennis Club. Multicoloured.

1981 10s. Type **573** 15 10

1982 10s. Francisco Segura Cano 15 10

1983 10s. Emblem (horiz) 15 10

574 Prawn

1986. Exports. Seafoods.

1984 **574** 35s. red and blue 35 20

1985 – 40s. green and red . . . 60 20

1986 – 45s. yellow & mauve . . 65 25

DESIGNS: 40s. Yellow-finned tuna; 45s. Pacific sardines in tin.

575 Goalkeeper diving for Ball

1986. World Cup Football Championship, Mexico. Multicoloured.

1988 5s. Type **575** 10 10

1989 10s. Player tackling 15 10

576 Betancourt and Cordero

1986. Rumichaca Meeting of Pres. Belisario Betancourt of Colombia and Pres. Leon Febres Cordero of Ecuador. Multicoloured.
1991 20s. Type **576** 20 15
1992 20s. Presidents embracing 20 15

577 Charles-Marie de La Condamine

1986. 250th Anniv of First Geodetic Expedition (to measure Arcs of Meridian).
1993 **577** 10s. green and light green 15 10
1994 – 15s. violet and lilac . . . 15 10
1995 – 20s. green and brown . . 20 10
DESIGNS: No. 1994, Maldonado; 1995, Centre of World Monument, Quito.

578 Emblem of Pichincha Chamber of Trade
579 National Railways Emblem

1986. 50th Anniversaries of Chambers of Trade.
1997 **578** 10s. black and brown . . 10 10
1998 – 10s. black and blue . . . 10 10
1999 – 10s. black and green . . 10 10
DESIGNS: No. 1998, Cuenca; 1999, Guayaquil.

1986. 57th Anniv of Ministry of Public Works and Communications. Multicoloured.
2000 5s. Type **579** . . . . 2·75 75
2001 10s. Post Office emblem . . 10 10
2002 15s. IETEL (telecommunications) emblem 15 10
2003 20s. Ministry of Public Works emblem 20 15

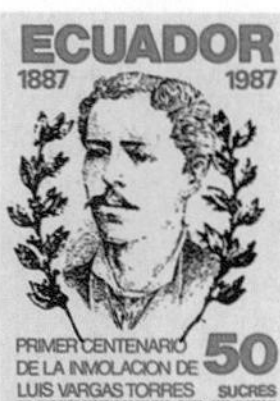
580 Emblem
581 Vargas

1987. 50th Anniv of First Zone Chamber of Agriculture.
2004 **580** 5s. multicoloured 10 10

1988. Death Centenary of Luis Vargas Torres (revolutionary).
2005 **581** 50s. black, gold & grn 40 20
2006 – 100s. blue, gold and red 1·00 35
DESIGN: No. 2006, Group of soldiers.

582 Las Penas Quarter

1988. 450th Anniv of Guayaquil City. Mult.
2008 15s. Type **582** 10 10
2009 30s. Rafael Mendoza Aviles Bridge of National Unity (horiz) 20 10
2010 40s. Federico de Orellana (founder) (horiz) 15 15

583 Family within Hands

1988. 60th Anniv of Social Security Work. Multicoloured.
2011 50s. Type **583** 30 20
2012 100s. Anniversary emblem 55 35

584 Yaguarcocha Lake

1988. Death Centenary of Dr. Pedro Moncayo y Esparza (politician). Multicoloured.
2013 10s. Type **584** 10 10
2014 15s. Dr. Moncayo 10 10
2015 20s. Dr. Moncayo's house 10 10

585 Junkers F-13 Seaplane

1988. 60th Anniv of Avianca National Airline. Multicoloured.
2017 10s. Type **585** 10 10
2018 20s. Dornier Wal flying boat 10 10
2019 30s. Ford "Tin Goose" . . 15 10
2020 40s. Boeing 247D 20 10
2021 50s. Boeing 720-059D . . . 25 15
2022 100s. Douglas DC-3 . . . . 45 25
2023 200s. Boeing 727-200 . . . 1·40 50
2024 300s. Sikorsky S-38 flying boat . . . . 2·00 1·00
2025 500s. Anniversary emblem (vert) . . . . 3·25 1·60

586 New Building

1988. 125th Anniv of San Gabriel College. Multicoloured.
2026 15s. Type **586** 10 10
2027 35s. Door of old building 25 10

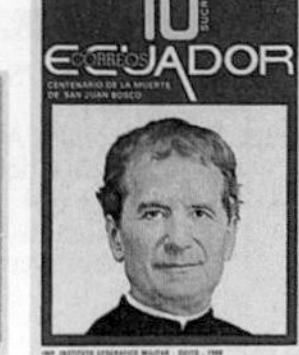
587 Institute
588 St. John Bosco

1988. 60th Anniv of Military Geographical Institute, Quito. Multicoloured.
2028 25s. Type **587** 25 10
2029 50s. Inside planetarium . . 35 20
2030 60s. Anniversary emblem . . 40 20
2031 500s. Mural by E. Kingman 3·25 1·60
No. 2028 was issued surcharged 800s. on 25 June 1996. Only a few sets were made available to the public at face value, the remainder sold by postal employees at considerably inflated prices.

1988. Centenary of Salesian Brothers in Ecuador and Death Centenary of St. John Bosco (founder). Multicoloured.
2033 10s. Type **588** 10 10
2034 50s. Group of Brothers . . 25 20

589 Dr. Francisco Campos Coello (founder)
590 Bank

1988. Cent of Guayaquil Welfare Society.
2036 **589** 15s. multicoloured . . . 10 10
2037 – 20s. multicoloured . . . 10 10
2038 – 45s. black, silver & blue 10 10
DESIGNS: 20s. Eduardo M. Arosemena (first Director); 45s. Emblem.
No. 2038 was issued surcharged 2600s. on 25 June 1996. Only a few sets were made available to the public at face value, the remainder sold by postal employees at considerably inflated prices.

1989. 75th Anniv (1988) of Azuay Bank, Cuenca. Multicoloured.
2040 20s. Type **590** 10 10
2041 40s. Bank (vert) 10 10

591 Athletics
592 "Bird" (sculpture, Joaquin Tinta)

1989. Olympic Games, Seoul (1988). Designs showing Hodori the Tiger (mascot).
2043 10s. Type **591** 10 10
2044 20s. Boxing 10 10
2045 30s. Cycling 10 10
2046 40s. Shooting 10 10
2047 100s. Swimming 20 10
2048 200s. Weightlifting 75 20
2049 300s. Taekwondo . . . . . 1·10 60

1989. 50th Anniv of Ruminahui State. Mult.
2051 50s. Type **592** 10 10
2052 70s. Sangolqui church (horiz) 15 15

593 Dr. Carrion Mora
594 "The Gilt Mirror" (Myrna Baez)

1989. Birth Centenary of Dr. Benjamin Carrion Mora (writer). Multicoloured.
2054 50s. Type **593** 10 10
2055 70s. Loja (horiz) 15 15
2056 1000s. Loja university (horiz) . . . . 3·75 1·90

1989. 2nd Art Biennale, Cuenca. Mult.
2058 40s. Type **594** 10 10
2059 70s. "Paraguay III" (Carlos Colombino) (vert) 15 15
2060 180s. "Modulation 892" (Julio Le Parc) (vert) . . 75 20

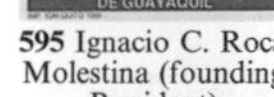

595 Ignacio C. Roca Molestina (founding President)
596 Emblems

1989. Centenary of Guayaquil Chamber of Commerce. Multicoloured.
2062 50s. Type **595** 10 10
2063 300s. Chamber building (horiz) . . . . 1·10 60
2064 500s. Trade and progress symbol (horiz) . . . . . 1·90 95

1989. 60th Anniv of Ministry of Public Works and Communications. Multicoloured.
2066 50s. Type **596** 90 40
2067 100s. IETEL emblem (telecommunications) . . 20 10
2068 200s. Ministry of Public Works emblem 75 20

597 Birds
598 Red Cross Worker

1989. Bicent of French Revolution. Mult.
2070 20s. Type **597** 10 10
2071 50s. Cathedral fresco (horiz) 10 10
2072 100s. French cock 20 10

1989. 125th Anniv of Red Cross in Ecuador. Multicoloured.
2074 10s. Type **598** 10 10
2075 30s. Emblem (horiz) 10 10
2076 200s. Masked Red Cross workers (horiz) 75 20

599 Montalvo's Tomb

1989. Death Cent of Juan Montalvo (writer).
2077 50s. Type **599** 10 10
2078 100s. Photograph of Montalvo 45 10
2079 200s. Statue of Montalvo . . 90 45

600 Dr. Jaramillo Leon (founder)

1990. 70th Anniv of Cuenca Chamber of Commerce. Multicoloured.
2081 100s. Type **600** 30 15
2082 100s. Federico Malo Andrade (first Honorary President) 30 15
2083 130s. Roberto Crespo Toral (first President) 40 20
2084 200s. Alfonso Jaramillo Leon (founder of savings and credit departments) 60 25

601 Tolita Head-shaped Censer
602 Mercedes de Jesus Molina

1990. America. Pre-Columbian Artefacts. Mult.
2086 200s. Type **601** 25 25
2087 300s. Carchi plate with warrior design (horiz) . . 65 20

1990. Anniversaries. Multicoloured.
2088 100s. Type **602** (centenary of Marianitas) 30 15
2089 200s. Clock tower and roses on open book (centenary of Santa Mariana de Jesus College) 60 25

603 Mascot, Quarter Finalists and Ball

1990. World Cup Football Championship, Italy. Multicoloured.
2090 100s. Type **603** 30 15
2091 200s. Finalists' flags and player (vert) 60 25
2092 300s. Mascot, map and trophy (vert) 90 45

604 Emblem
606 Members' Flags

605 Iguana (Galapagos)

1990. 5th Population Census and 4th Housing Census. Multicoloured.
2094 100s. Type **604** 25 10
2095 200s. Logo of National Statistics and Census Institute (horiz) 50 25
2096 300s. Pencil and population statistics 75 20

1990. Tourism. Multicoloured.
2098 100s. Type **605** 25 10
2099 200s. Church of Companionship (Quito) (vert) 50 25
2100 300s. Old man of Vilcabamba 75 20

1990. 30th Anniv of Organization of Petroleum Exporting Countries. Multicoloured.
2102 200s. Type **606** 50 25
2103 300s. Emblem 75 20

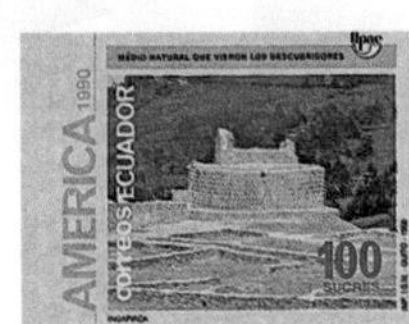
607 Anniversary Emblem
608 "Blakea sp."

1990. 25th Anniv of Organization for Preservation of Traditional Handicrafts. Multicoloured.
2104 200s. Type **607** 50 25
2105 300s. Carved and painted parrots 75 20

1990. Flowers. Multicoloured.
2107 100s. Type **608** . . 10 10
2108 100s. "Loasa sp." 10 10
2109 100s. "Cattleya sp." 10 10
2110 100s. "Sobralia sp." (horiz) 10 10

609 Ingapirca

1991. America. World found by the Discoverers. Multicoloured.
2111 100s. Type **609** 10 10
2112 200s. Forest pool 50 25

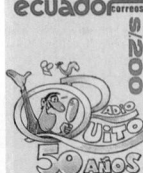

610 Globe and Means of Information
611 Broadcaster

1991. 50th Anniv of National Journalists' Federation. Multicoloured.
2113 200s. Type **610** 50 25
2114 300s. Eugenio Espejo . . . 75 20
2115 400s. Emblem . . . . . . 1·00 50

1991. 50th Anniv of Radio Quito. Mult.
2116 200s. Type **611** 20 20
2117 500s. Family listening to radio (horiz) 90 35

612 Suarez
613 Columbus's Ships

1991. Birth Cent of Dr. Pablo Arturo Suarez.
2118 **612** 70s. multicoloured . . . 15 10

1991. America. Multicoloured.
2119 200s. Type **613** 45 30
2120 500s. Columbus and landing party . . . . 1·25 55

614 Cat-shaped Censer
615 Hand and Woman's Face

1991. Archaeology. La Tolita Culture (1st series). Multicoloured.
2121 100s. Type **614** 10 10
2122 200s. Head of old man . . . 20 10
2123 300s. Human/animal statuette 60 20
See also No. 2144.

1991. No Violence to Women Day. Mult.
2124 300s. Type **615** 60 20
2125 500s. Woman's profile and hand 95 30

616 Presidents Borja and Paz Zamora

1991. Visit of President Jaime Paz Zamora of Bolivia.
2126 **616** 500s. multicoloured . . . 95 30

617 Jijon y Caamano

1991. Birth Centenary of Jacinto Jijon y Caamano (historian and geographer).
2127 **617** 200s. multicoloured . . . 20 10
2128 – 300s. blue, blk & mve . . 60 20
DESIGN—HORIZ: 300s. Books and Jijon y Caamano.

618 Pres. Borja

1992. President Rodrigo Borja's Speech to United Nations. Multicoloured.
2129 100s. Type **618** 10 10
2130 1000s. Map and flags of U.N. Security Council members . . . . 1·60 65

619 "Calderon" (gunboat) and Rafael Moran Valverde

1992. 50th Anniv (1991) of Battle of Jambeli. Multicoloured.
2131 300s. Type **619** 60 15
2132 500s. "Atahualpa" (despatch vessel) and Victor Naranjo Fiallo 95 30

620 Land Iguana

1992. Galapagos Islands Animals.
2134 100s. Type **620** 15 10
2135 100s. Giant tortoise 15 10
2136 100s. Swallow-tailed gull . . 55 30
2137 100s. Great frigate bird ("Fregata minor") 55 30
2138 100s. Galapagos penguin (vert) 55 30
2139 100s. Californian sea-lion (vert) 15 10

621 College

1992. 150th Anniv (1991) of Vicente Rocafuerte National College, Guayaquil. Multicoloured.
2140 200s. Type **621** 15 10
2141 400s. Vicente Rocafuerte (Ecuador President 1835–39 and College founder) 65 15

622 Alfaro
623 Ceremonial Mask

1992. 150th Birth Anniv of General Eloy Alfaro. Multicoloured.
2142 300s. Type **622** 20 10
2143 700s. Alfaro's house (horiz) 1·00 30

1992. Archaeology. La Tolita Culture (2nd series).
2144 **623** 400s. multicoloured . . . 60 15

624 "Santa Maria"

1992. America. 500th Anniv of Discovery of America by Columbus. Multicoloured.
2145 200s. Type **624** 60 20
2146 400s. Columbus and map of Americas (vert) 70 15

625 Cordova
626 Narcisa de Jesus

1992. Birth Centenary of Andres Cordova (President, 1940).
2147 **625** 300s. multicoloured . . . 45 10

1992. Beatification of Narcisa de Jesus.
2148 **626** 100s. multicoloured . . . 10 10

627 Infant Jesus
628 Velasco (statue)

1992. Christmas. Multicoloured.
2149 300s. Type **627** 45 10
2150 600s. Children, lamb and baby Jesus . . . . 1·00 25

1992. Death Bicentenary of Juan de Velasco.
2151 **628** 200s. multicoloured . . . 15 10

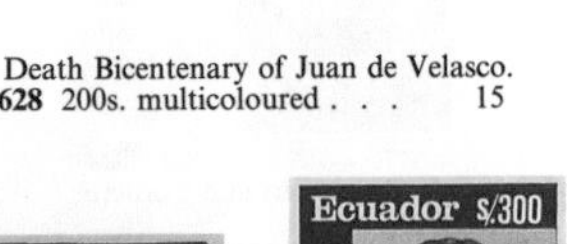

629 "Atelopus bomolochos"
630 Paez

1993. Frogs. Multicoloured.
2152 300s. Type **629** 20 10
2153 300s. Spurrell's tree frog ("Agalychnis spurrelli") 20 10
2154 600s. "Hyla picturata" . . . 40 20
2155 600s. "Gastrotheca plumbea" 40 20
2156 900s. Splendid poison-arrow frog ("Dendrobates" sp.) 60 25
2157 900s. "Sphaenorhynchus lacteus" 60 25

1993. Birth Centenary of J. Roberto Paez (co-founder of social security system and writer).
2158 **630** 300s. blue 20 10

631 1907 3c. Robles Stamp
632 Arms

1993. Death Centenary of Francisco Robles Garcia (President 1856–59).
2159 **631** 500s. multicoloured . . . 60 15

1993. National Police.
2160 **632** 300s. multicoloured . . . 45 10

633 Velasco

1993. Birth Centenary of Jose Maria Velasco Ibarra (President, 1934–35, 1944–47, 1952–56, 1960–61 and 1968–72).
2161 **633** 500s. multicoloured . . . 60 15

634 Lantern Fly

1993. Insects. Multicoloured.
2162 150s. Type **634** 10 10
2163 200s. "Semiotus ligneus" . . 15 10
2164 300s. "Taeniotes pulverulenta" 45 10
2165 400s. Orange tiger caterpillar 55 15
2166 600s. "Erotylus onagga" . . 85 20
2167 700s. Carpenter bee . . . . 1·00 20

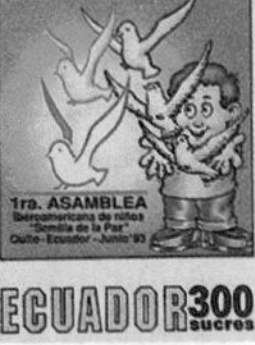
635 Cevallos Villacreces
636 Boy releasing Doves

1993. Death Centenary of Pedro Fermin Cevallos Villacreces (historian and founder of Language Academy).
2168 **635** 1000s. multicoloured . . 1·25 55

1993. 1st Latin-American Children's Peace Assembly, Quito.
2169 **636** 300s. multicoloured . . . 45 10

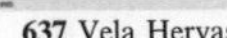

637 Vela Hervas

638 "Cinchonia cordifolia"

1993. 150th Birth Anniv of Juan Benigno Vela Hervas (politician).
2170 **637** 2000s. multicoloured . . 2·50 1·00

1993. 250th Anniv of Maldonado and La Condamine's Amazon Expedition. Multicoloured.
2171 150s. Type **638** 10 10
2172 250s. Pedro Maldonado . . 15 10
2173 1500s. Charles de la Condamine . . . . 1·75 65

639 Anniversary Emblem

1993. 300th Anniv of Faculty of Medical Sciences, Ecuador Central University.
2174 **639** 300s. multicoloured . . . 45 10

640 Bustamante

642 Arroyo del Rio

641 Pacarana

1993. Birth Centenary of Guillermo Bustamante (writer).
2175 **640** 1500s. multicoloured . . 2·10 75

1993. America. Endangered Animals. Mult.
2176 400s. Type **641** 30 15
2177 800s. Chestnut-fronted macaw (vert) . . . . . . 1·90 75

1993. Birth Centenary of Dr. Carlos Arroyo del Rio (President, 1939–44).
2178 **642** 500s. multicoloured . . . 60 15

643 "Nativity" (ivory nut carvings)

644 Scouts Emblem and Map on Wall

1993. Christmas. Multicoloured.
2179 600s. Type **643** 70 15
2180 900s. Madonna and Child in landscape (vert) . . . . . 1·10 45

1994. Scouting Movement.
2181 **644** 400s. multicoloured . . . 50 10

645 Emblem

646 Donoso

1994. International Year of the Family.
2182 **645** 300s. red, green & black 15 10

1994. Birth Cent of Dr. Julio Tobar Donoso.
2183 **646** 500s. multicoloured . . . 80 40

647 "Sobralia dichotoma"

648 Cabezas

1994. 1st Andean Orchid Conservation Convention. Multicoloured.
2184 150s. Type **647** 10 10
2185 150s. "Dracula hirtzii" . . . 10 10
2186 300s. "Encyclia pulcherrima" 40 10
2187 300s. "Lepanthes delhierroi" 40 10
2188 600s. "Masdevallia rosea" 70 40
2189 600s. "Telipogon andicola" 70 40

1994. Death Cent of Dr. Miguel Egas Cabezas.
2190 **648** 100s. multicoloured . . . 10 10

649 Gonzalez Suarez

650 Earth as Football

1994. 150th Birth Anniv of Federico Gonzalez Suarez, Archbishop of Quito.
2191 **649** 200s. multicoloured . . . 10 10

1994. World Cup Football Championship, U.S.A. Multicoloured.
2192 300s. Type **650** 50 10
2193 600s. Striker (mascot) . . . 1·10 45
2194 900s. Footballer . . . . . . 1·75 70

651 Cyclists on "Road" of National Colours to Equator Monument

652 Espinosa Polit

1994. International Junior Cycling Championship, Quito. Multicoloured.
2196 300s. Type **651** 15 10
2197 400s. Stylized cyclist and monument (vert) 20 10

1994. Birth Centenary of Father Aurelio Espinosa Polit (writer).
2198 **652** 200s. multicoloured . . . 35 10

653 Pedro Vicente Maldonado Research Station

1994. Ecuador's Presence in Antarctica. Mult.
2199 600s. Type **653** . . . . . . 1·10 45
2200 900s. "Orion" (survey ship) 1·75 70

654 Anniversary Emblem

1994. Centenary of National Lottery.
2201 **654** 1000s. multicoloured . . 2·00 80

655 Benjamon Carrion (founder)

1994. 50th Anniv of House of Ecuadorean Culture. Multicoloured.
2202 700s. Type **655** . . . . . . 1·25 60
2203 900s. House of Culture (horiz) . . . . 1·75 70

656 Worker and "75"

1994. 75th Anniv of I.L.O.
2204 **656** 100s. multicoloured . . . 10 10

657 Globe and Postal Emblem

1994. Christmas. Multicoloured.
2205 600s. Type **657** 25 10
2206 900s. Nativity (vert) 40 20

658 Airplane and Sack of Mail

659 Mera's Country Villa

1994. America. Postal Transport. Mult.
2207 600s. Type **658** 25 10
2208 600s. Airplane, ship and van (horiz) 40 10

1994. Death Centenary of Juan Leon Mera (author). Multicoloured.
2209 600s. Type **659** 50 10
2210 900s. Mera (after Victor Mideros) . . . . 1·25 60

660 Sucre

1995. Birth Bicent of Marshal Antonio Jose de Sucre (first Bolivian President). Multicoloured.
2211 1500s. Type **660** . . . . . 1·25 55
2212 2000s. Sucre (looking to left) 1·75 70

661 Escriva

663 Girl

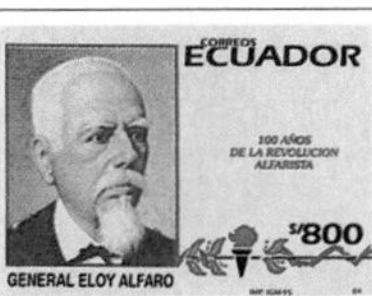

662 Eloy Alfaro (President 1897–1901 and 1907–11)

1995. 3rd Anniv of Beatification of Josemaria Escriva de Balaguer (founder of Opus Dei).
2214 **661** 900s. multicoloured . . . 75 20

1995. Centenary of Alfarist Revolution.
2215 **662** 800s. multicoloured . . . 70 15

1995. 50th Anniv of CARE (Co-operative for Assistance and Remittances Overseas).
2216 **663** 400s. black, grn & gold 20 10
2217 – 800s. multicoloured . . . 70 15
DESIGN—HORIZ: 800s. People working land.

664 Soldier thinking of Children

1995. "Peace with Dignity". Multicoloured.
2218 200s. Type **664** 10 10
2219 400s. Hand holding Ecuador flag (25 × 34 mm) 20 10
2220 800s. Soldier amongst bamboo 70 15

No. 2118 was issued surcharged 200s. on 25 June 1996. Only a few sets were made available to the public at face value, the remainder sold by postal employees at considerably inflated prices.

665 Anniversary Emblem

666 "Our Lady of Cisne" (statue, Diego de Robles)

1995. 25th Anniv of Andean Development Corporation.
2221 **665** 1000s. multicoloured . . 1·10 45

1995.
2222 **666** 500s. multicoloured . . . 45 10

667 Anniversary Emblem

668 Anniversary Emblem

1995. 35th Anniv of INNFA (child welfare organization).
2223 **667** 400s. multicoloured . . . 20 10

1995. 50th Anniv of U.N.O.
2224 **668** 1000s. blue, gold & blk 95 45

669 Man with Book (preparation for natural disasters)

1995. International Decade for the Reduction of Natural Disasters. Ecuador Civil Defence Organization. Multicoloured.
2225 1000s. Type **669** 90 45
2226 1000s. Family hiding beneath table (protection) 95 45
2227 1000s. Couple escaping from flooded house (maintenance of elevated refugee centres) 95 45
2228 1000s. Children planting sapling (reforestation) . . 95 45
2229 1000s. Family escaping erupting volcano (awareness of warning signs) 95 45

670 Emblem

1995. 50th Anniv of F.A.O.
2230 **670** 1300s. multicoloured . . 1·25 55

671 Woman, Piano and Book

1995. 50th Anniv of Women's Cultural Club.
2231 **671** 1500s. multicoloured . . 1·40 60

672 Emblem

1995. 39th Annual Assembly of Inter-American Philately Federation.
2232 **672** 1000s. blue and red . . . 95 40

673 Combat Planes flying over Mountains

674 Long-tailed Sylphs ("Aglaiocercus kingi")

1995. 75th Anniv of Ecuadorean Air Force.
2233 **673** 1000s. multicoloured . . 95 40

1995. Hummingbirds. Multicoloured.
2234 1000s. Type **674** . . . . . 1·00 40
2235 1000s. Collared incas ("Coeligena torquata") . . 1·00 40
2236 1000s. Long-tailed hermits ("Phaethornis superciliosus") . . . . . 1·00 40
2237 1000s. Booted racquet-tails ("Ocreatus underwoodii") 1·00 40
2238 1000s. Chimbarazo hillstars ("Oreotrochilus chimborazo") . . . . . . 1·00 40
2239 1000s. Violet-tailed sylphs ("Aglaiocercus coelestis") 1·00 40

675 "World Post" (Gishella Alejandro Reyes)

676 Jaramillo

1995. Christmas. Children's Painting Competition Winners. Multicoloured.
2240 2000s. Type **675** . . . . . 2·00 80
2241 2600s. "Procession" (Juan Jaramillo Leon) . . . . . 2·50 1·00

1996. National Music Year. 60th Birth Anniv of Julio Jaramillo (singer and composer). Multicoloured.
2242 **676** 2000s. multicoloured . . 2·00 80

677 Envelope (postal service)

1996. Modernization of the State. Multicoloured.
2244 1000s. Emblem . . . . . . 1·10 40
2245 1500s. Type **677** . . . . . 1·50 70
2246 2000s. Two-way arrow (customs clearance) . . . 2·10 90
2247 2600s. Telecommunications 2·50 1·00
2248 3000s. Ports . . . . 3·25 1·40

678 Table Tennis and Boxing

1996. 8th National Games, Esmeraldas. Multicoloured.
2249 400s. Type **678** 40 20
2250 400s. Basketball and football 40 20
2251 600s. Tennis and swimming 55 30
2252 800s. Weight-lifting and karate 75 35
2253 1000s. Volleyball and gymnastics 95 45
2254 1200s. Athletics and judo . . 1·10 55
2255 2000s. Chess and wrestling 2·00 90

679 Airplane and Emblem

1996. 50th Anniv of Civil Aviation Organization.
2257 **679** 2000s. multicoloured . . 2·00 90

680 Mascot

1996. Olympic Games, Atlanta. Multicoloured.
2258 1000s. Type **680** . . . . . 1·00 45
2259 2000s. Ecuador Olympic emblem . . . . 1·75 90
2260 3000s. Jefferson Perez (gold medal, 20km walk) (vert) 2·75 1·40

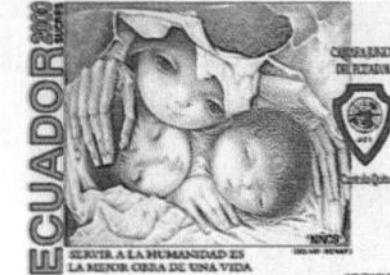

681 Mother and Children

1996. 40th Anniv of International Junior Chambers. Multicoloured.
2262 2000s. Type **681** . . . . . 1·25 1·25
2263 2600s. "Tree of Life" (relief, Eduardo Vega) (vert) . . 1·60 1·60

682 University Building (Munoz Marino)

1996. 50th Anniv of Catholic University of Ecuador. Multicoloured.
2264 400s. Type **682** 25 25
2265 800s. Window (Munoz Marino) (vert) 50 50
2266 2000s. University emblem 1·25 1·25

683 Gomez

684 Syringe and Outline Map of Ecuador

1996. Birth Centenary (1995) of Eduardo Salzar Gomez (lawyer and politician).
2267 **683** 1000s. multicoloured . . 60 60

1996. Anti-drugs Campaign.
2268 **684** 2000s. multicoloured . . 1·25 1·25

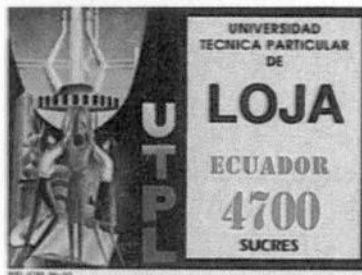

685 Emblem

1996. 25th Anniv of Private Technical University, Loja.
2269 **685** 4700s. multicoloured . . 2·75 2·75

686 Lorito (mascot)

1996. 50th Anniv of United Nations International Children's Emergency Fund.
2270 **686** 2000s. multicoloured . . 1·25 1·25

687 Headquarters

1996. 75th Anniv of *El Universo* (newspaper).
2271 **687** 2000s. multicoloured . . 1·25 1·25

688 Globe and Letters (Maria Belen Canas)

1996. Christmas. Designs showing winning entries in children's painting competition. Multicoloured.
2272 600s. Type **688** 35 35
2273 800s. Globe and dove (Beatriz Santana) 50 50
2274 2000s. Child in bed and bird (Oscar Perugachi) (54 × 34 mm) . . . . . . 1·25 1·25

689 Andean Condor *(Vultur grypus)*

1996. America (1995). Endangered Species. Multicoloured.
2275 1000s. Type **689** 65 65
2276 1500s. Harpy eagle and chick (*Harpia harpyja*) (vert) 95 95

690 Child in Traditional Dress

1996. America. National Costume. Multicoloured.
2277 2600s. Type **690** 95 95
2278 2600s. Child wearing hat . . 3·25 3·25

691 Jose Mejia Lequerica and Institute Facade

1997. Centenary of Mejia National Institute.
2279 **691** 1000s. multicoloured . . 85 55

692 Emblem

1997. 75th Anniv of Escula Politecnica del Ejercito (military school).
2280 **692** 400s. multicoloured . . . 40 25

693 College

1997. 50th Anniv of National Experimental College, Ambato.
2281 **693** 600s. multicoloured . . . 55 35

694 Rocafuerte

696 *Actinote equatoria*

695 Emblem

1997. 150th Death Anniv of Vicente Rocafuerte (President 1835–39).
2282 **694** 400s. multicoloured . . . 40 25

1997. 49th International Congress of Americanists, Quito.
2283 **695** 2000s. multicoloured . . 1·75 1·10

1997. Butterflies. Multicoloured.
2284 400s. Type **696** 40 25
2285 600s. Tiger pierid (*Dismorphia amphione*) . . 50 30
2286 800s. *Marpesia corinna* . . . 65 40
2287 2000s. *Marpesia berania* . . 1·75 1·00
2288 2600s. *Morpho helenor* . . . 2·40 1·40

697 Emblem

1997. 66th Anniv of Ecuador Flying Club.
2289 **697** 2600s. multicoloured . . 2·40 1·40

698 *Epidendrum secundum*

1997. Orchids of Mazan Forest. Multicoloured.
2290 400s. Type **698** 40 25
2291 600s. *Epidendrum sp.* 55 35
2292 800s. *Oncidium cultratrum* 70 40
2293 2000s. *Oncidium sp. mariposa* . . . . 1·75 1·10
2294 2600s. *Pleurothalis corrulensis* . . . . 2·40 1·40

699 Quartz

700 Santa Claus carrying Envelopes (Maria Daniela Delgado)

1997. International Mining Congress, Cuenca. Minerals. Multicoloured.
2295 400s. Type **699** 40 25
2296 600s. Chalcopyrite 55 35
2297 800s. Gold 70 40
2298 2000s. Petrified wood . . . 1·75 1·10
2299 2600s. Iron pyrites . . . . 2·40 1·40

1997. Christmas. "Design a Stamp" Competition Winners. Multicoloured.
2300 400s. Type **700** 40 25
2301 2600s. Star on Christmas tree holding envelopes (Dora Pinargote Tejena) 2·40 1·40
2302 3000s. Child dreaming of Christmas tree of envelopes (Christina Pazmino Montano) . . . 2·75 1·75

701 Postman with Wings on Heels

702 Matilde Hidalgo de Procel (first female politician)

1997. America. The Postman. Multicoloured.
2303 800s. Type **701** 70 45
2304 2000s. Postman on bicycle 1·75 1·10

1998. International Women's Day.
2305 **702** 2000s. multicoloured . . 1·60 95

703 Acosta Solis

1998. Misael Acosta Solis (botanist) Commemoration.
2306 **703** 2000s. multicoloured . . 2·75 1·75

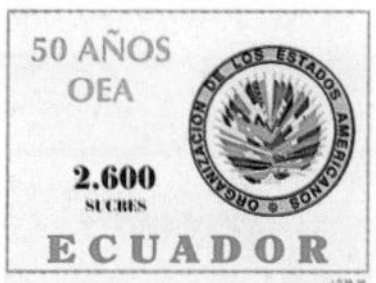

704 Emblem

1998. 50th Anniv of Organization of American States.
2307 **704** 2600s. multicoloured . . 2·00 1·25

705 Emblem and Trophy

1998. World Cup Football Championship, France. Multicoloured.
2308 2000s. Type **705** . . . . . 1·60 95
2309 2600s. Mascot and trophy (vert) . . . . 2·00 1·25
2310 3000s. Players and trophy 2·40 1·50

706 Red Roses and Gypsophila

707 Cactus (*Jasminocereus thouarsii var. delicatus*)

1998. Flowers. Multicoloured.
2311 600s. Type **706** 50 30
2312 800s. *Musa sp.* 65 40
2313 2000s. Yellow roses . . . . 1·60 95
2314 2600s. Asters and astilbes 2·00 1·25

1998. Galapagos Flora. Multicoloured.
2315 600s. Type **707** 50 30
2316 1000s. *Cordia lutea lamarck* 80 50
2317 2600s. *Montondica charantica* . . . . 2·00 1·25

708 San Agustin Church, Quito

1998. Tourism. Multicoloured.
2318 600s. Type **708** 50 30
2319 800s. Independence Monument, Guayaquil . . 65 40
2320 2000s. Mitad del Mundo Monument, Quito (horiz) 1·60 1·00
2321 2600s. Mojanda Lagoon (horiz) . . . . 2·00 1·25

709 Beatriz Cueva de Ayora Institute and Ortega Espinosa (founder)

1998. Birth Centenary of Emiliano Ortega Espinosa (teacher). Multicoloured.
2322 400s. Type **709** 40 25
2323 4700s. Ortega . . . . 4·25 2·75

710 Mascot

711 Cueva Tamariz

1998. 6th South American Games, Cuenca. Mult.
2324 400s. Type **710** 40 25
2325 1000s. Games emblems and sports pictograms 80 50
2326 2600s. Mascot and sports pictograms (different) . . 2·00 1·25

1998. Birth Centenary of Carlos Cueva Tamariz (United Nations ambassador).
2327 **711** 2600s. multicoloured . . 2·00 1·25

712 Emblem

713 "Ecuadorian Woman"

1998. 75th Anniv of Guayaquil Radio Club.
2328 **712** 600s. multicoloured . . . 50 30

1998. 85th Birth Anniv of Eduardo Kigman (artist). Multicoloured.
2329 600s. Type **713** 50 30
2330 800s. "World without Answer" (horiz) 65 40

714 Father Christmas reading Letters

1998. Christmas. Multicoloured.
2331 1000s. Type **714** 70 45
2332 2600s. Children holding letter (vert) . . . . 1·75 1·10
2333 3000s. Father Christmas and letters falling from sack (vert) . . . . 2·00 1·25

715 Manuelita Saenz

716 Caves

1999. Manuelita Saenz Commemoration.
2334 **715** 1000s. multicoloured . . 70 45

1999. Los Tayos Caves. Multicoloured.
2335 1000s. Type **716** 65 40
2336 2600s. Caves (horiz) . . . . 1·75 1·10

717 Man's Face

1999. 80th Birth Anniv of Oswaldo Guayasamin (artist).
2337 **717** 2000s. multicoloured . . 1·40 85

718 Women

1999. International Campaign to Prevent Violence Against Women.
2338 **718** 4000s. multicoloured . . 2·75 1·75

719 Building Facade

1999. Centenary of Eloy Alfaro Military College. Multicoloured.
2339 5200s. Type **719** . . . . . 3·50 2·10
2340 9400s. Soldier and college building . . . . 6·00 3·75

720 *Bromelia sp.*

1999. Centenary of Del Puyo Foundation. Mult.
2341 4000s. Type **720** . . . . . 2·75 2·00
2342 4000s. Scarlet macaws . . . 2·75 2·00

721 Barahona

1999. Death Centenary of Dr. Rafael Barahona.
2343 **721** 5200s. multicoloured . . 3·50 2·10

722 De Luzarraga

723 Wright

1999. 140th Death Anniv of Gen. Manuel Antonio de Luzarraga.
2344 **722** 2000s. multicoloured . . 1·40 85

No. 2344 is inscribed for the bicentenary of the birth of Gen. Manuel de Luzarraga, who was born in 1776.

1999. Birth Bicentenary of Gen. Tomas Carlos Wright.
2345 **723** 4000s. multicoloured . . 2·75 1·75

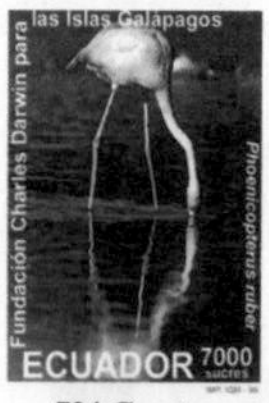

724 Greater Flamingo (*Phoenicopterus ruber*)

725 Emblem

1999. Charles Darwin Galapagos Islands Protection Foundation. Multicoloured.
2346 7000s. Type **724** . . . . . 3·00 1·90
2347 7000s. Galapagos hawk (*Buteo galapagoensis*) . . 3·00 1·90
2348 7000s. Marine iguana (*Amblyrhynchus cristatus*) 3·00 1·90
2349 7000s. Galapagos land iguana (*Conolophus subcristaus*) . . . . 3·00 1·90
2350 7000s. *Opuntia galapagela* (plant) . . . . 3·00 1·90
2351 7000s. Vermilion flycatcher (*Pyrocephalus rubinus*) . . 3·00 1·90
2352 7000s. Blue-footed booby (*Sula nebouxii*) . . . . . 3·00 1·90
2353 7000s. Blue-faced booby (*Sula dactylatra*) . . . . 3·00 1·90
2354 7000s. *Scalesia villosa* (plant) 3·00 1·90
2355 7000s. Galapagos giant tortoise (*G. elephantopus abingdoni*) . . . . 3·00 1·90
2356 15000s. *Brachycereus nesioticus* (coral) (horiz) 6·25 4·00
2357 15000s. Yellow warbler (*Dendroica petechia*) (horiz) . . . . 6·25 4·00
2358 15000s. Flightless cormorants (*Nannopterum harrisi*) (horiz) . . . . . 6·25 4·00
2359 15000s. Bottle-nosed dolphin (*Tursiops truncatus*) (horiz) . . . . 6·25 4·00
2360 15000s. *Pentaceraster cumingi* (starfish) (horiz) 6·25 4·00
2361 15000s. Galapagos giant tortoise (*G. elephantopus porteri*) (horiz) . . . . . 6·25 4·00
2362 15000s. Galapagos lava lizards (*Microlophus albemarlensis*) (horiz) . . 6·25 4·00
2363 15000s. Galapagos fur seal (*Arctocephalus galapagoensis*) (horiz) . . 6·25 4·00
2364 15000s. Galapagos penguins (*Spheniscus mendiculus*) (horiz) . . . . 6·25 4·00
2365 15000s. Cactus ground finch (*Geospiza scandens*) (horiz) 6·25 4·00

1999. International Year of the Older Person. Multicoloured.
2366 1000s. Type **725** 60 40
2367 1000s. Child and older person holding hands . . 60 40

726 Young Boys

1999. 50th Anniv of S.O.S. Children's Villages. Multicoloured.
2368 2000s. Type **726** 90 55
2369 2000s. Young girl 90 55

727 Postman

1999. 125th Anniv of Universal Postal Union. Multicoloured.
2370 1000s. Type **727** 35 20
2371 4000s. Dove carrying letter 1·40 80
2372 8000s. Emblem (horiz) . . . 2·75 1·75

728 World Map

1999. America. Millennium without Arms. Mult.
2373 4000s. Type **728** . . . . . 2·00 1·25
2374 4000s. Tree, Globe and bird 2·00 1·25

729 Cliff Face 730 Statue

1999. 5th Anniv of South Pacific Commission.
2375 **729** 7000s. multicoloured . . 3·00 1·90

1999. "Machala, City of Tourism and the Banana". Multicoloured.
2376 3000s. Type **730** . . . . . 1·25 75
2377 3000s. Building facade . . . 1·25 75
2378 3000s. View over city (horiz) 1·25 75

731 Jorge Bolanos 732 Society Headquarters

2000. 70th Anniv of Emelec Football Club (1999). Multicoloured.
2379 1000s. Type **731** 15 10
2380 1000s. Carlos Raffo 15 10
2381 2000s. Ivan Kavedes 30 20
2382 2000s. Team photograph (national championship winners, 1957 (horiz)) . . 30 20

2000. 150th Anniv (1999) of Guayas Philanthropic Society. Multicoloured.
2383 1000s. Type **732** 15 10
2384 2000s. Juan Maria Martinez Coello (founder) 30 20
2385 4000s. Emblem 55 35

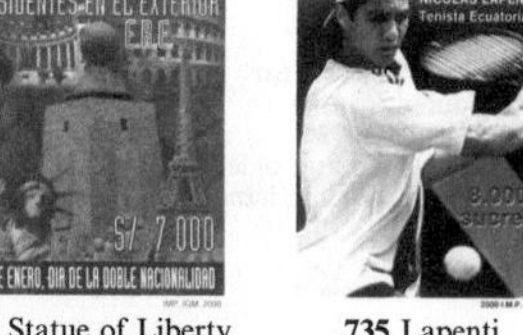

733 Statue of Liberty, New York, Equatorial Monument, Quito, Eiffel Tower, Paris and Coliseum, Rome 735 Lapenti

734 Buildings

2000. Ecuadorians living Abroad.
2386 **733** 7000s. multicoloured . . 1·00 60

2000. World Heritage Sites. Cuenca. Multicoloured.
2387 4000s. Type **734** 55 30
2388 4000s. Buildings and church tower (Puente Roto y Barranco del Rio Tomebamba) 55 30
2389 4000s. Monastery of the Conception Church . . . 55 30
2390 4000s. City view 55 30
2391 4000s. San Jose Church . . 55 30

2000. Nicolas Lapenti (tennis player).
2392 **735** 8000s. multicoloured . . 1·25 75

736 Masked Flowerpiercer (*Diglossa cyanea*) 737 Riobamba Cathedral

2000. Birds of Mazan. Multicoloured.
2393 8000s. Type **736** . . . . . 1·25 75
2394 8000s. Chimborazo hillstar (*Oreotrochilus chimborazo*) 1·25 75
2395 8000s. Masked trogon (*Trogon personatus*) . . . 1·25 75
2396 8000s. Sparkling violetear (*Colibri coruscans*) . . . . 1·25 75
2397 8000s. Rufus-naped brush finch (*Atlapetes rufinucha*) 1·25 75

2000. Bicentenary of the Rebuilding of Riobamba. Multicoloured.
2398 8000s. Type **737** . . . . . 1·25 75
2399 8000s. Pedro Vicente Maldonado (statue) . . . 1·25 75
2400 8000s. El Chimborazo mountain (horiz) . . . . 1·25 75

738 General Eloy Alfaro (founder) 739 *Guayas* (sail training ship) and Armed Forces Emblem

2000. Centenary of National Music Conservatory.
2401 **738** 10000s. multicoloured . . 1·20 75

2000. Ships. Multicoloured.
2402 68c. Type **739** 75 45
MS2403 91 × 111 mm. $1 As No. 2402 but with country name and emblem in gold. Imperf . . 1·10 70

740 Ivan Ricaurte 741 Dolores Sucre Lavayen

2000. 1st Anniv of Ivan Vallejo Ricaurte's Ascent of Everest without Oxygen.
2404 **740** 8000s. multicoloured . . 90 55

2000. 50th Anniv of Dolores Sucre Lavayen College.
2405 **741** 32c. multicoloured . . . 35 25

742 Commander Rafael Valverde and *Calderon* (battle ship) 743 Malecon 2000 and Emblem

2000. 59th Anniv of Jambeli Naval Battle. Day of the Armed Forces.
2406 **742** 16c. multicoloured . . . 20 15

2000. Opening of Malecon 2000 (waterside development), Guayaquil.
2407 **743** 84c. multicoloured . . . 95 60

744 Humpback Whale (*Megaptera novaeangliae*)

2000. Yaqu pacha (organization for the conservation of South American marine animals). Multicoloured.
2408 84c. Type **744** 95 60
MS2409 91 × 111 mm. $1 Humpback whales. Imperf . . . . 1·10 70

745 Flags encircling Map of Americas and Emblem

2000. Americas and Caribbean Dog Show.
2410 **745** 68c. multicoloured . . . 75 45

746 Club Emblem 747 Games Emblem

2000. 90th Anniv of Guayaquil Tennis Club.
2411 **746** 84c. multicoloured . . . 85 55

2000. Olympic Games, Sydney. Multicoloured.
2412 32c. Type **747** 35 25
2413 68c. Jefferson Perez (race walker) (1996 gold medallist) 75 45
2414 84c. Boris Burov (weightlifter) (gold medallist) (horiz) 85 55

748 Alberto Spencer 749 Lighthouse

2000. Alberto Spencer (footballer). Multicoloured.
2415 68c. Type **748** 75 45
MS2416 69 × 100 mm. $1 As No. 2415 but with design enlarged and reversed . . . . 1·10 70

2000. 60th Anniv of Salinas Yacht Club. Multicoloured.
2417 32c. Type **749** 35 25
2418 32c. Yacht with "60" on sail 35 25
2419 68c. Photo montage of yacht, water-skier and coast 75 45
MS2420 69 × 100 mm. $1 As. No. 2418 but with design enlarged 1·10 70

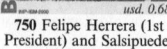

750 Felipe Herrera (1st President) and Salsipuedes Bridge 751 Dancer wearing Black Makeup and carrying Doll

2000. 40th Anniv of Inter-American Development Bank. Multicoloured.
2421 68c. Type **750** 75 45
2422 68c. Antonio Ortiz Mena Duale-Peripa dam 75 45
2423 84c. Enrique Inglesias and Ucubamba water treatment works 95 60
2424 84c. Bank emblem and Quito History Musuem 95 60
MS2425 151 × 91 mm. 25c. × 4, As Nos. 2422/4 but with designs enlarged . . . . 1·10 70

2000. La Mama Negra Festival, Latacunga. Multicoloured.
2426 32c. Type **751** 35 25
2427 32c. Bearded man (Rey Moro (moorish king)) . . 35 25
MS2428 100 × 68 mm. $1 Dancer wearing black makeup and doll (different). Imperf . . . . . . 1·10 70

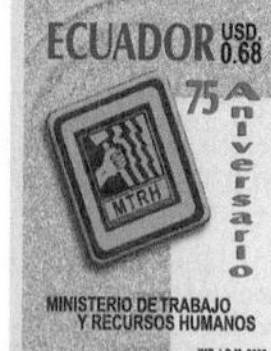

752 Emblem

2000. 75th Anniv of Works and Resources Ministry.
2429 **752** 68c. multicoloured . . . 70 45

753 Emblem

2000. National Union of Journalists.
2430 **753** 16c. multicoloured . . . 15 10

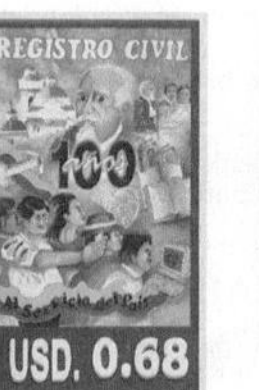

754 General Eloy Alfaro (president) and Crowd 755 Rose

2000. Centenary of Civil Register. Multicoloured.
2431 68c. Type **754** 70 45
2432 68c. Fingerprint and family 70 45

2000. Flower Export Campaign.
2433 **755** 68c. multicoloured . . . 70 45

756 "50" enclosing Ambato City

2000. 50th International Flower and Fruit Festival (2001). Multicoloured.
2434 32c. Type **756** 30 20
2435 32c. Volcano 30 20
2436 84c. Flower 85 55
2437 84c. Fruit 85 55
2438 84c. "50", emblem and stem (horiz) 85 55
MS2439 68 × 100 mm. $1 Enclosing view of Ambato city. Imperf 1·00 1·00

757 Angel, Stable and Holy Family 758 Arms

2000. Christmas. Children's Paintings. Multicoloured.
2440 68c. Type **757** (Ghiannina Rhor Isaias) 70 45
2441 68c. Nativity enclosed in tree and farm (Josue Remache Romero) . . . 70 45
2442 84c. Nativity at night (Maria Cedeno Bazurito) 85 55
2443 84c. Cattle and Holy Family (Juan Alban Salazar) . . 85 55
MS2444 100 × 69 mm. $1 Holy Family receiving gifts from children (Walther Carvache). Imperf . . . . 1·00 1·00

2000. 78th Anniv of Guayas Sports Federation.
2445 **758** 16c. multicoloured . . . 15 10

759 Museum Building

2000. Oswaldo Guayasamin (artist) "Chapel of Mankind" Museum.
2446 **759** 16c. multicoloured . . . 15 10

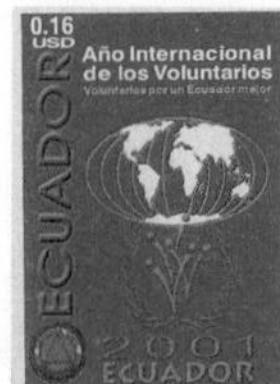

760 Emblem

2000. International Year of Volunteers.
2447 **760** 16c. multicoloured . . . 15 10

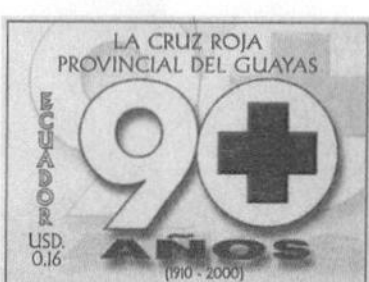

761 "90"

2000. 90th Anniv of Guayas Province Red Cross Society.
2448 **761** 16c. multicoloured . . . 15 10

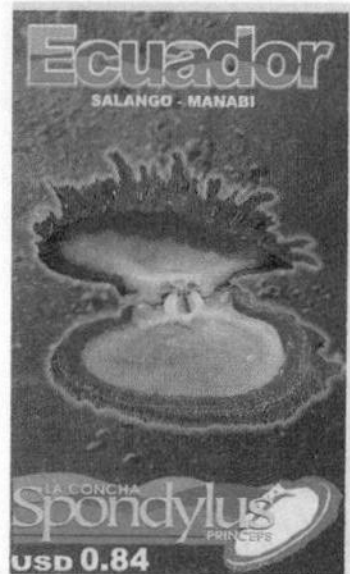

762 Pacific Thorny Oyster (*Spondylus princes*)

2000.
2449 **762** 84c. multicoloured . . . 85 55
MS2450 69 × 100 mm. **762** $1 multicoloured. Imperf . . . . 1·00 1·00

763 Restaurant
764 Map and Emblem

2000. Restoration of Bolivar Theatre. Multicoloured.
2451 16c. Type **763** 15 10
2452 32c. Auditorium (horiz) . . 30 20

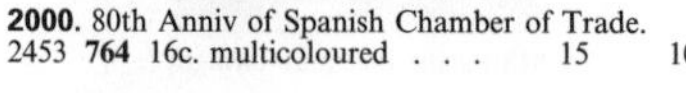
2000. 80th Anniv of Spanish Chamber of Trade.
2453 **764** 16c. multicoloured . . . 15 10

765 Veins, Arteries and Gender Symbols

767 Emblem

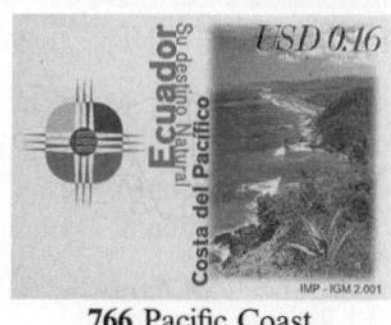

766 Pacific Coast

2000. America. AIDS Awareness Campaign. Multicoloured.
2454 84c. Type **765** 85 55
2455 84c. Globe described in blood 85 55

2001. Tourism. Multicoloured.
2456 16c. Type **766** 15 10
2457 16c. Andes 15 10
2458 32c. Emblem 30 20
2459 68c. Amazon basin 70 45
2460 84c. Galapagos Islands . . . 85 55

2001. 50th Anniv of Merchant Shipping.
2461 **767** 16c. multicoloured . . . 15 10

768 Rocks, Espanola Island

2001. UNESCO World Heritage Sites. Galapagos Islands. Multicoloured.
2462 16c. Type **768** 15 10
2463 16c. San Cristobal Island . . 15 10
2464 16c. Bartolome Island . . . 15 10
2465 16c. Inlet, Espanola Island 15 10
2466 16c. Bartolome and Santiago Island 15 10
MS2467 100 × 70 mm $1 Sea spray, Espanola Island. Imperf . . . 1·00 1·00

769 Emblem

2001. 50th Anniv (2000) of Guayas Football Association.
2468 **769** 68c. multicoloured . . . 70 45

770 Emblem (National Institute for Statistics and Census)

2001. National Census. Multicoloured.
2469 68c. Type **770** 70 45
2470 68c. Stylized crowd 70 45

771 Arms and Building Facade

2001. Centenary of Manuela Canizares College.
2471 **771** 84c. multicoloured . . . 85 55

772 Woman and Child

2001. International Women's Day. Multicoloured.
2472 84c. Type **772** 85 55
2473 84c. Woman with raised arms 85 55

773 Raul Huerta

2001. 10th Death Anniv of Raul Clemente Huerta (politician).
2474 **773** 68c. multicoloured . . . 70 45

774 Antonio Quevedo

2001. Birth Centenary (2000) of Antonio J. Quevedo (politician).
2475 **774** 84c. multicoloured . . . 85 55

775 Emblem

2001. 15th Anniv of ICAIM (women's education institute).
2476 **775** 84c. multicoloured . . . 85 55

776 Soldier and Building

2001. 55th Anniv of Military Geographic Institute. Multicoloured.
2477 68c. Type **776** 70 45
2478 68c. Computers and machinery 70 45

777 University Building

2001. 32nd Anniv of Ambato Technical University. Multicoloured.
2479 32c. Type **777** 30 20
2480 32c. Tree, couple and building 30 20

778 *Phragmipedium pearcei*

2001. 20th Anniv of Archidona Canton, Napo Province. Multicoloured.
2481 84c. Type **778** 85 55
2482 84c. Squirrel monkey (*Saimiri sciureus*) 85 55
2483 84c. *Brownea macrophylla* 85 55
2484 84c. Archidona church . . . 85 55
2485 84c. Native woman and children 85 55

779 Emblem

2001. 50th Anniv of ANETA (automobile club). Multicoloured.
2486 **780** 84c. multicoloured . . . 85 55

780 Flags forming Map

2001. Signing of Peace Treaty between Ecuador and Peru. Multicoloured.
2487 68c. Type **780** 70 45
2488 68c. Pioneer brigade emblem 70 45
2489 68c. Military observers emblem 70 45

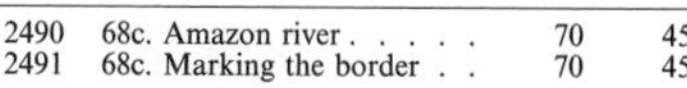
2490 68c. Amazon river 70 45
2491 68c. Marking the border . . 70 45

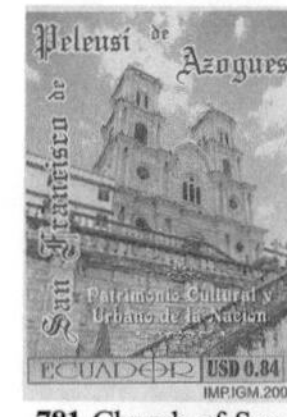

781 Church of San Francisco de Azogues

783 Alexander von Humboldt

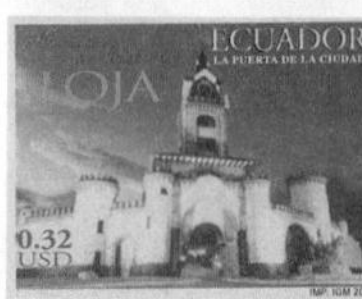

782 City Gates

2001. Cultural Heritage. San Francisco de Peleusi de Azogues.
2492 **781** 84c. multicoloured . . . 85 55

2001. Loja.
2493 **782** 32c. multicoloured . . . 30 20

2001. Bicentenary of Alexander von Humboldt's visit to Ecuador.
2494 **783** 84c. multicoloured . . . 85 55

784 Salvador Bustamante Celi

2001. 125th Birth Anniv of Salvador Bustamante Celi (musician and composer).
2495 **784** 68c. multicoloured . . . 70 45

785 Orchid Flower

2001. Banos State, Centre for Eco-Tourism. Multicoloured.
2496 86c. Type **785** 85 55
2497 86c. Nuestra Senora de Banos de Agua Santa basilica 85 55
2498 86c. Tungurahua volcano 85 55
2499 86c. Pailon de Diablo waterfalls 85 55
2500 86c. "Virgin del Rosario de Agua Santa" (statue) . . 85 55
MS2501 68 × 100 mm $1 Pailon de Diablo waterfalls (different). Imperf . . . . 1·00 1·00

786 Hand holding Chick and Condor

2001. Endangered Species. Andean Condor. Multicoloured.
2502 86c. Type **786** 85 55
2503 86c. Condor and FRAPZOO (animal protection organization) emblem 85 55
MS2504 68 × 100 mm. $1 Condor in flight. Imperf . . . . 1·00 1·00

787 Coastline

2001. Tourism. Esmeralda. Multicoloured.
2505 86c. Type **787** 85 55
2506 86c. Marimba band and dancers 85 55

788 Commission Emblem **790** Marcel Laniado de Wind

789 Emblem

2001. Atomic Energy Commission.
2507 **788** 70c. multicoloured . . . 70 45

2001. 30th Anniv of Guayas Educational Journalists Association.
2508 **789** 16c. multicoloured . . . 15 10

2001. 3rd Death Anniv of Marcel Laniado de Wind (banker).
2509 **790** 70c. multicoloured . . . 70 45

791 Emblem **792** Claudia Lars

2001. 15th Anniv of Agricultural Development Foundation.
2510 **791** 16c. multicoloured . . . 15 10

2001. Latin American Writers. Multicoloured.
2511 86c. Type **792** (poet) 85 55
2512 86c. Federico Proano (political journalist) . . . 85 55

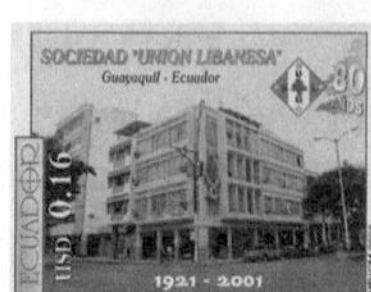

793 Union Building

2001. 80th Anniv of Lebanese Union, Guayaquil. Multicoloured.
2513 16c. Type **793** 15 10
2514 16c. Union emblem 15 10

794 Virgin del Carmen (statue)

2001. Cultural Heritage. Zaruma. Multicoloured.
2515 68c. Type **794** 70 45
2516 68c. Orchid flower 70 45

795 Emblem

2001. Manta Harbour Authority. Multicoloured.
2517 68c. Type **795** 70 45
2518 68c. Manta port 70 45

796 Davis Cup Tennis Trophy

2001. Tennis. Multicoloured.
2519 68c. Type **796** 70 45
2520 68c. Ecuador Davis Cup team, Wimbledon, 2000 70 45
2521 68c. Francisco Guzman and Miguel Olivera, 1967 . . 70 45
2522 68c. Francisco "Pancho" Segura Cano (80th birth anniv) 70 45
2523 68c. Andreas Gomez Santos 70 45

797 Students

2001. Wilson Popenoe (agricultural and horticultural) Foundation.
2524 **797** 16c. multicoloured . . . 15 10

798 Emblem **800** Jose Olmedo enclosed in Map and Clouds

799 Couple Planting

2001. Otonga Foundation (ecology charity). Multicoloured.
2525 16c. Type **798** 15 10
2526 16c. Weasel (Mustela frenata) 15 10

2001. 5th Anniv of World Food Summit (No. 2527). World Food Day (2528/9). Multicoloured.
2527 84c. Type **799** 85 50
2528 84c. Ears of corn 85 50
2529 84c. Baskets of crops . . . 85 50

2001. Jose Joaquin de Olmedo (writer and politician) Commemoration.
2530 **800** 84c. multicoloured . . . 85 50

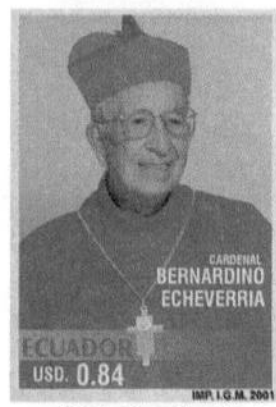

801 Cardinal Echeverria **802** Cupola, San Blas Church

2001. 1st Death Anniv of Cardinal Bernardino Echeverria.
2531 **801** 84c. multicoloured . . . 85 50

2001. Cultural Heritage. Multicoloured.
2532 25c. Type **802** 25 15
2533 25c. La Compania de Jesus church, Quito 25 15

803 "Composicion Espacial"

2001. Voroshilov Bazante (artist) Commemoration. Multicoloured.
2534 68c. Type **803** 70 45
2535 68c. "Absracto" 70 45
2536 68c. "Paisaje Urbano" . . . 70 45
2537 68c. "Abstracto" (different) 70 45
2538 68c. "Abstracto" (orange) 70 45

804 Andean Paramo (high altitude grasslands)

2001. La Angel Nature Reserve. Multicoloured.
2539 16c. Type **804** 15 10
2540 16c. "Frailejones" (Espeletia pycnophylla angelensis) 15 10

805 Children and Arms

2001. Social Security and Welfare Directorate, Quito.
2541 **805** 68c. multicoloured . . . 70 45

806 Aerial View of Race Track

2001. "CATI" (motoring club) and Yahuarcocha International Race Circuit, Imbabura. Multicoloured.
2542 68c. Type **806** 70 45
2543 68c. Aerial view (different) 70 45

807 International Rotary Emblem **808** Pedro Maldonado

2001. Anniv of Rotary Club (charitable organization) in Ecuador.
2544 **807** 84c. multicoloured . . . 85 50

2001. Pedro Vincente Maldonado (mathematician and cartographer) Commemoration.
2545 **808** 84c. multicoloured . . . 85 50

809 Microphone

2001. 70th Anniv of HCJB Radio Broadcasting Station. Multicoloured.
2546 68c. Type **809** 70 45
2547 68c. Station emblem 70 45

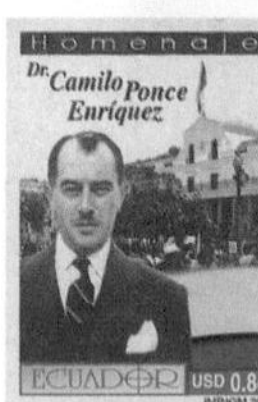

810 Camilo Ponce Enriquez **812** Nicolas Leoz (president of CSF)

811 Emblem

2001. Camilo Ponce Enriquez (politician) Commemoration.
2548 **810** 84c. multicoloured . . . 85 50

2002. Americas Judicial Summit Meeting (2001), Quito.
2549 **811** 68c. multicoloured . . . 70 45

2002. South American Football Association (CSF). Multicoloured.
2550 25c. Type **812** 25 15
2551 40c. Association emblem . . 40 25

813 Club Emblem **814** Porpoise, Leaves and Face

2002. Emelec Football Club. Fluorescent security markings.
2552 **813** 70c. blue 70 45

2002. World Conservation Union (UICN). Multicoloured.
2553 70c. Type **814** 70 45
2554 85c. Jaguar and conservation warden (horiz) 85 50
MS2555 100×70 mm. $1 Booby, giant otter, young women, spectacled bear and children. Imperf . . . . 1·00 1·00

815 Commission Emblem **817** Clock Tower

816 *Atelopus bomolochos*

2002. 50th Anniv of United Nations High Commissioner for Refugees.
2556 **815** 70c. blue and black . . . 70 45
2557 – 85c. multicoloured . . . 85 50
MS2558 100×70 mm. $1 multicoloured. Imperf . . . . 1·00 1·00
DESIGNS: 85c. Child; $1 Refugees. No. MS2558 has the UNHCR emblem foil embossed in top right corner.

2002. Frogs. Multicoloured.
2559 $1.05 Type **816** . . . . . . 1·10 65
2560 $1.05 *Atelopus longirostris* 1·10 65
2561 $1.05 *Atelopus pachydermus* 1·10 65
2562 $1.05 *Atelopus arthuri* . . . 1·10 65
2563 $1.05 *Atelopus* . . . . 1·10 65
MS2564 100×70 mm. $1 *Atelopus ignescens*. Imperf . . . . . . 1·00 1·00

2002. Imbabura Province. Multicoloured.
2565 40c. Type **817** 40 25
2566 40c. Atahualpa (last Inca ruler) (statue) 40 25

818 Pacific Beach at Twilight

2002. Tourism. Crucita State. Multicoloured.
2567 40c. Type **818** 40 25
2568 40c. Paragliding 40 25

819 "St. Francis" Church" (nave)

2002. Paintings by Wilfrido Martinez. Paintings. Multicoloured.
2569 90c. Type **819** 90 55
2570 90c. "Guapulo Church" . . 90 55
2571 90c. "St. Francis' Church" (apse) 90 55
2572 90c. "La Compana Church" 90 55
2573 90c. "El Rosario Church" 90 55

820 Team Members

2002. Cuenca Football Club. Multicoloured.
2574 25c. Type **820** 25 15
2575 25c. Club emblem 25 15

821 Altar Mountain

2002. Tourism. Chimborazo Province. Multicoloured.
2576 90c. Type **821** 90 55
2577 90c. Rounded peaks, Chimborazo 50 55
2578 90c. Three peaks, Carihuayrazo 90 55
2579 90c. Lake, forest and Altar mountain 90 55
2580 90c. Walker, scree and Cubillin mountain 90 55

822 Officer and Sniffer Dog
823 Club Emblem

2002. National Narcotics Police Force. Multicoloured.
2581 40c. Type **822** 40 25
2582 40c. Emblem 40 25

2002. 233rd Anniv of Club de la Union, Guayaquil.
2583 **823** 90c. blue and vermilion 90 55

824 Team Emblem
825 Student and Microscope

2002. World Cup Football Championships, Japan and South Korea. Multicoloured.
2584 90c. Type **824** 90 55
2585 $1.05 National team . . . . 1·10 65
MS2586 100 × 70 mm. $2 As. No. 2585. Imperf . . . . . . 2·00 2·00

2002. Institute for Financial Support for Education (IECE). Multicoloured.
2587 25c. Type **825** 25 15
2588 25c. Emblem 25 15

826 Blue Abstract

2002. Paintings by Milton Estrella Gavida. Paintings. Multicoloured.
2589 90c. Type **826** 90 55
2590 90c. Red abstract 90 55
2591 90c. Green abstract 90 55
2592 90c. Orange, bottle and vase of flowers 90 55
2593 90c. Fruit and vase 90 55

827 Servio Aguirre Villamagua

2002. Aguirre Protective Forest. Multicoloured.
2594 40c. Type **827** 40 25
2595 40c. Leaf 40 25

828 Organization Emblem

2002. 50th Anniv of FAO (UN food and agriculture organization).
2596 **828** $1.05 multicoloured . . 1·10 65

829 *Grapsus grapsus* (crab)

2002. Ibero-American Tourism and the Environment Conference. Galapagos Islands Fauna. Multicoloured.
2597 25c. Type **829** 25 15
2598 25c. Land iguana (*Conolophus subcristatus*) 25 15
2599 40c. Red-footed booby (*Sula sula*) (vert) 40 25
2600 40c. Greater flamingo (*Phoenicopterus rubber*) (vert) 40 25
2601 90c. Californian sea lion and pup (*Zalophus californianus*) (vert) . . . 90 55
2602 90c. Californian sea lion (vert) 90 55
2603 90c. Marine iguana (*Amblyrhynchus cristatus*) 90 55
2604 $1.05 Blue-faced booby (*Sula dactylatra*) (vert) . . 1·10 65
2605 $1.05 Emblem (vert) . . . . 1·10 65
2606 $1.05 Blue-footed booby (*Sula nebouxxi*)(vert) . . . 1·10 65
MS2607 100 × 70 mm. $2 Frigate bird, tourist and boat. Imperf 2·00 2·00

830 Carved Birds

2002. Directorate General for the Promotion of Exports and Bi-lateral Relations.
2608 **830** 90c. multicoloured . . . 90 55

831 Emblem and Building Facade

2002. 80th Anniv of Military Polytechnic College (ESPE).
2609 **831** 25c. multicoloured . . . 25 15

832 Engineering Centre, Quito

2002. Centenary of Military Engineers. Multicoloured.
2610 40c. Type **832** 40 25
2611 40c. Engineers (vert) 40 25
MS2612 100 × 70 mm. $2 Engineers, building and military emblems. Imperf . . . . 2·00 2·00

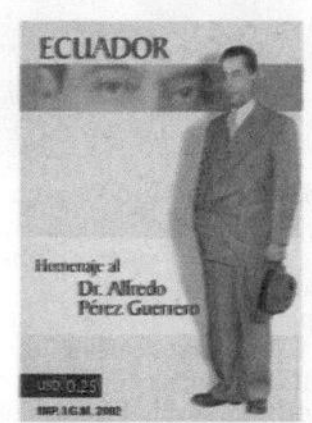

833 Alfredo Perez Guerrero

2002. Alfredo Perez Guerrero (language researcher) Commemoration.
2613 **833** 25c. multicoloured . . . 25 15

834 Duvan Canga and Jose Cedeno

2002. Duvan Canga and Jose Cedeno-1982 World Tae Kwon-do Championship Silver Medallists.
2614 **834** 40c. multicoloured . . . 40 25

835 Aboriginal Men

2002. Orellana Province. Multicoloured.
2615 25c. Type **835** 25 15
2616 25c. Climbing tree 25 15

836 Children and CARE Emblem
838 Flag and People

837 Emblem

2002. 40th Anniv of CARE (humanitarian organization). Multicoloured.
2617 90c. Type **836** 90 55
2618 90c. Smiling child 90 55

2002. Centenary of Macara Canton.
2619 **837** 40c. multicoloured . . . 40 25

2002. 50th Anniv of International Organization for Migration (IOM).
2620 **838** $1.05 multicoloured . . 1·10 65

839 Orchestra
840 Snow-capped Mountains

2002. 50th Anniv of Quito Philharmonic Orchestra.
2621 **839** 25c. multicoloured . . . 25 15

2002. 2nd International Mountain Peoples' Meeting. Multicoloured.
2622 90c. Type **840** 90 55
2623 90c. Indigenous mountain people 90 55
2624 90c. Village in valley 90 55
2625 90c. Mountains surrounding town 90 55
2626 90c. Conference emblem . . 90 55

841 "La Dolorosa"

2002. Paintings by Leonardo Hidalgo. Paintings. Multicoloured.
2627 90c. Type **841** 90 55
2628 90c. "El Hombre Cargano su Fruto" 90 55
2629 90c. "Frida Kahlo" (inscr "Kalo") 90 55
2630 90c. "El Hombre Fuerte del Mar" 90 55
2631 90c. "Jesus" 90 55

842 Dancer wearing Traditional Costume
844 Building and Emblem

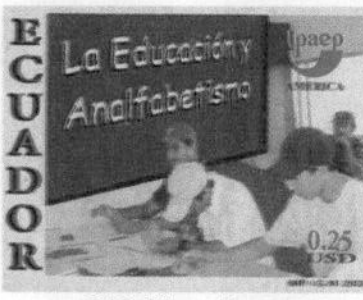

843 Class Room

2002. Pujili Dances.
2632 **842** $1.05 multicoloured . . 1·10 65

2002. America. Literacy Campaign. Multicoloured.
2633 25c. Type **843** 25 15
2634 25c. Toddler and open books 25 15

2002. 75th Anniv of National General Inspectorate.
2635 **844** 40c. multicoloured . . . 40 25

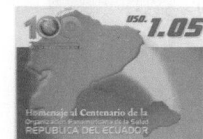

845 Anniversary Emblem and Map

2002. Centenary of Pan American Health Organization.
2636 **845** $1.05 multicoloured . . 1·10 65

846 Paintings of Pots displayed on Building

2002. Cultural Heritage. Multicoloured.
2637 25c. Type **846** 25 15
2638 25c. Paintings of flowers on buildings 25 15

847 University Building

2002. 40th Anniv of Catholic University, Guayaquil.
2639 **847** 40c. multicoloured . . . 40 25

848 Stars and Emblem

2003. 2nd (2002) South American Presidential Meeting, Guayaquil. Multicoloured.
2640 $1.05 Type **848** . . . . . . 1·10 65
2641 $1.05 President and flags . . 1·10 65

849 Pope John Paul II giving Blessing

850 Family (Huaita Sisa)

2003. Papal Benediction of Ecuadorian Emigrants. Multicoloured.

2642 $1.05 Type **849** . . . . . . 1·10 65
MS2643 68 × 100 mm. $2. As No. 2642. Imperf . . . . . . 2·10 2·10

2003. 25th Anniv of World Vision (humanitarian organization).

2644 **850** 40c. multicoloured . . . 40 25

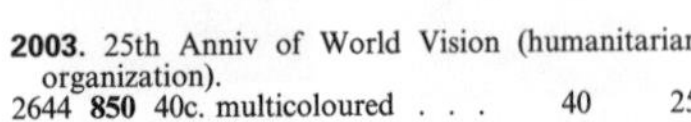

851 Women in Profile

852 Agustin Cueva Vallejo

2003. International Women's Day.

2645 **851** $1.05 multicoloured . . 1·10 65

2003. 130th Death Anniv of Agustin Cueva Vallejo (politician and journalist).

2646 **852** 40c. multicoloured . . . 40 25

853 Blasco Moscoso Cuesta (commentator)

2003. 50th Anniv of APDP (association of sports journalists), Pichincha Province.

2647 **853** 25c. multicoloured . . . 25 15

854 Dome and Cupola (Universidad del Azuay)

2003. Crafts. Multicoloured. Multicoloured.

2648 25c. Type **854** 25 15
2649 25c. Watering can (horticulture) 25 15
2650 25c. Pendant (jewellery) . . 25 15
2651 25c. Fireworks 25 15
2652 25c. Saddle (leatherwork) . . 25 15
2653 $1.05 Buckle (silverwork) . . 1·10 65
2654 $1.05 Weathervane (metalwork) . . . . . . 1·10 65
2655 $1.05 Basket . . . . . . 1·10 65
2656 $1.05 Shawl (needlework) 1·10 65
2657 $1.05 Pot (ceramics) . . . . 1·10 65
MS2658 100 × 68 mm. $2 Crafts. Imperf . . . . 2·10 2·10

Nos. 2648/52 and 2653/7, respectively, were issued in horizontal se-tenant strips of five stamps within the sheet.

855 Hands (painting, Eduardo Kingman)

2003. Centenary of Military Geographical Institute. Multicoloured.

2659 40c. Type **855** 40 25
2660 40c. Emblem (vert) 40 25
MS2661 100 × 69 mm. $2 As No. 2659. Imperf . . . . . . 2·10 2·10

856 *Curculionidae*

2003. Flora and Fauna. Multicoloured.

2662 $1.05 Type **856** . . . . . . 1·10 65
2663 $1.05 *Lycidae* . . . . 1·10 65
2664 $1.05 *Acridoidea* . . . . . 1·10 65
2665 $1.05 *Arachnida* (inscr "Arachnidae") . . . . . 1·10 65
2666 $1.05 *Liliaceae* . . . . . . 1·10 65

857 ECOCIENCIA (ecological organization) Emblem

2003. Galapagos Marine Reserve. Multicoloured.

2667 40c. Type **857** 40 25
2668 $1.05 Scalloped hammerhead shark (*Sphyrna lewini*) (horiz) 1·10 65
2669 $1.05 *Chelonia mydas agassisi* (horiz) . . . . . 1·10 65
2670 $1.05 Crosshatched triggerfish (*Xanthichthys mento*) (horiz) . . . . . 1·10 65
2671 $1.05 Moorish idol (*Zanclus cornutus*) (horiz) . . . . . 1·10 65
MS2672 100 × 68 mm. $2 *Tubastrea coccinea*. Imperf . . . . 2·10 2·10

858 Spider Monkey

2003. Tourism. Multicoloured.

2673 25c. Type **858** 25 15
2674 25c. Frigate bird 25 15
2675 25c. Embroidered cover . . 25 15
2676 25c. Cotopaxi volcano . . . 25 15
2677 25c. Basketwork seller . . . 25 15

859 Seated Figure

860 Golden Mask (bank emblem)

2003. Sierra Norte Pre-Colombian Artefacts. Multicoloured.

2678 25c. Type **859** 25 15
2679 25c. Three-legged pot . . . 25 15
2680 25c. Ball-shaped pot with figured handled 25 15
2681 25c. Tall decorated pot . . 25 15

2003. 75th Anniv of Central Bank. Multicoloured.

2682 25c. Type **860** 25 15
2683 25c. Window (Guayquil history park) 25 15
2684 $1.05 Inca figure (Pumapungo (archaeological site) museum, Cuenca) (horiz) 1·10 65

861 Envelope with British Consulate Stamp (1879)

2003. 33rd Anniv of Guayaquil Philatelic Club. Multicoloured.

2685 40c. Type **861** 40 25
2686 40c. Envelope with pre stamp postal mark . . . 40 25
2687 40c. Envelope with first SCADTA (internal airmail company) postmark (1928) 40 25
2688 40c. Envelope with French consulate stamp 40 25
2689 $1.05 Philatelic magazine covers (vert) . . . . . . 1·10 65
MS2690 100 × 69 mm. $2 Ecuador stamps and Guayquil philatelic club emblem. Imperf . . . . . 2·10 2·10

Nos. 2685/6 and 2687/8, respectively, were issued in se-tenant pairs within the sheets.

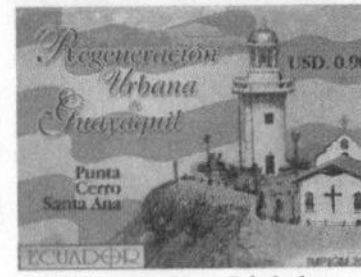

862 Santa Ana Lighthouse

2003. Preservation of Guayaquil Old Town. Multicoloured.

2691 90c. Type **862** 90 55
2692 90c. Colon plaza 90 55
2693 90c. Malecon gardens . . . 90 55
2694 90c. Crystal palace 90 55
2695 90c. San Francisco plaza . . 90 55

863 Black-chested Buzzard Eagle (*Geranoaetus melanoleucus*)

2003. International Bird Festival. Multicoloured.

2696 $1.05 Type **863** . . . . . . 1·00 60
2697 $1.05 Harpy eagle (Harpia harpyja) (vert) . . . . . 1·00 60

864 Porcupine

2003. 50th Anniv of Zamora Chinchipe Province. Multicoloured.

2698 25c. Type **864** 25 10
2699 25c. Tayra (*Eira barbata*) . . 25 10
2700 25c. Boa constrictor 25 10
2701 25c. Tapir (*Tapirus terrestris*) 25 10
2702 25c. Grey-winged trumpeter (*Psophia crepitans*) . . . 25 10

865 Toucan Barbet (*Semnornis ramphastinus*)

866 California Sea Lion (*Zalophus californianus*)

2003. America. Fauna and Flora. Multicoloured.

2703 $1.05 Type **865** . . . . . . 1·00 60
2704 $1.05 *Bomarea glaucescens* (flower) . . . . 1·00 60

2003. 25th Anniv of Galapagos Islands' UNESCO World Heritage Site Status. Multicoloured.

2705 40c. Type **866** 40 25
2706 40c. Great frigate bird (*Fregata minor palmerstoni*) 40 25
2707 40c. Blue footed booby (*Sula nebouxii*) (inscr "nebouxxi excisa") . . . 40 25
2708 40c. Bartolome island . . . 40 25
2709 40c. Anniversary emblem . . 40 25

867 El Sagrario Church

2003. World Heritage Sites, Quito. Churches. Multicoloured.

2710 40c. Type **867** 40 25
2711 90c. La Compania de Jesus 90 55
2712 90c. Santa Barbara 90 55
2713 $1.05 Convent of St. Francis (vert) . . . . 1·00 60

868 Tree, Child and Postman (Stephanie Patcheco)

2003. Christmas. Children's Drawings. Multicoloured.

2714 25c. Type **868** 25 10
2715 25c. Lorry, road and village (Sebastian Tejada) 25 10
2716 40c. Angel, envelope and people (Maria Claudia Ituralde) (vert) 40 25
2717 90c. Boy and bear posting letters to Santa (Luis Antonio Ortega) 90 55
2718 $1.05 Open window, presents and tree (Angel Andres Castro) (vert) . . 1·10 60

869 Open Book (Act of Independence for Guayaquil)

2003. Quayaquil Museum Artefacts. Multicoloured.

2719 40c. Type **869** 40 25
2720 40c. Punaes ceremonial stone 40 25
2721 40c. "Proclama Mariano Donoso" (medal struck for the coronation of King Carlos III of Spain) 40 25
2722 40c. Shrunken heads 40 25
2723 40c. Huancavilca totem pole 40 25

EXPRESS LETTER STAMPS

1928. Oblong Tobacco Tax stamp surch **"CORREOS EXPRESO"** and new value.

E457 2c. on 2c. blue . . . . . . 3·00 3·50
E458 5c. on 2c. blue . . . . . . 2·75 3·50
E459 10c. on 2c. blue . . . . . 2·75 2·25
E460 20c. on 2c. blue . . . . . 3·75 3·50
E461 50c. on 2c. blue . . . . . 4·50 3·50

1945. Surch **EXPRESO 20 Ctvs.**

E742 **194** 20c. on 5c. green 15 10

LATE FEE STAMP

1945. Surch **U. H. 10 Ctvs.**

L742 **194** 10c. on 5c. green 10 10

OFFICIAL STAMPS

1886. Stamps of 1881 optd **OFICIAL**.

O20 **5** 1c. brown 60 60
O21 2c. red 75 75
O22 5c. blue . . . . 1·50 1·90
O23 10c. orange . . . . 1·10 70
O24 20c. violet . . . . 1·10 1·10
O25 50c. green . . . . 3·25 2·75

1887. Stamps of 1887 optd **OFICIAL**.

O30 **13** 1c. green 75 10
O31 2c. red 75 10
O32 5c. blue . . . . 1·10 50
O33 80c. green . . . . 3·75 2·25

1892. Stamps of 1892 optd **FRANQUEO OFICIAL**.

O42 **15** 1c. blue 10 15
O43 2c. blue 10 15
O44 5c. blue 10 15
O45 10c. blue 10 10
O46 20c. blue 10 10
O47 50c. blue 10 25
O48 1s. blue 20 25

1894. Stamps of 1894 (dated "1894") optd **FRANQUEO OFICIAL**.

O65 **20** 1c. grey 25 25
O66 2c. grey 25 25
O67 5c. grey 25 25
O68 10c. grey 10 20
O69 20c. grey 30 35
O70 50c. grey 75 75
O71 1s. grey . . . . 1·10 1·10

This series was re-issued in 1897 optd "1897–1898".

1895. Postal Fiscals as Type F **1** but dated "1891–1892", optd **OFICIAL 1894 y 1895.**

O72 F **1** 1c. grey . . . . 6·25 4·00
O73 2c. red . . . . 6·25 4·00

1895. Stamps of 1895 (dated "1895") optd **FRANQUEO OFICIAL**.

O82 **20** 1c. grey . . . . 1·10 1·10
O83 2c. grey . . . . 1·60 1·60
O84 5c. grey 25 25
O85 10c. grey . . . . 1·60 1·60
O86 20c. grey . . . . 2·75 2·75

No.	Type	Description	Unused	Used
O87		50c. grey	6·75	6·75
O88		1s. grey	75	75

This series was re-issued in 1897 optd "1897–1898".

1896. Stamps of 1896 optd **FRANQUEO OFICIAL** in oval.

No.	Type	Description	Unused	Used
O 97	22	1c. bistre	20	15
O 98		2c. bistre	20	15
O 99		5c. bistre	25	15
O100		10c. bistre	25	15
O101		20c. bistre	25	15
O102		50c. bistre	25	15
O103		1s. bistre	50	35
O104		5s. bistre	85	80

F 10

O 245 Government Building, Quito

1898. Fiscal stamps as Type F **10**, surch **CORREOS OFICIAL** and value in frame.

No.	Type	Description	Unused	Used
O181	F 10	5c. on 50c. purple	15	15
O184		10c. on 20s. orange	15	40
O185		20c. on 50c. purple	1·25	1·25
O187		20c. on 50s. green	1·25	1·25

1899. Stamps as 1899 optd **OFICIAL**.

No.	Type	Description	Unused	Used
O201		2c. black and orange	25	55
O202		10c. black and orange	25	55
O203		20c. black and orange	25	85
O204		50c. black and orange	25	1·10

1913. Stamps of 1911 (except No. O396) optd **OFICIAL**.

No.	Type	Description	Unused	Used
O374	90	1c. black and red	50	50
O387		1c. orange	10	15
O388	91	2c. black and blue	55	55
O424		2c. green	15	15
O368	92	3c. black and orange	25	25
O390		3c. black	20	15
O437	98	4c. black and red	15	15
O369	93	5c. black and red	70	50
O393		5c. violet	25	10
O370	94	10c. black and blue	70	55
O395		10c. blue	10	10
O396	–	20c. blk & grn (No. 328)	1·50	60
O429	95	1s. black and green	1·90	1·90

1920. Stamps of 1920 (Nos. 381/400) optd **OFICIAL**.

No.	Type	Description	Unused	Used
O401	108	1c. green	40	40
O402	–	2c. red	30	30
O403	–	3c. bistre	30	30
O404	–	4c. green	10	10
O405	–	5c. blue	10	10
O406	–	6c. orange	40	40
O407	–	7c. brown	60	60
O408	–	8c. green	75	75
O409	–	9c. red	95	95
O410	109	10c. blue	60	60
O411	–	15c. black	3·00	3·00
O412	–	20c. purple	3·75	3·75
O413	–	30c. violet	4·50	4·50
O414	–	40c. sepia	6·25	6·25
O415	–	50c. green	3·75	3·75
O416	–	60c. blue	4·50	4·50
O417	–	70c. grey	4·50	4·50
O418	–	80c. yellow	5·75	5·75
O419	–	90c. green	6·25	6·25
O420	–	1s. blue	12·50	12·50

1924. Fiscal stamps of 1919 optd **OFICIAL**.

No.	Type	Description	Unused	Used
O421	103	1c. blue	60	60
O422		2c. green	3·25	3·25

1924. No. O204 optd **Acuerdo No 4.228**.

No.	Type	Description	Unused	Used
O430		50c. black and orange	70	70

1925. Stamps of 1925 optd **OFICIAL**.

No.	Type	Description	Unused	Used
O457	90	1c. blue	30	30
O439	93	5c. red	15	15
O440	94	10c. green	10	10

1928. Stamp of 1927 optd **OFICIAL**.

No.	Type	Description	Unused	Used
O463	123	20c. purple	1·10	75

1929. Official Air stamps. Air stamps of 1929 optd **OFICIAL**.

No.	Type	Description	Unused	Used
O466	130	2c. black	40	40
O467		5c. red	40	40
O468		10c. brown	40	40
O469		20c. purple	40	40
O470		50c. green	95	95
O474		50c. brown	75	85
O471		1s. blue	95	95
O475		1s. red	1·10	1·10
O472		5s. yellow	5·00	4·25
O476		5s. olive	2·25	2·25
O473		10s. red	55·00	42·00
O477		10s. black	5·75	5·75

1936. Stamps of 1936 (Nos. 520/4) optd **OFICIAL**.

No.	Type	Description	Unused	Used
O525		5c. olive	15	10
O526		10c. brown	15	10
O527		20c. purple	2·50	30
O528		1s. red	25	20
O529		2s. blue	40	60

1937. Stamps of 1937 optd **OFICIAL**.

No.	Type	Description	Unused	Used
O562	171	2c. green (postage)	10	10
O563	–	5c. red	10	10
O564	–	10c. blue	10	10
O565	–	20c. red	10	10
O566	–	1s. olive	10	10
O567	172	10c. brown (air)	25	25
O568		20c. olive	25	25
O569		70c. brown	35	25
O570		1s. slate	40	25
O571		2s. violet	1·40	40

1941. Air stamp of 1939 optd **OFICIAL**.

No.	Type	Description	Unused	Used
O638	184	5s. green	60	60

1946. Oblong Tobacco Tax stamp optd **CORRESPONDENCIA OFICIAL**. Roul.

No.	Type	Description	Unused	Used
O803		1c. red	12·00	3·50

1947.

No.	Type	Description	Unused	Used
O804	O 245	30c. blue	20	10
O805		30c. brown	20	10
O806		30c. violet	20	10

1964. Air. Nos. 1269/71 optd **Oficial**.

No.	Type	Description	Unused	Used
O1272	342	50c. multicoloured	70	70
O1273	–	80c. red, blue & yellow	70	70
O1274	–	1s.30 multicoloured	70	70

1964. No. 1272 optd **oficial** on each stamp.

No.	Type	Description	Unused	Used
O1275	344	80c. green and lake	1·50	30

The "OEA" overprint is across four stamps; the "oficial" overprint is on each stamp. The unused price is for a block of four.

POSTAGE DUE STAMPS

D 32

D 131

1896.

No.	Type	Description	Unused	Used
D105	D 32	1c. green	1·50	1·50
D106		2c. green	1·50	1·50
D107		5c. green	1·50	1·50
D108		10c. green	1·90	2·25
D109		20c. green	1·90	3·00
D110		50c. green	1·50	3·75
D111		100c. green	1·50	3·00

1929.

No.	Type	Description	Unused	Used
D466	D 131	5c. blue	10	10
D467		10c. yellow	10	10
D468		20c. red	20	15

D 335

1958.

No.	Type	Description	Unused	Used
D1128	D 335	10c. violet	10	10
D1129		50c. green	10	10
D1130		1s. brown	15	10
D1131		2s. red	25	15

APPENDIX

The following stamps have either been issued in excess of postal needs or have not been available to the public in reasonable quantities at face value. Such stamps may later be given full listing if there is evidence of regular postal use.

1966.

Cent of I.T.U. Postage 10, 10, 80c.; Air 1s.50, 3, 4s.

Space Achievements. Postage 10c., 1s.; Air 1s.30, 2s., 2s.50, 3s.50.

Dante and Galileo. Postage 10, 80c.; Air 2, 3s.

Pope Paul VI. Postage 10c.; Air 1s.30, 3s.50.

Famous Persons. Postage 10c., 1s.; Air 1s.50, 2s.50, 4s.

Olympic Games. Postage 10, 10, 80c.; Air 1s.30, 3s., 3s.50.

Winter Olympics. Postage 10c., 1s.; Air 1s.50, 2s., 2s.50, 4s.

Franco-American Space Research. Postage 10c.; Air 1s.50, 4s.

Italian Space Research. Postage 10c.; Air 1s.30, 3s.50.

Exploration of the Moon's Surface. Postage 10, 80c., 1s.; Air 2s., 2s.50, 3s.

1967.

Olympic Games, Mexico. Postage 10c., 1s.; Air 1s.30, 2s., 2s.50, 3s.50.

Olympic Games, Mexico. Postage 10, 10, 80c.; Air 1s.50, 3, 4s.

Eucharistic Conference. Postage 10, 60, 80c., 1s.; Air 1s.50, 2s.

Paintings of the Madonna. Postage 10, 40, 50c.; Air 1s.30, 2s.50, 3s.

Famous Paintings. Postage 10c., 1s.; Air 1s.50, 2s., 2s.50, 4s.

50th Birth Anniv of J. F. Kennedy. Postage 10, 10, 80c.; Air 1s.30, 3s., 3s.50.

Christmas Postage 10, 10, 40, 50, 60c.; Air 2s.50.

1968.

Religious Paintings and Sculptures. Postage 10, 80c., 1s.; Air 1s.30, 1s.50, 2s.

COTAL Tourist Organization Congress. Postage 20, 30, 40, 50, 60, 80c., 1s.; Air 1s.30, 1s.50, 2s.

1969.

Visit of Pope Paul VI to Latin America. Postage 40, 40c.; Air 1s.30.

39th Int Eucharistic Congress, Bogota. Postage 1s.; Air 2s.

Paintings of the Virgin Mary. Postage 40, 60c., 1s.; Air 1s.30, 2s.

EGYPT — Pt. 1, Pt. 19

Formerly a kingdom of N.E. Africa. Turkish till 1914, when it became a British Protectorate. Independent from 1922. A republic from 1953.

In 1958 the United Arab Republic was formed, comprising Egypt and Syria, but separate stamps continued to be issued for each territory as they have different currencies. In 1961 Syria became an independent Arab republic and left the U.A.R. but the title was retained by Egypt until a new federation was formed with Libya and Syria in 1971, when the country's name was changed to Arab Republic of Egypt.

1866. 40 paras = 1 piastre.
1888. 1000 milliemes = 1 piastre.
100 piastres = £1 Egyptian.

1

4

1866. Designs as T **1**. Imperf or perf.

No.	Type	Description	Unused	Used
1	1	5pa. grey	42·00	27·00
2		10pa. brown	55·00	29·00
3		20pa. blue	70·00	30·00
4		1pi. purple	60·00	4·75
5		2pi. yellow	90·00	42·00
6		5pi. pink	£250	£170
7		10pi. grey	£275	£250

1867.

No.	Type	Description	Unused	Used
11	4	5pa. yellow	28·00	8·00
12b		10pa. violet	55·00	9·50
13		20pa. green	£100	13·00
14		1pi. red	15·00	1·00
15		2pi. blue	£110	17·00
16		5pi. brown	£300	£180

On the piastre values the letters "P" and "E" appear on the upper corners.

7

10

1872.

No.	Type	Description	Unused	Used
28	7	5pa. brown	7·00	4·50
29		10pa. mauve	6·00	3·00
37d		20pa. blue	9·50	2·50
38		1pi. red	8·00	65
39c		2pi. yellow	5·50	6·00
40		2½pi. violet	8·50	5·00
41		5pi. green	60·00	19·00

1875. As T **7**, but "PARA" inscr at left-hand side and figure "5"'s inverted.

No.	Type	Description	Unused	Used
35	–	5pa. brown	9·50	3·75

1879. Surch in English and Arabic.

No.	Type	Description	Unused	Used
42	7	5pa on 2½pi. violet	6·00	6·00
43		10pa. on 2½pi. violet	11·00	10·00

1879. Various frames.

No.	Type	Description	Unused	Used
44	10	5pa. brown	2·50	30
45		10pa. lilac	50·00	3·00
50		10pa. purple	50·00	7·00
51		10pa. grey	10·00	1·75
52		10pa. green	2·00	1·25
46		20pa. blue	60·00	1·75
53a		20pa. red	15·00	50
47		1pi. pink	27·00	20
54b		1pi. blue	5·00	20
55b		2pi. brown	12·00	10
55ba		2pi. orange	22·00	1·00
49a		5pi. green	55·00	10·00
56a		5pi. grey	11·00	50

1884. Surch **20 PARAS** in English and Arabic.

No.	Type	Description	Unused	Used
57	10	20pa. on 5pi. green	7·00	1·25

18

1888. Various frames.

No.	Type	Description	Unused	Used
58	18	1m. brown	2·25	10
59		2m. green	1·50	10
60		3m. purple	3·25	1·00
61c		3m. yellow	2·50	10
62		4m. red	3·50	10
63		5m. red	3·50	10
64		10pi. mauve	15·00	80

29 Nile Feluccas

35 Archway of Ptolemy III, Karnak

41 Statue of Rameses II

42 Statue of Rameses II (different inscription)

1914.

No.	Type	Description	Unused	Used
73	29	1m. brown	1·25	40
74	–	2m. green	2·00	20
86	–	2m. red	3·50	80
75	–	3m. orange	1·50	35
76	–	4m. red	2·75	65
88	–	4m. green	5·00	6·00
77	–	5m. red	3·00	10
90	–	5m. pink	4·00	20
91	–	10m. blue	4·00	20
92	–	10m. lake	1·75	30
93	41	15m. blue	4·00	15
94	42	15m. blue	22·00	3·00
79	35	20m. olive	6·50	30
96	–	50m. purple	10·00	1·25
81	–	100m. grey	13·00	60
82	–	200m. purple	26·00	3·50

DESIGNS—AS Type **29**: 2m. Cleopatra; 3m. Ras-el-Tin Palace, Alexandria; 4m. Pyramids, Giza; 5m. Sphinx; 10m. Colossi of Amenophis III at Thebes. As Type **35**: 50m. Citadel, Cairo; 100m. Rock Temple, Abu Simbel; 200m. Aswan Dam.

1915. Surch **2 Milliemes** in English and Arabic.

No.	Type	Description	Unused	Used
83	29	2m. on 3m. orge (No. 75)	55	2·00

(43 "The Kingdom of Egypt, 15 March, 1922")

44 King Fuad I

1922. Stamps of 1914 optd with T **43**.

No.	Type	Description	Unused	Used
98	29	1m. brown	75	55
99	–	2m. red	75	35
100	–	3m. orange	1·00	65
101	–	4m. green	65	60
102	–	5m. pink	1·70	15
103	–	10m. lake	1·80	15
104	41	15m. blue	4·00	55
105	42	15m. blue	3·00	60
106	35	20m. olive	4·25	40
107	–	50m. purple	4·75	70
108	–	100m. grey	17·00	85
110	–	200m. purple	18·00	1·00

1923.

No.	Type	Description	Unused	Used
111	44	1m. orange	15	15
112		2m. black	55	15
113		3m. brown	65	40
114		4m. green	50	25
115		5m. brown	30	15
116		10m. pink	1·20	15
117		15m. blue	1·70	15
118		20m. green	3·75	15
119		50m. green	6·00	20
120		100m. purple	18·00	45
121		200m. mauve	29·00	1·30
122	–	£E1 violet and blue	£180	19·00

The 20m. to £E1 values are larger (22½ × 28 mm). The £E1 shows the King in military uniform.

46 Thoth writing name of King Fuad

1925. Int Geographical Congress, Cairo.

123	**46**	5m. brown	6·75	4·25
124		10m. red	14·00	8·75
125		15m. blue	14·00	9·75

47 Ploughing with Oxen

1926. 12th Agricultural Exhibition, Cairo.

126	**47**	5m. brown	1·40	1·20
127		10m. red	1·10	1·20
128		15m. blue	1·10	1·60
129		50m. green	11·00	5·50
130		100m. purple	14·00	12·00
131		200m. violet	20·00	26·00

49 De Havilland D.H.34 Biplane over Nile

1926. Air.

132	**49**	27m. violet	13·50	14·00
133		27m. brown	4·75	1·90

50 King Fuad

1926. King's 58th Birthday.

134	**50**	50p. purple	95·00	20·00

1926. Surch.

135	**47**	5m. on 50m. green	1·50	1·50
136		10m. on 100m. purple	1·50	1·50
137		15m. on 200m. violet	1·50	1·50

52 Ancient Egyptian Ship, Temple of Deir-el-Bahari

1926. International Navigation Congress.

138	**52**	5m. black and brown	1·90	1·30
139		10m. black and red	2·20	2·00
140		15m. black and blue	2·20	2·00

1926. Inauguration of Port Fuad. Optd **PORT FOUAD.**

141	**52**	5m. black and brown	£200	£140
142		10m. black and red	£200	£140
143		15m. black and blue	£200	£140
144	**50**	50p. purple	£1200	£950

55

1927. Int Cotton Congress, Cairo.

145	**55**	5m. green and brown	1·30	1·00
146		10m. green and red	2·20	1·50
147		15m. green and blue	2·20	1·50

56

57

58

1927.

148	**56**	1m. orange	20	15
149		2m. black	20	15
150		3m. brown	20	30
151		3m. green	35	15
153		4m. green	85	60
154		4m. brown	80	45
156		5m. brown	40	15
157		10m. red	95	15
158		10m. violet	2·50	15
159		13m. red	90	20
160a		15m. blue	1·40	15
161		15m. purple	3·75	15
162		20m. blue	6·75	15
163a	**57**	20m. olive	2·50	15
164		20m. blue	5·25	15
165		40m. brown	2·75	15
166a		50m. blue	2·30	15
167a		100m. purple	7·25	25
168a		200m. mauve	6·75	70
171	**58**	500m. blue and brown	75·00	7·00
172	–	£E1 brown and green	85·00	5·75

DESIGN—VERT: As Type **58**: £E1, King Fuad I.
See also Nos. 233/9.

60 Amenhotep

61 Imhotep

1927. Statistical Congress, Cairo.

173	**60**	5m. brown	75	90
174		10m. red	2·00	90
175		15m. blue	2·30	85

1928. Medical Congress, Cairo.

176	**61**	5m. brown	75	50
177	–	10m. red	80	45

DESIGN: 10m. Mohammed Ali Pasha.

63 King Farouk when Crown Prince

64 Ancient Agriculture

1929. Prince's 9th Birthday.

178	**63**	5m. grey and purple	1·90	1·10
179		10m. grey and red	2·30	1·10
180		15m. grey and blue	2·30	1·10
181		20m. grey and turquoise	2·30	1·10

1931. Agricultural and Industrial Exhibition, Cairo.

182	**64**	5m. brown	70	65
183		10m. red	1·00	1·10
184		15m. blue	1·40	1·10

1931. Air. Surch **GRAF ZEPPELIN AVRIL 1931** and value in English and Arabic.

185	**49**	50m. on 27m. brown	42·00	42·00
186		100m. on 27m. brown	42·00	47·00

1932. Surch in English and Arabic.

187	**50**	50m. on 50p. purple	10·50	1·50
188	–	100m. on £E1 violet and blue (No. 122)	£190	£180

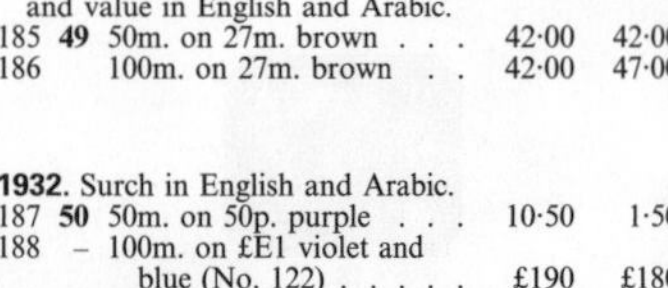

67 Locomotive No. 1, 1852

1933. International Railway Congress, Cairo.

189	**67**	5m. black and brown	9·75	5·50
190	–	13m. black and red	20·00	10·50
191	–	15m. black and violet	20·00	10·50
192	–	20m. black and blue	20·00	10·50

DESIGNS: 13m. Locomotive No. 41, 1859; 15m. Locomotive No. 68, 1862; 20m. Locomotive No. 787, 1932.

68 Handley Page H.P.42 over Pyramids

1933. Air.

193	**68**	1m. black and orange	15	35
194		2m. black and grey	75	1·10
195		2m. black and orange	3·50	2·30
196		3m. black and brown	50	25
197		4m. black and green	95	80
198		5m. black and brown	70	15
199		6m. black and green	1·40	1·10
200		7m. black and blue	1·10	80
201		8m. black and violet	60	20
202		9m. black and red	2·00	1·10
203		10m. brown and violet	50	55
204		20m. brown and green	60	15
205		30m. brown and blue	1·50	15
206		40m. brown and red	13·50	45
207		50m. brown and orange	12·00	15
208		60m. brown and grey	5·25	75
209		70m. green and blue	3·25	70
210		80m. green and sepia	3·25	75
211		90m. green and orange	4·00	75
212		100m. green and violet	7·75	45
213		200m. green and red	10·50	1·00

See also Nos. 285/8.

69 Armstrong-Whitworth Atalanta of Imperial Airways

1933. Int Aviation Congress. Inscr as in T **69**.

214	**69**	5m. brown	4·25	2·50
215		10m. violet	13·00	8·00
216	–	13m. red	14·50	10·50
217	–	15m. purple	14·50	9·50
218	–	20m. blue	18·00	12·00

DESIGNS: 13, 15m. Dornier Do-X flying boat; 20m. Airship "Graf Zeppelin".

72 Khedive Ismail Pasha

73

1934. 10th U.P.U. Congress, Cairo.

219	**72**	1m. orange	35	60
220		2m. black	40	60
221		3m. brown	45	70
222		4m. green	70	25
223		5m. brown	75	20
224		10m. violet	1·50	25
225		13m. red	2·40	1·30
226		15m. purple	2·30	1·00
227		20m. blue	1·90	40
228		50m. blue	5·75	50
229		100m. green	13·50	90
230		200m. violet	42·00	4·75
231	**73**	50p. brown	£170	70·00
232		£El blue	£275	£120

1936. As T **56** but inscribed "POSTES".

233	**56**	1m. orange	25	45
234		2m. black	1·30	15
235		4m. green	1·60	15
236		5m. brown	1·50	30
237		10m. violet	3·00	30
238		15m. purple	5·50	35
239		20m. blue	5·50	25

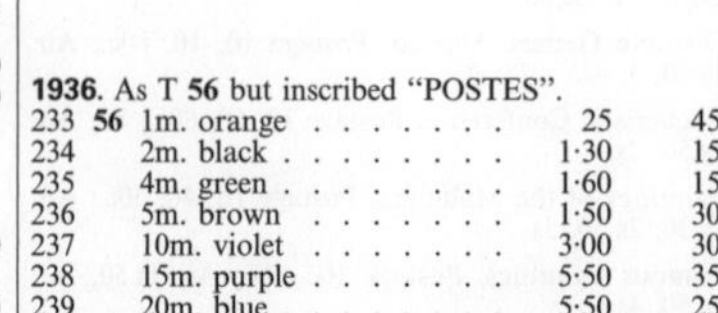

75 Exhibition Entrance

1936. 15th Agricultural and Industrial Exn, Cairo.

240	**75**	5m. brown	1·60	1·00
241	–	10m. violet	2·00	1·50
242	–	13m. red	3·00	3·00
243	–	15m. purple	1·60	1·40
244	–	20m. blue	4·25	3·50

DESIGN—HORIZ: 10m., 13m. Palace of Agriculture; 15m., 20m. Palace of Industry.

77 Nahas Pasha and Treaty Delegates

1936. Anglo-Egyptian Treaty.

245	**77**	5m. brown	65	85
246		15m. purple	80	90
247		20m. blue	1·30	1·10

78 King Farouk

79 Medal commemorating Abolition of Capitulations

1937. Investiture of King Farouk.

248	**78**	1m. orange	10	10
249		2m. red	10	10
250		3m. brown	10	10
251		4m. green	10	10
252		5m. brown	30	10
253		6m. green	45	15
254		10m. violet	20	10
255		13m. red	25	20
256		15m. purple	25	10
257		20m. blue	50	25
258		20m. violet	60	15

1937. Abolition of Capitulations at the Montreux Conference.

259	**79**	5m. brown	65	30
260		15m. purple	1·30	65
261		20m. blue	1·50	75

80 Nekhbet, Sacred Eye of Horus and Buto

1937. 15th Ophthalmological Congress, Cairo.

262	**80**	5m. brown	90	65
263		15m. purple	1·20	65
264		20m. blue	1·40	70

81 King Farouk and Queen Farida

1938. Royal Wedding.

265	**81**	5m. brown	5·50	4·25

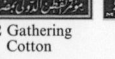

82 Gathering Cotton

83 Pyramids of Giza and Colossus of Thebes

1938. 18th International Cotton Congress, Cairo.
266 **82** 5m. brown . . . . 1·60 70
267 15m. purple . . . . 2·75 1·30
268 20m. blue . . . . 2·10 1·10

1938. Int Telecommunications Conf, Cairo.
269 **83** 5m. brown . . . . 1·90 1·00
270 15m. purple . . . . 2·75 1·10
271 20m. blue . . . . 2·40 1·20

1938. King Farouk's 18th Birthday. Portrait similar to T **81** with inscr "11 FEVRIER 1938" at foot.
272 – £E1 brown and green . . . £130 £140

84 Hydnocarpus

1938. Leprosy Research Congress.
273 **84** 5m. brown . . . . 1·80 90
274 15m. purple . . . . 2·50 95
275 20m. blue . . . . 2·50 95

85 King Farouk and Pyramids

86 King Farouk **87**

1939.
276a **85** 30m. grey 45 15
277 30m. green 50 15
278 – 40m. brown 65 15
279 – 50m. blue . . . . 1·10 15
280 – 100m. purple . . . . . 1·50 15
281 – 200m. violet . . . . . 5·50 15
282 **86** 50p. brown and green . . 10·50 1·10
283 **87** £E1 brown and blue . . . 20·00 2·50
DESIGNS (As Type **85**): 40m. Mosque; 50m. Cairo Citadel; 100m. Aswan Dam; 200m. Fuad I University, Giza.
For similar issue with portrait looking to left, see 1947 issue.

88 Princess Ferial (18 months old) **90** King Fuad I

1940. Child Welfare.
284 **88** 5m.+5m. red . . . . . . 1·00 45

1941. Air.
285 **68** 5m. red 30 25
286 10m. violet 40 25
287a 25m. purple 50 25
288 30m. green 55 25

1943. 5th Birthday of Princess Ferial. Optd **1943** in English and Arabic.
289 **88** 5m.+5m. red . . . . . . 6·75 5·50

1944. 8th Death Anniv of King Fuad.
290 **90** 10m. purple 30 15

91 King Farouk **92** King Farouk

1944.
291 **91** 1m. brown 15 15
292 2m. red 15 15
293 3m. brown 25 30
294 4m. green 20 15
295 5m. brown 20 15
296 10m. violet 40 15
297 13m. red . . . . 8·75 2·50
298 15m. purple 75 15
299 17m. olive 70 15
300 20m. violet 80 15
301 22m. blue 80 15

1945. 25th Birthday of King Farouk.
302 **92** 10m. violet 30 20

93 Khedive Ismail Pasha **94** Flags of the Arab Union

1945. 50th Death Anniv of Ismail Pasha.
303 **93** 10m. green 30 20

1945. Arab Union.
304 **94** 10m. violet 25 15
305 22m. green 35 25

95 Flags of Egypt and Saudi Arabia

1946. Visit of King of Saudi Arabia.
306 **95** 10m. green 25 15

96 Reproduction of First Egyptian Stamp

1946. 80th Anniv of First Egyptian Postage Stamp.
307 **96** 1m.+1m. grey 20 15
308 – 10m.+10m. purple 25 15
309 – 17m.+17m. brown 35 30
310 – 22m.+22m. green 45 40
MS311 - 129 × 171 mm. Nos. 307/10. Perf . . . . 65·00 60·00
MS312 - As last but imperf . . 65·00 60·00
DESIGNS: 10m. Khedive Ismail Pasha; 17m. King Fuad; 22m. King Farouk.

98 King Farouk, Egyptian Flag and Citadel

1946. Evacuation of Cairo Citadel.
313 **98** 10m. brown and green . . 30 30

1946. Air. Cairo Aviation Congress. Optd **Le Caire 1946** and Arabic characters.
314 **68** 30m. green (No. 288) . . . 30 20

100 King Farouk and Inshas Palace

1946. Arab League Congress. Portraits.
315 **100** 1m. green 40 15
316 – 2m. brown 40 15
317 – 3m. blue 40 15
318 – 4m. brown 40 15
319 – 5m. red 40 15
320 – 10m. grey 40 15
321 – 15m. violet 40 15
DESIGNS: 2m. Prince Abdullah of Yemen; 3m. President of Lebanon, Beshara al-Khoury; 4m. King Ibn Saud of Saudi Arabia; 5m. King Faisal II of Iraq; 10m. King Abdullah of Jordan; 15m. Pres of Syria, Shukri Bey al-Quwatli.

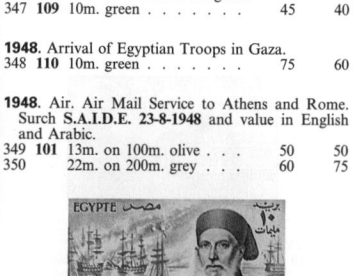

101 King Farouk, Delta Barrage and Douglas Dakota Transport **102** Triad of Mycerinus

1947. Air.
322 **101** 2m. red 15 45
323 3m. brown 15 50
324 5m. red 15 15
325 7m. orange 30 20
326 8m. green 30 45
327 10m. violet 30 20
328 20m. blue 50 20
329 30m. purple 60 20
330 40m. red 95 25
331 50m. blue . . . . 1·10 30
332 100m. olive . . . . . . 2·20 40
333 200m. grey . . . . 5·00 1·70

1947. International Exhibition of Fine Arts. Inscr "EXPOSITION INTERNATIONALE D'ART CONTEMPORIAN".
334 **102** 5m.+5m. grey 85 40
335 – 15m.+15m. blue . . . . . 1·00 70
336 – 30m.+30m. red . . . . . 1·30 90
337 – 50m.+50m. brown . . . . 2·00 1·60
DESIGNS—HORIZ: 15m. Temple of Rameses. VERT: 30m. Queen Nefertiti; 50m. Tutankhamun.

104 Egyptian Parliament Buildings **105** King Farouk hoisting Flag

1947. 36th International Parliamentary Union Conference, Cairo.
338 **104** 10m. green 25 20

1947. Withdrawal of British Troops from Nile Delta.
339 **105** 10m. purple and green . . 30 25

106 King Farouk and Sultan Hussein Mosque, Cairo **107** King Farouk

1947. Designs as 1939 issue but with portrait altered as T **106** and **107**.
340 – 30m. olive 50 10
341 **106** 40m. brown 40 10
342 – 50m. blue 65 10
343 – 100m. purple . . . . . . 4·25 60
344 – 200m. violet . . . . . . 9·75 1·10
345 **107** 50p. brown and green . . 24·00 11·00
346 – £El brown and blue . . . 31·00 2·75
DESIGNS—AS Type **106**: 30m. Pyramids; 50m. Cairo Citadel; 100m. Aswan Dam; 200m. Fuad I University, Cairo. As T **107**: £El, King Farouk (different).

109 Cotton Plant **110** Egyptian Soldiers Entering Palestine

1948. International Cotton Congress.
347 **109** 10m. green 45 40

1948. Arrival of Egyptian Troops in Gaza.
348 **110** 10m. green 75 60

1948. Air. Air Mail Service to Athens and Rome. Surch **S.A.I.D.E. 23-8-1948** and value in English and Arabic.
349 **101** 13m. on 100m. olive . . . 50 50
350 22m. on 200m. grey . . . 60 75

112 Ibrahim Pasha and Battle of Navarino, 1827

1948. Death Centenary of Ibrahim Pasha (statesman and General).
351 **112** 10m. green and red . . . 35 30

113 Reclining Male Figure symbolising River Nile

114 Protection of Industry and Agriculture by Army **115** Mohammed Ali and Map

1949. 16th Agricultural and Industrial Exn, Cairo.
352 **113** 1m. green 25 20
353 10m. violet 50 20
354 17m. red 50 25
355 22m. blue 55 30
356 **114** 30m. sepia 90 45
MS357 Two sheets. (a) 172 × 105 mm. Nos. 352/5 in new colours (b) 108 × 123 mm. 10m. as Type **114** and No. 356 in new colours. Imperf . . . . 6·00 10·50

1949. Death Centenary of Mohammed Ali (statesman and General).
358 **115** 10m. green and brown . . 30 25

116 Globe

1949. 75th Anniv of U.P.U.
359 **116** 10m. red 60 35
360 22m. violet 70 70
361 30m. blue 90 80

117 Scales of Justice

1949. Abolition of Mixed Courts.
362 **117** 10m. green & dp green . . 30 20

118 Camels by Water-hole

1950. Inaug of Fuad I Desert Institute.
363 **118** 10m. brown and violet . . 60 55

119 King Fuad University

1950. 25th Anniv of Fuad I University.
364 **119** 22m. purple and green . . 60 55

120 Khedive Ismail and Globe **121** Girl and Cotton

1950. 75th Anniv of Royal Egyptian Geographical Society.
365 **120** 30m. green and purple . . 65 60

1951. International Cotton Congress, Cairo.
366 **121** 10m. green 35 30

122 King Farouk and Queen Narriman

1951. Royal Wedding.
367 **122** 10m. brown and green . . 1·30 1·30
MS368 129 × 112 mm. No. 367 8·00 13·00

123 Triumphal Arch

1951. 1st Mediterranean Games, Alexandria.
369 **123** 10m. brown . . . . . . 80 1·10
370 – 22m. green . . . . 95 1·20
371 – 30m. blue and green . . . 95 1·20
MS372 189 × 117 mm. Nos. 369/71 9·75 13·00
DESIGNS—VERT: 22m. Badge of Alexandria and map of Mediterranean. HORIZ: 30m. King Farouk and waves.

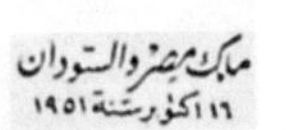
(**124** "King of Egypt and the Sudan 16th October 1951")

1952. Optd as T **124** (different sizes).
373 **91** 1m. brown (postage) . . . 50 60
374 2m. red 20 20
375 **78** 3m. brown 20 95
376 **91** 4m. green 20 20
377 **78** 6m. green . . . . . . 85 1·00
378 **91** 10m. violet 30 10
379 13m. red . . . . 95 1·00
380 15m. purple . . . . . . 1·90 1·10
381 17m. green . . . . . . 1·70 25
382 20m. violet . . . . . . 1·40 25
383 22m. blue . . . . . . 2·75 2·20
384 – 30m. green (No. 340) . . 1·50 60
386 **106** 40m. brown 75 20
387 – 50m. blue (No. 342) . . . 1·20 20
388 – 100m. purple (No. 343) . . 1·80 35
389 – 200m. violet (No. 344) . . 7·75 1·30
390 **107** 50p. brown and green . . 16·00 5·25
391 – £El brn & bl (No. 346) 33·00 6·00

392 **101** 2m. red (air) 25 20
393 3m. brown 85 80
394 5m. red 35 30
395 7m. brown 55 30
396 8m. green . . . . . . 1·20 95
397 10m. violet 70 80
398 20m. blue . . . . . . 2·50 1·90
399 30m. purple . . . . . . 1·10 1·10
400 40m. red . . . . 3·00 1·60
401 50m. blue . . . . . . 1·80 1·90
402 100m. green . . . . . . 4·25 2·50
403 200m. grey . . . . . . 9·00 4·25

125 "Egypt" **126** Egyptian Flag

1952. Abrogation of Anglo-Egyptian Treaty of 1936. Inscr "16 Oct. 1951".
404 **125** 10m. green 50 50
405 – 22m. green and purple . . 80 80
406 – 30m. green and brown . . 90 90
MS407 134 × 114 mm. Nos. 404/6 8·25 9·75
DESIGNS: 22m. King Farouk and map of Nile Valley; 30m. King Farouk and flag.

1952. Birth of Crown Prince Ahmed Fuad.
408 **126** 10m. green, yellow & blue 35 30
MS409 111 × 138 mm. No. 408 4·75 6·50

127 "Freedom, Hope and Peace"

1952. Revolution of 23 July 1952. Inscr "23 JUILLET 1952".
410 **127** 4m. orange and green . . 25 25
411 – 10m. brown and green . . 25 65
412 – 17m. brown and green . . 65 70
413 – 22m. green and brown . . 1·00 55
DESIGNS—HORIZ: 10m. Allegory of Egyptian freedom. VERT: 17m. Map of Nile Valley, and Egyptian citizens; 22m. Rejoicing crowd and Egyptian flag.

129 "Agriculture" **130** "Defence"

131 Sultan Hussein Mosque, Cairo **132** Queen Nefertiti

133 Douglas Dakota Transport over Delta Barrage

1953. Inscr "DEFENCE" (A) or "DEFENSE" (B).
414 **129** 1m. brown (postage) . . . 35 20
415 2m. purple 25 20
416 3m. blue 35 35
417 4m. green 25 25
418 **130** 10m. brown (A) 25 35
419 10m. brown (B) 45 20
420 15m. grey (B) 35 10
421 17m. blue (B) 45 25
422 20m. violet (B) 25 25
423 **131** 30m. green 30 20
424 32m. blue 60 25
425 35m. violet 75 25
426 37m. brown 85 70
427 40m. brown 65 25
428 50m. purple . . . . . . 1·40 20
429 **132** 100m. brown . . . . . . 1·90 25
430 200m. blue . . . . . . 5·00 45
431 500m. violet . . . . . 11·00 1·00
432 £El red and green . . . . 19·00 2·75

433 **133** 5m. brown (air) 35 50
434 15m. green 85 65
See also No. 619.

1953. Various issues of King Farouk with portrait obliterated by three horiz bars. (i) Stamps of 1937.
435 **78** 1m. orange . . . . . . 23·00 35·00
436 3m. brown 40 50
437 6m. green 25 25

(ii) Stamps of 1944.
438 **91** 1m. brown 25 25
439 2m. red 25 20
440 3m. brown 45 50
441 4m. green 25 20
442 10m. violet 25 20
443 13m. red 70 70
444 15m. purple 45 20
445 17m. green 45 25
446 20m. violet 55 20
447 22m. blue 80 25

(iii) Stamps of 1947.
448 – 30m. green (No. 340) . . 60 25
449 **106** 40m. brown . . . . . . 47·00 75·00
450 – 50m. blue (No. 342) . . . 1·00 25
451 – 100m. pur (No. 343) . . . 1·50 45
452 – 200m. violet (No. 344) . . 5·50 95
453 **107** 50p. brown and green . . 16·00 5·50
454 – £El brn & bl (No. 346) 18·00 3·50

(iv) Air stamps of 1947.
455 **101** 2m. red . . . . 1·50 1·60
456 3m. brown . . . . . . 1·20 2·20
457 5m. red . . . . 80 1·10
458 7m. brown 30 35
459 8m. green . . . . . . 1·00 1·50
460 10m. violet . . . . . . 34·00 47·00
461 20m. blue . . . . . . 1·20 45
462 30m. purple . . . . . . 1·60 95
463 40m. red . . . . 1·70 1·10
464 50m. blue . . . . . . 3·00 1·50
465 100m. green . . . . . . 4·50 3·00
466 200m. grey . . . . . . 55·00 75·00

(v) Stamps of 1952 with "Egypt-Sudan" opt T **124**.
467 **91** 1m. brown (postage) . . 7·75 11·50
468 2m. red . . . . 60 1·40
469 **78** 3m. brown . . . . . . 8·75 11·50
470 **91** 4m. green . . . . . . 9·50 11·50
471 **78** 6m. green . . . . . . 27·00 12·50
472 **91** 10m. violet . . . . . . 3·75 4·75
473 13m. red . . . . 95 1·30
474 15m. purple . . . . . . 19·00 23·00
475 17m. green . . . . . . 19·00 23·00
476 20m. violet . . . . . . 21·00 23·00
477 22m. blue . . . . . . 55·00 65·00
477a – 30m. green (No. 384) . . 26·00 26·00
478 **106** 40m. brown . . . . . . 3·00 1·30
479 – 200m. violet (No. 389) 4·50 2·50

480 **101** 2m. red (air) 45 30
481 3m. brown 85 70
482 5m. red 25 25
483 7m. brown . . . . . . 17·00 18·00
484 8m. green . . . . . . 50 1·40
485 10m. violet 45 95
486 20m. blue . . . . . . 65·00 80·00
487 30m. purple . . . . . . 1·00 95
488 40m. red . . . . 65·00 80·00
489 50m. blue . . . . . . 2·30 1·20
490 100m. green . . . . . . 3·75 3·00
491 200m. grey . . . . . . 7·00 7·25

135

1953. Electronics Exhibition, Cairo.
492 **135** 10m. blue 45 35

136 "Young Egypt" **137** "Agriculture"

1954. 1st Anniv of Republic.
493 **136** 10m. brown 50 25
494 – 30m. blue 75 60
DESIGN: 30m. Marching crowd, Egyptian flag and eagle.

1954.
495 **137** 1m. brown 25 20
496 2m. purple 25 20
497 3m. blue 25 25
498 4m. green 70 65
499 5m. red 25 25

138 Flag and Map showing Area watered by Canal **139**

1954. Evacuation of British Troops from Suez Canal. Inscr "EVACUATION".
500 **138** 10m. purple and green . . 40 25
501 – 35m. green and red . . . 60 50
DESIGN: 35m. Egyptian army bugler, machine-gunner and map.

1955. Arab Postal Union.
502 **139** 5m. brown 40 25
503 10m. green 40 35
504 37m. violet . . . . . . 75 1·20

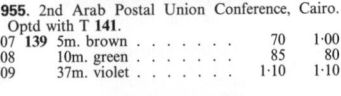

140 P. P. Harris and Rotary Emblem (**141**)

1955. 50th Anniv of Rotary International.
505 **140** 10m. purple 85 30
506 – 35m. blue . . . . . . 1·10 50
DESIGN: 35m. Globe and Rotary emblem.

1955. 2nd Arab Postal Union Conference, Cairo. Optd with T **141**.
507 **139** 5m. brown . . . . 70 1·00
508 10m. green 85 80
509 37m. violet . . . . . . 1·10 1·10

142 Scout Badge

1956. 2nd Arab Scout Jamboree, Aboukir (Alexandria). Inscr "2EME JAMBOREE ARABE", etc.
510 **142** 10m.+10m. green . . . . 50 1·10
511 – 20m.+10m. ultramarine 75 1·30
512 – 35m.+15m. blue . . . . . 95 1·40
MS513 120 × 160 mm. Nos. 510/2 £1000 £750
MS514 As last but imperf . . . £1000 £750
DESIGNS: 20m. Sea Scout badge; 35m. Air Scout badge.

143 Globes and Laurel Branch

1956. Afro-Asian Festival, Cairo. Inscr "FESTIVAL ASIATICO-AFRICAIN".
515 **143** 10m. green and brown . . 35 25
516 – 35m. purple and yellow 70 1·00
DESIGN—VERT: 35m. Globe, lamp, dove and ear of corn.

144 Freighter and Map of Suez Canal **145** Queen Nefertiti

1956. Nationalisation of Suez Canal.
517 **144** 10m. blue and buff . . . 40 35

1956. International Museum Week.
518 **145** 10m. green . . . . 80 1·00

146 Defence of Port Said

1956. "Port Said, Nov. 1956".
519 **146** 10m. purple 80 75

1957. Evacuation of British and French Troops from Port Said. Optd **EVACUATION 22-12-56** in English and Arabic.
520 **146** 10m. purple 55 80

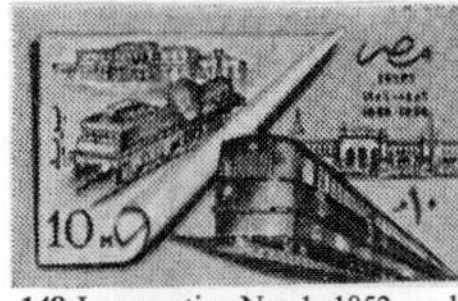
148 Locomotive No. 1, 1852, and Diesel Train

1957. Centenary of Egyptian Railways.
521 **148** 10m. purple and brown . . . . 75 1·10

149 Mother and Children

1957. Mothers' Day.
522 **149** 10m. red 50 75

150 Battle Scene

1957. 150th Anniv of Victory over British at Rosetta.
523 **150** 10m. blue 30 60

1957. Re-opening of Suez Canal. As T **144** but inscr "REOPENING 1957" in English and Arabic.
524 100m. blue and green . . . . 1·20 1·00

151 Al-Azhar University

152 Map of Gaza

1957. Millenary of Al-Azhar University, Cairo. Unissued stamps of 1942 as T **151** optd with the present Arabic year (1376).
525 **151** 10m. violet 40 50
526 15m. purple 55 45
527 20m. grey 80 70

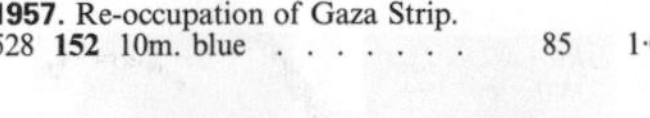

1957. Re-occupation of Gaza Strip.
528 **152** 10m. blue . . . . 85 1·00

153 Motor Ambulance

1957. 50th Anniv of Public Aid Society.
529 **153** 10m.+5m. red 40 50

154 Shepheard's Hotel

156 Egyptian Parliament Buildings

1957. Re-opening of Shepheard's Hotel, Cairo.
530 **154** 10m. violet 35 35

1957. Opening of National Assembly.
531 **156** 10m. brown & yellow . . 35 45

157 Avaris, 1580 B.C.

1957. 5th Anniv of 1952 Revolution.
532 **157** 10m. red 95 90
533 – 10m. green 95 90
534 – 10m. purple 95 90
535 – 10m. blue 95 90
536 – 10m. brown 95 90
DESIGNS—HORIZ: No. 533, Saladin at Hattin, A.D. 1187; 534, Ein Galout, A.D. 1260 (Middle East map); 536, Evacuation of Port Said, 1956. VERT: No. 534, Louis IX in chains at Mansourah, A.D. 1250.

159 Ahmed Arabi addressing Revolutionaries

1957. 75th Anniv of Arabi Revolution.
537 **159** 10m. violet 35 35

160 Rameses II

162 Ahmed Shawqi

1957.
540 – 1m. turquoise 25 25
541 – 5m. sepia 30 30
539 **160** 10m. violet 35 25
DESIGNS: 1m. Country woman and cotton plant; 5m. Factory skyline.
See also Nos. 553/9, 603/19 and 669/72.

1957. 25th Death Anniv of Ahmed Shawqi and Hafez Ibrahim (poets).
543 **162** 10m. olive 25 50
544 – 10m. brown (Hafez Ibrahim) 25 50

163 Vickers Viscount Airliner and Airline Badge

1957. 25th Anniv of Egyptian Civil Airlines "MISRAIR", and Air Force.
545 **163** 10m. green 45 45
546 – 10m. blue 45 45
DESIGN: No. 546, Ilyushin Il-28 bomber, two Mikoyan Gurevich MiG-17 jet fighters and Air Force emblem.

164 Pyramids, Dove of Peace and Globe

1957. Afro-Asian People's Conference, Cairo.
547 **164** 5m. brown 45 45
548 10m. green 30 30
549 15m. violet 35 35

165 Racing Cyclists

166 Mustapha Kamil

1958. 5th Egyptian International Cycle Race.
550 **165** 10m. brown 35 35

1958. 50th Death Anniv of Mustapha Kamil (patriot).
551 **166** 10m. slate 45 25

UNITED ARAB REPUBLIC

For stamps inscribed "UAR" but with value in piastres, see under Syria.

167 Congress Emblem

168 Princess Nofret

1958. 1st Afro-Asian Ophthalmology Congress.
552 **167** 10m.+5m. orange . . . . 1·00 70

1958. Inscr "U A R EGYPT".
553 – 1m. red (as No. 538) . . 25 25
554 – 2m. blue 20 15
555 **168** 3m. brown 20 15
556 – 4m. green 25 15
557 – 5m. sepia (as No. 541) . . 25 15
558 **160** 10m. violet 50 15
559 – 35m. blue . . . . 2·50 30
DESIGNS—VERT: 2m. Ahmed Ibn Toulon Mosque; 4m. Glass lamp and mosque; 35m. Ship and crate on hoist.
See also Nos. 603/19, 669/72 and 739.

169 Union of Egypt and Syria

170 Cotton Plant

1958. Birth of United Arab Republic.
560 **169** 10m. grn & yell (postage) 35 25
561 15m. brn & blue (air) . . 40 25

1958. International Cotton Fair, Cairo.
562 **170** 10m. turquoise 25 20

171 Qasim Amin

172 Dove of Peace

1958. 50th Death Anniv of Qasim Amin (reformer).
563 **171** 10m. blue 35 20

1958. 5th Anniv of Republic.
564 **172** 10m. violet 35 20

173 "Iron and Steel"

174 Sayed Darwich

173a UAR Flag

1958. 6th Anniv of 1952 Revolution. Egyptian Industries.
565 – 10m. brown 30 20
566 – 10m. green 30 20
567 **173** 10m. red 30 20
568 – 10m. myrtle 30 20
569 – 10m. blue 30 20
MS570 80 × 75 mm. **173a** green, red and black . . . . 15·00 15·00
DESIGNS: Industrial views representing: No. 565, "Cement"; No. 566, "Textiles"; No. 568, "Petroleum"; No. 569, "Electricity and Fertilizers".

1958. 35th Death Anniv of Sayed Darwich.
580 **174** 10m. purple 35 15

175 Torch and Broken Chains

1958. Republic of Iraq Commem.
581 **175** 10m. red 35 15

176 Cogwheels, Maps and Emblems of Productivity

1958. Afro-Asian Economic Conf, Cairo.
582 **176** 10m. blue 35 15

1958. Industrial and Agricultural Fair, Cairo. As No. 582 but colour changed, optd **INDUSTRIAL & AGRICULTURAL PRODUCTION FAIR** in Arabic and English.
583 **176** 10m. brown 35 20

178 Dr. Mahmoud Azmy (Egyptian U.N.O. representative)

1958. 10th Anniv of Declaration of Human Rights.
584 **178** 10m. violet 35 25
585 35m. green 70 50

179 "Learning"

1958. 50th Anniv of Cairo University.
586 **179** 10m. green 25 15

180 Egyptian Postal Emblem

1959. Post Day and Postal Employees Social Fund.
587 **180** 10m.+5m. red, black and turquoise 25 25

1959. Surch **UAR 55** and equivalent in Arabic.
588 **132** 55m. on 100m. red . . . 1·20 35

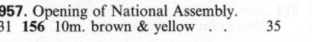

182

1959. Afro-Asian Youth Conf, Cairo.
589 **182** 10m. green 25 20

183 Nile Hilton Hotel

1959. Opening of Nile Hilton Hotel.
590 **183** 10m. brown 25 15

184 State Emblem

1959. 1st Anniv of United Arab Republic.
591 **184** 10m. red, black & green 25 15

185 "Telecommunications"

1959. Arab Telecommunications Union Commemoration.
592 **185** 10m. violet 25 15

186 U.A.R. and Yemeni Flags

1959. 1st Anniv of Proclamation of United Arab States (U.A.R. and Yemen).
593 **186** 10m. red and green . . . 25 20

187 Oil Derrick and Pipe-lines **189** "Migration"

188 "Railways" (Diesel-electric Train)

1959. 1st Arab Petroleum Congress.
594 **187** 10m. blue & turquoise . . 35 20

1959. 7th Anniv of Revolution and Transport and Communications Commemoration. Frames in slate. Centre colours given.
595 **188** 10m. lake 45 25
596 – 10m. green 45 25
597 – 10m. blue 45 25
598 – 10m. violet 45 25
599 – 10m. plum 45 25
600 – 10m. red 45 25
MS601 80 × 75 mm. 50m. green and red . . . . 10·50 10·50

DESIGNS: No. 596, "Highways" (bus passing bridge); 597, "Seaways" ("Al Mokattam" (freighter)); 598, "Nile Transport" (motorised river barge); 599, "Telecommunications" (telephone and radio mast); 600, "Postal Services" (Post Office H.Q., Cairo). 57 × 32 mm—**MS**601, Liner, diesel electric train, airliner and motorcycle mail carrier.

1959. 3rd Arab Emigrants' Association Convention, Middle East.
602 **189** 10m. lake 25 20

1959. As Types **132**, **160** and **168**, but inscr "UAR" only.
603 – 1m. red (as No. 553) . . 20 15
604 – 2m. blue (as No. 554) . . 20 15
605 **168** 3m. brown 20 15
606 – 4m. green (as No. 556) . . 20 15
607 – 5m. black (as No. 557) . . 20 15
608 **160** 10m. green 25 15
609 – 15m. brown 35 15
610 – 20m. red 65 15
611 – 30m. purple 45 15
612 – 35m. blue (as No. 559) . . 60 15
613 – 40m. brown 75 15
614 – 45m. blue . . . . 1·50 25
615 – 55m. green . . . . 1·20 20
616 – 60m. violet . . . . 1·90 20
617 – 100m. green & orange . . 1·80 25
618 – 200m. brown and blue . . 3·75 40
619 **132** 500m. red and blue . . . 11·50 1·20
DESIGNS—VERT: 15m. Omayad Mosque, Damascus; 20m. Tutankhamun's Lamp; 40m. Statue; 55m. Cotton and ears of corn; 60m. Barrage and plant; 100m. Egyptian eagle and hand holding agricultural products. HORIZ: 30m. Stone archway; 45m. Citadel Gate, Aleppo; 200m. Temple ruins.
See also Nos. 669/72 and No. 739.

191 Airplane over Pyramids

1959. Air.
620 **191** 5m. red 25 20
621 – 15m. purple 25 25
622 – 60m. green 60 40
623 – 90m. purple . . . . . . 1·30 80
DESIGNS: 15m. Boeing Flying Fortress bomber over Colossi of Thebes; 60m. Douglas DC-6B airliner over Al-Azhar University; 90m. Airplane over St. Catherine's Monastery, Sinai.
See also Nos. 758/62.

192 "Shield against Aggression" **193** Children and U.N. Emblem

1959. Army Day.
624 **192** 10m. red 25 20

1959. U.N. Day. UNICEF.
625 **193** 10m.+5m. purple 25 25
626 35m.+10m. blue 45 30

194 Cairo Museum

1959. Centenary of Cairo Museum.
627 **194** 10m. brown 30 20

195 Rock Temples of Abu Simbel

1959. UNESCO. Campaign for Preservation of Nubian Monuments (1st issue).
628 **195** 10m. brown 45 25
See also Nos. 650, 676, 728, 754/6, 825/7, 864/6 and 878/9.

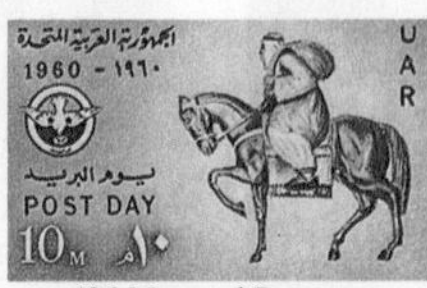
196 Mounted Postman

1960. Post Day.
629 **196** 10m. blue 25 15

197

198 View of projected Aswan High Dam

1960. Laying of Foundation Stone of Aswan High Dam.
630 **197** 10m. lake 45 45
631 **198** 35m. lake 70 50

199 Aswan Dam Hydro-electric Power Station

1960. Projected Aswan Dam Hydro-electric Power Station.
632 **199** 10m. black 25 20

200

1960. Industrial and Agricultural Fair.
633 **200** 10m. green 25 20

1960. No. 432 optd **UAR** and Arabic equivalent.
634 **132** £E1 red and green . . . . 19·00 3·75

202 State Emblem with U.A.R. Flag **203** Sculpture and Palette

1960. 2nd Anniv of U.A.R.
635 **202** 10m. red, black & green 25 15

1960. 3rd Fine Arts Biennale. Alexandria.
636 **203** 10m. sepia 25 15

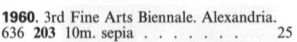

204 Arab League Centre, Cairo

1960. Inaug of Arab League Centre, Cairo.
637 **204** 10m. green and black . . 25 15

205 Mother and Child pointing to Map of Palestine

1960. World Refugee Year.
638 **205** 10m. red 25 20
639 35m. turquoise 55 45

206 Weightlifting

1960. Sports Campaign and Olympic Games.
640 **206** 5m. grey 20 20
641 – 5m. brown 20 20
642 – 5m. purple 20 20
643 – 10m. red 20 20
644 – 10m. green 20 20
645 – 30m. violet 40 35
646 – 35m. blue 55 40
MS647 79 × 75 mm. 100m. brown and carmine. Imperf . . . . . 3·00 2·75
DESIGNS—VERT: No. 641, Basketball; 642, Football; 643, Fencing; 644, Rowing. HORIZ: No. 645, Horse-jumping; 646, Swimming. LARGER (57 × 32 mm.)—**MS**647, Cairo stadium.

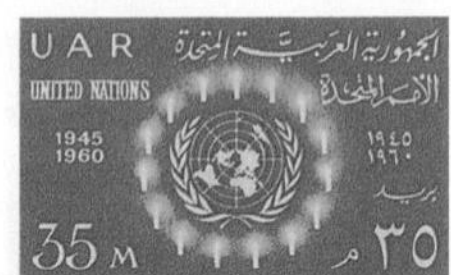
207 U.N. Emblem within 15 candles

1960. 15th Anniv of U.N.O.
648 – 10m. violet 25 20
649 **207** 35m. red 40 35
DESIGN—VERT: 10m. Dove and U.N. Emblem.

208 Rock Temples of Abu Simbel

1960. UNESCO. Campaign for Preservation of Nubian Monuments (2nd issue).
650 **208** 10m. brown 55 35

209 Modern Post Office

1961. Post Day.
651 **209** 10m. red 35 20

210 State Emblem and Wreath **211** Globe, Flags and Wheat

1961. 3rd Anniv of U.A.R.
652 **210** 10m. purple 25 15

1961. International Agricultural Exn, Cairo.
653 **211** 10m. red 25 20

212 Patrice Lumumba and Map of Africa **213** Hands "reading" Braille

1961. 3rd All African Peoples' Conf, Cairo.
654 **212** 10m. black 25 15

1961. World Health Organization Day.
655 **213** 10m. brown 30 20
656 35m.+15m. yellow & brn 75 55

214 Tower of Cairo **215** Refugee Mother and Child, and Map

1961. Inauguration of Tower of Cairo.
657 **214** 10m. blue 25 15

1961. Air. As No. 657, but with aircraft replacing inscr in upper corners and inscr "AIR MAIL" in English and Arabic.
658 **214** 50m. blue 75 40

1961. Palestine Day.
659 **215** 10m. green 30 15

216 "Transport and Communications"

216a Workers and Graph

1961. 9th Anniv of Revolution and Five Year Plan. Inscr "1961".
660 **216** 10m. purple 25 20
661 – 10m. red 25 20
662 – 10m. blue 25 20
663 – 35m. myrtle 50 30
664 35m. violet 50 30
MS665 80 × 75 mm. **216a** 100m. brown. Imperf . . . . 3·00 2·50
DESIGNS: No. 661, Worker turning cogwheel and pylons; No. 662, Apartment houses; No. 663, Cotton plant and dam; No. 664, Family moving towards lighted candle.

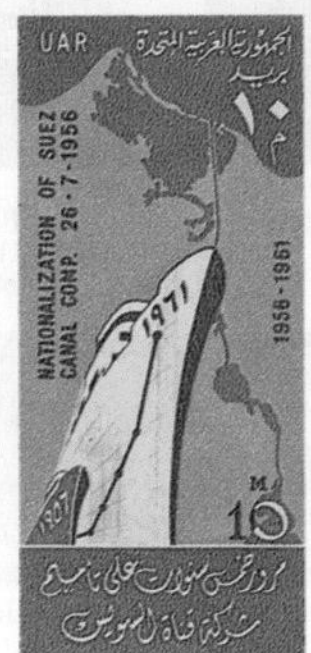

217 Ships and Map of Suez Canal

1961. 5th Anniv of Nationalization of Suez Canal.
666 **217** 10m. olive 35 25

218 Mehalla El Kobra Textile Factories

1961. Misr Bank Organization and 20th Death Anniv of Talaat Harb (founder).
667 **218** 10m. brown 25 15

219 Ship's Wheel and "Al Nasser" (destroyer) **220** "Industrial Worlds"

1961. Navy Day.
668 **219** 10m. blue 35 25

1961. As Nos. 553, etc. Inscr "UAR" only (in English). New colours.
669 1m. turquoise (as No. 603) 20 20
670 4m. olive (as No. 606) . . . 20 20
671 10m. violet 25 20
672 35m. slate (as No. 612) . . . 50 20
NEW DESIGN: 10m. Eagle of Saladin.
See also No. 739.

1961. U.N. Technical Co-operation. Programme and 16th Anniv of U.N.O.
674 – 10m. black and brown . . 25 20
675 **220** 35m. brown and green . . 40 30
DESIGN—VERT: 10m. Corncob, wheel and book ("Agriculture, Industry and Education").

221 Philae Temple

1961. 15th Anniv of UNESCO. and Preservation of Nubian Monuments Campaign (3rd issue).
676 **221** 10m. blue 60 35

222 "Fine Arts" **223** "Arts and Sciences"

1961. 4th Fine Arts Biennale, Alexandria.
677 **222** 10m. brown 25 20

1961. Education Day.
678 **223** 10m. purple 25 15

224 State Emblem, Torch and Olive Branch **225** Sphinx and Pyramid

1961. Victory Day.
679 **224** 10m. green and red . . . 25 20

1961. "Son et Lumiere" Display.
680 **225** 10m. black 35 25

226 Postal Authority Press Building, El Nasr

1962. Post Day.
681 **226** 10m. brown 30 20

227 King of Morocco and Map **229** Gaza Family with Egyptian Flag

228 Guide and Badge

1962. 1st Anniv of African Charter of Casablanca.
682 **227** 10m. blue 25 15

1962. Silver Jubilee of Egyptian Girl Guides Association.
683 **228** 10m. blue 45 25

1962. 5th Anniv of Egyptian Occupation of Gaza.
684 **229** 10m. myrtle 30 20

230 Mother and Child **231** League Centre, Cairo, and Emblem

1962. Mothers' Day.
694 **230** 10m. purple 25 20

1962. Arab League Week.
695 **231** 10m.+5m. black 35 30

232 W.M.O. Emblem and Weather-vane

1962. World Meteorological Day.
696 **232** 60m. blue and yellow . . 1·10 60

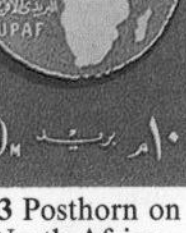

233 Posthorn on North Africa **235** Campaign Emblem

234 Cadets on Parade

1962. African Postal Union Commemoration.
697 **233** 10m. brown and red . . . 20 20
698 50m. brown and blue . . . 55 40

1962. 150th Anniv of Military Academy.
699 **234** 10m. green 25 15

1962. Malaria Eradication.
700 **235** 10m. red and sepia . . . 20 15
701 – 35m. blue and myrtle . . 40 35
DESIGN: 35m. As Type **235** but with laurel and inscription around emblem.

237 Bilharz and Microscope **238** Lumumba

1962. Death Centenary of Dr. Theodore Bilharz (discoverer of parasitic disease: bilharzia).
702 **237** 10m. brown 35 20

1962. Lumumba Commemoration.
703 **238** 10m. red (postage) . . . 25 20
704 – 35m. multicoloured (air) 50 40
DESIGN: 35m. Lumumba with laurel sprays and flaming torch.

239 "The Charter" **240** "Birth of the Revolution"

1962. Proclamation of National Charter.
705 **239** 10m. brown and blue . . 25 15

1962. 10th Anniv of 1952 Revolution.
706 **240** 10m. brown and pink . . 30 25
707 A 10m. sepia and blue . . . 30 25
708 B 10m. blue and sepia . . . 30 25
709 C 10m. blue and olive . . . 30 25
710 D 10m. red, black & green 30 25
711 E 10m. slate and brown . . 30 25
712 F 10m. purple and brown 30 25
713 G 10m. sepia and orange . . 30 25
MS714 70 × 80 mm. 100m. emerald, carmine, black and rose. Perf 2·20 1·70
MS715 As last. Imperf . . . . . 2·20 1·70
DESIGNS: A, Scroll and book; B, Agricultural Scene; C, Globe and dove; D, Flag and eagle emblem; E, Industrial scene and cogwheel; F, Dam construction; G, Eagle, building, cogwheel and ear of corn. **MS**714/15, Eagle emblem, Arab league emblem, United Nations emblems and maps of Africa and Aro-Asia.

241 M. Moukhtar (sculptor) and "La Vestale des Secrets"

1962. Moukhtar Museum Inaug.
716 **241** 10m. olive and blue . . . 25 20

242 Algerian Flag and map **243** Rocket

1962. Independence of Algeria.
717 **242** 10m. red, green & pink 25 15

1962. Launching of U.A.R. Rocket.
718 **243** 10m. red, black & green 30 20

244 Table Tennis Bat, Ball and Net

1962. 1st African Table Tennis Tournament, Alexandria, and 38th World Shooting Championships, Cairo.
719 **244** 5m. red and green 35 35
720 – 5m. red and green 35 35
721 **244** 10m. blue and ochre . . . 40 40
722 – 10m. blue and ochre . . . 40 40

723 **244** 35m. red and blue 85 85
724 – 35m. red and blue 85 85
DESIGN: Nos. 720, 722, 724, Rifle and target.

245 Dag Hammarskjold and U.N. Emblem

1962. 17th Anniv of U.N.O. and Dag Hammarskjold (Secretary-General, 1953–61) Commemoration.
725 **245** 5m. blue and violet . . . 20 20
726 10m. blue and green . . . 30 20
727 35m. blue & ultramarine 55 40

246 Coronation of Queen Nefertari (from small temple of Abu Simbel)

1962. UNESCO. Campaign for Preservation of Nubian Monuments (4th issue).
728 **246** 10m. brown and blue . . 55 30

247 Al Kahira Jet Trainer, College Emblem and De Havilland Tiger Moth Biplane

1962. Silver Jubilee of U.A.R. Air Force College.
729 **247** 10m. red and blue 30 20

248 Postal Authority Emblem

1963. Post Day and 1966 International Stamp Exhibition. Inscr "1866 1966".
736 **248** 20m.+10m. red & green 75 75
737 – 40m.+20m. sepia & brn 1·10 1·10
738 – 40m.+20m. brn & sepia 1·10 1·10
DESIGNS—TRIANGULAR: Egyptian stamps of 1866 – No. 737, 5 paras; No. 738, 10 paras.

1963. As No. 670 but inscr "1963" in English and Arabic and new colours.
739 4m. red, green and sepia . . 30 20

249 Yemeni Republican Flag and Torch

1963. Proclamation of Yemeni Arab Republic.
740 **249** 10m. red and olive . . . 25 20

250 Maritime Station, Alexandria

1963. Air.
741 **250** 20m. sepia 40 20
742 – 30m. mauve 50 30
743 – 40m. black 75 60
DESIGNS: 30m. International Airport, Cairo; 40m. Railway Station, Luxor.

251 Tennis-player

1963. 51st Int Lawn Tennis Championships held in U.A.R.
744 **251** 10m. brown and black . . 45 25

252 Cow and Emblems

1963. Freedom from Hunger.
745 **252** 5m. brown and violet . . 30 25
746 – 10m. yellow and blue . . 35 25
747 – 35m. yellow and blue . . 50 45
DESIGNS—VERT: 10m. Corncob and ear of wheat. HORIZ: 35m. Corncob, ear of wheat, U.N. and F.A.O. emblems.

253 Centenary Emblem within Red Crescent

254 "Arab Socialist Union"

1963. Centenary of Red Cross.
748 **253** 10m. red, purple & blue 25 15
749 – 35m. red and blue 50 50
DESIGN: 35m. Emblem, Red Crescent, olive branches and Globe.

1963. 11th Anniv of Revolution.
750 **254** 10m. mauve and blue . . 25 20
MS751 70 × 80 mm. 50m. ultramarine and yellow (Tools, torch and symbol of National Charter) . . . . 1·70 1·70
MS752 As last, imperf . . . . . 1·70 1·70

255 T.V. Building, Cairo, and Television Receiver

1963. 2nd Int Television Festival, Alexandria.
753 **255** 10m. yellow and blue . . 25 20

256 Queen Nefertari

257 Swimmer and Map

1963. UNESCO. Campaign for preservation of Nubian Monuments (5th issue).
754 **256** 5m. yellow and blue . . . 35 20
755 – 10m. orange and black . . 45 30
756 – 35m. yellow and black . . 80 55

DESIGNS—(28 × 61 mm): 10m. Great Hall of Pillars, Abu Simbel. As Type **256**: 35m. Heads of Colossi, Abu Simbel.

1963. Suez Canal Int Long-distance Swimming Race.
757 **257** 10m. red and blue 30 20

1963. Air.
758 50m. brown and blue . . . . 1·50 60
759 80m. purple and blue . . . . 1·90 90
761 115m. yellow and brown . . 2·10 80
762 140m. red and violet . . . . 2·20 1·30
DESIGNS—VERT: 50m. Cairo Tower and Arch. HORIZ: 80m. As No. 622; 115m. Colossi of Rameses II and Queen Nefertari, Abu Simbel; 140m. Seated colossi of Rameses II (Great Temple, Abu Simbel).

258 Ministry Building

1963. 50th Anniv of Egyptian Ministry of Agriculture.
763 **258** 10m. blue and brown . . 25 20

259 Map and Blocks of Flats

1963. Afro-Asian Housing Congress.
764 **259** 10m. blue and brown . . 25 20

259a Globe and Scales of Justice

1963. 15th Anniv of Declaration of Human Rights.
765 **259a** 5m. yellow and green . . 20 20
766 – 10m. black, brown & bl 25 20
767 – 35m. blk, pink & red . . 55 35
DESIGNS: 10, 35m. As Type **259a** but arranged differently.

259b Statuette, Palette and Arms of Alexandria

1963. 5th Fine Arts Biennale, Alexandria.
768 **259b** 10m. brown and blue . . 25 20

260 El Mitwalli Gate, Cairo

261 Glass and Enamel Urn

263 King Osircaf

1964.
769 – 1m. blue and green . . . 15 15
770 – 2m. bistre and purple . . 15 15
771 – 3m. blue, orge & salmon 15 15
772 – 4m. brown, black & blue 20 15
773 – 5m. brown, lt brn & blue 15 15
774 – 10m. lt brn, brn & grn . . 30 15
775 – 15m. yell, ultram & bl . . 30 15
776 – 20m. brown and blue . . 70 15
777 **260** 20m. green . . . . 1·40 20
778 **261** 30m. brown & yellow . . 65 15
779 – 35m. brown, bl & orge . . 65 15
780 – 40m. blue and yellow . . 1·50 30
781 – 55m. violet . . . . 1·90 15
782 – 60m. brown and blue . . 90 40
783 **263** 100m. blue and purple . . 2·75 60
784 – 200m. brown and blue . . 5·75 85
785 – 500m. orange and blue . . 12·50 2·50
DESIGNS—As Type **260**. 55m. Kiosk, Sultan Hussein Mosque. As Type **261**—VERT: 1m. 14th-century glass vase; 4m. Minaret and archway; 10m. Eagle emblem and pyramids; 35m. Queen Nefertari; 40m. Nile near Agouza; 60m. Al-Azhar Mosque. HORIZ: 2m. Ancient Egyptian headrest; 3m. Alabaster funerary barge; 5m. Aswan High Dam; 15m. Window, Ahmed ibn Toulon Mosque; 20m. (No. 776), Nile Hilton Hotel and Kasr el Nile Bridge. As Type **263**: 200m. Rameses; 500m. Tutankhamun.
For the 4m. in different colours, and with date "1964" added to design see No. 791.
For stamps as Nos. 777 and 781 but larger and in different colours, see Nos. 1042, 1044, 1134/5 and 1137.

264 Eagle and Pyramids

265 Emblems on Map of Africa

1964. Post Day.
786 **264** 10m.+5m. green & yell . . 1·60 90
787 80m.+40m. blk & bl . . . 3·00 1·90
788 115m.+55m. blk & brn . . 3·75 2·50

1964. 1st Health, Sanitation and Nutrition Commission Conference, Cairo.
789 **265** 10m. yellow and blue . . 25 20

266 League Emblem and Links

1964. Arab League Heads of State Council, Cairo.
790 **266** 10m. black and green . . 25 20

267 Arch and Minaret

269 King Akhnaton and Family (Tutankhamun's tomb)

268 Map and Old and New Houses

1964. Ramadan Festival.
791 **267** 4m. green, red & black . . 25 15

1964. Nubians' Resettlement.
792 **268** 10m. yellow & purple . . 25 20

1964. Mothers' Day.
793 **269** 10m. brown and blue . . 50 25

270 Diesel Train and Afro-Asian Map

1964. Asian Railways Conference.
794 **270** 10m. yellow and blue . . 70 20

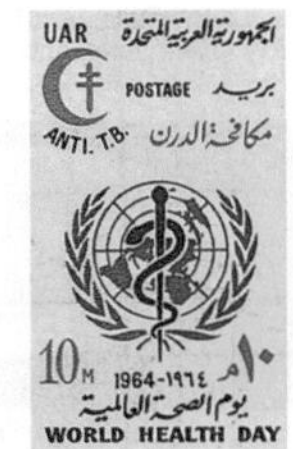

271 Office Emblem 272 W.H.O. Emblem

1964. 10th Anniv of Arab Postal Union's Permanent Office.
795 **271** 10m. blue and brown . . 25 20

1964. World Health Day.
796 **272** 10m. blue and red 25 20

273 Statue of Liberty, U.A.R. Pavilion and Pyramids

1964. New York World's Fair.
797 **273** 10m. green, brn & olive 20 15

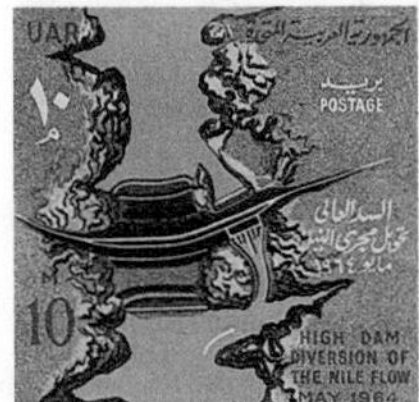

274 Site of Diversion

1964. Nile High Dam (Diversion of Flow).
798 **274** 10m. black and blue . . . 25 20

275 Map of Africa and Flags

1964. O.A.U. Assembly, Cairo.
799 **275** 10m. black, blue & brn 30 20

276 "Electricity"

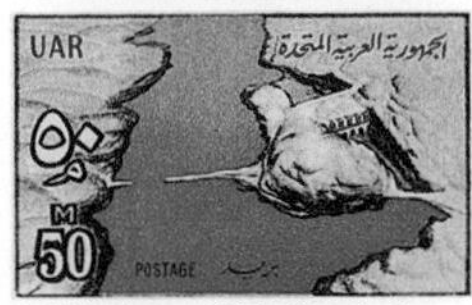

276a Aswan High Dam before Diversion of the Nile

1964. Aswan Dam Projects. (a) as Type **276**.
800 **276** 10m. blue and green . . . 35 25
801 – 10m. green and yellow . . 35 25
DESIGN: No. 801, "Land Reclamation" (tractor and symbols of land cultivation).

(b) Miniature sheet. Imperf.
MS802 102 × 82 mm. Two 50m. stamps in black and blue, T **276a** and similar design showing dam after diversion of the Nile. Imperf 3·00 3·00

277 Jamboree Badge

1964. 6th Pan Arab Scout Jamboree, Alexandria.
803 **277** 10m. green and red . . . 35 25
804 – 10m. red and green . . . 35 25
DESIGN: No. 804, Air Scout badge.

278 Algerian Flag

1964. 2nd Arab League Heads of State Council. Flags in national colours; inscr in green (except Sudan, in blue). Each with country name at foot.
805 10m. Type **278** 55 30
806 10m. Iraq 55 30
807 10m. Jordan 55 30
808 10m. Kuwait 55 30
809 10m. Lebanon 55 30
810 10m. Libya 55 30
811 10m. Morocco 55 30
812 10m. Saudi Arabia 55 30
813 10m. Sudan 55 30
814 10m. Syria 55 30
815 10m. Tunisia 55 30
816 10m. U.A.R. 55 30
817 10m. Yemen 55 30

279 Globe, Dove and Pyramids

1964. Non-aligned Countries Conf, Cairo.
818 **279** 10m. yellow and blue . . 25 20

280 Emblem and Map 281 Gymnastics

1964. 1st Afro-Asian Medical Congress.
819 **280** 10m. violet and yellow . . 25 20

1964. Olympic Games, Tokyo.
820 – 5m. orange and green . . 30 20
821 **281** 10m. ochre and blue . . . 30 20
822 – 35m. ochre and purple . . 75 50
823 – 50m. brown and blue . . 1·10 70
DESIGNS—As Type **281**. HORIZ: 5m. Gymnastics. VERT: 35m. Wrestling. LARGER (61 × 28 mm): 50m. Charioteer hunting lions.

282 Emblems of Posts and Telecommunications and Map 283 Rameses II

1964. Pan-African and Malagasy Posts and Telecommunications Congress, Cairo.
824 **282** 10m. sepia and green . . 25 20

1964. UNESCO. Campaign for Preservation of Nubian Monuments (6th issue).
825 – 5m. brown and blue . . . 25 20
826 **283** 10m. yellow and sepia . . 50 25
827 – 35m. blue and brown . . 1·40 90
MS828 106 × 63 mm. 50m. green and purple. Imperf . . . . 11·00 11·00
DESIGNS—SQUARE (40 × 40 mm): 5m. Horus and facade of Abu Simbel; 35m. Wall sculpture, Abu Simbel. HORIZ (42 × 25 mm)—50m. The Goddess Isis.

284 Handicrafts and Weaving 285 U.N. and UNESCO Emblems

1964. 25th Anniv of Ministry of Social Affairs.
829 **284** 10m. blue and yellow . . 25 20

1964. UNESCO Day.
830 **285** 10m. blue and yellow . . 25 20

286 Emblem and Posthorn

1965. Post Day and 1966 Int Stamp Exn.
831 **286** 10m.+5m. red, purple and green 60 50
832 – 10m.+5m. red, black and blue 60 50
833 – 80m.+40m. black, green and red . . . . . . 1·30 1·60
DESIGNS—As Type **286**: No. 832, Posthorn over emblem. As Type **248**: 80m. Bird carrying letter, inscr "STAMP CENTENARY EXHIBITION".

286a Al-Maridani Mosque Minaaret 287 Police Emblem

1965. Ramadan Festival.
834 **286a** 4m. brown and blue . . 35 25

1965. Police Day.
835 **287** 10m. yellow and sepia . . 50 20

288 Oil Derrick 289 Emblem and Flags

1965. 5th Arab Petroleum Congress and 2nd Petroleum Exhibition.
836 **288** 10m. sepia and yellow . . 40 25

1965. 20th Anniv of Arab League.
837 **289** 10m. green and red . . . 50 30
838 – 20m. brown and blue . . 65 40
DESIGN—HORIZ: 20m. Arab League emblem.

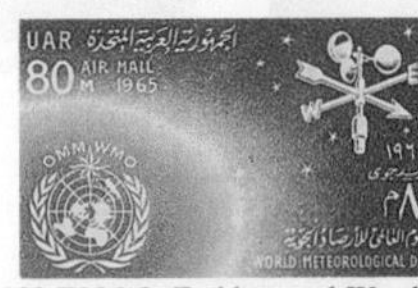

290 W.M.O. Emblem and Weather-vane

1965. Air. World Meteorological Day.
839 **290** 80m. purple and blue . . 1·90 90

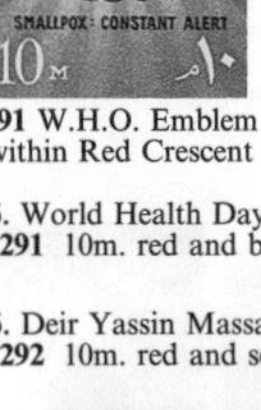

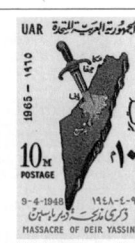

291 W.H.O. Emblem within Red Crescent 292 Dagger on Deir Yassin, Palestine

1965. World Health Day.
840 **291** 10m. red and blue 55 30

1965. Deir Yassin Massacre.
841 **292** 10m. red and sepia . . . 80 25

293 I.T.U. Emblem and Symbols

1965. Centenary of I.T.U.
842 **293** 5m. purple, yell & blk . . 30 25
843 10m. pink, yellow & red 35 25
844 35m. blue, yell & dp bl 1·00 80

294 Lamp and Burning Library

1965. Reconstitution of Algiers University Library.
845 **294** 10m. green, red & black 40 20

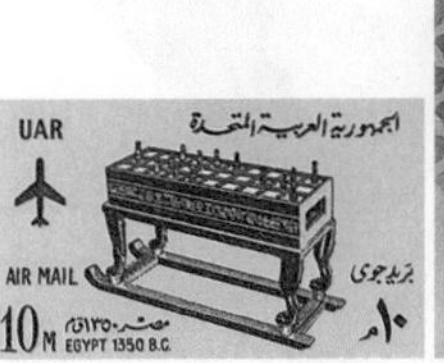

295 Senet Table of 1350 B.C. 296 Shaikh Mohamed Abdo

1965. Air. Re-establishment of Egyptian Civil Airlines, "MISRAIR".
846 **295** 10m. blue and yellow . . 1·20 30

1965. 60th Death Anniv of Shaikh Abdo (mufti).
847 **296** 10m. brown and blue . . 25 20

297 "Housing"

1965. 13th Anniv of Revolution.
848 **297** 10m. black and brown . . 50 35
849 – 10m. brown & yellow . . 50 35
850 – 10m. indigo and blue . . 50 35
851 – 100m. black and green . . 3·75 3·00
DESIGNS—SQUARE: No. 849, "Heavy Industry" (ladle and furnace); 850, "Petroleum and Mining" (refinery and oil rig "Discoverer"). 80 × 80 mm: No. 851, President Nasser.

298 Stadium, Flag and Torch

1965. 4th Pan-Arab Games, Cairo.
857 **298** 5m. blue & red on blue 30 30
858 – 10m. brown and blue . . 50 30
859 – 35m. brown and green . . 85 70
DESIGNS—As Type **298**: 35m. Horse "Saadoon". DIAMOND (56 × 56 mm): 10m. Map and emblems of Arab countries.

299 Swimmers Zeitun and Abd el Gelil

1965. Long-distance Swimming Championships, Alexandria.
860 **299** 10m. sepia and blue . . . 40 25

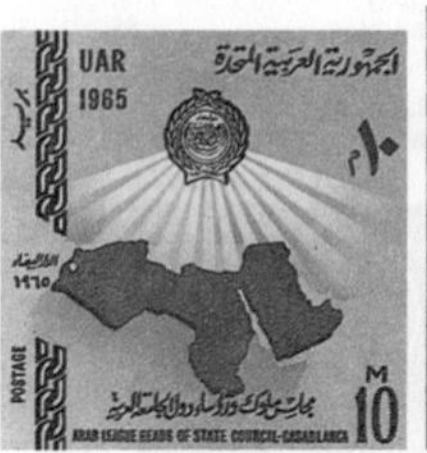

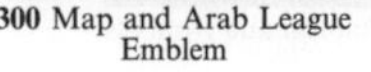
300 Map and Arab League Emblem
301 Land Forces Emblem

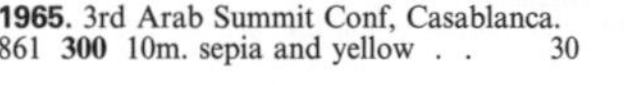
1965. 3rd Arab Summit Conf, Casablanca.
861 **300** 10m. sepia and yellow . . 30 20

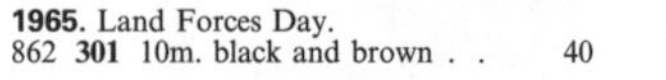
1965. Land Forces Day.
862 **301** 10m. black and brown . . 40 25

302 Flaming Torch on Africa

1965. O.A.U. Assembly, Accra.
863 **302** 10m. purple and red . . . 30 20

303 Rameses II, Abu Simbel

1965. UNESCO. Campaign for Preservation of Nubian Monuments (7th issue).
864 **303** 5m. blue and yellow . . . 60 35
865 – 10m. black and blue . . . 1·10 35
866 – 35m. violet and yellow . . 2·20 1·10
MS867 105 × 63 mm. 50m. brown and ultramarine. Imperf . . . 3·50 3·00
DESIGNS—As Type **303**: 35m. Colossi, Abu Simbel. VERT: (28 × 61½ mm): 10m. Hall of Pillars, Abu Simbel. HORIZ (42 × 25 mm.)—50m. Cartouche of Rameses II and ICY emblem.

304 Al-Maqrizi, Scrolls and Books
305 Bust and Flag

1965. 600th Birth Anniv of Al-Maqrizi (historian).
868 **304** 10m. blue and olive . . . 30 20

1965. 6th Fine Arts Biennale, Alexandria.
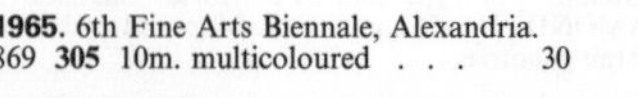
869 **305** 10m. multicoloured . . . 30 20

306 Pigeon, Parchment and Horseman
307 Glass Lamp

1966. Post Day.
870 **306** 10m. orange, yellow and blue (postage) 50 20
871 – 80m.+40m. purple, yellow and blue (air) . . . . . 2·30 1·90
872 – 115m.+55m. blue, yellow and purple . . . . . . 3·00 2·50
MS873 106 × 62 mm. 140m.+60m. black, blue and pink . . . . . 3·75 3·50
DESIGNS—As T **306**—80m. Pharaonic messengers; 115m. De Havilland D.H.34 airplane and 1926 27m. air stamps; **MS**873—5 and 10pi. Stamps of 1866.

1966. Ramadan Festival.
874 **307** 4m. orange and violet . . 30 20

308 Exhibition Emblem
309 Arab League Emblem

1966. Industrial Exhibition, Cairo.
875 **308** 10m. black, blue & lt bl 30 20

1966. Arab Publicity Week.
876 **309** 10m. violet and yellow . . 30 20

310 Torch and Newspapers
312 Traffic Signals

311 Rock Temples of Abu Simbel

1966. Centenary of Egyptian National Press.
877 **310** 10m. slate and orange . . 30 20

1966. Air. UNESCO. Campaign for Preservation of Nubian Monuments (8th issue).
878 **311** 20m. multicoloured . . . 60 40
879 80m. multicoloured . . . 1·40 1·10

1966. Traffic Day.
880 **312** 10m. red, emerald & grn 50 25

313 Torch
315 Emblem, People and City

314 "Labourers"

1966. U.A.R.–Iraq Union Agreement.
881 **313** 10m. red, grn & pur . . . 30 20

1966. 50th Session of I.L.O. Conference.
882 **314** 5m. black & turquoise . . 25 20
883 10m. green and purple . . 25 20
884 35m. black and orange . . 80 60

1966. 1st Population Census.
885 **315** 10m. purple and brown 25 15

316 Building "Salah-el-Deen"

317 Arab Dancers

1966. 14th Anniv of Revolution. (a) As T **316**
886 **316** 10m. black, blue & orge 40 25
887 – 10m. purple, yell & grn 40 25
888 – 10m. blue, yellow & blk 40 25
889 – 10m. turq, bl & red . . . 40 25

(b) Miniature sheets. Imperf.
MS890 115 × 67 mm. **317** 100m. vermilion, blue and brown . . 4·00 4·00
DESIGNS: No. 886, Type **316** (shipbuilding); 887, Transfer of first stones at Abu Simbel; 888, Map (development of Sinai); 889, El Mahdi hospital, nurse and patient.

318 Suez Canal H.Q., "Southern Cross" (liner), Freighter and Map

1966. 10th Anniv of Suez Canal Nationalization.
891 **318** 10m. red and blue 75 35

319 Jamboree Emblem and Camp

1966. Air. 7th Pan-Arab Scout Jamboree, Libya.
892 **319** 20m. red and olive . . . 75 35

320 Cotton

1966. Peasants' Day.
893 **320** 5m. violet, yell & blue . . 25 20
894 – 10m. brn & grn (Rice) . . 25 20
895 – 35m. orge & bl (Onions) 70 55

321 W.H.O. Building

1966. U.N. Day.
896 **321** 5m. violet and olive . . . 25 20
897 – 10m. violet and orange . . 25 20
898 – 35m. violet and blue . . . 65 45
DESIGNS: 10m. U.N.R.W.A. (Refugees) emblem; 35m. UNICEF emblem.

322 Globe and Festival Emblem

1966. 5th Int Television Festival.
899 **322** 10m. violet and yellow . . 35 20

323 St. Catherine's Monastery

1966. Air. 1400th Anniv of St. Catherine's Monastery, Mt. Sinai.
900 **323** 80m. red, yellow & blue 1·80 1·10

324 Eagle and Torch

1966. Victory Day.
901 **324** 10m. red and green . . . 35 20

325 Anubis (God)

1967. Post Day. Designs showing items from Tutankhamun's Tomb.
902 **325** 10m. multicoloured . . . 1·00 30
903 – 35m. brown. pur & bl . . 2·00 50
904 – 80m.+20m. brown, yellow and blue . . . . 2·40 1·80
905 – 115m.+40m. brown, black and blue . . . . 4·00 3·25
DESIGNS—As T **325**: 35m. Alabaster head (stopper from canopic urn); 27 × 60 mm: 80m. Ushabti figure; 115m. Statue of Tutankhamun.

326 Carnations
327 Tree-planting

1967. Ramadan Festival.
906 **326** 4m. violet and olive . . . 30 20

1967. Tree Festival.
907 **327** 10m. lilac and green . . . 30 20

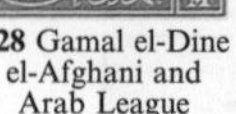
328 Gamal el-Dine el-Afghani and Arab League Emblem
329 Workers, Factories and Census Symbol

1967. Arab Publicity Week.
908 **328** 10m. brown and green . . 30 20

1967. 1st Industrial Census.
909 **329** 10m. green & orange . . 30 20

330 Hawker Siddeley Comet 4 Aircraft at Cairo Airport

1967. Air.
910 **330** 20m. blue and brown . . 65 30

331 "Workers" (rock-carving)

1967. Labour Day.
911 **331** 10m. orange and olive . . 35 25

332 Nefertari and Rameses II

1967. International Tourist Year.
912 **332** 10m. red, yellow and green (postage) 75 35
913 – 35m. orange, yell & bl . . 2·40 80
914 – 20m. lilac, black and orange (air) 95 30
915 – 80m. brown, yell & bl . . 1·90 95
916 – 115m. orange, bl & brn 3·50 1·40
DESIGNS—As T **332**: 35m. Shooting red-breasted geese; 40 × 40 mm: 20m. Hotel, El Alamein; 80m. Virgin's Tree; 115m. Hotel and fishes, Red Sea.

333 Pres. Nasser and Map

1967. Arab Solidarity for Palestine Defence.
917 **333** 10m. olive, yell & orge . . 1·70 1·00

334 "Petroleum" (oil rigs)

335 National Products (½-size illustration)

1967. Air. 15th Anniv of Revolution. (a) As Type **334**.
930 **334** 50m. black, orange and blue 80 50

(b) Miniature sheet. Imperf.
MS931 112 × 66 mm. **335** 100m. multicoloured (imperf) . . . . 3·25 3·25

336 Salama Higazi

337 Porcelain Dish

1967. 50th Death Anniv of Higazi (lyric stage impresario).
932 **336** 20m. brown and blue . . 50 20

1967. U.N. Day. Egyptian Art.
933 20m. blue & red (postage) . . 60 30
934 55m. multicoloured . . . . . 1·20 50
935 80m. red, yellow & blue (air) 1·60 65
DESIGNS: 20m. Type **337**. 55m. "Christ in Glory" (painting); 80m. Tutankhamun and Ankhesenamun (back of throne).

338 Savings Bank "Coffer"

1967. World Savings Day.
936 **338** 20m. blue and pink . . . 40 25

339 Ca d'Oro Palace (Venice) and Santa Maria Cathedral (Florence)

1967. "Save the Monuments of Florence and Venice".
937 **339** 80m.+20m. brown, yellow and green . . . . . . 1·30 1·20
938 – 115m.+30m. bl, yell & ol 2·00 1·80
DESIGN: 115m. Palace of the Doges and Campanile (Venice) and Vecchio Palace (Florence).

340 Rose

341 Isis

1967. Ramadan Festival.
939 **340** 5m. purple and green . . 35 20

1968. Post Day. Pharaonic Dress.
940 **341** 20m. sepia, green & yell 70 20
941 – 55m. brown, yellow & grn 1·40 60
942 – 80m. red, blue & blk . . 1·90 90
DESIGNS: 55m. Nefertari; 80m. Isis (different).
See also Nos. 970/3.

342 High Dam and Power Station

1968. Electrification of High Dam.
943 **342** 20m. purple, yellow & bl 35 20

343 Alabaster Vessel (Tutankhamun)

344 Head of Woman

1968. International Museums Festival.
944 **343** 20m. brown, yellow & bl 50 25
945 – 80m. grn, vio & emer . . 1·00 65
DESIGN—39 × 39 mm: 80m. Capital of Coptic limestone pillar.

1968. 7th Fine Arts Biennale, Alexandria.
946 **344** 20m. black and blue . . . 25 20

345 "The Glorious Koran" (½-size illustration)

1968. Air. 1400th Anniv of The Holy Koran.
947 **345** 30m. violet, blue & yell 75 75
948 80m. violet, blue & yell 1·00 1·00

346 Tending Cattle

1968. Arab Veterinary Congress.
949 **346** 20m. brown, grn & yell 50 20

347 St. Mark and St. Mark's Cathedral

1968. Air. 1900th Anniv of Martyrdom of St. Mark.
950 **347** 80m. sepia, mauve & grn 1·30 70

348 Human Rights Emblem

349 Open Book and Symbols

350 Marchers, Cogwheel and open book (½-size illustration)

1968. Human Rights Year.
951 **348** 20m. red, green & olive 35 20
952 60m. red, green & blue . . 75 60

1968. 16th Anniv of Revolution. (a) As T **349**.
953 **349** 20m. green and rose . . . 35 20

(b) Miniature sheet. Imperf.
MS954 117 × 69 mm. **350** 100m. plum, orange and green (imperf) 3·00 2·50

351 W.H.O. Emblem and Imhotep

352 Table Tennis Bats, Net and Ball

1968. 20th Anniv of W.H.O.
955 **351** 20m. sepia, yell & blue . . 75 40
956 – 20m. turq, sep & yell . . 75 40
DESIGN: No. 956, W.H.O. emblem and Avicenna.

1968. 1st Mediterranean Table Tennis Tournament.
957 **352** 20m. brown and green . . 60 25

353 Industrial Skyline

1968. International Industrial Fair, Cairo.
958 **353** 20m. red, indigo and blue 30 20

354 Philae Temple

355 Scout Badge

1968. United Nations Day.
959 – 20m. salmon, vio & blue 80 25
960 – 30m. blue, orge & yell . . 1·10 50
961 **354** 55m. purple, yell & blue 2·00 65
DESIGNS (62 × 29 mm): 20m. Philae Temples (aerial view); (As Type **354**): 30m. Refugee women and children.

1968. 50th Anniv of Egyptian Scout Movement.
962 **355** 10m. blue and orange . . 50 20

356 Ancient Games

1968. Olympic Games Mexico.
963 **356** 20m. violet, olive & orge 65 20
964 – 30m. violet, blue & buff 90 45
DESIGN: 30m. Ancient Games (different).

357 Boeing 707 Jetliner and Route Map

358 Ali Moubarek (educator)

1968. Air. 1st United Arab Airlines Boeing Flight, Cairo–London.
965 **357** 55m. red, blue & orange 1·00 55

1968. 75th Death Anniv of Ali Moubarek.
966 **358** 20m. lilac, orange & grn 35 20

359 Boy and Girl

360 Lotus

1968. World Children's Day.
967 **359** 20m.+10m. red, bl & brn 65 65
968 – 20m.+10m. bl, brn & grn 65 65
DESIGN: No. 968, Group of Children.

1968. Ramadan Festival.
969 **360** 5m. yellow, bl & grn . . . 40 20

1968. Post Day. Pharaonic Dress. As T **341**.
970 5m. brown, yellow and blue 55 25
971 20m. yellow, red and blue . . 85 40
972 20m. brown, cinnamon & bl 95 50
973 55m. orange, yellow & blue 2·20 1·10
DESIGNS: No. 970, Son of Ramess III; 971, Rameses III; 972, Maiden carrying offerings; 973, Queen Nefertari.

361 H. Nassef (poet and writer)

363 Teacher at Blackboard

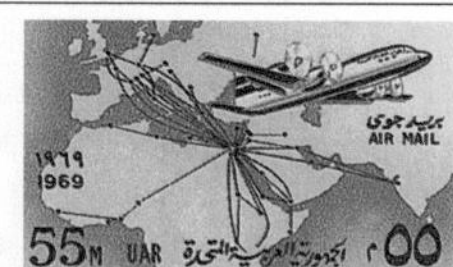
362 Ilyushin Il-18 and Route Map

1969. 50th Death Anniv of Hefni Nassef and Mohamed Farid.
974 **361** 20m. brown and violet . . 40 35
975 – 20m. brown and green . . 40 35
DESIGN: No. 975, M. Farid (politician).

1969. Air. Inauguration of Ilyushin Il-18 Aircraft by United Arab Airlines.
976 **362** 55m. purple, yellow & bl 80 55

1969. Arab Teachers' Day.
977 **363** 20m. multicoloured . . . 35 20

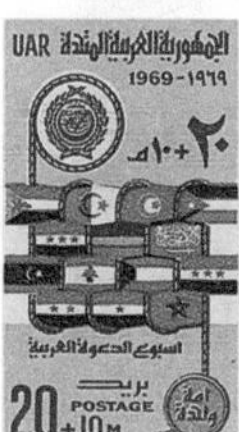
364 Flags of Arab Nations

365 I.L.O. Emblem and Factory Stacks

1969. Arab Publicity Week.
978 **364** 20m.+10m. red, bl & grn 40 40

1969. 50th Anniv of I.L.O.
979 **365** 20m. multicoloured . . . 35 20

366 Algerian Flag

1969. African Tourist Year. Flags of African Nations.
980 **366** 10m. red and green . . . 75 45
981 – 10m. black, blue & grn 75 45
982 – 10m. red and green . . . 75 45
983 – 10m. red, yellow & grn 75 45
984 – 10m. multicoloured . . . 75 45
985 – 10m. yellow, red & blue 75 45
986 – 10m. brown, red & grn 75 45
987 – 10m. red, yellow & blue 75 45
988 – 10m. brown, red & grn 75 45
989 – 10m. green, red & black 75 45
990 – 10m. multicoloured . . . 75 45
991 – 10m. multicoloured . . . 75 45
992 – 10m. yellow, grn & bl . . 75 45
993 – 10m. blue, red & green 75 45
994 – 10m. multicoloured . . . 75 45
995 – 10m. brown, red & grn 75 45
996 – 10m. orange & green . . 75 45
997 – 10m. black, red & green 75 45
998 – 10m. blue, red & green 75 45
999 – 10m. red and blue . . . 75 45
1000 – 10m. black, red & green 75 45
1001 – 10m. red and green . . . 75 45
1002 – 10m. red, black & green 75 45
1003 – 10m. brown, red & grn 75 45
1004 – 10m. yellow & green . . 75 45
1005 – 10m. multicoloured . . . 75 45
1006 – 10m. green and red . . . 75 45
1007 – 10m. orange & green . . 75 45
1008 – 10m. green 75 45
1009 – 10m. multicoloured . . . 75 45
1010 – 10m. green, brown & red 75 45
1011 – 10m. blue and green . . 75 45
1012 – 10m. blue and green . . 75 45
1013 – 10m. yellow, green & bl 75 45
1014 – 10m. multicoloured . . . 75 45
1015 – 10m. multicoloured . . . 75 45
1016 – 10m. yellow, grn & red 75 45
1017 – 10m. red and green . . . 75 45
1018 – 10m. black, yellow & red 75 45
1019 – 10m. black, red & green 75 45
1020 – 10m. multicoloured . . . 75 45
FLAGS: No. 981, Botswana. 982, Burundi. 983, Cameroun. 984, Central African Republic. 985, Chad. 986, Congo-Brazzaville. 987, Congo-Kinshasa. 988, Dahomey. 989, Egypt-U.A.R. 990, Equatorial Guinea. 991, Ethiopia. 992, Gabon. 993, Gambia. 994, Ghana. 995, Guinea. 996, Ivory Coast. 997, Kenya. 998, Lesotho. 999, Liberia. 1000, Libya. 1001, Malagasy Republic. 1002, Malawi. 1003, Mali. 1004, Mauritania. 1005, Mauritius. 1006, Morocco. 1007, Niger. 1008, Nigeria. 1009, Rwanda. 1010, Senegal. 1011, Sierra Leone. 1012, Somalia. 1013, Sudan. 1014, Swaziland. 1015, Tanzania. 1016, Togo. 1017, Tunisia. 1018, Uganda. 1019, Upper Volta. 1020, Zambia.

367 El Fetouh Gate

368 Development Bank Emblem

1969. Cairo Millenary.
1021 **367** 10m. brown, yellow & bl 45 20
1022 – 10m. multicoloured . . . 45 20
1023 – 10m. pink and blue . . . 45 20
1024 – 20m. multicoloured . . . 80 35
1025 – 20m. purple, yellow & bl 80 35
1026 – 20m. blue, yellow & brn 80 35
MS1027 128 × 70 mm. Four 20m. designs multicoloured . . . . 7·50 7·00
DESIGNS—HORIZ (38 × 22 mm)—No. 1021, T **367**; 1022 Al-Azhar University; 1023 Citadel. (57½ × 24½ mm)—No. 1024, Two Sculptures from Pharaonic period; 1025 Carved decorations, Coptic era; 1026 Glassware Fatimid dynasty. VERT (31½ × 21½)—**MS**1027, (a) Coptic dish, (b) Fatimid jewels, (c) Copper vase, Mameluke period, (d) Islamic coins.

1969. 5th Anniv of African Development Bank.
1028 **368** 20m. green, vio & yell 30 20

369 Mahatma Gandhi

370 "King and Queen" Abu Simbel (UNESCO)

1969. Air. Birth Cent of Mahatma Gandhi.
1029 **369** 80m. orange, brn & bl 2·75 95

1969. United Nations Day.
1030 **370** 5m. yellow, blue & brn 30 25
1031 – 20m. blue and yellow . . 80 25
1032 – 30m.+10m. mult 80 60
1033 – 55m. multicoloured . . . 1·10 50
DESIGNS—As T **370**: 20m. Ancient Egyptian Ship (I.M.C.O.); 36 × 36mm: 30m.+10m. Arab refugees (U.N.R.W.A.); 55m. Partly submerged temple, Philae (UNESCO).

371 Demonstrators

1969. Anniversaries.
1034 **371** 20m. purple, red & grn 60 25
1035 – 20m. brown, yellow & bl 1·00 40
1036 – 20m. multicoloured . . . 75 35
DESIGNS AND EVENTS: No. 1034, (50th anniv of 1919 Revolution). LARGER (58 × 25 mm); No. 1035, Labourers, merchant ships of 1869 and 1969 and map (Suez Canal Centenary); 1036, Performance of "Aida" (Cairo Opera-house Centenary).

372 "Ancient Egyptian Accountants"

1969. International Scientific Accounts Congress, Cairo.
1037 **372** 20m. purple, grn & yell 65 35

373 Poinsettia

1969. Ramadan Festival.
1038 **373** 5m. red, green & yellow 35 20

374 Step Pyramid, Sakkara

375 President Nasser

1969.
1039 **374** 1m. brown, ochre & bl 20 25
1040 – 5m. brown, yellow & bl 35 20
1041 – 10m. purple, ochre & bl 35 20
1042 **260** 20m. brown (22 × 27½ mm) . . . . 2·10 30
1043 – 50m. brn, ochre & bl . . 2·00 45
1044 – 55m. green . . . . . . 3·00 25
1045 **375** 200m. blue & purple . . 5·75 1·10
1046 500m. black and blue . . 13·00 3·75
1047 – £El green and orange . . 38·00 8·50
DESIGNS—As Type **374**: 5m. Al-Azhar Mosque, Cairo; 10m. Temple, Luxor; 50m. Qaitbay Fort, Alexandria. 22 × 27½ mm: 55m. As No. 781. As T **375**: £El, Khafre.
See also Nos. 1131/41.

376a Imam Mohamed El Boukhary

377 Azzahir Beybars Mosque

1969. Air. 1100th Death Anniv of Imam El Boukhary (philosopher and writer).
1048 **376a** 30m. brown and olive 50 20

1969. Air. 700th Anniv of Azzahir Beybars Mosque.
1049 **377** 30m. purple 50 20

378 "Three Veiled Women" (Mahmoud Said)

1970. Post Day.
1050 **378** 100m. multicoloured . . 2·50 2·00

379 Parliament Building and Emblems

1970. Int Conf on Middle East Crisis, Cairo.
1051 **379** 20m. ultram, brn & bl 50 20

380 Human Rights Emblem and "Three Races"

1970. Racial Equality Day.
1052 **380** 20m.+10m. yellow, brown and green . . . 85 55

381 Arab League Flag, Arms and Map

1970. 25th Anniv of Arab League.
1053 **381** 20m.+10m. green, brown and blue 65 45
1054 30m. grn, plum & orge 55 30

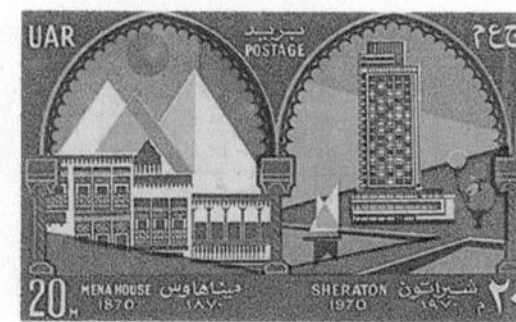
382 Mina House Hotel, Giza, and Sheraton Hotel, Cairo

1970. Centenary of Mina House Hotel and Opening of Sheraton Hotel.
1055 **382** 20m. green, orange & bl 55 25

383 Pharmacists

1970. 30th Anniv of Egyptian Pharmaceutical Industry.
1056 **383** 20m. blue, brown & yell 75 25

384 Mermaid

385 Lenin

1970. 8th Fine Arts Biennale, Alexandria.
1057 **384** 20m. blk, bl & orge . . 55 20

1970. Air. Birth Centenary of Lenin.
1058 **385** 80m. brown and green 1·10 75

386 Emblem and Bombed Factory

1970. Air. Attack on Abu Zaabal Factory.
1059 **386** 80m. purple, bl & yell 1·10 75

387 Talaat Harb (founder) and Bank

388 I.T.U. Emblem

1970. 50th Anniv of Misr Bank.
1060 **387** 20m. brn, ochre & bl . . 45 20

1970. World Telecommunications Day.
1061 **388** 20m. blue, yell & brn . . 50 20

389 New Headquarters Building

390 Basketball Player, Cup and Map

1970. New U.P.U. Headquarters Building, Berne.
1062 **389** 20m. purple, green and yellow (postage) . . . 50 25
1063 80m. black, green and yellow (air) 85 65

1970. 5th Africa Men's Basketball Championships.
1064 **390** 20m. blue, brn & yell . . 70 30

391 Emblems of U.P.U., U.N. and African Postal Union

1970. African Postal Union Seminar.
1065 **391** 20m. green, vio & orge 50 20

392 Footballer and Cup

393 Clenched Fists and Dove

1970. Africa Cup Football Championships.
1066 **392** 20m. brown, yellow & bl 65 30

1970. 18th Anniv of Revolution.
1067 **393** 20m. orge, blk & grn . . 60 25
MS1068 111 × 70 mm. **393** 100m. orange, black and blue. Imperf 3·25 3·00

394 Mosque in Flames

1970. 1st Anniv of Burning of Al Aqsa Mosque, Jerusalem.
1069 **394** 20m. brn, orge & grn . . 65 30
1070 60m. brown, red & blue 1·80 95

395 Globe, Wheat and Cogwheel

1970. World Standards Day.
1071 **395** 20m. brn, blue & grn . . 50 20

396 "Peace, Justice and Progress" (25th Anniv of U.N.)

1970. United Nations Day.
1072 **396** 5m. blue, lt bl & mve . . 20 15
1073 – 10m. bl, ochre & brn . . 20 20
1074 – 20m. multicoloured . . . 40 20
1075 – 20m.+10m. mult 70 60
1076 – 55m. brn, bl & ochre . . 90 70
1077 – 55m. brn, bl & ochre . . 90 70
DESIGNS AND EVENTS—37 × 37 mm: 10m. U.N. emblem; 55m. (2) Philae Temple (composite design) (UNESCO. Campaign for Preservation of Nubian Monuments); 36 × 36 mm: 20m. Frightened child and bombed school (Int Education Year); 41 × 25 mm: 20m.+10m. Palestinian guerrillas and refugees ("Int support for Palestinians").

397 President Nasser

398 Medical Association Building

1970. Pres. Gamal Nasser Memorial Issue.
1078 **397** 5m. black and bl (postage) 20 20
1079 – 20m. black and green . . 50 20
1080 – 30m. black & grn (air) 65 30
1081 – 80m. black & brown . . 2·00 75
DESIGN—46 × 27 mm: 30, 80m. Pres. Nasser and mosque.

1970. Egyptian Anniversaries.
1082 **398** 20m. brown, yellow and blue 50 35
1083 – 20m. brown, yellow and blue 50 35
1084 – 20m. brown and blue . . 50 35
1085 – 20m. brown, yellow and blue 50 35
1086 – 20m. brown, yellow and blue 50 35
DESIGNS AND EVENTS: No. 1082, Type **398** (50th anniv of Egyptian Medical Assn); 1083, Old and new library buildings (centenary of National Library); 1084, "The most significant victory..." Pres. Nasser text ("Egyptian Credo"); 1085, Old and new printing works (150th anniv of Govt. Printing Office); 1086, Old and new headquarters (50th anniv of Egyptian Engineering Society).

399 Map of Egypt, Libya and Sudan

1970. Signing of Tripoli Charter.
1087 **399** 20m. green, black & red 50 20

400 Minaret, Qalawun Mosque

402 Fair Emblem

401 Pres. Gamel Nasser

1970. Post Day. Mosque Minarets. Each brown, blue and yellow.
1088 5m. Type **400** 35 25
1089 10m. As-Salem Mosque . . 95 35
1090 20m. Isna Mosque . . . . 1·90 75
1091 55m. Al-Hakim Mosque . . 3·25 1·50
See also Nos. 1142/5 and 1189/92.

1971. Inauguration of Aswan High Dam. Sheet 135 × 80 mm.
MS1092 **401** (a) 100m. black and emerald; (b) 200m. black and blue 11·50 10·50

1971. Cairo International Fair.
1093 **402** 20m. yellow, blk & pur 45 20

403 Map of Arab States and A.P.U. Emblem

1971. 9th Arab Postal Union Congress, Cairo.
1094 **403** 20m. blue, orange and green (postage) . . . 45 20
1095 30m. brown, orange and green (air) 70 35

404 Globe and Cotton Symbols

1971. Egyptian Cotton Production.
1096 **404** 20m. brown, blue & grn 45 20

405 Army Emblem

406 Hesy Ra (ancient physician) and Papyrus

1971. Forces' Mail.
1097 **405** 10m. violet . . . . . . 1·70 1·30
The above stamp was issued for civilian use on letters addressed to servicemen and was not valid for any other purpose.

1971. World Health Day.
1098 **406** 20m. purple & yellow . . 65 20

407 Pres. Gamal Nasser

408 Map and I.T.U. Emblem

1971.
1099 **407** 20m. blue and purple . . 85 25
1100 55m. plum and blue . . 2·50 90

1971. African Telecommunications Year.
1101 **408** 20m. multicoloured . . . 55 20

409 El Rifaei and Sultan Hussein Mosques

1971. Air. Multicoloured.
1102 30m. Type **409** . . . . . . 1·20 45
1103 85m. Rameses Square, Cairo 2·75 80
1104 110m. Sphinx and Pyramids 3·25 1·60

410 "Industrial Progress"

411 A.P.U. Emblem

1971. 19th Anniv of Revolution. Mult.
1105 20m. Type **410** 40 25
1106 20m. Ear of Wheat and Laurel ("Land Reclamation") 40 25
MS1107 130 × 90 mm. 100m. Candle illuminating map of Africa (40 × 40 mm). Imperf . . . . . 4·25 1·70

1971. 25th Anniv of Founding of Arab Postal Union at Sofar Conference.
1108 **411** 20m. emerald, yellow and green (postage) . . 45 25
1109 30m. mult (air) 80 40

412 Federal Links

413 Pres. Gamal Nasser

1971. Inaug of Confederation of Arab Republics.
1110 **412** 20m. brown, black and purple (postage) . . . 50 30
1111 30m. green, black and purple (air) 80 40

1971. 1st Death Anniv of President Nasser.
1112 **413** 5m. blue and purple . . 30 20
1113 20m. purple and blue . . 40 20
1114 30m. blue and brown . . 80 45
1115 55m. brown and green 1·30 65

414 "Princess and Child"

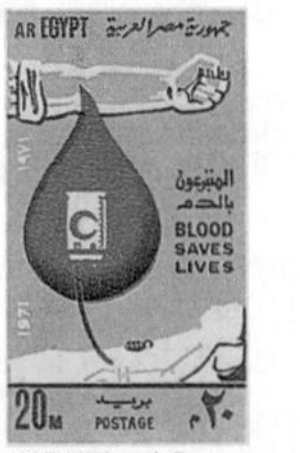

415 "Blood Saves Lives"

1971. United Nations Day.
1116 **414** 5m. black, brown and cinnamon (postage) . . 30 20
1117 – 20m. multicoloured . . . 70 25
1118 – 55m. multicoloured . . . 1·40 80
1119 – 30m. mult (air) . . . . 1·40 45
DESIGNS—As Type **414**. VERT: 5m. (UNICEF). HORIZ: 20m. Emblem and four heads (Racial Equality Year); 36 × 36 mm: 30m. Refugee and Al-Aqsa Mosque (U.N.R.W.A.); 24 × 58 mm: 55m. Partly submerged pillar, Philae (25th anniv of UNESCO).

1971. Blood Donors.
1120 **415** 20m. red and green . . . 75 20

416 New Post Office

417 Sunflower

1971. Opening of New Head Post Office, Alexandria.
1121 **416** 20m. brown and blue . . 70 25

1971. Ramadan Festival.
1122 **417** 5m. multicoloured . . . 30 15

418 Abdallah El Nadim

419 Globe and Earth's Strata

1971. 75th Death Anniv of Abdallah El Nadim (poet and journalist).
1123 **418** 20m. brown & green . . 45 20

1971. 75th Anniv of Egyptian Geological Survey.
1124 **419** 20m. multicoloured . . . 80 20

420 A.P.U. Emblem and Dove with Letter

1971. 10th Anniv of African Postal Union.
1125 **420** 5m. mult (postage) . . . 30 20
1126 20m. green, orge & blk 55 20
1127 – 55m. black, bl & red . . 85 70
1128 – 30m. mult (air) . . . . 1·00 40
DESIGN: 30m., 55m. A.P.U. emblem and airmail envelope.

421 "Savings Bank"

1971. 70th Anniv of Post Office Savings Bank.
1129 **421** 20m. multicoloured . . . 70 25

421a Victory Parade (scene from "Aida") **423** Cairo Citadel

1971. Air. Centenary of First Performance of Verdi's Opera "Aida", in Cairo.
1130 **421a** 110m. yell, grn & brn . . 4·00 2·30

1972. Inscr "A. R. EGYPT".
1131 **374** 1m. blue and brown . . 25 20
1131a 1m. brown 25 20
1132 – 5m. blue, yellow & brn (as No. 1040) 30 20
1132a – 5m. green 35 20
1132b – 5m. bistre 40 15
1133 – 10m. purple, brown & bl (as No. 1041) . . 50 20
1133a – 10m. brown 45 15
1134 **260** 20m. green (22 × 27½ mm) . . . 90 25
1135 20m. mauve (22 × 27½ mm) . . . 1·20 15
1136 – 50m. brown, ochre & blue (as No. 1043) 2·00 35
1136a – 50m. blue . . . . . . 2·20 30
1137 – 55m. mauve (as No. 1044) . . . . . 3·00 70
1137a – 55m. green . . . . . . 1·60 25
1138a **423** 100m. blk, red & bl . . 2·30 50
1139 – 200m. brown & grn . . 5·50 1·10
1140 – 500m. brown and blue (as No. 1046) . . . . 13·50 2·75
1141 – £El green & orange (as No. 1047) . . . . . 31·00 7·00
DESIGNS—As Type **423**: Nos. 1132a/b, Rameses II; 1133a, Head of Seti I; 1136a, Goddess Hathar; 1137a, Sphinx and pyramid. As Type **375**: No. 1139, Head of Userkaf.

1972. Post Day. Mosque Minarets. As T **400**. Multicoloured.
1142 5m. Western minaret, An-Nasir Mosque 35 15
1143 20m. Eastern minaret, An-Nasir Mosque . . . . . 1·00 15
1144 30m. Al-Gawli Mosque . . 2·30 35
1145 55m. Ahmed Ibn Toulon Mosque . . . . 3·25 1·00

424a Police Emblem and Activities

1972. Police Day.
1146 **424a** 20m. yellow, bl & brn 1·40 25

425 Book Year Emblem **426** Globe, Glider, Rocket and Emblem

1972. International Book Year.
1147 **425** 20m. violet, yellow & grn 70 25

1972. Air. International Aerospace Education Conference, Cairo.
1148 **426** 30m. brown, blue & yell 1·00 40

427 Monastery Aflame

1972. Air. Burning of St. Catherine's Monastery, Sinai.
1149 **427** 110m. black, brn & red 3·00 2·30

428 "Palette" (Seif Wanli)

1972. 9th Fine Arts Bienniale, Alexandria.
1150 **428** 20m. red, yellow & blk 70 20

429 Fair Emblem **430** Brig. Abdel Moniem Riad and Battle Scene

1972. Int Fair, Cairo.
1151 **429** 20m. multicoloured . . . 70 25

1972. 2nd Death Anniv of Brig. Abdel Moniem Riad.
1152 **430** 20m. brown, turq & bl 1·00 25

431 Birds in Tree

1972. Mother's Day.
1153 **431** 20m. multicoloured . . . 70 20

432 Head of Tutankhamun (wooden statuette)

1972. 50th Anniv of Discovery of Tutankhamun's Tomb.
1154 **432** 20m. mult (postage) . . 1·50 40
1155 – 55m. multicoloured . . . 4·25 1·00
1156 – 110m. grn brn & bl (air) 7·50 4·00
1157 – 110m. grn, brn & bl . . 7·50 4·00
MS1158 95 × 100 mm. 200m. multicoloured . . . . 27·00 25·00
DESIGNS—Square (As T **436**)—No. 1168, "Science and Faith" emblem. HORIZ: (42 × 25 mm)—110m. Confederation of Arab Republics flag.
Nos. 1156/7 were issued together, se-tenant, forming a composite design.

433 Nefertiti **434** Map of Africa

1972. 50th Anniv of Society of Friends of Art.
1159 **433** 20m. blk, gold & red . . 70 25

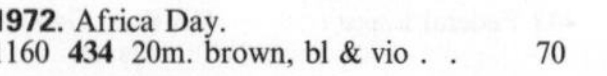

1972. Africa Day.
1160 **434** 20m. brown, bl & vio . . 70 25

436 Eagle Emblem

1972. 20th Anniv of Revolution.
1167 **436** 20m. gold, blk & grn (postage) 70 25
1168 20m. red, blk & blue . . 70 25
MS1169 70 × 110 mm. 110m. gold, red and black (air). Imperf . . 5·25 5·25

437 Al-Azhar Mosque and St. George's Church, Cairo

1972. Air.
1170 **437** 30m. brn, ochre & bl . . 1·40 35
1171 – 85m. brn, ochre & bl . . 2·40 1·10
1172 – 110m. brn, ochre & bl 2·75 1·10
DESIGNS: 85m. Temple, Abu Simbel; 110m. Pyramids, Giza.

438 Boxing

1972. Olympic Games, Munich.
1173 **438** 5m. mult (postage) . . . 25 20
1174 – 10m. yellow, blk & red 30 20
1175 – 20m. grn, red & orge . . 45 25
1176 – 30m. green, buff and red (air) 70 35
1177 – 30m. violet, red & turq 70 35
1178 – 50m. black, blue & grn 1·30 70
1179 – 55m. red, green & blue 1·60 80
DESIGNS—HORIZ: 10m. Wrestling; 20m. Basketball, VERT: 30m. (No. 1176), Weightlifting; 30m. (No. 1177), Handball; 50m. Swimming; 55m. Gymnastics.

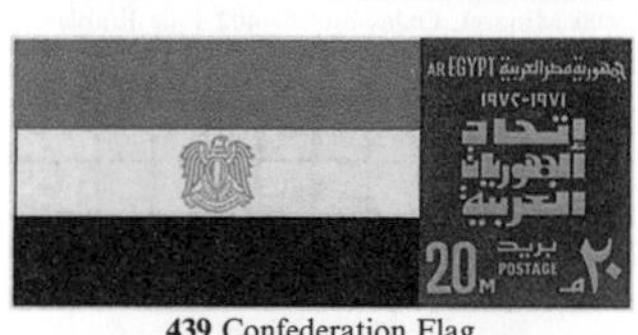

439 Confederation Flag

1972. 1st Anniv of Confederation of Arab Republics.
1180 **439** 20m. brown, red & blk 60 25

440 J. -F. Champollion and Rosetta Stone

1972. Air. 150th Anniv of Champollion's Translation of Egyptian Heiroglyphics.
1181 **440** 110m. grn, blk & brn . . 4·75 1·70

441 Heart (World Health Day)

1972. United Nations Day.
1182 – 10m. red, blue & brown 35 25
1183 **441** 20m. black, yell & grn 65 30
1184 – 30m. brown, vio & bl . 1·80 60
1185 – 55m. gold, brown & bl 2·20 75
DESIGNS—22 × 40 mm: 10m. Emblem of 14th Regional Tuberculosis Conference, Cairo. 47 × 28 mm: 30m. Refugees (U.N.R.W.A.). 37 × 37 mm: 55m. Flooded temple, Philae (UNESCO Campaign for Preservation of Nubian Monuments).

442 Hibiscus **443** Work Day Emblem

1972. Ramadan Festival.
1186 **442** 10m. purple, grn & brn 45 20

1972. Social Work Day.
1187 **443** 20m. blue, brown & grn 75 20

444 "Rowing Fours" on Nile

1972. 3rd Nile Rowing Festival, Luxor.
1188 **444** 20m. brown and blue . . 95 30

1973. Post Day. Mosque Minarets. As T **400**. Each brown, yellow and green.
1189 10m. Al-Maridani Mosque 65 15
1190 20m. Bashtak Mosque . . . 1·10 20
1191 30m. Qusun Mosque . . . 2·30 55
1192 55m. Al-Gashankir Mosque 3·25 1·40

445 Ears of Corn and Globe within Cogwheel

1973. International Fair, Cairo.
1193 **445** 20m. blue, black & grn 45 20

446 Symbolic Family

1973. Family Planning Week.
1194 **446** 20m. black, orge & grn 55 20

447 Telecommunications Map

1973. Air. 5th Int Telecommunications Day.
1195 **447** 30m. blue, black & brn 65 25

448 Temple Column, Karnak **449** Bloody Hand and Boeing 727 Jetliner

1973. Air. "Son et Lumiere", Karnak Temples, Luxor.
1196 **448** 110m. black, mve & bl 3·00 1·60

1973. Air. Attack on Libyan Airliner over Sinai.
1197 **449** 110m. red, black & bis 4·25 1·40

451 Rifaa el Tahtawi

452 Mrs. Hoda Sharawi and Sania Girls Secondary School

1973. Death Centenary of Rifaa el Tahtawi (educationist).
1200 **451** 20m. brn, grn & dp grn 60 25

1973. Centenary of Egyptian Female Education and 50th Anniv of Women's Union.
1201 **452** 20m. green, brn & bl . . 50 20

453 Mohamed Korayem

454 Refugees and Map of Palestine

1973. 21st Anniv of Revolution. Leaders of the 1798 Resistance Movement.
1202 **453** 20m. brown, blue & grn 55 25
1203 – 20m. brown, blue & grn 55 25
1204 – 20m. choc, pk & brn . . 55 25
MS1205 60 × 60 mm. 110m. gold, black and blue. Imperf . . . . 3·25 3·25
DESIGNS—As T **453**: No. 1202, Type **453**; No. 1203, Omar Makram; 1024, Abdel Rahman el Gaberti. (70 × 92 mm)—MS1205, Hands holding weapons and symbols.

1973. Air. Palestinian Refugees.
1206 **454** 30m. purple, brn & bl 2·10 40

455 Rose

456 "Light and Hope"

1973. Ramadan Festival.
1207 **455** 10m. red, yellow & blue 35 20

1973. 25th Anniv of W.H.O.
1208 **456** 20m.+10m. bl & gold . . 60 50

457 Bank Building

458 Emblem and Weather-vane

1973. 75th Anniv of National Bank of Egypt.
1209 **457** 20m. blk, grn & orge . . 50 25

1973. Air. Centenary of World Meteorological Organization.
1210 **458** 110m. gold, vio & bl . . 2·20 1·20

459 Global Emblem

1973. 10th Anniv of World Food Programme.
1211 **459** 10m. blue, grn & brn . . 45 25

460 Philae Temples

1973. UNESCO. Campaign for the Preservation of Nubian Monuments.
1212 **460** 55m. orge, blue & violet 2·75 80

461 Interpol Emblem

462 Flame Emblem

1973. Air. 50th Anniv of International Criminal Police Organization (Interpol).
1213 **461** 110m. multicoloured . . 2·75 1·20

1973. 25th Anniv of Declaration of Human Rights.
1214 **462** 20m. red, green & blue 50 20

463 Laurel and Map of Africa

464 "Donation"

1973. 10th Anniv of Organization of African Unity.
1215 **463** 55m.+20m. mult . . . . 1·90 1·70

1973. Social Work Day.
1216 **464** 20m.+10m. blue, lilac and red 60 50

465 Dr. Taha Hussein (scholar)

467 Egyptian Postal Services Emblem

466 Pres. Sadat and Flag

1973. Hussein Commemoration.
1217 **465** 20m. brown, blue & grn 45 20

1973. Crossing of the Suez Canal, 6 October 1973.
1218 **466** 20m. black, red & brn 1·10 60
See also No. 1233.

1973. Air. Post Day.
1219 **467** 20m. blk, red & grey . . 25 20
1220 – 30m. vio, orge & blk . . 30 20
1221 – 55m. mve, grn & blk . . 80 65
1222 – 110m. gold, bl & blk . . 1·50 1·10
DESIGNS—As T **467**: 30m. Arab Postal Union emblem; 55m. African Postal Union emblem; 37 × 37 mm: 110m. U.P.U. emblem.

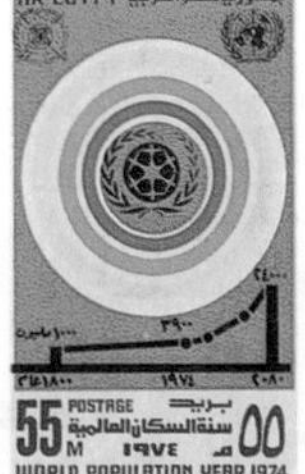

468 Cogwheel, Ear of Corn and Fair Emblem

470 Emblem and Graph

469 Madame Sadat with Patient

1974. International Fair, Cairo.
1223 **468** 20m. multicoloured . . . 45 20

1974. Society of Faith and Hope (for rehabilitation of the disabled).
1224 **469** 20m.+10m. purple, gold and green 80 65

1974. World Population Year.
1225 **470** 55m. black, orge & grn 85 45

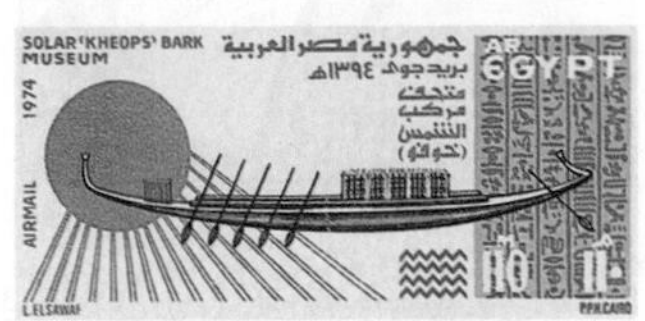

471 Solar Boat of Cheops

1974. Air. Inauguration of Solar Boat Museum.
1226 **471** 110m. brown, gold & bl 2·50 1·40

472 "Ancient Egyptian Workers" (carving from Queen Tee's tomb, Sakara)

1974. Labour Day (1 May).
1227 **472** 20m. black, yellow & bl 60 25

473 Nurse with Syringe

474 Troops crossing Barlev Line during October War

475 Scroll and Emblems (The October Working Paper)

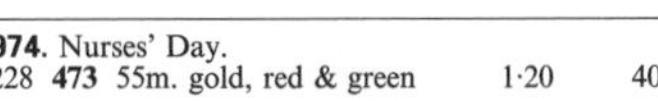

1974. Nurses' Day.
1228 **473** 55m. gold, red & green 1·20 40

1974. 22nd Anniv of Revolution.
1229 – 20m. gold, black & blue 70 30
1230 – 20m. silver, blk & pur 70 30
1231 **474** 20m. black, orge & bl . . 70 30
MS1232 72 × 108 mm. **475** 110m. gold, green and carmine. Imperf 3·50 3·00
DESIGNS—As T **474**: No. 1229, Map of Suez Canal and "Reconstruction". 36 × 36 mm: No. 1230, Sheet of aluminium.

476 Pres. Sadat and Flag

1974. 1st Anniv of Suez Crossing.
1233 **476** 20m. black, red & yell 1·20 60
See also No. 1218.

477 Teachers' Badge

478 Artists' Palette

1974. Teachers' Day.
1234 **477** 20m. brown, blk & bl . . 60 20

1974. 6th Plastic Arts Exhibition.
1235 **478** 30m. black, yellow & vio 75 30

479 Meridian Hotel

1974. Air. Opening of Meridian Hotel, Cairo.
1236 **479** 110m. multicoloured . . 1·40 75

1974. Centenary of Universal Postal Union. Sheet 76 × 101 mm.
MS1237 **480** 110m. multicoloured 5·50 5·25

480 U.P.U. Monument, Brene

1974. *Centenary of Universal Postal Union.* Sheet 76 × 101 mm. Imperf.
MS1237 **480** 110m. multicoloured 5·50 5·25

481 Child and Emblems

1974. Social Work Day.
1238 **481** 30m. green, brown & bl 85 30

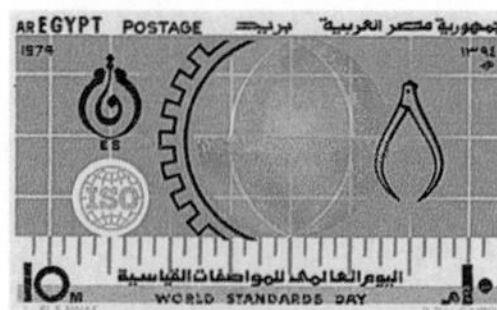
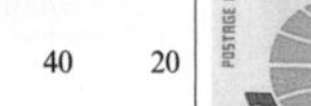
482 Emblems of Standardization

1974. World Standards Day.
1239 **482** 10m. orange, bl & blk 40 20

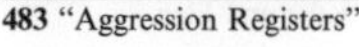
483 "Aggression Registers" 484 Philae Temples

1974. Refugees Propaganda.
1240 **483** 20m. blue and red . . . 65 25

1974. UNESCO. Campaign for Preservation of Nubian Monuments.
1241 **484** 55m. brn, stone & bl . . 2·20 55

485 Arum Lily 486 Pile of Coins

1974. Ramadan Festival.
1242 **485** 10m. multicoloured . . . 45 20

1974. International Savings Day.
1243 **486** 20m. grey, blue & grn 45 15

487 Organization Emblems and Cameos 487a Abbas Mahmoud El Akkad (writer)

1974. Health Insurance Organization.
1244 **487** 30m. violet, red & brn 65 25

1974. Famous Egyptians.
1245 **487a** 20m. blue and brown 40 25
1246 – 20m. brown and blue 40 25
DESIGNS: No. 1245, (10th death anniv); No. 1246, Mustafa Lutfy El Manfalouty (journalist).

488 Sacred Ibis

1975. Post Day. Ancient Treasures.
1247 **488** 20m. brown, bl & sil . . 65 25
1248 – 30m. bl, orge & mve . . 95 25
1249 – 55m. brn, gold & grn . . 1·30 60
1250 – 110m. yellow, brn & bl 2·20 1·40
DESIGNS—HORIZ: 30m. Glass "fish" vase. VERT: 55m. Pharaonic gold vase; 110m. Ankh-shaped mirror.

489 Om Kolthoum (Arab singer) 490 Crescent and Globe

1975. Om Kolthoum Commemoration.
1251 **489** 20m. brown 60 20

1975. Mohammed's Birthday.
1252 **490** 20m. violet, silver & bl 60 20

491 Fair Emblem 492 Kasr El Ainy Hospital

1975. Cairo International Fair.
1253 **491** 20m. green, blue & red 45 20

1975. World Health Day.
1254 **492** 20m. brown and blue . . 60 20

493 Children Reading Book 495 Belmabgoknis Flower

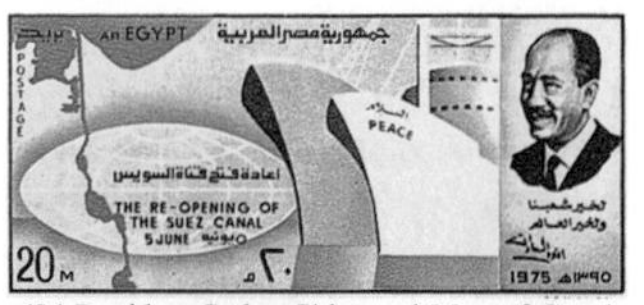
494 President Sadat, Ships and Map of Canal

1975. Science Day.
1255 **493** 20m. blue, red & yell . . 65 30
1256 – 20m. black & brown . . 65 30
DESIGN: No. 1256, Pupils and graph.

1975. Re-opening of Suez Canal.
1257 **494** 20m. brown, blue and black (postage) . . . 70 30
1258 30m. turquoise, green and blue (air) . . . . 1·20 40
1259 110m. bl blk & turq . . 1·90 1·10

1975. Festivals.
1260 **495** 10m. blue, grn & lt grn 45 20

496 I.C.I.D. Emblem 497 Spotlight on Village

1975. Air. 25th Anniv of International Commission on Irrigation and Drainage.
1261 **496** 110m. green, bl & orge 1·70 95

1975. 23rd Anniv of Revolution.
1262 **497** 20m. blue and brown . . 50 25
1263 – 20m. orge, blk & grn . . 50 25
1264 – 110m. multicoloured . . 5·00 4·25
DESIGNS—38 × 22 mm: No. 1263, "Tourism" (pyramids and sphinx). 70 × 79 mm: No. 1264, Tourist map of Egypt.

498 Volleyball 499 Flag and Tanks

1975. 6th Arab School Sports Tournament. Each blue, orange and green.
1265 20m. Type **498** 60 35
1266 20m. Running 60 35
1267 20m. Tournament emblem 60 35
1268 20m. Basketball 60 35
1269 20m. Football 60 45

1975. 2nd Anniv of Battle of 6 October.
1270 **499** 20m. multicoloured . . . 95 35

1975. International Symposium on October War, Cairo University. As T **499** but with additional commemorative inscription at foot and "M" above figures of value.
1271 20m. multicoloured 95 35

500 Schistosomiasis Conference Emblem 501 University Emblem

1975. United Nations Day.
1272 **500** 20m. blue, mauve and brown (postage) . . . 75 30
1273 – 55m. purple, yell & bl 1·90 75
1274 – 30m. brn, grn & pur (air) 1·60 40
1275 – 110m. blk, orge & grn 2·50 1·40
DESIGNS—27 × 47 mm: 55m. Wall relief (UNESCO Campaign for Preservation of Nubian Monuments). 48 × 40 mm: 30m. Refugees and barbed wire (U.N.R.W.A.). 22 × 40 mm: 110m. Women (International Women's Year).

1975. 25th Anniv of Ein Shams University.
1276 **501** 20m. blue, yell & grey 45 15

501a Al-Kanady 502 Ibex

1975. Arab Philosophers.
1277 **501a** 20m. brown, grn & bl 95 35
1278 – 20m. brown, grn & bl 95 35
1279 – 20m. brown, grn & bl 95 35
DESIGNS: No. 1278, Al-Farabi, and lute; No. 1279, Al-Biruni, and open book.

1976. Post Day. Treasures from Tutankhamun's Tomb. Multicoloured.
1280 20m. Type **502** . . . . . . 3·00 1·10
1281 30m. Lioness . . . . . . 4·75 1·40
1282 55m. Sacred Cow . . . . . 7·75 3·75
1283 110m. Hippopotamus . . . 11·00 7·50

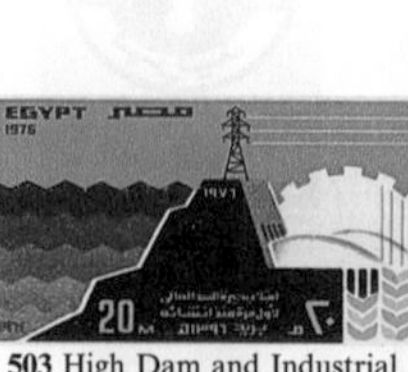
503 High Dam and Industrial Potential 504 Fair Emblem

1976. Filling of High Dam Lake.
1284 **503** 20m. multicoloured . . . 65 20

1976. Cairo International Fair.
1285 **504** 20m. violet & orange . . 35 15

505 Biennale Commemorative Emblem 506 Protective Hands

1976. 11th Fine Arts Biennale, Alexandria.
1286 **505** 20m. yellow, blk & grn 40 15

1976. Society of Faith and Hope.
1287 **506** 20m. yell, grn & dp grn 40 20

507 "Pharaonic Eye" and Emblem 508 Scales of Justice

1976. World Health Day.
1288 **507** 20m. brn, yell & grn . . 60 20

1976. 5th Anniv of Rectification Movement.
1289 **508** 20m. black, grn & red 55 20

509 Pres. Sadat and Emblem

1976. Centenary of Arbitration Service.
1290 **509** 20m. yellow, grn & ol . . 55 20

510 Front Page of First Issue

1976. Cent of Newspaper "Al-Ahram".
1291 **510** 20m. brown, blk & red 55 20

511 Pres. Sadat and World Map

1976. 24th Anniv of Revolution.
1292 **511** 20m. yellow, blue & black 55 30
MS1293 86 × 77 mm. **511** 110m. yellow and brown. Imperf . . 5·50 5·25

512 Amaryllis 513 Map of Red Sea, Pres. Sadat and Abu Redice Oil Refinery

1976. Festivals.
1294 **512** 10m. multicoloured . . . 35 15

1976. 3rd Anniv of Suez Canal Crossing. Mult.
1295 20m. Type **513** 65 50
1296 20m. Irrigation and reconstruction—map of Suez Canal (48 × 40 mm) 65 50
1297 110m. Monument to Soldiers of October 6th, 1973 (65 × 80 mm) . . . . 5·00 4·50

514 Animals on Papyrus Leaf ("Literature for Children")

1976. United Nations Day.
1298 **514** 20m. brown, stone & bl 45 20
1299 – 30m. brown, grn & blk 60 25
1300 – 55m. brown and blue . . 1·10 40
1301 – 110m. red, grn & vio . . 1·70 1·00

DESIGNS—39 × 22 mm: 30m. Dome of the Rock (Palestinian Refugees); 110m. UNESCO emblem on figure "30" (30th anniv of UNESCO). 25 × 59 mm: 55m. Relief showing goddess Isis, Philae Temple (UNESCO Campaign for Preservation of Nubian Monuments).

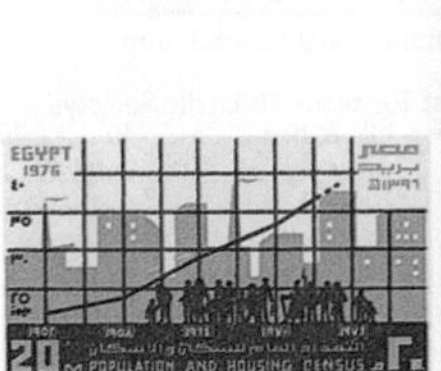
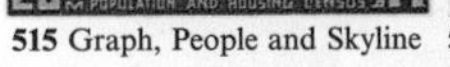

515 Graph, People and Skyline **516** Society Medal and Map of the Nile

1976. Population and Housing Census.

1302	**515**	20m. sepia, blue & brn	45	15

1976. Cent of Egyptian Geographical Society.

1303	**516**	20m. brown, green & bl	45	15

517 King Akhnaton **518** Patrolman, Police Car and Map

1977. Post Day.

1304	**517**	20m. brown & black . .	50	20
1305	–	30m. brown & black . .	60	20
1306	–	55m. brown & purple . .	85	30
1307	–	110m. brown & purple	2·30	85

DESIGNS: 30m. Head of Akhnaton's daughter; 55m. Head of Nefertiti, wife of Akhnaton; 110m. Bust of Akhnaton.

1977. Police Day.

1308	**518**	20m. red, blue & black	80	25

519 Pharaonic Ship **520** O.A.U. and Arab League Emblems on Map

1977. Cairo International Fair.

1309	**519**	20m. green, blk & red	50	20

1977. 1st Afro-Arab Summit Conference.

1310	**520**	55m. blue, blk & orge	75	35

521 King Faisal

522 Healthy Children and Paralysed Child

1977. King Faisal of Saudi Arabia Commemoration.

1311	**521**	20m. brown and blue . .	50	20

1977. National Campaign for Prevention of Poliomyelitis.

1312	**522**	20m. dp brn, brn & red	65	20

523 A.P.U. Emblem and National Flags

1977. Silver Jubilee of Arab Postal Union.

1313	**523**	20m. multicoloured . . .	35	20
1314		30m. multicoloured . . .	45	25

524 Children's Village **525** Earth and Satellite

1977. Inaug of S.O.S. Children's Village, Cairo.

1315	**524**	20m. brown, blue & grn	40	25
1316		55m. red, blue & green	1·10	45

1977. World Telecommunications Day.

1317	**525**	110m. blue, yell & blk	1·60	80

526 Loom, Spindle and Factories

1977. 50th Anniv of Egyptian Spinning and Weaving Company, El Mehalla El Kobra.

1318	**526**	20m. green, brn & bis . .	45	15

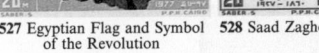

527 Egyptian Flag and Symbol of the Revolution **528** Saad Zaghoul

1977. 25th Anniv of Revolution.

1319	**527**	20m. black, red & silver	45	15
MS1320		76 × 85 mm. 110m. black, red and blue. Imperf	2·40	2·00

DESIGN: 110 mm. Egyptian flag on eagle silhouette.

1977. 50th Death Anniv of Saad Zaghoul (revolutionary).

1321	**528**	20m. brown & green . .	30	15

529 Archbishop Capucci and Map of Palestine

530 Bird of Paradise Flowers

1977. 3rd Anniv of Arrest of Archbishop Capucci.

1322	**529**	45m. blk, grey & grn . .	95	35

1977. Festivals.

1323	**530**	10m. multicoloured . . .	30	15

531 Title Deeds overshadowing Map of Egypt

532 Soldier, Tanks and 6th October Medal

1977. 25th Anniv of Agrarian Reform Law.

1324	**531**	20m. black, bl & grn . .	35	15

1977. 4th Anniv of Suez Canal Crossing.

1325	**532**	20m. brn, red & orge . .	40	20
1326	–	140m. brn, red & gold	8·25	7·00

DESIGN: 46 × 55 mm: 140m. President Sadat.

533 Diesel Locomotive, Electric Railcar and Steam Locomotive No. 1, 1852

1977. 125th Anniv of Egyptian Railways.

1327	**533**	20m. green, blue & vio	1·30	30

534 Refugees and the Al-Aqsa Mosque (U.N.R.W.A.)

1977. United Nations Day.

1328	**534**	45m. green, red & blk	60	30
1329	–	55m. yellow and blue . .	1·00	35
1330	–	140m. ochre & brown . .	2·10	95

DESIGNS—36 × 36 mm: 55m. Relief from Philae showing Horus and goddess Taueret. As T **534** but vert: 140m. Relief from Philae in frame of pharaonic column (UNESCO Campaign for Preservation of Nubian Monuments).

535 Ancient Egyptian Symbol for "Vision" and Film **536** Natural Gas Rig and Factories

1977. 50th Anniv of Egyptian Cinema.

1331	**535**	20m. blk, gold & grey	50	20

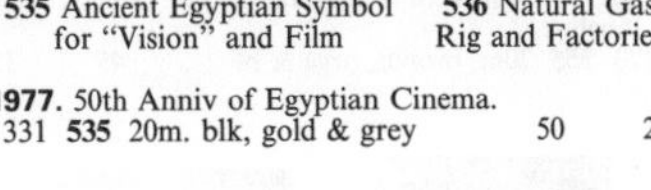

1977. National Petroleum Festival.

1332	**536**	20m. blue, blk & grn . .	85	25

537 President Sadat, Olive Branches and Dome of the Rock, Jerusalem

1977. President Sadat's Peace Mission to Israel.

1333	**537**	20m. brown, grn & blk	45	20
1334		140m. blk, grn & brn . .	1·90	1·00

538 The Three Pyramids at Giza

1978. Air.

1335	**538**	45m. yellow & brown	35	20
1335b		60m. brown	95	55
1336	–	115m. brown & blue . .	75	35
1337	–	140m. lilac and blue . .	1·10	55
1337a	–	185m. brown & blue . .	2·50	1·20

DESIGNS: 115, 185m. Step Pyramid and temple entrance, Sakkara. 140m. Nile feluccas.

539 Statue of Rameses II

1978. Post Day. Multicoloured.

1338	20m. Type **539**	60	30
1339	45m. Relief showing coronation of Queen Nefertari, Abu Simbel . .	1·30	60

540 Irrigation Wheels, Fayoum

541 Fair Emblem

1978.

1340	**540**	1m. blue	20	15
1341	–	5m. brown	20	15
1342	–	10m. green	20	15
1343	–	20m. brown	25	20
1343b	–	30m. brown	50	40
1344	–	50m. blue	35	20
1345	–	55m. brown	50	35
1346	–	70m. brown	60	25
1346a	–	80m. brown	80	20
1347	–	85m. purple	65	35
1348	–	100m. brown	1·30	30
1349	–	200m. indigo & blue . .	2·30	55
1350	–	500m. brn, bl & yell . .	6·00	1·90
1351	–	£E1 blue, yell & brn . .	9·25	3·25

DESIGNS—As T **540**: 5m. Pigeon-loft; 10m. Statue of Horus; 20, 30m. El Rifaei Mosque, Cairo; 50m. Syrian monastery, Wady el Netroon; 55m. Edfu temple; 70, 80m. October Bridge over Suez Canal; 85m. Medom pyramid; 100m. Facade of Abu el Abbas el Morsy Mosque, Alexandria; 200m. El Sawary column and sphinx, Alexandria; 37 × 45 mm: 500m. Arab horse; £E1, Bird (floor decoration from Akhnaton's palace).

1978. 11th Cairo International Fair.

1352	**541**	20m. grn, blk & orge . .	35	15

542 Old Kasr el Ainy Medical School and New Tower

543 Youssef el Sebai

1978. 150th Anniv of Kasr el Ainy Medical School.

1353	**542**	20m. brown, blue & gold	40	20

1978. Youssef el Sebai (assassination victim) and Commando Heroes Commemoration.

1354	–	20m. brown	35	25
1355	**543**	20m. black, brn & yell	35	25

DESIGN: No. 1354, Group of Commandos and emblems.

544 Bienniale Medal and Statue, Port Said

1978. 12th Fine Arts Biennale, Alexandria.

1356	**544**	20m. black, green & bl	40	20

545 Child with Smallpox

1978. World Health Day.

1357	**545**	20m. orge, blk & grn . .	55	30
1358	–	20m. red, orge & blk . .	55	30

DESIGN AND EVENT: No. 1357, Type **545** (World Year for the Eradication of Smallpox); 21 × 38 mm: No. 1358, Heart and downwards pointing arrow (World Hypertension Month).

546 President Sadat

1978. 7th Anniv of Rectification Movement.
1359 **546** 20m. brn, grn & gold . . 35 15

547 Emblem, Beneficiaries and Olive-branch

1978. 25th Anniv of General Organization of Insurance and Pensions.
1360 **547** 20m. brown and green 30 15

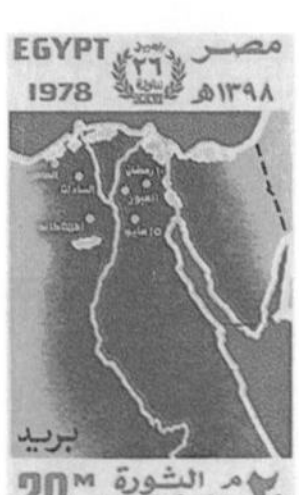

548 Map showing New Cities and Regions suitable for Cultivation (The Green Revolution)

549 Wall of Ministerial Emblems

1978. 26th Anniv of Revolution.
1361 **548** 20m. green, yellow & bl 50 25
1362 – 45m. orange, grn & brn 1·10 35
DESIGN: 45m. Map of Egypt and Sudan with ear of wheat (Economic integration of Egypt and Sudan).

1978. Cent of Egyptian Ministerial System.
1363 **549** 20m. violet, grn & yell 40 15

550 President Sadat, Statue of the Crossing and Factories

1978. 5th Anniv of Suez Canal Crossing.
1364 **550** 20m. yellow, brn & grn 45 15

551 Anti-Apartheid Emblem

552 Tahtib Folk-dance on Horseback

1978. United Nations Day.
1365 **551** 20m. orge, blk & grn . . 35 20
1366 – 45m. yell, brn & grn . . 70 35
1367 – 55m. orange, brn & bl 80 45
1368 – 140m. orge, blk & grn 1·90 75
DESIGNS—As T **551**. HORIZ: 55m. Philae temples (UNESCO Campaign for Preservation of Nubian Monuments). VERT: 140m. Dove, flame and olive branch (30th anniv of Declaration of Human Rights); 37 × 37 mm: 45m. Kobet al-Sakhra Mosque, refugee camp and U.N. emblem (U.N.R.W.A.).

1978. Festivals.
1369 **552** 10m. orange, brn & bl 25 15
1370 20m. bistre, brn & bl . . 35 20

553 Pilgrims at Mount Arafat and Script of Islamic Prayer

1978. Islamic Pilgrimage.
1371 **553** 45m. brown, yell & bl 75 30

554 U.N. and Conference Emblems

1978. U.N. Conference on Technical Co-operation amongst Developing Countries.
1372 **554** 20m. black, grn & yell 35 15

555 Oil Pipeline "Sumed", Badge and Map

1978. 1st Anniv of Inauguration of "Sumed" Oil Pipeline.
1373 **555** 20m. brown, orge & bl 45 15

556 Mastheads and Editors

557 Ibn Roshd

1978. 150th Anniv of "El Wakaea el Massreya" Newspaper.
1374 **556** 20m. black & brown . . 45 15

1978. 800th Death Anniv of Ibn Roshd (philosopher).
1375 **557** 45m. blue, emer & grn 55 20

558 Old and Modern Observatories and Chart of Planet Movements

1978. 75th Anniv of Helwan Observatory.
1376 **558** 20m. blue, brn & yell . . 60 25

559 Wright Brothers' Type A Biplane and I.C.A.O. Emblem

560 Daughter of Rameses II

1978. Air. 75th Anniv of First Powered Flight.
1377 **559** 140m. brown, bl & blk 1·50 95

1979. Post Day.
1378 **560** 20m. yellow & brown . . 50 25
1379 – 140m. yellow, brn & bl 1·80 50
DESIGN—(37½ × 43 mm). 140m. Small temple and statues of Rameses II, Abu Simbel.

561 Open Book, Globe and Reader

1979. 11th Cairo International Book Fair.
1380 **561** 20m. brown and green 35 15

562 Fair Emblem and Symbols of Industry and Agriculture

1979. Cairo International Fair.
1381 **562** 20m. brown, orge & bl 35 15

563 Poppy and Skull

1979. 50th Anniv of Anti-narcotics General Administration.
1382 **563** 70m. green, red & yell 1·30 40

564 Isis and Horus

566 Doves, President Sadat's Signature and "Peace"

565 World Map, Koran and Symbols of Arab Accomplishments

1979. Mother's Day.
1383 **564** 140m. yell, brn & blue 2·20 70

1979. The Arabs.
1384 **565** 45m. sep, yell & turq . . 45 20

1979. Signing of Egyptian-Israeli Peace Treaty.
1385 **566** 20m. violet & yellow . . 40 15
1386 70m. red and green . . . 1·00 70
1387 140m. red and green . . 1·90 1·00

567 Honeycomb of Food Projects

1979. Food Security.
1388 **567** 20m. yellow, grn & blk 30 15

568 Examining 1979 Peace Stamp

1979. 50th Anniv of Egyptian Philatelic Society.
1389 **568** 20m. emer, blk & brn . . 40 20

569 Coins of 1954 and 1979

1979. 25th Anniv of Egyptian Mint.
1390 **569** 20m. grey and yellow . . 35 15

570 "Sun of Freedom" and Open Book

1979. 27th Anniv of Revolution.
1391 **570** 20m. brown, orge & bl 35 15
MS1392 50 × 62 mm. 140m. brown and emerald. Imperf . . . . . 3·00 3·00
DESIGN: 140m. Decorative inscription "23 July 1952".

571 Musicians playing Rabab and Arghoul

572 Dove and Map of Sinai

1979. Festivals.
1393 **571** 10m. blk, brn & orge . . 25 15

1979. 6th Anniv of Suez Canal Crossing.
1394 **572** 20m. brown and blue . . 45 15

573 Skeleton of "Arsinotherium zittelli"

1979. 75th Anniv of Egyptian Geological Museum.
1395 **573** 20m. brown, yell & bl 1·20 25

574 Symbols of Engineering

1979. Engineers' Day.
1396 **574** 20m. pur, yell & emer 50 15

575 Human Rights Flame over Globe

1979. United Nations Day.
1397 **575** 45m. orange, bl & grn . . . 50 25
1398 – 140m. brn, yell & red . . 1·20 80
DESIGN: 140m. Child with flower (International Year of the Child).

576 Buildings and Hand placing Coin in Box

1979. International Savings Day.
1399 **576** 70m. multicoloured . . . 75 35

577 Championship Emblem
578 Figure clothed in Palestinian Flag

1979. 20th International Military Sports Council Shooting Championship.
1400 **577** 20m. red, blue & yellow 40 15

1979. International Day of Solidarity with Palestinian People.
1401 **578** 45m. multicoloured . . . 75 25

579 Dove, Globe and Rotary Club Emblem

1979. 50th Anniv of Cairo Rotary Club and 75th Anniv (1980) of Rotary International.
1402 **579** 140m. green, blue and yellow . . . . 1·20 70

580 Cogs and Factories
581 Ali el Garem (educational writer, 1881–1949)

1979. 25th Anniv of Military Factories.
1403 **580** 20m. green and brown 35 15

1979. Writers.
1404 **581** 20m. brown & dp brn 40 20
1405 – 20m. dp brown & brn 40 20
DESIGN: No. 1405, Mahmoud el Baroudy (poet, 1839–1904).

582 Capital of Pharaonic Column
583 Goddess of Writing and Fair Emblem

1980. Post Day. Pharaonic Capitals.
1406 **582** 20m. brown and violet 30 25
1407 – 45m. brown and violet 50 40
1408 – 70m. brown and violet 65 50
1409 – 140m. brown and violet 1·80 1·20
DESIGNS: 45m. Head capital; 70m. Leaf capital; 140m. Capital with cartouche.

1980. 12th Cairo International Book Fair.
1410 **583** 20m. brown, blue & yell 40 15

584 Exhibition Catalogue and Medal
585 Fair Emblem and Branch

1980. 13th Fine Arts Bienniale, Alexandria.
1411 **584** 20m. multicoloured . . . 45 15

1980. 13th Cairo International Fair.
1412 **585** 20m. blk, grn & orge . . 45 15

586 Trajan Monument

1980. 20th Anniv of Nubian Monuments Preservation Campaign.
1413 **586** 70m. orange, brn & bl 85 50
1414 – 70m. orange, brn & bl 85 50
1415 – 70m. orange, brn & bl 85 50
1416 – 70m. orange, brn & bl 85 50
DESIGNS: No. 1414, Qortasi monument; 1415, Kalabasha monument; 1416, Philae temple.

587 Doctors' Day Medal
588 President Sadat

1980. Doctors' Day.
1417 **587** 20m. green, blk & brn 45 15

1980. 9th Anniv of Rectification Movement.
1418 **588** 20m. green, blk & red 45 15

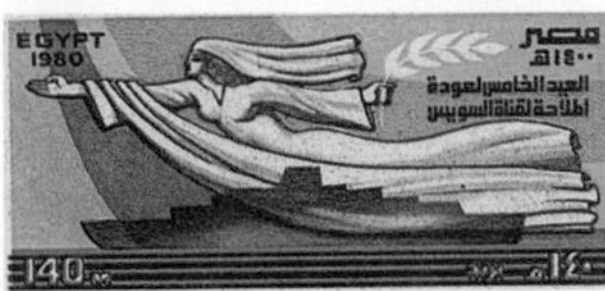

589 Ship and Figure symbolizing Peace and Freedom

1980. 5th Anniv of Re-opening of Suez Canal.
1419 **589** 140m. black, orge & bl 1·20 70

590 Pharaonic Cat

1980. Centenary of Society for the Prevention of Cruelty to Animals.
1420 **590** 20m. grey and green . . 70 20

591 Worker pushing Cogwheel

1980. Industry Day.
1421 **591** 20m. orange, brn & bl 35 15

592 Symbolic Tree
593 Erksous Seller and Nakrazan Player

1980. 28th Anniv of Revolution. Social Security Year.
1422 **592** 20m. purple, grn & brn 35 15
MS1423 57×67 mm. 140m. brown, emerald and black. Imperf . . 3·00 2·75

1980. Festivals 1980.
1424 **593** 10m. multicoloured . . . 30 15
DESIGN: 140m. Cupped hands holding family.

594 "6 October", Building Construction and Doves

1980. 7th Anniv of Suez Crossing.
1425 **594** 20m. multicoloured . . . 50 15

595 Islamic and Coptic Capitals

1980. United Nations Day.
1426 **595** 70m. yellow and blue . . 65 40
1427 – 140m. red, grn & brn . . 1·20 80
DESIGN: 140m. I.T.U. emblem (International Telecommunications Day).

596 Spider's Web, Dove and Olive Branch

1980. 1400th Anniv of Hegira.
1428 **596** 45m. yellow, brn & grn 55 25

597 Tankers

1980. Opening of Third Channel of Suez Canal.
1429 **597** 70m. blue, turq & grn 75 40

598 Mustafa Sadek el Rafai (writer)
599 Scarab from Tutankhamun Collection

1980. Arab Personalities. Brown and green.
1430 20m. Type **598** (birth cent) 40 25
1431 20m. Dr. Ali Mustafa Mousharafa (scientist, 30th death anniv) 40 25
1432 20m. Dr. Ali Ibrahim (surgeon, birth centenary) 40 35

1981. Post Day.
1433 **599** 70m. multicoloured . . . 80 35
1434 – 70m. yell, brn & grn . . 80 35
DESIGN: No. 1434, Other side of scarab.

600 Heinrich von Stephan
602 Symbols of Agriculture and Industry

601 Fair Emblem, Globe and Books

1981. 150th Birth Anniv of Heinrich von Stephen (founder of U.P.U.).
1435 **600** 140m. brown & blue . . 1·20 75

1981. 13th Cairo International Book Fair.
1436 **601** 20m. green, yell & brn 35 15

1981. 14th Cairo International Fair.
1437 **602** 20m. pink, brown & grn 30 15

603 R.E.A. Emblem, Pylon and Village

1981. 10th Anniv of Rural Electrification Authority.
1438 **603** 20m. yellow, grn & blk 40 15

604 Soldier, Olive Branch and Veteran's Association Emblem
605 Conference Emblem

1981. Veteran's Day.
1439 **604** 20m. green, red & brn 35 15

1981. International Dentistry Conference, Cairo.
1440 **605** 20m. brown and red . . 35 15

606 Confederation Emblem

607 Nurse

1981. 25th Anniv of International Confederation of Arab Trade Unions.
1441 **606** 20m. brown and blue . . 30 15

1981. Nurses' Day.
1442 **607** 20m. orange, grn & red 30 15

608 Irrigation Spray

609 Rocket and Military Equipment

1981. 10th Anniv of Rectification Movement.
1443 **608** 20m. green, brn & yell 40 15

1981. Air Defence Day.
1444 **609** 20m. green, blue & red 40 15

610 Map of Afghanistan

1981. Solidarity with Afghan People.
1445 **610** 20m.+10m. brn, red & black (37 × 36 mm) . . 60 35
1446 20m.+10m. brn, red & black (27 × 22 mm) . . 3·00 2·75

611 "29" and Social Defence Badge

612 Water Lilies

1981. 29th Anniv of Revolution.
1447 **611** 20m. yellow, grn & brn 35 20
1448 – 20m. blue, black & red 35 20
DESIGN: No. 1448, Map of Suez Canal and ships on graph surrounded by Egyptian flag (25th anniv of Suez Canal nationalization).

1981. Festivals 1981.
1449 **612** 10m. multicoloured . . . 30 15

613 Kemal Ataturk

614 Ahmed Arabi

1981. Birth Centenary of Kemal Ataturk (Turkish statesman).
1450 **613** 140m. brown & green . . 1·40 80

1981. Centenary of Arabi Revolution.
1451 **614** 20m. brown and green 30 15

615 Muscular Athlete, Sphinx and Pyramids

616 Factory on Graph and Atomic Symbol

1981. World Muscular Athletics Championship, Cairo.
1452 **615** 45m. yell, blk & brn . . 60 25

1981. 25th Anniv of Ministry of Industry.
1453 **616** 45m. yellow, bl & red . . 35 20

617 Congress Emblem and Imhotep (god of Medicine)

1981. 20th International Medical Industries Congress, Cairo.
1454 **617** 20m. green, blk & orge 35 15

618 Eye

1981. Air.
1455 **618** 230m. bl, orge & brn . . 2·00 80

619 Olive, Dove, Canal and Wheat

1981. 8th Anniv of Suez Crossing.
1456 **619** 20m. green, stone & bl 45 15

620 I.T.U. and W.H.O. Emblems

1981. United Nations Day.
1457 – 10m. yellow, bl & brn 25 15
1458 **620** 20m. blue, orge & blk 25 20
1459 – 45m. purple, grn & blk 50 30
1460 – 230m. orange, grn & blk 2·75 1·40
DESIGNS—HORIZ: 10m. Food and Agriculture Organization Emblem (World Food Day); 230m. Olive branches (Racial Discrimination Day). VERT: 20m. Type **620** (World Telecommunications Day); 45m. International Year of Disabled Persons emblem.

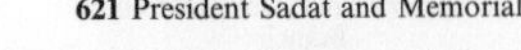

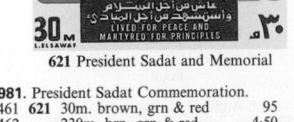

621 President Sadat and Memorial

1981. President Sadat Commemoration.
1461 **621** 30m. brown, grn & red 95 40
1462 230m. brn, grn & red . . 4·50 3·25

622 Dome of Shura Council, Hands and Candle

623 Bank Emblem

1981. 1st Anniv of Shura Council.
1463 **622** 45m. yellow & lilac . . . 45 20

1981. 50th Anniv of Bank for Development and Agricultural Credit.
1464 **623** 20m. buff, grn & blk . . 30 10

624 Ali el Gayati

625 Dove and Globe forming Figure "20"

1981. Celebrities.
1465 **624** 30m. brown & green . . 30 20
1466 – 60m. brown & green . . 50 35
DESIGNS: Type **624** (journalist, 25th death anniv). 60m. Omar Ebn el Fared (poet, 1181–1234).

1981. 20th Anniv of African Postal Union.
1467 **625** 60m. yellow, bl & red . . 65 25

626 Book and Writing Materials

627 Federation Emblem

1982. 14th Cairo International Book Fair.
1468 **626** 3p. brown and yellow . . 35 10

1982. 25th Anniv of Egyptian Trade Unions Federation.
1469 **627** 3p. blue and green . . . 25 10

628 Map, "25" and Dome of University

1982. 25th Anniv of Cairo University, Khartoum Branch.
1470 **628** 6p. green and blue . . . 55 30

629 Fair Emblem

630 Hilton Ramses Hotel

1982. 15th Cairo International Fair.
1471 **629** 3p. black, green & orge 25 10

1982. Air. Opening of Hilton Ramses Hotel.
1472 **630** 18½p. brown, yell & bl 1·40 75

631 Long-finned Batfish

1982. International Conference on Marine Science and 50th Anniv of Marine Biological Station, El Ghardaka. Multicoloured.
1473 10m. Type **631** 55 35
1474 30m. Blue-lined snapper . . 75 40
1475 60m. Yellow boxfish 90 60
1476 230m. Lined butterflyfish . . 3·00 1·40

632 Map of Sinai, Olive Branch and Dove

1982. Sinai Restoration.
1477 **632** 3p. brown, stone & grn 45 15

633 De Havilland D.H.86B Dragon Express Biplane and Boeing 737 Jetliner

1982. 50th Anniv of Egyptair (state airline).
1478 **633** 23p. blue, mauve & yell 2·10 1·40

634 Minaret

635 Dove

1982. Millenary of El Azhar Mosque.
1479 **634** 6p. yellow, brn & grn . . 65 40
1480 – 6p. yellow, brn & grn . . 65 40
1481 – 6p. yellow, brn & grn . . 65 40
1482 – 6p. yellow, brn & grn . . 60 40
MS1483 60 × 59 mm. 23p. brown, blue and emerald. Imperf . . . 4·25 4·00
DESIGNS: No. 1479 Type **634**; 1480, Dome and minaret (different); 1481, Minaret with three stages and one ball on top; 1482, Minaret with two balls on top; **MS**1483, General view of mosque.

1982. 30th Anniv of Revolution.
1484 **635** 3p. grn, dp grn & orge 35 20
MS1485 55 × 73 mm. 23p. black, rosine and emerald. Imperf . . 3·75 3·00
DESIGN: 23p. Flag arranged to form flower.

636 Hotel, Citadel, Sphinx, Pyramid and St. Catherine's

1982. International Tourism Day.
1486 **636** 23p. blue, orge & brn . . 2·40 1·60

637 Martyrs' Monument, Egyptian Flag and Map

1982. 9th Anniv of Suez Crossing.
1487 **637** 3p. black, pink & blue 45 20

638 Biennale Emblem and Sailboat

639 Trees and Factory Pollution (World Environment Day)

1982. 14th Fine Arts Biennale, Alexandria.
1488 **638** 3p. orange, blue & lilac 35 15

1982. United Nations Day.
1489 **639** 3p. brown, yell & grn . . 30 15
1490 – 6p. blue and green . . . 55 30
1491 – 6p. blue and brown . . . 55 30
1492 – 8p. brown, blue & red 80 45
DESIGNS—HORIZ: No. 1490, Olive branch and dove encircling globe (2nd Conference on the Exploration and Peaceful Uses of Outer Space, Vienna); 1492, Dr. Robert Koch and bacillus (centenary of discovery of tubercle bacillus); 36 × 36 mm: No. 1491, Lord Baden-Powell and scout emblems (125th birth anniv of Lord Baden-Powell (founder) and 75th anniv of boy scout movement).

640 Avro Type 618 Ten and General Dynamics Fighting Falcon

1982. 50th Anniv of Egyptian Air Force.
1493 **640** 3p. blue and black . . . 50 15

641 Ahmed Shawqi and Hafez Ibrahim

1982. 50th Death Annivs of Ahmed Shawqi and Hafez Ibrahim (poets).
1494 **641** 6p. blue and brown . . . 55 35

642 Jubilee Emblem

643 Hands holding Flower

1982. 25th Anniv of National Research Centre.
1495 **642** 3p. blue and red 40 15

1982. Aged People Year.
1496 **643** 23p. green, red & blue 2·10 1·30

644 "Academy" on Open Books

1982. 50th Anniv of Arab League Academy.
1497 **644** 3p. brown, stone & blue 50 30

645 Postal Emblem and Postcoded Letter

647 Emblem, Globe and Open Book

646 Police Emblem

1983. Post Day.
1498 **645** 3p. blue, red and blk . . 40 15

1983. Police Day.
1499 **646** 3p. blue, black & grn . . 50 15

1983. 15th Cairo International Book Fair.
1500 **647** 3p. blue and red 45 20

648 Satellite and Map of Africa

649 Conference Emblem

1983. 5th U.N. Regional Conference for African Maps, Cairo.
1501 **648** 3p. green and blue . . . 40 20

1983. 3rd African Ministers of Transport, Communication and Planning Conference, Cairo.
1502 **649** 23p. blue and green . . 1·30 75

650 Emblem, Olive Branch and Cogwheel

651 Footballer heading Ball

1983. 16th Cairo International Fair.
1503 **650** 3p. green, black & red 40 15

1983. Egyptian Football Victories in Africa Cup and African Cup-winners Cup.
1504 **651** 3p. stone, brown & red 40 20
1505 – 3p. stone, brown & red 40 20
DESIGNS: No. 1504, Type **651** (African Cup-winners Cup, Arab Contractors Club); No. 1505, Footballer kicking ball (Africa Cup, National Club).

652 Emblem within Heart

1983. World Health Day. Blood Donation.
1506 **652** 3p. black, red & green 45 15

653 Organization Emblem

1983. 10th Anniv of Trade Union Unity Organization.
1507 **653** 3p. blue and green . . . 40 15

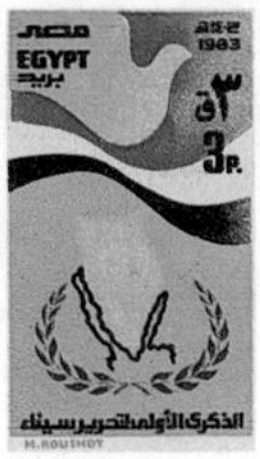

654 Map Dove and Flag

655 Scarab and Microscope

1983. 1st Anniv of Restoration of Sinai.
1508 **654** 3p. green, black & red 40 15

1983. 75th Anniv of Egyptian Entomological Society.
1509 **655** 3p. black and blue . . . 45 15

656 Chrysanthemums

1983. Festivals.
1510 **656** 20m. red and green . . . 25 15

657 Stadium, Player and Championship Emblem

1983. 5th African Handball Championship, Cairo.
1511 **657** 6p. brown and green . . 40 20

658 Ears of Wheat and "23"

659 Simon Bolivar (statue)

1983. 31st Anniv of Revolution.
1512 **658** 3p. green, yell & brn . . 30 15

1983. Birth Bicentenary of Simon Bolivar (South American revolutionary leader).
1513 **659** 23p. brown and blue . . 95 65

660 Arabi Pasha, Maps of Egypt and Ceylon and House

1983. Centenary of Exile to Ceylon of Arabi Pasha.
1514 **660** 3p. brown, grn & orge 35 15

661 Jar and Museum

1983. Reopening of Islamic Museum.
1515 **661** 3p. lt brown & brown 45 15

662 Monument, Martyrs, Cogwheel, Wheat and Oil Well

663 Rally Cars

1983. 10th Anniv of Suez Crossing.
1516 **662** 3p. green, red & blk . . 45 15

1983. 2nd International Pharaonic Motor Rally.
1517 **663** 23p. brown, bl & stone 1·60 75

664 Radar, Modern Freighter and Pharaonic Ship

1983. United Nations Day.
1518 **664** 3p. blue and black . . . 50 15
1519 – 6p. green and blue . . . 50 35
1520 – 6p. green, orge & blk . . 50 35
1521 – 23p. blue and brown . . 2·40 1·20
DESIGNS: No. 1518, Type **664** (25th anniv of International Maritime Organization); 1519, Emblems and concentric circles (World Communications Year); 1520, Ear of wheat and emblems (20th anniv of World Food Programme); 1521, Fishing boat and fish (Fishery Resources).

665 Karate, Pyramids and Sphinx

1983. 4th World Karate Championship, Cairo.
1522 **665** 3p. multicoloured . . . 40 20

666 Dome of the Rock, Jerusalem

1983. International Day of Solidarity with Palestinian People.
1523 **666** 6p. brown, ochre & grn 95 20

667 Artist's Palette

668 Statue and Cairo University

1983. 75th Anniv of Faculty of Fine Arts, Helwan University.
1524 **667** 3p. yellow, red & blue 30 15

1983. 75th Anniv of Cairo University.
1525 **668** 3p. lt brn, brn & bl . . . 30 15

669 "Mother and Child" and Emblem

1983. International Egyptian Maternity and Child Care Society.
1526 **669** 2p. blue, black & orge 30 15

670 Emblem and Maps

671 Rameses II, Thebes

1983. 20th Anniv of Organization of African Unity.
1527 **670** 3p. green and red . . . 30 15

1983. 10th Anniv (1982) of World Heritage Convention. Each stone, brown and green.
1528 3p. Type **671** 40 30
1529 3p. Coptic weaving (detail) 40 30
1530 3p. Islamic carved wooden panel 40 30

672 Qaitbay Fort

1984. Post Day. Multicoloured.
1531 6p. Type **672** 50 30
1532 23p. Mohammed Ali Mosque, Saladin's Citadel 1·40 90

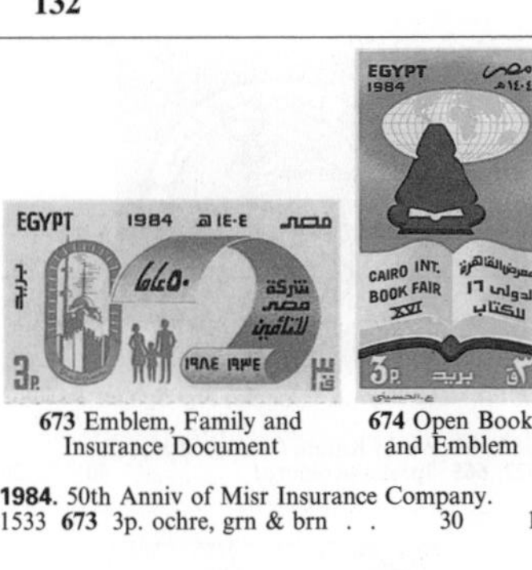

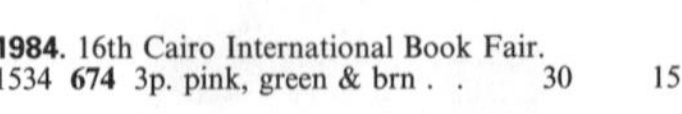

673 Emblem, Family and Insurance Document
674 Open Book and Emblem

1984. 50th Anniv of Misr Insurance Company.
1533 **673** 3p. ochre, grn & brn . . 30 15

1984. 16th Cairo International Book Fair.
1534 **674** 3p. pink, green & brn . . 30 15

675 Fair Emblem within Pyramids
676 University Emblem and Map

1984. 17th Cairo International Fair.
1535 **675** 3p. orange, brn & grn 35 15

1984. 25th Anniv of Assiout University.
1536 **676** 3p. orange, blue and lilac 30 15

677 Emblem
678 Curtains, Masks and Globe

1984. 75th Anniv of Egyptian Co-operatives.
1537 **677** 3p. orange, blue & grn 30 15

1984. World Theatre Day.
1538 **678** 3p. brown, blue and red 30 15

679 Mahmoud Moukhtar and Sculptures

1984. 50th Death Anniv of Mahmoud Moukhtar (sculptor).
1539 **679** 3p. brown and green . . 30 15

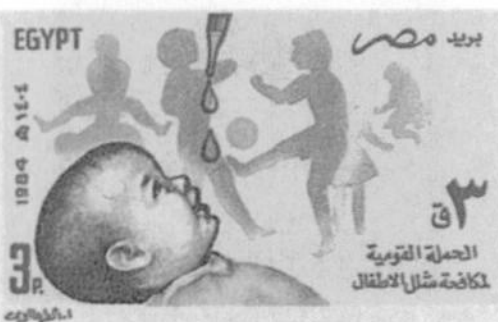

680 Baby receiving Oral Vaccine

1984. World Health Day. Anti-poliomyelitis Campaign.
1540 **680** 3p. yellow, brn & grn . . 60 20

681 Doves over Sinai
682 Map of Africa showing Namibia

1984. 2nd Anniv of Restoration of Sinai.
1541 **681** 3p. stone, green & blue 35 15

1984. Africa Day.
1542 **682** 3p. blue and brown . . . 30 15

683 Globe and Transmitter
684 Carnation

1984. 50th Anniv of Egyptian Broadcasting.
1543 **683** 3p. blue, black and red 30 15

1984. Festivals.
1544 **684** 2p. red and green . . . 25 10

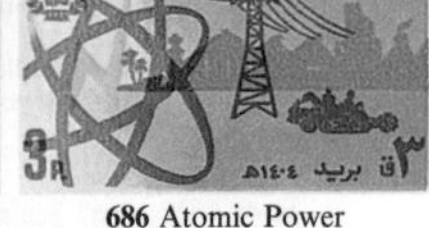

685 Decorated Mask
686 Atomic Power

1984. 1st Cairo International Biennale.
1545 **685** 3p. multicoloured . . . 30 15

1984. 32nd Anniv of Revolution.
1546 **686** 3p. blue, yellow and red 30 15

687 Boxing
688 Conference Emblem

1984. Olympic Games, Los Angeles.
1547 **687** 3p. green, blue and red 30 15
1548 – 3p. green, blue and red 30 15
1549 – 3p. green, blue and red 30 15
1550 – 3p. green, blue and red 30 15
MS1551 130 × 80 mm. 30p. As Nos. 1547/50 but without values and each 17½ × 30½ mm. Each green, blue and magenta. Imperf 3·50 3·25
DESIGNS: No. 1548, Basketball; 1549, Volleyball; 1550, Football.

1984. 2nd Egyptians Abroad Conference, Cairo.
1552 **688** 3p. brn, bl & blk 35 15
1553 23p. brn, grn & blk . . 1·60 90

689 Couple and Emblem
690 Emblem and Sphinx

1984. 30th Anniv of Egyptian Youth Hostels Association.
1554 **689** 3p. green, blk & orge . . 30 15

1984. 50th Anniv of Misr Travel Company.
1555 **690** 3p. brown, yellow & bl 35 15

691 Eagle's Head and Map of Sinai
692 Map of Nile Valley and Integration Badge

1984. 11th Anniv of Suez Crossing.
1556 **691** 3p. green, red and black 35 20

1984. 2nd Anniv of Signing of Egypt–Sudan Co-operation Treaty.
1557 **692** 3p. red, black and green 35 15

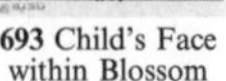

693 Child's Face within Blossom
694 Tank, Anti-aircraft Gun and Emblem

1984. United Nations Children's Fund.
1558 **693** 3p. multicoloured . . . 30 15

1984. Defence Equipment Exhibition, Cairo.
1559 **694** 3p. yellow, black and red 30 15

695 Kamel Kilany and Books
696 Ahmed ibn Toulon Mosque

1984. 25th Death Anniv of Kamel Kilany (children's author and poet).
1560 **695** 3p. brown, yell & bl . . 30 15

1984. 1100th Death Anniv of Ahmed ibn Toulon (governor of Egypt).
1561 **696** 3p. lt brn, bl & brn . . . 35 15

697 Congress Emblem
698 Emblem and Spotlights

1984. 29th International History of Medicine Congress, Cairo.
1562 **697** 3p. blue, black & red . . 30 15

1984. 25th Anniv of Academy of Art.
1563 **698** 3p. multicoloured . . . 30 15

699 Pharaoh receiving Letter (monument) and Postal Museum

1985. Post Day.
1564 **699** 3p. blue, brown & red 35 20

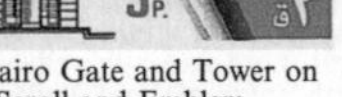

700 Cairo Gate and Tower on Scroll and Emblem
701 Scribe (statue) and Emblem

1985. 15th International Union of Architects Conference.
1565 **700** 3p. lilac and blue 30 20

1985. 17th Cairo International Book Fair.
1566 **701** 3p. blue and orange . . 40 20

702 Edfu Temple
703 Ear of Wheat, Cogwheels and Emblem

1985. Air.
1567 **702** 6p. green and blue . . . 60 25
1568 15p. brown and blue . . 1·00 40
1569 – 18p.50 grn, yell & brn 1·20 85
1570 – 23p. brown, yell & bl . . 1·60 1·10
1571 – 25p. blue, yell & brn . . 1·30 70
1572 – 30p. brown, orge & bl 1·30 65
DESIGNS—HORIZ: 23, 30p. Giza Pyramids. VERT: 18p. 50, 25p. Akhnaton.

1985. 18th Cairo International Fair.
1573 **703** 3p. multicoloured . . . 35 20

704 Woman holding Heart
705 Priest of god Mout

1985. 3rd Anniv of Restoration of Sinai.
1574 **704** 5p. multicoloured . . . 60 20

1985. (a) Size 22 × 27 mm.
1575 **705** 1p. brown 20 10
1576 – 2p. blue 20 10
1577 – 3p. brown 25 15
1578 – 5p. purple 40 15
1579 – 8p. brown and green . . 55 35
1580 – 10p. blue and purple . . 30 15
1581 – 11p. purple 70 50
1582 – 15p. brown and ochre 1·10 55
1583 – 20p. green . . . . 1·60 55
1584 – 20p. green and yellow . . 45 30
1585 – 30p. brn & cinnamon . . 45 25
1586 – 35p. yellow & brown . . 3·00 1·30
1587 – 50p. lilac and brown . . 95 45

(b) Mosques. Size 22 × 39 mm.
1588 – £E1 brown and orange . . 2·75 90
1589 – £E2 brown and yellow . . 5·50 1·50
DESIGNS: 2, 20p. (1583) Wading birds (relief sculpture); 3, 5p. Statue of Rameses II, Luxor; 8, 15p. Slave kneeling with tray and fruit (wall painting); 10p. Vase; 11p. Carved head; 20p. (1584) Jug; 30p. Flagon; 35p. Capitals of pharaonic columns; 50p. Flask; £E1, Al-Maridani Mosquel; £E2, Al-Azhar Mosque, Cairo.
For designs size 18 × 22 mm, see Nos. 1772/5.

707 Treble Clef
708 El Moulid Bride (doll)

1985. 50th Anniv of Helwan University Musical Faculty.
1595 **707** 5p. blue and yellow . . . 45 20

1985. Festivals 1985.
1596 **708** 2p. violet, orge & yell . . 30 10
1597 5p. red, blue & green . . 35 20

709 Player and Cup

710 Television Headquarters and Radio Waves

1985. Egyptian Football Victories. Mult.
1598 5p. Cairo Stadium (left-hand) 45 30
1599 5p. Cairo Stadium (right-hand) 45 30
1600 5p. El Zamalek Club player and Africa Cup (winners, 1984) 45 30
1601 5p. National Club player (red shirt) and African Cup-winners Cup (winners 1984) 45 30
1602 5p. Type **709** (Arab Contractors Club, African Cup-winners Cup winners, 1983) 45 30
Nos. 1598/9 were printed together, se-tenant, forming a composite design.

1985. Anniversaries. Multicoloured.
1603 5p. Type **710** (25th anniv of Egyptian television) . . . 45 20
1604 5p. Flag and olive branch entwined. ships and maps of world and Suez Canal (10th anniv of re-opening) (horiz) 45 20
1605 5p. Cars in Ahmed Hamdi Tunnel under Suez Canal (33rd anniv of revolution) 45 20
MS1606 97×79 mm. 30p. Aswan High Dam (25th anniv) (53×50 mm) . . . . 3·50 3·00
Nos. 1604 and **MS**1606 also bear 33rd anniv of revolution emblem.

711 Map within Heart and Emblem

1985. 3rd Egyptians Abroad Conference, Cairo.
1607 **711** 15p. multicoloured . . . 1·00 50

712 Akhnaton worshipping Aton and Emblem

1985. 50th Anniv of Tourism Organization.
1608 **712** 5p. multicoloured . . . 35 20

713 Flag and Olive Branch on Map of Sinai

1985. 12th Anniv of Suez Crossing.
1609 **713** 5p. multicoloured . . . 35 20

714 Air Scouts Emblem

1985. 30th Anniv of Air Scouts.
1610 **714** 5p. blue, red & yellow 45 20

715 International Youth Year Emblem

716 Conference and Association Emblems

1985. United Nations Day.
1611 **715** 5p. lilac, yellow & grn 35 20
1612 – 5p. multicoloured . . . 35 20
1613 – 15p. blue, yellow and red 90 60
1614 – 15p. blue & light blue . . 90 60
DESIGNS: No. 1612, Meteorological map of Egypt (World Meteorology Day); 1613, Dove and U.N. emblem (40th Anniv of United Nations Organization); 1614, International communications development programme emblem.

1985. 2nd International Conference of Egyptian Association of Dental Surgeons, Cairo.
1615 **716** 5p. blue and brown . . . 40 20

717 Conference Banner and Koran

718 Squash Player

1985. 4th International Conference of Biography and Sunna (sayings) of Prophet Mohammed.
1616 **717** 5p. blue, yellow & brn 35 20

1985. World Squash Championships, Cairo.
1617 **718** 5p. green, yellow & brn 45 20

719 Emblem, Flag and Hand holding Tools

720 Emblem and Tomb Paintings

1985. 1st Technical Industrial Education Conference.
1618 **719** 5p. blue, red & black . . 40 20

1985. 75th Anniv of Egyptian Olympic Committee.
1619 **720** 5p. multicoloured . . . 50 25

721 Narmer Board

722 Emblem and Relief of Scribe

1986. Air. Post Day. Multicoloured.
1620 15p. Type **721** . . . . . . 1·00 1·00
1621 15p. Narmer Board (opposite side) . . . . . 1·00 1·00

1986. 18th Cairo International Book Fair.
1622 **722** 5p. brown, yellow & bl 40 20

723 Conference Emblem

1986. 3rd International Conference for Transport in Developing Countries, Cairo.
1623 **723** 5p. blue, green & red . . 35 20

724 Emblem on Islamic Ornament

1986. 25th Anniv of Central Bank.
1624 **724** 5p. multicoloured . . . 25 20

725 Globe, Sorting Office and Map

1986. Inauguration of Cairo Postal Sorting Centre.
1625 **725** 5p. blue and brown . . . 25 15

726 Tomb Painting, Sakkara

1986. 75th Anniv of Cairo University Commerce Faculty.
1626 **726** 5p. yellow, brown & pur 50 20

727 Wheat, Cogwheel, Flags and Emblem

728 Map of Sudan and dead Tree

1986. 19th Cairo International Fair.
1627 **727** 5p. multicoloured . . . 35 20

1986. Relief of Drought Victims in Sudan.
1628 **728** 15p.+5p. bl, brn & yell 1·10 85

729 Map of Africa, Boeing 707 and Emblem

1986. 18th Annual General Assembly of African Airlines Association.
1629 **729** 15p. blue, yell & blk . . 85 40

730 Ankh, Red Crescent and Hands

1986. 50th Anniv of Ministry of Health.
1630 **730** 5p. multicoloured . . . 35 20

731 Queen Nefertari and Map of Sinai

1986. 4th Anniv of Restoration of Sinai.
1631 **731** 5p. blue, red & green . . 45 20

732 Profiles and Map

1986. Census.
1632 **732** 15p. brown, yell & bl . . 80 45

733 Map, Cup and Emblem

734 Roses

1986. Victory in African Nations Cup Football Championship. Multicoloured.
1633 5p. Type **733** 40 25
1634 5p. As No. 1633 but emblem inscr in Arabic 40 25

1986. Festivals 1986.
1635 **734** 5p. purple, green & lilac 35 20

735 Smoke issuing from Factory

737 Road on Map of Africa

736 Eagle and "23 July"

1986. World Environment Day.
1636 **735** 15p. black, green & blue 85 50

1986. 34th Anniv of Revolution.
1637 **736** 5p. yellow, green & red 30 20

1986. 6th African Road Conference, Cairo.
1638 **737** 15p. multicoloured . . . 80 45

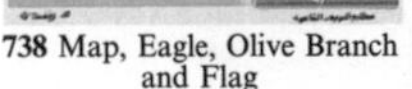

738 Map, Eagle, Olive Branch and Flag

739 Workers holding Books and Tools

1986. 13th Anniv of Suez Crossing.
1639 **738** 5p. multicoloured . . . 60 20

1986. 25th Anniv of Workers' Cultural Association.
1640 **739** 5p. orange and lilac . . 35 15

740 Syndicate Emblem and Engineering Symbols

741 Dove and Emblem (International Peace Year)

1986. Engineers' Day. 40th Anniv of Engineers' Syndicate.
1641 **740** 5p. green, brown & blue 30 15

1986. United Nations Day.
1642 **741** 5p. green, blue & red . . 25 20
1643 – 15p. yellow, grn & brn 80 55
1644 – 15p. multicoloured . . . 80 55
DESIGNS—HORIZ: As T **741**: No. 1643, Harvester and ears of wheat (40th anniv of Food and Agriculture Organization). 46×27 mm: 1644, Emblem, globe and "UNESCO" in Arabic (40th anniv of UNESCO).

742 Map and Old and New Drilling Towers

1986. Centenary of First Egyptian Oilwell, Gemsa.
1645 **742** 5p. green, yellow & blk 35 20

743 Children holding Flower

1986. Children's Day.
1646 **743** 5p. multicoloured . . . 35 20

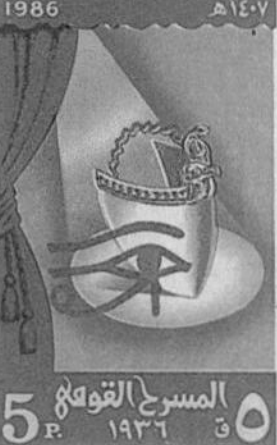

744 Ahmed Amin

745 Mask and Eye in Spotlight

1986. Birth Centenary of Ahmed Amin (literary researcher).
1647 **744** 5p. yellow, brn & grn . . 30 20

1986. 50th Anniv of National Theatre.
1648 **745** 5p. multicoloured . . . 35 20

746 Statue of King Zoser and Step Pyramid, Sakkara

1987. Post Day.
1649 **746** 5p. multicoloured . . . 40 20

747 Book and Pencil as "19"

1986. 19th Cairo International Book Fair.
1650 **747** 5p. multicoloured . . . 35 20

748 Emblem

749 Medal

1987. 5th International Conference on Islamic Education.
1651 **748** 5p. multicoloured . . . 30 20

1987. 20th Cairo International Fair.
1652 **749** 5p. black, gold & red . . 30 20

750 Olive Branch, Profile and National Colours

1987. Veterans' Day.
1653 **750** 5p. red, green & gold . . 30 20

751 Plants and Emblem

1987. Air. International Garden Festival, Cairo.
1654 **751** 15p. multicoloured . . . 80 50

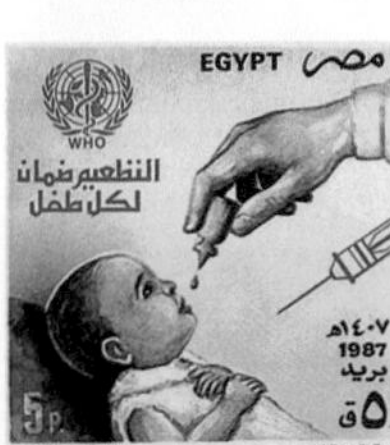

752 Oral Vaccination

1987. International Health Day.
1655 **752** 5p. multicoloured . . . 30 20
1656 – 5p. yellow, grn & blk . . 30 20
DESIGN: No. 1656, Woman giving baby oral rehydration therapy.

753 Africa Cup

754 Saladin's Citadel and Map

1987. Egyptian Victories in Football Championships. Multicoloured.
1657 5p. Type **753** (El Zamalek team) 40 30
1658 5p. African Nations Cup (national team) 40 30
1659 5p. African Cup Winners Cup (El Ahly team) . . . 40 30
MS1660 115×85 mm. 30p. Flag, Cairo International Stadium and Cups (from left to right). Imperf 3·50 3·00

1987. 5th Anniv of Restoration of Sinai.
1661 **754** 5p. blue and brown . . . 35 20

755 Dahlia

1987. Festivals 1987.
1662 **755** 5p. blue, yellow & mauve 30 15

756 Pyramid and Camel Train

1987. "Saudi Arabia—Yesterday and Today" Exhibition, Cairo.
1663 **756** 15p. multicoloured . . . 90 50

757 El Sawary Column and Sphinx and Qaitbay Fort, Alexandria

1987. Tourism. Multicoloured.
1664 15p. Type **757** 80 70
1665 15p. St. Catherine's Monastery, Sinai 80 70
1666 15p. Colossi of Thebes . . . 80 70
1667 15p. Temple, Luxor 80 70
MS1668 140×90 mm. 30p. As Nos. 1664/7. Imperf . . . . . 3·75 3·50
Nos. 1664/7 were printed together, se-tenant, forming a composite design of a map with each illustrated subject pinpointed.

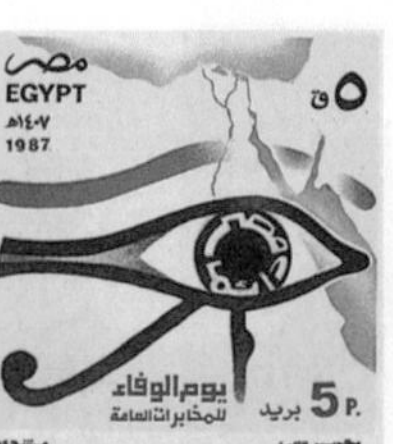

758 Pharaonic Eye on Map

1987. Loyalty Day. 32nd Anniv of General Intelligence Service.
1669 **758** 5p. multicoloured . . . 30 15

759 Ears of Wheat and Emblem

1987. Industrial and Agricultural Exhibition, Alexandria.
1670 **759** 5p. black, grn & orge . . 35 20

760 Emblems

1987. International Year of Shelter for the Homeless. World Architects' Day.
1671 **760** 5p. yellow, brn & grn . . 35 20

761 Scene from Opera and Sphinx

1987. Performance of Verdi's "Aida" (opera) at the Pyramids. Multicoloured.
1672 15p. Type **761** 90 30
MS1673 70×70 mm. 30p. As No. 1672. Imperf . . . . . . 7·25 7·00

762 Train in Station

1987. Inauguration of Cairo Underground Railway.
1674 **762** 5p. multicoloured . . . 70 20

763 Head composed of Industrial Symbols

764 Horseman and Map

1987. Production Day.
1675 **763** 5p. multicoloured . . . 35 15

1987. 800th Anniv of Battle of Hattin.
1676 **764** 5p. multicoloured . . . 40 20

765 U.P.U. Emblem

1987. 40th Anniv of Executive Council and 30th Anniv of Consultative Council of U.P.U.
1677 **765** 5p. black, orange & bl 30 15

766 Eye and Art Materials

1987. 16th Fine Arts Biennale. Alexandria.
1678 **766** 5p. multicoloured . . . 25 15

767 Emblem and Ancient Egyptians making Weapons

1987. 2nd International Defence Equipment Exhibition, Cairo.
1679 **767** 5p. multicoloured . . . 35 15

768 Profile and Emblem

1987. 2nd Pan-Arab Anaesthesia and Intensive Care Congress.
1680 **768** 5p. multicoloured . . . 40 20

769 Globe and Emblem on Skeleton

770 Selim Hassan (archaeologist) and Hieroglyphics

1987. International Orthopaedic and Traumatology Conference, Luxor.
1681 **769** 5p. grey, brown & blue 30 15

1987. Birth Centenaries. Multicoloured.
1682 5p. Type **770** 35 15
1683 5p. Abdel Hamid Badawi (politician and International Court of Justice judge) 35 15

771 Mycerinus and Left-hand Pyramid, Giza

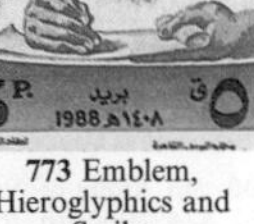
773 Emblem, Hieroglyphics and Scribe

772 Map

1988. Post Day. Multicoloured.
1684 15p. Type **771** 80 65
1685 15p. Chefren (with beard) and middle pyramid . . . 80 65
1686 15p. Cheops and righthand pyramid 80 65

1988. 30th Anniv of Asia–Africa Organization.
1687 **772** 15p. multicoloured . . . 65 45

1988. 20th Cairo International Book Fair.
1688 **773** 5p. multicoloured . . . 35 15

774 Container Ship

1988. 25th Anniv of Martrans Shipping Line.
1689 **774** 5p. multicoloured . . . 50 15

775 Fair Facade, Globe and Emblem

1988. 21st Cairo International Fair.
1690 **775** 5p. multicoloured . . . 30 15

776 Bowl of Sugar and Emblem

777 Prince Ossrite and Fig Tree

1988. World Health Day. Diabetic Care.
1691 **776** 5p. multicoloured . . . 35 15

1988. Festivals 1988.
1692 **777** 5p. orange, grn & brn 30 15

778 Letters and Emblem

1988. 25th Anniv of African Postal Union.
1693 **778** 15p. blue 65 45

779 Hands of Different Races reaching for Torch

1988. Anti-racism Campaign.
1694 **779** 5p. multicoloured . . . 25 25

780 Maps of Africa around Emblem

1988. 25th Anniv of Organization of African Unity.
1695 **780** 15p.+10p. mult 80 70

781 Tawfek el Hakem

1988. 1st Death Anniv of Tawfek el Hakem (dramatist).
1696 **781** 5p. brown and blue . . . 25 20

782 Cubic Art (M. el Razaz)

1988. 50th Anniv of Faculty of Art Education.
1697 **782** 5p. multicoloured . . . 25 15

783 Games Emblem

1988. Air. Olympic Games, Seoul. Multicoloured.
1698 15p. Type **783** 55 30
MS1699 94 × 90 mm. 30p. Various sports. Imperf . . . . 5·50 5·25

784 Torch, Flag and Palestinians

1988. Air. Palestinian "Intifida" Movement.
1700 **784** 25p. multicoloured . . . 85 60

785 Soldier and Flag

1988. 15th Anniv of Suez Crossing.
1701 **785** 5p. multicoloured . . . 30 15

786 Model of Opera House

1988. Inauguration of Opera House. Multicoloured.
1702 5p. Type **786** 30 20
MS1703 **786** 112 × 74 mm. 50p. View of Opera House. Imperf . . . 2·75 2·50

787 Red Crescent and Red Cross (125th Anniv of Red Cross)

1988. U.N. Day.
1704 **787** 5p. black, red and green (postage) 25 20
1705 – 20p. yellow, blue and orange 75 55
1706 – 25p. mult (air) 75 40
DESIGNS—22 × 39 mm. 20p. Anniversary emblem (40th anniv of W.H.O.); 47 × 28 mm. 25p. Globes on scales (40th anniv of Human Rights Declaration).

788 Naguib Mahfouz

1988. Award of Nobel Prize for Literature to Naguib Mahfouz.
1707 **788** 5p. mult (postage) . . . 25 25
1708 25p. mult (air) 80 35

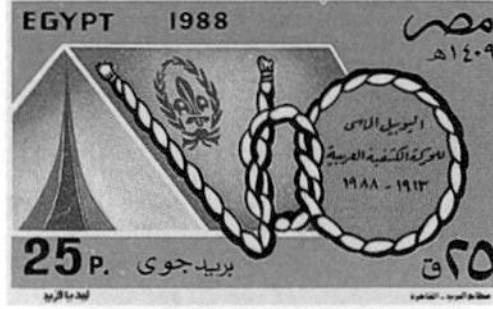
789 Tent and "75"

1988. 75th Anniv of Arab Scout Movement.
1709 **789** 25p. multicoloured . . . 80 60

790 Ein Shams University and Association Emblems

1988. Egyptian Orthopaedic Association International Conference, Cairo.
1710 **790** 5p. yellow, brn & grn . . 35 10

791 Pharaonic Eye and Map

1988. Restoration of Taba.
1711 **791** 5p. multicoloured . . . 25 10

792 "75" in Sun above Plant

793 Mohamed Hussein Hekal (writer and politician)

1988. 75th Anniv of Ministry of Agriculture.
1712 **792** 5p. blue, yell & orge . . 25 10

1988. Anniversaries. Each brown and green.
1713 5p. Type **793** (birth cent) . . 25 15
1714 5p. Ahmed Lofty el Sayed (philosopher and politician) (25th death anniv) 25 15

794 Priest (5th dynasty)

795 Nehru

1989. Post Day. Statues. Multicoloured.
1715 5p. Type **794** 30 15
1716 25p. Princess Nefert (4th dynasty) . . . . 1·10 45
1717 25p. Prince Ra-Hoteb (4th dynasty) . . . . 1·10 45

1989. Birth Centenary of Jawaharlal Nehru (Indian statesman).
1718 **795** 5p. green 25 10

796 Nile Hilton

1989. 30th Anniv of Nile Hilton Hotel.
1719 **796** 5p. multicoloured . . . 25 10

797 Route Map and Train leaving Tunnel

1989. Inauguration of Second Stage of Cairo Underground Railway.
1720 **797** 5p. multicoloured . . . 60 15

798 Arms and Map

799 Balcony

1989. Restoration of Taba.
1721 **798** 5p. multicoloured . . . 25 10

1989. Air.

1722	**799**	20p. purple, brn & bl	50	25
1723	–	25p. brn, yell & grn . .	70	35
1724	–	35p. pur, orge & bl . .	85	40
1725	–	45p. yell, blk & red . .	1·00	55
1725a	–	45p. pur, orge & grn	85	35
1726	–	50p. bl, stone & pur . .	1·20	65
1726a	–	55p. brn, buff & bl . .	1·20	55
1727	–	60p. pur, stone & bl . .	1·50	70
1727a	–	65p. pur, brn & grn . .	1·20	55
1728	**799**	70p. pur, brn & orge	1·40	60
1729	–	85p. yellow, light yellow and brown	1·50	75

DESIGNS: 25, 35, 45p. (1725a) Lantern; 45p. (1725) Carpet; 50, 60, 65p. Dish with gazelle motif; 55, 85p. Dish with fluted edge.

800 Lamp

801 Members' Flags

1989. Festivals 1989.
1730 **800** 5p. multicoloured . . . 20 10

1989. Air. Formation of Arab Co-operation Council. Multicoloured.
1731 25p. Type **801** 95 35
MS1732 89 × 80 mm. 50p. Members' flags (Egypt, Iraq, Jordan, Yemen Arab Republic) . . . . 3·00 3·00

802 Olympic Rings, Map and Sports

1989. 1st Arab Olympic Day.
1733 **802** 5p. green, brown & blk 20 10

803 Pyramids and Parliament Building

1989. Cent of Interparliamentary Union.
1734 25p. Type **803** 85 35
MS1735 85 × 70 mm. 25p. Pyramids, globe and Parliament building 1·50 1·50

804 Egyptian and French Flags

1989. Air. Bicentenary of French Revolution.
1736 **804** 25p. multicoloured . . . 40 15

805 Bank Emblem

1989. 25th Anniv of African Development Bank.
1737 **805** 10p. blue, yellow & pur 60 25

806 Conference Centre

1989. Cairo International Conference Centre.
1738 **806** 5p. brown, green & blue 25 10

807 October Panorama

808 Mohammed Ali Mosque, Saladin's Citadel

1989. 16th Anniv of Suez Crossing. Mult.
1739 10p. Egyptians in El Qantara (47 × 28 mm) . . 25 20
1740 10p. Type **807** 25 20
1741 10p. Crossing the Suez (47 × 28 mm) 25 20
See also No. 1766.

1989. Aga Khan Architecture Prize.
1742 **808** 35p. brown, grn & pur 85 40

809 Emblem sheltering Family

810 Envelopes forming World Map

1989. 25th Anniv of Health Insurance Scheme.
1743 **809** 10p. red, grey & black 25 10

1989. World Post Day.
1744 **810** 35p. black, blue & yell 75 40

811 Colossi of Thebes

1989. International Congress and Convention Association Meeting, Cairo.
1745 **811** 10p. lilac, green & blk 30 15

812 Faculty Emblem

814 University Emblem

813 Children at Crossings

1989. Centenary of Faculty of Agriculture, Cairo University.
1746 **812** 10p. purple, grn & yell 25 10

1989. 20th Anniv of Egyptian Road Safety Society.
1747 **813** 10p. multicoloured . . . 30 10

1989. 50th Anniv of Alexandria University.
1748 **814** 10p. brown and blue . . 25 10

815 Abdel Kader el Mazni (writer)

816 Statue of Priest Renofr

1989. Birth Anniversaries.
1749 **815** 10p. ochre and brown 25 15
1750 – 10p. olive and green . . 25 15
1751 – 10p. multicoloured . . . 25 15
DESIGNS—VERT: No. 1750, Abdel Rahman el Rafei (historian and politician). HORIZ: No. 1751, Ibrahim Pasha and statue in Opera Square, Cairo (son of Mohammed Ali and Viceroy of Egypt, July-November 1848).

1990. Post Day. Multicoloured.
1752 30p. Type **816** 70 40
1753 30p. Relief of Betah Hoteb from Sakkara 70 40

817 Emblem

1990. 1st Anniv of Arab Co-operation Council.
1754 **817** 10p. multicoloured . . . 30 20
1755 35p. multicoloured . . . 75 45

818 Emblem

819 Road Sign and Steering Wheel

1990. African Parliamentary Union Conference.
1756 **818** 10p. black, red & green 25 10
MS1757 80 × 59 mm 30p. multicoloured . . . . 1·10 1·00

1990. International Conference. Road Safety and Accidents in Developing Countries.
1758 **819** 10p. multicoloured . . . 25 10

820 Daisies

821 Doves and Map

1990. Festivals 1990.
1759 **820** 10p. multicoloured . . . 30 10

1990. 8th Anniv of Restoration of Sinai.
1760 **821** 10p. blue, yellow & blk 30 10

822 Trophy and Ball

824 Figures forming Pyramid

823 Pyramid, Sphinx, Mascot and Ball in Basket

1990. World Cup Football Championship, Italy. Multicoloured.
1761 10p. Type **822** 30 10
MS1762 80 × 60 mm. 50p. Trophy 1·50 1·50

1990. World Basketball Championship, Argentina.
1763 **823** 10p. black, blue & orge 30 10

1990. 5th Anniv of National Population Council.
1764 **824** 10p. brn, lt grn & grn 25 10

825 Battlefield

1990. 17th Anniv of Suez Crossing. Mult.
1765 10p. Type **825** 25 15
1766 10p. As Type **807** but dated "1990" 25 15
1767 10p. Egyptian soldiers with flamethrower 25 15

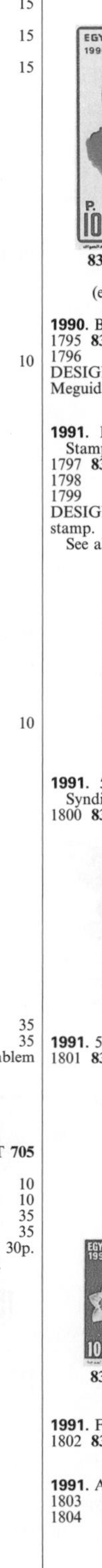

826 Anniversary Emblem

1990. 125th Anniv of Egyptian Post.
1768 **826** 10p. black, red & blue 25 10

827 Faculty Emblem and Al-Azhar Mosque, Cairo

1990. Centenary of Dar el Eloum Faculty.
1769 **827** 10p. multicoloured . . . 25 10

828 Emblem and Map (40th anniv of U.N. Development Programme)

1990. United Nations Day.
1770 **828** 30p. blue, grn & yell . . 60 35
1771 – 30p. multicoloured . . . 60 35
DESIGN—VERT: No. 1771, Cables and emblem forming Arabic "125" (125th anniv of I.T.U.).

1990. As previous designs and new design as T **705** but size 18 × 22 mm.
1772 5p. buff and brown 25 10
1773 10p. blue and lilac 25 10
1774 30p. brown and ochre . . . 45 35
1775 50p. brown and yellow . . . 60 35
DESIGNS: 5p. Jar; 10p. Vase (as No. 1580); 30p. Flagon (as No. 1585); 50p. Flask (as No. 1587).

829 Pictogram, Hand and Disabled Person

1990. Disabled Persons' Day.
1790 **829** 10p. multicoloured . . . 30 10

830 Crown Butterflyfish and Coral

1990. Ras Mohamed National Park. Mult.
1791 10p. Type **830** 35 20
1792 10p. Zebra lionfish 35 20
1793 20p. Two-banded anemonefish and emperor angelfish 40 25
1794 20p. Coral hind 40 25

831 Nabaweya Moussa (educationist)

832 1866 5pa. Stamp

1990. Birth Centenaries.
1795 **831** 10p. orge, grey & grn . . 25 15
1796 – 10p. orange, brn & bl . . 25 15
DESIGN: No. 1796, Dr. Mohamed Fahmy Abdel Meguid (pioneer of free medical care).

1991. Post Day. 125th Anniv of First Egyptian Stamps (1st issue).
1797 **832** 5p. grey and black . . . 20 10
1798 – 10p. brown and black . . 30 15
1799 – 20p. blue and black . . 35 25
DESIGNS: 10p. 1866 10pa. stamp; 20p. 1866 20pa. stamp.
See also Nos. 1815/17 and 1831, **MS**1832.

833 Birth of Calf

1991. 50th Anniv (1990) of Veterinary Surgeons' Syndicate.
1800 **833** 10p. multicoloured . . . 30 10

834 Newspaper, Quill, Ink and Lens

1991. 50th Anniv of Journalists' Syndicate.
1801 **834** 10p. multicoloured . . . 25 10

835 Narcissi

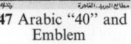

836 "Procession" and Mohamed Nagi

1991. Festivals 1991.
1802 **835** 10p. multicoloured . . . 25 10

1991. Artists' Anniversaries. Multicoloured.
1803 10p. Type **836** (35th death) 25 15
1804 10p. Mahmoud Mokhtar and sculptures (birth centenary) (horiz) 25 15

837 Riverbank Wildlife (½-size illustration)

1991. Centenary of Giza Zoo. Sheet 80 × 62 mm.
MS1805 **837** 50p. multicoloured 2·10 1·90

838 Saladin's Citadel and Faculty Building

1991. Centenary of Technical Faculty, University of Cairo.
1814 **838** 10p. multicoloured . . . 25 10

1991. 125th Anniv of First Egyptian Stamps (2nd issue) and "Cairo 1991" Stamp Exhibition (1st issue). As T **832**.
1815 10p. orange and black . . . 25 15
1816 10p. yellow and black . . . 25 15
1817 10p. purple and black . . . 25 15
MS1818 80 × 60 mm. 50p. multicoloured. Imperf . . . . 1·50 1·30
DESIGNS: No. 1815, 1866 5pi. Stamp; 1816, 1866 2pi. Stamp; 1817, 1866 1pi. Stamp; **MS**1818, Sphinx, pyramid and 1866 10pi. Stamp.

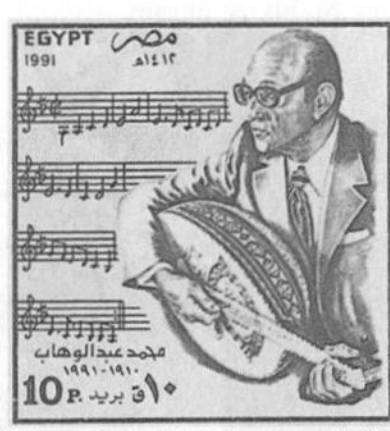

839 Score and Mohamed Abdel el Wahab

1991. Mohamed Abdel el Wahab (composer) Commemoration.
1819 **839** 10p. multicoloured . . . 30 10

840 Session Emblem

1991. 48th Session of International Statistics Institute, Nasr.
1820 **840** 10p. multicoloured . . . 25 10

841 Horus (mascot)

842 New Building

1991. 5th African Games, Cairo. Mult.
1821 10p. Type **841** 25 20
1822 10p. Running, gymnastics and swimming pictograms (horiz) 25 20
1823 10p. Football, basketball and shooting pictograms (horiz) 25 20
1824 10p. Taekwondo, karate and judo pictograms (horiz) 25 20
1825 10p. Table tennis, hockey and tennis pictograms (horiz) 25 20
1826 10p. Boxing, wrestling and weightlifting pictograms (horiz) 25 20
1827 10p. Handball, cycling and volleyball pictrograms (horiz) 25 20
MS1828 80 × 60 mm. 50p. Mascot, games emblem, torch and running track. Imperf . . . . 1·40 1·20

1991. Opening of Dar El Eftaa's New Building.
1829 **842** 10p. multicoloured . . . 25 10

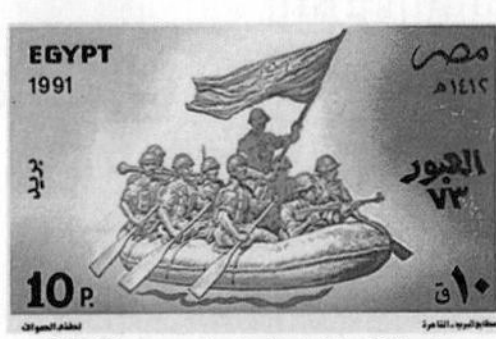

843 Troops in Inflatable Dinghy

1991. 18th Anniv of Suez Crossing.
1830 **843** 10p. multicoloured . . . 35 15

1991. 1st Anniv of Egyptian Stamps (3rd issue) and "Cairo 1991" Stamp Exhibition (2nd issue). As T832.
1831 10p. black and blue 25 10
MS1832 90 × 59 mm. £E1 multicoloured. Imperf . . . . 5·25 5·00
DESIGN: As Type **832**—10p. 188. 10pi stamp. 80 × 52mm. £E1 Exhibition emblem, hieroglyphics, pyramids and sphinx.

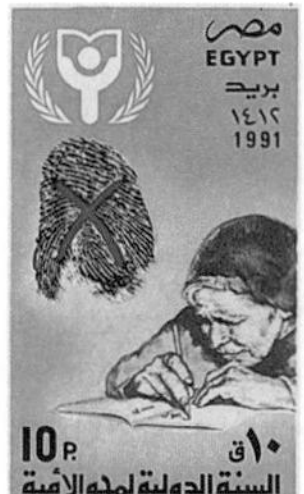

844 Woman writing

845 Dr. Zaki Mubarak (poet, birth centenary)

1991. United Nations Day. Multicoloured.
1833 10p. Type **844** (Int Literacy Year) 25 15
1834 10p. Brick "hands" sheltering people (World Shelter for the Homeless Day) (horiz) 25 15
1835 10p. Egyptian and International Standards Organizations emblems (World Standardization Day) (horiz) 25 15

1991. Writers' Anniversaries.
1836 **845** 10p. brown 25 15
1837 – 10p. grey 25 15
DESIGN: No. 1837, Abd el Kader Hamza (journalist and historian, 50th death anniv).

846 Scarab Pectoral (from Tutankhamun's tomb)

1992. Post Day. Multicoloured.
1838 10p. Type **846** (postage) . . 30 25
1839 45p. Eagle pectoral (from Tutankhamun's tomb) (air) 95 85
1840 70p. Golden saker falcon head (27 × 47 mm) . . . 1·50 1·30

847 Arabic "40" and Emblem

849 Darwish and Opening Bars of "Stand up O Egyptian"

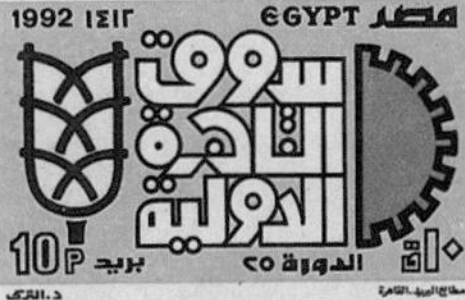

848 Ear of Wheat and Cogwheel

1992. Police Day.
1841 **847** 10p. multicoloured . . . 20 10

1992. 25th Cairo International Fair.
1842 **848** 10p. multicoloured . . . 20 10

1992. Birth Centenary of Sayed Darwish (composer).
1843 **849** 10p. green and yellow . . 20 10

850 Hoopoe

1992. Festivals 1992.
1844 **850** 10p. orange, blk & grn 25 10

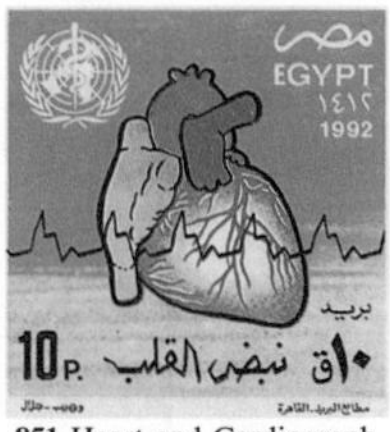

851 Heart and Cardiograph

1992. World Health Day.
1845 **851** 10p. multicoloured . . . 25 10

852 Tent, Emblem and Map

1992. 20th Arab Scout Jamboree.
1846 **852** 10p. multicoloured . . . 20 10

853 Games Emblem, Mascot and Pictograms
855 "Dar El Helal"

854 U.A.R. 1960 60m. Dam Stamp

1992. Olympic Games, Barcelona. Multicoloured.
1847 10p. Type **853** 20 10
MS1848 80 × 60 mm. 70p. Games emblem. Imperf . . . . 1·40 1·20

1992. 90th Anniv of Aswan Dam.
1849 **854** 10p. mauve, yell & blk 25 10

1992. Centenary of "El Helal" (periodical).
1850 **855** 10p. brown, gold & blk 45 20

856 Sphinx and Pyramids

1992. Federation of Travel Companies International Congress, Cairo.
1851 **856** 70p. multicoloured . . . 1·10 40

857 World Map, Lighthouse and Pharaonic Ship

1992. Alexandria World Festival.
1852 **857** 70p. multicoloured . . . 45 20

858 U.P.U. Emblem

1992. World Post Day.
1853 **858** 10p. bl, blk & ultram . . 25 10

859 Girl **860** Emblem

1992. United Nations Day. Multicoloured.
1854 10p. Type **859** (Children's Day) 30 10
1855 70p. Wall paintings of agriculture and medicine (International Food, Agriculture and World Health Conference) (36 × 37 mm) 80 50

1992. 20th Arab Scout Conference, Cairo.
1856 **860** 10p. multicoloured . . . 25 10

861 Mohamed Taymour **862** Sesostris I

1992. Birth Anniversaries.
1857 **861** 10p. blue, dp blue & bis 20 15
1858 – 10p. blue, dp blue & bis 20 15
1859 – 10p. brown, orge & bl 20 15
DESIGNS: No. 1857, Type **861** (dramatist and theatre critic, centenary); 1851, Ahmed Zaki Abu Shadi (physician and poet, centenary); 1859, Talaat Harb (economist, 125th anniv).

1993. Post Day. Statues of Pharaohs. Mult.
1860 10p. Type **862** 20 15
1861 45p. Amenemhet III 55 40
1862 70p. Hur I 85 60

863 Book and Statue of Scribe **864** Bust

1993. 25th Cairo International Book Fair.
1863 **863** 15p. multicoloured . . . 20 10

1993. Size 18 × 22 mm.
1864 **864** 5p. orange and black . . 35 15
1865 – 15p. brown and ochre 35 15
1866 – 15p. brown and ochre 20 10
1867 – 25p. lt brown & brown 30 20
1868 – 55p. blue and black . . 55 40
DESIGNS—15p. Sphinx*; 25p. Bust of woman; 55p. Bust of Pharaoh.
*On No. 1865 the illustration of the sphinx countinues behind the face value; on No. 1866 the sphinx is cropped so that the value appears on a white background.
For same designs but larger, 21 × 26 mm, see Nos. 1916/19.

865 Plan and Set Square on Drawing Board

1993. 75th Anniv (1992) of Architects' Association.
1869 **865** 15p. black, orange & bl 20 10

866 Gold Mask of Tutankhamun

1993.
1870 – £E1 brown and blue (postage) . . . . . . 2·00 1·10
1871 – £E2 green and brown . . 4·75 2·10
1872 – £E5 gold and brown . . 8·25 3·75
1873 **866** 55p. gold and brown (air) 95 50
1874 – 80p. gold and brown . . 1·70 65
DESIGNS: 80p. Side view of Tutankhamun's mask; £E1, Bust of woman; £E2, Head of Queen Tiye; £E5, Carved head capital.

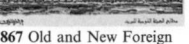

867 Old and New Foreign Ministry Buildings and Globe **868** Cactus

1993. (a) Egyptian Diplomacy Day.
1875 **867** 15p. multicoloured . . . 25 15
(b) Air. Inauguration of New Foreign Ministry Building. As T **867** but inscr "AIR MAIL MINISTRY OF FOREIGN AFFAIRS".
1876 **867** 80p. multicoloured . . . 90 55

1993. Festivals 1993.
1877 **868** 15p. multicoloured . . . 20 10

869 First Issue and Emblem

1993. Centenary of "Le Progres Egyptien" (newspaper).
1878 **869** 15p. multicoloured . . . 20 10

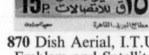

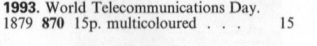

870 Dish Aerial, I.T.U. Emblem and Satellite **871** Globe

1993. World Telecommunications Day.
1879 **870** 15p. multicoloured . . . 15 10

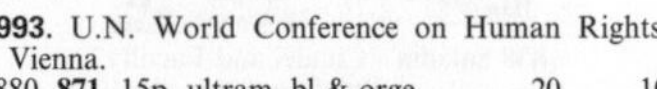

1993. U.N. World Conference on Human Rights, Vienna.
1880 **871** 15p. ultram, bl & orge 20 10

872 Emblem, Map of Africa and Stars

1993. 30th Anniv of Organization of African Unity.
1881 **872** 15p. black, silver and green (postage) . . . 20 15
1882 80p. black, gold and mauve (air) 60 30

873 Conference Emblem

1993. International Post, Telegraph and Telecommunications Union Conference, Cairo.
1883 **873** 15p. multicoloured . . . 20 10

874 Saladin and Dome of the Rock, Jerusalem

1993. 800th Death Anniv of Saladin.
1884 **874** 55p. multicoloured . . . 55 40

875 Soldiers **876** Pres. Mubarak

1993. 20th Anniv of Suez Crossing.
1885 **875** 15p. blk, mve & orge . . 20 10

1993. Mohammed Hosni Mubarak's 3rd Consecutive Term as President.
1886 **876** 15p. multicoloured . . . 20 15
1887 55p. multicoloured . . . 55 40
1888 80p. multicoloured . . . 75 60
MS1889 90 × 70 mm. 80p. Portrait and national flag as in Type **876**. Imperf . . . . 1·30 1·30

877 Map of Egypt and Electricity Symbol **878** Emblem and Caring Hands

1993. Centenary of Electricity in Egypt.
1890 **877** 15p. multicoloured . . . 20 10

1993. Air. International Decade for Natural Disaster Reduction.
1891 **878** 80p. violet, blue & red 55 35

879 Pyramids, Sphinx and Dam (congress emblem)

1993. 2nd International Large Dams Congress, Cairo.
1892 **879** 15p. yellow, mve & blk . . . 20 10

880 Trophy and Emblem

1993. Egyptian Victories in International Sports Competitions. Multicoloured.
1893 15p. Type **880** (Junior Men's World Handball Championship) 25 15
1894 15p. Trophy and emblem (World Military Football Championship) 25 15

881 Abdel Aziz al Bishry (50th death)
882 Amenhotep III

1993. Writers' Anniversaries.
1895 **881** 15p. blue 25 35
1896 – 15p. turquoise 25 35
1897 – 15p. green 25 35
1898 – 15p. mauve 25 35
DESIGNS: No. 1896, Mohamed Fareed Abu Hadeed (birth centenary); 1897, Ali Moubarak (death centenary); 1898, M. Beram al Tunisy (birth centenary).

1994. Post Day. Statues of Pharaohs. Multicoloured.
1899 15p. Type **882** 30 15
1900 55p. Queen Hatshepsut . . 65 15
1901 85p. Thutmose III . . . . . 1·10 25

883 Pyramids

1994. Egyptian Sedimentary Society Congress.
1902 **883** 15p. multicoloured . . . 20 15

884 Firecrests
885 Scout Salute and Emblem

1994. Festivals 1994. Multicoloured.
1903 15p. Type **884** 20 10
1904 15p. Barn swallows (one perching, one flying) . . . 20 10
1905 15p. Alexandrine parakeets (on tree trunk and branch) 20 10
1906 15p. Eurasian goldfinches (on blossoming branch) 20 10
Nos. 1903/6 were issued together, se-tenant, forming a composite design.

1994. 40th Anniv of Arab Scout Movement.
1907 **885** 15p. black, yell & grn . . 20 15

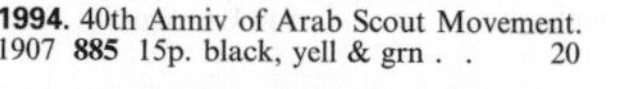

886 Emblem
887 Radio Waves over Map of Africa

1994. 27th Cairo International Fair.
1908 **886** 15p. multicoloured . . . 15 10

1994. "Africa Telecom 94" Exhibition, Cairo.
1909 **887** 15p. green and brown . . 15 10

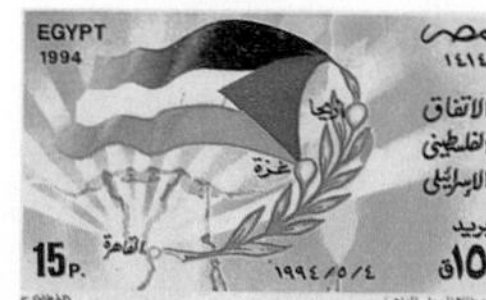

888 Map, Palestine Flag and Olive Branch

1994. Signing in Cairo of Israel-Palestine Agreement on Self-rule for Gaza and Jericho.
1910 **888** 15p. multicoloured . . . 15 10

889 Conference Emblem and Oil Well

1994. 5th Arab Energy Conference, Cairo.
1911 **889** 15p. multicoloured . . . 15 10

890 Emblem

1994. 18th Mediterranean Countries' Biennial Art Exhibition, Alexandria.
1912 **890** 15p. lilac, yellow & blk 15 10

891 Map of Africa and Dove
892 Campaign Emblem Magnfied

1994. Africa Day.
1913 **891** 15p. multicoloured . . . 15 10

1994. Tree Planting Campaign.
1914 **892** 15p. blue, green & black 15 10

893 Library, Family and Open Book

1994. "Reading for All" Summer Festival.
1915 **893** 15p. multicoloured . . . 15 10

1994. As previous designs but size 21 × 26 mm.
1916 **864** 5p. red and purple . . . 30 15
1917 – 15p. brown and cinnamon (as No. 1866) 30 15
1918 – 25p. orange and brown (as No. 1867) 40 20
1919 – 55p. blue and black (as No. 1868) 65 20

894 Emblem

1994. 75th Anniv of I.L.O.
1925 **894** 15p. grey, blue & black 15 10

895 Conference and United Nations Emblems

1994. U.N. International Conference on Population and Development, Cairo. Multicoloured.
1926 15p. Type **895** (postage) . . 15 15
1927 80p. Emblems and pharaonic murals (vert) (air) 60 40

896 Player and Trophy

1994. Egyptian Victories in Junior World Squash Championship.
1928 **896** 15p. multicoloured . . . 15 10

897 Anniversary Emblem

1994. Air. 50th Anniv of Signing of Int Civil Aviation Agreement, Chicago.
1929 **897** 80p. blue, yellow & blk 50 40

898 Map on Envelopes

1994. World Post Day.
1930 **898** 15p. multicoloured . . . 15 10

899 Akhenaten and Nefertiti (International Year of the Family)

1994. United Nations Day.
1931 **899** 80p. lilac, red and black (postage) 50 40
1932 – 80p. mult (air) 75 45
DESIGN—VERT: No. 1931, Nurses (75th anniv of International Red Crescent/Red Cross Union).

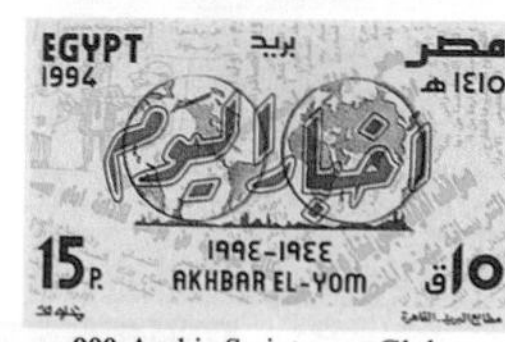

900 Arabic Script over Globes

1994. 50th Anniv of "Akhbar El Yom" (newspaper).
1933 **900** 15p. multicoloured . . . 20 10

901 Emblem, Trophy and Ancient Egyptian Players

1994. African Clubs Hockey Championship.
1934 **901** 15p. multicoloured . . . 20 15

902 Pharaoh and Radames
903 Centenary Emblem

1994. Performance of Verdi's "Aida" (opera) at Deir al-Bahari temple, Luxor. Multicoloured.
1935 15p. Type **902** (postage) . . 20 15
MS1936 68 × 80 mm. 80p. Aida, Great Priest and Pharaoh (air). Imperf . . . . 1·30 1·30

1994. Cent of Int Olympic Committee.
1937 **903** 15p. multicoloured . . . 15 10

904 Map showing Hostels and Association Emblem
906 Emblem as Flower

905 Player and Globe

1994. 40th Anniv of Egyptian Youth Hostels Association.
1938 **904** 15p. multicoloured . . . 15 10

1994. 10th Anniv of International Speedball Federation.
1939 **905** 15p. multicoloured . . . 15 10

1994. 30th Anniv of African Development Bank.
1940 **906** 15p. multicoloured . . . 15 10

907 Route Maps through Canal and around Africa

1994. 125th Anniv of Suez Canal. Mult.
1941 15p. Type **907** 40 15
1942 80p. Inauguration ceremony, 1869 . . . . 50 35

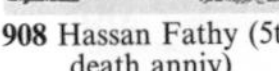

908 Hassan Fathy (5th death anniv) **910** Akhenaten (statuette)

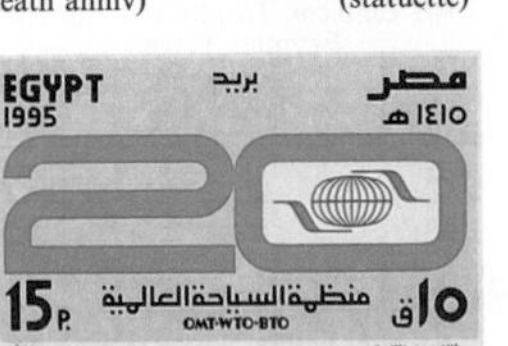

909 Anniversary Emblem

1994. Anniversaries.
1943 **908** 15p. brown and flesh . . 20 10
1944 – 15p. red and pink . . . 20 10
DESIGN: No. 1944, Mahmoud Taimour (birth centenary).

1995. 20th Anniv of World Tourism Organization.
1945 **909** 15p. multicoloured . . . 15 10

1995. Post Day. Multicoloured.
1946 15p. Type **910** 35 10
1947 55p. Gold mask of Tutankhamun 75 20
1948 80p. Nefertiti (bust) . . . . 1·10 30

911 Flowers

1995. Festivals 1995.
1949 **911** 15p. multicoloured . . . 15 10

912 Demonstration, 1919

1995. National Women's Day.
1950 **912** 15p. multicoloured . . . 15 10

913 Emblem and Map **915** Misr Bank

914 Hotel

1995. 50th Anniv of Arab League.
1951 **913** 15p. green, bl & gold . . 15 10
1952 55p. multicoloured . . . 45 40

1995. 25th Anniv of Cairo Sheraton Hotel.
1953 **914** 15p. multicoloured . . . 15 10

1995. 75th Anniv of Misr Bank.
1954 **915** 15p. multicoloured . . . 15 10

916 Dish Aerial and Globe

1995. International Telecommunications Day.
1955 **916** 80p. orange, blk & bl . . 55 30

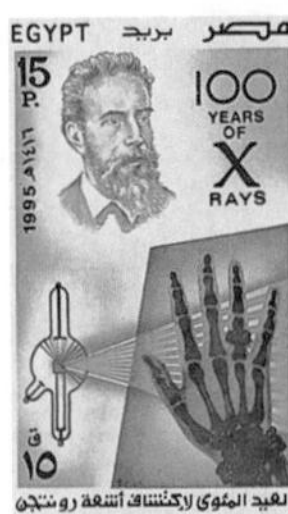

917 Rontgen and X-ray of Hand **918** Goddess Hathor

1995. Centenary of Discovery of X-rays by Wilhelm Rontgen.
1956 **917** 100p. multicoloured . . 15 10

1995. 20th Anniv of Membership of World Heritage Committee. Luxor Statues. Multicoloured.
1957 15p. Type **918** (postage) . . 30 15
1958 15p. God Atoum 30 15
1959 80p. God Amon with Horemheb (air) 85 25
Nos. 1957/8 were issued together, se-tenant, forming a composite design.

919 Emblem

1995. Air. 25th Anniv of Arab Educational, Scientific and Cultural Organization.
1960 **919** 55p. multicoloured . . . 45 20

920 Children as Flowers **921** Ozone Bands over Globe

1995. 21st Int Pediatrics Conf, Cairo.
1961 **920** 15p. multicoloured . . . 15 10

1995. International Ozone Day.
1962 **921** 15p. multicoloured . . . 30 20
1963 55p. multicoloured . . . 70 25
1964 – 80p. multicoloured . . . 95 30
DESIGNS: 80p. As Type **921** but inscribed "The Ozonaction Protection Programme".
See also Nos. 1994/5.

922 Pharaonic Ship and Globe

1995. World Tourism Day.
1965 **922** 15p. multicoloured . . . 60 15

923 Emblem and Works, Imbaba

1995. 175th Anniv of Government Printing Offices.
1966 **923** 15p. multicoloured . . . 15 10

924 Sun illuminating Statue

1995. Overhead Sun Festival, Abu Simbel.
1967 **924** 15p. multicoloured . . . 55 15

925 Gold Mask of Tutankhamun **926** Dam and Ship

1995. Air. United Nations Day. 50th Anniversaries.
1968 **925** 80p. multicoloured . . . 80 35
1969 – 80p. lilac, blue & violet 80 35
1970 – 80p. multicoloured . . . 80 35
DESIGNS—VERT: No. 1968, Type **925** (UNESCO). HORIZ: No. 1969, Globe, dove, emblem and "50" (U.N.O.); 1970, Farmer and wife working in field (ancient Egyptian mural) (F.A.O.).

1995. Inauguration of Esna Dam.
1971 **926** 15p. black, blue & grn 35 15

927 Emblem and Pharaonic Mural **928** Youssef Wahby

1995. 75th Anniv of Egyptian Engineers Society.
1972 **927** 15p. multicoloured . . . 20 10

1995. Artists.
1973 **928** 15p. blue and black . . 20 10
1974 – 15p. green 20 10
1975 – 15p. red and yellow . . 20 10
DESIGNS: No. 1974, Nagib el Rihany; 1975, Abdel Hallim Hafez.

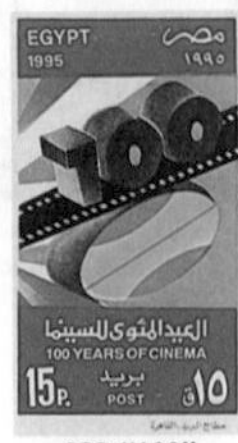

929 "100" **930** Pharaonic Mural (left detail)

1995. Centenary of Motion Pictures.
1976 **929** 15p. multicoloured . . . 15 10

1996. Post Day. Multicoloured.
1977 55p. Type **930** 75 20
1978 80p. Right detail of Pharaonic mural . . . . 1·00 25
MS1979 99 × 81 mm. 100p. Women playing musical instruments and dancing (mural). Imperf . . . 2·10 2·10
Nos. 1977/8 were issued together, se-tenant, forming a composite design.

931 Convolvulus **932** Summit Emblem

1996. Festivals 1996. Multicoloured.
1980 15p. Type **931** 25 15
1981 15p. Poppies 25 15

1996. Middle East Peace Process Summit, Sharm el Shaikh.
1982 **932** 15p. multicoloured . . . 30 15
1983 80p. multicoloured . . . 75 30

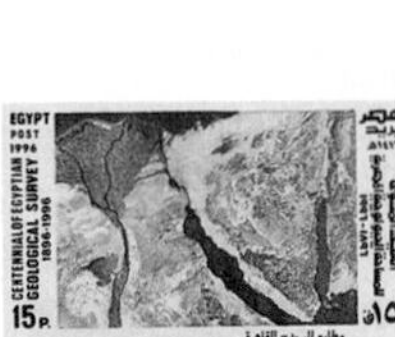

933 Geological Map **934** Fair Emblem

1996. Centenary of Egyptian Geological Survey Authority.
1984 **933** 15p. multicoloured . . . 30 15

1996. 29th Cairo International Fair.
1985 **934** 15p. multicoloured . . . 35 15

935 Emblem **936** Emblem, Calculator, Computer and Abacus

1996. Signing of Pelindaba Treaty declaring Africa a Nuclear Weapon-free Zone, Cairo.
1986 **935** 15p. multicoloured . . . 30 15
1987 80p. multicoloured . . . 70 50

1996. 50th Anniv of Egyptian Society of Accountants and Auditors.
1988 **936** 15p. multicoloured . . . 35 15

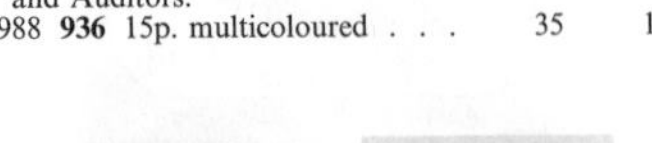

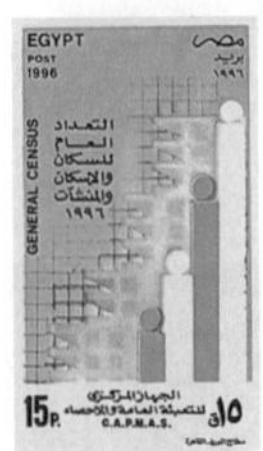

937 "People" forming Graph **938** Emblem

1996. General Population and Housing Census.
1989 **937** 15p. multicoloured . . . 35 15

1996. Arab Summit, Cairo.
1990 **938** 55p. multicoloured . . . 55 20

939 Games Emblem **940** Emblems

1996. Olympic Games, Atlanta.
1991 **939** 15p. multicoloured . . . 35 15
MS1992 80 × 116 mm. £E1 Sports pictograms around games emblem 1·20 1·20

1996. Air. 16th International Congress on Irrigation and Drainage, Cairo.
1993 **940** 80p. multicoloured . . . 60 25

1996. International Ozone Day. As T **921** but inscr "2nd ANNUAL OZONE INTERNATIONAL DAY".
1994 **921** 15p. mult (postage) . . . 15 10
1995 80p. multicoloured (air) 60 25

941 Fireworks over City

942 Test Tube, Microscope and Atomic Symbol

1996. 2nd Alexandria World Festival.
1996 **941** 80p. multicoloured . . . 55 45

1996. 25th Anniv of Academy of Scientific Research and Technology.
1997 **942** 15p. multicoloured . . . 25 10

943 Pharaonic Boat (Rowing Festival)

1996. International Tourism Day.
1998 **943** 15p. mult (postage) . . . 55 15
1999 – 55p. grey, black and green (air) 55 20
2000 – 80p. multicoloured . . . 1·10 25
DESIGNS: 20 × 36 mm—55p. Arab horse (Arabian Horse Festival); 47 × 26 mm—80p. Egyptian figure and hieroglyphs (Tourism Day).

944 Route Map and Train

945 U.P.U. Emblem and Stylized Postal Messengers

1996. Inauguration of Second Greater Cairo Metro Line.
2001 **944** 15p. multicoloured . . . 25 15

1996. Air. World Post Day.
2002 **945** 80p. multicoloured . . . 90 25

946 Emblems and Map

947 Mother and Child (statue)

1996. Air. Cairo, Cultural Capital of Arab Region.
2003 **946** 55p. blue, orange & blk 45 20

1996. Air. 50th Anniv of UNICEF.
2004 **947** 80p. multicoloured . . . 80 25

948 Council of State Courts

949 Emblem

1996. 50th Anniv of Council of State.
2005 **948** 15p. lilac, ultram & bl 25 20

1996. 25th Conference of International Federation of Training Development Organizations.
2006 **949** 15p. black, blue & yell 25 15

950 Emblem

951 Emblem and Ear of Wheat

1996. Economic Summit, Cairo.
2007 **950** 15p. multicoloured. (postage) 25 15
MS2008 80 × 60 mm. £E1 Emblem, globe, cogwheel, ear of wheat and olive branch . . . . 1·00 1·00

1996. International Nutrition Conf, Rome.
2009 **951** 15p. green, yell & red . . 25 15

952 Al-Said Ahmed el Badawi Mosque, Tanta

953 George Abyad

1996. National Day. El Gharbia Governate.
2010 **952** 15p. multicoloured . . . 25 15

1996. Artists.
2011 **953** 20p. rose and pink . . . 20 15
2012 – 20p. black and grey . . 20 15
2013 – 20p. deep brown and brown 20 15
2014 – 20p. black and grey . . 20 15
DESIGNS: No. 2012, Ali el Kassar; 2013, Mohamed Kareem; 2014, Fatma Roshdi.

954 Tutankhamun and Ankhesenamun (painted ivory plaque)

1996. Post Day. 75th Anniv of Discovery of Tutankaumun's Tomb. Multicoloured.
2015 20p. Type **954** (postage) . . 25 15
MS2016 60 × 80 mm. £E1 Tutankhamun and Ankhesenamun (chair back) (air). Imperf . . . . 1·30 1·30
See also No. 2056/**MS**2057.

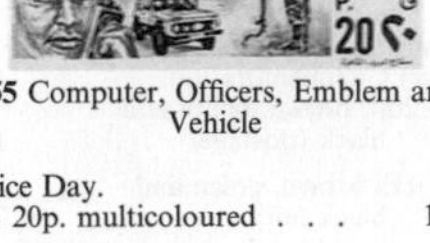

955 Computer, Officers, Emblem and Vehicle

1997. Police Day.
2017 **955** 20p. multicoloured . . . 15 10

956 Pink Asters

957 Queen Tiye

1997. Festivals 1997. Multicoloured.
2018 20p. Type **956** 15 10
2019 20p. White asters 15 10

1997.
2020 **957** 5p. brown and sepia (postage) 20 10
2020a – 10p. yellow and mauve 15 10
2021 – 20p. brown, ochre and grey 20 15
2022 – 20p. black and grey . . 20 10
2023 – 25p. yellow and green 20 15
2023a – 30p. yellow, brown and blue 20 15
2024 – 75p. black and orange 55 55
2025 – £E1 multicoloured . . . 85 75
2026 – £E2 multicoloured . . . 1·80 1·30
2027 – £E5 green, lilac and black . . . . 4·00 3·50
2029 – 25p. blue, buff and brown (air) 30 15
2030 – 75p. black, grey and blue 60 50
2031 – 125p. brown, yellow and green 75 60
2032 – £E1 brown, yellow and black . . . . 1·20 75
DESIGNS—POSTAGE—21 × 26 mm: No. 2020a, 2023, 2023a, Goddess Silakht. 23 × 27 mm: No. 2021, Queen Nofret. 21 × 26 mm: No. 2022, Horemheb; 75p. Amenhotep III. 21 × 38 mm: £E1 Queen Nefertari; £E5 Thutmose V ("Thotmes IV"). 22 × 38 mm: £E2 Mummiform coffin of Tutankhamun. AIR—22 × 40 mm: 25p. Akhnaton. 21 × 39 mm: 75p. Thutmose III ("Thotmes III"); 125p. Wooden statue of Tutankhamun; £E1 Gilded wooden statue of Tutankhamun.

958 Globe and Emblem

959 Emblem and Colours

1997. World Civil Defence Day.
2035 **958** 20p. multicoloured . . . 15 10

1997. 30th Cairo International Fair.
2036 **959** 20p. multicoloured . . . 15 10

960 Compass Rose and Wind Vane

961 Said

1997. Air. World Meteorological Day.
2037 **960** £E1 multicoloured . . . 1·30 60

1997. Birth Centenary of Mahmoud Said (artist). Multicoloured.
2038 20p. Type **961** (postage) . . 15 10
MS2039 80 × 60 mm. £E1 "The City" (air). Imperf . . . . . . 1·00 1·00

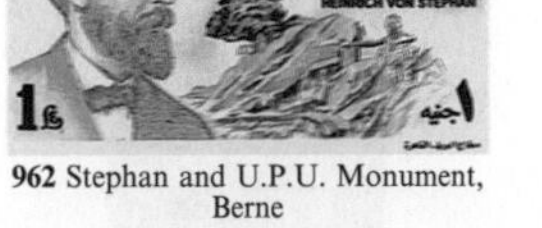

962 Stephan and U.P.U. Monument, Berne

1997. Death Cent of Heinrich von Stephan (founder of Universal Postal Union).
2040 **962** £E1 multicoloured . . . 1·10 60

963 Emblem

1997. 50th Anniv of Institute of African Research and Studies.
2041 **963** 75p. multicoloured . . . 55 55

964 Emblem, Building and Satellite

1997. Inauguration of State Information Service's New Headquarters.
2042 **964** 20p. multicoloured . . . 15 10

965 Emblem, Mascot and Trophy

966 Mascot with Torch and Gold Medal

1997. Under-17 Football World Championship, Egypt.
2043 **965** 20p. mult (postage) . . . 15 10
2044 75p. mult (air) 60 45
MS2045 81 × 60 mm. £E1 multicoloured (air). Imperf . . 1·00 1·00
DESIGN: £E1 Mascot, pitch and emblems.

1997. Air. Egypt's Winning Medal Tally at Eighth Pan-Arab Games, Beirut.
2046 **966** 75p. multicoloured (wrongly inscr "Ban Arab Games") 60 45

967 Emblem

968 Emblem

1997. Air. 98th Interparliamentary Union Conference, Cairo.
2047 **967** £E1 multicoloured . . . 75 60

1997. 10th Anniv of Montreal Protocol (on reduction of use of chlorofluorocarbons).
2048 **968** 20p. mult (postage) . . . 30 15
2049 £E1 mult (air) . . . . . 1·10 60

969 Train

970 Sarabas

1997. Inauguration of Second Stage of Underground Railway.
2050 **969** 20p. multicoloured . . . 30 15

1997. Air. "Fayoum's Portraits" Exhibition.
2051 **970** £E1 multicoloured . . . 1·20 60

971 Pharaonic Musician and Queen Hatshepsut's Temple

1997. 125th Anniv of First Performance of "Aida" (opera by Verdi), at Old Opera House, Cairo.
2052 **971** 20p. multicoloured . . . 40 15
MS2053 80×74 mm. **971** £E1 multicoloured (54×54 mm) (air). Imperf . . . . 2·75 2·75

972 Open Book showing Emblem

1997. Air. World Book and Copyright Day.
2054 **972** £E1 green, black & blue 1·10 60

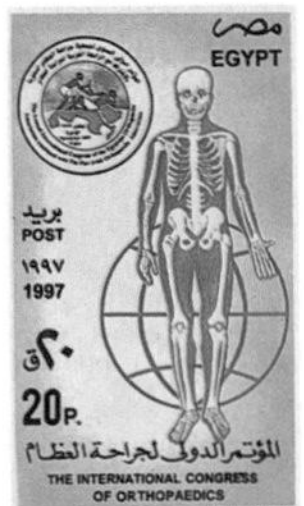
973 Skeleton and Globe

974 Goddess Serket (statuette protecting canopic chest)

1997. Int Orthopaedics Congress, Cairo.
2055 **973** 20p. multicoloured . . . 15 10

1997. 75th Anniv of Discovery of Tutankhamun's Tomb (2nd issue). Multicoloured.
2056 20p. Type **974** (postage) . . 25 15
MS2057 80×70 mm. £E1 Decoration with scarab in centre (air). Imperf . . . . . . 1·00 1·00

975 Conference Emblem

977 Emblem and Scout Bugler

976 Museum

1997. Air. 11th African Transport and Communications Ministers' Conference, Cairo.
2058 **975** 75p. multicoloured . . . 60 45

1997. Inaug of Nubia Monuments Museum.
2059 **976** 20p. multicoloured . . . 55 15

1997. Air. 85th Anniv of Arab Scout Movement.
2060 **977** 75p. multicoloured . . . 60 45

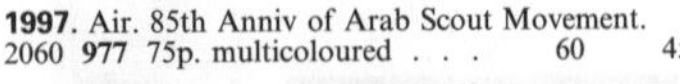

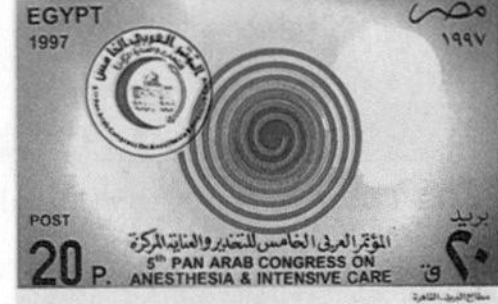
978 Emblem

1997. 5th Pan-Arab Anaesthesia and Intensive Care Congress.
2061 **978** 20p. multicoloured . . . 15 10

979 Emblem

980 "Egypt is the Cradle of Arts throughout the Ages"

1997. 50th Anniv of Arab Land Bank.
2062 **979** 20p. multicoloured . . . 15 10

1997. Dramatic Arts.
2063 **980** 20p. blue 20 15
2064 – 20p. black 20 15
2065 – 20p. black 20 15
2066 – 20p. black 20 15
2067 – 20p. black 20 15
DESIGNS: No. 2064, Zaky Tolaimat (founder and director of Institute of Drama); 2065, Ismael Yassen (actor); 2066, Zaky Roustom (actor); 2067, Soliman Naguib (actor and director of Opera House).

981 Map showing Canal

1997. 15th Anniv of Restoration of Sinai. Inaug of El Salaam ("Peace") Canal.
2068 **981** 20p. multicoloured . . . 15 10

982 Guard to Tutankhamun (statue)

983 Flowers

1998. Post Day. Multicoloured.
2069 20p. Type **982** 30 15
2070 75p. "Coronation of Rameses III" (sculpture) 85 35
2071 £E1 Mummiform coffin of Tutankhamun (29×49 mm) . . . . . . 1·10 60

1998. Festivals 1998. Multicoloured.
2072 20p. Type **983** 20 15
2073 20p. Pale pink flowers . . . 20 15

984 Emblem

985 New and Old Headquarters

1998. Cairo International Fair.
2074 **984** 20p. multicoloured . . . 15 10

1998. Centenary of National Bank of Egypt.
2075 **985** 20p. multicoloured . . . 15 10

986 Ancient Egyptians supporting Trophy

1998. Victory of Egypt in 21st African Nations Cup Football Championship. Multicoloured.
2076 20p. Type **986** (postage) . . 30 15
2077 75p. mult (air) 85 45
MS2078 80×60 mm. £E1 Map of Africa, flags of competing nations, mascot and trophy (air).Imperf 1·10 1·10

987 Emblem

988 Lighthouse of Alexandria and Bust of Alexander the Great

1998. Air. 8th Summit Meeting of G-15 Countries, Cairo.
2079 **987** £El multicoloured . . . 75 60

1998. Air.
2080 **988** £El multicoloured . . . 95 60

989 Satellite over Earth

1998. Egyptian "Nile Sat" Satellite.
2081 **989** 20p. multicoloured . . . 15 10

990 Emblem of Environment Agency within Pharaonic Eye

1998. World Environment Day. Multicoloured.
2082 20p. Type **990** (postage) . . 40 15
MS2083 49×70 mm. £E1 Endangered flora and fauna (air) 1·90 1·90

991 Zewail

992 Mohamed el Shaarawi

1998. Receipt of Franklin Institute Award by Dr. Ahmed Zewail.
2084 20p. Type **991** (postage) . . 15 10
2085 £E1 black & yell (air) . . . 70 55

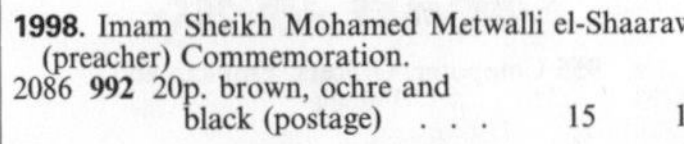

1998. Imam Sheikh Mohamed Metwalli el-Shaarawi (preacher) Commemoration.
2086 **992** 20p. brown, ochre and black (postage) . . . 15 10
2087 £El brown, green and black (air) 70 55

993 Ornament

994 Pharaonic Mermaid

1998. Air. Arab Post Day.
2088 **993** £El multicoloured . . . 70 55

1998. Nile Flood Day.
2089 **994** 20p. multicoloured . . . 25 15

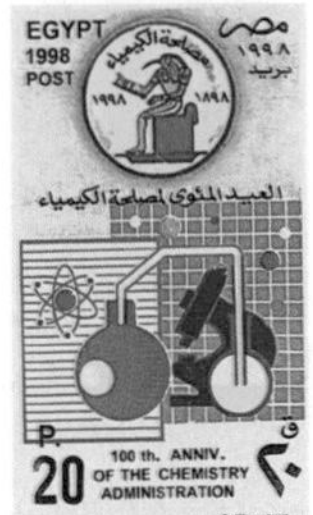
995 Emblem and Scientific Equipment

996 Anniversary Emblem

1998. Cent of Chemistry Administration.
2090 **995** 20p. multicoloured . . . 15 10

1998. 25th Anniv of Suez Crossing. Multicoloured.
2091 20p. Type **996** (postage) . . 15 10
MS2092 50×70 mm. £E2 Motif as in Type **969** (air) . . . . . . 2·10 2·10

997 Globe in Envelope

1998. Air. World Post Day.
2093 **997** 125p. multicoloured . . 90 70

998 Pharaonic Survey

1998. Centenary of Egyptian Survey Authority.
2094 **998** 20p. multicoloured . . . 30 15

999 Emblems in Handcuffs

1000 Anniversary Emblem

1998. Air. 67th Interpol Meeting, Cairo.
2095 **999** 125p. multicoloured . . 1·00 1·00

1998. Air. 50th Anniv of Universal Declaration of Human Rights.
2096 **1000** 125p. multicoloured . . 90 70

1001 Woman and University

1998. 90th Anniv of Cairo University.
2097 **1001** 20p. multicoloured . . 15 10

1002 Emblem and Pharaonic Workers

1003 Pharaonic Mural (19th Dynasty)

1998. Centenary of Trade Union Movement.
2098 **1002** 20p. multicoloured . . 30 15

1999. Post Day. Multicoloured.
2099 20p. Type **1003** 30 20
MS2100 50×70 mm. 125p. Wall carving . . . . 1·20 1·20

1004 Flowers

1006 Emblem and Colour Spectrum

1005 Emblem and Globe

1999. Festivals 1999. Multicoloured.
2101 20p. Type **1004** 20 20
2102 20p. Gladioli 20 20

1999. International Women's Day.
2103 **1005** 20p. multicoloured . . 15 10

1999. Cairo International Fair.
2104 **1006** 20p. multicoloured . . 15 10

1007 Train passing under Nile

1999. Inauguration of El Tahrir–Cairo University Section of Underground Railway.
2105 **1007** 20p. multicoloured . . 20 10

1008 U.P.U. Emblem and Messenger

1999. 125th Anniv of Universal Postal Union. Multicoloured.
2106 20p. Type **1008** (postage) . . 30 15
2107 £E1 Type **1008** (air) 90 55
2108 125p. Messenger delivering letter (painting) (vert) . . 1·20 70
MS2109 50×70 mm. 125p. Painting as in No. 2108 and U.P.U. emblem 1·60 1·60

1009 Hands supporting Pyramid and Egyptian Red Crescent Emblem

1010 Emblems

1999. 50th Anniv of Geneva Conventions.
2110 **1009** 20p. multicoloured (postage) 15 10
2111 125p. multicoloured (air) 90 70

1999. 35th Annual Board of Governors Meeting of African Development Bank.
2112 **1010** 20p. multicoloured (postage) 15 10
2113 £E1 multicoloured (air) 70 55

1011 Player and Pyramids

1999. 16th World Men's Handball Championship. Multicoloured.
2114 20p. Type **1011** (postage) . . 15 10
2115 £E1 Games mascot and pyramids (air) 70 55
2116 125p. Mascot and goalkeeper 90 70

1012 Emblem

1999. 50th Anniv of S.O.S. Children's Villages.
2117 **1012** 20p. blue, green and black (postage) . . . 15 10
2118 125p. blue, stone and black (air) 90 70

1013 Sameera Moussa

1014 Touny

1999. Personalities. Multicoloured.
2119 20p. Type **1013** 20 15
2120 20p. Aisha Abdel Rahman 20 15

1999. 2nd Death Anniv of Ahmed Eldemerdash Touny.
2121 **1014** 20p. multicoloured . . 15 10

1015 President Mubarak

1016 Harpist and Sphinx

1999. Re-election of Mohammed Hosni Mubarak to Fourth Consecutive Term as President. Multicoloured.
2122 20p. Type **1015** (postage) . . 15 10

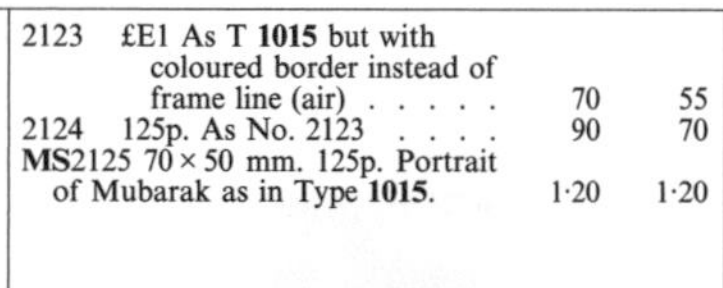

2123 £E1 As T **1015** but with coloured border instead of frame line (air) 70 55
2124 125p. As No. 2123 . . . . 90 70
MS2125 70×50 mm. 125p. Portrait of Mubarak as in Type **1015**. 1·20 1·20

1999. Air. Performance of Verdi's Opera "Aida" at the Pyramids.
2126 **1016** 125p. multicoloured . . 1·20 70

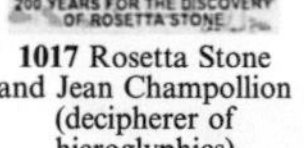

1017 Rosetta Stone and Jean Champollion (decipherer of hieroglyphics)

1018 Globe, Elderly Couple, Open Hands and Heart

1999. Air. Bicentenary of the Discovery of Rosetta Stone.
2127 **1017** 125p. black, brown and cream . . . . 1·20 70

1999. International Year of the Elderly. Mult.
2128 20p. Type **1018** (postage) . . 15 10
2129 £E1 As T **1018**, but inscription below motif in English (air) 70 55
2130 125p. As No. 2129 . . . . 90 70

1019 Children and Jigsaw Pieces

1021 Assia Dagher (film producer)

1020 Zewail and Pyramids (½-size illustration)

1999. Children's Day.
2131 **1019** 20p. multicoloured . . 15 10

1999. Air. Ahmed Zewail, Winner of 1999 Nobel Prize for Chemistry. Sheet 70×50 mm. Imperf.
MS2132 **1020** 125p. multicoloured 1·20 1·20

1999. Personalities. Each black, grey and blue.
2133 20p. Type **1021** 20 15
2134 20p. Anwar Wagdi (actor) 20 15
2135 20p. Farid el Attrash (musician) 20 15
2136 20p. Laila Mourad (singer and actress) 20 15

1022 Corner of Paper Revealing "2000"

1023 King and Prince on Thrones

2000. New Millennium. Multicoloured.
2137 20p. Type **1022** (postage) . . 15 10
2138 125p. Year dates culminating in "2000" (air) 85 70
MS2139 70×50 mm. £E2 "The Virgin Tree in Mataria" (painting). Imperf . . . . . . 1·90 1·90

2000. Post Day. 19th Dynasty Murals. Multicoloured.
2140 20p. Type **1023** 20 15
2141 20p. Woman making offering to Queen 20 15
MS2142 70×51 mm. 125p. Rameses II in war chariot. Imperf . . . 1·20 1·20

1024 Emblem and Main Building

2000. 50th Anniv of Ain Shams University, Cairo.
2143 **1024** 20p. multicoloured . . 15 10

1025 Flower

1026 Emblem

2000. Festivals 2000. Multicoloured.
2144 20p. Type **1025** 20 15
2145 20p. Roses 20 15
Nos. 2144/5 were issued together, se-tenant, forming a composite design.

2000. 25th Anniv of Islamic Development Bank.
2146 **1026** 20p. multicoloured . . 15 10

1027 Emblem and Pyramids

1028 Thoum

2000. 1st Common Market for Eastern and Southern Africa Regional Economic Conference.
2147 **1027** 125p. multicoloured . . 85 70

2000. 25th Death Anniv of Omkol Thoum.
2148 **1028** 20p. black and green 15 10

1029 Congress Emblem and Pyramids

2000. 8th International Congress of Egyptologists, Cairo.
2149 **1029** 20p. multicoloured . . 20 10

1030 Emblem

2000. Europe—Africa Summit, Cairo.
2150 **1030** 125p. multicoloured . . 85 70

1031 Emblem and Pyramids

2000. 10th Group 15 Summit, Cairo.
2151 **1031** 125p. multicoloured . . 85 70

1032 Skull and Syringe

2000. International Day Against Drug Abuse.
2152 **1032** 20p. multicoloured . . 20 15
See also No. 2202.

1033 Emblem and Arabic Inscription

2000. Centenary of the National Insurance Company. Multicoloured.
2153 20p. Type **1033** 30 15
MS2154 91 × 70 mm. 125p. Emblem and different Arabic inscriptions. Imperf . . . . 1·20 1·20

1034 Emblem

1036 Emblem

1035 Pottery

2000. Olympic Games, Sydney. Multicoloured.
2155 20p. Type **1034** (postage) . . 20 15
2156 15p. As No. 2155 (air) . . . 85 70
There are some minor differences in the designs of Nos. 2155/6.

2000. 25th Anniv of Co-operative Production Union.
2157 **1035** 20p. multicoloured . . 20 15

2000. Air. World Tourism Day.
2158 **1036** 125p. multicoloured . . 85 70

1037 Train and Pyramids

2000. Inaug of Fourth Stage of Second Metro Line.
2159 **1037** 20p. multicoloured . . 20 15

1038 Emblem and Olive Branch

2000. World Post Day.
2160 **1038** 125p. green, mauve and black 80 70

1039 Flag and Dome of the Rock

2000. Solidarity.
2161 **1039** 20p. mult (postage) . . 20 15
2162 125p. mult (horiz) . . . 85 70
2163 125p. mult (air) 85 70

1040 Map and Train on Bridge

2000. Inauguration of El Ferdan Bridge.
2164 **1040** 20p. multicoloured . . 25 15

1041 Disabled Sign and Olympic Medal

1042 Emblem

2000. Disabled Persons' Day.
2165 **1041** 20p. multicoloured . . 20 15

2000. Air. 50th Anniv of United Nations High Commission for Refugees.
2166 **1042** 125p. multicoloured . . 85 70

1043 Building

2000. Inauguration of New Al Azhar Professoriate Building.
2167 **1043** 20p. multicoloured . . 20 15

1044 Red and Yellow Flowers

1045 Karem Mahmoud

2000. Festivals 2001. Multicoloured.
2168 20p. Type **1044** 20 15
2169 20p. Mauve flowers 20 15

2000. Artists.
2170 **1045** 20p. black and ochre 20 15
2171 – 20p. black and green 20 15
2172 – 20p. black and pink . . 20 15
2173 – 20p. black and lilac . . 20 15
2174 – 20p. black and blue . . 20 15
DESIGNS: No. 2171, Mahmoud el Miligi; 2172, Mohamed Fawzi; 2173, Hussein Riyad; 2174, Abdel Wares Asser.

1046 Buildings (½-size illustration)

2001. Jerusalem. Sheet 80 × 80 mm. Imperf.
MS2175 **1046** £E2 multicoloured 1·50 1·50

1047 Mural

2001. Post Day. Multicoloured.
2176 20p. Type **1047** (postage) . . 35 20
2178 125p. Mural including pair of scales (air) 80 70
MS2177 79 × 61 mm. 125p. Mural depicting charioteers. Imperf 1·50 1·50

1048 Emblem

1049 Pass Book

2001. Arab Labour Organization.
2179 **1048** 20p. multicoloured . . 20 15

2001. Centenary of Postal Savings Bank.
2180 **1049** 20p. multicoloured . . 20 15

1050 Emblem

2001. 1st Anniv of National Council of Women.
2181 **1050** 30p. mult (postage) . . 20 20
2182 **1050** 125p. mult (air) 80 70

1051 Emblem

2001. Cairo International Fair.
2183 **1051** 30p. multicoloured . . 20 15

1052 Emblem

2001. 25th Anniv of Helwan University.
2195 **1052** 30p. multicoloured . . 20 15

1053 New Library Building

2001. Ancient Library of Alexandria Project.
2196 **1053** 12p. multicoloured . . 80 70

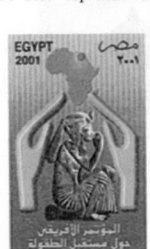

1054 Emblem

1055 Globe on Sunflower

2001. Pan-African Conference on Future of Children, Cairo. Multicoloured.
2197 30p. Type **1054** (postage) . . 20 20
2198 125p. As Type **1054** but with English inscr (air) . . 80 70

2001. World Environment Day.
2199 **1055** 125p. multicoloured . . 80 70

1056 Mascot

2001. World Military Football Championship, Cairo. Multicoloured.
2200 30p. Type **1056** 20 15
2201 125p. Mascot and emblem 80 70

2001. International Day against Drug Abuse.
2202 **1032** 30p. multicoloured . . 20 15

1057 Trophy and Emblem (⅔-size illustration)

2001. Egyptian Victory in 39th World Military Football Championship, Cairo.
MS2203 **1057** 125p. multicoloured 95 95

1058 Steam Locomotive

2001. 150th Anniv of Egyptian Railways.
2204 **1058** 30p. multicoloured . . 20 15

1059 Aziz Abaza Pasha (28th anniv)

1060 Emblem

2001. Poets' Death Anniversaries.
2205 **1059** 30p. black and blue . . 20 15
2206 – 30p. black and pink . . 20 15
DESIGN: No. 2206, Ahmed Rami (20th anniv).

2001. International Year of Volunteers.
2207 **1060** 125p. yellow and blue 80 70

1061 Couple dancing

2001. Ismaelia Folklore Festival.
2208 **1061** 30p. multicoloured . . 20 15

1062 Building and Satellite Dish

2001. 25th Anniv of First Telecommunications Ground Station.
2209 **1062** 30p. multicoloured . . 20 15

1063 Bridge spanning Suez Canal

2001. Inauguration of Suez Canal Road Bridge. Multicoloured.
2210 30p. Type **1063** 20 15
2211 125p. Bridge spanning road 80 70
MS2212 81 × 60 mm. 125p. Bridge spanning Suez Canal. Imperf 95 95
Nos. 2210/11 were issued together, se-tenant, forming a composite design.

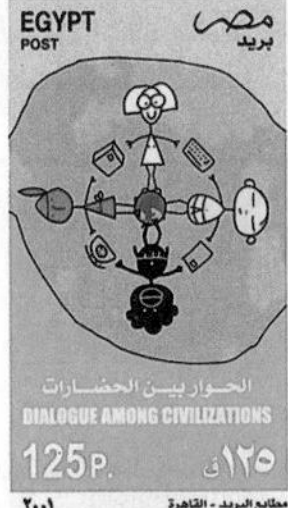

1064 Children encircling Globe

2001. United Nations Year of Dialogue Among Civilizations. Multicoloured.
2213 125p. Type **1064** 80 70
2214 125p. Globe and symbols of Egypt (horiz) 80 70

1065 Mask of San Xing Dui

2001. Egypt–China Joint Issue. Golden Masks. Multicoloured.
2215 30p. Type **1065** 30 25
2216 30p. Mask of Tutankhamun 30 25

1066 Cars leaving Tunnel

1067 Emblem

2001. Inauguration of Al Azhar Road Tunnel, Cairo.
2217 **1066** 30p. multicoloured . . 20 15

2001. 25th Anniv of El Menoufia University.
2218 **1067** 30p. multicoloured . . 20 15

1068 Zakareya Ahmed

2001. Composers' Death Anniversaries. Each black and lilac.
2219 30p. Type **1068** (40th anniv) 20 15
2220 30p. Riyadh el Sonbati (20th anniv) 20 15
2221 30p. Mahmoud el Sherif (11th anniv) 20 15
2222 30p. Mohamed el Kasabgi (35th anniv) 20 15

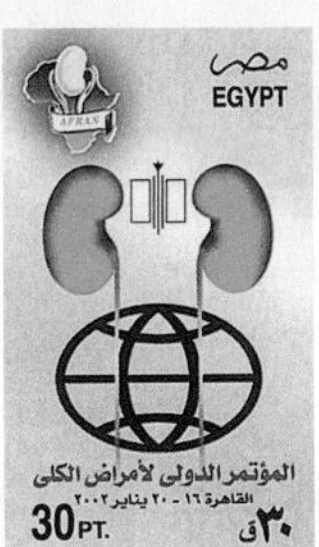

1069 Bird

2001. Festivals 2002. Birds. Multicoloured.
2223 30p. Type **1069** 20 15
2224 30p. Gulls 20 15
2225 30p. Parrot 20 15
2226 30p. Blue bird 20 15

1070 Tomb of Anhur Khawi (mural, 20th dynasty)

2002. Post Day. Multicoloured.
2227 30p. Type **1070** 20 15
MS2228 80 × 59 mm. 125p. Tomb of Irinefer (mural). Imperf 85 85

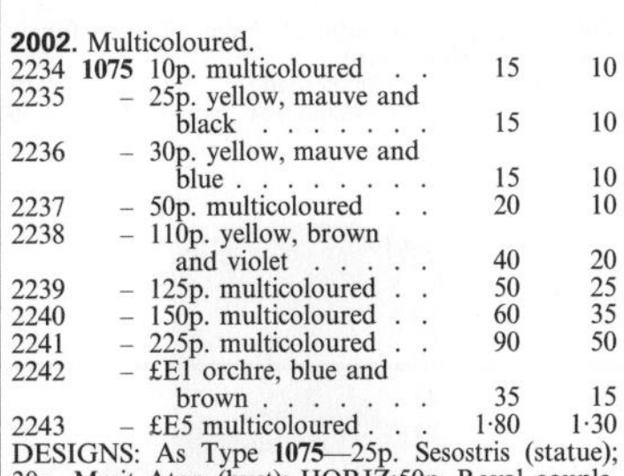

1071 Emblems and Kidneys

2002. International Nephrology Congress.
2229 **1071** 30p. multicoloured . . 20 15

1072 Emblem

2002. 50th Anniv of Police Day.
2230 **1072** 30p. multicoloured . . 20 15
MS2231 79 × 50 mm. **1072** 30p. multicoloured. Imperf . . . . 1·30 1·30

1073 Wind-surfers and Diver

2002. 20th Anniv of Return of Sinai to Egypt.
2232 **1073** 30p. multicoloured . . 15 10

1074 Facade

1075 Man wearing Animal Skin and Couple Enthroned (20th Dynasty wall painting)

2002. 50th Anniv of Cairo Bank.
2233 **1074** 30p. multicoloured . . 15 10

2002. Multicoloured.
2234 **1075** 10p. multicoloured . . 15 10
2235 – 25p. yellow, mauve and black 15 10
2236 – 30p. yellow, mauve and blue 15 10
2237 – 50p. multicoloured . . 20 10
2238 – 110p. yellow, brown and violet 40 20
2239 – 125p. multicoloured . . 50 25
2240 – 150p. multicoloured . . 60 35
2241 – 225p. multicoloured . . 90 50
2242 – £E1 orchre, blue and brown 35 15
2243 – £E5 multicoloured . . . 1·80 1·30
DESIGNS: As Type **1075**—25p. Sesostris (statue); 30p. Merit Aton (bust); HORIZ:50p. Royal couple, children and musicians (20th Dynasty wall painting); £E1 Snefru's pyramid, Dahshur. 24 × 41 mm:110p. Wife of Ka-Aper ("Sheikh el Balad") (bust); 125p. Psusennes I (bust); 150p. Tutankhamun holding spear (statue); 225p. Ramses II obelisk, Luxor; £E5 Karnak Temple ruins.

1076 Ibrahim Shams (1948)

2002. Olympic Gold Medal Weightlifters. Multicoloured.
2244 30p. Type **1076** 15 10
2245 30p. Khidre El Tourney (1936) 15 10

1077 Building and World Map

2002. 50th Anniv of *Al Akhba* (newspaper).
2246 **1077** 30p. multicoloured . . 15 10

1078 Stamps of 1952 (½-size illustration)

2002. 50th Anniv of Revolution of 23 July 1952. Sheet 80 × 95 mm. Imperf.
MS2247 **1078** 125p. multicoloured 60 60

1079 Aswan Dam

2002. Centenary of Aswan Dam. Multicoloured.
2248 30p. Type **1079** 15 10
2249 30p. Part of dam and shoreline 15 10
Nos. 2248/9 were issued together, se-tenant, forming a composite design.

1080 Globe encircled by Snake

1081 Man with Bandaged Head and Traffic Lights

2002. International Ozone Day.
2250 **1080** 125p. multicoloured . . 55 35

2002. International Road Safety Conference.
2251 **1081** 30p. multicoloured . . 15 10

1082 Cross Section of Head showing Cavities

1083 UPU Emblem

2002. 17th Oto-Rhino Laryngological Societies (IFOS) Congress, Cairo.
2252 **1082** 30p. multicoloured . . 15 15

2002. World Post Day. 125th Anniv of Universal Postal Union.
2253 **1083** 125p. multicoloured . . 15 10

1084 Library Building

2002. Inauguration of Bibliotheca Alexandrina (library), Alexandrina. Multicoloured.
2254 30p. Type **1084** 15 10
2255 125p. Inscribed column and sunset (vert) 55 35
MS2256 60 × 81 mm. 125p. Interior of ancient Alexandria library. Imperf 60 60

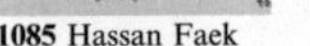

1085 Hassan Faek **1086** Bee-eater

2002. Actors. Each pink and grey.
2257 30p. Type **1085** 15 10
2258 30p. Aziza Amir 15 10
2259 30p. Farid Shawki 15 10
2260 30p. Mary Mounib 15 10

2002. Festivals 2003. Multicoloured.
2261 30p. Type **1086** 15 10
2262 30p. Swallow 15 10
2263 30p. Red-throated bee-eater 15 10
2264 30p. Roller 15 10
Nos. 2261/4 were issued together, se-tenant, forming a composite design.

1087 Face (sculpture)

2002. Centenary of Egyptian Museum, Cairo. Multicoloured.
2265 30p. Type **1087** 15 10
MS2266 80 × 60 mm. 125p. Building facade and statue. Imperf . . . 60 60

1088 Bridge

2002. Inauguration of Aswan Suspension Bridge. Multicoloured.
2267 30p. Type **1088** 15 10
2268 30p. Bridge right 15 10
Nos. 2267/8 were issued together, se-tenant, forming a composite design of the bridge.

1089 University Emblem

2002. 25th Anniv of Suez Canal University, Ismailia.
2269 **1089** 30p. multicoloured . . 15 10

1090 Pumping Station

2002. Inauguration of Toshka Irrigation Project.
2270 **1090** 30p. multicoloured . . 15 10

1091 Pharaonic Tomb Mural

2003. Post Day. Multicoloured.
2271 30p. Type **1091** 15 10
2272 30p. Mural showing wings 15 10
2273 125p. Mural showing pharaoh and goddess . . 55 35

1092 Emblem

2003. International Communications and Information Technology Fair, Cairo.
2274 **1092** 30p. multicoloured . . 15 10

1093 Festival Emblem

2003. 4th International Nile Children's Song Festival.
2275 **1093** 30p. multicoloured . . 15 10
2276 125p. multicoloured . . 55 35

1094 Association Emblem, Bat and Ball

2003. Egypt International Open Table Tennis Championship, Cairo.
2277 **1094** 30p. multicoloured . . 15 10
2278 125p. multicoloured . . 55 35

1095 Exhibition Emblem and Construction Workers

2003. 10th International Building and Construction Conference.
2279 **1095** 30p. multicoloured . . 15 10
2280 125p. multicoloured . . 55 35

1096 Emblem

2003. 80th Anniv of Arab Lawyers Union.
2281 **1096** 30p. multicoloured . . 15 10
2282 125p. multicoloured . . 55 35

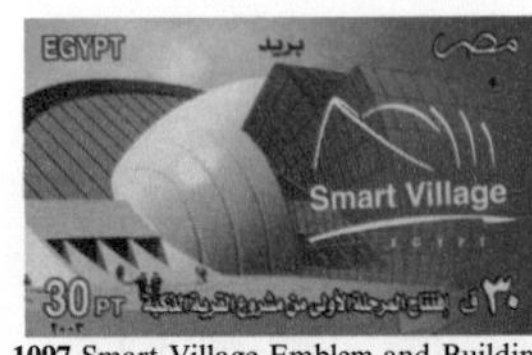

1097 Smart Village Emblem and Building

2003. Smart Village (technology business park), Cairo. Multicoloured.
2283 30p. Type **1097** 15 10
2284 125p. No. 2283 . . . . . . 55 35
MS2285 80 × 59 mm. 100p. Smart Village and environs. Imperf 50 50

1098 Ihsan Abdul Qudous **1099** Hand, Ball and Net

2003. Writers. Multicoloured.
2286 30p. Type **1098** 15 10
2287 30p. Youssef Idris 15 10

2003. Men's African Nations Basketball Championship.
2288 **1099** 30p. multicoloured . . 15 10
2289 125p. multicoloured . . 55 35

1100 Planets and Emblem

2003. Centenary of National Institute for Astrological and Geophysical Research.
2290 **1100** 30p. multicoloured . . 15 10

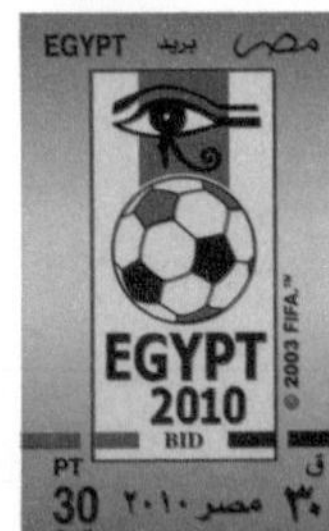

1101 Emblem

2003. Egypt's Bid to Host 2010 World Cup Football Championship. Multicoloured.
2291 30p. Type **1101** 15 10
2292 125p. Emblem and Tutankhamen (vert) . . . 55 35

1102 Tent Maker and Market

2003. World Tourism Day.
2293 **1102** 30p. multicoloured . . 15 10
2294 125p. multicoloured . . 55 35

1103 Soldier **1104** UPU Emblem and Computer

2003. 30th Anniv of October War.
2295 **1103** 30p. multicoloured . . 15 10

2003. World Post Day.
2296 **1104** 125p. multicoloured . . 55 35

1105 Emblem **1106** Alstromeria

2003. 91st Anniv of Bar Association.
2297 **1105** 30p. multicoloured . . 15 10

2003. Festivals 2004. Multicoloured.
2298 30p. Type **1106** 15 10
2299 30p. White rose 15 10
2300 30p. Red rose 15 10
2301 30p. Sunflower 15 10
Nos. 2298/2301 were issued together, se-tenant, forming a composite design.

1107 Salah Abou Seif **1109** Emblem and Building

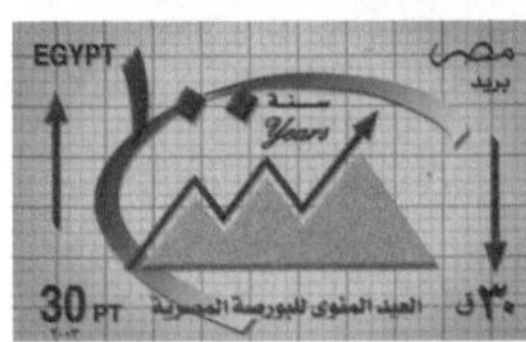

1108 Emblem

2003. Cinema Directors. Each black and azure.
2302 30p. Type **1107** 15 10
2303 30p. Kamal Selim 15 10
2304 30p. Henri Bakarat 15 10
2305 30p. Hassan el Emam . . . 15 10

2003. Centenary of Cairo Bourse (stock exchange).
2306 **1108** 30p. multicoloured . . 15 10

2003. 50th Anniv of El Gomhoreya Newspaper.
2307 **1109** 30p. multicoloured . . 15 10

1110 Mrs. Suzanne Mubarak

2003. 5th E-9 Ministerial Meeting.
2308 **1110** 30p. multicoloured . . 15 10
2309 125p. multicoloured . . 55 35
MS2310 80 × 60 mm. **1110** £E2 multicoloured. Imperf 90 90

1111 Emblems

2004. 25th Anniv of Delta International Bank.

2311 **1111** 30p. multicoloured . . 15 10

2312 125p. multicoloured . . 55 35

MS2313 81 × 60 mm. **1111** £E2 multicoloured (horiz) Imperf 90 90

1112 Post Emblem

2004. World Post Day.

2314 **1112** 30p. multicoloured . . 15 10

2315 125p. multicoloured . . 55 35

1113 Conference Emblem

2004. 8th International Telecommunication Conference.

2316 **1113** 30p. multicoloured . . 15 10

1114 First President

2004. 98th Anniv of National Bar Association.

2317 **1114** 30p. blue and black . . 15 10

2318 – 30p. blue and black . . 15 10

2319 – 30p. blue and black . . 15 10

2320 – 30p. blue and black . . 15 10

2321 – 30p. blue and black . . 15 10

2322 – 30p. rose and black . . 15 10

2323 – 30p. rose and black . . 15 10

2324 – 30p. rose and black . . 15 10

2325 – 30p. rose and black . . 15 10

2326 – 30p. rose and black . . 15 10

2327 – 30p. salmon and black 15 10

2328 – 30p. salmon and black 15 10

2329 – 30p. salmon and black 15 10

2330 – 30p. salmon and black 15 10

2331 – 30p. salmon and black 15 10

2332 – 30p. green, vermilion and black 15 10

2333 – 30p. green and black 15 10

2334 – 30p. green and black 15 10

2335 – 30p. green and black 15 10

2336 – 30p. green and black 15 10

2337 – 30p. blue, vermilion and black 15 10

2338 – 30p. blue and black . . 15 10

2339 – 30p. blue and black . . 15 10

2340 – 30p. blue and black . . 15 10

2341 – 30p. blue and black . . 15 10

DESIGNS: Nos. 2317/31 Presidents of association; No. 2332 Emblem; Nos. 2333/6 Presidents of association; No. 2337 Emblem; Nos. 2338/41 Presidents of association.

1115 Anniversary Emblem

1116 Club and Anniversary Emblems

2004. 50th Anniv of IBM (computer company) in Egypt.

2342 **1115** 30p. multicoloured . . 15 10

2004. 75th Anniv of Cairo Rotary Club.

2343 **1116** 30p. multicoloured . . 15 10

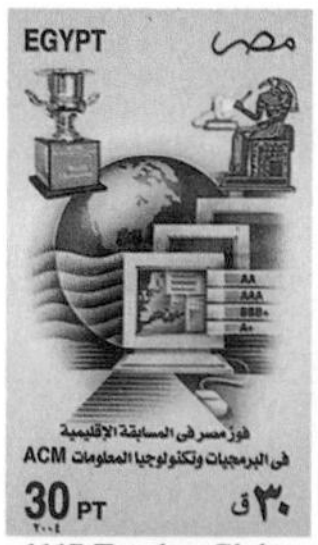

1117 Trophy, Globe and Computers

1118 Council Emblem

2004. Egypt, Winners of Regional Information Technology Competition.

2344 **1117** 30p. multicoloured . . 15 10

2004. 4th National Council for Women Conference, Alexandria.

2345 **1118** 30p. multicoloured . . 15 10

2346 125p. multicoloured . . 55 35

1119 Poppy Head and Emblem

2004. 75th Anniv of Anti-Narcotic Administration.

2347 **1119** 30p. multicoloured . . 15 10

MS2348 80 × 60 mm. **1119** 125p. multicoloured. Imperf 55 55

1120 Flower and Boy

1122 Society Emblem

1121 Map of Africa, Conference Emblem and Satellite

2004. Orphans' Day.

2349 **1120** 30p. multicoloured . . 15 10

2004. Telecom Africa Fair and Conference, Cairo.

2350 **1121** 30p. multicoloured . . 15 10

2004. 75th Anniv of Egyptian Philatelic Society. Multicoloured.

2351 30p. Type **1122** 15 10

MS2352 80 × 60 mm. 125p. Magnifying glass, stamp and emblem (horiz) Imperf 55 55

1123 Information Service Building

2004. 50th Anniv of State Information Service.

2353 **1123** 30p. multicoloured . . 15 10

1124 President Mubarak

2004. Arab Regional Conference. Multicoloured.

2354 30p. Type **1124** 15 10

2355 125p. Type **1124** 55 35

2356 125p. Sunrise and stylized couple (vert) 55 35

MS2357 80 × 60 mm. £E2 As Type **1124** but with design enlarged. Imperf . . . . 1·00 1·00

1125 Anniversary Emblem

1126 Bank and Anniversary Emblems

2004. 10th Television Festival. Multicoloured.

2358 30p. Type **1125** 15 10

2359 £E1 Type **1125** 50 20

2360 125p. Sphinx, emblem and film (horiz) 55 35

MS2361 80 × 60 mm. £E2 As No. 2360 but with design enlarged. Imperf . . . . 1·00 1·00

2004. 25th Anniv of Housing and Construction Bank.

2362 **1126** 30p. multicoloured . . 15 10

1127 Olympic Emblems

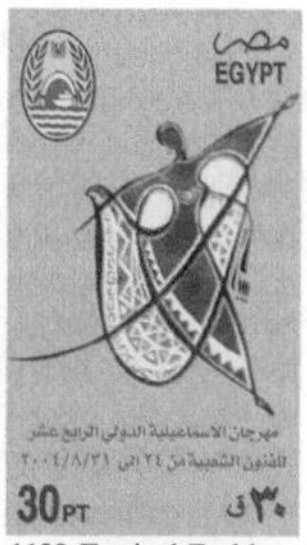

1129 Festival Emblem

1128 Scout Emblem

2004. Olympic Games, Athens 2004.

2363 **1127** 30p. multicoloured . . 15 10

2364 125p. multicoloured . . 55 35

2004. 90th Anniv of Egyptian Scouting Movement.

2365 **1128** 30p. multicoloured . . 15 10

2004. 14th Ismaelia Folklore Festival.

2366 **1129** 30p. multicoloured . . 15 10

1130 Blind Justice and Anniversary Emblem

2004. 50th Anniv of Administrative Attorney Establishment.

2367 **1130** 30p. multicoloured . . 15 10

MS2368 60 × 80 mm. **1130** £E1 multicoloured. Imperf 45 45

1131 Tugra (Imperial Ottoman monogram)

2004. 175th Anniv of Egyptian Archive. 50th Anniv of National Archive.

2369 **1131** 30p. multicoloured . . 15 10

1132 Emblems as Spectacles

2004. 50th Anniv of Light and Hope Society (charitable organization).

2370 **1132** 30p. multicoloured . . 15 10

1133 Pen Nib enclosing Union Emblem

2004. 10th General Arab Journalists Union Conference.

2371 **1133** 125p. multicoloured . . 55 35

1134 Chariot

2004. 50th Anniv of Military Production Day.

2372 **1134** 30p. multicoloured . . 15 10

1135 Post Horn and UPU Emblem

2004. World Post Day.

2373 **1135** 150p. multicoloured . . 60 40

1136 Association Emblem

1137 Rose

2004. 50th Anniv of Egypt Youth Hostel Association.

2374 **1136** 30p. multicoloured . . 15 10

2004. Festivals 2005. Multicoloured.

2375 30p. Type **1137** 15 10

2376 30p. Songbird (horiz) . . . 15 10

1138 Scouts

2004. 24th Arab Scouting Conference.

2377 **1138** 30p. multicoloured . . 15 10

1139 Anniversary Emblems

2004. 50th Anniv of Arab Scouting Association.
2378 **1139** 30p. multicoloured . . 15 10

1140 Decorated Pot

1142 Abd El Rahman El Sharquawi

1141 Anniversary Emblems

2004. Centenary of Islamic Art Foundation.
2379 **1140** 30p. multicoloured . . 15 10

2004. Centenary of FIFA (Federation Internationale de Football Association).
2380 **1141** 150p. multicoloured . . 60 40

2004. Personalities. Multicoloured.
2381 30p. Type **1142** (writer) . . 15 10
2382 30p. Fekri Abaza (journalist) 15 10

1143 Emblems

2004. 150th Anniv of First Telegraph Cable between Cairo and Alexandria.
2383 **1143** 30p. vermillion and black 15 10
2384 125p. vermillion and black 55 35

1144 Pipeline

2005. Inauguration of Gas Pipeline from Egypt to Jordan.
2385 **1144** 30p. multicoloured . . 15 10

1145 Post Box

2005. Post Day.
2386 **1145** 30p. multicoloured . . 15 10

1146 Metro Line and Train

2005. Inauguration of Fifth Phase of Metro Underground Rail Line.
2387 **1146** 30p. multicoloured . . 15 10
MS2388 80 × 60 mm. **1146** 150p. multicoloured. Imperf 60 40

1147 President Mubarak

1148 Emblem

2005. Police Day.
2389 **1147** 30p. multicoloured . . 15 10
MS2390 80 × 60 mm. **1147** £E1 multicoloured. Imperf 45 45

2005. 25th Anniv of El Mohandes Insurance Company.
2391 **1148** 30p. multicoloured . . 15 10

EXPRESS LETTER STAMPS

E 52 Postman on Motor-cycle

1926.
E138 E **52** 20m. green . . . . . . 21·00 7·00
E139 20m. black and red . . 4·25 1·20

1943. As Type E **52**, but inscr "POSTES".
E289 E **52** 26m. black and red . . 4·25 5·50
E290 40m. black and brown 3·50 3·00

1952. No. E290 optd as T **124**.
E404 E **52** 40m. black & brown 1·90 1·70

OFFICIAL STAMPS

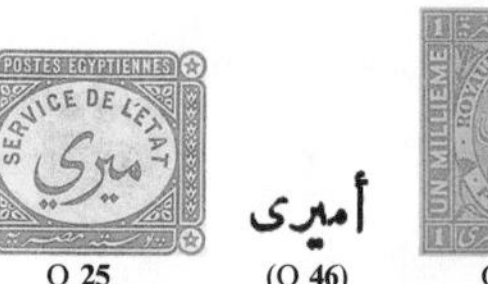

O 25 (O 46) O 52

1893.
O64 O **25** (–) brown . . . . . . 2·75 10

1907. Stamps of 1879 and 1888 optd **O.H.H.S.** and Arabic equivalent.
O73 **18** 1m. brown . . . . 1·75 30
O74 2m. green . . . . 4·00 10
O75 3m. yellow . . . . 2·75 1·25
O86 4m. red . . . . 4·75 2·25
O76 5m. red . . . . 5·00 10
O77 **10** 1p. blue . . . . 2·00 20
O78 5p. grey . . . . 16·00 3·50

1913. No. 63 optd in English only. (a) Optd **"O.H.H.S."** (with inverted commas).
O79 **18** 5m. pink . . . . — £300

(b) Optd **O.H.H.S.** (without inverted commas).
O80 **18** 5m. pink . . . . 8·00 60

1915. Stamps of 1914 optd **O.H.H.S.** and Arabic equivalent.
O 83 **29** 1m. sepia . . . . 1·50 3·75
O 99 – 2m. red . . . . 8·00 17·00
O 85 – 3m. orange . . . . . . 2·25 4·00
O 87 – 5m. lake . . . . 4·00 1·00
O101 – 5m. pink . . . . 17·00 4·25

1922. Stamps of 1914 optd **O.H.E.M.S.** and Arabic equivalent.
O111 **29** 1m. brown . . . . 1·40 2·50
O112 2m. red . . . . 1·90 3·25
O113 3m. orange . . . . 2·75 3·50
O114 4m. green . . . . 5·75 6·75
O115 5m. pink . . . . 2·75 90
O116 10m. blue . . . . 5·00 5·00
O117 10m. red . . . . 6·75 2·50
O118 **41** 15m. blue . . . . 6·25 4·50
O119 **42** 15m. blue £110 £110
O120 – 50m. purple . . . . . . 18·00 16·00

1923. Stamps of 1923 optd with Type O **46**.
O123 **44** 1m. orange . . . . . . 1·20 1·90
O124 2m. black . . . . . . 1·70 3·00
O125 3m. brown . . . . . . 4·25 5·25
O126 4m. green . . . . . . 4·75 5·75
O127 5m. brown . . . . . . 1·50 70
O128 10m. red . . . . 3·00 2·50
O129 15m. blue . . . . 5·50 6·00
O130 – 50m. green . . . . . . 17·00 12·00

1926.
O138 O **52** 1m. orange 60 30
O139 2m. black 40 25
O140 3m. brown . . . . . 1·10 95
O141 4m. green . . . . . 1·10 1·10
O142 5m. brown . . . . . 1·20 30
O143 10m. lake . . . . . 3·25 30
O144 10m. violet . . . . . 2·00 40
O145 15m. blue . . . . . 3·25 80
O146 15m. purple . . . . . 3·25 70
O147 20m. blue . . . . . . 4·50 1·30
O148 20m. olive . . . . . . 4·25 1·40
O149 50m. green . . . . . . 7·00 1·50
Nos. O148/9 are larger, 22½ × 27¼ mm.

O 85

O 174

1938.
O276 O **85** 1m. orange 25 85
O277 2m. red 25 30
O278 3m. brown . . . . . 1·10 1·40
O279 4m. green . . . . . 75 1·20
O280 5m. brown 35 40
O281 10m. mauve 45 60
O282 15m. purple . . . . . 1·10 1·10
O283 20m. blue . . . . . 1·10 1·10
O284 50m. green . . . . . 3·00 2·30

1952. Optd as T **124**.
O404 O **85** 1m. orange . . . . . 1·40 1·60
O405 2m. red . . . . . . 1·30 1·60
O406 3m. brown . . . . . 1·70 1·70
O407 4m. green . . . . . 1·70 1·70
O408 5m. brown . . . . . 1·70 1·70
O409 10m. mauve . . . . . 1·70 1·70
O410 15m. purple . . . . . 2·10 1·90
O411 20m. blue . . . . . 2·50 2·10
O412 50m. green . . . . . 5·50 4·75

1958.
O685 O **174** 1m. orange 25 35
O686 4m. green 50 55
O687 5m. brown 50 15
O571 10m. purple 60 20
O688 10m. brown 55 20
O572 35m. blue . . . . . 1·40 25
O689 35m. violet . . . . . 2·00 40
O690 50m. green . . . . . 3·00 50
O691 100m. lilac . . . . . 6·25 1·50
O692 200m. red . . . . . 13·00 7·25
O693 500m. black . . . . 19·00 13·00

O 334 Eagle

O 435 Eagle

1967.
O918 O **334** 1m. blue 15 20
O919 4m. brown 20 20
O920 5m. olive 25 10
O921 10m. brown 85 60
O922 10m. purple 90 35
O923 20m. purple 50 20
O924 35m. violet 75 30
O925 50m. orange 90 35
O926 55m. violet . . . . . 1·00 35
O927 100m. red and green 2·00 70
O928 200m. red and blue 4·00 1·80
O929 500m. red and olive 8·25 5·25

1972.
O1161a O **435** 1m. blue & black 20 15
O1162a 10m. red & black 20 15
O1163 20m. green & blk 85 30
O1165 20m. brown & vio 50 10
O1166 30m. brown & lilac 30 30
O1294 50m. orange & blk 35 30
O1295 55m. lilac & black 2·50 90
O1169 60m. orange & blk 55 30
O1170 70m. green & blk 65 40
O1171 80m. green & blk 40 30

O 706 Eagle

1985. Size 20 × 25 mm.
O1589 O **706** 1p. red 20 15
O1590 2p. brown 20 10
O1591 3p. brown 20 15
O1592a 5p. orange 30 30
O1593 8p. green 50 30
O1594 10p. brown 20 15
O1595 15p. lilac . . . . . 1·10 60
O1596 20p. blue 65 65
O1597 25p. red . . . . . 1·10 80
O1598 30p. purple 65 55
O1599 50p. green . . . . 1·90 1·90
O1600 60p. green . . . . 1·30 1·10

1991. As Nos. O1589/1600 but smaller, 17 × 22 mm.
O1806 O **706** 5p. orange 15 10
O1807 10p. brown 20 15
O1808 15p. brown 20 10
O1808a 20p. blue 15 10
O1808b 20p. violet 15 10
O1809 25p. lilac 30 20
O1810 30p. lilac 40 25
O1811 50p. green 65 45
O1812 55p. red 55 45
O1812a 75p. brown 60 50
O1813 £E1 blue 90 70
O1814 £E2 green . . . . 1·90 1·40

POSTAGE DUE STAMPS

D 16

D 24

1884.
D57 D **16** 10pa. red . . . . . . 45·00 9·00
D58 20pa. red . . . . . . £110 28·00
D64 1pi. red . . . . 30·00 8·00
D65 2pi. red . . . . 30·00 3·75
D61 5pi. red . . . . 14·00 42·00

1888. As Type D **16**, but values in "Milliemes" and "Piastres".
D66 D **16** 2m. green . . . . . . 13·00 21·00
D67 5m. red . . . . 32·00 20·00
D68 1p. blue . . . . £130 35·00
D69 2p. orange . . . . . . £150 12·00
D70 5p. grey £200 £180

1889. Inscr "A PERCEVOIR POSTES EGYPTIENNES".
D71 D **24** 2m. green . . . . . 7·00 50
D72 4m. purple . . . . . 2·25 50
D73 1p. blue . . . . . . 5·50 50
D74bw 2p. orange . . . . . 5·00 70

1898. Surch **3 Milliemes** in English and Arabic.
D75 D **24** 3m. on 2p. orange . . . 1·25 4·00

1921. As Type D **24**, but inscr "POSTAGE DUE EGYPT POSTAGE".
D 98 D **23** 2m. green . . . . . . 2·75 4·00
D 99 2m. red . . . . 1·00 1·50
D100 4m. red . . . . 5·00 14·00
D101 4m. green . . . . . . 4·50 1·00
D102 – 10m. blue . . . . . . 6·50 18·00
D103 – 10m. red . . . . . . 5·50 70
The 10m. values have "MILLIEMES" in a bar across the figure of value.

1922. Optd with T **43** inverted.
D111 D **24** 2m. red (No. D99) . . 50 1·50
D112 4m. green (No. D101) 80 1·60
D113 10m. red (No. D103) 1·20 90
D114 2p. orge (No. D74) . . 5·00 6·25

D 59

D 298

1927.
D173 D **59** 2m. black 55 30
D730 2m. orange 45 65
D175a 4m. green 55 30
D176 4m. sepia . . . . . 5·25 3·50
D177 5m. brown . . . . . 3·00 75
D575 6m. green . . . . . 2·30 1·50
D179 8m. purple . . . . . 1·00 40
D180a 10m. lake 85 25
D732 10m. brown . . . . 1·70 1·00
D181 12m. red . . . . . . 1·30 2·50
D182 20m. brown . . . . 1·60 2·00
D183 30m. violet . . . . . 3·25 2·40
The 30m. is larger, 22 × 27½ mm.

1952. Optd as T **124**.
D404 D **59** 2m. orange 80 90
D405 4m. green . . . . . 80 1·00
D406 6m. green . . . . . 95 1·40
D407 8m. purple . . . . . 1·10 1·10
D408 10m. lake . . . . . 2·00 1·00
D410 12m. red . . . . . . 1·20 1·20
D411 30m. violet . . . . . 1·80 1·70

1965.
D852 D **298** 2m. violet on orange 65 65
D853 8m. blue on lt blue 1·00 80
D854 10m. green on yell . . 1·50 80
D855 20m. violet on lt bl 1·90 1·30
D856 40m. green on orge 3·25 2·40

ELOBEY, ANNOBON AND CORISCO Pt. 9

A group of Spanish islands off the west coast of Africa in the Gulf of Guinea. In 1909 became part of Spanish Guinea. In 1959 Annobon became part of Fernando Poo, and Elobey and Corisco part of Rio Muni.

100 centimos = 1 peseta.

1903. "Curly Head" key-type inscr "ELOBEY, ANNOBON Y CORISCO". Dated "1903".
1 Z ¼c. red 55 35
2 ½c. purple 55 35
3 1c. black 55 35
4 2c. red 55 35
5 3c. green 55 35
6 4c. green 55 35
7 5c. lilac 55 35
8 10c. red 1·10 1·10
9 15c. orange 3·25 1·10
10 25c. blue 5·25 4·25
11 50c. brown 7·00 7·75
12 75c. brown 7·00 9·75
13 1p. red 11·00 14·00
14 2p. brown 30·00 41·00
15 3p. green 45·00 50·00
16 4p. purple £100 70·00
17 5p. green £120 70·00
18 10p. blue £225 £120

1905. "Curly Head" key-type inscr "ELOBEY, ANNOBON Y CORISCO" and dated "1905".
19 Z 1c. pink 95 55
20 2c. purple 4·00 55
21 3c. black 95 55
22 4c. red 95 55
23 5c. green 95 55
24 10c. green 3·25 70
25 15c. lilac 4·00 3·50
26 25c. red 4·00 3·50
27 50c. orange 7·00 5·50
28 75c. blue 7·00 5·50
29 1p. brown 14·00 12·00
30 2p. brown 16·00 17·00
31 3p. red 16·00 17·00
32 4p. brown £120 60·00
33 5p. green £120 60·00
34 10p. red £300 £200

1906. Preceding issue surch **1906** and value, with or without ornamental frame.
35d Z 10c. on 1c. pink 10·50 5·25
36 15c. on 2c. purple 10·50 8·50
38 25c. on 3c. black 10·50 8·50
40 50c. on 4c. red 10·50 8·50

3 King Alfonso XIII

1907.
41 3 1c. purple 35 35
42 2c. black 35 35
43 3c. red 35 35
44 4c. green 35 35
45 5c. green 35 35
46 10c. lilac 3·50 4·00
47 15c. pink 1·30 1·30
48 25c. buff 1·30 1·30
49 50c. blue 1·30 1·30
50 75c. brown 4·00 1·90
51 1p. brown 6·25 3·25
52 2p. red 8·75 5·75
53 3p. brown 8·75 5·75
54 4p. green 8·75 5·75
55 5p. red 12·50 5·75
56 10p. pink 31·00 18·00

1908. Surch **HABILITADO PARA 05 CTMS.**
57 3 05c. on 1c. purple 2·75 1·50
58 05c. on 2c. black 3·00 1·50
59 05c. on 3c. red 3·00 1·50
60 05c. on 4c. green 3·00 1·50
61 05c. on 10c. lilac 5·75 5·25
62 25c. on 10c. lilac 26·00 14·50

1909. Fiscal stamps inscr "POSESIONES ESPANOLES DE AFRICA OCCIDENTAL", surch **1909 CORREOS 10 cen de peseta.**
63 10c. on 50c. green 22·00 14·50
64 10c. on 1p.25 lilac 33·00 18·00
65 10c. on 2p. brown £130 £100
66 10c. on 2p.50 blue £130 £100
67 10c. on 10p. brown £140 £100
68 10c. on 15p. grey £130 £100
69 10c. on 25p. brown £130 £100

For later issues see **SPANISH GUINEA.**

EL SALVADOR Pt. 15

A republic of C. America, independent since 1838.

1867. 8 reales = 100 centavos = 1 peso.
1912. 100 centavos = 1 colon.

1 San Miguel Volcano
4

1867.
1 1 ½r. blue 90 90
2 1r. red 90 90
3 2r. green 1·75 2·50
4 4r. brown 4·25 4·00

1874. Optd **CONTRA SELLO 1874** and arms in circle.
5 1 ½r. blue 4·00 4·00
6 1r. red 4·00 4·00
7 2r. green 4·00 4·00
8 4r. brown 11·00 10·50

1879.
9 4 1c. green 1·25 75
15 2c. red 1·75 1·75
16 5c. blue 3·00 1·50
12 10c. black 6·00 4·00
13 20c. purple 15·00 12·00

8
9

10
14

1887.
18 8 3c. brown (perf) 40 40
19 9 5c. blue (roul) 40 30
20 10 10c. orange (perf) 4·00 1·10

1889. Surch **1 centavo.**
21 8 1c. on 3c. brown 1·00 60

A number of postage stamps listed above are found overprinted **1889.**

1889. As T 8, but with bar at top. Perf.
22 8 1c. green 50 50

1890.
30 14 1c. green 15 20
31 2c. brown 15 25
32 3c. yellow 15 25
33 5c. blue 15 25
34 10c. violet 15 25
35 20c. orange 15 30
36 25c. red 15 40
37 50c. purple 15 80
38 1p. red 15 2·00

15
19 Landing of Columbus

1891.
39 15 1c. red 40 20
40 2c. green 40 20
41 3c. violet 40 30
42 5c. red 40 30
43 10c. blue 40 30
44 11c. violet 40 85
45 20c. green 40 1·10
46 25c. brown 40 1·25
47 50c. blue 40 2·50
48 1p. brown 45 5·00

1891. Surch **1 centavo.**
49 15 1c. on 2c. green 8·50 6·00

1891. Surch **UN CENTAVO.**
50 15 1c. on 2c. green 3·50 4·50

1891. Surch **5 CENTAVOS.**
51 15 5c. on 3c. violet 7·50 6·00

1892.
52 19 1c. green 15 15
53 2c. brown 15 15
54 3c. blue 15 15
55 5c. grey 15 15
56 10c. red 15 20
57 11c. brown 15 1·00
58 20c. orange 15 1·00
59 25c. purple 15 1·50
60 50c. yellow 15 2·00
61 1p. red 15 3·00

1892. Surch.
62a 19 1c. on 5c. grey 75 80
64 1c. on 20c. orange 1·00 1·10
66 1c. on 25c. purple 1·50 90

23 Gen. Ezeta
24 Founding the City of Isabella

1893. Dated "1893".
67 23 1c. blue 15 20
68 2c. red 15 20
69 3c. violet 15 20
70 5c. brown 15 25
71 10c. brown 15 25
72 11c. red 15 30
73 20c. green 15 40
74 25c. black 15 50
75 50c. orange 15 60
76 1p. black 15 90
77 24 2p. green 50
78 – 5p. violet 50
79 – 10p. red 50
DESIGNS—VERT: 5p. Columbus Statue, Genoa; 10p. Departure from Palos.

1893. Surch **UN CENTAVO.**
80 23 1c. on 2c. red 60 60

28 Liberty
29 Columbus before the Council

1894. Dated "1894".
81 28 1c. brown 15 20
82 2c. blue 15 20
83 3c. purple 15 20
84 5c. brown 15 30
85 10c. violet 15 30
86 11c. red 15 30
87 20c. blue 15 40
88 25c. orange 15 50
89 50c. black 15 80
90 1p. blue 15 1·10
91 29 2p. blue 40
92 – 5p. red 50
93 – 10p. brown 50
DESIGNS—HORIZ: 5p. Columbus protecting hostages; 10p. Columbus received by King and Queen.

1894. Surch **1 Centavo.**
94 28 1c. on 11c. red 90 60

31
34

1895. Optd with Arms obliterating portrait. Various frames.
95 31 1c. olive 15
96 2c. green 15
97 3c. brown 15
98 5c. blue 15
99 10c. orange 15
100 12c. red 15
101 15c. red 15
102 20c. yellow 15
103 24c. violet 15
104 30c. blue 15
105 50c. red 15
106 1p. black 15

1895. Various frames.
115 34 1c. olive 90 60
116 2c. green 20 20
117 3c. brown 20 20
118 5c. blue 20 20
119 10c. orange 80 40
120 12c. red 80 40
121 15c. red 25 40
122 20c. green 30 60
123 24c. lilac 40 60
124 30c. blue 25 60
125 50c. red 1·25 1·50
126 1p. brown 1·50 2·25

1895. Surch.
132 34 1c. on 12c. red 1·25 1·10
133 1c. on 24c. lilac 1·25 1·10
134 1c. on 30c. blue 1·25 1·10
135 2c. on 20c. green 1·25 1·10
136 3c. on 30c. blue 1·50 1·40

37 Peace
38 Arms
39 Government Building

1896.
137 37 1c. brown 15 15
138 2c. brown 15 30
139 3c. green 15 20
140 5c. olive 15 30
141 10c. yellow 15 30
142 12c. blue 90 1·10
143 15c. violet 15 30
144 20c. red 70 60
145 24c. red 15 30
146 30c. orange 15 50
147 50c. black 15 60
148 1p. red 15 1·10

1896. Dated "1896".
158 38 1c. green 15 15
159 39 2c. lake 15 15
160 – 3c. orange 25 35
161 – 5c. blue 15 15
162 – 10c. brown 30 25
163 – 12c. grey 30 30
164 – 15c. green 15 30
165 – 20c. red 20 40
166 – 24c. violet 15 50
167 – 30c. green 15 50
168 – 50c. orange 15 50
169 – 100c. blue 15 1·00
DESIGNS: 3c. Locomotive; 5c. Mt. San Miguel; 10, 12c. Steamship; 15c. Post Office; 20c. Lake Ilopango; 24c. Magra Falls; 30, 50c. Arms; 100c. Columbus.

1896. No. 166 surch **Quince centavos.**
218 15c. on 24c. violet 5·00 5·00

1897. As Nos. 158/69. New colours.
220 1c. red 15 15
221 2c. green 15 15
222 3c. brown 25 30
223 5c. orange 15 15
224 10c. green 15 20
225 12c. blue 50 40
226 15c. black 2·50 2·50
227 20c. slate 15 40
228 24c. yellow 15 50
229 30c. red 15 40
230 50c. violet 25 80
231 100c. lake 3·50 3·50

55
57 Union of Central America

1897. Federation of Central America.
270 55 1c. multicoloured 75 3·00
271 5c. multicoloured 75 3·50

1897. Nos. 228/31 surch **TRECE centavos.**
272 13c. on 24c. yellow 3·00 3·00
273 13c. on 30c. red 3·00 3·00
274 13c. on 50c. violet 3·00 3·00
275 13c. on 100c. lake 3·00 3·00

1898.
276 57 1c. red 10 15
277 2c. red 10 15
278 3c. green 15 20
279 5c. green 15 15
280 10c. blue 15 20
281 12c. violet 25 30
282 13c. lake 15 20
283 20c. blue 15 40
284 24c. blue 15 50
285 26c. brown 15 50
286 50c. orange 15 90
287 1p. yellow 25 1·25
Some values of the above set exist optd with a wheel as Type **58**.

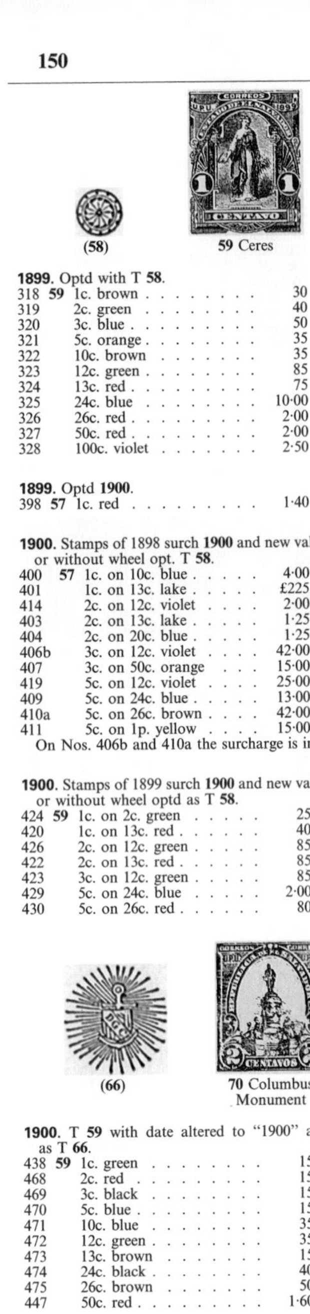

(58) 59 Ceres

1899. Optd with T **58**.
318 **59** 1c. brown 30 15
319 2c. green 40 10
320 3c. blue 50 25
321 5c. orange 35 15
322 10c. brown 35 15
323 12c. green 85 60
324 13c. red 75 70
325 24c. blue 10·00 10·00
326 26c. red 2·00 1·75
327 50c. red 2·00 1·75
328 100c. violet 2·50 1·25

1899. Optd **1900**.
398 **57** 1c. red 1·40 1·00

1900. Stamps of 1898 surch **1900** and new value, with or without wheel opt. T **58**.
400 **57** 1c. on 10c. blue 4·00 3·50
401 1c. on 13c. lake £225
414 2c. on 12c. violet 2·00 2·00
403 2c. on 13c. lake 1·25 1·10
404 2c. on 20c. blue 1·25 1·25
406b 3c. on 12c. violet 42·00 42·00
407 3c. on 50c. orange 15·00 15·00
419 5c. on 12c. violet 25·00 25·00
409 5c. on 24c. blue 13·00 13·00
410a 5c. on 26c. brown 42·00 42·00
411 5c. on 1p. yellow 15·00 15·00
On Nos. 406b and 410a the surcharge is inverted.

1900. Stamps of 1899 surch **1900** and new value, with or without wheel optd as T **58**.
424 **59** 1c. on 2c. green 25 15
420 1c. on 13c. red 40 40
426 2c. on 12c. green 85 60
422 2c. on 13c. red 85 70
423 3c. on 12c. green 85 70
429 5c. on 24c. blue 2·00 90
430 5c. on 26c. red 80 60

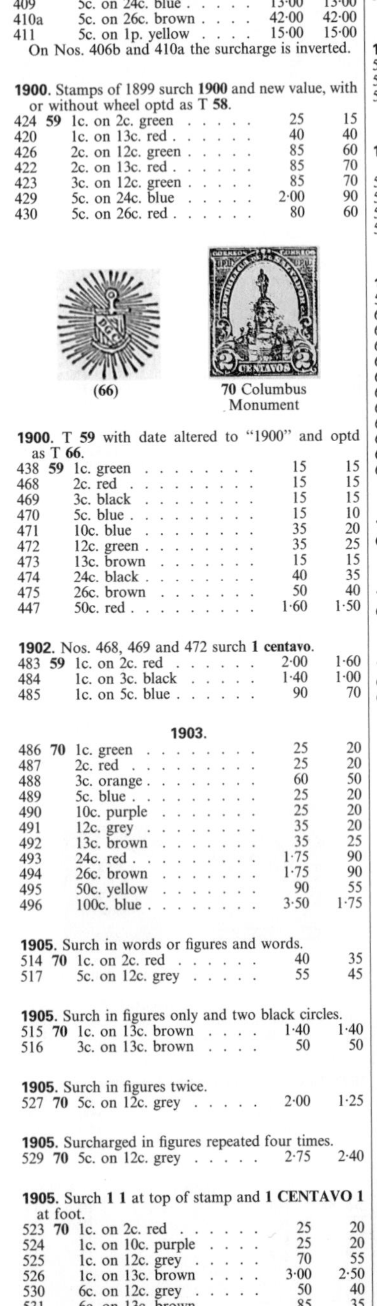

(66) 70 Columbus Monument

1900. T **59** with date altered to "1900" and optd as T **66**.
438 **59** 1c. green 15 15
468 2c. red 15 15
469 3c. black 15 15
470 5c. blue 15 10
471 10c. blue 35 20
472 12c. green 35 25
473 13c. brown 15 15
474 24c. black 40 35
475 26c. brown 50 40
447 50c. red 1·60 1·50

1902. Nos. 468, 469 and 472 surch **1 centavo**.
483 **59** 1c. on 2c. red 2·00 1·60
484 1c. on 3c. black 1·40 1·00
485 1c. on 5c. blue 90 70

1903.
486 **70** 1c. green 25 20
487 2c. red 25 20
488 3c. orange 60 50
489 5c. blue 25 20
490 10c. purple 25 20
491 12c. grey 35 20
492 13c. brown 35 25
493 24c. red 1·75 90
494 26c. brown 1·75 90
495 50c. yellow 90 55
496 100c. blue 3·50 1·75

1905. Surch in words or figures and words.
514 **70** 1c. on 2c. red 40 35
517 5c. on 12c. grey 55 45

1905. Surch in figures only and two black circles.
515 **70** 1c. on 13c. brown 1·40 1·40
516 3c. on 13c. brown 50 50

1905. Surch in figures twice.
527 **70** 5c. on 12c. grey 2·00 1·25

1905. Surcharged in figures repeated four times.
529 **70** 5c. on 12c. grey 2·75 2·40

1905. Surch **1 1** at top of stamp and **1 CENTAVO 1** at foot.
523 **70** 1c. on 2c. red 25 20
524 1c. on 10c. purple 25 20
525 1c. on 12c. grey 70 55
526 1c. on 13c. brown 3·00 2·50
530 6c. on 12c. grey 50 40
531 6c. on 13c. brown 85 35

1905. Stamps dated "1900", with or without opt T **66**, and optd **1905** or **01905**.
552 **59** 1c. green 3·25 2·25
546 2c. red 30 25
543 3c. black 3·50 2·10
547 5c. blue 90 50
548 10c. blue 50 40

1906. Stamps dated "1900", with or without opt T **66**, and optd **1906** or surch also.
560 **59** 2c. on 26c. brown 40 35
562 3c. on 26c. brown 2·40 2·00
564 10c. blue 90 90

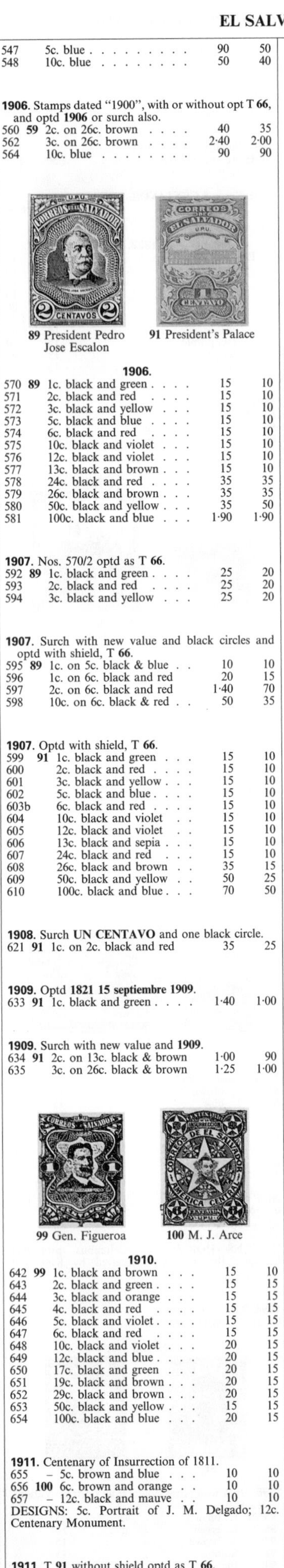

89 President Pedro Jose Escalon 91 President's Palace

1906.
570 **89** 1c. black and green 15 10
571 2c. black and red 15 10
572 3c. black and yellow 15 10
573 5c. black and blue 15 10
574 6c. black and red 15 10
575 10c. black and violet 15 10
576 12c. black and violet 15 10
577 13c. black and brown 15 10
578 24c. black and red 35 35
579 26c. black and brown 35 35
580 50c. black and yellow 35 50
581 100c. black and blue 1·90 1·90

1907. Nos. 570/2 optd as T **66**.
592 **89** 1c. black and green 25 20
593 2c. black and red 25 20
594 3c. black and yellow 25 20

1907. Surch with new value and black circles and optd with shield, T **66**.
595 **89** 1c. on 5c. black & blue 10 10
596 1c. on 6c. black and red 20 15
597 2c. on 6c. black and red 1·40 70
598 10c. on 6c. black & red 50 35

1907. Optd with shield, T **66**.
599 **91** 1c. black and green 15 10
600 2c. black and red 15 10
601 3c. black and yellow 15 10
602 5c. black and blue 15 10
603b 6c. black and red 15 10
604 10c. black and violet 15 10
605 12c. black and violet 15 10
606 13c. black and sepia 15 10
607 24c. black and red 15 10
608 26c. black and brown 35 15
609 50c. black and yellow 50 25
610 100c. black and blue 70 50

1908. Surch **UN CENTAVO** and one black circle.
621 **91** 1c. on 2c. black and red 35 25

1909. Optd **1821 15 septiembre 1909**.
633 **91** 1c. black and green 1·40 1·00

1909. Surch with new value and **1909**.
634 **91** 2c. on 13c. black & brown 1·00 90
635 3c. on 26c. black & brown 1·25 1·00

99 Gen. Figueroa 100 M. J. Arce

1910.
642 **99** 1c. black and brown 15 10
643 2c. black and green 15 15
644 3c. black and orange 15 15
645 4c. black and red 15 15
646 5c. black and violet 15 15
647 6c. black and red 15 15
648 10c. black and violet 20 15
649 12c. black and blue 20 15
650 17c. black and green 20 15
651 19c. black and brown 20 15
652 29c. black and brown 20 15
653 50c. black and yellow 15 15
654 100c. black and blue 20 15

1911. Centenary of Insurrection of 1811.
655 – 5c. brown and blue 10 10
656 **100** 6c. brown and orange 10 10
657 – 12c. black and mauve 10 10
DESIGNS: 5c. Portrait of J. M. Delgado; 12c. Centenary Monument.

1911. T **91** without shield optd as T **66**.
658 **91** 1c. red 10 10
659 2c. brown 35 35
660 13c. green 15 15
661 24c. yellow 20 20
662 50c. brown 20 20

101 Jose Matias Delgado

107 Independence Monument

108 National Palace

110 National Arms

1912.
663 **101** 1c. black and blue 15 10
664 – 2c. black and brown 20 15
665 – 5c. black and red 20 15
666 – 6c. black and green 15 15
667 – 12c. black and olive 60 25
668 – 17c. grey and purple 50 20
669 **107** 19c. grey and red 75 20
670 **108** 29c. grey and orange 90 25
671 – 50c. grey and blue 1·10 50
672 **110** 1col. grey and black 1·50 70
DESIGNS—As Type **101**: 2c. M. J. Arce; 5c. F. Morazan; 6c. R. Campo; 12c. T. Cabanas; 17c. Barrios Monument. As Type **108**: 50c. Rosales Hospital.

111 J. M. Rodriguez

1914.
673 **111** 10c. brown and orange 1·50 70
674 – 25c. brown and violet 1·50 70
PORTRAIT: 25c. Dr. M. E. Araujo.

1915. Re-issue of T **91**. No shield. Optd **1915**.
675 **91** 1c. grey 15 10
676 2c. red 15 10
677 5c. blue 15 10
678 6c. blue 15 10
679 10c. yellow 55 40
680 12c. brown 40 20
681 50c. purple 20 15
682 100c. brown 85 85

113 National Theatre

114 Pres. Carlos Melendez

1916. Various frames.
683 **113** 1c. green 1·50 30
684 2c. red 1·50 30
685 5c. blue 1·50 20
686 6c. violet 2·00 20
687 10c. brown 3·00 25
688 12c. purple 5·25 1·50
689 17c. orange 1·50 45
690 25c. brown 3·75 1·25
691 29c. black 7·50 2·00
692 50c. grey 4·50 2·00
693 **114** 1col. black and blue 1·50 90

1917. Official stamps of 1915, with word "OFICIAL" cancelled with five bars.
694 **91** 2c. red (No. O686) 40 25
695 5c. blue (No. O687) 50 35

1918. Official stamps of 1915 optd **CORRIENTE** and bar.
696 **91** 1c. grey (No. O685) 1·10 90
697 2c. red 1·10 90
698 5c. blue 7·00 4·50
699 6c. blue 70 50
700 10c. yellow 75 40
701 12c. brown 60 50
702 50c. purple 50 50

1918. Official stamps of 1916 optd **CORRIENTE** and bar or surch also.
704 **113** 1c. on 6c. violet (No. O696) 6·50 4·75
705 5c. blue 8·50 6·50
706 6c. violet 11·00 8·00

1919. Surch with new value and square or circles or bars.
710 **113** 1c. on 6c. violet 6·50 4·75
711 1c. on 12c. purple 4·25 2·75
712 1c. on 17c. orange 5·50 4·00
713 2c. on 10c. brown 4·25 3·25
714 5c. on 50c. grey 6·50 4·00
715 6c. on 25c. brown 5·50 4·50
716 15c. on 29c. black 2·75 2·25
717 26c. on 29c. black 7·00 8·00
719 35c. on 50c. grey 8·00 10·00
720 60c. on 1col. blk & bl 95 90

1919. No. O699 surch **1 CENTAVO 1**.
721 **113** 1c. on 12c. purple 4·25 3·45

1920. Municipal stamps (Arms) surch **Correos Un centavo 1919**.
722 1c. olive 10 10
723 1c. on 5c. yellow 10 10
724 1c. on 10c. blue 15 10
725 1c. on 25c. green 10 10
726 1c. on 50c. olive 15 15
727 1c. on 1p. black 25 25

130 F. Menendez

131 Confederation Coin

132 Delgado Speaking

133 Arms of the Confederation

135 Independence Monument

139 J. S. Canas

1921. Portraits are as T **130**.
728 **130** 1c. green 25 10
729 – 2c. black (M. J. Arce) 25 10
730 **131** 5c. orange 60 15
731 **132** 6c. red 50 10
732 **133** 10c. blue 50 10
733 – 25c. grn (F. Morazan) 1·50 15
734 **135** 60c. violet 3·75 50
735 – 1col. sepia (Columbus) 6·00 50

1921. Centenary of Independence. Nos. 728/31 optd **CENTENARIO**.
735a **130** 1c. green 4·50 2·40
735b – 2c. black 4·50 2·40
735c **131** 5c. orange 4·50 2·40
735d **132** 6c. red 4·50 2·40

1923. As last, surch.
745 **131** 1c. on 5c. orange 35 25
741 – 1c. on 25c. green 15 15
746 **131** 2c. on 5c. orange 35 35
737 **132** 5c. on 6c. red 25 20
747 **133** 6c. on 10c. blue 35 25
742 – 6c. on 25c. green 20 15
738 – 10c. on 2c. black 50 20
739 **132** 20c. on 6c. red 35 35
743 – 20c. on 25c. green 45 35
744 – 20c. on 1col. sepia 55 25

1923. Centenary of Abolition of Slavery.
740 **139** 5c. blue 50 35

1924. U.P.U. Commemoration. Surch **15 Sept. 1874 – 1924 5 5 U.P.U. CINCO CENTAVOS**.
749 **135** 5c. on 60c. violet 3·25 3·00

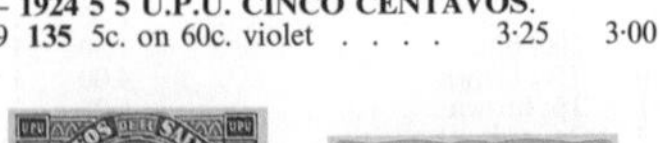

141 Daniel Hernandez

146 Central America

150

1924.
750 **141** 1c. purple 10 10
751 – 2c. red 25 10
752 – 3c. brown 20 10
753 – 5c. black 20 10
754 – 6c. blue 3·25 25
755 **146** 10c. orange 55 20
756 – 20c. green 70 35
757 – 35c. green and red 1·75 30
758 – 50c. brown 1·50 40
759 **150** 1col. blue and green 2·25 40

DESIGNS—VERT: 2c. National Gymnasium; 3c. Atlacatl; 20c. Balsam tree; 35c. Senora T. S. Morazan. HORIZ: 5c. Conspiracy of 1811; 6c. Bridge over R. Lempa; 50c. Columbus at La Rabida.

1925. 400th Anniv of San Salvador. Surch **1525 2 2 1925 Dos centavos.**
760 **135** 2c. on 60c. violet . . . . 1·60 1·50

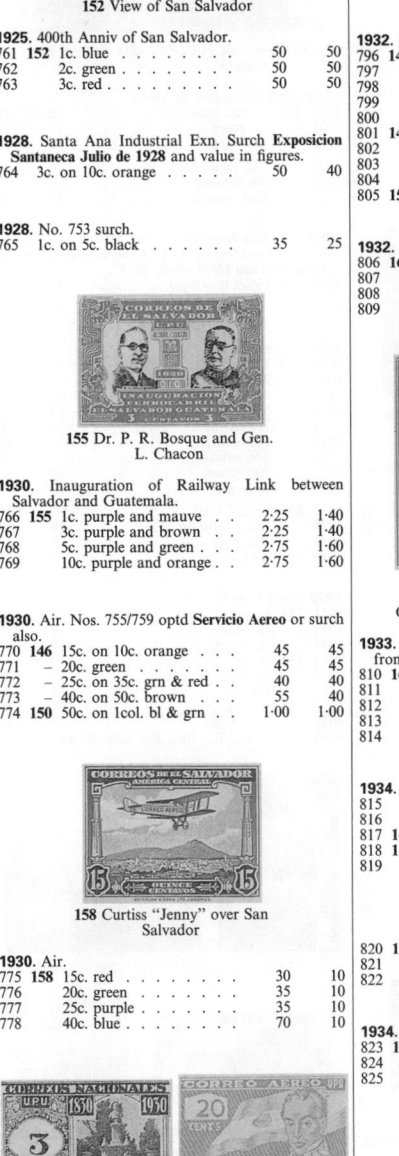

152 View of San Salvador

1925. 400th Anniv of San Salvador.
761 **152** 1c. blue 50 50
762 2c. green 50 50
763 3c. red 50 50

1928. Santa Ana Industrial Exn. Surch **Exposicion Santaneca Julio de 1928** and value in figures.
764 3c. on 10c. orange 50 40

1928. No. 753 surch.
765 1c. on 5c. black 35 25

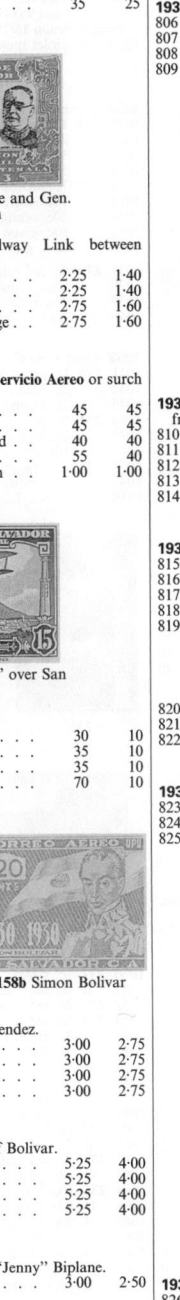

155 Dr. P. R. Bosque and Gen. L. Chacon

1930. Inauguration of Railway Link between Salvador and Guatemala.
766 **155** 1c. purple and mauve . . 2·25 1·40
767 3c. purple and brown . . 2·25 1·40
768 5c. purple and green . . . 2·75 1·60
769 10c. purple and orange . . 2·75 1·60

1930. Air. Nos. 755/759 optd **Servicio Aereo** or surch also.
770 **146** 15c. on 10c. orange . . . 45 45
771 – 20c. green 45 45
772 – 25c. on 35c. grn & red . . 40 40
773 – 40c. on 50c. brown . . . 55 40
774 **150** 50c. on 1col. bl & grn . . 1·00 1·00

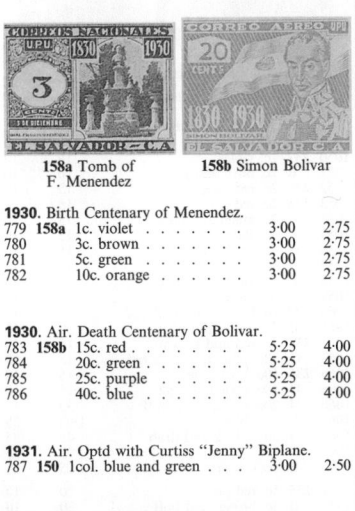

158 Curtiss "Jenny" over San Salvador

1930. Air.
775 **158** 15c. red 30 10
776 20c. green 35 10
777 25c. purple 35 10
778 40c. blue 70 10

158a Tomb of F. Menendez **158b** Simon Bolivar

1930. Birth Centenary of Menendez.
779 **158a** 1c. violet . . . . 3·00 2·75
780 3c. brown . . . . 3·00 2·75
781 5c. green . . . . 3·00 2·75
782 10c. orange . . . . . . 3·00 2·75

1930. Air. Death Centenary of Bolivar.
783 **158b** 15c. red . . . . 5·25 4·00
784 20c. green . . . . 5·25 4·00
785 25c. purple . . . . 5·25 4·00
786 40c. blue . . . . 5·25 4·00

1931. Air. Optd with Curtiss "Jenny" Biplane.
787 **150** 1col. blue and green . . . 3·00 2·50

1931. New G.P.O. Building Fund. Nos. 756 and 758 surch **EDIFICIOS POSTALES** and value.
790 1c. on 20c. green 15 15
788 1c. on 50c. brown 15 15
789 2c. on 20c. green 15 15
791 2c. on 50c. brown 15 15

162 Church of Mercy, San Salvador **164** Jose Matias Delgado

1931. Air. 120th Anniv of Independence.
792 **162** 15c. red . . . . 3·50 3·00
793 20c. green . . . . 3·50 3·00
794 25c. purple . . . . 3·50 3·00
795 40c. blue . . . . 3·50 3·00

1932. Issues of 1924–26 optd **1932.**
796 **141** 1c. purple 15 10
797 – 2c. red 20 15
798 – 3c. brown 25 10
799 – 5c. black 25 10
800 – 6c. blue . . . . 3·75 1·50
801 **146** 10c. orange 85 20
802 – 20c. green . . . . 1·10 45
803 – 35c. green and red . . . 1·60 55
804 – 50c. brown . . . . 2·25 70
805 **150** 1col. blue and green . . . 4·00 1·60

1932. Air. Death Centenary of J. M. Delgado.
806 **164** 15c. red and violet . . . 1·00 1·00
807 20c. green and blue . . . 1·50 1·50
808 25c. violet and red . . . 1·50 1·50
809 40c. blue and green . . . 1·75 1·75

166 Ford "Tin Goose" over Columbus's Fleet **169** Police Headquarters

1933. Air. 441st Anniv of Departure of Columbus from Palos.
810 **166** 15c. orange . . . . 6·00 1·75
811 20c. green . . . . 8·00 3·75
812 25c. mauve . . . . 8·00 3·75
813 40c. blue . . . . 8·00 3·75
814 1col. bronze . . . . . . 8·00 3·75

1934. Issues of 1924 and 1926 surch.
815 – 2 on 5c. blk (No. 753) . . 15 10
816 – 2 on 50c. brn (No. 758) 25 15
817 **146** 3 on 10c. orange 15 10
818 **150** 8 on 1col. blue & green 15 15
819 – 15 on 35c. green and red (No. 757) 25 25

1934.
820 **169** 2c. brown 20 10
821 5c. red 20 10
822 8c. blue 20 10

1934. Air. Inscr "SERVICIO AEREO".
823 **169** 25c. violet 45 20
824 30c. brown 65 30
825 1col. black . . . . 1·75 55

171 Discus Thrower

172 Runner breasting the Tape

1935. 3rd Central American Athletic Games.
826 **171** 5c. red (postage) . . . . 3·00 2·40
827 8c. blue . . . . 3·25 2·75
828 10c. yellow . . . . 4·00 3·00
829 15c. brown . . . . 4·75 3·25
830 37c. green . . . . 6·00 4·75
831 **172** 15c. red (air) . . . . . . 4·00 4·00
832 25c. violet . . . . 4·00 4·00
833 30c. brown . . . . 3·50 3·00
834 55c. blue . . . . 17·00 15·00
835 1col. black . . . . 13·00 12·00

1935. Nos. 826/35 optd **HABILITADO.**
836 **171** 5c. red (postage) . . . . 4·00 3·00
837 8c. blue . . . . 6·00 3·00
838 10c. yellow . . . . 6·00 3·50
839 15c. brown . . . . 6·00 3·50
840 37c. green . . . . 9·50 6·00
841 **172** 15c. red (air) . . . . . . 4·00 1·75
842 25c. violet . . . . 4·00 1·75
843 30c. brown . . . . 4·00 1·75
844 55c. blue . . . . 26·00 22·00
845 1col. black . . . . 13·00 12·00

174 National Flag **175** The Settlers' Oak

1935.
846 **174** 1c. blue (postage) 15 10
847 2c. grey 15 10
848 3c. purple 15 10
849 5c. red 25 10
850 8c. blue 35 15
851 15c. brown 40 15
852 30c. black (air) 60 25

1935. Tercentenary of San Vicente. Value in black.
853 **175** 2c. grn & brn (postage) 35 25
854 3c. green 40 25
855 5c. green and red 55 35
856 8c. green and blue 55 40
857 15c. green and brown . . 55 50
858 10c. green & yell (air) . . 1·25 90
859 15c. green and brown . . 1·25 90
860 20c. green . . . . 1·25 90
861 25c. green and violet . . . 1·25 90
862 30c. green and brown . . 1·25 90

178 Cutuco Harbour **179** D. Vasconcelos

181 Sugar Refinery **182** Coffee Cargo

1935.
863 – 1c. violet 15 10
864 **178** 2c. brown 90 35
865 **179** 3c. green 15 10
866 – 5c. red 40 10
867 – 8c. blue 15 10
868 **181** 10c. yellow 25 10
869 **182** 15c. bistre 40 20
870 – 50c. blue . . . . 1·25 75
871 – 1col. black . . . . 3·50 2·25
DESIGNS—As Type **178**: 1c. Mt. Izalco; 5c. Campo de Marte playing-fields. As Type **179**: 8c. T. G. Palomo. As Type **181**: 1col. Dr. M. Araujo; 50c. Balsam tree.

1937. Air. Optd **AEREO** in frame.
872 **182** 15c. bistre 40 25

1937. Air. No. 844 surch **30** in frame.
873 **172** 30 on 55c. blue . . . . . 1·25 55

186 Panchimalco Church

1937. Air.
874 **186** 15c. orange 30 15
875 20c. green 30 15
876 25c. violet 30 15
877 30c. brown 25 10
878 40c. blue 45 35
879 1col. black 85 35
880 5col. red . . . . 3·75 2·50

1938. Surch.
881 **178** 1c. on 2c. brown . . . . 1·60 90
882 – 1c. on 5c. red (No. 866) 15 10
883 **181** 3c. on 10c. yellow 15 10
884 **182** 8c. on 15c. bistre 20 15

1938. Death Cent of J. Simeon Canas. Surch **3.**
885 **139** 3 on 5c. blue 25 30

190 Flags and Book of Constitution

1938. 150th Anniv of U.S. Constitution. (a) Postage (without airliner).
886 **190** 8c. red, yellow and blue 60 50

(b) Air.
887 **190** 30c. multicoloured . . . . 1·50 1·00

191 J. S. Canas **192** Native Women at Washing Pool

1938. Air. Death Centenary of J. S. Canas.
888 **191** 15c. orange . . . . 1·00 1·00
889 20c. green . . . . 1·25 1·00
890 30c. brown . . . . 1·25 1·00
891 1col. black . . . . 4·00 3·50

1938.
892 – 1c. violet 15 10
893 **192** 2c. green 15 10
894 – 3c. brown 25 10
895 – 5c. red 25 10
896 – 8c. blue 90 20
897 – 10c. orange . . . . 1·50 20
898 – 20c. brown . . . . 1·25 25
899 – 50c. violet . . . . 1·60 35
900 – 1col. black . . . . 1·50 60
DESIGNS: 1c. Native sugar-mill; 3c. Girl at spring; 5c. Native ploughing; 8c. Yucca plant; 10c. Champion cow; 20c. Extraction of Peruvian balsam; 50c. Maquilishuat tree in flower; 1col. G.P.O., San Salvador.

195 Golden Gate Bridge

1939. Air. Golden Gate Int Exn, San Francisco.
901 **195** 15c. black and yellow . . 30 15
902 30c. black and brown . . 45 15
903 40c. black and blue . . . 65 35

1939. Centenary of Battle of San Pedro Perulapan. Surch **25 Sept 1839 1939 BATALLA SAN PEDRO PERULAPAN** and value.
904 – 8c. on 50c. bl (No. 870) 35 20
905 – 10c. on 1col. black (No. 871) 50 20
906 **150** 50c. on 1col. bl & grn . . 2·75 2·75

197 Sir Rowland Hill **199** Coffee Tree in Bloom

198 Western Hemisphere and "Peace"

1940. Cent of 1st Adhesive Postage Stamps.
907 **197** 8c. black & blue (postage) 3·00 60
908 30c. black & brown (air) 4·75 1·75
909 80c. black and red 12·00 9·00

1940. Air. 50th Anniv of Pan-American Union.
910 **198** 30c. blue and brown 50 35
911 80c. black and red 75 50

1940. Air.
912 **199** 15c. orange 75 25
913 20c. green 90 15
914 25c. violet 1·10 30
915 – 30c. brown 1·25 25
916 – 1col. black 4·75 35
DESIGN: 30c., 1col. Coffee tree in fruit.

200 Dr. Lindo, Gen. Mallespin and New National University of El Salvador

1941. Air. Cent of El Salvador University.
917 **200** 20c. red and green 75 50
918 – 40c. orange and blue 75 50
919 – 60c. brown and violet 75 50
920 – 80c. green and red 2·75 2·00
921 – 1col. orange and black 2·75 2·00
922 **200** 2col. purple and orange 2·75 2·00
PORTRAITS: 40c., 80c. Dr. N. Monterey and A. J. Canas; 60c., 1col. Dr. I. Menendez and Dr. C. Salazar.

201 Map of El Salvador

1942. 1st National Eucharistic Congress. Inscr "NOVIEMBRE 1942".
923 – 8c. blue (postage) 40 25
924 **201** 30c. orange (air) 40 30
DESIGN 8c. Patron Saint and Cathedral of San Salvador, in medallions.

1943. Air. Surch in large figures.
925 **195** 15 on 15c. black & yellow 35 30
926 20 on 30c. black & brown 40 30
927 25 on 40c. black & blue 50 35

1944. Air. Surch in small figures.
928 **195** 15 on 15c. black & yell 25 20
929 20 on 30c. black & brn 40 30
930 25 on 40c. black & blue 50 30

205 Cuscatlan Bridge

1944. Optd with small shield.
931 **205** 8c. black & blue (postage) 20 15
932 30c. black & red (air) 45 25

206 Presidential Palace **207** Gen. J. J. Canas

1944. Air.
933 **206** 15c. mauve 15 10
934 – 20c. green 25 10
935 – 25c. purple 25 10
936 – 30c. red 25 10
937 – 40c. blue 35 25
938 – 1col. black 75 35
DESIGNS: 20c. National Theatre; 25c. National Palace; 30c. Mayan Pyramid; 40c. Public Gardens; 1col. Aeronautics School.

1945. Gen. J. J. Canas (author of National Anthem).
939 **207** 8c. blue 15 10

1945. No. 893 surch **1**.
940 1c. on 2c. green 15 10

1945. Air. Optd **Aereo**.
942 1col. black (No. 900) 65 25

210 Juan Ramon Uriarte **211** Alberto Masferrer

1945. Air. J. R. Uriarte, former Director General of Posts.
943 **210** 12c. blue 25 15
944 14c. orange 25 10

1945. Air. Alberto Masferrer (writer).
945 **211** 12c. red 25 15
946 14c. green 25 10

212 Lake Ilopango **215** Isidro Menendez

1946.
947 **212** 1c. blue 10 10
948 – 2c. green 25 10
949 – 5c. red 15 10
DESIGNS: 2c. Ceiba tree; 5c. Water carriers (larger).

1947.
950 **215** 1c. red 10 10
951 – 2c. yellow (Salazar) 10 10
952 – 3c. violet (Bertis) 10 10
953 – 5c. grey (Duenas) 10 10
954 – 8c. blue (Belloso) 10 10
955 – 10c. bistre (Trigueros) 15 10
956 – 20c. green (Gonzalez) 25 15
957 – 50c. black (Castaneda) 45 25
958 – 1col. red (Castro) 1·00 35

217 Alfredo Espino **218** M. J. Arce

1947. Air.
959 – 12c. brown (F. Soto) 25 15
960 **217** 14c. blue 20 10

1948. Death Centenary of M. J. Arce.
961 **218** 8c. blue (postage) 20 15
962 12c. green (air) 20 15
963 14c. red 25 15
964 1col. purple 2·00 1·60

219 Mackenzie King, Roosevelt and Churchill

220 Franklin D. Roosevelt

1948. 3rd Death Anniv of Franklin D. Roosevelt.
965 – 5c. black & bl (postage) 15 10
966 – 8c. black and green 15 10
967 **220** 12c. black and violet 25 10
968 **219** 15c. black and red 25 15
969 – 20c. black and lake 35 30
970 – 50c. black and grey 55 45
971 **220** 12c. black & grn (air) 40 25
972 – 14c. black and olive 40 25
973 – 20c. black and brown 40 35
974 – 25c. black and red 40 40
975 **219** 1col. black and purple 1·00 60
976 – 2col. black and lilac 2·00 1·25

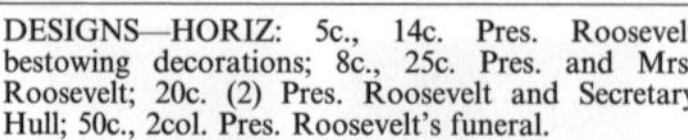
DESIGNS—HORIZ: 5c., 14c. Pres. Roosevelt bestowing decorations; 8c., 25c. Pres. and Mrs. Roosevelt; 20c. (2) Pres. Roosevelt and Secretary Hull; 50c., 2col. Pres. Roosevelt's funeral.

1948. Air. Optd **Aereo**.
977 5c. grey (No. 953) 10 10
978 10c. bistre (No. 955) 15 10
979 1col. red (No. 958) 1·40 80

1949. Air. No. 936 surch **10**.
980 10c. on 30c. red 20 10

222 Torch and Wings

1949. 75th Anniv of U.P.U.
981 **222** 8c. blue (postage) 50 25
982 5c. brown (air) 15 10
983 10c. black 25 10
984 1col. violet 8·50 8·50

223 Civilian and Soldier **224** Flag and Arms

1949. 1st Anniv of Revolution. (a) Postage.
985 **223** 8c. blue 30 10

(b) Air. Centres in blue and yellow.
986 **224** 5c. brown 15 10
987 10c. green 25 10
988 15c. violet 30 10
989 1col. red 40 25
990 5col. purple 3·75 2·75

225 Isabella the Catholic

1951. Air. 500th Birth Anniv of Isabella the Catholic. Backgrounds in blue, red and yellow.
991 **225** 10c. green 40 10
992 20c. violet 40 20
993 40c. red 40 20
994 1col. brown 90 40

226 **227**

1952. 1948 Revolution and 1950 Constitution. (a) Postage. Wreath in green.
995 **226** 1c. green 10 10
996 2c. purple 10 10
997 5c. brown 10 10
998 10c. yellow 10 10
999 20c. green 20 15
1000 1col. red 70 55

(b) Air. Flag in blue.
1001 **227** 10c. blue 10 10
1002 15c. brown 20 10
1003 20c. blue 20 10
1004 25c. grey 20 10
1005 40c. violet 40 30
1006 1col. orange 50 30
1007 2col. brown 1·75 1·25
1008 5col. blue 1·75 65

1952. Surch in figures and words (No. 1009) or in figures only (remainder). (a) Postage.
1009 – 2c. on 3c. violet (952) 10 10
1010 – 2c. on 8c. blue (954) 15 10
1011 – 2c. on 12c. brn (959) 15 10
1012 **217** 2c. on 14c. blue 15 10
1013 – 3c. on 8c. blue (954) 15 10
1014 – 5c. on 8c. blue (954) 15 10
1015 – 5c. on 12c. brn (959) 15 10
1016 – 7c. on 8c. blue (954) 15 10
1017 **217** 10c. on 14c. blue 15 15
1018 – 10c. on 50c. blk (957) 20 15

(b) Air.
1019 – 20c. on 25c. pur (935) 25 20

230 Jose Marti **232** Signing Act of Independence

233 Campanile of Our Saviour **234** General Barrios

1953. Birth Centenary of Marti.
1020 **230** 1c. red (postage) 10 10
1021 2c. green 15 10
1022 10c. blue 15 10
1023 10c. violet (air) 20 15
1024 20c. brown 20 15
1025 1col. orange 50 30

1953. 4th Pan-American Social Medicine Congress. Nos. 952 and 953 optd **"IV Congreso Medico Social Panamericano 16/19 Abril, 1953"**.
1026 3c. violet (postage) 15 10
1027 25c. purple (air) 40 25

1953. Independence.
1028 **232** 1c. red (postage) 10 10
1029 2c. turquoise 10 10
1030 3c. violet 10 10
1031 5c. blue 10 10
1032 7c. brown 10 10
1033 10c. ochre 20 10
1034 20c. orange 25 20
1035 50c. green 60 25
1036 1col. grey 90 65
1037 **233** 5c. red (air) 10 10
1038 10c. turquoise 10 10
1039 20c. blue 20 15
1040 1col. violet 50 35

1953. Optd **C de C**.
1041 **234** 1c. green 10 10
1042 2c. blue 10 10
1043 – 3c. green 10 10
1044 **234** 5c. red 10 10
1045 – 7c. blue 15 10
1046 – 10c. red 15 10
1047 **234** 20c. violet 20 15
1048 – 22c. violet 25 20
PORTRAIT: 3c., 7c., 10c., 22c. Gen. Morazan.

235 **236**

237 General Barrios Square **238** Balboa Park

1954.
1049 A 1c. red & olive (postage) 10 10
1050 **237** 1c. violet 10 10
1051 B 1c. olive and green 10 10
1052 **235** 2c. red 15 10
1053 **236** 2c. red 15 10
1054 **237** 2c. green and blue 15 10
1055 F 3c. slate and blue 15 10
1056 C 3c. green and blue 15 10
1057 I 3c. lake 15 10
1058 F 5c. violet and blue 15 10
1059 I 5c. green 15 10
1060 C 7c. brown and buff 15 10
1061 B 7c. green and blue 20 10
1062 **238** 7c. red and brown 15 10
1063 G 10c. blue, brown & red 15 10
1064 **236** 10c. turquoise 15 10
1065 D 10c. lake and pink 15 10
1066 H 20c. orange and buff 35 15
1067 E 22c. blue 1·00 35
1068 J 50c. black and drab 45 35
1069 G 1col. blue, brn & chest 90 55
1070 E 1col. blue 1·25 35
1071 **235** 5c. red (air) 20 10
1072 B 5c. brown and buff 30 10
1073 G 10c. blue, green & emer 25 10
1074 **237** 10c. olive and grey 25 10
1075 E 10c. red 55 10
1076 **238** 10c. violet and brown 25 10
1077 I 10c. blue 30 10
1078 D 15c. slate and blue 40 15

1079 A 20c. violet and slate 45 15
1080 E 25c. green and blue 90 15
1081 H 30c. red and pink 45 15
1082 J 40c. chestnut & brown 50 35
1083 **236** 80c. lake 1·00 65
1084 C 1col. red and pink 1·25 65
1085 **236** 2col. orange 2·25 65

DESIGNS—$32\frac{1}{2}\times22\frac{1}{2}$ mm: A, Litoral Bridge; B, Fishing boats; C, Izalco Volcano and Atecosol Baths; D, Lake Ilopango and Apulo Baths; E, "Fle-Ja-Lis" (coastguard cutter). $37\frac{1}{2}\times22\frac{1}{2}$ mm: F, Guayabo Dam; G, Six Prime Ministers and flag of O.D.E.C.A.; H, Workers' houses. $22\frac{1}{2}\times32\frac{1}{2}$ mm: I, Gen. Arce. $21\times35\frac{1}{2}$ mm: J, Sonsonate–Puerto Acajutla Highway.

239 Captain General Barrios

240 Gathering Coffee Beans

1956.
1086 **239** 1c. red (postage) 10 10
1087 2c. green 15 10
1088 3c. blue 15 10
1089 20c. violet 20 15
1090 20c. brown (air) 20 15
1091 30c. lake 25 25

1956. Centenary of Santa Ana.
1092 **240** 3c. brown (postage) 10 10
1093 5c. orange 15 10
1094 10c. blue 20 15
1095 2col. red 1·25 75
1096 5c. brown (air) 10 10
1097 10c. green 10 10
1098 40c. purple 25 20
1099 80c. green 45 30
1100 5col. slate 2·50 1·50

241

1956. Centenary of Chalatenango Province.
1101 **241** 2c. blue (postage) 15 10
1102 7c. red 35 25
1103 50c. brown 55 40
1104 10c. red (air) 10 10
1105 15c. orange 15 10
1106 20c. olive 15 10
1107 25c. lilac 35 25
1108 50c. brown 55 35
1109 1col. blue 60 50

242 Arms of Nueva San Salvador

1957. Centenary of Nueva San Salvador City.
1110 **242** 1c. red (postage) 10 10
1111 2c. green 10 10
1112 3c. violet 10 10
1113 7c. orange 35 35
1114 10c. blue 15 10
1115 50c. brown 40 40
1116 1col. red 60 50
1117 10c. salmon (air) 15 10
1118 20c. red 20 10
1119 50c. red 35 30
1120 1col. green 60 35
1121 2col. red 1·50 90

1957. Surch.
1121a **242** 1c. on 2c. green 10 10
1121b 5c. on 7c. orange 20 15
1122 C 6c. on 7c. brown and buff (No. 1060) 25 15
1123 B 6c. on 7c. green and blue (No. 1061) 30 15
1124 **241** 6c. on 7c. red 20 10
1125 **242** 6c. on 7c. orange 25 15

244 Salvador Hotel

1958. Salvador Hotel Commem. Centre mult, frame colour below.
1126 **244** 3c. brown 10 10
1127 6c. red 10 10
1128 10c. blue 10 10
1129 15c. green 15 10
1130 20c. violet 25 15
1131 30c. green 35 25

245 Presidents Eisenhower and Lemus

1959. Visit of Pres. Lemus to U.S. Flags in red and blue. Portraits in brown.
1132 **245** 3c. pink & blue (postage) 15 10
1133 6c. green and blue 15 10
1134 10c. red and blue 20 10
1135 15c. orge & blue (air) 20 15
1136 20c. green and blue 25 15
1137 30c. red and blue 30 25

1960. 20th Anniv of Salvador Philatelic Society. Optd **5 Enero 1960 XX Aniversario Fundacion Sociedad Filatelica de El Salvador**.
1138 **242** 2c. green 10 10

1960. Air. World Refugee Year. Optd **ANO MUNDIAL DE LOS REFUGIADOS 1959-1960**.
1139 **240** 10c. green 25 20

248 Block of Flats

249 Poinsettias

1960. "I.V.U." Building Project. Centres multicoloured.
1140 **248** 10c. red 10 10
1141 15c. purple 15 10
1142 25c. green 20 15
1143 30c. turquoise 25 15
1144 40c. olive 35 25
1145 80c. blue 55 45

1960. Christmas. Flowers in yellow, red and green. Background colours given.
1146 **249** 3c. yellow (postage) 10 10
1147 6c. orange 15 10
1148 10c. blue 20 10
1149 15c. blue 25 15
1150 20c. mauve (air) 35 15
1151 30c. grey 40 25
1152 40c. grey 40 35
1153 50c. salmon 65 35

250 Fathers Nicolas, Vincent and Manuel Aguilar

1961. 150th Anniv of Revolution against Spain.
1154 **250** 1c. sepia and grey 10 10
1155 2c. brown and pink 10 10
1156 – 5c. green and brown 15 10
1157 – 6c. sepia and mauve 15 10
1158 – 10c. sepia and blue 15 10
1159 – 20c. sepia and violet 25 10
1160 – 30c. mauve and blue 35 15
1161 – 40c. sepia and brown 50 20
1162 – 50c. sepia & turquoise 70 40
1163 – 80c. blue and grey 1·00 60

DESIGNS: 5c., 6c. Manuel Arce, Jose Delgado and Juan Rodriguez; 10c., 20c. Pedro Castillo, Domingo de Lara and Santiago Celis; 30c., 40c. Parochial Church of San Salvador, 1808; 50c., 80c. Monument, Plaza Libertad.

1962. 3rd Central American Industrial Exn. Nos. 1048, 1069, 1116 and 1121 optd **"III Exposicion Industrial Centroamericana Diciembre de 1962"**. Nos. 1166/7 additionally optd **AEREO**.
1165 – 22c. violet (postage) 20 15
1166 G 1col. blue, brown and chestnut (air) 50 45
1167 **242** 1col. red 50 45
1168 2col. red 1·00 85

1962. Nos. 1161/2, 1141 and 1070 surch.
1169 – 6c. on 40c. sep & brn 25 10
1170 – 6c. on 50c. sep & turq 25 10
1164 **248** 10c. on 15c. purple 25 10
1171 E 10c. on 1col. blue 40 10

1963. Surch in figures.
1172 **248** 6c. on 15c. purple (postage) 25 10
1173 – 10c. on 50c. sepia and turquoise (No. 1162) 25 10
1174 – 10c. on 80c. blue and grey (No. 1163) (air) 25 10
1175 **242** 10c. on 1col. green 1·10 15
1176 **249** 10c. on 30c. grey 15 10
1177 **242** 10c. on 1col. red (No. 1167) 15 15
1178 10c. on 2col. red (No. 1168) 1·10 10

1963. Freedom from Hunger. No. 1161 optd **CAMPANA MUNDIAL CONTRA EL HAMBRE** and Campaign emblem.
1179 40c. sepia and brown 60 40

259 Coyote

260 Statue of Christ on Globe

1963. Fauna. Multicoloured.
1180 1c. Type **259** (postage) 25 10
1181 2c. Black spider monkey (vert) 25 10
1182 3c. Common racoon 25 10
1183 5c. King vulture (vert) 1·10 25
1184 6c. Northern coati 25 10
1185 10c. Kinkajou 25 10
1186 5c. As No. 1183 (vert) (air) 1·10 25
1187 6c. Yellow-headed amazon (vert) 1·10 25
1188 10c. Spotted-breasted oriole 1·10 25
1189 20c. Turquoise-browed motmot 1·60 35
1190 30c. Great-tailed grackle 2·10 50
1191 40c. Great curassow (vert) 3·75 60
1192 50c. White-throated magpie-jay 4·00 70
1193 80c. Golden-fronted woodpecker (vert) 6·50 1·75

1964. 2nd National Eucharistic Congress, San Salvador.
1194 **260** 6c. bl & brn (postage) 10 10
1195 10c. blue and bistre 10 10
1196 10c. slate & blue (air) 10 10
1197 25c. blue and red 20 15

261 President Kennedy

262 Water-lily

1964. Pres. Kennedy Commem.
1198 **261** 6c. blk & stone (postage) 10 10
1199 10c. black and drab 15 10
1200 50c. black and pink 50 30
1201 15c. black & grey (air) 20 15
1202 20c. black and green 25 15
1203 40c. black and yellow 40 30

1965. Flora. Multicoloured.
1204 3c. Type **262** (postage) 10 10
1205 5c. "Maquilishuat" 10 10
1206 6c. "Cinco Negritos" 10 10
1207 30c. Hydrangea 20 15
1208 50c. "Maguey" 60 25
1209 60c. Geranium 70 25
1210 10c. Rose (air) 10 10
1211 15c. "Platanillo" 15 10
1212 25c. "San Jose" 20 15
1213 40c. Hibiscus 25 25
1214 45c. Bougainvillea 40 25
1215 70c. "Flor de Fuego" 55 45

263 I.C.Y. Emblem

1965. International Co-operation Year. Laurel in gold.
1216 **263** 5c. brn & yell (postage) 10 10
1217 6c. brown and red 10 10
1218 10c. brown and grey 10 10
1219 15c. brn & blue (air) 10 10
1220 30c. brown and violet 25 15
1221 50c. brown and orange 35 30

1965. Death Centenary of Captain General Barrios. No. 1163 optd **1er. Centenario Muerte Cap. Gral. Gerardo Barrios 1865 29 de Agosto 1965**.
1222 80c. blue and grey 70 40

265 F. A. Gavidia (philosopher)

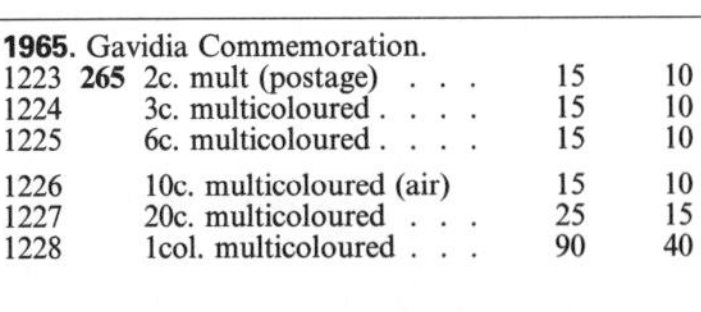

1965. Gavidia Commemoration.
1223 **265** 2c. mult (postage) 15 10
1224 3c. multicoloured 15 10
1225 6c. multicoloured 15 10
1226 10c. multicoloured (air) 15 10
1227 20c. multicoloured 25 15
1228 1col. multicoloured 90 40

1965. Birth Centenary of Dr. M. E. Araujo. Optd **1865 12 de Octubre 1965 Dr. Manuel Enrique Araujo.** Laurel in gold.
1229 **263** 10c. brn & grey (postage) 10 10
1230 50c. brown & orge (air) 45 30

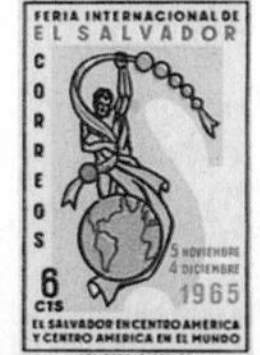

267 Fair Emblem

268 W.H.O. Building

1965. International Fair, El Salvador.
1231 **267** 6c. mult (postage) 10 10
1232 10c. multicoloured 10 10
1233 20c. multicoloured 20 15
1234 20c. multicoloured (air) 15 10
1235 80c. multicoloured 50 30
1236 5col. multicoloured 2·50 1·75

1966. Inaug of W.H.O. Headquarters, Geneva.
1237 **268** 15c. mult (postage) 15 10
1238 50c. multicoloured (air) 45 30

1966. Air. 150th Birth Anniv of St. Juan Bosco. No. 1197 optd **1816 1966 150 anos Nacimiento San Juan Bosco**.
1239 **260** 25c. blue and red 35 25

1966. Civic Commem of Independence Month. No. 1163 optd **Mes de Conmemoracion Civica de la Independencia Centroamericana 15 Sept. 1821 1966**.
1240 80c. ultramarine and grey 55 45

271 UNESCO Emblem

1966. 20th Anniv of UNESCO.
1241 **271** 20c. blue, grey and black (postage) 15 15
1242 1col. blue, green & blk 60 30
1243 30c. blue, brown and black (air) 35 15
1244 2col. blue, green & blk 1·25 75

272 Map, Cogwheels and Flags

1966. 2nd International Fair, El Salvador.
1245 **272** 6c. mult (postage) 10 10
1246 10c. multicoloured 10 10
1247 15c. multicoloured (air) 15 10
1248 20c. multicoloured 20 15
1249 60c. multicoloured 50 35

1967. Air. 9th International Catholic Education Congress. No. 1197 optd **IX-Congreso Interamericano de Educacion Catolica 4 Enero 1967**.
1250 **260** 25c. blue and red 35 20

274 Father Canas pleading for Slaves

1967. Birth Centenary of Father J. S. Canas y Villacorta (slavery emancipator).
1251 **274** 6c. mult (postage) 10 10
1252 10c. multicoloured 10 10

1253 5c. mult (air) 10 10
1254 45c. multicoloured . . . 55 35

1967. 15th Lions Convention, El Salvador. No. 1161 optd **"XV Convencion de Clubes de Leones,** etc.
1255 40c. sepia and brown . . . 45 20

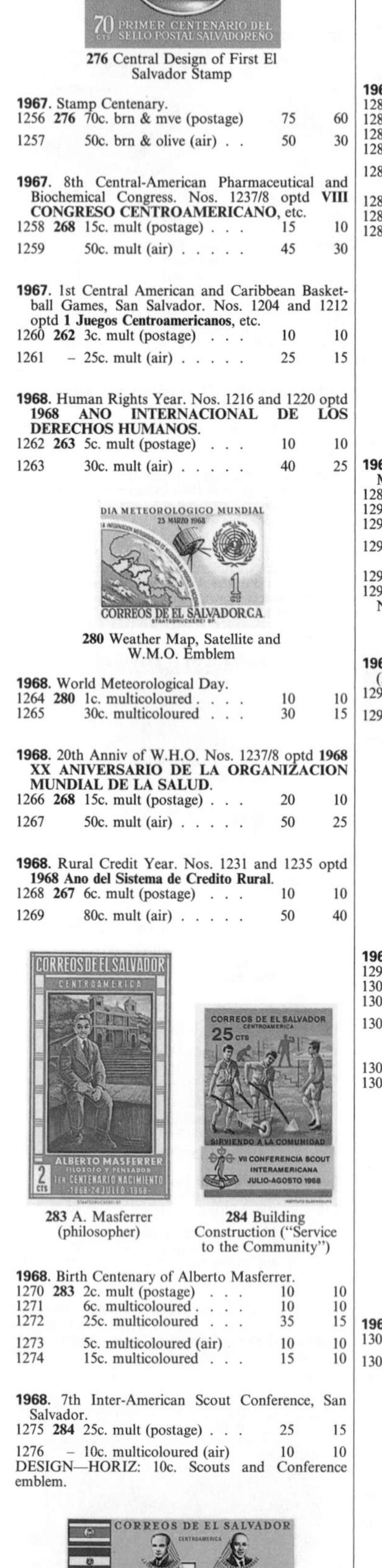

276 Central Design of First El Salvador Stamp

1967. Stamp Centenary.
1256 **276** 70c. brn & mve (postage) 75 60
1257 50c. brn & olive (air) . . 50 30

1967. 8th Central-American Pharmaceutical and Biochemical Congress. Nos. 1237/8 optd **VIII CONGRESO CENTROAMERICANO,** etc.
1258 **268** 15c. mult (postage) . . . 15 10
1259 50c. mult (air) 45 30

1967. 1st Central American and Caribbean Basketball Games, San Salvador. Nos. 1204 and 1212 optd **1 Juegos Centroamericanos,** etc.
1260 **262** 3c. mult (postage) . . . 10 10
1261 – 25c. mult (air) 25 15

1968. Human Rights Year. Nos. 1216 and 1220 optd **1968 ANO INTERNACIONAL DE LOS DERECHOS HUMANOS.**
1262 **263** 5c. mult (postage) . . . 10 10
1263 30c. mult (air) 40 25

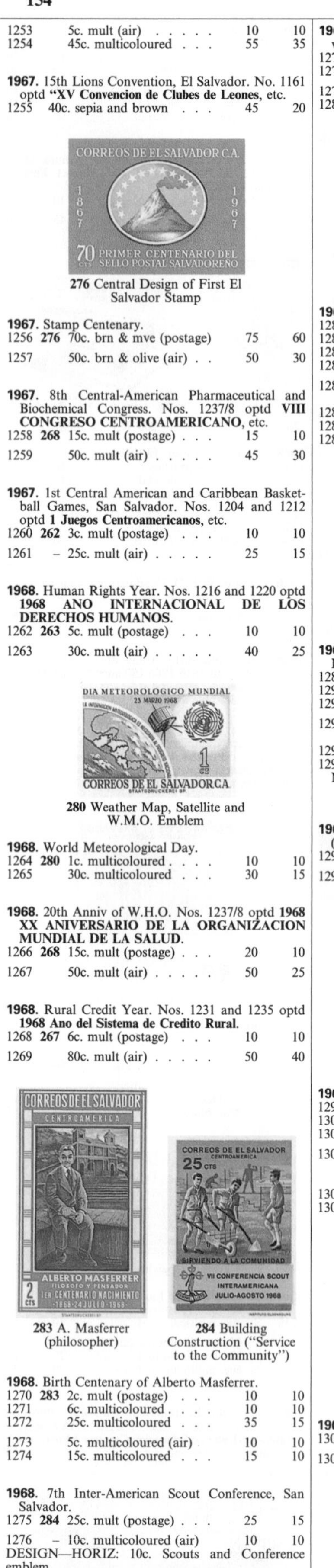

280 Weather Map, Satellite and W.M.O. Emblem

1968. World Meteorological Day.
1264 **280** 1c. multicoloured 10 10
1265 30c. multicoloured . . . 30 15

1968. 20th Anniv of W.H.O. Nos. 1237/8 optd **1968 XX ANIVERSARIO DE LA ORGANIZACION MUNDIAL DE LA SALUD.**
1266 **268** 15c. mult (postage) . . . 20 10
1267 50c. mult (air) 50 25

1968. Rural Credit Year. Nos. 1231 and 1235 optd **1968 Ano del Sistema de Credito Rural.**
1268 **267** 6c. mult (postage) . . . 10 10
1269 80c. mult (air) 50 40

283 A. Masferrer (philosopher)
284 Building Construction ("Service to the Community")

1968. Birth Centenary of Alberto Masferrer.
1270 **283** 2c. mult (postage) . . . 10 10
1271 6c. multicoloured 10 10
1272 25c. multicoloured . . . 35 15
1273 5c. multicoloured (air) 10 10
1274 15c. multicoloured . . . 15 10

1968. 7th Inter-American Scout Conference, San Salvador.
1275 **284** 25c. mult (postage) . . . 25 15
1276 – 10c. multicoloured (air) 10 10
DESIGN—HORIZ: 10c. Scouts and Conference emblem.

285 Map, Presidents and Flags

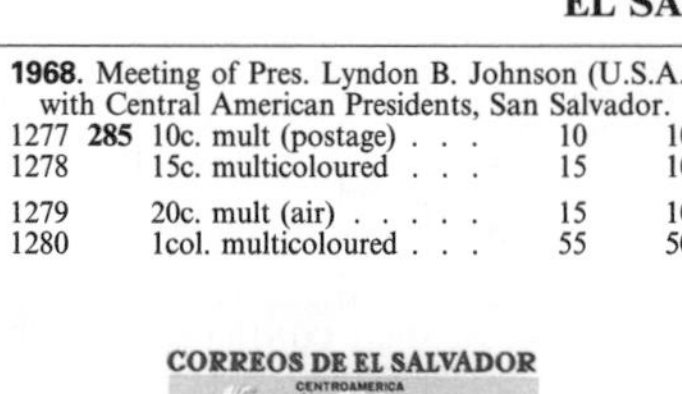

1968. Meeting of Pres. Lyndon B. Johnson (U.S.A.) with Central American Presidents, San Salvador.
1277 **285** 10c. mult (postage) . . . 10 10
1278 15c. multicoloured . . . 15 10
1279 20c. mult (air) 15 10
1280 1col. multicoloured . . . 55 50

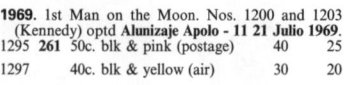

286 "Heliconius charithonius"

1969. Butterflies. Multicoloured.
1281 5c. Type **286** (postage) . . . 10 10
1282 10c. "Diaethria astala" . . . 15 10
1283 30c. "Heliconius hortense" 40 20
1284 50c. "Pyrrhogyra arge" . . 55 35
1285 20c. "Ageronia amphinome" (air) 25 10
1286 1col. "Smyrna karkwinskii" 1·10 50
1287 2col. "Papilio photinus" . . 2·10 1·10
1288 10col. "Papilio consus" . . 9·75 5·00

287 Red Cross Activities

1969. 50th Anniv of League of Red Cross Societies. Multicoloured.
1289 10c. Type **287** (postage) . . 10 10
1290 20c. Type **287** 15 10
1291 40c. Type **287** 25 15
1292 30c. Red Cross emblems (air) 25 15
1293 1col. As No. 1292 . . . . . 60 45
1294 4col. As No. 1292 . . . . . 2·40 1·75
Nos. 1292/4 are smaller, size 34 × 25 mm.

1969. 1st Man on the Moon. Nos. 1200 and 1203 (Kennedy) optd **Alunizaje Apolo - 11 21 Julio 1969.**
1295 **261** 50c. blk & pink (postage) 40 25
1297 40c. blk & yellow (air) 30 20

289 Social Security Hospital

1969. Salvador Hospitals. Multicoloured.
1299 6c. Type **289** (postage) . . . 10 10
1300 10c. Type **289** 10 10
1301 30c. Type **289** 25 15
1302 1col. Benjamin Bloom Children's Hospital, San Salvador (air) 60 45
1303 2col. As No. 1302 . . . . . 1·25 70
1304 5col. As No. 1302 . . . . . 3·00 1·75

290 I.L.O. Emblem

1969. 50th Anniv of I.L.O.
1305 **290** 10c. mult (postage) . . . 10 10
1306 50c. multicoloured (air) 40 25

291 Los Chorros Baths

1969. Tourism. Multicoloured.
1307 10c. Type **291** (postage) . . 10 10
1308 40c. Jaltepeque estuary . . . 60 25
1309 80c. Fountains, Amapulapa 70 45
1310 20c. Devil's Gate (air) . . . 15 10
1311 35c. Gardens, Ichanmichen 25 15
1312 60c. Port of Acajutla . . . 50 25

292 "Euchroma gigantea"

1970. Insects. Multicoloured.
1313 5c. Type **292** (postage) . . . 10 10
1314 25c. "Pterophylla" sp. . . . 15 15
1315 30c. "Chlorion cyaneum" 30 20
1316 2col. "Eulema dimidiata" (air) . . . . 2·00 95
1317 3col. "Elaterida" . . . . . 2·75 1·50
1318 4col. "Tenodora sinensis" 3·50 2·00

293 Map, Emblem and Arms

1970. "Human Rights".
1319 **293** 10c. mult (postage) . . . 10 10
1320 40c. multicoloured . . . 45 20
1321 – 20c. multicoloured (air) 15 10
1322 – 80c. multicoloured . . . 50 40
DESIGN—VERT: Nos. 1321/2 are similar to Type **293**.

294 Infantry with National Flag

1970. Army Day. Multicoloured.
1323 10c. Type **294** (postage) . . 10 10
1324 30c. Anti-aircraft gun position 30 15
1325 20c. Fighter aircraft (air) . . 15 10
1326 40c. Artillery gun and crew 35 15
1327 50c. "Nohaba" (coastguard patrol boat) . . . . . . 2·00 35

295 Brazilian Team

1970. Air. World Cup Football Championship, Mexico. National Teams. Multicoloured.
1328 1col. Belgium 70 50
1329 1col. Type **295** 70 50
1330 1col. Bulgaria 70 50
1331 1col. Czechoslovakia 70 50
1332 1col. El Salvador 70 50
1333 1col. England 70 50
1334 1col. West Germany 70 50
1335 1col. Israel 70 50
1336 1col. Italy 70 50
1337 1col. Mexico 70 50
1338 1col. Morocco 70 50
1339 1col. Peru 70 50
1340 1col. Rumania 70 50
1341 1col. Russia 70 50
1342 1col. Sweden 70 50
1343 1col. Uruguay 70 50

296 Lottery Building
297 Education Year and U.N. Emblems

1970. Centenary of National Lottery.
1344 **296** 20c. mult (postage) . . . 20 10
1345 80c. multicoloured (air) 50 35

1970. International Education Year.
1346 **297** 50c. mult (postage) . . . 40 15
1347 1col. multicoloured . . . 60 40
1348 20c. multicoloured (air) 15 10
1349 2col. multicoloured . . . 1·25 70

298 Globe and Fair Symbols

1970. 4th International Fair, El Salvador.
1350 **298** 5c. mult (postage) . . . 10 10
1351 10c. multicoloured . . . 10 10
1352 20c. multicoloured (air) 25 10
1353 30c. multicoloured . . . 35 15

1970. Cent of National Library. Nos. 1212/3 optd **Ano del Centenario de la Biblioteca Nacional 1970.**
1354 **283** 25c. mult (postage) . . . 20 15
1355 5c. mult (air) 10 10

300 Beethoven and Music

1971. 2nd Int Music Festival, San Salvador.
1356 **300** 50c. brown, yellow and green (postage) . . . 45 25
1357 – 40c. multicoloured (air) 45 25
DESIGN: 40c. Bach, manuscript and harp.

301 Maria Elena Sol
302 Michelangelo's "Pieta"

1971. Maria Elena Sol's Election as "World Tourism Queen", Punta del Este, Uruguay.
1358 **301** 10c. mult (postage) . . . 10 10
1359 30c. multicoloured . . . 25 15
1360 20c. mult (air) 15 10
1361 60c. multicoloured . . . 40 30

1971. Mothers' Day.
1362 **302** 10c. pur & pink (post) 10 10
1363 40c. pur & grn (air) . . 45 20

1971. 104th Anniv of National Police Force. Nos. 1320/1 optd **1867 CIV Aniversario Fundacion de la Policia Nacional 6-Julio 1971.**
1364 **293** 40c. mult (postage) . . . 45 25
1365 – 20c. mult (air) 25 10

304 Tiger Shark

1971. Fishes. Multicoloured.
1366 10c. Type **304** (postage) . . 15 10
1367 40c. Swordfish 35 15
1368 30c. Small-toothed sawfish (air) 35 15
1369 1col. Sailfish 70 50

305 Izalco Church

1971. Churches. Multicoloured.
1370 20c. Type **305** (postage) . . 25 10
1371 30c. Sonsonate Church . . . 40 15

1372 15c. Metapan Church (air) 15 10
1373 70c. Panchimalco Church 45 25

1971. Air. 20th Anniv of El Salvador Navy. No. 1327 optd **1951-12 Octubre-1971 XX Aniversario MARINA NACIONAL.**
1374 50c. multicoloured 85 30

307 Declaration of Independence

1971. 150th Anniv of Central American Independence.
1375 **307** 5c. blk & grn (postage) 10 10
1376 – 10c. black and purple 10 10
1377 – 15c. black and red 10 10
1378 – 20c. black and mauve 15 10
1379 – 30c. black & blue (air) 25 15
1380 – 40c. black and brown 40 20
1381 – 50c. black and yellow 30 25
1382 – 60c. black and grey 40 35
DESIGNS: Nos. 1376/82 as Type **307**, but showing different manuscripts.

1972. Air. 5th Int Fair, El Salvador. No. 1235 optd **V Feria Internacional 3-20 Noviembre de 1972.**
1384 **267** 80c. multicoloured 1·25 40

1972. American Tourist Year. No. 1359 optd **1972 Ano del Turismo de las Americas.**
1385 **301** 30c. multicoloured 25 10

1972. Air. 30th Anniv of Inter-American Agricultural Science Institute. No. 1221 optd **1972 - XXX Aniversario Creacion Instituto Interamericano de Ciencias Agricolas.**
1386 **263** 50c. multicoloured 30 25

1973. 3rd Int Music Festival. Nos. 1356/7 optd **III Festival Internacional de Musica 9 - 25 Febrero - 1973.**
1387 **300** 50c. brown, yellow and green (postage) 35 20
1388 – 40c. multicoloured (air) 40 20

312 Lions Emblem **318** Institute Emblem

314 Hurdling

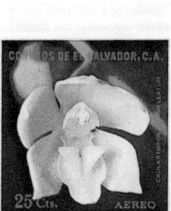

1973. 31st Convention of Lions International District D.
1389 **312** 10c. mult (postage) 10 10
1390 25c. multicoloured 15 10
1391 – 20c. mult (air) 20 10
1392 – 40c. multicoloured 40 15
DESIGN: 20c., 40c. Map of Central America.

1973. 50th Anniv of El Salvador Air Force. No. 1324 optd **1923 1973 50 ANOS FUNDACION FUERZA AEREA.**
1393 30c. multicoloured 25 15

1973. Olympic Games, Munich (1972). Mult.
1394 5c. Type **314** (postage) 10 10
1395 10c. High-jumping 10 10
1396 25c. Running 15 10
1397 60c. Pole-vaulting 35 20
1398 20c. Throwing the javelin (air) 15 10
1399 80c. Throwing the discus 45 35
1400 1col. Throwing the hammer 55 40
1401 2col. Putting the shot 1·10 65

1973. Nos. 1256/7 surch.
1402 **276** 10c. on 70c. brown and mauve (postage) 10 10
1403 25c. on 50c. brown and olive (air) 15 10

1973. 150th Anniv of Slaves' Liberation in Central America. Nos. 1251 and 1254 surch **1823 – 1973 150 Aniversario Liberacion Esclavos en Centroamerica** and value.
1404 **274** 5c. on 6c. multicoloured 10 10
1405 10c. on 45c. mult 10 10
No. 1405 has the word "AEREO" obliterated.

1974. Nos. 1198 and 1238 surch.
1407 **261** 5c. on 6c. black and stone (postage) 10 10
1408 **268** 25c. on 50c. mult (air) 15 10

1974. 10th Anniv of Institute for the Rehabilitation of Invalids.
1409 **318** 10c. mult (postage) 10 10
1410 25c. multicoloured (air) 15 10

1974. Air. No. 1235 surch.
1411 **267** 10c. on 80c. mult 10 10

1974. Air. West Germany's Victory in World Cup Football Championship. Nos. 1328/43 optd **ALEMANIA 1974.**
1412 1col. Belgium 60 50
1413 1col. Type **158** 60 50
1414 1col. Bulgaria 60 50
1415 1col. Czechoslovakia 60 50
1416 1col. El Salvador 60 50
1417 1col. England 60 50
1418 1col. West Germany 60 50
1419 1col. Israel 60 50
1420 1col. Italy 60 50
1421 1col. Mexico 60 50
1422 1col. Morocco 60 50
1423 1col. Peru 60 50
1424 1col. Rumania 60 50
1425 1col. Russia 60 50
1426 1col. Sweden 60 50
1427 1col. Uruguay 60 50

1974. No. 1271 surch.
1428 **283** 5c. on 6c. multicoloured 10 10

322 Interpol Headquarters, Paris **323** F.A.O. and W.F.P. Emblems

1974. 50th Anniv of International Criminal Police Organization (Interpol).
1429 **322** 10c. mult (postage) 10 10
1430 25c. multicoloured (air) 15 10

1974. 10th Anniv of World Food Programme.
1431 **323** 10c. gold, turquoise and blue (postage) 10 10
1432 25c. gold, turquoise and blue (air) 15 10

1974. Surch.
1432a **271** 25c. on 1col. blue, green & black (postage) 15 10
1433 **276** 10c. on 50c. brown and olive (air) 10 10
1434 **271** 25c. on 2col. blue, green and black 45 25

1974. 12th Central American and Caribbean Chess Tournament. Surch **XII Serie Ajedrez de Centro America y del Caribe Oct. 1974.**
1435 **265** 5c. on 6c. mult 10 10

1974. Surch.
1436 **289** 5c. on 6c. mult (postage) 10 10
1437 **265** 10c. on 3c. mult 10 10
1438 – 10c. on 45c. mult (No. 1214) (air) 10 10
1439 – 10c. on 70c. mult (No. 1215) 10 10
1440 – 25c. on 2col. mult (No. 1287) 20 10
1441 – 25c. on 1col. mult (No. 1293) 20 15
1442 – 25c. on 4col. mult (No. 1294) 20 15
1443 – 25c. on 5col. mult (No. 1304) 20 15

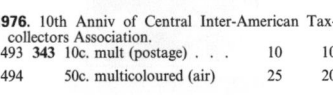

327 25-cent Silver Coin, 1914

1974. El Salvador Coins. Multicoloured.
1445 10c. Type **327** (postage) 10 10
1446 15c. 50-cent silver coin, 1953 10 10
1447 25c. 25-cent silver coin, 1943 15 10
1448 30c. 1-centavo copper coin, 1892 15 10
1449 20c. 1-peso silver coin, 1892 (air) 10 10
1450 40c. 20-cent silver coin, 1828 20 15
1451 50c. 20-peso gold coin, 1892 25 20
1452 60c. 20-col. gold coin, 1925 35 25

328 U.P.U. Emblem

1975. Centenary of U.P.U.
1453 **328** 10c. mult (postage) 10 10
1454 60c. multicoloured 35 20
1455 25c. mult (air) 15 10
1456 30c. multicoloured 15 15

329 Acajutla Harbour

1975. Opening of Acajutla Port.
1457 **329** 10c. mult (postage) 10 10
1458 15c. mult (air) 10 10

331 Central Post Office, San Salvador

1975.
1459 **331** 10c. mult (postage) 10 10
1460 25c. mult (air) 15 10

332 Map of El Salvador and the Americas

1975. "Miss Universe" Contest.
1461 **332** 10c. mult (postage) 10 10
1462 40c. multicoloured 35 25
1463 25c. mult (air) 25 15
1464 60c. multicoloured 50 35

333 Claudia Lars (poet) **334** Nurses with Patient

1975. International Women's Year.
1465 **333** 10c. blue & yellow (post) 10 10
1466 15c. blue & lt blue (air) 10 10
1467 – 25c. blue & green 15 10
DESIGN: 25c. I.W.Y. emblem.

1975. Honouring Nursing Profession.
1468 **334** 10c. mult (postage) 10 10
1469 25c. mult (air) 25 15

335 Conference Emblem **337** Congress Emblem and Flags

1975. 15th Conference of Inter-American Security Printers Federation, San Salvador.
1470 **335** 10c. mult (postage) 10 10
1471 30c. mult (air) 15 15

1975. 16th Central American Medical Congress, San Salvador. Optd **XVI CONGRESO MEDICO CENTROAMERICANO SAN SALVADOR, EL SALVADOR DIC. 10-13, 1975.**
1472 **268** 15c. multicoloured 15 10

1975. 8th Iberian and Latin-American Dermatological Congress, El Salvador.
1473 **337** 15c. mult (postage) 10 10
1474 50c. multicoloured 25 20
1475 20c. mult (air) 15 10
1476 30c. multicoloured 15 15

338 Congress Emblem **339** UNICEF Emblem

1975. 7th Latin-American Charity Congress, San Salvador.
1477 **338** 10c. brn & red (postage) 10 10
1478 20c. lt blue & blue (air) 15 10

1975. Air. 25th Anniv (1971) of UNICEF.
1479 **339** 15c. silver and green 10 10
1480 20c. silver and red 15 10

1976. Air. Nos. 1316/18 surch.
1481 25c. on 2col. multicoloured 20 15
1482 25c. on 3col. multicoloured 20 15
1483 25c. on 4col. multicoloured 20 15

341 "Caularthron bilamellatum" **343** Map of El Salvador

1976. Air. Orchids. Multicoloured.
1484 25c. Type **341** 20 10
1485 25c. "Oncidium oliganthum" 20 10
1486 25c. "Epidendrum radicans" 20 10
1487 25c. "Cyrtopodium punctatum" 20 10
1488 25c. "Epidendrum vitellinum" 20 10
1489 25c. "Pleurothallis schiedei" 20 10
1490 25c. "Lycaste cruenta" 20 10
1491 25c. "Spiranthes speciosa" 20 10

1976. "Cencamex '76" 3rd Nurses' Congress. Surch **III CONGRESO ENFERMERIA CENCAMEX 76.**
1492 **334** 10c. multicoloured 10 10

1976. 10th Anniv of Central Inter-American Tax-collectors Association.
1493 **343** 10c. mult (postage) 10 10
1494 50c. multicoloured (air) 25 20

344 Torch and Flags of El Salvador and U.S.A.

1976. Bicent of American Revolution. Mult.
1495 10c. Type **344** (postage) 10 10
1496 40c. "Spirit of '76" (A. M. Willard) (vert) 20 15
1497 25c. Type **344** (air) 15 10
1498 5col. As 40c. 2·25 1·50

345 "Crocodylus acutus"

1976. Reptiles. Multicoloured.
1499 10c. Type **345** (postage) . . 10 10
1500 20c. "Iguana iguana rhinolopha" 10 10
1501 30c. "Ctenosaura similis" . . 20 15
1502 15c. "Sceloporus malachiticus" (air) 10 10
1503 25c. "Basiliscus vittatus" . . 15 10
1504 60c. "Anolis sp." 35 25

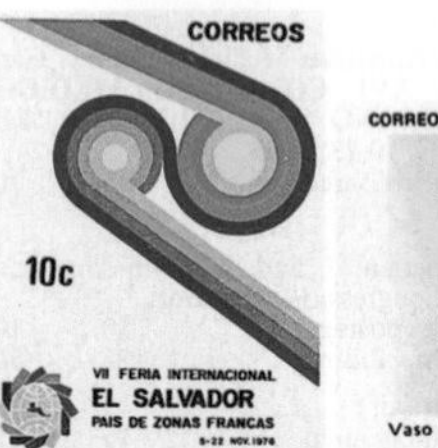

346 Fair Emblem **347** Post-classical Lead Vase (San Salvador)

1976. 7th International Fair.
1505 **346** 10c. mult (postage) . . . 10 10
1506 30c. multicoloured . . . 15 10
1507 25c. multicoloured (air) 15 10
1508 70c. multicoloured . . . 35 25

1976. Pre-Columbian Art. Multicoloured.
1509 10c. Type **347** (postage) . . 10 10
1510 15c. Brazier with classical effigy (Tazumal) 10 10
1511 40c. Vase with classical effigy (Tazumal) 20 15
1512 25c. Brazier with pre-classical effigy (El Trapiche) (air) 15 10
1513 50c. Kettle with pre-classical effigy (Atiquizaya) 25 20
1514 70c. Classical whistling vase (Tazumal) 35 30

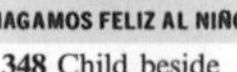

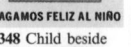

348 Child beside Christmas Tree **349** Rotary Emblem on Map of El Salvador

1976. Christmas.
1515 **348** 10c. mult (post) 10 10
1516 15c. multicoloured . . . 10 10
1517 30c. multicoloured . . . 15 10
1518 40c. multicoloured . . . 20 15
1519 25c. multicoloured (air) 15 10
1520 50c. multicoloured . . . 25 20
1521 60c. multicoloured . . . 35 25
1522 75c. multicoloured . . . 40 30

1977. 50th Anniv of San Salvador Rotary Club.
1523 **349** 10c. gold, bl & blk (post) 10 10
1524 15c. multicoloured . . . 15 10
1525 25c. mult (air) 25 15
1526 1col. multicoloured . . . 60 50

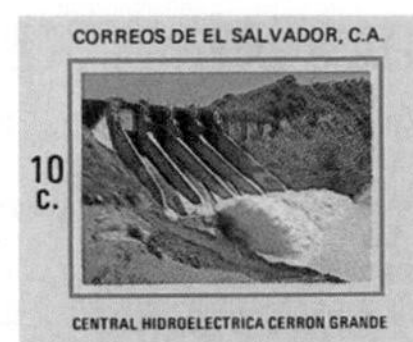

350 Hydro-electric Station, Cerron Grande

1977. Industrial Development. Multicoloured.
1527 10c. Type **350** (postage) . . 10 10
1528 10c. Sugar refinery, Jiboa 10 10
1529 15c. As No. 1528 . . . . . 10 10
1530 30c. Radar station, Izalco (vert) 15 10
1531 25c. As No. 1530 (air) . . . 15 10
1532 50c. As No. 1528 . . . . . 25 20
1533 75c. Type **192** 40 30

1977. Surch.
1534 **283** 15c. on 2c. mult (postage) 10 10
1535 **274** 25c. on 6c. mult 15 10
1536 – 25c. on 80c. mult (No. 1322) (air) . . . 30 15
1537 **274** 30c. on 5c. mult 20 15
1538 40c. on 5c. mult 25 15
1539 50c. on 5c. mult 25 20

352 Microphone and A.S.D.E.R. Emblem

1977. 50th Anniv of Broadcasting in El Salvador.
1540 **352** 10c. mult (postage) . . . 10 10
1541 15c. multicoloured . . . 10 10
1542 20c. multicoloured (air) 20 10
1543 25c. multicoloured . . . 25 15

353 King, Pawn and Championship Emblem **354** Basketball

1977. Air. El Salvador's Victory in Arab Chess Olympiad, Tripoli.
1544 **353** 25c. multicoloured . . . 15 10
1545 50c. multicoloured . . . 25 25

1977. Air. 2nd Central American Games, San Salvador. Multicoloured.
1546 10c. Type **354** 10 10
1547 10c. Football 10 10
1548 15c. Javelin throwing . . . 10 10
1549 15c. Weightlifting 10 10
1550 20c. Boxing (horiz) 10 10
1551 20c. Volleyball 10 10
1552 25c. Baseball 15 10
1553 25c. Softball (horiz) 15 10
1554 30c. Swimming (horiz) . . . 15 10
1555 30c. Fencing (horiz) 15 10
1556 40c. Cycle-racing (horiz) . . 20 15
1557 50c. Rifle-shooting (horiz) 25 20
1558 50c. Tennis (horiz) 25 20
1559 60c. Judo 35 25
1560 75c. Wrestling (horiz) . . . 40 30
1561 1col. Gymnastics (horiz) . . 55 40
1562 1col. Horse-jumping (horiz) 55 40
1563 2col. Table-tennis (horiz) . . 1·10 80

1978. Air. Centenary of Chalchuapa City. No. 1514 optd **CENTENARIO CIUDAD DE CHALCHUAPA 1878-1978.**
1565 70c. Classical whistling vase (Tazumal) 35 30

356 Map of South America and Emblem

1978. Air. World Cup Football Championship, Argentina.
1566 **356** 25c. multicoloured . . . 15 10
1567 60c. multicoloured . . . 35 20
1568 5col. multicoloured . . . 2·40 2·00

357 Wooden Drum

1978. Musical Instruments. Multicoloured.
1569 5c. Type **357** (postage) . . . 10 10
1570 10c. Flutes 10 10
1571 25c. Drum (vert) (air) . . . 15 10
1572 50c. Rattles 25 20
1573 80c. Xylophone 45 30

358 "Man and Engineering"

1978. 4th Nat Engineers' Congress, San Salvador.
1574 **358** 10c. mult (postage) . . . 10 10
1575 25c. multicoloured (air) 15 10

359 Dish Aerials

1978. Inauguration of Izalco Satellite Earth Station.
1576 **359** 10c. mult (postage) . . . 10 10
1577 75c. multicoloured (air) 40 30

360 Softball, Bat and Hemispheres

1978. Air. 4th Women's Softball Championships, San Salvador.
1578 **360** 25c. multicoloured . . . 15 10
1579 1col. multicoloured . . . 55 40

361 Henri Dunant

1978. 150th Birth Anniv of Henri Dunant (founder of Red Cross).
1580 **361** 10c. yellow, black and red (postage) 10 10
1581 25c. turquiose, black and red (air) 15 10

362 Fair Poster

1978. 8th International Fair.
1582 **362** 10c. mult (postage) . . . 10 10
1583 20c. multicoloured . . . 10 10
1584 15c. multicoloured (air) 10 10
1585 25c. multicoloured . . . 15 10

363 Globe as Cotton Boll

1978. 37th Plenary Session of Cotton Growers' Association, San Salvador.
1586 **363** 15c. mult (postage) . . . 10 10
1587 40c. multicoloured (air) 25 15

364 "Nativity with Angel" (stained glass window)

1978. Christmas.
1588 **364** 10c. mult (postage) . . . 10 10
1589 15c. multicoloured . . . 10 10
1590 25c. multicoloured (air) 15 10
1591 1col. multicoloured . . . 55 40

365 Arms of Salvador Athenium

1978. Millenary of Castilian Language.
1592 **365** 5c. mult (postage) . . . 10 10
1593 25c. mult (air) 15 10

366 Four Candles

1979. Four Year Plan "Welfare for All".
1594 **366** 10c. mult (postage) . . . 10 10
1595 15c. multicoloured . . . 10 10
1596 25c. multicoloured (air) 15 10
1597 1col. multicoloured . . . 55 40

367 Torch and Letter beside U.P.U. Statue

1979. Centenary of U.P.U. Membership.
1598 **367** 10c. mult (postage) . . . 10 10
1599 75c. multicoloured (air) 40 30

368 Emblem and "75"

1979. 75th Anniv of Pan-American Health Organization.
1600 **368** 10c. turq & yell (postage) 10 10
1601 25c. turq & rose (air) . . 15 10

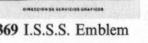

369 I.S.S.S. Emblem **370** Pope John Paul II and Map of Americas

1979. Air. 25th Anniv of Social Insurance Institute (I.S.S.S.).
1602 **369** 25c. blue and black . . . 15 10
1603 60c. mauve and black . . 35 25

1979. Pope John Paul II. Multicoloured.
1604 10c. Type **370** (postage) . . 10 10
1605 20c. Type **370** 15 10
1606 60c. Pope John Paul II and Aztec pyramid (air) . . . 35 25
1607 5col. As 60c. . . . . 2·75 2·10

371 Games Emblem

1979. Air. 8th Pan-American Games, Puerto Rico.
1608 **371** 25c. multicoloured . . . 15 10
1609 40c. multicoloured . . . 25 20
1610 70c. multicoloured . . . 40 30

372 Mastodon **373** J. Cauas (lyric writer) and Chorus of Anthem

1979. Prehistoric Animals. Multicoloured.
1611 10c. Type **372** (postage) . . 10 10
1612 20c. Sabre-toothed tiger . . 15 10
1613 30c. Toxodon 15 15
1614 15c. Mammoth (air) 10 10
1615 25c. Giant sloth (vert) . . . 15 15
1616 2col. Hyenas . . . . 1·10 70

1979. Centenary of National Anthem.
1617 10c. Type **373** (postage) . . 10 10
1618 40c. J. Aberle (composer) and score (air) 25 15

374 Cogwheel encircling Central America **376** Map of Central and South America

375 Children of Different Races

1979. 8th Mechanical, Electrical and Allied Trade Engineers' Congress, San Salvador.
1619 **374** 10c. mult (postage) . . . 10 10
1620 50c. multicoloured (air) 30 20

1979. International Year of the Child.
1621 **375** 10c. mult (postage) . . . 10 10
1622 – 15c. multicoloured . . . 10 10
1623 – 25c. yell, red & blk (air) 15 15
1624 – 30c. blue and black . . 15 15
DESIGNS—HORIZ: 30c. S.O.S. Children's Village emblem. VERT: 15c. Children with nurses; 25c. Children dancing in circle.

1979. 5th Latin-American Clinical Biochemistry Congress, San Salvador.
1625 **376** 10c. orange, red and black (postage) . . . 10 10
1626 25c. yellow, red and black (air) 15 10

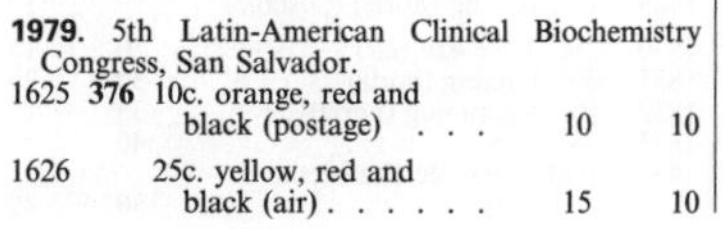

377 Coffee Bushes in Bloom

1979. 50th Anniv of Salvador Coffee Association. Multicoloured.
1627 10c. Type **377** (postage) . . 10 10
1628 30c. Planting coffee bushes (vert) 15 15
1629 40c. Coffee beans 25 15
1630 50c. Picking coffee beans (air) 30 20
1631 75c. Drying coffee beans (vert) 45 30
1632 1col. Coffee exports . . . . 1·00 45

378 Dove, Star and Children holding Candles

1979. Christmas.
1633 **378** 10c. multicoloured . . . 10 10

379 Diseased Animal

1980. Campaign against Foot and Mouth Disease.
1634 **379** 10c. mult (postage) . . . 10 10
1635 60c. multicoloured (air) 35 25

380 Grand Ark

1980. Shells. Multicoloured.
1636 10c. Type **380** (postage) . . 15 10
1637 30c. "Ostrea iridescens" . . 30 15
1638 40c. White-mouthed turritella 50 20
1639 15c. Regal murex (air) . . . 20 10
1640 25c. Spiral moon 30 15
1641 75c. Jenner's cowrie 85 45
1642 1col. Prostitute venus . . . 1·00 65

381 Resplendent Quetzal

1980. Birds. Multicoloured.
1643 10c. Type **381** (postage) . . 1·10 15
1644 20c. Highland guan . . . . 1·75 30
1645 25c. Emerald toucanet (air) 2·10 50
1646 50c. Fulvous owl . . . . . 3·00 75
1647 75c. Slate-coloured solitaire 3·75 1·10

382 "Porthidium godmani" **383** Corporation Emblem

1980. Snakes. Multicoloured.
1648 10c. Type **382** (postage) . . 10 10
1649 20c. "Agkistrodon bilineatus" 15 10
1650 25c. "Crotalus durissus" (air) 15 10
1651 50c. "Micrurus nigrocinctus" 30 20

1980. 50th Anniv of Corporation of Auditors.
1652 **383** 15c. mult (postage) . . . 10 10
1653 20c. multicoloured . . . 15 10
1654 50c. multicoloured (air) 30 20
1655 75c. multicoloured . . . 45 30

384 Hands releasing Dove (cartoon by "Nando")

1980. "Man and Peace" Caricature Contest Winner.
1656 **384** 5c. bl, blk & brn (post) 10 10
1657 10c. blue, black & yellow 10 10
1658 25c. bl, blk & grn (air) 15 10
1659 60c. blue, black & orge 35 25

385 Decade Emblem **386** Black-handed Spider Monkey

1981. Air. International Decade for Women.
1660 **385** 25c. black and green . . 15 10
1661 1col. black & orange . . 55 45

1981. Air. Protected Animals. Multicoloured.
1662 25c. Type **386** 15 10
1663 40c. Tropical gar 35 20
1664 50c. Common iguana 30 20
1665 60c. Hawksbill turtle 35 25
1666 75c. Ornate hawk eagle . . 3·25 60

387 Heinrich von Stephan **389** Dental Association Emblems

1981. Air. 150th Birth Anniv of Heinrich von Stephan (founder of U.P.U.).
1667 **387** 15c. pink and black . . 10 10
1668 2col. blue and black . . 1·10 70

1981. Air. Nos. 1573 and 1610 surch.
1669 – 50c. on 80c. mult . . . 30 20
1670 **371** 1col. on 70c. mult . . . 55 45

1981. 50th Anniv of El Salvador Dental Society, and 25th Anniv of Odontological Federation of South America and Panama.
1671 **389** 15c. grn & blk (postage) 10 10
1672 5col. blue & blk (air) . . 2·40 2·10

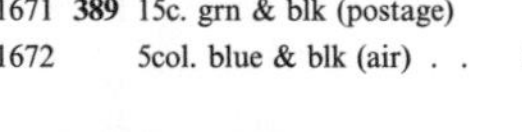

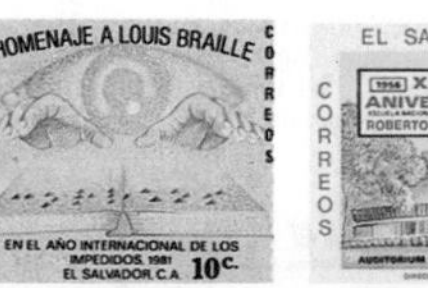

390 Eye, Hands and Braille Book **391** Los Proceres Auditorium

1981. International Year of Disabled People.
1673 **390** 10c. mult (postage) . . . 10 10
1674 25c. multicoloured (air) 15 10
1675 – 50c. green and blue . . . 30 20
1676 **390** 75c. multicoloured . . . 45 30
1677 – 1col. black and blue . . 55 40
DESIGN: 50c., 1col. I.Y.D.P. emblem.

1981. 25th Anniv of Roberto Quinonez National Agricultural College.
1678 **391** 10c. mult (postage) . . . 10 10
1679 50c. multicoloured (air) 30 20

392 Map of El Salvador and Hand holding Maize **393** Open Book and El Salvador Flags of 1881 and 1981

1981. World Food Day.
1680 **392** 10c. mult (postage) . . . 10 10
1681 25c. multicoloured (air) 15 10

1981. Air. Centenary of Land Registry Office.
1682 **393** 1col. black, bl & red . . 55 40

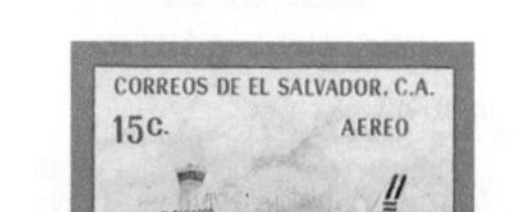

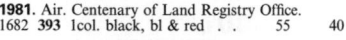

394 Boeing 737

1981. Air. 50th Anniv of "TACA" National Airline.
1683 **394** 15c. multicoloured . . . 15 10
1684 25c. multicoloured . . . 30 15
1685 75c. multicoloured . . . 90 50

395 Goalkeeper

1981. World Cup Football Preliminary Round, Honduras. Multicoloured.
1686 10c. Type **395** (postage) . . 10 10
1687 40c. World Cup, football and flags of competing countries 25 20
1688 25c. Type **395** (air) 15 10
1689 75c. As No. 1687 . . . . . 45 30

396 Salvador Lyceum

1981. Centenary of Salvador Lyceum.
1690 **396** 10c. mult (postage) . . . 10 10
1691 25c. multicoloured (air) 15 10

397 Ceremonial Axe

1982. Pre-Columbian Stone Sculptures. Mult.
1692 10c. Type **397** (postage) . . 10 10
1693 20c. Sun disc 15 10
1694 40c. Stela of Tazumal . . . 25 20
1695 25c. Ehecatl (god of the winds) (air) 15 10
1696 30c. Rock mask of jaguar 15 15
1697 80c. Flint sculpture 50 35

398 Scout Salute, Flag and Globe **399** Dr. Robert Koch

1982. Boy Scout and Girl Guide Movements. Multicoloured.
1698 10c. Type **398** (Scout Movement, 75th anniv) (postage) 10 10
1699 30c. Girl guide helping old lady 15 10

1700	25c. Scout and Lord Baden-Powell (125th birth anniv) (air)	15	10
1701	50c. Girl Guide with emblem and national flag	30	20

1982. Air. Cent of Discovery of Tubercle Bacillus.

1702	**399** 50c. multicoloured	30	20

400 Emblem and Soldier

1982. Armed Forces.

1703	**400** 10c. black, green and brown (postage)	10	10
1704	25c. multicoloured (air)	15	10

401 Converging Lines

402 Hexagonal Pattern

1982. Air. 25th Anniv of Confederation of Latin American Tourist Organizations.

1705	**401** 75c. yellow, grn & blk	45	30

1982. Air. World Telecommunications Day.

1706	**402** 15c. multicoloured	10	10
1707	2col. multicoloured	1·10	60

403 Salvador Football Team

1982. World Cup Football Championship, Spain (1st issue). Multicoloured.

1708	10c. Type **403** (postage)	10	10
1709	25c. As 10c. but different logo (air)	15	10
1710	60c. Trophy and map of El Salvador	35	25
1711	2col. National team and results of qualifying rounds (66×45 mm)	1·10	60

404 Flag of Italy

405 Fair Poster

1982. Air. World Cup Football Championship, Spain (2nd issue). Multicoloured. (a) Flags.

1712	15c. Type **404**	10	10
1713	15c. West Germany	10	10
1714	15c. Argentine Republic	10	10
1715	15c. England	10	10
1716	15c. Spain	10	10
1717	15c. Brazil	10	10
1718	15c. Poland	10	10
1719	15c. Algeria	10	10
1720	15c. Belgium	10	10
1721	15c. France	10	10
1722	15c. Honduras	10	10
1723	15c. Russia	10	10
1724	15c. Peru	10	10
1725	15c. Chile	10	10
1726	15c. Hungary	10	10
1727	15c. Czechoslovakia	10	10
1728	15c. Yugoslavia	10	10
1729	15c. Scotland	10	10
1730	15c. Cameroun	10	10
1731	15c. Austria	10	10
1732	15c. El Salvador	10	10
1733	15c. Kuwait	10	10
1734	15c. Northern Ireland	10	10
1735	15c. New Zealand	10	10

(b) Coat of Arms.

1736	25c. Italy	15	10
1737	25c. Poland	15	10
1738	25c. West Germany	15	10
1739	25c. Algeria	15	10
1740	25c. Argentine Republic	15	10
1741	25c. Belgium	15	10
1742	25c. Peru	15	10
1743	25c. Cameroun	15	10
1744	25c. Chile	15	10
1745	25c. Austria	15	10
1746	25c. Hungary	15	10
1747	25c. El Salvador	15	10
1748	25c. England	15	10
1749	25c. France	15	10
1750	25c. Spain	15	10
1751	25c. Honduras	15	10
1752	25c. Brazil	15	10
1753	25c. Russia	15	10
1754	25c. Czechoslovakia	15	10
1755	25c. Kuwait	15	10
1756	25c. Yugoslavia	15	10
1757	25c. Northern Ireland	15	10
1758	25c. Scotland	15	10
1759	25c. New Zealand	15	10

(c) 89 × 67 mm.

1760	5col. El Salvador team, World Cup and flags of competing countries	2·40	1·50

1982. 10th International Fair. Multicoloured.

1761	10c. Type **405** (postage)	10	10
1762	15c. Fair emblem (air)	10	10

406 Hand supporting Family

407 St. Francis with Wolf

1983. Air. World Food Day.

1763	**406** 25c. multicoloured	15	10

1982. Air. 800th Birth Anniv of St. Francis of Assisi.

1764	**407** 1col. multicoloured	55	45

408 Campaign Emblem

409 Christmas Retable

1982. Air. National Labour Campaign.

1765	**408** 50c. multicoloured	30	20

1982. Christmas. Multicoloured.

1766	5c. Type **409** (postage)	10	10
1767	25c. Christmas triptych (air)	15	10

410 Dance

1983. Pre-Columbian Ceramics. Mult.

1768	10c. Type **410** (postage)	10	10
1769	20c. The sower	15	10
1770	25c. Flying man	15	10
1771	60c. Archer hunting (left) (air)	35	30
1772	60c. Archer hunting (right)	35	30
1773	1col. Procession (left)	55	45
1774	1col. Procession (right)	55	45

Nos. 1771/2 and 1773/4 were issued together, each pair forming a composite design.

411 Papal Arms and Maria Auxiliadora Church

1983. Papal Visit. Multicoloured.

1775	25c. Type **411**	15	10
1776	60c. Pope John Paul II and Christ on Globe monument	35	30

412 Ricardo Aberle

1983. 50th Anniv of Air Force. Mult.

1777	10c. Type **412**	10	10
1778	10c. Air Force emblem	10	10
1779	10c. Enrico Massi	10	10
1780	10c. Juan Ramon Munes	20	10
1781	10c. American Airforces Co-operation emblem	10	10
1782	10c. Belisario Salazar	20	10

413 "Papilio torquatus" (male)

414 Simon Bolivar

1983. Butterflies. Multicoloured.

1783	5c. Type **413**	10	10
1784	5c. "Metamorpha steneles"	10	10
1785	10c. "Papilio torquatus" (female)	10	10
1786	10c. "Anaea marthesia"	10	10
1787	15c. "Prepona brooksiana"	15	10
1788	15c. "Caligo atreus"	15	10
1789	25c. Emperor	30	15
1790	25c. "Dismorphia praxinoe"	30	15
1791	50c. "Morpho polyphemus"	70	25
1792	50c. "Metamorpha epaphus"	70	25

1983. Birth Bicentenary of Simon Bolivar.

1793	**414** 75c. multicoloured	45	30

415 Dr. Jose Mendoza (founder)

417 David J. Guzman (founder)

416 "Rural School" (L. A. Caceres Madrid)

1983. 40th Anniv of Medical College.

1794	**415** 10c. pink, black & grn	10	10

1983. Air. Paintings. Multicoloured.

1795	25c. "Potters of Paleca" (M. Ortiz Villacorta)	15	10
1796	25c. Type **416**	15	10
1797	75c. "To the Wash" (Julia Diaz) (vert)	45	30
1798	75c. "La Pancha" (Mejia Vides) (vert)	45	30
1799	1col. "Meanguera del Golfo" (Elas Reyes) (vert)	1·40	60
1800	1col. "The Muleteers" (Noe Canjura) (vert)	55	45

1983. Centenary of David J. Guzman National Museum. Multicoloured.

1801	10c. Type **417** (postage)	10	10
1802	50c. Guzman and Museum (air)	30	20

418 Gen. Juan Jose Canas and Dr. Francisco Duenas

1983. World Communications Year. Mult.

1803	10c. Type **418** (postage)	10	10
1804	25c. Postman delivering letter (vert) (air)	15	10
1805	50c. Central sorting office	30	20

419 Dove and Globe

420 Bus emitting Exhaust Fumes

1983. Christmas. Multicoloured.

1806	10c. Type **419** (postage)	10	10
1807	25c. Christmas crib (air)	15	10

1983. Environmental Protection. Mult.

1808	10c. Type **420** (postage)	10	10
1809	15c. Fig tree (air)	10	10
1810	25c. Paca	20	15

421 Fisherman with Catch

1983. Air. Fishery Resources. Multicoloured.

1811	25c. Type **421**	70	30
1812	75c. Fish farming	70	30

422 Tweezers holding First Stamp of El Salvador

1984. Philatelists' Day.

1813	**422** 10c. blue, blk & orge	10	10

423 Maize

424 Caluco Church

1984. Agricultural Products. Multicoloured.

1814	10c. Type **423**	10	10
1815	15c. Cotton	10	10
1816	25c. Coffee	20	15
1817	50c. Sugar	35	25
1817a	55c. Cotton	20	20
1817b	70c. Type **423**	25	20
1818	75c. Kidney bean	25	20
1818a	90c. Sugar cane	25	20
1819	1col. Agave	30	25
1819a	2col. Beans	60	50
1820	5col. Balsam	2·40	1·75
1820c	10col. Agave	4·75	3·50

1984. Colonial Churches. Multicoloured.

1821	5c. Type **424** (postage)	10	10
1822	10c. Salcoatitan	10	10
1823	15c. Huizucar (air)	10	10
1824	25c. Santo Domingo	20	15
1825	50c. Pilar	35	25
1826	75c. Nahuizalco	40	30

425 Banknote

426 Running

1984. 50th Anniv of General Reserve Bank. Multicoloured.

1827	10c. Type **425** (postage)	10	10
1828	25c. Bank Building (air)	20	15

1984. Olympic Games, Los Angeles. Multicoloured.

1829	10c. Boxing (horiz) (postage)	10	10
1830	25c. Type **426** (air)	20	15
1831	40c. Cycling (horiz)	30	20
1832	50c. Swimming (horiz)	35	25
1833	75c. Judo	40	30
1834	1col. Pierre de Coubertin (horiz)	50	40

427 New Building

1984. New Servicios Graficos (Government printer) Building.
1835 **427** 10c. multicoloured . . . 10 10

428 "5th November" Hydro-electric Plant

1984. National Energy Resources. Mult.
1836 20c. Type **428** (postage) . . 10 10
1837 55c. "Cerron Grande" hydro-electric plant . . . 30 20
1838 70c. Ahuachapan geothermal plant (air) . . 40 30
1839 90c. Mural, Guajoyo hydro-electric plant 45 35
1840 2col. "15th September" hydro-electric plant . . . 60 50

429 Playing Marbles

1984. Children's Games. Multicoloured.
1841 55c. Type **429** 30 20
1842 70c. Spinning a top 40 30
1843 90c. Flying a kite 45 35
1844 2col. "Capirucho" 60 50

430 Fair Emblem

1984. 11th International Fair, El Salvador. Mult.
1845 25c. Type **430** (postage) . . 15 10
1846 70c. Fair building and flags (air) 40 30

431 Los Chorros Tourist Centre

1984. Tourism. Multicoloured.
1847 15c. Type **431** 10 10
1848 25c. The Americas Square 15 10
1849 70c. El Salvador International Airport . . 70 30
1850 90c. El Tunco beach 45 35
1851 2col. Sihuatehucan Tourist Centre 60 50

432 "The White Nun" (Salarrue)

1984. Paintings. Multicoloured.
1852 20c. Type **432** (postage) . . 10 10
1853 55c. "The Paper of Papers" (Roberto Antonio Galicia) (horiz) (air) . . 30 20
1854 70c. "Supreme Elegy to Masferrer" (Antonio Garcia Ponce) (wrongly inscr "Figuras en Palco") 40 30
1854a 70c. "Supreme Elegy to Masferrer" (correct inscription) 40 30
1855 90c. "Transmutation" (Armando Solis) (horiz) 45 35
1856 2col. "Figures in Theatre Box" (Carlos Canas) (wrongly inscr "Suprema Elegia a Masferrer") . . 1·10 90
1856a 2col. "Figures in Theatre Box" (correct inscription) 1·10 90

Nos. 1854a and 1856a are overprinted with the correct inscription.

433 Christmas Tree Decoration

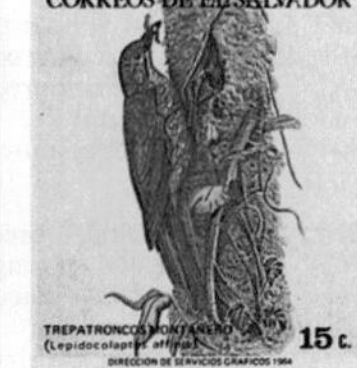

434 Spot-crowned Woodcreeper

1984. Christmas. Multicoloured.
1857 25c. Type **433** (postage) . . 15 10
1858 70c. Christmas tree decorations and dove (air) 40 30

1984. Birds. Multicoloured.
1859 15c. Type **434** (postage) . . 50 20
1860 25c. Slaty finch 80 45
1861 55c. Purple-breasted ground dove (air) . . . . 2·00 85
1862 70c. Tody-motmot . . . . 2·40 1·50
1863 90c. Belted flycatcher . . . 2·00 1·00
1864 1col. Red-faced warbler . . 3·00 1·75

435 Emblem and Share Certificate

1985. Centenary of El Salvador Bank.
1865 **435** 25c. multicoloured . . . 15 10

436 Share Certificate and Emblem

1985. 50th Anniv of El Salvador Mortgage Bank.
1866 **436** 25c. multicoloured . . . 15 10

437 I.Y.Y. Emblem

1985. International Youth Year.
1867 **437** 25c. blk & grn (postage) 15 10
1868 – 55c. mult (air) 30 20
1869 – 70c. multicoloured . . . 40 30
1870 – 1col.50 multicoloured . . 50 40

DESIGNS: 55c. Woodwork class; 70c. Boys raising tray of equipment by pulley; 1col.50, Parade.

438 Pre-classic seated Figurine

439 Red Cross and Hand holding "100"

1985. Archaeological Finds. Multicoloured.
1871 15c. Type **438** (postage) . . 10 10
1872 20c. Late classic engraved vase 10 10
1873 25c. Post-classic lead animal pot 15 10
1874 55c. Post-classic figurine (air) 30 20
1875 70c. Late post-classic figurine of Xipe Totec . . 40 30
1876 1col. Late post-classic clay animal on wheels 30 25

1985. Cent of El Salvador Red Cross. Mult.
1878 25c. Type **439** (postage) . . 15 10
1879 55c. Red Cross workers and inflatable inshore lifeboat (horiz) (air) . . . . . . 1·00 30
1880 70c. Blood donor and Red Cross workers (horiz) . . 40 30
1881 90c. Tending injured man 45 35

440 Hand holding Pin Figures and Houses

1985. Child Welfare. Multicoloured.
1882 25col. Type **440** (postage) 15 10
1883 55c. Children outside house (air) 30 20
1884 70c. Children dancing . . . 40 30
1885 80c. Oral vaccination . . . 45 35

441 Child and Soldiers on Map

1985. El Salvador Army. Multicoloured.
1886 25c. Type **441** (postage) . . 15 10
1887 70c. Armed soldier and flag (air) 40 30

442 Flag, Open Book and Laurel

1985. Election of President Duarte.
1888 **442** 25c. multicoloured 15 10
1889 – 70c. black & yellow . . 40 30

DESIGN: 70c. Extract from constitution.

443 Hydro-electric Station and Emblem

1985. 25th Anniv of Inter-American Development Bank. Multicoloured.
1890 25c. Type **443** (postage) . . 15 10
1891 70c. Emblem and map (air) 25 30
1892 1col. Emblem and arms . . 30 25

1985. Air. No. 1829 surch.
1893 1col. on 10c. mult 55 45

445 Three-spotted Cichlid

1985. Fresh Water Fishes. Multicoloured.
1894 25c. Type **445** (postage) . . 25 15
1895 55c. Guatemalan long-whiskered catfish (air) . . 60 30
1896 70c. Black molly 80 40
1897 90c. Convict cichlid 90 50
1898 1col. Banded astyanax . . . 1·10 60
1899 1col.50 Pacific fat sleeper . . 1·90 1·10

446 Food spilling from Basket

1985. 40th Anniv of Food and Agriculture Organization. Multicoloured.
1900 20c. Type **446** 10 10
1901 40c. Centeotl, Nahuat god of maize 20 15

447 "Cordulegaster godmani mclachlan"

1985. Dragonflies. Multicoloured.
1902 25c. Type **447** (postage) . . 20 15
1903 55c. "Libellula herculea karsch" (air) 45 30
1904 70c. "Cora marina selys" . . 65 45
1905 90c. "Aeshna cornigera braver" 70 50
1906 1col. "Mecistogaster ornata rambur" 90 60
1907 1col.50 "Hetaerina smaragdalis de marmels" 1·50 1·00

448 "Summer Holiday" (Roberto Huezo)

449 St. Vicente Tower

1985. Paintings. Multicoloured.
1908 25c. "Profiles" (Rosa Mena Valenzuela) (vert) (postage) 15 10
1909 55c. Type **448** (air) 30 20
1910 70c. "La Entrega" (Fernando Llort) 35 25
1911 90c. "For Decorating Pots" (Pedro Acosta Garcia) . . 45 35
1912 1col. "Still Life" (Miguel Angel Orellana) (vert) . . 55 45

1985. 350th Anniv of City of St. Vicente de Austria y Lorenzana. Multicoloured.
1913 15c. Type **449** 10 10
1914 20c. St. Vicente Cathedral 10 10

450

1986. International Peace Year. Mult.
1915 15c. Type **450** (postage) . . 10 10
1916 70c. People reaching towards peace dove (air) 20 15

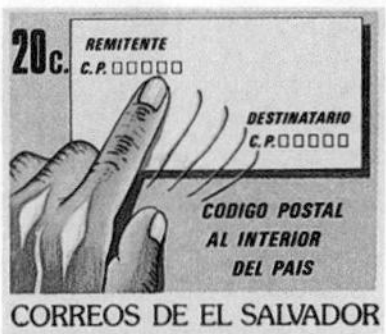

451 Hand and Interior Mail Envelope

1986. Introduction of Post Codes. Mult.
1917 20c. Type **451** 10 10
1918 25c. Hand and airmail envelope 10 10

452 Microphone

1986. 60th Anniv of Radio El Salvador. Multicoloured.

No.	Description	Mint	Used
1919	25c. Type **452** (postage)	10	10
1920	70c. "60", map and radio waves (air)	20	15

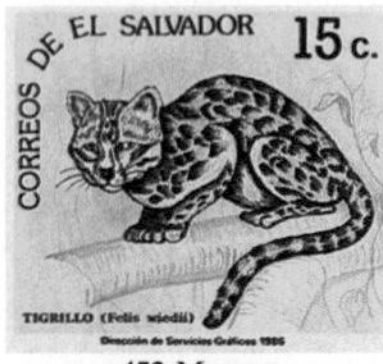

453 Margay

1986. Mammals. Multicoloured.

No.	Description	Mint	Used
1921	15c. Type **453** (postage)	10	10
1922	20c. Tamandua	10	10
1923	1col. Nine-banded armadillo (air)	30	25
1924	2col. Collared peccary	95	75

454 Flags and Mascot

1986. World Cup Football Championship, Mexico. Multicoloured.

No.	Description	Mint	Used
1925	70c. Type **454**	20	15
1926	1col. Footballers and Trophy (vert)	30	25
1927	2col. Footballer (vert)	95	75
1928	5col. Goal and emblem	2·40	1·90

455 Dr. Dario Gonzalez (medicine) **456** Tlaloc Seal

1986. Teachers (1st series). Multicoloured.

No.	Description	Mint	Used
1929	20c. Type **455** (postage)	10	10
1930	20c. Valero Lecha (art)	10	10
1931	40c. Prof. Marcelino Garcia Flamenco	10	10
1932	40c. Camilo Campos	10	10
1933	70c. Prof. Saul Flores (educationist) (air)	20	15
1934	70c. Prof. Jorge Larde (law)	20	15
1935	1col. Prof. Francisco Moran	30	25
1936	1col. Mercedes Maiti de Luarca	30	25

See also Nos. 1973/80.

1986.

No.	Description	Mint	Used
1937	**456** 25c. mult (postage)	10	10
1938	55c. mult (air)	15	15
1939	70c. multicoloured	20	15
1940	90c. multicoloured	25	20
1941	1col. multicoloured	30	25
1942	1col.50 multicoloured	45	40

457 Open Book on "100" as Stand **458** "Spathiphyllum phryniifolium"

1986. Air. Centenary of Constitution.

No.	Description	Mint	Used
1943	**457** 1col. multicoloured	30	25

1986. Flowers. Multicoloured.

No.	Description	Mint	Used
1944	20c. Type **458** (postage)	10	10
1945	25c. "Asclepias curassavica" (horiz)	10	10
1946	70c. "Tagetes tenuifolia" (horiz) (air)	20	15
1947	1col. "Ipomoea lilacea"	30	25

459 Unloading Fishing Boat

1986. World Food Day.

No.	Description	Mint	Used
1948	**459** 20c. multicoloured	40	15

460 Hugo Lindo **461** Emblem

1986. Air. 1st Death Anniv of Hugo Lindo (writer and poet).

No.	Description	Mint	Used
1949	**460** 1col. multicoloured	30	25

1986. Air. 25th Anniv of Central American Economic Integration Bank.

No.	Description	Mint	Used
1950	**461** 1col.50 blk, bl & mve	45	40

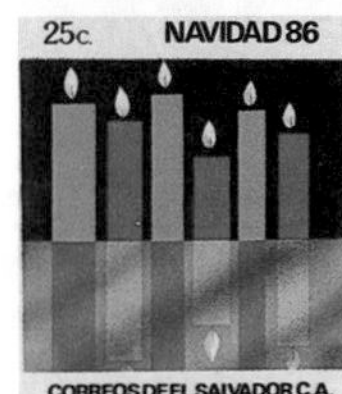

462 Candles

1986. Christmas. Multicoloured.

No.	Description	Mint	Used
1951	25c. Type **462** (postage)	10	10
1952	70c. Birds flying towards light (air)	20	15

463 Baskets

1986. Traditional Crafts. Multicoloured.

No.	Description	Mint	Used
1953	25c. Type **463**	10	10
1954	55c. Pottery	15	15
1955	70c. Guitars (vert)	20	15
1956	1col. Eastern reed baskets	30	25

464 "Church" (Mario Araujo Rajo) **465** Emblem

1986. Paintings. Multicoloured.

No.	Description	Mint	Used
1957	25c. Type **464** (postage)	10	10
1958	70c. "Landscape" (Francisco Reyes) (air)	20	15

1987. Air. 12th International Fair, El Salvador.

No.	Description	Mint	Used
1959	**465** 70c. multicoloured	20	15

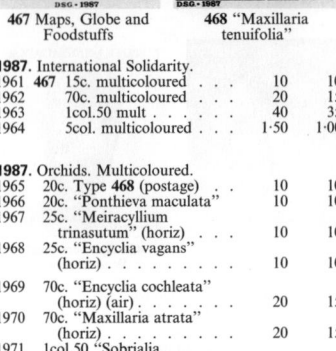

466 Stamps

1987. Philately.

No.	Description	Mint	Used
1960	**466** 25c. multicoloured	15	10

467 Maps, Globe and Foodstuffs **468** "Maxillaria tenuifolia"

1987. International Solidarity.

No.	Description	Mint	Used
1961	**467** 15c. multicoloured	10	10
1962	70c. multicoloured	20	15
1963	1col.50 mult	40	35
1964	5col. multicoloured	1·50	1·00

1987. Orchids. Multicoloured.

No.	Description	Mint	Used
1965	20c. Type **468** (postage)	10	10
1966	20c. "Ponthieva maculata"	10	10
1967	25c. "Meiracyllium trinasutum" (horiz)	10	10
1968	25c. "Encyclia vagans" (horiz)	10	10
1969	70c. "Encyclia cochleata" (horiz) (air)	20	15
1970	70c. "Maxillaria atrata" (horiz)	20	15
1971	1col.50 "Sobrialia xantholeuca" (horiz)	40	35
1972	1col.50 "Encyclia microcharis" (horiz)	40	35

469 C. de Jesus Alas (music)

1987. Teachers (2nd series).

No.	Description	Mint	Used
1973	**469** 15c. black & bl (postage)	10	10
1974	– 15c. black and blue	10	10
1975	– 20c. black and brown	10	10
1976	– 20c. black and brown	10	10
1977	– 70c. black & orange (air)	20	15
1978	– 70c. black and orange	20	15
1979	– 1col.50 black & green	40	35
1980	– 1col.50 black & green	40	35

DESIGNS: No. 1974, Dr. Luis Edmundo Vasquez (medicine); 1975, Dr. David Rosales (law); 1976, Dr. Guillermo Trigueros (medicine); 1977, Manuel Farfan Castro; 1978, Iri Sol (singing); 1979, Carlos Arturo Imendia (primary education); 1980, Dr. Benjamin Orozco (chemistry).

470 Man on Roof above Houses

1987. Air. Int Year of Shelter for the Homeless.

No.	Description	Mint	Used
1981	**470** 70col. multicoloured	20	15
1982	– 1col. blue	25	20

DESIGN: 1p. Emblem.

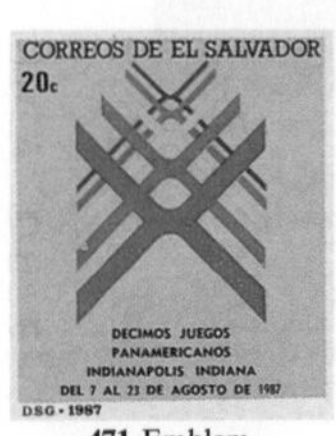

471 Emblem **472** Nicolas Aguilar

1987. 10th Pan-American Games, Indianapolis, U.S.A. Multicoloured.

No.	Description	Mint	Used
1983	20c. Type **471** (postage)	10	10
1984	20c. Table tennis	10	10
1985	25c. Wrestling (horiz)	10	10
1986	25c. Fencing (horiz)	10	10
1987	70c. Softball (horiz) (air)	20	15
1988	70c. Showjumping (horiz)	20	15
1989	5col. Weightlifting	1·40	1·10
1990	5col. Hurdling	1·40	1·10

1987. Independence Leaders. Multicoloured.

No.	Description	Mint	Used
1991	15c. Type **472** (postage)	10	10
1992	20c. Domingo Antonio de Lara	10	10
1993	70c. Juan Manuel Rodriguez (air)	20	15
1994	1col.50 Pedro Pablo Castillo	40	35

473 Man tending Crops

1987. World Food Day.

No.	Description	Mint	Used
1995	**473** 50c. multicoloured	15	10

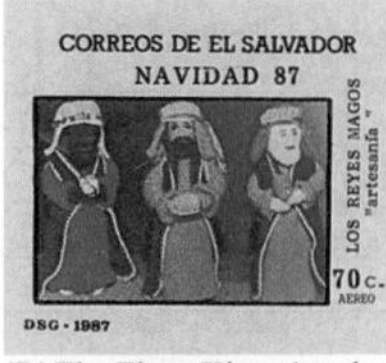

474 The Three Kings (crochet)

1987. Christmas. Multicoloured.

No.	Description	Mint	Used
1996	25c. Stained glass window from Church of Virgin of the Everlasting Succour (postage)	10	10
1997	70c. Type **474** (air)	20	15

475 "Self-portrait"

1987. Salvador Salazar Arrue (writer and painter). Multicoloured.

No.	Description	Mint	Used
1998	25c. Type **475** (postage)	10	10
1999	70c. "Lake" (air)	20	15

476 Man with Ceramic Drum

1987. Pre-Columbian Musical Instruments. Mult.

No.	Description	Mint	Used
2000	20c. Type **476** (postage)	10	10
2001	70c. Parade of musicians from Saluan ceramic vase (left) (air)	20	15
2002	70c. Parade of musicians from Saluan ceramic vase (right)	20	15
2003	1col.50 Conch shell trumpet	65	45

Nos. 2001/2 are each 31 × 30 mm.

477 King Ferdinand of Spain

1987. 500th Anniv (1992) of Discovery of America by Columbus (1st issue). Multicoloured.

No.	Description	Mint	Used
2004	1col. Type **477**	25	20
2005	1col. Queen Isabella of Spain	25	20
2006	1col. Banner and North America	25	20
2007	1col. Islands, coat of arms and ships	25	20
2008	1col. Caribbean	25	20
2009	1col. Ships and South America	25	20
2010	1col. Native figure and South America	25	20
2011	1col. South America and compass rose	25	20
2012	1col. Anniversary logo	25	20
2013	1col. Columbus	25	20

Nos. 2004/13 were printed together in se-tenant sheetlets, Nos. 2006/11 forming a composite design of a contemporary map.

See also Nos. 2040/9, 2065/70, 2116/21, 2166/71 and 2206/9.

478 Words and Stamps

1988. Philately.
2014 **478** 25c. multicoloured . . . 10 10

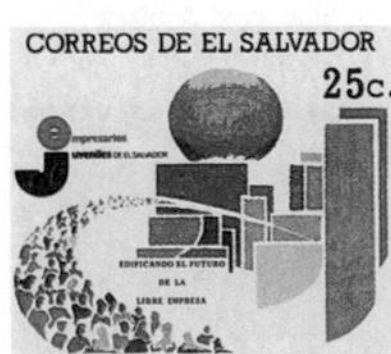

479 Crowd and Emblem

1988. Empesarios Juveniles (youth education programme).
2015 **479** 25c. multicoloured . . . 10 10

480 Bosco (after N. Musio)

1988. Death Centenary of St. John Bosco (founder of Salesian Brothers).
2016 **480** 20c. multicoloured . . . 10 10

481 Felling of Trees and Children Planting Saplings

1983. Environmental Protection. Mult.
2017 20c. Type **481** (postage) . . 10 10
2018 70c. Rubbish in river and monkey in forest (air) . . 20 15

482 High Jumping

1988. Olympic Games, Seoul (1988) and Barcelona (1992). Multicoloured.
2019 1col. Type **482** 25 20
2020 1col. Throwing the javelin 25 20
2021 1col. Pistol shooting 25 20
2022 1col. Wrestling 25 20
2023 1col. Basketball 25 20

483 Rural Youth

1988. World Food Day.
2025 **483** 20c. multicoloured . . . 10 10

484 Fair Emblem

486 Father and Son flying Heart-shaped Kite

1988. 13th International Fair, El Salvador.
2026 **484** 70c. multicoloured . . . 20 15

1988. "Prenfil '88" International Philatelic Literature and Press Exhibition, Buenos Aires. No. 1905 surch **C5.00 PRENFIL '88 EXPOSICION MUNDIAL DE LITERATURA Y PRENSA FILATELICA BUENOS AIRES ARGENTINA DEL 25 DE NOVIEMBRE AL 2 DE DICEMBRE** and emblem.
2027 5col. on 90c. multicoloured 1·40 1·25

1988. Infant Protection Campaign. Mult.
2028 15c. Type **486** 10 10
2029 20c. Happy child hugging adult's leg 10 10

487 "Virgin and Child with St. John and St. Anthony"

1988. Christmas. 500th Birth Anniv of Titian (painter). Multicoloured.
2030 25c. Type **487** (postage) . . 10 10
2031 70c. "Virgin and Child in Glory with St. Francis and St. Alvise" (vert) (air) 20 15

488 Emblems

1988. Air. 18th Organization of American States General Assembly.
2032 **488** 70c. multicoloured . . . 20 15

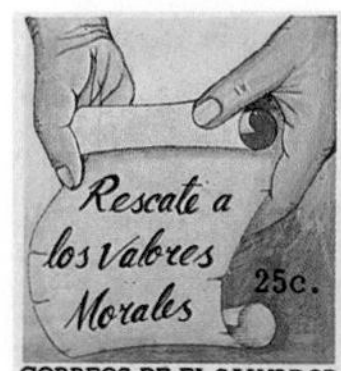

489 Hands holding Scroll

1988. "Return to Moral Values".
2033 **489** 25c. multicoloured . . . 10 10

490 "Esperanza de los Soles" (Victor Rodriguez Preza)

491 Emblem within Laurel Wreath, People and Map

1988. Paintings. Multicoloured.
2034 40c. Type **490** (postage) . . 10 10
2035 1col. "Pastoral" (Luis Angel Salinas) (horiz) (air) . . . 25 20
2036 2col. "Children" (Julio Hernandez Aleman) (horiz) 60 45
2037 5col. "El Nino de las Alcancias" (Camilo Minero) . . . . 1·50 1·25

1988. 40th Anniv of Declaration of Human Rights. Multicoloured.
2038 25c. Type **491** (postage) . . 10 10
2039 70c. U.N. and Human Rights emblems and map (air) (horiz) 20 15

492 El Tazumal

1988. 500th Anniv (1992) of Discovery of America by Columbus (2nd issue). Multicoloured.
2040 1col. Type **492** 25 20
2041 1col. Earthenware bowl . . 25 20
2042 1col. San Andres 25 20
2043 1col. Dish for burning aromatic substances . . . 25 20
2044 1col. Sihuatan 25 20
2045 1col. Effigy of rain god . . 25 20
2046 1col. Cara Sucia 25 20
2047 1col. Monkey-shaped pot . . 25 20
2048 1col. San Lorenzo 25 20
2049 1col. Round pot with monkey-head spout . . . 25 20

493 Margay

1989. Endangered Animals. Multicoloured.
2051 25c. Type **493** 10 10
2052 25c. Margay (different) . . . 10 10
2053 55c. Ocelot in tree 15 10
2054 55c. Ocelot resting 15 10

494 Flag, Map and Compass Rose

1989. Centenary of El Salvador Meteorological Services. Multicoloured.
2055 15c. Type **494** 10 10
2056 20c. Sea, land and measuring equipment . . 20 10

495 El Salvador Philatelic Society Emblem

496 Basketball

1989. Philately.
2057 **495** 25c. grey, black & bl . . 10 10

1989. Olympic Games, Barcelona (1992). Mult.
2058 20c. Type **496** (postage) . . 10 10
2059 25c. Boxing 10 10
2060 25c. Athletics 10 10
2061 40c. Showjumping 10 10
2063 55c. Badminton (horiz) (air) 15 10
2064 55c. Handball (horiz) . . . 15 10

497 1893 10p. Columbus Stamp

1989. 500th Anniv (1992) of Discovery of America by Columbus (3rd issue). El Salvador Stamps featuring Columbus.
2065 **497** 50c. orange 15 10
2066 – 50c. blue 15 10
2067 – 50c. green 15 10
2068 – 50c. red 15 10
2069 – 50c. violet 15 10
2070 – 50c. brown 15 10

DESIGNS: No. 2066, 1894 2p. stamp; 2067, 1893 2p. stamp; 2068, 1894 5p. stamp; 2069, 1893 5p. stamp; 2070, 1894 10p. stamp.

498 Fire Engine

1989. 106th Anniv of Fire Service. Mult.
2072 25c. Type **498** 10 10
2073 70c. Firemen fighting fire . . 15 10

499 Birds

1989. Bicent of French Revolution. Mult.
2074 90c. Type **499** 25 20
2075 1col. Storming the Bastille 25 20

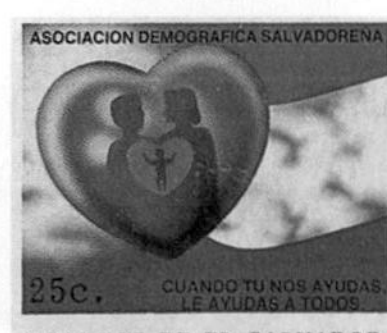

500 People within Heart

1989. 27th Anniv of El Salvador Demographic Association.
2076 **500** 25c. multicoloured . . . 10 10

501 "Signing the Act of Independence" (Luis Vergara Ahumada)

1989. 168th Anniv of Independence. Mult.
2077 25c. Type **501** (postage) . . 10 10
2078 70c. Flag, independence leaders and arms (air) . . 15 10

502 Flags of El Salvador and United States

1989. World Cup Football Championship, Italy (1990) (1st issue). Preliminary Rounds. Multicoloured.
2079 20c. Type **502** 10 10
2080 20c. Flags of El Salvador and Guatemala 10 10
2081 25c. Flags of El Salvador and Costa Rica 10 10
2082 25c. Flags of El Salvador and Trinidad and Tobago 10 10
2083 55c. Flags and ball 15 10
2084 1col. Ball and Cuscatlan Stadium 25 20
See also Nos. 2109/15.

503 Marcelino Champagnat and Arms of Order

1989. Birth Bicent of Jose Benito Marcelino Champagnat (founder of Maristas Brothers).
2085 **503** 20c. multicoloured . . . 10 10

504 "The Farmer" (bowl decoration)

1989. America. Multicoloured.
2086 25c. Type **504** 10 10
2087 70c. Pre-Columbian pottery production 15 10

505 Man tending Crops

1989. World Food Day. "One Land, One Community, One Future". Multicoloured.
2088 15c. Type **505** 10 10
2089 55c. Food production activities in chain links . . 15 10

506 Children under Umbrella

507 Holy Family in Stable

1989. Children's Rights.
2090 **506** 25c. multicoloured . . . 10 10

1989. Christmas. Multicoloured.
2091 25c. Type **507** 10 10
2092 70c. Holy Family 15 10

508 King Vulture

1989. Birds. Multicoloured.
2093 70c. Type **508** 35 25
2094 1col. Common caracara (horiz) 65 50
2095 2col. Sharp-shinned hawk 1·40 90
2096 10col. Ferruginous pygmy owl (horiz) . . . . 7·00 5·25

509 Treasury, Map and "50"

1990. 50th Anniv of Treasury.
2097 **509** 50c. blue, gold & black 15 10

510 Baden-Powell

1990. 133rd Birth Anniv of Lord Baden-Powell (founder of Boy Scouts Movement).
2098 **510** 25c. multicoloured . . . 10 10

511 Young Girl

1990. International Women's Day.
2099 **511** 25c. multicoloured . . . 10 10

512 Hourglass

1990. 50th Anniv of El Salvador Philatelic Society.
2100 **512** 25c. mult (postage) . . . 10 10
2101 55c. mult (air) 10 10

513 "No to Alcoholic Drinks"

1990. Problems of Addiction. Multicoloured.
2103 20c. Type **513** (postage) . . 10 10
2104 25c. "No to Tobacco" . . . 10 10
2105 1col.50 "No to Drugs" (air) 25 20

514 Player

515 First Page and Map

1990. Air. Victory by El Salvador at Fourth International Football Championship for Amputees (1989).
2106 **514** 70c. multicoloured . . . 15 10

1990. 75th Anniv of "La Prensa Grafica" (newspaper). Multicoloured.
2107 15c. Type **515** 10 10
2108 25c. Newspaper as diamond and "75" 10 10

516 Group A

1990. World Cup Football Championship, Italy (2nd issue). Multicoloured.
2109 55c. Type **516** 10 10
2110 55c. Group B 10 10
2111 70c. Group C 15 10
2112 70c. Group D 15 10
2113 1col. Group E 15 10
2114 1col. Group F 15 10
2115 1col.50 Winner's medal (vert) 25 20

517 Ferdinand the Catholic

1990. 500th Anniv (1992) of Discovery of America by Columbus (4th issue). Multicoloured.
2116 1col. Type **517** 15 10
2117 1col. Isabella the Catholic 15 10
2118 1col. Arms and topsail . . . 15 10
2119 1col. Anniversary emblem 15 10
2120 1col. "Santa Maria" 50 15
2121 1col. "Pinta" and "Nina" 50 15

1990. Germany, World Cup Football Championship Winner. No. 2112 surch **90c. ALEMANIA CAMPEON**.
2123 90c. on 70c. multicoloured 15 10

519 Globe and Figures

1990. World Summit on Children, New York.
2124 **519** 5col. blue, bis & blk . . 85 80

520 Sir Rowland Hill (instigator of first postage stamps)

1990. 150th Anniv of the Penny Black.
2125 **520** 2col. multicoloured . . . 30 25
2126 – 2col. multicoloured . . . 30 25
2127 – 2col. multicoloured . . . 30 25
2128 – 2col. multicoloured . . . 30 25
2129 – 2col. multicoloured . . . 30 25
2130 – 2col. multicoloured . . . 30 25
DESIGNS: No. 2126, 1d. Black; 2127, El Salvador 1889 1c. stamp; 2128, Post Headquarters; 2129, United Kingdom and El Salvador flags; 2130, El Salvador 1949 1col. U.P.U. stamp.

521 Chichontepec Volcano

1990. America. Natural World. Multicoloured.
2131 25c. Type **521** 40 25
2132 70c. Coatepeque Lake . . . 90 25

522 "Food for the Future"

1990. World Food Day.
2133 **522** 5col. multicoloured . . . 85 80

523 Light Bulb

1990. Centenary of San Salvador Electric Light Company. Multicoloured.
2134 20c. Type **523** 10 10
2135 90c. Maintenance of overhead power lines . . 15 10

524 Road Signs

1990. 8th Anniv of National Commission for Education and Road Safety. Multicoloured.
2136 25c. Type **524** 10 10
2137 40c. Family at road junction (horiz) 10 10

525 Anniversary Emblem

1990. 75th Anniv of Chamber of Trade and Commerce.
2138 **525** 1col. blue, gold & black 15 10

526 "Papilio garamas amerias"

1990. Butterflies. Multicoloured.
2139 15c. "Eurytides calliste" . . 10 10
2140 20c. Type **526** 10 10
2141 25c. "Papilio garamas" . . 10 10
2142 55c. "Hypanartia godmani" (vert) 10 10
2143 70c. "Anaea (Consul) excellens" (vert) 10 10
2144 1col. "Papilio pilumnus" (vert) 15 10

527 Children

1990. Christmas. Multicoloured.
2146 25c. Type **527** 10 10
2147 70c. Nativity (vert) 10 10

528 Elderly Couple

529 University Emblem

1991. Month of the Third Age.
2148 **528** 15c. black and violet . . 10 10

1991. 150th Anniv of El Salvador University.
2149 **529** 25c. black and silver . . 10 10
2150 – 70c. multicoloured . . . 10 10
2151 – 1col.50 multicoloured . . 20 15
DESIGNS: 70c. Footsteps leading to light; 1col.50, Pencil, pen and dove on globe.

530 Auditorium

1991. Restoration of Santa Ana Theatre. Mult.
2152 20c. Type **530** 10 10
2153 70c. Facade 10 10

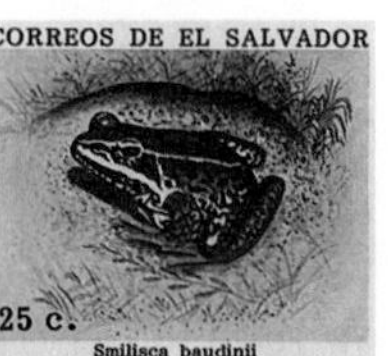

531 Mexican Tree Frog

1991. Frogs. Multicoloured.
2154 25c. Type **531** 10 10
2155 70c. Robber frog 10 10

2156 1col. "Plectrohyla guatemalensis" 15 10
2157 1col.50 Morelet's frog 20 15

532 National Colours, Map and Child

1991. S.O.S. Children's Villages. Mult.
2158 20c. Type **532** 10 10
2159 90c. Children playing in village 15 10

533 Family building Map

534 Blue and White Mockingbird

1991. Family Unity Month.
2160 **533** 50c. multicoloured 10 10

1991. Birds. Multicoloured.
2161 20c. Type **534** 30 35
2162 25c. Red-winged blackbird 30 40
2163 70c. Rufous-naped wren 30 40
2164 1col. Bushy-crested jay 55 40
2165 5col. Long-tailed manakin 3·00 1·75

535 Hourglass and Atlas

1991. 500th Anniv (1992) of Discovery of America by Columbus (5th issue). Multicoloured.
2166 1col. Type **535** 15 10
2167 1col. "Santa Maria's" sails and atlas 50 15
2168 1col. Map and caravel 50 15
2169 1col. Caravels and edge of atlas 50 15
2170 1col. Compass rose and map 15 10
2171 1col. Map and anniversary emblem 15 10
Nos. 2166/71 were issued together, se-tenant, forming a composite design.

536 Battle of Acaxual

537 Tree-globe and Plant and Animal Life

1991. America. Voyages of Discovery. Mult.
2173 25c. Type **536** 10 10
2174 70c. First Mass in Cuzcatlan 10 10

1991. World Food Day. "The Tree, Fountain of Life for the World".
2175 **537** 50c. multicoloured 35 20

538 Manuscript and Mozart

1991. Death Bicentenary of Wolfgang Amadeus Mozart (composer).
2176 **538** 1col. multicoloured 15 10

539 Nativity

1991. Christmas. Multicoloured.
2177 25c. Type **539** 10 10
2178 70c. Carol singers (horiz) 10 10

540 Moon and Left Half of Eclipse

1991. Total Eclipse of the Sun. Mult.
2179 70c. Type **540** 10 10
2180 70c. Right half of eclipse and Moon 10 10
Nos. 2179/80 were issued together, se-tenant, forming a composite design.

541 Lifeguards with rescued Swimmer

1992. Red Cross Lifeguards. Multicoloured.
2181 3col. Type **541** 45 30
2182 4col.50 Lifeguards in sea 1·00 45

542 St. Vincent de Paul and Sick Man

543 Anniversary Emblem

1992. Centenary of St. Vincent de Paul Society of Sisters of Charity.
2183 **542** 80c. multicoloured 10 10

1992. 50th Anniv of Lions International in El Salvador.
2184 **543** 90c. multicoloured 15 10

544 Cyclist ("Non-polluting Transport")

545 Roberto Orellana Valdes (gynaecologist)

1992. Ecology. Multicoloured.
2185 60c. Type **544** 10 10
2186 80c. Children and butterfly ("Fauna, ecology and education") 10 10
2187 1col.60 Man working on allotment ("Harmony with nature") 15 10
2188 2col.20 Animals beside clean river ("Do not pollute rivers") 30 20
2189 3col. Fruits ("Eat natural foods") 45 30
2190 5col. Recycling bins ("Energy without contamination") 75 50
2191 10col. Landscape ("Conserve nature") 1·50 1·00
2192 25col. Wild animals ("Do not destroy fauna") 3·50 2·40

1992. Doctors. Multicoloured.
2193 80c. Type **545** 10 10
2194 1col. Carlos Gonzalez Bonilla (surgeon) 15 10
2195 1col.60 Andres Gonzalez Funes (paediatrician) 25 20
2196 2col.20 Joaquin Coto (anaesthetist) 30 20

546 Mascot and Census Document

548 Simon Bolivar

1992. 5th Population and Fourth Housing Census. Multicoloured.
2197 60c. Type **546** 10 10
2198 80c. Graph and globe 10 10

1992.
2205 **548** 2col.20 multicoloured 30 20

549 Carvings

1992. 500th Anniv of Discovery of America by Columbus (6th series). Multicoloured.
2206 1col. Type **549** 15 10
2207 1col. Caravel reflected in human eye 40 15
2208 1col. Caravel and Mexican pyramids 40 15
2209 1col. "500", caravel and satellite 40 15

550 Footprints on Globe

1992. Emigration. Multicoloured.
2211 2col.20 Type **550** 30 20
2212 2col.20 Happy cloud and footprints 30 20

551 Morazan

552 Radio Waves on Map

1992. Birth Bicent of General Francisco Morazan.
2213 **551** 1col. multicoloured 15 10

1992. Salvadoran and Int Broadcasting Day.
2214 **552** 2col.20 multicoloured 30 20

553 Cross, Pyramid, Church and Carving

1992. America. 500th Anniv of Discovery of America by Columbus. Multicoloured.
2215 80c. Type **553** 10 10
2216 2col.20 Map and stern of caravel 70 25

554 Map and Sails

1992. "Exfilna '92" National Stamp Exn.
2217 **554** 5col. multicoloured 75 50

555 Sun and Stylized Dove

1992. Peace.
2218 **555** 50c. blue, yellow & blk 10 10

556 Christmas Tree and Children

1992. Christmas. Multicoloured.
2219 80c. Type **556** 10 10
2220 2col.20 Holy Family (vert) 30 20

557 Baird's Tapir

1993. Mammals. Multicoloured.
2221 50c. Type **557** 10 10
2222 70c. Water opossum 10 10
2223 1col. Tayra 15 10
2224 3col. Jaguarundi 45 30
2225 4col.50 White-tailed deer 65 45

558 Head

1993. "Third Age" Month.
2226 **558** 80c. black 10 10
2227 – 2col.20 multicoloured 30 20
DESIGN: 2col.20, Young boy beside elderly man holding tree.

559 Church of the Divine Providence

1993. AGAPE (social organization). Mult.
2228 1col. Type **559** 15 10
2229 1col. Family and AGAPE emblem 15 10

560 Secretary

1993. Secretary's Day. 25th Anniv of Salvadoran Association of Executive Secretaries.
2230 **560** 1col. multicoloured 15 10

561 Hospital

1993. Inauguration of Reconstructed Benjamin Bloom Children's Hospital.
2231 **561** 5col. multicoloured . . . 80 55

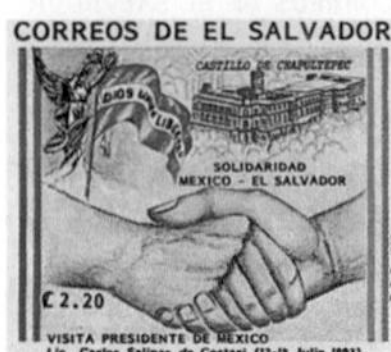

562 Flags, Clasped Hands and Chapultepec Castle

1993. State Visit of Pres. Carlos Salinas de Gortari of Mexico.
2232 **562** 2col.20 multicoloured . . 35 25

563 White Ibis

1993. Birds. Multicoloured.
2233 80c. Type **563** 30 25
2234 1col. American wood ibis 45 25
2235 2col.20 Great blue heron . . 1·10 60
2236 5col. Roseate spoonbill . . 2·50 1·25

564 Anniversary Emblem

1993. Centenary of Pharmaceutical Industry Standards Council.
2237 **564** 80c. mauve, blk & yell 10 10

565 Agouti

1993. America. Endangered Animals. Mult.
2238 80c. Type **565** 10 10
2239 2col.20 Common racoon . . 30 20

566 Pulgarcito (mascot)

567 Holy Family

1993. 5th Central American Games, El Salvador (1994). Multicoloured.
2240 50c. Type **566** 10 10
2241 1col.60 Games emblem, flags and Olympic rings 25 20
2242 2col.20 Mascot and map of Central America (horiz) 30 20
2243 4col.50 Mascot and map of El Salvador (horiz) . . . 65 45

1993. Christmas. Multicoloured.
2244 80c. Type **567** 10 10
2245 2col.20 Nativity scene and Christmas tree 30 20

1993. 125th Birth Anniv of Alberto Masferrer (sociologist).
2246 **568** 2col.20 multicoloured . . 30 20

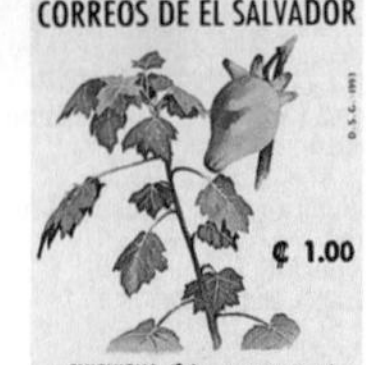

569 "Solanum mammosum"

1993. Medicinal Plants. Multicoloured.
2247 1col. Type **569** 15 10
2248 1col. "Hamelia patens" . . 15 10
2249 1col. "Tridax procumbens" 15 10
2250 1col. "Calea urticifolia" . . 15 10
2251 1col. "Ageratum conyzoides" 15 10
2252 1col. "Pluchea odorata" . . 15 10

570 I.Y.F. and United Nations Emblems

1994. International Year of the Family.
2253 **570** 2col.20 multicoloured . . 30 20

571 Hospital

1994. Centenary of Military Hospital. Mult.
2254 1col. Type **571** 15 10
2255 1col. Medical corps soldier treating wounded 15 10

572 Santa Ana Arms

1994. Centenary of Uprising of the 44 at Santa Ana. Multicoloured.
2256 60c. Type **572** 10 10
2257 80c. Commemorative inscription, laurel wreath and ribbon 10 10

573 Goalkeeper and Flags of U.S.A., Switzerland, Colombia and Rumania

1994. World Cup Football Championship, U.S.A. Various footballing scenes and flags of participating countries. Multicoloured.
2258 60c. Type **573** 10 10
2259 80c. Brazil, Russia, Cameroun and Sweden 10 10
2260 1col. Germany, Bolivia, South Korea and Spain 15 10
2261 2col.20 Argentina, Greece, Nigeria and Bulgaria . . 30 20
2262 4col.50 Italy, Ireland, Norway and Mexico . . . 65 45
2263 5col. Belgium, Morocco, Holland and Saudi Arabia 75 50

574 Order of Malta Square, Santa Elena, Cuscatlan

1994. Work of Sovereign Military Order of Malta in El Salvador.
2264 **574** 2col.20 multicoloured . . 30 20

575 Tiger and the Stag (San Juan Nonualco)

1994. Traditional Dances. Multicoloured.
2265 1col. Type **575** 15 10
2266 2col.20 The Speckled Bull (Santa Cruz Analquito and Estanzuelas) 30 20

576 Sweet Pepper

1994. Edible Plants. Multicoloured.
2267 70c. Type **576** 10 10
2268 80c. Cacao 10 10
2269 1col. Sweet potato 15 10
2270 5col. Pacaya 75 50

577 Mail Van

1994. America. Postal Vehicles. Mult.
2271 80c. Type **577** 10 10
2272 2col.20 Steam mail train . . 2·75 1·50

578 Cyclists **579** National Colours and Globe as Crate

1994. 22nd Tour of El Salvador Cycling Championship.
2273 **578** 80c. multicoloured . . . 10 10

1994. 16th International Fair.
2274 **579** 5col. multicoloured . . . 75 50

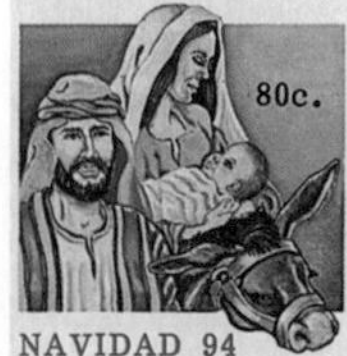

580 Holy Family and Donkey

1994. Christmas. Multicoloured.
2275 80c. Type **580** 10 10
2276 2col.20 Wise men and baby Jesus 30 20

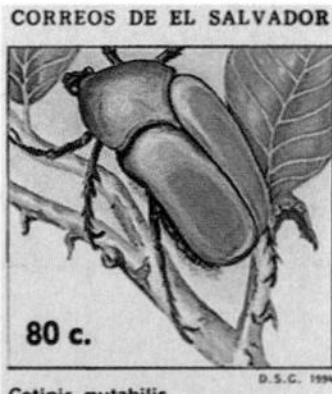

581 "Cotinis mutabilis"

1994. Beetles. Multicoloured.
2277 80c. Type **581** 10 10
2278 1col. "Phyllophaga sp." . . 15 10
2279 2col.20 "Galofa sp." 30 20
2280 5col. Longhorn beetle . . . 75 50

582 Books

1995. 40th Anniv of Cultural Centre. Anniversary emblems. Multicoloured.
2281 70c. Type **582** 10 10
2282 1col. "40" and arrows . . . 15 10

583 Vase **584** Menendez

1995. World Heritage Site. Joya de Ceren. Multicoloured.
2283 60c. Type **583** 10 10
2284 70c. Three-footed dish . . . 10 10
2285 80c. Two-handled pot . . . 10 10
2286 2col.20 Jug 35 25
2287 4col.50 Building No. 3 . . . 65 45
2288 5col. Building No. 4 . . . . 75 50

1995. Birth Bicent of Isidro Menendez (politician).
2289 **584** 80c. multicoloured . . . 10 10

585 Anniversary Emblem

1995. 80th Anniv of La Centro Americana, S.A. (welfare organization). Multicoloured.
2290 80c. Type **585** (safeguarding the future of the child) . . 10 10
2291 2col.20 "Child in Fancy Dress" (Jorge Driottez) (first "Expresiones" painting competition) . . 35 25

586 College and Map of Founding Sisters' Voyage

1995. Cent of College of the Sacred Heart.
2292 **586** 80c. multicoloured . . . 30 10

587 Emblem

1995. 50th Anniv of F.A.O.
2293 **587** 2col.20 multicoloured . . 35 25

588 Los Almendros Beach, Sonsonate

1995. 20th Anniv of World Tourism Organization. Multicoloured.
2294 50c. Type **588** 10 10
2295 60c. Apaneca Lake 10 10
2296 2col.20 Guerrero Beach, La Union 35 25
2297 5col. Usulutan Volcano . . 3·25 1·25

589 National Arms and Symbols of Development

1995. 174th Anniv of Central American Independence. Multicoloured.
2298 80c. Type **589** 30 10
2299 25col. El Salvador exports (sustained economic development) . . . . . . 3·75 2·50

590 "Lemboglossum stellatum"

1995. Orchids. Multicoloured.
2300 60c. "Pleurothallis glandulosa" 10 10
2301 60c. "Pleurothallis grobyi" 10 10
2302 70c. Type **590** 10 10
2303 70c. "Pleurothallis fuegii" 10 10
2304 1col. "Pleurothallis hirsuta" 15 10
2305 1col. "Lepanthes inaequalis" 15 10
2306 3col. "Hexadesmia micrantha" 45 30
2307 3col. "Pleurothallis segoviense" 45 30
2308 4col.50 "Stelis aprica" . . . 65 45
2309 4col.50 "Platystele stenostachya" 65 45
2310 5col. "Stelis barbata" . . . 75 50
2311 5col. "Pleurothallis schiedeii" 75 50

591 Pygmy Kingfisher

1995. America. Conservation. Multicoloured.
2312 80c. Type **591** 60 45
2313 2col. Green kingfisher . . . 1·75 90

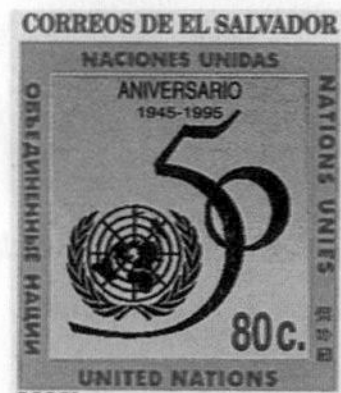

592 Anniversary Emblem

1995. 50th Anniv of U.N.O. Multicoloured.
2314 80c. Type **592** 10 10
2315 2col.20 Hands supporting emblem 35 25

593 Children with Sparklers

1995. Christmas. Multicoloured.
2316 80c. Type **593** 10 10
2317 2col.20 Family celebrating at midnight 35 25

594 Great Horned Owl ("Bubo virginianus")

1995. Wildlife of Montecristo. Multicoloured.
2318 80c. Type **594** 10 10
2319 80c. Kinkajou ("Potos flavus") 10 10
2320 80c. "Porthidium godmani" (snake) 10 10
2321 80c. Ocelot ("Felis pardalis") 10 10
2322 80c. "Deliathis bifurcata" (longhorn beetle) 10 10
2323 80c. Puma ("Felis concolor") 10 10
2324 80c. Red brocket ("Mazama americana") 10 10
2325 80c. "Leptophobia aripa" (butterfly) 10 10
2326 80c. Salamander ("Bolitoglossa salvinii") 10 10
2327 80c. Rivoli's hummingbird ("Eugenes fulgens") . . . 10 10
Nos. 2318/27 were issued together, se-tenant, forming a composite design of a forest.

595 Pope John Paul II in Mitre

1996. 2nd Papal Visit. Multicoloured.
2328 1col.50 Type **595** 20 15
2329 5col.40 Pope and Metropolitan Cathedral 75 50

596 Arrival of Spaniards

1996. 450th Anniv of Grant of City Status to San Salvador. Multicoloured.
2330 2col.50 Type **596** 35 25
2331 2col.70 Diego de Holguin (first governor) and chapel 40 30
2332 3col.30 Former National Palace, 1889 . . . . . . 45 30
2333 4col. Boulevard de los Heroes 55 40

597 ANTEL Emblem incorporating Globes

1996. Telecommunications Workers' Day. Mult.
2334 1col.50 Dish aerial and hand holding optic fibres (horiz) 20 15
2335 5col. Type **597** 70 50

598 Rey Avila (El Chele) (singer)

1996. Entertainers' Death Anniversaries. Mult.
2336 1col. Type **598** (1st death) 15 10
2337 1col.50 Maria Moreira (Dona Teresfora) (singer, 1st death) 20 15
2338 2col.70 Francisco Lara (Pancho Lara) (musician and composer, 7th death) 40 30
2339 4col. Carlos Pineda (Aniceto Porsisoca) (singer, 3rd death) 55 40

599 Anniversary Emblem

1996. 40th Anniv of YSKL Radio Station.
2340 **599** 1col.40 multicoloured . . 20 15

600 Throwing the Discus

1996. Centenary of Modern Olympic Games and Olympic Games, Atlanta. Ancient Greek athletes. Multicoloured.
2341 1col.50 Type **600** 20 15
2342 3col. Hurdling 45 30
2343 4col. Wrestling 55 40
2344 5col. Throwing the javelin 70 50

601 Northern Oriole ("Icterus galbula")

1996. Migratory Birds. Multicoloured.
2345 1col.50 Type **601** 20 15
2346 1col.50 American kestrel ("Falco sparverius") . . . 20 10
2347 1col.50 Yellow warbler ("Dendroica petechia") 20 15
2348 1col.50 Kingbird ("Tyrannus forficatus") 20 15
2349 1col.50 Rose-breasted grosbeak ("Pheucticus ludovicianus") 20 15

602 Printed Hand releasing Letters

1996. 60th Anniv of "El Diario de Hoy" (newspaper).
2350 **602** 5col.20 multicoloured . . 70 50

603 Station Emblem

1996. 30th Anniv of Channel 2 (television station).
2351 **603** 10col. multicoloured . . 1·40 95

604 Child and Anniversary Emblem

1996. 50th Anniv of UNICEF.
2352 **604** 1col. multicoloured . . . 15 10

605 Nahuizalco Woman

1996. America. Costumes. Multicoloured.
2353 1col.50 Type **605** 20 15
2354 4col. Panchimalco woman 55 40

606 Christmas Eve Mass (Doris Landaverde)

1996. Christmas. Children's Paintings. Mult.
2355 2col.50 Type **606** 35 25
2356 4col. Christmas morning (Isabel Perez) 55 40

607 Jerusalem

1996. 3000th Anniv of Jerusalem.
2357 **607** 1col. multicoloured . . . 15 10

608 White-nosed Sharks ("Nasolamia velox")

1996. Marine Life. Multicoloured.
2358 1col. Type **608** 15 10
2359 1col. Pacific sierra ("Scomberomorus sierra") 15 10
2360 1col. Common dolphins ("Delphinus delphis") . . 15 10
2361 1col. Hawksbill turtle ("Eretmochelys imbricata") 15 10
2362 1col. Starry grouper ("Epinephelus labriformis") 15 10
2363 1col. Cortez angelfish ("Pomacanthus zonipectus") 15 10
2364 1col. Mexican parrotfish ("Scarus perrico") 15 10
2365 1col. Pacific seahorse ("Hippocampus ingens") 15 10
Nos. 2358/65 were issued together, se-tenant, forming a composite design.

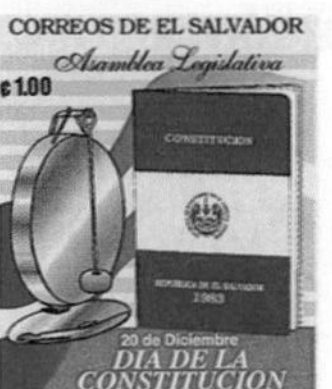

609 Gong and 1983 Constitution

1996. Constitution Day.
2366 **609** 1col. multicoloured . . . 15 10

610 Newspapers and Computer

1997. 30th Anniv of "El Mundo" (newspaper).
2367 **610** 10col. multicoloured . . 1·40 95

611 Steam Locomotive No. 58441, 1925

1997. "Exfilna 97" National Stamp Exhibition, San Salvador.
2368 **611** 4col. multicoloured . . . 1·40 90

612 Church and Mother Clara

1997. 80th Anniv of Foundation of Carmelite Order of St. Joseph.
2369 **612** 1col. multicoloured . . . 15 10

613 Anniversary Emblem

1997. 50th Anniv of American School.
2370 **613** 25col. multicoloured . . 3·50 2·40

614 Custard Apple ("Annona diversifolia")

1997. Tropical Fruits. Multicoloured.
2371 1col.50 Type **614** 20 15
2372 1col.50 Cashew ("Anacardium occidentale") 20 15
2373 1col.50 Melon ("Cucumis melo") 20 15
2374 1col.50 Sapodilla ("Pouteria mammosa") 20 15

615 Anniversary Emblem

1997. 55th Anniv of Lions International in El Salvador.
2376 **615** 4col. multicoloured . . . 55 40

616 Hand protecting Ecosystem

1997. Int Ozone Layer Day (2377) and Int-American Water Day (2378). Multicoloured.
2377 1col.50 Type **616** 20 15
2378 4col. Boy drinking clean water 55 40

617 Flag, Duck, Face and Wreath

1997. 176th Anniv of Independence. Mult.
2379 2col.50 Type **617** 35 25
2380 5col.20 National flag, celebrating crowd and peace dove 70 50

618 Cervantes, Book and Don Quixote and Sancho

1997. 450th Birth Anniv of Miguel de Cervantes (writer).
2381 **618** 4col. multicoloured . . . 55 40

619 Emblem

620 Postman handing Letter to Woman

1997. 75th Anniv of Scout Movement in El Salvador.
2382 **619** 1col.50 multicoloured . . 20 15

1997. America. The Postman. Multicoloured.
2383 1col. Type **620** 15 10
2384 4col. Dog chasing postman on scooter 55 40

621 Motor Car

1997. 26th Anniv of El Salvador Automobile Club.
2385 **621** 10col. multicoloured . . 1·40 95

622 Open-air Feast

1997. Christmas. Children's paintings. Mult.
2386 1col.50 Type **622** 20 15
2387 1col.50 Family gathering . . 20 15

623 Map and St. John Bosco (founder)

1997. Centenary of Salesian Brothers in El Salvador. Multicoloured.
2388 1col.50 Type **623** 20 15
2389 1col.50 St. Cecilia College, Santa Tecla 20 15
2390 1col.50 St. Joseph College, Santa Ana 20 15
2391 1col.50 Ricaldone Technical College 20 15
2392 1col.50 Maria Auxiliadora Church and statue 20 15
2393 1col.50 Don Bosco Citadel, Soyapango, and electronics class 20 15

624 Standard, 1946

1997. Motor Cars. Multicoloured.
2394 2col.50 Type **624** 35 25
2395 2col.50 Chrysler, 1936 . . . 35 25
2396 2col.50 Jaguar, 1954 . . . . 35 25
2397 2col.50 Ford, 1930 . . . . 35 25
2398 2col.50 Mercedes Benz, 1953 35 25
2399 2col.50 Porsche, 1956 . . . 35 25

625 St. Joseph's Church, Ahuachapan

1998. 125th Anniv of St. Joseph's Order. Mult.
2400 1col. Type **625** 15 10
2401 4col. Jose Vilaseca and Cesarea Esparza (founders) 55 40

626 Air Traffic Control Tower

1998. Modernisation of El Salvador International Airport.
2402 **626** 10col. multicoloured . . 1·40 95

627 Player with Ball and Sacre Coeur, Paris

1998. World Cup Football Championship, France. Multicoloured.
2403 1col.50 Type **627** 20 15
2404 1col.50 Player and Eiffel Tower, Paris 20 15
2405 1col.50 Player and the Louvre, Paris 20 15
2406 1col.50 Goalkeeper and Notre Dame Cathedral, Paris 20 15

628 Sun around Map of Americas

1998. 50th Anniv of Organization of American States.
2408 **628** 4col. multicoloured . . . 55 40

629 Swimming, Tennis and Water Polo Medals

1999. El Salvador, Champion of Sixth Central American Games. Multicoloured.
2409 1col.50 Type **629** 20 15
2410 1col.50 Body-building, judo and shooting medals . . . 20 15
2411 1col.50 Gymnastics, weightlifting and karate medals 20 15
2412 1col.50 Discus, volleyball and netball medals . . . 20 15

630 Guerrero

1998. 40th Death Anniv of Dr. Jose Gustano Guerrero (former President of Tribunal of Justice, The Hague).
2413 **630** 1col. multicoloured . . . 15 10

631 Maps on Cubes

1998. 18th International Fair.
2414 **631** 4col. multicoloured . . . 55 40

632 Arce's Deathbed

1998. 150th Death Anniv of Manuel Jose Arce (President of United Provinces of Central America, 1825–29).
2415 **632** 4col. multicoloured . . . 55 40

633 Ruby-throated Hummingbird

1998. Hummingbirds. Multicoloured.
2416 1col.50 Type **633** 20 15
2417 1col.50 Cinnamon hummingbird ("Amazilia rutila") 20 15
2418 1col.50 Blue-throated hummingbird ("Hylocharis eliciae") . . 20 15
2419 1col.50 Green violetear ("Colibri thalassinus") . . 20 15

2420 1col.50 Violet sabrewing ("Campylopterus hemileucurus") 20 15
2421 1col.50 Amethyst-throated hummingbird ("Lampornis amethystinus") 20 15

634 House and Figure

635 Scroll

1998. 25th Anniv of Housing Social Fund.
2422 **634** 10col. multicoloured . . 1·40 95

1998. 50th Anniv of National Archives.
2423 **635** 1col.50 multicoloured . . 20 15

636 Alice Larde de Venturino (writer)

1998. America. Famous Women. Multicoloured.
2424 1col. Type **636** 15 10
2425 4col. Maria de Baratta (composer) 55 40

637 Nativity

1998. Christmas. Children's Paintings. Mult.
2426 1col. Type **637** 15 10
2427 4col. Angels and shepherds going to church 55 40

638 Planets and Philatelic Emblems on Pyramid

1998. World Post Day.
2428 **638** 1col. multicoloured . . . 15 10

639 C47T Transport and Badge

1998. 75th Anniv of El Salvador Air Force. Mult.
2429 1col.50 Type **639** 20 15
2430 1col.50 TH-300 training helicopter and badge . . 20 15
2431 1col.50 UH-1H utility helicopter and badge . . 20 15
2432 1col.50 Cessna A-37B Dragonfly bomber and badge 20 15

640 Papaw and Palm Leaf Salad

1998. Traditional Dishes. Multicoloured.
2433 1col.50 Type **640** 20 15
2434 1col.50 Black pudding soup ("Sopa de Mondongo") 20 15
2435 1col.50 Alhuaiste prawns . . 20 15
2436 1col.50 Panela honey fritters 20 15
2437 1col.50 Chilled salad ("Refresco de Ensalada") 20 15
2438 1col.50 Avocado salad ("Ensalada de Aguacate") 20 15
2439 1col.50 Water rice and cabbage soup ("Sopa de Arroz ...") 20 15
2440 1col.50 Typical El Salvador dish 20 15
2441 1col.50 Banana rissoles ("Empanadas de Platano") 20 15
2442 1col.50 Barley water ("Horchata") 20 15

641 Roberto d'Aubuisson signing Constitution

1998. 15th Anniv of Constitution.
2443 **641** 25col. black and blue . . 3·50 2·40

642 "Salvador" (steamship)

1999. 1st National Thematic Stamps Exhibition, San Salvador.
2444 **642** 2col.50 multicoloured . . 35 25

643 Anniversary Emblem

1999. 40th Anniv of National Television.
2445 **643** 4col. multicoloured . . . 55 40

644 Moorhen

1999. Water Birds. Multicoloured.
2446 1col. Type **644** 15 10
2447 1col. American purple gallinule ("Porphyrula martinica") 15 10
2448 1col. Spotted rail ("Pardirallus maculatus") 15 10
2449 1col. Blue-winged teal ("Anas discors") 15 10
2450 1col. Red-billed whistling duck ("Dendrocygna autumnalis") 15 10
2451 1col. American coot ("Fulica americana") . . 15 10
2452 1col. Northern jacana ("Jacana spinosa") . . . 15 10
2453 1col. Sora crake ("Porzana carolina") 15 10
2454 1col. Limpkin ("Aramus guarauna") 15 10
2455 1col. Masked duck ("Oxyura dominica") . . 15 10

645 E.U. and El Salvador Flags

1999. Co-operation between European Union and El Salvador. Multicoloured.
2457 5col.20 Type **645** 70 50
2458 10col. Handshake, El Salvador arms and E.U. emblem . . . . 1·40 95

646 Flags and Arms of El Salvador and U.S.A.

1999. Visit of U.S. President William Clinton to El Salvador. Multicoloured.
2459 5col. Type **646** 70 50
2460 5col. Presidents Armando Calderon Sol and Clinton 70 50

Nos. 2459/60 were issued together, se-tenant, forming a composite design.

647 Stylized People and Globe

1999. 5th Anniv of Salvadoran Institute for Professional Development.
2461 **647** 5col.40 multicoloured . . 75 50

648 Common Long-tongued Bat

1999. Bats. Multicoloured.
2462 1col.50 Type **648** 20 15
2463 1col.50 Common vampire bat ("Desmodus rotundus") 20 15
2464 1col.50 Mexican bulldog bat (Noctilio leporinus) . . . 20 15
2465 1col.50 False vampire bat ("Vampyrum spectrum") 20 15
2466 1col.50 Honduran white bat ("Ectophylla alba") . . . 20 15
2467 1col.50 Black-whiskered bat ("Myotis nigricans") . . . 20 15

649 Drilling Tower, Ahuachapan

1999. Energy in the 21st Century. Geothermal Technology. Multicoloured.
2468 1col. Type **649** 15 10
2469 4col. Geothermal power station, Berlin, Usulutan 55 40

650 Globe and Items for Export

1999. 24th Anniv of Corporation of Exporters.
2470 **650** 4col. multicoloured . . . 55 40

651 Dove, Typewriter and Map

1999. National Journalists' Day.
2471 **651** 1col.50 multicoloured . . 20 15

652 "Cattleya skinneri var. alba"

1999. Orchids. Multicoloured.
2472 1col.50 Type **652** 20 15
2473 1col.50 "Cattleya skinneri var. coerulea" 20 15
2474 1col.50 "Cattleya skinneri" 20 15
2475 1col.50 "Cattleya guatemalensis" 20 15
2476 1col.50 "Cattleya aurantiaca var. flava" 20 15
2477 1col.50 "Cattleya aurantiaca" 20 15

653 Self-portrait

1999. 120th Birth Anniv of Tono Salazar (caricaturist). Each blue and black.
2478 1col.50 Type **653** 20 15
2479 1col.50 Salarrue 20 15
2480 1col.50 Claudia Lars 20 15
2481 1col.50 Francisco Gavidia 20 15
2482 1col.50 Miguel Angel Asturias 20 15

654 Flask, Computer and Children eating

1999. Central American Institute of Nutrition, Panama. Multicoloured.
2483 5col.20 Type **654** 80 50
2484 5col.40 Foodstuffs 85 55

655 Gen. Manuel Jose Arce and Capt. Gen. Gerardo Barrios

1999. 175th Anniv of the Army. Multicoloured.
2485 1col. Type **655** 15 10
2486 1col.50 Soldier and flag . . 25 15

656 Emblem

1999. International Year of the Elderly.
2487 **656** 10col. multicoloured . . 1·60 1·10

657 Dove, Globe and Children

1999. America. A New Millennium without Arms. Multicoloured.
2488 1col. Type **657** 15 10
2489 4col. Globe and sign crossing out gun 65 40

658 Emblem

1999. 125th Anniv of Universal Postal Union. Mult.
2490 4col. Type **658** 65 40
2491 4col. Mail and modes of transport 65 40
Nos. 2490/1 were issued together, se-tenant, forming a composite design.

659 Star and Temples (Delmy Guandique)

1999. Christmas. Paintings. Multicoloured.
2492 1col.50 Type **659** 25 15
2493 1col.50 Woman holding poinsettias (Margarita Orellana) 25 15
2494 4col. The Holy Family (Lolly Sandoval) 65 40
2495 4col. The Nativity (Jose Francisco Guadron) . . . 65 40

660 Emblem

1999. 40th Anniv of International Development Bank.
2496 **660** 25col. multicoloured . . 3·25 2·10

661 Golden-fronted Woodpecker

1999. Woodpeckers. Multicoloured.
2497 1col.50 Type **661** 25 15
2498 1col.50 Golden-olive woodpecker (*Piculus rubiginosus*) 25 15
2499 1col.50 Yellow-bellied sapsucker (*Sphyrapicus varius*) 25 15
2500 1col.50 Lineated woodpecker (*Dryocopus lineatus*) 25 15
2501 1col.50 Acorn woodpecker (*Melanerpes formicivorus*) 25 15

662 Emblem

1999. 70th Anniv of Coffee Farmers' Association.
2502 **662** 10col. multicoloured . . 1·60 1·10

663 Emblem

2000. New Year.
2503 **663** 1col.50 multicoloured . . 25 15

664 Fireman rescuing Child

2000. 25th Anniv of National Fire Service. Mult.
2504 2col.50 Type **664** 40 25
2505 25col. Fire service emblem 3·25 2·10

665 Children, Books and Map of El Salvador

2000. 30th Anniv of Educational Work.
2506 **665** 1col. multicoloured . . . 15 10

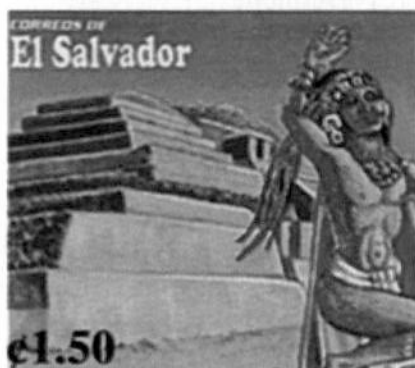

666 Temple and Dancer

2000. New Millennium (1st series). Multicoloured.
2507 1col.50 Type **666** 25 15
2508 1col.50 *Santa Maria* and Columbus (discovery of America by Columbus) 25 15
2509 1col.50 Soldier and native 25 15
2510 1col.50 Court room (Declaration of Independence, 1841) . . . 25 15
See also Nos. 2533/6.

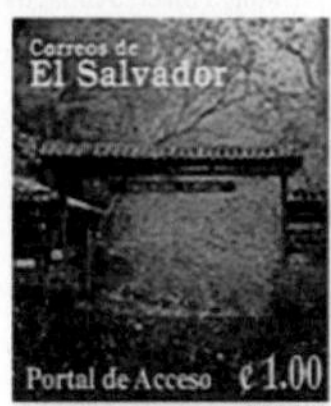

667 Acceso Gate

2000. El Imposible National Park, Ahuachapan. Multicoloured.
2511 1col. Type **667** 15 10
2512 1col. Ocelot cub 15 10
2513 1col. Paca 15 10
2514 1col. Venado River falls . . 15 10
2515 1col. Great curassow . . . 15 10
2516 1col. Tree with yellow leaves 15 10
2517 1col. Orchid 15 10
2518 1col. Blue-crowned motmot 15 10
2519 1col. Painted bunting . . . 15 10
2520 1col. Plant 15 10
2521 1col. Information centre . . 15 10
2522 1col. White-eared ground sparrow 15 10
2523 1col. Green frog 15 10
2524 1col. Fungi growing on branch 15 10
2525 1col. Flower (Guaco de Tierra) 15 10
2526 1col. Emerald toucanet . . . 15 10
2527 1col. View over park . . . 15 10
2528 1col. Brazilian agouti . . . 15 10
2529 1col. Tamandua 15 10
2530 1col. El Imposible River falls 15 10

668 Ink Pen, Text and Emblem

2000. 85th Anniv of *La Prensa Grafica* (bilingual newspaper).
2531 **668** 5col. multicoloured . . . 80 50

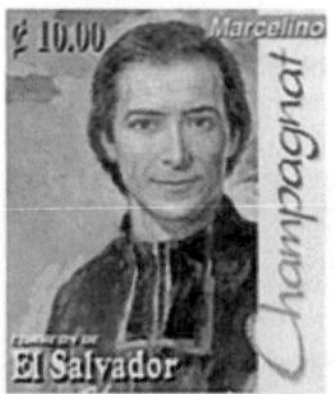

669 Champagnat

2000. Canonization (1999) of Marcelino Champagnat (Catholic priest).
2532 **669** 10col. multicoloured . . 1·60 1·00

670 Casa Blanca, San Salvador, 1890

2000. New Millennium (2nd series). Each black and brown.
2533 1col.50 Type **670** 25 15
2534 1col.50 Market, 1920 . . . 25 15
2535 1col.50 Tram outside Nuevo Mundo Hotel, 1924 . . . 25 15
2536 1col.50 Motor cars, 2a South Avenue, 1924 . . . 25 15

671 Athletics

2000. Olympic Games, Sydney. Multicoloured.
2537 1col. Type **671** 15 10
2538 1col. Gymnastics 15 10
2539 1col. High-jumping 15 10
2540 1col. Weightlifting 15 10
2541 1col. Fencing 15 10
2542 1col. Cycling 15 10
2543 1col. Swimming 15 10
2544 1col. Shooting 15 10
2545 1col. Archery 15 10
2546 1col. Judo 15 10

672 Baldwin Steam Locomotive

2000. Trains. Multicoloured.
2547 1col.50 Type **672** 25 15
2548 1col.50 General Electric Corporation locomotive 25 15
2549 1col.50 Open-sided carriage 25 15
2550 1col.50 Presidential carriage 25 15

673 Globe, Envelope and Computer

2000. World Post Day.
2551 **673** 5col. multicoloured . . . 80 50

674 Snowman

2000. Christmas. Multicoloured.
2552 1col. Type **674** 15 10
2553 1col. Bells 15 10
2554 1col. Baubles 15 10
2555 1col. Candy stick 15 10
2556 1col. Candles 15 10
2557 1col. Sleigh 15 10
2558 1col. Presents 15 10
2559 1col. Father Christmas . . . 15 10
2560 1col. Christmas hat 15 10
2561 1col. Boot 15 10

675 "The Traveller" (Roberto Mejia Ruiz)

2000. Paintings. Multicoloured.
2562 4col. Type **675** 65 40
2563 4col. Man kneeling (Alex Cuchilla) 65 40
2564 4col. Woman wearing hat (Nicolas Fredy Shi Quan) 65 40
2565 4col. Swallows (Jose Bernardo Pacheco) . . . 65 40
2566 4col. Man on Globe (Oscar Soles) 65 40

676 West Highland White Terriers

2001. Pets. Multicoloured.
2567 1col.50 Type **676** 20 15
2568 1col.50 West highland white terrier and cat 20 15
2569 2col.50 Budgerigars 35 20
2570 2col.50 Rough-coated terrier and English toy terrier . . 35 20

677 Children's Playground

2001. 25th Anniv of Saburo Hirao Park, San Salvador. Multicoloured.
2571 5col. Type **677** 75 45
2572 25col. Japanese garden . . . 3·75 1·50

678 Claudia Lars and Federico Proano

2001. Latin American Writers.
2573 **678** 10col. multicoloured . . 1·40 85

679 Building, Nun and Children

2001. 125th Anniv of Hogar del Nino San Vicente de Paul (children's home), Quito, Ecuador.
2574 **679** 4col. multicoloured . . . 60 35

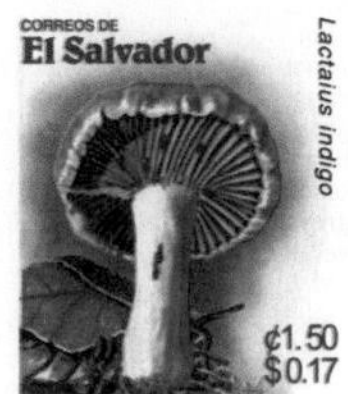

680 Indigo Milky (*Lactarius indigo*)

2001. Fungi. Multicoloured.
2575 1col.50 Type **680** (inscr Lactaius) 20 15
2576 1col.50 Oyster mushroom (*Pleurotus ostreatus*) . . . 20 15
2577 1col.50 *Ramaria sp.* 20 15
2578 1col.50 White worm coral fungus (*Clavaria vermicularis*) 20 10
2579 4col. Fly agaric (*Amanita muscaria*) 60 35
2580 4col. *Phillipsia sp.* 60 35
2581 4col. Emetic russula (*Russula*) 60 35
2582 4col. Collared earthstar (*Geastrum triplex*) 60 35

681 Josemaria Escriva de Balaguer

2002. Birth Centenary of Josemaria Escriva de Balaguer (founder of Opus Dei (religious organization)). Multicoloured.
2583 1col. Type **681** 15 10
2584 5col. Facing left 60 35

682 Clasped Hands

2002. 10th Anniv of Peace Accord. Multicoloured.
2585 2col.50 Type **682** 30 20
2586 2col.50 Sun and dove . . . 30 20
MS2587 150 × 120 mm. 2col.50 × 2, Dove holding olive branch; Dove as flag 60 60

683 Weightlifter, Archer and Show Jumper

2002. 19th Central America and Caribbean Games. Multicoloured.
2588 1col. Type **683** 15 10
2589 1col. Cyclists 15 10
2590 1col. Blocks containing stylized sportsmen 15 10
2591 1col. Young gymnast . . . 15 10
MS2592 120 × 90 mm. 4col. Stylized birds 50 20

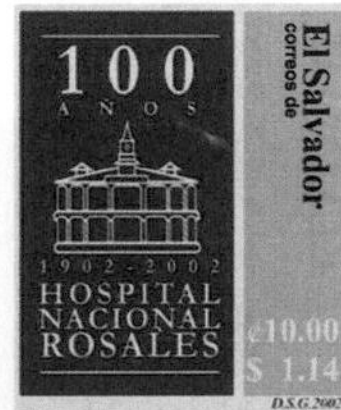

684 Anniversary Emblem

2002. Rosales Hospital Centenary.
2593 **684** 10col. ultramarine and black . . . . 1·20 70

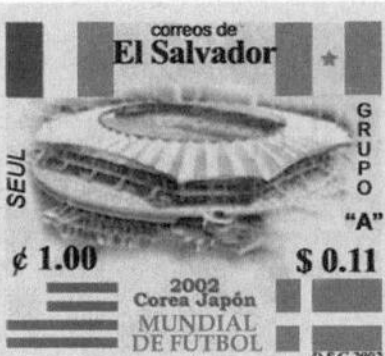

685 Seoul Stadium

2002. World Cup Football Championships, Japan and South Korea. Designs showing stadia. Multicoloured.
2594 1col. Type **685** 15 10
2595 1col. Busan 15 10
2596 1col. Incheon 15 10
2597 1col. Suwon 15 10
2598 1col.50 Niigata 20 15
2599 1col.50 Saitama 20 15
2600 1col.50 Miyagi 20 15
2601 1col.50 Osaka 20 15
MS2602 110 × 85 mm. 4col. Brazilian flag 50 30

686 Lion Club Emblem

2002. 50th Anniv (2001) of San Miguel Lion's Club (charitable organization).
2603 **686** 5col. multicoloured . . . 60 35

687 Academy Emblem

2002. 10th Anniv of National Public Security Academy.
2604 **687** 1col. multicoloured . . . 15 10

688 Parliamentary Emblem

2002. 10th Anniv (2001) of Central American Parliament.
2605 **688** 25col. blue and black . . 3·00 1·80

689 Organization Building

2002. Centenary of Pan American Health Organization. Multicoloured.
2606 2col. 70 Type **689** 35 20
2607 2col. 70 Anniversary emblem 35 20

690 Stylized Child standing on Open Book

2002. America. Literacy Campaign. Multicoloured.
2608 1col. Type **690** 15 10
2609 1col.50 Classroom 20 15

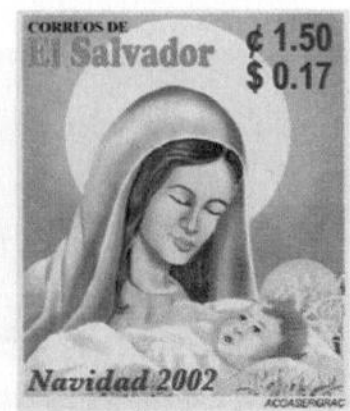

691 Mary and Jesus

2002. Christmas. Multicoloured.
2610 1col.50 Type **691** 20 15
2611 2col.50 Joseph and Jesus . . 30 20

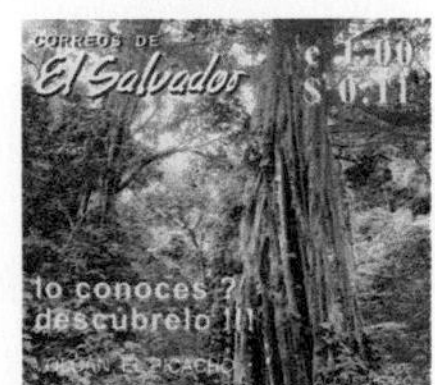

692 El Picacho, San Salvador Volcano

2002. Tourism. Multicoloured.
2612 1col. Type **692** 15 10
2613 1col. Jiquilisco Bay 15 10
2614 4col. Joya de Ceren archaeological site 50 30
2615 4col. Juayua, Sonsonate . . 50 30

693 Emblem and Scouts

2002. 80th Anniv of El Salvador Scouting Movement.
2616 **693** 25col. multicoloured . . 3·00 1·80

694 Women seated at Desks

2003. Centenary of Daughters of Mary (religious organization). Multicoloured.
2617 70c. Type **694** 10 10
2618 1col.50 Mary and Jesus (statue) 20 15

695 Early Family

2003. 450th Anniv of Sonsonate City.
2619 **695** 1col. 60 multicoloured 20 15

696 Leafless Tree

2003. 40th Anniv of Grupo Roble (entrepreneurial group). Multicoloured.
2620 1col.50 Type **696** 20 15
2621 1col.50 Fruiting tree 20 15
MS2622 75 × 100 mm. 40col. Bird on nest 50 50

697 Anniversary Emblem

2003. 50th Anniv of Regional Organization for Farming Health (OIRSA).
2623 **697** 25col. multicoloured . . 3·00 1·80

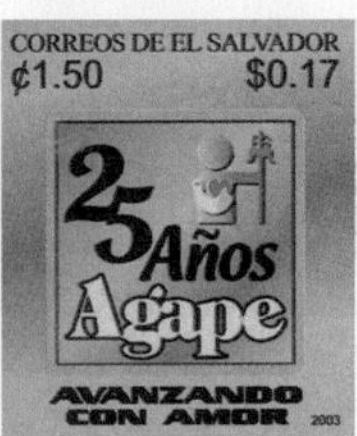

698 Emblem

2003. 25th Anniv of AGAPE (Catholic social organization).
2624 **698** 1col.50 multicoloured . . 20 15

699 Maria Felipe Aranzamendi

2003. Women of the Independence Movement. Multicoloured.
2625 2col.50 Type **699** 30 20
2626 2col. 70 Manuela Arce de Lara 35 20
MS2627 75 × 100 mm. 4col. Celebration 50 50

700 Children, Farmers and Produce

2003. 25th Anniv of United Nations Food and Agriculture Organization in El Salvador. Multicoloured.
2628 1col.50 Type **700** 20 15
MS2629 100 × 75 mm. 4col. Girl behind tree and food workers 50 50

701 Bee (inscr "Abejorro")

2003. Flora and Fauna (1st issue). Multicoloured.
2630 1col.50 Type **701** 20 15
2631 1col.50 *Chrysina quetzalcoatli* 20 15
2632 1col.50 *Anartia Fatima* . . . 20 15
2633 1col.50 *Manduca* 20 15
2634 1col.50 *Manduca sexta* . . . 20 15

2635 1col.50 *Tabebuia chrysantha* 20 15
2636 1col.50 *Alpina purpurata* 20 15
2637 1col.50 *Tecoma stans* 20 15
2638 1col.50 *Tabebuia rosea* 20 15
2639 1col.50 *Passiflora edulis* 20 15
MS2640 100 × 75 mm. 4col. *Tabebuia rosea* and Anartia Fatima (vert) 50 50
See also Nos. 2653/4.

702 Mary and Jesus

2003. Christmas. Multicoloured.
2641 1col.50 Type **702** 20 15
2642 4col. Holy Family 50 30

703 Church of the Immaculate Conception, Citalia

2003. Churches. Multicoloured.
2643 4col. Type **703** 50 30
2644 4col. St. James Apostle, Chalchuapa 50 30
2645 4col. St. Peter Apostle, Metapan 50 30
2646 4col. Our Lady Santa Ana, Chapeltique 50 50
2647 4col. St. James Apostle, Conchagua 50 30
MS2648 75 × 100 mm. 5col. El Cavario, San Salvador (vert) 60 60

704 Procession of Brotherhood of Panchimalco

2003. Tourism. Multicoloured.
2649 1col.50 Type **704** 20 15
2650 1col.50 Church cupola, Juayua 20 15
2651 1col.50 Shalpa beach, La Libertad 20 15
2652 1col.50 Maya ruins, Tazumal 20 15

705 *Fernaldia pandurata*

2003. Flora and Fauna (2nd issue). Multicoloured.
2653 1col.50 Type **705** 20 15
2654 4col. *Lepidophyma smithii* 50 30

706 Panama and El Salvador Flags

2004. Centenary of Panama Independence. Centenary of Panama—El Salvador Diplomatic Relations. Multicoloured.
2655 10col. Type **706** 1·20 80
2656 25col. Ship in canal 3·00 1·80

707 Stars

2004. Europe Day (2657). Enlargement of European Union (2658). Multicoloured.
2657 2col. 70 Type **707** 35 20
2658 5col. Stars and map of Europe 60 35

708 "La Siguanaba"

2004. Legends. Multicoloured.
2659 1col. Type **708** 15 10
2660 1col. "La Carreta Chillona" 15 10
2661 1col. 60 "El Cipitio" 20 15
2662 1col. 60 "Justo Juez de la Noche" 20 15

709 Flasks

2004. Centenary of Pharmaceutical College. Litho.
2663 **709** 10col. multicoloured 1·20 80

710 Adalberto Guirola Children's Home

2004. 150th Anniv of Santa Tecla (town).
2664 **710** 1col.50 multicoloured 20 15

711 Wilbur and Orville Wright

2004. Centenary of Powered Flight (2003). Aviation pioneers. Multicoloured.
2665 1col.50 Type **711** 20 15
2666 1col.50 Alberto Santos Dumont 20 15
2667 1col.50 Louis Bleriot 20 15
2668 1col.50 Glenn Curtiss 20 15
2669 1col.50 Hugo Junkers 20 15
2670 4col. Charles Lindbergh 50 30
2671 4col. Amelia Earhart 50 30
2672 4col. Chuck Yeagar 50 30
2673 4col. Robert With 50 30
2674 4col. Richard Rutan and Jeana Yeagar 50 30
MS2675 70 × 93 mm. 4col. Wilbur and Orville Wright (34 × 40 mm) 50 50

712 The Nativity

2004. Christmas. Multicoloured.
2676 1col.50 Type **712** 20 15
2677 2col.50 Shepherd and star 30 20
2678 4col. Three Wise Men 50 30
2679 5col. Flight into Egypt 60 35

713 *Akko rossi*

2004. America. Fauna. Multicoloured.
2680 1col. 40 Type **713** 15 10
2681 2col. 20 *Chromodoris sphoni* 25 15

ACKNOWLEDGEMENT OF RECEIPT STAMP

AR 53

1897.
AR264 AR **53** 5c. green 15

EXPRESS STAMPS

E **547** Throwing the Hammer

1992. Olympic Games, Barcelona. Mult.
E2199 60c. Type E **547** 10 10
E2200 80c. Volleyball 10 10
E2201 90c. Putting the shot (decathlon) 15 10
E2202 2col.20 Long jumping 30 20
E2203 3col. Gymnastics (vaulting) 45 30
E2204 5col. Gymnastics (floor exercise) 75 50

OFFICIAL STAMPS

1896. Stamps of 1896 (first issue) optd **FRANQUEO OFICIAL** in oval.
O170 **37** 1c. blue 10
O171 2c. brown 10
O172 3c. green 40
O173 5c. olive 10
O174 10c. yellow 10
O175 12c. blue 20
O176 15c. violet 10
O177 20c. red 40
O178 24c. red 10
O179 30c. orange 40
O180 50c. black 30
O181 1p. red 20

1896. Stamps of 1896 (second issue) optd **FRANQUEO OFICIAL** in oval.
O182 **38** 1c. green 10
O183 **39** 2c. lake 10
O184 3c. orange 50
O185 5c. blue 20
O186 10c. brown 10
O187 12c. grey 25
O188 15c. green 25
O189 20c. red 25
O190 24c. violet 25
O191 30c. green 15
O192 50c. orange 25
O193 100c. blue 30

1896. Stamps of 1895 (first issue) optd **CORREOS DE EL SALVADOR DE OFICIO** in circle and band.
O194 **37** 1c. blue 8·50
O195 2c. brown 8·50
O196 3c. green 8·50
O197 5c. olive 8·50
O198 10c. yellow 10·00
O199 12c. blue 13·00
O200 15c. violet 13·00
O201 20c. red 13·00
O202 24c. red 13·00
O203 30c. orange 13·00
O204 50c. black 17·00
O205 1p. red 17·00

1896. Stamps of 1896 (second issue) optd **CORREOS DE EL SALVADOR DE OFICIO** in circle and band.
O206 **38** 1c. green 7·00
O207 **39** 2c. lake 7·00
O208 3c. orange 30·00
O209 5c. blue 7·00
O210 10c. brown 7·00
O211 12c. grey 12·00
O212 15c. green 12·00
O219 15c. on 24c. violet (No. 218) 12·00
O213 20c. red 12·00
O214 24c. violet 12·00
O215 30c. green 12·00
O216 50c. orange 12·00
O217 100c. blue 12·00

1897. Stamps of 1897 optd **FRANQUEO OFICIAL** in oval.
O232 1c. red 10 10
O233 2c. green 70
O234 3c. brown 60
O235 5c. orange 20 25
O236 10c. green 25
O237 12c. blue 30
O238 15c. black 35 45
O239 20c. grey 15
O240 24c. yellow 25 35
O241 30c. red 25 65
O242 50c. violet 90
O243 100c. lake 80 1·75

1897. Stamps of 1897 optd **CORREOS DE EL SALVADOR DE OFICIO** in circle and band.
O244 1c. red 9·00 9·00
O245 2c. green 9·00 9·00
O246 3c. brown 30·00 32·00
O247 5c. orange 9·00 9·00
O248 10c. green 10·00 10·00
O249 12c. blue 13·00
O250 15c. black 13·00
O251 20c. grey 15·00
O252 24c. yellow 20·00
O253 30c. red 17·00
O254 50c. violet 22·00
O255 100c. lake 20·00

1898. Stamps of 1898 optd **FRANQUEO OFICIAL** in oval.
O288 **57** 1c. red 10
O289 2c. red 15
O290 3c. green 1·75
O291 5c. green 15
O292 10c. blue 10
O293 12c. violet 1·75
O294 13c. lake 15
O295 20c. blue 15
O296 24c. blue 10
O297 26c. brown 15
O298 50c. orange 15
O299 1p. yellow 15

1899. Stamps of 1899, with wheel opt as T **58** optd **FRANQUEO OFICIAL** in curved type.
O329 **59** 1c. brown 40 40
O330 2c. green 70 70
O331 3c. blue 40 40
O332 5c. orange 40 40
O333 10c. brown 50 50
O334 12c. green
O335 13c. red 95 95
O336 24c. blue 18·00 18·00
O337 26c. red 50 50
O338 50c. red 1·00 1·00
O339 100c. violet 1·00 1·00

1900. Federation issue of 1897 optd **CORREOS DE EL SALVADOR DE OFICIO** in circle and band.
O355 **55** 1c. multicoloured 20·00 20·00
O356 5c. multicoloured 20·00 20·00

1900. Stamps of 1900, dated "1900", optd **FRANQUEO OFICIAL** in oval, and with or without shield opt T **66**.
O448 **59** 1c. green (No. 438) 35 35
O449 2c. red 40 35
O450 3c. black 25 25
O451 5c. blue 25 25
O452 10c. blue 50 50
O453 12c. green 50 50
O454 13c. brown 50 50
O455 24c. black 30 50
O461 26c. brown 35 35
O462 50c. red 55 40

1903. As T **70**, but inscr "FRANQUEO OFICIAL" across statue.
O497 1c. green 35 25
O498 2c. red 35 15
O499 3c. orange 70 60
O500 5c. blue 35 15
O501 10c. purple 50 35
O502 13c. brown 50 35
O503 15c. brown 2·50 1·25
O504 24c. red 35 35
O505 50c. brown 50 25
O506 100c. blue 50 55

1905. Nos. O500/502 surch with new value and two black circles.
O518 2c. on 5c. blue 2·40 2·00
O519 3c. on 5c. blue
O520 3c. on 10c. purple 6·50 4·50
O521 3c. on 13c. brown 60 50

1905. No. O450 optd **1905**.
O558 **59** 3c. black 1·25 1·10

1906. Nos. O449/50 optd **1906**.
O567 **59** 2c. red
O568 3c. black 90 70

1906. As T **89**, but inscr "FRANQUEO OFICIAL" at foot of portrait.
O582 1c. black and green 15 10
O583 2c. black and red 15 10
O584 3c. black and yellow 15 10
O585 5c. black and blue 15 35
O586 10c. black and violet 15 10
O587 13c. black and brown 15 10
O588 15c. black and red 20 10
O589 24c. black and red 25 25

O590 50c. black and orange 25 50
O591 100c. black and blue 25 1·50

1908. As T **91**, but inscr "FRANQUEO OFICIAL" below building.
O611 1c. black and green 10 10
O612 2c. black and red 10 10
O613 3c. black and yellow 10 10
O614 5c. black and blue 10 10
O615 10c. black and violet 10 10
O616 13c. black and violet 15 15
O617 15c. black and sepia 15 15
O618 24c. black and red 15 15
O619 50c. black and yellow 15 15
O620 100c. black and blue 25 15
These stamps also exist optd with shield, Type **66**.

1910. As T **99**, but inscr "OFICIAL" below portrait.
O655 2c. black and green 15 15
O656 3c. black and orange 15 15
O657 4c. black and red 15 15
O658 5c. black and violet 15 15
O659 6c. black and red 15 15
O660 10c. black and violet 15 15
O661 12c. black and blue 15 15
O662 17c. black and green 15 15
O663 19c. black and brown 15 15
O664 29c. black and brown 15 15
O665 50c. black and yellow 15 15
O666 100c. black and blue 15 15

1911. Stamps of 1900, dated "1900", optd **OFICIAL** and black circles or surch also.
O667 **59** 1c. green 10 10
O668 3c. on 13c. brown 10 10
O669 5c. on 10c. green 10 10
O670 10c. green 10 10
O671 12c. green 10 10
O672 13c. brown 10 10
O673 50c. on 10c. green 10 10
O674 1col. on 13c. brown 15 15

O 112 **O 113**

1914. Words of background in green, shield and word "PROVISIONAL" in black.
O675 **O 112** 2c. brown 10 10
O676 3c. yellow 10 10
O677 5c. blue 10 10
O678 10c. red 10 10
O679 12c. green 10 10
O680 17c. violet 10 10
O681 50c. brown 10 10
O682 100c. brown 10 10

1915.
O683 **O 113** 2c. green 10 10
O684 3c. orange 10 10

1915. Stamps of 1915, with opt **1915** optd **OFICIAL**.
O685 **91** 1c. grey (No. 675) 25 20
O686 2c. red 25 20
O687 5c. blue 25 20
O688 6c. blue 50 40
O689 10c. yellow 25 25
O690 12c. brown 60 60
O691 50c. purple 60 50
O692 100c. brown 90 70

1916. Stamps of 1916 optd **OFICIAL**.
O694 **113** 1c. green 1·10 1·10
O695 2c. red 6·00 3·00
O696 5c. blue 5·50 3·00
O697 6c. violet 1·10 1·10
O698 10c. brown 1·10 1·10
O699 12c. purple 7·25 5·50
O700 17c. orange 1·10 1·10
O701 25c. brown 1·10 1·10
O702 29c. black 1·10 1·10
O703 50c. grey 1·10 1·10

1922. Stamps of 1921 optd **OFICIAL**.
O736 **130** 1c. green 15 10
O737 – 2c. black 15 10
O738 **131** 5c. orange 20 15
O739 **132** 6c. red 15 10
O740 **133** 10c. blue 25 20
O741 – 25c. green 40 35
O742 **135** 60c. sepia 50 50
O743 – 1col. sepia 50 60

1925. Stamps of 1924 optd **OFICIAL**.
O768 **141** 1c. purple 15 10
O769 – 2c. red 35 10
O770 – 5c. black 15 10
O765 – 6c. blue 35·00 18·00
O766 **146** 10c. orange 35 15
O767 **150** 1col. blue and green 1·10 70

1947. Stamps of 1947 optd **OFICIAL**.
O959 **155** 1c. red 30·00 14·00
O960 – 2c. yellow 30·00 14·00
O961 – 5c. grey 30·00 14·00
O962 – 10c. yellow 30·00 14·00
O963 – 20c. green 30·00 14·00
O964 – 50c. black 30·00 14·00

1964. No. O963 further surch **1 CTS. X X.**
O1198 1c. on 20c. green

OFFICIAL REGISTRATION STAMP

1897. Registration stamp optd **FRANQUEO OFICIAL** in oval.
OR268 **R 54** 10c. blue 20

PARCEL POST STAMPS

P 35 Hermes

1895.
P127 **P 35** 5c. orange 30 50
P128 10c. blue 30 50
P129 15c. red 30 75
P130 20c. orange 30 75
P131 50c. green 30 75

POSTAGE DUE STAMPS

D 33 **D 72** Columbus Monument

1895.
D107 **D 33** 1c. green 10 15
D108 2c. green 10 15
D109 3c. green 10 15
D110 5c. green 10 20
D111 10c. green 10 20
D112 15c. green 10 25
D113 25c. green 10 50
D114 50c. green 30 50

1896.
D150 **D 33** 1c. red 10 15
D151 2c. red 10 15
D152 3c. red 10 15
D153 5c. red 10 15
D154 10c. red 10 20
D155 15c. red 15 30
D156 25c. red 15 30
D157 50c. red 15 40

1897.
D256 **D 33** 1c. blue 10 15
D257 2c. blue 10 15
D258 3c. blue 10 15
D259 5c. blue 10 15
D260 10c. blue 15 20
D261 15c. blue 15 25
D262 25c. blue 10 30
D263 50c. blue 10 40

1898.
D302 **D 33** 1c. violet 15 15
D303 2c. violet 15 15
D304 3c. violet 15 15
D305 5c. violet 15 15
D306 10c. violet 30 50
D307 15c. violet 15 20
D308 25c. violet 15 25
D309 50c. violet 20 50

1899. Optd with T **35**.
D347 **D 33** 1c. orange 35 35
D348 2c. orange 35 35
D349 3c. orange 35 35
D350 5c. orange 55 55
D351 10c. orange 70 70
D352 15c. orange 70 70
D353 25c. orange 90 90
D354 50c. orange 1·00 1·00

1903.
D507 **D 72** 1c. green 90 70
D508 2c. red 1·50 1·10
D509 3c. orange 1·50 1·10
D510 5c. blue 1·50 1·10
D511 10c. purple 1·50 1·10
D512 25c. green 1·50 1·10

1908. Stamps of 1907 optd **Deficiencia de franqueo**.
D623 **91** 1c. black and green 20 20
D624 2c. black and red 20 20
D625 3c. black & yellow 25 25
D626 5c. black & blue 40 40
D627 10c. black & violet 70 70

1908. Stamps of 1907 optd **DEFICIENCIA DE FRANQUEO.**
D628 **91** 1c. black and green 30 30
D629 2c. black and red 20 20
D630 5c. black and blue 55 40
D631 10c. black & mauve 80 70
D632 – 3c. blk & yell (No. O613) 55 50

1910. As T **99**, but inscr "FRANQUEO DEFICIENTE" below portrait.
D655 1c. black and brown 15 15
D656 2c. black and green 15 15
D657 3c. black and yellow 15 15
D658 4c. black and red 15 15
D659 5c. black and violet 15 15
D660 12c. black and blue 15 15
D661 24c. black and red 15 15

REGISTRATION STAMP

R 54 Gen. R. A. Gutierrez

1897.
R266 **R 54** 10c. lake 20 30

EQUATORIAL GUINEA Pt. 12

The former Spanish Overseas Provinces of Fernando Poo and Rio Muni united on 12 October 1968, to become the Republic of Equatorial Guinea.

1968. 100 centimos = 1 peseta.
1973. 100 centimos = 1 ekuele (plural: bipkwele).
1985. 100 centimos = 1 franc (CFA).

1 Clasped Hands **2** President Macias Nguema

1968. Independence.
1 **1** 1p. sepia, gold and blue 10 10
2 1p.50 sepia, gold & green 10 10
3 6p. sepia, gold and red 15 10

1970. 1st Anniv (12.10.69) of Independence.
4 **2** 50c. red, purple & orange 10 10
5 1p. purple, green & mauve 10 10
6 1p.50 green and purple 10 10
7 2p. green and buff 10 10
8 2p.50 blue and green 10 10
9 10p. purple, blue & brown 60 10
10 25p. brown, black & grey 1·10 15

3 Pres. Macias Nguema and Cockerel

1971. 2nd Anniv of Independence.
11 **3** 3p. multicoloured 10 10
12 5p. multicoloured 15 10
13 10p. multicoloured 25 10
14 25p. multicoloured 40 20

5 Flaming Torch

1972. 3rd Year of Independence.
17 **5** 50p. multicoloured 1·00 35

Issues of 1972–79. These are listed at the end of Equatorial Guinea in the Appendix.

6 Pres. Macias Nguema, Hands and Fruit

1979. 4th Anniv of Independence (1972). Mult.
18 1p.50 Type **6** 10 10
19 2p. Classroom 10 10
20 3p. Soldiers and sailors on parade 10 10
21 4p. As No. 19 10 10
22 5p. As No. 20 15 10

7 Party Emblem

1979. United National Workers' Party.
23 **7** 1p. multicoloured 10 10
24 1p.50 multicoloured 10 10
25 2p. multicoloured 10 10
26 4p. multicoloured 10 10
27 5p. multicoloured 15 10

8 Ekuele Coin

1979. 5th Anniv of Independence (1973) (1st issue).
28 **8** 1e. multicoloured 10 10

9 State Palace **10** Pres. Macias Nguema

1979. Independence (1973) (2nd issue). National Enterprises. Multicoloured.
29 1e. Bata harbour 30 10
30 1e.50 Type **9** 10 10
31 2e. Bata Central Bank 10 10
32 2e.50 Nguema Biyogo bridge 10 10
33 3e. Pres. Nguema and scenes as on Nos. 29/32 15 10

1979. 3rd Congress of United National Workers' Party.
34 **10** 1e.50 multicoloured 10 10

11 Salvador Ndongo Ekang **12** Hands cupping Seedling

1979. Martyrs of Independence. Mult.
35 1e. Enrique Nvo 10 10
36 1e.50 Type **11** 10 10
37 2e. Acacio Mane 10 10

1979. Experimental Agriculture Year.
38 **12** 1e. multicoloured 10 10
39 1e.50 multicoloured 10 10

12a Boy and Bells

1980. Christmas.
39b **12a** 25b. multicoloured 70 50

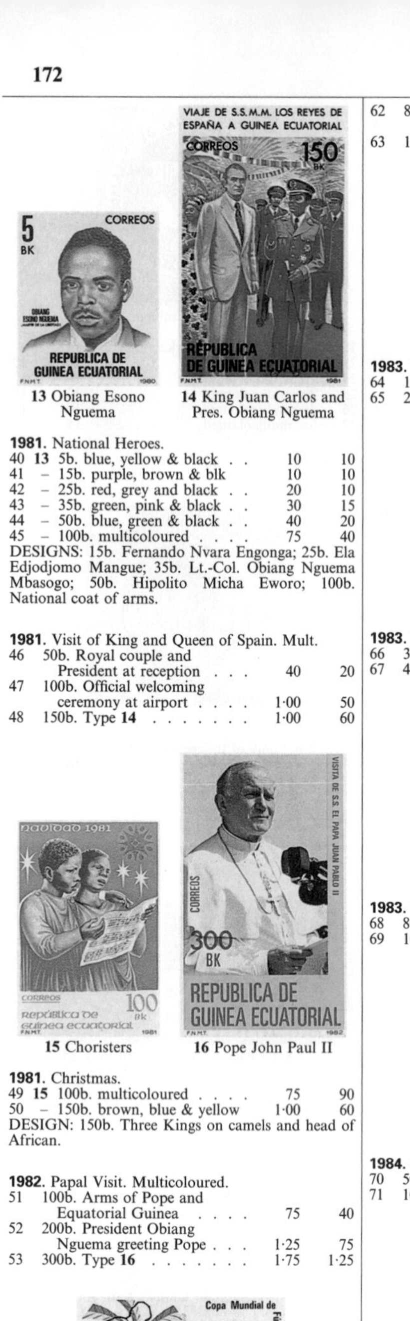

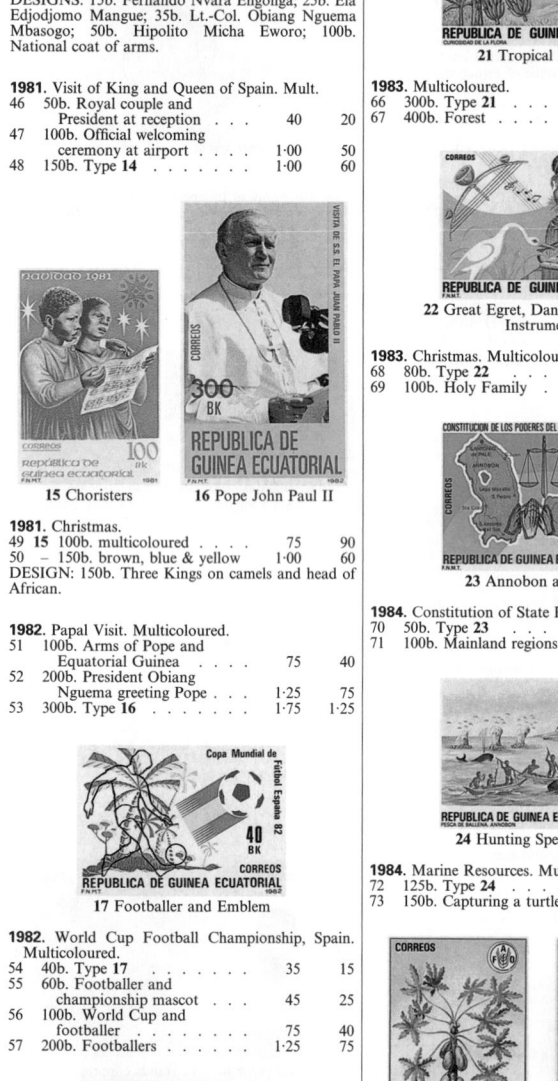

13 Obiang Esono Nguema

14 King Juan Carlos and Pres. Obiang Nguema

1981. National Heroes.
40 **13** 5b. blue, yellow & black . . 10 10
41 – 15b. purple, brown & blk 10 10
42 – 25b. red, grey and black . . 20 10
43 – 35b. green, pink & black . . 30 15
44 – 50b. blue, green & black . . 40 20
45 – 100b. multicoloured 75 40
DESIGNS: 15b. Fernando Nvara Engonga; 25b. Ela Edjodjomo Mangue; 35b. Lt.-Col. Obiang Nguema Mbasogo; 50b. Hipolito Micha Eworo; 100b. National coat of arms.

1981. Visit of King and Queen of Spain. Mult.
46 50b. Royal couple and President at reception . . . 40 20
47 100b. Official welcoming ceremony at airport . . . . 1·00 50
48 150b. Type **14** . . . . 1·00 60

15 Choristers

16 Pope John Paul II

1981. Christmas.
49 **15** 100b. multicoloured 75 90
50 – 150b. brown, blue & yellow 1·00 60
DESIGN: 150b. Three Kings on camels and head of African.

1982. Papal Visit. Multicoloured.
51 100b. Arms of Pope and Equatorial Guinea 75 40
52 200b. President Obiang Nguema greeting Pope . . . 1·25 75
53 300b. Type **16** . . . . 1·75 1·25

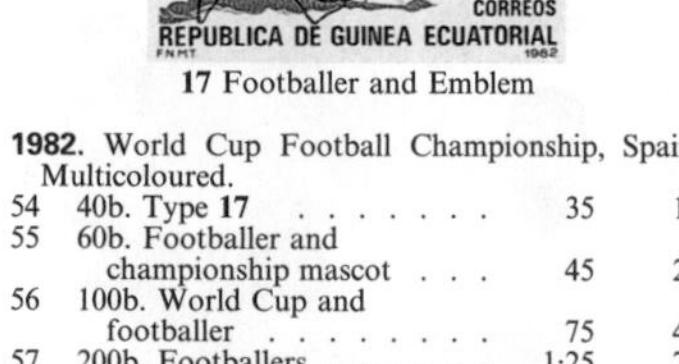

17 Footballer and Emblem

1982. World Cup Football Championship, Spain. Multicoloured.
54 40b. Type **17** 35 15
55 60b. Footballer and championship mascot . . . 45 25
56 100b. World Cup and footballer 75 40
57 200b. Footballers . . . . . . 1·25 75

18 Stars

1982. Christmas. Multicoloured.
58 100b. Type **18** 75 40
59 200b. King offering gift . . . 1·25 75

19 Gorilla

1982. Protected Animals. Multicoloured.
60 40b. Type **19** 40 15
61 60b. Hippopotamus 55 30
62 80b. African brush-tailed porcupine 65 35
63 120b. Leopard 90 60

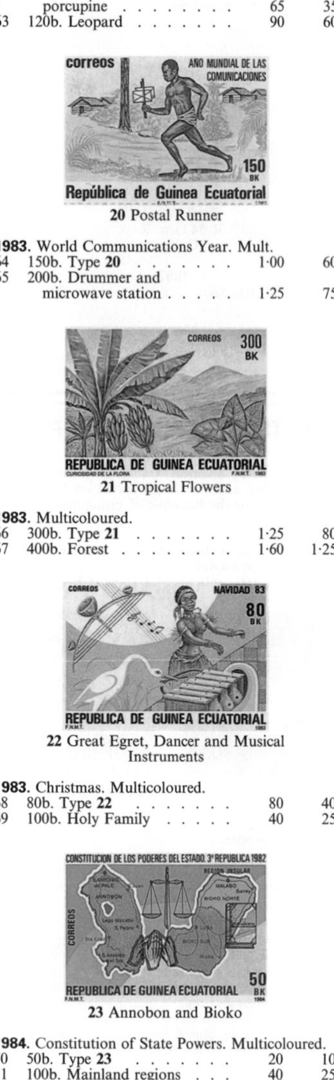

20 Postal Runner

1983. World Communications Year. Mult.
64 150b. Type **20** . . . . 1·00 60
65 200b. Drummer and microwave station . . . . . 1·25 75

21 Tropical Flowers

1983. Multicoloured.
66 300b. Type **21** . . . . 1·25 80
67 400b. Forest . . . . 1·60 1·25

22 Great Egret, Dancer and Musical Instruments

1983. Christmas. Multicoloured.
68 80b. Type **22** 80 40
69 100b. Holy Family 40 25

23 Annobon and Bioko

1984. Constitution of State Powers. Multicoloured.
70 50b. Type **23** 20 10
71 100b. Mainland regions . . . 40 25

24 Hunting Sperm Whales

1984. Marine Resources. Multicoloured.
72 125b. Type **24** . . . . 1·40 75
73 150b. Capturing a turtle . . . 1·40 75

25 Pawpaw

26 Mother and Child

1984. World Food Day. Multicoloured.
74 60b. Type **25** 30 20
75 80b. Malanga 40 25

1984. Christmas. Multicoloured.
76 60b. Type **26** 30 20
77 100b. Musical instruments . . 50 30

27 "Black Gazelle" and "Anxiety" (wood carvings)

1985. Art.
78 **27** 25b. multicoloured 15 10
79 – 30b. multicoloured 15 10
80 – 60b. multicoloured 30 20
81 – 75b. black, red & yellow . . 40 25
82 – 100b. multicoloured 50 30
83 – 150b. multicoloured 75 45
DESIGNS—HORIZ: 30b. "Black Gazelle" (different) and "Woman" (wood carvings); 150b. "Man and Woman" and "Bust of Woman" (wood carvings). VERT: 60b. "Man and Woman" (different); 75b. Poster; 100b. "Mother and Child" (wood carving).

28 Mission Emblem

29 Postal Emblem

1985. Immaculate Conception Mission. Centenary. Multicoloured.
84 50f. Type **28** 20 15
85 60f. Nun teaching children in African village 20 15
86 80f. First Guinean nuns . . . 30 20
87 125f. Nuns landing on Bata beach 45 25

1985. Postal Service. Multicoloured.
88 50f. Type **29** 20 15
89 80f. Jose Mavule Ndjong, first Guinean postman 30 20

30 Nativity

1985. Christmas. Multicoloured.
90 40f. Type **30** 15 10
91 70f. Musicians, dancer and woman with baby 30 20

31 Crab and Snail

1986. Nature Protection. Multicoloured.
92 15f. Type **31** 20 10
93 35f. Butterflies, bees, chaffinch and grey-headed kingfisher 1·25 55
94 45f. Plants 20 15
95 65f. Men working on cacao crop 30 20

32 Mekuyo Dancers

1986. Folk Customs. Multicoloured.
96 10f. Type **32** 10 10
97 50f. Kokom dancers 20 15
98 65f. Bisila girl 30 20
99 80f. Ndong-Mba man 35 20

33 Footballers and Emblem

1986. World Cup Football Championship, Mexico. Designs showing various footballing scenes.
100 **33** 50f. multicoloured 20 15
101 – 100f. multicoloured 45 25
102 – 150f. mult (vert) 65 40
103 – 200f. mult (vert) 85 50

34 Musical Instruments

1986. Christmas. Multicoloured.
104 100f. Type **34** 40 25
105 150f. Mother breast-feeding baby 60 35

35 Map and Member Countries' Flag

1986. Union of Central African States Conference. Multicoloured.
106 80f. Type **35** 35 20
107 100f. Maps 40 25

36 Coins and Hen with Chick

1987. Campaign against Hunger.
108 **36** 60f. purple, orange & blk 25 15
109 – 80f. blue, orange & black 35 20
110 – 100f. brown, orange & blk 40 25
DESIGNS: 80f. Coins and fish in net; 100f. Coins and ear of wheat.

37 Dove and Open Door

1987. International Peace Year. Mult.
111 100f. Type **37** 40 25
112 200f. Hands holding dove . . 80 50

38 Night Sky and Envelope

1987. World Stamp Day. Multicoloured.
113 150f. Type **38** 60 35
114 300f. Banner of national colours and envelope . . . 1·10 75

39 Mother and Child

40 Man climbing Palm Tree

1987. Christmas. Wood Sculptures. Mult.
115 80f. Type **39** 30 15
116 100f. Mother and child (different) 40 20

1988. International Labour Day. Mult.
117 50f. Type **40** 20 15
118 75f. Woman with catch of fish 40 20
119 150f. Chopping down tree . . 60 35

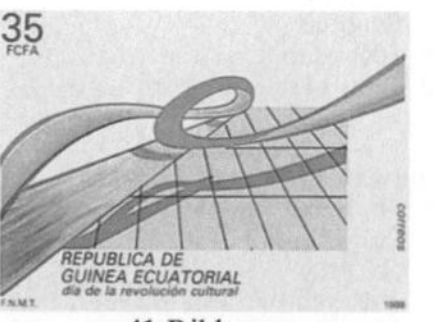

41 Ribbons

1988. Cultural Revolution Day. Mult.
120 35f. Type **41** 15 10
121 50f. Cubes and sphere . . . 20 15
122 100f. Stylized dove 40 25

42 Party Badge

43 Musician

1988. 1st Anniv of Democratic Party of Equatorial Guinea. Multicoloured.
123 40f. Type **42** 15 10
124 75f. Torch and concentric circles (horiz) 30 20
125 100f. Torch (horiz) 40 25

1988. Christmas. Multicoloured.
126 50f. Type **43** 20 15
127 100f. Mother, child and stars 40 25

44 Lorry loaded with Logs

1989. 20th Anniv of Independence. Mult.
128 10f. Type **44** 10 10
129 35f. Traditional folk gathering 15 10
130 45f. President at official function 20 15

45 Bathers at Ilachi Waterfall

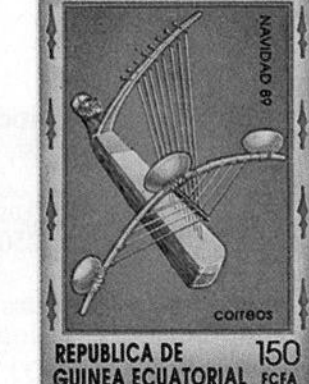

47 Stringed Instrument

46 Palace of Congresses

1989. Water. Multicoloured.
131 15f. Type **45** 10 10
132 25f. La Selva waterfall . . . 10 10
133 60f. Boy drinking from green coconut and youths in water 25 15

1989. 1st Democratic Party Congress. Mult.
134 25f. Type **46** 10 10
135 35f. Torch (party emblem) (vert) 15 10
136 40f. Pres. Obiang Nguema Mbasogo (vert) 15 10

1989. Christmas. Multicoloured.
137 150f. Type **47** 60 35
138 300f. Mother with child and drummer (horiz) . . . . . 1·25 80

48 Sir Robert Baden-Powell (founder)

1990. Boy Scout Movement. Multicoloured.
139 100f. Type **48** 40 25
140 250f. Scout saluting . . . . 1·00 70
141 350f. Scout with bugle . . . 1·40 90

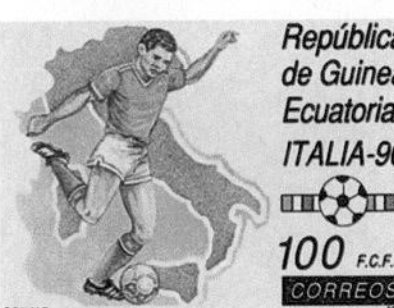

49 Player and Map of Italy

1990. World Cup Football Championship, Italy. Multicoloured.
142 100f. Type **49** 40 25
143 250f. Goalkeeper and ball in net . . . . 1·00 70
144 350f. Trophy and globe . . . 1·40 90

50 Drums and Horn (Ndowe tribe)

1990. Musical Instruments. Multicoloured.
145 100f. Type **50** 40 25
146 250f. Drums, horn, pipes and stringed instruments (Fang) 1·00 70
147 350f. Flute and cup, bell and horn (Bubi) . . . . 1·40 90

51 Arrival in America of Columbus

1990. 500th Anniv (1992) of Discovery of America by Columbus (1st issue). Multicoloured.
148 170f. Type **51** . . . . 1·10 55
149 300f. "Santa Maria", "Pinta" and "Nina" . . . . 1·90 1·10
See also Nos. 165/7.

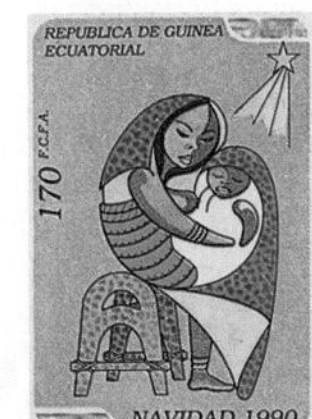

52 Mother and Child

1990. Christmas. Multicoloured.
150 170f. Type **52** 70 40
151 300f. Bubi man ringing handbell . . . . 1·25 80

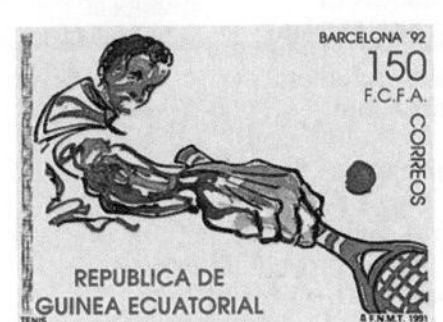

53 Tennis

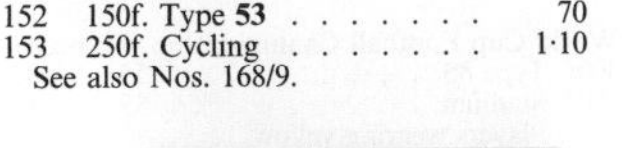

1991. Olympic Games, Barcelona (1992) (1st issue). Multicoloured.
152 150f. Type **53** 70 45
153 250f. Cycling . . . . 1·10 70
See also Nos. 168/9.

54 "The Naked Maja" (Francisco de Goya)

1991. Paintings. Multicoloured.
155 100f. Type **54** 45 25
156 250f. "Eve" (Albrecht Durer) (vert) . . . . 1·10 70
157 350f. "The Three Graces" (Peter Paul Rubens) (vert) 1·60 1·00

55 Mandrill

1991. The Mandrill. Multicoloured.
158 25f. Type **55** 10 10
159 25f. Close-up of face 10 10
160 25f. On all fours (horiz) . . . 10 10
161 25f. With foreleg raised . . . 10 10

56 Class EF53 Electric Locomotive, 1932, Japan

1991. Railway Locomotives. Multicoloured.
162 150f. Type **56** . . . . 1·50 25
163 250f. Steam locomotive, 1873, U.S.A. . . . . 3·25 35

57 Vicente Pinzon and "Nina"

1991. 500th Anniv (1992) of Discovery of America by Columbus (2nd issue). Multicoloured.
165 150f. Type **57** . . . . 1·00 45
166 250f. Martin Pinzon and "Pinta" . . . . 1·10 70
167 350f. Christopher Columbus and "Santa Maria" . . . . 1·90 1·00

58 Basketball

1992. Olympic Games, Barcelona (2nd issue). Multicoloured.
168 200f. Type **58** 90 60
169 300f. Swimming . . . . . . 1·40 90

60 Blue-breasted Kingfisher and Black-winged Stilt

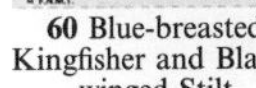

62 "Termitomyces globulus"

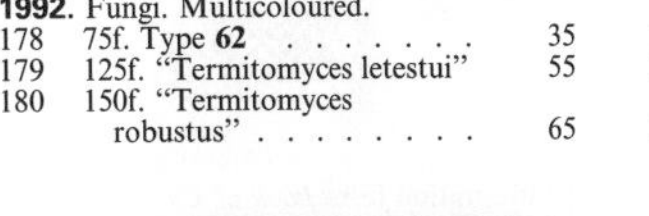

61 Scene from "Casablanca"

1992. Nature Protection. Multicoloured.
172 150f. Type **60** 40 25
173 250f. Great blue turaco and grey parrot 65 40

1992. Centenary of Motion Pictures.
175 **61** 100f. blue and black . . . 25 15
176 – 250f. green and black . . . 65 40
177 – 350f. brown and black . . 90 60
DESIGNS: 250f. Scene from "Viridiana"; 350f. Scene from "A Couple of Gypsies".

1992. Fungi. Multicoloured.
178 75f. Type **62** 35 15
179 125f. "Termitomyces letestui" 55 30
180 150f. "Termitomyces robustus" 65 35

63 "Virgin and Child amongst the Saints" (Claudio Coello)

1993. Painters' Anniversaries. Multicoloured.
181 200f. Type **63** (300th death anniv) 50 30
182 300f. "Apollo, Conqueror of Marsyas" (Jacob Jordaens) (400th birth anniv) 80 50

64 Scene from "Romeo and Juliet" and Pyotr Ilyich Tchaikovsky

1993. Composers' Death Centenaries. Mult.
184 100f. Type **64** 25 15
185 200f. Scene from "Faust" (opera) and Charles Gounod 50 30

65 Quincy Watts (400 m)

1993. Gold Medal Winners at Olympic Games, Barcelona, and Winter Olympic Games, Albertville. Multicoloured.
186 100f. Type **65** 25 15
187 250f. Martin Lopez Zubero (200 m backstroke) 65 40
188 350f. Petra Kronbreger (slalom and combined) . . 90 60
189 400f. "Flying Dutchman" class yacht (Luis Doreste and Domingo Manrique) 1·50 65

66 Ford's First Motor Car

1993. 130th Birth Anniv of Henry Ford (motor car manufacturer).
190 **66** 200f. multicoloured 50 30
191 – 300f. multicoloured 80 50
192 – 400f. black and red . . . . 1·00 65
DESIGNS—HORIZ: 300f. Model "T" motor car. VERT: 400f. Henry Ford.

67 Pres. Obiang Nguema Mbasogo

1993. 25th Anniv of Independence. Mult.
193 150f. Type **67** 40 25
194 250f. Oil refinery, ship, map and radio mast (horiz) . . 90 40
195 300f. Hydro-electric station, Riaba, and waterfall (horiz) 80 50
196 350f. Woman, bridge and man (horiz) 90 60

68 Lunar Module "Eagle"

1994. 25th Anniv of First Manned Moon Landing. Multicoloured.
197 500f. Type **68** . . . . 1·25 80
198 700f. Buzz Aldrin, Michael Collins and Neil Armstrong (astronauts) . . 1·75 1·10
199 900f. Footprint on Moon and module reflected in astronaut's visor . . . . . 2·25 1·50

69 German Team (1990 champions)

1994. World Cup Football Championship, U.S.A. Multicoloured.
200 200f. Type **69** 50 30
201 300f. Rose Bowl Stadium, Los Angeles 75 45
202 500f. Player dribbling ball (vert) . . . . 1·25 80

70 "Chasmosauraus belli"

1994. Prehistoric Animals. Multicoloured.
203 300f. Type **70** 75 45
204 500f. "Tyrannosaurus rex" 1·25 80
205 700f. "Triceratops horridus" 1·75 1·10

71 Gold Calcite

1994. Minerals. Multicoloured.
207 300f. Type **71** 75 45
208 400f. Pyromorphite 95 60
209 600f. Fluorite . . . . 1·40 90
210 700f. Halite . . . . 1·75 1·10

72 Poster for "Elena y los Hombres" and Jean Renoir (film director)

1994. Anniversaries. Multicoloured.
211 300f. Type **72** (birth cent) . . 75 45
212 500f. Map and Ferdinand Marie de Lesseps (director of Suez Canal development, death centenary) . . . . 1·25 80
213 600f. Illustration from "The Little Prince" and Antoine de Saint-Exupery (pilot and writer, 50th death anniv) 1·40 90
214 700f. Bauhaus (75th anniv) and Walter Gropius (architect) . . . . 1·75 1·10

73 Kitten

1995. Domestic Animals. Multicoloured.
215 500f. Type **73** . . . . 1·25 80
216 500f. Pekingese . . . . . . 1·25 80
217 500f. Pig . . . . 1·25 80

74 Blue Diadem ("Hypolimnas salmacis")

1995. Butterflies. Multicoloured.
218 400f. Type **74** . . . . 1·00 65
219 400f. Fig-tree blue ("Myrina silenus") . . . . 1·00 65
220 400f. "Palla ussheri" . . . . 1·00 65
221 400f. Boisduval's false acraea ("Pseudacraea boisduvali") 1·00 65

75 Steam Locomotive, Great Britain

1995. Railways. Multicoloured.
222 500f. Type **75** . . . . 1·25 80
223 500f. Diesel locomotive, Germany . . . . 1·25 80
224 500f. "Hikari" express train, Japan . . . . 1·25 80

76 Signing of Japanese Surrender Document

1995. Anniversaries. Multicoloured.
226 350f. Type **76** (50th anniv of end of Second World War) 90 60
227 450f. Palais des Nations, Geneva (50th anniv of U.N.O.) . . . . 1·10 70
228 600f. Basel 1845 2½r. stamp and Sir Rowland Hill (birth bicentenary) . . . . 1·50 1·00

77 J. Manuel Fangio (1951 and 1954–7)

1996. Formula 1 Racing Champions. Mult.
229 400f. Type **77** . . . . 1·00 65
230 400f. Ayrton Senna (1988, 1990, 1991) . . . . 1·00 65
231 400f. Jim Clark (1963, 1965) 1·00 65
232 400f. Jochen Rindt (1970) . . 1·00 65

78 Alfred Nobel (chemist)

1996. Anniversaries. Multicoloured.
233 500f. Type **78** (death centenary) 90 60
234 500f. Anton Bruckner (composer, death centenary) 90 60
235 500f. "Abraham and the Three Angels" (Giovanni Tiepolo), (painter, birth tercentenary) 90 60

79 Marilyn Monroe (actress)

1996. Personalities. Multicoloured.
237 350f. Type **79** 60 40
238 350f. Elvis Presley (entertainer) 60 40
239 350f. James Dean (actor) . . 60 40
240 350f. Vittorio de Sica (actor and film director) 60 40

80 Illustration from *Book of Chess, Dice and Tablings* by King Alfonso X of Castile and Leon

1996. Chess Competitions. Multicoloured.
241 400f. Type **80** (32nd Chess Olympiad, Yerevan, Armenia) 70 45
242 400f. Girl playing chess (World Junior Chess Championship, Minorca, Spain) 70 45
243 400f. Chess pieces (Women's World Chess Championship, Jaen, Spain) 70 45
244 400f. Anatoly Yevgenievich Karpov (World Chess Championship title match, Elisa, Russian Federation) 70 45

81 19th-century Sail/Steam Warship

1996. Ships. Multicoloured.
245 500f. Type **81** 90 60
246 500f. *Galatea* (cadet ship) . . 90 60
247 500f. Modern ferry 90 60

82 Olympic Stadium, Athens, 1896

1996. Olympic Games, Atlanta. Centenary of Modern Olympic Games. Multicoloured.
248 400f. Type **82** 70 45
249 400f. Cycling 70 45
250 400f. Tennis 70 45
251 400f. Show jumping 70 45

83 False Blusher

1997. Fungi. Multicoloured.
252 400f. Type **83** 70 45
253 400f. Common morel (*Morchella esculenta*) . . . 70 45
254 400f. Orange peel fungus (*Aleuria aurantia*) 70 45
255 400f. *Sparassis laminosa* . . . 70 45

84 Franz Schubert and Score

85 Players

1997. Anniversaries and Events. Multicoloured.
256 500f. Type **84** (composer, birth bicentenary) 90 60
257 500f. Head of ox (Chinese New Year—Year of the Ox) 90 60
258 500f. Johannes Brahms and score (composer, death centenary) 90 60

1997. World Cup Football Championship, France.
260 300f. Type **85** 55 35
261 300f. Stadium 55 35
262 300f. Players wearing yellow and blue shirts 55 35

86 Snake

1998. Fauna. Multicoloured.
263 400f. Type **86** 70 45
264 400f. Snail 70 45
265 400f. Turtle 70 45
266 400f. Lizard 70 45

87 French Infantry, Alsace Regiment, 1767

88 "The Crucifixion" (Velazquez)

1998. Military Uniforms. Multicoloured.
267 400f. Type **87** 70 45
268 400f. 18th-century British Admiral 70 45
269 400f. 18th-century Georgian Hussars, Russia 70 45
270 400f. 19th-century Prussian field artillery 70 45

1999. Birth Bimillenary (2000) of Jesus Christ.
271 500f. Type **88** 90 60
272 500f. "Adoration of the Magi" (Peter Paul Rubens) 90 60
273 500f. "The Holy Family" (Miguel Angel Buonarroti) 90 60

89 *Cattleya leopoldii*

1999. Orchids. Multicoloured.
274 400f. Type **89** 70 45
275 400f. *Angraecum eburneum* 70 45
276 400f. *Paphiopedilum insigne* 70 45
277 400f. *Ansellia africana* . . . 70 45

90 "The Coronation of Thorns" (Anthony van Dyck)

91 Golden Conure

1999. Anniversaries. Multicoloured.
278 100f. Type **90** (artist, 400th birth anniv) 15 10
279 250f. Johann Wolfgang Goethe (writer, 250th birth anniv) 45 30
280 500f. Bust of Jacques-Etienne Montgolfier (balloonist, death bicentenary) 90 60
281 750f. Frederic Chopin (composer, 150th death anniv) . . . . 1·40 90

1999. Birds. Multicoloured.
282 500f. Type **91** 90 60
283 500f. Buffon's macaw (*Ara ambigua*) 90 60
284 500f. Hyacinth macaw (*Anodorhynchus hyacinthinus*) 90 60

92 Purple Emperor (*Apatura iris*)

1999. Butterflies. Multicoloured.
286 400f. Type **92** 85 40
287 400f. Peacock (*Inachis io*) . . 85 40
288 400f. Purple-edged copper (*Palaeochrysophanus hippothoe*) 85 40
289 400f. Niobe fritillary (*Fabriciana niobe*) 85 40

93 Swiss Electric Locomotive, Linares–Almeria Line, Spain

1999. Railway Locomotives. Multicoloured.
290 500f. Type **93** . . . . 1·10 55
291 500f. German diesel locomotive . . . . 1·10 55
292 500f. Japanese series 269 electric locomotive . . . . 1·10 55
MS293 82 × 106 mm. 800f. A.V.E. (Spanish high-speed train) . . 1·75 85

94 Anniversary Emblem

2000. 125th Anniv of UPU.

294	94	40f. multicoloured	10	10

FAUNA PREHISTÓRICA REPÚBLICA DE GUINEA ECUATORIAL correos 500 F.C.F.A.

95 Carnotaurus

2001. Prehistoric Fauna. Multicoloured.

295	500f. Type **95**	1·00	60
296	500f. Iberomesornis	1·00	60
297	500f. Troodon	1·00	60
MS298	107 × 78 mm. 800f. Diplodocus	1·60	1·00

96 Indigo Boletus (*Gyroporus cyanescens*)

2001. Fungi. Multicoloured.

299	400f. Type **96**	80	50
300	400f. *Terfezia arenaria*	80	50
301	400f. *Battarrea stevenii*	80	50
302	400f. Fly agaric (*Amanita muscaria*)	80	50

97 Merryweather Fire Appliance (1915)

2001. Fire Engines. Multicoloured.

303	400f. Type **97**	80	50
304	400f. De Dion Bouton appliance TE-450 (1943)	80	50
305	400f. Magirus appliance E-2 (1966)	80	50
306	400f. Merryweather appliance (1888)	80	50

98 Infantry Officer, 1700

2001. Military Uniforms. Multicoloured.

307	400f. Type **98**	80	50
308	400f. Arquebusier, 1534	80	50
309	400f. 17th-century musketeer	80	50
310	400f. Fusilier, 1815	80	50

EXPRESS LETTER STAMPS

E **4** Guinea Archer

1971. 3rd Anniv of Independence.

E15	E **4**	4p. multicoloured	10	10
E16		8p. multicoloured	10	10

APPENDIX

The following stamps have either been issued in excess of postal needs or have not been available to the public in reasonable quantities at face value. Such stamps may later be given full listing if there is evidence of regular postal use.

1972.

Space Flight of "Apollo 15". Postage 1, 3, 5, 8, 10p.; Air 15, 25p.

Winter Olympic Games, Sapporo, Japan. Postage 1, 2, 3, 5, 8p.; Air 15, 50p.

Christmas 1971. Paintings. Postage 1, 3, 5, 8, 10p.; Air 15, 25p.

Easter. Postage 1, 3, 5, 8, 10p.; Air 15, 25p.

Olympic Games, Munich 1972. Augsburg Events. Postage 1, 2, 3, 5, 8p.; Air 15, 50p.

Winter Olympic Games, Sapporo, Japan. Gold medal winners. Postage 1, 2, 3, 5, 8p.; Air 15, 50p.

Olympic Games, Munich 1972. Buildings and previous medal winners. Postage 1, 2, 3, 5, 8p.; Air 15, 50p.

Olympic Games. Sailing and rowing, Kiel. Postage 1, 2, 3, 5, 8p.; Air 15, 50p.

Olympic Games Munich. Modern sports. Postage 1, 2, 3, 5, 8p.; Air 15, 50p.

Olympic Games, Munich. Equestrian events. Postage 1, 2, 3, 5, 8p.; Air 15, 50p.

Centenary of Japanese Railway. Various steam locomotives. Postage 1, 3, 5, 8, 10p.; Air 15, 25p.

Olympic Games, Munich. Gold medal winners. Postage 1, 2, 3, 5, 8p.; Air 15, 50p.

Christmas 1972. Paintings by Cranach. Postage 1, 3, 5, 8, 10p.; Air 15, 25p.

Cosmonauts Memorial. Designs with black borders. Postage 1, 3, 5, 8, 10p.; Air 15, 25p.

1973.

Transatlantic Yacht Race 1972. Postage 1, 2, 3, 5, 8p.; Air 15, 50p.

Renoir Paintings. Postage 1, 2, 3, 5, 8p.; Air 15, 50p.

Conquest of Venus. Postage 1, 3, 5, 8, 10p.; Air 15, 25p.

Easter. Religious Paintings by Old Masters. Postage 1, 3, 5, 8, 10p.; Air 15, 25p.

"Tour de France" Cycle Race. Postage 1, 2, 3, 5, 8p.; Air 15, 50p.

Paintings by European Old Masters. Postage 1, 2, 3, 5, 8p.; Air 15, 50p.

World Football Cup Championship, West Germany (1974) (1st issue). Previous Finals. Postage 5, 10, 15, 20, 25, 60c.; Air 5, 70p.

Paintings by Rubens. Postage 1, 2, 3, 5, 8p.; Air 15, 50p.

Christmas. Religious Paintings. Postage 1, 3, 5, 8, 10p.; Air 15, 25p.

World Cup Football Championship, West Germany (1974) (2nd issue). Famous players. Postage 30, 35, 40, 45, 50, 65, 70c.; Air 8, 60p.

Paintings by Picasso. Postage 30, 35, 40, 45, 50c.; Air 8, 60e.

1974.

500th Birth Anniv of Nicolas Copernicus (astronomer). Postage 5, 10, 15, 20c.; Air 4, 10, 70e.

World Cup Football Championship, West Germany (3rd issue). Venues of Qualifying Matches. Postage 75, 80, 85, 90, 95c., 1e., 1e.25; Air 10, 50e.

Easter. Postage 1, 3, 5, 8, 10p.; Air 15, 25p.

Holy Year. Postage 5, 10, 15, 20c., 3e.50; Air 10, 70e.

World Cup Football Championship, West Germany (4th issue). Famous Players. Postage 1e.50, 1e.75, 2e., 2e.25, 2e.50, 3e., 3e.50; Air 10, 60e.

Centenary of U.P.U. (1st issue). Postage 60, 70, 80c., 1e.50; Air 30, 50e.

First Death Anniv of Picasso. Postage 55, 60, 65, 70, 75c.; Air 10, 50e.

"The Wild West". Postage 30, 35, 40, 45, 50c.; Air 8, 60p.

Protected Flowers. Postage 5, 10, 15, 20, 25c., 1, 3, 5, 8, 10p.; Air 5, 15, 25, 70p.

Christmas. Postage 60, 70, 80c., 1e., 1e.50; Air 30, 50e.

75th Anniv of FC Barcelona. Postage 1, 3, 5, 8, 10e.; Air 15, 60e.

Centenary of U.P.U. (2nd issue) and "Espana '75" International Stamp Exhibition, Madrid. Postage 1e.25, 1e.50, 1e.75, 2e., 2e.25; Air 35, 60e.

Nature Protection (1st series). Australian Animals. Postage 80, 85, 90, 95c., 1e.; Air 15, 40e.

Nature Protection (2nd series). African Animals. Postage 50, 60, 65, 70, 75c.; Air 10, 70e.

Nature Protection (3rd series). South American and Australian Birds. Postage 1p.25, 1p.50, 1p.75, 2p., 2p.25, 2p.50, 2p.75, 3p., 3p.50, 4p.; Air 20, 25, 30, 35p.

Nature Protection (4th series). Endangered Species. Postage 10, 15, 20, 25, 30, 35, 40, 45, 50, 55, 60c., 1e.; Air 2, 10, 70e.

1975.

Paintings by Picasso. Postage 5, 10, 15, 20, 25c.; Air 5, 70e.

Easter. Postage 60, 70, 80c., 1e., 1e.50; Air 30, 50e.

Winter Olympic Games, Innsbruck (1976). 5, 10, 15, 20, 25, 30, 35, 40, 45c., 25, 70e.

Paintings of Don Quixote. Postage 30, 35, 40, 45, 50c.; Air 25, 60e.

Bicent of American Revolution (1st issue). Postage 5, 20, 40, 75c., 2, 5, 8e.; Air 25, 30e.

Bullfighting. Postage 80, 85, 90c., 8e.; Air 35, 40e.

"Apollo–Soyuz" Space Test Project. Postage 1, 2, 3, 5e., 5e.50, 7e., 7e.50, 9, 15e.; Air 20, 30e.

Bicent of American Revolution (2nd issue). Postage 10, 30, 50c., 1, 3, 6, 10e.; Air 12, 40e.

Nude Paintings. Postage 5, 10, 15, 20, 25, 30, 35, 40, 45, 50, 55, 60c., 1, 2e.; Air 10, 70e.

Ships. Postage 30, 35, 40, 45, 50, 55, 60, 65, 70, 75c.; Air 8, 10, 50, 60e.

Christmas. Postage 60, 70, 80c., 1e., 1e.50; Air 30, 50e.

Olympic Games, Montreal (1st issue). Postage 50, 60, 70, 80, 90, c.; Air 35, 60e.

Bicent of American Revolution (3rd issue). Presidents. Postage 5, 10, 20, 30, 40, 50, 75c., 1, 2, 3, 5, 6, 8, 10e.; Air 12, 25, 30, 40e.

Monkeys. Postage 5, 10, 15, 20, 25, 30, 35, 40, 45, 50, 55, 60c., 1, 2e.; Air 10, 70e.

Butterflies (1st series). Postage 5, 10, 15, 20, 25, 30, 35, 40, 45, 50, 55, 60c., 1, 2e.; Air 10, 70e.

Fishes (1st series). Postage 5, 10, 15, 20, 25, 30, 35, 40, 45, 50, 55, 60c., 1, 2e.; Air 10, 70e.

Cats (1st series). Postage 5, 10, 15, 20, 25, 30, 35, 40, 45, 50, 55, 60c., 1, 2e.; Air 10, 70e.

Pres. Francisco Macias Nguema. Postage 1e.50, 3e.50, 7e.; Air 300e.

Arms. Postage 3e.; Air 100e.

Government House. 5e.

International Women's Year. 10e.

1976.

Winter Olympic Games, Innsbruck (1st issue). Postage 50, 55, 60, 65, 70, 75, 80, 85, 90c.; Air 35, 60e.

Winter Olympic Games, Innsbruck (2nd issue). Postage 3, 5, 50e.; Air 200e.

Bicent of American Revolution (4th issue). Flora and Fauna. Postage 1e.50, 3, 5, 7, 25, 100e.; Air 200e.

Apollo–Soyuz Project. Optd on Arms issue. Air 100e.

Concorde's First Commercial Flight. Optd on Arms issue. Air 100e.

Nude Paintings. 7, 10, 25e.

Easter. Air 200e.

Olympic Games, Montreal (2nd issue). Postage 7, 10, 25e.; Air 200e.

Apollo–Soyuz Project, Concorde, and Telephone Centenary. Postage 3, 5, 50e.; Air 200e.

Bicent of American Revolution (5th issue). Fauna. Postage 1e.50, 3, 5, 7, 25, 100e.; Air 200e.

Cavalry Officers. Postage 5, 10, 15, 20, 25c.; Air 5, 70p.

Paintings by El Greco. Postage 1, 3, 5, 8, 10p.; Air 15, 25p.

Olympic Games, Montreal (3rd issue). Rowing and Sailing events. Postage 50, 60, 70, 80, 90c.; Air 30, 60e.

Olympic Games, Montreal (4th issue). Postage 50, 55, 60, 65, 70, 75, 80, 85, 90c.; Air 35, 60e.

Veteran Cars. Postage 1, 3, 5, 8, 10p.; Air 15, 25p.

Nature Protection (5th series). European animals. Postage 5, 10, 15, 20, 25c.; Air 5, 70p.

Racing Motorcyclists. 1, 2, 3, 4, 5, 10, 30, 40e.

Nature Protection (6th series). Flowers of South America and Oceania. Postage 30, 35, 40, 45, 50, 80, 85, 90, 95c., 1p.; Air 8, 15, 40, 60p.

Nature Protection (7th series). Asian animals and birds. Postage 30, 35, 40, 45, 55, 60, 65, 70, 75c., 8p.; Air 50c., 10, 50, 60p.

Chess Pieces. 1, 3, 5, 8, 15, 30, 60, 100e.

Nature Protection (8th series). African birds and flowers. Postage 30, 35, 40, 45, 50, 55, 60, 65, 70, 75c.; Air 8, 10, 50, 60p.

Steamships. Postage 80, 85, 90, 95c., 1p.; Air 15, 40p.

Nature Protection (9th series). European birds. Postage 5, 10, 15, 20, 25c.; Air 5, 70p.

Paintings of Ships. Postage 5, 10, 15, 20, 25, 30e.; Air 50, 60, 65, 70e.

1977.

Nature Protection (10th series). Birds of North America. Postage 80, 85, 90, 95c., 1p.; Air 15, 40p.

Cats (2nd series). Postage 5, 10, 15, 20, 25c.; Air 15, 70e.

Silver Jubilee of Queen Elizabeth II. Postage 2, 4, 5, 8, 10, 15e.; Air 20, 35e.

Nude Drawings. Postage 5, 10, 50, 50e.; Air 15, 200e.

Dogs (1st series). Postage 5, 10, 15, 20, 25, 30, 35, 40, 45, 50, 55, 60c., 1, 2e.; Air 10, 70e.

World War Air Aces. Postage 5, 10, 15, 20, 25, 30, 35, 40, 45, 50, 55, 60c.; Air 10, 70e.

Football. Postage 2, 4, 5, 8, 10, 15e.; Air 20, 35e.

Butterflies (2nd series). Postage 80, 85, 90, 95c., 8e.; Air 35, 40e.

Cars. Postage 5, 10, 15, 20, 25, 30, 35, 40, 45, 50, 55, 60c., 1, 2e.; Air 10, 70e.

Chinese Art. Postage 60, 70, 80c., 1e., 1e.50; Air 30, 50e.

African Masks. Postage 5, 10, 15, 20, 25c.; Air 5, 70e.

Nature Protection (11th series). Animals of North America. Postage 1e.25, 1e.50, 1e.75, 2e., 2e.25; Air 20, 50e.

Napoleon. Scenes from his life. Postage 5, 10, 15, 20, 25, 30, 35, 40, 45, 50, 55, 60c., 1, 2e.; Air 10, 70e.

Napoleon. Military uniforms. Postage 5, 10, 15, 20, 25, 30, 35, 40, 45, 50, 55, 60c., 1, 2e.; Air 10, 70e.

Nature Protection (12th series). Animals of South America. Postage 2e.50, 2e.75, 3e., 3e.50, 4e.; Air 25, 35e.

Nature Protection (13th series). European flowers. Postage 2e.50, 2e.75, 3e.50, 4e.; Air 25, 30e.

1978.

25th Anniv of Queen Elizabeth II's Coronation. Members of Royal Family. Postage 2, 5, 8, 10, 12, 15e.; Air 30, 50, 150e.

Knights. Postage 5, 10, 15, 20, 25c.; Air 15, 70e.

Cats (3rd series). 1, 3, 5, 8, 15, 30, 60, 100e.

American Astronauts. 1, 3, 5, 8, 15, 30, 60, 100e.

25th Anniv of Queen Elizabeth II's Coronation. Medals. 1, 3, 5, 8, 25, 50, 75, 200e.

Queen Elizabeth II's Coronation. 25th Anniv Scenes from previous coronations. Air 1, 3, 5, 8, 15, 30, 60, 100e.

Dogs (2nd series). 1, 3, 5, 8, 15, 30, 60, 100e.

World Famous Paintings. 1, 3, 5, 8, 25, 50, 75, 200e.

Butterflies (3rd series). 1, 3, 5, 8, 15, 30, 60, 100e.

Nature Protection (14th series). Asian flowers. Postage 1e.25, 1e.50, 1e.75, 2e., 2e.25; Air 20, 50e.

Flowers. 1, 3, 5, 8, 15, 30, 60, 100e.

Water Birds. 1, 3, 5, 8, 15, 30, 60, 100e.

World Cup Football Championship. Air 150e.

Belgrade Conference. Air 250e.

"Eurphila 78" Exhibition. Air 250e.

Winter Olympic Games, Lake Placid (1980). Postage 5, 10, 20, 25e.; Air 70e.

150th Death Anniv of Goya. Air 150e.

Christmas. Painting by Titian. Air 150e.

Prehistoric Animals. Postage 30, 35, 40, 45, 50c.; Air 25, 60e.

Cats (4th series). Postage 2e.50, 2e.75, 3e., 3e.50, 4e.; Air 25, 40e.

1979.

Death Centenary of Sir Rowland Hill (1st series). 3, 5, 8, 15, 30, 75, 220e.

Wright Brothers, 1, 3, 5, 8, 15, 30, 60, 100e.

Death Bicentenary of Capt. James Cook. Air 100e.

Fishes (2nd series). Postage 5, 10, 20, 25c., 1e.50; Air 15, 70e.

Death Centenary of Sir Rowland Hill (2nd series). Stamps. Postage 8, 15, 20, 20, 30e.; Air 50e.

International Year of the Child (1st series). Postage 5, 7, 11, 24e.; Air 75e.

Death Anniversaries of Schubert, Voltaire, Rousseau and Cranach. Air 100, 100, 100, 100e.

10th Anniv (1972) of "Apollo XI" Space Flight. "Apollo 15" stamps each surch 50e. and inscription. Postage 50e. on 1, 3, 5, 8, 10p.; Air 50e. on 15, 25p.

European Space Agency Satellite. 200e.

Fairy Tales. Postage 2, 3, 5, 10, 15, 18e.; Air 24, 35e.

Automobiles. Air 35, 50e.

Fishes (3rd series). 5, 10, 15, 20, 25, 30, 35, 40, 45, 50, 55, 60, 70c., 1, 2, 10e.

International Year of the Child (2nd series). Various 1978 stamps optd with I.Y.C. emblem. On Cats (3rd series). 1, 3, 5, 8, 15, 30, 60, 100e. On Dogs. 1, 3, 5, 8, 15, 30, 60, 100e. On Butterflies. 1, 3, 5, 8, 15, 30, 60, 100e. On Water Birds. 1, 3, 5, 8, 15, 30, 60, 100e.

"London 1980" Stamp Exhibition. Rowland Hill (1st series) stamps optd 1, 3, 5, 8, 15, 30, 75, 200e.

Olympic Games, Moscow (1st series). Postage 2, 3, 5, 8, 10, 15e.; Air 30, 50e.

Olympic Games, Moscow (2nd series). Water sports. Postage 5, 10, 20, 25e.; Air 70e.

ERITREA Pt. 8

A former Italian colony on the Red Sea, north-east Africa. Under British Administration from 1942 to September 1952, when Eritrea was federated with Ethiopia.

Eritrea was declared an independent state in May 1993.

1893. 100 centesimi = 1 lira.
1991. 100 cents = 1 birr.
1997. Nakfa.

ITALIAN COLONY

1893. Stamps of Italy optd **Colonia Eritrea** (1 to 5c.) or **COLONIA ERITREA** (others).

1	**4**	1c. green	4·00	2·00
2	**5**	2c. brown	1·40	85
3	**23**	5c. green	45·00	2·75
4	**12**	10c. red	55·00	2·75
5		20c. orange	£120	2·00
6		25c. blue	£400	14·50
7	**14**	40c. brown	4·50	6·50
8		45c. green	4·50	9·75
9		60c. mauve	4·50	20·00
10		1l. brown and orange	13·00	20·00
11	**29**	5l. red and blue	£225	£160

1895. Stamps of Italy optd **Colonia Eritrea** (1 to 5c.) or **COLONIA ERITREA** (others).

12	**21**	1c. brown	8·00	4·75
13	**22**	2c. brown	85	85
14	**24**	5c. green	85	85
15	**25**	10c. lake	85	85
16	**26**	20c. orange	1·25	1·00
17	**27**	25c. blue	1·40	1·60
18		45c. olive	11·50	11·50

1903. Stamps of Italy optd **Colonia Eritrea**.

19	**30**	1c. brown	30	75
20	**31**	2c. brown	30	45
21		5c. green	26·00	45
22	**33**	10c. red	32·00	45
30		15c. on 20c. orange	24·00	5·25
23		20c. orange	2·00	75
24		25c. blue	£200	9·00
25		40c. brown	£275	13·00
26		45c. olive	2·75	5·50
27		50c. violet	80·00	15·00

28 34 1l. brown and green 2·75 60
29 5l. blue and red 16·00 21·00

1908. Stamps of Italy optd **ERITREA** (20c.) or **Colonia Eritrea** (others).
31 37 5c. green 80 75
32 10c. red 80 75
41 15c. grey 13·00 5·75
42 41 20c. orange 3·00 7·25
33 39 25c. blue 3·75 1·50
43 40c. brown 24·00 21·00
44 50c. violet 8·00 1·60
45 60c. red 16·00 14·00
46 34 10l. green and red £225 £325

3 Ploughing

1910.
34 3 5c. green 65 1·60
35 10c. red 3·00 2·40
40 – 15c. grey 32·00 29·00
37 – 25c. blue 4·00 6·50
DESIGN: 15, 25c. Government Palace, Massawa.

1916. Red Cross Society stamps of Italy optd **ERITREA.**
47 53 10c.+5c. red 2·00 8·00
48 54 15c.+5c. grey 10·50 18·00
49 20c. on 15c.+5c. grey 10·50 18·00
50 20c.+5c. orange 3·25 18·00

1916. No. 40 surch with new value and bars or crosses.
51 – 5c. on 15c. grey 5·00 8·50
52 – 20c. on 15c. grey 2·40 2·10

1922. Victory stamps of Italy optd **ERITREA.**
53 62 5c. green 1·25 5·00
54 10c. red 1·25 5·00
55 15c. grey 1·25 6·50
56 25c. blue 1·25 6·50

1922. Stamps of Somalia optd **ERITREA** and bars.
57 1 2c. on 1b. brown 3·75 9·75
58 5c. on 2b. green 3·75 6·50
59 2 10c. on 1a. red 3·75 1·60
60 15c. on 2a. brown 3·75 1·60
61 25c. on 2½a. blue 3·75 1·60
62 50c. on 5a. orange 11·50 6·50
63 1l. on 10a. lilac 13·00 11·50

1923. Propagation of the Faith stamps of Italy optd **ERITREA.**
64 66 20c. orange and green 4·00 18·00
65 30c. orange and red 4·00 18·00
66 50c. orange and violet 2·75 20·00
67 1l. orange and blue 2·75 26·00

1923. Fascist March on Rome stamps of Italy optd **ERITREA.**
68 73 10c. green 4·25 7·25
69 30c. violet 4·25 7·25
70 50c. red 4·25 8·25
71 74 1l. blue 4·25 21·00
72 2l. brown 4·25 24·00
73 75 5l. black and blue 4·25 35·00

1924. Manzoni stamps of Italy optd **ERITREA.**
74 77 10c. black and purple 5·00 20·00
75 – 15c. black and green 5·00 20·00
76 – 30c. black 5·00 20·00
77 – 50c. black and brown 5·00 20·00
78 – 1l. black and blue 40·00 £150
79 – 5l. black and purple £400 £1300

1924. Stamps of Italy optd **ERITREA.**
80 30 1c. brown 5·75 6·50
81 31 2c. orange 3·25 5·50
82 37 5c. green 5·75 6·00

1925. Holy Year stamps of Italy optd **ERITREA.**
90 – 20c.+10c. brown & green 2·50 11·50
91 81 30c.+15c. brown & dp brn 2·50 13·00
92 – 50c.+25c. brown & violet 2·50 11·50
93 – 60c.+30c. brown & red 2·50 14·50
94 – 1l.+50c. purple and blue 2·50 20·00
95 – 5l.+2l.50 purple & red 2·50 29·00

1925. Stamps of Italy optd **Colonia Eritrea.**
123 92 7½c. brown 11·50 38·00
124 39 20c. purple 3·25 2·75
96 20c. green 9·75 7·25
97 30c. grey 9·75 9·00
125 92 50c. mauve 38·00 23·00
126 39 60c. orange 65·00 75·00
127 34 75c. red and carmine 48·00 4·50
128 1l.25 blue & ultramarine 23·00 2·75
98 2l. green and orange 45·00 42·00
129 2l.50 green and orange £100 32·00

1925. Royal Jubilee stamps of Italy optd **ERITREA.**
99 82 60c. red 65 3·00
100 1l. blue 65 5·00
101 1l.25 blue 4·00 16·00

1926. St. Francis of Assisi stamps of Italy optd **ERITREA** (20 to 60c.) or **Eritrea** (others).
102 83 20c. green 1·50 6·50
103 – 40c. violet 1·50 6·50
104 – 60c. red 1·50 11·50
105 – 1l.25 blue 1·50 18·00
106 – 5l.+2l.50 brown 4·00 38·00

1926. Colonial Propaganda stamps Nos. 30/5 of Cyrenaica, but inscr "ERITREA".
107 5c.+5c. brown 60 4·00
108 10c.+5c. olive 60 4·00
109 20c.+5c. green 60 4·00
110 40c.+5c. red 60 4·00
111 60c.+5c. orange 60 4·00
112 1l.+5c. blue 60 4·00

1926. Portrait stamps of Italy optd **ERITREA.**
113 34 75c. red and carmine 38·00 7·25
114 1l.25 blue & ultramarine 23·00 7·25
115 2l.50 green and orange 75·00 21·00

1927. 1st National Defence issue of Italy optd **ERITREA.**
116 89 40c.+20c. black & brn 1·90 14·50
117 60c.+30c. brown & red 1·90 14·50
118 1l.25+60c. black and blue 1·90 29·00
119 5l.+2l.50 blk & grn 2·75 40·00

1927. Centenary of Volta issue of Italy optd **Eritrea.**
120 90 20c. violet 5·00 18·00
121 50c. orange 6·50 11·50
122 1l.25 blue 9·75 26·00

1928. Portrait stamps of Italy optd Eritrea (130) or **ERITREA** (others).
130 91 50c. grey and brown 10·50 3·25
131 92 50c. mauve 29·00 23·00
132 91 1l.75 brown 48·00 16·00

1928. 45th Anniv of the Italian-African Society. As Nos. 43/6 of Cyrenaica but inscr "ERITREA".
133 20c.+5c. green 1·60 5·25
134 30c.+5c. red 1·60 5·25
135 50c.+10c. violet 1·60 9·00
136 1l.25+20c. blue 1·75 10·50

1929. 2nd National Defence issue of Italy (colours changed) optd **ERITREA.**
137 89 30c.+10c. black & red 3·00 10·50
138 50c.+20c. grey & lilac 3·00 12·00
139 1l.25+50c. blue & brn 3·75 20·00
140 5l.+2l. black and green 3·75 38·00

1929. Montecassino stamps of Italy (colours changed) optd Eritrea (10l.) or **ERITREA** (others).
141 104 20c. green 3·75 8·00
142 – 25c. red 3·75 8·00
143 – 50c.+10c. red 3·75 9·75
144 – 75c.+15c. brown 3·75 9·75
145 104 1l.25+25c. purple 7·25 16·00
146 – 5l.+1l. blue 7·25 23·00
147 – 10l.+2l. brown 7·25 26·00

1930. Royal Wedding stamps of Italy (colours changed) optd **ERITREA.**
148 109 20c. green 1·00 3·00
149 50c.+10c. red 85 4·00
150 1l.25+25c. red 85 9·25

21 Telegraph Linesman
22
24 King Victor Emmanuel III

1930.
151 – 2c. black and blue 1·00 4·75
152 – 5c. black and violet 1·40 65
153 – 10c. black and brown 1·40 35
154 21 15c. black and green 1·40 50
155 – 25c. black and green 1·40 35
156 – 35c. black and red 4·50 8·75
157 – 1l. black and blue 1·40 35
158 – 2l. black and brown 4·50 8·75
159 – 5l. black and green 8·00 14·50
160 – 10l. black and blue 11·50 26·00
DESIGNS—VERT: 2, 35c. Lancer; 5, 10c. Postman; 25c. Rifleman. HORIZ: 1l. Massawa; 2l. Railway Bridge; 5l. Asmara Deghe Selam; 10l. Camel transport.

1930. Ferrucci issue of Italy (colours changed) optd **ERITREA.**
161 114 20c. violet 1·60 1·60
162 – 25c. green (283) 1·60 1·60
163 – 50c. black (284) 1·60 3·25
164 – 1l.25 blue (285) 1·60 6·50
165 – 5l.+2l. red (286) 5·00 13·00

1930. 3rd National Defence issue of Italy (colours changed) optd **ERITREA.**
166 89 30c.+10c. grn & dp grn 13·00 16·00
167 50c.+10c. purple & grn 13·00 20·00
168 1l.25+30c. lt brn & brn 13·00 29·00
169 5l.+1l.50 green & blue 42·00 65·00

1930. 25th Anniv of Italian Colonial Agricultural Institute.
170 22 50c.+20c. brown 2·25 9·75
171 1l.25+20c. blue 2·25 9·75
172 1l.75+20c. green 2·25 12·00
173 2l.55+50c. violet 3·25 20·00
174 5l.+1l. red 3·25 28·00

1930. Bimillenary of Virgil issue of Italy (colours changed) optd **ERITREA.**
175 15c. grey 85 4·00
176 20c. brown 85 2·00
177 25c. green 85 1·60
178 30c. brown 85 2·00
179 50c. purple 85 1·60
180 75c. red 85 3·00
181 1l.25 blue 85 4·00
182 5l.+1l.50 purple 3·00 21·00
183 10l.+2l.50 brown 3·00 32·00

1931. St. Antony of Padua issue of Italy (colours changed) optd **ERITREA.**
184 121 20c. brown 1·40 8·00
185 – 25c. green 1·40 3·25
186 – 30c. brown 1·40 3·25
187 – 50c. purple 1·40 3·25
188 – 75c. grey 1·40 8·00
189 – 1l.25 blue 1·40 16·00
190 – 5l.+2l.50 brown 3·75 38·00

1931.
191 24 7½c. brown 45 1·50
192 20c. red and blue 35 10
193 30c. purple and olive 45 10
194 40c. green and blue 50 10
195 50c. olive and brown 10 10
196 75c. red 1·50 10
197 1l.25 blue and purple 2·40 1·00
198 2l.50 green 2·40 3·25

25 Dromedary

1933.
199 25 2c. blue 50 2·25
200 – 5c. black 65 25
201 25 10c. brown 1·00 10
202 – 15c. brown 1·25 1·25
203 – 25c. green 80 10
204 – 35c. violet 3·00 4·25
205 – 1l. blue 10 10
206 – 2l. olive 11·50 2·00
207 – 5l. red 5·75 3·25
208 – 10l. orange 8·00 13·00
DESIGNS—HORIZ: 5c., 15c. Fish wharf; 25c. Baobab tree; 35c. Native village; 2l. African Elephant. VERT: 1l. Ruins at Cholloe; 5l. Eritrean man; 10l. Eritrean woman.

1934. Honouring the Duke of the Abruzzi. Designs as Nos. 201/2 and 204/8 optd **ONORANZE AL DUCA DEGLI ABRUZZI.**
209 25 10c. blue 7·75 11·50
210 – 15c. blue 5·75 11·50
211 – 35c. green 3·75 11·50
212 – 1l. red 3·75 11·50
213 – 2l. red 10·50 11·50
214 – 5l. violet 6·00 16·00
215 – 10l. green 6·00 20·00

30 Grant's Gazelle

1934. 2nd International Colonial Exn, Naples.
216 30 5c. brown & grn (postage) 2·75 9·00
217 10c. black and brown 2·75 9·00
218 20c. slate and red 2·75 7·25
219 50c. brown and violet 2·75 7·25
220 60c. blue and brown 2·75 9·75
221 1l.25 green and blue 2·75 16·00

222 – 25c. orange & blue (air) 2·75 9·00
223 – 50c. blue and green 2·75 7·25
224 – 75c. orange and brown 2·75 7·25
225 – 80c. green and brown 2·75 9·00
226 – 1l. green and red 2·75 9·75
227 – 2l. brown and blue 2·75 16·00
DESIGNS—36×43 mm: Nos. 222/4, Caproni Ca 101 airplane over landscape; 225/7, Savoia Marchetti S-66 flying boat over globe.

31 King Victor Emmanuel III and Caproni Ca 101 Airplane

1934. Air. Rome–Mogadiscio Flight.
228 31 25c.+10c. green 3·25 5·00
229 50c.+10c. brown 3·25 5·00
230 75c.+15c. red 3·25 5·00
231 80c.+15c. black 3·25 5·00
232 1l.+20c. brown 3·25 5·00
233 2l.+20c. blue 3·25 5·00
234 3l.+25c. violet 16·00 40·00
235 5l.+25c. red 16·00 40·00
236 10l.+30c. purple 16·00 40·00
237 25l.+2l. green 16·00 40·00

33 Macchi Castoldi MC-94 Flying Boat over Zebu-drawn Plough

1936. Air.
238 33 25c. green 85 2·25
239 – 50c. brown 50 10
240 – 60c. orange 1·40 5·25
241 – 75c. brown 1·25 1·00
242 – 1l. blue 10 10
243 33 1l.50 violet 80 35
244 – 2l. blue 1·00 2·00
245 – 3l. lake 18·00 8·75
246 – 5l. green 6·50 4·00
247 – 10l. red 16·00 8·75
DESIGNS: 50c., 2l. Caproni Ca 101 airplane over Massawa–Asmara Railway; 60c., 5l. Savoia Marchetti S-74 airplane over Dom palm trees; 75c., 10l. Savoia Marchetti S-73 airplane over roadway through cactus trees; 1, 3l. Caproni Ca 101 airplane over bridge.

INDEPENDENT STATE

35 Soldier with Flag and Scales of Justice
36 Map on Ballot Box

1991. 30th Anniv of Liberation Struggle. (a) As T **35**. Size 26×36 mm.
250 5c. black, orange and blue
251 15c. black, orange & green
252 20c. black, orange & yellow

(b) As T **35**, but redrawn with dates added either side of "30". Size 24×33 mm.
253 3b. black, orange & silver
254 5b. black, orange and gold

1993. Independence Referendum.
255 36 15c. multicoloured 10 10
256 – 60c. red, violet & green 15 10
257 – 75c. black, red and blue 15 10
258 – 1b. multicoloured 20 15
259 – 2b. blue, black & green 45 30
DESIGNS: 60c. Arrows; 75c. "YES" and "NO" signpost; 1b. Candle; 2b. Dove, posthorn and map.

38 Eritrean Flag

1993. Multicoloured, colour of frame given.
260 38 5c. brown 10 10
261 5c. blue 10 10
262 15c. red 10 10
263 20c. gold 10 10
264 20c. blue 10 10
265 25c. blue 10 10
266 35c. blue 10 10
267 40c. blue 10 10
268 50c. blue 10 10
269 60c. yellow 15 10
270 70c. mauve 15 10
271 70c. blue 15 10
272 80c. blue 20 15
273 3b. green 65 45
274 5b. silver 1·10 80

39 National Flag and Map

1994. Multicoloured, colour of frame given.
275 39 5c. yellow 10 10
276 10c. green 10 10
277 20c. orange 10 10
278 25c. red 10 10
279 40c. mauve 10 10
280 60c. turquoise 15 10
281 70c. green 15 10
282 1b. orange 20 15
283 2b. orange 45 30
284 3b. blue 65 45
285 5b. mauve 1·10 80
286 10b. lilac 2·25 1·60

40 Fishermen

1995. 20th Anniv of World Tourism Organization. Multicoloured.

287	10c. Type **40**	10	10
288	35c. Monument (vert)	10	10
289	85c. Mountain road	1·00	65
290	2b. Archaeological site (vert)	45	30

41 Red Sea Bannerfish

1995. Marine Life. Multicoloured.

291	30c. Type **41**	15	10
292	55c. Hooded butterflyfish	15	10
293	70c. Shrimp and lobster	15	10
294	1b. Blue-lined snapper	35	15

42 Mountain and broken Manacles

1995. Independence Day. Multicoloured.

295	25c. Type **42**	10	10
296	40c. Planting national flag on mountain top (vert)	10	10
297	70c. Men with national flag and scimitar (vert)	15	10
298	3b. National flag and fireworks (vert)	65	45

43 Construction Works

44 Dove flying around Map

1995. "Towards the Bright Future".

299 **43**	60c. black, orange & red	15	10
300 –	80c. multicoloured	20	15
301 –	90c. black, orange & red	20	15
302 –	1b. brown, orange & red	20	15

DESIGNS: 80c. Tree; 90c. Village; 1b. Camels.

1995. Council for Mutual Economic Assistance in Africa. Multicoloured.

303	40c. Type **44**	10	10
304	50c. Tree with member countries' names on leaves	10	10
305	60c. Emblem and handshake	15	10
306	3b. Emblem and flags of member countries (horiz)	65	45

45 Headquarters, New York, and Anniversary Emblem

46 Bowl and Spoon

1995. 50th Anniv of U.N.O. Multicoloured.

307	40c. Type **45**	10	10
308	60c. U.N. Emblem forming tree	15	10
309	70c. Anniversary emblem and peace dove	15	10
310	2b. Type **45**	45	30

1995. 50th Anniv of F.A.O. Multicoloured.

311	5c. Type **46**	10	10
312	25c. Agriculture	10	10
313	80c. Bird feeding young	20	15
314	3b. Cornucopia of crops	65	45

47 Eritreans raising Flag

1996. Martyrs' Day. Multicoloured.

315	40c. Type **47**	10	10
316	60c. Man laying wreath on grave	10	10
317	70c. Breast-feeding	15	10
318	80c. Planting seedlings	15	10

48 Adult and Young

1996. Endangered Animals. Multicoloured.

(a) Gemsbok.

319	3b. Type **48**	60	45
320	3b. Adult eating	60	45
321	3b. Encounter between two males	60	45
322	3b. Gemsbok	60	45
	(b) Mammals.		
323	3b. Savanna (inscr "Green") monkey	60	45
324	3b. Aardwolf	60	45
325	3b. Dugong	60	45
326	3b. Maned rat	60	45
	(c) White-eyed Gull.		
327	3b. Preening	60	45
328	3b. Flying	60	45
329	3b. Pair of gulls on rock	60	45
330	3b. Gull on rock	60	45

49 Emblem and Mother and Child

1996. 50th Anniv of UNICEF. Designs showing Fund emblem. Multicoloured.

331	40c. Type **49**	10	10
332	55c. Nurse and child	10	10
333	60c. Weighing baby	10	10
334	95c. Amputee beside bed	15	10

50 Taking Oath of Allegiance

52 Volleyball

51 Track-laying

1996. National Service. Multicoloured.

335	40c. Type **50**	10	10
336	55c. National rebuilding programmes	10	10
337	60c. Road-building (horiz)	10	10
338	95c. Man with club (horiz)	15	10

1997. Revival of Eritrean Railways. Mult.

339	40c. Type **51**	35	20
340	55c. Steam locomotive on seafront line	45	30
341	60c. Seafront tourist diesel locomotive	50	35
342	95c. Railway tunnel through mountain	80	55

1997. Olympic Games, Atlanta (1996). Mult.

343	2b. Type **52**	35	25
344	2b. Laurel wreath and stars	35	25
345	2b. Basketball (three players reaching for ball)	35	25
346	2b. Torch (with flame to right)	35	25
347	2b. Cycling (facing forward)	35	25
348	2b. Torch (with flame to left)	35	25
349	2b. Cycling (facing right)	35	25
350	2b. Gold medal	35	25
351	2b. Football	35	25
352	3b. Football match (horiz)	55	40
353	3b. Cycling road race (horiz)	55	40
354	3b. Volleyball match	55	40
355	3b. Basketball match	55	40

53 "Heliconius melpomerie cytherea"

1997. Butterflies and Moths. Multicoloured.

357	1b. Mustard white	20	15
358	2b. Type **53**	35	25
359	3b. "Papilio polymnestor"	55	40
360	3b. Paradise birdwing ("Ornithoptera paradisea")	55	40
361	3b. "Graphium marcellus"	55	40
362	3b. Jersey tiger moth ("Panaxia quadripunctaria")	55	40
363	3b. "Cardui japonica"	55	40
364	3b. "Papilio childrence"	55	40
365	3b. "Philosamea cynthis"	55	40
366	3b. Luna moth ("Actias luna")	55	40
367	3b. "Heticopis acit"	55	40
368	3b. "Psaphis eusehemoides" (vert)	55	40
369	3b. "Papilio brookiana" (vert)	55	40
370	3b. "Parnassius charitonius" (vert)	55	40
371	3b. Blue morpho ("Morpho cypris") (vert)	55	40
372	3b. Monarch ("Danaus plexippus") (vert)	55	40
373	3b. Gaudy commodore ("Precis octavia") (vert)	55	40
374	3b. Kaiser-i-hind ("Teinopalpus imperialis") (vert)	55	40
375	3b. "Samia gloreri" (moth) (vert)	55	40
376	3b. "Automeris nyctimene" (vert)	55	40
377	4b. "Ornithoptera goliath"	75	55
378	8b. "Heliconius astraea rondonia"	1·40	1·00

Nos. 359/67 and 368/76 respectively were issued together, se-tenant, the backgrounds forming composite designs.

There are some errors in the Latin inscriptions.

54 Agricultural Land

1997. Environmental Conservation. Mult.

380	60c. Type **54**	10	10
381	90c. Hillside tree plantation	15	10
382	95c. Terraced hillside	15	10

55 Local Meeting

57 Village Weaver

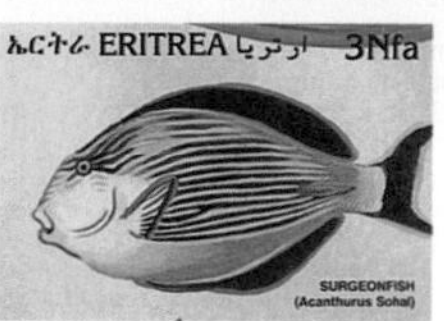

56 Red Sea Surgeonfish

1997. Adoption of National Constitution. Mult.

383	10c. Type **55**	10	10
384	40c. Dove holding open book	10	10
385	85c. Open book in hands	15	10

1997. Marine Life. Multicoloured.

386	3n. Sergeant major and white-tipped reef shark	50	35
387	3n. Hawksbill turtle and manta ("Devil") ray	50	35
388	3n. Type **56**	50	35
389	3n. Needlefish ("Red Sea Houndfish") and humpback whale	50	35
390	3n. Manta ("Devil") ray	50	35
391	3n. Manta ("Devil") ray and two-banded anemonefishes ("Clownfishes")	50	35
392	3n. Forceps ("Long-nosed") butterflyfish	50	35
393	3n. Needlefish ("Red Sea Houndfish") and yellow sweetlips	50	35
394	3n. White moray eel	50	35
395	3n. Blue-cheeked ("Masked") butterflyfishes	50	35
396	3n. Shark sucker ("Suckerfish") and whale shark	50	35
397	3n. Sunrise dottyback and bluefin trevally	50	35
398	3n. Moon wrasse, purple moon angel and yellow-tailed ("Two-banded") anemonefish	50	35
399	3n. Lionfish	50	35
400	3n. White-tipped reef shark and Niki's sanddiver	50	35
401	3n. Golden trevallys ("Golden Jacks") and yellow-edged lyretail ("Lunar tailed grouper")	50	35
402	3n. Narrow-banded batfishes	50	35
403	3n. Red-toothed ("Black") triggerfish	50	35

Nos. 386/94 and 395/403 respectively were issued together, se-tenant, forming a composite design.

1998. Birds. Multicoloured.

405	3n. Type **57** (inscr "Black Headed Weaver")	50	35
406	3n. Abyssinian roller	50	35
407	3n. Abyssinian ground hornbills	50	35
408	3n. Lichtenstein's sandgrouse	50	35
409	3n. Erckel's francolin	50	35
410	3n. Arabian bustard	50	35
411	3n. Chestnut-backed sparrow-lark ("Chestnut-backed Finchlark")	50	35
412	3n. Desert lark	50	35
413	3n. Hoopoe lark ("Bifasciated Lark")	50	35
414	3n. African darter	50	35
415	3n. White-headed vulture	50	35
416	3n. Egyptian vultures	50	35
417	3n. Yellow-billed hornbill	50	35
418	3n. Helmet guineafowl	50	35
419	3n. Secretary bird	50	35
420	3n. Martial eagle	50	35
421	3n. Bateleur	50	35
422	3n. Red-billed quelea	50	35

Nos. 405/13 and 414/22 were respectively issued together, se-tenant, forming a composite design.

58 Highland Dwelling

59 Cunama Hair Style

1998. Traditional Houses. Multicoloured.

424	50c. Type **58**	10	10
425	60c. Lowland dwelling	10	10
426	85c. Danakil dwelling	15	10

1998. Traditional Hair Styles. Multicoloured.

427	10c. Type **59**	10	10
428	50c. Tigrinya	10	10
429	85c. Bilen	15	10
430	95c. Tigre	15	10

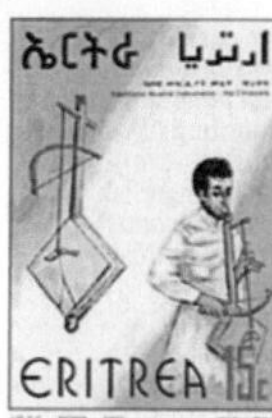

60 Chirawata

1998. Traditional Musical Instruments. Mult.

431	15c. Type **60**	10	10
432	60c. Imbilta, malaket and shambeko (wind instruments)	10	10
433	75c. Kobero (drum)	10	10
434	85c. K'rar (stringed instrument)	15	10

61 Planting Flag

1999. 8th Anniv of Independence.

435 **61**	60c. multicoloured	10	10
436	1n. multicoloured	15	10
437	3n. multicoloured	45	35

62 1 Nafka Banknote

1999. 2nd Anniv of Currency Reform. Multicoloured.

438	10c. Type **62**	10	10
439	60c. 5 nafka banknote	10	10
440	80c. 10 nafka banknote	15	10
441	1n. 20 nafka banknote	20	15
442	2n. 50 nafka banknote	40	30
443	3n. 100 nafka banknote	50	40

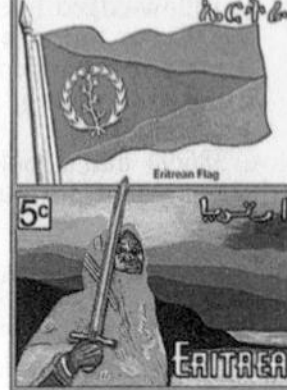

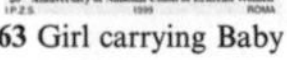

63 Girl carrying Baby **64** Flag and Man

1999. 20th Anniv of National Union of Eritrean Women. Multicoloured.

444	5c. Type **63**	10	10
445	10c. Women reading (horiz)	10	10
446	25c. Crowd (horiz)	10	10
447	1n. Soldier using binoculars (horiz)	1·75	1·25

2000. Millennium. Designs showing the Eritrean Flag and a local scene. Multicoloured.

448	5c. Type **64**	10	10
449	10c. *Denden Assab* (freighter)	10	10
450	25c. Procession in stadium	10	10
451	60c. Soldiers and camp	10	10
452	1n. Raised hand and names of indigenous language groups	20	15
453	2n. Crowd sitting beneath tree	35	25
454	3n. Hand posting ballot paper	55	40
455	5n. Military equipment	90	65
456	7n. State emblem	1·25	90
457	10n. Eritrean 10n. banknote	1·75	1·25

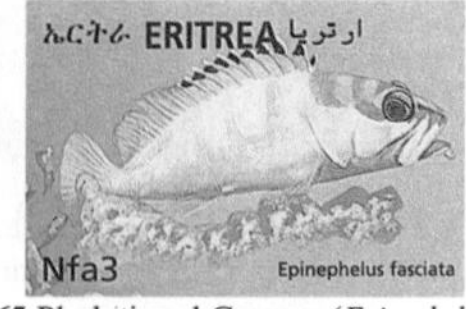

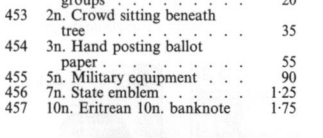

65 Black-tipped Grouper (*Epinephelus fasciata*)

2000. Marine Life. Multicoloured.

458	3n. Type **65**	55	40
459	3n. Regal angelfish (*Pygoplites diacanthus*)	55	40
460	3n. Coral hind (*Cephalopholis miniata*)	55	40
461	3n. Eibl's angelfish (*Centropyge eibli*)	55	40
462	3n. Yellow boxfish (*Ostracion cubicus*)	55	40
463	3n. Pennant coralfish (*Heniochus acuminatus*)	55	40
464	3n. *Chilomycterus spilostylus*	55	40
465	3n. Gray humbug (*Dascyllus marginatus*)	55	40
466	3n. Undulate triggerfish (*Balistapus undulatus*)	55	40
467	3n. Semicircle angelfish (*Pomacanthus semicirculatus*)	55	40
468	3n. Picasso triggerfish (*Rhinecanthus assasi*)	55	40
469	3n. Millepora (coral)	55	40
470	3n. Coachwhip ray	55	40
471	3n. Sulfur damselfish	55	40
472	3n. Grey moray	55	40
473	3n. Sabre squirrelfish	55	40
474	3n. Rusty parrotfish	55	40
475	3n. Striped eel catfish	55	40
476	3n. Spangled emperor	55	40
477	3n. Devil scorpionfish	55	40
478	3n. Crown squirrelfish	55	40
479	3n. Vanikoro sweeper	55	40
480	3n. Sergeant major	55	40
481	3n. Giant manta	55	40

66 Women talking

2001. 10th Anniv of Independence. Multicoloured.

483	20c. Type **66**	10	10
484	60c. Flag and doves (vert)	10	10
485	1n. Emblem (vert)	15	15
486	3n. Celebrating (vert)	45	35
MS487	200 × 115 mm. Nos. 483/6	80	80

67 Adult lying down

2001. Aardwolf (*Proteles cristatus*). Multicoloured.

488	3n. Type **67**	45	35
489	3n. Cubs	45	35
490	3n. Adult walking	45	35
491	3n. Adult head	45	35

68 Aardvark

2001. Wild Animals. Two sheets, each 149 × 83 mm, containing T **68** and similar horiz designs. Multicoloured.

MS492 (a) 3n. Type **68**; 3n. Black-backed jackal; 3n. Striped hyaena; 3n. Spotted hyaena; 3n. Leopard; 3n. African elephant; (b) 3n. Salts dik-dik (inscr "Dick Dick"); 3n. Klipspringer; 3n. Greater kudu (inscr "Tragelophus"); 3n. Soemmerring's gazelle (inscr "soemmering"); 3n. Dorcas gazelle; 3n. African ass (inscr "Equu") Set of 2 sheets 5·50 4·75

CONCESSIONAL LETTER POST

1939. No. CL267 of Italy optd **ERITREA**.

CL248	CL **109**	10c. brown	13·00	16·00

EXPRESS LETTER STAMPS

1907. Express Letter stamps of Italy optd **Colonia Eritrea.**

E31	E **35**	25c. red	14·50	11·50
E34	E **41**	30c. blue and red	75·00	90·00
E53	E **35**	50c. red	2·00	13·00

E 13

1924.

E83	E **13**	60c. brown and red	5·00	14·50
E84		2l. pink and blue	11·50	18·00

1926. Surch.

E113	E **13**	70 on 60c. brn & red	5·00	9·00
E116		1l.25 on 60c. brown and red	9·00	2·25
E114		2l.50 on 2l. pink and blue	11·50	17·00

OFFICIAL AIR STAMP

1934. Optd **SERVIZIO DI STATO** and Crown.

O238	**31**	25l.+2l. red	£1600	

PARCEL POST STAMPS

PRICES: Unused prices are for complete stamps, used prices for a half stamp.

1916. Parcel Post stamps of Italy optd **ERITREA** on each half of stamp.

P61	P **53**	5c. brown	1·60	1·60
P62		10c. blue	1·60	1·60
P63		20c. black	1·60	1·60
P64		25c. red	1·60	1·60
P65		50c. orange	3·25	1·10
P66		1l. violet	3·25	1·10
P67		2l. green	3·25	1·40
P68		3l. yellow	3·25	1·40
P69		4l. grey	3·25	1·60
P70		10l. purple	45·00	4·50
P71		12l. brown	£110	6·00
P72		15l. green	£110	9·00
P73		20l. purple	£110	18·00

1927. Parcel Post stamps of Italy optd **ERITREA** on each half of stamp.

P123	P **92**	10c. blue	£3500	4·25
P124		25c. red	£180	80
P125		30c. blue	85	60
P126		50c. orange	£180	1·00
P127		60c. red	80	30
P128		1l. violet	£160	30
P129		2l. green	£130	30
P130		3l. yellow	3·25	30
P131		4l. grey	3·25	30
P132		10l. mauve	£275	6·00
P133		20l. purple	£275	9·50

POSTAGE DUE STAMPS

1903. Postage Due stamps of Italy optd **Colonia Eritrea.**

D 53	D **12**	5c. mauve & orange	1·00	5·00
D 54		10c. mauve & orge	2·00	5·00
D 32		20c. mauve & orge	7·25	11·50
D 33		30c. mauve & orge	9·75	14·50
D 57		40c. mauve & orge	26·00	18·00
D 58		50c. mauve & orge	11·50	14·50
D 59		60c. mauve & orge	14·50	18·00
D116		60c. brown & orge	65·00	70·00
D 37		1l. mauve and blue	8·00	16·00
D 38		2l. mauve and blue	80·00	65·00
D 39		5l. mauve and blue	£160	£120
D 63		10l. mauve and blue	25·00	29·00
D 41	D **13**	50l. yellow	£375	£120
D 42		100l. blue	£225	60·00

1934. Postage Due stamps of Italy optd **ERITREA.**

D216	D **141**	5c. brown	25	3·25
D217		10c. blue	25	85
D218		20c. red	2·00	1·60
D219		25c. green	2·00	2·00
D220		30c. orange	2·00	3·75
D221		40c. brown	2·00	3·75
D222		50c. violet	2·00	65
D223		60c. blue	4·00	6·50
D224	D **142**	1l. orange	2·00	80
D225		2l. green	9·75	18·00
D226		5l. violet	21·00	21·00
D227		10l. blue	23·00	25·00
D228		20l. red	28·00	28·00

For British Administration see **BRITISH OCCUPATION OF ITALIAN COLONIES.**

ESTONIA Pt. 10

A former province of the Russian Empire on the S. Coast of the Gulf of Finland. Under Russian rule until 1918 when it became an independent republic. The area was incorporated into the Soviet Union from 1940; for issues made during 1941 see GERMAN OCCUPATION OF ESTONIA.

Estonia once again became independent in 1991.

1918. 100 kopeks = 1 rouble.
1919. 100 penni = 1 Estonian mark.
1928. 100 senti = 1 kroon.
1991. 100 kopeks = 1 rouble.
1992. 100 senti = 1 kroon.

Note. An asterisk * after the date indicates that the stamps have a network background in colour.

2 **4** Seagulls

1918. Imperf.

1	**2**	5k. pink	65	50
2		15k. blue	65	50
3		35p. brown	90	75
4		70p. olive	2·00	2·00

1919. Imperf.

5	**4**	5p. yellow	2·00	2·00

5 **6**

7 **9** Viking Longship

1919. Imperf (10p., 15m. and 25m. also perf).

6	**5**	5p. orange	10	10
7		10p. green	20	10
8	**6**	15p. red	15	10
9	**7**	35p. blue	25	10
10		70p. lilac	30	20
11a	**9**	1m. blue and brown	40	25
12a		5m. yellow and black	1·25	20
33		15m. green and violet	2·75	50
34		25m. blue and brown	4·00	2·00

10 L.V.G. Schneider Biplane

1920. Air. Imperf.

15	**10**	5m. black, blue & yellow	4·00	4·00

11 Tallinn **12** Wounded Soldier **13**

1920. Imperf.

16	**11**	25p. green	30	15
17		25p. yellow	25	40
18		35p. red	40	15
19		50p. green	30	15
20		1m. red	90	20
21		2m. blue	70	40
23		2m.50 blue	1·00	30

1920. War Victims' Fund. Imperf.

24	**12**	35+10p. grey and red	60	1·50
25	**13**	70+15p. bistre and blue	60	1·50

1920. Surch.

26	**6**	1m. on 15p. red	40	40
27	**11**	1m. on 35p. red	50	50
29	**12**	1m. on 35+10p. grey and red	50	35
28	**7**	2m. on 70p. lilac	75	40
30	**13**	2m. on 70+15p. bistre and blue	50	35

17 **18** Weaver **19** Blacksmith

1921. Red Cross. Imperf or perf.

31	**17**	2½–3½m. brn, red & orge	1·00	5·00
32		5–7m. brn, red & blue	1·00	5·00

1922. Imperf or perf.

35	**18**	½m. orange	75	30
36		1m. brown	1·25	30
37		2m. green	1·40	15
38		2½m. red	3·00	30
39		3m. green	1·50	20
40	**19**	5m. red	1·75	10
41		9m. red	2·50	1·50
42		10m. blue	3·50	10
72		10m. grey	3·00	5·50
42a		12m. red	4·00	1·50
42b		15m. purple	3·00	60
42c		20m. blue	10·00	30

20 Map of Estonia

1923.*

43	**20**	100m. blue and olive	16·00	2·00
43a		300m. blue and brown	35·00	10·00

1923. Air. No. 15 optd **1923** or surch **15 Marka 1923.**

44	**10**	5m. black, blue & yellow	7·00	20·00
45		15m. on 5m. blk, bl & yell	13·00	30·00

1923. Air. Pairs of No. 15 surch **1923** and new value.

46	**10**	10m. on 5m.	8·50	25·00
47		20m. on 5m.	18·00	35·00
48		45m. on 5m.	60·00	£170

1923. Red Cross stamps optd **Aita hadalist**. Imperf or perf.

49	**17**	2½–3½m. brn, red & orge	25·00	75·00
50		5–7m. brown, red & blue	25·00	75·00

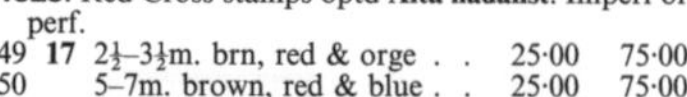

24 Junkers F-13 with Floats

1924.* Air. Various aircraft. Imperf or perf.

51	–	5m. black and yellow	1·25	4·00
52	–	10m. black and blue	1·25	4·00
53	**24**	15m. black and red	1·25	6·00
54	–	20m. black and green	1·25	4·00
55	–	45m. black and violet	1·25	8·00

DESIGNS: 5m. Sabaltnig PIII; 10m. Sabaltnig PIII with floats; 20m. Junkers F-13 with wheels; 45m. Junkers F-13 with skis.

25 National Theatre

1924.* Perf.
57 **25** 30m. black and violet . . . 10·00 3·00
58 – 40m. sepia and blue . . . . 8·00 2·00
59 **25** 70m. black and red . . . . 12·00 5·00
DESIGN: 40m. Vanemuine Theatre, Tartu.

1926. Red Cross stamps surch in figures only. Perf.
60 **17** 5–6 on 2½–3½ brown, red and orange . . . . 3·00 5·00
61 10–12 on 5–7m. brown, red and blue . . . . 3·00 5·00

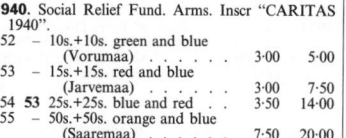

28 Kuressaare Castle
30 Tallinn

1927. Liberation War Commemoration Fund.
62 **28** 5m.+5m. brown & green . . 75 3·00
63 – 10m.+10m. brown & blue 75 3·00
64 – 12m.+12m. green & red . . 75 3·00
65 – 20m.+20m. purple & blue 85 5·00
66 **30** 40m.+40m. grey & brown 90 5·00
DESIGNS—As Type **28**: 10m. Tartu Cathedral; 12m. Parliament House, Tallinn. As Type **30**: 20m. Narva Fortress.

1928. 10th Anniv of Independence. Surch **1918 24/11 1928 S. S.** Perf.
67 **18** 2s. on 2m. green . . . . . 1·00 75
68 **19** 5s. on 5m. red . . . . . . 1·00 75
69 10s. on 10m. blue . . . . . 1·75 75
70 15s. on 15m. purple . . . . 2·50 1·00
71 20s. on 20m. blue . . . . . 2·25 75

32 Arms of Estonia
35 "Succour"

1928.*
73 **32** 1s. grey 40 10
74 2s. green 40 10
75 4s. green . . . . 1·25 15
76 5s. red 90 10
77 8s. purple . . . . 3·00 20
78 10s. blue . . . . 1·00 10
79 12s. red . . . . 2·00 10
80 15s. yellow . . . . 2·50 10
80a 15s. red . . . . 15·00 1·00
81 20s. blue . . . . 2·75 10
82 25s. mauve . . . . 10·00 15
83 25s. blue . . . . 18·00 1·00
84 40s. orange . . . . 6·50 60
86 60s. grey . . . . 8·50 50
87 80s. sepia . . . . 11·00 1·10

1930.* Surch in **KROON.**
88 **25** 1k. on 70m. black & red . . 8·00 5·00
89 **20** 2k. on 300m. blue & brown 18·00 10·00
90 3k. on 300m. blue & brown 35·00 25·00

1931. Red Cross Fund.
91 **35** 2s.+3s. green and red . . . 4·50 7·50
92 – 5s.+3s. rose and red . . . . 4·50 7·50
93 – 10s.+3s. blue and red . . . 4·50 7·50
94 **35** 20s.+3s. blue and red . . . 8·50 14·00
DESIGN: 5s., 10s. "The Light of Hope".

37 Tartu Observatory
39 Narva Falls

1932.* 300th Anniv of Tartu University.
95 **37** 5s. red . . . . 4·50 40
96 – 10s. blue . . . . 1·25 30
97 **37** 12s. red . . . . 10·00 4·00
98 – 20s. blue . . . . 3·50 1·00
DESIGN: 10s., 20s. Tartu University.

1933.
99 **39** 1k. black . . . . 5·00 2·00
99a 1k. green . . . . 1·00 7·50

40 Ancient Bard
41 Invalid and Nurse

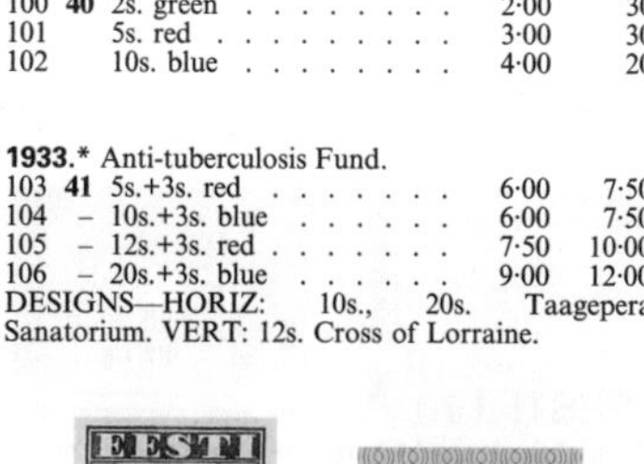

1933.* 10th All-Estonian Choral Festival.
100 **40** 2s. green . . . . 2·00 30
101 5s. red . . . . 3·00 30
102 10s. blue . . . . 4·00 20

1933.* Anti-tuberculosis Fund.
103 **41** 5s.+3s. red . . . . 6·00 7·50
104 – 10s.+3s. blue . . . . 6·00 7·50
105 – 12s.+3s. red . . . . 7·50 10·00
106 – 20s.+3s. blue . . . . . . 9·00 12·00
DESIGNS—HORIZ: 10s., 20s. Taagepera Sanatorium. VERT: 12s. Cross of Lorraine.

43 Harvesting
44 Arms of Narva

1935.
107 **43** 3k. brown . . . . 1·25 3·00

1936.* Charity. Social Relief Fund.
108 **44** 10s.+10s. blue & green . . 3·75 7·50
109 – 15s.+15s. blue and red . . 4·00 9·00
110 – 25s.+25s. orange & blue . . 6·00 12·50
111 – 50s.+50s. yellow & blk . . 16·00 38·00
DESIGNS—Arms of Parnu (15s.), Tartu (25s.) and Tallinn (50s.).

45 Pres. Konstantin Pats
46 Restored Portal

1936.
112 **45** 1s. brown 50 20
113 2s. green 50 20
113a 3s. orange . . . . 7·50 8·00
114 4s. purple . . . . 1·75 50
115 5s. green . . . . 1·00 20
116 6s. red . . . . 1·25 20
117 6s. green . . . . 30·00 38·00
118 10s. blue . . . . 1·50 20
119 15s. red . . . . 2·50 40
119a 15s. blue . . . . 4·00 45
120 18s. red . . . . 18·00 7·50
121 20s. mauve . . . . 2·25 20
122 25s. blue . . . . 10·00 1·00
123 30s. yellow . . . . . . 14·00 1·25
123a 30s. blue . . . . 20·00 6·00
124 50s. brown . . . . 7·00 1·50
125 60s. mauve . . . . 15·00 5·00

1936.* 500th Anniv of St. Brigitte Abbey.
126 **46** 5s. green 60 40
127 – 10s. blue 60 50
128 – 15s. red . . . . 1·75 4·00
129 – 25s. blue . . . . 2·00 5·50
DESIGNS: 10s. Ruins of the Abbey; 15s. Ruined facade; 25s. Old seal.

47 Paide
48 Paldiski (Port Baltic)

1937.* Social Relief Fund. Inscr "CARITAS 1937".
130 **47** 10s.+10s. green . . . . . 3·00 5·00
131 – 15s.+15s. red . . . . . 3·00 6·00
132 – 25s.+25s. blue . . . . . 5·50 10·00
133 – 50s.+50s. purple . . . . 10·00 22·00
DESIGNS—Arms of: Rakvere (15s.); Valga (25s.); Viljandi (50s.).

1938.* Social Relief Fund. Inscr "CARITAS 1938".
134 **48** 10s.+10s. brown . . . . . 3·00 5·00
135 – 15s.+15s. grn & red . . . 3·00 6·00
136 – 25s.+25s. red & blue . . . 4·25 12·00
137 – 50s.+50s. yell & blue . . . 14·00 30·00
MS138 106 × 150 mm. Nos. 134/7 32·00 60·00
DESIGNS: Arms of: Voru (15s.); Haapsalu (25s.); Kuresaare (50s.).

49 Cargo Liner "Aegna" in Tallinn Harbour

1938.
139 **49** 2k. blue . . . . 1·25 5·00

50 Dr. F. R. Faehlmann
51 Arms of Viljandi

1938. Centenary of Estonian Literary Society. Designs showing Society founders.
140 **50** 5s. green 30 40
141 – 10s. brown 55 50
142 – 15s. red . . . . 1·00 5·00
143 **50** 25s. blue . . . . 1·75 7·50
MS143a 90 × 40 mm. Nos. 140/3 12·00 55·00
DESIGN: 10s., 15s. Dr. F. R. Kreutzwald.

1939.* Social Relief Fund. Inscr "CARITAS 1939".
144 **51** 10s.+10s. green . . . . . 3·25 4·50
145 – 15s.+15s. red (Parnu) . . . 3·25 5·00
146 – 25s.+25s. blue (Tartu) . . 7·50 12·00
147 – 50s.+50s. pur (Harju) . . . 12·50 30·00
MS147a 90 × 137 mm. Nos. 144/7 45·00 90·00

52 Sanatorium, Parnu
53 Laanemaa

1939. Centenary of Parnu.
148 **52** 5s. green . . . . 1·00 50
149 – 10s. violet 75 50
150 **52** 18s. red . . . . 2·00 5·00
151 – 30s. blue . . . . 2·75 6·00
MS151a 137 × 90 mm. Nos. 148/51 20·00 65·00
DESIGN—10s., 30s. Beach Hotel, Parnu.

1940. Social Relief Fund. Arms. Inscr "CARITAS 1940".
152 – 10s.+10s. green and blue (Vorumaa) . . . . . . 3·00 5·00
153 – 15s.+15s. red and blue (Jarvemaa) . . . . . . 3·00 7·50
154 **53** 25s.+25s. blue and red . . 3·50 14·00
155 – 50s.+50s. orange and blue (Saaremaa) . . . . . . 7·50 20·00

54 Carrier Pigeon and Airplane
55 State Arms

1940. Cent of 1st Adhesive Postage Stamps.
156 **54** 3s. orange 30 45
157 10s. violet 30 15
158 15s. brown 30 15
159 30s. blue . . . . 1·90 1·25

1991.
161 **55** 5k. red and orange 10 10
162 10k. green & emerald . . . 10 10
163 15k. blue and light blue . . 10 10
164 30k. black and grey . . . 20 15
165 50k. brown and orange . . 30 20
166 70k. purple and mauve . . 40 20
167 90k. magenta & mauve . . 50 30
168 1r. brown (21 × 27 mm) . . 60 40
169 2r. blue (21 × 27 mm) . . . 1·25 60
See also Nos. 194/205.

56 Flag
57 State Arms

1991.
170 **56** 1r.50 multicoloured 75 75
171 – 2r.50 black, grey & green 1·40 1·40
DESIGN—HORIZ: 2r.50, Map of Europe showing Estonia.

1992. Value expressed by letter.
172 **57** E (1r.) green and yellow . . 10 10
173 R (10r.) red and pink . . . 25 15
174 I (20r.) green & blue . . . 50 30
175 A (40r.) blue & lt blue . . 1·10 70
See also Nos. 179/81 and 182/4.

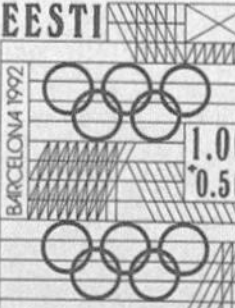

58 Olympic Rings and Pattern
59 Osprey ("Pandion haliaetus")

1992. Olympic Games, Barcelona.
176 **58** 1k.+50s. red 20 20
177 – 3k.+1k.50 green 60 60
178 – 5k.+2k.50 black & blue . . 1·25 1·25
DESIGNS: 3k. Olympic rings and pattern (different); 5k. Estonian flag, rings and pattern.

1992. As Nos. 172 and 174/5 but colours changed.
179 **57** E (10s.) orange & yellow 10 10
180 I (1k.) green 20 20
181 A (2k.) blue 30 30

1992. Value expressed by letter. Size 21 × 27 mm.
182 **57** X (10s.) brown 20 10
183 X (10s.) green 20 10
184 X (10s.) black 20 10

1992. Birds of the Baltic.
185 **59** 1k. black and red 65 65
186 – 1k. brown, black & red . . 65 65
187 – 1k. sepia, brown & red . . 65 65
188 – 1k. brown, black & red . . 65 65
DESIGNS: No. 186, Black-tailed godwit ("Limosa limosa"); 187, Goosander ("Mergus merganser"); 188, Common shelducks ("Tadorna tadorna").

1992. Value expressed by letter. Size 21 × 27 mm.
189 **57** Z (30s.) mauve 20 10
190 Z (30s.) red 20 10
191 Z (30s.) black 20 10

60 Decorated Christmas Tree
61 Birds, Flowers and Envelope within Heart

1992. Christmas.
192 **60** 30s. multicoloured 10 10
193 2k. multicoloured 15 15

1993. As Nos. 161/9 but face values in senti.
194 **55** 10s. grey and blue (18 × 21 mm) 10 10
194a 10s. brown and blue (18 × 21 mm) 10 10
195 20s. black and green (21 × 27 mm) 10 10
196 30s. purple and grey (21 × 27 mm) 10 10
197 50s. blue and brown (18 × 21 mm) 10 10
198 60s. green and purple (18 × 21 mm) 10 10
209 60s. brn (21 × 27 mm) . . 10 10
199 80s. blue and mauve (21 × 27 mm) 15 10
200 2k.50 turquoise and green (18 × 21 mm) 20 10
201 3k.10 red and violet . . . 25 10
202 3k.30 lilac and violet (18 × 21 mm) 30 15
203 3k.60 blue & cobalt . . . 35 15
203a 3k.60 violet and blue (18 × 21 mm) 30 15
204 4k.50 brown & lt brn . . 40 20
205 5k. mauve and brown (23 × 28 mm) 40 20
205a 5k. mauve and yellow (23 × 28 mm) 40 20
206 10k. green and blue (23 × 28 mm) 85 45
207 20k. green and lilac (23 × 28 mm) . . . . . 1·75 1·00

1993. Friendship.
210 **61** 1k. multicoloured 15 10

62 Anniversary Emblem
64 Wrestling

1993. 75th Anniv of Republic.
211 **62** 60s. multicoloured 10 10
212 1k. multicoloured 15 10
213 2k. multicoloured 30 15

1993. No. 163 surch **0.60**.
214 **55** 60s. on 15k. blue & lt blue 10 10

1993. Baltic Sea Games. Multicoloured.
215 60s. Type **64** 10 10
216 1k.+25s. Ship with map of Baltic on sail and colours of participating countries as shields 25 10
217 2k. Athlete putting the rock and sports pictograms . . 30 20

65 Toompea Castle, Tallinn

66 1918 5k. Stamp and Anniversary Emblem

1993.
218 – 1k. black and brown . . 10 10
219 **65** 2k. brown & lt brown . . 15 10
219a – 2k.50 deep lilac and lilac 25 15
219b – 2k.50 grey 20 15
220 – 2k.70 blue and cobalt . . 25 15
221 – 2k.90 dp green & green 25 15
222 – 3k. brown and pink . . . 25 15
222a – 3k.20 dp green & green 25 15
223 – 4k. violet and lilac . . . 35 20
224 – 4k.80 brown and pink . . 40 20
DESIGNS—HORIZ: 1k. Toolse Castle; 2k.70, Hermann's Castle, Narva; 2k.90, Haapsalu Castle; 3k.20, Rakvere Castle; 4k. Kuressaare Castle; 4k.80, Viljandi Castle. VERT: 2k.50 (219a), Paide Castle; 2k.50 (219b), Purtse Castle; 3k. Kiiu Castle.

1993. 75th Anniv of First Estonian Stamps.
225 **66** 1k. multicoloured 15 10
MS226 74×91 mm. 4k. Type **66** against enlarged background of posthorn blower (sold at 5k.) 1·75 1·75

1993. "Mare Balticum" Stamp Exhibition. No. **MS**226 optd **FILATEELIANAITUS MARE BALTICUM '93 24. – 28. NOVEMBER 1993**.
MS227 **66** 4k. multicoloured . . 3·25 3·25

68 Haapsalu Church

69 Lydia Koidula

1993. Christmas.
228 **68** 80s. red 10 10
229 – 2k. blue 25 15
DESIGN—VERT: 2k. Tallinn church.

1993. 150th Birth Anniv of Lydia Koidula (writer).
230 **69** 1k. multicoloured 10 10

70 Ski Jumping

71 Tartu 1869 Emblem

1994. Winter Olympic Games, Lillehammer, Norway. Multicoloured.
231 1k.+25s. Type **70** 20 15
232 2k. Speed skating 30 20

1994. 125th Song Festival. Multicoloured.
233 **71** 1k.+25s. yell, brn & grn . . 20 15
234 – 2k. brown and blue 30 20
235 – 3k. bistre, brown and stone 45 30
MS236 120×95 mm. 15k. multicoloured . . . . 2·50 2·50
DESIGNS: 2k. Tallinn 1923 emblem; 3k. Tallinn 1969 emblem; 15k. 1994 emblem.

72 Squirrel

73 Mill (Patent No. 1. Aleksander Mikiver)

1994. The Siberian Flying Squirrel. Mult.
237 1k. Type **72** 15 10
238 2k. Squirrel on broad-leafed branch 30 20
239 3k. Squirrel on pine branch 45 30
240 4k. Squirrel with young . . . 65 40

1994. Europa. Inventions. Multicoloured.
241 1k. Type **73** 15 10
242 2k.70 "Minox" mini camera (Patent No. 2628, Walter Zapp) 35 20

74 Mustjala Woman

75 Kadriorg Palace

1994. Costumes (1st series). Multicoloured.
243 1k. Type **74** 15 10
244 1k. Jamaja couple 15 10
See also Nos. 254/5, 274/5, 298/9, 316/17, 340/1, 377/8 and 411/12.

1994. 75th Anniv of Estonian Art Museum, Tallinn.
245 **75** 1k.70 multicoloured . . . 30 15

76 "The Holy Family" (Lichtenstein Master)

77 Ruhnu Church

1994. International Year of the Family.
246 **76** 1k.70 multicoloured . . . 30 15

1994. Christmas.
247 **77** 1k.20 brown 20 10
248 – 2k.50 green 40 25
DESIGN—HORIZ: 2k.50, Urvaste Church.

1994. Victims of the "Estonia" Ferry Disaster Fund. No. 248 surch **+20 kr 28. 09. 1994 59°23' POHJALAIUST 21°42' IDAPIKKUST "ESTONIA" laevahuku ohvrite fondi**.
249 2k.50+20k. green . . . . . . 3·00 2·50

79 Gustav II Adolphus

80 Barnacle Geese

1994. 400th Birth Anniv of King Gustav II Adolphus of Sweden.
250 **79** 2k.50 purple 35 20

1995. Matsalu Wetland Reserve. Mult.
251 1k.70 Type **80** 25 25
252 3k.20 Greylag geese 50 50

81 "Labourer's Family at Table" (Efraim Allsalu)

82 Beach Hotel, Parnu (Estonia)

1995. 50th Anniv of F.A.O.
253 **81** 2k.70 multicoloured . . . 35 20

1995. Costumes (2nd series). As T **74**. Mult.
254 1k.70 Muhu couple 25 15
255 1k.70 Muhu women 25 15

1995. Via Baltica Motorway Project. Multicoloured.
256 1k.70 Type **82** 20 15
MS257 99×109 mm. 3k.20 Type **82**; 3k.20 Bauska Castle (Latvia); 3k.20 Kaunas (Lithuania) . . . 1·50 1·50

83 Broken Barbed Wire

84 U.N. Emblem and Landscape

1995. Europa. Peace and Freedom.
258 **83** 2k.70 brown and mauve . . 35 30

1995. 50th Anniv of U.N.O.
259 **84** 4k. multicoloured 55 45

85 Lighthouse and Chart

86 Vanemuine Theatre

1995. Pakri Lighthouse.
260 **85** 1k.70 multicoloured . . . 25 15

1995. 125th Anniv of Vanemuine Theatre.
261 **86** 1k.70 orange, black & grn 25 15

87 White-tailed Sea Eagle

88 Pasteur and Bacteria

1995. "Keep the Estonian Sea Clean".
262 **87** 2k.+25s. black and blue . . 30 30

1995. Death Cent of Louis Pasteur (chemist).
263 **88** 2k.70 multicoloured . . . 30 30

89 Bronze Bear Amulet (Samoyedic group)

90 Kunileid and Music

1995. Finno-Ugric Peoples. Multicoloured.
264 2k.50 Shaman's drum (Saami group) 30 15
265 2k.50 Karelian writing (Baltic-Finnic group) . . . 30 15
266 3k.50 Duck brooch of Kama area (Volga group) 40 20
267 3k.50 Type **89** 40 20
268 4k.50 Duck-feet pendant (Permic group) 55 25
269 4k.50 Khanty band ornament (Ugric group) 55 25

1995. 150th Birth Anniv of Aleksandr Kunileid (composer).
270 **90** 2k. blue 20 15

91 St. Martin's Church, Turi

92 "Lembit" (submarine)

1995. Christmas.
271 **91** 2k. yellow 20 15
272 – 3k.50 red 40 20
DESIGN: 3k.50, Charles's Church, Tallinn.

1996. 60th Anniv of "Lembit".
273 **92** 2k.50 multicoloured . . . 25 15

1996. Costumes (3rd series). As T **74**. Mult.
274 2k.50 Emmaste mother and bride 25 15
275 2k.50 Reigi women 25 15

93 1896 Gold Medal

1996. Centenary of Modern Olympic Games and Olympic Games, Atlanta. Sheet 110×66 mm containing T **93** and similar vert designs. Mult.
MS276 2k.50 Type **93**; 3k.50 Alfred Neuland (weightlifter and first Estonian gold medal winner, 1920); 4k. Cycling . . . . . . 1·00 1·00

94 Marie Under (poet)

95 Marconi and Wireless Telegraph

1996. Europa. Famous Women.
277 **94** 2k.50 multicoloured . . . 25 15

1996. Centenary of Guglielmo Marconi's Patented Wireless Telegraph.
278 **95** 3k.50 multicoloured . . . 50 25

96 "Suur Toll"

97 Lighthouse and Chart

1996. 82nd Anniv of "Suur Toll" (ice-breaker).
279 **96** 2k.50 multicoloured . . . 30 15

1996. 125th Anniv of Vaindloo Lighthouse.
280 **97** 2k.50 multicoloured . . . 25 15

98 Class Gk Steam Locomotive

99 Elf and Mother and Child

1996. Cent of Narrow-gauge Railway. Mult.
281 3k.20 Type **98** 60 20
282 3k.50 Class DeM diesel railcar 65 25
283 4k.50 Class Sk steam locomotive 75 30

1996. Christmas (1st issue).
284 **99** 2k.50 multicoloured . . . 25 15

100 Harju-Madise Church

101 Map and Lighthouse

1996. Christmas (2nd issue).
285 **100** 3k.30 blue 30 20
286 – 4k.50 purple 50 30
DESIGNS: 4k.50, Church of the Holy Spirit, Tallinn.

1997. 120th Anniv of Ruhnu Lighthouse.
287 **101** 3k.30 multicoloured . . . 30 15

102 Steller's Sea Eagle

103 Von Stephan (after Anton Weber)

1997. Captive Breeding Programmes at Tallinn Zoo. Multicoloured.
288 3k.30 Type **102** 50 20
289 3k.30 European mink 30 20
290 3k.30 Cinereous vulture . . . 50 20
291 3k.30 Amur leopard 30 20
292 3k.30 Black rhinoceros . . . 30 20
293 3k.30 East Caucasian tur . . 30 20

1997. Death Cent of Heinrich von Stephan (founder of Universal Postal Union).
294 **103** 7k. gold and black . . . 60 30

104 Goldspinner

105 Maasilinn Ship

1997. Europa. Tales and Legends. "The Goldspinners".
295 **104** 4k.80 multicoloured . . . 40 20

1997. Baltic Sailing Ships.
296 **105** 3k.30 multicoloured . . . 50 20

1997. Costumes (4th series). Folk Costumes of Swedish Communities in Estonia. As T **74**. Multicoloured.
298 3k.30 Couple, Ruhnu Island 25 15
299 3k.30 Family, Vormsi Island 25 15

106 1 Kroon Coin **107** "Tormilind"

1997.
299a **106** 10k. silver, black & red 80 40
300 25k. silver, black & grn 2·10 1·10
301 50k. silver, black & grn 4·50 2·50
302 100k. gold, black & blue 8·50 4·25

1997. 75th Anniv of Completion of "Tormilind" (barquentine).
305 **107** 5k.50 multicoloured . . . 60 30

108 "Stone Bridge, Tartu" (Tiina Tarve)

1997.
306 **108** 3k.30 multicoloured . . . 30 15

109 Title Page **110** St. Anne's Church, Halliste

1997. 311th Anniv of Publication of "Wastne Testament" (first translation, by Andreas Verginius, into South Estonian dialect of New Testament).
307 **109** 3k.50 black, ochre & bl 30 15

1997.
308 **110** 3k.30 brown 30 15

111 Dwarves **112** Cross-country Skier

1997. Christmas.
309 **111** 2k.90 multicoloured . . . 30 15

1998. Winter Olympic Games, Nagano, Japan.
310 **112** 3k.60 multicoloured . . . 30 15

113 Arms **114** "Porgu", 1932

1998. 80th Anniv of 1918 Declaration of Independence. Sheet 68 × 58 mm. Imperf.
MS311 **113** 7k. multicoloured . . 60 60

1998. Birth Centenary of Eduard Wiiralt (artist). Sheet 79 × 94 mm containing T **114** and similar vert designs. Each black.
MS312 3k.60 Type **114**; 3k.60 "Porgu", 1930; 5k.50 "Enfer", 1932 . . . . 1·50 1·50

115 Chart and Lighthouse **116** Players

1998. 99th Anniv of Kunda Lighthouse.
313 **115** 3k.60 multicoloured . . . 30 15

1998. World Cup Football Championship, France.
314 **116** 7k. black, red and violet 65 30

117 St. John's Eve Bonfire **118** Tallinn Codex, 1282

1998. Europa. National Festivals.
315 **117** 5k.20 multicoloured . . . 45 25

1998. 750th Anniv of Adoption by Tallinn of Lubeck Law in Charter by King Erik IV of Denmark.
316 **118** 4k.80 multicoloured . . . 40 40

119 Barn Swallow over House **120** Yacht

1998. Beautiful Homes Year.
317 **119** 3k.60 multicoloured . . . 30 15

1998. World 470 Class Junior Yachting Championships, Tallinn Bay.
318 **120** 5k.50 dp blue, bl & red 45 25

1998. Costumes (5th series). As T **74**. Mult.
319 3k.60 Couple, Kihnu Island 30 15
320 3k.60 Family, Kihnu Island 30 15

121 "The Bottle Genie" (illustrated by Eduard Jarv) **122** Siberian Tiger

1998. 50th Death Anniv of Juhan Jaik (children's writer).
321 **121** 3k.60 yellow, blue & blk 30 15

1998. Tallinn Zoo.
322 **122** 3k.60 multicoloured . . . 30 15

123 1923 9m. Stamp **124** Freedom Cross

1998. 80th Anniv of Estonian Post.
323 **123** 3k.60 red, orange & blk 30 15

1998. Estonian–Finnish Friendship.
324 **124** 4k.50 multicoloured . . . 40 20

125 Father Christmas and Boy **126** Faehlmann

1998. Christmas. Multicoloured.
325 3k.10 Type **125** 25 15
326 5k. Angels and Christmas tree 40 20

1998. Birth Bicentenary of Friedrich Robert Faehlmann (writer and founder of Learned Estonian Society).
327 **126** 3k.60 multicoloured . . . 30 15

127 Chart and Lighthouse **128** Snow Leopards

1999. 190th Anniv of Vilsandi Lighthouse.
328 **127** 3k.60 multicoloured . . . 30 15

1999. Tallinn Zoo.
329 **128** 3k.60 multicoloured . . . 30 15

129 Emblem and Palais de l'Europe, Strasbourg **130** Meri

1999. 50th Anniv of Council of Europe.
330 **129** 5k.50 multicoloured . . . 45 25

1999. 70th Birth Anniv of President Lennart Meri.
331 **130** 3k.60 multicoloured . . . 30 15

131 Tolkuse Bog, Parnu

1999. Europa. Parks and Gardens.
332 **131** 5k.50 multicoloured . . . 45 25

132 Emblem and Bank Headquarters, Tallinn

1999. 80th Anniv of Bank of Estonia.
333 **132** 5k. multicoloured 40 20

133 Olustvere Hall

1999.
334 **133** 3k.60 multicoloured . . . 30 15

134 Band and Score

1999. 130th Anniv of National Anthem.
335 **134** 3k.60 multicoloured . . . 30 15

135 Observation Tower **136** Family and State Flag

1999. 60th Anniv of Observation Tower on Suur Munamagi (highest point in Baltics).
336 **135** 5k.20 multicoloured . . . 45 25

1999. 10th Anniv of Baltic Chain (human chain uniting the Capitals of Estonia, Latvia and Lithuania). Multicoloured.
337 3k.60 Type **136** 30 15
MS338 110 × 72 mm. 5k.50 Type **136** (28 × 38 mm); 5k.50 Family and Latvian flag (28 × 38 mm); 5k.50 Family and Lithuanian flag (28 × 38 mm) . . . . 1·40 1·40

137 U.P.U. Emblem **138** State Arms

1999. 125th Anniv of Universal Postal Union.
339 **137** 7k. multicoloured 80 40

1999. Costumes (6th series). Setu Costumes of South-east Estonia. As T **74**. Multicoloured.
340 3k.60 Bride and bridegroom 30 15
341 5k. Two young men 40 20

1999.
342 **138** 10s. red and pink . . . 10 10
343 20s. brown and grey . . 10 10
344 30s. light blue and blue 10 10
346 1k. brown and pink . . 10 10
348 2k. black 15 10
352 3k.60 blue and turquoise 30 15
354 4k.40 deep green and green 35 20
355 5k. green and light green 40 20
355a 5k. deep green and green 40 20
355b 5k. 50 deep green and green 40 20
356 6k. brown and yellow . . 45 25
357 6k.50 brown and yellow 50 25
359 8k. brown and pink . . 60 30

139 Santa's Helpers

1999. Christmas. Multicoloured.
360 3k.10 Type **139** 25 15
361 7k. Christmas tree (558th anniv of first public Christmas tree in Tallinn) (vert) 80 40

1999. New Year Lottery. As No. 360 but with additional premium and lottery numbers.
362 **139** 3k.10+1k.90 mult 40 20

140 Hands of Clock **141** Faces

1999. Year 2000.
363 **140** 5k.50 multicoloured . . . 45 20

2000. Population and Housing Census.
364 **141** 3k.60 multicoloured . . . 30 15

142 Signatures on Treaty

2000. 80th Anniv of Tartu Peace Treaty (between Estonia and Russia).
365 **142** 3k.60 multicoloured . . . 30 15

143 Ristna Lighthouse and Chart

2000. Lighthouses on Kopu Peninsula. Mult.
366 3k.60 Type **143** 30 15
367 3k.60 Kopu lighthouse and chart 30 15

Nos. 366/7 were issued together, se-tenant, forming a composite design.

144 State Arms and Emblem

145 Cornflower

2000. 10th Anniv of Estonian Congress.
368 **144** 3k.60 multicoloured . . . 25 15

2000. National Flower.
369 **145** 4k.80 multicoloured . . . 35 20

146 "E" and Text

147 Building Europe

2000. National Book Year. 475th Anniv of Publication of Lutheran Catechism (oldest known publication in Estonian).
370 **146** 3k.60 multicoloured . . . 25 15

2000. Europa.
371 **147** 4k.80 multicoloured . . . 35 20

148 Palmse Hall

2000.
372 **148** 3k.60 multicoloured . . . 25 15

149 Amur Long-tailed Goral

2000. Tallinn Zoo (1st series).
373 **149** 3k.60 multicoloured . . . 25 15
See also No. 409.

150 Locomotive

2000. Centenary of Viljandi–Tallinn Narrow Gauge Railway.
374 **150** 4k.50 multicoloured . . . 35 20

151 Hand-woven Girdle

152 Discus thrower

2000. 9th Finno–Ugric Congress, Tartu.
375 **151** 5k. multicoloured 35 20

2000. Olympic Games, Sydney.
376 **152** 8k. multicoloured 60 30

2000. Costumes (7th series). As T **74**. Mult.
377 4k.40 Family, Hargla 30 15
378 8k. Women, Polva 60 30

153 Malk

2000. Birth Centenary of August Malk (author).
379 **153** 4k.40 multicoloured . . . 60 30

154 European Smelt (*Osmerus eperlanus spirinchus*) and Vendace (*Coregonus albula*)

2000. Fish from Lake Peipsi. Multicoloured.
380 6k.50 Type **154** 50 25
381 6k.50 Zander (*Stizostedion lucioperca*) and whitefish (*Coregonus lavaretus manaenoides*) 50 25

155 Illustration and Emblem

2000. Centenary of National Bookplate. Sheet 80 × 58 mm containing T **155** and similar vert design. Multicoloured.
MS382 6k. Type **155**; 6k. Man ploughing and emblem 50 25

156 Horn with Ribbon

2000. Christmas. Multicoloured.
383 3k.60 Type **156** 30 15
384 6k. Tree decorations 50 25

157 Nool celebrating

2001. Olympic Games, Sydney. Erki Nool (decathlete, gold medallist).
385 **157** 4k.40 multicoloured . . . 35 20

158 Mohni Lighthouse, Lahemaa National Park, Cape Purekkari

159 Couple kissing

2001.
386 **158** 4k.40 multicoloured . . . 35 20

2001. St. Valentines Day.
387 **159** 4k.40 yellow, blue & red 35 20

160 Facade

2001. Inauguration (2000) of Stenbock House as Seat of Government and State Chancellery.
388 **160** 6k.50 multicoloured . . . 50 25

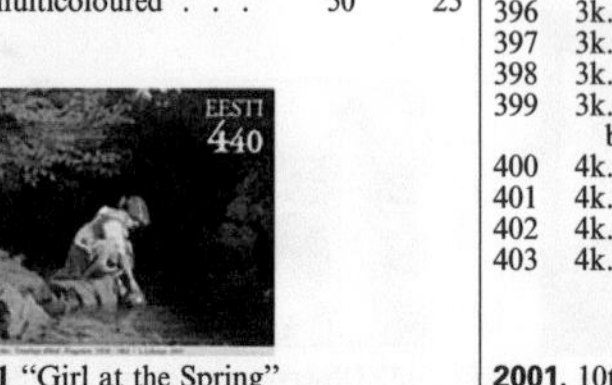

161 "Girl at the Spring" (detail)

2001. 175th Birth Anniv of Johann Koler (artist). Sheet 58 × 83 mm containing T **161** and similar horiz design. Multicoloured.
MS389 4k.40 Type **161**; 4k.40 "Eve of the Pomegranate" (detail) 70 35

162 Text and Emblem

2001. European Year of Languages.
390 **162** 4k.40 multicoloured . . . 35 20

163 Northern Lapwing

2001. Northern Lapwing (*Vanellus vanellus*).
391 **163** 4k.40 multicoloured . . . 35 20

164 Laupa Hall

2001.
392 **164** 4k.40 multicoloured . . . 35 20

165 Sluice, Lake Soodla

166 Emblem

2001. Europa. Water Resources.
393 **165** 6k.50 multicoloured . . . 50 25

2001. Cent of Kalev (Estonian Sports Association).
394 **166** 6k.50 multicoloured . . . 50 25

167 Mud Baths Main Building

2001. 750th Anniv of Parnu.
395 **167** 4k.40 multicoloured . . . 35 20

168 Pockus beside Lake

169 Barn Swallow

2001. *Pokuland* (children's book by Edgar Valter). Multicoloured.
396 3k.60 Type **168** 30 15
397 3k.60 Pocku and owl 30 15
398 3k.60 Pocku and stork . . . 30 15
399 3k.60 Pocku on branch and bird in nest 30 15
400 4k.40 Two Pockus on fence 35 20
401 4k.40 Pocku smelling flower 35 20
402 4k.40 Pocku hugging dog . . 35 20
403 4k.40 Pocku watching moon 35 20

2001. 10th Anniv of Independence.
404 **169** 4k.40 multicoloured . . . 35 20

170 Virgin and Child (wooden altarpiece)

171 1991 5k. State Arms Stamp

2001. 800th Anniv of St. Mary's Land (conversion to Christianity of Estonia, Livonia and Courland).
405 **170** 6k.50 multicoloured . . . 50 25

2001. 10th Anniv of Re-adoption of Estonian Stamps.
406 **171** 4k.40 multicoloured . . . 35 20

172 Rocky Coastline, Lahemaa, Estonia

2001. Baltic Sea Coast. Multicoloured.
407 4k.40 Type **172** 40 20
MS408 125 × 60 mm. 6k. As Type **172** (36 × 30 mm); 6k. Beach, Vidzeme, Latvia (36 × 30 mm); 6k. Sand dunes, Palanga, Lithuania (36 × 30 mm) . . . . 1·60 80
Stamps in similar designs were issued by Latvia and Lithuania.

173 Chinese Alligator (*Alligator sinenesis*)

2001. Tallinn Zoo (2nd series).
409 **173** 4k.40 multicoloured . . . 40 20

174 Estonia 26-9 Racing Car

175 Snowflake

2001.
410 **174** 6k. multicoloured 55 30

2001. Costumes (8th series). As T **74**. Multicoloured.
411 4k.40 Woman, Paistu 40 20
412 7k.50 Man, Tarvastu 70 35

2001. Christmas. Multicoloured.
413 3k.60 Type **175** 30 15
414 6k.50 Dove (horiz) 60 30

176 First Radio Station Building and Felix Moor (presenter)

2001. 75th Anniv of National Radio Broadcasting.
415 **176** 4k.40 multicoloured . . . 40 20

177 Skier

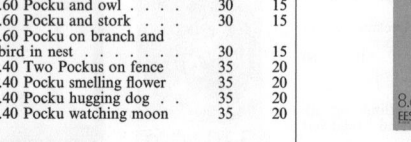

2002. Winter Olympic Games, Salt Lake City.
416 **177** 8k. multicoloured 70 35

178 Sangaste Hall

179 Laidunina Lighthouse, Saaremaa Island, Gulf of Riga

2002.
417 **178** 4k.40 multicoloured . . . 40 20

2002.
418 **179** 4k.40 multicoloured . . . 40 20

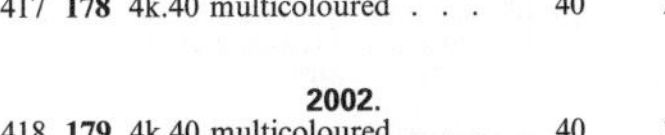

180 Eurasian Tree Sparrow (*Passer montanus*) and House Sparrow(*Passer domesticus*)

2002.
419 **180** 4k.40 multicoloured . . . 40 20

181 Apple Blossom

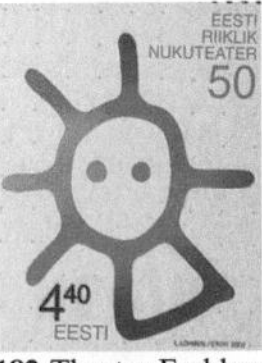
182 Theatre Emblem (E. Kivi)

2002.
420 **181** 4k.40 multicoloured . . . 40 20

2002. 50th Anniv Estonian Puppet Theatre, Tallinn.
421 **182** 4k.40 multicoloured . . . 40 20

183 PTO-4 Training Aircraft

2002.
422 **183** 6k. multicoloured 50 25

184 Andrus Veerpalu

2002. Andrus Veerpalu Nordic Skiing Olympic Gold Medallist.
423 **184** 4k.40 multicoloured . . . 40 20

185 University Building

2002. 370th Anniv of Tartu University. Bicentenary of Re-opening. Multicoloured.
424 4k.40 Type **185** 40 20
425 4k.40 Library building . . . 40 20

186 Acrobat

2002. Europa. Circus.
426 **186** 6k.50 multicoloured . . . 55 25

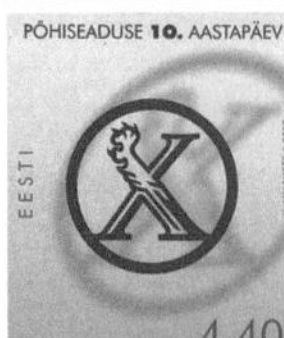
187 Emblem

188 Ancient Coin and Modern Arms

2002. 10th Anniv of New Constitution.
427 **187** 4k.40 ultramarine and blue 40 20

2002. 700th Anniv of Granting of Lubek Charter to Rakvere.
428 **188** 4k.40 multicoloured . . . 40 20

189 Lydia Koidula (poet)

2002. 10th Anniv of Re-introduction of the Kroon (currency). Sheet 53 × 76 mm containing T **189** and similar horiz design. Multicoloured.
MS429 4k.40 Type **189**; 4k.40 Carl Robert Jackson (writer) . . . 75 75

190 Top Left Quarter of Decorated Plate

2002. Birth Centenary of Adamson-Eric (artist). Sheet 86 × 75 mm containing T **190** and similar horiz designs. Multicoloured.
MS430 4k.40 Type **190**; 4k.40 Top right; 4k.40 Bottom left; 4k.40 Bottom right . . . . 1·50 1·50
The stamps in No. **MS**430 form a composite design of a decorated plate.

191 Wild Boar (*Sus scofa*)

2002.
431 **191** 4k.40 multicoloured . . . 40 20

192 Limestone Cliff, Cape Pakri

2002. Limestone (National Stone).
432 **192** 4k.40 multicoloured . . . 40 20

193 Women, Kolga-Jaani Region

194 Lamb wearing Ribbon

2002. Folk Costumes. Multicoloured.
433 4k.40 Type **193** 40 20
434 5k.50 Couple dancing, Suure-Janni region 45 20

2002. Christmas. Multicoloured.
435 3k.60 Type **194** 30 15
436 6k.50 Tree covered in snow (vert) 55 25

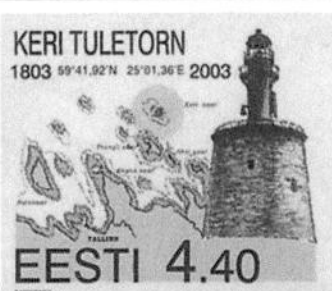
195 Keri Lighthouse, Prangli Island, Gulf of Riga

2003.
437 **195** 4k.40 multicoloured . . . 40 20

196 Anton Tammsaare (sculpture, Jaak Soans and Rein Luup)

2003. 125th Birth Anniv of Anton Hansen Tammsaare (writer).
438 **196** 4k.40 multicoloured . . . 40 20

197 Magpie (*Pica pica*)

2003.
439 **197** 4k.40 multicoloured . . . 40 20

198 Tulips (*Tulipa*)

199 Alatskivi Hall

2003. Flowers. Sheet 130 × 67 mm containing T **198** and similar vert designs. Multicoloured.
MS440 4k.40 × 4, Type **198**; Hellebore (*Helleborus purpurascens*); Pheasant's eye daffodil (*Narcissus poeticus*) (inscr "Nartcissus"); Crocus (*Crocus vernus*) . . . . 1·60 1·60

2003.
441 **199** 4k.40 multicoloured . . . 40 20

200 President Ruutel

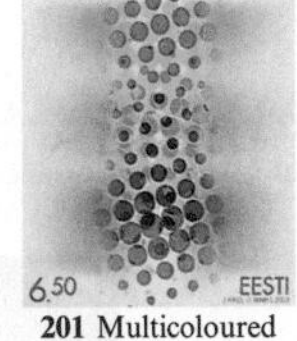
201 Multicoloured Printing Raster

2003. 75th Birth Anniv of Arnold Ruutel, President of Estonia.
442 **200** 4k.40 multicoloured . . . 40 20

2003. Europa. Poster Art.
443 **201** 6k.50 multicoloured . . . 55 25

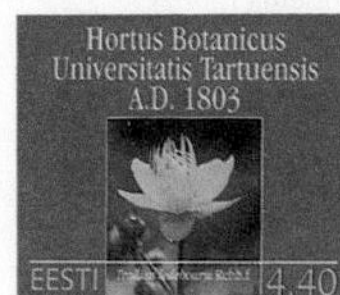
202 Globe Flower (*Trollius ledebourii*)

2003. Bicentenary of Tartu University Botanic Garden.
444 **202** 4k.40 multicoloured . . . 40 20

203 Championship Emblem

2003. 14th World Under 21 Orienteering Championship, Polva.
445 **203** 7k.50 multicoloured . . . 65 30

204 Adam von Krusenstern and *Neva* and *Nadezhda*

2003. Bicentenary of Adam Johann von Krusenstern's Circumnavigation of the World.
446 **204** 8k. multicoloured 70 35

205 Ringed Seal (*Phoca hispida*)

2003.
447 **205** 4k.40 multicoloured . . . 40 20

206 *Vostok* and Fabian von Bellingshausen

2003. 225th Birth Anniv of Fabian Gottlieb von Bellingshausen (explorer).
448 **206** 8k. blue, sepia and ochre 70 35

207 Danish Coin and "Arrival of Scandinavian Seamen" (detail)

2003. Ancient Trade Route along Gulf of Finland and Dnieper River, Ukraine. Multicoloured.
449 6k.50 Type **207** 55 25
450 6k.50 11th-century silver coin and Viking ship 55 25

2003. Folk Costumes. As T **193**. Multicoloured.
451 4k.40 Aksi women, Tartu . . 40 20
452 5k.50 Family, Otep region . . 45 20

208 Great Tit holding Rose

209 "Voyage to the End of the World" (book illustration, Kristjan Raud)

2003. Christmas. Multicoloured.
453 3k.60 Type **208** 30 15
454 6k. Mary and Jesus (stained glass) 50 25

2003. Birth Bicentenary of Friedrich Reinhold Kreutzwald (writer). Sheet 100 × 73 mm containing T **209** and similar vert design.
MS455 4k.40 blue and black; 6k.50 multicoloured 95 95
DESIGNS: Type **209**; 6k.50 Friedrich Reinhold Kreutzwald.

210 Lighthouse, Sorgu Island, Gulf of Riga

2004. Centenary of Sorgu Lighthouse.
456 **210** 4k.40 multicoloured . . . 40 20

211 Wolf (*Canis lupus*)

2004.
457 **211** 4k.40 multicoloured . . . 40 20

212 Map and Wheel **213** Violet (*Viola riviniana*)

2004. 150th Anniv of *Hioma* (Estonian barque) Voyage around Cape Horn.
458 **212** 8k. multicoloured 70 35

2004. Flowers. Sheet 130 × 66 mm containing T **213** and similar vert designs. Multicoloured.
MS459 4k.40 × 4, Type **213**; Wood anemone (*Anemone nemorosa*); Hepatica nobilis; Globeflower (*Trollius europaeus*) . . . . . 1·50 1·50

214 Adult and Chicks

2004. Endangered Species. White Stork (*Ciconia ciconia*).
460 **214** 4k.40 multicoloured . . . 40 20

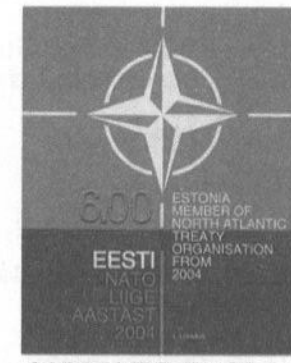

215 NATO Emblem

2004. Accession to NATO (North Atlantic Treaty Organization).
461 **215** 6k. blue, ultramarine and orange 55 25

216 New Member Flags and EU Emblem

2004. Accession to European Union.
462 **216** 6k.50 multicoloured . . . 60 30

217 Sailing (½-size illustration)

2004. Europa. Holidays.
463 **217** 6k.50 multicoloured . . . 60 30

218 Town Hall

2004. 600th Anniv of Tallinn Town Hall.
464 **218** 4k.40 multicoloured . . . 40 20

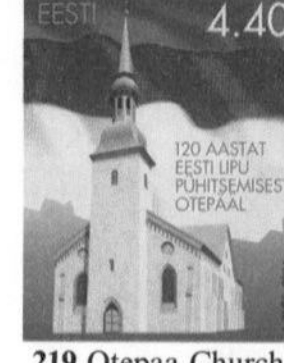

219 Otepaa Church and Flag **220** Vasalemma Hall

2004. 120th Anniv of National Flag.
465 **219** 4k.40 multicoloured . . . 40 20

2004.
466 **220** 4k.40 multicoloured . . . 40 20

221 Runner carrying Torch **222** Dragon ClassYacht

2004. Olympic Games, Athens 2004.
467 **221** 8k. multicoloured 70 35

2004. 75th Dragon Class European Championship, Tallin, Estonia.
468 **222** 6k. multicoloured 55 25

223 Dandelion

2004. Self-adhesive gum.
469 **223** 30s. multicoloured 10 10

224 Harjumaa

2004. Town Arms (1st series). Each emerald, scarlet and black. Self-adhesive gum.
470 4k.40 Type **224** 40 20
471 4k.40 Hiiumaa 40 20
See also Nos. 481/2.

2004. Folk Costumes. As T **193**. Multicoloured.
472 4k.40 Couple, Viru-Jaagupi 40 20
473 7k.50 Johvi women 70 35

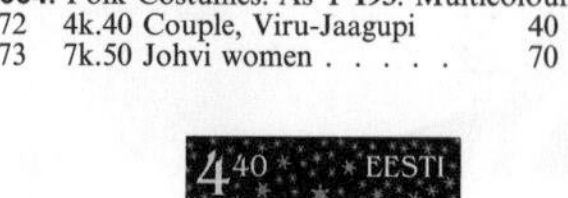

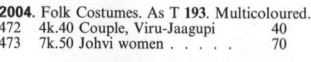

225 Candle and Fir Twigs

2004. Christmas. Multicoloured.
474 4k.40 Type **225** 40 20
475 6k.50 Poinsettia (horiz) . . . 60 30

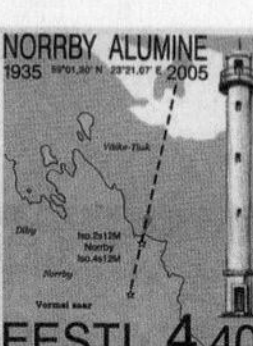

226 Norrby Alumine Lighthouse

2005. 70th Anniv of Norrby Lighthouses, Vormsi Islands. Multicoloured.
476 4k.40 Type **226** 40 20
477 4k.40 Norrby Ulemine . . . 40 20

227 Beaver (*Castor fiber*)

2005.
478 **227** 4k.40 multicoloured . . . 40 20

228 Rotary Emblem **229** National Flag flying from Pikk Herman Tower

2005. Centenary of Rotary International (charitable organisation).
479 **228** 8k. multicoloured 80 40

2005.
480 **229** 5k. multicoloured 50 25

2005. Town Arms (2nd series). As T **224**. Multicoloured. Self-adhesive gum.
481 4k.40 Ida-Virumaa 40 20
482 4k.40 Jarvamaa 40 20

230 Two Swans

2005. Spring. Sheet 89 × 69 mm containing T **230** and similar horiz designs. Multicoloured.
MS483 4k.40 × 4, Type **230**; Swan and bulrushes; Swan and pondweed: Two swans (different) 1·60 1·60

231 Goshawk (*Accipiter gentiles*)

2005.
484 **231** 4k.40 multicoloured . . . 40 20

232 Hands exchanging Flower

2005. Mothers' Day.
485 **232** 4k.40 multicoloured . . . 40 20

233 Vegetable Cornucopia

2005. Europa. Gastronomy. Multicoloured.
486 6k. Type **233** 55 25
487 6k.50 Vegetables as rainbow 60 30

ETHIOPIA Pt. 12

Formerly called Abyssinia. An ancient empire on the E. coast of Africa. From 1936 to 1941, part of Italian East Africa. Federated with Ethiopia from 1952 to 1993. In 1974 Emperor Haile Selassie was deposed and a republic proclaimed.

1894. and 1907. 16 guerche = 1 Maria Theresa-Thaler.
1905. 100 centimes = 1 franc.
1908. 16 piastres = 1 thaler.
1928. 16 mehaleks = 1 thaler.
1936. 100 centimes = 1 thaler.
1936. 100 centesimi = 1 lira.
1946. 100 cents = 1 Ethiopian dollar.
1976. 100 cents = 1 birr.

INDEPENDENT EMPIRE

1 Menelik II **2** Lion of the Tribe of Judah

1894.
1 **1** ¼g. green . . . . 3·25 5·00
2 ½g. red . . . . 1·90 3·75
3 1g. blue . . . . 1·90 3·75
4 2g. brown . . . . 1·90 5·00
5 **2** 4g. red . . . . 1·90 5·00
6 8g. mauve . . . . 1·90 5·00
7 16g. black . . . . 2·75 5·00

1901. Optd **Ethiopie**.
15 **1** ¼g. green . . . . 9·25 9·25
16 ½g. red . . . . 9·25 9·25
17 1g. blue . . . . 10·00 10·00
18 2g. brown . . . . 10·00 10·00
19 **2** 4g. red . . . . 10·00 10·00
20 8g. mauve . . . . 13·50 13·50
21 16g. black . . . . 18·00 18·00

በሰጣ። (4) መልክት። (5)

1902. Optd with T **4**.
22 **1** ¼g. green . . . . 5·25 5·25
23 ½g. red . . . . 5·25 5·25
24 1g. blue . . . . 7·25 7·25
25 2g. brown . . . . 7·25 7·25
26 **2** 4g. red . . . . 11·50 11·50
27 8g. mauve . . . . 15·00 15·00
28 16g. black . . . . 30·00 30·00

1903. Optd with T **5**.
29 **1** ¼g. green . . . . 4·50 4·50
30 ½g. red . . . . 4·50 4·50
31 1g. blue . . . . 7·00 7·00
32 2g. brown . . . . 8·25 8·25
33 **2** 4g. red . . . . 8·25 8·25
34 8g. mauve . . . . 20·00 20·00
35 16g. black . . . . 28·00 28·00

ምልክት (6) ምኒልክ (10)

1904. Optd with T **6**.
36 **1** ¼g. green . . . . 8·25 8·25
37 ½g. red . . . . 10·00 10·00
38 1g. blue . . . . 13·50 13·50
39 2g. brown . . . . 15·00 15·00
40 **2** 4g. red . . . . 17·00 17·00
41 8g. mauve . . . . 32·00 32·00
42 16g. black . . . . 50·00 50·00

1905. Surch in figures.
43 **1** 05 on ¼g. green . . . . . . 6·00 6·00
44 10 on ½g. red . . . . 6·00 6·00
45 20 on 1g. blue . . . . . . 6·00 6·00
46 40 on 2g. brown . . . . . 7·75 8·00
47 **2** 80 on 4g. red . . . . 13·50 13·50
48 1.60 on 8g. mauve . . . . 12·00 17·00
49 3.20 on 16g. black . . . . . 24·00 24·00
The above surcharge was also applied to some stamps optd with **Ethiopie** and Types **4**, **5** and **6**.

1905. Surch in figures and words.
90 **2** 5c. on 16g. blk (No. 28) . . . 85·00 £100

1905. No. 2 divided diagonally and surch **5c/m**.
86 **1** 5c. on half of ½g. red . . . . 4·25 4·25

1905. Surch **5c/m**.
71 **1** 5c. on ¼g. grn (No. 22) . . . 10·00 11·50

1906. Optd with T **10** and surch in figures.
94 **1** 05 on ¼g. green . . . . . . 5·25 5·25
95 10 on ½g. red . . . . 7·00 7·00
96 20 on 1g. blue . . . . . . 7·00 7·00
97 40 on 2g. brown . . . . . 7·00 7·00
98 **2** 80 on 4g. red . . . . 8·75 8·75
99 1.60 on 8g. mauve . . . . . 12·00 12·00
100 3.20 on 16g. black . . . . . 32·00 32·00

1906. Surch with figures and Amharic characters.
101 **1** 05 on ¼g. green . . . . . . 5·75 5·75
102 10 on ½g. red . . . . 7·00 7·00
103 20 on 1g. blue . . . . . . 9·75 9·75
104 40 on 2g. brown . . . . . 9·75 9·75
105 **2** 80 on 4g. red . . . . 13·50 13·50
106 1.60 on 8g. mauve . . . . . 13·50 13·50
107 3.20 on 16g. black . . . . . 32·00 32·00

ዳግማዊ።

(13)

1907. Optd with T **13** and surch in figures between stars.

No.	Type	Description	Mint	Used
115	**1**	¼ on ¼g. green	6·00	6·00
116		½ on ½g. red	6·00	6·00
117		1 on 1g. blue	7·25	7·25
118		2 on 2g. brown	8·75	8·75
119	**2**	4 on 4g. red	8·75	8·75
120		8 on 8g. mauve	18·00	18·00
121		16 on 16g. black	25·00	25·00

1908. Entry into U.P.U. Nos. 1/7 surch in figures and words.

No.	Type	Description	Mint	Used
133	**1**	¼pi. on ¼g. green	2·10	2·10
134		½pi. on ½g. red	2·10	2·10
129		1pi. on ½g. red	7·75	7·75
135		1pi. on 1g. blue	2·75	2·75
136		2pi. on 2g. brown	4·75	4·75
137	**2**	4pi. on 4g. red	6·75	6·75
138		8pi on 8g. mauve	13·50	13·50
139		16pi. on 16g. black	18·00	18·00

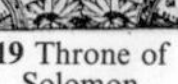

19 Throne of Solomon   **20** Emperor Menelik

1909.

No.	Type	Description	Mint	Used
147	**19**	¼g. green	85	85
148		½g. red	85	65
149		1g. orange and green	2·75	2·75
150	**20**	2g. blue	3·25	2·75
151		4g. red and green	5·00	4·25
152	–	8g. grey and red	8·25	5·75
153	–	16g. red	12·50	9·25

DESIGN: 8g., 16g. Another portrait.

1911. T **1** and **2** optd **AFF EXCEP FAUTE TIMB** and surch in manuscript.

No.	Type	Description	Mint	Used
154	**1**	¼g. on ¼g. green	£110	60·00
155		½g. on ½g. red	£110	60·00
156		1g. on 1g. blue	£110	60·00
157		2g. on 2g. brown	£110	60·00
158	**2**	4g. on 4g. red	£110	60·00
159		8g. on 8g. mauve	£110	60·00
160		16g. on 16g. black	£110	60·00

(22)

11/2/1917.

(24)

1917. Coronation. Optd with T **22** (and similar type).

No.	Type	Description	Mint	Used
161	**19**	¼g. green	4·25	5·00
162		½g. red	4·25	5·00
163	**20**	2g. blue	5·00	6·00
164		4g. red and green	8·25	8·25
165	–	8g. grey and red (No. 152)	15·00	15·00
166	–	16g. red (No. 153)	23·00	25·00

1917. Optd with **T 24** (and similar type).

No.	Type	Description	Mint	Used
168	**19**	¼g. green	25	25
169		½g. red	25	25
170		1g. orange and green	2·10	2·10
171	**20**	2g. blue	70	70
174		4g. red and green	1·40	1·40
175	–	8g. grey & red (No. 152)	1·10	1·10
176	–	16g. red (No. 153)	2·10	2·10

1917. Nos. 175/6 surch with large figure.

No.	Type	Description	Mint	Used
177		¼ on 8g. grey and red	3·00	3·00
178		½ on 8g. grey and red	3·00	3·00
179		1 on 16g. red	7·00	7·00
180		2 on 16g. red	7·00	7·00

28 Gerenuk

29 Ras Tafari, later Emperor Haile Selassie

30 African Buffalo

1919.

No.	Type	Description	Mint	Used
181	**28**	⅛g. brown and violet	15	10
182	–	¼g. grey and green	15	10
183	–	½g. green and red	15	10
184	–	1g. black and purple	10	10
185	**29**	2g. brown and blue	10	10
186	–	4g. orange and blue	20	20
187	–	6g. orange and blue	25	25
188	–	8g. black and olive	40	40
189	–	12g. grey and purple	90	90
190	–	$1 black and red	1·40	1·10
191	**30**	$2 brown and black	3·25	3·00
192	–	$3 red and green	5·00	5·00
193	–	$4 pink and brown	5·00	5·00
194	–	$5 grey and red	6·75	6·75
195	–	$10 yellow and olive	10·00	10·00

DESIGNS—VERT: As Type **28**: ¼g. Giraffes; ½g. Leopard. As Type **29**: 1g., 4g. Ras Tafari (different portraits); $4, $5, $10, Empress Zauditu (different portraits). HORIZ: As Type **30**: 6g. St. George's Cathedral, Addis Ababa; 8g. Black rhinoceros; 12g. Ostriches; $1, African elephant; $3, Lions.

1919. Stamps of 1919 variously surch.

No.	Type	Description	Mint	Used
197	**28**	½g. on ⅛g. brn & violet	50	50
207	–	½g. on 8g. blk & olive	1·00	80
202	–	½g. on $1 black and red	50	50
203	–	½g. on $5 grey and red	1·00	1·00
198	–	1g. on ¼g. grey & green	1·40	1·40
204	–	1g. on 6g. orge & blue	85	85
208	–	1g. on 12g. grey & pur	1·60	1·50
205	–	1g. on $3 red and green	90	90
206	–	1g. on $10 yell & olive	1·40	1·40
198c	–	2g. on 1g. black & pur	50	50
199	–	2g. on $4 pink & brown	18·00	18·00
200	–	2½g. on ½g. grn & red	90	90
201	**29**	4g. on 2g. brn & blue	90	90
196	–	4g. on $4 pink & brown	1·40	1·40

39 Ras Tafari, later Emperor Haile Selassie   **40** Empress Zauditu

(41)

(**46** "The Emperor of the Kings of Ethiopia, 2 Nov., 1930, Haile Selassie")

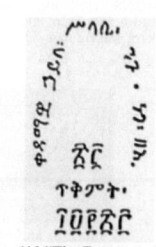

1928. Opening of P.O. at Addis Ababa. Optd with T **41**.

No.	Type	Description	Mint	Used
213	**39**	⅛m. blue and orange	1·60	2·50
214	**40**	¼m. red and blue	1·60	2·50
215	**39**	½m. black and green	1·60	2·50
216	**40**	1m. black and red	1·60	2·50
217	**39**	2m. black and blue	1·60	2·50
218	**40**	4m. olive and yellow	1·60	2·50
219	**39**	8m. olive and mauve	1·60	2·40
220	**40**	1t. mauve and brown	2·00	3·00
221	**39**	2t. brown and green	2·75	4·25
222	**40**	3t. green and purple	2·75	4·25

1928.

No.	Type	Description	Mint	Used
223	**39**	⅛m. blue and orange	85	95
224	**40**	¼m. red and blue	50	85
225	**39**	½m. black and green	95	1·10
226	**40**	1m. black and red	45	50
227	**39**	2m. black and blue	45	50
228	**40**	4m. olive and yellow	45	50
229	**39**	8m. olive and mauve	1·40	1·75
230	**40**	1t. mauve and brown	1·75	2·10
231	**39**	2t. brown and green	2·50	2·75
232	**40**	3t. green and purple	3·25	4·25

1928. Elevation of Ras Tafari to Negus. Optd with crown, Amharic characters and **NEGOUS TEFERI**.

No.	Type	Description	Mint	Used
233	**39**	⅛m. blue and orange	2·75	5·00
234		½m. black and green	2·75	5·00
235		2m. black and blue	2·75	6·75
236		8m. olive and mauve	2·75	6·75
237		2t. brown and green	2·75	6·75

1929. Air. Arrival of First Airplane of the Ethiopian Government. Optd with airplane and Amharic text (= "16 Aug 1929. Ethiopian Government Air Mail").

No.	Type	Description	Mint	Used
238	**39**	⅛m. blue and orange	1·40	1·90
239	**40**	¼m. red and blue	1·40	1·90
240	**39**	½m. black and green	1·50	2·00
241	**40**	1m. black and red	1·50	2·00
242	**39**	2m. black and blue	1·50	2·00
243	**40**	4m. olive and yellow	1·50	2·00
244	**39**	8m. olive and mauve	1·50	2·00
245	**40**	1t. mauve and brown	2·00	3·25
246	**39**	2t. brown and green	3·25	4·25
247	**40**	3t. green and purple	3·25	4·25

1930. Accession of Ras Taffari as Emperor Haile Selassie. Optd **HAYLE** (or **HAILE**) **SELASSIE 1er 3 Avril 1930** and Amharic text.

No.	Type	Description	Mint	Used
248	**39**	⅛m. blue and orange	65	65
249	**40**	¼m. red and blue	65	65
250	**39**	½m. black and green	65	65
261	**40**	1m. black and red	50	50
262	**39**	2m. black and blue	50	50
263	**40**	4m. olive and yellow	1·00	1·00
264	**39**	8m. olive and mauve	1·40	1·40
265	**40**	1t. mauve and brown	2·40	2·40
266	**39**	2t. brown and green	2·75	2·75
267	**40**	3t. green and purple	4·25	4·25

1930. Coronation of Emperor Haile Selassie (1st issue). Optd with T **46**.

No.	Type	Description	Mint	Used
268	**39**	⅛m. blue and orange	50	70
269	**40**	¼m. red and blue	50	70
270	**39**	½m. black and green	50	70
271	**40**	1m. black and red	50	70
272	**39**	2m. black and blue	50	70
273	**40**	4m. olive and yellow	50	70
274	**39**	8m. olive and mauve	85	85
275	**40**	1t. mauve and brown	1·40	1·40
276	**39**	2t. brown and green	2·10	2·10
277	**40**	3t. green and purple	3·25	3·25

47 The Ethiopian Lion and Symbols

1930. Coronation of Emperor Haile Selassie (2nd issue).

No.	Type	Description	Mint	Used
278	**47**	1g. orange	25	25
279		2g. blue	25	25
280		4g. purple	40	50
281		8g. green	40	55
282		1t. brown	50	65
283		3t. green	1·10	1·10
284		5t. brown	1·50	1·50

1931. Issue of 1928 surch in mehaleks.

No.	Type	Description	Mint	Used
285	**40**	⅛m. on 1m. black & red	45	85
286	**39**	⅛m. on 2m. black & blue	45	85
287	**40**	⅛m. on 4m. green & yell	45	85
288		¼m. on 1m. black & red	45	85
289	**39**	¼m. on 2m. black & blue	1·00	1·40
290	**40**	¼m. on 4m. green & yell	1·00	1·40
291		½m. on 1m. black & red	1·00	1·40
292	**39**	½m. on 2m. black & blue	1·00	1·40
293	**40**	½m. on 4m. green & yell	1·00	1·40
294		½m. on 3t. green & purple	6·75	8·25
295	**39**	1m. on 2m. black & blue	1·40	1·60

49 Potez 25A2 over Map of Ethiopia

50 Ras Makonnen

1931. Air.

No.	Type	Description	Mint	Used
296	**49**	1g. red	30	50
297		2g. blue	30	50
298		4g. mauve	45	65
299		8g. green	1·00	1·10
300		1t. brown	1·60	1·60
301		2t. red	4·00	5·25
302		3t. green	6·00	7·25

1931.

No.	Type	Description	Mint	Used
303	**50**	⅛g. red	15	40
304	–	¼g. olive	65	55
305	**50**	½g. purple	45	45
306	–	1g. orange	45	45
307	–	2g. blue	45	45
308	–	4g. lilac	95	1·00
309	–	8g. green	2·00	2·00
310	–	1t. brown	5·25	5·25
311	–	3t. green	5·75	6·00
312	–	5t. brown	8·25	8·25

DESIGNS—HORIZ: ¼g. Railway Bridge over R. Awash. VERT: 1g. Empress Menen (profile); 2g., 8g. Haile Selassie (profile); 4g., 1t. Statue of Menelik II; 3t. Empress Menen (full face); 5t. Haile Selassie (full face).

1936. Red Cross. As T **50** optd with red cross.

No.	Type	Description	Mint	Used
313		1g. green	90	90
314		2g. pink	90	90
315		4g. blue	90	90
316		8g. brown	1·10	1·10
317		1t. violet	1·10	1·10

1936. As T **50** surch with value and Amharic text.

No.	Type	Description	Mint	Used
318	**50**	1c. on ⅛g. red	1·40	1·40
319	–	2c. on ¼g. green	1·40	1·00
320	**50**	3c. on ½g. purple	1·40	1·40
321	–	5c. on 1g. orange	1·10	1·10
322	–	10c. on 2g. blue	1·10	1·00

54 King Victor Emmanuel III

56 Haile Selassie I in Coronation Robes

ITALIAN COLONY

1936. Annexation of Ethiopia.

No.	Type	Description	Mint	Used
322a	**54**	10c. brown	8·00	4·75
322b	–	20c. violet	7·25	1·90
322c	–	25c. green	3·50	45
322d	–	30c. brown	3·50	90
322e	–	50c. red	2·00	20
322f	–	75c. orange	16·00	4·00
322g	–	1l.25 blue	16·00	5·75

DESIGNS—VERT: 25c., 30c., 50c. Victor Emmanuel III. HORIZ: Victor Emmanuel III and: 20c. Mountain scenery; 75c. Gonder Castle; 1l.25, Tomb of Scec Hussen and Dordola Hills.

INDEPENDENCE RESTORED

1942. 1st issue. "Centimes" with capital initial and small letters.

No.	Type	Description	Mint	Used
323	**56**	4c. black and green	1·40	75
324		10c. black and red	2·75	1·10
325		20c. black and blue	4·00	2·00

1942. 2nd issue. "CENTIMES" in block capital letters.

No.	Type	Description	Mint	Used
326	**56**	4c. black and green	85	25
327		8c. black and orange	90	25
328		10c. black and red	1·25	30
329		12c. black and violet	1·25	60
330		20c. black and blue	1·60	85
331		25c. black and green	2·40	1·40
332		50c. black and brown	4·00	1·60
333		60c. black and mauve	5·25	2·40

1943. Restoration of Obelisk and 13th Anniv of Coronation of Haile Selassie. Stamps of 1942 inscr "CENTIMES" surch **OBELISK 3 NOV. 1943** and value.

No.	Type	Description	Mint	Used
334	**56**	5c. on 4c. black & grn	50·00	50·00
335		10c. on 8c. black & orge	50·00	50·00
336		15c. on 10c. black & red	50·00	50·00
337		20c. on 12c. black & vio	50·00	50·00
338		30c. on 20c. black & bl	50·00	50·00

In No. 338 the figure "3" is surcharged on the "2" of "20" to make "30" and this value is confirmed by the Amharic characters.

58 Royal Palace, Addis Ababa

59 Menelik II

1944. Birth Cent of Emperor Menelik II.

No.	Type	Description	Mint	Used
339	**58**	5c. green	1·60	85
340	**59**	10c. red	2·50	1·25
341	–	20c. blue	4·75	3·00
342	–	50c. violet	5·25	3·25
343	–	65c. orange	9·25	4·25

DESIGNS—VERT: 20c. Equestrian statue of Menelik II; 65c. Menelik in royal robes. HORIZ: 50c. Menelik's mausoleum.

60 Patient and Nurse (Amharic characters = "Victory")

63 Lion of the Tribe of Judah

64 Postal Transport by Mule and by Bus

1945. Victory. Optd **V** in red.

No.	Type	Description	Mint	Used
344	–	5c. green	3·25	2·00
345	–	10c. red	4·00	3·25
346	**60**	25c. blue	5·00	4·75

347 – 50c. brown . . . . 6·75 5·00
348 – 1t. violet . . . . 8·25 8·25
DESIGNS: 5c. Nurse and baby; 10c. Native soldier; 50c. Nurse and child; 1t. "Supplication".
The above stamps without the "V" were not issued for postal purposes.

1946. Air. Resumption of National Air Mail Services.
(a) Surch at sides and top in Amharic, with **20-4-39** and value below.
349 **56** 12c. on 4c. blk & grn . . . 55·00 55·00

(b) Surch **REPRISE POSTE AERIENNE ETHIOPIENNE** at sides and top, with **29.12.46** and values below.
350 **56** 0.50 on 25c. black & green 55·00 55·00
351 $2 on 60c. black & mauve 75·00 75·00

1947. 50th Anniv of Postal Service.
352 **63** 10c. yellow . . . . 2·50 2·00
353 – 20c. blue . . . . 3·25 2·40
354 **64** 30c. brown . . . . 4·75 3·25
355 – 50c. green . . . . 12·50 6·75
356 – 70c. mauve . . . . 19·00 10·50
DESIGNS—VERT: 20c. Menelik II (as in Type **1**). HORIZ: 50c. G.P.O., Addis Ababa; 70c. Menelik and Haile Selassie.

65 Negus Sahle Selassie

1947. 150th Anniv of Selassie Dynasty.
357 **65** 20c. blue . . . . 2·50 1·60
358 – 30c. purple . . . . 3·25 2·75
359 – $1 green . . . . 9·25 4·00
DESIGNS—HORIZ: 30c. View of Ancober. VERT: $1, Negus Sahle Selassie.

67 Emperor Haile Selassie and Pres. Roosevelt

1947. 2nd Death Anniv of Pres. Roosevelt.
360 **67** 12c. green & red (postage) 1·40 1·60
361 25c. red and blue . . . . 2·75 3·25
362 – 65c. blue, red and black . . 5·00 6·25
363 – $1 brown & purple (air) . . 10·00 12·00
364 – $2 blue and red . . . . . 20·00 23·00
DESIGNS—HORIZ: 65c. Pres. Roosevelt and U.S. flags. VERT: $1, Pres. Roosevelt; $2, Haile Selassie.

1947. Surch **12 centimes** in French and Amharic with six bars.
365 **56** 12c. on 25c. black & grn 50·00 50·00

69 Lake Tana

70 Douglas DC-3 over Zoquala Volcano

1947. Views with medallion portrait of Haile Selassie inset. (a) Postage.
366 – 1c. purple 15 10
367 – 2c. violet 15 15
368 – 4c. green 20 15
369 – 5c. green 15 10
370 **69** 8c. orange 50 15
371 – 12c. red 40 15
371a – 15c. olive 50 25
372 – 20c. blue 65 30
373 – 30c. brown . . . . 1·10 50
373a – 60c. red . . . . 1·90 60
374 – 70c. mauve . . . . 2·40 65
375 – $1 red . . . . 4·75 55
376 – $3 blue . . . . 12·00 3·25
377 – $5 olive . . . . 18·00 5·75
DESIGNS: 1c. Amba Alagi; 2c. Trinity Church, Addis Ababa; 4c. Debra Sina; 5c. Mecan mountain pathway, near Ashangi; 12c., 15c. Parliament Building, Addis Ababa; 20c. Aiba mountain scenery, near Mai Chio; 30c. Nile Bridge; 60c., 70c. Canoe on Lake Tana; $1, Omo Falls; $3, Mt. Alamata; $5, Ras Dashan Mountains.

(b) Air.
378 – 8c. purple 15 10
379 **70** 10c. green 25 10
379a – 25c. purple 50 20
380 – 30c. orange 75 25
380a – 35c. blue . . . . 1·00 40
380b – 65c. purple 75 35
381 – 70c. red . . . . 1·75 40
382 – $1 blue . . . . 2·75 65
383 – $3 mauve . . . . 8·25 4·00
384 – $5 brown . . . . 13·00 6·50
385 – $10 violet . . . . 24·00 16·00
DESIGNS: 8c. Ploughing with oxen; 30c., 35c. Tehis Isat Falls, Blue Nile; 65c., 70c. Amba Alagi; $1, Sacala source of River Nile; $3, Gorgora and Dembia on Lake Tana; $5, Magdala Fort; $10, Ras Dasnan Mountains and Lake.

72 Emperor, Empress, Lion and Map

1949. 8th Anniv of Liberation.
386 – 20c. blue . . . . 1·40 30
387 **72** 30c. orange . . . . 1·40 65
388 – 50c. violet . . . . 3·00 1·60
389 – 80c. green . . . . 4·25 2·10
390 – $1 red . . . . 7·00 3·25
DESIGNS: 20c. Emperor and Empress with sceptres and orb; 50c. Coat of arms; 80c. Shield and spears; $1, Star of Solomon.

1949. Industrial and Agricultural Exn. Nos. 370/1 and 373/5 surch **EXPOSITION 1949**, and new value and two lines of Amharic characters.
391 8c.+8c. orange . . . . 3·25 3·25
392 12c.+5c. red . . . . 3·25 3·25
393 30c.+15c. brown . . . . . . 6·75 6·75
394 70c.+70c. mauve . . . . . . 17·00 17·00
395 $1+80c. red . . . . 20·00 20·00

74 Emperor and U.P.U. Monument, Berne

1950. Air. 75th Anniv of U.P.U.
396 **74** 5c. red and green 90 70
397 15c. red and blue . . . . 1·10 70
398 25c. green and yellow . . . 1·75 90
399 50c. blue and red . . . . 3·00 2·10

1950. Red Cross Fund. As Nos. 344/8 but without **V** opt and surch **+ 10 ct.** below a cross.
399a 5c.+10c. green . . . . . . 1·40 1·40
399b 10c.+10c. red . . . . 1·60 1·60
399c 25c.+10c. blue . . . . . . 3·25 3·25
399d 50c.+10c. brown . . . . . 5·25 5·25
399e $1+10c. violet . . . . . . 12·50 12·50

75 Lion of the Tribe of Judah

76 Emperor and Abbaye Bridge

1950. 20th Anniv of Coronation.
400 – 5c. violet . . . . 1·40 45
401 – 10c. mauve . . . . 2·75 1·00
402 – 20c. red . . . . 3·25 1·50
403 **75** 30c. green . . . . 4·00 2·00
404 – 50c. blue . . . . 5·00 3·25
DESIGNS—HORIZ: 5c. Dejach Balcha Hospital; 50c. Emperor, Empress and palace. VERT: 10c. Abuna Petros; 20c. Emperor hoisting flag.

1951. Opening of Abbaye Bridge.
405 **76** 5c. brown and green . . . 3·25 1·00
406 10c. black and orange . . 5·00 1·60
407 15c. brown and blue . . . 6·75 2·50
408 30c. mauve and olive . . . 10·00 3·25
409 60c. blue and brown . . . 13·50 5·00
410 80c. green and violet . . . 20·00 6·75

1951. 55th Anniv of Battle of Adwa. As T **76**, but Emperor and Tomb of Ras Makonnen.
411 5c. black and green . . . . . 1·60 1·00
412 10c. black and blue . . . . . 2·00 1·40
413 15c. black and blue . . . . . 3·00 2·00
414 30c. black and red . . . . . 4·00 2·40
415 80c. black and red . . . . . 6·00 3·25
416 $1 black and brown . . . . 10·00 4·00

1951. Industrial and Agricultural Exhibition. Nos. 391/5 further optd **1951** with Amharic characters above.
417 8c.+8c. orange . . . . 1·00 1·00
418 12c.+5c. red . . . . 1·00 1·00
419 30c.+15c. brown . . . . . . 1·40 1·40
420 70c.+70c. mauve . . . . . . 11·50 11·50
421 $1+80c. red . . . . 18·00 18·00

79 "Tree of Health" **80** Haile Selassie I

1951. Anti-tuberculosis Fund. Cross and inscr in red.
422 **79** 5c.+2c. green 55 55
423 10c.+3c. orange 55 55
424 15c.+3c. blue . . . . . . 1·00 1·00
425 30c.+5c. red . . . . 1·60 1·60
426 50c.+7c. brown . . . . . 2·50 2·50
427 $1+10c. purple . . . . . . 4·00 4·00

1952. Emperor Haile Selassie's 60th Birthday.
428 **80** 5c. green 25 25
429 10c. orange 45 30
430 15c. black . . . . 1·00 40
431 25c. blue . . . . 1·40 45
432 30c. violet . . . . 2·00 1·00
433 50c. red . . . . 2·75 65
434 65c. sepia . . . . 5·25 2·00

81 Ethiopian Flag over the Sea

1952. Celebration of Federation of Eritrea with Ethiopia.
435 – 15c. lake . . . . 1·00 85
436 – 25c. brown . . . . 1·60 1·10
437 – 30c. brown . . . . 2·40 1·50
438 – 50c. purple . . . . 2·75 1·60
439 – 65c. black . . . . 7·50 2·00
440 – 80c. green . . . . 5·00 3·00
441 – $1 red . . . . 8·25 4·00
442 **81** $2 blue . . . . 15·00 6·75
443 – $3 mauve . . . . 27·00 10·00
DESIGNS: 15c., 30c. Port Assab; 25c., 50c. Port Massawa; 65c. Map; 80c. Allegory of Federation; $1, Emperor raising flag; $3, Emperor in 1936.

82 Emperor and Massawa Harbour

1953. 1st Anniv of Federation of Ethiopia and Eritrea.
444 **82** 10c. brown and red . . . . 4·75 2·00
445 – 15c. green and blue . . . 3·25 2·50
446 **82** 25c. brown and orange . . 13·00 7·50
447 – 30c. green and brown . . . 6·75 4·25
448 **82** 50c. brown and purple . . 13·00 7·50
DESIGN—HORIZ: 15c., 30c. Emperor aboard freighter at sea.

83 Princess Tsahai tending sick Child

1953. 20th Anniv of Ethiopian Red Cross Society. Cross in red.
449 **83** 15c. blue and brown . . . 1·60 50
450 20c. orange and green . . 2·50 1·00
451 30c. green and blue . . . . 4·25 1·60

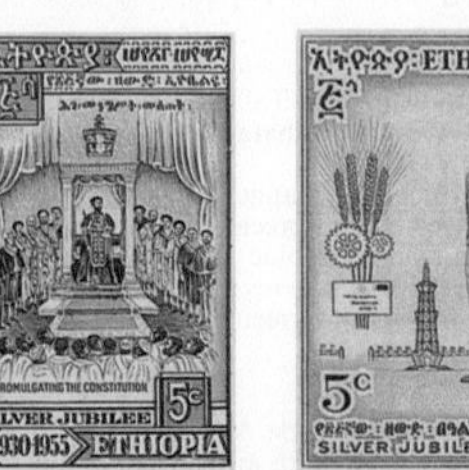

84 Promulgating the Constitution **85** Emperor Haile Selassie

1955. Silver Jubilee of Emperor. Inscr "1930–1955".
452 **84** 5c. brown and green . . . 50 20
453 – 20c. green and red . . . . 1·60 40
454 – 25c. black and mauve . . . 2·00 50
455 – 35c. red and brown . . . . 2·50 1·00
456 – 50c. blue and brown . . . 7·75 2·25
457 – 65c. red and lilac . . . . 5·25 3·00
DESIGNS—HORIZ: 20c. Bishop's consecration; 25c. Emperor presenting standard to troops; 50c. Emperor, Empress and symbols of progress; 65c. Emperor and Empress in coronation robes. VERT: 35c. Allegory of re-union of Ethiopia and Eritrea.

1955. Silver Jubilee Fair, Addis Ababa.
458 **85** 5c. olive and green 65 15
459 10c. blue and red . . . . 1·00 25
460 15c. green and black . . . 1·40 40
461 50c. lake and mauve . . . 2·10 1·60

86 Convair CV 240 Airliner

1955. Air. 10th Anniv of Ethiopian Airlines.
462 **86** 10c. multicoloured 75 25
463 15c. multicoloured . . . . 1·10 85
464 20c. multicoloured . . . . 1·50 90

87 Promulgating the Constitution **89** Amharic "A"

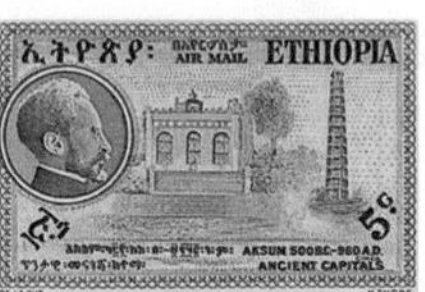

88 Aksum

1956. Air. 25th Anniv of Constitution.
465 **87** 10c. blue and brown . . . 65 35
466 15c. green and red 90 45
467 20c. orange and blue . . . 1·25 60
468 25c. green and lilac . . . . 1·60 75
469 30c. brown and green . . . 2·10 85

1957. Air. Ancient Capitals of Ethiopia. Centres in green.
470 **88** 5c. brown 60 15
471 – 10c. red (Lalibela) 60 50
472 – 15c. orange (Gondar) . . . 80 65
473 – 20c. blue (Makalle) . . . . 1·40 1·00
474 – 25c. mauve (Ankober) . . . 2·10 1·40

1957. Air. 70th Anniv of Addis Ababa. Amharic characters in red and miniature views of buildings as in T **89**.
475 **89** 5c. blue on salmon 50 15
476 – 10c. green on flesh 30 25
477 – 15c. purple on buff 45 35
478 – 20c. green on buff . . . . 1·10 50
479 – 25c. mauve on lavender . . 1·40 65
480 – 30c. brown on green . . . 1·60 1·10
AMHARIC CHARACTERS: 10c. "DD1"; 15c. "S"; 20c. "A"; 25c. "BE"; 30c. "BA".
The set spells out "Addis Ababa" in Amharic.

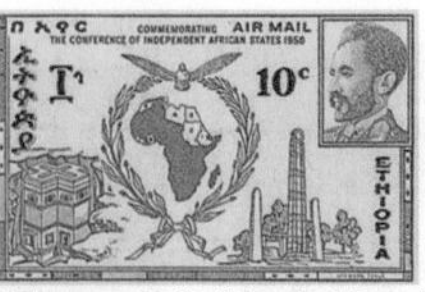

90 Emperor Haile Selassie, Map of Africa, Building and Monument

1958. Air. Conference of Independent African States, Accra.
481 **90** 10c. green 30 20
482 20c. red 85 85
483 30c. blue . . . . 1·40 1·00

1958. Anti-tuberculosis Fund. As Nos. 422/7 but new values.
483a **79** 20c.+3c. purple & red . . 50 65
483b 25c.+4c. green & red . . 65 85
483c 35c.+5c. purple & red . . 1·25 1·25
483d 60c.+7c. blue and red . . 2·00 2·00
483e 65c.+7c. violet & red . . 2·75 2·75
483f 80c.+9c. carmine & red . . 4·50 4·50

91 Emperor Haile Selassie, Map of Africa and U.N. Emblem

96 Woman with Torch

1958. Air. 1st Session of U.N. Economic Conference for Africa, Addis Ababa.
484 **91** 5c. green 20 15
485 20c. red 35 25
486 25c. blue 50 35
487 50c. purple . . . . 1·00 50

1959. Red Cross Commem. Surch **RED CROSS CENTENARY 1859-1959** in English and Amharic and premium. Colours changed. Cross in red.
488 **83** 15c.+2c. red & brown . . . 70 70
489 20c.+3c. green & violet . . 1·50 1·50
490 30c.+5c. blue and red . . . 2·00 2·00

1959. Air. 30th Anniv of Air Mail Service in Ethiopia. Nos. 378/81 optd **30th Airmail Ann. 1929-1959**.
491 8c. purple 40 25
492 10c. green 50 40
493 25c. purple 65 50
494 30c. orange . . . . 1·10 65
495 35c. blue . . . . 1·50 1·00
496 65c. violet . . . . 2·00 1·10
497 70c. red . . . . 2·25 1·25

1960. World Refugee Year. Optd **World Refugee Year 1959-1960** in English and Amharic.
498 20c. blue (No. 372) . . . . . 1·00 1·00
499 60c. red (No. 373a) . . . . . 1·60 1·60

1960. Ethiopian Red Cross Society's Silver Jubilee. As Nos. 344/8 but without **V** opt surch **Silver Jubilee 1960** in English and Amharic and premium.
500 5c.+1c. green 20 15
501 10c.+2c. red 55 55
502 25c.+3c. blue . . . . 1·00 1·00
503 50c.+4c. brown . . . . . . 2·10 2·10
504 $1+5c. violet . . . . 4·25 4·25

1960. 2nd Independent African States Conf, Addis Ababa.
505 **96** 20c. green and red 40 50
506 80c. violet and red . . . . 1·50 65
507 $1 lake and red . . . . . 3·00 2·10

97 Emperor Haile Selassie

98 Africa Hall, Addis Ababa

1960. 30th Anniv of Emperor's Coronation.
508 **97** 10c. brown and blue . . . 65 65
509 25c. violet and green . . . 1·10 1·10
510 50c. blue and buff . . . . 2·00 2·00
511 65c. green and salmon . . 2·75 2·75
512 $1 blue and purple . . . . 4·25 4·25

1961. Africa Day.
513 **98** 80c. blue . . . . 2·00 1·10

99 Emperor Haile Selassie and Map of Ethiopia

1961. 20th Anniv of Liberation.
514 **99** 20c. green 40 30
515 30c. blue 55 45
516 $1 brown . . . . 1·40 85

100 African Ass

1961. Ethiopian Fauna.
517 **100** 5c. black and green . . . 50 15
518 – 15c. brown and green . . 50 20
519 – 25c. sepia and green . . . 65 30
520 – 35c. brown and green . . 1·50 40
521 – 50c. red and green . . . 1·40 50
522 – $1 brown and green . . . 3·00 1·50
DESIGNS: 15c. Eland; 25c. African elephant; 35c. Giraffe; 50c. Gemsbok; $1, Lion and lioness.
See also Nos. 641/5.

101 Emperor Haile Selassie I and Empress Menen

1961. Golden Wedding of Emperor and Empress.
523 **101** 10c. green 45 20
524 50c. blue . . . . 1·10 45
525 $1 red . . . . 1·60 1·40

102 Guks (jousting)

1962. Sports.
526 **102** 10c. red and green 40 30
527 – 15c. brown and red . . . 50 45
528 – 20c. black and red 70 50
529 – 30c. purple and blue . . . 80 65
530 – 50c. green and buff . . . 1·50 75
DESIGNS: 15c. Ganna (Ethiopian hockey); 20c. Cycling; 30c. Football (3rd Africa Cup game); 50c. Abbebe Bikila (Marathon winner, Olympic Games Rome, 1960).

103 Mosquito on World Map

1962. Malaria Eradication.
531 **103** 15c. black 25 15
532 30c. purple 40 30
533 60c. brown . . . . 1·40 60

104 Abyssinian Ground Hornbill

105 "Collective Security"

1962. Ethiopian Birds (1st series). Mult.
534 5c. Type **104** (postage) . . . 85 20
535 15c. Abyssinian roller . . . . 1·40 45
536 30c. Bateleur (vert) . . . . . 1·75 1·00
537 50c. Double-toothed barbet (vert) . . . . 3·00 1·25
538 $1 Didric cuckoo . . . . . . 7·25 2·10
539 10c. Dark-headed oriole (air) 85 15
540 15c. Broad-tailed paradise whydah (vert) . . . . . . 1·25 45
541 20c. Lammergeier (vert) . . . 1·50 55
542 50c. White-cheeked turaco . . 3·00 1·25
543 80c. Village indigobird . . . 3·50 1·40
See also Nos 633/7 and 673/7.

1962. Air. 2nd Anniv of Ethiopian U.N. Forces in Congo and 70th Birthday of Emperor.
544 **105** 15c. multicoloured 25 20
545 50c. multicoloured 60 35
546 60c. multicoloured . . . . 1·10 45

106 Assab Hospital

108 Telephone and Communications Map

107 Bazan, "The Nativity" and Bethlehem

1962. 10th Anniv of Federation of Ethiopia and Eritrea.
547 **106** 3c. purple 10 10
548 – 15c. blue 15 15
549 – 20c. green 25 15
550 – 50c. brown 50 25
551 – 60c. red . . . . 1·00 40
DESIGNS: 15c. Assab school; 20c. Massawa church; 50c. Massawa mosque; 60c. Assab port.

1962. Ethiopian Rulers (1st issue). Mult.
552 10c. Type **107** 15 10
553 15c. Ezana and monuments, Aksum 25 15
554 20c. Kaleb and fleet in Adulis port 90 20
555 50c. Lalibela, Christian figures from Lalibela churches (vert) 90 40
556 60c. Yekuno Amlak and Abuna Tekle Haimanot preaching in Ankober . . . 1·10 50
557 75c. Zara Yacob and ceremonial pyre . . . . . 1·40 90
558 $1 Lebna Bengel and battle against Mohammed Gragn 2·10 1·10

1963. 10th Anniv of Ethiopian Imperial Telecommunications Board.
559 **108** 10c. red 50 25
560 – 50c. blue . . . . 1·40 65
561 – 60c. brown . . . . 1·60 1·00
DESIGNS: 50c. Radio aerial; 60c. Telegraph pole.

109 Campaign Emblem

110 "African Solidarity"

1963. Freedom from Hunger.
562 **109** 5c. red 10 10
563 10c. mauve 15 10
564 15c. violet 25 15
565 30c. green 40 20

1963. Air. Conference of African Heads of States, Addis Ababa.
566 **110** 10c. black and purple . . 40 10
567 40c. black and green . . . 90 40
568 60c. black and blue . . . 1·40 45

111 Disabled Boy

112 Bishop Abuna Salama

1963. "Aid for the Disabled" Fund.
569 **111** 10c.+2c. blue 25 25
570 15c.+3c. red 45 45
571 50c.+5c. green . . . . . 1·10 1·10
572 60c.+5c. purple . . . . . 2·40 2·40

1964. Ethiopian Spiritual Leaders.
573 **112** 10c. blue 25 20
574 – 15c. green (Abuna Aregawi) 40 30
575 – 30c. lake (Abuna Tekle Haimanot) . . . . . . 1·10 50
576 – 40c. blue (Yared) . . . . 1·40 1·10
577 – 60c. brn (Zara Yacob) . . 2·10 1·60

113 Queen Sheba

114 Priest teaching Alphabet

1964. Ethiopian Empresses. Multicoloured.
578 10c. Type **113** 30 35
579 15c. Helen 65 50
580 50c. Seble Wongel . . . . . 1·10 85
581 60c. Mentiwab . . . . 2·50 1·50
582 80c. Taitu . . . . 3·25 2·00

1964. "Education".
583 **114** 5c. brown 15 10
584 – 10c. green 15 10
585 – 15c. purple 20 15
586 – 40c. blue 50 35
587 – 60c. purple . . . . 1·10 50
DESIGNS—HORIZ: 10c. Pupils in classroom. VERT: 15c. Teacher with pupil; 40c. Students in laboratory; 60c. Graduates in procession.

115 Swimming

116 Eleanor Roosevelt

1964. Air. Olympic Games, Tokyo. Mult.
588 5c. Type **115** 15 10
589 10c. Basketball (vert) 25 20
590 15c. Throwing the javelin . . 30 25
591 80c. Football at Addis Ababa stadium . . . . 1·60 1·10

1964. Eleanor Roosevelt Commem.
592 **116** 10c. blue and bistre . . . 15 15
593 60c. blue and brown . . . 1·00 75
594 80c. blue, gold and green 1·40 1·00

1964. Ethiopian Rulers (2nd issue). As T **107**. Multicoloured.
595 5c. Serse Dengel and view of Gondar, 1563 . . . . . . 10 10
596 10c. Fasiladas and Gondar, 1632 . . . . 20 15
597 20c. Yassu the Great and Gondar, 1682 . . . . . . 40 20
598 25c. Theodore II and map of Ethiopia 45 25
599 60c. John IV and Battle of Gura, 1876 . . . . 1·25 95
600 80c. Menelik II and Battle of Adwa, 1896 . . . . . . 1·40 1·00

118 Queen Elizabeth II and Emperor Haile Selassie

1965. Air. Visit of Queen Elizabeth II.
601 **118** 5c. multicoloured 10 10
602 35c. multicoloured 50 50
603 60c. multicoloured . . . . 1·00 75

119 Abyssinian Rose

120 I.T.U. Emblem and Symbols

1965. Ethiopian Flowers. Multicoloured.
604 5c. Type **119** 15 10
605 10c. Kosso tree 20 15
606 25c. St. John's wort 75 50
607 35c. Parrot tree . . . . . . 1·10 90
608 60c. Maskal daisy . . . . . 2·00 1·50

1965. Centenary of I.T.U.
609 **120** 5c. yellow, indigo & blue 15 10
610 10c. orange, dp blue & bl 20 10
611 60c. mauve, dp blue & bl 1·25 85

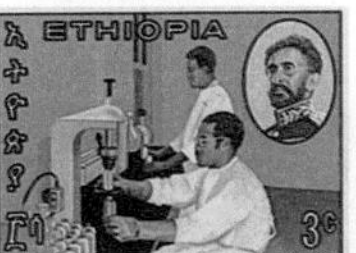

121 Laboratory Technicians

1965. Multicoloured.
612 3c. Type **121** (postage) . . . 10 30
613 5c. Textile mill 15 10
614 10c. Sugar factory 10 10
615 20c. Mountain highway . . . 40 15
616 25c. Motor coach 45 10
617 30c. Diesel locomotive . . . 1·75 35
618 35c. Railway Station, Addis Ababa . . . . 1·75 35

619 15c. Sisal (inscr "SUGAR CANES") (air) 25 15
620 40c. Koka Dam 45 25
621 50c. Blue Nile Bridge 70 40
622 60c. Gondar castles 75 35
623 80c. Coffee tree . . . . . . 1·00 40
624 $1 Cattle . . . . 1·50 45
625 $3 Camels . . . . 4·75 2·10
626 $5 Boeing 720B airliner . . . 9·00 4·25

122 I.C.Y. Emblem

1965. I.C.Y.
627 **122** 10c. red and turquoise . . 25 15
628 50c. red and blue 90 65
629 80c. red and blue . . . . 1·40 75

123 Commercial Bank's Seal

1965. Ethiopian National and Commercial Banks.
630 **123** 10c. black, blue and red 25 25
631 – 30c. black, blue & ultram 85 60
632 – 60c. yellow, blue & black 1·10 85
DESIGNS: 30c. National Bank's Seal; 60c. Banking halls and main building.

1966. Air. Ethiopian Birds (2nd series). As T **104**. Multicoloured.
633 10c. White-collared kingfisher 80 35
634 15c. Blue-breasted bee eater 1·10 50
635 25c. African paradise fly-catcher . . . . 1·40 65
636 40c. Village weaver . . . . . 2·50 90
637 60c. White-collared pigeon 3·25 1·25

124 Press Building

1966. Inauguration of "Light and Peace" Printing Press, Addis Ababa.
638 **124** 5c. black and red 10 10
639 15c. black and green . . . 25 25
640 30c. black and yellow . . 45 45

125 Black Rhinoceros 126 Kebero Drum

1966. Air. Animals.
641 **125** 5c. black, grey & green 15 10
642 – 10c. brown, black & grn 50 15
643 – 20c. black, green & ol . . 80 20
644 – 30c. ochre, black & green 1·40 60
645 – 60c. brown, black & grn 2·40 1·25
ANIMALS: 10c. Leopard; 20c. Eastern black and white colobus; 30c. Mountain nyala; 60c. Ibex.

1966. Musical Instruments.
646 **126** 5c. black and green . . . 15 10
647 – 10c. black and blue . . . 25 10
648 – 35c. black and orange . . 75 60
649 – 50c. black and yellow . . 1·50 90
650 – 60c. black and red . . . . 2·00 1·25
INSTRUMENTS: 10c. Begena harp; 35c. Mesenko stringed instrument; 50c. Krar lyre; 60c. Washent flutes.

127 Emperor Haile Selassie

1966. "Fifty Years of Leadership".
651 **127** 10c. multicoloured 15 10
652 15c. multicoloured 20 20
653 40c. black, grey & gold 1·00 75

128 UNESCO Emblem and Map of Africa

1966. 20th Anniv of UNESCO.
654 **128** 15c. red, black and blue 25 25
655 60c. blue, brown & green 1·10 70

129 W.H.O. Building 130 Ethiopian Pavilion

1966. Inaug of W.H.O. Headquarters, Geneva.
656 **129** 5c. green, sepia & blue . . 25 15
657 40c. sepia, green & violet 95 65

1967. World Fair, Montreal.
658 **130** 30c. multicoloured 80 50
659 45c. multicoloured 90 65
660 80c. multicoloured . . . . 1·60 1·10

131 Diesel Train and Route-Map

1967. 50th Anniv of Completion of Djibouti–Addis Ababa Railway.
661 **131** 15c. multicoloured 75 30
662 30c. multicoloured . . . . 1·75 1·00
663 50c. multicoloured . . . . 3·00 1·75

132 "Papilio aethiops" (inscr "Papilionidae")

1967. Butterflies (1st series). Multicoloured.
664 5c. Type **132** 10 10
665 10c. "Charaxes epijasius" . . 20 25
666 20c. "Charaxes varans" . . . 45 45
667 35c. "Euphaedra neophron" 1·10 90
668 40c. "Salamis aethiops" . . . 1·40 1·10
See also Nos. 915/19.

133 Haile Selassie I

1967. Emperor Haile Selassie's 75th Birthday.
669 **133** 10c. multicoloured 25 25
670 15c. multicoloured 40 35
671 $1 multicoloured . . . . 2·00 1·50

1967. Air. Birds (3rd series). As T **104**. Mult.
673 10c. Blue-winged goose (vert) 80 75
674 15c. African yellow-bill . . . 1·00 30
675 20c. Wattled ibis . . . . . . 1·40 55
676 25c. Lesser striped swallow 2·10 65
677 40c. Black-winged lovebird (vert) . . . . 3·50 1·00

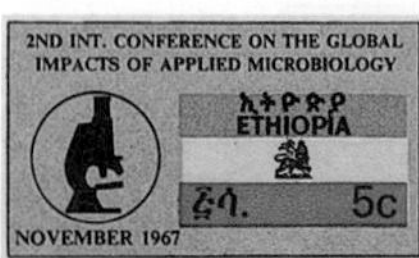

134 Microscope and Flag

1967. 2nd International Conference on Global Impacts of Applied Microbiology, Addis Ababa.
678 **134** 5c. multicoloured 10 10
679 30c. multicoloured 35 20
680 $1 multicoloured . . . . 1·90 1·50

135 Wall Painting, Gondar

1967. International Tourist Year. Multicoloured.
681 15c. Type **135** 60 45
682 25c. Ancient votive stone and statuary, Atsbe Dera (vert) 1·25 65
683 35c. Cave paintings of animals, Harrar Province 90 75
684 50c. Prehistoric stone tools, Melke Kontoure (vert) . . 1·60 1·00

136 Cross of Biet-Maryam (bronze) 137 Emperor Theodore II with Lions

1967. Crosses of Lalibela (1st series). Crosses in black and silver.
685 **136** 5c. black and lemon . . . 15 10
686 – 10c. black and orange . . 15 15
687 – 15c. black and violet . . 20 10
688 – 20c. black and red 50 40
689 – 50c. black and yellow . . 1·50 1·10
CROSSES: 10c. "Zagwe King's" cross; 15c. Copper, Biet-Maryam; 20c. Typical cross of Lalibela region; 50c. Copper, Medhani Alem.
See also Nos. 737/40.

1968. Death Cent of Emperor Theodore II.
690 – 10c. brown, lilac & yellow 20 10
691 **137** 20c. lilac, brown & mauve 35 20
692 – 50c. red, orange & green 1·10 85
DESIGNS—VERT: 10c. Emperor Theodore; 50c. Imperial crown.

138 Human Rights Emblem

1968. Human Rights Year.
693 **138** 15c. black and red 55 15
694 $1 black and blue . . . . 2·40 1·60

139 Shah of Iran and Haile Selassie I

1968. State Visit of Shah of Iran.
695 **139** 5c. multicoloured 20 10
696 15c. multicoloured 35 20
697 30c. multicoloured . . . . 1·00 75

140 Haile Selassie I and Addressing League of Nations, 1936

1968. "Ethiopia's Struggle for Peace".
698 **140** 15c. multicoloured 20 20
699 – 35c. multicoloured 40 45
700 – $1 multicoloured . . . . 2·40 1·40
HAILE SELASSIE and: 35c. Africa Hall; $1, World map ("International Relations").

141 W.H.O. Emblem

1968. 20th Anniv of W.H.O.
701 **141** 15c. black and green . . . 20 15
702 60c. black and purple . . 1·00 65

142 Running

1968. Olympic Games, Mexico. Multicoloured.
703 10c. Type **142** 15 10
704 15c. Football 20 15
705 20c. Boxing 25 20
706 40c. Basketball 85 55
707 50c. Cycling . . . . 1·10 85

143 Arrussi Costume

1968. Ethiopian Costumes (1st series). Mult.
708 5c. Type **143** 10 10
709 15c. Gemu Gofa 20 10
710 20c. Godjam 25 10
711 30c. Kaffa 30 20
712 35c. Harar 45 25
713 50c. Illubabor 95 35
714 60c. Eritrea . . . . 1·10 85
See also Nos. 768/74.

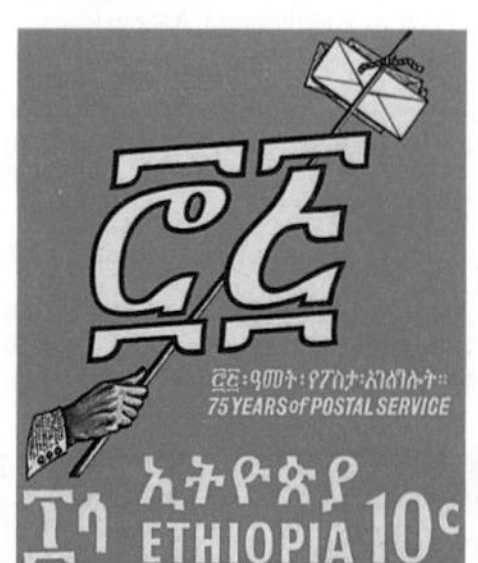

144 Postal Service Emblem and Initials

1969. 75th Anniv of Ethiopian Postal Service.
715 **144** 10c. black, brown & green 15 10
716 15c. black, brown & yell 50 50
717 35c. black, brown & red 90 90

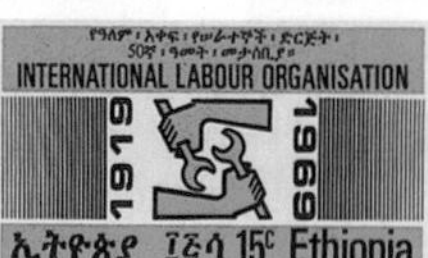

145 I.L.O. Emblem

1969. 50th Anniv of I.L.O.
718 **145** 15c. orange and black . . 25 15
719 60c. green and black . . . 1·40 1·40

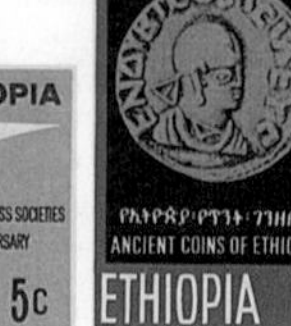

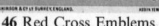

146 Red Cross Emblems 147 Silver Coin of Endybis (3rd cent)

1969. 50th Anniv of League of Red Cross Societies.
720 **146** 5c. red, black and blue . . 20 15
721 15c. red, green & blue . . 65 50
722 30c. red, ultram & blue 1·10 1·00

1969. Ancient Ethiopian Coins.
723 **147** 5c. silver, black & blue . . 15 15
724 – 10c. gold, black & red . . 30 25
725 – 15c. gold, black & brown 25 35
726 – 30c. bronze, black & red 85 65
727 – 40c. bronze, black & grn 95 85
728 – 50c. silver, black & violet 1·25 1·10
COINS: 10c. Gold coin of Ezana (4th century); 15c. Gold coin of Kalob (6th century); 30c. Bronze coin of Armah (7th century); 40c. Bronze coin of Wazena (7th century); 50c. Silver coin of Gersem (8th century);

148 "Hunting"

1969. African Tourist Year. Multicoloured.

729	5c. Type **148**	10	10
730	10c. "Camping"	10	10
731	15c. "Fishing"	55	10
732	20c. "Watersports"	65	65
733	25c. "Mountaineering" (vert)	1·10	1·00

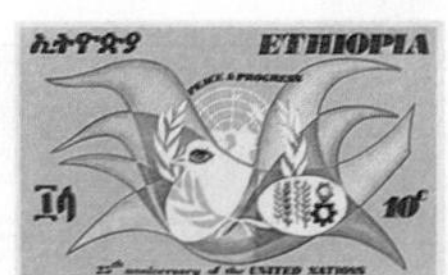

149 Dove of Peace

1969. 25th Anniv of U.N. Multicoloured.

734	10c. Type **149**	10	10
735	30c. Stylized flowers (vert)	50	65
736	60c. Peace dove and emblem	1·25	1·25

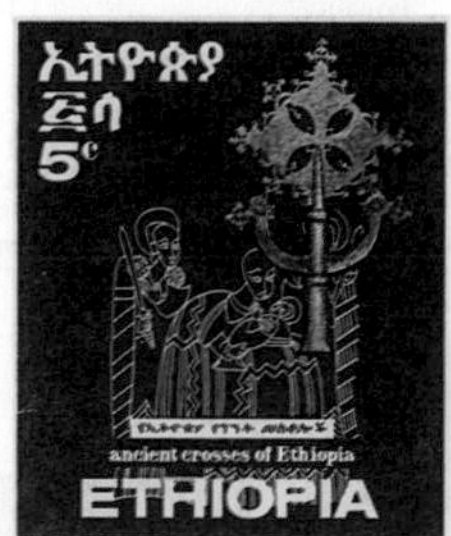

150 Ancient Cross and "Holy Family"

1969. Ancient Ethiopian Crosses (2nd series).

737 **150**	5c. black, yellow & green	10	10
738 –	10c. black and yellow	10	10
739 –	25c. black, green & yell	75	60
740 –	60c. black and yellow	1·90	1·40

DESIGNS—VERT: 10c., 25c. and 60c. show different crosses and drawings similar to Type **150**.

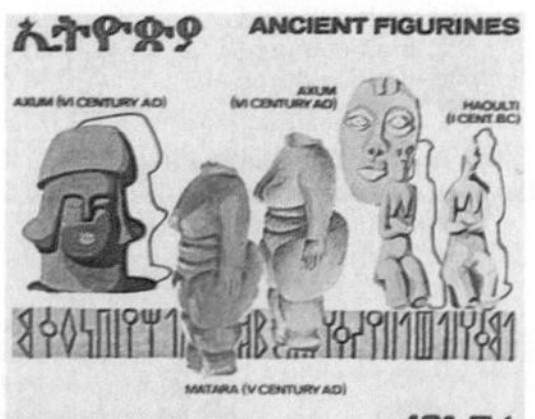

151 Ancient Figurines

1970. Ancient Ethiopian Pottery. Mult.

741	10c. Type **151**	10	10
742	20c. Decorated jar, Yeha	45	45
743	25c. Axum Pottery	60	60
744	35c. "Bird" jug, Matara	75	75
745	60c. Christian pottery, Adulis	1·40	1·40

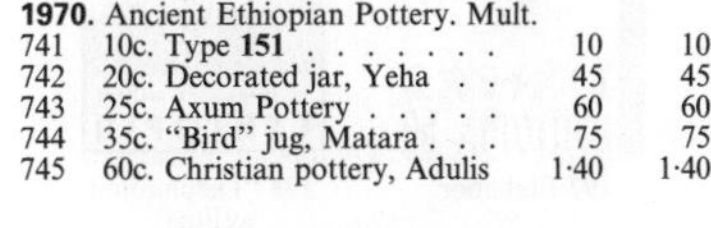

152 Medhane Alem Church

1970. Rock Churches of Lalibela. Mult.

746	5c. Type **152**	10	10
747	10c. Bieta Amanuel	10	10
748	15c. Four churches	20	35
749	20c. Bieta Mariam	55	55
750	50c. Bieta Giorgis	1·40	1·40

153 Sail-finned Tang

1970. Fishes. Multicoloured.

751	5c. Type **153**	15	15
752	10c. Undulate triggerfish	35	35
753	15c. Blue-cheeked butterflyfish	65	65
754	25c. Hooded butterflyfish	1·10	1·10
755	50c. Emperor angelfish	1·60	1·60

154 I.E.Y. Emblem

156 Haile Selassie I

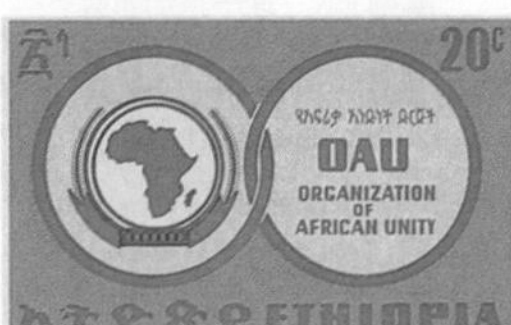

155 O.A.U. Emblem

1970. International Education Year.

756 **154**	10c. multicoloured	15	10
757	20c. multicoloured	25	15
758	50c. multicoloured	65	85

1970. Organization of African Unity. Mult.

759	20c. Type **155**	20	15
760	30c. O.A.U. flag	50	50
761	40c. O.A.U. Headquarters, Addis Ababa	85	85

1970. 40th Anniv of Haile Selassie's Coronation.

762 **156**	15c. multicoloured	15	10
763	50c. multicoloured	70	70
764	60c. multicoloured	1·25	1·25

157 Ministry Buildings

1970. Inauguration of New Posts and Telecommunications Buildings, Addis Ababa.

765 **157**	10c. multicoloured	15	10
766	50c. multicoloured	95	95
767	80c. multicoloured	1·25	1·25

1971. Ethiopian Costumes (2nd series). As T **143**. Multicoloured.

768	5c. Begemedir and Semain Costume	10	10
769	10c. Bale	15	10
770	15c. Wolega	20	10
771	20c. Showa	40	40
772	25c. Sidamo	50	50
773	40c. Tigre	75	75
774	50c. Wello	95	95

159 Tail of Boeing 707

160 "Fountain of Life" (15th-cent Gospel)

1971. Air. 25th Anniv of Ethiopian Airlines. Multicoloured.

775	5c. Type **159**	10	10
776	10c. "Ethiopian Life"	10	10
777	20c. Nose of Boeing 707 and control tower	40	40
778	60c. Airliner's flight deck and jet engine	1·10	1·10
779	80c. Route map	1·60	1·60

1971. Ethiopian Paintings. Multicoloured.

780	5c. Type **160**	10	10
781	10c. "King David" (15th-cent manuscript)	10	10
782	25c. "St. George" (17th-cent canvas)	45	45
783	50c. "King Kaleb" (18th-cent triptych, Lalibela)	95	95
784	60c. "Yared singing to King Kaleb" (18th-cent mural, Axum)	1·60	1·60

161 Black and White Heads

1971. Racial Equality Year.

785 **161**	10c. black, red & orange	15	10
786 –	60c. multicoloured	75	75
787 –	80c. multicoloured	1·25	1·25

DESIGN: 60c. Black and white hands holding Globe; 80c. Heads of four races.

162 Emperor Menelik II and Proclamation

1971. 75th Anniv of Victory of Adwa. Mult.

788	10c. Type **162**	15	10
789	30c. Ethiopian army on the march	55	55
790	50c. Battle of Adwa	85	85
791	60c. Ethiopian soldiers	90	1·00

163 Emperor Menelik II, Ras Makonnen and Early Telephones

1971. 75th Anniv of Ethiopian Telecommunications. Multicoloured.

792	5c. Type **163**	10	10
793	10c. Emperor Haile Selassie and radio masts	10	10
794	30c. T.V. set and Ethiopians	55	55
795	40c. Microwave equipment	65	65
796	60c. Telephone dial and part of Globe	1·00	1·00

164 Mother and Child

1971. 25th Anniv of UNICEF. Mult.

797	5c. Type **164**	10	10
798	10c. Refugee children	10	10
799	15c. Man embracing child	35	35
800	30c. Children with toys	60	60
801	50c. Students	90	90

165 Lion's Head

1971. Tourism. Embossed on gold foil.

802 **165**	$15 gold	20·00	
803 –	$15 gold	20·00	

DESIGN: No. 803, Visit of Queen of Sheba to King Solomon.

1972. 1st U.N. Security Council Meeting in Africa (1st issue). Nos. 615/8 Optd **U.N. SECURITY COUNCIL FIRST MEETING IN AFRICA 1972** in English and Amharic.

804	20c. multicoloured	25	15
805	25c. multicoloured	40	25
806	30c. multicoloured	3·25	2·00
807	35c. multicoloured	3·25	1·75

See also Nos. 832/4.

167 Reed Raft, Lake Haik

1972. Ethiopian River Craft. Multicoloured.

808	10c. Type **167**	10	10
809	20c. Canoes, Lake Abaya	45	45
810	30c. Punts, Lake Tana	75	75
811	60c. Dugout canoes, Baro River	1·75	1·75

168 Cuneiform Proclamation of Cyrus the Great

1972. 2500th Anniv of Persian Empire.

812 **168**	10c. multicoloured	20	20
813	60c. multicoloured	1·00	1·00
814	80c. multicoloured	1·50	1·50

169 "Beehive" Hut, Sidamo Province

1972. Architecture of Ethiopian Provinces.

815 **169**	5c. multicoloured	10	10
816 –	10c. black, grey & brown	10	10
817 –	20c. multicoloured	55	55
818 –	40c. multicoloured	90	90
819 –	80c. multicoloured	1·60	1·60

DESIGNS: 10c. Two-storey houses, Tigre Province; 20c. House with veranda, Eritrea Province; 40c. Town house, Addis Ababa; 80c. Thatched huts, Shoa Province.

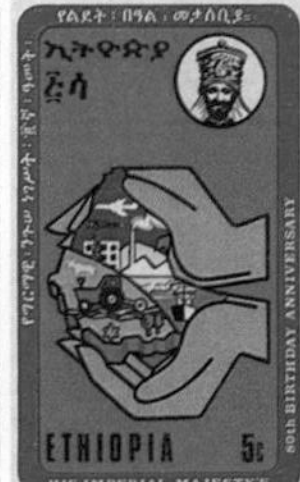

170 "Development" within Cupped Hands

171 Running

1972. Emperor Haile Selassie's 80th Birthday. Multicoloured.

820	5c. Type **170**	10	10
821	10c. Ethiopians within cupped hands	10	10
822	25c. Map, hands and O.A.U. emblem	45	45
823	50c. Handclasp and U.N. emblem	90	90
824	60c. Peace dove within hands	1·25	1·25

1972. Olympic Games, Munich. Mult.

825	10c. Type **171**	20	20
826	30c. Football	60	60
827	50c. Cycling	95	95
828	60c. Boxing	1·40	1·40

172 Cross and Open Bible

1972. World Assembly of United Bible Societies, Addis Ababa. Multicoloured.

829	20c. Type **172**	35	35
830	50c. First office of B.F.B.S., and new H.Q. (vert)	75	75
831	80c. Amharic Bible	1·40	1·40

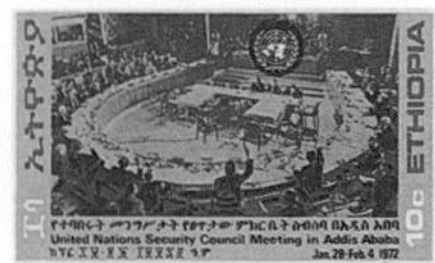
173 Council in Session

1972. 1st U.N. Security Council Meeting in Africa (2nd issue). Multicoloured.
832 10c. Type **173** 10 10
833 60c. Africa Hall, Addis Ababa . . . . 1·00 1·00
834 80c. Map of Africa and flags 1·50 1·50

174 "Polluted Waters"

1973. World Campaign against Sea Pollution. Multicoloured.
835 20c. Type **174** 25 10
836 30c. Fishing in polluted sea 40 25
837 80c. Beach pollution . . . . 1·10 1·10

175 Interpol and Ethiopian Police Badges

1973. 50th Anniv of International Criminal Police Organization (Interpol).
838 **175** 40c. black and orange . . 65 65
839 – 50c. black, brown & bl . . 85 85
840 – 60c. black and red . . . . 1·00 1·00
DESIGNS: 50c. Interpol badge and Headquarters, Paris; 60c. Interpol badge.

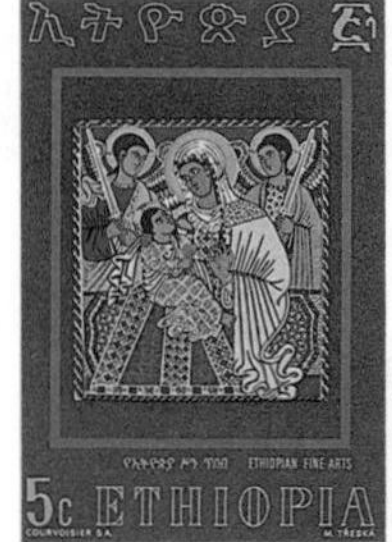
176 "The Virgin and Child" (Fere Seyoum Zana Yacob period)

1973. Ethiopian Fine Arts. Multicoloured.
841 5c. Type **176** 10 10
842 15c. "The Crucifixion" (Zara Yacob period) 15 15
843 30c. "St. Mary" (Entoto Mariam church painting) 65 65
844 40c. "Saint" mosaic (Addis Ababa Art School) 75 75
845 80c. Sculptured relief (Addis Ababa Art School) . . . . 1·60 1·60

177 African Colonial Maps, 1963 and 1973
178 Ethiopian Scout Flags

1973. 10th Anniv of Organization of African Unity. Multicoloured.
846 5c. Type **177** 15 15
847 10c. Map, Headquarters and flags 10 10
848 20c. Map and emblems . . . 40 40
849 40c. Map and "population" ranks 85 85
850 80c. Map on globe, O.A.U. and U.N. emblems . . . . 1·60 1·60

1973. 40th Anniv of Scouting in Ethiopia. Mult.
851 5c. Type **178** 10 10
852 15c. "Scout" sign on highway 15 15
853 30c. Guide teaching old man to read 65 65
854 40c. "First Aid" 90 90
855 60c. Ethiopian scout . . . . 1·90 1·90

179 W.M.O. Emblem
180 Old Wall, Harar

1973. Cent of World Meteorological Organization.
856 **179** 40c. black, blue & lt blue 75 75
857 – 50c. black and blue . . . 95 95
858 – 60c. multicoloured . . . . 1·10 1·10
DESIGNS: 50c. Wind gauge and emblem; 60c. Weather satellite.

1973. Inauguration of Prince Makonnen Memorial Hospital. Multicoloured.
859 5c. Type **180** 10 10
860 10c. Prince Makonnen, equipment and patients . . . 10 10
861 20c. Operating theatre . . . 40 40
862 40c. Scouts giving first-aid . . 70 70
863 80c. Prince Makonnen . . . 1·40 1·40

181 Haile Selassie I
182 Flame Emblem

1973.
864 **181** 5c. multicoloured 10 10
865 10c. multicoloured 10 10
866 15c. multicoloured 10 10
867 20c. multicoloured 15 10
868 25c. multicoloured 20 10
869 30c. multicoloured 25 15
870 35c. multicoloured 30 15
871 40c. multicoloured 35 15
872 45c. multicoloured 35 20
873 50c. multicoloured 40 20
874 55c. multicoloured 50 35
875 60c. multicoloured 65 45
876 70c. multicoloured 70 45
877 90c. multicoloured . . . . 1·10 60
878 $1 multicoloured . . . . 1·40 1·00
879 $2 multicoloured . . . . 3·25 1·90
880 $3 multicoloured . . . . 4·75 2·40
881 $5 multicoloured . . . . 8·00 4·25

1973. 25th Anniv of Declaration of Human Rights.
882 **182** 40c. gold, green & yell . . 65 65
883 50c. gold, grn & emerald 85 85
884 60c. gold, grn & orge . . 1·00 1·00

183 Wicker Furniture
184 Cow, Calf and Syringe

1974. Ethiopian Wickerwork. Various Wicker handicrafts.
885 **183** 5c. multicoloured 10 10
886 – 10c. multicoloured 10 10
887 – 30c. multicoloured 45 45
888 – 50c. multicoloured 80 80
889 – 60c. multicoloured . . . . 1·00 1·00

1974. Campaign Against Rinderpest. Mult.
890 5c. Type **184** 10 10
891 15c. Inoculation 10 10
892 20c. Bullock and syringe . . 40 40
893 50c. Laboratory technician 95 95
894 60c. Symbolic map . . . . . 1·40 1·40

185 Umbrella Manufacture

1974. 20th Anniv of Haile Selassie I Foundation. Multicoloured.
895 10c. Type **185** 10 10
896 30c. Weaving 50 50
897 50c. Children with books and toys 95 95
898 60c. Foundation building . . 1·10 1·10

186 Bitwoded Robe

1974. Traditional Ceremonial Robes. Mult.
899 15c. Type **186** 10 10
900 25c. Wagseyoum 25 20
901 35c. Ras 35 35
902 40c. Leol Ras 45 45
903 60c. Negusenegest . . . . . 1·00 1·00

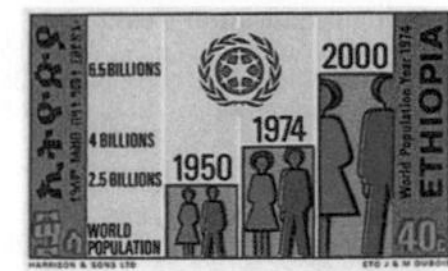
187 "Population Growth"

1974. World Population Year. Multicoloured.
904 40c. Type **187** 35 35
905 50c. Diagram with large family 45 45
906 60c. "Rising Population" . . 1·00 1·00

188 U.P.U. and Ethiopian P.T.T. Emblems

1974. Centenary of Universal Postal Union. Multicoloured.
907 15c. Type **188** 10 10
908 50c. Emblem and letters . . . 75 75
909 60c. U.P.U. emblem 90 90
910 70c. U.P.U. emblem and H.Q., Berne . . . . 1·00 1·00

189 Landscape
190 "Nymphalidae precis clelia CR"

1974. Meskel Festival.
911 **189** 5c. multicoloured 10 10
912 – 10c. multicoloured 10 10
913 – 20c. multicoloured 20 20
914 – 80c. multicoloured . . . . 1·10 1·10
DESIGNS: Nos. 912/4, Various festive scenes similar to Type **189**.

1975. Butterflies (2nd series). Multicoloured.
915 10c. Type **190** 15 15
916 25c. "Nymphalidae charaxes achaemenes F." 30 30
917 45c. "Papilionidae P. dardanus" 80 80
918 50c. "Nymphalidae charaxes druceanus B." . . . . . . 1·10 1·10
919 60c. "Papilionidae P. demodocus" . . . . 1·25 1·25

191 "The Magi"
192 Warthog

1975. Religious Paintings in Ethiopian Churches. Multicoloured.
920 5c. Type **191** 10 10
921 10c. "The Entombment" . . 10 10
922 15c. "Christ with the Apostles" 10 10
923 30c. "The Miracle of the Blind" 25 20
924 40c. "The Crucifixion" . . . 55 55
925 80c. "Christ in Majesty" . . 1·10 1·10

1975. Animals. Multicoloured.
926 5c. Type **192** 10 10
927 10c. Aardvark 10 10
928 20c. Simien jackal 20 15
929 40c. Gelada 85 85
930 80c. African civet . . . . . 1·60 1·60

193 Dove crossing Globe
194 Reception Desk

1975. International Women's Year. Mult.
931 40c. Type **193** 50 50
932 50c. I.W.Y. emblem and symbols 65 65
933 90c. "Equality" . . . . . . 1·10 1·10

1975. Opening of National Postal Museum.
934 **194** 10c. multicoloured 10 10
935 – 30c. multicoloured 25 15
936 – 60c. multicoloured 85 85
937 – 70c. multicoloured . . . . 1·00 1·00
DESIGNS: 30c. to 70c. Views of museum display area.

195 Map Emblem
196 U.N. Emblem

1975. 1st Anniv of Socialist Government.
938 **195** 5c. multicoloured 10 10
939 10c. multicoloured 10 10
940 25c. multicoloured 15 15
941 50c. multicoloured 65 65
942 90c. multicoloured . . . . 1·10 1·10

1975. 30th Anniv of United Nations.
943 **196** 40c. multicoloured 55 55
944 50c. multicoloured 65 65
945 90c. multicoloured . . . . 1·10 1·10

197 Illubabor
198 "Delphinium wellbyi"

1975. Regional Hairstyles (1st series). Mult.
946 5. c. Type **197** 10 10
947 15c. Arussi 10 10
948 20c. Eritrea 20 15
949 30c. Bale 25 20
950 35c. Kaffa 45 45
951 50c. Begemder 55 65
952 60c. Shoa 85 85
See also Nos. 1027/33.

1975. Ethiopian Flowers. Multicoloured.
953 5c. Type **198** 10 10
954 10c. "Plectocephalus varians" 10 10
955 20c. "Brachystelma asmarensis" (horiz) 35 35
956 40c. "Ceropegia inflata" . . . 80 80
957 80c. "Erythrina brucei" . . . 1·25 1·25

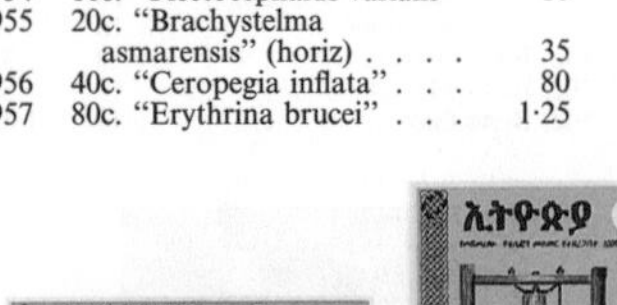

199 Goalkeeper diving
200 Early and Modern Telephones

1976. 10th African Football "Cup of Nations" Championship. Multicoloured.
958 5c. Type **199** 10 10
959 10c. Footballers in tackle . . 10 10
960 25c. Player shooting at goal 15 15

961 50c. Defender clearing ball 85 85
962 90c. Ball and Ethiopian flag 1·40 1·40

1976. Telephone Centenary. Multicoloured.
963 30c. Type **200** 25 15
964 60c. A. Graham Bell 90 90
965 90c. Aerial complex 1·10 1·10

201 Amulets **202** Boxing

1976. Ethiopian Jewellery.
966 **201** 5c. multicoloured 10 10
967 – 10c. multicoloured 10 10
968 – 20c. multicoloured 35 35
969 – 40c. multicoloured 65 65
970 – 80c. multicoloured 1·10 1·10
Nos. 967/70 are similar to Type **201** showing models with jewellery.

1976. Olympic Games, Montreal. Mult.
971 10c. Type **202** 10 10
972 80c. Shot-putting 1·10 1·10
973 90c. Cycling 1·10 1·10

203 Campaign Emblem **204** Map Emblem

1976. "Development Through Co-operation" Campaign.
974 **203** 5c. multicoloured 10 10
975 10c. multicoloured 10 10
976 25c. multicoloured 15 15
977 50c. multicoloured 65 65
978 90c. multicoloured 1·00 1·00

1976. 2nd Anniv of Republic.
979 **204** 5c. multicoloured 10 10
980 10c. multicoloured 10 10
981 25c. multicoloured 30 30
982 50c. multicoloured 65 65
983 90c. multicoloured 1·00 1·00

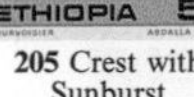

205 Crest with Sunburst **206** Donkey Boy and Aircraft

1976.
984 **205** 5c. gold, green & black 10 10
985 10c. gold, orange & blk 10 10
986 15c. gold, blue & black 10 10
987 20c. gold, lilac & black 15 10
988 25c. gold, green & blk 15 10
989 30c. gold, red & black 20 15
990 35c. gold, yellow & blk 25 15
991 40c. gold, green & blk 55 20
992 45c. gold, green & blk 65 50
993 50c. gold, mauve & blk 75 55
994 55c. gold, blue & black 85 65
995 60c. gold, brown & blk 90 65
996 70c. gold, pink & black 1·00 75
997 90c. gold, blue & black 1·10 85
998 $1 gold, green & black 1·40 1·00
999 $2 gold, grey & black 2·50 2·00
1000 $3 gold, purple & black 3·75 2·75
1001 $5 gold, blue & black 6·75 4·75
See also Nos. 1263a/c.

1976. 30th Anniv of Ethiopian Airlines. Multicoloured.
1002 5c. Type **206** 10 10
1003 10c. Crescent on globe 15 15
1004 25c. "Star" of crew and passengers 35 35
1005 50c. Propeller and jet engines 65 65
1006 90c. Aircraft converging on map 1·10 1·10

207 Tortoise **208** Cessna 170A dropping Supplies

1976. Reptiles. Multicoloured.
1007 10c. Type **207** 10 10
1008 20c. Chameleon 15 10
1009 30c. Python 25 45
1010 40c. Monitor (lizard) 75 75
1011 80c. Crocodile 1·25 1·25

1976. Relief and Rehabilitation. Mult.
1012 5c. Type **208** 10 10
1013 10c. Carved hand with hammer 10 10
1014 45c. Child supported by banknote 65 65
1015 60c. Map of Ogaden region and desert tracks 85 85
1016 80c. Waif within broken eggshell, camera & film 1·10 1·10

209 Dengour Ruins and Elephant Figurine **210** Route Map

1977. Ethiopian Archaeology. Multicoloured.
1017 5c. Type **209** 10 10
1018 10c. Yeha temple and bronze ibex 10 10
1019 25c. Sourre Kabanawa dolmen and ancient pot 20 10
1020 50c. Melka Kontoure site and stone axe 75 75
1021 80c. Omo Valley, skull and jawbone 1·10 1·10

1977. Inauguration of Trans-East African Highway.
1022 **210** 10c. multicoloured 10 10
1023 20c. multicoloured 20 15
1024 40c. multicoloured 50 50
1025 50c. multicoloured 65 65
1026 60c. multicoloured 85 85

1977. Regional Hairstyles (2nd series). As T **197**. Multicoloured.
1027 5c. Wollega 10 10
1028 10c. Godjam 10 10
1029 15c. Tigre 10 10
1030 20c. Harrar 40 40
1031 25c. Gemu Gofa 40 40
1032 40c. Sidamo 80 80
1033 50c. Wollo 90 90

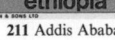

211 Addis Ababa **212** "Terebratula abyssinica"

1977. Ethiopian Towns. Multicoloured.
1034 5c. Type **211** 10 10
1035 10c. Asmara 10 10
1036 25c. Harrar 20 15
1037 50c. Jimma 75 75
1038 90c. Dessie 1·25 1·25

1977. Fossil Shells. Multicoloured.
1039 5c. Type **212** 10 10
1040 10c. "Terebratula subalata" 10 10
1041 25c. "Cuculloea lefeburiaua" 40 40
1042 50c. "Ostrea (gryphea) plicatissima" 75 75
1043 90c. "Trigonia cousobrina" 1·40 1·40

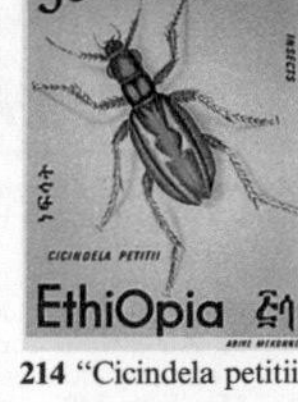

213 Shattered Imperial Crown **214** "Cicindela petitii"

1977. 3rd Anniv of Republic. Mult.
1044 5c. Type **213** 10 10
1045 10c. Emblem of revolutionary regime 10 10
1046 25c. Warriors with hammer and sickle 20 15
1047 60c. Soldiers and map 50 40
1048 80c. Crest of revolutionary regime 1·10 1·10

1977. Insects. Multicoloured.
1049 5c. Type **214** 10 10
1050 10c. "Heliocopris dillonii" 10 10
1051 25c. "Poekilocerus vignaudii" 30 20
1052 50c. "Pepsis heros" 80 80
1053 90c. "Pepsis dedjaz" 1·40 1·40

215 Lenin, Globe and Map of Ethiopia **216** Moon Wrasse

1977. 60th Anniv of Russian Revolution.
1054 **215** 5c. multicoloured 10 10
1055 10c. multicoloured 10 10
1056 25c. multicoloured 20 15
1057 50c. multicoloured 65 65
1058 90c. multicoloured 1·10 1·10

1978. Fishes. Multicoloured.
1059 5c. Type **216** 10 10
1060 10c. Yellow boxfish 10 10
1061 25c. Summan grouper 50 50
1062 50c. Sea perch 1·00 1·00
1063 90c. Northern pufferfish 1·90 1·90

217 Cattle **218** Emblem and Weapons

1978. Domestic Animals. Multicoloured.
1064 5c. Type **217** 10 10
1065 10c. Donkeys 10 10
1066 25c. Sheep 20 15
1067 50c. Camels 85 85
1068 90c. Horses 1·40 1·40

1978. "Call of the Motherland". Mult.
1069 5c. Type **218** 10 10
1070 10c. Armed workers 10 10
1071 25c. Map of Africa 20 15
1072 60c. Soldiers 50 65
1073 80c. Nurse and blood donor 70 90

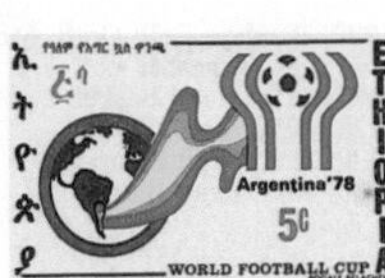

219 Ibex **220** Globe and Emblem

1978. Ancient Bronzes. Multicoloured.
1074 5c. Type **219** 10 10
1075 10c. Lion (horiz) 10 10
1076 25c. Lamp 40 40
1077 50c. Goat (horiz) 90 90
1078 90c. Axe, chisel and sickle 1·50 1·50

1978. World Cup Football Championship, Argentina. Multicoloured.
1079 5c. Type **220** 10 10
1080 20c. Player kicking ball 20 15
1081 30c. Ball in net 25 20
1082 55c. F.I.F.A. emblem and ball 80 80
1083 70c. World Cup emblem and pitch (vert) 90 90

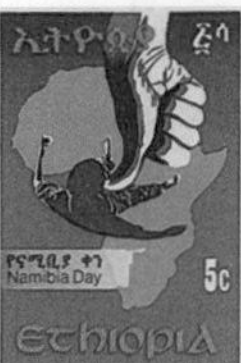

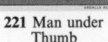

221 Man under Thumb **222** Armed Forces

1978. Namibia Day. Multicoloured.
1084 5c. Type **221** 10 10
1085 10c. Man with pistol 10 10
1086 25c. Soldier 20 20
1087 60c. Bound figure 65 65
1088 80c. Head of African 90 90

1978. 4th Anniv of Revolution. Mult.
1089 80c. Type **222** 90 90
1090 1b. Revolutionaries 1·10 1·10

223 Open Globe filled with Tools

1978. U.N. Conference on Technical Co-operation among Developing Countries. Multicoloured.
1091 10c. Type **223** 10 10
1092 15c. Symbols 10 10
1093 25c. World map and gear wheels 20 20
1094 60c. Hands passing spanner over globe 65 65
1095 70c. Geese and tortoise over world map 85 85

224 Human Rights Emblem **225** Manacled Hands and Anti-Apartheid Emblem

1978. 30th Anniv of Human Rights Declaration.
1096 **224** 5c. multicoloured 10 10
1097 15c. multicoloured 10 10
1098 25c. multicoloured 20 20
1099 35c. multicoloured 40 40
1100 1b. multicoloured 1·25 1·25

1978. International Anti-Apartheid Year.
1101 **225** 5c. multicoloured 10 10
1102 20c. multicoloured 15 10
1103 30c. multicoloured 20 20
1104 55c. multicoloured 65 65
1105 70c. multicoloured 75 75

226 Stone Monument at Osole

1979. Ancient Carved Stones from Soddo. Mult.
1106 5c. Type **226** 10 10
1107 10c. Garashino 10 10
1108 25c. Wado 20 20
1109 60c. Ambeut 90 90
1110 80c. Detail of decoration, Tiya 1·00 1·00

227 Cotton Plant **228** Grar

1979. Cotton Industry. Multicoloured.
1111 5c. Type **227** 10 10
1112 10c. Women spinning cotton 10 10
1113 20c. Reeling cotton onto poles 45 45
1114 65c. Weaving 90 90
1115 80c. Shemma work 1·10 1·10

1979. Trees. Multicoloured.
1116 5c. Type **228** 10 10
1117 10c. Weira 10 10
1118 25c. Tidh 20 20
1119 50c. Shola 75 75
1120 90c. Zigba 1·10 1·10

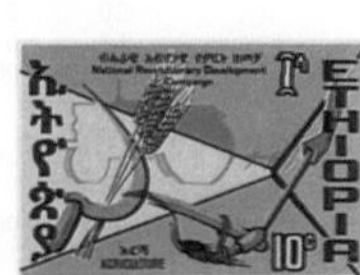
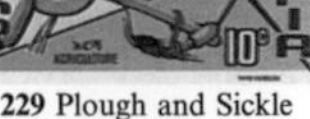
229 Plough and Sickle (agriculture)

230 Family holding Hands

1979. National Revolutionary Development Campaign. Multicoloured.
1121 10c. Type **229** 10 10
1122 15c. Industry 10 10
1123 25c. Transport and communications . . . . . 2·25 75
1124 60c. Education and Health 85 85
1125 70c. Commerce 90 90

1979. International Year of the Child. Mult.
1126 10c. I.Y.C. Emblem 10 10
1127 15c. Type **230** 10 10
1128 25c. Helping a crippled child 40 40
1129 60c. Circle of children . . . 90 90
1130 70c. Black and white children embracing . . . 1·00 1·00

231 Revolutionaries and Emblem

1979. 5th Anniv of Revolution. Mult.
1131 10c. Type **231** 10 10
1132 15c. Soldiers and agriculture 10 10
1133 25c. Emblem of revolution 20 20
1134 60c. Students with torch . . 65 65
1135 70c. Citizens and emblems 75 75

232 "Communications"

233 Incense Container

1979. 3rd World Telecommunications Exhibition, Geneva.
1136 **232** 5c. blue, mauve & blk 10 10
1137 – 30c. multicoloured . . . 50 50
1138 – 35c. multicoloured . . . 50 50
1139 – 45c. multicoloured . . . 70 70
1140 – 65c. multicoloured . . . 90 90
DESIGN: 30c. Telephone handset; 35c. Communications satellite; 45c. Ground receiving aerial; 65c. Television camera.

1979. Wickerwork. Multicoloured.
1141 5c. Type **233** 10 10
1142 10c. Flower vase 10 10
1143 25c. Earthenware cover . . 40 40
1144 60c. Milk container 90 90
1145 80c. Storage container . . . 1·10 1·10

234 Dish

235 Lappet-faced Vulture

1980. Woodwork. Multicoloured.
1146 5c. Type **234** 10 10
1147 30c. Table and chair 50 50
1148 35c. Pestles and mortars . . 50 50
1149 45c. Stools 70 70
1150 65c. Pots 90 90

1980. Birds of Prey. Multicoloured.
1151 10c. Type **235** 70 70
1152 15c. Long-crested eagle . . 80 80
1153 25c. Secretary bird . . . . 1·00 1·00
1154 60c. Abyssinian long-eared owl . . . . 2·75 2·75
1155 70c. Lanner falcon . . . . 3·25 3·25

236 W.H.D. Emblem and Cigarette

237 Lenin in Hiding at Rasliv

1980. Anti-smoking Campaign. Multicoloured.
1156 20c. Skull superimposed on cigarette packet 40 40
1157 60c. Type **236** 85 85
1158 1b. Pipe, cigarette and infected lungs . . . . . . 1·25 1·25

1980. 110th Birth Anniv of Lenin. Mult.
1159 5c. Lenin's House, Pskov . . 10 10
1160 15c. Type **237** 10 10
1161 20c. Lenin as student . . . 20 15
1162 40c. Lenin returns to Russia 50 50
1163 1b. Lenin speaking on the Goerlo plan . . . . . . 1·10 1·10

238 Grevy's Zebra

239 Running

1980. Endangered Animals. Multicoloured.
1164 10c. Type **238** 10 10
1165 15c. Dibatag 15 10
1166 25c. Hunting dog 40 40
1167 60c. Hartebeest . . . . . . 1·00 1·00
1168 70c. Cheetahs . . . . 1·10 1·10

1980. Olympic Games, Moscow. Multicoloured.
1169 30c. Type **239** 45 45
1170 70c. Cycling 95 95
1171 80c. Boxing . . . . 1·10 1·10

240 Man cutting Blindfold

241 Meal Basket

1980. 6th Anniv of Revolution. Mult.
1172 30c. Type **240** 35 35
1173 40c. Crowd 50 50
1174 50c. Woman cutting chain 65 65
1175 70c. Crowd and flags . . . 1·00 1·00

1980. Bamboo Folk Craft. Multicoloured.
1176 5c. Type **241** 10 10
1177 15c. Hand basket 10 10
1178 25c. Stool 40 40
1179 35c. Fruit compote 65 65
1180 1b. Lamp shade . . . . . . 1·40 1·40

242 Mekotkocha (weeding tool)

1980. Traditional Cultivating and Harvesting Tools. Multicoloured.
1181 10c. Type **242** 10 10
1182 15c. Layda 10 10
1183 40c. Mensh 50 50
1184 45c. Medekdekia 60 60
1185 70c. Mofer and kenber . . . 1·00 1·00

243 Baro River

1981. Baro River Bridge. Multicoloured.
1186 15c. Type **243** 20 10
1187 65c. Bridge under construction 90 90
1188 1b. Bridge . . . . 1·40 1·40

244 Wawel Castle, Poland

1981. World Heritage (1st series). Mult.
1189 5c. Type **244** 10 10
1190 15c. Quito Cathedral, Ecuador 10 10
1191 20c. Island of Goree, Senegal 10 10
1192 30c. Messa Verde, U.S.A. 35 35
1193 80c. Simien National Park, Ethiopia . . . . 1·00 1·00
1194 1b. L'Anse aux Meadows, Canada . . . . 1·10 1·10
See also Nos. 1200/1205.

245 Drinking Vessel

1981. Ancient Pottery. Multicoloured.
1195 20c. Type **245** 15 10
1196 25c. Spice container 15 10
1197 35c. Jug 45 45
1198 40c. Cooking apparatus . . 55 55
1199 60c. Animal figurine 90 90

246 Biet Medhani Alem Church, Ethiopia

1981. World Heritage (2nd series). Mult.
1200 10c. Type **246** 10 10
1201 15c. Nehanni National Park, Canada 10 10
1202 20c. Lower Falls of the Yellowstone River, U.S.A. 15 10
1203 30c. Aachen Cathedral, West Germany 45 45
1204 80c. Kicker Rock, San Cristobel Island, Ecuador 1·00 1·00
1205 1b. Holy Cross Chapel, Poland (vert) . . . . . . 1·40 1·40

247 Disabled Child learning to write

248 Children at Work and Play

1981. International Year of Disabled Persons. Multicoloured.
1206 5c. Disabled, artificial limbs and crutch 10 10
1207 15c. Type **247** 10 10
1208 20c. Artificial limbs 15 15
1209 40c. Disabled hands learning to knit 50 50
1210 1b. Disabled people learning to weave . . . . 1·25 1·25

1981. 7th Anniv of Revolution. Mult.
1211 20c. Type **248** 15 15
1212 60c. Disabled revolutionaries 75 75
1213 1b. Printing and distributing "Serto Ader Gazette" . . 1·10 1·10

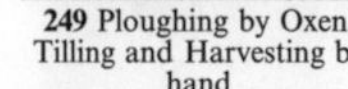
249 Ploughing by Oxen, Tilling and Harvesting by hand

250 Animal-shaped Pitcher

1981. World Food Day. Multicoloured.
1214 5c. Air-drop of food and starving Ethiopians . . . 10 10
1215 15c. Type **249** 10 10

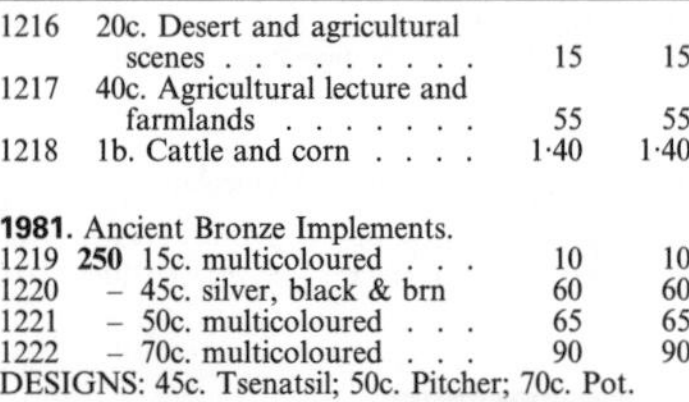
1216 20c. Desert and agricultural scenes 15 15
1217 40c. Agricultural lecture and farmlands 55 55
1218 1b. Cattle and corn . . . . 1·40 1·40

1981. Ancient Bronze Implements.
1219 **250** 15c. multicoloured . . . 10 10
1220 – 45c. silver, black & brn 60 60
1221 – 50c. multicoloured . . . 65 65
1222 – 70c. multicoloured . . . 90 90
DESIGNS: 45c. Tsenatsil; 50c. Pitcher; 70c. Pot.

251 Cup

252 Coffee Plantation

1981. Horn Work. Multicoloured.
1223 10c. Tobacco container . . 10 10
1224 15c. Type **251** 10 10
1225 40c. Tej container 50 50
1226 45c. Goblet 60 60
1227 70c. Spoon . . . . 1·00 1·00

1982. Ethiopian Coffee. Multicoloured.
1228 5c. Type **252** 10 10
1229 15c. Coffee bush 10 10
1230 25c. Mature plantation . . . 15 10
1231 35c. Picking coffee 45 45
1232 1b. Pouring and drinking coffee . . . . 1·40 1·40

253 Players and Football

1982. World Cup Football Championship, Spain. Multicoloured.
1233 5c. Type **253** 10 10
1234 15c. Player with ball 10 10
1235 20c. Goalkeeper saving ball 15 15
1236 40c. Player kicking ball . . 60 60
1237 1b. Ball, clasped hands and shirts . . . . 1·40 1·40

254 Cattle

255 Preventing Theft

1982. Centenary of Discovery of Tubercle Bacillus. Multicoloured.
1238 15c. Type **254** 10 10
1239 20c. Magnifying glass and bacillus 15 15
1240 30c. Koch with microscope 20 15
1241 35c. Dr. Robert Koch . . . 45 45
1242 80c. T.B. patient and Dr. Koch . . . . 1·10 1·10

1982. 8th Anniv of Revolution. Mult.
1243 80c. Type **255** . . . . . . 1·00 1·00
1244 1b. Voting . . . . 1·25 1·25

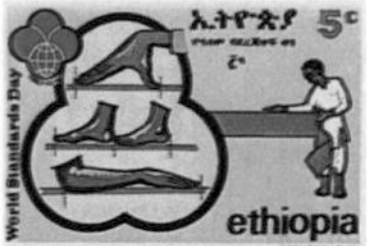
256 Primitive Measurements of Length

1982. World Standards Day. Multicoloured.
1245 5c. Type **256** 10 10
1246 15c. Primitive balance . . . 10 10
1247 20c. Metric measurement . . 15 10
1248 40c. Weights and scales . . 50 50
1249 1b. Ethiopian standards emblem . . . . 1·40 1·40

257 Wildlife Conservation

1982. 10th Anniv of U.N. Environment Programme. Multicoloured.
1250 5c. Type **257** 10 10
1251 15c. Village (Environmental health and settlement) . . 10 10

1252 20c. Forest protection 15 10
1253 40c. National literacy campaign 50 50
1254 1b. Soil and water conservation 1·40 1·40

258 Grand Gallery

1983. Sof Omar Caves. Multicoloured.
1255 5c. Type **258** 10 10
1256 10c. Chamber of Columns 10 10
1257 15c. Route through cave 10 10
1258 70c. Map of caves 90 90
1259 80c. Entrance to cave 1·00 1·00

259 "25" on Emblem **260** I.M.O. Emblem and Waves

1983. 25th Anniv of Economic Commission for Africa.
1260 **259** 80c. multicoloured 1·10 1·10
1261 1b. multicoloured 1·40 1·40

1983. 25th Anniv of International Maritime Organization. Multicoloured.
1262 85c. Type **260** 1·10 1·10
1263 1b. Lighthouse and liner 3·75 1·60

1983. As Nos. 998/1000 but with value expressed in "BIRR".
1263a **205** 1b. grn, gold & blk
1263b 2b. grey, gold & blk
1263c 3b. pur, gold & blk

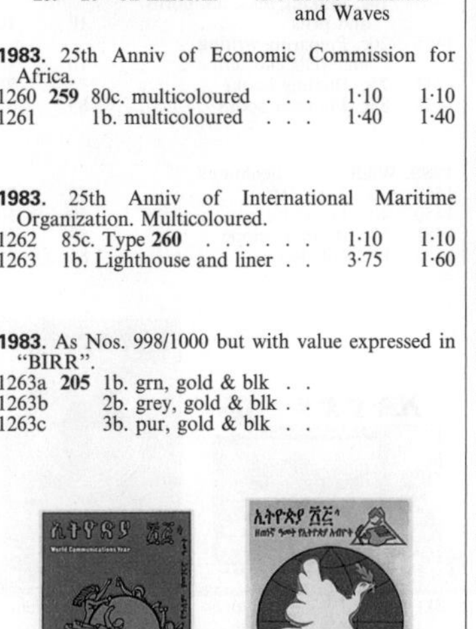

261 U.P.U. Monument, Berne **262** Peace Dove on Globe

1983. World Communications Year. Mult.
1264 25c. Type **261** 15 10
1265 55c. Antenna, satellite and drum 65 65
1266 1b. River bridge and railway tunnel 12·00 13·00

1983. 9th Anniv of Revolution. Mult.
1267 25c. Type **262** 15 10
1268 55c. Red star 75 75
1269 1b. Crest 1·10 1·10

263 Hura and Shepherd **264** "Charaxes galawadiwosi"

1983. Musical Instruments. Multicoloured.
1270 5c. Type **263** 10 10
1271 15c. Dinke and funeral 10 10
1272 20c. Meleket and announcing royal proclamation 35 35
1273 40c. Embilta and royal procession 65 65
1274 1b. Tom and dancers 1·50 1·50

1983. Butterflies. Multicoloured.
1275 10c. Type **264** 15 10
1276 15c. "Epiphora elianae" 30 10
1277 55c. "Batiama rougeoti" 1·00 1·00
1278 1b. "Achaea saboeaereginae" 1·90 1·90

265 I.A.A.Y. Emblem **266** "Protea gaguedi"

1984. International Anti-Apartheid Year.
1279 **265** 5c. multicoloured 10 10
1280 15c. multicoloured 10 10
1281 20c. multicoloured 15 10
1282 40c. multicoloured 55 55
1283 1b. multicoloured 1·40 1·40

1984. Flowers. Multicoloured.
1284 5c. Type **266** 10 10
1285 25c. "Sedum epidendrum" 55 55
1286 50c. "Echinops amplexicaulis" 95 95
1287 1b. "Canarina eminii" 1·90 1·90

267 Konso House **268** Torch on Map and Crowd of Workers

1984. Ethiopian House Architecture. Mult.
1288 15c. Type **267** 15 15
1289 65c. Dorze house 95 95
1290 1b. Harer houses 1·50 1·50

1984. 10th Anniv of Revolution. Mult.
1291 5c. Type **268** 10 10
1292 10c. Countrywoman and ploughing with oxen 10 10
1293 15c. Crowd with flag 15 10
1294 20c. Pres. Mengistu, flag, map and crowd 20 15
1295 25c. Soldiers ploughing with oxen 25 20
1296 40c. Workers writing 60 60
1297 45c. Pres. Mengistu addressing Party conference 65 65
1298 50c. Schoolchildren 75 75
1299 70c. Pres. Mengistu and statue 1·00 1·00
1300 1b. Pres. Mengistu addressing Organization of African Unity meeting 1·40 1·40

269 "Gugs" **270** Harwood's Francolin

1984. Traditional Games. Multicoloured.
1301 5c. Type **269** 10 10
1302 25c. Tigil (wrestling) 35 35
1303 50c. Gerna (hockey) 75 75
1304 1b. Gebeta (board game) 1·40 1·40

1985. Birds. Multicoloured.
1305 5c. Type **270** 35 35
1306 15c. Rouget's rail 50 50
1307 80c. Little bee eater 2·75 2·25
1308 85c. Red-headed weaver 3·25 3·25

271 Hippopotamuses

1985. Mammals. Multicoloured.
1309 20c. Type **271** 20 15
1310 25c. Gerenuk 20 15
1311 40c. Common duiker 65 65
1312 1b. Gunther's dik-dik 1·90 1·90

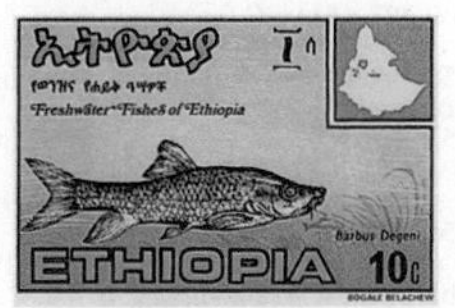

272 Degen's Barb

1985. Fishes. Multicoloured.
1313 10c. Type **272** 20 15
1314 20c. Cylinder labeo 35 15
1315 55c. Toothed tetra 1·75 1·40
1316 1b. African lungfish 3·25 2·75

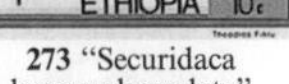

273 "Securidaca longepedunculata" **274** "50" and First Aid

1985. Medicinal Plants. Multicoloured.
1317 10c. Type **273** 10 10
1318 20c. "Plumbago zeylanicum" 15 10
1319 55c. "Brucea antidysenteric" 85 85
1320 1b. "Dorstenia barminiana" 1·60 1·60

1985. 50th Anniv of Ethiopian Red Cross. Multicoloured.
1321 35c. Type **274** 50 50
1322 55c. Community aid scenes 85 85
1323 1b. Nursing scenes 1·60 1·60

275 Kombolcha Textile Mills **276** U.N. Emblem

1985. 11th Anniv of Revolution. Mult.
1324 10c. Type **275** 10 10
1325 80c. Mugher cement factory 1·10 1·10
1326 1b. Views of famine and drought and resettlement of victims 1·60 1·60

1985. 40th Anniv of U.N.O.
1327 **276** 25c. multicoloured 15 10
1328 55c. multicoloured 85 85
1329 1b. multicoloured 1·60 1·60

277 Man with Caliper, Boy, Microscope and Crutch

1986. Anti-polio Campaign. Multicoloured.
1330 5c. Type **277** 10 10
1331 10c. Child on crutches 10 10
1332 20c. Doctor fitting child with caliper 15 10
1333 55c. Man with caliper working sewing machine 85 85
1334 1b. Doctor vaccinating baby 1·60 1·60

278 "Millettia ferruginea" **279** Ginger

1986. Trees. Multicoloured.
1335 10c. Type **278** 10 10
1336 30c. "Syzygium guineense" 45 45
1337 50c. "Cordia africana" 80 80
1338 1b. "Hagenia abyssinica" 1·60 1·60

1986. Spices and Herbs. Multicoloured.
1339 10c. Type **279** 10 10
1340 15c. Basil 10 10
1341 55c. Mustard 85 85
1342 1b. Cumin 1·60 1·60

280 One Cent Coin

1986. Coins. Multicoloured.
1343 5c. Type **280** 10 10
1344 10c. 25 cents 10 10
1345 35c. 5 cents 50 50
1346 50c. 50 cents 75 75
1347 1b. 10 cents 1·60 1·60

281 Globe, Map and Skeleton

1986. 12th Anniv of Discovery of Oldest Known Hominid Skeleton.
1348 **281** 2b. multicoloured 3·75 3·75

282 Military Training

1986. 12th Anniv of Revolution. Mult.
1349 20c. Type **282** 15 10
1350 30c. Tiglachin Monument, Addis Ababa 40 40
1351 55c. Emblem of Delachin Historical Exhibition 85 85
1352 85c. Merti food-processing plant 1·10 1·10

283 Boeing 767 **284** Emblem

1986. 40th Anniv of Ethiopian Airlines. Mult.
1353 10c. Type **283** 15 10
1354 20c. Douglas DC-3 20 10
1355 30c. Emblem on tail-fin of airplane and crew 20 40
1356 40c. Mechanic working on engine 60 60
1357 1b. Map and Boeing 727 airliner 1·60 1·60

1986. International Peace Year.
1358 **284** 10c. multicoloured 15 15
1359 80c. multicoloured 1·10 1·10
1360 1b. multicoloured 1·60 1·60

285 Mother breastfeeding Baby

1986. UNICEF. Child Survival Campaign. Multicoloured.
1361 10c. Type **285** 10 10
1362 35c. Doctor vaccinating child and vaccination chart 50 50
1363 50c. Fly on feeding bottle and oral rehydration therapy formula 75 75
1364 1b. Baby on scales and growth chart 1·60 1·60

286 Auxum, Tigray **287** "Affar"

1987. Traditional Umbrellas. Multicoloured.
1365 35c. Type **286** 50 50
1366 55c. Negele-Borena, Sidamo 85 85
1367 1b. Jimma, Kafa 1·50 1·50

1987. "Defender of his Country". Paintings by Afewerk Tekle. Multicoloured.
1368 50c. Type **287** 75 75
1369 2b. "Adwa" 2·75 2·75

288 People behind Man holding Torch

1987. "The Struggle of the African People" (stained glass windows) by Afewerk Tekle. Multicoloured.

1370	50c. Type **288**	75	75
1371	80c. Robed skeleton, dragon and men covering their faces (23 × 36 mm)	1·10	1·10
1372	1b. Robed skeleton, man killing dragon and people on map of Africa (23 × 36 mm)	1·50	1·50

289 Simien Fox

1987.

1373 **289**	5c. multicoloured	10	10
1374	10c. multicoloured	10	10
1375	15c. multicoloured	10	10
1376	20c. multicoloured	25	20
1377	25c. multicoloured	15	10
1378	45c. multicoloured	60	45
1379	55c. multicoloured	75	55

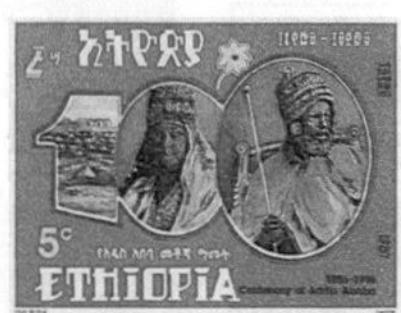

290 Finfine, Empress Taitu and Emperor Menelik II in "100"

1987. Centenary of Addis Ababa. Mult.

1380	5c. Type **290**	10	10
1381	10c. Traditional housing	10	10
1382	80c. Central Addis Ababa	1·10	1·10
1383	1b. Aerial view of city	1·50	1·50

291 Newspaper and People on Map

1987. 13th Anniv of Revolution. Mult.

1384	5c. Type **291**	10	10
1385	10c. People queuing by ballot box and open book	10	10
1386	80c. Ballot paper and map	1·10	1·10
1387	1b. Boeing 727 airliner on runway at Bahir Dar airport	1·50	1·50

292 Spoon fron Hurso, Hararge

1987. Wooden Spoons. Multicoloured.

1388	85c. Type **292**	95	95
1389	1b. Spoon from Borena, Sidamo	1·10	1·10

293 Village Programme

1988. International Year of Shelter for the Homeless (1987). Multicoloured.

1390	10c. Type **293**	10	10
1391	35c. Resettlement programme	20	15
1392	50c. Urban improvement programme	50	50
1393	1b. Co-operative and Government housing	1·00	1·00

294 Lenin and Delegates

1988. 70th Anniv of Russian Revolution.

1394 **294**	1b. multicoloured	1·10	1·10

295 Bow and Arrows **296** Anniversary Emblem

1988. Traditional Hunting Weapons. Mult.

1395	85c. Type **295**	90	90
1396	1b. Double-pronged spear	1·10	1·10

1988. 125th Anniv of Red Cross.

1397 **296**	85c. multicoloured	85	85
1398	1b. multicoloured	1·10	1·10

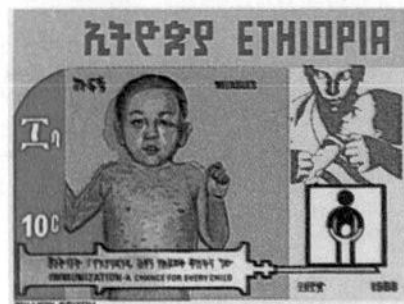

297 Measles

1988. UNICEF. Child Vaccination Campaign. Multicoloured.

1399	10c. Type **297**	10	10
1400	35c. Tetanus	20	15
1401	50c. Whooping cough	45	45
1402	1b. Diphtheria	85	85

298 "Let there be Peace in Africa and the World" (detail, Afewerk Tekle) **299** Mikoyan Gurevich MiG-23 above Simien Mountains and Farmland

1988. 25th Anniv of Organization of African Unity.

1403 **298**	2b. multicoloured	1·90	1·90

1988. "The Victory of Ethiopia" (triptych) by Afewerk Tekle. Details of the mural in Heroes' Centre, Debre Zeit. Multicoloured.

1404	10c. Type **299**	20	10
1405	20c. Coffee plantation, rural homelife and farmers going to work	15	10
1406	35c. New Ethiopia rising above flags and people	20	15
1407	55c. Mikoyan Gurevich MiG-21 over port of Assab (horiz)	40	45
1408	80c. Worker in foundry (horiz)	50	65
1409	1b. Villagers engaged in cottage industries (horiz)	85	85

300 Sidamo Bracelet

1988. Bracelets. Multicoloured.

1410	15c. Type **300**	10	10
1411	85c. Arsi bracelet	85	85
1412	1b. Hararge bracelet	1·00	1·00

301 Dollars on Map

1988. International Agricultural Development Fund. Multicoloured.

1413	15c. Type **301**	10	10
1414	85c. Agricultural activities	85	85
1415	1b. Farmer and produce	1·00	1·00

302 First Session of National Shengo (assembly)

1988. 1st Anniv of People's Democratic Republic of Ethiopia. Multicoloured.

1416	5c. Type **302**	10	10
1417	10c. President Lt.-Col. Mengistu Haile Mariam	10	10
1418	80c. State emblem and flag	85	85
1419	1b. State Council building	1·00	1·00

303 One Birr Note

1988. Banknotes. Multicoloured.

1420	5c. Type **303**	10	10
1421	10c. Five birr note	10	10
1422	20c. Ten birr note	15	10
1423	75c. 50 birr note	75	75
1424	85c. 100 birr note	85	85

1988. World Aids Day. Nos. 1376/9 optd **WORLD AIDS DAY.**

1425 **289**	20c. multicoloured	15	10
1426	25c. multicoloured	15	10
1427	45c. multicoloured	60	60
1428	55c. multicoloured	75	75

305 Emblem within "40"

1988. 40th Anniv of W.H.O.

1429 **305**	50c. multicoloured	50	50
1430	65c. multicoloured	65	65
1431	85c. multicoloured	85	85

306 Gambella Gere (leg rattle)

1989. Musical Instruments. Multicoloured.

1432	30c. Type **306**	35	35
1433	40c. Konos fanfa (pipes)	40	40
1434	50c. Konso chancha (waist rattle)	50	50
1435	85c. Gendeberet negareet (drum)	85	85

307 "Abyot" (container ship)

1989. 25th Anniv of Ethiopian Shipping Lines. Multicoloured.

1436	15c. Type **307**	80	20
1437	30c. "Wolwol" (container ship)	95	25
1438	55c. "Queen of Sheba" (freighter)	1·10	40
1439	1b. "Abbay Wonz" under construction	1·75	90

308 Yellow-faced Parrot

1989. Birds. Multicoloured.

1440	10c. Type **308**	15	15
1441	35c. White-winged chiffchat	75	75
1442	50c. Yellow-rumped seedeater	95	95
1443	1b. Dark-headed oriole	2·10	2·10

309 Making Vellum **310** Greater Kudu

1989. Ethiopian Manuscripts. Multicoloured.

1444	5c. Type **309**	10	10
1445	10c. Making inks, ink horns and pens	10	10
1446	20c. Preparing writing materials and scribe	10	10
1447	75c. Binding books	75	75
1448	85c. Finished books	85	85

1989. Wildlife. Multicoloured.

1449	30c. Type **310**	40	40
1450	40c. Lesser kudu	50	50
1451	50c. Roan antelope	50	50
1452	85c. Nile lechwe	85	85

311 Melka Wakana Hydro-electric Power Station **312** Bank Emblem

1989. 2nd Anniv of People's Democratic Republic of Ethiopia. Multicoloured.

1453	15c. Type **311**	10	10
1454	75c. Adea Berga Dairy Farm	75	75
1455	1b. Pawe Hospital	1·00	1·00

1989. 25th Anniv of African Development Bank.

1456 **312**	20c. multicoloured	15	10
1457	80c. multicoloured	85	85
1458	1b. multicoloured	1·00	1·00

313 Emblem **314** Unhappy Man with Newspaper Upside Down

1990. 10th Anniv of Pan-African Postal Union.

1459 **313**	50c. multicoloured	50	50
1460	70c. multicoloured	70	70
1461	80c. multicoloured	80	80

1990. International Literacy Year. Mult.

1462	15c. Type **314**	10	10
1463	85c. Adults learning to read	90	90
1464	1b. Happy man reading newspaper	1·00	1·00

315 Marathon Race

1990. Abebe Bikila (marathon runner). Mult.

No.	Description	Unused	Used
1465	5c. Type **315**	10	10
1466	10c. Bikila carrying national flag during Olympic opening ceremony	10	10
1467	20c. Bikila running in number 11 vest	10	10
1468	75c. Bikila running in number 69 vest	80	80
1469	85c. Bikila with medals and cups (vert)	90	90

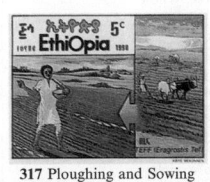

316 Revolutionary Flag

1990.

No.	Description	Unused	Used
1470 **316**	5c. multicoloured	10	10
1471	10c. multicoloured	10	10
1472	15c. multicoloured	10	10
1473	20c. multicoloured	10	10
1474	25c. multicoloured	15	10
1475	30c. multicoloured	15	10
1476	35c. multicoloured	15	15
1477	40c. multicoloured	20	15
1478	45c. multicoloured	40	40
1479	50c. multicoloured	40	40
1480	55c. multicoloured	45	45
1481	60c. multicoloured	50	50
1482	70c. multicoloured	60	60
1483	80c. multicoloured	65	65
1484	85c. multicoloured	70	70
1485	90c. multicoloured	75	75
1486	1b. multicoloured	85	85
1487	2b. multicoloured	1·60	1·60
1488	3b. multicoloured	2·50	2·50

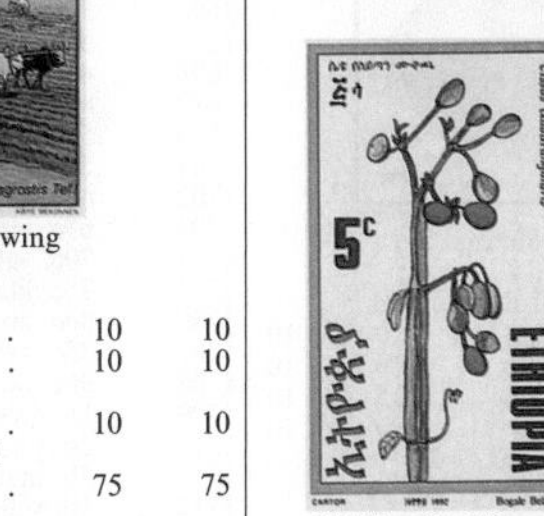

317 Ploughing and Sowing

1990. Teff. Multicoloured.

No.	Description	Unused	Used
1489	5c. Type **317**	10	10
1490	10c. Harvesting	10	10
1491	20c. Oxen threshing grain underfoot	10	10
1492	75c. Grinding teff flour and making starter batter	75	75
1493	85c. Family eating baked injera	85	85

318 Male and Female Ibexes **319** Deterioration in Victim's Health

1990. Walia Ibex. Multicoloured.

No.	Description	Unused	Used
1494	5c. Type **318**	10	10
1495	15c. Male ibex	10	10
1496	20c. Male ibex (different)	10	10
1497	1b. Male ibexes fighting (horiz)	1·00	1·00

1991. World Aids Day. Multicoloured.

No.	Description	Unused	Used
1498	15c. Type **319**	10	10
1499	85c. Aids education	80	80
1500	1b. Preventive measures and family sheltered by umbrella	95	95

320 Volcano

1991. International Decade for Natural Disaster Reduction. Multicoloured.

No.	Description	Unused	Used
1501	5c. Type **320**	10	10
1502	10c. Earthquake	10	10
1503	15c. Drought	10	10
1504	30c. Flood	15	10
1505	50c. W.H.O. hygiene instruction	30	45
1506	1b. Red Cross workers helping disaster victims	95	95

321 Constructing Cannon

1991. Emperor Theodor's Cannon "Sevastopol". Multicoloured.

No.	Description	Unused	Used
1507	15c. Type **321**	10	10
1508	85c. Completed cannon on carriage	80	80
1509	1b. Hauling cannon uphill	95	95

322 Diadem Squirrelfish **323** Balambaras

1991. Fishes. Multicoloured.

No.	Description	Unused	Used
1510	5c. Type **322**	20	20
1511	15c. Blue-cheeked butterflyfish	20	20
1512	80c. Regal angelfish	1·50	1·50
1513	1b. Grey reef shark	2·00	2·00

1992. Traditional Ceremonial Robes (military group). Multicoloured.

No.	Description	Unused	Used
1514	5c. Type **323**	10	10
1515	15c. Kegnazmatch	10	10
1516	80c. Fitawurari (Army Commander)	75	75
1517	1b. Dedjazmatch	90	90

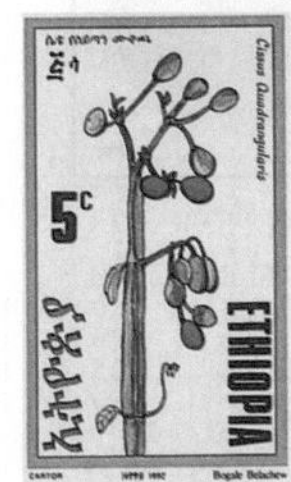

324 Devil's Mortar **326** Plate

325 Afar House

1992. Flowers. Multicoloured.

No.	Description	Unused	Used
1518	5c. Type **324**	10	10
1519	15c. "Delphinium dasycaulon"	10	10
1520	80c. Cow's salt	65	65
1521	1b. Red hot poker	85	85

1992. Ethiopian Houses. Multicoloured.

No.	Description	Unused	Used
1522	15c. Type **325**	10	10
1523	35c. Anuak house	20	15
1524	50c. Gimira house	30	20
1525	1b. Oromo house	85	85

1992. Pottery from Sixth Tomb, Yeha. Mult.

No.	Description	Unused	Used
1526	15c. Type **326**	10	10
1527	85c. Milk jar	50	35
1528	1b. Wine vessel	55	40

327 Campaign Emblem **328** Catchel (hand rattle)

1992. Pan-African Rinderpest Campaign.

No.	Description	Unused	Used
1529 **327**	20c. gold, green & black	10	10
1530	80c. multicoloured	45	30
1531	1b. multicoloured	55	40

1993. Traditional Musical Instruments. Mult.

No.	Description	Unused	Used
1532	15c. Type **328**	10	10
1533	35c. Huldudwa (wind instrument)	10	10
1534	50c. Dita (stringed instrument)	15	10
1535	1b. Atamo (drum)	30	20

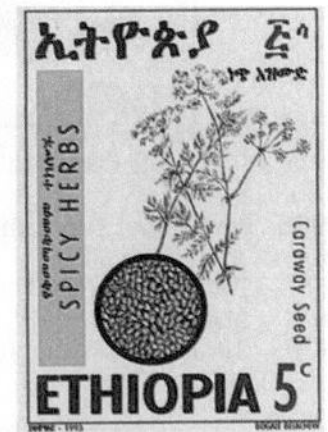

329 Banded Barbets **331** Caraway Seed

330 Honey Badger

1993. Birds. Multicoloured.

No.	Description	Unused	Used
1536	15c. Type **329**	45	45
1537	35c. Ruppell's chats	45	45
1538	50c. Abyssinian catbirds	65	65
1539	1b. White-billed starling	1·40	1·40

1993. Mammals. Multicoloured.

No.	Description	Unused	Used
1540	15c. Type **330**	10	10
1541	35c. Spotted-necked otter	10	10
1542	50c. Rock hyrax	15	10
1543	1b. White-tailed mongoose	30	20

1993. Spicy Herbs. Multicoloured.

No.	Description	Unused	Used
1544	5c. Type **331**	10	10
1545	15c. Garlic	10	10
1546	80c. Turmeric	20	15
1547	1b. Capsicum peppers	30	20

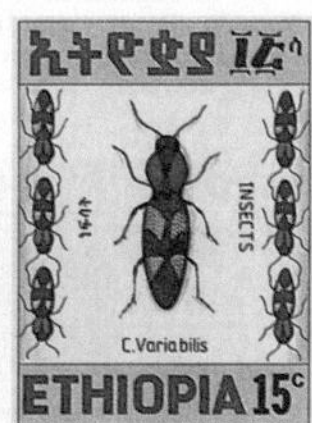

332 Southern White-banded Papilio **333** "C. variabilis"

1993. Butterflies. Multicoloured.

No.	Description	Unused	Used
1548	20c. Type **332**	10	10
1549	30c. King swallowtail	10	10
1550	50c. Small striped swallowtail	15	10
1551	1b. Veined swallowtail	30	20

1993. Beetles. Multicoloured.

No.	Description	Unused	Used
1552	15c. Type **333**	10	10
1553	35c. "Lycus trabeatus"	10	10
1554	50c. "Malachius bifasciatus"	15	10
1555	1b. "Homoeogryllus xanthographus"	30	20

334 "Euphorbia amliphylla"

1993. Trees. Multicoloured.

No.	Description	Unused	Used
1556	15c. Type **334**	10	10
1557	35c. "Erythrina brucei"	10	10
1558	50c. "Draceana steudneri"	15	10
1559	1b. "Allophylus abbyssinicus"	30	20

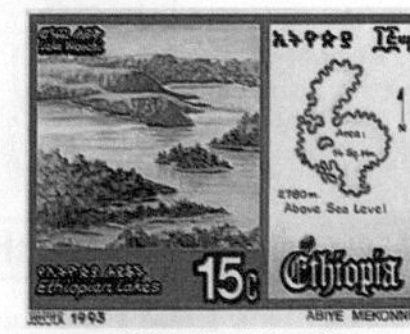

335 Lake Wonchi

1993. Lakes. Multicoloured.

No.	Description	Unused	Used
1560	15c. Type **335**	10	10
1561	35c. Lake Zuquala	10	10
1562	50c. Lake Ashengi	10	10
1563	1b. Lake Tana	25	15

336 Simien Fox

1994. Dated "1991". Mult, frame colours given.

No.	Description
1564 **336**	5c. lilac
1565	10c. brown
1566	15c. yellow
1567	20c. pink
1568	40c. pink
1569	55c. green
1570	60c. blue
1571	80c. blue
1572	85c. green
1573	1b. green

For similar stamps dated "1993" see Nos. 1596/1615.

337 Flag and Fighter **338** Emblem

1994. 3rd Anniv of Ethiopian People's Revolutionary Democratic Front Transitional Government. Multicoloured.

No.	Description	Unused	Used
1574	15c. Type **337** (control of Addis Ababa, May 1991)	10	10
1575	35c. Peaceful and Democratic Transition Conference, Addis Ababa, July 1991	10	10
1576	50c. Elections, June 1994	10	10
1577	1b. Flag and Government arms	25	15

1994. International Year of the Family.

No.	Description	Unused	Used
1578 **338**	15c. multicoloured	10	10
1579	85c. multicoloured	20	15
1580	1b. multicoloured	25	15

339 Postal Messengers

1994. Centenary of Postal Services in Ethiopia. Multicoloured.

No.	Description	Unused	Used
1581	60c. Postal workers, magnifying glass over 1st Ethiopian stamp and early postal messenger	15	10
1582	75c. Type **339**	20	15
1583	80c. Old post office and early mechanized post transport	2·00	40
1584	85c. Rural service	20	15
1585	1b. Express Mail Service	2·00	40

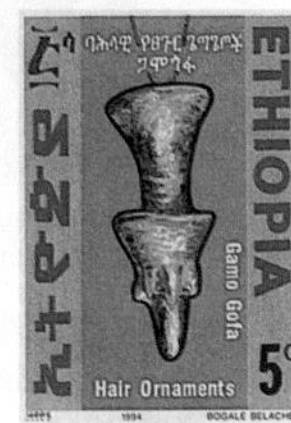

340 Plant **341** Iron Ornament, Gamo Gofa

1994. The Enset Plant. Multicoloured.

No.	Description	Unused	Used
1587	10c. Type **340**	10	10
1588	15c. Enset growing beside house	10	10
1589	25c. Gathering and preparation	10	10
1590	50c. Plantation	10	10
1591	1b. Prepared food	20	15

1994. Hair Ornaments. Multicoloured.

No.	Description	Unused	Used
1592	5c. Type **341**	10	10
1593	15c. Aluminium beads, Sidamo	10	10
1594	80c. Metal ornament, Gamo Gofa (different)	20	15
1595	1b. Silver hairpin, Wello	20	15

342 Simien Fox

1994. Dated "1993". Mult, frame colours given.

1596 **342** 5c. lilac 10 10
1597 10c. brown 10 10
1598 15c. yellow 10 10
1599 20c. pink 10 10
1600 25c. yellow 15 10
1601 30c. yellow 15 10
1602 35c. orange 20 15
1603 40c. pink 25 20
1604 45c. orange 25 20
1605 50c. mauve 30 25
1606 55c. green 30 25
1607 60c. blue 35 30
1608 65c. lilac 35 30
1609 70c. green 40 35
1610 75c. green 45 40
1611 80c. blue 45 40
1612 85c. green 50 45
1614 1b. green 55 50
1615 2b. brown . . . . 1·10 95

344 Anniversary Emblem

1994. 50th Anniv of I.C.A.O.

1620 **344** 20c. blue, yell & mve . . 10 10
1621 80c. blue and yellow . . 20 15
1622 1b. bl, yell & ultram . . 20 15

1994. 30th Anniv of African Development Bank. Nos. 1608/10 and 1612 optd with map of Africa and **30TH ANNIVERSARY OF BANQUE AFRICAINE DE DEVELOPPEMENT AFRICAN DEVELOPMENT BANK.**

1623 **342** 65c. multicoloured . . .
1624 70c. multicoloured . . .
1625 75c. multicoloured . . .
1626 95c. multicoloured . . .

346 Erbo (dish)

1995. Traditional Food Serving Utensils. Multicoloured.

1627 30c. Type **346** 10 10
1628 70c. Sedieka (round table) 15 10
1629 1b. Tirar (rectangular table) 20 15

347 Kuncho (young boys and girls)

1995. Traditional Hairstyles. Multicoloured.

1630 25c. Type **347** 10 10
1631 75c. Gamme (unmarried women) 15 10
1632 1b. Sadulla (married women until birth of first child) 20 15

348 Anniversary Emblem

1995. 50th Anniv of F.A.O.

1633 **348** 20c. multicoloured . . . 10 10
1634 80c. multicoloured . . . 15 10
1635 1b. multicoloured . . . 20 15

349 Dangora (digging tool)

1995. Traditional Agricultural Tools. Mult.

1636 15c. Type **349** 10 10
1637 35c. Gheso (hoe) 10 10
1638 50c. Akafa (hoe) 10 10
1639 1b. Ankasse (digging tool) 20 15

350 Anniversary Emblem

1995. 50th Anniv of U.N.O.

1640 **350** 20c. multicoloured . . . 10 10
1641 80c. multicoloured . . . 15 10
1642 1b. multicoloured . . . 20 10

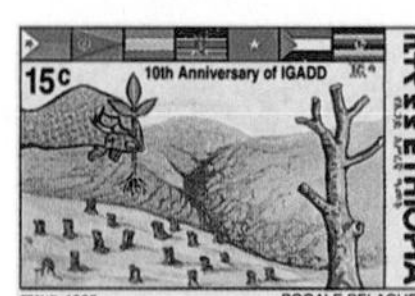
351 Reforestation

1995. 10th Anniv of Intergovernmental Authority on Drought and Development. Multicoloured.

1643 15c. Type **351** 10 10
1644 35c. People moving from drought area 10 10
1645 50c. Boy picking fruit . . . 10 10
1646 1b. Member countries' flags and map of East Africa 20 15

352 Map of Battle Site

1996. Cent of Victory at Battle of Adwa. Mult.

1647 40c. Type **352** 10 10
1648 50c. Map of Africa and emblem 10 10
1649 60c. Ship and Italian soldiers 30 10
1650 70c. Battle scenes 15 10
1651 80c. Soldiers surrendering and frontline 15 10
1652 1b. Emperor Menelik II and Empress Zauditu 20 10

353 Village

1996. 25th Anniv of United Nations Volunteers' Service. Multicoloured.

1654 20c. Type **353** 10 10
1655 30c. Planting 10 10
1656 50c. Teacher and pupils . . 10 10
1657 1b. Parents and child . . . 20 10

354 Boxing

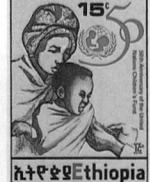

355 Child Vaccination

1996. Olympic Games, Atlanta. Unissued stamps (for 1984 Olympics) optd with Atlanta Olympics emblem as in T **354**. Multicoloured.

1658 15c. Type **354** 10 10
1659 20c. Swimming 10 10
1660 40c. Cycling 10 10
1661 85c. Running 20 10
1662 1b. Football 20 10

1996. 50th Anniv of UNICEF. Mult.

1663 10c. Anniversary emblem . . 10 10
1664 15c. Type **355** 10 10
1665 25c. Girl carrying water bottle and boy drinking from tap 10 10
1666 50c. School children writing 10 10
1667 1b. Mother breastfeeding . . 20 15

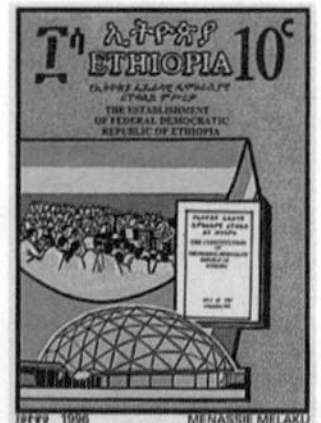
356 Discussion of Constitution

1996. Establishment of Federal Democratic Republic (August 1995). Multicoloured.

1668 10c. Type **356** 10 10
1669 20c. Ballot papers and boxes 10 10
1670 30c. Voting methods and Parliament building . . . 10 10
1671 40c. Parliament building, ballot paper and meeting of legislature 10 10
1672 1b. New national flag, President and Prime Minister, Parliament Building and legislature 20 10

357 Baskets from Jimma

1997. Basketwork (1st series). Multicoloured.

1673 5c. Type **357** 10 10
1674 15c. Containers from Wello 10 10
1675 80c. Baskets from Welega 15 10
1676 1b. Bags from Shewa . . . 20 10

See also Nos. 1677/9 and 1718/20.

1997. Basketwork (2nd series). As T **357**. Mult.

1677 35c. Baskets from Arssi (vert) 10 10
1678 65c. Baskets from Gojam (vert) 10 10
1679 1b. Baskets from Harer (vert) 20 10

358 Emblem

1997. United Nations Decade against Drug Abuse and Trafficking.

1680 **358** 20c. multicoloured . . . 10 10
1681 80c. multicoloured . . . 15 10
1682 1b. multicoloured . . . 15 10

359 Bitweded Haile Giorgis's House

1997. Historic Buildings of Addis Ababa (1st series). Multicoloured.

1683 45c. Type **359** 10 10
1684 55c. Alfred Elg's house (vert) 10 10
1685 3b. Menelik's elfign 50 35

360 Ras Biru W/Gabriel's House

1997. Historic Buildings of Addis Ababa (2nd series). Multicoloured.

1686 60c. Type **360** 10 10
1687 75c. Sheh Hojele Alhassen's house 10 10
1688 80c. Fitawrari H/Giorgis Dinegde's house 10 10
1689 85c. Etege Taitu Hotel . . . 15 10
1690 1b. Dejazmach Wube Atnafseged's house . . . 15 10

361 Golden-mantled Woodpecker ("Golden-backed Woodpecker")

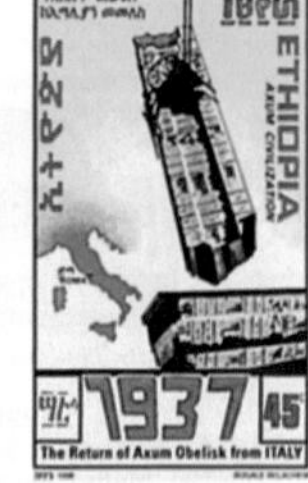
363 Map of Italy and Removal of Obelisk

362 Emblem and Bushbuck

1998. Multicoloured, colour of panel at right given.

1691 **361** 5c. blue 10 10
1692 10c. yellow 10 10
1693 15c. blue 10 10
1694 20c. orange 10 10
1695 25c. violet 10 10
1696 30c. blue 10 10
1697 35c. red 10 10
1698 40c. mauve 10 10
1699 45c. green 10 10
1700 50c. pink 10 10
1701 55c. blue 10 10
1702 60c. red 10 10
1703 65c. violet 10 10
1704 70c. yellow 10 10
1705 75c. lilac 10 10
1706 80c. green 10 10
1707 85c. grey 15 10
1708 90c. orange 15 10
1709 1b. green 15 10
1710 2b. pink 30 20
1711 3b. mauve 45 30
1712 5b. yellow 75 55
1713 10b. yellow . . . . . . 1·50 1·10

1998. 18th Anniv of Pan-African Postal Union. Multicoloured.

1714 45c. Type **362** (inscr "Deculla Bushback") . . 10 10
1715 55c. Soemmerring's gazelle 10 10
1716 1b. Defassa waterbuck . . . 15 10
1717 2b. African ("Black") buffalo 30 20

1998. Basketwork (3rd series). As T **357**. Mult.

1718 45c. Baskets from Gonder 10 10
1719 55c. Baskets from Harere 10 10
1720 3b. Baskets from Tigray . . 45 30

1998. Project to Return the Axum Obelisk from Rome to Ethiopia. Multicoloured.

1721 45c. Type **363** 10 10
1722 55c. Axum obelisk in Rome 10 10
1723 3b. Map of Ethiopia, obelisk and Axum 45 30

364 Workers carrying Rail

1998. Centenary (1997) of Addis Ababa–Djibouti Railway. Multicoloured.

1724 45c. Type **364** 10 10
1725 55c. Steam locomotive No. 404 . . . . 10 10
1726 1b. Railway station, Addis Ababa 15 10
1727 2b. Diesel locomotive . . . 30 20

365 Anniversary Emblem and Globe of People

1998. 50th Anniv of Universal Declaration of Human Rights.

1728	**365**	45c. multicoloured . . .	10	10
1729		55c. multicoloured . . .	10	10
1730		1b. multicoloured . . .	15	10
1731		2b. multicoloured . . .	30	20

366 Mother Teresa

1999. Mother Teresa (founder of Missionaries of Charity) Commemoration. Multicoloured.

1732	45c. Type **366**	10	10
1733	55c. Praying	10	10
1734	1b. Carrying child	15	10
1735	2b. Smiling	30	20

367 Head of Fish

1999. International Year of the Ocean.

1736	**367**	45c. multicoloured . . .	10	10
1737		55c. multicoloured . . .	10	10
1738		1b. multicoloured . . .	15	10
1739		2b. multicoloured . . .	30	20

368 Emblem and Globe

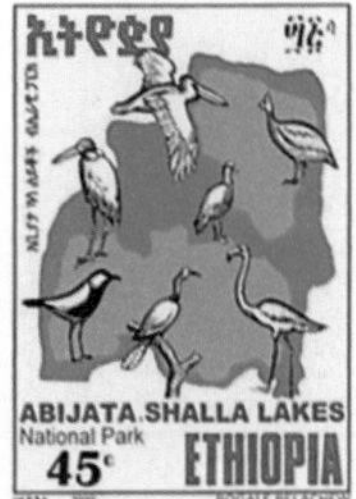

369 Abijata-Shalla Lakes National Park

1999. World Environment Day.

1740	**368**	45c. multicoloured . . .	10	10
1741		55c. multicoloured . . .	10	10
1742		1b. multicoloured . . .	15	10
1743		2b. multicoloured . . .	30	20

1999. National Parks (1st series). Multicoloured.

1744	45c. Type **369**	10	10
1745	70c. Nechisar National Park	10	10
1746	85c. Bale Mountains National Park	15	10
1747	2b. Awash National Park (horiz)	30	20

See also Nos 1752/5.

370 "125" and Emblem

371 Omo National Park

1999. 125th Anniv of Universal Postal Union.

1748	**370**	20c. multicoloured . . .	10	10
1749		80c. multicoloured . . .	10	10
1750		1b. multicoloured . . .	15	10
1751		2b. multicoloured . . .	30	20

1999. National Parks (2nd series). Multicoloured.

1752	50c. Type **371**	15	10
1753	70c. Mago National Park	15	10
1754	80c. Yangudi-Rassa National Park	20	15
1755	2b. Gambella National Park (horiz)	25	15

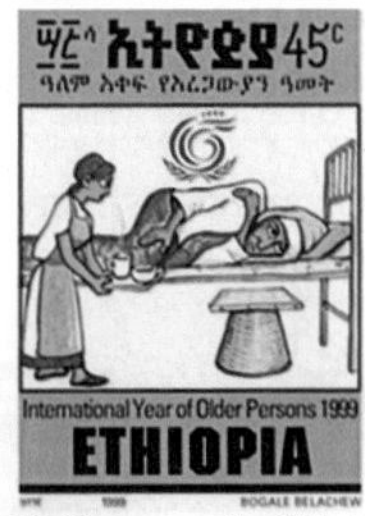

372 Woman nursing Elderly Man

1999. International Year of the Elderly. Mult.

1756	45c. Type **372**	15	10
1757	70c. Elderly couple gardening	15	10
1758	85c. Elderly man with three youths	20	15
1759	2b. Elderly man with two youths	25	15

373 Aleksandr Pushkin

2000. Birth Bicentenary of Aleksandr Pushkin (Russian writer). Multicoloured.

1760	45c. Type **373**	10	10
1761	70c. With folded arms . . .	10	10
1762	85c. Wearing hat	10	10
1763	2b. Facing right	25	15

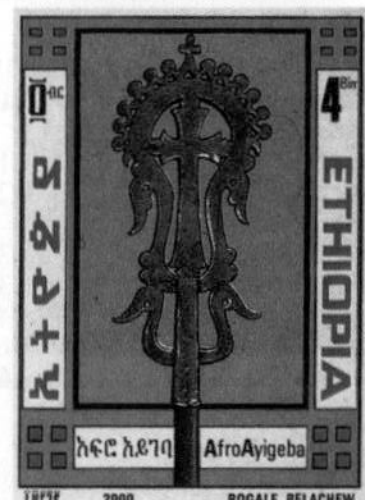

374 Afro Ayigeba

2000. The Cross of Lalibela (Afro Ayigeba).

1764	**374**	4b. multicoloured . . .	50	30

376 Meeting

2000. "Operation Sunset". Multicoloured.

1789	45c. Type **376**	10	10
1790	55c. Soldiers	10	10
1791	1b. Families returning home	15	10
1792	2b. Farmer ploughing and villagers	25	15

377 "50" enclosing Emblem

2000. 50th Anniv of World Meteorological Organization.

1793	**377**	40c. multicoloured . . .	10	10
1794		75c. multicoloured . . .	10	10
1795		85c. multicoloured . . .	10	10
1796		2b. multicoloured . . .	25	15

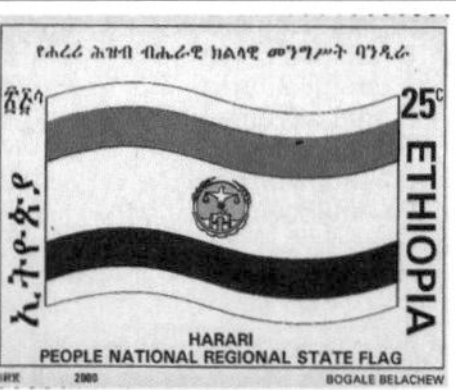

378 Harari

2000. Flags of Ethiopia. Multicoloured.

1797	25c. Type **378**	10	10
1798	30c. Oromia	10	10
1799	50c. Amhara	10	10
1800	60c. Tigrai	10	10
1801	70c. Benishangul Gumuz . .	10	10
1802	80c. Somale	10	10
1803	90c. Southern Nation Nationalities	10	10
1804	95c. Gambella	10	10
1805	1b. Afar	15	10
1806	2b. Federal Democratic Republic of Ethiopia . .	25	15

379 Haile Gebreselassie

2000. Haile Gebreselassie (athlete and Olympic Gold Medal winner). Designs showing Haile Gebreselassie running. Multicoloured.

1807	50c. Type **379**	10	10
1808	60c. With left arm raised . .	10	10
1809	90c. With right arm raised	10	10
1810	2b. Winning pose and flag	25	15

380 Anniversary Emblem

2000. 50th Anniv of Addis Ababa University.

1811	**380**	4b. multicoloured . . .	50	30

381 Anniversary Emblem and "We thank you for your support"

2000. 50th Anniv of United Nations High Commissioner for Refugees.

1812	**381**	40c. chestnut and gold	10	10
1813		75c. emerald and gold	10	10
1814		85c. new blue and gold	10	10
1815		2b. gold and black . . .	25	15

Nos. 1813/15 were printed without the inscription "We thank you for your support".

382 Grazing Zebra

2001. Endangered Species. Grevy's Zebra. Multicoloured.

1816	45c. Type **382**	10	10
1817	55c. Galloping	10	10
1818	1b. Lying down	10	10
1819	3b. Head	10	10

383 Sharp-toothed Catfish (*Clarius gariepinus)*

2001. Freshwater Fish. Multicoloured.

1820	45c. Type **383**	10	10
1821	55c. Nile mouthbrooder (inscr "Tilapia") (*Oreochromis niloticus*) . .	10	10
1822	3b. Nile perch (*Lates niloticus*)	35	25

384 Rider and Cart

2001. Traditional Transport. Multicoloured.

1823	40c. Type **384**	10	10
1824	60c. Camels	10	10
1825	1b. Rider and laden mule	15	10
1826	2b. Mules carrying hay . .	25	15

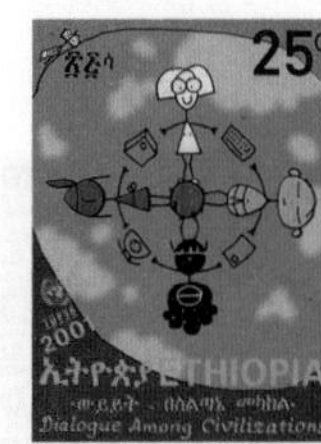

385 Children encircling Globe

2001. United Nations Year of Dialogue Among Civilizations.

1827	**385**	25c. multicoloured . . .	10	10
1828		75c. multicoloured . . .	10	10
1829		1b. multicoloured . . .	15	10
1830		2b. multicoloured . . .	25	15

386 Inscr "White-tailed Swallow"

2001. Birds. Multicoloured.

1831	50c. Type **386**	10	10
1832	60c. Inscr "Spot-breasted plover"	10	10
1833	90c. Inscr "Abyssinian long claw"	10	10
1834	2b. Inscr "Prince Ruspoli's Turaco"	25	15

387 Beehives

2002. Traditional Beehives (1st issue). Multicoloured.

1835	40c. Type **387**	10	10
1836	70c. Straw covered hives . .	10	10
1837	90c. Barrel-shaped hive . .	10	10
1838	2b. Conical hive in tree . .	25	15

See also Nos. 1851/4.

388 Storage Jar

2002. Traditional Grain Storage. Multicoloured.

1839	30c. Type **388**	10	10
1840	70c. Raised hut	10	10
1841	1b. Conical hut	15	10
1842	2b. Hut supported by branches	25	15

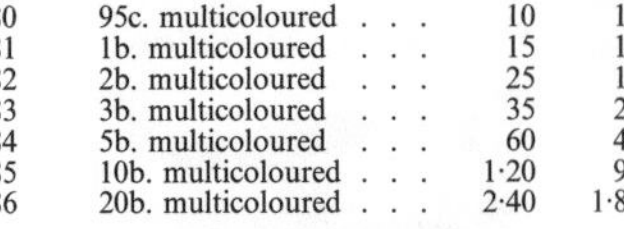

389 Lions International Emblem

2002. Lions Club International (charitable organization). Multicoloured.

1843	45c. Type **389**	10	10
1844	55c. Solar-powered water pump	10	10
1845	1b. Medical symbols	15	10
1846	2b. Wheelchair user	25	15

390 *Acacia abyssinica*

2002. Trees. Multicoloured.

1847	50c. Type **390**	10	10
1848	60c. *Boswellia papyrifera* (vert)	10	10
1849	90c. *Aningeria adolfi-friederici* (vert)	10	10
1850	2b. *Prunus africanus* (vert)	25	15

391 Cone-shaped Hive

2002. Traditional Beehives (2nd issue). Multicoloured.

1851	45c. Type **391**	10	10
1852	55c. Narrow log hive	10	10
1853	1b. Woven straw hive	15	10
1854	2b. Large log hive	25	15

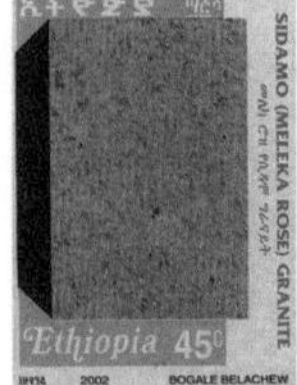

392 Sidamo Granite

394 Menelik's Bushbuck

393 Men, Women and Warrior

2002. Granite. Multicoloured.

1855	45c. Type **392**	10	10
1856	55c. Harrar	10	10
1857	1b. Tigray	15	10
1858	2b. Wollega	25	15

2002. Konso Waka (memorial wood carvings). Multicoloured, background colour given.

1859	40c. Type **393**	10	10
1860	60c. Carvings (blue)	10	10
1861	1b. Carvings (yellow)	15	10
1862	2b. Carvings (red)	25	15

DESIGNS: 60c. to 2b. Different carvings.

2002. Menelik's Bushbuck (2nd series).

1863	**394**	5c. multicoloured	10	10
1864		10c. multicoloured	10	10
1865		15c. multicoloured	10	10
1866		20c. multicoloured	10	10
1867		25c. multicoloured	10	10
1868		30c. multicoloured	10	10
1869		35c. multicoloured	10	10
1870		40c. multicoloured	10	10
1871		45c. multicoloured	10	10
1872		50c. multicoloured	10	10
1873		55c. multicoloured	10	10
1874		65c. multicoloured	10	10
1875		70c. multicoloured	10	10
1876		75c. multicoloured	10	10
1877		80c. multicoloured	10	10
1878		85c. multicoloured	10	10
1879		90c. multicoloured	10	10
1880		95c. multicoloured	10	10
1881		1b. multicoloured	15	10
1882		2b. multicoloured	25	15
1883		3b. multicoloured	35	25
1884		5b. multicoloured	60	45
1885		10b. multicoloured	1·20	90
1886		20b. multicoloured	2·40	1·80

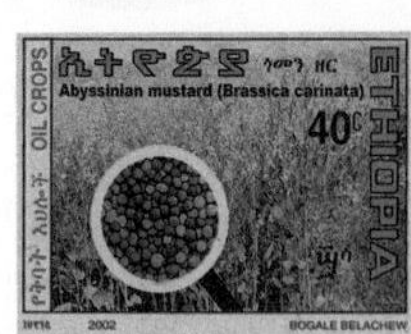

395 Abyssinian Mustard (*Brassica carinata*)

2002. Oil Producing Seeds. Multicoloured.

1887	40c. Type **395**	10	10
1888	60c. Linseed (*Linum usitatissimum*)	10	10
1889	3b. Niger (*Guizotia abyssinica*)	35	25

396 Emblem

397 Milk Opal

2003. 23rd Anniv of Pan African Postal Union.

1890	**396**	20c. multicoloured	10	10
1891		80c. multicoloured	10	10
1892		1b. multicoloured	15	10
1893		2b. multicoloured	25	15

2003. Opals. Multicoloured.

1894	45c. Type **397**	10	10
1895	60c. Brown	10	10
1896	95c. Fire	10	10
1897	2b. Yellow	25	15

398 Amulet

399 *Kniphofia isoetfolia*

2003. 1st Anniv of Return of Emperor Tewodro's (Ethiopian ruler) Amulet. Multicoloured.

1898	40c. Type **398**	10	10
1899	60c. Leather pouch	10	10
1900	3b. Amulet and pouch	35	25

2003. Plants. Multicoloured.

1901	45c. Type **399**	10	10
1902	55c. *Kniphofia insignis*	10	10
1903	1b. *Crinum bambusetum*	15	10
1904	2b. *Crinum abyssinicum* (horiz)	25	15

400 Village, Terraces and Produce

2003. Konso Terracing System. Multicoloured.

1905	40c. Type **400**	10	10
1906	60c. Field of crop and couple	10	10
1907	1b. Terraces	15	10
1908	2b. Men hoeing	25	15

EXPRESS LETTER STAMPS

E 65 Motor-cycle Messenger

1947. Inscr "EXPRESS".

E357	**E 65**	30c. brown	2·75	75
E358	–	50c. blue	3·25	90

DESIGN: 50c. G.P.O., Addis Ababa.

POSTAGE DUE STAMPS

(D 3)

D 77

1896. Optd with Type D **3**.

D 8	**1**	¼g. green	1·25
D 9		½g. red	1·25
D10		1g. blue	1·25
D11		2g. brown	1·25
D12		4g. red	90
D13		8g. mauve	90
D14		16g. black	90

1905. Optd **TAXE a PERCEVOIR T.**

D108	**1**	¼g. green	10·00	10·00
D109		½g. red	10·00	10·00
D110		1g. blue	10·00	10·00
D111		2g. brown	10·00	10·00
D112	**2**	4g. red	10·00	10·00
D113		8g. mauve	15·00	15·00
D114		16g. black	17·00	17·00

1907. As above further optd with value in figures between stars.

D122	**1**	¼g. green	17·00	17·00
D123		½g. red	17·00	17·00
D124		1g. blue	17·00	17·00
D125		2g. brown	17·00	17·00
D126	**2**	4g. red	17·00	17·00
D127		8g. mauve	17·00	17·00
D128		16g. black	25·00	25·00

1908. Optd with Amharic inscription and large **T** in triangle.

D140	**1**	¼g. green	1·60	1·60
D141		½g. red	1·60	1·60
D142		1g. blue	1·60	1·60
D143		2g. brown	2·00	2·00
D144	**2**	4g. red	3·00	3·00
D145		8g. mauve	7·50	7·50
D146		16g. black	13·50	13·50

1913. Stamps of 1909 and the 1g. of 1919 optd with Amharic inscription and large **T** in triangle.

D161	**19**	¼g. green	75	75
D162		½g. red	1·10	1·10
D163		1g. orange and green	2·50	2·50
D210	–	1g. black & pur (No. 184)	3·75	3·75
D164	**20**	2g. blue	3·00	3·00
D165		4g. red and green	4·75	4·75
D166	–	8g. grey & red (No. 152)	6·00	6·00
D167	–	16g. red (No. 153)	16·00	16·00

1951.

D417	**D 77**	1c. green	10	15
D418		5c. red	20	20
D419		10c. violet	55	55
D420		20c. brown	80	85
D421		50c. blue	2·00	2·25
D422		$1 purple	4·00	4·00

FALKLAND ISLANDS Pt. 1

A British colony in the South Atlantic.

1878. 12 pence = 1 shilling;
20 shillings = 1 pound.
1971. 100 (new) pence = 1 pound.

3

6

1878.
17b 3 ½d. green . . . . 2·00 3·00
23 1d. red to brown . . . . . 6·50 2·25
26 2d. purple . . . . 5·00 11·00
30 2½d. blue . . . . 28·00 11·00
32 4d. black . . . . 10·00 21·00
3 6d. green . . . . 80·00 70·00
34 6d. yellow . . . . 35·00 45·00
35 9d. orange . . . . 40·00 55·00
38 1s. brown . . . . 50·00 48·00
41 – 2s.6d. blue £250 £250
42 6 5s. red £200 £225
DESIGN: 2s.6d. As Type **6**, but different frame.

1891. No. 23 bisected diagonally and each half surch ½d.
13 3 ½d. on half of 1d. brown . . £550 £300

7

8

1904.
43 7 ½d. green . . . . 4·25 1·50
44b 1d. red . . . . 1·00 2·50
45 2d. purple . . . . 17·00 26·00
46 2½d. blue . . . . 29·00 7·50
47 6d. orange . . . . 38·00 48·00
48 1s. brown . . . . 40·00 32·00
49b 8 3s. green £130 £150
50 5s. red £200 £150

1912. As T **7/8** but portrait of King George V.
60 ½d. green . . . . 2·75 3·50
74 1d. red . . . . 5·00 1·25
75 2d. purple . . . . 16·00 7·00
76b 2½d. blue . . . . 6·50 16·00
77 2½d. purple on yellow . . . . 4·50 38·00
64 6d. orange . . . . 14·00 20·00
65 1s. brown . . . . 32·00 30·00
66 3s. green . . . . 85·00 80·00
67 5s. red £100 £100
67b 5s. purple . . . . 80·00 £110
68 10s. red on green £160 £250
69 £1 black on red £450 £500

1918. As 1912, optd **WAR STAMP**.
70b ½d. green . . . . 50 6·50
71c 1d. red . . . . 50 3·75
72a 1s. brown . . . . 4·00 48·00

1928. No. 75 surch **2½D**.
115 2½d. on 2d. purple £900 £900

13 Fin Whale and Gentoo Penguins

15 Romney Marsh Ram

1929.
116 13 ½d. green . . . . 1·25 3·00
117 1d. red . . . . 3·75 80
118 2d. grey . . . . 2·75 2·75
119 2½d. blue . . . . 2·75 2·25
120 4d. orange . . . . 16·00 13·00
121 6d. purple . . . . 16·00 13·00
122 1s. black on green . . . . . 23·00 35·00
123 2s.6d. red on blue . . . . . 50·00 50·00
124 5s. green on yellow . . . . 80·00 95·00
125 10s. red on green £150 £180
126 £1 black on red £300 £375

1933. Centenary of British Administration. Inscr "1833–1933".
127 15 ½d. black and green . . . 1·75 7·00
128 – 1d. black and red . . . . 3·50 2·25
129 – 1½d. black and blue . . . 15·00 17·00
130 – 2d. black and brown . . . 10·00 22·00
131 – 3d. black and violet . . . 16·00 20·00
132 – 4d. black and orange . . . 17·00 17·00
133 – 6d. black and grey . . . . 50·00 65·00
134 – 1s. black and olive . . . . 48·00 75·00
135 – 2s.6d. black and violet . . £170 £200
136 – 5s. black and yellow . . . £600 £800
137 – 10s. black and brown . . . £600 £900
138 – £1 black and red £1700 £2250
DESIGNS—HORIZ: 1d. Iceberg; 1½d. Whale-catcher; 2d. Port Louis; 3d. Map of Falkland Islands; 4d. South Georgia; 6d. Fin whale; 1s. Government House, Stanley. VERT: 2s.6d. Battle Memorial; 5s. King penguin; 10s. Arms; £1 King George V.

1935. Silver Jubilee. As T **10a** of Gambia.
139 1d. blue and red . . . . . . 3·25 40
140 2½d. brown and blue . . . . 11·00 1·75
141 4d. green and blue . . . . . 11·00 4·50
142 1s. grey and purple . . . . . 8·00 3·50

1937. Coronation. As T **10b** of Gambia.
143 ½d. green 30 10
144 1d. red . . . . 1·00 50
145 2½d. blue . . . . 1·50 1·40

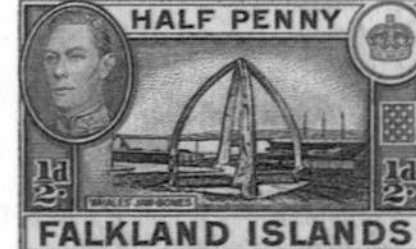
27 Whales' Jaw Bones

1938.
146 27 ½d. black and green . . . 30 75
147a A 1d. black and red . . . . 3·75 85
148 B 1d. black and violet . . . 2·50 1·75
149 2d. black and violet . . . 1·25 50
150 A 2d. black and red . . . . 1·00 2·25
151 C 2½d. black and blue . . . 1·25 30
152 D 2½d. black and blue . . . 6·50 7·00
153 C 3d. black and blue . . . . 6·50 2·50
154 D 4d. black and purple . . . 3·25 1·00
155 E 6d. black and brown . . . 2·50 1·50
156 6d. black . . . . 6·50 4·25
157 F 9d. black and blue . . . 22·00 1·75
158a G 1s. blue . . . . 21·00 3·25
159 H 1s.3d. black and red . . . 2·50 1·40
160 I 2s.6d. black . . . . . . 55·00 14·00
161 J 5s. blue and brown . . . £120 70·00
162 K 10s. black and orange . . £110 40·00
163 L £1 black and violet . . . £130 55·00
DESIGNS—HORIZ: A, Black-necked swan; B, Battle memorial; C, Flock of sheep; D, Magellan goose; E, "Discovery II" (polar supply vessel); F, "William Scoresby" (research ship); G, Mount Sugar Top; H, Turkey vultures; I, Gentoo penguins; J, Southern sealion; K, Deception Is.; L, Arms of Falkland Islands.

1946. Victory. As T **11a** of Gambia.
164 1d. violet 30 50
165 3d. blue 45 50

1948. Silver Wedding. As T **11b/c** of Gambia.
166 2½d. blue . . . . 2·00 1·00
167 £1 mauve . . . . 90·00 60·00

1949. U.P.U. As T **11d/g** of Gambia.
168 1d. violet . . . . 1·50 1·00
169 3d. blue . . . . 5·00 2·25
170 1s.3d. green . . . . 3·00 2·25
171 2s. blue . . . . 3·00 8·00

39 Sheep

1952.
172 39 ½d. green . . . . 1·00 70
173 – 1d. red . . . . 2·50 40
174 – 2d. violet . . . . 4·50 2·50
175 – 2½d. black and blue . . . 1·25 50
176 – 3d. blue . . . . 2·25 1·00
177 – 4d. purple . . . . 8·00 1·50
178 – 6d. brown . . . . 12·00 1·00
179 – 9d. yellow . . . . 9·00 2·00
180 – 1s. black . . . . 24·00 80
181 – 1s.3d. orange . . . . . . 15·00 5·00
182 – 2s.6d. olive . . . . 20·00 11·00
183 – 5s. purple . . . . 14·00 9·00
184 – 10s. grey . . . . 26·00 13·00
185 – £1 black . . . . 27·00 17·00
DESIGNS—HORIZ: 1d. "Fitzroy" (supply ship); 2d. Magellan goose; 2½d. Map; 4d. Auster Autocrat aircraft; 6d. "John Biscoe I" (research ship); 9d. View of the Two Sisters; 1s.3d. Kelp goose and gander; 10s. Southern sealion and South American fur seal; £1 Hulk of "Great Britain". VERT: 3d. Arms; 1s. Gentoo penguins; 2s.6d. Sheep shearing; 5s. Battle Memorial.

1953. Coronation. As T **11h** of Gambia.
186 1d. black and red . . . . . 80 1·50

1955. As 1952 issue but with portrait of Queen Elizabeth II.
187 ½d. green . . . . 70 1·25
188 1d. red . . . . 1·25 1·25
189 2d. violet . . . . 3·25 4·50
190 6d. brown . . . . 7·00 60
191 9d. yellow . . . . 10·00 17·00
192 1s. black . . . . 6·00 1·25

54 Austral Thrush

1960. Birds.
227 54 ½d. black and green . . . 30 40
194 – 1d. black and red . . . . 2·50 1·25
195 – 2d. black and blue . . . . 4·50 1·25
196 – 2½d. black and bistre . . . 2·50 75
197 – 3d. black and olive . . . . 1·25 50
198 – 4d. black and red . . . . 1·50 1·25
199 – 5½d. black and violet . . . 3·25 2·50
200 – 6d. black and sepia . . . . 3·50 30
201 – 9d. black and orange . . . 2·50 1·25
202 – 1s. black and purple . . . 1·25 40
203 – 1s.3d. black and blue . . . 10·00 13·00
204 – 2s. black and brown . . . 29·00 2·50
205 – 5s. black and turquoise . . 27·00 11·00
206 – 10s. black and purple . . . 48·00 16·00
207 – £1 black and yellow . . . 48·00 27·00
BIRDS: 1d. Southern black-backed gull; 2d. Gentoo penguins; 2½d. Long-tailed meadow lark; 3d. Magellan goose; 4d. Falkland Island flightless steamer ducks; 5½d. Rock-hopper penguins; 6d. Black-browed albatross; 9d. Silver grebe; 1s. Magellanic oystercatcher; 1s.3d. Chilean teal; 2s. Kelp geese; 5s. King cormorants; 10s. Common caracara; £1 Black-necked swan.

69 Morse Key

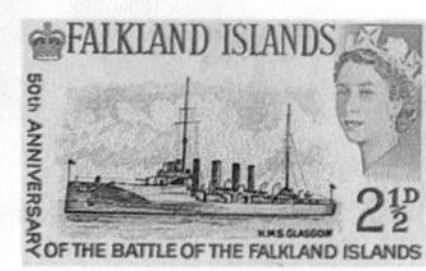
72 H.M.S. "Glasgow"

1962. 50th Anniv of Establishment of Radio Communications.
208 69 6d. red and orange 75 40
209 – 1s. green and olive 80 40
210 – 2s. violet and blue . . . . 90 1·75
DESIGNS: 1s. One-valve receiver; 2s. Rotary spark transmitter.

1963. Freedom from Hunger. As T **20a** of Gambia.
211 1s. blue . . . . 10·00 1·50

1963. Centenary of Red Cross. As T **20b** of Gambia.
212 1d. red and black . . . . . 3·00 75
213 1s. red and blue . . . . . . 13·00 4·75

1964. 400th Birth Anniv of Shakespeare. As **22a** of Gambia.
214 6d. black . . . . 1·50 50

1964. 50th Anniv of Battle of the Falkland Islands.
215 72 2½d. black and red . . . . 11·00 3·25
216 – 6d. black and blue 50 25
217 – 1s. black and red . . . . . 50 1·00
218 – 2s. black and blue 35 75
DESIGNS—HORIZ: 6d. H.M.S. "Kent"; 1s. H.M.S. "Invincible". VERT: 2s. Battle Memorial.

1965. Centenary of I.T.U. As T **44** of Gibraltar.
219 1d. light blue and deep blue . . 50 30
220 2s. lilac and yellow . . . . . 4·50 1·75

1965. I.C.Y. As T **45** of Gibraltar.
221 1d. purple and turquoise . . . 1·50 40
222 1s. green and lavender . . . 4·00 1·10

1966. Churchill Commemoration. As T **46** of Gibraltar.
223 ½d. blue . . . . 65 1·25
224 1d. green . . . . 1·75 15
225 1s. brown . . . . 6·00 2·50
226 2s. violet . . . . 4·00 2·50

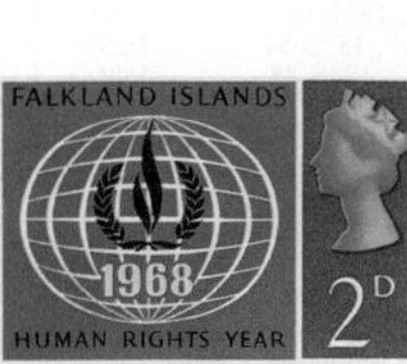
76 Globe and Human Rights Emblem

77 Dusty Miller

1968. Human Rights Year.
228 76 2d. multicoloured 40 20
229 6d. multicoloured 40 20
230 1s. multicoloured 50 20
231 2s. multicoloured 50 30

1968. Flowers. Multicoloured.
232 ½d. Type **77** . . . . 15 1·75
233 1½d. Pig vine 40 15
234 2d. Pale maiden 50 15
235 3d. Dog orchid . . . . . . 6·00 1·00
236 3½d. Sea cabbage 30 75
237 4½d. Vanilla daisy . . . . . 1·50 2·00
238 5½d. yellow, brown and green (Arrowleaf marigold) . . . 1·50 2·00
239 6d. red, black and green (Diddle dee) 75 20
240 1s. Scurvy grass . . . . . 75 1·50
241 1s.6d. Prickly burr . . . . 4·50 12·00
242 2s. Fachine . . . . 5·50 6·50
243 3s. Lavender . . . . 8·00 8·00
244 5s. Felton's flower . . . . 29·00 13·00
245 £1 Yellow orchid . . . . . 13·00 2·50
Nos. 233, 236, 238/40 and 244 are horiz.

91 De Havilland Beaver Seaplane

1969. 21st Anniv of Government Air Services. Multicoloured.
246 2d. Type **91** 50 30
247 6d. Noorduyn Norseman V . . 50 35
248 1s. Auster Autocrat 50 35
249 2s. Arms of the Falkland Islands . . . . 1·50 2·00

92 Holy Trinity Church, 1869

1969. Centenary of Bishop Stirling's Consecration.
250 92 2d. black, grey and green 40 60
251 – 6d. black, grey and red . . 40 60
252 – 1s. black, grey and lilac . . 40 60
253 – 2s. multicoloured 50 75
DESIGNS: 6d. Christ Church Cathedral, 1969; 1s. Bishop Stirling; 2s. Bishop's Mitre.

96 Mounted Volunteer

1970. Golden Jubilee of Defence Force. Mult.
254 2d. Type **96** . . . . 1·50 70
255 6d. Defence Post (horiz) . . . 1·50 70
256 1s. Corporal in No. 1 Dress uniform . . . . 1·50 70
257 2s. Badge (horiz) . . . . . . 1·50 75

97 S.S. "Great Britain" (1843)

1970. S.S. "Great Britain" Restoration. Stamps show S.S. "Great Britain" in year given. Multicoloured.
258 2d. Type **97** 80 40
259 4d. 1845 . . . . 80 75
260 9d. 1876 . . . . 80 75
261 1s. 1886 . . . . 80 75
262 2s. 1970 . . . . 1·10 75

1971. Decimal Currency. Nos. 232/44 surch.
263 ½p. on ½d. multicoloured . . 25 20
264 1p. on 1½d. multicoloured . . 30 15
265 1½p. on 2d. multicoloured . . 30 15
266 2p. on 3d. multicoloured . . 50 20
267 2½p. on 3½d. multicoloured . . 30 20
268 3p. on 4½d. multicoloured . . 30 20
269 4p. on 5½d. yellow, brn & grn 30 20
270 5p. on 6d. red, black and green 30 20
271 6p. on 1s. multicoloured . . 7·50 7·00
272 7½p. on 1s.6d. multicoloured 7·00 7·50
273 10p. on 2s. multicoloured . . 7·50 3·00
274 15p. on 3s. multicoloured . . 4·50 2·75
275 25p. on 5s. multicoloured . . 5·00 3·25

1972. Decimal Currency. Nos. 232/44 inscr in decimal currency.
276 ½p. multicoloured . . . . . 35 4·75
277 1p. multicoloured 30 40
278 1½p. multicoloured . . . . . 30 4·50
279 2p. multicoloured . . . . . 13·00 1·25
280 2½p. multicoloured . . . . . 35 4·50
281 3p. multicoloured . . . . . 35 1·25
282 4p. yellow, brown and green 40 1·00
283 5p. red, black and green . . 40 55
295 6p. multicoloured . . . . . 1·50 2·25
285 7½p. multicoloured . . . . . 1·50 4·00
286 10p. multicoloured . . . . . 9·00 4·50
287 15p. multicoloured . . . . . 3·25 5·00
288 25p. multicoloured . . . . . 3·25 6·00

1972. Royal Silver Wedding. As T **98** of Gibraltar but with Romney Marsh Sheep and Giant Sea Lions in background.
289 1p. green 40 40
290 10p. blue 85 85

1973. Royal Wedding. As T **101a** of Gibraltar. Background colour given. Multicoloured.
291 5p. mauve 25 10
292 15p. brown 35 20

101 South American Fur Seal

1974. Tourism. Multicoloured.

296	2p. Type **101**	2·25	1·25
297	4p. Trout-fishing	3·00	1·25
298	5p. Rockhopper penguins	9·50	2·50
299	15p. Long-tailed meadow lark ("Military Starling")	12·00	4·50

102 19th-century Mail-coach

1974. U.P.U. Multicoloured.

300	2p. Type **102**	20	25
301	5p. Packet ship, 1841	25	45
302	8p. First U.K. aerial post, 1911	30	55
303	16p. Ship's catapult mail, 1920s	35	75

103 Churchill and Houses of Parliament

1974. Birth Centenary of Sir Winston Churchill. Multicoloured.

304	16p. Type **103**	80	1·25
305	20p. Churchill with H.M.S. "Inflexible" and H.M.S. "Invincible", 1914	80	1·25
MS306	108 × 83 mm. Nos. 304/5	9·00	8·00

104 H.M.S. "Exeter"

1974. 35th Anniv of Battle of the River Plate. Multicoloured.

307	2p. Type **104**	3·00	1·60
308	6p. H.M.N.Z. "Achilles"	4·50	3·50
309	8p. "Admiral Graf Spee"	5·00	4·50
310	16p. H.M.S. "Ajax"	8·50	15·00

105 Seal and Flag Badge

1975. 50th Anniv of Heraldic Arms. Multicoloured.

311	2p. Type **105**	80	35
312	7½p. Coat of arms, 1925	1·60	1·40
313	10p. Coat of arms, 1948	1·75	1·60
314	16p. Arms of the Dependencies, 1952	2·50	3·25

106 ½p. Coin and Brown Trout

1975. New Coinage. Multicoloured.

316	2p. Type **106**	1·00	50
317	5½p. 1p. coin and Gentoo penguin	1·75	1·50
318	8p. 2p. coin and Magellan goose	2·25	1·75
319	10p. 5p. coin and Black-browed albatross	2·25	2·00
320	16p. 10p. coin and Southern sealion	2·75	3·00

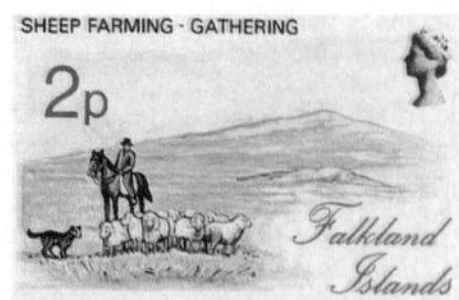

107 Gathering Sheep

1976. Sheep Farming Industry. Multicoloured.

321	2p. Type **107**	50	40
322	7½p. Shearing	75	1·50
323	10p. Dipping	1·00	1·60
324	20p. Shipping	1·50	3·00

108 The Queen awaiting Anointment

1977. Silver Jubilee. Multicoloured.

325	6p. Visit of Prince Philip, 1957	1·50	1·00
326	11p. The Queen, ampulla and anointing spoon	20	60
327	33p. Type **108**	30	75

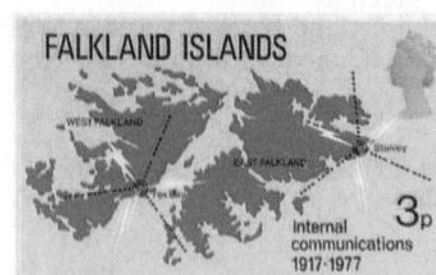

109 Map of Falkland Islands

1977. Telecommunications. Multicoloured.

328	3p. Type **109**	75	15
329	11p. Ship to shore communications	1·00	40
330	40p. Telex and telephone service	1·75	1·75

110 "A.E.S.", 1957–74

1978. Mail Ships. Multicoloured.

331A	1p. Type **110**	20	30
332A	2p. "Darwin", 1957–73	30	30
333A	3p. "Merak-N", 1951–52	25	1·25
334A	4p. "Fitzroy", 1936–57	30	1·25
335A	5p. "Lafonia", 1936–41	30	30
336A	6p. "Fleurus", 1924–33	30	50
337A	7p. "Falkland", 1914–34	30	2·50
338A	8p. "Oravia", 1900–12	35	1·25
339A	9p. "Memphis", 1890–97	35	50
340A	10p. "Black Hawk", 1873–80	35	50
341B	20p. "Foam", 1863–72	1·00	3·00
342B	25p. "Fairy", 1857–61	1·00	3·00
343B	50p. "Amelia", 1852–54	1·25	3·75
344B	£1 "Nautilus", 1846–48	1·40	4·50
345B	£3 "Hebe", 1842–46	3·50	9·50

Nos. 331/45 come with and without date imprint.

111 Short Hythe at Stanley **112** Red Dragon of Wales

1978. 26th Anniv of First Direct Flight, Southampton–Port Stanley. Multicoloured.

346	11p. Type **111**	3·25	2·50
347	33p. Route map and Short Hythe flying boat	3·75	3·00

1978. 25th Anniv of Coronation. Multicoloured.

348	**112** 25p. brown, blue and silver	60	1·00
349	– 25p. multicoloured	60	1·00
350	– 25p. brown, blue and silver	60	1·00

DESIGNS: No. 349, Queen Elizabeth II; 350, Hornless ram.

113 First Fox Bay P.O. and 1d. Stamp of 1878 **114** "Macrocystis pyrifera"

1978. Centenary of First Falkland Islands Postage Stamp. Multicoloured.

351	3p. Type **113**	25	20
352	11p. Second Stanley P.O. and 4d. stamp of 1878	30	50
353	15p. New Island P.O. and 6d. stamp of 1878	40	60
354	22p. First Stanley P.O. and 1s. stamp of 1878	60	1·00

1979. Kelp and Seaweed. Multicoloured.

355	3p. Type **114**	30	25
356	7p. "Durvillea sp."	40	45
357	11p. "Lessonia sp." (horiz)	50	60
358	15p. "Callophyllis sp." (horiz)	60	80
359	25p. "Iradaea sp."	75	1·40

115 Britten Norman Islander over Falkland Islands

1979. Opening of Stanley Airport. Multicoloured.

360	3p. Type **115**	40	20
361	11p. Fokker F.27 Friendship over South Atlantic	70	60
362	15p. Fokker F.28 Fellowship over Airport	75	60
363	25p. Cessna 172 Skyhawk, Britten Norman Islander, Fokker F.27 Friendship and Fokker F.28 Fellowship over runway	1·25	80

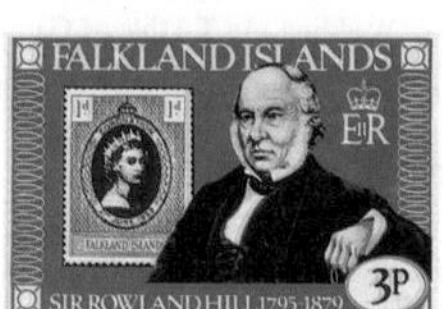

116 Sir Rowland Hill and 1953 Coronation 1d. Commemorative

1979. Death Centenary of Sir Rowland Hill.

364	3p. Type **116**	25	25
365	11p. 1878 1d. stamp (vert)	40	70
366	25p. Penny Black	60	85
MS367	137 × 98 mm. 33p. 1916 5s. stamp (vert)	85	1·50

117 Mail Drop by De Havilland Beaver Aircraft

1979. Centenary of U.P.U. Membership. Multicoloured.

368	3p. Type **117**	20	20
369	11p. Mail by horseback	40	55
370	25p. Mail by schooner "Gwendolin"	50	1·00

118 Peale's Porpoise

1980. Dolphins and Porpoises. Multicoloured.

371	3p. Type **118**	30	45
372	6p. Commerson's dolphin (horiz)	35	55
373	7p. Hour-glass dolphin (horiz)	35	55
374	11p. Spectacled porpoise	40	70
375	15p. Dusky dolphin (horiz)	40	80
376	25p. Killer whale (horiz)	55	1·40

119 1878 Falkland Islands Postmark

1980. "London 1980" International Stamp Exhibition.

377	**119** 11p. black, gold and blue	20	30
378	– 11p. black, gold and yellow	20	30
379	– 11p. black, gold and green	20	30
380	– 11p. black, gold and purple	20	30
381	– 11p. black, gold and red	20	30
382	– 11p. black, gold and flesh	20	30

POSTMARKS: No. 378, 1915 New Island; 379, 1901 Falkland Islands; 380, 1935 Port Stanley; 381, 1952 Port Stanley first overseas airmail; 382, 1934 Fox Bay.

120 Queen Elizabeth the Queen Mother at Ascot, 1971

1980. 80th Birthday of Queen Mother.

383	**120** 11p. multicoloured	40	30

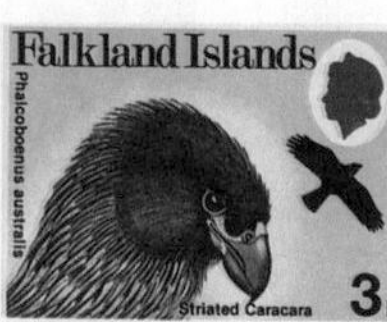

121 Forster's Caracara

1980. Birds of Prey. Multicoloured.

384	3p. Type **121**	50	25
385	11p. Red-backed buzzard	60	45
386	15p. Common caracara	70	55
387	25p. Peregrine falcon	75	75

122 Stanley

1981. Early Settlements. Multicoloured.

388	3p. Type **122**	15	15
389	11p. Port Egmont	20	35
390	25p. Port Louis	45	65
391	33p. Mission House, Keppel Island	50	80

123 Sheep

1981. Farm Animals. Multicoloured.

392	3p. Type **123**	15	30
393	11p. Cattle	20	55
394	25p. Horse	40	1·00
395	33p. Dogs	50	1·25

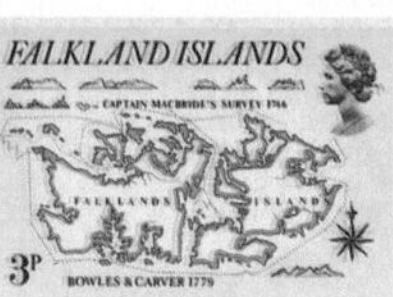

124 Bowles and Carver, 1779

1981. Early Maps.

396	**124** 3p. multicoloured	25	30
397	– 10p. multicoloured	35	50
398	– 13p. multicoloured	35	60
399	– 15p. multicoloured	35	60
400	– 25p. multicoloured	40	80
401	– 26p. black, pink and stone	40	80

MAPS: 10p. J. Hawkesworth, 1773; 13p. Eman Bowen, 1747; 15p. T. Boutflower, 1768; 25p. Philippe de Pretot, 1771; 26p. Bellin "Petite Atlas Maritime", Paris, 1764.

125 Wedding Bouquet from Falkland Islands

126 "Handicrafts"

1981. Royal Wedding. Multicoloured.
402 10p. Type **125** 25 30
403 13p. Prince Charles riding . . 30 35
404 25p. Prince Charles and Lady Diana Spencer 55 90

1981. 25th Anniv of Duke of Edinburgh Award Scheme. Multicoloured.
405 10p. Type **126** 15 20
406 13p. "Camping" 20 30
407 15p. "Canoeing" 30 40
408 52p. Duke of Edinburgh . . 35 60

127 "The Adoration of the Holy Child" (16th-century Dutch Artist)

1981. Christmas. Paintings. Multicoloured.
409 3p. Type **127** 20 20
410 13p. "The Holy Family in an Italian Landscape" (17th-century Genoan artist) 35 45
411 26p. "The Holy Virgin" (Reni) 55 75

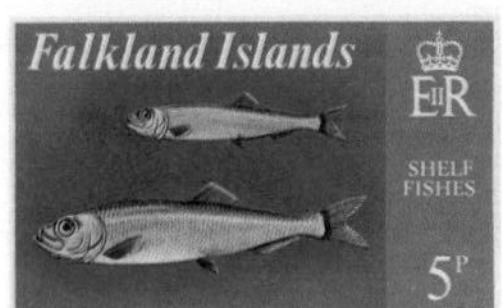

128 Patagonian Sprat

1981. Shelf Fishes. Multicoloured.
412 5p. Type **128** 15 20
413 13p. Gunther's rockcod (vert) 20 35
414 15p. Argentine hake 20 40
415 25p. Southern blue whiting 35 75
416 26p. Grey-tailed skate (vert) 35 75

129 "Lady Elizabeth", 1913

1982. Shipwrecks. Multicoloured.
417 5p. Type **129** 20 50
418 13p. "Capricorn", 1882 . . . 25 70
419 15p. "Jhelum", 1870 . . . . 30 85
420 25p. "Snowsquall", 1864 . . 40 1·10
421 26p. "St. Mary", 1890 . . . 40 1·10

130 Charles Darwin

1982. 150th Anniv of Charles Darwin's Voyage. Multicoloured.
422 5p. Type **130** 30 25
423 17p. Darwin's microscope . . 35 60
424 25p. Falkland Islands wolf 55 80
425 34p. H.M.S. "Beagle" . . . 75 1·10

131 Falkland Islands Coat of Arms

134 Blackish Cinclodes ("Tussock Bird")

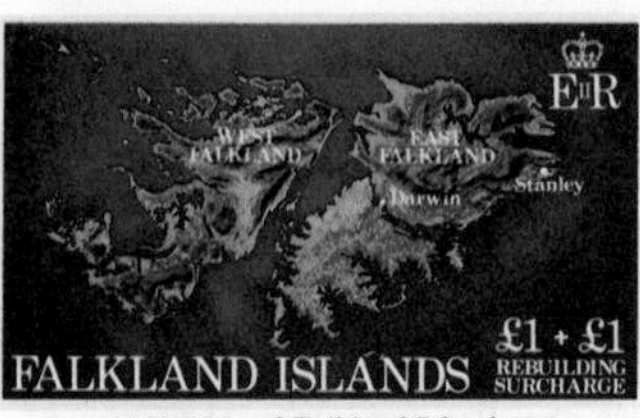

132 Map of Falkland Islands

1982. 21st Birthday of Princess of Wales. Multicoloured.
426 5p. Type **131** 15 20
427 17p. Princess at Royal Opera House, Covent Garden, November, 1981 . . . . . 30 40
428 37p. Bride and groom in doorway of St. Paul's . . . 50 70
429 50p. Formal portrait 65 90

1982. Rebuilding Fund.
430 **132** £1+£1 multicoloured . . . 1·50 4·00

1982. Commonwealth Games, Brisbane. Nos. 335 and 342 optd **1st PARTICIPATION COMMONWEALTH GAMES 1982**.
431 5p. "Lafonia", 1936–41 . . . 15 30
432 25p. "Fairy", 1857–61 . . . 35 1·10

1982. Birds of the Passerine Family. Multicoloured.
433 5p. Type **134** 25 35
434 10p. Black-chinned siskin . . 30 45
435 13p. Sedge wren ("Grass Wren") 30 55
436 17p. Black-throated finch . . 30 65
437 25p. Correndera pipit ("Falkland-Correndera Pipit") 35 85
438 34p. Dark-faced ground-tyrant . . . . 40 1·10

135 Raising Flag, Port Louis, 1833

1983. 150th Anniv of British Administration. Multicoloured.
439 1p. Type **135** 20 30
440 2p. Chelsea pensioners and barracks, 1849 (horiz) . . . 25 40
441 5p. Development of wool trade, 1874 . . . . 25 40
442 10p. Ship-repairing trade, 1850–1890 (horiz) 35 70
443 15p. Government House, early 20th century (horiz) 35 80
444 20p. Battle of Falkland Islands, 1914 . . . . . . 45 1·25
445 25p. Whalebone Arch (horiz) 45 1·25
446 40p. Contribution to War effort, 1939–45 . . . . . . 50 1·25
447 50p. Duke of Edinburgh's visit, 1957 (horiz) . . . . 60 1·25
448 £1 Royal Marine uniforms 75 1·75
449 £2 Queen Elizabeth II . . . 1·50 2·25

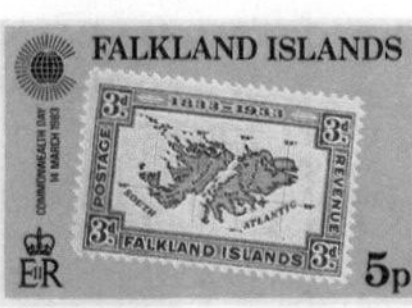

136 1933 British Administration Centenary 3d. Commemorative

1983. Commonwealth Day. Multicoloured.
450 5p. Type **136** 15 15
451 17p. 1933 British Administration Centenary ½d. commemorative 20 35
452 34p. 1933 British Administration Centenary 10s. commemorative (vert) 40 80
453 50p. 1983 British Administration 150th anniv £2 commemorative (vert) 60 1·00

137 British Army advancing across East Falkland

1983. 1st Anniv of Liberation. Multicoloured.
454 5p. Type **137** 25 30
455 13p. S.S. "Canberra" and M.V. "Norland" at San Carlos 40 60
456 17p. R.A.F. Hawker Siddeley Harrier fighter 45 70
457 50p. H.M.S. "Hermes" (aircraft carrier) . . . . . 1·00 1·40
MS458 169 × 130 mm. Nos. 454/7 1·60 2·75

138 Diddle Dee

1983. Native Fruits. Multicoloured.
459 5p. Type **138** 15 20
460 17p. Tea berry 25 35
461 25p. Mountain berry 35 50
462 34p. Native strawberry . . . 45 70

139 Britten Norman Islander

1983. Bicentenary of Manned Flight. Mult.
463 5p. Type **139** 15 20
464 13p. De Havilland Beaver . . 25 35
465 17p. Noorduyn Norseman V 30 40
466 50p. Auster Autocrat . . . . 70 1·00

1984. Nos. 443 and 445 surch.
467 17p. on 15p. Government House, early 20th century 60 45
468 22p. on 25p. Whalebone Arch, 1933 . . . . 65 55

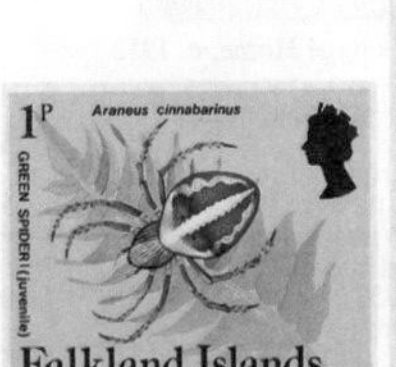

141 "Araneus cinnabarinus" (juvenile spider)
142 "Wavertree" (sail merchantman)

1984. Insects and Spiders. Multicoloured.
469A 1p. Type **141** 20 80
470A 2p. "Alopophion occidentalis" (fly) . . . . 2·00 2·00
471A 3p. "Pareuxoina falklandica (moth) 40 80
472A 4p. "Lissopterus quadrinotatus" (beetle) 30 80
473A 5p. "Issoria cytheris" (butterfly) 30 80
474A 6p. "Araneus cinnabarinus" (adult spider) 30 80
475A 7p. "Trachysphyrus penai" (fly) 30 65
476A 8p. "Caphornia ochricraspia" (moth) . . 30 65
477A 9p. "Caneorhinus biangulatus" (weevil) . . 30 65
478A 10p. "Syrphus octomaculatus" (fly) . . 30 65
479A 20p. "Malvinius compressi-ventris" (weevil) . . . . 2·00 75
480A 25p. "Metius blandus" (beetle) 50 90
481A 50p. "Parudenus falklandicus" (cricket) . . 80 1·50
482A £1 "Emmenomma beauchenieus" (spider) . . 1·00 2·25
483A £3 "Cynthia carye" (butterfly) . . . . 2·75 6·00

No. 470 comes with or without imprint date.

1984. 250th Anniv of "Lloyd's List" (newspaper). Multicoloured.
484 6p. Type **142** 55 40
485 17p. "Bjerk" (whale catcher) at Port Stanley 80 50
486 22p. "Oravia" (liner) stranded 80 55
487 52p. "Cunard Countess" (liner) . . . . 1·25 1·75

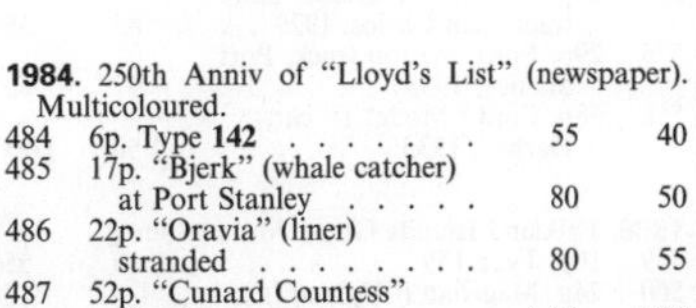

143 Ship, Lockheed Hecules Aircraft and U.P.U. Logo

1984. Universal Postal Union Congress, Hamburg.
488 **143** 22p. multicoloured . . . 55 75

144 Great Grebe

145 Black-browed Albatross, Wilson's Storm Petrel and South American Tern

1984. Grebes. Multicoloured.
489 17p. Type **144** . . . . . . 1·10 1·00
490 22p. Silvery grebe ("Silver Grebe") . . . . 1·25 1·10
491 52p. White-tufted grebe ("Rolland's Grebe") . . . 1·75 3·25

1984. Nature Conservation. Multicoloured.
492 6p. Type **145** . . . . 1·00 60
493 17p. Tussock grass 75 70
494 22p. Dusky dolphin and Southern sea lion 80 80
495 52p. Rockcod (fish) and krill 1·25 2·25
MS496 130 × 90 mm. Nos. 492/5 4·00 7·00

146 Technical Drawing of Class "Wren" Locomotive

1985. 70th Anniv of Camber Railway. Each black, brown and light brown.
497 7p. Type **146** 35 30
498 22p. Sail-propelled trolley . . 60 90
499 27p. Class "Wren" locomotive at work . . . . 65 1·25
500 54p. "Falkland Islands Express" passenger train (76 × 25 mm) . . . . . . 1·10 2·00

147 Construction Workers' Camp

1985. Opening of Mount Pleasant Airport. Multicoloured.
501 7p. Type **147** 75 40
502 22p. Building construction . . 1·00 75
503 27p. Completed airport . . . 1·25 80
504 54p. Lockheed TriStar 500 airliner over runway . . . 1·50 1·75

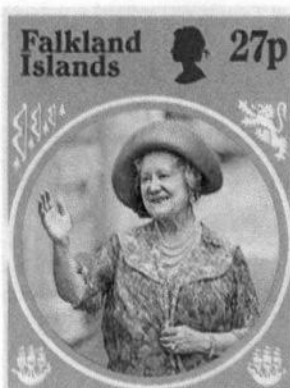

148 The Queen Mother on 84th Birthday

149 Captain J. McBride and H.M.S. "Jason", 1765

1985. Life and Times of Queen Elizabeth the Queen Mother. Multicoloured.
505 7p. Attending reception at Lancaster House 25 20
506 22p. With Prince Charles, Mark Phillips and Princess Anne at Falklands Memorial Service 60 50
507 27p. Type **148** 70 60
508 54p. With Prince Henry at his christening (from photo by Lord Snowdon) . . . . . 1·25 1·25
MS509 91 × 73 mm. £1 With Princess Diana at Trooping the Colour 3·25 2·25

1985. Early Cartographers. Multicoloured.
510 7p. Type **149** 60 40
511 22p. Commodore J. Byron and H.M.S. "Dolphin" and "Tamar", 1765 . . . . . 1·00 80

512 27p. Vice-Admiral R. FitzRoy and H.M.S. "Beagle", 1831 . . . . . . 1·10 85
513 54p. Admiral Sir B. J. Sullivan and H.M.S. "Philomel", 1842 . . . . . 1·75 1·75

149a Philibert Commerson and Commerson's Dolphin

1985. Early Naturalists. Multicoloured.
514 7p. Type **149a** 60 40
515 22p. Rene Primevere Lesson and "Lessonia sp." (kelp) 75 85
516 27p. Joseph Paul Gaimard and Common diving petrel ("Diving Petrel") . . . . . 1·40 1·50
517 54p. Charles Darwin and "Calceolaria darwinii" . . 1·50 2·50

150 Painted Keyhole Limpet

1986. Seashells. Multicoloured.
518 7p. Type **150** 75 60
519 22p. "Provocator palliata" 1·25 1·10
520 27p. Patagonian or Falkland scallop . . . . 1·40 1·60
521 54p. Rough thorn drupe . . 2·25 3·00

1986. 60th Birthday of Queen Elizabeth II. As T **120a** of Hong Kong. Multicoloured.
522 10p. With Princess Margaret at St. Paul's, Walden Bury, Welwyn, 1932 . . . . . . 15 25
523 24p. Queen making Christmas television broadcast, 1958 . . . . . 25 50
524 29p. In robes of Order of the Thistle, St. Giles Cathedral, Edinburgh, 1962 . . . . . 25 60
525 45p. Aboard Royal Yacht "Britannia", U.S.A., 1976 1·00 1·25
526 58p. At Crown Agents Head Office, London, 1983 . . . 60 1·50

151 S.S. "Great Britain" crossing Atlantic, 1845

1986. "Ameripex '86" International Stamp Exhibition, Chicago. Centenary of Arrival of S.S. "Great Britain" in Falkland Islands. Multicoloured.
527 10p. Type **151** 25 60
528 24p. Beached at Sparrow Cove, 1937 . . . . 30 80
529 29p. Refloated on pontoon, 1970 . . . . 35 90
530 58p. Undergoing restoration, Bristol, 1986 . . . . 50 2·25
MS531 109 × 100 mm. Nos. 527/30 1·10 2·75

152 Head of Rockhopper Penguin

153 Prince Andrew and Miss Sarah Ferguson presenting Polo Trophy, Windsor

1986. Rockhopper Penguins. Multicoloured.
532 10p. Type **152** . . . . . . 1·00 70
533 24p. Rockhopper penguins at sea . . . . 1·75 1·75
534 29p. Courtship display . . . 2·00 2·00
535 58p. Adult with chick . . . 2·50 4·50

1986. Royal Wedding. Multicoloured.
536 17p. Type **153** . . . . . . 1·00 50
537 22p. Prince Andrew and Duchess of York on wedding day . . . . 1·10 65
538 29p. Prince Andrew in battledress at opening of Fox Bay Mill . . . . . . 1·40 90

154 Survey Party, Sapper Hill

1987. Bicentenary of Royal Engineers' Royal Warrant. Multicoloured.
539 10p. Type **154** . . . . 1·25 80
540 24p. Mine clearance by robot 1·75 1·50
541 29p. Boxer Bridge, Stanley 2·00 2·50
542 58p. Unloading mail, Mount Pleasant Airport . . . . . 2·75 4·00

155 Southern Sea Lion

1987. Seals. Multicoloured.
543 10p. Type **155** 85 55
544 24p. Falkland fur seal . . . 1·50 90
545 29p. Southern elephant seal 1·60 1·50
546 58p. Leopard seal . . . . . 2·25 3·00

156 "Suillus luteus"

1987. Fungi. Multicoloured.
547 10p. Type **156** . . . . . . 1·75 85
548 24p. "Mycena sp." . . . . . 2·75 2·00
549 29p. "Hygrophorus adonis" ("Camarophyllus adonis") 3·00 3·00
550 58p. "Gerronema schusteri" 4·50 5·00

157 Victoria Cottage Home, c. 1912

1987. Local Hospitals. Multicoloured.
551 10p. Type **157** 50 25
552 24p. King Edward VII Memorial Hospital, c. 1914 85 55
553 29p. Churchill Wing, King Edward VII Memorial Hospital, c. 1953 . . . . . 95 60
554 58p. Prince Andrew Wing, New Hospital, 1987 . . . 1·50 1·25

158 Morris Truck, Fitzroy, 1940

159a Silver from Lloyd's Nelson Collection

159 Kelp Goose

1988. Early Vehicles. Multicoloured.
555 10p. Type **158** 50 25
556 24p. Citroen "Kegresse" half-track, San Carlos, 1929 . . 85 55
575 29p. Ford one ton truck, Port Stanley, 1933 . . . . 95 60
558 58p. Ford "Model T" car, Darwin, 1935 . . . . . . 1·50 1·25

1988. Falkland Islands Geese. Multicoloured.
559 10p. Type **159** . . . . . . 2·00 55
560 24p. Magellan ("Upland") goose . . . . 2·75 70
561 29p. Ruddy-headed goose . . 3·00 90
562 58p. Ashy-headed goose . . . 4·50 2·00

1988. 300th Anniv of Lloyd's of London. Mult.
563 10p. Type **159a** 40 30
564 24p. Falkland Islands hydroponic market garden (horiz) 75 65
565 29p. "A.E.S." (mail ship) (horiz) . . . . 1·25 75
566 58p. "Charles Cooper" (full-rigged ship), 1866 . . . . 1·50 1·25

160 "Padua" (barque)

1989. Cape Horn Sailing Ships. Multicoloured.
567 1p. Type **160** . . . . 1·75 80
613 2p. "Priwall" (barque) (vert) 1·00 1·00
614 3p. "Passat" (barque) . . . . 1·00 1·00
570 4p. "Archibald Russell" (barque) (vert) . . . . . . 2·50 80
571 5p. "Pamir" (barque) (vert) 2·50 80
617 6p. "Mozart" (barquentine) 1·50 1·25
573 7p. "Pommern" (barque) . . 2·50 1·00
574 8p. "Preussen" (full-rigged ship) . . . . 2·50 1·00
620 9p. "Fennia" (barque) . . . 1·50 1·40
576 10p. "Cassard" (barque) . . 2·50 1·00
577 20p. "Lawhill" (barque) . . . 4·00 2·00
578 25p. "Garthpool" (barque) 4·00 2·00
579 50p. "Grace Harwar" (full-rigged ship) . . . . 5·00 3·00
625 £1 "Criccieth Castle" (full-rigged ship) . . . . 3·75 3·75
581 £3 "Cutty Sark" (full-rigged ship) (vert) . . . . . . 14·00 8·50
582 £5 "Flying Cloud" (full-rigged ship) . . . . 15·00 9·00

161 Southern Right Whale

1989. Baleen Whales. Multicoloured.
583 10p. Type **161** . . . . . . 1·25 40
584 24p. Minke whale . . . . . 2·00 85
585 29p. Humpback whale . . . 2·25 1·25
586 58p. Blue whale . . . . . . 3·50 2·50

162 "Gymkhana" (Sarah Gilding)

1989. Sports Associations' Activities. Children's Drawings. Multicoloured.
587 5p. Type **162** 20 20
588 10p. "Steer Riding" (Karen Steen) 30 30
589 17p. "Sheep Shearing" (Colin Shepherd) 45 45
590 24p. "Sheepdog Trials" (Rebecca Edwards) 60 70
591 29p. "Horse Racing" (Dilys Blackley) 70 80
592 45p. "Sack Race" (Donna Newell) . . . . 1·00 1·10

163 Vice-Admiral Sturdee and H.M.S. "Invincible" (battle cruiser)

164 Southern Sea Lions on Kidney Island

1989. 75th Anniv of the Battle of the Falkland Islands and 50th Anniv of Battle of the River Plate. Mult.
593 10p. Type **163** 80 30
594 24p. Vice-Admiral Graf von Spee and "Scharnhorst" (German cruiser) . . . . . 1·50 75
595 29p. Commodore Harwood and H.M.S. "Ajax" (cruiser) . . . . 1·60 85
596 58p. Captain Langsdorff and "Admiral Graf Spee" (German pocket battleship) 2·25 2·00

1990. Nature Reserves and Sanctuaries. Mult.
597 12p. Type **164** 60 35
598 26p. Black-browed albatrosses on Beauchene Island . . . . 1·40 70
599 31p. Penguin colony on Bird Island . . . . 1·40 90
600 62p. Tussock grass on Elephant Jason Island . . 1·50 1·75

165 Supermarine Spitfire Mk. I "Falkland Islands I"

1990. "Stamp World London 90" International Stamp Exhibition, London. Presentation Spitfires. Multicoloured.
601 12p. Type **165** 65 45
602 26p. Supermarine Spitfire Mk. I "Falkland Islands VII" . . . . 1·25 80
603 31p. Cockpit and wing of "Falkland Islands I" . . . 1·25 1·10
604 62p. Squadron scramble, 1940 . . . . 1·75 2·50
MS605 114 × 100 mm. £1 Supermarine Spitfire Mk I in action, 1940 . . . . 4·00 2·50
For No. **MS**605 with additional inscription see No. **MS**628.

165a Queen Mother in Dover

166 Black-browed Albatrosses

1990. 90th Birthday of Queen Elizabeth the Queen Mother.
606 **165a** 26p. multicoloured . . . 1·00 65
607 – £1 black and red . . . . 2·75 2·75
DESIGN: £1 On bridge of liner "Queen Elizabeth", 1946 (29 × 33 mm).

1990. Black-browed Albatrosses. Multicoloured.
608 12p. Type **166** 75 50
609 26p. Female with egg . . . 1·40 1·00
610 31p. Adult and chick . . . . 1·60 1·25
611 62p. Black-browed albatrosses in flight . . . . 2·75 3·00

1991. 2nd Visit of H.R.H. The Duke of Edinburgh. As No. **MS**605, but with Exhibition emblem replaced by "SECOND VISIT OF HRH THE DUKE OF EDINBURGH".
MS628 144 × 100 mm. £1 Spitfire Mk. I in action . . . . 6·50 8·50
The margin of No. **MS**628 also shows the exhibition emblem omitted and has the same commemorative inscription added.

167 "Gavilea australis"

168 Heads of Two King Penguins

1991. Orchids. Multicoloured.
629 12p. Type **167** 75 70
630 26p. Dog orchid . . . . . . 1·25 1·00
631 31p. "Chlorea gaudichaudii" 1·40 1·50
632 62p. Yellow orchid . . . . . 2·50 3·75

1991. Endangered Species. King Penguin. Mult.
633 2p. Type **168** 70 70
634 6p. Female incubating egg . . 90 90
635 12p. Female with two chicks 1·25 1·00
636 20p. Penguin underwater . . 1·50 1·25
637 31p. Parents feeding their chick . . . . 1·60 1·90
638 62p. Courtship dance . . . . 2·25 2·75
Nos. 637/8 do not include the W.W.F. panda emblem.

169 ½d. and 2½d. Stamps of September, 1891

1991. Cent of Bisected Surcharges. Mult.
639 12p. Type **169** 60 50
640 26p. Cover of March, 1891 franked with strip of five ½d. bisects 1·00 1·00
641 31p. Unsevered pair of ½d. surcharge 1·25 1·50
642 62p. "Isis" (mail ship) 2·00 3·25

169a Map of Re-enactment Voyages and "Eye of the Wind" (cadet brig)

1991. 500th Anniv of Discovery of America by Columbus. Re-enactment Voyages. Multicoloured.
643 14p. Type **169a** 60 60
644 29p. Compass rose and "Soren Larsen" (cadet brigantine) 1·25 1·40
645 34p. "Santa Maria", "Pinta" and "Nina" 1·50 1·75
646 68p. Columbus and "Santa Maria" 2·50 4·00

1992. 40th Anniv of Queen Elizabeth II's Accession. As T **179a** of Gibraltar. Multicoloured.
647 7p. "Stanley through the Narrows" (A. Asprey) 45 35
648 14p. "Hill Cove" (A. Asprey) 70 60
649 29p. "San Carlos Water" (A. Asprey) 1·10 95
650 34p. Three portraits of Queen Elizabeth 1·25 1·25
651 68p. Queen Elizabeth II 1·75 2·00

170 Laying Foundation Stone, 1890
170a San Carlos Cemetery

1992. Centenary of Christ Church Cathedral, Stanley. Multicoloured.
652 14p. Type **170** 75 55
653 29p. Interior of Cathedral, 1920 1·40 1·00
654 34p. Bishop's chair 1·60 1·25
655 68p. Cathedral in 1900 (horiz) 2·00 1·90

1992. 10th Anniv of Liberation. Multicoloured.
656 14p.+6p. Type **170a** 75 1·60
657 29p.+11p. War Memorial, Port Stanley 1·40 2·25
658 34p.+16p. South Atlantic medal 1·60 2·25
659 68p.+32p. Government House, Port Stanley 2·75 3·25
MS660 115 × 115 mm. Nos. 656/9 6·00 7·00
The premiums on Nos. 656/9 were for the S.S.A.F.A.

171 Captain John Davis and Backstaff

1992. 400th Anniv of First Sighting of the Falkland Islands. Multicoloured.
661 22p. Type **171** 1·25 80
662 29p. Captain John Davis 1·50 1·10
663 34p. Queen Elizabeth I and Queen Elizabeth II 1·75 1·50
664 68p. "Desire" sighting Falkland Islands 2·75 3·00

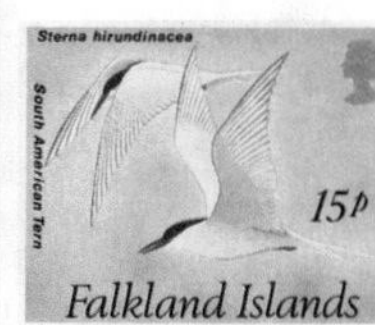

172 Private, Falkland Islands Volunteers, 1892
173 South American Tern

1992. Centenary of Falkland Islands Defence Force and 50th Anniv of Affiliation to West Yorkshire Regiment. Multicoloured.
665 7p. Type **172** 45 30
666 14p. Officer, Falkland Islands Defence Corps, 1914 70 50
667 22p. Officer, Falkland Islands Defence Force, 1920 90 70
668 29p. Private, Falkland Islands Defence Force, 1939–45 1·10 90
669 34p. Officer, West Yorkshire Regiment, 1942 1·40 1·25
670 68p. Private, West Yorkshire Regiment, 1942 2·40 2·10

1993. Gulls and Terns. Multicoloured.
671 15p. Type **173** 1·00 75
672 31p. Brown-hooded gull ("Pink-breasted Gull") 1·25 1·25
673 36p. Magellan gull ("Dolphin Gull") 1·75 1·75
674 72p. Southern black-backed gull ("Dominican Gull") 2·75 5·00

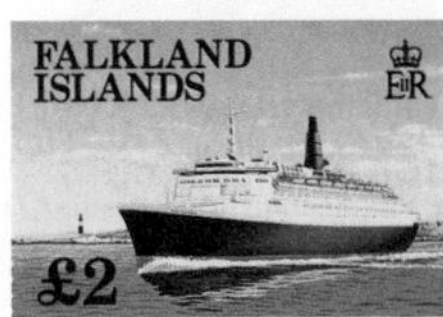

174 "Queen Elizabeth 2"

1993. Visit of "Queen Elizabeth 2". Cruise liner. Sheet 60 × 42 mm.
MS675 **174** £2 multicoloured 7·00 7·50

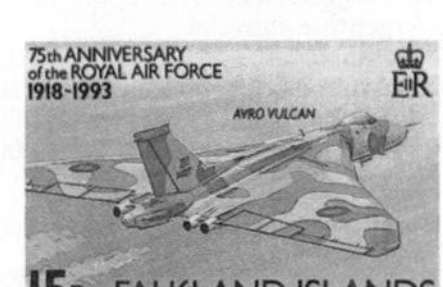

174a Avro Vulcan B.1A

1993. 75th Anniv of Royal Air Force. Multicoloured.
676 15p. Type **174a** 75 85
677 15p. Lockhead Hercules 75 85
678 15p. Boeing-Vertol Chinook 75 85
679 15p. Lockhead TriStar 500 75 85
MS680 110 × 77 mm. 36p. Hawker Siddeley Andover CC.2; 36p. Westland Wessex HC-2 helicopter; 36p. Panavia Tornado F Mk 3; 36p. McDonnell Douglas F-4M Phantom II 3·75 4·75

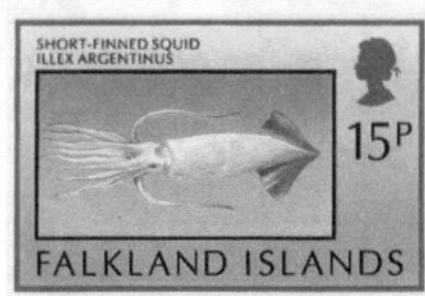

175 Short-finned Squid

1993. Fisheries. Multicoloured.
681 15p. Type **175** 60 60
682 31p. Catch of whip-tailed hake 1·25 1·40
683 36p. "Falklands Protector" (fisheries patrol vessel) 1·50 1·75
684 72p. Britten Norman Islander patrol aircraft and "Pomorze" (fish factory ship) 2·25 4·50

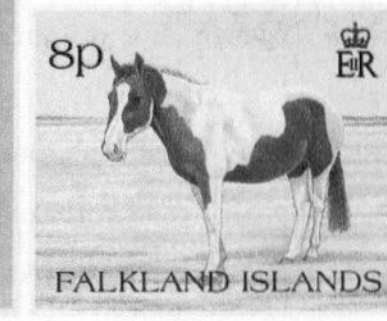

176 "Great Britain" in Dry Dock, Bristol
178 Pony

177 "Explorer" (liner)

1993. 150th Anniv of Launch of "Great Britain" (liner). Multicoloured.
685 8p. Type **176** 75 50
686 £1 "Great Britain" at sea 2·75 4·50

1993. Tourism. Multicoloured.
687 16p. Type **177** 1·25 70
688 34p. Rockhopper penguins 2·00 1·50
689 39p. "World Discoverer" (liner) 2·25 2·00
690 78p. "Columbus Caravelle" (liner) 2·75 4·50

1993. Pets. Multicoloured.
691 8p. Type **178** 60 60
692 16p. Lamb 75 75
693 34p. Puppy and cat 1·75 1·75
694 39p. Kitten (vert) 2·00 2·00
695 78p. Collie dog (vert) 2·75 4·00

1994. "Hong Kong '94" International Stamp Exhibition. Nos. 691/5 optd **HONG KONG '94** and emblem.
696 8p. Type **178** 80 90
697 16p. Lamb 1·00 1·10
698 34p. Puppy and cat 2·25 2·50
699 39p. Kitten (vert) 2·50 2·75
700 78p. Collie dog (vert) 3·25 5·00

179 Goose Barnacles

1994. Inshore Marine Life. Multicoloured.
701 1p. Type **179** 65 50
702 2p. Painted shrimp (horiz) 1·25 50
703 8p. Patagonian copper limpet (horiz) 1·50 75
704 9p. Eleginops ("Mullet") (horiz) 1·50 75
705 10p. Sea anemones (horiz) 1·50 60
706 20p. Flathead eelpout (horiz) 2·25 90
707 25p. Spider crab (horiz) 2·25 90
708 50p. Lobster krill 2·50 2·00
709 80p. Falkland skate (horiz) 2·50 2·50
710 £1 Centollon crab (horiz) 2·50 2·50
711 £3 Wilton's notothen ("Rock Cod") (horiz) 7·50 6·25
712 £5 Octopus 12·00 10·50

180 Dockyard Blacksmith's Shop and Sir James Clark Ross (explorer)

1994. 150th Anniv of Founding of Stanley. Multicoloured.
713 9p. Type **180** 60 50
714 17p. 21 Fitzroy Road (home of Chaplain James Moody) 85 60
715 30p. Stanley Cottage (built by Dr. Henry Hamblin) 1·40 1·25
716 35p. Pioneer Row and Sgt.-Maj. Henry Felton 1·60 1·75
717 40p. Government House (designed by Governor R. Moody) 1·75 1·90
718 65p. View of Stanley and Edward Stanley, Earl of Derby (Secretary of State for Colonies) 2·50 3·00

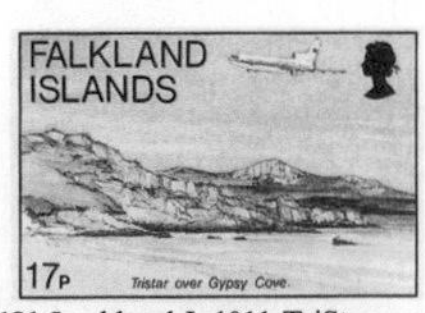

181 Lockheed L-1011 TriStar over Gypsy Cove

1994. Falkland Beaches. Multicoloured.
719 17p. Type **181** 85 70
720 35p. "Explorer" (liner) off Sea Lion Island 1·60 1·40
721 40p. Britten Norman Islander aircraft at Pebble Island 2·00 2·00
722 65p. Landrover at Volunteer Beach 2·25 3·50

182 Mission House, Keppel Island

1994. 150th Anniv of South American Missionary Society. Multicoloured.
723 5p. Type **182** 35 40
724 17p. Thomas Bridges (compiler of Yahgan dictionary) 65 65
725 40p. Fuegian Indians 1·40 1·75
726 65p. Capt. Allen Gardiner and "Allen Gardiner" (schooner) 1·75 2·50

183 "Lupinus arboreus"

1995. Flowering Shrubs. Multicoloured.
727 9p. Type **183** 50 50
728 17p. "Hebe elliptica" 70 70
729 30p. "Fuschia magellanica" 95 95
730 35p. "Berberis ilicifolia" 1·10 1·10
731 40p. "Ulex europaeus" 1·25 1·25
732 65p. "Hebe x franciscana" 2·00 2·75

184 Magellanic Oystercatcher

1995. Shore Birds. Multicoloured.
733 17p. Type **184** 1·25 85
734 35p. Rufous-chested dotterel 1·75 1·50
735 40p. Blackish oystercatcher 1·90 1·90
736 65p. Two-banded plover 3·50 6·00

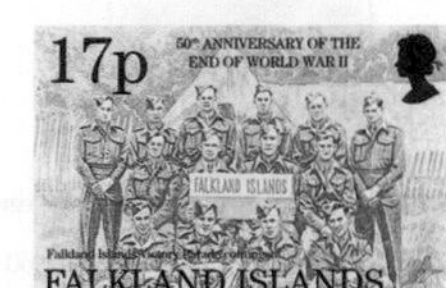

184a Falkland Islands Contingent in Victory Parade

1995. 50th Anniv of End of Second World War. Multicoloured.
737 17p. Type **184a** 90 75
738 35p. Governor Sir Alan Cardinall on Bren gun-carrier 1·60 1·40
739 40p. H.M.A.S. "Esperance Bay" (troopship) 1·75 1·75
740 65p. H.M.S. "Exeter" (cruiser) 3·25 3·75
MS741 75 × 85 mm. £1 Reverse of 1939–45 War Medal (vert) 3·50 3·75

185 Ox and Cart

1995. Transporting Peat. Multicoloured.
742 17p. Type **185** 60 60
743 35p. Horse and cart 1·10 1·10
744 40p. Caterpillar tractor pulling sleigh 1·25 1·25
745 65p. Lorry 2·25 3·50

186 Kelp Geese

1995. Wildlife. Multicoloured.
746 35p. Type **186** 1·50 1·25
747 35p. Black-browed albatross 1·50 1·25
748 35p. Blue-eyed cormorants 1·50 1·25
749 35p. Magellanic penguins 1·50 1·25

750 35p. Fur seals . . . . 1·50 1·25
751 35p. Rockhopper penguins 1·50 1·25
Nos. 746/51 were printed together, se-tenant, forming a composite design.

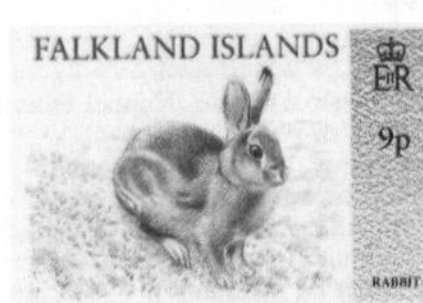

187 Cottontail Rabbit

1995. Introduced Wild Animals. Multicoloured.
752 9p. Type **187** 65 65
753 17p. Brown hare 90 75
754 35p. Guanacos . . . . 1·40 1·40
755 40p. Fox . . . . 1·60 1·60
756 65p. Otter . . . . 2·50 3·00

188 Princess Anne and Government House

1996. Royal Visit. Multicoloured.
757 9p. Type **188** 70 45
758 19p. Falklands War Memorial, San Carlos Cemetery 80 65
759 30p. Christ Church Cathedral 1·10 1·10
760 73p. Helicopter over Goose Green . . . . 4·00 3·00

188a Steeple Jason

1996. 70th Birthday of Queen Elizabeth II. Each incorporating a different photograph of the Queen. Multicoloured.
761 17p. Type **188a** 60 50
762 40p. "Tamar" (container ship) . . . . 1·50 1·25
763 45p. New Island . . . . . . 1·50 1·40
764 65p. Falkland Islands Community School . . . . 1·60 1·60
MS765 64 × 66 mm. £1 Queen Elizabeth II . . . . 2·75 3·25

189 Mounted Postman, c. 1890

1996. "CAPEX '96" International Stamp Exhibition. Mail Transport. Multicoloured.
766 9p. Type **189** 75 60
767 40p. Noorduyn Norseman V seaplane . . . . 1·75 1·50
768 45p. "Forrest" (freighter) at San Carlos . . . . 1·75 1·60
769 76p. De Havilland D.H.C.2 Beaver seaplane . . . . . 2·75 2·75
MS770 110 × 80 mm. £1 L.M.S. Class "Jubilee" steam locomotive No. 5606 "Falkland Islands" (47 × 31 mm) . . . . 2·40 3·50

190 Southern Bottlenose Whale

1996. Beaked Whales. Multicoloured.
771 9p. Type **190** 55 45
772 30p. Cuvier's beaked whale 1·10 1·10
773 35p. Straptoothed beaked whale . . . . 1·25 1·25
774 75p. Gray's beaked whale . . 2·40 2·40

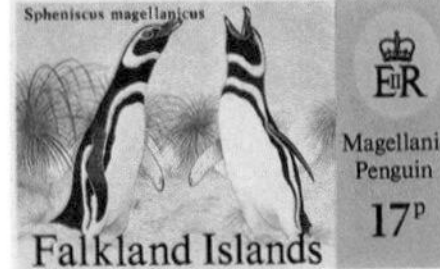

191 Magellanic Penguins performing Courtship Dance

1997. Magellanic Penguins. Multicoloured.
775 17p. Type **191** . . . . . . 1·00 55
776 35p. Penguins in burrow . . 1·75 1·00
777 40p. Adult and chick . . . . 1·75 1·25
778 65p. Group of Penguins swimming . . . . 2·50 1·75

192 Black Pejerry

1997. "HONG KONG '97" International Stamp Exhibition. Sheet 130 × 90 mm.
MS779 **192** £1 multicoloured . . 2·50 2·50

193 Coral Fern **193a** Queen Elizabeth II

1997. Ferns. Multicoloured.
780 17p. Type **193** 80 45
781 35p. Adder's tongue fern . . 1·40 1·00
782 40p. Fuegian tall fern . . . . 1·60 1·10
783 65p. Small fern . . . . . . 2·00 1·75

1997. Return of Hong Kong to China. Sheet 130 × 90 mm, containing design as No. 710.
MS784 £1 Centolln crab . . . . 2·50 2·50

1997. Golden Wedding of Queen Elizabeth II and Prince Philip. Multicoloured.
785 9p. Type **193a** . . . . . . 1·00 60
786 9p. Prince Philip and horse, 1995 . . . . 1·00 60
787 17p. Queen Elizabeth in phaeton at Trooping the Colour, 1996 . . . . . . 1·25 80
788 17p. Prince Philip in R.A.F. uniform . . . . 1·25 80
789 40p. Queen Elizabeth wearing red coat, 1986 . . . . . 1·60 1·10
790 40p. Prince William and Princess Beatrice on horseback . . . . 1·60 1·10
MS791 110 × 71 mm. £1.50, Queen Elizabeth and Prince Philip in landau (horiz) . . . . 6·50 3·75
Nos. 785/6, 787/8 and 789/90 respectively were printed together, se-tenant, with the backgrounds forming composite designs.

194 Bull Point Lighthouse

1997. Lighthouses. Multicoloured.
792 9p. Type **194** 75 40
793 30p. Cape Pembroke Lighthouse . . . . 1·50 1·25
794 £1 Cape Meredith Lighthouse 3·00 3·00

195 Forster's Caracara ("Johnny Rock")

1997. Endangered Species. Multicoloured.
795 17p. Type **195** . . . . . . 1·25 70
796 19p. Southern sealion . . . . 1·00 85
797 40p. Felton's flower . . . . 1·75 1·50
798 73p. Trout . . . . 2·50 4·00

196 Merryweather and Son Greenwich Gem Fire Engine **196a** Wearing Black Jacket, 1990

1998. Centenary of Falkland Islands Fire Service. Multicoloured.
799 9p. Type **196** . . . . 1·25 55
800 17p. Merryweather's Hatfield trailer pump . . . . 1·75 70
801 40p. Coventry Climax Godiva trailer pump . . . 2·75 1·50
802 65p. Carmichael Bedford "Type B" water tender . . 3·00 3·25

1998. Diana, Princess of Wales Commemoration.
MS803 145 × 70 mm. 30p. Type **196a**, 30p. Wearing red dress, 1988; 30p. Resting head on hand, 1991; 30p. Wearing landmine protection clothing, Angola (sold at £1.20 + 20p. charity premium) . . . . . . 3·25 3·25

197 Tawny-throated Dotterel

1998. Rare Visiting Birds. Multicoloured. (a) Designs $39\frac{1}{2} \times 23\frac{1}{2}$ mm.
804 1p. Type **197** . . . . 50 1·00
805 2p. Hudsonian godwit . . . 50 1·00
806 5p. Eared dove . . . . . . 60 1·00
807 9p. Great grebe 80 80
808 10p. Southern lapwing . . . 80 80
809 16p. Buff-necked ibis . . . . 1·25 1·00
810 30p. Ashy-headed goose . . . 1·75 1·25
811 65p. Red-legged cormorant ("Red-legged Shag") . . . 2·50 2·00
812 88p. Argentine shoveler ("Red Shoveler") . . . . 3·25 3·25
813 £1 Red-fronted coot . . . . 3·50 4·00
814 £3 Chilian flamingo . . . . 7·00 8·50
815 £5 Fork-tailed flycatcher . . 11·00 15·00

(b) Designs 35 × 22 mm.
816 9p. Roseate spoonbill 60 85
817 17p. Austral conure ("Austral Parakeet") . . . . 1·00 1·10
818 35p. American kestrel . . . . 1·60 2·25

198 "Penelope" (auxillary ketch) **200** Marine at Port Egmont, Saunders Island, 1766

199 First Medivac Air Ambulance Service, 1948

1998. Local Vessels. Multicoloured.
819 17p. Type **198** . . . . . . 1·00 55
820 35p. "Ilen" (auxillary ketch) 1·75 1·25
821 40p. "Weddell" (schooner) 1·90 1·40
822 65p. "Lively" (tug) (31 × 22 mm) . . . . . . 2·50 2·50

1998. 50th Anniv of Falkland Islands Government Air Service. Multicoloured.
823 17p. Type **199** . . . . . . 2·25 50
824 £1 F.I.G.A.S. Beaver and Islander aircraft over map 4·50 3·25

1998. Royal Marine Uniforms. Multicoloured.
825 17p. Type **200** . . . . . . 1·50 75
826 30p. Officer at Port Louis, East Falklands, 1833 . . . 2·00 1·75
827 35p. Corporal and H.M.S. "Kent" (cruiser), 1914 . . 2·00 1·75
828 65p. Bugler at Government House, 1976 . . . . 3·50 4·00

201 Altar, St. Mary's Church

1999. Centenary of St. Mary's Roman Catholic Church, Stanley. Multicoloured.
829 17p. Type **201** . . . . . . 1·50 70
830 40p. St. Mary's Church . . . 2·25 2·00
831 75p. Laying of foundation stone, 1899 . . . . 3·75 5·00

202 H.M.S. "Beagle" (Darwin)

1999. "Australia '99" World Stamp Exhibition, Melbourne. Maritime History. Multicoloured.
832 25p. Type **202** . . . . . . 1·75 1·25
833 35p. H.M.A.S. "Australia" (battle cruiser) . . . . . . 2·00 1·25
834 40p. "Canberra" (liner) . . . 2·25 1·60
835 50p. "Great Britain" (steam/sail) . . . . 2·50 3·25
836 50p. All-England Cricket Team, 1861–62 . . . . . 2·50 3·25

203 Prince of Wales (from photo by Clive Arrowsmith) **203a** Prince Edward and Miss Sophie Rhys-Jones

1999. Royal Visit.
837 **203** £2 multicoloured . . . . 7·50 6·50

1999. Royal Wedding. Multicoloured.
838 80p. Type **203a** . . . . . . 3·75 2·25
839 £1.20 Engagement photograph . . . . 4·75 3·75

204 "Jeanne d'Arc" (French cruiser)

1999. "PHILEXFRANCE '99", International Stamp Exhibition, Paris. First Flight over Falkland Islands, 1931. Multicoloured.
840 35p. Type **204** . . . . . . 1·75 1·75
841 40p. CAMS 37 (flying boat) taking off . . . . 1·75 1·75
MS842 115 × 63 mm. £1 CAMS 37 over Port Stanley (47 × 31 mm) 5·00 4·50

204a On Board Ship, Port of London, 1939

1999. "Queen Elizabeth the Queen Mother's Century". Multicoloured.
843 9p. Type **204a** . . . . . . 1·00 60
844 20p. With Queen Elizabeth II, 1996 . . . . 1·60 90
845 30p. With Prince Charles and his sons, 1995 . . . . . . 1·75 1·25
846 67p. Presenting colours to Queen's Royal Hussars . . 3·25 5·00
MS847 145 × 70 mm. £1.40, Duchess of York, 1936, and Shackleton, Scott and Wilson in the Antarctic, 1902 . . . . 8·00 8·00

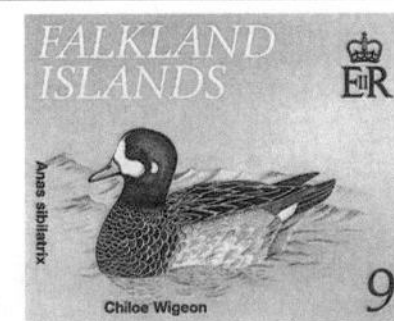

205 Chiloe Wigeon

1999. Waterfowl. Multicoloured.
848 9p. Type **205** . . . . 1·25 80
849 17p. Crested duck . . . . . 1·50 1·00
850 30p. Georgian teal ("Brown Pintail") . . . . 2·25 1·75
851 35p. Versicolor teal ("Silver Teal") . . . . 2·25 1·75
852 40p. Chilean teal ("Yellow-billed Teal") . . . . 2·25 1·75
853 65p. Falkland Islands flightless steamer duck . . 3·25 4·25

206 Hulk of "Vicar of Bray", 1999

1999. 150th Anniv of California Goldrush. Mult.
854 9p. Type **206** . . . . 1·50 80
855 35p. Panning for gold, 1849 2·25 1·75
856 40p. Gold rocking cradle, 1849 . . . . 2·25 1·75
857 80p. "Vicar of Bray" (barque) at sea, 1849 . . . 3·75 5·00
MS858 105 × 63 mm. £1 "Vicar of Bray" in San Francisco (47 × 31 mm) . . . . 5·50 6·50

207 Magellan Goose ("Upland Goose") on Nest

1999. New Millennium. Multicoloured.
859 9p. Type **207** . . . . 90 1·10
860 9p. Southern black-backed gull ("Kelp Gull") at sunrise . . . . 90 1·10
861 9p. Christ Church Cathedral, Stanley . . . . 90 1·10
862 30p. Black-crowned night heron ("Night Heron") at sunset . . . . 1·60 1·75
863 30p. Family and Christmas tree . . . . 1·60 1·75
864 30p. King penguins . . . . . 1·60 1·75

208 Princess Alexandra and Meadow

2000. Visit of Princess Alexandra. Multicoloured.
865 9p. Type **208** . . . . 1·00 65
866 £1 Princess Alexandra and plantation of saplings . . . 4·25 5·00

208a "Endurance" off Caird Coast

2000. Shackleton's Trans-Antarctic Expedition, 1914–1917, Commemoration.
867 **208a** 17p. multicoloured . . . 1·50 75
868 – 45p. blue and black . . . 2·50 2·00
869 – 75p. multicoloured . . . 3·75 5·00
DESIGNS: 45p. "Endurance" beset in the Weddell Sea pack-ice; 75p. Sir Ernest Shackleton and "Yelcho" (Chilean resone tug).

208b Queen Elizabeth I **208c** Wearing Fireman's helmet, 1988

2000. "Stamp Show 2000" International Stamp Exhibition, London. Kings and Queens of England. Multicoloured.
870 40p. Type **208b** . . . . . . 1·75 1·75
871 40p. King James II . . . . . 1·75 1·75
872 40p. King George I . . . . . 1·75 1·75
873 40p. King William IV . . . . 1·75 1·75
874 40p. King Edward VIII . . . 1·75 1·75
875 40p. Queen Elizabeth II . . . 1·75 1·75

2000. 18th Birthday of Prince William. Mult.
876 10p. Type **208c** 70 60
877 20p. At Eton, 1995 . . . . . 85 75
878 37p. Prince William in Cardiff, 2000 (horiz) . . . 1·40 1·40
879 43p. Prince William in 1998 (horiz) . . . . 1·40 1·60
MS880 175 × 95 mm. 50p. With golden retriever, 1997 (horiz) and Nos. 876/9 . . . . 6·00 7·00

2000. Queen Elizabeth the Queen Mother's 100th Birthday. No. **MS**847 optd **100 birthday.**
MS881 145 × 70 mm. £1.40, Duchess of York, 1936, and Shackleton, Scott and Wilson in the Antarctic, 1902 . . . . 5·50 6·50

210 Malo River Bridge

2000. Bridges. Multicoloured.
882 20p. Type **210** . . . . . . 1·50 85
883 37p. Bodie Creek Bridge . . 2·00 1·75
884 43p. Fitzroy River Bridge . . 2·25 2·25

211 Shepherd with Lamb

2000. Christmas. Multicoloured.
885 10p. Type **211** 70 55
886 20p. Angel with Shepherds 1·10 60
887 33p. The Nativity . . . . . 1·50 90
888 43p. Angel with Wise Men 1·75 1·10
889 78p. Camel . . . . 2·75 4·50
MS890 160 × 75 mm. Nos. 885/9 7·50 7·50

212 Sunset over Islands

2001. Sunrise and Sunsets. Multicoloured.
891 10p. Type **212** 65 60
892 20p. Sunset over Stanley . . 1·00 80
893 37p. Sunset over Stanley Harbour . . . . 1·60 1·40
894 43p. Sunrise over islands . . 1·75 1·75

213 Forster's Caracara ("Striated caracara")

2001. "HONG KONG 2001" Stamp Exhibition. Sheet 150 × 90 mm, containing T **213** and similar horiz design showing bird of prey. Multicoloured.
MS895 37p. Type **213**; 37p. Hodgsons hawk eagle ("Mountain hawk") . . . . 3·75 4·25

214 1878 1d. Claret Stamp

2001. Death Centenary of Queen Victoria. Multicoloured.
896 3p. Type **214** 50 60
897 10p. *Great Britain* (steam/sail) (horiz) 90 60
898 20p. Stanley Harbour, 1888 (horiz) . . . . 1·10 70
899 43p. Cape Pembroke Lighthouse and first telephone line, 1897 . . . 2·00 1·25
900 93p. Royal Marines, 1900 . . 3·25 3·50
901 £1.50 "Queen Victoria, 1859" (Franz Winterhalter) . . . 4·00 4·75
MS902 105 × 80 mm. £1 Queen Victoria's funeral cortege in the streets of Windsor . . . . . . 3·75 4·50

215 *Welfare* (first British landing on Falkland Islands, 1690)

2001. Royal Navy Connections with the Falkland Islands. Multicoloured.
903 10p. Type **215** 70 60
904 17p. H.M.S. *Invincible* (battle cruiser), 1914 . . . . . . 1·00 65
905 20p. H.M.S. *Exeter* (cruiser), 1939 . . . . 1·10 75
906 37p. SR N6 hovercraft, 1967 1·50 1·25
907 43p. H.M.S. *Protector* (ice patrol ship) . . . . 1·60 1·40
908 68p. *Desire* (Cavendish and Davis), 1592 . . . . . . 2·50 3·25

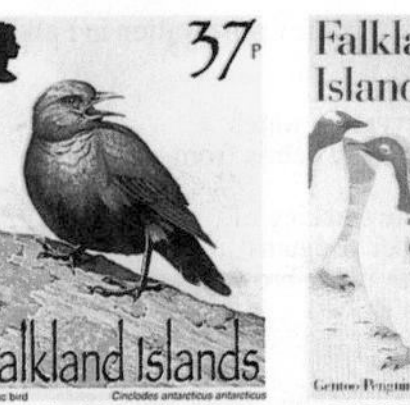

216 Blackish Cinclodes ("Tussac Bird") **217** Young Gentoo Penguins

2001. Off-shore Islands (1st series). Carcass Island. Multicoloured.
909 37p. Type **216** . . . . . . 1·50 1·60
910 37p. Yellow violet . . . . . 1·50 1·60
911 43p. Black-crowned night heron . . . . 1·60 1·75
912 43p. Carcass Island settlement . . . . 1·60 1·75
See also Nos. 941/4, 972/5 and 993/6.

2001. Gentoo Penguins. Multicoloured.
913 10p. Type **217** 65 60
914 33p. Adult feeding chick . . 1·25 1·10
915 37p. Adult on eggs . . . . . 1·40 1·40
916 43p. Group of penguins . . . 1·50 1·60

218 Rounding-up Wild Cattle

2002. 150th Anniv of Falkland Islands Company. Multicoloured.
917 10p. Type **218** 75 60
918 20p. *Amelia*, (postal schooner), 1852 . . . . . 1·50 75
919 43p. F. E. Cobb (Colonial Manager), 1867 . . . . . 1·75 1·00
920 £1 W. W. Bertrand, (sheep farmer) and sheep dipping 3·25 4·00

219 Princess Elizabeth reading, 1945

2002. Golden Jubilee.
921 **219** 20p. agate, violet and gold 90 70
922 – 37p. multicoloured . . . 1·40 1·00
923 – 43p. brown, violet and gold . . . . 1·50 1·10
924 – 50p. multicoloured . . . 1·75 2·00
MS925 162 × 95 mm. Nos. 921/4 and 50p. multicoloured . . . . . . 7·00 8·00
DESIGNS—HORIZ: 37p. Queen Elizabeth, New Zealand, 1977; 43p. Princess Elizabeth with Prince Charles at his christening, 1949; 50p. Queen Elizabeth in Garter robes, Windsor, 1994. VERT (38 × 51 mm)—50p. Queen Elizabeth after Annigoni.
Designs as Nos. 921/4 in No. **MS**925 omit the gold frame around each stamp and the "Golden Jubilee 1952–2002" inscription.

220 H.M.S. *Hermes* (aircraft carrier), 1982

2002. 20th Anniv of Liberation. Multicoloured.
926 22p. Type **220** . . . . 85 1·00
927 22p. *Dorada* (fishery patrol vessel), 2002 . . . . 85 1·00
928 40p. Troops landing, 1982 . . 1·50 1·60
929 40p. Mine clearing, 2002 . . 1·50 1·60
930 45p. Harrier jet on H.M.S. *Hermes*, 1982 . . . . . . 1·60 1·75
931 45p. R.A.F. Tristar, 2002 . . 1·60 1·75

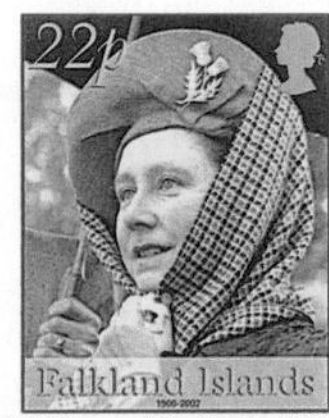

221 Queen Elizabeth visiting Royal Farms, Windsor, 1946

2002. Queen Elizabeth the Queen Mother Commemoration.
932 **221** 22p. brown, gold and purple . . . . 1·00 75
933 – 25p. multicoloured . . . 1·00 75
934 – 95p. black, gold and purple . . . . 3·00 3·25
935 – £1.20 multicoloured . . . 3·50 4·00
MS936 145 × 70 mm. Nos. 934/5 8·00 8·50
DESIGNS: 25p. Queen Mother at Guildhall lunch for Queen's Golden Wedding, 1997; 95p. Queen Elizabeth at a garden party, 1947; £1.20, Queen Mother at Scrabster, 1986.
Designs as Nos. 934/5 in No. **MS**936 omit the "1900–2002" inscription and the coloured frame.

222 Rockhopper Penguin

2002. Endangered Species. Penguins. Multicoloured.
937 36p. Type **222** . . . . 1·25 1·25
938 40p. Magellanic penguin . . 1·40 1·40
939 45p. Gentoo penguin . . . . 1·50 1·50
940 70p. Macaroni penguin . . . 2·25 2·75

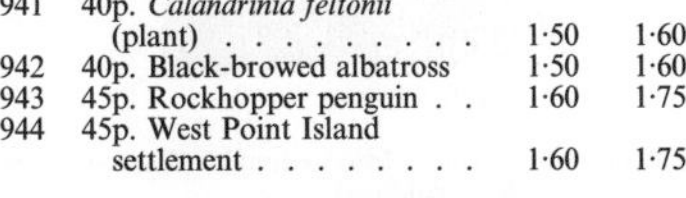

2002. Off-shore Islands (2nd series). West Point Island. As T **216**, but horiz. Multicoloured.
941 40p. *Calandrinia feltonii* (plant) . . . . 1·50 1·60
942 40p. Black-browed albatross 1·50 1·60
943 45p. Rockhopper penguin . . 1·60 1·75
944 45p. West Point Island settlement . . . . 1·60 1·75

FALKLAND ISLANDS
223 Prince Andrew as Naval Helicopter Pilot, 1982

2002. Visit of Duke of York to Falkland Islands.
945 **223** 22p. black and blue . . . 1·50 75
946 – £1.52 multicoloured . . . 5·00 5·50
DESIGN: £1.52, Duke of York and San Carlos Cemetery.

224 Gun Hill Shanty, Little Chartres

2003. Shepherds' Houses. Multicoloured.
947 10p. Type **224** 40 40
948 22p. Paragon House, Lafonia 65 55
949 45p. Dos Lomas, Lafonia . . 1·25 1·00
950 £1 The Old House, Shallow Bay Farm . . . . 2·40 2·75

225 Queen Elizabeth II

226 Prince William at Queen Mother's 101st Birthday and at Eton College

2003.
951 **225** £2 black, orange and brown . . . . 5·00 5·50

2003. 21st Birthday of Prince William of Wales. Multicoloured.
952 95p. Type **226** . . . . 3·50 3·50
953 95p. With Prince Harry at polo match and at Sighthill Community Education Centre . . . . 3·50 3·50

227 Chiloe Wigeon

2003. Birds. Multicoloured.
954 1p. Type **227** 10 10
955 2p. Dolphin gull (vert) . . . 15 15
956 5p. Falkland Islands flightless steamer duck 20 20
957 10p. Black-throated finch (vert) 35 35
958 22p. White-tufted grebe . . . 65 65
959 25p. Rufous-chested dotterel (vert) 70 70
960 45p. Magellan goose ("Upland Goose") . . . . 1·25 1·25
961 50p. Dark-faced ground tyrant (vert) . . . . 1·40 1·50
962 95p. Black-crowned night heron . . . . 2·75 3·00
963 £1 Red-backed buzzard ("Red-backed Hawk") (vert) . . . . 2·75 3·00
964 £3 Black-necked swan . . . 7·50 8·00
965 £5 Short-eared owl (vert) . . 12·00 13·00

(b) Self-adhesive.
966 (–) Rockhopper penguins . . 80 80

No. 966 was inscribed "Airmail Postcard".

228 Albatross on Nest

2003. Bird Life International. Black-browed Albatross. Multicoloured.
967 22p. Type **228** 75 75
968 22p. Nestling 75 75
969 40p. Adults displaying (vert) 1·50 1·50
970 £1 Immature bird (grey beak) on nest (vert) . . . . . . 3·00 3·50
MS971 175 × 80 mm. 16p. Albatrosses in flight and Nos. 967/70 . . . . 6·50 7·00

2003. Off-shore Islands (3rd series). New Island. Multicoloured. As T **216**, but horiz.
972 40p. Forster's caracara ("Striated Caracara") . . . 1·50 1·60
973 40p. Lady's slipper orchids 1·50 1·60
974 45p. The Stone Cottage . . . 1·60 1·70
975 45p. King penguin . . . . . 1·60 1·70

229 Pale Maiden Flowers

2003. Christmas. National Flower. Pale Maiden (*Olysnium filifolium*). Multicoloured.
976 16p. Type **229** 70 45
977 30p. Bouquet of Pale Maiden flowers . . . . 1·25 90
978 40p. Pale Maiden plant . . . 1·50 1·10
979 95p. Pale Maiden plant growing on moorland . . . 3·00 3·75

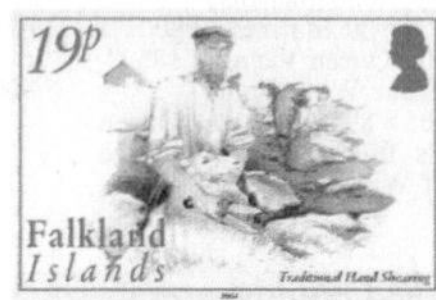

230 Hand Shearing

2004. History of Sheep Farming in the Falklands. Multicoloured.
980 19p. Type **230** 40 45
981 22p. Driving flock of sheep 45 50
982 45p. The "Big House", Hill Cove 90 95
983 70p. Woman in Victorian-style dress . . . . 1·40 1·40
984 £1 *Fitzroy* (supply ship) collecting wool . . . . . . 2·00 2·00

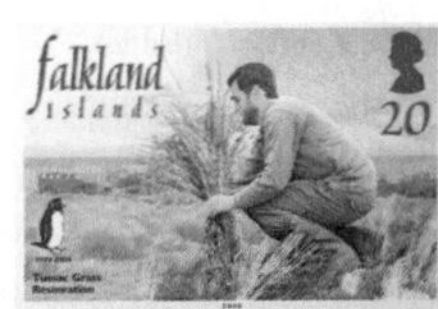

231 Volunteer planting Tussac

2004. 25 Years of Wildlife Conservation in Falklands. Multicoloured.
985 20p. Type **231** 40 45
986 24p. Conservation watch group clearing debris from beach 50 55
987 50p. Satellite tracking of rockhopper penguins . . . 1·00 1·10
988 £1 Weighing black-browed albatross chick . . . . . . 2·00 2·00

232 Sir Rowland Hill and 1898 Falkland Islands Stamp

2004. 125th Death of Sir Rowland Hill (postal reformer). Showing Sir Rowland Hill and early Falkland Islands stamps. Multicoloured.
989 24p. Type **232** 50 55
990 50p.5s. King penguin (No. 136) . . . . 1·00 1·10
991 75p.5s. Southern sealion (No. 161) . . . . 1·50 1·60
992 £1 6d. HMS *Glasgow* (No. 216 error) . . . . . 2·00 2·10

2004. Off-shore Islands (4th series). Sea Lion Island. As T **216** but horiz. Multicoloured.
993 42p. King cormorant 85 90
994 42p. Dog orchid 85 90
995 50p. Magellanic penguin . . 1·00 1·10
996 50p. Sea Lion Lodge . . . . 1·00 1·10

233 Short-eared Owl

2004. Owls. Multicoloured.
997 18p. Type **233** 35 40
998 45p. Short-eared owl on rock 90 95
999 50p. Barn owl in flight . . . 1·00 1·10
1000 £1.50 Barn owl on fence . . 3·00 3·25
MS1001 74 × 54 mm. £2 Barn owl flying . . . . 4·00 4·00

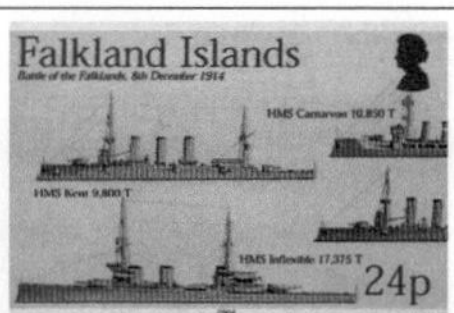

234 HMS *Kent*, HMS *Inflexible* and HMS *Carnarvon*

2004. 90th Anniv of the Battle of the Falkland Islands. Multicoloured.
1002 24p. Type **234** 50 55
1003 24p. HMS *Cornwall*, HMS *Glasgow* and HMS *Invincible* 50 55
1004 24p. HMS *Invincible* and two medals 50 55
1005 50p. SMS *Scharnhorst* and two coins . . . . 1·00 1·10
1006 50p. SBS *Scharnhorst*, SMS *Leipzig* and SMS *Dresden* 1·00 1·10
1007 50p. SMS *Nurnberg* and SMS *Gneisenau* . . . . . 1·00 1·10

Nos. 1002/4 and 1005/7 were each printed together, se-tenant, with the backgrounds forming composite designs.

235 The Old Track Bed

2005. 90th Anniv of the Camber Railway. Multicoloured.
1008 3p. Type **235** 10 10
1009 24p. Kerr Stuart "Wren" Class locomotive at Camber depot (horiz) . . 50 55
1010 50p. Falkland Islands Express (horiz) . . . . . 1·00 1·10
1011 £2 Camber Sailing Wagon 4·00 4·25

236 Prince Charles and Mrs. Camilla Parker-Bowles

2005. Royal Wedding. Multicoloured.
1012 24p. Type **236** 50 55
1013 50p. Prince Charles and Mrs. Camilla Parker-Bowles at evening reception (vert) . . . . . 1·00 1·10
MS1014 120 × 65 mm. £2 Prince Charles and Mrs. Camilla Parker-Bowles and Windsor Castle . . 4·00 2·25

POSTAGE DUE STAMPS

D **1** King Penguin

1991.
D1 D **1** 1p. red and mauve . . . 10 10
D2 2p. orange and light orange 10 10
D3 3p. ochre and yellow . . 10 10
D4 4p. green and light green 10 15
D5 5p. blue and light blue . . 10 15
D6 10p. deep blue and blue 20 25
D7 20p. violet and lilac . . . 40 45
D8 50p. green and light green 1·00 1·10

FALKLAND ISLANDS DEPENDENCIES — Pt. 1

Four groups of Islands situated between the Falkland Is. and the South Pole. In 1946 the four groups ceased issuing separate issues which were replaced by a single general issue. From 1963 the stamps of British Antarctic Territory were used in all these islands except South Georgia and South Sandwich for which separate stamps were issued inscribed "SOUTH GEORGIA" from 1963 until 1980.

Under the new constitution effective on 3 October 1985, South Georgia and South Sandwich Islands ceased to be dependencies of the Falkland Islands.

1944. 12 pence = 1 shilling;
20 shillings = 1 pound.
1971. 100 (new) pence = 1 pound.

GRAHAM LAND

1944. Stamps of Falkland Islands of 1938 optd **GRAHAM LAND DEPENDENCY OF.**
A1 **27** ½d. black and green . . . . 30 1·75
A2 – 1d. black and violet . . . . 30 1·00
A3 – 2d. black and red . . . . . 50 1·00
A4 – 3d. black and blue . . . . 50 1·00
A5 – 4d. black and purple . . . 2·00 1·75
A6 – 6d. black and brown . . . 16·00 2·25
A7 – 9d. black and blue . . . . 1·00 1·25
A8 – 1s. blue . . . . 1·00 1·25

SOUTH GEORGIA

1944. Stamps of Falkland Islands of 1938 optd **SOUTH GEORGIA DEPENDENCY OF.**
B1 **27** ½d. black and green . . . . 30 1·75
B2 – 1d. black and violet . . . . 30 1·00
B3 – 2d. black and red . . . . . 50 1·00
B4 – 3d. black and blue . . . . 50 1·00
B5 – 4d. black and purple . . . 2·00 1·75
B6 – 6d. black and brown . . . 16·00 2·25
B7 – 9d. black and blue . . . . 1·00 1·25
B8 – 1s. blue . . . . 1·00 1·25

SOUTH ORKNEYS

1944. Stamps of Falkland Islands of 1938 optd **SOUTH ORKNEYS DEPENDENCY OF.**
C1 **27** ½d. black and green . . . . 30 1·75
C2 – 1d. black and violet . . . . 30 1·00
C3 – 2d. black and red . . . . . 50 1·00
C4 – 3d. black and blue . . . . 50 1·00
C5 – 4d. black and purple . . . 2·00 1·75
C6 – 6d. black and brown . . . 16·00 2·25
C7 – 9d. black and blue . . . . 1·00 1·25
C8 – 1s. blue . . . . 1·00 1·25

SOUTH SHETLANDS

1944. Stamps of Falkland Islands of 1938 optd **SOUTH SHETLAND DEPENDENCY OF.**
D1 **27** ½d. black and green . . . . 30 1·75
D2 – 1d. black and violet . . . . 30 1·00
D3 – 2d. black and red . . . . . 50 1·00
D4 – 3d. black and blue . . . . 50 1·00
D5 – 4d. black and purple . . . 2·00 1·75
D6 – 6d. black and brown . . . 16·00 2·25
D7 – 9d. black and blue . . . . 1·00 1·25
D8 – 1s. blue . . . . 1·00 1·25

GENERAL ISSUES

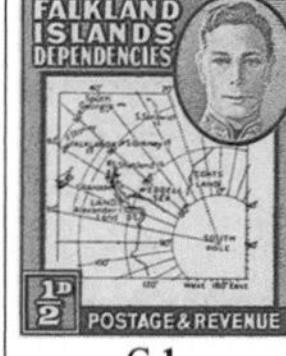

G **1**

G **3** "Trepassey", 1945–47

1946.
G 1 G **1** ½d. black and green . . 1·00 3·50
G 2 1d. black and violet . . 1·25 1·75
G 3 2d. black and red . . . 1·25 2·50
G11a 2½d. black and blue . . 6·50 5·00
G 4 3d. black and blue . . . 1·25 5·00
G 5 4d. black and red . . . 2·25 4·75
G 6 6d. black and orange 3·25 4·75
G 7 9d. black and brown . . 2·00 3·75
G 8 1s. black and purple . . 2·00 4·25

1946. Victory. As T **11a** of Gambia.
G17 1d. violet 50 50
G18 3d. blue 75 50

1949. Silver Wedding. As T **11b/c** of Gambia.
G19 2½d. blue . . . . 2·50 2·50
G20 1s. blue . . . . 1·75 2·50

1949. U.P.U. As T **11d/g** of Gambia.
G21 1d. violet . . . . 1·00 2·25
G22 2d. red . . . . 5·00 3·50
G23 3d. blue . . . . 3·25 1·25
G24 6d. orange . . . . 4·00 3·00

1953. Coronation. As T **11h** of Gambia.
G25 1d. black and violet . . . . 1·10 1·25

1954. Ships.
G26 – ½d. black and green . . 30 2·75
G27 G **3** 1d. black and sepia . . . 1·75 1·50
G28 – 1½d. black and olive . . 2·00 2·75
G29 – 2d. black and red . . . 1·75 1·25
G30 – 2½d. black and yellow . . 1·25 35
G31 – 3d. black and blue . . . 1·25 35
G32 – 4d. black and purple . . 4·25 1·50
G33 – 6d. black and lilac . . . 4·75 1·50
G34 – 9d. black . . . . 4·50 2·25
G35 – 1s. black and brown . . 4·50 1·75
G36 – 2s. black and red . . . . 19·00 11·00
G37 – 2s.6d. black and turquoise . . . . . 20·00 8·50
G38 – 5s. black and violet . . . 42·00 9·50
G39 – 10s. black and blue . . . 55·00 20·00
G40 – £1 black . . . . 90·00 48·00

SHIPS—VERT: 1½d. "John Biscoe"; 6d. "Discovery"; 9d. "Endurance"; 2s.6d. "Francais"; 5s. "Scotia"; £1 "Belgica". HORIZ: 1½d. "Wyatt Earp"; 2d. "Eagle"; 2½d. "Penola"; 3d. "Discovery II"; 4d. "William Scoresby"; 1s. "Deutschland"; 2s. "Pourquoi pas?"; 10s. "Antarctic".

1956. Trans-Antarctic Expedition. Nos. G27, G30/1 and G33 optd **TRANS-ANTARCTIC EXPEDITION 1955-1958.**

G41 G **3** 1d. black and sepia . . . 10 35
G42 – 2½d. black and yellow . . 50 60
G43 – 3d. black and blue . . . 50 30
G44 – 6d. black and lilac . . . 50 30

For later issues see **BRITISH ANTARCTIC TERRITORIES** and **SOUTH GEORGIA**.

ISSUES FOR SOUTH GEORGIA AND SOUTH SANDWICH ISLANDS

In 1980 stamps were again inscribed "FALKLAND ISLANDS DEPENDENCIES" for use in the above area.

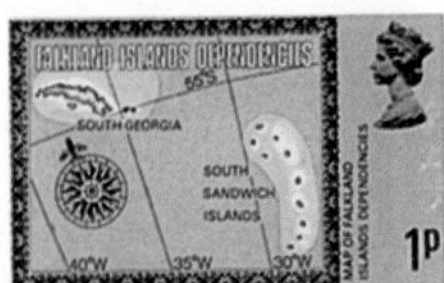

14 Map of Falkland Islands Dependencies

1980. Multicoloured.

74A 1p. Type **14** 30 30
75A 2p. Shag Rocks 30 30
76A 3p. Bird and Willis Islands 30 30
77A 4p. Gulbrandsen Lake . . . 30 30
78A 5p. King Edward Point . . . 30 30
79A 6p. Sir Ernest Shackleton's memorial cross, Hope Point 40 30
80A 7p. Sir Ernest Shackleton's grave, Grytviken 40 40
81A 8p. Grytviken Church . . . 30 40
82A 9p. Coaling Hulk "Louise" at Grytviken 30 45
83A 10p. Clerke Rocks 30 45
84B 20p. Candlemas Island . . . 1·50 1·50
85B 25p. Twitcher Rock and Cook Island, Southern Thule . . . . 1·50 2·50
86A 50p. R.R.S. "John Biscoe II" in Cumberland Bay . . . 70 1·50
87A £1 R.R.S. "Bransfield" in Cumberland Bay . . . . 75 2·25
88A £3 H.M.S. "Endurance" in Cumberland Bay . . . . 2·00 4·50

These stamps come with or without date imprint.

15 Magellanic Clubmoss

16 Wedding Bouquet from Falkland Islands Dependencies

1981. Plants. Multicoloured.

89 3p. Type **15** 10 25
90 6p. Alphine cat's-tail 10 30
91 7p. Greater burnet 10 30
92 11p. Antarctic bedstraw . . . 15 30
93 15p. Brown rush 15 35
94 25p. Antarctic hair grass . . . 25 50

1981. Royal Wedding. Multicoloured.

95 10p. Type **16** 15 30
96 13p. Prince Charles dressed for skiing 20 35
97 52p. Prince Charles and Lady Diana Spencer 65 85

17 Introduced Reindeer during Calving, Spring

1982. Reindeer. Multicoloured.

98 5p. Type **17** 20 65
99 13p. Bull at rut, Autumn . . . 20 85
100 25p. Reindeer and mountains, Winter . . . . 30 1·10
101 26p. Reindeer feeding on tussock, late Winter . . . 30 1·10

18 "Gamasellus racovitzai" (tick)

19 Lady Diana Spencer at Tidworth, Hampshire, July 1981

1982. Insects. Multicoloured.

102 5p. Type **18** 10 25
103 10p. "Alaskozetes antarcticus" (mite) 15 35
104 13p. "Cryptopygus antarcticus" (spring-tail) . . 15 40
105 15p. "Notiomaso australis" (spider) 15 40
106 25p. "Hydromedion sparsutum" (beetle) 25 50
107 26p. "Parochlus steinenii" (midge) 25 50

1982. 21st Birthday of Princess of Wales. Multicoloured.

108 5p. Falkland Islands Dependencies coat of arms 10 15
109 17p. Type **19** 40 35
110 37p. Bride and groom on steps of St. Paul's 45 80
111 50p. Formal portrait . . . . 1·00 1·10

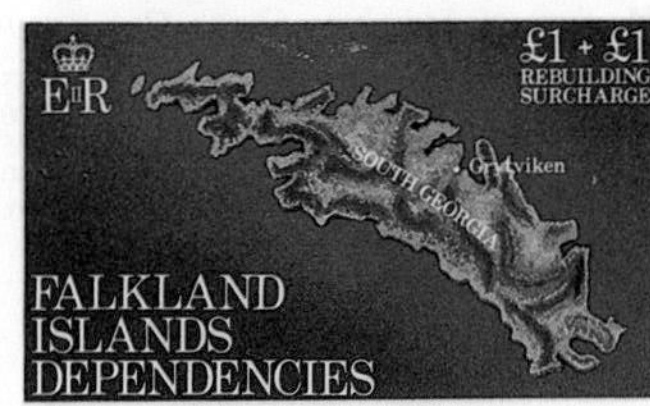

20 Map of South Georgia

1982. Rebuilding Fund.

112 **20** £1+£1 multicoloured . . . 1·50 3·25

21 Westland Whirlwind

1983. Bicentenary of Manned Flight. Multicoloured.

113 5p. Type **21** 25 35
114 13p. Westland Wasp helicopter 35 60
115 17p. Vickers Supermarine Walrus II 35 60
116 50p. Auster Autocrat . . . . 70 1·25

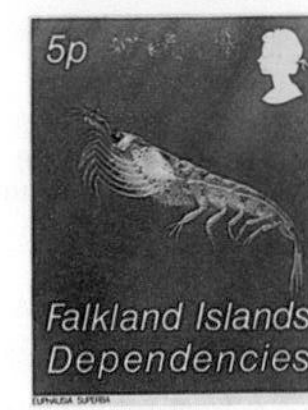

22 "Euphausia superba"

1983. Crustacea. Multicoloured.

117 5p. Type **22** 40 20
118 17p. "Glyptonotus antarcticus" 50 50
119 25p. "Epimeria monodon" 60 60
120 34p. "Serolis pagenstecheri" 70 80

23 Zavodovski Island

1984. Volcanoes of South Sandwich Islands. Mult.

121 6p. Type **23** 65 80
122 17p. Mt. Michael, Saunders Island . . . . 1·50 1·60
123 22p. Bellingshausen Island . . 1·50 1·75
124 52p. Bristol Island . . . . . 2·00 3·25

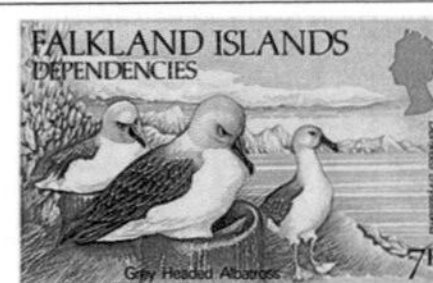

24 Grey-headed Albatross

1985. Albatrosses. Multicoloured.

125 7p. Type **24** . . . . 1·25 85
126 22p. Black-browed albatross 1·50 1·40
127 27p. Wandering albatross . . 1·75 1·60
128 54p. Light-mantled sooty albatross . . . . 2·00 2·50

25 The Queen Mother

1985. Life and Times of Queen Elizabeth the Queen Mother. Multicoloured.

129 7p. At Windsor Castle on Princess Elizabeth's 14th Birthday, 1940 . . . . . 30 30
130 22p. With Princess Anne, Lady Sarah Armstrong-Jones and Prince Edward at Trooping the Colour . . 60 70
131 27p. Type **25** 70 80
132 54p. With Prince Henry at his christening (from photo by Lord Snowdon) . . . . . 1·25 1·40
MS133 91 × 73 mm. £1 Disembarking from Royal Yacht *Britannia* . . . . 2·75 2·75

1985. Early Naturalists. As T **149a** of Falkland Islands. Multicoloured.

134 7p. Dumont d'Urville and "Durvillea antarctica" (kelp) . . . . 75 1·00
135 22p. Johann Reinhold Forster and king penguin . . . . 1·50 1·75
136 27p. Johann Georg Adam Forster and tussock grass 1·50 2·00
137 54p. Sir Joseph Banks and dove prion . . . . 2·00 3·00

For later issues see **SOUTH GEORGIA AND THE SOUTH SANDWICH ISLANDS**.

FARIDKOT Pt. 1

A state of the Punjab, India. Now uses Indian stamps.

1879. 1 folus = 1 paisa = ¼ anna.
1886. 12 pies = 1 anna; 16 annas = 1 rupee.

N **1** (1 folus) N **2** (1 paisa)

1879. Imperf.

N5 N **1** 1f. blue . . . . 3·25 3·75
N6 N **2** 1p. blue . . . . 3·75 9·00

1887. Stamps of India (Queen Victoria) optd **FARIDKOT STATE.**

17 **40** 3p. red . . . . 1·50 40·00
1 **23** ½a. turquoise . . . . 1·75 1·40
3 – 1a. purple . . . . 2·00 1·75
4 – 2a. blue . . . . 2·75 5·50
7 – 3a. orange . . . . 3·25 4·50
8 – 4a. green (No. 96) . . . . . 7·50 15·00
11 – 6a. brown (No. 80) . . . . 2·00 15·00
12 – 8a. mauve . . . . 12·00 38·00
14 – 12a. purple on red . . . . 40·00 £400
15 – 1r. grey . . . . 42·00 £375
16 **37** 1r. green and red . . . . . 35·00 95·00

OFFICIAL STAMPS

1886. Stamps of India (Queen Victoria) optd **SERVICE FARIDKOT STATE.**

O 1 **23** ½a. turquoise 30 60
O 2 – 1a. purple . . . . 1·00 1·60
O 4 – 2a. blue . . . . 1·75 9·00
O 6 – 3a. orange . . . . 6·50 8·50
O 8 – 4a. green (No. 96) . . . . 4·25 24·00
O11 – 6a. brown (No. 80) . . . . 21·00 26·00
O12 – 8a. mauve . . . . 7·00 27·00
O14 – 1r. grey . . . . 48·00 £200
O15 **37** 1r. green and red . . . . . 80·00 £550

FAROE ISLANDS Pt. 11

A Danish possession in the North Atlantic Ocean. Under British Administration during the German Occupation of Denmark, 1940/5.

100 ore = 1 krone.

1940. Stamps of Denmark surch with new value (twice on Type **43**).

2 **43** 20ore on 1ore green . . . . 36·00 55·00
3 20ore on 5ore purple . . . . 36·00 23·00
1 **40** 20ore on 15ore red . . . . . 55·00 12·50
4 **43** 50ore on 5ore purple . . . . £275 55·00
5 60ore on 6ore orange £110 £170

2 1673 Map of the Faroe Islands

3 "Vidoy and Svinoy" (E. Nohr)

1975.

6 **2** 5ore brown 20 15
7 – 10ore blue and green 20 15
8 **2** 50ore blue 20 20
9 – 60ore brown and blue . . . 90 75
10 – 70ore black and blue 90 75
11 – 80ore brown and blue . . . 45 45
12 **2** 90ore red 85 75
13 – 120ore blue and deep blue . . 45 30
14 – 200ore black and blue . . . 70 70
15 – 250ore green, brown & blue 75 60
16 – 300ore green, brown & blue 3·75 1·90
17 **3** 350ore multicoloured 90 85
18 – 450ore multicoloured . . . . 1·00 95
19 – 500ore multicoloured . . . . 1·10 1·00

DESIGNS—As Type **2** but HORIZ: 10, 60, 80, 120ore Northern map (A. Ortelius); 70, 200ore West Sandoy; 250, 300ore Streymoy and Vagar. As Type **3**: 450ore "Nes" (R. Smith); 500ore "Hvitanes and Skalafjordur" (S. Joensen-Mikines).

4 Rowing Boat

5 Motor Fishing Boat

1976. Inauguration of Faroese Post Office.

20 **4** 125ore red . . . . 2·00 1·30
21 – 160ore multicoloured 40 35
22 – 800ore green . . . . 1·40 95

DESIGNS—24 × 34 mm: 160ore Faroese flag. 24 × 31 mm: 800ore Faroese postman.

1977. Faroese Fishing Vessels.

23 **5** 100ore black, lt green & green . . . . 5·00 4·25
24 – 125ore black, rose and red 65 70
25 – 160ore black, lt blue & blue 1·00 90
26 – 600ore black, ochre & brown 1·40 90

DESIGNS: 125ore "Niels Pauli" (inshore fishing cutter); 160ore "Krunborg" (seine fishing boat); 600ore "Polarfisk" (deep-sea trawler).

6 Common Snipe

7 Atlantic Puffins over North Coast

1977. Birds. Multicoloured.

27 70ore Type **6** 35 20
28 180ore Oystercatcher 45 45
29 250ore Whimbrel 50 55

1978. Views of Mykines Island. Multicoloured.

30 100ore Type **7** 25 25
31 130ore Mykines village (horiz) 35 25
32 140ore Cultivated fields (horiz) 45 40
33 150ore Aerial view of Mykines 45 35
34 180ore Map of Mykines (37 × 26 mm) 45 40

8 Northern Gannet

9 Old Library Building

1978. Sea Birds. Multicoloured.
35 140ore Type **8** 60 50
36 180ore Atlantic puffin 80 65
37 400ore Common guillemot 85 70

1978. 150th Anniv of National Library.
38 **9** 140ore olive and blue 50 45
39 – 180ore brown and flesh 50 50
DESIGN: 180ore New National Library building.

10 Guide, Tent and Campfire
11 Ram 

1978. 50th Anniv of Girl Guides.
40 **10** 140ore multicoloured 50 60

1979. Sheep-rearing.
41 **11** 25k. multicoloured 5·00 3·75

12 Bisect of Denmark 4ore Blue, 1919
13 Girl in Festive Costume 

1979. Europa. Multicoloured.
42 **12** 140ore bl & yell on stone 50 50
43 – 180ore ol & mve on stone 50 50
DESIGN: 180ore Denmark 1919 2ore surcharge on 5ore.

1979. International Year of the Child. Multicoloured designs showing childrens' drawings.
44 110ore Type **13** 35 25
45 150ore Man fishing from boat 35 35
46 200ore Two friends 50 45

14 Sea Plantain
15 Jakob Jakobsen (linguist and folklorist) 

1980. Flowers. Multicoloured.
47 90ore Type **14** 20 25
48 110ore Glacier buttercup 20 25
49 150ore Purple saxifrage 35 25
50 200ore Starry saxifrage 60 35
51 400ore Faroese lady's mantle 1·00 70

1980. Europa.
52 **15** 150ore green 35 35
53 – 200ore brown 45 35
DESIGN: 200ore Vensel Ulrich Hammershaimb (theologian and linguist).

16 Virgin and Child
17 Timber Houses, Torshavn 

1980. Pews of Kirkjubour Church (1st series).
54 **16** 110ore multicoloured 45 30
55 – 140ore multicoloured 45 25
56 – 150ore multicoloured 45 30
57 – 200ore black and buff 50 35
DESIGNS: 140ore St. John the Baptist; 150ore St. Peter; 200ore St. Paul.
See also Nos. 90/3.

1981. Old Torshavn. Designs show different views.
58 **17** 110ore green 45 25
59 – 140ore black 45 30
60 – 150ore brown 45 30
61 – 200ore blue 45 40

18 Garter Dance

1981. Europa.
62 **18** 150ore green and brown 30 30
63 – 200ore brown and green 40 45
DESIGN: 200ore Ring dance.

19 Rune Stone
20 Map of Viking Voyages in North Atlantic 

1981. Historic Writings of the Faroes.
64 **19** 10ore blue, black and grey 15 15
65 – 1k. lt brown, black & brn 35 25
66 – 3k. grey, black and red 1·00 55
67 – 6k. red, black and grey 1·40 1·10
68 – 10k. stone, brown and black 2·50 2·40
DESIGNS: 1k. Score of folksong, 1846; 3k. Manuscript of Sheep Farming Law, 1298; 6k. Seal showing heraldic ram, 1533; 10k. Title page of "Faeroae et Faeroa Reserata" and library.

1982. Europa.
69 **20** 1k.50 blue 30 40
70 – 2k. black 55 45
DESIGN: 2k. Archaeological excavations at Kvivik village.

21 Gjogv
22 Elinborg's Promise to remain Faithful 

1982. Villages.
71 **21** 180ore black and blue 50 40
72 – 220ore black and brown 1·00 50
73 – 250ore black and brown 80 50
DESIGNS: 220ore Hvalvik; 250ore Kvivik.

1982. The Ballad of Harra Paetur and Elinborg. Multicoloured.
74 220ore Type **22** 70 40
75 250ore Elinborg longing for Paetur 70 45
76 350ore Paetur in disguise greets Elinborg 1·00 65
77 450ore Elinborg and Paetur sail away 1·30 95

23 "Arcturus"
24 King 

1983. Old Cargo Liners on the Faroes Run. Multicoloured.
78 220ore Type **23** 65 55
79 250ore "Laura" 85 60
80 700ore "Thyra" 2·30 1·90

1983. 19th-century Chess Pieces by Pol i Bud from Nolsoy.
81 **24** 250ore brown and black 1·50 1·40
82 – 250ore blue and black 1·50 1·40
DESIGN: No. 82, Queen.

25 Niels R. Finsen (founder of phototherapy)

1983. Europa.
83 **25** 250ore blue 70 65
84 – 400ore purple 1·30 1·00
DESIGN: 400ore Sir Alexander Fleming (discoverer of penicillin).

26 Torsk

1983. Fishes. Multicoloured.
85 250ore Type **26** 60 45
86 280ore Haddock 80 65
87 500ore Atlantic halibut 1·40 1·20
88 900ore Atlantic wolffish 2·50 2·20

27 Greenland, Halsingland (Sweden) and Iceland Costumes

1983. Inauguration of Nordic House (cultural centre), Torshavn. Sheet 120 × 67 mm containing T **27** and similar horiz designs.
MS89 250ore Type **27**; 250ore Finnmark (Norway), Funen (Denmark) and Aland costumes; 250ore Telemark (Norway), Faroes and Ostra Nyland (Finland) costumes 7·00 8·00

1984. Pews of Kirkjubour Church (2nd series). As T **16**.
90 250ore multicoloured 80 65
91 300ore lt brown, black & brn 1·30 1·00
92 350ore brown, grey & black 90 85
93 400ore multicoloured 1·50 1·30
DESIGNS: 250ore St. John; 300ore St. Jacob; 350ore St. Thomas; 400ore Judas Taddeus.

28 Bridge

1984. Europa. 25th Anniv of European Post and Telecommunications Conference.
94 **28** 250ore red 70 70
95 500ore blue 1·40 1·30

29 Sverri Patursson
30 Fisherman 

1984. Writers.
96 **29** 200ore green 60 50
97 – 250ore red 80 70
98 – 300ore blue 90 75
99 – 450ore violet 1·30 1·10
DESIGNS: 250ore Joannes Patursson; 300ore Janus Djurhuus; 450ore Hans Andrias Djurhuus.

1984. Fishing Industry.
100 – 280ore blue 70 75
101 – 300ore brown 85 85
102 **30** 12k. green 3·00 3·25
DESIGNS—HORIZ: 280ore Fishing ketch "Westward Ho". VERT: 300ore Fishermen on deck.

31 "Beauty of the Veils"
32 Torshavn 

1984. Fairy Tales. Designs showing woodcuts by Elinborg Lutzen.
103 **31** 140ore blue, green & brn 4·00 4·25
104 – 280ore green and brown 4·00 4·25
105 – 280ore dp green, grn & brn 4·00 4·25
106 – 280ore brown and green 4·00 4·25
107 – 280ore dp green, grn & brn 4·00 4·25
108 – 280ore brn, grn & dp brn 4·00 4·25
DESIGNS: No. 104, "Beauty of the Veils" (different); 105, "The Shy Prince"; 106, "The Glass Sword"; 107, "Little Elin"; 108, "The Boy and the Ox".

1985. J. T. Stanley's Expedition to the Faroes, 1789. Paintings by Edward Dayes.
109 **32** 250ore brown and blue 80 70
110 – 280ore brown, green & bl 75 85
111 – 550ore green, brown & bl 1·50 1·70
112 – 800ore brown, green & bl 2·50 2·40
DESIGNS: 280ore Mount Skaeling; 550ore Hoyvik; 800ore The Rocking Stones, Eysturoy.

33 Cellist, Pianist and Flautist

1985. Europa. Music Year. Multicoloured.
113 280ore Type **33** 75 80
114 550ore Drummer, guitarist and saxophonist 2·10 2·10

34 "Self-portrait" (Ruth Smith)

1985. Paintings. Multicoloured.
115 280ore "The Garden, Hoyvik" (Tummas Arge) (horiz) 1·00 80
116 450ore Type **34** 1·60 1·50
117 550ore "Winter's Day in Nolsoy" (Steffan Danielsen) (horiz) 2·50 2·00

35 Nolsoy Lighthouse

1985. Lighthouses. Multicoloured.
118 270ore Type **35** 1·20 1·30
119 320ore Torshavn 1·30 1·50
120 350ore Mykines 1·40 1·60
121 470ore Map of the Faroes showing lighthouse sites 2·00 2·00

36 Douglas DC-3, Faroe Airways

1985. Aircraft. Multicoloured.
122 300ore Type **36** 2·40 2·20
123 300ore Fokker F.27 Friendship, Flugfelag Islands 2·40 2·20
124 300ore Boeing 737 Special, Maersk Air 2·40 2·20
125 300ore Beech 50 Twin Bonanza, Bjorum Fly 2·40 2·20
126 300ore Bell 212 helicopter, Snipan 2·40 2·20

37 Peasant in Forest
38 Ship dumping Dangerous Canisters at Sea 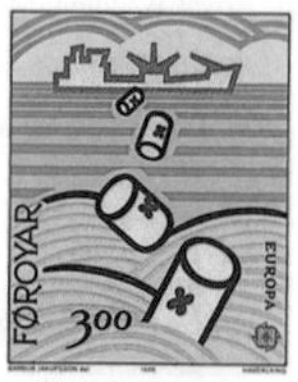

1986. Skrimsla (dancing ballad). Mult.
127 300ore Type **37** 1·00 85
128 420ore Giant challenges peasant to chess game 1·30 1·40
129 550ore Peasant beats giant 2·00 1·90
130 650ore Peasant and castle 2·30 2·10

1986. Europa. Multicoloured.
131 3k. Type **38** 1·30 1·50
132 5k.50 Contents of damaged canister escaping into sea 2·20 2·50

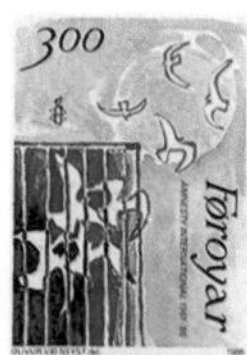

39 Birds escaping from Cage 40 Ship at Anchor in Bay

1986. 25th Anniv of Amnesty International. Multicoloured.
133 3k. Type **39** . . . . 1·20 1·00
134 4k.70 Faces (horiz) . . . . . 1·40 1·40
135 5k.50 Man behind bars and woman with children . . . 2·00 1·90

1986. "Hafnia 87" International Stamp Exhibition, Copenhagen (1st issue). Sheet 108 × 76 mm containing T **40** and similar vert designs showing "Torshavn East Bay" (watercolour) by Christian Rosenmeyer. Multicoloured.
MS136 3k. Type **40**; 4k.70 Rowing boat in bay; 6k.50 Houses (sold at 20k.) . . . . 8·75 8·50
See also No. **MS**154.

41 Glyvrar Bridge, Eysturoy

1986. Bridges.
137 **41** 2k.70 brown . . . . 2·00 1·90
138 – 3k. blue . . . . 2·10 1·80
139 – 13k. green . . . . 5·00 4·25
DESIGNS—VERT: 3k. Leypanagjogv, Vagar. HORIZ: 13k. Skaelingur, Streymoy.

42 Farmhouse, Depli 43 Windows

1987. Farm Buildings.
140 **42** 300ore dp blue & blue . . 1·00 90
141 – 420ore brown & lt brown 2·30 1·90
142 – 470ore green & lt green . . 2·50 1·70
143 – 650ore black & grey . . . 2·75 2·30
DESIGNS: 420ore Barn, Depli; 470ore Cowshed and blacksmith's, Frammi vid Gjonna; 650ore Farmhouse, Frammi vid Gjonna.

1987. Europa. Architecture. Details of Nordic House, Torshavn (by O. Steen and K. Ragnarsdottir).
144 **43** 300ore blue . . . . 1·30 1·20
145 – 550ore brown . . . . . . 2·30 2·20
DESIGN: 550ore Entrance.

44 "Joannes Patursson" 45 Map

1987. Trawlers. Multicoloured.
146 300ore Type **44** . . . . . . 1·20 85
147 550ore "Magnus Heinason" (side trawler) . . . . . . 2·50 2·20
148 800ore "Sjurdarberg" (stern trawler) . . . . 4·50 3·00

1987. Hestur Island. Multicoloured.
149 270ore Type **45** . . . . . . 1·00 1·00
150 300ore Harbour (horiz) . . . 90 90
151 420ore Alvastakkur needle . . 1·40 1·50
152 470ore Fagradalsvatn Lake (horiz) . . . . 1·60 1·50
153 550ore Bygdin village . . . . 2·00 1·80

46 Ships in Bay

1987. "Hafnia 87" International Stamp Exhibition, Copenhagen (2nd issue). Sheet 75 × 54 mm showing "Torshavn West Bay" (watercolour) by Christian Rosenmeyer.
MS154 **46** 3k. multicoloured (sold at 4k.) . . . . 2·75 3·25

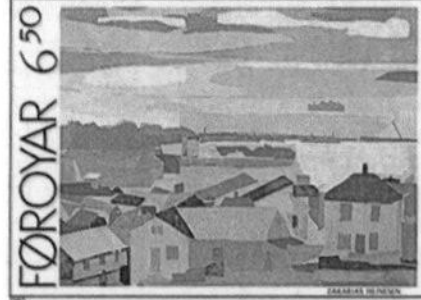

47 "West Bay"

1987. Torshavn Views. Collages by Zacharias Heinesen. Multicoloured.
155 4k.70 "East Bay" . . . . . 2·00 1·80
156 6k.50 Type **47** . . . . . . 2·20 2·40

48 Daisy 49 Container Ship and Dockside Scene

1988. Flowers. Multicoloured.
157 2k.70 Type **48** . . . . . . 1·20 90
158 3k. Heath spotted orchid . . 1·00 90
159 4k.70 Tormentil . . . . . . 1·60 1·60
160 9k. Common butterwort . . 3·25 2·75

1988. Europa. Transport and Communications. Multicoloured.
161 3k. Dish aerial and satellite 1·10 1·40
162 5k.50 Type **49** . . . . . . 2·40 2·30

50 Jorgen-Frantz Jacobsen 51 Notice of Christmas Meeting and Conveners

1988. Writers.
163 **50** 270ore green . . . . . . 1·30 1·40
164 – 300ore red 90 85
165 – 470ore blue . . . . 2·20 1·80
166 – 650ore brown . . . . . . 3·00 2·40
DESIGNS: 300ore Christian Matras; 470ore William Heinesen; 650ore Hedin Bru.

1988. Centenary of Christmas Meeting to Establish National Movement. Multicoloured.
167 3k. Type **51** . . . . 1·00 90
168 3k.20 Drawing by William Heinesen of a People's Meeting, 1908, and conveners . . . . 1·30 1·30
169 12k. Opening words of Joannes Patursson's poem "Now the Hour has Come", conveners and oystercatcher . . . . . . 5·00 4·25

52 Exterior View of Cathedral

1988. Kirkjubour Cathedral Ruins.
170 **52** 270ore green . . . . . . 1·40 1·70
171 – 300ore blue . . . . 1·20 1·10
172 – 470ore brown . . . . . . 2·30 1·30
173 – 550ore purple . . . . . . 2·50 2·10
DESIGNS—VERT: 300ore Window; 470ore Crucifixion (relief). HORIZ: 550ore Nave.

53 Church

1989. Bicentenary of Torshavn Church.
174 **53** 350ore green . . . . . . 1·30 1·10
175 – 500ore brown . . . . . . 1·80 1·80
176 – 15k. blue . . . . 5·75 5·00
DESIGNS—VERT: 500ore "The Last Supper" (altarpiece); 15k. Bell from "Norske Love" (shipwreck).

54 Wooden Toy Boat 55 Sjostuka Man

1989. Europa. Children's Toys. Multicoloured.
177 3k.50 Type **54** . . . . . . 1·30 1·40
178 6k. Wooden horse . . . . . 2·30 2·30

1989. Nordic Countries' Postal Co-operation. Traditional Costumes. Multicoloured.
179 350ore Type **55** . . . . . 1·10 1·30
180 600ore Stakkur woman . . . . 2·10 2·10

56 Rowing 57 Tvoran

1989. Sports. Multicoloured.
181 200ore Type **56** 90 95
182 350ore Handball . . . . . . 1·30 1·20
183 600ore Football . . . . . . 2·30 2·00
184 700ore Swimming . . . . . 2·50 2·30

1989. Bird Cliffs of Suduroy. Each brown, green and blue.
185 320ore Type **57** . . . . . . 1·00 95
186 350ore Skuvanes . . . . . . 1·40 1·20
187 500ore Beinisvord . . . . . 1·70 1·60
188 600ore Asmundarstakkur . . 2·50 2·00

58 Unloading Boxes of Fish from Trawler 59 Old Post Office, Gjogv

1990. Fish Processing Industry. Mult.
189 3k.50 Type **58** . . . . . . 1·00 90
190 3k.70 Cleaning Atlantic cod 1·40 1·20
191 5k. Filleting fish . . . . . 2·20 1·60
192 7k. Packed processed fish . . 2·50 2·20

1990. Europa. Post Office Buildings. Mult.
193 3k.50 Type **59** . . . . . . 1·40 1·60
194 6k. Klaksvik post office . . . 2·50 2·20

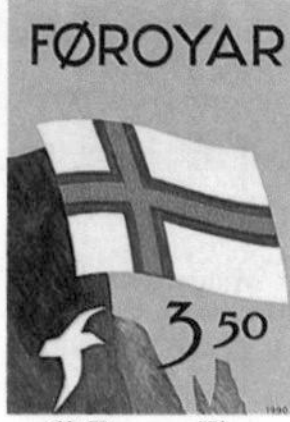

60 Faroese Flag

1990. 50th Anniv of Official Recognition of Faroese Flag. Sheet 116 × 75 mm containing T **60** and similar vert designs. Multicoloured.
MS195 3k.50 Type **60**; 3k.50 "Nyggjaberg" (trawler); 3k.50 "Sanna" (schooner) . . . . . 4·75 3·75

61 Sowerby's Beaked Whale

1990. Whales. Multicoloured.
196 320ore Type **61** . . . . . . 1·20 1·10
197 350ore Bowhead whale . . . 1·30 1·50
198 600ore Black right whale . . 2·50 2·10
199 700ore Northern bottle-nosed whale . . . . 3·50 2·20

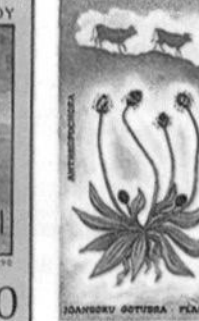

62 Nolsoy from Hilltop 63 Ribwort Plantain

1990. Nolsoy. Paintings by Steffan Danielsen. Multicoloured.
200 50ore Type **62** 15 25
201 350ore Church . . . . 1·20 90
202 500ore Village . . . . 2·00 1·80
203 1000ore Cliffs by moonlight 4·25 3·00

1991. Anthropochora. Multicoloured.
204 3k.70 Type **63** . . . . . . 1·80 1·20
205 4k. Northern dock . . . . . 2·10 1·20
206 4k.50 Black beetle . . . . . 2·50 2·00
207 6k.50 Earthworm . . . . . 3·50 2·50

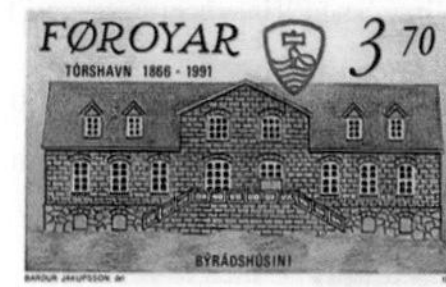

64 Town Hall

1991. 125th Anniv of Torshavn as Capital. Multicoloured.
208 3k.70 Type **64** . . . . . . 1·50 1·70
209 3k.70 Eastern Tinganes (old part of Torshavn) . . . . 1·40 1·40

65 Satellite, Earth and Weather Map 66 Arctic Terns

1991. Europa. Europe in Space. Mult.
210 3k.70 Type **65** . . . . . . 1·60 1·40
211 5k.50 Chart of Plough constellation and Pole Star, and sailors navigating by stars . . . . 2·50 2·50

1991. Birds. Multicoloured.
212 3k.70 Type **66** . . . . . . 1·60 1·30
213 3k.70 Black-legged kittiwakes 1·60 1·30

67 Saksun

1991. Nordic Countries' Postal Co-operation. Tourism. Multicoloured.
214 370ore Type **67** . . . . . . 1·30 1·20
215 650ore Vestmanna cliffs . . . 2·50 2·30

68 "Handanagardur"

1991. 85th Birth Anniv of Samal Joensen-Mikines (painter). Multicoloured.
216 340ore "Funeral Procession" 1·70 1·30
217 370ore "The Farewell" . . . 1·60 1·20
218 550ore Type **68** . . . . . . 2·00 1·70
219 1300ore "Winter Morning" 5·75 4·25

69 "Ruth"

1991. Mail Ships. Multicoloured.
220 200ore Type **69** . . . . . . 1·00 1·00
221 370ore "Ritan" . . . . 1·60 1·10
222 550ore "Sigmundur" . . . . 2·30 1·20
223 800ore "Masin" . . . . . . 3·25 2·30

70 Map and Viking Ship (Leif Eriksson)

1992. Europa. 500th Anniv of Discovery of America by Columbus. Multicoloured.
224 3k.70 Type **70** . . . . . . 1·40 1·40
225 6k.50 Map and "Santa Maria" . . . . 2·20 2·10
MS226 85 × 67 mm. Nos. 224/5 5·75 4·75

71 Grey Seal ("Halichoerus grypus")

1992. Seals. Multicoloured.
227 3k.70 Type **71** . . . . . . 1·50 1·20
228 3k.70 Common seal ("Phoca vitulina") . . . . 1·50 1·20

72 Desmine 73 Glyvra Hanus's House

1992. Minerals. Multicoloured.
229 370ore Type **72** . . . . . . 1·20 2·00
230 650ore Mesolite . . . . . . 2·30 2·20

1992. Old Houses in Nordragota, Eysturoy. Multicoloured.
231 3k.40 Type **73** . . . . . . 1·30 1·20
232 3k.70 Village and church . . 1·60 1·40
233 6k.50 Blasastova . . . . . . 2·75 2·10
234 8k. Jakupsstova . . . . . . 3·25 2·50

74 Musicians at Jazz, Folk and Blues Festival

1993. 10th Anniv of Nordic House, Torshavn. Multicoloured.
235 400ore "The Lost Musicians" (William Heinesen) . . . . 1·60 1·30
236 400ore Joannes Andreassen (pianist) . . . . 1·60 1·30
237 400ore Type **74** . . . . . . 1·60 1·30
MS238 140 × 80 mm. Nos. 235/7 3·75 4·00

75 Landscape 76 "Reflection"

1993. Nordic Countries' Postal Co-operation. Gjogv. Multicoloured.
239 4k. Type **75** . . . . 1·50 1·30
240 4k. Village . . . . 1·50 1·30

1993. Europa. Contemporary Art. Bronzes by Hans Pauli Olsen. Multicoloured.
241 4k. Type **76** . . . . 1·50 1·30
242 7k. "Movement" . . . . . . 2·30 2·20

77 Horse's Head

1993. Horses.
243 **77** 400ore brown . . . . . . 1·40 1·00
244 – 20k. lilac . . . . 7·00 6·00
DESIGN—HORIZ: 20k. Mare and foal.

78 "Apamea zeta"

1993. Butterflies and Moths. Multicoloured.
245 350ore Type **78** . . . . . . 1·30 1·00
246 400ore "Hepialus humuli" . . 1·40 1·00
247 700ore Red admiral . . . . 2·75 2·20
248 900ore "Perizoma albulata" 3·75 2·75

79 Three-spined Stickleback

1994. Fishes. Multicoloured.
249 10ore Type **79** 20 15
250 4k. False boarfish . . . . . 2·20 1·40
251 7k. Brown trout . . . . . . 2·50 2·00
252 10k. Orange roughy . . . . 5·00 3·00

80 St. Brendan discovering Faroe Islands

1994. Europa. St. Brendan's Voyages. Mult.
253 4k. Type **80** . . . . 1·60 1·30
254 7k. St. Brendan visiting Iceland . . . . 2·40 2·00
MS255 81 × 76 mm. Nos. 253/4 4·25 3·00

81 Sailing Ship and Sailor using Sextant

1994. Centenary (1993) of Faroese Nautical School, Torshavn. Multicoloured.
256 3k.50 Type **81** . . . . . . 5·00 1·40
257 7k. Modern ship and sailor using modern equipment 2·20 1·90

82 Dog and Sheep

1994. Sheepdogs. Multicoloured.
258 4k. Type **82** . . . . 1·50 1·30
259 4k. Dog's head (18 × 25 mm) 1·50 1·40

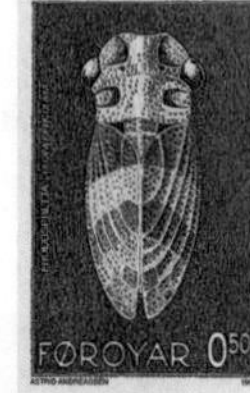

83 Viking Ship 85 "Ulopa reticulata"

84 First to Tenth Days

1994. "Brusajokil's Lay" (traditional song). Multicoloured.
260 1k. Type **83** 40 40
261 4k. Asbjorn at entrance to Brusajokil's cave . . . . . 1·50 1·30
262 6k. Trolls appearing after Ormar had killed cat . . . 1·00 1·80
263 7k. Ormar pulling off Brusajokil's beard . . . . 2·50 2·10

1994. Christmas. Designs illustrating "On the First Day of Christmas St. Martin gave to Me". Multicoloured.
264 400ore Type **84** . . . . . . 1·50 1·50
265 400ore 11th to 15th days . . 1·40 1·40

1995. Leafhoppers. Multicoloured.
266 50ore Type **85** 20 20
267 4k. "Streptanus sordidus" . . 1·40 1·30
268 5k. "Anoscopus flavostriatus" 1·60 1·50
269 13k. "Macrosteles alpinus" 5·25 4·00

86 Vatnsdalur

1995. Nordic Countries' Postal Co-operation. Tourism. Multicoloured.
270 400ore Type **86** . . . . . . 1·50 1·10
271 400ore Fomjin . . . . 1·50 1·10

87 Vidar, Vali and Baldur

1995. Europa. Peace and Freedom. Mult.
272 4k. Type **87** . . . . 1·40 1·30
273 7k. Liv and Livtrasir . . . . 2·20 2·00

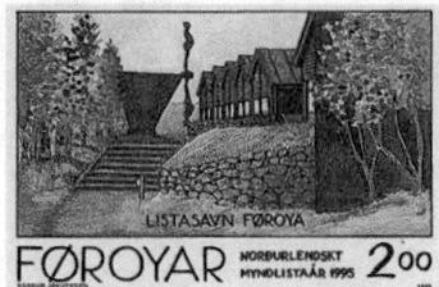

88 Museum of Art, Torshavn

1995. 50th Anniv of Nordic Artists Association. Multicoloured.
274 2k. Type **88** 80 65
275 4k. "Woman" (Frimod Joensen) (vert) . . . . . . 1·40 1·30
276 5k.50 Self-portrait (Joensen) (vert) . . . . 2·10 1·80

89 Common Raven

1995. The Raven. Multicoloured.
277 400ore Type **89** . . . . . . 1·20 1·30
278 400ore White speckled raven 1·20 1·30

90 St. Olaf

1995. Birth Millenary of St. Olaf.
279 **90** 4k. multicoloured . . . . 1·20 1·20

91 Dairy Maids

92 St. Mary's Catholic Church

1995. Rural Life.
280 **91** 4k. green . . . . 1·30 1·20
281 – 6k. brown . . . . 2·50 1·80
282 – 15k. blue . . . . 5·00 4·75

DESIGNS—VERT: 6k. Sheep shearing; 15k. Fishermen.

1995. Christmas. Multicoloured.
283 400ore Type **92** . . . . . . 1·30 1·20
284 400ore Stained glass window, St. Mary's Church . . . . 1·30 1·20

93 Risin and Kellingin (rocks) 94 "Ptilota plumosa"

1996.
285 **93** 450ore multicoloured . . . 1·30 1·20

1996. Seaweed. Multicoloured.
286 4k. Type **94** . . . . 1·40 1·10
287 5k.50 Flat wrack . . . . . . 2·10 1·60
288 6k. Knotted wrack . . . . . 2·50 2·00
289 9k. Forest kelp . . . . . . 3·00 2·40

95 "Young Girl"

96 Bohemian Waxwing

1996. Europa. Famous Women. Paintings by Samal Joensen-Mikines. Multicoloured.
290 4k.50 Type **95** . . . . . . 1·60 1·30
291 7k.50 "Old Woman" (vert) 2·00 2·00

1996. Birds (1st series). Multicoloured.
292 4k.50 Type **96** . . . . . . 1·30 1·40
293 4k.50 Red crossbill ("Loxia curvirostra") . . . . 1·30 1·40
See also Nos. 321/2, 336/7 and 355/6.

97 Faroe Islands and Compass Rose 98 Boy Playing with Hoop (Bugvi)

1996. Maps.
301 **97** 10k. multicoloured . . . . 2·30 2·40
302 11k. multicoloured . . . . 2·75 2·50
303 14k. multicoloured . . . . 3·50 3·50
304 15k. multicoloured . . . . 3·75 3·50
305 16k. multicoloured . . . . 4·25 4·25
306 18k. multicoloured . . . . 4·25 4·50
309 22k. multicoloured . . . . 4·50 4·50

1996. "Nordatlantex 96" Stamp Exhibition, Torshavn. Children's Drawings. Sheet 98 × 61 mm containing T **98** and similar vert designs. Mult.
MS314 4k.50 Type **98**; 4k.50 Girls and traffic lights (Gudrid); 4k.50 Street and child on bicycle (Herborg) . . . . 3·75 4·00

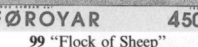

99 "Flock of Sheep" 100 Klaksvik Church

1996. Paintings by Janus Kamban. Mult.
315 4k.50 Type **99** . . . . . . 1·40 1·20
316 6k.50 "Fishermen on way Home" . . . . 2·00 1·70
317 7k.50 "View from Torshavn's Old Quarter" . . . . . . 2·30 2·20

1996. Christmas. Multicoloured.
318 4k.50 Type **100** . . . . . . 1·20 1·20
319 4k.50 Altarpiece depicting biblical scenes (21 × 38 mm) 1·20 1·20

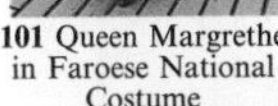

101 Queen Margrethe in Faroese National Costume

102 "Hygrocybe helobia"

1997. Silver Jubilee of Queen Margrethe. Sheet 81 × 61 mm.
MS320 **101** 450ore multicoloured 1·80 1·50

1997. Birds (2nd series). As T **96**. Mult.
321 4k.50 Redpolls ("Carduelis flammea") 1·10 1·10
322 4k.50 Northern bullfinches ("Pyrrhula pyrrhula") 1·10 1·10

1997. Fungi. Multicoloured.
323 4k.50 Type **102** 1·40 1·30
324 6k. "Hygrocybe chlorophana" 2·10 1·60
325 6k.50 Snowy wax cap 2·30 1·90
326 7k.50 Parrot wax cap 2·50 2·10

103 Seal

104 "Temptations of Saint Anthony"

1997. 600th Anniv of Kalmar Union (of Denmark, Norway and Sweden).
327 **103** 4k.50 violet 1·30 1·10

1997. Europa. Tales and Legends. Illustrations by William Heinesen. Multicoloured.
328 4k.50 Type **104** 1·20 1·20
329 7k.50 "The Merman" (eating fish bait) 1·90 1·90

105 Hvalvik Church

106 Arrival of Poul Aggerso

1997. Christmas. Multicoloured.
330 4k.50 Type **105** 1·30 1·20
331 4k.50 Church interior 1·30 1·30

1997. "Barbara" (film from novel by Jorgen-Frantz Jacobsen). Scenes from the film. Multicoloured.
332 4k.50 Type **106** 1·20 1·20
333 6k.50 Annike van der Lippe and Lars Simonsen as Barbara and Aggerso 1·75 1·60
334 7k.50 Barbara and men in boat 2·30 1·80
335 9k. Barbara in rowing boat 2·50 2·20

107 Blackbird

108 Wall of Fire around King Budle and Brynhild

1998. Birds (3rd series). Multicoloured.
336 4k.50 Type **107** 1·20 1·00
337 4k.50 Common starling ("Sturnus vulgaris") 1·20 1·00

1998. "Brynhild's Ballad" (traditional poem). Multicoloured.
338 450ore Type **108** 1·20 1·00
339 650ore Sigurd on his horse Grane jumps through the flames 1·80 1·50
340 750ore Golden rings around Sigurd and Brynhild 2·10 1·80
341 1000ore Gudrun (Sigurd's widow) leading Grane 2·50 2·40

109 Atlantic White-sided Dolphin

1998. International Year of the Ocean. Whales and Dolphins. Multicoloured.
342 4k. Type **109** 1·20 1·00
343 4k.50 Killer whale 1·20 1·10
344 7k. Bottle-nosed dolphin 2·20 1·80
345 9k. White whale 2·50 2·40

110 Procession with Flags

111 Hands cradling Family

1998. Europa. National Festivals. St. Olav's Day. Multicoloured.
346 4k.50 Type **110** 1·10 1·00
347 7k.50 Members of Parliament and clergy processing through the streets 1·90 1·90

1998. 50th Anniv of Universal Declaration of Human Rights.
348 **111** 750ore multicoloured 1·90 1·90

112 Interior of Frederik's Church, Nes

113 "Hagamynd"

1998. Christmas. Multicoloured.
349 4k.50 Type **112** 1·20 1·10
350 4k.50 Exterior of church 1·20 1·10

1998. Paintings by Hans Hansen. Mult.
351 4k.50 Type **113** 1·20 1·10
352 5k.50 "Bygdarmynd" 1·70 1·40
353 6k.50 "Portrait of a Man" 2·00 1·60
354 8k. "Self-portrait" 2·50 2·00

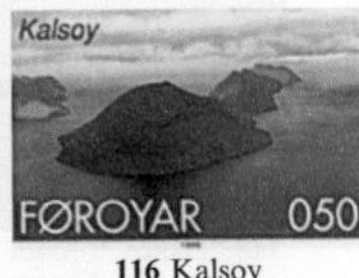

114 Winter Wren

116 Kalsoy

115 "Smiril" (ferry), 1896

1999. Birds (4th series). Multicoloured.
355 4k.50 Type **114** 1·10 1·10
356 4k.50 House sparrow ("Passer domesticus") 1·10 1·10

1999. Suduroy–Torshavn Passenger Ferries. Mult.
357 4k.50 Type **115** 1·00 1·10
358 5k. "Smiril", 1932 1·20 1·30
359 8k. "Smyril", 1967 2·10 2·00
360 13k. "Smyril" (car ferry), 1975 3·00 3·50

1999. Islands of the Faroes. Multicoloured.
361 50ore Type **116** 20 15
362 100ore Vidoy 25 25
363 200ore Skuvoy 50 60
365 400ore Svinoy 1·30 1·00
366 450ore 50 Fugloy 1·60 1·30
367 500ore Bour 1·60 1·30
368 500ore Gasadalur 1·60 1·30
368a 550ore Stora Dimun 1·70 1·30
369 600ore Kunoy 1·60 1·60
370 650ore Hestoy 2·00 1·30
370a 700ore Litla Dimun 1·90 1·60
371 750ore Koltur 2·30 1·60
372 800ore Bardoy 2·30 2·00
375 1000ore Nolsoy 3·25 2·30

117 Svartifossur, Hoydalar

118 Adam and Eve

1999. Europa. Waterfalls. Multicoloured.
379 6k. Type **117** 1·60 1·50
380 8k. Foldarafossur, Hov 2·00 2·00

1999. Christmas. Multicoloured.
381 450ore Type **118** 1·10 1·10
382 600ore The Annunciation 1·20 1·40

119 "Bygd"

120 Rasmus Rasmussen and Simun av Skardi (founders)

1999. Paintings by Ingalvur av Renyi. Mult.
383 4k.50 Type **119** 2·20 1·10
384 6k. "Husavik" 1·70 1·30
385 8k. "Reytt regn" (vert) 1·70 2·00
386 20k. "Genta" (vert) 4·00 4·50

2000. Centenary (1999) of Folk High School, Torshavn. Multicoloured.
387 4k.50 Type **120** 1·90 1·10
388 4k.50 Sanna av Skardi and Anna Suffia Rasmussen (housekeepers and teachers) 1·00 1·10

121 Arrival of Sigmundur

122 "Building Europe"

2000. One Thousand Years of Christianity on the Faroe Islands. Multicoloured.
389 4k.50 Type **121** 1·20 1·00
390 5k.50 Killing of bishop by rebels 1·20 1·30
391 8k. People with flags of Denmark and Faroe Islands 1·80 1·80
392 16k. Children on shore and sun rising 4·25 3·75

2000. Europa.
393 **122** 8k. multicoloured 1·90 1·80

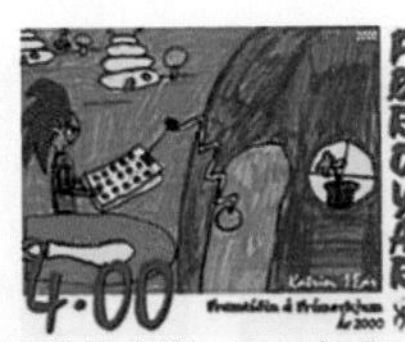

123 Girl unlocking Door by Remote Control and House (Katrin Mortensen)

2000. "Stampin' the Future". Winning Entries in Children's International Painting Competition Multicoloured.
394 4k. Type **123** 1·00 95
395 4k.50 Boy dreaming of future (Sigga Andreassen) 1·20 1·10
396 6k. Offshore oil rig (Steingrimur Joensen) 1·40 1·20
397 8k. Spaceman and television (Dion Dam Frandsen) 2·10 1·60

124 Mary and Joseph

125 Apostle holding Cross

2000. Christmas. Multicoloured.
398 4k.50 Type **124** 95 1·00
399 6k. Mary holding Jesus 1·20 1·30

2001. Pew Gables, St. Olav's Church, Kirkjubour.
400 **125** 450ore buff, black & grey 95 1·40
401 – 650ore buff, black & cinn 1·50 1·50
402 – 800ore buff, black & grn 1·60 2·00
403 – 18k. buff, black and brown 3·75 4·25

DESIGNS: 650ore Apostle holding knife; 800ore Apostle holding book in right hand; 18k. Apostle holding book in left hand.

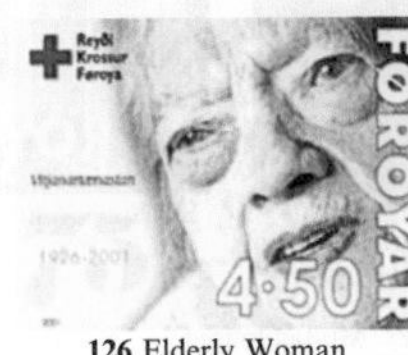

126 Elderly Woman

2001. 75th Anniv of Faroese Red Cross. Multicoloured.
404 4k.50 Type **126** 95 1·00
405 6k. Red Cross volunteers carrying patient on stretcher 1·20 1·20

127 Skjuts (early postal service) Boat

2001. 25th Anniv of Faroese Postal Administration. Sheet 138 × 101 mm containing T **127** and similar vert designs. Each buff, black and silver.
MS406 4k.50 Type **127**; 4k.50 First Post Office, Torshavn; 4k50 Postman 4·25 4·00

128 Hognis and Tidrik Tatteson ("Hognis Ballad")

2001. Nordic Myths and Legends. Multicoloured.
407 6k. Type **128** 1·40 1·40
408 6k. Tree and birds nests ("The Tree of the Year") 1·40 1·40
409 6k. Woman beside river ("The Harp") 1·40 1·40
410 6k. Sigurd the Dragonslayer's horse Grane and sword Gram 1·40 1·40
411 6k. Sigurd fighting dragon ("Ballad of Nornagest") 1·40 1·40
412 6k. Hogni Jukeson and brothers on ship ("Hognis Ballad") 1·40 1·40

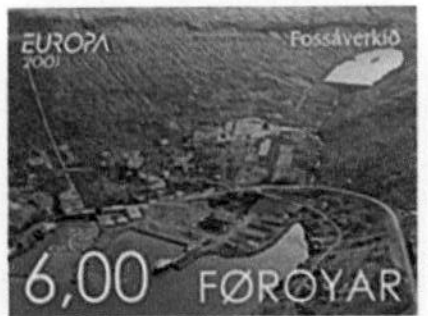

129 Hydro-electric Power Station, Fossaverkio, Vestmanna

2001. Europa. Water Resources. Multicoloured.
413 6k. Type **129** 1·20 1·20
414 8k. Hydro-electric power station, Eidisverkio, Eysturoy 1·60 1·50

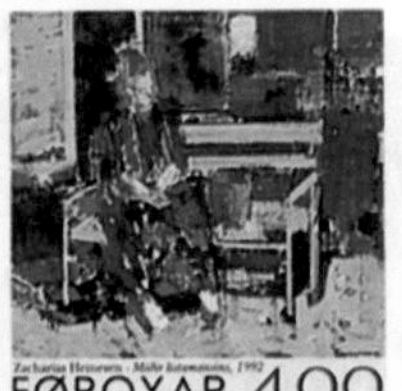
130 "The Artist's Mother"

2001. Paintings by Zacharias Heinesen. Multicoloured.
415 4k. Type **130** 70 90
416 4k.50 "Uti a Reyni" . . . . 75 1·00
417 10k. "Ur Vagunum" . . . . 1·90 1·70
418 15k. "Sunrise" . . . . 2·75 2·75

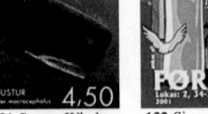

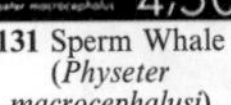
131 Sperm Whale (*Physeter macrocephalusi*)
132 Simeon and Mary

2001. Whales. Multicoloured.
419 4k.50 Type **131** . . . . . . 80 1·00
420 6k.50 Fin whales (*Balaenoptera physalus*) . . 1·60 1·60
421 9k. Blue whales (*Balaenoptera musculus*) . . . . 2·00 2·10
422 20k. Sei whales (*Balaenoptera borealis*) . . . . 4·25 4·75

2001. Christmas. Multicoloured.
423 5k. Type **132** . . . . 1·00 1·10
424 6k.50 Flight into Egypt . . . 1·40 1·30

133 Atlantic Bob-tailed Squid (*Sepiola atlantica*)
134 Primitive Compass

2002. Molluscs. Multicoloured.
425 5k. Type **133** . . . . 1·30 1·10
426 7k. Horse mussel (*Modiolus modiolus*) . . . . 1·30 1·40
427 7k.50 Sea slug (*Polycera faeroensis*) . . . . 1·30 1·50
428 18k. Common northern whelk (*Buccinum undatum*) 3·00 3·50

2002. Viking Voyages. Sheet 160×70 mm containing T **134** and similar vert designs. Multicoloured.
MS429 6k.50 Type **134**; 6k.50 Viking sailor using compass; 6k.50 Viking ship . . . . 4·75 4·75

135 "Depths of the Ocean"

2002. Nordic Countries' Postal Co-operation. Art by Trondur Patursson. Multicoloured.
430 5k. Type **135** . . . . 1·00 1·10
431 6k.50 "Cosmic Space" . . . 1·10 1·20

136 Clowns (Anna Katrina Olsen)

2002. Europa. Circus. Showing winning designs in children's painting competition. Multicoloured.
432 6k.50 Type **136** . . . . . . 1·20 1·20
433 8k. Animals in Circus Tent (Sara Zachariasardottir) . . 1·50 1·60

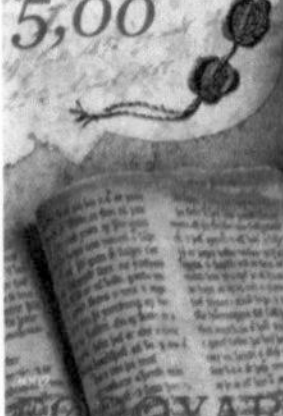

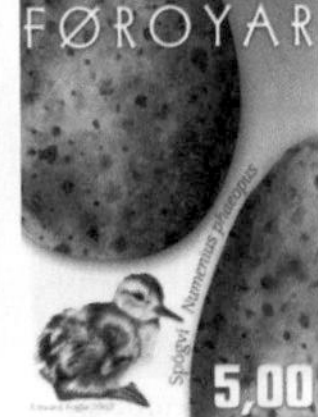
137 Kongsbokin (Royal Book)
138 Whimbrel (*Numenius phaeopus*)

2002. 150th Anniv of Foroya Logting (Faroese Representative Council). Sheet 100×70 mm containing T **137** and similar vert design. Multicoloured.
MS434 5k. Type **137**; 6k.50, Introduction of the 1852 Logting protocol . . . . 2·20 2·30

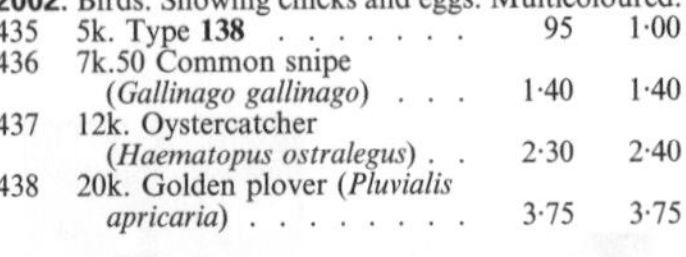

2002. Birds. Showing chicks and eggs. Multicoloured.
435 5k. Type **138** . . . . 95 1·00
436 7k.50 Common snipe (*Gallinago gallinago*) . . . 1·40 1·40
437 12k. Oystercatcher (*Haematopus ostralegus*) . . 2·30 2·40
438 20k. Golden plover (*Pluvialis apricaria*) . . . . 3·75 3·75

139 Church
140 Cliffs and Blue Whiting (*Micromesistius poutassou*)

2002. Gøta Church. Multicoloured.
439 5k. Type **139** . . . . 90 1·00
440 6k.50 Church interior . . . . 1·20 1·30

2002. Centenary of International Council for the Exploration of the Sea. Sheet 186×61 mm, containing T **140** and similar vert design. Multicoloured.
MS441 8k. Type **140**; 8k. *Magnus Heinason* (trawler) and blue whiting . . . . 3·00 3·25
Stamps of a similar design were issued by Denmark and Greenland.

141 Male Merlin (*Falco columbarius subaesalon*)

2002.
442 **141** 30k. multicoloured . . . 5·75 5·75

142 Engine Drilling

2003. Completion of Vagatunnilin (tunnel under Vestmannasund). Multicoloured.
443 5k. Type **142** 90 90
444 5k. Miners and equipment . . 90 90

143 Heid
144 "Omma Ludvik"

2003. Norse Myths and Legends. Voluspa. Multicoloured.
445 6k.50 Type **143** . . . . . . 1·20 1·20
446 6k.50 Creation of the universe . . . . 1·20 1·20
447 6k.50 Creation of humans . . 1·20 1·20
448 6k.50 Norns (deities of fate) and Yggdrasil (world tree) 1·20 1·20
449 6k.50 Thor with raised hammer . . . . 1·20 1·20
450 6k.50 Odin hurling spear . . 1·20 1·20
451 6k.50 Baldur dying and his infant brother Hodlyn . . 1·20 1·20
452 6k.50 Ship and Nidhog (giant serpent) . . . . 1·20 1·20
453 6k.50 Hodlyn killing serpent 1·20 1·20
454 6k.50 Hodur and Baldur . . 1·20 1·20

2003. Children's Songs. Sheet 166×80 mm containing T **144** and similar vert designs. Multicoloured.
MS455 5k.×10, Type **144** and nine different designs depicting children's songs . . . . 9·00 9·00

145 "Fish Tree" (tapestry) (Astrid Andreasen)
147 Jesper Rasmussen Brochmand

146 Fuglafjordur

2003. Europa. Poster Art. Multicoloured.
456 6k.50 Type **145** . . . . . . 1·20 1·20
457 8k. "Chrysalis", "Reclining Form" and "Jazz III" (ceramics) (Gudrid Poulsen) . . . . 1·40 1·40

2003. Island Post Office Centenaries. Sheet 170×120 mm containing T **146** and similar horiz designs. Each black and grey.
MS458 5k. Type **146**; 5k. Strendur; 5k. Sandur; 5k. Eidi; 5k. Vestmanna; 5k. Vagur; 5k. Midvagur; 5k. Hvalba . . . . 7·25 7·25

2003. Theologians. Multicoloured.
459 5k. Type **147** 90 90
460 6k.50 Thomas Kingo . . . . 1·20 1·20

148 "Dance in Main Room" (Emil Krause)

2003. Czeslaw Slania's 100th Stamp for Faroese Posts. Sheet 88×72 mm.
MS461 **148** 25k. multicoloured 4·50 4·50

149 Sandvok

2004. Settlements on Suduroy Island. Sheet 135×204 mm containing T **149** and similar horiz designs. Multicoloured.
MS462 5k.×10, Type **149**; Hvalba; Frodba; Oravok; Fámjin; Hov; Porkeri; Akrar; Sumba; Akraberg 9·00 9·00

150 Thor (god) and the Midgard Serpent

2004. Nordic Mythology. Sheet 105×70 mm containing T **150** and similar vert design. Multicoloured.
MS463 6k.50×2, Type **150**; Ran (sea goddess) . . . . 2·25 2·25
Stamps of a similar theme were issued by Aland Islands, Denmark, Finland, Greenland, Iceland, Norway and Sweden.

151 Gasholmur and Tindholmur

2004. 150th Anniv of *Journal of Cruise of Maria* (yacht) by Samuel Rathbone and E. H. Greig. Sheet 176×140 mm containing T **151** and similar horiz designs showing illustrations from the journal. Multicoloured.
MS464 6k.50×8, Type **151**; *Diamantunum* (yacht); Houses; Mylingur; Mylingur (different); Kalsoyggin; Yacht and rowing boats; Kunoynni . . . . . . 10·00 10·00

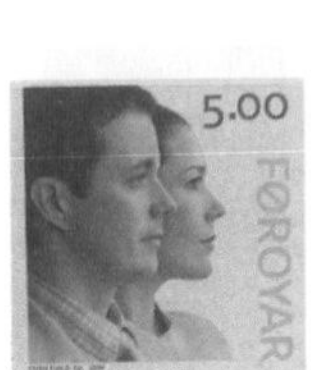

152 Prince Frederik and Mary Donaldson
153 Club Emblems and Players

2004. Marriage of Crown Prince Frederik and Mary Elizabeth Donaldson. Multicoloured.
MS465 130×65 mm. 5k. Type **152**; 6k.50 As 5k. but with design reversed . . . . 2·20 2·20
Stamps of same design were issued by Denmark and Greenland.

2004. Football Centenaries. Multicoloured.
466 5k. Type **153** (KI) (Klasvik) and HB (Torshavn) football clubs 95 95
467 6k.50 Tackling for ball (FIFA) . . . . 1·10 1·10

154 Cliffs and Yacht, Hestur

2004. Europa. Holidays. Multicoloured.
468 6k.50 Type **154** . . . . . . 1·10 1·10
469 8k. Walking on foreshore, Stora Dimun . . . . . . 1·50 1·50

155 Vagur Church

2004. Christmas. Churches. Multicoloured.
470 5k.50 Type **155** 15 15
471 7k.50 Tvoroyri church . . . 1·40 1·40

156 Sea, Woman and Columns

2004. Poems by Jens Hendrik Oliver (Janus) Djurhuus. Sheet 158 × 126 mm containing T **156** and similar vert designs. Multicoloured.
MS472 7k.50 × 10, Type **156** ("Atlantis"); Woman, children, man and ship ("Grimur Kamban"); Face in storm ("Gandkvædi Trondar"); Seated man ("Til Faroya I-II"); Woman and sea ("Min sorg"); Snake, woman and man ("Loki"); Birds, wren and crows ("I buri og Slatur"); Giantess and ship at sea ("Heimferd Nolsyar Pals"); Moses and stone tablets ("Moses a Sinai fjalli"); Cello and man wearing raincoat and hat ("Cello") . . 14·00 14·00

157 Vikar

2005. Settlements on Vagar Island. Sheet 135 × 206 mm containing T **157** and similar horiz designs. Multicoloured.
MS473 5k.50 × 10, Type **157**; Gasadalur; Bour; Slaettanes; Kvigandalsa; Sorvagur; Sandavagur; Vatnsoyrar; Fjallavatn; Miovagur . . . . . 5·50 5·50

158 Farmers and Sheep

2005. Everyday Life in Viking Age. Sheet 161 × 70 mm containing T **158** and similar vert designs. Multicoloured.
MS474 7k.50 × 3, Type **158**; Making hay; Woman milking cow . . . 4·25 4·25
The stamps and margin of **MS**474 form a composite design of a Viking community.

FEDERATED MALAY STATES Pt. 1

A British protectorate in South East Asia, comprising the States of Negri Sembilan (with Sungei Ujong), Pahang, Perak and Selangor.
Separate issues for each of these states appeared in 1936.

100 cents = $1 (Straits).

1900. Stamps of Negri Sembilan optd **FEDERATED MALAY STATES** and bar.
1 **3** 1c. purple and green . . . . 3·00 7·00
2 2c. purple and brown . . . . 29·00 65·00
3 3c. purple and black . . . . 2·75 4·00
4 5c. purple and yellow . . . . 70·00 £170
5 10c. purple and orange . . . 8·00 28·00
6 20c. green and olive . . . . 85·00 £100
7 25c. green and red £250 £350
8 50c. green and black . . . . 90·00 £130

1900. Stamps of Perak optd **FEDERATED MALAY STATES** and bar.
9 **31** 5c. purple and yellow . . . 16·00 55·00
10 10c. purple and orange . . . 75·00 65·00
11 **32** $1 green £170 £225
12 $2 green and red £140 £225
13 $5 green and blue £375 £550
14 $25 green and orange . . . £8000

3

4

1900.
15 a **3** 1c. black and green . . . 3·50 1·00
29 1c. green . . . . 5·50 20
30 1c. brown . . . . 2·25 90
53 1c. black 75 20
31 2c. green . . . . 2·50 30
54 2c. brown . . . . 6·50 7·00
16 b 3c. black and brown . . . 4·75 20
58 3c. brown . . . . 1·75 50
34 3c. red . . . . 3·25 10
35 3c. grey . . . . 2·00 20
57 3c. green . . . . 1·25 1·50
36 d 4c. black and red . . . . 5·50 80
38 4c. red . . . . 1·75 15
60 4c. orange . . . . 1·50 10
18 5c. green and red on yellow . . . . 2·25 3·00
61 5c. mauve on yellow . . . 1·00 20
62 5c. brown . . . . 3·50 10
63 6c. orange . . . . 1·00 45
64 6c. red . . . . 1·50 10
41bb 8c. black and blue . . . . 8·50 4·75
42 8c. blue . . . . 13·00 1·00
43 b 10c. black and mauve . . 25·00 65
44 a 10c. blue . . . . 6·50 1·00
66 10c. black and blue . . . 2·00 75
67 10c. purple and yellow . . 3·75 40
68 12c. blue . . . . 1·25 10
69 20c. mauve and black . . 4·00 1·25
70 25c. purple and mauve . . 2·75 1·50
71 30c. purple and orange . . 3·25 3·50
46 35c. red on yellow . . . . 5·50 12·00
73 35c. red and purple . . . 13·00 14·00
74 50c. black and orange . . 13·00 9·50
75 50c. black on green . . . 4·00 2·50
76 a **4** $1 green . . . . 17·00 45·00
77 **3** $1 black and red on blue 12·00 3·50
78 **4** $2 green and red . . . . . 19·00 70·00
79 **3** $2 green and red on yellow 38·00 35·00
80 **4** $5 green and blue £100 £170
81 **3** $5 green and red on green £150 £160
82 **4** $25 green and orange . . . £850 £650

POSTAGE DUE STAMPS

D **1**

1924.
D1 **D 1** 1c. violet . . . . 4·75 29·00
D2 2c. black . . . . 1·75 4·75
D3 4c. green . . . . 2·25 5·00
D4 8c. red . . . . 5·50 29·00
D5 10c. orange . . . . 9·00 17·00
D6 12c. blue . . . . 9·00 27·00

FERNANDO POO Pt. 9

A Spanish island off the west coast of Africa, in the Gulf of Guinea. Became part of Spanish Guinea in 1909. In 1959 Fernando Poo became an overseas province of Spain, comprising the island and Annobon. On 12 October 1968 became independent and joined Rio Muni to form Equatorial Guinea.

1868. Currencies stated below issue.
1894. 1000 milesimas = 100 centavos = 1 peso.
1901. 100 centimos = 1 peseta.

1 Isabella II (**3**)

1868.
1 **1** 20c. brown £450 £130
The face value of No. 1 is expressed in centimos de escudo. It was in use until Dec 1868. Stamps of Cuba were then used until 1879.

1879. "Alfonso XII" key-type inscr "FERNANDO POO".
5 X 1c. green . . . . 8·25 5·00
6 2c. red . . . . 12·00 8·75
2 5c. green . . . . 45·00 12·00
7 5c. lilac . . . . 40·00 12·00
3 10c. red . . . . 22·00 12·00
8 10c. brown . . . . 60·00 6·25
4 50c. blue . . . . 80·00 12·00
Nos. 2, 3 and 4 have face values expressed in centimos de peseta and the remainder are in centavos de peso.

1884. Nos. 5, 6 and 7 surch as T **3**.
9 X 50c. on 1c. green . . . . . 85·00 23·00
10 50c. on 2c. red . . . . . . 24·00 6·75
11 50c. on 5c. lilac . . . . . 95·00 30·00

1893. On plain paper.
12 **3** 50c. on blue . . . . 11·00 9·50

1894. "Baby" key-type inscr "FERNANDO POO".
13 Y ⅛c. grey . . . . 21·00 3·75
14 2c. red . . . . 15·00 2·75
15 5c. green . . . . 15·00 2·75
16 6c. purple . . . . 12·50 3·75
18 10c. red . . . . 46·00 10·50
19 10c. brown . . . . 9·50 2·75
20 12½c. brown . . . . 11·00 3·25
21 20c. blue . . . . 11·00 3·25
22 25c. red . . . . 21·00 3·25

1896. Nos. 13/22 surch **HABILITADO 5 C. DE PESO** in circle.
23 Y 5c. on ⅛c. grey . . . . . 80·00 28·00
24 5c. on 2c. red . . . . . . 39·00 17·00
25 5c. on 6c. purple . . . . . £120 46·00
26a 5c. on 10c. brown . . . . 50·00 46·00
28 5c. on 12½c. brown . . . . 29·00 13·50
29 5c. on 20c. blue . . . . . £120 46·00
30 5c. on 25c. red . . . . . . £120 37·00

7

1896. Fiscal stamps optd **HABILITADO PARA CORREOS** (Nos. 60/1) or surch **CORREOS 5 CENTAVOS** (59).
59 **7** 5c. on 10c. red . . . . 22·00 11·00
60 10c. red . . . . 22·00 11·00
61 15c. on 10c. green . . . . . 25·00 13·00

1897. Nos. 13 etc surch **5 Cen.** in circle.
31 Y 5c. on ⅛c. grey . . . . . . 23·00 12·50
32 5c. on 2c. red . . . . . . 23·00 12·50
33a 5c. on 5c. green . . . . . £110 40·00
34c 5c. on 6c. purple . . . . . 17·00 24·00
35 5c. on 10c. brown . . . . £130 48·00
36 5c. on 10c. red £300 £120
38 5c. on 12½c. brown . . . . 49·00 20·00
39a 5c. on 20c. blue . . . . . 29·00 18·00
40 5c. on 25c. red . . . . . . 29·00 20·00

1898. Nos. 13 etc surch as T **3**.
41 Y 50c. on ⅛c. grey . . . . . . £225 85·00
42 50c. on 2c. red . . . . . . 60·00 21·00
43 50c. on 5c. green . . . . . £160 60·00
44 50c. on 10c. brown . . . . £140 60·00
45a 50c. on 10c. red . . . . . £160 60·00
47 50c. on 12½c. brown . . . £120 37·00
48 50c. on 25c. red . . . . . £140 50·00

10

1899. Fiscal stamps variously optd. (a) Surch **Fernando Poo 1899 Habilitado para Corrreos** and new value.
62 **10** 10c. on 25c. green . . . . . 65·00 44·00
63 15c. on 25c. green . . . . . 95·00 60·00

(b) Optd or surch **CORREOS**.
65 **10** 15c. on 25c. green £1800 £1400
64 25c. green £350 £170

1899. "Curly Head" key-type inscr "FERNANDO POO 1899".
66 Z 1m. brown . . . . 1·80 65
67 2m. brown . . . . 1·80 65
68 3m. brown . . . . 1·80 65
69 4m. brown . . . . 1·80 65
70 5m. brown . . . . 1·80 65
71 1c. purple . . . . 1·80 65
72 2c. green . . . . 1·80 65
73 3c. brown . . . . 1·80 65
74 4c. orange . . . . 10·50 1·60
75 5c. red . . . . 1·80 65
76 6c. blue . . . . 1·80 65
77 8c. brown . . . . 6·50 65
78 10c. red . . . . 4·25 65
79 15c. grey . . . . 4·25 65
80 20c. purple . . . . 11·50 1·60
81 40c. lilac . . . . 80·00 28·00
82 60c. black . . . . 80·00 28·00
83 80c. brown . . . . 80·00 28·00
84 1p. green £275 £140
85 2p. blue £275 £140

1900. No. 80 surch **HABILITADO 5 C. DE PESO**.
86 Z 5c. on 20c. purple . . . . . £250 17·00

1900. No. 80 surch **5 Cen.** in circle.
87 Z 5c. on 20c. purple . . . . . 8·25 4·50

1900. No. 80 surch with T **3**.
88 Z 50c. on 20c. purple . . . . . 10·50 4·50

1900. "Curly Head" key-type inscr "FERNANDO POO 1900".
91 Z 1m. black . . . . 2·75 65
92 2m. black . . . . 2·75 65
93 3m. black . . . . 2·75 65
94 4m. black . . . . 2·75 65
95 5m. black . . . . 2·75 65
96 1c. green . . . . 2·75 65
97 2c. lilac . . . . 2·75 65
98 3c. pink . . . . 2·75 65
99 4c. brown . . . . 2·75 65
100 5c. blue . . . . 2·75 65
101 6c. orange . . . . 2·75 2·75
102 8c. green . . . . 2·75 2·75
103 10c. red . . . . 2·75 65
104 15c. purple . . . . 2·75 65
105 20c. brown . . . . 2·75 65
106 40c. brown . . . . 6·75 3·00
107 60c. green . . . . 15·00 3·00
108 80c. blue . . . . 15·00 5·00
109 1p. brown . . . . 85·00 37·00
110 2p. orange . . . . £140 80·00

1900. Fiscal stamps as T **7** but dated 1900 optd or surch. (a) **CORREOS** and **5 Cen.** in circle.
111 **7** 5c. on 10c. blue . . . . . . 55·00 28·00

(b) **CORREOS CORREOS** and **5 Cen.** in circle.
113 **7** 5c. on 10c. blue . . . . . . £140 85·00

(c) **CORREOS**.
114a **7** 10c. blue . . . . 32·00 8·25

1900. Fiscal stamp as T **7** but dated 1900 surch **CORREOS 5 CENTAVOS**.
115 **7** 5c. on 10c. blue £550 £400

1900. Nos. 74 and 105 surch with T **3**.
116a Z 50c. on 4c. orange . . . . 12·00 6·50
117 50c. on 20c. brown . . . . 9·50 4·00

14a

1900. Fiscal stamp surch. (a) **CORREOS** and **5 Cen.** in circle.
118 **14a** 5c. on 25c. brown £600 £350

(b) **CORREOS HABILITADO 5 C. DE PESO**.
119 **14a** 5c. on 25c. brown £650 £350

1901. "Curly Head" key-type inscr "FERNANDO POO 1901".
124 Z 1c. black . . . . 1·90 1·10
125 2c. brown . . . . 1·90 1·10
126 3c. purple . . . . 1·90 1·10
127 4c. lilac . . . . 1·90 1·10
128 5c. red . . . . 1·20 1·10
129 10c. brown . . . . 1·20 1·10
130 25c. blue . . . . 1·20 1·10
131 50c. purple . . . . 1·90 1·10
132 75c. brown . . . . 1·40 1·10
133 1p. green . . . . 41·00 8·75
134 2p. brown . . . . 25·00 13·50
135 3p. green . . . . 25·00 19·00
136 4p. red . . . . 25·00 19·00
137 5p. green . . . . 32·00 19·00
138 10p. orange . . . . 70·00 55·00

1902. "Curly Head" key-type inscr "FERNANDO POO 1902". With control figures on back.
140 Z 5c. green . . . . 1·70 30
141 10c. grey . . . . 1·70 30
142 25c. red . . . . 4·00 85
143 50c. brown . . . . 9·25 3·25
144 75c. lilac . . . . 9·25 3·25
145 1p. red . . . . 12·00 4·75
146 2p. green . . . . 24·00 12·00
147 5p. red . . . . 37·00 28·00

1903. "Curly Head" key-type inscr "FERNANDO POO PARA 1903". With control figures on back.
154 Z ¼c. purple 25 25
155 ½c. black 25 25
156 1c. red 25 25
157 2c. green 25 25
158 3c. green 25 25
159 4c. lilac 25 25
160 5c. red 35 25
161 10c. orange 45 35
162 15c. green . . . . 1·80 1·20
163 25c. brown . . . . 1·90 1·80
164 50c. brown . . . . 3·25 3·25
165 75c. red . . . . 11·50 6·00
166 1p. brown . . . . 17·00 8·75
167 2p. green . . . . 22·00 13·50
168 3p. purple . . . . 22·00 13·50
169 4p. blue . . . . 27·00 24·00
170 5p. blue . . . . 40·00 28·00
171 10p. orange . . . . 85·00 44·00

1905. "Curly Head" key-type inscr "FERNANDO POO PARA 1905". With control figures on back.
172 Z 1c. purple 30 30
173 2c. black 30 30
174 3c. red 30 30
175 4c. green 30 30
176 5c. green 35 30
177 10c. lilac . . . . 1·20 60
178 15c. red . . . . 1·20 60
179 25c. orange . . . . 10·00 2·00
180 50c. green . . . . 6·75 3·25
181 75c. brown . . . . 8·75 8·75
182 1p. brown . . . . 10·00 8·75
183 2p. red . . . . 18·00 13·00
184 3p. brown . . . . 27·00 15·00
185 4p. green . . . . 32·00 20·00
186 5p. red . . . . 50·00 30·00
187 10p. blue . . . . 80·00 44·00

17 King Alfonso XIII

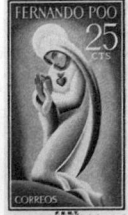

24 Woman at Prayer

1907. With control figures on back.
188 **17** 1c. black 15 15
189 2c. pink 15 15
190 3c. purple 15 15
191 4c. black 15 15
192 5c. buff 15 15
193 10c. purple 1·00 55
194 15c. black 25 25
195 25c. brown 16·00 12·50
196 50c. green 15 15
197 75c. red 20 15
198 1p. blue 1·70 60
199 2p. brown 6·00 5·00
200 3p. pink 6·00 5·00
201 4p. lilac 6·00 5·00
202 5p. brown 6·00 5·00
203 10p. brown 6·00 5·00

1908. Surch **HABILITADO PARA 05 CTMS.**
204 **17** 05c. on 10c. purple 3·25 2·10

1929. Seville and Barcelona Exhibition stamps of Spain (Nos. 504, etc) optd **FERNANDO POO.**
209 5c. red 20 20
210 10c. green 20 20
211 15c. blue 20 20
212 20c. violet 20 20
213 25c. red 20 20
214 30c. brown 20 20
215 40c. blue 60 60
216 50c. orange 1·30 1·30
217 1p. grey 4·75 4·75
218 4p. red 24·00 24·00
219 10p. brown 31·00 31·00

1960.
220 **24** 25c. grey 15 15
221 50c. drab 15 15
222 75c. brown 15 15
223 1p. red 15 15
224 1p.50 turquoise 15 15
225 2p. purple 15 15
226 3p. blue 1·80 55
227 5p. brown 20 15
228 10p. olive 25 20

25 De Falla (composer)

1960. Child Welfare.
229 **25** 10c.+5c. purple 20 20
230 – 15c.+5c. brown 20 20
231 – 35c. green 20 20
232 **25** 80c. green 20 20
DESIGNS—VERT: (De Falla's ballets): 15c. Spanish dancer ("Love, the Magician"); 35c. Tricorne, stick and windmill ("Three-cornered Hat").

26 Sperm Whale **27** "The Blessing"

1960. Stamp Day.
233 **26** 10c.+5c. red 20 20
234 – 20c.+5c. green 20 20
235 **26** 30c.+10c. brown 20 20
236 – 50c.+20c. brown 20 20
DESIGN: 20, 50c. Natives harpooning humpback whale.

1961. Child Welfare. Inscr "PRO-INFANCIA 1961".
237 **27** 10c.+5c. lake 20 20
238 – 25c.+10c. violet 20 20
239 **27** 80c.+20c. green 20 20
DESIGN: 25c. African kneeling before Cross.

28

1961. 25th Anniv of Gen. Franco as Head of State.
240 – 25c. grey 20 20
241 **28** 50c. brown 20 20
242 – 70c. green 20 20
243 **28** 1p. orange 20 20
DESIGNS—VERT: 25c. Map; 70c. St. Isabel Cathedral.

29 Great Turtle

1961. Stamp Day. Inscr "DIA DEL SELLO 1961".
244 **29** 10c.+5c. red 20 20
245 – 25c.+10c. plum 20 20
246 **29** 30c.+10c. purple 20 20
247 – 1p.+10c. orange 20 20
DESIGN: 25c., 1p. Native porters, palm trees and shore.

30 Spanish Freighter "Okume"

1962. Child Welfare. Inscr "PRO-INFANCIA 1962".
248 **30** 25c. violet 20 20
249 – 50c. olive 20 20
250 **30** 1p. brown 20 20
DESIGN: 50c. Spanish freighter "San Francisco".

31 Postman **32** Native Shrine

1962. Stamp Day. Inscr "DIA DEL SELLO 1962".
251 **31** 15c. green 20 20
252 – 35c. mauve 65 90
253 **31** 1p. brown 20 20
DESIGN—HORIZ: 35c. Mail transport.

1963. Seville Flood Relief.
254 **32** 50c. brown 20 20
255 1p. purple 20 20

33 Sister and Child

1963. Child Welfare.
256 – 25c. purple 20 20
257 **33** 50c. green 20 20
258 – 1p. red 20 20
DESIGN—HORIZ: 25c., 1p. Two sisters.

34 Child and Arms

1963. "For Barcelona".
259 **34** 50c. brown 20 20
260 1p. red 20 20

35 Governor Chacon **36** Canoe

1964. Stamp Day.
261 **35** 25c. violet 20 20
262 – 50c. brown 20 20
263 **35** 1p. red 20 20
DESIGN—VERT: 50c. Orange blossom.

1964. Child Welfare. Inscr "PRO INFANCIA 1964".
264 **36** 25c. violet 20 20
265 – 50c. olive (Pineapple) 20 20
266 **36** 1p. purple 20 20

37 Ring-necked Francolin **38** "The Three Kings"

1964. Birds.
267 **37** 15c. brown 15 15
268 – 25c. violet 15 15
269 – 50c. green 15 15
270 **37** 70c. green 15 15
271 – 1p. brown 15 15
272 – 1p.50 blue 15 15
273 **37** 3p. blue 35 15
274 – 5p. purple 95 15
275 – 10p. green 1·50 45
DESIGNS: 25c., 1, 5p. Mallard; 50c., 1p.50, 10p. Great blue turaco.

1964. Stamp Day.
276 – 50c. green 20 20
277 **38** 1p. red 20 20
278 – 1p.50 green 20 20
279 **38** 3p. blue 90 90
DESIGN—VERT: 50c., 1p.50, King presenting gift to Infant Jesus.

39 Native **40** "Metopodontus savagei" (stag beetle)

1965. 25th Anniv of End of Spanish Civil War.
280 **39** 50c. blue 20 20
281 – 1p. red 20 20
282 – 1p.50 turquoise 20 20
DESIGNS: 1p. "Agriculture" (fruit farming); 1p.50, "Education" (child writing).

1965. Child Welfare. Insects.
283 – 50c. green 20 20
284 **40** 1p. red 20 20
285 – 1p.50 blue 20 20
DESIGN—VERT: 50c., 1p.50, "Plectrocnemia cruciata" (squashbug).

41 Pole Vaulting

1965. Stamp Day.
286 **41** 50c. green 20 20
287 – 1p. brown 20 20
288 **41** 1p.50 blue 20 20
DESIGN—VERT: 1p. Arms of Fernando Poo.

42 European and African Women

1966. Child Welfare.
289 **42** 50c. green 20 20
290 1p. red 20 20
291 – 1p.50 blue 20 20
DESIGN—VERT: 1p.50, St. Isabel of Hungary.

43 Greater White-nosed Monkey **44** Flowers

1966. Stamp Day.
292 **43** 10c. blue and yellow 20 20
293 – 40c. blue and brown 20 20
294 **43** 1p.50 olive and brown 20 20
295 – 4p. brown and green 20 20
DESIGN—VERT: 40c., 4. p. Moustached monkey.

1967. Child Welfare and similar floral design.
296 **44** 10c. red and green 20 20
297 – 40c. brown and orange 20 20
298 **44** 1p.50 purple & brown 20 20
299 – 4p. blue and green 20 20

45 African Linsang **47** Libra (scales)

46 Arms of San Carlos and Stamp of 1868

1967. Stamp Day.
300 **45** 1p. black and bistre 20 20
301 – 1p.50 brown and olive 20 20
302 – 3p.50 purple and green 30 30
DESIGNS—VERT: 1p.50, Western needle-clawed bush-baby. HORIZ: 3p.50, Lord Derby's flying squirrel.

1968. Stamp Centenary.
303 **46** 1p. brown and purple 20 20
304 – 1p.50 brown and blue 20 20
305 – 2p.50 chestnut & brown 30 30
DESIGNS—Each with stamp of 1868: 1p.50, Arms of Santa Isabel; 2p.50, Arms of Fernando Poo.

1968. Child Welfare. Signs of the Zodiac.
306 **47** 1p. mauve on yellow 20 20
307 – 1p.50 brown on pink 20 20
308 – 2p.50 violet on yellow 30 30
DESIGNS: 1p.50, Lion (Leo); 2p.50, Water carrier (Aquarius).

For later issues see **EQUATORIAL GUINEA**.

FEZZAN Pt. 6

A desert territory in N. Africa taken from Turkey by Italy and captured by French forces in 1943. Algerian stamps used from April 1944, until 1946, and then under French control until the end of 1951 when it was incorporated in the independent kingdom of Libya.

100 centimes = 1 franc.

(a) Issues For Fezzan And Ghadames

1943. Optd **FEZZAN Occupation Francaise** or surch in addition. (a) Postage. No. 247 of Italy optd.
1 **103** 50c. violet 48·00 48·00

Stamps of Libya surch.
2 **4** 0f.50 on 5c. green & black £100 95·00
3 **5** 1f. on 10c. pink and black £140 £140
4 **6** 2f. on 30c. brown & black £275 £275
5 **9** 3f. on 20c. green 65·00 55·00
6 **5** 3f.50 on 25c. blue & dp blue 80·00 70·00
7 **6** 5f. on 50c. green & black 19·00 19·00
8 10f. on 1l.25 blue and indigo £900 £800
9 **9** 20f. on 1l.75 orange £2750 £2750
10 **7** 50f. on 75c. red & purple £3250 £3250

(b) Air. No. 271 of Italy optd.
11 **10** 50c. brown 70·00 70·00

(c) Air. No. 72 of Libya surch.
12 **18** 7f.50 on 50c. red 75·00 75·00

1943. Handstamped locally. (a) Postage. No. 247 of Italy handstamped **R.F. 0,50 FEZZAN** around circle and within dotted circle.
13 **103** 0f.50 on 50c. violet £2750 £275

(b) Postage. No. 27 of Libya handstamped **R.F. 1 Fr FEZZAN** in two lines.
14 **5** 1f. on 25c. blue & dp blue £3000 £250

(c) Air. No. 271 of Italy handstamped as No. 13.
15 **110** 0f.50 on 50c. brown – £750

1943. Parcel Post stamps of Libya handstamped across each half as No. 14.
16 **P 53** 1f. on 5c. brown £500 £200
17 **P 92** 1f. on 10c. blue £500 £200
18 1f. on 50c. orange £500 £200
19 1f. on 1l. violet £500 £200
20 1f. on 2l. green – £1000
21 1f. on 3l. bistre – £1400
22 1f. on 4l. black – £1000
The prices are for each half of the parcel post stamps.

4 Fort of Sebha

6 Map and Fort of Sebha

1946.

23 4 10c. black . . . . 15 2·75
24 50c. red . . . . 50 3·00
25 1f. brown . . . . 35 3·00
26 1f.50 green . . . . 55 3·00
27 2f. blue . . . . 40 3·25
28 – 2f.50 violet . . . . 65 3·50
29 – 3f. red . . . . 60 3·50
30 – 5f. brown . . . . 60 3·75
31 – 6f. green . . . . 80 3·50
32 – 10f. blue . . . . 55 3·50
33 6 15f. violet . . . . 1·50 3·75
34 20f. red . . . . 1·25 4·50
35 25f. brown . . . . 1·75 4·50
36 40f. green . . . . 2·25 4·75
37 50f. blue . . . . 1·75 4·75
DESIGN—36 × 21½ mm: 2f.50 to 10f. Turkish fort and mosque at Murzuk.

(b) Issues For Fezzan Only

7 Douglas C-47B Skytrain at Fezzan Airfield

1948. Air.
38 7 100f. red . . . . 2·50 11·00
39 – 200f. blue . . . . 5·00 16·00
DESIGN—VERT: 200f. Airplane over Fezzan.

9 Djerma 10 Well at Gorda

1949.
40 9 1f. black . . . . 1·25 3·50
41 2f. pink . . . . 1·40 3·50
42 – 4f. brown . . . . 1·60 4·50
43 – 5f. green . . . . 1·75 4·50
44 10 8f. blue . . . . 1·75 4·25
45 10f. brown . . . . 1·90 5·50
46 12f. green . . . . 1·75 10·00
47 – 15f. red . . . . 2·75 11·00
48 – 20f. black . . . . 2·25 6·25
49 – 25f. blue . . . . 1·75 7·75
50 – 50f. red . . . . 3·00 11·00
DESIGNS—HORIZ: 4f., 5f. Beni Khettab tombs; 15f., 20f. Col. Colonna d'Ornano and fort; 25f., 50f. Gen. Leclerc and map of Europe and N. Africa.

11 "Charity" 12 Mother and Child

1950. Charity.
51 11 15f.+5f. lake . . . . 1·75 4·75
52 12 25f.+5f. blue . . . . 2·25 4·75

14 Camel Breeding 15 Ahmed Bey

1951.
59 14 30c. brown (postage) . . . 3·00 3·75
60 1f. blue . . . . 2·50 3·75
61 2f. red . . . . 2·75 3·75
62 – 4f. red . . . . 3·00 3·75
63 – 5f. green . . . . 3·00 4·00
64 – 8f. blue . . . . 2·50 4·00
65 – 10f. brown . . . . 5·50 8·25
66 – 12f. green . . . . 5·75 8·75
67 – 15f. red . . . . 6·75 10·50
68 15 20f. brown . . . . 2·00 10·50
69 25f. blue and deep blue . . 2·75 14·00
70 50f. brown and blue . . . . 2·50 14·00
71 – 100f. blue (air) . . . . . . 12·50 21·00
72 – 200f. red . . . . 12·00 24·00
DESIGNS—HORIZ: 4f. to 8f. Arab hoeing; 100f. Brak Oasis; 200f. Sebha Fort. VERT: 10f. to 15f. Artesian well.

POSTAGE DUE STAMPS

1943. Postage Due stamps of Libya optd **FEZZAN Occupation Francaise** or surch in addition with bars obliterating old inscr and values.
D13 D 141 0f.50 on 5c. brown . . £850 £750
D14 1f. on 10c. blue . . . £850 £750
D15 2f. on 25c. green . . . £850 £750
D16 3f. on 50c. violet . . . £900 £850
D17 D 142 5f. on 1l. orange . . . £7500 £7500

D 13 Brak Oasis

1950.
D53 D 13 1f. black . . . . 2·50 3·75
D54 2f. green . . . . 1·90 3·75
D55 3f. lake . . . . 2·25 4·00
D56 5f. violet . . . . 2·75 4·25
D57 10f. red . . . . 3·00 6·50
D58 20f. blue . . . . 3·25 10·00

FIJI Pt. 1

A British colony in the South Pacific, which became independent within the Commonwealth during October 1970. Following a military coup on 25 September 1987 Fiji was declared a republic on 7 October. The Governor-General resigned on 15 October 1987 and Fiji's Commonwealth membership lapsed until 1 October 1997 when the country was readmitted following further constitutional changes.

1870. 12 pence = 1 shilling;
20 shillings = 1 pound.
1969. 100 cents = 1 dollar.

1 2

1870.
5 1 1d. black on pink £900 £1800
6 3d. black on pink £1500 £2750
7 6d. black on pink £1100 £1800
8 9d. black on pink £1900 £3000
9 1s. black on pink £1200 £1400

1871.
10 2 1d. blue . . . . 50·00 £120
11 3d. green £110 £350
12 6d. red £140 £300

1872. Surch in words.
13a 2 2c. on 1d. blue . . . . . . 35·00 50·00
14 6c. on 3d. green . . . . . . 70·00 70·00
15 12c. on 6d. red . . . . . . 95·00 80·00

V.R. (5) (8)

1874. Optd as T **5**.
16 2 2c. on 1d. blue £900 £250
17 6c. on 3d. green £1500 £650
18 12c. on 6d. red £650 £200

1875. Nos. 17 and 18 surch **2d.**
22 2 2d. on 6c. on 3d. green . . . £550 £180
26 2d. on 12c. on 6d. red . . . £1900 £800

1876. Optd with T **8**, and the 3d. surch in words also.
31 2 1d. blue . . . . 19·00 30·00
29a 2d. on 3d. green . . . . . 48·00 55·00
34 4d. on 3d. mauve . . . . . 85·00 25·00
33 6d. red . . . . 50·00 28·00

10 12

1878. Surch on Nos. 36 and 41/2 in words.
35 10 1d. blue . . . . 9·50 9·50
40 2d. green . . . . 16·00 1·00
36 2d. on 3d. green . . . . . 7·00 22·00
54 4d. mauve . . . . 12·00 13·00
41 4d. on 1d. mauve . . . . . 45·00 32·00
42 4d. on 2d. mauve . . . . . 75·00 12·00
59a 6d. red . . . . 9·00 3·75
67 12 1s. brown . . . . 38·00 9·50
69 5s. red and black . . . . . 55·00 28·00

1891. Surch in figures or words.
72a 10 ½d. on 1d. blue . . . . . 48·00 70·00
70 2½d. on 2d. green . . . . 48·00 50·00
73 5d. on 4d. mauve . . . . 50·00 70·00
74a 5d. on 6d. red . . . . . . 55·00 60·00

20 21 Native Canoe 23

1891.
99 20 ½d. grey . . . . 1·00 3·50
87 21 1d. black . . . . 5·50 5·50
101 1d. mauve . . . . 6·00 1·00
89 2d. green . . . . 6·50 80
103a 10 2½d. brown . . . . 5·00 5·00
85 21 5d. blue . . . . 13·00 7·50

1903.
104 23 ½d. green . . . . 2·25 2·00
105 1d. purple and black on red . . . . 13·00 55
119 1d. red . . . . 11·00 10
106 2d. purple and orange . . 3·75 1·25
107 2½d. purple and blue on blue . . . . 14·00 3·50
120 2½d. blue . . . . 6·50 7·50
108 3d. purple . . . . 1·50 4·00
109 4d. purple and black . . . 1·50 2·50
110 5d. purple and green . . . 1·50 2·75
111 6d. purple and red . . . . 1·50 1·75
121 6d. purple . . . . 14·00 29·00
112 1s. green and red . . . . 11·00 65·00
122 1s. black on green . . . . 4·50 10·00
113 5s. green and black . . . . 60·00 £140
123 5s. green and red on yellow 55·00 65·00
114 £1 black and blue £325 £375
124 £1 purple and black on red £300 £275

1912. As T **23**, but portrait of King George V.
125a ¼d. brown . . . . 1·50 40
126b ½d. green . . . . 1·25 50
127 1d. red . . . . 2·00 10
231 1d. violet . . . . 1·25 10
232 1½d. red . . . . 4·00 1·50
233 2d. grey . . . . 1·25 10
129 2½d. blue . . . . 3·00 3·50
130 3d. purple on yellow . . . 4·25 5·50
234 3d. blue . . . . 2·75 1·00
235 4d. black and red on yellow 5·50 7·00
236 5d. purple and olive . . . 1·50 1·50
237 6d. purple . . . . 2·00 1·25
134a 1s. black on green . . . . . 1·00 11·00
239 2s. purple and blue on blue 25·00 60·00
240 2s.6d. black and red on blue 11·00 32·00
136 5s. green and red on yellow 32·00 40·00
137 £1 purple and black on red £275 £275

1916. Nos. 126/7 optd **WAR STAMP**.
138b ½d. green . . . . 75 2·75
139a 1d. red . . . . 1·75 75

1935. Silver Jubilee. As T **10a** of Gambia.
242 1½d. blue and red . . . . . 1·00 8·00
243 2d. blue and grey . . . . . 1·50 35
244 3d. brown and blue . . . . 2·50 3·25
245 1s. grey and purple . . . . 5·00 7·00

1937. Coronation. As T **10b** of Gambia.
246 1d. violet . . . . 60 1·75
247 2d. grey . . . . 60 2·00
248 3d. blue . . . . 60 2·00

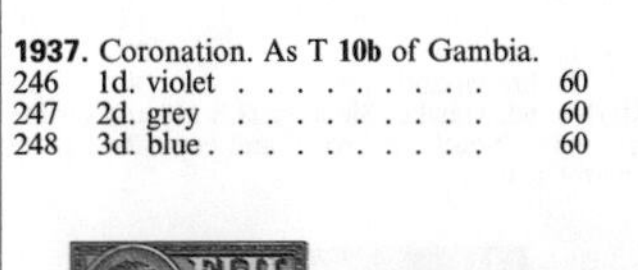

28 Native Sailing Canoe 29 Native Village

32 Government Offices

1938.
249 28 ½d. green 20 75
250 29 1d. brown and blue . . . 50 20
252c – 1½d. red . . . . 1·00 1·25
254 – 2d. brown and green . . . 16·00 16·00
255 32 2d. green and mauve . . 40 60
256i – 2½d. brown and green . . 70 80
257 – 3d. blue . . . . 1·00 30
258 – 5d. blue and red . . . . 42·00 10·00
259 – 5d. green and red 20 30
261b – 6d. black . . . . 1·50 1·50
261c – 8d. red . . . . 1·00 2·25
262 – 1s. black and yellow . . . 75 70
263 – 1s.5d. black and red . . . 20 10
263a – 1s.6d. blue . . . . 3·50 2·75
264 – 2s. violet and orange . . 2·50 40
265 – 2s.6d. green and brown . 2·75 1·50
266 – 5s. green and purple . . . 2·75 1·75
266a – 10s. orange and green . . 35·00 40·00
266b – £1 blue and red . . . . . 48·00 50·00
DESIGNS—HORIZ (As Type **32**): 1½d. Camakua (canoe); 2d. (No. 254), 2½d., 6d. Map of Fiji Is. HORIZ (As Type **29**): 3d. Canoe and arms; 8d., 1s.5d., 1s.6d. Arms; 2s. Suva Harbour; 2s.6d. River scene; 5s. Chief's hut. VERT (As Type **29**): 5d. (Nos. 258/9), Sugar cane; 1s. Spearing fish; 10s. Pawpaw tree; £1 Police bugler.

1941. No. 254 surch **2½d.**
267 2½d. on 2d. brown and green 2·00 30

1946. Victory. As T **11a** of Gambia.
268 2½d. green . . . . 1·25 1·00
269 3d. blue 10 10

1948. Silver Wedding. As T **11b/c** of Gambia.
270 2½d. green . . . . 40 1·50
271 5s. blue . . . . 14·00 7·50

1949. U.P.U. As T **11d/g** of Gambia.
272 2d. purple 30 50
273 3d. blue . . . . 2·00 2·75
274 8d. red . . . . 30 2·75
275 1s.6d. blue . . . . 35 1·25

43 Children Bathing

1951. Health stamps. Inscr "HEALTH".
276 43 1d.+1d. brown . . . . . . 10 1·00
277 – 2d.+1d. green . . . . . . 30 1·00
DESIGNS—VERT: 2d. Rugby footballer.

1953. Coronation. As T **11h** of Gambia.
278 2½d. black and green . . . . 1·25 50

1953. Royal Visit. As No. 261c, but with portrait of Queen Elizabeth II and inscr "ROYAL VISIT 1953".
279 8d. red 30 15

46 Queen Elizabeth II (after Annigoni) 48 Loading Copra

1954. Queen Elizabeth II. (I) inscr "FIJI". (II) Inscribed "Fiji".
280 28 ½d. green . . . . 15 1·50
298 46 ½d. green . . . . 15 2·00
281 1d. turquoise (I) . . . . . 1·75 10
299 1d. blue (II) . . . . 2·50 2·00
282 1½d. sepia (I) . . . . . . 1·00 65
300 1½d. sepia (II) . . . . . . 2·25 1·75
283 32 2d. green and mauve . . 1·25 40
312 46 2d. red (I) 50 10
284 2½d. violet (I) . . . . . . 3·00 10
302 2½d. brown (I) . . . . . . 1·50 3·00
285 48 3d. brown and purple . . 3·25 20
287 – 6d. black (As No. 261) . . 2·50 85
303 A 6d. red and black . . . . 1·25 10
288 – 8d. red (As No. 261d) . . 4·25 1·25
316 B 10d. brown and red . . . 60 50
289 – 1s. black and yellow (As No. 262) . . . . 2·50 10
306 C 1s. blue . . . . 1·50 10
290 D 1s.6d. blue and green . . 19·00 1·00
291 E 2s. black and red . . . . . 5·50 50
292a – 2s.6d. green and brown (As No. 265) . . . . 1·25 10
320 F 2s.6d. black and purple . . 2·50 90
293 G 5s. ochre and blue . . . . 13·00 1·25
294 – 10s. orange and green (As No. 266a) . . . . . . 7·00 20·00
309 H 10s. green and sepia . . . 3·50 1·50
295 – £1 bl & red (As No. 266b) 38·00 19·00
310 I £1 black and orange . . . 11·00 4·00

DESIGNS—HORIZ (As Type **48**): A, Fijian beating lali; B, Yaqona ceremony; C, Location map; D, Sugar cane train; E, Preparing bananas for export; F, Nadi Airport; G, Gold industry; H, Cutting sugar-cane; I, Arms of Fiji.

52 River Scene **56** Hibiscus

1954. Health stamps.
296 **52** 1½d.+½d. brown and green . . . 10 50
297 – 2½d.+½d. orange and black . . . 10 10
DESIGN: 2½d. Queen's portrait and Cross of Lorraine inscribed "FIJI WAR MEMORIAL" and "ANTI-TUBERCULOSIS CAMPAIGN".

1959.
313 – 3d. multicoloured 25 10
304 **56** 8d. multicoloured 50 25
315 9d. multicoloured 90 65
318 – 1s.6d. multicoloured . . . 1·50 90
319 – 2s. yellow, green and copper . . . . 13·00 3·50
308 – 4s. multicoloured . . . . 1·75 1·50
323 – 5s. red, yellow and grey . . 12·00 35
DESIGNS—HORIZ: 1s.6d. International date line; 4s. Kandavu shining parrot ("Kandavu Parrot"); 5s. Orange dove. VERT: 2s. White orchid. 23 × 28 mm: 3d. Queen Elizabeth II.

1963. Royal Visit. Optd **ROYAL VISIT 1963**.
326 – 3d. mult (No. 313) 40 20
327 C 1s. blue (No. 306) 60 20

1963. Freedom from Hunger. As T **20a** of Gambia.
328 – 2s. blue . . . . 1·00 1·25

69 Running

1963. 1st South Pacific Games, Suva. Inscr as in T **69**.
329 **69** 3d. brown, yellow and black 25 10
330 – 9d. brown, violet and black 25 1·50
331 – 1s. brown, green and black 25 10
332 – 2s.6d. brown, blue and black 60 60
DESIGNS—VERT: 9d. Throwing the discus; 1s. Hockey. HORIZ: 2s.6d. High-jumping.

1963. Centenary of Red Cross. As T **20b** of Gambia.
333 2d. red and black 35 10
334 2s. red and blue . . . . . . 75 2·50

1963. Opening of COMPAC (Trans-Pacific Telephone Cable). No. 306 optd **COMPAC CABLE IN SERVICE DECEMBER 1963** and ship.
335 C 1s. blue 55 10

74 Jamborette Emblem **76** Flying-boat "Aotearoa"

1964. 50th Anniv of Fijian Scout Movement.
336 **74** 3d. multicoloured 15 25
337 – 1s. violet and brown . . . 15 30
DESIGN: 1s. Scouts of three races.

1964. 25th Anniv of 1st Fiji–Tonga Airmail Service.
338 **76** 3d. black and red 40 10
339 – 6d. red and blue . . . . . 70 1·00
340 – 1s. black and turquoise . . 70 1·00
DESIGNS—VERT: 6d. De Havilland Heron 2. HORIZ (37½ × 25 mm): 1s. "Aotearoa" and map.

1965. Centenary of I.T.U. As T **44** of Gibraltar.
341 3d. blue and red 20 10
342 2s. yellow and bistre 50 25

1965. I.C.Y. As T **45** of Gibraltar.
343 2d. purple and turquoise . . 20 10
344 2s.6d. green and lavender . . 80 25

1966. Churchill Commemoration. As T **46** of Gibraltar.
345 3d. blue 70 10
346 9d. green 90 85
347 1s. brown 90 10
348 2s.6d. violet . . . . 1·00 85

1966. World Cup Football Championships. As T **47** of Gibraltar.
349 2d. multicoloured 25 10
350 2s. multicoloured 75 20

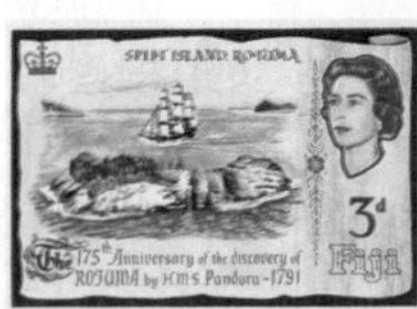

79 H.M.S. "Pandora" approaching Split Island, Rotuma

1966. 175th Anniv of Discovery of Rotuma. Mult.
351 3d. Type **79** 30 10
352 10d. Rotuma chiefs 30 10
353 1s.6d. Rotumans welcoming H.M.S. "Pandora" 50 30

1966. Inauguration of W.H.O. Headquarters, Geneva. As T **54** of Gibraltar.
354 6d. black, green and blue . . 1·25 25
355 2s.6d. black, purple and ochre . . . . 2·75 2·50

82 Running

1966. 2nd South Pacific Games.
356 **82** 3d. black, brown and green 10 10
357 – 9d. black, brown and blue 15 15
358 – 1s. multicoloured 15 15
DESIGNS—VERT: 9d. Putting the shot. HORIZ: 1s. Diving.

85 Military Forces Band

1967. International Tourist Year. Multicoloured.
360 3d. Type **85** 40 10
361 9d. Reef diving 15 10
362 1s. Beqa fire walkers 15 10
363 2s. "Oriana" (cruise liner) at Suva 40 15

89 Bligh (bust), H.M.S. "Providence" and Chart

1967. 150th Death Anniv of Admiral Bligh.
364 **89** 4d. multicoloured 10 10
365 – 1s. multicoloured 10 10
366 – 2s.6d. multicoloured . . . 15 15
DESIGNS (As Type **89**): 2s.6d. Bligh's tomb. (54 × 20 mm): 1s. "Bounty's longboat being chased in Fiji waters".

92 Simmonds Spartan Seaplane

1968. 40th Anniv of Kingsford Smith's Pacific Flight via Fiji.
367 **92** 2d. black and green . . . 15 10
368 – 6d. blue, black and lake . . 15 10
369 – 1s. violet and green 20 10
370 – 2s. brown and blue 30 15
DESIGNS: 6d. Hawker Siddeley H.S.748 and airline insignias; 1s. "Southern Cross" and crew; 2s. "Lady Southern Cross".

96 Bure Huts

1968.
371 **96** ½d. multicoloured 10 10
372 – 1d. blue, red and yellow . . 10 10
373 – 2d. blue, brown and ochre 10 10
374 – 3d. green, blue and ochre 35 10
375 – 4d. multicoloured . . . . 80 1·75
376 – 6d. multicoloured 25 10
377 – 9d. multicoloured . . . . 15 1·75
378 – 10d. blue, orange and brown . . . . 1·25 20
379 – 1s. blue and red 20 10
380 – 1s.6d. multicoloured . . . 4·50 4·25
381 – 2s. turquoise, black and red . . . . 75 2·00
382 – 2s.6d. multicoloured . . . 75 30
383 – 3s. multicoloured . . . . . 2·25 6·00
384 – 4s. ochre, black and olive 6·00 2·75
385 – 5s. multicoloured . . . . . 3·00 1·50
386 – 10s. brown, black and ochre . . . . 1·00 2·25
387 – £1 multicoloured . . . . . 1·25 3·00
DESIGNS—As T **96**: 1d. Passion flowers; 2d. Chambered or pearly nautilus; 4d. "Psilogramma jordana" (moth); 6d. Pennant coralfish; 9d. Bamboo raft; 10d. "Asota woodfordi" (moth); 3s. Golden cowrie shell. 33 × 22 mm: 2s. Sea snake; 2s.6d. Outrigger canoes; 5s. Bamboo orchids; £1 Queen Elizabeth and Arms of Fiji. 23 × 33 mm: 3d. Reef heron; 1s. Black marlin; 1s.6d. Orange-breasted honeyeaters ("Sun Birds"); 4s. Mining industry; 10s. Ceremonial whale's tooth.

113 Map of Fiji, W.H.O. Emblem and Nurses

1968. 20th Anniv of W.H.O. Multicoloured.
388 3d. Type **113** 15 10
389 9d. Transferring patient to medical ship "Vuniwai" . . 20 15
390 3s. Recreation 25 30

116 Passion Flowers **120** Javelin Throwing

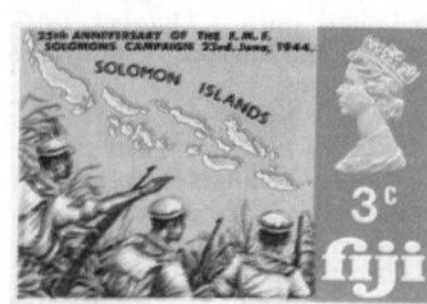

117 Fijian Soldiers overlooking the Solomon Islands

1969. Decimal Currency. Designs as T **96** etc, but with values inscr in decimal currency as in T **116**.
391 **116** 1c. blue, red and yellow 10 10
392 – 2c. blue, brown and ochre (As 373) 10 10
393 – 3c. green, blue and ochre (As 374) . . . . 1·25 1·25
394 – 4c. multicoloured (As 375) 1·50 1·25
395 – 5c. multicoloured (As 376) 20 10
396 **96** 6c. multicoloured 10 10
397 – 8c. multicoloured (As 377) 10 10
398 – 9c. blue, orange and brown (As 378) . . . . 1·50 2·50
399 – 10c. blue and red (As 379) 20 10
400 – 15c. multicoloured (As 380) . . . . 9·00 4·50
401 – 20c. turquoise, black and red (As 381) . . . . . 1·25 80
402 – 25c. multicoloured (As 382) . . . . 1·00 20
403 – 30c. multicoloured (As 383) . . . . 6·50 1·50
404 – 40c. ochre, black and olive (As 384) . . . . 7·50 4·00
405 – 50c. multicoloured (As 385) . . . . 4·50 20
406 – $1 brown, black and ochre (As 386) . . . . 1·50 40
407 – $2 multicoloured (As 387) 1·50 1·50

1969. 25th Anniv of Fijian Military Forces' Solomons Campaign.
408 **117** 3c. multicoloured 20 10
409 – 10c. multicoloured 25 10
410 – 25c. multicoloured 35 20
DESIGNS: 10c. Regimental flags and soldiers in full dress and battledress; 25c. Sefanaia Sukanai-valu and Victoria Cross.

1969. 3rd South Pacific Games, Port Moresby.
411 **120** 4c. black, brown and red 10 10
412 – 8c. black, grey and blue 10 10
413 – 20c. multicoloured 20 20
DESIGNS: 8c. Sailing dinghy; 20c. Games medal and winner's rostrum.

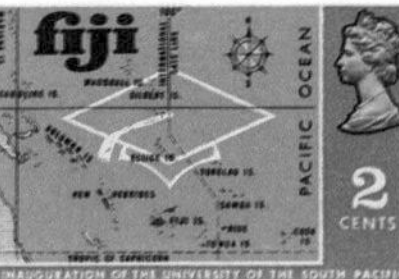

123 Map of South Pacific and "Mortar-board"

1969. Inauguration of University of the South Pacific. Multicoloured.
414 2c. Type **123** 10 15
415 8c. R.N.Z.A.F. Badge and Short S25 Sunderland flying boat over Laucala Bay (site of University) . . 15 10
416 25c. Science students at work 25 15

1970. Royal Visit. Nos. 392, 399 and 402 optd **ROYAL VISIT 1970**.
417 2c. blue, brown and ochre . . 10 20
418 10c. blue and red 10 10
419 25c. multicoloured 20 10

127 Chaulmugra Tree, Makogai

1970. Closing of Leprosy Hospital, Makogai.
420 **127** 2c. multicoloured 10 30
421 – 10c. green and black (vert) 15 30
422 – 10c. blue, black and mauve (vert) 15 30
423 – 30c. multicoloured 20 50
DESIGNS: 10c. (No. 421) "Cascade" (Semisi Maya); 10c. (No. 422) "Sea Urchins" (Semisi Maya); 30c. Makogai Hospital.

131 Abel Tasman and Log, 1643

1970. Explorers and Discoverers.
424 **131** 2c. black, brown & turq 30 25
425 – 3c. multicoloured 60 25
426 – 8c. multicoloured 60 15
427 – 25c. multicoloured 30 15
DESIGNS: 3c. Captain Cook and H.M.S. "Endeavour", 1774; 8c. Captain Bligh and long-boat, 1789; 25c. Fijian and ocean-going Canoe.

135 King Cakobau and Cession Stone

1970. Independence. Multicoloured.
428 2c. Type **135** 10 10
429 3c. Children of the world . . 10 10
430 10c. Prime Minister and Fijian flag 10 10
431 25c. Dancers in costume . . 20 20

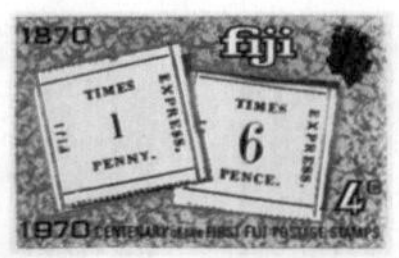

139 1d. and 6d. Stamps of 1870

1970. Stamp Centenary. Multicoloured.
432 4c. Type **139** 15 10
433 15c. Fijian stamps of all reigns (61 × 21 mm) 40 15
434 20c. "Fiji Times" office and modern G.P.O. 40 15

140 Grey-backed White-eye **142** Women's Basketball

1971. Birds and Flowers. Multicoloured.
435 1c. "Cirrhopetalum umbellatum" 15 30
436 2c. Cardinal honeyeater . . . 30 10

437 3c. "Calanthe furcata" . . . 85 20
438 4c. "Bulbophyllum sp. nov." 75 1·75
439 5c. Type **140** 35 10
510 6c. "Phaius tancarvilliae" . . 2·75 20
441 8c. Blue-headed flycatcher ("Blue-crested Broadbill") 35 10
442 10c. "Acanthephippium vitiense" 40 10
513 15c. "Dendrobium tokai" . . 2·50 40
444 20c. Slaty flycatcher . . . . 1·50 30
468 25c. Yellow-faced honeyeater ("Kandavu Honeyeater") 1·75 90
516 30c. "Dendrobium gordonii" 5·00 1·00
517 40c. Masked shining parrot ("Yellow-breasted Musk Parrot") . . . . 4·50 60
448 50c. White-throated pigeon 3·50 50
449 $1 Collared lory . . . . . . 4·00 1·00
520 $2 "Dendrobium platygastrium" . . . . . . 1·25 1·25
The 25c. to $2 are larger, $22\frac{1}{2} \times 35\frac{1}{2}$ mm.

1971. 4th South Pacific Games, Tahiti.
451 **142** 8c. multicoloured 10 10
452 – 10c. blue, black and brown 10 10
453 – 25c. green, black and brown 30 25
DESIGNS: 10c. Running; 25c. Weightlifting.

143 Community Education
144 "Native Canoe"

1972. 25th Anniv of South Pacific Commission. Multicoloured.
454 2c. Type **143** 10 25
455 4c. Public health 10 10
456 50c. Economic growth . . . 70 80

1972. South Pacific Festival of Arts, Suva.
457 **144** 10c. black, orange and blue 10 10

145 Flowers, Conch and Ceremonial Whale's Tooth

1972. Royal Silver Wedding. Multicoloured. Background colour given.
474 **145** 10c. green 20 15
475 25c. purple 30 15

1972. Hurricane Relief. Nos. 400 and 403 surch **HURRICANE RELIEF +** and premium.
476 15c.+5c. multicoloured . . . 15 15
477 30c.+10c. multicoloured . . . 15 15

147 Line Out

149 Christmas

148 Forestry Development

1973. Diamond Jubilee of Rugby Union. Mult.
478 2c. Type **147** . . . . 45 2·50
479 8c. Body tackle 85 10
480 25c. Conversion . . . . . . 1·50 40

1973. Development Projects. Multicoloured.
481 5c. Type **148** 10 35
482 8c. Rice irrigation scheme . . 10 10
483 10c. Low income housing . . . 10 10
484 25c. Highway construction 20 30

1973. Festivals of Joy. Multicoloured.
485 3c. Type **149** 10 10
486 10c. Diwali 10 10
487 20c. Id-Ul-Fitar 15 25
488 25c. Chinese New Year . . . 15 25

150 Athletics
151 Bowler

1974. Commonwealth Games, Christchurch, New Zealand. Multicoloured.
489 3c. Type **150** 15 10
490 8c. Boxing 15 10
491 50c. Bowling 50 75

1974. Centenary of Cricket. Multicoloured.
492 3c. Type **151** 40 15
493 25c. Batsman and wicket-keeper 60 15
494 40c. Fielder (horiz) . . . . . 70 1·10

152 Fiji Postman

1974. Centenary of U.P.U. Multicoloured.
495 3c. Type **152** 10 10
496 8c. Loading mail onto "Fijian Princess" 10 10
497 30c. Fijian post office and mailbus 20 40
498 50c. B.A.C. One Eleven 200/400 modern aircraft . . 35 2·50

153 Cubs lighting Fire

1974. 1st National Scout Jamboree, Lautoka. Multicoloured.
499 3c. Type **153** 15 10
500 10c. Scouts reading map . . 20 10
501 40c. Scouts and Fijian flag (vert) . . . . 65 3·00

154 Cakobau Club and Flag

155 "Diwali" (Hindu Festival)

1974. Centenary of Deed of Cession and 4th Anniv of Independence. Multicoloured.
502 3c. Type **154** 10 10
503 8c. King Cakobau and Queen Victoria 10 10
504 50c. Raising the Royal Standard at Nasova Ovalau . . . . 30 1·75

1975. "Festivals of Joy". Multicoloured.
521 3c. Type **155** 10 10
522 15c. "Id-Ul-Fitar" (Muslim Festival) 10 10
523 25c. Chinese New Year . . . 15 15
524 30c. Christmas . . . . 20 1·90
MS525 121 × 101 mm. Nos. 521/4 1·00 6·00

156 Steam Locomotive No. 21

1976. Sugar Trains. Multicoloured.
526 4c. Type **156** 25 20
527 15c. Diesel loco No. 8 . . . 45 40
528 20c. Diesel loco No. 1 . . . 50 1·00
529 30c. Free passenger train . . 60 2·75

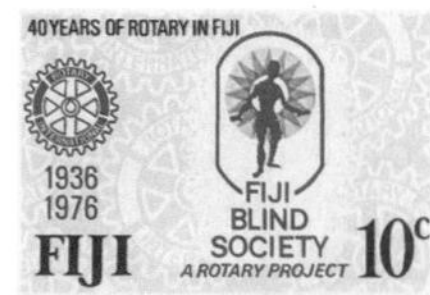
157 Fiji Blind Society and Rotary Symbols

1976. 40th Anniv of Rotary in Fiji.
530 **157** 10c. blue, green and black 15 25
531 – 25c. multicoloured 40 75
DESIGN: 25c. Ambulance and Rotary Symbol.

158 De Havilland Drover 1

1976. 25th Anniv of Air Services. Multicoloured.
532 4c. Type **158** 40 20
533 15c. B.A.C. One Eleven 200/400 . . . . 75 1·50
534 25c. Hawker Siddeley H.S.748 . . . . 80 1·50
535 30c. Britten Norman "long nose" Trislander . . . . . 90 3·50

159 The Queen's Visit to Fiji, 1970

1977. Silver Jubilee. Multicoloured.
536 10c. Type **159** 10 10
537 25c. King Edward's Chair . . 15 10
538 30c. The Queen wearing cloth of gold supertunica 25 15

160 Map of the World

1977. E.E.C./A.C.P.* Council of Ministers Conference. Multicoloured.
539 4c. Type **160** 10 10
540 30c. Map of Fiji group . . . 30 1·75
*A.C.P. = African, Caribbean, Pacific Group.

161 "Hibiscus rosa-sinensis"

1977. 21st Anniv of Fiji Hibiscus Festival.
541 **161** 4c. multicoloured 10 10
542 – 15c. multicoloured 15 15
543 – 30c. multicoloured 25 30
544 – 35c. multicoloured . . . . 40 1·25
Nos. 542/44 show different varieties of "Hibiscus rosa-sinensis".

162 Drua

1977. Canoes. Multicoloured.
545 4c. Type **162** 15 10
546 15c. Tabilai 25 20
547 25c. Takai 30 25
548 40c. Camakua 40 80

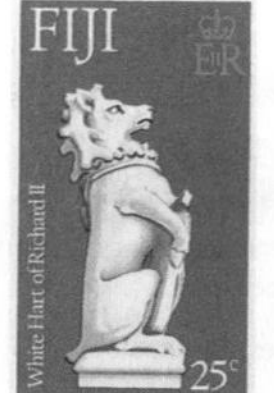

163 White Hart of Richard II

165 Shallow Wooden Oil Dish in Shape of Human Figure

164 Defence Force surrounding "Southern Cross", Suva

1978. 25th Anniv of Coronation. Multicoloured.
549 **163** 25c. brown, green and silver 15 20
550 – 25c. multicoloured 15 20
551 – 25c. brown, green and silver 15 20
DESIGNS: No. 550, Queen Elizabeth II; No. 551, Banded iguana.

1978. Aviation Anniversaries. Multicoloured.
552 4c. Type **164** 30 10
553 15c. "Southern Cross" prior to leaving Naselai Beach 50 30
554 25c. Wright Flyer I 60 60
555 30c. Bristol F2B Brisfit . . . 60 1·25
The 25c. value commemorates the 75th anniv of Powered Flight, the 30c. the 60th anniv of R.A.F. and the other values the 50th anniv of First Trans-Pacific Flight by Kingsford-Smith.

1978. Fijian Artifacts. Multicoloured.
556 4c. Type **165** 10 10
557 15c. Necklace of cachalot teeth (horiz) 10 10
558 25c. Double water bottle (horiz) 15 10
559 30c. Finely carved Ula or throwing club 15 15

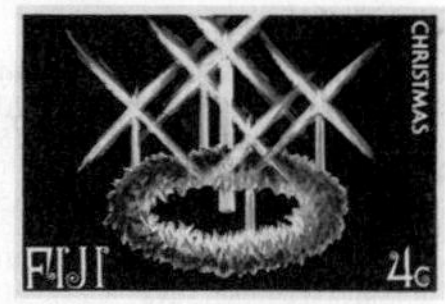
166 Advent Crown with Candles (Christmas)

1978. Festivals. Multicoloured.
560 4c. Type **166** 10 10
561 15c. Lamps (Diwali) 15 10
562 25c. Coffee pot, cups and fruit (Id-Ul-Fitr) 20 10
563 40c. Lion (Chinese New Year) 35 40

167 Banded Iguana

1979. Endangered Wildlife. Multicoloured.
564 4c. Type **167** 60 10
565 15c. Tree frog . . . . 1·10 15
566 25c. Long-legged warbler . . 4·25 40
567 30c. Pink-billed parrot finch 4·25 2·40

168 Women with Dholak

1979. Centenary of Arrival of Indians. Multicoloured.
568 4c. Type **168** 10 10
569 15c. Men sitting around tanoa 10 10
570 30c. Farmer and sugar cane plantation 15 10
571 40c. Sailing ship "Leonidas" 40 25

169 Soccer

1979. 6th South Pacific Games. Multicoloured.
572 4c. Type **169** 30 10
573 15c. Rugby Union 70 20
574 30c. Lawn tennis 80 80
575 40c. Weightlifting . . . . . 80 1·40

170 Indian Child and Map of Fiji

1979. International Year of the Child. Multicoloured.
576 4c.+1c. Type **170** 10 10
577 15c.+2c. European child . . . 15 15
578 30c.+3c. Chinese child . . . 15 15
579 40c.+4c. Fijian child 15 20

171 Old Town Hall, Suva

1979. Architecture. Multicoloured.
580A 1c. Type **171** 15 60
581Bc 2c. Dudley Church, Suva 30 20
582A 3c. Fiji International Telecommunications Building, Suva 35 80
722 4c. Lautoka Mosque . . . 30 30
583A 5c. As 4c. 15 10
584B 6c. General Post Office, Suva 15 10
724 8c. Public School, Levuka 1·75 2·25
585A 10c. Fiji Visitors Bureau, Suva 20 10
586A 12c. As 8c. . . . . 20 2·50
726 15c. Colonial War Memorial Hospital, Suva 30 20
588A 18c. Labasa sugar mill . . 20 30
589A 20c. Rewa Bridge, Nausori 55 30
590A 30c. Sacred Heart Cathedral, Suva (vert) 65 50
591A 35c. Grand Pacific Hotel, Suva . . . . 30 1·00
592A 45c. Shiva Temple, Suva 30 45
593A 50c. Serua Island Village 30 40
594A $1 Solo Rock Lighthouse (30 × 46 mm) . . . . . 75 2·25
595A $2 Baker Memorial Hall, Nausori (46 × 30 mm) 75 1·60
595cA $5 Government House (46 × 30 mm) . . . . . 1·00 2·75
Most values come with or without date imprint.

172 "Southern Cross", 1873

1980. "London 1980" Int Stamp Exhibition. Mult.
596 6c. Type **172** 25 10
597 20c. "Levuka", 1910 . . . . 35 10
598 45c. "Matua", 1936 . . . . 40 50
599 50c. "Oronsay", 1951 . . . . 40 70

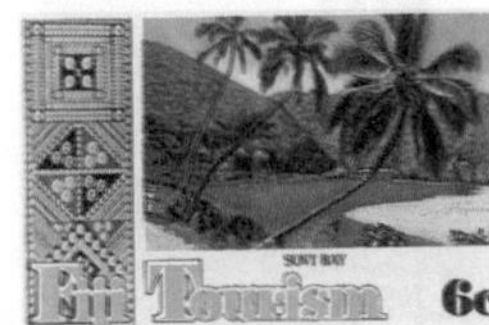

173 Sovi Bay

1980. Tourism. Multicoloured.
600 6c. Type **173** 10 10
601 20c. Evening scene, Yanuca Island 15 15
602 45c. Dravuni Beach 20 40
603 50c. Wakaya Island 20 45

174 Official Opening of Parliament, 1979

1980. 10th Anniv of Independence. Multicoloured.
604 6c. Type **174** 10 10
605 20c. Fiji coat of arms (vert) 15 10
606 45c. Fiji flag 20 20
607 50c. Queen Elizabeth II (vert) 25 35

175 "Coastal Scene" (painting, Semisi Maya)

1981. Int Year for Disabled Persons. Mult.
608 6c. Type **175** 10 10
609 35c. "Underwater Scene" (Semisi Maya) 35 30
610 50c. Semisi Maya (disabled artist) at work (vert) . . . 40 40
611 60c. "Peacock" (Semisi Maya) (vert) 45 45

176 Prince Charles Sailing

1981. Royal Wedding. Multicoloured.
612 6c. Wedding bouquet from Fiji 10 10
613 45c. Type **176** 30 15
614 $1 Prince Charles and Lady Diana Spencer 50 60

177 Operator Assistance Centre

1981. Telecommunications. Multicoloured.
615 6c. Type **177** 10 10
616 35c. Microwave station . . . 35 50
617 50c. Satellite earth station . . 40 75
618 60c. Cable ship "Retriever" 55 90

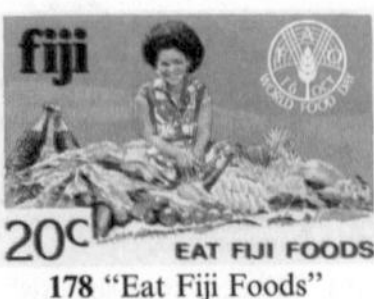

178 "Eat Fiji Foods"

1981. World Food Day.
619 **178** 20c. multicoloured 30 10

179 Ratu Sir Lala Sukuna (first Speaker, Legislative Council)

1981. Commonwealth Parliamentary Association Conference, Suva.
620 **179** 6c. black, buff and brown 10 10
621 – 35c. multicoloured 20 30
622 – 50c. multicoloured 30 45
MS623 73 × 53 mm. 60c. mult . . 70 1·00
DESIGNS: 35c. Mace of the House of Representatives; 50c. Suva Civic Centre; 60c. Flags of C.P.A. countries.

180 Bell P-39 Airacobra

1981. World War II Aircraft. Multicoloured.
624 6c. Type **180** . . . . 1·00 10
625 18c. Consolidated PBY-5 Catalina . . . . 1·75 40
626 35c. Curtiss P-40E Warhawk 2·25 95
627 60c. Short Singapore III . . 2·75 6·00

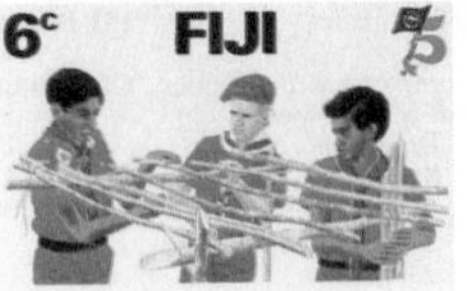

181 Scouts constructing Shelter

1982. 75th Anniv of Boy Scout Movement. Mult.
628 6c. Type **181** 15 10
629 20c. Scouts sailing (vert) . . 35 30
630 45c. Scouts by campfire . . . 40 50
631 60c. Lord Baden-Powell (vert) 50 1·00

182 Fiji Soldiers at U.N. Checkpoint

1982. Disciplined Forces. Multicoloured.
632 12c. Type **182** 50 10
633 30c. Soldiers engaged on rural development 60 45
634 40c. Police patrol . . . . . 1·75 1·25
635 70c. "Kiro" (minesweeper) 1·75 5·50

183 Footballers and Fiji Football Association Logo

1982. World Cup Football Championship, Spain.
636 **183** 6c. red, black and yellow 10 10
637 – 18c. multicoloured 25 20
638 – 50c. multicoloured 70 70
639 – 90c. multicoloured . . . . 1·10 2·00
DESIGNS: 18c. Footballers and World Cup emblem; 50c. Football and Bernabeu Stadium; 90c. Footballers and Naranjito (mascot).

184 Bride and Groom leaving St. Paul's

185 Prince Philip

1982. 21st Birthday of Princess of Wales. Mult.
640 20c. Fiji coat of arms 20 15
641 35c. Lady Diana Spencer at Broadlands, May 1981 . . 35 25
642 45c. Type **184** 40 40
643 $1 Formal portrait . . . . . 1·25 2·25

1982. Royal Visit. Muticoloured.
644 6c. Type **185** 75 25
645 45c. Queen Elizabeth II . . . 1·25 3·00
MS646 128 × 88 mm. Nos. 644/5 and $1 Royal Yacht "Britannia" (horiz) . . . . 2·00 3·00

186 Baby Jesus with Mary and Joseph

187 Red-throated Lorikeet ("Red-throated Lory")

1982. Christmas. Multicoloured.
647 6c. Type **186** 10 10
648 20c. Three Wise Men presenting gifts 30 20
649 35c. Carol-singing 45 35
MS650 94 × 42 mm. $1 "Faith" (from the "Three Virtues" by Raphael) . . . . 1·25 1·50

1983. Parrots. Multicoloured.
651 20c. Type **187** . . . . 1·25 20
652 40c. Blue-crowned lory . . . 1·50 50
653 55c. Masked shining parrot ("Sulphur-breasted Musk Parrot") . . . . 1·75 1·50
654 70c. Kandavu shining parrot ("Red-breasted Musk Parrot") . . . . 2·25 4·75

188 Bure in Traditional Village

1983. Commonwealth Day. Multicoloured.
655 8c. Type **188** 10 10
656 25c. Barefoot firewalkers . . 20 15
657 50c. Sugar industry 30 35
658 80c. Kava "Yagona" ceremony 55 70

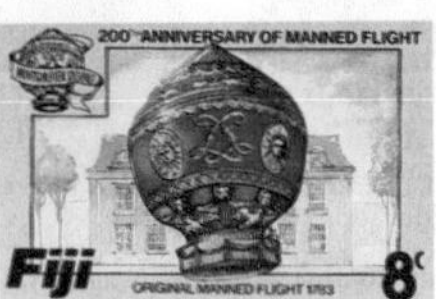

189 First Manned Balloon Flight, 1783

1983. Bicentenary of Manned Flight. Multicoloured.
659 8c. Type **189** 25 10
660 20c. Wright brothers' Flyer I 35 30
661 25c. Douglas Super DC-3 . . 40 40
662 40c. De Havilland Comet 1 60 60
663 50c. Boeing 747 . . . . . . 70 70
664 58c. Space shuttle 80 80

190 Nawanawa

191 Fijian beating Lali and Earth Satellite Station

1983. Flowers (1st series). Multicoloured.
665 8c. Type **190** 10 10
666 25c. Rosawa 25 30
667 40c. Warerega 30 50
668 $1 Saburo . . . . 50 1·40
See also Nos. 680/3.

1983. World Communications Year.
669 **191** 50c. multicoloured . . . . 50 1·25

192 "Dacryopinax spathularia"

193 "Tui Lau" (freighter) on Reef

1984. Fungi. Multicoloured.
670 8c. Type **192** 85 15
671 15c. "Podoscypha involuta" 1·25 25
672 40c. "Lentinus squarrosulus" 2·25 1·00
673 50c. "Scleroderma cepa" ("Scleroderma flavidum") (horiz) . . . . 2·25 1·25
674 $1 "Phillipsia domingensis" (horiz) . . . . 2·75 3·50

1984. 250th Anniv of "Lloyd's List" (newspaper). Multicoloured.
675 8c. Type **193** 70 10
676 40c. "Tofua" (cargo liner) . . 1·50 80
677 55c. "Canberra" (liner) . . . 1·50 1·50
678 60c. "Nedlloyd Madras" (freighter) at Suva wharf 1·50 1·75

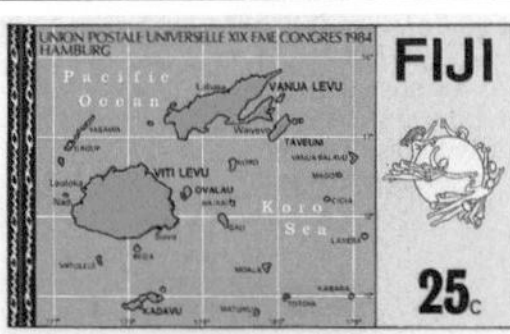

194 Map of Fijian Islands

1984. Universal Postal Union Congress, Hamburg. Sheet 77 × 65 mm.
MS679 **194** 25c. multicoloured . . . 2·75 2·25

1984. Flowers (2nd series). As T **190**. Multicoloured.
680 15c. Dravidrivi 25 25
681 20c. Vesida 30 40
682 50c. Vuga 40 90
683 70c. Qaiqi . . . . 45 1·40

195 Prize Bull, Yalavou Cattle Scheme

1984. "Ausipex" International Stamp Exhibition, Melbourne. Multicoloured.
684 8c. Type **195** 15 10
685 25c. Wailoa Power Station (vert) 30 40
686 40c. Air Pacific Boeing 737 airliner . . . . 1·50 1·25
687 $1 Container ship "Fua Kavenga" . . . . 1·10 3·75

196 The Stable at Bethlehem

1984. Christmas. Children's Paintings. Mult.
688 8c. Type **196** 10 10
689 20c. Outrigger canoe 30 20
690 25c. Father Christmas and Christmas tree 30 25
691 40c. Going to church 30 70
692 $1 Decorating Christmas tree (vert) . . . . 45 1·75

197 "Danaus plexippus"

1985. Butterflies. Multicoloured.
693 8c. Type **197** . . . . 1·50 15
694 25c. "Hypolimnas bolina" . . 2·50 60
695 40c. "Lampides boeticus" (vert) . . . . 3·25 2·25
696 $1 "Precis villida" (vert) . . 4·50 7·00

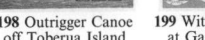

198 Outrigger Canoe off Toberua Island

199 With Prince Charles at Garter Ceremony

1985. "Expo '85" World Fair, Japan. Multicoloured.
697 20c. Type **198** 55 30
698 25c. Wainivula Falls . . . . 1·00 40
699 50c. Mana Island . . . . . 1·10 1·10
700 $1 Sawa-I-Lau Caves . . . . 1·40 2·50

1985. Life and Times of Queen Elizabeth the Queen Mother. Multicoloured.
701 8c. With Prince Andrew on her 60th Birthday 20 10
702 25c. Type **199** 50 40
703 40c. The Queen Mother at Epsom Races . . . . . . 1·25 80
704 50c. With Prince Henry at his christening (from photo by Lord Snowdon) . . . . . . 1·25 1·25
MS705 91 × 73 mm. $1 With Prince Andrew at Royal Wedding, 1981 3·50 2·00

200 Horned Squirrelfish

1985. Shallow Water Marine Fishes. Multicoloured.
706 40c. Type **200** . . . . 1·00 55
707 50c. Yellow-banded goatfish 1·25 1·10
708 55c. Yellow-edged lyretail ("Fairy cod") . . . . . . 1·25 1·75
709 $1 Peacock hind . . . . . . 1·75 5·00

201 Collared Petrel

202 Children and "Peace for Fiji and the World" Slogan

1985. Seabirds. Multicoloured.
710 15c. Type **201** . . . . 2·00 50
711 20c. Lesser frigate bird . . . 2·00 50
712 50c. Brown booby . . . . . 3·75 3·75
713 $1 Crested tern . . . . . . 5·50 8·00

1986. 60th Birthday of Queen Elizabeth II. As T **120a** of Hong Kong. Multicoloured.
714 20c. With Duke of York at Royal Tournament, 1936 20 25
715 25c. Royal Family on Palace balcony after Princess Margaret's wedding, 1960 20 25
716 40c. Queen inspecting guard of honour, Suva, 1982 . . 25 45
717 50c. In Luxembourg, 1976 . . 30 60
718 $1 At Crown Agents Head Office, London, 1983 . . . 45 1·60

1986. International Peace Year. Multicoloured.
736 8c. Type **202** 40 25
737 40c. Peace dove and houses 1·00 1·00

203 Halley's Comet in Centaurus Constellation and Newton's Reflector

1986. Appearance of Halley's Comet. Multicoloured.
738 25c. Type **203** . . . . 2·00 40
739 40c. Halley's Comet over Lomaiviti . . . . 2·25 85
740 $1 "Giotto" spacecraft photographing comet nucleus . . . . 3·25 7·00

204 Ground Frog

1986. Reptiles and Amphibians. Multicoloured.
741 8c. Type **204** 55 10
742 20c. Burrowing snake . . . . 1·00 30
743 25c. Spotted gecko . . . . . 1·10 35
744 40c. Crested iguana . . . . 1·25 90
745 50c. Blotched skink . . . . . 1·40 3·25
746 $1 Speckled skink . . . . . 1·75 6·00

205 Gatawaka

206 Weasel Cone

1986. Ancient War Clubs. Multicoloured.
747 25c. Type **205** 90 35
748 40c. Siriti . . . . 1·25 60
749 50c. Bulibuli . . . . 1·40 1·60
750 $1 Culacula . . . . 2·50 3·00

1987. Cone Shells of Fiji. Multicoloured.
751 15c. Type **206** 75 30
752 20c. Pertusus cone 80 40
753 25c. Admiral cone 85 40
754 40c. Leaden cone . . . . . . 1·00 1·40
755 50c. Imperial cone . . . . . 1·00 2·75
756 $1 Geography cone . . . . . 1·25 5·00

207 Tagimoucia Flower

1987. Tagimoucia Flower. Sheet 72 × 55 mm.
MS757 **207** $1 multicoloured . . 2·75 2·00

1987. "Capex '87" International Stamp Exhibition, Toronto. No. MS757 optd **CAPEX '87**.
MS758 72 × 55 mm. $1 Type **207** 9·00 9·00
Stamps from Nos. **MS**757 and **MS**758 are identical as the overprint on **MS**758 appears on the margin of the sheet.

209 Traditional Fijian House

1987. Int Year of Shelter for the Homeless. Mult.
759 55c. Type **209** 45 50
760 70c. Modern bungalows . . . 55 60

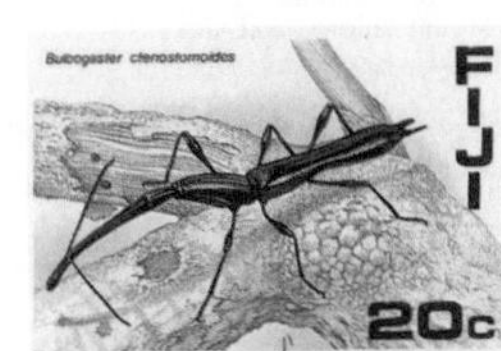

210 "Bulbogaster ctenostomoides" (stick insect)

1987. Fijian Insects. Multicoloured.
761 20c. Type **210** . . . . 2·50 50
762 25c. "Paracupta flaviventris" (beetle) . . . . 2·50 50
763 40c. "Cerambyrhynchus schoenherri" (beetle) . . . 3·25 1·75
764 50c. "Rhinoscapha lagopyga" (weevil) . . . . 3·25 3·75
765 $1 "Xixuthrus heros" (beetle) 4·25 10·00

211 The Nativity

1987. Christmas. Multicoloured.
766 8c. Type **211** . . . . 1·00 10
767 40c. The Shepherds (horiz) 2·50 40
768 50c. The Three Kings (horiz) 3·00 1·50
769 $1 The Three Kings presenting gifts . . . . . 3·75 4·50

212 Windsurfer and Beach

1988. "Expo '88" World Fair, Brisbane.
770 **212** 30c. multicoloured . . . . 1·50 1·40

213 Woman using Fiji "Nouna" (stove)

1988. Centenary of International Council of Women.
771 **213** 45c. multicoloured . . . . 1·00 1·25

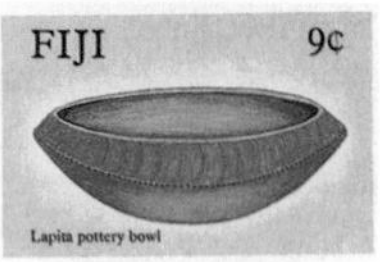

214 Pottery Bowl

1988. Ancient Fijian Pottery. Multicoloured.
772 9c. Type **214** 15 10
773 23c. Cooking pot 25 25
774 58c. Priest's drinking vessel 50 1·25
775 63c. Drinking vessel . . . . 55 1·60
776 69c. Earthenware oil lamp . . 60 1·75
777 75c. Cooking pot with relief pattern (vert) . . . . . . 70 1·75

215 Fiji Tree Frog

216 "Dendrobium mohlianum"

1988. Fiji Tree Frog. Multicoloured.
778 18c. Type **215** . . . . 2·75 1·50
779 23c. Frog climbing grass stalks . . . . 3·00 1·50
780 30c. On leaf . . . . 3·50 3·50
781 45c. Moving from one leaf to another . . . . 4·00 5·00

1988. Native Flowers. Multicoloured.
782 9c. Type **216** 65 15
783 30c. "Dendrobium cattilare" 90 45
784 45c. "Degeneria vitiensis" . . 90 70
785 $1 "Degeneria roseiflora" . . 1·60 2·75

217 Battle of Solferino, 1859

1989. 125th Anniv of International Red Cross.
786 **217** 58c. multicoloured . . . . 1·10 80
787 – 63c. multicoloured . . . . 1·10 1·00
788 – 69c. multicoloured . . . . 1·40 1·25
789 – $1 black and red . . . . 1·50 1·50
DESIGNS—VERT: 63c. Henri Dunant (founder); $1 Anniversary logo. HORIZ: 69c. Fijian Red Cross worker with blood donor.

218 Plan of "Bounty's" Launch

1989. Bicent of Capt. Bligh's Boat Voyage. Mult.
790 45c. Type **218** . . . . 1·75 50
791 58c. Cup, bowl and Bligh's journal . . . . 1·90 1·25
792 80c. Bligh and extract from journal . . . . 3·00 2·75
793 $1 "Bounty's" launch and map of Fiji . . . . 4·00 3·00

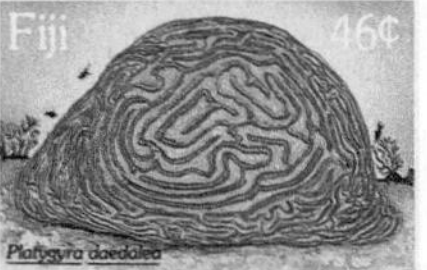

219 "Platygyra daedalea"

1989. Corals. Multicoloured.
794 46c. Type **219** . . . . 2·00 75
795 60c. "Caulastrea furcata" . . 2·25 1·75

796 75c. "Acropora echinata" (vert) . . . 2·50 2·25
797 90c. "Acropora humilis" (vert) . . . 2·75 2·75

220 Goalkeeper

1989. World Cup Football Championship, Italy (1990). Multicoloured.
798 35c. Type **220** . . . 1·25 40
799 63c. Goalkeeper catching ball 2·00 2·25
800 70c. Player with ball . . . 2·25 2·50
801 85c. Tackling . . . 2·25 3·00

221 Congregation in Church

1989. Christmas. Multicoloured.
802 9c. Type **221** . . . 25 10
803 45c. "Delonix regia" (Christmas tree) . . . 75 35
804 $1 The Nativity . . . 1·50 2·00
805 $1.40 Fijian children under tree . . . 1·75 4·50

222 River Snapper

1990. Freshwater Fishes. Multicoloured.
806 50c. Type **222** . . . 2·25 70
807 70c. Kner's grunter ("Orange-spotted Therapon") . . . 2·75 3·00
808 85c. Spotted scat . . . 3·25 3·50
809 $1 Rock flagtail . . . 3·50 4·00

223 1968 3d. Reef Heron Definitive

1990. "Stamp World London 90" International Stamp Exhibition, London. Sheet 120×70 mm, containing T **223** and similar vert design. Multicoloured.
MS810 $1 Type **223**; $2 1968 1s.6d. Orange-breasted honeyeaters definitive . . . 6·50 8·00

224 Vertiver Grass Contours

225 "Dacrydium nidulum"

1990. Soil Conservation. Multicoloured.
811 50c. Type **224** . . . 1·50 50
812 70c. Mulching . . . 1·75 1·75
813 90c. Hillside contour cultivation . . . 1·90 2·25
814 $1 Land use rotation (vert) 2·00 2·50

1990. Timber Trees. Multicoloured.
815 25c. Type **225** . . . 75 20
816 35c. "Decussocarpus vitiensis" . . . 85 30
817 $1 "Agathis vitiensis" . . . 2·50 3·00
818 $1.55 "Santalum yasy" . . . 3·50 5·00

226 "Hark the Herald Angels sing"

1990. Christmas. Carols. Multicoloured.
819 10c. Type **226** . . . 30 10
820 35c. "Still the Night, Holy the Night" . . . 75 30
821 65c. "Joy to the World!" . . 1·25 1·75
822 $1 "The Race that long in Darkness pined" . . . 2·00 2·75

227 Sigatoka Sand Dunes

1991. Environmental Protection. Multicoloured.
823 35c. Type **227** . . . 1·00 30
824 50c. Monu and Monuriki Islands . . . 1·75 1·00
825 65c. Ravilevu Nature Reserve, Taveuni . . . 2·00 2·75
826 $1 Colo-I-Suva Forest Park 3·00 4·25

228 H.M.S. "Pandora" (frigate)

1991. Bicentenary of Discovery of Rotuma Island. Multicoloured.
827 54c. Type **228** . . . 2·00 90
828 70c. Map of Rotuma . . . 2·25 2·50
829 75c. Natives welcoming H.M.S. "Pandora" . . . 2·25 2·50
830 $1 Mount Soloroa and Uea Island . . . 3·50 4·00

229 "Scylla serrata"

1991. Mangrove Crabs. Multicoloured.
831 38c. Type **229** . . . 90 35
832 54c. "Metopograpsus messor" 1·25 85
833 96c. "Parasesarma erythrodactyla" . . . 2·25 3·00
834 $1.65 "Cardisoma carnifex" 3·25 5·00

230 Mary and Joseph travelling to Bethlehem

1991. Christmas. Multicoloured.
835 11c. Type **230** . . . 40 10
836 75c. Manger scene . . . 1·50 1·25
837 96c. Presentation in the Temple . . . 1·75 3·00
838 $1 Infant Jesus with symbols 1·75 3·00

231 De Havilland D.H.89 Dragon Rapide of Fiji Airways

1991. 40th Anniv of Air Pacific. Multicoloured.
839 54c. Type **231** . . . 1·75 1·00
840 75c. Douglas DC-3 . . . 2·25 2·25
841 96c. Aerospatial/Aeritalia ATR42 . . . 2·50 3·25
842 $1.40 Boeing 767 . . . 3·50 4·50

232 Ethnic Dancers

1992. "Expo 92" World's Fair, Seville, Spain. Multicoloured.
843 27c. Type **232** . . . 65 45
844 75c. Peoples of Fiji . . . 1·40 1·75
845 96c. Gold bars and sugar cane train . . . 7·00 5·50
846 $1.40 "Queen Elizabeth 2" (cruise liner) at Suva . . . 7·50 7·00

233 "Tabusoro"

1992. Inter-Islands Shipping. Multicoloured.
847 38c. Type **233** . . . 2·25 55
848 54c. "Degei II" . . . 2·75 1·40
849 $1.40 "Dausoko" . . . 4·75 4·25
850 $1.65 "Nivanga" . . . 4·75 4·25

234 Running

235 European War Memorial, Levuka

1992. Olympic Games, Barcelona. Multicoloured.
851 20c. Type **234** . . . 1·00 20
852 86c. Dinghy sailing . . . 3·00 2·50
853 $1.34 Swimming . . . 3·50 3·75
854 $1.50 Judo . . . 3·50 3·75

1992. Historic Levuka (former capital). Mult.
855 30c. Type **235** . . . 30 30
856 42c. Map of Fiji . . . 45 55
857 59c. Beach Street . . . 65 1·00
858 77c. Sacred Heart Church (vert) . . . 80 1·50
859 $2 Deed of Cession site (vert) 1·75 3·50

236 The Nativity

1992. Christmas. Multicoloured.
860 12c. Type **236** . . . 75 10
861 77c. Shepherds and family giving presents . . . 2·25 1·60
862 83c. Shepherds at manger and giving presents to pensioners . . . 2·25 1·75
863 $2 Wise Men and collecting Fiji produce . . . 3·75 5·50

237 International Planned Parenthood Federation Logo

1992. 40th Anniv of International Planned Parenthood Federation. Multicoloured.
864 77c. Type **237** . . . 1·00 85
865 $2 Man weeping and pregnant mother with children . . . 2·75 3·50

238 Dove and Peace Corps Emblem

1993. 25th Anniv of Peace Corps in Fiji. Mult.
866 59c. Type **238** . . . 1·10 75
867 77c. Handshake . . . 1·40 1·40
868 $1 Educational symbols . . . 1·75 1·75
869 $2 Symbols of home businesses scheme . . . 3·00 4·50

239 Fijian Players performing Cibi (traditional dance)

1993. Hong Kong Rugby Sevens Competition. Multicoloured.
870 77c. Type **239** . . . 2·00 1·40
871 $1.06 Players and map of Pacific . . . 2·75 2·75
872 $2 Scrum and stadium . . . 4·50 5·50

1993. 75th Anniv of Royal Air Force. As T **173** of Falkland Islands. Multicoloured.
873 59c. Gloster Gauntlet II . . . 1·25 75
874 77c. Armstrong Whitworth Whitley Mk V . . . 1·50 1·40
875 83c. Bristol F2B "Brisfit" . . 1·60 1·60
876 $2 Hawker Tempest Mk V 2·50 3·50
MS877 110×77 mm. $1 Vickers Vildebeest III; $1 Handley Page Hampden; $1 Vickers FB-27 Vimy; $1 British Aerospace Hawk T.1 . . . 6·50 6·50

240 "Chromodoris fidelis"

1993. Nudibranchs. Multicoloured.
878 12c. Type **240** . . . 65 10
879 42c. "Halgerda carlsoni" . . 1·40 55
880 53c. "Chromodoris lochi" . . 1·50 1·25
881 83c. Blue sea lizard . . . 2·25 2·25
882 $1 "Phyllidia bourguini" . . 2·50 2·50
883 $2 Spanish dancer . . . 3·75 6·00

241 Mango

242 "Anaphaesis java"

1993. Tropical Fruits. Multicoloured.
884 30c. Type **241** . . . 1·60 45
885 42c. Guava . . . 1·75 80
886 $1 Lemon . . . 3·25 2·50
887 $2 Soursop . . . 5·50 7·00

1994. "Hong Kong '94" International Stamp Exhibition. (a) No. **MS**877 optd **HONG KONG '94** and emblem on each stamp.
MS888 110×77 mm. $1 Vickers Vildebeest III; $1 Handley Page Hampden; $1 Vickers FB-27 Vimy; $1 British Aerospace Hawk T.1 . . . 4·50 6·00

(b) Sheet 122×85 mm containing T **242** and similar vert designs showing butterflies. Multicoloured.
MS889 $1 Type **242**; $1 *Euploea leucostictos*; $1 *Vagrans egista*; $1 *Acraea andromache* . . . 4·50 6·00

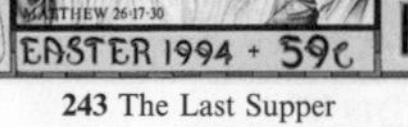

243 The Last Supper

1994. Easter. Multicoloured.
890 59c. Type **243** . . . 1·25 60
891 77c. The Crucifixion (vert) . . 1·50 1·25
892 $1 The Resurrection . . . 2·00 2·25
893 $2 Examining Christ's wounds (vert) . . . 3·50 6·50

244 Sagati

245 White-collared Kingfisher on Branch

1994. Edible Seaweeds. Multicoloured.
894 42c. Type **244** 90 45
895 83c. Nama . . . . 1·75 2·00
896 $1 Lumicevata . . . . 2·00 2·50
897 $2 Lumiwawa . . . . 3·50 6·50

1994. White-collared Kingfisher. Sheet 98 × 84 mm, containing T **245** and similar vert design. Multicoloured.
MS898 $1.50, Type **245**; $1.50, Kingfisher with crab in beak 7·50 8·00

246 "Neoveitchia storckii"

247 Father Ioane Batita

1994. "Singpex '94" International Stamp Exhibition. Endemic Palm. Sheet 97 × 69 mm, containing T **246** and similar vert design. Multicoloured.
MS899 $1.50, Type **246**; $1.50, Palm flowers . . . . 7·50 8·50

1994. 150th Anniv of Arrival of Catholic Missionaries in Fiji. Multicoloured.
900 23c. Type **247** 35 25
901 31c. Local catechist 45 30
902 44c. Sacred Heart Cathedral, Suva 60 70
903 63c. Lomary Church . . . . 80 1·10
904 81c. Pope Gregory XVI . . . 1·50 1·75
905 $2 Pope John Paul II . . . . 3·00 4·25

248 Waterfall and Banded Iguana

249 Red-headed Parrot Finch

1995. Eco-Tourism in Fiji. Sheet 140 × 80 mm, containing T **248** and similar square designs. Multicoloured.
MS906 81c. Type **248**; 81c. Mountain trekkers and Fiji Tree Frog; 81c. Bilibili River trip and White-collared kingfisher ("Kingfisher"); 81c. Historic sites and Flying Fox . . . . 4·50 5·50

1995. 50th Anniv of End of Second World War. As T **184a** of Falkland Islands. Multicoloured.
907 13c. Fijian soldiers guarding crashed Japanese Mitsubishi A6M Zero-Sen aircraft 60 20
908 63c. American spotter plane landing on Kameli Airstrip, Solomon Islands . . . . . 1·75 1·50
909 87c. Corporal Sukanaivalu and Victoria Cross . . . . 2·00 2·50
910 $1.12 H.M.S. "Fiji" (cruiser) 2·50 2·75
MS911 75 × 85 mm. $2 Reverse of 1939–45 War Medal (vert) . . 2·25 2·75

1995. Birds. Multicoloured.
912 1c. Type **249** 10 10
913 2c. Golden whistler 10 10
914 3c. Ogea flycatcher 10 10
915 4c. Peale's pigeon 10 10
916 6c. Blue-headed flycatcher ("Blue-crested Broadbill") 15 10
917 13c. Island thrush 25 10
918 23c. Many-coloured fruit dove 15 30
919 31c. Green-backed heron ("Mangrove heron") . . . 20 35
920 44c. Purple swamphen . . . 45 35
921 63c. Fiji goshawk 65 45
922 81c. Kandavu fantail ("Kadavu Fantail") . . . 80 55
923 87c. Collard lory 90 60
924 $1 Scarlet robin . . . . . . 1·00 70
925 $2 Peregrine falcon . . . . . 1·75 1·40
926 $3 Barn owl . . . . 2·50 2·00
927 $5 Masked shining parrot ("Yellow-breasted musk parrot") . . . . 3·75 3·50

1995. "JAKARTA '95" Stamp Exhibition, Indonesia. No. **MS**898 optd "JAKARTA '95" and emblem on sheet margin.
MS928 $1.50, Type **245**; $1.50, White-collared kingfisher with crab in beak . . . . 7·50 9·00

250 "Arundina graminifolia"

1995. Orchids. Sheet 100 × 80 mm, containing T **250** and similar vert design.
MS929 $1 Type **250**; $1 "Phaius tankervilliae" . . . . 4·50 6·00
No. **MS**929 also includes "Singapore '95" and emblem on the sheet margin.

251 Pres. Ratu Sir Kamisese Mara, Parliament Building and National Flag

1995. 25th Anniv of Independence. Multicoloured.
930 81c. Type **251** . . . . 1·25 1·00
931 87c. Young citizens of Fiji . . 1·00 1·10
932 $1.06 Rugby players . . . . 1·75 2·25
933 $2 Boeing 747 "Island of Viti Levu" . . . . 3·25 5·00

252 "Praying Madonna with the Crown of Stars" (workshop of Correggio)

253 Trolling Lure

1995. Christmas. Multicoloured.
934 10c. Type **252** 25 10
935 63c. "Madonna and Child with Crowns" (on porcelain) 90 80
936 87c. "The Holy Virgin with Holy Child and St. John" (after Titian) . . . . . . 1·25 1·25
937 $2 "The Holy Family and St. John" (workshop of Rubens) . . . . 2·75 5·00

1996. 50th Anniv of Resettlement of Banabans (inhabitans of Ocean Island) in Fiji. Multicoloured.
938 81c. Type **253** . . . . 1·00 1·10
939 87c. Banaban fishing canoes 1·25 1·25
940 $1.12 Banaban warrior (vert) 1·40 2·00
941 $2 Great frigate bird (vert) 5·00 6·00

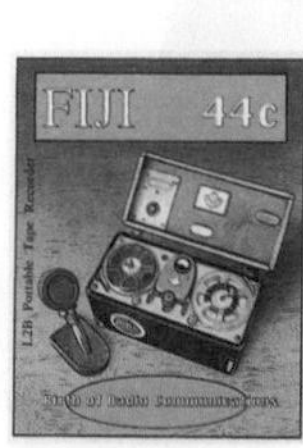

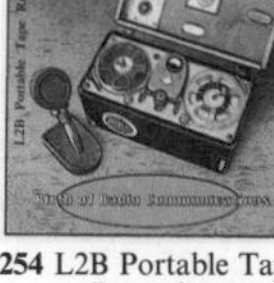

254 L2B Portable Tape Recorder

255 Winged Monster and Ring (bronze), c. 450 B.C.

1996. Centenary of Radio. Multicoloured.
942 44c. Type **254** 70 45
943 63c. Broadcasting House, Fiji 90 70
944 81c. Communications satellite 1·40 1·25
945 $3 Guglielmo Marconi . . . 4·00 6·50

1996. "CHINA '96" 9th Asian International Stamp Exhibition, Peking. Multicoloured.
946 63c. Type **255** 85 65
947 81c. Archer (terracotta sculpture), 210 B.C . . . . 1·10 1·10
948 $1 Dragon plate, 1426–35 . . 1·40 1·50
949 $2 Central Asian horseman (sculpture), 706 . . . . . 2·75 5·00
MS950 81 × 127 mm. 30c. "Yan Deng Mountains" (painting) (48½ × 76 mm) . . . . 2·00 2·50

256 Hurdling

1996. Cent of Modern Olympic Games. Mult.
951 31c. Type **256** 65 30
952 63c. Judo . . . . 1·25 80
953 87c. Sailboarding . . . . . . 1·40 1·75
954 $1.12 Swimming . . . . . . 1·60 2·50
MS955 59 × 99 mm. $2 Winning athlete, 1896 . . . . 2·50 3·25

257 Computerized Telephone Exchange

1996. Inauguration of Independent Postal and Telecommunications Companies. Multicoloured.
956 31c. Type **257** 40 30
957 44c. Unloading mail from aircraft 80 65
958 81c. Manual telephone exchange (vert) . . . . . 1·00 1·50
959 $1 Postman on motorbike (vert) . . . . 1·75 2·00
MS960 120 × 77 mm. $1.50, Fiji 1938 ½d. Sailing canoe stamp (vert); $1.50, Fiji 1985 20c. "Expo '85" stamp (vert) . . . . 9·00 9·50

258 "Our Children Our Future"

1996. 50th Anniv of UNICEF. Children's Paintings. Multicoloured.
961 81c. Type **258** . . . . 1·50 1·25
962 87c. "Village Scene" . . . . 1·50 1·25
963 $1 "Living in Harmony the World over" . . . . 1·60 1·60
964 $2 "Their Future" . . . . . 2·50 5·00

259 First Seaplane in Fiji, 1921

1996. 50th Anniv of Nadi International Airport. Multicoloured.
965 31c. Type **259** 65 30
966 44c. Nadi Airport in 1946 . . 80 50
967 63c. Arrival of first jet airliner, 1959 . . . . 1·25 1·00
968 87c. Airport entrance . . . . 1·40 1·50
969 $1 Control tower . . . . . . 1·60 1·75
970 $2 Diagram of Global Positioning System . . . . 2·75 5·00

260 The Annunciation and Fijian beating Lali (drum)

1996. Christmas. Multicoloured.
971 13c. Type **260** 40 15
972 81c. Shepherds with sheep, and canoe . . . . 1·40 85
973 $1 Wise men on camels, and people on cross . . . . . 1·60 1·40
974 $3 The Nativity, and Fijian blowing conch . . . . . . 4·75 6·50

261 Brahman

1997. "HONG KONG '97" International Stamp Exhibition. Cattle. Sheet 130 × 92 mm, containing T **261** and similar horiz designs. Multicoloured.
MS975 $1 Type **261**; $1 Friesian (Holstein); $1 Hereford; $1 Fiji draught bullock . . . . 5·00 6·50
No. **MS**975 is inscribed "FREISIAN" in error.

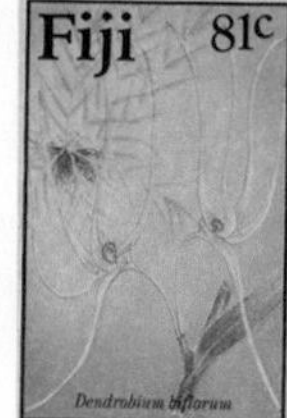

262 Black-throated Shrikebill

263 "Dendrobium biflorum"

1997. "SINGPEX '97" Stamp Exhibition, Singapore. Sheet 92 × 78 mm.
MS976 **262** $2 multicoloured . . 2·40 3·00

1997. Orchids. Multicoloured.
977 81c. Type **263** . . . . 1·50 1·25
978 87c. "Dendrobium dactylodes" . . . . 1·50 1·25
979 $1.06 "Spathoglottis pacifica" 1·75 2·00
980 $2 "Dendrobium macropus" 3·00 4·00

264 Hawksbill Turtle laying Eggs

1997. Life Cycle of Hawksbill Turtle. Sheet 140 × 85 mm, containing T **264** and similar horiz designs. Multicoloured.
MS981 63c. Type **264**; 81c. Turtles hatching; $1.06, Young turtles swimming; $2 Adult turtle . . 7·00 7·50

265 Branching Hard Coral

1997. Year of the Coral Reef. Multicoloured.
982 63c. Type **265** . . . . 1·00 55
983 87c. Massive hard coral . . . 1·40 1·25
984 $1 White soft coral . . . . . 1·60 1·60
985 $3 Pink soft coral . . . . . 4·25 6·50

266 Fijian Monkey-faced Bat

267 Waisale Serevi (Captain)

1997. Endangered Species. Fijian Monkey-faced Bat.
986 **266** 44c. multicoloured 70 40
987 – 63c. multicoloured 90 60
988 – 81c. multicoloured . . . . 1·25 1·10
989 – $2 multicoloured . . . . 2·50 4·50
MS990 157 × 106 mm. Nos. 986/9 × 2 8·00 10·00
DESIGNS: 63c. to $2 Showing different bats.

1997. Fiji Rugby Club's Victory in Hong Kong Rugby Sevens Competition. Multicoloured.
991 50c. Type **267** 65 80
992 50c. Taniela Qauqau 65 80
993 50c. Jope Tuikabe 65 80
994 50c. Leveni Duvuduvukula 65 80
995 50c. Inoke Maraiwai 65 80
996 50c. Aminiasi Naituyaga . . 65 80

997 50c. Lemki Koroi 65 80
998 50c. Marika Vunibaka . . . 65 80
999 50c. Luke Erenavula 65 80
1000 50c. Manasa Bari 65 80
1001 $1 Fijian rugby team (56×42 mm) . . . . . . 80 1·00

268 Shepherd and Angel

1997. Christmas. Multicoloured.
1002 13c. Type **268** 25 10
1003 31c. Mary, Joseph and baby Jesus 50 30
1004 87c. The Three Kings . . . 1·25 90
1005 $3 Mary and baby Jesus . . 3·50 6·00

269 Chief in War Dress

270a Diana, Princess of Wales, 1990

270 Man in Wheelchair using Computer

1998. Traditional Chiefs' Costumes. Multicoloured.
1006 81c. Type **269** 85 75
1007 87c. Formal dress 95 90
1008 $1.12 Presentation dress . . 1·40 1·75
1009 $2 War dress of Highland chief . . . . 2·00 3·25

1998. Asian and Pacific Decade of Disabled People. Multicoloured.
1010 63c. Type **270** . . . . . . 1·25 60
1011 87c. Woman with child . . 1·40 80
1012 $1 Man at desk . . . . . . 1·60 1·40
1013 $2 Wheelchair race . . . . 2·50 3·75

1998. Diana, Princess of Wales Commemoration.
1014 **270a** 81c. multicoloured . . . 1·00 1·00
MS1015 145×70 mm. 81c. As No. 1014; 81c. Wearing blue jacket, 1991; 81c. Wearing high-necked blouse, 1990; 81c. Carrying bouquet. Sold at $3.24 + 50c. charity premium . . . . 2·75 3·25

270b R34 Airship

1998. 80th Anniv of Royal Air Force. Multicoloured.
1016 44c. Type **270b** 70 30
1017 63c. Handley Page Heyford 1·00 60
1018 87c. Supermarine Swift FR.5 1·40 1·00
1019 $2 Westland Whirlwind . . 2·25 3·00
MS1020 110×77 mm. $1 Sopwith Dolphin; $1 Avro 504K; $1 Vickers Warwick V; $1 Shorts Belfast . . . . 3·75 4·50

271 Pod of Sperm Whales Underwater

1998. Sperm Whales. Multicoloured.
1021 63c. Type **271** . . . . . . 1·00 55
1022 81c. Female and calf . . . . 1·25 90
1023 87c. Pod on surface . . . . 1·40 1·00
1024 $2 Ceremonial whale tooth 2·00 3·00
MS1025 90×68 mm. No. 1024 3·00 3·25

272 Athletics

1998. 16th Commonwealth Games, Kuala Lumpur. Multicoloured.
1026 44c. Type **272** 75 30
1027 63c. Lawn bowls . . . . . 1·00 45
1028 81c. Throwing the javelin 1·40 1·10
1029 $1.12 Weightlifting . . . . 1·60 2·25
MS1030 63×77 mm. $2 Waisale Serevi (Fiji rugby captain) . . 2·50 3·00

273 Takia (traditional raft)

1998. Maritime Past and Present (1st series). Multicoloured.
1031 13c. Type **273** 25 10
1032 44c. Camakau (outrigger canoe) 50 30
1033 87c. Drua (outrigger canoe) 1·00 90
1034 $3 "Pioneer" (inter-island ship) . . . . 4·25 6·00
MS1035 105×75 mm. $1.50, Camakau (outrigger canoe) . . 2·25 2·75
See also Nos. 1044/48.

274 "Jesus in a Manger" (Grace Lee)

1998. Christmas. Children's Paintings. Multicoloured.
1036 13c. Type **274** 40 10
1037 50c. "A Time with Family and Friends" (Brian Guevara) 90 35
1038 $1 "What Christmas Means to Me" (Naomi Tupou) (vert) . . . . 1·50 1·00
1039 $2 "The Joy of Christmas" (Lauretta Ah Sam) (vert) 2·00 3·75

275 Women's Sitting Dance

1999. Traditional Fijian Dances. Multicoloured.
1040 13c. Type **275** 50 10
1041 81c. Club dance . . . . . . 1·75 1·00
1042 87c. Women's fan dance . . 1·75 1·00
1043 $3 Kava-serving dance . . . 4·50 6·00

1999. Maritime Past and Present (2nd series). As T **273**. Multicoloured.
1044 63c. "Tofua I" (cargo liner) 1·00 45
1045 81c. "Adi Beti" (government launch) . . . . 1·25 65
1046 $1 "Niagara" (liner) . . . . 1·50 1·25
1047 $2 "Royal Viking Sun" (liner) . . . . 2·25 3·00
MS1048 105×75 mm. $1.50, "Makatea" (inter-island freighter) 2·75 3·00

276 Wandering Whistling Duck

1999. "iBRA '99" International Stamp Exhibition, Nuremberg. Sheet 100×95 mm, containing T **276** and similar vert design. Multicoloured.
MS1049 $2 Type **276**; $2 Pacific black duck . . . . 3·75 4·25

277 "Calanthe ventilabrum"

277a Astronaut preparing to enter Module

1999. Orchids. Multicoloured.
1050 44c. Type **277** 85 35
1051 63c. "Dendrobium prasinum" . . . . 1·10 45
1052 81c. "Dendrobium macrophyllum" . . . . . 1·40 70
1053 $3 "Dendrobium tokai" . . 3·00 4·50

1999. 30th Anniv of First Manned Landing on Moon. Multicoloured.
1054 13c. Type **277a** 35 10
1055 87c. Third stage rockets firing near Moon . . . . 1·00 70
1056 $1 Buzz Aldrin on Moon's surface . . . . 1·10 1·00
1057 $2 Command module returning to Earth . . . . 1·75 2·50
MS1058 90×80 mm. $2 Earth as seen from Moon (circular, 40 mm diam) . . . . 2·00 2·50

1999. "Queen Elizabeth the Queen Mother's Century." As T **204a** of Falkland Islands. Mult.
1059 13c. Inspecting bomb damage, Hull, 1940 . . . . 50 10
1060 63c. With Prince Charles, 1950 . . . . 1·00 55
1061 81c. Meeting soldiers from the Light Infantry . . . . 1·50 85
1062 $3 Saying goodbye to Prince Charles, 1986 . . . . . . 2·75 3·75
MS1063 145×70 mm. $2 Lady Elizabeth Bowes-Lyon, 1923 and Armistice Day celebrations, 1918 2·75 3·25

278 Sugar Mills Diesel Locomotive

1999. 125th Anniv of U.P.U. Sugar Mill Locomotives. Multicoloured.
1064 50c. Type **278** 65 35
1065 87c. Steam locomotive . . . 1·00 75
1066 $1 Diesel locomotive "Hunsley" . . . . 1·10 90
1067 $2 Free passenger service . . 2·00 3·25

279 Exchanging Gifts

1999. Christmas. Multicoloured.
1068 13c. Type **279** 20 15
1069 31c. Two angels over Earth 40 30
1070 63c. Open Bible 70 45
1071 87c. Joseph and Mary on donkey (vert) 85 70
1072 $1 The Nativity (vert) . . . 95 80
1073 $2 Children and Father Christmas (vert) . . . . . 1·60 3·00

280 Sun rising over Islands and Hands holding Ceremonial Objects

2000. New Millennium. Multicoloured.
1074 $5 Type **280** . . . . 3·25 4·00
1075 $5 Traditional sailing canoe and globe (vert) . . . . . 3·25 4·00
1076 $5 Fijian warrior beating drum, palm trees and hut 3·25 4·00
1077 $5 Fijian flag and map of islands (vert) . . . . . . 3·25 4·00
MS1078 133×93 mm. $10 Macgillivary's petrel; $10 Crested iguana; $10 Prawns; $10 Indigenous flowers . . . . . . 24·00 27·00

281 *Paracupta sulcata* (beetle)

2000. Beetles. Multicoloured.
1079 15c. Type **281** 35 10
1080 87c. *Agrilus* sp. . . . . . . 1·00 65
1081 $1.06 *Cyphogastra abdominalis* . . . . . . 1·25 1·25
1082 $2 *Paracupta* sp. . . . . . 2·00 2·75

282 Big Bird

2000. *Sesame Street* (children's T.V. programme). Multicoloured.
1083 50c. Type **282** 60 70
1084 50c. Oscar the Grouch in dustbin 60 70
1085 50c. Cookie Monster eating cookie 60 70
1086 50c. Grover (turquoise background) 60 70
1087 50c. Elmo (blue background) 60 70
1088 50c. Ernie (yellow background) 60 70
1089 50c. Zoe (pink background) 60 70
1090 50c. The Count (blue background) 60 70
1091 50c. Bert (green background) 60 70
MS1092 Two sheets, each 139×86 mm. (a) $2 Bert and birthday cake (horiz). (b) $2 Big Bird, Elmo and Ernie in tree house (horiz) Set of 2 sheets . . . . 3·00 3·50

283 President Ratu Sir Kamisese Mara and Forestry Plantation

284 Swimming

2000. 80th Birthday of President Ratu Sir Kamisese Mara. Multicoloured.
1093 15c. Type **283** 25 15
1094 81c. Pres. Mara and Fijians 70 55
1095 $1 Pres. Mara and harvesting sugar 80 65
1096 $3 Wearing naval uniform and patrol boats . . . . 3·25 4·25

2000. 18th Birthday of Prince William. As T **208c** of Falkland Islands. Multicoloured.
1097 $1 Prince William wearing fireman's helmet . . . . 1·25 1·25
1098 $1 At Clarence House, 1995 1·25 1·25
1099 $1 Prince William waving (horiz) . . . . 1·25 1·25
1100 $1 At Christmas service, 1998 (horiz) . . . . . . 1·25 1·25
MS1101 175×95 mm. $1 Wearing Parachute Regiment uniform and Nos. 1097/1100 . . . . 6·50 6·50

2000. Olympic Games, Sydney. Multicoloured.
1102 44c. Type **284** 60 35
1103 87c. Judo 95 60
1104 $1 Running (horiz) . . . . 1·10 90
1105 $2 Windsurfing (horiz) . . . 2·00 3·00

285 Top Left Leaf Fronds of *Alsmithia longipipes*

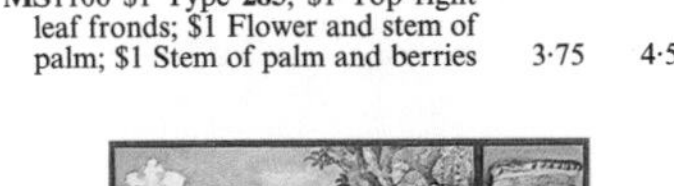

2000. *Alsmithia longpipes* (Endemic Palm of Fiji). Sheet 121 × 85 mm, containing T **285** and similar horiz designs forming a complete palm.
MS1106 $1 Type **285**; $1 Top right leaf fronds; $1 Flower and stem of palm; $1 Stem of palm and berries 3·75 4·50

286 Pottery Fragment and Site on Yanuca Island, Nadroga

2000. Lapita Pottery. Showing excavation sites and pottery fragments. Multicoloured.
1107 44c. Type **286** 55 35
1108 63c. Vutua, Mago Island . . 75 55
1109 $1 Ugaga Island, Beqa . . . 1·10 1·10
1110 $2 Sigatoka Sand Dunes . . 1·75 2·50

287 Three Kings in Jungle
288 Orange Dove

2000. Christmas. Journey of the Three Kings in Fijian Setting. Multicoloured.
1111 15c. Type **287** 30 10
1112 81c. Three Kings on precipice 95 55
1113 87c. Three Kings by lagoon 1·00 60
1114 $3 Three Kings on canoe . . 2·75 3·75

2001. Taveuni Rainforest. Sheet 122 × 86 mm, containing T **288** and similar vert design. Multicoloured.
MS1115 $2 Type **288**; $2 *Xisuthrus heyrovskyi* (beetle) . . . . . . 3·50 4·25

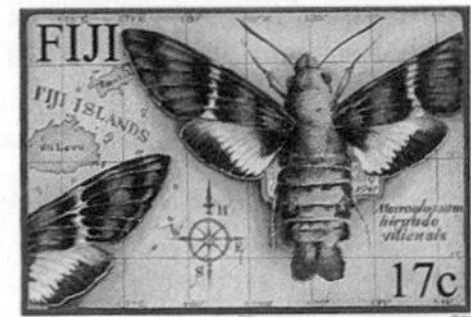

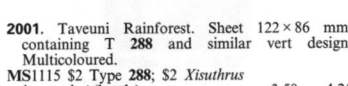

289 *Macroglossum hirundo vitiensis* (moth)

2001. Hawk Moths of Fiji. Multicoloured.
1116 17c. Type **289** 30 10
1117 48c. *Hippotion celerio* . . . 55 40
1118 69c. *Gnatholhlibus erotus eras* 75 65
1119 89c. *Theretra pinastrina intersecta* 85 85
1120 $1.17 *Deilephila placida torenia* . . . . 95 1·10
1121 $2 *Psilogramma jordana* . . 1·50 2·25

290 Red Junglefowl Hen

2001. Jungle Fowl of Fiji. Sheet 122 × 86 mm, containing T **290** and similar horiz dseign. Multicoloured.
MS1122 $2 Type **290**; $2 Red junglefowl cock . . . . 4·50 4·50

291 Girl with "Mile-a-Minute" (cat)

2001. Fijian Society for the Prevention of Cruelty to Animals. Multicoloured.
1123 34c. Type **291** 40 30
1124 96c. Boy with two puppies 90 90
1125 $1.23 Girl with "Twistie" (cat) . . . . 1·00 1·10
1126 $2 Boy with "Rani" (dog) 1·50 2·25

292 White-throated Pigeon

2001. Pigeons. Multicoloured.
1127 69c. Type **292** 70 70
1128 89c. Pacific pigeon (vert) . . 85 85
1129 $1.23 Peale's pigeon (vert) 1·00 1·10
1130 $2 Rock pigeon . . . . . . 1·50 2·25
No. 1129 is inscribed "PEAL'S PIGEON" in error.

293 Bank of New South Wales (1901)

2001. Centenary of the Westpac Bank. Multicoloured.
1131 48c. Type **293** 45 40
1132 96c. Bank of New South Wales (1916) 80 75
1133 $1 Bank of New South Wales (1934) 80 75
1134 $2 Westpac Bank (2001) . . 1·50 2·25

294 Yellow-finned Tuna

2001. Game Fish. Multicoloured.
1135 50c. Type **294** 65 55
1136 96c. Wahoo 90 75
1137 $1.17 Dolphin fish . . . . 1·00 1·10
1138 $2 Blue marlin . . . . . . 1·75 2·50

295 Angel appearing to Mary on Beach

2001. Christmas. The Nativity Story in a Fijian setting. Multicoloured.
1139 17c. Type **295** 40 10
1140 34c. Birth of Jesus in stable 55 15
1141 48c. Local shepherds visiting the baby 70 45
1142 69c. Fijian wise men bringing gifts 95 70
1143 89c. Holy family boarding canoe . . . . 1·10 75
1144 $2 Jesus with purple-capped fruit dove . . . . 2·25 3·00

296 Colonial Building

2001. 125th Anniv of Colonial Mutual Life Assurance Ltd in Fiji. Multicoloured.
1145 17c. Type **296** 35 10
1146 48c. Women at Colonial cash point 70 45
1147 $1 Private hospital, Suva . . 1·25 90
1148 $3 Deed of Cession ceremony, 1874 . . . . . 2·75 3·50

297 Fiji Airways De Havilland Drover Aircraft (1950s)
298 Pepper

2001. 50th Anniv of Air Pacific. Multicoloured.
1149 89c. Type **297** . . . . . . 1·10 1·25
1150 96c. Hawker Siddeley 748 (1967) . . . . 1·25 1·40
1151 $1 Douglas DC-10 (1980s) 1·25 1·40
1152 $2 Boeing 747-200 (1985) . . 1·60 1·75
Nos. 1149/52 were printed together, se-tenant, with the backgrounds forming a composite design.

2002. Spices. Multicoloured.
1153 69c. Type **298** 80 55
1154 89c. Nutmeg . . . . 1·00 70
1155 $1 Vanilla . . . . 1·25 1·10
1156 $2 Cinnamon . . . . 1·75 2·50

299 Balaka Palm Tree with Bird and Butterfly

2002. Seemann's Balaka Palm. Sheet 97 × 107 mm, containing T **299** and similar vert design. Multicoloured.
MS1157 $2 Type **299**; $2 Balaka palm in fruit with lizard on trunk 3·25 3·75

300 *Redigobius sp.*

2002. Freshwater Fish. Multicoloured.
1158 48c. Type **300** 65 35
1159 96c. Spotted flagtail . . . . 1·25 85
1160 $1.23 Silver-stripe mudskipper . . . . . . 1·40 1·40
1161 $2 Snakehead gudgeon . . . 1·75 2·25

301 Breadfruit
302 Saul's Murex Shell

2002. Tropical Fruit. Multicoloured.
1162 25c. Type **301** 40 20
1163 34c. Wi fruit 50 25
1164 $1 Jakfruit . . . . 1·25 80
1165 $3 Avocado . . . . 2·75 3·50

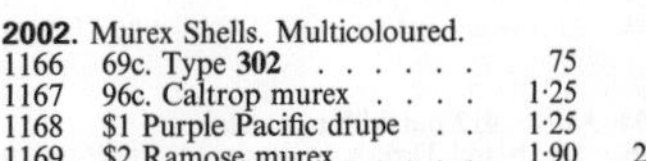

2002. Murex Shells. Multicoloured.
1166 69c. Type **302** 75 50
1167 96c. Caltrop murex . . . . 1·25 90
1168 $1 Purple Pacific drupe . . 1·25 90
1169 $2 Ramose murex . . . . . 1·90 2·25

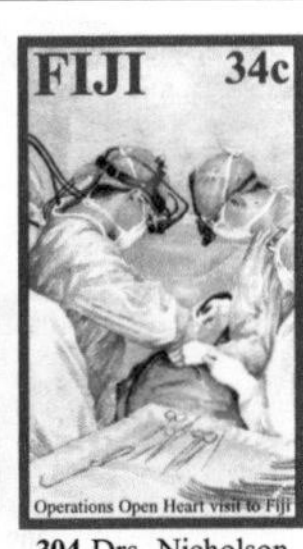

303 Adult Fiji Goshawk and Eggs
304 Drs. Nicholson and Menzie operating on Patient

2002. Fiji Goshawk. Multicoloured.
1170 48c. Type **303** 65 35
1171 89c. Chicks in nest . . . . 1·00 75
1172 $1 Juvenile Fiji goshawk on branch . . . . 1·25 85
1173 $3 Adult Fiji goshawk . . . 2·75 3·25

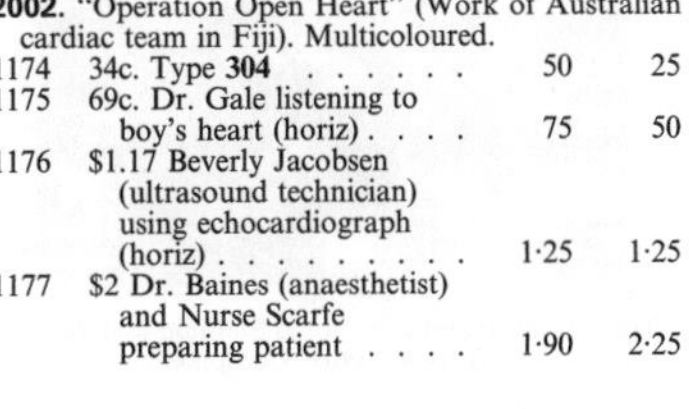

2002. "Operation Open Heart" (Work of Australian cardiac team in Fiji). Multicoloured.
1174 34c. Type **304** 50 25
1175 69c. Dr. Gale listening to boy's heart (horiz) 75 50
1176 $1.17 Beverly Jacobsen (ultrasound technician) using echocardiograph (horiz) . . . . 1·25 1·25
1177 $2 Dr. Baines (anaesthetist) and Nurse Scarfe preparing patient . . . . 1·90 2·25

305 Bottle of Fiji Natura Artesian Water
306 Methodist Church, Wakaya Island

2002. Fiji Natural Water Industry. Multicoloured.
1178 25c. Type **305** 40 20
1179 48c. Bottling plant, Viti Levu (horiz) 65 35
1180 $1 Local delivery van (horiz) 1·25 85
1181 $3 Fijian children with bottled water . . . . . . 2·75 3·25

2002. Christmas. Religious Buildings. Mult.
1182 17c. Type **306** 30 15
1183 89c. Mosque, Yaqara . . . 1·00 60
1184 $1 Hindu temple, Suva . . . 1·25 75
1185 $3 Methodist church, Suva 2·75 3·25

307 General Post Office, Suva

2003. Opening of New Mail Centre. Multicoloured.
1186 48c. Type **307** 60 35
1187 96c. Mail Centre . . . . . 1·10 90
1188 $1 Postal Logistics Centre 1·10 90
1189 $2 Smart Mail installation 1·90 2·25

308 Orchids and Waterfall

2003. International Year of Fresh Water. Sheet 86 × 104 mm containing T **308** and similar horiz design. Multicoloured.
MS1190 $2 Type **308**; $2 Butterfly on vegetation and waterfall plunging into pool . . . . . . 4·00 4·50

309 Athlete

2003. South Pacific Games, Fiji (1st issue). Multicoloured.

1191 10c. Type **309** 20 10
1192 14c. Baseball 25 10
1193 20c. Netball 35 20
1194 $5 Shot put . . . . 4·25 4·75

310 Netball Players, National Stadium and Multi-Purpose Sports Complex

2003. South Pacific Games, Fiji (2nd issue). Sheet 120 × 85 mm. Imperf.

MS1195 **310** $5 multicoloured . . 5·50 6·00

311 Uspi Rabbitfish

2003. Uspi Rabbitfish. Multicoloured.

1196 58c. Type **311** 65 35
1197 83c. Two rabbitfish 95 60
1198 $1.15 Rabbitfish, coral and moorish idols . . . . . . 1·25 1·25
1199 $3 Rabbitfish feeding on algae . . . . 2·75 3·25

312 Long-legged Warbler

2003. Bird Life International. Fiji's Rarest Land Birds. Multicoloured.

1200 41c. Type **312** 75 50
1201 60c. Silktail . . . . 1·00 70
1202 $1.07 Red-throated lorikeet 1·50 1·40
1203 $3 Pink-billed parrot finch 3·75 4·25

313 Pacific Slender-toed Gecko

2003. Geckos. Multicoloured.

1204 83c. Type **313** 95 70
1205 $1.07 Indopacific tree gecko 1·25 1·00
1206 $1.15 Mann's gecko . . . . 1·25 1·00
1207 $2 Voracious gecko . . . . 2·10 2·40

314 Christmas Tree and Children (Shalini Amrita Nand)

2003. Christmas. Showing winning entries from Christmas "United Fiji for all" stamp design competition. Multicoloured.

1208 18c. Type **314** 15 15
1209 41c. Children with Fiji flag (Kelerayani Gavidi) . . . 40 40
1210 58c. Santa and children in reindeer-drawn sleighs (Ronald Patrick) (vert) . . 55 55
1211 83c. Christmas presents and Santa on chimney (Cadillac Graphics) (vert) 90 90
1212 $1.07 Children with candles and Christmas tree (Shuetal Shamlee) (vert) 1·10 1·10
1213 $1.15 Santa with children (Roselyn Roshika) (vert) 1·20 1·20
MS1214 100 × 75 mm. $1.41 Handshake and cross (Viliame Vosabeci) . . . . 1·50 1·50

315 Tagimoucia (The Flower of Fiji)

2003. Fiji's First Personalised Stamps. Sheet 296 × 210 mm.

MS1215 **315** 50c. multicoloured 50 50

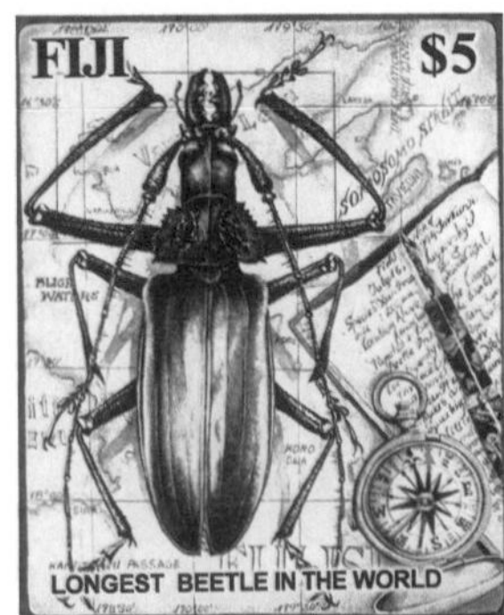

316 Longhorn Beetle (½-size illustration)

2004. Longest Beetle in the World. Sheet 80 × 95 mm. Imperf.

MS1216 **316** $5 multicoloured . . 3·25 3·25

317 Skipjack Tuna

2004. Endangered Species. Tuna. Sheet 130 × 90 mm containing T **317** and similar horiz designs. Multicoloured.

MS1217 58c. Type **317**; 83c. Albacore tuna; $1.07 Yellowfin tuna; $3 Bigeye tuna . . . . . 3·50 3·50

318 *Malleated Placostyle*

2004. Land Snails. Multicoloured.

1218 18c. Type **318** 10 15
1219 41c. *Kandavu Placostyle* . . 30 35
1220 $1.15 *Fragile Orpiella* . . . 75 80
1221 $3 Thin Fijian Placostyle . . 1·90 2·00

319 Boxer Shrimp

2004. Coral Reef Shrimps. Multicoloured.

1222 58c. Type **319** 35 40
1223 83c. Bumblebee shrimp . . 55 60
1224 $1.07 Mantis shrimp 70 75
1225 $3 Anemone shrimp . . . . 1·90 2·00

2004. As No. 917 but with new value.

1226 18c. Island Thrush 10 10

320 Wandering Tattler

2004. Migrating Shorebirds. Multicoloured.

1229 41c. Type **320** 30 35
1230 58c. Whimbrel ("Wimbrel") 35 40
1231 $1.15 Pacific golden plover 75 80
1232 $3 Bristle-thighed curlew . . 1·90 2·00

321 Swimming

2004. Olympic Games, Athens. Multicoloured.

1233 41c. Type **321** 30 35
1234 58c. Judo (vert) 35 40
1235 $1.41 Weight lifting (vert) 95 1·00
1236 $2 Sprinting . . . . 1·30 1·40

322 Yachts Racing

2004. 25th Anniv of the Musket Cove—Port Vila Yacht Race. Multicoloured.

1237 83c. Type **322** 55 60
1238 $1.07 Two catamarans (vert) 70 75
1239 $1.15 Two yachts with white sails 75 80
1240 $2 One yacht (vert) . . . . 1·30 1·40
MS1241 100 × 70 mm. $2 As No. 1240 . . . . 1·30 1·30

Stamps of a similar design were issued by Vanuatu.

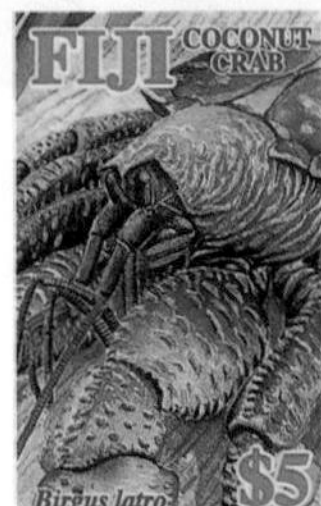

323 Coconut Crab

2004. Coconut Crab. Sheet 74 × 89 mm.

MS1242 **323** $5 multicoloured . . 3·25 3·25

324 New Adult Swallowtail Butterfly

2004. Swallowtail Butterflies. Multicoloured.

1243 58c. Type **324** 35 40
1244 83c. Larva (horiz) 55 60
1245 $1.41 Adult feeding on nectar (horiz) . . . . . . 95 1·00
1246 $3 Pupa . . . . 1·90 2·00

325 Mary and Archangel Gabriel

2004. Christmas. Multicoloured.

1247 18c. Type **325** 10 10
1248 58c. Baby Jesus 35 40
1249 $1.07 Mary and Jesus . . . 70 75
1250 $3 The Shepherds with Mary and Jesus . . . . . 1·90 2·00

326 Green-backed Heron

2005. Herons and Egrets.Multicoloured.

1251 $1 Type **326** 70 75
1252 $1 Great egret ("Great White Egret") 70 75
1253 $1 White-faced egret ("White-faced Heron") . . 70 75
1254 $1 Reef heron ("Pacific Reef Heron") 70 75

Nos. 1251/4 were printed together, se-tenant, forming a composite background design.

327 *Cananga odorata*

2005. Perfumed Flowers of Fiji. Multicoloured.

1255 58c. Type **327** 35 40
1256 $1.15 *Euodia hortensis* . . . 75 80
1257 $1.41 *Pandannus tecorius* . . 95 1·00
1258 $2 *Santalum yasi* . . . . . 1·30 1·40

POSTAGE DUE STAMPS

D 1

D 3

1917.

D5a D 1 ½d. black £475 £275
D2 1d. black . . . . £350 90·00
D3 2d. black . . . . £300 75·00
D4 3d. black . . . . £350 90·00
D5 4d. black £800 £400

1918.

D 6 D 3 ½d. black . . . . 3·00 21·00
D 7 1d. black . . . . 3·50 5·00
D 8 2d. black . . . . 3·25 7·50
D 9 3d. black . . . . 3·25 48·00
D10 4d. black . . . . 6·00 27·00

D 4

1940.

D11 D 4 1d. green . . . . 7·00 60·00
D12 2d. green . . . . 9·00 60·00
D13 3d. green . . . . 13·00 65·00
D14 4d. green . . . . 15·00 70·00
D15 5d. green . . . . 17·00 70·00
D16 6d. green . . . . 19·00 75·00
D17 1s. red . . . . 22·00 £100
D18 1s.6d. red . . . . 23·00 £150

FINLAND Pt. 11

A country to the east of Scandinavia. A Russian Grand-Duchy until 1917, then a Republic.

1856. 100 kopeks = 1 rouble.
1865. 100 pennia = 1 markka.
2002. 100 cents = 1 euro.

1

2

1856. Imperf.

1	1	5k. blue	£4750	£800
2		10k. pink	£6000	£275

Used prices are for stamps with penmark cancellation only. Stamps with postmark as well are worth more.

1860. Values in "KOP". Roul.

10	2	5k. blue on blue	£475	£120
13		10k. pink on pink	£450	50·00

1866. As T 2, but values in "PEN" and "MARK". Roul.

19	2	5p. brown on grey	£250	£140
46		8p. black on green	£180	£120
31		10p. black on buff	£550	£250
36		20p. blue on blue	£425	50·00
40		40p. pink on lilac	£375	50·00
49		1m. brown	£1500	£600

5 6

1875. Perf.

81	5	2p. grey	12·00	9·50
82		5p. yellow	50·00	4·50
83		5p. red	50·00	9·50
97		5p. green	13·00	40
71		8p. green	£150	47·00
85		10p. brown	75·00	15·00
99		10p. pink	21·00	2·00
87		20p. blue	55·00	1·30
102		20p. orange	28·00	30
89		25p. red	£250	17·00
103		25p. blue	41·00	1·60
79		32p. red	£225	26·00
90		1m. mauve	£250	31·00
105		1m. grey and pink	28·00	14·00
106		5m. green and pink	£350	£275
107		10m. brown and pink	£450	£450

1889.

108	6	2p. grey	65	50
148		5p. green	75	20
149		10p. red	90	25
150		20p. yellow	90	25
151		25p. blue	90	30
119		1m. grey and pink	3·00	2·50
120a		5m. green and red	26·00	36·00
122		10m. brown and red	36·00	65·00

7

8

9

10 11

1891. Similar to Russian types, but with circles added in designs.

133	7	1k. yellow	4·25	7·25
134		2k. green	5·50	6·75
135		3k. pink	9·75	11·00
136	8	4k. pink	13·50	10·50
137	7	7k. blue	7·25	1·30
138	8	10k. blue	14·00	9·50
139	9	14k. red and blue	20·00	18·00
140	8	20k. red and blue	17·00	12·50
141	9	35k. green and purple	22·00	31·00
142	8	50k. green and purple	30·00	24·00
143	10	1r. orange and brown	90·00	65·00
144	11	3½r. grey and black	£300	£300
145		7r. yellow and black	£250	£160

12

13

14 15

1901. Similar to Russian types, but value in Finnish currency.

161	12	2p. orange	55	75
162b		5p. green	1·50	30
169a	13	10p. red	35	25
170	12	20p. blue	35	25
165a	14	1m. green and purple	75	25
166	15	10m. grey and black	£130	38·00

16 17 18

1911.

176	16	2p. orange	30	30
177		5p. green	35	15
180	17	10p. red	45	20
181	16	20p. blue	30	15
182	18	40p. blue and purple	25	20

19 20 23

1917.

187a	19	5p. green	20	20
188		5p. grey	20	20
189		10p. red	25	20
190		10p. green	1·60	35
191a		10p. blue	30	20
192		20p. orange	25	20
193		20p. red	45	20
194		20p. brown	80	40
195		25p. blue	30	20
196		25p. brown	20	20
234		30p. green	35	30
198a		40p. purple	25	20
246		40p. green	25	90
200		50p. brown	45	30
201		50p. blue	4·00	25
247		50p. green	25	45
237		60p. purple	45	30
204		75p. yellow	25	35
205		1m. black and pink	12·00	20
248		1m. orange	25	35
207		1½m. purple and green	20	30
208a		2m. black and green	3·50	45
250		2m. blue	25	35
251		3m. black and blue	25	30
242		5m. black and purple	40	40
212		10m. black and bistre	95	80
213		25m. orange and red	55	15·00

1918. With white circle round figure of value.

214	20	5p. green	30	55
215		10p. pink	30	55
216		30p. grey	75	1·50
217		40p. lilac	35	50
218		50p. brown	50	1·70
219		70p. brown	2·00	10·50
220		1m. black and red	40	80
221		5m. black and lilac	47·00	55·00

1919. Surch with new figure of value three times.

222	19	10 on 5p. green	25	30
223		20 on 10p. red	30	25
224		50 on 25p. blue	90	30
225		75 on 20p. orange	25	25

1921. Surch with value, P and bars.

226	19	30p. on 10p. green	75	25
227		60p. on 40p. purple	2·75	40
228		90p. on 20p. red	25	25
229		1½m. on 50p. blue	1·60	20

1922. Red Cross.

230	23	1m.+50p. red and grey	80	6·75

26

28 Freighter "Bore" leaving Turku (Abo)

1927. 10th Anniv of Independence.

255	26	1½m. mauve	15	30
256		2m. blue	20	1·10

1928. Philatelic Exhibition. Optd **Postim. naytt. 1928 Frim. utstalln.**

258	19	1m. orange	6·50	10·50
259		1½m. purple and green	7·25	10·50

1929. 700th Anniv of Abo.

260	28	1m. olive	1·80	3·25
261	–	1½m. brown	2·00	2·20
262	–	2m. grey	55	3·50

DESIGNS—VERT: 1½m. Cathedral. HORIZ: 2m. Castle.

31

32 Olavinlinna

1930.

263	31	5p. brown	20	20
264		10p. lilac	20	20
265		20p. green	55	30
266		25p. brown	20	15
267		40p. green	2·75	15
268		50p. yellow	70	30
268a		50p. green	20	15
269		60p. grey	55	35
371		75p. orange	35	35
270		1m. orange	75	25
372		1m. green	25	20
271		1m.20 red	45	55
271a		1m.25 yellow	30	25
272		1½m. mauve	3·25	15
272a		1½m. red	30	25
272b		1½m. grey	25	15
272c		1m.75 yellow	50	30
273		2m. blue	35	20
273a		2m. mauve	6·50	15
273b		2m. red	30	15
373		2m. orange	25	20
373a		2m. green	35	20
273c		2½m. blue	2·50	20
374		2½m. red	20	15
425		2½m. green	35	20
273d		2m.75 purple	15	15
427		3m. green	1·60	20
375		3m. red	40	20
375a		3m. yellow	45	50
426		3m. grey	45	40
274a		3½m. blue	8·00	20
376		3½m. green	20	15
377		4m. green	50	15
378		4½m. blue	25	20
275	32	5m. blue	35	20
379	31	5m. blue	75	15
379a		5m. violet	75	25
379b		5m. yellow	80	15
379c		6m. red	60	20
429		6m. green	75	40
430		7m. red	45	20
379d		8m. violet	30	15
431		8m. green	85	1·30
432		9m. red	85	25
433		9m. orange	1·10	25
276b	–	10m. lilac	85	25
379e	31	10m. blue	1·10	20
434		10m. violet	1·40	20
435		10m. brown	3·25	20
436		10m. green	1·70	20
437		12m. blue	1·70	20
438		12m. red	65	20
410	32	15m. purple	1·00	20
439	31	15m. blue	3·00	20
440		15m. purple	8·50	20
441		15m. red	2·40	20
442		20m. blue	3·50	20
443		24m. purple	95	30
277	–	25m. brown	2·30	30
444	31	25m. blue	2·75	20
445	32	35m. violet	4·25	25
445a	–	40m. brown	3·25	25

DESIGNS—As Type 32: 10m. Lake Saimaa; 25, 40m. Wood-cutter.

35

1930. Red Cross Fund.

278	35	1m.+10p. red & orange	1·10	7·25
279	–	1½m.+15p. red & green	75	5·50
280	–	2m.+20p. red and blue	1·70	27·00

DESIGNS: 1½m. Drapery; 2m. Viking longship.

1930. Air. No. 276b optd **ZEPPELIN 1930**.

281		10m. lilac	90·00	£110

39 Church at Hattula

40 Elias Lonnrot

1931. Red Cross Fund.

282	39	1m.+10p. green & red	1·50	5·75
283	–	1½m.+15p. brown & red	4·75	9·50
284	–	2m.+20p. blue & red	95	12·50

DESIGNS: 1½m. Hameen Castle; 2m. Viipuri Castle.

1931. Finnish Literary Society's Centenary.

285	40	1m. brown	4·00	3·00
286	–	1½m. blue	10·50	3·75

DESIGN—HORIZ: 1½m. Society's seal with inscr as T 40.

42

1931. 75th Anniv of First Finnish Postage Stamps.

287	42	1½m. red	2·50	4·25
288		2m. blue	2·50	4·25

43

45

1931. Granberg Collection Fund.

289	43	1m.+4m. black	14·50	30·00

1931. Surch.

290	31	50PEN. on 40p. green	1·00	30
291		1,25 MK. on 50p. yellow	3·50	1·00

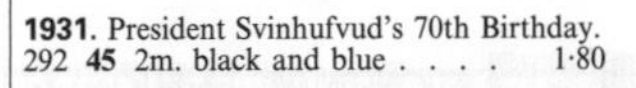

1931. President Svinhufvud's 70th Birthday.

292	45	2m. black and blue	1·80	1·80

47 St. Nicholas Cathedral

48 Magnus Tawast

1932. Red Cross Fund.

293	–	1½m.+10p. bistre & red	1·20	11·00
294	47	2m.+20p. purple & red	65	5·50
295	–	2½m.+25p. blue & red	80	18·00

DESIGNS—HORIZ: 1½m. University Library, Helsinki; 2½m. Houses of Parliament.

1933. Red Cross Fund.

296	48	1½m.+10p. brown & red	4·00	7·50
297	–	2m.+20p. purple & red	70	2·00
298	–	2½m.+25p. blue & red	90	3·50

DESIGNS: 2m. Michael Agricola; 2½m. Isacus Rothovius.

51 Evert Horn

52 Aleksis Kivi, after medallion by V. Aaltonen

1934. Red Cross Fund.

299	51	1½m.+10p. brown & red	50	1·90
300	–	2m.+20p. mauve & red	1·90	4·25
301	–	2½m.+25p. blue & red	65	2·75

DESIGNS: 2m. Torsten Stalhandske; 2½m. Jacob de la Gardie ("Lazy Jack").

1934. Birth Centenary of Kivi (poet).

302	52	2m. purple	2·20	2·50

53 Calonius 54 Finnish Bards

1935. Red Cross Fund. Cross in red.
303 **53** 1¼m.+15p. brown . . . . 50 1·50
304 – 2m.+20p. mauve . . . . . 1·20 4·25
305 – 2½m.+25p. blue . . . . . 70 1·30
PORTRAITS: 2m. H. G. Porthan. 2½m. A. Chydenius.

1935. Centenary of Publication of "Kalevala" (Finnish National Poems).
306 **54** 1¼m. red . . . . 1·20 1·30
307 – 2m. brown . . . . 3·00 85
308 – 2½m. blue . . . . 3·00 1·20
DESIGNS: 2m. Louhi's failure to recover the "Sampo"; 2½m. Kullervo's departure to war.

57 R. H. Rehbinder 58 "Lodbrok", 1771 60 Marshal Mannerheim

1936. Red Cross Fund. Cross in red.
309 **57** 1¼m.+15p. brown . . . . 50 2·10
310 – 2m.+20p. purple . . . . . 2·00 4·75
311 – 2½m.+25p. blue . . . . . 50 2·10
PORTRAITS: 2m. G. M. Armfeldt. 2½m. Arvid Horn.

1937. Red Cross Fund. Warships. Cross in red.
312 – 1¼m.+15p. brown . . . . 90 1·60
313 **58** 2m.+20p. red . . . . . . 12·00 3·25
314 – 3½m.+35p. blue . . . . . 1·20 2·10
DESIGNS—HORIZ: 1¼m. "Thorborg" (inscr "Uusiman"); 3½m. "Styrbjorn" (inscr "Hameenmaa").

1937. Surch **2 MARKKAA**.
315 **31** 2m. on 1¼m. red . . . . . 4·50 50

1937. Marshal Mannerheim's 70th Birthday.
316 **60** 2m. blue 55 70

61 A. Makipeska 62 Cross-country Skiing 63 War Veteran

1938. Red Cross Fund. Cross in red.
317 **61** 50p.+5p. green . . . . . . 25 1·20
318 – 1¼m.+15p. brown . . . . . 50 1·70
319 – 2m.+20p. red . . . . . . 5·00 5·50
320 – 3½m.+35p. blue . . . . . 40 2·40
PORTRAITS: 1¼m. R. I. Orn. 2m. E. Bergenheim, 3½m. J. M. Nordenstam.

1938. International Skiing Contest, Lahti.
321 **62** 1m.25+75p. black . . . . 2·30 7·25
322 – 2m.+1m. red . . . . . . 2·50 6·75
323 – 3m.50+1m.50 blue and light blue . . . . . . 2·50 6·75
DESIGNS: 2m. Ski jumping; 3m.50, Downhill skiing contest.

1938. Disabled Soldiers' Relief Fund. 20th Anniv of Independence.
324 **63** 2m.+½m. blue . . . . . . 1·80 2·75

64 Colonizers felling Trees 65 Ahvenkoski P.O., 1787

1938. Tercentenary of Scandinavian Settlement in America.
325 **64** 3½m. brown . . . . 1·10 1·70

1938. Tercentenary of Finnish Postal Service.
326 **65** 50p. green 25 60
327 – 1¼m. blue . . . . 1·10 2·10
328 – 2m. red . . . . 1·10 65
329 – 3½m. grey . . . . 3·50 5·00
DESIGNS: 1¼m. Sledge-boat; 2m. Junkers Ju 52/3m mail plane; 3½m. G.P.O., Helsinki.

66 Battlefield of Solferino 67 G.P.O., Helsinki

1939. Red Cross Fund and 75th Anniv of International Red Cross. Cross in red.
330 **66** 50p.+5p. green . . . . . . 60 1·50
331 1¼m.+15p. brown . . . . 90 2·20
332 2m.+20p. red . . . . . . 8·25 9·50
333 3½m.+35p. blue . . . . . 60 2·30

1939.
334 **67** 4m. brown 30 25
See also Nos. 382/4.

68 Crossbowman 69 Lion of Finland

1940. Red Cross Fund. Cross in red.
335 **68** 50p.+5p. green . . . . . . 50 1·50
336 – 1¼m.+15p. brown . . . . 50 2·20
337 – 2m.+20p. red . . . . . . 85 2·20
338 – 3½m.+35p. blue . . . . . 80 3·25
DESIGNS: 1¼m. Mounted cavalrymen; 2m. Unmounted cavalrymen; 3½m. Officer and infantryman.

1940. National Defence Fund.
339 **69** 2m.+2m. blue . . . . . . 25 1·00

70 Helsinki University 72 Builder

1940. 300th Anniv of Founding of Helsinki University.
340 **70** 2m. deep blue and blue . . 35 80

1940. Surch.
341 **31** 1m.75 on 1m.25 yellow . . 1·10 1·40
342 2m.75 on 2m. red . . . . 3·00 35

1941. Red Cross Fund. Cross in red.
343 **72** 50p.+5p. green 25 60
344 – 1m.75+15p. sepia . . . . 65 1·30
345 – 2m.75+25p. brown . . . . 3·00 7·25
346 – 3m.50+35p. blue . . . . 70 2·10
DESIGNS: 1m.75, Farmer; 2m.75, Mother and child; 3m.50, Flag.
See also Nos. 405/8.

73 Farewell Review 74 Knight

1941. President Kallio Memorial.
347 **73** 2m.75 black 35 65

1941. "Brothers-in-Arms" Welfare Fund.
348 **74** 2m.75+25p. blue 35 85

75 Viipuri Castle

1941. Reconquest of Viipuri.
349 **75** 1m.75 orange 30 85
350 2m.75 purple 25 60
351 3m.50 blue . . . . 65 1·30

76 Pres. Risto Ryti 77 Marshal Mannerheim

1941. (a) President Ryti.
352 **76** 50p. green 40 90
353 1m.75 brown . . . . . . 50 1·10
354 2m. red . . . . 40 1·10
355 2m.75 violet . . . . . . 55 1·10
356 3m.50 blue . . . . . . 45 1·10
357 5m. grey . . . . 45 1·10

(b) Marshal Mannerheim.
358 **77** 50p. green 40 80
359 1m.75 brown . . . . . . 40 1·20
360 2m. red . . . . 40 1·20
361 2m.75 violet . . . . . . 60 1·20
362 3m.50 blue . . . . . . 60 1·20
363 5m. grey . . . . 60 1·20

79 Aland 80 Tampere

1942. Red Cross Fund. Cross in red.
364 **79** 50p.+5p. green . . . . . . 25 1·20
365 – 1m.75+15p. brown . . . . 65 2·30
366 – 2m.75+25p. red . . . . . 95 2·30
367 – 3m.50+35p. blue . . . . . 65 2·30
368 – 4m.75+45p. grey . . . . . 45 2·30
ARMS: 1m.75, Uusimaa (Nyland); 2m.75, Finland Proper; 3m.50, Karelia; 4m.75, Satakunta.

1942.
369 **80** 50m. violet . . . . 1·20 20
370 – 100m. blue . . . . 1·70 20
DESIGN: 100m. Helsinki Harbour.
For 100m. in green without "mk" see No. 557b.

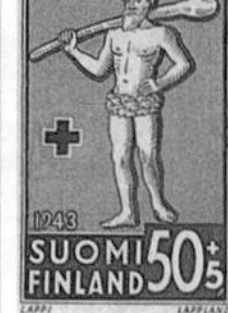
81 New Testament 82 Mediaeval Press 83 Lapland

1942. Tercentenary of Introduction of Printing into Finland.
380 **81** 2m.75 brown 25 75
381 **82** 3m.50 blue . . . . 40 1·30

1942.
382 **67** 7m. brown 40 20
383 9m. mauve 45 20
384 20m. brown 80 15

1943. Red Cross Fund. Cross in red.
385 **83** 50p.+5p. green 20 70
386 – 2m.+20p. brown . . . . . 40 1·90
387 – 3m.50+35p. red . . . . . 40 1·90
388 – 4m.50+45p. blue . . . . . 1·40 4·25
ARMS: 2m. Hame (Tavastland); 3m.50, Pohjanmaa (Osterbotten); 4m.50, Savo (Savolaks).

1943. Surch **3½mk**.
389 **31** 3½m. on 2m.75 purple . . 20 20

85 Military Tokens

1943. National Relief Fund.
390 **85** 2m.+50p. brown 25 60
391 – 3m.50+1m. purple 25 80
DESIGN—VERT: 3m.50, Widow and Orphans.

87 Red Cross Train

1944. Red Cross Fund. Inscr "1944". Cross in red.
392 **87** 50p.+25p. green 25 35
393 – 2m.+50p. violet 20 70
394 – 3m.50+75p. red 20 70
395 – 4m.50+1m. blue . . . . . 50 2·50
DESIGNS: 2m. Ambulance; 3m.50, Hospital, Helsinki; 4m.50, Airplane.

88 Minna Canth 89 Douglas DC-2 Mail Plane

1944. Birth Cent of Minna Canth (authoress).
396 **88** 3m.50 green 30 65

1944. Air. 20th Anniv of Air Mail Service.
397 **89** 3m.50 brown 30 70

90 Pres. Svinhufvud 91 92 Wrestling

1944. Mourning for Pres. P. E. Svinhufvud.
398 **90** 3½m. black 30 65

1944. National Relief Fund.
399 **91** 3m.50+1m.50 brown . . . 30 70

1945. Sports Fund.
400 **92** 1m.+50p. green 15 55
401 – 2m.+1m. red 15 55
402 – 3m.50+1m.75 violet . . . 15 65
403 – 4m.50+2m.25 blue 15 55
404 – 7m.+3m.50 brown . . . . 45 1·60
DESIGNS: 2m. Vaulting; 3m.50, Running; 4m.50, Skiing; 7m. Throwing the javelin.

1945. Red Cross Fund. As Nos. 343/6, but dated "1945". Cross in red.
405 1m.+25p. green 15 40
406 2m.+50p. brown 15 50
407 3m.50+75p. brown 15 50
408 4m.50+1m. blue . . . . . . 45 1·00
DESIGNS: 1m. Builder; 2m. Farmer; 3m.50, Mother and child; 4m.50, Flag.

93 Pres. Stahlberg 94 Sibelius 95 Fishermen

1945. 80th Birth Anniv of Pres. K. J. Stahlberg.
409 **93** 3m.50 violet 35 45

1945. 80th Birthday of Sibelius (composer).
411 **94** 5m. green 25 25

1946. Red Cross Fund. Cross in red.
412 **95** 1m.+25p. green 20 35
413 – 3m.+75p. purple 20 35
414 – 5m.+1m.25 red 20 35
415 – 10m.+2m.50 blue 20 50
DESIGNS: 3m. Butter-making; 5m. Harvesting; 10m. Logging.

1946. Surch with bold figures and bars.
416 **31** 8m. on 5m. violet 30 25
416a 12m. on 10m. violet . . . 75 25

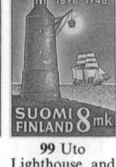

97 Athletes 98 Nurse and Children 99 Uto Lighthouse, and Sailing Ship

1946. National Games.
417 **97** 8m. purple 35 50

1946. Anti-tuberculosis Fund.
418 **98** 5m.+1m. green 25 45
419 – 8m.+2m. purple 25 45
DESIGN: 8m. Lady doctor examining child.

1946. 250th Anniv of Foundation of Pilotage Institution.
420 **99** 8m. violet 35 45

100 Postal Motor Coach 101 Town Hall

1946.
421 **100** 16m. black 45 70
421a 30m. black . . . . 1·50 25

1946. 600th Anniv of Founding of Porvoo (Borga).
422 **101** 5m. black 25 35
423 – 8m. purple 25 35
DESIGN—VERT: 8m. Bridge and church.

103 Tammisaari

104 Pres. Paasikivi

1946. 400th Anniv of Tammisaari (Ekenas).
424 **103** 8m. green 35 40

1947.
446 **104** 10m. black 35 35

1947. Anti-tuberculosis Fund. Nos. 418/19 surch.
447 **98** 6+1 on 5m.+1m. grn . . . 30 65
448 – 10+2 on 8m.+2m. pur . . 30 65

106 Bank Emblem

107 Athletes

1947. 60th Anniv of Finnish Postal Savings Bank.
449 **106** 10m. purple 35 40

1947. National Sports Festival.
450 **107** 10m. blue 35 40

108 Ilmarinen Ploughing

109 Emblem of Savings Bank Association

1947. Conclusion of Peace Treaty.
451 **108** 10m. black 35 40

1947. 125th Anniv of Savings Bank Assn.
452 **109** 10m. brown 35 50

110 Physical Exercise

111 Sower

1947. Anti-tuberculosis Fund.
453 **110** 2m.50+1m. green 35 95
454 – 6m.+1m.50 red . . . . . 35 1·00
455 – 10m.+2m.50 brown . . . 35 1·00
456 – 12m.+3m. blue . . . . . 50 1·50
457 – 20m.+5m. mauve . . . . 50 1·90
DESIGNS—VERT: 6, 10, 20m. Various infant exercises. HORIZ: 12m. Mme. Paasikivi and child.

1947. 150th Anniv of Central League of Agricultural Societies.
458 **111** 10m. grey 35 40

112 Heights of Koli

113 Z. Topelius

1947. 60th Anniv of Tourist Society.
459 **112** 10m. blue 35 40

1948. Red Cross Fund. Dated "1948". Cross in red.
460 **113** 3m.+1m. green 25 50
461 – 7m.+2m. red 35 95
462 – 12m.+3m. blue . . . . . 35 1·00
463 – 20m.+5m. violet . . . . 40 1·30
PORTRAITS: 7m. Fr. Pacius; 12m. J. L. Runeberg; 20m. F. R. Cygnaeus.

1948. Anti-tuberculosis Fund. Nos. 454/5 and 457 surch.
464 7m.+2m. on 6m.+1m.50 red 65 1·70
465 15m.+3m. on 10m.+2m.50 brown . . . . 85 1·70
466 24m.+6m. on 20m.+5m. mauve . . . . 1·20 3·00

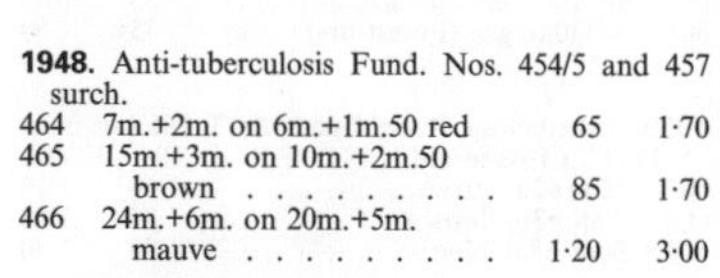

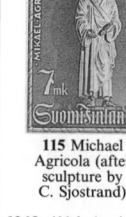

115 Michael Agricola (after sculpture by C. Sjostrand)

116 King's Gate, Suomenlinna

1948. 400th Anniv of Translation of New Testament into Finnish by Michael Agricola.
467 **115** 7m. purple . . . . 75 1·20
468 – 12m. blue . . . . 75 1·30
DESIGN: 12m. Agricola translating New Testament (after painting by A. Edelfelt).

1948. Bicentenary of Suomenlinna (Sveaborg).
469 **116** 12m. green . . . . 1·00 1·60

117 Finnish Mail-carrier's Badge

118 Girl Bundling Twigs

119 Anemone

1948. Helsinki Philatelic Exhibition.
470 **117** 12m. green . . . . 4·50 9·50
Sold only at the Exhibition, at 62m. (including 50m. entrance fee).

1949. Red Cross Fund. Inscr "SAUNA BASTU 1949". Cross in red.
471 **118** 5m.+2m. green 40 55
472 – 9m.+3m. red 40 85
473 – 15m.+5m. blue 55 75
474 – 30m.+10m. brown . . . . 40 2·30
DESIGNS: 9m. Bathing scene; 15m. Heating sauna in winter; 30m. Bathers leaving sauna for plunge in lake.

1949. Tuberculosis Relief Fund.
475 **119** 5m.+2m. green 45 55
476 – 9m.+3m. red 45 80
477 – 15m.+5m. brown 65 80
DESIGNS: 9m. Rose; 15m. Coltsfoot.

120 Trees and Papermill

121 Girl with Torch

1949. 3rd World Forestry Congress. Inscr "IIIE CONGRES FORESTIER MONDIAL 1949".
478 **120** 9m. brown . . . . 1·40 2·40
479 – 15m. green (Tree and Globe) . . . . 1·40 2·30

1949. 50th Anniv of Labour Movement.
480 **121** 5m. green . . . . 3·00 8·25
481 – 15m. red (Man with mallet) . . . . 3·00 8·25

122 Kristiinankaupunki

123 "Salmetar" (lake steamer), Lappeenranta

1949. Tercent of Kristiinankaupunki (Kristinestad).
482 **122** 15m. blue . . . . 1·10 2·10

1949. Tercent of Lappeenranta (Villmanstrand).
483 **123** 5m. green 75 65

124 Church, Raahe

125 Seal of Technical High School

126 Hannes Gebhard (founder)

1949. Tercentenary of Raahe (Brahestad).
484 **124** 9m. purple 80 95

1949. Cent of Technical High School, Helsinki.
485 **125** 15m. blue 90 90

1949. 50th Anniv of Finnish Co-operative Movement.
486 **126** 15m. green 85 70

127

128 Douglas DC-6

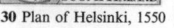

129 White Water-lily

1949. 75th Anniv of U.P.U.
487 **127** 15m. blue . . . . 85 1·10

1950. Air.
488 **128** 300m. blue . . . . 7·25 4·75
For 300m. stamp without "mk" see No. 585 and for 3m. stamp see No. 679.

1950. Tuberculosis Relief Fund.
489 **129** 5m.+2m. green . . . . . 1·20 1·50
490 – 9m.+3m. mauve . . . . . 95 1·40
491 – 15m.+5m. blue . . . . . 95 1·40
DESIGNS: 9m. Pasque flower; 15m. Clustered bellflower.

130 Plan of Helsinki, 1550

131 President Paasikivi

1950. 400th Anniv of Helsinki.
492 **130** 5m. green 25 50
493 – 9m. brown . . . . 40 1·00
494 – 15m. blue 40 65
DESIGNS: 9m. J. A. Ehrenstrom and C. L. Engel; 15m. Town Hall and Cathedral.

1950. President's 80th Birthday.
495 **131** 20m. blue 45 35

132 Hospital, Helsinki

133 Town Hall

134 Western Capercaillie

1951. Red Cross Fund. Cross in red.
496 **132** 7m.+2m. brown 55 80
497 – 12m.+3m. violet 55 85
498 – 20m.+5m. red . . . . . 75 1·50
DESIGNS: 12m. Blood donor and nurse; 20m. Blood donor's badge.

1951. 300th Anniv of Kajaani (Kajana).
499 **133** 20m. brown 45 55

1951. Tuberculosis Relief Fund.
500 **134** 7m.+2m. green . . . . . 1·40 2·20
501 – 12m.+3m. lake . . . . . 1·40 2·20
502 – 20m.+5m. blue . . . . . 1·40 2·20
DESIGNS: 12m. Common Cranes; 20m. Caspian Terns.

135 Diving

138 Marshal Mannerheim

139 Arms of Pietarsaari

1951. 15th Olympic Games, Helsinki.
503 **135** 12m.+2m. red . . . . . 45 1·00
504 – 15m.+2m. green . . . . . 45 1·00
505 – 20m.+3m. blue . . . . . 1·10 1·10
506 – 25m.+4m. brown . . . . 1·40 1·50
DESIGNS—HORIZ: 15m. Football; 25m. Running. VERT: 20m. Olympic stadium.

1952. Red Cross Fund. Cross in red.
507 **138** 10m.+2m. black . . . . . 75 1·40
508 15m.+3m. purple . . . . 75 1·60
509 25m.+5m. blue . . . . . 75 1·40

1952. 300th Anniv of Founding of Pietarsaari (Jakobstad).
510 **139** 25m. blue 55 70

140 Vaasa

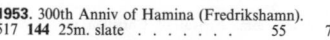

141 Knight, Rook and Chessboard

142 Great Tit

1952. Centenary of Fire of Vaasa (Vasa).
511 **140** 25m. brown 55 75

1952. 10th Chess Olympiad, Helsinki.
512 **141** 25m. black . . . . 1·20 1·80

1952. Tuberculosis Relief Fund. Birds.
513 **142** 10m.+2m. green . . . . . 1·60 1·90
514 – 15m.+3m. red . . . . . 1·60 1·90
515 – 25m.+5m. blue . . . . . 1·60 1·90
BIRDS: 15m. Spotted Flycatchers; 25m. Eurasian Swifts.

143 "Flame of Temperance"

144 Aerial view of Hamina

1953. Cent of Finnish Temperance Movement.
516 **143** 25m. blue 65 80

1953. 300th Anniv of Hamina (Fredrikshamn).
517 **144** 25m. slate 55 75

145 Eurasian Red Squirrel

1953. Tuberculosis Relief Fund.
518 **145** 10m.+2m. brown . . . . 1·80 2·20
519 – 15m.+3m. violet . . . . 1·80 2·20
520 – 25m.+5m. green . . . . . 1·80 2·20
DESIGNS: 15m. Brown bear; 25m. Elk.

146 Wilskman

147 Mother and Children

1954. Birth Centenary of Ivar Wilskman (gymnast).
521 **146** 25m. blue 55 75

1954. Red Cross Fund. Cross in red.
522 **147** 10m.+2m. green . . . . . 55 1·10
523 – 15m.+3m. blue . . . . . 75 1·00
524 – 25m.+5m. brown . . . . 75 1·00
DESIGNS: 15m. Old lady knitting; 25m. Blind man and dog.

148

149 "In the Outer Archipelago" (after Edelfelt)

1954.
525 **148** 1m. brown 30 30
526 2m. green 30 20
527 3m. orange 25 20
527a 4m. grey 35 30
528 5m. blue 45 20
529 10m. green 55 25
530 15m. red . . . . 2·40 20
530a 15m. orange . . . . . . 4·00 20
531 20m. purple . . . . . . 6·00 25
531a 20m. red . . . . 1·10 20

532 25m. blue . . . . 2·20 20
532a 25m. purple . . . . . . 6·25 20
532b 30m. blue . . . . 1·30 20
See also Nos. 647, etc.

1954. Birth Centenary of A. Edelfelt (painter).
533 **149** 25m. black 55 65

150 White-tailed Bumble Bees collecting Pollen

151 J. J. Nervander

1954. Tuberculosis Relief Fund. Cross in red.
534 **150** 10m.+2m. brown . . . . 1·20 1·10
535 – 15m.+3m. red . . . . . 1·40 1·40
536 – 25m.+5m. blue . . . . . 1·50 1·40
DESIGNS: 15m. Apollo (butterfly) and wild rose; 25m. "Aeshna juncea" (dragonfly).

1955. 150th Birth Anniv of Nervander (astronomer and poet).
537 **151** 25m. blue 65 80

152 Parliament Building

153 St. Henry

1955. National Philatelic Exhibition, Helsinki.
538 **152** 25m. black . . . . 5·75 10·00

1955. 800th Anniv of Establishment of Christianity in Finland.
539 **153** 15m. purple 55 60
540 – 25m. green 55 65
DESIGN: 25m. Arrival of Christian preachers in 1155.

154 Conference in Session

155 Barque "Ilma" and Cargo

1955. Interparliamentary Conference, Helsinki.
541 **154** 25m. green . . . . 75 1·10

1955. 350th Anniv of Oulu (Uleaborg).
542 **155** 25m. brown . . . . . . 1·00 1·10

156 Eurasian Perch

157 Town Hall, Lahti

1955. Tuberculosis Relief Fund. Cross in red.
543 **156** 10m.+2m. green . . . . . 1·00 1·10
544 – 15m.+3m. brown (Northern pike) . . . . 1·30 1·20
545 – 25m.+5m. blue (Atlantic salmon) . . . . 1·30 1·20

1955. 50th Anniv of Lahti.
546 **157** 25m. blue . . . . 75 1·30

158 J. Z. Duncker

159 "Telegraphs"

1955. Red Cross. Cross in red.
547 – 10m.+2m. blue 45 90
548 **158** 15m.+3m. brown . . . . 65 1·10
549 – 25m.+5m. green . . . . . 65 1·10
DESIGNS: 10m. Von Dobeln on horseback; 25m. Young soldier.

1955. Centenary of Telegraphs in Finland. Inscr "1855–1955 Telegrafen".
550 **159** 10m. green 90 95
551 – 15m. violet 75 80
552 – 25m. blue . . . . 75 1·20
DESIGNS: 15m. Otto Nyberg; 25m. Telegraph pole.

160 Lighthouse at Porkkala

161 Lammi Church

1956. Return of Porkkala to Finland.
553 **160** 25m. blue 45 60

1956. Value expressed as "5" etc.
553a – 5m. green 20 15
554 **161** 30m. green 55 30
555 – 40m. lilac . . . . 1·60 20
556 **161** 50m. green . . . . . . 4·00 20
557 – 60m. purple . . . . . . 5·50 20
557a – 75m. black . . . . . . 2·30 20
557b – 100m. green . . . . . . 13·00 20
557c – 125m. green . . . . . . 12·50 40
DESIGNS: 5m. View of lake, Keuru; 40m. Houses of Parliament; 60m. Olavinlinna; 75m. Pyhakoski Dam; 100m. Helsinki Harbour; 125m. Turku Castle.
No. 557b differs from No. 370 in that "FINLAND" is without the scroll, the figures "100" are upright and "mk" is omitted.
See also Nos. 660, etc.

162 J. V. Snellman (after sculpture by E. Wikstrom)

163 Athletes

1956. 150th Birth Anniv of Snellman (statesman).
558 **162** 25m. brown 65 60

1956. Finnish Games.
559 **163** 30m. blue 65 70

164

165 Bohemian Waxwing

1956. Centenary of First Finnish Postage Stamp and International Philatelic Exhibition, Helsinki. Roul.
560 **164** 30m. blue . . . . 2·10 3·25

1956. Tuberculosis Relief Fund. Cross in red.
561 **165** 10m.+2m. brown . . . . 1·00 75
562 – 20m.+3m. green . . . . . 1·20 1·30
563 – 30m.+5m. blue . . . . . 1·70 1·50
DESIGNS: 20m. Eagle Owl; 30m. Mute Swan.

166 Vaasa Town Hall

167 P. Aulin

1956. 350th Anniv of Vaasa.
564 **166** 30m. blue 65 75

1956. Northern Countries' Day. As T **100** of Denmark.
565 20m. red . . . . 2·10 1·00
566 30m. blue . . . . 5·75 1·00

1956. Red Cross. Inscr "1956". Cross in red.
567 **167** 5m.+1m. green . . . . . 2·50 60
568 – 10m.+2m. brown . . . . 1·00 1·10
569 – 20m.+3m. red . . . . . 1·00 1·70
570 – 30m.+5m. blue . . . . . 1·00 1·30
PORTRAITS: 10m. L. von Pfaler; 20m. G. Johansson; 30m. V. M. von Born.

168 University Hospital, Helsinki

169 Scout Badge and Saluting Hand

1956. Bicentenary of National Health Service.
571 **168** 30m. green . . . . 1·00 70

1957. 50th Anniv of Boy Scout Movement.
572 **169** 30m. blue . . . . 1·20 95

171 "In Honour of Work"

172 "Lex" (sculpture by W. Runeberg)

1957. 50th Anniv of Finnish Trade Union Movement.
573 **171** 30m. red 65 75

1957. 50th Anniv of Finnish Parliament.
574 **172** 30m. olive 95 80

173 Wolverine

174 Factories within Cogwheel

1957. Tuberculosis Relief Fund. Inscr "1957". Cross in red.
575 **173** 10m.+2m. purple . . . . 1·00 90
576 – 20m.+3m. sepia . . . . . 1·50 1·20
577 – 30m.+5m. blue . . . . . 65 1·20
DESIGNS: 20m. Lynx; 30m. Reindeer.
See also Nos. 642/4.

1957. 50th Anniv of Central Federation of Finnish Employers.
578 **174** 20m. blue 55 60

175 Red Cross Flag

176 Ida Aalberg (after Edelfelt)

1957. Red Cross Fund and 80th Anniv of Finnish Red Cross. Cross in red.
579 **175** 10m.+2m. green . . . . . 1·00 1·70
580 20m.+3m. lake . . . . . 1·00 1·60
581 30m.+5m. blue . . . . . 1·00 1·60

1957. Birth Cent of Ida Aalberg (actress).
582 **176** 30m. maroon & purple . . 65 70

177 Arms of Finland

178 Bust of Sibelius (Waino Aaltonen)

1957. 40th Anniv of Independence.
583 **177** 30m. blue 65 75

1957. Death of Sibelius (composer).
584 **178** 30m. black . . . . 1·00 90

1958. Air. As No. 488 but with "mk" omitted.
585 **128** 300m. blue . . . . 19·00 70
See also No. 679.

179 Ski Jumping

180 "March of the Bjorneborgienses" (after Edelfelt)

1958. World Ski Championships.
586 **179** 20m. green . . . . 75 1·00
587 – 30m. blue 60 65
DESIGN—VERT: 30m. Cross-country skiing.

1958. 400th Anniv of Founding of Pori (Bjorneborg).
588 **180** 30m. purple . . . . . . 1·00 65

181 Lily of the Valley

182 Lyceum Seal

1958. Tuberculosis Relief Fund. Cross in red.
589 **181** 10m.+2m. green . . . . . 95 1·00
590 – 20m.+3m. red . . . . . 1·40 1·50
591 – 30m.+5m. blue . . . . . 1·40 1·50
DESIGNS: 20m. Red clover; 30m. Anemone.

1958. Centenary of Jyvaskyla Lyceum (secondary school).
592 **182** 30m. red 85 90

183 Convair CV 340 over Lakes

184 Cloudberry

1958. Air.
593 **183** 34m. blue 60 65
594 45m. blue . . . . 1·40 1·10
See also Nos. 678/a.

1958. Red Cross Fund. Cross in red.
595 **184** 10m.+2m. orange 75 95
596 – 20m.+3m. red . . . . . 1·10 1·30
597 – 30m.+5m. blue . . . . . 1·10 1·40
DESIGNS: 20m. Cowberry; 30m. Blueberry.

185 Missionary Emblem and Globe

186 Opening of Diet, 1809

1959. Centenary of Finnish Missionary Society.
598 **185** 30m. purple 55 50

1959. 150th Anniv of Re-convening of Finnish Diet at Porvoo.
599 **186** 30m. blue 55 50

1959. Air. No. 593 surch **45.**
600 45m. on 34m. blue . . . . . 1·30 2·75

188 Multiple Saws

189 Gymnast

1959. Centenaries of Kestila Sawmill (10m.) and Finnish Forestry Department (30m.).
601 **188** 10m. brown 35 45
602 – 30m. grn (Forest firs) . . 35 50

1959. Tuberculosis Relief Fund. As T **181** but inscr "1959". Cross in red.
603 10m.+2m. green . . . . . . 1·40 1·10
604 20m.+3m. brown . . . . . . 1·80 1·80
605 30m.+5m. blue . . . . . . 1·80 1·80

DESIGNS: 10m. Marguerite; 20m. Cowslip; 30m. Cornflower.

1959. Birth Centenary of Elin Oihonna Kallio (Women's Gymnastics pioneer).
606 **189** 30m. purple 65 60

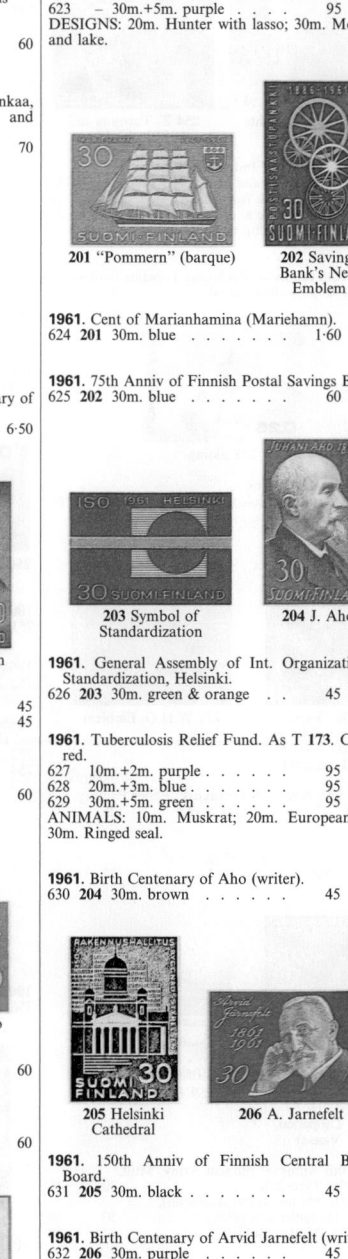

190 Oil Lamp **191** Arms of the Towns

1959. Cent of Trade Freedom in Finland.
607 **190** 30m. blue 55 60

1960. Extra Privileges for Finnish Towns–Hyvinkaa, Kouvola, Riihimaki, Rovaniemi, Salo and Seinajoki.
608 **191** 30m. violet 55 70

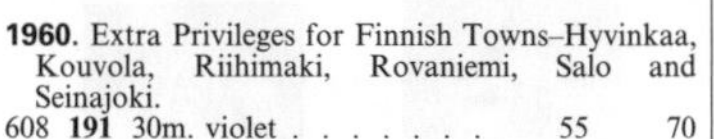

192 5k. "Serpentine Roulette" Stamp of 1860

1960. Stamp Exhibition, Helsinki, and Centenary of "Serpentine Roulette" stamps. Roul.
609 **192** 30m. blue and grey . . . 3·50 6·50

193 Refugees and Symbol **194** J. Gadolin

1960. World Refugee Year.
610 **193** 30m. red 30 45
611 40m. blue 30 45

1960. Birth Bicent of Johan Gadolin (chemist).
612 **194** 30m. brown 45 60

195 H. Nortamo **196** European Cuckoo

1960. Birth Cent of H. Nortamo (writer).
613 **195** 30m. green 45 60

1960. Karelian National Festival, Helsinki.
614 **196** 30m. red 55 60

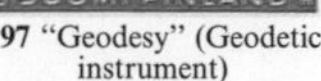

197 "Geodesy" (Geodetic instrument) **198** Pres. Kekkonen

1960. 12th International Geodesy and Geophysics Union Assembly, Helsinki.
615 **197** 10m. sepia and blue . . . 35 45
616 – 30m. brn, red & verm . . 35 55
DESIGN: 30m. "Geophysics" (representation of Northern Lights).

1960. President Kekkonen's 60th Birthday.
617 **198** 30m. blue 55 35

1960. Europa. As T **373** of Belgium but size 31 × 20½ mm.
618 30m. blue and ultramarine . . 40 50
619 40m. purple and sepia . . . 40 50

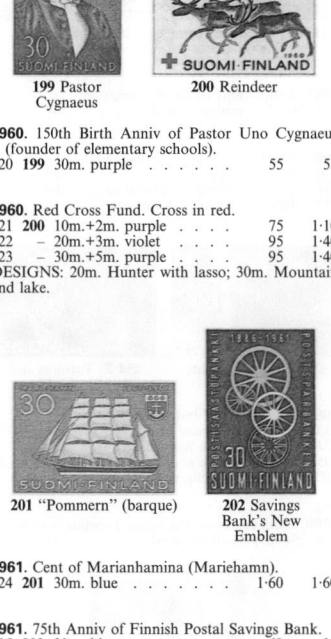

199 Pastor Cygnaeus **200** Reindeer

1960. 150th Birth Anniv of Pastor Uno Cygnaeus (founder of elementary schools).
620 **199** 30m. purple 55 55

1960. Red Cross Fund. Cross in red.
621 **200** 10m.+2m. purple . . . . 75 1·10
622 – 20m.+3m. violet . . . . 95 1·40
623 – 30m.+5m. purple . . . . 95 1·40
DESIGNS: 20m. Hunter with lasso; 30m. Mountain and lake.

201 "Pommern" (barque) **202** Savings Bank's New Emblem

1961. Cent of Marianhamina (Mariehamn).
624 **201** 30m. blue . . . . 1·60 1·60

1961. 75th Anniv of Finnish Postal Savings Bank.
625 **202** 30m. blue 60 35

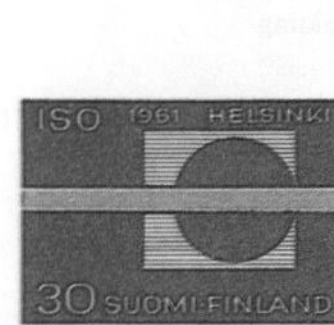

203 Symbol of Standardization **204** J. Aho

1961. General Assembly of Int. Organization for Standardization, Helsinki.
626 **203** 30m. green & orange . . 45 50

1961. Tuberculosis Relief Fund. As T **173**. Cross in red.
627 10m.+2m. purple . . . . . 95 1·10
628 20m.+3m. blue . . . . . . 95 1·30
629 30m.+5m. green . . . . . 95 1·50
ANIMALS: 10m. Muskrat; 20m. European otter; 30m. Ringed seal.

1961. Birth Centenary of Aho (writer).
630 **204** 30m. brown 45 50

205 Helsinki Cathedral **206** A. Jarnefelt

1961. 150th Anniv of Finnish Central Building Board.
631 **205** 30m. black 45 50

1961. Birth Centenary of Arvid Jarnefelt (writer).
632 **206** 30m. purple 45 50

207 Bank Facade **208** First locomotive, "Ilmarinen"

1961. 150th Anniv of Bank of Finland.
633 **207** 30m. purple 45 50

1962. Centenary of Finnish Railways.
634 **208** 10m. green 95 40
635 – 30m. blue . . . . 1·30 50
636 – 40m. purple . . . . . . 2·75 45
LOCOMOTIVES: 30m. Class Hr-1 steam locomotive and Type Hk wagon; 40m. Class Hr-12 diesel locomotive and passenger carriages.

209 Mora Stone **210** Senate Place, Helsinki

1962. 600th Anniv of Finnish People's Political Rights.
637 **209** 30m. purple 45 60

1962. 150th Anniv of Proclamation of Helsinki as Finnish Capital.
638 **210** 30m. brown 45 55

211 Customs Board Crest **212** Emblem of Commerce

1962. 150th Anniv of Finnish Customs Board.
639 **211** 30m. red 45 55

1962. Cent of 1st Finnish Commercial Bank.
640 **212** 30m. green 45 50

213 S. Alkio **214** Finnish Labour Emblem on Conveyor Belt

1962. Birth Cent of Santeri Alkio (writer and founder of Young People's Societies' Movement).
641 **213** 30m. purple 45 55

1962. Tuberculosis Relief Fund. As T **173**. Cross in red.
642 10m.+2m. black . . . . . . 1·10 1·10
643 20m.+3m. purple . . . . . . 1·30 1·40
644 30m.+5m. blue . . . . 1·30 1·40
DESIGNS: 10m. Brown hare; 20m. Pine marten; 30m. Stoat.

1962. Home Production.
645 **214** 30m. purple 45 30

215 Hunting Pembroke making Aerial Survey **216**

1962. 150th Anniv of Finnish Land Survey Board.
646 **215** 30m. green 55 60

Currency reform. 100 (old) markkaa = 1 (new) markka.

1963. (a) Lion Type.
647 **216** 1p. brown 20 25
648 2p. green 20 15
649 4p. grey 55 30
650c 5p. blue 35 15
651c 10p. green 35 30
652 15p. orange 95 25
653 20p. red 95 30
654a 25p. purple 55 30
656a 30p. blue 90 30
657 35p. blue . . . . . . 1·00 15
657a 35p. yellow 55 25
658 40p. blue 95 30
658b 40p. orange 80 30
659 50p. blue . . . . . . 1·60 15
659a 50p. purple 65 25
659b 60p. blue 55 25

(b) Views. Values expressed as "0,05" (pennia values) or "1,00" (mark values).
660 – 5p. green (As No. 553a) (postage) 35 15
661 – 25p. multicoloured . . . 20 25
662 – 30p. multicoloured . . . 95 25
663 – 40p. lilac (As No. 555) 2·40 15
664 **161** 50p. green . . . . . . 3·75 15
665 – 60p. purple (As No. 557) 4·25 15
666 – 65p. purple (As No. 557) 55 25
667 – 75p. black (As No. 557a) 1·40 15
668 – 80p. multicoloured . . . 3·00 25
669 – 90p. multicoloured . . . 95 40
670 – 1m. green (As No. 557b) 70 20
671 – 1m.25 green (As No. 557c) . . . . . . 1·30 25
672 – 1m.30 multicoloured . . 60 30
673 – 1m.50 green 95 15
674 – 1m.75 blue 95 15
675 – 2m. green . . . . 6·00 20
676 – 2m.50 blue & yellow . . 3·25 35
677 – 5m. green . . . . 9·25 25
678 **183** 45p. blue (air) 95 25
678a 57p. blue . . . . 1·10 85
679 – 3m. blue (585) . . . . . 1·90 25
NEW DESIGNS: As Type **161**—VERT: 30p. Nasinneula Tower, Tampere; 80p. Keuruu church; 1m.30, Helsinki Railway Station. HORIZ: 25p. Country mail bus; 90p. Hameen Bridge, Tampere; 1m.50, Loggers afloat; 1m.75, Parainen Bridge; 2m. Country house by lake; 2m.50, Aerial view of Punkaharju; 5m. Ristikallio Gorge.
No. 679 is as No. 585, but with a comma after "3".

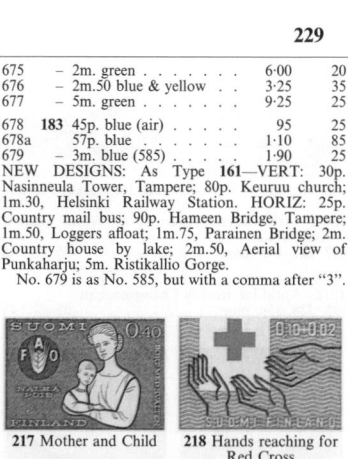

217 Mother and Child **218** Hands reaching for Red Cross

1963. Freedom from Hunger.
680 **217** 40p. brown 25 40

1963. Centenary of Red Cross.
681 **218** 10p.+2p. brn & red . . . 35 65
682 20p.+3p. violet & red . . 45 1·20
683 30p.+5p. green & red . . 45 1·30

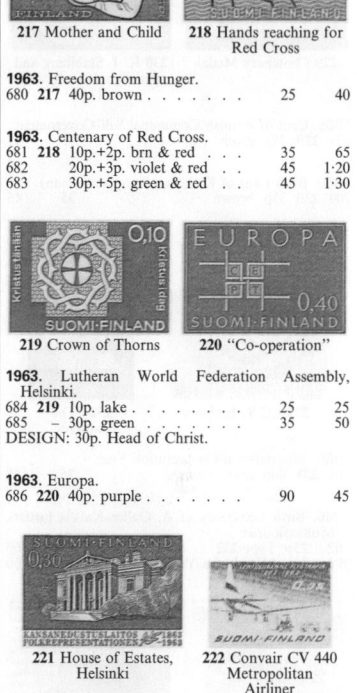

219 Crown of Thorns **220** "Co-operation"

1963. Lutheran World Federation Assembly, Helsinki.
684 **219** 10p. lake 25 25
685 – 30p. green 35 50
DESIGN: 30p. Head of Christ.

1963. Europa.
686 **220** 40p. purple 90 45

221 House of Estates, Helsinki **222** Convair CV 440 Metropolitan Airliner

1963. Cent of Finnish Representative Assembly.
687 **221** 30p. purple 35 45

1963. 40 Years of Finnish Civil Aviation.
688 **222** 35p. green 45 50
689 – 40p. blue 45 40
DESIGN: 40p. Sud-Aviation SE 210 Caravelle in flight.

223 M. A. Castren (after E. J. Lofgren) **224** Soapstone Elk's Head

1963. 150th Birth Anniv of M. A. Castren (explorer and scholar).
690 **223** 35p. blue 35 40

1964. "For Art" (centenary of Finnish Artists' Society).
691 **224** 35p. green and buff . . . 35 30

225 E. N. Setala **226** Doctor tending Patient on Sledge

1964. Birth Centenary of Emil Setala (philologist and statesman).
692 **225** 35p. brown 35 45

1964. Red Cross Fund. Cross in red.
693 **226** 15p.+3p. blue 35 65
694 – 25p.+4p. green 65 90
695 – 35p.+5p. purple 50 90
696 – 40p.+7p. green 50 90
DESIGNS: 25p. Red Cross hospital ship; 35p. Military sick parade; 40p. Distribution of Red Cross parcels.

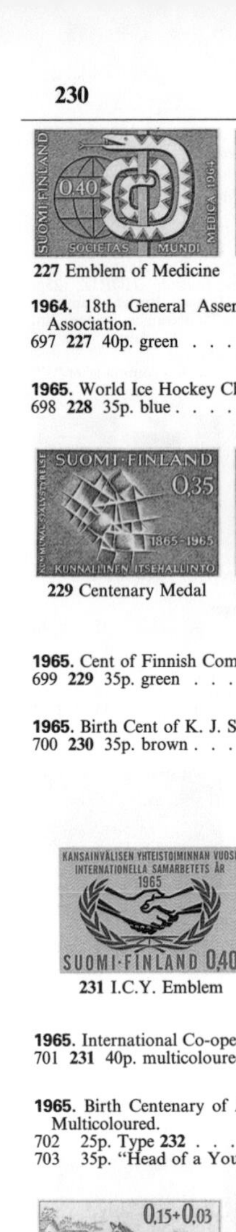

227 Emblem of Medicine   228 Ice Hockey Players

1964. 18th General Assembly of World Medical Association.
697 **227** 40p. green 35 45

1965. World Ice Hockey Championships.
698 **228** 35p. blue 35 45

229 Centenary Medal   230 K. J. Stahlberg and Runeberg's sculpture, "Lex"

1965. Cent of Finnish Communal Self-Government.
699 **229** 35p. green 35 45

1965. Birth Cent of K. J. Stahlberg (statesman).
700 **230** 35p. brown 35 45

231 I.C.Y. Emblem   232 "The Fratricide"

1965. International Co-operation Year.
701 **231** 40p. multicoloured . . . 35 45

1965. Birth Centenary of A. Gallen-Kallela (artist). Multicoloured.
702 25p. Type **232** 80 60
703 35p. "Head of a Young Girl" 80 60

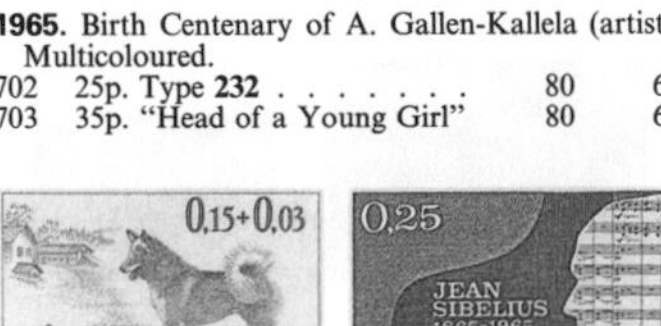

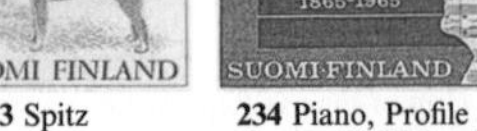

233 Spitz   234 Piano, Profile and Score of "Finlandia"

1965. Tuberculosis Relief Fund. Dogs.
704 **233** 15p.+3p. brn & red . . . 80 1·00
705 – 25p.+4p. blk & red . . . 1·00 1·50
706 – 35p.+5p. sep & red . . . 1·00 1·50
FINNISH DOGS: 25p. Karelian bear dog. 35p. Finnish stovare.

1965. Birth Centenary of Sibelius (composer).
707 **234** 25p. violet 55 45
708 – 35p. green 55 60
DESIGN: 35p. Part of score of "Finlandia" and dove.

235 Dish Aerial   236 "Winter Day" (after P. Halonen)

1965. Centenary of I.T.U.
709 **235** 35p. blue 35 50

1965. Birth Cent of Pekka Halonen (painter).
710 **236** 35p. multicoloured . . . 35 35

237 Europa "Sprig"   238 "Kiss of Life"

1965. Europa.
711 **237** 40p. multicoloured . . . 90 35

1966. Red Cross Fund. Multicoloured.
712 15p.+3p. Type **238** 45 80
713 25p.+4p. Diver and submerged car 45 95
714 35p.+5p. Sud-Aviation SE 3130 Alouette II Red Cross helicopter 45 95

239 "Growing Up"   240 Old Post Office

1966. Cent of Finnish Elementary School Decree.
715 **239** 35p. bl & ultramarine . . 35 35

1966. "Nordia 1966" Stamp Exn., Helsinki, and Centenary of 1st Postage Stamps in Finnish Currency.
716 **240** 35p. blue, brown & yell 2·40 4·25

241 Globe and UNESCO Emblem   242 Police Emblem

1966. 20th Anniv of UNESCO.
717 **241** 40p. multicoloured . . . 35 45

1966. 150th Anniv of Finnish Police Force.
718 **242** 35p. silver, black & blue 35 45

243 Anniversary Medal (after K. Kallio)   244 U.N.I.C.E.F Emblem

1966. 150th Anniv of Finnish Insurance.
719 **243** 35p. olive and lake . . . 35 45

1966. 20th Anniv of UNICEF.
720 **244** 15p. violet, green & blue 25 25

245 FINEFTA Symbol   246 Windmill

1967. Abolition of Industrial Customs Tariffs by European Free Trade Association.
721 **245** 40p. blue 35 30

1967. 350th Anniv of Uusikaupunki (Nystad).
722 **246** 40p. multicoloured . . . 35 30

247 Birch Tree and Foliage   248 Mannerheim Statue (A. Tukiainen)

1967. Tuberculosis Relief Fund. Mult.
723 20p.+3p. Type **247** 35 70
724 25p.+4p. Pine and foliage . . 35 80
725 40p.+7p. Spruce and foliage 35 80
See also Nos. 753/5.

1967. Birth Cent of Marshal Mannerheim.
726 **248** 40p. multicoloured . . . 35 35

249 "Solidarity"   250 Watermark of Thomasbole Factory

1967. Finnish Settlers in Sweden.
727 **249** 40p. multicoloured . . . 35 30

1967. 300th Anniv of Finnish Paper Industry.
728 **250** 40p. blue and bistre . . . 35 35

251 Martin Luther (from painting by Lucas Cranach the Elder)   252 Horse-drawn Ambulance

1967. 450th Anniv of the Reformation.
729 **251** 40p. multicoloured . . . 35 30

1967. Red Cross Fund. Multicoloured.
730 20p.+3p. Type **252** 40 90
731 25p.+4p. Modern ambulance 60 85
732 40p.+7p. Red Cross emblem 60 85

253 Northern Lights   254 Z. Topelius and "Bluebird"

1967. 50th Anniv of Independence.
733 **253** 20p. green and blue . . . 30 30
734 – 25p. blue & light blue . . 30 25
735 – 40p. mauve and blue . . 30 25
DESIGNS: 25p. Flying swan; 40p. Ear of wheat.

1968. 150th Anniv of Zacharias Topelius (writer).
736 **254** 25p. multicoloured . . . 35 45

255 Skiing

1968. Winter Tourism.
737 **255** 25p. multicoloured . . . 35 65

256 "Paper-making" (from wood relief by H. Autere)   257 W.H.O. Emblem

1968. 150th Anniv of Tervakoski Paper Factory.
738 **256** 45p. brown, buff & red 25 35

1968. 20th Anniv of W.H.O.
739 **257** 40p. multicoloured . . . 35 30

258 "Infantryman" (statue by L. Leppanen, Vaasa)   259 Holiday Camp

1968. 50th Anniv of Finnish Army. Mult.
740 20p. Type **258** 30 40
741 25p. Memorial (V. Aaltonen), Hietaniemi cemetery . . . 30 40
742 40p. Modern soldier 30 40

1968. Tourism.
743 **259** 25p. multicoloured . . . 35 75

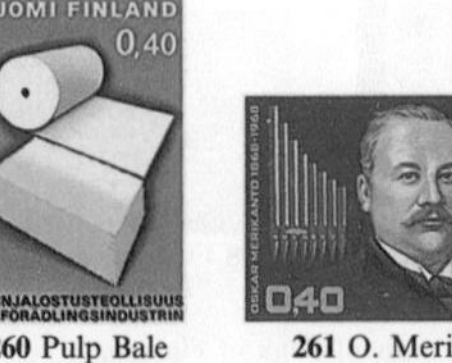

260 Pulp Bale (with outline of tree in centre) and Paper Reel   261 O. Merikanto

1968. Finnish Wood-processing Industry.
744 **260** 40p. multicoloured . . . 35 40

1968. Birth Cent of Oskar Merikanto (composer).
745 **261** 40p. multicoloured . . . 35 35

262 Mustola Lock   263 Dock Cranes, "Ivalo" (container ship) and Chamber of Commerce Emblem

1968. Opening of Saima Canal.
746 **262** 40p. multicoloured . . . 35 35

1968. "Finnish Economic Life". 50th Anniv of Finnish Central Chamber of Commerce.
747 **263** 40p. multicoloured . . . 35 30

264 Welding   265 Lyre Emblem

1968. Finnish Metal Industry.
748 **264** 40p. multicoloured . . . 35 25

1968. Finnish Student Unions.
749 **265** 40p. brn, bl & ultram . . 35 30

1969. 50th Anniv of Northern Countries' Union. As T **159** of Denmark.
750 40p. blue 65 40

266 City Hall and Arms, Kemi   267 Colonnade

1969. Centenary of Kemi (Kemin).
751 **266** 40p. multicoloured . . . 35 30

1969. Europa.
752 **267** 40p. multicoloured . . . 2·50 55

1969. Tuberculosis Relief Fund. As T **247**, but inscr "1969". Multicoloured.
753 20p.+3p. Juniper and berries 35 75
754 25p.+4p. Aspen and catkins 40 85
755 40p.+7p. Wild cherry and flowers 40 85

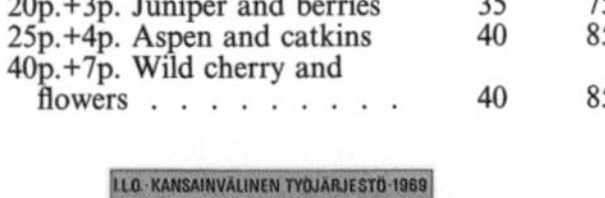

268 I.L.O. Emblem

1969. 50th Anniv of I.L.O.
756 **268** 40p. blue, lt blue & red 35 30

269 A. Jarnefelt (after V. Sjostrom)   270 Fairs Symbol

1969. Birth Cent of Armas Jarnefelt (composer).
757 **269** 40p. multicoloured . . . 35 25

1969. Finnish National and Int. Fairs.
758 **270** 40p. multicoloured . . . 35 25

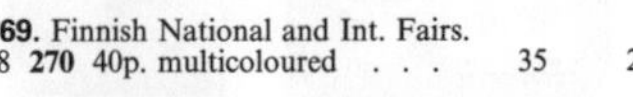

271 J. Linnankoski   272 Board Emblems

1969. Birth Centenary of Johannes Linnankoski (writer).
759 **271** 40p. multicoloured . . . 35 30

1969. Centenary of Central Schools Board.
760 **272** 40p. violet, green & grey 35 30

273 Douglas DC-8-62F over Helsinki Airport

274 Golden Eagle and Eyrie

1969. Aviation.
761 **273** 25p. multicoloured . . . 35 70

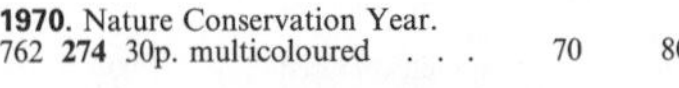

1970. Nature Conservation Year.
762 **274** 30p. multicoloured . . . 70 80

275 "Fabric" Factories

276 "Molecular Structure" and Factories, Nysta

1970. Finnish Textile Industry.
763 **275** 50p. multicoloured . . . 35 35

1970. Finnish Chemical Industry.
764 **276** 50p. multicoloured . . . 35 35

277 UNESCO Emblem and Lenin

278 "The Seven Brothers"

1970. Finnish Co-operation with United Nations.
765 **277** 30p. multicoloured . . . 35 35
766 – 30p. multicoloured . . . 45 30
767 – 50p. gold, ultram & bl . . 35 30
DESIGNS—VERT: 30p. (No. 765), Type **277** (Lenin Symposium of UNESCO, Tampere); 30p. (No. 766), "Nuclear data" (Int. Atomic Energy Agency Conference, Otaniemi). HORIZ: 50p. U. N. emblem and globe (United Nations 25th Anniv).

1970. Red Cross Fund. Multicoloured.
768 25p.+5p. Type **278** 30 75
769 30p.+6p. "Juhani on top of Impivaara" (vert) 30 80
770 50p.+10p. "The Pale Maiden" 30 80

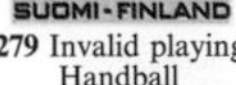
279 Invalid playing Handball

280 "Aurora Society Meeting" (E. Jarnefelt)

1970. 30th Anniv of Finnish Invalids League.
771 **279** 50p. black, red & orange 35 35

1970. Bicentenary of Aurora Society.
772 **280** 50p. multicoloured . . . 35 30

281 City Hall and Old Schoolhouse, Uusikaarlepyy

282 Pres. Kekkonen (from medal by A. Tukiainen)

1970. 350th Anniv of Uusikaarlepyy (Nykarleby) and Kokkola (Gamlakarleby) (towns). Mult.
773 50p. Type **281** 35 35
774 50p. Kokkola and arms . . . 35 35

1970. President Urho Kekkonen's 70th Birthday.
775 **282** 50p. silver and blue . . . 35 30

283 "S.A.L.T." and Globe

284 Pres. Paasikivi (after sculpture by E. Renvall)

1970. Strategic Arms Limitation Talks, Helsinki.
776 **283** 50p. multicoloured . . . 35 30

1970. Birth Centenary of President Paasikivi.
777 **284** 50p. black, blue & gold 35 25

285 Cogwheels

286 Felling Trees

1971. Finnish Industry.
778 **285** 50p. multicoloured . . . 35 35

1971. Tuberculosis Relief Fund. Timber Industry. Multicoloured.
779 25p.+5p. Type **286** 25 70
780 30p.+6p. Tug and log raft . . 35 75
781 50p.+10p. Sorting logs . . . 35 85

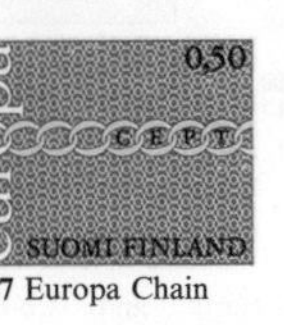
287 Europa Chain

288 Tornio Church

1971. Europa.
782 **287** 50p. yellow, pink & blk 3·00 55

1971. 350th Anniv of Tornio (Torneaa).
783 **288** 50p. multicoloured . . . 35 35

289 "Front-page News" (in Swedish, Finnish and French)

290 Hurdling, High-jumping and Discus-throwing

1971. Bicentenary of Finnish Press.
784 **289** 50p. multicoloured . . . 35 35

1971. European Athletic Championships, Helsinki. Multicoloured.
785 30p. Type **290** 55 55
786 50p. Throwing the javelin and running 65 55
These two designs form a composite picture when placed side by side.

291 "Lightning" Dinghies

292 Silver Pot, Seal and Tools

1971. Int "Lightning" Class Sailing Championships, Helsinki.
787 **291** 50p. multicoloured . . . 45 50

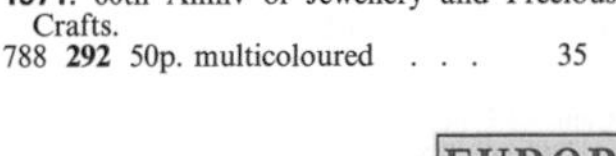

1971. 60th Anniv of Jewellery and Precious-metal Crafts.
788 **292** 50p. multicoloured . . . 35 30

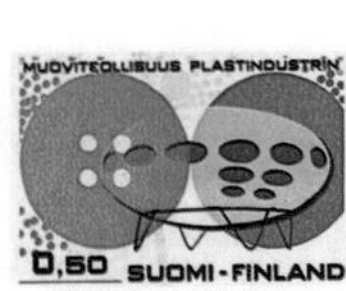
293 Plastic Buttons

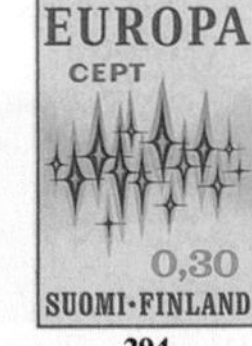
294 "Communications"

1971. Finnish Plastics Industry.
789 **293** 50p. multicoloured . . . 35 35

1972. Europa.
790 **294** 30p. multicoloured . . . 2·20 50
791 50p. multicoloured . . . 2·40 50

295 National Theatre Building

296 Globe

1972. Centenary of Finnish National Theatre.
792 **295** 50p. multicoloured . . . 35 45

1972. Conclusion of the Strategic Arms Limitation Talks, Helsinki.
793 **296** 50p. multicoloured . . . 35 30

297 Map and Arms

298 Cadet Ship "Suomen Joutsen"

1972. 50th Anniv of Local Self-government for the Aland Islands.
794 **297** 50p. multicoloured . . . 1·10 65

1972. Start of the Tall Ships' Race, Helsinki.
795 **298** 50p. multicoloured . . . 1·10 35

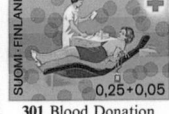

299 Post Office, Tampere

301 Blood Donation

1972. Multicoloured.
797 40p. Type **299** 25 20
798 60p. National Museum (28 × 40 mm) 35 35
799 70p. Market Place, Helsinki (39 × 27 mm) 30 20
800 80p. As 70p. 35 25

1972. Red Cross Fund. Blood Service. Mult.
820 25p.+5p. Type **301** 45 85
821 30p.+6p. Laboratory research (vert) 50 85
822 50p.+10p. Blood transfusion 50 1·00

302 Voyri Man

303 "European Co-operation"

1972. Ancient and National Costumes. Multicoloured.
823 50p. Pernio woman . . . . . 1·10 30
824 50p. Married couple, Tenala 1·10 30
825 50p. Nastola girl . . . . . . 1·10 30
826 50p. Type **302** . . . . . . 1·10 30
827 50p. Lapp winter costumes 1·10 30
828 60p. Kaukola girl . . . . . 2·75 25
829 60p. Jaaski woman . . . . . 2·75 25
830 60p. Koivisto couple . . . . 2·75 25
831 60p. Mother and son, Sakyla 2·75 25
832 60p. Heinavesi girl . . . . . 2·75 25

1972. European Security and Co-operation Conf, Helsinki (1st issue).
833 **303** 50p. multicoloured . . . 75 45
See also No. 839.

304 "Treaty" and National Colours

305 Pres. K. Kallio

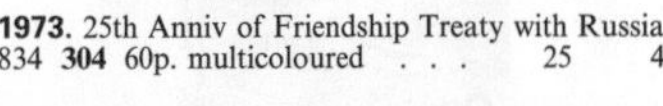

1973. 25th Anniv of Friendship Treaty with Russia.
834 **304** 60p. multicoloured . . . 25 40

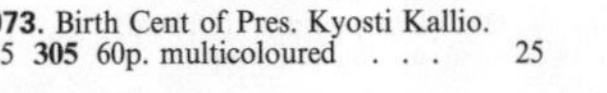

1973. Birth Cent of Pres. Kyosti Kallio.
835 **305** 60p. multicoloured . . . 25 25

306 Europa "Posthorn"

307 "EUROPA" on Map

1973. Europa.
836 **306** 60p. green, turq & blue 1·10 45

1973. Nordic Countries' Postal Co-operation. As T **201** of Denmark.
837 60p. multicoloured 30 25
838 70p. multicoloured 30 25

1973. European Security and Co-operation Conf, Helsinki (2nd issue).
839 **307** 70p. multicoloured . . . 40 40

308 Canoe Paddle

309 Radiosonde Balloon

1973. World Canoeing Championships, Tampere.
840 **308** 60p. multicoloured . . . 35 35

1973. Cent of World Meteorological Organization.
841 **309** 60p. multicoloured . . . 25 35

310 E. Saarinen

1973. Birth Cent of Eliel Saarinen (architect).
842 **310** 60p. multicoloured . . . 25 45

311 "Young Girl with Lamb" (H. Simberg)

312 Douglas DC-10-30

1973. Tuberculosis Relief Fund. Artists' Birth Centenaries. Multicoloured.
843 30p.+5p. Type **311** 65 85
844 40p.+10p. "Summer Evening" (W. Sjostrom) . . 85 1·10
845 60p.+15p. "At a Mountain Spring" (J. Rissanen) . . . 85 1·10

1973. 50th Annivs. of Finnair (airline) and Regular Air Services in Finland.
846 **312** 60p. multicoloured . . . 35 35

313 Santa Claus

1973. Christmas.
847 **313** 30p. multicoloured . . . 40 25

314 Scene from "The Barber of Seville"

1973. Centenary of Finnish State Opera Company.
848 **314** 60p. multicoloured . . . 25 35

315 Porcelain Products

316 "Paavo Nurmi" (Statue by W. Aaltonen)

1973. Finnish Porcelain Industry.
849 **315** 60p. green, blk & bl . . . 25 35

1973. Paavo Nurmi (Olympic athlete) Commem.
850 **316** 60p. multicoloured . . . 35 35

317 Hanko Casino, Harbour and Map

318 Arms of Finland, 1581

1974. Centenary of Hanko (Hango).
851 **317** 60p. multicoloured . . . 35 35

1974.
852 **318** 10m. multicoloured . . . 1·90 30
852a – 20m. multicoloured . . . 4·75 50
DESIGN: 20m. Arms as in T **318** but different border.

319 Ice Hockey Players

1974. World and European Ice Hockey Championships.
853 **319** 60p. multicoloured . . . 35 25

320 Herring Gulls

1974. Baltic Area Marine Environmental Conference, Helsinki.
854 **320** 60p. multicoloured . . . 35 30

321 "Goddess of Victory bestowing Wreath on Youth" (W. Aaltonen)

322 Ilmari Kianto

1974. Europa.
855 **321** 70p. multicoloured . . . 2·50 45

1974. Birth Centenary of Ilmari Kianto ("Iki Kianto") (writer).
856 **322** 60p. multicoloured . . . 30 35

323 Society Emblem

324 "Rationalization"

1974. Finnish Society for Popular Education.
857 **323** 60p. multicoloured . . . 30 35

1974. Finnish Rationalization in Social Development.
858 **324** 60p. multicoloured . . . 30 35

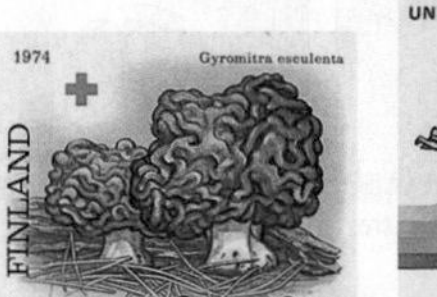

325 Beefsteak Morel

326 U.P.U. Emblem

1974. Red Cross Fund. Mushrooms (1st series). Multicoloured.
859 35p.+5p. Type **325** . . . . . 1·10 80
860 50p.+10p. Chanterelle . . . . 95 1·00
861 60p.+15p. Cep . . . . 95 1·00
See also Nos. 937/9 and 967/9.

1974. Centenary of Universal Postal Union.
862 **326** 60p. multicoloured . . . 25 25
863 70p. multicoloured . . . 25 25

327 Christmas Gnomes

328 Aunessilta Granite Bridge and Modern Reinforced Concrete Bridge

1974. Christmas.
864 **327** 35p. multicoloured . . . 1·10 45

1974. 175th Anniv of Finnish Road and Waterways Board.
865 **328** 60p. multicoloured . . . 35 30

329 National Arms

330 Finnish 32p. Stamp of 1875

1975.
865a **329** 10p. purple 25 20
865c 20p. yellow 25 20
865d 30p. red 25 25
866 40p. orange 25 20
867 50p. green 25 20
868 60p. blue 25 20
869 70p. brown 25 20
870 80p. red and green . . 25 20
871 90p. violet 25 20
872 1m. brown 30 20
873 1m.10 yellow 35 20
874 1m.20 blue 35 30
875 1m.30 green 35 30
875a 1m.40 violet 45 20
875b 1m.50 blue 45 25
875c 1m.60 red 45 20
875d 1m.70 grey 45 20
875e 1m.80 green 55 25
875f 1m.90 orange 50 20
1161 2m. green 55 45

1975. "Nordia 1975" Stamp Exhibition.
876 **330** 70p. brown, black & buff 1·40 2·20

331 "A Girl Combing Her Hair" (M. Enckell)

332 Office Seal

1975. Europa. Multicoloured.
877 70p. Type **331** . . . . . . 1·10 25
878 90p. "Washerwomen" (T. Sallinen) . . . . 1·40 25

1975. 150th Anniv of State Economy Controllers' Office.
879 **332** 70p. multicoloured . . . 30 25

333 "Niilo Saarinen" (lifeboat) and Sinking Ship

1975. 12th International Salvage Conference, Helsinki.
880 **333** 70p. multicoloured . . . 30 25

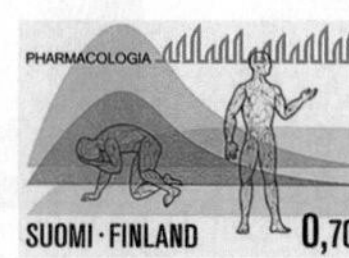

334 "Pharmacology"

1975. 6th International Pharmacological Congress, Helsinki.
881 **334** 70p. multicoloured . . . 30 25

335 Olavinlinna Castle

1975. 500th Anniv of Olavinlinna Castle.
882 **335** 70p. multicoloured . . . 30 25

336 Finlandia Hall (Conference Headquarters) and Barn Swallow

337 "Echo" (E. Thesleff)

1975. European Security and Co-operation Conference, Helsinki.
883 **336** 90p. multicoloured . . . 35 25

1975. Tuberculosis Relief Fund. Paintings by female artists. Multicoloured.
884 40p.+10p. Type **337** 35 70
885 60p.+15p. "Portrait of Hilda Wiik" (Maria Wiik) . . . 65 95
886 70p.+20p. "At Home" (Helene Schjerfbeck) . . . 65 80

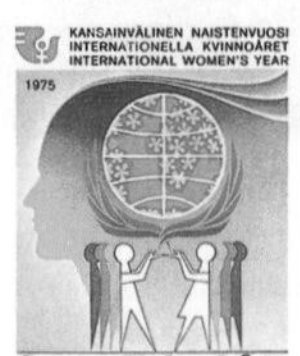

338 Men and Women supporting Globe

339 Graphic Quarter-circle

1975. International Women's Year.
887 **338** 70p. multicoloured . . . 30 30

1975. Centenary of Finnish Society of Industrial Art.
888 **339** 70p. multicoloured . . . 30 30

340 Nativity Play

341 State Debenture

1975. Christmas.
889 **340** 40p. multicoloured . . . 30 25

1975. Cent. of Finnish State Treasury.
890 **341** 80p. multicoloured . . . 30 25

342 Finnish Glider

343 Disabled Ex-servicemen's Association Emblem

1976. 15th World Gliding Championships, Rayskala.
891 **342** 80p. multicoloured . . . 35 30

1976. Finnish War Invalids Fund.
892 **343** 70p.+30p. mult 35 50

344 Cheese Frames

345 Heikki Klemetti

1976. Traditional Finnish Arts.
893 – 1m.50 multicoloured . . 35 25
893a – 2m. multicoloured . . . 45 25
893b – 2m.20 multicoloured . . 65 30
894 **344** 2m.50 multicoloured . . 65 35
895 – 3m. multicoloured . . . 95 35
896 – 4m.50 multicoloured . . 1·00 35
896b – 4m.80 multicoloured . . 1·40 45
897 – 5m. multicoloured . . . 1·60 30
898 – 6m. multicoloured . . . 1·30 25
899 – 7m. multicoloured . . . 1·90 35
899a – 8m. brown and black . . 1·90 30
899b – 9m. black and blue . . . 2·50 55
899c – 12m. ochre, drab & brn 2·75 60
DESIGNS—VERT: 1m.50, Rusko drinking bowl, 1542; 4m.50, Spinning distaffs; 5m. Weathercock, Kirvu (metalwork); 6m. Kaspaikka (Karelian towel); 7m. Bridal rug, 1815; 8m. Arsenal door, Hollola church (iron forging). HORIZ: 2m., 4m.80, Old-style sauna; 2m.20, Kerimaki Church and belfry (peasant architecture); 3m. Shuttle and raanu (patterned cover); 9m. Four-pronged fish spear, c. 1000; 12m. Damask with tulip pattern.

1976. Birth Centenary of Professor Heikki Klemetti (composer).
900 **345** 80p. multicoloured . . . 30 25

346 Map of Finnish Dialect Regions

347 "Aino Ackte in Paris" (A. Edelfelt)

1976. Centenary of Finnish Language Society.
901 **346** 80p. multicoloured . . . 30 25

1976. Birth Cent of Aino Ackte (opera singer).
902 **347** 70p. multicoloured . . . 35 30

348 Ancient Knives and Belts

1976. Europa.
903 **348** 80p. multicoloured . . . 2·10 35

349 "Radio Broadcasting"

1976. 50th Anniv of Radio Broadcasting in Finland.
904 **349** 80p. multicoloured . . . 30 25

350 Wedding Dance

1976. Tuberculosis Relief Fund. Traditional Wedding Customs. Multicoloured.
905 50p.+10p. Wedding procession (horiz) 35 55
906 70p.+15p. Type **350** 45 85
907 80p.+20p. Wedding breakfast (horiz) 45 85

351 Sleigh arriving at Church

1976. Christmas.
908 **351** 50p. multicoloured . . . 30 25

352 Medieval Seal and Text

1976. 700th Anniv of Cathedral Chapter, Turku.
909 **352** 80p. multicoloured . . . 30 25

353 Hugo Alvar Aalto and Finlandia Hall, Helsinki

1976. Hugo Alvar Aalto (architect) Commem.
910 **353** 80p. multicoloured . . . 30 30

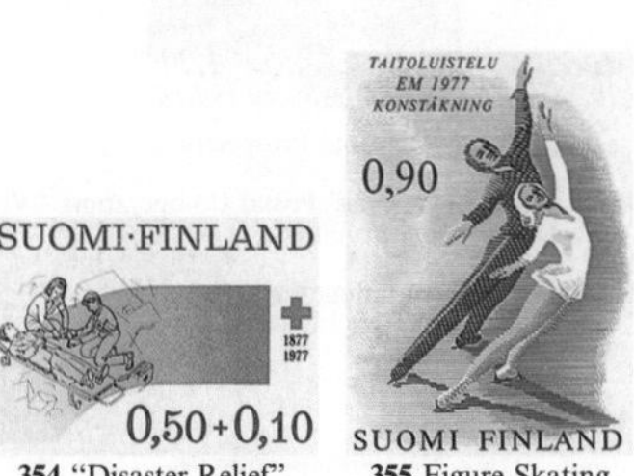

354 "Disaster Relief" 355 Figure Skating

1977. Red Cross Fund. Centenary of Finnish Red Cross. Multicoloured.
911 50p.+10p. Type **354** 30 75
912 80p.+15p. "Community Work" 35 75
913 90p.+20p. "Blood Transfusion Service" . . . 35 75

1977. European Figure Skating Championships, Helsinki.
914 **355** 90p. multicoloured . . . 35 25

1977. Northern Countries' Co-operation in Nature Conservation and Environment Protection. As T **229** of Denmark.
915 90p. multicoloured 35 30
916 1m. multicoloured 35 30

356 "Urho" (ice-breaker) and Freighter

1977. Centenary of Winter Navigation between Finland and Sweden.
917 **356** 90p. multicoloured . . . 50 25

357 "Nuclear Reactor"

1977. Inauguration of Hastholm Island Nuclear Power Station.
918 **357** 90p. multicoloured . . . 30 25

358 Autumn Landscape

1977. Europa.
919 **358** 90p. multicoloured . . . 1·60 35

359 Tree with Nest 360 New Church of Valamo Cloister, Heinavesi

1977. 75th Anniv of Co-operative Banks.
920 **359** 90p. multicoloured . . . 30 25

1977. 800th Anniv of Finnish Orthodoxy and Inauguration of Valamo Cloister.
921 **360** 90p. multicoloured . . . 30 25

361 Paavo Ruotsalainen 362 "Defence and Protection"

1977. Birth Centenary of Paavo Ruotsalaninen (leader of Pietistic Movement).
922 **361** 90p. multicoloured . . . 30 25

1977. Civil Defence.
923 **362** 90p. multicoloured . . . 30 25

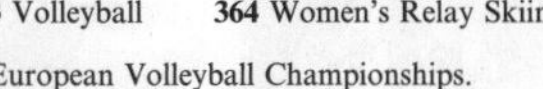
363 Volleyball 364 Women's Relay Skiing

1977. European Volleyball Championships.
924 **363** 90p. multicoloured . . . 30 25

1977. World Ski Championships, Lahti. Mult.
925 80p.+40p. Type **364** . . . . 75 1·60
926 1m.+50p. Ski jumper . . . . 75 1·50

365 Children taking Water to the Sauna 366 Finnish Flag

1977. Christmas.
927 **365** 50p. multicoloured . . . 40 25

1977. 60th Anniv of Independence.
928 **366** 80p. multicoloured . . . 35 25
929 1m. multicoloured (37 × 25½ mm) 50 25

367 Early and Modern Telephones 368 Kotka Harbour

1977. Centenary of Finnish Telephone.
930 **367** 1m. multicoloured 30 25

1978. Centenary of Kotka.
931 **368** 1m. multicoloured 30 30

369 Sanatorium, Paimio

1978. Europa. Multicoloured.
932 1m. Type **369** . . . . 2·10 80
933 1m.20 Studio House, Hvittrask (37 × 25½ mm) 5·75 6·50

370 Buses

1978. Provincial Bus Service.
934 **370** 1m. multicoloured 35 25

371 Eino Leino

1978. Birth Cent of Eino Leino (poet).
935 **371** 1m. multicoloured 35 25

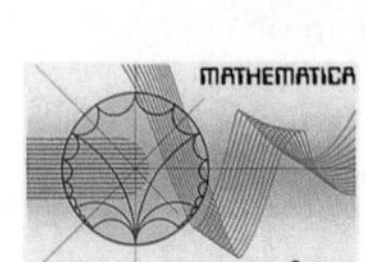

372 Function Theory Diagram 373 Girl feeding Corn to Great Tits

1978. International Congress of Mathematicians, Finland.
936 **372** 1m. multicoloured 35 25

1978. Red Cross Fund. Mushrooms (2nd series). As T **325**. Multicoloured.
937 50p.+10p. "Lactarius deterrimus" 50 65
938 80p.+15p. Parasol mushroom (vert) . . . . 70 1·00
939 1m.+20p. The gypsy . . . . 70 1·00

1978. Christmas.
940 **373** 50p. multicoloured . . . 40 25

374 Child, Hearts and Flowers 375 Orienteer

1979. International Year of the Child.
941 **374** 1m.10 multicoloured . . . 60 25

1979. 8th World Orienteering Championships.
942 **375** 1m.10 multicoloured . . . 35 30

376 Old Training College, Hamina, and Academy Flag 377 Turku Buildings

1979. Bicentenary of Officer Training.
943 **376** 1m.10 multicoloured . . . 35 25

1979. 750th Anniv of Turku (Abo).
944 **377** 1m.10 multicoloured . . . 35 25

378 Tram in City Street 379 "Tammerkoski Waterfall" (lithograph, P. Gaimard)

1979. Helsinki Tram Service.
945 **378** 1m.10 multicoloured . . . 35 25

1979. Bicent of Tampere (Tammerfors) (1st issue).
946 **379** 90p. brown, buff & black 35 30
See also No. 953.

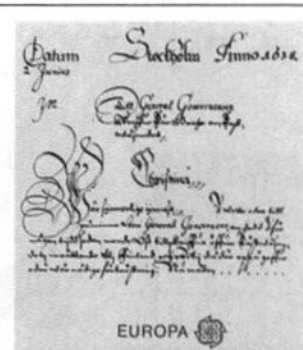

380 Letter establishing Finnish Postal Service, 1638

1979. Europa.
947 **380** 1m.10 blk, brn and ochre 1·40 25
948 – 1m.30 blk, brn and grey 2·75 1·10
DESIGN—HORIZ: 1m.30, A. E. Edelcrantz's optical telegraph, 1796.

381 Pehr Kalm and Title Page 382 Town Street with Trade-signs

1979. Tuberculosis Relief Fund. Finnish Scientists. Multicoloured.
949 60p.+10p. Type **381** 35 55
950 90p.+15p. Wheat and title page of Pehr Gadd's "Svenska Landt-skot-selen" (vert) 35 80
951 1m.10+20p. Petter Forsskaal and title page 35 80

1979. Centenary of Business and Industry Law.
952 **382** 1m.10 multicoloured . . . 35 25

383 Stylized View of Tampere

1979. Bicentenary of Tampere (2nd issue).
953 **383** 1m.10 multicoloured . . . 35 25

384 Early and Modern Cars at Pedestrian Crossing

1979. The Private Car.
954 **384** 1m.10 multicoloured . . . 35 30

385 House of Korppi, Lapinjarvi, Uusimaa

1979. Peasant Architecture. Mult.
955 1m.10 Type **385** 40 35
956 1m.10 House of Syrjala, Tammela, Hame (left-hand part) 40 35
957 1m.10 House of Syrjala (right-hand part) 40 35
958 1m.10 House of Murtovaarsa, Valtimo, North Karelia . . 40 35
959 1m.10 House of Antila, Lapua, Pohjanmaa 40 35
960 1m.10 Gable loft of Luukila, Haukipudas and loft of Keskikangas, Yliharma, Pohjanmaa 40 35
961 1m.10 Gate, house of Kanajarvi, Kalvola, Hame 40 35
962 1m.10 Porch, house of Havuselka, Kauhajoki, Pohjanmaa 40 35
963 1m.10 Dinner bell and House of Maki-Rasinpera, Kuortane, Pohjanmaa . . 40 35
964 1m.10 Gable and eaves of granary of Rasula, Kuortane, Pohjanmaa . . 40 35
See also Nos. 1024/33.

386 "Brownies" feeding Horse

387 Maria Jotuni

1979. Christmas.
965 **386** 60p. multicoloured . . . 30 25

1980. Birth Centenary of Maria Jotuni (writer).
966 **387** 1m.10 multicoloured . . . 35 25

1980. Finnish Red Cross Fund. Mushrooms (3rd series). As T **325**. Multicoloured.
967 60p.+10p. Woolly milk cap 45 70
968 90p.+15p. Red cap . . . . . 70 1·00
969 1m.10+20p. "Russula paludosa" . . . . 60 1·00

388 Frans Eemil Sillanpaa

1980. Europa. Finnish Nobel Prize Winners. Multicoloured.
970 1m.10 Type **388** (Literature, 1939) 85 30
971 1m.30 Artturi Ilmari Virtanen (Chemistry, 1945) (vert) . . 1·60 95

389 Pres. Kekkonen

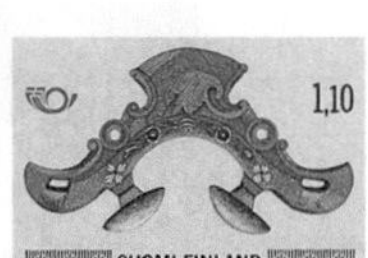

390 Back-piece Harness

1980. President Urho Kekkonen's 80th Birthday.
973 **389** 1m.10 multicoloured . . . 35 25

1980. Nordic Countries' Postal Co-operation. Multicoloured.
974 1m.10 Type **390** 35 30
975 1m.30 Collar harness (vert) 35 30

391 Biathlon

392 Trials of Strength

1980. Biathlon World Championship, Lahti.
976 **391** 1m.10 multicoloured . . . 35 30

1980. Christmas. Multicoloured.
977 60p. Type **392** 40 25
978 1m.10 "To put out the shoe maker's eye" (children's game) 35 25

393 Kauhaneva Swamps, Kauhajoki

1981. National Parks.
979 **393** 70p. pink, brown & grn 25 30
980 – 1m.60 multicoloured . . . 45 40
981 – 1m.80 multicoloured . . . 65 30
982 – 2m.40 multicoloured . . . 65 30
983 – 4m.30 multicoloured . . . 1·10 80
DESIGNS—VERT: 1m.60, Forest of Multiharju, Seitseminen National Park. HORIZ: 1m.80, Razorbills, Eastern Gulf National Park; 2m.40, Urho Kekkonen National Park; 4m.30, Archipelago National Park.

394 Boxing

395 Glass-blowing and 19th-century Bottle

1981. European Boxing Championships, Tampere.
990 **394** 1m.10 multicoloured . . . 35 35

1981. 300th Anniv of Finnish Glass Industry.
991 **395** 1m.10 multicoloured . . . 35 30

396 "Furst Menschikoff" (paddle-steamer)

1981. "Nordia 1981" Stamp Exhibition, Helsinki.
992 **396** 1m.10 brown & stone . . 1·50 2·50

397 Rowing to Church

1981. Europa. Multicoloured.
993 1m.10 Type **397** 90 30
994 1m.50 Midsummer Eve celebrations . . . . 1·10 60

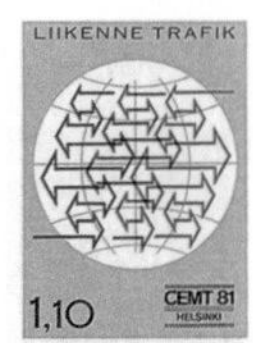

398 "International Traffic Movement"

399 Children on Winged Horse

1981. Council Session of European Conference of Ministers of Transport, Finland.
995 **398** 1m.10 multicoloured . . . 35 25

1981. Centenary of Finnish Youth Associations.
996 **399** 1m. multicoloured 30 30

400 Fuchsia

401 Face on Graph

1981. Tuberculosis Relief Fund. Potted Plants. Multicoloured.
997 70p.+10p. Type **400** 35 65
998 1m.+15p. African violet ("Saintpaulia ionantha") 35 70
999 1m.10+20p. Pelargonium . . 35 70

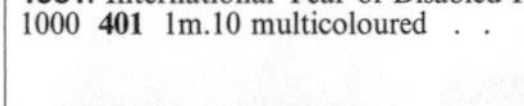

1981. International Year of Disabled Persons.
1000 **401** 1m.10 multicoloured . . 35 30

402 Children bringing Home Christmas Tree

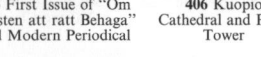

405 First Issue of "Om konsten att ratt Behaga" and Modern Periodical

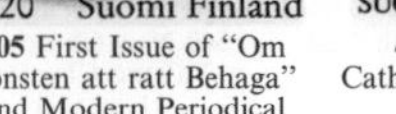

406 Kuopio Cathedral and Puijo Tower

1982. Bicentenary of Finnish Periodicals.
1015 **405** 1m.20 multicoloured . . 35 25

1982. Bicentenary of Kuopio.
1016 **406** 1m.20 multicoloured . . 35 25

407 Neck of Stringed Instrument and Staves of Music

408 Flats, Factories and Houses

1982. Music Jubilee.
1017 **407** 1m.20 multicoloured . . 35 30

1982. Centenary of Electricity in Finland.
1018 **408** 1m.20 multicoloured . . 35 30

409 Vegetable and Fruit Garden

410 Cover of "Abckiria" and sculpture of M. Agricola by O. Jauhiainen

1982. Cent of First Finnish Horticultural Society.
1019 **409** 1m.10 multicoloured . . 35 30

1982. Europa. Multicoloured.
1020 1m.20 Type **410** . . . . . 1·10 25
1021 1m.50 "Turku Academy Inaugural Procession in 1640" (fresco copied by Johannes Gebhard from painting by Albert Edelfelt) (47 × 31 mm) . . 1·60 55

411 Emblems and Symbolic Design

1982. International Monetary Fund and World Bank Committees' Meetings, Helsinki.
1022 **411** 1m.60 multicoloured . . 45 35

412 Interior of Parliament and "Future" (sculpture by W. Aaltonen)

1982. 75th Anniv of Single Chamber Parliament.
1023 **412** 2m.40 blue, dp bl & blk 65 65

1982. Manor Houses. As T **385**. Mult.
1024 1m.20 Kuitia, 1490s 45 40
1025 1m.20 Louhisaari, 1655 . . 45 40
1026 1m.20 Frugard, 1780 . . . 45 40
1027 1m.20 Jokioinen, 1798 . . 45 40
1028 1m.20 Moisio, 1820 . . . . 45 40
1029 1m.20 Sjundby, 1560s . . . 45 40
1030 1m.20 Fagervik, 1773 . . . 45 40
1031 1m.20 Mustio, 1792 . . . . 45 40
1032 1m.20 Fiskars, 1818 . . . . 45 40
1033 1m.20 Kotkaniemi, 1836 . . 45 40

1981. Christmas. Multicoloured.
1001 70p. Type **402** 30 25
1002 1m.10 Decorating the Christmas tree (vert) . . . 30 25

404 Hame Castle

1982.
1007 **404** 90p. brown 30 30
1008 – 1m. brown and blue . . 35 35
DESIGN—VERT: 1m. Windmill, Harrstrom.

413 Garden Dormouse

1982. Red Cross Fund. Endangered Mammals. Multicoloured.
1034 90p.+10p. Type **413** 50 60
1035 1m.10+15p. Siberian flying squirrel (vert) 65 90
1036 1m.20+20p. European mink 65 90

414 Brownie Children feeding Forest Animals

1982. Christmas. Multicoloured.
1037 90p. Type **414** 40 25
1038 1m.20 Brownie children eating porridge 40 25

415 Gold Prospector

1983. Nordic Countries' Postal Co-operation. "Visit the North". Multicoloured.
1039 1m.20 Type **415** 30 25
1040 1m.30 Descending the Kitajoki river rapids . . . 45 25

416 Postman, Letters and Computer

1983. World Communications Year. Mult.
1041 1m.30 Type **416** 40 25
1042 1m.70 Modulated wave, pulse stream and optical cables 40 40

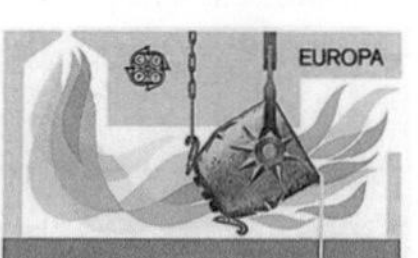

418 Flash Smelting

1983. Europa. Multicoloured.
1044 1m.30 Type **418** . . . . . 2·75 25
1045 1m.70 Interior of Temppeliaukio Church (Timo and Tuomo Suomalainen) . . . . . . 3·75 95

419 President Relander

420 Throwing the Javelin

1983. Birth Centenary of Lauri Kristian Relander (President, 1925–1931).
1046 **419** 1m.30 multicoloured . . 35 25

1983. World Athletics Championships, Helsinki. Multicoloured.
1047 1m.20 Type **420** 35 25
1048 1m.30 Running (vert) . . . 35 25

421 Kuula and Ostrobothnia

422 Chickweed Wintergreen

1983. Birth Cent of Toivo Kuula (composer).
1049 **421** 1m.30 multicoloured . . 35 25

1983. Tuberculosis Relief Fund. Wild Flowers. Multicoloured.
1050 1m.+20p. Type **422** 35 65
1051 1m.20+25p. Marsh Violet 40 65
1052 1m.30+30p. Marsh Marigold 40 65

423 "Santa Claus" (Eija Myllyviita)

1983. Christmas. Children's Drawings.
1053 **423** 1m. blue & deep blue . . 35 25
1054 – 1m.30 multicoloured . . 35 25
DESIGN—VERT: 1m.30, "Two Candles" (Camilla Lindberg).

424 Koivisto

1983. President Mauno Henrik Koivisto's 60th Birthday.
1055 **424** 1m.30 bl, blk & dp bl . . 35 25

425 Second Class Letters

426 Hydraulic Turbine Manufacture

1984. Re-classification of Postal Items.
1056 **425** 1m.10 green 35 20
1057 – 1m.40 orange & red . . 35 20
DESIGN—VERT: 1m.40, First class letter.

1984. "Work and Skill" Centenary of Workers' Associations.
1058 **426** 1m.40 multicoloured . . 45 25

427 Crossbow, Pot and Chalice

428 Bridge

1984. Museum Activities.
1059 **427** 1m.40 multicoloured . . 45 25

1984. Europa. 25th Anniv of European Post and Telecommunications Conference.
1060 **428** 1m.40 orange, deep orange and black . . . 1·50 25
1061 2m. blue, violet and black . . . . 3·25 1·00

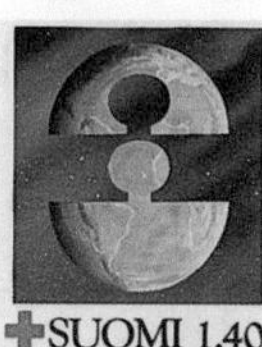

429 Globe as Jigsaw Puzzle

430 Teeth and Dentist treating Patient

1984. Finnish Red Cross Fund. Multicoloured.
1062 1m.40+35p. Type **429** . . . 45 70
1063 2m.+40p. Spheres around globe 45 75

1984. International Dental Federation Congress, Helsinki.
1064 **430** 1m.40 multicoloured . . 35 25

431 Observatory, Planets and Sun

432 Statute Book and Title Page

1984. Cent of University of Helsinki Observatory.
1065 **431** 1m.10 multicoloured . . 35 30

1984. 250th Anniv of 1734 Common Law.
1066 **432** 2m. multicoloured . . . 55 50

433 "Mother and Child" (Waino Aaltonen) and Lines from "Song of my Heart"

1984. 150th Birth Anniv of Aleksis Kivi (writer).
1067 **433** 1m.40 grey and black . . 45 25

434 Father Christmas and Brownie

1984. Christmas.
1068 **434** 1m.10 multicoloured . . 35 25

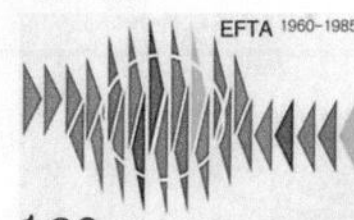

435 Symbolic Representation of International Trade

1985. 25th Anniversary of European Free Trade Association.
1069 **435** 1m.20 multicoloured . . 35 35

436 Medal of Johan Ludwig Runeberg (by Walter Runeberg) and Emblem

437 "Saints Sergei and Herman" (icon, Petros Sasaki)

1985. Centenary of Society of Swedish Literature in Finland.
1070 **436** 1m.50 multicoloured . . 45 25

1985. Centenary of Saint Sergei and Saint Herman Order (home missionary organization of Finnish Orthodox Church).
1071 **437** 1m.50 multicoloured . . 45 25

438 Pedri Semeikka (rune singer)

439 "Mermaid" (Ville Vallgren)

1985. 150th Anniv of "Kalevala" (Karelian poems collected by Elias Lonnrot). Multicoloured.
1072 1m.50 Type **438** 35 35
1073 2m.10 Larin Paraske (legend teller) (after Albert Edelfelt) 55 50

1985. "Nordia 1985" International Stamp Exhibition, Helsinki.
1074 **439** 1m.50 black, grey and blue . . . . 2·20 3·25

440 1886 5m. Banknote

441 Children playing Recorders

1985. Centenary of Finnish Banknote Printing. Multicoloured.
1075 1m.50 Type **440** 55 50
1076 1m.50 1909 50m. banknote showing sailing ship (horiz) 55 50
1077 1m.50 50m. banknote showing waterfall 55 50
1078 1m.50 1000m. banknote showing lake (left side) . . 55 50
1079 1m.50 1000m. banknote showing lake (right side) 55 50
1080 1m.50 500m. banknote showing harvesters . . . 55 50
1081 1m.50 1000m. banknote showing arms and tree, and part of 50m. banknote (horiz) 55 50
1082 1m.50 1955 5000m. banknote showing J. V. Snellman 55 50

1985. Europa. Music Year. Multicoloured.
1083 1m.50 Type **441** . . . . . 3·25 25
1084 2m.10 Cathedral columns and score of "Ramus Virens Olivarum" . . . . 3·10 1·10

442 Finlandia Hall and Barn Swallow

443 Provincial Arms and Seal of Per Brahe

1985. 10th Anniv of European Security and Co-operation Conference, Helsinki.
1085 **442** 2m.10 multicoloured . . 55 55

1985. 350th Anniv of Provincial Administration.
1086 **443** 1m.50 multicoloured . . 45 25

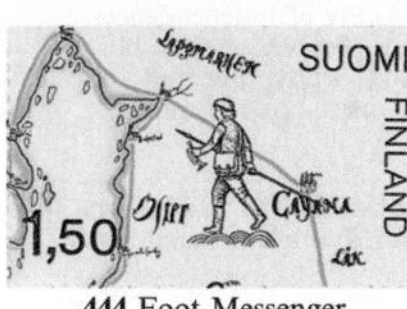

444 Foot Messenger

1985. "Finlandia 88" International Stamp Exhibition, Helsinki (1st issue). Sheet 135×90 mm containing T **444** and similar multicoloured designs forming a composite design of 1698 postal map of Sweden and Finland.
MS1087 1m.50 Type **444**; 1m.50 Raft; 1m.50 Mounted messanger (vert); 1m.50 Iceboat (sold at 8m.) 5·50 7·25
See also Nos. **MS**1107, **MS**1122, 1149 and **MS**1152.

445 I.Y.Y. Emblem

446 Bird Decoration and Tulips

1985. International Youth Year.
1088 **445** 1m.50 multicoloured . . 45 25

1985. Christmas. Multicoloured.
1089 1m.20 Type **446** 35 25
1090 1m.20 St. Thomas's cross and hyacinths 35 25

447 Orbicular Granite

449 Baghdad Conference Palace (Kaija and Heikki Siren)

448 Saimaa Ringed Seal

1986. Centenary of Geological Society. Mult.
1091 1m.30 Type **447** 40 35
1092 1m.60 Rapakivi (granite) . . 40 25
1093 2m.10 Veined gneiss 40 35

1986. Europa. Multicoloured.
1094 1m.60 Type **448** . . . . . 2·50 25
1095 2m.20 Landscape seen through window . . . . 3·25 80

1986. Modern Architecture. Multicoloured.
1096 1m.60 Type **449** 45 45
1097 1m.60 Lahti Theatre (Pekka Salminen and Esko Koivisto) (value in blue) 45 45
1098 1m.60 Kuusamo Municipal Offices (Marja and Keijo Petaja) (value in red) . . 45 45
1099 1m.60 Hamina police and court building (Timo and Tuomo Suomalainen) and Greek church (value in green) 45 45
1100 1m.60 Finnish Embassy, New Delhi (Raili and Reima Pietila) (value in green) 45 45
1101 1m.60 Day care centre, Western Sakyla (Kari Jarvinen and Timo Airas) (value in red) 45 45

450 Orange-tip

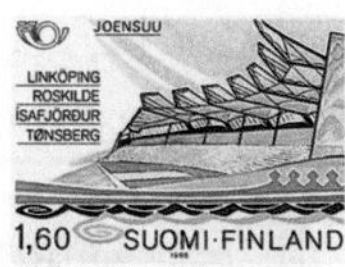

451 Auditorium, Joensuu

1986. Finnish Red Cross Fund. Butterflies. Multicoloured.
1102 1m.60+40p. Type **450** . . . 75 75
1103 2m.10+45p. Camberwell beauty . . . . 1·20 1·50
1104 5m.+50p. Apollo . . . . . 2·00 2·30

1986. Nordic Countries' Postal Co-operation. Twinned Towns. Multicoloured.
1105 1m.60 Type **451** 45 25
1106 2m.20 Emblem of University of Jyvaskyla 55 70

452 Paddle-steamer "Aura"

1986. "Finlandia 88" International Stamp Exhibition, Helsinki (2nd issue). Sheet 135×90 mm containing T **452** and similar designs, each deep brown and buff.
MS1107 1m.60 Type **452**; 1m.60 Steamship "Alexander"; 2m.20 Steamship "Nicolai"; 2m.20 Ice-breaker "Express II" (vert) (sold at 10m.) . . . . 5·50 7·25

453 Maupertuis, Globe, Quadrant and Sledge

1986. 250th Anniv of Measurement of Arcs of Meridian.
1108 **453** 1m.60 bl, ultram & blk 45 25

454 Kekkonen

455 Cloud, Rainbow and Emblem

1986. Urho Kekkonen (President, 1956–81). Commemoration.
1109 **454** 5m. black . . . . 1·20 65

1986. International Peace Year.
1110 **455** 1m.60 multicoloured . . 45 25

456 Angels and Garland

1986. Christmas. Multicoloured.
1111 1m.30 Type **456** 55 25
1112 1m.30 Angels and garland (different) 55 25
1113 1m.60 Brownies and garland 45 25

457 Microchip

458 Prototype Metre Measuring Bar as Parcel

1987. Centenary of Postal Savings Bank.
1114 **457** 1m.70 multicoloured . . 45 30

1987. Centenary of Metric System in Finland.
1115 **458** 1m.40 multicoloured . . 35 45

459 "Borea" (liner), Diesel Train, Snow Scene and Skier

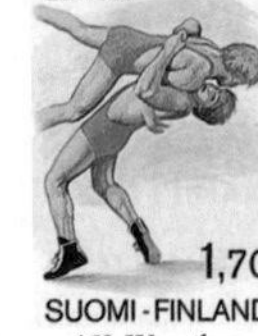

460 Wrestlers

1987. Tourism. Multicoloured.
1116 1m.70 Type **459** 45 25
1117 2m.30 Douglas DC-10 airplane, bus, yachts on lake and hiker 55 70

1987. European Wrestling Championships, Helsinki.
1118 **460** 1m.70 multicoloured . . 60 30

461 Madetoja and Score of Cradlesong

462 Balls and Pins

1987. Birth Centenary of Leevi Madetoja (composer).
1119 **461** 2m.10 multicoloured . . 55 30

1987. 11th World Ten Pin Bowling Championships.
1120 **462** 1m.70 multicoloured . . 45 30

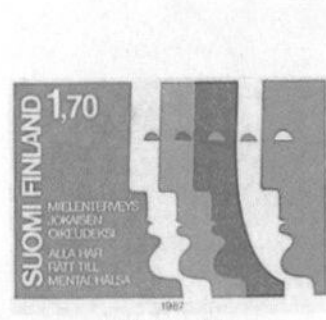

463 Profiles

465 "Strawberry Girl" (Nils Schillmark)

464 Locomotive "Lemminkainen", 1862

1987. 90th Anniv of Finnish Association for Mental Health.
1121 **463** 1m.70 multicoloured . . 45 25

1987. "Finlandia 88" International Stamp Exhibition, Helsinki (3rd issue). Sheet 135 × 90 mm containing T **464** and similar horiz designs, depicting trains on the Helsinki–Hameenlinna and Riihimaki–St. Petersburg routes.
MS1122 1m.70 green, orange and blue (Type **464**); 1m.70 multicoloured (Mail van No. 9935, 1871); 1m.70 multicoloured (Mail van No. 9991, 1899); 2m.30 green and blue (Locomotive No. 57, 1874) (sold at 10m.) . . . . . 5·50 7·25

1987. Centenary of Ateneum Art Museum. Paintings. Multicoloured.
1123 1m.70 Type **465** . . . . . 1·00 55
1124 1m.70 "Still Life on a Lady's Work-table" (Ferdinand von Wright) 1·00 55
1125 1m.70 "Old Woman with Basket" (Albert Edelfelt) 1·00 55
1126 1m.70 "Boy and Crow" (Akseli Gallen-Kallela) . . 1·00 55
1127 1m.70 "Late Winter" (Tyko Sallinen) . . . . 1·00 55

466 Tampere Main Library (Railia and Reima Pietila)

467 Arrows

1987. Europa. Art and Architecture. Mult.
1128 1m.70 Type **466** . . . . . 2·75 30
1129 2m.30 "Stoa" (Hannu Siren) 3·75 1·00

1987. 7th European Physics Society General Conference.
1130 **467** 1m.70 multicoloured . . 45 25

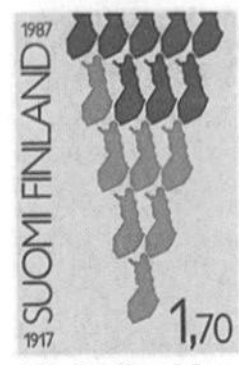

468 Outline Maps of Finland

469 Baby with Ball and Prof. Ylppo

1987. 70th Anniv of Independence.
1131 **468** 1m.70 silver, grey & bl 45 25
1132 10m. silver, blue and azure (26 × 37 mm) . . 2·30 1·30

1987. 100th Birthday of Arvo Ylppo (paediatrician).
1133 **469** 1m.70 multicoloured . . 55 25

470 Father Christmas and Brownies

471 Birds flying from Globe to Finland

1987. Christmas. Multicoloured.
1134 1m.40 Type **470** 45 25
1135 1m.70 Mother Christmas and brownie (vert) . . . 40 25

1987. Centenary of Finnish News Agency.
1136 **471** 2m.30 multicoloured . . 55 75

472 Pihkala

473 Telephone and Mail Boxes

1988. Birth Centenary of Lauri Pihkala ("Tahko") (writer and sport organizer).
1137 **472** 1m.80 deep blue, blue and black 45 25

1988. 350th Anniv of Posts and Telecommunications Services (1st issue). Multicoloured.
1138 1m.80 Type **473** 90 25
1139 1m.80 Airplane and lorry 90 25
1140 1m.80 Fork-lift truck carrying parcels 90 25
1141 1m.80 Postman 90 25
1142 1m.80 Woman receiving letter 90 25

Nos. 1138/42 were printed together, se-tenant, Nos. 1141/2 forming a composite design.

See also Nos. 1165/70.

474 Conifer Branches (Christmas)

475 Weather Chart and Measuring Equipment

1988. Finnish Red Cross Fund. Festivals. Multicoloured.
1143 1m.40+40p. Type **474** . . . 45 55
1144 1m.80+45p. Narcissi (Easter) 45 65
1145 2m.40+50p. Rose (Midsummer) . . . . . . 80 1·00

1988. 150th Anniv of Meteorological Institute.
1146 **475** 1m.40 multicoloured . . 45 25

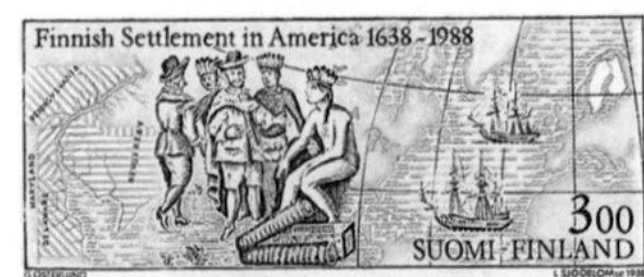

476 Map, Settlers, Indians, "Calmare Nyckel" and "Fagel Grip"

1988. 350th Anniv of Founding of New Sweden (Finnish and Swedish settlement in North America).
1147 **476** 3m. multicoloured . . . 90 55

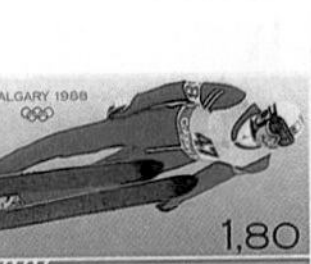

477 Matti Nykanen (triple gold medal winner)

478 Agathon Faberge (philatelist)

1988. Finnish Success at Winter Olympic Games, Calgary.
1148 **477** 1m.80 multicoloured . . 45 30

1988. "Finlandia 88" International Stamp Exhibition, Helsinki.
1149 **478** 5m. multicoloured . . . 11·00 12·00

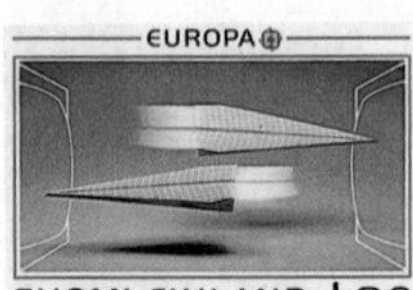

479 Paper Airplanes between VDUs

1988. Europa. Transport and Communications. Multicoloured.
1150 1m.80 Type **479** . . . . . 3·25 25
1151 2m.40 Horse tram, 1890 . . 3·75 95

480 Breguet 14 Biplane with Skis

1988. "Finlandia 88" International Stamp Exhibition, Helsinki (5th issue). Sheet 135 × 90 mm containing T **480** and similar horiz designs.
MS1152 1m.80 blue and red (Type **480**); 1m.80 blue and mauve (Junkers F-13); 1m.80 blue and orange (Douglas DC-3); 2m.40 ultramarine and blue (Douglas DC-10-30) (sold at 11m.) . . . 6·50 8·50

481 Steam-driven Fire Pump, Turku Fire Brigade

482 "Missale Aboense" and Illuminated Page

1988. 150th Anniv of Fire Brigades in Finland.
1163 **481** 2m.20 multicoloured . . 55 45

1988. 500th Anniv of Publishing of "Missale Aboense" (first printed book for Finland).
1164 **482** 1m.80 multicoloured . . 45 25

483 1638 Postal Tariffs

484 Teacher with Children

1988. 350th Anniv of Posts and Telecommunications Services (2nd issue). Multicoloured.
1165 1m.80 Type **483** 55 35
1166 1m.80 Rural postman, 1860s 55 35
1167 1m.80 Postman delivering from mail van 55 35
1168 1m.80 Malmi Post Office . . 55 35
1169 1m.80 Skiers using mobile telephone 55 35
1170 1m.80 Communications satellite 55 35

1988. Church Playgroups.
1171 **484** 1m.80 multicoloured . . 45 25

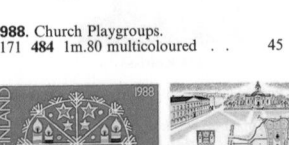

485 Decorations

486 Market Place, Town Plan and Arms

1988. Christmas.
1172 **485** 1m.40 multicoloured . . 45 25
1173 1m.80 multicoloured . . 45 25

1989. 350th Anniv of Hameenlinna Town Charter.
1174 **486** 1m.90 multicoloured . . 55 25

487 Skier

488 Photographer with Box Camera on Tripod

1989. World Skiing Championships, Lahti.
1175 **487** 1m.90 multicoloured . . 45 25

1989. 150th Anniv of Photography.
1176 **488** 1m.50 multicoloured . . 45 35

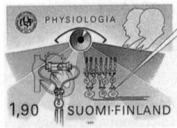

489 Christmas Collection

490 Professors Tigerstedt and Granit and Research Fields

1989. Cent of Salvation Army in Finland.
1177 **489** 1m.90 multicoloured . . 55 25

1989. 31st International Physiological Sciences Congress, Helsinki.
1178 **490** 1m.90 multicoloured . . 45 25

491 Skiing

1989. Sport. Multicoloured.
1179 1m.90 Type **491** 55 40
1180 1m.90 Jogging 55 40
1181 1m.90 Cycling 55 40
1182 1m.90 Canoeing 55 40

492 Lapponian Herder

1989. Centenary of Finnish Kennel Club. Sheet 114×90 mm containing T **492** and similar horiz designs. Multicoloured.
MS1183 1m.90 Type **492**; 1m.90 Finnish spitz; 1m.90 Karelian bear dog; 1m.90 Finnish hound . . 3·25 3·25

493 Hopscotch

1989. Europa. Children's Activities. Mult.
1184 1m.90 Type **493** . . . . . 1·40 25
1185 2m.50 Sledging . . . . . . 2·30 65

494 Man from Sakyla

495 Foxglove and Pharmaceutical Equipment

1989. Nordic Countries' Postal Co-operation. Traditional Costumes. Multicoloured.
1186 1m.90 Type **494** 55 25
1187 2m.50 Woman from Veteli 65 65

1989. 300th Anniv of Pharmacies in Finland.
1188 **495** 1m.90 multicoloured . . 55 25

496 Snow Leopard

497 Savonlinna

1989. Cent of Helsinki Zoo. Multicoloured.
1189 1m.90 Type **496** 55 25
1190 2m.50 Markhor goat . . . 65 60

1989. 350th Anniv of Savonlinna.
1191 **497** 1m.90 multicoloured . . 45 25

498 Brown Bear

499 Open Book and Mercury's Staff

1989.
1192 **498** 50m. multicoloured . . . 11·00 8·00

1989. 150th Anniv of Commercial Studies in Finland.
1193 **499** 1m.50 multicoloured . . 45 35

500 Emblem and Columns in Finland's Parliament

1989. Cent of Interparliamentary Union.
1194 **500** 1m.90 multicoloured . . 55 30

501 Bridges

1989. Accession of Finland to, and 40th Anniv of Council of Europe.
1195 **501** 2m.50 multicoloured . . 65 55

502 Kolehmainen winning 5000 m, Olympic Games, 1912

503 Students, Open Book and Keyboard

1989. Birth Cent of Hannes Kolehmainen (runner).
1196 **502** 1m.90 multicoloured . . 55 25

1989. Centenary of Folk High Schools.
1197 **503** 1m.90 multicoloured . . 45 30

504 Decorated Street

505 Emblem and Lake Paijanne

1989. Christmas. Multicoloured.
1198 1m.50 Type **504** 40 25
1199 1m.90 Sodankyla Church, Lapland 70 25

1990. Formation of Posts and Telecommunications into State Commercial Company.
1200 **505** 1m.90 multicoloured . . 60 75
1201 2m.50 multicoloured . . 65 1·10

506 Wood Anemone (Uusimaa province)

507 Erik Ferling (first orchestra leader) conducting

1990. Provincial Plants. Multicoloured.
1205 2m. Type **506** 55 25
1206 2m.10 Rowan (Northern Savo) 55 25
1207 2m.70 Heather (Kainuu) . . 70 25
1208 2m.90 Shrub sea buck-thorn (Satakunta) 75 25
1209 3m.50 Oak (Varsinais Suomi) 95 35
No. 1206 also comes self-adhesive and imperforate.
See also Nos. 1273/4, 1303, 1309, 1327 and 1354.

1990. Bicentenary of Foundation of Turku Musical Society (first Finnish orchestra).
1220 **507** 1m.90 multicoloured . . 55 30

508 Snowflake

509 Disabled Ex-serviceman

1990. 50th Anniv of End of Russo–Finnish Winter War.
1221 **508** 2m. blue & ultramarine 45 25

1990. 50th Anniv of Disabled Ex-servicemen's Association.
1222 **509** 2m. multicoloured . . . 55 25

510 Nuvvus Postal Agency

1990. Europa. Post Office Buildings. Mult.
1223 2m. Type **510** . . . . . . 1·60 25
1224 2m.70 Turku Postal Centre 2·50 40

511 Queen Christina

1990. 350th Anniv of Grant of Charter to Turku Academy (later Helsinki University). Mult.
1225 2m. Type **511** 55 30
1226 3m.20 Main building of Helsinki University . . . 80 70

512 Scarce Copper on Goldrod

1990. Finnish Red Cross Fund. Butterflies. Multicoloured.
1227 1m.50+40p. Type **512** . . . 45 70
1228 2m.+50p. Amanda's blue on meadow vetchling 65 95
1229 2m.70+60p. Peacock on tufted vetch . . . . . . 95 1·10
See also Nos. 1279/81.

513 Postman at Larsmo, 1890, and Modern Address Sign

514 "Ali Baba and the Forty Thieves"

1990. Compilation of Address Register and Centenary of Rural Postal Service.
1230 **513** 2m. multicoloured . . . 55 25

1990. Birth Centenary of Rudolf Koivu (artist). Designs showing Koivu's illustrations of fairy tales. Multicoloured.
1231 2m. Type **514** 45 35
1232 2m. "The Great Musician" (Raul Roine) 45 35
1233 2m. "The Giants, the Witches and the Daughter of the Sun" (Koivu) . . . 45 35
1234 2m. "The Golden Bird, the Golden Horse and the Princess" (Grimm Brothers) 45 35
1235 2m. "Lamb Brother" (Koivu) 45 35
1236 2m. "The Snow Queen" (Hans Christian Andersen) 45 35

515 Youth feeding Horse

1990. Youth Hobbies. Horse Riding. Sheet 118×63 mm containing T **515** and similar vert designs. Multicoloured.
MS1237 2m. Type **515**; 2m. Two riders; 2m. Girl saddling pony; 2m. Girl grooming horse . . . . . 4·25 4·50

516 Brownies dealing with Father Christmas's Mail

517 Player and Turku Castle

1990. Christmas. Multicoloured.
1238 1m.70 Type **516** 55 25
1239 2m. Father Christmas and reindeer 60 25

1991. World Ice Hockey Championship, Turku, Tampere and Helsinki.
1246 **517** 2m.10 multicoloured . . 55 30

518 Teacher and Pupils preparing Meal

519 "Green Still Life"

1991. Cent of Domestic Science Teacher Training.
1247 **518** 2m.10 multicoloured . . 55 25

1991. Pro Filatelia. Paintings by Helene Schjerfbeck. Multicoloured.
1248 2m.10+50p. Type **519** . . . 90 1·50
1249 2m.10+50p. "The Little Convalescent" . . . . . 90 1·70

520 Great Tit

521 Fly-fishing for RainbowTrout

1991. Birds (1st series). Multicoloured.
1250 10p. Type **520** 20 25
1251 60p. Pair of chaffinches . . 75 30
1252 2m.10 Northern bullfinch . . 45 25
See also Nos. 1282/4 and 1322/4.

1991. Centenary of Central Fishery Organization. Multicoloured.
1253 2m.10 Type **521** 50 35
1254 2m.10 Stylized Eurasian perch and float 50 35
1255 2m.10 Stylized fish and crayfish 50 35
1256 2m.10 Trawling for Baltic herring 50 35
1257 2m.10 Restocking with whitefish from lorry . . . 50 35

522 Seurasaari Island

523 Map of Europe and Human Figures

1991. Nordic Countries' Postal Co-operation. Multicoloured.
1258 2m.10 Type **522** 55 25
1259 2m.90 Saimaa ferry 75 50

1991. Europa. Europe in Space. Mult.
1260 2m.10 Type **523** . . . . . 2·30 30
1261 2m.90 Map of Europe, satellites and dish aerials 3·25 55

524 Iris Vase

525 Kittens and "Kiss-Kiss" Sweet

1991. 61st Death Anniv of Alfred Finch (painter and ceramic artist). Multicoloured.
1262 2m.10 Type **524** 65 25
1263 2m.90 "The English Coast at Dover" 90 55

1991. Centenary of Opening of Karl Fazer's Confectionery (beginning of Finnish Sweet Industry).
1264 **525** 2m.10 multicoloured . . 55 25

526 "Sun" (Kaisa Niemi)

527 Leisure Skiing

1991. Children's Stamp Design Competition Winners. Sheet 100 × 60 mm containing T **526** and similar horiz design. Multicoloured.

MS1265 2m.10 Type **526**; 2m.10 "Rainbow" (Elina Aro); 2m.10 "Cows grazing" (Noora Kaunisto) 2·75 2·75

1991. Youth Hobbies. Skiing. Sheet 118 × 64 mm containing T **527** and similar vert designs. Mult.

MS1266 2m.10 Type **527**; 2m.10 Ski-boarding; 2m.10 Freestyle skiing; 2m.10 Speed skating . . . . . 3·25 3·25

528 Iisalmi

1991. Centenary of Granting of Town Rights to Iisalmi.

1267 **528** 2m.10 multicoloured . . 55 30

529 Forest Animals and Elf

1991. Christmas. Multicoloured.

1268 1m.80 Type **529** 45 25

1269 2m.10 Father Christmas in sleigh over new Arctic Circle post office (vert) . . 70 25

530 Camphor Molecule and Erlenmeyer Flask

1991. Cent of Organized Chemistry in Finland.

1270 **530** 2m.10 multicoloured . . 75 25

No. 1270 covers either of two stamps which were issued together as a horizontal gutter pair, the stamps differing very slightly in the diagram of the molecule. The gutter pair is stated to produce a three-dimensional image without use of a special viewer.

531 Skiing

1992. Winter Olympic Games, Albertville (1271) and Summer Games, Barcelona (1272). Multicoloured.

1271 2m.10 Type **531** 70 25

1272 2m.90 Swimming 80 40

532 Globe Flower (Lapland)

533 Finnish Exhibition Emblem

1992. Provincial Plants. With service indicator. Multicoloured.

1273 2KLASS (1m.60) Type **532** 75 25

1274 1KLASS (2m.10) Hepatica (Hame) 95 25

See also Nos. 1303, 1309, 1327 and 1354.

1992. "Expo '92" World's Fair, Seville.

1275 **533** 3m.40 multicoloured . . 85 75

534 Map of Europe

1992. 3rd Meeting of Council of Foreign Ministers of European Security and Co-operation Conference, Helsinki.

1276 **534** 16m. multicoloured . . . 4·50 3·25

535 Church of the Holy Cross, Town Hall and Brigantine

536 Thoughts within Head

1992. 550th Anniv of Rauma Town Charter.

1277 **535** 2m.10 multicoloured . . 60 25

1992. Healthy Brains Campaign.

1278 **536** 3m.50 multicoloured . . 90 1·00

1992. Finnish Red Cross Fund. Centenary of Training of Visually Handicapped. Moths. As T **512**. Multicoloured.

1279 1m.60+40p. Taiga dart . . . 80 90

1280 2m.10+50p. Fjeld tiger . . . 90 1·10

1281 5m.+60p. Baneberry looper moth . . . . 1·80 2·30

537 Pied Wagtail

538 "Santa Maria" and Route Map

1992. Birds (2nd series). Multicoloured.

1282 10p. Type **537** 20 35

1283 60p. European robin . . . . 1·00 85

1284 2m.10 Three Bohemian waxwings 55 40

1992. Europa. 500th Anniv of Discovery of America by Columbus. Multicoloured.

1285 2m.10 Type **538** . . . . . 1·20 25

1286 2m.10 Route map and Columbus . . . . 1·20 25

Nos. 1285/6 were issued together, se-tenant, forming a composite design.

539 Blowing Machine (first Finnish patent, 150th anniv)

540 Currant Harvesting

1992. Technology. Multicoloured.

1287 2m.10 Type **539** (50th anniv of National Board of Patents and Registration of Trademarks) 55 65

1288 2m.90 Triangles and circuits (Finnish chairmanship of EUREKA (European technology development scheme)) 75 75

1289 3m.40 Inverted triangles (50th anniv of Government Technology Research Centre) 95 80

1992. Cent of National Board of Agriculture.

1290 **540** 2m.10 multicoloured . . 60 25

541 Aurora Karamzin

1992. Notable Finnish Women. Mult.

1291 2m.10 Type **541** (founder of Helsinki Deaconesses' Institution) 75 50

1292 2m.10 Sophie Mannerheim (nursing pioneer) 75 50

1293 2m.10 Laimi Leidenius (Professor of Obstetrics and Gynaecology, Helsinki University) . . . 75 50

1294 2m.10 Miina Sillanpaa (first woman Cabinet Minister) 75 50

1295 2m.10 Edith Sodergran (poet) 75 50

1296 2m.10 Kreetta Haapasalo (folk singer) 75 50

542 Flag in Garden (Niina Pennanen)

1992. 75th Anniv of Independence.

1297 **542** 2m.10 multicoloured . . 60 25

MS1298 116 × 53 mm. 2m.10 Birds and birch grove (29 × 36 mm) 95 85

543 Moomin looking into River ("Moominland Midwinter")

544 Rosebay Willowherb (Etela-Pohjanmaa)

1992. "Nordia 1993" International Stamp Exhibition. Stamp Day. Designs showing illustrations from her stories by Tove Jansson. Multicoloured.

1299 2m.10 Type **543** . . . . . 1·90 50

1300 2m.10 Moomin and trolls ("Moominland Midwinter") . . . . . . 1·90 50

1301 2m.10 Theatre performance on water ("Moomin Summer Madness") . . . 1·90 50

1302 2m.10 Moomin and inhabitants ("Tales from Moomin Valley") . . . . 1·90 50

1992. Provincial Plants. With service indicator. Self-adhesive. Imperf.

1303 **544** 1KLASS (2m.10) mult 95 25

545 Computerized and Hot Metal Typesetting

546 St. Lawrence's Church, Vantaa

1992. 350th Anniv of Printing in Finland.

1304 **545** 2m.10 multicoloured . . 55 25

1992. Christmas. Multicoloured.

1305 1m.80 Type **546** 60 25

1306 2m.10 Stained glass window, Karkkila Church (vert) . . 60 25

547 Couple

1993. 75th Anniv of Central Chamber of Commerce.

1307 **547** 1m.60 multicoloured . . 45 45

548 Birds, Flowers and Envelope within Heart

1993. Friendship.

1308 **548** 1KLASS (2m.10) mult 95 25

549 Iris (Kymenlaakso)

550 Fox in Winter Coat

1993. Provincial Plants. With service indicator. Self-adhesive. Imperf.

1309 **549** 2KLASS (1m.90) mult 80 30

1993. Endangered Species. The Arctic Fox. Multicoloured.

1310 2m.30 Type **550** 95 60

1311 2m.30 Two foxes in winter coat 95 60

1312 2m.30 Mother with young in summer coat 95 60

1313 2m.30 Two foxes in summer coat 95 60

551 "Autumn Landscape of Lake Pielisjarvi" (left half)

1993. Pro Filatelia. 130th Birth Anniv of Eero Jarnefelt (painter). Multicoloured.

1314 2m.30+70p. Type **551** . . . 85 1·20

1315 2m.30+70p. "Autumn Landscape of Lake Pielisjarvi" (right half) . . 85 1·20

Nos. 1314/15 were issued together, se-tenant, forming a composite design of the entire painting.

552 "Rumba" (Martti Aiha)

553 Burnet Rose

1993. Europa Contemporary Art. Sculptures. Multicoloured.

1316 2m. Type **552** 95 25

1317 2m.90 "Complete Works" (Kari Caven) . . . . . . 1·40 55

1993. Centenary of Helsinki Philatelic Association.

1318 **553** 2m.30 multicoloured . . 75 55

554 Castle and Courier Route Map

1993. 700th Anniv of Vyborg Castle.

1319 **554** 2m.30 multicoloured . . 55 25

555 Naantali

556 Tengmalm's Owl

1993. Nordic Countries' Postal Co-operation. Tourism. Multicoloured.

1320 2m.30 Type **555** 65 25

1321 2m.90 Imatra 80 50

1993. Birds (3rd series). Multicoloured.

1322 10p. Type **556** 20 50

1323 20p. Common redstart . . . 2·20 1·50

1324 2m.30 White-backed woodpecker 55 50

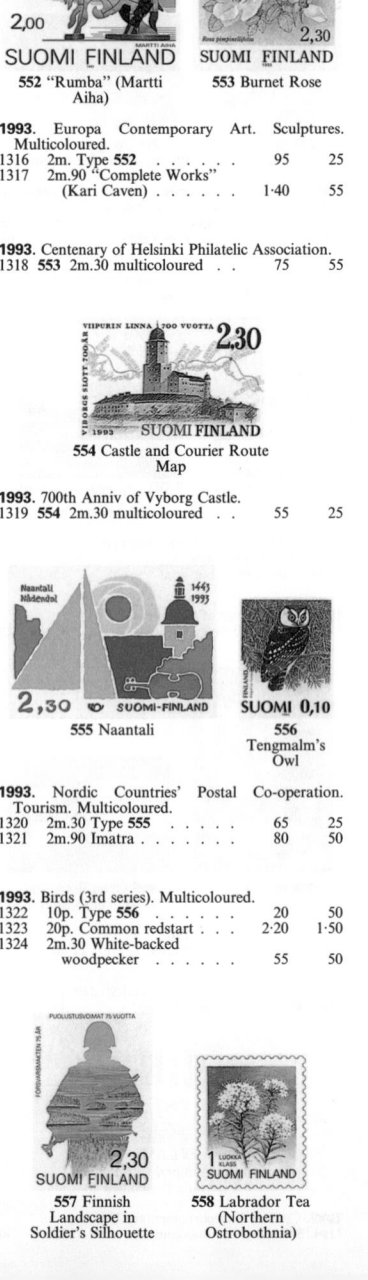

557 Finnish Landscape in Soldier's Silhouette

558 Labrador Tea (Northern Ostrobothnia)

1993. 75th Anniv of Military Forces. Mult.
1325 2m.30 Type **557** 55 25
1326 3m.40 Checkpoint of Finnish soldiers serving with U.N. peacekeeping force . . . . 1·00 75

1993. Provincial Plants. With service indicator. Self-adhesive. Imperf.
1327 **558** 1KLASS (2m.30) mult 1·00 25

559 Child skiing (cover illustration from "Kotiliesi")

561 Gymnastics and Football

560 Flock of Black-throated Divers

1993. Birth Centenary of Martta Wendelin (artist). Multicoloured.
1328 2m.30 Type **559** 80 40
1329 2m.30 Mother and daughter knitting (illustration from "First Book of the Home and School") 80 40
1330 2m.30 Children making snowman (illustration from "First Book of the Home and School") . . . 80 40
1331 2m.30 Rural scene (postcard) 80 40
1332 2m.30 Young girl and lamb (cover illustration from "Kotiliesi") 80 40

1993. Water Birds. Multicoloured.
1333 2m.30 Type **560** 95 80
1334 2m.30 Pair of black-throated divers ("Gavia arctica") (53 × 28 mm) 95 80
1335 2m.30 Goosander ("Mergus merganser") (26 × 39 mm) 95 80
1336 2m.30 Mallards ("Anas platy rhynchos") (26 × 39 mm) 95 80
1337 2m.30 Red-breasted merganser ("Mergus serrator") (26 × 39 mm) 95 80

1993. 150th Anniv of Compulsory Physical Education in Schools.
1338 **561** 2m.30 multicoloured . . 55 25

562 "Ostobothnians" (Leevi Madetoja)

1993. Inauguration of New National Opera House. Sheet 120 × 80 mm containing T **562** and similar horiz designs showing scenes from operas and ballets. Multicoloured.
MS1339 2m.30 Type **562**; 2m.30 "The Faun" (Claude Debussy, choreographed by Jorma Uotinen); 2m.90 "The Magic Flute" (Mozart); 3m.40 "Giselle" (Adolphe Adam) . . . . . . 4·25 4·00

563 Brownies and Christmas Tree (Anna Kymalainen)

564 Koivisto

1993. Christmas. Children's Drawings. Mult.
1340 1m.80 Type **563** 55 25
1341 2m.30 Three angels and star (Taina Tuomola) 55 25

1993. 70th Birthday of President Mauno Koivisto.
1342 **564** 2m.30 multicoloured . . 55 30

565 "Moominland Winter"

566 Marja-Liisa Kirvesniemi and Marjo Matikainen

1994. Moomin. With service indicator. Illustrations from her stories by Tove Jansson. Multicoloured.
1343 1klass (2m.30) Type **565** . . 95 25
1344 1klass (2m.30) "Moominland Storm" . . 95 25

1994. "Finlandia 95" International Stamp Exhibition, Helsinki (1st issue) and Centenary of International Olympic Committee. Sheet 120 × 80 mm containing T **566** and similar vert designs showing Finnish Winter Olympic Games Competitors. Multicoloured.
MS1345 4m.20 Type **566**; 4m.20 Clas Thunberg; 4m.20 Veikko Kankkonen; 4m.20 Veikko Hakulinen . . . . 5·50 6·25

567 "Peace"

1994. Birth Centenary of Waino Aaltonen (sculptor). Multicoloured.
1346 2m. Type **567** 60 25
1347 2m. "Muse" 60 25

568 Postal Clerk and Customer

1994. Centenary of Postal Service Civil Servants Federation.
1348 **568** 2m.30 multicoloured . . 55 25

569 Ploughing

1994. Finnish Red Cross Fund. Horses. Multicoloured.
1349 2m. Type **569** 50 85
1350 2m.30 Marinka (trotting horse) 60 95
1351 4m.20 Cavalry horses (vert) 1·40 1·80

570 Paper Roll, Nitrogen-fixing Technique, Padlock and "Fennica" (ice-breaker)

571 Rose (North Karelia)

1994. Europa. Discoveries and Inventions. Multicoloured.
1352 2m.30 Type **570** 65 40
1353 4m.20 Balloon, radiosonde, mobile telephone, fishing lure and lake oxygenation equipment . . . . 1·60 1·30

1994. Provincial Plants. With service indicator. Self-adhesive. Imperf.
1354 **571** 1KLASS (2m.30) mult 95 30

572 Riitta Salin and Pirjo Haggman (runners)

1994. "Finlandia 95" International Stamp Exhibition (2nd issue) and European Athletics Championships, Helsinki. Sheet 120 × 80 mm containing T **572** and similar vert designs showing Finnish athletes. Multicoloured.
MS1355 4m.20 Type **572**; 4m.20 Lasse Viren (runner); 4m.20 Tiina Lillak (javelin thrower); 4m.20 Pentti Nikula (pole vaulter) . . 5·50 6·25

573 Seven-spotted Ladybirds

1994. "Finlandia 95" International Stamp Exhibition, Helsinki.
1356 **573** 16m. multicoloured . . . 5·25 5·00
See also No. 1393.

574 Perforate St. John's Wort ("Hypericum perforatum")

575 Patrik Sjoberg (high jump)

1994. Flowers. With service indicator. Mult.
1357 1klass (2m.30) Type **574** . . 95 35
1358 1klass (2m.30) Sticky catchfly ("Lychnis viscaria") 95 35
1359 1klass (2m.30) Harebell ("Campanula rotundifolia") 95 35
1360 1klass (2m.30) Clustered bellflower ("Campanula glomerata") 95 35
1361 1klass (2m.30) Bloody cranesbill ("Geranium sanguineum") 95 35
1362 1klass (2m.30) Wild strawberry ("Fragaria vesca") 95 35
1363 1klass (2m.30) Germander speedwell ("Veronica chamaedrys") 95 35
1364 1klass (2m.30) Meadow saxifrage ("Saxifraga granulata") 95 35
1365 1klass (2m.30) Wild pansy ("Viola tricolor") 95 35
1366 1klass (2m.30) Silver-weed ("Potentilla anserina") . . 95 35

1994. Sweden–Finland Athletics Meeting, Stockholm. Multicoloured.
1367 2m.40 Sepo Raty (javelin) 55 30
1368 2m.40 Type **575** 55 30

576 Crowd on Registration List

577 Emblem

1994. 450th Anniv of Population Registers.
1369 **576** 2m.40 multicoloured . . 65 25

1994. International Year of the Family.
1370 **577** 3m.40 multicoloured . . 95 65

578 Postman greeting Woman

1994. Stamp Day. Dog Hill Kids (cartoon characters) at the Post Office. Sheet 112 × 88 mm containing T **578** and similar horiz designs. Mult.
MS1371 2m.80 Type **578**; 2m.80 Postmaster handing letter to postman; 2m.80 Messenger playing bugle; 2m.80 Couple posting letters . . . . 3·75 5·25

579 Northern Bullfinches on Reindeer's Antlers

580 Postman delivering Letter to Alien

1994. Christmas. Multicoloured.
1372 2m.10 Type **579** 60 25
1373 2m.80 Father and son selecting Christmas tree (vert) 70 30

1995. Greetings stamps. Multicoloured.
1374 2m.80 Type **580** 95 40
1375 2m.80 Cat writing letter . . 95 40
1376 2m.80 Postman delivering letter to elderly dog . . . 95 40
1377 2m.80 Teenage dog writing letter 95 40
1378 2m.80 Dog receiving postcard 95 40
1379 2m.80 Dog on train reading letter 95 40
1380 2m.80 Guitarist dog with Valentine greeting 95 40
1381 2m.80 Baby dog 95 40

581 Paivi Ikola (Pesapallo)

1995. "Finlandia 95" International Stamp Exhibition, Helsinki (4th issue). Team Sports. Sheet containing T **581** and similar vert designs. Multicoloured.
MS1382 3m.40 Type **581**; 3m.40 Jari Kurri (ice hockey); 3m.40 Jari Litmanen (football); 3m.40 Lea Hakala (basketball) . . . . . 4·75 5·25

582 Shooting Star and Stars

584 Figures forming Parachute

583 "Boys playing on the Shore"

1995. Admission of Finland to European Union.
1383 **582** 3m.50 blue, yell & blk 95 60

1995. Pro Filatelia. Paintings by Albert Edelfelt. Multicoloured.
1384 2m.40+60p. Type **583** . . . 95 1·10
1385 2m.40+60p. "Queen Blanche" (21 × 30½ mm) 95 1·10

1995. Europa. Peace and Freedom.
1386 **584** 2m.90 multicoloured . . 1·10 80

585 Lynx

586 Daisy (Keski-Suomi)

1995. Endangered Animals. Multicoloured.

1387 2m.90 Type **585** 80 95
1388 2m.90 Landscape 80 95
1389 2m.90 Shoreline 80 95
1390 2m.90 Ringed seal 80 95

1995. Provincial Plants. With service indicator. Self-adhesive. Imperf.

1391 **586** 1KLASS (2m.80) mult 95 25

587 Mini

1995. "Finlandia 95" International Stamp Exhibition, Helsinki (5th issue). Motor Sports. Sheet 120 × 80 mm containing T **587** and similar vert designs. Multicoloured.

MS1392 3m.50 Type **587** (Timo Makinen, rally driver); 3m.50 Rally car (Juha Kankkunen, rally driver); 3m.50 Tommi Ahvala on motor cycle (trials); 3m.50 Heikki Mikkola on motor cycle (motocross) . . . . 4·75 5·25

588 Dung Beetle

1995. "Finlandia 95" International Stamp Exhibition, Helsinki.

1393 **588** 19m. multicoloured . . . 6·00 6·50

589 Linnanmaki Amusement Park, Helsinki

590 Loviisa Market and Church

1995. Nordic Countries' Postal Co-operation. Tourism. Multicoloured.

1394 2m.80 Type **589** 80 25
1395 2m.90 Mantyharju church (400th anniv of parish) . . 85 75

1995. 250th Anniv of Loviisa.

1396 **590** 3m.20 multicoloured . . 75 70

591 Silver Birch (incorrectly inscr "Betula pendula")

592 Rontgen Tube and X-Ray Theory

1995. 20th International Union of Forestry Research Organizations World Congress, Tampere. Leaves and flowers of trees. Multicoloured.

1397 2m.80 Type **591** 80 40
1398 2m.80 Scots pine ("Pinus sylvestris") 80 40
1399 2m.80 Norway spruce ("Picea abies") 80 40
1400 2m.80 Propagating tree from needle 80 40

1995. Centenary of Discovery of X-Rays by Wilhelm Rontgen.

1401 **592** 4m.30 multicoloured . . 1·20 85

593 Somali

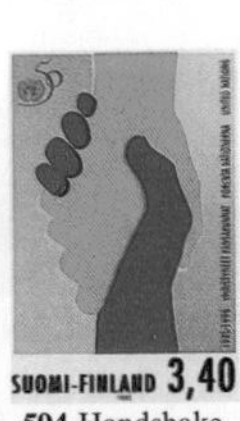

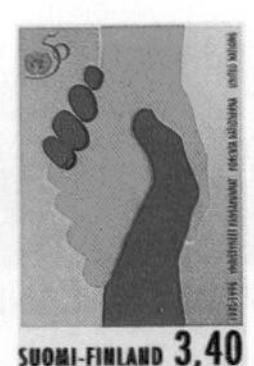

594 Handshake

1995. Cats. Multicoloured.

1402 2m.80 Type **593** . . . . . 1·20 45
1403 2m.80 Siamese . . . . . . 1·20 45
1404 2m.80 Domestic cat in grass (58 × 35 mm) . . . . . . 1·20 45
1405 2m.80 Norwegian forest cat 1·20 45
1406 2m.80 Colourpoint Persian 1·20 45
1407 2m.80 Kittens playing in grass (58 × 35 mm) . . . 1·20 45

Nos. 1404 and 1407 form a composite design.

1995. 50th Anniv of U.N.O.

1408 **594** 3m.40 multicoloured . . 85 70

595 Father Christmas on Skates

596 "O"

1995. Christmas. Multicoloured.

1409 2m. Type **595** 55 25
1410 2m.80 Poinsettias in snow (horiz) 45 35

1996. Greeting Stamps. Letters of the Alphabet.

1411 **596** 1m. vio, grn & blk ("M") 35 40
1412 1m. bl, mauve and black (Type **596**) 35 40
1413 1m. red, yell & blk ("i") 35 40
1414 1m. bl, red & blk ("H") 35 40
1415 1m. red, grn & blk ("E") 35 40
1416 1m. yell, bl & blk ("J") 35 40
1417 1m. grn, red & blk ("A") 35 40
1418 1m. yellow, mauve and black ("N") 35 40
1419 1m. yell, grn & blk ("T") 35 40
1420 1m. red, bl & blk ("P") 35 40
1421 1m. lt bl, bl & blk ("U") 35 40
1422 1m. yell, mve & blk ("S") 35 40

Nos. 1411/22 were intended to be arranged on envelopes to spell out a desired message.

597 "Smile" (Mauno Paavola)

1996. 50th Anniv of UNICEF.

1423 **597** 2m.80 multicoloured . . 65 30

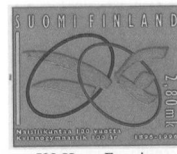

598 Hoop Exercise

1996. Centenary of Women's Gymnastics Associations in Finland.

1424 **598** 2m.80 multicoloured . . 75 30

599 Mother and Children at Polling Station

1996. Europa. 90th Anniv of Women's Suffrage in Finland.

1425 **599** 3m.20 multicoloured . . 1·00 80

600 Chicks

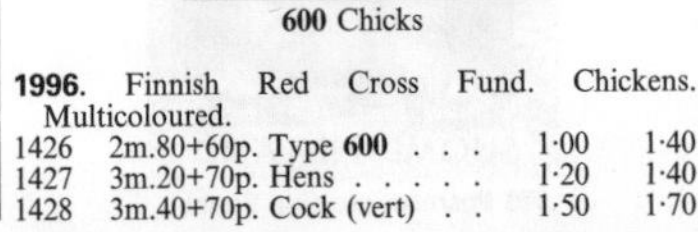

1996. Finnish Red Cross Fund. Chickens. Multicoloured.

1426 2m.80+60p. Type **600** . . . 1·00 1·40
1427 3m.20+70p. Hens . . . . . 1·20 1·40
1428 3m.40+70p. Cock (vert) . . 1·50 1·70

601 J. Gronroos (circus director) at Film Projector

1996. Centenary of Motion Pictures. Mult.

1429 2m.80 Valle Saikko and Irma Seikkula in "Juha" 75 45
1430 2m.80 Alli Riks and Theodor Tugai in "Wide Road" ("Den Breda Vagen") 75 45
1431 2m.80 Ake Lindman in "The Unknown Soldier" ("Okana Soldat") 75 45
1432 2m.80 Type **601** 75 45
1433 2m.80 Antti Litja in "Year of the Hare" ("Harens Ar") 75 45
1434 2m.80 Mirjami Kuosmanen in "The White Forest" ("Den Vita Renen") . . . 75 45
1435 2m.80 Ansa Ikonen and Tauno Palo in "Complete Love" ("Alla Alskar") . . 75 45
1436 2m.80 Matti Pellonpaa in "Shadow in Paradise" ("Skuggor i Paradiset") 75 45

602 Radio Waves

1996. Centenary (1995) of First Radio Transmission.

1437 **602** 4m.30 multicoloured . . 1·00 1·20

603 Canoeing

604 White Water Lily (Southern Savonia)

1996. Centenary of Modern Olympic Games. Watersports. Multicoloured.

1438 3m.40 Type **603** . . . . . 95 1·10
1439 3m.40 Sailing . . . . 95 1·10
1440 3m.40 Rowing . . . . . . 95 1·10
1441 3m.40 Swimming . . . . . 95 1·10

1996. Provincial Plants. With service indicator. Self-adhesive. Imperf.

1442 **604** 1KLASS (2m.80) mult 95 25

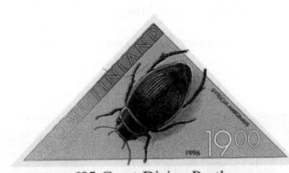

605 Great Diving Beetle

1996.

1443 **605** 19m. multicoloured . . . 6·00 6·25

606 Common Snipe ("Gallinago gallinago")

607 Professor Itikaisen (Ilmari Vainio)

1996. Stamp Day. Wading Birds. Sheet 121 × 72 mm containing T **606** and similar vert designs. Multicoloured.

MS1444 2m.80 Curlew ("Numenius arquata") (29 × 53 mm); 2m.80 Type **606**; 2m.80 Oystercatcher ("Haematopus ostralegus"); 2m.80 Woodcock ("Scolopax rusticola"); 2m.80 Lapwing ("Vanellus vanellus") . . . . 4·75 5·00

1996. Centenary of Comic Strips. Each red and black.

1445 2m.80 Type **607** 75 50
1446 2m.80 Pekka Puupaa (Peter Blockhead) receiving letter from booth (Ola Fogelberg) 75 50
1447 2m.80 Joonas resting chin on hand (Veikko Savolainen) 75 50
1448 2m.80 Posti-Aune from "Mammila" in motor cycle helmet (Tarmo Koivisto) 75 50
1449 2m.80 Rymy-Eetu smoking pipe (Erkki Tanttu) . . . 75 50
1450 2m.80 Kieku (duck) writing letter (Asmo Alho) . . . 75 50
1451 2m.80 Pikku Risunen from "Hyvissa naimisissa" (Well-married) in headdress with big ears (Riitta Uusitalo) 75 50
1452 2m.80 Kiti from "Vihrea Rapsodia" (Green Rhapsody) holding pencil (Kati Kovacs) 75 50

608 Father Christmas and Musicians

609 Player

1996. Christmas. Multicoloured.

1453 2m. Type **608** 55 25
1454 2m.80 Reindeer and hare . . 65 30
1455 3m.20 Father Christmas reading letters (vert) . . . 85 50

1997. World Ice Hockey Championship, Helsinki, Turku and Tampere.

1456 **609** 2m.80 multicoloured . . 75 25

610 Parcel

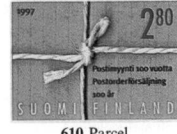

1997. Cent of Mail Order Sales in Finland.

1457 **610** 2m.80 multicoloured . . 65 60

611 Angels

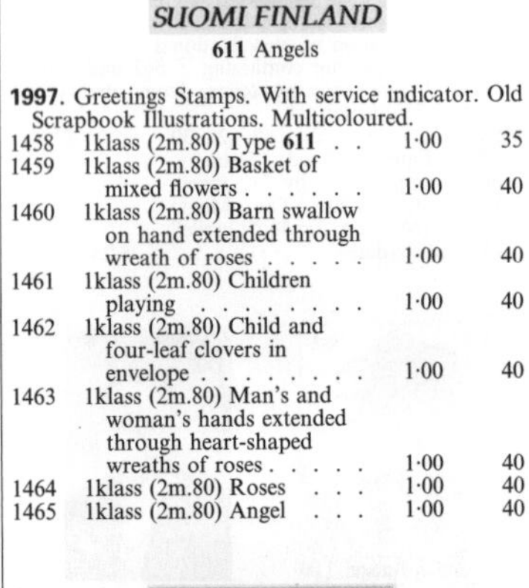

1997. Greetings Stamps. With service indicator. Old Scrapbook Illustrations. Multicoloured.

1458 1klass (2m.80) Type **611** . . 1·00 35
1459 1klass (2m.80) Basket of mixed flowers . . . . . . 1·00 40
1460 1klass (2m.80) Barn swallow on hand extended through wreath of roses . . . . . 1·00 40
1461 1klass (2m.80) Children playing . . . . 1·00 40
1462 1klass (2m.80) Child and four-leaf clovers in envelope . . . . 1·00 40
1463 1klass (2m.80) Man's and woman's hands extended through heart-shaped wreaths of roses . . . . 1·00 40
1464 1klass (2m.80) Roses . . . 1·00 40
1465 1klass (2m.80) Angel . . . 1·00 40

612 Arctic Hares

1997. Easter.

1466 **612** 2m.80 multicoloured . . 70 30

613 Golden Merganser casting Reflection of Girl
614 Bird Cherry (Birkaland)

1997. Europa. Tales and Legends. "The Girl who turned into a Golden Merganser" (folktale). Illustrations by Mika Launis. Multicoloured.
1467 3m.20 Type **613** . . . . . 1·00 30
1468 3m.40 Girl falling into water 1·40 85

1997. Provincial Plants. With service indicator. Self-adhesive. Imperf.
1469 **614** 1KLASS (2m.80) mult 95 50

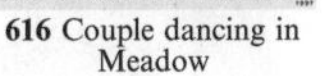

615 Nurmi running 3000 m (Olympic Games, Paris, 1924)
616 Couple dancing in Meadow

1997. Birth Cent of Paavo Nurmi (runner).
1470 **615** 3m.40 multicoloured . . 95 55

1997. The Tango. With service indicator.
1471 **616** 1klass (2m.80) black and pink 95 50

617 "Astrid" (galeasse)
618 Globe and Ahtisaari

1997. Centenary of Finnish Lifeboat Society. Sailing Ships. Multicoloured.
1472 2m.80 Type **617** 80 40
1473 2m.80 "Jacobstads Wapen" (replica of schooner) . . . 80 55
1474 2m.80 "Suomen Joutsen" (cadet ship) (48 × 25 mm) 80 55
1475 2m.80 "Tradewind" (brigantine) 80 55
1476 2m.80 "Merikokko" (lifeboat) 80 55
1477 2m.80 "Sigyn" (barque) (48 × 25 mm) 80 55

1997. 60th Birthday of President Martii Ahtisaari.
1478 **618** 2m.80 multicoloured . . 65 25

619 Clouds (Summer)
620 Crane with Chick

1997. 80th Anniv of Independence. The Four Seasons. Multicoloured.
1479 2m.80 Lily of the valley (Spring) 85 50
1480 2m.80 Type **619** 85 50
1481 2m.80 Leaves (Autumn) . . 85 50
1482 2m.80 Snowflakes (Winter) 85 50

1997. The Common Crane (Grus grus). Sheet 120 × 80 mm containing T **620** and similar multicoloured designs.
MS1483 2m.80 Type **620**; 2m.80 Adults, one with frog in beak; 2m.80 Courting dance; 2m.80 Adults in flight (31 × 34 mm) 3·75 3·75

621 Vainamoinen proposing to Aino
622 "Seven Brothers" (Aleksis Kivi)

1997. Pro Filatelia. "Aino" (triptych) by Akseli Gallen-Kallela. Multicoloured.
1484 2m.80+60p. Type **621** . . . 1·30 1·10
1485 2m.80+60p. Aino in water escaping from Vainamoinen (33 × 47 mm) . . . . . . 1·30 1·10
1486 2m.80+60p. Mermaids luring Aino into water . . 1·30 1·10

1997. Centenary of Finnish Writers' Association. Book Covers. Multicoloured.
1487 2m.80 Type **622** 75 50
1488 2m.80 "Sinuhe the Eyptian" (Mika Waltari) 75 50
1489 2m.80 "Under the North Star" (Vaino Linna) . . . 75 50
1490 2m.80 "Farewell River Iijoki" (Kalle Paatalo) . . 75 50
1491 2m.80 "Eagle, My Beloved" (Kaari Utrio) 75 50
1492 2m.80 "Midsummer Dance" (Hannu Salama) 75 50
1493 2m.80 "Manilla Rope" (Veijo Meri) 75 50
1494 2m.80 "Uppo-Nalle ja Kumma" (Elina Karjalainen) 75 50

623 Church and Houses

1997. Christmas. Multicoloured.
1495 2m. Type **623** 55 25
1496 2m.80 Candelabra, Petajavesi Church (vert) 75 35
1497 3m.20 St. John's Church, Eira, Helsinki (35 × 24 mm) 85 50

624 Zander

1998. Provincial Birds and Fish (1st series). Uusimaa. With service indicator. Mult. Self-adhesive.
1498 2klass (2m.40) Type **624** . . 75 70
1499 1KLASS (2m.80) Blackbird 95 25

625 Moominpappa writing Play
626 Nurses of 1898 and 1998

1998. Moomin. Illustrations from her stories by Tove Jansson. With service indicator. Multicoloured.
1500 1klass (2m.80) Type **625** . . 1·30 40
1501 1klass (2m.80) Moomin-mamma making jam . . . 1·30 40
1502 1klass (2m.80) Too-ticky playing barrel organ and Littly My dancing . . . . 1·30 40
1503 1klass (2m.80) Moomintroll dancing with the Snork Maiden . . . . 1·30 40

1998. Cent of Finnish Federation of Nurses.
1504 **626** 2m.80 multicoloured . . 70 25

627 Gold Heart and Musical Notes
628 Harebell (Central Ostrobothnia)

1998. St. Valentine's Day. With service indicator. Multicoloured.
1505 1klass (2m.80) Type **627** . . 1·00 50
1506 1klass (2m.80) Gold heart and elephant . . . . . 1·00 50
1507 1klass (2m.80) Gold heart and puppy on blanket . 1·00 50
1508 1klass (2m.80) Gold heart and kittens . . . . 1·00 50
1509 1klass (2m.80) Gold heart and dog . . . . 1·00 50
1510 1klass (2m.80) Gold heart and flowers . . . . 1·00 50

The gold hearts could be scratched off to reveal a complete design.

1998. Provincial Plants. With service indicator. Self-adhesive. Imperf.
1511 **628** 1KLASS (2m.80) mult 95 25

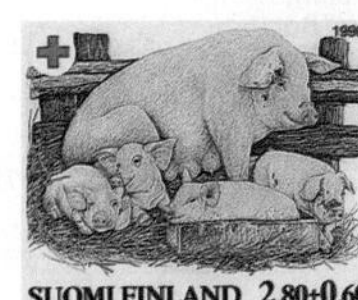

629 Sow and Litter
630 Coltsfoot

1998. Finnish Red Cross Fund. Pigs. Mult.
1512 2m.80+60p. Type **629** . . . 1·00 1·30
1513 3m.20+70p. Three piglets . . 1·30 1·50
1514 3m.40+70p. Boar . . . . . 1·30 1·50

1998. Spring.
1515 **630** 2m.80 multicoloured . . 70 25

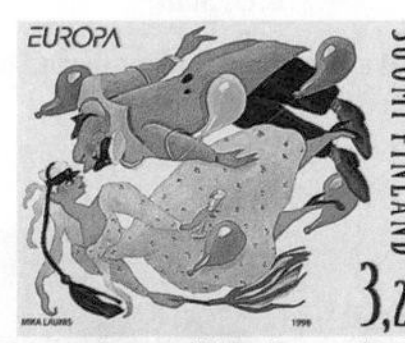

631 Students with Balloons (Labour Day)

1998. Europa. National Festivals. Mult.
1516 3m.20 Type **631** 95 40
1517 3m.40 Couple by lake (Midsummer) . . . . . . 1·30 1·20

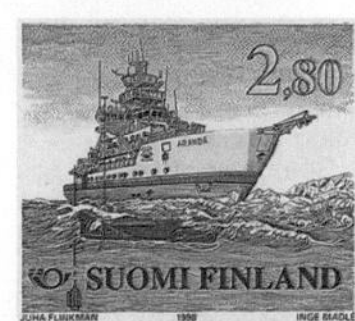

632 "Aranda" (research vessel)

1998. Nordic Countries' Postal Co-operation. Shipping. Multicoloured.
1518 2m.80 Type **632** (80th anniv of Finnish Marine Research Institute) . . . 75 30
1519 3m.20 "Vega" (120th anniv of Nils Nordenskjold's navigation of the North-east Passage) 95 70

633 Flag and Score

1998. 150th Anniv of First Performance of "Our Country" (national anthem).
1520 **633** 5m. multicoloured . . . 1·40 90

634 Bernese Mountain Dog
635 Downhill Competitor and 19th-century Cyclist

1998. World Dog Show, Helsinki. With service indicator. Multicoloured.
1521 1klass (2m.80) Type **634** . . 1·00 50
1522 1klass (2m.80) Pumis . . . 1·00 50
1523 1klass (2m.80) Boxers . . . 1·00 50
1524 1klass (2m.80) Bichon frises 1·00 50
1525 1klass (2m.80) Finnish lapphounds . . . . . . 1·00 50
1526 1klass (2m.80) Dachshunds 1·00 50
1527 1klass (2m.80) Cairn terriers 1·00 50
1528 1klass (2m.80) Labrador retrievers . . . . 1·00 50

1998. Centenary of Cycling Union of Finland.
1529 **635** 3m. multicoloured . . . 85 65

636 Eagle Owl "Bubo bubo"
638 Children and Christmas Tree

637 Kilta Tableware (Kaj Franck)

1998. Stamp Day. Owls. Sheet 120 × 80 mm containing T **636** and similar multicoloured designs.
MS1530 3m. Type **636**; 3m. Wing-tip of eagle owl (25 × 49 mm); 3m. Tengmalm's owl ("Aegolius funereus") (23 × 42 mm); 3m. Great grey owl ("Stris nebulosa") (24 × 42 mm); 3m. Snowy owl ("Nyctea scandiaca") (29 × 42 mm) . . . . 4·75 4·75

1998. Finnish Industrial Design. Mult.
1531 3m. Savoy Vase (Alvar Aalto) 95 70
1532 3m. Karuselli 412 chair (Yrjo Kukkapuro) (29 × 34 mm) 95 70
1533 3m. Tasaraita T-shirts (Annika Rimala) (29 × 34 mm) 95 70
1534 3m. Type **637** 95 70
1535 3m. Cast-iron cooking pot (Timo Sarpaneva) (29 × 34 mm) 95 70
1536 3m. Carelia cutlery (Bertel Gardberg) (29 × 34 mm) 95 70

1998. Christmas. Multicoloured.
1537 2m. Type **638** 55 25
1538 3m. Children tobogganing (horiz) 75 35
1539 3m.20 Snow-bound cottage on island (horiz) 95 50

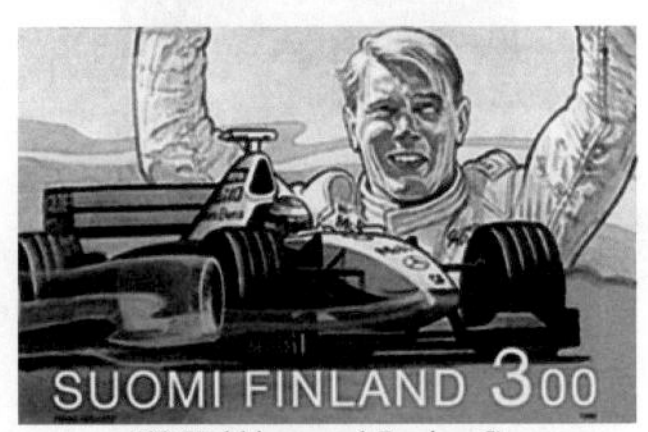

639 Hakkinen and Racing Car

1999. Mika Hakkinen, Formula 1 World Champion 1998. Sheet 115 × 70 mm.
MS1540 **639** 3m. multicoloured 1·40 1·20

640 Atlantic Salmon

1999. Provincial Birds and Fish (2nd series). Lapland. With service indicator. Multicoloured. Self-adhesive.
1541 2klass (2m.40) Type **640** . . 75 55
1542 1KLASS (3m.) Bluethroat (vert) 95 35

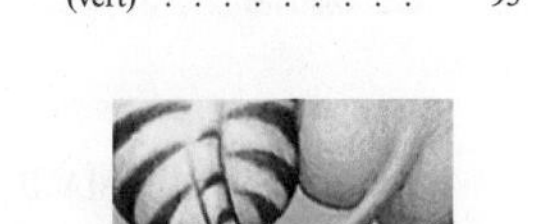

641 Zebra and Lion Tails

1999. Friendship. Multicoloured. Self-adhesive.
1543 3m. Type **641** 95 70
1544 3m. Cat and dog tails . . . 95 70

642 Monument to Eetu Salin (founder) (Aimo Tukiainen)

1999. Centenary of Founding of Finnish Labour Party (predecessor of Social Democrat Party).
1545 **642** 4m.50 multicoloured . . 1·20 1·30

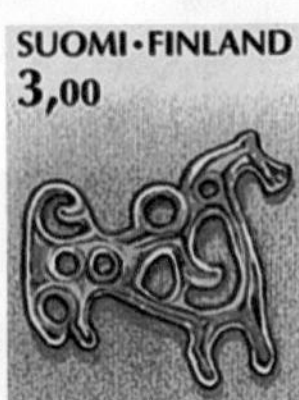

643 Horse Brooch

1999. 150th Anniv of New Kalevala (Karelian poems collected by Elias Lonnrot). Sheet 120×74 mm containing T **643** and similar vert designs. Multicoloured.
MS1546 3m. Type **643**; 3m. Kuhmoinen Cocks brooch; 3m. Virusmaki brooch . . . . . . 2·75 3·00

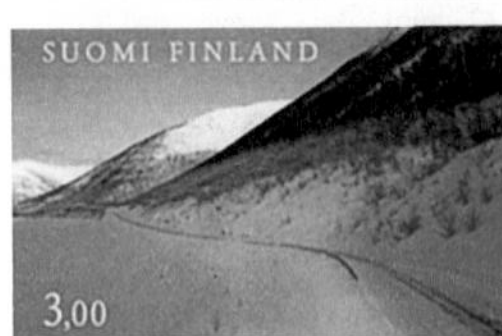

644 Road by River Tenojoki, Utsjoki

1999. Bicentenary of National Road Administration. Multicoloured.
1547 3m. Type **644** 95 55
1548 3m. Motorway intersection, Jyvaskyla 95 55
1549 3m. Raippaluoto bridge, Vaasa 95 55
1550 3m. North Karelian forest road, Kitee 95 55

645 Esplanade, Helsinki

1999. Europa. Parks and Gardens. Multicoloured.
1551 2m.70 Type **645** 95 80
1552 3m.20 Ruissalo island, Turku . . . . 1·10 65

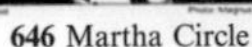

646 Martha Circle **647** Crocuses

1999. Centenary of Martha Organization (for education and development of women).
1553 **646** 3m. multicoloured . . . 75 70

1999. Easter.
1554 **647** 3m. multicoloured . . . 75 35

648 Cowslip (Aland Islands) **649** Nightingale ("Luscinia luscinia")

1999. Provincial Plants. With service indicator. Self-adhesive. Imperf.
1555 **648** 1KLASS (3m.) mult . . 95 25

1999. Nocturnal Summer Birds. Sheet 120×80 mm containing T **649** and similar multicoloured designs.
MS1556 3m. Type **649**; 3m. European cuckoo ("Cuculus canorus) (24×39½ mm); 3m. Eurasian bittern ("Botaurus stellaris") (44×29 mm); 3m. European nightjar ("Caprimulgus europaeus") (24½×36 mm); 3m. Corncrake ("Crex crex") (24½×37 mm) . . . . 4·75 4·75

650 Figure reaching for E.U. Stars

1999. Finland's Presidency of European Union.
1557 **650** 3m.50 multicoloured . . 95 45

651 Harmony Sisters

1999. Entertainers. Multicoloured.
1558 3m.50 Type **651** . . . . . 1·00 70
1559 3m.50 Olavi Virta (tango and jazz singer) (29×34 mm) . . . . . . 1·00 70
1560 3m.50 Georg Malmsten (composer and band leader) (29×34 mm) . . . 1·00 70
1561 3m.50 Topi Karki (composer) and Reino Helismaa (lyricist) . . . . 1·00 70
1562 3m.50 Tapio Rautavaara (composer and folk singer) (29×34 mm) . . . 1·00 70
1563 3m.50 Esa Pakarinen (folk artist and actor) (29×34 mm) . . . . . . 1·00 70

652 "Garden of Death" **654** Santa Claus

653 Fiskars Secateurs and Pruning Shears Designed by Olavi Linden

1999. Pro Filatelia. Paintings by Hugo Simberg. Multicoloured.
1564 3m.50+50p. Type **652** . . . 1·00 1·30
1565 3m.50+50p. "Wounded Angel" . . . . 1·00 1·30

1999. Finnish Industrial Design. Multicoloured.
1566 3m.50 Type **653** . . . . . 1·00 70
1567 3m.50 Zoel Versoul guitar (Kari Nieminen) (29×34½mm) . . . . . . 1·00 70
1568 3m.50 Ergo II Silenta hearing protectors (Jyrki Jarvinen) (29×34½ mm) 1·00 70
1569 3m.50 Ponsse Cobra HS10 harvester (Pentti Hukkanen, Jorma Hyvonen, Jouko Kelppe and Heikki Koivurova) 1·00 70
1570 3m.50 Suunto sailing compass (Heikki Metsa-Ketela and Erikki Vainio) (29×34½ mm) . . . . . 1·00 70
1571 3m.50 Exel Avanti QLS ski stick (Pasi Jarvinen, Matti Lyly and Mika Vesalainen) (29×34½ mm) 1·00 70

1999. Christmas. Multicoloured.
1572 2m.50 Type **654** 75 30
1573 3m. "Nativity" (Giorgio de Chirico) (horiz) 75 55
1574 3m.50 Two hares (horiz) . . 95 45

655 Earth, Sun and Moon

2000. Friendship. Multicoloured.
1575 3m.50 Type **655** . . . . . 1·10 65
1576 3m.50 Painting a smile on Jupiter . . . . 1·10 65
1577 3m.50 Birds using Neptune as balloon . . . . 1·10 65
1578 3m.50 Martian using magnet to rescue traveller from Mars . . . . 1·10 65
1579 3m.50 People on Saturn's rings . . . . 1·10 65
1580 3m.50 Pluto as igloo and polar bear . . . . 1·10 65

656 Herring Market

2000. 450th Anniv of Helsinki (European City of Culture, 2000). Multicoloured.
1581 3m.50 Type **656** . . . . . 1·00 95
1582 3m.50 Museum of Contemporary Art, Kiasma (24×48 mm) . . 1·00 1·00
1583 3m.50 Statue and Cathedral, Senate Square (42×24 mm) . . . . . . 1·00 1·00
1584 3m.50 Finlandia Hall (42×24 mm) . . . . . . 1·00 1·00
1585 3m.50 Glass Palace Film and Media Centre (24×48 mm) . . . . . . 1·00 1·00
1586 3m.50 "Looking for the Lost Crown" (children's tour), Suomenlin Sea Fortress (24×48 mm) . . 1·00 1·00
1587 3m.50 Type **656** . . . . . 1·00 1·00
1588 3m.50 "Forces of Light" celebration (42×24 mm) 1·00 1·00
1589 3m.50 Open-air concert, Kaivopuisto Park (24×48 mm) 85 80

657 Fortifications at Sveaborg **659** Marsh Marigold

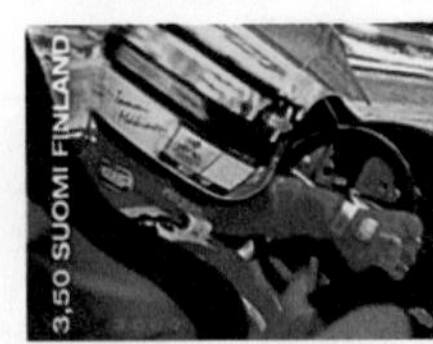

658 Makinen at Wheel of Rally Car

2000. Sveaborg Fortress.
1590 **657** 7m.20 multicoloured . . 1·80 1·40

2000. Tommi Makinen, Rally World Champion (1999). Sheet 109×80 mm containing T **658** and similar horiz design. Multicoloured.
MS1591 3m.50 Type **658**; 3m.50 Mitsubishi Lancer rally car . . 2·20 2·20

2000. Spring.
1592 **659** 3m.50 multicoloured . . 95 45

660 Interior of Turku Cathedral

2000. Holy Year 2000. 700th Anniv of Turku Cathedral. Multicoloured.
1593 3m.50 Type **660** . . . . . 1·00 90
1594 3m.50 Woman lighting candle . . . . 1·00 1·00
1595 3m.50 "Transfiguration of Christ" (altarpiece) . . . 1·00 1·00
1596 3m.50 Christening . . . . . 1·00 90

661 Emma the Theatre Rat and Moomins at Table **662** Bull

2000. Moomin. Illustrations from her stories by Tove Jansson. With service indicator. Multicoloured.
1597 1klass (3m.50) Type **661** . . 1·00 55
1598 1klass (3m.50) Park keeper and Hattifatteners growing from the grass 1·00 55
1599 1klass (3m.50) Snufkin walking through forest . . 1·00 55
1600 1klass (3m.50) Snufkin surrounded by forest children . . . . 1·00 55

2000. Finnish Red Cross Fund. Cattle. Multicoloured.
1601 3m.50+70p. Type **662** . . . 1·30 1·10
1602 4m.80+80p. Cow and calf (horiz) . . . . 1·50 1·50

663 "Building Europe" **664** Spring Anemone (South Karelia)

2000. Europa.
1603 **663** 3m.50 multicoloured . . 1·00 55

2000. Provincial Plants. With service indicator. Self-adhesive. Imperf.
1604 **664** 1KLASS (3m.50) mult 95 25

665 Girls in Laboratory

2000. Heureka Science Centre. Sheet 120×80 mm containing T **665** and similar multicoloured designs.
MS1605 3m.50 Type **665**; 3m.50 DNA double helix and man's face (parallelogram, 20×20 mm); 3m.50 Man's face and Sierinski Triangle aerial (27×27 mm) . . 3·25 3·25

666 Common Whitefish

2000. Provincial Birds and Fish (3rd series). Southern Lapland. With service indicator. Multicoloured. Self-adhesive.
1606 2klass (2m.70) Type **666** . . 75 60
1607 1KLASS (3m.30) Willow grouse 95 65

667 "Flame" Rug (Akseli Gallen-Kallela)

2000. Finnish Industrial Design. Multicoloured.
1608 3m.50 Type **667** 90 65
1609 3m.50 Pearl Bird (Birger Kaipiainen) (29 × 34 mm) 90 65
1610 3m.50 Pot (Kyllikki Salmenhaara) (29 × 34 mm) 90 65
1611 3m.50 "Leaf" platter (Tapio Wirkkala) 90 65
1612 3m.50 "Lichen" (furnishing fabric pattern, Dora Jung) (29 × 34 mm) 90 65
1613 3m.50 Glass vase (Valter Jung) (29 × 34 mm) . . . 90 65

668 Three Wise Men and Star

2000. Christmas. Multicoloured. Self-adhesive.
1614 2m.50 Type **668** 70 30
1615 3m.50 Northern bullfinch sitting on wreath (vert) . . 95 45

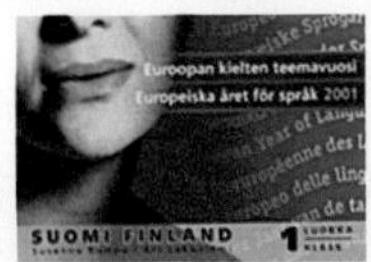
669 Woman's Head

2001. European Year of Languages. With service indicator.
1616 **669** 1KLASS (3m.50) mult 95 35

670 Janne Ahonen (ski jumper)

2001. Nordic World Skiing Championships, Lahti. Multicoloured.
1617 3m.50 Type **670** 65 40
1618 3m.50 Mika Myllyla 65 40

671 Garland of Flowers

672 Cover of First Magazine published in Finland, 1951

2001. Greetings Stamps. Flowers. Multicoloured. Self-adhesive.
1619 1KLASS (3m.50) Type **671** 90 55
1620 1KLASS (3m.50) Basket of flowers 90 55
1621 1KLASS (3m.50) Heart-shaped garland 90 55
1622 1KLASS (3m.50) Bouquet 90 55
1623 1KLASS (3m.50) Flowers, cake and cups 90 55
1624 1KLASS (3m.50) Flowers and heart-shaped cake . . 90 55

2001. 50th Anniv of The Donald Duck Magazine in Finland. Sheet 130 × 80 mm containing T **672** and similar vert designs. Multicoloured.
MS1625 1klass Type **672**; 1klass Silhouette of boy and page from magazine; 1klass Toy carrying flag and Chip and Dale (24 × 30 mm); 1klass Silhouette of Donald Duck and Vainamoinen; 1klass Donald Duck and Helsinki Cathedral 5·50 3·75

673 Father Christmas in Sleigh

2001. Santa Claus. With service indicator. Self-adhesive.
1630 **673** 1klass (3m.50) multicoloured . . . . 1·00 75

674 Haapavitja Rapids, Ruunaa

2001. Europa. Water Resources.
1631 **674** 5m.40 multicoloured . . 1·60 1·40

675 Face of Chick

676 Roof of Mill and Trees

2001. Easter. Multicoloured.
1632 3m.60 Type **675** 90 45
1633 3m.60 Easter egg 90 45

2001. Verla Groundwood and Board Mill Museum, Jaala. Sheet 80 × 120 mm containing T **676** and similar vert designs. Multicoloured.
MS1634 3m.60 Type **676**; 3m.60 Mill manager's house, mill building and river; 3m.60 Main mill building and trees; 3m.60 Mill building and river . . . . 4·75 3·00

677 Lesser Spotted Woodpecker (*Dendrocopos minor*)

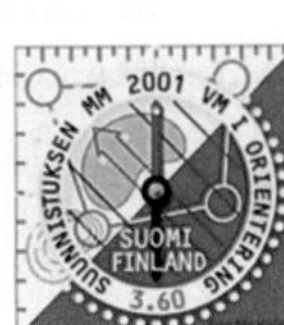
678 Compass and Emblem

2001. Woodpeckers. Sheet 79 × 119 mm containing T **677** and similar vert designs. Mult.
MS1635 3m.60 Type **677**; 3m.60 Three-toed woodpecker (*Picoides tridactylus*) (28 × 35 mm); 3m.60 White-backed woodpecker (*Dendrocopos leucotos*) (32 × 41 mm); 3m.60 Great spotted woodpecker (*Dendrocopos major*) (28 × 41 mm); 3m.60 Grey-headed green woodpecker (*Picus canus*) (32 × 41 mm); 3m.60 Black woodpecker (*Dryocopus martius*) (28 × 41 mm) . . . . 6·50 6·50

2001. Orienteering World Championship, Tampere.
1636 **678** 3m.60 multicoloured . . 1·10 45

679 Cornflower (Pajat-Hame)

680 Lampern (*Lampetra fluviatilis*)(Satakunta)

2001. Provincial Flowers. With service indicator. Self-adhesive.
1637 1KLASS (3m.50) Type **679** 80 45
1638 1KLASS (3m.50) Pasque flower (Kanta-Hame) . . 80 45

2001. Provincial Fish. With service indicator. Multicoloured. Self-adhesive.
1639 2klass (2m.70) Type **680** . . 65 65
1640 2klass (2m.70) Asp (*Aspius aspius*) (Pirkanmaa) . . . 65 65
1641 2klass (2m.70) Vendace (*Coregonus albula*) (Savonia) 65 65

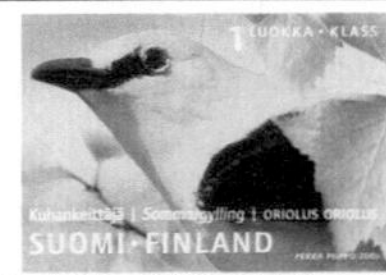
681 Golden Oriole (*Oriolus oriolus*) (Satakunta)

2001. Provincial Birds. With service indicator. Multicoloured. Self-adhesive.
1642 1KLASS (3m.60) Type **681** 85 50
1643 1KLASS (3m.60) Blue tit (*Parus caeruleus*) (Pirkanmaa) 85 50
1644 1KLASS (3m.60) Pied wagtail (*Motacilla alba*) (South Savonia) 85 55

682 18th-century Captain's Quarters, Merchant Ship

2001. Gulf of Finland (1st series). Multicoloured.
1645 1KLASS (3m.60) Type **682** 90 60
1646 1KLASS (3m.60) Uto Lighthouse (32 × 27 mm) 90 60
1647 1KLASS (3m.60) *Sankt Mikael* (Dutch sailing ship) (33 × 27 mm) . . . 90 60
1648 1KLASS (3m.60) Diver on *Sankt Mikael* and treasure (33 × 27 mm) 90 60
1649 1KLASS (3m.60) Opossum shrimp, isopod and bladder wrack (33 × 27 mm) 90 60
See also Nos. 1675/9 and 1753/7.

683 Elf Girl reading

684 Water Forget-me-not (*Myosotis scorpoides*)

2001. Christmas. Multicoloured. Self-adhesive.
1650 2m.50 Type **683** 85 30
1651 3m.60 Elf boy sledding (horiz) . . . . 1·00 45

New currency. 100cents = 1 euro

2002. Flowers. Showing water forget-me-nots (5c.) or lily-of-the-valley (10c.). Multicoloured. Self-adhesive.
1652 5c. Type **684** 15 20
1653 5c. Four flowers 15 20
1654 5c. One open flower and four buds 15 20
1655 5c. Spray of flowers 15 20
1656 5c. Five flower heads . . . 15 20
1657 10c. Spray of five lily-of-the-valley flowers (*Convallaria majallis*) 25 20
1658 10c. Spray of eight flowers between two leaves . . . 25 20
1659 10c. Two flowers 25 20
1660 10c. Spray of six flowers against leaf 25 20
1661 10c. Lily-of-the-valley growing through grass . . 25 20

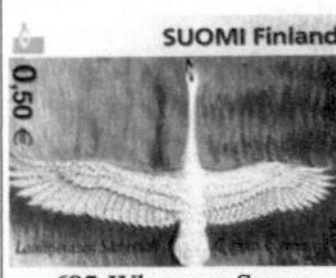
685 Whooper Swan (*Cygnus cygnus*)

686 Birch (*Betula pendula*)

2002. Self-adhesive.
1662 **685** 50c. multicoloured . . . 75 55

2002. Trees. Self-adhesive.
1663 60c. Type **686** 85 30
1664 €2.50 Norway spruce (*Picea abies*) . . . . . . 3·75 2·20
1665 €3.50 Scots pine (*Pinus sylvestris*) . . . . 5·00 3·50

687 National Flag .

2002. With service indicator. Self-adhesive.
1666 **687** 1klass (60c.) multicoloured 95 70
No. 1666 was for use on domestic first class mail.

688 "Kymintehtaalta" (Victor Westerholm)

689 Heraldic Lion

2002. Finnish Landscapes. Self-adhesive. Multicoloured.
1667 90c. Type **688** . . . . . . 1·30 1·20
1668 €1.30 Granite substrata . . 1·90 1·40

2002. Winning entry in Stamp Design Competition. Multicoloured. Self- adhesive.
1669 €1 Type **689** . . . . 1·40 1·10
1670 €5 No. 1668 . . . . 7·00 4·75

690 Witch riding Broomstick

2002. Easter. Self-adhesive.
1671 **690** 60c. multicoloured . . . 95 65

691 Plantain

693 Circus Performers

692 Houses

2002. Birth Bicentenary of Elias Lonnrot (linguist, botanist and physician). Sheet 120 × 80 mm, containing T **691** and similar vert designs. Multicoloured.
MS1672 60c. Type **691**; 60c. Tip of feather and text; 60c. Base of feather and text; 60c. Elias Lonnrot . . . . 3·50 3·75

2002. UNESCO World Heritage Site. 560th Anniv of Rauma. Sheet 82 × 122 mm, containing T **692** and similar vert designs. Multicoloured.
MS1673 60c. Type **692**; 60c. Church of the Holy Cross; 60c. Left side of Rauma museum (face value at left); 60c. Right side of museum (face value at right) . . . . . 3·50 3·75

2002. Europa. Circus.
1674 **693** 60c. multicoloured . . . 95 65

694 Fishing Boat and Net

2002. Gulf of Finland (2nd series). Multicoloured.
1675 1KLASS (60c.) Type **694** . . 85 80
1676 1KLASS (60c.) Arctic terns, island and perch (fish) (32 × 27 mm) 85 80
1677 1KLASS (60c.) Island, dinghy and buoy (32 × 27 mm) 85 80
1678 1KLASS (60c.) Flounder (32 × 27 mm) 85 80
1679 1KLASS (60c.) Zooplankton, herring and cod (32 × 27 mm) 85 80
Nos. 1675/9 were issued together, se-tenant, forming a composite design.

695 "Passio Muscicae" (Sibelius Monument) (sculpture, Eila Hiltunen)

2002. Nordic Countries' Postal Co-operation. Modern Art.
1680 **695** 60c. multicoloured . . . 95 40

696 Juniper (*Juniperus communis*)

2002. Self-adhesive.
1681 **696** 60c. multicoloured . . . 95 50

697 Reindeer, Lapland

2002. Self-adhesive.
1682 **697** 60c. multicoloured . . . 95 65

698 Horse-drawn Sleigh

2002. Christmas. Multicoloured. Self-adhesive.
1683 45c. Type **698** 65 60
1684 60c. Angel (vert) 95 70

699 Northern Pike (*Esox lucius*)

2003. Provincial Fish. With service indicator. Multicoloured. Self-adhesive.
1685 2KLASS (50c.) Type **699** . . 95 95
1686 2KLASS (50c.) Bream (*Abramis brama*) 95 95
1687 2KLASS (50c.) Lake trout (*Salmo trutta lacustris*) . . 95 95

700 European Cuckoo (*Cuculus canorus*)

2003. Provincial Birds. With service indicator. Multicoloured. Self-adhesive.
1688 1KLASS (60c.) Type **700** . . 1·10 1·10
1689 1KLASS (60c.) Eurasian sky lark (*Alauda arvensis*) . . 1·10 1·10
1690 1KLASS (60c.) Siberian jay (*Perisoreus infaustus*) . . . 1·10 1·10

701 Viivi and Wagner

2003. Friendship. With service indicator. Showing Viivi and Wagner (cartoon characters). Multicoloured. Self-adhesive.
1691 1KLASS (60c.) Type **701** . . 1·10 1·10
1692 1KLASS (60c.) Dancing . . 1·10 1·10
1693 1KLASS (60c.) Viivi writing letter . . . . 1·10 1·10
1694 1KLASS (60c.) In bed . . . 1·10 1·10
1695 1KLASS (60c.) Kissing . . 1·10 1·10
1696 1KLASS (60c.) Wagner receiving letter . . . . . 1·10 1·10

702 Games Mascot

703 Pansy (*Viola wittrockiana*)

2003. World Ice Hockey Championships, Helsinki, Tampere and Turku.
1697 **702** 65c. multicoloured . . . 1·20 1·20

2003. Self-adhesive.
1698 **703** 65c. multicoloured . . . 1·20 1·20

704 St. Birgitta (Bridget) (detail, altar screen, Naantali Convent Church)

705 Super Caravelle

2003. 700th Birth Anniv of St. Birgitta.
1699 **704** 65c. multicoloured . . . 1·20 1·20

2003. Centenary of First Powered Flight. 80th Anniv of Finnair. Multicoloured.
1700 65c. Type **705** . . . . . . 1·20 1·20
1701 65c. Airbus 320 . . . . . . 1·20 1·20
1702 65c. Junkers Ju 52/3m . . . 1·20 1·20
1703 65c. Douglas DC-3 . . . . 1·20 1·20

706 "The Fighting Capercailles" (Ferdinand von Wright)

707 Heart (Lasse Hietala)

2003. Self-adhesive.
1704 **706** 90c. multicoloured . . . 1·70 1·70

2003. Europa. Poster Art. Design showing "Someone is waiting for your letter" posters by Lasse Hietala. Multicoloured.
1705 65c. Type **707** . . . . . . 1·20 1·20
1706 65c. Mother . . . . 1·20 1·20

708 Butterfly

709 Moomin Family

2003. Summer. T **708** and similar multicoloured designs.
MS1707 65c. Type **708**; 65c. Dragonfly (45 × 35 mm); 65c. Flowers and caterpillar; 65c. Frog (45 × 36 mm); 65c. Magpie (36 × 46 mm) (vert); 65c. Hedgehogs (45 × 29 mm) . . . 7·50 7·50

2003. Moomins. With service indicator. Illustrations from Moominland Midwinter by Tove Jansson. Multicoloured. Self-adhesive.
1708 1klass (65c.) Type **709** . . . 1·20 1·20
1709 1klass (65c.) Tooticky, Little My and Moomintroll sitting by stove . . . . . 1·20 1·20
1710 1klass (65c.) Moomintroll performing handstand and Little My . . . . 1·20 1·20
1711 1klass (65c.) Moonmintroll and squirrel . . . . . . 1·20 1·20
1712 1klass (65c.) Tooticky, Moominmamma and Little My in snow . . . . 1·20 1·20
1713 1klass (65c.) Snufkin walking through forest . . 1·20 1·20

710 Ligonberry (*Vaccinium vitis-idaea*)

711 Russaro Lighthouse

2003. Self-adhesive.
1714 **710** 65c. multicoloured . . . 95 35

2003. Lighthouses. With service indicator. Sheet 120 × 80 mm containing T **711** and similar vert designs. Multicoloured.
MS1715 1klass (65c.) Bengtskar (29 × 40 mm); 1klass (65c.) Type **711**; 1klass (65c.) Ronnskar; 1klass (65c.) Harmaja Grahara; 1klass (65c.) Soderskar . . . . 6·75 6·75

712 Maria and Juho Lallukka

2003. Scientific and Cultural Patrons. Multicoloured.
1716 65c. Type **712** . . . . . . 1·20 1·20
1717 65c. Emil Aaltonen (vert) . . 1·20 1·20
1718 65c. Heikki Huhtamaki (vert) . . . . 1·20 1·20
1719 65c. Jenny and Antti Wihuri 1·20 1·20
1720 65c. Alfred Kordelin (vert) 1·20 1·20
1721 65c. Amos Andersson (vert) 1·20 1·20

713 Elf Boy posting Letters

714 President Halonen

2003. Christmas. Multicoloured. Self-adhesive.
1722 45c. Type **713** 60 60
1723 65c. Elf girl holding ginger bread on tray (vert) . . . 85 85

2003. 60th Birth Anniv of Tarja Halonen, President of Finland.
1724 **714** 65c. multicoloured . . . 85 85

715 *Linnaea borealis*

716 Jean Sibelius' Hands playing Piano

2004. Self-adhesive.
1725 **715** 30c. multicoloured . . . 40 40

2004. Ainola Museum (Jean Sibelius (composer)'s house). Multicoloured. Self-adhesive.
1726 2klass (55c.) Type **716** . . . 75 75
1727 2klass (55c.) Swans and score 75 75
1728 2klass (55c.) *En Saga Jean Sibelius* (painting, Akseli Gallen-Kalhla) 75 75
1729 1klass (65c.) *Voices Intimae* score (detail) . . . . . . 1·20 1·20
1730 1klass (65c.) Drawing of Ainola . . . . 1·20 1·20
1731 1klass (65c.) *Aino Sibelius* (Eero Jrnfelt) and *Jean Sibelius* (Albert Edelfelt) 1·20 1·20

717 Silhouette of Johan Runeberg

718 Rose

2004. Birth Bicentenary of Johan Ludvig Runeberg (writer). Sheet 118 × 80 mm containing T **717** and similar vert designs. Each stone, black and red.
MS1732 65c. × 4, Type **717**; Sven Dufa at the Battle of Koljonvirta (Albert Edelfelt) Landscape (Albert Edelfelt) and Vrt Land (national anthem); Johan Runeberg (statue, Walter Runeberg) . . . . 1·70 1·70

2004. Greetings Stamps. Each black and red. Self-adhesive.
1733 1klass (65c.) Type **718** . . . 1·20 1·20
1734 1klass (65c.) Pursed lips . . 1·20 1·20
1735 1klass (65c.) Eye . . . . . 1·20 1·20
1736 1klass (65c.) Man and woman . . . . 1·20 1·20
1737 1klass (65c.) Elderly woman 1·20 1·20
1738 1klass (65c.) Hand and flower . . . . 1·20 1·20

719 Bear Cub **720** Rose

2004. Self-adhesive.
1739 **719** 2klass (55c.) multicoloured 75 75

2004. Self-adhesive.
1740 **720** 1klass (65c.). multicoloured 90 90

721 Daffodils, Narcissi and Grape Hyacinths

2004. Easter. Self-adhesive.
1741 **721** 65c. multicoloured . . . 90 90

2004. As T **689**. Self-adhesive.
1742 **689** €3 multicoloured . . . 4·00 4·00

722 Orchid

2004. Greetings Stamps. Multicoloured. Self-adhesive gum.
1743 1 klass (65c.) Type **722**. . . 90 90
1744 1 klass (65c.) Swallow and martins 90 90

723 "Luonnotar" (detail) (Akseli Gallen-Kallela)

2004. Nordic Mythology. Sheet 105×70 mm containing T **723** and similar multicoloured design.
MS1745 65c.×2, Type **723**; "Luonnotar" (different) (22×42 mm) . . . . 1·80 1·80
Stamps of a similar theme were issued by Aland Islands, Denmark, Faroe Islands, Greenland, Iceland, Norway and Sweden.

724 Wild Strawberry

2004. Self-adhesive.
1746 **724** 65c. multicoloured . . . 90 90

725 "From the Luxembourg Gardens" (Albert Edelfelt)

2004. Self-adhesive.
1747 **725** 1 klass (65c.) multicoloured 90 90

726 Fire on Beach

2004. Europa. Holidays. Multicoloured.
1748 65c. Type **726** 90 90
1749 65c. Rowers 90 90

727 Red Squirrel

2004. Fauna. Sheet 80×120 mm containing T **727** and similar multicoloured designs.
MS1750 65c.×6, Type **727**; Crow (40×31 mm); Rabbit; Weasels; Lizard; Fox (40×40 mm) . . . 5·50 5·50

728 Snufkin and Moomin Troll

2004. 90th Birth Anniv of Tove Jansson (artist and writer). 50th Anniv of Moomins (cartoon strip by Tove Jansson).
1751 **728** 1 klass (65c.) multicoloured 90 90

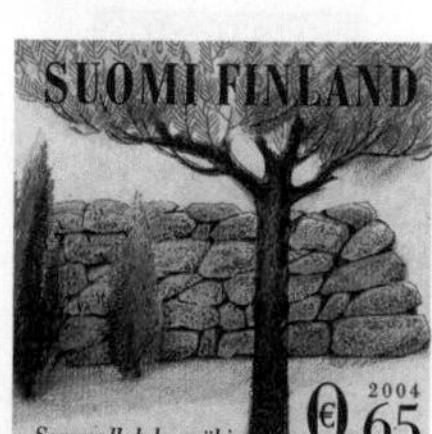

729 Trees and Stone Wall

2004. UNESCO World Heritage Sites. Sammallahdenmki Bronze Age Ruins. Sheet 120×80 mm containing T **729** and similar square design. Multicoloured.
MS1752 65c.×2, Type **729**; Lichen covered stones . . . . 1·80 1·80

730 Jug (*Egelskar*)

2004. Gulf of Finland (3rd series). Showing artefacts from ships. Multicoloured.
1753 1 klass (65c.) Type **730** . . . 90 90
1754 1 klass (65c.) Seal (*Vrouw Maria*) 90 90
1755 1 klass (65c.) Gold watch (*St. Michael*) 90 90
1756 1 klass (65c.) Figurehead (*St. Nikolai*) (24×40 mm) 90 90
1757 1 klass (65c.) Powder box (*Mulan*) 90 90

731 Child writing Letter (Martta Wendelin)

2004. Christmas. Drawings by Martta Wendelin. Self-adhesive.
1758 45c. Type **731** 60 60
1759 65c. Tree decorations (vert) 90 90

732 Two Girls

2004. 25th Anniv of United Nations Convention on Rights of the Child. Multicoloured.
1760 65c. Type **732** 90 90
1761 65c. Boy painting 90 90

733 World Map of Rotary Emblems

2005. Centenary of Rotary International (charitable organization).
1762 **733** 65c. ultramarine and gold 90 90

734 Child with Bucket and Spade

2005. 400th Anniv of Oulu City. Multicoloured.
1763 65c. Type **734** 90 90
1764 65c. Cyclist 90 90
Nos. 1763/4 were issued together, se-tenant, pairs forming a composite design.

735 Sibelius Concert Hall

736 Lion and Tiger

2005. Centenary of Lahti City. Multicoloured.
1765 65c. Type **735** 90 90
1766 65c. Radio masts 90 90

2005. Toys. Multicoloured. Self-adhesive.
1767 1 klass (65c.) Type **736** . . . 90 90
1768 1 klass (65c.) Elephant and dog 90 90
1769 1 klass (65c.) Airplane, car and train 90 90
1770 1 klass (65c.) Teddy bear and rabbit 90 90

737 Earth and Moon (waxing moon)

738 Door Decoration

2005. 300th Anniv of First Finnish Almanac. Self-adhesive.
1771 **737** 65c. multicoloured . . . 90 90

2005. Hvittrask (Art Nouveau house), Kirkkonummi.Multicoloured. Self-adhesive.
1772 2 klass (55c.) Type **738** (Eliel Saarinen and Santtu Hartman) 75 75
1773 2 klass (55c.) Copper stove door 75 75
1774 2 klass (55c.) Chair (detail) 75 75
1775 1 klass (65c.) Stained glass window (Olga Gummerus-Ehrstrom) 90 90
1776 1 klass (65c.) Living room 90 90
1777 1 klass (65c.) Faade 90 90

739 Woman Auxiliary feeding Soldier and Veteran Organization Emblems

740 Apple Blossom

2005. 65th Anniv of End of 105-day Winter War.
1778 **739** 65c. multicoloured . . .

2005. Self-adhesive.
1779 **740** 1 klass (65c.) multicoloured 90 90

741 Easter Witch carrying Bouquet

2005. Easter. Self-adhesive.
1780 **741** 65c. multicoloured . . . 90 90

MILITARY FIELD POST

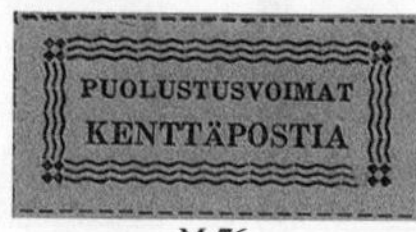

M 76

1941. No value indicated. Imperf.
M352 **M 76** (–) black on red . . . 30 60

M 86 **M 222**

1943. No value indicated.
M392 **M 86** (–) green 30 30
M393 (–) purple 30 30

1943. Optd **KENTTA-POSTI FALTPOST.**
M394 **31** 2m. orange 25 40
M395 3½m. blue 25 40

1944. As Type **M 86**, but smaller (20×16 mm) and inscr "1944".
M396 (–) violet 20 25
M397 (–) green 20 30

1963. No value indicated.
M688 **M 222** (–) violet . . . . . 90·00 £100

1983. No. M688 optd **1983.**
M1043 **M 222** (–) violet £130 £100

PARCEL POST STAMPS

P 118

1949. Printed in black on coloured backgrounds. Roul.
P471 **P 118** 1m. green . . . . . . 1·80 2·25
P472 5m. red . . . . 13·00 11·00
P473 20m. orange . . . . . 24·00 19·00
P474 50m. blue . . . . . . 11·50 11·00
P475 100m. brown . . . . 11·00 11·00

P 137

P 216

1952.
P507 **P 137** 5m. red . . . . 2·20 2·50
P508 20m. orange . . . . . 7·00 4·00
P509 50m. blue . . . . . . 12·50 9·00
P510 100m. brown . . . . 18·00 16·00

1963. Figures of value in black.
P647 **P 216** 5p. mauve . . . . . 2·40 2·00
P648 20p. orange . . . . . 2·75 3·25
P649 50p. blue . . . . . . 2·75 3·00
P650 1m. brown . . . . . 1·80 5·50

P 403 "SISU" Bus

1981. Figures of values in black.
P1003 **P 403** 50p. blue . . . . . 90 3·75
P1004 1m. brown . . . . . 1·10 4·00
P1005 5m. green . . . . . 3·50 8·00
P1006 10m. purple . . . . 4·25 18·00

FINNISH OCCUPATION OF AUNUS Pt. 10

The Russian town of Olonets was occupied by Finnish troops from April 1919 to May 1919.

1919. Arms of Finland optd **Aunus.**
1 **19** 5p. green . . . . 5·50 8·75
2 10p. pink . . . . 5·50 8·75
3 20p. orange . . . . 5·50 8·75
4 40p. violet . . . . 5·50 8·75
5 50p. brown . . . . 75·00 £110
6 1m. black and pink . . . . . 85·00 £120
7 5m. black and lilac £325 £450
8 10m. black and brown . . . £800 £1100

FINNISH OCCUPATION OF EASTERN KARELIA Pt. 10

Part of Russia, extending East to Lake Onega, occupied by Finland from 1941 to 1944.

100 penni = 1 markka.

1941. Types of Finland in unissued colours optd **ITA-KARJALA Sot.hallinto.** (a) Arms and pictorial issue.
1 **31** 50p. green 50 75
2 1m.75 grey . . . . 1·00 1·10
10 2m. orange . . . . 2·00 2·25
11 2m.75 orange . . . . . . 85 1·10
12 3½m. blue . . . . 2·10 6·25
13 **32** 5m. purple . . . . 5·25 8·25
14 – 10m. brown (as No. 276b) 5·25 7·25
15 – 25m. green (as No. 277) . . 4·25 7·25

(b) President Ryti.
16 **76** 50p. green . . . . 50 1·25
17 1m.75 slate . . . . 50 1·25
18 2m. red . . . . 75 1·25
19 2m.75 brown . . . . 75 1·10
20 3m.50 blue . . . . 75 1·10
21 5m. purple . . . . 75 1·10

(c) Marshal Mannerheim.
22 **77** 50p. green . . . . 75 1·25
23 1m.75 slate . . . . 75 1·25
24 2m. red . . . . 75 1·25
25 2m.75 brown . . . . 55 1·25
26 3m.50 blue . . . . 55 1·25
27 5m. purple . . . . 55 1·25

4 Arms of E. Karelia

1943. National Relief Fund.
28 4 3m.50+1m.50 olive 60 1·75

FIUME Pt. 8

A seaport and territory on the Adriatic Sea formerly belonging to Hungary and occupied by the Allies in 1918/19. Between 1919 and 1924 the territory was a Free State, controlled by D'Annunzio and his legionaries, until annexation to Italy in 1924. For later issues see Fiume and Kupa Zone; Venezia Giulia. Ceded to Yugoslavia in 1947 and now known as Rijeka.

1918. 100 filler = 1 krone.
1919. 100 centesimi = 1 corona.
1920. 100 centesimi = 1 lira.

1918. Various issues of Hungary optd **FIUME**. On "Harvesters" and "Parliament" issue of 1916.
1 18 2f. brown 2·50 1·25
2 3f. red 2·50 1·25
3 5f. green 2·50 1·25
4 6f. green 2·50 1·25
5 10f. red (No. 250) 35·00 16·00
6 10f. red (No. 243) 50·00 24·00
7 15f. violet (No. 251) 2·50 1·25
8 15f. violet (No. 244) 22·00 16·00
9 20f. brown 2·50 1·25
10 25f. blue 1·60 1·50
11 35f. brown 4·50 2·50
12 40f. olive 23·00 13·00
13 19 50f. purple 3·25 1·90
14 75f. blue 7·25 2·50
15 80f. green 7·25 1·90
16 1k. lake 19·00 5·75
17 2k. brown 3·25 1·90
18 3k. grey and violet 22·00 9·50
19 5k. brown 50·00 13·00
20 10k. lilac and brown £190 £140

On "Charles" and "Zita" issue of 1918.
21 27 10f. red 1·90 1·60
22 20f. brown 1·25 1·25
23 28 40f. olive 14·50 5·00

On War charity issue of 1916.
24 20 10+2f. red 3·25 2·25
25 – 15+2f. violet 3·25 2·25
26 22 40+2f. lake 5·00 2·25

On Newspaper issue of 1900.
27 N 9 (2f.) orange 2·40 95

On Express Letter stamp of 1916.
28 E 18 2f. olive and red 2·40 95

On Saving Bank stamp and surch **FRANCO** and value.
29 B 17 15 on 10f. purple 9·50 6·50

On Postage Due stamps of 1915 with figures in red and surch **FRANCO** and value.
30 D 9 45 on 6f. green 6·50 6·50
31 45 on 20f. green 16·00 6·50

2 Liberty

3 Clock Tower over Market in Fiume

4

5 Port of Fiume

1919. Inscr "FIUME".
32 2 2c. blue 50 50
33 3c. brown 50 50
35 5c. green 65 50
36 3 10c. red 14·50 4·50
57 15c. violet 50 50
39 20c. green 80 95
59 4 25c. blue 1·25 50
60 5 30c. violet 80 50
43 4 40c. brown 85 1·10
62 45c. orange 1·10 80
63 5 50c. green 80 50
46 60c. lake 1·10 50
65 1cor. brown 2·50 80
48 2cor. blue 2·50 1·10
49 3cor. red 3·25 1·25
50 5cor. brown 16·00 11·50
51 10cor. olive 13·00 32·00

6 Statue of Romulus, Remus and Wolf

9 Dr. Grossich

1919. Students' Education Fund. 200th Day of Peace.
71 6 5c.+5l. green 8·75 5·00
72 10c.+5l. red 8·75 5·00
73 15c.+5l. grey 8·75 5·00
74 20c.+5l. orange 8·75 5·00
75 – 45c.+5l. olive 8·75 5·00
76 – 60c.+5l. red 8·75 5·00
77 – 80c.+5l. violet 8·75 5·00
78 – 1cor.+5l. grey 8·75 5·00
79 – 2cor.+5l. red 8·75 5·00
80 – 3cor.+5l. brown 8·75 5·00
81 – 5cor.+5l. brown 8·75 5·00
82 – 10cor.+5l. violet 8·75 5·00
DESIGNS—HORIZ: 45, 60, 80c., 1cor. 13th-century Venetian war galley; 2, 3, 5, 10cor. Piazza of St. Mark, Venice.

1919. As T 2 to 5, but inscr "POSTA FIUME".
83 2 5c. green 65 50
84 3 10c. red 65 50
85 5 30c. violet 3·75 1·40
86 4 40c. brown 95 1·10
87 45c. orange 3·75 1·90
88 5 50c. green 3·75 2·25
89 60c. lake 3·75 2·25
90 10cor. olive 3·50 6·50

1919. Dr. Grossich Foundation.
91 9 25c. (+2cor.) blue 1·60 1·60

1919. Stamps of 1919 surch **FRANCO** and value.
(a) Inscr "FIUME".
92 3 5 on 20c. green 30 30
93 4 10 on 45c. orange 1·90 30
94 5 25 on 50c. green 9·50 14·50
95 55 on 1cor. brown 19·00 14·50
96 55 on 2cor. blue 3·25 4·75
97 55 on 3cor. red 3·25 3·75
98 55 on 5cor. brown 3·25 3·75

(b) Inscr "POSTA FIUME".
99 4 5 on 25c. blue 3·25 35
100 5 15 on 30c. violet 3·25 35
101 4 15 on 45c. orange 3·25 35
102 5 15 on 60c. lake 50 50
103 25 on 50c. green 50 50
104 55 on 10cor. olive 14·50 13·00

1919. Nos. 71/82 and 91 surch **Valore globale** and value.
105 6 5c. on 5c. green 60 60
106 10c. on 10c. red 60 60
107 15c. on 15c. grey 60 60
108 20c. on 20c. orange 60 60
122 9 25c. on 25c. blue 30 30
109 – 45c. on 45c. green 80 80
110 – 60c. on 60c. red 80 80
111 – 80c. on 80c. violet 1·10 1·10
112 – 1cor. on 1cor. grey 1·10 1·10
113 – 2cor. on 2cor. brown 1·10 1·10
114 – 3cor. on 3cor. brown 2·50 2·50
115 – 5cor. on 5cor. brown 3·25 3·25
130 – 10cor. on 10cor. violet 1·10 1·10

16 Gabriele d'Annunzio

21 Medieval Ship

1920. Background in ochre.
131 16 5c. green 50 50
132 10c. red 50 50
133 15c. grey 50 50
134 20c. orange 60 60
135 25c. blue 80 80
136 30c. brown 90 90
137 45c. olive 1·40 1·40
138 50c. lilac 1·40 1·40
139 55c. yellow 1·40 1·40
140 1l. black 8·00 11·00
141 2l. red 8·00 11·00
142 3l. green 8·00 11·00
143 5l. brown 40·00 20·00
144 10l. lilac 8·00 11·50

1920. Nos. M145/8 optd **Reggenza Italiana del Carnaro** or surch also.
146 M 17 1 on 5c. green 95 40
147 – 2 on 25c. blue 40 40
148 M 17 5c. green 13·00 1·10
149 – 10c. red 13·00 1·10
150 – 15 on 10c. red 95 50
151 – 15 on 20c. brown 40 50
152 – 15 on 25c. blue 50 65
153 – 20c. brown 65 65
154 – 25c. blue 65 65
155 – 25 on 10c. red 1·60 1·90
156 – 55 on 20c. brown 3·50 1·25
157 M 17 55 on 5c. green 13·00 2·25
158 – 1l. on 10c. red 21·00 13·00
159 – 1l. on 25c. blue 50·00 50·00
160 M 17 2l. on 5c. green 21·00 13·00
161 – 5l. on 10c. red 85·00 90·00
162 – 10l. on 20c. brown £375 £275

1921. Issue of d'Annunzio optd **Governo Provvisorio** or also surch **LIRE UNA** (No. 173).
163 16 5c. green 30 30
164 10c. red 30 30
165 15c. grey 30 40
166 20c. orange 1·10 80
167 25c. blue 1·10 80
168 30c. brown 1·10 80
169 45c. olive 65 65
170 50c. lilac 1·25 95
171 55c. yellow 1·10 75
172 1l. black 70·00 65·00
173 1l. on 30c. brown 65 65
174 2l. red 16·00 14·50
175 3l. green 16·00 14·50
176 5l. brown 16·00 14·50
177 10l. lilac 16·00 14·50

1921. Charity Stamps of 1919 optd **24 - IV - 1921 Costituente Fiumana** (and **L** over "Cor." in high values).
178 5c. green 1·60 1·60
179 10c. red 1·60 1·60
180 15c. grey 1·60 1·60
181 20c. orange 1·60 1·60
182 45c. green 4·50 3·50
183 60c. red 4·50 3·50
184 80c. violet 5·75 4·75
185 1l. on 1cor. grey 7·75 6·50
186 1l. on 2cor. brown 35·00 95
187 3l. on 3cor. brown 35·00 35·00
188 5l. on 5cor. brown 35·00 1·60
189 10l. on 10cor. violet 42·00 40·00

1922. Charity Stamps of 1919 optd **24 - IV - 1921 Costituente Fiumana 1922** (and **L** over "Cor." in high values).
190 5c. green 3·00 1·25
191 10c. red 30 30
192 15c. grey 10·00 4·50
193 20c. orange 95 95
194 45c. green 7·75 4·75
195 60c. red 65 1·40
196 80c. violet 65 1·40
197 1l. on 1cor. grey 95 95
198 2l. on 2cor. brown 10·00 6·50
199 3l. on 3cor. brown 95 1·25
200 5l. on 5cor. brown 65 1·25

1923.
201 21 5c. green 30 30
202 10c. mauve 30 30
203 15c. brown 30 30
204 – 20c. red 30 30
205 – 25c. grey 30 30
206 – 30c. green 30 30
207 – 50c. blue 30 30
208 – 60c. red 50 1·10
209 – 1l. blue 50 1·40
210 – 2l. brown 32·00 8·00
211 – 3l. olive 22·00 16·00
212 – 5l. brown 22·00 19·00
DESIGNS: 20, 25, 30c. Roman Arch; 50, 60c., 1l. St. Vitus; 2, 3, 5l. Tarsatic Column.

1924. Issue of 1923 optd **REGNO D'ITALIA** in frame.
213 21 5c. green 65 3·00
214 10c. mauve 65 3·00
215 15c. brown 80 3·00
216 – 20c. red 80 3·00
217 – 25c. grey 80 3·00
218 – 30c. green 80 3·00
219 – 50c. blue 80 3·00
220 – 60c. red 80 3·00
221 – 1l. blue 80 3·00
222 – 2l. brown 2·10 7·00
223 – 3l. olive 3·25 8·25
224 – 5l. brown 3·25 8·25

1924. Issue of 1923 optd **ANNESSIONE ALL'ITALIA** in frame with **22 Febb 1924** below.
225 21 5c. green 30 1·25
226 10c. mauve 30 1·25
227 15c. brown 30 1·25
228 – 20c. red 30 1·25
229 – 25c. grey 30 1·25
230 – 30c. green 30 1·25
231 – 50c. blue 30 1·25
232 – 60c. red 30 1·25
233 – 1l. blue 30 1·25
234 – 2l. brown 65 2·50
235 – 3l. olive 65 2·50
236 – 5l. brown 65 2·50

EXPRESS LETTER STAMPS

E 17

1920.
E145 E 17 30c. green 16·00 12·00
E146 50c. red 16·00 12·00

1920. Nos. M147 and M145 surch **Reggenza Italiana del Carnaro ESPRESSO** and new value.
E163 30c. on 20c. bistre 60·00 60·00
E164 50c. on 5c. green 85·00 48·00

1921. Optd **Governo Provvisorio**.
E178 E 17 30c. blue 6·50 8·00
E179 50c. red 9·50 8·00

E 25 Fiume in 16th Century

1923.
E213 E 25 60c. red 12·00 7·25
E214 2l. blue 12·00 8·75

1924. Optd **REGNO D'ITALIA** in frame with arms between the two words.
E225 E 25 60c. red 80 4·00
E226 2l. blue 80 4·00

1924. Optd **ANNESSIONE ALL'ITALIA** in frame with **22 Febbraio 1924** below.
E237 E 25 60c. red 80 3·25
E238 2l. blue 80 3·25

MILITARY POST STAMPS

M 17 Severing the Gordian Knot

1920. 1st Anniv of Capture of Fiume by D'Annunzio's "Legionaries".
M145 M 17 5c. green 35·00 16·00
M146 – 10c. red 21·00 13·00
M147 – 20c. bistre 35·00 13·00
M148 – 25c. blue 65·00 65·00
DESIGNS: 10c. Arms of Fiume; 20c. "Crown of Thorns"; 25c. Daggers raised in clenched fists.

NEWSPAPER STAMPS

N 9

1919.
N91 N 9 2c. brown 4·75 6·50

N 17 Mail Steamer

1920.
N145 N 17 1c. green 1·60 95

POSTAGE DUE STAMPS

1918. Postage Due stamps of Hungary of 1903 (figures in black), optd **FIUME**.
D29 D 9 6f. green (D21) £225 85·00
D30 12f. green (D31) £350 £140
D31 50f. green (D33) 70·00 55·00

1918. Postage Due stamps of Hungary of 1915 (figures in red), optd **FIUME**.
D32 D 9 1f. green 80·00 70·00
D33 2f. green 50 40
D34 5f. green 3·25 3·25
D35 6f. green 50 40
D36 10f. green 6·40 1·90
D37 12f. green 65 50
D38 15f. green 14·50 13·00
D39 20f. green 65 50
D40 30f. green 14·50 11·00

D 9

1919.
D91 D 9 2c. brown 1·10 95
D92 5c. brown 1·40 95

1921. Nos. 105/30 surch **Segnatasse**, new value and device obliterating old surch.
D191 6 2c. on 15c. grey 80 80
D192 4c. on 10c. red 65 55
D193 9 5c. on 25c. blue 65 55
D194 6 6c. on 20c. orange 65 55
D195 10c. on 20c. orange 95 95

D188 – 20c. on 45c. green 1·10 1·60
D183 – 30c. on 1cor. grey 1·25 1·60
D184 – 40c. on 80c. violet 65 80
D185 – 50c. on 60c. red 65 80
D189 – 60c. on 45c. green 1·10 1·60
D190 – 80c. on 45c. green 1·10 1·60
D187 – 1l. on 2cor. brown 1·60 1·90

For stamps of Italy surch **3-V-1945 FIUME RIJEKE** and new value, see Venezia Giulia and Istria, Nos 18/24.

FIUME AND KUPA ZONE Pt. 3

The zone comprised Fiume (Rijeka), Susak and the Kupa River area.

100 pares = 1 dinar.

1941. Nos 414, etc. of Yugoslavia optd **ZONA OCCUPATA FIUMANO KUPA.**
1 **99** 25p. black 2·40 2·50
2 50p. orange 1·25 1·40
3 1d. green 1·25 1·40
4 1d.50 red 1·25 1·40
5 3d. brown 1·60 1·75
6 4d. blue 2·75 3·50
7 5d. blue 5·50 6·00
8 5d.50 violet 5·50 6·00
9 6d. blue 20·00 20·00
10 8d. brown 14·00 16·00
11 12d. violet £300 £325
12 16d. purple 95·00 £100
13 20d. blue £1100 £1100
14 30d. pink £6000 £6000

1941. Maternity and Child Welfare Fund. Nos 2/4 further optd **O.N.M.I.**
15 **99** 50p. orange 2·25 5·00
16 1d. green 2·25 5·00
17 1d.50 red 2·25 5·00

1941. Italian Naval Exploit at Buccari (Bakar), 1918. No. 415 of Yugoslavia surch **MEMENTO AVDERE SEMPER L1 BVCCARI.**
18 **99** 1l. on 50p. orange 14·00 32·00

1942. Maternity and Child Welfare. Nos 15/17 further optd **Pro Maternita e Infanzia.**
19 **99** 50p. orange 5·25 12·00
20 1d. green 5·25 12·00
21 1d.50 red 5·25 12·00

Nos. 1/21 were valid until 26.5.42 after which unoverprinted Italian stamps were used until the Italian Occupation ended.

FRANCE Pt. 6

A republic in the W. of Europe.

1849. 100 centimes = 1 franc.
2002. 100 cents = 1 euro.

NOTE. Stamps in types of France up to the 1877 issue were also issued for the French Colonies and where the values and colours are the same they can only be distinguished by their shade or postmark or other minor differences which are outside the scope of this Catalogue. They are priced here by whichever is the lower of the quotations under France or French Colonies in the Stanley Gibbons Catalogue, Part 6 (France). Numbers with asterisks are French Colonies numbers.

1 Ceres

2 Louis Napoleon, President

3 Napoleon III, Emperor of the French

1849. Imperf.
157 **1** 5c. green £180 £110
15* 10c. bistre £325 £120
4 15c. green £13000 £650
6 20c. black £225 27·00
17* 20c. blue £400 95·00
18* 25c. blue £140 11·00
22* 30c. brown 90·00 18·00
19* 40c. orange £210 10·00
23* 80c. red £500 £130
17 1f. orange £32000 £9500
19 1f. red £5000 £500

For 10c. brown on pink and 15c. bistre, imperf, see French Colonies Nos. 16 and 20.

1852. Imperf.
37a **2** 10c. yellow £27000 £450
39 25c. blue £2000 30·00

1853. Imperf.
42 **3** 1c. olive £140 46·00
45 5c. green £400 45·00
50a 10c. yellow £375 11·00
51 20c. blue £120 2·00
63 25c. blue £2000 £180
64 40c. orange £2000 10·50
70 80c. red £1700 33·00
72 1f. red £4250 £2500

1862. Perf.
87 **3** 1c. green £110 26·00
89 5c. green £130 7·25
91 10c. bistre £825 3·00
95 20c. blue £200 60
97 40c. orange £1000 4·00
98 80c. pink £850 21·00

4 Head with Laurel Wreath

5 Head with Laurel Wreath

1863. Perf.
102 **4** 1c. green 17·00 8·50
104 2c. brown 50·00 18·00
109 4c. grey £140 43·00
113a **5** 10c. bistre £375 4·50
115a 20c. blue £160 1·30
116 30c. brown £600 11·00
120 40c. orange £700 6·50
122 80c. pink £800 13·00

For imperforate stamps in these designs see French Colonies.

6

7 Ceres

1869.
131 **6** 5f. lilac £4000 £1000

1870. Imperf.
148 **7** 1c. green 80·00 80·00
152 2c. brown £180 £180
156 4c. grey £180 £180

For 1c. green on blue, 2c. brown on yellow and 5c. green as Type **7** and imperf, see French Colonies.

1870. Perf.
185 **7** 1c. green 29·00 8·75
187 2c. brown 60·00 8·75
189 4c. grey £200 25·00
192 5c. green £130 5·00
136 **1** 10c. bistre £450 00
194 10c. bistre on pink £225 7·50
204 15c. bistre £250 2·50
137 20c. blue £200 5·00
198 25c. blue £100 85
205 30c. brown £400 5·00
140 40c. orange £350 3·50
142 40c. red £425 5·00
208 80c. red £500 10·50

10 Peace and Commerce

11 "Blanc" type

12 "Mouchon" type

13 "Olivier Merson" type

1876.
212 **10** 1c. green £120 50·00
245 1c. black on blue 2·75 1·40
225 2c. green 85·00 9·25
248 2c. brown on buff 5·00 1·40
249 3c. brown on yellow £190 29·00
251 3c. grey 2·00 1·10
214 4c. green £110 36·00
252 4c. brown on grey 2·75 1·50
254 4c. purple on blue 5·00 2·30
282 5c. green 9·00 90
216 10c. green £500 14·00
284 10c. black on lilac 13·50 2·00
232 15c. lilac £550 1·70
279 15c. blue 9·00 1·40
219 20c. brown on yellow £350 11·50
260 20c. red on green 40·00 2·50
234 25c. blue £325 1·20
262 25c. black on red £650 15·00
263 25c. bistre on yellow £225 3·25
267 25c. black on pink 50·00 70
237 30c. brown 85·00 95
268 35c. brown on yellow £325 23·00
269 40c. red on yellow 85·00 1·50
273 50c. red £190 1·60
223 75c. red £550 7·75
274 75c. brown on orange £200 27·00
240 1f. green £120 4·50
287 2f. brown on blue 60·00 26·00
277 5f. mauve on lilac £350 48·00

For imperforate stamps in this design see French Colonies.

For 5f. red, perf, see No. 412.

1900.
288 **11** 1c. grey 70 20
289 2c. purple 90 20
290 3c. red 80 30
292a 4c. brown 3·25 1·00
295 5c. green 1·20 20
300 **12** 10c. red 20·00 1·00
301 15c. orange 8·00 25
297 20c. brown 50·00 5·50
302 25c. blue 90·00 1·00
299 30c. mauve 50·00 4·50
303 **13** 40c. red and blue 11·00 35
304 45c. green and blue 16·00 1·30
305 50c. brown and lilac 50·00 55
306 1f. red and green 25·00 40
369 1f. red and yellow 55·00 90
307 2f. lilac and buff £850 60·00
308 5f. blue and buff 85·00 2·75

For further values in these designs, see 1920 issues (following No. 379).

14 "Mouchon" type redrawn

15 Sower

1902.
309 **14** 10c. red 30·00 85
310 15c. red 12·00 30
311 20c. brown 90·00 11·50
312 25c. blue £100 1·40
313 30c. mauve £225 11·00

1903.
314 **15** 10c. red 9·50 25
316 15c. green 3·50 20
317 20c. purple 75·00 2·10
320 25c. blue 90·00 1·10
321 30c. lilac £150 5·50

16 Ground below Feet

18 No Ground

20

1906.
325 **16** 10c. red 2·75 2·50

1906.
331 **18** 5c. green 1·70 15
335 10c. red 2·00 15
337 20c. brown 4·00 40
341 25c. blue 3·50 20
343 30c. orange 18·00 1·20
346 35c. violet 7·50 1·10

See also Nos. 497 etc. and 454/a.

1914. Red Cross Fund. Surch with red cross and **5c.**
351 **18** 10c.+5c. red 5·00 5·25

1914. Red Cross Fund.
352 **20** 10c.+5c. red 26·00 3·00

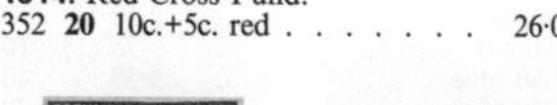

21 War Widow

26 Spirit of War

23 Woman replaces Man

27 Sinking of "Charles Roux" Hospital Ship, and Bombed Hospital

1917. War Orphans' Fund.
370 **21** 2c.+3c. red 4·25 4·25
371 – 5c.+5c. green 15·00 9·25
372 **23** 15c.+10c. green 24·00 21·00
373 25c.+15c. blue 80·00 48·00
374 – 35c.+25c. violet and grey £130 £100
375 – 50c.+50c. brown £200 £150
376 **26** 1f.+1f. red £325 £325
377 5f.+5f. blue and black £1200 £1100

DESIGNS—As Type **21**: 5c. Orphans. As Type **26**: 35c. Front line trench; 50c. Lion of Belfort.

See also Nos. 450/3.

1918. Red Cross Fund.
378 **27** 15c.+5c. red & green £110 50·00

1919. Surch ½ **centime.**
379 **11** ½c. on 1c. grey 25 35

1920.
497 **18** 1c. bistre 15 20
497a 1c. brown 15 35
498 2c. green 15 20
499 3c. red 15 25
380 5c. orange 1·70 25
500 5c. mauve 15 20
413 **11** 7½c. mauve* 80 85
381 **18** 10c. green 50 20
501 10c. blue 1·70 20
413a **11** 10c. lilac 4·75 35
414 **18** 15c. brown 25 20
415 20c. mauve 25 20
415b 25c. brown 10 15
503 30c. red 50 30
382a 30c. mauve 1·00 75
416 30c. blue 3·50 25
505 35c. green 75 45
417 40c. green 1·20 40
418 40c. red 2·00 35
418a 40c. violet 1·90 70
418b 40c. blue 1·20 20
419 **15** 45c. violet 6·25 1·30
592 50c. blue 1·20 35
420 50c. green 6·25 1·00
421 50c. red 1·20 35
384 **13** 60c. violet and blue 90 60
385 **15** 60c. violet 6·25 1·40
385a 65c. red 2·75 1·30
422 65c. green 6·00 1·50
423 75c. mauve 5·25 30
424 80c. red 25·00 7·50
386 85c. red 12·00 2·10
425 1f. blue 6·00 40
426 **18** 1f.05 red 14·00 5·00
427 1f.10 mauve 10·50 2·20
428 1f.40 mauve 20·00 21·00
387 **13** 2f. orange and green 48·00 40
428a **18** 2f. green 12·50 1·20
429 **13** 3f. violet and blue 25·00 6·00
430 3f. mauve and red 48·00 3·00
431 10f. green and red £100 14·00
432 20f. mauve and green £160 29·00

***PRECANCEL.** No. 413 was issued only precancelled. The "unused" price is for stamp with full gum and the used price for stamp without gum.

1922. War Orphans' Fund. Nos. 370/7 surch with new value, cross and bars.
388 **21** 1c. on 2c.+3c. red 40 65
389 – 2½c. on 5c.+5c. green 65 85
390 **23** 5c. on 15c.+10c. green 1·10 1·30
391 5c. on 25c.+15c. blue 2·00 2·30
392 – 5c. on 35c.+25c. violet and grey 12·00 14·00
393 – 10c. on 50c.+50c. brn 18·00 17·00
394 **26** 25c. on 1f.+1f. red 29·00 29·00
395 1f. on 5f.+5f. blue and black £140 £140

30 Pasteur

31 Stadium and Arc de Triomphe

1923.
396 **30** 10c. green 65 20
396a 15c. green 1·30 25
396b 20c. green 2·50 80
397 30c. red 80 1·40
397a 30c. green 70 35
398 45c. red 2·00 2·00
399 50c. blue 3·75 25
400 75c. blue 4·00 85
400a 90c. red 11·00 3·25
400b 1f. blue 20·00 20
400c 1f.25 blue 23·00 8·00
400d 1f.50 blue 5·25 20

1923. Optd **CONGRES PHILATELIQUE DE BORDEAUX 1923.**
400e **13** 1f. red and green £325 £425

1924. Olympic Games.
401 **31** 10c. green & light green 2·00 1·00
402 – 25c. deep red and red 2·75 70
403 – 30c. red and black 8·50 10·50
404 – 50c. ultramarine & blue 24·00 4·00

DESIGNS—HORIZ: 25c. Notre Dame and Pont Neuf. VERT: 30c. Milan de Crotone (statue); 50c. The victor.

35 Ronsard

36

1924. 400th Birth Anniv of Ronsard.
405 **35** 75c. blue 1·80 1·50

1924. International Exhibition of Modern Decorative Arts. Dated "1925".
406 **36** 10c. yellow and green 65 70
407 – 15c. green & deep green 65 80
408 – 25c. red and purple 65 40
409 – 25c. mauve and blue 1·30 70
410 – 75c. blue and grey 3·00 1·90
411 **36** 75c. blue and deep blue 16·00 6·00

DESIGNS—HORIZ: 25c. (No. 408); 75c. (No. 410) Potter and vase; 25c. (No. 409), Chateau and steps. VERT: 15c. Stylized vase.

1925. Paris Int Philatelic Exhibition.
412 **10** 5f. red . . . . 95·00 95·00
MS412a 140×220 mm. No. 412 in block of four £800 £800

1926. Surch with new value and bars.
433 **18** 25c. on 30c. blue 25 40
434 25c. on 35c. violet 25 40
436 **15** 50c. on 60c. violet . . . . 1·20 1·00
437 50c. on 65c. red 70 60
438 **30** 50c. on 75c. blue . . . . . 3·00 1·50
439 **15** 50c. on 80c. red . . . . . 1·20 1·00
440 50c. on 85c. red . . . . . 2·00 90
441 **18** 50c. on 1f.05 red . . . . . 1·20 60
442 **30** 50c. on 1f.25 blue . . . . 2·50 2·00
443 **15** 55c. on 60c. violet* . . . . £130 49·00
444 **18** 90c. on 1f.05 red . . . . . 2·50 2·75
445 1f.10 on 1f.40 red 90 90
***PRECANCEL.** No. 443 was issued only precancelled. The "unused" price is for stamp with full gum and the used price for stamp without gum.

1926. War Orphans' Fund.
450 **21** 2c.+1c. purple . . . . . . 1·60 1·50
451 – 50c.+10c. brn (as No. 375) 22·00 11·50
452 **26** 1f.+25c. red . . . . 49·00 37·00
453 5f.+1f. blue and black . . 95·00 85·00

1927. Strasbourg Philatelic Exhibition.
454 **18** 5f. blue £250 £275
454a 10f. red £250 £275
MS454b 110×140 mm. 5f.+10f. and label inscr "STRASBOURG 1927" £750 £750

1927. Air. 1st International Display of Aviation and Navigation, Marseilles. Optd with Bleriot XI airplane and **Poste Aerienne**.
455 **13** 2f. red and green £180 £200
456 5f. blue and yellow £150 £200

44 Marcelin Berthelot

45 Lafayette, Washington, "Paris" (liner) and Lindbergh's Airplane "Spirit of St. Louis"

1927. Birth Centenary of Berthelot.
457 **44** 90c. red . . . . 1·90 45

1927. Visit of American Legion.
458 **45** 90c. red . . . . 1·30 1·50
459 1f.50 blue . . . . 4·00 1·70

1927. Sinking Fund. Surch **Caisse d'Amortissement** or **C A** and premium.
460 **18** 40c.+10c. blue . . . . . . 5·25 5·75
461 **15** 50c.+25c. green . . . . . 8·25 8·50
462 **30** 1f.50+50c. orange . . . . 13·00 13·50
See also Nos. 466/8, 476/8, 485/7 and 494/6.

48

50 Joan of Arc

1928. Sinking Fund.
463 **48** 1f.50+8f.50 blue £100 £120

1928. Air ("Ile de France"). Surch **10 FR.** and bars.
464 **44** 10f. on 90c. red £1600 £1600
465 **30** 10f. on 1f.50 blue £11000 £11000

1928. Sinking Fund. Surch as Nos. 460/2.
466 **18** 40c.+10c. violet . . . . . 9·25 10·00
467 **15** 50c.+25c. red . . . . . . 29·00 29·00
468 **30** 1f.50+50c. mauve . . . . 45·00 39·00

1929. 500th Anniv of Relief of Orleans.
469 **50** 50c. blue . . . . 2·00 25

1929. Optd **EXPOSITION LE HAVRE 1929 PHILATELIQUE.**
470 **13** 2f. red and green £500 £500

52 Reims Cathedral

53 Mont St. Michel

1929. Views.
470a – 90c. mauve . . . . 3·25 85
471 – 2f. red . . . . 36·00 55
472 **52** 3f. blue . . . . 80·00 2·30
473a **53** 5f. brown . . . . 22·00 45
474b – 10f. blue . . . . 75·00 9·50
475 – 20f. brown . . . . £250 34·00

DESIGNS—HORIZ: 90c. Le Puy-en-Velay; 2f. Arc de Triomphe; 10f. Port de la Rochelle; 20f. Pont du Gard.

1929. Sinking Fund. Surch as Nos. 460/2.
476 **18** 40c.+10c. green . . . . . 17·00 16·00
477 **15** 50c.+25c. mauve . . . . . 31·00 28·00
478 **30** 1f.50+50c. brown . . . . 60·00 55·00

54 Bay of Algiers

1930. Centenary of French Conquest of Algeria.
479 **54** 50c. red and blue . . . . 2·75 40

55 "Le Sourire de Reims"

1930. Sinking Fund.
480 **55** 1f.50+3f.50 purple . . . . 70·00 75·00

1930. I.L.O. Session, Paris. Optd **CONGRES DU B.I.T. 1930.**
481 **15** 50c. red . . . . 2·40 2·00
482 **30** 1f.50 blue . . . . 20·00 14·50

57 Notre Dame de la Garde, Marseilles

1930. Air.
483 **57** 1f.50 red . . . . 21·00 2·75
484 1f.50 blue . . . . 19·00 1·60

1930. Sinking Fund. Surch as Nos. 460/2.
485 **18** 40c.+10c. red . . . . . . 20·00 17·00
486 **15** 50c.+25c. brown . . . . . 38·00 35·00
487 **18** 1f.50+50c. violet . . . . . 65·00 60·00

58 Woman of the Fachi tribe

59 "French Colonies"

1930. International Colonial Exhibition.
488 **58** 15c. black . . . . 1·00 30
489 40c. brown . . . . 2·50 30
490 50c. red 75 10
491 1f.50 blue . . . . 9·50 40
492 **59** 1f.50 blue . . . . 42·00 1·70

60 "French Provinces"

1931. Sinking Fund.
493 **60** 1f.50+3f.50 green £120 £120

1931. Sinking Fund. Surch as Nos. 460/2.
494 **18** 40c.+10c. green . . . . . 37·00 35·00
495 **15** 50c.+25c. violet . . . . . 90·00 90·00
496 **18** 1f.50+50c. red . . . . . . 90·00 90·00

61 Peace

62 Briand

65 Dove of Peace

1932.
502 **61** 30c. green 85 45
506 40c. mauve 25 25
507 45c. brown . . . . 1·80 1·00
508 50c. red 15 10
508d 55c. violet 70 25
508e 60c. bistre 30 35
509 65c. purple 45 40
509a 65c. blue 35 15
510 75c. green 15 15
510a 80c. orange 55 25
511 90c. red . . . . 30·00 1·80
511a 90c. green 55 45
511b 90c. blue 70 35
512 1f. orange . . . . 2·75 20
512a 1f. pink . . . . 3·25 20
513 1f.25 olive . . . . 65·00 4·50
513a 1f.25 red . . . . 1·70 1·80
513b 1f.40 mauve . . . . 6·25 6·25
514 1f.50 blue 25 20
515 1f.75 mauve . . . . 4·00 30

1933. Surch $\frac{1}{2}$ **centime**.
515a **18** $\frac{1}{2}$c. on 1c. bistre 20 55
515b $\frac{1}{2}$c. on 1c. brown . . . . 90 1·40

1933. Portraits.
516 **62** 30c. green . . . . 17·00 8·00
517 – 75c. mauve (Doumer) . . . 25·00 1·20
518 – 1f.25 red (Victor Hugo) . . 7·00 1·90

1934.
519 **65** 1f.50 blue . . . . 45·00 13·00

66 J. M. Jacquard

67 Jacques Cartier, "Grande Hermine" and "Petite Hermine"

1934. Death Centenary of Jacquard.
520 **66** 40c. blue . . . . 3·25 85

1934. 4th Cent of Cartier's Discovery of Canada.
521 **67** 75c. mauve . . . . 23·00 1·70
522 1f.50 blue . . . . 40·00 3·00

68 Bleriot XI

1934. Air. 25th Anniv of Channel Flight.
523 **68** 2f.25 violet . . . . 19·00 6·25

1934. Surch in figures and bars.
524 **61** 50c. on 1f.25 olive . . . . 3·50 50
524a 80c. on 1f. orange 45 55

69 Breton River Scene

1935.
525 **69** 2f. green . . . . 33·00 65

70 "Normandie"

71 St. Trophime, Arles

1935. Maiden Trip of Liner "Normandie".
526 **70** 1f.50 blue . . . . 13·00 1·50

1935.
527 **71** 3f.50 brown . . . . 27·00 3·50

72 B. Delessert

73 Victor Hugo

1935. Opening of Int Savings Bank Congress.
528 **72** 75c. green . . . . 18·00 1·10

1935. 50th Death Anniv of Victor Hugo.
529 **73** 1f.25 purple . . . . 4·25 1·70

74 Cardinal Richelieu

1935. Tercentenary of French Academy by Richelieu.
530 **74** 1f.50 red . . . . 20·00 1·20

75 Jacques Callot

77 Symbolic of Art

1935. Death Tercentenary of Callot (engraver).
531 **75** 75c. red . . . . 10·50 45

1935. Unemployed Intellectuals' Relief Fund. Inscr "POUR L'ART ET LA PENSEE".
532 – 50c.+10c. blue . . . . . . 2·75 2·75
533 **77** 50c.+2f. red . . . . 45·00 47·00
DESIGN—HORIZ: No. 532, Help for intellectuals (inscr "POUR LES CHOMEURS INTELLECTUELS").

78 Caudron C-635 Simoun over Paris

1936. Air.
534 **78** 85c. green . . . . 2·75 2·40
535 1f.50 blue . . . . 9·25 4·75
536 2f.25 violet . . . . 20·00 6·50
537 2f.50 red . . . . 30·00 10·50
538 3f. blue . . . . 24·00 1·70
539 3f.50 brown . . . . 60·00 23·00
540 50f. green £650 £375

79 Caudron C-635 Simoun over Paris

1936. Air.
541 **79** 50f. blue and pink £650 £300

80 Statue of Liberty

81 Andre-Marie Ampere

1936. Nansen (Refugee) Fund.
541a **80** 50c.+25c. blue . . . . . 3·50 4·00
542 75c.+50c. violet . . . . . 8·50 9·25

1936. Death Centenary of Ampere.
543 **81** 75c. brown . . . . 16·00 1·70

82 Daudet's Mill, Fontvieille

1936.
544 **82** 2f. blue . . . . 3·50 35

83 Children of the Unemployed

84 Pilatre de Rozier

1936. Children of the Unemployed Fund.
545 **83** 50c.+10c. red . . . . . . 4·25 4·75

1936. 150th Death Anniv of Pilatre de Rozier.
546 **84** 75c. blue . . . . 16·00 2·50

85 Rouget de Lisle 87 Canadian War Memorial, Vimy

1936. Death Centenary of Rouget de Lisle, Composer of the "Marseillaise."
547 **85** 20c. green . . . . 3·25 1·70
548 – 40c. brown . . . . 5·00 2·50
DESIGN—HORIZ: 40c. Female figure inscr "LA MARSEILLAISE".

1936. Unveiling of Canadian War Memorial, Vimy Ridge.
549 **87** 75c. red . . . . 13·00 3·50
550 1f.50 blue . . . . 12·50 7·50

88 Jean Jaures as an Orator

1936. Jaures Commemoration.
551 **88** 40c. brown . . . . 3·25 1·20
552 – 1f.50 blue . . . . 11·50 2·40
The 1f.50 has a head and shoulders portrait of Jaures.

91 Latecoere 300 Flying Boat

1936. 100th Flight between France and S. America.
553 – 1f.50 blue . . . . 15·00 3·00
554 **91** 10f. green £275 £110
DESIGN—VERT: 1f.50, Airplane and old-time sailing ship.

92 Herald 93 "World Exhibition"

1936. Paris International Exhibition.
555 **92** 20c. mauve 40 50
556 30c. green . . . . 2·50 1·60
557 40c. blue . . . . 1·10 60
558 50c. orange . . . . 1·30 25
559 **93** 90c. red . . . . 11·00 7·50
560 1f.50 blue . . . . 30·00 3·25

94 "Vision of Peace"

1936. Universal Peace Propaganda.
561 **94** 1f.50 blue . . . . 14·50 2·75

1936. Unemployed Intellectuals' Fund. No. 533 surch **+ 20c.**
562 **77** 20c. on 50c.+2f. red . . . 3·00 3·25

96 Jacques Callot

1936. Unemployed Intellectuals' Fund. Inscr as in T **96**.
563 **96** 20c.+10c. lake . . . . . . 2·50 2·75
564 – 40c.+10c. green . . . . . 2·75 3·25
565 – 50c.+10c. red . . . . . . 3·00 3·25
566 – 1f.50+50c. blue . . . . . 19·00 18·00
DESIGNS: 40c. Hector Berlioz; 50c. Victor Hugo; 1f.50, Louis Pasteur.
See also Nos. 603/5 and 607.

97 Ski Jumper

1937. Chamonix-Mont Blanc Skiing Week.
567 **97** 1f.50 blue . . . . 5·75 1·40

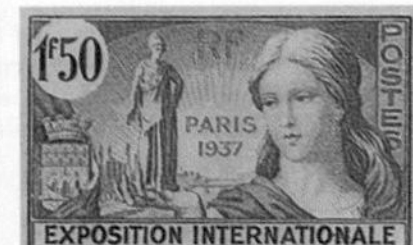
98 Pierre Corneille (author) 99 France and Minerva

1937. 300th Anniv of First Performance of "Le Cid" (play).
568 **98** 75c. red . . . . 1·90 1·10

1937. Paris International Exhibition.
569 **99** 1f.50 blue . . . . 2·10 85

100 Mermoz 101 Jean Mermoz Memorial

1937. Mermoz Commemoration.
570 **100** 30c. green 45 60
571 **101** 3f. violet . . . . 5·50 3·25

102 Paris–Orleans Midi Electric Train

1937. 13th International Railway Congress, Paris.
572 **102** 30c. green . . . . 95 1·20
573 – 1f.50 blue . . . . 6·25 6·25
DESIGN: 1f.50, Nord streamlined steam locomotive.

103 Rene Descartes

1937. 300th Anniv of Publication of "Discours".
(a) Wrongly inscr "DISCOURS SUR LA METHODE".
574 **103** 90c. red . . . . 1·90 1·30

(b) Corrected to "DISCOURS DE LA METHODE".
575 **103** 90c. red . . . . 5·75 1·60

104 Anatole France 107 Ramblers

1937. Unemployed Intellectuals' Relief Fund.
576 **104** 30c.+10c. green . . . . . 2·20 2·50
577 – 90c.+10c. red . . . . . . 5·25 5·75
DESIGN—HORIZ: 90c. Auguste Rodin.
See also Nos. 602 and 606.

1937. Postal Workers' Sports Fund.
578 – 20c.+10c. brown . . . . 1·70 2·00
579 – 40c.+10c. lake . . . . . 1·70 2·00
580 **107** 50c.+10c. purple . . . . 1·70 2·00

DESIGNS—HORIZ: 20c. Tug-of-War; 40c. Runners and discus thrower.

1937. Inter Philatelic Ex, Paris. As T **1**, printed in miniature sheets of four (5⅞ × 8⅜ ins.) inscr "PEXIP PARIS 1937" between stamps.
MS581 5c. brown and blue; 15c. carmine and red; 30c. red and blue; 50c. brown and red . . . £275 £275

108 Pierre Loti and Constantinople 109 "Victory" of Samothrace

1937. Pierre Loti Memorial Fund.
585 **108** 50c.+20c. red . . . . . . 3·50 4·00

1937. National Museums.
586 **109** 30c. green . . . . 65·00 39·00
587 55c. red . . . . 65·00 39·00

110 "France" and Child

1937. Public Health Fund.
588 **110** 65c.+25c. purple . . . . 2·75 2·50
588a 90c.+30c. blue . . . . . 2·50 2·50

111 France congratulating U.S.A.

1937. 150th Anniv of U.S. Constitution.
589 **111** 1f.75 blue . . . . 2·10 1·30

112 Iseran Pass 113 Ceres

1937. Opening of Col de l'Iseran Road.
590 **112** 90c. green . . . . 1·90 35

1938.
591 **113** 1f.75 blue 65 45
591a 2f. red 20 20
591b 2f.25 blue . . . . 8·50 65
591c 2f.50 green . . . . . . 1·30 50
591d 2f.50 blue 65 60
591e 3f. mauve 60 30

1938. Shipwrecked Mariners Society. As T **104** but portrait of Jean Charcot.
593 65c.+35c. green . . . . . . 1·80 2·50
593a 90c.+35c. purple . . . . . 10·50 11·50

113a Gambetta 113b Champagne Girl

1938. Birth Centenary of Leon Gambetta (politician).
594 **113a** 55c. lilac 45 50

1938.
594a – 90c. red on blue . . . . 1·00 1·10
595 **113b** 1f.75 blue . . . . 3·25 3·00
596 – 2f. brown 70 85
597 – 2f.15 purple . . . . . . 4·00 70
598 – 3f. red . . . . 11·00 3·50
599 – 5f. blue 50 40
600 – 10f. purple on blue . . 1·20 1·30
601 – 20f. green . . . . 41·00 16·00

DESIGNS—VERT: 2f.15, Coal miners; 10f. Vincennes. HORIZ: 90c. Chateau de Pau; 2f. Arc de Triomphe at Orange; 3f. Papal Palace, Avignon; 5f. Carcassonne; 20f. St. Malo.

1938. Unemployed Intellectuals' Relief Fund. As Nos. 563/6 and 576/7, inscr "POUR LES CHOMEURS INTELLECTUELS".
602 30c.+10c. red . . . . 2·10 2·20
603 35c.+10c. green . . . . . . 2·50 2·50
604 55c.+10c. violet . . . . . . 5·75 4·50
605 65c.+10c. blue . . . . . . 5·75 4·75
606 1f.+10c. red . . . . 5·25 5·00
607 1f.75+25c. blue . . . . . . 16·00 17·00
PORTRAITS—As Type **96**: 35c. Callot; 55c. Berlioz; 65c. Victor Hugo; 1f.75, Louis Pasteur. As No. 577: 1f. Auguste Rodin. As Type **104**: 30c. Anatole France.

114 Palais de Versailles 115 Soldier in Trench

1938. French National Music Festivals.
608 **114** 1f.75+75c. blue . . . . . 18·00 18·00

1938. Infantry Monument Fund.
609 **115** 55c.+70c. purple . . . . 4·50 4·75
610 65c.+1f.10 blue . . . . . 4·50 4·75

116 Medical Corps Monument at Lyons 117 Saving a Goal

1938. Military Medical Corps' Monument Fund.
611 **116** 55c.+45c. red . . . . . . 9·75 10·50

1938. World Football Cup.
612 **117** 1f.75 blue . . . . 11·50 9·50

117a Clement Ader 118 Jean de La Fontaine

1938. Clement Ader (air pioneer).
612a **117a** 50f. blue . . . . 85·00 65·00

1938. La Fontaine (writer of fables).
613 **118** 55c. green . . . . 1·20 95

1938. Reims Cathedral Restoration Fund. As T **52**, but inscr "REIMS 10.VII.1938".
614 65c.+35c. blue . . . . 7·75 10·50

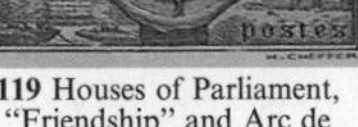

119 Houses of Parliament, "Friendship" and Arc de Triomphe 120 "France" welcoming Frenchmen repatriated from Spain

1938. Visit of King George VI and Queen Elizabeth to France.
615 **119** 1f.75 blue 60 90

1938. French Refugees' Fund.
616 **120** 65c.+60c. red . . . . . . 3·75 5·25

121 Pierre and Marie Curie

1938. International Anti-cancer Fund. 40th Anniv of Discovery of Radium.
617 **121** 1f.75+50c. blue . . . . . 8·50 10·50

122 Arc de Triomphe and Allied Soldiers

123 Mercury

1938. 20th Anniv of 1918 Armistice.
618 **122** 65c.+35c. red . . . . . . 3·25 4·25

1938. Inscr "REPUBLIQUE FRANCAISE".

No.	Type	Description	Unused	Used
618a	**123**	1c. brown	25	25
619		2c. green	25	25
620		5c. red	10	15
621		10c. blue	10	15
622		15c. orange	15	30
622a		15c. brown	60	70
623		20c. mauve	10	15
624		25c. green	10	15
625		30c. red	10	15
626		40c. violet	10	15
627		45c. green	65	70
627b		50c. green	40	45
627c		50c. blue	10	15
628		60c. orange	15	25
629		70c. mauve	15	20
629a		75c. brown	4·25	3·25

For similar stamps inscr "POSTES FRANCAISES", see Nos. 750/3.

124 Nurse and Patient

125 Blind Radio Listener

1938. Students' Fund.
630 **124** 65c.+60c. blue . . . . . 6·75 7·75

1938. "Radio for the Blind" Fund.
631 **125** 90c.+25c. purple . . . . 6·75 8·00

126 Monument to Civilian War Victims, Lille

127 Paul Cezanne

1939. War Victims' Monument Fund.
632 **126** 90c.+35c. brown . . . . 7·50 8·75

1939. Birth Cent of Paul Cezanne (painter).
633 **127** 2f.25 blue . . . . 3·25 2·75

128 Red Cross Nurse

129 Military Engineer

1939. 75th Anniv of Red Cross Society. Cross in red.
634 **128** 90c.+35c. blue & black . . 5·50 6·75

1939. To the Glory of French Military Engineers.
635 **129** 70c.+50c. red . . . . . . 5·75 6·75

130 Ministry of Posts, Telegraphs and Telephones

1939. P.T.T. Orphans' Fund.
636 **130** 90c.+35c. blue . . . . . 18·00 18·00

131 "Dunkerque" Class Battleship

1939. Laying down Keel of Battleship "Clemenceau".
637 **131** 90c. blue 60 75

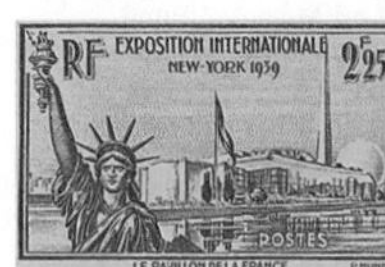
132 French Pavilion, New York Exhibition

1939. New York World's Fair.
638 **132** 2f.25 blue . . . . 7·25 5·75
638a 2f.50 blue . . . . 7·25 7·75

133 Mother and Child

134 Niepce and Daguerre

1939. Children of the Unemployed Fund.
639 **133** 90c.+35c. red . . . . . . 2·50 2·50

1939. Photographic Centenary.
640 **134** 2f.25 blue . . . . 5·75 5·00

135 Eiffel Tower

136 Iris

1939. 50th Anniv of Erection of Eiffel Tower.
641 **135** 90c.+50c. purple . . . . 7·25 7·75

1939.

No.	Type	Description	Unused	Used
642	**136**	80c. brown	25	35
643		1f. green	65	20
643a		1f. red	25	20
643b		1f.30 blue	15	35
643c		1f.50 orange	15	30

See also Nos. 861/8.

137 Marly Water Works

1939. International Water Exhibition, Liege.
644 **137** 2f.25 blue . . . . 9·50 4·00

138 Balzac

1939. Unemployed Intellectuals' Fund.

No.	Type	Description	Unused	Used
645	–	40c.+10c. red	80	1·20
646	–	70c.+10c. purple	3·75	2·75
647	**138**	90c.+10c. mauve	3·25	2·75
648	–	2f.25+25c. blue	15·00	12·50

PORTRAITS—VERT: 40c. Puvis de Chavannes. HORIZ: 70c. Claude Debussy; 2f.25, Claude Bernard.
See also Nos 667b/d.

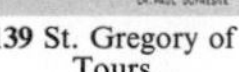
139 St. Gregory of Tours

140 Mother and Children

1939. 1400th Birth Anniv of St. Gregory of Tours.
649 **139** 90c. red 45 65

1939. Birth-rate Development Fund.
650 – 70c.+80c. vio, bl & grn 3·75 4·25
651 **140** 90c.+60c. brn, pur & sep 4·75 5·75
DESIGN: 70c. Mother and children admiring infant in cot.

141 Oath of the Tennis Court

142 Strasbourg Cathedral

1939. 150th Anniv of French Revolution.
652 **141** 90c. green . . . . 1·80 1·70

1939. 5th Centenary of Completion of Strasbourg Cathedral Spire.
653 **142** 70c. red . . . . 90 1·20

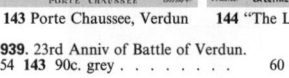

143 Porte Chaussee, Verdun

144 "The Letter"

1939. 23rd Anniv of Battle of Verdun.
654 **143** 90c. grey 60 95

1939. Postal Museum Fund.
655 **144** 40c.+60c. brown & pur 2·75 3·50

145 Statue to Sailors lost at Sea

146 Languedoc

1939. Boulogne Monument Fund.
656 **145** 70c.+30c. plum . . . . . 11·00 11·50

1939.
657 **146** 70c. black on blue 45 50

147 Lyons

1939.
658 **147** 90c. purple 60 80

148 French Soldier and Strasbourg Cathedral

1940. Soldiers' Comforts Fund.
659 **148** 40c.+60c. purple . . . . 2·10 2·50
660 – 1f.+50c. blue . . . . . . 2·30 2·50
DESIGN: 1f. Veteran French colonial soldier and African village.

149 French Colonial Empire

1940. Overseas Propaganda Fund.
661 **149** 1f.+25c. red . . . . . . 1·90 2·40
See also Nos. 708 and 953.

150 Marshal Joffre

1940. War Charities. Inscr as in T **150**.

No.	Type	Description	Unused	Used
662	**150**	80c.+45c. brown	4·75	6·00
663	–	1f.+50c. violet	4·00	6·00
664	–	1f.50+50c. red	4·00	4·75
665	–	2f.50+50c. blue	8·50	10·50

DESIGNS—HORIZ: 1f.50, General Gallieni; 2f.50, Ploughing. VERT: 1f. Marshal Foch.

151 Nurse and Wounded Soldier

1940. Red Cross. Cross in red.
666 – 80c.+1f. green . . . . . 4·75 6·25
667 **151** 1f.+2f. brown . . . . . . 5·75 6·25
DESIGN: 80c. Doctor, nurse, soldier and family.

152 G. Guynemer (pilot)

153 Nurse, wounded Soldier and Family

1940.
667a **152** 50f. blue . . . . 9·00 8·75

1940. Unemployed Intellectuals' Fund. As T **138**. Inscr "POUR LES CHOMEURS INTELLECTUELS".
667b 80c.+10c. brown . . . . . 4·50 7·25
667c 1f.+10c. purple . . . . . . 4·50 7·25
667d 2f.50+25c. blue . . . . . . 4·50 7·00
PORTRAITS: 80c. Debussy; 1f. Balzac.; 2f.50, Bernard.

1940. War Victim's Fund.
667e **153** 1f.+2f. violet . . . . . . 85 1·10

154 Harvesting

1940. National Relief Fund. Inscr "SECOURS NATIONAL".

No.	Type	Description	Unused	Used
668	**154**	80c.+2f. sepia	1·90	2·20
669	–	1f.+2f. brown	1·90	2·20
670	–	1f.50+2f. violet	1·90	2·20
671	–	2f.50+2f. green	2·50	2·20

DESIGNS: 1f. Sowing; 1f.50, Gathering grapes; 2f.50, Cattle.

1940. Surch with new value and with bars on all except T **113**.

No.	Type	Description	Unused	Used
672	**18**	30c. on 35c. green	15	30
673	**61**	50c. on 55c. violet	15	30
674		50c. on 65c. blue	15	15
675		50c. on 75c. green	25	30
676	**123**	50c. on 75c. brown	25	30
677	**61**	50c. on 80c. orange	20	35
678		50c. on 90c. blue	15	15
679		1f. on 1f.25 red	25	35
680		1f. on 1f.40 mauve	20	35
681		1f. on 1f.50 blue	75	1·20
682	**113**	1f. on 1f.75 blue	15	25
683	–	1f. on 2f.15 purple (No. 597)	25	40
684	**113**	1f. on 2f.25 blue	15	25
685		1f. on 2f.50 green	90	1·10
686	–	2f.50 on 5f. blue (No. 599)	25	40
687	–	5f. on 10f. purple on blue (No. 600)	1·50	2·10
688	–	10f. on 20f. green (No. 601)	1·30	1·90
689	**117a**	20f. on 50f. blue	35·00	39·00

155 Marshal Petain 156 Prisoners of War

1940.
690 155 40c. brown 35 50
691 80c. green 40 55
692 1f. red 20 30
693 2f.50 blue . . . . 95 1·30
See also Nos. 774/5.

1941. Prisoners of War Fund.
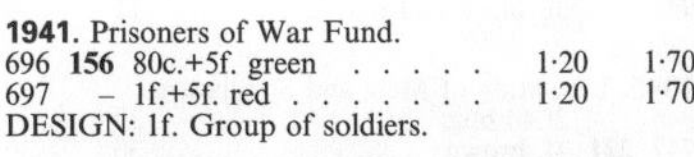
696 156 80c.+5f. green . . . . . 1·20 1·70
697 – 1f.+5f. red . . . . 1·20 1·70
DESIGN: 1f. Group of soldiers.

157 Frederic Mistral 158 Science against Cancer

1941. Frederic Mistral (poet).
698 157 1f. red 20 30

1941. Anti-cancer Fund.
699 158 2f.50+50c. blk and brn . . 1·10 1·60

159 Beaune Hospital, 1443

1941. Views.
700 159 5f. brown 25 30
701 – 10f. violet 35 55
702 159 15f. red 50 75
703 – 20f. brown . . . . 80 1·20
DESIGNS: 10f. Angers; 20f. Ramparts of St. Louis, Aigues-Mortes.

1941. National Relief Fund. Surch **+ 10c**.
704 155 1f.+10c. red 15 20

160

1941. Winter Relief Fund. Inscr as in T **160**.
705 160 1f.+2f. purple . . . . . . 1·60 1·80
706 – 2f.50+7f.50 blue . . . . . 5·50 4·25
DESIGN: 2f.50, "Charity" helping a pauper.

162 Liner "Pasteur"

1941. Seamen's Dependants Relief Fund. Surch.
707 162 1f.+1f. on 70c. green . . . 30 40

1941. As No. 661, but without "R.F." and dated "1941".
708 149 1f.+1f. multicoloured . . 40 60

163 164 Marshal Petain 165

1941. Frame in T **164** is $17 \times 20\frac{1}{2}$ mm.
709 163 20c. purple 20 40
710 30c. red 15 30
711 40c. blue 20 30
712 164 50c. green 15 20
713 60c. violet 15 20
714 70c. blue 15 20
715 70c. orange 15 20
716 80c. brown 20 20
717 80c. green 15 20
718 1f. red 15 20
719 1f.20 brown 15 20
720 165 1f.50 pink 20 20
721 1f.50 brown 15 20
722 2f. green 15 20
723 2f.40 red 15 45
724 2f.50 blue . . . . 65 1·10
725 3f. orange 20 20
725a 164 4f. blue 20 35
725b 4f.50 green 65 70
See also Nos. 740/1.

166 Fisherman 167 Arms of Nancy

1941. National Seamen's Relief Fund.
726 166 1f.+9f. green . . . . . . 80 1·00

1942. National Relief Fund.
727 167 20c.+30c. black . . . . . 1·80 2·75
728 – 40c.+60c. brown . . . . 1·80 2·75
729 – 50c.+70c. blue . . . . . 1·90 3·00
730 – 70c.+80c. red . . . . . 2·50 3·00
731 – 80c.+1f. red . . . . . 2·50 3·00
732 – 1f.+1f. black . . . . . 2·50 3·00
733 – 1f.50+2f. blue . . . . . 2·50 3·00
734 – 2f.+2f. violet . . . . . 2·50 3·00
735 – 2f.50+3f. green . . . . 2·50 3·00
736 – 3f.+5f. brown . . . . . 2·50 3·00
737 – 5f.+6f. blue . . . . . 2·50 3·00
738 – 10f.+10f. red . . . . . 2·75 3·00
DESIGNS—As Type **167**. Nos. 728/38 show respectively the Arms of Lille, Rouen, Bordeaux, Toulouse, Clermont-Ferrand, Marseilles, Lyons, Rennes, Reims, Montpellier and Paris.
See also Nos. 757/68.

168 Jean-Francois de La Perouse, "L'Astrolabe" and "La Boussole"

1942. Birth Bicentenary of La Perouse (navigator and explorer) and National Relief Fund.
739 168 2f.50+7f.50 blue . . . . . 1·20 1·80

1942. Frame $18 \times 21\frac{1}{2}$ mm.
740 164 4f. blue 25 35
741 4f.50 green 25 35

169 Potez 63-11 Bombers

1942. Air Force Dependants Relief Fund.
742 169 1f.50+3f.50 violet . . . . 1·60 2·75

170 Alexis Emmanuel Chabrier

1942. Birth Centenary of Chabrier (composer) and Musicians' Mutual Assistance Fund.
743 170 2f.+3f. brown . . . . . . 85 1·40

171 Symbolical of French Colonial Empire

1942. Empire Fortnight and National Relief Fund.
744 171 1f.50+8f.50 black . . . . 75 1·30

172 Marshal Petain 173 Marshal Petain

1942.
745 172 5f. green 25 30
746 173 50f. black . . . . 3·75 4·50
See also Nos. 772/3.

174 Jean de Vienne 175 Jules Massenet

1942. 600th Birth Anniv of Jean de Vienne (admiral) and Seamen's Relief Fund.
748 174 1f.50+8f.50 brown . . . . 70 1·20

1942. Birth Centenary of Massenet (composer).
749 175 4f. green 20 30

1942. As T **123**, but inscr "POSTES FRANCAISES".
750 10c. blue 15 20
751 30c. red 15 20
752 40c. violet 15 25
753 50c. blue 15 20

1942. National Relief Fund. Surch **+ 50 S N**.
754 165 1f.50+50c. blue 10 15

177 Stendhal (Marie Henri Beyle) 178 Andre Blondel

1942. Death Centenary of Stendhal (novelist).
755 177 4f. brown and red 45 65

1942. Andre Blondel (physicist).
756 178 4f. blue 50 60

1942. National Relief Fund. Arms of French towns as T **167**.
757 50c.+60c. black . . . . . 2·50 4·50
758 60c.+70c. green . . . . . 2·50 3·25
759 80c.+1f. red . . . . 2·50 3·50
760 1f.+1f.30 green . . . . . 2·75 3·50
761 1f.20+1f.50 red . . . . . 3·00 3·75
762 1f.50+1f.80 blue . . . . . 3·00 3·75
763 2f.+2f.30 red . . . . . . 3·00 4·00
764 2f.40+2f.80 green . . . . 3·00 4·00
765 3f.+3f.50 violet . . . . . 3·00 4·00
766 4f.+5f. blue . . . . 3·00 4·25
767 4f.50+6f. red . . . . . . 3·00 4·25
768 5f.+7f. lilac . . . . . . 3·50 4·50
DESIGNS: Nos. 757/68 respectively show the Arms of Chambery, La Rochelle, Poitiers, Orleans, Grenoble, Angers, Dijon, Limoges, Le Havre, Nantes, Nice and St. Etienne.

179 Legionary and Grenadiers 180 Belfry, Arras Town Hall

1942. Tricolor Legion.
769 179 1f.20+8f.80 blue . . . . 8·00 11·00
770 1f.20+8f.80 red . . . . . 8·00 11·00

1942.
771 180 10f. green 25 30

1943. National Relief Fund.
772 173 1f.+10f. blue . . . . . . 2·30 3·25
773 1f.+10f. red . . . . . . 2·30 3·25
774 155 2f.+12f. blue . . . . . . 2·30 3·25
775 2f.+12f. red . . . . . . 2·30 3·25

182 Arms of Lyonnais

1943. Provincial Coats of Arms.
776 182 5f. red, blue & yellow . . 30 40
777 – 10f. black and brown . . 45 55
778 – 15f. yellow, blue & red . . 1·40 1·60
779 – 20f. yellow, blue & brn . 1·10 1·60
ARMS: 10f. "Bretagne"; 15f. "Provence"; 20f. "Ile-de-France".
For other provinces in this series, see Nos. 814/7, 971/4, 1049/53, 1121/5, 1178/83, 1225/31, 1270/3.

For arms of French towns, see Nos. 1403/10, etc.

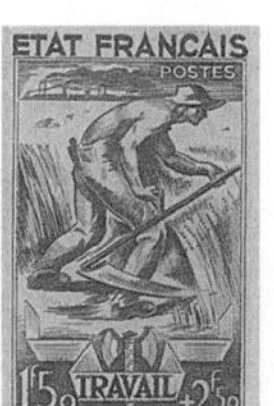

183 "Work" 184 Marshal Petain

1943. National Relief Fund.
780 – 1f.20+1f.40 purple . . . . 13·00 18·00
781 183 1f.50+2f.50 red . . . . . 13·00 18·00
782 – 2f.40+7f. brown . . . . . 13·00 18·00
783 – 4f.+10f. violet . . . . . 13·00 18·00
784 184 5f.+15f. brown . . . . . 13·00 18·00
DESIGNS: 1f.20, Marshal Petain bareheaded; 2f.40, "Family"; 4f. "Country".

185 Lavoisier 186 Lake Lerie and the Meije Peak

1943. Birth Bicentenary of Lavoisier (chemist).
785 185 4f. blue 45 35

1943.
786 186 20f. green 70 85

187 Nicholas Rolin and Guisone de Salins 188 Victims of Bombed Towns

1943. 500th Anniv of Beaune Hospital.
787 187 4f. blue 15 30

1943. National Relief Fund.
788 188 1f.50+3f.50 black 45 70

189 Prisoners' Families' Relief Work 190 Chevalier de Bayard

1943. Prisoners' Families Relief Fund. Inscr as in T **189**.
789 – 1f.50+8f.50 brown . . . . 85 1·20
790 189 2f.40+7f.60 green . . . . 85 1·40
DESIGN—VERT: 1f.50, Prisoner's family.

1943. National Relief Fund.
791 – 60c.+80c. green . . . . . 1·50 2·10
792 – 1f.20+1f.50 black . . . . 1·50 2·10
793 – 1f.50+3f. blue . . . . . 1·50 2·10
794 190 2f.40+4f. red . . . . . . 1·70 2·10
795 – 4f.+6f. brown . . . . . . 1·70 2·30
796 – 5f.+10f. green . . . . . 1·70 2·40
PORTRAITS: 60c. Michel de Montaigne (essayist); 1f.20, Francois Clouet (painter); 1f.50, Ambroise Pare (surgeon); 4f. Due de Sully (King Henri IV's finance minister); 5f. King Henri IV.

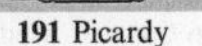
191 Picardy 196 Admiral de Tourville

1943. National Relief Fund. Provincial costumes.
797 191 60c.+1f.30 brown . . . . 1·70 2·20
798 – 1f.20+2f. violet . . . . . 1·70 2·20
799 – 1f.50+4f. blue . . . . . 1·70 2·20
800 – 2f.40+5f. red . . . . . . 1·70 2·20
801 – 4f.+6f. blue . . . . . . 2·00 3·25
802 – 5f.+7f. red . . . . 2·00 3·25

DESIGNS: 1f.20, "Bretagne"; 1f.50, "Ile de France"; 2f.40, "Bourgogne"; 4f. "Auvergne"; 5f. "Provence".

1944. 300th Birth Anniv of Admiral de Tourville.
810 **196** 4f.+6f. red 70 90

197 Branly **198** Gounod

1944. Birth Centenary of Branly (physicist).
811 **197** 4f. blue 25 40

1944. 50th Death Anniv of Gounod (composer).
812 **198** 1f.50+3f.50 brown . . . . 75 1·00

200 Flanders **202** Petain gives France Workers' Charter

201 Marshal Petain

1944. Provincial Coats of Arms.
814 **200** 5f. black, orange & red 25 40
815 – 10f. yellow, red & brown 25 40
816 – 15f. yellow, blue & brown 55 1·10
817 – 20f. yellow, red & blue . . 95 1·30
ARMS: 10f. "Languedoc"; 15f. "Orleanais"; 20f. "Normandie".

1944. Petain's 88th Birthday.
818 **201** 1f.50+3f.50 brown . . . . 2·40 4·25
819 – 2f.+3f. blue 60 70
820 **202** 4f.+6f. red 60 70
DESIGN—As Type **202**: 2f. inscr "Le Marechal institua la Corporation Paysanne" (Trans. "The Marshal set up the Peasant Corporation").

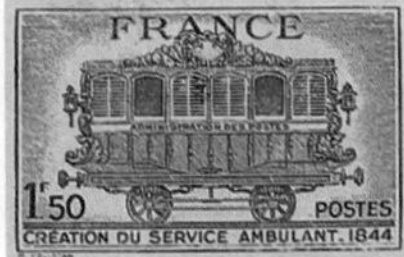

203 Paris–Rouen Travelling Post Office Van, 1844

1944. Centenary of Mobile Post Office.
821 **203** 1f.50 green 45 75

204 Chateau of Chenonceaux

1944.
822 **204** 15f. brown 45 60
823 25f. black 45 70
The 15f. is inscr "FRANCE".

205 Louis XIV **206** Old and Modern Locomotives

1944. National Relief Fund.
824 – 50c.+1f.50 red . . . . . 1·30 1·90
825 – 80c.+2f.20 green . . . . 1·10 1·80
826 – 1f.20+2f.80 black . . . . 1·10 1·70
827 – 1f.50+3f.50 blue . . . . 1·10 1·80
828 – 2f.+4f. brown . . . . . 1·10 1·80
829 **205** 4f.+6f. orange . . . . . 1·10 2·10
DESIGNS: 50c. Moliere (dramatist); 80c. Jean Hardouin-Manzart (scholar); 1f.20, Blaise Pascal (mathematician); 1f.50, Louis, Prince de Conde; 2f. Jean-Baptiste Colbert (King Louis XIV's chief minister).

1944. National Relief Fund. Centenary of Paris–Orleans and Paris–Rouen Railways.
830 **206** 4f.+6f. black . . . . . . 1·40 2·40

207 Claude Chappe **208** Gallic Cock **209** "Marianne"

1944. 150th Anniv of Invention of Semaphore Telegraph.
831 **207** 4f. blue 15 30

1944.
832 **208** 10c. green 10 15
833 30c. lilac 20 50
834 40c. blue 10 25
835 50c. red 10 15
836 **209** 60c. brown 10 25
837 70c. mauve 10 15
838 80c. green . . . . 95 1·30
839 1f. violet 10 25
840 1f.20 red 10 25
841 1f.50 blue 10 15
842 **208** 2f. blue 10 25
843 **209** 2f.40 red . . . . 1·30 1·70
844 3f. green 20 30
845 4f. blue 20 30
846 4f.50 black 20 20
847 5f. blue . . . . 4·00 4·25
848 **208** 10f. violet . . . . . . 4·25 5·25
849 15f. brown . . . . . . 4·25 5·25
850 20f. green . . . . . . 4·25 4·25

210 Arc de Triomphe, Paris **211** "Marianne"

1944.
851 **210** 5c. purple 15 15
852 10c. grey 15 15
853 25c. brown 15 15
854 50c. green 15 15
855 1f. green 15 15
856 1f.50 pink 15 15
857 2f.50 violet 15 35
858 4f. blue 15 35
859 5f. black 15 35
860 10f. orange . . . . . . 25·00 27·00
See also Nos. 936/45.

1944. New colours and values.
861 **136** 80c. green 15 45
862 1f. blue 15 15
863 1f.20 violet 15 15
864 1f.50 brown 15 15
865 2f. brown 15 15
866 2f.40 red 20 30
867 3f. orange 20 20
868 4f. blue 20 35

1944.
869 **211** 10c. blue 10 10
870 30c. brown 10 10
871 40c. blue 10 10
872 50c. orange 10 10
873 60c. blue 10 10
874 70c. brown 10 10
875 80c. green 10 10
876 1f. lilac 10 10
877 1f.20 green 10 10
878 1f.50 red 10 10
879 2f. brown 10 15
880 2f.40 red 15 15
881 3f. olive 15 20
882 4f. blue 15 30
883 4f.50 grey 15 30
884 5f. orange 15 30
885 10f. green 20 35
886 15f. red 25 35
887 20f. orange . . . . . . 1·30 1·80
888 50f. violet . . . . . . 2·75 3·00

212 St. Denis Basilica

1944. 8th Centenary of St. Denis Basilica.
889 **212** 2f.40 brown 30 45

213 Marshal Bugeaud **214** Angouleme Cathedral

1944. Centenary of Battle of Isly.
890 **213** 4f. green 15 30

1944. Cathedrals of France (1st issue).
891 **214** 50c.+1f.50 black 45 85
892 – 80c.+2f.20 purple 45 85
893 – 1f.20+2f.80 red 60 85
894 – 1f.50+3f.50 blue 60 85
895 – 4f.+6f. red 60 85
DESIGNS: 80c. Chartres; 1f.20, Amiens; 1f.50, Beauvais; 4f. Albi.

1944. Nos. 750/3 optd **RF**.
896 10c. blue 10 15
897 30c. red 10 15
898 40c. violet 10 15
899 50c. blue 10 15

215 Arms of De Villayer **216** "France" exhorting Resistance Forces

1944. Stamp Day.
900 **215** 1f.50+3f.50 brown 15 25

1945. Liberation.
901 **216** 4f. blue 35 45

217 Shield and Broken Chains **218** Ceres **219** Marianne

220 Marianne **221** Arms of Strasbourg

1945.
902 **217** 10c. brown 15 15
903 30c. green 15 20
904 40c. mauve 25 30
905 50c. blue 15 15
906 **218** 60c. blue 15 15
907 80c. green 15 15
908 90c. green* 85 85
909 1f. red 15 15
910 1f.20 black 25 35
997 1f.30 blue 25 25
911 1f.50 purple 15 15
912 **219** 1f.50 red 15 25
913 2f. green 20 15
914 **218** 2f. green 15 15
915 **219** 2f.40 red 50 50
916 **218** 2f.50 brown 15 15
997a **219** 2f.50 brown* . . . . . . 2·10 1·70
917 3f. brown 15 15
918 3f. red 15 10
998 3f. green . . . . . . 1·90 40
999 3f. mauve 25 20
1000 3f.50 red 75 60
919 4f. blue 25 20
920 4f. violet 15 20
1001 4f. green 30 30
1001a 4f. orange . . . . . . 3·25 95
1002 4f.50 blue 15 10
921 5f. green 20 10
1003 5f. red 15 10
1004 5f. blue 25 20
1004b 5f. violet 40 10
922 6f. blue 35 40
1005 6f. red 25 10
1005a 6f. green . . . . . . 6·75 45
1006 8f. blue 40 20
924 10f. orange 75 65
928 10f. blue . . . . . . 1·40 50
1007 10f. violet 30 10
1007a 12f. blue . . . . . . 3·00 35
1007b 12f. orange 70 80

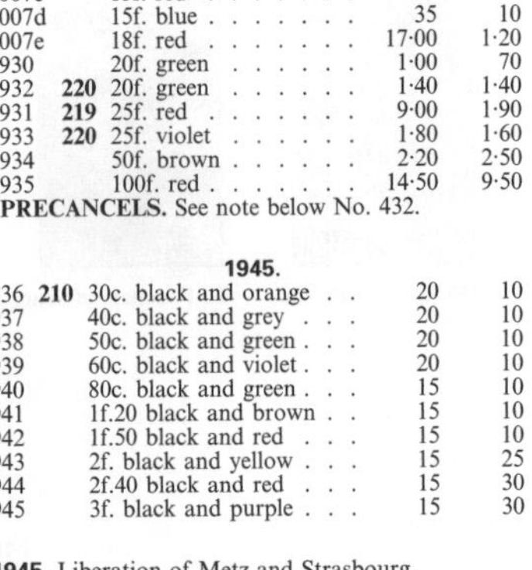

926 15f. purple . . . . . . 4·25 2·30
1007c 15f. red 95 20
1007d 15f. blue 35 10
1007e 18f. red . . . . . . 17·00 1·20
930 20f. green . . . . . . 1·00 70
932 **220** 20f. green . . . . . . 1·40 1·40
931 **219** 25f. red . . . . . . 9·00 1·90
933 **220** 25f. violet . . . . . . 1·80 1·60
934 50f. brown . . . . . . 2·20 2·50
935 100f. red . . . . . . 14·50 9·50
***PRECANCELS.** See note below No. 432.

1945.
936 **210** 30c. black and orange . . 20 10
937 40c. black and grey . . 20 10
938 50c. black and green . . . 20 10
939 60c. black and violet . . . 20 10
940 80c. black and green . . . 15 10
941 1f.20 black and brown . . 15 10
942 1f.50 black and red . . . 15 10
943 2f. black and yellow . . . 15 25
944 2f.40 black and red . . . 15 30
945 3f. black and purple . . . 15 30

1945. Liberation of Metz and Strasbourg.
946 – 2f.40 blue 30 30
947 **221** 4f. brown 30 30
DESIGN: 2f.40, Arms of Metz.

222 Patient in Deck Chair **223** Refugee Employee and Family

1945. Anti-tuberculosis Fund.
948 **222** 2f.+1f. orange 25 30

1945. Postal Employees War Victims' Fund.
949 **223** 4f.+6f. brown 25 30

224 Sarah Bernhardt **225** Alsatian and Lorrainer in Native Dress

1945. Birth Cent of Sarah Bernhardt (actress).
950 **224** 4f.+1f. brown 40 45

1945. Liberation of Alsace-Lorraine.
951 **225** 4f. brown 25 30

226 Children in Country **227** Destruction of Oradour

1945. Fresh Air Crusade.
952 **226** 4f.+2f. green 30 30

1945. As No. 661 but incorporating Cross of Lorraine and inscr "1945".
953 **149** 2f. blue 30 30

1945. Destruction of Oradour-sur-Glane.
954 **227** 4f.+2f. brown 30 30

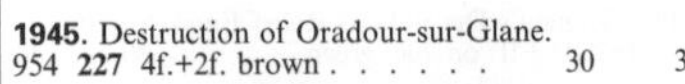

228 Louis XI

1945. Stamp Day.
955 **228** 2f.+3f. blue 60 60

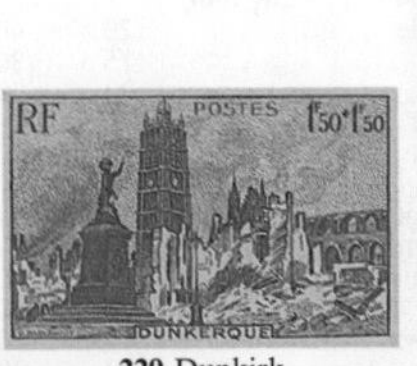

229 Dunkirk **230** Alfred Fournier

1945. Devastated Towns.
956 **229** 1f.50+1f.50 red 65 60
957 – 2f.+2f. violet 65 55
958 – 2f.40+2f.60 blue 80 75
959 – 4f.+4f. black 80 75
DESIGNS: 2f. Rouen; 2f.40c. Caen; 4f. St. Malo.

1946. Prophylaxis Fund.
960 **230** 2f.+3f. red 40 45
961 2f.+3f. blue 45 40

231 Henri Becquerel **233** "Les Invalides"

1946.
962 **231** 2f.+3f. violet 40 35

1946. Surcharged **3F.**
963 **222** 3f. on 2f.+1f. orange . . . 25 30

1946. War Invalids' Relief Fund.
964 **233** 4f.+6f. brown 40 45

234 "Emile Bertin" (cruiser) and "Lorraine" (battleship) **235** "The Letter"

1946. Naval Charities.
965 **234** 2f.+3f. black 80 80

1946. Postal Museum Fund.
966 **235** 2f.+3f. red 70 60

236 Iris **237** Jupiter carrying off Egine

1946. Air.
967 – 40f. green 60 40
968 **236** 50f. pink 60 25
969 **237** 100f. blue . . . . 8·50 90
970 – 200f. red . . . . 6·25 1·40
DESIGNS—VERT: 40f. Centaur. HORIZ: 200f. Apollo and chariot.

239 Arms of Corsica **241** Fouquet de la Varane

1946. Provincial Coats of arms.
971 **239** 10c. black and blue . . . 15 15
972 – 30c. black, red and yellow 15 15
973 – 50c. brown, yellow & red 15 15
974 – 60c. red, blue & black . . 15 15
DESIGNS: 30c. Alsace; 50c. Lorraine; 60c. Nice.

1946. Stamp Day.
975 **241** 3f.+2f. brown 75 75

244 Luxembourg Palace **245** Roc-Amadour

1946. Views.
976 – 5f. mauve 25 15
977 – 6f. red . . . . 1·50 65
978 **244** 10f. blue 30 15
979 12f. red . . . . 3·00 60
980 **245** 15f. purple . . . . . . 5·00 45
980a **244** 15f. red 75 80
981 – 20f. blue . . . . 1·40 20
982 – 25f. brown . . . . . . 5·00 25
982a – 25f. blue . . . . . . 12·50 80
DESIGNS—HORIZ: 5f. Vezelay; 6f. Cannes; 20f. Pointe du Raz; 25f. (both) Stanislas Place, Nancy.

248 "Peace"

1946. Peace Conference.
983 **248** 3f. green 30 30
984 – 10f. blue 30 30
DESIGN: 10f. Woman releasing dove.

250 Francois Villon **251**

1946. National Relief Fund. 15th-century Figures.
985 **250** 2f.+1f. blue . . . . . . 1·70 1·70
986 – 3f.+1f. blue . . . . . . 1·70 1·70
987 – 4f.+3f. red . . . . . . 1·70 1·70
988 – 5f.+4f. blue . . . . . . 1·90 1·90
989 – 6f.+5f. brown . . . . . 1·90 2·00
990 – 10f.+6f. orange . . . . . 1·90 2·00
DESIGNS: 3f. Jean Fouquet; 4f. Philippe de Commynes; 5f. Joan of Arc; 6f. Jean Gerson; 10f. Charles VII.

1946. UNESCO Conference, Paris.
991 **251** 10f. blue 30 30

252 St. Julien Cathedral, Le Mans **253** Louvois

1947. National Relief Fund. Cathedrals of France (2nd issue). As T **214** and **252**.
992 – 1f.+1f. red . . . . 1·10 1·30
993 – 3f.+2f. black . . . . . . 3·25 3·75
994 – 4f.+3f. red . . . . 1·70 1·80
995 **252** 6f.+4f. blue . . . . . . 1·70 1·80
996 – 10f.+6f. green . . . . . . 3·25 3·75
DESIGNS—VERT: 1f. St. Sernin, Toulouse; 3f. Notre-Dame du Port, Clermont-Ferrand; 10f. Notre-Dame, Paris. HORIZ: 4f. St. Front, Perigueux.

1947. Stamp Day.
1008 **253** 4f.50+5f.50 red . . . . 1·50 1·60

254 The Louvre Colonnade

255 Herring Gull over Ile de la Cite

1947. 12th U.P.U. Congress.
1009 **254** 3f.50 purple (postage) . . 50 45
1010 – 4f.50 grey 60 60
1011 – 6f. red . . . . 1·20 1·00
1012 – 10f. blue . . . . 1·30 1·10
1013 **255** 500f. green (air) . . . . 60·00 55·00

DESIGNS—As Type **254**: 4f.50, La Conciergerie; 6f. La Cite; 10f. Place de la Concorde.

256 Auguste Pavie **257** Fenelon

1947. Birth Cent of Auguste Pavie (explorer).
1014 **256** 4f.50 purple 45 50

1947. Fenelon, Archbishop of Cambrai.
1015 **257** 4f.50 brown 45 45

258 St. Nazaire Monument **259**

1947. 5th Anniv of British Commando Raid on St. Nazaire.
1016 **258** 6f.+4f. blue 75 60

1947. Boy Scouts' Jamboree.
1017 **259** 5f. brown 60 50

260 Milestone on Road of Liberty **261** "Resistance"

1947. Road Maintenance Fund.
1018 **260** 6f.+4f. green . . . . . 1·20 1·20

1947. Resistance Movement.
1019 **261** 5f. purple 75 70

1947. No. 997 surch **1F.**
1020 **218** 1f. on 1f.30 blue 30 30

263 Conques Abbey **264** Louis Braille

1947.
1021 **263** 15f. red . . . . 5·25 65
1022 18f. blue . . . . 3·50 25
No. 1022 is inscribed "FRANCE".

1948. Louis Braille (inventor of system of writing and printing for the blind).
1023 **264** 6f.+4f. violet 45 50

265 A. de Saint-Exupery (pilot and writer) **267** Etienne Arago

1948. Air. Famous Airmen.
1026 – 40f.+10f. blue . . . . . 1·60 1·70
1024 **265** 50f.+30f. purple . . . . 3·50 3·75
1025 – 100f.+70f. blue . . . . . 4·25 4·50
DESIGNS: 40f. "Avion III" and Douglas DB-7 (Clement Ader); 100f. Jean Dagnaux.

1948. Stamp Day and Centenary of First French Adhesive Postage Stamps.
1027 **267** 6f.+4f. violet 65 65

268 Lamartine **269** Dr. Calmette

1948. National Relief Fund and Cent of 1848 Revolution. Dated "1848 1948".
1028 **268** 1f.+1f. green . . . . . 1·50 1·60
1029 – 3f.+2f. red . . . . . . 1·50 1·60
1030 – 4f.+3f. purple . . . . . 1·60 1·60
1031 – 5f.+4f. blue . . . . . . 3·75 3·50
1032 – 6f.+5f. blue . . . . . . 2·75 2·75
1033 – 10f.+6f. red . . . . . . 2·75 2·75
1034 – 15f.+7f. blue . . . . . 3·50 3·75
1035 – 20f.+8f. violet . . . . . 3·75 3·75
PORTRAITS: 3f. Alexandre-Auguste Ledru-Rollin; 4f. Louis Blanc; 5f. A. M. Albert; 6f. Pierre Joseph Proudhon; 10f. Louis-Auguste Blanqui; 15f. Armand Barbes; 20f. Denis-Auguste Affre.

1948. 1st International B.C.G. (Vaccine) Congress.
1036 **269** 6f.+4f. slate 65 65

270 Gen. Leclerc

1948. Gen. Leclerc Memorial.
1037 **270** 6f. black 45 45
See also Nos. 1171/a.

271 Chateaubriand

1948. Death Centenary of Chateaubriand.
1038 **271** 18f. blue 45 45

272 Genissiat Barrage

1948. Inauguration of Genissiat Barrage.
1039 **272** 12f. red 75 80

273 Aerial View of Chaillot Palace **274** Paul Langevin

1948. U.N. Assembly, Paris.
1040 – 12f. red 55 55
1041 **273** 18f. blue 60 60
DESIGN: 12f. Ground level view of Chaillot Palace.

1948. Transfer of Ashes of Paul Langevin and Jean Perrin to the Pantheon.
1042 **274** 5f. brown 40 35
1043 – 8f. green (Perrin) 35 30

1949. Surch **5F.**
1044 **219** 5f. on 6f. red 30 30

276 Ploughing **277** Arms of Burgundy

1949. Workers.
1045 **276** 3f.+1f. purple . . . . . 1·10 90
1046 – 5f.+3f. blue . . . . . . 1·10 1·00
1047 – 8f.+4f. blue . . . . . . 1·10 1·10
1048 – 10f.+6f. red . . . . . . 1·40 1·30

DESIGNS: 5f. Fisherman; 8f. Miner; 10f. Industrial worker.

1949. Provincial Coats of Arms.
1049 **277** 10c. red, yellow & blue . . . 15 15
1050 – 50c. yellow, red & blue . . . 15 15
1051 – 1f. red and brown . . . 70 35
1052 – 2f. red, yellow & green . . . 70 20
1053 – 4f. blue, yellow & red . . 50 45
ARMS: 50c. "Guyenne"; 1f. "Savoie"; 2f. "Auvergne"; 4f. "Anjou".
See also Nos. 1121/5, 1178/83, 1225/31 and 1270/3.

278 Due de Choiseul

279 Lille

279a Paris

1949. Stamp Day.
1054 **278** 15f.+5f. green . . . . . 1·30 1·30

1949. Air. Views.
1055 **279** 100f. purple . . . . . 1·40 20
1056 – 200f. green . . . . . . 16·00 90
1057 – 300f. violet . . . . . . 20·00 11·50
1058 – 500f. red . . . . 70·00 5·75
1059 **279a** 1000f. purple & black £120 23·00
DESIGNS—As Type **279**: 200f. Bordeaux; 300f. Lyons; 500f. Marseilles.

280 Polar Scene

281 Collegiate Church of St. Bernard, Romans

1949. Polar Expeditions.
1060 **280** 15f. blue 45 45

1949. French Stamp Centenary. (a) Imperf.
1061 **1** 15f. red . . . . 7·25 5·75
1062 25f. blue . . . . 7·25 5·75

(b) Perf.
1063 **219** 15f. red . . . . 7·25 5·75
1064 25f. blue . . . . 7·25 5·75

1949. 600th Anniv of Cession of Dauphiny to King of France.
1065 **281** 12f. brown 45 45

282 Emblems of U.S.A. and France

1949. Franco-American Amity.
1066 **282** 25f. blue and red 95 75

284 St. Wandrille Abbey

285 Jean Racine

1949. Views.
1067 – 20f. red 30 20
1068 **284** 25f. blue 40 20
1068a 30f. blue . . . . 5·75 4·50
1068b – 30f. blue . . . . 1·10 25
1069 – 40f. green . . . . . . 16·00 45
1070 – 50f. purple . . . . . . 2·50 20
DESIGNS: 20f. St. Bertrand de Comminges; 30f. (1068b) Arbois (Jura); 40f. Valley of the Meuse (Ardennes); 50f. Mt. Gerbier-de-Jone, Vivarais.

1949. 250th Death Anniv of Racine (dramatist).
1071 **285** 12f. purple 55 50

1949. French Stamp Centenary ("CITEX"). T **1** with dates "1849 1949" below, repeated ten times (2 × 5) with "1849–1949" centred above.
MS1071a 280 × 155 mm. 10f. (+100f.) red. Complete sheet of ten £400 £400

286 Claude Chappe

288 Allegory of Commerce

287 Alexander III Bridge and "Petit Palais"

1949. International Telephone and Telegraph Congress, Paris.
1072 **286** 10f. red (postage) . . . 1·10 1·00
1073 – 15f. violet . . . . 1·20 1·10
1074 – 25f. red . . . . 2·75 2·50
1075 – 50f. blue . . . . 7·00 5·00
1076 **287** 100f. red (air) . . . . . 8·25 7·50
PORTRAITS—As Type **286**: 15f. Arago and Ampere; 25f. Emile Baudot; 50f. Gen. Ferrie.

1949. French Chambers of Commerce.
1077 **288** 15f. red 30 30

289 Allegory

290 Montesquieu

1949. 75th Anniv of U.P.U.
1078 **289** 5f. green 40 35
1079 15f. red 40 35
1080 25f. blue . . . . 1·50 1·00

1949. National Relief Fund.
1081 **290** 5f.+1f. green . . . . . 3·50 3·50
1082 – 8f.+2f. blue . . . . . . 3·50 3·50
1083 – 10f.+3f. brown . . . . . 4·50 4·50
1084 – 12f.+4f. violet . . . . . 4·50 4·50
1085 – 15f.+5f. red . . . . . . 6·00 5·50
1086 – 25f.+10f. blue . . . . . 7·25 7·25
PORTRAITS: 8f. Voltaire; 10f. Watteau; 12f. Buffon; 15f. Dupleix; 25f. Turgot.

291 "Spring"

1949. National Relief Fund. Seasons.
1087 **291** 5f.+1f. green . . . . . 1·90 1·90
1088 – 8f.+2f. yellow . . . . . 2·75 2·75
1089 – 12f.+3f. violet . . . . . 2·75 2·75
1090 – 15f.+4f. blue . . . . . 4·25 4·50
DESIGNS: 8f. "Summer"; 12f. "Autumn"; 15f. "Winter".

292 Postman

293 Raymond Poincare

1950. Stamp Day.
1091 **292** 12f.+3f. blue . . . . . 4·25 3·25

1950. Honouring Poincare.
1092 **293** 15f. blue 45 50

294 Charles Peguy

295 Francois Rabelais

1950. Honouring Charles Peguy (writer).
1093 **294** 12f. purple 45 50

1950. Honouring Francois Rabelais (writer).
1094 **295** 12f. lake 80 70

296 Andre Chenier

297 Chateaudun

1950. National Relief Fund (revolutionaary celebrities). Frames in blue.
1095 **296** 5f.+2f. purple . . . . . 10·50 10·50
1096 – 8f.+3f. sepia . . . . . . 10·50 10·50
1097 – 10f.+4f. red . . . . . . 11·50 12·00
1098 – 12f.+5f. brown . . . . . 13·00 13·50
1099 – 15f.+6f. green . . . . . 14·00 14·00
1100 – 20f.+10f. blue . . . . . 14·00 14·00
PORTRAITS: 8f. Louis David; 10f. Lazare Carnot; 12f. Danton; 15f. Robespierre; 20f. Hoche.

1950.
1101 **297** 8f. brown & lt brown . . 75 70
1102 – 12f. brown . . . . . . 1·00 85
DESIGN: 12f. Palace of Fontainebleau.

298 Madame Recamier

299 "L'Amour" (after Falconet)

1950.
1103 **298** 12f. green 55 55
1104 – 15f. blue 55 55
PORTRAIT: 15f. Madame de Sevigne.

1950. Red Cross. Cross in red.
1105 – 8f.+2f. blue . . . . . . 2·75 2·50
1106 **299** 15f.+3f. purple . . . . . 3·25 3·00
DESIGN: 8f. Bust of Alexandre Brongniart (after Houdon).

300 T.P.O. Sorting Van

301 J. Ferry (statesman)

1951. Stamp Day.
1107 **300** 12f.+3f. violet . . . . . 3·75 4·50

1951.
1108 **301** 15f. red 60 60

302 Shuttle

303 De La Salle

1951. Textile Industry.
1109 **302** 25f. blue 95 75

1951. Birth Tercentenary of Jean Baptiste de la Salle (educational reformer).
1110 **303** 15f. brown 65 55

304 Anchor and Map

1951. 50th Anniv of Formation of Colonial Troops.
1111 **304** 15f. blue 70 60

305 Vincent D'Indy

1951. Birth Centenary of Vincent D'Indy (composer).
1112 **305** 25f. green . . . . 2·20 2·10

306 A. de Musset

307 Nocard, Bouley and Chauveau

1951. National Relief Fund. Frames in sepia.
1113 **306** 5f.+1f. green . . . . . 7·25 7·25
1114 – 8f.+2f. purple . . . . . 8·75 8·75
1115 – 10f.+3f. green . . . . . 7·25 7·25
1116 – 12f.+4f. brown . . . . . 8·75 8·50
1117 – 15f.+5f. red . . . . . . 8·75 8·50
1118 – 30f.+10f. blue . . . . . 14·00 16·00
PORTRAITS: 8f. Delacroix; 10f. Gay-Lussac; 12f. Surcouf; 15f. Talleyrand; 30f. Napoleon.

1951. French Veterinary Research.
1119 **307** 12f. mauve 65 65

308 Picque, Roussin and Villemin

309 St. Nicholas

1951. Military Health Service.
1120 **308** 15f. purple 75 60

1951. Provincial Coats of Arms as T **277**.
1121 10c. yellow, blue and red . . 15 20
1122 50c. black, red and green . . 15 20
1123 1f. red, yellow and blue . . 30 25
1124 2f. yellow, blue and red . . 1·00 35
1125 3f. yellow, blue and red . . 90 45
ARMS: 10c. "Artois"; 50c. "Limousin"; 1f. "Bearn"; 2f. "Touraine"; 3f. "Franche-Comte".

1951. Popular Pictorial Art Exhibition, Epinal. Multicoloured centre.
1126 **309** 15f. blue . . . . 1·30 90

310 Seal of Mercantile Guild

311 M. Nogues

1951. Bimillenary of Paris.
1127 **310** 15f. brown, blue & red 65 50

1951. M. Nogues (aviator).
1128 **311** 12f. indigo and blue . . 1·00 80

312 C. Baudelaire

1951. Famous French Poets.
1129 **312** 8f. violet 65 65
1130 – 12f. grey 65 65
1131 – 15f. green 65 65
DESIGNS: 12f. Paul Verlaine; 15f. Arthur Rimbaud.

313 Eiffel Tower and Chaillot Palace

314 L. G. Clemenceau (statesman)

1951. U.N.O. General Assembly.
1132 **313** 18f. red . . . . 1·40 80
1133 30f. blue . . . . 2·40 1·10

1951. 110th Birth Anniv of Clemenceau and 33rd Anniv of Armistice.
1134 **314** 15f. sepia 55 50

315 Chateau Clos-Vougeot

316 15th-century Child

1951. 400th Anniv of Chateau Clos-Vougeot.
1135 **315** 30f. dp brown & brown 5·75 2·50

1951. Red Cross. Cross in red.
1136 **316** 12f.+3f. brown . . . . . 3·50 3·25
1137 – 15f.+5f. blue . . . . . 4·50 4·25
DESIGN: 15f. 18th-century child (De La Tour).

317 Observatory, Pic du Midi de Bigorre

1951.
1138 **317** 40f. violet . . . . 6·25 15
1139 – 50f. brown . . . . . . 5·25 15
VIEW—VERT: 50f. Church of St. Etienne, Caen.

319 19th-cent Mail Coach

1952. Stamp Day.
1140 **319** 12f.+3f. green . . . . . 5·00 4·50

320 Marshal de Lattre de Tassigny

321 Gate of France, Vaucouleurs

1952.
1140a **320** 12f. indigo and blue . . 2·40 1·50
1141 15f. brown . . . . . . 1·00 70

1952.
1142 **321** 12f. brown . . . . . . 1·50 1·30

322 French Monument, Narvik

1952. Battle of Narvik.
1143 **322** 30f. blue . . . . 3·25 2·20

323 Chambord Chateau

1952.
1144 **323** 20f. violet 60 15

324 Council of Europe Building, Strasbourg

1952. Council of Europe Assembly.
1145 **324** 30f. green . . . . 8·25 6·25

325 Bir Hakeim Monument

326 Abbey of the Holy Cross, Poitiers

1952. 10th Anniv of Battle of Bir Hakeim.
1146 **325** 30f. lake . . . . 3·75 2·40

1952. 1400th Anniv of Abbey of the Holy Cross, Poitiers.
1147 **326** 15f. red 55 50

327 Medaille Militaire, in 1852 and 1952

328 Garabit Railway Viaduct

1952. Centenary of Medaille Militaire.
1148 **327** 15f. brown, yell & grn 55 50

1952.
1149 **328** 15f. blue 80 65

329 Leonardo, Amboise Chateau and Town of Vinci

330 Flaubert (after E. Giraud)

1952. 500th Birth Anniv of Leonardo da Vinci.
1150 **329** 30f. blue . . . . 8·50 7·50

1952. National Relief Fund. Frames in sepia.
1151 **330** 8f.+2f. blue . . . . . . 6·25 7·25
1152 – 12f.+3f. blue . . . . . 7·75 7·75
1153 – 15f.+4f. green . . . . . 7·75 7·75
1154 – 18f.+5f. sepia . . . . . 10·50 10·00
1155 – 20f.+6f. red . . . . . . 10·50 10·00
1156 – 30f.+7f. violet . . . . . 10·50 10·00
PORTRAITS: 12f. Manet; 15f. Saint-Saens; 18f. H. Poincare; 20f. Haussmann (after Yvon); 20f. Thiers.

331 R. Laennec (physician)

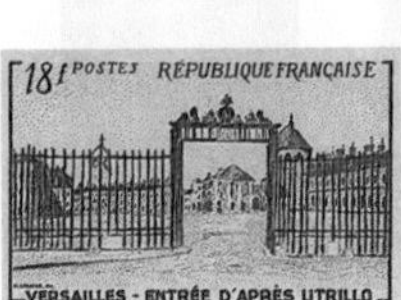
332 "Cherub" (bas-relief)

1952.
1157 **331** 12f. green 70 55

1952. Red Cross Fund. Sculptures from Basin of Diana, Versailles. Cross in red.
1158 **332** 12f.+3f. green . . . . . 5·50 5·25
1159 – 15f.+5f. blue . . . . . 5·50 5·25
DESIGN: 15f. "Cherub" (facing left).

333 Versailles Gateway

334 Count D'Argenson

1952.
1160 **333** 18f. purple . . . . . . 2·75 2·10
1160a 18f. indigo, blue & brn 11·50 7·00

1953. Stamp Day.
1161 **334** 12f.+3f. blue . . . . . 3·25 3·25

335 "Gargantua" (Rabelais)

337 Mannequin and Place Vendome, Paris

1953. Literary Figures and National Industries.
1162 **335** 6f. lake and red 45 20
1163 – 8f. blue and indigo . . 25 15
1164 – 12f. green and brown 25 15
1165 – 18f. sepia and purple 70 30
1166 – 25f. sepia, red & brown 15·00 40
1166a – 25f. blue and black . . 85 20
1167 **337** 30f. violet and blue . . 1·00 20
1167a – 30f. blue & turquoise 1·90 15
1168 – 40f. brown & chocolate 5·00 15
1169 – 50f. brn, turq & blue 1·60 15
1170 – 75f. lake and red . . . 16·00 1·00
DESIGNS—As Types **335/337**: 8f. "Celimene" (Moliere); 12f. "Figaro" (Beaumarchais); 18f. "Hernani" (Victor Hugo); 25f. (No. 1166) Tapestry; 25f. (No. 1166a) Mannequin modelling gloves; 30f. (No. 1167a) Rare books and book-binding; 40f. Porcelain and cut-glass; 50f. Gold plate and jewellery; 75f. Flowers and perfumes.

1953. General Leclerc. As T **270** but inscr "GENERAL LECLERC MARECHAL DE FRANCE".
1171 **270** 8f. brown . . . . . . 1·10 80
1171a 12f. turquoise & green 3·50 1·90

338 Olivier de Serres

339 Cyclists and Map

1953. National Relief Fund.
1172 – 8f.+2f. blue . . . . . . 6·25 6·50
1173 **338** 12f.+3f. green . . . . . 6·25 6·50
1174 – 15f.+4f. lake . . . . . 10·50 10·00
1175 – 18f.+5f. blue . . . . . 11·50 11·00
1176 – 20f.+6f. violet . . . . 11·50 11·00
1177 – 30f.+7f. brown . . . . 13·00 12·50
PORTRAITS: 8f. St. Bernard; 15f. Rameau; 18f. Monge; 20f. Michelet; 30f. Marshal Lyautey.

1953. Provincial Coats of Arms as T **277**.
1178 50c. yellow, red and blue . . 25 30
1179 70c. yellow, blue and red . . 30 30
1180 80c. yellow, red and blue . . 30 30
1181 1f. yellow, red and black . . 30 25
1182 2f. yellow, blue and brown 50 30
1183 3f. yellow, blue and red . . 75 40

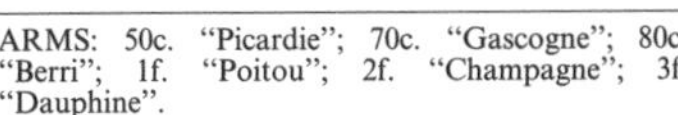
ARMS: 50c. "Picardie"; 70c. "Gascogne"; 80c. "Berri"; 1f. "Poitou"; 2f. "Champagne"; 3f. "Dauphine".

1953. 50th Anniv of "Tour de France" Cycle Race.
1184 **339** 12f. black, blue & red . . 2·30 1·40

340 Swimming

341 Mme. Vigee-Lebrun and Daughter (self-portrait)

1953. Sports.
1185 **340** 20f. brown and red . . . 2·75 20
1186 – 25f. brown and green . . 14·50 60
1187 – 30f. brown and blue . . 2·75 40
1188 – 40f. indigo and brown 13·00 55
1189 – 50f. brown and green . . 7·75 30
1190 – 75f. lake and orange . . 39·00 14·50
SPORTS: 25f. Running; 30f. Fencing; 40f. Canoeing; 50f. Rowing; 75f. Horse-jumping.
See also Nos. 1297/1300.

1953. Red Cross Fund. Cross in red.
1191 **341** 12f.+3f. brown . . . . . 7·50 7·25
1192 – 15f.+5f. blue . . . . . 11·00 9·75
DESIGN: 15f. "The Return from the Baptism" (L. Le Nain).

1953. Surch **15F.**
1193 **219** 15f. on 18f. red 70 55

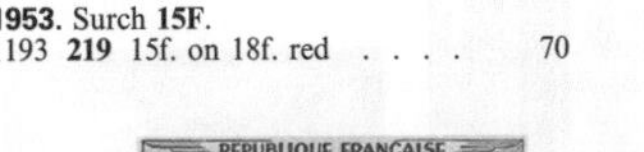

343 Air Fouga Magister

1954. Air.
1194 – 100f. brown and blue . . 3·25 20
1195 – 200f. purple and blue . . 12·00 35
1196 **343** 500f. red and orange . . £160 13·50
1197 – 1000f. blue, pur & turq £130 19·00
AIRCRAFT: 100f. Dassault Mystere IVA; 200f. Nord 2501 Noratlas; 1000f. Breguet Provence.
See also No. 1457.

344 Harvester

345 Gallic Cock

346 Lavallette

1954. (a) Precancelled*.
1198 **344** 4f. blue 30 20
1198a **345** 5f. brown 40 35
1199 **344** 8f. red . . . . 5·25 1·60
1199a **345** 8f. violet 65 50
1199b 10f. blue . . . . . . 2·30 60
1200 12f. mauve . . . . . . 4·50 1·10
1200b 15f. purple . . . . . . 2·50 1·10
1200c 20f. green . . . . . . 2·10 1·50
1201 24f. green . . . . . . 23·00 7·50
1201a 30f. red . . . . . . 8·75 4·50
1201b 40f. red . . . . . . 5·25 4·00
1201c 45f. green . . . . . . 35·00 30·00
1201d 55f. green . . . . . . 30·00 25·00
(b) Without precancel.
1201e **344** 6f. brown 15 10
1201f 10f. green 65 10
1201g 12f. purple 25 15
***PRECANCELS.** See note below No. 432. See also Nos. 1470/3.

1954. Stamp Day.
1202 **346** 12f.+3f. green & brown 5·00 4·00

347 Exhibition Buildings

348 "D-Day"

1954. 50th Anniv of Paris Fair.
1203 **347** 15f. lake and blue . . . 45 45

1954. 10th Anniv of Liberation.
1204 **348** 15f. red and blue . . . . 2·10 1·40

349 Lourdes **350** Jumieges Abbey

1954. Views.
1205 **349** 6f. indigo, blue & grn 40 20
1206 – 8f. green and blue . . . 30 15
1207 – 10f. brown and blue . . 35 10
1208 – 12f. lilac and violet . . 40 10
1209 – 12f. brown & chocolate 1·70 1·60
1210 – 18f. indigo, blue & grn 3·25 85
1211 – 20f. brn, chestnut & bl 3·25 15
1211a **349** 20f. brown and blue . . 40 25
VIEWS—HORIZ: 8f. Seine Valley at Andelys; 10f. Royan; 12f. (No. 1209), Limoges; 18f. Cheverny Chateau; 20f. (No. 1211), Ajaccio Bay. VERT: 12f. (No. 1208), Quimper.

1954. 13th Centenary of Jumieges Abbey.
1212 **350** 12f. indigo, blue & grn 1·70 1·40

351 Abbey Church of St. Philibert, Tournus **352** Stenay

1954. 1st Conference of Romanesque Studies, Tournus.
1213 **351** 30f. blue and indigo . . 6·00 4·50

1954. Tercent of Return of Stenay to France.
1214 **352** 15f. brown and sepia . . 90 80

353 St. Louis **354** Villandry Chateau

1954. National Relief Fund.
1215 **353** 12f.+4f. blue . . . . . 21·00 19·00
1216 – 15f.+5f. violet . . . . . 21·00 21·00
1217 – 18f.+6f. sepia . . . . . 21·00 19·00
1218 – 20f.+7f. red . . . . . . 28·00 29·00
1219 – 25f.+8f. blue . . . . . 28·00 27·00
1220 – 30f.+10f. purple . . . . 28·00 25·00
PORTRAITS: 15f. Bossuet; 18f. Sadi Carnot; 20f. A. Bourdelle; 25f. Dr. E. Roux; 30f. Paul Valery.

1954. Four Centuries of Renaissance Gardens.
1221 **354** 18f. green and blue . . . 4·75 4·00

355 Cadet and Flag

1954. 150th Anniv of St. Cyr Military Academy.
1222 **355** 15f. indigo, blue & red 1·40 1·40

356 Napoleon Conferring Decorations **357** "Basis of Metric System"

1954. 150th Anniv of First Legion of Honour Presentation.
1223 **356** 12f. red . . . . 1·50 1·20

1954. 150th Anniv of Metric System.
1224 **357** 30f. sepia and blue . . . 6·50 4·75

1954. Provincial Coats of Arms as T **277**.
1225 50c. yellow, blue and black 30 35
1226 70c. yellow, red and green 30 35
1227 80c. yellow, blue and red . . 30 35
1228 1f. yellow, blue and red . . 20 15
1229 2f. yellow, red and black . . 15 15
1230 3f. yellow, red and brown 15 15
1231 5f. yellow and blue 15 10
ARMS: 50c. "Maine"; 70c. "Navarre"; 80c. "Nivernais"; 1f. "Bourbonnais"; 2f. "Angoumois"; 3f. "Aunis"; 5f. "Saintonge".

359 "Young Girl with Doves" (J.-B. Greuze) **360** Saint-Simon

1954. Red Cross Fund. Cross in red.
1232 – 12f.+3f. indigo & blue 12·00 10·50
1233 **359** 15f.+5f. brn & dp brn 13·00 12·00
DESIGN: 12f. "The Sick Child" (E. Carriere).

1955. Death Bicentenary of Saint-Simon (writer).
1234 **360** 12f. purple & brown . . 85 65

361 "Industry", "Agriculture" and Rotary Emblem **362** "France"

1955. 50th Anniv of Rotary International.
1235 **361** 30f. orange, blue and deep blue . . . . . . 2·50 1·60

1955.
1236 **362** 6f. brown . . . . . . 3·25 2·40
1237 12f. green . . . . . . 3·50 1·70
1238 15f. red 35 10
1238a 18f. green 15 25
1238b 20f. blue 30 10
1238c 25f. red . . . . 1·40 10

363 Thimonnier and Sewing-machines

1955. French Inventors (1st series).
1239 – 5f. blue & light blue . . 85 70
1240 **363** 10f. brown & chestnut 1·10 1·10
1241 – 12f. green . . . . 1·80 1·20
1242 – 18f. blue and grey . . . 3·00 2·50
1243 – 25f. violet and plum . . 3·25 2·75
1244 – 30f. vermilion & red . . 3·25 2·75
DESIGNS: 5f. Le Bon (gaslight); 12f. Appert (food canning); 18f. Sainte-Claire Deville (aluminium); 25f. Martin (steel); 30f. Chardonnet (artificial silk).
See also Nos. 1324/7.

364 Mail Balloon "Armand Barbes", 1870

1955. Stamp Day.
1245 **364** 12f.+3f. brown, green and blue . . . . . . 5·25 4·75

365 Florian and Pastoral scene

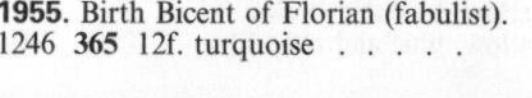

1955. Birth Bicent of Florian (fabulist).
1246 **365** 12f. turquoise 80 75

366 Eiffel Tower and Television Aerials

1955. Television Development.
1247 **366** 15f. blue & deep blue . . 1·10 1·00

367 Observation Tower and Fence

1955. 10th Anniv of Liberation of Concentration Camps.
1248 **367** 12f. black and grey . . . 1·10 1·10

368 Electric Locomotive **369** The "Jacquemart" (campanile), Moulins

1955. Electrification of Valenciennes–Thionville Railway Line.
1249 **368** 12f. brown and grey . . 2·40 1·40

1955.
1250 **369** 12f. brown . . . . . . 1·70 1·30

370 Jules Verne and Capt. Nemo on the "Nautilus"

1955. 50th Death Anniv of Jules Verne (author).
1251 **370** 30f. blue . . . . 7·75 5·75

371 Maryse Bastie (airwoman) **372** Vauban

1955. Air. Maryse Bastie Commemoration.
1252 **371** 50f. claret and red . . . 7·75 5·25

1955. National Relief Fund.
1253 – 12f.+5f. violet . . . . . 15·00 14·00
1254 – 15f.+6f. blue . . . . . 15·00 14·00
1255 **372** 18f.+7f. green . . . . . 17·00 17·00
1256 – 25f.+8f. slate . . . . . 22·00 22·00
1257 – 30f.+9f. lake . . . . . 25·00 24·00
1258 – 50f.+15f. turquoise . . . 29·00 29·00
PORTRAITS: 12f. King Philippe-Auguste; 15f. Malherbe; 25f. Vergennes; 30f. Laplace; 50f. Renoir.

373 A. and L. Lumiere

1955. 60th Anniv of French Cinema Industry.
1259 **373** 30f. brown . . . . . . 6·50 4·75

374 Jacques Coeur (merchant prince)

1955.
1260 **374** 12f. violet . . . . 2·40 1·60

375 "La Capricieuse"

1955. Centenary of Voyage of "La Capricieuse" (sail warship).
1261 **375** 30f. blue & turquoise . . 5·75 4·75

376 Marseilles **377** Gerard de Nerval

1955. Views.
1262 – 6f. red . . . . 8·25 15
1263 **376** 8f. blue 55 15
1264 – 10f. blue 30 10
1265 – 12f. brown and grey . . 30 10
1265a – 15f. indigo and blue . . 65 65
1266 – 18f. blue and green . . 80 20
1267 – 20f. violet & dp violet 3·75 15
1268 – 25f. brown & chestnut 1·20 15
1268a – 35f. turquoise & green 4·75 70
1268b – 70f. black and green . . 20·00 2·30
DESIGNS—HORIZ: 6f., 35f. Bordeaux; 10f. Nice; 12f., 70f. Valentre Bridge, Cahors; 18f. Uzerche; 20f. Mount Pele, Martinique; 25f. Ramparts of Brouage. VERT: 15f. Douai Belfry.

1955. Death Centenary of De Nerval (writer).
1269 **377** 12f. sepia and red . . . 60 50

1955. Provincial Coats of Arms as T **277**.
1270 50c. multicoloured 20 20
1271 70c. yellow, blue and red . . 20 20
1272 80c. yellow, red & brown . . 20 20
1273 1f. yellow, red and blue . . 20 10
ARMS: 50c. "Comte de Foix"; 70c. "Marche"; 80c. "Roussillon"; 1f. "Comtat Venaissin".

379 "Child and Cage" (after Pigalle) **380**

1955. Red Cross Fund. Cross in red.
1274 **379** 12f.+3f. lake . . . . . 7·75 7·00
1275 – 15f.+5f. blue . . . . . 4·75 5·00
DESIGN: 15f. "Child and goose" (Greek sculpture).

1956. National Deportation Memorial.
1276 **380** 15f. sepia and brown . . 65 55

381 Colonel Driant **382** Trench Warfare

1956. Birth Centenary of Col. Driant.
1277 **381** 15f. blue 45 40

1956. 40th Anniv of Battle of Verdun.
1278 **382** 30f. blue and brown . . 2·10 1·60

383 Francis of Taxis

1956. Stamp Day.
1279 **383** 12f.+3f. brn, grn & bl 2·75 3·25

384 J. H. Fabre (entomologist)

1956. French Scientists.
1280 **384** 12f. dp brown & brn . . 90 75
1281 – 15f. black and grey . . . 1·20 65
1282 – 18f. blue . . . . 1·70 1·90
1283 – 30f. green & dp green . . 4·50 3·50
DESIGNS: 15f. C. Tellier (refrigeration engineer); 18f. C. Flammarion (astronomer); 30f. P. Sabatier (chemist).

385 Grand Trianon, Versailles

1956.
1284 **385** 12f. brown, green & blk 1·60 1·30

386 "Latin America" and "France"

1956. Franco-Latin American Friendship.
1285 **386** 30f. brown and sepia . . 2·20 1·60

387 "Reims" and "Florence" **388** Order of Malta and Leper Colony

1956. Reims-Florence Friendship.
1286 **387** 12f. green and black . . 90 80

1956. Order of Malta Leprosy Relief.
1287 **388** 12f. red, brown & sepia 60 55

389 St. Yves de Treguier

390 Marshal Franchet d'Esperey

1956. St. Yves de Treguier Commemoration.
1288 **389** 15f. black and grey . . . 45 50

1956. Birth Centenary of Marshal d'Esperey.
1289 **390** 30f. purple . . . . . . 2·50 1·90

391 Monument

392 Bude

1956. Centenary of Montceau-les-Mines.
1290 **391** 12f. sepia 60 55

1956. National Relief Fund.
1291 **392** 12f.+3f. blue . . . . . 7·75 5·25
1292 – 12f.+3f. grey . . . . . 7·75 5·25
1293 – 12f.+3f. red . . . . . . 7·75 5·25
1294 – 15f.+5f. green . . . . . 8·75 8·75
1295 – 15f.+5f. brown . . . . . 8·75 8·75
1296 – 15f.+5f. violet . . . . . 8·75 8·75
PORTRAITS: No. 1292, Goujon; No. 1293, Champlain; No. 1294, Chardin; No. 1295, Barres; No. 1296, Ravel.

393 Pelota **395** Donzere-Mondragon Barrage

1956. Sports.
1297 – 30f. black and grey . . . 1·60 15
1298 **393** 40f. purple and brown 6·00 35
1299 – 50f. violet and purple . . 2·10 15
1300 – 75f. grn, black & blue 12·50 2·20
DESIGNS: 30f. Basketball; 50f. Rugby; 75f. Alpine climbing.

1956. Europa. As T **320** of Belgium.
1301 15f. red and pink . . . . . 1·00 20
1302 30f. ultramarine and blue 5·00 1·00

1956. Technical Achievements.
1303 **395** 12f. grey and brown . . 1·70 1·20
1304 – 18f. blue . . . . 2·75 2·40
1305 – 30f. blue and indigo . . 14·00 7·00
DESIGNS—VERT: 18f. Aiguille du Midi cable railway. HORIZ: 30f. Port of Strasbourg.

396 A. A. Parmentier (agronomist)

397 Petrarch

1956. Parmentier Commemoration.
1306 **396** 12f. brown and sepia . . 70 70

1956. Famous Men.
1307 **397** 8f. green 75 70
1308 – 12f. purple (Lully) . . . 75 65
1309 – 15f. red (Rousseau) . . . 1·00 90
1310 – 18f. blue (Franklin) . . . 2·75 2·30
1311 – 20f. violet (Chopin) . . . 4·00 1·90
1312 – 30f. turq (Van Gogh) . . 6·00 3·50

398 Pierre de Coubertin (reviver of Olympic Games)

399 "Jeune Paysan" (after Le Nain)

1956. Coubertin Commemoration.
1313 **398** 30f. purple and grey . . 1·90 1·20

1956. Red Cross Fund. Cross in red.
1314 **399** 12f.+3f. olive . . . . . 3·00 3·25
1315 15f.+5f. lake . . . . . . 3·00 3·25
DESIGN: 15f. "Gilles" (after Watteau).

400 Pigeon and Loft

1957. Pigeon-fanciers' Commemoration.
1316 **400** 15f. blue, indigo & pur 40 40

401 Sud Aviation Caravelle

402 Victor Schoelcher (slavery abolitionist)

1957. Air.
1318 – 300f. olive & turquoise 16·00 3·25
1319 **401** 500f. black and blue . . 33·00 3·50
1320 – 1000f. black, vio & sep 55·00 21·00
AIRCRAFT: 300f. Morane Saulnier Paris I airplane; 1000f. Sud Aviation Alouette II helicopter.
See also Nos. 1458/60.

1957. Schoelcher Commem.
1321 **402** 18f. mauve 70 70

403 18th-century Felucca

1957. Stamp Day.
1322 **403** 12f.+3f. black & grey . . 1·90 1·50

404 "La Baigneuse" (after Falconet) and Sevres Porcelain

1957. Bicentenary of National Porcelain Industry at Sevres.
1323 **404** 30f. blue and light blue 85 70

405 Plante and Accumulators

1957. French Inventors (2nd series).
1324 **405** 8f. purple and sepia . . 45 45
1325 – 12f. black, blue & green 60 55
1326 – 18f. lake and red . . . . 1·40 1·40
1327 – 30f. myrtle and green . . 2·50 2·50
DESIGNS: 12f. Beclere (radiology); 18f. Terrillon (antiseptics); 30f. Oehmichen (helicopter).

406 Uzes Chateau

407 Jean Moulin

1957.
1334 – 8f. green 20 15
1328 **406** 12f. black, brown & bl 50 45
1335 – 15f. black and green . . 20 10
DESIGNS—VERT: 8f., 15f. Le Quesnoy.

1957. Heroes of the Resistance (1st issue). Inscr as in T **407**.
1329 **407** 8f. chocolate & brown 1·20 60
1330 – 10f. blue and black . . . 1·20 60
1331 – 12f. green and brown . . 1·40 1·10
1332 – 18f. black and violet . . 2·00 1·70
1333 – 20f. blue & turquoise . . 1·80 1·10
PORTRAITS: 10f. H. d'Estienne d'Orves; 12f. R. Keller; 18f. P. Brossolette; 20f. J.-B. Lebas.
See also Nos. 1381/4, 1418/22, 1478/82 and 1519/22.

409 Emblems of Auditing **410** Joinville

1957. 150th Anniv of Court of Accounts.
1336 **409** 12f. blue and green . . . 35 25

1957. National Relief Fund.
1337 **410** 12f.+3f. olive & sage . . 2·50 2·50
1338 – 12f.+3f. black & turq . . 2·75 2·75
1339 – 15f.+5f. red & verm . . 3·25 3·25
1340 – 15f.+5f. bl & ultram . . 3·50 3·50
1341 – 18f.+7f. black & grn . . 4·25 4·25
1342 – 18f.+7f. choc & brn . . 4·25 4·50
PORTRAITS: No. 1338, Bernard Palissy; No. 1339, Quentin de la Tour; No. 1340, Lamennais; No. 1341, George Sand; No. 1342, Jules Guesde.
See also Nos. 1390/5.

411 "Public Works"

1957. French Public Works.
1343 **411** 30f. brn, dp brn & grn 2·00 1·30

412 Port of Brest

1957.
1344 **412** 12f. green and brown . . 1·00 1·20

413 Leo Lagrange (founder) and Stadium **414** Auguste Comte

1957. Universities World Games.
1345 **413** 18f. black and grey . . . 60 55

1957. Death Centenary of Auguste Comte (philosopher).
1346 **414** 35f. sepia and brown . . 50 50

415 "Agriculture and Industry"

416 Roman Theatre, Lyons

1957. Europa.
1347 **415** 20f. green and brown . . 55 30
1348 35f. blue and sepia . . . 1·30 75

1957. Bimillenary of Lyons.
1349 **416** 20f. purple & brown . . 45 55

417 Sens River, Guadeloupe

418 Copernicus

1957. Tourist Publicity Series.
1350 **417** 8f. brown and green . . 15 10
1351 – 10f. chocolate & brown 15 10
1351a – 15f. multicoloured . . . 55 50
1352 – 18f. brown and blue . . 25 15
1353 – 25f. brown and grey . . 70 15
1353a – 30f. green . . . . . . 2·50 15
1354 – 35f. mauve and red . . 25 10
1355 – 50f. brown & green . . 60 15
1356 – 65f. blue and indigo . . 75 30
1356a – 85f. purple . . . . . . 4·00 25
1356b **417** 100f. violet . . . . . 31·00 40
DESIGNS—HORIZ: 10f., 30f., Palais de l'Elysee, Paris; 15f. Chateau de Foix; 25f. Chateau de Valencay; 50f. Les Antiques, Saint Remy; 65f., 85f. Evian-les-Bains. VERT: 18f. Beynac-Cazenac (Dordogne); 35f. Rouen Cathedral.

1957. Famous Men.
1357 **418** 8f. brown 80 70
1358 – 10f. green 80 70
1359 – 12f. violet 85 90
1360 – 15f. brown & dp brown 90 95
1361 – 18f. blue . . . . 1·60 1·30
1362 – 25f. purple and lilac . . 1·60 1·20
1363 – 35f. blue . . . . 1·90 1·60
PORTRAITS: 10f. Michelangelo; 12f. Cervantes; 15f. Rembrandt; 18f. Newton; 25f. Mozart; 35f. Goethe.
See also Nos. 1367/74.

419 L.-J. Thenard

420 "The Blind Man and the Beggar" (after J. Callot)

1957. Death Centenary of Thenard (chemist).
1364 **419** 15f. green and bistre . . 45 45

1957. Red Cross Fund. Cross in red.
1365 **420** 15f.+7f. blue . . . . . 3·75 4·25
1366 – 20f.+8f. brown . . . . . 4·75 5·25
DESIGN: 20f. "The Beggar and the One-eyed Woman" (after J. Callot).

1958. French Doctors. As T **418**.
1367 8f. brown 85 80
1368 12f. violet 75 80
1369 15f. blue . . . . 1·50 1·00
1370 35f. black . . . . 1·90 1·40
PORTRAITS: 8f. Dr. Pinel; 12f. Dr. Widal; 15f. Dr. C. Nicolle; 35f. Dr. R. Leriche.

1958. French Scientists. As T **418**.
1371 8f. violet and blue 85 75
1372 12f. grey and brown . . . . 1·10 90
1373 15f. green and deep green 2·00 90
1374 35f. red and lake . . . . . 2·50 1·50
PORTRAITS: 8f. Lagrange (mathematician); 12f. Le Verrier (astronomer); 15f. Foucault (physicist); 35f. Berthollet (chemist).

421 Rural Postal Services

1958. Stamp Day.
1375 **421** 15f.+5f. deep green, green and brown . . . 1·80 1·50

422 Le Havre

1958. Municipal Reconstruction.
1376 **422** 12f. red and olive . . . 75 65
1377 – 15f. brown and violet . . 75 60
1378 – 18f. indigo and blue . . 1·20 1·00
1379 – 25f. brown, turq & blue 1·50 1·00
DESIGNS—VERT: 15f. Maubeuge; 18f. Saint-Die. HORIZ: 25f. Sete.

423 French Pavilion

1958. Brussels International Exhibition.
1380 **423** 35f. green, blue & brn 25 30

1958. Heroes of the Resistance (2nd issue). Portraits inscr as in T **407**.
1381 8f. black and violet 65 80
1382 12f. green and blue 65 80
1383 15f. grey and sepia . . . . 2·10 1·40
1384 20f. blue and brown . . . . 1·60 1·40
PORTRAITS: 8f. Jean Cavailles; 12f. Fred Scamaroni; 15f. Simone Michel-Levy; 20f. Jacques Bingen.

424 Boules

425 Senlis Cathedral

1958. French Traditional Games.
1385 **424** 12f. brown and red . . . 1·30 1·00
1386 – 15f. dp grn, grn & bl . . 1·50 1·00
1387 – 18f. brown and green . . 2·30 1·40
1388 – 25f. blue and brown . . 3·50 2·30
DESIGNS—HORIZ: 15f. Nautical jousting. VERT: 18f. Archery; 25f. Breton wrestling.

1958. Senlis Cathedral Commemoration.
1389 **425** 15f. blue and indigo . . 45 50

1958. Red Cross Fund. French Celebrities as T **410**.
1390 12f.+4f. green . . . . . . 1·90 2·00
1391 12f.+4f. blue . . . . 1·90 2·00
1392 15f.+5f. purple . . . . . . 2·20 2·30
1393 15f.+5f. blue . . . . 2·50 2·50
1394 20f.+8f. red . . . . 2·50 2·50
1395 35f.+15f. green . . . . . . 2·75 2·75
PORTRAITS: No. 1390, J. du Bellay; No. 1391, Jean Bart; No. 1392, D. Diderot; No. 1393, G. Courbet; No. 1394, J. B. Carpeaux; No. 1395, Toulouse-Lautrec.

426 Fragment of the Bayeux Tapestry

1958.
1396 **426** 15f. red and blue 40 45

1958. Europa. As T **345** of Belgium. Size 22 × 36 mm.
1397 20f. red 25 20
1398 35f. blue 70 70

427 Town Halls of Paris and Rome

1958. Paris–Rome Friendship.
1399 **427** 35f. grey, blue & red . . 40 45

428 UNESCO Headquarters, Paris

429 Flanders Grave

1958. Inauguration of UNESCO Building.
1400 **428** 20f. bistre and turq . . . 15 15
1401 – 35f. red and myrtle . . . 30 30
DESIGN: 35f. Different view of building.

1958. 40th Anniv of First World War Armistice.
1402 **429** 15f. blue and green . . . 50 40

430 Arms of Marseilles

431 St. Vincent de Paul

1958. Arms of French Towns.
1403 **430** 50c. blue & deep blue . . 15 25
1404 – 70c. multicoloured . . . 15 25
1405 – 80c. red, yellow & bl . . 15 25
1406 – 1f. red, yellow & blue . . 15 15
1407 – 2f. red, green & blue . . 15 15
1408 – 3f. multicoloured 15 15
1409 – 5f. red and brown . . . 15 15
1410 – 15f. multicoloured . . . 30 15
ARMS: 70c. "Lyon"; 80c. "Toulouse"; 1f. "Bordeaux"; 2f. "Nice"; 3f. "Nantes"; 5f. "Lille"; 15f. "Alger".
See also Nos. 1452, 1454, 1498a/99f, 1700/1 and 1735.

1958. Red Cross Fund. Cross in red.
1411 **431** 15f.+7f. green . . . . . 1·40 1·50
1412 – 20f.+8f. violet . . . . . 1·40 1·50
PORTRAIT: 20f. J. H. Dunant (founder).

432 Arc du Carrousel and Flowers

433 Symbols of Learning and "Academic Palms"

1959. Paris Flower Festival.
1413 **432** 15f. multicoloured . . . 50 40

1959. 150th Anniv of "Academic Palms".
1414 **433** 20f. black, vio & lake . . 30 30

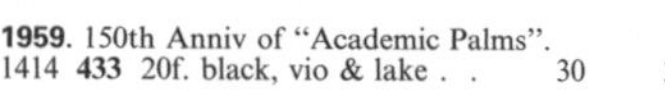

434 Father Charles de Foucauld (missionary)

1959. Charles de Foucauld Commem.
1415 **434** 50f. multicoloured . . . 60 55

435 Douglas DC-3 Mail Plane making Night-landing

1959. Stamp Day.
1416 **435** 20f.+5f. mult 60 60
See also No. 1644.

436 Miner's Lamp, Picks and School Building

437 "Five Martyrs"

1959. 175th Anniv of School of Mines.
1417 **436** 20f. turq, blk & red . . 30 30

1959. Heroes of the Resistance (3rd series).
1418 **437** 15f. black and violet . . 50 35
1419 – 15f. violet and purple . . 50 35
1420 – 20f. brown & chestnut 55 55
1421 – 20f. turquoise & green 50 50
1422 – 30f. violet and purple . . 75 65
PORTRAITS—As T **407**: No. 1419, Yvonne Le Roux; No. 1420, Martin Bret; No. 1421, Mederic-Vedy; No. 1422, Moutardier.

438 Foum el Gherza Dam

1959. French Technical Achievements.
1423 **438** 15f. turq and brown . . 40 35
1424 – 20f. purple, red & brn 55 60
1425 – 30f. brn, turq & blue . . 55 60
1426 – 50f. blue and green . . . 1·10 75
DESIGNS—VERT: 20f. Marcoule Atomic Power Station; 30f. Oil derrick and pipe-line at Hassi-Messaoud, Sahara. HORIZ: 50f. National Centre of Industry and Technology, Paris.

439 C. Goujon and C. Rozanoff (test pilots)

1959. Goujon and Rozanoff Commem.
1427 **439** 20f. brown, red & blue 50 50

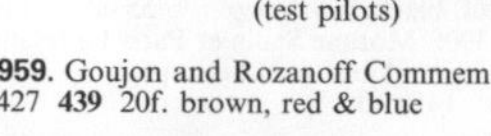

440 Villehardouin (chronicler)

1959. Red Cross Fund.
1428 **440** 15f.+5f. blue . . . . . 1·70 1·40
1429 – 15f.+5f. myrtle . . . . . 1·40 1·40
1430 – 20f.+10f. bistre . . . . 1·40 1·60
1431 – 20f.+10f. grey . . . . . 1·70 1·60
1432 – 30f.+10f. lake . . . . . 1·70 1·50
1433 – 30f.+10f. brown . . . . 2·00 1·70
PORTRAITS: No. 1429, Le Notre (Royal gardener); No. 1430, D'Alembert (philosopher); No. 1431, D'Angers (sculptor); No. 1432, Bichat (physiologist); No. 1433, Bartholdi (sculptor).

441 M. Desbordes-Valmore

442 "Marianne" in Ship of State

1959. Death Centenary of Marceline Desbordes-Valmore (poetess).
1434 **441** 30f. brown, blue & grn 25 25

1959.
1437 **442** 25f. red and black . . . 40 10
See also No. 1456.

443 Tancarville Bridge

1959. Inauguration of Tancarville Bridge.
1438 **443** 30f. green, brown & blue 40 40

444 Jean Jaures

445 "Giving Blood"

1959. Birth Centenary of Jean Jaures (socialist leader).
1439 **444** 50f. brown 40 30

1959. Europa. As T **360** of Belgium but size 22 × 36 mm.
1440 25f. green 30 15
1441 50f. violet . . . . 1·00 65

1959. Blood Donors.
1442 **445** 20f. grey and red 30 25

446 Clasped Hands of Friendship

447 Youth throwing away Crutches

1959. Tercent of Treaty of the Pyrenees.
1443 **446** 50f. red, blue & mauve 45 45

1959. Infantile Paralysis Relief Campaign.
1444 **447** 20f. blue 35 30

448 Henri Bergson

449 Avesnes-sur-Helpe

1959. Birth Centenary of Bergson (philosopher).
1445 **448** 50f. brown 40 40

1959.
1446 **449** 20f. blue, brown & blk 40 30
1447 – 30f. brown, purple & bl 40 40
DESIGN: 30f. Perpignan Castle.

450 Abbe C. M. de l'Epee (teacher of deaf mutes) **451** N.A.T.O. Headquarters, Paris

1959. Red Cross Fund. Cross in red.
1448 **450** 20f.+10f. purple & blk 2·20 2·30
1449 – 25f.+10f. black & blue 2·50 2·50
PORTRAIT: 25f. V. Hauy (teacher of the blind).

1959. 10th Anniv of N.A.T.O.
1450 **451** 50f. brown, green & bl 65 55

1959. Frejus Disaster Fund. Surch **FREJUS + 5f.**
1451 **442** 25f.+5f. red & black . . 30 35

(New currency. 100 (old) francs = 1 (new) franc.)

453 Sower **454** Laon Cathedral

1960. T **453** and previous designs but new currency.
1452 – 5c. red & brn (as 1409) 7·25 20
1453 **344** 10c. green 55 10
1454 – 15c. mult (as 1410) . . 85 20
1455 **453** 20c. red & turquoise . . 25 10
1456 **442** 25c. blue and red . . . 2·50 10
1456a **453** 30c. blue and indigo . . 1·70 35

1960. Air. As previous designs but new currency and new design (No. 1457b).
1457 – 2f. pur & blk (as 1195) 1·50 20
1457b – 2f. indigo and blue . . 90 20
1458 – 3f. brn & bl (as 1318) 1·60 15
1459 **401** 5f. black and blue . . . 2·75 60
1460 – 10f. black, violet and brown (as 1320) . . 13·00 2·20
DESIGN: No. 1457b, Mystere "20" jetliner.

1960. Tourist Publicity.
1461 **454** 15c. indigo and blue . . 40 35
1462 – 30c. pur, grn & blue . . 3·00 35
1463 – 45c. vio, pur & sepia . . 65 20
1464 – 50c. purple and green . . 2·00 10
1465 – 65c. brn, grn & blue . . 1·50 40
1466 – 85c. sepia, grn & blue . . 2·75 45
1467 – 1f. violet, grn & turq . . 2·75 20
DESIGNS—HORIZ: 30c. Fougeres Chateau; 65c. Valley of the Sioule; 85c. Chaumont Railway Viaduct. VERT: 45c. Kerrata Gorges, Algeria; 50c. Tlemcen Mosque, Algeria; 1f. Cilaos Church and Great Bernard Mountains, Reunion.
See also Nos. 1485/7.

455 Pierre de Nolhac

1960. Birth Centenary (1959) of Pierre de Nolhac (historian).
1468 **455** 20c. black 65 55

456 St. Etienne Museum

1960. Museum of Art and Industry, St. Etienne.
1469 **456** 30c. brown, red & blue 70 65

1960. As T **345** but with values in new currency.
1470 **345** 8c. violet 60 15
1471 20c. green . . . . 2·00 75
1472 40c. red . . . . 8·50 3·25
1473 55c. green . . . . 30·00 25·00
Nos. 1470/3 were only issued precancelled (see note below No. 432).

457 Assembly Emblem and View of Cannes

1960. 5th Meeting of European Mayors Assembly.
1474 **457** 50c. brown and green . . 85 90

458 "Ampere" (cable-laying ship)

1960. Stamp Day.
1475 **458** 20c.+5c. blue & turq . . 1·50 1·60

459 Girl of Savoy **460** Child Refugee

1960. Centenary of Attachment of Savoy and Nice to France.
1476 **459** 30c. green 65 75
1477 – 50c. brown, red and yellow (Girl of Nice) 55 55

1960. Heroes of the Resistance (4th series). Portraits as T **407**.
1478 20c. black and brown . . . 2·50 1·80
1479 20c. lake and red . . . . . 2·00 1·80
1480 30c. violet & deep violet . . 2·00 1·80
1481 30c. blue and indigo . . . 3·00 2·50
1482 50c. brown and green . . . 3·50 3·50
PORTRAITS: No. 1478, E. Debeaumarche; No. 1479, P. Masse; No. 1480, M. Ripoche; No. 1481, L. Vieljeux; No. 1482, Abbe Rene Bonpain.

1960. World Refugee Year.
1483 **460** 25c.+10c. bl, brn & grn 40 45

461 "The Road to Learning"

1960. 150th Anniv of Strasbourg Teachers' Training College.
1484 **461** 20c. violet, pur & blk . . 35 30

1960. Views as T **454**.
1485 15c. sepia, grey and blue 45 40
1485a 20c. blue, green and buff 35 35
1486 30c. sepia, green and blue 85 75
1487 50c. brown, green & red 75 75
DESIGNS: 15c. Lisieux Basilica; 20c. Bagnoles de l'Orne; 30c. Chateau de Blois; 50c. La Bourboule.

462 L'Hospital (statesman) **463** "Marianne"

1960. Red Cross Fund.
1488 **462** 10c.+5c. violet & red . . 2·50 2·75
1489 – 20c.+10c. turq & grn . . 3·25 3·50
1490 – 20c.+10c. green & brn 3·25 3·50
1491 – 30c.+10c. blue & vio . . 5·50 6·00
1492 – 30c.+10c. crim & red . . 5·00 5·25
1493 – 50c.+15c. blue and slate 6·50 6·25
DESIGNS: No. 1489, Boileau (poet); No. 1490, Turenne (military leader); No. 1491, Bizet (composer); No. 1492, Charcot (neurologist); No. 1493, Degas (painter).

1960.
1494 **463** 25c. grey and red . . . 25 10

464 Cross of Lorraine **465** Jean Bouin and Olympic Stadium

1960. 20th Anniv of De Gaulle's Appeal.
1495 **464** 20c. brown, grn & sep 70 40

1960. Olympic Games.
1496 **465** 20c. brown, red & blue 40 45

1960. Europa. As T **373** of Belgium, but size $36 \times 22\frac{1}{2}$ mm.
1497 25c. turquoise and green . . 15 10
1498 50c. purple and red 35 35

1960. Arms. As T **430**.
1498a 1c. blue and yellow 10 10
1498b 2c. yellow, green and blue 10 10
1499 5c. multicoloured 20 15
1499a 5c. red, yellow and blue . . 10 10
1499b 10c. blue, yellow and red 10 10
1499c 12c. red, yellow and black 10 10
1499d 15c. yellow, blue and red 10 10
1499e 18c. multicoloured 40 40
1499f 30c. red and blue 50 10
ARMS: 1c. "Niort"; 2c. "Gueret"; 5c. (No. 1499) "Oran"; 5c. (No. 1499a) "Amiens"; 10c. "Troyes"; 12c. "Agen"; 15c. "Nevers"; 18c. "Saint-Denis (Reunion)"; 30c. "Paris".

466 Madame de Stael (after Gerard) **467** Gen. Estienne, Morane Saulnier Type L Airplane and Tank

1960. Madame de Stael (writer).
1500 **466** 30c. olive and purple . . 35 35

1960. Birth Centenary of Gen. Estienne.
1501 **467** 15c. sepia and lilac . . . 40 45

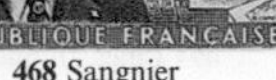

468 Sangnier **469** Order of the Liberation

1960. 10th Death Anniv of Marc Sangnier (patriot).
1502 **468** 20c. black, violet & blue 25 30

1960. 20th Anniv of Order of the Liberation.
1503 **469** 20c. green and black . . 40 45

470 Atlantic Puffins at Les Sept Iles

1960. Nature Protection.
1504 **470** 30c. multicoloured . . . 30 30
1505 – 50c. multicoloured . . . 85 45
DESIGN: 50c. European bee eaters, Camargue.

471 A. Honnorat **472** Mace of St. Martin's Brotherhood

1960. 10th Death Anniv of Andre Honnorat (philanthropist).
1506 **471** 30c. black, green & blue 30 30

1960. Red Cross Fund. Cross in red.
1507 **472** 20c.+10c. lake . . . . . 3·00 3·25
1508 – 25c.+10c. blue . . . . . 3·00 3·25
DESIGN: 25c. St. Martin (after 16th-cent. wood-carving).

473 St. Barbe and College

1960. 500th Anniv of St. Barbe College.
1509 **473** 30c. multicoloured . . . 40 40

474 Northern Lapwings

1960. Study of Bird Migration. Inscr "ETUDE DES MIGRATIONS".
1510 **474** 20c. multicoloured . . . 35 35
1511 – 45c. multicoloured . . . 95 1·00
DESIGN: 45c. Green-winged teal.

475 "Mediterranean" (after Maillol) **476** "Marianne"

1961. Birth Cent of Aristide Maillol (sculptor).
1512 **475** 20c. blue and red 25 30

1961.
1513 **476** 20c. red and blue 25 10

477 Orly Airport

1961. Opening of New Installations at Orly Airport.
1514 **477** 50c. turq, blue & blk . . 45 45

478 Georges Melies **479** Postman of Paris "Little Post" 1760

1961. Birth Centenary of Georges Melies (cinematograph pioneer).
1515 **478** 50c. blue, brown & vio 80 70

1961. Stamp Day and Red Cross Fund.
1516 **479** 20c.+5c. grn, red & brn 90 95

480 Jan Nicquet and Tobacco Flowers and Leaves **481** Father Lacordaire (after Chasseriau)

1961. 400th Anniv of Introduction of Tobacco into France.
1517 **480** 30c. red, brown & grn 25 30

The portrait on No. 1517 is of Jan Nicquet, a Flemish merchant, and not Jean Nicot as inscribed.

1961. Death Centenary of Father Lacordaire (theologian).
1518 **481** 30c. black and brown . . 40 40

1961. Heroes of the Resistance (5th issue). Portrait inscr as in T **407**.
1519 20c. violet and blue 80 80
1520 20c. blue and green . . . . 1·00 85
1521 30c. black and brown . . . 1·40 1·00
1522 30c. black and blue . . . . 1·30 1·10
PORTRAITS: No. 1519, J. Renouvin; No. 1520, L. Dubray; No. 1521, P. Gateaud; No. 1522, Mother Elisabeth.

482 Dove, Globe and Olive Branch

483 Deauville, 1861

1961. World Federation of Old Soldiers Meeting, Paris.
1523 **482** 50c. red, blue & green 40 40

1961. Centenary of Deauville.
1524 **483** 50c. lake . . . . 1·90 1·60

484 Du Guesclin (Constable of France)

485 Champmesle ("Roxane")

1961. Red Cross Fund.
1525 **484** 15c.+5c. black & pur . . 2·40 2·50
1526 – 20c.+10c. green & blue 2·40 2·50
1527 – 20c.+10c. crimson & red 2·40 2·50
1528 – 30c.+10c. black & brn 3·75 3·25
1529 – 45c.+10c. brown & grn 4·00 4·00
1530 – 50c.+15c. violet & red 4·25 4·00
PORTRAITS: No. 1526, Puget (sculptor); No. 1527, Coulomb (physicist); No. 1528, General Drouot; No. 1529, Daumier (caricaturist); No. 1530, Apollinaire (writer).

1961. French Actors and Actresses. Frames in red.
1531 **485** 20c. brown and green . . 75 45
1532 – 30c. brown and red . . . 95 65
1533 – 30c. myrtle and green . . 95 65
1534 – 50c. brown & turquoise 1·40 75
1535 – 50c. brown and olive . . 1·20 65
PORTRAITS: No. 1532, Talma ("Oreste"); No. 1533, Rachel ("Phedre"); No. 1534, Raimu ("Cesar"); No. 1535, Gerard Philipe ("Le Cid").

486 Mont Dore, Snow Crystal and Cable Rly

487 Thann

1961. Mont Dore.
1536 **486** 20c. purple and orange 25 30

1961. 800th Anniv of Thann.
1537 **487** 20c. violet, brn & grn . . 65 60

488 Pierre Fauchard

489 Doves

1961. Birth Bicentenary of Pierre Fauchard (dentist).
1538 **488** 50c. black and green . . 55 55

1961. Europa.
1539 **489** 25c. red 20 15
1540 50c. blue 40 40

490 Sully-sur-Loire

1961. Tourist Publicity.
1541 – 15c. slate, pur & turq . . 10 10
1542 – 20c. brown and green . . 30 30
1543 – 30c. blue, grn & sepia . . 25 25
1544 – 30c. black, grey & grn 1·80 1·40
1545 **490** 45c. brown, green & blue 25 10
1546 – 50c. myrt, turq & grn . . 1·10 15
1547 – 65c. blue, brown & myrt 40 15
1548 – 85c. blue, brown & myrt 65 25
1549 – 1f. brown, blue & myrt 4·50 15
1550 – 1f. brown, green & blue 40 10
VIEWS—HORIZ: 15c. Saint-Paul; 30c. (No. 1543), Arcachon; 30c. (No. 1544), Law Courts, Rennes; 50c. Cognac; 65c. Dinan; 85c. Calais; 1f. (No. 1549), Medea, Algeria; 1f. (No. 1550), Le Touquet-Paris-Plage, golf-bag and Handley Page Dart Herald airplane. VERT: 20c. Laval, Mayenne.
See also Nos. 1619/23, 1654/7, 1684/8, 1755/61, 1794, 1814/18, 1883/5, 1929/33, 1958/61, 2005/8, 2042/4, 2062/4, 2115/20, 2187/97, 2258/64, 2310/15, 2360/5, 2403/10, 2503/8, 2566/70, 2630/4, 2652/6, 2710/14, 2762/6, 2834/6, 2883/6, 2973/6, 3024/6, 3077/80, 3124/9, 3180/3, 3240/3, 3330/3, 3375/9, 3487/91, 3580/3, 3642/5, 3720/3, 3800/1, 3908/11 and 3946/9.

491 "14th July" (R. de la Fresnaye)

1961. Modern French Art.
1551 – 50c. multicoloured . . . 2·75 1·90
1552 – 65c. blue, green & violet 4·25 2·75
1553 – 85c. red, bistre and blue 2·00 2·20
1554 **491** 1f. multicoloured . . . . 4·25 3·25
PAINTINGS: 50c. "The Messenger" (Braque); 65c. "Blue Nudes" (Matisse); 85c. "The Cardplayers" (Cezanne).
See also Nos. 1590/2, 1603/6, 1637/9, 1671/4, 1710/4, 1742/5, 1786/9, 1819/22, 1877/80, 1908/10, 1944/7, 1985/8, 2033/6, 2108/13, 2159/60, 2243, 2290/2, 2338/41, 2398/9, 2531/4, 2580/2, 2608/12, 2672/6, 2721/5, 2773/6, 2850/3, 2858/60, 2966/8, 3008/9, 3085, 3245/7, 3306/7, 3368/9, 3483/6, 3561/3, 3638/4, 3702/5, 3899, 3990, 3902, 3951/4 and 4074.

493 "It is so sweet to love" (Wood-carving from Rouault's "Miserere")

494 Liner "France"

1961. Red Cross Fund. Cross in red.
1555 **493** 20c.+10c. black & pur 2·40 2·75
1556 – 25c.+10c. black & pur 3·25 2·75
DESIGN: 25c. "The blind leading the blind" (from Rouault's "Miserere").

1962. Maiden Voyage of Liner "France".
1557 **494** 30c. black, red & blue 70 55

495 Skier at Speed

496 M. Bourdet

1962. World Ski Championships, Chamonix.
1558 **495** 30c. violet and blue . . . 25 25
1559 – 50c. green, blue & vio 45 35
DESIGN: 50c. Slalom-racer.

1962. 60th Birth Anniv of Maurice Bourdet (journalist and radio commentator).
1560 **496** 30c. grey 25 30

497 Dr. P.-F. Bretonneau

498 Gallic Cock

1962. Death Centenary of Dr. Pierre-Fidele Bretonneau (medical scientist).
1561 **497** 50c. violet and blue . . . 40 40

1962.
1562 **498** 25c. red, blue & brown 45 10
1562a 30c. red, green & brn 75 10

499 Royal Messenger of late Middle Ages

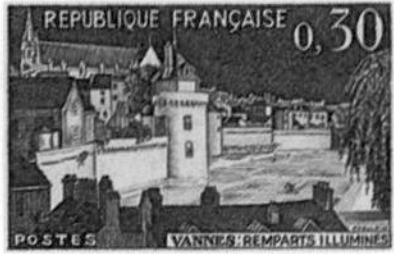

500 Vannes

1962. Stamp Day.
1563 **499** 20c.+5c. brn, bl & red 85 90

1962.
1564 **500** 30c. blue 80 90

501 Globe and Stage Set

503 Mount Valerien Memorial

504 Emblem and Swamp

502 Harbour Installations

1962. World Theatre Day.
1565 **501** 50c. lake, grn & ochre 65 40

1962. 300th Anniv of Cession of Dunkirk to France.
1566 **502** 95c. purple, brown & green . . . . 1·00 55

1962. Resistance Fighters' Memorials (1st issue).
1567 **503** 20c. myrtle and drab . . 85 65
1568 – 30c. blue 80 65
1569 – 50c. indigo and blue . . 1·00 75
MEMORIALS—VERT: 30c. Vercors; 50c. Ile de Sein.
See also Nos. 1609/10.

1962. Malaria Eradication.
1570 **504** 50c. red, blue & green 40 40

505 Nurses and Child

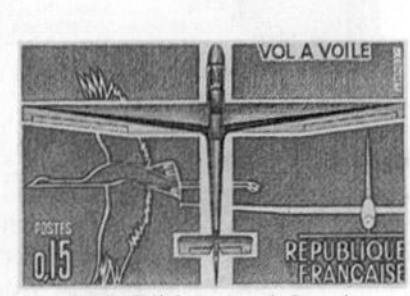

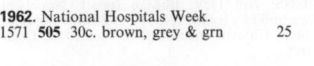

506 Gliders and Stork

1962. National Hospitals Week.
1571 **505** 30c. brown, grey & grn 25 30

1962. Civil and Sports Aviation.
1572 **506** 15c. brown and chest . . 45 50
1573 – 20c. red and purple . . . 45 50
DESIGN: 20c. Jodel Ambassadeur and early aircraft.

507 Emblem and School of Horology

508 "Selecting a Tapestry"

1962. Cent of School of Horology, Besancon.
1574 **507** 50c. vio, brown & red 45 50

1962. Tercentenary of Manufacture of Gobelin Tapestries.
1575 **508** 50c. turq, red & grn . . 50 50

509 Pascal

510 Denis Papin (inventor)

1962. Death Tercent of Pascal (philosopher).
1576 **509** 50c. red and green . . . 50 50

1962. Red Cross Fund.
1577 15c.+5c. sepia & turquoise 2·30 2·50
1578 20c.+10c. brown and red . . 2·75 3·00
1579 20c.+10c. blue and grey . . 2·75 2·50
1580 30c.+10c. indigo and blue 3·75 4·00
1581 45c.+15c. pur and brown . . 4·50 4·00
1582 50c.+20c. black and blue . . 3·75 4·00
DESIGNS: No. 1577, Type **510**; 1578, Edme Bouchardon (sculptor); 1579, Joseph Lakanal (politician); 1580, Gustave Charpentier (composer); 1581, Edouard Estauni (writer); 1582, Hyacinthe Vincent (scientist).

511 "Modern" Rose

512 Europa "Tree"

1962. Rose Culture.
1583 **511** 20c. red, green & olive 55 40
1584 – 30c. red, myrt & olive 60 55
DESIGN: 30c. "Old fashioned" rose.

1962. Europa.
1585 **512** 25c. violet 20 15
1586 50c. brown 40 45

513 Telecommunications Centre, Pleumeur-Bodou

1962. 1st Trans-Atlantic Telecommunications Satellite Link.
1587 **513** 25c. buff, green & grey 25 30
1588 – 50c. bl, grn & indigo . . 50 40
1589 – 50c. brown and blue . . 50 45
DESIGNS: 50c. (No. 1588), "Telstar" satellite, globe and television receiver; 50c. (No. 1589), Radio telescope, Nancay (Cher).

1962. French Art. As T **491**.
1590 50c. multicoloured . . . . . 3·25 2·50
1591 65c. multicoloured . . . . . 2·50 2·10
1592 1f. multicoloured . . . . . 5·50 4·00
PAINTINGS—HORIZ: 50c. "Bonjour, Monsieur Courbet" (Courbet); 65c. "Madame Manet on a Blue Sofa" (Manet). VERT: 1f. "Officer of the Imperial Horse Guards" (Gericault).

514 "Rosalie Fragonard" (after Fragonard) **515** Bathyscaphe "Archimede"

1962. Red Cross Fund. Cross in red.
1593 **514** 20c.+10c. brown . . . . 1·60 1·60
1594 – 25c.+10c. green . . . . 2·20 2·30
PORTRAIT: 25c. "Child as Pierrot" (after Fragonard).

1963. Record Undersea Dive.
1595 **515** 30c. black and blue . . . 25 30

516 Flowers and Nantes Chateau

1963. Nantes Flower Show.
1596 **516** 30c. blue, red & green 25 30

517 Jacques Amyot (Bishop of Auxerre)

1963. Red Cross Fund.
1597 **517** 20c.+10c. purple, violet and grey . . . . . 1·00 1·30
1598 – 20c.+10c. deep brown, brown and blue . . . 1·70 1·60
1599 – 30c.+10c. grn & pur . . 1·00 1·20
1600 – 30c.+10c. black, green and brown . . . . . 1·30 1·30
1601 – 50c.+20c. grn, brn & bl 1·20 1·30
1602 – 50c.+20c. blk, bl & brn 2·20 2·20
DESIGNS: No. 1598, Etienne Mehul (composer); No. 1599 Pierre de Marivaux (dramatist); No. 1600, N.-L. Vauquelin (chemist); No. 1601, Jacques Daviel (oculist); No. 1602, Alfred de Vigny (poet).

1963. French Art. As T **491**.
1603 50c. multicoloured . . . . . 3·50 2·75
1604 85c. multicoloured . . . . . 2·10 1·50
1605 95c. multicoloured 65 80
1606 1f. multicoloured . . . . . 5·00 4·25
DESIGNS—VERT: 50c. "Jacob's Struggle with the Angel" (Delacroix); 85c. "The Married Couple of the Eiffel Tower" (Chagall); 95c. "The Fur Merchants" (stained glass window, Chartres Cathedral); 1f. "St. Peter and the Miracle of the Fishes" (stained glass window, Church of St. Foy de Conches).

518 Roman Post Chariot

1963. Stamp Day.
1607 **518** 20c.+5c. purple & brn 35 40

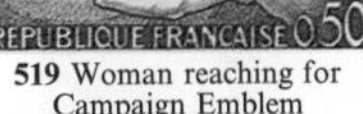

519 Woman reaching for Campaign Emblem **520** Glieres Memorial

1963. Freedom from Hunger.
1608 **519** 50c. brown & myrtle . . 40 40

1963. Resistance Fighters' Memorials (2nd issue).
1609 **520** 30c. olive and brown . . 55 55
1610 – 50c. black 55 55
DESIGN: 50c. Deportees Memorial, Ile de la Cite (Paris).

521 Beethoven (West Germany)

1963. Celebrities of European Economic Community Countries.
1611 **521** 20c. blue, brown & grn 40 45
1612 – 20c. black, violet & red 40 45
1613 – 20c. blue, pur & olive . . 40 45
1614 – 20c. brown, pur & brn 40 45
1615 – 30c. sepia, violet & brn 40 45
PORTRAITS AND VIEWS: No. 1611, Birthplace and modern Bonn; No. 1612, Emile Verhaeren (Belgium: Family grave and residence, Roisin); No. 1613, Giuseppe Mazzini (Italy: Marcus Aurelius statue and Appian Way, Rome); No. 1614, Emile Mayrisch (Luxembourg: Colpach Chateau and Steel Plant, Esch); No. 1615, Hugo de Groot (Netherlands: Palace of Peace, The Hague, and St. Agatha's Church, Delft).

522 Hotel des Postes, Paris **523** College Building

1963. Centenary of Paris Postal Conference.
1616 **522** 50c. sepia 40 40

1963. 400th Anniv of Louis the Great College, Paris.
1617 **523** 30c. myrtle 25 25

524 St. Peter's Church and Castle Keep, Caen

1963. 36th French Philatelic Societies Federation Congress, Caen.
1618 **524** 30c. brown and blue . . 35 35

1963. Tourist Publicity. As T **490**. Inscr "1963".
1619 30c. ochre, blue & green . . 35 15
1620 50c. red, blue & turquoise 35 10
1621 60c. red, turquoise & blue 65 30
1622 85c. purple, turquoise & grn 1·50 30
1623 95c. black 65 30
DESIGNS—HORIZ: 30c. Amboise Chateau; 50c. Cote d'Azur, Var; 85c. Vittel. VERT: 60c. Saint-Flour; 95c. Church and cloisters, Moissac.

525 Water-skiing

1963. World Water-skiing Championships, Vichy.
1624 **525** 30c. black, red & turq 25 30

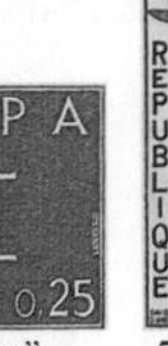

526 "Co-operation" **527** "Child with Grapes" (Angers)

1963. Europa.
1625 **526** 25c. brown 25 20
1626 50c. green 35 35

1963. Red Cross Fund. Cross in red.
1627 **527** 20c.+10c. black 85 95
1628 – 25c.+10c. green 85 95
DESIGN: 25c. "The Piper" (Manet).

528 "Philately"

1963. "PHILATEC 1964" International Stamp Exhibition, Paris (1st issue).
1629 **528** 25c. red, green & grey 25 15
See also Nos. 1640/3 and 1651.

529 Radio-T.V. Centre

1963. Opening of Radio-T.V. Centre, Paris.
1630 **529** 20c. slate, ol & brn . . . 25 15

530 Emblems of C.P. Services **531** Paralytic at Work in Invalid Chair

1964. Civil Protection.
1631 **530** 30c. blue, red & orange 40 45

1964. Professional Rehabilitation of Paralytics.
1632 **531** 30c. brn, chestnut & grn 25 30

532 18th-century Courier **533** "Deportation"

1964. Stamp Day.
1633 **532** 20c.+5c. myrtle 25 30

1964. 20th Anniv of Liberation (1st issue).
1634 **533** 20c.+5c. slate 75 75
1635 – 50c.+5c. green 95 95
DESIGN: 50c. "Resistance" (memorial).
See also Nos. 1652/3 and 1658.

534 Pres. Rene Coty **535** "Blanc" 2c. Stamp of 1900

1964. Pres. Coty Commemoration.
1636 **534** 30c.+10c. brown & red 40 45

1964. French Art. As T **491**.
1637 1f. multicoloured . . . . . 2·10 1·70
1638 1f. multicoloured . . . . . 1·50 1·40
1639 1f. multicoloured 95 80
DESIGNS—VERT: No. 1637, Jean le Bon (attributed to Girard of Orleans); No. 1638, Tomb plaque of Geoffrey IV (12th-century "champleve" (grooved) enamel from Limousin); No. 1639, "The Lady with the Unicorn" (15th-century tapestry).

1964. "PHILATEC 1964" International Stamp Exhibition, Paris (2nd issue).
1640 – 30c. blue, black & brn 45 45
1641 **535** 25c. purple and bistre . . 45 45
1642 – 25c. blue and bistre . . . 45 45
1643 – 30c. red, black & blue 45 45
DESIGNS: No. 1640, "Postal Mechanization" (letter-sorting equipment and parcel conveyor); No. 1642, "Mouchon" 25c. stamp of 1900; No. 1643, "Telecommunications" (telephone dial, teleprinter and T.V. tower).

1964. 25th Anniv of Night Airmail Service. As T **435** but additionally inscr "25E ANNIVERSAIRE" and colours changed.
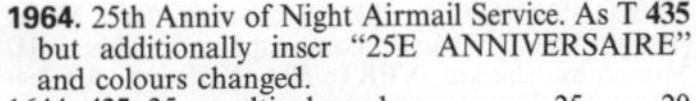
1644 **435** 25c. multicoloured . . . 25 20

536 Stained Glass Window **537** Calvin

1964. 800th Anniv of Notre Dame, Paris.
1645 **536** 60c. multicoloured . . . 60 60

1964. 400th Death Anniv of Calvin (reformer).
1646 **537** 30c.+10c. brown, sepia and turquoise 35 45

538 Gallic Coin **539** Pope Sylvester II

1964. Pre-cancels.
1647 **538** 10c. brown and green 55 30
1647a 15c. brown & orange 30 30
1647b 22c. violet and green 70 60
1647c 25c. brown and violet 65 65
1647d 26c. brown & purple 65 55
1647e 30c. brn & lt brown . . 75 75
1647f 35c. blue and red . . . 1·60 1·30
1648 45c. brown and green 1·70 1·50
1648a 50c. brown and blue . . 1·20 1·20
1648b 70c. brown and blue . . 7·50 7·50
1649 90c. brown and red . . 2·30 3·00
See note below No. 432 (1920).
For stamps as Type **538** but inscribed "FRANCE", see Nos. 2065a/1.

1964. Pope Sylvester II Commemoration.
1650 **539** 30c.+10c. pur & grey . . 35 45

540 Rocket and Horseman

1964. "PHILATEC 1964" International Stamp Exhibition, Paris (3rd issue).
1651 **540** 1f. blue, red & brown . . 23·00 24·00
MS1651a 145×285 mm. No. 1651 ×8 plus labels bearing "PHILATEC" emblem £180 £140
Sold at 4f. incl. entrance fee to Exhibition.

541 Landings in Normandy and Provence

1964. 20th Anniv of Liberation (2nd issue).
1652 **541** 30c.+5c. sep, brn & bl 85 90
1653 – 30c.+5c. red, sep & brn 90 95
DESIGN: No. 1653, Taking prisoners in Paris, and tank in Strasbourg.

1964. Tourist Publicity. As T **490**. Inscr "1964".
1654 40c. brown, green & chest 25 15
1655 70c. purple, turquoise & blue 35 10
1656 1f.25 green, blue & bistre . . 70 50
1657 1f.30 chestnut, choc & brn 1·20 50
DESIGNS—HORIZ: 40c., 1f.25, Notre-Dame Chapel, Haut-Ronchamp (Haute-Saone). VERT: 70c. Caesar's Tower, Provins; 1f.30, Joux Chateau (Doubs).

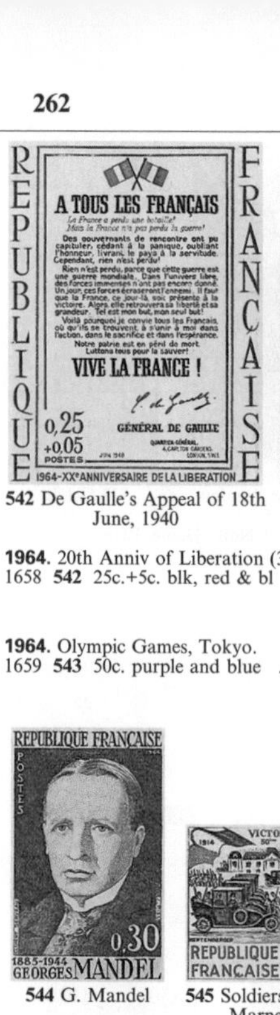

542 De Gaulle's Appeal of 18th June, 1940 543 Judo

1964. 20th Anniv of Liberation (3rd issue).
1658 **542** 25c.+5c. blk, red & bl 90 1·00

1964. Olympic Games, Tokyo.
1659 **543** 50c. purple and blue . . 40 40

544 G. Mandel 545 Soldiers departing for the Marne by Taxi-cab

1964. 20th Death Anniv of Georges Mandel (statesman).
1660 **544** 30c. purple 25 15

1964. 50th Anniv of Victory of the Marne.
1661 **545** 30c. black, red & blue 35 25

546 Europa "Flower" 547 Co-operation

1964. Europa.
1662 **546** 25c. red, brown & grn 15 10
1663 50c. red, green & vio . . 35 25

1964. French, Africa and Malagasy Co-operation.
1664 **547** 25c. choc, blue & brn . . 25 20

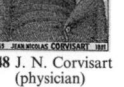

548 J. N. Corvisart (physician) 549 La Rochefoucauld

1964. Red Cross Fund.
1665 **548** 20c.+10c. black and red 45 45
1666 – 25c.+10c. black and red 45 45
DESIGN: 25c. D. Larrey (military surgeon).

1965. Red Cross Fund. Inscr "1965".
1667 **549** 30c.+10c. blue & brn . . 50 50
1668 – 30c.+10c. brown & red 65 65
1669 – 40c.+10c. slate and brown 65 70
1670 – 40c.+10c. brown, blue and chestnut 65 65
PORTRAITS: No. 1668, Nicolas Poussin (painter); No. 1669, Paul Dukas (composer); No. 1670, Charles d'Orleans.

1965. French Art. As T **491**.
1671 1f. multicoloured 80 75
1672 1f. multicoloured 40 45
1673 1f. multicoloured 40 45
1674 1f. black, rose and red . . . 40 45
DESIGNS—VERT: No. 1671, "L'Anglaise du 'Star' au Havre" (Toulouse-Lautrec); No. 1673, "The Apocalypse" (14th-century tapestry). HORIZ: No. 1672, "Hunting with Falcons" (miniature from manuscript "Les Tres Riches Heures du Duc de Berry", by the Limbourg brothers); No. 1674, "The Red Violin" (R. Dufy).

550 "La Guienne" (steam packet) 551 Deportees

1965. Stamp Day.
1675 **550** 25c.+10c. blk, grn & bl 80 80

1965. 20th Anniv of Return of Deportees.
1676 **551** 40c. green 60 50

552 Youth Club 553 Girl with Bouquet

1965. 20th Anniv of Youth Clubs ("Maisons des Jeunes et de la Culture").
1677 **552** 25c. blue, brn & grn . . 25 30

1965. "Welcome and Friendship" Campaign.
1678 **553** 60c. red, orge & grn . . 35 35

554 Allied Flags and Broken Swastika 555 I.T.U. Emblem, "Syncom", Morse Key and Pleumeur-Bodou Centre

1965. 20th Anniv of Victory in World War II.
1679 **554** 40c. red, blue & black 40 30

1965. Centenary of I.T.U.
1680 **555** 60c. brown, black & bl 50 55

556 Croix de Guerre 557 Bourges Cathedral

1965. 50th Anniv of Croix de Guerre.
1681 **556** 40c. brown, red & green 50 55

1965. National Congress of Philatelic Societies, Bourges.
1682 **557** 40c. brown and blue . . 35 30

558 Stained Glass Window

1965. 800th Anniv of Sens Cathedral.
1683 **558** 1f. multicoloured 65 55

1965. Tourist Publicity. As T **490**. Inscr "1965".
1684 50c. blue, green and bistre 35 15
1685 60c. brown and blue 70 15
1686 75c. brown, green & blue . . 1·00 95
1687 95c. brown, green & blue . . 5·50 1·00
1688 1f. grey, green and brown 1·10 15
DESIGNS—HORIZ: 50c. Moustiers Ste. Marie (Basses-Alpes); 95c. Landscape, Vendee; 1f. Monoliths, Carnac. VERT: 60c. Yachting, Aix-les-Bains; 75c. Tarn gorges.

559 Mont Blanc from Chamonix 560 Europa "Sprig"

1965. Opening of Mont Blanc Road Tunnel.
1689 **559** 30c. violet, blue & plum 30 25

1965. Europa.
1690 **560** 30c. red 35 25
1691 60c. grey 80 80

561 Etienne Regnault and "Le Taureau" 562 "One Million Hectares"

1965. Tercent of Colonisation of Reunion.
1692 **561** 30c. blue and red 25 30

1965. Reafforestation.
1693 **562** 25c. brown, yellow & grn 25 25

563 Atomic Reactor and Emblems 564 Aviation School, Salon-de-Provence

1965. 20th Anniv of Atomic Energy Commission.
1694 **563** 60c. black and blue . . . 60 45

1965. 30th Anniv of Aviation School.
1695 **564** 25c. green, indigo & blue 30 25

565 Rocket "Diamant"

1965. Launching of 1st French Satellite.
1696 **565** 30c. blue, turq & ind . . 25 30
1697 – 60c. blue, turq & ind . . 30 40
DESIGN: 60c. Satellite "A1".

566 "Le Bebe a la Cuiller" 568 St. Pierre Fourier and Basilica, Mattaincourt (Vosges)

1965. Red Cross Fund. Paintings by Renoir.
1698 **566** 25c.+10c. blue and red 35 30
1699 – 30c.+10c. brown & red 45 35
DESIGN: 30c. "Coco ecrivant" (portrait of Renoir's small son writing).

1966. Arms. As T **430**.
1700 5c. red and blue 20 10
1701 25c. blue and brown 80 15
DESIGNS: 5c. "Auch"; 25c. "Mont-de-Marsan".

1966. Red Cross Fund.
1702 **568** 30c.+10c. brown & grn 50 55
1703 – 30c.+10c. purple & grn 50 55
1704 – 30c.+10c. bl, brn & grn 50 55
1705 – 30c.+10c. blue & brn . . 45 50
1706 – 30c.+10c. brown & grn 50 50
1707 – 30c.+10c. black & brn 45 50
DESIGNS: No. 1703, F. Mansart (architect) and Carnavalet House, Paris; No. 1704, M. Proust (writer) and St. Hilaire Bridge, Illiers (Eure-et-Loir); No. 1705, G. Faure (composer), statuary and music; No. 1706, Hippolyte Taine (philosopher) and birthplace; No. 1707, Elie Metchnikoff (scientist), microscope and Pasteur Institute.

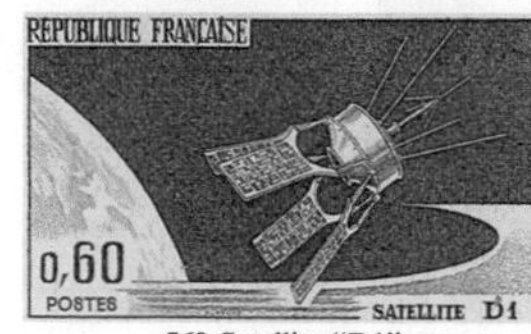
569 Satellite "D1"

1966. Launching of Satellite "D1".
1708 **569** 60c. red, blue & green 25 30

570 Engraving a die 571 Knight and Chessboard

1966. Stamp Day.
1709 **570** 25c.+10c. deep brown, grey and brown . . . 35 35

1966. French Art. As T **491**.
1710 1f. bronze, green & purple 40 45
1711 1f. multicoloured 45 45
1712 1f. multicoloured 45 50
1713 1f. multicoloured 45 50
1714 1f. multicoloured 45 50
DESIGNS—HORIZ: No. 1710, Detail of Vix Crater (wine-bowl); No. 1711, "The New-born Child" (G. de la Tour); No. 1712, "Baptism of Judas" (stained glass window, Sainte Chapelle, Paris); No. 1714, "Crispin and Scapin" (after H. Daumier). VERT: No. 1713, "The Moon and the Bull" (Lurcat tapestry).

1966. International Chess Festival, Le Havre.
1715 **571** 60c. grey, brown & vio 60 50

572 Pont St. Esprit Bridge 573 St. Michel

1966. 700th Anniv of Pont St. Esprit.
1716 **572** 25c. black and blue . . . 25 15

1966. Millenary of Mont St. Michel.
1717 **573** 25c. multicoloured . . . 25 25

574 King Stanislas, Arms and Palace

1966. Bicentenary of Reunion of Lorraine and Barrois with France.
1718 **574** 25c. brown, grn & blue 25 15

575 Niort 576 "Angel of Verdun"

1966. National Congress of Philatelic Societies, Niort.
1719 **575** 40c. slate, green & blue 25 25

1966. 50th Anniv of Verdun Victory.
1720 **576** 30c.+5c. slate, bl & grn 30 35

577 Fontenelle

1966. Tercentenary of Academy of Sciences.
1721 **577** 60c. brown and lake . . 40 40

578 William the Conqueror, Castle and Landings

1966. 900th Anniv of Battle of Hastings.
1722 **578** 60c. brown and blue . . 40 45

579 Globe and Railway Track

1966. 19th International Railway Congress, Paris.
1723 **579** 60c. brown, blue & lake 1·00 65

580 Oleron Bridge 581 Europa "Ship"

1966. Opening of Oleron Bridge.
1724 **580** 25c. brown, green & bl 25 30

1966. Europa.
1725 **581** 30c. blue 25 20
1726 60c. red 60 50

582 Vercingetorix

1966. History of France (1st series). Inscr "1966".
1727 **582** 40c. brown, blue & grn 35 35
1728 – 40c. brown and black . . 35 35
1729 – 60c. red, brown & violet 45 40
DESIGNS—VERT: 40c. (No. 1728), Clovis. 60c. Charlemagne.
See also Nos. 1769/71, 1809/11, 1850/2, 1896/8, 1922/4, 1975/7 and 2017/19.

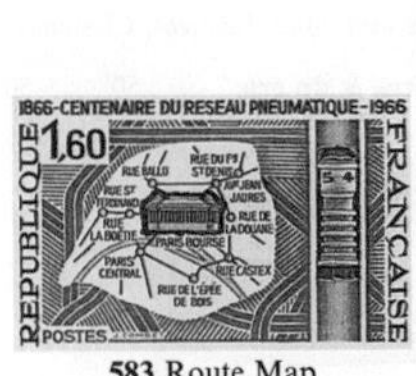

583 Route Map 584 Chateau de Val

1966. Centenary of Paris Pneumatic Post.
1730 **583** 1f.60 blue, lake & brn 80 65

1966. Chateau de Val.
1731 **584** 2f.30 brown, grn & bl 1·40 30

585 Rance Barrage 586 Nurse tending wounded soldier (1859)

1966. Inauguration of Rance River Tidal Power Station.
1732 **585** 60c. slate, grn & brn . . 50 50

1966. Red Cross Fund. Cross in red.
1733 **586** 25c.+10c. green 45 45
1734 – 30c.+10c. blue 45 45
DESIGN: 30c. Nurse tending young girl (1966).

1966. Arms. As T **430**. Multicoloured.
1735 20c. "Saint-Lo" 10 10

588 Beaumarchais (playwright) 589 Congress Emblem

1967. Red Cross Fund.
1736 **588** 30c.+10c. violet & red 40 40
1737 – 30c.+10c. blue & indigo 40 45
1738 – 30c.+10c. purple & brn 40 40
1739 – 30c.+10c. violet & bl . . 45 45
PORTRAITS: No. 1737, Emile Zola (writer); No. 1738, A. Camus (writer); No. 1739, St. Francois de Sales (reformer).

1967. 3rd International Congress of European Broadcasting Union (U.E.R.).
1740 **589** 40c. red and blue 25 30

590 Postman of the Second Empire 591 Winter Olympics Emblem

1967. Stamp Day.
1741 **590** 25c.+10c. grn, red & bl 25 30

1967. French Art. As T **491**.
1742 1f. multicoloured 50 50
1743 1f. multicoloured 50 50
1744 1f. brown, blue and black 50 50
1745 1f. multicoloured 50 50
DESIGNS—HORIZ: No. 1742, "Old Juniet's Trap" (after H. Rousseau); No. 1745, "The Window-makers" (stained glass window, St. Madeleine's Church, Troyes). VERT: No. 1743, "Francois I" (after Jean Clouet); No. 1744, "The Bather" (Ingres).

1967. Publicity for Winter Olympic Games, Grenoble (1968).
1746 **591** 60c. red, lt blue & bl . . 35 45

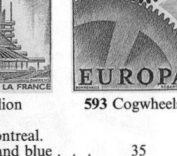

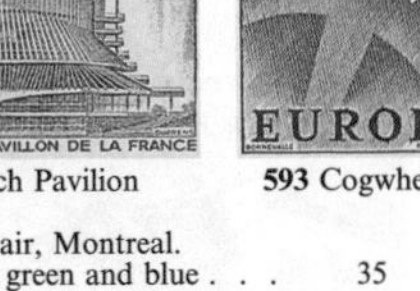
592 French Pavilion 593 Cogwheels

1967. World Fair, Montreal.
1747 **592** 60c. green and blue . . . 35 35

1967. Europa.
1748 **593** 30c. blue and grey . . . 25 25
1749 60c. brown and blue . . 85 50

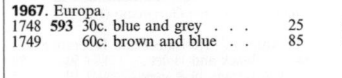

594 Nungesser, Coli and "L'Oiseau Blanc"

1967. 40th Anniv of Trans-Atlantic Flight Attempt by Nungesser and Coli.
1750 **594** 40c. blue, brown & pur 50 35

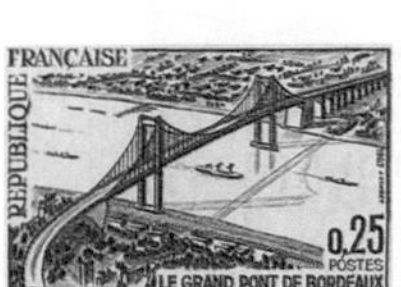

595 Great Bridge, Bordeaux 596 Gouin Mansion, Tours

1967. Inauguration of Great Bridge, Bordeaux.
1751 **595** 25c. black, olive & brn 25 25

1967. National Congress of Philatelic Societies, Tours.
1752 **596** 40c. brown, blue & red 60 55

597 Gaston Ramon (vaccine pioneer) and College Gates

1967. Bicentenary of Alfort Veterinary School.
1753 **597** 25c. brown, green & bl 25 20

598 Esnault-Pelterie, Rocket and Satellite

1967. 10th Death Anniv of Robert Esnault-Pelterie (rocket pioneer).
1754 **598** 60c. indigo and blue . . 50 50

1967. Tourist Publicity. As T **490**. Inscr "1967".
1755 50c. brown, dp blue & blue 35 15
1756 60c. brown, dp blue & blue 60 40
1757 70c. brown, blue and red . . 35 15
1758 75c. blue, red and brown . . 2·40 1·40
1759 95c. violet, green & blue . . 1·60 1·40
1760 1f. blue 65 10
1761 1f.50 red, blue and green . . 1·10 35
DESIGNS—VERT: 50c. Town Hall, St. Quentin (Aisne); 60c. Clock-tower and gateway, Vire (Calvados); 1f. Rodez Cathedral; 1f.50, Morlaix-views and carved buttress. HORIZ: 70c. St. Germain-en-Laye Chateau; 75c. La Baule; 95c. Boulogne-sur-Mer.

599 Orchids 600 Scales of Justice

1967. Orleans Flower Show.
1762 **599** 40c. red, purple & violet 85 70

1967. 9th Int Accountancy Congress, Paris.
1763 **600** 60c. brown, blue & pur 85 70

601 Servicemen and Cross of Lorraine 602 Marie Curie and Pitchblende

1967. 25th Anniv of Battle of Bir-Hakeim.
1764 **601** 25c. ultramarine, bl & brn 25 25

1967. Birth Centenary of Marie Curie.
1765 **602** 60c. ultramarine & blue 40 45

603 Lions Emblem 604 "Republique"

1967. 50th Anniv of Lions International.
1766 **603** 40c. violet and lake . . . 1·10 55

1967.
1767 **604** 25c. blue 50 40
1768 30c. purple 45 10
1843 30c. green 45 10
1768b 40c. red 45 10
See also No. 1882.

1967. History of France (2nd series). As T **582**, but inscr "1967".
1769 40c. ultramarine, grey & bl 40 40
1770 40c. black and slate 40 35
1771 60c. green and brown . . . 45 45
DESIGNS—HORIZ: No. 1769, Hugues Capet elected King of France. VERT: No. 1770, Philippe-Auguste at Bouvines; 1771, Saint-Louis receiving poor.

605 "Flautist" 606 Anniversary Medal

1967. Red Cross Fund. Ivories in Dieppe Museum. Cross in red.
1772 **605** 25c.+10c. brown & vio 50 60
1773 – 30c.+10c. brown & grn 50 60
DESIGNS: 30c. "Violinist".

1968. 50th Anniv of Postal Cheques Service.
1774 **606** 40c. bistre and green . . 25 25

607 Cross-country Skiing and Ski Jumping 608 Road Signs

1968. Winter Olympic Games, Grenoble.
1775 30c.+10c. brown, grey & red 40 40
1776 40c.+10c. pur, bis & dp pur 40 45
1777 60c.+20c. red, purple & grn 50 50
1778 75c.+25c. brown, grn & pur 65 75
1779 95c.+35c. brown, mve & bl 65 75
DESIGNS: 30c. Type **607**; 40c. Ice hockey; 60c. Olympic flame; 75c. Figure skating; 95c. Slalom.

1968. Road Safety.
1780 **608** 25c. red, blue and purple 25 30

609 Rural Postman of 1830 610 F. Couperin (composer) and Concert Instruments

1968. Stamp Day.
1781 **609** 25c.+10c. indigo, blue and red 25 30

1968. Red Cross Fund. Inscr "1968".
1782 **610** 30c.+10c. lilac & vio . . 25 30
1783 – 30c.+10c. brown & grn 25 30
1784 – 30c.+10c. red & brown 25 30
1785 – 30c.+10c. purple & lil . . 25 30
DESIGNS: No. 1783, General Desaix, and death scene at Marengo; No. 1784, Saint Pol-Roux (poet) and "Evocation of Golgotha"; No. 1785, Paul Claudel (poet) and "Joan of Arc".

1968. French Art. As T **491**.
1786 1f. multicoloured 50 55
1787 1f. multicoloured 65 55
1788 1f. olive and red 65 50
1789 1f. multicoloured 85 60
DESIGNS—HORIZ: No. 1786, Wall painting, Lascaux; No. 1787, "Arearea" (Gauguin). VERT: No. 1788, "La Danse" (relief by Bourdelle in Champs-Elysees Theatre, Paris); No. 1789, "Portrait of a Model" (Renoir).

611 Congress Palace, Royan

1968. World Co-operation Languages Conf, Royan.
1790 **611** 40c. blue, brown & grn 45 30

612 Europa "Key" **613** Alain R. Le Sage

1968. Europa.
1791 **612** 30c. brown and purple 20 15
1792 60c. red and brown . . . 95 60

1968. 300th Birth Anniv of Le Sage (writer).
1793 **613** 40c. purple and blue . . 25 30

1968. Tourist Publicity. As T **490**, but inscr "1968".
1794 60c. blue, purple & green . . 65 60
DESIGN—HORIZ: 60c. Langeais Chateau.

614 Pierre Larousse (encyclopedist) **615** Forest Trees

1968. Larousse Commem.
1795 **614** 40c. brown & violet . . 35 40

1968. Link of Black and Rambouillet Forests.
1796 **615** 25c. brown, green & blue 40 40

616 Presentation of the Keys, and Map

1968. 650th Anniv of Papal Enclave, Valreas.
1797 **616** 60c. violet, bistre & brn 50 55

617 Louis XIV, and Arms of Flanders and France

1968. 300th Anniv of (First) Treaty of Aix-la-Chapelle.
1798 **617** 40c. lake, bistre & grey 25 25

618 Martrou Bridge, Rochefort

1968. Inauguration of Martrou Bridge.
1799 **618** 25c. black, brown & blue 25 30

619 Letord Lorraine Bomber and Route Map **620** Tower of Constance, Aigues-Mortes

1968. 50th Anniv of 1st Regular Internal Airmail Service.
1800 **619** 25c. indigo, blue & red 50 45

1968. Bicent. of Release of Huguenot Prisoners.
1801 **620** 25c. purple, brown & bl 25 30

621 Cathedral and Old Bridge, Beziers

1968. National Congress of Philatelic Societies, Beziers.
1802 **621** 40c. ochre, green & blue 90 60

622 "Victory" and White Tower, Salonika **623** Louis XV and Arms of Corsica and France

1968. 50th Anniv of Armistice on Salonika Front.
1803 **622** 40c. purple & lt purple 25 25

1968. Bicent of Union of Corsica and France.
1804 **623** 25c. blue, green & blk 25 25

624 Relay-racing **626** "Ball of the Little White Beds" (opera) and Bailby

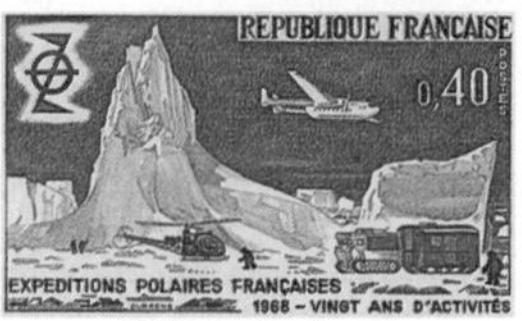

625 Polar Landscape

1968. Olympic Games, Mexico.
1805 **624** 40c. blue, green & brn 50 50

1968. French Polar Exploration.
1806 **625** 40c. turq, red & blue . . 40 45

1968. 50th Anniv of "Little White Beds" Children's Hospital Charity.
1807 **626** 40c. red, orge & brn . . 25 30

627 "Angel of Victory" over Arc de Triomphe **628** "Spring"

1968. 50th Anniv of Armistice on Western Front.
1808 **627** 25c. blue and red 25 30

1968. History of France (3rd series). Designs as T **582**, but inscr "1968".
1809 40c. green, grey and red . . 40 45
1810 40c. blue, green & brown . . 40 45
1811 60c. brown, blue & ultram 60 55
DESIGNS—HORIZ: No. 1809, Philip the Good presiding over States-General. VERT: No. 1810, Death of Du Guesclin; No. 1811, Joan of Arc.

1968. Red Cross Fund. Cross in red.
1812 **628** 25c.+10c. blue & vio . . 35 45
1813 – 30c.+10c. red & brown 35 45
DESIGN: 30c. "Autumn".
See also Nos. 1853/4.

1969. Tourist Publicity. Similar to T **490** but inscr "1969".
1814 45c. green, brown and blue 35 20
1815 70c. brown, indigo and blue 40 40
1816 80c. brown, purple & bistre 40 15
1817 85c. grey, blue and green . . 1·00 1·10
1818 1f.15 lt brown, brown & blue 95 75
DESIGNS—HORIZ: 45c. Brou Church, Bourg-en-Bresse (Ain); 70c. Hautefort Chateau; 80f. Vouglans Dam, Jura; 85f. Chantilly Chateau; 1f.15, La Trinite-sur-Mer, Morbihan.

1969. French Art. As T **491**.
1819 1f. brown and black 55 55
1820 1f. multicoloured 55 55
1821 1f. multicoloured 55 55
1822 1f. multicoloured . . . . . 1·00 75
DESIGNS—VERT: No. 1819, "February" (bas-relief, Amiens Cathedral); No. 1820, "Philippe le Bon" (Rogier de la Pasture, called Van der Weyden); No. 1822, "The Circus" (Georges Seurat). HORIZ: No. 1821, "Savin and Cyprien appearing before Ladicius" (Romanesque painting, Church of St. Savin, Vienne).

629 Concorde in Flight

1969. Air. 1st Flight of Concorde.
1823 **629** 1f. indigo and blue . . . 90 75

630 Postal Horse-bus of 1890

1969. Stamp Day.
1824 **630** 30c.+10c. green, brown and black 25 30

631 A. Roussel (composer) **632** Irises

1969. Red Cross Fund. Celebrities.
1825 **631** 50c.+10c. blue 50 60
1826 – 50c.+10c. red 50 60
1827 – 50c.+10c. grey 50 60
1828 – 50c.+10c. brown 60 65
1829 – 50c.+10c. purple 60 65
1830 – 50c.+10c. green 60 65
PORTRAITS: No. 1826, General Marceau; No. 1827, C. A. Sainte-Beuve (writer); No. 1828, Marshal Lannes; No. 1829, G. Cuvier (anatomist and naturalist); No. 1830, A. Gide (writer).

1969. International Flower Show, Paris.
1831 **632** 45c. multicoloured . . . 40 45

633 Colonnade

1969. Europa.
1832 **633** 40c. mauve 25 15
1833 70c. blue 40 35

634 Battle of the Garigliano (Italy)

1969. 25th Anniv of "Resistance and Liberation".
1834 **634** 45c. black and violet . . 50 55
1835 – 45c. ultram, bl & grey 1·10 55
1836 – 45c. grey, blue & green 80 70
1837 – 45c. brown and grey . . 1·10 60
1838 – 45c. indigo, blue & red 1·10 75
1839 – 45c.+10c. green & grey 1·10 1·30
1840 – 70c.+10c. grn, pur & brn 3·00 3·25
DESIGNS—VERT: No. 1835, Parachutists and Commandos ("D-Day Landings"); 1836, Memorial and Resistance fighters (Battle of Mont Mouchet). HORIZ: No. 1837, Troops storming beach (Provence Landings); 1838, French pilot, Soviet mechanic and Yakovlev Yak-9 fighter aircraft (Normandy-Niemen Squadron); 1839, General Leclerc, troops and Les Invalides (Liberation of Paris); 1840, As No. 1839 but showing Strasbourg Cathedral (Liberation of Strasbourg).

635 "Miners" (I.L.O. Monument, Geneva) and Albert Thomas (founder) **636** Chalons-sur-Marne

1969. 50th Anniv of I.L.O.
1841 **635** 70c. brn, bl & dp brn . . 40 45

1969. National Congress of Philatelic Societies, Chalons-sur-Marne.
1842 **636** 45c. ochre, blue & grn 45 45

637 Canoeing **639** "Diamond Crystal" in Rain Drop

638 Napoleon as Young Officer, and Birthplace

1969. World Kayak-Canoeing Championships, Bourg-St. Maurice.
1844 **637** 70c. brown, green & blue 45 45

1969. Birth Bicent of Napoleon Bonaparte.
1845 **638** 70c. grn, violet & blue 45 50

1969. European Water Charter.
1846 **639** 70c. black, green & bl 55 45

640 Mouflon **641** Aerial View of College

1969. Nature Conservation.
1847 **640** 45c. black, brn & grn . . 90 90

1969. College of Arts and Manufactures, Chatenay-Malabry.
1848 **641** 70c. grn, orge & dp grn 50 50

642 "Le Redoutable"

1969. 1st French Nuclear Submarine "Le Redoutable".
1849 **642** 70c. green, emer & bl . . 40 45

1969. History of France (4th series). As T **582** but inscr "1969".
1850 80c. bistre, brown & green 50 50
1851 80c. brown, blk & lt brn . . 50 50
1852 80c. blue, black and violet 55 55
DESIGNS—HORIZ: No. 1850, Louis XI and Charles the Bold; 1852, Henry IV and Edict of Nantes, VERT: No. 1851, Bayard at the Battle of Brescia.

1969. Red Cross Fund. Paintings by N. Mignard. As T **628**. Cross in red.
1853 40c.+15c. brown & choc . . 50 60
1854 40c.+15c. blue & violet . . 50 60
DESIGNS: No. 1853, "Summer"; 1854, "Winter".

643 Gerbault aboard "Firecrest"

1970. Alain Gerbault's World Voyage, 1923–29.
1855 **643** 70c. indigo, grey & blue 70 70

644 Gendarmerie Badge and Activities

1970. National Gendarmerie.
1856 **644** 45c. blue, green & brown 1·30 55

645 L. Le Vau (architect) 646 Handball Player

1970. Red Cross Fund.
1857 **645** 40c.+10c. lake 50 65
1858 – 40c.+10c. blue 50 65
1859 – 40c.+10c. green 50 65
1860 – 40c.+10c. brown 50 65
1861 – 40c.+10c. slate 50 65
1862 – 40c.+10c. blue 50 65
DESIGNS: No. 1858, Prosper Merimee (writer); 1859, Philbert de l'Orme (architect); 1860, Edouard Branly (scientist); 1861, Maurice de Broglie (physicist); 1862, Alexandre Dumas (pere) (writer).

1970. 7th World Handball Championship.
1863 **646** 80c. green 45 50

647 Marshal Alphonse Juin and Les Invalides, Paris

1970. Marshal Juin Commem.
1864 **647** 45c. brown and blue . . 35 35

648 Gas-turbine Monorail Aerotrain "Orleans 1-80" 649 Postman of 1830 and Paris Scene

1970. 1st Aerotrain in Service.
1865 **648** 80c. drab and violet . . 65 55

1970. Stamp Day.
1866 **649** 40c.+10c. black, blue and red 45 50

650 P.-J. Pelletier and J. B. Caventou with Formula

1970. 150th Anniv of Discovery of Quinine.
1870 **650** 50c. green, mauve & bl 40 45

651 Greater Flamingo 652 Rocket and Dish Aerial

1970. Nature Conservation Year.
1871 **651** 45c. mauve, grey & grn 35 30

1970. Launching of "Diamant B" Rocket from Guyana.
1872 **652** 45c. green 60 55

653 "Health and Sickness" 654 "Flaming Sun"

1970. W.H.O. "Fight Cancer" Day (7th April).
1873 **653** 40c.+10c. mauve, brown and blue 35 45

1970. Europa.
1874 **654** 40c. red 30 30
1875 80c. blue 50 50

655 Marshal de Lattre de Tassigny and Armistice Meeting

1970. 25th Anniv of Berlin Armistice.
1876 **655** 40c.+10c. blue & turq . . 85 85

1970. French Art. As T **491**.
1877 1f. multicoloured 50 55
1878 1f. chestnut 60 55
1879 1f. multicoloured . . . . . 1·20 80
1880 1f. multicoloured . . . . . 1·10 80
DESIGNS—VERT: No. 1877, 15-cent. Savoy Primitive painting on wood; No. 1880, "The Ballet-dancer" (Degas). HORIZ: No. 1878, "The Triumph of Flora" (sculpture by J. B. Carpeaux); No. 1879, "Diana's Return from the Hunt" (F. Boucher).

656 Arms of Lens, Miner's Lamp and Pithead

1970. 43rd French Federation of Philatelic Societies Congress, Lens.
1881 **656** 40c. red 25 30

657 "Republique" and Perigueux 658 Javelin-thrower in Wheel-chair

1970. Transfer of French Govt Printing Works to Perigueux.
1882 **657** 40c. red 40 40
The above stamp and label which together comprise No. 1882 were issued together se-tenant in sheets for which special printing plates were laid down. The stamp is virtually indistinguishable from the normal 40c. definitive, No. 1768b.

1970. Tourist Publicity. As T **490**, but inscr "1970".
1883 50c. purple, blue & green . . 35 20
1884 95c. brown, red and olive 1·70 1·20
1885 1f. green, blue and red . . . 45 15
DESIGNS: 50c. Diamond Rock, Martinique; 95c. Chancelade Abbey (Dordogne); 1f. Gosier Island, Guadeloupe.

1970. World Games for the Physically Handicapped, St.-Etienne.
1886 **658** 45c. red, green & blue 45 45

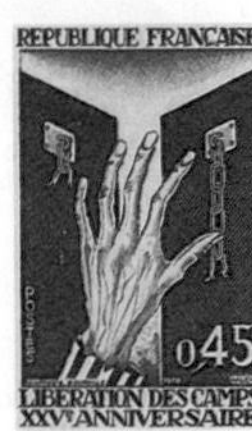

659 Hand and Broken Chain 660 Observatory and Nebula

1970. 25th Anniv of Liberation from Concentration Camps.
1887 **659** 45c. brown, ultram & bl 45 40

1970. Haute-Provence Observatory.
1888 **660** 1f.30 violet, blue & grn 2·20 1·40

661 Pole Vaulting 663 Bath-House, Arc-et-Senans (Doubs)

662 Didier Daurat, Raymond Vanier and Douglas DC-4

1970. 1st European Junior Athletic Championships, Paris.
1889 **661** 45c. indigo, blue & purple 50 45

1970. Air. Pioneer Aviators.
1890 **662** 5f. brown, green & blue 1·90 25
1891 – 10f. grey, violet & red 4·00 45
1892 – 15f. grey, mauve & brn 6·00 95
1893 – 20f. indigo and blue . . 8·00 95
DESIGNS: 10f. Helene Boucher, Maryse Hilsz and De Havilland Gipsy Moth and Caudron aircraft; 15f. Henri Guillaumet, Paul Codos, "Lieutenant de Vaisseau Paris" (flying boat) and wreck of Potez 25A2 airplane; 20f. Jean Mermoz, Antoine de Saint-Exupery and Concorde airplane.

1970. Royal Salt Springs, Chaux (founded by N. Ledoux).
1895 **663** 80c. brown, grn & bl . . 1·50 85

1970. History of France (5th series). As T **582**, but inscr "1970".
1896 45c. mauve, grey & black 85 60
1897 45c. brown, green & yellow 70 60
1898 45c. grey, brown & orange 70 70
DESIGNS: No. 1896, Richelieu and siege of La Rochelle, 1628; 1897, King Louis XIV; 1898, King Louis XV at Battle of Fontenoy (after painting by H. Vernet).

664 U.N. Emblem, New York Headquarters and Palais des Nations, Geneva

1970. 25th Anniv of United Nations.
1899 **664** 80c. violet, green & blue 50 50

665 Bordeaux and "Ceres" Stamp

1970. Centenary of Bordeaux "Ceres" Stamp Issue.
1900 **665** 80c. violet and blue . . . 50 50

666 Col. Denfert-Rochereau and "Lion of Belfort" (after Bartholdi)

1970. Centenary of Belfort Siege.
1901 **666** 45c. blue, brown & grn 40 45

667 "Lord and Lady" (c. 1500) 668 "Marianne"

1970. Red Cross Fund. Frescoes from Dissay Chapel, Vienne. Cross in red.
1902 **667** 40c.+15c. green 70 75
1903 – 40c.+15c. red 70 75
DESIGN: No. 1903, "Angel with instruments of mortification".

1971.
1904 **668** 45c. blue 50 10
1905 50c. red 20 10
1904ap 60c. green . . . . . . 1·90 25
1905bp 80c. red 50 20
1904b 80c. green 40 20
1905d 1f. red 45 40

669 Balloon "Ville d'Orleans" leaving Paris 670 Ice Skaters

1971. Air. Centenary of Paris Balloon Post.
1907 **669** 95c. multicoloured . . . 95 90

1971. French Art. As T **491**.
1908 1f. brown . . . . 1·00 75
1909 1f. multicoloured 80 70
1910 1f. multicoloured 65 65
DESIGNS: No. 1908, "St. Matthew" (sculpture, Strasbourg Cathedral); No. 1909, "The Winnower" (Millet); No. 1910, "Songe Creux" (G. Rouault).

1971. World Ice Skating Championships, Lyon.
1911 **670** 80c. ultramarine, blue and indigo 50 55

671 Diver and Bathysphere 672 General D. Brosset and Fourviere Basilica, Lyon

1971. "Oceanexpo" Exhibition, Bordeaux.
1912 **671** 80c. turquoise & blue . . 45 45

1971. Red Cross Fund. Celebrities.
1913 **672** 50c.+10c. brown & grn 65 65
1914 – 50c.+10c. brn & choc . . 75 65
1915 – 50c.+10c. brown & red 75 60
1916 – 50c.+10c. lilac & blue . . 75 60
1917 – 50c.+10c. pur & plum 85 75
1918 – 50c.+10c. bl & indigo . . 85 75
DESIGNS: No. 1914, Esprit Auber (composer) and manuscript of "Fra Diavolo"; 1915, Victor Grignard (chemist) and Nobel Prize for Chemistry; 1916, Henri Farman (aviation pioneer) and Farman Voisin No. 1 bis (airplane); 1917, General C. Delestraint (Resistance leader) and "Secret Army" proclamation; 1918, J. Robert-Houdin (magician) and levitation act.

673 Field Post Office, World War I

1971. Stamp Day.
1919 **673** 50c.+10c. blue, brown and bistre 55 55

674 Barque "Antoinette"

1971. French Sailing Ships.
1920 **674** 80c. violet, indigo & bl 1·20 1·00
See also Nos. 1967, 2011 and 2100.

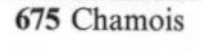
675 Chamois **676** Basilica of Santa Maria, Venice

1971. Inaug of Western Pyrenees National Park.
1921 **675** 65c. brown, bl & choc 60 60

1971. History of France (6th series). As T **582** but inscr "1971".
1922 45c. purple, blue & red . . 55 60
1923 45c. red, brown & blue . . 60 60
1924 65c. brown, purple & blue 90 95
DESIGNS: No. 1922, Cardinal, noble and commoner (Opening of the States-General, 1789); No. 1923, Battle of Valmy, 1792; No. 1924, Fall of the Bastille, 1789.

1971. Europa.
1925 **676** 50c. brown and blue . . 45 40
1926 – 80c. purple 55 55
DESIGN: 80c. Europa chain.

677 View of Grenoble **678** A.F.R. Emblem and Town

1971. 44th French Federation of Philatelic Societies Congress, Grenoble.
1927 **677** 50c. red, pink & brown 1·00 30

1971. 25th Anniv (1970) of Rural Family Aid.
1928 **678** 40c. blue, violet & green 30 30

1971. Tourist Publicity. As T **490**, but inscr "1971".
1929 60c. black, blue and green 35 20
1930 65c. black, violet & brown 55 30
1931 90c. brown, green & ochre 45 20
1932 1f.10 brown, blue & green 70 70
1933 1f.40 purple, blue & green 65 30
DESIGNS—VERT: 60c. Sainte Chapelle, Riom; 65c. Church and fountain, Dole; 90c. Gate-tower and houses, Riquewihr; 1f.40, Ardeche gorges. HORIZ: 1f.10, Fortress, Sedan.

679 Bourbon Palace, Paris

1971. 59th Interparliamentary Union Conference, Paris.
1934 **679** 90c. blue 80 70

680 Embroidery and Instrument-making

1971. 40th Anniv of 1st Meeting of Crafts Guilds Association.
1935 **680** 90c. purple and red . . . 55 45

681 Reunion Chameleon **682** De Gaulle in Uniform (June 1940)

1971. Nature Conservation.
1936 **681** 60c. green, brn & yell . . 1·00 85

1971. 1st Death Anniv of General Charles de Gaulle.
1937 **682** 50c. black . . . . 1·20 95
1938 – 50c. blue . . . . 1·20 95
1939 – 50c. red . . . . 1·20 95
1940 – 50c. black . . . . . . 1·20 95
DESIGNS: No. 1938, De Gaulle at Brazzaville, 1944; No. 1939, Liberation of Paris, 1944; No. 1940, De Gaulle as President of the French Republic, 1970.

683 Baron Portal (1st President) and First Assembly

1971. 150th Anniv of National Academy of Medicine.
1941 **683** 45c. plum and purple . . 40 40

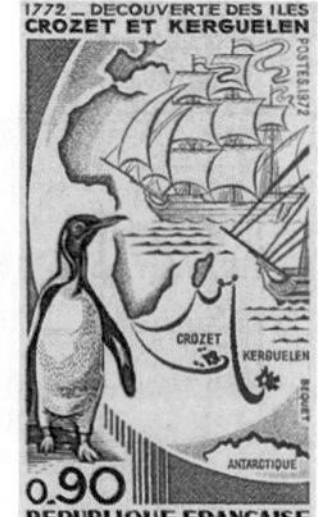
684 "Young Girl with Little Dog" **685** King Penguin, Map and "Le Mascarin" (Dutresne)

1971. Red Cross Fund. Paintings by J.-B. Greuze. Cross in red.
1942 **684** 30c.+10c. blue 70 80
1943 – 50c.+10c. red 70 80
DESIGN: No. 1943. "The Dead Bird".

1972. French Art. As T **491**. Multicoloured.
1944 1f. "L'Etude" (portrait of a young girl) (Fragonard) (vert) 95 95
1945 1f. "Women in a Garden" (Monet) (vert) . . . . . 1·80 85
1946 2f. "St. Peter presenting Pierre de Bourbon" (Master of Moulins) (vert) 1·80 1·40
1947 2f. "The Barges" (A. Derain) . . . . 2·75 1·70

1972. Bicentenary of Discovery of Crozet Islands and Kerguelen (French Southern and Antarctic Territories).
1948 **685** 90c. black, blue & orge 65 60

686 Skier and Emblem **687** Aristide Berges (hydro-electric engineer)

1972. Winter Olympic Games, Sapporo, Japan.
1949 **686** 90c. red and green . . . 60 45

1972. Red Cross Fund. Celebrities.
1950 **687** 50c.+10c. black, emerald and green 70 90
1951 – 50c.+10c. black, blue and ultramarine . . . 70 90
1952 – 50c.+10c. black, purple and plum 70 90
1953 – 50c.+10c. black, red and crimson 70 90
1954 – 50c.+10c. black, chestnut and brown 95 90
1955 – 50c.+10c. black, orange and red 85 90
DESIGNS: No. 1951, Paul de Chomedey, Sieur de Maisonneuve (founder of Montreal); No. 1952, Edouard Belin (communications scientist); No. 1953, Louis Bleriot (pioneer airman); No. 1954, Theophile Gautier (writer); No. 1955, Admiral Francois de Grasse.

688 Rural Postman of 1894 **689** Heart and W.H.O. Emblems

1972. Stamp Day.
1956 **688** 50c.+10c. blue, drab and yellow . . . . 1·00 1·00

1972. World Heart Month.
1957 **689** 45c. red, orange & grey 40 45

1972. Tourist Publicity. As Type **490**, but inscr "1972".
1958 1f. brown and yellow . . . 60 30
1959 1f.20 blue and brown . . . 60 25
1960 2f. purple and green 80 30
1961 3f.50 brown, red and blue 1·50 55
DESIGNS—VERT: 1f. Red deer stag and forest, Sologne Nature Reserve. HORIZ: 1f.20, Charlieu Abbey; 2f. Bazoches-du-Morvand Chateau; 3f.50, St. Just Cathedral, Narbonne.

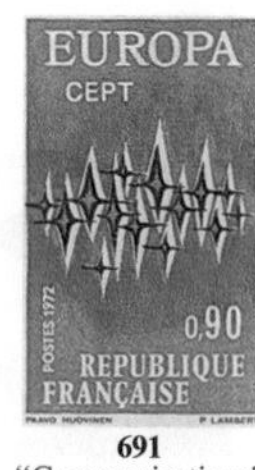
690 Eagle Owl **691** "Communications"

1972. Nature Conservation.
1962 – 60c. black, green & bl 2·20 1·30
1963 **690** 65c. brown, bis & grey 95 80
DESIGN—HORIZ: 60c. Atlantic salmon.

1972. Europa.
1964 – 50c. purple, yellow & brn 40 30
1965 **691** 90c. multicoloured . . . 55 55
DESIGN: 50c. Aix-la-Chapelle Cathedral.

692 "Tree of Hearts" **693** "Cote d'Emeraude" Grand Banks Fishing barquentine

1972. 20th Anniv of Post Office Employees' Blood-donors Association.
1966 **692** 40c. red 35 35

1972. French Sailing Ships.
1967 **693** 90c. blue, green & orge 1·10 90

694 St.-Brieuc Cathedral (from lithograph of 1840)

1972. 45th French Federation of Philatelic Societies Congress, St.-Brieuc.
1968 **694** 50c. red 35 35

695 Hand and Code Emblems **696** Old and New Communications

1972. Postal Code Campaign.
1969 **695** 30c. red, black & green 15 15
1970 50c. yellow, black & red 35 20

1972. 21st World Congress of Post Office Trade Union Federation (I.P.T.T.), Paris.
1971 **696** 45c. blue and grey . . . 35 30

697 Hurdling **698** Hikers on Road

1972. Olympic Games, Munich.
1972 **697** 1f. green 60 40

1972. "Walking Tourism Year".
1973 **698** 40c. multicoloured . . . 1·50 1·00

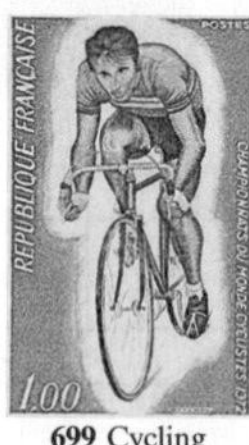

699 Cycling **701** Nicholas Desgenettes (military physician)

700 J.-F. Champollion and Hieroglyphics

1972. World Cycling Championships.
1974 **699** 1f. brown, purple & grey 1·80 1·00

1972. History of France (7th series). The Directory. As T **582** but dated "1972".
1975 45c. purple, olive & green 40 50
1976 60c. blue, red and black . . 80 65
1977 65c. purple, brown & blue 90 85
DESIGNS—VERT: 45c. "Incroyables et Merveilleuses" (fashionable Parisians), 1794; 60c. Napoleon Bonaparte at the Bridge of Arcole, 1796; 65c. Discovery of antiquities, Egyptian Expedition, 1798.

1972. 150th Anniv of Champollion's Translation of Egyptian Hieroglyphics.
1978 **700** 90c. brown, blue & blk 50 45

1972. Red Cross Fund. Doctors of the 1st Empire. Cross in red.
1979 **701** 30c.+10c. green and bronze 70 80
1980 – 50c.+10c. red & brown 70 75
DESIGN: No. 1980, Francois Broussais (pathologist).

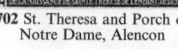

702 St. Theresa and Porch of Notre Dame, Alencon **703** Anthurium

1973. Birth Centenary of St. Theresa of Lisieux.
1981 **702** 1f. indigo & turquoise 65 55

1973. Martinique Flower Cultivation.
1982 **703** 50c. multicoloured . . . 40 45

704 National Colours of France and West Germany

1973. 10th Anniv of Franco-German Co-operation Treaty.
1983 **704** 50c. multicoloured . . . 40 45

705 Polish Immigrants

1973. 50th Anniv of Polish Immigration.
1984 **705** 40c. red, green & brown 25 30

1973. French Art. As T **491**.
1985 2f. multicoloured . . . . . 1·60 1·30
1986 2f. red and yellow . . . . . 1·60 1·40
1987 2f. maroon and brown . . . 1·60 1·50
1988 2f. multicoloured . . . . . 1·90 1·30
DESIGNS: No. 1985, "The Last Supper" (carved capital, St. Austremoine Church, Issoire); No. 1986, "Study of a Kneeling Woman" (Charles le Brun); No. 1987, Wood-carving, Moutier d'Ahun; No. 1988, "La Finette" (girl with lute) (Watteau).

706 Admiral G. de Coligny (Protestant leader)

707 Mail Coach, c. 1835

1973. Red Cross Fund. Celebrities' Annivs.
1989 **706** 50c.+10c. blue, brown and purple . . . . . 85 1·10
1990 – 50c.+10c. mauve, grey and orange . . . . . 85 1·10
1991 – 50c.+10c. green, purple and yellow . . . . . 85 1·10
1992 – 50c.+10c. red, purple and bistre . . . . . . 85 1·10
1993 – 50c.+10c. grey, purple and brown . . . . . 85 1·10
1994 – 50c.+10c. brown, lilac and blue . . . . . . 95 1·00
1995 – 50c.+10c. blue, purple and brown . . . . . 95 1·00
DESIGNS: No. 1989, 400th death anniv (1972); 1990, Ernest Renan (philologist and writer, 150th birth anniv); 1991, Santos-Dumont (pioneer aviator, birth centenary); 1992, Colette (writer, birth centenary); 1993, Duguay-Trouin (naval hero, 300th birth anniv); 1994, Louis Pasteur (scientist, 150th birth anniv 1972); 1995, Tony Garnier (architect, 25th death anniv).

1973. Stamp Day.
1996 **707** 50c.+10c. blue 45 50

708 Tuileries Palace and New Telephone Exchange

709 Town Hall, Brussels

1973. French Technical Achievements.
1997 **708** 45c. blue, grey & green 25 30
1998 – 90c. black, blue & pur 65 50
1999 – 3f. black, blue & grn . . 1·50 1·00
DESIGNS: 90c. Francois I Lock, Le Havre; 3f. Airbus Industrie A300B2-100 airplane.

1973. Europa.
2000 **709** 50c. brown and red . . . 35 25
2001 – 90c. multicoloured . . . 1·60 85
DESIGN—HORIZ: 90c. Europa "Posthorn".

710 Guadeloupe Racoon

1973. Nature Conservation.
2002 **710** 40c. mauve, grn & pur 40 30
2003 – 60c. black, red & blue 55 55
DESIGN: 60c. White storks.

711 Masonic Emblem

712 Globe and "Heart"

1973. Bicentenary of Masonic Grand Orient Lodge of France.
2004 **711** 90c. blue and purple . . 55 45

1973. Tourist Publicity. As T **490**, but inscr "1973".
2005 60c. blue, green and light blue 35 15
2006 65c. violet and red 35 25
2007 90c. brown, dp blue & bl . . 40 15
2008 1f. green, brown and blue 40 15
DESIGNS—VERT: 60c. Waterfall, Doubs; 1f. Clos-Luce Palace, Amboise; HORIZ: 65c. Palace of the Dukes of Burgundy, Dijon; 90c. Gien Chateau.

1973. 50th Anniv of Academy of Overseas Sciences.
2009 **712** 1f. green, brown & pur 50 45

713 Racing-car at Speed

715 Bell-tower, Toulouse

714 Five-masted Barque "France II"

1973. 50th Anniv of Le Mans 24-hour Endurance Race.
2010 **713** 60c. blue and brown . . 70 55

1973. French Sailing Ships.
2011 **714** 90c. lt blue, indigo & bl 1·10 75

1973. 46th French Federation of Philatelic Societies Congress, Toulouse.
2012 **715** 50c. brown and violet . . 40 30

716 Dr. G. Hansen

717 Eugene Ducretet (radio pioneer)

1973. Centenary of Hansen's Identification of Leprosy Bacillus.
2013 **716** 45c. brown, olive & grn 35 25

1973. 75th Anniv of Eiffel Tower–Pantheon Experimental Radio Link.
2014 **717** 1f. green and red 55 55

718 Moliere as "Sganarelle"

719 Pierre Bourgoin (parachutist) and Philippe Kieffer (Marine Commando)

1973. 300th Death Anniv of Moliere (playwright).
2015 **718** 1f. brown and red . . . 60 50

1973. Heroes of World War II.
2016 **719** 1f. claret, blue & red . . 50 45

1973. History of France (8th series). As Type **582**, but inscr "1973".
2017 45c. purple, grey and blue 45 45
2018 60c. brown, bistre & green 55 65
2019 1f. red, brown and green . . 65 65
DESIGNS—HORIZ: 45c. Napoleon and Portalis (Preparation of Civil Code, 1800–1804); 60c. Paris Industrial Exhibition, Les Invalides, 1806. VERT: 1f. "The Coronation of Napoleon, 1804" (David).

720 Eternal Flame, Arc de Triomphe

721 "Mary Magdalene"

1973. 50th Anniv of Tomb of the Unknown Soldier, Arc de Triomphe.
2020 **720** 40c. red, blue and lilac 40 35

1973. Red Cross Fund. Tomb Figures, Tonnerre.
2021 **721** 30c.+10c. grn & red . . 55 65
2022 – 50c.+10c. blk & red . . 65 65
DESIGN: 50c. Female saint.

722 Weathervane

723 Figure and Human Rights Emblem

1973. 50th Anniv of French Chambers of Agriculture.
2023 **722** 65c. black, blue & green 40 50

1973. 25th Anniv of Declaration of Human Rights.
2024 **723** 45c. brown, orge & red 25 30

724 Facade of Museum

725 Exhibition Emblem

1973. Opening of New Postal Museum Building.
2025 **724** 50c. lt brown, pur & brn 25 30

1974. "ARPHILA 75" International Stamp Exhibition, Paris.
2026 **725** 50c. brown, blue & pur 25 30

726 St. Louis-Marie Grignion de Montfort

727 Automatic Letter-sorting

1974. Red Cross Fund. Celebrities.
2027 **726** 50c.+10c. brown, green and red . . . . 1·10 1·10
2028 – 50c.+10c. red, purple and blue 85 90
2029 – 80c.+15c. purple, deep purple & blue 80 90
2030 – 80c.+15c. blue, black and purple 80 90
DESIGNS: No. 2028, Francis Poulenc (composer); No. 2029, Jean Giraudoux (writer); No. 2030, Jules Barbey d'Aurevilly (writer).

1974. Stamp Day.
2031 **727** 50c.+10c. brn, red & grn 40 45

728 Concorde over Airport

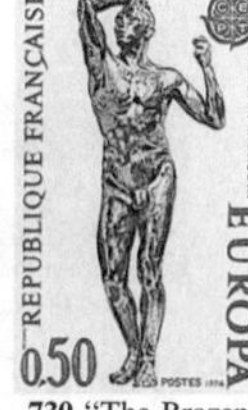
730 "The Brazen Age" (Rodin)

729 French Alps and Gentian

1974. Opening of Charles de Gaulle Airport, Roissy.
2032 **728** 60c. violet and brown . . 40 45

1974. "Arphila 1975" Stamp Exhibition. French Art. As Type **491**. Multicoloured.
2033 2f. "Cardinal Richelieu" (P. de Champaigne) . . . . 1·40 1·40
2034 2f. "Abstract after Original Work" (J. Miro) . . . . 1·70 1·60
2035 2f. "Loing Canal" (A. Sisley) . . . . 1·70 1·60
2036 2f. "Homage to Nicolas Fouquet" (E. de Mathieu) 1·70 1·60

1974. Centenary of French Alpine Club.
2037 **729** 65c. vio, grn & blue . . 45 45

1974. Europa. Sculptures.
2038 **730** 50c. black and purple . . 35 30
2039 – 90c. brown and bistre . . 70 60
DESIGN—HORIZ: 90c. "The Expression" (reclining woman) (A. Maillol).

731 Shipwreck and "Pierre Loti" (lifeboat)

1974. French Lifeboat Service.
2040 **731** 90c. blue, red & brown 50 40

732 Council Headquarters, Strasbourg

1974. 25th Anniv of Council of Europe.
2041 **732** 45c. blue, lt blue & brn 40 40

733 "Cornucopia of St. Florent" (Corsica)

1974. Tourist Publicity.
2042 – 65c. brown and green . . 40 45
2043 – 1f.10 brown & green . . 55 50
2044 – 2f. purple and blue . . . 80 30
2045 **733** 3f. blue, red & green . . 1·00 50
DESIGNS—As Type **490**. HORIZ: 65c. Salers; 1f.10, Lot Valley; VERT: 2f. Basilica of St. Nicolas-de-Port.

734 European Bison

1974. Nature Conservation.
2046 **734** 40c. purple, bl & brn . . 40 30
2047 – 65c. grey, green & blk 40 45
DESIGN: 65c. Giant Armadillo of Guiana.

735 Normandy Landings

1974. 30th Anniv of Liberation.
2048 **735** 45c. blue, red & green 65 60
2049 – 1f. red, brown & violet 50 50
2050 – 1f. brown, blk & red . . 65 65
2051 – 1f.+10c. brn, grn & blk 75 85
DESIGNS—HORIZ: No. 2050, Resistance medal and torch; 2051, Order of Liberation and honoured towns. VERT: No. 2049, General Koenig and liberation monuments.

736 Colmar **737** Board and Chess Pieces

1974. 47th Congress of French Philatelic Societies.
2052 **736** 50c. red, purple & brn 25 35

1974. 21st Chess Olympiad, Nice.
2053 **737** 1f. red, brown & blue . . 65 45

738 Commemorative Medallion

1974. 300th Anniv of "Hotel des Invalides".
2054 **738** 40c. black, brn & bl . . 25 30

739 French Turbotrain TGV 001

1974. Completion of Turbotrain TGV 001 Project.
2055 **739** 60c. red, black & blue 95 75

740 "Nuclear Power"

1974. Completion of Phenix Nuclear Generator.
2056 **740** 65c. brown, mve & red 40 45

741 Peacocks with Letter

1974. Centenary of Universal Postal Union.
2057 **741** 1f.20 red, green & blue 45 50

742 Copernicus and Heliocentric System

1974. 500th Birth Anniv (1973) of Nicolas Copernicus (astronomer).
2058 **742** 1f.20 mauve, brn & blk 45 45

743 Children playing on Beach **744** Dr. Albert Schweitzer

1974. Red Cross Fund. Seasons. Cross in red.
2059 **743** 60c.+15c. red, brown and blue 55 65
2060 – 80c.+15c. red, brown and blue 65 80
DESIGN: 80c. Child in garden looking through window.
See also 2098/9.

1975. Birth Centenary of Dr. Albert Schweitzer.
2061 **744** 80c.+20c. brown, red and green 55 75

1975. Tourist Publicity. As Type **490** but inscr "1975".
2062 85c. blue and brown 45 30
2063 1f.20 brown, dp brn & bl 40 20
2064 1f.40 blue, brown & green 55 35
DESIGNS—HORIZ: 85c. Law Courts, Rouen; 1f.40, Chateau de Rochechouart. VERT: 1f.20, St. Pol-de-Leon.

745 Little Egrets **746** Edmond Michelet (politician)

1975. Nature Conservation.
2065 **745** 70c. brown and blue . . 40 50

1975. Precancels. As T **538**, but inscribed "France".
2065a 42c. red and orange . . . 2·75 2·10
2065b 48c. red and turquoise . . 2·50 2·00
2065c 50c. brown & turquoise . . 2·50 2·00
2065d 52c. brown and red . . . 1·50 1·10
2065e 60c. brown and mauve . . 3·50 3·50
2065f 62c. brown & mauve . . . 2·20 2·20
2065g 70c. red and mauve . . . 4·50 4·50
2065h 90c. brown and pink . . . 4·50 4·50
2065i 95c. brown and sepia . . . 2·75 2·10
2065j 1f.35 red and green . . . . 4·50 4·50
2065k 1f.60 brown and violet . . 7·00 7·00
2065l 1f.70 brown and blue . . . 5·00 5·00
See note below No. 432 (1920).

1975. Red Cross Fund. Celebrities.
2066 **746** 80c.+20c. ind & bl . . . 55 60
2067 – 80c.+20c. blk & bl . . . 80 90
2068 – 80c.+20c. blk & bl . . . 55 60
2069 – 80c.+20c. blk, turq & bl 55 65
DESIGNS—VERT: No. 2067, Robert Schuman (statesman); No. 2068, Eugene Thomas (former Telecommunications Minister). HORIZ: No, 2069, Andre Siegfried (geographer and humanist).

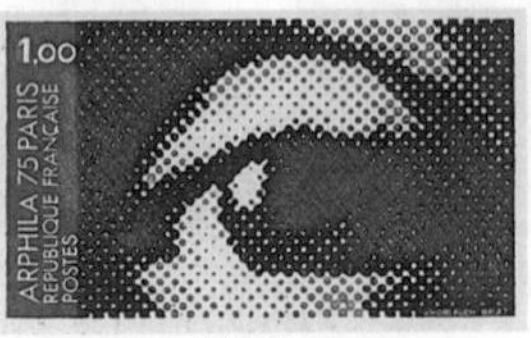

747 Eye

1975. "Arphila 75" International Stamp Exhibition, Paris.
2070 **747** 1f. orange, vio & red . . 45 50
2071 – 2f. black, red & green . . 90 75
2072 – 3f. green, grey & brown 1·10 1·00
2073 – 4f. green, red & orange 1·70 1·60
MS2074 152 × 143 mm. 2f. blue and red (Type **747**); 3f. deep blue, red and blue (as No. 2071); 4f. blue, deep blue and red (as No. 2072); 6f. deep blue, blue and red (as No. 2073) . . . . 8·00 8·00
DESIGNS: 2f. Capital; 3f. "Arphila 75 Paris"; 4f. Head of Ceres.

748 Postman's Badge **749** Pres. G. Pompidou

1975. Stamp Day.
2075 **748** 80c.+20c. blk, yell & bl 60 60

1975. Pres. Georges Pompidou Commem.
2076 **749** 80c. black and blue . . . 40 30

750 "Paul as Harlequin" (Picasso)

1975. Europa. Multicoloured.
2077 80c. Type **750** 45 35
2078 1f.20 "In the Square" or "Woman leaning on Balcony" (Van Dongen) (horiz) 80 75

751 Machine Tools and Emblem

1975. 1st World Machine-Tools Exhibition, Paris.
2079 **751** 1f.20 black, red & blue 50 50

752 First Assembly at Luxembourg Palace

1975. Centenary of French Senate.
2080 **752** 1f.20 bistre, brn & red 50 50

753 Seals, Signatures and Symbols

1975. Centenary of Metre Convention.
2081 **753** 1f. purple, mve & brn . . 50 45

754 Sud Aviation Gazelle Helicopter **755** Youth and Health Symbols

1975. Development of Gazelle Helicopter.
2082 **754** 1f.30 green and blue . . 65 60

1975. Students' Health Foundation.
2083 **755** 70c. black, purple & red 40 40

756 Underground Train

1975. Opening of Metro Regional Express Service.
2084 **756** 1f. deep blue and blue 75 50

757 Bussang Theatre and M. Pottecher (founder) **758** Picardy Rose

1975. 80th Anniv of People's Theatre, Bussang.
2085 **757** 85c. lilac, brown & blue 40 40

1975. Regions of France.
2086 **758** 85c. orange, turq & blue 70 45
2087 – 1f. lake, red & yellow . . 70 45
2088 – 1f.15 green, bl & ochre 70 50
2089 – 1f.30 black, red & blue 75 60
2090 – 1f.90 blue, bistre & blk 90 55
2091 – 2f.80 blue, red, & black 1·60 1·30
DESIGNS—VERT: 1f. Bourgogne agriculture emblems; 1f.15, Loire scene; 1f.30, Auvergne (bouquet of carnations); 1f.90, Allegory, Poitou-Charentes. HORIZ: 2f.80, "Nord-Pas-de-Calais".
See also Nos. 2102/6, 2150/7, 2246/8, 2329, 2508, 2555 and 2613.

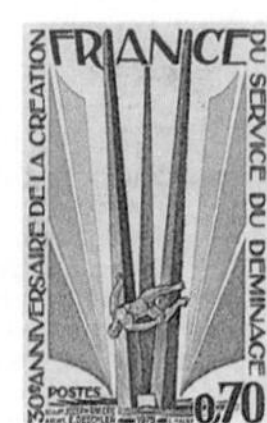

759 Concentration Camp Victims **760** "Ballon d'Alsace" (Mine-clearers Monument)

1975. 30th Anniv of Liberation of Concentration Camps.
2092 **759** 1f. green, blue and red 50 55

1975. 30th Anniv of Mine Clearance Service.
2093 **760** 70c. green, bistre & blue 40 30

761 "Urban Development"

1975. New Towns.
2094 **761** 1f.70 blue, grn & brn . . 80 75

762 St. Nazaire Bridge **763** Rainbow over Women's Faces

1975. Opening of St. Nazaire Bridge.
2095 **762** 1f.40 black, bl & grn . . 65 45

1975. International Women's Year.
2096 **763** 1f.20 multicoloured . . . 50 55

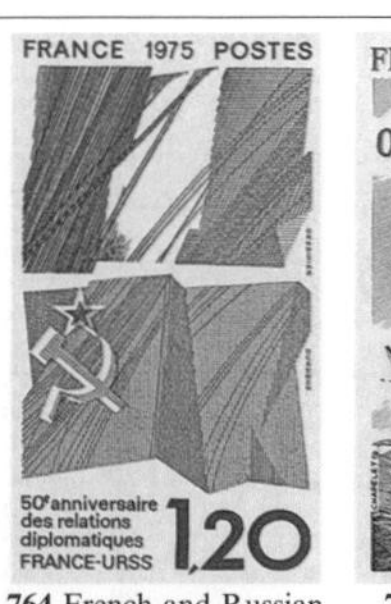

764 French and Russian Flags

765 Cadet Ship "La Melpomene"

1975. 50th Anniv of Franco-Soviet Diplomatic Relations.
2097 **764** 1f.20 yellow, red & blue 45 45

1975. Red Cross Fund. "The Seasons". As T **743**.
2098 60c.+15c. red and green . . 60 65
2099 80c.+20c. brn, orge & red 70 70
DESIGNS: 60c. Child on swing; 80c. Rabbits under umbrella.

1975. French Sailing Ships.
2100 **765** 90c. blue, orge & red . . 1·10 70

766 Concorde

767 French Stamp Design of 1876

1976. Air. Concorde's First Commercial Flight, Paris–Rio de Janeiro.
2101 **766** 1f.70 black, blue & red 85 65

1976. Regions of France. As T **758**.
2102 25c. green and blue 25 30
2103 60c. green, blue & purple . 25 30
2104 70c. blue, green, & black . . 50 45
2105 1f.25 blue, brown & green 80 85
2106 2f.20 multicoloured . . . . 1·30 1·20
DESIGNS—HORIZ: 25c. Industrial complex in the Central region; 60c. Aquitaine; 2f.20, Pyrenees. VERT: 70c. Limousin; 1f.25, Guiana.

1976. French Art. As T **491**.
2108 2f. grey and blue . . . . . 1·30 1·00
2109 2f. yellow and brown . . . 1·20 1·10
2110 2f. multicoloured . . . . . 1·30 1·20
2111 2f. multicoloured 85 95
2112 2f. multicoloured . . . . . 1·00 95
2113 2f. multicoloured . . . . . 1·10 95
DESIGNS—VERT: No. 2108, "The Two Saints", St.-Genis-des-Fontaines (wood-carving); No. 2109, "Venus of Brassempouy" (ivory sculpture); No. 2110, "La Joie de Vivre" (Robert Delaunay). HORIZ: No. 2111, Rameses II in war-chariot (wall-carving); No. 2112, Painting by Carzou; No. 2113, "Still Life with Fruit" Maurice de Vlaminck).

1976. International Stamp Day.
2114 **767** 80c.+20c. lilac & blk . . 50 50

1976. Tourist Publicity. As T **490**, but dated "1976".
2115 1f. brown, green and red . . 35 30
2116 1f.10 blue 50 45
2117 1f.40 blue, green & brown 55 30
2118 1f.70 purple, green & blue 60 25
2119 2f. mauve, red and brown 75 30
2120 3f. brown, blue and green 1·00 30
DESIGNS—HORIZ: 1f. Chateau Bonaguil; 1f.40, Basque coast, Biarritz. 3f. Chateau de Malmaison. VERT: 1f.10, Lodeve Cathedral; 1f.70, Thiers. 2f. Ussel.

768 Old Rouen

769 "Duguay Trouin VIII" (cruiser), "Duguay Trouin IX" (destroyer) and Naval Emblem

1976. 49th Congress of French Philatelic Societies.
2121 **768** 80c. green and brown . . 40 35

1976. 50th Anniv of Central Marine Officers' Reserve Association.
2122 **769** 1f. yellow, blue & red . . 50 45

770 Youth

771 Strasbourg Jug

1976. "Juvarouen 76" Youth Stamp Exhibition, Rouen.
2123 **770** 60c. indigo, blue & red 35 35

1976. Europa. Multicoloured.
2124 80c. Type **771** 35 30
2125 1f.20 Sevres plate 70 65

772 Vergennes and Franklin

1976. Bicentenary of American Revolution.
2126 **772** 1f.20 black, red & blue 50 45

773 Marshal Moncey

774 People talking

1976. Red Cross. Celebrities.
2127 **773** 80c.+20c. purple, black and brown 60 70
2128 – 80c.+20c. grn & brn . . 60 70
2129 – 80c.+20c. mve & grn . . 60 70
2130 – 1f.+20c. black, light blue and blue 65 75
2131 – 1f.+20c. blue, mauve and purple 65 75
2132 – 1f.+20c. grey & red . . . 65 75
DESIGNS: No. 2128, Max Jacob (poet); 2129, Mounet-Sully (tragedian); 2130, General Daumesnil; 2131, Eugene Fromentin (writer and painter); 2132, Anna de Noailles.

1976. "Communication".
2133 **774** 1f.20 black, red & yell 50 55

775 Verdun Memorial

776 Troncais Forest

1976. 60th Anniv of Verdun Offensive.
2134 **775** 1f. red, brown & green 45 45

1976. Nature Conservation.
2135 **776** 70c. brown, green & blue 45 35

777 Cross of Lorraine Emblem

778 Satellite "Symphonie"

1976. 30th Anniv of Free French Association.
2136 **777** 1f. red, dp blue & blue 65 45

1976. Launch of "Symphonie No. 1" Satellite.
2137 **778** 1f.40 brn, choc & vio . . 60 55

779 Carnival Figures

780 Yachting

1976. "La Fete" (Summer Festivals Exhibition, Tuileries, Paris).
2138 **779** 1f. red, green & blue . . 65 40

1976. Olympic Games, Montreal.
2139 **780** 1f.20 ind, ultram & bl 60 45

781 Officers in Military and Civilian Dress

1976. Centenary of Reserve Officers Corps.
2140 **781** 1f. grey, red & blue . . . 40 30

782 Early and Modern Telephones

1976. Telephone Centenary.
2141 **782** 1f. grey, brown & blue 40 30

783 Bronze Statue and Emblem

784 Police and Emblems

1976. 10th Anniv of International Tourist Film Association.
2142 **783** 1f.40 brown, red & grn 65 55

1976. 10th Anniv of National Police Force.
2143 **784** 1f.10 green, red & blue 50 50

785 Symbol of Nuclear Science

1976. European Research into Nuclear Science.
2144 **785** 1f.40 multicoloured . . . 80 70

786 Fair Emblem

787 St. Barbara

1976. 50th Anniv of French Fairs and Exhibitions Federation.
2145 **786** 1f.50 blue, green & brn 75 55

1976. Red Cross Fund. Statuettes in Brou Church.
2146 **787** 80c.+20c. vio & red . . 60 65
2147 – 1f.+25c. brn & red . . 90 95
DESIGN: 1f. Cumaean Sybil.

788 "Douane" Symbol

1976. French Customs Service.
2148 **788** 1f.10 multicoloured . . . 55 55

789 Museum and "Duchesse Anne" (cadet ship)

1976. Atlantic Museum, Port Louis.
2149 **789** 1f.45 brown, blue & blk 65 65

1977. Regions of France. As T **758**.
2150 1f.45 mauve and green . . . 60 50
2151 1f.50 multicoloured 65 55
2152 2f.10 yellow, blue & green 1·00 90
2153 2f.40 brown, green & blue 1·00 55
2154 2f.50 multicoloured . . . . 1·10 85
2155 2f.75 green . . . . 1·60 1·00
2156 3f.20 brown, green & blue 1·60 1·20
2157 3f.90 red, brown and blue 2·10 1·30
DESIGNS—HORIZ: 1f.45, Birds and flowers (Reunion); 2f.40, Coastline (Bretagne); 2f.75, Mountains (Rhone-Alpes). VERT: 1f.50, Banana tree (Martinique); 2f.10, Arms and transport (Franche-Comte); 2f.50, Fruit and yachts (Languedoc-Roussillon); 3f.20, Champagne and scenery (Champagne-Ardenne); 3f.90, Village church (Alsace).

790 Centre Building

1977. Opening of Georges Pompidou National Centre of Arts and Culture, Paris.
2158 **790** 1f. red, blue & green . . 40 30

1977. French Art. As T **491**.
2159 2f. multicoloured . . . . . 1·00 90
2160 2f. multicoloured . . . . . 1·20 1·10
DESIGNS—HORIZ: No. 2159, "Mantes Bridge" (Corot). VERT: No. 2160, "Virgin and Child" (Rubens).

791 Dunkirk Harbour

792 Torch and Dagger Emblem

1977. Dunkirk Port Extensions.
2161 **791** 50c. blue, indigo & brn 25 30

1977. 90th Anniv of "Le Souvenir Francais" (French War Graves Organization).
2162 **792** 80c. brown, red & blue 50 45

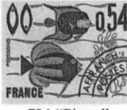

793 Marckolsheim Post Relay Sign

794 "Pisces"

1977. Stamp Day.
2163 **793** 1f.+20c. grey & blue . . 55 65

1977. Precancels. Signs of the Zodiac.
2164 **794** 54c. violet 65 65
2165 – 58c. green . . . . 1·60 1·60
2166 – 61c. blue 70 70
2167 – 68c. brown . . . . . . 1·10 1·10
2168 – 73c. red . . . . 2·50 2·50
2169 – 78c. orange . . . . . . 1·30 1·30
2170 – 1f.05 mauve . . . . . . 2·40 2·40
2171 – 1f.15 orange . . . . . . 4·00 4·00
2172 – 1f.25 green . . . . . . 1·80 1·80
2173 – 1f.85 green . . . . . . 5·00 5·00
2174 – 2f. turquoise . . . . . 5·00 5·00
2175 – 2f.10 mauve . . . . . . 2·50 2·50

DESIGNS: 58c. Cancer; 61c. Sagittarius; 68c. Taurus; 73c. Aries; 78c. Libra; 1f.05, Scorpio; 1f.15, Capricorn; 1f.25, Leo; 1f.85, Aquarius; 2f. Virgo; 2f.10, Gemini.

See note below No. 432 (1920).

795 "Geometric Design" (Victor Vasarely)

1977. Philatelic Creations. Works of Art by Modern Artists.

2176 **795** 3f. green and lilac . . . 1·40 95
2177 – 3f. black and red . . . . 2·00 1·80
2178 – 3f. multicoloured . . . . 1·90 1·50

DESIGNS—VERT: No. 2177, Profile heads of man and hawk (Pierre-Yves Tremois). HORIZ: No. 2178, Abstract in Blue (R. Excoffon).

See also Nos. 2249, 2331/2, 2346/8, 2434/5, 2547 and 2578/9.

796 Flowers and Ornamental Garden

1977. 50th Anniv of National Horticultural Society.

2179 **796** 1f.70 red, brown & grn 80 55

797 Provencal Village

1977. Europa.

2180 **797** 1f. red, brown & blue . . 50 30
2181 – 1f.40 blk, brn & grn . . 85 35

DESIGN: 1f.40, Breton port.

798 Stylized Plant

1977. International Flower Show, Nantes.

2182 **798** 1f.40 mve, yell & bl . . 70 70

799 Battle of Cambrai

1977. 300th Anniv of Reunification of Cambrai with France.

2183 **799** 80c. mauve, brown & bl 55 45

800 Church, School and Map **801** Modern Constructions

1977. Centenary of French Catholic Institutes.

2184 **800** 1f.10 brown, bl & choc 55 65

1977. Meeting of European Civil Engineering Federation, Paris.

2185 **801** 1f.10 red, bistre & blue 60 45

802 Annecy

1977. 50th Congress of French Philatelic Societies.

2186 **802** 1f. brown, grn & olive 55 40

1977. Tourist Publicity. As T **490**.

2187 1f.25 grey, brown & red . . 50 45
2188 1f.40 blue, purple & pink . . 60 40
2189 1f.45 sepia, brown & blue 60 40
2190 1f.50 olive, red & brown . . 60 30
2191 1f.90 yellow and black . . . 70 55
2192 2f.40 bistre, green & black 90 50

DESIGNS—HORIZ: 1f.25, Premontres Abbey, Pont-a-Mousson; 1f.50, Statue and cloisters, Fontenay Abbey, Cote d'Or; 2f.40, Chateau de Vitre. VERT: 1f.40, Abbey tower of St. Amand-les-Eaux, Nord; 1f.45, Le Dorat Church, Haute-Vienne; 1f.90, Bayeux Cathedral.

803 School Building

1977. Polytechnic School, Palaiseau.

2193 **803** 1f.70 green, red & blue 70 50

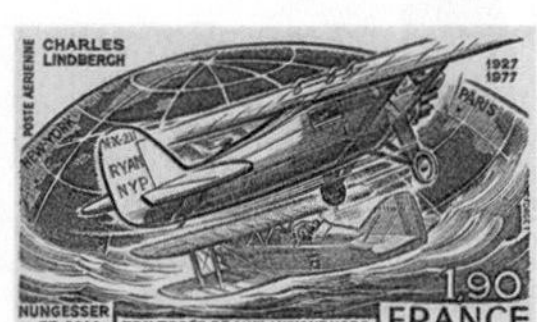

804 "Spirit of St. Louis" and "L'Oiseau Blanc"

1977. Air. 50th Anniv of North Atlantic Flights.

2194 **804** 1f.90 indigo, blue & grn 95 75

805 French Football Cup and Players

1977. 60th Anniv of French Football Cup.

2195 **805** 80c. bistre, blue & red 1·00 65

806 De Gaulle Memorial **807** "Map of France"

1977. 5th Anniv of General de Gaulle Memorial.

2196 **806** 1f. multicoloured . . . . 1·00 65

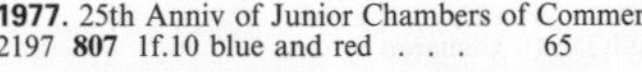

1977. 25th Anniv of Junior Chambers of Commerce.

2197 **807** 1f.10 blue and red . . . 65 50

808 Battle of Nancy **809** Seal of Burgundy

1977. 500th Anniv of Battle of Nancy.

2198 **808** 1f.10 slate and blue . . . 90 70

1977. 500th Anniv of Union of Burgundy with France.

2199 **809** 1f.25 green and olive . . 50 50

810 Compass on Globe **811** Red Cicada

1977. 10th Anniv of International Association of French Language Parliaments.

2200 **810** 1f.40 red and blue . . . 60 55

1977. Nature Protection.

2201 **811** 80c. multicoloured . . . 50 50

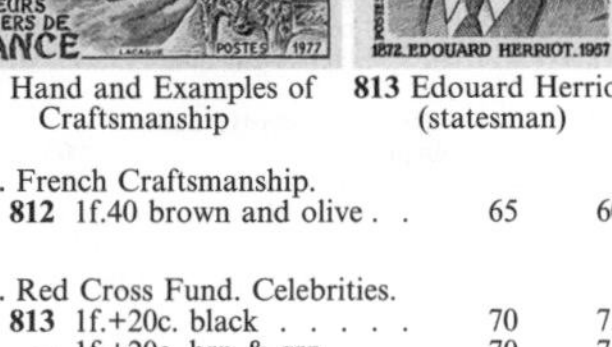

812 Hand and Examples of Craftsmanship **813** Edouard Herriot (statesman)

1977. French Craftsmanship.

2202 **812** 1f.40 brown and olive . . 65 60

1977. Red Cross Fund. Celebrities.

2203 **813** 1f.+20c. black 70 75
2204 – 1f.+20c. brn & grn . . . 70 75
2205 – 1f.+20c. brn, bis & grn 70 75
2206 – 1f.+20c. bl, lt bl & red 70 75

DESIGNS: No. 2204, Abbe Breuil (archaeologist); 2205, Guillaume de Machault (poet); 2206, Charles Cros (poet).

814 "Agriculture and Industry" **815** "Old Man"

1977. 30th Anniv of Economic and Social Council.

2207 **814** 80c. bistre, green & brn 35 30

1977. Red Cross Fund. Carved Christmas Crib Figures from Provence.

2208 **815** 80c.+20c. black & red 55 65
2209 – 1f.+25c. green & red . . 70 75

DESIGN: 1f. "Old Woman".

816 "Sabine" (after Louis David) **817** Table Tennis

1977. Inscr "FRANCE".

2210 **816** 1c. black 15 30
2211 2c. blue 15 30
2212 5c. green 10 10
2213 10c. red 10 15
2214 15c. blue 40 45
2215 20c. green 10 20
2216 30c. orange 10 10
2216a 40c. brown 25 25
2217 50c. violet 20 15
2217a 60c. red 30 40
2218 70c. blue 25 30
2219 80c. green 75 45
2220 80c. yellow 25 35
2221 90c. mauve 35 40
2222 1f. red 60 20
2223 1f. emerald 40 15
2224 1f. olive 25 15
2225 1f.10 green 55 20
2226 1f.20 red 40 15
2226a 1f.20 green 40 20
2227 1f.30 red 55 10
2228 1f.40 blue . . . . . . 1·20 60
2228a 1f.40 red 55 15
2229 1f.60 violet 80 45
2230 1f.70 blue 75 55
2230a 1f.80 brown 80 60
2231 2f. green 55 15
2232 2f.10 purple 60 45
2233 3f. brown 80 45
2233a 3f.50 green . . . . . . 1·30 90
2234 4f. red . . . . 1·50 80
2234a 5f. blue . . . . 1·70 70

For values inscr "REPUBLIQUE FRANCAISE" see Nos. 2423/5.

1977. 50th Anniv of French Table Tennis Federation.

2240 **817** 1f.10 grn, pur & orge . . 2·30 1·90

818 Percheron

1978. Nature Conservation.

2241 **818** 1f.70 multicoloured . . . 1·00 95
2242 – 1f.80 brn, olive & grn . . 85 70

DESIGN—VERT: (23 × 37 mm) 1f.80, Osprey.

1978. French Art. As T **491**.

2243 2f. black . . . . 2·40 1·80

DESIGN: 2f. Tournament under Louis XIV, Les Tuileries, 1662.

819 Flags of France and Sweden of 1878 **820** College Building

1978. Centenary of Return of St. Barthelemy Island to France.

2244 **819** 1f.10 brn, red & mve . . 50 45

1978. Centenary of National Telecommunications College.

2245 **820** 80c. blue 35 30

1978. Regions of France. As T **758**.

2246 1f. red, blue and black . . . 40 35
2247 1f.40 blue, orange & green 70 55
2248 1f.70 gold, red and black . . 1·00 80

DESIGNS—VERT: 1f. Symbol of Ile de France. HORIZ: 1f.40, Flower and port (Haute-Normandie); 1f.70, Ancient Norman ship (Basse-Normandie).

1978. "Philatelic Creations". As T **795**.

2249 3f. multicoloured . . . . . 2·30 1·50
2250 3f. multicoloured . . . . . 1·80 1·20

DESIGNS—HORIZ: No. 2249 "Institut de France and Pont des Arts, Paris" (B. Buffet); 2250, "Camargue Horses" (Yves Brayer).

821 Marie Noel (poet) **822** Jigsaw Map of France

1978. Red Cross Fund. Celebrities.

2251 **821** 1f.+20c. indigo & bl . . 75 80
2252 – 1f.+20c. green, brown and blue 75 80
2253 – 1f.+20c. mve & vio . . 75 80
2254 – 1f.+20c. green & brn . . 75 80
2255 – 1f.+20c. mve & red . . . 75 80
2256 – 1f.+20c. black, brown and red 75 80

DESIGNS: No. 2252, Georges Bernanos (writer); 2253, Leconte de Lisle (poet); 2254, Leo Tolstoy (novelist); 2255, Voltaire and J.-J. Rousseau; 2256, Claude Bernard (physician).

1978. 15th Anniv of Regional Planning Boards.
2257 **822** 1f.10 green & violet . . 45 35

1978. Tourist Publicity. As T **490**.
2258 50c. green, blue & dp green 30 25
2259 80c. dp green, blue & grn 35 35
2260 1f. black 35 35
2261 1f.10 violet, brown & grn 55 50
2262 1f.10 brown, blue & green 50 50
2263 1f.25 brown and red 70 50
2264 1f.70 black and brown . . . 85 80
DESIGNS—VERT: 50c. Verdon Gorge; 1f. Church of St. Saturnin, Puy de Dome. HORIZ: 80c. Pont-Neuf, Paris; 1f.10 (No. 2261), Notre-Dame du Bec-Hellouin Abbey; 1f.10 (No. 2262), Chateau d'Esquelbecq; 1f.25, Abbey Church of Aubazine; 1f.70, Fontevraud Abbey.

823 Head of Girl

824 Postman emptying Pillar Box, 1900

1978. "Juvexniort" Youth Philately Exhibition, Niort.
2265 **823** 80c. brn, choc & mve . . 35 35

1978. Stamp Day.
2266 **824** 1f.+20c. grn & blue . . . 50 60

825 Underwater Scene and Rainbow Wrasse

826 Floral Arch and Garden

1978. Port Cros National Park.
2267 **825** 1f.25 multicoloured . . . 1·10 1·20

1978. "Make France Bloom".
2268 **826** 1f.70 red, blue & green 1·60 65

827 Hands encircling Sun

828 War Memorial, Notre Dame de Lorette

1978. Energy Conservation.
2269 **827** 1f. yellow, brn & bistre 55 40

1978. Hill of Notre Dame de Lorette (War Cemetery).
2270 **828** 2f. brown and bistre . . 90 50

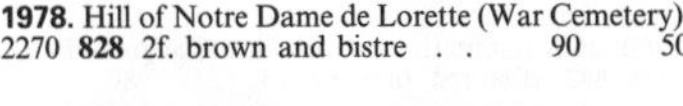

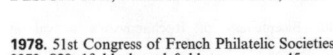

829 Fontaine des Innocents, Paris

830 Hotel de Mauroy, Troyes

1978. Europa. Fountains.
2271 **829** 1f. blk, bistre & blue . . 50 30
2272 – 1f.40 brn, grn & blue . . 75 50
DESIGN: 1f.40, Fontaine du Parc Floral, Paris.

1978. 51st Congress of French Philatelic Societies.
2273 **830** 1f. black, red & blue . . 45 45

831 Tennis Player and Stadium

1978. 50th Anniv of Roland Garros Tennis Stadium.
2274 **831** 1f. grey, brown & blue 1·90 55

832 Open Hand

833 Citadel and Church

1978. Handicrafts.
2275 **832** 1f.30 brown, grn & red 55 50

1978. 300th Anniv of Reunification of Franche-Comte with France.
2276 **833** 1f.20 grey, blue & grn 50 35

834 Emblem

835 Valenciennes and Maubeuge

1978. State Printing Office.
2277 **834** 1f. green, black & blue 45 35

1978. 300th Anniv of Return of Valenciennes and Maubeuge to France.
2278 **835** 1f.20 brown, vio & grey 55 45

836 Sower

837 Morane-Saulnier Type H and Route

1978. 50th Anniv of Academie de Philatelie.
2279 **836** 1f. blue, purple & violet 45 50

1978. Air. 65th Anniv of First Airmail Flight Villacoublay–Pauillac.
2280 **837** 1f.50 brown, blue & grn 85 55

838 Gymnasts, White Stork and Strasbourg Cathedral

839 Sporting Activities

1978. 19th World Gymnastics Championships, Strasbourg.
2281 **838** 1f. red, sepia & brown 55 50

1978. Sport for All.
2282 **839** 1f. violet, mauve & blue 95 80

840 "Freedom holding Dying Warrior" (A. Greck)

841 Railway Carriage, Rethondes, and Armistice Monument

1978. Polish Fighters' War Memorial.
2283 **840** 1f.70 lake, red & green 85 80

1978. 60th Anniv of Armistice.
2284 **841** 1f.20 black 55 50

842 Symbols of Readaptation

1978. Help for Convalescents.
2285 **842** 1f. red, brown & orge . . 45 50

843 "The Hare and the Tortoise"

844 Human Figures balanced on Globe

1978. Red Cross Fund. Fables of La Fontaine.
2286 **843** 1f.+25c. brown, red and green 80 85
2287 – 1f.20+30c. green, red and brown 80 85
DESIGN: 1f.20, "The Town and the Country Mouse".

1978. 30th Anniv of Human Rights.
2288 **844** 1f.70 blue and brown . . 70 45

845 Seated Child

846 Marshal de Bercheny (Cavalry leader)

1979. International Year of the Child.
2289 **845** 1f.70 red, vio & brn . . 3·00 2·75

1979. French Art. As T **491**.
2290 2f. multicoloured . . . . . 1·40 1·20
2291 2f. brown, black & dp brn 1·40 1·10
2292 2f. multicoloured . . . . . 3·75 1·50
DESIGNS—HORIZ: No. 2290, "Music" (15th century miniature by Robinet Testart). VERT: No. 2291, "Diana in her Bath" (mantelpiece originally from Chalons-sur-Marne, now in Chateau d'Ecouen); 2292, "Auvers-sur-Oise Church" (Vincent van Gogh).

1979. Red Cross Fund. Celebrities.
2293 **846** 1f.20+30c. brown, blue and deep blue 85 90
2294 – 1f.20+30c. black and yellow 90 90
2295 – 1f.20+30c. deep brown, red & brown 85 90
2296 – 1f.20+30c. blue, mauve and red 85 90
2297 – 1f.30+30c. red and brown 90 90
2298 – 1f.30+30c. blue and ultramarine 90 90
DESIGNS: No. 2294, Leon Jouhaux (Nobel Peace Prize winner); 2295, Abelard and Heloise; 2296, Georges Courteline (playwright); 2297, Simone Weil (social philosopher); 2298, Andre Malraux (writer and politician).

847 "Amanita caesarea"

848 Segalen, Pirogue, Pagoda and "Durance"

1979. Precancelled. Mushrooms.
2299 **847** 64c. red 55 55
2300 – 83c. brown 60 60
2301 – 1f.30 yellow 95 95
2302 – 2f.25 lilac . . . . 1·50 1·50
DESIGNS: 83c. "Craterellus cornucopioides"; 1f.30, "Omphalotus olearius"; 2f.20, "Ramaria botrytis".
See note below No. 432 (1920).

1979. 60th Death Anniv of Victor Segalen (writer and explorer).
2303 **848** 1f.50 turq, brn & red . . 60 40

849 Hibiscus Flower

850 Seated Buddha

1979. International Flower Show, Martinique.
2304 **849** 35c. lilac, mve & grn . . 25 30

1979. Borobudur Temple Preservation.
2305 **850** 1f.80 turquoise & green 70 50

851 Head Post Office, Paris

852 Street Urchin

1979. Stamp Day.
2306 **851** 1f.20+30c. blue, red and brown 65 60

1979. Birth Centenary of Francisque Poulbot (artist).
2307 **852** 1f.30 multicoloured . . . 50 45

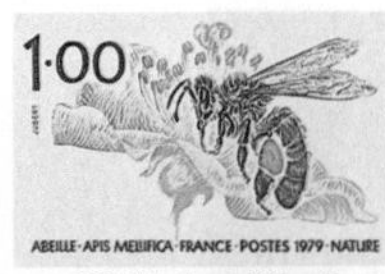

853 "Apis mellifera"

1979. Nature Conservation.
2308 **853** 1f. green, brown & orge 70 50

854 St.-Germain-des-Pres Abbey

1979. St.-Germain-des-Pres Abbey Restoration.
2309 **854** 1f.40 red, grey and blue 60 50

1979. Tourist Publicity. As T **490**.
2310 45c. violet, blue & ultram 30 30
2311 1f. green, dp grn & lt grn 40 40
2312 1f. sepia, brown and lilac . . 40 35
2313 1f.20 brown, blue and green 45 40
2314 1f.50 sepia, red & brown . . 60 45
2315 1f.70 blue and brown . . . 75 80
DESIGNS—VERT: No. 2311, Interiors of Abbeys of Bernay and St. Pierre-sur-Dives, Normandy; 2312, Auray; 2313, Windmill at Steenvoorde, Dunkirk (after Pierre Spas). HORIZ: No. 2310, Chateau de Maisons-Laffitte; 2314, Niaux Grotto; 2315, Palace of Kings of Majorca, Perpignan.

855 Caudron C.635 Monoplanes

1979. Europa.
2316 **855** 1f.20 blue, grn & turq 70 35
2317 – 1f.70 green, turq & red 1·10 75
DESIGN: 1f.70, Boule de Moulins (floating container used to carry letters during the Siege of Paris).

856 Sailing Ship at Nantes

1979. Federation of French Philatelic Societies Congress, Nantes.
2318 **856** 1f.20 blue, vio & grey . . 50 45

857 "Camille Desmoulins addressing Crowd" (engraving by Huyot)

1979. 190th Anniv of Palais Royal, Paris.
2319 **857** 1f. red and violet 35 35

858 Flags of Member Countries and Strasbourg Cathedral

1979. First Direct Elections to European Assembly.
2320 **858** 1f.20 multicoloured . . . 45 35

859 Joan of Arc Monument, Rouen

1979. National Monument.
2321 **859** 1f.70 mauve 75 60

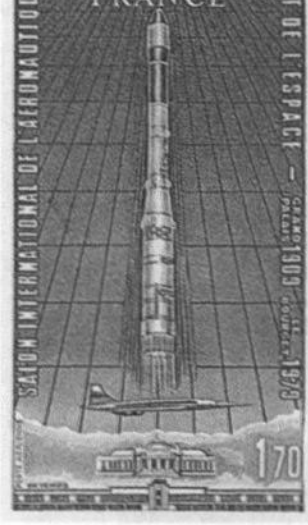

860 "Ariane" Rocket and Concorde over Grand Palais, Paris and Le Bourget Airport

862 Lantern Tower, La Rochelle

861 Felix Guyon (urologist)

1979. Air. International Aeronautics and Space Exhibition, Le Bourget.
2322 **860** 1f.70 bl, orge & brn . . 1·10 1·20

1979. 18th Congress of International Society of Urologists, Paris.
2323 **861** 1f.80 blue and brown . . 70 50

1979. Pre-cancelled. Historic Monuments (1st series).
2324 **862** 68c. lilac 50 50
2325 – 88c. blue 60 60
2326 – 1f.40 green 95 95
2327 – 2f.35 brown . . . . . . 1·30 1·30
DESIGNS: 88c. Cathedral towers, Chartres; 1f.40, Cathedral towers, Bourges; 2f.35, Cathedral towers, Amiens.
See note below No. 432 (1920).
See also Nos. 2342/5, 2383/6 and 2509/12.

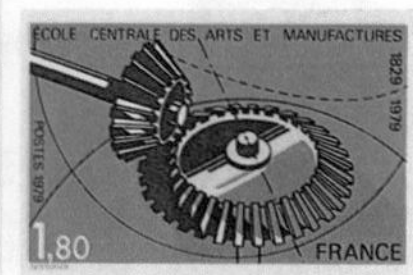

863 "Telecom 79" **864** Gear-wheels

1979. Third World Telecommunications Exhibition, Geneva.
2328 **863** 1f.10 brn, turq & grn . . 40 35

1979. Regions of France. As T **758**.
2329 2f.30 black, yellow & red . . 90 50
DESIGN: 2f.30, Thistle, Lorraine.

1979. 150th Anniv of Central Technical School, Paris.
2330 **864** 1f.80 yellow, blk & grn 85 75

1979. "Philatelic Creations". As T **795**.
2331 3f. multicoloured . . . . . 1·40 1·20
2332 3f. brown and green . . . . 1·40 1·20
DESIGNS: No. 2331, "Marianne" (Salvador Dali); 2332, "Fire Dancer from 'The Magic Flute'" (Chapelain-Midy).

865 Judo **866** Women's Head

1979. World Judo Championships, Paris.
2333 **865** 1f.60 blk, lt grn & grn 65 45

1979. Red Cross Fund. Stained Glass Windows, Church of St. Joan of Arc, Rouen.
2334 **866** 1f.10+30c. brown, green and red 70 75
2335 – 1f.30+30c. brown, green and red 80 80
DESIGN: 1f.30, Simon the Magician.
The windows came originally from the Church of St. Vincent, Rouen, destroyed during the Second World War.

867 Violins **868** Eurovision Satellite

1979. Handicrafts. Violin Manufacture.
2336 **867** 1f.30 blk, red & lake . . 55 45

1980. 25th Anniv of Eurovision (European Broadcasting Union).
2337 **868** 1f.80 bl, dp bl & blk . . 95 95

1980. French Art. Design similar to T **491**.
2338 3f. brown, ochre & green . . 1·40 1·10
2339 3f. multicoloured . . . . . 1·40 1·10
2340 3f. multicoloured . . . . . 1·40 1·10
2341 4f. multicoloured . . . . . 2·20 1·40
DESIGNS—VERT: No. 2338, "Woman with Fan" (sculpture by Ossip Zadkine); 2340, "The Peasant Family" (Louis le Nain); 2341, "Woman with Blue Eyes" (Modigliani). HORIZ: No. 2339, "Homage to J. S. Bach" (tapestry by Jean Picart Le Doux).

1980. Pre-cancelled. Historic Monuments (2nd series). Designs as T **862**.
2342 76c. turquoise 35 35
2343 99c. green 55 55
2344 1f.60 red 85 85
2345 2f.65 brown . . . . 1·40 1·40
DESIGNS: 76c. Chateau d'Angers; 99c. Chateau de Kerjean; 1f.60, Chateau de Pierrefonds; 2f.65, Chateau de Tarascon.
See note below No. 432 (1920).

1980. Philatelic Creations. Design similar to T **795**.
2346 3f. blue, black and brown 1·50 1·20
2347 4f. multicoloured . . . . . 2·75 1·70
2348 4f. black and blue . . . . . 1·90 1·70
DESIGNS—As T **795**: HORIZ: No. 2346, Abstract (Raoul Ubac). VERT: No. 2348, Abstract (Hans Hartung). 43 × 49 mm: No. 2347, "Message of Peace" (Yaacov Agam).

869 Processional Figures and Carnival Crowd **870** Viollet-le-Duc (architect and writer)

1980. "Giants of the North" Festival.
2349 **869** 1f.60 red, grn & blue . . 60 50

1980. Red Cross Fund. Celebrities.
2350 **870** 1f.30+30c. black and grey 85 90
2351 – 1f.30+30c. brown and green . . . . 1·10 1·30
2352 – 1f.40+30c. deep blue and blue 85 90
2353 – 1f.40+30c. black 85 90
2354 – 1f.40+30c. grey and black 85 90
2355 – 1f.40+30c. turquoise and green 85 90
DESIGN—VERT: No. 2351, Jean Monnet (statesman); 2352, Jean-Marie de la Mennais (Christian educationalist) (portrait after Paulin-Guerin); 2353, Frederic Mistral (poet); 2355, Saint-John Perse (poet and diplomat). HORIZ: No. 2354, Pierre Paul de Riquet (constructor of Canal du Midi).

871 French Cuisine **873** "Woman Embroidering" (Toffoli)

872 "The Letter to Melie" (Mario Avati)

1980. French Gastronomical Exn, Paris.
2356 **871** 90c. brown and red . . . 95 75

1980. Stamp Day.
2357 **872** 1f.30+30c. mult 75 80

1980. Handicrafts. Embroidery.
2358 **873** 1f.10 blue, yell & brn . . 50 45

874 Smoker and Non-smoker (poster) **875** Aristide Briand (statesman)

1980. Anti-smoking Campaign.
2359 **874** 1f.30 blue, red & black 45 35

1980. Tourist Publicity. Designs as T **490**.
2360 1f.50 orange, brown & blue 55 35
2361 2f. black and red 75 55
2362 2f.20 brown, blue & green 75 45
2363 2f.30 green, brown & blue 90 55
2364 2f.50 blue, violet and mauve 85 35
2365 3f.20 brown and blue . . . 1·20 75
DESIGNS—VERT: 1f.50, Cordes; 2f.30, Montauban; 2f.50, Praying nun and St. Peter's Abbey, Solesmes; 3f.20, Puy Cathedral. HORIZ: 2f. Chateau de Maintenon; 2f.20, Chateau de Rambouillet.

1980. Europa.
2366 **875** 1f.30 multicoloured . . . 50 35
2367 – 1f.80 red and brown . . 80 70
DESIGN: 1f.80, St. Benedict (illuminated letter from manuscript).

876 La Rouchefoucauld-Liancourt (founder) and Map

1980. Bicentenary of National Technical High School.
2368 **876** 2f. green and violet . . . 70 55

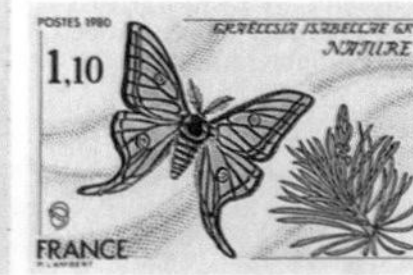

877 Town Hall and Cranes, Dunkirk **878** Isabel

1980. Federation of French Philatelic Societies Congress, Dunkirk.
2369 **877** 1f.30 bl, red & ultram 45 40

1980. Nature Conservation.
2370 **878** 1f.10 multicoloured . . . 75 50

879 Albert Durer (self portrait) **880** Symbolic Design

1980. "Philexfrance 82" International Stamp Exhibition, Paris (1st issue).
2371 **879** 2f. multicoloured . . . . 1·50 1·50
See also Nos. 2415/16, 2520/1 and **MS**2539.

1980. 25th Anniv of International Public Relations Association.
2372 **880** 1f.30 blue and red . . . 55 45

881 "Marianne" and Architecture

1980. Heritage Year.
2373 **881** 1f.50 blue and black . . 60 50

882 Sources of Energy

1980. 26th International Geological Congress, Paris.
2374 **882** 1f.60 red, brown & ol . . 80 50

883 Rochambeau landing at Newport

1980. Bicentenary of Rochambeau's arrival at Newport, Rhode Island.
2375 **883** 2f.50 mve, red & grey . . 1·20 95

884 Breguet 19 Super TR "Point d'Interrogation"

1980. Air. 50th Anniv of First Non-stop Paris–New York Flight.
2376 **884** 2f.50 purple and blue . . 95 60

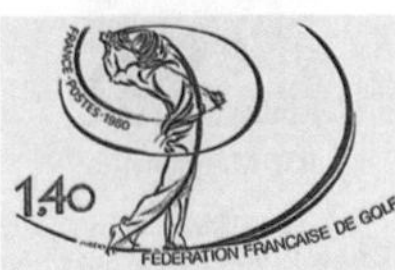

885 Golf

1980. French Golf Federation.
2377 **885** 1f.40 brown & green . . 65 50

886 Comedie-Francaise

1980. 300th Anniv of Comedie-Francaise.
2378 **886** 2f. blue, red and grey . . 80 55

887 Abstract based on Lorraine Cross and French Flag

1980. 40th Anniv of Appeal by, and 10th Death Anniv of, General de Gaulle.
2379 **887** 1f.40 multicoloured . . . 1·00 50

888 Guardsman **889** "Filling the Granaries"

1980. Centenary of Reorganization and Naming of Republican Guard.
2380 **888** 1f.70 blue and red . . . 90 60

1980. Red Cross Fund. Stall Carvings from Amiens Cathedral.
2381 **889** 1f.20+30c. brown and red 75 85
2382 – 1f.40+30c. brown and red 75 85
DESIGN: 1f.40, "Grapes from the Promised Land".

1981. Pre-cancelled. Historic Monuments (3rd series). Horiz designs as T **862**.
2383 88c. mauve 45 45
2384 1f.14 blue 50 50
2385 1f.84 green 90 90
2386 3f.05 brown . . . . 1·40 1·40
DESIGNS: 88c. Imperial Chapel, Ajaccio; 1f.14, Astronomical Clock, Besancon; 1f.84, Castle ruins, Coucy-le-Chateau; 3f.05, Cave paintings, Font-de Gaume, Les Eyzies-de Tayac.
See note below No. 432 (1920).

890 Micro-electronics **891** Louis Armand (engineer and Academician)

1981. Technology.
2387 **890** 1f.20 multicoloured . . . 60 45
2388 – 1f.20 multicoloured . . . 50 35
2389 – 1f.40 multicoloured . . . 60 40
2390 – 1f.80 dp bl, bl & yell . . 80 65
2391 – 2f. blue, red and black 1·00 80
DESIGNS: No. 2388, Biology; 2389, New energy sources; 2390, Sea bed exploitation; 2391, Telematics.

1981. Red Cross Fund. Celebrities.
2392 **891** 1f.20+30c. green and brown 80 85
2393 – 1f.20+30c. mult 80 85
2394 – 1f.40+30c. deep green and green 90 95
2395 – 1f.40+30c. blue and black 90 95
2396 – 1f.40+30c. blue and violet . . . . 90 1·00
2397 – 1f.40+30c. brown and bistre . . . . 1·00 1·10
DESIGNS—VERT: No. 2393, Louis Jouvet (theatre and film director and actor); 2396, R. P. Pierre Teilhard de Chardin (palaeontologist and philosopher). HORIZ: No. 2394, Anne-Marie Javouhey (missionary); 2395, Jacques Offenbach (composer); 2397, Pastor Marc Boegner.

1981. French Art. As T **491**. Multicoloured.
2398 2f. "The Footpath" (Camille Pissarro) (horiz) . . . . 1·10 1·10
2399 4f. "Composition 1920/23" (Albert Gleizes) (vert) . . 1·80 1·20

892 "The Love Letter" (Goya)

1981. Stamp Day.
2400 **892** 1f.40+30c. mult . . . . 95 1·00

893 Angel pouring Water on France **894** Bookbinding Press

1981. Water.
2401 **893** 1f.40 red, blue & blk . . 65 40

1981. Tourist Publicity. Designs similar to T **490**.
2403 1f.40 brown and red 60 35
2404 1f.70 brown, green & blue 90 55
2405 2f. black and red 85 55
2406 2f.20 black and blue 95 60
2407 2f.20 sepia and brown . . . 85 55
2408 2f.50 brown, blue & green 90 55
2409 2f.60 red and green . . . . 1·00 60
2410 2f.90 green . . . . 1·00 45
DESIGNS—VERT: 1f.40, St. John's Cathedral, Lyon; 1f.70, Maison Carree, Nimes; 2f.20 (2406), St. Anne's Church, Auray; 2f.90, Crest. HORIZ: 2f. Interior, Notre Dame Abbey, Vaucelles; 2f.20 (2407), Notre Dame Church, Louviers; 2f.50, Chateau de Sully, Rosny-sur-Seine; 2f.60, Saint-Emilion.

1981. Handicrafts. Bookbinding.
2411 **894** 1f.50 olive and red . . . 80 55

895 Bourree Croisee dance **896** Military and Sporting Scenes

1981. Europa.
2412 **895** 1f.40 brown, blk & grn 50 35
2413 – 2f. black, brn & blue . . 1·00 55
DESIGN: 2f. Sardane (Catalan dance).

1981. Cent of Saint-Maixent Military Academy.
2414 **896** 2f.50 mauve, blue & vio 80 55

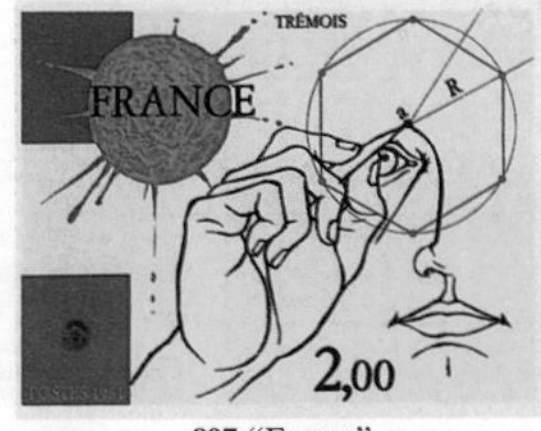

897 "France"

1981. "Philexfrance 82" International Stamp Exhibition, Paris (2nd issue). Multicoloured.
2415 2f. Type **897** . . . . 1·50 1·40
2416 2f. "Paris" . . . . 1·50 1·50

898 Theophraste Renaudot and Emile de Girardin **899** Thermal Waters of Vichy

1981. 350th Anniv of First French Newspaper "La Gazette", Death Centenary of Emile de Girardin (founder of newspaper "La Presse") and Cent of Law on Freedom of the Press.
2417 **898** 2f.20 black and red . . . 85 75

1981. Federation of French Philatelic Societies Congress, Vichy.
2418 **899** 1f.40 brown, bl & grn 65 50

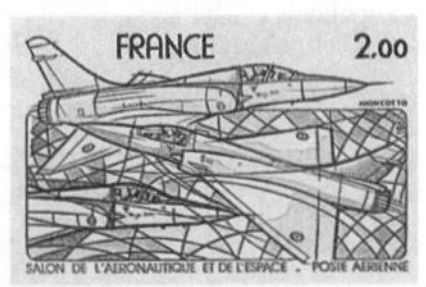

900 Dassault Mirage 2000 Aircraft

1981. Air. 34th International Aeronautics and Space Exhibition.
2419 **900** 2f. mauve, blue & violet 1·60 55

901 "HEC"

1981. Centenary of Paris Commercial College.
2420 **901** 1f.40 blue, green & red 60 50

902 Grey Heron and La Palissade, Camargue

1981. Conservation of Littoral Regions.
2421 **902** 1f.60 green, brn & red 80 65

903 Fencing

1981. World Fencing Championships, Clermont-Ferrand.
2422 **903** 1f.80 black & brown . . 85 75

1981. Vert designs as T **816** but inscr "REPUBLIQUE FRANCAISE".
2423 1f.40 green 45 25
2424 1f.60 red 55 25
2425 2f.30 blue . . . . 1·90 1·10

904 Car colliding with Glass

1981. Campaign against Drinking and Driving.
2428 **904** 1f.60 brown, red & olive 75 50

905 Costes, Le Brix and Breguet 19 "Nungesser et Coli"

1981. Air. Dieudonne Costes and Joseph Le Brix (pilots of first non-stop South Atlantic flight) Commemoration.
2429 **905** 10f. black, brn & red . . 4·00 1·10

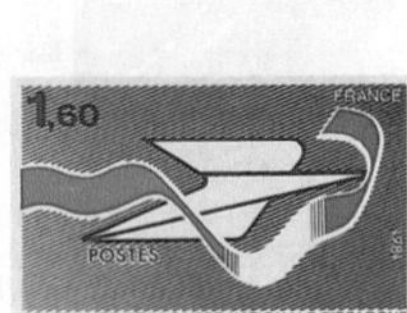

906 Bird **907** Stylized Bird

1981. 45th International Congress of P.E.N. Club, Lyon and Paris.
2430 **906** 2f. black, violet & grn 85 55

1981. Centenary of National Savings Bank.
2431 **907** 1f.40 green, bl & red . . 55 35
2432 1f.60 carmine, blue & red 65 40

908 Jules Ferry (education reformer) **909** "Borda" (warship) and Naval School, Lanveoc-Poulmic

1981. Cent of National Education System.
2433 **908** 1f.60 vio, brn & blk . . 75 40

1981. Philatelic Creations. As T **795**. Mult.
2434 4f. "The Divers" (Edouard Pignon) (horiz) . . . . . 1·70 1·20
2435 4f. "Alleluia" (Alfred Manessier) . . . . 1·70 1·20

1981. 150th Anniv of Naval School.
2436 **909** 1f.40 brown, blue & red 70 50

910 "Vision of St. Hubert" (15th-cent sculpture) **911** J. Moulin, J. Jaures, V. Schoelcher and Pantheon

1981. Hunting and Nature Museum, Hotel de Guenegaud, Paris.
2437 **910** 1f.60 brown & stone . . 75 40

1981. Pantheon.
2438 **911** 1f.60 purple and blue . . 70 35

912 Disabled Draughtsman

1981. International Year of Disabled Persons.
2439 **912** 1f.60 black, bl & red . . 65 45

REPUBLIQUE FRANÇAISE HOMMAGE A VIRGILE 2,00

913 Pastoral Scene (2nd-century mosaic)

1981. 2000th Death Anniv of Virgil (poet).
2440 **913** 2f. multicoloured . . . . 1·20 1·00

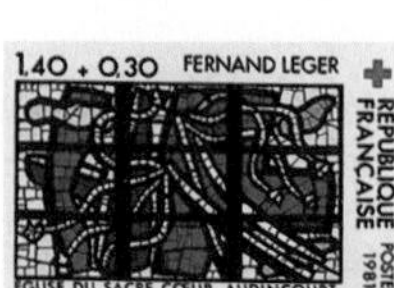

914 "Scourges of the Passion" **915** Memorial (Antoine Rohal)

1981. Red Cross Fund. Stained Glass Windows by Fernand Leger from the Church of the Sacred Heart, Audincort. Multicoloured.
2441 1f.40+30c. Type **914** . . . 85 95
2442 1f.60+30c. "Peace" 85 95

1981. Martyrs of Chateaubriant (Second World War victims).
2443 **915** 1f.40 black, purple & bl 55 45

916 "Liberty" (from "Liberty guiding the People" by Delacroix) **918** Guillaume Postel (scholar)

1982.
2444 **916** 5c. green 20 15
2445 10c. red 10 10
2446 15c. purple 35 40
2447 20c. green 10 10
2448 30c. orange 10 10
2449 40c. brown 20 20
2450 50c. mauve 25 10
2451 60c. brown 25 15
2452 70c. blue 30 25
2453 80c. green 35 20
2454 90c. mauve 35 30
2455 1f. green 40 15
2456 1f.40 green 65 25
2457 1f.60 red 55 20
2458 1f.60 green 65 10
2484 1f.70 green 95 65
2460 1f.80 red 65 20
2461 1f.80 green 75 35
2487 1f.90 green . . . . . . 1·10 65
2465 2f. green 00 30
2464 2f. red 65 10
2466 2f.10 red 65 10
2467 2f.20 red 65 10
2468 2f.30 blue . . . . 2·20 1·20
2469 2f.60 blue . . . . 2·00 1·20
2470 2f.80 blue . . . . 1·70 1·10
2471 3f. brown 95 35
2472 3f. blue . . . . 1·70 90
2473 3f.20 blue . . . . 1·90 85
2474 3f.40 blue . . . . 2·20 1·10
2475 3f.60 blue . . . . 1·30 85
2476 3f.70 purple . . . . . . 1·30 65
2477 4f. red . . . . 1·30 55
2478 5f. blue . . . . 1·70 45
2479 10f. violet . . . . 2·75 85

1982. Tourist Publicity. As T **490**.
2503 1f.60 blue, green and black 70 40
2504 2f. red and mauve 85 55
2505 2f.90 green, dp brn & brn 1·20 90
2506 3f. deep blue and blue . . . 1·10 70
2507 3f. red, yellow and blue . . 1·00 65
DESIGNS—VERT: No. 2503, Fishing boats and map of St. Pierre et Miquelon. HORIZ: No. 2504, Aix-en-Provence; 2505, Chateau de Ripaille, Haute-Savoie; 2506, Chateau Henri IV, Pau; 2507, Collonges-la-Rouge.

1982. Regions of France. As T **758**.
2508 1f.90 blue and red 75 45
DESIGN: 1f.90, Map of Corsica, containing sun and sea, superimposed on mountain.

1982. Pre-cancelled. Historic Monuments (4th series). As T **862**.
2509 97c. green 50 45
2510 1f.25 red 60 60
2511 2f.03 brown 95 95
2512 3f.36 blue . . . . 1·40 1·40
DESIGNS: 97c. Chateau de Tanlay; 1f.25, Salses Fort; 2f.03, Montlhery Tower; 3f.36, Chateau d'If.
See note below No. 432 (1920).

1982. Red Cross Fund. Celebrities.
2513 **918** 1f.40+30c. black and brown 85 95
2514 – 1f.40+30c. brown and grey 85 95
2515 – 1f.60+30c. lilac, violet and purple 95 95
2516 – 1f.60+40c. blue and brown 85 90
2517 – 1f.60+40c. blue 85 90
2518 – 1f.80+40c. brown . . . 1·20 1·30
DESIGNS: No. 2514, Henri Mondor (doctor and writer); 2515, Andre Chantemesse (doctor and bacteriologist); 2516, Louis Pergaud (writer); 2517, Robert Debre (professor of medicine); 2518, Gustave Eiffel (engineer).

919 St. Francis of Assisi

1982. 800th Birth Anniv of St. Francis of Assisi.
2519 **919** 2f. black and blue . . . 80 60

920 "The Post and Man"

1982. "Philexfrance 82" International Stamp Exhibition, Paris (3rd issue). Multicoloured.
2520 2f. Type **920** . . . . 3·75 3·25
2521 2f. Cogwheels ("The Post and Technology") . . . . 3·75 3·25

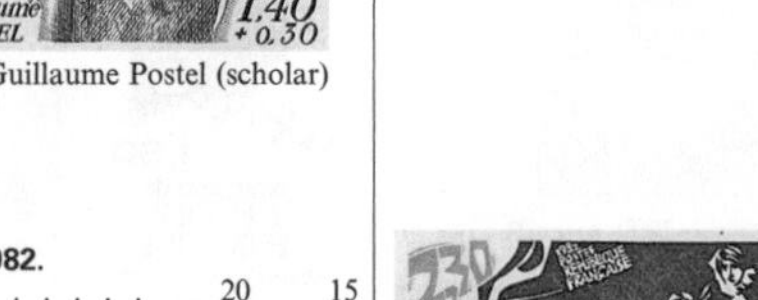

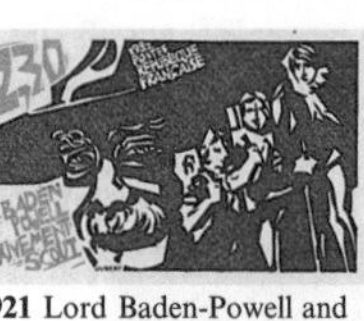

921 Lord Baden-Powell and Scouts **922** "Marianne" on Map of France

1982. 75th Anniv of Boy Scout Movement and 125th Birth Anniv of Lord Baden-Powell (founder).
2522 **921** 2f.30 black & green . . . 85 60

1982. Population Census.
2523 **922** 1f.60 multicoloured . . . 55 40

923 Basel-Mulhouse Airport

1982.
2524 **923** 1f.90 blue, brn & red . . 95 60

924 Clasped Wrists

1982. Anti-racism Campaign.
2525 **924** 2f.30 orange & brown 95 65

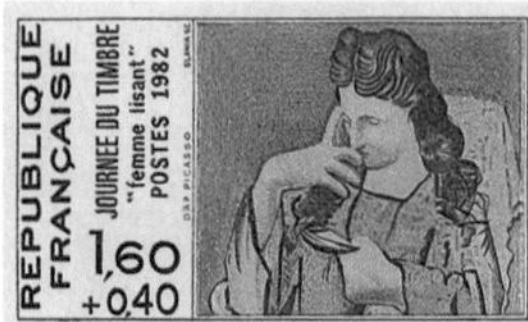

925 "Woman Reading" (Picasso)

1982. Stamp Day.
2526 **925** 1f.60+40c. mult 95 85

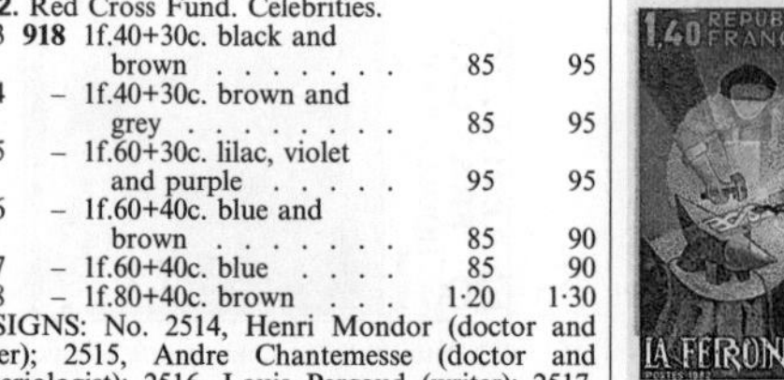

926 "Blacksmith" (Toffoli) **927** Map of Europe and Seal (Treaty of Rome)

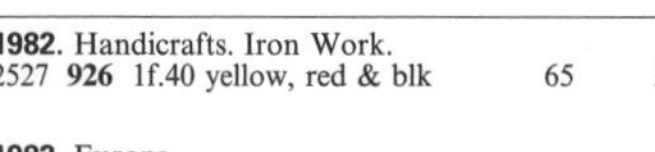

1982. Handicrafts. Iron Work.
2527 **926** 1f.40 yellow, red & blk 65 55

1982. Europa.
2528 **927** 1f.60 blue 75 45
2529 – 2f.30 brn, blk & grn . . 95 65
DESIGN: 2f.30, Seal of Charles the Bald (Treaty of Verdun, 843).

928 Goalkeeper and Stadium

1982. World Cup Football Championship, Spain.
2530 **928** 1f.80 green, red & bl . . 1·20 55

1982. Art. Designs as T **491**.
2531 4f. yellow, blue and brown 1·80 1·30
2532 4f. multicoloured . . . . . 1·80 1·20
2533 4f. multicoloured . . . . . 1·90 1·30
2534 4f. pink and grey . . . . . 1·80 1·30
DESIGNS—VERT: No. 2531, "Ephebus of Agde" (ancient Greek bronze sculpture); 2533, "The Lacemaker" (Vermeer); 2534, "The Family" (sculpture, Marc Boyan). HORIZ: 2532, "Embarkation of St. Paul at Ostia" (Claude Gellee (Le Lorrain)).

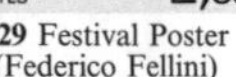

929 Festival Poster (Federico Fellini) **930** "Eole" Satellite, "Ariane" Rocket and Antenna

1982. 35th International Film Festival, Cannes.
2535 **929** 2f.30 multicoloured . . . 95 90

1982. 20th Anniv of National Space Studies Centre.
2536 **930** 2f.60 dp blue, bl & red 95 85

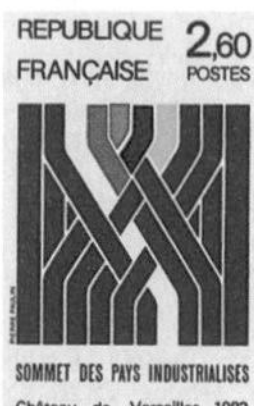

931 Interlocking Lines **932** Valles

1982. Industrialized Countries Summit, Versailles.
2537 **931** 2f.60 multicoloured . . . 1·00 90

1982. 150th Birth Anniv of Jules Valles (journalist).
2538 **932** 1f.60 dp green & green 70 40

933 "Marianne" **934** The Joliot-Curies

1982. "Philexfrance 82" International Stamp Exhibition, Paris (4th issue). Sheet 100 × 71 mm.
MS2539 **933** 4f. blue and red; 6f. red and blue . . . . 15·00 15·00

1982. Frederic and Irene Joliot-Curie (nuclear physicists) Commemoration.
2540 **934** 1f.80 pur, mve & vio . . 75 50

935 Grenoble Street Scene **936** Firemen

1982. Centenary of Electric Street Lighting.
2541 **935** 1f.80 purple, bl & vio . . 70 40

1982. Cent of National Federation of Fire Fighters.
2542 **936** 3f.30 brown and red . . 1·40 75

937 Marionnettes

1982.
2543 **937** 1f.80 red, blue & lilac . . 75 50

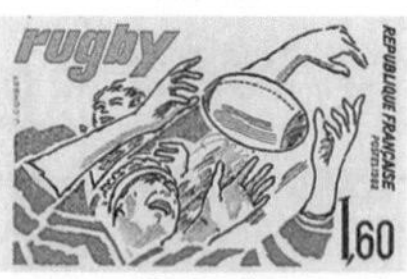

938 Rugby

1982.
2544 **938** 1f.60 blue, grn & red . . 1·60 55

939 Lecture Room **940** Lille

1982. Teacher Training Colleges.
2545 **939** 1f.80 grey & brown . . . 75 50

1982.
2546 **940** 1f.80 red and green . . . 75 40

1982. Philatelic Creations. As T **795**. Mult.
2547 4f. "The Turkish Room" (Balthus) . . . . 1·80 1·30

941 Dr. Robert Koch, Microscope and Bacillus **942** "Five Weeks in a Balloon"

1982. Cent of Discovery of Tubercle Bacillus.
2548 **941** 2f.60 black and red . . . 95 65

1982. Red Cross Fund. Works by Jules Verne.
2549 **942** 1f.60+30c. brown & red 85 85
2550 – 1f.80+40c. green & red 75 75
DESIGN: 1f.80, "20,000 Leagues Under the Sea".

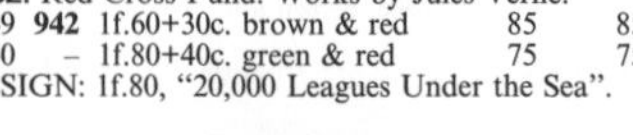

943 St. Theresa of Avila

1982. 400th Death Anniv of St. Theresa of Avila.
2551 **943** 2f.10 brn, blk & grn . . 80 50

944 Latecoere 300 Flying Boat "Croix du Sud"

1982. Air. 46th Anniv of Disappearance of "Croix du Sud".
2552 **944** 1f.60 lilac and blue . . . 85 90

945 Cavelier de la Salle and Map of Louisiana

946 Leon Blum

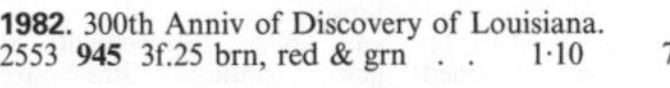

1982. 300th Anniv of Discovery of Louisiana.
2553 **945** 3f.25 brn, red & grn . . 1·10 75

1982. 110th Birth Anniv of Leon Blum (politician).
2554 **946** 1f.80 brown & lt brn . . 70 35

1983. Regions of France. As T **758**.
2555 1f. multicoloured 45 25
DESIGN—HORIZ: 1f. Map and coastline, Provence, Alpes, Cote d'Azur.

947 Andre Messager (composer)

948 Budding Plant (spring)

1983. Red Cross Fund. Celebrities.
2556 **947** 1f.60+30c. blk & bl . . . 1·00 1·00
2557 – 1f.60+30c. blk & yell . . 95 95
2558 – 1f.80+40c. blk & vio . . 1·10 1·10
2559 – 1f.80+40c. blk & red . . 1·10 1·10
2560 – 2f.+40c. blk & grn . . . 1·10 1·10
2561 – 2f.+40c. black & bl . . 1·10 1·10
DESIGNS: No. 2557, Jacques-Ange Gabriel (architect); 2558, Hector Berlioz (composer); 2559, Max-Pol Fouchet (writer); 2560, Rene Cassin (diplomat); 2561, Stendhal (writer).

1983. Pre-cancelled. The Four Seasons.
2562 **948** 1f.05 green 45 45
2563 – 1f.35 red 60 60
2564 – 2f.19 brown 90 90
2565 – 3f.63 violet . . . . . . 1·50 1·50
DESIGNS: 1f.35, Wheat (summer); 2f.19, Berries (autumn); 3f.63, Tree in snow (winter).
See note below No. 432 (1920).

949 Charleville Mezieres (½-size illustration)

1983. Tourist Publicity.
2566 – 1f.80 brown, grn & bl 65 40
2567 – 2f. brown and black . . 70 55
2568 – 3f. brown and blue . . . 1·10 80
2569 **949** 3f.10 brown and red . . 1·30 95
2570 – 3f.60 black, brn & bl . . 1·20 70
DESIGNS—As T **490**: 1f.80, Brantome, Perigord; 2f. Jarnac; 3f. Concarneau; 3f.60, Noirlac Abbey.
See also Nos. 2838 and 3642/5.

950 Martin Luther

951 Woman reading and Globe

1983. 500th Birth Anniv of Martin Luther (Protestant reformer).
2571 **950** 3f.30 brown & stone . . 1·20 75

1983. Centenary of French Alliance (language-teaching and cultural institute).
2572 **951** 1f.80 blue, red & brn . . 70 40

952 "Man dictating Letter" (Rembrandt)

1983. Stamp Day.
2573 **952** 1f.80+40c. stone and black . . . . 1·10 1·10

953 Danielle Casanova (resistance leader)

1983. International Women's Day.
2574 **953** 3f. brown and black . . 1·00 55

954 Figure within Globe releasing Dove

955 Montgolfier Brothers' Hot-air Balloon

1983. World Communications Year.
2575 **954** 2f.60 multicoloured . . . 1·00 85

1983. Bicentenary of Manned Flight. Mult.
2576 2f. Type **955** (first manned flight by Pilatre de Rozier and Marquis d'Arlandes, Nov 1783) . . . . 1·00 1·10
2577 3f. Hydrogen balloon over Tuileries, Paris (flight by J. Charles and M. N. Robert, Dec 1783) . . . . 1·30 1·40

1983. Philatelic Creations. As T **795**. Mult.
2578 4f. "Aurora-Set" (Dewasne) (horiz) . . . . 1·90 1·50
2579 4f. "Marianne" licking envelope (Jean Effel) (vert) . . . . 1·80 1·50

1983. Art. As T **491**.
2580 4f. brown and buff . . . . 1·90 1·50
2581 4f. black and red . . . . . 1·90 1·50
2582 4f. multicoloured . . . . . 1·70 1·20
DESIGNS—VERT: No. 2580, "Venus and Psyche" (preparatory sketch for fresco, Raphael); 2581, "Blue-beard giving Keys to his wife" from Perrault's "Tales" (engraving by Gustave Dore). HORIZ: 2582, "The agile Rabbit Inn" (Utrillo).

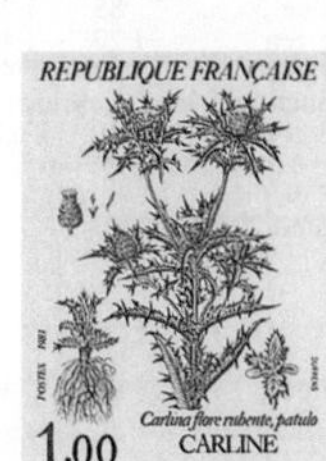

956 Thistle

957 Camera Diaphragm (photography)

1983. Flowers. Engravings from Paris Natural History Museum Library. Multicoloured.
2583 1f. Type **956** 40 30
2584 2f. Turk's cap lily (after Nicolas Robert) 75 45
2585 3f. Aster (after Nicolas Robert) . . . . 1·10 75
2586 4f. Aconite . . . . 1·60 85

1983. Europa. Each brown and deep brown.
2587 1f.80 Type **957** . . . . . . 1·80 65
2588 2f.60 Light rays entering eye and film (cinema) . . . . 2·10 1·10

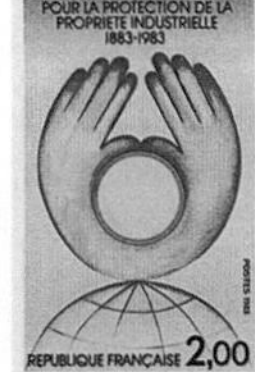

958 Hands on Globe

959 Marseille

1983. Centenary of Paris Convention for the Protection of Industrial Property.
2589 **958** 2f. multicoloured 65 40

1983. Federation of French Philatelic Societies Congress, Marseille.
2590 **959** 1f.80 red and blue . . . 70 50

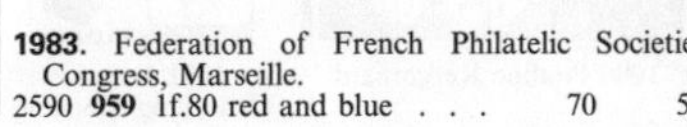

960 Air France Colours and Emblem

1983. 50th Anniv of Air France.
2591 **960** 3f.45 blue, red & black 1·40 1·10

961 "France defending U.S.A. from England" (medal by Augustin Dupre)

1983. Bicentenary of Treaties of Versailles and Paris.
2592 **961** 2f.80 brown & black . . 1·00 85

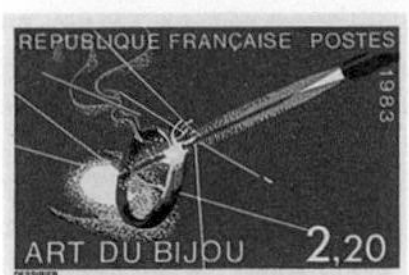

962 Forging a Ring

1983. Handicrafts. Jewellery.
2593 **962** 2f.20 multicoloured . . . 80 50

963 Customs Museum, Bordeaux

1983. 30th Anniv of Customs Co-operation Council.
2594 **963** 2f.30 blk, dp grn & grn 90 60

964 Pierre and Ernest Michaux's Bicycle

965 Globe and Weather-Satellite and Map

1983. The Bicycle.
2595 **964** 1f.60 black, blue & red 1·10 50

1983. National Meteorology.
2596 **965** 1f.50 dp blue, brn & bl 70 40

966 Renee Levy

967 Virgin and Child, Baillon

1983. Heroines of the Resistance.
2597 **966** 1f.60 brown & blue . . . 50 55
2598 – 1f.60 brown and green 65 45
DESIGN: No. 2598, Berthie Albrecht.

1983. Red Cross Fund. Wood Sculptures.
2599 **967** 1f.60+40c. brn & red . . 85 90
2600 – 2f.+40c. blue & red . . . 85 90
DESIGN: 2f. Virgin and Child, Genainville.

968 Pierre Mendes France

969 Emile Littre (lexicographer and writer)

1983. 1st Death Anniv of Pierre Mendes France (statesman).
2601 **968** 2f. black and red 65 40

1984. Red Cross Fund. Celebrities.
2602 **969** 1f.60+40c. purple and black 85 90
2603 – 1f.60+40c. green and black 85 90
2604 – 1f.70+40c. violet and black . . . . 1·00 1·10
2605 – 2f.+40c. grey and black 1·00 1·10
2606 – 2f.10+40c. brown and black . . . . 1·00 1·10
2607 – 2f.10+40c. blue and black . . . . 1·00 1·10
DESIGNS: No. 2603, Jean Zay (politician); 2604, Pierre Corneille (dramatist); 2605, Gaston Bachelard (philosopher and poet); 2606, Jean Paulhan (writer); 2607, Evariste Galois (mathematician).

1984. Art. As T **491**. Multicoloured.
2608 4f. "Cesar" film award (Cesar Baldaccini) (vert) 1·70 1·30
2609 4f. "The Four Corners of Heaven" (Jean Messagier) (horiz) . . . . 1·70 1·30
2610 4f. "Corner of Dining Room at Cannet" (Pierre Bonnard) (horiz) . . . . 1·70 1·40
2611 5f. "Pythia" (Andre Masson) (vert) . . . . . 2·10 1·40
2612 5f. "The Painter trampled by his Model" (Jean Helion) (vert) . . . . . . 2·10 1·40

1984. Regions of France. As T **758**.
2613 2f.30 violet, purple & red . . 90 50
DESIGN—HORIZ: 2f.30, Map and dancers, Guadeloupe.

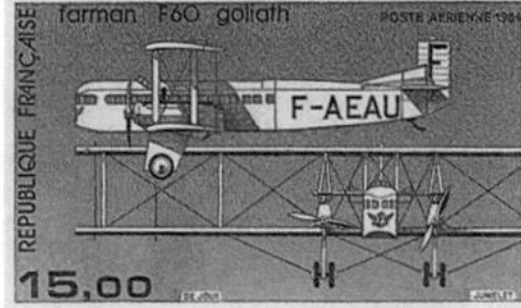

970 Farman F60 Goliath

1984. Air.
2614a **970** 15f. blue . . . . . . 2·75 90
2614ba – 20f. red . . . . 3·75 1·10
2614ca – 30f. violet . . . . . 8·25 3·75
2614d – 50f. green . . . . . 13·50 9·50
DESIGNS: 20f. CAMS 53 flying boat; 30f. Wibault 283 trimotor; 50f. Dewoitine D-338 trimotor.

971 Flora Tristan

1984. International Women's Day.
2615 **971** 2f.80 purple and black 1·00 65

972 "Diderot" (L. M. van Loo)

1984. Stamp Day.
2616 **972** 2f.+40c. blue & blk . . . 1·10 1·20

973 Pierre Waldeck-Rousseau (politician)

974 Emblem

1984. Centenary of Trade Union Legislation.
2617 **973** 3f.60 black and blue . . 1·10 70

1984. 2nd Direct Elections to European Parliament.
2618 **974** 2f. orange, yell & bl . . 70 40

975 Hearts **976** Jacques Cartier and "Grande Hermine"

1984. Precancels. Playing Cards.
2619 **975** 1f.14 violet and red . . . 55 55
2620 – 1f.47 blue and black . . 75 75
2621 – 2f.38 brown and red . . 1·30 1·30
2622 – 3f.95 green and black . . 1·90 1·90
DESIGNS: 1f.47, Spades; 2f.38, Diamonds; 3f.95, Clubs.
See note below No. 432 (1920).

1984. 450th Anniv of Jacques Cartier's Voyage to Canada.
2623 **976** 2f. multicoloured 70 35

977 Children and "Sower" Stamp

1984. "Philex-Jeunes 84" Stamp Exhibition, Dunkirk.
2624 **977** 1f.60 brn, red & vio . . 65 50

978 Bridge

1984. Europa. 25th Anniv of European Post and Telecommunications Conference.
2625 **978** 2f. red 95 50
2626 2f.80 blue . . . . 1·20 80

979 Legionnaires at Camerone, Mexico, 1863

1984. Foreign Legion.
2627 **979** 3f.10 red, grn & blk . . 1·10 75

980 Resistance Fighter

1984. 40th Anniv of Liberation.
2628 **980** 2f. red, brown and black 1·10 1·00
2629 – 3f. red, brown and black 1·30 1·40
DESIGN: 3f. Soldiers disembarking.

1984. Tourist Publicity. As T **490**.
2630 1f.70 blue and red 70 40
2631 2f.10 brown, green & red . . 80 40
2632 2f.50 brown, green & blue 70 60
2633 3f.50 purple and black . . . 1·50 80
2634 3f.70 purple, violet & red . . 1·20 80
DESIGNS—HORIZ: 1f.70, Monastery of Grande, Chartreuse; 2f.10, Cheval's Ideal Palace, Hauterives; 2f.50, Vauban's Citadel, Belle-Ile-en-Mer, Brittany; 3f.70, Chateau de Montsegur. VERT: 3f.50, Cordouan lighthouse, Gironde.

981 Olympic Sports (½-size illustration)

1984. Olympic Games, Los Angeles, and 90th Anniv of International Olympic Committee.
2635 **981** 4f. lilac, blue & green . . 1·50 1·20

982 Engraver **983** Bordeaux

1984. Handicrafts. Engraving.
2636 **982** 2f. brown, blk & grn . . 70 40

1984. Federation of French Philatelic Societies Congress, Bordeaux.
2637 **983** 2f. red 70 40

984 Anniversary Emblem

1984. 40th Anniv of National Centre for Telecommunications Studies.
2638 **984** 3f. blue and deep blue 1·00 55

985 Contour Map of Alps (½-size illustration)

1984. 25th International Geography Congress, Paris.
2639 **985** 3f. blue, black & orge . . 1·00 80

986 "Telecom 1"

1984. "Telecom 1" Communications Satellite.
2640 **986** 3f.20 multicoloured . . . 1·30 85

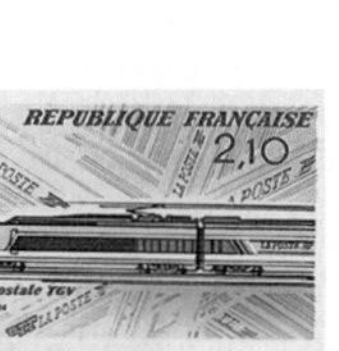

987 TGV Mail Train **988** Marx Dormoy

1984. Inauguration of TGV High-speed Paris–Lyon Mail Service.
2641 **987** 2f.10 multicoloured . . . 95 40

1984. Marx Dormoy (politician) Commemoration.
2642 **988** 2f.40 black and blue . . 85 40

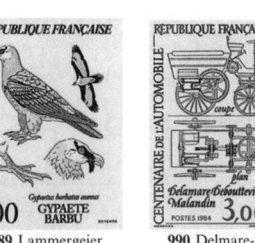

989 Lammergeier **990** Delmare-Debouteville Malandin Automobile

1984. Birds of Prey. Multicoloured.
2643 1f. Type **989** 35 35
2644 2f. Short-toed eagle 90 45
2645 3f. Northern sparrowhawk 1·20 95
2646 5f. Peregrine falcon . . . . 1·60 95

1984. Centenary of Motor Car.
2647 **990** 3f. brown, blue & red . . 1·30 65

991 Vincent Auriol **992** "The Pink Basket" (Caly)

1984. Birth Centenary of Vincent Auriol (President, 1947–54).
2648 **991** 2f.10 brown & green . . 75 45

1984. Red Cross Fund.
2649 **992** 2f.10+50c. mult . . . . 1·10 1·20

993 Emblem **994** Four Heads

1984. 9th Five-year Plan.
2650 **993** 2f.10 blue, red and black 80 40

1985. Promotion of French Language.
2651 **994** 3f. deep blue & blue . . 1·00 65

1985. Tourist Publicity. As T **490**.
2652 1f.70 green, olive & brown 85 40
2653 2f.10 brown and orange . . 1·00 50
2654 2f.20 multicoloured . . . . 1·00 45
2655 3f. brown, red and blue . . 1·30 70
2656 3f.90 brown, red and blue 1·70 75
DESIGNS—HORIZ: 1f.70, Vienne, Isere; 2f.10, Montpellier Cathedral; 3f. Talmont Church; 3f.90, Solutre. VERT: 2f.20, St. Michael of Cuxa Abbey.

995 Coloured Dots

1985. 50th Anniv of French Television.
2657 **995** 2f.50 multicoloured . . . 1·10 60

996 Snowflake (January) **997** Couple, Heart-shaped Letter-box and Cherubs

1985. Precancels. Months of the Year (1st series).
2658 **996** 1f.22 violet and lilac . . 75 75
2659 – 1f.57 grey and blue . . . 85 1·20
2660 – 2f.55 brown & green . . 1·20 1·40
2661 – 4f.23 green & orange . . 1·90 2·40
DESIGNS: 1f.57, Bare branch and bird (February); 2f.55, Rain-drops and sun-rays (March); 4f.23, Flowers (April).
See note below No. 432 (1920).
See also Nos. 2699/2702 and 2750/3.

1985. St. Valentine's Day.
2662 **997** 2f.10 multicoloured . . . 1·00 40

998 Jean-Paul Sartre

1985. Red Cross Fund. Writers.
2663 **998** 1f.70+40c. violet and purple . . . . 2·50 2·75
2664 – 1f.70+40c. purple and violet . . . . 2·50 2·75
2665 – 1f.70+40c. violet and deep violet . . . . . 2·50 2·75
2666 – 2f.10+50c. deep violet and violet . . . . . . 2·50 2·75
2667 – 2f.10+50c. violet and purple . . . . 2·50 2·75
2668 – 2f.10+50c. purple and violet . . . . 2·50 2·75
DESIGNS: No. 2664, Romain Rolland; 2665, Jules Romains; 2666, Francois Mauriac; 2667, Victor Hugo; 2668, Roland Dorgeles.

1000 Pauline Kergomard **1001** Daguin Cancelling Machine

1985. International Women's Day. 60th Death Anniv of Pauline Kergomard (reformer of infant schools).
2670 **1000** 1f.70 blue and brown 85 40

1985. Stamp Day.
2671 **1001** 2f.10+50c. brown, grey and black . . . . . 1·10 1·20

1985. Art. As T **491**.
2672 5f. multicoloured . . . . . 3·75 1·50
2673 5f. multicoloured . . . . . 3·25 1·50
2674 5f. multicoloured . . . . . 2·40 1·40
2675 5f. red, green and black . . 2·40 1·40
2676 5f. black and yellow . . . . 2·40 1·40
DESIGNS—VERT: No. 2672, "Judgement of Solomon" (stained glass window, Strasbourg Cathedral); 2675, Painting by Pierre Alechinsky. HORIZ: No. 2673, "Still Life with Candlestick" (Nicholas de Stael); 2674, Painting by Dubuffet; 2676, "The Dog" (sculpture by Alberto Giacometti).

1002 Landevennec Abbey

1985. 1500th Anniv of Landevennec Abbey.
2677 **1002** 1f.70 green & purple . . 85 40

1003 Modern Housing, Givors (Jean Renaudie)

1985. Contemporary Architecture.
2678 **1003** 2f.40 blk, grn & orge 1·10 60

1004 Adam de la Halle (composer) **1005** Soldier with Rifle

1985. Europa. Music Year.
2679 **1004** 2f.10 dp bl, bl & blk . . 1·10 50
2680 – 3f. black, bl & dp bl . . 1·70 85
DESIGN: 3f. Darius Milhaud (composer).

1985. 40th Anniv of V.E. (Victory in Europe) Day.
2681 **1005** 2f. black, red & blue . . 90 80
2682 – 3f. black, red & blue . . 1·20 1·00
DESIGN: 3f. Prisoners of war.

1006 Tours Cathedral **1007** Vaccinating Patient (after Le Riverend)

1985. Federation of French Philatelic Societies Congress, Tours.
2683 **1006** 2f.10 indigo and blue 90 50

1985. Centenary of Anti-rabies Vaccination.
2684 **1007** 1f.50 brn, grn & red . . 75 40

1008 Dassault Breguet Mystere Falcon 900

1985. 36th International Aeronautics and Space Exhibition, Le Bourget.
2685 **1008** 10f. blue . . . . 4·75 2·75

1009 Capsized Boat and Lifeboat   1010 U.N. Emblem

1985. Centenary of Lake Geneva International Life-Saving Society.
2686 **1009** 2f.50 black, red & bl . . 1·00 55

1985. 40th Anniv of U.N.O.
2687 **1010** 3f. blue, grey & dp bl 1·20 65

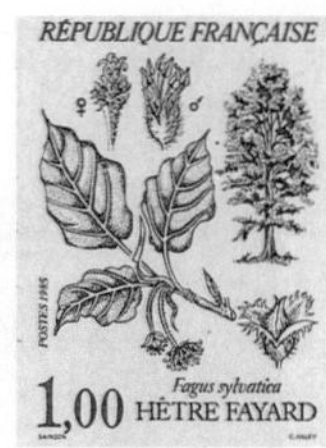

1011 Huguenot Cross   1012 Beech

1985. French Huguenots (300th Anniv of Revocation of Edict of Nantes).
2688 **1011** 2f.50 brown, red & bl 1·10 60

1985. Trees.
2689 **1012** 1f. black, green & blue 55 30
2690 – 2f. black, green & red 1·10 45
2691 – 3f. black, green & violet 1·40 90
2692 – 5f. black, green & brn 2·30 1·00
DESIGNS: 2f. Scotch elm; 3f. Pedunculate oak; 5f. Norwegian spruce.

1013 "Marianne"   1014 Dullin and Theatre

1985. National Memorial Day.
2693 **1013** 1f.80 pur, orge & blk 90 40

1985. Birth Centenary of Charles Dullin (actor).
2694 **1014** 3f.20 black & blue . . . 1·30 65

1015 World Map on Open Book and Keyboard   1016 "Concert of Angels" (M. Grunewald) (detail, Isenheim Altarpiece)

1985. 40th Anniv of French Information Service.
2695 **1015** 2f.20 black and red . . 90 40

1985. Red Cross Fund.
2696 **1016** 2f.20+50c. mult . . . . 1·10 1·10

1017 Siamese Envoys before King Louis XIV   1019 Masked Revellers

1018 "Leisure Activities" (Fernand Leger)

1986. 300th Anniv of Diplomatic Relations with Thailand.
2697 **1017** 3f.20 purple & black . . 1·30 95

1986. 50th Anniv of Popular Front.
2698 **1018** 2f.20 multicoloured . . 1·00 40

1986. Precancels. Months of the Year (2nd series). As T **996**.
2699 1f.28 pink and green 90 95
2700 1f.65 green & turquoise . . 1·10 1·10
2701 2f.67 blue and red . . . . . 1·40 1·50
2702 4f.44 orange and brown . . 2·30 2·50
DESIGNS: 1f.28, Butterflies (May); 1f.65, Flowers (June); 2f.67, Phrygian cap (July); 4f.44, Sun (August). See note below No. 432 (1920).

1986. Venetian Carnival in Paris.
2703 **1019** 2f.20 multicoloured . . 1·00 40

1020 Francois Arago (physicist and politician)   1021 Woman's Head

1986. Red Cross Fund. Celebrities.
2704 **1020** 1f.80+40c. black, blue & turquoise 85 95
2705 – 1f.80+40c. black, blue & turquoise 85 95
2706 – 1f.80+40c. black, blue & turquoise 85 95
2707 – 2f.20+50c. black, turquoise & blue . . 95 1·10
2708 – 2f.20+50c. black, turquoise & blue . . 1·10 1·20
2709 – 2f.20+50c. brown . . . 2·40 2·30
DESIGNS: No. 2705, Henri Moissan (chemist); 2706, Henri Fabre (engineer); 2707, Marc Seguin (locomotive engineer); 2708, Paul Heroult (chemist); 2709, Pierre Cot (politician).

1986. Tourist Publicity. As T **490** and **949**.
2710 1f.80 multicoloured 85 40
2711 2f. blue and black 90 60
2712 2f.20 brown, blue & green 1·00 50
2713 2f.50 dp brown & brown . . 1·20 50
2714 3f.90 orange and black . . . 2·10 1·20
DESIGNS: As T **490**—HORIZ: 1f.80, Filitosa, Corsica; 2f. Chateau de Loches; 2f.20, Manor of St. Germain de Livet, Calvados. VERT: 2f.50, Cloisters, Notre Dame en Vaux, Marne. As T **949**: 3f.90, Monpazier, Dordogne.

1986. Typography.
2715 **1021** 5f. black and red . . . 2·50 1·40

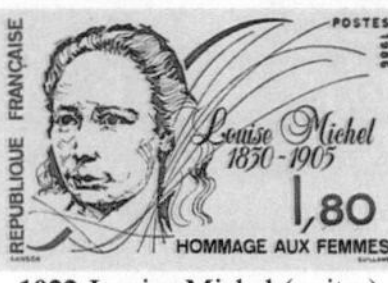

1022 Louise Michel (writer)

1986. International Women's Day.
2716 **1022** 1f.80 black and red . . 85 40

1023 La Villette

1986. Science and Industry City, La Villette.
2717 **1023** 3f.90 multicoloured . . 1·70 85

1024 Britska Mail Coach

1986. Stamp Day.
2718 **1024** 2f.20+60c. pink and brown . . . . 1·30 1·20
2719 2f.20+60c. yellow and black . . . . 1·40 1·50

1025 Map and Latitude Lines

1986. 50th Anniv of African and Asian Studies Centre.
2720 **1025** 3f.20 multicoloured . . 1·40 80

1986. Art. As T **491**.
2721 5f. multicoloured . . . . . 2·40 1·50
2722 5f. multicoloured . . . . . 2·40 1·60
2723 5f. multicoloured . . . . . 2·50 1·30
2724 5f. multicoloured . . . . . 2·50 1·40
2725 5f. grey, black & violet . . . 2·50 1·40
DESIGNS—HORIZ: No. 2721, "Skibet" (Maurice Esteve); 2722, "Virginia" (Alberto Magnelli); 2725, Abstract by Pierre Soulages. VERT: 2723, "The Dancer" (Hans Arp); 2724, "Isabelle d'Este" (Leonardo da Vinci).

1026 Genet   1027 Victor Basch

1986. Europa.
2726 **1026** 2f.20 black and red . . 1·20 45
2727 – 3f.20 black and red . . 1·70 75
DESIGN: 3f.20, Lesser horseshoe bat.

1986. International Peace Year.
2728 **1027** 2f.50 black & green . . 1·10 55

1028 Vianney   1029 City Gate

1986. Birth Bicentenary of Saint J. M. B. Vianney, Cure d'Ars.
2729 **1028** 1f.80 brown, deep brown and orange . . 85 40

1986. Federation of French Philatelic Societies Congress, Nancy.
2730 **1029** 2f. blue and green . . . 90 40

1030 Players   1031 Head of Statue

1986. Men's World Volleyball Championships.
2731 **1030** 2f.20 purple, vio & red 90 50

1986. Centenary of Statue of Liberty.
2732 **1031** 2f.20 blue and red . . . 1·00 50

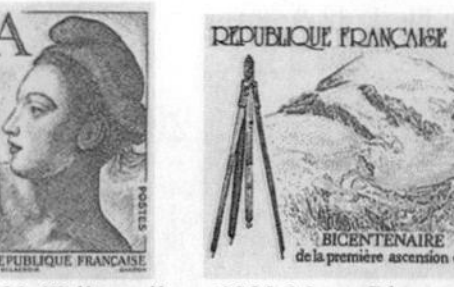

1032 "Liberty" (after Delacroix)   1033 Mont Blanc, J. Balmat and M. G. Paccard

1986. No value expressed.
2733 **1032** (1f.90) green 85 40
See also Nos. 2784 and 2949/50.

1986. Bicentenary of First Ascent of Mont Blanc.
2734 **1033** 2f. blue, dp bl & brn 90 60

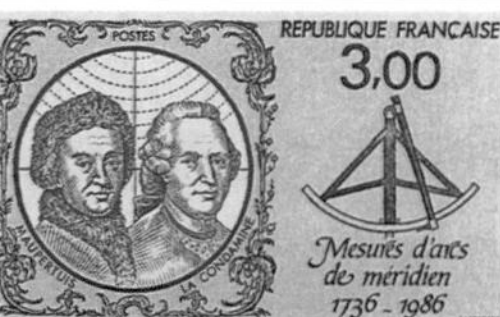

1034 Maupertuis and La Condamine

1986. 250th Anniv of Measurement of Arcs of Meridian.
2735 **1034** 3f. black, lt bl & bl . . 1·30 70

1035 Marcasite   1037 Woman's Head, Printed Circuit and Drawing Instruments

1036 Musidora in "The Vampires" (dir. Louis Feuillade)

1986. Minerals.
2736 **1035** 2f. multicoloured . . . 95 45
2737 – 3f. multicoloured . . . 1·20 60
2738 – 4f. blue, brown & mve 1·80 1·20
2739 – 5f. turq, mve & bl . . . 2·20 1·20
DESIGNS: 3f. Quartz; 4f. Calcite; 5f. Fluorite.

1986. 50th Anniv of French Film Institute. Sheet 143 × 179 mm containing T **1036** and similar horiz designs, each black, deep grey and deep grey-brown.
MS2740 2f.20 Type **1036**; 2f.20 Max Linder; 2f.20 Sacha Guitry in "Story of a Cheat" (dir. Guitry); 2f.20 Pierre Fresnay and Eric von Stroheim in "The Great Illusion" (dir. Jean Renoir); 2f.20 Raimu and Ginette Leclerc in "The Baker's Wife" (dir. Marcel Pagnol); 2f.20 Rene Ferte in "The Triple Mirror" (dir. Jean Epstein); 2f.20 Gerard Philipe and Martine Carol in "Beauties in the Night" (dir. Rene Clair); 2f.20 Jean Gabin and Mireille Balin in "Face of Love" (dir. Jean Gremillon); 2f.20 Simone Signoret in "Casque d'Or" (Golden Marie) (dir. Jacques Becker); 2f.20 Francois Truffaut and Jean-Pierre Cargol in "The Wild Child" (dir. Truffaut) . . 9·50 9·50

1986. Centenary of Technical Education.
2741 **1037** 1f.90 blue & mauve . . 85 40

1038 Scene from "Le Grand Meaulnes"   1039 Emblem

1986. Birth Centenary of Henri Alain-Fournier (writer).
2742 **1038** 2f.20 brown & red . . 90 45

1986. World Energy Conference, Cannes.
2743 **1039** 3f.40 blue, mve & red 1·40 85

1041 Detail of Window by Vieira da Silva, St. John's Church, Rheims   1042 Car, Steam Locomotive and Carpet

1986. Red Cross Fund.
2745 **1041** 2f.20+60c. mult 1·20 1·30

1986. Mulhouse Technical Museums.
2746 **1042** 2f.20 red, black & blue 1·70 50

1043 Museum Facade

1986. Quai d'Orsay Museum.
2747 **1043** 3f.70 dp blue & blue 1·50 85

1044 Underground Train in Tunnel

1045 Raoul Follereau

1987. 50th Death Anniv (1986) of Fulgence Bienvenue (designer of Paris Metro).
2748 **1044** 2f.50 pur, grn & brn 1·20 60

1987. 10th Death Anniv of Raoul Follereau (leprosy pioneer).
2749 **1045** 1f.90 dp grn & grn 85 40

1987. Precancels. Months of the Year (3rd series). As T **996**.
2750 1f.31 brown and orange 95 1·00
2751 1f.69 orange and purple 1·20 1·40
2752 2f.74 grey and blue 1·40 1·50
2753 4f.56 green and mauve 2·40 2·75
DESIGNS: 1f.31, Grapes (September); 1f.69, Posthorn (October); 2f.74, Falling leaves (November); 4f.56, Christmas tree (December).
See note below No. 432 (1920).

1046 Charles Richet (physiologist)

1047 Grinding Blades

1987. Red Cross Fund. Medical Celebrities.
2754 **1046** 1f.90+50c. blue 1·00 1·10
2755 – 1f.90+50c. lilac 1·00 1·10
2756 – 1f.90+50c. grey 1·00 1·10
2757 – 2f.20+50c. grey 1·10 1·30
2758 – 2f.20+50c. blue 1·10 1·30
2759 – 2f.20+50c. lilac 1·10 1·30
DESIGNS: No. 2755, Eugene Jamot (sleeping sickness pioneer); 2756, Bernard Halpern (immunologist); 2757, Alexandre Yersin (bacteriologist, discoverer of plague bacillus); 2758, Jean Rostand (geneticist); 2759, Jacques Monod (molecular biologist).

1987. Handicrafts. Thiers Cutlery.
2760 **1047** 1f.90 black and red 80 40

1048 "Liberty" and "Philexfrance 89"

1987. "Philexfrance 89" International Stamp Exhibition, Paris (1st issue).
2761 **1048** 2f.20 red 1·00 45
The stamp and label which together comprise No. 2761 were printed together se-tenant. For stamp without label, see No. 2466.
See also No. 2821.

1987. Tourist Publicity. As T **490** and **949**.
2762 2f.20 green, grey & mauve 1·10 45
2763 2f.20 multicoloured 1·10 55
2764 2f.50 green and blue 1·20 70
2765 2f.50 black, red and blue 1·10 65
2766 3f. brown and violet 1·30 85
2767 3f.70 blue, lilac & brown 3·00 1·80
DESIGNS—As T **490**: No. 2762, Redon Abbey; 2763, Etretat (after Eugene Delacroix); 2764, Azay-le-Rideau Chateau; 2765, Montbenoit le Saugeais; 2766, Les Baux-de-Provence. As T **949**: No. 2767, Cotes de Meuse.

1049 Berlin

1987. Stamp Day.
2768 **1049** 2f.20+60c. brown and yellow 1·20 1·20
2769 2f.20+60c. deep blue and blue 1·30 1·40

1050 "Divine Proportion"

1987. Birth Centenary of Charles-Edouard Jeanneret "Le Corbusier" (architect).
2770 **1050** 3f.70 multicoloured 1·60 85

1051 "57 Metal", Boulogne-Billancourt (Claude Vasconi)

1052 Gaspard of the Mountains

1987. Europa. Architecture.
2771 **1051** 2f.20 blue and green 1·70 55
2772 – 3f.40 brown & green 2·50 80
DESIGN: 3f.40, Rue Mallet-Stevens, Paris (Robert Mallet-Stevens).

1987. Art. As T **491**.
2773 5f. multicoloured 2·40 1·50
2774 5f. multicoloured 2·40 1·50
2775 5f. multicoloured 2·40 1·50
2776 5f. brn, lt brn & blk 2·40 1·50
DESIGNS—HORIZ: No. 2773, "Abstract" (Bram van Velde); 2774, "Woman with Parasol" (Eugene Boudin); 2776, "World" (sculpture, Antoine Pevsner). VERT: No. 2775, "Pre-Cambrian" (Camille Bryen).

1987. Birth Centenary of Henri Pourrat (writer).
2777 **1052** 1f.90 brown and green 85 40

1053 Lens

1987. Federation of French Philatelic Societies Congress, Lens.
2778 **1053** 2f.20 red & brown 1·10 65

1054 Gen. Pershing, Soldiers and U.S. Flag

1055 Cable Cars

1987. 70th Anniv of Entry of U.S. Troops into First World War.
2779 **1054** 3f.40 red, blue & green 1·40 90

1987. 6th International Cable Transport Congress, Grenoble.
2780 **1055** 2f. black, bl & grn 85 65

1056 Noyon Cathedral and Symbol

1057 Prytanee

1987. Millenary of Election of Hugues Capet as King of France.
2781 **1056** 1f.90 black and blue 80 50

1987. Prytanee National Military School (for French Soldiers' Children), La Fleche.
2782 **1057** 2f.20 black, grn & red 90 50

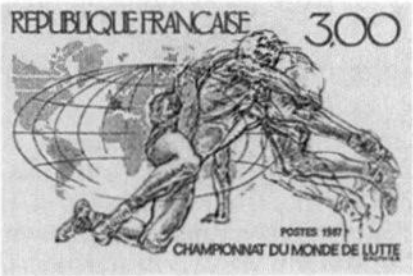

1058 Black Footprints on Map of France

1059 Globe and Wrestlers

1987. "25 Years After" World Assembly of Repatriated French-Algerians, Nice.
2783 **1058** 1f.90 multicoloured 85 60

1987. No value expressed. As T **1032** but inscr "B".
2784 (2f.) green 85 55

1987. World Wrestling Championship, Clermont-Ferrand.
2785 **1059** 3f. brown, grey & vio 1·30 85

1060 "Gyroporus cyanescens"

1061 Bayeux Tapestry (detail)

1987. Fungi.
2786 **1060** 2f. multicoloured 1·10 55
2787 – 3f. multicoloured 1·40 80
2788 – 4f. black, bistre & brn 1·90 1·40
2789 – 5f. multicoloured 2·40 1·20
DESIGNS: 3f. "Gomphus clavatus"; 4f. "Morchella conica"; 5f. "Russula virescens".

1987. 900th Death Anniv of William the Conqueror.
2790 **1061** 2f. multicoloured 85 50

1062 Institute

1063 Cendrars (after Modigliani)

1987. Centenary of Pasteur Institute.
2791 **1062** 2f.20 red and blue 1·00 45

1987. Birth Centenary of Blaise Cendrars (writer).
2792 **1063** 2f. buff, black and green 85 50

1064 "Flight into Egypt" (Melchior Broederlam) (detail, Champmol Charterhouse retable)

1987. Red Cross Fund.
2793 **1064** 2f.20+60c. mult 1·00 1·20

1065 Leclerc, Oasis, Tank, Pantheon and Strasbourg Cathedral

1066 Treaty Document, Brunehaut, Childebert II and King Guntram of Burgundy

1987. 40th Death Anniv of Marshal Leclerc.
2794 **1065** 2f.20 blk, brn & dp brn 1·10 45

1987. 1400th Anniv of Treaty of Andelot.
2795 **1066** 3f.70 blk, dp bl & bl 1·60 80

1067 Dr. Konrad Adenauer (West German Chancellor) and Charles de Gaulle (French President)

1988. 25th Anniv of Franco–German Co-operation Treaty.
2796 **1067** 2f.20 purple & black 1·20 50

1068 Dassault and Aircraft

1988. 2nd Death Anniv of Marcel Dassault (aircraft engineer).
2797 **1068** 3f.60 brown, red & bl 2·10 1·10

1069 People on Airplane flying around Globe (Rene Pellos)

1070 Bird flying (Air)

1988. Communications. Designs by comic strip artists. Multicoloured.
2798 2f.20 Type **1069** 90 1·00
2799 2f.20 Monkey writing in light from table lamp (Jean-Marc Reiser) 90 1·00
2800 2f.20 Sitting Bull and smoke signals (Marijac (Jacques Dumas)) 90 1·00
2801 2f.20 Couple with love letter (Fred (Othon Aristides)) 90 95
2802 2f.20 Man watching levitating letter (Moebius (Jean Giraud)) 90 1·00
2803 2f.20 Globe and astronaut (Paul Gillon) 90 1·00
2804 2f.20 Man playing letter and pen "guitar" (Claire Bretecher) 90 1·00
2805 2f.20 Hand posting letter in talking letter-box (Jean-Claude Forest) 90 1·00
2806 2f.20 Rocket behind astronaut reading letter (Jean-Claude Mezieres) 90 1·00
2807 2f.20 Woman with mystery letter (Jacques Tardi) 90 1·00
2808 2f.20 Baby reading letter in pram with attached letter-box (Jacques Lob) 90 1·00
2809 2f.20 Woman pilot with letters (Enki Bilal) 90 1·00

1988. Precancels. The Elements.
2810 **1070** 1f.36 blue and black 1·00 95
2811 – 1f.75 blue and black 1·20 1·20
2812 – 2f.83 red and black 1·50 1·60
2813 – 4f.75 green & black 2·75 3·00
DESIGNS: 1f.70, Splash of water (Water); 2f.83, Flames (Fire); 4f.75, Tree (Earth).
See note below No. 432 (1920).

1071 Dove and Interior **1072** Abraham Duquesne and Map

1988. Rue Victoire Synagogue, Paris.
2814 **1071** 2f. black and gold . . . 85 60

1988. Red Cross Fund. Explorers. Each blue, brown and black.
2815 2f.+50c. Type **1072** . . . . 95 1·00
2816 2f.+50c. Pierre Andre de Suffren Saint Tropez . . 95 1·00
2817 2f.+50c. Jean Francois de Galaup, Comte de La Perouse . . . . 95 1·00
2818 2f.+50c. Bertrand Francois Mahe de La Bourdonnais 95 1·10
2819 2f.20+50c. Louis Antoine de Bougainville . . . . . . 95 1·10
2820 2f.20+50c. Jules Dumont d'Urville . . . . 95 1·10

1073 "Liberty" and Emblem

1988. "Philexfrance 89" International Stamp Exhibition, Paris (2nd issue).
2821 **1073** 2f.20 red, black & bl . . 90 45

1074 Mail Coach

1988. Stamp Day.
2822 **1074** 2f.20+60c. purple and mauve . . . . 1·20 1·30
2823 2f.20+60c. brown and flesh . . . . 1·20 1·30

1075 Emblem

1988. Centenary of Post Office National College.
2824 **1075** 3f.60 bl, grn & red . . 1·40 85

1076 "Stamps"

1988. "Philex-Jeunes 88" Stamp Exhibition, Nevers.
2825 **1076** 2f. blue, violet & mve 85 40

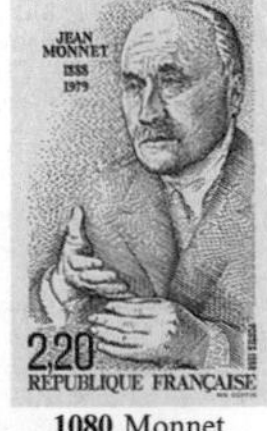

1077 Blood Drop **1080** Monnet

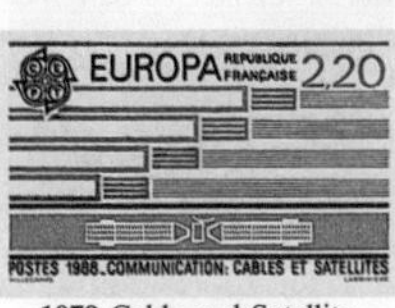

1079 Cable and Satellite Communications

1988. Blood Donation Service.
2826 **1077** 2f.50 red, blk & yell . . 1·10 60

1988. No. 2467 surch **ECU 0,31..**
2827 **916** 0.31ECU on 2f.20 red 1·10 50
ECU stands for European Currency Unit.

1988. Europa. Transport and Communications.
2828 **1079** 2f.20 grey, black & bl 1·90 50
2829 – 3f.60 pur, blk & lt pur 2·50 85
DESIGN: 3f.60, Two-car electric train.

1988. Birth Centenary of Jean Monnet (statesman).
2830 **1080** 2f.20 blue and brown 1·10 45

1081 Town Hall and Roman Carved Stone Heads

1988. Federation of French Philatelic Societies Congress, Valence.
2831 **1081** 2f.20 orge, dp bl & bl 90 55

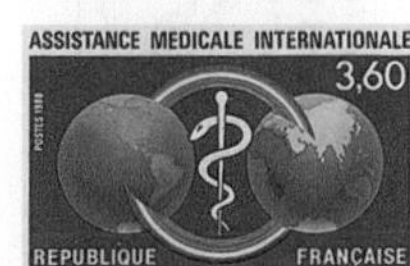

1082 Rod of Aesculapius, Globes and Rainbows

1988. International Medical Assistance.
2832 **1082** 3f.60 multicoloured . . 1·40 90

1083 Typical Access Routes

1988. Easy Access for the Handicapped.
2833 **1083** 3f.70 multicoloured . . 1·50 90

1988. Tourist Publicity.
2834 2f. multicoloured 90 40
2835 2f.20 brown, bl & turq . . . 90 50
2836 2f.20 blue, turq & grn . . . 95 45
2837 3f. violet, green and brown 1·30 65
2838 3f.70 black, blue and red . . 1·80 1·10
DESIGNS—As T **490**. HORIZ: No. 2834, Ship Museum, Douarnenez; 2836, Perouges; 2837, Cirque de Gavarnie (rock formation). VERT: No. 2835, Sedieres Chateau, Correze. As T **949**: No. 2838, "Double-headed Hermes of Frejus" (Roman sculpture).

1084 Otters **1086** Soldiers of 1888 and 1988

1085 "Assembly of the Three Estates, Vizille" (Alexandre Debelle)

1988. Animals. Illustrations from "Natural History" by Comte de Buffon.
2839 **1084** 2f. black and green . . 90 45
2840 – 3f. black and red . . . 1·30 70
2841 – 4f. black and mauve . . 1·70 1·20
2842 – 5f. black and blue . . . 2·20 1·00
DESIGNS: 3f. Stag; 4f. Fox; 5f. Badger.

1988. Bicentenary of French Revolution (1st issue). Each black, blue and red.
2843 3f. Type **1085** . . . . . . 1·30 1·40
2844 4f. "Day of the Tiles, Grenoble" (Alexandre Debelle) . . . . 1·50 1·50

See also Nos. 2857, 2863/8, 2871/3, **MS**2889, **MS**2890, **MS**3005 and **MS**3083.

1988. Centenary of Alpine Troops.
2845 **1086** 2f.50 dp bl, bl & red . . 1·20 85

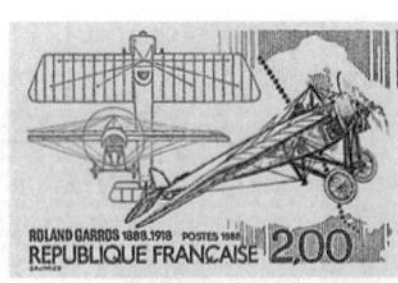

1087 Bleriot XI

1988. Birth Centenary of Roland Garros (aviator).
2846 **1087** 2f. green, olive and blue 1·00 40

1088 Soldiers

1988. 70th Anniv of Armistice.
2847 **1088** 2f.20 multicoloured . . 95 45

1089 "Tribute to Leon Degand" (Robert Jacobsen)

1988. French–Danish Cultural Year.
2848 **1089** 5f. red & black on grey 2·40 1·40

1090 City Arms **1091** Activities at Spas

1988. 2000th Anniv of Strasbourg.
2849 **1090** 2f.20 multicoloured . . 95 45

1988. Art. As T **491**.
2850 5f. brown . . . . 2·40 1·50
2851 5f. multicoloured . . . . . 2·40 1·50
2852 5f. multicoloured . . . . . 3·50 1·60
2853 5f. multicoloured . . . . . 2·50 1·60
DESIGNS—48 × 38 mm: No. 2850, St. Mihiel's Sepulchre (Ligier Richier); 2851, "Composition" (Serge Poliakoff); 2852, "Meta" (Tinguely). 48 × 43 mm: No. 2853, "Pieta de Villeneuve-les-Avignon" (Enguerrand Quarton).

1988. Thermal Spas.
2854 **1091** 2f.20 red, blue & grn 95 45

1092 Cross

1988. Red Cross Fund.
2855 **1092** 2f.20+60c. red, blue and black . . . . 1·10 1·10

1093 Earth

1988. 40th Anniv of Universal Declaration of Human Rights.
2856 **1093** 2f.20 dp blue & blue . . 1·40 50

1094 Birds

1989. Bicentenary of French Revolution (2nd issue).
2857 **1094** 2f.20 blue, red & blk 95 50

1989. Art. As T **491**. Multicoloured.
2858 5f. "Anthropometry of the Blue Era" (Yves Klein) 2·30 1·50
2859 5f. "Oath of the Tennis Court" (sketch, David) . . 2·20 1·40
2860 5f. "Regetta with Wind Astern" (Lapicque) (vert) 2·40 1·60

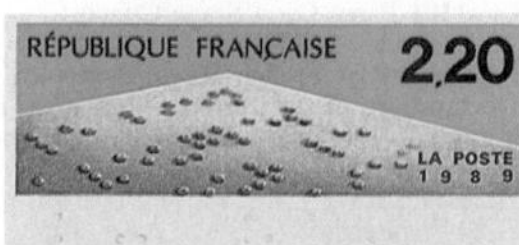

1095 Page of Braille

1989. The Blind.
2861 **1095** 2f.20 bl, orge & mve . . 95 75

1096 "E"

1989. Centenary of Estienne School.
2862 **1096** 2f.20 blk, grey & red 95 50

1097 Comte de Sieyes

1989. Red Cross Fund. Bicentenary of French Revolution (3rd issue). Personalities. Mult.
2863 2f.20+50c. Type **1097** . . . 1·00 1·20
2864 2f.20+50c. Comte de Mirabeau . . . . 1·00 1·20
2865 2f.20+50c. Vicomte de Noailles . . . . 1·00 1·20
2866 2f.20+50c. Marquis de Lafayette . . . . 1·00 1·20
2867 2f.20+50c. Antoine Barnave 1·00 1·20
2868 2f.20+50c. Jean Baptiste Drouet . . . . 1·00 1·20

1098 Emblem on Spectrum

1989. Direct Elections to European Parliament.
2869 **1098** 2f.20 multicoloured . . 95 45

1099 Flags, Astronauts and Satellite

1989. French–Soviet Space Flight.
2870 **1099** 3f.60 multicoloured . . 1·90 95

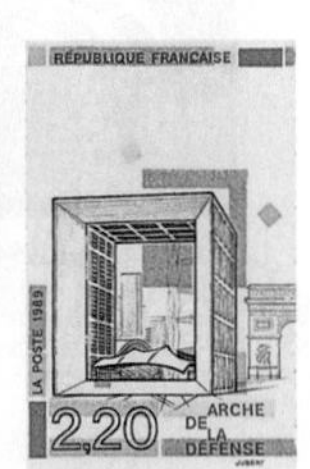

1100 "Liberty" **1102** Arche de la Defense

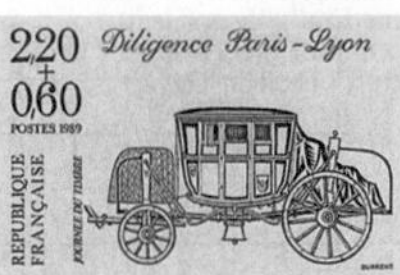

1101 Paris–Lyon Stage Coach

1989. Bicentenary of French Revolution (4th issue) and Declaration of Rights of Man (1st issue). Paintings by Roger Druet. Multicoloured.

2871 2f.20 Type **1100** 95 45
2872 2f.20 "Equality" 95 45
2873 2f.20 "Fraternity" 95 45

1989. Stamp Day.

2874 **1101** 2f.20+60c. deep blue and blue . . . . . . 1·30 1·30
2875 2f.20+60c. lilac and mauve . . . . 1·30 1·30

1989. Paris Panorama. Multicoloured.

2876 2f.20 Type **1102** . . . . . 1·10 1·10
2877 2f.20 Eiffel Tower . . . . . 1·10 1·10
2878 2f.20 Pyramid, Louvre . . . . 1·10 1·10
2879 2f.20 Notre Dame Cathedral 1·10 1·10
2880 2f.20 Bastille Opera House 1·10 1·10

1103 Hopscotch

1989. Europa. Children's Games. Mult.

2881 2f.20 Type **1103** 95 50
2882 3f.60 Ball game . . . . . . 1·70 95

1989. Tourist Publicity. As T **490** and **949**.

2883 2f.20 green, brown & orge 95 45
2884 3f.70 red, blue and black . . 1·50 90
2885 3f.70 black and brown . . . 1·50 1·00
2886 4f. blue . . . . 1·80 1·10

DESIGNS—As T **490**. HORIZ: No. 2883, Fontainebleau forest. VERT: No. 2884, Malestroit. As T **949**: No. 2885, Chateau of Vaux-le-Vicomte; 2886, La Brenne.

1104 Emblems and Buildings

1989. International Telecommunications Union Plenipotentiaries Conference, Nice.

2887 **1104** 3f.70 red, blue & orge 1·40 85

1105 Cyclists

1989. International Cycling Championships, Chambery.

2888 **1105** 2f.20 multicoloured . . 1·10 45

1106 Madame Roland

1989. Bicentenary of French Revolution (5th issue). Personalities. Sheet 78 × 105 mm containing T **1106** and similar vert designs. Multicoloured.

MS2889 2f.20 Type **1106**; 2f.20 Camille Desmoulins; 2f.20 Marquis de Condorcet; 2f.20 Major-Gen. Francois Kellerman 3·50 3·50

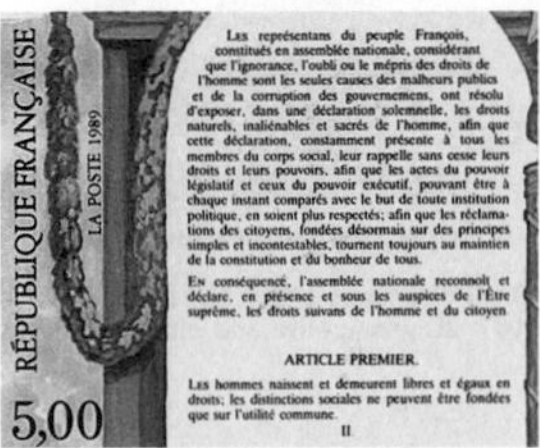

1107 "LES repesentans du people Francois,..."

1989. Bicentenary of French Revolution (6th issue) and Declaration of Rights of Man (2nd issue). Sheet 130 × 143 mm containing T **1107** and similar horiz designs. Multicoloured.

MS2890 5f. Type **1107**; 5f. "NUL home ne peut etre accuse..."; 5f. "LE but de toute association politique..."; 5f. "LA garantie des droits de l'homme..." (sold at 50f.) 15·00 15·00

1108 Arche de la Defense

1989. Summit Conference of Industrialised Countries, Paris.

2891 **1108** 2f.20 multicoloured . . 95 55

1109 Preamble

1989. Bicentenary of Declaration of Rights of Man (3rd issue). Multicoloured.

2892 2f.50 Type **1109** . . . . . 1·10 1·30
2893 2f.50 Articles II to VI . . . 1·30 1·30
2894 2f.50 Articles VII to XI . . 1·30 1·30
2895 2f.50 Articles XII to XVII 1·30 1·30

1110 Harp **1111** Train

1989. Precancels. Musical Instruments (1st series).

2896 **1110** 1f.39 lt blue & blue . . 90 95
2897 – 1f.79 brn & lt brn . . 1·00 1·00
2898 – 2f.90 orange & brn . . 2·10 2·40
2899 – 4f.84 orange & brn . . 2·75 2·75

DESIGNS: 1f.79, Piano; 2f.90, Trumpet; 4f.84, Violin.

See note below No. 432 (1920).

See also Nos. 2993/9, 3052/62, 3095/8 and 3145/8.

1989. TGV "Atlantique" Express Train.

2900 **1111** 2f.50 blue, silver & red 2·00 50

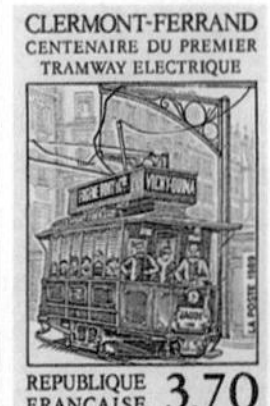

1112 Tram **1113** King Francois I

1989. Cent of Clermont-Ferrand Electric Tramway.

2901 **1112** 3f.70 black & brown . . 1·70 90

1989. 450th Anniv of Villers-Cotterets Ordinance.

2902 **1113** 2f.20 red and black . . 95 50

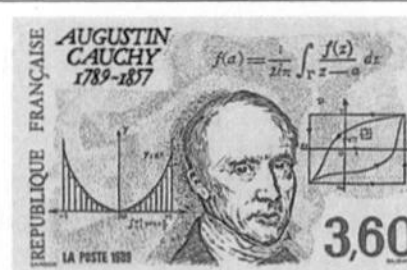

1114 Cauchy, Graphs and Formula

1989. Birth Bicentenary of Augustin Louis Cauchy (mathematician).

2903 **1114** 3f.60 blue, blk & red 1·60 90

1115 Marshal Lattre de Tassigny

1989. Birth Centenary of Marshal Jean de Lattre de Tassigny.

2904 **1115** 2f.20 black, blue & red 95 50

1116 Bird feeding Chicks (18th-century silk painting)

1989. Red Cross Fund.

2905 **1116** 2f.20+60c. mult . . . . 1·10 1·20

1117 Harkis **1118** "Marianne"

1989. Harkis (French North African troops).

2906 **1117** 2f.20 multicoloured . . 1·20 45

1989. Imperf (2943), perf or imperf (2910, 2915, 2916), perf (others).

2907 **1118** 10c. brown 20 10
2908 20c. green 20 10
2909 50c. violet 25 10
2943b 70c. brown . . . . . 5·00 3·00
2910 1f. orange 40 20
2911 2f. green 85 25
2912 2f. blue 75 20
2913 2f.10 green . . . . . 1·00 40
2914 2f.20 green . . . . . 1·20 35
2916 2f.30 red . . . . . . 1·00 30
2917 2f.40 green . . . . . 1·20 65
2918 2f.50 red . . . . . . 1·30 45
2919 2f.70 green . . . . . 1·40 60
2920 3f.20 blue . . . . . . 1·50 80
2921 3f.40 blue . . . . . . 1·40 75
2922 3f.50 green . . . . . 1·70 65
2923 3f.80 mauve . . . . . 1·60 75
2924 3f.80 blue . . . . . . 1·70 80
2925 4f. mauve . . . . . . 1·90 75
2926 4f.20 mauve . . . . . 1·60 80
2927 4f.40 blue . . . . . . 1·80 95
2928 4f.50 mauve . . . . . 2·75 80
2929 5f. blue . . . . 1·80 70
2930 10f. violet . . . . . . 3·50 1·30

The imperforate stamps are self-adhesive.

For designs as T **1118** but inscr "D" for face value, see Nos. 3036/7, and with no value at all see No. 3122b.

1990. No value expressed. As T **1032** but inscr "C".

2949 (2f.10) green 95 65
2950 (2f.30) red . . . . 1·10 65

1119 Lace

1990.

2951 **1119** 2f.50 white and red . . 1·10 55

1990. Winter Olympic Games, Albertville (1992) (1st issue).

2952 **1120** 2f.50 multicoloured . . 1·10 45

See also Nos. 2953/62 and 3048.

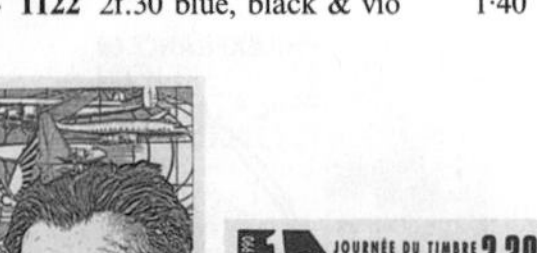

1121 Emblem and Ice Skaters **1122** Cross of Lorraine and De Gaulle

1990. Winter Olympic Games, Albertville (1992) (2nd issue). Each black, blue and red.

2953 2f.30+20c. Type **1121** . . . 1·10 1·00
2954 2f.30+20c. Ski jumping . . 1·10 90
2955 2f.30+20c. Speed skiing . . 1·10 90
2956 2f.30+20c. Slalom . . . . . 1·10 95
2957 2f.30+20c. Cross-country skiing . . . . 1·10 95
2958 2f.30+20c. Ice hockey . . . 1·10 95
2959 2f.50+20c. Luge . . . . . . 1·10 95
2960 2f.50+20c. Curling . . . . 1·10 95
2961 2f.50+20c. Artistic skiing . . 1·20 95
2962 2f.50+20c. Downhill skiing 1·20 95
MS2963 143 × 126 mm. 10 × 2f.50+20c. As Nos. 2953/62 13·00 13·00

1990. Birth Centenary of Charles de Gaulle (President, 1959–69).

2964 **1122** 2f.30 blue, black & vio 1·40 45

1123 Aircraft and Hymans **1124** Eyes and Keyboard

1990. 90th Birth Anniv of Max Hymans (civil aviation pioneer).

2965 **1123** 2f.30 green, violet & bl 1·00 50

1990. Art. As T **491**.

2966 5f. multicoloured . . . . . 2·30 1·60
2967 5f. blue, brown and ochre 2·30 1·60
2968 5f. multicoloured . . . . . 2·75 1·60
2969 5f. multicoloured . . . . . 2·30 1·70

DESIGNS—VERT: No. 2966, "Woman's Profile" (Odilon Redon); 2967, "Seated Cambodian Woman" (Auguste Rodin); 2968, "Head of Christ of Wissembourg"; 2969, "Yellow and Grey" (Roger Bissiere).

1990. Stamp Day.

2970 **1124** 2f.30+60c. blue, ultramarine and yellow . . . . 1·20 1·40
2971 2f.30+60c. deep green, green, blue and yellow . . . . 1·30 1·30

1125 Guehenno **1126** Macon Post Office

1990. Birth Cent of Jean Guehenno (writer).

2972 **1125** 3f.20 brown & lt brn 1·40 75

1990. Tourist Publicity. As T **490**.

2973 2f.30 orange, blue & black 1·00 60
2974 2f.30 black, blue & green . . 1·00 55
2975 3f.80 brown and green . . . 1·70 90
2976 3f.80 purple, brown & blue 1·50 90

DESIGNS: No. 2973, Cluny; 2974, Aqueduct, Briare Canal; 2975, Flaran-Gers Abbey; 2976, Cap Canaille Cassis.

1990. Europa. Post Office Buildings.

2978 **1126** 2f.30 black, ochre and blue . . . . 1·20 60
2979 – 3f.20 multicoloured . . 2·00 1·20

DESIGN: 3f.20, Cerizay post office.

1127 Crowd

1990. Centenary of Labour Day.

2980 **1127** 2f.30 multicoloured . . 1·00 50

1128 Quimper Faience Plate **1129** Institute Building

1990. Red Cross Fund.
2981 **1128** 2f.30+60c. mult . . . . 1·20 1·30

1990. Arab World Institute.
2982 **1129** 3f.80 dp blue, bl & red 1·60 1·00

1130 Detail of Stonework, Notre Dame des Marais **1131** "La Poste"

1990. Federation of French Philatelic Societies Congress, Villefranche-sur-Saone.
2983 **1130** 2f.30 black, grn & red 1·00 55

1990. Round the World Yacht Race.
2984 **1131** 2f.30 multicoloured . . 1·00 50

1132 Georges Brassens **1133** Cross of Lorraine and Marianne

1990. Red Cross Fund. French Singers. Mult.
2985 2f.30+50c. Aristide Bruant 1·10 1·30
2986 2f.30+50c. Maurice Chevalier . . . . 1·10 1·30
2987 2f.30+50c. Tino Rossi . . . 1·10 1·30
2988 2f.30+50c. Edith Piaf . . . 1·10 1·30
2989 2f.30+50c. Jacques Brel . . 1·10 1·30
2990 2f.30+50c. Type **1132** . . . 1·10 1·30

1990. 50th Anniv of De Gaulle's Call to Resist.
2991 **1133** 2f.30 red, blue & blk 1·10 55

1134 Aerial View of House

1990. 5th Anniv of France–Brazil House, Rio de Janeiro.
2992 **1134** 3f.20 multicoloured . . 1·40 1·10

1990. Precancels. Musical Instruments (2nd series). As T **110**.
2993 1f.46 emerald and green . . 1·10 1·10
2994 1f.80 brown and orange . . 1·40 1·20
2995 1f.93 green & deep green . . 1·40 1·30
2996 2f.39 mauve and purple . . 1·70 1·50
2997 2f.74 violet and blue . . . . 2·30 2·10
2998 3f.06 blue and deep blue . . 2·40 2·20
2999 5f.10 violet and purple . . . 3·25 3·25
DESIGNS: 1 f 46, Accordion; 1f.89, Breton bagpipe; 1f.93, Harp; 2f.39, Piano; 2f.74, Violin; 3f.06, Provencal drum; 5f.10, Hurdy-gurdy.
See note below No. 432 (1920).

1135 Relief Map of France **1136** Roach

1990. 50th Anniv of National Geographical Institute.
3000 **1135** 2f.30 multicoloured . . 1·10 65

1990. Freshwater Fishes. Multicoloured.
3001 2f. Type **1136** 90 50
3002 3f. Eurasian perch . . . . . 1·20 95
3003 4f. Atlantic salmon . . . . 1·90 1·30
3004 5f. Northern pike . . . . . 2·00 1·30

1137 Gaspard Monge (Navy Minister)

1990. Bicentenary of French Revolution (7th issue). Sheet 79 × 106 mm containing T **1137** and similar vert designs.
MS3005 2f.50 Type **1137**; 2f.50 Abbe Henri Gregorie; 2f.50 Creation of national flag; 2f.50 Creation of departments . . . . 3·50 3·50

1138 Genevoix **1139** World Map

1990. Birth Centenary of Maurice Genevoix (writer).
3006 **1138** 2f.30 green & black . . 1·00 45

1990. 30th Anniv of Organization for Economic Co-operation and Development.
3007 **1139** 3f.20 blue & ultram . . 1·30 90

1991. Art. As T **491**.
3008 5f. multicoloured . . . . . 2·30 1·60
3009 5f. black and stone . . . . 2·30 1·60
3010 5f. black . . . . 2·30 1·70
3011 5f. multicoloured . . . . . 2·30 1·70
DESIGNS—VERT: No. 3008, "The Swing" (Auguste Renoir); 3009, "The Black Knot" (Georges Seurat); 3010, "Volta faccia" (Francois Rouan). HORIZ: No. 3011, "Oh Black Painting" (Roberto Matta).

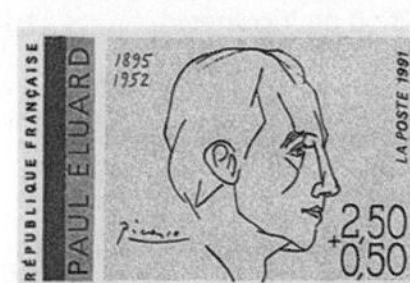

1140 Paul Eluard (after Pablo Picasso)

1991. Red Cross Fund. French Poets. Each grey, black and blue.
3013 2f.50+50c. Type **1140** . . . 1·20 1·30
3014 2f.50+50c. Andre Breton (after Man Ray) . . . . 1·20 1·30
3015 2f.50+50c. Louis Aragon (after Henri Matisse) . . 1·20 1·30
3016 2f.50+50c. Francis Ponge (after Stella Mertens) . . 1·20 1·30
3017 2f.50+50c. Jacques Prevert (after Picasso) . . . . . 1·20 1·30
3018 2f.50+50c. Rene Char (after Valentine Hugo) . . . . 1·20 1·30

1141 Mail Sorting by Hand and by Machine

1991. Stamp Day. Multicoloured, colour of machine given.
3019 **1141** 2f.50+60c. blue . . . . 1·30 1·30
3020 2f.50+60c. violet . . . 1·40 1·50

1142 Children, Bicycle and Dove

1991. "Philexjeunes 91" Youth Stamp Exhibition, Cholet.
3021 **1142** 2f.50 multicoloured . . 1·10 70

1143 Mozart and Globe **1144** Eyes and Forms of Writing

1991. Death Bicentenary of Wolfgang Amadeus Mozart (composer).
3022 **1143** 2f.50 black, blue & red 1·10 75

1991. 350th Anniv of State Printing Office.
3023 **1144** 4f. multicoloured . . . 1·60 1·00

1991. Tourist Publicity. As T **490**.
3024 2f.50 multicoloured . . . . 1·10 50
3025 2f.50 multicoloured . . . . 1·30 65
3026 4f. lilac . . . . 1·60 95
DESIGNS—VERT: No. 3024, Chevire Bridge, Nantes. HORIZ: No. 3025, Carennac; 3026, Munster Valley.

1145 Poster **1146** "Ariane" Rocket and Map of French Guiana

1991. 90th Anniv of Concours Lepine (French Association of Small Manufacturers and Inventors).
3028 **1145** 4f. multicoloured . . . 1·60 1·10

1991. Europa. Europe in Space. Each blue, red and green.
3029 2f.50 Type **1146** . . . . . 1·50 55
3030 3f.50 "TDF-1" broadcasting satellite, eyes and globe 2·10 1·00

1147 Perpignan **1148** Painting by Joan Miro

1991. Federation of French Philatelic Societies Congress, Perpignan.
3031 **1147** 2f.50 red, grey & blue 1·10 50

1991. Centenary of French Open Tennis Championships.
3032 **1148** 3f.50 multicoloured . . 1·60 80

1149 La Tour d'Auvergne ("First Grenadier of France")

1991. Bicentenary of French Revolution (8th issue). Sheet 105 × 80 mm containing T **1149** and similar horiz designs. Multicoloured.
MS3033 2f.50 Type **1149**; 2f.50 Tree of Liberty; 2f.50 Mounted gendarme; 2f.50 Louis Saint-Just 4·00 4·00

1150 Organ Pipes **1151** Illustration from Gaston's "Book of Hunting"

1991. Organ of St. Nicholas's, Wasquehal.
3034 **1150** 4f. buff and brown . . 1·60 95

1991. 600th Death Anniv of Gaston III Phoebus, Count of Foix.
3035 **1151** 2f.50 multicoloured . . 1·10 65

1991. No value expressed. As T **1118** but inscr "D". Imperf (self-adhesive) or perf (3037), perf (3036).
3036 (2f.20) green . . . . 1·10 55
3037 (2f.50) red . . . . 1·10 50

1152 Brown Bear

1991. Nature. Multicoloured.
3039 2f. Type **1152** 95 60
3040 3f. Hermann's tortoise . . . 1·20 75
3041 4f. Eurasian beaver . . . . 1·60 1·20
3042 5f. River kingfisher . . . . 2·10 1·60

1153 Forest

1991. 10th World Forestry Congress, Paris.
3043 **1153** 2f.50 green, bl & blk . . 1·10 50

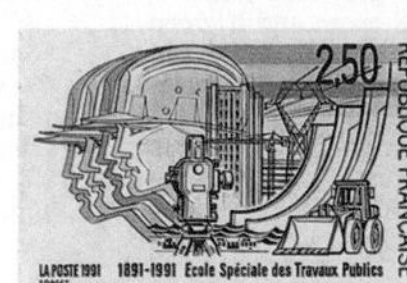

1154 Aspects of Public Works

1991. Centenary of School of Public Works.
3044 **1154** 2f.50 multicoloured . . 1·10 70

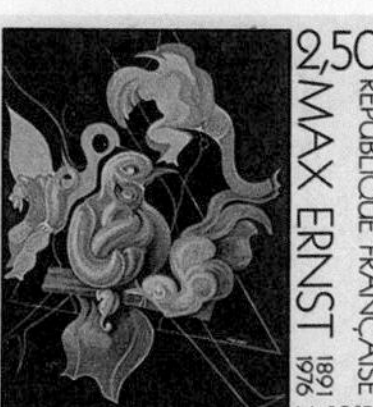

1155 "Bird Monument" (detail)

1991. Birth Centenary of Max Ernst (painter).
3045 **1155** 2f.50 multicoloured . . 1·30 90

1156 Cerdan

1991. 75th Birth Anniv of Marcel Cerdan (boxer).
3046 **1156** 2f.50 black and red . . 1·10 60

1157 "Amnesty International" **1158** Stylized Flame

1991. 30th Anniv of Amnesty International.
3047 **1157** 3f.40 bl, mve & blk . . 1·50 90

1991. Winter Olympic Games, Albertville (1992) (3rd issue).
3048 **1158** 2f.50 blue, blk & red 1·10 50

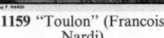

1159 "Toulon" (Francois Nardi) **1160** Bird

1991. Red Cross Fund.
3049 **1159** 2f.50+60c. mult . . . . 1·20 1·20

1991. 5th Paralympic Games, Tignes (1992).
3050 **1160** 2f.50 blue . . . . . . 1·10 60

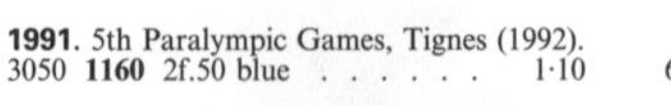

1161 Shore

1991. 150th Anniv of Voluntary Adhesion of Mayotte to France.
3051 **1161** 2f.50 multicoloured . . 1·10 50

1992. Precancels. Musical Instruments (3rd series). As T **1110**.
3052a 1f.60 brown and orange . . 6·50 5·75
3053 1f.98 bistre and ochre . . . 3·50 4·00
3054 2f.08 orange and yellow . . 1·80 2·10
3055 2f.46 violet . . . . 1·80 2·10
3056 2f.98 lilac and mauve . . . 1·80 2·10
3057 3f.08 purple and red . . . 5·50 5·50
3058 3f.14 green and turquoise 2·40 2·75
3059 3f.19 grey and black . . . 5·50 5·75
3060 5f.28 green and lt green . . 4·75 4·75
3061 5f.30 ultramarine & blue 3·00 3·50
3062 5f.32 brown & dp brown 3·00 3·50
DESIGNS: 1f.60, Guitar; 1f.98, Accordion; 2f.08, Saxophone; 2f.46, Breton bagpipe; 2f.98, Banjo; 3f.08, Provencal drum; 3f.14, Hurdy-gurdy; 3f.19, Harp; 5f.28, Xylophone; 5f.30, Piano; 5f.32, Violin.
See note below No. 432 (1920).

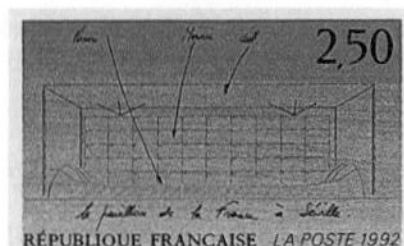

1162 Plan of French Pavilion

1992. "Expo '92" World's Fair, Seville.
3063 **1162** 2f.50 blue, blk & grn 1·10 50

1163 Post Office, Reception Area and Postal Self-service Machines

1992. Stamp Day.
3064 **1163** 2f.50+60c. black, blue and yellow . . . . 1·20 1·20
3065 2f.50+60c. red, blue, black & yell . . . . 1·30 1·30

1164 Runner **1165** Cesar Franck

1992. Olympic Games, Barcelona.
3066 **1164** 2f.50 multicoloured . . 1·50 50

1992. Red Cross Fund. Composers. Mult.
3067 2f.50+50c. Type **1165** . . . 1·20 1·30
3068 2f.50+50c. Erik Satie . . . 1·20 1·30
3069 2f.50+50c. Florent Schmitt 1·20 1·30
3070 2f.50+50c. Arthur Honegger 1·20 1·30
3071 2f.50+50c. Georges Auric 1·20 1·30
3072 2f.50+50c. Germaine Tailleferre . . . . 1·20 1·30

1166 Marguerite d'Angouleme (after Clouet) **1167** "Madonna, Child and Angel" (Botticelli)

1992. 500th Birth Anniv of Marguerite d'Angouleme, Queen of Navarre.
3073 **1166** 3f.40 multicoloured . . 1·40 1·10

1992. 500th Anniv of Ajaccio.
3074 **1167** 4f. multicoloured . . . 1·70 1·00

1168 Navigational Instruments and Map **1169** Wheat, Poppies and Loaves

1992. Europa. 500th Anniv of Discovery of America by Columbus. Multicoloured.
3075 2f.50 Type **1168** . . . . . 1·20 50
3076 3f.40 Caravel, map and compass rose . . . . . . 2·10 90

1992. Tourist Publicity. As T **490**.
3077 2f.50 brown, blue & green 1·10 50
3078 3f.40 brown, green & blue 1·50 95
3079 4f. blue, black and green . . 1·60 85
3080 4f. green, lt green & brown 1·60 1·00
DESIGNS—VERT: No. 3077, Chateau de Biron, Dordogne; 3078, Mont Aiguille, Isere (500th anniv of first ascent). HORIZ: No. 3079, 4f. L'Ourcq Canal; 3080, Lorient.

1992. International Bread and Cereals Congress.
3081 **1169** 3f.40 multicoloured . . 1·50 1·50

1170 Couple leaping through Stamp

1992. Federation of French Philatelic Societies Congress, Niort.
3082 **1170** 2f.50 multicoloured . . 1·10 50

1171 Olympic Rings

1992. Winter Olympic Games, Albertville, and Summer Games, Barcelona.
3083 **1171** 2f.50 multicoloured . . 1·70 60

1172 Tautavel Man

1992.
3084 **1172** 3f.40 multicoloured . . 1·50 1·00

1992. Art. As T **491**.
3085 5f. black and stone . . . . 2·30 1·70
DESIGN—VERT: 5f. "Portrait of Claude Deruet" (Jacques Callot).

1173 Sand Lily

1992. Flowers. Multicoloured.
3086 2f. Type **1173** 85 50
3087 3f. Sundew . . . . 1·30 80
3088 4f. "Orchis palustris" . . . 1·60 1·10
3089 5f. Yellow water lily . . . . 2·00 1·50

1174 Marianne and National Colours **1175** Marianne

1992. Bicentenary of Year One of First Republic.
3090 **1174** 2f.50 multicoloured . . 1·10 50

1992. Bicentenary of Declaration of First Republic. Each red.
3091 2f.50 Type **1175** . . . . . 1·00 55
3092 2f.50 Tree of Liberty . . . 1·00 55
3093 2f.50 Marianne as cockerel 1·00 55
3094 2f.50 "Republique Francaise" . . . . 1·00 55

1992. Precancels. Musical Instruments (4th series). As T **1110**.
3095 1f.73 deep green & green . . 85 80
3096 2f.25 red and orange . . . 1·10 1·10
3097 3f.51 ultramarine & blue . . 2·10 1·90
3098 5f.40 red and mauve . . . . 2·50 2·75
DESIGNS: 1f.73, Guitar; 2f.25, Saxophone; 3f.51, Banjo; 5f.40, Xylophone.
See note below No. 432 (1920).

1176 Symbol of Market

1992. European Single Market.
3099 **1176** 2f.50 multicoloured . . 1·10 60

1177 Farman HF16 and Boeing 737-500

1992. 80th Anniv of Nancy–Luneville Air Mail Service.
3100 **1177** 2f.50 multicoloured . . 1·10 65

1178 Paul and Electricity Pylon **1180** Birds holding Strings (T. Ungerer)

1179 "Woman at Window" (Paul Delvaux)

1992. 10th Death Anniv of Marcel Paul (politician).
3101 **1178** 4f.20 blue & purple . . 1·90 80

1992. Contemporary Art.
3102 **1179** 5f. multicoloured . . . 2·10 1·40
3103 – 5f. multicoloured . . . 2·10 1·40
3104 – 5f. black, mauve & yell 2·10 1·40
3105 – 5f. black and yellow . . 2·10 1·40
DESIGNS: No. 3103, "Portrait of Man" (Francis Bacon); 3104, Abstract (Alberto Burri); 3105, Abstract (Antoni Tapies).
See also Nos. 3154, 3176, 3285 and 3301/2.

1992. Red Cross Fund. Mutual Aid Meeting, Strasbourg.
3106 **1180** 2f.50+60c. mult . . . . 1·20 1·30

1181 Horse, Guitar and Dancer **1182** Smew Pair

1992. Gypsies.
3107 **1181** 2f.50 multicoloured . . 1·10 60

1993. Ducks. Multicoloured.
3108 2f. Type **1182** 90 45
3109 3f. Ferruginous duck and drake . . . . 1·40 65
3110 4f. Common sheldrake pair 1·80 1·00
3111 5f. Red-breasted merganser pair . . . . 2·20 1·10

1183 "La Poste" (yacht) and Globe

1993. "Postmen around the World". Post Office Team Participation in Around the World Yacht Race.
3112 **1183** 2f.50 yell, ultram & bl 1·20 65
3113 2f.80 yell, ultram & bl 1·60 80

1184 Memorial

1993. Indo–China Wars Memorial, Frejus.
3114 **1184** 4f. multicoloured . . . 1·70 85

1185 Postman with Bicycle **1186** Yacht and Runner

1993. Stamp Day.
3115 **1185** 2f.50 multicoloured . . 1·90 1·70
3116 2f.50+60c. mult . . . . 1·30 1·30

1993. Mediterranean Games, Agde and Roussillon (Languedoc).
3117 **1186** 2f.50 multicoloured . . 1·10 55

1187 Maria Deraismes and Georges Martin (founders) **1189** Guy de Maupassant

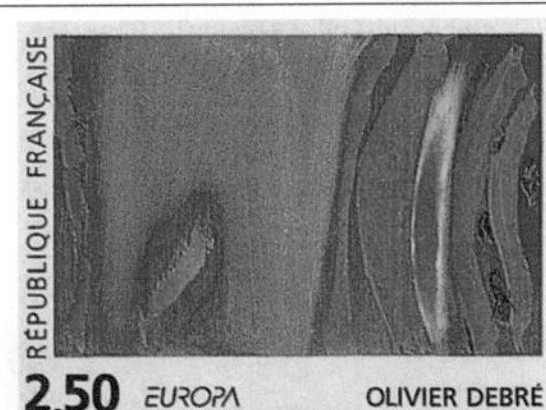

1188 "Red Rhythm Blue" (Olivier Debre)

1993. Centenary of Le Droit Humain (International Mixed Freemasons Order).
3118 **1187** 3f.40 black and blue . . 1·50 1·00

1993. Europa. Contemporary Art. Mult.
3119 2f.50 Type **1188** . . . . . 1·20 65
3120 3f.40 "Le Griffu" (bronze, Germaine Richier) (vert) 1·70 1·10

1993. As T **1118** but no value expressed. Imperf (self-adhesive) or perf.
3122b **1118** (–) red . . . . 1·10 25
No. 3122b was sold at the current inland rate (at time of issue 2f.50).

1993. Tourist Publicity. As T **490** and **949**.
3124 2f.80 green, brown and blue 1·30 65
3125 3f.40 red, green and blue . . 1·60 75
3126 4f.20 dp green, green & brn 1·60 1·00
3127 4f.20 brown and green . . . 1·80 1·00
3128 4f.40 black, green and red 2·00 1·10
3129 4f.40 multicoloured . . . . 2·00 1·10
DESIGNS—As T **490**. HORIZ: No. 3124, La Chaise-Dieu Abbey, Haute-Loire; 3128, Montbeliard-Doubs. VERT: No. 3125, Artouste train, Laruns; 3126, Minerve-Herault; 3129, Le Jacquemard, Lambesc. As T **949**: No. 3127, Chinon.

1993. Red Cross Fund. Writers. Mult.
3131 2f.50+50c. Type **1189** . . . 1·30 1·30
3132 2f.50+50c. Alain . . . . . 1·30 1·30
3133 2f.50+50c. Jean Cocteau . . 1·30 1·30
3134 2f.50+50c. Marcel Pagnol 1·30 1·30
3135 2f.50+50c. Andre Chamson 1·30 1·30
3136 2f.50+50c. Marguerite Yourcenar . . . . 1·30 1·30

1190 Map of Europe and Liberty

1993. 9th European Constitutional Court Conference on Human Rights.
3137 **1190** 2f.50 multicoloured . . 1·10 55

1191 Reinhardt 1192 Weiss

1993. 40th Death Anniv of Django Reinhardt (guitarist).
3138 **1191** 4f.20 multicoloured . . 1·80 1·00

1993. Birth Centenary of Louise Weiss (women's rights campaigner).
3139 **1192** 2f.50 blk, orge & red 1·10 60

1193 TGV and Eurostar Trains at Lille

1993. Federation of French Philatelic Societies Congress, Lille.
3140 **1193** 2f.50 lt bl, bl & mve . . 1·10 55

1194 Emblem

1993. Bicentenary of National Natural History Museum, Paris.
3141 **1194** 2f.50 multicoloured . . 1·10 50

1195 Bas-relief (Georges Jeanclos) (left half) 1196 Central Telegraph Tower, Paris

1993. Martyrs and Heroes of the Resistance. Multicoloured.
3142 2f.50 Type **1195** . . . . . 1·40 1·20
3143 4f.20 Right half of bas-relief 1·80 1·70
Nos. 3142/3 were issued together, se-tenant, forming a composite design.

1993. Bicentenary of Chappe's Optical Telegraph.
3144 **1196** 2f.50 black, stone and blue . . . . 1·10 50

1993. Precancels. Musical Instruments (5th series). As T **1110**.
3145 1f.82 grey and black 85 80
3146 2f.34 brown and orange . . 1·10 1·10
3147 3f.86 red and pink . . . . 2·00 1·90
3148 5f.93 violet and mauve . . . 2·50 2·75
DESIGNS: 1f.82, Trumpet; 2f.34, Drum; 3f.86, Hurdy-gurdy; 5f.93, Xylophone.

1197 Map of Corsica and "Casabianca" (submarine) 1198 Le Val-de-Grace, Paris

1993. 50th Anniv of Liberation of Corsica.
3149 **1197** 2f.80 black, red & bl . . 1·30 60

1993. Art. As T **491**. Multicoloured.
3150 5f. "Saint Thomas" (Georges de la Tour) (vert) . . . . 2·30 1·70
3151 5f. "The Muses" (Maurice Denis) (vert) . . . . . . 2·40 1·80

1993. Bicentenary of Conversion of Monastery of Le Val-de-Grace to Military Hospital (now museum).
3152 **1198** 3f.70 black, grn & brn 1·60 75

1199 Clowns 1200 Girl studying Flower ("Happy Holiday") (C. Wendling)

1993. National Centre for Circus Arts, Chalons-sur-Marne.
3153 **1199** 2f.80 multicoloured . . 1·30 50

1993. Contemporary Art. As T **1179**.
3154 5f. red and black . . . . . 2·30 1·80
3155 5f. multicoloured . . . . . 2·30 1·80
DESIGNS: No. 3154, Abstract (Takis); 3155, "Enhanced Engraving" (Maria Elena Vieira da Silva).

1993. Greetings Stamps. "The Pleasure of Writing". Designs by comic strip artists. Multicoloured.
3156A 2f.80 Type **1200** . . . . 1·30 85
3157A 2f.80 Clowns ("Happy Holiday") (B. Olivie) . . 1·30 85
3158A 2f.80 Cat on birthday cake ("Happy Birthday") (S. Colman) . . . . . . 1·30 85
3159A 2f.80 Girl with cake ("Happy Birthday") (G. Sorel) . . . . . . 1·30 85
3160A 2f.80 Man courting woman on balcony ("With Passion") (J. M. Thiriet) . . . . 1·30 85
3161A 2f.80 Man playing large fountain pen ("Pleasure of Writing") (E. Davodeau) . . . . 1·30 85
3162A 2f.80 Pig with letter ("Greetings") (J. de Moor) . . . . 1·30 85
3163A 2f.80 Jester in horseshoe ("Good Luck") (Mezzo) 1·30 85
3164A 2f.80 Clowns running ("Best Wishes") (N. de Crecy) . . . . 1·30 85
3165A 2f.80 Girl and cat watching tree fairy ("Best Wishes") (F. Magnin) . . . . . 1·30 85
3166A 2f.80 Cards tumbling from Santa Claus's sack ("Happy Christmas") (T. Robin) . . . . . . 1·30 85
3167A 2f.80 Mouse dressed as Santa Claus ("Happy Christmas") (P. Prugne) 1·30 85

1201 Rhododendron

1993. 1st European Stamp Salon, Flower Gardens, Paris (1994) (1st issue). Sheet 106 × 78 mm containing T **1201** and similar horiz design. Multicoloured.
MS3168 2f.40 Type **1201**; 2f.40 View of Gardens (sold at 15f.) . . . 12·00 12·00

1202 Louvre, 1793

1993. Bicentenary of Louvre Museum. Mult.
3169 2f.80 Type **1202** . . . . . 1·30 1·10
3170 4f.40 Louvre, 1993 . . . . 2·10 1·60
Nos. 3169/70 were issued together, se-tenant, forming a composite design.

1203 "St. Nicholas" 1204 Cast-iron Sign at Metro Entrance, Paris (detail, Hector Guimard)

1993. Red Cross Fund. Metz Engravings.
3171 **1203** 2f.80+60c. mult . . . . 1·40 1·30

1994. Art Nouveau. Multicoloured.
3172 2f.80 Type **1204** . . . . . 1·30 55
3173 2f.80 "Roses of France Cup" (vase, Emile Galle) 1·30 55
3174 4f.40 Drawing-room table with bronze water-lily decoration (Louis Majorelle) . . . . 2·00 95
3175 4f.40 Stoneware teapot (Pierre-Adrien Dalpayrat) 2·00 95

1994. Contemporary Art. As T **1179**. Mult.
3176 6f.70 Abstract (Sean Scully) 3·00 1·90
3177 6f.70 "Couple" (Georg Baselitz) . . . . 3·00 2·10

1205 "Death of St. Stephen"

1994. 12th-century Stained Glass Window, Le Mans Cathedral.
3179 **1205** 6f.70 multicoloured . . 3·00 2·00

1994. Tourist Publicity. As T **490**.
3180 2f.80 multicoloured . . . . 1·20 50
3181 2f.80 blue . . . . 1·20 50
3182 3f.70 brown, dp green & grn 1·60 1·10
3183 4f.40 brown and blue . . . 1·80 1·10
3184 4f.40 brown and red . . . . 1·80 1·10
DESIGNS—HORIZ: No. 3180, "Mount Sainte Victoire" (Paul Cezanne); 3181, Bridge at Rupt aux Nonains, Saulx Region, Meuse; 3184, Argentat. VERT: No. 3182, La Grand Cascade, Saint-Cloud Park; 3183, Old port and St. John the Baptist Church, Bastia.

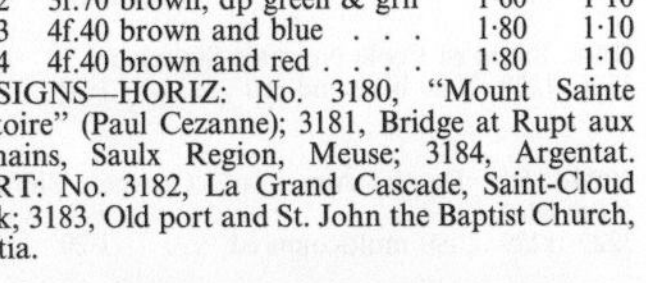

1206 European Union Flag

1994. European Parliament Elections.
3185 **1206** 2f.80 blue, yell & grey 1·20 50

1207 Mourguet and Guignol

1994. 150th Death Anniv of Laurent Mourguet (creator of Guignol (puppet)).
3186 **1207** 2f.80 multicoloured . . 1·20 60

1208 Emblem

1994. Bicent of Polytechnic Institute, Paris.
3187 **1208** 2f.80 multicoloured . . 1·20 75

1209 "Marianne" 1210 "The Vikings" (detail, Bayeux Tapestry)

1994. Stamp Day. 50th Anniv of Edmond Dulac's "Marianne" Design.
3188 **1209** 2f.80 red and blue . . . 1·60 1·60
3190 2f.80+60c. red & bl . . . 1·80 2·10

1994. Franco–Swedish Cultural Relations. Mult.
3191 2f.80 Type **1210** . . . . . 2·75 2·40
3192 2f.80 Viking longships (different detail) . . . . . 2·75 2·40
3193 2f.80 Costume design for sailor by Fernand Leger in Swedish Ballet production of "Skating Rink" . . . . 2·75 2·40
3194 2f.80 Costume design for gentleman in "Skating Rink" . . . . 2·75 2·40
3195 3f.70 "Banquet for Gustav III at the Trianon, 1784" (Niclas Lafrensen the younger) . . . . 4·50 3·00
3196 3f.70 Swedish and French flags . . . . 4·50 3·00
Nos. 3195/6 are larger, 49 × 37 mm.

1211 Mountain Ambush 1212 Pompidou

1994. 50th Anniv of Liberation. The Maquis (resistance movement).
3197 **1211** 2f.80 multicoloured . . 1·20 50

1994. 20th Death Anniv of Georges Pompidou (Prime Minister 1962–68, President 1969–74).
3198 **1212** 2f.80 brown . . . . . 1·20 60

1213 Boy netting Stamps

1994. "Philex Jeunes 94" Youth Stamp Exhibition, Grenoble.
3199 **1213** 2f.80 multicoloured . . 1·20 50

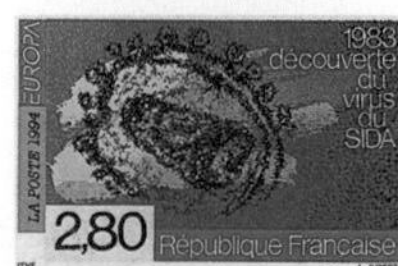
1214 AIDS Virus

1994. Europa. Discoveries. Multicoloured.
3200 2f.80 Type **1214** (11th anniv of discovery) . . . . . . 1·40 60
3201 3f.70 Wavelength formula (70th anniv of Louis de Broglie's proof of undulatory theory of matter) . . . . 1·70 1·20

1215 Bank Emblem

1994. 27th Assembly of Asian Development Bank, Nice.
3202 **1215** 2f.80 multicoloured . . 1·20 55

1216 British Lion and French Cockerel over Tunnel

1994. Opening of Channel Tunnel. Mult.
3203 2f.80 Type **1216** . . . . . 1·10 65
3204 2f.80 Symbolic hands over Eurostar express train . . 1·20 65
3205 4f.30 Type **1216** . . . . . 1·70 1·60
3206 4f.30 As No. 3204 . . . . . 1·70 1·60

1217 Martigues inside Fish

1994. Federation of French Philatelic Societies Congress, Martigues.
3207 **1217** 2f.80 violet, bl & grn 1·20 50

1218 Court Building, Ile de la Cite, Paris

1994. Court of Cassation.
3208 **1218** 2f.80 multicoloured . . 1·20 50

1219 Landing Forces and Beach Defences

1994. 50th Anniv of Normandy Landings.
3209 **1219** 4f.30 red, ind & bl . . 1·90 95

1220 Allied Forces

1994. 50th Anniv of Liberation.
3210 **1220** 4f.30 multicoloured . . 1·90 1·10

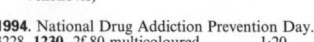

1221 Sorbonne University and Pierre de Coubertin (founder) **1222** Organ Pipes

1994. Centenary of International Olympic Committee.
3211 **1221** 2f.80 multicoloured . . 1·40 60

1994. Poitiers Cathedral Organ.
3212 **1222** 4f.40 multicoloured . . 1·80 1·10

1223 Flag, Map and Soldier **1224** Oak

1994. 50th Anniv of Allied Landings in Southern France.
3213 **1223** 2f.80 multicoloured . . 1·20 55

1994. Precancels. Leaves.
3321 – 1f.87 brown & green . . 1·00 95
3214 **1224** 1f.91 olive & green . . 85 85
3322 – 2f.18 red and lake . . . 1·20 1·10
3215 – 2f.46 green & lt green 1·10 1·00
3216 – 4f.24 red and orange . . 1·90 1·90
3323 – 4f.66 yellow & green . . 2·00 2·00
3217 – 6f.51 turquoise & blue 3·00 3·00
3324 – 7f.11 turquoise & blue 3·00 3·25
DESIGNS: 1f.87, Ash; 2f.18, Beech; 2f.46, Plane; 4f.24, Chestnut; 4f.66, Walnut; 6f.51, Holly; 7f.11, Elm.

1225 "Moses and the Daughters of Jethro" (drawing) (½-size illustration)

1994. 400th Birth Anniv of Nicolas Poussin (artist).
3218 **1225** 4f.40 brown & black . . 1·90 1·30

1226 Yvonne Printemps (singer and actress) **1227** Map and Foucault's Pendulum

1994. Entertainers. Multicoloured.
3219 2f.80+60c. Type **1226** . . . 1·40 1·60
3220 2f.80+60c. Fernandel (Fernand Contandin) (actor) . . . . 1·40 1·60
3221 2f.80+60c. Josephine Baker (music hall performer) . . 1·40 1·60
3222 2f.80+60c. Bourvil (Andre Raimbourg) (actor) . . . 1·40 1·60
3223 2f.80+60c. Yves Montand (singer and actor) . . . 1·40 1·60
3224 2f.80+60c. Coluche (Michel Colucci) (comedian) . . . 1·40 1·60

1994. Bicentenary of National Conservatory of Arts and Craft.
3225 **1227** 2f.80 pur, bl & red . . 1·20 55

1228 Doorway **1229** Simenon and Quai des Orfevres, Paris

1994. Bicent of Ecole Normale Superieure.
3226 **1228** 2f.80 blue and red . . . 1·20 55

1994. 5th Death Anniv of Georges Simenon (novelist).
3227 **1229** 2f.80 multicoloured . . 1·20 65

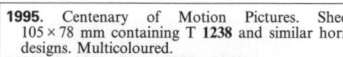

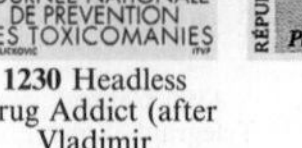
1230 Headless Drug Addict (after Vladimir Velickovic) **1231** Gardens

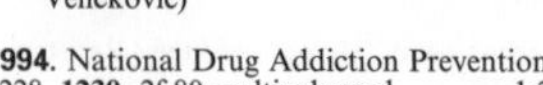
1994. National Drug Addiction Prevention Day.
3228 **1230** 2f.80 multicoloured . . 1·20 65

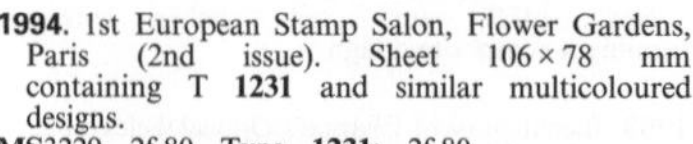
1994. 1st European Stamp Salon, Flower Gardens, Paris (2nd issue). Sheet 106 × 78 mm containing T **1231** and similar multicoloured designs.
MS3229 2f.80 Type **1231**; 2f.80 Dahlias (25 × 39 mm) (sold at 16f.) 12·00 12·00

1232 Lodge Emblem and Symbols of Freemasonry

1994. Centenary of Grand Lodge of France.
3230 **1232** 2f.80 brown, red & bl 1·20 60

1233 Stormy Sea and Colas

1994. 16th Death Anniv of Alain Colas (yachtsman).
3231 **1233** 3f.70 blk, grn & emer 1·70 1·10

1234 St. Vaast

1994. Red Cross Fund. 15th-century Arras Tapestry.
3232 **1234** 2f.80+60c. mult . . . . 1·40 1·50

1235 AIDS Virus (½-size illustration)

1994. AIDS Day.
3233 **1235** 2f.80 multicoloured . . 1·50 95
The stamp and se-tenant label, as illustrated, comprise No. 3233. For stamp without attached label, see No. 3200.

1236 Slogan

1994. 50th Anniv of National Press Federation.
3234 **1236** 2f.80 purple & yellow 1·20 55

1237 Champs Elysees (½-size illustration)

1994. New Year.
3235 **1237** 4f.40 multicoloured . . 2·10 1·40

1238 Projector and Scene from Film

1995. Centenary of Motion Pictures. Sheet 105 × 78 mm containing T **1238** and similar horiz designs. Multicoloured.
MS3236 2f.80 Type **1238**; 2f.80 Projector and head of man in cap; 2f.80 Projector and monster's head; 2f.80 Reel of films and Indian's head . . . . 4·50 4·50

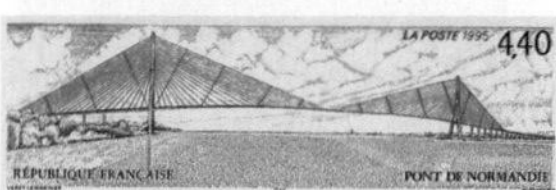
1239 Normandy Bridge (½-size illustration)

1995. Inauguration of Normandy Bridge (over Seine between Le Havre and Honfleur).
3237 **1239** 4f.40 multicoloured . . 2·40 1·20

1240 Emblem **1241** Pasteur

1995. European Public Notaries.
3238 **1240** 2f.80 multicoloured . . 1·20 55

1995. Death Centenary of Louis Pasteur (chemist).
3239 **1241** 3f.70 multicoloured . . 1·60 1·20

1995. Tourist Publicity. As T **490**.
3240 2f.80 green and olive . . . 1·20 55
3241 2f.80 green, brown & blue 1·20 55
3242 4f.40 multicoloured . . . . 2·00 1·10
3243 4f.40 black, lilac & green . . 2·00 1·10
DESIGNS—HORIZ: No. 3240, Malt works, Stenay; 3241, Remiremont, Vosges; 3242, Nyons Bridge, Drome. VERT: No. 3243, Margot gate and St. Martial's Church, Correze.

1995. Art. As T **491**.
3245 6f.70 black, yellow & red . . 3·00 2·10
3246 6f.70 black, blue & dp blue 3·00 2·10
3247 6f.70 multicoloured . . . . 3·00 2·10
3248 6f.70 multicoloured . . . . 2·75 2·00
DESIGNS—VERT: No. 3245, Reliquary of St. Taurin, Evereux; 3248, "The Cradle" (Berthe Morisot). HORIZ: No. 3246, Study for "The Dream of Happiness" (Pierre Prud'hon); 3247, Seascape (Zao Wou-Ki).

1242 Band-tailed Pigeons

1995. Bird Paintings by John James Audubon (ornithologist). Multicoloured.
3249 2f.80 Type **1242** . . . . . 1·30 65
3250 2f.80 Snowy egret . . . . . 1·30 65
3251 4f.30 Common tern . . . . 2·10 1·20
3252 4f.40 Rough-legged buzzards 2·10 1·30
MS3253 113 × 120 mm. Nos. 2149/52 4·50 4·50

1243 "Marianne"

1995. Stamp Day. 50th Anniv of Pierre Gandon's "Marianne" Design.
3255 **1243** 2f.80 green, bl & red . . 4·00 3·75
3254 2f.80+60c. green, ultramarine & red . . 1·80 1·80

1244 Hour Glass **1245** Means of Communications

1995. 50th Anniv of Works Councils.

3257 **1244** 2f.80 brown, lt bl & bl 1·20 55

1995. Centenary (1994) of Advanced Institute of Electricity.

3258 **1245** 3f.70 lt blue, bl & red 1·60 1·20

1246 Forms of Writing

1995. Bicentenary of School of Oriental Languages.

3259 **1246** 2f.80 multicoloured . . 1·20 65

1247 Giono

1248 "Ariane" Rocket and Map of French Guiana

1995. Birth Centenary of Jean Giono (writer).

3260 **1247** 3f.70 blk, blue & red 1·60 1·20

1995. French Space Centre in French Guiana.

3261 **1248** 2f.80 blue, grn & red 1·30 55

1249 Steel and Worker

1995. Lorraine's Iron and Steel Industry.

3262 **1249** 2f.80 multicoloured . . 1·20 55

1250 "Freedom"

1995. Europa. Peace and Freedom. Mult.

3263 2f.80 Type **1250** . . . . . 1·30 55
3264 3f.70 "Peace" . . . . 1·80 1·10

1251 Lumberjack

1252 Paris Landmarks and Charles de Gaulle

1995. Forestry in the Ardennes.

3265 **1251** 4f.40 brn, blk & grn . . 2·00 1·20

1995. 50th Anniv of End of Second World War.

3266 **1252** 2f.80 multicoloured . . 1·20 65

1253 Marianne in Assembly Building

1995. National Assembly.

3267 **1253** 2f.80 multicoloured . . 1·20 75

1254 "King Louis XIII on Horseback" (Saumur tapestry)

1995. Red Cross Fund.

3268 **1254** 2f.80+60c. mult . . . . 1·40 1·30

1255 Winged Hand

1256 Brittany

1995. 50th Anniv of French People's Relief Association (welfare organization).

3270 **1255** 2f.80 multicoloured . . 1·20 75

1995. Landscapes.

3271 **1256** 2f.40 green . . . . . . 1·10 50
3272 – 2f.40 green . . . . . . 1·10 50
3273 – 2f.80 red . . . . . . 1·30 50
3274 – 2f.80 red . . . . 1·30 50

DESIGNS: No. 3272, Vosges; 3273, Auvergne; 3274, Camargue.

1257 Orleans

1258 "The Grasshopper and The Ant"

1995. Federation of French Philatelic Societies Congress, Orleans.

3275 **1257** 2f.80 multicoloured . . 1·20 55

1995. 300th Death Anniv of Jean de la Fontaine (writer of fables). Multicoloured.

3276 2f.80 Type **1258** . . . . . 2·00 1·10
3277 2f.80 "The Fat Frog and the Ox" . . . . 2·00 1·10
3278 2f.80 "The Wolf and the Lamb" . . . . 2·00 1·10
3279 2f.80 "The Raven and the Fox" . . . . 2·00 1·10
3280 2f.80 "The Cat, the Weasel and the Little Rabbit" . . 2·00 1·10
3281 2f.80 "The Hare and the Tortoise" . . . . 2·00 1·10

1259 Flower, Star and Wire

1260 Maginot and Roof

1995. 53rd Anniv of Internment of Jews in Velodrome d'Hiver, Paris.

3282 **1259** 2f.80 multicoloured . . 1·20 70

1995. 63rd Death Anniv of Andre Maginot (politician and instigator of Maginot Line (fortifications on French–German border)).

3283 **1260** 2f.80 brown, grn & red 1·20 55

1261 Lodge Emblem

1262 Apothecary and Molecules

1995. 50th Anniv of Women's Grand Masonic Lodge of France.

3284 **1261** 2f.80 multicoloured . . 1·20 55

1995. Contemporary Art. As T **1179**. Mult.

3285 6f.70 Abstract (Kirkeby) . . 2·75 2·10

1995. 500th Anniv of Hospital Pharmacies.

3286 **1262** 2f.80 multicoloured . . 1·20 55

1263 "Thatched Cottages in Barbizon" (Narcisse Diaz de a Pena)

1264 Institute Emblem

1995. 170th Anniv of Barbizon School (artists' settlement).

3287 **1263** 4f.40 multicoloured . . 2·00 1·00

1995. 50th Anniv of National Civil Servants' Training Institute, Paris.

3288 **1264** 2f.80 multicoloured . . 90 40

1265 Institute Building

1266 New and Old Motor Vehicles and Headquarters

1995. Bicentenary of French Institute, Paris.

3289 **1265** 2f.80 black, red & grn 90 40

1995. Centenary of French Automobile Club.

3290 **1266** 4f.40 black, bl & red . . 1·50 85

1267 Dove, Blue Helmet and Anniversary Emblem

1268 Shepherd

1995. 50th Anniv of U.N.O.

3291 **1267** 4f.30 multicoloured . . 1·50 95

1995. Red Cross Fund. Crib Figures from Provence. Multicoloured.

3292 2f.80+60c. Type **1268** . . . 1·20 1·20
3293 2f.80+60c. Miller . . . . . 1·20 1·20
3294 2f.80+60c. Simpleton and tambourine player . . . . 1·20 1·20
3295 2f.80+60c. Fishmonger . . . 1·20 1·20
3296 2f.80+60c. Knife grinder . . 1·20 1·20
3297 2f.80+60c. Elderly couple . . 1·20 1·20

1269 Jammes

1995. 127th Birth Anniv of Francis Jammes (poet).

3298 **1269** 3f.70 black and blue . . 1·20 95

1270 Architect's Plans

1271 Pitch and Balls

1995. Completion of Evry Cathedral.

3299 **1270** 2f.80 multicoloured . . 95 40

1995. World Cup Football Championship, France (1998).

3300 **1271** 2f.80 multicoloured . . 95 45

1996. Contemporary Art. As T **1179**.

3301 6f.70 black, red and blue . . 2·20 1·60
3302 6f.70 multicoloured . . . . 2·20 1·60

DESIGNS: No. 3301, "Sculpture" (Lucien Wercollier); 3302, "Horizon" (Jan Dibbets).

1272 Pottery Dog

1273 "St. Patrick" (stained glass window, Evie Hone)

1996. Completion of Archaeological Excavations in Saint-Martin Island, Guadeloupe.

3305 **1272** 2f.80 multicoloured . . 95 50

1996. Art. As T **491**.

3306 6f.70 multicoloured . . . . 2·30 1·60
3307 6f.70 multicoloured . . . . 2·20 1·50
3308 6f.70 gold, copper & blk . . 1·90 1·20

DESIGNS—HORIZ: No. 3306, "Narni Bridge" (Camille Corot); 3308, "Cellos" (Arman). VERT: No. 3307, Bronze horse (found at Neuvy-en-Sullias).

1996. "L'imaginaire Irlandais" Festival of Contemporary Irish Arts, France.

3311 **1273** 2f.80 multicoloured . . 95 55

1274 "The Sower"

1276 Descartes (after Frans Hals)

1275 Rueff and New 1 Franc Coin of 1960

1996. Stamp Day. 93rd Anniv of Louis-Oscar Roty's "The Sower" design.

3312 **1274** 2f.80+60c. mauve and violet . . . . 1·30 1·10
3313 2f.80 mauve & violet 3·50 3·25

1996. Birth Centenary of Jacques Rueff (economist).

3315 **1275** 2f.80 black, bl & brn 85 50

1996. 400th Birth Anniv of Rene Descartes (philosopher and scientist).

3316 **1276** 4f.40 red . . . . 1·40 1·10

1277 Lightbulb and Flame

1996. 50th Anniv of Electricite de France and Gaz de France.

3317 **1277** 3f. multicoloured . . . 1·00 55

1278 Eurasian Beaver and Columbine, Cevennes

1280 Mme. de Sevigne (writer)

1996. National Parks. Multicoloured.
3318 3f. Type **1278** 1·00 60
3319 4f.40 Lammergeier and saxifrage, Mercantour 1·50 95
3320 4f.40 Ibex and gentian, Vanoise 1·50 95
See also Nos. 3380/3.

1996. Europa. Famous Women.
3325 **1280** 3f. multicoloured 1·00 70

1281 Test Tubes and Flower held with Tweezers

1996. 50th Anniv of National Institute for Agronomic Research.
3326 **1281** 3f.80 multicoloured 1·30 90

1282 Joan of Arc's Cottage, Domremy la Pucelle, Vosges

1996. 75th Anniv (1995) of Canonization of Joan of Arc.
3327 **1282** 4f.50 multicoloured 1·60 85

1283 Fishes, Sea and Coastline

1996. 20th Anniv of Ramoge Agreement on Environmental Protection of the Mediterranean.
3328 **1283** 3f. multicoloured 1·10 50

1284 Notre-Dame de Clermont and the Jacquemart (Cathedral clock)

1996. Federation of French Philatelic Societies Congress, Clermont-Ferrand.
3329 **1284** 3f. green, brown & red 1·00 55

1996. Tourist Publicity. As T **490**.
3330 3f. multicoloured 1·00 55
3331 3f. multicoloured 1·00 55
3332 3f.80 brown and mauve 1·20 80
3333 4f.50 multicoloured 1·50 85
DESIGN—HORIZ: 3f. (No. 3330), Bitche Castle, Moselle; 3f. (No. 3331), Sanguinaries Islands, Corsica; 3f.80, Cloisters, Thoronet Abbey, Var; 4f.50, Detail of trompe l'oeil by Casimir Vicario, Chambery Cathedral.

1285 Lens

1286 Throwing the Discus

1996. World Cup Football Championship, France (1998) (1st issue). Host Cities. Multicoloured.
3335 3f. Type **1285** 1·00 55
3336 3f. Montpellier 1·00 55
3337 3f. Saint-Etienne 1·00 55
3338 3f. Toulouse 1·00 55
See also Nos. 3401/4, 3464/5 and 3472.

1996. Centenary of Modern Olympic Games.
3339 **1286** 3f. multicoloured 1·00 55

1287 Marette

1288 Diesel Railcar Set

1996. 12th Death Anniv of Jacques Marette (journalist and politician).
3340 **1287** 4f.40 lilac 1·50 90

1996. Centenary of Ajaccio–Vizzavona Railway, Corsica.
3341 **1288** 3f. multicoloured 1·00 55

1289 Basilica

1996. Centenary of Our Lady of Fourviere Basilica, Lyon.
3342 **1289** 3f. black and yellow 1·00 50

1290 Baptism of Clovis (illus from "Grandes Chroniques de France")

1291 Arsene Lupin (Maurice Leblanc)

1996. Inauguration of Committee for Commemoration of Origins: from Gaul to France. 1500th Anniv of Baptism of Clovis.
3343 **1290** 3f. multicoloured 1·00 50

1996. Red Cross Fund. Heroes of Crime Novels. Multicoloured.
3344 3f.+60c. Rocambole (Pierre Ponson du Terrail) 1·20 1·20
3345 3f.+60c. Type **1291** 1·20 1·20
3346 3f.+60c. Joseph Rouletabille (Gaston Leroux) 1·20 1·20
3347 3f.+60c. Fantomas (Pierre Souvestre and Marcel Allain) 1·20 1·20
3348 3f.+60c. Commissioner Maigret (Georges Simenon) 1·20 1·20
3349 3f.+60c. Nestor Burma (Leo Malet) 1·30 1·10

1292 School Building

1293 Children of Different Nations

1996. Bicentenary of Henri IV School, Paris.
3350 **1292** 4f.50 blue, brn & grn 1·50 85

1996. 50th Anniv of UNICEF.
3351 **1293** 4f.50 multicoloured 1·50 85

1294 Iena Palace (headquarters)

1295 Headquarters, Paris

1996. 50th Anniv of Economic and Social Council.
3352 **1294** 3f. black, red & blue 1·00 50

1996. 50th Anniv of UNESCO.
3353 **1295** 3f.80 multicoloured 1·20 80

1296 Magnifying Glass over Eiffel Tower

1297 "Woman"

1996. 50th Anniv of Autumn Stamp Show, Paris.
3354 **1296** 3f. multicoloured 1·00 65

1996. 50th Anniv of Creation of French Overseas Departments of Martinique, Guadeloupe, Guiana and La Reunion.
3355 **1297** 3f. multicoloured 1·00 55

1298 Snowman and Polar Bear in Hot-air Balloon

1996. Red Cross Fund. Christmas.
3356 **1298** 3f.+60c. mult 1·10 1·00

1299 Temple, Delphi

1996. 150th Anniv of French School in Athens.
3357 **1299** 3f. multicoloured 1·00 55

1300 Malraux

1996. 20th Death Anniv of Andre Malraux (writer and politician).
3358 **1300** 3f. blue 1·00 50

1301 Clapperboard, Camera and Golden Palm

1996. 50th Int Film Festival, Cannes.
3359 **1301** 3f. multicoloured 1·00 50

1302 New Building

1996. Inauguration of New National Library Building, Paris.
3360 **1302** 3f. yellow, blue & red 1·00 50

1303 Mitterrand

1304 Wire Figures

1997. Francois Mitterrand (President, 1981–95) Commemoration.
3361 **1303** 3f. multicoloured 1·00 50

1997. "Participatory Innovation" (suggestions schemes).
3362 **1304** 3f. multicoloured 1·00 50

1305 Detail of Building

1997. 20th Anniv of Georges Pompidou National Centre of Art and Culture.
3363 **1305** 3f. multicoloured 1·00 50

1306 "bonne fete" (Happy Holiday)

1997. Greetings stamps. Multicoloured.
3364 3f. Type **1306** 1·00 50
3365 3f. "joyeux anniversaire" (Happy Birthday) 1·00 50

1307 New Building, Marne-la-Vallee

1997. 250th Anniv of National School of Bridges and Highways.
3366 **1307** 3f. multicoloured 1·00 50

1308 Gateway and Buildings

1997. National Historic Landmark Status of Former Penal Colony, Saint-Laurent-du-Maroni, French Guiana.
3367 **1308** 3f. multicoloured 1·00 50

1997. Art. As T **491**.
3368 6f.70 Fresco (detail), St. Nicholas's Church, Tavant (Indre et Loire) (vert) 2·20 1·50
3369 6f.70 Abstract (Bernard Moninot) 2·20 1·50
3370 6f.70 "The Thumb" (sculpture, Cesar Baldaccini) (vert) 2·20 1·70
3371 6f.70 "Grapes and Pomegranates" (Jean Baptiste Chardin) 2·20 1·70

1309 "Mouchon" type

1310 "Puss in Boots" (engraving by Gustav Dore)

1997. Stamp Day. 97th Anniv of Louis-Eugene Mouchon's Design.
3374 **1309** 3f. blue, mauve & silver 1·60 1·70
3372 3f.+60c. blue, mauve and silver 1·20 1·20

1997. Tourist Publicity. As T **490**.
3375 3f. emerald, dp green & grn 1·00 45
3376 3f. green, red and orange 1·00 45
3377 3f. brown, blue and green 1·00 50
3378 3f. brown, choc & green 1·00 50
3379 3f. green, blue and brown 1·00 50
DESIGN—VERT: No. 3375, Millau, Aveyron; 3376, Buttress of "Calvary" and church, Guimiliau. HORIZ: No. 3377, Sable-sur-Sarthe; 3378, St. Maurice's Cathedral, Epinal; 3379, Sceaux estate.

1997. National Parks. As T **1278**. Mult.
3380 3f. Golden eagle and blue thistle, Ecrins 1·10 60
3381 3f. Racoon and La Soufriere (volcano), Guadeloupe 1·20 75

3382 4f.50 Manx shearwater and coves, Port-Cros 1·30 85
3383 4f.50 Chamois and mountain, Pyrenees 1·30 85

1997. Europa. Tales and Legends.
3384 **1310** 3f. blue 1·00 60

1311 Teenager "flying" Stamp

1997. "Philexjeunes 97" Youth Stamp Exhibition, Nantes.
3385 **1311** 3f. multicoloured 1·50 1·20

1312 Envelope writing Letter

1997. The Journey of a Letter. Multicoloured. Ordinary or self-adhesive gum.
3386 3f. Type **1312** 1·80 1·30
3387 3f. Smiling letter climbing up to post box 1·30 1·20
3388 3f. Letter as van 1·80 1·20
3389 3f. Letters holding hands and postman carrying letter 1·80 1·20
3390 3f. Girl kissing letter 1·80 1·20
3391 3f. Girl reading long letter 1·30 65

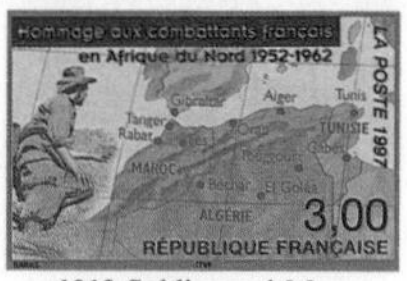

1313 Soldier and Map

1997. French Army Operations in North Africa, 1952–62.
3398 **1313** 3f. multicoloured 1·00 50

1314 Palace of Versailles (½-size illustration)

1997. 70th Federation of French Philatelic Societies Congress, Versailles.
3399 **1314** 3f. multicoloured 1·20 75

1315 Chateau du Plessis-Bourre

1997.
3400 **1315** 4f.40 multicoloured 1·30 70

1997. World Cup Football Championship, France (1998) (2nd issue). Host Cities. As T **1285**. Multicoloured.
3401 3f. Lyon 1·00 50
3402 3f. Marseille 1·00 50
3403 3f. Nantes 1·00 50
3404 3f. Paris 1·20 55

1316 Detail of Fresco

1997. Restoration of Frescoes in St. Eutrope's Church, Les Salles-Lavauguyon.
3405 **1316** 4f.50 multicoloured 1·50 70

1317 St. Martin (from Tours Missal)

1997. 1600th Death Anniv of St. Martin, Bishop of Tours.
3406 **1317** 4f.50 multicoloured 1·50 75

1318 "Marianne of 14 July"

1319 Rowers

1997. No value expressed.
3407 **1318** (3f.) red 1·00 40

1997.
3415 **1318** 10c. brown 10 10
3416 20c. green 10 15
3417 50c. violet 20 20
3417a 50c. red 25 20
3418 1f. orange 35 25
3419 2f. blue 70 35
3420 2f.70 green 90 35
3423 3f.50 green 1·10 50
3425 3f.80 blue 1·20 65
3427 4f.20 red 1·40 65
3428 4f.40 blue 1·60 75
3429 4f.50 mauve 1·60 60
3430 5f. blue 1·70 65
3431 6f.70 green 2·30 80
3432 10f. violet 3·25 1·10
MS3439 (a) Nos. 3415/19, 3430 and 3432; (b) Nos. 3407, 3420/9 and 3431 12·00 12·00

1997. World Rowing Championships, Lake Aiguebelette, Savoie.
3440 **1319** 3f. mauve, bl & red 1·00 45

1320 Sailors and Privateer Ship

1997. Basque Corsairs.
3441 **1320** 3f. multicoloured 1·00 50

1321 Horse-drawn Fish Cart

1997. Fresh Fish Merchants from Boulogne.
3442 **1321** 3f. green, violet & blue 1·00 50

1322 Kudara Kannon (statue from Horyu Temple, Nara) and Japanese Cultural Centre, Paris

1997. Japan Year.
3443 **1322** 4f.90 blue, orge & blk 1·60 1·10

1323 Contest

1997. World Judo Championships, Paris.
3444 **1323** 3f. multicoloured 1·00 50

1324 Emblem

1997. Sar-Lor-Lux (Saarland–Lorraine–Luxembourg) European Region.
3445 **1324** 3f. multicoloured 1·00 50

1325 College and King Francois I (founder)

1326 Team with Coloured Ribbons

1997. Le College de France.
3446 **1325** 4f.40 green, brn & blk 1·40 85

1997. French Movement for Quality.
3447 **1326** 4f.50 multicoloured 1·40 90

1327 Lancelot (Chretien de Troyes)

1997. Red Cross Fund. Literary Heroes. Multicoloured.
3448 3f.+60c. Type **1327** 1·20 1·30
3449 3f.+60c. Pardaillan (Michel Zevaco) 1·20 1·30
3450 3f.+60c. D'Artagnan ("The Three Musketeers" by Alexandre Dumas) 1·20 1·30
3451 3f.+60c. Cyrano de Bergerac (Edmond Rostand) 1·20 1·30
3452 3f.+60c. Captain Fracasse (Theophile Gautier) 1·20 1·30
3453 3f.+60c. Lagardere as Le Bossu (Paul Feval) 1·20 1·30

1328 Teddy Bear with Gifts in Spaceship

1329 Mouse giving Gift to Cat

1997. Red Cross Fund. Christmas.
3454 **1328** 3f.+60c. mult 1·20 1·20

1997. "Best Wishes".
3455 **1329** 3f. multicoloured 1·00 50

1330 Breguet 14 Biplane

1997. Air.
3456 **1330** 20f. multicoloured 6·75 4·25

1331 Teddy Bear holding Toy Windmill

1997. Protection of Abused Children Campaign.
3457 **1331** 3f. multicoloured 1·00 50

1332 Flying Postman

1997. "Best Wishes".
3458 **1332** 3f. multicoloured 1·00 50

1333 Cross of Lorraine on Map of France and Leclerc

1997. 50th Death Anniv of Marshal Leclerc.
3459 **1333** 3f. multicoloured 1·00 50

1334 "Marianne of 14 July" and Emblem

1997. "Philexfrance 99" International Stamp Exhibition, Paris.
3460 **1334** 3f. red and blue 1·20 65

1335 Carving and Buildings

1997. Millenary of Foundation of Moutier D'Ahun Monastery, Creuse.
3461 **1335** 4f.40 multicoloured 1·60 95

1336 Debre

1998. 2nd Death Anniv of Michel Debre (Prime Minister, 1958–62).
3462 **1336** 3f. black, blue & red 1·00 50

1337 Anniversary Emblem

1338 Cherub with Letter and Flowers

1998. Bicentenary of National Assembly.
3463 **1337** 3f. red and blue 1·00 50

1998. World Cup Football Championship, France (3rd issue). Host Cities. As T **1285**. Multicoloured.
3464 3f. Bordeaux 1·00 55
3465 3f. Saint-Denis, Paris 1·00 55
MS3466 148 × 140 mm. Nos. 3335/8, 3401/4 and 3464/5 9·00 9·00

1998. St. Valentine's Day.
3467 **1338** 3f. multicoloured 1·00 50

1339 Mediator and People

1998. 25th Anniv of Mediator of the Republic (ombudsman).
3468 **1339** 3f. multicoloured 1·00 50

1340 "Blanc" Type

1341 Football

1998. Stamp Day. 98th Anniv of Joseph Blanc's Design.
3470 **1340** 3f. red, grn & silver . . 3·25 3·25
3469 3f.+60c. red, green and silver . . . . 1·20 1·10

1998. World Cup Football Championship, France (4th issue). Ordinary or self-adhesive gum.
3472 **1341** 3f. multicoloured . . . 1·00 50
MS3474 No. 3472 plus 7 labels showing the World Cup mascot demonstrating various shots . . 3·00 3·00

1342 Stock 1343 "Happy Birthday"

1998. 50th Death Anniv of Father Franz Stock (wartime prison chaplain).
3475 **1342** 4f.50 blue . . . . . . 1·40 1·00

1998. Greeting Stamp.
3476 **1343** 3f. multicoloured . . . 1·00 50

1344 Citeaux Abbey

1998. 900th Anniv of Founding of Citeaux Abbey.
3477 **1344** 3f. multicoloured . . . 1·00 50

1345 Mulhouse, 1798

1998. Bicentenary of Union of Mulhouse with France.
3478 **1345** 3f. multicoloured . . . 1·00 50

1346 Sub-prefect's Residence, Saint-Pierre

1998. Reunion's Architectural Heritage.
3479 **1346** 3f. multicoloured . . . 1·00 50

1347 "The Return"

1998. Birth Centenary of Rene-Ghislain Magritte (painter).
3480 **1347** 3f. multicoloured . . . 1·00 55

1348 King Henri IV

1998. 400th Anniv of Edict of Nantes.
3481 **1348** 4f.50 multicoloured . . 1·50 95

1349 Slave wearing Cap of Liberty

1998. 150th Anniv of Abolition of Slavery by France.
3482 **1349** 3f. multicoloured . . . 1·00 50

1998. Art. As T **491**. Multicoloured.
3483 6f.70 "The Crusaders' Arrival in Constantinople" (detail, Eugene Delacroix) (vert) 2·20 1·70
3484 6f.70 "Spring" (Pablo Picasso) . . . . 2·20 1·60
3485 6f.70 "Nine Idiot Bachelors" (Marcel Duchamp) . . . 2·20 1·70
3486 6f.70 "Vision after the Sermon" (Paul Gaugin) 2·20 1·70

1998. Tourist Publicity. As T **490**.
3487 3f. multicoloured . . . . . 1·00 55
3488 3f. multicoloured . . . . . 1·00 50
3489 3f. green, blue and cream 1·00 50
3490 3f. multicoloured . . . . . 1·00 50
3491 4f.40 multicoloured . . . . 1·50 1·00
DESIGNS—As Type **490**: No. 3487, Le Gois Causeway, Noirmoutiers Island; 3489, Crussol Chateau, Ardeche; 3490, Liberty Tower, Saint-Die, Vosges. 26 × 38 mm: No. 3488, Bay of Somme. 26 × 36 mm: No. 3491, Mantes-la-Jolie collegiate church, Yvelines.

1350 Dove Carrying Letter to Noah's Ark 1351 Figure with Butterfly Wings

1998. History of the Letter. Multicoloured. Ordinary or self-adhesive gum.
3492 3f. Type **1350** . . . . . . 1·80 95
3493 3f. Egyptian carving tablet 1·80 95
3494 3f. Ancient Greek carrying letter from Marathon to Athens . . . . 1·80 95
3495 3f. Knight on horseback carrying letter and pen . . 1·80 95
3496 3f. Man writing with quill 1·80 95
3497 3f. Spaceman posting letter 1·80 95

1998. Cent of League of Human Rights.
3504 **1351** 4f.40 multicoloured . . 1·50 80

1352 Collet

1998. 47th Death Anniv of Henri Collet (composer).
3505 **1352** 4f.50 black & stone . . 1·50 85

1353 Statue of Jean Bart, Cathedral and "Sandettie II" (light-ship)

1998. Federation of French Philatelic Societies Congress, Dunkirk.
3506 **1353** 3f. red, orange & blue 1·00 45

1354 Mont Saint Michel 1355 Pan playing Flute (Festival of Music)

1998.
3507 **1354** 3f. multicoloured . . . 1·00 50

1998. Europa. National Festivals.
3508 **1355** 3f. multicoloured . . . 1·00 50

1998. France, World Cup Football Champion. As No. 3472 but additionally inscribed "Champion du Monde FRANCE".
3509 3f. multicoloured . . . . . 1·00 50

1356 Potez 25 Biplane

1998. Air.
3510 **1356** 30f. multicoloured . . . 10·50 8·75

1357 Convolvulus 1358 Mallarme

1998. Precancels. Flowers. Multicoloured.
3511 1f.87 Type **1357** 65 60
3512 2f.18 Poppy 95 90
3513 4f.66 Violet . . . . 1·70 1·70
3514 7f.11 Buttercup . . . . . . 1·90 2·00

1998. Death Centenary of Stephane Mallarme (poet).
3515 **1358** 4f.40 multicoloured . . 1·40 1·00

1359 Balloon and Early Airplane 1360 The Little Prince

1998. Centenary of Aero Club of France.
3516 **1359** 3f. multicoloured . . . 1·00 50

1998. "Philexfrance 99" International Stamp Exhibition, Paris (1st issue). "The Little Prince" (novel) by Antoine de Saint-Exupery. Multicoloured.
3517 3f. Type **1360** . . . . . . 1·20 80
3518 3f. On wall watching snake (vert) . . . . 1·00 70
3519 3f. On planet (vert) . . . . 1·00 70
3520 3f. Watering flower (vert) . . 1·00 70
3521 3f. On hillside with fox . . 1·00 70
MS3522 111 × 157 mm. Nos. 3517/21 (sold at 25f.) . . . . 7·50 7·50
See also No. **MS**3576.

1361 Hall of Supreme Harmony, Forbidden City, Peking, China

1998. Cultural Heritage. Multicoloured.
3523 3f. Type **1361** . . . . . . 1·00 50
3524 4f.90 Louvre Palace, Paris 1·50 1·00

1362 Violin and Ballet Dancer

1998. National Opera House, Paris.
3525 **1362** 4f.50 multicoloured . . 1·40 95

1363 Camargue

1998. Horses. Multicoloured.
3526 2f.70 Type **1363** 95 55
3527 3f. French trotter . . . . . 1·00 50
3528 3f. Pottok . . . . 1·00 50
3529 4f.50 Ardennais . . . . . . 1·50 90

1364 Dion-Bouton and Racing Cars

1998. Centenary of Paris Motor Show.
3530 **1364** 3f. multicoloured . . . 90 55

1365 Marianne and Flag 1366 Romy Schneider

1998. 40th Anniv of Constitution of Fifth Republic.
3531 **1365** 3f. multicoloured . . . 1·00 50

1998. Film Stars. Multicoloured.
3532 3f.+60c. Type **1366** . . . . 1·30 1·30
3533 3f.+60c. Simone Signoret . . 1·30 1·40
3534 3f.+60c. Jean Gabin . . . . 1·30 1·40
3535 3f.+60c. Louis de Funes . . 1·30 1·40
3536 3f.+60c. Bernard Blier . . . 1·30 1·40
3537 3f.+60c. Lino Ventura . . . 1·30 1·40

1367 State Flags

1998. 80th Anniv of Signing of First World War Armistice.
3538 **1367** 3f. multicoloured . . . 1·00 50

1368 Flora and Fauna, Child and Emblem

1998. 50th Anniv of International Union for the Conservation of Nature and Natural Resources.
3539 **1368** 3f. multicoloured . . . 1·00 50

1369 Elf on Christmas Bauble 1370 Father Christmas Snowboarding

1998. Red Cross Fund. Christmas.
3540 **1369** 3f.+60c. mult . . . . . 1·20 95

1998. Christmas and New Year. Multicoloured.
3541 3f. Type **1370** (violet background) . . . . . . 1·10 45
3542 3f. Decorated house (daytime) . . . . 1·10 45
3543 3f. Type **1370** (bright yellow background) . . . . . . 1·10 45
3544 3f. Decorated house (night-time) . . . . 1·10 45
3545 3f. Type **1370** (green background) . . . . . . 1·10 45

1371 Child expressing Ambition and People of Different Nations

1998. Medecins sans Frontieres (volunteer medical and relief organization).

3546 **1371** 3f. multicoloured . . . 1·00 55

1372 Architectural Drawing

1998. Construction of New European Parliament Building, Strasbourg (designed by Architecture Studio Europe).

3547 **1372** 3f. multicoloured . . . 1·00 55

1373 Rene Cassin, Eleanor Roosevelt and Palais de Chaillot

1998. 50th Anniv of Universal Declaration of Human Rights. Multicoloured.

3548 3f. Type **1373** . . . . . . 1·00 50

3549 3f. Globe and people of different races . . . . . 1·00 50

1374 Radium

1998. Centenary of Discovery of Radium by Marie and Pierre Curie and 50th Anniv of ZOE Reactor, Chatillon.

3550 **1374** 3f. multicoloured . . . 1·00 50

1375 1849 Ceres Design

1376 Euro Symbol

1999. 150th Anniv of First French Postage Stamp (1st issue).

3551 **1375** 3f. black and red . . . 4·00 3·00

3552 – 3f. black and red . . . 95 35

DESIGN: No. 3552, As Type **1375** but with stamp and text transposed.

See also No. 3596.

1999. Introduction of the Euro (European currency). Ordinary or self-adhesive gum.

3553 **1376** 3f. red and blue 95 40

No. 3553 is denominated both in French francs and in euros.

1377 Open Hands

1378 Flags of France and Israel

1999. 150th Anniv of Public Welfare Hospitals of Paris (administration of Paris health services).

3555 **1377** 3f. blue, mve & grn . . 1·10 50

1999. 50th Anniv of Diplomatic Relations between France and Israel.

3556 **1378** 4f.40 multicoloured . . 1·50 1·00

1379 Heart

1999. St. Valentine's Day. Multicoloured. Ordinary and self-adhesive gum.

3557 3f. Type **1379** . . . . 1·30 55

3558 3f. Heart-shaped rose . . . 1·30 55

1999. Art. As T **491**.

3561 6f.70 brown and orange . . 2·40 2·00

3562 6f.70 multicoloured . . . . 2·20 1·70

3563 6f.70 multicoloured . . . . 2·40 1·90

3564 6f.70 multicoloured . . . . 2·40 1·90

DESIGNS—VERT: No. 3561, "St. Luke the Evangelist" (sculpture, Jean Goujon); 3562, Stained glass window (Arnaud de Moles), Chapelle de la Compassion, Auch Cathedral; 3564, "Charles I, King of England" (Anton van Dyck). HORIZ: No. 3563, "Water Lilies, Effect of Evening" (Claude Monet).

1380 Flowers on Map of France

1382 Asterix

1381 "The Capture of Europa" (mosaic from Byblos)

1999. 33rd Population Census.

3565 **1380** 3f. multicoloured . . . 1·10 55

1999. Cultural Heritage of Lebanon.

3566 **1381** 4f.40 multicoloured . . 1·50 1·00

1999. Stamp Day. Asterix the Gaul (cartoon character) by Albert Uderzo and Rene Goscinny.

3567 **1382** 3f. multicoloured . . . 95 50

3569 3f.+60c. mult . . . . . 2·10 1·60

MS3570 102×77 mm. No. 3569 1·50 1·50

1383 Council Emblem on World Map

1999. 50th Anniv of Council of Europe.

3571 **1383** 3f. multicoloured . . . 1·00 50

1384 Two Doves and Hearts (wedding)

1999. Greetings Stamps. Multicoloured.

3572 3f. Type **1384** . . . . . . 1·00 50

3573 3f. "Thank you" in different languages . . . . 1·50 1·00

3574 3f. Stork carrying blue bundle ("It's a boy") . . 1·00 50

3575 3f. Stork carrying pink bundle ("It's a girl") . . . 1·00 50

1385 "Venus de Milo" (statue)

1999. "Philexfrance 99" International Stamp Exhibition, Paris (2nd issue). Art. Sheet 159×111 mm containing T **1385** and similar designs.

MS3576 5f. sepia (Type **1385**); 5f. multicoloured ("Mona Lisa" (Leonardo da Vinci)) (37×49 mm); 10f. multicoloured ("Liberty guiding the People" (Eugene Delacroix)) (36×37 mm) (sold at 50f.) . . . . 25·00 25·00

1386 Branches and Hand reaching for Star

1387 Richard the Lion Heart (from "Historia Anglorum")

1999. European Parliament Elections.

3577 **1386** 3f. multicoloured . . . 1·00 50

1999. 800th Death Anniv of King Richard I of England.

3578 **1387** 3f. multicoloured . . . 1·00 50

1388 Airbus A300-B4

1999. Air.

3579 **1388** 15f. multicoloured . . . 3·50 3·50

1389 Dieppe Castle

1999. Tourist Publicity.

3580 **1389** 3f. multicoloured . . . 1·00 50

3581 – 3f. multicoloured . . . 1·00 60

3582 – 3f. multicoloured . . . 1·00 50

3583 – 3f. multicoloured . . . 1·00 50

DESIGNS—As T **949**: No. 3581, Haut-Koenigsbourg Castle, Lower Rhine. As T **490**: No. 3582, Place des Ecritures, Figeac; 3583, Arnac-Pompadour Chateau.

No. 3583 is denominated in both francs and euros.

1390 The Camargue

1999. Europa. Parks and Gardens.

3584 **1390** 3f. multicoloured . . . 1·00 50

1391 Cake and Music Notes ("Happy Birthday")

1999. Greetings Stamps. Multicoloured.

3585 3f. Type **1391** . . . . . . 1·00 50

3586 3f. Seagull and sun wearing sunglasses ("Have a nice holiday") . . . 1·00 50

3587 3f. Float on water ("Long live holidays") (vert) . . . 1·00 50

1392 St. Pierre and Mt. Pelee

1999. Heritage of Martinique.

3588 **1392** 3f. multicoloured . . . 1·00 50

1393 "Noctuelles" Dish (detail, Emile Galle)

1999. Nancy School (art movement).

3589 **1393** 3f. multicoloured . . . 1·00 50

1394 "Mme. Alfred Carriere"

1999. Old Roses. Sheet 111×160 mm containing T **1394** and similar vert designs. Multicoloured.

MS3590 3f. Type **1394**; 4f.50 "Mme. Caroline Testout"; 4f.50 "La France" . . . . 4·50 4·50

1395 Ruins, Grape Vines and Seal

1999. 800th Anniv of Granting of City Rights to Saint-Emilion and 50th Anniv of Re-institution of the Jurade (controllers of St.-Emilion wine appellation).

3591 **1395** 3f.80 multicoloured . . 1·20 1·00

1396 The Mint, Paris

1999.

3592 **1396** 4f.50 red, blue & black 1·50 95

1397 Model Girls

1398 Sun and Doves in Mosaic

1999. Birth Bicentenary of Countess de Segur (children's writer).

3593 **1397** 3f. multicoloured . . . 1·00 50

1999. Post Office "Pleasure to Welcome" Customer Campaign.

3594 **1398** 3f. multicoloured . . . 1·00 65

1399 Caillie

1999. Birth Bicentenary of Rene Caillie (explorer).

3595 **1399** 4f.50 violet, yellow and orange . . . . 1·50 1·00

1400 1849 Ceres Design

1999. 150th Anniv of First French Postage Stamp (2nd issue).
3596 **1400** 6f.70 multicoloured . . 1·80 1·30

DENOMINATION. From No. 3597 French stamps are denominated both in francs and in euros. As no cash for the latter is in circulation, the catalogue continues to use the franc value.

1401 Spinning Globe

1999. Year 2000.
3597 **1401** 3f. multicoloured . . . 1·00 55

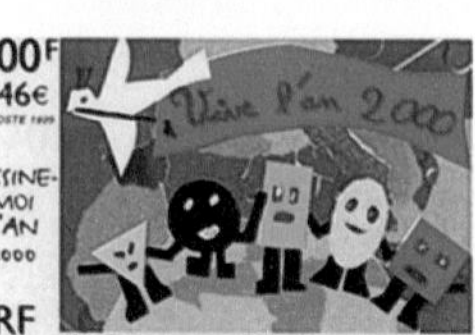

1402 Winning Entry by Morgane Toulouse

1999. "Design a Stamp for Year 2000" Children's Drawing Contest.
3598 **1402** 3f. multicoloured . . . 1·00 50

1403 Total Eclipse

1999. Solar Eclipse (11 August).
3599 **1403** 3f. multicoloured . . . 75 65

1404 "Simon Bolivar" (Venezuelan cadet barque)

1999. "Armada of the Century", Rouen. Sailing Ships. Multicoloured.
3600 1f. Type **1404** 35 40
3601 1f. "Iskra" (Polish cadet ship) 35 40
3602 1f. "Statsraad Lehmkuhl" (barque) 35 40
3603 1f. "Asgard II" (cadet brigantine) 35 40
3604 1f. "Belle Poule" (sail frigate) 35 40
3605 1f. "Belem" (barque) . . . 35 40
3606 1f. "Amerigo Vespucci" (cadet ship) 35 40
3607 1f. "Sagres" (cadet barque) 35 40
3608 1f. "Europa" (barque) . . . 35 40
3609 1f. "Cuauhtemoc" (barque) 35 40

1405 "School, 1956" (Robert Doisneau)

1999. French Photographers. Multicoloured.
3610 3f.+60c. Type **1405** . . . . 1·30 1·40
3611 3f.+60c. "St. James's Tower, View of Notre Dame, 1936" (Gilberte Brassai) 1·30 1·40
3612 3f.+60c. "Renee on the way to Paris, Aix-les-Bains" (Jacques Henri Lartigue) 1·30 1·40
3613 3f.+60c. "Hyeres, France, 1932" (Henri Cartier-Bresson) . . . . 1·30 1·40
3614 3f.+60c. "Travelling Salesman" (Eugene Atget) 1·30 1·40
3615 3f.+60c. "Debureau at the Camera" (Nadar) . . . . 1·30 1·40

1406 Players

1999. 4th World Cup Rugby Championship, Great Britain, Ireland and France.
3616 **1406** 3f. multicoloured . . . 1·20 70

1407 Ozanam (after Louis Janmot)

1999. 146th Death Anniv of Frederic Ozanam (historian and social campaigner).
3617 **1407** 4f.50 deep green, brown and red . . . . . . 1·30 70

1408 People holding Hands

1999. 50th Anniv of Emmaus Movement (welfare organization).
3618 **1408** 3f. multicoloured . . . 1·00 50

1409 Chartreuse Cat

1999. Domestic Pets. Multicoloured.
3619 2f.70 Type **1409** . . . . . 1·00 60
3620 3f. European tabby cat . . . 1·00 60
3621 3f. Pyrenean mountain dog 1·30 75
3622 4f.50 Brittany spaniel . . . 1·50 1·20

1410 Chopin (after George Sand)

1999. 150th Death Anniv of Frederic Chopin (composer).
3623 **1410** 3f.80 blue, deep violet and orange . . . . . 1·40 1·10

1411 Star playing Drum with Clock Face

1999. Red Cross Fund. New Year.
3624 **1411** 3f.+60c. mult . . . . . 1·40 1·10

1412 "2000"

1999. Year 2000. Multicoloured.
3625 3f. Type **1412** . . . . . . 1·00 55
3626 3f. Half-unwrapped parcel (vert) . . . . 1·00 55

1413 Metro Signs

1999. Centenary of Paris Metro.
3627 **1413** 3f. multicoloured . . . 1·00 55

1414 Column and Pediment

1999. Bicentenary of Council of State.
3628 **1414** 3f. blue and grey . . . 1·10 55

1415 San Juan de Salvamento and La Rochelle Lighthouses

2000. Reconstruction of San Juan de Salvamento Lighthouse, Staten Island.
3629 **1415** 3f. multicoloured . . . 1·00 60

1416 Snakes forming Heart **1417** Bank Entrance

2000. Yves St. Laurent (couturier). Multicoloured. Ordinary or self-adhesive gum.
3630 3f. Type **1416** . . . . . . 1·10 50
3631 3f. Woman's face . . . . . 1·00 50
MS3632 95 × 150 mm. Nos. 3630 × 3 and No. 3631 × 2 . . . . . . 5·25 5·25

2000. Bicentenary of Bank of France.
3635 **1417** 3f. multicoloured . . . 95 50

1418 Couzinet 70 *Arc en Ciel*

2000. Air.
3636 **1418** 50f. multicoloured . . . 15·00 15·00

1419 Emblem **1420** Tintin and Snowy

2000. Bicentenary of Prefectorial Corps.
3637 **1419** 3f. multicoloured . . . 1·00 50

2000. Art. As T **491**.
3638 6f.70 multicoloured (vert) 1·80 1·30
3639 6f.70 multicoloured (vert) 2·40 1·90
3640 6f.70 multicoloured (vert) 2·30 1·70
DESIGNS: No. 3638, Detail of "Venus and the Graces offering Gifts to a Young Girl" (Sandro Botticelli); 3639, "The Waltz" (sculpture, Camille Claudel); 3640, "Visage Rouge" (Gaston Chaissac).

2000. Tourist Publicity. As T **949**.
3642 3f. multicoloured 95 55
3643 3f. multicoloured 95 50
3644 3f. multicoloured 95 50
3645 3f. multicoloured . . . . . 1·00 50
DESIGNS: No. 3642, Carcassonne. As Type **490**: 37 × 27 mm—No. 3643, Saint Guilhem le Desert, Herault; 3644, Valley of the Lakes, Gerardmer. 36 × 23 mm—No. 3645, Ottmarsheim Abbey church.

2000. Tintin (cartoon character) by Georges Renu (Herge).
3646 **1420** 3f. multicoloured . . . 1·00 55
3648 3f.+60c. mult . . . . . 2·30 1·30
MS3649 101 × 76 mm. No. 3648 1·20 1·20

1421 Parliament Building

2000. Restoration of Breton Regional Parliament, Rennes.
3650 **1421** 3f. multicoloured . . . 95 50

1422 Periwinkle

2000.
3651 **1422** 4f.50 multicoloured . . 1·50 85

1423 "Congratulations"

2000. Greetings Stamp. Multicoloured.
3652 3f. Type **1423** . . . . . . 1·10 60
3653 3f. "bonnes vacances" . . . 95 50

1424 Football World Cup Trophy (France, World Champions, 1998) **1426** "Building Europe"

1425 Bugatti 35

2000. The Twentieth Century (1st series). Sporting Achievements. Sheet 185 × 245 mm containing five different 3f. designs as T **1424**, each × 2. Multicoloured.
MS3654 3f. Type **1424**; 3f. Marcel Cerdan (World Middleweight Champion, 1948); 3f. Carl Lewis (Olympic Gold medallist 100m, 200m, 100m relay and long jump, 1984) (vert); 3f. Charles Lindbergh and *Spirit of St. Louis* (First solo Atlantic crossing,1927); 3f. Jean-Claude Killy (Winter Olympic Gold medallist downhill, giant slalom and special slalom, 1968) (vert) . . . . 6·50 6·50

See also No. **MS**3687, **MS**3710, **MS**3756, **MS**3814 and **MS**3861.

2000. "Philexjeunes 2000" International Youth Stamp Exhibition, Annely. Vintage Cars. Multicoloured.
3655 1f. Type **1425** 45 45
3656 1f. Citroen Traction 45 45
3657 1f. Renault 4CV 45 40
3658 1f. Simca Chamord 45 45
3659 1f. Hispano Suiza K6 . . . 45 45
3660 2f. Volkswagen Beetle . . . 70 55
3661 2f. Cadillac 62 . . . . . . 70 55
3662 2f. Peugeot 203 . . . . . . 70 55
3663 2f. Citroen DS19 . . . . . 70 55
3664 2f. Ferrari 250 GTO 70 55

2000. Europa.
3665 **1426** 3f. multicoloured . . . 80 45

1427 Du Monceau

2000. 300th Birth Anniv of Henry-Louis Duhamel du Monceau (technologist and natural scientist).
3666 **1427** 4f.50 multicoloured . . 1·40 90

1428 Porte du Croux and Earthenware Jug
1429 Mountaineers

2000. 73rd French Philatelic Federation Congress, Nevers.
3667 **1428** 3f. multicoloured . . . 95 50

2000. 50th Anniv of French Ascent of Mt. Annapurna, Himalayas.
3668 **1429** 3f. multicoloured . . . 95 50

1430 *Agrias sardanapalus*

2000. National Museum of Natural History. Mult.
3669 2f.70 Type **1430** 95 50
3670 3f. Giraffe (vert) . . . . . 1·00 55
3671 3f. Allosaurus . . . . . . 1·00 55
3672 4f.50 *Tulipa lutea* (vert) . . 1·50 1·00
MS3673 110 × 160 mm. Nos. 3669/72 3·25 3·25

1431 Saint-Exupery
1432 Train

2000. Birth Centenary of Antoine de Saint-Exupery (aviator and writer).
3674 **1431** 3f. multicoloured . . . 95 50

2000. Centenary of the Yellow Train (Villefranch de Conflent–Latourde Card service), Cerdagne.
3675 **1432** 3f. multicoloured . . . 80 50

1433 "Folklores" and Characters

2000.
3676 **1433** 4f.50 multicoloured . . 1·50 75

1434 Cycling, Fencing and Relay

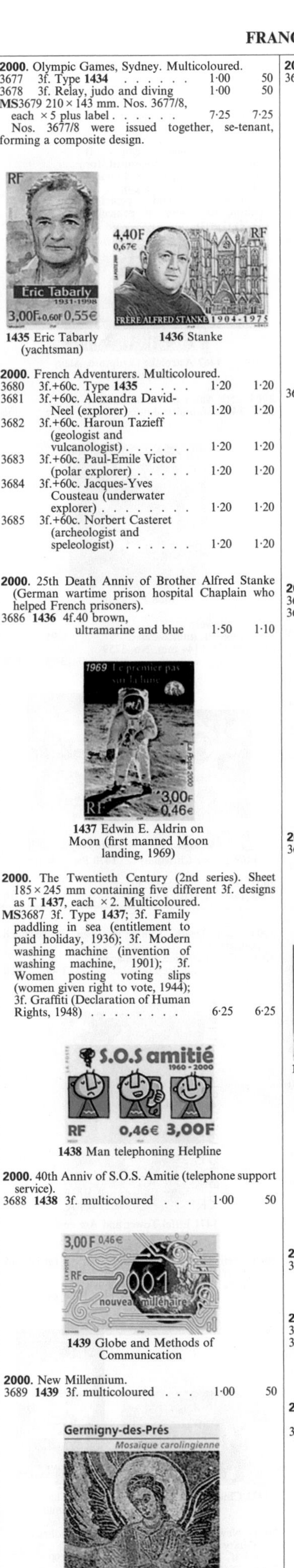

2000. Olympic Games, Sydney. Multicoloured.
3677 3f. Type **1434** . . . . . . 1·00 50
3678 3f. Relay, judo and diving 1·00 50
MS3679 210 × 143 mm. Nos. 3677/8, each × 5 plus label . . . . . . 7·25 7·25
Nos. 3677/8 were issued together, se-tenant, forming a composite design.

1435 Eric Tabarly (yachtsman)
1436 Stanke

2000. French Adventurers. Multicoloured.
3680 3f.+60c. Type **1435** . . . . 1·20 1·20
3681 3f.+60c. Alexandra David-Neel (explorer) . . . . . 1·20 1·20
3682 3f.+60c. Haroun Tazieff (geologist and vulcanologist) . . . . . . 1·20 1·20
3683 3f.+60c. Paul-Emile Victor (polar explorer) . . . . . 1·20 1·20
3684 3f.+60c. Jacques-Yves Cousteau (underwater explorer) . . . . 1·20 1·20
3685 3f.+60c. Norbert Casteret (archeologist and speleologist) . . . . . . 1·20 1·20

2000. 25th Death Anniv of Brother Alfred Stanke (German wartime prison hospital Chaplain who helped French prisoners).
3686 **1436** 4f.40 brown, ultramarine and blue 1·50 1·10

1437 Edwin E. Aldrin on Moon (first manned Moon landing, 1969)

2000. The Twentieth Century (2nd series). Sheet 185 × 245 mm containing five different 3f. designs as T **1437**, each × 2. Multicoloured.
MS3687 3f. Type **1437**; 3f. Family paddling in sea (entitlement to paid holiday, 1936); 3f. Modern washing machine (invention of washing machine, 1901); 3f. Women posting voting slips (women given right to vote, 1944); 3f. Graffiti (Declaration of Human Rights, 1948) . . . . 6·25 6·25

1438 Man telephoning Helpline

2000. 40th Anniv of S.O.S. Amitie (telephone support service).
3688 **1438** 3f. multicoloured . . . 1·00 50

1439 Globe and Methods of Communication

2000. New Millennium.
3689 **1439** 3f. multicoloured . . . 1·00 50

1440 Detail of Mosaic

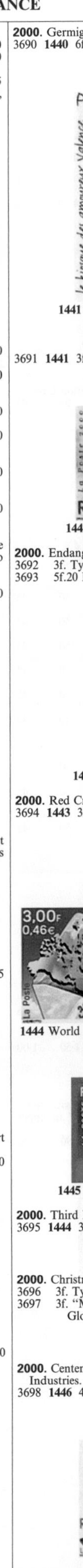

2000. Germigny-des-Pres Mosaic, Loire Valley.
3690 **1440** 6f.70 multicoloured . . 2·30 1·70

1441 Young Couple and Bandstand (R. Peynet)

2000.
3691 **1441** 3f. multicoloured . . . 1·20 50

1442 Brown Kiwi (New Zealand)

2000. Endangered Species. Multicoloured.
3692 3f. Type **1442** 90 40
3693 5f.20 Lesser kestrel (France) 1·50 1·10

1443 Toy Aeroplane and Gifts

2000. Red Cross Fund. New Year.
3694 **1443** 3f.+60c. mult . . . . . 1·10 90

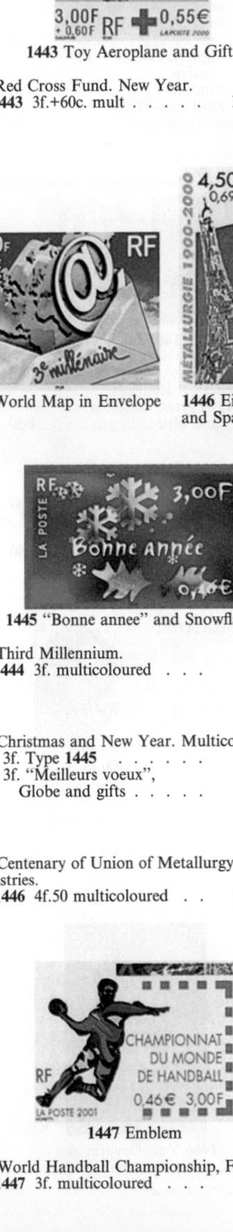

1444 World Map in Envelope
1446 Eiffel Tower and Space Rocket

1445 "Bonne annee" and Snowflakes

2000. Third Millennium.
3695 **1444** 3f. multicoloured . . . 95 50

2000. Christmas and New Year. Multicoloured.
3696 3f. Type **1445** 95 50
3697 3f. "Meilleurs voeux", Globe and gifts 95 50

2000. Centenary of Union of Metallurgy and Mining Industries.
3698 **1446** 4f.50 multicoloured . . 1·50 1·00

1447 Emblem

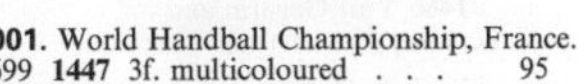

2001. World Handball Championship, France.
3699 **1447** 3f. multicoloured . . . 95 45

1448 Stone covered Heart

2001. St. Valentine's Day.
3700 **1448** 3f. multicoloured . . . 95 50
MS3701 136 × 143 mm. No. 3700 × 5 . . . . 4·00 4·00

2001. Art. As T **491**.
3702 6f.70 multicoloured . . . . 2·20 1·70
3703 6f.70 multicoloured . . . . 2·20 1·70
3704 6f.70 multicoloured . . . . 2·10 1·90
3705 6f.70 multicoloured . . . . 2·10 1·90
DESIGNS—Horiz: No. 3702, "The Peasant Dance" (Pieter Brugel the Elder); 3703, St. James of Compostela and Angel (mural, hospital of Order of St. John of Jerusalem, Toulouse), 3705, "Honfleur at Low Tide" (Johan Barthold Jongkind). VERT: 3704, "Yvette Guilbert singing Linger, Longer Loo" (Henri Toulouse-Lautrec).

1449 Gaston Lagaffe

2001. Gaston Lagaffe (cartoon character) by Andre Franquin.
3706 **1449** 3f. multicoloured . . . 1·00 50
3708 3f.+60c. multicoloured 2·20 1·40
MS3709 101 × 75 mm. No. 3708 1·20 1·20

1450 Nounours, Pimprenelle and Nicolas from "Bonne Nuit les Petits" (chilren's televison programme, 1965)

2001. The Twentieth Century (3rd series). Forms of Communication. Sheet 186 × 245 mm containing five different 3f. designs as T **1450**, each × 2. Multicoloured.
MS3710 3f. Type **1450**; 3f. Hand holding compact disc (development of analogue technology); 3f. The Little Miner and road sign (cinema advertising character created by Jean Mineur, 1950); 3f. Couple dancing and early radio (*Salut les Copians* (first broadcast by popular radio programme, 1959)); 3f. Baby, mobile phone and globe (development of digital mobile phone technology, 1991) . . . 7·25 7·25

1451 Flower ("merci")

2001. Greetings Stamps. Multicoloured.
3711 3f. Type **1451** 95 45
3712 3f. Teddy bear wearing bow tie ("c'est un garcon") . . 95 50
3713 3f. Teddy bear wearing yellow ribbon ("c'est une fille") 95 50
3714 4f.50 Two hearts ("oui") . . 1·50 1·20

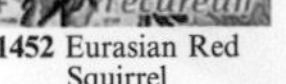

1452 Eurasian Red Squirrel
1453 Water Droplet and Globe

2001. Animals. Multicoloured.
3715 2f.70 Type **1452** 95 50
3716 3f. Roe deer (horiz) . . . . 1·00 55

3717 3f. West European hedgehog (horiz) . . . . 1·10 55
3718 4f.50 Stoat . . . . 1·50 95
MS3719 161 × 111 mm. Nos. 3715/18 3·00 3·00

2001. Tourist Publicity. As T **490**. Multicoloured.
3720 3f. Nogent-le-Rotrou (vert) 95 45
3721 3f. Besancon, Doubs 95 45
3722 3f. Calais 95 45
3723 3f. Chateau de Grignan, Drome 95 55

2001. Europa. Water Resources.
3724 **1453** 3f. multicoloured . . . 95 45

1454 Gardens (½-size illustration)

2001. Versailles Palace Gardens.
3725 **1454** 4f.40 multicoloured . . 1·50 1·30

1455 Lyon **1456** Claude Francois

2001.
3726 **1455** 3f. multicoloured . . . 95 45

2001. Singers. Multicoloured.
3727 3f. Type **1456** . . . . . . 1·00 60
3728 3f. Leo Ferre . . . . 1·00 60
3729 3f. Serge Gainsbourg . . . 1·00 60
3730 3f. Dalida . . . . 1·00 60
3731 3f. Michel Berger . . . . . 1·00 60
3732 3f. Barbara . . . . 1·00 60
MS3733 135 × 143 mm. Nos. 3727/32 (sold at 28f.) . . . . 7·25 7·25

1457 Craftsman, Wilson Bridge and St. Gatien Cathedral

2001. 74th French Philatelic Federation Congress, Tours.
3734 **1457** 3f. multicoloured . . . 95 45

1458 Vilar

2001. 30th Death Anniv of Jean Vilar (theatre director).
3735 **1458** 3f. multicoloured . . . 95 45

1459 Footprint in Sand

2001. Greetings Stamps. Holidays. Ordinary or self-adhesive gum.
3736 **1459** 3f. multicoloured . . . 95 50

1460 1 Euro Coin

2001. The European Currency.
3738 **1460** 3f. multicoloured . . . 95 45

1461 Caquot, Airship and Bridge

2001. 120th Birth Anniv of Albert Caquot (civil engineer).
3739 **1461** 4f.50 multicoloured . . 1·40 90

1462 Jigsaw Pieces

2001. Centenary of Freedom of Association Law.
3740 **1462** 3f. multicoloured . . . 95 45

1463 Eurostar Express Train

2001. Locomotives. Multicoloured.
3741 1f.50 Type **1463** 50 45
3742 1f.50 American 220 steam locomotive 50 45
3743 1f.50 Ae 6/8 "Crocodile" locomotive 50 45
3744 1f.50 Crampton steam locomotive 50 45
3745 1f.50 Garratt type 59 steam locomotive 50 45
3746 1f.50 Pacific Chapelon steam locomotive 50 45
3747 1f.50 LNER Class A4 steam locomotive No. 4468 *Mallard*, 1938, Great Britain 50 45
3748 1f.50 Capitole electric locomotive 50 45
3749 1f.50 Autorail 50 45
3750 1f.50 230 Class P8 type 230 steam locomotive 50 45

1464 Emblem

2001. 50th Anniv of United Nations High Commissioner for Refugees.
3751 **1464** 4f.50 green, magenta and blue . . . . . . 1·50 1·00

2001. No value expressed. As T **1318** but with "RF" in lower left corner and "LA POSTE" in upper right corner.
3752 (3.f) red 90 40

1465 Fermat and Mathematical Equations

2001. 400th Birth Anniv of Pierre de Fermat (mathematician).
3755 **1465** 4f.50 multicoloured . . 1·50 90

1466 Yuri Gagarin and Vostok 1 (first man in space, 1961)

2001. The Twentieth Century (4th issue). Science. Sheet 185 × 244 mm containing five different 3f. designs as T **1466**, each × 2. Multicoloured.
MS3756 3f. Type **1466**; 3f. Human body and DNA double helix (identification of DNA molecule, 1953); 3f. Hand holding credit card (development of chip card) (horiz); 3f. Laser treatment for correcting eye sight (development of laser technology); 3f. Bacteriologist and penicillin culture (discovery of penicillin, 1928) (horiz) . . . . 7·25 7·25

1467 Astrolabe (sculpture, Alain Le Boucher)

2001. 25th Anniv of Val-de-Reuil.
3757 **1467** 3f. multicoloured . . . 95 55

1468 Pumpkin

2001. Halloween.
3758 **1468** 3f. multcoloured . . . 95 55
MS3759 135 × 144 mm. No. 3759 × 5 . . . . 3·75 3·75

1469 Father Christmas **1470** Pierre-Bloch

2001. Red Cross Fund. Christmas.
3760 **1469** 3f.+60c. multicoloured 1·10 1·10

2001. 2nd Death Anniv of Jean Pierre-Bloch (politician).
3761 **1470** 4f.50 blue, ultramarine and deep blue . . . 1·40 1·20

1471 Eiffel Tower and Arc de Triomphe dancing

2001. Birth Centenary of Albert Decaris (artist and engraver).
3762 **1471** 3f. violet, brown and blue 85 70

1472 Children and Snowman **1473** Chaban-Delmas

2001. New Year. Multicoloured. Self-adhesive or ordinary gum.
3763 3f. Type **1472** 90 55
3764 3f. Children and wheelbarrow 90 55

2001. Jacques Chaban-Delmas (politician) Commemoration.
3767 **1473** 3f. multicoloured . . . 95 45

1474 Nejjarine Fountain, Fez, Morocco **1475** *Orchis insularis*

2001. French–Moroccan Cultural Heritage. Fountains. Multicoloured.
3768 3f. Type **1474** 95 50
3769 3f.80 Wallace Fountain, Paris . . . . 1·20 1·10

After the adoption by France of the euro currency on 1 January 2002, No. 3752 were sold at 46c.

2002. As T **1318** but with "RF" in lower left corner, "LAPOSTE" in upper right corner and values expressed in euros. (a) Sheet stamps.
3770 1c. yellow 10 10
3771 2c. brown 10 10
3772 5c. green 10 10
3773 10c. violet 20 15
3774 20c. orange 30 20
3775 41c. green 95 45
3776 50c. blue . . . . 1·80 55
3777 53c. green . . . . 1·50 60
3778 58c. blue 85 55
3778a 58c. green 90 20
3779 64c. orange 95 70
3780 67c. blue . . . . 1·30 75
3781 69c. mauve . . . . 1·00 50
3782 70c. green 95 15
3783 75c. blue . . . . 1·00 25
3784 90c. blue . . . . 1·20 30
3785 €1 turquoise . . . . . . 1·40 35
3786 €1.02 green . . . . . . 1·40 35
3787 €1.11 purple . . . . . . 1·50 40
3788 €1.90 purple . . . . . . 2·50 65
3789 €2 violet . . . . 2·75 70

(b) Coil stamp. (i) No Value expressed.
3790 (41c.) green . . . .
3791 (46c.) red 60 15

(ii).
3792 41c. green 55 15

(c) Miniature sheets. Two sheets, each 145 × 143 mm.
MS3794 (a) Nos. 3770/4, 3776, 3785 and 3789; (b) Nos. 3775, 3752, 3777/8, 3779/81 and 3789 . . . 13·50 13·50

2002. Orchids. Multicoloured.
3795 29c. Type **1475** . . . . . . 1·50 1·10
3796 33c. *Orphrys fuciflora* . . . 1·30 1·10
Nos. 3795/6 were only issued precancelled.

1476 Heart Shape in Landscape, New Caledonia

2002. St. Valentine's Day.
3797 **1476** 46c. multicoloured . . . 90 35
MS3798 135 × 142 mm. No. 3797 × 5 3·50 5·25

1477 Snowboarder **1478** Bosquet

2002. Winter Olympic Games, Salt Lake City, U.S.A.
3799 **1477** 46c. multicoloured . . . 1·00 35

2002. Art. Designs as T **491**. Multicoloured.
3800 €1.02 "The Kiss" (Gustav Klimt) . . . . 1·50 1·80
3801 €1.02 "The Dancers" (painting, Fernando Botero) . . . . 1·90 1·80

2002. 4th Death Anniv of Alain Bosquet (Anatole Bisk) (writer).
3804 **1478** 58c. brown, orange and blue . . . . 90 1·10

1479 Bee wearing Crown ("c'est une fille")

2002. Greetings Stamps. Multicoloured.
3805 46c. Type **1479** 90 35
3806 46c. Bee wearing cap ("c'est un garcon") 90 35
3807 69c. "Oui" in flowers . . . 1·20 1·10

1481 Elephant, Performers and Horse

1482 Boule, Bill and Birds

2002. Europa. Circus.
3808 **1481** 46c. multicoloured . . . 85 35

2002. Boule and Bill (cartoon characters) by Jean Roba. Multicoloured.
3809 46c. Type **1482** 85 40
3811 46c. + 9c. Boule, Bill and ball . . . . 1·10 1·40
MS3812 100 × 75 mm. As No. 3811 1·40 1·40

1483 Amphitheatre, Nimes

2002.
3813 **1483** 46c. multicoloured . . . 85 35

1484 Concorde (first flight, 1969)

2002. The Twentieth Century (5th series).Transport. Sheet 185 × 245 mm, containing five different 46c. designs as T **1484**, each × 2. Multicoloured.
MS3814 46c. Type **1484**; 46c. TGV train (high speed passenger train); 46c. "La Mobylette" (motorcycle) (vert); 46c. *France* (transatlantic passenger liner) (vert); 46c. 2CV (motor car) (vert) . . . . . . 13·50 11·50

1485 Matthew Flinders, Map of Australia and H.M.S. *Investigator* (ship of the line)

2002. France—Australia Joint Issue. Bicentenary of Nicolas Baudin–Matthew Flinders Meeting at Encounter Bay, Australia. Multicoloured.
3815 46c. Type **1485** 85 35
3816 79c. *Geographie* (corvette), map of Australia and Nicolas Baudin . . . . . 1·80 1·40

1486 La Charite-sur-Loire Church, Nievre

2002. UNESCO. World Heritage Site.
3817 **1486** 46c. multicoloured . . . 85 35

1487 Butterflies and Gift ("Anniversaire")

1488 Cyclists

2002. Greetings Stamps. Multicoloured.
3818 46c. Type **1487** 85 40
3819 46c. Bird and envelopes ("Invitation") 85 40

2002. 100th Paris–Roubaix Cycle Race.
3820 **1488** 46c. multicoloured . . . 85 70

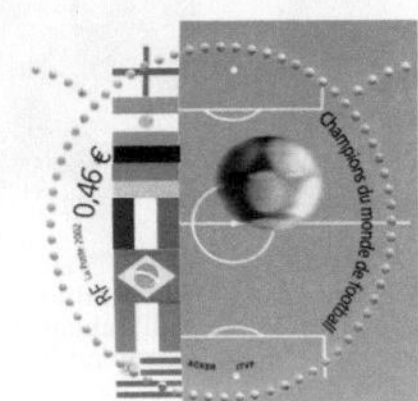

1489 Winners' Flags and Football

2002. World Cup Football Championship, Japan and South Korea. Multicoloured.
3821 46c. Type **1489** 85 40
3822 46c. Footballer 85 40
MS3823 143 × 210 mm. Nos. 3821/2, each × 5 . . . . 9·00 10·50

No. **MS**3823 was inscribed on the back, with the groups around the edge and with facilities for recording the results between the stamps, over the gum.

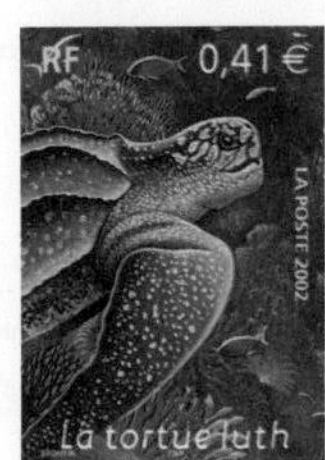

1490 Leatherback Turtle

2002. Animals. Multicoloured.
3824 41c. Type **1490** 70 40
3825 46c. Killer whale (horiz) . . 85 35
3826 46c. Bottle-nosed dolphin (horiz) 85 30
3827 69c. Common seal . . . . . 1·20 70
MS3828 109 × 160 mm. Nos. 3824/7 4·25 4·25

1491 Old Port, Marseille (½-size illustration)

2002. 75th French Federation of Philatelic Societies Congress, Marseille.
3829 **1491** 46c. multicoloured . . . 85 45

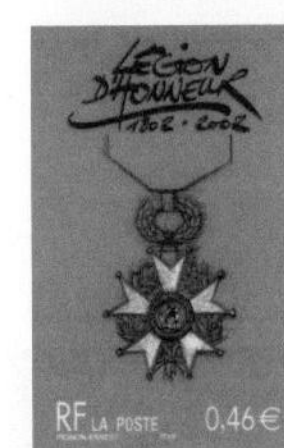

1492 Medal

1493 Rocamadour, Lot

2002. Bicentenary of Legion d'Honneur (medal).
3830 **1492** 46c. multicoloured . . . 85 35

2002.
3831 **1493** 46c. multicoloured . . . 85 35

1494 Delgres

2002. Death Bicentenary of Louis Delgres (soldier and anti-slavery campaigner).
3832 **1494** 46c. multicoloured . . . 85 40

1495 Woman in Hammock

2002. Holidays. Ordinary or self-adhesive gum.
3833 **1495** 46c. multicoloured . . . 85 40

1496 Wheelchair Racers

2002. World Disabled Athletics Championship, Lille-Villeneuve-d'Ascq.
3835 **1496** 46c. multicoloured . . . 85 35

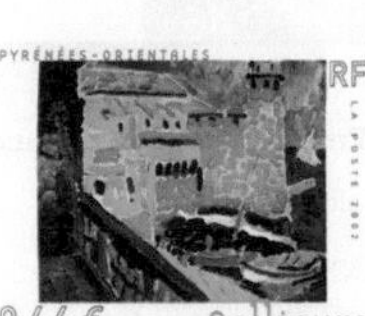

1497 Collioure Lighthouse (painting, Andre Derain)

1498 Chapel

2002. Collioure, Pyrenees.
3836 **1497** 46c. multicoloured . . . 85 35

2002. Saint-Ser Chapel, Puyloubier, Bouches-du-Rhone.
3837 **1498** 46c. multicoloured . . . 85 35

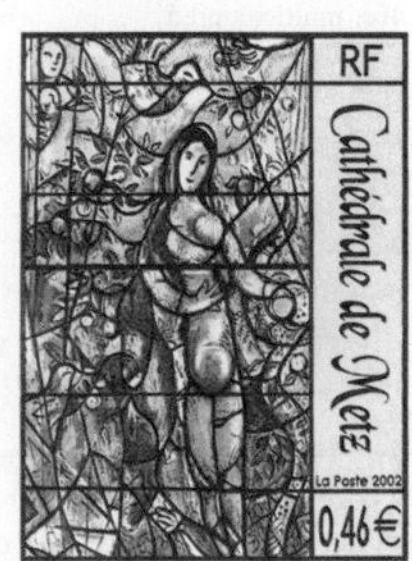

1499 Stained Glass Window (Mark Chagall)

2002. Metz Cathedral.
3838 **1499** 46c. multicoloured . . . 85 50

2002. Tourist Publicity. As Type **490**. Multicoloured.
3839 46c. Lacronan, Finistere (vert) 85 25
3840 46c. Neufchateau, Vosges 85 45

1500 Louis Armstrong

1501 Building Facade

2002. Jazz. Multicoloured.
3841 46c. Type **1500** 85 40
3842 46c. Ella Fitzgerald 85 40
3843 46c. Duke Ellington 85 40
3844 46c. Stephane Grappelli . . 85 40
3845 46c. Michel Petrucciani (horiz) 85 40
3846 46c. Sidney Bechet (horiz) 85 40
MS3847 135 × 143 mm. Nos. 3841/6 (sold at €4.36) . . . . 8·50 10·50

No. **MS**3847 was sold with a premium of €1.60 for the benefit of the Red Cross.

2002. 150th Anniv of Notre-Dame de la Salette, Isere.
3848 **1501** 46c. multicoloured . . . 90 40

1502 Hands (½-size illustration)

2002. Choreography.
3849 **1502** 53c. multicoloured . . . 1·10 1·20

1503 Honda CB 750 Four

2002. Motorcycles. Multicoloured.
3850 16c. Type **1503** 30 40
3851 16c. Terrot 500 RGST . . . 30 40
3852 16c. Majestic 350 . . . . . 30 40
3853 16c. Norton Commando 750 30 40
3854 16c. Voxon 1000 Cafe Racer 30 75
3855 30c. BMW R 90 S 60 55
3856 30c. Harley Davidson FL Hydra-Glide 60 60
3857 30c. Triumph T120 Bonneville 650 . . . . . 60 60
3858 30c. Ducati 916 . . . . . . 60 60
3859 30c. Yamaha 500 XT . . . 60 60

1504 Perec

1505 Family on Motor Scooter

2002. 20th Death Anniv of Georges Perec (writer).
3860 **1504** 46c. multicoloured . . . 90 40

2002. The Twentieth Century (6th series). Everyday Life. Sheet 185 × 243 mm, containing five different 46c. designs as T **1505**, each × 2. Multicoloured.
MS3861 46c. Type **1505**; 46c. Man with horse and cart (horiz); 46c. Woman ironing (horiz); 46c. Boy at water pump; 46c. Girl at school desk . . . . 4·75 8·00

1506 Zola

2002. Death Centenary of Emile Zola (writer).
3862 **1506** 46c. multicoloured . . . 95 45

1507 Self-portrait (Uffizi museum, Florence)

2002. 160th Death Anniv of Elisabeth Vigee-Lebrun (artist).
3863 **1507** €1.02 multicoloured 1·80 2·10

1508 Airbus

2002. 30th Anniv of First Flight of Airbus A 300-B1.
3864 **1508** €3 multicoloured . . . 5·00 2·50

1509 "Sleeping Jesus" (Giovanni Battista Salvi)
1510 Trevi Fountain

2002. Red Cross Fund. Christmas.
3865 **1509** 46c.+9c. multicoloured 1·10 1·20

2002. European Capitals. Rome. Sheet 144 × 36 mm containing T **1510** and similar multicoloured designs.
MS3866 46c. Type **1510**; 46c. Coliseum (horiz); 46c. Trinita dei Monti church; 46c. St. Peter's Basilica (horiz) . . . . 3·50 4·00

1511 World embedded in Computer Circuit

2002. Enterprise.
3867 **1511** 46c. multicoloured . . . 90 45

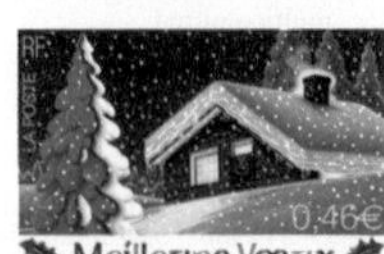

1512 Snow-covered House

2002. New Year. Ordinary or Self-adhesive gum.
3868 **1512** 46c. multicoloured . . . 90 45

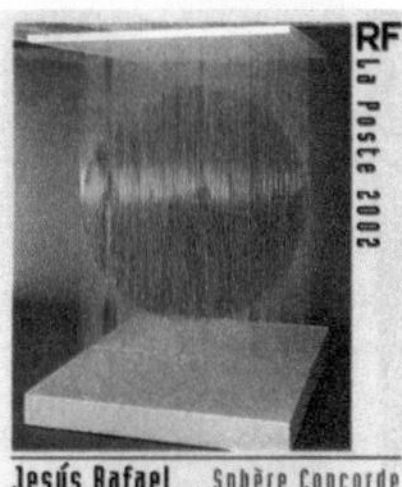

1513 "Sphere Concorde" (Jesus Rafael)

2002.
3870 **1513** 75c. multicoloured . . . 1·40 1·70

1514 Dumas

2002. Birth Bicentenary of Alexandre Dumas (writer).
3871 **1514** 46c. multicoloured . . . 90 45

1515 Senghor

2002. 1st Death Anniv of Leopold Sedar Senghor (writer and linguist).
3872 **1515** 46c. multicoloured . . . 1·10 45

1516 Baby and "naissance"

2003. Greetings Stamps. Multicoloured.
3873 46c. Type **1516** 65 20
3874 46c. "MERCI" and oak leaf 65 20

1517 Heart

2003. St. Valentine's Day. Multicoloured.
3875 46c. Type **1517** 65 20
3876 69c. Heart and roses 95 25
MS3877 136 × 144 mm. As No. 3875 × 5 . . . . 3·25 3·25

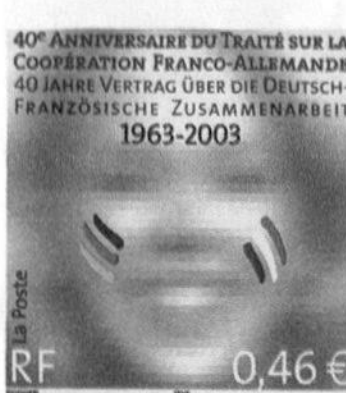

1518 Face

2003. 40th Anniv of French–German Co-operation Treaty.
3878 **1518** 46c. multicoloured . . . 65 20

1519 Map

2003. 40th Anniv of Delegation for Land Use Planning and Regional Action (DATAR).
3879 **1519** 46c. multicoloured . . . 65 20

1520 Genevieve De Gaulle Anthioniz
1521 Eiffel Tower

2003. 1st Death Anniv of Genevieve De Gaulle Anthioniz (resistance fighter and writer).
3880 **1520** 46c. multicoloured . . . 65 20

2003. Bicentenary of Chamber of Commerce and Industry.
3881 **1521** 46c. multicoloured . . . 65 20

1522 Lucky Luke

2003. Lucky Luke (cartoon character) by Morris. Multicoloured.
3882 46c. Type **1522** 65 20
3884 46c.+9c. Lucky Luke and Rantanplan (dog) 65 20
MS3885 101 × 75 mm. 46c. As No. 3882 . . . . 65 65

1523 Blue-headed Hummingbird

2003. Birds. Multicoloured.
3886 41c. Type **1523** 55 15
3887 46c. Toucan 65 20
3888 46c. Purple-throated carib 65 20
3889 69c. Mascarene paradise fly-catcher 90 25
MS3890 110 × 160 mm. Nos. 3886/9 2·75 2·75

1524 Tram and Nantes Town Hall

2003. Nantes City.
3891 **1524** 46c. multicoloured . . . 65 20

1525 Pierre Beregovoy
1527 Monsavon Cow and Dubonnet Man (Raymond Savignac)

1526 Milan Stefanik

2003. 10th Death Anniv of Pierre Beregovoy (resistance fighter and politician).
3892 **1525** 46c. multicoloured . . . 65 20

2003. Milan Rastislav Stefanik Commemoration (founder of Czechoslovakia).
3893 **1526** 50c. multicoloured . . . 65 20

2003. Europa. Poster Art.
3894 **1527** 50c. multicoloured . . . 65 20

1528 *Charles de Gaulle* (aircraft carrier)

2003.
3895 **1528** 50c. multicoloured . . . 65 20

1529 Figure with Winged Shadow
1531 Marsupilami (cartoon character) (Andre Franquin)

1530 Beach Huts

2003. European Union Charter of Fundamental Rights.
3896 **1529** 50c. multicoloured . . . 65 20

2003. Regions (1st issue). Sheet 286 × 110 mm containing T **1530** and similar multicoloured designs.
MS3897 50c. Type **1530**; 50c. Fishing hut; 50c. Vinyards; 50c. Camembert cheese (vert); 50c. Foie gras; 50c. Petanque; 50c. "Guignol" (puppet) (vert); 50c. Crepes (vert); 50c. Cassoulet (casserole); 50c. Porcelain . . . 6·75 6·75
See also No. **MS**3926, **MS**3962 and **MS**3996.

2003. Art. Design as T **491**. Multicoloured.
3898 75c. "La Boulee Rouge" (Paul Signac) . . . . . . 1·00 25
3899 75c. "The Dying Slave" and "The Rebel Slave" (sculptures, Michelangelo) 1·00 25
3900 €1.11 "Untitled" (Vassily Kandinsky) . . . . 1·50 40

2003. Greetings Stamp. Birthday.
3902 **1531** 50c. multicoloured . . . 65 20

2003. Orchids. As T **1475**. Multicoloured.
3903 30c. *Platanthera chlorantha* 40 10
3904 35c. *Dactylorhiza savogiensis* 45 15

1532 Mulhouse Museums Building and Car
1533 Woman and Children Bugatti Sunbathing

2003. 76th French Federation of Philatelic Associations Congress.
3905 **1532** 50c. multicoloured . . . 65 20

2003. Holidays. Ordinary or self-adhesive gum.
3906 **1533** 50c. multicoloured . . . 65 20

2003. Tourist Publicity. As T **490**.
3908 50c. multicoloured 65 20
3909 50c. lilac, orange and green 65 20
3910 50c. multicoloured 65 20
3911 50c. multicoloured 65 20
DESIGNS: No. 3908, Tulle (35 × 26 mm); No. 3909, Notre-Dame de l'Epine (vert). 50c. Arras (80 × 24 mm). 50c. Pontarlier (25 × 39 mm).

1534 Jaqueline Auriol and Dassault Mirage III Fighter

2003. Air. 3rd Death Anniv of Jaqueline Auriol (aviation pioneer).
3912 **1534** €4 multicoloured . . . 5·50 1·50

1535 Square and Compass

2003. 1275th Anniv of French Freemasonry.
3913 **1535** 50c. blue, orange and red 65 20

1536 Maurice Garin (1903 race winner)

2003. Centenary of Tour de France Cycle Race. Multicoloured.
3914 50c. Type **1536** 65 20
3915 50c. Modern competitor . . 65 20

1537 Saint-Pere-sous-Vezelay Church, Yonne

1539 Eugene-Francois Vidocq (undercover police officer and writer)

1538 Athletes

2003.
3916 **1537** 50c. multicoloured . . . 65 20

2003. 9th IAAF World Athletics Championships, Paris and Saint Denis.
3917 **1538** 50c. multicoloured . . . 65 20

2003. Literature. Multicoloured.
3918 50c. Type **1539** 65 20
3919 50c. Esmeralda (character from *The Hunchback of Notre Dame*, Victor Hugo) 65 20
3920 50c. Claudine (character from Claudine novels, *Colette*) 65 20
3921 50c. Nana (character from *Nana*, Emile Zola) 65 20
3922 50c. Edmond Dantes (character from *The Count of Monte-Cristo*, Alexandre Dumas) . . . 65 20
3923 50c. Gavroche (character from Les *Miserables*, Victor Hugo) 65 20
MS3924 135 × 144 mm. 50c. × 6 Nos. 3918/23 . . . . 2·00 2·00
No. **MS**3924 was sold with a premium of €1.60 for the benefit of the Red Cross.

1540 Ahmad Massoud

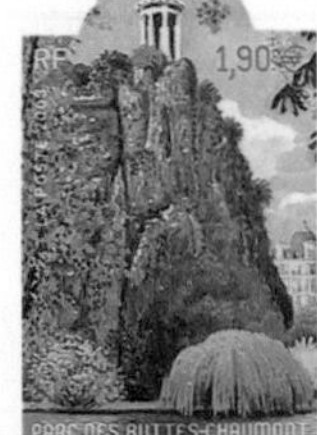
1541 Buttes-Chaumont Park, Paris

2003. 50th Birth Anniv of Ahmad Shah Massoud (Afghan resistance fighter).
3925 **1540** 50c. multicoloured . . . 65 20

2003. Regions (2nd issue). Sheet 286 × 110 mm containing multicoloured designs as T **1530**.
MS3926 50c. Chenonceau Chateau; 50c. Alsatian house; 50c. Dormer windows, Hospices de Beaune; 50c. Genoese tower, Cap Corse (vert); 50c. Arc de Triomphe, Paris (vert); 50c. Mas (country house), Provence; 50c. Pointe de Raz (vert); 50c. Mont Blanc (vert); 50c. Basque house; 50c. Pont du Gard (Roman bridge) . . . . 6·75 6·75

2003. French Gardens. Sheet 286 × 109 mm containing T **1541** and similar design. Multicoloured.
MS3927 €1.90 Type **1541**; €1.90 Luxembourg Gardens . . . . 2·75 2·75
See also No. **MS**3978.

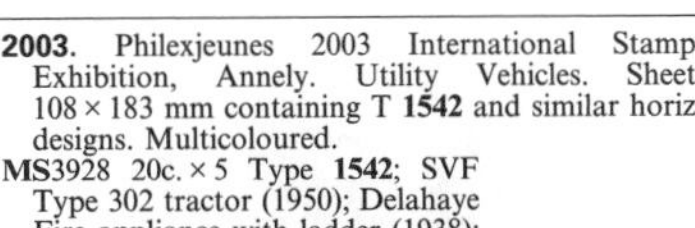
1542 Isobloc Type 648 DP 102 Coach (1954)

2003. Philexjeunes 2003 International Stamp Exhibition, Annely. Utility Vehicles. Sheet 108 × 183 mm containing T **1542** and similar horiz designs. Multicoloured.
MS3928 20c. × 5 Type **1542**; SVF Type 302 tractor (1950); Delahaye Fire appliance with ladder (1938); Renault Kangoo postal van; Renault Type TN6 coach (1932); 30c. × 5 Berliet 22 HP Type M delivery truck (1910); Berliet T 100 (1957); Citroen Police van (1960); Heuliez and Citroen DS ambulance; Hotchkiss Type PL 50 rescue truck (1964) 3·50 3·50

1543 "Meilleurs Voeux"

2003. New Year.
3929 **1543** 50c. multicoloured . . . 65 20
No. 3929 was intended for use by corporate customers.

1544 Robin

2003. New Year. Ordinary or Self-adhesive gum.
3930 **1544** 50c. multicoloured . . . 65 20

1545 "The Virgin of the Grapes" (Pierre Mignard)

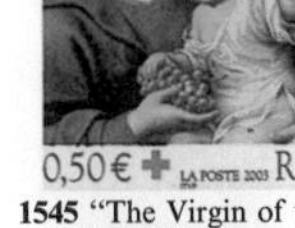
1546 "The Sower"

2003. Red Cross Fund. Christmas.
3932 **1545** 50c. multicoloured . . . 65 20

2003. Centenary of "The Sower" (sculpture, O. Roty). Self-adhesive.
3933 **1546** 50c. red 65 20

1547 Notre-Dame Cathedral

2002. European Capitals. Luxembourg. Sheet 144 × 136 mm containing T **1547** and similar multicoloured designs.
MS3934 50c. × 4, Type **1547**; Saint Esprit plateau (vert); Grand Ducal Palace; Adolphe Bridge (vert) 2·75 2·75

1548 "Marilyn"

2003. 16th Death Anniv of Andy Warhol (artist).
3935 **1548** €1.11 multicoloured 1·50 40

1549 Cockerel amongst Foliage

2003. 15th-century Illuminations. Multicoloured.
3936 50c. Type **1549** 65 20
3937 90c. Peacock . . . . 1·20 40
Stamps of a similar design were issued by India.

1550 *Queen Mary 2*

2003. Launch of *Queen Mary 2* (ocean liner).
3938 **1550** 50c. multicoloured . . . 65 20

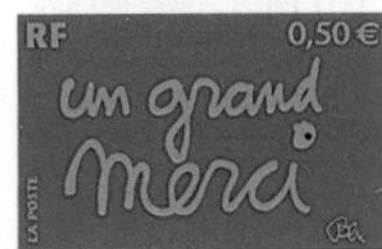
1551 "ceci est une invitation"

2004. Greetings Stamps. Multicoloured.
3939 50c. Type **1551** 65 20
3940 50c. "un grand merci" . . . 65 20
See also Nos. 4072/3.

1552 Baby wearing Bee Costume ("c'est une fille")

2004. Greetings Stamps. Multicoloured. Self-adhesive.
3941 50c. Type **1552** 65 20
3942 50c. Baby wearing butterfly costume ("c'est un garcon") 65 20

1553 Perfume Bottle

2004. St. Valentine's Day. Multicoloured.
3943 50c. Type **1553** 65 20
3944 75c. Eiffel tower and woman 1·00 40
MS3945 135 × 143 mm. No. 3944 × 5 5·00 5·00

2004. Tourist Publicity. As T **490**. Multicoloured.
3946 50c. Lille (European capital of culture, 2004) 65 20
3947 50c. Bridge and tram, Gironde, Bordeaux (79 × 25mm) 65 20
3948 50c. Vaux sur Mer, Charente–Maritime . . . 65 20
3949 50c. Lucon cathedral, Vendee 65 20

2004. Art. As T **491**.
3951 75c. multicoloured . . . . . 1·40 40
3952 90c. green, red and gold . . 1·40 90
3953 € 1.11 multicoloured . . . 1·60 50
3954 € 1.11 multicoloured . . . 1·60 50
DESIGN:No.3951, "La Meridienne d'apres Millet" (Vincent van Gogh); 3952, " The statue of Liberty" (sculpture, Auguste Barthodli) (horiz); 3953, € 1.11 "Cock Fight" (Jean–Leon Gerome); 3954 "Galatee aux Spheres" (Salvador Dali).

1554 Eleanor of Aquitaine

1555 Mickey Mouse

2004. 600th Death Anniv of Eleanor of Aquitaine (wife of King Henry II of England).
3955 **1554** 50c. multicoloured . . . 65 20

2004. 75th Anniv of Mickey Mouse (cartoon character). Multicoloured.
3956 45c. Donald Duck 60 15
3957 50c. Type **1555** 65 20
3958 75c. Minnie Mouse . . . . 1·00 40

1556 Emblem

2004. Bicentenary of Civil Code.
3959 **1556** 50c. blue, black and red 65 20

1557 George Sand

2004. Birth Bicentenary of George Sand (Aurore Dupin) (writer).
3960 **1557** 50c. multicoloured . . . 65 20

1558 Vercingetorix (Gaullist leader) (statue) (Auguste Bartholdi)

2004. Clermont-Ferrand, Puy-de-Dome, Auvergne.
3961 **1558** 50c. multicoloured . . . 65 20

2004. Regions (3rd issue). Sheet 286 × 110 mm containing multicoloured designs as T **1530**.
MS3962 50c. × 10 Cutlery; Vegetables of Provence (vert); Grapes, Beaujolais (vert); Bread; Madras cotton Creole headdress (vert); Oyster (vert); Quiche Lorraine; Course Landes, Aquitaine; Clafoutis (fruit flan); Pipe band . . . . 6·50 6·50

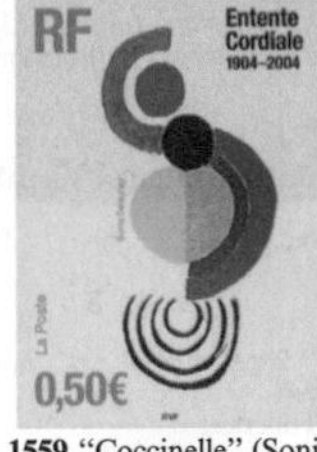
1559 "Coccinelle" (Sonia Delaunay)

1560 Heart-shaped Seat Belt Buckle and Body as Map

2004. Centenary of the Entente Cordiale. Contemporary Paintings.
3963 **1559** 50c. grey, black and rose 65 20
3964 – 75c. multicoloured . . . 1·00 25
DESIGN: 75c. "Lace 1 (trial proof) 1968" (Sir Terry Frost). Stamps of similar designs were issued by Great Britain.

2004. Road Safety. Two phosphor bands.
3965 **1560** 50c. multicoloured . . . 65 20

1561 Rabbit

2004. Farm Animals. Multicoloured.
3966 45c. Type **1561** 65 15
3967 50c. Hen and chicks 70 15
3968 50c. Cow (vert) 70 15
3969 75c. Donkey (vert) . . . . 1·10 25
MS3970 160 × 110 mm. Nos. 3966/9 3·25 3·25

1562 Map of EU as Flags

2004. Enlargement of European Union.
3971 **1562** 50c. multicoloured . . . 70 15

1563 Soldiers

2004. 50th Anniv of Battle of Dien Bieen Phu.
3972 **1563** 50c. multicoloured . . . 70 15

1564 Yachts (painting) (Raoul Dufy)

2004. Europa. Holidays. Ordinary or self-adhesive gum.
3973 **1564** 50c. multicoloured . . . 70 15

1565 Emblem as Graffiti and Blake and Mortimer
1566 FIFA Emblem

2004. Birth Centenary of Edgar Pierre Jacobs (creator of Blake and Mortimer (comic strip)). Multicoloured.
3975 50c. Type **1565** 70 15
3976 €1 Blake and Mortimer (horiz) . . . . 1·40 35
Stamps of a similar design were issued by Belgium.

2004. Centenary of FIFA (Federation Internationale de Football Association).
3977 **1566** 50c. multicoloured . . . 70 15

2004. French Gardens. Sheet 286 × 109 mm containing designs as T **1541**. Multicoloured.
MS3978 €1.90 Jardin des Tuileries; €1.90 Parc Floral de Paris . . 5·50 5·50

1567 Woman throwing Flowers to Soldiers
1568 Smiling Hand and Organs

2004. 60th Anniv of Liberation of France.
3979 **1567** 50c. multicoloured . . . 70 15

2004. Organ Donation Campaign.
3980 **1568** 50c. multicoloured . . . 70 15

1569 Mounted Rifleman
1570 Pierre Dugua de Mons (founder of Arcadia)

2004. Napoleon I's Imperial Guard. Multicoloured.
3981 50c. Type **1569** 70 15
3982 50c. Gunner (horiz) 70 15
3983 50c. Dragoon 70 15
3984 50c. Mameluk 70 15
3985 50c. Napoleon I 70 15
3986 50c. Bombardier 70 15
MS3987 135 × 143 mm. Nos. 3981/6 6·00 6·00
No. MS3987 was sold at €4.60, the premium for the benefit of the Red Cross.

2004. 400th Anniv of French Landing in Maine, USA and Nova Scotia.
3988 **1570** 90c. blue and ochre . . 1·30 30

1571 Eiffel Tower holding Postcard

2004. 77th French Federation of Philatelic Associations Congress.
3989 **1571** 50c. multicoloured . . . 70 15

1572 Canoeist, Tennis Player and Show Jumper

2004. Olympic Games Athens 2004. Sheet 183 × 108 mm containing T **1572** and similar horiz designs. Multicoloured.
MS3990 50c. × 10, Type **1572** × 5; Early Greek athletes × 5 . . . 7·00 7·00

1573 Marie Marvingt

2004. 40th Death Anniv (2003) of Marie Marvingt (aviation pioneer).
3991 **1573** €5 multicoloured . . . 7·00 1·75

1574 Waiter carrying Candlelit Cake

2004. Greetings Stamp.
3992 **1574** 50c. multicoloured . . . 70 15
MS3993 135 × 143 mm. No. 3992 × 5 5·00 5·00

1575 Marianne and Emblem

2004. Campaign to Combat AIDS, Tuberculosis and Malaria.
3994 **1575** (50c.) bright scarlet . . 70 15

1576 Skateboarding

2004. Sport. Multicoloured.
MS3995 108 × 184 mm. 20c. × 5, Type **1576**; Parachuting; Windsurfing; Surfing; Tobogganing; 30c. × 5, BMX cycling; Paragliding; Jet skiing; Snowboarding; Roller skating 3·50 3·50

2004. Regions (4th issue). Sheet 286 × 110 mm containing multicoloured designs as T **1530**.
MS3996 50c. × 10 Thatched house, Normandy; Chateau, Chambord; Gorge, Tarn (vert); Notre Dame cathedral, Paris (vert); Northern windmill (vert); Troglodyte houses; Stream, Cassis (vert); Lighthouse, Cap Ferrat (vert); Cathar chateau; Alpine chalet

1577 Pumpkin and Witch
1578 Felix Eboue

2004. Halloween.
3997 **1577** 50c. multicoloured . . . 75 15

2004. 120th Birth Anniv of Felix Eboue (politician).
3998 **1578** 50c. multicoloured . . . 75 15

1579 Lighthouse, Ouistreham
1580 Virgin and Child (15th-century Cretan school)

2004.
3999 **1579** 50c. multicoloured . . . 75 15

2004. Red Cross Fund. Christmas.
4000 **1580** 50c. multicoloured . . . 75 15

2004. 60th Anniv of "Marianne d'Alger". Two phosphor bands. Self-adhesive.
4001 **209** 50c. scarlet 75 15

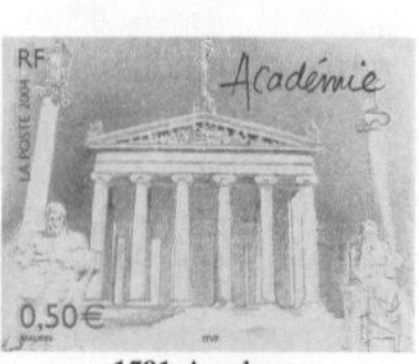

1581 Academy

2004. European Capitals. Athens. Sheet 144 × 134 mm containing T **1581** and similar multicoloured designs.
MS4002 50c. × 4, Type **1581**; Parthenon; Odeon of Herode Atticus; Church of the Holy Apostles (vert) . . . . 3·00 3·00

1582 "Meilleurs Voeux"

2004. Christmas and New Year.
4003 **1582** 50c. multicoloured . . . 75 15

1583 "Meilleurs Voeux" and Bird
1584 Henri Wallon

2004. Christmas and New Year. Multicoloured. Ordinary gum or self-adhesive gum.
4004 50c. Type **1583** 75 15
4005 50c. Baubles hanging from branch 75 15
4006 50c. Stars holding snowballs 75 15
4007 50c. Star holding flower . . 75 15
4008 50c. Stars 75 15

2004. Death Centenary of Henri Wallon (politician).
4014 **1584** 50c. multicoloured . . . 75 15

1585 Millau Viaduct (⅔-size illustration)

2004.
4015 **1585** 50c. multicoloured . . . 75 15

1586 "Marianne de Francais"
1587 "Solidarite Asie"

2005. (i) With face value.
4016 **1586** 1c. yellow 10 10
4016a 5c. agate 10
4017 10c. violet 10 10
4017a 55c. uiltramarine . . .
4018 58c. yellow 75 15
4018a 64c. green 85 20
4019 70c. green 90 20
4020 75c. blue . . . . . . 1·00 25
4020a 82c. rose . . . . . . 1·10 25
4021 90c. indigo . . . . . 1·20 30
4022 €1 orange . . . . . 1·30 35
4023 €1.11 purple . . . . 1·50 45
4023a €1.22 purple . . . . 1·60 50
4024 €1.90 brown . . . . 2·50 75
4024a €1.98 purple . . . . 2·70 80

(ii) Without face value
4025 (45c.) emerald 60 10
4026 (50c.) scarlet 75 15

2005. Red Cross Fund. For Victims of the Tsunami Disaster.
4060 **1587** (50c.)+20c. scarlet . . . 90 90

1588 Rashi

2005. 900th Death Anniv of Rabbi Solomon bar Isaac (Rashi) of Troyes (Biblical and Talmudic scholar).
4061 **1588** 50c. ultramarine, green and brown 75 15

1589 Rooster

2005. New Year. "Year of the Rooster".
4062 **1589** (50c.) multicoloured . . 75 15

1590 Heart

2005. St. Valentine's Day. Multicoloured.
4063 53c. Type **1590** 70 15
4064 82c. Heart containing bird 1·10 25
MS4065 136 × 144 mm. 53c. × 5, As No. 4063 × 5 . . . .

2005. Orchids. Aas T **1475**.
4066 **1475** 39c. multicoloured . . . 55 10
No. 4066 was only issued pre-cancelled in black

1591 Emblem 1592 Manu

2005. Centenary of Rotary International (charitable organization).
4067 **1591** 53c. lemon, ultramarine and vermilion 70 15

2005. Titeuf (cartoon created by Philippe Chappuis (Zep). Multicoloured.
4068 (50c.) Titeuf 75 15
4069 (45c.) Type **1592** 65 15
4071 (90c.) Nadia . . . . 1·30 30

2005. Greetings Stamps. As T **1551**. Multicoloured.
4072 (53c.) As No. 3939 . . . . 70 10
4073 (53c.) As No. 3940 . . . . 70 10
Nos. 4072/3 were for use on mail within France weighing 20 grams or less.

2005. Art. As T **491**.
4074 €1.22 multicoloured . . .
DESIGN: "Sicile" (painting, Nicolas de Stael) (48 × 38 mm).

FRANK STAMP

1939. Optd **F.**
F652 **61** 90c. blue . . . . 1·60 2·75

MILITARY FRANK STAMPS

1901. Optd **F. M.**
M309 **12** 15c. orange . . . . . . 48·00 6·50

1903. Optd **F. M.**
M314 **14** 15c. red . . . . 50·00 5·25

1904. Optd **F. M.**
M323 **15** 10c. red . . . . 26·00 6·50
M324 15c. green . . . . 32·00 6·00

1907. Optd **F. M.**
M348 **18** 10c. red . . . . 2·00 65

1929. Optd **F. M.**
M471 **15** 50c. red . . . . 4·00 60

1933. Optd **F. M.**
M516 **61** 50c. red . . . . 3·00 65
M517 65c. blue 35 40
M518 90c. blue 70 45

M 236 M 545 Flag

1946. No value indicated.
M967 **M 236** green . . . . 1·80 1·00
M968 red 45 50

1964. No value indicated.
M1661 **M 545** multicoloured . . . 45 50

NEWSPAPER STAMPS

J 6

1868. With or without gum. (a) Imperf.
J131 **J 6** 2c. mauve . . . . £275 65·00
J132 2c. blue £550 £275

(b) Perf.
J133 **J 6** 2c. mauve . . . . 40·00 15·00
J134 2c. blue . . . . 65·00 28·00
J135 2c. pink . . . . £170 85·00
J136 5c. mauve £1000 £600

POSTAGE DUE STAMPS

D 4 D 11 D 19

1859.
D 87 **D 4** 10c. black . . . . . . 27·00 13·00
D 88 15c. black . . . . . . 30·00 13·00
D212 25c. black . . . . . . 90·00 40·00
D213 30c. black £140 £100
D214 40c. blue £180 £300
D216 60c. yellow £350 £700
D217 60c. blue . . . . 32·00 80·00

1882.
D279 **D 11** 1c. black . . . . . . 1·30 1·30
D280 2c. black . . . . . . 18·00 19·00
D281 3c. black . . . . . . 18·00 18·00
D282 4c. black . . . . . . 35·00 25·00
D283 5c. black . . . . . . 65·00 21·00
D297 5c. blue . . . . 30 1·60
D284 10c. black . . . . . . 65·00 1·30
D298 10c. brown 30 30
D285 15c. black . . . . . . 50·00 7·00
D317 15c. green . . . . . . 19·00 1·00
D286 20c. black . . . . . . £250 95·00
D300 20c. green . . . . . . 5·00 50
D301 25c. red . . . . 5·00 3·50
D287 30c. black . . . . . . £160 1·60
D302 30c. red 30 25
D288 40c. black . . . . . . £100 36·00
D304 40c. red . . . . 6·00 5·25
D305 45c. green . . . . . . 5·50 4·00
D289 50c. black £450 £150
D306 50c. purple 70 55
D307 60c. green . . . . . . 1·50 80
D290 60c. black . . . . . . £450 40·00
D291 1f. black £600 £275
D310 1f. brown . . . . 1·10 75
D308 1f. pink on yellow . . £400 £350
D309 1f. brown on yellow . 5·50 70
D293 2f. black £1100 £650
D294 2f. brown £180 £120
D311 2f. red . . . . £170 50·00
D312 2f. mauve . . . . 1·20 90
D313 3f. mauve . . . . 2·10 95
D295 5f. black £2500 £1600
D296 5f. brown £300 £225
D314 5f. orange . . . . 1·70 2·50

1908.
D348 **D 19** 1c. olive . . . . . . 1·90 1·70
D349 10c. violet 95 60
D350 20c. bistre . . . . . . 32·00 1·20
D351 30c. bistre . . . . . . 21·00 40
D352 50c. red . . . . £225 55·00
D353 60c. red . . . . 4·00 4·00

1917. Surch.
D378 **D 19** 20c. on 30c. bistre . . 20·00 3·00
D379 40c. on 50c. red . . . 9·00 2·75
D433 50c. on 10c. violet . . 3·25 3·75
D434 60c. on 1c. olive . . . 5·50 4·00
D435 1f. on 60c. red . . . . 17·00 10·50
D436 2f. on 60c. red . . . . 17·00 10·50

D 43 D 187 Wheat Sheaves D 457

1927.
D454 **D 43** 1c. green . . . . . . 1·30 2·10
D455 10c. red . . . . 1·80 1·90
D456 30c. bistre . . . . . . 5·50 75
D457 60c. red . . . . 4·75 95
D458 1f. purple . . . . . . 12·50 2·75
D459 1f. green . . . . . . 15·00 1·10
D460 2f. blue . . . . 48·00 32·00
D461 2f. brown . . . . . . £120 24·00

1929. Surch.
D471 **D 43** 1f.20 on 2f. blue . . . 34·00 8·50
D472 5f. on 1f. purple . . . 45·00 9·00

1931. Surch **UN FRANC**.
D494 **D 43** 1f. on 60c. red . . . . 25·00 1·80

1943. Inscr "CHIFFRE-TAXE".
D787 **D 187** 10c. brown 10 55
D788 30c. purple 10 90
D789 50c. green 10 55
D790 1f. blue 10 45
D791 1f.50 red 15 75
D792 2f. blue 15 65
D793 3f. red 15 55
D794 4f. violet . . . . . 4·50 3·25
D795 5f. pink 35 70
D796 10f. orange . . . . 3·25 2·10
D797 20f. bistre . . . . 9·00 2·75

1946. As Type **D 187** but inscr "TIMBRE TAXE".
D985 10c. brown . . . . 1·00 1·50
D986 30c. purple . . . . 85 1·30
D987 50c. green . . . . 20·00 8·25
D988 1f. blue 35 45
D989 2f. blue 35 45
D990 3f. red 30 65
D991 4f. violet 30 75
D992 5f. pink 30 90
D993 10f. red 40 50
D994 20f. brown . . . . 1·00 55
D995 50f. green . . . . 18·00 1·60
D996 100f. green . . . . 55·00 7·50

1960. New Currency.
D1474 **D 457** 5c. mauve . . . . . 3·00 85
D1475 10c. red . . . . . . 4·50 65
D1476 20c. brown . . . . . 4·25 1·00
D1477 50c. green . . . . . 12·00 1·50
D1478 1f. green . . . . . 50·00 2·30

D 539 Poppies D 917 "Ampedus cinnabarinus"

1964.
D1650 – 5c. red, grn & pur 15 15
D1651 – 10c. bl, grn & pur 15 40
D1652 **D 539** 15c. red, green & brown 35 40
D1653 – 20c. pur, grn & turq 25 30
D1654 – 30c. bl, grn & brn 15 70
D1655 – 40c. yell, red & turq 45 45
D1656 – 50c. red, grn & bl 45 35
D1657 – 1f. vio, grn & bl . . 80 45
DESIGNS: 5c. Knapweed; 10c. Gentian; 20c. Little periwinkle; 30c. Forget-me-not; 40 c Columbine; 50c. Clover; 1f. Soldanella.

1982. Beetles.
D2493 **D 917** 10c. brown & black 50 40
D2494 – 20c. black 35 30
D2495 – 30c. red, brn & blk 35 45
D2496 – 40c. bl, brn & blk 55 50
D2497 – 50c. red and black 55 55
D2498 – 1f. black 60 60
D2499 – 2f. yellow and black 80 80
D2500 – 3f. black and red . . 1·10 60
D2501 – 4f. brown and black 1·30 65
D2502 – 5f. bl, red & blk . . 1·80 75
DESIGNS: 20c. "Dorcadion fuliginator"; 30c. "Leptura cordigera"; 40c. "Paederus littoralis"; 50c. "Pyrochroa coccinea"; 1f. "Scarites laevigatus"; 2f. "Trichius gallicus"; 3f. "Adalia alpina"; 4f. "Apoderus coryli"; 5f. "Trichodes alvearius".

COUNCIL OF EUROPE STAMPS

Until March 25th, 1960, these stamps could only be used by delegates and permanent officials of the Council of Europe on official correspondence at Strasbourg. From that date they could be used on all correspondence posted within the Council of Europe building.

1950. No. 1354 optd **CONSEIL DE L'EUROPE**.
C1 35f. mauve and red . . . . . 1·30 2·00

C 2 Council Flag

1958.
C2 **C 2** 8f. blue, orange & pur 50 50
C3 20f. blue, yellow & brn . . 55 55
C4 25f. blue, pur & myrtle . . 1·40 1·30
C5 35f. blue and red 95 90
C6 50f. blue and purple . . . 1·90 1·90

(New currency. 100 (old) francs = 1 (new) franc).

1963.
C 7 **C 2** 20c. blue, yellow & brn 95 1·00
C 8 25c. blue, pur & myrt . . 2·20 2·10
C 9 25c. multicoloured . . . 1·10 1·10
C10 30c. blue, yellow & red 1·20 1·10
C11 40c. multicoloured . . . 1·40 1·40
C12 50c. blue and purple . . 2·10 2·00
C13 50c. multicoloured . . . 2·50 2·00
C14 60c. multicoloured . . . 1·30 1·50
C15 70c. multicoloured . . . 2·50 3·25

1975. As Type **C 2**, but inscr "FRANCE".
C16 60c. multicoloured . . . . . 1·40 1·50
C17 80c. yellow, blue and red . . 1·60 1·70
C18 1f. multicoloured . . . . . 3·50 4·25
C19 1f.20 multicoloured . . . . 5·00 4·50

C 3 New Council of Europe Building, Strasbourg

1977.
C20 **C 3** 80c. red, lt brn & brn . . 1·10 1·10
C21 1f. brown, blue & grn . . 40 55
C22 1f.40 grey, grn & brn . . 2·75 2·30
C23 1f.40 green 60 80
C24 2f. blue 70 85

1978. 25th Anniv of European Convention on Human Rights. As Type **C 3** with the addition of the Human Rights emblem.
C25 1f.20 black, purple & grn . . 55 65
C26 1f.70 turquoise, blue & grn 75 75

C 5 Exterior and Interior of New Council Building, Strasbourg

1981.
C27 **C 5** 1f.40 violet, blue & pur 65 60
C28 1f.60 green & brown . . 65 60
C29 1f.70 green 65 80
C30 1f.80 red, green & pur . . 80 90
C31 2f. red, green & blue . . 75 80
C32 2f.10 red . . . . 90 1·00
C33 2f.30 green, turq & bl . . 1·10 80
C34 2f.60 purple, bl & grey 1·00 95
C35 2f.80 brown, dp bl & bl 1·10 1·20
C36 3f. blue . . . . 1·30 1·40

C 6 Foot Breaking through Shell

1985.
C37 **C 6** 1f.80 green 75 95
C38 2f.20 red 85 95
C39 3f.20 blue . . . . 1·20 1·50

C 7 Council of Europe Building, Strasbourg

1986.
C40 **C 7** 1f.90 green . . . . . . 95 1·00
C41 2f. green . . . . 1·10 1·30
C42 2f.20 red . . . . 95 1·00
C43 3f.40 blue . . . . . . 1·70 1·90
C44 3f.60 blue . . . . . . 2·10 2·40

C 8 Stars, Doves and Girl

1989. 40th Anniv of Council of Europe.
C45 **C 8** 2f.20 multicoloured . . . 1·40 1·60
C46 3f.60 multicoloured . . . 2·20 2·75

C 9 Map of Europe

C 10 "36 Heads" (Friedensreich Hundertwasser)

1990.

C47 C 9 2f.30 multicoloured . . . 1·40 1·30
C48 2f.50 multicoloured . . . 1·10 1·30
C49 3f.20 multicoloured . . . 2·00 1·80
C50 3f.40 multicoloured . . . 1·50 1·70

1994.

C51 C 10 2f.80 multicoloured . . 1·00 1·00
C52 3f.70 multicoloured . . 1·90 1·90

C 11 Palace of Human Rights, Strasbourg

1996.

C53 C 11 3f. multicoloured . . . 1·30 1·40
C54 3f.80 multicoloured . . 1·70 1·90

C 12 "Charioteer of Delphi" (replica of ancient Greek statue)

C 14 "Walking on Stars" (drawing, Tom Ungerer)

C 13 "I am black, I am white, I am black and white" (drawing, Tom Ungerer)

1999. Sculptures presented by Member states.

C55 3f. Type C **12** . . . . . . 1·10 1·30
C56 3f.80 "Nike" (Petras Mazuras) . . . . 1·40 1·50

2001.

C57 C **13** 3f. multicoloured . . . 1·10 1·10
C58 3f.80 multicoloured . . 1·50 1·50

2003.

C59 C **14** 50c. multicoloured . . . 65 20
C60 75c. multicoloured . . . 1·40 40

UNESCO STAMPS

For use on correspondence posted within the UNESCO headquarters building.

U 1 Buddha and Hermes

1961.

U1 U **1** 20c. bistre, blue & brown 45 55
U2 25c. purple, green & blk 45 55
U3 30c. brown & dp brown 1·50 1·40
U4 50c. red, violet & black 1·60 1·70
U5 60c. brown, mauve & bl 2·75 2·50

U 2 Open Book and Globe

U 3 "Human Rights"

1966.

U6 U **2** 25c. brown 55 55
U7 30c. red 80 80
U8 60c. green . . . . 1·00 1·30

1969.

U 9 U **3** 30c. red, green & brown 75 70
U10 40c. red, mauve & brn 90 95
U11 50c. red, blue & brown 2·10 2·10
U12 70c. red, violet & blue 3·00 3·25

1975. As Type U **3**, but inscribed "France".

U13 60c. red, green and brown 80 1·20
U14 80c. red, brown and lake . . 1·30 1·40
U15 1f.20 red, blue and purple 4·25 4·50

U 4 "Leaf"

1976.

U16 U **4** 80c. blue, brown & pur 85 95
U17 1f. orange, green & blue 35 60
U18 1f.20 blue, red & green 50 65
U19 1f.40 brn, mve & orge 2·00 2·10
U20 1f.70 red, green & brn 70 80

U 5 Old Slave Dungeons, Goree, Senegal

U 6 Gateway, Fez, Morocco

1980. Sites in Need of Protection.

U21 U **5** 1f.20 blue, green & red 60 60
U22 – 1f.40 mauve, blue & grn 75 70
U23 – 2f. violet, green & red 90 80

DESIGNS: 1f.40, Moenjodaro, Pakistan; 2f. Palace of Sans-Souci, Haiti.

1981. Sites in Need of Preservation.

U24 U **6** 1f.40 brown, blue & red 70 75
U25 – 1f.60 blue, red & grn . . 70 75
U26 – 1f.80 violet, pur & bl . . 80 75
U27 – 2f.30 brown, grn & bl . . 90 95
U28 – 2f.60 black, bl & red . . 80 1·20

DESIGNS—VERT: 1f.60, Seated Buddha Sukhotai, Thailand; 1f.80, Hue, Vietnam; 2f.60, Sao Miguel Cathedral, Brazil. HORIZ: 2f.30, Fort St. Elmo, Malta.

U 7 Chinguetti Mosque, Mauritania

U 8 Amphitheatre, Carthage

1983. Sites in Need of Preservation.

U29 – 1f.70 brown and green 75 80
U30 U **7** 2f. brown, blue & blk . . 75 75
U31 – 2f.10 brown, bl & turq 65 85
U32 – 2f.80 black, bl & brn . . 1·10 1·10
U33 – 3f. orange, brn & grn . . 1·20 1·40

DESIGNS: 1f.70, Lalibela Church, Ethiopia; 2f.10, Sana'a, Yemen Arab Republic; 2f.80, City walls, Istanbul, Turkey; 3f. St. Mary's Church, Kotor, Yugoslavia.

1985. Protected Sites. Each grey, green and blue.

U34 1f.80 Type U **8** . . . . . . 90 1·20
U35 2f.20 Old Square, Havana, Cuba . . . . 95 1·20
U36 3f.20 Temple of Anuradhapura, Sri Lanka 1·80 2·20

U 9 Temple of Tikal, Guatemala

U 10 Acropolis, Athens

1986. Protected Sites. Each grey, brown and green.

U37 1f.90 Type U **9** . . . . . . 1·30 1·30
U38 3f.40 Bagerhat Mosque, Bangladesh . . . . 1·90 2·20

1987. Protected Sites. Each brown, chestnut and blue.

U39 2f. Type U **10** . . . . . . 1·10 1·20
U40 3f.60 Philae Temple, Egypt 2·10 2·10

U 11 St. Francis's Monastery, Lima, Peru

U 12 Temple of Bagdaon, Nepal

1990. Protected Sites.

U41 U **11** 2f.30 brn, grn & blk . . 1·00 1·20
U42 – 3f.20 brn, orge & bl . . 1·40 1·60

DESIGN—HORIZ: 3f.20 Shibam, People's Democratic Republic of Yemen.

1991. Protected Sites.

U43 U **12** 2f.50 brown and red . . 1·10 1·30
U44 – 3f.40 brown & green . . 1·60 1·70

DESIGN—HORIZ: 3f.40, Herat Fort, Afghanistan.

U 13 Angkor, Cambodia

U 14 Ayers Rock, Uluru, Australia

1993. Protected Sites. Multicoloured.

U45 2f.80 Type U **13** . . . . . 1·30 1·40
U46 3f.70 Cave paintings, Tassili n'Ajjer National Park, Algeria (horiz) . . . . . 1·70 1·80

1996. Protected Sites. National Parks. Mult.

U47 3f. Type U **14** . . . . . . 1·30 1·30
U48 3f.80 Glacier, Los Glaciares, Argentine Republic . . . 1·60 1·60

U 15 Detail of Fresco from Villa of Mysteries, Pompeii

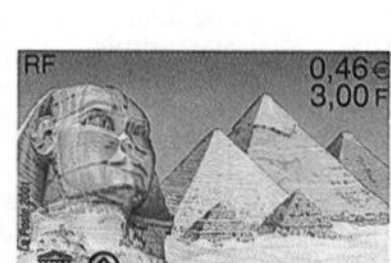

U 16 Sphinx and Pyramids, Giza, Egypt

1998. Protected Sites. Multicoloured.

U49 3f. Type U **15** . . . . . . 1·30 1·40
U50 3f.80 Statues, Easter Island (horiz) . . . . 1·60 1·70

2001. Protected Sites. Multicoloured.

U51 3f. Type U **16** . . . . 1·30 1·30
U52 3f.80 Komodo National Park, Indonesia . . . . . 1·60 1·60

U 17 Reindeer, Lapland

2003. Protected Sites. Multicoloured.

U53 50c. Type U **17** 65 20
U54 75c. Church of the Resurrection, St. Petersburg (300th anniv) (vert) . . . . . . 1·40 40

FREE FRENCH FORCES IN THE LEVANT Pt. 19

After British and Free French troops had occupied Syria and Lebanon in June 1941 the following stamps were issued for the use of Free French forces in those areas.

100 centimes = 1 franc.

1942. Surch with Lorraine Crosses, **FORCES FRANCAISES LIBRES LEVANT** and value. (i) On No. 252 of Syria.
1 – 50c. on 4p. orange . . . . . 7·50 13·50

(ii) On Nos. 251 and 212 of Lebanon.
2 **16a** 1f. on 5p. blue . . . . . . 3·50 13·00
3 **22** 2f.50 on 12½p. blue . . . . 4·25 12·00

1942. Air. Nos. 269/70 of Syria surch with Lorraine Crosses, **LIGNES AERIENNES F.A.F.L.** and value.
4 4f. on 50p. black . . . . . . 5·50 11·50
5 6f.50 on 50p. black . . . . . . 5·50 8·25
6 8f. on 50p. black . . . . . . 5·00 8·25
7 10f. on 100p. mauve . . . . . 5·25 13·50

3 Camelry and Ruins at Palmyra

4 Wings bearing Lorraine Crosses

1942. Buff background.
8 **3** 1f. red (postage) . . . . . . 80 3·00
9 1f.50 violet . . . . 80 4·25
10 2f. orange . . . . 70 4·50
11 2f.50 brown . . . . 70 4·50
12 3f. blue . . . . 70 4·75
13 4f. green . . . . 55 5·50
14 5f. purple . . . . 50 5·00
15 **4** 6f.50 red (air) . . . . . . 50 5·75
16 10f. purple and blue . . . . 30 5·25
MS17 106 × 16 mm. Nos. 15/16. No gum . . . . 19·00 50·00

1942. Air. No. 15 surch **4** and bars.
17 **4** 4f. on 6f.50 red . . . . . . 1·10 5·75

1943. Surch **RESISTANCE** and premium.
18 **3** 1f.+9f. red (postage) . . . . 4·50 4·75
19 5f.+20f. purple . . . . 4·50 5·75
20 **4** 6f.50+48f.50 red (air) . . . . 38·00 55·00
21 10f.+100f. pur & bl . . . . . 44·00 55·00

1943. Air. No. 12 surch **4F**, bars and airplane.
22 **3** 4f. on 3f. blue and buff . . . 1·40 3·00

FRENCH COLONIES Pt. 6

General issues for use in French Colonies which had no special stamps.

100 centimes = 1 franc.

NOTE. For other stamps issued for French Colonies see the note at the beginning of France.

A Eagle B Laureated D Laureated

1859. Imperf.
1 A 1c. green . . . . 16·00 14·00
2 5c. green . . . . 20·00 11·00
3 10c. brown . . . . 23·00 7·25
4a 20c. blue . . . . 25·00 10·50
5 40c. orange . . . . 19·00 5·50
6 80c. red . . . . 80·00 42·00

1871. Imperf.
7 B 1c. green . . . . 48·00 48·00
9 D 30c. brown . . . . £110 36·00
10 80c. red . . . . £750 85·00

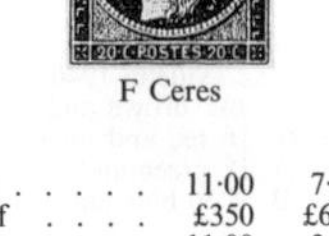
E Ceres F Ceres

1871. Imperf.
11 E 1c. green on blue . . . . . 11·00 7·75
12 2c. brown on buff £350 £600
14a 5c. green . . . . 11·00 3·75
20 F 10c. brown on pink . . . . £170 11·00
16 15c. bistre . . . . £250 8·75

H Peace and Commerce J Commerce

1877. Imperf.
24 H 1c. green . . . . 22·00 34·00
25 2c. green . . . . 11·00 9·00
26 4c. green . . . . 13·00 9·75
27 5c. green . . . . 13·50 1·90
28 10c. green . . . . 65·00 8·25
29 15c. grey . . . . £200 55·00
30 20c. brown on yellow . . . 48·00 3·75
31a 25c. blue . . . . 30·00 3·75
32 30c. brown . . . . 30·00 30·00
33 35c. black on yellow . . . . 34·00 21·00
34 40c. red on yellow . . . . . 19·00 17·00
35a 75c. red . . . . 60·00 48·00
36 1f. green . . . . 42·00 13·50

1878. Imperf.
37 H 1c. black on blue . . . . . 14·00 14·00
38 2c. brown on buff . . . . . 13·50 10·00
39 4c. brown on grey . . . . . 18·00 18·00
40 10c. black on lilac . . . . . 85·00 16·00
41 15c. blue on blue . . . . . 22·00 7·00
42 20c. red on green . . . . . 60·00 11·00
43 25c. black on red £425 £225
44 25c. brown on yellow . . . . £525 30·00

1881. Perf.
45 J 1c. black on blue . . . . . 2·00 2·50
46 2c. brown on buff . . . . . 4·50 2·50
47 4c. brown on grey . . . . . 3·50 3·75
48a 5c. green on green . . . . . 6·75 85
49 10c. black on lilac . . . . . 7·75 2·50
50 15c. blue on blue . . . . . 12·00 1·40
51 20c. red on green . . . . . 40·00 12·00
52 25c. brown on yellow . . . . 10·00 2·25
53 25c. black on pink . . . . . 10·50 90
54 30c. brown on drab . . . . 15·00 14·50
55 35c. black on orange . . . . 30·00 20·00
56 40c. red on yellow . . . . . 29·00 32·00
57 75c. red on pink . . . . . 75·00 42·00
58 1f. green . . . . 55·00 26·00

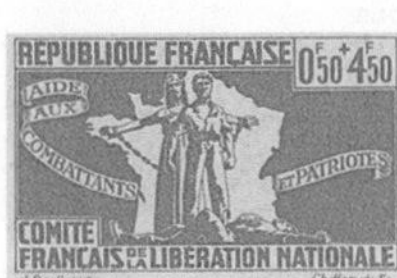

K Map of France

L Colonies offering France Aid

1943. Aid to Resistance Movement.
82 K 50c.+4f.50 green . . . . . . 2·00 3·25
83 1f.50+8f.50 red . . . . . . 1·40 3·25
84 3f.+12f. blue . . . . 1·10 3·25
85 5f.+15f. grey . . . . 1·50 3·50
86 L 9f.+41f. purple . . . . . . 2·50 4·50

M Resisters

1943. Aid to Resistance Movement. Roul.
87 M 1f.50+98f.50 bl & grey . . . 30·00 44·00

N O

1943. French Solidarity Fund.
88 N 10f.+40f. blue . . . . 4·25 8·75

1944. Air. Aviation Fund.
89 O 10f.+40f. green . . . . . . 5·25 9·50

POSTAGE DUE STAMPS

U V

1884. Imperf.
D59 U 1c. black . . . . 1·40 3·50
D60 2c. black . . . . 1·40 3·50
D61 3c. black . . . . 1·60 2·25
D62 4c. black . . . . 2·25 2·75
D63 5c. black . . . . 2·50 1·40
D64 10c. black . . . . 6·25 2·25
D65 15c. black . . . . 6·00 3·75
D66 20c. black . . . . 7·25 4·50
D67 30c. black . . . . 10·00 3·00
D68 40c. black . . . . 14·00 8·25
D69 60c. black . . . . 22·00 14·00
D70 1f. brown . . . . 26·00 19·00
D71 2f. brown . . . . 16·00 12·50
D72 5f. brown . . . . 70·00 48·00

1893. Imperf.
D73 U 5c. blue 40 25
D74 10c. brown 30 25
D75 15c. green . . . . 1·40 1·10
D76 20c. olive . . . . 90 2·75
D77 30c. red . . . . 1·50 1·10
D78 50c. red . . . . 1·25 1·90
D79 60c. brown on yellow . . . 3·00 2·75
D81 1f. red on yellow . . . . . 4·75 6·25

1945. Perf.
D 90 V 10c. blue . . . . 15 2·75
D 91 15c. green . . . . 70 2·75
D 92 25c. orange . . . . 95 2·75
D 93 50c. black . . . . 2·25 3·00
D 94 60c. brown . . . . 2·75 3·00
D 95 1f. red . . . . 2·50 3·00
D 96 2f. red . . . . 2·75 3·00
D 97 4f. grey . . . . 4·00 4·50
D 98 5f. blue . . . . 4·75 4·75
D 99 10f. violet . . . . 16·00 12·50
D100 20f. brown . . . . 4·75 5·00
D101 50f. green . . . . 8·00 8·25

FRENCH CONGO Pt. 6

A French colony in central Africa, in 1903 divided into Gabon, Middle Congo, Ubangi-Shari and Chad.

100 centimes = 1 franc.

1891. Stamps of French Colonies, "Commerce" type, surch **Congo francais** and value in figures.
2 J 5c. on 1c. black on blue . . . £110 80·00
3 5c. on 15c. blue £200 £110
4 5c. on 25c. black on red . . . £100 32·00
11 10c. on 25c. black on red . . £150 95·00
12 15c. on 25c. black on red . . £200 75·00

1892. Stamps of French Colonies. "Commerce" type, surch **COngo Francais** and value in figures.
5 J 5c. on 20c. red on green . . . £850 £300
6 5c. on 25c. black on red . . . £120 75·00
7 10c. on 25c. black on red . . . £130 50·00
8 10c. on 40c. red on yellow . . £1600 £275
9 15c. on 25c. black on red . . . £130 35·00

1892. Postage Due stamps of French Colonies surch **Congo francais Timbre poste** and value in figures.
13 U 5c. on 5c. black £120 £110
14 5c. on 20c. black £110 £110
15 5c. on 30c. black £160 £110
16 10c. on 1f. brown £130 £120

1892. "Tablet" key-type inscr "CONGO FRANCAIS" in red (1, 5, 15, 25, 50 (No. 31), 75c. and 1f.) or blue (others).
17 D 1c. black on blue . . . . . 85 1·25
18 2c. brown on buff . . . . . 2·50 3·25
19 4c. brown on grey . . . . . 1·90 3·50
20 5c. green on light green . . 3·50 5·25
21 10c. black on lilac . . . . . 11·00 9·75
22 10c. red . . . . 1·50 1·60
23 15c. blue . . . . 48·00 8·00
24 15c. grey . . . . 6·25 10·00
25 20c. red on green . . . . . 11·00 14·00
26 25c. black on pink . . . . . 18·00 8·25
27 25c. blue . . . . 8·00 10·50
28 30c. brown on drab . . . . . 20·00 16·00
29 40c. red on yellow . . . . . 35·00 20·00
30 50c. red on pink . . . . . . 48·00 16·50
31 50c. brown on blue . . . . 5·75 8·75
32 75c. brown on orange . . . 34·00 20·00
33 1f. green . . . . 50·00 25·00

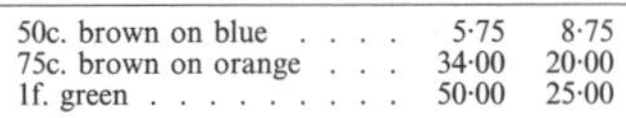

6 Leopard in Ambush 8 Woman of the Bakalois Tribe

1900.
36c **6** 1c. brown and grey . . . . 95 1·60
37 2c. brown and yellow . . . 1·25 65
38 4c. red and grey . . . . . . 1·90 1·40
39 5c. green and light green . . 1·40 80
40 10c. red and light red . . . 5·50 2·50
41 15c. violet and green . . . . 2·00 1·10
42 **8** 20c. green and red . . . . . 2·50 2·75
43 25c. blue and light blue . . . 3·00 3·00
44 30c. red and yellow . . . . 3·00 2·50
45 40c. brown and green . . . . 3·75 2·75
46 50c. violet and lilac . . . . 3·50 3·00
47 75c. red and orange . . . . 9·00 9·25
48 – 1f. grey and green . . . . . 16·00 13·00
49 – 2f. red and brown . . . . . 27·00 21·00
50 – 5f. orange and black . . . . 75·00 80·00
DESIGN—28 × 40 mm: 1, 2, 5f. Coconut palms, Libreville.

1903. Surch in figures.
51 **8** 5c. on 30c. red & yellow . . £225 £110
52 – 0,10 on 2f. red & brn (No. 49) £275 £110

PARCEL POST STAMPS

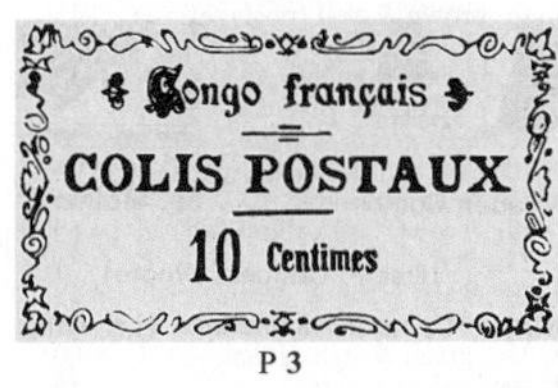

P 3

1891.
P13 P 3 10c. black on blue £180 £120

1893. Receipt stamp of France optd **Congo Francais COLIS POSTAUX**.
P34 10c. grey £130 £120

FRENCH EQUATORIAL AFRICA Pt. 6

In 1910 Gabon, Middle Congo and Ubangi-Shari-Chad were federated to form French Equatorial Africa: each colony continued to issue its own stamps until 1936.

In 1958 the four constituent colonies became autonomous republics as Gabon, Congo Republic, Central African Republic (formerly Ubangi-Shari) and Chad.

100 centimes = 1 franc.

1936. Middle Congo stamps of 1933 optd **AFRIQUE EQUATORIALE FRANCAISE**.
1 **15** 1c. brown . . . . 30 2·50
2 2c. blue . . . . 15 2·75
3 4c. green . . . . 1·50 3·00
4 5c. purple . . . . 1·25 3·25
5 10c. green . . . . 2·75 3·25
6 15c. purple . . . . 2·75 3·00
7 20c. red on pink . . . . . 2·50 3·50
8 25c. orange . . . . 4·00 4·25
9 – 40c. brown . . . . 3·75 4·00
10 – 50c. purple . . . . 3·25 1·25
11 – 75c. black on pink . . . . 4·25 3·25
12 – 90c. red . . . . 3·75 4·25
13 – 1f.50 blue . . . . 3·00 3·00
14 – 5f. blue . . . . 42·00 25·00
15 – 10f. black . . . . 22·00 17·00
16 – 20f. brown . . . . 24·00 20·00

1936. Gabon Stamps of 1933 optd **AFRIQUE EQUATORIALE FRANCAISE**.
17 **21** 1c. red . . . . 15 2·75
18 2c. black on pink . . . . . 15 2·75
19 4c. green . . . . 1·40 3·25
20 5c. blue . . . . 1·75 2·75
21 10c. red on yellow . . . . . 2·00 2·75
22 **22** 40c. purple . . . . 2·75 3·75
23 50c. brown . . . . 2·75 1·50
24 1f. green on blue . . . . . 20·00 11·00
25 1f.50 blue . . . . 4·00 3·50
26 2f. red . . . . 10·00 6·00

1937. International Exhibition, Paris. As **T58a** of Guadeloupe.
27 20c. violet . . . . 1·60 4·00
28 30c. green . . . . 1·75 3·50
29 40c. red . . . . 65 3·25
30 50c. brown and blue . . . . . 50 3·00
31 90c. red . . . . 95 2·00
32 1f.50 blue . . . . 1·25 4·75

MS33 120×100 mm. 3f. red. Imperf . . . 9·00 18·00

8 Logging near Mayumba

9 Chad Family

10 Count Savorgnan de Brazza

12 Savoia Marchetti S-73 over Stanley Pool

1937.

34 8 1c. brown & yell (postage) 15 2·75
35 2c. violet and green 15 2·75
36 3c. blue and yellow 55 3·00
37 4c. mauve and blue 15 2·75
38 5c. deep green & green 20 2·25
39 9 10c. mauve and blue 15 1·90
40 15c. blue and pink 15 10
41 20c. brown and yellow 60 1·25
42 25c. red and blue 85 65
44 10 30c. deep green & green 1·60 2·75
45 30c. blue and pink 65 2·75
46 9 35c. green & light green 1·00 2·25
47 10 40c. red and blue 15 70
48 45c. blue and green 3·75 4·50
49 45c. green & light green 1·00 3·25
50 50c. brown and yellow 15 10
51 55c. violet and blue 1·25 2·25
52 60c. purple and blue 1·00 3·00
53 A 65c. blue and green 80 70
54 70c. violet and orange 1·10 3·00
55 75c. black and yellow 5·25 5·25
56 80c. brown and yellow 65 1·60
57 90c. red and orange 90 1·25
58 1f. violet and green 2·50 50
59 10 1f. red and orange 2·00 1·10
60 A 1f. green and blue 85 2·00
61 B 1f.25 red and orange 2·00 1·90
62 1f.40 brown and green 1·10 2·25
63 1f.50 blue and light blue 2·50 2·50
64 1f.60 violet and orange 90 3·00
65 1f.75 brown and yellow 1·75 2·00
66 A 1f.75 blue and light blue 1·10 2·75
67 B 2f. green and light green 1·00 20
68 C 2f.15 violet and yellow 1·50 2·75
69 2f.25 blue and light blue 2·25 3·25
70 2f.50 purple and orange 1·00 1·25
71 3f. blue and pink 35 15
72 5f. green and light green 1·10 80
73 10f. violet and blue 2·50 2·75
74 20f. black and yellow 3·00 2·50

75 D 1f.50 black & yellow (air) 65 3·00
76 2f. mauve and blue 2·25 3·25
77 2f.50 green and pink 35 80
78 3f.75 brown and green 2·00 3·00
79 12 4f.50 red and blue 2·25 1·90
80 6f.50 blue and green 2·50 3·50
81 8f.50 red and orange 2·50 3·00
82 10f.75 violet and green 2·50 3·00

DESIGNS: A, Emile Gentil; B, Paul Crampel; C, Victor Liotard; D, Latecoere 300 flying boat over Pointe Noire.

1938. Anti-cancer Fund. As T **58b** of Guadeloupe.
94 1f.75+50c. blue 5·25 27·00

1938. Social Welfare. Surch with premium in figures.
95 A 65c.+35c. (No. 53) 75 3·50
96 1f.75+50c. (No. 66) 1·00 4·00

16 Bouet-Willaumez and "La Malouine"

1938. Centenary of Landing of Bouet-Willaumez in Gabon.
97 16 65c. brown 65 2·25
98 1f. red 70 2·00
99 1f.75 blue 1·00 3·50
100 2f. violet 1·40 1·10

1939. New York World's Fair. As T **58c** of Guadeloupe.
101 1f.25 red 1·75 2·75
102 2f.25 blue 2·50 3·75

1939. 150th Anniv of French Revolution. As T **58d** of Guadeloupe.
103 45c.+25c. green and black (postage) 8·50 22·00
104 70c.+30c. brown & black 6·50 22·00
105 90c.+35c. orange & black 6·50 22·00
106 1f.25+1f. red and black 6·50 22·00
107 2f.25+2f. blue and black 6·50 22·00

108 4f.50+4f. blk & orge (air) 12·50 45·00

1940. Adherence to General de Gaulle. A. Postage stamps of 1936 and 1937. (a) Optd **AFRIQUE FRANCAISE LIBRE.**
109 8 1c. brown and yellow 90 3·25
110 2c. violet and green 1·25 3·50
111 3c. blue and yellow 1·40 3·25
112 5c. green & light green 70 3·50
113 9 10c. mauve and blue 85 2·75
114 15c. blue and pink 85 2·75
115 20c. brown and yellow 80 1·50
116 25c. red and blue 2·00 8·50
117 35c. green & lt green 1·00 2·75

(b) Optd **LIBRE**.
118 – 4c. green (No. 3) 11·50 8·50
119a 10 30c. dp green & green 4·00 1·25
120a 30c. blue and pink 8·25 11·00
121 40c. red and blue 40 20
122 45c. green & lt green 40 2·25
123a 50c. brown and yellow 2·25 2·75
124 55c. violet and blue 45 70
125 60c. purple and blue 30 65
126 A 65c. blue and green 60 1·40
127 70c. violet and orange 80 2·50
128 75c. black and yellow 48·00 38·00
129 80c. brown and yellow 50 1·40
130 90c. red and orange 40 90
131 10 1f. red and orange 80 1·90
132 A 1f. green and blue 1·50 7·75
133 B 1f.40 brown and green 40 1·40
134 1f.50 blue & light blue 50 1·50
135 1f.60 violet & orange 50 1·75
136 1f.75 brown & yellow 75 2·50
137 C 2f.15 violet and yellow 75 2·50
138 2f.25 blue & light blue 60 1·75
139 2f.50 purple & orange 60 35
140 3f. blue and pink 1·10 2·75
141 5f. green & light green 1·00 70
142 10f. violet and blue 1·00 40
143 20f. black and yellow 75 60

(c) Surch **LIBRE** and value in figures.
144 10 75c. on 50c. brn & yell 75 90
145 A 1f. on 65c. blue & green 45 10

(d) Optd **Afrique Francaise Libre**.
146 8 1c. brown and yellow 2·25 45
147 2c. violet and green 2·25 1·60
148 3c. blue and yellow 2·75 2·50
149 5c. blue and green 2·50 1·75
150 9 10c. mauve and blue 2·25 45
151 15c. blue and pink 2·00 45
152 20c. brown and yellow 1·40 45
153 25c. red and blue 4·25 4·00
154 35c. green & light green 3·50 1·60

B. Air stamps of 1937 optd **Afrique Francaise Libre** or surch also.
155 D 1f.50 black and yellow £150 £150
156 2f.50 green and pink 1·25 1·60
157 3f.75 brown and green £160 £160
158 12 4f.50 red and blue 1·25 1·90
159 6f.50 blue and green 1·90 3·00
160 8f.50 red and orange 1·75 2·75
161 D 10f. on 2f.50 grn & pk 70·00 70·00
162 12 50f. on 10f.75 vio & grn 6·00 17·00

C. No. 71 of Middle Congo optd **AFRIQUE FRANCAISE LIBRE.**
163 15 4c. green 40·00 32·00

22 Phoenix

24 Count Savorgnan de Brazza and Stanley Pool

1941. Free French Issue. (a) Postage.
164 22 5c. brown 10 2·25
165 10c. blue 10 2·50
166 25c. green 10 2·75
167 30c. orange 10 2·25
168 40c. green 20 2·00
169 80c. purple 20 2·25
170 1f. mauve 90 40
171 1f.50 red 90 45
172 2f. black 90 50
173 2f.50 blue 1·25 90
174 4f. violet 55 15
175 5f. yellow 90 55
176 10f. brown 85 30
177 20f. green 1·25 65

(b) Air. As T **63a** of Guadeloupe.
178 – 1f. orange 70 1·75
179 – 1f.50 red 1·60 2·75
180 – 5f. purple 2·00 2·50
181 – 10f. black 2·00 2·25
182 – 25f. blue 1·90 2·75
183 – 50f. green 1·75 2·25
184 – 100f. red 2·00 2·75

1941. De Brazza Memorial Fund.
185 24 1f.+2f. brown and red 1·90 3·50

1942. Commemorating the Arrival of Gen. de Gaulle at Brazzaville in 1940. Optd **LIBRE 24-10-40.**
186 A 80c. brown and yellow 22·00 11·50
187 10 1f. red and orange 22·00 11·50
188 A 1f. green and blue 22·00 11·50
189 B 1f.50 blue and pale blue 22·00 11·50

1943. Free French Funds. Nos. 69, 73 and 82 surch **Afrique Francaise Combattante**, cross and value.
190 2f.25+50f. bl & lt bl (postage) 11·00 13·50
191 10f.+100f. violet and blue 35·00 42·00

192 10f.75+200f. vio & grn (air) £120 £130

1944. French Aid Fund. Various stamps surch **RESISTANCE** and value.
195 22 5c.+10f. brn (No. 164) 8·50 9·00
196 10c.+10f. blue (No. 165) 7·50 9·00
197 25c.+10f. grn (No. 166) 7·50 9·00
198 30c.+10f. orge (No. 167) 7·50 9·00
199 40c.+10f. grn (No. 168) 7·50 9·00
193 A 80c.+10f. brown and yellow (No. 169) 27·00 32·00
200 22 1f.+10f. mve (No. 170) 28·00 32·00
194 B 1f.50+15f. blue and light blue (No. 171) 28·00 32·00
201 22 2f.+20f. black (No. 172) 7·50 8·75
202 2f.50+25f. bl (No. 173) 8·00 8·75
203 4f.+40f. violet (No. 174) 7·50 8·75
204 5f.+50f. yellow (No. 175) 7·50 5·75
205 10f.+100f. brn (No. 176) 12·00 12·50
206 20f.+200f. grn (No. 177) 12·00 12·50

1944. French Aid Fund. Nos. 164/8, 170, 172/3, 186 and 189 surch **LIBERATION** and value.
209 22 5c.+10f. brown 8·50 10·00
210 10c.+10f. blue 8·50 10·00
211 25c.+10f. green 8·50 10·00
212 30c.+10f. orange 8·50 10·00
213 40c.+10f. green 8·75 10·00
207 A 80c.+10f. brown & yell 27·00 32·00
214 22 1f.+10f. mauve 8·50 10·00
208 B 1f.50+15f. bl & lt blue 28·00 32·00
215 22 2f.+20f. black 8·75 10·00
216 2f.50+25f. blue 8·75 10·00

1944. Mutual Aid and Red Cross Funds. As T **58e** of Guadeloupe.
217 5f.+20f. blue 1·10 3·00

1945. Surch with new values and bars.
218 22 50c. on 5c. brown 1·75 3·25
219 60c. on 5c. brown 1·75 3·25
220 70c. on 5c. brown 1·90 3·25
221 1f.20 on 5c. brown 2·25 3·25
222 2f.40 on 25c. green 2·25 3·50
223 3f. on 25c. green 2·00 3·50
224 4f.50 on 25c. green 2·50 3·50
225 15f. on 2f.50 blue 2·75 3·50

1945. Eboue. As T **58f** of Guadeloupe.
226 2f. black 20 25
227 25f. green 1·25 3·75

1946. Air. Victory. As T **63b** of Guadeloupe.
228 8f. red 35 80

1946. Air. From Chad to the Rhine. As Nos. 226/31 of Cameroun.
229 5f. purple 2·75 3·50
230 10f. green 1·50 3·75
231 15f. blue 2·50 4·25
232 20f. red 3·00 4·00
233 25f. black 2·50 4·25
234 50f. red 2·75 4·00

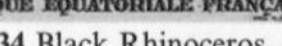

34 Black Rhinoceros

36 Boatman

37 Caudron Goeland over Beach

1947.

235 34 10c. blue (postage) 10 2·75
236 30c. violet 10 2·75
237 40c. orange 45 2·50
238 – 50c. blue 50 2·50
239 – 60c. red 15 2·75
240 – 80c. green 25 3·00
241 – 1f. orange 1·00 10
242 – 1f.20 red 40 2·50
243 – 1f.50 green 1·60 2·50
244 – 2f. brown 1·60 35
245 – 3f. red 1·25 80
246 – 3f.60 brown 2·75 4·50
247 – 4f. blue 1·40 20
248 36 5f. purple 1·50 30
249 6f. blue 1·25 55
250 10f. black 1·40 55
251 – 15f. brown 1·60 25
252 – 20f. red 1·75 10
253 – 25f. black 1·00 10

254 – 50f. brown (air) 2·25 1·25
255 37 100f. green 4·00 2·25
256 – 200f. blue 5·75 3·50

DESIGNS—As Type **36**: 50c. to 80c. Palms and cataract; 1f. to 1f.50, River view; 2f. to 4f. Tropical forest; 15f. to 25f. Bakongo girl. As Type **37**: 50f. Savoia Marchetti S.M.75 airplane over village; 200f. Savoia Marchetti S.M.75 over column of porters.

39 People of Five Races, Aircraft and Globe

1949. Air. 75th Anniv of U.P.U.
267 39 25f. green 4·50 17·00

40 Doctor and Patient

1950. Colonial Welfare Fund.
268 40 10f.+2f. purple & green 3·50 7·50

42 De Brazza and Landscape

1951. Birth Cent of Count Savorgnan de Brazza.
269 – 10f. green & blue (postage) 80 10

270 42 15f. red, blue & brn (air) 3·25 1·90

DESIGN—22×31½ mm: 10f. De Brazza.

43 Monseigneur Augouard

1952. Air. Birth Centenary of Mgr. Augouard (First Bishop of the Congo).
271 43 15f. sepia, purple & olive 4·50 3·25

44

1952. Centenary of Military Medal.
272 44 15f. multicoloured 5·50 7·50

45 Sailing Canoe

1953. Air.
273 – 50f. brown, green & blue 1·60 90
274 45 100f. grn, turq & sepia 4·25 65
275 – 200f. red and lake 3·75 2·00
276 – 500f. blue, black & grn 30·00 6·00

DESIGNS: 50f. Logs in river; 200f. Native driver and docks; 500f. African darters.

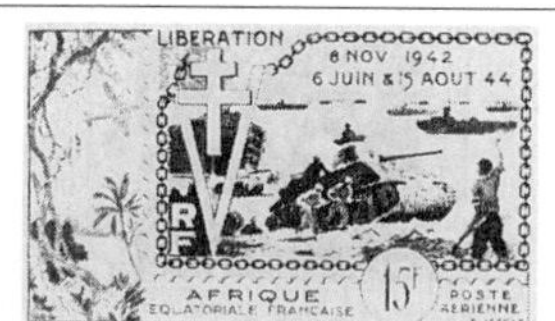
46 Normandy Landings, 1944

1954. Air. 10th Anniv of Liberation.
277 **46** 15f. brown and violet . . . 4·75 4·75

47 Lieut.-Governor Cureau

1954.
278 **47** 15f. brown and green . . . 90 25

48 Felix Eboue

1955. Air. Governor-General Eboue Commem.
279 **48** 15f. sepia, brown & blue 2·25 1·40

49 Lizard

1955. Nature Protection.
280 **49** 8f. green and purple . . . 1·00 1·25

50 Boali Waterfall and Power Station

1956. Economic and Social Development Fund.
281 **50** 5f. purple and sepia . . . 70 10
282 – 10f. green and black . . . 55 15
283 – 15f. grey and blue . . . 25 10
284 – 20f. vermilion and red . . . 65 20
DESIGNS: 10f. Cotton production, Chad; 15f. Brazzaville Hospital, Middle Congo; 20f. Libreville harbour, Gabon.

51 Coffee

1956. Coffee.
285 **51** 10f. violet and lilac 90 60

52 Riverside Hospital

1957. Order of Malta Leprosy Relief.
286 **52** 15f. turquoise, grn & red 1·40 95

53 Gen. Faidherbe and African Trooper

54 Lion and Lioness

1957. Air. Centenary of African Troops.
287 **53** 15f. brown & chestnut . . 3·25 4·75

1957.
288 – 1f. brown and green . . . 95 2·75
289 **54** 2f. olive and green . . . . 1·00 2·50
290 – 3f. black, blue & green . . 1·40 2·25
291 – 4f. brown and grey . . . . 1·50 1·90
DESIGNS—HORIZ: 1f. Giant eland. VERT: 3f. African elephant; 4f. Greater kudu.

55 Regional Bureau, Brazzaville 56 "Euadania"

1958. 10th Anniv of W.H.O.
292 **55** 20f. brown and green . . . 1·10 1·25

1958. Tropical Flora.
293 **56** 10f. yellow, grn & violet 35 55
294 – 25f. red, yellow & green . . 35 30
DESIGN: 25f. "Spathodea".

57 "Human Rights"

1958. 10th Anniv of Declaration of Human Rights.
295 **57** 20f. turquoise and blue . . 55 1·10

POSTAGE DUE STAMPS

D 13

D 38

1937.
D83 D **13** 5c. blue and purple . . 10 2·75
D84 10c. pink and red . . . 10 2·75
D85 20c. lt green & green 10 2·75
D86 25c. pink and brown . . 10 2·75
D87 30c. blue and red . . . 10 2·75
D88 45c. green & mauve . . 35 3·00
D89 50c. pink and green . . 20 3·00
D90 60c. yellow & purple . . 80 3·25
D91 1f. yellow and brown 30 3·25
D92 2f. pink and blue . . . 65 2·75
D93 3f. blue and brown . . 85 2·75

1947.
D257 D **38** 10c. red . . . . . . 10 2·75
D258 30c. orange . . . . . 10 2·75
D259 50c. black . . . . . 25 2·75
D260 1f. red . . . . . . 10 2·75
D261 2f. green . . . . . 1·25 2·75
D262 3f. mauve . . . . . 1·75 3·00
D263 4f. blue . . . . . 2·25 3·25
D264 5f. brown . . . . . 2·00 2·50
D265 10f. blue . . . . . 2·75 3·50
D266 20f. brown . . . . . 2·50 3·75

FRENCH GUIANA Pt. 6

Formerly a French colony on the N.E. coast of S. America, now an overseas department using the stamps of France.

100 centimes = 1 franc.

Nos. 1 to 32 and 51 are all stamps of French Colonies surcharged or overprinted.

1886. "Peace and Commerce" and "Commerce" types surch **Dec. 1886. GUY. FRANC. 0f 05.**
2 H 0f.05 on 2c. green £425 £425
4 J 0f.05 on 2c. brown on buff £425 £375

1887. "Ceres" and "Peace and Commerce" types surch **Avril 1887. GUY. FRANC.** and value.
6 H 0f.05 on 2c. green £110 £110
7b 0f.20 on 35c. blk on yell . . 50·00 42·00
8 F 0f.25 on 30c. brown . . . . 30·00 35·00

No. 7b has the "Av" of "Avril" inverted; stamps with these letters normal are worth more.

1887. "Ceres" and "Peace and Commerce" types surch **DEC. 1887. GUY. FRANC. 5c.**
9 F 5c. on 30c. brown £120 £110
10 H 5c. on 30c. brown £850 £850

1888. "Ceres" and "Peace and Commerce" types surch **Fevrier 1888 GUY. FRANC.** and value.
11 F 5 on 30c. brown £110 £110
12 H 10 on 75c. red £170 £170

1892. Optd **GUYANE.** (a) On "Ceres" type.
14 F 30c. brown £120 £120

(b) On "Peace and Commerce" type.
15 H 2c. green £600 £600
16 35c. black on orange £1700 £1800
17 40c. red on yellow £100 £100
18 75c. red £110 £100
19 1f. green £120 £120

(c) On "Commerce" type.
20 J 1c. black on blue . . . . . . 45·00 35·00
21 2c. brown on buff . . . . . 25·00 35·00
22 4c. brown on grey . . . . . 35·00 35·00
23 5c. green on light green . . . 38·00 32·00
24 10c. black on lilac . . . . . 60·00 40·00
25 15c. blue on light blue . . . 60·00 35·00
26 20c. red on green . . . . . 32·00 20·00
27 25c. black on pink . . . . . 65·00 29·00
28 30c. brown on drab . . . . 26·00 35·00
29 35c. black on orange £160 £160
30 40c. red on yellow £110 £100
31 75c. red on pink £110 £100
32 1f. green £170 £160

1892. "Tablet" key-type inscr "GUYANE" in red (1, 5, 15, 25, 50 (No. 56), 75c., 1, 2f.) or blue (others).
38 D 1c. black on blue . . . . . 35 1·75
39 2c. brown on buff 80 60
40 4c. brown on grey . . . . . 1·90 2·75
52 5c. green . . . . 1·10 1·25
42 10c. black on lilac . . . . . 11·50 5·75
53 10c. red . . . . 3·25 1·10
43 15c. blue . . . . 42·00 4·25
54 15c. grey . . . . 95·00 85·00
44 20c. red on green . . . . . 18·00 14·00
45 25c. black on red . . . . . 17·00 4·75
55 25c. blue . . . . 17·00 19·00
46 30c. brown on drab . . . . 16·00 15·00
47 40c. red on yellow . . . . . 27·00 12·50
48 50c. red on pink . . . . . . 30·00 13·00
56 50c. brown on blue . . . . . 29·00 22·00
49 75c. brown on yellow . . . 38·00 20·00
50 1f. green . . . . 13·00 10·50
57 2f. violet on pink . . . . . £160 5·25

1892. "Commerce" type surch **DEC. 92. 0f05 GUYANE.**
51 J 0.05 on 15c. blue on blue . . 26·00 28·00

8 Giant Anteater

9 Gold-washer

10 Plantation of Coconut Palms, Cayenne

1904.
58 **8** 1c. black 15 15
59 2c. blue 15 40
60 4c. brown . . . . 15 1·40
61 5c. green . . . . 1·00 1·25
83 5c. orange . . . . 30 2·40
62 10c. red . . . . 1·10 15
84 10c. green . . . . 65 2·50
104 10c. red on blue . . . . . 55 1·40
63 15c. violet . . . . 1·25 75
64 **9** 20c. brown . . . . 85 2·25
65 25c. blue . . . . 2·50 55
85 25c. violet . . . . 1·10 1·00
66 30c. black . . . . 1·60 1·40
86 30c. red . . . . 65 2·75
105 30c. orange . . . . 25 2·50
106 30c. green . . . . 2·00 3·25
66a 35c. black on yellow . . . 1·60 1·25
67 40c. red . . . . 30 1·60
87 40c. black . . . . 1·75 2·75
68 45c. brown . . . . 2·00 3·00
69 50c. lilac . . . . 3·00 2·75
88 50c. blue . . . . 25 2·50
107 50c. grey . . . . 1·60 1·25
108 60c. mauve on pink . . . . 1·50 2·75
109 65c. green . . . . 2·25 3·00
70 75c. green . . . . 2·25 2·50
110 85c. purple . . . . 30 2·75
71 **10** 1f. red . . . . 1·40 1·25
111 1f. blue on light blue . . . 2·25 3·00
112 1f. blue on green . . . . . 2·75 4·25
113 1f.10 pink . . . . 2·00 3·25
72 2f. blue . . . . 2·00 2·25
114 2f. red on yellow . . . . . 2·50 3·75
73 5f. black . . . . 7·00 6·00
115 10f. green on yellow . . . 13·00 18·00
116 20f. red . . . . 19·00 23·00

1912. "Tablet" key-type surch in figures.
74 D 05 on 2c. brown on buff . . 1·60 3·00
75 05 on 4c. brown on grey . . 15 2·75
76 05 on 20c. red on green . . 35 3·25
77 05 on 25c. black on pink . . 3·50 4·75
78 05 on 30c. brown on drab 40 3·50
79 10 on 40c. red on yellow . . 70 3·00
80 10 on 50c. red . . . . . . 3·50 4·25

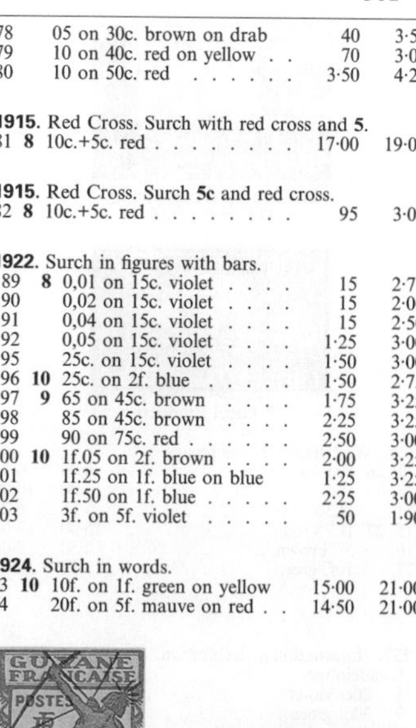

1915. Red Cross. Surch with red cross and **5.**
81 **8** 10c.+5c. red . . . . 17·00 19·00

1915. Red Cross. Surch **5c** and red cross.
82 **8** 10c.+5c. red . . . . 95 3·00

1922. Surch in figures with bars.
89 **8** 0,01 on 15c. violet . . . . 15 2·75
90 0,02 on 15c. violet . . . . 15 2·00
91 0,04 on 15c. violet . . . . 15 2·50
92 0,05 on 15c. violet . . . . 1·25 3·00
95 25c. on 15c. violet . . . . 1·50 3·00
96 **10** 25c. on 2f. blue . . . . . 1·50 2·75
97 **9** 65 on 45c. brown . . . . 1·75 3·25
98 85 on 45c. brown . . . . 2·25 3·25
99 90 on 75c. red . . . . . 2·50 3·00
100 **10** 1f.05 on 2f. brown . . . . 2·00 3·25
101 1f.25 on 1f. blue on blue 1·25 3·25
102 1f.50 on 1f. blue . . . . . 2·25 3·00
103 3f. on 5f. violet . . . . . 50 1·90

1924. Surch in words.
93 **10** 10f. on 1f. green on yellow 15·00 21·00
94 20f. on 5f. mauve on red . . 14·50 21·00

20 Carib Archer 21 Shooting the Rapids, R. Maroni

22 Government Building, Cayenne

1929.
117 **20** 1c. blue and lilac . . . . . 15 2·50
118 2c. green and red . . . . . 15 2·00
119 3c. green and violet . . . . 15 2·50
120 4c. mauve and brown . . . 15 2·50
121 5c. red and blue . . . . . 40 2·25
122 10c. brown and mauve . . 15 1·40
123 15c. red and brown . . . . 80 2·50
124 20c. green and blue . . . . 15 2·50
125 25c. brown and red . . . . 85 2·25
126 **21** 30c. lt green & green . . . 70 2·50
127 30c. brown and green . . . 15 2·50
128 35c. green and blue . . . . 2·00 3·00
129 40c. drab and brown . . . 25 2·50
130 45c. brown and green . . . 2·10 3·00
131 45c. green and olive . . . 1·25 2·50
132 50c. brown and blue . . . 40 30
133 55c. red and blue . . . . 2·25 3·25
134 60c. green and red . . . . 85 2·50
135 65c. green and red . . . . 85 2·75
136 70c. green and blue . . . 1·00 3·00
137 75c. light blue and blue . . 2·50 3·25
138 80c. blue and black . . . . 2·10 2·50
139 90c. red and carmine . . . 2·00 2·75
140 90c. brown and mauve . . 2·00 3·00
141 1f. brown and mauve . . . 40 2·50
142 1f. red and carmine . . . 3·00 4·00
143 1f. blue and black . . . . 85 3·00
144 **22** 1f.05 green and red . . . 4·25 7·00
145 1f.10 mauve and brown . . 3·25 6·25
146 1f.25 green and brown . . 2·00 3·25
147 1f.25 red and carmine . . . 1·50 2·75
148 1f.40 mauve and brown . . 2·00 3·00
149 1f.50 light blue & blue . . 1·40 2·75
150 1f.60 green and brown . . 1·60 2·75
151 1f.75 brown and red . . . 2·75 3·00
152 1f.75 ultramarine & bl . . 2·25 3·00
153 2f. red and green . . . . . 1·40 1·50
154 2f.25 ultramarine & bl . . 1·25 3·25
155 2f.50 brown and red . . . 1·25 2·75
156 3f. mauve and brown . . . 2·00 2·75
157 5f. green and violet . . . 1·60 2·50
158 10f. blue and brown . . . 2·00 2·50
159 20f. red and blue . . . . . 3·00 4·00

1931. "Colonial Exhibition" key-types inscr "GUYANE FRANCAISE".
160 E 40c. black and green . . . 3·50 5·75
161 F 50c. black and mauve . . . 3·50 5·50
162 G 90c. black and red . . . . 3·75 6·00
163 H 1f.50 black and blue . . . 4·25 6·00

25 Cayenne

1933. Air.
164 **25** 50c. brown 85 70
165 1f. green 25 70
166 1f.50 blue 25 90
167 2f. orange 75 80
168 3f. black . . . . 1·25 2·75
169 5f. violet . . . . 70 1·25
170 10f. olive . . . . 35 1·60
171 20f. red . . . . 65 1·25

26 Cayenne recaptured by D'Estrees, 1676

27 Local Products

1935. West Indies Tercentenary.
172 **26** 40c. brown 6·00 6·75
173 50c. red 13·00 10·00
174 1f.50 blue 5·75 6·25
175 **27** 1f.75 red 16·00 17·00
176 5f. brown 12·50 9·00
177 10f. green 13·50 12·00

1937. International Exhibition, Paris. As **58a** of Guadeloupe.
178 20c. violet 30 3·00
179 30c. green 25 2·75
180 40c. red 25 2·75
181 50c. brown and agate 25 2·75
182 90c. red 40 3·25
183 1f.50 blue 50 3·25
MS183a 120 × 100 mm. 3f. violet. Imperf 8·25 13·00

1938. International Anti-cancer Fund. As T **58b** of Guadeloupe.
184 1f.75+50c. blue 7·25 16·00

1939. New York World's Fair. As T **58c** of Guadeloupe.
185 1f.25 red 1·10 3·25
186 2f.25 blue 1·40 3·00

1939. 150th Anniv of French Revolution. As T **58d** of Guadeloupe.
187 45c.+25c. grn & blk (post) 7·50 13·00
188 70c.+30c. brown & black 7·50 13·00
189 90c.+35c. orange & black 7·50 13·00
190 1f.25+1f. red & black 7·75 14·00
191 2f.25+2f. blue & black 8·25 13·00
192 5f.+4f. black & orange (air) 11·50 23·00

28 View of Cayenne and Marshal Petain

1941. Marshal Petain Issue.
192a **28** 1f. purple 35 3·00
192b 2f.50 blue 15 3·00

1944. Mutual Aid and Red Cross Funds. As T **58e** of Guadeloupe.
193 5f.+20f. purple 80 3·00

1945. Felix Eboue. As T **58f** of Guadeloupe.
194 2f. black 20 3·00
195 25f. green 50 3·25

28a Arms of French Guiana

1945.
196 **28a** 10c. blue 1·00 2·75
197 30c. brown 15 2·75
198 40c. blue 70 2·75
199 50c. purple 70 2·75
200 60c. yellow 20 2·75
201 70c. brown 20 2·75
202 80c. green 65 2·75
203 1f. blue 60 2·75
204 1f.20 lilac 1·00 2·75
205 1f.50 orange 1·25 2·75
206 2f. black 1·10 3·00
207 2f.40 red 1·10 3·00
208 3f. pink 85 3·00
209 4f. blue 1·40 3·00
210 4f.50 green 60 3·00
211 5f. brown 50 3·00
212 10f. violet 55 2·75
213 15f. red 70 3·25
214 20f. olive 1·75 3·25

1945. Air. As T **63a** of Guadeloupe.
215 50f. green 1·00 3·00
216 100f. red 1·75 3·50

1946. Air. Victory. As T **63b** of Guadeloupe.
217 8f. black 30 3·75

1946. Air. From Chad to the Rhine. As T **63c** of Guadeloupe.
218 5f. blue 85 3·00
219 10f. red 55 3·00
220 15f. purple 40 3·00
221 20f. green 85 3·50
222 25f. purple 75 3·50
223 50f. mauve 1·60 4·00

29 Hammock

33 Red-billed Toucans

35 Yellow-throated Caracara

1947.
224 **29** 10c. green (postage) 15 2·75
225 30c. red 15 2·75
226 50c. purple 15 2·75
227 – 60c. grey 15 2·75
228 – 1f. brown 15 2·75
229 – 1f.50 brown 15 2·75
230 – 2f. green 30 3·00
231 – 2f.50 blue 50 3·00
232 – 3f. brown 85 3·00
233 – 4f. brown 2·25 3·25
234 – 5f. blue 2·00 3·00
235 – 6f. brown 1·75 3·25
236 **33** 10f. blue 4·50 3·75
237 15f. brown 4·50 4·00
238 20f. brown 6·75 4·00
239 – 25f. green 8·00 6·00
240 – 40f. brown 6·75 6·00
241 **35** 50f. green (air) 13·50 13·50
242 – 100f. lake 11·50 22·00
243 – 200f. blue 25·00 24·00
DESIGNS—As Types **29** and **33**—HORIZ: 60c. to 1f.50, Riverside village; 2f. to 3f. Pirogue; 25f., 40f. Blue and yellow macaw, military macaw and white-eyed conure. VERT: 4f. to 6f. Girl. As Type **35**—VERT: 100f. Airplane over peccary and palms. HORIZ: 200f. Sud Ouest Corse II airplane, channel-billed toucan, red-billed toucan and black-necked aracari.

POSTAGE DUE STAMPS

1925. Postage Due stamps of France optd **GUYANE FRANCAISE** or surch also **centimes a percevoir** and value in figures.
D117 **D 11** 5c. blue 15 3·00
D118 10c. brown 15 2·75
D119 15c. on 20c. olive 15 3·00
D120 20c. olive 75 3·00
D121 25c. on 5c. blue 1·25 3·00
D122 30c. on 20c. olive 70 3·25
D123 45c. on 10c. brown 1·40 2·75
D124 50c. red 85 3·25
D125 60c. on 5c. blue 1·00 3·00
D126 1f. on 20c. olive 1·00 3·50
D127 2f. on 50c. red 1·25 3·75
D128 3f. mauve 7·00 12·50

D 23 Palm Trees

D 36

1929.
D160 **D 23** 5c. blue & dp blue 15 2·50
D161 10c. blue & brown 15 2·50
D162 20c. red and green 20 2·50
D163 30c. red and brown 45 2·50
D164 50c. brown & mauve 1·60 2·50
D165 60c. brown and red 1·60 2·75
D166 – 1f. red and blue 1·75 3·00
D167 – 2f. green and red 2·50 4·00
D168 – 3f. grey and mauve 2·75 4·50
DESIGN: 1f. to 3f. Creole girl.

1947.
D244 **D 36** 10c. red 15 2·50
D245 30c. green 15 2·50
D246 50c. black 15 2·50
D247 1f. blue 20 3·00
D248 2f. lake 25 3·00
D249 3f. violet 30 3·00
D250 4f. red 45 3·25
D251 5f. purple 60 3·50
D252 10f. green 1·00 4·25
D253 20f. purple 1·75 4·75

FRENCH GUINEA Pt. 6

A French colony on the W. coast of Africa incorporated in French West Africa in 1944. Became completely independent in 1958 (see Guinea).

100 centimes = 1 franc.

1892. "Tablet" key-type inscr "GUINEE FRANCAISE" in red (1, 5, 15, 50 (No. 17), 75c., 1f.) or blue (others).
1 D 1c. black on blue 1·60 2·25
2 2c. brown on buff 1·40 2·50
3 4c. brown on grey 2·25 2·50
4 5c. green on light green 3·50 4·00
5 10c. black on lilac 5·50 5·25
14 10c. red 30·00 35·00
6 15c. blue 5·50 3·75
15 15c. grey £100 90·00
7 20c. red on green 14·50 14·00
8 25c. black on pink 6·75 3·75
16 25c. blue 13·00 18·00
9 30c. brown on drab 17·00 20·00
10 40c. red on yellow 22·00 21·00
11 50c. red on pink 28·00 30·00
17 50c. brown on blue 24·00 24·00
12 75c. brown on yellow 55·00 65·00
13 1f. green 48·00 35·00

1 Fulas Shepherd

3 Ford at Kitim

1904.
18 **1** 1c. black on green 45 35
19 2c. brown on yellow 20 20
20 4c. red on blue 85 1·50
21 5c. green on light green 1·25 35
22 10c. red 2·50 80
23 15c. lilac on pink 4·25 3·00
24 20c. red on green 7·50 11·00
25 25c. blue 10·00 11·00
26 30c. brown 10·00 15·00
27 40c. red on yellow 18·00 22·00
28 50c. brown on green 17·00 15·00
29 75c. blue on yellow 21·00 28·00
30 1f. green 45·00 32·00
31 2f. red on orange 85·00 80·00
32 5f. blue on green £110 £110

1906. "Faidherbe", "Palms" and "Balay" key-types inscr "GUINEE" in blue (10c., 5f.) or red (others).
33 I 1c. slate 15 25
34 2c. brown 1·75 90
35 4c. brown on blue 75 80
36 5c. green 2·50 95
37 10c. red 12·00 80
38 J 20c. black on blue 2·25 3·75
39 25c. blue 3·25 3·75
40 30c. brown on pink 3·75 4·25
41 35c. black on yellow 1·25 1·40
43 45c. brown on green 3·00 4·00
44 50c. violet 7·25 9·25
45 75c. green on orange 4·50 4·25
46 K 1f. black on blue 13·00 11·00
47 2f. blue on pink 32·00 38·00
48 5f. red on yellow 35·00 50·00

1912. Surch in figures.
49 D 05 on 2c. brown on buff 90 2·50
50 05 on 4c. brown on grey 1·25 2·00
51 05 on 15c. blue 50 50
52 05 on 20c. red on green 2·00 5·00
53 05 on 30c. brown on drab 2·75 6·00
54 10 on 40c. red on yellow 75 5·25
55 10 on 75c. brown on yellow 4·00 9·50

1912. Surch in figures.
56 **1** 05 on 2c. brown on yellow 70 1·90
57 05 on 4c. red on blue 25 70
58 05 on 15c. lilac on pink 30 1·60
59 05 on 20c. red on green 35 1·60
60 05 on 25c. blue 60 1·25
61 05 on 30c. brown 70 2·00
62 10 on 40c. red on yellow 50 2·50
63 10 on 50c. brown on green 1·90 4·50

1913.
64 **3** 1c. blue and violet 10 10
65 2c. chocolate and brown 10 10
66 4c. black and grey 10 85
67 5c. green and light green 50 30
83 5c. green and purple 10 2·00
68 10c. pink and red 95 70
84 10c. green & light green 1·00 1·75
85 10c. red and lilac 10 55
69 15c. red and purple 50 95
86 15c. green & light green 40 1·75
87 15c. mauve and purple 1·10 1·40
70 20c. violet and brown 10 1·75
88 20c. green 75 3·00
89 20c. brown and red 80 1·10
71 25c. blue & ultramarine 2·25 1·90
90 25c. violet and black 45 20
72 30c. green and purple 2·00 2·75
91 30c. pink and red 1·25 2·25
92 30c. green and red 50 1·75
93 30c. green and olive 2·00 2·00
73 35c. pink and blue 1·25 2·50
74 40c. grey and green 1·75 1·25
75 45c. red and brown 2·00 2·75
76 50c. black and blue 5·50 3·75
94 50c. blue & ultramarine 1·10 2·25
95 50c. green and brown 1·90 15
96 60c. violet on pink 95 2·50
97 65c. blue and brown 2·25 2·75
77 75c. blue and pink 1·60 3·00
98 75c. light blue and blue 60 2·50
99 75c. green and mauve 2·00 2·00
100 85c. purple and green 90 3·25
101 90c. mauve and red 3·00 6·75
78 1f. black and violet 1·60 1·10
102 1f.10 brown and violet 4·50 8·75
103 1f.25 brown and violet 2·25 3·50
104 1f.50 light blue and blue 4·50 3·00
105 1f.75 mauve and brown 1·10 1·75
79 2f. brown and orange 3·25 2·50
106 3f. mauve on pink 7·25 6·75
80 5f. violet and black 8·50 16·00
107 5f. black and blue 1·40 3·00

1915. Surch **5c** and red cross.
81 **3** 10c.+5c. pink and red 1·75 2·75

1922. Surch in figures and bars.
108 **3** 25c. on 2f. brown & orange 95 2·75
109 25c. on 5f. black & blue 90 2·75
110 60 on 75c. violet on pink 1·50 3·00
111 65 on 75c. blue and pink 1·25 4·00
112 85 on 75c. blue and pink 1·60 4·00
113 90c. on 75c. mve & red 60 3·75
114 1f.25 on 1f. ultram & bl 1·25 3·00
115 1f.50 on 1f. lt blue & blue 75 1·75
116 3f. on 5f. grey & mauve 3·00 5·75
117 10f. on 5f. green & blue 7·00 8·25
118 20f. on 5f. brown and mauve on pink 17·00 27·00

1931. "Colonial Exhibition" key-types inscr "GUINEE FRANCAISE".
119 E 40c. black and green 3·25 4·50
120 F 50c. black and purple 3·25 4·75
121 G 90c. black and red 4·00 5·25
122 H 1f.50 black and blue 4·00 4·50

1937. International Exhibition, Paris. As T **58a** of Guadeloupe.
123 20c. violet 50 2·25
124 30c. green 90 2·75
125 40c. red 80 2·50
126 50c. brown and agate 25 1·75
127 90c. red 30 1·40
128 1f.50 blue 30 1·00
MS128a 120 × 100 mm. 3f. green and deep green. Imperf 6·75 13·00

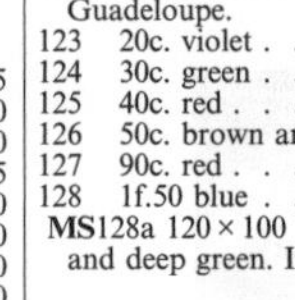
4 Native Village

7 Ford at Kitim and Marshal Petain

6a Airplane over Jungle

1938.
129 **4** 2c. red 10 95
130 3c. blue 10 1·40
131 4c. green 10 95
132 5c. red 65 40
133 10c. blue 10 65
134 15c. purple 10 1·50
135 – 20c. red 15 25
136 – 25c. blue 70 85
137 – 30c. blue 15 10
138 – 35c. green 1·25 1·25
139 – 40c. brown 30 2·75
140 – 45c. green 1·90 2·75
141 – 50c. red 30 1·25
142 – 55c. blue 55 1·75
143 – 60c. blue 1·75 3·00
144 – 65c. green 55 1·00
145 – 70c. green 2·25 3·00
146 – 80c. purple 85 2·50
147 – 90c. purple 2·00 3·00
148 – 1f. red 2·50 2·50
149 – 1f. brown 60 1·60
150 – 1f.25 red 2·25 3·25
151 – 1f.40 brown 2·00 2·25
152 – 1f.50 brown 1·50 1·75
153 – 1f.60 red 2·25 1·75
154 – 1f.75 blue 50 55
155 – 2f. mauve 90 55
156 – 2f.25 blue 1·60 2·50
157 – 2f.50 brown 2·00 65
158 – 3f. blue 65 40
159 – 5f. purple 65 60
160 – 10f. green 45 55
161 – 20f. brown 1·75 1·75

DESIGNS—HORIZ: 20c. to 50c. Wooden pot makers; 55c. to 1f.50, Waterfall. VERT: 1f.60 to 20f. Native women.

1938. International Anti-cancer Fund. As T **58b** of Guadeloupe.
162 1f.75+50c. blue . . . . . . 4·25 13·50

1939. Death Centenary of R. Caillie. As T **21** of French Sudan.
163 90c. orange . . . . 25 1·60
164 2f. violet 25 90
165 2f.25 blue . . . . 40 3·25

1939. New York World's Fair. As T **58c** of Guadeloupe.
166 1f.25 red . . . . 2·25 3·25
167 2f.25 blue . . . . 2·00 3·00

1939. 150th Anniv of French Revolution. As T **58d** of Guadeloupe.
168 45c.+25c. green & black . . . 7·00 10·00
169 70c.+30c. brown & black . . 5·25 10·00
170 90c.+35c. orange & black . . 6·00 10·00
171 1f.25+1f. red and black . . . 6·25 10·00
172 2f.25+2f. blue and black . . 6·50 10·00

1940. Air.
173 **6a** 1f.90 blue . . . . 1·25 2·50
174 2f.90 red . . . . 30 2·75
175 4f.50 green . . . . 1·25 3·00
176 4f.90 olive . . . . 1·10 3·25
177 6f.90 orange . . . . 1·40 3·50

1941. National Defence Fund. Surch **SECOURS NATIONAL** and value.
178 +1f. on 50c. (No. 141) . . . 1·25 3·50
179 +2f. on 80c. (No. 146) . . . 6·00 6·25
180 +2f. on 1f.50 (No. 152) . . . 5·50 7·50
181 +3f. on 2f. (No. 155) . . . . 6·00 7·25

1941.
182 **7** 1f. green . . . . 35 2·75
183 2f.50 blue . . . . 40 2·75

8 Dakar Maternity Hospital

1942. Air. Colonial Child Welfare.
184 **8** 1f.50+3f.50 green . . . . . 45 3·25
185 2f.+6f. brown . . . . . . 65 3·25
186 3f.+9f. red . . . . 90 3·25

9a "Vocation"

1942. Air.
187 **9a** 50f. olive and green . . . 1·75 4·00

POSTAGE DUE STAMPS

D **2** Woman of Futa Jallon

D **7** Native Idol

1905.
D33 D **2** 5c. blue . . . . 1·00 70
D34 10c. brown . . . . . . 1·60 1·00
D35 15c. green . . . . . . 2·75 2·75
D36 30c. red . . . . 3·25 3·25
D37 50c. black . . . . . . 5·50 6·25
D38 60c. orange . . . . . . 9·75 7·50
D39 1f. lilac . . . . 32·00 34·00

1906. "Natives" key-type inscr "GUINEE".
D49 L 5c. green . . . . 7·00 6·00
D50 10c. purple . . . . . . 1·50 2·75
D51 15c. blue on blue . . . . 1·75 4·00
D52 20c. black on yellow . . . 1·75 4·50
D53 30c. red on cream . . . 13·00 30·00
D54 50c. violet . . . . . . 5·75 30·00
D55 60c. black on buff . . . 5·25 28·00
D56 1f. black on pink . . . . 3·00 17·00

1914. "Figure" key-type inscr "GUINEE".
D81 M 5c. green . . . . 15 2·50
D82 10c. red . . . . 20 2·50
D83 15c. grey . . . . 1·10 2·75
D84 20c. brown . . . . 1·00 2·75
D85 30c. blue . . . . 75 2·75
D86 50c. black . . . . 85 3·00
D87 60c. orange . . . . 1·60 3·50
D88 1f. violet . . . . 1·10 3·50

1927. Surch in figures.
D119 M 2F. on 1f. mauve . . . . 4·00 10·50
D120 3F. on 1f. brown . . . . 2·50 12·00

1938.
D162 D **7** 5c. violet . . . . 10 2·50
D163 10c. red . . . . 10 2·50
D164 15c. green . . . . . . 10 2·50
D165 20c. brown . . . . . . 10 2·75
D166 30c. purple . . . . . . 40 2·75
D167 50c. brown . . . . . . 40 3·00
D168 60c. blue . . . . 60 3·25
D169 1f. red . . . . 55 3·25
D170 2f. blue . . . . 1·25 3·50
D171 3f. black . . . . 85 3·75
For later issues see **GUINEA**.

FRENCH INDIAN SETTLEMENTS

Pt. 6

A group of five small French settlements in India. The inhabitants voted to join India in 1954.

1892. 100 centimes = 1 franc.
1923. 24 caches = 1 fanon;
8 fanons = 1 rupee.

1892. "Tablet" key-type inscr "ETABLISSEMENTS DE L'INDE" in red (1, 5, 15, 25, 35, 45, 50 (No. 19), 75c., 1f.) or blue (others).
1 D 1c. black on blue 70 95
2 2c. brown on buff . . . . . 1·40 1·25
3 4c. brown on grey . . . . . 2·75 3·00
4 5c. green on light green . . 4·25 3·50
5 10c. black on lilac . . . . . 9·25 3·25
14 10c. red . . . . 3·00 2·25
6 15c. blue . . . . 5·25 5·25
15 15c. grey . . . . 25·00 27·00
7 20c. red on green . . . . . 6·00 6·00
8 25c. black on pink . . . . . 3·50 3·75
16 25c. blue . . . . 16·00 16·00
9 30c. brown on drab . . . . 45·00 40·00
17 35c. black on yellow . . . . 12·00 9·00
10 40c. red on yellow . . . . . 4·50 6·00
18 45c. black on green . . . . 5·00 5·00
11 50c. red on pink . . . . . . 5·25 6·00
19 50c. brown on blue . . . . 11·00 13·00
12 75c. brown on yellow . . . 7·25 11·00
13 1f. green . . . . 4·75 10·00

1903. Surch in figures.
20 D 0,05 on 25c. blk on pink . . £225 £160
21 0,10 on 25c. blk on pink . . £250 £170
22 0,15 on 25c. blk on pink . . 70·00 85·00
23 0,40 on 50c. red on pink . . £400 £325

1903. Fiscal stamp bisected and each half surch **Inde Fcaise POSTES 0,05**.
24 0.05 black and blue . . . . . 19·00 22·00

3 Brahma

4 Temple near Pondicherry

1914.
26 **3** 1c. black and grey 70 15
27 2c. black and purple . . . . 15 1·00
52 2c. purple and green . . . . 40 3·00
28 3c. black and brown . . . . 20 1·50
29 4c. black and orange . . . . 90 2·00
30 5c. black and green . . . . 40 2·25
53 5c. black and purple . . . . 1·25 2·75
31 10c. black and red . . . . . 2·10 2·50
54 10c. black and green . . . . 1·40 3·00
32 15c. black and violet . . . . 2·25 2·50
33 20c. black and red . . . . . 2·75 3·25
34 25c. black and blue . . . . . 2·75 2·75
55 25c. red and blue . . . . . 2·50 2·75
35 30c. black and blue . . . . . 2·75 3·25
56 30c. black and red . . . . . 1·50 3·00
36 **4** 35c. black and brown . . . . 2·75 3·25
37 40c. black and red . . . . . 3·00 3·25
38 45c. black and green . . . . 3·00 3·50
39 50c. black and red . . . . . 2·50 3·25
57 50c. blue and ultramarine . . 1·60 3·25
40 75c. black and blue . . . . . 3·25 4·00
41 1f. black and yellow . . . . 3·50 4·00
42 2f. black and violet . . . . . 6·00 7·00
43 5f. black and blue . . . . . 3·25 4·00
58 5f. black and red . . . . . . 3·00 4·50
See also Nos. 88/107.

1915. Red Cross surch with plain cross and premium.
44 **3** 10c.+5c. black and red . . . 85 3·25

1916. Surch **5** and Maltese cross.
48 **3** 10c.+5c. black and red . . . 5·75 21·00

1916. Surch with Maltese cross and **5 C**.
49 **3** 10c.+5c. black and red . . . 45 4·25

1922. Surch in figures and bars.
59 **3** 0.01 on 15c. black & violet 75 3·00
60 0.02 on 15c. black & violet 10 3·00
61 0.05 on 15c. black & violet 10 3·00

1923. Surch in new currency (caches, fanons and rupees) in figures and words.
62 **3** 1ca. on 1c. black and grey . . 15 2·75
63 2ca. on 5c. black & purple 20 2·00
64 3ca. on 3c. black & brown 40 2·75
65 4ca. on 4c. black & orange 40 2·40
66 6ca. on 10c. black & green 1·40 2·25
67 **4** 6ca. on 45c. black & green 40 3·00
68 **3** 10ca. on 20c. green & red . . 3·25 3·75
69 12ca. on 15c. black & violet 1·90 2·75
70 15ca. on 20c. black & red . . 65 3·00
71 **4** 16ca. on 35c. brown & blue 3·25 3·75
72 **3** 18ca. on 30c. black & red . . 2·25 75
73 **4** 20ca. on 45c. pink & green 2·50 2·75
74 **3** 1fa. on 25c. red and green . . 3·25 4·50
75 **4** 1fa.3ca. on 35c. blk & brn . . 80 2·50
76 1fa.6ca. on 40c. black & red 2·25 2·25
77 1fa.12ca. on 50c. blue and ultramarine . . . . 2·40 2·75
78 1fa.12ca. on 75c. black & bl 70 3·25
79 1fa.16ca. on 75c. grn & red 3·25 3·75
80 **3** 2fa.9ca. on 25c. red & blue 1·60 3·25
81 **4** 2fa.12ca. on 1f. brn & mve 3·50 4·00
82 3fa.3ca. on 1f. black & yell 1·60 3·25
83 6fa.6ca. on 2f. black & vio 5·00 5·75
84 1r. on 1f. blue and green . . 7·50 7·50
85 2r. on 5f. black and red . . . 7·75 7·50
86 3r. on 2f. violet and grey . . 12·00 16·00
87 5r. on 5f. blk & pink on green . . . . 26·00 24·00

1929. As T **3** and **4** but with value in caches, fanons or rupees.
88 **3** 1ca. black and brown . . . 15 2·50
89 2ca. black and purple . . . 20 2·25
90 3ca. black and brown . . . 15 2·50
91 4ca. black and orange . . . 25 3·25
92 6ca. green and deep green 35 1·75
93 10ca. green and red . . . . 1·40 2·50
94 **4** 12ca. green & deep green . . 20 2·75
95 **3** 16ca. black and blue . . . . 1·25 3·25
96 18ca. red and carmine . . . 1·60 3·25
97 20ca. green & bl on azure 40 30
98 **4** 1fa. red and green . . . . . 55 2·25
99 1fa.6ca. black and orange 1·60 3·00
100 1fa.12ca. blue and dp blue 1·10 2·75
101 1fa.16ca. green and red . . 1·40 3·25
102 2fa.12ca. brown and mauve 60 1·75
103 6fa.6ca. black and violet . . 1·50 3·25
104 1r. blue and green . . . . 1·50 2·25
105 2r. black and red . . . . . 1·40 1·90
106 3r. lilac and black . . . . . 2·75 2·50
107 5r. black & red on green . . 2·75 2·75

1931. "Colonial Exhibition" key-types inscr "ETS FRANCAIS DANS L'INDE".
108 E 10ca. green . . . . 3·50 4·25
109 F 12ca. mauve . . . . 3·25 3·75
110 G 18ca. red . . . . 4·25 4·75
111 H 1fa.12 blue . . . . 3·50 4·00

1937. International Exhibition, Paris. As T **58a** of Guadeloupe.
112 8ca. violet . . . . 70 3·50
113 12ca. green . . . . 2·10 3·50
114 16ca. red . . . . 1·00 3·50
115 20ca. brown . . . . 90 3·50
116 1fa.12 red . . . . 65 3·50
117 2fa.12 blue . . . . 75 3·50
MS117a 120 × 100 mm. 5fa. purple. Imperf . . . . 7·50 14·00

1938. International Anti-cancer Fund. As T **58b** of Guadeloupe.
118 2fa.12ca.+20ca. blue . . . . 7·00 15·00

1939. New York World's Fair. As T **58c** of Guadeloupe.
119 1fa.12 red . . . . 2·75 3·25
120 2fa.12 blue . . . . 3·00 3·75

1939. 150th Anniv of French Revolution. As T **58d** of Guadeloupe.
121 18ca.+10ca. green & black . . 6·75 10·00
122 1fa.6ca.+12ca. brn & blk . . 6·75 10·00
123 1fa.12ca.+16ca. orge & blk 6·50 10·00
124 1fa.16ca.+1fa.16ca. red & blk 6·50 10·00
125 2fa.12ca.+3fa. blue & blk . . 6·75 10·00

1941. Optd **FRANCE LIBRE**. (a) Stamps of 1923.
126 **3** 15ca. on 20ca. black & red 65·00 85·00
127 18ca. on 30ca. black & red 2·75 4·25
128a **4** 1fa.3 on 35ca. black & brn 55·00 65·00
132 **3** 2fa.9 on 25ca. red & blue £700 £700

(b) Stamps of 1929.
133 **3** 2ca. black and purple . . . 7·00 12·50
134 3ca. black and brown . . . 1·40 4·00
135 4ca. black and orange . . . 5·50 7·50
136 6ca. green and deep green 2·25 3·75
137 10ca. green and red . . . . 3·00 4·00
139 **4** 12ca. green & deep green . . 2·00 4·00
140 **3** 16ca. black and blue . . . . 2·00 4·00
141 18ca. red and carmine . . . £450 £450
142 20ca. green & bl on azure 2·50 3·75
143 **4** 1fa. red and green . . . . . 1·90 3·75
144 1fa.6 black and red . . . . 2·00 4·00
145 1fa.12 blue and deep blue 3·50 5·75
146 1fa.16 green and red . . . . 2·50 3·50
147 2fa.12 brown and mauve . . 2·00 75
148 6fa.6 black and violet . . . 2·50 4·00
149 1r. blue and green . . . . . 3·00 3·75
150 2r. black and red . . . . . 2·75 4·00
151 3r. lilac and black . . . . . 3·00 4·25
152 5r. black & red on green . . 7·25 10·50

(c) Paris Exhibition stamps of 1937.
154 8ca. violet . . . . 4·50 9·50
157 12ca. green . . . . 3·50 6·00
158 16ca. red . . . . 2·50 6·00
159 1fa.12 red . . . . 2·50 6·00
160 2fa.12 blue . . . . 2·50 6·00
MS160a 5fa. bright purple (**MS**117a) £575 £575

(d) New York World's Fair stamps of 1939.
161 1fa.12 red . . . . 2·75 4·75
162 2fa.12 blue . . . . 2·75 4·75

1941. Various issues optd **FRANCE TOUJOURS** and Cross of Lorraine. (a) On Nos. 70, 72 and 75.
162a **3** 15ca. on 20c. black & red £600 £160
162b 18ca. on 30c. black & red £900 £425
162c **4** 1fa.3 on 35c. black & brn £600 £160

(b) On Nos. 89/90, 92 and 94/107.
162d **3** 2ca. black and purple . . £600 £140
162e 3ca. black and brown . . £600 £140
162f 6ca. green and deep green £600 £140
162g **4** 12ca. green and deep green £600 £140
162h **3** 16ca. black and blue . . . £600 £140
162i 18ca. red and carmine . . £900 £550
162j 20ca. green & bl on azure £550 £130
162k **4** 1fa. red and green £550 £130
162l 1fa.6 black and orange . . £550 £130
162m 1fa.12 blue and deep blue £550 £130
162n 1fa.16 green and red . . . £550 £130
162o 2fa.12 brown and mauve £550 £130
162p 6fa.6 black and violet . . £550 £140
162q 1r. blue and green £550 £140
162r 2r. black and red £550 £140
162s 3r. lilac and black £550 £140
162t 5r. black and red on green £550 £140

(c) On Nos. 112/14 and 116/17.
162u 8ca. violet £550 £160
162v 12ca. green £550 £160
162w 16ca. red £550 £160
162x 1fa.12 red £550 £160
162y 2fa.12 blue £550 £160

(d) On Nos. 119/20.
162z 1fa.12 red £550 £160
162za 2fa.12 blue £550 £160

1942. Optd **FRANCE LIBRE** and Cross of Lorraine. (a) Nos. 72 and 88/107.
164 **3** 2ca. black and purple . . . 1·25 3·00
165 3ca. black and brown . . . 30 3·25
166 6ca. green and deep green 2·00 3·00
167 **4** 12ca. green & deep green 2·75 4·50
168 **3** 16ca. black and blue . . . 2·25 3·25
169 18ca. red and carmine . . 35 3·25
163 18ca. on 30c. black and red (No. 72) £200 £160
171 20ca. green & bl on azure 35 3·25
172 **4** 1fa. red and green . . . . 35 3·25
173a 1fa.6 black and red . . . . 3·00 3·75
174 1fa.12 blue and deep blue 2·50 3·50
175 1fa.16 green and red . . . 55 65
176 2fa.12 brown and mauve 1·75 85
177 6fa.6 black and violet . . . 3·25 4·50
178 1r. blue and green . . . . 5·25 8·75
179 2r. black and red . . . . . 4·00 7·25
180a 3r. lilac and black . . . . 4·50 8·25
181 5r. black & red on green . . 4·50 9·25

(b) Paris Exhibition stamps of 1937.
189 8ca. violet . . . . 6·50 9·00
190 12ca. green . . . . 6·00 9·00
191 16ca. red £850 £850
192 1fa.12 red . . . . 2·25 3·25
193 2fa.12 blue . . . . 3·00 4·75

(c) New York World's Fair stamps of 1939.
194 1fa.12 red . . . . 3·25 4·00
195 2fa.12 blue . . . . 4·25 5·25

1942. No. 103 surch with value only.
203 1ca. on 6fa.6 black and violet 27·00 21·00
204 4ca. on 6fa.6 black and violet 27·00 21·00
205 10ca. on 6fa.6 black & violet 13·50 9·50
206 15fa. on 6fa.6 black & violet 13·50 9·50
207 1fa.3 on 6fa.6 black & violet 21·00 20·00
208 2fa.9 on 6fa.6 black & violet 14·00 21·00
209 3fa.3 on 6fa.6 black & violet 18·00 20·00

1942. Stamps of 1929 surch **FRANCE LIBRE**, Cross of Lorraine and new value.
196 **3** 1ca. on 16ca. black & blue 60·00 40·00
210 **4** 1ca. on 6fa.6 black & violet 3·00 11·00
211 1ca. on 1r. blue and green 1·50 6·50
212 2ca. on 1r. blue and green 40 3·25
197 **3** 4ca. on 16ca. black & blue 60·00 40·00
213 **4** 4ca. on 6fa.6 black & violet 3·50 16·00
214 4ca. on 1r. blue and green 40 3·50
215 6ca. on 2r. black and red . . 35 3·25
198 **3** 10ca. on 16ca. black & blue 38·00 25·00
216 10ca. on 6fa.6 black & vio 80 4·00
217 10ca. on 2r. black and red 50 3·50
218 12ca. on 2r. black and red 35 3·25
199 15ca. on 16ca. black & blue 35·00 20·00
219 **4** 15ca. on 6f.6 black & violet 1·60 3·75
220 15ca. on 3r. lilac and black 30 3·25
221 16c. on 3r. lilac and black 30 3·25
200 **3** 1fa.3ca. on 16ca. black and blue . . . . 65·00 42·00
222 **4** 1fa.3 on 6fa.6 black & vio 2·50 5·50
223 1fa.3 on 3r. lilac and black 35 3·75
224 1fa.6 on 5r. black and red on green . . . . 50 3·75
225 1fa.12 on 5r. black and red on green . . . . 50 3·75
226 1fa.16 on 5r. black and red on green . . . . 50 3·50
201 **3** 2fa.9ca. on 16ca. black and blue . . . . 60·00 55·00

227 4 2fa.9 on 6fa.6 black & vio 1·90 7·25
202 3 3fa.3ca. on 16ca. black and blue 42·00 28·00
228 3fa.3 on 6fa.6 black & vio 3·00 8·25

20 Lotus Flowers 22 Apsara

1942. Free French issue. (a) Postage.
229 20 2ca. brown 15 2·75
230 3ca. blue 15 1·75
231 4ca. green 35 2·75
232 6ca. orange 35 1·90
233 12ca. green 1·40 1·90
234 16ca. purple 1·60 2·75
235 20ca. purple 1·50 2·25
236 1fa. red 1·60 2·00
237 1fa.18 black 1·40 1·25
238 6fa.6 blue 1·60 3·25
239 1r. violet 1·75 3·25
240 2r. bistre 1·90 3·25
241 3r. brown 1·75 3·50
242 5r. green 1·90 4·50

(b) Air. As T **63a** of Guadeloupe.
243 4fa. orange 75 3·25
244 1r. red 1·10 3·25
245 2r. purple 1·25 3·75
246 5r. black 1·25 3·75
247 8r. blue 1·90 5·00
248 10r. green 1·90 5·00

1944. Mutual Aid and Red Cross Funds. As T **58e** of Guadeloupe.
249 3fa.+1r.4fa. bistre 1·10 3·50

1945. Eboue. As T **58f** of Guadeloupe.
250 3fa.8 black 20 3·00
251 5r.1fa.16 green 80 3·50

1946. Air. Victory. As T **63b** of Guadeloupe.
252 4fa. green 25 3·50

1946. Air. From Chad to the Rhine. As Nos. 226/31 of Cameroun.
253 2fa.12 brown 90 3·50
254 5fa. blue 90 3·50
255 7fa.12 violet 65 3·50
256 1r.2fa. green 1·00 3·75
257 1r.4fa.12 red 1·25 4·00
258 3r.1fa. purple 1·40 4·00

1948.
259 22 1ca. olive 15 2·75
260 2ca. brown 15 2·75
261 4ca. violet on cream 15 2·50
262 A 6ca. orange 35 2·75
263 8ca. slate 55 2·50
264 10ca. green on green 90 3·00
265 B 12ca. purple 90 2·25
266 15ca. blue 1·10 2·75
267 C 18ca. lake 3·00 3·50
268 B 1fa. violet on red 1·10 2·25
269 D 1fa.6 red 1·25 3·00
270 C 1fa.15 violet 3·25 4·00
271 D 2fa. green 1·10 65
272 2fa.2 blue on cream 1·50 3·25
273 E 2fa.12 brown 1·75 3·00
274 3fa. red 1·75 1·10
275 C 4fa. olive 3·25 4·25
276 E 5fa. purple on red 1·40 2·25
277 F 7fa.12 brown 1·40 3·50
278 1r.2fa. black 3·00 6·00
279 1r.4fa.12c. green 2·00 7·00
DESIGNS—As Type **22**: A, Dvarabalagar standing erect; B, Vishnu; C, Brahmin idol; D, Dvarabalagar with leg raised; E, Temple Guardian; F, One of the Tigoupalagar.

25 Douglas DC-4 and Bas-relief

1949. Air.
281 25 1r. red and yellow 4·75 5·25
282 – 2r. deep green & green 6·00 8·00
283 – 5r. purple and blue 18·00 12·50
DESIGNS—VERT: 2r. Wing and temple; 5r. Short-toed eagle and palm trees.

1949. Air. 75th Anniv of U.P.U. As T **39** of French Equatorial Africa.
284 6fa. red 3·00 11·00

1950. Colonial Welfare Fund. As T **40** of French Equatorial Africa.
285 1fa.+10ca. blue & grey 1·90 3·50

1952. Centenary of Military Medal. As T **44** of French Equatorial Africa.
286 1fa. brown, yellow & green 2·75 5·50

1954. Air. 10th Anniv of Liberation. As T **46** of French Equatorial Africa.
287 1fa. purple and sepia 6·75 8·50

POSTAGE DUE STAMPS

1923. Postage Due stamps of France surch in figures and letters.
D88 D 11 4ca. on 20c. violet 60 3·25
D89 6ca. on 10c. brown 95 3·25
D90 12ca. on 25c. red 65 3·25
D91 15ca. on 20c. olive 85 3·50
D92 1fa. on 30c. orange 1·75 3·75
D93 1fa.6 on 30c. red 5·25 15·00
D94 1fa.12 on 50c. purple 1·50 4·00
D95 1fa.15 on 5c. blue 75 4·75
D96 1fa.16 on 5c. black 2·00 4·00
D97 3fa. on 1f. green 2·50 4·50
D98 3fa.3 on 1f. brn on yell 90 4·50

D 14

D 24

1929.
D108 D 14 4ca. red 20 3·00
D109 6ca. blue 20 3·25
D110 12ca. green 30 3·25
D111 1fa. brown 1·10 3·50
D112 1fa.12 violet 1·40 3·50
D113 1fa.16 brown 1·90 3·50
D114 3fa. mauve 2·50 4·25

1948.
D280 D 24 1ca. violet 15 2·75
D281 2ca. brown 15 2·75
D282 6ca. green 15 2·75
D283 12ca. red 20 2·75
D284 1fa. mauve 70 2·75
D285 1fa.12 brown 1·25 3·25
D286 2fa. blue 1·25 3·50
D287 2fa.12 lake 85 3·50
D288 5fa. green 1·50 4·25
D289 1r. violet 1·60 5·00

FRENCH MOROCCO Pt. 6

Part of the Sultanate of Morocco, which was a French protectorate from 1912 until independence was granted on 2 March 1956. For issues before 1912 see French Post Offices in Morocco, and for stamps used in the International Zone see French Post Offices in Tangier.

100 centimes = 1 franc.

1914. Surcharged "Blanc", "Mouchon" and "Merson" key-types of French Post Offices in Morocco optd **PROTECTORAT FRANCAIS**.
40 A 1c. on 1c. grey 15 65
41 2c. on 2c. red 15 60
42 3c. on 3c. orange 55 1·40
43 5c. on 5c. green 50 10
44 B 10c. on 10c. red 35 10
45 15c. on 15c. orange 45 10
46 20c. on 20c. red 1·75 2·00
47 25c. on 25c. blue 1·25 10
48 25c. on 25c. brown 1·50 10
49 30c. on 30c. brown 18·00 12·00
50 35c. on 35c. lilac 2·25 1·25
51 C 40c. on 40c. red and blue 5·00 4·75
52 45c. on 45c. green & blue 40·00 50·00
53 50c. on 50c. brn & lilac 1·40 15
54 1p. on 1f. red and green 1·10 15
55 2p. on 2f. lilac and yellow 1·60 50
56 5p. on 5f. blue & yellow 6·50 7·75

1914. Surch **5c** and red cross. (a) No. 32 of French Post Offices in Morocco.
65 5 10c.+5c. on 10c. red 1·90 3·75

(b) As No. 43 but without previous surcharge.
62 4 5c.+5c. green 45 1·75

(c) No. 44.
59 5 10c.+5c. on 10c. red 2·00 5·00

1915. No. 352 of France optd **MAROC** and in Arabic.
63 20 10c.+5c. red 2·25 5·50

13

1915. Optd **PROTECTORAT FRANCAIS**.
64 13 10c.+5c. red 1·75 2·25

15 Tower of Hassan, Rabat

16 Fez

1917.
76 15 1c. black 50 1·60
123 1c. green 25 35
124 2c. purple 25 35
125 3c. brown 10 55
79 16 5c. green 20 10
126 5c. yellow 25 10
80 10c. red 20 10
127 10c. green 35 10
128 15c. grey 65 45
129 A 20c. purple 45 10
131 25c. blue 25 10
84 30c. lilac 4·25 4·50
132 30c. red 25 10
133 30c. blue 40 15
85 B 35c. orange 3·00 4·00
134 35c. purple 60 1·75
86 40c. blue 80 30
135 40c. orange 25 10
136 45c. green 35 70
88 C 50c. brown 6·00 2·75
137 50c. blue 1·40 90
138 B 50c. green 1·60 10
139 C 60c. mauve 30 45
140a 75c. purple 35 15
89 1f. grey 6·50 6·50
141 1f. brown 30 80
142 1f.05 brown 1·40 2·25
143 1f.40 pink 30 65
144 1f.50 blue 80 10
145 D 2f. brown 60 55
146 3f. red 1·75 25
147 5f. green 85 1·75
148 10f. brown 3·25 5·50
DESIGNS—VERT: A, Chella; B, Marrakesh. Horiz: C, Meknes; D, Volubilis.

22 Breguet 14T Biplane over Casablanca

1922. Air.
112 22 5c. orange 55 40
113 25c. blue 60 1·10
114 50c. blue 45 45
115 75c. blue 75·00 9·00
116 75c. green 1·10 65
117 80c. brown 20 75
118 1f. red 1·10 15
119 1f.40 red 60 2·25
120 1f.90 blue 2·25 4·00
121 2f. violet 2·25 1·40
122 3f. black 1·50 2·25

23 Ploughing with Camel and Donkey

1928. Air. Flood Relief.
149 – 5c. blue 4·25 7·50
150 23 25c. orange 4·75 7·25
151 – 50c. red 3·75 6·50
152 – 75c. brown 3·25 7·75
153 – 80c. green 4·00 7·00
154 – 1f. orange 3·75 7·75
155 – 1f.50 blue 3·50 7·75
156 – 2f. brown 3·50 7·75
157 – 3f. purple 4·00 3·75
158 – 5f. black 3·75 7·75
DESIGNS: 5c. Moorish tribesmen; 50c. Caravan nearing Safi; 75c. Walls of Marrakesh; 80c. Sheep grazing at Azrou; 1f. Gateway at Fez; 1f.50, Aerial view of Tangier; 2f. Aerial view of Casablanca; 3f. White storks at Rabat; 5f. "La Hedia", a Moorish entertainment.

1930. Stamps of 1917 surch.
163 B 15c. on 40c. orange 35 90
164 A 25c. on 30c. blue 2·50 3·50
165 C 50c. on 60c. mauve 35 10
166 1f. on 1f.40 pink 2·50 1·40

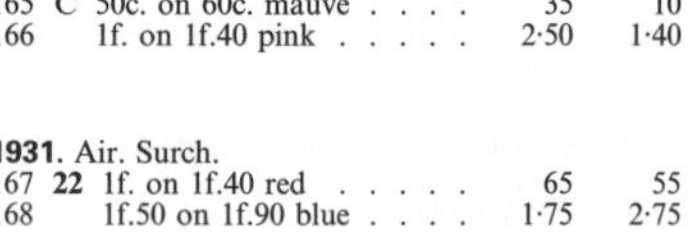

1931. Air. Surch.
167 22 1f. on 1f.40 red 65 55
168 1f.50 on 1f.90 blue 1·75 2·75

27 Sultan's Palace, Tangier

28 Saadian Tombs, Marrakesh

1933.
169 27 1c. black 40 10
170 2c. mauve 45 1·25
171 – 3c. brown 25 1·90
172 – 5c. lake 35 45
173 – 10c. green 25 10
174 – 15c. black 55 10
175 – 20c. purple 1·75 10
176 – 25c. blue 1·40 10
177 – 30c. green 1·40 10
178 – 40c. sepia 35 10
179 – 45c. purple 40 1·25
180 – 50c. green 1·75 10
181 – 65c. red 35 10
182 – 75c. purple 25 10
183 – 90c. red 65 25
184 – 1f. brown 1·00 10
185 – 1f.25 black 60 95
186 – 1f.50 blue 1·25 10
187 – 1f.75 green 55 10
188 – 2f. brown 2·50 10
189 – 3f. red 45·00 3·75
190 28 5f. lake 1·50 75
191 10f. black 4·75 4·00
192 20f. grey 4·25 11·50
DESIGNS—HORIZ: 3c., 5c. Agadir Bay; 10c. to 20c. G.P.O., Casablanca; 25c. to 40c. Moulay Idriss; 45c. to 65c. Rabat; 1f.50 to 3f. Quarzazat. VERT: 75c. to 1f.25, Attarine College, Fez.

29 Hassan Tower, Rabat

30 Marshal Lyautey

1933. Air.
193 29 50c. blue 2·10 2·50
194 80c. brown 2·10 50
195 1f.50 lake 1·25 40
196 – 2f.50 red 2·25 1·25
197 – 5f. violet 3·50 1·75
198 – 10f. green 2·10 3·25
DESIGN: 2f.50 to 10f. Casablanca.

1935. Lyautey Memorial Fund.
199 30 50c.+50c. red (postage) 10·00 16·00
200 1f.+1f. green 7·50 16·00
201 5f.+5f. brown 35·00 65·00
202 – 1f.50+1f.50 blue (air) 14·00 14·00
DESIGN—HORIZ: 1f.50, Lyautey in profile.

1938. Child Welfare Fund. Stamps of 1933 surch **O.S.E.** and premium.
203 27 2c.+2c. mauve (postage) 1·75 7·50
204 – 3c.+3c. brown 1·60 7·50
205 – 20c.+20c. purple 1·75 7·50
206 – 40c.+40c. sepia 1·60 7·50
207 – 65c.+65c. red 3·50 10·50
208 – 1f.25+1f.25 black 1·75 7·50
209 – 2f.+2f. brown 1·75 7·50
210 28 5f.+5f. lake 1·75 7·50
211 29 50c.+50c. blue (air) 2·75 7·25
212 – 10f.+10f. green 2·75 7·50

1939. No. 180 surch **40c**.
213 40c. on 50c. green 2·00 30

34 Mosque at Sale

36 Shepherd and Arganier Trees

42 Dewoitine D-338 Trimotor over Morocco

1939.
214 **34** 1c. mauve (postage) . . . 30 1·50
215 A 2c. green . . . 30 1·75
216 3c. blue . . . 35 1·50
217 **34** 5c. green . . . 20 60
218 A 10c. purple . . . 10 10
219 B 15c. green . . . 30 1·50
220 20c. brown . . . 10 15
221 **36** 30c. blue . . . 10 10
222 40c. brown . . . 30 20
223 45c. green . . . 40 2·50
224 E 50c. red . . . 1·90 2·00
293 50c. green . . . 60 10
226 60c. blue . . . 60 80
227 60c. brown . . . 30 10
228 C 70c. violet . . . 25 25
229 F 75c. green . . . 25 3·00
230 80c. blue . . . 10 45
231 80c. green . . . 30 1·25
232 E 90c. blue . . . 60 1·10
233 B 1f. brown . . . 55 10
234 F 1f.20 mauve . . . 30 2·25
295 1f.20 brown . . . 40 15
235 1f.25 red . . . 35 2·25
296 A 1f.30 blue . . . 1·25 2·50
236 F 1f.40 purple . . . 60 2·50
238 E 1f.50 pink . . . 40 75
297 1f.50 red . . . 20 25
239 D 2f. green . . . 55 10
240 2f.25 blue . . . 50 65
241 **34** 2f.40 red . . . 40 50
242 2f.50 red . . . 35 85
243 2f.50 blue . . . 30 70
299 D 3f. brown . . . 20 10
300 **36** 3f.50 red . . . 85 45
245 **34** 4f. blue . . . 50 50
246 F 4f.50 green . . . 10 20
301 C 4f.50 mauve . . . 65 30
302 5f. blue . . . 40 45
303 F 6f. blue . . . 10 10
248 C 10f. red . . . 1·75 1·60
305 15f. green . . . 1·10 45
306 20f. purple . . . 1·75 3·50
307 25f. brown . . . 1·25 1·25
DESIGNS—VERT: A, Mosque at Sefrou; B,Horseman and Cedar tree; C, Scimitar oryxes; D, Fez. HORIZ: E, Ramparts at Sale; F, Draa Valley.

251 G 80c. green (air) . . . 50 1·10
252 1f. brown . . . 30 80
253 **42** 1f.90 blue . . . 20 1·40
254 2f. purple . . . 20 55
255 3f. brown . . . 40 20
256 G 5f. violet . . . 65 2·75
257 **42** 10f. blue . . . 80 1·75
DESIGN—VERT: G, Storks and Mosque at Chella.

1940. No. 181 surch **35c.**
258a 35c. on 65c. red . . . 2·25 3·50

1942. French Child Refugees in Morocco Fund. Types of 1939 surch **Enfants de France au Maroc** and premium.
259 **36** 45c.+2f. green . . . 2·40 7·50
260 E 90c.+4f. blue . . . 4·00 7·00
261 F 1f.25+6f. red . . . 2·40 7·00
262 **34** 2f.50+8f. red . . . 2·40 7·50

45 "La Marseillaise"

46 Tower of Hassan

1943.
263 **45** 1f.50 blue . . . 1·90 3·25

1943.
264 **46** 10c. lilac . . . 10 75
265 30c. blue . . . 10 2·25
266 40c. red . . . 10 10
267 50c. green . . . 10 10
268 60c. brown . . . 10 10
269 70c. lilac . . . 15 10
270 80c. green . . . 10 10
271 1f. red . . . 10 15
272 1f.20 violet . . . 10 10
273 1f.50 red . . . 10 10
274 2f. green . . . 30 1·25
275 2f.40 red . . . 25 90
276 3f. brown . . . 20 60
277 4f. blue . . . 35 10
278 4f.50 black . . . 25 95
279 5f. blue . . . 30 10
280 10f. brown . . . 30 75
281 15f. green . . . 10 10
282 20f. purple . . . 40 25

47 Sud Est Languedoc over Desert

49 Potez 56 over Minarets

1944. Air.
283 **47** 50c. green . . . 70 1·10
284 2f. blue . . . 35 80
285 5f. red . . . 30 10
286 10f. violet . . . 25 20
287 50f. black . . . 35 2·75
288 100f. blue and red . . . 5·00 15·00

1944. Air. Mutual Aid Fund. Surch **ENTR'AIDE FRANCAISE +98F 50.**
289 **47** 1f.50+98f.50 red & bl . . . 2·00 3·75

1945. Air.
290 **49** 50f. brown . . . 1·75 3·00

1945. Anti-tuberculosis Fund. No. 239 surch **AIDEZ LES TUBERCULEUX + 1f.**
308 D 2f.+1f. green . . . 40 2·75

51 Mausoleum

54 Marshal Lyautey Statue, Casablanca

1945. Solidarity Fund. Marshal Lyautey's Mausoleum.
309a **51** 2f.+3f. blue . . . 95 1·25

1946. No. 308 surch **3f** and bars.
310 D 3f. on 2f.+1f. green . . . 50 2·00

1946. Air. 6th Anniv of Gen. De Gaulle's Call to Arms. Surch **+ 5 F 18 Juin 1940 18 Juin 1946.**
311 **47** 5f.+5f. red . . . 1·40 2·25

1946. Solidarity Fund.
312 **54** 2f.+10f. black (postage) . . 95 3·50
313 3f.+15f. red . . . 35 3·50
314 10f.+20f. blue . . . 35 4·00

315 10f.+30f. green (air) . . . 1·00 4·00

1947. Stamp Day. No. 301 surch **JOURNEE DU TIMBRE 1947 +5F50.**
316 C 4f.50+5f.50 mauve . . . 2·50 3·25

56 Coastline and Symbols of Prosperity

1947. 25th Anniv of Sherifian Phosphates Office.
317 **56** 3f.50+5f.50 green . . . 1·25 3·25

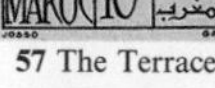
57 The Terraces

58 Coastal Fortress

59 Barracks on the Mountains

65 La Medina Barracks

1947. (a) Postage.
318 **57** 10c. brown . . . 10 2·00
319 30c. red . . . 10 2·75
320 30c. violet . . . 10 2·75
321 50c. blue . . . 10 15
322 60c. purple . . . 10 2·25
323 **58** 1f. black . . . 10 10
324 1f.50 blue . . . 15 40
325 **59** 2f. green . . . 45 30
325a **58** 2f. purple . . . 2·00 30
326 **59** 3f. lake . . . 40 10
327 – 4f. violet . . . 1·10 50
328 – 4f. green . . . 1·40 1·60
329 – 5f. green . . . 25 90
329a – 5f. green . . . 60 20
330 – 6f. red . . . 60 10
330a – 8f. orange . . . 50 60
331 – 10f. blue . . . 1·10 15
332a – 10f. red . . . 1·25 15
333 **58** 12f. red . . . 90 20
334 – 15f. green . . . 70 1·25
334a – 15f. red . . . 50 20
335 – 18f. blue . . . 95 30
336 – 20f. red . . . 10 20
337 – 25f. violet . . . 90 1·50
337a – 25f. blue . . . 45 30
337b – 25f. violet . . . 2·50 3·50
337c – 30f. blue . . . 95 65
337d – 35f. brown . . . 1·00 55
337e – 50f. slate . . . 1·75 10
DESIGNS—HORIZ: 4f., 6f. Marrakesh; 5f. (No. 329), 8f., 10f. blue, The Gardens, Fez; 5f. (No. 329a) Fortified oasis; 15f. red, 25f. (Nos. 337a/b), Walled city; 30f., 35f., 50f. Todra Valley. VERT: 10f. red, 15f. green, 18f., 20f., 25f. (No. 337) Barracks in oasis.

(b) Air.
338 – 9f. red . . . 1·25 10
339 – 40f. blue . . . 1·25 35
340 – 50f. purple . . . 1·40 20
341 **65** 100f. blue . . . 1·10 1·40
342 200f. red . . . 1·50 1·10
342a – 300f. violet . . . 6·75 8·75
DESIGNS—VERT: 9, 40, 50f. Sud Est Languedoc airplane over Moulay Idriss. HORIZ: 300f. Oudayas Kasbah, Rabat.

67 "Energy"

68 Marshal Lyautey's Mausoleum

1947. Solidarity Fund. Inscr "SOLIDARITE 1947".
343 **67** 6f.+9f. red (postage) . . . 90 4·00
344 – 10f.+20f. blue . . . 50 4·25

345 – 9f.+16f. green (air) . . . 2·50 4·50
346 – 20f.+35f. brown . . . 1·60 4·00
DESIGNS—VERT: 10f. Red Cross unit ("Health"). HORIZ: 9f. Freighter at quayside and Sud Est Languedoc airplane ("Supplies"); 20f. Sud Est Languedoc airplane over landscape ("Agriculture").

1948. Stamp Day. View of Meknes (as No. 88) inscr "JOURNEE DU TIMBRE 1948" below central vignette.
347 6f.+4f. brown . . . 30 3·00

1948. Air. Lyautey Exhibition, Paris.
348 **68** 10f.+25f. green . . . 1·75 3·25

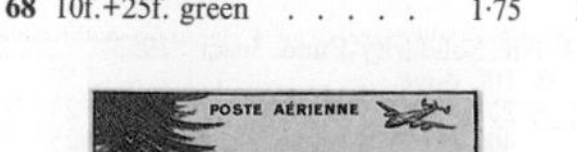

69 P.T.T. Clubhouse, Ifrane

1948. Air. P.T.T. Employees' Holiday Camp Fund.
349 **69** 6f.+34f. green . . . 1·75 4·00
350 9f.+51f. red . . . 1·60 4·00

70 "Dunkerque" (battleship) and Coastline

1948. Naval Charities.
351 **70** 6f.+9f. violet . . . 1·60 3·75

1948. Stamp of 1939 surch **8f.**
352 C 8f. on 20f. purple (No. 306) 15 2·25

72 Wheat and View of Meknes

1949. Solidarity Fund. Inscr "SOLIDARITE 1948".
353 **72** 1f.+2f. orange (postage) . . 25 3·25
354 – 2f.+5f. red . . . 25 3·50
355 – 3f.+7f. blue . . . 30 3·50
356 – 5f.+10f. purple . . . 30 3·50
MS356a 120×96 mm. Nos. 353/6 16·00 30·00

357 – 5f.+5f. green (air) . . . 70 3·50
358 – 6f.+9f. red . . . 60 3·50
359 – 9f.+16f. brown . . . 50 3·50
360 – 15f.+25f. slate . . . 70 3·50
MS360a 96×120 mm. Nos. 357/60 13·50 30·00
DESIGNS—HORIZ: (postage): 2f. Olive grove and Taroudant; 3f. Trawling; 5f. Plums and Aguedal Gardens, Marrakesh. VERT: (air): Airplane over—5f. Agadir; 6f. Fez; 9f. Atlas Mountains; 15f. Draa Valley.

74 Gazelle Hunter

75 Soldiers with Flag

1949. Stamp Day and 50th Anniv of Mazagan-Marrakesh Local Postage Stamp.
361 **74** 10f.+5f. red and purple . . 1·60 3·75

1949. Army Welfare Fund.
362 **75** 10f.+10f. red . . . 95 3·50

76 Oudayas Gate, Rabat

77 Nejjarine Fountain, Fez

78 Gardens at Meknes

1949.
363 **76** 10c. black . . . 10 2·50
364 50c. lake . . . 15 2·75
365 1f. violet . . . 20 10
366 **77** 2f. red . . . 10 10
367 3f. blue . . . 10 10
368 5f. green . . . 10 10
369 **78** 8f. green . . . 10 10
370 10f. red . . . 10 10

79 Post Office, Meknes

80 Breguet 14T Biplane over Globe

1949. 75th Anniv of U.P.U.
371 **79** 5f. green . . . 1·75 2·50
372 15f. red . . . 1·60 3·75
373 25f. blue . . . 1·60 4·00

1950. Air. Stamp Day and 25th Anniv of First Mail Flight from Casablanca to Dakar.
374 **80** 15f.+10f. blue, grn & red 1·25 4·50

81 Carpets

83 Ruins of Sala-Colonia (Chella)

1950. Solidarity Fund. Inscr "SOLIDARITE 1949".
375 **81** 1f.+2f. red (postage) . . . 40 4·00
376 – 2f.+5f. blue . . . 40 3·75
377 – 3f.+7f. violet . . . 40 3·75
378 – 5f.+10f. brown . . . 55 4·00
MS378a 96×120 mm. Nos. 375/8 13·00 32·00

379 – 5f.+5f. blue (air) . . . 70 3·75
380 – 6f.+9f. green . . . 40 3·50
381 – 9f.+16f. brown . . . 35 3·75
382 – 15f.+25f. brown . . . 40 3·50
MS382a 120×96 mm. Nos. 379/82 16·00 32·00
DESIGNS—VERT: Postage: 2f. Pottery; 3f. Books; 5f. Copperware. HORIZ: Air—(Maps of Morocco): 5f. N.W.; 6f. N.E.; 9f. S.W.; 15f. S.E.

1950. Army Welfare Fund. Inscr "OUVRES SOCIALES DE L'ARMEE".
383 **83** 10f.+10f. red (postage) . . 55 3·25
384 15f.+15f. slate . . . 55 3·50

385 – 10f.+10f. sepia (air) . . . 2·00 3·75
386 – 15f.+15f. green . . . 2·25 3·75

DESIGN: 10f., 15f. Triumphal Arch of Caracalla, Volubilis.

1950. Stamps of 1939 and 1947 surch.
387 F 1f. on 1f.20 brn (No. 295) 10 15
388 A 1f. on 1f.30 blue (No. 296) 10 15
389 – 5f. on 6f. red (No. 330) . . 10 10

84 General Leclerc

85 New Hospital, Meknes

1951. Gen. Leclerc Monument, Casablanca.
390 **84** 10f. green (postage) . . . . 85 3·50
391 15f. red . . . . 65 3·75
392 25f. blue . . . . 75 4·00
393 50f. violet (air) . . . . . . 1·90 4·25

1951. Solidarity Fund. Inscr "SOLIDARITE 1950".
394 – 10f. violet & blue (postage) 25 3·00
395 **85** 15f. brown and green . . . 25 3·50
396 – 25f. blue and brown . . . 20 2·40
397 – 50f. green & violet (air) . . 65 2·75
DESIGNS: 10f. Loustau Hospital, Oujda; 25f. New Hospital, Rabat; 50f. Sanatorium, Ben Smine.

86 Fountain and Doves

87 Karaouine Mosque, Fez

88 Old Moroccan Courtyard

1951.
398 **86** 5f. purple (A) 10 10
434 5f. purple (B) . . . . . . 2·50 2·25
399 **87** 6f. green . . . . 45 1·25
400 **86** 8f. brown 15 25
401 **87** 10f. red . . . . 1·25 15
402 12f. blue . . . . 1·10 10
403 – 15f. brown (A) 70 30
404 – 15f. brown (B) 30 10
405 – 15f. violet (A) . . . . . . 1·25 15
435 – 15f. violet (B) . . . . . . 1·60 1·50
406 **86** 15f. green . . . . 1·40 15
407 – 18f. red . . . . 2·50 2·75
408 **88** 20f. blue 85 20
DESIGNS—As Type **86/7**: 15f. brown (2) Oudayas Courtyard; 15f. violet (2), 18f. Oudayas Point, Rabat.
Two types each of: 5f. (A) 18×22 mm, (B) 17×21½ mm: 15f. brown (A) "MAROC" not in tablet, (B) "MAROC" in white tablet; 15f. violet (A) 18×22½ mm, (B) 16½×21½ mm.

89 Casablanca P.O. and Reproduction of Type **22**

90 Saadian Capital

1952. Air. Stamp Day and 30th Anniv of First Moroccan Air Stamps.
409 **89** 15f.+5f. blue & brown . . 4·50 7·50

1952. Solidarity Fund. Inscr "SOLIDARITE 1951". Column capitals as T **90**.
410 – 15f. blue (Omeiyad) . . . 80 4·50
411 – 20f. red (Almohad) . . . . 80 4·25
412 – 25f. violet (Merinid) . . . 70 3·75
413 **90** 50f. green . . . . 70 3·00

91 Ramparts of Chella, Rabat

92 War Memorial, Casablanca

1952. Air.
414 **91** 10f. green . . . . 1·25 1·25
415 – 40f. red . . . . 1·25 20
416 – 100f. brown . . . . 1·40 30
417 – 200f. violet . . . . 2·75 3·25

DESIGN: Lockheed Constellation over—HORIZ: 40f. Marrakesh. VERT: 100f. Fort in Anti-Atlas Mts.; 200f. Fez.

1952. Centenary of Military Medal.
418 **92** 15f. brown, yellow & green 50 3·75

93 Jewellery from Fez

94 Arab Courier and Scribe

1953. Solidarity Fund. Inscr "SOLIDARITE 1952".
419 – 15f. red (postage) . . . . 85 4·25
420 **93** 20f. brown . . . . 1·10 3·50
421 – 25f. blue . . . . 80 3·50
422 – 50f. green (air) . . . . . 2·00 4·25
DESIGNS: 15f. Daggers from S. Morocco; 25f. Jewellery from Anti-Atlas; 50f. Jewellery from N. Morocco.

1953. Stamp Day.
423 **94** 15f. purple . . . . 1·10 4·00

95 Bine el Ouidane Barrage

96 Mogador Battlements

1953. Inauguration of Barrage.
424 **95** 15f. blue . . . . 60 3·75
424a 15f. blue and brown . . . 50 50

1953. Army Welfare Fund.
425 **96** 15f. green . . . . 75 3·50
426 – 30f. brown . . . . 40 3·50
DESIGN: 30f. Moorish horsemen.

1954. Nos. 324 and 335 surch.
427 **58** 1f. on 1f.50 blue 10 20
428 – 15f. on 18f. blue . . . . . 20 1·75

98 Meknes

1954. Air. Solidarity Fund. Inscr "1953".
429 **98** 10f. olive . . . . 2·50 3·00
430 – 20f. violet (Rabat) . . . . 2·25 4·00
431 – 40f. brn (Casablanca) . . . 2·25 4·00
432 – 50f. green (Fedala) . . . . 1·90 2·40

99 Mail Van and Postmen

1954. Stamp Day.
433 **99** 15f. green . . . . 1·60 3·50

100 Schooner and Destroyer

101 Marshal Lyautey at Khenifra

1954. Air. Naval Welfare Fund.
436 **100** 15f. green . . . . 2·50 2·25
437 30f. blue . . . . 1·60 1·50

1954. Birth Centenary of Marshal Lyautey.
438 – 5f. blue . . . . 2·50 4·25
439 **101** 15f. green . . . . 2·25 4·25
440 – 30f. lake . . . . 1·75 4·50
441 – 50f. brown . . . . 1·75 3·75
DESIGNS—HORIZ: 5f. Lyautey receiving Moroccan notables at Rabat. VERT: 30f. Lyautey in dockyards; 50f. Portrait of Lyautey (after Laszlo).

102 Moroccan Scholar

103 Mazagan P.O.

1955. Solidarity Fund.
442 – 5f. blue . . . . 35 1·90
443 **102** 15f. red . . . . 40 3·50
444 – 30f. brown . . . . 55 1·75
445 – 50f. green . . . . 50 2·75
DESIGNS—HORIZ: 5f. French and Moroccan schoolchildren; 30f. Muslim School, Camp-Boulhaut. VERT: 50f. Moulay Idriss College, Fez.

1955. Day of the Stamp.
446 **103** 15f. red . . . . 1·40 3·50

104 Map of Morocco

105 Bab el Mrissa, Sale

106 Mahakma, Casablanca

107 Bou Regreg Estuary

1955. 50th Anniv of Rotary International.
447 **104** 15f. blue and brown . . . 60 4·25

1955.
448 **105** 50c. purple . . . . 10 1·75
449 1f. blue 10 10
450 2f. purple 10 10
451 3f. blue 30 20
452 – 5f. red . . . . 1·25 20
453 – 6f. green 55 50
454 – 8f. brown . . . . 1·60 3·00
455 – 10f. purple 45 50
456 – 12f. turquoise 55 25
457 – 15f. lake . . . . 1·50 10
458 **106** 18f. myrtle 55 60
459 20f. lake 20 10
460 – 25f. blue . . . . 1·75 65
461 – 30f. green . . . . 1·10 25
462 – 40f. red 35 15
463 – 50f. sepia 60 20
464 – 75f. turquoise . . . . . . 1·25 80
DESIGNS—As Type **105**: 5f., 6f., 8f. Bab Chorfa, Fez; 10f., 12f., 15f. Chella Minaret, Rabat. As Type **106**—HORIZ: 25f. Coastal castle, Safi; 30f. Menara, Marrakesh; 40f. Tafraout; 50f. Portuguese cistern, Mazagan. VERT: 75f. Oudaya gardens, Rabat.

1955. Air.
465 – 100f. violet . . . . 3·25 35
466 **107** 200f. red . . . . 4·25 75
467 – 500f. blue . . . . 4·25 2·75
DESIGNS—VERT: 100f. Village in the Anti-Atlas. HORIZ: 500f. Ksar es Souk.

PARCEL POST STAMPS

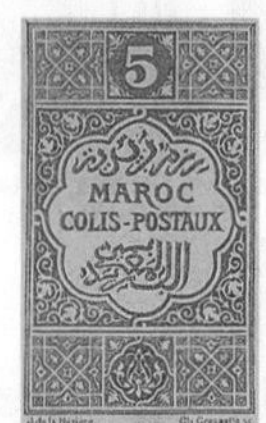

P 21

1917.
P101 **P 21** 5c. green . . . . 35 1·40
P102 10c. red . . . . 40 1·25
P103 20c. brown . . . . . . 1·10 1·60
P104 25c. blue . . . . 1·10 80
P105 40c. brown . . . . . . 2·25 1·40
P106 50c. red . . . . 3·00 1·40
P107 75c. grey . . . . 2·75 2·25
P108 1f. blue . . . . 3·50 80
P109 2f. grey . . . . 3·00 35
P110 5f. violet . . . . 4·25 55
P111 10f. black . . . . 6·50 60

POSTAGE DUE STAMPS

1915. Postage Due stamps of France surch with figure and Arabic word, and further optd **PROTECTORAT FRANCAIS**.
D66 D **11** 1c. on 1c. black . . . . 95 2·40
D67 5c. on 5c. blue . . . . 1·10 2·75
D68 10c. on 10c. brown . . 2·75 3·50
D69 20c. on 20c. green . . . 1·50 2·50
D70 30c. on 30c. red . . . . 1·90 6·75
D71 50c. on 50c. purple . . 1·75 3·75

1915. Postage Due stamps of France with surch and optd as above.
D72 D **19** 1c. on 1c. olive . . . . 70 2·75
D73 10c. on 10c. violet . . . 2·50 3·50
D74 30c. on 30c. bistre . . . 1·90 4·00
D75 50c. on 50c. red . . . . 2·10 3·75

D 21

1917.
D 93 D **21** 1c. black 10 75
D 94 5c. blue . . . . 10 1·75
D 95 10c. brown 10 20
D 96 20c. green 50 25
D 97 30c. red 20 15
D 98 50c. brown 10 10
D 99 1f. purple on yellow 15 20
D308 1f. red . . . . 85 3·00
D100 2f. violet 20 20
D310 3f. blue . . . . 85 2·00
D311 4f. orange . . . . . . 1·75 2·25
D312 5f. green . . . . . . 1·00 25
D313 10f. bistre . . . . . . 1·40 15
D314 20f. red . . . . 2·75 2·00
D315 30f. brown . . . . . 3·00 4·00

1944. Surch.
D289 D **21** 50c. on 30c. red . . . 4·25 7·50
D290 1f. on 10c. brown . . 4·75 7·50
D291 3f. on 10c. brown . . 12·00 18·00

For later issues see **MOROCCO**.

FRENCH OCCUPATION OF HUNGARY — Pt. 2

ARAD

Arad later became part of Rumania.

100 filler = 1 korona.

1919. Stamps of Hungary Optd **Occupation francaise** or surch also. (a) War Charity stamps of 1916.
1 **20** 11f. (+2f.) red . . . . . . 22·00 22·00
2 – 15f. (+2f.) lilac . . . . . . 1·60 1·60
3 **22** 40f. (+2f.) red . . . . 2·25 2·25

(b) Harvesters and Parliament Types.
4 **18** 2f. brown 95 85
5 3f. red 85 85
6 5f. green . . . . 1·60 1·60
7 6f. blue 95 95
8 10f. red . . . . 1·10 1·10
9 15f. purple 95 95
10 15f. violet (No. 244) . . . 45·00 45·00
11 20f. brown . . . . 9·00 9·00
12 35f. brown . . . . 23·00 23·00
13 40f. green . . . . 7·50 78·50
14 45 on 2f. brown . . . . . 1·60 1·60
15a 45 on 3f. red . . . . . . 19·00
16 50 on 3f. red . . . . . . 1·60 1·60
18 **19** 50f. purple . . . . 1·40 1·40
19 75f. blue . . . . 1·10 1·10
20 80f. green . . . . 1·25 1·25
21 1k. red . . . . 4·25 4·25
22 2k. brown . . . . 1·40 1·40
23 3k. grey and violet . . . . 4·00 4·00
24 5k. brown . . . . 4·00 4·00
25 10k. mauve and brown . . 45·00 45·00

(c) Charles and Zita stamps.
26 **27** 10f. red . . . . 12·50 12·50
27 20f. brown 85 85
28 25f. blue . . . . 1·10 1·10
29 **28** 40f. green . . . . 1·25 1·25

(d) Harvester stamps inscr "MAGYAR POSTA".
30 **18** 5f. green . . . . 10·00 10·00
31 10f. red . . . . 1·40 1·40
32 20f. brown . . . . 7·00 7·00

(e) Stamps of 1919 optd **KOZTARSASAG**. (i) Harvesters and Parliament Types.
33 **18** 2f. brown . . . . 1·10 1·10
34 3f. red . . . . 3·00 3·00
35 4f. grey . . . . 1·10 1·10
36 5f. green 85 85
37 6f. blue . . . . 2·50 2·50
38 10f. red . . . . 23·00 23·00
39 20f. brown . . . . 4·00 4·00
40 40f. green . . . . 1·10 1·10
41 **19** 1k. red . . . . 1·10 1·10
42 3k. grey and violet . . . . 4·00 4·00
43 10(k)on 1k. red . . . . . 4·00 4·00

(ii) Charles and Zita stamps.
44 **27** 25f. blue . . . . 1·10 1·10
45 **28** 40f. green . . . . 21·00 21·00
46 50f. violet . . . . 1·10 1·10

EXPRESS LETTER STAMP

1919. No. E245 optd **Occupation francaise**.
E48 E **18** 2f. green and red . . . 85 85

NEWSPAPER STAMP

1919. No. N136 optd **Occupation francaise**.
N47 N **9** (2f.) orange 85 85

POSTAGE DUE STAMPS

1919. (a) No. D191 of Hungary optd **Occupation francaise**.
D49 D **9** 2f. red and green . . . . 1·25 1·25
D50 10f. red and green . . . 1·10 1·10
D51 12f. red and green . . . 10·00 10·50
D52 15f. red and green . . . 10·00 10·50
D53 20f. red and green . . . 6·00 7·00

(b) No. N47 of Arad surch **Porto** and new value.
D54 N **9** 12 on (2f.) orange . . . 2·40 2·40
D55 15 on (2f.) orange . . . 2·40 2·40
D56 30 on (2f.) orange . . . 2·40 2·40
D57 50 on (2f.) orange . . . 2·40 2·40
D58 100 on (2f.) orange . . . 2·40 2·40

FRENCH POLYNESIA Pt. 6

The French Settlements in the South Pacific, formerly called Oceanic Settlements.

100 centimes = 1 franc.

1 Girl playing Guitar 2 Polynesian

3 "The Women of Tahiti" (after Gauguin)

1958.
1 **1** 10c. brn, grn & turq (postage) . . . . 40 3·00
2 25c. purple, red and green . . 20 2·75
3 1f. sepia, red and blue . . . 1·90 1·25
4 2f. violet, choc & brown . . . 3·00 2·50
5 **2** 4f. myrtle, green & yellow . . 3·00 2·00
6 – 5f. brown, violet & green . . 4·00 3·25
7 **2** 7f. brown, green & orange . . 4·25 3·50
8 9f. purple, green & orange . . 5·50 3·75
9 – 10f. red, blue and brown . . 8·00 4·00
10 – 16f. multicoloured . . . . . 9·00 4·00
11 – 17f. brown, blue & turquoise 9·75 2·25
12 – 20f. brown, violet & pink . . 15·00 3·50
13 – 13f. brn, grn & drab (air) . . 9·50 5·75
14 **3** 50f. multicoloured . . . . . 9·75 8·25
15 – 100f. multicoloured . . . . . 14·50 10·50
16 – 200f. slate and lilac . . . . . 36·00 23·00
DESIGNS: As Types **1/2**—VERT: 5f. Spearfishing; 10f., 20f. Polynesian girl on beach. HORIZ: 16f. Post Office, Papeete; 17f. Tahitian dancers. As Type **3**—VERT: 13f. Mother-of-pearl engraver; 100f. "The White Horse" (after Gauguin). HORIZ: 200f. Night-fishing off Moorea.

1958. 10th Anniv of Declaration of Human Rights. As T **57** of French Equatorial Africa.
17 7f. grey and blue . . . . . . 6·25 14·00

1959. Tropical Flora. As T **56** of French Equatorial Africa. Multicoloured.
18 4f. "Artocarpus" . . . . . . 3·00 6·00

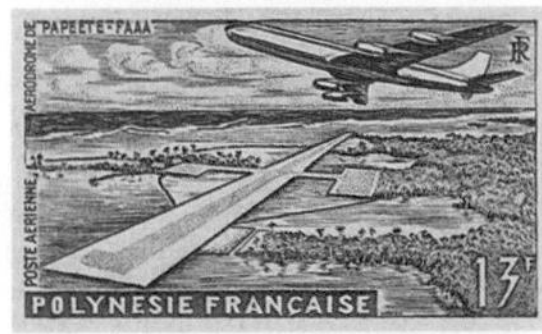

7 Douglas DC-8 over Papeete Airport

1960. Air. Inauguration of Papeete Airport.
19 **7** 13f. violet, purple & green . . 3·75 3·25

8 "Saraca indica"

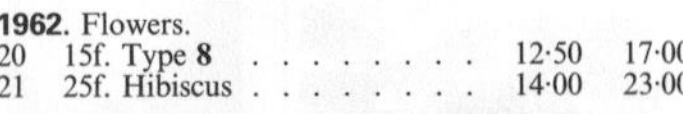

1962. Flowers.
20 15f. Type **8** . . . . 12·50 17·00
21 25f. Hibiscus . . . . 14·00 23·00

9 Pacific Map and Palms

1962. 5th South Pacific Conference, Pago-Pago.
22 **9** 20f. multicoloured . . . . . 10·50 10·00

10 "Telstar" Satellite

1962. Air. 1st Trans-Atlantic T.V. Satellite Link.
23 **10** 50f. blue, brown and purple 9·50 8·75

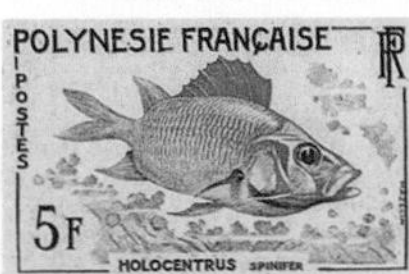

11 Spined Squirrelfish

1962. Fishes. Multicoloured.
24 5f. Type **11** . . . . 5·50 2·50
25 10f. Teardrop butterflyfish . . 5·50 3·25
26 30f. Radial lionfish . . . . . 10·00 6·25
27 40f. Long-horned cowfish . . 19·00 12·00

12 Football

1962. 1st South Pacific Games, Suva, Fiji.
28 **12** 20f. brown and blue . . . . 9·50 12·00
29 – 50f. blue and red . . . . . 12·50 12·00
DESIGN: 50f. Throwing the javelin.

13 Centenary Emblem 14 Globe and Scales of Justice

1963. Centenary of Red Cross.
30 **13** 15f. red, grey and purple . . 10·50 16·00

1963. 15th Anniv of Declaration of Human Rights.
31 **14** 7f. violet and green . . . . 11·50 8·75

1964. "PHILATEC 1964" International Stamp Exhibition, Paris. As T **528** of France.
32 25f. red, black and green . . . 13·50 17·00

16 Dancer 17 Tahitian Volunteers

1964. Tahitian Dancers.
33 **16** 1f. multicoloured (postage) 90 75
34 3f. orange, sepia & purple 1·00 1·10
35 – 15f. multicoloured (air) . . 4·00 2·50
DESIGN—VERT: (27 × 46½ mm): 15f. Dancer in full costume.

1964. Polynesia's War Effort in Second World War. Multicoloured.
36 5f. Type **17** (postage) . . . . 8·00 8·75
37 16f. Badges and map of Tahiti (48 × 27 mm) (air) . . . . . 12·50 12·50

18 Tuamotu Lagoon (after J. D. Lajoux)

1964. Landscapes. Multicoloured.
38 2f. Type **18** (postage) . . . . 1·75 95
39 4f. Bora-Bora (after Lajoux) 1·40 1·10
40 7f. Papeete (after A. Sylvain) 2·50 1·75
41 8f. Marquesas (Gauguin's grave) . . . . 2·75 1·75
42 20f. Gambier (after Mazellier) 5·50 2·25
43 23f. Moorea (after Sylvain) (48 × 27 mm) (air) . . . . . 10·00 4·25

19 "Syncom" Communications Satellite, Telegraph Poles and Morse Key

1965. Air. Centenary of I.T.U.
44 **19** 50f. brown, blue & violet . . 65·00 50·00

20 Museum Buildings

1965. Air. Gauguin Museum.
45 **20** 25f. green . . . . 8·50 8·00
46 – 40f. turquoise . . . . 13·50 12·00
47 – 75f. brown . . . . 25·00 19·00
DESIGNS: 40f. Statues and hut; 75f. Gauguin.

21 Skin-diver with Harpoon

1965. Air. World Under-water Swimming Championships, Tuamotu.
48 **21** 50f. blue, brown & green . . 80·00 £100

22 Tropical Foliage 23 Aerial, Globe and Palm

1965. Schools Canteen Art.
49 **22** 20f. red, green and brown (postage) . . . . 18·00 23·00
50 – 80f. red, blue and brown (27 × 48 mm) (air) . . . . 22·00 32·00
DESIGN: 80f. Totem, and garland in harbour.

1965. Air. 50th Anniv of 1st Radio Link with France.
51 **23** 60f. brown, green & orge . . 18·00 30·00

1966. Air. Launching of 1st French Satellite. As Nos. 1696/7 (plus se-tenant label) of France.
52 7f. brown, purple & green . . 9·25 12·00
53 10f. brown, purple & green . . 9·25 12·00

1966. Air. Launching of Satellite "D1". As T **569** of France.
54 20f. red, brown and green . . 6·50 8·75

26 Papeete Port

1966. Air.
55 **26** 50f. multicoloured . . . . . 14·00 22·00

27 Pirogue

1966. Polynesian Boats.
56 **27** 10f. red, green and blue . . 3·25 2·25
57 – 11f. red, green and blue . . 3·00 2·75
58 – 12f. purple, green & blue . . 4·50 3·50
59 – 14f. brown, blue & green . . 6·25 3·00
60 – 19f. green, red and blue . . 7·00 4·00
61 – 22f. green, blue & purple . . 10·00 4·75
DESIGNS—VERT: 11f. Schooner; 19f. Early schooner. HORIZ: 12f. Fishing launch; 14f. Pirogues; 22f. Coaster "Oiseau des Iles II".

28 Tahitian Dancer and Band

1966. Air. "Vive, Tahiti!" (tourist publicity).
62 **28** 13f. multicoloured . . . . . 9·25 11·00

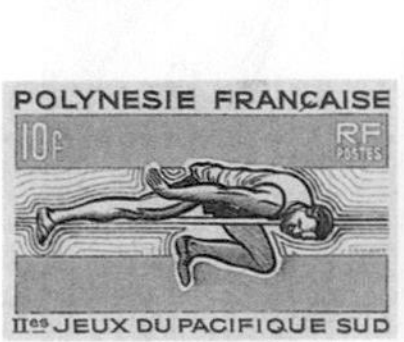

29 High-jumping 30 Stone Pestle

1966. 2nd South Pacific Games, Noumea.
63 **29** 10f. bistre and red . . . . . 3·00 4·00
64 – 20f. green and blue . . . . 6·00 3·25
65 – 40f. purple and green . . . 10·00 3·00
66 – 60f. blue and brown . . . . 12·50 16·50
DESIGNS—VERT: 20f. Pole-vaulting; 40f. Basketball. HORIZ: 60f. Hurdling.

1967. 50th Anniv of Oceanic Studies Society.
67 **30** 50f. blue and orange . . . . 14·50 11·00

31 Spring Dance

1967. July Festival.
68 **31** 5f. blue, purple and drab . . 3·25 2·75
69 – 13f. purple, violet & green 4·25 3·00
70 – 15f. brown, purple & green 5·75 3·00
71 – 16f. purple, green & blue . . 5·00 3·50
72 – 21f. brown, green & blue . . 7·25 8·00
DESIGNS—VERT: 13f. Javelin-throwing; 16f. Fruit-porters' race. HORIZ: 15f. Horse-racing; 21f. Pirogue-racing.

32 Earring

34 Bouquet, Sun and W.H.O. Emblem

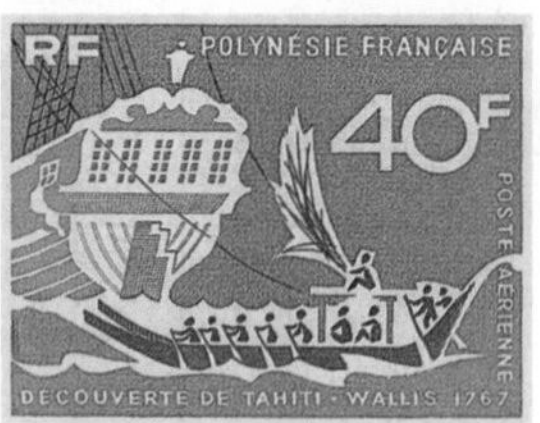

33 Ship's Stern and Canoe ("Wallis, 1767")

1967. Ancient Art of the Marquesas Islands.
73 – 10f. blue, red & purple . . . 3·75 2·75
74 – 15f. black and green . . . . 4·50 3·25
75 **32** 20f. brown, green & lake . . 4·00 3·75
76 – 23f. brown and ochre . . . 6·25 7·00
77 – 25f. brown, purple & blue 7·00 4·75
78 – 30f. brown and purple . . . 8·25 7·75
79 – 35f. blue and brown . . . . 11·00 12·50
80 – 50f. brown, blue & green . . 10·00 12·00
DESIGNS: 10f. Sculpture on mother-of-pearl; 15f. Paddle-blade; 23f. Receptacle for anointing oil; 25f. Hunting stirrups; 30f. Fan handles; 35f. Tattooed man; 50f. "Tikis".

1968. Air. Bicentenary of Discovery of Tahiti.
81 **33** 40f. brown, blue & green . . 13·00 9·50
82 – 60f. orange, black & blue 16·00 11·50
83 – 80f. salmon, lake & purple 17·00 15·00
MS84 180 × 100 mm. Nos. 81/3 £170 £180
DESIGNS—HORIZ: 60f. Ship and witch-doctor ("Cook, 1769"). VERT: 80f. "Bougainville, 1768" (portrait).

1968. 20th Anniv of World Health Organization.
85 **34** 15f. violet, red and green . . 8·00 10·00
86 16f. green, purple & orange 8·00 14·00

35 "The Meal" (Gauguin)

1968. Air.
87 **35** 200f. multicoloured . . . . 38·00 50·00

36 Human Rights Emblem

37 Putting the Shot

1968. Human Rights Year.
88 **36** 15f. red, blue and brown . . 7·25 9·75
89 16f. blue, brown & purple 8·00 9·50

1968. Air. Olympic Games, Mexico.
90 **37** 35f. green, purple & red . . 14·00 15·00

38 Tiare Apetahi

1969. Flowers. Multicoloured.
91 9f. Type **38** . . . . 3·75 3·00
92 17f. Tiare Tahiti . . . . . . 11·00 8·50

39 Concorde in Flight

1969. Air. 1st Flight of Concorde.
93 **39** 40f. brown and red . . . . 60·00 60·00

40 Polynesian with Guitar

1969. Air. Pacific Area Travel Association (P.A.T.A.) Congress, Tahiti (1970) (1st issue).
94 **40** 25f. multicoloured . . . . . 26·00 13·00
See also Nos. 109/11.

41 Diver and Fish

1969. Air. World Underwater Hunting Championships.
95 **41** 48f. black, purple & turq . . 30·00 18·00
96 – 52f. black, red and blue . . 40·00 35·00
DESIGN—VERT: 52f. "Flag" Fish.

42 Boxing

1969. 3rd South Pacific Games, Port Moresby, New Guinea.
97 **42** 9f. brown and violet . . . 4·25 4·50
98 – 17f. brown and red . . . . 5·00 4·00
99 – 18f. brown and blue . . . 6·75 5·50
100 – 22f. purple and green . . . 10·00 9·25
DESIGNS—VERT: 17f. High jumping; 18f. Running; 22f. Long jumping.

43 "Bonaparte as Commander-in-Chief, Italy" (Rouillard)

1969. Air. Birth Bicentenary of Napoleon Bonaparte.
101 **43** 100f. multicoloured . . . . 80·00 £120

44 I.L.O. Building, Geneva

1969. 50th Anniv of International Labour Organization.
102 **44** 17f. drab, green & orange 9·25 10·50
103 18f. blue, brown & orange 10·00 13·00

45 Territorial Assembly Building

46 Tiki holding P.A.T.A. Emblem

1969. Polynesian Buildings. Multicoloured.
104 13f. Type **45** . . . . 3·25 4·00
105 14f. Governor's residence . . 4·25 4·00
106 17f. Tourist offices . . . . . 6·00 4·50
107 18f. Maeva Hotel . . . . . 8·50 4·50
108 24f. Taharaa Hotel . . . . . 11·00 7·00

1970. P.A.T.A. Congress (2nd issue).
109 **46** 20f. blue, brown & purple 8·00 6·00
110 – 40f. blue, purple & green 12·50 9·50
111 – 60f. dp brown, blue & brn 16·00 15·00
DESIGNS—HORIZ: 40f. Globe, airliner and "tourists". VERT: 60f. Polynesian holding globe.

47 New U.P.U. Building, Berne

1970. New U.P.U. Headquarters Building.
112 **47** 18f. lt brown, violet & brn 10·00 6·25
113 20f. blue, brown & purple 10·00 8·00

48 Tower of the Sun and Mt. Fuji

1970. Air. "EXPO 70" World Fair, Osaka, Japan. Multicoloured.
114 30f. Type **48** . . . . 12·00 12·00
115 50f. Eiffel Tower and Torii Gate (vert) . . . . 29·00 18·00

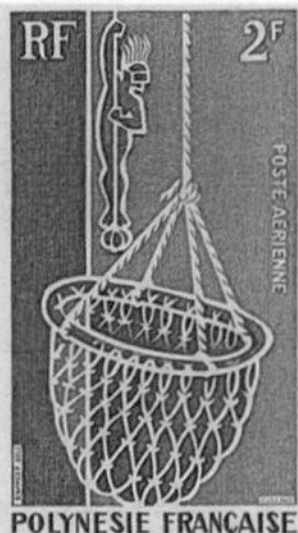

49 Diver and Basket

1970. Air. Pearl-diving.
116 **49** 2f. brown, indigo & blue 2·00 1·25
117 – 5f. ultramarine, orge & bl 4·00 2·00
118 – 18f. grey, orange & purple 5·00 4·00
119 – 27f. lilac, brown & purple 9·00 6·25
120 – 50c. orange, grey & brown 19·00 13·00
DESIGNS—VERT: 5f. Diver gathering black-lipped pearl oysters; 27f. Pearl in opened oyster; 50f. Woman with pearl jewellery. HORIZ: 18f. Opening oyster-shell.

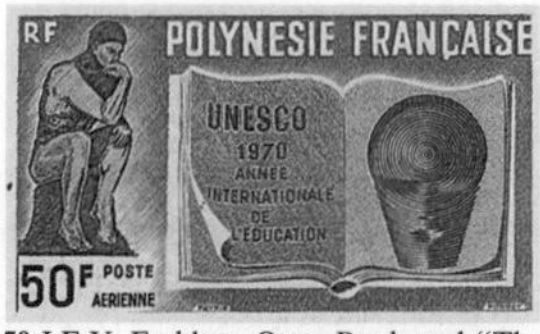

50 I.E.Y. Emblem, Open Book and "The Thinker" (statue)

1970. Air. International Education Year.
121 **50** 50f. blue, brown & lt blue 17·00 18·00

51 "Polynesian Woman" (Y. de St. Front)

1970. Air. Paintings by Polynesian Artists (1st series). Multicoloured.
122 20f. Type **51** . . . . 10·00 7·00
123 40f. "Harbour Scene" (F. Fay) . . . . 12·00 12·00
124 60f. "Niu" (abstract, J. Guillois) . . . . 20·00 9·00
125 80f. "Beach Hut" (J. Masson) 23·00 25·00
126 100f. "Polynesian Girl" (J. C. Bouloc) (vert) . . . . . 48·00 36·00
See also Nos. 147/51, 160/4, 172/6, 189/93 and 205/9.

52 Games Emblem

53 Flame of Remembrance

1971. Air. 4th South Pacific Games, Tahiti (1st issue).
127 **52** 20f. multicoloured . . . . 8·25 9·50

1971. Air. Erection of General de Gaulle Monument.
128 **53** 5f. multicoloured . . . . . 9·75 6·50

54 Volunteer, Crest and Tricolour

1971. Air. 30th Anniv of Departure of Tahitian "Free French" Volunteers.
129 **54** 25f. multicoloured . . . . 12·00 12·50

55 Marara Fisherman

1971. Water Sports. Multicoloured.
130 10f. Type **55** (postage) . . . 10·50 8·25
131 15f. Surfing (vert) (air) . . . 6·75 6·50
132 16f. Skin-diving (vert) . . . . 8·25 8·25
133 20f. Paragliding . . . . . . 10·00 8·50

56 Red Flower

57 Yachting

1971. "Day of the 1,000 Flowers". Mult.
134 8f. Type **56** . . . . 2·50 2·00
135 12f. Hibiscus (horiz) . . . . 2·75 2·50
136 22f. Porcelain rose . . . . . 6·00 3·50

1971. Air. 4th South Pacific Games, Tahiti (2nd issue). Multicoloured.
137 15f. Type **57** . . . . 9·00 6·50
138 18f. Golf . . . . 10·50 8·00
139 27f. Archery . . . . 10·50 10·50
140 53f. Tennis . . . . 45·00 40·00
MS141 138 × 170 mm. Nos. 137/40 £200 £200

58 Water-skiing

1971. 1st World Water-ski Championships, Papeete.
142 **58** 10f. red, green & brown . . 8·75 5·00
143 – 20f. red, brown & green . . 13·00 8·50
144 – 40f. purple, brown & grn 28·00 15·00
DESIGNS—VERT: 20f. Ski-jumping. HORIZ: 40f. Acrobatics on one ski.

1971. 1st Death Anniv of General de Gaulle. As Nos. 1937 and 1940 of France.
145 30f. black and purple . . . . 13·00 13·00
146 50f. black and purple . . . . 18·00 19·00

1971. Air. Paintings by Polynesian Artists (2nd series). As T **51**. Multicoloured.
147 20f. "Polynesian Village" (I. Wolf) . . . . 7·50 9·50
148 40f. "Lagoon" (A. Dobrowolski) . . . . 11·00 12·50
149 60f. "Polynesian Woman" (F. Seli) (vert) . . . . . . 18·00 18·00
150 80f. "The Holy Family" (P. Heymann) (vert) . . . 25·00 20·00
151 100f. "Faces in a Crowd" (N. Michoutouchkine) . . 32·00 45·00

60 Cross Emblem

1971. 2nd French Pacific Scouts and Guides Rally, Taravao.
152 **60** 28f. multicoloured . . . . 12·50 14·00

61 Harbour, Papeete

1972. Air. 10th Anniv of Autonomous Port of Papeete.
153 **61** 28f. multicoloured . . . . 16·00 13·00

62 Figure-skating

1972. Air. Winter Olympic Games, Sapporo, Japan.
154 **62** 20f. red, green & violet . . 14·00 11·50

63 Commission H.Q., Noumea, New Caledonia

1972. Air. 25th Anniv of South Pacific Commission.
155 **63** 21f. multicoloured . . . . 12·50 9·75

64 Alcoholic behind Bars

65 Floral Emblem

1972. Campaign Against Alcoholism.
156 **64** 20f. multicoloured . . . . 11·00 7·25

1972. Air. South Pacific Arts Festival, Fiji.
157 **65** 36f. orange, green & blue 10·00 10·00

66 Raft "Kon-Tiki" and Route-map

1972. Air. 25th Anniv of Arrival of "Kon-Tiki" Expedition in French Polynesia.
158 **66** 16f. multicoloured . . . . 8·75 7·50

67 De Gaulle and Monument

1972. Air. Completion of De Gaulle Monument.
159 **67** 100f. grey . . . . 60·00 70·00

1972. Air. Paintings by Polynesian Artists (3rd series). As Type **51**. Multicoloured.
160 20f. "Horses" (G. Bovy) . . 9·00 5·50
161 40f. "Harbour" (R. Juventin) (vert) . . . . 15·00 10·50
162 60f. "Landscape" (A. Brooke) . . . . . . 27·00 15·00
163 80f. "Polynesians" (D. Adam) (vert) . . . . 30·00 24·00
164 100f. "Dancers" (A. Pilioko) (vert) . . . . 32·00 45·00

68 St. Theresa and Lisieux Basilica

1973. Air. Birth Centenary of St. Theresa of Lisieux.
165 **68** 85f. multicoloured . . . . 30·00 32·00

69 Copernicus and Planetary System

1973. Air. 500th Birth Anniv of Nicolas Copernicus (astronomer).
166 **69** 100f. violet, brown & pur 30·00 35·00

70 Aeroplane and Flying Fish

1973. Air. Inauguration of "Air France" Round-the-World Service via Tahiti.
167 **70** 80f. multicoloured . . . . 26·00 26·00

71 Douglas DC-10 over Papeete Airport

1973. Air. Inauguration of "DC-10" Service.
168 **71** 20f. blue, green & lt blue 24·00 12·00

72 "Ta Matete" (Gauguin)

1973. Air. 125th Birth Anniv of Gauguin.
169 **72** 200f. multicoloured . . . . 32·00 35·00

73 Loti, Fishermen and Polynesian Girl

1973. Air. 50th Death Anniv of Pierre Loti (writer).
170 **73** 60f. multicoloured . . . . 50·00 35·00

74 Polynesian Mother and Child

75 "Teeing Off"

1973. Opening of Tahitian Women's Union Creche.
171 **74** 28f. multicoloured . . . . 12·00 7·50

1973. Air. Paintings by Polynesian Artists (4th series). As Type **51**. Multicoloured.
172 20f. "Sun God" (J.-F. Favre) (vert) . . . . 6·75 6·25
173 40f. "Polynesian Girl" (E. de Gennes) (vert) . . . . . 13·00 10·50
174 60f. "Abstract" (A. Sidet) (vert) . . . . 17·00 15·00
175 80f. "Bus Passengers" (F. Ravello) (vert) . . . . 30·00 26·00
176 100f. "Boats" (J. Bourdin) . . 32·00 35·00

1974. Atimaono Golf Course, Tahiti. Mult.
177 16f. Type **75** . . . . 8·25 4·00
178 24f. View of golf course . . . 9·50 4·75

76 "A Helping Hand"

1974. Polynesian Animal Protection Society.
179 **76** 21f. multicoloured . . . . 13·50 7·50

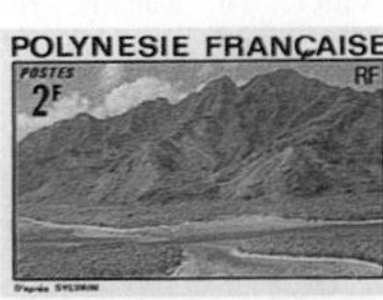
77 Mountains and Lagoon

1974. Polynesian Landscapes. Multicoloured.
180 2f. Type **77** . . . . 1·90 2·25
181 5f. Beach games . . . . . . 2·50 1·25
182 6f. Canoe fishing . . . . . . 2·25 2·75
183 10f. Mountain peak (vert) . . 3·25 2·50
184 15f. "Regina Maris" (schooner) in sunset scene 5·25 3·25
185 20f. Island and lagoon . . . 5·00 2·75

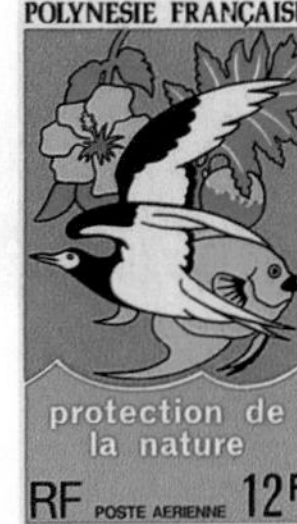
78 Bird, Stylized Angelfish, Leaf and Flower

1974. Air. Protection of Nature.
186 **78** 12f. multicoloured . . . . 11·00 9·50

79 Catamarans

80 Polynesian Woman

1974. Air. 2nd World Catamaran Sailing Championships, Papeete.
187 **79** 100f. multicoloured . . . . 23·00 26·00

1974. Centenary of Universal Postal Union.
188 **80** 65f. multicoloured . . . . 10·00 13·00

1974. Air. Paintings by Polynesian Artists (5th series). As Type **51**. Multicoloured.
189 20f. "Flower arrangement" (R. Temarui-Masson) (vert) 13·00 13·00
190 40f. "Palms on Beach" (M. Chardon) (vert) . . . 25·00 14·00
191 60f. "Portrait of Man" (M. F. Avril) (vert) . . . . 42·00 20·00
192 80f. "Polynesian Girl" (H. Robin) (vert) . . . . . 55·00 27·00
193 100f. "Lagoon at Night" (D. Farsi) . . . . 80·00 50·00

81 "The Travelling Gods"

1975. Air. "50 Years of Tahitian Aviation".
194 **81** 50f. violet, red & brown . . 9·50 9·50
195 – 75f. blue, red & green . . . 16·00 16·00
196 – 100f. brown, mve & grn . . 24·00 26·00
DESIGNS: 75f. Tourville's flying boat; 100f. Boeing 707 airliner.

82 Polynesian Girl and French "Ceres" Stamp of 1870

83 Tahiti Lions' Emblem

1975. Air. "Arphila 75" International Stamp Exhibition, Paris.
197 **82** 32f. red, brown & black . . 9·75 7·50

1975. 15th Anniv of Tahiti Lions' Club.
198 **83** 26f. multicoloured . . . . 20·00 11·50

84 "Protect Nature"

1975. Nature Protection.
199 **84** 19f. blue and green . . . . 7·75 8·25

85 Putting the Shot

1975. Air. 5th South Pacific Games, Guam. Mult.
200 25f. Type **85** . . . . 5·25 15·00
201 30f. Volleyball . . . . 7·25 7·25
202 40f. Swimming . . . . 9·00 9·50

86 Athlete and View of Montreal

1975. Air. Olympic Games, Montreal (1976).
203 **86** 44f. black, blue and red . . 10·00 9·50

87 Boeing 737 Airliner and Letters

1975. Air. World U.P.U. Day.
204 **87** 100f. blue, olive & brn . . 23·00 24·00

1975. Air. Paintings by Polynesian Artists (6th series). As T **51**. Multicoloured.
205 20f. "Beach Scene" (R. Marcel-Marius) . . . . 3·25 3·75
206 40f. "Rooftop Aerials" (M. Anglade) . . . . . . 6·75 5·50
207 60f. "Street Scene" (J. Day) 10·00 8·00
208 80f. "Tropical Waters" (J. Steimetz) (vert) . . . . 15·00 12·00
209 100f. "Portrait of a Woman" (A. van der Heyde) (vert) 21·00 18·00

88 Concorde

1976. Air. Concorde's First Commercial Flight.
210 **88** 100f. dp blue, blue & mve 28·00 24·00

89 President Pompidou **91** King Pomare 1

90 Battle of the Saints

1976. 2nd Death Anniv of Georges Pompidou (President of France, 1969–74).
211 **89** 49f. grey and blue . . . . 9·50 12·00

1976. Air. Bicentenary of American Revolution.
212 **90** 24f. blue, brown & black 6·50 5·00
213 – 31f. purple, red & brown 7·50 6·00
DESIGN: 31f. Sea battle of The Chesapeake.

1976. Air. Pomare Dynasty. Multicoloured.
214 18f. Type **91** . . . . 3·00 2·25
215 21f. King Pomare II . . . . 3·50 2·50
216 26f. Queen Pomare IV . . . 3·50 2·25
217 30f. King Pomare V . . . . 3·25 4·00
See also Nos. 234/7.

92 Gerbault and "Firecrest"

1976. 50th Anniv of Alain Gerbault's Arrival at Bora-Bora.
218 **92** 90f. multicoloured . . . . 22·00 18·00

93 Turtle

1976. World Ecology Day. Multicoloured.
219 18f. Type **93** . . . . 9·50 8·25
220 42f. Doves in hand . . . . . 16·00 14·50

94 Legs of Runner

1976. Air. Olympic Games, Montreal.
221 **94** 26f. brown, purple & blue 4·00 4·00
222 – 34f. purple, brown & blue 6·00 5·00
223 – 50f. brown, blue & purple 10·00 9·50
MS224 181 × 101 mm. Nos. 222/24 85·00 £100
DESIGNS—VERT: 34f. Runners. HORIZ: 50f. Olympic Flame and flowers.

95 A. Graham Bell, early Telephone and Dish Aerial

1976. Telephone Centenary.
225 **95** 37f. red, blue & brown . . 11·50 8·25

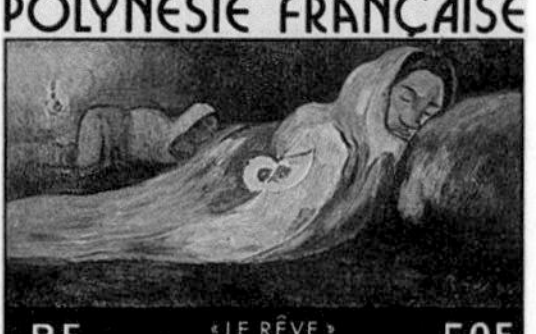

96 "The Dream" (Gauguin)

1976. Air.
226 **96** 50f. multicoloured . . . . 22·00 13·00

97 Marquesas Pirogue

1976. Ancient Pirogues. Multicoloured.
227 25f. Type **97** . . . . 4·00 3·25
228 30f. Raiatea pirogue . . . . 4·75 4·00
229 75f. Tahiti pirogue . . . . . 10·50 6·50
230 100f. Tuamotu pirogue . . . 12·00 8·50

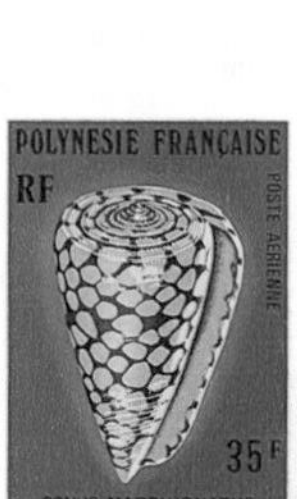

98 Marquesas Cone **101** Dancer

99 "Acropora"

1977. Air. Sea Shells (1st series). Mult.
231 25f. Maurus murex . . . . . 3·25 2·75
232 27f. Gaugin's cone . . . . . 4·25 3·00
233 35f. Type **98** . . . . 5·00 3·50
See also Nos. 268/70 and 307/9.

1977. Air. "Sovereigns of Archipelago". As T **91**. Multicoloured.
234 19f. Maputeoa (Mangareva) 2·00 2·25
235 33f. Tamatoa V (Raiatea) . . 2·25 2·50
236 39f. Vaekehu (Marquesas) . . 3·00 3·50
237 43f. Teuruarii III (Rurutu) 3·25 3·50

1977. Air. 3rd Coral Reefs Symposium, Miami.
238 25f. Type **99** . . . . 3·00 2·50
239 33f. "Pocillopora" (vert) . . 3·75 3·75

1977. Air. 5th Anniv of General de Gaulle Memorial. As T **806** of France.
255 40f. multicoloured . . . . . 5·25 5·50

1977. Air. Polynesian Dancer.
256 **101** 27f. multicoloured . . . . 5·75 3·75

102 Lindbergh and "Spirit of St. Louis"

1977. Air. 50th Anniv of Lindbergh's Transatlantic Flight.
257 **102** 28f. multicoloured . . . . 8·75 7·25

103 "Hibiscus tiliaceus" **104** Palm Tree

1977. Air. Polynesian Flowers (1st series). Multicoloured.
258 8f. Type **103** . . . . 2·00 2·75
259 12f. "Plumeria acuminata" 2·75 2·50
See also Nos. 276/7 and 288/9.

1977. Air. Forest Conservation.
260 **104** 32f. multicoloured . . . . 9·00 6·00

105 "Portrait of Rubens' Son, Albert"

1977. Air. 400th Birth Anniv of Peter Paul Rubens.
261 **105** 100f. red and blue . . . . 10·50 14·50

106 Cutter

1977. Sailing Ships. Multicoloured.
262 20f. Type **106** . . . . 3·75 3·50
263 50f. "Tiare Taporo" (schooner) . . . . 4·75 4·00
264 85f. Barque . . . . 6·75 5·50
265 120f. Full-rigged ship . . . . 9·75 7·25

107 Captain Cook and H.M.S. "Discovery"

1978. Air. Bicent of Discovery of Hawaii.
266 **107** 33f. mauve, red and blue 5·50 4·25
267 – 39f. green, blue & mauve 6·75 4·75
DESIGN: 39f. Captain Cook and H.M.S. "Resolution".

1978. Air. Sea Shells (2nd series). As T **98**. Multicoloured.
268 22f. Walled cowrie . . . . . 2·50 2·50
269 24f. Ventral cowrie . . . . . 2·50 2·50
270 31f. False scorpion conch . . 3·75 3·50

108 "Tahitian Woman and Boy" (Gauguin)

1978. Air. 75th Death Anniv of Paul Gauguin.
271 **108** 50f. multicoloured . . . . 14·00 11·00

109 Microwave Antenna

1978. Air. World Telecommunications Day.
272 **109** 80f. multicoloured . . . . 7·00 7·25

110 Match Scene

1978. Air. World Cup Football Championship, Argentina.
273 **110** 28f. multicoloured . . . . 3·25 3·75

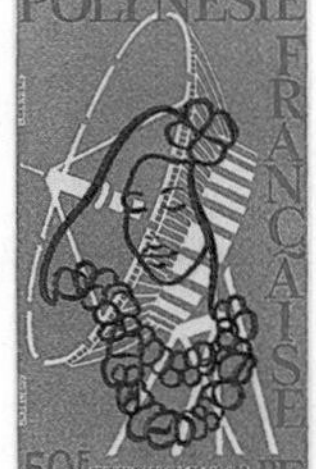

111 Fungia **112** "Hibiscus aros sinensis"

1978. Air. Coral (1st series). Multicoloured.
274 26f. Type **111** . . . . 2·75 3·25
275 34f. Millepora (vert) . . . . 3·25 3·25
See also Nos. 292/3.

1978. Flowers (2nd series). Multicoloured.
276 13f. Type **112** . . . . 2·75 3·00
277 16f. "Fagraea berteriana" . . 3·25 3·50

113 Polynesian Girl and Aerial **115** Polynesian Girl on Beach

114 Bird and Rainbow over Tropical Island

1978. Air. Papenoo Ground Receiving Station.
278 **113** 50f. black and blue . . . 5·25 3·75

1978. Air. Nature Protection.
279 **114** 23f. multicoloured . . . . 3·25 3·50

1978. 20th Anniv of First French Polynesian Stamps.
280 **115** 20f. brown, violet & red 3·75 3·50
281 – 28f. brown, green & yell 4·75 4·00
282 – 36f. brown, red and blue 5·75 4·25
MS283 130 × 100 mm. Nos. 280/82 in different colours . . . . . . 28·00 29·00
DESIGNS: 28f. Polynesian (as T **2**); 36f. Girl playing guitar (as T **1**).

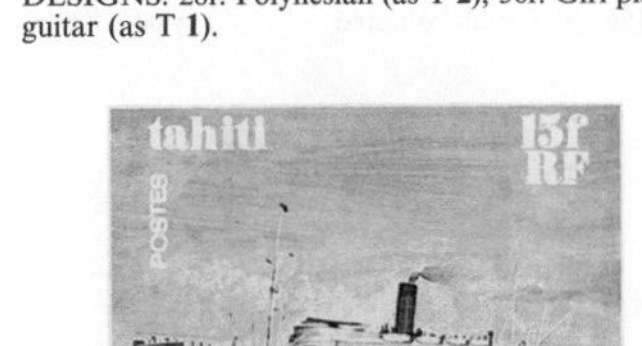

116 "Tahiti" (inter-island ship)

1978. Ships. Multicoloured.
284 15f. Type **116** . . . . 2·00 3·00
285 30f. "Monowai" (liner) . . . 2·75 2·50
286 75f. "Tahitien" (inter-island ship) . . . . 4·25 3·75
287 100f. "Mariposa" (cargo liner) . . . . 6·00 5·75

1979. Flowers (3rd series). As T **112**. Mult.
288 10f. "Vanda sp." . . . . 2·75 2·50
289 22f. "Gardenia tahitensis" (vert) . . . . 3·25 2·50

1979. Air. Death Bicentenary of Captain James Cook (explorer). Nos. 266/7 optd **"1779-1979" BICENTENAIRE DE LA MORT DE.**
290 **107** 33f. mauve, red & blue . . 4·75 3·50
291 – 39f. green, blue & mauve 5·00 3·25

1979. Coral (2nd series). As T **111**. Mult.
292 32f. Porytes . . . . 2·50 3·00
293 37f. Montipora and white-tailed damselfish . . . . . 3·50 3·50

118 Raiatea

1979. Landscapes.
294 1f. Bora Bora . . . . 70 1·25
469 2f. Ua Pou . . . . 60 1·25
470 3f. Motu Tapu 75 90
470a 4f. Type **118** . . . . 1·25 1·25
471 5f. Motu . . . . 1·00 1·25
472 6f. Case au Taumotu . . . 60 1·25

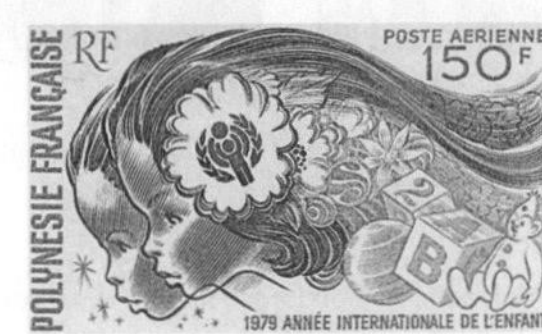

119 Children and Toys

1979. Air. International Year of the Child.
300 **119** 150f. mauve, blue & turq 9·75 9·25

120 "You are waiting for a Letter?" (Gauguin)

1979. Air.
301 **120** 200f. multicoloured . . . 17·00 12·50

121 Conch and Stone Head of a Tiki

1979. Air. Tahiti and the Islands Museum.
302 **121** 44f. brown, red & lake . . 5·75 4·75

122 Fetia

1979. Traditional Dancing Costumes. Multicoloured.
303 45f. Type **122** . . . . 2·25 3·00
304 51f. Teanuanua . . . . . . 2·50 3·00
305 74f. Temaeva . . . . 4·75 3·75

123 Sir Rowland Hill, British and Polynesian Stamps

1979. Death Centenary of Sir Rowland Hill.
306 **123** 100f. mauve, violet & grn 5·75 5·75

1979. Sea Shells (3rd series). As T **98**. Mult.
307 20f. Strigate auger . . . . . 1·75 2·50
308 28f. Snake mitre . . . . . . 2·50 2·00
309 35f. Wavy-edge spindle . . . 3·25 3·50

124 Arrows converging on Tahiti

1979. Air. 19th South Pacific Conference, Tahiti.
310 **124** 23f. multicoloured . . . . 2·75 3·50

125 Carving and Rotary Emblem

1979. 20th Anniv of Papeete Rotary Club.
311 **125** 47f. multicoloured . . . . 4·75 4·75

126 Short Sandringham 7 Bermuda Flying Boat

1979. Air. Aircraft (1st series). Multicoloured.
312 24f. Type **126** . . . . 2·25 1·25
313 40f. Douglas DC-4 . . . . . 3·25 2·75
314 60f. Britten Norman Islander 4·00 3·25
315 80f. Fokker/Fairchild Friendship . . . . 5·50 4·50
316 120f. Douglas DC-8 . . . . . 7·00 4·50
See also Nos. 335/8.

127 Emperor Angelfish

1980. Fishes (1st series). Multicoloured.
317 7f. Big-eyed soldierfish . . . 1·75 2·75
318 8f. Hump-headed wrasse . . 1·75 2·75
319 12f. Type **127** . . . . 2·25 2·75
See also Nos. 339/41, 360/2 and 386/8.

128 "Window in Tahiti"

1980. Air. 50th Anniv of Henri Matisse's Visit to Tahiti.
320 **128** 150f. multicoloured . . . 8·50 7·00

1980. 75th Anniv of Rotary International. No. 311 surch **75eme ANNIVERSAIRE 1905-1980 77F.**
321 **125** 77f. on 47f. mult . . . . 6·00 5·75

130 National Centre for Exploitation of Oceans

1980. Aquaculture (1st series). Multicoloured.
322 15f. Type **130** . . . . 1·60 2·50
323 22f. Sea-water shrimp . . . . 1·90 2·25
See also Nos. 343/4.

131 General Post Office, Papeete

1980. Opening of New General Post Office.
324 **131** 50f. multicoloured . . . . 2·50 2·50

132 Tiki Statuette, Marquesas Islands

1980. 3rd South Pacific Arts Festival, Papua New Guinea.
325 34f. Type **132** . . . . 2·25 1·50
326 39f. Pahu (drum), Marquesas Islands . . . . 2·25 3·00
327 49f. Adze, Society Islands . . 2·50 3·50
MS328 136 × 100 mm. Nos. 325/7 18·00 18·00

133 "Tehamana's Ancestors" (Gauguin)

1980. Air.
329 **133** 500f. multicoloured . . . 24·00 22·00

134 Sydney Town Hall and 1955 Oceanic Settlements 9f. stamp

1980. Air. "Sydpex 80" Stamp Exhibition, Sydney.
330 **134** 70f. multicoloured . . . . 8·50 9·75

135 White Tern **136** Charles de Gaulle

1980. Birds (1st series). Multicoloured.
331 25f. Type **135** . . . . 2·75 1·75
332 35f. Tahitian lory (vert) . . . 3·75 2·25
333 45f. Great frigate bird . . . 4·00 2·75
See also Nos. 350/52 and 379/81.

1980. 10th Death Anniv of Charles de Gaulle (French statesman).
334 **136** 100f. multicoloured . . . 4·50 4·00

1980. Air. Aircraft (2nd series). As T **126**. Mult.
335 15f. Consolidated Catalina amphibian . . . . 1·25 2·25
336 26f. De Havilland Twin Otter 1·60 1·00
337 30f. CAMS 55 flying boat . . 1·75 1·75
338 50f. Douglas DC-6 . . . . . 3·75 2·50

1981. Fishes (2nd series). As T **127**. Mult.
339 13f. Zebra unicornfish . . . 2·00 2·25
340 16f. Black-tailed snapper . . 2·00 2·25
341 24f. Purple-spotted grouper 2·50 2·50

137 "And the Gold of their Bodies" (Gauguin)

1981. Air.
342 **137** 100f. multicoloured . . . 7·00 4·50

1981. Aquaculture (2nd series). As T **130**. Mult.
343 23f. Shrimp hatching room, National Centre for Exploitation of Oceans . . 1·40 2·50
344 41f. Green mussels . . . . . 1·90 2·25

138 Yuri Gagarin and Alan Shepard

1981. Air. 20th Anniv of First Men in Space.
345 **138** 300f. multicoloured . . . 10·00 9·25

139 Dancers

1981. Folklore. Multicoloured.
346 26f. Type **139** . . . . 2·50 1·50
347 28f. Drummer . . . . 1·90 2·00
348 44f. Two dancers (vert) . . . 3·50 3·00

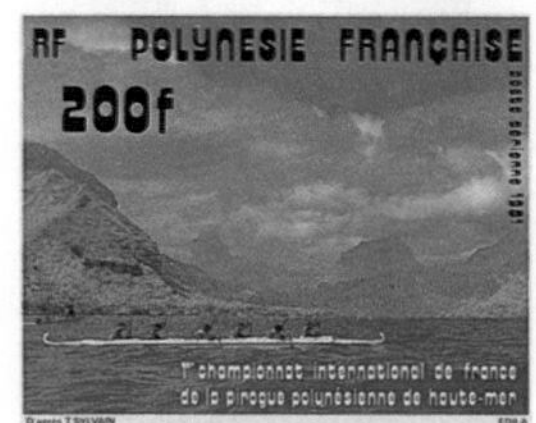

140 Racing Pirogue

1981. Air. 1st International Pirogue Championship, Polynesia.
349 **140** 200f. multicoloured . . . 9·00 7·00

141 Common Waxbill

1981. Birds (2nd series). Multicoloured.
350 47f. Crested terns . . . . . 1·50 1·00
351 53f. Grey-green fruit dove . . 1·75 1·00
352 65f. Type **141** . . . . 2·00 1·25

142 Huahine

1981. French Polynesian Islands (1st series). Multicoloured.
353 34f. Type **142** . . . . 2·00 2·25
354 134f. Maupiti . . . . 4·50 3·00
355 136f. Bora Bora . . . . . . 4·50 3·50
See also Nos. 376/8.

143 "Matavai Bay" (William Hodges)

1981. Air. 18th-century Paintings. Mult.
356 40f. Type **143** . . . . . . 2·75 2·50
357 60f. "Poedea" (John Webber) (wrongly inscr "Weber") (vert) . . . . 2·25 2·75
358 80f. "Omai" (Sir Joshua Reynolds) (vert) . . . . . 3·50 2·75
359 120f. "Point Venus" (Georges Tobin) . . . . 5·25 4·25

1982. Fishes (3rd series). As T **127**. Mult.
360 30f. Indo-Pacific hump-headed parrotfish . . . . 1·00 2·25
361 31f. Regal angelfish . . . . . 1·40 2·50
362 45f. Greasy grouper . . . . 1·50 2·50

144 Family, Bacillus and Dr Robert Koch

1982. Air. Centenary of Discovery of Tubercle Bacillus.
363 **144** 200f. blue, grey & brown 6·50 5·25

145 Oyster Farm

1982. Pearl Industry. Multicoloured.
364 7f. Type **145** . . . . 90 2·00
365 8f. Grafting oysters . . . . . 95 2·25
366 10f. Pearls . . . . 1·75 2·25

146 Girl and Tahiti 25c. stamp

1982. "Philexfrance 82" International Stamp Exhibition, Paris.
367 **146** 15f. brown, green & blue 8·00 10·00
MS368 122 × 95 mm. **146** 150f. rose, green and blue . . . . 21·00 22·00

147 Footballers **148** Priest

1982. Air. World Cup Football Championship, Spain.
369 **147** 250f. multicoloured . . . 7·25 8·75

1982. Polynesian Folklore. King's Enthroning. Multicoloured.
370 12f. Type **148** . . . . 80 1·25
371 13f. Enthroning ceremony . . 90 1·50
372 17f. Priest and King . . . . 1·10 1·60

149 "Hobie Cat 16" Class Catamaran

1982. 4th World "Hobie Cat" Championship, Tahiti.
373 **149** 90f. multicoloured . . . . 3·00 3·25

150 Island Scene **151** Sun, Man and Pacific Scene

1982. Air. Overseas Week.
374 **150** 110f. brown, blue & grn 4·00 3·50

1982. 1st South Pacific Commission Conference on New Energy Sources, Tahiti.
375 **151** 46f. multicoloured . . . . 2·00 2·75

1982. French Polynesian Islands (2nd series). As T **142**. Multicoloured.
376 20f. Motu . . . . 1·25 2·25
377 33f. Tupai Atoll . . . . . . 1·40 80
378 35f. Gambier . . . . 1·40 2·25

1982. Birds (3rd series). As T **141**. Mult.
379 37f. Reef heron (horiz) . . . 1·10 20
380 39f. Pacific golden plover . . 1·10 90
381 42f. Chestnut-breasted mannikins . . . . 2·25 1·10

152 "Tahitian Girl" (Maximilien Radiguet)

1982. Air. 19th-century Paintings. Mult.
382 50f. Type **152** . . . . 2·75 2·50
383 70f. "Tahiti Souvenir" (Charles Giraud) (horiz) . . 2·25 2·75
384 100f. "Pounding Material" (Jules Louis Le Jeune) (horiz) . . . . 3·00 3·25
385 160f. "Papeete Harbour" (Constance Gordon Cumming) (horiz) . . . . 5·00 5·50

1983. Fishes (4th series). As T **127**. Mult.
386 8f. Clown surgeonfish . . . . 1·25 2·00
387 10f. Blue-finned trevally . . . 2·00 2·00
388 12f. Black-finned reef shark 1·25 2·25

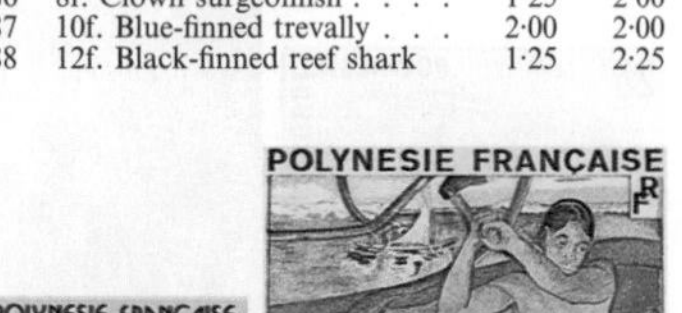

153 "The Way of the Cross" **154** "The Axeman"

1983. Religious Sculptures by Damien Haturau. Multicoloured.
389 7f. Type **153** . . . . 85 1·25
390 21f. "The Virgin and the Infant Jesus" . . . . . . 1·25 1·50
391 23f. "Christ" . . . . 1·50 2·25

1983. Air. 80th Death Anniv of Gauguin (painter).
392 **154** 600f. multicoloured . . . 17·00 16·00

155 Acacia and Pandanus Hat

1983. Polynesian Hats (1st series). Mult.
393 11f. Type **155** . . . . 1·25 1·90
394 13f. High-crowned hat made from coconut leaves . . . 1·25 1·75
395 25f. Coffee-coloured openwork hat . . . . . . 1·40 2·00
396 35f. Bamboo hat . . . . . . 1·40 2·25
See also Nos. 423/6.

156 Bligh, Route Map and Breadfruit

1983. Air. Re-enactment of Captain William Bligh's Open-boat Voyage after the "Bounty" Mutiny.
397 **156** 200f. multicoloured . . . 8·00 6·00

157 Chief of St. Christine

1983. Costumes (1st series). Multicoloured.
398 15f. Type **157** . . . . 75 1·50
399 15f. St. Christine man . . . 80 1·60
400 28f. St. Christine woman . . 1·25 2·00
See also Nos. 427/9 and 454/6.

158 Polynesian Girls

1983. Air. "Brasiliana 83" International Stamp Exhibition, Rio de Janeiro.
401 **158** 100f. multicoloured . . . 4·00 4·25
MS402 131 × 92 mm. No. 401 . . 5·00 6·50

159 Polynesian and Thai Girls

1983. Air. "Bangkok 1983" International Stamp Exhibition.
403 **159** 110f. multicoloured . . . 4·00 4·25
MS404 92 × 131 mm. No. 403 . . 6·25 6·50

160 Fragrant Fern Headdress

1983. Floral Headdresses (1st series). Multicoloured.
405 41f. Type **160** . . . . 2·25 2·50
406 44f. Gardenias . . . . 2·50 2·50
407 45f. Mixed flowers . . . . . 2·50 2·50
See also Nos. 433/5.

161 Luther and Church

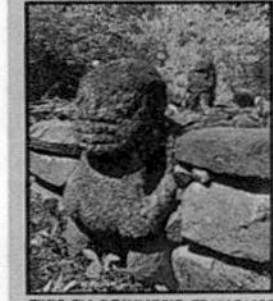

163 Me'ae of Peke, Nuku-Hiva

162 "Arrival of Escort Ship" (Nicolas Mordvinoff)

1983. 500th Birth Anniv of Martin Luther (Protestant reformer).
408 **161** 90f. black, blue & brown 3·50 3·25

1983. Air. 20th-century Paintings. Mult.
409 40f. "View of Moorea" (William MacDonald) (horiz) . . . . 2·50 2·50
410 60f. "Fei Porter" (Adrian Herman Gouwe) . . . . . 2·00 2·25
411 80f. Type **162** . . . . 3·25 3·00
412 100f. "Women on the Veranda" (Charles Lemoine) (horiz) . . . . . 3·00 2·75

1984. Marquesian Tikis. Multicoloured.
413 14f. Type **163** . . . . 80 1·50
414 16f. Me'ae of Paeke (different) . . . . 95 1·25
415 19f. Me'ae Oipona, Hiva-Oa 1·00 2·00

165 Island Canoeists

1984. Air. "Espana 84" International Stamp Exhibition, Madrid.
420 **165** 80f. red and blue . . . . 2·75 3·75
MS421 144 × 100 mm. **165** 200f. blue 10·00 12·00

166 "Woman with Mango" (Gauguin)

1984. Air.
422 **166** 400f. multicoloured . . . 17·00 12·00

1984. Polynesian Hats (2nd series). As T **155**. Multicoloured.
423 20f. Reed hat . . . . 1·40 70
424 24f. Pandanus leaves hat . . 1·60 1·60
425 26f. Fei and bamboo hat . . 1·60 1·60
426 33f. Pandanus hat decorated with toetoe flowers . . . . 2·00 1·75

1984. Costumes (2nd series). As T **157**. Mult.
427 34f. Tahitian boy playing nose flute . . . . 1·75 2·25
428 35f. Priest from Oei-Eitia . . 1·75 2·25
429 39f. Tahitian woman and her son . . . . 2·00 1·75

167 "Human Sacrifice" (detail, John Webber)

1984. Air. "Ausipex 84" International Stamp Exhibition, Melbourne. Multicoloured.
430 120f. Type **167** . . . . . . 7·75 5·50
431 120f. Different detail of "Human Sacrifice" . . . . 7·75 5·50
MS432 127 × 93 mm. 200f. Type **167** 17·00 21·00

1984. Floral Headdresses (2nd series). As T **160**. Multicoloured.
433 46f. Ylang ylang . . . . . . 2·25 2·25
434 47f. Garden vine . . . . . . 2·25 2·50
435 53f. Bougainvillea . . . . . 2·50 1·90

168 Tiki and Native

1984. 4th South Pacific Arts Festival, Noumea, New Caledonia.
436 **168** 150f. multicoloured . . . 4·75 4·25
See also No. 453.

169 "Tahitian Girls on the Beach" (Pierre Heyman)

1984. 20th-century Paintings. Multicoloured.
437 50f. "After Church" (Jacques Boulaire) (vert) . . . . . 2·50 2·50
438 65f. "Anaa Countryside" (Jean Masson) . . . . . . 2·25 2·25
439 75f. "Festival" (Robert Tatin) 3·00 3·00
440 85f. Type **169** . . . . 3·00 3·50

170 Pair of Tikis

171 Girl wearing Lei

1985. Wooden Tikis. Multicoloured.
441 30f. Type **170** . . . . 1·25 1·60
442 36f. Joined tikis . . . . . . 1·40 45
443 40f. Tiki . . . . 1·60 1·50

1985. Polynesian Faces (1st series). Multicoloured.
444 22f. Type **171** . . . . 85 1·50
445 39f. Girl's profile . . . . . . 1·25 1·75
446 44f. Girl wearing shell necklace . . . . 1·50 1·60
See also Nos. 473/5 and 498/500.

172 "Where Have We come From? What are We? Where are We Going?" (Gauguin) (½-size illustration)

1985. Air.
447 **172** 550f. multicoloured . . . 14·50 14·00

173 East Bridge, Papeete

1985. Tahiti in Olden Days (1st series). Mult.
448 42f. Type **173** . . . . 1·60 1·75
449 45f. Inhabitants of Papeete (vert) . . . . 1·25 1·75
450 48f. Papeete market . . . . 1·60 2·00
See also Nos. 477/9, 528/30, 703/5 and 742/4.

174 Coral Reef

1985. 5th International Coral Reefs Congress, Tahiti.
451 **174** 140f. multicoloured . . . 4·50 3·50

175 National Flag

1985.
452 **175** 9f. multicoloured . . . . 1·25 1·40

1985. 4th Pacific Arts Festival, Papeete. As T **168** but with "Sud Noumea" omitted, different emblem, inscr "29 juin au 15 juillet" and dated "1985".
453 200f. multicoloured . . . . . 5·50 4·25

The Festival was originally to be held in New Caledonia in 1984 but was cancelled and subsequently held in Tahiti in 1985.

1985. Costumes (3rd series). As T **157**. Mult.
454 38f. Tahitian dancer . . . . 1·60 1·75
455 55f. Tahitian couple . . . . 1·90 1·90
456 70f. Tahitian king . . . . . 2·75 1·10

176 Couple holding Blue-faced Booby

1985. Air. International Youth Year.
457 **176** 250f. multicoloured . . . 5·25 3·25

177 19th-century French Warship in Papeete Harbour

1985. Air. "Italia '85" International Stamp Exhibition, Rome.
458 **177** 130f. green . . . . 5·50 4·00
MS459 143 × 100 mm. **177** 240f. blue 11·00 11·50

178 Traditional Foods

1985. Tahitian Oven Pit. Multicoloured.
460 25f. Type **178** . . . . 1·40 1·60
461 35f. Man tending oven . . . 1·50 55

179 St. Michael's Cathedral, Rikitea (Gambier Island)

1985. Catholic Churches. Multicoloured.
462 90f. St Anne's Church, Otepipi (Anaa) . . . . . . 3·00 2·50
463 100f. Interior of St. Michael's Cathedral, Rikitea (Gambier Island) . . . . . 3·00 2·75
464 120f. Type **179** . . . . . . 4·00 3·25

180 Fiddler Crab

1986. Crabs. Multicoloured.
465 18f. Type **180** . . . . 90 1·50
466 29f. Hermit land crab . . . . 1·25 1·60
467 31f. Coconut crab . . . . . 1·25 1·60

181 Youth with Pufferfish

1986. Polynesian Faces (2nd series). Multicoloured.
473 43f. Type **181** . . . . 1·75 1·75
474 49f. Boy holding coral . . . 1·75 1·75
475 51f. Youth and turtle (vert) 1·90 1·75

182 Marlin and Emblem

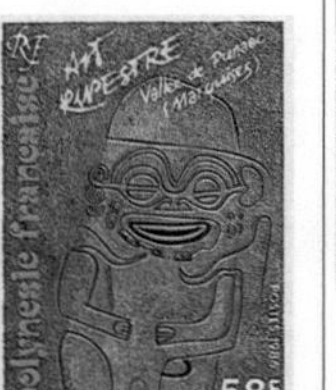
183 Tiki, Punaei Valley

1986. Air. 1st International Marlin Fishing Contest.
476 **182** 300f. multicoloured . . . 9·00 6·50

1986. Tahiti in Olden Days (2nd series). As T **173**. Multicoloured.
477 52f. Papeete . . . . 1·75 1·75
478 56f. Harpoon fishing . . . . 1·90 1·90
479 57f. King's Palace, Papeete 2·00 1·90

1986. Rock Carvings (1st series). Mult.
480 58f. Type **183** . . . . 1·90 1·90
481 59f. Human figure, Hane Valley . . . . 1·90 1·50
See also Nos. 507/8.

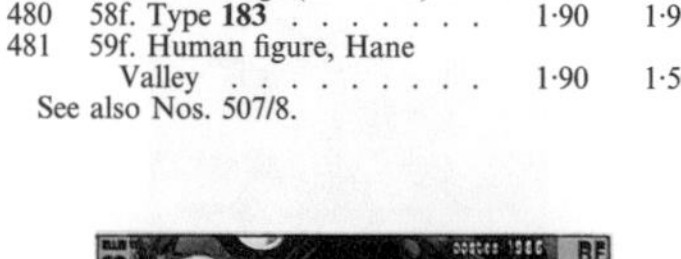
184 Fish in Coconut Milk

1986. Polynesian Food Dishes (1st series). Multicoloured.
482 80f. Type **184** . . . . 3·00 2·75
483 110f. Fafaru . . . . 4·00 3·25
See also Nos. 504/5 and 524/5.

185 Arrival of Sailing Ships, 1880

1986. Air.
484 **185** 400f. blue . . . . 10·00 8·50

186 "Tifaifai" (sewn collage)

1986. Polynesian Folklore. Traditional Crafts. Multicoloured.
485 8f. Type **186** . . . . 65 1·25
486 10f. Wickerwork . . . . . . 80 1·40
487 12f. Making "mores" (dance skirts) . . . . 90 1·40

187 Map of Tahiti, Daniel Carl Solander and Anders Sparrmann

1986. Air. "Stockholmia 86" International Stamp Exhibition.
488 **187** 150f. grn, dp bl & bl . . 5·00 4·00
MS489 143 × 105 mm. **187** 210f. green, turquoise and blue . . . 8·50 8·50

188 Building a Pirogue
189 Metuapua

1986. Pirogue Construction. Multicoloured.
490 46f. Type **188** . . . . 1·25 1·75
491 50f. Constructing the hull . . 1·40 1·90

1986. Medicinal Plants (1st series). Designs showing illustrations by Gilles Cordonnier.
492 **189** 40f. green . . . . 1·75 1·75
493 – 41f. green . . . . 1·75 1·75
494 – 60f. green . . . . 2·25 2·00
DESIGNS: 41f. Hotu; 60f. Miri.
See also Nos. 514/16 and 545/7.

190 Tiva Church

1986. Air. Protestant Churches. Mult.
495 80f. Type **190** . . . . 3·00 2·50
496 200f. Avera church . . . . . 5·50 4·00
497 300f. Papetoai church . . . . 8·75 5·25

191 Old Man

1987. Polynesian Faces (3rd series). Mult.
498 28f. Type **191** . . . . 1·60 1·60
499 30f. Girl holding baby . . . 1·60 1·60
500 37f. Elderly woman . . . . . 1·75 1·60

192 Reef Crab

1987. Crustaceans. Multicoloured.
501 34f. Type **192** . . . . 1·50 1·60
502 35f. "Parribacus antarcticus" 1·50 1·75
503 39f. "Justitia longimana" . . 1·75 1·90

1987. Polynesian Food Dishes (2nd series). As T **184**. Multicoloured.
504 33f. Papaya po'e . . . . . . 1·00 1·75
505 65f. Chicken fafa . . . . . . 1·75 2·25

193 Broche Barracks

1987. Air. Centenary of Broche Army Barracks.
506 **193** 350f. multicoloured . . . 9·75 8·50

1987. Rock Carvings (2nd series). As T **183**. Multicoloured.
507 13f. Double-headed figure, Tipaerui . . . . 80 1·40
508 21f. Turtle, Raiatea . . . . . 1·10 1·50

194 George Vancouver, Map of Rapa Island and Quotation

1987. Air. "Capex '87" International Stamp Exhibition, Toronto.
509 **194** 130f. brown and red . . . 4·50 3·25
MS510 143 × 100 mm. 260f. brown, blue and deep blue. Imperf . . 8·50 8·50
DESIGN: 260f. Motifs as T **194**, Polynesian, Red Indian, and Polynesian and Canadian scenes.

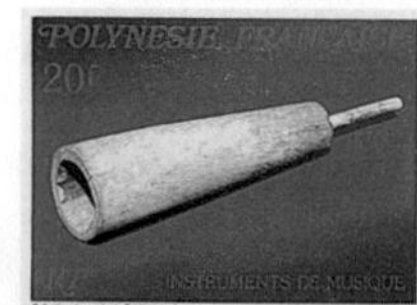
195 Marquesas Islands Miro Wood and Bamboo Horn

1987. Musical Instruments. Multicoloured.
511 20f. Type **195** . . . . 1·00 1·00
512 26f. Trumpet triton horn with coconut fibre cord . . . . 1·10 1·60
513 33f. Bamboo flutes . . . . . 1·40 1·75

1987. Medicinal Plants (2nd series). As T **189**, showing illustrations by Gilles Cordonnier.
514 46f. green . . . . 1·90 1·75
515 53f. mauve . . . . 2·00 1·90
516 54f. black . . . . 2·00 1·90
DESIGNS: 46f. Miro; 53f. Tiapito; 54f. Taataahiara.

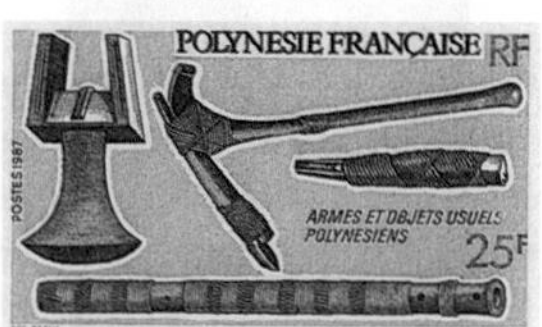
196 Penu, War Club, Adze and Nose Flute

1987. Tools and Weapons. Designs showing plates from "The Voyages of Captain Cook".
517 **196** 25f. black and green . . . 1·60 1·60
518 – 27f. blue & turquoise . . 1·60 1·60
519 – 32f. dp brn & brn . . . . 2·00 1·60
DESIGNS: 27f. War club, tattooing comb, paddle and chisels; 32f. Head bands, head and chest ornaments and adze.

197 "Soyez Mysterieuses" (wood sculpture, Paul Gauguin) (½-size illustration)

1987. Air.
520 **197** 600f. multicoloured . . . 17·00 13·50

198 Mgr. Rene Dordillon, Bishop of Marquesas Islands

1987. Catholic Missionaries. Multicoloured.
521 95f. Type **198** . . . . 2·75 2·75
522 105f. Mgr. Tepano Jaussen 3·00 2·75
523 115f. Mgr. Paul Maze, Archbishop of Papeete . . 4·00 3·00

1988. Polynesian Food Dishes (3rd series). As T **184**. Multicoloured.
524 40f. Crayfish (vert) . . . . . 1·40 1·75
525 75f. Bananas in coconut milk (vert) . . . . 3·00 2·50

199 James Norman Hall

1988. Birth Centenaries (1987) of Nordhoff and Hall (writers).
526 **199** 62f. black, cream & sil . . 2·25 2·00
527 – 85f. black, grey and silver 3·25 2·50
DESIGN: 85f. Charles Bernard Nordhoff.

1988. Tahiti in Olden Days (3rd series). As T **173**. Multicoloured.
528 11f. Taranpoo house raft, Raiatea . . . . 1·25 1·25
529 15f. Small Tahitian huts . . . 1·25 1·25
530 17f. Large Tahitian hut . . . 1·25 1·25

200 Lighthouse and Anchor

1988. 120th Anniv of Venus Point Lighthouse.
531 **200** 400f. multicoloured . . . 17·00 9·75

201 "River Scene"

1988. Tapa (cloth made from beaten bark) Paintings by Paul Engdahl. Multicoloured.
532 52f. Type **201** . . . . 2·25 2·00
533 54f. "River scene" (different) 2·25 2·00
534 64f. "Jungle" . . . . 2·50 2·50

202 Dish Aerial, Papenoo, Tahiti

1988. Polysat Satellite Communications Network.
535 **202** 300f. multicoloured . . . 10·00 8·00

203 Doll in More Skirt

1988. Polynesian Folklore. Tahitian Dolls. Mult.
536 42f. Type **203** . . . . 1·75 1·75
537 45f. Doll in city clothing . . 1·75 1·75
538 48f. Doll in city clothing (different) . . . . 1·90 2·00

204 Carved Figures (detail)

1988. "Sydpex 88" International Stamp Exhibition, Australia. Engraving by J. and E. Verreaux from Atlas by Baron von Krusenstern (explorer).
539 **204** 68f. brown . . . . 3·50 2·50
MS540 142 × 100 mm. 145f. red, green and ochre. Imperf . . . 6·75 6·75
DESIGN: 145f. Russian officer in marae (cemetery) at Nuku Hiva.

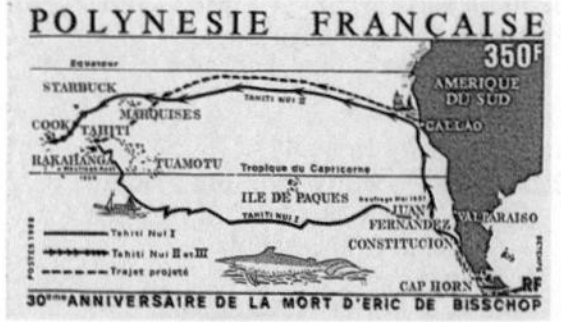
205 Route Map

1988. 30th Death Anniv of Eric de Bisschop (leader of "Tahiti Nui" expedition).

541	**205**	350f. blue, black & brown	14·50	8·00

206 "Kermia barnardi"

1988. Sea Shells (1st series). Multicoloured.

542	24f. Type **206**	1·25	1·50
543	35f. "Vexillum suavis"	1·40	1·75
544	44f. "Berthelinia" sp.	1·60	1·90

See also Nos. 573/5.

1988. Medicinal Plants (3rd series). As T **189**, showing illustrations by Gilles Cordonnier.

545	23f. red	1·25	1·25
546	36f. brown	1·60	1·75
547	49f. blue	2·00	1·90

DESIGNS: 23f. Tiatiamona; 36f. Patoa purahi; 49f. Haèhaa.

207 Henry Nott and "Duff"

1988. Protestant Missionaries. Multicoloured.

548	80f. Type **207**	3·50	2·50
549	90f. Papeiha	3·75	2·75
550	100f. Samuel Raapoto	4·25	2·75

208 Papeete Post Office, 1875

1989. Taihitian Postal History.

551	**208**	30f. brown, green & blue	1·75	1·50
552	–	40f. brown, green & blue	1·90	1·75

DESIGN: 40f. Papeete Post Office, 1915.

209 Bowl with Wooden Cover, Marquesas Islands

1989. 8th Anniv of Arts and Crafts Centre. Multicoloured.

553	29f. Type **209**	1·75	1·50
554	31f. Mother-of-pearl pendant, Marquesas Islands	1·75	1·50

210 Woman splitting Coconuts

211 Wooden Statue with Tapa Covering

1989. Copra Production. Multicoloured.

555	55f. Type **210**	90·00	75·00
556	70f. Drying copra (horiz)	3·00	2·50

1989. Tapa (bark of paper-mulberry tree) Decorations. Multicoloured.

557	43f. Type **211**	2·25	1·90
558	51f. Fern leaf decoration, Society Islands (horiz)	2·25	1·90
559	56f. Concentric circles decoration, Austral Islands (horiz)	2·50	2·00

212 Woman playing Ukulele

213 Lifting Stone

1989. Polynesian Environment. Mult.

560	120f. Type **212**	4·75	3·50
561	140f. Diver collecting marlin-spike auger shells	5·25	4·00

1989. Polynesian Folklore. July Festivals. Mult.

562	47f. Type **213**	2·50	1·90
563	61f. Dancer	2·75	2·00
564	67f. Group of singers (horiz)	3·25	2·25

214 "Mutineers casting Bligh adrift" (detail, Robert Dodd)

1989. Bicentenaries of French Revolution and Mutiny on the "Bounty".

565	**214**	100f. dp blue, blue & grn	4·25	3·25
MS566		140 × 100 mm. 200f. brown, green and black. Imperf	8·00	8·50

DESIGN: 200f. Complete painting by Dodd and French Colonies 1939 150th Anniv of Revolution omnibus issue.

215 Fr. O'Reilly

1989. 1st Death Anniv of Father Patrick O'Reilly (founder of Gauguin Museum).

567	**215**	52f. green and brown	2·50	1·90

216 "Get Well Soon"

1989. Greetings Stamps. Multicoloured.

568	42f. Type **216**	2·75	2·50
569	42f. Horseshoe ("Good Luck")	2·75	2·50
570	42f. Cake ("Happy Anniversary")	2·75	2·50
571	42f. Letters and telephone ("In Touch")	2·75	2·50
572	42f. Presents ("Congratulations")	2·75	2·50

1989. Sea Shells (2nd series). As T **206**. Mult.

573	60f. "Triphoridae"	2·25	2·00
574	69f. "Favartia"	2·50	2·25
575	73f. Checkerboard engina and grape drupe	2·75	2·25

217 "Te Faaturuma" (Paul Gauguin)

1989.

576	**217**	1000f. multicoloured	26·00	28·00

218 "Legend of Maui: Birth of the Islands"

1989. Polynesian Legends (1st series). Mult.

577	66f. Type **218**	2·75	2·00
578	82f. "Legend of the Pierced Mountain" (horiz)	3·50	2·50
579	88f. "Legend of Hina, the Eel from Lake Vaihiria"	3·25	2·50

See also Nos. 599/601.

219 Flower

1990. Traditional Resources. Vanilla. Mult.

580	34f. Type **219**	1·75	1·50
581	35f. Pods	1·75	1·50

220 Spotted Flagtail

1990. Fresh Water Animals. Multicoloured.

582	40f. Type **220**	2·00	1·75
583	50f. Shrimp	2·25	1·90

221 Sandwich Islands Man and Hawaiian Islands

1990. Maori World (1st series).

584	**221**	58f. black	2·50	1·90
585	–	59f. blue	28·00	21·00
586	–	63f. green	2·50	1·90
587	–	71f. blue	2·75	2·00

DESIGNS: 59f. Easter Island man and map; 63f. New Zealand man and map; 71f. Octopus and Tahiti.

See also Nos. 610/12 and 644/6.

222 Old Town Hall

1990. Centenary of Township of Papeete. Mult.

588	150f. Type **222**	4·75	3·50
589	250f. New Town Hall	8·75	5·75

223 Sooty Crake

224 Young People reading

1990. Birds. Multicoloured.

590	13f. Type **223**	80	25
591	20f. Ultramarine lory	70	30

1990. 30th Anniv of Papeete Lions Club.

592	**224**	39f. multicoloured	1·60	1·75

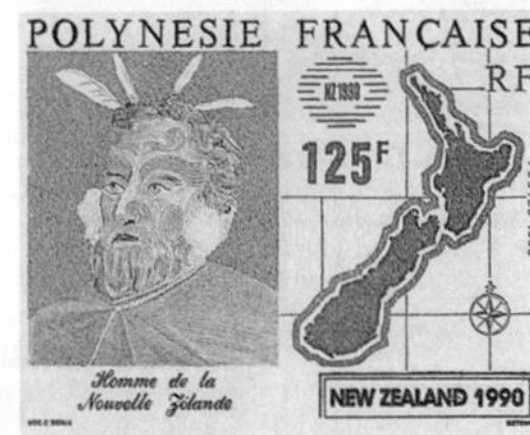

225 New Zealand Man and Map

1990. "New Zealand 1990" International Stamp Exhibition, Auckland.

593	**225**	125f. blue, green & purple	5·50	3·50
MS594		100 × 76 mm. **225** 230f. purple, olive and green. Imperf	10·00	10·50

226 De Gaulle and Globe

1990. Birth Centenary of Charles de Gaulle (French statesman).

595	**226**	200f. blue, brown & red	7·00	5·50

227 Girls in Pareos

228 Girl wearing Tiare Headdress

1990. World Tourism Day.

596	**227**	8f. multicoloured	1·00	1·10
597	–	10f. multicoloured	1·00	1·10
598	–	12f. multicoloured	1·10	1·25

DESIGNS: 10, 12f. Girls in pareos (different).

1990. Polynesian Legends (2nd series). As T **218**. Multicoloured.

599	170f. "Legend of Uru" (horiz)	5·75	4·75
600	290f. "Legend of Pipiri-Ma"	11·00	6·00
601	375f. "Legend of Hiro, God of Thieves"	12·50	9·75

1990. Tiare Flower. Multicoloured.

602	28f. Type **228**	1·40	1·50
603	30f. Tiare bush	1·40	1·50
604	37f. Girl wearing flower over ear and lei	1·60	1·50

229 Pineapple Plants

230 Doridian Nudibranch

1991. Traditional Resources. The Pineapple. Multicoloured. Self-adhesive. Backing paper perf.
605 42f. Type **229** . . . . 1·60 1·75
606 44f. Plantation . . . . 1·60 1·75

1991. Undersea Wonders. Multicoloured.
607 7f. Type **230** . . . . 70 1·10
608 9f. "Galaxaura tenera" (red alga) . . . . 70 1·10
609 11f. Cuming's cowrie . . . . 75 1·25

1991. Maori World (2nd series). As T **221** showing 18th-century engravings.
610 68f. green . . . . 38·00 35·00
611 84f. black . . . . 3·75 2·50
612 94f. brown . . . . 4·25 3·25
DESIGNS—VERT: 68f. Woman, child and statues, Easter Island. HORIZ: 84f. Sandwich Islands pirogue race; 94f. Maori village, New Zealand.

231 Basketball Players

1991. Centenary of Basketball.
613 **231** 80f. multicoloured . . . . 2·75 2·25

232 Tuamotu Kingfisher

234 "Tuava"

233 "Oranges of Tahiti" (Gauguin)

1991. Protected Birds. Multicoloured.
614 17f. Type **232** 40 40
615 21f. Kuhl's lory 60 35

1991. Centenary of Paul Gauguin's Arrival in Tahiti.
616 **233** 700f. multicoloured . . . 28·00 13·50

1991. Marquesas Islands Sculptures. Mult.
617 56f. Type **234** . . . . 1·90 1·75
618 102f. "Te Hina o Motu Haka" . . . . 3·25 2·50
619 110f. "Kooka" (horiz) . . . 3·50 2·75

235 Pianist's Hands, Conductor and Orchestra

1991. Death Bicentenary of Wolfgang Amadeus Mozart (composer).
620 **235** 100f. multicoloured . . . 4·00 2·50

236 Fishing Canoes

1991. Stone Fishing. Multicoloured.
621 25f. Type **236** . . . . 1·75 1·25
622 57f. Fisherman swinging stone (used to beat the water) . . . . 2·00 1·90
623 62f. Fish in entrapment area (horiz) . . . . 2·75 2·00

237 Sketches of Shells and Marine Life by Rene Lesson

1991. "Phila Nippon '91" International Stamp Exhibition, Tokyo.
624 **237** 50f. brown, red & violet 2·25 1·75
625 – 70f. blue, red & green . . 3·25 2·25
DESIGN—HORIZ: 70f. "View of Venus Point at Matavae, Tahiti".

238 Financed Projects

1991. 50th Anniv of Central Economic Co-operation Bank.
627 **238** 307f. multicoloured . . . 10·00 6·75

239 Father Christmas

1991. "Christmas under the Sea". Mult.
628 55f. Type **239** . . . . 2·50 1·75
629 83f. Corals decorated with baubles . . . . 3·50 2·25
630 86f. Crib among corals (vert) 3·50 2·50

240 Setting Nets along Shore

1992. Tourist Activities. Multicoloured.
631 1f. Type **240** . . . . 1·10 1·10
632 2f. Horse riding along beach 1·10 1·10
633 3f. Woman holding sailfish 1·10 1·10
634 4f. Exploring waterfall (vert) 1·10 1·10
635 5f. Yachting . . . . 1·25 1·10
636 6f. Sikorsky S-61N helicopter flight to waterfall (vert) . . 1·25 1·10

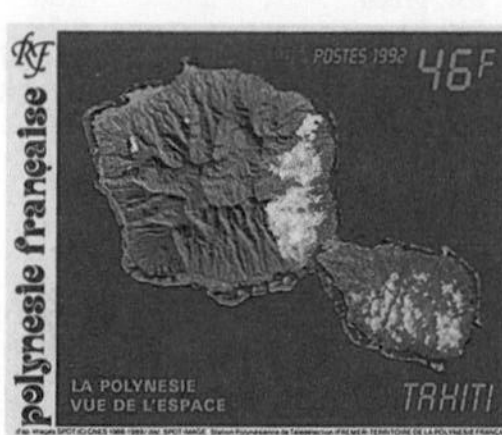

241 Tahiti

1992. "SPOT" Satellite Pictures of French Polynesia. Multicoloured.
637 46f. Type **241** . . . . 1·75 1·75
638 72f. Mataiva . . . . 2·50 2·00
639 76f. Bora-Bora . . . . 2·50 2·00
MS640 130 × 100 mm. 230f. Satellite highlighting Polynesian Islands. Imperf . . . . 7·00 7·25

242 "Orange Carriers" (L. Taerea)

1992. World Health Day. "Health in Rhythm with the Heart".
641 **242** 136f. multicoloured . . . 4·25 3·25

243 Sailor asking for Directions

1992. "World Columbian Stamp Expo '92" Exhibition, Chicago.
642 **243** 130f. multicoloured . . . 5·00 3·50
MS643 140 × 100 mm. 250f. Scene incorporating Type **243**. Imperf 6·75 8·00

244 Dancers, Tahiti

1992. Maori World (3rd series). Traditional Dances.
644 **244** 95f. brown . . . . 3·25 2·50
645 – 105f. brown . . . . 3·50 2·75
646 – 115f. green, brn & choc 3·75 2·75
DESIGNS: 105f. Hawaiian dancers; 115f. Night Dance by Tongan women.

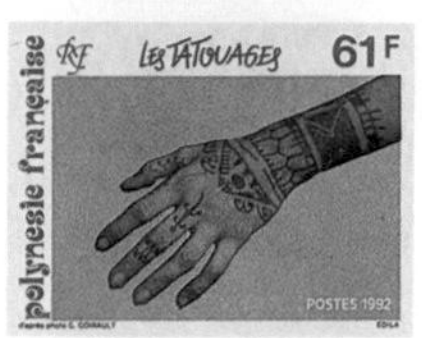

245 Tattooed Hand

1992. Tattoos. Multicoloured.
647 61f. Type **245** . . . . 2·50 1·90
648 64f. Tattooed man (vert) . . 2·50 2·00

246 Sailing Model Outrigger Canoes

1992. Children's Pastimes. Multicoloured.
649 22f. Type **246** . . . . 1·75 1·25
650 31f. String game . . . . . . 1·75 1·50
651 45f. Stilt walking (vert) . . . 2·00 1·75

247 Melville and Books

1992. Writers of the South Seas. 150th Anniv of Arrival in Polynesia of Herman Melville (novelist).
652 **247** 78f. multicoloured . . . . 3·75 2·00

248 Raft, Gambier Islands

1992. 6th Pacific Arts Festival, Rarotonga, Cook Islands.
653 **248** 40f. red . . . . 2·00 1·75
654 – 65f. blue . . . . 2·50 2·25
DESIGN: 65f. Pirogues off Taihiti.

249 Arrival of Mail at Cercle Bougainville Post Office, Papeete

1992. Centenary of First French Oceanic Settlements Stamp.
655 **249** 200f. multicoloured . . . 6·00 4·25

250 "Fare Tamarii" (Erhard Lux)

1992. Artists in Polynesia. Multicoloured.
656 55f. Type **250** . . . . 2·25 1·75
657 60f. "Symphonie de Monettes" (Uschi) . . . . 2·25 1·75
658 75f. "Spear Fisherman" (Pierre Kienlen) . . . . . 2·75 2·00
659 85f. "Maternity" (Octave Morillot) . . . . 2·75 2·25

252 Cast-net Fisherman

253 Hanging Skipjack Tuna on Rack

1993. Fishing in Couleur Lagoon. Self-adhesive. Imperf. (a) Size 26 × 36 mm.
670 **252** 46f. multicoloured . . . . 1·75 1·25

(b) Size 17 × 23 mm.
671 **252** 46f. multicoloured . . . . 1·75 1·25

1993. Bonito Fishing. Multicoloured.
672 68f. Bone hook and line . . . 2·25 1·60
673 84f. Fishing launch (horiz) . . 2·50 1·75
674 86f. Type **253** . . . . 2·75 2·00

254 U.S. Flag, Pilot and Airstrip

1993. 50th Anniv of Bora-Bora Airfield.
675 **254** 120f. multicoloured . . . 3·00 2·50

255 "Pahi Moorea"

1993. Birth Centenary of Jacques Boullaire (artist).
676 **255** 32f. brown . . . . 1·25 1·00
677 – 36f. orange . . . . 1·40 1·10
678 – 39f. violet . . . . 1·00 1·25
679 – 51f. brown . . . . 1·75 1·40
DESIGNS: 36f. "Pahi Tuamoto"; 39f. "Pahi Rurutu"; 51f. "Pahi Nuku-hiva".

256 Sportsman

1993. Sports Festival.
680 **256** 30f. multicoloured . . . . 1·25 1·00

257 Contestant

1993. 15th Anniv of Australian Mathematics Competition.
681 **257** 70f. multicoloured . . . . 2·25 1·75

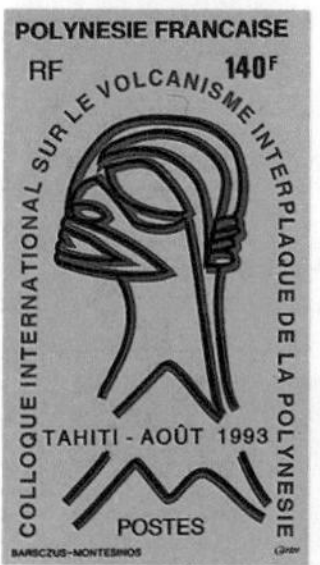

258 Pele, Goddess of Volcanoes

259 Red Junglefowl crowing

1993. International Symposium on Intra-plate Volcanism, Punaauia (Tahiti).
682 **258** 140f. pink, brown & blk 3·50 2·50

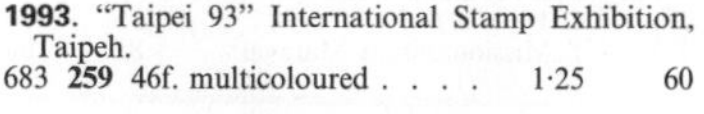

1993. "Taipei 93" International Stamp Exhibition, Taipeh.
683 **259** 46f. multicoloured . . . . 1·25 60

260 Sight-seeing Canoe Trip

1993. International Tourism Day. Mult.
684 14f. Type **260** 65 40
685 20f. Tahitian women decorating tourist (vert) . . 80 50
686 29f. Beach picnic . . . . . . 1·10 70

261 Municipal Guard of 1843 and Modern Gendarme

1993. 150th Anniv of Arrival of First Gendarme in Tahiti.
687 **261** 100f. multicoloured . . . 2·75 1·90

262 Gerbault and "Firecrest"

1993. Birth Centenary of Alain Gerbault (round the world sailor).
688 **262** 150f. blue, red & green . . 4·00 3·50

263 Woman Dancing to Guitar Music (Vaea Sylvain)

1993. Artists in Polynesia. Multicoloured.
689 40f. Type **263** . . . . 1·25 75
690 70f. Portrait of Polynesian woman (Andre Marere) (vert) . . . . 1·75 1·10
691 80f. Four generations of women (Jean Shelsher) . . 2·00 1·25
692 90f. Woman in hat (Paul-Emile Victor) (vert) . . . . 2·75 1·60

264 Relief (Vahineroo Terupe)

1993. 30th Anniv of French Pacific School.
693 **264** 200f. multicoloured . . . 5·00 3·25

265 Spinner Dolphins

1994. Marine Mammals. Multicoloured.
694 25f. Spinner dolphin 75 45
695 68f. Type **265** . . . . 1·90 1·25
696 72f. Humpback whales (vert) 2·10 1·40

266 Spaniel

267 Sister Germaine Bruel and Child

1994. "Hong Kong '94" Int Stamp Exhibition.
697 **266** 51f. multicoloured . . . . 1·60 90

1994. 150th Anniv of Arrival of Sisters of St. Joseph of Cluny Congregation.
698 **267** 180f. multicoloured . . . 4·50 3·00

268 Tahiti Temple

1994. 150th Anniv of Arrival in Polynesia of Church of Jesus Christ of Latter Day Saints.
699 **268** 154f. multicoloured . . . 3·75 2·75

269 Father Gregoire (founder) and Polynesians

1994. Bicentenary of National Conservatory of Arts and Crafts, Paris, and 15th Anniv of Papeete Regional Associated Centre.
700 **269** 316f. multicoloured . . . 7·50 4·50

270 Emblem and Polynesians

1994. 10th Anniv of Internal Autonomy.
701 **270** 500f. multicoloured . . . 12·00 8·00

271 "Fare Vana'a"

1994. 20th Anniv of Tahiti Academy.
702 **271** 136f. black, red & blue . . 3·50 2·25

272 Papara

1994. Tahiti in Olden Days (4th series). Mult.
703 22f. Type **272** 75 45
704 26f. Mataiea coast 90 60
705 51f. Bamboo forest, Taravao (vert) . . . . 1·40 75

273 "Faaturuma" (Paul Gauguin)

1994.
706 **273** 1000f. multicoloured . . . 23·00 15·00

274 "Epiphyllum oxipetalum"

1994. Beauty of the Night (cactus).
707 **274** 51f. multicoloured . . . . 1·40 75

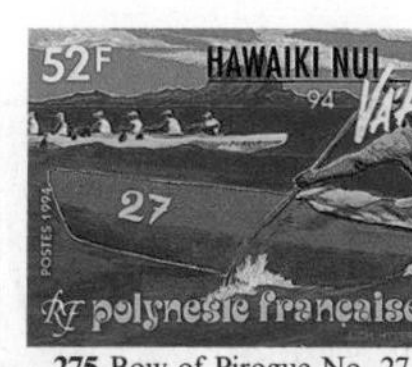

275 Bow of Pirogue No. 27

1994. "Hawaiki Nui Va'a 94" Pirogue Race. Multicoloured.
708 52f. Type **275** . . . . . . 1·25 75
709 76f. Pirogue (detail) . . . . 1·60 1·10
710 80f. Pirogue (different detail) 1·60 1·25
711 94f. Stern of pirogue and pirogue No. 60 . . . . . 2·00 1·40
Nos. 708/11 were issued together, se-tenant, forming a composite design.

276 Portrait by Michelle Villemin

1994. Artists in Polynesia. Paintings by artists named. Multicoloured.
712 62f. Type **276** . . . . 1·60 85
713 78f. Michele Dallet . . . . . 2·00 1·10
714 102f. Johel Blanchard . . . . 2·25 1·40
715 110f. P. Lacouture (horiz) . . 2·50 1·60

277 Don Domingo de Boenechea and Frigate

1995. 220th Anniv of Spanish Expeditions to Tautira.
716 **277** 92f. multicoloured . . . . 2·00 1·25

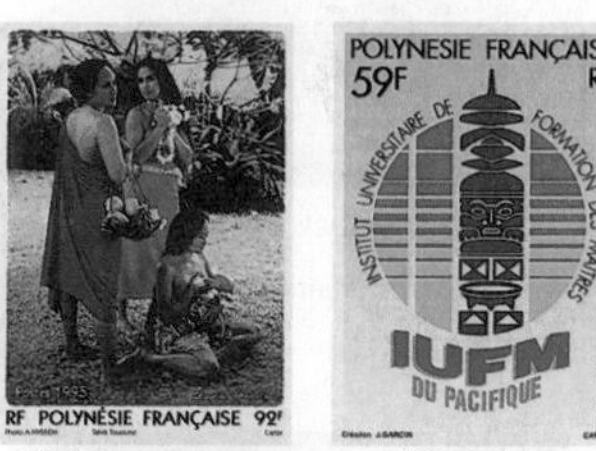

278 "Women on the Sea Shore" (Paul Gauguin)

280 Emblem

279 Pigs

1995. South Pacific Tourism Year.
717 **278** 92f. multicoloured . . . . 2·00 1·25

1995. Chinese New Year. Year of the Pig.
718 **279** 51f. multicoloured . . . . 1·40 75

1995. Pacific University Teachers' Training Institute.
719 **280** 59f. multicoloured . . . . 1·40 70

281 Head of Green Turtle

1995. Protected Species. Multicoloured.
720 22f. Type **281** 50 20
721 29f. Green turtle 75 40
722 91f. Black coral . . . . . . 2·00 1·25

282 Pasteur

1995. Death Centenary of Louis Pasteur (chemist).
723 **282** 290f. blue and lt blue . . 6·50 4·00

283 Scene from Novel

1995. 113th Anniv of Publication of "Le Mariage de Loti" by Pierre Loti.
724 **283** 66f. multicoloured . . . . 1·60 80

284 Woman with Bowl of Monoi **285** Rapa Island Fruit Dove

1995. Tahiti Monoi (blend of coconut oil and tiare flower).
725 **284** 150f. multicoloured . . . 3·25 1·75

1995. "Unique Birds of the World". Mult.
726 22f. Type **285** 55 40
727 44f. Marquesas pigeon . . . 1·25 55

286 Black Pearls

1995. Tahitian Pearls. Multicoloured.
728 66f. Type **286** . . . . 1·40 75
729 84f. Coloured pearls . . . . 1·90 1·10

287 Alvaro de Mendana de Neira and "Todos los Santos" (galleon)

1995. 400th Anniv of Discovery of Marquesas Islands. Multicoloured.
730 161f. Type **287** . . . . . . 3·00 1·75
731 195f. Pedro Fernandez de Quiros and map of islands 3·50 2·50

288 Games Mascot **289** Pandanus Tree

1995. 10th South Pacific Games, Tahiti.
732 **288** 83f. multicoloured . . . . 1·90 1·00

1995. "Singapore'95" International Stamp Exhibition. Multicoloured.
733 91f. Type **289** . . . . 2·00 1·25
734 91f. Pandanus (flower) . . . 2·00 1·25
735 91f. Pandanus (fruit) . . . . 2·00 1·25
736 91f. Plaiting leaves . . . . 2·00 1·25

290 Man and Woman wearing Headdresses and Emblem

1995. 50th Anniv of U.N.O.
737 **290** 420f. multicoloured . . . 7·25 4·75

291 "Paddler with Yellow Dog" (Philippe Dubois)

1996. Artists in Polynesia. Multicoloured.
738 57f. Type **291** . . . . 1·00 70
739 76f. "Afternoon in Vaitape" (Maui Seaman) . . . . . 1·50 95
740 79f. "Woman with White Hat" (Simone Testeguide) (horiz) . . . . 1·75 1·10
741 100f. "Kellum House in Moorea" (Christian Deloffre) (horiz) . . . . . 2·10 1·40

1996. Tahiti in Olden Days (5th series). As T **272**. Multicoloured.
742 18f. La Fautaua 40 25
743 30f. Punaauia Grove 60 35
744 35f. Coconut palm forest, Tautira 70 45

292 Rats **293** Queen Pomare

1996. Chinese New Year. Year of the Rat.
745 **292** 51f. multicoloured . . . . 1·10 55

1996. No value expressed. (a) Size 26 × 36 mm.
746 **293** (51f.) multicoloured . . . 80 50

(b) Size 17 × 23 mm. Self-adhesive.
747 **293** (51f.) multicoloured . . . 80 50

294 Victor and Hemispheres

1996. Paul-Emile Victor (polar explorer) Commemoration.
748 **294** 500f. multicoloured . . . 8·50 5·50

295 Pertusus Cone

1996. Sea Shells. Multicoloured.
749 10f. Type **295** 25 20
750 15f. "Cypraea alisonae" (cowrie) 30 20
751 25f. "Vexillum roseotinctum" (ribbed mitre) 45 30

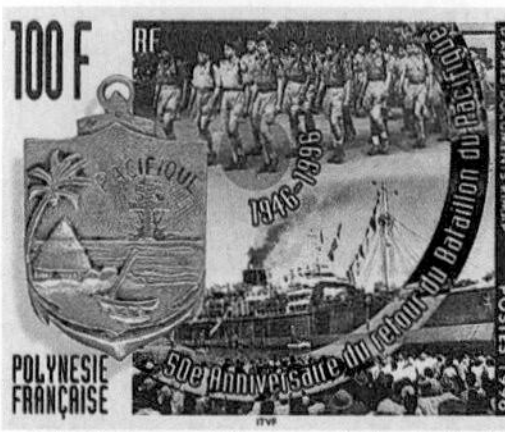

296 Badge, Soldiers and "Sagittaire" (troopship)

1996. 50th Anniv of Return of Pacific Battalion from Second World War.
752 **296** 100f. multicoloured . . . 2·00 1·40

297 Dancers

1996. "China'96" Int Stamp Exn, Peking.
753 **297** 50f. multicoloured . . . . 1·00 55
MS754 100 × 76 mm. 200f. Staff and pupils of Chinese school, Tahiti, 1940. Imperf . . . . 4·50 4·50

298 Red-footed Booby

1996. Marine Birds. Multicoloured.
755 66f. Type **298** . . . . 1·10 70
756 79f. Great frigate bird . . . 1·60 80
757 84f. Common noddy . . . . 1·75 90

299 Pahu, Ukulele and Toere

1996. Musical Instruments. Multicoloured.
758 5f. Type **299** 10 10
759 9f. Toere 20 20
760 14f. Pu and vivo (wind instruments) 25 20

300 Polynesian Cicada

1996.
761 **300** 66f. multicoloured . . . . 1·25 75

301 Ruahatu, God of the Ocean **302** Lemasson's 1913 Tahitian Girl Stamp Design

1996. 7th Pacific Arts Festival.
762 **301** 70f. black and blue . . . 1·40 90

1996. Stamp Day. 40th Death Anniv of Henri Lemasson (photographer and stamp designer).
763 **302** 92f. multicoloured . . . . 1·90 1·25

303 Assembly Building

1996. 50th Anniversaries of Territorial Assembly and Autumn Stamp Salon.
764 **303** 85f. multicoloured . . . . 1·60 1·10

304 "Woman sitting on Shore" (T. Becaud)

1996. Artists in Polynesia. Multicoloured.
765 70f. Type **304** . . . . 1·10 70
766 85f. "Woman with leaf headdress" (M. Noguier) (vert) . . . . 1·50 80
767 92f. "Woman with yellow headdress" (C. de Dinechin) (vert) . . . . . 1·60 1·10
768 96f. "Two women" (A. Lang) (vert) . . . . 1·90 1·25

305 Hand writing **306** Oxen

1997. 80th Anniv of Society for Oceanic Studies.
769 **305** 55f. brown 95 55

1997. Chinese New Year. Year of the Ox.
770 **306** 13f. multicoloured 25 20

307 Arrival of "Duff" (full-rigged missionary ship)

1997. Bicentenary of Evangelical Church of French Polynesia. Multicoloured.
771 43f. Type **307** 85 60
772 43f. Missionaries at Matavai 85 60

308 Uru Leaves

1997. Tifaifai. Multicoloured.
773 1f. Type **308** 10 10
774 5f. Tiare flower 15 10
775 70f. Hibiscus flowers . . . . 1·25 65

309 "Papeete-Zelee" (schooner) **311** Male Dancer

310 Tiare Flower

1997. "Pacific '97" International Stamp Exhibition, San Francisco. Maritime Link between San Francisco and Papeete. Mult.
790 92f. Type **309** . . . . 1·75 1·10
791 92f. "Tropic Bird" (barquentine) . . . . . . 1·75 1·10
MS792 100 × 75 mm. Nos. 790/1 (sold at 400f.) . . . . 7·25 7·25

1997. Tourism. Multicoloured.
793 85f. Type **310** . . . . 1·50 70
794 85f. Canoeing . . . . 1·50 70
795 85f. Spearman . . . . 1·50 70

796 85f. Tahiti . . . . 1·50 70
797 85f. Barrier reef anemone-fish 1·50 70
798 85f. Women on shore . . . . 1·50 70
799 85f. Shell . . . . 1·50 70
800 85f. Outrigger canoe at sunset 1·50 70
801 85f. Snorkelling . . . . . . 1·50 70
802 85f. Pineapples and bananas 1·50 70
803 85f. Palm tree on beach . . . 1·50 70
804 85f. Dancers . . . . 1·50 70

1997. Dance Costumes. Multicoloured.
805 4f. Type **311** 10 10
806 9f. Female dancer 20 15
807 11f. Couple 25 20

312 "Kon Tiki" (after Christian Faugerat)

1997. 50th Anniv of Thor Heyerdahl's "Kon Tiki" (replica of balsa raft) Expedition from Peru to Tuamoto Island, South Pacific.
808 **312** 88f. multicoloured . . . . 1·75 1·10

313 Man carrying Fruits on Yoke (Monique Garnier-Bissol)

1997. Artists in Polynesia. Multicoloured.
809 85f. Type **313** . . . . 1·00 70
810 96f. Mother-of-pearl mermaid and turtles (Camelia Maraea) . . . . 1·40 95
811 110f. Pot (Peter Owen) (vert) 1·50 1·10
812 126f. Coconut halves in water (Elisabeth Stefanovitch) . . 1·90 1·40

314 "Te arii vahine" (Paul Gauguin)

1997. Autumn Salon, Paris.
813 **314** 600f. multicoloured . . . 8·25 6·00

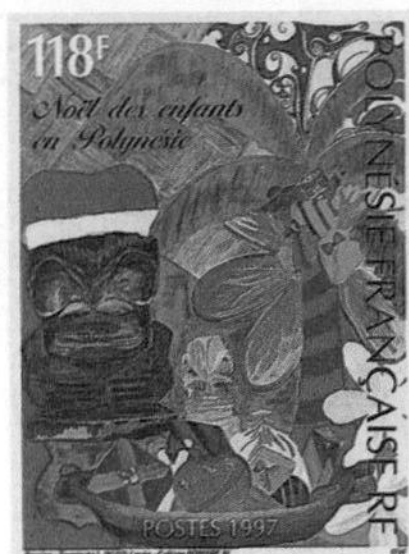

315 Santa Claus Hat on Statue, Candy-striped Palm Tree and Dish of Gifts

1997. Christmas.
814 **315** 118f. multicoloured . . . 1·75 1·25

316 Adult and Cub

1998. Chinese New Year. Year of the Tiger.
815 **316** 96f. multicoloured . . . . 1·60 1·00

317 Grumman Widgeon

1998. Aviation. Multicoloured.
816 70f. Type **317** . . . . 1·10 75
817 70f. Fairchild FH-227 . . . . 1·10 75
818 85f. De Havilland D.H.C.6 Twin Otter . . . . 1·25 90
819 85f. Aerospatiale ATR 42-500 1·25 90
No. 816 is wrongly inscribed "Grumann".

318 "Dendrobium" "Royal King"

1998. Orchids. Multicoloured.
820 5f. Type **318** 15 10
821 20f. "Oncidium" "Ramsey" (vert) 35 20
822 50f. "Ascocenda" "Laksi" (vert) 75 40
823 100f. "Cattleya" hybrid . . . 1·50 90

319 "The Lovers"

1998. 150th Birth Anniv of Paul Gauguin (artist).
824 **319** 1000f. multicoloured . . . 13·00 8·00

320 Boy in Football Strip

321 Woman wearing Shell Necklaces

1998. World Cup Football Championship, France.
825 **320** 85f. multicoloured . . . . 1·25 70

1998. Necklaces and Headdresses. Mult.
826 55f. Type **321** 75 45
827 65f. Woman wearing shell necklaces and bracelet . . 95 55
828 70f. Woman in floral headdress 95 55
829 80f. Woman with floral headdress and garland . . 1·25 65

322 Painting by Stanley Haumani

1998. Undersea Life.
830 **322** 200f. multicoloured . . . 3·00 1·60

323 "Papeete Bay"

1998. Autumn Stamp Salon, Paris. Paintings by R. Gillotin. Multicoloured.
831 250f. Type **323** . . . . . . 3·50 2·00
832 250f. "Papeete Bay" (different) . . . . 3·50 2·00
MS833 142 × 105 mm. Nos. 831/2. Imperf . . . . 7·50 7·50

1998. French Victory in World Cup Football Championship. As No. 825 but additionally inscr "FRANCE championne du monde" on boy's shirt and with colours of French flag forming frame around design.
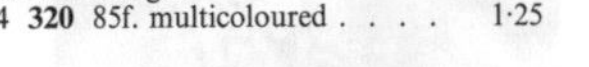
834 **320** 85f. multicoloured . . . . 1·25 65

324 "Return from the Market" (A. Deymonaz)

1998. Daily Life. Paintings by Andre Deymonaz. Multicoloured.
835 70f. Type **324** . . . . 1·10 55
836 100f. "Sellers of Skipjack Tuna" . . . . 1·40 90
837 102f. "Fishermen Departing" (horiz) . . . . 1·50 95
838 110f. "Women in Sunday Best" (horiz) . . . . . . 1·60 95

325 Hares

1999. Chinese New Year. Year of the Hare.
839 **325** 118f. multicoloured . . . 1·75 90

326 Couple

1999. St. Valentine's Day.
840 **326** 96f. multicoloured . . . . 1·25 75

327 Thorny Seahorse

1999. Marine Life. Multicoloured.
841 70f. Lionfish . . . . 1·10 55
842 85f. Type **327** . . . . 1·25 65
843 90f. Painted angler . . . . . 1·40 70
844 120f. Three-spined scorpionfish . . . . 1·75 95

328 Tattooed Man

329 Children

1999. Tattooes. Multicoloured.
845 90f. Type **328** . . . . 1·25 80
846 120f. Tattooed man with cloak . . . . 1·90 1·10

1999. Mothers' Day. Multicoloured.
847 85f. Type **329** . . . . 1·25 60
848 120f. Two children with heart of blossoms (horiz) . . . . 1·60 90

330 Papaya

1999. Fruits of Fenua (Tahiti) (1st series). Multicoloured.
849 85f. Type **330** . . . . 1·25 75
850 85f. Guava ("La goyave") . . 1·25 75
851 85f. Red mombin . . . . . 1·25 75
852 85f. Rambutan . . . . 1·25 75
853 85f. Star-apple ("La pomme-etoile") . . . . 1·25 75
854 85f. Gooseberry tree ("La seurette") . . . . 1·25 75
855 85f. Rose apple ("La pomme-rose") . . . . 1·25 75
856 85f. Five fingers ("La carambole") . . . . 1·25 75
857 85f. Spanish lime . . . . . . 1·25 75
858 85f. Sugar-apple ("La pomme-cannelle") . . . . 1·25 75
859 85f. Cashew ("La pomme de cajou") . . . . 1·25 75
860 85f. Passion fruit . . . . . . 1·25 75
See also Nos. 864/5.

331 Cancellation, 1997 9f. Stamp and Islanders

1999. 150th Anniv of First French Stamp.
861 **331** 180f. multicoloured . . . 2·75 1·60
MS862 101 × 70 mm. No. 861 . . 7·50 7·50

332 Chopin and Score

1999. 150th Death Anniv of Frederic Chopin (composer).
863 **332** 250f. multicoloured . . . 3·75 2·10

333 Breadfruit

1999. Fruit of Fenua (2nd series). Multicoloured.
864 85f. Type **333** . . . . 1·25 70
865 120f. Coconut (horiz) . . . . 1·75 1·00

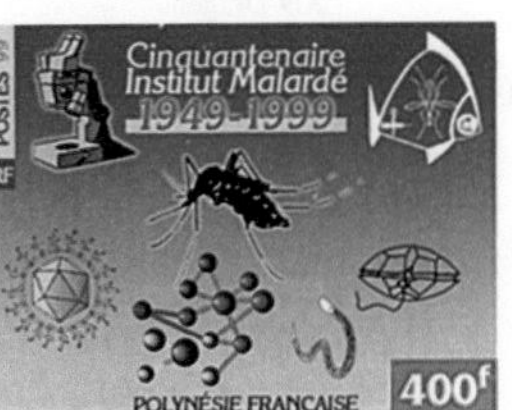

334 Microscope, Disease Carriers and Atomic Model

1999. 50th Anniv of Louis Malarde Institute (for research into public health).
866 **334** 400f. multicoloured . . . 5·25 3·00

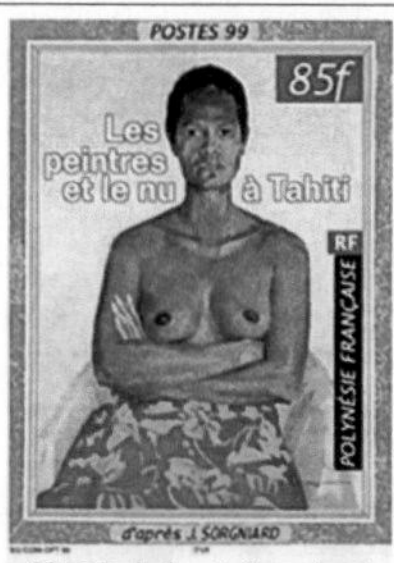

335 Nude by J. Sorgniard

1999. Painters and the Nude in Tahiti. Showing paintings by artists named. Multicoloured.
867 85f. Type **335** . . . . 1·25 70
868 120f. J. Dubrusk . . . . . . 1·60 1·00
869 180f. C. Deloffre . . . . . . 2·25 1·50
870 250f. J. Gandouin . . . . . 3·25 2·10

336 Woman blowing Conch

1999. Year 2000.
871 **336** 85f. multicoloured 90 60

337 Emblem

1999. 5th Marquesas Islands' Art Festival.
872 **337** 90f. multicoloured . . . . 1·00 70

338 Adult holding Baby's Hand

2000. New Millennium. Multicoloured.
873 85f. Type **338** 90 60
874 120f. Part of child's face (horiz) . . . . 1·25 85

339 Dragons

2000. Chinese New Year. Year of the Dragon.
875 **339** 180f. multicoloured . . . 2·00 1·40

340 Stamps and Postal Emblem

2000. Philately.
876 **340** 90f. multicoloured . . . . 1·00 70

341 Tattooed Hand

2000. 1st International Tattooing Festival, Raiatea. Multicoloured.
877 85f. Type **341** 90 60
878 120f. Woman with tattooed hand and ear . . . . . . 1·25 85
879 130f. Man with tattooed hands . . . . 1·40 90
880 160f. Man holding tattooed hand in front of eye . . . 1·60 1·10

342 Polynesian Women

2000. Polynesian Women.
881 **342** 300f. multicoloured . . . 4·00 2·50
MS882 106 × 80 mm. No. 881 (sold at 500f.) . . . . 6·50 4·25

343 White Dress

2000. Traditional Costumes. Showing women wearing different traditional dresses. Multicoloured.
883 85f. Type **343** 90 60
884 120f. Green and white floral dress with hat . . . . . . 1·25 85
885 160f. White lace tunic and long cap skirt . . . . . . 1·60 1·10
886 250f. Embroidered red dress 3·25 2·10

344 Mt. Aorai and Mt. Orohena

2000. Mountains over 2000 Metres on Tahiti. Mult.
887 90f. Type **344** . . . . 1·00 70
888 180f. Mt. Aorai and Mt. Orohena (different) . . . . 2·25 1·50

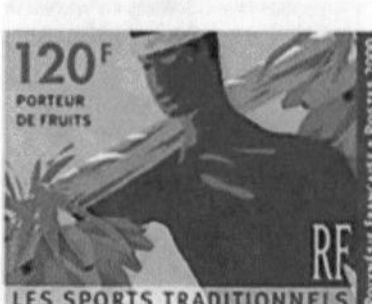

345 Fruit Carriers' Race

2000. Traditional Sports. Multicoloured.
889 120f. Type **345** . . . . . . 1·25 85
890 250f. Stone lifting (vert) . . . 3·25 2·10

346 Woven Fans

2000. Traditional Crafts. Multicoloured.
891 85f. Type **346** 90 60
892 85f. Woven hat 90 60

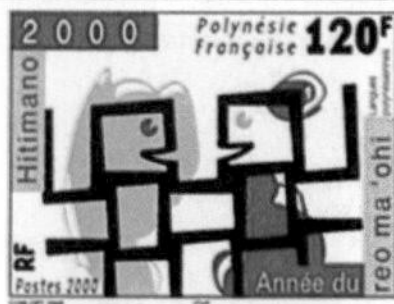

347 Stylized Couple

2000. National Tahitian Language Year.
893 **347** 120f. yellow, red & blk . . 1·25 85

348 Flower and Satellite

2000. New Millennium.
894 **348** 85f. multicoloured 90 60

349 Main Gateway

2001. Centenary of Ecole Centrale. Multicoloured.
895 85f. Type **349** 90 60
896 85f. Present day main building 90 60

350 Snake and Flower

351 Vaiharuru Waterfall, Papenoo, Tahiti

2001. Chinese New Year. Year of the Snake.
897 **350** 120f. multicoloured . . . 1·25 85

2001. Polynesian Nature. Multicoloured.
898 35f. Type **351** 35 30
899 50f. Lake Vaihiria, Tahiti (horiz) 55 45
900 90f. Hakaui Valley, Nuku Hiva, Marquesas Islands 95 75

352 Children

2001. Year of the Polynesian Child.
901 **352** 55f. multicoloured 60 50

353 Eddie Lund (pianist and songwriter)

2001. Entertainers. Multicoloured.
902 85f. Type **353** 85 70
903 120f. Charley Mauu (musician) . . . . 1·25 1·00
904 130f. Bimbo Moetrauri (musician) . . . . 1·40 1·10
905 180f. Marie Mariteragi (singer and dancer) and Emma Terangi (singer) (horiz) . . . . 1·90 1·50

354 *Monovai* (liner)

2001. 60th Anniv of Departure of Pacific Battalion Volunteers.
906 **354** 85f. multicoloured 85 70

355 Wave

2001. Teahupoo Wave.
907 **355** 120f. multicoloured . . . 1·25 1·00

356 Emblem

2001. 17th Anniv of Internal Autonomy.
908 **356** 250f. multicoloured . . . 2·50 2·00
MS909 142 × 105 mm. No. 908 2·50 2·00

357 Men racing

2001. "Heiva 2001" Traditional Arts and Sports Festival. Canoe Racing. Multicoloured.
910 85f. Type **357** 85 70
911 120f. Women racing . . . . 1·25 1·00
MS912 140 × 105 mm. Nos. 910/11. Imperf (sold at 250f.) . . . . 2·10 1·75

358 Tou

2001. Native Hardwood Trees. Multicoloured.
913 90f. Type **358** 90 75
914 130f. Ati . . . . 1·40 1·10
915 180f. Miro . . . . 2·00 1·60

359 Couple and Emblem

2001. A.I.D.S. Awareness Campaign.
916 **359** 55f. multicoloured 60 50

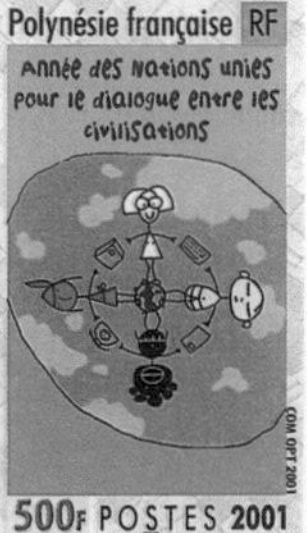

360 "Building Europe"

2001. U.N. Year of Dialogue among Civilizations.
917 **360** 500f. multicoloured . . . 5·50 4·50

361 Tiare (*Gardenia tahitensis*)

2001. Native Flowers. Multicoloured.

918 35f. Type **361** 35 30
919 50f. Pua (*Fagraea berteriana*) 55 40
920 85f. Taina (*Gardenia jasminoides*) 85 70

362 Polynesian Crib

2001.

921 **362** 120f. multicoloured . . . 1·25 1·00

363 Parcel and Flowers ("Joyeuses fetes")

2002. Greetings Stamps. Multicoloured.

922 55c. Type **363** 65 50
923 55c. Pink hibiscus ("Felicitations") 65 50
924 85c. As No. 922 but with blue background . . . . . 1·00 80
925 85c. Red hibiscus ("Felicitations") . . . . . 1·00 80

364 Horses

2002. Chinese New Year. Year of the Horse.

926 **364** 130f. multicoloured . . . 1·50 1·25

365 Canoeist and Emblem

2002. 10th World Outrigger Canoe Championship. Multicoloured.

927 120f. Type **365** . . . . 1·40 1·10
928 120f. Masked canoeist and emblem . . . . 1·40 1·10

366 Urchin (*Echinometra sp.*)

2002. Sea Urchins. Multicoloured.

929 35f. Type **366** 40 30
930 50f. *Heterocentrotus trigonarius* 60 50
931 90f. Banded urchin (*Echinothrix calamaris*) . . 1·10 90
932 120f. *Toxopneustes sp.* . . . 1·40 1·10

367 Couple holding Droplet of Blood **368** Children holding Football

2002. Blood Donation.

933 **367** 130f. multicoloured . . . 1·50 1·25

2002. World Cup Football Championship, Japan and South Korea.

934 **368** 85f. multicoloured . . . . 1·00 80

369 Coconut Pulp Peeling

2002. "Heiva 2002" Traditional Arts and Sports Festival. Multicoloured.

935 85f. Type **369** . . . . 1·00 80
936 120f. Fruit carrying races . . 1·40 1·10
937 250f. Javelin throwing . . . 3·00 2·40

370 James Norman Hall and House

2002. Inauguration of James Norman Hall House (museum).

938 **370** 90f. multicoloured . . . . 1·10 90

The museum commemorates the writer James Norman Hall.

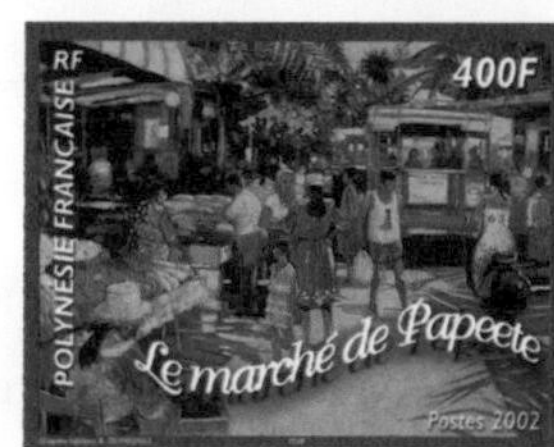

371 Market Place, Papeete (A. Deymonaz)

2002.

939 **371** 400f. multicoloured . . . 4·75 3·75
MS940 142 × 105 mm. No. 939 4·75 3·75

No. MS940 is inscribed for "Amphilex 2002" International Stamp Exhibition, Amsterdam in the margin.

372 Lagoon, Fish, Crustaceans and Bottles

2002. French Research Institute for Marine Exploitation. Multicoloured.

941 55f. Type **372** 65 50
942 90f. Aerial view of centre . . 1·10 90

373 Surfer

2002. "Taapuna Master 2002" Surfing Competition, Tahiti.

943 **373** 120f. multicoloured . . . 1·40 1·10

374 *Hibiscus tiliaceus*

2002. Seaside Flowers. Multicoloured.

944 85f. Type **374** . . . . 1·00 80
945 130f. *Scaveola sericea* . . . . 1·60 1·25
946 180f. *Guettarda speciosa* . . . 2·25 1·75

375 Bus and Dancers

2002. Festivals. Multicoloured.

947 55f. Type **375** 70 55
948 120f. Musicians (vert) . . . . 1·50 1·25

376 Goats **377** Two Women

2003. New Year. Year of the Goat.

949 **376** 120f. multicoloured . . . 1·40 1·10

2003. Polynesian Women.

950 **377** 55f. multicoloured 60 50

378 Waterfall, Trees and Lake

2003. Polynesian Waterfalls.

951 **378** 330f. multicoloured . . . 3·75 3·00

379 Building with Balcony **381** Pirogue

380 Fish

2003. Papeete in Old Photographs. Multicoloured.

952 55f. Type **379** 60 50
953 85f. Sailing ship (horiz) . . . 1·00 80
954 90f. Men with bicycles (52 × 32 mm) . . . . . . 1·00 80
955 120f. Tree-lined street (52 × 32 mm) . . . . . . 1·40 1·20
MS956 148 × 106 mm. Nos. 952/5 4·00 4·00

2003. Polynesian Marine Life.

957 **380** 460f. multicoloured . . . 5·25 4·25

2003. Pirogues (sailing canoes). Multicoloured.

958 85f. Type **381** . . . . 1·00 80
959 85f. Boy seated on sail beam 1·00 80
960 85f. Twin-sailed craft with hills behind (horiz) . . . . 1·00 80
961 85f. Craft with three crew members (horiz) . . . . . 1·00 80

382 Fire Walkers

2003.

962 **382** 130f. multicoloured . . . 1·50 1·20

383 Bi-valve

2003. Shellfish.

963 **383** 420f. multicoloured . . . 4·75 3·75

384 "Ahaoe Feii ou Quoi?" (Are you jealous?)

2003. Death Centenary of Paul Gauguin (artist).

964 **384** 250f. multicoloured . . . 2·75 2·20

385 Flag

2003.

965 **385** (60f.) multicoloured . . . 70 60

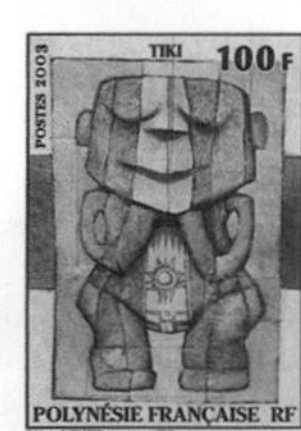

386 Figure

2003. Tiki (1st issue).

966 **386** 100f. multicoloured . . . 1·10 90

See also No. 969.

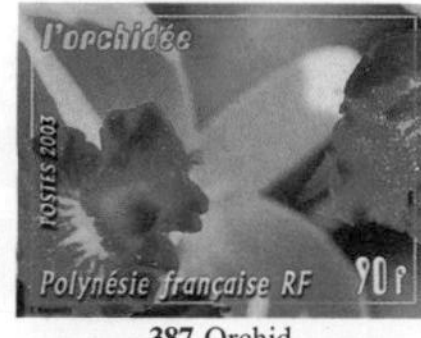

387 Orchid

2003. Flowers. Multicoloured.

967 90f. Type **387** . . . . 1·00 80
968 130f. Rose . . . . 1·60 1·30

388 Island and Trees

2003. Bora Bora. Multicoloured.

969 60f. Type **388** 70 60
970 60f. Aerial view of island . . 70 60

389 Face

2003. Tiki (2nd issue).
970 **389** 190f. multicoloured . . . 2·20 1·70

390 Landscape

2003.
972 **390** 90f. multicoloured . . . . 1·00 80

391 Monkeys
393 Woman seated in Cane Chair

392 Women ironing Cloth

2004. Year of the Monkey.
973 **391** 130f. multicoloured . . . 1·50 90

2004. Scenes from Daily Life. Multicoloured.
974 60f. Type **392** 70 45
975 90f. Street scene (vert) . . . 1·00 80

2004. Polynesian Women.
976 **393** 55f. multicoloured 60 50

394 Ceremonial Dance

2004.
977 **394** 500f. multicoloured . . . 6·00 4·75

395 Airplanes, Boules and Palm Trees

2004. Economic Development.
978 **395** 500f. multicoloured . . . 6·00 4·75

396 Mobile Cafe

2004.
979 **396** 300f. multicoloured . . . 3·75 3·00

397 Plaiting (Society Islands)

2004. Handicrafts. Multicoloured.
980 60f. Type **397** 70 55
981 60f. Carved shell (Tuamoto Islands) 70 55
982 90f. Plaited hat (Australs Islands) . . . . 1·10 90
983 90f. Wood carving(Marquesas Islands) . . . . 1·10 90

398 Globe and Island Sunset

2004. Expansion of South Pacific Post and Telecommunication Service. Multicoloured.
984 100f. Type **398** . . . . 1·20 1·00
985 130f. Satellite dish and resort 1·50 1·20

OFFICIAL STAMPS

O **100** Uru
O **251** 1840 French Colonies 40c. Stamps

1977. Native Fruits.
O240 O **100** 1f. multicoloured . . 2·25 2·25
O241 2f. multicoloured . . 1·90 2·25
O242 3f. multicoloured . . 1·90 2·25
O243 5f. multicoloured . . 2·50 2·00
O244 – 7f. multicoloured . . 2·25 2·25
O245 – 8f. multicoloured . . 2·25 2·25
O246 – 10f. multicoloured . . 2·25 2·25
O247 – 15f. multicoloured . . 2·75 2·75
O248 – 19f. multicoloured . . 2·75 2·75
O249 – 20f. multicoloured . . 3·00 2·75
O250 – 25f. multicoloured . . 3·75 3·25
O251 – 35f. multicoloured . . 4·25 3·75
O252 – 50f. multicoloured . . 4·75 4·75
O253 – 100f. multicoloured 9·00 8·25
O254 – 200f. multicoloured 16·00 12·00
DESIGNS: 7f., 8f., 10f., 15f. Vi Tahiti; 19f., 20f., 25f., 35f. Avocat; 50f., 100f., 200f. Vi Popaa.

1993.
O660 O **251** 1f. red, brown & blk 70 70
O777 – 2f. multicoloured . . 10 10
O662 – 3f. black, red & yell 70 70
O779 – 5f. black, red & yell 15 15
O780 – 9f. multicoloured . . 20 15
O781 – 10f. multicoloured 20 15
O782 – 20f. multicoloured 30 20
O666 – 46f. multicoloured 1·75 1·40
O666a – 51f. multicoloured 1·90 1·60
O785 – 70f. multicoloured 80 60
O786 – 85f. multicoloured 1·40 1·10
O787 – 100f. multicoloured 1·10 90
O788 – 200f. multicoloured 2·25 1·75
DESIGNS—HORIZ: 2f. French Colonies 1877 Peace and Commerce 40c. and 1872 Ceres 25c. stamps; 3f. French Colonies Peace and Commerce stamp with Papeete 1884 postmark; 5f. 1884 Papeete postmark; 9f. Pair of Oceanic Settlements 1948 15f. stamps with Papeete postmark; 10f. Oceanic Settlements 1892 5c. stamp and 1894 postmark; 20f. Oceanic Settlements 1892 10 and 15c. stamps with Tahiti postmark; 46f. Oceanic Settlements 1930 90c. Kanakas stamps; 51f. Oceanic Settlements 1942 5 and 10f. Free French stamps with Vaitepaua postmark; 70f. "Visit Tahiti" postmark; 100f. Oceanic Settlements 1956 3f. Dry dock stamp; 200f. Oceanic Settlements 1953 14f. Gauguin stamps. VERT: 85f. Oceanic Settlements 1921 25 on 15c. stamp.

POSTAGE DUE STAMPS

D **4** Polynesian Mask
D **164** Mother of Pearl Fish-hook

1958.
D17 D **4** 1f. green and brown . . 1·25 4·25
D18 3f. red and indigo . . . 1·25 4·50
D19 5f. blue and brown . . . 1·60 5·00

1984. Multicoloured.
D416 1f. Type D **164** . . . . . 1·40 1·90
D417 3f. Tahitian bowl (horiz) . . 1·40 1·90
D418 5f. Marquesian fan (horiz) 1·40 1·90
D419 10f. Lamp stand . . . . . 1·50 1·90
D420 20f. Wooden head-rest (horiz) . . . . 2·25 2·00
D421 50f. Scoop (horiz) . . . . 2·75 2·75

FRENCH POST OFFICES IN CHINA Pt. 6

General issues for the French post offices in China, which were closed in 1922.

1894. 100 centimes = 1 franc.
1907. 100 cents = 1 piastre.

Stamps of Indo-China optd **CHINE** are listed under Indo-Chinese Post Offices in China.

1894. Stamps of France optd **Chine**.
2 **10** 5c. green . . . . 1·60 75
4 10c. black on lilac . . . . . 4·50 1·60
6 15c. blue . . . . 5·75 1·25
8 20c. red on green . . . . . 4·50 2·75
9 25c. black on pink . . . . 5·50 80
10 30c. brown . . . . 4·00 4·50
11 40c. red on yellow . . . . . 6·75 4·25
12 50c. red . . . . 16·00 2·75
14 75c. brown on orange . . . 75·00 42·00
15 1f. green . . . . 9·25 2·25
16 2f. brown on blue . . . . . 29·00 23·00
17 5f. mauve on lilac . . . . . 80·00 48·00

1900. No. 15 surch **25**.
18 **10** 25 on 1f. green . . . . . . 65·00 48·00

1901. No. 9 surch.
19 **10** 2c. on 25c. black on pink £750 £200
20 4c. on 25c. black on pink £650 £200
21 6c. on 25c. black on pink £750 £300
22 16c. on 25c. black on pink £200 £160

1902. "Blanc", "Mouchon" and "Merson" key-types inscr "CHINE".
37a A 5c. green . . . . 3·50 70
38 B 10c. red . . . . 1·75 1·60
39 15c. red . . . . 2·25 1·50
40 20c. brown . . . . 4·50 5·00
41 25c. blue . . . . 3·75 1·60
42 30c. mauve . . . . 5·25 6·50
43 C 40c. red and blue . . . . . 11·00 12·00
44 50c. brown and lilac . . . 12·50 8·75
45 1f. red and green . . . . . 20·00 10·00
46 2f. lilac and buff . . . . . 52·00 30·00
47 5f. blue and buff . . . . . 70·00 42·00

1903. No. 39 surch **5**.
48 B 5 on 15c. red . . . . 15·00 9·25

1907. Stamps of 1902 surch with new value in French and Chinese.
92 A 1c. on 5c. orange . . . . . 3·25 3·50
84 2c. on 5c. green 95 20
93 B 2c. on 10c. green . . . . . 6·25 5·75
94 3c. on 15c. orange . . . . 8·75 8·25
77 4c. on 10c. red . . . . . . 2·25 85
95 4c. on 20c. brown . . . . 11·00 10·00
96 5c. on 25c. purple . . . . 7·50 4·50
78 6c. on 15c. red . . . . . . 1·75 50
97 6c. on 30c. red . . . . . . 15·00 12·50
87 8c. on 20c. brown . . . . . 1·40 1·00
80 10c. on 25c. blue . . . . . 1·25 15
98 10c. on 50c. blue . . . . . 16·00 12·00
81 C 20c. on 50c. brown & lilac 2·75 1·00
89 B 20c. on 50c. blue . . . . . 55·00 40·00
99 C 20c. on 1f. red and green 32·00 28·00
90 40c. on 1f. red and green 4·50 2·75
100 40c. on 2f. red and green 40·00 27·00
101 1pi. on 5f. blue and buff . . £110 £110
83 2pi. on 5f. blue and buff . . 24·00 17·00
91 $2 on 5f. blue and buff . . £120 £110

POSTAGE DUE STAMPS

1901. Postage Due stamps of France optd **Chine**.
D23 D **11** 5c. blue . . . . 3·50 1·90
D24 10c. brown . . . . . . 5·75 6·00
D25 15c. green . . . . . . 8·50 6·75
D26 20c. olive . . . . . . 6·00 9·25
D27 30c. red . . . . 12·50 9·00
D28 50c. red . . . . 16·00 12·00

1903. Stamps of 1894 and 1902 optd **A PERCEVOIR**.
D58 **10** 5c. green £1300 £250
D62 A 5c. green £900 £500
D51 **10** 10c. black on lilac £5000 £4500
D63 B 10c. red . . . . £325 60·00
D60 **10** 15c. blue . . . . £700 65·00
D64 B 15c. red . . . . £425 70·00
D61 **10** 30c. brown . . . . £350 55·00

1911. Postage Due stamps of France surch with new value in French and Chinese.
D102 D **11** 1c. on 5c. blue . . . . 60·00 60·00
D 92 2c. on 5c. blue . . . . 1·25 2·75
D103 2c. on 10c. brown . . 70·00 65·00
D 93 4c. on 10c. brown . . 1·90 2·25
D104 4c. on 20c. olive . . . 70·00 65·00
D 94 8c. on 20c. olive . . . 2·25 2·00
D105 10c. on 50c. red . . . 70·00 65·00
D 95 20c. on 50c. red . . . 3·00 2·00

FRENCH POST OFFICES IN CRETE Pt. 6

These offices were closed in 1914.

100 centimes = 1 franc.
25 centimes = 1 piastre.

1902. "Blanc", "Mouchon" and "Merson" key-types inscr "CRETE".
1 A 1c. grey . . . . 1·50 95
2 2c. red . . . . 70 1·50
3 3c. red . . . . 1·10 2·50
4 4c. brown . . . . 1·75 3·25
5 5c. green . . . . 1·75 1·60
6 B 10c. red . . . . 2·25 2·75
7 15c. orange . . . . 2·40 4·00
8 20c. red . . . . 2·25 4·25
9 25c. blue . . . . 4·00 2·75
10 30c. mauve . . . . 6·50 8·25
11 C 40c. red and blue . . . . . 12·00 13·00
12 50c. brown and lavender . . 9·50 14·00
13 1f. red and green . . . . . 14·00 14·00
14 2f. lilac and buff . . . . . 28·00 35·00
15 5f. blue and buff . . . . . 35·00 45·00

1903. Surch in figures and words.
16 B 1pi. on 25c. blue . . . . . . 38·00 38·00
17 C 2pi. on 50c. brown & lav . . 60·00 55·00
18 4pi. on 1f. red and green . . 85·00 85·00
19 8pi. on 2f. lilac and buff . . 85·00 85·00
20 20pi. on 5f. blue and buff . . £140 £130

FRENCH POST OFFICES IN ETHIOPIA Pt. 6

100 centimes = 1 franc.

1906. Perf or imperf.
25 A 25c. blue . . . . 40·00 40·00
26 B 50c. brown and lavender . . £160 £160
27 1f. red and green £375 £375

FRENCH POST OFFICES IN MOROCCO Pt. 6

French Post Offices were first established in Morocco in 1862, using the stamps of France. For stamps used by French Post Offices in Tangier after 1912 see under that heading.

100 centimos = 1 peseta.

1891. Stamps of France surch in Spanish currency (centimos on equivalent centime values).
1 **10** 5c. on 5c. green . . . . . 7·50 1·60
5 10c. on 10c. blk on lilac . . 27·00 1·25
6 20c. on 20c. red on grn . . 27·00 19·00
7 25c. on 25c. blk on pink 14·50 60
8a 50c. on 50c. red . . . . . 55·00 9·00
10 1p. on 1f. green . . . . . 50·00 38·00
11 2p. on 2f. brown on blue £150 £150

1893. Postage Due stamps of France optd **TIMBRE POSTE** and bar.
12 D **11** 5c. black £1500 £600
13 10c. black £1300 £400

1902. "Blanc", "Mouchon" and "Merson" key types inscr "MAROC" and surch in Spanish currency in figures and words.
14 A 1c. on 1c. grey 30 15
15 2c. on 2c. red 20 15
16 3c. on 3c. red . . . . . . 1·10 20
17 4c. on 4c. brown . . . . . 5·50 4·50
18a 5c. on 5c. green . . . . . 5·50 30
19 B 10c. on 10c. red . . . . . 3·50 15
20 20c. on 20c. red . . . . . 15·00 1·25
21 25c. on 25c. blue . . . . . 28·00 15
22 35c. on 35c. lilac . . . . . 16·00 7·00
23 C 50c. on 50c. brown & lilac 30·00 2·00
24 1p. on 1f. red and green . . 75·00 50·00
25 2p. on 2f. lilac and yellow 90·00 55·00

1903. Postage Due stamps of 1896 optd **P.P.** in box.
26 D **11** 5c. on 5c. blue £850
27 10c. on 10c. brown . . . £1700

1911. Key-types surch with figure of value and Arabic word.
28 A 1c. on 1c. grey 15 20
29 2c. on 2c. red 15 20
30 3c. on 3c. orange 15 85
31 5c. on 5c. green . . . . . 1·10 15
32 B 10c. on 10c. red 15 10
33 15c. on 15c. orange . . . . 1·75 2·00
34 20c. on 20c. red . . . . . 1·25 2·50
35 25c. on 25c. blue . . . . . 1·60 35
36 35c. on 35c. lilac . . . . . 3·50 20
37 C 40c. on 40c. red and blue . . 6·50 7·00
38 50c. on 50c. brown & lilac 9·50 3·50
39 1p. on 1f. red and green . . 4·25 9·50

POSTAGE DUE STAMPS

1896. Postage Due stamps of France surch in Spanish currency in figures and words.
D14 D **11** 5c. on 5c. blue . . . . 5·50 1·90
D15 10c. on 10c. brown . . . 9·00 1·75
D16 30c. on 30c. red . . . 11·00 2·75

D17a 50c. on 50c. red 27·00 13·50
D18 1p. on 1f. brown £275 £190

1909. Postage Due stamps of France surch in Spanish currency.
D28 D 19 1c. on 1c. olive 60 2·25
D29 10c. on 10c. violet 25·00 29·00
D30 30c. on 30c. bistre 24·00 30·00
D31 50c. on 50c. red 45·00 50·00

1911. Postage Due stamps of France surch with figure and Arabic word.
D40 D 11 5c. on 5c. blue 1·25 4·25
D41 10c. on 10c. brown 2·00 15·00
D42 50c. on 50c. purple 4·00 21·00

1911. Postage Due stamps of France surch in figures and Arabic.
D43 D 19 1c. on 1c. olive 65 65
D44 10c. on 10c. violet 1·60 4·25
D45 30c. on 30c. bistre 2·50 6·00
D46 50c. on 50c. red 3·50 18·00

For later issues see **FRENCH MOROCCO**.

FRENCH POST OFFICES IN TANGIER Pt. 6

By Franco-Spanish Treaty of 27 November 1912, Tangier was given a special status outside the protectorates. After the Tangier Convention of 1924 the zone was administered by an international commission. Tangier was occupied by Spain in 1940 and the French P.O.s closed in 1942.

100 centimes = 1 franc.

1918. "Blanc", "Mouchon" and "Merson" key-types of French Post Offices in Morocco optd **TANGER**.
1a A 1c. grey 20 2·25
2 2c. red 85 2·25
3 3c. orange 60 2·50
4 5c. green 1·10 1·25
5 5c. orange 2·25 2·75
6 B 10c. red 1·25 65
7 10c. green 1·75 2·75
8 15c. orange 1·25 1·10
9 20c. red 1·40 2·25
10 25c. blue 2·50 70
11 30c. red 3·50 4·50
12 35c. lilac 2·25 3·25
13 C 40c. red and blue 2·75 3·75
14 50c. brown and lilac 10·00 12·00
15 B 50c. blue 17·00 9·75
16 C 1f. red and green 4·75 7·75
17 2f. red and green 65·00 80·00
18 5f. blue and yellow 60·00 70·00

1928. Air. Nos. 149/58 of French Morocco optd **Tanger**.
30 5c. blue 1·75 7·50
31 25c. orange 2·25 7·00
32 50c. red 2·00 7·50
33 75c. brown 1·90 7·50
34 80c. green 2·25 7·50
35 1f. orange 2·00 7·50
36 1f.50 blue 1·90 7·50
37 2f. brown 2·25 7·50
38 3f. purple 4·00 4·00
39 5f. black 2·25 7·50

POSTAGE DUE STAMPS

1918. Postage Due stamps of France optd **TANGER**.
D19 D 11 1c. black 25 2·50
D20 5c. blue 1·25 3·00
D21 10c. brown 1·75 3·00
D22 15c. green 1·75 4·75
D23 20c. olive 3·00 5·75
D24 30c. red 6·50 16·00
D25 50c. purple 6·75 20·00

1918. Postage Due stamps of France optd **TANGER**.
D26 D 19 1c. olive 70 3·25
D27 10c. violet 2·75 3·25
D28 20c. bistre 6·50 9·50
D29 40c. red 16·00 22·00

FRENCH POST OFFICES IN TURKISH EMPIRE Pt. 6

General issues for the French Post Offices in the Turkish Empire.

1885. 25 centimes = 1 piastre.
1921. 40 paras = 1 piastre.

1885. Stamps of France surch in figures and words.
1 10 1pi. on 25c. bistre on yellow £350 3·50
4 1pi. on 25c. black on pink 3·00 15
5 2pi. on 50c. pink 18·00 70
2 3pi. on 75c. red 38·00 8·50
3 4pi. on 1f. green 35·00 3·00
7 8pi. on 2f. brown on blue 23·00 18·00
8 20pi. on 5f. mauve 80·00 45·00

1902. "Blanc", "Mouchon" and "Merson" key-types inscr "LEVANT".
9 A 1c. grey 10 25
10 2c. purple 15 60
11 3c. red 10 1·40
12 4c. brown 2·40 1·50
13a 5c. green 2·25 15
14 B 10c. red 4·75 20
15 15c. red 1·60 25
16 20c. brown 2·75 2·25
17 30c. lilac 4·25 3·50
18 C 40c. red and blue 5·50 4·25

1902. Surch in figures and words.
19 B 1pi. on 25c. blue 2·25 10
20 C 2pi. on 50c. brown & lav 3·00 65
21 4pi. on 1f. red & green 3·50 2·40
22 8pi. on 2f. lilac & yellow 23·00 12·50
23 20pi. on 5f. blue & yellow 6·00 4·75

1905. Surch **1 Piastre Beyrouth**.
24 B 1pi. on 15c. orange £1500 £225

1921. Stamps of France surch in figures and words.
28 18 30pa. on 5c. green 70 2·40
29 30pa. on 5c. orange 2·25 2·25
30 1pi.20 on 10c. red 60 1·40
31 1pi.20 on 10c. green 95 1·10
39 3pi.30 on 15c. green 25·00 26·00
32 3pi.30 on 25c. blue 60 30
33 4pi.20 on 30c. orange 50 1·10
40 7pi.20 on 35c. violet 26·00 28·00
34 15 7pi.20 on 50c. blue 35 45
35 13 15pi. on 1f. red & green 1·40 1·10
36 30pi. on 2f. red & green 7·25 9·50
37 75pi. on 5f. blue & yellow 7·75 6·00

For stamps issued by the Free French forces during 1942/3 see under **FREE FRENCH FORCES IN THE LEVANT**.

FRENCH POST OFFICES IN ZANZIBAR Pt. 6

The French post office in Zanzibar operated from 1889 to 1904.

16 annas = 1 rupee.

Stamps of France surcharged.

1894. Surch in figures and words.
1a 10 ½a. on 5c. green 7·00 5·50
3 1a. on 10c. black on lilac 13·00 9·00
4a 1½a. on 15c. blue 24·00 22·00
6 2a. on 20c. red on green 12·50 10·00
7 2½a. on 25c. black on red 11·50 6·25
8 3a. on 30c. brown 20·00 16·00
9 4a. on 40c. red on yellow 19·00 22·00
10 5a. on 50c. red 35·00 27·00
11 7½a. on 75c. brn on orge £350 £275
12a 10a. on 1f. olive 65·00 55·00
14 50a. on 5f. mve on lilac £200 £200

1894. Surch **ZANZIBAR** and value in Indian currency (in figures and words) and in corresponding French currency (in figures only on Nos. 15/18).
15 10 ½a. and 5 on 1c. black on blue £120 £120
16 1a. and 10 on 3c. grey 95·00 £100
17 2½a. and 25 on 4c. lilac on grey £140 £140
18 5a. and 50 on 20c. red on green £140 £150
19 10a. and 1f. on 40c. red on yellow £275 £275

1896. Surch **ZANZIBAR** and new value in Indian currency only.
22 10 ½a. on 5c. green 6·00 5·75
24 1a. on 10c. black on lilac 8·50 6·50
26 1½a. on 15c. blue 7·00 6·25
28 2a. on 20c. red on green 5·25 7·25
29 2½a. on 25c. black on red 10·50 6·50
30 3a. on 30c. brown 7·75 6·25
31 4a. on 40c. red on yellow 7·00 8·25
32 5a. on 50c. red 16·00 14·00
35 10a. on 1f. olive 25·00 14·00
37 20a. on 2f. brown on blue 17·00 20·00
38 50a. on 5f. mve on lilac 42·00 35·00

1897. Nos. 1/4 and 8/9 further surch with new figures of value in French and Indian currency and optd **ZANZIBAR** vert.
42 10 2½ and 25 on ½a. on 5c. £750 £100
43 2½ and 25 on 1a. on 10c. £2500 £550
44 2½ and 25 on 1½a. on 15c. £2500 £450
45 5 and 50 on 3a. on 30c. £2500 £425
46 5 and 50 on 4a. on 40c. £2500 £550

PosteFrance
5
Annas
50c
ZANZIBAR

(4)

1897.
47 4 2½a. and 25c. black on green and white — £650
48 2½a. and 25c. black on lilac and white — £2250
49 2½a. and 25c. black on blue and white — £2000
50 5a. and 50c. black on buff and white — £1800

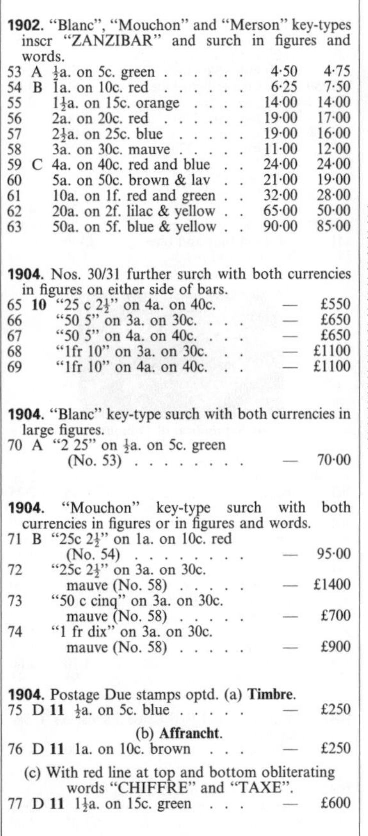

51 5a. and 50c. black on yellow and white — £2250
52 5a. and 50c. on white — £2250

1902. "Blanc", "Mouchon" and "Merson" key-types inscr "ZANZIBAR" and surch in figures and words.
53 A ½a. on 5c. green 4·50 4·75
54 B 1a. on 10c. red 6·25 7·50
55 1½a. on 15c. orange 14·00 14·00
56 2a. on 20c. red 19·00 17·00
57 2½a. on 25c. blue 19·00 16·00
58 3a. on 30c. mauve 11·00 12·00
59 C 4a. on 40c. red and blue 24·00 24·00
60 5a. on 50c. brown & lav 21·00 19·00
61 10a. on 1f. red and green 32·00 28·00
62 20a. on 2f. lilac & yellow 65·00 50·00
63 50a. on 5f. blue & yellow 90·00 85·00

1904. Nos. 30/31 further surch with both currencies in figures on either side of bars.
65 10 "25 c 2½" on 4a. on 40c. — £550
66 "50 5" on 3a. on 30c. — £650
67 "50 5" on 4a. on 40c. — £650
68 "1fr 10" on 3a. on 30c. — £1100
69 "1fr 10" on 4a. on 40c. — £1100

1904. "Blanc" key-type surch with both currencies in large figures.
70 A "2 25" on ½a. on 5c. green (No. 53) — 70·00

1904. "Mouchon" key-type surch with both currencies in figures or in figures and words.
71 B "25c 2½" on 1a. on 10c. red (No. 54) — 95·00
72 "25c 2½" on 3a. on 30c. mauve (No. 58) — £1400
73 "50 c cinq" on 3a. on 30c. mauve (No. 58) — £700
74 "1 fr dix" on 3a. on 30c. mauve (No. 58) — £900

1904. Postage Due stamps optd. (a) **Timbre**.
75 D 11 ½a. on 5c. blue — £250

(b) **Affrancht**.
76 D 11 1a. on 10c. brown — £250

(c) With red line at top and bottom obliterating words "CHIFFRE" and "TAXE".
77 D 11 1½a. on 15c. green — £600

POSTAGE DUE STAMPS

1897. Postage Due stamps of France surch **ZANZIBAR** and value in figures and words.
D39 D 11 ½a. on 5c. blue 21·00 5·00
D40 1a. on 10c. brown 21·00 9·00
D41 1½a. on 15c. green 28·00 10·00
D42 3a. on 30c. red 28·00 19·00
D43 5a. on 50c. purple 35·00 18·00

FRENCH SOMALI COAST Pt. 6

A French colony on the Gulf of Aden, E. coast of Africa. Renamed French Territory of the Afars and the Issas in 1967.

100 centimes = 1 franc.

23 Mosque at Tajurah
24 Mounted Somalis
25 Somali Warriors

1902.
121 23 1c. orange and purple 95 90
137 1c. black and brown 35 1·50
122 2c. green and brown 1·00 70
138 2c. black and brown 1·25 60
123 4c. red and blue 1·25 2·75
139 4c. black and red 2·25 1·50
124 5c. green & deep green 2·25 1·60
140a 5c. black and green 5·00 1·50
125 10c. orange and red 3·50 5·75
141a 10c. black and red 8·75 55
126 15c. blue and orange 3·75 4·00
142 15c. black and brown 17·00 14·00
127 24 20c. green and lilac 7·00 10·00
143 20c. black and lilac 14·00 32·00
128 25c. blue 10·00 11·00
129 25c. blue and indigo 15·00 19·00
144 25c. black and blue 5·75 4·25
130 30c. black and red 5·50 7·50
131 40c. blue and yellow 19·00 19·00
145 40c. black and orange 8·00 8·75
132 50c. red and green 38·00 45·00
146 50c. black and green 14·00 13·00
133 75c. mauve and orange 7·00 6·75
147 75c. black and brown 7·25 9·75
134 25 1f. purple and red 13·00 18·00
148 1f. black and red 10·00 22·00
135 2f. red and green 29·00 35·00
149 2f. black and green 6·25 9·00
136 5f. blue and orange 22·00 24·00
150 5f. black and orange 11·00 24·00

26 Mosque at Tajurah
27 Mounted Somalis

1909.
151 26 1c. brown and purple 20 20
152 2c. green and violet 20 20
153 4c. blue and brown 95 25
154 5c. olive and green 2·25 75
155 10c. orange and red 3·25 1·40
156 20c. brown and black 3·00 7·50
157 27 25c. blue and deep blue 5·25 1·75
158 30c. red and brown 5·00 9·25
159 35c. green and violet 7·00 4·50
160 40c. violet and pink 8·25 7·50
161 45c. green and brown 9·75 7·25
162 50c. brown and purple 8·50 8·50
163 75c. green and red 14·00 18·00
164 25 1f. brown and violet 17·00 28·00
165 2f. pink and brown 28·00 45·00
166 5f. green and brown 65·00 60·00

28 Drummer
29 Somali Woman

30 Railway Bridge at Holl-Holli

1915. No. 172 surch **5c** and red cross.
167 29 10c.+5c. red & carmine 4·00 8·50

1915.
168 28 1c. brown and violet 10 30
169 2c. blue and bistre 10 10
170 4c. red and brown 20 1·75
171 5c. green & light green 45 95
195 5c. red and orange 10 1·40
172 29 10c. red and carmine 1·10 2·25
196 10c. green & light green 30 3·00
214 10c. green and red 45 1·25
173 15c. pink and lilac 1·60 1·90
174 20c. brown and orange 15 1·60
215 20c. light green & green 20 2·00
216 20c. red and green 20 1·75
175 25c. blue & ultramarine 45 2·25
197 25c. green and black 15 20
176 30c. green and black 2·75 3·25
198 30c. brown and red 1·60 3·25
217 30c. green and violet 10 1·90
218 30c. olive and green 20 1·75
177 35c. pink and green 1·10 2·75
178 40c. lilac and blue 1·50 2·50
179 45c. blue and brown 2·25 3·00
180 50c. black and pink 14·50 9·75
199 50c. blue & ultramarine 1·50 3·50
219 50c. purple and brown 20 15
220 60c. purple and green 45 2·75
221 65c. green and red 35 1·75
181 75c. brown and lilac 1·00 2·25
222 75c. blue and deep blue 10 1·25
223 75c. brown and mauve 2·25 4·25
224 85c. green and purple 15 3·25
225 90c. carmine and red 4·50 5·50
182 30 1f. red and brown 1·40 30
226 1f.10 blue and brown 4·75 7·50
227 1f.25 brown and blue 12·00 12·00
228 1f.50 blue & light blue 70 55
229 1f.75 red and green 6·00 3·25
183 2f. black and violet 4·00 1·60
230 3f. mauve on pink 14·00 7·25
184 5f. black and red 9·50 3·00

1922. Surch **1922** and value in figures in frame.
193 28 10 on 5c. green & lt grn 15 1·50
194 29 50 on 25c. bl & ultram 15 2·50

1922. Surch in figures.
200 29 0.01 on 15c. pink and lilac 10 2·75
201 0.02 on 15c. pink and lilac 10 2·75
202 0.04 on 15c. pink and lilac 15 2·75
203 0.05 on 15c. pink and lilac 10 2·50
204 30 25c. on 5f. black & red 1·40 3·25
205 29 60 on 75c. violet & green 40 2·50
206 65 on 15c. pink and lilac 1·40 3·25
207 85 on 40c. lilac and blue 1·50 3·25
208 90 on 75c. red 1·25 3·75
209 30 1f.25 on 1f. ultram & bl 1·25 3·00
210 1f.50 on 1f. bl & lt bl 1·25 1·60
211 3f. on 5f. mauve & red 3·75 4·25
212 10f. on 5f. brown & red 8·75 9·75
213 20f. on 5f. pink & green 15·00 14·50

1931. "Colonial Exhibition" key-types inscr "COTE FR. DES SOMALIS".
233 E 40c. green and black 2·25 3·50
234 F 50c. mauve and black 3·75 5·75

235 G 90c. red and black 2·75 7·25
236 H 1f.50 blue and black 4·00 7·00

1937. Int Exn, Paris. As T **58a** of Guadeloupe.
237 20c. violet 55 2·75
238 30c. green 40 2·50
239 40c. red 30 2·25
240 50c. brown and blue 30 2·50
241 90c. red 80 2·50
242 1f.50 blue 35 2·00

1938. International Anti-cancer Fund. As T **58b** of Guadeloupe.
244 1f.75+50c. blue 95 10·50

34 Mosque at Djibouti **35** Somali Warriors

37 Djibouti

1938.
245 **34** 2c. purple 10 1·25
246 3c. green 10 1·10
247 4c. brown 10 2·75
248 5c. red 10 2·75
249 10c. blue 10 1·40
250 15c. black 10 2·75
251 20c. red 55 3·00
252 **35** 25c. brown 65 2·00
253 30c. blue 30 2·25
254 35c. green 35 3·00
255 **34** 40c. brown 75 2·75
256 45c. green 50 2·75
257 **35** 50c. red 55 2·50
258 55c. purple 80 3·00
259 60c. black 45 3·25
260 65c. brown 50 3·00
261 70c. violet 75 4·00
262 – 80c. black 1·00 4·00
263 **35** 90c. mauve 1·25 4·00
264 – 1f. red 60 2·75
265 – 1f. black 40 3·00
266 – 1f.25 red 1·40 3·75
267 – 1f.40 blue 2·25 3·75
268 – 1f.50 green 40 3·00
269 – 1f.60 red 2·75 3·75
270 – 1f.75 blue 70 3·00
271 – 2f. red 30 85
272 – 2f.25 blue 1·90 3·75
273 – 2f.50 brown 3·00 4·25
274 – 3f. purple 60 1·75
275 **37** 5f. brown & deep brown 1·25 3·00
276 10f. light blue and blue 85 3·75
277 20f. blue and red 1·00 3·00
DESIGN—VERT: 80c. and 1f. to 3f. Governor L. Lagarde.

1939. New York World's Fair. As T **58c** of Guadeloupe.
288 1f.25 red 1·25 3·75
289 2f.25 blue 2·50 1·60

1939. 150th Anniv of French Revolution. As T **58d** of Guadeloupe.
290 45c.+25c. green & black 5·25 12·00
291 70c.+30c. brown & black 5·25 12·00
292 90c.+35c. orange & black 6·25 12·00
293 1f.25+1f. red and black 7·50 14·00
294 2f.25+2f. blue and black 10·00 16·00

1941. Air. Free French Issue. As T **63a** of Guadeloupe, but inscr "DJIBOUTI".
295 **32** 1f. orange 55 65
296 1f.50 red 40 2·50
297 5f. purple 30 1·40
298 10f. black 85 2·25
299 25f. blue 80 4·00
300 50f. green 60 4·00
301 100f. red 85 3·00

1942. Optd or surch also **FRANCE LIBRE** or **France Libre**.
302 **28** 1c. brown and violet 2·25 3·50
303 2c. blue and bistre 2·75 3·75
304 **34** 2c. purple 1·25 3·50
305 3c. green 2·00 3·50
306 **28** 4c. red and brown 15·00 42·00
307 **34** 4c. brown 2·75 3·50
308 **28** 5c. red and orange 1·60 3·75
309 **34** 5c. red 1·25 4·00
310 10c. blue 50 2·50
311 **29** 15c. pink and lilac 4·50 11·00
312 **34** 15c. black 1·50 3·50
313 **29** 20c. red and green 1·50 4·00
314 **34** 20c. red 1·50 3·50
315 **35** 25c. brown 1·50 4·00
316 **29** 30c. olive and green 1·40 4·00
317 **35** 30c. blue 50 2·75
318 35c. green 2·50 3·75
319 **34** 40c. brown 50 2·75
320 45c. green 1·75 3·50
321 **29** 50c. purple and brown 85 4·00
322 **35** 50c. on 65c. brown 40 95
323 55c. purple 1·90 3·50
324 60c. black 45 2·25
325 **29** 65c. green and red 70 4·00
326 **35** 70c. violet 40 2·75
327 – 80c. black (No. 262) 40 2·75
328 **35** 90c. mauve 40 1·50
329 – 1f.25 red (No. 266) 95 2·75
330 – 1f.40 blue (No. 267) 50 2·75
331 **30** 1f.50 blue & light blue 90 3·50
332 – 1f.50 green (No. 268) 65 2·75
333 – 1f.60 red (No. 269) 1·00 2·75
334 **30** 1f.75 red and green 10·00 13·00
335 – 1f.75 blue (No. 270) 3·25 12·50
336 – 2f. red (No. 271) 40 2·25
337 – 2f.25 blue (No. 272) 90 3·25
338 – 2f.50 brown (No. 273) 1·10 3·50
339 – 3f. purple (No. 274) 85 4·75
340 **37** 5f. brown & deep brown 5·25 16·00
341 10f. light blue and blue £140 £150
342 20f. blue and red 5·50 7·50

41 Symbolical of Djibouti

1943. Free French issue.
361 **41** 5c. blue 15 2·50
362 10c. red 15 2·25
363 25c. green 15 2·75
364 30c. black 15 2·50
365 40c. violet 30 2·75
366 80c. purple 20 2·75
367 1f. blue 40 35
368 1f.50 red 60 50
369 2f. bistre 60 55
370 2f.50 blue 50 60
371 4f. orange 55 1·60
372 5f. mauve 55 1·25
373 10f. blue 1·10 1·60
374 20f. green 95 95

1944. Mutual Aid and Red Cross Funds. As T **58e** of Guadeloupe.
375 5f.+20f. green 1·00 4·00

1945. Eboue. As T **58f** of Guadeloupe.
376 2f. black 65 2·75
377 25f. green 1·25 3·50

1945. Surch.
378 **41** 50c. on 5c. blue 20 3·00
379 60c. on 5c. blue 15 2·75
380 70c. on 5c. blue 20 2·75
381 1f.20 on 5c. blue 1·50 3·00
382 2f.40 on 25c. green 90 3·00
383 3f. on 25c. green 55 3·00
384 4f.50 on 25c. green 1·40 2·50
385 15f. on 2f.50 blue 1·50 3·50

1946. Air. Victory. As T **63b** of Guadeloupe.
386 8f. blue 25 2·75

1946. Air. From Chad to the Rhine. As T **63c** of Guadeloupe.
387 5f. black 2·25 4·25
388 10f. red 1·00 4·00
389 15f. brown 1·00 4·00
390 20f. mauve 2·25 4·00
391 25f. green 1·00 4·00
392 50f. blue 1·50 4·50

43 Danakil Tent **45** Somali

44 Outpost at Khor-Angar

46 Government Palace, Djibouti

1947.
393 **43** 10c. orge & vio (postage) 10 2·75
394 30c. orange and green 10 2·75
395 40c. orange and purple 10 2·75
396 **44** 50c. orange and green 10 2·25
397 60c. yellow and brown 10 2·75
398 80c. orange and violet 15 2·75
399 – 1f. brown and blue 15 80
400 – 1f.20 green and grey 30 3·00
401 – 1f.50 blue and orange 35 3·00
402 – 2f. mauve and grey 20 20
403 – 3f. blue and brown 65 45
404 – 3f.60 brown and red 2·00 4·00
405 – 4f. brown and grey 60 35
406 – 5f. orange and brown 45 30
407 – 6f. blue and grey 85 70
408 – 10f. purple and blue 70 25
409 – 15f. brown, blue & buff 1·75 40
410 – 20f. blue, orange & blue 1·50 40
411 – 25f. red, blue & purple 1·60 35

412 **45** 50f. brown & blue (air) 1·75 75
413 – 100f. yellow and green 2·00 1·75
414 **46** 200f. green, yell & blue 2·50 2·75
DESIGNS—HORIZ: As Type **44**: 1f. to 1f.50, Obock Tajurah road; 2f. to 4f. Woman carrying dish; 5f. to 10f. Somali village; 15f. to 25f. Mosque. Djibouti. As Type **46**: 100f. Frontier post, Loyada.

1949. Air. 75th Anniv of U.P.U. As T **39** of French Equatorial Africa.
425 30f. multicoloured 1·50 15·00

1950. Colonial Welfare Fund. As T **40** of French Equatorial Africa.
426 10f.+2f. red and brown 2·75 7·50

1952. Centenary of Medaille Militaire. As T **44** of French Equatorial Africa.
427 15f. violet, yellow and green 4·50 6·75

1954. Air. 10th Anniv of Liberation. As T **46** of French Equatorial Africa.
428 15f. violet and blue 6·00 11·00

48 Ras-Bir Lighthouse **50** Freighter at Wharf, Djibouti

49 Aerial Map of Djibouti

1956.
429 **48** 40f. blue & dp bl (postage) 4·00 70
430 **49** 500f. purple & vio (air) 40·00 48·00

1956. Economic and Social Development Fund.
431 **50** 15f. violet 2·50 55

51 Warthog

1958. Animals, Fishes and Birds.
432 **51** 30c. brown & red (postage) 15 2·75
433 – 40c. brown and bistre 15 3·00
434 – 50c. purple, grey & green 15 2·75
435 – 1f. orge, blue & brown 30 30
436 – 2f. multicoloured 65 95
437 – 3f. brown and violet 1·40 70
438 – 4f. brn, orange & blue 1·25 2·25
439 – 5f. black and blue 2·25 1·10
440 – 10f. red, brown & green 2·10 1·00
441 – 15f. yellow, green & mve 3·25 1·40
442 – 20f. purple, red and blue 3·25 3·25
443 – 25f. blue, red and green 4·00 2·25
444 – 30f. black, red and blue 6·50 3·75
445 – 60f. green and blue 8·75 3·50
446 – 75f. yellow, brown & grn 11·00 7·00

447 – 100f. brown, grn & bl (air) 8·00 5·75
448 – 200f. brown, blk & orge 20·00 13·50
449 – 500f. multicoloured 23·00 21·00
DESIGNS—HORIZ: As Type **51**: 40c. Cheetah; 1f. Blue-barred orange parrotfish; 3f. Blue marlin; 4f. Blue spotted boxfish; 5f. African eagle ray; 15f. Little bee eater; 20f. Undulate triggerfish; 25f. Yellow-wedged triggerfish; 30f. Sacred ibis; 60f. Smooth hammerhead; 48 × 27 mm: 100f. Bohar reedbucks and airplane; 200f. Great bustard; 500f. Salt caravan, Lake Assal. VERT: As Type **51**: 50c. Gerenuks; 2f. Pennant coralfish; 10f. Greater flamingo; 75f. Pink-backed pelican.

1958. Tropical Flora. As T **56** of French Equatorial Africa.
450 10f. red, green and yellow 1·60 1·60
DESIGN—HORIZ: 10f. "Haemanthus".

1958. 10th Anniv of Declaration of Human Rights. As T **57** of French Equatorial Africa.
451 20f. violet and blue 60 2·25

53 Governor Bernard

1960. Air. 25th Death Anniv of Governor Bernard.
452 **53** 55f. brown, blue & red 1·90 2·25

54 "Forbin", Obock, 1862

1962. Air. Centenary of Obock.
453 **54** 100f. brown and blue 4·00 2·50

55 Dragon Tree **55a** Campaign Emblem

1962. Fauna and Flora.
454 **55** 2f. multicoloured 1·90 2·00
455 – 4f. brown and ochre 1·90 2·00
456 – 6f. multicoloured 3·00 3·00
457 – 25f. bistre, green and red 5·00 3·50
458 – 40f. brown, black & blue 10·50 6·25
459 – 50f. brown, purple & blue 8·25 9·25
DESIGNS—HORIZ: 4f. Large-toothed rock hyrax; 6f. Giant trevally (fish); 25f. Fennec foxes; 40f. Griffon vulture. VERT: 50f. Klipspringer.

1962. Malaria Eradication.
460 **55a** 25f.+5f. blue 6·25 8·25

56 Black-lip Pearl Oyster

1962. Shells of the Red Sea. Multicoloured.
(a) Postage. As T **56**.
461 8f. Type **56** 1·10 1·50
462 10f. Fluted giant clam (horiz) 1·10 1·40
463 25f. Three knobbed conch (horiz) 3·00 2·50
464 30f. Knobbed top 3·00 2·00
(b) Air. 50 × 28 mm.
465 60f. Arabian tibia 4·00 3·50
466 100f. Giant spider conch 5·75 4·00

1962. Air. 1st Trans-Atlantic TV Satellite Link. As T **10** of French Polynesia.
467 20f. purple and green 65 1·10

1963. Red Cross Centenary. As T **13** of French Polynesia.
468 50f. red, grey and brown 4·25 6·75

57 Large Star Coral

58 Houri

1963. Corals. Multicoloured. (a) Postage. As T **57**.
469 5f. Type **57** 1·25 1·75
470 6f. Organ-pipe coral 1·00 1·25

(b) Air. Horiz (48 × 27 mm).
471 40f. Stinging coral 2·50 1·40
472 55f. Brain coral 5·00 3·25
473 200f. Branched coral 9·00 6·25

1963. 15th Anniv of Declaration of Human Rights. As T **14** of French Polynesia.
474 70f. blue and brown 5·75 10·00

1964. "PHILATEC 1964" International Stamp Exhibition, Paris. As T **528** of France.
475 80f. brown, green & purple 6·00 10·00

1964. Local Dhows. Multicoloured. (a) Postage. As T **58**.
476 15f. Type **58** 2·00 1·90
477 25f. Sambuk 2·50 2·50

(b) Air. Size 48 × 27 mm.
478 50f. Building sambuk 3·50 2·75
479 85f. Zaruk 3·50 3·75
480 300f. Ziema 15·00 8·50

59 Rameses II and Nefertari Temple, Philae

1964. Air. Nubian Monuments Preservation.
481 **59** 25f.+5f. brown, green and red 5·25 11·50

60 "The Discus Thrower" (Ancient Greece)

1964. Air. Olympic Games, Tokyo.
482 **60** 90f. purple, red & black 10·00 11·50

1965. Air. Centenary of I.T.U. As T **19** of French Polynesia.
483 95f. blue, brown & purple 13·00 13·50

61 Ghoubet Kharab

1965. Landscapes.
484 – 6f. brn, bl & grn (postage) 1·10 1·75
485 – 20f. green, blue & brown 1·10 1·90
486 – 45f. brn, bl & dp bl (air) 2·25 3·75
487 **61** 65f. brown, ochre & blue 2·75 2·75
VIEWS—26 × 22 mm: 6f. Dadwayya; 20f. Tajurah. As Type **61**: 45f. Lake Abbe.

62 "Life and Death"

1965. Anti-tuberculosis Campaign.
488 **62** 25f.+5f. brn, grn & turq 2·75 3·00

1966. Air. Launching of 1st French Satellite. As Nos. 1696/7 of France.
489 25f. brown, bistre and red 3·75 3·75
490 30f. brown, bistre and red 4·50 4·50

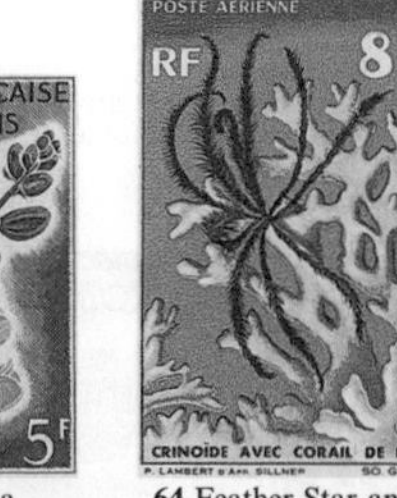

63 Senna **64** Feather Star and Flame Coral

1966. Flowers.
491 **63** 5f. orange, green and brown (postage) 1·25 1·50
492 – 8f. orange, green & brown 1·75 1·75
493 – 25f. red, blue and green 1·75 2·00
494 – 55f. lake, green and myrtle (air) 4·25 3·25
FLOWERS—VERT: 8f. Poinciana; 25f. Aloes. HORIZ: (48½ × 27 mm); 55f. Stapelia.

1966. Air. Marine Life. Multicoloured.
495 8f. Type **64** 2·75 2·75
496 25f. Regal angelfish 3·50 4·25
497 40f. Yellow-banded angelfish 5·00 6·75
498 50f. Saddle anemonefish 7·25 8·75
499 70f. Spined squirrelfish 12·00 15·00
500 80f. Red Sea surgeonfish 13·00 16·00
501 100f. Lunulate lionfish 18·00 24·00

1966. Air. Launching of Satellite "D1". As T **569** of France.
502 48f. green, brown and blue 2·75 3·50

65 Grey Monitor

1967. Somali Fauna.
503 **65** 20f. purple, chest & brn 3·00 3·50

POSTAGE DUE STAMPS

D 31 Somali Spears **D 47**

1915.
D278 **D 31** 5c. blue 10 2·75
D279 10c. red 10 2·75
D187 15c. black 45 2·25
D281 20c. violet 15 2·75
D282 30c. yellow 20 2·75
D190 50c. red 1·25 3·75
D283 50c. brown 20 3·00
D284 60c. green 75 3·25
D285 1f. blue 25 4·50
D286 2f. red 25 3·50
D287 3f. sepia 75 3·50

1927. Surch in figures.
D231 **D 31** 2f. on 1f. red 3·50 10·00
D232 3f. on 1f. mve 2·25 7·00

1942. (a) Optd **FRANCE LIBRE**.
D343 **D 31** 5c. blue 1·25 4·00
D344 10c. red 1·75 4·00
D345 15c. black 1·25 4·00
D346 20c. violet 1·75 4·00
D347 30c. yellow 1·75 4·00
D348 50c. red 1·75 4·00
D349 60c. green 1·75 4·00
D350 1f. blue 7·75 10·50

(b) Optd **France Libre**.
D351 **D 31** 5c. blue 1·50 4·00
D352 10c. red 1·50 4·00
D353 15c. black 1·50 4·00
D354 20c. violet 60 4·00
D355 30c. yellow 60 4·00
D356 50c. brown 60 4·00
D357 60c. green 70 4·00
D358 1f. blue 1·25 4·00
D359 2f. red 2·50 4·00
D360 3f. sepia 1·90 4·00

1947.
D415 **D 47** 10c. mauve 10 2·25
D416 30c. brown 10 2·75
D417 50c. green 10 2·75
D418 1f. brown 10 2·75
D419 2f. red 35 2·75
D420 3f. brown 80 2·75
D421 4f. blue 1·10 3·00
D422 5f. red 1·25 3·00
D423 10f. green 1·25 3·50
D424 20f. blue 1·00 3·50

For later issues see **FRENCH TERRITORY OF THE AFARS AND THE ISSAS**.

FRENCH SOUTHERN AND ANTARCTIC TERRITORIES Pt. 6

Stamps issued for use in the French settlements in the southern Indian Ocean and in the Antarctic.

100 centimes = 1 franc.

1955. No. 324 of Madagascar optd **TERRES AUSTRALES ET ANTARCTIQUES FRANCAISES**.
1 **39** 15f. blue and green 20·00 35·00

2 Rockhopper Penguins **5** Polar Camp and Meteorologist

4 Emperor Penguins, Snowy Petrel and South Pole

1956.
2 – 30c. brn, grn & bl (postage) 40 65
3 – 40c. blk, purple and blue 45 65
4 **2** 50c. blue, ochre & brown 40 65
5 – 1f. blue, orange and grey 1·40 1·60
6 – 2f. black, brown and blue 3·25 4·75
7 – 4f. brown, green and blue 15·00 20·00
8 – 5f. blue and light blue 1·90 7·50
9 – 8f. brown and grey 8·00 27·00
10 – 10f. blue 3·25 13·00
11 – 12f. black and blue 13·00 8·00
12 – 15f. purple and blue 3·75 16·00
13 – 20f. blue, yellow & lt blue 19·00 25·00
14 – 25f. black, brown & green £100 85·00
15 – 85f. orange, blue and black 21·00 14·00
16 **4** 50f. green and olive (air) 42·00 32·00
17 100f. indigo and blue 35·00 28·00
18 – 200f. black, blue & purple 42·00 50·00
DESIGNS—VERT: As Type **2**: 30c. Light-mantled sooty albatross; 2f. Black-faced sheathbills; 12f. Kerguelen cormorants; 20f. Territorial arms; 85f. King penguin. HORIZ: (36 × 22 mm). 40c. Antarctic skuas; 4f. Leopard seal; 5f., 8f. Kerguelen fur seal and settlement; 10f., 15f. Southern elephant-seal; 25f. Kerguelen fur seal. As Type **4**: 200f. Wandering albatross.
See also Nos. 26/34.

1957. International Geophysical Year.
19 **5** 5f. black and violet 4·00 7·50
20 10f. red 5·00 10·00
21 15f. blue 6·25 10·50

1959. Tropical Flora. As T **56** of French Equatorial Africa.
22 10f. multicoloured 3·75 15·00
DESIGN—HORIZ: 10f. "Pringlea".

6 Yves-Joseph Kerguelen-Tremarec and "Dauphine"

1960. Kerguelen Archipelago Discovery Commem.
23 **6** 25f. brown, chestnut & blue 35·00 29·00

7 Jean Charcot, Compass and "Pourquoi Pas?"

1962. 25th Anniv of Disappearance of Jean Charcot.
24 **7** 25f. brown, red and green 25·00 30·00

1962. Air. 1st Trans-Atlantic T.V. Satellite Link. As T **10** of French Polynesia.
25 50f. green, olive and blue 26·00 35·00

1963. Designs as T **2** and **4**.
26 5f. violet and blue (postage) 16·00 10·50
35 5f. brown, black and blue 65·00 35·00
27 8f. indigo, purple and blue 13·00 15·00
28 10f. black, blue and brown 30·00 25·00
29 12f. green, blue and brn 16·00 20·00
30 15f. blue, black and brown 11·00 9·00
31 20f. grey, orange and green £400 £225
32 45f. green, brown and blue 13·50 11·50
33 25f. purple, brown & bl (air) 25·00 14·00
34 50f. black, purple and blue 45·00 35·00
DESIGNS—HORIZ: As Type **2**: 5f. (No. 26) Blue whale; 5f. (No. 35) Crozet Archipelago; 8f. Southern elephant-seals in combat; 12f. Phylica (tree), New Amsterdam island; 15f. Killer whale, Crozet islands. As Type **4**: 50f. Adelie penguins. VERT: As Type **2**: 10f. Pintado petrel; 20f. Black-browed albatross; 45f. Kerguelen cabbage. As Type **4**: 25f. Ionospheric research pylon, Adelie Land.

9 Observation Station

1963. "International Year of the Quiet Sun".
36 **9** 20f. slate, brown and violet (postage) 50·00 40·00
37 – 100f. red, blue & black (air) £160 £120
DESIGN—VERT: (27 × 48 mm); 100f. Pylons and Adelie penguins.

10 Landfall of Dumont d'Urville

1965. Air. Discovery of Adelie Land, 1840.
38 **10** 50f. indigo and blue £110 £120

1965. Air. Centenary of I.T.U. As T **19** of French Polynesia.
39 30f. brown, mauve and blue £140 £140

1966. Air. Launching of 1st French Satellite. As Nos. 1696/7 of France.
40 25f. blue, green and brown 17·00 21·00
41 30f. blue, green and brown 17·00 21·00

1966. Air. Launching of Satellite "D1". As T **569** of France.
42 50f. violet, purple & orange 38·00 30·00

11 Space Probe **12** Dumont D'Urville, "L'Astrolabe" and "Zelee"

1967. Launching of 1st Space Probe, Adelie Land.
43 **11** 20f. black, purple & blue 17·00 16·00

1968. Dumont D'Urville Commem.
44 **12** 30f. brown, dp blue & lt bl £130 £120

13 Port-aux-Francais

1968. Air.
45 – 40f. slate and blue 38·00 40·00
46 **13** 50f. black, green & blue £160 £120
DESIGN: 40f. Aerial View of St. Paul Island.

14 Kerguelen and Rocket

1968. Air. Launching of "Dragon" Space Rockets.
47 **14** 25f. brown, green & blue 26·00 28·00
48 – 30f. blue, brown & green 26·00 28·00
DESIGN: 30f. Adelie Land and rocket.

1968. 20th Anniv of W.H.O. As T **34** of French Polynesia.
49 30f. blue, yellow and red 55·00 26·00

1968. Human Rights Year. As T **36** of French Polynesia.
50 30f. red, blue and brown 38·00 30·00

15 Eiffel Tower and Badge of Paris, and Ship in Antarctica

1969. Air. 5th Antarctic Treaty Consultative Meeting, Paris.
51 **15** 50f. blue . . . . 35·00 45·00

16 Antarctic Scene

1969. French Polar Exploration.
52 **16** 25f. blue, red & turquoise 24·00 29·00

1969. Air. 1st Flight of Concorde. As T **39** of French Polynesia.
53 85f. turquoise and blue . . . 38·00 45·00

17 Possession Island, Crozet Archipelago

1969. Air.
54 **17** 50f. green, red and blue . . 18·00 8·25
55 – 100f. black, grey and blue 55·00 75·00
56 – 200f. brown, green & blue 70·00 60·00
57 – 500f. blue . . . . 14·00 23·00
DESIGNS—HORIZ: 100f. Relief Map of Kerguelen. VERT: 200f. Cape Geology Archipelago map; 500f. Territorial arms.

1970. 50th Anniv of International Labour Organization. As T **44** of French Polynesia.
58 20f. purple, blue and red . . . 18·00 16·00

18 Relief Map of New Amsterdam Island

1970. Air. 20th Anniv of Meteorological Station, New Amsterdam Island.
59 **18** 30f. brown . . . . 16·00 10·00

1970. New U.P.U. Headquarters Building, Berne. As T **47** of French Polynesia.
60 50f. brown, purple and blue 38·00 16·00

19 Long-nosed Icefish

1971. Fishes.
61 **19** 5f. blue, yellow and green 4·00 1·90
62 – 10f. brown, violet and blue 6·00 3·00
63 – 20f. green, orange & purple 6·00 2·25
64 – 22f. red, violet and brown 8·50 9·75
65 – 25f. blue, yellow and green 5·25 2·25
66 – 30f. grey, blue and brown 7·00 4·75
67 – 35f. multicoloured . . . . . 7·25 6·00
68 – 135f. red, brown and blue 9·00 11·50
DESIGNS: 10f. Marbled rockcod; 20f. Antarctic rockcod; 22f. Hanson's rockcod; 25f. Orange-throated rockcod; 30f. Blue-gilled rockcod; 35f. Bernacchi's rockcod; 135f. Spiny pigfish.

20 Port-aux-Francais, 1950

1971. Air. 20th Anniv of Port-aux-Francais, Kerguelen.
69 **20** 40f. brown, green & blue . . 25·00 24·00
70 – 50f. green, blue & brown . . 30·00 29·00
DESIGN: 50f. Port-aux-Francais, 1970.

21 Treaty Emblem

22 "Christiansenia dreuxi"

1971. 10th Anniv of Antarctic Treaty.
71 **21** 75f. red . . . . 22·00 14·00

1972. Insects.
72 **22** 15f. brown, purple and red 11·50 8·00
73 – 22f. yellow, blue and green 11·50 9·75
74 – 25f. violet, purple & green 9·00 9·75
75 – 30f. multicoloured . . . . . 14·50 10·00
76 – 40f. black, brown & choc 9·50 8·50
77 – 140f. brown, green & blue 11·00 15·00
DESIGNS: 22f. "Phtirocoris antarcticus"; 25f. "Microzetia mirabilis" (midge); 30f. "Antarctophytosus atriceps" (rove beetle); 40f. "Paractora dreuxi"; 140f. "Pringleophaga kerguelenensis" (scavenger moth).

23 Landing on Crozet Islands

1972. Air. Bicentenary of Discovery of Crozet Islands and Kerguelen.
78 **23** 100f. black . . . . 35·00 20·00
79 – 250f. black and brown . . . 90·00 55·00
DESIGN: 250f. Hoisting the flag on Kerguelen.

1972. 1st Death Anniv of General De Gaulle. As Nos. 1937 and 1940 of France.
80 50f. black and green . . . . . 14·50 9·75
81 100f. black and green . . . . 19·00 11·00

24 "Gallieni"

1973. Air. Antarctic Voyages of the "Gallieni" (supply ship).
82 **24** 100f. black and blue . . . . 22·00 16·00

25 "Azorella selago"

1973. Plants.
83 **25** 61f. green, grey & brown . . 4·25 5·00
84 – 87f. green, blue and red . . 5·75 5·75
DESIGN: 87f. "Acaena ascendens".

26 "Mascarin", 1772

1973. Air. Antarctic Ships.
85 **26** 120f. brown . . . . 9·75 7·50
86 – 145f. blue . . . . 11·00 9·75
87 – 150f. blue . . . . 12·50 8·25
88 – 185f. brown . . . . 14·00 13·50
DESIGNS: 145f. "L'Astrolabe", 1840; 150f. "Roland", 1774; 185f. "Vitoria", 1522.
See also Nos. 93/4.

27 Part of Alfred Faure Base

1974. 10th Anniv of Alfred Faure Base, Crozet Archipelago.
89 **27** 75f. brown, blue & ultram 17·00 5·00
90 – 110f. brown, blue & ultram 17·00 6·25
91 – 150f. brown, blue & ultram 23·00 11·00
Nos. 89/91 were issued together se-tenant within the sheet, making a composite picture of the base.

28 Emperor Penguin, Globe and Letters

1974. Air. Centenary of Universal Postal Union.
92 **28** 150f. brown, black & blue 7·50 5·50

1974. Air. Charcot's Antarctic Voyages. As T **26**.
93 100f. blue . . . . 5·25 5·75
94 200f. red . . . . 6·25 7·50
DESIGN: 100f. "Francais" (1903–05 voyage); 200f. "Pourquoi Pas?" (1908–10 voyage).

29 Mail Ship "Sapmer"

1974. 25th Anniv of Postal Service.
95 **29** 75f. black, blue & mauve . . 6·50 5·00

30 Rockets over Kerguelen Islands

1975. Air. "ARAKS" Franco-Soviet Magnetosphere Research Project.
96 **30** 45f. red, blue and lilac . . . 8·00 5·25
97 – 90f. red, lilac and blue . . . 11·50 7·50
DESIGN: 90f. Map of North Coast of U.S.S.R.

31 Antarctic Tern

32 "La Curieuse" (topsail schooner)

1976.
98 **31** 40c. black, blue and orange (postage) . . . . 4·75 3·25
99 – 50c. brown, lt blue & blue 4·75 3·50
100 – 90c. brown and blue . . . 8·00 7·00
101 – 1f. brown, blue & violet . . 12·50 13·00
102 – 1f.20 green, blue & brown 13·50 10·50
103 – 1f.40 blue, green & orange 14·00 11·00
104 **32** 1f.90 bl, ultram & brn (air) 7·00 6·75
105 – 2f.70 brown, bl & ultram 8·50 8·75
106 – 4f. blue and red . . . . . 10·00 8·50
DESIGNS—As T **31**. HORIZ: 50c. Antarctic petrel; 90c. Kerguelen fur seal; 1f. Weddell seal. VERT: 1f.20, Kerguelen cormorant; 1f.40, Gentoo penguin. As T **32**: 2f.70, "Commandant Charcot" (ice patrol ship); 4f. "Marion Dufresne" (Antarctic supply ship).

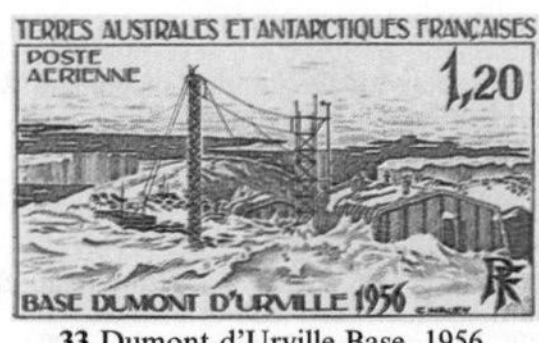

33 Dumont d'Urville Base, 1956

1976. Air. 20th Anniv of Dumont d'Urville Base, Adelie Land.
107 **33** 1f.20 brown, orge & blue 14·00 10·50
108 – 4f. orange, blue & brown 18·00 18·50
DESIGNS: 4f. Dumont d'Urville Base, 1976.

34 Kerguelen Island

1976. Air. Bicent of Cook's Passage to Kerguelen.
109 **34** 3f.50 slate and blue . . . . 10·00 9·00

35 Captain Cook

36 First Ascent of Mt. Ross (5 Jan 1975)

1976. Cook Commemoration.
110 **35** 70c. blue, brown & yellow 14·50 10·00

1976. Ross Commemoration.
111 **36** 30c. red, brown and blue 4·25 4·50
112 – 3f. violet, brown and blue 5·00 4·00
DESIGN: 3f. Sir James Clark Ross.

37 Blue Whale

1977. Marine Mammals.
113 **37** 1f.10 deep blue & blue . . 6·50 7·75
114 – 1f.50 indigo, blue & brown 6·50 7·75
DESIGN: 1f.50, Commerson's dolphin.

38 Seaweed, "Macrocystis"

1977.
115 **38** 40c. brown and bistre . . . 1·90 2·75
116 – 70c. green, brown & black 2·00 2·75
117 – 1f. grey . . . . 2·25 2·25
118 – 1f.20 red, green and blue 3·75 3·75
119 – 1f.40 red, blue and grey . . 4·00 5·75
DESIGNS—HORIZ: 70c. Seaweed, "Durvillea"; 1f.20, "Magga Dan" (Antarctic supply ship); 1f.40, "Thala Dan" (Antarctic supply ship). VERT: 1f. Oceanology.

39 Kerguelen Satellite

1977. Air. Satellites.
120 **39** 2f.70 multicoloured . . . . 4·25 5·00
121 – 3f. blue and light blue . . 5·50 6·75
DESIGN: 3f. Adelie Land satellite.
See also No. 143.

40 Polar Explorer with Flags — **42** R. Rallier du Baty

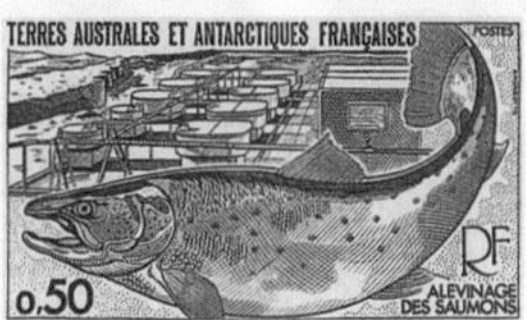

41 Atlantic Salmon and Breeding Tanks

1977. 30th Anniv of French Polar Expeditions.
122 **40** 1f.90 orange, red & blue 9·75 4·50

1977. Antarctic Fauna.
123 **41** 50c. violet & blue (postage) 2·25 3·25
124 – 90c. brown, blue & green 2·00 1·25
125 – 10f. brown, blue & red (air) . . . . 18·00 20·00
DESIGNS—As T **41**: 90c. Head of light-mantled sooty albatross. 36 × 48 mm: 10f. Kerguelen fur seal and cub.

1979. R. Rallier du Baty Commemoration.
126 **42** 1f.20 blue and bistre . . . 2·50 3·25

43 Memorial and Names of French Navigators

1979. French Navigators' Memorial, Hobart.
127 **43** 1f. brown, turq & blue . . 2·00 3·00

44 "Argos" Satellite and Geophysical Laboratory

1979. Air. Satellite Research.
128 **44** 70c. turquiose, vio & grn 2·25 3·00
129 – 1f.90 black, brown & mve 2·75 3·00
DESIGN: 1f.90, Satellite and Kerguelen Receiving Station.

45 Kerguelen Cormorant

1979. Antarctic Fauna.
130 **45** 1f.40 green, blue and sepia (postage) . . . . 1·75 1·25
131 – 4f. ultramarine, blue and green (air) . . . . 3·50 5·00
132 – 10f. brown, green & blk . . 7·25 13·00
DESIGNS—VERT: (36 × 48 mm): 4f. As No. 125, (27 × 48 mm): 10f. Southern elephant-seal.
See also Nos. 138/9.

46 Destroyer "Forbin"

1979. Ships.
133 **46** 40c. black, turquoise & grn 2·25 3·25
134 – 50c. black, turquoise & grn 2·25 2·25
DESIGN: 50c. Helicopter carrier "Jeanne d'Arc".
See also Nos. 136/7.

47 H.M.S. "Challenger" in the Antarctic (from engraving in "Illustrated London News")

1979. Air. Expedition of the "Challenger", 1872–6.
135 **47** 2f.70 black and blue . . . 3·50 3·50

1980. Frigates. As T **46**.
136 1f.10 blue, ultram & vio . . . 1·25 1·75
137 1f.50 black, blue & dp bl . . 1·25 3·00
DESIGNS—VERT: 1f.10, "Doudart de Lagree". HORIZ: 1f.50, "Commandant Bourdais".

1980. Antarctic Fauna. As T **45**.
138 70c. black, red and blue . . . 1·40 1·00
139 1f. brown and blue . . . . . 1·40 1·00
DESIGNS—VERT: 70c. Royal penguins. HORIZ: 1f. Head of soft-plumaged petrel.

50 Admiral d'Entrecasteaux — **51** El Cano

1980. Admiral d'Entrecasteaux Commemoration.
140 **50** 1f.20 black, violet & blue 1·75 1·60

1980. Sebastian de El Cano (discoverer of Amsterdam Island) Commemoration.
141 **51** 1f.40 grey, orange & red 1·40 3·00
142 – 4f. multicoloured . . . . . 2·50 4·00
DESIGN: 4f. El Cano's ship "Vitoria".

1980. Air. Kerguelen Satellite.
143 **39** 50c. grey, blue & brown . . 90 3·00

52 Lion Rock

1980. Air. Dumont d'Urville Base.
144 **52** 90c. multicoloured . . . . 1·25 2·75

53 "La Recherche" and "L'Esperance" (after Roux)

1980. Air. Arrival at Amsterdam Island of D'Entrecasteaux and De Kermadec Commemoration.
145 **53** 1f.90 blue . . . . 2·00 4·00

54 H.M.S. "Terror" (bomb ketch) at Arched Rock, Kerguelen (after Williams)

1980. Air.
146 **54** 2f.70 black, green & brn 1·75 3·50

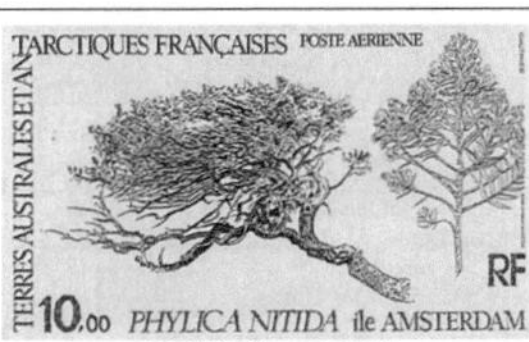

55 "Phylica nitida"

1980. Air.
147 **55** 10f. black, green & brown 4·75 10·00

56 Charles de Gaulle — **57** Adelie Penguins

1980. Air. 10th Death Anniv of Charles de Gaulle.
148 **56** 5f.40 purple, blue & red . . 10·00 20·00

1981. Antarctic Fauna.
149 **57** 50c. lilac . . . . 1·50 1·25
150 – 60c. blue, green & turq . . 2·75 1·00
151 **57** 1f.20 black, blue & violet 2·00 1·10
152 – 1f.30 black, brown & blue 1·50 2·75
153 – 1f.80 brown, green & bis 1·75 2·75
DESIGNS—HORIZ: 1f.30; 1f.80, Leopard seal. (48 × 28 mm) 60c. Head of Adelie penguin.

58 "HB 40 Castor"

1981. Air. Antarctic Transport.
154 **58** 2f.40 blue, orange & violet 2·50 3·00

59 "Saint Marcouf"

1981. Air. Antarctic Supply Ships.
155 **59** 3f.50 grey, blue & red . . . 1·60 3·00
156 – 7f.30 blue, turq & lilac . . 2·50 4·50
DESIGN: 7f.30, "Norsel".

60 Map of Antarctica

1981. 20th Anniv of Antarctic Treaty.
157 **60** 1f.80 blue, dp blue & brn 6·50 9·75

61 Sud Aviation Alouette II Helicopter

1981.
158 **61** 55c. blue, turq & brown . . 2·25 2·50
159 65c. turquoise, green & bl 2·25 2·50

62 Compacted Ice, Dumont d'Urville

1981. Air.
160 **62** 1f.30 dp blue, blue & grey 1·75 2·50

63 Loranchet

1981. Jean Loranchet Commemoration.
161 **63** 1f.40 dp green, green & ol 1·75 2·50

64 Black-faced Sheathbill

1981. Air.
162 **64** 1f.50 black 90 70

65 "Adele Dumont d'Urville" (Michele Garreau)

1981. Air.
163 **65** 2f. brown and black . . . 1·75 1·50

66 "Arcad III" Satellite over Antarctic

1981. Air.
164 **66** 3f.85 green, bl & dp bl . . 3·50 4·50

67 Charcot Station

1981. Air. 25th Anniv of Charcot Antarctic Station.
165 **67** 5f. red, blue and violet . . 3·25 4·25

68 "Antares" (dispatch vessel)

1981. Air.
166 **68** 8f.40 purple, grey & blue 3·25 4·50

69 Rockhopper, Gentoo and King Penguins

1982. Air. "Philexfrance 82" International Stamp Exhibition, Paris.
167 **69** 8f. brown, blue & black . . 4·25 4·50

70 "Commandant Charcot" (ice patrol ship)

1982. Air. Overseas Week.
168 **70** 5f. blue and green . . . . 3·50 4·50

71 Lighter "Le Gros Ventre"

1983.
169 **71** 55c. dp brown, green & bl 1·90 2·75

72 Apostles Islands

1983. Air.
170 **72** 65c. dp blue, brown & bl 1·75 2·75

73 Church and Statue of Virgin and Child

1983. Church of Our Lady of the Winds, Kerguelen.
171 **73** 1f.40 blue, brown & green 1·60 1·75

74 Pintails **75** Vivies

1983.
172 **74** 1f.50 dp brown, brn & bl 70 50
173 1f.80 brown and green . . 70 50

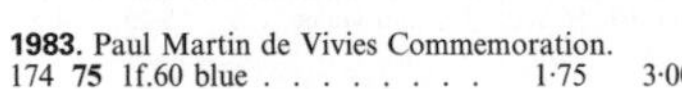
1983. Paul Martin de Vivies Commemoration.
174 **75** 1f.60 blue . . . . 1·75 3·00

76 Trawler "Austral"

1983.
175 **76** 2f.30 brown, blue & pur 2·50 3·25

77 Dog Sledge

1983. Air.
176 **77** 4f.55 blue . . . . 3·75 6·25

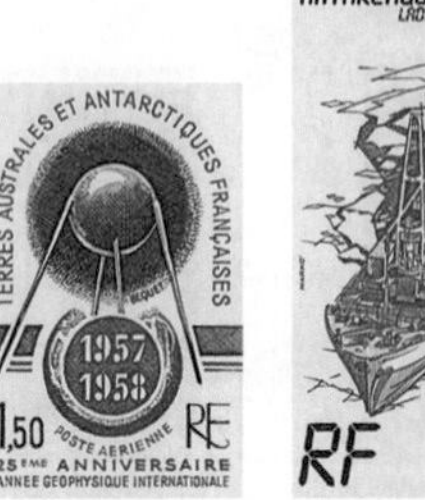

78 "Sputnik I" Satellite **80** "Lady Franklin" (Antarctic supply ship)

79 "Antarctica" (Georges Mathieu) (½-size illustration)

1983. Air. Anniversaries. Each black, blue and brown.
177 1f.50 Type **78** (25th anniv of International Geophysical Year) . . . . 1·10 2·00
178 3f.30 Orange Bay, Cape Horn (cent of first Polar Year) (49 × 36 mm) . . . . . . 1·50 2·50
179 5f.20 Scoresby Sound, Greenland (50th anniv of second Polar Year) (49 × 36 mm) . . . . . . 1·90 3·00

1983. Air.
180 **79** 25f. blue, black and red . . 13·00 18·00

1983.
181 **80** 5f. blue, dp blue & black 7·00 9·75

81 Drilling for Samples

1984. Glaciology.
182 **81** 15c. brown, orange & bl 1·75 1·75
183 1f.70 blue, orange & red 2·25 1·25

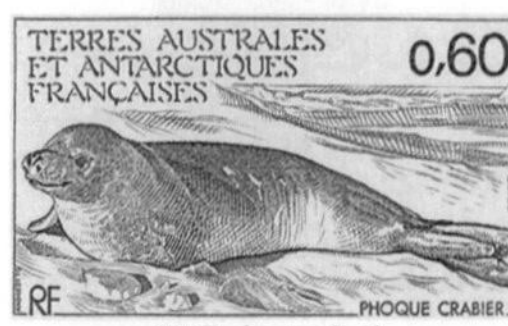

82 Crabeater Seal

1984. Antarctic Wildlife.
184 **82** 60c. green, grey & brown 1·75 2·75
185 – 70c. blue, dp blue & brown 60 50
186 – 2f. green, blue and brown 1·25 1·00
187 **82** 5f.90 black, blue and red 4·00 3·25
DESIGNS: 70 c, 2f. Rockhopper penguins.

83 Faure

1984. Alfred Faure Commemoration.
188 **83** 1f.80 black, brown & red 2·50 1·75

84 H.M.S. "Erebus" (bomb ketch) in Antarctic (after Davis)

1984. Air.
189 **84** 2f.60 deep blue & blue . . 1·75 3·25

85 Balloons and Airships

1984. Air. Bicentenary of Manned Flight.
190 **85** 3f.50 red, brown & blue . . 1·90 3·25
191 – 7f.80 brown, blue & violet 3·75 6·25
DESIGN: 7f.80, Montgolfier balloon, Renard and Krebs' airship "La France", balloon "Zodiac" and other balloons and airships

86 Polar Aurora

1984. Air.
192 **86** 3f.50 multicoloured . . . . 6·75 4·25

87 Port Jeanne d'Arc, Kerguelen, 1930

1984. Air.
193 **87** 4f.70 turquoise, bl & dp bl 3·00 5·25

88 "Albatros" **90** Mouflons

89 Survey Barquentine "Gauss"

1984. Air. Commissioning of Patrol Boat "Albatros".
194 **88** 11f.30 dp blue, red & bl . . 4·75 6·75

1984. Air. "Nordposta" International Stamp Exhibition, Hamburg.
195 **89** 9f. mauve and blue . . . . 5·50 4·75

1985. Antarctic Wildlife.
196 – 1f.70 black, brown and orange (postage) . . . . 1·10 90
197 – 2f.80 turquoise, blk & bl 1·40 1·25
198 **90** 70c. brown, bl & mve (air) 1·60 1·75
199 – 3f.90 brown, grey & orge 1·90 1·25
DESIGNS—HORIZ: 1f.70, Emperor penguins; 2f.80, Snow petrel. VERT: 3f.90, Amsterdam albatross.

91 Emblem, Humpback Whales, Krill and Research Vessel

1985. Biomass.
200 **91** 1f.80 dp blue, mve & bl . . 2·75 2·50
201 5f.20 blue, lt bl & red . . . 3·50 3·50

92 Liotard **93** Port Martin Base, Adelie Land

1985. Andre-Frank Liotard (explorer) Commem.
202 **92** 2f. purple and violet . . . 2·00 1·90

1985.
203 **93** 2f.20 blue, brn & dp bl . . 2·75 2·00

94 "La Novara" (frigate) at Saint Paul (after J. Noel)

1985. Air.
204 **94** 12f.80 black and orange . . 6·75 9·25

95 "Explorer and Fur Seal" (½-size illustration)

1985. Air.
205 **95** 30f. multicoloured . . . . 11·50 16·00

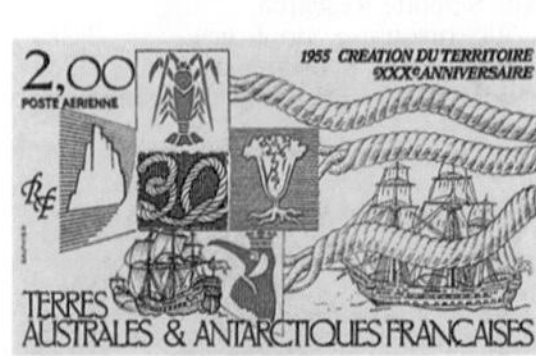

96 Various Motifs, Rope and Kerguelen's Ships

1985. Air. 30th Anniv of French Southern and Antarctic Territories. Each blue, green and black.
206 2f. Type **96** . . . . 1·50 2·50
207 12f.80 Motifs, rope and ships (different) . . . . 5·25 8·50

97 Southern Fulmars

1986. Birds.
208 **97** 1f. blue & black (postage) 55 70
209 – 1f.70 black, grn & brn . . 1·25 1·25
210 – 4f.60 brn, yell & red (air) 1·50 1·75
DESIGNS: 1f.70, Giant petrels; 4f.60. Southern black-backed gull.

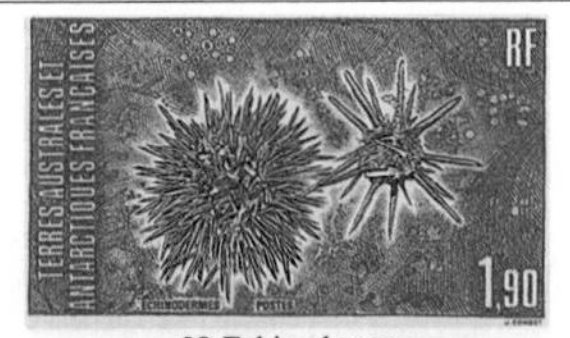

98 Echinoderms

1986.
211 **98** 1f.90 brown and blue . . . 2·50 1·75

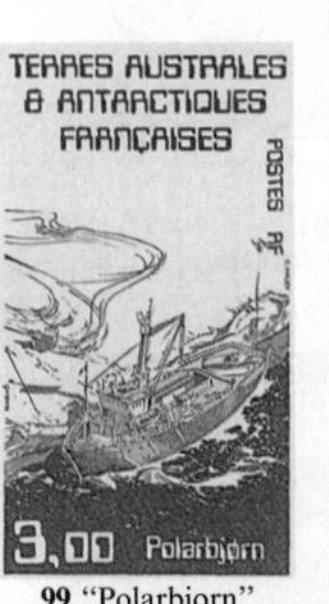

99 "Polarbjorn" (Antarctic supply ship) **101** "Cotula plumosa"

100 Charcot and "Pourquoi Pas?" leaving Harbour

1986. Ships.
212 – 2f.10 deep blue and blue 2·25 1·75
213 **99** 3f. red, light blue and blue 3·00 2·25
DESIGN: 2f.10, B.C.A. "Var A 608" (patrol boat).

1986. Air. 50th Death Anniv of Jean Charcot (explorer). Each brown, blue and red.
214 2f.10 Type **100** . . . . . . 1·75 2·75
215 14f. Charcot and "Pourquoi Pas?" in heavy seas . . . . 7·25 9·25

1986. Plants.
216 **101** 2f.30 green, yell & blk . . 1·75 2·75
217 – 6f.20 green and red . . . 3·25 3·50
DESIGN: 6f.20, "Lycopodium saururus."

102 Airplane, Parachutes and Aerial

1986. Scientific Research.
218 **102** 14f. red, black & orange 5·75 10·50

103 Satellite over Antarctic

1986. Air. "SPOT" Surveillance Satellite.
219 **103** 8f. brown, green & blue 4·00 7·00

104 Starfish

1987.
220 **104** 50c. blue, orange & green 1·75 1·75

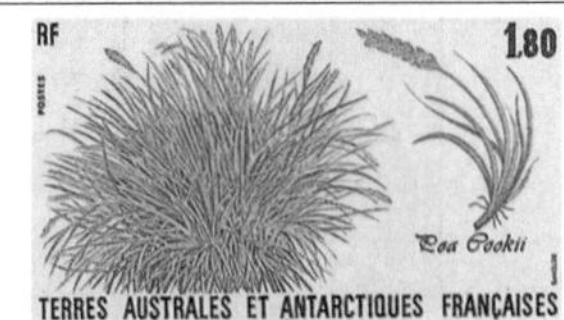

105 "Poa cookii"

1987. Plants.
221 **105** 1f.80 green and blue . . . 1·40 2·25
222 – 6f.50 green, red and blue 2·75 3·75
DESIGN: 6f.50, Lichen.

106 Marret Base, Adéelie Land

1987.
223 **106** 2f. brown, blue & purple 2·75 2·75

107 Admiral Mouchez

1987.
224 **107** 2f.20 blue, black & brown 2·75 2·75

108 Reindeer

1987. Antarctic Wildlife.
225 **108** 2f.50 black . . . . 2·75 2·50
226 – 4f.80 multicoloured . . . 2·00 1·50
DESIGN: 4f.80, Macaroni penguins.

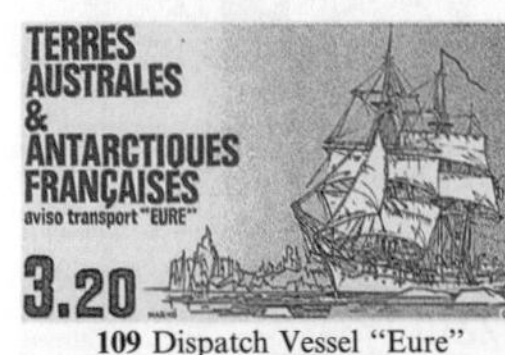

109 Dispatch Vessel "Eure"

1987.
227 **109** 3f.20 turquoise, bl & grn 2·75 2·75

110 "J. B. Charcot" (schooner)

1987. Air.
228 **110** 14f.60 purple, bl & brn 5·75 9·00

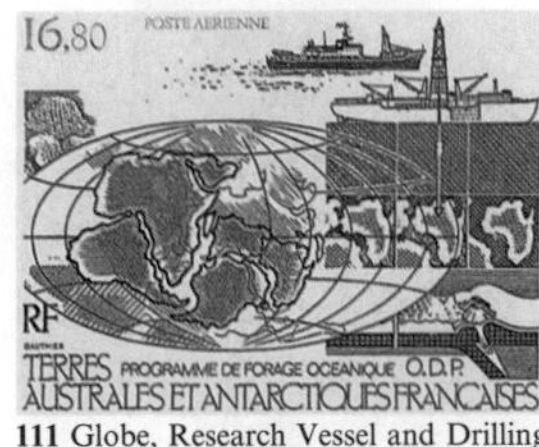

111 Globe, Research Vessel and Drilling Ship

1987. Air. Scientific Research.
229 **111** 16f.80 dp blue, bl & brn 5·25 9·00

112 "Inmarsat" Satellite

1987. Air.
230 **112** 16f.80 brown and black 5·50 9·00

113 Darrieus Wind Generator

1988.
231 **113** 1f. blue, indigo & lt bl . . 1·60 1·50

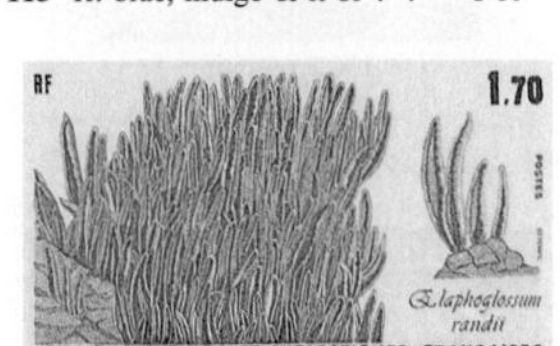

114 Elephant Grass

1988.
232 **114** 1f.70 green, bis & dp grn 1·75 1·50

115 Globe and Father Lejay **117** Gessain

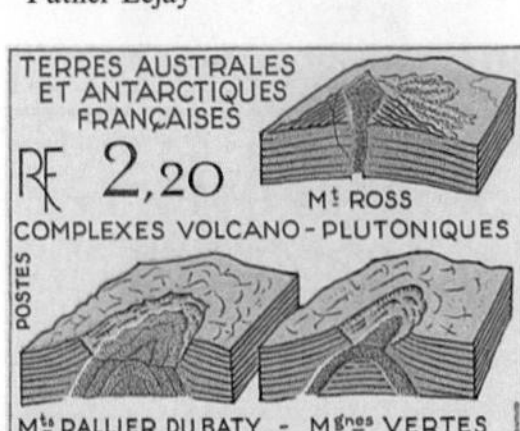

116 Geological Sections of Volcanoes

1988.
233 **115** 2f.20 black and violet . . 1·90 1·60

1988. Antarctic Geology. Multicoloured.
234 2f.20 Type **116** . . . . . . 1·50 1·50
235 15f.10 Geological map of Kerguelen Islands . . . . 6·75 6·00

1988. 2nd Death Anniv of Robert Gessain (explorer).
236 **117** 3f.40 red, grey and green 2·00 1·90

118 "Le Gros Ventre" (frigate)

1988. Ships.
237 **118** 3f.50 brown, grn & bl . . 1·75 1·75
238 – 4f.90 blue and black . . . 2·50 2·25
239 – 5f. blue and black . . . . 2·50 2·25
DESIGNS—HORIZ: 4f.90, Mermaid with anvil and "Jules Verne" (Antarctic supply ship). VERT: 5f. "La Fortune" (sail warship).

119 Penguin Island

1988. Air. Penguin Island.
240 **119** 3f.90 brown and blue . . 1·75 2·00
241 – 15f.10 blue, brown & grn 5·25 6·00
DESIGN: 15f.10, Views of island from sea and air.

120 Wilson's Storm Petrels

1988.
242 **120** 6f.80 blue, black & brn 2·75 2·00

121 Igloos

1988. Air. 40th Anniv of French Polar Expeditions.
243 **121** 20f. green, purple and red 7·50 8·00

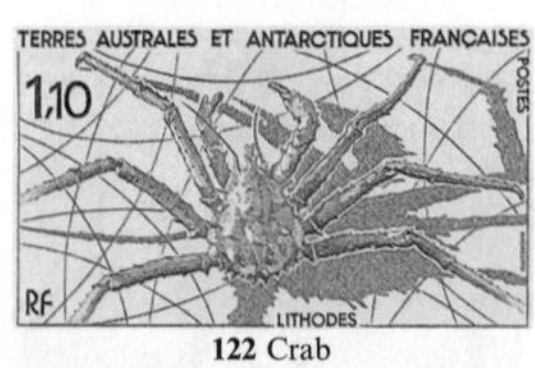

122 Crab

1989. Flora and Fauna.
244 **122** 1f.10 lt brown, bl & brn 1·00 1·10
245 – 2f. black, brn & grn . . . 1·25 1·50
246 – 2f.80 green, red & brn . . 1·60 1·50
247 – 3f.60 blue, dp bl & blk . . 1·40 80
DESIGNS: 2f. Kerguelen sheep; 2f.80, "Blechnum penna marina"; 3f.60, Blue petrel.

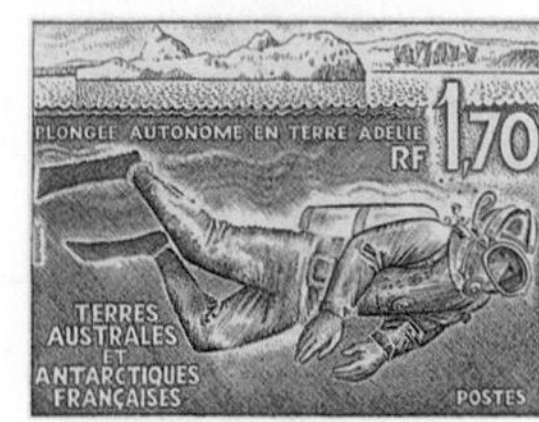

123 Diver

1989. Diving off Adelie Land.
248 **123** 1f.70 brown, green & bl 1·60 1·50

124 Henry and Rene Bossiere

1989. Kerguelen Islands Pioneers.
249 **124** 2f.20 brown, green & bl 1·60 1·50

125 "La Curieuse" (topsail schooner), 1913

1989. Air. Ships. Each blue, black and red.
250 2f.20 Type **125** . . . . . . 2·00 2·00
251 15f.50 "La Curieuse" (supply ship), 1989 . . . . 6·75 6·75

126 Mesotype

1989. Crystals.
252 **126** 5f.10 turquoise, blk & bl 2·25 2·50
253 – 7f.30 mauve, grn & grey 3·00 3·00
DESIGN: 7f.30, Analcime.

127 Map

1989. Air. Apostles Islands.
254 **127** 8f.40 blue, grey & green 3·75 2·75

128 Buildings

1989. Air. 40th Anniv of Establishment of Permanent Antarctic Bases.
255 **128** 15f.50 brown . . . . . . 5·50 5·25

129 Allegory

1989. Air. Bicentenary of French Revolution.
256 **129** 5f. blue, green & mauve 5·75 4·25
MS257 150 × 120 mm. **129** 5f. × 4 blue, red and light blue . . . . 12·50 13·50

130 Figures around Map

1989. Air. 15th Antarctic Treaty Consultative Meeting, Paris.
258 **130** 17f.70 red, purple & blue 6·25 6·75

131 "Chonotriches", "Copepodes" and Map of Kerguelen

1990. Protistology.
259 **131** 1f.10 blue, brown & black 65 55

132 Cattle

1990. Restoration of Amsterdam Island.
260 **132** 1f.70 brown, green & blue 75 55

133 Quoy and Decollate Planaxis (shell)
135 Dumont d'Urville

134 Yellow-nosed Albatrosses

1990. Birth Bicentenary of Jean Rene C. Quoy (doctor and naturalist).
261 **133** 2f.20 blue, dp brn & brn 1·00 85

1990.
262 **134** 2f.80 multicoloured . . . 1·10 70

1990. Birth Bicentenary of Jules Dumont d'Urville (explorer).
263 **135** 3f.60 brown and blue . . 1·50 1·25

136 Aragonite

1990. Minerals.
264 **136** 5f.10 brown and blue . . 2·25 2·00

137 Pigs Island

1990. Air.
265 **137** 7f.30 green, brown & blue 3·25 2·75

138 "Ranunculus pseudo trullifolius"

1990.
266 **138** 8f.40 green, blue & orge 3·50 3·00

139 "L'Astrolabe"

1990. Air. 150th Anniv of Discovery of Adelie Land by Dumont d'Urville.
267 **139** 15f.50 brown and red . . 5·50 4·50

140 "L'Astrolabe" (fishery control vessel), 1988

1990. Air. Ships. Each blue, green and red.
268 2f.20 Type **140** . . . . . . 1·75 1·75
269 15f.50 "L'Astrolabe" (Dumont d'Urville's ship), 1840 . . . . 7·00 7·00

141 Bird (½-size illustration)

1990. Air.
270 **141** 30f. multicoloured . . . . 12·00 8·00

142 Map, Emperor Penguin and Envelopes

1991. 30th Anniv of Postal Service to Crozet.
271 **142** 50c. blue, ultram & blk 1·00 60

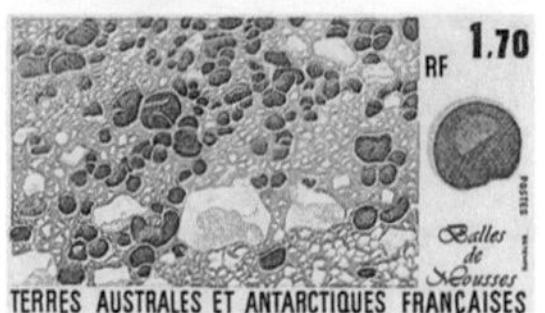

143 Moss Balls in Shingle

1991.
272 **143** 1f.70 grey, brown & blk 90 60

144 Wandering Albatrosses and "Argos" Satellite

1991. Air.
273 **144** 2f.10 brown, blue & red 90 55

145 Douguet and Flag

1991. Admiral Max Douguet Commemoration.
274 **145** 2f.30 blue, black & orge 90 65

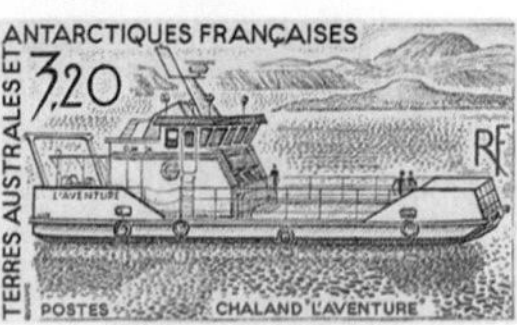

146 "L'Aventure" (landing craft)

1991.
275 **146** 3f.20 brown, blue & grn 1·90 2·00

147 Fur Seals

1991.
276 **147** 3f.60 brown and blue . . 2·00 1·60

148 Infra-red Image and Measuring Equipment (study of ozone layer)

1991. Air. Climatic Research. Each green, violet and orange.
277 3f.60 Type **148** . . . . . . 2·00 2·00
278 20f. Research vessel and rock samples (palaeoclimatology) . . . . 8·50 8·50

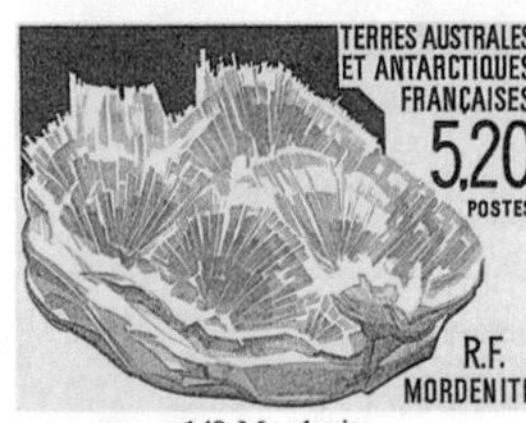

149 Mordenite

1991.
279 **149** 5f.20 blue, green & black 2·00 1·50

150 Mackerel Icefish

1991.
280 **150** 7f.80 green and blue . . . 3·50 2·75

151 Map **152** De Gaulle and Map

1991. 30th Anniv of Antarctic Treaty.
281 **151** 9f.30 grn, dp grn & red 3·25 3·00

1991. Air. Birth Centenary of Charles de Gaulle (French statesman).
282 **152** 18f.80 black, blue & red 8·00 4·75

153 Research Worker greeting Penguin (Antarctic)

1991. Air. French Institute for Polar Research and Technology. Multicoloured.
283 15f. Type **153** . . . . . . 6·25 6·25
284 15f. Research worker greeting polar bear (Arctic) . . . . 6·25 6·25
Nos. 283/4 were printed together, se-tenant, forming a composite design.

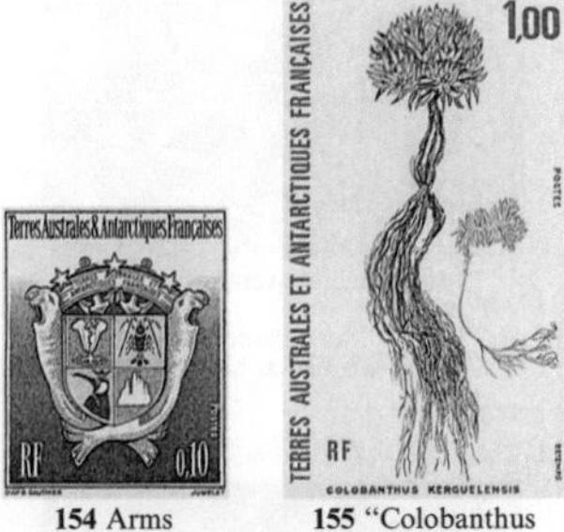

154 Arms **155** "Colobanthus kerguelensis"

1992.
285 **154** 10c. black 10 10
286 20c. blue 10 10
287 30c. red 10 10
288 40c. green 10 10
289 50c. orange 10 10

1992.
295 **155** 1f. brown, green & blue 55 40

156 "Groupe Safap-Helvim" (yacht) and Antarctic Route

1992. "Globe Challenge" Round the World Sailing Race.
296 **156** 2f.20 multicoloured . . . 1·25 1·25

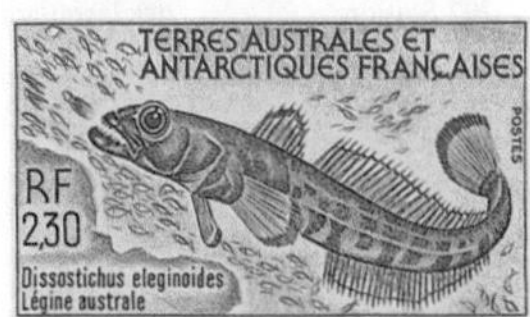
157 Blenny Rockcod

1992.
297 **157** 2f.30 green, blue & brn 1·50 1·25

158 Paul Tchernia (scientist)

1992.
298 **158** 2f.50 grn, brn & dp brn 1·40 1·25

159 Pintado Petrels 160 Marion-Dufresne (after Meryon)

1992. Air.
299 **159** 3f.40 brown, blk & grn 1·40 65

1992. 220th Death Anniv of Marion-Dufresne (explorer).
300 **160** 3f.70 black, red & blue . . 1·75 1·40

161 "Tottan" (supply ship)

1992.
301 **161** 14f. brown, turq & blue 6·00 6·00

162 Columbus's Fleet, Montgolfier Balloon and Columbus

1992. Air. 500th Anniv of Discovery of America by Columbus.
302 **162** 22f. brown, pur & dp brn 10·50 10·50

163 Satellite in Orbit

1992. Air. "Topex Poseidon" Satellite.
303 **163** 24f.50 red, black & blue 10·00 4·25

164 Ocean Currents, Research Vessel and Pipes

1992. WOCE Research Programme.
304 **164** 25f.40 brown, orge & bl 11·00 11·00

165 Adelie and Emperor Penguins on Landing Strip (½-size illustration)

1992. Air. Completion of Landing Strip at Dumont D'Urville Research Station, Adelie Land.
305 **165** 25f.70 multicoloured . . . 9·25 5·25

166 Violet-tinted Garnet

1993.
306 **166** 1f. purple, green & black 30 20

167 Radio Equipment, Handshake and Globe

1993. Air. Amateur Radio Enthusiasts.
307 **167** 2f. black, red & mauve . . 70 35

168 "Marion Dufresne" 169 "Lyallia kerguelensis"

1993. 20th Anniv of the "Marion Dufresne" (Antarctic supply ship).
308 **168** 2f.20 mauve, black & bl 1·00 60

1993.
309 **169** 2f.30 blue, green & yell 75 50

170 Killer Whale

1993.
310 **170** 2f.50 black and purple . . 85 50

171 Antarctic Skuas

1993.
311 **171** 2f.50 black . . . . 1·75 70

172 Andre Prud'homme (meteorologist)

1993. 43rd Anniv of Meteo France (weather service) in the Antarctic. Each black, blue and red.
312 2f.50 Type **172** 75 50
313 22f. Meteorologists recording wind speed on Adelie Land (35 × 37 mm) . . . . . . 6·00 4·50

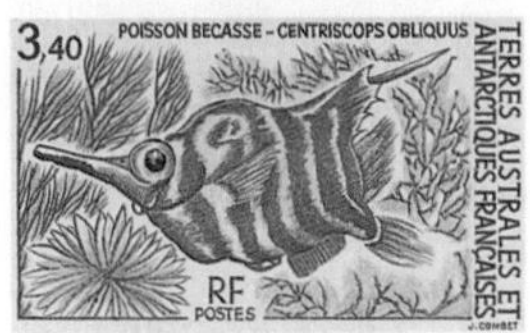
173 Red-banded Snipefish

1993.
314 **173** 3f.40 red, brown & blue 1·00 75

174 "Italo Marsano"

1993. 43rd Anniv of Chartering of the "Italo Marsano" (freighter).
315 **174** 3f.70 purple, brown & bl 1·10 80

175 King Penguins on Television and Platform

1993. ECOPHY Research Programme.
316 **175** 14f. brown, blue & black 5·00 2·75

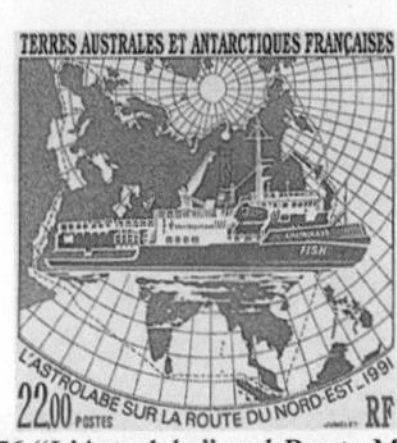
176 "L'Astrolabe" and Route Map

1993. Voyage of "L'Astrolabe" (fishery control ship) through North-East Passage.
317 **176** 22f. red and blue . . . . 6·50 4·00

177 Scientists examining Arctic Tern and using Microscope

1993. Air. Animal Biology Laboratory, Adelie Land.
318 **177** 25f.40 brn, grn & dp grn 9·00 6·00

178 Camp, Snow Vehicles and Map

1993. Air. Antarctic Expedition Base D 10.
319 **178** 25f.70 brown, red & blue 7·50 5·50

179 Lockheed Hercules over Adelie Land

1993. Air. Inauguration of Air Strip, Adelie Land.
320 **179** 30f. black, blue & green 8·50 6·50

180 Cordierite

1994.
321 **180** 1f. blue, green & black . . 45 25

181 Domestic Cat

1994.
322 **181** 2f. black, green & emer 70 50

182 Lowering Probe into Sea

1994. 1000th Sea-bed Sample.
323 **182** 2f.40 black and blue . . . 1·10 60

183 Pommier and Dog

1994. 75th Birth Anniv of Robert Pommier (explorer).
324 **183** 2f.80 blue, pur & orge . . 1·25 75

184 Salvin's Prion

1994.
325 **184** 2f.80 blue . . . . 1·10 80

185 C. A. Vincendon Dumoulin (hydrographic engineer)

1994. Navy Hydrographic and Oceanographic Service. Each black and blue.
326 2f.80 Type **185** . . . . . . 1·00 75
327 23f. Measuring magnetic force (35 × 36 mm) . . . . 8·00 5·50

186 Rascasse Scorpionfish

1994.
328 **186** 3f.70 orange and green . . 1·40 90

187 "Kerguelen de Tremarec" (trawler)

1994.
329 **187** 4f.30 lilac, red & green . . 1·50 1·00

188 "Copepoda"

1994. Air.
330 **188** 15f. black . . . . 4·75 3·25

189 Trawler and Chart of Fishing Sectors around Kerguelen Islands

1994. Air. Scientific Management of Fishing Industry.
331 **189** 23f. purple, blue & red . . 7·50 5·50

190 Map of Antarctic, Satellite and Earth Station

1994. Air. National Centre for Space Study Satellite Station, Kerguelen.
332 **190** 26f.70 lilac, bl & ultram 8·50 6·00

191 Lidar Station and Map

1994. Air. Lidar Research Station, Adelie Land.
333 **191** 27f.30 blue, green & mve 9·00 6·50

192 Penguins (½-size illustration)

1994. Air. Migration of Emperor Penguins.
334 **192** 28f. black and blue . . . 10·00 6·50

193 Olivine

1995.
335 **193** 1f. olive, green and lilac 35 20

194 Southern Flounder

1995.
336 **194** 2f.40 brown, blue & mve 1·00 55

195 Andree and Edgar Aubert de la Rue (naturalists)

1995.
337 **195** 2f.80 brown, blue & mve 95 65

196 SODAR Station (wind study centre)

1995.
338 **196** 2f.80 mauve, red & violet 95 65

197 Mont d'Alsace, Kerguelen

1995.
339 **197** 3f.70 brown, violet & bl 1·40 1·10

198 "Antarctica" (research vessel)

1995. Air. Mt. Erebus Expedition.
340 **198** 4f.30 blue, green & mve 1·75 1·00

199 Waving Farewell

1995. Air. Departure of Winter Residents from Charcot Station.
341 **199** 15f. multicoloured . . . . 5·50 3·25

200 Minke Whale

1995.
342 **200** 23f. dp blue, blue & pur 8·50 5·00

201 "Tamaris" and Tagged Grey-headed Albatross

1995. Voyage of "Tamaris" (full-rigged ship).
343 **201** 25f.80 brn, turq & bl . . 9·25 5·50

202 "Heroine" (full-rigged ship)

1995. Expedition of "Heroine" to Crozet Islands in 1837.
344 **202** 27f.30 blue . . . . 10·00 6·25

203 Seals (½-size illustration)

1995. 165th Death Anniv of G. Lesquin.
345 **203** 28f. multicoloured . . . . 10·50 6·50

204 Amazonite

1996.
347 **204** 1f. blue, green and black 40 30

205 White-chinned Petrel

1996.
348 **205** 2f.40 blue 90 75

206 "Yves de Kerguelen" (expedition ship)

1996.
349 **206** 2f.80 brown, blue & pur 1·25 80

207 Station

209 Jacquinot

208 Victor crossing Greenland, 1936

1996. Benedict Point Scientific Research Station, Amsterdam Island.
350 **207** 2f.80 brn, dp grn & grn 1·10 80

1996. Paul-Emile Victor Commemoration. Each black, blue and red.
351 2f.80 Type **208** . . . . . . 1·00 70
352 23f. Victor, emperor penguins and Dumont d'Urville Base, Terre Adelie . . . . 9·00 6·50

1996. Birth Bicentenary of Admiral Jacquinot.
353 **209** 3f.70 ultramarine & blue 1·40 90

210 "Austral" (trawler)

1996.
354 **210** 4f.30 black, blue & grn 1·60 1·25

211 "Lycopodium magellanicum"

1996.
355 **211** 7f.70 green and purple . . 2·75 1·50

212 Drilling and Micrometeorite

1996. Micrometeorites of Cape Prudhomme.
356 **212** 15f. black, violet & blue 6·00 4·00

213 East Island

1996. Air.
357 **213** 20f. brown, blue & lt brn 7·50 5·00

214 Tractor and Camp

1996. Air. Raid Dome/C.
358 **214** 23f. blue . . . . 6·00 5·50

215 Blue Rorqual and Map of Sanctuary Area

1996. Air. Southern Whale Sanctuary.
359 **215** 26f.70 purple, bl & orge 9·50 6·00

216 Port-Couvreux

1996. Air.
360 **216** 27f.30 blue, green & brn 9·50 6·00

217 Amethyst

1997.
361 **217** 1f. mauve, grey & blue . . 40 20

218 Grey-backed Stormy Petrels

1997.
362 **218** 2f.70 grey, blue & green 1·00 70

219 Ships (½-size illustration)

1997. Refit of "Marion Dufresne" (Antarctic supply ship).
363 **219** 3f. multicoloured . . . . 1·00 70

220 Garcia

1997. 2nd Death Anniv of Rene Garcia (explorer).
364 **220** 3f. black, blue & brown 1·00 70

221 Turquet **222** Spiny Lobster

1997. 130th Birth Anniv of Jean Turquet.
365 **221** 4f. brown and black . . . 1·40 1·00

1997. Air.
366 **222** 5f.20 multicoloured . . . 1·90 1·25

223 Antarctic Terns, Bell Tower and Church **224** Service Emblem and Operation

1997. Church of Our Lady of the Birds, Crozet.
367 **223** 5f.20 brown, blue & red 1·90 1·25

1997. Forces Health Service.
368 **224** 8f. red, brown & purple 2·75 2·00

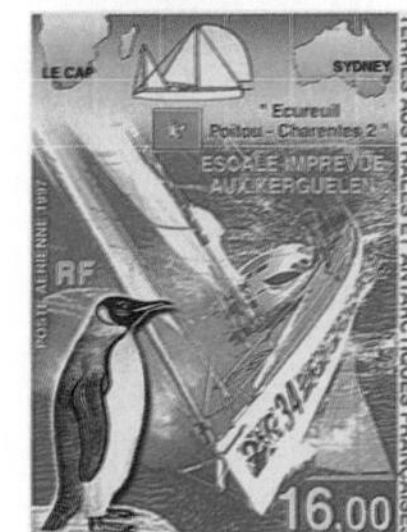

225 Map, "Ecureuil Poitou-Charantes 2" and King Penguin

1997. Air. Unscheduled Stop at Kerguelen by Contestant in BOC Challenge Yacht Race.
369 **225** 16f. multicoloured . . . . 6·00 3·50

226 Nunn at Hope Cottage, Point Charlotte

1997. Air. John Nunn (shipwreck survivor).
370 **226** 20f. red, purple & brown 6·50 4·00

227 Lighter, Nets, Antarctic Dragonfish and Crocodile Icefish

1997. Air. Icota Programme (fish research project).
371 **227** 24f. green, blue and red 8·00 5·50

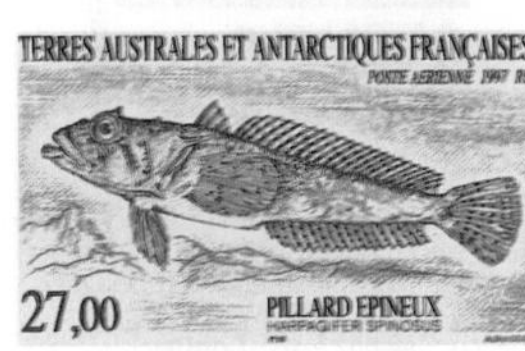

228 Spiny Plunderfish

1997. Air.
372 **228** 27f. black, purple & blue 9·00 7·00

229 "Poa kerguelensis" **231** Kerguelen-Tremarec

230 Snow Tractors, Greenland

1997.
373 **229** 29f.20 brown, grn & mve 10·00 7·50

1997. 50th Anniv of First French Polar Expedition. Multicoloured.
374 1f. Type **230** 35 35
375 1f. Port Martin and Marret Bases, Adelie Land 35 35
376 1f. Dumont d'Urville Base in 1956 and 1997 and Charcot Station 35 35
Nos. 374/6 were issued together, se-tenant, forming a composite design.

1997. Bicentenary of Disappearance of Admiral Yves Kerguelen-Tremarec (discoverer of Kerguelen Land). Each black, green and red.
377 3f. Type **231** . . . . 1·00 70
378 24f. Christmas Harbour (from "Atlas of Cook's Voyages") (37 × 38 mm) . . 8·00 5·50

232 Rock-crystal

1998.
379 **232** 1f. blue, violet & black . . 30 20

233 Launch approaching Trawlers

1998. Fisheries Control.
380 **233** 2f.60 blue, black & brn 95 60
381 – 2f.60 blue, black & red . . 95 60
DESIGN: No. 381, Inspectors measuring fish and checking records.

234 Grey-headed Albatrosses

1998.
382 **234** 2f.70 multicoloured . . . 90 70

235 Broad-billed Prion and Helicopter over Saint Paul Island

1998. Ecological Rehabilitation of Saint Paul Island (rat and rabbit eradication).
383 **235** 3f. blue, green & brown 95 70

236 Peau **237** Laclavere

1998. Etienne Peau (Antarctic researcher) Commemoration.
384 **236** 3f. blue, mauve & black 95 70

1998. 4th Death Anniv of Georges Laclavere (geographer and head of French National Antarctic Research Committee).
385 **237** 4f. brown, orange & blk 1·25 90

238 Preparation for Deep Boring and Map

1998. Air. Epica Dome C Programme.
386 **238** 5f.20 brown and mauve 1·75 1·40

239 Station Buildings

1998. Air. 1st Meteorological Radio Station, Port-aux-Francais.
387 **239** 8f. black, blue and red . . 2·75 2·75

240 "Argos" Satellite and King Penguins with Radio Transmitters

1998. Air. Penguin Research.
388 **240** 16f. multicoloured . . . . 5·50 3·75

241 "Ranunculus moseleyi"

1998.
389 **241** 24f. green, lt green & yell 7·50 5·50

242 Porbeagle Shark pursuing Fish

1998.
390 **242** 27f. grey, blue and green 8·50 6·00

243 "Le Cancalais" (schooner)

1998.
391 **243** 29f.20 sepia, blue & brn 10·00 7·00

244 Antarctic Base (½-size illustration)

1998. 40th Anniv of International Geophysical Year.
392 **244** 5f.20 blue, red and black 1·60 1·00

245 Epidote

1999.
393 **245** 1f. emerald, green & blk 30 20

246 Bearded Penguins

1999.
394 **246** 2f.70 indigo, blue & brn 80 60

247 King Penguins (½-size illustration)

1999. Crozet Penguin Colony.
395 **247** 3f. multicoloured 90 70

248 Sicaud

1999. Death Commemoration (1998) of Pierre Sicaud (scientist).
396 **248** 3f. green and black . . . 90 70

249 Martin

1999. 50th Death Anniv of Jacques-Andre Martin (scientist).
397 **249** 4f. ultramarine, blk & bl 1·25 90

250 Ray

1999.
398 **250** 5f.20 brown, blue & pur 1·60 1·25

251 "Floreal" (frigate)

1999.
399 **251** 5f.20 multicoloured . . . 1·60 1·25

252 Cats, Scientists and Map

1999. Cat Research Programme, Kerguelen Islands.
400 **252** 8f. green, blue and red . . 2·40 1·60

253 Amsterdam Island Albatrosses and Ornithologist

1999. Artificial Nests, Amsterdam Island.
401 **253** 16f. green, black and olive 4·75 3·50

254 "Festuca contracta"

1999.
402 **254** 24f. blue, green & dp grn 7·00 5·50

255 Geologist, Fishery Control Vessel and Map

1999. Geoleta Programme, Adelie Land.
403 **255** 29f.20 blue, black and red 9·00 6·50

256 Research Base, Amsterdam Island

1999. 50th Anniv of Research Bases on Kerguelen and Amsterdam Islands. Each red, blue and green.
404 3f. Type **256** . . . . . . 1·00 75
405 24f. Research base, Kerguelen 6·50 5·25

257 Loading Ship at La Reunion

1999. Tourism. Booklet Stamps. No value expressed. Multicoloured.
406 (5f.20) Type **257** . . . . . . 2·75 2·25
407 (5f.20) Diners on board the "Marion Dufresne" (Antarctic supply ship) . . 2·75 2·25
408 (5f.20) King penguin colony 2·75 2·25
409 (5f.20) Handstamping letters, Crozet (vert) . . . . 2·75 2·25
410 (5f.20) Research station, Port-aux-Francais, Kerguelen 2·75 2·25
411 (5f.20) Port Couvreux, Kerguelen . . . . 2·75 2·25
412 (5f.20) Unloading ships, Port-aux-Francais, Kerguelen 2·75 2·25
413 (5f.20) Port Jeanne d'Arc, Kerguelen . . . . 2·75 2·25
414 (5f.20) St. Paul Island . . . . 2·75 2·25
415 (5f.20) Remains of crayfish canning industry, St. Paul Island . . . . 2·75 2·25
416 (5f.20) Martin de Vivies base, Amsterdam Island . . . . 2·75 2·25
417 (5f.20) Unloading ships, Amsterdam Island . . . . 2·75 2·25

258 Madagascar 1946 5f. Stamp and Kerguelen Islands Handstamp

1999. "Philexfrance 99" International Stamp Exhibition, Paris. Sheet 148 × 81 mm containing T **258** and similar multicoloured designs.
MS418 5f.20 Type **258**; 5f.20 French Southern and Antarctic Territories 1961 25f. stamp and Crozet Islands handstamp; 5f.20 Madagascar 1946 10f. stamp and Amsterdam Island handstamp (39 × 51 mm); 5f.20 Madagascar 1948 100f. overprinted stamp and Adelie Land handstamp (39 × 51 mm) (sold at 25f.) . . 7·50 7·50

259 Mica

2000.
419 **259** 1f. black, green and blue 30 20

260 Pale-footed Shearwaters

2000.
420 **260** 2f.70 multicoloured . . . 55 40

261 Beauge

2000. 3rd Death Anniv of Andre Beauge (scientist).
421 **261** 3f. black, brn & dp brn 60 45

262 Penguins (Crozet Island)

2000. "Third Millennium on French Southern and Antarctic Territories". Sheet 138 × 190 mm containing T **262** and similar vert designs.
MS422 3f. Type **262**; 3f. Walruses (Kerguelen Island); 3f. Lobster (St. Paul and Amsterdam Islands); 3f. Exploration vehicle (Adelie Land) . . . . 2·50 2·50

263 Yves Joseph Kerguelen-Tremarec

264 Abby Jane Morrell

2000. Explorers. Multicoloured.
423 3f. Type **263** 60 45
424 3f. Dumont D'Urville 60 45
425 3f. Raymond Rallier du Baty 60 45
426 3f. E. Aubert de la Rue . . . 60 45
427 3f. Paul-Emile Victor 60 45

2000.
428 **264** 4f. black, yellow & brn 80 60

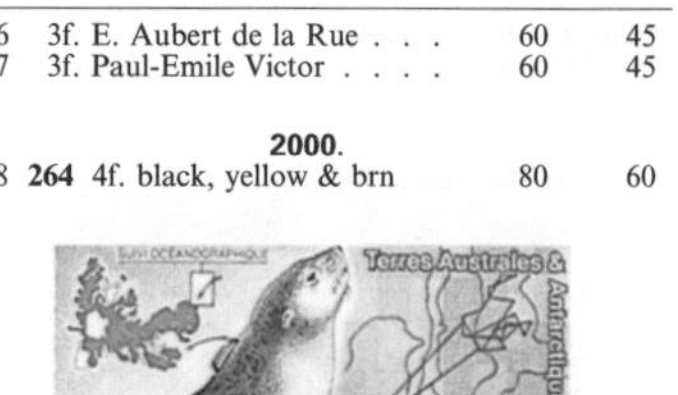

265 Seal and Maps

2000. Oceanographic Survey (seal tracking).
429 **265** 4f.40 multicoloured . . . 90 65

266 Hobbs (sledge dog)

267 Yellow-nosed Albatross

2000.
430 **266** 5f.20 black, blue & orge 1·00 75

2000. Demographic Database of Birds. Mult.
431 5f.20 Type **267** . . . . . . 1·00 75
432 8f. Wandering albatross and graph (Crozet Island) (50 × 28 mm) . . . . 1·60 1·25
433 16f. Emperor penguins and graph (Adélie Land) (50 × 28 mm) . . . . . . 3·25 2·25
Nos. 431/3 were issued together, se-tenant, forming a composite design.

268 Map of Antarctica and Computer Images (½-size illustration)

2000. Sleep Research.
434 **268** 8f. multicoloured . . . . 1·60 1·10

269 *La Perouse* (supply frigate)

2000.
435 **269** 16f. deep blue, blue & grn 3·25 2·25

270 Lantern Fishes

2000.
436 **270** 24f. black, blue & purple 4·75 3·50

271 Penguins

2000. Larose Bay Penguin Colony.
437 **271** 27f. multicoloured . . . . 5·50 3·75

272 Old and New Headquarters

2000. Relocation of Administrative Headquarters.
438 **272** 27f. multicoloured . . . . 5·50 3·75

273 Magnetite

2001.
439 **273** 1f. grey, green & turquoise 30 20

274 Common Diving Petrels

2001.
440 **274** 2f.70 blue, violet & black 55 40

275 Richert **276** Man pulling Sledge

2001. 9th Death Anniv of Xavier-Charles Richert.
441 **275** 3f. black, blue and indigo 60 45

2001. Armee de Terre's Expedition to Adelie Land.
442 **276** 3f. multicoloured 60 45

277 L'Arche des Kerguelen, Christmas Harbour

2001.
443 **277** 3f. black 60 45

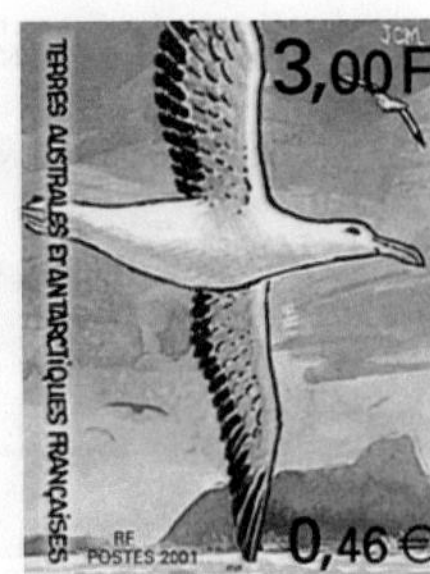

278 Albatrosses (Kerguelen Island)

2001. Wildlife on French Southern and Antarctic Territories. Sheet 138 × 190 mm containing T **278** and similar multicoloured designs.
MS444 3f. Type **278**; 3f. Emperor penguins (Adelie Land) (horiz); 3f. Eared seals (St. Paul and Amsterdam Islands) (horiz); 3f. Killer whale (Crozet Island) . . 2·50 2·50

279 Jean Coulomb

2001.
445 **279** 4f. multicoloured 80 60

280 *Carmen* (brigantine)

2001. Ships. Sheet 143 × 102 mm containing T **280** and similar horiz designs.
MS446 5f.20 azure, blue and brown (Type **280**); 5f.20 chestnut, ochre and blue (*Austral* (supply ship)); 5f.20 ochre, chestnut and blue (*Ramuntcho* (ketch)); 5f.20 azure, blue and brown (*Sapmer 1* (supply ship)) . . . . 4·00 4·00

281 Memorial Plaque

2001. 127th Anniv of French Astronomers' Visit to St. Paul Island to Observe Transit of Venus across the Sun.
447 **281** 8f. brown and black . . . 1·60 1·10

282 *La Fayette* (frigate)

2001.
448 **282** 16f. multicoloured . . . . 3·25 2·25

283 Squid

2001.
449 **283** 24f. multicoloured . . . . 4·75 3·50

284 "Mir", Earth and Computer

2001. Amateur Radio Link between "Mir" Space Station and Crozet Island.
450 **284** 27f. multicoloured . . . . 5·50 3·75

285 *Bryum laevigatum*

2001.
451 **285** 29f.20 multicoloured . . . 5·75 4·00

286 Map of Antarctica and Compass

2001. 40th Anniv of Antarctic Treaty.
452 **286** 5f.20 blue and indigo . . 1·10 90

287 Map of Antarctica and Fish

2001. 20th Anniv of Commission for the Conservation of Antarctic Marine Living Resources.
453 **287** 5f.20 multicoloured . . . 1·10 90

288 Ship in Pack Ice

2001. Adelie Land. No value expressed. Multicoloured.

454	(5f.20) Type **288**	1·10	90
455	(5f.20) Statue of Dumont d'Urville (explorer), Dumont d'Urville Base . .	1·10	90
456	(5f.20) Adelie penguin colony	1·10	90
457	(5f.20) Astrolabe glacier . . .	1·10	90
458	(5f.20) Geology Point Archipelago	1·10	90
459	(5f.20) Releasing weather balloon	1·10	90
460	(5f.20) Convoy of equipment	1·10	90
461	(5f.20) Helicopter delivering supplies	1·10	90
462	(5f.20) Emperor penguins . .	1·10	90
463	(5f.20) Radio communications centre	1·10	90
464	(5f.20) Statue of Paul Emile Victor (explorer)	1·10	90
465	(5f.20) Cap Prud'homme . .	1·10	90
466	(5f.20) *Astrolabe* (fishery control vessel) and penguins	1·10	90
467	(5f.20) Men leaving by helicopter	1·10	90

New Currency. 100 cents = 1 euro

2002. As T **154** but with face values expressed in euros.

468	1c. black	10	10
469	2c. blue	10	10
470	5c. red	10	10
471	10c. green	15	10
472	20c. orange	30	20

289 Nepheline **290** Albatross

2002.
480 **289** 15c. multicoloured 20 15

2002.
481 **290** 41c. black, yellow and blue 55 45

291 *Marion Dufresne* (Antarctic supply ship)

2002.
482 **291** 46c. blue, red and black 65 50

292 Shed and Pylon

2002. Cable Cars on Crozet Island (1963–1983).
483 **292** 46c. multicoloured 65 50

293 Albatrosses and Rock (Kerguelen Islands)

2002. "The French Southern Antarctic Olympic Games". Sheet 139 × 191 mm containing T **293** and similar multicoloured designs.
MS484 46c. Type **293**; 46c. Lobsters diving (St. Paul and Amsterdam Islands); 46c. Emperor penguins sliding (Adelie Land) (vert); 46c. Killer whales leaping (Crozet Island) (vert) . . . . 1·90 1·90

294 Geological Diagram

2002. 11th Anniv (2001) of Cartoker Geological Survey of Kerguelen Islands. Multicoloured.
485 46c. Type **294** 65 50
486 €3.66 Map of Kerguelen Islands . . . . 5·00 4·00

295 Dubois and Scientific Equipment

2002. 2nd Death Anniv of Jacques Dubois (Antarctic researcher).
487 **295** 61c. multicoloured 85 70

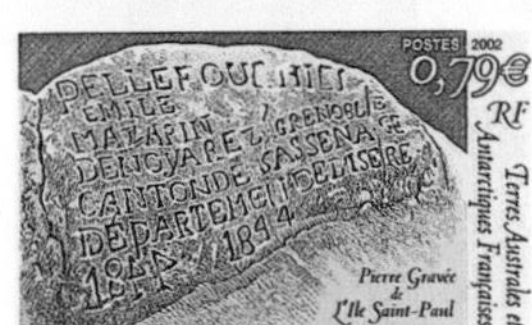

296 Engraved Rock, St. Paul Island

2002.
488 **296** 79c. sepia, blue and green 1·10 85

297 Emperor Penguin and Chicks

2002. Antarctic Animals and their Young. Sheet 104 × 143 mm, containing T **297** and similar vert designs. Multicoloured.
MS489 79c. Type **297**; 79c. Grey seal and pup; 79c. Abatross and chick; 79c. Elephant seal and pups . . 4·50 4·50

298 Kerguelen Cabbage

2002.
490 **298** €1.22 multicoloured . . 1·70 1·40

299 Ship

2002. Centenary of Visit of *Guass* (survey barquentine) to Kerguelen Islands.
491 **299** €2.44 multicoloured . . 3·50 3·00

300 Crab

2002.
492 **300** €3.66 multicoloured . . 5·00 4·00

301 Diatoms and Pack Ice

2002. Diatoms (microscopic algae) of the Antarctic Pack Ice.
493 **301** €4.12 multicoloured . . 5·75 5·25

302 Door and Facade

2002. 181st Anniv of French Geographical Society.
494 **302** €4.45 multicoloured . . 6·25 5·00

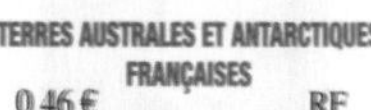

303 Penguins incubating "€"

2002. Introduction of the Euro.
495 **303** 46c. black and blue . . . 65 50

304 Apatite

2003.
496 **304** 15c. mauve, blue and black 20 15

305 Factory, St. Paul Island

2003.
497 **305** 41c. black, green and blue 55 45

306 Emperor Penguins

2003.
498 **306** 46c. multicoloured 60 50

307 Glaciers

2003. Luc Marie Bayle (artist) Commemoration.
499 **307** 46c. multicoloured 60 50

308 Louis XV and Penguins wearing Neckties on Crozet Island

2003. 18th-century French Personalities transposed to Southern Antarctic Territories. Sheet 139 × 191 mm containing T **308** and similar vert designs. Multicoloured.
MS500 Type **308**; 46c. "Triumph of Venus" on St. Paul and Amsterdam Islands; 46c. Dumont and Adele D'urville on Adelie Land; 46c. Le Chavalier Yves de Kerguelen on Kerguelen Island 2·00 2·00

309 Map, Satellite and Hydrophone

2003. Research Station, Crozet Island.
501 **309** 61c. green and blue . . . 80 65

310 Damaged and Restored Buildings

2003. Restoration of Port Jeanne d'Arc.
502 **310** 79c. multicoloured . . . . 1·00 80

311 Man wearing Furs, 1898 **313** *Bougainville* (research ship)

312 Phylica (tree), Amsterdam Island

2003. Polar Clothing. Multicoloured.
503 79c. Type **311** . . . . 1·00 80
504 79c. Man wearing brown hat, 1912 . . . . 1·00 80
505 79c. Penguins and man wearing yellow parka, 2002 1·00 80
506 79c. Dogs and man wearing blue jacket, 1980 . . . . . 1·00 80
507 79c. Snowmobiles and man wearing red all-in-one suit, 1996 . . . . 1·00 80

2003.
508 **312** €1.22 multicoloured . . 1·60 1·30

2003.
509 **313** €2.44 multicoloured . . 3·25 2·75

314 Penguin Island

2003.
510 **314** €3.66 black . . . . . . 4·75 3·75

315 Cabot

2003.
511 **315** €3.66 multicoloured . . 4·75 3·75

316 Super Dual Auroral Radar Network (Super DARN)

2003.
512 **316** €4.12 multicoloured . . 5·50 4·25

317 Jean-Baptiste Charcot (scientist and expedition leader)

2003. Centenary of Expedition to Antarctic Territories.
513 **317** 79c. brown, blue and violet . . . . 1·00 80
514 – €1.22 brown, blue and pink (48 × 27 mm) . . . 1·80 1·40
515 – €2.44 violet, blue and orange (48 × 27 mm) . . 3·25 2·50
DESIGNS: 79c. Type **317**; €1.22, *Le Francais* at anchor; €2.44, *Le Francais* in port.

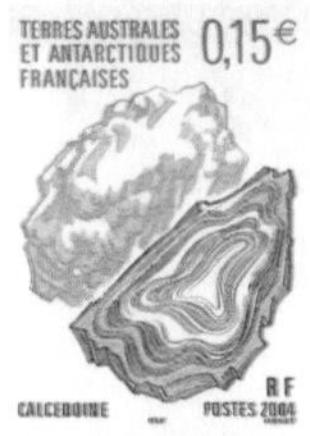

318 Calcedone **319** Mario Marret

2004.
516 **318** 15c. purple, ochre and blue 20 15

2004. Mario Marret (Antarctic explorer and writer) Commemoration.
517 **319** 41c. blue, red and green 55 45

320 Base Camp Buildings (½-size illustration)

2004. 40th Anniv of Alfred-Faure Base, Crozet Island.
518 **320** 50c. multicoloured 65 50

321 Robert Genty

2004. Colonel Robert Genty (pilot) Commemoration.
519 **321** 50c. black, red and green 65 50

322 Whaling Museum, Jeanne d'Arc Port, Kerguelen Island

2004. Fantasy Tourist Attractions in Southern Antarctic Territories. Sheet 139 × 191 mm containing T **322** and similar horiz designs. Multicoloured.
MS520 50c. × 4, Type **322**; Showgirls and sea lions on St. Paul and Amsterdam Islands; Couple with ice creams (Ice palace on Adelie Land); Girl sunbathing amongst penguins (Hotel Marina on Crozet Island) . . . . 2·75 2·75

323 Southern Right-whale Dolphin

2004.
521 **323** 75c. multicoloured . . . . 1·00 80

324 De Havilland Twin Otter Airplane and Map of Antarctica

2004.
522 **324** 90c. multicoloured . . . . 1·20 1·00

325 Amsterdam Island Postal Buildings

2004. Antarctic Postal Buildings. Sheet 162 × 114 mm containing T **325** and similar horiz designs. Multicoloured.
MS523 90c. × 4, Type **325**; Crozet Island; Kerguelen Island; Adelie Island . . . . 4·75 3·25

326 Iceberg

2004.
524 **326** €1.30 blue and lilac . . . 1·75 1·40

327 Cairn and Cross

2004. *Volage* (British sail training ship) Sailor's Grave.
525 **327** €2.50 blue, indigo and red . . . . 3·25 2·50

328 Krill (*Euphausia superba*)

2004.
526 **328** €4 blue, orange and brown . . . . 5·25 4·25

329 *Dives*

2004.
527 **329** €4.50 multicoloured . . 6·00 4·75

330 Scientists taking Readings from Sea Bed

2004. Hydrographic Surveys in Adelie Land. Sheet 107 × 81 mm.
MS528 **330** €4.90 multicoloured 6·50 6·50

331 Penguin holding Sea-lion Mask

2004.
529 **331** €4.50 multicoloured . . 6·00 4·75

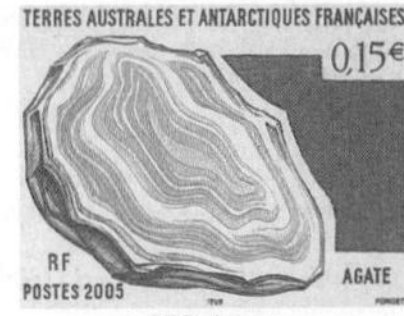

332 Agate

2005.
530 **332** 15c. green, blue and black 20 15

333 Albert Bauer **334** Roger Barberot

2005. Albert Bauer (explorer) Commemoration.
531 **333** 45c. brown and blue . . . 60 50

2005. 90th Birth Anniv of Roger Barberot (administrator).
532 **334** 50c. black, brown and blue 70 55

335 *Cap Horn*

2005.
533 **335** 50c. multicoloured 70 55

336 Cauldron

2005.
534 **336** 50c. multicoloured 70 55

337 MacGillivray's Prion (Prion de MacGillivray)

2005.
535 **337** 75c. black, yellow and blue . . . . 1·00 80

338 Studer Valley

2005.
536 **338** 90c. multicoloured . . . . 1·20 1·00

339 "Peigne de Neriedes"

2005.
537 **339** €2.50 multicoloured . . 3·25 2·60

340 *Harpovoluta charcoti*

2005.
538 **340** €4 multicoloured . . . . 5·50 4·50

341 Murray's Skate ("Raie de Murray")

2005.
539 **341** €4.50 multicoloured . . 6·00 4·75

342 Elephant Seal and Oceanographic Chart (½-size illustration)

2005.
540 **342** €4.90 multicoloured . . 6·50 5·25

343 Concordia, French—Italian Base (½-size illustration)

2005.
541 **343** 50c. multicoloured 70 55

344 Jean-Baptiste Charcot and Penguins

2005. Centenary of the Return of *Le Francais* (exploration ship).
542 **344** €4.50 multicoloured . . 6·00 4·75

345 Paul-Emile Victor

2005. 10th Death Anniv of Paul-Emile Victor (polar explorer and writer).
543 **345** 50c. multicoloured 70 55

FRENCH SUDAN Pt. 6

A territory in central Africa. In 1899 parts of the colony were detached and added to neighbouring coastal colonies with the remainder becoming Senegambia and Niger (subsequently renamed Upper Senegal and Niger). In 1920 Niger became a separate colony and Upper Senegal reverted to the name of French Sudan.

From 1944 to 1959 French Sudan used the stamps of French West Africa. In 1959 French Sudan combined with Senegal to form the Mali Federation.

100 centimes = 1 franc.

1894. Stamps of French Colonies, "Commerce" type, surch **SOUDAN Fais** and value.
1 J 0.15 on 75c. red £3000 £1500
2 0.25 on 1f. olive £3250 £1100

1894. "Tablet" key-type inscr "SOUDAN FRANCAIS" in red (1, 5, 15, 25, 50 (No. 21), 75c., 1f.) or blue (others).
3 D 1c. black on blue . . . . . 2·00 3·75
4 2c. brown on buff . . . . . 2·00 1·50
5 4c. brown on grey . . . . . 3·00 6·00
6 5c. green on light green . . 3·00 4·00
7 10c. black on lilac . . . . . 13·00 6·50
18 10c. red . . . . 5·50 6·25
8 15c. blue . . . . 3·25 4·00
19 15c. grey . . . . 7·75 9·75
9 20c. red on green . . . . . 16·00 22·00
10 25c. black on pink . . . . . 20·00 21·00
20 25c. blue . . . . 7·00 8·25
11 30c. brown on drab . . . . 42·00 40·00
12 40c. red on yellow . . . . . 28·00 28·00
13 50c. red on pink . . . . . . 45·00 45·00
21 50c. brown on blue . . . . 11·50 12·00
14 75c. brown on yellow . . . 20·00 20·00
15 1f. green . . . . 4·50 5·50

1921. Stamps of Upper Senegal and Niger optd **SOUDAN FRANCAIS**.
85 **7** 1c. violet and purple . . . . 10 2·75
86 2c. purple and grey . . . . 10 2·50
87 4c. blue and black . . . . . 15 2·50
88 5c. chocolate and brown . . 25 2·50
89 10c. green and light green 1·10 2·25
121 10c. blue and mauve . . . . 50 1·10
90 15c. orange and purple . . . 1·50 2·50
122 15c. green and light green 30 2·25
123 15c. mauve and brown . . . 1·50 3·25
91 20c. black and purple . . . 75 1·40
92 25c. green and black . . . . 2·00 75
93 30c. carmine and red . . . 2·25 2·75
124 30c. black and green . . . . 1·75 2·00
125 30c. green and olive . . . . 1·40 4·00
94 35c. violet and red . . . . 85 2·50
95 40c. red and grey . . . . . 2·25 2·50
96 45c. brown and blue . . . . 2·50 2·75
97 50c. blue and ultramarine 1·25 1·90
126 50c. blue and orange . . . 2·00 65
127 60c. violet on pink . . . . 2·00 3·00
128 65c. blue and brown . . . . 3·50 3·50
98 75c. brown and yellow . . . 2·50 2·75
129 90c. carmine and red . . . 6·50 7·75
99 1f. purple and brown . . . 2·75 2·75
130 1f.10 mauve and blue . . . 3·25 3·75
131 1f.50 blue . . . . 6·25 7·50
100 2f. blue and green . . . . . 3·25 3·50
132 3f. mauve on pink . . . . . 10·00 12·00
101 5f. black and violet . . . . 6·50 6·50

1922. Surch in figures and bars.
110 **7** 25c. on 45c. brown & blue 2·00 3·25
111 60 on 75c. violet on pink . . 1·75 2·25
112 65 on 75c. brown & yellow 2·25 3·50
113 85 on 2f. blue and green . . 2·25 3·75
114 85 on 5f. black and violet 2·00 4·00
115 90c. on 75c. red & carmine 2·50 4·00
116 1f.25 on 1f. lt bl & blue . . 2·25 3·50
117 1f.50 on 1f. ultram & bl . . 2·50 1·60
118 3f. on 5f. buff and pink . . 5·00 4·50
119 10f. on 5f. green and red . . 18·00 23·00
120 20f. on 5f. red and violet . . 20·00 30·00

14 Sudanese Woman marketing **15** Djenne Gateway

1931.
135 **14** 1c. black and red . . . . 20 1·75
136 2c. red and blue . . . . . 10 2·25
137 3c. black and red . . . . 30 2·50
138 4c. red and lilac . . . . . 1·25 2·25
139 5c. green and blue . . . . 35 1·25
140 10c. red and green . . . . 20 1·25
141 15c. violet and black . . . 55 75
142 20c. blue and brown . . . 25 1·25
143 25c. pink and mauve . . . 40 45
144 **15** 30c. light green and green 35 1·10
145 30c. red and blue . . . . 70 3·00
146 35c. green and olive . . . 80 2·25
147 40c. red and green . . . . 15 1·75
148 45c. red and blue . . . . 2·00 1·90
149 45c. green and olive . . . 75 2·75
150 50c. black and red 85 15

151 55c. red and blue . . . . 95 2·75
152 60c. brown and blue . . . 95 2·50
153 65c. black and violet . . . 1·00 1·75
154 70c. red and blue . . . . 1·25 3·00
155 75c. brown and blue . . . 2·25 2·50
156 80c. brown and red . . . . 50 2·00
157 90c. orange and red . . . 75 2·50
158 90c. black and violet . . . 1·40 3·25
159 1f. green and blue . . . . 8·00 2·25
160 1f. red . . . . 4·25 1·75
161 1f. brown and red . . . . 70 2·50
162 – 1f.25 mauve and violet . . 2·00 2·75
163 – 1f.25 red and scarlet . . . 1·25 2·25
164 – 1f.40 black and violet . . . 1·40 2·75
165 – 1f.50 blue and indigo . . . 2·00 2·75
166 – 1f.60 blue and brown . . . 1·50 2·75
167 – 1f.70 blue and brown . . . 2·50 1·90
168 – 1f.75 blue . . . . 1·90 3·25
169 – 2f. green and brown . . . 1·40 1·25
170 – 2f.25 ultramarine & blue 75 2·50
171 – 2f.50 brown . . . . . . 2·75 3·00
172 – 3f. brown and green . . . 75 35
173 – 5f. black and red . . . . 1·10 2·00
174 – 10f. green and blue . . . . 2·00 3·75
175 – 20f. brown and mauve . . 4·00 4·50
DESIGN: 1f.25 to 20f. Niger boatman.

1931. "Colonial Exhibition" key-types inscr "SOUDAN FRANCAIS".
186 E 40c. green and black . . . 3·25 4·00
187 F 50c. mauve and black . . . 3·50 4·00
188 G 90c. red and black . . . 3·00 3·25
189 H 1f.50 blue and black . . . 2·50 3·75

1937. International Exhibition, Paris. As T **58a** of Guadeloupe.
190 20c. violet . . . . 40 2·00
191 30c. green . . . . 1·60 3·25
192 40c. red . . . . 80 2·50
193 50c. brown and agate . . . . 40 2·75
194 90c. red . . . . 35 1·75
195 1f.50 blue . . . . 45 2·75

1938. International Anti-cancer Fund. As T **58b** of Guadeloupe.
197 1f.75+50c. blue . . . . . . 3·00 11·00

21 Rene Caillie

1939. Caillie.
198 **21** 90c. orange . . . . 50 2·50
199 2f. violet . . . . 75 1·25
200 2f.25 blue . . . . 50 2·75

1939. New York World's Fair. As T **58c** of Guadeloupe.
201 1f.25 red . . . . 1·25 2·75
202 2f.25 blue . . . . 2·25 3·25

1939. 150th Anniv of French Revolution. As T **58d** of Guadeloupe.
203 45c.+25c. green and black . . 4·50 8·25
204 70c.+30c. brown and black 8·00 12·00
205 90c.+35c. orange and black 5·00 12·00
206 1f.25+1f. red and black . . . 4·25 10·50
207 2f.25+2f. blue and black . . 4·25 12·00

1940. Air. As T **6a** of French Guinea.
208 1f.90 blue . . . . 1·25 3·00
209 2f.90 red . . . . 75 3·00
210 4f.50 green . . . . 1·25 2·25
211 4f.90 olive . . . . 1·25 2·25
212 6f.90 orange . . . . 1·25 2·50

1941. National Defence Fund. Surch **SECOURS NATIONAL** and value.
213 +1f. on 50c. (No. 150) . . . 4·25 5·00
214 +2f. on 80c. (No. 156) . . . 7·00 9·50
215 +2f. on 1f.50 (No. 165) . . . 8·00 9·25
216 +3f. on 2f. (No. 169) . . . . 8·25 9·50

1941. Marshal Petain Issue. As T **16a** of Ivory Coast.
217 1f. green . . . . 40 3·00
218 2f.50 blue . . . . 55 2·50
DESIGNS—VERT: Gate at Djenne and Marshal Petain.

1942. Air. Colonial Child Welfare Fund. As T **8** of French Guinea.
219 1f.50+3f.50 green . . . . . 50 2·50
220 2f.+6f. brown . . . . 15 3·50
221 3f.+9f. red . . . . 15 3·50

1942. Air. Imperial Fortnight. As T **9a** of French Guinea.
222 1f.20+1f.80 blue and red . . 40 3·50

27 Airplane over Camel Caravan

1942. Air.
223 **27** 50f. blue and green . . . . 90 1·40

POSTAGE DUE STAMPS

1921. Postage Due stamps of Upper Senegal and Niger optd **SOUDAN FRANCAIS**.
D102 M 5c. green . . . . 20 2·75
D103 10c. red . . . . 20 1·75
D104 15c. grey . . . . 75 2·50
D105 20c. brown . . . . 1·10 2·25
D106 30c. blue . . . . 95 3·25
D107 50c. black . . . . 1·90 3·50
D108 60c. orange . . . . 1·75 3·50
D109 1f. violet . . . . 1·60 4·00

1927. Postage Due stamps of Upper Senegal and Niger surch **SOUDAN FRANCAIS** and value.
D133 M "2F." on 1f. mauve . . . 2·75 6·00
D134 "3F." on 1f. brown . . . 2·75 7·25

1931. "Figure" key-type inscr "SOUDAN FRANCAIS".
D176 M 5c. green . . . . 10 2·50
D177 10c. red . . . . 10 1·75
D178 15c. grey . . . . 10 2·75
D179 20c. brown . . . . 10 2·75
D180 30c. blue . . . . 15 2·25
D181 50c. black . . . . 40 3·00
D182 60c. orange . . . . 60 2·75
D183 1f. violet 60 90
D184 2f. mauve . . . . 1·75 2·25
D185 3f. brown . . . . 1·75 3·25

FRENCH TERRITORY OF THE AFARS AND THE ISSAS Pt. 6

Formerly French Somali Coast. Became independent in 1977 as Djibouti Republic.

100 centimes = 1 franc.

66 Grey-headed Kingfisher

1967. Fauna.
504 **66** 10f. mult (postage) . . . . 3·00 2·10
505 – 15f. multicoloured . . . . 3·75 3·00
506 – 50f. purple, brown & grn 10·00 7·50
507 – 55f. blue, violet and grey 12·50 11·50
508 – 60f. orange, emer & grn . . 22·00 19·00
509 – 200f. sepia, bistre & bl (air) 32·00 9·50
DESIGNS—HORIZ: 15f. Oystercatcher; 50f. Common greenshank; 55f. Abyssinian roller. VERT: (22 × 36 mm); 60f. Unstriped ground squirrel. (27 × 48 mm): 200f. Tawny eagles.

67 Footballers

1967. Sports.
510 **67** 25f. brn, grn & bl (postage) 2·50 2·25
511 – 30f. brown, blue & purple 4·25 3·75
512 – 48f. pur, bl & bistre (air) 4·25 2·75
513 – 85f. brown, blue & bistre 4·00 8·00
DESIGNS—HORIZ: 30f. Basketball. VERT: (27 × 48 mm) 48f. Parachute-jumping; 85f. Aquatic sports.

1968. 20th Anniv of W.H.O. As T **34** of French Polynesia.
514 15f. multicoloured . . . . . 2·25 2·25

68 Damerdjog Fort

1968. Administrative Outposts.
515 **68** 20f. blue, brown & green 1·75 1·90
516 – 25f. blue, green & brown 1·75 1·90
517 – 30f. blue, bistre & orange 2·00 2·25
518 – 40f. blue, brown & green 3·25 2·75
DESIGNS—FORTS: 25f. Ali Adde; 30f. Dorra; 40f. Assamo.

1968. Human Rights Year. As T **36** of French Polynesia.
519 10f. red, violet and yellow . . 2·25 2·25
520 70f. purple, green & orange 3·00 3·00

69 Broadcasting Station

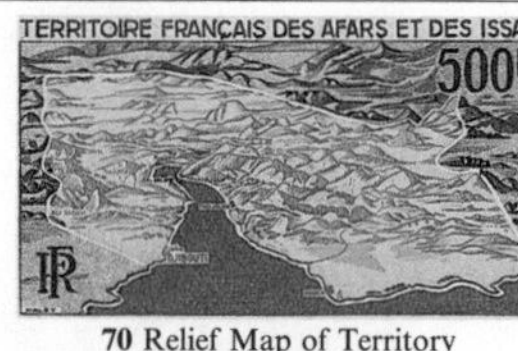

70 Relief Map of Territory

1968. Buildings and Landmarks.
521 **69** 1f. bl, turq & red (postage) 1·25 1·10
522 – 2f. blue, green & lt blue . . 1·25 1·10
523 – 5f. brown, green & blue . . 1·50 1·25
524 – 8f. brown, blue & green . . 1·50 1·40
525 – 15f. brown, green & blue 4·00 2·50
526 – 40f. grey, brown & turq . . 3·25 2·50
527 – 60f. multicoloured . . . . 3·25 2·75
528 – 70f. brown, green & grey 4·50 3·50
529 – 85f. green, blue & brn . . 6·75 4·50
530 – 85f. grey, blue & green . . 5·50 5·00
531 – 100f. brown, grn & bl (air) 4·25 2·50
532 – 200f. blue, brown & purple 8·25 4·00
533 **70** 500f. orange, brown & bl 32·00 14·50
DESIGNS—As T **69**: HORIZ: 2f. Courts of Justice; 5f. Chamber of Deputies; 8f. Great Mosque; 40f. Post Office, Djibouti; 70f. Governor's Residence, Obock; 85f. (No. 529) Port Administration Building, Djibouti; 85f. (No. 530) Airport. VERT: 15f. Free French Forces' Monument. As T **70**: HORIZ: 60f. French High Commission, Djibouti. VERT: 100f. Djibouti Cathedral; 200f. Sayed Hassan Mosque.

1969. Air. 1st Flight of Concorde. As T **39** of French Polynesia.
534 100f. red and drab . . . . . 30·00 18·00

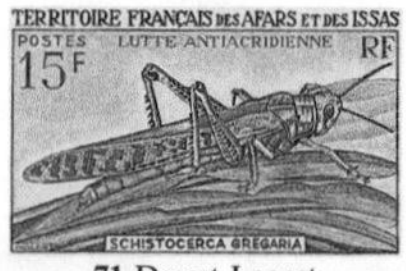

71 Desert Locust

1969. Anti-Locust Campaign.
535 **71** 15f. brown, slate & green 3·25 2·25
536 – 50f. brn, green & blue . . 3·50 2·00
537 – 55f. brown, blue & lake . . 3·75 2·75
DESIGNS: 50f. Sud Aviation Alouette II helicopter spraying crops; 55f. Piper Super Cub spraying crops.

1969. 50th Anniv of International Labour Organization. As T **44** of French Polynesia.
538 30f. mauve, slate and red . . 2·75 2·00

73 Afar Dagger 74 Ionospheric Station, Arta

1970.
543 **73** 10f. brown, grn & myrtle 1·75 1·25
544 15f. brown, green & blue 1·90 1·40
545 20f. brown, green & red . . 2·25 1·75
546 25f. brown, green & violet 2·50 1·60

1970. Air. Opening of Ionospheric Station, Arta.
547 **74** 70f. red, green and blue . . 5·25 4·00

1970. New U.P.U. Headquarters Building. As T **47** of French Polynesia.
548 25f. brown, green & bistre . . 2·50 2·25

75 Clay-pigeon Shooting

1970. Sports.
549 **75** 30f. brown, blue & green 3·00 2·00
550 – 48f. brown, purple & blue 3·25 2·50
551 – 50f. red, violet and blue . . 3·50 1·75
552 – 55f. brown, bistre & blue 3·25 2·75
553 – 60f. black, brown & green 5·00 3·75
DESIGNS—HORIZ: 48f. Speedboat racing; 50f. Show jumping; 60f. Pony-trekking. VERT: 55f. Yachting.

76 "Fish" Sword-guard

1970. Air "Expo 70" World Fair, Osaka, Japan.
554 **76** 100f. vio, bl & grn on gold 11·50 7·50
555 – 200f. vio, grn & red on gold . . . . 14·50 9·00
DESIGN: 200f. "Horse" sword-guard.

77 "Goubet"

1970. Inauguration of Car Ferry, Tajurah.
556 **77** 48f. brown, blue & green 3·25 2·75

78 Dolerite Basalt

1971. Geology. Multicoloured.
557 10f. Type **78** . . . . 1·75 1·60
558 15f. Olivine basalt . . . . . 2·00 2·50
559 25f. Volcanic geode . . . . . 3·50 2·00
560 40f. Diabase and chrysolite 4·00 2·75

79 Manta Rays

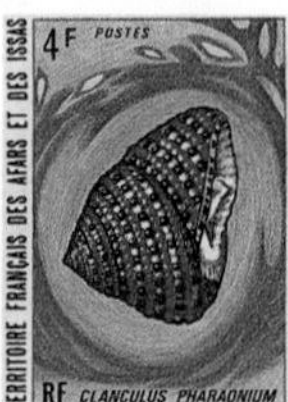

81 Mantle Clanculus

80 Aerial View of Port

1971. Marine Fauna. Multicoloured. (a) Postage. As T **79**.
561 4f. Type **79** . . . . 2·25 1·25
562 5f. Dolphin (fish) . . . . . . 2·25 1·75
563 9f. Small-toothed sawfish . . 2·75 2·00

(b) Air. Size 46 × 27 mm (30f.) or 48 × 27 mm (others).
564 30f. Queen parrotfish . . . . 4·25 3·50
565 40f. Long-armed octopus . . 2·50 2·50
566 60f. Dugong . . . . 5·00 3·25

1971. De Gaulle Commemoration. As Nos. 1937 and 1940 of France.
567 60f. black and blue . . . . . 4·75 3·50
568 85f. black and blue . . . . . 6·75 4·25

1971. Air. New Harbour, Djibouti.
569 **80** 100f. multicoloured . . . . 6·75 4·25

1972. Sea Shells. Multicoloured.
570 4f. Type **81** . . . . 1·60 1·10
571 9f. Panther cowrie . . . . . 1·75 1·75
572 20f. Bull-mouth helmet . . . 3·25 2·25
573 50f. Melon shell . . . . . . 4·25 2·75

82 Lichtenstein's Sandgrouse

1972. Air. Birds. Multicoloured.

574 30f. Type **82** . . . . 1·75 2·00
575 49f. Hoopoe . . . . 3·25 2·00
576 66f. Great snipe . . . . 6·00 3·50
577 500f. Pale-bellied francolin . . 33·00 12·00

83 Swimming

1972. Air. Olympic Games, Munich.

578 – 5f. brown, green & violet 1·50 1·40
579 – 10f. brown, green & red . . 1·50 1·40
580 **83** 55f. brown, blue & green 3·00 1·75
581 – 60f. violet, red and green 3·50 2·25

DESIGNS—VERT: 5f. Running; 10f. Basketball. HORIZ: 60f. Olympic flame, rings and ancient frieze.

84 Pasteur and Equipment

1972. Air. "Famous Medical Scientists".

582 **84** 20f. brown, green & red . . 2·50 1·75
583 – 100f. brown, green & red 5·25 4·00

DESIGN: 100f. Calmette and Guerin (B.C.G. pioneers).

85 Mosque, Map and Transport

1973. Air. Visit of President Pompidou. Mult.

584 30f. Type **85** . . . . 8·00 4·75
585 200f. Mosque and street scene, Djibouti (vert) . . . 14·50 11·50

86 Gemsbok

1973. Air. Wild Animals. Multicoloured.

587 30f. Type **86** . . . . 3·00 2·50
588 50f. Salt's dik-dik . . . . . 4·50 2·75
590 66f. Caracal . . . . 5·25 3·75

See also Nos. 603/5, 641/3, 659/60 and 662/4.

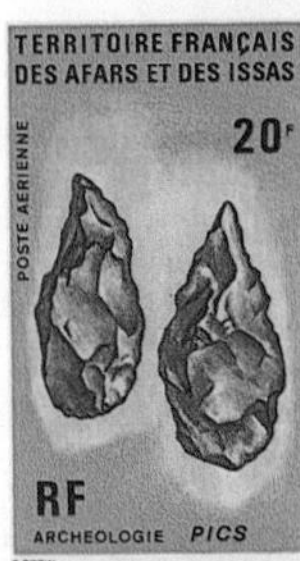

87 Flint Pick-heads

89 Nicolas Copernicus (500th birth anniv)

88 Shepherd watering Sheep

1973. Air. Archaeological Discoveries. Mult.

592 20f. Type **87** . . . . 2·75 2·25
593 40f. Arrow-heads and blade (horiz) . . . . 3·00 2·50
594 49f. Biface flint tool . . . . 5·25 3·25
595 60f. Flint axe-head and scraper (horiz) . . . . . . 4·00 3·25

1973. Pastoral Economy. Multicoloured.

596 9f. Type **88** . . . . 1·75 1·75
597 10f. Camel herd . . . . . . 1·75 1·75

1973. Air. Celebrities' Anniversaries.

598 **89** 8f. black, brown & purple 1·75 1·50
599 – 9f. purple, orange & brn 1·75 1·25
600 – 10f. purple, brown & red 1·75 1·60
615 – 10f. maroon, blue & pur 1·75 1·10
601 – 49f. purple, grn & dp grn 4·00 2·75
658 – 50f. brown, blue & green 3·25 2·00
611 – 55f. indigo, brown & blue 3·00 2·75
602 – 85f. dp blue, blue & violet 5·50 3·50
607 – 100f. purple, blue & green 5·00 2·50
657 – 150f. turq, blue & brn . . 5·75 2·75
656 – 250f. brn, lt brn & grn . . 8·75 3·75

DESIGNS: 9f. Wilhelm Rontgen (X-ray pioneer) (50th death anniv); 10f. (600) Edward Jenner (smallpox vaccination pioneer) (150th death anniv); 10f. (615) Marie Curie (physicist) (40th death anniv); 49f. Robert Koch (bacteriologist) (130th birth anniv); 50f. Clement Ader (aviation pioneer) (50th death anniv); 55f. Guglielmo Marconi (radio pioneer) (birth centenary); 85f. Moliere (playwright) (300th death anniv); 100f. Henri Farman (aviation pioneer) (birth centenary); 150f. Ampere (physicist) (birth bicentenary); 250f. Michelangelo (500th birth anniv).

1973. Air. Wild Animals (2nd series). As Type **86**. Multicoloured.

603 20f. Olive baboon (vert) . . . 2·25 1·90
604 50f. Large-spotted genet . . . 3·50 2·50
605 66f. Abyssinian hare (vert) 4·75 3·25

90 Afar Dagger

1974.

606 **90** 30f. purple and green . . . 2·50 1·75

91 Greater Flamingos

1974. Lake Abbe. Multicoloured.

608 5f. Type **91** . . . . 1·60 30
609 15f. Two greater flamingos 1·50 1·00
610 50f. Greater flamingos in flight . . . . 2·50 1·75

92 Underwater Hunting

1974. Air. 3rd Underwater Hunting Trophy.

612 **92** 200f. blue, green & red . . 10·00 8·00

No. 612 has part of the original inscription blocked out.

93 Various Animals

1974. Air. Balho Rock Paintings.

613 **93** 200f. black and red . . . . 10·50 8·75

94 Football and Emblem

1974. World Cup Football Championship, West Germany.

614 **94** 25f. green and black . . . 2·75 2·25

95 U.P.U. Emblem and Letters

97 "Oleo chrysophylla"

96 Sunrise over Lake

1974. Centenary of Universal Postal Union.

616 **95** 20f. violet, blue & indigo 2·50 1·40
617 100f. brown, lt brn & red 4·25 3·25

1974. Air. Lake Assal. Multicoloured.

618 49f. Type **96** . . . . 2·50 2·25
619 50f. Rocky shore . . . . . . 2·75 2·25
620 85f. Crystallisation on dead wood . . . . 4·75 3·75

1974. Forest Plants. Multicoloured.

621 10f. Type **97** . . . . 1·90 1·25
622 15f. "Fiscus" (tree) . . . . . 2·25 1·75
623 20f. "Solanum adoense" (shrub) . . . . 3·50 2·25

1975. Surch **40F.**

624 **90** 40f. on 30f. purple & grn 2·75 2·25

99 Treasury Building

1975. Administrative Buildings, Djibouti.

625 **99** 8f. grey, blue and red . . . 1·75 1·60
626 – 25f. grey, blue and red . . 2·25 1·90

DESIGN: 25f. "Government City" complex.

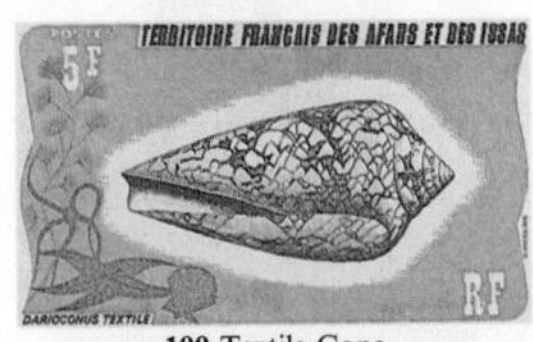

100 Textile Cone

1975. Sea Shells.

627 **100** 5f. brown and green . . . 1·60 1·60
628 – 5f. brown and blue . . . 1·60 1·40
629 – 5f. brown, mve & vio . . 1·75 1·75
630 – 10f. brown and purple . . 1·75 1·60
631 – 15f. brown and blue . . . 2·25 1·75
632 – 20f. brown and violet . . 3·00 1·75
633 – 20f. brown and green . . 1·75 1·60
634 – 30f. brown, pur & grn . . 2·00 1·75
635 – 40f. brown and green . . 3·75 2·75
636 – 45f. brown, green & blue 3·00 2·50
637 – 55f. brown and blue . . . 2·50 2·25
638 – 60f. black and brown . . 3·00 2·75
639 – 70f. brown, blue & black 4·00 3·00
640 – 85f. purple, blue & black 6·00 4·25

DESIGNS: 5f. (628) Rose-branch murex; 5f. (629) Tiger cowrie; 10f. Sumatran cone; 15f. Lovely cowrie; 20f. (632), 45f. Woodcock murex; 20f. (633) Burnt cowrie; 30f. Beech cowrie; 40f. Spiny frog shell; 55f. Red Sea cowrie; 60f. Ringed cone; 70f. Striate cone; 85f. Humpback cowrie.

1975. Wild Animals (3rd series). As T **86**. Mult.

641 50f. White-tailed mongoose 3·50 2·75
642 60f. North African crested porcupine (vert) . . . . . 4·25 3·00
643 70f. Zorilla . . . . 5·75 3·75

101 African Monarch

1975. Butterflies and Moths (1st series). Mult.

644 25f. Type **101** . . . . 2·50 2·25
645 40f. Narrow blue-banded swallowtail . . . . 3·00 2·25
646 70f. Citrus butterfly . . . . 4·50 3·00
647 100f. Mocker swallowtail . . 5·50 4·25

See also Nos. 666/7 and 675/6.

102 Speckled Pigeon

103 Palm Trees

1975. Birds. Multicoloured.

648 20f. Pin-tailed whydah (postage) . . . . 1·75 85
649 25f. Rose-ringed parakeet . . 2·00 1·00
650 50f. Variable sunbird . . . . 3·00 1·50
651 60f. Goliath heron . . . . . 4·25 2·10
652 100f. Hammerkop . . . . . 6·00 3·00
653 100f. Namaqua dove . . . . 4·00 2·00
654 300f. African spoonbill . . . 10·00 5·00
655 500f. Type **102** (air) . . . . 25·00 13·00

1975. Wild Animals (4th series). As T **86**. Mult.

659 15f. Savanna monkeys (vert) 1·90 1·75
660 200f. Aardvarks . . . . . . 8·50 5·00

1975.

661 **103** 20f. multicoloured . . . . 1·90 1·60

1976. Wild Animals (5th series). As T **86**. Multicoloured.

662 10f. Striped hyena . . . . . 1·75 1·50
663 15f. African ass (vert) . . . . 1·90 1·75
664 30f. Beira antelope . . . . . 2·50 1·90

104 Alexander Graham Bell and Satellite

1976. Telephone Centenary.

665 **104** 200f. blue, green & orge 5·50 4·25

1976. Butterflies and Moths (2nd series). As T **101**. Multicoloured.

666 65f. Variable prince . . . . 3·50 2·75
667 100f. "Balachowsky gonimbrasia" . . . . . . 4·75 3·25

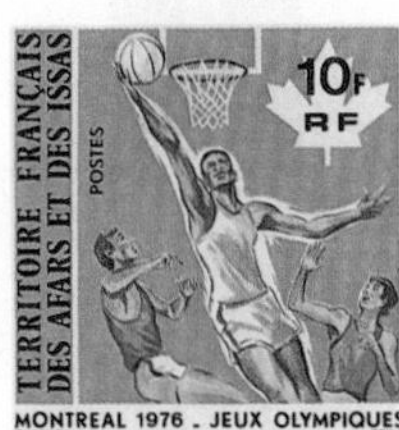

105 Basketball

1976. Olympic Games, Montreal. Mult.

668 10f. Type **105** . . . . 1·50 1·50
669 15f. Cycling . . . . 1·60 1·60
670 40f. Football . . . . 2·25 1·90
671 60f. Running . . . . 2·75 2·25

106 Radial Lionfish

1976. Marine Life.

672 **106** 45f. multicoloured . . . . 2·75 2·75

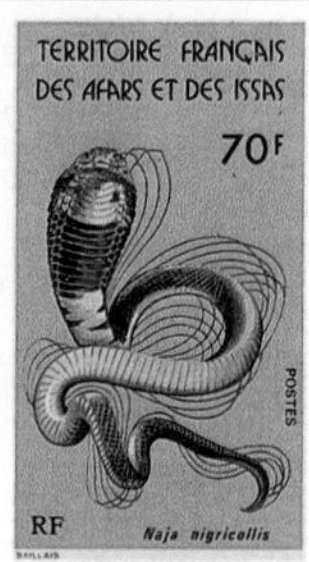

107 Black-necked Cobra

108 Motor Cyclist on Course

1976. Snakes. Multicoloured.
673 70f. Type **107** . . . . 3·50 3·00
674 80f. Elegant sand snake . . . 4·25 3·25

1976. Butterflies and Moths (3rd series). As T **101**. Multicoloured.
675 50f. Broad bordered acraea 3·00 2·75
676 150f. Painted lady . . . . . 5·00 4·25

1977. Moto-Cross.
677 **108** 200f. multicoloured . . . 7·50 4·50

109 Air Terminal

1977. Air. Inauguration of New Djibouti Airport.
678 **109** 500f. multicoloured . . . 16·00 12·50

110 Black-spotted Sweetlips

1977. Fishes. Multicoloured.
679 15f. Type **110** . . . . 1·90 1·90
680 65f. Great barracuda . . . . 3·00 2·25

111 Edison and Phonograph

1977. Air. Celebrities.
681 **111** 55f. red, slate and green 4·00 3·00
682 – 75f. red, brown & green 7·75 5·75
DESIGN: 75f. Volta and TGV express train, France.

POSTAGE DUE STAMPS

D 72 Nomadic Milk-Jug

1969.
D539 D **72** 1f. slate, brn & pur . . 1·40 1·40
D540 2f. slate, brn & grn . . 1·40 1·40
D541 5f. slate, brn & blue 1·75 1·75
D542 10f. slate, lake & brn 2·10 2·10

For later issues see **DJIBOUTI REPUBLIC**.

FRENCH WEST AFRICA Pt. 6

The territory in north-west Africa comprising Senegal, French Guinea, Ivory Coast, Dahomey, French Sudan, Mauritania, Niger and Upper Volta. French Sudan and Senegal became the Mali Federation and the rest independent republics.

100 centimes = 1 franc.

1944. Mutual Aid and Red Cross Funds. As T **58e** of Guadeloupe.
1 5f.+20f. purple . . . . 2·50 9·25

1945. Eboue. As T **58f** of Guadeloupe.
2 2f. black . . . . 30 1·10
3 25f. green . . . . 1·25 3·75

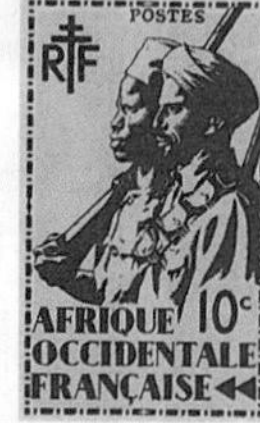

1 Soldiers

1945.
4 **1** 10c. blue and pink . . . . . 70 1·25
5 30c. olive and cream . . . . 1·10 2·75
6 40c. blue and pink . . . . . 90 2·75
7 50c. orange and grey 65 60
8 60c. olive and grey . . . . . 1·00 3·00
9 70c. mauve and cream . . . 1·40 3·00
10 80c. green and cream . . . . 80 2·25
11 1f. purple and olive 35 10
12 1f.20 brown and olive . . . . 1·40 4·00
13 1f.50 brown and red 75 15
14 2f. yellow and grey 95 25
15 2f.40 red and grey . . . . . 1·10 2·25
16 3f. red and olive 60 10
17 4f. blue and red 65 20
18 4f.50 brown and olive . . . . 1·40 1·25
19 5f. violet and olive . . . . . 1·00 10
20 10f. green and red 60 25
21 15f. brown and cream . . . 90 65
22 20f. green and grey . . . . . 1·25 95

1945. Stamp Day. As T **228** of France (Louis XI) but optd **A O F**.
23 2f.+3f. red . . . . 30 3·25

1945. Air. As T **63a** of Guadeloupe.
24 5f.50 blue . . . . 1·50 2·25
25 50f. green . . . . 1·25 55
26 100f. red . . . . 1·40 1·40

1946. Air. Victory. As T **63b** of Guadeloupe.
27 8f. mauve 30 35

1946. Air. From Chad to the Rhine. As T **63c** of Guadeloupe.
28 5f. red . . . . 2·75 4·25
29 10f. blue . . . . 2·75 4·00
30 15f. mauve . . . . 2·50 4·00
31 20f. green . . . . 2·50 4·25
32 25f. brown . . . . 2·50 4·25
33 50f. brown . . . . 2·50 4·75

3 War Dance

6 Sudanese Carving

9 Natives and Airplane

1947.
34 **3** 10c. blue (postage) . . . . . 10 2·25
35 – 30c. brown . . . . 10 2·75
36 – 40c. green . . . . 45 2·75
37 – 50c. red . . . . 35 1·90
38 – 60c. grey . . . . 1·00 2·75
39 – 80c. lilac . . . . 60 3·25
40 – 1f. red 10 10
41 – 1f.20 green . . . . 1·40 3·50
42 – 1f.50 blue . . . . 1·75 3·25
43 **6** 2f. orange 55 10
68 – 3f. brown . . . . 1·25 90
45 – 3f.60 red . . . . 2·00 3·75
46 – 4f. blue . . . . 1·25 15
47 – 5f. green . . . . 1·10 10
48 – 6f. blue 75 15
49 – 10f. red 75 15
50 – 15f. brown . . . . 1·90 75
51 – 20f. brown 90 15
52 – 25f. black 40 25

53 – 8f. red (air) . . . . 1·75 80
54 – 50f. violet . . . . 2·75 1·25
55 – 100f. blue . . . . 8·50 3·50
56 **9** 200f. grey . . . . 3·50 2·25

DESIGNS—As Type **3/6**—HORIZ: 30c. Girl and bridge; 40c. Canoe; 50c. Niger landscape; 80c. Dahomey weaver; 1f. Donkey caravan; 1f.20, Crocodile and hippopotamus; 10f. Djenne Mosque; 15f. Renault model ABH railcar. VERT: 60c. Coconuts; 1f.50, Palm trees; 3f. Togo girl; 3f.60, Sudanese market; 4f. Dahomey labourer; 5f. Mauritanian woman; 6f. Guinea headdress; 20f. Ivory Coast girl; 25f. Niger washerwoman. As Type **9**—VERT: 8f. Antoine de Saint-Exupery. HORIZ: 50f. Caudron Goeland airplane over Dakar (Senegal); 100f. Flight of great egrets (Niger).

1949. 75th Anniv of U.P.U. As T **39** of French Equatorial Africa.
69 25f. multicoloured . . . . . . 1·75 5·00

1950. Colonial Welfare Fund. As T **40** of French Equatorial Africa.
70 10f.+2f. dp brown & brown 3·00 8·00

10 Medical Research

11 T. Laplene and Map of Ivory Coast

12 Logging Camp

1951.
71 – 8f. blue & brown (postage) 1·25 90
72 **10** 15f. green, brown & sepia 60 10
73 – 20f. myrtle and turquoise . . 1·75 4·00
74 – 25f. sepia, blue and purple 95 15
75 **11** 40f. red . . . . 1·25 20

76 **12** 50f. brown and green (air) 2·50 85
77 – 100f. brown, blue & green 4·00 90
78 – 200f. green, turq & lake . . 12·50 2·50
79 – 500f. green, blue & orange 20·00 5·25
DESIGNS—As Type **11**: 8f. Governor-General Ballay; 20f. Houphouet-Boigny Bridge, Abidjan; 25f. Africans, animals and sailing canoe. As Type **12**: 100f. Telephonist, Lockheed Constellation airplane and pylons; 200f. Baobab trees; 500f. Vridi Canal, Abidjan.

1952. Centenary of Military Medal. As T **44** of French Equatorial Africa.
80 15f. sepia, yellow and green 3·25 3·00

1954. Air. 10th Anniv of Liberation. As T **46** of French Equatorial Africa.
81 15f. blue and indigo . . . . . 3·75 3·50

13 Chimpanzee

14

1955. Nature Protection. Inscr as in T **13**.
82 **13** 5f. sepia and grey . . . . . 1·50 30
83 – 8f. sepia and green . . . . 75 1·25
DESIGN—HORIZ: 8f. Giant ground pangolin.

1955. 50th Anniv of Rotary International.
84 **14** 15f. blue 30 25

15 Mossi Railways

1955. Economic and Social Development Fund. Inscr "F.I.D.E.S.".
85 – 1f. green and myrtle . . . . 60 1·75
86 – 2f. myrtle and turquoise . . 1·25 2·75
87 **15** 3f. sepia and brown . . . . 2·00 2·50
88 – 4f. red . . . . 1·25 85
89 – 15f. blue and indigo 80 20
90 – 17f. blue and indigo . . . . 1·10 2·00
91 – 20f. purple . . . . 90 1·10
92 – 30f. purple and lilac . . . . 1·25 95
DESIGNS—HORIZ: 1f. Date palms; 2f. Milo River bridge; 4f. Herdsman and cattle; 15f. Combine harvester; 17f. Woman and aerial view; 20f. Palm oil factory; 30f. Abidjan-Abengourou road.

1956. Coffee. As T **51** of French Equatorial Africa.
93 15f. green and turquoise . . . 35 20

16 Medical Station and Ambulance

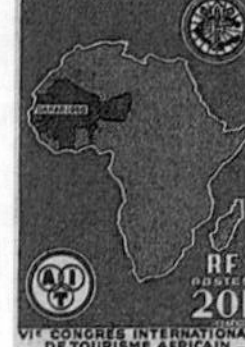

17 Map of Africa

1957. Order of Malta Leprosy Relief.
94 **16** 15f. claret, purple & red . . 75 2·50

1957. Air. Centenary of African Troops. As T **53** of French Equatorial Africa.
95 15f. blue and indigo . . . . . 1·25 2·75

1958. 6th African International Tourist Congress.
96 **17** 20f. red and green . . . . . 30 2·50

18 "Communication"

1958. Stamp Day.
97 **18** 15f. brown, blue & orange 30 2·75

19 Isle of Goree and West African

1958. Air. Dakar Centenary. Inscr "CENTENAIRE DE DAKAR".
98 **19** 15f. multicoloured . . . . 1·25 1·60
99 – 20f. red, brown and blue 2·00 2·75
100 – 25f. multicoloured 75 75
101 – 40f. brown, green & blue 65 55
102 – 50f. violet, brown & green 95 1·25
103 – 100f. green, blue & brown 3·25 2·50
MS104 185 × 125 mm. Nos. 98/103 with view of Dakar . . . . . 18·00 30·00
DESIGNS: 20f. Map of Dakar, liner, freighters and Lockheed Super Constellation and Douglas DC-6 aircraft; 25f. Town construction; 40f. Council house; 50f. Groundnuts, artisan and "L'Arachide" (freighter) at quayside; 100f. Bay of N'Gor.

20 Banana Plant and Fruit

1958. Banana Production.
105 **20** 20f. purple, green & olive 60 20

1958. Tropical Flora. As T **56** of French Equatorial Africa.
118 10f. multicoloured 60 15
119 25f. yellow, green and red . . 85 25
120 30f. brown, green and blue 1·40 45
121 40f. yellow, green & brown 1·60 2·25
122 65f. multicoloured . . . . . 1·75 2·00
DESIGNS—VERT: 10f. "Gloriosa"; 25f. "Adenopus"; 30f. "Cyrtosperma"; 40f. "Cistanche"; 65f. "Crinum moorei".

22 Moro Naba Sagha and Map of Upper Volta

1958. 10th Anniv of Upper Volta Scheme.
123 **22** 20f. multicoloured . . . . 2·75 2·75

23 Native Chief and Musician

1958. Air. Inauguration of Nouakchott, Capital of Mauritania.
124 23 20f. sepia, brown & grey 1·75 2·75

1958. 10th Anniv of Declaration of Human Rights. As T 14 of French Polynesia.
125 20f. purple and blue 35 3·25

1959. Stamp Day. As T 18 but inscr "DAKAR-ABIDJAN" in place of "AFRIQUE OCCIDENTALE FRANÇAISE".
126 20f. green, blue and red 3·25 4·50
No. 126 was for use in Ivory Coast and Senegal.

OFFICIAL STAMPS

O 21

1958. Inscr "OFFICIEL".
O106 O 21 1f. brown 2·00 1·75
O107 3f. green 2·25 3·00
O108 5f. red 2·00 90
O109 10f. blue 2·00 2·50
O110 – 20f. red 2·25 1·60
O111 – 25f. violet 2·25 85
O112 – 30f. green 2·00 2·25
O113 – 45f. black 1·60 1·60
O114 – 50f. red 3·25 90
O115 – 65f. blue 1·60 2·25
O116 – 100f. olive 3·50 2·50
O117 – 200f. green 11·00 4·25
DESIGNS—VERT: 20f. to 45f. Head as Type O 21 but with female face; 50f. to 200f. Head as Type O 21 but with hooped headdress, portrait being diagonal on stamp.

POSTAGE DUE STAMPS.

D 10

1947.
D57 D 10 10c. red 10 2·50
D58 30c. orange 10 2·25
D59 50c. black 10 2·50
D60 1f. red 80 2·50
D61 2f. green 85 2·50
D62 3f. mauve 1·50 2·75
D63 4f. blue 1·75 3·00
D64 5f. brown 1·75 3·00
D65 10f. blue 1·10 4·00
D66 20f. brown 1·90 5·00

FUJEIRA Pt. 19

One of the Trucial States in the Persian Gulf.
With six other sheikdoms formed the State of the United Arab Emirates on 18 July 1971. Fujeira stamps were replaced by issues of United Arab Emirates on 1 January 1973.

1964. 100 naye paise = 1 rupee.
1967. 100 dirhams = 1 riyal.

1 Shaikh Mohamed bin Hamad al Sharqi and Great Crested Grebe

1964. Multicoloured. (a) Size as T 1.
1 1n.p. Type 1 15 15
2 2n.p. Arabian oryx 15 15
3 3n.p. Hoopoe 15 15
4 4n.p. Asiatic wild ass 15 15
5 5n.p. Great Egrets 15 15
6 10n.p. Arab horses 15 15
7 15n.p. Cheetah 15 15
8 20n.p. Dromedaries 15 15
9 30n.p. Lanner falcon 15 15

(b) Size 43½ × 28½ mm.
10 40n.p. Type 1 35 15
11 50n.p. Arabian oryx 35 15
12 70n.p. Hoopoe 50 30
13 1r. Asiatic wild ass 60 50
14 1r.50 Great egrets 1·00 60
15 2r. Arab horses 1·30 1·00

(c) Size 53½ × 35½ mm.
16 3r. Leopard 1·80 2·00
17 5r. Dromedaries 3·25 3·75
18 10r. Lanner falcon 6·75 5·25

2 Shaikh Mohamed and Putting the Shot

1964. Olympic Games, Tokyo. Multicoloured. (a) Size as T 2.
19 25n.p. Type 2 15 15
20 50n.p. Throwing the discus 35 35
21 75n.p. Fencing 50 50
22 1r. Boxing 60 60
23 1r.50 Relay-racing 1·00 1·00
24 2r. Football 1·30 1·30

(b) Size 53 × 35½ mm.
25 3r. High jumping 1·80 1·80
26 5r. Hurdling 3·00 3·00
27 7r.50 Horse-riding 4·50 4·50

3 Kennedy as a Boy

1965. Pres. Kennedy Commem. Each black and gold on coloured paper as given below.
28 3 5n.p. blue 15 10
29 – 10n.p. yellow 15 10
30 – 15n.p. pink 15 10
31 – 20n.p. green 15 15
32 – 25n.p. blue 25 15
33 – 50n.p. flesh 35 25
34 – 1r. lilac 1·10 90
35 – 2r. yellow 1·70 1·40
36 – 3r. blue 2·75 2·20
37 – 5r. buff 5·00 4·25
DESIGNS (Kennedy): 10n.p. As student. 15n.p. As cadet. 20n.p. As Senator. 25n.p. Sailing. 50n.p. As President. 33 × 51 mm: 1r. With Mrs. Kennedy and guest. 2r. With Pres. Eisenhower. 3r. With family. 5r. Full face portrait.

1965. Air. Designs similar to Nos. 1/9, but with "FUJEIRA" and value transposed, and inscr "AIR MAIL". Mult. (a) Size 43½ × 28½ mm.
39 15n.p. Type 1 15 10
40 25n.p. Arabian oryx 25 10
41 35n.p. Hoopoe 40 10
42 50n.p. Asiatic wild ass 40 15
43 75n.p. Great egrets 65 10
44 1r. Arab horses 75 40

(b) Size 53½ × 35½ mm.
45 2r. Leopard 1·70 65
46 3r. Dromedaries 3·25 1·10
47 5r. Lanner falcon 4·00 1·30
MS38 90 × 80 mm. Nos. 36/7 in new colours, but size 28½ × 44 mm 10·00 5·00

4 Queen Nefertiti

1966. Stamp Centenary Exn, Cairo. Mult.
57 3n.p. Type 4 10 10
58 5n.p. Colossi, Abu Simbel 10 10
59 10n.p. Tutankhamun's mask 10 10
60 15n.p. Sphinx, Gezir 10 15
61 25n.p. Statues of Prince Rahotep and his wife Nofret 15 15
62 50n.p. Ancient Church (horiz) 25 15
63 1r. Colonnade, Great Temple of Isis, Philae (horiz) 60 25
64 2r. Nile sphinxes (horiz) 1·30 60
65 5r. Pyramids, Giza (horiz) 3·75 1·40
MS66 120 × 75 mm. Nos. 64/5 but size 44 × 29 mm 6·25 6·25

5 Sir Winston Churchill as Harrow Schoolboy

1966. Churchill Commem. Each design black and gold; frame in colours given.
67 5 10n.p. yellow (postage) 10 15
68 – 15n.p. blue 10 15
69 – 25n.p. buff 15 15
70 – 50n.p. blue 25 15
71 – 75n.p. mauve 40 25
72 – 1r. blue 60 30
73 – 2r. gold (air) 1·30 55
74 – 3r. gold 1·80 1·20
MS75 105 × 75 mm. Nos. 73/4 in new colours but size 32 × 44 mm and inscr "POSTAGE" instead of "AIR MAIL" 4·25 4·25
DESIGNS—Churchill: 15n.p. Wearing Hussars' uniform; 25n.p. As Boer War correspondent; 50n.p. In morning dress; 75n.p. With Eisenhower; 1r. Painting; 2r. With grandson; 3r. Giving "V" sign.

6 Lunar Satellite

1966. Space Achievements. Multicoloured.
76 5n.p. Type 6 10 15
77 10n.p. Satellite approaching Moon 10 15
78 15n.p. Satellite and planets 10 15
79 25n.p. Satellite and Solar System 25 15
80 50n.p. Communications satellite 35 15
81 75n.p. Venus probe 60 15
82 1r. "Telstar" 75 30
83 2r. "Relay" 1·70 70
MS84 130 × 90 mm. Nos. 82/3 3·25 2·75

1967. Various stamps with currency names changed by overprinting. (i) Nos. 1/18 (Definitives).
85 1d. on 1n.p. 25 10
86 2d. on 2n.p. 25 10
87 3d. on 3n.p. 25 10
88 4d. on 4n.p. 25 10
89 5d. on 5n.p. 25 10
90 10d. on 10n.p. 25 10
91 15d. on 15n.p. 25 10
92 20d. on 20n.p. 25 10
93 30d. on 30n.p. 15 15
94 40d. on 40n.p. 25 25
95 50d. on 50n.p. 25 25
96 70d. on 70n.p. 35 35
97 1r. on 1r. 50 50
98 1r.50 on 1r.50 85 85
99 2r. on 2r. 1·10 1·10
100 3r. on 3r. on 3r. 1·70 1·70
101 5r. on 5r. 2·75 2·75
102 10r. on 10r. 5·75 5·75

(ii) Air. Nos. 39/47 (Definitives).
123 15d. on 15n.p. 15 10
124 25d. on 25n.p. 15 10
125 35d. on 35n.p. 50 25
126 50d. on 50n.p. 50 25
127 75d. on 75n.p. 85 40
128 1r. on 1r. 1·00 50
129 2r. on 2r. 2·00 1·00
130 3r. on 3r. 3·25 1·70
131 5r. on 5r. 5·50 2·75
Nos. 19/37 and 57/83 were also surcharged in the new currency in limited quantities, but they had little local usage.

9 "Pararge felix"

1967. Butterflies. Multicoloured. (a) Postage. (i) Size 32 × 32 mm.
167 1d. Type 9 10 10
168 2d. African clouded yellow (male) 10 10
169 3d. African clouded yellow (female) 10 10
170 4d. "Spindasis scotti" 10 10
171 5d. "Pararge felix" (different) 10 10
172 10d. "Lepidochrysops arabicus" 10 10
173 15d. "Eumenis tewfiki" 10 10
174 20d. "Euchrysops philbyi" 10 10
175 30d. "Mylothris arabicus" 15 10

(ii) Size 40 × 40 mm.
176 40d. Type 9 15 10
177 50d. As No. 168 25 10
178 70d. As No. 169 25 15
179 1r. As No. 170 40 25
180 1r.50 As No. 171 65 40
181 2r. As No. 172 85 70

(iii) Size 42 × 42 mm.
182 3r. As No. 173 1·30 80
183 5r. As No. 174 2·10 1·30
184 10r. As No. 175 4·50 2·75

(b) Air. Size 45 × 45 mm.
185 15d. Type 9 10 15
186 25d. As No. 168 10 15
187 35d. As No. 169 15 15
188 50d. As No. 170 25 15
189 75d. As No. 171 25 20
190 1r. As No. 172 40 25
191 2r. As No. 173 85 50
192 3r. As No. 174 1·30 70
193 5r. As No. 175 2·10 1·30

10 Shaikh Mohamed bin Hamad al Sharqi and Veil-tailed Goldfish

1971. Multicoloured.
194 5d. Type 10 (postage) 10 25
195 20d. Shaikh and semicircle angelfish (air) 10 15
196 35d. Shaikh and paradise fish 15 15
197 40d. Shaikh and moorish idol 15 15
198 60d. Shaikh and daisy 25 15
199 1r. Shaikh and rose 50 15
200 2r. Shaikh and gentian 1·00 40
201 3r. Shaikh and wild rose 1·50 65

OFFICIAL STAMPS

1965. Designs similar to Nos. 1/9, but with "FUJEIRA" and value transposed, additionally inscr "ON STATE'S SERVICE". Multicoloured. (a) Postage. Size 43½ × 28½ mm.
O48 25n.p. Type 1 15 10
O49 40n.p. Arabian oryx 25 10
O50 50n.p. Hoopoe 35 15
O51 75n.p. Asiatic wild ass 60 25
O52 1r. Great egrets 75 40

(b) Air. (i) Size 43½ × 28½ mm.
O53 75n.p. Arab horses 50 25

(ii) Size 53½ × 35½ mm.
O54 2r. Leopard 1·50 65
O55 3r. Dromedaries 2·20 1·00
O56 5r. Lanner falcon 3·75 1·80

1967. Nos. 48/56 with currency name changed by overprinting.
O158 25d. on 25n.p. (postage) 15 15
O159 40d. on 40n.p. 25 25
O160 50d. on 50n.p. 35 35
O161 75d. on 75n.p. 50 50
O162 1r. on 1r. 75 75
O163 75d. on 75n.p. (air) 50 50
O164 2r. on 2r. 1·50 1·50
O165 3r. on 3r. 2·20 2·20
O166 5r. on 5r. 3·75 3·75

APPENDIX

The following stamps have either been issued in excess of postal needs or have not been available to the public in reasonable quantities at face value. Such stamps may later be given full listing if there is evidence of regular postal use.

1967.

"One Thousand and One Nights". Postage 10, 15, 30, 75d., 1r., 1r.50; Air 25, 50, 75d., 1r., 1r.25, 2r.

Famous Paintings. Postage 25, 50, 75d., 1, 1r.50; Air 2, 3, 5r.

Cats. Postage 10, 35, 50d., 1, 1r.50; Air 1r.25, 2r.75, 3r.50.

1968.

Winter Olympic Games, Grenoble. 25, 50, 75d., 1, 1r.50, 2, 3r.

Famous Paintings (square designs). Postage 50, 75d., 1, 2, 3r.; Air 1r.50, 2r.50, 3r.50, 4, 5r.

Ships. Postage 15, 25, 50, 75d., 1r.; Air 2, 3, 4, 5r.

Olympic Games, Mexico. Optd on Nos. 22/6 and four values of 1968 Winter Olympics issue. Postage 1, 1r.50, 2, 3, 5r.; Air 1, 1r.50, 2, 3r.

Prehistoric Animals. Postage 15, 25, 50, 75d., 1r.50; Air 1, 2r.50, 3, 4, 5r.

Robert Kennedy Memorial issue. Optd on Nos. 34/7. 1, 2, 3, 5r.

Olympic Games, Mexico. Postage 15, 25, 35, 50, 75d., 1r.; Air 1r.50, 2, 3, 5r.

International Letter-writing Week. Paintings. Postage 25, 50, 75d., 1r.; Air 1r.50, 2, 3, 5r.

"EFIMEX" International Stamp Exhibition, Mexico. Optd on 1968 Letter-writing Week issue. Postage 25, 50, 75d.; 1r. Air 1r.50, 2, 3, 5r.

Gold Medal Winners, Olympic Games, Mexico. Optd on 1968 Olympic Games, Mexico issue. Postage 15, 25, 35, 50 75d., 1r.; Air 1r.50, 2, 3, 5r.

1969.

Wild Animals of the World. Postage 15, 25, 50, 75d., 1r.; Air 1r.50, 2, 3, 5r.

Scenes from Shakespeare's Plays. Postage 25, 50, 75d., 1, 2r.; Air 1r.25, 2r.50, 3, 5r.

Olympic Games, Munich (1969). Optd on 1968 Olympic Games, Mexico issue. Postage 15, 25, 35, 50, 75d., 1r.; Air 1r.50, 2r.50, 3, 5r.

Famous Railway Locomotives. Postage 15, 25, 50, 75d., 1r.; Air 2, 3, 5r.

Moon Flight of "Apollo 8". Optd or surch on Nos. 76/83. 50, 75n.p., 1, 2, 2r.50 on 25n.p., 3r. on 15n.p., 4r. on 10n.p. 5r. on 5n.p.

Winter Olympic Games, Sapporo, Japan (1972). Optd on 1968 Winter Olympic Games, Grenoble issue. 25, 50, 75d., 1, 1r.50, 2, 3r.

Birds. Postage 25, 50d., 1r., 1r.50, 2r.; Air 1r.25, 2r.50, 3, 5r.

Pres. Eisenhower Memorial issue. Postage 25, 50d., 1r., 1r.50, 2r.; Air 1r.25, 2r.50, 3, 5r.

Champions of Peace. 25, 50, 75d., 1, 2, 3, 5r.

Human Rights Year. Optd on 1969 Champions of Peace issue. 25, 50, 75d., 1, 2, 3, 5r.

Flowers. Postage 25, 50d., 1, 1r.50, 2r.; Air 1r.25, 2r.50, 3, 5r.

"Apollo" Space Flights. Postage 10, 25, 50d., 1, 2r.; Air 2r.50, 3, 4, 5r.

Space Flight of "Apollo 10". Optd on 1969 "Apollo" Space Flights issue. Postage 10, 25, 50d., 1, 2r.; Air 2r.50, 3, 4, 5r.

Moon Landing. Optd on 1969 "Apollo" Space Flights issue. Postage 10, 25, 50d., 1, 2r.; Air 2r.50, 3, 4, 5r.

First Man on the Moon. 1969 "Apollo" Space Flights issue optd with various commemoration inscriptions. Postage 10, 25, 50d., 1, 2r.; Air 2r.50, 3, 4, 5r.

1970.

Birth Bicentenary of Napoleon Bonaparte. 15, 25, 50, 75d., 1, 1r.50, 2r.

General De Gaulle Commemoration. Air 35, 60, 75d., 1r.25, 2r.50, 3, 5r.

Bible Stories. Postage 15d., 1r.; Air 35, 75d., 1r.25, 1r.50, 2r.50, 3r.

"Expo 70" World Fair, Osaka, Japan. Japanese Art. Postage 15, 25, 50, 75d., 1, 2r.; Air 75d., 1r.25, 2r.50, 4r.

Exploration of the Moon. 25, 50d., 1, 2, 3, 4, 5r.

Space Flight of "Apollo 13". Optd on 1970 Moon Exploration issue. 25, 50d., 1, 2, 3, 4, 5r.

Moon Mission of "Apollo 14". Optd on 1970 Moon Exploration issue. 25, 50d., 1, 2, 3, 4, 5r.

"Expo 70" World Fair, Osaka, Japan. Pavilions. 10, 20, 70d., 1r. × 2, 2r.

World Football Cup, Mexico. 10, 20, 70d., 1r. × 2, 2r.

Pres. Gamal Nasser Memorial issue. Postage 10, 20, 30, 40, 50d.; Air 5r.

Horses. Postage 10, 20d.; Air 70d., 1, 2r.

Cats. Postage 30, 70d.; Air 1, 2, 3r.

Dogs. Postage 30, 70d.; Air 1, 2, 3r.

Paintings of the Madonna. 30, 70d., 1, 2, 3r.

Stations of the Cross. 1r. × 15.

Christmas. Paintings. Postage 30, 70d., 1r.; Air 2, 3r.

1971.

American and European Cars. Postage 5, 20, 30d., 4r.; Air 30, 50, 70d., 1r.50, 2r.50, 4r.

Space Exploration. Air 40, 60d., 1, 2, 5r.

History of Railways. 10, 20, 70d., 2, 3r.

General De Gaulle Memorial issue. Air 30, 70d. 1, 2, 3r.

Moon Mission of "Apollo 14" Air 70d., 1, 2, 3, 4r.

Wild Animals. Air 20, 40, 60d., 1, 2, 3r.

Olympic Games, Munich (1972) (square designs). Postage 50d., 1r.; Air 2, 3, 4r.

Winter Olympic Games, Sapporo, Japan (1972). Postage 5, 10, 15, 20, 30, 50d.; Air 70d., 4r.

500th Birth Anniv of Durer. Paintings. Air 70d., 1, 2, 3, 4r.

Birth Bicentenary of Beethoven. Portraits and instruments. Postage 30, 70d.; Air 1, 3, 4r.

Mozart Commem. Postage 30, 70d.1r.; Air 3, 4r.

Frazier v Mohammed Ali World Heavyweight Boxing Championship Fight. Air 1, 2, 3r.

World Scout Jamboree, Asagiri, Japan. Postage 20, 30, 50, 70d., 1r. × 2, 2r. × 2; Air 3, 4r.

Butterflies. Air. 70d., 1, 2, 3, 5r.

Cats and Dogs. 10, 20, 30d., 1, 2, 3r.

Monkeys. 30, 70d., 1, 2, 3r.

Wild Animals. 30, 70d., 1, 2, 3r.

Horses. 70d., 1, 2, 3, 4r.

Olympic Games, Munich. Sports. 1, 2, 3, 4, 5, 6, 7, 8, 9, 10, 11, 12, 13, 14, 15, 16, 17, 18, 19, 20, 21, 22, 23, 24, 25, 26, 27, 28, 29, 30d.

Olympic Games, Munich. Sports and Arenas. Postage 35, 60d., 2, 3r.; Air 4r.

Christmas. Postage 40, 60d., 2r.; Air 3, 4r.

International Labour Day. Paintings. Postage 40, 60d., 2, 3r.; Air 2, 3, 4r.

1972.

400th Birth Anniv of Kepler. Postage 35, 75d., 1, 2r.; Air 3, 5r.

Moon Mission of "Apollo 15". Postage 30, 70d.; Air 1, 2, 5r.

2500th Anniv of The Persian Empire. Postage 35, 65, 75d.; Air 1r.25, 2, 3r.

Historical Costumes. 30, 70d., 1, 2, 3r.

Winter Olympic Games, Sapporo, Japan. Postage 25, 30, 70d.; Air 1r.25, 2, 3r.

Tropical Birds 30, 70d., 1, 2, 3r.

Children's Day. Paintings. Postage 10, 30, 60d.; Air 4, 5r.

Sculptures. Postage 30, 70d.; Air 1, 2, 6r.

Paintings of the Madonna. Postage 20, 30 50d.; Air 4, 5r.

Nude Paintings. 50d., 1, 2, 3, 4r.

Gold Medal Winners, Winter Olympic Games, Sapporo. Optd on 1972 Winter Olympic Games, Sapporo issue. Postage 25, 30, 70d.; Air 1r.25, 2, 3r.

Olympic Games, Munich. Discus-thrower. Air 8r.

Space Exploration. Postage 5, 10, 15, 20, 25, 30, 35, 40, 45, 50, 55, 60d.; Air 65, 70, 75d., 1, 2, 3, 4, 5r.

Walt Disney Cartoon Characters. Postage 1, 2, 3, 4, 5, 10, 15, 20, 25, 30d.; Air 45, 55, 65, 70d., 1, 1r.50, 2, 3, 4, 5r.

History of the Olympic Games Postage 1, 2, 3, 4, 5, 10, 15, 20, 25, 30, 45, 55d.; Air 65, 70d., 1, 1r.50, 2, 3, 5r.

Summit Meeting of Pres. Nixon and Mao Tse-tung. Air 2, 3, 5r.

Pres. Nixon's Visit of Russia. Optd on 1972 Nixon–Mao Tse-tung Meeting issue. Air 2, 3, 5r.

150th Death Anniv (1971) of Napoleon Bonaparte. Air 10r.

2nd Death Anniv of General De Gaulle. Air 10r.

Olympic Games, Munich, Javelin-thrower. Air 10r.

Gold Medal Winners, Olympic Games, Munich. Optd on 1972 Discus-thrower issue. Air 8r.

Moon Mission of "Apollo 16". Air 10r.

European Birds. 30, 70d., 1, 2, 3r.

A number of issues on gold and silver foil also exist, but it is understood that these were mainly for presentation purposes, although valid for postage.

During 1970 a number of other sets came on to the market, but their official status is in doubt.

The United Arab Emirates Ministry of Communications took over the Fujeira postal service on 1 August 1972. Further stamps were released without authority and had no validity.

FUNCHAL Pt. 9

The District of Funchal (the chief town) was the administrative title of Madeira from 1892 to 1905. From 1905 the name reverted to Madeira.

1000 reis = 1 milreis.

4

1892.

No.	Type	Description	Unused	Used
85	4	5r. yellow	3·25	2·00
86		10r. mauve	2·75	2·00
87		15r. brown	3·75	3·25
89		20r. lilac	4·00	2·75
83		25r. green	7·00	1·80
84		50r. blue	5·25	2·75
92		75r. pink	8·25	7·00
93		80r. green	16·00	12·50
95		100r. brown on buff	10·00	5·25
107		150r. red on pink	60·00	34·00
96		200r. blue on blue	70·00	48·00
97		300r. blue on brown	70·00	60·00

1897. "King Carlos" key-type inscr "FUNCHAL". Name and value in red (Nos. 123, 130) or black (others).

No.	Type	Description	Unused	Used
110	S	2½r. grey	55	40
111		5r. red	55	40
112		10r. green	55	40
113		15r. brown	6·50	5·25
126		15r. green	3·75	3·00
114		20r. lilac	1·60	90
115		25r. green	3·00	90
127		25r. red	1·60	70
128		50r. blue	6·50	5·25
129		65r. blue	1·40	1·10
117		75r. pink	1·70	1·20
130		75r. brown on yellow	2·10	1·40
118		80r. mauve	1·70	1·50
119		100r. blue on blue	1·70	1·40

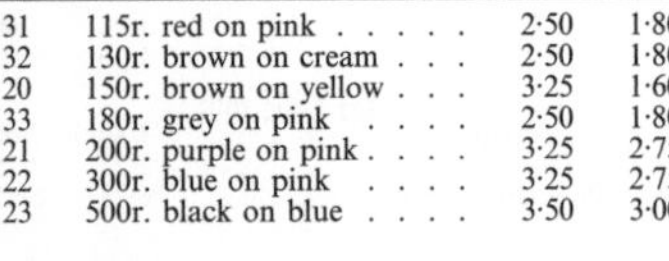

No.	Type	Description	Unused	Used
131		115r. red on pink	2·50	1·80
132		130r. brown on cream	2·50	1·80
120		150r. brown on yellow	3·25	1·60
133		180r. grey on pink	2·50	1·80
121		200r. purple on pink	3·25	2·75
122		300r. blue on pink	3·25	2·75
123		500r. black on blue	3·50	3·00

GABON Pt. 6; Pt. 13

A French colony on the W. coast of equatorial Africa. Became part of Fr. Equatorial Africa in 1937 and a republic within the French Community in 1958.

100 centimes = 1 franc.

1886. Stamps of French Colonies, "Commerce" type, surch **GAB** surrounded by dots, and value in figures.

No.	Type	Description	Unused	Used
1	J	5c. on 20c. red on green	£325	£325
2		10c. on 20c. red on green	£325	£325
3		25c. on 20c. red on green	50·00	35·00
4		50c. on 15c. blue on light blue	£1100	£1100
5		75c. on 15c. blue on light blue	£1300	£1400

1888. Stamps of French Colonies, "Commerce" type, surch in figures.

No.	Type	Description	Unused	Used
6	J	15c. on 10c. black on lilac	£4000	£800
7		15c. on 1f. olive	£1600	£650
8		25c. on 5c. green	£950	£170
9		25c. on 10c. black on lilac	£4000	£1200
10		25c. on 75c. red	£2500	£1000

1889. Postage Due stamps of French Colonies surch **GABON TIMBRE** and value in figures.

No.	Type	Description	Unused	Used
11	U	15c. on 5c. black	£190	£170
12		15c. on 30c. black	£3750	£2500
13		25c. on 20c. black	80·00	70·00

6

1889. Imperf.

No.	Type	Description	Unused	Used
14	6	15c. black on pink	£1100	£700
15		25c. black on green	£700	£575

1904. "Tablet" key-type inscr "GABON" in red (1, 5, 15, 25, 35, 45, 75c., 1, 2f.) or blue (others).

No.	Type	Description	Unused	Used
16	D	1c. black on blue	80	75
17		2c. brown on buff	80	65
18		4c. brown on grey	1·00	1·25
19		5c. green	1·50	80
20		10c. red	3·50	40
21		15c. grey	6·00	1·50
22		20c. red on green	8·00	6·25
23		25c. blue	5·00	2·25
24		30c. brown on drab	10·50	8·00
25		35c. black on yellow	27·00	18·00
26		40c. red on yellow	14·50	10·00
27		45c. black on green	32·00	30·00
28		50c. brown on blue	9·00	9·50
29		75c. brown on orange	18·00	19·00
30		1f. green	35·00	32·00
31		2f. violet on pink	60·00	65·00
32		5f. mauve on lilac	£100	£100

7 Gabon Warrior 9 Bantu Woman

8 View of Libreville

1910.

No.	Type	Description	Unused	Used
33	7	1c. brown and orange	1·10	70
34		2c. black and brown	2·25	1·40
35		4c. violet and blue	65	90
36		5c. olive and green	35	80
37		10c. red and lake	2·25	1·25
38		20c. brown and violet	1·25	5·00
39	8	25c. brown and blue	1·90	4·75
40		30c. red and grey	19·00	30·00
41		35c. green and violet	18·00	14·00
42		40c. blue and brown	17·00	26·00
43		45c. violet and red	21·00	32·00
44		50c. grey and green	50·00	65·00
45		75c. brown and orange	80·00	85·00
46	9	1f. yellow and brown	80·00	85·00
47		2f. brown and red	£225	£200
48		5f. brown and blue	£200	£225

1910. As last but inscr "AFRIQUE EQUATORIALE GABON".

No.	Type	Description	Unused	Used
49	7	1c. brown and orange	10	10
50		2c. black and brown	10	40
51		4c. violet and blue	20	25
52		5c. grey and green	40	95
82		5c. black and yellow	90	2·75
53		10c. red and lake	1·75	75
83		10c. light green and green	35	3·00
54		15c. purple and pink	50	2·75
55		20c. brown and violet	7·00	9·50
56	8	25c. brown and blue	1·40	2·00
84		25c. black and green	2·25	3·50
57		30c. red and grey	1·75	2·75
85		30c. red and carmine	1·60	2·75
58		35c. green and violet	2·25	2·25
59		40c. blue and brown	2·50	2·75
60		45c. violet and red	1·75	3·75
86		45c. red and black	1·60	3·25
61		50c. grey and green	2·00	3·00
87		50c. blue and deep blue	55	1·25
62		75c. brown and red	2·75	6·50
63	9	1f. bistre and brown	3·25	4·50
64		2f. brown and red	3·75	5·50
65		5f. brown and blue	7·25	10·00

1912. "Tablet" key-type surch in figures.

No.	Type	Description	Unused	Used
66	D	05 on 2c. brown on buff	45	1·75
67		05 on 4c. brown on grey	40	2·25
68		05 on 15c. grey	15	15
69		05 on 20c. red on green	25	1·40
70		05 on 25c. blue	20	25
71		05 on 30c. brown on drab	40	2·75
72		10 on 40c. red on yellow	25	75
73		10 on 45c. black on green	45	90
74		10 on 50c. brown on blue	40	1·25
75		10 on 75c. brown on orange	60	2·25
76		10 on 1f. green	35	1·40
77		10 on 2f. violet on pink	20	2·25
78		10 on 5f. mauve on lilac	2·00	4·50

1915. Surch with red cross and **5c**.

No.	Type	Description	Unused	Used
79	7	10c.+5c. (No. 37)	19·00	22·00
81		10c.+5c. (No. 53)	25	2·00

1924. Inscr "AFRIQUE EQUATORIALE GABON" and optd **AFRIQUE EQUATORIALE FRANCAISE.**

No.	Type	Description	Unused	Used
88	7	1c. brown and orange	10	95
89		2c. black and brown	10	2·25
90		4c. violet and blue	10	2·75
91		5c. black and yellow	10	1·10
92		10c. light green and green	60	2·50
93		10c. blue and brown	50	15
94		15c. purple and pink	30	2·50
95		15c. pink and purple	1·25	3·00
96		20c. brown and violet	70	2·75
97	8	25c. black and green	45	35
98		30c. red and carmine	95	2·50
99		30c. yellow and black	15	2·50
100		30c. green	2·25	2·75
101		35c. green and violet	50	2·75
102		40c. blue and brown	1·40	25
103		45c. red and black	1·25	2·75
104		50c. blue and deep blue	85	2·75
105		50c. green and red	1·10	15
106		65c. red and blue	2·50	5·00
107		75c. brown and orange	80	2·50
108		90c. red and scarlet	3·50	3·75
109	9	1f. bistre and brown	1·25	1·10
110		1f.10 red and green	5·25	8·75
111		1f.50 blue and light blue	3·25	2·00
112		2f. brown and red	80	1·40
113		3f. mauve on pink	5·75	10·00
114		5f. brown and blue	6·25	9·50

1925. As last, surch in figures.

No.	Type	Description	Unused	Used
115	9	65 on 1f. brown and green	85	3·00
116		85 on 1f. brown and green	60	3·00
117	8	90c. on 75c. pink and red	55	3·50
118	9	1f.25 on 1f. ultram & bl	25	1·40
119		1f.50 on 1f. dp blue & blue	1·25	2·75
120		3f. on 5f. brown and mauve	3·00	9·50
121		10f. on 5f. green and brown	11·50	20·00
122		20f. on 5f. red and purple	14·00	18·00

1931. "Colonial Exn" key-type inscr "GABON".

No.	Type	Description	Unused	Used
123	E	40c. green	2·75	4·50
124	F	50c. mauve	65	3·75
125	G	90c. orange	1·90	4·50
126	H	1f.50 blue	4·75	5·50

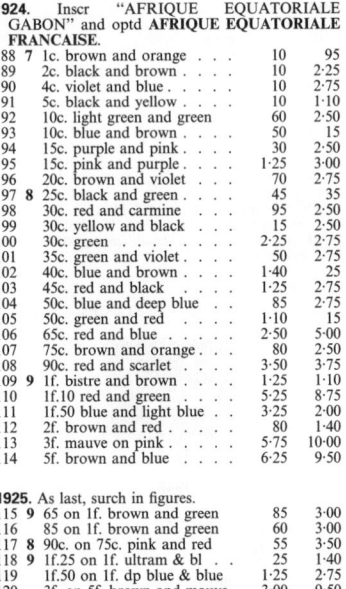

21 Log Raft on the River Ogowe

22 Count de Brazza

1932.

No.	Type	Description	Unused	Used
127	21	1c. red	15	2·25
128		2c. black on red	45	30
129		4c. green	20	2·75
130		5c. blue	35	2·25
131		10c. red on yellow	60	1·75
132		15c. red on green	2·50	3·00
133		20c. red	2·75	3·25
134		25c. brown	1·75	1·60
135	22	30c. green	3·00	3·50
136		40c. purple	2·75	3·25
137		45c. black on green	2·75	3·50
138		50c. brown	2·50	1·60
139		65c. blue	7·00	7·50
140		75c. black on orange	4·00	4·75
141		90c. red	4·00	4·75
142		1f. green on blue	11·00	24·00
143	–	1f.25 violet	3·50	3·25
144	–	1f.50 blue	4·25	3·50
145	–	1f.75 green	3·75	3·00
146	–	2f. red	23·00	23·00
147	–	3f. green on blue	5·50	6·00

148 – 5f. brown . . . . 8·75 10·00
149 – 10f. black on orange . . . 27·00 35·00
150 – 20f. purple . . . . 45·00 45·00
DESIGN—HORIZ: 1f.25 to 20f. Gabon village.

25 Prime Minister Leon Mba

26 CCTA Emblem

1959. 1st Anniv of Republic.
161 **25** 15f. brown 65 85
162 – 25f. green and sepia . . . 1·60 10
PORTRAIT: 25f. Prime Minister Mba (profile).

1960. 10th Anniv of African Technical Co-operation Commission.
163 **26** 50f. blue and purple . . . 2·25 2·75

27 Dr. Albert Schweitzer (philosopher and missionary), Organ and View of Lambarene

1960. Air.
164 **27** 200f. brown, green and blue . . . . 5·50 2·50

1960. Air. Olympic Games. No. 192 of French Equatorial Africa surch with Olympic rings, **XVIIe OLYMPIADE 1960 REPUBLIQUE GABONAISE 250F** and bars.
165 250f. on 500f. blue, blk & grn 6·75 6·75

29 Tree Felling

1960. Air. 5th World Forestry Congress, Seattle.
166 **29** 100f. brown, black & green 3·00 1·40

30 Flag, Map and U.N. Emblem

32 Combretum

33 President Mba

1962.
181 **33** 15f. blue, red and green . . 20 10
182 20f. sepia, red and green 35 15
183 25f. brown, red and green 40 15

34 Airliners, European and African

1962. Air. "Air Afrique" Airline.
184 **34** 500f. green, ochre & black 9·50 5·50

36 Start of Race

1962. Malaria Eradication. As T **55a** of French Somali Coast.
185 25f.+5f. green 80 80

1962. Sports. Multicoloured.
186 20f. Type **36** (postage) . . . 45 20
187 50f. Football 95 60
188 100f. Long jump (26 × 47 mm) (air) . . . . 2·50 1·10

37 Breguet 14 Biplane

1962. Air. Evolution of Air Transport.
189 **37** 10f. blue and red 50 20
190 – 20f. indigo, blue and brown 70 35
191 – 60f. blue, purple and green 1·60 85
192 – 85f. indigo, blue and orange . . . . 2·75 1·40
AIRCRAFT: 20f. De Havilland Dragon Rapide; 60f. Sud Aviation Caravelle; 85f. Rocket.

38 Union Flag

1962. 1st Anniv of Union of African and Malagasy States.
194 **38** 30f. green . . . . 1·10 80

31 Lyre-tailed Honeyguide in flight

1961. Admission into U.N.
167 **30** 15f. multicoloured 30 20
168 25f. multicoloured 35 25
169 85f. multicoloured . . . . 1·25 80

1961. Air. Birds. Multicoloured.
170 50f. Type **31** . . . . 2·50 1·10
171 100f. Madame Verreaux's sunbird . . . . 4·50 1·60
172 200f. Blue-headed bee eater (vert) . . . . 7·50 3·75
173 250f. Crowned eagle (vert) . . 9·75 5·25
174 500f. Narina's trogon (vert) 22·00 10·25

1961.
175 **32** 50c. red, purple and green 10 10
176 – 1f. red, turquoise and bistre 10 10
177 – 2f. yellow and green . . . 10 10
178 – 3f. yellow, green and olive 20 15
179 – 5f. multicoloured 25 20
180 **32** 10f. red, green & turquoise 30 25
FLOWERS—VERT: 1f., 5f. Gabonese tulip (tree). HORIZ: 2f., 3f. Yellow cassia.

39 Capt. Ntchorere and Flags

1962. Capt. Ntchorere Commemoration.
195 **39** 80f. multicoloured . . . . 1·10 70

41 Globe and Emblem

1963. Freedom from Hunger.
196 **41** 25f.+5f. green, brown and red 60 60

1963. Air. 50th Anniv of Arrival of Dr Schweitzer in Gabon. Surch **100F JUBILE GABONAIS 1913-1963**.
197 **27** 100f. on 200f. brown, green and blue . . . . 2·75 1·40

43 Libreville Post Office

1963. Air. Cent of Gabon Postal Services.
198 **43** 100f. multicoloured . . . . 1·40 85

44 "Posts and Telecommunications"

1963. Air. African and Malagasy Posts and Telecommunications Union.
199 **44** 85f. multicoloured . . . . 1·40 80

45 "Telecommunications"

1963. Space Telecommunications.
200 **45** 25f. orange, blue and green 40 35
201 100f. brown, green & blue 1·60 1·40

46 Airline Emblem

1963. Air. 1st Anniv of "Air Afrique" and Inauguration of "DC-8" Service.
202 **46** 50f. multicoloured 90 55

47 "Europafrique"

1963. Air. European–African Economic Convention.
203 **47** 50f. multicoloured . . . . 1·25 65

48 UNESCO Emblem, Scales of Justice and Tree

1963. 15th Anniv of Declaration of Human Rights.
204 **48** 25f. slate, green and brown 45 30

49 Rameses and Gods, Wadi-es-Sebua

1964. Air. Nubian Monuments.
205 **49** 10f.+5f. brown and blue 85 85
206 25f.+5f. blue and red . . . 1·00 1·00
207 50f.+5f. purple & myrtle 1·50 1·50

50 Barograph

1964. World Meteorological Day.
208 **50** 25f. green, blue and bistre 55 35

51 Arms of Gabon

52 Map and African Heads of State

1964.
209 **51** 25f. multicoloured 50 30

1964. Air. 5th Anniv of Equatorial African Heads of State Conf.
210 **52** 100f. multicoloured . . . . 1·50 85

53 Atlantic Tarpon

1964. Gabon Fauna.
211 **53** 30f. black, blue and brown 90 45
212 – 60f. brown, chestnut & grn 1·50 60
213 – 80f. brown, green and blue 1·60 85
DESIGNS—VERT: 60f. Gorilla. HORIZ: 80f. African buffalo.

54 Ear of Wheat, Cogwheel and Globe

1964. Air. 1st Anniv of "Europafrique".
214 **54** 50f. blue, olive and red . . 1·25 80

55 Start of Race

1964. Air. Olympic Games, Tokyo.
215 **55** 25f. green, brown & orange 60 35
216 – 50f. brown, orange & green 1·10 45
217 – 100f. violet, purple & olive 2·25 90
218 – 200f. brown, purple and red . . . . 3·50 2·25
DESIGNS—VERT: 50f. Massaging athlete; 100f. Anointing before the Games. HORIZ: 200f. Athletes.

56 Posthorns, Envelope and Radio Mast

1964. Air. Pan-African and Malagasy Posts and Telecommunications Congress, Cairo.
220 **56** 25f. sepia, red and green . . . 55 30

57 "Co-operation"

1964. French, African and Malagasy Co-operation.
221 **57** 25f. brown, blue and slate . . . 55 40

58 "Dissotis rotundifolia" **59** Pres. Kennedy

1964. Flowers. Multicoloured.
222 3f. Type **58** 20 10
223 5f. "Gloriosa superba" . . . 30 15
224 15f. "Eulophia horsfallii" . . 55 25

1964. Air. Pres. Kennedy Commem.
225 **59** 100f. black, orange & green 1·60 1·40

60 Women in Public Service

1964. Air. Social Evolution of Gabonese Women.
227 **60** 50f. brown, blue and red 85 45

61 Sun and IQSY Emblem

1965. International Quiet Sun Year.
228 **61** 85f. multicoloured . . . . 1·40 85

62 Globe and ICY Emblem

1965. Air. International Co-operation Year.
229 **62** 50f. orange, turquoise & bl 85 45

63 17th-century Merchantman

1965. Air. Old Ships. Multicoloured.
230 25f. 16th-century galleon (vert) . . . . 1·25 55
231 50f. Type **63** . . . . 2·10 85
232 85f. 18th-century frigate (vert) 3·75 1·40
233 100f. 19th-century brig . . . 5·25 1·60

64 Morse Telegraph Apparatus

1965. Centenary of ITU.
234 **64** 30f. green, orange and blue 55 35

65 Manganese Mine, Moanda **67** Football

66 Nurse holding Child

1965. "Mining Riches".
235 **65** 15f. red, violet and blue . . 40 20
236 – 60f. red and blue . . . . . 1·25 60
DESIGN: 60f. Uranium mine, Mounana.

1965. Air. Gabon Red Cross.
237 **66** 100f. brown, red and green 1·60 85

1965. 1st African Games, Brazzaville.
238 **67** 25f. black, red & grn (post) 55 35
239 – 100f. purple, red and brown (air) . . . . . . 1·90 85
DESIGN (27 × 48½ mm): 100f. Basketball.

68 "Globe", Pylon and "Sun"

1965. Air. "Europafrique".
240 **68** 50f. multicoloured . . . . 1·40 55

69 President Mba

1965. Air. 5th Anniv of Independence.
241 **69** 25f. multicoloured 50 30

70 Okoukoue Dance **71** Abraham Lincoln

1965. Gabon Dances.
242 **70** 25f. yellow, brown & green 45 20
243 – 60f. black, red and brown 1·25 60
DESIGN: 60f. Makudji dance.

1965. Death Cent of Abraham Lincoln.
244 **71** 50f. multicoloured 80 45

72 Sir Winston Churchill

1965. Air. Churchill Commem.
245 **72** 100f. multicoloured . . . . 1·60 85

73 Dr. A. Schweitzer and Map

1965. Air. Schweitzer Commem.
246 **73** 1000f. gold . . . . 48·00 48·00

74 Pope John XXIII

1965. Air. Pope John Commem.
247 **74** 85f. multicoloured . . . . 1·10 80

75 Mail Carrier, Post Office and Van

1965. Stamp Day.
248 **75** 30f. brown, green and blue 50 40

76 Nurse and Patients

1966. Air. Red Cross. Multicoloured.
249 50f. Type **76** 95 55
250 100f. Bandaging patient . . . 1·90 85

77 Balumbu Mask **78** WHO Building

1966. World Festival of Negro Arts, Dakar. Multicoloured.
253 5f. Type **77** 20 15
254 10f. Statuette—"Ancestor of the Fang (tribe), Byeri" . . 30 20
255 25f. Fang mask 70 30
256 30f. Okuyi Myene mask . . . 90 50
257 85f. Bakota copper mask . . 2·10 1·10

1966. Inaug of WHO Headquarters, Geneva.
258 **78** 50f. black, yellow and blue 85 40

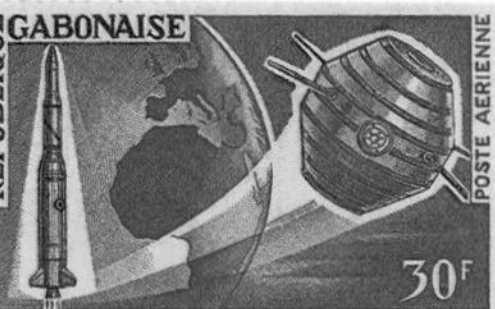

79 Satellite "A1" and Rocket

1966. Air. "Conquest of Space".
259 **79** 30f. lake, plum and blue 55 30
260 – 90f. plum, red and purple 1·40 60
DESIGN: 90f. Satellite "FR1" and rocket.

80 "Learning the Alphabet" **81** Footballer

1966. UNESCO Literacy Campaign.
261 **80** 30f. multicoloured 55 30

1966. World Cup Football Championship, England.
262 **81** 25f. bl, grn & lake (postage) 40 20
263 – 90f. purple and blue . . . 1·60 70
264 – 100f. slate and red (air) . . 1·90 90
DESIGNS—VERT: 90f. Footballer (different). HORIZ: 100f. Footballers on world map (47½ × 27 mm).

82 Industrial Scenes within leaves of "Plant" **83** Plywood Mill

1966. Air. "Europafrique".
265 **82** 50f. multicoloured . . . . 2·75 65

1966. Economic Development.
266 **83** 20f. lake, purple and green 45 30
267 – 85f. brown, blue and green 3·50 1·40
DESIGN: 85f. "Roger Butin" (oil rig).

84 Aircraft and "Air Afrique" Emblem

1966. Air. Inauguration of Douglas DC-8F Air Services.
268 **84** 30f. grey, black and orange 40 20

85 Making Deposit

1966. Savings Bank.
269 **85** 25f. brown, green and blue 55 30

86 Scouts and Camp Fire

1966. Scouting.
270 **86** 30f. brown, red and slate 55 35
271 – 50f. brown, lake and blue 1·00 45
DESIGN—VERT: 50f. Scouts taking oath.

87 Gabonese Scholar

1966. Air. 20th Anniv of UNESCO.

272	**87**	100f. black, buff and blue	1·40	65

88 Libreville Airport

1966. Air.

273	**88**	200f. brown, red and blue	3·25	1·10

89 Sikorsky S-43 Amphibian, Map and Flag (Aeromaritime's First Airmail Service, 1937)

1966. Stamp Day.

274	**89**	30f. multicoloured	80	50

90 Hippopotami

1967. Gabon Fauna. Multicoloured.

275	1f. Type **90**	10	10
276	2f. Crocodiles	15	10
277	3f. Water chevrotains	15	10
278	5f. Chimpanzees	20	10
279	10f. African elephants	65	30
280	20f. Leopards	1·25	40

91 Lions Emblem and Anniversary Dates

1967. 50th Anniv of Lions Int. Mult.

281	30f. Type **91**	55	30
282	50f. Lions emblem, map and globe	90	40

92 Masked Faces 93 ITY Emblem and Transport

1967. Libreville Carnival.

283	**92**	30f. blue, brown and yellow	60	30

1967. Int Tourist Year.

284	**93**	30f. multicoloured	1·25	40

94 Diving-board (Mexico City) 96 Atomic Symbol, Dove and Globe

95 Farman F.190

1967. Publicity for 1968 Olympic Games, Mexico.

285	**94**	25f. turquoise, blue & violet	45	20
286	–	30f. purple, lake and green	65	30
287	–	50f. blue, green and purple	1·10	60

DESIGNS: 30f. Sun and snow crystal; 50f. Ice rink, Grenoble.

1967. Air. Famous Aircraft.

288	**95**	200f. plum, blue & turq	3·25	1·10
289	–	300f. blue, purple & brown	5·50	1·40
290	–	500f. blue, purple and green	9·50	4·25

AIRCRAFT: 300f. De Havilland Heron 2; 500f. Potez 56.

1967. International Atomic Energy Agency.

291	**96**	30f. red, blue and green	65	30

97 Aircraft on Flight-paths

1967. Air. ICAO Commem.

292	**97**	100f. purple, blue and green	1·50	70

98 Pope Paul VI

1967. Papal Encyclical "Populorum Progressio".

293	**98**	30f. black, blue and green	65	35

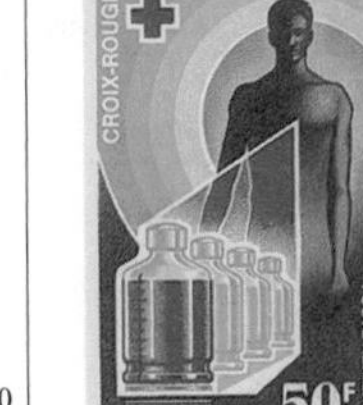

99 Blood Donor and Bank 100 Indigenous Emblems

1967. Air. Red Cross.

294	**99**	50f. multicoloured	1·10	45
295	–	100f. multicoloured	2·25	95

DESIGN: 100f. Heart and blood-transfusion apparatus.

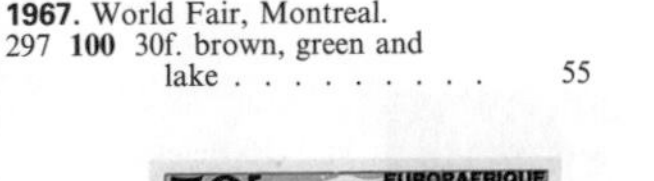

1967. World Fair, Montreal.

297	**100**	30f. brown, green and lake	55	30

101 "Europafrique"

1967. Europafrique.

298	**101**	50f. multicoloured	85	35

102 Orientation Diagram and Sun

1967. Air. World Scout Jamboree, Idaho.

299	**102**	50f. green, orange and blue	80	50
300	–	100f. red, green and blue	1·40	90

DESIGN: 100f. U.S. scout greeting Gabon scout on map.

103 U.N. Emblem, Gabon Women and Child

1967. U.N. Status of Women Commission.

301	**103**	75f. blue, green and brown	1·40	55

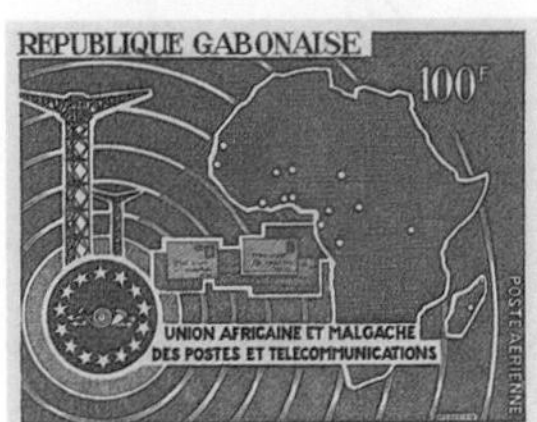

104 Map of Africa, Letters and Pylons

1967. Air. 5th Anniv of UAMPT.

302	**104**	100f. red, blue and olive	1·40	65

105 Baraka Mission, Libreville

1967. Air. 125th Anniv of American Missionaries Arrival.

303	**105**	100f. black, green and blue	1·60	85

106 U.N. Emblem and Book with Supporters 107 "Draconea fragans"

1967. Air. U.N. Int Rights Commission.

304	**106**	60f. multicoloured	90	55

1967. Gabon Trees.

305	**107**	5f. brown, green and blue (postage)	20	15
306	–	10f. green, bronze and blue	35	20
307	–	20f. red, green and brown	55	30
308	–	50f. green, bistre and blue (air)	95	40
309	–	100f. multicoloured	1·90	70

DESIGNS: 10f. "Pycnanthus angolensis"; 20f. "Disthemonanthus benthamianus". (27 × 48 mm): 50f. "Baillonella toxisperma"; 100f. "Aucoumea klaineana".

108 "Belgrano" and "Jean Guiton" (19th-century steam packets)

1967. Stamp Day. Multicoloured.

311	30f. Type **108**	1·25	45
312	30f. "Ango" and "Lucie Delmas" (modern mail carriers)	1·25	45

Nos. 311/12 were issued together, se-tenant, forming a composite design.

109 Chancellor Adenauer

1968. Air. Adenauer Commem.

313	**109**	100f. sepia, red and yellow	1·90	65

110 African WHO Building

1968. 20th Anniv of WHO.

315	**110**	20f. purple, blue and green	55	30

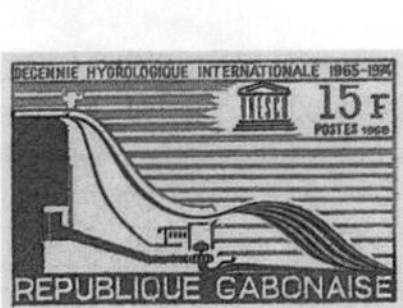

111 Dam and Power-station 112 President Bongo

1968. International Hydrological Decade.

316	**111**	15f. blue, orange and lake	45	20

1968.

317	**112**	25f. black, yellow & green	40	20
318	–	30f. black, turquoise & pur	45	20

DESIGN: 30f. Pres. Bongo (half-length portrait).

113 "Madonna and Child with Rosary" (Murillo)

1968. Air. Religious Paintings. Multicoloured.

319	60f. Type **113**	90	45
320	90f. "Christ in Bonds" (Luis de Morales)	1·40	65
321	100f. "St. John at Patmos" (Juan Mates) (horiz)	1·60	85

114 Beribboned Rope

1968. Air. 5th Anniv of Europafrique.
322 **114** 50f. multicoloured 80 40

115 Refinery and Tanker

1968. Inauguration of Petroleum Refinery, Port Gentil, Gabon.
323 **115** 30f. multicoloured 70 30

116 Distribution to the Needy

1968. Air. Red Cross. Multicoloured.
324 50f. Type **116** 85 35
325 100f. "Support the Red Cross" . . . . 1·90 65

117 High-jumping

1968. Air. Olympic Games, Mexico.
327 **117** 25f. brown, slate and red 50 30
328 – 30f. brown, blue and red 60 35
329 – 100f. brown, yellow & blue . . . . 1·60 80
330 – 200f. brown, slate & green 3·00 1·40
DESIGNS—VERT: 30f. Cycling; 100f. Judo. HORIZ: 200f. Boxing.

118 Open Book **120** Coffee

1968. Literacy Day.
332 **118** 25f. brown, red and blue 40 20

1968. Agricultural Produce.
333 **120** 20f. red, myrtle and green 45 15
334 – 40f. orange, brown & grn 75 35
DESIGNS: 40f. Cocoa.

121 "Junon" (sail/steam warship) **123** Advocate holding "Charter"

122 President Mba and Flag

1968. Stamp Day.
335 **121** 30f. violet, green & orange . . . . 1·10 55

1968. Air. 1st Death Anniv of Pres. Mba.
336 **122** 1,000f. multicoloured . . 18·00 18·00

1968. Human Rights Year.
337 **123** 20f. black, green and red 45 30

124 President Bongo, Maps of Gabon and Owendo Port

1968. Air. "Laying of 1st Stone", Owendo Port. Multicoloured.
338 25f. Type **124** 60 25
339 30f. Harbour Project 75 20

125 "The Cloisters of Ste. Marie des Anges" (F. M. Granet)

1969. Air. "Philexafrique" Stamp Exhibition, Abidjan, Ivory Coast (1st issue).
340 **125** 100f. multicoloured . . . 2·75 2·75
See also No. 346.

126 Mahatma Gandhi

1969. Air. "Apostles of Peace".
341 **126** 25f. black and pink . . . 45 15
342 – 30f. black and green . . . 55 30
343 – 50f. black and blue . . . 85 35
344 – 100f. black and mauve . . 1·50 60
DESIGNS: 30f. J. F. Kennedy; 50f. R. F. Kennedy; 100f. Martin Luther King.

127 Oil Refinery. Port Gentil and Gabon Stamp of 1932

1969. Air. "Philexafrique" Stamp Exhibition, Abidjan, Ivory Coast (2nd issue).
346 **127** 50f. blue, red and green 1·50 1·50

128 View of Okanda Gates

1969. African Tourist Year.
347 **128** 10f. brown, green and blue 20 10
348 – 15f. blue, green and red 1·25 25
349 – 25f. purple, blue & brown 40 20
350 – 30f. brown, choc & blue 85 35
DESIGNS—HORIZ: 15f. Great barracuda. VERT: 25f. Kinguele Falls; 30f. Hunting trophies.

129 "Battle of Rivoli" (Philippoteaux)

1969. Air. Birth Bicentenary of Napoleon Bonaparte. Multicoloured.
351 50f. Type **129** . . . . 1·60 1·10
352 100f. "Oath of the Army" (J. L. David) . . . . . . 1·90 1·60
353 250f. "The Emperor Napoleon I on the Terrace at St. Cloud" (Ducis) . . . 7·50 4·50

130 Mvet **132** "Aframomum polyanthum"

131 Refugees and Red Cross Plane

1969. Traditional Musical Instruments from Folk Art Museum, Libreville.
354 **130** 25f. lake, drab and purple 40 15
355 – 30f. brown, drab and red 45 20
356 – 50f. lake, drab and purple 85 35
357 – 100f. brown, drab and red 1·60 65
DESIGNS: 30f. Ngombi harp; 50f. Ebele and Mbe drums; 100f. Medzang xylophone.

1969. Air. Red Cross. Aid for Biafra. Multicoloured.
359 15f. Type **131** 40 20
360 20f. Hospital and supplies van 45 25
361 25f. Doctor and nurse tending children 50 25
362 30f. Children and hospital . . 60 30

1969. Flowers. Multicoloured.
364 1f. Type **132** 10 10
365 2f. "Chlamydocola chlamydantha" 15 10
366 5f. "Costus dinklagei" . . . 20 10
367 10f. "Cola rostrata" 45 20
368 20f. "Dischistocalyx grandifolius" 70 45

133 Astronauts and Module on Moon

1969. Air. 1st Man on the Moon. Embossed on gold foil.
369 **133** 1000f. gold . . . . 18·00 18·00

134 Tree and Insignia **135** Oil Derrick

1969. "National Renovation".
370 **134** 25f. multicoloured 40 30

1969. 20th Anniv of Elf/Spafe Petroleum Consortium.
371 25f. Type **135** 35 10
372 50f. Oil rig 90 30

136 African Workers **137** Arms of Lambarene

1969. 50th Anniv of ILO.
373 **136** 30f. green, blue and red 55 30

1969. Town Arms (1st series).
374 **137** 20f. multicoloured 50 15
375 – 25f. gold, black and blue 80 15
376 – 30f. multicoloured 90 45
ARMS: 25f. Port-Gentil; 30f. Libreville.
See also Nos. 405/7, 460/2, 504/6, 510/12, 539/41, 596/8, 618/20, 669/71, 684/6, 729/31, 800/2, 898/900, 953/4, 1083 and 1128.

138 Adoumas Mail Pirogue

1969. Stamp Day.
377 **138** 30f. brown, emerald & grn 80 35

139 Satellite and Globe

1970. World Telecommunications Day.
378 **139** 25f. blue, black and lake 55 35

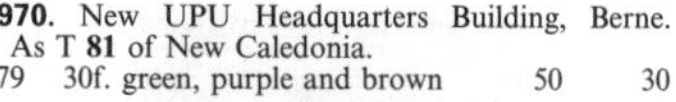

1970. New UPU Headquarters Building, Berne. As T **81** of New Caledonia.
379 30f. green, purple and brown 50 30

140 Japanese Geisha and African

1970. "EXPO 70" World Fair, Osaka, Japan.
380 **140** 30f. multicoloured 50 30

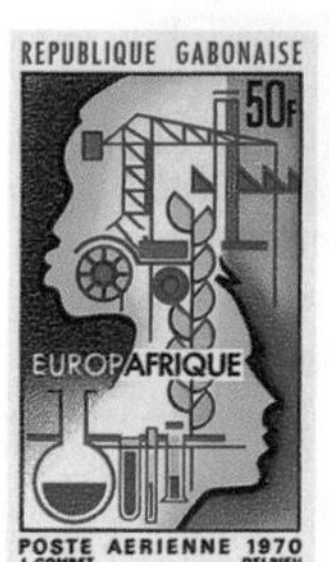

141 "Co-operation" **142** Icarus and the Sun

1970. Air. "Europafrique".
381 **141** 50f. multicoloured 85 35

1970. Air. History of Flight.
382 **142** 25f. blue, yellow and red 55 35
383 – 100f. green, brown & pur 1·40 70
384 – 200f. blue, red and slate 3·00 1·40
DESIGNS: 100f. Leonardo da Vinci's design for wings; 200f. Jules Verne's rocket approaching Moon.

143 UAMPT Emblem

1970. Air. UAMPT Conference, Libreville.
386 **143** 200f. gold, green and blue 2·75 1·25

144 Throwing-knives

1970. Air. Gabonaise Weapons, Folk Art Museum, Libreville. All values blue, red and green.
387 25f. Type **144** 45 30
388 30f. Assegai and crossbow (vert) 55 35
389 50f. War knives (vert) 80 40
390 90f. Dagger and sheath . . . 1·60 55

145 Japanese Masks, Gateway and Mt. Fuji

1970. Air. "Expo 70" World Fair, Osaka, Japan. Embossed on gold foil.
392 **145** 1000f. red, black and green . . . . 17·00 17·00

146 President Bongo

1970. Air. 10th Anniv of Independence.
393 **146** 200f. multicoloured . . . 3·25 1·60

147 Aircraft, Map and Airport

1970. 10th Anniv (1969) of Aerial Navigation Security Agency for Africa and Madagascar.
394 **147** 100f. green and blue . . . 1·40 65

148 "Portrait of Young Man" (School of Raphael)

1970. Air. 450th Death Anniv of Raphael. Multicoloured.
395 50f. Type **148** 90 40
396 100f. "Jeanne d'Aragon" (Raphael) . . . . 1·60 70
397 200f. "The Virgin of the Blue Diadem" (Raphael) . . . . 3·25 1·60

149 U.N. Emblem, Globe, Dove and Wheat

1970. 25th Anniv of United Nations.
398 **149** 30f. multicoloured 55 35

150 Bushbucks

1970. Wild Fauna. Multicoloured.
399 5f. Type **150** 35 25
400 15f. Pel's flying squirrel . . . 55 30
401 25f. White-cheeked mangabey (vert) . . . . 1·40 55
402 40f. African golden cat . . . 2·25 1·10
403 60f. Servaline genet . . . . . 3·25 1·40

151 Presidents Bongo and Pompidou

1971. Air. Visit of Pres. Pompidou of France to Gabon.
404 **151** 50f. multicoloured . . . . 1·60 85

1971. Town Arms (2nd series). As T **137**. Multicoloured.
405 20f. multicoloured 40 15
406 25f. black, green and gold . . 40 15
407 30f. multicoloured 55 20
ARMS: 20f. Mouila; 25f. Bitam; 30f. Oyem.

152 Four Races and Emblem

154 Freesias

153 Telecommunications Map

1971. Racial Equality Year.
408 **152** 40f. black, orange & yell 55 30

1971. Pan-African Telecommunications Network.
409 **153** 30f. multicoloured 50 30

1971. Air. "Flowers by Air". Mult.
410 15f. Type **154** 35 20
411 25f. Carnations 50 20
412 40f. Roses 85 35
413 55f. Daffodils 95 35
414 75f. Orchids . . . . 1·90 60
415 120f. Tulips . . . . 2·25 80

155 Napoleon's Death Mask

1971. Air. 150th Death Anniv of Napoleon. Multicoloured.
417 100f. Type **155** . . . . . . 2·25 60
418 200f. "Longwood House" (after Marchand) (horiz) 3·25 1·40
419 500f. Napoleon's Tomb . . . 8·25 4·00

156 "Charaxes smaragdalis"

157 Hertzian Communications Centre, Nkol Ogoum

1971. Butterflies. Multicoloured.
420 5f. Type **156** 40 30
421 10f. "Euxanthe crossleyi" . . 90 40
422 15f. "Epiphora rectifascia" 1·60 45
423 25f. "Imbrasia bouvieri" . . 2·00 70

1971. World Telecommunications Day.
424 **157** 40f. red, blue and green 60 35

159 Red Crosses

1971. Air. Red Cross.
426 **159** 50f. multicoloured 95 40

160 Uranium

1971. Air. Minerals. Multicoloured.
427 85f. Type **160** . . . . 3·25 1·90
428 90f. Manganese . . . . . . 4·00 2·25

161 Landing Module above Moon's Surface

1971. Air. Moon Flight of "Apollo 15". Embossed on gold foil.
429 **161** 1500f. multicoloured . . . 19·00 19·00

162 Mother feeding Child

1971. 15th Anniv of Social Welfare Fund.
430 **162** 30f. brown, bistre & mve 50 30

163 U.N. Emblem and New York Headquarters

1971. 10th Anniv of Gabon's Admission to United Nations.
431 **163** 30f. multicoloured 45 30

164 Great Egret

1971. Birds. Multicoloured.
432 30f. Type **164** . . . . 1·50 80
433 40f. Grey parrot . . . . . . 2·25 1·10
434 50f. Woodland kingfisher . . 2·50 1·40
435 75f. Grey-necked bald crow 3·75 1·50
436 100f. Green turaco . . . . . 5·50 2·25

166 UAMPT Building, Brazzaville and Bakota copper mask

1971. Air. 10th Anniv of African and Malagasy Posts and Telecommunications Union.
439 **166** 100f. multicoloured . . . 1·40 65

167 Ski-jumping

1972. Air. Winter Olympic Games, Sapporo, Japan.
440 **167** 40f. violet, brown & green 65 35
441 – 130f. green, violet & brn 1·90 80
DESIGN: 130f. Speed-skating.

168 "Santa Maria della Salute" (Vanvitelli)

1972. Air. UNESCO "Save Venice" Campaign. Multicoloured.
443 60f. "The Basin and Grand Canal" (Vanvitelli) (horiz) 1·10 55
444 70f. "Rialto Bridge" (Canaletto) . . . . 1·60 85
445 140f. Type **168** . . . . . 2·75 1·10
On the stamp the design of No. 445 wrongly attributed to Caffi.

170 Hotel Intercontinental

1972. Air. Opening of Hotel Intercontinental.
447 **170** 40f. brown, green and blue 60 30

1972. Air. Visit of the Grand Master, Sovereign Order of Malta. No. 289 surch **VISITE OFFICIELLE GRAND MAITRE ORDRE SOUVERAIN DE MALTE 3 MARS 1972 50F** and emblem.
448 50f. on 300f. blue, pur & brn 80 40

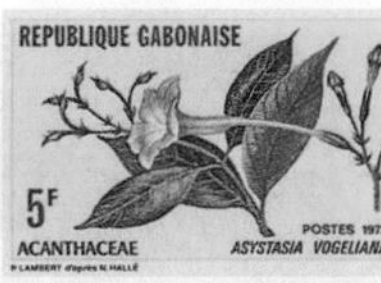
172 "Asystasia vogeliana"

1972. Flowers. Varieties of Acanthus. Multicoloured.
449 5f. Type **172** 20 20
450 10f. "Stenandriopsis guineensis" 35 25
451 20f. "Thomandersia hensii" 55 35
452 30f. "Thomandersia laurifolia" 85 50
453 40f. "Physacanthus batanganus" . . . . 1·40 65
454 65f. "Physacanthus nematosiphon" . . . . . 2·25 85

173 "The Discus-thrower" (Alcamene)

174 Pasteur with Microscope

1972. Air. Olympic Games, Munich. Ancient Sculptures.
455 **173** 30f. grey and red 60 50
456 – 100f. grey and red . . . . 1·40 70
457 – 140f. grey and red . . . . 1·90 1·00

DESIGNS: 100f. "Doryphoros" (Polyclete); 140f. "Gladiator" (Agasias).

1972. 150th Anniv of Louis Pasteur (scientist).
459 **174** 80f. purple, green & red 65 35

1972. Town Arms (3rd series). Vert designs as T **137**. Multicoloured.
460 30f. multicoloured 40 20
461 40f. multicoloured 55 20
462 60f. silver, black and green 90 30
ARMS: 30f. Franceville; 40f. Makokou; 60f. Tchibanga.

175 Global Emblem

1972. World Telecommunications Day.
463 **175** 40f. black, orange & yell 55 30

176 Nat King Cole

1972. Famous Negro Musicians. Mult.
464 40f. Type **176** 60 30
465 60f. Sidney Bechet 90 45
466 100f. Louis Armstrong . . . 1·60 65

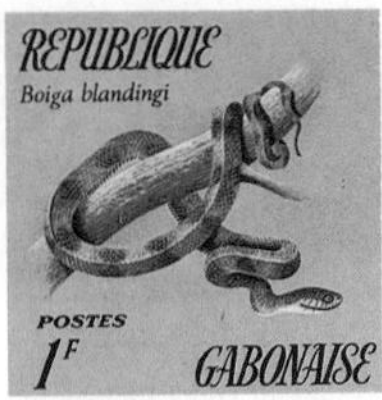

177 "Boiga blandingi"

1972. Reptiles. Multicoloured.
467 1f. Type **177** 10 10
468 2f. Sand snake 15 10
469 3f. Egg-eating snake 20 15
470 15f. Pit viper 70 25
471 25f. Jameson's tree asp . . . 1·40 30
472 50f. Gabon viper . . . . . . 2·25 50

178 "The Adoration of the Magi" (Bruegel the Elder)

1972. Air. Christmas. Multicoloured.
473 30f. Type **178** 60 35
474 40f. "Madonna and Child" (Basaiti) (vert) 85 45

1972. Air. Olympic Gold Medal Winners. Nos. 455/7 surch as listed below.
475 **125** 40f. on 30f. grey and red 70 40
476 – 120f. on 100f. grey & red 1·40 65
477 – 170f. on 140f. grey & red 2·10 90
SURCHARGES: No. 475, **MORELON**; 476, **KEINO**; 477, **SPITZ**.

180 Dr. G. A. Hansen and Hospital, Lambarene

182 "Charaxes candiope"

181 "Thematic Collecting"

1973. Centenary of Dr. Hansen's Discovery of Leprosy Bacillus.
478 **180** 30f. brown, green and blue 65 35

1973. Air. "PHILEXGABON 73" International Stamp Exhibition, Libreville.
479 **181** 100f. multicoloured . . . 2·40 85

1973. Butterflies. Multicoloured.
481 10f. Type **182** 40 15
482 15f. "Eunica pechueli" . . . 50 15
483 20f. "Cyrestis camillus" . . . 80 30
484 30f. "Charaxes castor" . . . 1·10 40
485 40f. "Charaxes ameliae" . . 1·25 55
486 50f. "Pseudacrea boisduvali" 1·40 80

183 Douglas DC-10-30 over Libreville Airport

1973. Air. Libreville-Paris Air Service by "Air Afrique" "DC 10 Libreville". No gum.
487 **183** 40f. multicoloured . . . . 1·10 55

184 Montgolfier's Balloon, 1783

186 Interpol Emblem

185 Power Station

1973. History of Flight.
488 **184** 1f. green, myrtle & brown 10 10
489 – 2f. green and blue . . . 10 10
490 – 3f. new blue, blue & orge 10 10
491 – 4f. violet & reddish violet 25 15
492 – 5f. green and orange . . 30 20
493 – 10f. purple and blue . . 45 20
493a – 10f. blue 45 45
DESIGNS—HORIZ: 2f. Santos-Dumont's airship "Ballon No. 6", 1901; 3f. Chanute's glider, 1896; 4f. Clement Ader's "Avion III" flying-machine, 1897; 5f. Bleriot's cross-Channel flight, 1909; 10f. (both) Fabre's seaplane "Hydravion", 1910.

1973. Air. Kinguele Hydro-electric Project.
494 **185** 30f. green and brown . . 50 25
495 – 40f. blue, green and brown 60 25
DESIGN: 40f. Dam.

1973. 50th Anniv of International Criminal Police Organization (Interpol).
496 **186** 40f. blue and red 55 35

187 Dish Aerial and Station

188 Gabon Woman

1973. Inauguration of "2 Decembre" Satellite Earth Station.
497 **187** 40f. brown, blue and green 55 30

1973. Air. M'Bigou Stone Sculptures.
498 **188** 100f. brown, blue & black 1·50 80
499 – 200f. green and brown . . 2·75 1·40
DESIGN: 200f. Gabon man wearing head-dress.

1973. Air. Pan-African Drought Relief. No. 426 surch **SECHERESSE SOLIDARITE AFRICAINE 100F**.
500 **159** 100f. on 50f. mult . . . . 1·40 85

190 Party Headquarters

1973. Gabonaise Democratic Party Headquarters, Libreville.
501 **190** 30f. multicoloured 40 20

191 Astronauts and Lunar Rover

1973. Air. Moon Flight of "Apollo 17".
502 **191** 500f. multicoloured . . . 6·75 3·25

192 Crane with Letter and Telecommunications Emblem

1973. 12th Anniv of African and Malagasy Posts and Telecommunications Union.
503 **192** 100f. plum, purple & blue 90 55

1973. Town Arms (4th series). As T **137** dated "1973". Multicoloured.
504 30f. Kango 55 20
505 40f. Booue 65 30
506 60f. Koula-Moutou . . . . . 1·00 35

193 St. Theresa of Lisieux

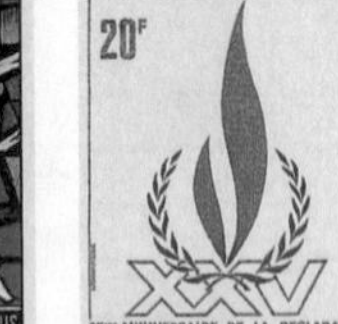

194 Flame Emblem

1973. Birth Cent of St. Theresa of Lisieux. Stained-glass windows in the Basilica at Lisieux. Multicoloured.
507 30f. Type **193** 55 25
508 40f. "St. Theresa with Saviour" 65 30

1973. 25th Anniv of Declaration of Human Rights.
509 **194** 20f. red, blue and green 40 20

1974. Town Arms (5th series). As T **137** dated "1974". Multicoloured.
510 5f. Gamba 15 10
511 10f. Ogooue-Lolo 15 10
512 15f. Fougamou 20 15

195 White-collared Mangabey

1974. Monkeys. Multicoloured.
513 40f. Type **195** 55 30
514 60f. Moustached monkey . . 85 35
515 80f. Mona monkey . . . . . 1·40 50

196 De Gaulle and Houphouet-Boigny

1974. Air. 30th Anniv of Brazzaville Conference.
516 **196** 40f. blue and purple . . . 1·00 55

197 "Pleasure Boats" (Monet)

1974. Air. Impressionist Paintings. Multicoloured.
517 40f. Type **197** 90 45
518 50f. "End of an Arabesque" (Degas) (vert) . . . . . . 1·40 65
519 130f. "Young Girl with Flowers" (Renoir) (vert) 2·25 1·10

198 American Bald Eagle, and Astronaut on Moon

1974. Air. 5th Anniv of First Manned Moon Landing.
520 **198** 200f. blue, brown & indigo . . . . 3·00 1·75

199 Ogooue River, Lambarene

1974. Gabon Views. Multicoloured.
521 30f. Type **199** 35 25
522 50f. Cape Esterias 50 30
523 75f. Rope bridge, Poubara 85 45

200 UPU Emblem and Letters

1974. Air. Centenary of UPU.
524 **200** 150f. turquoise and blue 1·90 80
525 – 300f. red and orange . . 3·25 1·60
DESIGN: 300f. Similar to Type **200**, but with design reversed.

201 "Apollo" and "Soyuz" Spacecraft, Flight Badge and Maps of U.S.A. and U.S.S.R.

1974. Air. Soviet-American Co-operation in Space.
526 **201** 1000f. green, red and blue 7·75 5·50

202 Ball and Footballers

1974. Air. World Cup Football Championship, West Germany.
527 **202** 40f. red, green and brown 50 30
528 – 65f. green, brown and red 65 40
529 – 100f. brown, red and green 1·10 65
DESIGNS: 65f., 100f. Football scenes similar to Type **202**.

203 Manioc Plantation

1974. Agriculture. Multicoloured.
531 40f. Type **203** 50 20
532 50f. Palm-tree grove 60 20

204 African Leaders, UDEAC Headquarters and Flags

1974. 10th Anniv of Central African Customs and Economic Union. Multicoloured.
533 40f. Type **204** (postage) 50 30
534 100f. African leaders, UDEAC Headquarters Building (air) 85 45

205 "The Visitation"

1974. Air. Christmas. Details from 15th-century tapestry of Notre Dame, Beaune. Multicoloured.
535 40f. Type **205** 80 35
536 50f. "The Annunciation" (horiz) 90 45

206 Dr. Schweitzer and Lambarene Hospital

1975. Air. Birth Centenary of Dr. Albert Schweitzer.
537 **206** 500f. green, lilac & brown 5·50 3·25

207 Dialogue Hotel

1975. Inauguration of "Hotel du Dialogue", Libreville.
538 **207** 50f. multicoloured 55 30

1975. Town Arms (6th series). As T **137** dated "1975". Multicoloured.
539 5f. Ogoouе-Ivindo 10 10
540 10f. Moabi 15 10
541 15f. Moanda 25 10

208 "The Crucifixion" (Bellini)

1975. Air. Easter. Multicoloured.
542 140f. Type **208** 1·40 55
543 150f. "The Resurrection" (Burgundian School) (36 × 49 mm) 1·90 80

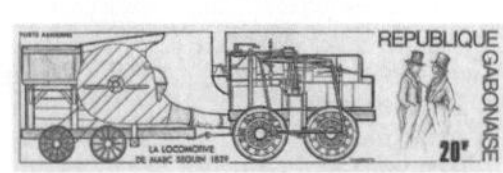

209 Marc Seguin Locomotive, 1829, France (⅓-size illustration)

1975. Air. Scale Drawings of Steam Locomotives.
544 **209** 20f. blue, brown & brt bl 1·10 40
545 – 25f. red, yellow and blue 1·50 50
546 – 40f. blue, purple and green 1·90 80
547 – 50f. purple, blue and green 2·75 1·10
LOCOMOTIVES: 25f. "Iron Duke", 1847, Great Britain; 40f. "Thomas Rogers", 1855, U.S.A. (inscr "1895"); 50f. Class AA steam locomotive, 1934, Russia.

210 Congress Emblem

1975. 17th Lions Club Congress, Libreville.
548 **210** 50f. multicoloured 70 30

211 Aerial and Network Map

1975. Gabonese Development of Hertzian Wave Radio Links.
549 **211** 40f. green, brown and blue 55 35

212 Man and Woman and IWY Emblem

1975. International Women's Year.
550 **212** 50f. brown, red and blue 1·75 35

213 Ange M'ba (founder of Gabonaise Scouts)

1975. "Nordjamb 75" World Scout Jamboree, Norway.
551 **213** 40f. black, purple & green 45 30
552 – 50f. purple, green and red 55 30
DESIGN: 50f. Scout camp.

214 Pink Snapper

1975. Fishes. Multicoloured.
553 30f. Type **214** 70 25
554 40f. Guinean threadfin 85 40
555 50f. Round sardinella 1·50 40
556 120f. West African parrot-fish 2·50 85

215 Swimming Pool

1975. Air. Olympic Games, Montreal (1976) (1st issue). Multicoloured.
557 100f. Type **215** 1·00 45
558 150f. Boxing ring 1·40 65
559 300f. Aerial view of Games complex 2·75 1·40
See also Nos. 591/3.

1975. Air. "Apollo–Soyuz" Space Link. No. 526 optd **JONCTION 17 Juillet 1975**.
561 **201** 1000f. green, red and blue 7·25 4·00

217 "The Annunciation" (M. Denis)

1975. Air. Christmas. Multicoloured.
562 40f. Type **217** 60 30
563 50f. "Virgin and Child with Two Saints" (Fra Filippo Lippi) 80 40

218 Franceville Complex

1975. Inauguration of Agro-Industrial Complex, Franceville.
564 **218** 60f. multicoloured 65 35

219 Concorde

1975. Air.
565 **219** 500f. ultramarine, bl & red 7·75 4·50

1975. Air. Concorde's First Commercial Flight. Surch **1000F 21 Janv. 1976 1er Vol Commercial de CONCORDE**.
566 **219** 1000f. on 500f. ultram, blue and red 14·00 9·00

221 Tchibanga Bridge

1975. Gabon Bridges. Multicoloured.
567 5f. Type **221** 15 10
568 10f. Mouila Bridge 20 15
569 40f. Kango Bridges 45 20
570 50f. Lambarene Bridges (vert) 60 30

222 A. G. Bell and Early and Modern Telephones

1976. Telephone Centenary.
571 **222** 60f. grey, green and blue 60 30

223 Skiing (slalom)

1976. Air. Winter Olympic Games, Innsbruck.
572 **223** 100f. brown, blue & black 95 45
573 – 250f. brown, blue & black 2·10 1·25
DESIGN: 250f. Speed skating.

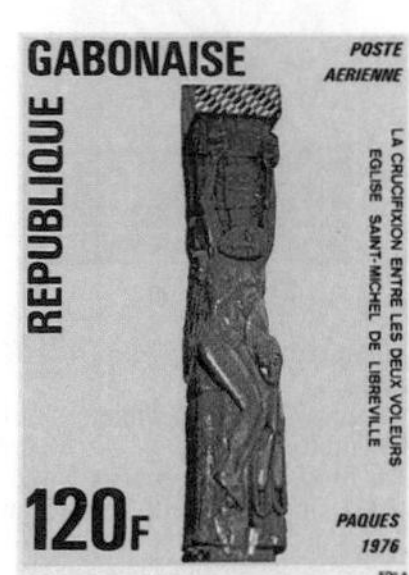

224 "The Crucifixion between Thieves" (wood-carving)

1976. Air. Easter. Multicoloured.
575 120f. Type **224** 1·10 60
576 130f. "Thomas placing finger in Jesus' wounds" (wood-carving) 1·40 80

225 Monseigneur Jean-Remy Bessieux

1976. Death Centenary of Bessieux.
577 **225** 50f. brown, blue & green 50 30

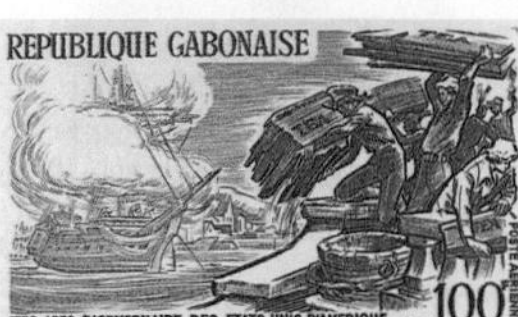

226 Boston Tea Party

1976. Air. Bicent of American Revolution.
578 **226** 100f. brown, orange & bl 90 50
579 – 150f. brown, orange & bl 1·40 65
580 – 200f. brown, orange & bl 2·00 1·00
DESIGNS: 150f. Battle scenes at Hudson Bay and New York; 200f. Wrecking of King George III's statue in New York.

227 Games Emblem

1976. 1st Central African Games.

581	227	50f. multicoloured	45	20
582		60f. multicoloured	55	30

1976. Air. U.S. Independence Day. Nos. 578/80 optd **4 JUILLET 1976**.

583	226	100f. brown, orange & bl	95	55
584	–	150f. brown, orange & bl	1·40	65
585	–	200f. brown, orange & bl	2·00	1·00

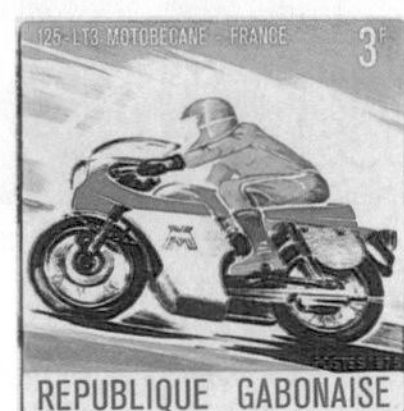
229 Motobecane 125-LT3 (France)

1976. Motorcycles.

586	229	3f. black, green and blue	15	10
587	–	5f. black, mauve & yellow	15	15
588	–	10f. black, green and blue	35	15
589	–	20f. black, green and red	65	15
590	–	100f. black, blue and red	2·00	70

MOTORCYCLES: 5f. Bultaco 125 (Spain); 10f. Suzuki 125 (Japan); 20f. Kawasaki H2R (Japan); 100f. Harley-Davidson 750-TX (USA).

230 Running

1976. Air. Olympic Games, Montreal (2nd issue). Multicoloured.

591	230	100f. brown, blue & violet	85	45
592	–	200f. multicoloured . . .	1·60	90
593	–	260f. brown, grn & myrtle	2·25	1·10

DESIGNS: 200f. Football; 260f. High Jumping.

231 Presidents Giscard d'Estaing and Bongo

1976. Air. Visit of Pres. Giscard d'Estaing to Gabon.

595	231	60f. multicoloured	90	40

1976. Town Arms (7th series). As T **137** dated "1976".

596	15f. multicoloured	15	10
597	25f. multicoloured	20	10
598	50f. black, gold and red . . .	50	15

ARMS: 15f. Nyanga; 25f. Mandji; 50f. Mekambo.

232 Ricefield and Plant

1976. Agriculture. Multicoloured.

599	50f. Type **232**	55	20
600	60f. Pepper grove and plant	65	30

233 "Presentation at the Temple"

1976. Air. Christmas. Wood-carvings. Mult.

601	50f. Type **233**	60	30
602	60f. "The Nativity"	70	35

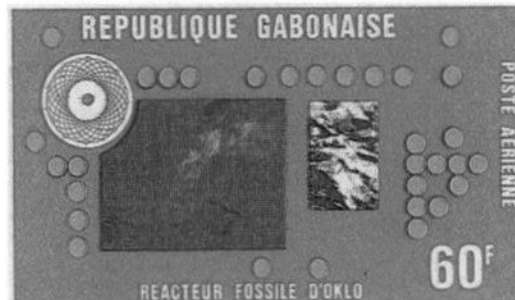
234 Photograph of Site

1976. Air. Discovery of Oklo Fossil Reactor.

603	234	60f. multicoloured	65	35

235 "The Last Supper" (Juste de Gand)

1977. Air. Easter. Multicoloured.

604	50f. Type **235**	80	45
605	100f. "The Deposition" (N. Poussin)	1·40	65

1977. Agriculture. As T **232** but dated "1977". Multicoloured.

606	50f. Banana plantation . . .	55	20
607	60f. Groundnuts and market	65	30

236 Printed Circuit and Telephone

1977. 9th World Telecommunications Day.

608	236	60f. multicoloured	55	30

237 "Air Gabon" Insignia and Boeing 747

1977. Air. 1st "Air Gabon" Intercontinental Air Service.

609	237	60f. blue, yellow and green	70	40

238 Cap Lopez

1977. Gabon Views and Features. Mult.

610	50f. Type **238**	45	20
611	60f. Oyem	45	20
612	70f. Lebamba grotto	60	25

239 Beethoven and Musical Score

1977. Air. 150th Death Anniv of Beethoven.

613	239	260f. blue	2·25	1·40

240 Palais des Congres

1977. Organization of African Unity Conference.

614	240	100f. multicoloured . . .	85	55

241 Gabon Coat of Arms

1977.

615	241	50f. blue (22 × 36 mm) . .	65	30
616		60f. orange	60	30
617		80f. red	70	35

1977. Town Arms (8th series). As T **137** but dated "1977". Multicoloured.

618	50f. Omboue	45	20
619	60f. Minvoul	50	20
620	90f. Mayumba	85	35

242 Parliament Building, Libreville

1977. National Festival.

621	242	50f. multicoloured	50	20

243 Renault "Voiturette" of 1902

1977. Birth Centenary of Louis Renault (motor pioneer).

622	243	5f. blue, red and brown	20	15
623	–	10f. brown and red . . .	20	15
624	–	30f. red, green and drab	65	30
625	–	40f. green, yellow & brown	1·10	35
626	–	100f. black, turquoise & bl	2·25	1·00

DESIGNS: 10f. Coupe of 1921; 30f. "Torpedo Scaphandrier" of 1925; 40f. "Reinastella" of 1929; 100f. "Nerva Grand Sport" of 1937.

244 Lindbergh and "Spirit of St. Louis"

1977. Air. 50th Anniv of Lindbergh's Transatlantic Flight.

628	244	500f. blue, brown & lt bl	5·50	3·25

245 Footballer

1977. Air. World Cup Football Championship Qualifying Rounds.

629	245	250f. multicoloured . . .	2·25	1·25

246 "Viking" on Mars

1977. Air. "Operation Viking".

630	246	1000f. multicoloured . . .	8·25	8·25

1977. Air. 1st Commercial Paris–New York Flight by "Concorde". Optd **PARIS NEW YORK PREMIER VOL 22.11.77**.

631	219	500f. ultramarine, bl & red	7·25	5·00

248 "Study of a Head"

1977. Air. 400th Birth Anniv of Peter Paul Rubens. Multicoloured.

632	60f. "Lion Hunt" (horiz) . .	65	25
633	80f. "Hippopotamus Hunt" (horiz)	85	40
634	200f. Type **248**	2·25	1·00

249 "Adoration of the Magi" (Rubens)

1977. Air. Christmas. Multicoloured.

636	60f. Type **249**	65	35
637	80f. "The Flight into Egypt" (Rubens)	90	45

250 "Still Life and Maori Statue"

1978. Air. 75th Death Anniv of Paul Gauguin. Multicoloured.

638	150f. Type **250**	1·90	65
639	300f. "Self-Portrait"	3·25	1·40

251 Globe

1978. World Leprosy Day.

640	251	80f. green, blue and red	55	30

252 Boeing 747 Airplane, Diesel Locomotive and President

1978. 10th Anniv of National Renewal.
641 **252** 500f. multicoloured . . . 10·00 5·25

253 Citroen "Cabriolet", 1922

1978. Birth Centenary of Andre Citroen (motor pioneer).
642 **253** 10f. purple, green and red 30 15
643 – 50f. green, blue & turq . . 65 20
644 – 60f. grey, brown and blue 1·00 40
645 – 80f. blue, slate and lilac 1·10 45
646 – 200f. brown, slate & orge 2·75 1·00
DESIGNS: 50f. "B14" Taxi, 1927; 60f. 8 h.p. "Berline", 1932; 80f. 7 h.p. "Berline" saloon, 1934; 200f. 2 h.p. "Berline", 1948.

254 Ndjole and L'Ogooue

1978. Views of Gabon. Multicoloured.
648 30f. Type **254** 20 15
649 40f. Lambarene, Lake District 35 15
650 50f. Owendo Port 60 15

255 "Sternotomis mirabilis"

1978. Beetles. Multicoloured.
651 20f. Type **255** 20 15
652 60f. "Analeptes trifasciata" 65 40
653 75f. "Homoderus mellyi" . . 85 45
654 80f. "Stephanorrhina guttata" 1·00 55

257 Players heading Ball

1978. Air. World Cup Football Championship, Argentina.
660 **257** 100f. brown, red and green 70 35
661 – 120f. brown, red and green 85 45
662 – 200f. brown and red . . . 1·50 70
DESIGNS: 120f. Players tackling. VERT: 200f. F.I.F.A. World Cup.

258 Anti-Apartheid Emblem

1978. International Anti-Apartheid Year.
664 **258** 80f. orange, brown & blue 55 35

1978. Air. Argentina's Victory in World Cup Football Championship. Nos. 660/2 optd.
665 **257** 100f. brown, red and green 70 40
666 – 120f. brown, red and green 90 50
667 – 200f. brown and red . . . 1·40 80
OVERPRINTS: 100f. **ARGENTINE HOLLAND 3 - 1**; 120f. **BRESIL ITALIE 2 - 1**; 200f. **CHAMPION DU MONDE 1978 ARGENTINE**.

1978. Town Arms (9th series). As T **137**, but dated "1978".
669 5f. multicoloured 15 10
670 40f. multicoloured 30 15
671 60f. gold, black and blue . . 45 15
DESIGNS: 5f. Oyem; 40f. Okandja; 60f. Mimongo.

260 "Self-portrait at 13 years"

1978. Air. 450th Death Anniv of Albrecht Durer (artist).
672 **260** 100f. grey and red 85 40
673 – 250f. red and grey . . . . 2·50 1·00
DESIGN: 250f. "Lucas de Leyde".

261 Parthenon

1978. UNESCO Campaign for the Preservation of the Acropolis.
674 **261** 80f. brown, orange & blue 55 35

262 White Stork and Saxony 1850 3f. Stamp

1978. Air. "Philexafrique" Exhibitions, Libreville, Gabon and International Stamp Fair, Essen, W. Germany. Multicoloured.
675 100f. Type **262** . . . . . . 1·75 1·50
676 100f. Gorilla and Gabon 1971 40f. Grey Parrot stamp . . . . 1·75 1·50

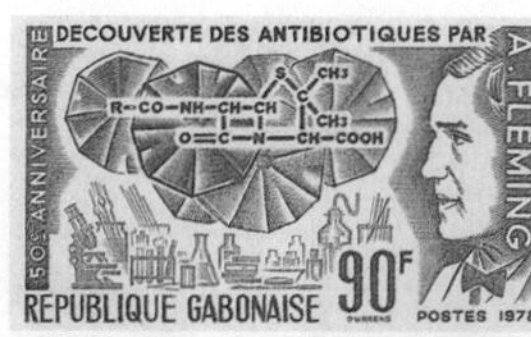

263 Sir Alexander Fleming, Chemical Formula and Laboratory Equipment

1978. 50th Anniv of Fleming's Discovery of Antibiotics.
677 **263** 90f. brown, orange & grn 80 40

264 "The Visitation"

1978. Christmas. Sculptures from the Church of St. Michel de Libreville. Multicoloured.
678 60f. Type **264** 50 20
679 80f. "Massacre of the Innocents" 60 35

265 Wright Brothers and Flyer I

1978. Air. 75th Anniv of First Powered Flight.
680 **265** 380f. brown, blue and red 3·25 1·40

266 Diesel Train

1978. Inauguration of First Section of Trans-Gabon Railway, Libreville-Njole.
681 **266** 60f. multicoloured . . . . 1·40 45

267 Pope John Paul II

1979. Air. The Popes of 1978. Multicoloured.
682 100f. Type **267** . . . . . . 1·40 65
683 200f. Popes Paul VI and John Paul I with St. Peter's . . 2·50 90

1979. Town Arms (10th series). As T **137**, but dated "1979". Multicoloured.
684 5f. Ogooue-Maritime 15 10
685 10f. Lastoursville 15 10
686 15f. M'Bigou 20 10

268 "The Two Disciples"

1979. Air. Easter. Wood-carvings from St. Michel de Libreville Church. Multicoloured.
687 100f. Type **268** 75 55
688 150f. "Jesus appearing to Mary Magdalene" . . . . 1·25 65

269 Long Jumping

1979. Pre-Olympic Year.
689 – 60f. red, brown & turq . . 45 15
690 **269** 80f. brown, turq & red . . 55 30
691 – 100f. turquoise, red & brn 65 35
DESIGNS—HORIZ: 60f. Horse riding; 100f. Yachting.

270 Sir Rowland Hill, Postal Messenger and Stamp

1979. "Philexafrique 2" Exhibition, Libreville.
693 **270** 50f. multicoloured 70 55
694 – 80f. multicoloured . . . . 1·25 85
695 – 150f. green, blue & brown 1·90 1·40
DESIGNS—VERT: 80f. Bakota mask and tulip flower. HORIZ: 150f. Canoeist, mail van, UPU emblem and stamps.

272 Child holding Bird

1979. International Year of the Child.
697 **272** 100f. brown, violet & blue 80 40

273 Captain Cook

1979. Air. Death Bicent of Captain Cook.
698 **273** 500f. multicoloured . . . 4·50 2·25

274 Louis Bleriot and Channel Flight Route

1979. Air. Aviation History. Multicoloured.
699 250f. Type **274** (First Channel Flight, 70th anniv) . . . . 2·25 1·40
700 1000f. Astronauts and module on Moon and Gabon S.G. 369 (Moon Landing, 10th anniv) . . . 7·25 4·00

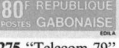

275 "Telecom 79" 276 Carved Head, Map and Rotary Emblem

1979. 3rd World Telecommunications Exhibition, Geneva.
701 **275** 80f. blue, orange & dp bl 50 30

1979. Air. 75th Anniv of Rotary International.
702 **276** 80f. multicoloured 60 35

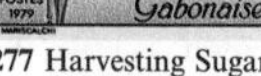

277 Harvesting Sugar Cane 278 Judo

1979. Agriculture. Multicoloured.
703 25f. Type **277** 25 10
704 30f. Igname 35 10

1979. World Judo Championships, Paris.
705 **278** 40f. olive, brown & orange . . . . 1·00 45

279 Eugene Jamot and Tsetse Fly

1979. Air. Birth Centenary of Eugene Jamot (discovery of sleeping sickness cure).
706 **279** 300f. black, brown & vio 2·75 1·40

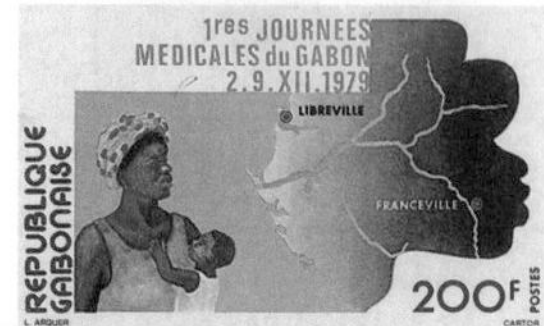

280 Mother with Child and Map of Gabon

1979. 1st Gabon Medical Days.
707 **280** 200f. multicoloured . . . 1·50 65

281 "The Flight into Egypt" 282 Statue of President Bongo

1979. Christmas. Carvings from St. Michael's Church, Libreville. Multicoloured.
708 60f. Type **281** 50 30
709 80f. "The Circumcision" . . 60 30

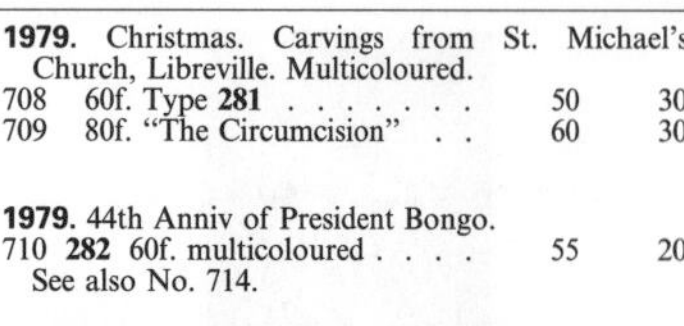

1979. 44th Anniv of President Bongo.
710 **282** 60f. multicoloured 55 20
See also No. 714.

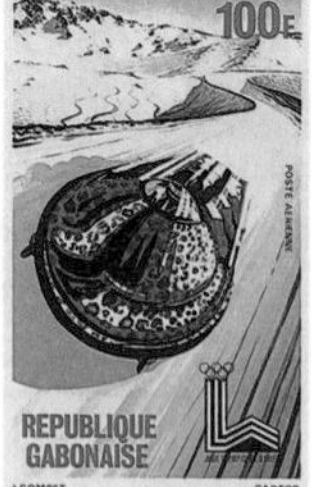

283 Bob Sleighing 284 Oil Derrick

1980. Air. Winter Olympic Games, Lake Placid. Multicoloured.
711 100f. Type **283** 70 40
712 200f. Ski jumping . . . . . 1·50 70

1980. Investiture of President. As No. 710 but inscr "INVESTITURE 27 FEVRIER 1980".
714 **282** 80f. multicoloured . . . . 1·60 1·00

1980. 20th Anniv of OPEC.
715 **284** 50f. multicoloured 60 30

285 Donguila Church

1980. Easter. Multicoloured.
716 60f. Type **285** 45 15
717 80f. Bizangobibere Church 55 30

286 Dominique Ingres (artist)

1980. Air. Celebrities' Anniversaries.
718 **286** 100f. sepia, green & brown 85 40
719 – 200f. brown, pur & grey 2·25 1·00
720 – 360f. brown, green & sepia . . . . 2·50 1·40
DESIGNS: 100f. Type **286** (birth cent); 200f. Jacques Offenbach (composer, death cent); 360f. Gustave Flaubert (author, death cent).

287 Telephone

1980. Air. World Telecommunications Day.
721 **287** 80f. multicoloured 60 30

288 Savorgnan de Brazza and Map

1980. Centenary of Franceville.
722 **288** 165f. multicoloured . . . 1·40 80

289 Dieudonne Costes, Maurice Bellonte and "Point d'Interrogation"

1980. Air. Aviation Anniversaries.
723 **289** 165f. red, blue and green 1·10 55
724 – 1000f. green, red and blue 7·25 3·25
DESIGNS: 165f. Type **289** (50th anniv of first North Atlantic flight); 1000f. Jean Mermoz and seaplane "Comte de la Vaulx" (50th anniv of first South Atlantic airmail).

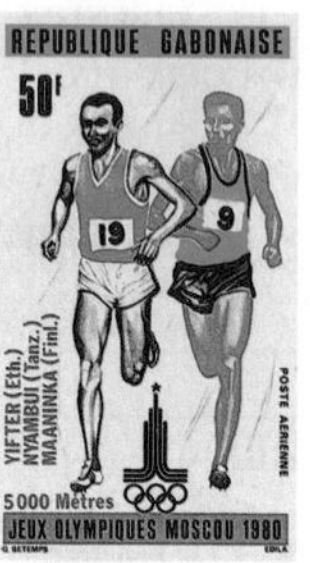

290 Running

1980. Air. Olympic Games, Moscow.
725 **290** 50f. multicoloured 40 15
726 – 100f. black, red and green 70 40
727 – 250f. multicoloured . . . 1·60 85
DESIGNS: 100f. Pole vaulting; 250f. Boxing.

1980. District Arms (1st series). As T **137** but dated "1980".
729 10f. silver, black and gold . . 15 10
730 20f. multicoloured 20 15
731 30f. black, silver and red . . 20 15
DESIGNS: 10f. Haut-Ogooue; 20f. L'Estuaipe; 30f. Bitam.

291 Leon Mba and El Hadj Omar Bongo

1980. 20th Anniv of Independence.
732 **291** 60f. multicoloured 60 30

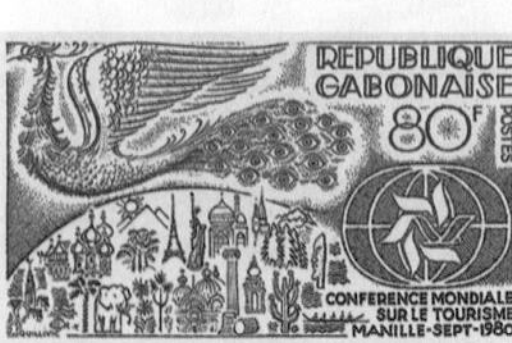

292 Peacock Emblem and Tourist Attractions

1980. World Tourism Conference, Manila.
733 **292** 80f. blue, violet and brown 60 30

293 Figures supporting OPEC Emblem 295 African River Martin

1980. 20th Anniv of Organization of Petroleum Exporting Countries. Multicoloured.
734 90f. Globe and OPEC Emblem (horiz) 85 35
735 120f. Type **293** . . . . . . 1·10 50

1980. Air. Olympic Medal Winners. Nos. 725/7 optd.
736 50f. **YIFTER (Eth.) NYAMBUI (Tanz.) MAANINKA (Finl.) 5000 Metres** 40 20
737 100f. **KOZIAKIEWICZ (Pol.) (record du monde) VOLKOV (Urss) et SLUSARSKI (Pol.)** . . . 70 45
738 250f. **WELTERS ALDAMA (Cuba) MUGABI (Oug.) KRUBER (Rda) et SZCZERDA (Pol.)** . . . 1·60 1·00

1980. Birds. Multicoloured.
740 50f. Type **295** . . . . 1·75 60
741 60f. White-fronted bee eater 2·25 90
742 80f. African pitta . . . . . . 2·75 1·10
743 150f. Pel's fishing owl . . . . 4·75 2·40

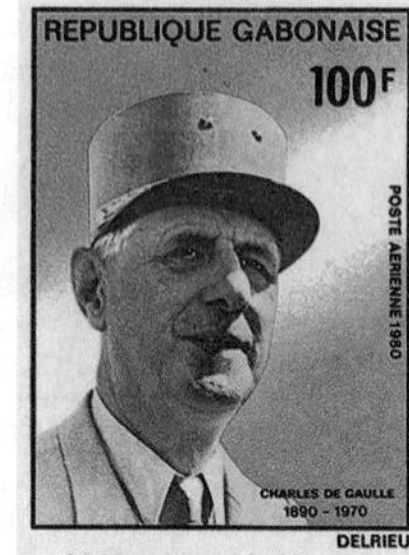

296 Charles de Gaulle

1980. Air. 10th Death Anniv of Charles de Gaulle. Multicoloured.
744 100f. Type **296** 95 55
745 200f. Charles and Mme. de Gaulle . . . . 1·90 95

297 St. Matthew

1980. Christmas. Carvings from Bizangobibere Church. Multicoloured.
747 60f. St. Luke 45 20
748 80f. Type **297** 65 35

298 Heinrich von Stephan 299 Shooting at Goal

1981. 150th Birth Anniv of Heinrich von Stephan (founder of UPU).
749 **298** 90f. dp brn, lt brn & brn 65 35

1981. Air. World Cup Football Championship Eliminators. Multicoloured.
750 60f. Type **299** 45 30
751 190f. Players with ball . . . 1·40 85

300 Palais Renovation

1981. 13th Anniv of National Renewal.
752 **300** 60f. multicoloured 55 20

301 W. Herschel (Discovery of Uranus Bicent)

302 Lion (St. Mark)

1981. Air. Space Anniversaries. Mult.
753 150f. Type **301** . . . . . . 1·10 45
754 250f. Yuri Gagarin, first man in space (20th anniv) . . . 1·60 95
755 500f. Alan Shepard, first American in space (20th anniv) . . . . 3·25 1·60

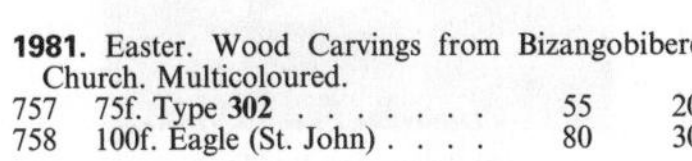

1981. Easter. Wood Carvings from Bizangobibere Church. Multicoloured.
757 75f. Type **302** 55 20
758 100f. Eagle (St. John) 80 30

303 Port Gentil

304 Caduceus

1981. 23rd Congress of Lions Club District 403 Libreville. Multicoloured.
759 60f. Type **303** 45 20
760 75f. District 403 . . . . . . 55 20
761 80f. Libreville Cocotiers . . . 55 30
762 100f. Libreville Hibiscus . . . 80 35
763 165f. Ekwata . . . . 1·25 55
764 200f. Haute-Ogooue . . . . 1·40 65

1981. World Telecommunications Day.
765 **304** 125f. multicoloured . . . 80 40

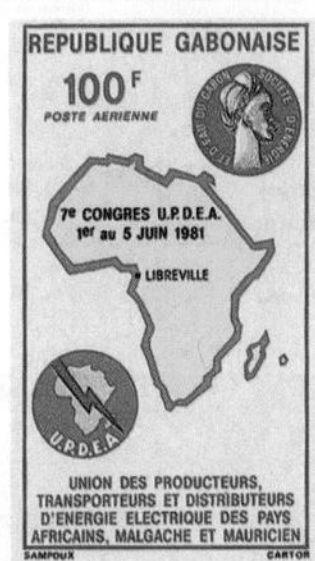
305 Map of Africa and Emblems of Gabon Electricity and Water Society and UPDEA

1981. Air. 7th Congress of African Electricity Producers and Suppliers.
766 **305** 100f. multicoloured . . . 70 40

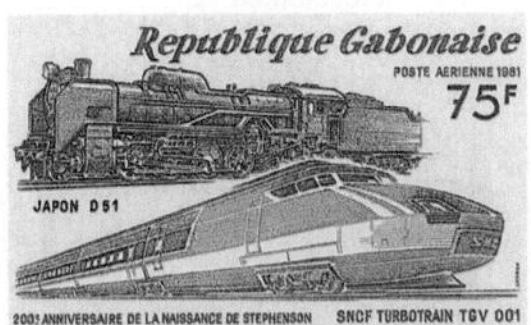
306 Japanese D-51 Locomotive and French Turbotrain TGV 001

1981. Air. Birth Bicent of George Stephenson.
767 **306** 75f. grey, orange & brown 1·50 40
768 – 100f. green, black & blue 1·75 55
769 – 350f. green, brown & red 4·25 1·60
DESIGNS: 100f. Baltimore & Ohio Mallet 7100 and Prussian State Railway T-3 locomotives; 350f. George Stephenson, his locomotive "Rocket" (1829) and Alsthom diesel locomotive.

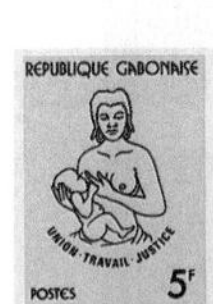

307 Mother Breast-feeding Child

308 R. P. Klaine (70th death anniv)

1981.
772 **307** 5f. brown and black . . 10 10
773 10f. mauve and black . . 10 10
774 15f. green and black . . 10 10
775 20f. pink and black . . . 10 10
776 25f. blue and black . . . 15 10
777 40f. pink and black . . . 25 10
778 50f. green and black . . 35 10
779 75f. brown and black . . 45 20
779a 90f. blue and black . . . 55 20
780 100f. yellow and black 60 25
780a 125f. green and black . . 85 30
780b 150f. purple and black 1·00 25

1981. Religious Personalities. Multicoloured.
781 70f. Type **308** 50 20
782 90f. Mgr. Walker (110th birth anniv) 70 30

309 Scout Badge on Map of Gabon

311 "Helping the Disabled"

1981. 4th Pan-African Scout Congress, Abidjan.
783 **309** 75f. multicoloured 60 30

1981. 28th World Scout Conference, Dakar. Optd **DAKAR 28e CONFERENCE MONDIALE DU SCOUTISME.**
784 **309** 75f. multicoloured 60 30

1981. International Year of Disabled People.
785 **311** 100f. red, dp green & grn 65 35

312 "Hypolimnas salmacis"

1981. Butterflies. Multicoloured.
786 75f. Type **312** 90 45
787 100f. "Euphaedra themis" . . 1·10 45
788 150f. "Amauris niavius" . . 1·40 90
789 250f. "Cymothoe lucasi" . . 2·50 1·25

313 "Paul as Harlequin"

1981. Birth Centenary of Pablo Picasso.
790 **313** 500f. multicoloured . . . 4·50 1·90

314 Hand holding Pen

316 Traditional Hairstyle

315 Agricultural Scenes, Wheat and FAO Emblem

1981. Air. International Letter-writing Week.
791 **314** 200f. multicoloured . . . 1·40 65

1981. World Food Day.
792 **315** 350f. brown, dp brn & bl 2·75 1·40

1981. Traditional Hairstyles.
793 **316** 75f. red, yellow and black 70 35
794 – 100f. green, lilac and black 85 40
795 – 125f. lt green, green & blk 1·10 60
796 – 200f. pink, violet and black . . . . 1·75 90
DESIGNS: 100f. to 200f. Different hairstyles. See also Nos. 964a and 1046.

317 Dancers around Fire

1981. Christmas. Multicoloured.
798 75f. Type **317** 55 20
799 100f. Christmas meal 80 35

1982. District Arms (2nd series). As T **137** but dated "1982". Multicoloured.
800 75f. Moyen-Ogooue 50 15
801 100f. Woleu-N'tem 65 15
802 150f. N'Gounie . . . . . . 1·00 30

318 Pope John Paul II

319 Alfred de Musset

1982. Papal Visit.
803 **318** 100f. multicoloured . . . 1·10 65

1982. 125th Death Anniv of Alfred de Musset (writer).
804 **319** 75f. black 55 20

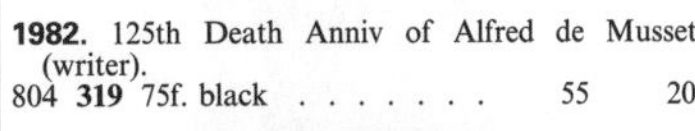

320 "Leonce Veilvieux" (freighter)

1982. Merchant Ships. Multicoloured.
805 75f. Type **320** 90 55
806 100f. "Correze" (container ship) . . . . 1·10 55
807 200f. Oil tanker . . . . . . 1·90 85

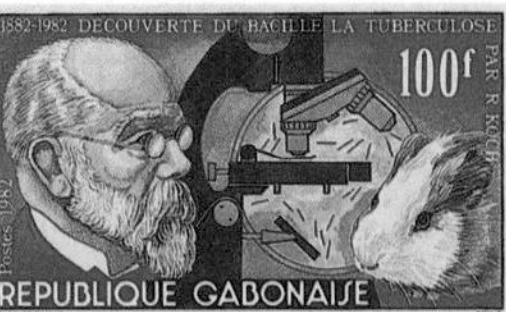
321 Dr. Robert Koch, Microscope, Bacillus and Guinea Pig

1982. Centenary of Discovery of Tubercle Bacillus.
808 **321** 100f. multicoloured . . . 90 45

322 Rope Bridge, Poubara

324 Footballer (Brazil)

323 Hexagonal Pattern

1982. "Philexfrance 82" International Stamp Exhibition, Paris. Multicoloured.
809 100f. Type **322** 65 35
810 100f. Bapounou sculpture . . 1·40 55

1982. World Telecommunications Day.
811 **323** 75f. multicoloured 60 35

1982. World Cup Football Championship, Spain. Multicoloured.
812 100f. Type **324** 65 30
813 125f. Footballer (Argentina) 85 35
814 200f. Footballer (England) . . 1·25 50

325 "Caprice des Dames" (Morning)

1982. Flower "Caprice des Dames". Mult.
816 75f. Type **325** 60 35
817 100f. Midday 80 35
818 175f. Evening . . . . 1·40 65

326 Satellites

1982. Second U.N. Conference on Exploration and Peaceful Uses of Outer Space.
819 **326** 250f. blue, deep blue & red . . . . 1·90 1·10

1982. World Cup Football Championship Winners. Nos. 812/14 optd.
821 **324** 100f. multicoloured . . . 65 35
822 – 125f. multicoloured . . . 85 40
823 – 200f. multicoloured . . . 1·40 60
OPTS: 100f. **DEMIE-FINALE POLOGNE 0—ITALIE 2**; 125f. **DEMIE-FINALE R. F. ALLEMAGNE 3—FRANCE 3**; 200f. **FINALE ITALIE 3—R. F. ALLEMAGNE 1.**

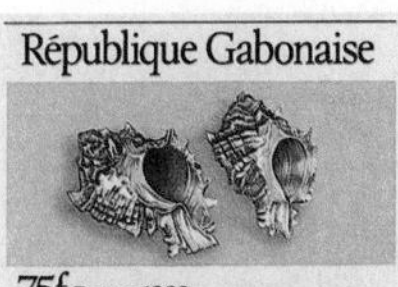
329 Duplex Murex

1982. Shells. Multicoloured.
825 75f. Type **329** 80 50
826 100f. "Chama crenulata" . . 1·40 60
827 125f. "Cardium hians" . . . 2·00 1·10

330 "Still-life with Mandolin" (Braque, birth centenary)

1982. Painters' Anniversaries. Mult.
828 300f. Type **330** . . . . . . 2·25 70
829 350f. "Boy blowing Soap Bubbles" (Manet, death cent) (vert) . . . . 3·25 1·10

331 Okouyi Mask 332 St. Francis Xavier Church, Lambarene

1982. Artifacts. Multicoloured.
830 75f. Type **331** 45 20
831 100f. Ondoumbo reliquary . . 65 20
832 150f. Tsogho statuette . . . 1·10 40
833 250f. Forge bellows . . . . . 1·60 60

1982. Christmas.
834 **332** 100f. multicoloured . . . 65 35

333 Presidents Bongo and Mitterand, Route Map and Diesel Train

1983. Inauguration of Second Stage of Trans-Gabon Railway.
835 **333** 75f. multicoloured . . . . 1·50 50

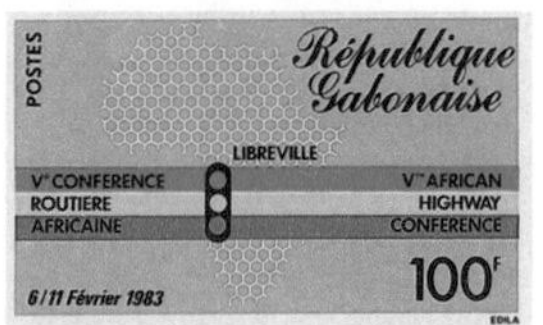

334 Stylized Highway and Map of Africa

1983. 5th African Highway Conference.
836 **334** 100f. multicoloured . . . 65 30

335 Gymnast with Hoop 336 "Epitorium trochiformis" (Estuaire)

1983. Air. Olympic Games, Los Angeles. Multicoloured.
837 90f. Type **335** 60 30
838 350f. Wind-surfing . . . . . 2·50 1·00

1983. Provinces. Multicoloured.
839 75f. Bakota mask (Ogooue Ivindo) 50 25
840 90f. African buffalo (Nyanga) 60 30
841 90f. "Charaxes druceanus" (Ogooue Lolo) 60 30
842 100f. Isogho hairstyle (Ngounie) 65 35
843 125f. Manganese (Haut Ogooue) 85 45
844 125f. Crocodiles (Moyen Ogooue) 85 45
845 125f. Atlantic tarpon (Ogooue Maritime) . . . . 1·40 60

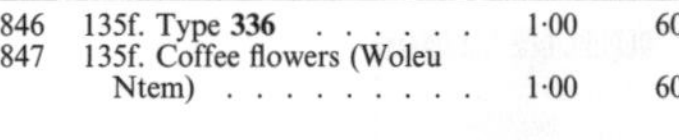

846 135f. Type **336** . . . . . . 1·00 60
847 135f. Coffee flowers (Woleu Ntem) . . . . 1·00 60

337 "Ville de Rouen" (container ship) and IMO Emblem

1983. 25th Anniv of International Maritime Organization.
848 **337** 125f. multicoloured . . . 1·25 45

338 Water Chevrotain

1983. Fauna. Multicoloured.
849 90f. Type **338** 60 30
850 125f. Pink-backed pelican ("Pelican") . . . . 1·50 60
851 225f. African elephant . . . 1·90 70
852 400f. Iguana . . . . 2·75 1·40

339 ECA Anniversary Emblem

1983. 25th Anniv of Economic Commission for Africa.
854 **339** 125f. multicoloured . . . 85 40

340 Telephones

1983. World Telecommunications Day. Mult.
855 90f. Type **340** 85 45
856 90f. As No. 855 but design inverted 85 45

341 "Double Eagle II" crossing Atlantic

1983. Air. Ballooning Anniversaries.
857 100f. grey, orange and blue 80 45
858 125f. green, purple and blue 90 55
859 350f. blue, green & light green . . . . 2·75 1·40

DESIGNS: 100f. Type **341** (5th anniv of first Atlantic crossing); 125f. Hot-air balloons (Bicentenary of Montgolfier Brothers' balloon); 350f. Pilatre de Rozier and Montgolfier balloon (Bicentenary of manned flight).

342 "Lady with Unicorn"

1983. Air. 150th Birth Anniv of Raphael.
860 **342** 1000f. multicoloured . . . 7·25 3·25

343 Nkoltang Satellite Receiving Station

1983. World Communications Year.
861 **343** 125f. multicoloured . . . 85 35

344 Rapids on the Ivindo River

1983. Tourism.
862 **344** 90f. blue, brown and green 55 30
863 – 125f. brown, green & grey 85 45
864 – 185f. grey, orange & green 1·25 45
865 – 350f. brown, green & blue 2·40 1·10

DESIGNS: 125f. Pirogue on the Ogooue River; 185f. Wonga Wongue Game Reserve; 350f. Coastal beach.

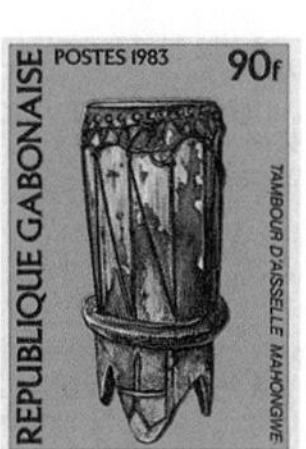

345 Mahongwe Drum

1983. Music and Dance. Multicoloured.
866 90f. Type **345** 55 30
867 125f. Okoukoue dance . . . 85 45
868 135f. Ngomi bateke . . . . 1·00 45
869 260f. Ndoumou dancer . . . 1·90 90

346 "Glossinidae" 347 "The Adulterous Woman"

1983. Harmful Insects. Multicoloured.
870 90f. Type **346** 90 45
871 125f. "Belonogaster junceus" 1·10 50
872 300f. "Aedes aegypti" . . . . 2·25 1·25
873 350f. "Mylabris" . . . . . . 3·25 1·40

1983. Christmas. Wood carvings from St. Michel Church, Libreville. Multicoloured.
874 90f. Type **347** 55 30
875 125f. "Parable of the Good Samaritan" 85 40

348 Boeing 747-200 Airliner and Gabon Stamp of 1966

1984. World Post Congress Stamp Exhibition, Hamburg. Multicoloured.
876 125f. Type **348** 95 45
877 225f. Douglas DC-10 and German airmail stamp of 1919 . . . . 1·90 90

349 Pylons and Buildings

1984. 3rd Anniv of "Africa 1".
878 **349** 125f. multicoloured . . . 85 35

350 Ice Hockey

1984. Air. Winter Olympic Games, Sarajevo.
879 **350** 125f. green, purple & blk 1·10 55
880 – 350f. blue, brown & black 2·50 1·10

DESIGN: 350f. Ice-dancing.

351 Coconut

1984. Fruit Trees. Multicoloured.
881 90f. Type **351** 70 35
882 100f. Pawpaw 80 35
883 125f. Mango . . . . 1·00 45
884 250f. Banana . . . . 1·90 85

352 Robin Dauphin and Piper Cherokee Six Aircraft

1984. Air. Paris–Libreville Air Rally.
885 **352** 500f. multicoloured . . . 3·25 1·90

353 "Racehorses"

1984. Air. 150th Birth Anniv of Degas.
886 **353** 500f. multicoloured . . . 4·50 2·25

354 Water Lily 356 Basketball

355 Spectrum

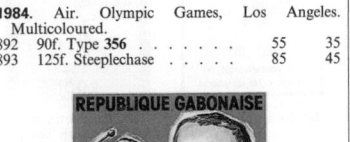

1984. Flowers. Multicoloured.
887 90f. Type **354** 80 30
888 125f. Water hyacinth 80 40
889 135f. Hibiscus . . . . 1·10 45
890 350f. Bracteate orchid . . . 2·50 1·40

1984. World Telecommunications Day.
891 **355** 125f. multicoloured . . . 85 35

1984. Air. Olympic Games, Los Angeles. Multicoloured.
892 90f. Type **356** 55 35
893 125f. Steeplechase 85 45

358 Lionel Hampton

1984. Jazz Musicians. Multicoloured.
895 90f. Type **358** . . . . 1·10 55
896 125f. Charlie Parker . . . . 1·40 55
897 260f. Erroll Garner . . . . 2·75 1·40

1984. District Arms (3rd series). As T **137** but dated "1984". Multicoloured.
898 90f. Cocobeach 55 15
899 125f. Mouila 80 15
900 135f. N'Djole 90 20

359 Medouneu

1984. Tourism. Multicoloured.
901 90f. Type **359** 65 35
902 125f. Sunset over Ogooue . . 1·00 50
903 165f. Trans-Gabon train . . 3·50 1·10

360 Globe, Post and Emblem 360a Kota Reliquary

1984. Universal Postal Union Day.
905 **360** 125f. multicoloured . . . 85 35

1984. Traditional Art. Multicoloured.
905a 90f. Kouble mask . . . . .
905b 125f. Pounou fan . . . . .
905c 150f. Mahongoue reliquary
905d 250f. Type **360a** . . . . .

361 "Icarus" (Hans Herni)

1984. 40th Anniv of International Civil Aviation Organization.
906 **361** 125f. dp blue, green & bl 85 35

362 Tympanum of Saint Michael's Church (left side)

1984. Christmas. Multicoloured.
907 90f. Type **362** 55 25
908 125f. Tympanum of Saint Michael's church (right side) 85 35

Nos. 907/8 were printed together, se-tenant, forming a composite design.

363 South African Crowned Cranes

1984. Birds. Multicoloured.
909 90f. Type **363** . . . . 1·40 75
910 125f. Snowy-breasted hummingbird . . . . . . 2·40 1·40
911 150f. Keel-billed toucan . . . 2·75 1·50

364 Leper Colony, Libreville

1985. World Lepers' Day.
912 **364** 125f. multicoloured . . . 85 40

365 I.Y.Y. Emblem

1985. International Youth Year.
913 **365** 125f. multicoloured . . . 85 35

367 Profiles and Emblem

1985. 15th Anniv of Cultural and Technical Co-operation Agency.
914 **367** 125f. blue, red & dp blue 85 35

368 Water Rat

1985. Animals. Multicoloured.
915 90f. Type **368** 90 35
916 100f. Porcupine 90 35
917 125f. Giant pangolin . . . . 1·25 55
918 350f. Antelope . . . . 3·00 1·40

369 Score and Aleka

1985. Georges Damas Aleka (composer) Commemoration.
920 **369** 90f. multicoloured 80 35

370 Emblem and Coloured Lines 371 Shield

1985. World Telecommunications Day.
921 **370** 125f. multicoloured . . . 85 35

1985. 30th Anniv of Christian Youth Workers' Movement in Gabon.
922 **371** 90f. multicoloured 60 30

372 "La Mpassa" (freighter)

1985.
923 **372** 185f. multicoloured . . . 2·25 85

373 Building and Dish Aerials

1985. 25th Anniv of Posts and Telecommunications Administration.
924 **373** 90f. multicoloured 60 30

374 President Bongo

1985. 25th Anniv of Independence.
925 **374** 250f. multicoloured . . . 2·25 1·10
926 500f. multicoloured . . . 4·50 2·75

375 Dr. Albert Schweitzer

1985. Air. 20th Death Anniv of Dr. Albert Schweitzer.
928 **375** 350f. multicoloured . . . 2·75 1·25

376 Hand holding U.N. and Gabon Flags

1985. Air. 20th Anniv of Membership of United Nations Organization.
929 **376** 225f. multicoloured . . . 1·50 70

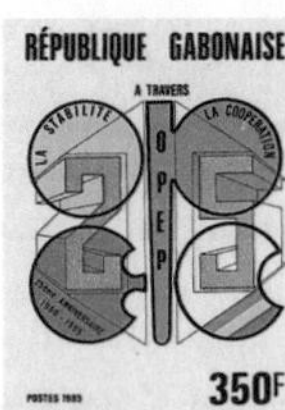

377 OPEC Emblem

1985. 25th Anniv of Organization of Petroleum Exporting Countries.
930 **377** 350f. multicoloured . . . 2·50 1·40

378 Boy Scouts around Campfire and Elephant

1985. Air. "Philexafrique" Stamp Exhibition, Lome, Togo. Multicoloured.
931 100f. Type **378** 85 45
932 150f. Diesel train, satellite and dish aerial . . . . . . 3·75 80

379 Central Post Office, Libreville, Gabon Posts and UPU Emblems

1985. Air. World Post Day.
933 **379** 300f. multicoloured . . . 2·25 1·00

380 Hand holding Globe

1985. Air. 40th Anniv of UNO.
934 **380** 350f. multicoloured . . . 2·50 1·10

381 Centre

1985. International Centre of Bantu Civilisations.
935 **381** 185f. multicoloured . . . 1·40 60

381a Interior of Church

1985. Christmas. St. Andrew's Church, Libreville. Multicoloured.
935a 90f. Exterior of church . . .
935b 125f. Type **381a** . . . . .

382 Young People within Laurel Wreath

1986. 25th Anniv of UNESCO National Commission.
936 **382** 100f. multicoloured . . . 65 30

383 "Mother and Child"

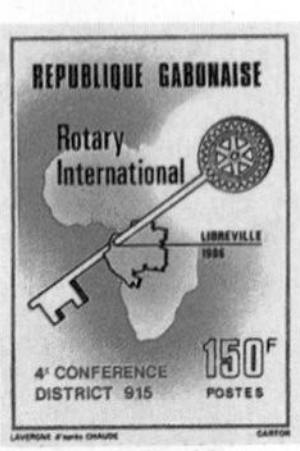
385 Key as Emblem and Map

384 Savorgnan de Brazza and Canoe

1986. Air. Gabon's Gift to United Nations Organization.
937 **383** 350f. multicoloured . . . 2·50 1·10

1986. Air. Centenary of Lastoursville.
938 **384** 100f. multicoloured . . . 85 45

1986. 4th Rotary International District 915 Conference, Libreville.
939 **385** 150f. multicoloured . . . 1·10 50

386 Communications Equipment

1986. World Telecommunications Day.
940 **386** 300f. multicoloured . . . 2·00 1·00

387 Goalkeeper saving Ball

1986. Air. World Cup Football Championship, Mexico. Multicoloured.
941 100f. Type **387** 65 35
942 150f. Footballers and Mexican statue . . . . . 1·00 45
943 250f. World Cup trophy, footballers and map . . . 1·60 65
944 350f. Flags, ball and stadium 2·25 1·00

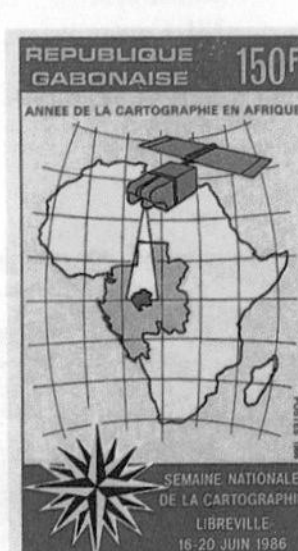
388 Map and Satellite

1986. African Cartography Year and National Cartography Week, Libreville.
946 **388** 150f. multicoloured . . . 1·10 55

389 "L'Abanga" (container ship)

1986.
947 **389** 250f. multicoloured . . . 2·25 1·10

390 River and Gabon 1886 50c. Stamp

1986. Centenary of First Gabon Stamps.
948 **390** 500f. multicoloured . . . 4·50 2·25

391 "Allamanda neriifolia"

392 Arms of Lambarn

1986. Flowers. Multicoloured.
949 100f. Type **391** 65 35
950 150f. "Musa cultivar" . . . . 1·00 50
951 350f. "Dissotis decumbens" 1·10 55
952 350f. "Campylospermum laeve" . . . . 2·50 1·10

1986. District Arms (4th series). Mult.
953 100f. Type **392** 65 20
954 160f. Leconi . . . . 1·10 35

393 Coffee Berries, Flowers and Beans

1986. 25th Anniv of African and Malagasy Coffee Producers Organization.
955 **393** 125f. multicoloured . . . 95 55

394 "Machaon"

1986. Butterflies. Multicoloured.
956 150f. Type **394** . . . . . . 1·90 1·25
957 290f. "Urania" . . . . . . 2·75 2·25

395 Dove and UPU Emblem

1986. Air. World Post Day.
958 **395** 500f. multicoloured . . . 3·25 1·60

1986. Air. World Cup Football Championship Winners. Nos 941/4 optd **ARGENTINE 3-R.F.A. 2.** Multicoloured.
959 100f. Type **387** 65 45
960 150f. Footballers and Mexican statue . . . . . 1·00 55
961 250f. World Cup trophy, footballers and map . . . 1·60 1·00
962 350f. Flags, ball and stadium 2·25 1·60

397 St. Peter's Church, Libreville

1986. Christmas.
963 **397** 500f. multicoloured . . . 3·25 1·60

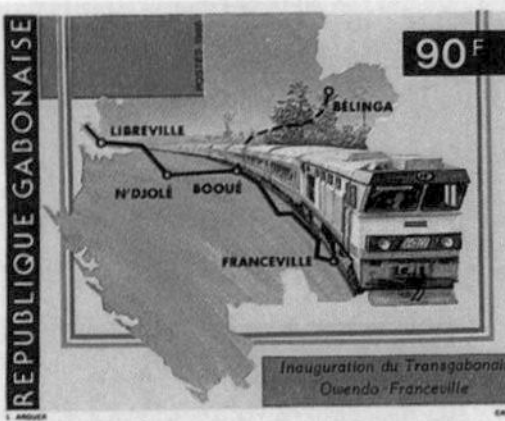
398 Diesel Train and Route Map

1986. Inauguration of Owendo–Franceville Trans-Gabon Railway.
964 **398** 90f. multicoloured . . . . 3·00 1·10

1986. Traditional Hairstyles. As T **316**.
964a 150f. black, red and grey . . 3·25 1·10

399 West African Squirrelfish

1987. Fishes. Multicoloured.
966 90f. Type **399** 85 45
967 125f. West African parrotfish 1·10 65
968 225f. Flying gurnard . . . . 2·00 1·10
969 350f. Marbled stingray . . . 3·25 2·00

400 Raoul Follereau (leprosy pioneer)

1987. World Leprosy Day.
971 **400** 125f. multicoloured . . . 1·00 65

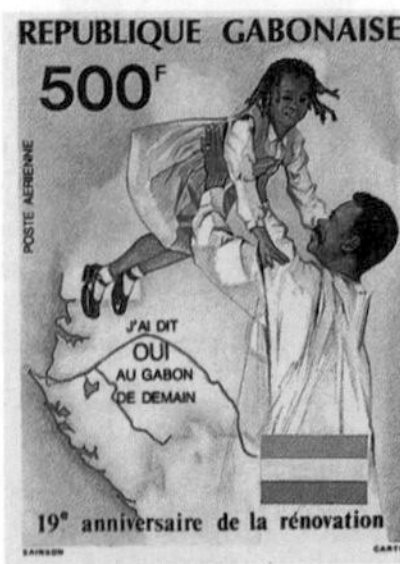
401 Man and Child in front of Map

1987. Air. 19th Anniv of National Renewal.
972 **401** 500f. multicoloured . . . 4·00 1·60

402 Pres. Bongo receiving Prize

1987. Award of Dag Hammarskjold Peace Prize to Pres. Omar Bongo.
973 **402** 125f. multicoloured . . . 85 55

403 Konrad Adenauer

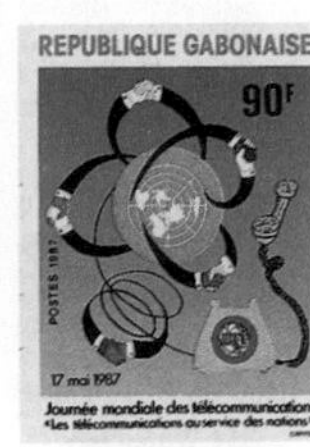
404 Symbols of Communication

1987. Air. 20th Death Anniv of Konrad Adenauer (German statesman).
974 **403** 300f. multicoloured . . . 2·75 1·25

1987. World Telecommunications Day.
975 **404** 90f. multicoloured 60 35

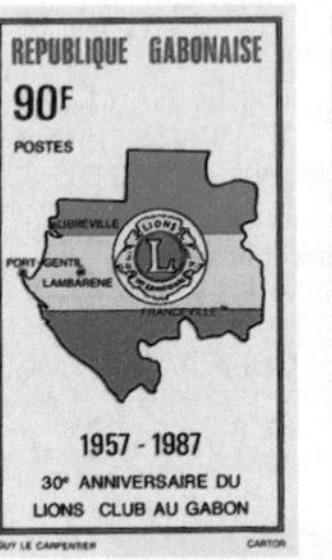
405 Emblem on Map

406 Coubertin and Runner with Torch

1987. 30th Anniv of Lions Club of Gabon.
976 **405** 90f. multicoloured 60 35

1987. 50th Death Anniv of Pierre de Coubertin (founder of modern Olympic Games).
977 **406** 200f. multicoloured . . . 1·40 65

407 Map, Emblems and People

408 Globe in Envelope

1987. 70th Anniv of Lions International.
978 **407** 165f. multicoloured . . . 1·25 65

1987. World Post Day.
979 **408** 125f. multicoloured . . . 85 35

409 Pres. Bongo and Sam Nujoma

1987. Solidarity with South-West African Peoples' Organization.
980 **409** 225f. multicoloured . . . 1·40 55

410 Fanel Moon

1987. Sea Shells. Multicoloured.
981 90f. Type **410** . . . . 1·25 70
982 125f. Lightning moon ("Natica fulminea cruentata") . . . . 1·50 70

See also Nos. 1018a/b.

411 Man, House and Machinery

1987. International Year of Shelter for the Homeless. World Shelter Day.
984 **411** 90f. multicoloured 60 35

412 Mission

1987. Centenary of St. Anne of Odimba Mission.
985 **412** 90f. multicoloured 65 35

413 Nurse vaccinating Child

1987. Universal Vaccination for Children.
986 **413** 100f. multicoloured . . . 80 40

414 President making Address

1987. 20th Anniv of Installation of President Omar Bongo.
987 **414** 1000f. multicoloured . . . 6·75 3·25

415 St. Theresa's Church, Oyem

1987. Christmas.
988 **415** 90f. multicoloured 65 35

416 Skier

1987. Winter Olympic Games, Calgary (1988).
989 **416** 125f. multicoloured . . . 85 45

417 "Cassia occidentalis"

1988. Medicinal Plants. Multicoloured.
990 90f. Type **417** 65 45
991 125f. "Tabernanthe iboga" 90 45
992 225f. "Cassia alata" . . . . 1·50 80
993 350f. "Anthocleista schweinfurthii" . . . . . 2·75 1·60

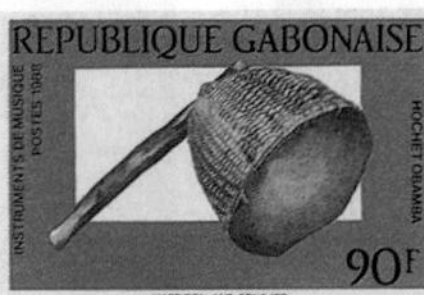

418 Obamba Rattle

1988. Traditional Musical Instruments. Mult.
995 90f. Type **418** 60 35
996 100f. Fang sanza (vert) . . . 80 45
997 125f. Mitsogho harp (vert) . . 90 55
998 165f. Fang xylophone . . . . 1·40 65

419 Elephant with raised Trunk

1988. Endangered Animals. African Elephant. Multicoloured.
1000 25f. Type **419** 30 15
1001 40f. Elephant family 70 20
1002 50f. Elephant in vegetation 90 20
1003 100f. Elephant . . . . . . 1·40 55

420 Postal Delta Building

1988. Inauguration of Postal Delta.
1004 **420** 90f. multicoloured . . . 65 35

421 Village and Dr. Schweitzer

1988. Air. 75th Anniv of Arrival in Gabon of Dr. Albert Schweitzer.
1005 **421** 500f. multicoloured . . . 4·00 1·60

422 Players

1988. World Cup Rugby Championship (1987).
1006 **422** 350f. multicoloured . . . 2·75 1·60

423 Opposing Arrows

1988. World Telecommunications Day.
1007 **423** 125f. multicoloured . . . 85 40

424 Storming the Bastille, 1789

1988. "Philexfrance 89" Stamp Exhibition, Paris.
1008 **424** 125f. multicoloured . . . 1·10 55

425 Crops and Agricultural Activities

1988. 10th Anniv of International Agricultural Development Fund.
1009 **425** 350f. multicoloured . . . 2·75 1·10

426 Emblem and Theatre Staff

1988. 125th Anniv of Red Cross.
1010 **426** 125f. multicoloured . . . 85 35

427 Refinery

1988. Air. 20th Anniv of Port Gentil Oil Refinery.
1011 **427** 350f. multicoloured . . . 2·50 1·10

428 Tennis

1988. Olympic Games, Seoul. Multicoloured.
1012 90f. Type **428** 65 35
1013 100f. Swimming 65 35
1014 350f. Running . . . . . . 2·50 1·00
1015 500f. Hurdling . . . . . . 4·00 1·10

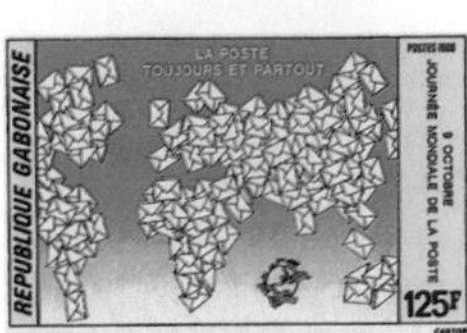

429 Envelopes forming World Map

1988. World Post Day.
1017 **429** 125f. black, blue & yell 85 35

430 Medouneu Church

431 Map and Emblem

1988. Christmas.
1018 **430** 200f. multicoloured . . . 1·40 65

1988. Sea Shells. As T **410**. Multicoloured.
1018a 90f. Fanel moon ("Natica fanel var") . . . . . . 1·60 1·10
1018b 125f. "Natica variolaria" (inscr "Natica sp.") . . 2·75 1·60

1989. 10th Anniv of Chaine de Rotisseurs in Gabon.
1019 **431** 175f. multicoloured . . . 1·10 65

432 Map

434 White-crested Tiger Bittern

433 Boys playing

1989. Inauguration of Rabi Kounga Oil Field.
1020 **432** 125f. multicoloured . . . 85 50

1989. Traditional Games.
1021 **433** 90f. multicoloured . . . 60 40

1989. Birds. Multicoloured.
1022 100f. Type **434** 85 45
1023 175f. Grey parrot . . . . . 1·50 75
1024 200f. Red-billed dwarf hornbill . . . . 2·00 80
1025 500f. Blue-breasted kingfisher . . . . 4·25 2·40

435 Map and Emblem

436 Arrows and Dish Aerials

1989. 8th Lions Club International Multidistrict 403 Convention, Libreville.
1027 **435** 125f. multicoloured . . . 85 45

1989. World Telecommunications Day.
1028 **436** 300f. multicoloured . . . 2·25 90

437 Palm-nuts

1989. Fruits. Multicoloured.
1029 90f. Type **437** 60 35
1030 125f. Cabosse 85 35
1031 175f. Pineapple . . . . . . 1·40 55
1032 250f. Breadfruit . . . . . . 2·00 1·00

438 "Apples and Oranges"

1989. 150th Birth Anniv of Paul Cezanne (painter).
1034 **438** 500f. multicoloured . . . 4·00 2·75

439 Phrygian Cap on Tree of Liberty and Sans-culotte

1989. "Philexfrance '89" International Stamp Exhibition, Paris.
1035 **439** 175f. multicoloured . . . 1·60 65

440 Soldier and Sans-culotte

1989. Bicentenary of French Revolution.
1036 **440** 500f. multicoloured . . . 4·50 2·75

441 Town Hall

1989. 10th Anniv of International Association of French-speaking Town Halls.
1037 **441** 100f. multicoloured . . . 90 40

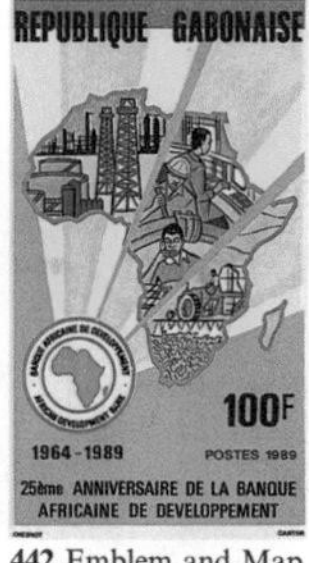

442 Emblem and Map showing Development Programmes

1989. 25th Anniv of African Development Bank.
1038 **442** 100f. multicoloured . . . 65 40

443 Post Office

1989. 125th Anniv (1987) of Gabon Postal Service.
1039 **443** 90f. multicoloured . . . 65 35

444 Footballers

1989. World Cup Football Championship, Italy (1990). Multicoloured.
1040 100f. Type **444** 65 35
1041 175f. Player tackling . . . . 1·25 55
1042 300f. Goalkeeper catching ball . . . . 2·00 80
1043 500f. Goalkeeper catching ball (different) . . . . . 3·25 1·40

445 Woman and Child posting Letter

1989. World Post Day.
1045 **445** 175f. multicoloured . . . 1·10 45

1989. Traditional Hairstyles. As T **316**.
1046 175f. black, lilac and grey 1·40 55

447 St. Louis' Church, Port-Gentil

1989. Christmas.
1047 **447** 100f. multicoloured . . . 65 30

448 L'Ogooue, N'Gomo

1989.
1048 **448** 100f. multicoloured . . . 50 25

449 Axehead

1990. Prehistory. Stone Weapons. Mult.
1049 100f. Type **449** 90 45
1050 175f. Paring knife . . . . . 1·40 65
1051 300f. Flint arrowhead . . . 2·25 1·10
1052 400f. Double-edged knife . . 3·50 2·25

450 Arms of Libreville

1990. 22nd Anniv of National Renovation.
1054 **450** 100f. multicoloured . . . 65 30

451 Penny Black and Beach

1990. 150th Anniv of the Penny Black.
1055 **451** 500f. multicoloured . . . 4·50 2·75

452 Doctor and Nurse examining Patient **453** Monkey

1990. World Health Day.
1056 **452** 400f. multicoloured . . . 2·75 1·40

1990. Animals of Gabon. Multicoloured.
1057 100f. Type **453** 90 45
1058 175f. Bush pig (horiz) . . . 1·40 65
1059 200f. Antelope (horiz) . . . 1·60 1·10
1060 500f. Mandrill . . . . . . 4·50 2·75

454 De Gaulle and Map

1990. Air. 50th Anniv of De Gaulle's Call to Resist.
1062 **454** 500f. multicoloured . . . 4·50 2·25

455 Map and Arms on Flag

1990. 30th Anniv of Independence.
1063 **455** 100f. multicoloured . . . 65 45

456 "Phallus indusiatus"

1990. Fungi.
1064 100f. Type **456** . . . . . . 1·10 55
1065 175f. "Panaeolus sphinctrinus?" . . . . . 2·25 1·10
1066 300f. "Agaricus bitorquis" 3·25 2·25
1067 500f. "Termitomyces" sp. 4·50 3·25

457 Flags of Member Countries **458** Envelopes as World Map

1990. 30th Anniv of Organization of Petroleum Exporting Countries.
1068 **457** 200f. multicoloured . . . 1·40 80

1990. World Post Day.
1069 **458** 175f. blue, yellow & blk 1·25 65

459 Makokou Church

1990. Christmas.
1070 **459** 100f. multicoloured . . . 65 45

460 Frangipani

1991. Flowers. Multicoloured.
1071 100f. Type **460** 90 45
1072 175f. Burning bush . . . . 1·40 65
1073 200f. Flame tree . . . . . 1·75 90
1074 300f. Porcelain rose . . . . 2·25 1·40

461 "Marseilles Harbour"

1991. Air. Death Centenary of Johan Barthold Jongkind (artist).
1076 **461** 500f. multicoloured . . . 4·00 1·60

462 Lizard

1991. Prehistory. Petroglyphs. Multicoloured.
1077 100f. Type **462** 70 45
1078 175f. Triangular figure . . . 1·10 65
1079 300f. Abstract pattern . . . 2·10 1·10
1080 500f. Circles and chains . . 3·50 2·25

463 Collecting Resin from Rubber Trees **465** Basket Weaving

464 Couple and Arrows

1991. Agriculture.
1082 **463** 100f. multicoloured . . . 65 45

1991. District Arms (5th series). As T **392**.
1083 100f. silver, black and green 65 20
DESIGN: 100f. Port-Gentil.

1991. World Telecommunications Day.
1084 **464** 175f. multicoloured . . . 1·10 55

1991. Arts and Crafts. Multicoloured.
1085 100f. Type **465** 65 45
1086 175f. Stone carving . . . . 1·40 80
1087 200f. Weaving . . . . . . 1·40 80
1088 500f. Straw plaiting . . . . 3·50 1·90

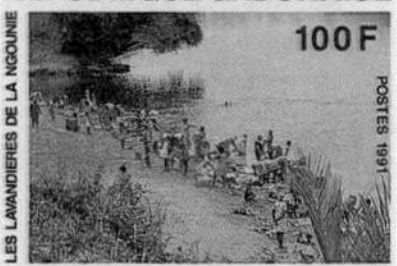

466 Women at Riverbank

1991. Washerwomen of the Ngounie.
1089 **466** 100f. multicoloured . . . 65 45

467 Knight

469 Post Box and Globe

468 Inspecting Fish Traps

1991. Order of the Equatorial Star. Mult.
1090 100f. Type **467** 65 45
1091 175f. Officer . . . . 1·10 65
1092 200f. Commander . . . . . 1·40 90

1991. Fishing. Multicoloured.
1093 100f. Type **468** 65 45
1094 175f. Fishing from canoe . . 1·10 65
1095 200f. Casting net . . . . . 1·40 90
1096 300f. Pulling in net . . . . 2·75 1·90

1991. World Post Day.
1098 **469** 175f. blue, black and red 1·10 45

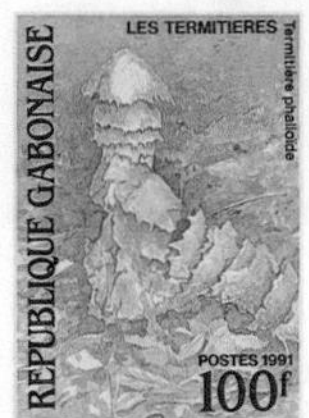

470 "Phalloid"

1991. Termitaries. Multicoloured.
1099 100f. Type **470** 85 55
1100 175f. "Cathedral" . . . . . 1·40 85
1101 200f. "Mushroom" . . . . 1·60 1·10
1102 300f. "Treehouse" . . . . . 2·25 2·00

471 Dibwangui Church

1991. Christmas.
1103 **471** 100f. multicoloured . . . 65 45

472 Neolithic Ceramic Pot

473 Stripping Wood

1992. Prehistory. Pottery. Multicoloured.
1104 100f. Type **472** 65 45
1105 175f. Ceramic bottle (8th century) . . . . 1·10 65
1106 200f. Ceramic vase (late 8th century) . . . . 1·40 90
1107 300f. Ceramic vase (early 8th century) . . . . . . 2·25 1·40

1992. Arts and Crafts. Multicoloured.
1109 100f. Type **473** 65 45
1110 175f. Metalwork . . . . . 1·10 65
1111 200f. Boat building . . . . 1·40 80
1112 300f. Hairdressing . . . . . 2·25 1·40

474 Grand Officer of Order of Equatorial Star

475 Konrad Adenauer

1992. Gabonese Honours. Multicoloured.
1114 100f. Type **474** 65 45
1115 175f. Grand Cross of Order of Equatorial Star . . . . 1·10 65
1116 200f. Order of Merit . . . . 1·40 90

1992. 25th Death Anniv of Konrad Adenauer (German statesman).
1117 **475** 500f. black, stone & grn 4·00 2·75

476 Earth and Moon

477 Small Striped Swallowtail

1992. World Telecommunications Day.
1118 **476** 175f. multicoloured . . . 1·10 45

1992. Butterflies. Multicoloured.
1119 100f. Type **477** 65 45
1120 175f. "Acraea egina" . . . 1·10 65

478 Fang Mask

479 Cycling

1992. Gabonese Masks. Multicoloured.
1121 100f. Type **478** 65 45
1122 175f. Mpongwe mask . . . 1·10 65
1123 200f. Kwele mask . . . . . 1·40 95
1124 300f. Pounou mask . . . . 1·90 1·40

1992. Olympic Games, Barcelona. Mult.
1125 100f. Type **479** 65 45
1126 175f. Boxing . . . . 1·10 65
1127 200f. Pole vaulting . . . . 1·40 90

1992. District Arms (6th series). As T **392**.
1128 100f. silver, black and blue 65 20
DESIGN: 100f. Medouneu.

1992. World Post Day. As No. 1098 but dated "1992".
1129 **469** 175f. multicoloured . . . 1·10 55

480 Columbus and Fleet

1992. Air. 500th Anniv of Discovery of America by Columbus.
1130 **480** 500f. multicoloured . . . 3·25 1·90

481 African Owl

1992. Birds. Multicoloured.
1131 100f. Type **481** . . . . . . 1·10 50
1132 175f. Speckled mousebird 1·75 75
1133 200f. Palm-nut vulture . . . 2·50 1·10
1134 300f. Giant kingfisher . . . 4·00 2·00

482 Cattle

1992. Beef Production.
1136 **482** 100f. multicoloured . . . 65 45
1137 – 175f. multicoloured . . . 1·10 65
1138 – 200f. multicoloured . . . 1·40 85
DESIGNS: 175, 200f. Cattle (different).

483 Tchibanga Church

1992. Christmas.
1139 **483** 100f. multicoloured . . . 65 35

484 Emblems

1992. International Nutrition Conference, Rome.
1140 **484** 100f. multicoloured . . . 65 45

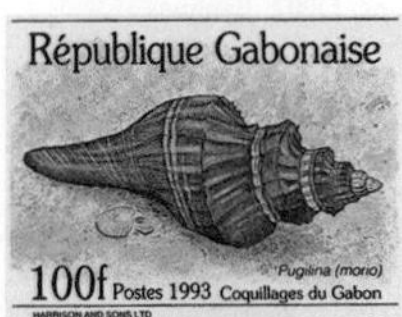

485 "Giant Hairy Melongena"

1993. Shells. Multicoloured.
1141 100f. Type **485** 50 30
1142 175f. Butterfly cone . . . . 1·10 60
1143 200f. Carpat's spindle . . . 1·25 70
1144 300f. "Cymatium linatella" 2·00 1·10

486 Crowd with Banner outside Hospital

1993. World Leprosy Day.
1146 **486** 175f. multicoloured . . . 1·10 50

487 Fritz the Elephant

1993. Fernan-Vaz Mission.
1147 **487** 175f. multicoloured . . . 1·40 90

488 Claude Chappe

489 Schweitzer feeding Animals

1993. Bicentenary of Chappe's Optical Telegraph. Multicoloured.
1148 100f. Type **488** 45 25
1149 175f. Signals and table of signs . . . . 1·10 50
1150 200f. Emile Baudot (inventor of five-unit code telegraph printing system) 1·25 80
1151 300f. Satellite and fibre-optics . . . . 2·00 1·10

1993. 80th Anniv of First Visit of Albert Schweitzer (medical missionary) to Lambarene. Multicoloured.
1153 250f. Type **489** . . . . . . 2·00 1·10
1154 250f. Schweitzer holding babies . . . . 2·00 1·10
1155 500f. Schweitzer (36 × 49 mm) . . . . . . 3·75 2·25

490 Copernicus (astronomer) and illustration from "De Revolutionibus"

491 Emblem

1993. "Polska'93" International Stamp Exhibition, Poznan.
1156 **490** 175f. multicoloured . . . 1·10 50

1993. World Telecommunications Day.
1157 **491** 175f. multicoloured . . . 1·10 50

492 Making Sugar-cane Wine

493 Lobster

1993. Traditional Wine-making. Mult.
1158 100f. Type **492** 70 25
1159 175f. Filling bottle with palm wine . . . . 1·10 50
1160 200f. Gathering ingredients for palm wine . . . . . 1·40 55

1993. Crustaceans. Multicoloured.
1162 100f. Type **493** 70 25
1163 175f. Crab . . . . 1·10 50
1164 200f. Crayfish . . . . . . 1·25 80
1165 300f. Sea spider . . . . . . 2·00 1·10

494 Magnifying Glass, Flowers, Stamp and Emblem

1993. 1st European Stamp Salon, Flower Gardens, Paris.
1166 **494** 100f. multicoloured . . . 70 50

495 Squirrel Trap

1993. Trapping. Multicoloured.
1167 100f. Type **495** 70 25
1168 175f. Small game trap . . . 1·10 50
1169 200f. Large game trap . . . 1·25 80
1170 300f. Palm squirrel trap . . 2·00 1·10

496 Post Box and Globe

1993. World Post Day.
1171 **496** 175f. multicoloured . . . 80 50

497 Making Model Airplane **499** Mandji Catholic Mission

498 Leconi Canyon

1993. Bamboo Toys.
1172 **497** 100f. multicoloured . . . 70 50

1993. Tourism. Multicoloured.
1173 100f. Type **498** 70 25
1174 175f. La Lope tourist site 1·10 50

1993. Christmas.
1175 **499** 100f. multicoloured . . . 70 50

OFFICIAL STAMPS

O **119** Map of Gabon River

1968.
O333 O **119** 1f. multicoloured . . 10 10
O334 2f. multicoloured . . 10 10
O335 5f. multicoloured . . 10 10
O336 10f. multicoloured . . 15 10
O337 – 25f. multicoloured . . 35 15
O338 – 30f. multicoloured . . 40 20
O339 – 50f. multicoloured . . 55 20
O340 – 85f. multicoloured . . 1·10 40
O341 – 100f. multicoloured 1·40 55
O342 – 200f. multicoloured 2·50 1·10
DESIGNS: 25f., 30f. Gabon flag; 50f. to 200f. Gabon coat of arms.

O **165** Gabon Flag

1971. Flag in actual colours; inscription in blue; background as below.
O436 O **165** 5f. blue 10 10
O437 10f. grey 15 15
O437a 20f. orange 15 10
O437b 25f. yellow 20 15
O438 30f. cobalt 30 10
O439 40f. orange 55 30
O440 50f. red 60 20
O441 60f. brown 70 30
O441a 75f. grey 55 15
O442 80f. mauve . . . . 1·10 50
O443 100f. mauve 80 30
O444 500f. green . . . . 4·50 1·40

POSTAGE DUE STAMPS

1928. Postage Due type of French Colonies optd **GABON A. E. F.**
D123 U 5c. blue . . . . 10 2·50
D124 10c. brown . . . . . . 10 2·50
D125 20c. olive . . . . . . 55 3·00
D126 25c. red . . . . 25 3·25
D127 30c. red . . . . 15 2·75
D128 45c. green . . . . . . 1·00 3·25
D129 50c. red . . . . 15 2·50
D130 60c. brown . . . . . . 25 3·25
D131 1f. purple . . . . . . 60 3·00
D132 2f. red . . . . 1·00 3·25
D133 3f. violet . . . . . . 1·10 3·75

D **19** Local Chief D **24** Pahquin Woman

1930.
D134 D **19** 5c. drab and blue . . 1·00 3·00
D135 10c. brown and red . . 1·60 3·25
D136 20c. brown and green 1·90 3·50
D137 25c. brown and blue 2·00 3·75
D138 30c. green and brown 2·00 3·75
D139 45c. drab and green 1·40 2·75
D140 50c. brown and mauve 2·00 5·25
D141 60c. black and violet 1·50 9·00
D142 – 1f. black and brown 2·00 12·50
D143 – 2f. brown and mauve 5·00 19·00
D144 – 3f. brown and red . . 5·25 21·00
DESIGN—VERT: 1f. to 3f. Count Savorgnan de Brazza.

1932.
D151 D **24** 5c. blue on blue . . . 10 2·00
D152 10c. brown . . . . . 40 2·75
D153 20c. brown . . . . . 2·25 3·75
D154 25c. green on blue . . 2·00 3·25
D155 30c. red . . . . . . 3·25 5·00
D156 45c. red on yellow . . 5·25 9·25
D157 50c. purple . . . . . 3·75 6·75
D158 60c. blue . . . . . . 4·00 6·75
D159 1f. black on orange . . 2·75 6·25
D160 2f. green . . . . . . 13·50 16·00
D161 3f. red . . . . 10·50 16·00

D **40** Pineapple

1962. Fruits.
D196 50c. red, yellow and green 10 10
D197 50c. red, yellow and green 10 10
D198 1f. mauve, yellow and green 10 10
D199 1f. mauve, yellow and green 10 10
D200 2f. yellow, brown and green 10 10
D201 2f. yellow, brown and green 10 10
D202 5f. yellow, green and brown 30 30
D203 5f. yellow, green and brown 30 30
D204 10f. multicoloured 60 60
D205 10f. multicoloured 60 60
D206 25f. yellow, green and purple 80 80
D207 25f. yellow, green and purple 80 80
FRUITS: No. D196, Type D **40**; D197, Mangoes; D198, Mandarin oranges; D199, Avocado pears; D200, Grapefruit; D201, Coconuts; D202. Oranges; D203, Papaws; D204, Breadfruit; D205, Guavas; D206, Lemons; D207, Bananas.

D **256** "Charaxes candiope"

1978. Butterflies. Multicoloured.
D655 5f. Type D **256** 10 10
D656 10f. "Charaxes ameliae" . . 10 10
D657 25f. "Cyrestis camillus" . . 30 15
D658 50f. "Charaxes castor" . . 60 35
D659 100f. "Pseudacrea boisduvali" . . . . . . 1·10 65

GALAPAGOS ISLANDS Pt. 20

These islands, noted for their fauna and flora, were annexed by Ecuador, and later (1973) became a province of that country.

100 centavos = 1 sucre.

1 Californian Sealions

1957. Inscr "ISLAS GALAPAGOS".
1 **1** 20c. brown (postage) 40 15
2 – 50c. violet 40 15
3 – 1s. green . . . . 1·25 45
4 – 1s. blue (air) 30 15
5 – 1s.80 purple 65 30
6 – 4s.20 black . . . . 1·75 75
DESIGNS—VERT: 50c. Map of Ecuador coastline. HORIZ: 1s. (No. 3) Iguana; 1s. (No. 4) Santa Cruz Island; 1s.80, Map of Galapagos Is; 4s.20, Giant tortoise.

1959. Air. United Nations Commem. Triangular design as T **316** of Ecuador but inscr "ISLAS GALAPAGOS".
7 2s. green 50 35

GAMBIA Pt. 1

A British colony and protectorate on the West coast of Africa. Granted full internal self-government on 4 October 1963, and achieved indepedence on 18 February 1965. Became a republic within the Commonwealth on 24 April 1970.

1869. 12 pence = 1 shilling;
20 shillings = 1 pound.
1971. 100 butut = 1 dalasi.

1 2

1869. Imperf.
5 **1** 4d. brown £375 £190
8 6d. blue £325 £190

1880. Perf.
11B **1** ½d. orange . . . . 8·50 15·00
12B 1d. purple . . . . 4·50 6·00
13B 2d. pink . . . . 26·00 11·00
14cB 3d. blue . . . . 50·00 26·00
30 4d. brown . . . . 7·00 2·00
17B 6d. blue . . . . 85·00 45·00
19B 1s. green £225 £130

1886.
21 **1** ½d. green . . . . 3·00 2·25
23 1d. red . . . . 6·00 8·00
25 2d. orange . . . . 1·60 8·00
27 2½d. blue . . . . 3·50 1·25
29 3d. grey . . . . 5·00 15·00
34 6d. green . . . . 12·00 45·00
35 1s. violet . . . . 3·25 17·00

1898.
37 **2** ½d. green . . . . 2·75 1·75
38 1d. red . . . . 2·00 75
39 2d. orange and mauve . . . 6·00 3·50
40 2½d. blue . . . . 1·75 2·50
41 3d. purple and blue . . . . 25·00 12·00
42 4d. brown and blue . . . . 9·50 30·00
43 6d. green and red . . . . 10·00 28·00
44 1s. mauve and green . . . . 30·00 65·00

1902. As T **2**, but portrait of King Edward VII.
57 ½d. green . . . . 4·50 30
46 1d. red . . . . 4·50 1·00
47 2d. orange and mauve . . . . 3·25 2·00
74 2d. grey . . . . 1·75 11·00
60 2½d. blue . . . . 6·50 4·75
61 3d. purple and blue . . . . . 7·50 2·00
75 3d. purple on yellow . . . . 3·75 1·00
50 4d. brown and blue . . . . . 3·25 24·00
76 4d. black and red on yellow 1·25 65
63 5d. grey and black . . . . . 14·00 19·00
77 5d. orange and purple . . . . 1·50 1·25
51 6d. green and red . . . . . 5·00 12·00
78 6d. purple . . . . 2·25 2·25
65 7½d. green and red . . . . . 11·00 40·00
79 7½d. brown and blue . . . . 2·50 2·50
80 10d. green and red . . . . . 2·50 7·00
67 1s. mauve and green . . . . 23·00 48·00
81 1s. black on green . . . . . 3·25 17·00
53 1s.6d. green and red on yellow 7·00 18·00
82 1s.6d. violet and green . . . . 15·00 60·00
54 2s. grey and orange . . . . . 48·00 60·00
83 2s. purple and blue on blue . . 14·00 20·00
55 2s.6d. purple & brown on yell 15·00 60·00
84 2s.6d. black and red on blue 21·00 20·00
56 3s. red and green on yellow . . 20·00 60·00
85 3s. yellow and green . . . . 24·00 48·00

1906. Surch in words.
69 ½d. on 2s.6d. (No. 55) . . . . 50·00 60·00
70 1d. on 3s. (No. 56) . . . . . 55·00 30·00

1912. As T **2**, but portrait of King George V.
86 ½d. green . . . . 1·75 1·50
87a 1d. red . . . . 2·50 30
88 1½d. olive and green 50 30
111 2d. grey . . . . 1·00 2·25
112 2½d. blue . . . . 50 6·50
91 3d. purple on yellow 50 30
92c 4d. black and red on yellow 1·50 6·50
93 5d. orange and purple . . . 1·00 2·00
94 6d. purple . . . . 1·00 2·50
95 7½d. brown and blue . . . . 1·25 6·50
96a 10d. green and red . . . . 2·00 15·00
97 1s. black on green . . . . . 2·00 1·00
98 1s.6d. violet and green . . . 11·00 10·00
99 2s. purple and blue on blue 3·50 6·00
100 2s.6d. black and red on blue 3·25 14·00
101 3s. yellow and green . . . . 8·50 28·00
117 4s. black and red . . . . . 80·00 £140
102 5s. green and red on yellow 85·00 £140

9 10

1922.
122 **9** ½d. black and green . . . 55 55
124 1d. black and brown . . . 80 20
125 1½d. black and red 80 20
126 2d. black and grey . . . . 1·00 3·50
127 2½d. black and orange . . 1·00 11·00
128 3d. black and blue . . . . 1·00 20
118 4d. black and red on yellow . . . . 2·75 3·50
130 5d. black and olive . . . . 2·00 10·00
131 6d. black and red . . . . 1·25 30
119 7½d. black & purple on yell 3·50 6·50
133 10d. black and blue . . . 4·50 18·00
134 **10** 1s. black & purple on yell 2·50 1·25
135 1s.6d. black and blue . . . 11·00 14·00
136 2s. black and purple on blue . . . . 4·50 4·25
137 2s.6d. black and green . . 4·75 9·50
138 3s. black and violet . . . . 13·00 50·00
140 4s. black and brown . . . 6·50 16·00
141 5s. black and green on yellow . . . . 13·00 40·00
142 10s. black and olive . . . 70·00 £100

10a Windsor Castle

1935. Silver Jubilee.
143 **10a** 1½d. blue and red 60 80
144 3d. brown and blue . . . 65 80
145 6d. blue and olive . . . 1·00 3·75
146 1s. grey and purple . . . 5·00 8·00

10b King George VI and Queen Elizabeth

1937. Coronation.
147 **10b** 1d. brown . . . . 30 1·00
148 1½d. red 30 50
149 3d. blue . . . . 55 1·25

11 Elephant (from Colony Badge)

1938.
150 **11** ½d. black and green . . . 15 70
151 1d. purple and brown . . 20 50
152b 1½d. lake and red . . . . 30 2·00
152c 1½d. blue and black . . . 30 1·50
153 2d. blue and black . . . 7·00 3·25
153a 2d. lake and red . . . . 60 2·25
154 3d. blue 30 10
154a 5d. green and purple . . 50 50
155 6d. olive and red . . . . 1·50 35
156 1s. blue and purple . . . 2·00 10
156a 1s.3d. purple and blue . . 3·00 2·50
157 2s. red and blue . . . . 4·50 3·25
158 2s.6d. brown and green . . 12·00 2·50
159 4s. red and purple . . . . 21·00 2·50
160 5s. blue and red . . . . 21·00 4·00
161 10s. orange and black . . 21·00 7·00

11a Houses of Parliament, London

1946. Victory.
162 **11a** 1½d. black 10 25
163 3d. blue 10 40

11b King George VI and Queen Elizabeth **11c** King George VI and Queen Elizabeth

1948. Silver Wedding.
164 **11b** 1½d. black 25 10
165 **11c** £1 mauve . . . . . . 15·00 15·00

11d Hermes, Globe and Forms of Transport

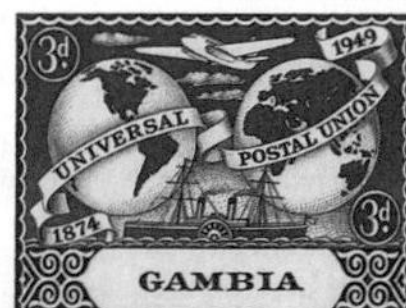

11e Hemispheres, Jet-powered Vickers Viking Airliner and Steamer

11f Hermes and Globe

11g UPU Monument

1949. UPU.
166 **11d** 1½d. black 30 1·50
167 **11e** 3d. blue 1·25 2·00
168 **11f** 6d. mauve 50 1·25
169 **11g** 1s. violet 35 60

11h Queen Elizabeth II

12 Tapping for Palm Wine

1953. Coronation.
170 **11h** 1½d. black and blue 50 1·00

1953. Queen Elizabeth II.
171 **12** ½d. red and green 30 20
172 – 1d. blue and brown 40 50
173 – 1½d. brown and black 20 70
174 – 2½d. black and red 45 70
175 – 3d. blue and lilac 35 10
176 – 4d. black and blue 60 2·25
177 **12** 6d. brown and purple 35 15
178 – 1s. brown and green 60 60
179 – 1s.3d. ultramarine and blue 10·00 60
180 – 2s. blue and red 7·00 3·50
181 – 2s.6d. green and brown 4·00 1·50
182 – 4s. blue and brown 11·00 3·00
183 – 5s. brown and blue 2·50 1·50
184 – 10s. blue and green 21·00 8·50
185 – £1 green and black 20·00 9·00
DESIGNS—HORIZ: 1d., 1s.3d. Cutter (sailing ship); 1½d., 5s. Wollof woman; 2½d., 2s. Barra canoe; 3d., 10s. S.S. "Lady Wright"; 4d., 4s. James Island; 1s., 2s.6d. Woman hoeing; £1 As Type **11**.

20 Queen Elizabeth II and Palm

20a Protein Foods

1961. Royal Visit.
186 **20** 2d. green and purple 30 20
187 – 3d. turquoise and sepia 75 15
188 – 6d. blue and red 75 70
189 **20** 1s.3d. violet and green 75 2·25
DESIGN: 3d., 6d. Queen Elizabeth II and West African map.

1963. Freedom from Hunger.
190 **20a** 1s.3d. red 55 15

20b Red Cross Emblem

1963. Centenary of Red Cross.
191 **20b** 2d. red and black 20 10
192 1s.3d. red and blue 40 45

22 Beautiful Sunbird

36 Gambia Flag and River

22a Shakespeare and Memorial Theatre, Stratford-upon-Avon

1963. Birds. Multicoloured.
193 ½d. Type **22** 50 1·00
194 1d. Yellow-mantled whydah 75 30
195 1½d. Cattle egret 2·00 70
196 2d. Senegal parrot 2·00 70
197 3d. Rose-ringed parakeet 2·00 1·00
198 4d. Violet starling 2·00 80
199 6d. Village weaver 2·00 10
200 1s. Rufous-crowned roller 2·00 10
201 1s.3d. Red-eyed dove 14·00 1·50
202 2s.6d. Double-spurred francolin 9·00 2·50
203 5s. Palm-nut vulture 9·00 3·50
204 10s. Orange-cheeked waxbill 14·00 7·00
205 £1 African emerald cuckoo 29·00 14·00

1963. New Constitution. Nos. 194, 197 and 200/1 optd **SELF GOVERNMENT 1963**.
206 1d. multicoloured 10 40
207 3d. multicoloured 25 20
208 1s. multicoloured 25 10
209 1s.3d. multicoloured 30 45

1964. 400th Birth Anniv of Shakespeare.
210 **22a** 6d. blue 20 10

1965. Independence. Multicoloured.
211 ½d. Type **36** 10 40
212 2d. Arms 15 10
213 7½d. Type **36** 40 35
214 1s.6d. Arms 50 30

1965. Nos 193/205 optd **INDEPENDENCE 1965**.
215 ½d. Type **22** 30 1·00
216 1d. Yellow-mantled whydah 30 20
217 1½d. Cattle egret 60 1·00
218 2d. Senegal parrot 70 30
219 3d. Rose-ringed parakeet 70 15
220 4d. Violet starling 70 1·75
221 6d. Village weaver 70 10
222 1s. Rufous-crowned roller 70 10
223 1s.3d. Red-eyed dove 70 10
224 2s.6d. Double-spurred francolin 70 60
225 5s. Palm-nut vulture 70 75
226 10s. Orange-cheeked waxbill 1·75 2·50
227 £1 African emerald cuckoo 7·50 8·50

39 ITU Emblem and Symbols

1965. Centenary of ITU.
228 **39** 1d. silver and blue 25 10
229 1s.6d. gold and violet 1·00 40

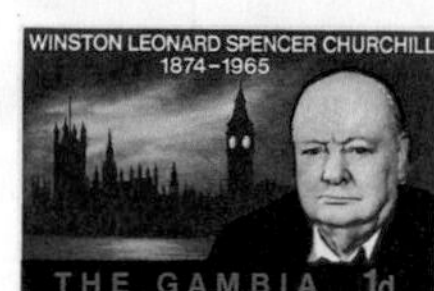

40 Sir Winston Churchill and Houses of Parliament

1966. Churchill Commemoration.
230 **40** 1d. multicoloured 15 10
231 6d. multicoloured 35 15
232 1s.6d. multicoloured 60 75

41 Red-cheeked Cordon-bleu

1966. Birds. Multicoloured.
233 ½d. Type **41** 90 40
234 1d. White-faced whistling duck 30 50
235 1½d. Red-throated bee eater 30 40
236 2d. Lesser pied kingfisher 4·25 75
237 3d. Golden bishop 30 10
238 4d. African fish eagle 50 30
239 6d. Yellow-bellied green pigeon 40 10
240 1s. Blue-bellied roller 40 10
241 1s.6d. African pygmy kingfisher 50 30
242 2s.6d. Spur-winged goose 50 70
243 5s. Cardinal woodpecker 50 75
244 10s. Violet turaco 50 2·75
245 £1 Pin-tailed whydah (25×39½ mm) 75 6·50

54 Arms, Early Settlement and Modern Buildings

1966. 150th Anniv of Bathurst.
246 **54** 1d. silver, brown and orange 10 10
247 2d. silver, brown and blue 10 10
248 6d. silver, brown and green 10 10
249 1s.6d. silver, brn & pur 15 15

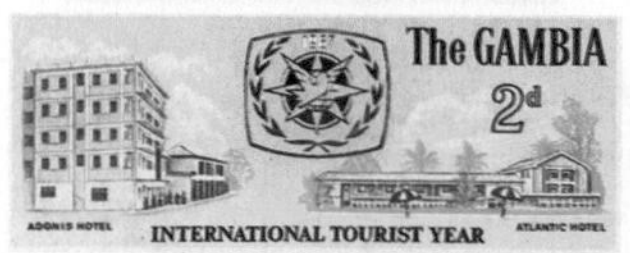

55 ITY Emblem and Hotels

1967. International Tourist Year.
250 **55** 2d. silver, brown and green 10 10
251 1s. silver, brown and orange 10 10
252 1s.6d. silver, brn & mve 15 25

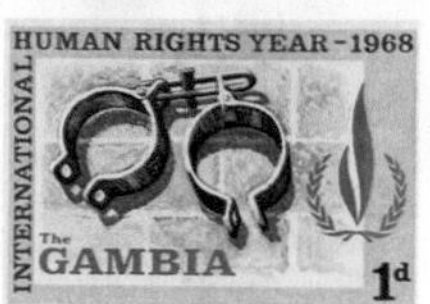

56 Handcuffs

1968. Human Rights Year. Multicoloured.
253 1d. Type **56** 10 10
254 1s. Fort Bullen 10 10
255 5s. Methodist Church 30 60

59 Queen Victoria, Queen Elizabeth II and 4d. Stamp of 1869

1969. Gambia Stamp Centenary.
256 **59** 4d. sepia and ochre 20 10
257 6d. blue and green 20 10
258 – 2s.6d. multicoloured 70 1·40
DESIGN: 2s.6d. Queen Elizabeth II with 4d. and 6d. stamps of 1869.

61 Catapult-ship "Westfalen" launching Dornier Wal

1969. 35th Anniv of Pioneer Air Service. Mult.
259 2d. Type **61** 35 20
260 1s. Dornier Wal flying boat "Boreas" 35 20
261 1s.6d. Airship "Graf Zeppelin" 40 1·40

63 Athlete and Gambian Flag

1970. 9th British Commonwealth Games, Edinburgh.
262 **63** 1d. multicoloured 10 10
263 1s. multicoloured 10 10
264 5s. multicoloured 30 90

64 President Sir Dawda Kairaba Jawara and State House

1970. Republic Day. Multicoloured.
265 2d. Type **64** 10 10
266 1s. President Sir Dawda Jawara (vert) 15 10
267 1s.6d. President and flag of Gambia (vert) 30 35

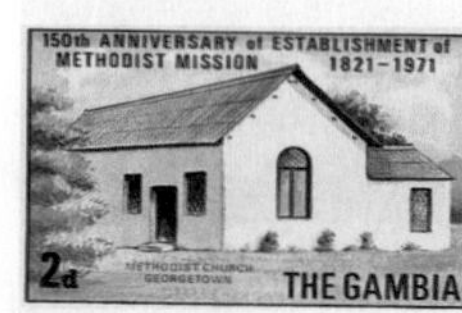

65 Methodist Church, Georgetown

1971. 150th Anniv of Establishment of Methodist Mission. Multicoloured.
268 2d. Type **65** 10 10
269 1s. Map of Africa and Gambian flag (vert) 15 15
270 1s.6d. John Wesley and scroll 15 1·00

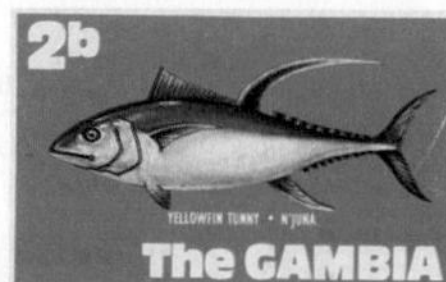

66 Yellow-finned Tunny

1971. New Currency. Fishes. Multicoloured.
271 2b. Type **66** 10 75
272 4b. Peter's mormyrid 10 20
273 6b. Four-winged flyingfish 15 75
274 8b. African sleeper goby 15 75
275 10b. Yellow-tailed snapper 20 20
276 13b. Rock hind 20 60
277 25b. West African eel catfish 35 60
278 38b. Tiger shark 55 45
279 50b. Electric catfish 70 55
280 63b. Black swampeel 80 1·75
281 1d.25 Small-toothed sawfish 1·40 2·50
282 2d.50 Great barracuda 1·50 4·50
283 5d. Brown bullhead 1·75 7·00

67 Mungo Park in Scotland

1971. Birth Centenary of Mungo Park (explorer). Multicoloured.
284 4b. Type **67** 20 10
285 25b. Dug-out canoe 45 35
286 37b. Death of Mungo Park, Busa Rapids 75 1·50

68 Radio Gambia

1972. 10th Anniv of Radio Gambia.
287 **68** 4b. brown and black 10 10
288 – 25b. blue, orange and black 10 30
289 **68** 37b. green and black 20 1·25
DESIGN: 25b. Broadcast-area map.

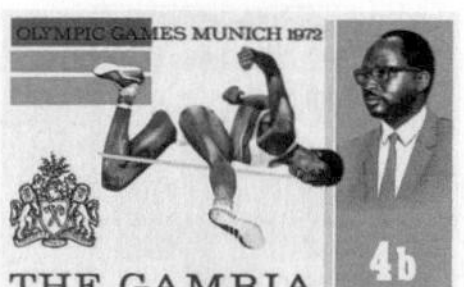

69 High Jumping

1972. Olympic Games, Munich.
290 **69** 4b. multicoloured 10 10
291 25b. multicoloured 20 15
292 37b. multicoloured 25 20

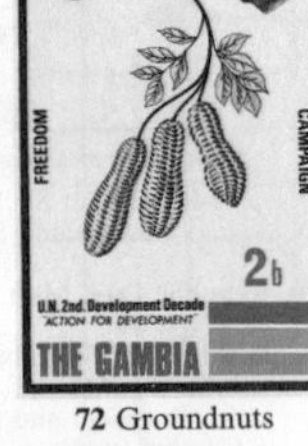
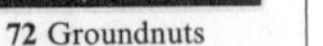

70 Manding Woman **72** Groundnuts

71 Children carrying Fanal

1972. International Conference on Manding Studies. Multicoloured.
293 2b. Type **70** 10 10
294 25b. Musician playing the Kora 15 15
295 37b. Map of Mail Empire . . 25 25

1972. Fanals (Model Boats). Multicoloured.
296 2b. Type **71** 10 10
297 1d.25 Fanal with lanterns . . 30 45

1973. Freedom from Hunger Campaign.
298 **72** 2b. multicoloured 10 10
299 25b. multicoloured 15 10
300 37b. multicoloured 25 20

73 Planting and Drying Rice **74** Oil Palm

1973. Agriculture (1st series). Multicoloured.
301 2b. Type **73** 10 10
302 25b. Guinea corn 20 15
303 37b. Rice 25 25

1973. Agriculture (2nd series). Multicoloured.
304 2b. Type **74** 10 10
305 25b. Limes 30 30
306 37b. Oil palm (fruits) 40 40

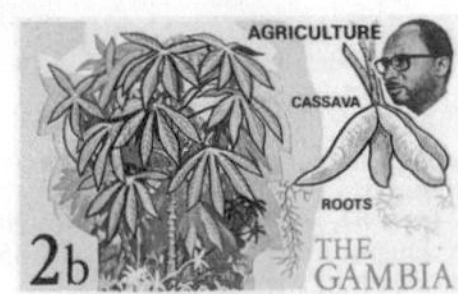

75 Cassava

1973. Agriculture (3rd series). Multicoloured.
307 2b. Type **75** 10 10
308 50b. Cotton 40 25

76 OAU Emblem

1973. 10th Anniv of OAU.
309 **76** 4b. multicoloured 10 10
310 25b. multicoloured 15 10
311 37b. multicoloured 15 20

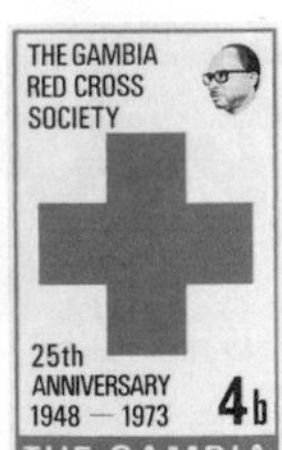

77 Red Cross

1973. 25th Anniv of Gambian Red Cross.
312 **77** 4b. red and black 10 10
313 25b. red, black and blue 15 15
314 37b. red, black and green 20 20

78 Arms of Banjul

1973. Change of Bathurst's Name to Banjul.
315 **78** 4b. multicoloured 10 10
316 25b. multicoloured 15 15
317 37b. multicoloured 15 20

79 UPU Emblem

1974. Centenary of UPU.
318 **79** 4b. multicoloured 10 10
319 37b. multicoloured 20 30

80 Churchill as Harrow Schoolboy

1974. Birth Cent of Sir Winston Churchill. Mult.
320 4b. Type **80** 10 10
321 37b. Churchill as 4th Hussars officer 20 15
322 50b. Churchill as Prime Minister 30 60

81 "Different Races"

1974. World Population Year. Multicoloured.
323 4b. Type **81** 10 10
324 37b. "Multiplication and Division of Races" 15 15
325 50b. "World Population" . . 20 25

82 Dr. Schweitzer and River Scene

1975. Birth Centenary of Dr. Albert Schweitzer. Multicoloured.
326 10b. Type **82** 20 10
327 50b. Surgery scene 40 25
328 1d.25 River journey 75 55

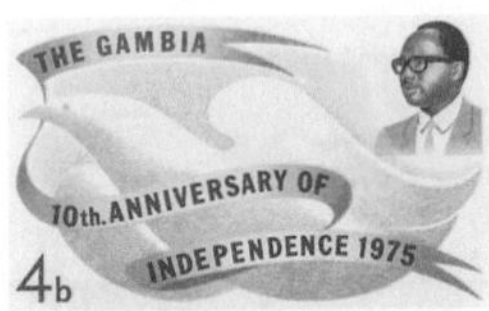

83 Dove of Peace

1975. 10th Anniv of Independence. Multicoloured.
329 4b. Type **83** 10 10
330 10b. Gambian flag 10 10
331 50b. Gambian arms 15 10
332 1d.25 Map of The Gambia 35 40

84 Development Graph **85** Statue of "David" (Michelangelo)

1975. 10th Anniv of African Development Bank. Multicoloured.
333 10b. Type **84** 10 10
334 50b. Symbolic plant 20 15
335 1d.25 Bank emblem and symbols 55 60

1975. 500th Birth Anniv of Michelangelo. Mult.
336 10b. Type **85** 15 10
337 50b. "Madonna of the Steps" 30 15
338 1d.25 "Battle of the Centaurs" (horiz) . . . . 50 1·25

86 School Building

1975. Centenary of Gambia High School. Mult.
339 10b. Type **86** 10 10
340 50b. Pupil with scientific apparatus 15 10
341 1d.50 School crest 35 35

87 "Teaching"

1975. International Women's Year. Multicoloured.
342 4b. Type **87** 10 10
343 10b. "Planting rice" 10 10
344 50b. "Nursing" 35 15
345 1d.50 "Directing traffic" . . 85 35

88 Woman playing Golf

1975. 11th Anniv of Independence. Mult.
346 10b. Type **88** 55 10
347 50b. Man playing golf . . . 1·50 30
348 1d.50 President playing golf 2·25 70

89 American Militiaman **90** Mother and Child

1976. Bicentenary of American Revolution. Mult.
349 25b. Type **89** 20 10
350 50b. Soldier of the Continental Army 30 20
351 1d.25 Independence Declaration 40 60
MS352 110 × 80 mm. Nos. 349/51 1·00 4·00

1976. Christmas.
353 **90** 10b. multicoloured 10 10
354 50b. multicoloured 15 10
355 1d.25 multicoloured . . . 50 45

91 Serval Cat

1976. Abuko Nature Reserve (1st series). Mult.
356 10b. Type **91** . . . . 3·50 20
357 20b. Bushbuck . . . . 4·50 20
358 50b. Sitatunga (deer) . . . . 8·00 40
359 1d.25 Leopard . . . . 13·00 2·50
MS360 137 × 110 mm. Nos. 356/9 32·00 12·00
See also Nos. 400/3, 431/5 and 460/3.

92 Festival Emblem and Gambian Weaver

1977. 2nd World Black and African Festival of Arts and Culture, Nigeria.
361 **92** 25b. multicoloured 15 10
362 50b. multicoloured 20 15
363 1d.25 multicoloured . . . 50 70
MS364 118 × 114 mm. Nos. 361/3 1·75 3·75

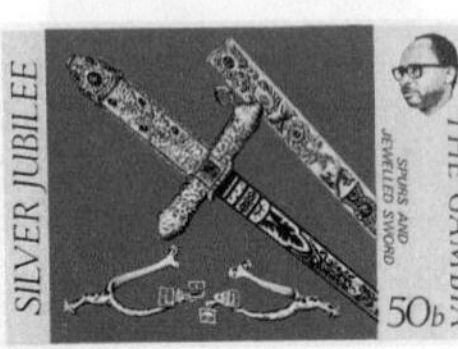

93 The Spurs and Jewelled Sword

1977. Silver Jubilee. Multicoloured.
365 25b. The Queen's visit, 1961 15 20
366 50b. Type **93** 15 20
367 1d.25 Oblation of the Sword 20 30

94 Stone Circles, Kuntaur

1977. Tourism. Multicoloured.
368 25b. Type **94** 10 10
369 50b. Ruined Fort, James Island 15 20
370 1d.25 Mungo Park Monument 40 80

95 Widow of Last Year

1977. Flowers and Shrubs. Multicoloured.
371 2b. Type **95** 10 15
372 4b. White water-lily 10 30
373 6b. Fireball lily (vert) . . . 10 30
374 8b. Cocks-comb (vert) . . . 10 15
375 10b. Broad leaved ground orchid (vert) . . . . . . 2·00 30
376 13b. Fibre plant (yellow background) (vert) . . . 15 40
376a 13b. Fibre plant (grey background) (vert) . . . 1·25 4·00
377 25b. False kapok (vert) . . 15 15
378 38b. Baobab (vert) 25 55
379 50b. Coral tree 35 35
380 63b. Gloriosa lily 40 70
381 1d.25 Bell-flowered mimosa (vert) . . . . 45 1·00
382 2d.50 Kindin dolo (vert) . . 50 1·00
383 5d. African tulip tree . . . 60 2·00

96 Endangered Animals **97** "Flight into Egypt"

1977. Banjul Declaration.
384 **96** 10b. black and blue . . . 25 10
385 – 25b. multicoloured 30 10
386 – 50b. multicoloured 45 20
387 – 1d.25 black and red . . . 1·50 75
DESIGNS: 25b. Extract from Declaration; 50b. Declaration in full; 1d.25, Endangered insects and flowers.

1977. 400th Birth of Rubens. Multicoloured.
388 10b. Type **97** 15 10
389 25b. "The Education of the Virgin" 20 10

390 50b. "Clara Serena Rubens" 30 30
391 1d. "Madonna with Saints" 45 90

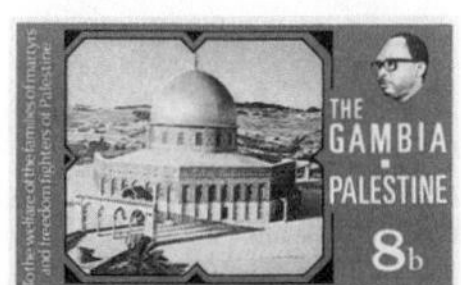

98 Dome of the Rock, Jerusalem

1978. Palestinian Welfare.
392 **98** 8b. multicoloured 50 15
393 25b. multicoloured . . . . 1·50 85

99 Walking on a Greasy Pole **100** Lion

1978. 13th Anniv of Independence. Multicoloured.
394 10b. Type **99** 10 10
395 50b. Pillow fighting 20 10
396 1d. Long boat rowing . . . 45 45

1978. 25th Anniv of Coronation.
397 – 1d. black, brown and yellow 20 45
398 – 1d. multicoloured 20 45
399 **100** 1d. black, brown and yellow 20 45
DESIGNS: No. 397, White Greyhound of Richmond; 398, Queen Elizabeth II.

101 Verreaux's Eagle Owl

1978. Abuko Nature Reserve (2nd series). Multicoloured.
400 20b. Type **101** . . . . . . 10·00 65
401 25b. Lizard buzzard . . . . 10·00 65
402 50b. African harrier hawk . . 13·00 2·25
403 1d.25 Long-crested eagle . . 17·00 9·00

102 M.V. "Lady Wright"

1978. Launching of River Vessel "Lady Chilel Jawara". Multicoloured.
404 8b. Type **102** 15 10
405 25b. Sectional view of "Lady Chilel Jawara" 40 25
406 1d. "Lady Chilel Jawara" . . 1·25 1·40

103 Police Service

1979. 14th Anniv of Independence. Multicoloured.
407 10b. Type **103** 60 10
408 50b. Fire service . . . . . . 1·10 25
409 1d.25 Ambulance service . . 1·40 80

1979. Nos. 376 and 380/1 surch **25b**.
410 25b. on 13b. Fibre plant . . 15 35
411 25b. on 63b. Gloriosa lily . . 10 20
412 25b. on 1d.25 Bell-flowered mimosa 10 20

105 "Ramsgate Sands" (detail showing children playing on beach)

1979. International Year of the Child. "Ramsgate Sands" (William Powell Frith). Multicoloured.
413 10b. Type **105** 10 10
414 25b. Detail showing child paddling (vert) 20 10
415 1d. Complete painting (60 × 23 mm) 60 60

106 1883 2½d. Stamp

1979. Death Centenary of Sir Rowland Hill. Multicoloured.
416 10b. Type **106** 10 10
417 25b. 1869 4d. stamp 10 10
418 50b. 1965 Independence 7½d. commemorative 15 20
419 1d.25 1935 Silver Jubilee 1½d. commemorative 35 50
MS420 109 × 83 mm. No. 419 . . 65 1·00

107 Satellite Earth Station under Construction

1979. Abuko Satellite Earth Station. Multicoloured.
421 25b. Type **107** 20 10
422 50b. Satellite Earth Station (completed) 30 20
423 1d. "Intelsat" satellite 65 60

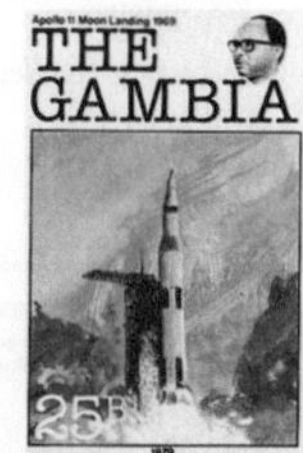

108 "Apollo 11" leaving Launch Pad

1979. 10th Anniv of Moon Landing. Multicoloured.
424 25b. Type **108** 20 10
425 38b. "Apollo 11" in Moon orbit 25 20
426 50b. Splashdown 30 40
430 2d. Lunar module on Moon 1·50 2·25
Nos. 424/6 also exist self-adhesive from booklet panes. No. 430 only exists in this form.

109 "Acraea zetes"

1980. Abuko Nature Reserve (3rd series). Butterflies. Multicoloured.
431 25b. Type **109** . . . . . . 5·00 20
432 50b. "Precis hierta" . . . . 6·00 50
433 1d. "Graphium leonidas" . . 8·50 1·40
434 1d.25 "Charaxes jasius" . . . 8·50 2·00
MS435 145 × 122 mm. Nos. 431/4 38·00 8·50

110 Steam Launch "Vampire"

1980. "London 1980" International Stamp Exhibition. Multicoloured.
436 10b. Type **110** 20 10
437 25b. T.S.S. "Lady Denham" 25 10
438 50b. T.S.C.M.Y. "Mansa Kila Ba" 30 20
439 1d.25 T.S.S. "Prince of Wales" 50 60
Nos. 438 and 439 are larger, 49 × 26 mm.

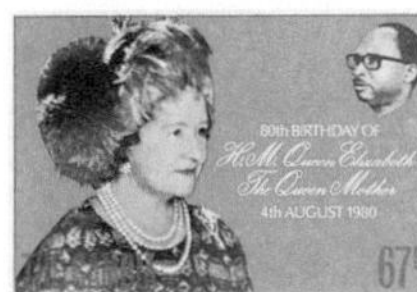

111 Queen Elizabeth the Queen Mother

1980. 80th Birthday of Queen Elizabeth The Queen Mother.
440 **111** 67b. multicoloured . . . 30 60

112 Phoenician Trading Vessel

1980. Early Sailing Vessels. Multicoloured.
441 8b. Type **112** 10 10
442 67b. Egyptian sea-going vessel 30 20
443 75b. Portuguese caravel . . . 35 30
444 1d. Spanish galleon 40 50

113 "Madonna and Child" (Francesco de Mura)

1980. Christmas. Multicoloured.
445 8b. Type **113** 10 10
446 67b. "Praying Madonna with Crown of Stars" (workshop of Correggio) 25 25
447 75b. "La Zingarella" (workshop replica of Correggio painting) 25 30

114 New Atlantic Hotel

1981. World Tourism Conference, Manila. Mult.
448 25b. Type **114** 15 10
449 75b. Ancient stone circles . . 20 40
450 85b. Conference emblem . . 30 60

115 1979 Abuko Satellite Earth Station 50b. Commemorative

1981. World Telecommunications Day.
451 **115** 50b. multicoloured . . . 45 20
452 – 50b. multicoloured . . . 45 20
453 – 85b. black and brown . . 50 45
DESIGNS: No. 452, 1975 Birth centenary of Schweitzer 50b. commemorative; 453 ITU and WHO emblems.

116 Prince Charles in Naval Uniform

1981. Royal Wedding. Multicoloured.
454 75b. Wedding bouquet from Gambia 20 20
455 1d. Type **116** 25 30
456 1d.25 Prince Charles and Lady Diana Spencer . . . 30 35

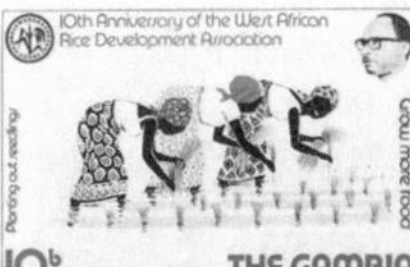

117 Planting-out Seedlings

1981. 10th Anniv of West African Rice Development Association. Multicoloured.
457 10b. Type **117** 10 10
458 50b. Care of the crops . . . 25 35
459 85b. Winnowing and drying 40 55

118 Bosc's Monitor

1981. Abuko Nature Reserve (4th series). Reptiles. Multicoloured.
460 40b. Type **118** . . . . . . 7·00 30
461 60b. Dwarf crocodile . . . . 7·50 80
462 80b. Royal python . . . . . 9·50 1·25
463 85b. Chameleon . . . . . . 9·50 1·25

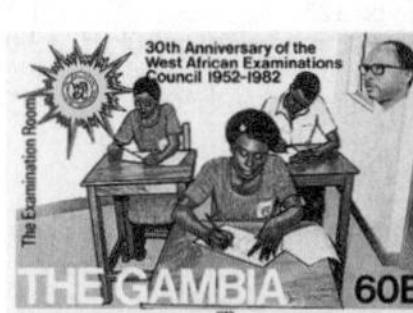

119 Examination Room

1982. 30th Anniv of West African Examinations Council. Multicoloured.
464 60b. Type **119** 50 30
465 85b. First high school 65 45
466 1d.10 Council's office 85 55

1982. No. 454 surch **60B**.
467 60b. on 75b. Wedding bouquet from Gambia . . 75 1·60

121 Tree-planting ("Conservation")

1982. 75th Anniv of Boy Scout Movement. Multicoloured.
468 85b. Type **121** . . . . . . 1·50 1·25
469 1d.25 Woodworking . . . . 1·75 2·50
470 1d.27 Lord Baden-Powell . . 2·00 3·25

122 Gambia Football Team

1982. World Cup Football Championship, Spain. Multicoloured.
471 10b. Type **122** 20 10
472 1d.10 Gambian team practice 1·10 70
473 1d.25 Bernabeu Stadium, Madrid . . . . 1·10 75
474 1d.55 FIFA World Cup . . . 1·25 80
MS475 114 × 85 mm. Nos. 471/4 4·00 4·50

123 Gambia Coat of Arms

1982. 21st Birthday of Princess of Wales. Multicoloured.
476 10b. Type **123** 10 10
477 85b. Princess at City Hall, Cardiff, October 1981 . . . 30 20
478 1d.10 Bride and groom returning to Buckingham Palace 35 35
479 2d.50 Formal portrait . . . . 1·25 1·00

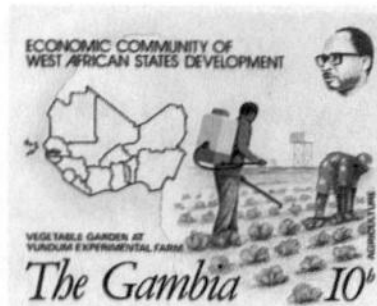

124 Vegetable Garden at Yundum Experimental Farm

1982. Economic Community of West African States Development. Multicoloured.

480 10b. Type **124** 30 15
481 60b. Banjul/Kaolack microwave tower . . . . . 2·00 2·25
482 90b. Soap factory, Denton Bridge, Banjul . . . . . . 2·00 3·00
483 1d.25 Control tower, Yundum Airport . . . . . 3·00 3·50

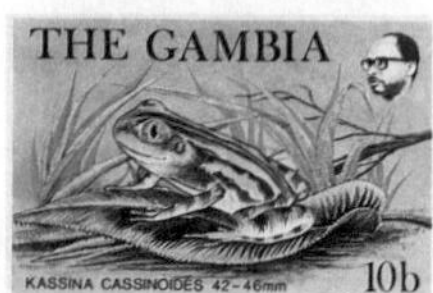

125 "Kassina cassinoides"

1982. Frogs. Multicoloured.

484 10b. Type **125** . . . . . . 1·75 20
485 20b. "Hylarana galamensis" 3·00 30
486 85b. "Euphlyctis occipitalis" 4·25 2·00
487 2d. "Kassina senegalensis" 6·50 11·00

126 Satellite View of Gambia

1983. Commonwealth Day. Multicoloured.

488 10b. Type **126** 10 10
489 60b. Batik cloth 20 45
490 1d.10 Bagging groundnuts . . 35 65
491 2d.10 Gambia flag . . . . . 55 1·25

127 Blessed Anne Marie Javouhey (foundress of Order)

1983. Centenary of Sisters of St. Joseph of Cluny's Work in Gambia. Multicoloured.

492 10b. Type **127** 10 10
493 85b. Bathurst Hospital, nun and school children (horiz) 45 50

128 Canoes

1983. River Craft. Multicoloured.

494 1b. Type **128** 15 60
495 2b. Upstream ferry 20 60
496 3b. Dredger 20 60
497 4b. "Sir Dawda" (harbour launch) 30 60
498 5b. Cargo liner 30 60
499 10b. "Lady Dale" (60ft. launch) 30 20
500 20b. "Shonga" (container ship) 45 55
501 30b. Large sailing canoe . . 45 55
502 40b. "Lady Wright" (river steamer) 65 75
503 50b. Container ship (different) 65 75
504 75b. Fishing boats . . . . . 75 1·00
505 1d. Tug with groundnut barges . . . . 90 1·00
506 1d.25 Groundnut canoe . . . 1·00 1·50
507 2d.50 "Banjul" (car ferry) . . 1·75 2·50
508 5d. "Bintang Bolong" (freighter) . . . . 2·50 4·00
509 10d. "Lady Chilel Jawara" (river vessel) . . . . 4·00 6·50

129 Osprey in Tree

1983. The Osprey. Multicoloured.

510 10b. Type **129** . . . . . . 1·50 50
511 60b. Osprey . . . . 2·75 2·50
512 85b. Osprey with catch . . . 3·25 3·00
513 1d.10 In flight . . . . 3·50 5·00

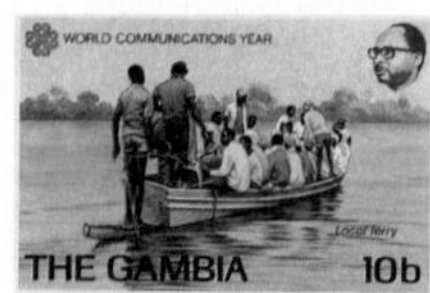

130 Local Ferry

1983. World Communications Year. Multicoloured.

514 10b. Type **130** 10 10
515 85b. Telex operator 45 50
516 90b. Radio Gambia 45 50
517 1d.10 Loading mail onto Douglas DC-9-80 aircraft 1·50 65

131 "St. Paul preaching at Athens" (detail)

1983. 500th Birth Anniv of Raphael.

518 **131** 60b. multicoloured . . . 35 40
519 – 85b. multicoloured . . . 45 50
520 – 1d. multicoloured 50 55
MS521 105 × 83 mm. 2d. multicoloured (vert) . . . . . 1·25 1·25

Nos. 519/20 show different details of "St. Paul preaching at Athens".

132 Montgolfier Balloon and Siege of Paris Cover

1983. Bicentenary of Manned Flight. Multicoloured.

522 60b. Type **132** 35 40
523 85b. Douglas DC-10 aircraft and flown cover 45 50
524 90b. Junkers seaplane "Atlantis" and Hans Bertram cover 45 50
525 1d.25 Lunar module and H. E. Sieger's space cover 50 70
526 4d. Airship "Graf Zeppelin" 2·25 3·00

133 Shot-putting **134** Goofy

1984. Olympic Games, Los Angeles (1st issue). Multicoloured.

527 60b. Type **133** 25 30
528 85b. High jumping (horiz) . . 35 40
529 90b. Wrestling 35 40
530 1d. Gymnastics 40 45
531 1d.25 Swimming (horiz) . . . 50 55
532 2d. Diving 80 85
MS533 100 × 80 mm. 5d. Yachting 2·00 2·75

See also Nos. 555/8.

1984. Easter. Multicoloured.

534 1b. Type **134** 10 10
535 2b. Mickey Mouse 10 10
536 3b. Huey, Dewey and Louie 10 10
537 4b. Goofy (different) 10 10
538 5b. Donald Duck 10 10
539 10b. Chip 'n' Dale 10 10
540 60b. Pluto 35 40
541 90b. Scrooge McDuck 50 60
542 5d. Morty and Ferdie . . . . 2·25 2·75
MS543 125 × 100 mm. 5d. Donald Duck (different) . . . . 3·50 3·50

Nos. 534/42 show Walt Disney cartoon characters painting eggs.

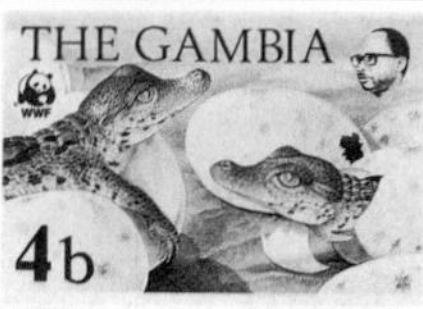

135 Young Crocodiles Hatching

1984. Endangered Species. The Nile Crocodile. Multicoloured.

544 4b. Type **135** . . . . 1·25 65
545 6b. Adult carrying young . . 1·25 65
546 90b. Adult . . . . 9·00 3·25
547 1d.50 Crocodile at riverbank 10·00 8·00
MS548 126 × 94 mm. As Nos. 544/7, but without W.W.F. logo . . . 5·50 8·00

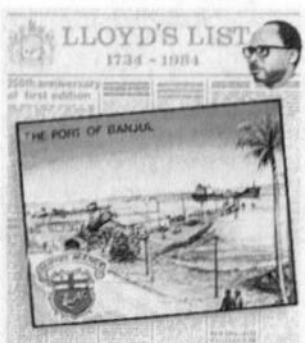

136 Port Banjul

1984. 250th Anniv of "Lloyd's List" (newspaper). Multicoloured.

549 60b. Type **136** 60 50
550 85b. Bulk carrier 75 80
551 90b. Sinking of the "Dagomba" 75 90
552 1d.25 19th-century frigate . . 1·25 1·60

1984. Universal Postal Union Congress, Hamburg. Nos. 507/8 optd **19th UPU CONGRESS HAMBURG**.

553 2d.50 "Banjul" (car ferry) . . 1·00 1·50
554 5d. "Bintang Bolong" (ferry) 1·75 2·50

138 Sprinting

1984. Olympic Games, Los Angeles (2nd issue). Multicoloured.

555 60b. Type **138** 25 30
556 85b. Long jumping 35 40
557 90b. Long-distance running 35 40
558 1d.25 Triple jumping 50 55

139 Airship "Graf Zeppelin"

1984. 50th Anniv of Gambia–South America Trans-Atlantic Flights. Multicoloured.

559 60b. Type **139** . . . . . . 1·10 1·00
560 85b. Dornier Wal on S.S. "Westfalen" . . . . 1·60 1·75
561 90b. Dornier Do-18 . . . . 1·75 2·50
562 1d.25 Dornier Wal . . . . . 1·75 2·75

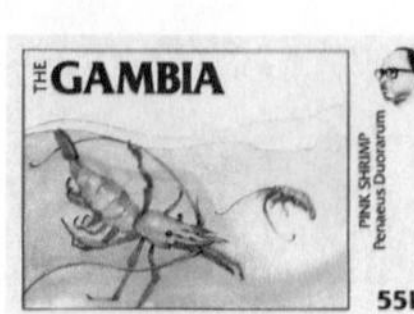

140 Pink Shrimp

1984. Marine Life. Multicoloured.

563 55b. Type **140** 35 30
564 75b. Atlantic loggerhead turtle 55 40
565 1d.50 Portuguese man-of-war 90 1·00
566 2d.35 Fiddler crab . . . . . 1·40 1·60
MS567 105 × 70 mm. 5d. Cowrie snail . . . . 2·75 4·00

141 "Antanartia hippomene"

1984. Butterflies. Multicoloured.

568 10b. Type **141** 30 20
569 85b. "Pseudacraea eurytus" 80 90
570 90b. "Charaxes lactitinctus" 80 90
571 3d. "Graphium pylades" . . 2·00 3·75
MS572 105 × 75 mm. 5d. "Eurema hapale" . . . . 10·00 9·50

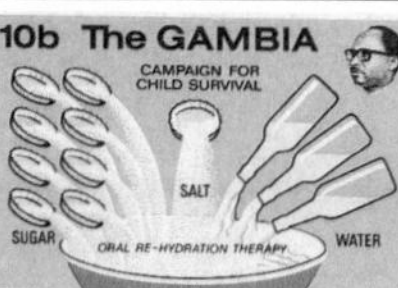

142 Oral Re-hydration Therapy

1985. Campaign for Child Survival.

573 **142** 10b. black, blue and brown 10 10
574 – 85b. multicoloured . . . 35 45
575 – 1d.10 multicoloured . . . 45 65
576 – 1d.50 multicoloured . . . 60 80

DESIGNS: 85b. Growth monitoring; 1d.10, Health care worker with women and babies ("Promotion of breast feeding"); 1d.50, Universal immunization.

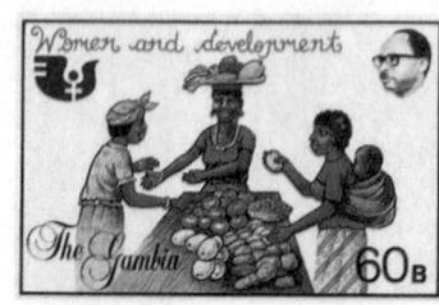

143 Women at Market

1985. Women and Development. Multicoloured.

577 60b. Type **143** 25 35
578 85b. Type **143** 35 50
579 1d. Woman office worker . . 40 60
580 1d.25 As 1d. 50 90

144 Turkey Vulture **145** The Queen Mother

1985. Birth Bicentenary of John J. Audubon (ornithologist). Designs showing original paintings. Multicoloured.

581 60b. Type **144** . . . . . . 1·40 75
582 85b. American darter ("American Anhinga") . . 1·60 1·50
583 1d.50 Green-backed heron ("Green Heron") . . . . . 2·00 3·25
584 5d. Wood duck . . . . . . 3·25 5·50
MS585 100 × 70 mm. 10d. Great northern diver ("Common Loon") 6·50 4·00

1985. Life and Times of Queen Elizabeth the Queen Mother. Multicoloured.

586 85b. The Queen Mother and King George VI reviewing Home Guard . . . . . . 1·25 30
587 3d. Type **145** . . . . 1·75 1·50
588 5d. The Queen Mother with posy . . . . 2·50 2·25
MS589 56 × 85 mm. 10d. The Queen Mother in Garter robes . . . . 4·25 3·25

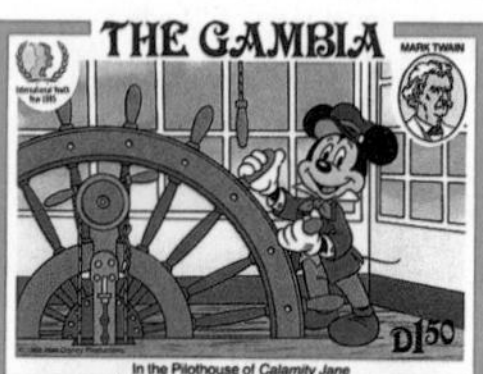

145a Mickey Mouse steering the "Calamity Jane"

1985. 150th Birth Anniv of Mark Twain (author). Designs showing Walt Disney cartoon characters in scenes from "Life on the Mississippi". Multicoloured.

590 1d.50 Type **145a** . . . . . 2·00 2·00
591 2d. Mickey and Minnie Mouse at antebellum mansion . . . . 2·25 2·25
592 2d.50 Donald Duck and Goofy heaving the lead . . 2·50 2·50
593 3d. Poker game aboard the "Gold Dust" . . . . . . 2·75 2·75
MS594 126 × 101 mm. 10d. Mickey Mouse and riverboat . . . . . 7·50 4·75

145b The King (Mickey Mouse) and Portrait of the Princess (Minnie Mouse)

1985. Birth Bicentenaries of Grimm Brothers (folklorists). Designs showing Walt Disney cartoon characters in scenes from "Faithful John". Multicoloured.

595 60b. Type **145b** 75 40
596 85b. The King showing the Princess his treasures . . . 95 50
597 2d.35 Faithful John (Goofy) playing trumpet . . . . . 2·25 1·40
598 5d. Faithful John turned to stone . . . . 3·25 2·50
MS599 126 × 101 mm. 10d. Faithful John after recovery . . . . . 7·50 5·00

1985. Olympic Gold Medal Winners, Los Angeles. Nos. 527/32 optd.

600 60b. Type **133** (optd **GOLD MEDALLIST CLAUDIA LOCH WEST GERMANY**) 40 40
601 85b. High jumping (optd **GOLD MEDALLIST ULRIKE MEYFARTH WEST GERMANY**) . . . 50 50
602 90b. Wrestling (optd **GOLD MEDALLIST PASQUALE PASSARELLI WEST GERMANY**) 50 50
603 1d. Gymnastics (optd **GOLD MEDALLIST LI NING CHINA**) 55 55
604 1d.25 Swimming (optd **GOLD MEDALLIST MICHAEL GROSS WEST GERMANY**) 70 70
605 2d. Diving (optd **GOLD MEDALLIST SYLVIE BERNIER CANADA**) . . 1·00 1·00
MS606 100 × 80 mm. 5d. Yachting (optd **GOLD MEDAL STAR CLASS U.S.A.**) . . . . 2·00 2·00

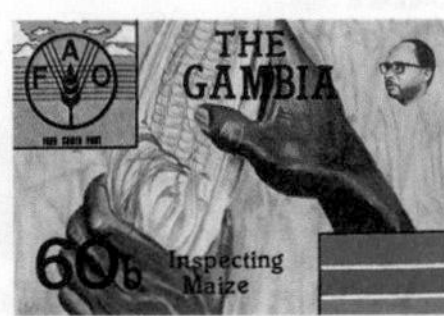

147 Inspecting Maize

1985. United Nations Anniversaries. Multicoloured.

607 60b. Type **147** 40 35
608 85b. Football match, Independence Stadium, Banjul 50 40
609 1d.10 Rice fields 60 60
610 2d. Central Bank of The Gambia . . . . 85 1·00
611 3d. Cow and calf . . . . . . 1·50 1·75
612 4d. Banjul harbour . . . . . 2·00 2·25
613 5d. Gambian fruits . . . . . 2·25 2·50
614 6d. Oyster Creek Bridge . . . 2·50 3·00

Nos. 607, 609, 611 and 613 commemorate the 40th anniv of the Food and Agriculture Organization and Nos. 608, 610, 612 and 614 the 40th anniv of the United Nations Organization.

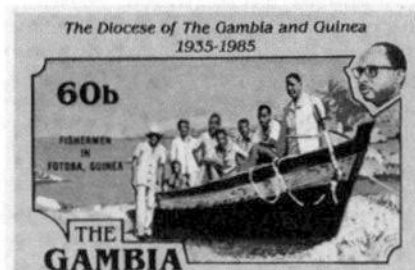

148 Fishermen in Fotoba, Guinea

1985. 50th Anniv of Diocese of The Gambia and Guinea. Multicoloured.

615 60b. Type **148** 40 30
616 85b. St. Mary's Primary School, Banjul 40 40
617 1d.10 St. Mary's Cathedral, Banjul 40 65
618 1d.50 Mobile dispensary at Christy Kunda . . . . . . 1·10 85

149 "Virgin and Child" (Dieric Bouts)

1985. Christmas. Religious Paintings. Multicoloured.

619 60b. Type **149** 20 25
620 85b. "The Annunciation" (Robert Campin) 25 30
621 1d.50 "Adoration of the Shepherds" (Gerard David) 45 50
622 5d. "The Nativity" (Gerard David) . . . . 1·60 1·75
MS623 106 × 84 mm. 10d. "Adoration of the Magi" (Hieronymus Bosch) . . . . . 3·50 4·00

150 Enrolment Card

1985. 75th Anniv of Girl Guide Movement. Multicoloured.

624 60b. Type **150** 40 30
625 85b. 2nd Bathurst Company centre 50 35
626 1d.50 Lady Baden-Powell (vert) . . . . 70 1·00
627 5d. Miss Rosamond Fowlis (Gambian Guide Association leader) (vert) 2·00 3·75
MS628 97 × 67 mm. 10d. Gambian girl guides (vert) . . . . 4·50 6·00

151 Girl and Village Scene

1985. International Youth Year. Multicoloured.

629 60b. Type **151** 30 30
630 85b. Youth and wrestling bout 35 35
631 1d.10 Girl and Griot storyteller . . . . 45 1·00
632 1d.50 Youth and crocodile pool . . . . 70 1·40
MS633 106 × 76 mm. 5d. Herdsman with cattle . . . . 2·00 3·00

151a Maria Mitchell (astronomer) and Kitt Peak National Observatory, Arizona

1986. Appearance of Halley's Comet (1st issue). Multicoloured.

634 10b. Type **151a** 40 20
635 20b. Neil Armstrong, first man on Moon, 1969 . . . 55 25
636 75b. "Skylab 4" and Comet Kohoutek, 1973 . . . . . 85 65
637 1d. N.A.S.A.'s infra-red astronomical satellite and Halley's Comet . . . . . 1·00 80
638 2d. Comet of 1577 from Turkish painting . . . . . 1·50 1·50
639 10d. N.A.S.A.'s International Cometary Explorer . . . . 4·00 5·50
MS640 102 × 70 mm. 10d. Halley's Comet . . . . 5·00 6·00

See also Nos. 679/84.

151b Duke of York and Family, Royal Tournament, 1936

1986. 60th Birthday of Queen Elizabeth II.

641 **151b** 1d. black and yellow . . 25 30
642 – 2d.50 multicoloured . . . 65 70
643 – 10d. multicoloured . . . 2·50 3·50
MS644 120 × 85 mm. 10d. black and brown . . . . 3·00 3·00

DESIGNS: Nos. 642, Queen attending christening, 1983; 643, In West Germany, 1978; **MS**644, Duchess of York with her daughters, Balmoral, 1935.

152 Two Players competing for Ball

1986. World Cup Football Championship, Mexico. Multicoloured.

645 75b. Type **152** 75 60
646 1d. Player kicking ball . . . 1·00 85
647 2d.50 Player kicking ball (different) . . . . 2·00 2·25
648 10d. Player heading ball . . . 5·00 6·00
MS649 100 × 70 mm. 10d. Goalkeeper saving goal . . . . 7·50 7·00

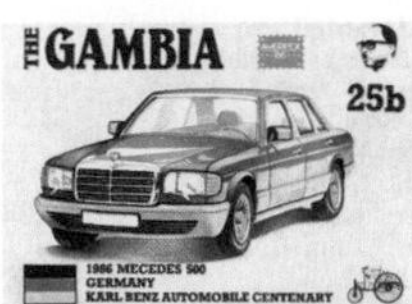

153 Mercedes "500" (1986)

1986. "Ameripex" International Stamp Exhibition, Chicago. Centenary (1985) of First Benz Motor Car. Multicoloured.

650 25b. Type **153** 20 10
651 75b. Cord "810" (1935) . . . 35 40
652 1d. Borgward "Isabella Coupe" (1957) 40 60
653 1d.25 Lamborghini "Countach" (1985/6) . . . 50 70
654 2d. Ford "Thunderbird" (1955) . . . . 50 1·25
655 2d.25 Citroen "DS19" (1956) 50 1·60
656 5d. Bugatti "Atlante" (1936) 70 3·00
657 10d. Horch "853" (1936) . . 80 5·00
MS658 Two sheets, each 100 × 70 mm. (a) 12d. Benz "8/20" (1913). (b) 12d. Steiger "10/50" (1924) Set of 2 sheets . . . . . 4·75 12·00

The 25b. value is inscribed "MECEDES" and the 10d. "LARL BENZ".

153a John Jacob Astor (financier)

1986. Centenary of Statue of Liberty (1st issue). Multicoloured. Designs showing Statue of Liberty and immigrants to the U.S.A.

659 20b. Type **153a** 10 10
660 1d. Jacob Riis (journalist) . . 40 50
661 1d.25 Igor Sikorsky (aeronautics engineer) . . . 60 60
662 5d. Charles Boyer (actor) . . 2·50 2·50
MS663 114 × 80 mm. 10d. Statue of Liberty (vert) . . . . 4·00 4·50

See also Nos. 705/14.

153b Prince Andrew and Miss Sarah Ferguson

1986. Royal Wedding. Multicoloured.

664 1d. Type **153b** 40 45
665 2d.50 Prince Andrew . . . . 1·00 1·40
666 4d. Prince Andrew as helicopter pilot . . . . . . 2·50 2·00
MS667 88 × 88 mm. 7d. Prince Andrew and Miss Sarah Ferguson (different) . . . . 4·75 3·50

1986. World Cup Football Championship Winners, Mexico. Nos. 645/8 optd **WINNERS Argentina 3 W.Germany 2**.

668 75b. Type **152** 30 40
669 1d. Player kicking ball . . . 40 55
670 2d.50 Player kicking ball (different) . . . . 1·00 1·25
671 10d. Player heading ball . . . 4·25 4·75
MS672 100 × 70 mm. Goalkeeper saving goal . . . . 4·50 4·50

154 Minnie Mouse (Great Britain)

1986. Christmas. Designs showing Walt Disney cartoon characters posting letters in various countries. Multicoloured.

673 1d. Type **154** 75 60
674 1d.25 Huey (U.S.A.) 80 80
675 2d. Huey, Dewey and Louie (France) . . . . 1·25 1·40
676 2d.35 Kanga and Roo (Australia) . . . . 1·40 1·75
677 5d. Goofy (Germany) . . . . 2·25 3·00
MS678 127 × 101 mm. 10d. Goofy (Sweden) . . . . 7·50 6·00

Nos. 673/7 also show the "Stockholmia '86" International Stamp Exhibition emblem.

1986. Appearance of Halley's Comet (2nd issue). Nos. 634/9 optd **HALLEYS COMET 1985-OFFICIAL-1986.**

679 10b. Maria Mitchell (astronomer) and Kitt Peak National Observatory, Arizona 30 15
680 20b. Neil Armstrong, first man on Moon, 1969 . . . 50 20
681 75b. "Skylab 4" and Comet Kohoutek, 1973 . . . . . 75 50
682 1d. N.A.S.A.'s infra-red astronomical satellite and Halley's Comet 85 60
683 2d. Comet of 1577 from Turkish painting . . . . . 1·40 1·75
684 10d. N.A.S.A.'s International Cometary Explorer . . . . 3·75 6·00
MS685 102 × 70 mm. 10d. Halley's Comet . . . . 3·00 4·25

155 Bugarab and Tabala

1987. Manding Musical Instruments. Multicoloured.

686 75b. Type **155** 15 20
687 1d. Balaphong and fiddle . . 15 25
688 1d.25 Bolongbato and konting (vert) 20 35
689 10d. Antique and modern koras (vert) . . . . . . 1·60 3·00
MS690 100 × 70 mm. 12d. Sabarr 1·90 2·50

156 "Snowing"

1987. Birth Centenary of Marc Chagall (artist). Multicoloured.

691 75b. Type **156** 40 40
692 85b. "The Boat" 50 50
693 1d. "Maternity" 65 65
694 1d.25 "The Flute Player" . . 75 75
695 2d.35 "Lovers and the Beast" 1·00 1·25
696 4d. "Fishes at Saint Jean" . . 1·25 2·00
697 5d. "Entering the Ring" . . . 1·50 2·50
698 10d. "Three Acrobats" . . . 2·25 3·75
MS699 Two sheets. (a) 110 × 68 mm. 12d. "The Cattle Driver" (104 × 61 mm). (b) 109 × 95 mm. 12d. "The Sabbath" (104 × 89 mm). Imperf Set of 2 sheets . . . . 7·50 8·50

157 "America", 1851

1987. America's Cup Yachting Championship. Multicoloured.
700 20b. Type **157** 20 15
701 1d. "Courageous", 1974 . . . 35 35
702 2d.50 "Volunteer", 1887 . . 75 1·10
703 10d. "Intrepid", 1967 . . . . 2·25 3·25
MS704 114 × 89 mm. 12d. "Australia II", 1983 . . . . 4·00 3·00

158 Arm of Statue of Liberty **159** "Lantana camara"

1987. Centenary of Statue of Liberty (1986) (2nd issue). Multicoloured.
705 1b. Type **158** 10 10
706 2b. Launch passing Statue (horiz) 10 10
707 3b. Schooner passing Statue (horiz) 10 10
708 5b. U.S.S. "John F. Kennedy" (aircraft carrier) and "Queen Elizabeth 2" (liner) (horiz) 10 10
709 50b. Checking Statue for damage 40 40
710 75b. Cleaning in progress . . 55 55
711 1d. Working on Statue . . . 70 70
712 1d.25 Statue and fireworks 80 80
713 10d. Statue illuminated . . . 4·25 4·75
714 12d. Statue and fireworks (different) . . . . 4·50 5·00

1987. Flowers of Abuko Nature Reserve. Multicoloured.
715 75b. Type **159** 20 15
716 1d. "Clerodendrum thomsoniae" 20 20
717 1d.50 "Haemanthus multiflorus" 30 30
718 1d.70 "Gloriosa simplex" . . 30 35
719 1d.75 "Combretum microphyllum" 35 40
720 2d.25 "Eulophia quineensis" 50 60
721 5d. "Erythrina senegalensis" 1·10 1·25
722 15d. "Dichrostachys glomerata" . . . . 2·75 3·50
MS723 Two sheets, each 100 × 70 mm. (a) 15d. "Costus spectabilis". (b) 15d. "Strophanthus preussii" Set of 2 sheets . . . . 5·50 7·50

160 Front of Mail Bus **161** Basketball

1987. "Capex '87" International Stamp Exhibition, Toronto and 10th Anniv of Gambia Public Transport Corporation. Mail Buses. Mult.
724 20b. Type **160** 60 20
725 75b. Bus in Banjul (horiz) . . 90 45
726 1d. Passengers queueing for bus (horiz) 90 45
727 10d. Two buses on rural road 3·50 6·50
MS728 77 × 70 mm. 12d. Parked bus fleet (horiz) . . . . 4·50 4·50

1987. Olympic Games, Seoul (1988) (1st issue). Multicoloured.
729 50b. Type **161** 35 20
730 1d. Volleyball 50 35
731 3d. Hockey (horiz) . . . . . 1·10 85
732 10d. Handball (horiz) . . . . 2·50 2·25
MS733 100 × 85 mm. 15d. Football (horiz) . . . . 3·00 2·75
See also Nos. 779/83.

162 "A Partridge in a Pear Tree" **163** Campfire Singsong

1987. Christmas. Designs showing a Victorian couple in scenes from carol "The Twelve Days of Christmas". Multicoloured.
734 20b. Type **162** 60 50
735 40b. "Two turtle doves" . . 65 55
736 60b. "Three French hens" . . 70 60
737 75b. "Four calling birds" . . 70 60
738 1d. "Five golden rings" . . . 70 60
739 1d.25 "Six geese a-laying" . . 80 65
740 1d.50 "Seven swans a-swimming" 80 65
741 2d. "Eight maids a-milking" 90 75
742 3d. "Nine ladies dancing" . . 95 85
743 5d. "Ten lords a-leaping" . . 1·25 1·25
744 10d. "Eleven pipers piping" 1·90 2·00
745 12d. "Twelve drummers drumming" . . . . 2·25 2·25
MS746 100 × 70 mm. 15d. Exchanging presents (horiz) . . 2·40 3·25

1987. World Scout Jamboree, Australia. Multicoloured.
747 75b. Type **163** 50 30
748 1d. Scouts examining African katydid 70 40
749 1d.25 Scouts watching Red-tailed tropic bird . . . . . 1·50 85
750 12d. Scouts helping bus passenger . . . . 3·75 4·50
MS751 72 × 98 mm. 15d. Scouts on field trip . . . . 6·50 7·50

163a Morty and Ferdie examining Trevithick's Locomotive, 1804

1987. 60th Anniv of Mickey Mouse (Walt Disney cartoon character) (1st issue). Multicoloured.
752 60b. Type **163a** 25 25
753 75b. Clarabelle Cow in "Empire State Express", 1893 . . . . 30 30
754 1d. Donald Duck inspecting Stephenson's "Rocket", 1829 . . . . 40 40
755 1d.25 Piglet and Winnie the Pooh with Santa Fe Railroad locomotive, 1920 45 45
756 2d. Donald and Daisy Duck with Pennsylvania Railroad Class GG1 electric locomotive, 1933 . . . . . 70 70
757 5d. Mickey Mouse in "Stourbridge Lion", 1829 1·60 1·75
758 10d. Goofy in "Best Friend of Charleston", 1830 . . . 2·75 3·25
759 12d. Brer Bear and Brer Rabbit with Union Pacific diesel locomotive No. M10001, 1934 . . . . . . 3·00 3·50
MS760 Two sheets, each 127 × 101 mm. (a) 15d. Chip n'Dale in "The General", 1855. (b) 15d. Donald Duck and Mickey Mouse in modern French "TGV" train Set of 2 sheets . . . . . 7·50 8·00
See also Nos. 849/58.

164 Common Duiker and Acacia **165** Wedding Portrait, 1947

1988. Flora and Fauna. Multicoloured.
761 50b. Type **164** 20 10
762 75b. Red-billed hornbill and casuarina (vert) 65 30
763 90b. West African dwarf crocodile and rice 30 20
764 1d. Leopard and papyrus (vert) 30 20
765 1d.25 Crowned crane ("Crested Crane") and millet 65 45
766 2d. Waterbuck and baobab tree (vert) 40 60
767 3d. Oribi and Senegal palm 50 1·25
768 5d. Hippopotamus and papaya (vert) . . . . . . 90 1·75
MS769 98 × 69 mm. (a) 12d. Red-throated bee eater and acacia (vert). (b) 12d. Eastern white pelican ("Great White Pelican") Set of 2 sheets . . . . 2·75 4·50

1988. Royal Ruby Wedding.
770 **165** 75b. brown, black orange 30 15
771 – 1d. brown, black and blue 40 20
772 – 3d. multicoloured . . . . 90 1·00
773 – 10d. multicoloured . . . 2·25 3·25
MS774 100 × 75 mm. 15d. multicoloured . . . . 3·00 3·25
DESIGNS: 1d. Engagement photograph; 3d. Wedding portrait, 1947 (different); 10d. Queen Elizabeth II and Prince Philip (photo by Karsh), 1986; 15d. Wedding portrait with page, 1947.

1988. Stamp Exhibitions. Nos. 689, 703, 722 and 726 optd.
775 1d. Passengers queueing for bus (optd **Independence 40**, Israel) 25 25
776 10d. Antique and modern koras (optd **FINLANDIA 88**, Helsinki) . . . . 2·00 2·50
777 10d. "Intrepid" (yacht), 1967 (optd **Praga '88**, Prague) 2·00 2·50
778 15d. "Dichrostachys glomerata" (optd **OLYMPHILEX '88**, Seoul) 2·75 3·00

1988. Olympic Games, Seoul (2nd issue). As T **161**. Multicoloured.
779 1d. Archery 50 20
780 1d.25 Boxing 50 25
781 5d. Gymnastics . . . . . . 1·25 1·10
782 10d. Start of 100 metre race (horiz) . . . . 2·00 2·25
MS783 74 × 102 mm. 15d. Medal winners on rostrum . . . . . 2·40 3·25

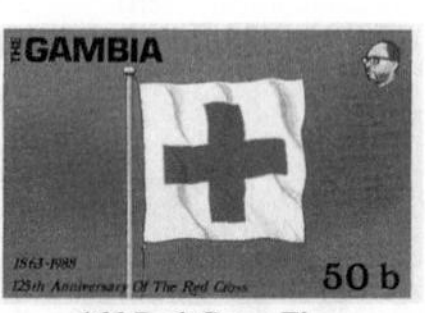

166 Red Cross Flag

1988. Anniversaries and Events. Multicoloured.
784 50b. Type **166** (125th anniv) 75 55
785 75b. "Friendship 7" spacecraft (25th anniv of first American manned Earth orbit) 85 60
786 1d. British Airways Concorde (10th anniv of Concorde London–New York service) 2·00 1·00
787 1d.25 "Spirit of St. Louis" (60th anniv of first solo transatlantic flight) . . . . 1·25 1·00
788 2d. North American X-15 (20th anniv of fastest aircraft flight) . . . . . . 1·60 1·40
789 3d. Bell "XS-1" rocket plane (40th anniv of first supersonic flight) . . . . . 1·75 1·50
790 10d. English and Spanish galleons (400th anniv of Spanish Armada) . . . . 3·75 3·75
791 12d. "Titanic" (75th anniv of sinking) . . . . 5·50 4·25
MS792 Two sheets. (a) 113 × 85 mm. 15d. Kaiser Wilhelm Memorial Church, Berlin (vert) (750th anniv of Berlin). (b) 121 × 90 mm. 15d. Kangaroo (Bicentenary of Australian Settlement) Set of 2 sheets . . . . 4·75 7·00

166a "Emperor Charles V"

1988. 500th Birth Anniv of Titian (artist). Mult.
793 25b. Type **166a** 20 20
794 50b. "St. Margaret and the Dragon" 35 35
795 60b. "Ranuccio Farnese" . . 40 40
796 75b. "Tarquin and Lucretia" 55 55
797 1d. "The Knight of Malta" 70 70
798 5d. "Spain succouring Faith" 2·25 2·50
799 10d. Doge Francesco Venier" 3·50 3·50
800 12d. "Doge Grimani before the Faith" (detail) . . . . 3·75 3·75
MS801 110 × 95 mm. (a) 15d. "Jealous Husband" (detail). (b) 15d. "Venus blindfolding Cupid" Set of 2 sheets . . . . 4·75 7·00

167 John Kennedy sailing

1988. 25th Death Anniv of President John F. Kennedy. Multicoloured.
802 75b. Type **167** 15 15
803 1d. Kennedy signing Peace Corps legislation, 1962 . . 15 20
804 1d.25 Speaking at U.N., New York (vert) 20 25
805 12d. Grave and eternal flame, Arlington National Cemetery (vert) . . . . . 1·90 2·75
MS806 99 × 72 mm. 15d. John F. Kennedy (vert) . . . . . . 2·40 3·50

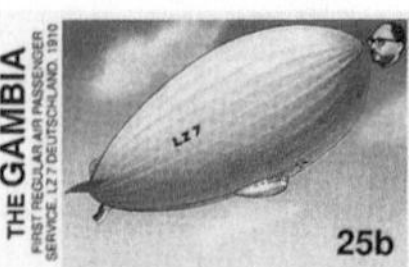

168 Airship "Graf Zeppelin" (first regular air passenger service), 1910

1988. Milestones of Transportation. Multicoloured.
807 25b. Type **168** 80 35
808 50b. Stephenson's "Locomotion" (first permanent public railway), 1825 . . . . 1·50 50
809 75b. G.M. "Sun Racer" (first world solar challenge), 1987 . . . . 1·25 65
810 1d. Sprague's "Premiere" (first operational electric tramway), 1888 . . . . . 1·50 80
811 1d.25 "Gold Rush" Bicycle (holder of man-powered land speed record), 1986 2·25 85
812 2d.50 Robert Goddard and rocket launcher (first liquid fuel rocket), 1925 . . . . 2·00 1·25
813 10d. "Orukter Amphibolos" (first steam traction engine), 1805 . . . . . . 4·00 3·25
814 12d. "Sovereign of the Seas" (largest cruise liner), 1988 4·00 3·50
MS815 Two sheets, each 71 × 92 mm. (a) 15d. U.S.S. "Nautilus" (first nuclear-powered submarine), 1954 (vert). (b) 15d. Fulton's "Nautilus" (first fish-shaped submarine), 1800's (vert) Set of 2 sheets . . . . 8·00 8·50

169 Emmett Kelley **170** Prince Henry the Navigator and Caravel

1988. Entertainers. Multicoloured.
816 20b. Type **169** 10 10
817 1d. Gambia National Ensemble 25 25
818 1d.25 Jackie Gleason 30 30
819 1d.50 Laurel and Hardy . . . 40 40
820 2d.50 Yul Brynner 75 75
821 3d. Cary Grant 95 95
822 10d. Danny Kaye . . . . . 3·00 3·00
823 20d. Charlie Chaplin . . . . 5·50 5·50
MS824 Two sheets. (a) 110 × 77 mm. 15d. Marx Brothers (horiz). (b) 70 × 99 mm. 15d. Fred Astaire and Rita Hayworth (horiz) Set of 2 sheets . . . . 9·50 9·50

1988. Exploration of West Africa. Multicoloured.
825 50b. Type **170** 80 60
826 75b. Jesse Ramsden's sextant, 1785 . . . . 85 70
827 1d. 15th-century hourglass . . 90 80
828 1d.25 Prince Henry the Navigator and Vasco da Gama . . . . 1·40 95
829 2d.50 Vasco da Gama and ship . . . . 2·25 1·60
830 5d. Mungo Park and map of Gambia River (horiz) . . . 3·50 2·50
831 10d. Map of West Africa, 1563 (horiz) . . . . . . 4·50 3·75
832 12d. Portuguese caravel (horiz) . . . . 4·50 4·00
MS833 Two sheets, each 65 × 100 mm. (a) 15d. Ship from Columbus's fleet off Gambia. (b) 15d. 15th-century ship moored off Gambia Set of 2 sheets . . . . 7·00 6·50

171 Projected Space Plane and Ernst Mach (physicist)

1988. 350th Anniv of Publications of Galileo's "Discourses". Space Achievements. Mult.

834 50b. Type **171** 70 30
835 75b. OAO III astronomical satellite and Niels Bohr (physicist) 80 40
836 1d. Space shuttle, projected space station and Robert Goddard (physicist) (horiz) 90 45
837 1d.25 Jupiter probe, 1979, and Edward Barnard (astronomer) (horiz) . . . 1·25 60
838 2d. Hubble Space Telescope and George Hale (astronomer) . . . . . . 1·75 75
839 3d. Earth-to-Moon laser measurement and Albert Michaelson (physicist) (horiz) . . . . 1·75 85
840 10d. HEAO-2 "Einstein" orbital satellite and Albert Einstein "physicist" . . . 3·25 2·75
841 20d. "Voyager" (first non-stop round-the-world flight), 1987, and Wright Brothers (aviation pioneers) (horiz) . . . . 5·50 5·00
MS842 Two sheets. (a) 99 × 75 mm. 15d. Great Red Spot on Jupiter (horiz). (b) 88 × 71 mm. 15d. Neil Armstrong (first man on Moon), 1969 Set of 2 sheets . . . . . 6·00 8·00

172 Passing Out Parade

1989. Army Day. Multicoloured.

843 75b. Type **172** 25 25
844 1d. Standards of The Gambia Regiment 25 25
845 1d.25 Side drummer in ceremonial uniform (vert) 30 30
846 10d. Marksman with Atlantic Shooting Cup (vert) . . . 2·00 2·00
847 15d. Soldiers on assault course (vert) . . . . 2·75 2·75
848 20d. Gunner with 105 mm field gun . . . . 3·00 3·00

173 Mickey Mouse, 1928

1989. 60th Birthday of Mickey Mouse (2nd issue). Multicoloured.

849 2d. Type **173** . . . . 1·00 90
850 2d. Mickey Mouse, 1931 . . 1·00 90
851 2d. Mickey Mouse, 1936 . . 1·00 90
852 2d. Mickey Mouse, 1955 . . 1·00 90
853 2d. Mickey Mouse, 1947 . . 1·00 90
854 2d. Mickey Mouse as magician, 1940 . . . . 1·00 90
855 2d. Mickey Mouse with palette, 1960 . . . . 1·00 90
856 2d. Mickey Mouse as Uncle Sam, 1976 . . . . 1·00 90
857 2d. Mickey Mouse, 1988 . . 1·00 90
MS858 138 × 109 mm. 15d. Mickey Mouse at 60th birthday party (132 × 103 mm) Imperf . . . . 4·25 4·00
Nos. 849/57 were printed together, se-tenant, forming a composite design.

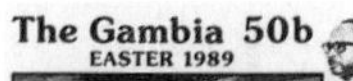

174 "Le Coup de Lance" (detail)

176 "Druryia antimachus"

175 African Emerald Cuckoo

1989. Easter. Religious Paintings by Rubens. Multicoloured.

859 50b. Type **174** 45 25
860 75b. "Flagellation of Christ" 55 35
861 1d. "Lamentation for Christ" 55 35
862 1d.25 "Descent from the Cross" 60 40
863 2d. "Holy Trinity" 90 70
864 5d. "Doubting Thomas" . . 1·75 1·75
865 10d. "Lamentation over Christ" . . . . 2·50 2·75
866 12d. "Lamentation with Virgin and St. John" . . . 2·50 3·00
MS867 Two sheets, each 96 × 110 mm. (a) 15d. "The Last Supper". (b) 15d. "Raising of the Cross" Set of 2 sheets . . . . 4·50 5·50

1989. West African Birds. Multicoloured.

868 20b. Type **175** 90 30
869 60b. Grey-headed bush shrike 1·40 50
870 75b. South African crowned crane ("Crowned Crane") 1·40 55
871 1d. Secretary bird . . . . . 1·60 60
872 2d. Red-billed hornbill . . . 2·25 1·00
873 5d. Superb sunbird . . . . . 3·00 3·00
874 10d. Pearl-spotted owlet ("Little owl") . . . . . . 4·00 4·25
875 12d. Bateleur ("Bateleur Eagle") . . . . 4·00 4·25
MS876 Two sheets, each 115 × 86 mm. (a) 15d. Ostrich. (b) 15d. Red-billed fire finch Set of 2 sheets . . . . 7·50 8·00

1989. Butterflies of Gambia. Multicoloured.

877 50b. Type **176** 65 30
878 75b. "Euphaedra neophron" 75 45
879 1d. "Aterica rabena" 75 45
880 1d.25 "Salamis parhassus" 85 55
881 5d. "Precis rhadama" . . . . 2·25 2·25
882 10d. "Papilio demodocus" . . 3·00 3·00
883 12d. "Charaxes etesipe" . . . 3·25 3·50
884 15d. "Danaus formosa" . . . 3·25 3·75
MS885 Two sheets, each 99 × 68 mm. (a) 15d. "Euptera pluto". (b) 15d. "Euphaedra ceres" Set of 2 sheets . . . . . 11·00 12·00

177 Class "River" Steam Locomotive No. 021, 1959, Nigeria

1989. African Steam Locomotive. Multicoloured.

886 50b. Type **177** 70 35
887 75b. Class 14A steam locomotive, Rhodesia . . . 80 45
888 1d. British-built steam locomotive No. 120, Sudan 85 55
889 1d.25 Steam locomotive, 1925, U.S.A. 95 65
890 5d. North British steam locomotive, 1955 . . . . . 2·50 1·75
891 7d. Scottish-built steam locomotive No. 120, 1926 2·75 2·75
892 10d. East African Railways Class 1T steam tank locomotive . . . . 3·00 3·00
893 12d. American-built steam locomotive, Ghana . . . . 3·25 3·75
MS894 Two sheets, each 82 × 58 mm. (a) 15d. East African Railways Class 25 steam locomotive No. 2904 (vert). (b) 15d. East African Railways Class 25 steam locomotive No. 3700A (vert) Set of 2 sheets . . . . . 9·50 10·00

1989. "Philexfrance '89" Int Stamp Exhibition, Paris. Nos. 686/9 optd **PHILEXFRANCE '89**.

895 75b. Type **155** 15 15
896 1d. Balaphong and fiddle . . 20 20
897 1d.25 Bolongbato and konting (vert) 25 25
898 10d. Antique and modern koras (vert) . . . . 1·75 2·50
MS899 100 × 70 mm. 12d. Sabarr 1·75 2·25

177a "Sparrow and Bamboo" (Hiroshige)

1989. Japanese Art. Multicoloured.

900 50b. Type **177a** 50 30
901 75b. "Peonies and a Canary" (Hokusai) 65 40
902 1d. "Crane and Marsh Grasses" (Hiroshige) . . . 75 45
903 1d.25 "Crossbill and Thistle" (Hokusai) 85 60
904 2d. "Cuckoo and Azalea" (Hokusai) . . . . 1·25 80
905 5d. "Parrot on a Pine Branch" (Hiroshige) . . . 2·00 2·00
906 10d. "Mandarin Ducks in a Stream" (Hiroshige) . . . 2·75 3·00
907 12d. "Bullfinch and Drooping Cherry" (Hokusai) . . . . 2·75 3·25
MS908 Two sheets, each 102 × 77 mm. (a) 15d. "Tit and Peony" (Hiroshige). (b) 15d. "Peony and Butterfly" (Shigenobou) Set of 2 sheets 9·00 9·50

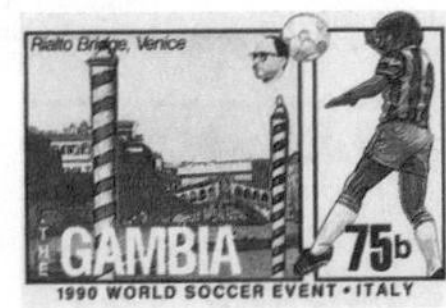

179 Rialto Bridge, Venice

1989. World Cup Football Championship, Italy (1990) (1st issue). Designs showing landmarks and players. Multicoloured.

909 75b. Type **179** 45 45
910 1d.25 The Baptistery, Pisa . . 60 60
911 7d. Casino, San Remo . . . 2·25 2·75
912 12d. Colosseum, Rome . . . 3·00 3·50
MS913 Two sheets, each 104 × 78 mm. (a) 15d. St. Mark's Cathedral, Venice. (b) 15d. Piazza Colonna, Rome Set of 2 sheets 9·50 10·00
See also Nos. 1064/8.

180 "Vitex doniana"

1989. Medicinal Plants. Multicoloured.

914 20b. Type **180** 20 20
915 50b. "Ricinus communis" . . 30 30
916 75b. "Palisota hirsuta" . . . 45 45
917 1d. "Smilax kraussiana" . . 55 55
918 1d.25 "Aspilia africana" . . . 65 65
919 5d. "Newbouldia laevis" . . 1·75 2·00
920 8d. "Monodora tenuifolia" . 1·90 2·50
921 10d. "Gossypium arboreum" 2·00 2·50
MS922 Two sheets, each 87 × 72 mm. (a) 15d. "Kigelia africana". (b) 15d. "Spathodea campanulata" Set of 2 sheets 11·00 11·00

181 Lookdown Fish

1989. Fishes. Multicoloured.

923 20b. Type **181** 25 25
924 75b. Boarfish 55 55
925 1d. Grey triggerfish 65 65
926 1d.25 Skipjack tuna 75 75
927 2d. Striped rudderfish 95 95
928 4d. Atlantic manta . . . . . 1·60 1·75
929 5d. Flat-headed grey mullet 1·75 1·90
930 10d. Ladyfish . . . . 2·75 3·25
MS931 Two sheets, each 104 × 72 mm. (a) 15d. Porcupinefish. (b) 15d. Shortfin mako Set of 2 sheets . . . . 12·00 12·00

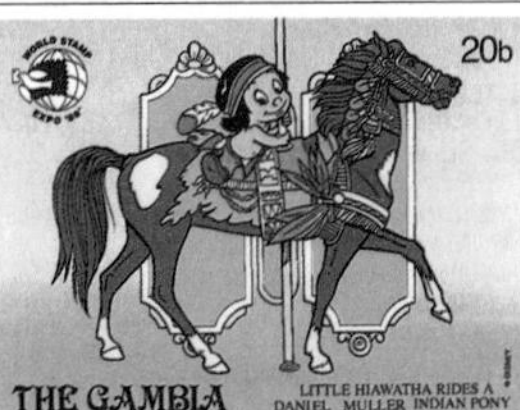

181a Little Hiawatha on Daniel Muller Indian Pony

1989. "World Stamp Expo '89" International Stamp Exhibition, Washington. Designs showing Walt Disney cartoon characters and American carousel horses. Multicoloured.

932 20b. Type **181a** 70 30
933 50b. Morty on Herschell-Spillman stander 90 50
934 75b. Goofy on Gustav Dentzel stander . . . . . 1·10 65
935 1d. Mickey Mouse on Daniel Muller armoured stander 1·25 70
936 1d.25 Minnie Mouse on jumper from Smithsonian Collection . . . . 1·40 80
937 2d. Webby on Illion "American Beauty" . . . 2·00 1·25
938 8d. Donald Duck on Zalar jumper . . . . 4·25 4·50
939 10d. Mickey Mouse on Parker bucking horse . . . 4·25 4·50
MS940 Two sheets, each 127 × 102 mm. (a) 12d. Donald, Mickey and Goofy in carousel car. (b) 12d. Donald's nephews on Roman chariot horses Set of 2 sheets . . . . 9·50 10·00

182 White House

1989. "World Stamp Expo '89" International Stamp Exhibition, Washington (2nd issue). Landmarks of Washington. Sheet 78 × 61 mm.

MS941 10d. multicoloured . . . 1·40 2·00

183 Mickey and Minnie Mouse in Pierce-Arrow, 1922

1989. Christmas. Designs showing Walt Disney cartoon characters with cars. Multicoloured.

942 20b. Type **183** 80 25
943 50b. Goofy in Spyker, 1919 1·00 45
944 75b. Donald and Grandma Duck with Packard, 1929 1·10 55
945 1d. Mickey Mouse driving Daimler, 1920 . . . . . . 1·25 65
946 1d.25 Mickey Mouse in Hispano "Suiza", 1924 . . 1·40 90
947 2d. Mickey and Minnie Mouse in Opel "Laubfrosch", 1924 . . . 1·90 1·25
948 10d. Donald Duck driving Vauxhall "30/98", 1927 . . 4·00 4·50
949 12d. Goofy with Peerless, 1923 . . . . 4·00 4·50
MS950 Two sheets, each 127 × 102 mm. (a) 15d. Mickey and Minnie Mouse picnicking by Stutz "Blackhawk Speedster", 1928. (b) 15d. Donald Duck, Mickey and Minnie Mouse in Bentley "Supercharged", 1930 Set of 2 sheets . . . . 11·00 13·00

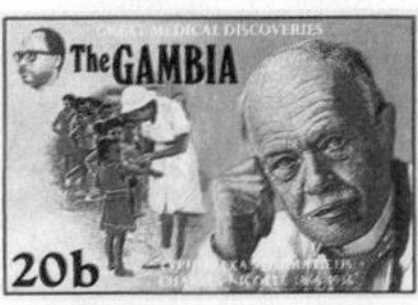

184 Charles Nicolle (typhus transmission) and Vaccination

1989. Great Medical Discoveries. Multicoloured.

951 20b. Type **184** 85 20
952 50b. Paul Ehrlich (immunization pioneer) and medical examination . . . 1·25 30
953 75b. Selman Waksman (discoverer of streptomycin) and T.B. clinic . . . . . . 1·40 40
954 1d. Edward Jenner (smallpox vaccination), and Jenner conducting experiment, 1796 . . . . 1·60 50

955 1d.25 Robert Koch (developer of tuberculin test) and Gambian using vaccination gun 1·90 75
956 5d. Sir Alexander Fleming (discoverer of penicillin) and doctor giving injection 2·50 2·75
957 8d. Max Theiler (developer of yellow fever vaccine) and child clinic 3·25 4·00
958 10d. Louis Pasteur (bacteriologist) and health survey 3·25 4·00
MS959 Two sheets, each 121 × 86 mm. (a) 15d. Hughes 369 Viking medical helicopter. (b) 15d. B.A.C. One Eleven Nightingale C.9 medical relief plane Set of 2 sheets 8·00 8·50

No. **MS**959a is incorrectly inscribed "Vicking".

185 "Bulbophyllum lepidum"

186 John Newcombe

1989. Orchids. Multicoloured.
960 20b. Type **185** 30 30
961 75b. "Tridactyle tridactylites" 55 55
962 1d. "Vanilla imperialis" 70 70
963 1d.25 "Oeceoclades maculata" 80 90
964 2d. "Polystachya affinis" 1·10 1·25
965 4d. "Ancistrochilus rothschildianus" 1·90 2·25
966 5d. "Angraecum distichum" 2·00 2·25
967 10d. "Liparis guineensis" 3·50 4·00
MS968 Two sheets, each 99 × 67 mm. (a) 15d. "Plectrelminthus caudatus". (b) 15d. "Eulophia guineensis" Set of 2 sheets 8·50 8·50

1990. Wimbledon Tennis Champions. Multicoloured.
969 20b. Type **186** 10 10
970 20b. Mrs. G. W. Hillyard 10 10
971 50b. Roy Emerson 20 20
972 50b. Dorothy Chambers 20 20
973 75b. Donald Budge 30 30
974 75b. Suzanne Lenglen 30 30
975 1d. Laurence Doherty 35 35
976 1d. Helen Wills Moody 35 35
977 1d.25 Bjorn Borg 40 40
978 1d.25 Maureen Connolly 40 40
979 4d. Jean Borotra 1·00 1·00
980 4d. Maria Bueno 1·00 1·00
981 5d. Anthony Wilding 1·00 1·00
982 5d. Louise Brough 1·00 1·00
983 7d. Fred Perry 1·40 1·40
984 7d. Margaret Court 1·40 1·40
985 10d. Bill Tilden 2·00 2·00
986 10d. Billie Jean King 2·00 2·00
987 12d. Rod Laver 2·25 2·25
988 12d. Martina Navratilova 2·25 2·25
MS989 Two sheets, each 101 × 76 mm. (a) 15d. Rod Laver (different). (b) 15d. Martina Navratilova (different) Set of 2 sheets 8·50 9·50

187 Lunar Module "Eagle"

1990. 20th Anniv (1989) of First Manned Landing on Moon. Multicoloured.
990 20b. Type **187** 85 20
991 50b. Lift-off of "Apollo 11" (vert) 1·10 30
992 75b. Neil Armstrong stepping on to Moon 1·25 45
993 1d. Buzz Aldrin and American flag 1·40 55
994 1d.25 "Apollo 11" emblem (vert) 1·60 60
995 1d.75 Crew of "Apollo 11" 1·90 1·40
996 8d. Lunar Module "Eagle" on Moon 3·50 4·00
997 12d. Recovery of "Apollo 11" after splashdown 3·75 4·50
MS998 Two sheets, each 110 × 89 mm. (a) 15d. Neil Armstrong (vert). (b) 15d. View of Earth from Moon (vert) Set of 2 sheets 7·00 7·50

188 Bristol Type 142 Blenheim Mk I

1990. R.A.F. Aircraft of Second World War. Multicoloured.
999 10b. Type **188** 85 50
1000 20b. Fairey Battle 1·10 50
1001 50b. Bristol Type 142 Blenheim Mk IV 1·40 50
1002 60b. Vickers-Armstrong Wellington Mk 1c 1·50 50
1003 75b. Armstrong Whitworth Whitley Mk V 1·50 50
1004 1d. Handley Page Hampden Mk 1 1·50 50
1005 1d.25 Supermarine Spitfire Mk 1A and Hawker Hurricane Mk I 1·50 55
1006 2d. Avro Manchester 1·90 90
1007 3d. Short Stirling Mk I 1·90 1·60
1008 5d. Handley Page Halifax Mk I 2·25 2·25
1009 10d. Avro Lancaster Mk III 3·25 3·75
1010 12d. De Havilland Mosquito Mk IV 3·25 3·75
MS1011 Two sheets, each 107 × 77 mm. (a) 15d. Supermarine Spitfire Mk 1A. (b) 15d. Avro Type 683 Lancaster Mk III (different) Set of 2 sheets 8·50 9·00

189 White-faced Scops Owl

191 Flag and National Assembly Building

190 Penny Black

1990. African Birds. Multicoloured.
1012 1d.25 Type **189** 70 70
1013 1d.25 Village weaver 70 70
1014 1d.25 Red-throated bee eater 70 70
1015 1d.25 Brown snake eagle ("Brown Harrier Eagle") 70 70
1016 1d.25 Red bishop 70 70
1017 1d.25 Scarlet-chested sunbird 70 70
1018 1d.25 Red-billed hornbill 70 70
1019 1d.25 Mosque swallow 70 70
1020 1d.25 White-faced whistling duck 70 70
1021 1d.25 African fish eagle 70 70
1022 1d.25 Eastern white pelican 70 70
1023 1d.25 Carmine bee eater 70 70
1024 1d.25 Hadada ibis 70 70
1025 1d.25 Egyptian plover 70 70
1026 1d.25 Variable sunbird 70 70
1027 1d.25 African skimmer 70 70
1028 1d.25 Woodland kingfisher 70 70
1029 1d.25 African jacana 70 70
1030 1d.25 African pygmy goose 70 70
1031 1d.25 Hammerkop 70 70

Nos. 1012/31 were printed together, se-tenant, forming a composite design of birds at a lake.

1990. 150th Anniv of the Penny Black.
1032 **190** 1d.25 black and blue 1·50 50
1033 12d. black and red 4·50 4·50
MS1034 79 × 73 mm. **190** 15d. black, silver and orange 6·00 7·00

The design of No. **MS**1034 is without the additional stamps behind the Penny Black as shown on Type **190**.

1990. 25th Anniv of Independence. Multicoloured.
1035 1d. Type **191** 50 25
1036 3d. President Sir Dawda Jawara 50 50
1037 12d. Map of Yundum airport and Boeing 707 airliner 6·50 6·50
MS1038 100 × 69 mm. 18d. State arms 5·00 6·50

192 Baobab Tree

1990. Gambian Life. Multicoloured.
1039 5b. Type **192** 65 65
1040 10b. Woodcarving, Albert Market, Banjul 10 30
1041 20b. President Jawara planting seedling (vert) 10 10
1042 50b. Sailing canoe and map 1·50 25
1043 75b. Batik fabric 20 10
1044 1d. Hibiscus and Bakau beach 30 20
1045 1d.25 Bougainvillea and Tendaba Camp 30 20
1046 2d. Shrimp fishing and sorting 45 35
1047 5d. Groundnut oil mill, Denton Bridge 80 1·25
1048 10d. Handicraft pot and kora (musical instrument) 1·50 2·50
1049 15d. "Ansellia africana" (orchid) (vert) 7·00 8·00
1050 30d. "Euriphene gambiae" (butterfly) and ancient stone ring near Georgetown 9·00 12·00

193 Daisy Duck at 10 Downing Street

1990. "Stamp World London 90" International Stamp Exhibition. Walt Disney cartoon characters in England. Multicoloured.
1051 20b. Type **193** 70 30
1052 50b. Goofy in Trafalgar Square 90 35
1053 75b. Mickey Mouse on White Cliffs of Dover (horiz) 1·00 50
1054 1d. Mickey Mouse at Tower of London 1·00 50
1055 5d. Mickey Mouse and Goofy at Hampton Court Palace (horiz) 2·75 2·50
1056 8d. Mickey Mouse by Magdalen Tower, Oxford 3·25 3·50
1057 10d. Mickey Mouse on Old London Bridge (horiz) 3·25 3·50
1058 12d. Scrooge McDuck and Rosetta Stone, British Museum (horiz) 3·50 4·00
MS1059 Two sheets, each 125 × 100 mm. (a) 18d. Mickey Mouse and Donald Duck at Piccadilly Circus (horiz). (b) 18d. Mickey Mouse steering tug on River Thames (horiz) Set of 2 sheets 13·00 14·00

194 Lady Elizabeth Bowes-Lyon in High Chair

195 Vialli, Italy

1990. 90th Birthday of Queen Elizabeth the Queen Mother.
1060 **194** 6d. black, mve & yell 1·40 1·75
1061 – 6d. black, mve & yell 1·40 1·75
1062 – 6d. black, mve & yell 1·40 1·75
MS1063 90 × 75 mm. 18d. mult 4·50 5·00

DESIGNS: No. 1061, **MS**1063, Lady Elizabeth Bowes-Lyon as a young girl; 1062, Lady Elizabeth Bowes-Lyon with wild flowers.

1990. World Cup Football Championship, Italy (2nd issue). Multicoloured.
1064 1d. Type **195** 35 30
1065 1d.25 Cannegia, Argentina 40 35
1066 3d. Marchena, Costa Rica 90 1·00
1067 5d. Shaiba, United Arab Emirates 1·25 1·75
MS1068 Two sheets, each 75 × 92 mm. (a) 18d. Hagi, Rumania. (b) 18d. Van Basten, Netherlands Set of 2 sheets 13·00 13·00

195a Men's Discus

1990. Olympic Games, Barcelona (1992) (1st issue). Multicoloured.
1069 20b. Type **195a** 45 15
1070 50b. Men's 100 m 55 20
1071 75b. Women's 400 m 65 30
1072 1d. Men's 200 m 70 40
1073 1d.25 Women's rhythmic gymnastics 75 50
1074 3d. Football 1·25 1·50
1075 10d. Men's marathon 2·50 3·50
1076 12d. "Tornado" class yachting 2·50 3·50
MS1077 Two sheets, each 101 × 71 mm. (a) 15d. Parade of national flags (horiz). (b) 15d. Opening ceremony (horiz) Set of 2 sheets 12·00 13·00

See also Nos. 1289/97 and 1351/63.

195b "The Annunciation with St. Emidius" (detail) (Crivelli)

1990. Christmas. Paintings by Renaissance Masters. Multicoloured.
1078 20b. Type **195b** 45 10
1079 50b. "The Annunciation" (detail) (Campin) 65 10
1080 75b. "The Solly Madonna" (detail) (Raphael) 80 25
1081 1d.25 "The Tempi Madonna" (Raphael) 1·00 30
1082 2d. "Madonna of the Linen Window" (detail) (Raphael) 1·25 50
1083 7d. "The Annunciation, with St. Emidius" (different detail) (Crivelli) 2·75 3·50
1084 10d. "The Orleans Madonna" (Raphael) 3·00 3·50
1085 15d. "Madonna and Child" (detail) (Crivelli) 3·50 5·00
MS1086 72 × 101 mm. 15d. "Niccolini-Cowper Madonna" (Raphael) 6·00 7·00

195c "The Lion Hunt" (detail)

1990. 350th Death Anniv of Rubens. Multicoloured.
1087 20b. Type **195c** 20 15
1088 75b. "The Lion Hunt" (detail) 35 25
1089 1d. "The Tiger Hunt" (detail) 40 30
1090 1d.25 "The Tiger Hunt" (different detail) 40 35
1091 3d. "The Tiger Hunt" (different detail) 90 1·00
1092 5d. "The Boar Hunt" (detail) 1·40 1·75
1093 10d. "The Lion Hunt" (different detail) 2·00 2·50
1094 15d. "The Tiger Hunt" (different detail) 2·75 3·75
MS1095 Four sheets. (a) 100 × 71 mm. 15d. "The Boar Hunt". (b) 100 × 71 mm. 15d. "The Lion Hunt". (c) 100 × 71 mm. 15d. "The Crocodile and Hippopotamus Hunt". (d) 71 × 100 mm. 15d. "St. George slays the Dragon" (vert) Set of 4 sheets 12·00 13·00

196 Summit Logo

1991. World Summit for Children, New York.
1096 **196** 1d. multicoloured 80 55

196a Sir Kay and Wart searching for Lost Arrow

1991. International Literacy Year (1990). Designs showing scenes from Disney cartoon film "The Sword in the Stone". Multicoloured.

1097 3d. Type **196a** 1·75 1·50
1098 3d. Merlin the Magician 1·75 1·50
1099 3d. Merlin teaching Wart 1·75 1·50
1100 3d. Wart writing on blackboard 1·75 1·50
1101 3d. Wart transformed into bird and Madame Mim 1·75 1·50
1102 3d. Merlin and Madame Mim 1·75 1·50
1103 3d. Madame Mim transformed into dragon 1·75 1·50
1104 3d. Wart pulling sword from stone 1·75 1·50
1105 3d. King Arthur on throne 1·75 1·50
MS1106 Two sheets, each 131 × 106 mm. (a) 20d. Sword in stone. (b) 20d. Merlin Set of 2 sheets 16·00 15·00

197 "Bebearia senegalensis"

1991. Wildlife. Multicoloured.

1107 1d. Type **197** 60 65
1108 1d. "Graphium ridleyanus" (butterfly) 60 65
1109 1d. "Precis antilope" (butterfly) 60 65
1110 1d. "Charaxes ameliae" (butterfly) 60 65
1111 1d. Addax 60 65
1112 1d. Sassaby 60 65
1113 1d. Civet 60 65
1114 1d. Green monkey 60 65
1115 1d. Spur-winged goose 60 65
1116 1d. Red-billed hornbill 60 65
1117 1d. Osprey 60 65
1118 1d. Glossy ibis 60 65
1119 1d. Egyptian plover 60 65
1120 1d. Golden-tailed woodpecker 60 65
1121 1d. Green wood hoopoe 60 65
1122 1d. Gaboon viper 60 65
1123 1d.50 Red-billed fire finch 60 65
1124 1d.50 Leaf-love 60 65
1125 1d.50 Piapiac 60 65
1126 1d.50 African emerald cuckoo 60 65
1127 1d.50 Red colobus monkey 60 65
1128 1d.50 African elephant 60 65
1129 1d.50 Duiker 60 65
1130 1d.50 Giant eland 60 65
1131 1d.50 Oribi 60 65
1132 1d.50 Western African dwarf crocodile 60 65
1133 1d.50 Crowned crane 60 65
1134 1d.50 Jackal 60 65
1135 1d.50 Yellow-throated longclaw 60 65
1136 1d.50 Abyssinian ground hornbill 60 65
1137 1d.50 "Papilio hesperus" 60 65
1138 1d.50 "Papilio antimachus" 60 65
1139 5d. Martial eagle 1·00 1·10
1140 5d. Red-cheeked cordon-bleu 1·00 1·10
1141 5d. Red bishop 1·00 1·10
1142 5d. Eastern white pelican 1·00 1·10
1143 5d. Patas monkey 1·00 1·10
1144 5d. Vervet monkey 1·00 1·10
1145 5d. Roan antelope 1·00 1·10
1146 5d. Western hartebeest 1·00 1·10
1147 5d. Waterbuck 1·00 1·10
1148 5d. Warthog 1·00 1·10
1149 5d. Spotted hyena 1·00 1·10
1150 5d. Olive baboon 1·00 1·10
1151 5d. "Palla decius" 1·00 1·10
1152 5d. "Acraea pharsalus" 1·00 1·10
1153 5d. "Neptidopsis ophione" 1·00 1·10
1154 5d. "Acraea caecilia" 1·00 1·10
MS1155 Three sheets, each 101 × 69 mm. (a) 18d. African spoonbill (vert). (b) 18d. White-billed buffalo weaver ("Buffalo Weaver") (vert). (c) 18d. Lion (vert) Set of 3 sheets 16·00 15·00

Nos. 1107/22, 1123/38 and 1139/54 respectively were issued together, se-tenant, forming composite designs.

198 "Papilio dardanus"

1991. Butterflies. Multicoloured.

1156 20b. Type **198** 60 30
1157 50b. "Bematistes poggei" 80 40
1158 1d. "Vanessa cardui" 90 55
1159 1d.50 "Amphicallia tigris" 1·00 85
1160 3d. "Hypolimnas dexithea" 1·75 1·25
1161 8d. "Acraea egina" 2·25 3·00
1162 10d. "Salamis temora" 2·25 3·00
1163 15d. "Precis octavia" 2·75 4·00
MS1164 Four sheets, each 100 × 70 mm. (a) 18d. "Danaus chrysippus". (b) 18d. "Charaxes jasius" (male). (c) 18d. "Papilio demodocus". (d) 18d. "Papilio nireus" Set of 4 sheets 16·00 15·00

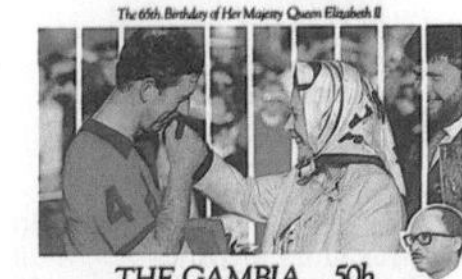

198a The Queen and Prince Charles at Windsor Polo Match

1991. 65th Birthday of Queen Elizabeth II. Mult.

1165 50b. Type **198a** 65 20
1166 1d. The Queen and Princess Anne at the Derby, 1988 80 35
1167 1d.25 The Queen at the Royal London Hospital, 1970 90 50
1168 12d. The Queen and Prince Philip at Balmoral, 1976 3·50 4·00
MS1169 68 × 90 mm. 18d. Separate photographs of The Queen and Prince Philip 4·25 5·00

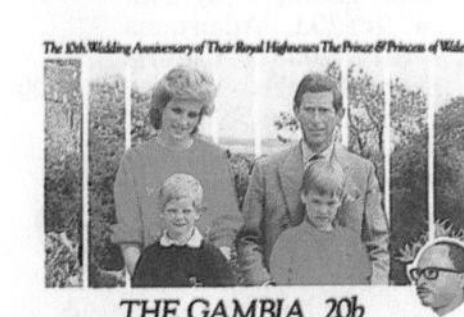

198b Prince and Princess with Sons in June, 1989

1991. 10th Wedding Anniv of Prince and Princess of Wales. Multicoloured.

1170 20b. Type **198b** 70 25
1171 75b. Separate photographs of Prince, Princess and sons 1·25 50
1172 1d.50 Prince Henry on first day of school, 1987, and Prince William at polo match 1·50 85
1173 15d. Separate photographs of Prince and Princess of Wales 5·50 6·00
MS1174 68 × 90 mm. 18d. The family in Italy, 1985 6·00 6·50

198c Donald Duck and Mickey Mouse playing "Go"

1991. "Phila Nippon '91" International Stamp Exhibition, Tokyo. Designs showing Walt Disney cartoon characters playing Japanese sports and games. Multicoloured.

1175 50b. Type **198c** 80 30
1176 75b. Morty, Ferdie and Pete as Sumo wrestlers 90 40
1177 1d. Minnie Mouse, Clarabelle Cow and Daisy Duck playing battledore and shuttlecock 1·00 45
1178 1d.25 Goofy and Mickey at Okinawa bullfight (vert) 1·10 55
1179 5d. Mickey flying hawk (vert) 2·75 2·50
1180 7d. Mickey, Minnie and Donald playing "jan-ken-pon" (vert) 2·75 3·25
1181 10d. Goofy as archer 3·00 3·25
1182 15d. Morty and Ferdie flying kites (vert) 4·00 4·50
MS1183 Four sheets, each 127 × 102 mm. (a) 20d. Mickey climbing Mt. Fuji. (b) 20d. Mickey fishing. (c) 20d. Scrooge McDuck and Mickey playing football. (d) 20d. Goofy playing baseball Set of 4 sheets 14·00 15·00

198d "How the Whale got his Throat"

1991. International Literacy Year (1990). Designs showing Walt Disney cartoon characters in Kipling's "Just So" stories. Multicoloured.

1184 50b. Type **198d** 85 30
1185 75b. "How the Camel got his Hump" 95 40
1186 1d. "How the Leopard got his Spots" 1·10 45
1187 1d.25 "The Elephant's Child" 1·40 55
1188 1d.50 "The Singsong of Old Man Kangaroo" 1·50 1·00
1189 7d. "The Crab that played with the Sea" 3·00 3·25
1190 10d. "The Cat that walked by Himself" 3·25 3·25
1191 15d. "The Butterfly that Stamped" 4·00 4·50
MS1192 Four sheets, each 127 × 102 mm. (a) 20d. Mickey Mouse reading story to Morte and Ferdie (horiz). (b) 20d. "How the Rhinoceros got his Skin" (horiz). (c) 20d. "How the Alphabet was made". (d) 20d. "How the first Letter was written" Set of 4 sheets 14·00 15·00

199 Canadian Pacific Steel Cupola Caboose

1991. Railway Brake-vans. Multicoloured.

1193 1d. Type **199** 65 65
1194 1d. Cumberland and Pennsylvania four-wheeled caboose, U.S.A. 65 65
1195 1d. Ferrocarril Interoceanico caboose, Mexico 65 65
1196 1d. Northern Pacific Railroad steel cupola caboose, U.S.A. 65 65
1197 1d. Morristown and Erie Railroad four-wheeled caboose, U.S.A. 65 65
1198 1d. Burlington Northern Railroad streamlined cupola caboose, U.S.A. 65 65
1199 1d. McCloud River Railroad caboose-coach, U.S.A. 65 65
1200 1d. Santa Fe Railroad wide-vision caboose, U.S.A. 65 65
1201 1d. Frisco Railroad wide-vision caboose, U.S.A. 65 65
1202 1d.50 Colorado and Southern Railroad four-wheeled caboose, U.S.A. 65 65
1203 1d.50 Santa Fe Railroad transfer caboose, U.S.A. 65 65
1204 1d.50 Canadian National wooden cupola caboose 65 65
1205 1d.50 Union Pacific steel transfer caboose, U.S.A. 65 65
1206 1d.50 Virginia and Truckee Railroad caboose-coach, U.S.A. 65 65
1207 1d.50 British Railways standard brake van 65 65
1208 1d.50 International Railways of Central America caboose 65 65
1209 1d.50 Northern Pacific Railroad steel cupola caboose, U.S.A. 65 65
1210 1d.50 Burlington Northern Railroad wooden caboose, U.S.A. 65 65
1211 2d. Oahu Railway caboose, Hawaii 65 65
1212 2d. British Railways standard brake van 65 65
1213 2d. Union Pacific steel wide-view caboose, U.S.A. 65 65
1214 2d. Belt Railway of Chicago four-wheeled caboose, U.S.A. 65 65
1215 2d. McCloud River Railroad four-wheeled caboose, U.S.A. 65 65
1216 2d. Angelina County Lumber Co caboose, U.S.A. 65 65
1217 2d. Coahuila Zacateca caboose, Mexico 65 65
1218 2d. United Railways of Yucatan caboose, Mexico 65 65
1219 2d. Rio Grande Railroad steel cupola caboose, U.S.A. 65 65
MS1220 Three sheets, each 79 × 56 mm. (a) 20d. Wooden caboose on steam goods train. (b) 20d. Pennsylvania Railroad steel caboose on electric goods train (vert). (c) 20d. Wooden caboose on passenger train and railwayman with flag (vert) Set of 3 sheets 13·00 14·00

200 Tiger Shark

1991. Fishes. Multicoloured.

1221 20b. Type **200** 25 15
1222 25b. Common jewelfish 25 15
1223 50b. Five-spotted cichlid 35 25
1224 75b. Small-toothed sawfish 35 25
1225 1d. Spotted tilapia 40 30
1226 1d.25 Dwarf jewelfish 40 35
1227 1d.50 Five-spotted jewelfish 45 40
1228 3d. Lion-headed cichlid 65 65
1229 10d. Egyptian mouthbrooder 2·00 2·50
1230 15d. Burton's mouthbrooder 2·75 3·50
MS1231 Two sheets, each 118 × 83 mm. (a) 18d. Great barracuda. (b) 18d. Yellow-tailed snapper Set of 2 sheets 12·00 13·00

200a Children waving

1991. Hummel Figurines. Multicoloured.

1232 20b. Type **200a** 10 10
1233 75b. Children under umbrella 15 15
1234 1d. Girl kissing friend 20 20
1235 1d.50 Children at window 30 30
1236 2d.50 Two girls in aprons 45 45
1237 5d. Two boys in bow ties 85 85
1238 10d. Two girls sitting on fence with birds 1·75 2·00
1239 15d. Boy and girl in Swiss costume 2·50 3·00
MS1240 Two sheets, each 98 × 128 mm. (a) 4d. × 4 As Nos. 1233/5 and 1239. (b) 5d. × 4 As Nos. 1232 and 1236/8 Set of 2 sheets 7·00 8·00

200b "The Old Cemetery Tower at Nuenen in the Snow"

1991. Death Centenary of Vincent van Gogh (artist). Multicoloured.

1241 20b. Type **200b** 40 25
1242 25b. "Head of Peasant Woman with White Cap" (vert) 40 25
1243 50b. "The Green Parrot" (vert) 50 25
1244 75b. "Vase with Carnations" (vert) 55 30
1245 1d. "Vase with Red Gladioli" (vert) 65 30
1246 1d.25 "Beach at Scheveningen in Calm Weather" 75 35
1247 1d.50 "Boy cutting Grass with Sickle" 85 40
1248 2d. "Coleus Plant in a Flowerpot" (detail) (vert) 90 40
1249 3d. "Self-portrait 1887" (vert) 1·10 60
1250 4d. "Self-portrait" (different) (vert) 1·40 90
1251 5d. "Self-portrait" (different) (vert) 1·60 1·25
1252 6d. "Self-portrait 1887" (different) (vert) 1·90 1·90
1253 8d. "Still Life with Bottle, Two Glasses, Cheese and Bread" (detail) (vert) 2·50 2·50
1254 10d. "Still Life with Cabbage, Clogs and Potatoes" 2·75 2·75
1255 12d. "Montmartre: The Street Lamps" (vert) 3·00 3·50
1256 15d. "Head of Peasant Woman with Brownish Cap" (vert) 3·25 4·00
MS1257 Four sheets, each 127 × 102 mm. (a) 20d. "The Potato Eaters" (horiz). (b) 20d. "Montmartre: Quarry and Mills" (horiz). (c) 20d. "Autumn Landscape" (horiz). (d) 20d. "Arles: View from the Wheat Fields" (detail) (horiz). Imperf Set of 4 sheets 19·00 20·00

200c "The Madonna of Humility"

1991. Christmas. Religious Paintings by Fra Angelico. Multicoloured.

No.	Description		
1258	20b. Type **200c**	15	10
1259	50b. "Madonna and Child with Angels"	25	20
1260	75b. "Virgin and Child with Angels"	30	25
1261	1d. "The Annunciation"	35	30
1262	1d.25 "Presentation in the Temple"	40	35
1263	5d. "The Annunciation" (different)	1·50	1·50
1264	10d. "Madonna della Stella"	2·25	3·00
1265	15d. "Naming of St. John the Baptist"	2·75	4·00
MS1266	Two sheets, each 102 × 128 mm. (a) 20d. "Coronation of the Virgin". (b) 20d. "Annunciation and Adoration of the Magi" Set of 2 sheets	7·50	8·50

201 Son House

1992. Famous Blues Singers. Multicoloured.

No.	Description		
1267	20b. Type **201**	15	15
1268	25b. W. C. Handy	15	15
1269	50b. Muddy Waters	30	30
1270	75b. Lightnin Hopkins	40	40
1271	1d. Ma Rainey	45	45
1272	1d.25 Mance Lipscomb	50	50
1273	1d.50 Mahalia Jackson	60	60
1274	2d. Ella Fizgerald	70	70
1275	3d. Howlin Wolf	85	85
1276	5d. Bessie Smith	1·25	1·25
1277	7d. Leadbelly	1·50	1·75
1278	10d. Joe Willie Wilkins	2·00	2·25
MS1279	Three sheets, each 110 × 78 mm. (a) 20d. String drum. (b) 20d. Elvis Presley. (c) 20d. Billie Holiday Set of 3 sheets	13·00	14·00

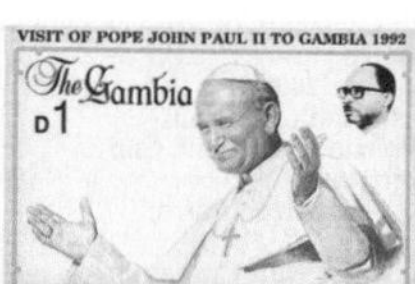

202 Pope John Paul II

1992. Papal Visit. Multicoloured.

No.	Description		
1280	1d. Type **202**	40	40
1281	1d.25 Pope John Paul II and Pres. Sir Dawda Jawara	50	50
1282	20d. Gambian and Papal flags	4·75	6·00
MS1283	104 × 70 mm. 25d. Pope giving blessing	6·00	8·00

202a Pottery Market

1992. 40th Anniv of Queen Elizabeth II's Accession. Multicoloured.

No.	Description		
1284	20b. Type **202a**	25	10
1285	50b. Ruins of early fort	35	20
1286	1d. Fishing boat	50	30
1287	15d. Canoes on beach	4·50	5·50
MS1288	Two sheets, each 75 × 97 mm. (a) 20d. "Lady Chilel Jawara" (river vessel). (b) 20d. River ferry being loaded Set of 2 sheets	9·50	10·00

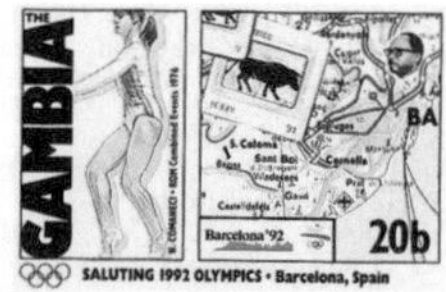

203 Nadia Comaneci (Rumania) (combined gymnastic events) and Map of Barcelona

1992. Olympic Games, Barcelona (2nd issue). Past Medal Winners. Multicoloured.

No.	Description		
1289	20b. Type **203**	35	20
1290	50b. D. Moorcroft (G.B.) (5000 m) and map	45	20
1291	75b. M. Nemeth (Hungary) (javelin) and decorative tiles	45	25
1292	1d. J. Pedraza (Mexico) (20 km walk) and decorative plate	45	30
1293	1d.25 "Soling" class yachting (Brazil), state arms and flag	90	40
1294	1d.50 Women's hockey (G.D.R.) and Barcelona building	1·00	60
1295	12d. M. Jordan (U.S.A.) (basketball) and map	4·00	4·00
1296	15d. V. Borzov (U.S.S.R.) (100 m) and galleon	4·00	4·25
MS1297	Two sheets. (a) 82 × 112 mm. 20d. Silhouette of flamenco dancer on map (vert). (b) 112 × 82 mm. 20d. Silhouette of bull on map Set of 2 sheets	8·50	9·00

204 Mickey Mouse as Christopher Columbus

1992. International Stamp Exhibitions. Walt Disney cartoon characters. Multicoloured. (a) "Granada '92", Spain. Voyage of Columbus.

No.	Description		
1298	20b. Type **204**	50	15
1299	75b. Mickey's plans derided	65	25
1300	1d.50 Mickey lands in America	85	60
1301	15d. Mickey presents treasure to Minnie	3·75	4·75
MS1302	127 × 102 mm. 18d. Mickey embarks for America	5·00	5·50

(b) World Columbian Stamp "Expo '92". Chicago Landmarks.

No.	Description		
1303	50b. Navy Pier	60	10
1304	1d. Wrigley Building	75	25
1305	1d.25 University of Chicago	85	30
1306	12d. Alder Planetarium	4·00	4·75
MS1307	127 × 102 mm. 18d. Goofy hanging over Chicago (horiz)	5·00	5·50

204a "Christ presented to the People" (Rembrandt)

1992. Easter. Religious Paintings. Multicoloured.

No.	Description		
1308	20b. Type **204a**	10	10
1309	50b. "Christ carrying the Cross" (Grunewald)	20	20
1310	75b. "The Crucifixion" (Grunewald)	25	25
1311	1d. "The Crucifixion" (Rubens)	30	30
1312	1d.25 "The Road to Calvary" (detail) (Tintoretto)	35	35
1313	1d.50 "The Road to Calvary" (Tintoretto) (different)	40	40
1314	15d. "The Crucifixion" (Masaccio)	2·75	3·75
1315	20d. "The Descent from the Cross" (Rembrandt)	3·50	4·50
MS1316	Two sheets, each 72 × 101 mm. (a) 25d. "The Crowning with Thorns" (detail) (Van Dyck). (b) 25d. "The Crowning with Thorns" (detail) (Titian) Set of 2 sheets	8·50	9·50

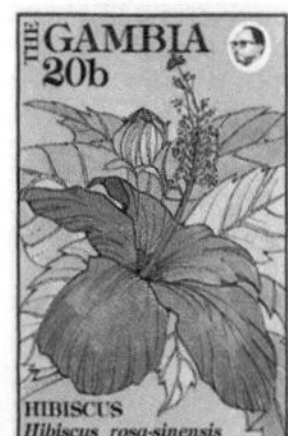

205 "Hibiscus rosa-sinensis"

1992. Flowers. Multicoloured.

No.	Description		
1317	20b. Type **205**	10	10
1318	50b. "Monodora myristica"	20	20
1319	75b. "Bombax costatum"	25	25
1320	1d. "Oncoba spinosa"	30	30
1321	1d.25 "Combretum grandiflorum"	35	35
1322	1d.50 "Rothmannia longiflora"	40	40
1323	2d. "Clerodendrum splendens"	55	55
1324	5d. "Mussaenda erythrophylla"	1·10	1·25
1325	10d. "Nauclea latifolia"	1·75	2·00
1326	12d. "Clerodendrum capitatum"	1·90	2·50
1327	15d. "Costus spectabilis"	2·50	3·25
1328	18d. "Strophanthus preussii"	2·75	3·50
MS1329	Four sheeets, each 102 × 71 mm. (a) 20d. "Bougainvillea glabra". (b) 20d. "Nymphaea". (c) 20d. "Adansonia digitata". (d) 20d. "Clitoria ternatea" Set of 4 sheets	12·00	13·00

206 "Joven Antonia" (River Gambia)

1992. River Boats of the World. Multicoloured.

No.	Description		
1330	20b. Type **206**	15	10
1331	50b. "Dresden" (River Elbe)	25	20
1332	75b. "Medway Queen" (River Medway)	30	25
1333	1d. "Lady Wright" (River Gambia)	35	30
1334	1d.25 "Devin" (River Vltava)	40	35
1335	1d.50 "Lady Chilel Jawara" (River Gambia)	45	50
1336	5d. "Robert Fulton" (River Hudson)	1·25	1·25
1337	10d. "Coonawarra" (River Murray)	2·00	2·25
1338	12d. "Nakusp" (River Columbia)	2·25	3·00
1339	15d. "Lucy Ashton" (Firth of Clyde)	2·75	3·50
MS1340	Two sheets, each 107 × 69 mm. (a) 20d. "City of Cairo" (Mississippi). (b) 20d. "Rüdesheim" (Rhine) Set of 2 sheets	9·00	10·00

206a U.S.S. "Pennsylvania" (battleship)

1992. 50th Anniv of Japanese Attack on Pearl Harbor. Multicoloured.

No.	Description		
1341	2d. Type **206a**	1·50	1·10
1342	2d. Japanese Mitsubishi A6M Zero-Sen aircraft over Pearl Harbor	1·50	1·10
1343	2d. U.S.S. "Ward" (destroyer) sinking midget submarine	1·50	1·10
1344	2d. Ford Naval Station under attack	1·50	1·10
1345	2d. Agency report of Japanese attack	1·50	1·10
1346	2d. Newspaper headline	1·50	1·10
1347	2d. Japanese troops on Guam	1·50	1·10
1348	2d. U.S. forces regaining Wake Island	1·50	1·10
1349	2d. North American B-25B Mitchell bomber raid on Japan	1·50	1·10
1350	2d. American Douglas Dauntless dive bomber attacking Japanese carrier, Midway	1·50	1·10

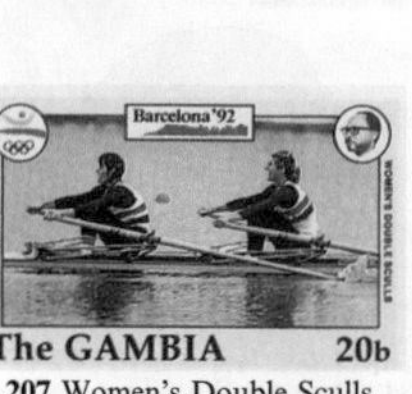

207 Women's Double Sculls

1992. Winter Olympic Games, Albertville, and Olympic Games, Barcelona (3rd issue). Multicoloured.

No.	Description		
1351	20b. Type **207**	25	15
1352	50b. Men's kayak (vert)	35	20
1353	75b. Women's rapid precision pistol shooting	50	30
1354	1d. Judo (vert)	55	30
1355	1d.25 Men's javelin (vert)	65	35
1356	1d.50 Men's vaulting horse (vert)	80	40
1357	2d. Men's downhill skiing (vert)	1·00	55
1358	3d. Windsurfing (vert)	1·10	90
1359	5d. Men's high jump	1·50	1·50
1360	10d. Four-man bobsled (vert)	2·50	2·75
1361	12d. 90 m ski-jump (vert)	2·75	3·00
1362	15d. Men's slalom skiing	3·00	4·00
MS1363	Four sheets, each 100 × 70 mm. (a) 18d. Table tennis (vert). (b) 18d. Men's 500 metre speed skating. (c) 18d. Women's 200 metre backstroke. (d) 18d. Pairs figure skating (vert) Set of 4 sheets	13·00	14·00

207a Immigration Centre, Ellis Island

1992. Postage Stamp Mega Event, New York. Sheet 100 × 70 mm.

No.	Description		
MS1363	18d. multicoloured	3·75	4·25

207b Dryosaurus

1992. "Genova '92" International Thematic Stamp Exhibition. Dinosaurs. Multicoloured.

No.	Description		
1364	20b. Type **207b**	30	10
1365	25b. Saurolophus	30	10
1366	50b. Allosaurus	35	20
1367	75b. Fabrosaurus	40	25
1368	1d. Deinonychus	40	30
1369	1d.25 Cetiosaurus	50	35
1370	1d.50 Camptosaurus	50	35
1371	2d. Ornithosuchus	55	45
1372	3d. Spinosaurus	60	60
1373	5d. Ornithomimus	1·00	1·25
1374	10d. Kentrosaurus	1·75	2·25
1375	12d. Schlermochus	1·90	2·50
MS1376	Three sheets, each 104 × 75 mm. (a) 25d. As No. 1366. (b) 25d. As No. 1369. (c) 25d. As No. 1371 Set of 3 sheets	14·00	15·00

207c "The Holy Family" (Raphael)

1992. Christmas. Religious Paintings. Multicoloured.

No.	Description		
1378	50b. Type **207c**	25	20
1379	75b. "The Little Holy Family" (Raphael)	30	25
1380	1d. "The Little Holy Family" (detail) (Raphael)	35	30
1381	1d.25 "Escape to Egypt" (Melchior Broederlam)	40	35
1382	1d.50 "Flight into Egypt" (Adriaen Isenbrant)	40	35
1383	2d. "The Holy Family" (El Greco)	55	55
1384	2d. "Flight into Egypt" (detail) (Cosimo Tura)	55	55
1385	2d. "Flight into Egypt" (detail) (Master of Hoogstraelen)	55	55
1386	4d. "The Holy Family" (Bernard van Orley)	90	1·00
1387	5d. "Holy Family with Infant Jesus Sleeping" (detail) (Charles Le Brun)	1·10	1·25

1388 10d. "Rest on The Flight to Egypt" (Orazio Gentileschi) . . . . . . 1·90 2·50
1389 12d. "Rest on The Flight to Egypt" (detail) (Orazio Gentileschi) . . . . . . 2·25 2·75
MS1390 Three sheets, each 102 × 77 mm. (a) 25d. "The Holy Family" (detail) (Giorgione). (b) 25d. "Flight into Egypt" (detail) (Vittore Carpaccio). (c) 25d. "Rest on The Flight to Egypt" (detail) (Simone Cantarino) Set of 3 sheets 11·00 12·00

207d Goofy in "Orphan's Benefit", 1934

1992. 60th Anniv of Goofy (Disney cartoon character). Multicoloured.
1391 50b. Type **207d** 30 20
1392 75b. Goofy and Donald Duck in "Moose Hunters", 1937 . . . . . 40 30
1393 1d. Goofy in "Mickey's Amateurs", 1937 . . . . 50 40
1394 1d.25 Goofy, Donald and Mickey Mouse in "Lonesome Ghosts", 1937 55 55
1395 5d. Goofy, Donald and Mickey in "Boat Builders", 1938 . . . . . 1·40 1·40
1396 7d. Goofy, Donald and Mickey in "The Whalers", 1938 . . . . 1·75 2·00
1397 10d. Goofy and Wilbur the grasshopper in "Goofy and Wilbur", 1939 . . . 2·00 2·25
1398 15d. Goofy in "Saludos Amigos", 1941 . . . . . 2·50 2·75
MS1399 Two sheets, each 127 × 102 mm. (a) 20d. Goofy in "The Band Concert", 1935 (vert). (b) 20d. Goofy today (vert) Set of 2 sheets . . . . 10·00 11·00

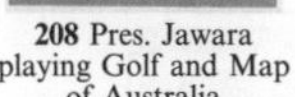

208 Pres. Jawara playing Golf and Map of Australia

209 Launch of European "Ariane 4"

1992. Open Golf Championships. Multicoloured.
1400 20b. Type **208** 55 20
1401 1d. Pres. Jawara and Gambia Open trophy . . 85 45
1402 1d.50 Pres. Jawara (winner of Gambia Open, 1985) 1·00 55
1403 2d. Pres. Jawara and map of Japan . . . . 1·50 70
1404 3d. Pres. Jawara and map of U.S.A. . . . . 1·75 1·00
1405 5d. Gambia Open trophy . . 2·00 1·75
1406 10d. Pres. Jawara and map of Scotland . . . . 3·25 3·75
1407 12d. Pres. Jawara and map of Italy . . . . 3·25 3·75
MS1408 Two sheets. (a) 106 × 71 mm. 10d. Pres. Jawara playing shot. (b) 67 × 99 mm. 18d. Flag of Gambia (horiz) Set of 2 sheets . . . . 11·00 12·00

1993. Anniversaries and Events. Multicoloured.
1409 2d. Type **209** 70 70
1410 2d. Konrad Adenauer and Berlin Airlift (horiz) . . . 70 70
1411 2d. Airship "Hindenburg", 1928 (horiz) 70 70
1412 5d. "Santa Maria" (horiz) 1·75 1·25
1413 6d. Jentink's duiker (horiz) 1·40 1·40
1414 7d. World map and emblem (horiz) . . . . 2·25 1·60
1415 9d. Wolfgang Amadeus Mozart . . . . 3·00 2·50
1416 10d. Lions Club emblem . . 1·75 2·50
1417 10d. "Enterprise" (yacht), 1930 . . . . 1·75 2·50
1418 10d. Imperial amazon (Imperial "Sisserou Parrot") . . . . 3·00 2·50
1419 12d. American space shuttle 3·00 3·25
1420 12d. Fleet of Columbus (horiz) . . . . 3·00 3·25
1421 15d. Adenauer and returning prisoners of war (horiz) . . . . 3·00 3·25
1422 18d. Airship LZ-1, 1900 (horiz) . . . . 3·50 3·75
MS1423 Six sheets. (a) 104 × 76 mm. 18d. Nose of projected European space station "Hermes". (b) 113 × 87 mm. 18d. Konrad Adenauer. (c) 85 × 65 mm. 18d. Count von Zeppelin. (d) 103 × 75 mm. 18d. Green-winged Macaw and bow of ship. (e) 85 × 65 mm. 18d. Globe. (f) 99 × 69 mm. 18d. Dancers from "The Marriage of Figaro". Set of 6 sheets . . . . 20·00 22·00

ANNIVERSARIES AND EVENTS: Nos. 1409, 1419, **MS**1423a, International Space Year; 1410, 1421, **MS**1423b, 25th death anniv of Konrad Adenauer (German statesman); 1411, 1422, **MS**1423c, 75th death anniv of Count Ferdinand von Zeppelin; 1412, 1420, **MS**1423d, 500th anniv of discovery of America by Columbus; 1413, 1418, **MS**1423e, Earth Summit '92, Rio; 1414, International Nutrition Conference, Rome; 1415, **MS**1423f, Death bicentenary of Mozart; 1416, 75th anniv of International Association of Lions Clubs; 1417, Americas Cup Yachting Championship.

209a Elvis Presley

1993. 15th Death Anniv (1992) of Elvis Presley (singer). Multicoloured.
1424 3d. Type **209a** 70 70
1425 3d. Elvis with guitar 70 70
1426 3d. Elvis with microphone 70 70

209b "St. John the Baptist" (Da Vinci)

1993. Bicentenary of the Louvre, Paris. Paintings. Multicoloured.
1427 3d. Type **209b** 65 70
1428 3d. "Virgin of the Rocks" (Da Vinci) 65 70
1429 3d. "Bacchus" (Da Vinci) 65 70
1430 3d. "Lady of the Court, Milan" (Da Vinci) 65 70
1431 3d. "Virgin of the Rocks" (detail) (Da Vinci) 65 70
1432 3d. "Mona Lisa" (Da Vinci) 65 70
1433 3d. "Mona Lisa" (detail) (Da Vinci) 65 70
1434 3d. Sketches for "Two Horsemen" (Da Vinci) . . 65 70
1435 3d. "The Oath of Horatii" (left detail) (David) . . . 65 70
1436 3d. "The Oath of Horatii" (right detail) (David) . . . 65 70
1437 3d. "The Love of Paris and Helen" (detail) (David) . . 65 70
1438 3d. "The Sabine Women" (detail) (David) 65 70
1439 3d. "Leonidas at Thermopylae" (detail) (David) 65 70
1440 3d. "The Coronation of Napoleon" (left detail) (David) 65 70
1441 3d. "The Coronation of Napoleon" (centre detail) (David) 65 70
1442 3d. "The Coronation of Napoleon" (right detail) (David) 65 70
1443 3d. "Peasant Family at Home" (detail) (L. le Nain) 65 70
1444 3d. "Smoking Room" (left detail) (L. le Nain) . . . 65 70
1445 3d. "Smoking Room (right detail) (L. le Nain) . . . 65 70
1446 3d. "The Cart" (detail) (L. le Nain) 65 70
1447 3d. "Peasants' Repast" (detail) (L. le Nain) . . . 65 70
1448 3d. "Portrait in an Interior" (detail) (L. le Nain) 65 70
1449 3d. "Portrait in an Interior" (different detail) (L. le Nain) 65 70
1450 3d. "The Forge" (L. le Nain) 65 70
MS1451 Two sheets, each 70 × 100 mm. (a) 20d. "Allegory of Victory" (M. le Nain) (52 × 86 mm). (b) 20d. "Madame Vigee-Le Brun and Daughter" (Le Brun) (52 × 86 mm) Set of 2 sheets 10·00 11·00
Nos. 1432/3 are incorrectly inscr "Monna Lisa".

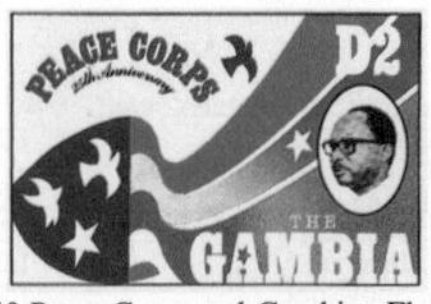

210 Peace Corps and Gambian Flags

1993. 25th Anniv of U.S. Peace Corps.
1452 **210** 2d. multicoloured . . . 1·00 1·00

211 Jackie Robinson and Ruby Dee ("The Jackie Robinson Story")

1993. Baseball Films. Multicoloured.
1453 3d. Type **211** 75 80
1454 3d. Robert De Niro ("Bang the Drum Slowly") . . . 75 80
1455 3d. James Earl Jones and Billy Dee Williams ("The Bingo Long Travelling All-Stars and Motor Kings") 75 80
1456 3d. Kevin Costner and Susan Sarandon ("Bull Durham") 75 80
1457 3d. Cast photograph ("Eight Men Out") 75 80
1458 3d. Ray Liotta ("Field of Dreams") 75 80
1459 3d. Charlie Sheen ("Major League") 75 80
1460 3d. Tom Selleck ("Mr. Baseball") 75 80
1461 3d. Wallace Beery, 1927, and Elliott Gould, 1986 ("Casey at the Bat") . . . 75 80
1462 3d. Anna Nilsson and Babe Ruth ("Babe comes Home") 75 80
1463 3d. Joe Brown ("Elmer the Great") 75 80
1464 3d. Bud Abbott and Lou Costello ("The Naughty Nineties") 75 80
1465 3d. Frank Sinatra, Gene Kelly and Esther Williams ("Take Me Out to the Ball Game") 75 80
1466 3d. Tab Hunter and Gwen Verdon ("Damn Yankees") 75 80
1467 3d. Dan Dailey ("The Pride of St. Louis") 75 80
1468 3d. John Candy and Richard Pryor ("Brewster's Millions") . . 75 80
MS1469 Four sheets, each 132 × 107 mm. (a) 20d. John Goodman ("The Babe"). (b) 20d. Ronald Reagan ("The Winning Team"). (c) 20d. Tom Hanks and Madonna ("A League of Their Own") (vert). (d) 20d. Robert Redford ("The Natural") (vert) Set of 4 sheets . . . . 15·00 17·00

212 Giraffe

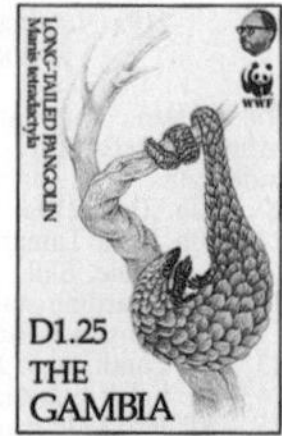

213 Long-tailed Pangolin hanging by Tail

1993. Animals of West Africa. Multicoloured.
1470 2d. Type **212** 55 60
1471 2d. Baboon 55 60
1472 2d. Caracal 55 60
1473 2d. Large-spotted genet . . 55 60
1474 2d. Bushbuck 55 60
1475 2d. Red-fronted gazelle . . 55 60
1476 2d. Red-flanked duiker . . . 55 60
1477 2d. Cape buffalo 55 60
1478 2d. African civet 55 60
1479 2d. Side-striped jackal . . 55 60
1480 2d. Ratel 55 60
1481 2d. Striped polecat 55 60
1482 5d. Vervet 85 90
1483 5d. Blackish-green guenon 85 90
1484 5d. Long-tailed pangolin . . 85 90
1485 5d. Leopard 85 90
1486 5d. Elephant 85 90
1487 5d. Hunting dog 85 90
1488 5d. Spotted hyena 85 90
1489 5d. Lion 85 90
1490 5d. Hippopotamus 85 90
1491 5d. Nile crocodile 85 90
1492 5d. Aardvark 85 90
1493 5d. Warthog 85 90
MS1494 101 × 72 mm. 20d. As No. 1483 . . . . 3·75 4·50
Nos. 1470/81 and 1482/93 were each printed together, se-tenant, with the backgrounds forming composite designs.

1993. Endangered Species. Long-tailed Pangolin. Multicoloured.
1495 1d.25 Type **213** 45 25
1496 1d.50 Sitting on branch . . 55 40
1497 2d. Climbing up branch . . 65 60
1498 5d. Climbing down branch 1·60 2·00

214 Osprey

215 Rose-ringed Parakeet

1993. Birds of Prey. Multicoloured.
1500 1d.25 Type **214** . . . . . 1·40 50
1501 1d.50 Egyptian vulture (horiz) . . . . 1·60 50
1502 2d. Martial eagle . . . . . 1·75 55
1503 3d. Ruppell's griffon ("Ruppell's Griffon Vulture") (horiz) . . . . 2·25 75
1504 5d. Augur buzzard ("Auger Buzzard") . . . . 2·50 1·25
1505 8d. Greater kestrel . . . . 2·75 3·00
1506 10d. Secretary bird . . . . 2·75 3·00
1507 15d. Bateleur ("Bateleur Eagle") (horiz) . . . . . 3·25 4·00
MS1508 Two sheets, each 108 × 80 mm. (a) 20d. Owl sp. ("Tawny Owl") (57 × 42½ mm). (b) 20d. Verreaux's eagle (57 × 42½ mm) Set of 2 sheets 13·00 13·00

1993. African Birds. Multicoloured.
1509 2d. Type **215** . . . . . . 1·25 1·25
1510 2d. Variable sunbird . . . . 1·25 1·25
1511 2d. Red-billed hornbill . . . 1·25 1·25
1512 2d. Red-billed fire finch . . 1·25 1·25
1513 2d. Go-away bird ("Common Go-away Bird") . . . . 1·25 1·25
1514 2d. Burchell's gonolek ("Crimson-breasted shrike") . . . . 1·25 1·25
1515 2d. Grey-headed bush shrike ("Gray-headed Bush shrike") . . . . 1·25 1·25
1516 2d. Western nicator ("Nicator") . . . . 1·25 1·25
1517 2d. Egyptian plover . . . . 1·25 1·25
1518 2d. Congo peafowl ("Congo Peacock") . . . . 1·25 1·25
1519 2d. Painted snipe ("Greater Painted Snipe") . . . . . 1·25 1·25
1520 2d. South African crowned crane ("Crowned Crane") 1·25 1·25

215a Queen Elizabeth II (photograph by Cecil Beaton)

1993. 40th Anniv of Coronation.
1521 **215a** 2d. multicoloured . . . 95 1·00
1522 – 5d. multicoloured . . . 1·60 1·75
1523 – 8d. brown and black . . 1·75 1·90
1524 – 10d. multicoloured . . 1·90 2·00
MS1525 70 × 100 mm. 20d. mult 6·00 6·50
DESIGNS—(38 × 47 mm): 5d. Orb and sceptre; 8d. Sir Winston Churchill; 10d. Queen Elizabeth II at Trooping the Colour (28½ × 42½ mm); 20d. "Elizabeth II, 1972" (detail) (Joe King).

216 Hugo Eckener and "Graf Zeppelin"

1993. Aviation Anniversaries. Multicoloured.
1526 2d. Type **216** 55 50
1527 2d. Guyot's balloon, 1785 (vert) 55 50
1528 5d. Airship "Luftschiffe 3" and crowd . . . . 1·00 1·00
1529 5d. Sopwith Snipe (fighter) 1·00 1·00
1530 8d. Eckener and "Graf Zeppelin" . . . . 1·60 1·75
1531 10d. "Comte d'Artois" (hot air balloon), 1785 (vert) 1·90 2·00
1532 15d. Royal Aircraft Factory S.E.5 (fighter) . . . . . . 2·40 3·00
MS1533 Three sheets. (a) 105 × 84 mm. 20d. Eckener and LZ-127 "Graf Zeppelin" (airship). (b) 84 × 105 mm. 20d. Blanchard's balloon, 1785 (vert). (c) 84 × 105 mm. 20d. Avro 504k (biplane) Set of 3 sheets . . . 16·00 16·00

ANNIVERSARIES: Nos. 1526, 1528, 1530, **MS**1533a, Birth anniv of Hugo Eckener (airship pioneer); 1527, 1531, **MS**1533b, Bicentenary of first airmail flight; 1529, 1532, **MS**1533c, 75th anniv of Royal Air Force.

217 Henry Ford and "Model T", 1910

1993. Centenaries of Henry Ford's First Petrol Engine (Nos. 1534/45) and Karl Benz's First Four-wheeled Car (Nos. 1546/57). Multicoloured.
1534 2d. Type **217** 45 50
1535 2d. Car of 1896 . . . . . . 45 50
1536 2d. Henry Ford with Barney Oldfield and "999", 1902 45 50
1537 2d. Henry Ford, 1893, and car of 1896 . . . . . . 45 50
1538 2d. "Model A", 1903 . . . 45 50
1539 2d. "Model T" with roof lowered, 1908 . . . . . . 45 50
1540 2d. "Model T" with roof raised, 1908 . . . . . . 45 50
1541 2d. "Model K", 1906 . . . 45 50
1542 2d. "Model A", 1931 . . . 45 50
1543 2d. "Model A", 1906 . . . 45 50
1544 2d. "Model N", 1906 . . . 45 50
1545 2d. "Model F", 1905 . . . 45 50
1546 2d. Benz "Velo", 1894 . . . 45 50
1547 2d. Car of 1894 . . . . . . 45 50
1548 2d. Three-wheeled car of 1885 from side 45 50
1549 2d. "Mannheim", 1905 . . . 45 50
1550 2d. Car of 1892 . . . . . . 45 50
1551 2d. Car of 1900 from front 45 50
1552 2d. Racing car of 1911 from side 45 50
1553 2d. "Velo", 1893 . . . . . 45 50
1554 2d. Black car of 1900 from side 45 50
1555 2d. Red car of 1900 from side 45 50
1556 2d. Racing car of 1911 from front 45 50
1557 2d. Three-wheeled car of 1885 from back 45 50
MS1558 Two sheets, each 132 × 115 mm. (a) 20d. Ford car of 1896. (b) 20d. Benz car of 1900 Set of 2 sheets . . . . 8·50 9·00

Nos. 1534/45 and 1546/57 were each printed together, se-tenant, with the backgrounds forming composite designs.

218 Marilyn Monroe

220 "Woman with a Comb" (Picasso)

219 Siamese

1993. Musical Entertainers.
1559/93 3d. × 35 multicoloured . . 38·00 32·00

Nos. 1559/93 were issued as four sheetlets, three of nine different designs (Nos. 1559/85) and one of eight (Nos. 1586/93), depicting Marilyn Monroe (Nos. 1559/67), Elvis Presley (Nos. 1568/76), Madonna (Nos. 1577/85) and Buddy Holly, Otis Redding, Bill Haley, Dinah Washington, musical instruments, Ritchie Valens, Clyde McPhatter, Elvis Presley (Nos. 1586/93).

1993. Oriental Cats. Multicoloured.
1594 2d. Type **219** . . . . . . 1·25 1·00
1595 2d. Colourpoint longhair sitting . . . . 1·25 1·00
1596 2d. Burmese . . . . 1·25 1·00
1597 2d. Birman . . . . 1·25 1·00
1598 2d. Snowshoe . . . . 1·25 1·00
1599 2d. Tonkinese . . . . 1·25 1·00
1600 2d. Foreign shorthair stretching . . . . 1·25 1·00
1601 2d. Balinese . . . . 1·25 1·00
1602 2d. Oriental shorthair . . . 1·25 1·00
1603 2d. Foreign shorthair lying 1·25 1·00
1604 2d. Colourpoint longhair with black face standing 1·25 1·00
1605 2d. Colourpoint longhair with white face standing 1·25 1·00
MS1606 Two sheets, each 121 × 90 mm. (a) 20d. Colourpoint shorthair (vert). (b) 20d. Burmese (vert) Set of 2 sheets . . . . . 9·00 9·50

Nos. 1594/1605 were printed together, se-tenant, with the background forming a composite design.

1993. Royal Dogs. As T **219**. Multicoloured.
1607 2d. Shih tzu (Emperor of China) . . . . 1·25 1·00
1608 2d. Skye terrier (Queen Victoria) . . . . 1·25 1·00
1609 2d. Berner laufhund (King Louis XVI, France) . . . 1·25 1·00
1610 2d. Boxer (King Francis I, France) . . . . 1·25 1·00
1611 2d. Welsh corgi (Queen Elizabeth II) . . . . . . 1·25 1·00
1612 2d. Dumfriesshire (Princess Anne) . . . . 1·25 1·00
1613 2d. Lurcher (King George VI) . . . . 1·25 1·00
1614 2d. Welsh corgi (Princess Anne) . . . . 1·25 1·00
1615 2d. Pekinese (Empress Ts'Eu-Hi, China) . . . . 1·25 1·00
1616 2d. Papillon (King Louis XIII, France) . . . 1·25 1·00
1617 2d. Otterhound (King John) 1·25 1·00
1618 2d. Pug (Napoleon I, France) . . . . 1·25 1·00
MS1619 Two sheets, each 120 × 90 mm. (a) 20d. Cairn terrier (Mary, Queen of Scots). (b) 20d. Long-haired dachshund (Queen Victoria) Set of 2 sheets . . . 9·00 9·50

Nos. 1607/18 were printed together, se-tenant, with the backgrounds forming a composite design.

219a National Monument and Statue, Jakarta

1993. Asian International Stamp Exhibitions. Multicoloured. (a) "Indopex '93", Surabaya, Indonesia.
1620 20b. Type **219a** 20 20
1621 20b. Pura Taman Ayun Temple, Bali 20 20
1622 2d. Guardian statue, Singosari Palace, Java . . 60 60
1623 2d. Candi Jawi, Java . . . 60 60
1624 5d. Telek Luh mask . . . . 1·40 1·40
1625 5d. Jero Gde mask . . . . 1·40 1·40
1626 5d. Barong Macan mask . . 1·40 1·40
1627 5d. Monkey mask . . . . . 1·40 1·40
1628 5d. Mata Gde mask . . . . 1·40 1·40
1629 5d. Jauk Kras mask . . . . 1·40 1·40
1630 5d. "Tree Mask" (Soedibio) 1·40 1·40
1631 5d. "Dry Lizard" (Hendra Gunawan) . . . . 1·40 1·40
1632 5d. "The Corn Eater" (Sudjana Kerton) . . . . 1·40 1·40
1633 5d. "Night Watchman" (Djoko Pekik) . . . . . 1·40 1·40
1634 5d. "Hunger" (Kerton) . . 1·40 1·40
1635 5d. "Arje Player" (Soedjojono) . . . . 1·40 1·40
1636 5d. Central Temple, Lara Djonggrang . . . . . . 1·40 1·40
1637 5d. Irian Jaya Monument, Jakarta . . . . 1·40 1·40
1638 15d. Brahma and Siva Temples, Java . . . . . 2·75 3·25
1639 15d. Date of the Year Temple, Java . . . . . . 2·75 3·25
MS1640 Two sheets, each 135 × 105 mm. (a) 18d. Tomb effigies, Torajaland (horiz). (b) 18d. Relief from Borobudur, Java (horiz) Set of 2 sheets . . . . 7·50 8·00

(b) "Taipei '93", Taiwan.
1641 20b. Fawang Si Pagoda, Henan 20 20
1642 20b. Wanshoubao Pagoda, Shashi 20 20
1643 2d. Red Pavilion, Shibaozhai 60 60
1644 2d. Songyue Si Pagoda, Henan 60 60
1645 5d. Pottery camel (walking) 1·40 1·40
1646 5d. Pottery horse and rider 1·40 1·40
1647 5d. Pottery camel (standing with mouth closed) . . . 1·40 1·40
1648 5d. Yellow-glazed pottery horse . . . . 1·40 1·40
1649 5d. Pottery camel (standing with mouth open) . . . . 1·40 1·40
1650 5d. Pottery saddled horse 1·40 1·40
1651 5d. Qianlong vase . . . . . 1·40 1·40
1652 5d. Small wine cup . . . . 1·40 1·40
1653 5d. Mei-ping vase . . . . . 1·40 1·40
1654 5d. Urn vase . . . . 1·40 1·40
1655 5d. Tureen . . . . 1·40 1·40
1656 5d. Lidded potiche . . . . 1·40 1·40
1657 5d. Tianning Si Pagoda, Beijing . . . . 1·40 1·40
1658 5d. Bond Centre, Hong Kong . . . . 1·40 1·40
1659 15d. Forbidden City pavilion, Beijing . . . . 2·75 3·25
1660 15d. Xuanzhuang Pagoda, Shenxi . . . . 2·75 3·25
MS1661 Two sheets, each 135 × 105 mm. (a) 18d. Seated Buddha, Shanhua Temple, Shanxi. (b) 18d. Statues, Upper Huayan Si Temple, Datong (horiz) Set of 2 sheets . . . . 7·50 8·00

(c) "Bangkok '93", Thailand.
1662 20b. Sanctuary of Prasat Phanom Wan 20 20
1663 20b. Lai Kham Vihan, Chiang Mai 20 20
1664 2d. Upmarket spirit shrine, Bangkok 60 60
1665 2d. Walking Buddha statue, Wat Phra Si Ratana Mahathat 60 60
1666 5d. "Early Fruit Stand" . . 1·40 1·40
1667 5d. "Scene Rendered in Chinese Style" . . . . . 1·40 1·40
1668 5d. "Buddha descends from Tauatimsa" . . . . . . 1·40 1·40
1669 5d. "Sang Thong Tales" (detail) . . . . 1·40 1·40
1670 5d. "The Damned in Hell" 1·40 1·40
1671 5d. "King Sanjaya travels on Elephant" . . . . . . 1·40 1·40
1672 5d. U Thong C Buddha (bronze) . . . . 1·40 1·40
1673 5d. Seated Buddha (bronze) 1·40 1·40
1674 5d. Phra Chai Buddha (ivory and gold) . . . . . 1·40 1·40
1675 5d. Buddha (bronze) . . . . 1·40 1·40
1676 5d. U Thong A Buddha (bronze) . . . . 1·40 1·40
1677 5d. Crowned Buddha (bronze) . . . . 1·40 1·40
1678 5d. Statue of Buddha, Wat Mahathat . . . . 1·40 1·40
1679 5d. The Gopura of Prasat Phanom Rung . . . . . 1·40 1·40
1680 15d. Slender Chedis, Mongkon . . . . 2·75 3·25
1681 15d. The Prang of Prasat Hin Phimai . . . . . . 2·75 3·25
MS1682 Two sheets, each 135 × 105 mm. (a) 18d. Khon (Thai dance drama). (b) 18d. Ceramics (horiz) Set of 2 sheets 7·50 8·00

1993. Anniversaries and Events. Mult.
1683 2d. Type **220** 75 75
1684 2d. "Niedzica Castle" (horiz) 75 75
1685 5d. "The Mirror" (Picasso) 1·40 1·40
1686 5d. Early astronomical instrument . . . . 1·40 1·40
1687 7d. "Woman on a Pillow" (Picasso) . . . . 1·60 2·00
1688 10d. "Pont-Neuf in Paris" (Hanna Rudza-Cybisowa) (horiz) . . . . 2·50 3·00
1689 10d. "Honegger's Liturgical Symphony" (Marian Bogusz) (horiz) . . . . 2·50 3·00
1690 10d. Modern telescope . . . 2·50 3·00
MS1691 Three sheets. (a) 75 × 105 mm. 18d. "The Three Dancers" (detail) (Picasso). P 14. (b) 105 × 75 mm. 18d. "When You enter here, Whisper my Name soundlessly" (detail) (Henryk Waniek) (horiz). P 14. (c) 102 × 74 mm. 18d. Copernicus Set of 3 sheets . . . . 14·00 14·00

ANNIVERSARIES AND EVENTS: Nos. 1683, 1685, 1687, **MS**1691a, 20th death anniv of Picasso (artist); 1684, 1688/9, **MS**1691b, "Polska '93" International Stamp Exhibition, Poznan; 1686, 1690, **MS**1691c, 450th death anniv of Copernicus (astronomer).

The captions on Nos. 1684 and 1689 are transposed in error.

No. **MS**1691b is inscribed "WHISPERT" in error.

221 Mudville Player at the Plate

1993. "Casey at the Bat". Scenes from Walt Disney's cartoon film. Multicoloured.
1692 2d. Type **221** 95 90
1693 2d. Mudville player out . . 95 90
1694 2d. Umpire and player arguing 95 90
1695 2d. Fans applauding 95 90
1696 2d. Casey reading newspaper at plate . . . 95 90
1697 2d. Casey letting second pitch go by 95 90
1698 2d. Over-confident Casey . . 95 90
1699 2d. Casey striking out . . . 95 90
1700 2d. Casey striking out at night 95 90
MS1701 Two sheets, each 129 × 103 mm. (a) 20d. Mudville manager. (b) 20d. Pitcher (vert) Set of 2 sheets . . . . 10·00 11·00

221a Hannich (Hungary) and Stopyra (France)

1993. World Cup Football Championship, 1994, U.S.A. (1st issue). Multicoloured.
1702 1d.25 Type **221a** . . . . . 1·00 40
1703 1d.50 Labd (Morocco) and Gary Lineker (England) 1·25 50
1704 2d. Segota (Canada) and Morozov (Russia) . . . . 1·40 65
1705 3d. Roger Milla (Cameroun) 1·60 1·25
1706 5d. Rodax (Austria) and Weiss (Czechoslovakia) 2·00 1·75
1707 10d. Claesen (Belgium), Bossis and Amoros (France) . . . . 2·75 2·75
1708 12d. Candida (Brazil) and Ramirez (Costa Rica) . . 2·75 3·00
1709 15d. Silva (Brazil) and Michel Platini (France) 3·00 3·50
MS1710 Two sheets, each 100 × 70 mm. (a) 25d. Muller (Brazil) and McDonald (Ireland) (horiz). (b) 25d. Diego Maradona (Argentina) and Matthaeus (Germany) (horiz) Set of 2 sheets 12·00 13·00

See also Nos. 1882/90.

221b "The Adoration of the Magi" (detail) (Rubens)

1993. Christmas. Religious Paintings. Black, yellow and red (Nos. 1712/13 and 1715/17) or multicoloured (others).
1711 25b. Type **221b** 30 20
1712 1d. "The Holy Family with Joachim and Anna" (Durer) 70 20
1713 1d.50 "The Annunciation" (Durer) 90 30
1714 2d. "The Adoration of the Magi" (different detail) (Rubens) . . . . 1·00 60
1715 2d. "The Virgin Mary worshipped by Albrecht Bonstetten" (Durer) . . . 1·00 60
1716 7d. "The Holy Family with Two Angels in a Portico" (detail) (Durer) . . . . . 2·50 3·25
1717 10d. "Virgin on a Throne, crowned by an Angel" (Durer) . . . . 2·75 3·25
1718 15d. "The Adoration of the Magi" (different detail) (Rubens) . . . . 3·00 4·25
MS1719 Two sheets, each 102 × 127 mm. (a) 20d. "The Adoration of the Magi" (different detail) (Rubens). (b) 20d. "The Holy Family with Two Angels in a Portico" (different detail) (Durer) (horiz) Set of 2 sheets 9·00 10·00

221c "A Man in a Cap" (Rembrandt)

1993. Famous Paintings by Rembrandt and Matisse. Multicoloured.

1720 50b. Type **221c** 65 20
1721 1d.50 "Pierre Matisse" (Matisse) 1·00 40
1722 2d. "Man with a Gold Helmet" (Rembrandt) 1·25 85
1723 2d. "Auguste Pellerin" (Matisse) 1·25 85
1724 5d. "Andre Derain" (Matisse) 2·25 2·25
1725 7d. "A Franciscan Monk" (Rembrandt) 2·75 3·25
1726 12d. "The Young Sailor (II)" (Matisse) 3·25 4·00
1727 15d. "The Apostle Paul" (Rembrandt) 3·25 4·50
MS1728 Two sheets, each 127 × 102 mm. (a) 20d. "Dr. Tulp demonstrating the Anatomy of the Arm" (detail) (Rembrandt) (horiz). (b) 20d. "Pianist and Draughts Players" (detail) (Matisse) Set of 2 sheets 10·00 11·00

222 Mickey Mouse performing Ski Ballet

1993. Winter Sports. Walt Disney cartoon characters. Multicoloured.

1729 50b. Type **222** 40 15
1730 75b. Clarabelle and Horace ice dancing 50 15
1731 1d. Donald Duck and Dale speed skating 55 20
1732 1d.25 Donald in biathlon 60 20
1733 4d. Donald and nephews in bob-sled 1·60 1·60
1734 5d. Goofy on luge 1·75 1·75
1735 7d. Minnie Mouse figure skating 2·25 2·75
1736 10d. Goofy downhill skiing 2·50 2·75
1737 15d. Goofy playing ice hockey 2·75 3·25
MS1738 Two sheets, each 128 × 102 mm. (a) 20d. Minnie mogul skiing. (b) 20d. Goofy cross-country skiing Set of 2 sheets 8·50 9·50

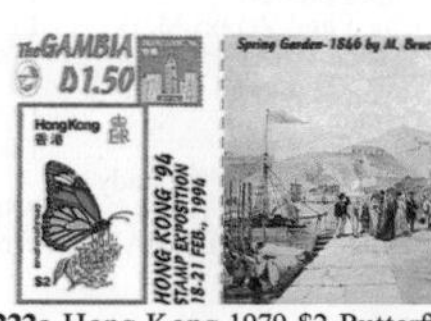

222a Hong Kong 1979 $2 Butterflies Stamp and "Spring Garden" (M. Bruce)

1994. "Hong Kong '94" International Stamp Exhibition (1st issue). Multicoloured.

1739 1d.50 Type **222a** 65 75
1740 1d.50 Gambia 1990 50d. Gambian Life stamp and "Spring Garden" (M. Bruce) 65 75
MS1741 82 × 117 mm. 20d. Hong Kong 1970 Chinese New Year 10c. stamp 3·50 4·00

Nos. 1739/40 were printed together, se-tenant, forming the complete painting.

See also Nos. 1742/7.

222b Warriors and Horses

1994. "Hong Kong '94" International Stamp Exhibition (2nd issue). Qin Dynasty Terracotta Figures. Multicoloured.

1742 1d.50 Type **222b** 60 55
1743 1d.50 Head of warrior 60 55
1744 1d.50 Kneeling warrior 60 55
1745 1d.50 Chariot driver 60 55
1746 1d.50 Dog 60 55
1747 1d.50 Warriors as excavated 60 55

223 Pluto the Racer, 1934–35

1994. Chinese New Year ("Year of the Dog"). Walt Disney cartoon dogs. Multicoloured.

1748 25b. Type **223** 55 20
1749 50b. Fifi, 1933 70 30
1750 75b. Pluto Jnr, 1942 90 30
1751 1d.25 Goofy and Bowser 1·25 30
1752 1d.50 Butch, 1940 1·25 45
1753 2d. Toliver, 1936 1·50 60
1754 3d. Ronnie, 1946 1·75 1·00
1755 5d. Primo, 1950 2·00 1·40
1756 8d. Pluto's kid brother, 1946 2·25 2·25
1757 10d. The army mascot, 1942 2·25 2·50
1758 12d. Pluto and Fifi's puppies, 1937 2·25 3·00
1759 18d. Bent Tail Jnr, 1949 2·75 4·00
MS1760 Three sheets, each 127 × 102 mm. (a) 20d. Pluto and Fifi's puppies, 1937 (different). (b) 20d. Pluto and Dinah, 1950. (c) 20d. Pflip (horiz) Set of 3 sheets 12·00 13·00

Nos. 1758 and **MS**1760a are inscribed "DINAH'S PUPPIES" in error.

224 Ludwig von Drake and Easter Bunny

1994. Easter. Walt Disney cartoon characters. Multicoloured.

1761 25b. Type **224** 40 10
1762 50b. Minnie Mouse and Daisy Duck carrying banner 55 10
1763 3d. Mickey Mouse wearing top hat 1·50 85
1764 4d. Von Drake holding hatching egg 1·75 1·25
1765 5d. Donald Duck pushing trolley full of eggs 2·00 1·75
1766 8d. Bunny taking photograph of Von Drake 2·25 2·50
1767 10d. Goofy dressed as Easter Bunny 2·25 2·75
1768 12d. Von Drake holding dinosaur egg 2·50 3·25
MS1769 Two sheets. (a) 102 × 123 mm. 20d. Mickey and Minnie. (b) 123 × 102 mm. 20d. Ludwig von Drake Set of 2 sheets 8·50 9·50

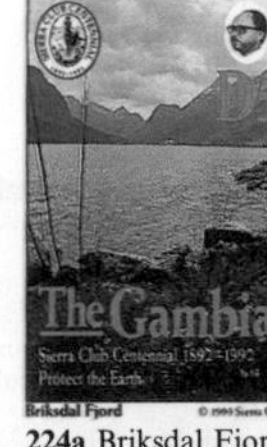

224a Briksdal Fjord

1994. Centenary (1992) of Sierra Club (environmental protection society). Endangered Environments. Multicoloured.

1770 5d. Type **224a** 1·00 1·10
1771 5d. Glacier, Briksdal Fjord 1·00 1·10
1772 5d. Waterfall, Briksdal Fjord 1·00 1·10
1773 5d. Frozen lake, Yosemite 1·00 1·10
1774 5d. Cliffs and river, Yosemite 1·00 1·10
1775 5d. Forest, Yosemite 80 90
1776 5d. Mother and child, Tibetan Plateau 80 90
1777 5d. Yellowstone in winter 80 90
1778 5d. Ross Island 80 90
1779 5d. Mount Erebus 80 90
1780 5d. Tibetan Plateau 80 90
1781 5d. Waterfall, Yellowstone 80 90
1782 5d. Sunset on the Serengeti 80 90
1783 5d. Dead trees, Ansel Adams Wilderness 80 90
1784 5d. Ansel Adams Wilderness in winter (horiz) 80 90
1785 5d. Ansel Adams Wilderness in summer (horiz) 80 90
1786 5d. Ridge on Mount Erebus (horiz) 80 90
1787 5d. Mount Erebus from a distance (horiz) 80 90
1788 5d. Prince William Sound (horiz) 80 90
1789 5d. Geysers, Yellowstone (horiz) 80 90
1790 5d. Local dwelling, Tibetan Plateau (horiz) 80 90
1791 5d. Sierra Club Centennial emblem (horiz) 80 90
1792 5d. Frozen lake, Prince William Sound (horiz) 1·00 1·10
1793 5d. Forest, Prince William Sound (horiz) 1·00 1·10
1794 5d. Baobab Tree, Serengeti (horiz) 1·00 1·10
1795 5d. Plains, Serengeti (horiz) 1·00 1·10
1796 5d. Volcano, Ross Island (horiz) 1·00 1·10
1797 5d. Mountains, Ross Island (horiz) 1·00 1·10

225 "Oeceoclades maculata" **226** "Girl with a Kitten" (Perronneau)

1994. Orchids. Multicoloured.

1798 1d. Type **225** 35 20
1799 1d.25 "Angraecum distichum" (horiz) 45 30
1800 2d. "Plectrelminthus caudatus" 60 35
1801 5d. "Tridactyle tridactylites" (horiz) 1·25 1·25
1802 8d. "Bulbophyllum lepidum" (horiz) 1·40 1·50
1803 10d. "Angraecum eburneum" 1·60 1·90
1804 12d. "Eulophia guineensis" 1·75 2·00
1805 15d. "Angraecum eichleranum" (horiz) 2·00 2·50
MS1806 Two sheets, each 100 × 70 mm. (a) 25d. "Vanilla imperialis". (b) 25d. "Ancistrochilus rothschildianus" (horiz) Set of 2 sheets 9·00 10·00

1994. Cats. Paintings of Cats. Multicoloured.

1807 5d. Type **226** 1·40 1·40
1808 5d. "Still Life with Cat and Fish" (Chardin) 1·40 1·40
1809 5d. "Tinkle a Cat" 1·40 1·40
1810 5d. "Naughty Puss!" (advertisement) 1·40 1·40
1811 5d. "Cats" (T.-A. Steinlen) 1·40 1·40
1812 5d. "Girl in Red with Cat and Dog" (Phillips) 1·40 1·40
1813 5d. "Cat, Butterfly and Begonia" (Harunobu) 1·40 1·40
1814 5d. "Cat and Kitten" (Pamela Higgins) 1·40 1·40
1815 5d. "Woman with a Cat" (Renoir) 1·40 1·40
1816 5d. "Minnie from Outskirts of the Village" (Thrall) 1·40 1·40
1817 5d. "The Fisher" (Raphael Tuck postcard) 1·40 1·40
1818 5d. "Artist and His Family" (detail) (Vaenius) 1·40 1·40
1819 5d. "The Arena" (Harold Weston) (horiz) 1·40 1·40
1820 5d. "Cat killing a Bird" (Picasso) (horiz) 1·40 1·40
1821 5d. "Cat and Butterfly" (Hokusai) (horiz) 1·40 1·40
1822 5d. "Winter: Cat on a Cushion" (Steinlen) (horiz) 1·40 1·40
1823 5d. "Rattown Tigers" (Prang) (horiz) 1·40 1·40
1824 5d. "Cat on the Floor" (Steinlen) (horiz) 1·40 1·40
1825 5d. "Cat and Kittens" (horiz) 1·40 1·40
1826 5d. "Cats looking over Fence" (Prang) (horiz) 1·40 1·40
1827 5d. "Little White Kittens into Mischief" (Ives) (horiz) 1·40 1·40
1828 5d. "Cat Bathing" (Hiroshige) (horiz) 1·40 1·40
1829 5d. "Playtime" (Tuck postcard) (horiz) 1·40 1·40
1830 5d. "Summer: Cat on a Balustrade" (Steinlen) (horiz) 1·40 1·40
MS1831 Two sheets, each 100 × 70 mm. (a) 20d. "The Graham Children" (detail) (William Hogarth). (b) 20d. "The Morning Rising" (detail) (Michel Lepicie) (horiz) Set of 2 sheets 9·00 10·00

227 Patas Monkey

1994. Monkeys. Multicoloured.

1832 1d. Type **227** 45 20
1833 1d.50 Collared mangabey 65 30
1834 2d. Black and white colobus 75 35
1835 5d. Mona monkey 1·25 1·10
1836 8d. Kirk's colobus 1·50 2·00
1837 10d. Vervet 1·75 2·25
1838 12d. Red colobus 2·00 2·50
1839 15d. Guinea baboon 2·25 2·75
MS1840 Two sheets, each 106 × 77 mm. (a) 25d. Head of Guinea baboon. (b) 25d. Head of Collared mangabey Set of 2 sheets 12·00 13·00

227a Yuri Gagarin (first cosmonaut)

1994. 25th Anniv of First Manned Moon Landing. Multicoloured.

1841 2d. Type **227a** 75 75
1842 2d. Valentina Tereshkova (first woman in Space) 75 75
1843 2d. Ham (first chimpanzee in Space) 75 75
1844 2d. Aleksei Leonov (first man to walk in Space) 75 75
1845 2d. Neil Armstrong (first man on Moon) 75 75
1846 2d. Svetlana Savitskaya (first woman to walk in Space) 75 75
1847 2d. Marc Garneau (first Canadian in Space) 75 75
1848 2d. Vladimir Komarov (first Soviet Space casualty) 75 75
1849 2d. Ulf Merbold (first German in Space) 75 75
MS1850 81 × 81 mm. 30d. "Apollo 11" crew at news conference 7·00 7·50

227b Daley Thompson (Great Britain) (decathlon), 1980 and 1984 **227d** Soldiers on Horses

227c "Soema" (Dutch Sloop)

1994. Centenary of International Olympic Committee. Gold Medal Winners. Multicoloured.
1851 1d.50 Type **227b** 50 40
1852 5d. Heide Marie Rosendohl (Germany) (long jump), 1972 . . . . 1·25 1·50
MS1853 106 × 76 mm. 20d. Sweden (ice hockey), 1994 . . . . . . 6·00 6·50

1994. 50th Anniv of D-Day. Multicoloured.
1854 50b. Type **227c** 70 50
1855 75b. H.M.S. "Belfast" (cruiser) 80 60
1856 1d. U.S.S. "Texas" (battleship) 90 70
1857 2d. "Georges Leygues" (French cruiser) . . . . . 1·40 1·40
MS1858 105 × 76 mm. 20d. H.M.S. "Ramillies" (battleship) firing broadside . . . . 4·25 4·50

1994. "Philakorea '94" International Stamp Exhibition, Seoul. Screen paintings of the "Sanguozhi". Multicoloured.
1859 50b. Kungnakchon Hall (38 × 25 mm) 45 30
1860 1d. Type **227d** 55 60
1861 1d. Soldiers defending fort 55 60
1862 1d. Archers 55 60
1863 1d. General on horse . . . 55 60
1864 1d. Three soldiers in battle 55 60
1865 1d. Army in retreat 55 60
1866 1d. Archers using fire arrows 55 60
1867 1d. Horsemen attacking fort 55 60
1868 1d. Women in summer house 55 60
1869 1d. Old man, child and house 55 60
1870 2d. Kettle of Popchusa (38 × 25 mm) 80 85
1871 3d. Pomun tourist resort (38 × 25 mm) . . . . . . 90 1·10
MS1872 98 × 68 mm. 20d. Tomb guardian, Taenung (38 × 25 mm) 4·50 5·50

228 "Mylothris rhodope"

1994. Butterflies. Multicoloured.
1873 1d. Type **228** 50 25
1874 1d.25 "Iolaphilus menas" 65 35
1875 2d. "Neptis nemetes" . . . 75 40
1876 5d. "Antanartia delius" . . 1·25 1·10
1877 8d. "Acraea caecilia" . . . 1·50 2·00
1878 10d. "Papilio nireus" . . . 1·50 2·00
1879 12d. "Papilio menestheus" 1·75 2·50
1880 15d. "Iolaphilus julus" . . . 2·00 2·75
MS1881 Two sheets, each 97 × 68 mm. (a) 25d. "Bematistes epaea". (b) 25d. "Colotis evippe" Set of 2 sheets . . . . 11·00 12·00

229 Bobby Charlton (England)

1994. World Cup Football Championship, U.S.A. (2nd issue). Multicoloured.
1882 50b. Type **229** 50 30
1883 75b. Ferenc Puskas (Hungary) 60 30
1884 1d. Paolo Rossi (Italy) . . . 75 30
1885 2d. Biri Biri (Spain) . . . . 1·00 40
1886 3d. Diego Maradona (Argentina) . . . . 1·25 80
1887 8d. Johann Cruyff (Netherlands) . . . . . . 2·00 2·25
1888 10d. Franz Beckenbauer (Germany) . . . . 2·00 2·25
1889 15d. Thomas Dooley (U.S.A.) . . . . 2·25 3·25
MS1890 Two sheets, each 70 × 100 mm. (a) 25d. Pelé (Brazil). (b) 25d. Gordon Banks (England) Set of 2 sheets . . . . 11·00 11·00

230 "Suillus luteus"

231 Marilyn Monroe

230a "Expectant Madonna with St. Joseph" (French 15th-century)

1994. Fungi. Multicoloured.
1891 5d. Type **230** 90 90
1892 5d. "Bolbitius vitellinus" . . 90 90
1893 5d. "Clitocybe nebularis" . . 90 90
1894 5d. "Omphalotus olearius" 90 90
1895 5d. "Auricularia auricula" 90 90
1896 5d. "Macrolepiota rhacodes" 90 90
1897 5d. "Volvariella volvacea" 90 90
1898 5d. "Psilocybe coprophila" 90 90
1899 5d. "Suillus granulatus" . . 90 90
1900 5d. "Agaricus campestris" 90 90
1901 5d. "Lepista nuda" 90 90
1902 5d. "Podaxis pistillaris" . . 90 90
1903 5d. "Oudemansiella radicata" 90 90
1904 5d. "Schizophyllum commune" 90 90
1905 5d. "Chlorophyllum molybdites" 90 90
1906 5d. "Hypholoma fasciculare" 90 90
1907 5d. "Mycena pura" 90 90
1908 5d. "Ganoderma lucidum" 90 90
MS1909 Two sheets, each 100 × 70 mm. (a) 20d. "Leucoagaricus naucinus". (b) 20d. "Cyathus striatus" Set of 2 sheets . . . . 11·00 11·00

1994. Christmas. Religious Paintings. Multicoloured.
1910 50b. Type **230a** 30 10
1911 75b. "Rest of the Holy Family" (Louis le Nain) 40 20
1912 1d. "Rest on the Flight into Egypt" (Antoine Watteau) 55 20
1913 2d. "Rest on the Flight into Egypt" (Jean-Honore Fragonard) 70 70
1914 2d. "Rest on the Flight into Egypt" (Francois Boucher) 70 70
1915 2d. "Noon" (Claude Lorrain) 70 70
1916 10d. "The Holy Family" (Nicolas Poussin) . . . . 2·50 3·25
1917 12d. "Mystical Marriage of St. Catherine" (Pierre-Francois Mignard) . . . 2·50 3·50
MS1918 Two sheets, each 122 × 87 mm. (a) 25d. "Adoration of the Shepherds" (detail) (Mathieu le Nain). (b) 25d. "The Nativity by Torchlight" (detail) (Louis le Nain) Set of 2 sheets 10·00 11·00

1995. Marilyn Monroe (American entertainer) Commemoration. Multicoloured.
1919 4d. Type **231** 90 90
1920 4d. Wearing pendant necklace 90 90
1921 4d. In blue jacket 90 90
1922 4d. With sun-glasses on head 90 90
1923 4d. Looking over right arm 90 90
1924 4d. Wearing gold beret and jacket 90 90
1925 4d. Wearing hooped earrings 90 90
1926 4d. Smiling 90 90
1927 4d. Laughing 90 90
MS1928 Two sheets, each 70 × 100mm. (a) 25d. Marilyn Monroe in red dress. (b) 25d. With pendant earrings Set of 2 sheets 8·50 9·00

232 Elvis as a Child

1995. 60th Birth Anniv of Elvis Presley (singer). Multicoloured.
1929 4d. Type **232** . . . . . . 1·00 90
1930 4d. Wearing white shirt . . 1·00 90
1931 4d. With his mother Gladys 1·00 90
1932 4d. With his wife Priscilla 1·00 90
1933 4d. With large gold medallion . . . . 1·00 90
1934 4d. In army uniform . . . . 1·00 90
1935 4d. In purple shirt . . . . . 1·00 90
1936 4d. Wearing stetson . . . . 1·00 90
1937 4d. With his daughter Lisa-Marie . . . . 1·00 90

233 Pteranodon

1995. Prehistoric Animals. Multicoloured.
1938 2d. Type **233** 65 65
1939 2d. Archaeopteryx 65 65
1940 2d. Rhamphorhynchus . . . 65 65
1941 2d. Ornithomimus 65 65
1942 2d. Stegosaurus 65 65
1943 2d. Heterodontosaurus . . . 65 65
1944 2d. Lystrosaurus 65 65
1945 2d. Euoplocephalus 65 65
1946 2d. Coelophysis 65 65
1947 2d. Staurikosaurus 65 65
1948 2d. Giantoperis 65 65
1949 2d. Diarthrognathus 65 65
1950 3d. Archaeopteryx 65 65
1951 3d. Vangehuanosaurus . . . 65 65
1952 3d. Celophysis 65 65
1953 3d. Plateosaurus 65 65
1954 3d. Baryonyx 65 65
1955 3d. Ornitholestes 65 65
1956 3d. Dryosaurus 65 65
1957 3d. Estemmenosuchus . . . 65 65
1958 3d. Macroplata 65 65
1959 3d. Shonisaurus 65 65
1960 3d. Muraeonosaurus 65 65
1961 3d. Archelon 65 65
MS1962 Four sheets, each 100 × 70 mm. (a) 20d. Bactrosaurus. (b) 22d. Tyrannosaurus rex (vert). (c) 25d. Triceratops (vert). (d) 25d. Spinosaurus Set of 4 sheets . . 20·00 20·00
Nos. 1938/49 and 1950/61 respectively were printed together, se-tenant, forming composite designs.

234 Pig (Chinese characters in green)

236 Rural Road

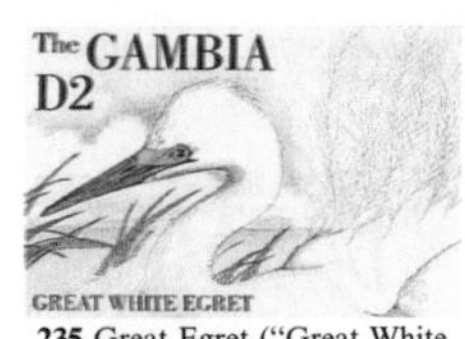

235 Great Egret ("Great White Egret")

1995. Chinese New Year ("Year of the Pig").
1963 **234** 3d. red, black and green 65 65
1964 – 3d. multicoloured (characters in blue) . . 65 65
1965 – 3d. orange, red and black (characters in white) 65 65
1966 – 3d. pink, red and black (characters in black) 65 65
MS1967 76 × 100 mm. 10d. mauve and red (three pigs) . . . . . 2·25 2·50
DESIGNS: Nos. 1964/6, Different symbolic pigs.

1995. Water Birds. Multicoloured.
1968 2d. Type **235** 80 60
1969 3d. Pintails 80 80
1970 3d. Fulvous whistling duck ("Fulvous Tree Duck") 80 80
1971 3d. Garganey 80 80
1972 3d. White-faced whistling duck ("White-faced Tree Duck") 80 80
1973 3d. White-backed duck . . . 80 80
1974 3d. Egyptian goose 80 80
1975 3d. African pygmy geese ("Pygmy Goose") 80 80
1976 3d. Little bitterns 80 80
1977 3d. Common redshanks ("Redshank") 80 80
1978 3d. Ringed plovers 80 80
1979 3d. Black-winged stilt . . . 80 80
1980 3d. Squacco herons 80 80
1981 8d. Hammerkop . . . . . 2·00 2·50
1982 10d. Common shovelers ("Shoveler") . . . . . . 2·00 2·50
1983 12d. Crowned crane . . . . 2·25 2·75
MS1984 Two sheets, each 106 × 76 mm. (a) 25d. Ferruginous ducks. (b) 25d. Moorhen Set of 2 sheets . . . . 11·00 12·00
Nos. 1969/80 were printed together, se-tenant, forming a composite design.

1995. 20th Anniv of Economic Community of West African States (ECOWAS). Multicoloured.
1985 2d. Type **236** 50 25
1986 5d. Pres. Yayah Jammeh . . 1·25 1·50

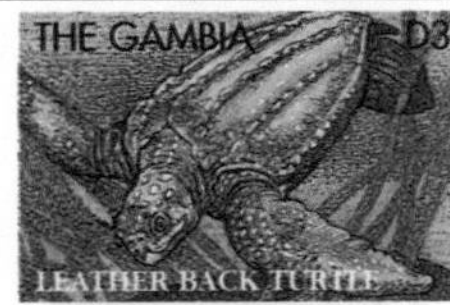

237 Leather Back Turtle

1995. Marine Life. Multicoloured.
1987 3d. Type **237** 70 75
1988 3d. Tiger shark 70 75
1989 3d. Powder-blue surgeonfish 70 75
1990 3d. Emperor angelfish . . . 70 75
1991 3d. Blue parrotfish 70 75
1992 3d. Clown triggerfish . . . 70 75
1993 3d. Sea horses 70 75
1994 3d. Lionfish 70 75
1995 3d. Moray eel 70 75
1996 3d. Melon butterflyfish . . . 70 75
1997 3d. Octopus 70 75
1998 3d. Common stingray . . . 70 75
1999 8d. Stoplight parrotfish ("Multicoloured Parrot Fish") (vert) . . . . . . 1·75 2·00
2000 8d. Stoplight parrotfish ("Sparisoma Viride") (vert) . . . . 1·75 2·00
2001 8d. Queen parrotfish (vert) 1·75 2·00
2002 8d. Bicoloured parrotfish (vert) . . . . 1·75 2·00
MS2003 Two sheets, each 98 × 68 mm. (a) 25d. Queen angelfish ("Angelicthys isabelita"). (b) 25d. Rock beauty ("Holacanthus ciliaris") Set of 2 sheets . . . . 13·00 13·00
Nos. 1987/98 and 1999/2002 respectively were printed together, se-tenant, forming composite designs.
No. 1991 is inscribed "BLUE PARRO FISH" in error.

238 First stage of Lariat Knot

1995. 18th World Scout Jamboree, Netherlands. T **238** amd similar vert designs. Multicoloured.
MS2004 Two sheets, each 101 × 65 mm. (a) 2d. Type **238**; 2d. Second stage of knot with ropes end at right; 2d. Completed Lariat knot. (b) 5d. Completed Bowline knot; 10d. Second stage of knot; 12d. First stage of knot Set of 2 sheets . . . . 7·00 8·00
MS2005 Two sheets, each 72 × 102 mm. (a) 25d. Scout in rope using Hitch knot. (b) 25d. Injured scout supported by Bowline knot Set of 2 sheets 8·50 9·50

238a Peter Lawford

1995. 50th Anniv of End of Second World War in Europe. Film Stars. Black and red (Nos. 2008 and 2010) or multicoloured (others).
2006 3d. Type **238a** . . . . . 1·00 1·00
2007 3d. Gene Tierney and Dana Andrews . . . . 1·00 1·00
2008 3d. Groucho and Harpo Marx . . . . 1·00 1·00
2009 3d. James Stewart . . . . . 1·00 1·00
2010 3d. Chico and Zeppo Marx 1·00 1·00
2011 3d. Tyrone Power . . . . . 1·00 1·00
2012 3d. Cary Grant and Ingrid Bergman . . . . 1·00 1·00
2013 3d. Veronica Lake . . . . . 1·00 1·00
MS2014 105 × 75 mm. 25d. "A Lady Fights Back" film poster (vert) 7·50 8·50
No. 2012 is inscribed "BERMAN" in error.

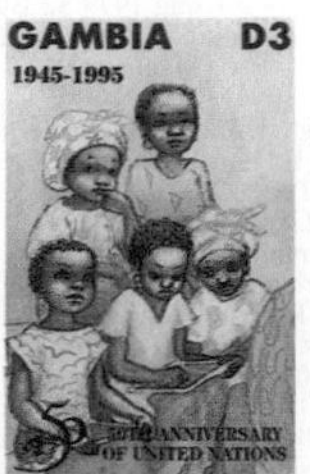

238b Children in Class

1995. 50th Anniv of United Nations. Multicoloured.
2015 3d. Type **238b** . . . . . . 95 1·10
2016 3d. Teacher helping child . . 95 1·10
2017 3d. Child writing on blackboard . . . . 95 1·10
MS2018 104 × 74 mm. 25d. Nurse weighing baby . . . . 3·75 4·50
Nos. 2015/17 were printed together, se-tenant, forming a composite design.

238c Woman carrying Sack

1995. 50th Anniv of FAO Multicoloured.
2019 3d. Type **238c** . . . . . . 95 1·10
2020 3d. Two men carrying sacks 95 1·10
2021 3d. Man carrying sack . . . 95 1·10
MS2022 104 × 74 mm. 25d. Fisherman with net . . . . . 3·75 4·50
Nos. 2019/21 were printed together, se-tenant, forming a composite design.

239 Paul Harris (founder) and Rotary Emblem

1995. 90th Anniv of Rotary International.
2023 **239** 15d. multicoloured . . . 2·00 2·50
MS2024 75 × 105 mm. 20d. National flag and Rotary emblem . . . 3·00 3·50

239a Queen Elizabeth the Queen Mother (pastel drawing)

1995. 95th Birthday of Queen Elizabeth the Queen Mother.
2025 **239a** 5d. brown, lt brn & blk 1·60 1·60
2026 – 5d. multicoloured . . . 1·60 1·60
2027 – 5d. multicoloured . . . 1·60 1·60
2028 – 5d. multicoloured . . . 1·60 1·60
MS2029 102 × 126 mm. 25d. multicoloured . . . . 6·50 5·50
DESIGNS: Nos. 2026, Wearing blue hat and dress; 2027, At desk (oil painting); 2028, Wearing green hat and dress; **MS**2029 Wearing lavender hat and dress.

239b Fairey Firefly

1995. 50th Anniv of End of Second World War in the Pacific. Multicoloured.
2030 5d. Type **239b** . . . . . . 1·25 1·25
2031 5d. Fairey Barracuda Mk III . . . . 1·25 1·25
2032 5d. Supermarine Seafire II 1·25 1·25
2033 5d. H.M.S. "Repulse" (battle cruiser) . . . . . 1·25 1·25
2034 5d. H.M.S. "Illustrious" (aircraft carrier) . . . . . 1·25 1·25
2035 5d. H.M.S. "Exeter" (cruiser) . . . . 1·25 1·25
MS2036 108 × 76 mm. 25d. Kamikaze aircraft heading for British "County" class cruiser 4·75 4·75

240 Kenichi Fukui (1981 Chemistry)

1995. Centenary of Nobel Prize Trust Fund. Past Prize Winners. Multicoloured.
2037 2d. Type **240** 55 40
2038 3d. Gustav Stresemann (1929 Peace) 65 50
2039 5d. Thomas Mann (1929 Literature) . . . . 1·00 1·10
2040 5d. Marie Curie (1911 Chemistry) . . . . 1·00 1·10
2041 5d. Adolf Butenandt (1939 Chemistry) . . . . 1·00 1·10
2042 5d. Susumu Tonegwa (1987 Medicine) . . . . 1·00 1·10
2043 5d. Nelly Sachs (1966 Literature) . . . . 1·00 1·10
2044 5d. Yasunari Kawabata (1968 Literature) . . . . 1·00 1·10
2045 5d. Hideki Yukawa (1949 Physics) . . . . 1·00 1·10
2046 5d. Paul Ehrlich (1908 Medicine) . . . . 1·00 1·10
2047 5d. Bisaku Sato (1974 Peace) . . . . 1·00 1·10
2048 5d. Carl von Ossietsky (1935 Peace) . . . . 1·00 1·10
2049 8d. Albert Schweitzer (1952 Peace) . . . . 2·00 2·00
2050 12d. Leo Esaki (1973 Physics) . . . . 2·00 2·50
2051 15d. Lech Walesa (1983 Peace) . . . . 2·25 3·00
MS2052 75 × 105 mm. 25d. Willy Brandt (1971 Peace) . . . . . 4·25 5·00
Nos. 2040/8 were printed together, se-tenant, forming a composite design.
No. 2048 is dated "1974" and No. 2051 inscribed "Lech Walsea", both in error.

241 Bruce Jenner (U.S.A.) (decathlon)

1995. Olympic Games, Atlanta (1996) (1st issue). Multicoloured.
2053 1d. Type **241** 50 30
2054 1d.25 Greg Louganis (U.S.A.) (diving) 55 30
2055 1d.50 Michael Gross (Germany) (50 m butterfly) 55 30
2056 2d. Vasily Alexeev (Russia) (weightlifting) 60 30
2057 3d. Ewing (U.S.A.) and Corbalan (Spain) (basketball) . . . . 1·25 80
2058 3d. Stefano Cerioni (Italy) (fencing) (vert) . . . . . 1·25 1·25
2059 3d. Alberto Cova (Italy) (10,000 m) (vert) . . . . 1·25 1·25
2060 3d. Mary Lou Retton (U.S.A.) (gymnastics) (vert) . . . . 1·25 1·25
2061 3d. Vladimir Artemov (Russia) (gymnastics) (vert) . . . . 1·25 1·25
2062 3d. Florence Griffith-Joyner (U.S.A.) (400 m relay) (vert) . . . . 1·25 1·25
2063 3d. Brazil (football) (vert) 1·25 1·25
2064 3d. Nelson Vails (U.S.A.) (sprint cycling) (vert) . . 1·25 1·25
2065 3d. Cheryl Miller (U.S.A.) (basketball) (vert) . . . 1·25 1·25
2066 5d. U.S.A. v Brazil (men's volleyball) . . . . 1·50 1·75
2067 10d. Svenden (West Germany) and Fernandez (U.S.A.) (water polo) . . . 2·00 2·25
2068 15d. Pertii Karppinen (Finland) (single sculls) 2·75 3·50
MS2069 Two sheets, each 71 × 101 mm. (a) 25d. Karen Stives (U.S.A.) (equestrian) (vert). (b) 25d. Edwin Moses (U.S.A.) (400 metre hurdles) (vert) Set of 2 sheets . . . . 10·00 11·00
No. 2059 is inscribed "Alberto Covo" and No. 2064 "Nelson Valis", both in error.
See also Nos. 2281/2303.

242 Rotary Emblem and Rotarians supporting School for the Deaf

1995. Local Rotary and Boy Scout Projects. Multicoloured.
2070 2d. Type **242** 55 30
2071 5d. Scout wood badge course, 1980 . . . . . . 1·25 1·40
2072 5d. Scout Commissioner M. J. E. Sambou (vert) 1·25 1·40

243 "Zantedeschia rehmannii"

1995. African Flowers. Multicoloured.
2073 2d. Type **243** 55 45
2074 3d. "Kigelia africana" . . . 60 65
2075 3d. "Hibiscus schizopelatus" 60 65
2076 3d. "Dombeya mastersii" . . 60 65
2077 3d. "Agapanthus orientalis" 60 65
2078 3d. "Strelitzia reginae" . . . 60 65
2079 3d. "Spathodea campanulata" 60 65
2080 3d. "Rhodolaena bakeriana" 60 65
2081 3d. "Gazania rigens" . . . 60 65
2082 3d. "Ixianthes retzioides" . . 60 65
2083 3d. "Canarina abyssinica" . 60 65
2084 3d. "Nerine bowdenii" . . . 60 65
2085 3d. "Zantedeschia aethiopica" 60 65
2086 3d. "Aframomum sceptrum" 60 65
2087 3d. "Schotia brachypetala" 60 65
2088 3d. "Catharanthus roseus" 60 65
2089 3d. "Protea grandiceps" . . 60 65
2090 3d. "Plumbago capensis" . . 60 65
2091 3d. "Uncarina grandidieri" 60 65
2092 5d. "Euadenia eminens" . . 1·10 1·25
2093 10d. "Passiflora vitifolia" . . 1·75 2·00
2094 15d. "Dietes grandiflora" . . 2·50 3·00
MS2095 Two sheets, each 106 × 75 mm. (a) 25d. "Eulophia quartiniana". (b) 25d. "Gloriosa simplex" Set of 2 sheets . . . 9·50 10·00
Nos. 2074/82 and 2083/91 respectively were printed together, se-tenant, forming composite background designs.

244 Children outside Huts

1995. Kinderdorf International SOS Children's Villages. Multicoloured.
2096 2d. Type **244** 50 50
2097 2d. Charity worker with children (vert) 50 50
2098 5d. Children at party . . . 1·25 1·50

245 Roy Orbison

1995. History of Rock 'n' Roll Music. Multicoloured.
2099 3d. Type **245** 75 75
2100 3d. Mick Jagger 75 75
2101 3d. Bruce Springsteen . . . 75 75
2102 3d. Jimi Hendrix 75 75
2103 3d. Bill Haley 75 75
2104 3d. Gene Vincent 75 75
2105 3d. Buddy Holly 75 75
2106 3d. Jerry Lee Lewis 75 75
2107 3d. Chuck Berry 75 75
MS2108 116 × 86 mm. 25d. Elvis Presley . . . . 7·00 6·00
Nos. 2099/2107 were printed together, se-tenant, forming a composite design.

1995. Centenary of Cinema. As T **245** but depicting James Dean. Multicoloured.
2109 3d. As a boy 75 75
2110 3d. On motorbike 75 75
2111 3d. With sports car and trophy 75 75
2112 3d. Close-up portrait . . . 75 75
2113 3d. Facing left 75 75
2114 3d. Holding girl 75 75
2115 3d. "Rebel without a Cause" (film) 75 75
2116 3d. "Giant" (film) 75 75
2117 3d. "East of Eden" (film) 75 75
MS2118 116 × 86 mm. 25d. James Dean in "Rebel without a Cause" 4·50 4·50

Nos. 2109/17 were printed together, se-tenant, forming a composite design.

245a "Madonna and Child" (Maria della Vallicella)

1995. Christmas. Religious Paintings. Multicoloured.
2119 75b. Type **245a** 45 15
2120 1d. "Madonna" (Giotto) . . 45 15
2121 2d. "The Flight into Egypt" (Luca Giordano) 65 25
2122 5d. "The Epiphany" (Bordone) . . . . 1·50 1·00
2123 8d. "Virgin and Child" (Burgkmair) . . . . . . 2·25 2·50
2124 12d. "Madonna" (Bellini) 2·50 3·25
MS2125 Two sheets, each 101 × 127 mm. (a) 25d. "Christ" (Carpaccio). (b) 25d. "Madonna and Child" (Rubens) Set of 2 sheets . . . . 10·00 11·00

246 Terminal Building

1995. Opening of New Terminal Building, Banjul International Airport.
2126 **246** 1d. multicoloured . . . 40 10
2127 2d. multicoloured . . . 55 25
2128 3d. multicoloured . . . 70 55
2129 5d. multicoloured . . . 1·10 1·25

247 UPU Emblem

1995. 121st Anniv of Universal Postal Union.
2130 **247** 1d. black and violet . . 30 10
2131 2d. black and blue . . . 50 25
2132 3d. black and red . . . 70 45
2133 7d. black and green . . 1·50 2·25

248 Commerson's Dolphin

1995. Whales and Dolphins. Multicoloured.
2134 2d. Type **248** 40 25
2135 3d. Bryde's whale 50 55
2136 3d. Sperm whale 50 55
2137 3d. Humpback whale . . . 50 55
2138 3d. Sei whale 50 55
2139 3d. Blue whale 50 55
2140 3d. Grey whale 50 55
2141 3d. Fin whale 50 55
2142 3d. Killer whale 50 55
2143 3d. Right whale 50 55
2144 3d. Northern right whale dolphin 75 75
2145 3d. Spotted dolphin 75 75
2146 3d. Common dolphin . . . 75 75
2147 3d. Pacific white-sided dolphin 75 75
2148 3d. Atlantic humpbacked dolphin 75 75
2149 3d. Atlantic white-sided dolphin 75 75
2150 3d. White-beaked dolphin 75 75
2151 3d. Striped dolphin 75 75
2152 3d. Risso's dolphin 75 75
2153 5d. Narwhal 80 80
2154 8d. True's beaked whale . . 1·25 1·50
2155 10d. Rough-toothed dolphin 1·40 1·60
MS2156 Two sheets, each 110 × 80 mm. (a) 25d. Beluga and clymene dolphin. (b) 25d. Bowhead whale and blue shark (vert) Set of 2 sheets . . . . . 10·00 11·00
Nos. 2135/43 and 2144/52 respectively were printed together, se-tenant, forming composite designs.

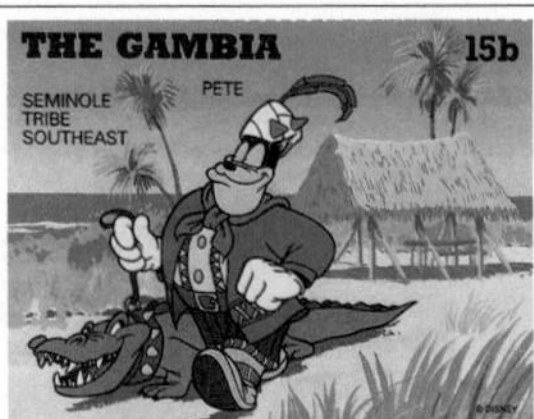

249 Big Pete as Seminole with Alligator

1995. Disney Cowboys and Indians. Walt Disney cartoon characters. Multicoloured.
2157 15b. Type **249** 20 20
2158 20b. Donald Duck as Chinook fisherman . . . 20 20
2159 25b. Huey, Dewey and Louie as Blackfoot braves 20 20
2160 30b. Minnie Mouse shooting bottles 20 20
2161 40b. Donald riding bull . . 20 20
2162 50b. Mickey Mouse branding steer 20 20
2163 2d. Donald in Tlingit mask 70 25
2164 3d. Mickey bronco-busting 80 40
2165 12d. Grandma Duck with lasso . . . . 2·75 2·75
2166 15d. Mickey in Pomo canoe 3·00 3·25
2167 15d. Goofy as ranch hand 3·00 3·25
2168 20d. Goofy and Minnie with Navaho weaving . . . . 3·25 3·50
MS2169 Four sheets, each 127 × 102 mm. (a) 25d. Minnie as Massachusetts squaw. (b) 25d. Minnie as Shoshoni squaw (vert). (c) 25d. Pluto singing to the Moon (vert). (d) 25d. Donald and steer (vert) Set of 4 sheets . . . . . 19·00 20·00

250 Rat

1996. Chinese New Year ("Year of the Rat").
2170 **250** 63b. multicoloured . . . 35 25
2171 – 75b. multicoloured . . . 40 30
2172 – 1d.50 multicoloured . . 70 60
2173 – 4d. multicoloured . . . 1·50 1·50
MS2174 84 × 88 mm. 3d. × 4 As Nos. 2170/3 . . . . 2·50 2·75
MS2175 76 × 106 mm. 10d. red, violet and brown . . . . . . 1·60 1·90
DESIGNS: 75b. to 10d. Different stylized rats.

251 "Don Tiburcio Perez y Cuervo" (detail) (Goya)

1996. 125th Anniv of Metropolitan Museum of Art, New York. Multicoloured.
2176/83 4d. × 8 (Type **251**: "Jean Antoine Moltedo" (Ingres); "The Letter" (Corot); "General Etienne Gerard" (David); "Portrait of the Artist" (Van Gogh); "Joseph Henri Altes" (Degas); "Princess de Broglie" (Ingres); "Lady at the Table" (Cassatt)) . . . . .
2184/91 4d. × 8 ("Broken Eggs" (Greuze); "Johann Joachim Winckleman" (Mengs); "Col. George Coussmaker" (Reynolds); "Self Portrait with Pupils" (Labille-Guiard); "Courtesan holding a Fan" (Utamaro); "The Woodgatherers" (Gainsborough); "Mrs Grace Elliott" (Gainsborough); "The Drummond Children" (Raeburn))
2192/9 4d. × 8 ("Sunflowers" (Monet); "Still Life with Pansies" (Fantin-Latour); "Parisians enjoying the Parc" (Monet); "La Mere Larcheveque" (Pissarro); "Rue de L'Epicerie, Rouen" (Pissarro); "The Abduction of Rebecca" (Delacroix); "Daughter, Abraham- Ben-Chimol" (Delacroix); "Christ on Lake of Gennesaret" (Delacroix)) . . . .
2200/7 4d. × 8 ("Henry Prince of Wales" (Peake); "Saints Peter, Martha, Mary and Leonard" (Correggio); "Marriage Feast at Cana" (Juan de Flandes); "Portrait of One of Wedigh Family" (Holbein); "Guillaume Bude" (Clouet); "Portrait of a Cardinal" (El Greco); "St. Jerome as a Cardinal" (El Greco); "Portrait of a Man" (Titian)) . .
2176/2207 Set of 32 . . . . 24·00 26·00
MS2208 Four sheets, each 95 × 70 mm, containing horiz designs, 81 × 53 mm. (a) 25d. "Israelites gathering Manna in the Desert" (Rubens). (b) 25d. "Henry IV at the Battle of Ivry" (Rubens). (c) 25d. "The Creation of the World and the Expulsion from Paradise" (Giovanni di Paolo). (d) 25d. "The Harvesters" (Bruegel) Set of 4 sheets . . . . 17·00 19·00

252 Fire-eater **253** Bruce Lee

1996. Fire-eating in the Gambia.
2209 **252** 1d. multicoloured . . . 25 15
2210 – 2d. multicoloured . . . 40 30
2211 – 3d. multicoloured . . . 55 50
2212 – 7d. multicoloured . . . 1·25 1·50
DESIGNS: 2d. to 7d. Various fire-eating scenes, the 2d. and 7d. being horiz.

1996. Bruce Lee (film star) Commemoration. Different portraits. Multicoloured.
2213 3d. Wearing cap and mask 70 60
2214 3d. Type **253** 70 60
2215 3d. Facing left 70 60
2216 3d. Wearing blue jumper and with hand to face . . 70 60
2217 3d. Wearing buff jacket . . 70 60
2218 3d. Wearing brown jacket (Chinese characters in brown) 70 60
2219 3d. Wearing black shirt (Chinese characters in lilac) 70 60
2220 3d. Wearing white shirt . . 70 60
2221 3d. Bare-chested 70 60
MS2222 Two sheets. (a) 140 × 85 mm. 5d. Deng Xiao Ping (Chinese leader) (78 × 51 mm). (b) 70 × 100 mm. 25d. Bruce Lee Set of 2 sheets . . . . 9·50 9·50

254 Donald Duck and Big Pete giving Blood

1996. Voluntary Activities. Walt Disney cartoon characters. Multicoloured.
2223 1d. Type **254** 35 30
2224 4d. Daisy Duck and Minnie Mouse adopting pets . . 1·00 75
2225 5d. Goofy as one-man band raising money for the needy . . . . 1·25 85
2226 10d. Goofy teaching outdoor skills . . . . . . 2·00 2·25
2227 15d. Minnie teaching reading . . . . 2·50 3·00
2228 20d. Donald, Mickey and Goofy as volunteer fire fighters . . . . 2·50 3·00
MS2229 Two sheets, each 127 × 102 mm. (a) 25d. Minnie counting whales. (b) 25d. Mickey planting roadside sapling Set of 2 sheets . . . . 8·50 9·00

255 Roan Antelope

1996. Wildlife. Multicoloured.
2230 3d. Type **255** 50 55
2231 3d. Lesser bushbaby 50 55
2232 3d. Black leopard 50 55
2233 3d. Guinea forest red colobus 50 55
2234 3d. Kobs 50 55
2235 3d. Common eland 50 55
2236 4d. African buffalo 55 60
2237 4d. Herd of topi 55 60
2238 4d. Vervet 55 60
2239 4d. Hippopotamuses 55 60
2240 4d. Waterbuck 55 60
2241 4d. Senegal chameleon . . . 55 60
2242 4d. Western green mamba 55 60
2243 4d. Slender-snouted crocodile 55 60
2244 4d. Adanson's mud turtle 55 60
2245 15d. African civet . . . . . 2·00 2·50
MS2246 Two sheets, each 98 × 68 mm. (a) 25d. Lion (vert). (b) 25d. Chimpanzee (vert) Set of 2 sheets . . . . 7·50 8·00
Nos. 2230/5 and 2236/44 respectively were printed together, se-tenant, Nos. 2236/44 forming a composite design.

255a Queen Elizabeth II

1996. 70th Birthday of Queen Elizabeth II. Mult.
2247 8d. Type **255a** . . . . . . 1·60 1·60
2248 8d. Wearing tiara facing right . . . . 1·60 1·60
2249 8d. Wearing tiara facing left 1·60 1·60
MS2250 125 × 104 mm. 25d. Buckingham Palace (horiz) . . 5·00 5·50

256 Pumper Hose Cart, U.S.A. (1850)

1996. Classic Road Transport. Fire Engines (Nos. 2251/6) or Cars (Nos. 2257/62). Multicoloured.
2251 4d. Type **256** 75 75
2252 4d. Steam fire engine, U.S.A. (1891) 75 75
2253 4d. Lausitzer engine, Germany (1864) 75 75
2254 4d. Chemical engine, Great Britain (1902) 75 75
2255 4d. Motor fire engine, Great Britain (1904) 75 75
2256 4d. Colonia No. 5 engine, Germany (1860) 75 75
2257 4d. Fiat Tipo 510, Italy (1912) 75 75
2258 4d. Toyota Model 4B Phaeton, Japan (1936) . . 75 75
2259 4d. Nag C4B, Germany (1924) 75 75
2260 4d. Cadillac, U.S.A. (1903) 75 75
2261 4d. Bentley, Great Britain (1925) 75 75
2262 4d. Renault Model AX, France (1909) 75 75
MS2263 Two sheets. (a) 76 × 58 mm. 25d. Amoskeag Steamer (fire engine), U.S.A. (1865). (b) 81 × 59 mm. 25d. Mitsubishi Model A, Japan (1917) Set of 2 sheets . . . . 8·00 8·50

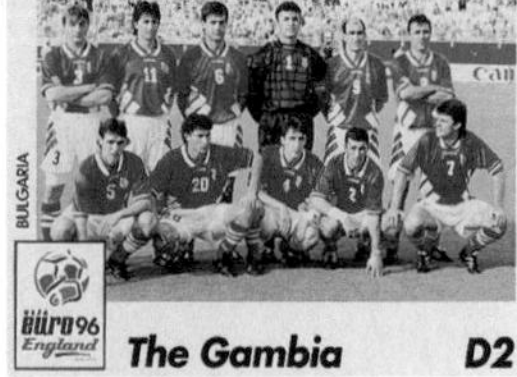

257 Bulgarian Team

1996. European Football Championship, England. Multicoloured.
2264 2d. Type **257** 45 45
2265 2d. Croatian team 45 45
2266 2d. Czech Republic team . . 45 45
2267 2d. Danish team 45 45
2268 2d. English team 45 45
2269 2d. French team 45 45
2270 2d. German team 45 45
2271 2d. Dutch team 45 45
2272 2d. Italian team 45 45
2273 2d. Portuguese team 45 45
2274 2d. Rumanian team 45 45
2275 2d. Russian team 45 45
2276 2d. Scottish team 45 45
2277 2d. Spanish team 45 45
2278 2d. Swiss team 45 45
2279 2d. Turkish team 45 45
MS2280 Sixteen sheets. (a) 115 × 85 mm. 25d. Danish team celebrating (43 × 28 mm). (b) 85 × 115 mm. 25d. Ruud Gullit (Netherlands) (28 × 43 mm). (c) 85 × 115 mm. 25d. Gary McAllister (Scotland) (28 × 43 mm). (d) 115 × 85 mm. 25d. Oleg Salenko (Russia) (28 × 43 mm). (e) 85 × 115 mm. 25d. Hami Mandirali (Turkey) (28 × 43 mm). (f) 85 × 115 mm. 25d. Hristo Stoitchkov (Bulgaria) (28 × 43 mm). (g) 115 × 85 mm. 25d. European Championship Trophy (28 × 43 mm). (h) 85 × 115 mm. 25d. Davor Suker (Croatia) (28 × 43 mm). (i) 115 × 85 mm. 25d. Jurgen Klinsmann (Germany) (43 × 28 mm). (j) 85 × 115 mm. 25d. Juan Goikoetxea (Spain) (28 × 43 mm). (k) 85 × 115 mm. 25d. Eusebio (Portugal) (28 × 43 mm). (l) 115 × 85 mm. 25d. Bryan Robson (England) (28 × 43 mm). (m) 85 × 115 mm. 25d. Roberto Baggio (Italy) (28 × 43 mm). (n) 85 × 115 mm. 25d. Christophe Ohrel (Switzerland) (28 × 43 mm). (o) 85 × 115 mm. 25d. Pavel Hapal (Czech Republic) (43 × 28 mm). (p) 85 × 115 mm. 25d. Gheorge Hagi (Rumania) (28 × 43 mm). P 14 Set of 16 sheets . . . . 65·00 65·00

258 Ray Ewry (U.S.A.) (standing high jump), 1912 **258a** Boy holding Shoes

1996. Olympic Games, Atlanta (2nd issue). Previous Gold Medal Winners. Multicoloured.
2281 1d. Type **258** 25 15
2282 2d. Fanny Durack (Australia) (100 m freestyle swimming), 1912 . . . . 35 20
2283 3d. Fu Mingxia (China) (platform diving), 1992 . . 40 45
2284 3d. H. Henkel (Germany) (high jump), 1992 . . . . 40 45
2285 3d. Spanish team (soccer), 1992 . . . . 40 45
2286 3d. Jackie Joyner-Kersee (U.S.A.) (heptathlon), 1988 and 1992 . . . . . 40 45
2287 3d. T. Gutsu (Russia) (gymnastics), 1992 . . . . 40 45
2288 3d. M. Johnson (U.S.A.) (400 m running), 1992 . . 40 45
2289 3d. Lin Li (China) (200 m medley swimming), 1992 . . . . 40 45
2290 3d. G. Devers (U.S.A.) (100 m running), 1992 . . 40 45
2291 3d. Michael Powell (U.S.A.) (long jump), 1992 . . . . 40 45
2292 3d. Japanese volleyball team, 1964 . . . . 40 45
2293 3d. Li Neng (China) (floor exercises), 1984 . . . . . 40 45
2294 3d. S. Bubka (U.S.S.R.) (pole vault), 1988 . . . . 40 45
2295 3d. Nadia Comaneci (Romania) (gymnastics), 1976 . . . . 40 45
2296 3d. Edwin Moses (U.S.A.) (400 m hurdles), 1984 . . 40 45
2297 3d. Victor Scherbo (Russia) (gymnastics), 1992 . . . . 40 45

2298 3d. Evelyn Ashford (U.S.A.) (100 m running), 1984 . . 40 45
2299 3d. Mohammed Ali (U.S.A.) (light heavyweight boxing), 1960 . . . . . . 40 45
2300 3d. Carl Lewis and C. Smith (U.S.A.) (400 m relay), 1984 . . . . 40 45
2301 5d. Stockholm Olympic arena, 1912 . . . . 70 75
2302 10d. Jim Thorpe (U.S.A.) (decathalon and pentathlon), 1912 . . . . 1·25 1·40
MS2303 Two sheets, each 100 × 70 mm. 25d. Michael Gross (Germany) (butterfly swimming), 1984 and 1988 (horiz). 25d. Ulrike Meyfarth (Germany) (high jump), 1972 and 1984 Set of 2 sheets 8·50 9·00

1996. 50th Anniv of UNICEF Multicoloured.
2304 63b. Type **258a** 15 15
2305 3d. Girl being inoculated . . 40 35
2306 8d. Boy holding ladle . . . 1·00 1·25
2307 10d. Child with blanket . . 1·25 1·40
MS2308 105 × 75 mm. 25d. Boy being inoculated (horiz) . . . 3·25 3·75

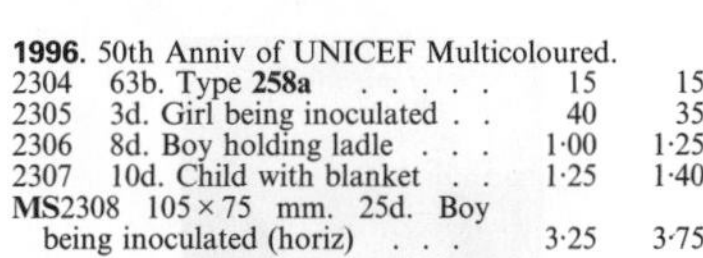

259 Roman Officer and Pillar of Absalom

1996. 3000th Anniv of Jerusalem. Multicoloured.
2309 1d.50 Type **259** 45 25
2310 2d. Turk and Gate of Mercy 50 30
2311 3d. Ancient Greek and Church of the Holy Sepulchre 60 40
2312 10d. Modern Hasidic Jew at Wailing Wall . . . . . . 1·75 1·75
MS2313 100 × 70 mm. 25d. City coat of arms (vert) . . . . 4·25 4·25

259a Glenn Miller

1996. Centenary of Radio. Entertainers. Mult.
2314 1d. Type **259a** 20 20
2315 4d. Louis Armstrong . . . 60 45
2316 5d. Nat "King" Cole . . . 70 75
2317 10d. The Andrew Sisters . . 1·25 1·50
MS2318 105 × 74 mm. 25d. President Truman . . . . 3·25 3·75
No. 2314 is inscribed "Glen Miller" in error.

260 Jacqueline Kennedy Onassis in Wedding Dress

1996. Famous People of the 20th Century. Multicoloured.
2319 5d. Type **260** 75 75
2320 5d. Jaqueline Kennedy and White House 75 75
2321 5d. Jaqueline Kennedy wearing pink hat 75 75
2322 5d. Jaqueline Kennedy and motor yacht 75 75
2323 5d. Jacqueline Kennedy wearing red jumper . . . 75 75
2324 5d. Jacqueline Kennedy and horse 75 75
2325 5d. Jacqueline Kennedy on book 75 75
2326 5d. Jacqueline Kennedy in blue dress and three rows of pearls 75 75
2327 5d. Jacqueline Kennedy and corner of fountain 75 75
2328 5d. President John Kennedy 75 75
2329 5d. Jacqueline Kennedy (inscr in capitals) 75 75
2330 5d. Willy Brandt 75 75
2331 5d. Marilyn Monroe 75 75
2332 5d. Mao Tse-tung 75 75
2333 5d. Sung Ching Ling . . . 75 75
2334 5d. Charles De Gaulle . . . 75 75
2335 5d. Marlene Dietrich . . . 75 75
MS2336 105 × 74 mm. 25d. Jacqueline Kennedy (different) 3·25 3·75
No. 2330 is inscr "WILLIE BRANDT", No. 2331 "MARYLYN MONROE" and No. 2332 "MAO TSE TONG", all in error.

261 Richard Petty's 1969 Ford

1996. Richard Petty (stock car driver) Commem. Multicoloured.
2337 5d. Type **261** 90 80
2338 5d. Richard Petty 90 80
2339 5d. Dodge Magnum, 1978 90 80
2340 5d. Pontiac, 1987 . . . . . 90 80
2341 5d. Pontiac, 1989 . . . . . 90 80
2342 5d. Dodge Daytona, 1975 90 80
MS2343 104 × 74 mm. 25d. Plymouth, 1972 (84 × 27 mm) 4·00 4·25

1996. Results of European Football Championship, England. As Nos. 2265/6, 2268, 2270, 2272, 2275 and **MS**2280 (d, h, i, l, m, o), but each additionally inscribed with date and match result. Multicoloured.
2344 2d. Croatian team ("23/6/96 Germany 2, Croatia 1") 45 45
2345 2d. Czech Republic team ("9/6/96 Germany 2, Czech Rep. 0") 45 45
2346 2d. English team ("26/6/96 Germany 6, England 5") 45 45
2347 2d. German team ("30/6/96 Germany 2, Czech Rep. 1") 45 45
2348 2d. Italian team ("19/6/96 Germany 0, Italy 0") . . 45 45
2349 2d. Russian team ("16/6/96 Germany 3, Russia 0") 45 45
MS2350 Six sheets. (a) 114 × 84 mm. 25d. Oleg Salenko (Russia) (28 × 43 mm) ("16/6/96 Germany 3, Russia 0"). (b) 84 × 114 mm. 25d. Davor Suker (Croatia) (28 × 43 mm) ("23/6/96 Germany 2, Croatia 1"). (c) 114 × 84 mm. 25d. Jurgen Klinsmann (Germany) (43 × 28 mm) ("Final 30/6/96 Germany 2, Czech Republic 1"). (d) 114 × 84 mm. 25d. Bryan Robson (England) (28 × 43 mm) ("26/6/96 Germany 6 England 5"). (e) 84 × 114 mm. 25d. Roberto Baggio (Italy) (28 × 43 mm) ("19/6/96 Germany 0 Italy 0"). (f) 84 × 114 mm. 25d. Pavel Hapal (Czech Rep) (43 × 28 mm) ("9/6/96 Germany 2 Czech Republic 0") Set of 6 sheets . . . . 24·00 26·00

262 Elvis Presley with Microphone **263** Bob Dylan

1996. Elvis Presley Commemoration. Different Portraits. Multicoloured.
2351 5d. Type **262** 90 90
2352 5d. In dinner jacket 90 90
2353 5d. In Mexican outfit . . . 90 90
2354 5d. Wearing blue jumper . . 90 90
2355 5d. In leather jacket 90 90
2356 5d. Wearing lei 90 90

1996. Rock and Roll Legends. Bob Dylan.
2357 **263** 5d. multicoloured . . . 1·25 1·00

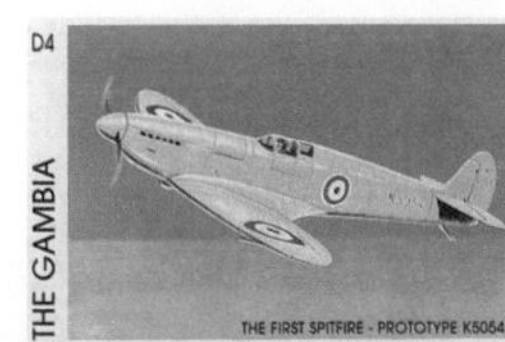

264 Supermarine Spitfire Prototype K5054

1996. 65th Anniv of Britain's Victory in Schneider Trophy Air Race. Multicoloured.
2358 4d. Type **264** 80 80
2359 4d. First production Spitfire K9787 . . . . 80 80
2360 4d. Spitfire Mk 1A in Battle of Britain 80 80
2361 4d. Spitfire LF Mk IXE with D-Day markings . . 80 80
2362 4d. Spitfire Mk XII (first with "Griffon" engine) . . 80 80
2363 4d. Spitfire Mk XIVC with jungle markings 80 80
2364 4d. Spitfire XIX of Royal Swedish Air Force . . . 80 80
2365 4d. Spitfire Mk XIX 80 80
2366 4d. Spitfire F Mk 22/24 (final variant) 80 80
2367 4d. Spitfire Mk XIX of Royal Swedish Air Force (from below) 80 80
2368 4d. Spitfire Mk VB of United States Army Air Corps 80 80
2369 4d. Spitfire Mk VC of French Air Force 80 80
2370 4d. Spitfire Mk VB of Soviet Air Force 80 80
2371 4d. Spitfire Mk IXE of Netherlands East Indies Air Force 80 80
2372 4d. Spitfire Mk IXE of Israeli Air Force 80 80
2373 4d. Spitfire Mk VIII of Royal Australian Air Force 80 80
2374 4d. Siptfire Mk VB of Turkish Air Force 80 80
2375 4d. Spitfire Mk XI of Royal Danish Air Force 80 80
MS2376 Two sheets, each 97 × 67 mm. (a) 25d. Supermarine S 6B S1595 seaplane taking off (42 × 29 mm). (b) 25d. Supermarine S 6B S1595 in flight (42 × 29 mm) Set of 2 sheets . . 9·00 9·00

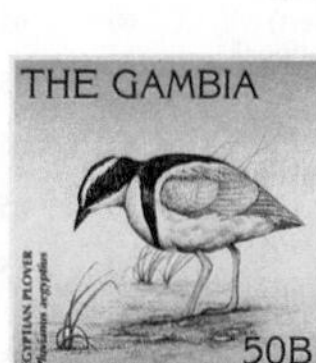

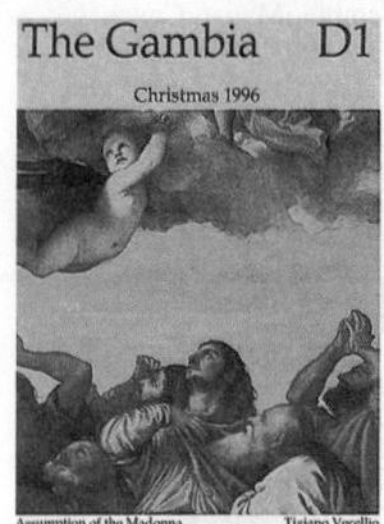

265 Egyptian Plover **266** Sylvester Stallone as Rocky Balboa

265a "Assumption of the Madonna" (detail)

1996. Birds. Multicoloured.
2377 50b. Type **265** 30 20
2378 63b. Painted-snipe 35 20
2379 75b. Golden-breasted bunting 35 20
2380 1d. Bateleur 40 25
2381 1d.50 Didric cuckoo 50 30
2382 2d. Turtle dove ("European Turtle Dove") 55 30
2383 3d. Village weaver 65 35
2384 4d. European roller 75 50
2385 5d. Cut-throat weaver ("Cut-throat") 80 60
2386 10d. Hoopoe . . . . 1·75 1·50
2387 15d. White-faced scops owl 2·00 2·00
2388 20d. Narina's trogon . . . 2·25 2·50
2389 25d. Lesser pied kingfisher 2·75 3·00
2390 30d. Common kestrel . . . 3·25 3·50
2391 40d. Temminck's courser 3·75 4·25
2392 50d. European bee eater 4·50 5·00
2392a 100d. Green-winged teal . . 8·00 9·50
No. 2388 is inscribed "TROGAN" in error.

1996. Christmas. Religious Paintings.
2393 **265a** 1d. multicoloured . . . 25 10
2394 – 1d.50 multicoloured . . 30 15
2395 – 2d. multicoloured . . . 35 20
2396 – 3d. multicoloured . . . 50 30
2397 – 10d. multicoloured . . 1·50 1·75
2398 – 15d. multicoloured . . 2·00 2·50
MS2399 Two sheets, each 76 × 106 mm. (a) 25d. deep brown, black and brown ("Adoration of the Magi" (Filippo Lippi)) (horiz). (b) 25d. red, black and rose ("Virgin and Child with Infant St. John" (Raphael)) Set of 2 sheets . . . . 7·50 8·50
DESIGNS: 1d.50 to 15d. Different details of "Assumption of the Madonna" (Tiziano Vecellio).
No. **MS**2399a is inscribed "Flippo Lippi" in error.

1996. 20th Anniv of *Rocky* (film). Sheet 143 × 182 mm.
MS2400 **266** 10d. × 3 multicoloured 4·25 4·50

267 Ox **268** "Arch 22" Monument

1997. Chinese New Year ("Year of the Ox").
2401 **267** 63b. multicoloured . . . 30 25
2402 – 75b. multicoloured . . . 30 25
2403 – 1d.50 multicoloured . . 50 35
2404 – 4d. multicoloured . . . 1·00 1·10
MS2405 84 × 68 mm. 3d. × 4. As Nos. 2401/4 . . . . 2·25 2·50
MS2406 76 × 106 mm. 10d. multicoloured (ox and sleeping peasant) ($39\frac{1}{2} \times 24\frac{1}{2}$mm) . . . . 1·60 1·75
DESIGNS: 75b. to 4d. Symbolic oxen.

1997. Economic Development. Multicoloured.
2407 63b. Type **268** 20 15
2408 1d. Tractor (horiz) 25 15
2409 1d.50 Man planting rice . . 30 20
2410 2d. As Type **268**, but with white panel at top 40 25
2411 3d. Model of Banjul International Airport terminal building (horiz) 75 60
2412 5d. Chamoi Bridge (horiz) 90 1·00
MS2413 Two sheets. (a) 106 × 76 mm. 20d. Workers in rice field (horiz). (b) 76 × 106 mm. 25d. As Type **268** Set of 2 sheets . . 7·00 8·00

269 Monkey King extinguishing Fire on Flame Mountain

1997. Mickey Mouse's Journey to the West. Disney cartoon characters. Multicoloured.
2414 2d. Type **269** 70 70
2415 2d. Demon Ox and Monkey King fighting 70 70
2416 2d. Mickey, Donald, Monkey King and Master San Tsang 70 70
2417 2d. Fighting the Spider Demon 70 70
2418 2d. Fighting the White Skeleton Demon 70 70
2419 2d. The real and the fake Monkey King 70 70
2420 3d. Monkey King trapped in furnace 70 70
2421 3d. Monkey King with magic weapon 70 70
2422 3d. Type **269** 70 70
2423 3d. At the Gate of South Heaven 70 70
2424 3d. Tasting the celestial peaches 70 70
2425 3d. Monkey King rescued from Five-Finger Mountain 70 70
MS2426 Four sheets, each 134 × 109 mm. (a) 5d. Mickey and Donald with Master San Tsang (vert). (b) 10d. Monkey King, Mickey and monkeys. (c) 10d. Monkey King, Mickey and tortoise (vert). (d) 15d. Mickey and Minnie with Buddhist scriptures Set of 4 sheets . . . 14·00 14·00

270 Jackie Chan

1997. "HONG KONG '97" International Stamp Exhibition. Jackie Chan (film star). Multicoloured.
2427 4d. Type **270** 75 75
2428 4d. Wearing red jacket . . . 75 75
2429 4d. In open-necked shirt . . 75 75
2430 4d. Bare-chested 75 75
2431 4d. Wearing black jacket . . 75 75
2432 4d. Wearing black and white spotted shirt 75 75
2433 4d. Wearing white T-shirt and red anorak 75 75
2434 4d. Wearing white sleeveless T-shirt 75 75
MS2435 76 × 106 mm. 25d. Jackie Chan in action (horiz) . . . . 4·50 4·75

271 Clouded Leopard

1997. Endangered Species. Multicoloured.
2436 1d.50 Type **271** 40 40
2437 1d.50 Audouin's gull 40 40
2438 1d.50 Leatherback turtle 40 40
2439 1d.50 White-eared pheasant 40 40
2440 1d.50 Kakapo 40 40
2441 1d.50 Right whale 40 40
2442 1d.50 Black-footed ferret 40 40
2443 1d.50 Dwarf lemur 40 40
2444 1d.50 Palawan peacock-pheasant ("Peacock-Pheasant") 40 40
2445 1d.50 Brown hyena 40 40
2446 1d.50 Cougar 40 40
2447 1d.50 Gharial 40 40
2448 1d.50 Monk seal 40 40
2449 1d.50 Mountain gorilla 40 40
2450 1d.50 Blyth's tragopan 40 40
2451 1d.50 Malayan tapir 40 40
2452 1d.50 Black rhinoceros 40 40
2453 1d.50 Polar bear 40 40
2454 1d.50 Red colobus 40 40
2455 1d.50 Tiger 40 40
2456 1d.50 Arabian oryx 40 40
2457 1d.50 Baiji 40 40
2458 1d.50 Ruffed lemur 40 40
2459 1d.50 California condor 40 40
2460 1d.50 Blue-headed quail dove 40 40
2461 1d.50 Numbat 40 40
2462 1d.50 Congo peafowl ("Congo Peacock") 40 40
2463 1d.50 White uakari 40 40
2464 1d.50 Eskimo curlew 40 40
2465 1d.50 Gouldian finch 40 40
2466 1d.50 Coelacanth 40 40
2467 1d.50 Toucan barbet 40 40
2468 1d.50 Snow leopard 40 40
2469 1d.50 Queen Alexandra's birdwing 40 40
2470 1d.50 Dalmatian pelican 40 40
2471 1d.50 Chaco tortoise 40 40
2472 1d.50 Mekong catfish 40 40
2473 1d.50 Helmeted hornbill 40 40
2474 1d.50 White-eyed river martin 40 40
2475 1d.50 Fluminense swallowtail 40 40
MS2476 Three sheets, each 103 × 72 mm. (a) 25d. Giant panda. (b) 25d. Humpback whale. (c) 25d. Manchurian crane ("Japanese Crane") Set of 3 sheets 13·00 13·00

272 Monkey

1997. "The Jungle Book" by Rudyard Kipling. Multicoloured.
2477 3d. Type **272** 60 60
2478 3d. Baloo (bear) 60 60
2479 3d. Elephant 60 60
2480 3d. Monkey and temple 60 60
2481 3d. Bagheera (panther) 60 60
2482 3d. Buffalo 60 60
2483 3d. Mandrill 60 60
2484 3d. Shere Khan (tiger) 60 60
2485 3d. Rama (wolf) 60 60
2486 3d. Kaa (cobra) 60 60
2487 3d. Mongoose 60 60
2488 3d. Mowgli 60 60
Nos. 2477/88 were printed together, se-tenant, with the backgrounds forming a composite design.

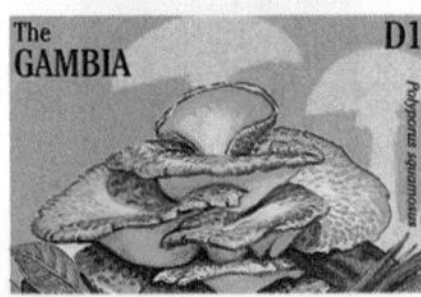

273 "Polyporus squamosus"

1997. Fungi. Multicoloured.
2489 1d. Type **273** 35 25
2490 3d. "Armillaria tabescens" 65 40
2491 4d. "Amanita caesarea" (vert) 75 80
2492 4d. "Lepiota procera" (vert) 75 80
2493 4d. "Hygrophorus psittacinus" (vert) 75 80
2494 4d. "Russula xerampelina" (vert) 75 80
2495 4d. "Laccaria amethystina" (vert) 75 80
2496 4d. "Coprinus micaceus" (vert) 75 80
2497 4d. "Boletus edulis" (vert) 75 80
2498 4d. "Morchella esculenta" (vert) 75 80
2499 4d. "Otidea auricula" (vert) 75 80
2500 5d. "Collybia velutipes" 85 85
2501 10d. "Sarcoscypha coccinea" 1·40 1·50
MS2502 76 × 106 mm. 25d. "Volvariella bombycina" 5·50 5·50

273a Cloister, Horyu-ji, Japan

1997. 50th Anniv of UNESCO Multicoloured.
2503 1d. Type **273a** 30 25
2504 2d. Great Wall, China 50 35
2505 3d. Statues, Ayutthaya, Thailand 55 40
2506 4d. Ascension Convent, Santa Maria, Philippines 60 65
2507 4d. Mount Nimba Nature Reserve, Guinea (vert) 60 65
2508 4d. Banc d'Argun National Park, Mauritania (vert) 60 65
2509 4d. Doorway, Marrakesh, Morocco (vert) 60 65
2510 4d. Ichkeul National Park, Tunisia (vert) 60 65
2511 4d. Village pottery, Mali (vert) 60 65
2512 4d. Hippopotamus, Salonga National Park, Zaire (vert) 60 65
2513 4d. Timgad Roman Ruins, Algeria (vert) 60 65
2514 4d. Wooden statue, Benin (vert) 60 65
2515 4d. Temple, Magao Caves, China (vert) 60 65
2516 4d. Statue, Magao Caves (vert) 60 65
2517 4d. Domes, Magao Caves (vert) 60 65
2518 4d. Great Wall from air, China (vert) 60 65
2519 4d. Statue, Great Wall (vert) 60 65
2520 4d. Bronze Bird, Imperial Palace, China (vert) 60 65
2521 4d. Temples, Imperial Palace, China (vert) 60 65
2522 4d. Dragon statue, Imperial Palace (vert) 60 65
2523 4d. Kyoto Gardens, Japan (vert) 60 65
2524 4d. Himeji Castle, Japan (vert) 60 65
2525 4d. Horyu-ji Temple, Japan (vert) 60 65
2526 4d. Buddha, Horyu-ji, Japan (vert) 60 65
2527 4d. Yakushima Forest, Japan (vert) 60 65
2528 4d. Ancient tree, Yakushima Forest, Japan (vert) 60 65
2529 4d. Temple, Kyoto, Japan (vert) 60 65
2530 4d. Pavilion, Kyoto, Japan (vert) 60 65
2531 5d. Riverside houses, Inselstadt, Germany 70 75
2532 5d. Rosaleda Gardens, Bamberg, Germany 70 75
2533 5d. Bamberg Cathedral, Germany 70 75
2534 5d. Timbered house, Maulbronn, Germany 70 75
2535 5d. Maulbronn Monastry, Germany 70 75
2536 5d. Ruins at Delphi, Greece 70 75
2537 5d. Rhodes waterfront, Greece 70 75
2538 5d. Knights' Hospital, Rhodes, Greece 70 75
2539 5d. Temple, Delphi, Greece 70 75
2540 5d. Delphi from air, Greece 70 75
2541 5d. Foliage, Shirakami-Sanchi, Japan 70 75
2542 5d. Notice board, Shirakami-Sanchi, Japan 70 75
2543 5d. Tower, Himeji Castle, Japan 70 75
2544 5d. Roof tops, Himeji Castle, Japan 70 75
2545 5d. Gateway, Himeji Castle, Japan 70 75
2546 10d. Komodo Dragons, Indonesia 1·40 1·50
2547 15d. Ancient hut, Timbuktu, Mali 1·90 2·25
MS2548 Four sheets, each 127 × 102 mm. (a) 25d. Plitvice Lakes National Park, Croatia. (b) 25d. Ruins of Kilwa Kisiwani, Tanzania. (c) 25d. Santa Maria de Alcobaca cloisters, Portugal. (d) 25d. Watergarden, Kyoto, Japan Set of 4 sheets 13·00 14·00

274 Minnie Mouse, 1928

1997. Minnie Mouse Through the Years. Designs showing Disney cartoon character in years stated. Multicoloured.
2549 4d. Type **274** 1·00 1·00
2550 4d. In 1933 1·00 1·00
2551 4d. In 1934 1·00 1·00
2552 4d. In 1937 1·00 1·00
2553 4d. In 1938 1·00 1·00
2554 4d. In 1941 1·00 1·00
2555 4d. In 1950 1·00 1·00
2556 4d. In 1990 1·00 1·00
2557 4d. In 1997 1·00 1·00
MS2558 133 × 108 mm. 25d. In 1987 6·50 7·00

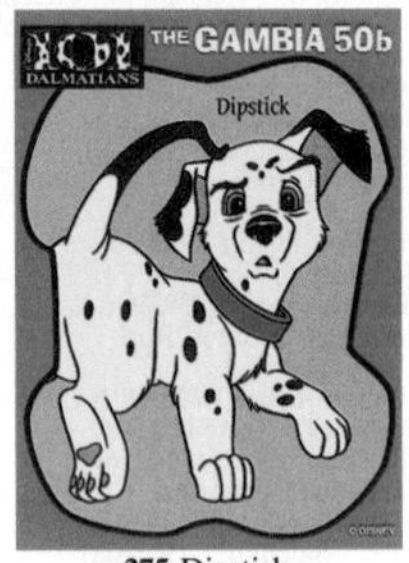

275 Dipstick

1997. "101 Dalmatians". Disney cartoon characters. Multicoloured.
2559 50b. Type **275** 55 55
2560 50b. Fidget 55 55
2561 50b. Jewel 55 55
2562 50b. Lucky 55 55
2563 50b. Two-Tone 55 55
2564 50b. Wizzer 55 55
2565 2d. Two puppies playing (horiz) 55 55
2566 2d. Puppy and pig (horiz) 55 55
2567 2d. Two puppies with butterfly (horiz) 55 55
2568 2d. Puppy lying on back (horiz) 55 55
2569 2d. Puppy with ball (horiz) 55 55
2570 2d. Puppy with bone (horiz) 55 55
2571 2d. One puppy pulling another puppy's tail (horiz) 55 55
2572 2d. Two puppies pulling third puppy's ears (horiz) 55 55
2573 2d. Puppy with teddy bear (horiz) 55 55
2574 3d. Puppy asleep on biscuit box (horiz) 55 55
2575 3d. Puppy with hose (horiz) 55 55
2576 3d. Puppy and bottle (horiz) 55 55
2577 3d. Puppy and biscuit bowl (horiz) 55 55
2578 3d. Puppy wearing hat (horiz) 55 55
2579 3d. Three puppies with lipstick (horiz) 55 55
2580 3d. Puppy tying another up with string (horiz) 55 55
2581 3d. Two puppies and lunch box (horiz) 55 55
2582 3d. Three puppies and computer (horiz) 55 55
MS2583 Six sheets, each 127 × 103 mm. (a) 25d. Sheep and puppies (horiz). (b) 25d. Cruella de Vil (horiz). (c) 25d. Puppy looking at photograph (horiz). (d) 25d. Puppies in mail sack. (e) 25d. Two puppies covered in paint (horiz). (f) 25d. Two puppies playing computer game (horiz) Set of 6 sheets 30·00 30·00

276 Juventus Team, 1897

1997. Centenary of Juventus Football Team. Multicoloured.
2584 5d. Type **276** 80 80
2585 5d. Centenary emblem and player 80 80
2586 5d. Giampiero Boniperti 80 80
2587 5d. Roberto Bettega 80 80
2588 5d. Juventus team, 1996 80 80
2589 5d. Juventus '97 logo 80 80

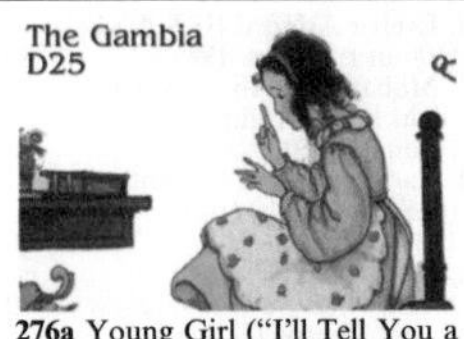

276a Young Girl ("I'll Tell You a Story")

1997. 300th Anniv of Mother Goose Nursery Rhymes. Sheet 72 × 102 mm.
MS2590 **276a** 25d. multicoloured 3·75 4·00

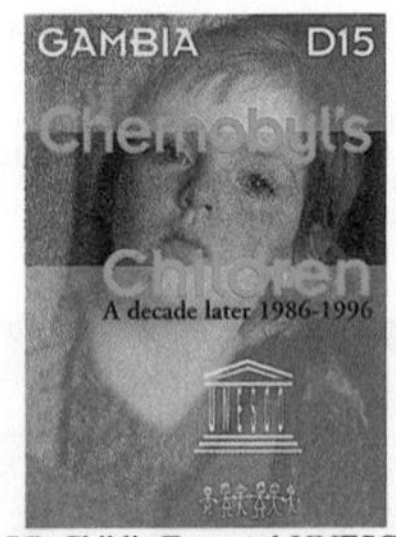

276b Child's Face and UNESCO Emblem

1997. 10th Anniv of Chernobyl Nuclear Disaster. Multicoloured.
2591 15d. Type **276b** 1·90 2·25
2592 15d. As No. 2591 but inscribed "CHABAD'S CHILDREN OF CHERNOBYL" 1·90 2·25

276c Rotary President Sydney Pascall planting Tree of Friendship

1997. 50th Death Anniv of Paul Harris (founder of Rotary International).
2593 10d. Type **276c** 1·40 1·75
MS2594 78 × 108 mm. 25d. Paul Harris and Preserve Planet Earth emblem 3·25 3·75

276d Queen Elizabeth II

1997. Golden Wedding of Queen Elizabeth and Prince Philip. Multicoloured.
2595 4d. Type **276d** 80 80
2596 4d. Royal coat of arms 80 80
2597 4d. Queen Elizabeth and Prince Philip applauding 80 80
2598 4d. Queen Elizabeth and Prince Philip taking the salute 80 80
2599 4d. Royal Yacht "Britannia" 80 80
2600 4d. Prince Philip 80 80
MS2601 100 × 70 mm. 20d. Princess Elizabeth, 1948 4·00 4·25

276e Von Stephan and Otto von Bismarck

1997. "Pacific '97" International Stamp Exhibition, San Francisco. Death Centenary of Henrich von Stephan (founder of UPU).
2602 **276e** 5d. mauve 90 1·00
2603 – 5d. brown 90 1·00
2604 – 5d. green and black 90 1·00
MS2605 82 × 118 mm. 25d. green and black 4·25 4·75
DESIGNS: Nos. 2603, Von Stephan and Mercury; 2604, Mail wagon, Boston, 1900; **MS**2605, Von Stephan and Hamburg–Lubeck postilion.

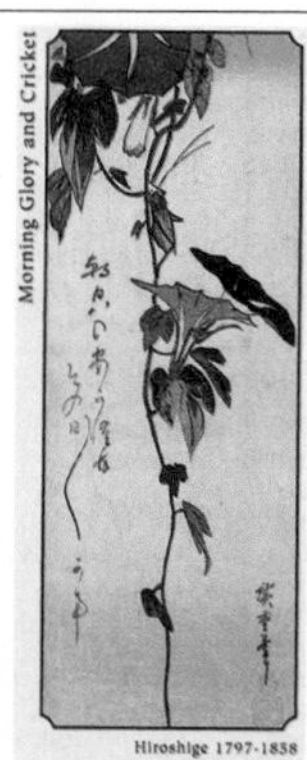

277 "Morning Glory and Cricket"

1997. Birth Bicentenary of Hiroshige (Japanese painter). Multicoloured.
2606/11 4d. × 6 (Type **277**: "Dragonfly and Begonia"; "Two Ducks swimming among Reeds"; "A Black-naped Oriole perched on a Stem of Rose Mallow"; "A Pheasant on a Snow-covered Pine"; "A Cuckoo flying through the Rain") . . . . . .
2612/17 4d. × 6 ("An Egret among Rushes"; "Peacock and Peonies"; "Three Wild Geese flying across the Moon"; "A Cock in the Snow"; "A Pheasant and Bracken"; "Peonies") . . . . . .
2618/23 4d. × 6 ("Sparrow and Bamboo"; "Mandarin Ducks on an Icy Pond with Brown Leaves falling"; "Blossoming Plum Tree"; "Java Sparrow and Magnolia"; "Chinese Bellflowers and Miscanthus"; "A Small Black Bird clinging to a Tendril of Ivy") . . .
2624/9 5d. × 6 ("Sparrows and Camellia in Snow"; "Parrot on a Branch of Pine"; "A Long-tailed Blue Bird on a Branch of Flowering Plum"; "Sparrow and Bamboo"; "Bird in a Tree"; "A Wild Duck swimming beneath Snow-laden reeds") . .
2630/5 5d. × 6 ("Kingfisher above a Yellow-flowered Water Plant"; "Wagtail and Roses"; "A Mandarin Duck on a Snowy Bank"; "A Japanese White-eye on a Persimmon Branch"; "Sparrows and Camellia in Snow"; "Kingfisher and Moon above a Yellow-flowered Water Plant")
2636/41 5d. × 6 ("Sparrow and Bamboo by Night"; "Birds Flying over Waves"; "Blossoming Plum Tree with Full Moon"; "Kingfisher and Iris"; "A Blue-and-White Flycatcher on a Hibiscus Flower"; "Mandarin Ducks in Snowfall") . . . . . .
2606/41 Set of 35 . . . . 26·00 27·00
MS2642 Six sheets, each 95 × 120 mm. (a) 25d. Hawk on perch. (b) 25d. Two green birds on branch. (c) 25d. Kingfisher hovering. (d) 25d."Three Wild Geese flying across moon". (e) 25d. Red parrot on branch. (f) 25d. White bird on flowering bush Set of 6 sheets . . . . 35·00 38·00

277a Grandma's Cottage

1997. 175th Anniv of Brothers Grimm's Third Collection of Fairy Tales. Little Red Riding Hood. Multicoloured.
2643 10d. Type **277a** . . . . . 1·75 1·90
2644 10d. Little Red Riding Hood . . . . 1·75 1·90
2645 10d. The Wolf . . . . . . 1·75 1·90
MS2646 126 × 96 mm. 10d. Little Red Riding Hood (horiz) . . . 2·25 2·50

278 Coelophysis chasing Ornitholestes

1997. Dinosaurs. Multicoloured.
2647 50b. Type **278** 30 20
2648 63b. Spinosaurus 35 20
2649 75b. Kentrosaurs 40 25
2650 1d. Ceratosaurus 40 25
2651 1d.50 Stygimoloch 50 35
2652 2d. Troodon 60 35
2653 3d. Velociraptor 70 45
2654 4d. Triceratops 80 80
2655 4d. Anurognathus 80 80
2656 4d. Pteranodon 80 80
2657 4d. Pterosaurus 80 80
2658 4d. Saltasaurus 80 80
2659 4d. Agathaumus 80 80
2660 4d. Stegosaurus 80 80
2661 4d. Albertosaurus libratus 80 80
2662 4d. Three Lesothosauruses running 80 80
2663 4d. Five Lesothosauruses running 80 80
2664 4d. Tarbosaurus bataar . . 80 80
2665 4d. Brachiosaurus 80 80
2666 4d. Styracosasaurus 80 80
2667 4d. Baryonyx 80 80
2668 4d. Coelophysis 80 80
2669 4d. Carnotaurus 80 80
2670 4d. Compsognathus longipes 80 80
2671 4d. Compsognathus "Elegant Jaw" 80 80
2672 4d. Stenonychosaurus . . . 80 80
2673 4d. Protoceratops 80 80
2674 10d. Ornithomimus . . . . 1·50 1·50
2675 15d. Stegosaurus . . . . . 1·90 2·25
2676 20d. Ankylosaurus saichania 2·25 2·50
MS2677 Two sheets, each 106 × 81 mm. (a) 25d. Head of Deinonychus (50 × 37 mm). (b) 25d. Seismosaurus (88 × 27 mm) Set of 2 sheets . . . . 9·00 10·00
Nos. 2655/63 and 2664/72 respectively were printed together, se-tenant, with the backgrounds forming composite designs.

279 Margaret Thatcher and Deng Xiaoping toasting Joint Declaration, 1984

1997. Return of Hong Kong to China. Multicoloured.
2678 3d. Type **279** 60 60
2679 3d. Signing Joint Declaration on Hong Kong, 1984 . . . . . . 60 60
2680 3d. Signing Joint Declaration on Macao, 1987 . . . . 60 60
2681 3d. Deng Xiaoping toasting Prime Minister Anibal Silva of Portugal 60 60
2682 4d. Hong Kong in 1843 and Governor Sir Henry Pottinger 75 75
2683 4d. Kowloon in 1860 and Governor Sir Hercules Robinson 75 75
2684 4d. Reception in New Territories, 1898, and Governor Sir Henry Blake 75 75
2685 5d. Governor Sir Henry Pottinger and British warship 85 85
2686 5d. Governor Christopher Patten and Lantau Bridge 85 85
2687 5d. Chief Executive C. H. Tung and Hong Kong by night 85 85
2688 6d. Signing the Treaty of Nanking, 1842 . . . . . 1·00 1·10
2689 6d. Signing the Japanese Surrender of Hong Kong, 1945 . . . . 1·00 1·10
2690 6d. Signing of the Sino-British Joint Declaration, 1984 . . . . 1·00 1·10

280 Great Mosque, Samarra, Iran

1997. Natural and Man-made Wonders of the World. Multicoloured.
2691 63b. Type **280** 40 20
2692 75b. Moai statues, Easter Island (horiz) 50 20
2693 1d. Golden Gate Bridge, San Francisco (horiz) . . 50 20
2694 1d.50 The Statue of Liberty, New York 50 25
2695 2d. The Parthenon, Athens (horiz) 50 30
2696 3d. Pyramid of the Sun, Mexico (horiz) 60 40
2697 5d. The Rock of Gibraltar (horiz) . . . . 80 1·00
2698 5d. St. Peter's Basilica, Rome (horiz) . . . . . 1·00 1·00
2699 5d. Santa Sophia, Istanbul (horiz) . . . . 80 1·00
2700 5d. "Gateway to the West" monument, St. Louis (horiz) . . . . 80 1·00
2701 5d. Great Wall of China (horiz) . . . . 80 1·00
2702 5d. City of Carcassonne, France (horiz) . . . . . 80 1·00
2703 5d. Stonehenge, England (horiz) . . . . 1·00 1·00
2704 5d. Hughes HK-1 "Spruce Goose" flying boat (World's largest aircraft) (horiz) . . . . 1·00 1·00
2705 5d. Hoverspeed "Seacat" catamaran (fastest Atlantic crossing by a commercial catamaran) (horiz) . . . . 1·00 1·00
2706 5d. "Thrust 2" car (official land speed record) (horiz) 1·00 1·00
2707 5d. Stepped Pyramid, Egypt (horiz) . . . . 1·00 1·00
2708 5d. L.N.E.R. Clas A4 "Mallard" (fastest steam locomotive), 1938 (horiz) 1·00 1·00
MS2709 Three sheets, each 98 × 68 mm. (a) 5d. Mount Everest (42 × 28 mm). (b) 25d. The Grand Canyon, Colorado (42 × 28 mm). (c) 25d. Washington Monument (33 × 51 mm) Set of 3 sheets . . 12·00 13·00
No. 2702 is inscribed "CARCASSONNNE" in error.

281 Downhill Skiing

1997. Winter Olympic Games, Nagano (1998). Multicoloured.
2710 5d. Type **281** 90 90
2711 5d. Two-man bobsleigh (vert) 90 90
2712 5d. Freestyle skiing (vert) . . 90 90
2713 5d. Speed skating (vert) . . 90 90
2714 5d. Slalom skiing (No. 8 on bib) (vert) 90 90
2715 5d. Womens figure skating (vert) 90 90
2716 5d. Downhill skiing (No. 4 on bib) (vert) 90 90
2717 5d. Pairs figure skating (vert) 90 90
2718 5d. Cross-country (vert) . . 90 90
2719 5d. Ski jumping (vert) . . . 90 90
2720 5d. One-man luge 90 90
2721 5d. Ice hockey 90 90
2722 5d. Four-man bobsleigh . . 90 90
2723 5d. Ski-jumping 90 90
2724 5d. Curling 90 90
2725 5d. Figure skating 90 90
2726 5d. Speed skating 90 90
2727 5d. Biathlon 90 90
2728 5d. Downhill skiing (different) 90 90
2729 10d. One-man luge . . . . 1·60 1·75
2730 15d. Speed skating . . . . 2·25 2·50
2731 20d. Ice hockey . . . . . . 3·00 3·25
MS2732 Two sheets. (a) 97 × 67 mm. 25d. Bobsleigh. (b) 67 × 97 mm. 25d. Pairs figure skating (vert) Set of 2 sheets . . . . 9·50 10·00

282 Brown Pelican

1997. Sea Birds. Multicoloured.
2733 3d. Type **282** 85 85
2734 3d. Galapagos penguin . . . 85 85
2735 3d. Red-billed tropic bird 85 85
2736 3d. Little tern 85 85
2737 3d. Dunlin 85 85
2738 3d. Black-legged kittiwake 85 85
2739 3d. Atlantic puffin 85 85
2740 3d. Wandering albatross . . 85 85
2741 3d. Blue-faced booby ("Masked Booby") . . . 85 85
2742 3d. Glaucous-winged gull . . 85 85
2743 3d. Arctic tern 85 85
2744 3d. Piping plover 85 85
2745 5d. Roseate tern . . . . . 1·00 1·00
2746 10d. Red-legged cormorant 1·50 1·60
2747 15d. Blue-footed booby . . 2·25 2·50
2748 20d. Sanderling . . . . . . 2·50 2·75
MS2749 Two sheets, each 106 × 76 mm. (a) 23d. Long-tailed skua (vert). (b) 23d. Osprey (vert) Set of 2 sheets . . . . . . 7·50 8·00
No. 2743 is inscribed "ARTIC TERN" and the captions on Nos. 2745/6 are transposed, both in error.

283 Scottish Fold Cat

1997. Cats and Dogs. Multicoloured.
2750 63b. Type **283** 30 20
2751 75b. Dalmatian 35 20
2752 1d. Rottweiler 35 20
2753 1d.50 American curl cat . . 45 25
2754 2d. British bi-colour cat . . 50 25
2755 3d. Newfoundland 60 35
2756 3d. Devon Rex cat 60 35
2757 4d. Great Dane 75 50
2758 5d. Burmilla cat 85 85
2759 5d. Blue Burmese cat . . . 85 85
2760 5d. Korat cat 85 85
2761 5d. British tabby cat 85 85
2762 5d. Foreign white cat . . . 85 85
2763 5d. Somali cat 85 85
2764 5d. Akita 85 85
2765 5d. Welsh corgi 85 85
2766 5d. German shepherd . . . 85 85
2767 5d. Saint Bernard 85 85
2768 5d. Bullmastiff 85 85
2769 5d. Malamute 85 85
2770 6d. Silver tabby cat 95 95
2771 10d. Old English sheepdog 1·40 1·50
2772 15d. Queensland heeler . . . 1·90 2·25
2773 20d. Abyssinian cat . . . . 2·25 2·50
MS2774 Four sheets, each 107 × 78 mm. (a) 25d. Cornish Rex cat. (b) 25d. Siamese cat. (c) 25d. Boxer. (d) Dobermann pinscher Set of 4 sheets . . . . 17·00 17·00

283a Uruguay Team, 1950

1997. World Cup Football Championship, France (1998).
2775 **283a** 1d. black 40 20
2776 – 1d.50 black . . . 50 25
2777 – 2d. black 55 30
2778 – 3d. black 70 40
2779/86 – 4d. × 8 mult or brown (Nos. 2782/3) 5·00
2787/94 – 4d. × 8 mult or black (No. 2788) 5·00
2795/2802 – 4d. × 8 brown (Nos. 2795/6, 2800 and 2802) or mult . . . . 5·00
2803/10 – 4d. × 8 mult . . . 5·00
2811 – 5d. black 80 80
2812 – 10d. black . . . . 1·40 1·50
MS2813 Four sheets, each 102 × 127 mm. (a) 25d. multicoloured. (b) 25d. multicoloured. (c) 25d. black. (d) 25d. brown Set of 4 sheets . . 17·00 17·00
DESIGNS—HORIZ: No. 2776, West German team, 1954; 2777, Brazilian team, 1970; 2778, Brazilian team, 1962; 2779, Brazilian team, 1994; 2780, Argentine team, 1986; 2781, Brazilian team, 1970; 2782, Italian team, 1934; 2783, Uruguay team, 1958; 2784, English team, 1966; 2785, Brazilian team, 1962; 2786, West German team, 1990; 2787, Mario Kempes, Argentina (1978); 2788, Joseph Gaetjens, U.S.A. (1950) (inscr "ADEMIR BRAZIL" in error); 2789, Muller, West Germany (1970); 2790, Lineker, England (1986); 2791, Eusebio, Portugal (1966); 2792, Schillaci, Italy (1990); 2793, Lato, Poland (1974); 2794, Rossi, Italy (1982); 2811, Italian team, 1938; 2812, Uruguay team, 1930; **MS**2813a, Philippe Albert, Belgium; **MS**2813b, Juninho, Brazil; **MS**2813c, Eusebio, Portugal; **MS**2813d, Pele, Brazil. VERT:

No. 2795, Moore, England (1966); 2796, Fritzwalter, West Germany (1954); 2797, Beckenbauer, West Germany (1974); 2798, Zoff, Italy (1982); 2799, Maradona, Argentina (1986); 2800, Passarella, Argentina (1978); 2801, Matthaus, West Germany (1990); 2802, Dunga, Brazil (1994); 2803, Kinkladze, Georgia; 2804, Shearer, England; 2805, Dani, Portugal; 2806, Weah, Portugal; 2807, Ravanelli, Italy; 2808, Raducioiu, Rumania; 2809, Schmeichel, Denmark; 2810, Bergkamp, Holland.

284 Diana, Princess of Wales **285** Tiger

284a "Angel" (Rembrandt)

1997. Diana, Princess of Wales Commemoration. Each brown and black.

2814 10d. Type **284** . . . . . . 1·50 1·60
2815 10d. Wearing open-necked shirt . . . . 1·50 1·60
2816 10d. Wearing polo-neck jumper . . . . 1·50 1·60
2817 10d. Wearing diamond-drop earrings . . . . 1·50 1·60
MS2818 76 × 106 mm. 25d. Diana, Princess of Wales (multicoloured) 4·25 4·50

1997. Christmas. Paintings. Multicoloured.

2819 1d. Type **284a** 40 15
2820 1d.50 "Initiation into the Rites of Dionysus" at Villa dei Misteri 50 15
2821 2d. "Pair of Erotes with Purple Cloaks" 65 20
2822 3d. "The Ecstasy of Saint Theresa" (Gianlorenzo Bernini) 80 35
2823 5d. "Virgin and Child with Angels" (Matthias Grunewald) . . . . . . 1·00 90
2824 10d. "Angel playing the Organ" (Stefan Lochner) 1·75 2·25
MS2825 Two sheets, each 105 × 95 mm. (a) 25d. "The Rest on the Flight into Egypt" (Caravaggio). (b) 25d. "The Education of Cupid" (Titian) Set of 2 sheets . . . . 8·00 9·00

No. **MS**2825a is inscribed "THE REST OF THE FLIGHT INTO EGYPT" and No. **MS**2825b "TITAN", both in error.

1998. Chinese New Year ("Year of the Tiger"). Multicoloured.

2826 3d. Type **285** ("GAMBIA" in green) 15 20
2827 3d. Tiger ("GAMBIA" in mauve) 15 20
2828 3d. Tiger ("GAMBIA" in lilac) 15 20
2829 3d. Tiger ("GAMBIA" in blue) 15 20
MS2830 73 × 100 mm. 10d. Tiger (42 × 28 mm) 55 60

286 Class 91 Electric Train, Great Britian

1998. Trains of the World. Multicoloured.

2831 5d. Type **286** 25 30
2832 5d. Class 26 steam locomotive No. 3450 "Red Devil", South Africa 25 30
2833 5d. TGV express train, France 25 30
2834 5d. People Mover railcar, Great Britain 25 30
2835 5d. ICE high speed train, Germany 25 30
2836 5d. Montmartre funicular car, France 25 30
2837 5d. Burlington Northern SD70 diesel locomotive No. 9716, U.S.A. 25 30
2838 5d. L.N.E.R. Class A4 steam locomotive "Mallard", 1938 . . . . 25 30
2839 5d. Baldwin steam locomotive, Peru 25 30
2840 5d. Amtrak Class ARM-7 electric locomotive, U.S.A. 25 30
2841 5d. Rack steam locomotive No. B2503, Amberawa, Java 25 30
2842 5d. Beyer-Peacock steam locomotive No. 3108, Pakistan 25 30
MS2843 Two sheets, each 84 × 110 mm. (a) 25d. Futuristic monorail train, Great Britain. (b) 25d. Southern Pacific GS4 streamlined steam locomotive, U.S.A. Set of 2 sheets . . . . 2·75 3·00

No. 2832 is inscribed "BEACONSFIELD CHINA", No. 2836 "MOUNTMAETRE FUNICULAR" and No. 2840 "SWEDEN RAIL 125 MPH", all in error.

287 Yellow Orchid **289** Mulan

288 Wright "Flyer I", 1903

1998. African Flowers. Multicoloured.

2844 75b. Type **287** 10 10
2845 1d.50 Transvaal daisy . . . 10 15
2846 3d. Torch lily 15 20
2847 4d. "Ancistrochilus rothschildianus" 20 25
2848 5d. "Adenium multiflorum" (horiz) 25 30
2849 5d. "Huernia namaquensis" (horiz) 25 30
2850 5d. "Gloriosa superba" (horiz) 25 30
2851 5d. "Strelitzia reginae" (horiz) 25 30
2852 5d. "Passiflora mollissima" (horiz) 25 30
2853 5d. "Bauhinia variegata" (horiz) 25 30
2854 10d. "Polystachya vulcanica" 55 60
2855 15d. Gladiolus 80 85
MS2856 Two sheets, each 106 × 76 mm. (a) 25d. "Aerangis rhodosticta". (b) 25d. "Ansella gigantea" Set of 2 sheets . . . 2·75 3·00

Nos. 2848/53 were printed together, se-tenant, forming a composite background design.

1998. History of Aviation. Multicoloured.

2857 5d. Type **288** 25 30
2858 5d. Curtiss A-1 seaplane, 1910 . . . . 25 30
2859 5d. Farman biplane, 1907 25 30
2860 5d. Bristol monoplane, 1911 25 30
2861 5d. Antoinette IV, 1908 . . 25 30
2862 5d. Sopwith "Bat Boat" amphibian, 1912 . . . . 25 30
2863 5d. Short Type 38, 1913 . . 25 30
2864 5d. Fokker F.VIIb/3m, 1925 25 30
2865 5d. Junkers J.13, 1919 . . . 25 30
2866 5d. Pitcairn "Mailwing", 1927 . . . . 25 30
2867 5d. Douglas, 1920 . . . . . 25 30
2868 5d. Curtiss T-32 Condor II airliner, 1934 . . . . . 25 30
MS2869 Two sheets, each 106 × 76 mm. (a) 25d. Albatross, 1913 (84 × 28 mm). (b) 25d. Boeing 247 airliner, 1932 (84 × 28 mm) Set of 2 sheets . . . . 2·75 3·00

Nos. 2857/62 and 2863/8 respectively were printed together, se-tenant, forming composite background designs.

No. 2857 is dated "1902" in error.

1998. "Mulan" (film). Multicoloured.

2870 4d. Type **289** . . . . . . 1·10 1·10
2871 4d. Mushu . . . . 1·10 1·10
2872 4d. Little Brother . . . . . 1·10 1·10
2873 4d. Cri-kee . . . . 1·10 1·10
2874 4d. Grandmother Fa . . . . 1·10 1·10
2875 4d. Fa Li . . . . 1·10 1·10
2876 4d. Fa Zhou . . . . 1·10 1·10
2877 4d. Mulan and Khan . . . 1·10 1·10
2878 5d. Mulan riding Khan . . 1·10 1·10
2879 5d. Shang . . . . 1·10 1·10
2880 5d. Chi-fu . . . . 1·10 1·10
2881 5d. Chien-po . . . . 1·10 1·10
2882 5d. Yao . . . . 1·10 1·10
2883 5d. Ling . . . . 1·10 1·10
2884 5d. Shan-yu . . . . 1·10 1·10
2885 5d. Mulan, Shang and Mushu . . . . 1·10 1·10
MS2886 Four sheets. (a) 102 × 127 mm. 25d. Mulan and Khan. (b) 127 × 102 mm. 25d. Mulan and firework. (c) 127 × 102 mm. 25d. Mulan in front of house. (d) 127 × 102 mm. 25d. Mulan performing karate kick Set of 4 sheets . . . . 20·00 22·00

289a Sidney Bechet

1998. Millennium Series. Famous People of the Twentieth Century. Multicoloured. (a) Famous Jazz Musicians.

2887 4d. Type **289a** 20 25
2888 4d. Sidney Bechet playing saxophone (53 × 38 mm) 20 25
2889 4d. Duke Ellington conducting (53 × 38 mm) 20 25
2890 4d. Duke Ellington 20 25
2891 4d. Louis Armstrong . . . 20 25
2892 4d. Louis Armstrong playing trumpet (53 × 38 mm) 20 25
2893 4d. Charlie "Bird" Parker playing saxophone (53 × 38 mm) 20 25
2894 4d. Charlie "Bird" Parker 20 25

(b) Famous Theatrical Composers.

2895 4d. Cole Porter 20 25
2896 4d. "Born to Dance" (Cole Porter) (53 × 38 mm) . . . 20 25
2897 4d. "Porgy and Bess" (George Gershwin) (53 × 38 mm) 20 25
2898 4d. George Gershwin . . . 20 25
2899 4d. Rogers and Hammerstein 20 25
2900 4d. "The King and I" (Rogers and Hammerstein) (53 × 38 mm) 20 25
2901 4d. "West Side Story" (Leonard Bernstein) (53 × 38 mm) 20 25
2902 4d. Leonard Bernstein . . . 20 25
MS2903 Two sheets, each 76 × 106 mm. (a) 25d. Ella Fitzgerald. (b) 25d. "Oh How I Hate to Get Up in the Morning" (Irving Berlin) Set of 2 sheets 2·75 3·00

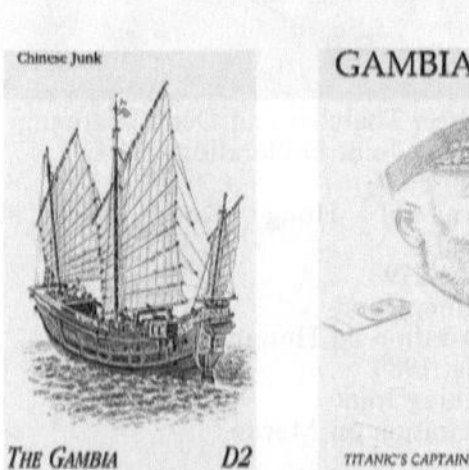

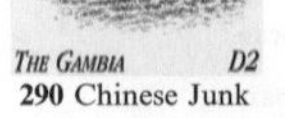

290 Chinese Junk **291** Captain Edward Smith

1998. Ships. Multicoloured.

2904 2d. Type **290** 10 15
2905 3d. H.M.S. "Victory" (ship of the line, 1765) 15 20
2906 5d. "Santa Maria" (Columbus) 25 30
2907 5d. "Mary Rose" (galleon) 25 30
2908 5d. "Mayflower" (Pilgrim Fathers) 25 30
2909 5d. "Ark Royal" (galleon, 1587) 25 30
2910 5d. H.M.S. "Beagle" (Darwin) 25 30
2911 5d. H.M.S. "Bounty" (Bligh) 25 30
2912 5d. H.M.S. "Dreadnought" (battleship) 25 30
2913 5d. American "Truxton" Class cruiser 25 30
2914 5d. "Queen Mary" (liner) 25 30
2915 5d. "Canberra" (liner) . . . 25 30
2916 5d. "Queen Elizabeth" (liner) 25 30
2917 5d. "Queen Elizabeth II" (liner) 25 30
2918 10d. British "County" Class destroyer 55 60
2919 15d. Viking longship 80 85
MS2920 Two sheets. (a) 70 × 100 mm. 25d. "Cutty Sark" (clipper) (41 × 56 mm). (b) 100 × 70 mm. 25d. "Sovereign of the Seas" (liner) (56 × 41 mm) Set of 2 sheets . . . . 2·75 3·00

1998. "Titanic" Commemoration.

2921 **291** 5d. brown, black and blue 25 30
2922 – 5d. brown, black and blue 25 30
2923 – 5d. brown and black . . 25 30
2924 – 5d. blue and black . . 25 30
2925 – 5d. mauve and black . . 25 30
2926 – 5d. mauve and black . . 25 30
MS2927 Three sheets, each 110 × 85 mm. (a) 25d. multicoloured. (b) 25d. sepia and black. (c) 25d. multicoloured Set of 3 sheets . . . . . . 4·00 4·25

DESIGNS—VERT: No. 2922, Mrs. J. J. "Molly" Brown (passenger); 2923, Newspaper boy with placard; 2924, Benjamin Guggenheim (passenger); 2925, Isidor Strauss (passenger); 2926, Ida Strauss (passenger). HORIZ: No. **MS**2927a, "Titanic" on postcard; **MS**2927b, "Titanic sinking"; **MS**2927c, Wreckage of "Titanic" on seabed.

291a "Death of Casagemas"

1998. 25th Death Anniv of Pablo Picasso (painter). Multicoloured.

2928 3d. Type **291a** 15 20
2929 5d. "Seated Woman" (vert) 25 30
2930 10d. "Mother and Child" (vert) 55 60
MS2931 102 × 126 mm. 25d. "Child playing with Toy Truck" (vert) 1·40 1·50

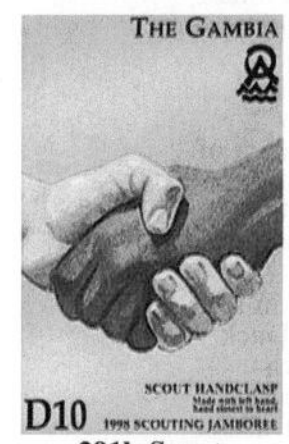

291b Scout Handshake **292** Mahatma Gandhi

1998. 19th World Scout Jamboree, Chile. Mult.

2932 10d. Type **291b** 55 60
2933 10d. Dinghy sailing 55 60
2934 10d. Scout salute 55 60
MS2935 47 × 61 mm. 25d. Lord Baden-Powell (brown and black) 1·40 1·50

1998. 50th Death Anniv of Mahatma Gandhi. Multicoloured.

2936 10d. Type **292** 55 60
2937 10d. Gandhi on Salt March with Mrs. Sarojini Naidu (53 × 38 mm) 55 60
2938 10d. Gandhi spinning yarn (53 × 38 mm) 55 60
2939 10d. Gandhi in 1916 . . . . 55 60
MS2940 53 × 71 mm. 25d. Gandhi writing . . . . 1·40 1·50

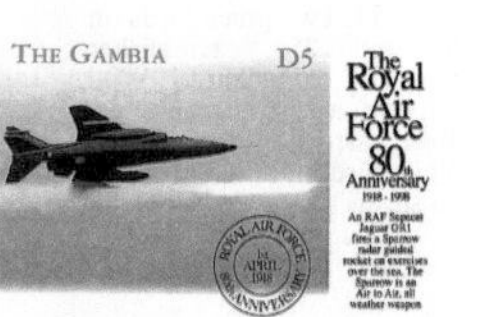

292a Sepecat Jaguar GR1A

1998. 80th Anniv of Royal Air Force. Multicoloured.

2941 5d. Type **292a** 25 30
2942 5d. Panavia Tornado GR1A 25 30
2943 5d. Sepecat Jaguar GR1A (side view) 25 30
2944 5d. BAe Hawk 200 . . . . 25 30
2945 5d. Sepecat Jaguar GR1A firing Sparrow missile . . 25 30
2946 5d. BAe Harrier GR7 firing SNEB rockets 25 30
2947 5d. Panavia Tornado GR1 firing AIM-9L missile . . 25 30
2948 5d. Panavia Tornado GR1 in low level flight 25 30
2949 7d. Panavia Tornado GR1 (facing left) 35 40
2950 7d. BAe Hawk T1A 35 40

2951 7d. Sepecat Jaguar GR1A 35 40
2952 7d. Panavia Tornado GR1 (facing right) 35 40
MS2953 Six sheets, each 90 × 68 mm. (a) 20d. EF-2000 Eurofighter. (b) 25d. Bristol F2B Fighter and bird of prey in flight. (c) 25d. Falcon's head and Bristol F2B Fighter. (d) 25d. Bristol F2B Fighter and Golden Eagle (bird). (e) 25d. Lancaster and EF-2000 Eurofighter. (f) 25d. Lightning and EF-2000 Eurofighter Set of 6 sheets 8·00 8·25

293 "Mule-drivers from Tetuan"

1998. Birth Bicentenary of Eugene Delacroix (painter). Multicoloured.
2954 4d. Type **293** 20 25
2955 4d. "Encampment of Arab Mule-drivers" 20 25
2956 4d. "An Orange Seller" 20 25
2957 4d. "The Banks of the River" 20 25
2958 4d. "View of Tangier from the Seashore" 20 25
2959 4d. "Arab Horses fighting in a Stable" 20 25
2960 4d. "Horses at the Trough" 20 25
2961 4d. "The Combat of Giaour and Hassan" 20 25
2962 4d. "Turk on a Sofa, Smoking" 20 25
2963 4d. "View of Tangier" 20 25
2964 4d. "The Spanish Coast at Salobrena" 20 25
2965 4d. "The Aissaouas" 20 25
2966 4d. "The Sea from the Cliffs of Dieppe" 20 25
2967 4d. "The Fanatics of Tangier" 20 25
2968 4d. "Arab Musicians" 20 25
2969 4d. "An Arab Camp at Night" 20 25
2970 4d. "Moroccan from Tangier, standing" (vert) 20 25
2971 4d. "A Man of Tangier" (vert) 20 25
2972 4d. "Young Arab standing with a Rifle" (vert) 20 25
2973 4d. "Moroccan Chieftain" (vert) 20 25
2974 4d. "Jewish Bride, Tangier" (vert) 20 25
2975 4d. "Seated Jewess from Morocco" (vert) 20 25
2976 4d. "Young Arab seated by a Wall" (vert) 20 25
2977 4d. "Arab Dancer" (vert) 20 25
MS2978 Three sheets. (a) 100 × 85 mm. 25d. "Massacre at Chios". (b) 100 × 85 mm. 25d. "Women of Algiers in their Apartment". (c) 85 × 100 mm. 25d. "Self-portrait" (vert) Set of 3 sheets 4·00 4·25

293a Diana, Princess of Wales

1998. 1st Death Anniv of Diana, Princess of Wales.
2979 **293a** 10d. multicoloured 55 60

294 Puppy in Stocking

295 Rabbit

1998. Christmas. Multicoloured.
2980 1d. Type **294** 10 10
2981 2d. Giraffe in Christmas wreath 10 15
2982 3d. Australian bee eater ("Rainbow Bee Eater") (bird) with bauble 15 20
2983 4d. Deer 20 25
2984 5d. Fawn 25 30
2985 10d. Puppy in gift box 55 60
MS2986 Two sheets, each 105 × 76 mm. (a) 25d. Brown classic tabby. (b) 25d. Basset hound and Rough collie Set of 2 sheets 2·75 3·00

1999. Chinese New Year ("Year of the Rabbit"). Multicoloured.
2987 3d. Type **295** 15 20
2988 3d. Rabbit looking over shoulder 15 20
2989 3d. Rabbit facing left 15 20
2990 3d. Rabbit running 15 20
MS2991 73 × 103 mm. 10d. Rabbit (42 × 28 mm) 55 60

296 Mowgli and Baloo (bear)

1999. "The Jungle Book" (film). Walt Disney cartoon characters. Multicoloured.
2992 5d. Type **296** 1·25 1·25
2993 5d. Kaa (snake) and Mowgli 1·25 1·25
2994 5d. King Louie at ruined temple 1·25 1·25
2995 5d. Monkey playing leaf "guitar" 1·25 1·25
2996 5d. Village girl collecting water 1·25 1·25
2997 5d. King Louie on throne with Mowgli 1·25 1·25
2998 5d. Mowgli and vultures 1·25 1·25
2999 5d. Shere Khan (tiger) 1·25 1·25
MS3000 Two sheets, each 127 × 102 mm. (a) 25d. Baloo (bear) (50 × 37 mm). (b) 25d. Baby elephant (50 × 37 mm) Set of 2 sheets 8·00 9·00

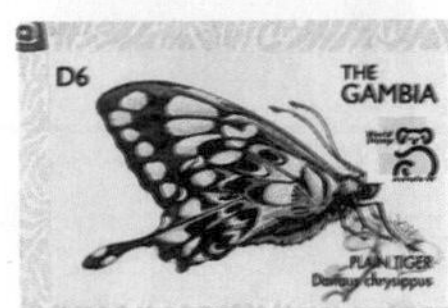

297 "Danaus chrysippus"

1999. "Australia '99" World Stamp Exhibition, Melbourne. African Butterflies. Multicoloured.
3001 6d. Type **297** 30 35
3002 6d. "Papilio zalmoxis" 30 35
3003 6d. "Papilio menestheus" 30 35
3004 6d. "Poecilmitis thysbe" 30 35
3005 6d. "Euxanthe wakefieldii" 30 35
3006 6d. "Pseudacraea boisduvali" 30 35
3007 6d. "Eurytela dryope" 30 35
3008 6d. "Papilio demodocus" 30 35
3009 6d. "Hemiolaus coeculus" 30 35
3010 6d. "Charaxes jasius" 30 35
3011 6d. "Junonia orithya" 30 35
3012 6d. "Kallimoides rumia" 30 35
MS3013 Two sheets, each 106 × 76 mm. (a) 25d. "Charaxes jasius" (vert). (b) 25d. "Catacroptera cloanthe" (vert) Set of 2 sheets 2·75 3·00
No. 3003 is inscribed "Papilio mnestheus" in error.

298 Prince Edward and Miss Sophie Rhys-Jones

1999. Royal Wedding. Multicoloured.
3014 10d. Type **298** 55 60
3015 10d. Prince Edward and Miss Sophie Rhys-Jones (with long hair) 55 60
3016 10d. Prince Edward and Miss Sophie Rhys-Jones (wearing a red jacket) 55 60
MS3017 78 × 78 mm. 25d. Prince Edward and Miss Sophie Rhys-Jones (39 × 29 mm) 1·40 1·50

299 Cannon and Freedom Post, Jaffureh

1999. *Roots* Homecoming Festival. Multicoloured.
3018 1d. Type **299** 10 10
3019 2d. Fort Bullen 10 15
3020 3d. James Island 15 20

299a Railway locomotive "Adler", 1835, and Samoa 1914 G.R.I. 2½d. on 20pf. variety

1999. "iBRA '99" International Stamp Exhibition, Nuremberg. Multicoloured.
3021 4d. Type **299a** 20 25
3022 5d. Railway locomotive "Adler", 1835, and Samoa 1900 25pf. optd on Germany 25 30
3023 10d. "Friedrech August" (full-rigged ship) and Samoa 1900 Yacht type 50pf. and 80pf. stamps 55 60
3024 15d. "Friedrech August" (full-rigged ship) and Samoa 1900 Yacht type 2m. stamp 80 85
MS3025 162 × 107 mm. 25d. Samoa 1900 Yacht type 3m. stamp postmarked Palauli (60 × 40 mm) 1·40 1·50

299b "Exotic Beauty"

1999. 150th Death Anniv of Katsushika Hokusai (Japanese artist). Multicoloured.
3026 5d. Type **299b** 25 30
3027 5d. "Wind" (two people) 25 30
3028 5d. "Dancing Monkey" 25 30
3029 5d. "Lady and Maiden on an Outing" 25 30
3030 5d. "Wind" (three people) 25 30
3031 5d. "Courtesan with Fan" 25 30
3032 5d. "Bunshosei" 25 30
3033 5d. "Overthrower of Castles, Overthrower of Nations" 25 30
3034 5d. "Bee on Wild Rose" 25 30
3035 5d. "Sei Shonagon" 25 30
3036 5d. "Kuan-yu" 25 30
3037 5d. "The Fifth Month" 25 30
MS3038 Two sheets, each 72 × 103 mm. (a) 25d. "People on the Balcony of the Sazaido". (b) 25d. "Caocao before the Battle of Chibi" Set of 2 sheets 2·75 3·00

299c Child asleep

1999. 10th Anniv of United Nations Rights of the Child Convention. Multicoloured.
3039 10d. Type **299c** 55 60
3040 10d. Child drinking 55 60
3041 10d. Child drawing 55 60
MS3042 112 × 85 mm. 25d. Child laughing 1·40 1·50
Nos. 3039/41 were printed together, se-tenant, forming a composite design.

299d Road Carriage on Wagon

1999. "PhilexFrance 99" International Stamp Exhibition, Paris. Railway Transport. Two sheets, each 106 × 81 mm, containing T **299d** and similar designs. Multicoloured.
MS3043 (a) 25d. Type **299d**. (b) 25d. Passenger locomotive, 1846 Set of 2 sheets 2·75 3·00

299e Faust quaffs the Spirit's Nectar

1999. 250th Birth Anniv of Johann von Goethe (German writer).
3044 **299e** 15d. violet, black & pur 80 85
3045 – 15d. blue and black 80 85
3046 – 15d. brown, blk & grn 80 85
MS3047 76 × 106 mm. 25d. blue, black and brown 1·40 1·50
DESIGNS—HORIZ: No. 3045, Goethe and Schiller; 3046, Faust contemplates mortality. VERT: No. MS3047, Johann von Goethe.

299f Bell X-14A VTOL Aircraft

1999. 30th Anniv of First Manned Landing on Moon. Multicoloured.
3048 6d. Type **299f** 30 35
3049 6d. Lunar landing practice rig 30 35
3050 6d. Early prototype lander 30 35
3051 6d. Astronaut during zero gravity training 30 35
3052 6d. Jet pack training 30 35
3053 6d. Lunar lander pilot training 30 35
MS3054 Two sheets. (a) 76 × 105 mm. 25d. "Apollo 11" splashdown. (b) 85 × 110 mm. 25d. Lunar module "Eagle" Set of 2 sheets 2·75 3·00
Nos. 3048/53 were printed together, se-tenant, forming a composite design.

300 Swallow-tailed Gull

1999. Marine Life of the Galapagos Islands. Multicoloured.
3055 1d.50 Type **300** 10 15
3056 1d.50 Magnificent frigate birds ("Frigate Bird") 10 15
3057 1d.50 Red-footed booby 10 15
3058 1d.50 Galapagos hawk 10 15
3059 1d.50 Great blue heron 10 15
3060 1d.50 Blue-faced booby ("Masked Booby") 10 15
3061 1d.50 Bottlenose dolphins 10 15
3062 1d.50 Black grunts 10 15
3063 1d.50 Surgeonfish 10 15
3064 1d.50 Stingray 10 15
3065 1d.50 Short-finned pilot whales 10 15
3066 1d.50 Pacific green sea turtle 10 15
3067 1d.50 Great white shark 10 15
3068 1d.50 Sealion 10 15
3069 1d.50 Marine iguana 10 15
3070 1d.50 Pacific manta ray 10 15
3071 1d.50 Moorish idol 10 15
3072 1d.50 Galapagos penguins 10 15
3073 1d.50 Silver grunts 10 15
3074 1d.50 Sea urchin 10 15
3075 1d.50 Wrasse 10 15
3076 1d.50 Almaco amber jack 10 15
3077 1d.50 Blue parrotfish 10 15
3078 1d.50 Yellow sea urchin 10 15
3079 1d.50 Lobster 10 15
3080 1d.50 Grouper 10 15
3081 1d.50 Scorpionfish 10 15
3082 1d.50 Squirrelfish 10 15
3083 1d.50 Octopus 10 15
3084 1d.50 King angelfish 10 15

3085 1d.50 Horned shark 10 15
3086 1d.50 Galapagos hogfish 10 15
3087 1d.50 Pufferfish 10 15
3088 1d.50 Moray eel 10 15
3089 1d.50 Orange tube coral 10 15
3090 1d.50 Whitestripe chromis 10 15
3091 1d.50 Long-nosed hawkfish 10 15
3092 1d.50 Sea cucumbers 10 15
3093 1d.50 Spotted hawkfish 10 15
3094 1d.50 Zebra moray eel 10 15
MS3095 106 × 76 mm. 25d. Emperor penguins 1·40 1·50

Nos. 3055/94 respectively were printed together, se-tenant, forming a composite design.

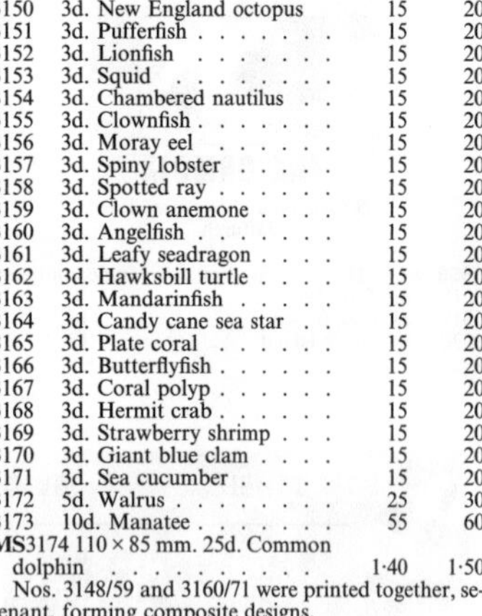

301 "Telstar 1" Satellite, 1962

1999. History of Space Exploration. Multicoloured.
3096 1d. Type **301** 10 10
3097 1d.50 "Skylab", 1973 (vert) 10 15
3098 2d. "Mars 3" spacecraft, 1971 (vert) 10 15
3099 3d. "Cobe", 1989 (vert) 15 20
3100 6d. "Mariner 4", 1964 30 35
3101 6d. "Viking" Mars Orbiter, 1975 30 35
3102 6d. Giotto, 1985 30 35
3103 6d. "Luna 9", 1966 30 35
3104 6d. "Voyager 1", 1977 30 35
3105 6d. Galileo, 1989 30 35
3106 6d. Soviet "Vostok 1", 1961 30 35
3107 6d. "Apollo" command and service module, 1968 30 35
3108 6d. "Mercury" capsule, 1961 30 35
3109 6d. "Apollo 16" lunar module, 1972 30 35
3110 6d. "Gemini 8", 1966 30 35
3111 6d. Soviet "Soyuz", 1975 30 35
3112 6d. German "V 2" rocket, 1942 (vert) 30 35
3113 6d. "Delta Straight 8", 1972 (vert) 30 35
3114 6d. "Ariane 4", 1988 (vert) 30 35
3115 6d. "Mercury MA-A Atlas", 1962 (vert) 30 35
3116 6d. "Saturn 1B", 1975 (vert) 30 35
3117 6d. "Cassini", 1997 (vert) 30 35
3118 10d. Bruce McCandless outside shuttle, 1984 (vert) 55 60
3119 15d. "Apollo 13" after splashdown, 1970 (vert) 80 85
MS3120 Two sheets. (a) 85 × 110 mm. 25d. "Mars Pathfinder", 1997 (56 × 41 mm). (b) 110 × 85 mm. 25d. "Apollo" and "Soyuz" joint mission, 1975 (56 × 41 mm) Set of 2 sheets 2·75 3·00

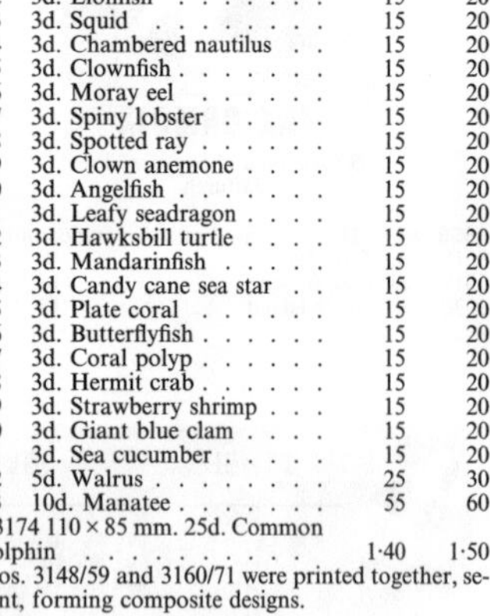

302 Carnotaurus

1999. Prehistoric Animals. Multicoloured.
3121 3d. Type **302** 15 20
3122 3d. Quetzalcoatlus 15 20
3123 3d. Peteinosaurus 15 20
3124 3d. Prenocephale 15 20
3125 3d. Hesperornis 15 20
3126 3d. Coelophysis 15 20
3127 3d. Camptosaurus 15 20
3128 3d. Panderichthys 15 20
3129 3d. Garudimimus 15 20
3130 3d. Cacops 15 20
3131 3d. Ichthyostega 15 20
3132 3d. Scutellosaurus 15 20
3133 3d. Diatryma 15 20
3134 3d. Pteranodon 15 20
3135 3d. Stegodon 15 20
3136 3d. Icaronycthris 15 20
3137 3d. Archaeopteryx 15 20
3138 3d. Chasmatosaurus 15 20
3139 3d. Tytthostonyx 15 20
3140 3d. Hyaenodon 15 20
3141 3d. Uintatherium 15 20
3142 3d. Hesperocyon 15 20
3143 3d. Ambelodon 15 20
3144 3d. Indricotherium 15 20
MS3145 Four sheets, each 110 × 85 mm. (a) 25d. Deinonychus. (b) 25d. Sabre-tooth Tiger. (c) 25d. Lepisosteus. (d) 25d. Microceratops Set of 4 sheets 5·50 5·75

Nos. 3121/32 and 3133/44 were printed together, se-tenant, forming composite designs.

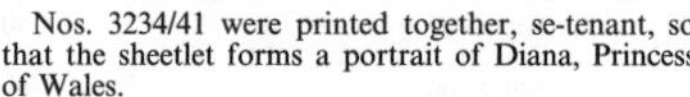

303 Seagull

1999. Marine Life. Multicoloured.
3146 1d. Type **303** 10 10
3147 1d.50 Portuguese man-o-war 10 15
3148 3d. Whale shark 15 20
3149 3d. Grey reef shark 15 20
3150 3d. New England octopus 15 20
3151 3d. Pufferfish 15 20
3152 3d. Lionfish 15 20
3153 3d. Squid 15 20
3154 3d. Chambered nautilus 15 20
3155 3d. Clownfish 15 20
3156 3d. Moray eel 15 20
3157 3d. Spiny lobster 15 20
3158 3d. Spotted ray 15 20
3159 3d. Clown anemone 15 20
3160 3d. Angelfish 15 20
3161 3d. Leafy seadragon 15 20
3162 3d. Hawksbill turtle 15 20
3163 3d. Mandarinfish 15 20
3164 3d. Candy cane sea star 15 20
3165 3d. Plate coral 15 20
3166 3d. Butterflyfish 15 20
3167 3d. Coral polyp 15 20
3168 3d. Hermit crab 15 20
3169 3d. Strawberry shrimp 15 20
3170 3d. Giant blue clam 15 20
3171 3d. Sea cucumber 15 20
3172 5d. Walrus 25 30
3173 10d. Manatee 55 60
MS3174 110 × 85 mm. 25d. Common dolphin 1·40 1·50

Nos. 3148/59 and 3160/71 were printed together, se-tenant, forming composite designs.

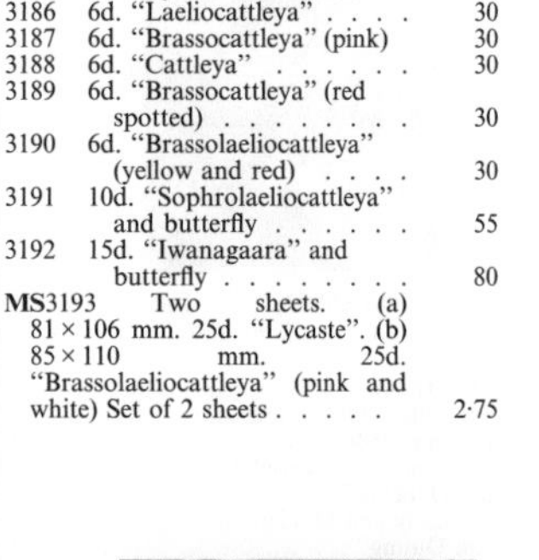

304 "Sophrocattleya"

1999. Orchids of the World. Multicoloured.
3175 2d. Type **304** 10 15
3176 3d. "Cattleya" and butterfly 15 20
3177 4d. "Brassolaeliocattleya" (pink) 20 25
3178 5d. "Brassoepidendrum" 25 30
3179 6d. "Brassolaeliocattleya" (yellow) 30 35
3180 6d. "Cattleytonia" 30 35
3181 6d. "Lacliocattleya" 30 35
3182 6d. "Miltonia" 30 35
3183 6d. "Cattleya forbesii" 30 35
3184 6d. "Odontoglossum cervantesii" 30 35
3185 6d. "Lycaste macrobulbon" 30 35
3186 6d. "Laeliocattleya" 30 35
3187 6d. "Brassocattleya" (pink) 30 35
3188 6d. "Cattleya" 30 35
3189 6d. "Brassocattleya" (red spotted) 30 35
3190 6d. "Brassolaeliocattleya" (yellow and red) 30 35
3191 10d. "Sophrolaeliocattleya" and butterfly 55 60
3192 15d. "Iwanagaara" and butterfly 80 85
MS3193 Two sheets. (a) 81 × 106 mm. 25d. "Lycaste". (b) 85 × 110 mm. 25d. "Brassolaeliocattleya" (pink and white) Set of 2 sheets 2·75 3·00

305 American Black Oystercatcher

1999. Sea Birds. Multicoloured.
3194 2d. Type **305** 10 15
3195 3d. Blue-footed booby 15 20
3196 4d. Atlantic puffin 20 25
3197 4d. Red-billed tropic birds ("Red-tailed Tropic Bird") 20 25
3198 4d. Reddish egret 20 25
3199 4d. Laughing gull 20 25
3200 4d. Great egret 20 25
3201 4d. Northern gannet 20 25
3202 4d. Forster's tern 20 25
3203 4d. Common cormorant 20 25
3204 4d. Razorbill (perched on rocks) 20 25
3205 4d. Adelie penguin 20 25
3206 4d. Black skimmer 20 25
3207 4d. Big crested penguin ("Erect-crested Penguin") 20 25
3208 4d. Heermann's gull 20 25
3209 4d. Glaucous-winged gull 20 25
3210 4d. Laysan albatross 20 25
3211 4d. American white pelican 20 25
3212 4d. Tufted puffin 20 25
3213 4d. Black guillemot 20 25
3214 5d. Razorbill (in flight) 25 30
3215 5d. Common shelduck ("Shelduck") 25 30
3216 5d. Sandwich tern 25 30
3217 5d. Arctic skua 25 30
3218 5d. Northern gannet ("Gannet") 25 30
3219 5d. Mew gull ("Common Gull") 25 30
3220 10d. Western gull 55 60
3221 15d. Brown pelican 80 85
MS3222 Three sheets. (a) 110 × 85 mm. 25d. American white pelican ("Pelican"). (b) 105 × 76 mm. 25d. Gentoo penguin. (c) 106 × 76 mm. 25d. California gull Set of 3 sheets 4·00 4·25

Nos. 3196/3204, 3205/13 and 3214/19 were printed together, se-tenant, forming a composite design.

Nos. 3205 and 3210 are inscribed "ADELIES PENGUIN" or "LAYSON ALBATROSS", both in error.

305a Duchess of York and Princess Elizabeth, 1928

1999. "Queen Elizabeth the Queen Mother's Century".
3223 **305a** 10d. multicoloured 55 60
3224 – 10d. black and gold 55 60
3225 – 10d. black and gold 55 60
3226 – 10d. multicoloured 55 60
MS3227 153 × 155 mm. 25d. mult 1·40 1·50

DESIGNS: No. 3224, Lady Elizabeth Bowes-Lyon, 1923; 3225, Queen Elizabeth, 1946; 3226, Queen Mother and Prince Harry. (37 × 50 mm)—**MS**3227, Queen Mother on 89th Birthday, 1989.

306 Temple of A-Ma

1999. "China '99" International Stamp Exhibition, Beijing. Return of Macao to China. Multicoloured.
3228 7d. Type **306** 35 40
3229 7d. Border Gate 35 40
3230 7d. Ruins of St. Paul's 35 40

307 John F. Kennedy Jr. as Baby, 1961

1999. John F. Kennedy Jr. Commemoration. Each brown, blue and black.
3231 15d. Type **307** 80 85
3232 15d. John F. Kennedy Jr. as teenager 80 85
3233 15d. John F. Kennedy Jr. in 1997 80 85

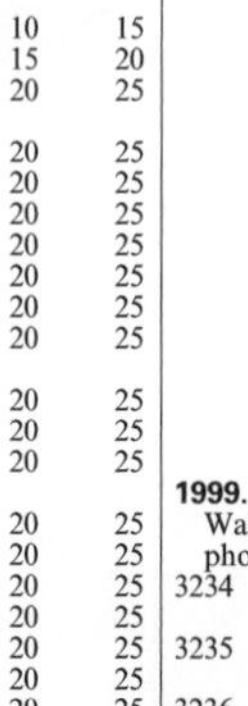

307a Flowers forming Top of Head

1999. Faces of the Millennium: Diana, Princess of Wales. Designs showing collage of miniature flower photographs. Multicoloured.
3234 3d. Type **307a** (face value at left) 15 20
3235 3d. Top of head (face value at right) 15 20
3236 3d. Ear (face value at left) 15 20
3237 3d. Eye and temple (face value at right) 15 20
3238 3d. Cheek (face value at left) 15 20
3239 3d. Cheek (face value at right) 15 20
3240 3d. Blue background (face value at left) 15 20
3241 3d. Chin (face value at right) 15 20

Nos. 3234/41 were printed together, se-tenant, so that the sheetlet forms a portrait of Diana, Princess of Wales.

308 Betty Boop

2000. Betty Boop (cartoon character). Mult.
3242 5d. Type **308** 25 30
3243 5d. In full-length gown 25 30
3244 5d. In T-shirt and dungarees 25 30
3245 5d. In cropped trousers, sleeveless shirt and tie 25 30
3246 5d. Sitting in wicker chair 25 30
3247 5d. In ripped purple trousers, orange T-shirt and gilet 25 30
3248 5d. In fur coat 25 30
3249 5d. In pink crinoline 25 30
3250 5d. In the gym 25 30
MS3251 Two sheets, each 140 × 89 mm. (a) 25d. In the bath. (b) 25d. With chin on hand Set of 2 sheets 2·75 3·00

309 Lucille Ball on Sofa

2000. Scenes from *I Love Lucy* (American T.V. comedy series). Multicoloured.
3252 5d. Type **309** 25 30
3253 5d. Lucy and Desi Arnaz talking 25 30
3254 5d. Lucy holding ball of string 25 30
3255 5d. Lucy in blue coat standing in front of lamp 25 30
3256 5d. Lucy and Desi kissing 25 30
3257 5d. Lucy in front of mirror 25 30
3258 5d. Lucy excited with hands clenched 25 30
3259 5d. Lucy sitting on Desi's knee 25 30
3260 5d. Lucy looking in purse 25 30
3261 5d. Lucy clutching shelf 25 30
3262 5d. Lucy leaning against wall with arms raised 25 30
3263 5d. Lucy with right fist in the air 25 30
3264 5d. Lucy sitting on shelf (front view) 25 30
3265 5d. Lucy smoothing hair with right hand 25 30
3266 5d. Lucy sitting on shelf (side view) 25 30
3267 5d. Desi Arnaz with Lucy bound 25 30
3268 5d. Lucy lying on sofa 25 30
3269 5d. Lucy being held by masked man 25 30
3270 5d. Lucy singing in Austrian costume 25 30
3271 5d. Lucy playing tambourine 25 30
3272 5d. Lucy and Desi in uniform singing 25 30
3273 5d. Lucy with stage trees 25 30
3274 5d. Lucy seated at organ with Desi 25 30
3275 5d. Desi with blonde girl sitting on bench 25 30
3276 5d. Lucy typing 25 30
3277 5d. Blonde girl with chorus 25 30
3278 5d. Lucy being carried off on bench 25 30
MS3279 Six sheets. (a) 100 × 140 mm. 25d. As No. 3256 (vert). (b) 100 × 140 mm. 25d. As No. 3257 (vert). (c) 103 × 130 mm. 25d. As No. 3269 (vert). (d) 130 × 98 mm. 25d. As No. 3270 (vert). (e) 130 × 100 mm. 25d. As No. 3273 (vert). (f) 130 × 100 mm. 25d. Lucy bound and gagged (vert) Set of 6 sheets 8·00 8·25

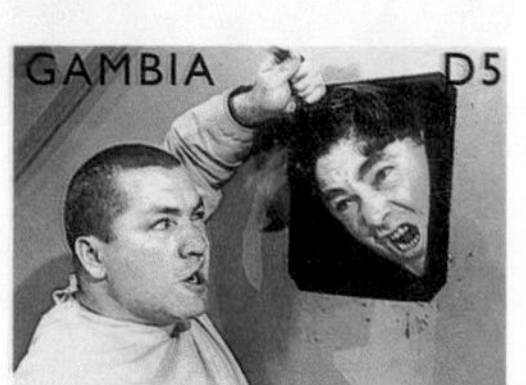

310 Curly pulling Moe through Hole

2000. Scenes from *The Three Stooges* (American T.V. comedy series). Multicoloured.
3280 5d. Type **310** 25 30
3281 5d. Curly with hands in mangle 25 30
3282 5d. Moe giving Curly a bottle 25 30
3283 5d. Larry having hair tugged 25 30
3284 5d. Moe with arms outstretched 25 30
3285 5d. Curly with finger up nose 25 30
3286 5d. Larry, Moe and Curly pointing 25 30
3287 5d. Moe biting Curly's nose with skull 25 30
3288 5d. Moe in yellow shirt and brown jacket 25 30
3289 5d. Moe in Heaven 25 30
3290 5d. Larry, Moe and Curly in Elizabethan costume 25 30
3291 5d. Larry, Moe and Curly in chemist shop 25 30
3292 5d. Moe with shotgun 25 30
3293 5d. With belly dancer 25 30
3294 5d. Larry and Moe in Scottish costume 25 30
3295 5d. Larry and Moe behind wheel 25 30
3296 5d. As postmen 25 30
3297 5d. Curly attacking Larry and Moe with stick 25 30
MS3298 Four sheets. (a) 89×140 mm. 25d. Larry wearing crown and leopard skin. (b) 140×89 mm. 25d. Curly using phone (inscr "GAMBIA") (vert). (c) 124×96 mm. 25d. Curly using phone (inscr "The Gambia") (vert). (d) 124×96 mm. 25d. Moe and Curly as postmen (vert) Set of 4 sheets 5·50 5·75

Nos. 3280/8 were printed together, se-tenant, forming a composite design.

310a Leonardo da Vinci's First Design for Flying Machine, 1480

310b Max Planck (Quantum Theory of Energy, 1900)

2000. New Millennium. People and Events of Fifteenth Century (1450–1500). Multicoloured.
3299 2d. Type **310a** 10 15
3300 2d. Johannes Gutenberg (first printed Bible, 1455) 10 15
3301 2d. Capital "B" (first colour printing, 1457) 10 15
3302 2d. Ivan III ("the Great") becomes Grand Prince of Moscow, 1462 10 15
3303 2d. Walls under attack (Fall of Constantinople, 1453) 10 15
3304 2d. Great Wall of China rebuilt, 1488 10 15
3305 2d. Lorenzo de Medici (ruler of Florence) and "Pieta" (sculpture), 1479 10 15
3306 2d. King Henry VII of England (Foundation of Tudor dynasty, 1485) 10 15
3307 2d. Sailing ship and meeting with Indians (Vasco da Gama's voyage to India, 1497) 10 15
3308 2d. King Ferdinand V and Queen Isabella I (Union of Aragon and Castile, 1479) 10 15
3309 2d. Foetus (birth of Erasmus (Dutch scholar), 1466) 10 15
3310 2d. Sailing ship and Cross of St. George (John Cabot's voyage to North America, 1497) 10 15
3311 2d. King Henry VI and Richard, Duke of Gloucester (Wars of the Roses, 1455) 10 15
3312 2d. Bartolomeu Dias and map (Discovery of Cape of Good Hope, 1487) 10 15
3313 2d. Matthias Hunyadi (crowned King of Hungary, 1458) 10 15
3314 2d. Christopher Columbus (Discovery of the Americas, 1492) (59×39 mm) 10 15
3315 2d. Girolamo Savonarola (religious reformer) (executed 1498) 10 15

2000. New Millennium. People and Events of Twentieth Century (1900–09). Multicoloured.
3316 3d. Type **310b** 15 20
3317 3d. Zeppelin in hangar (invention of rigid airship, 1900) 15 20
3318 3d. Guglielmo Marconi (first transatlantic radio message, 1901) 15 20
3319 3d. Funeral of Queen Victoria, 1901 15 20
3320 3d. Alfred Nobel (first Nobel Prizes awarded, 1901) 15 20
3321 3d. British infantry advancing (end of Boer War, 1902) 15 20
3322 3d. Wright Brothers and aircraft (first flight, 1903) 15 20
3323 3d. Early teddy bear, 1903 15 20
3324 3d. Panama Canal locks under construction, 1904 15 20
3325 3d. Albert Einstein (Theory of Relativity, 1905) 15 20
3326 3d. Crowd with flags (unrest in Russia, 1905) 15 20
3327 3d. Rescue squad and collapsed building, San Francisco earthquake, 1906 15 20
3328 3d. Louis Lumiere (development of colour photography, 1907) 15 20
3329 3d. "Les Demoiselles d'Avignon" (Pablo Picasso), 1907 15 20
3330 3d. Robert Peary (conquest of North Pole, 1909) 15 20
3331 3d. Henry Ford and first Model T, 1908 (59×39 mm) 15 20
3332 3d. Planting sapling (foundation of first Jewish kibbutz in Palestine, 1909) 15 20

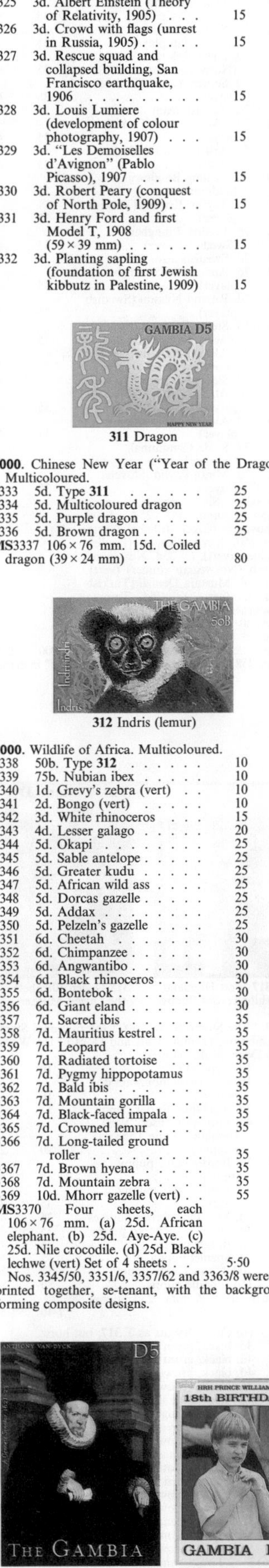

311 Dragon

2000. Chinese New Year ("Year of the Dragon"). Multicoloured.
3333 5d. Type **311** 25 30
3334 5d. Multicoloured dragon 25 30
3335 5d. Purple dragon 25 30
3336 5d. Brown dragon 25 30
MS3337 106×76 mm. 15d. Coiled dragon (39×24 mm) 80 85

312 Indris (lemur)

2000. Wildlife of Africa. Multicoloured.
3338 50b. Type **312** 10 10
3339 75b. Nubian ibex 10 10
3340 1d. Grevy's zebra (vert) 10 10
3341 2d. Bongo (vert) 10 15
3342 3d. White rhinoceros 15 20
3343 4d. Lesser galago 20 25
3344 5d. Okapi 25 30
3345 5d. Sable antelope 25 30
3346 5d. Greater kudu 25 30
3347 5d. African wild ass 25 30
3348 5d. Dorcas gazelle 25 30
3349 5d. Addax 25 30
3350 5d. Pelzeln's gazelle 25 30
3351 6d. Cheetah 30 35
3352 6d. Chimpanzee 30 35
3353 6d. Angwantibo 30 35
3354 6d. Black rhinoceros 30 35
3355 6d. Bontebok 30 35
3356 6d. Giant eland 30 35
3357 7d. Sacred ibis 35 40
3358 7d. Mauritius kestrel 35 40
3359 7d. Leopard 35 40
3360 7d. Radiated tortoise 35 40
3361 7d. Pygmy hippopotamus 35 40
3362 7d. Bald ibis 35 40
3363 7d. Mountain gorilla 35 40
3364 7d. Black-faced impala 35 40
3365 7d. Crowned lemur 35 40
3366 7d. Long-tailed ground roller 35 40
3367 7d. Brown hyena 35 40
3368 7d. Mountain zebra 35 40
3369 10d. Mhorr gazelle (vert) 55 60
MS3370 Four sheets, each 106×76 mm. (a) 25d. African elephant. (b) 25d. Aye-Aye. (c) 25d. Nile crocodile. (d) 25d. Black lechwe (vert) Set of 4 sheets 5·50 5·75

Nos. 3345/50, 3351/6, 3357/62 and 3363/8 were each printed together, se-tenant, with the backgrounds forming composite designs.

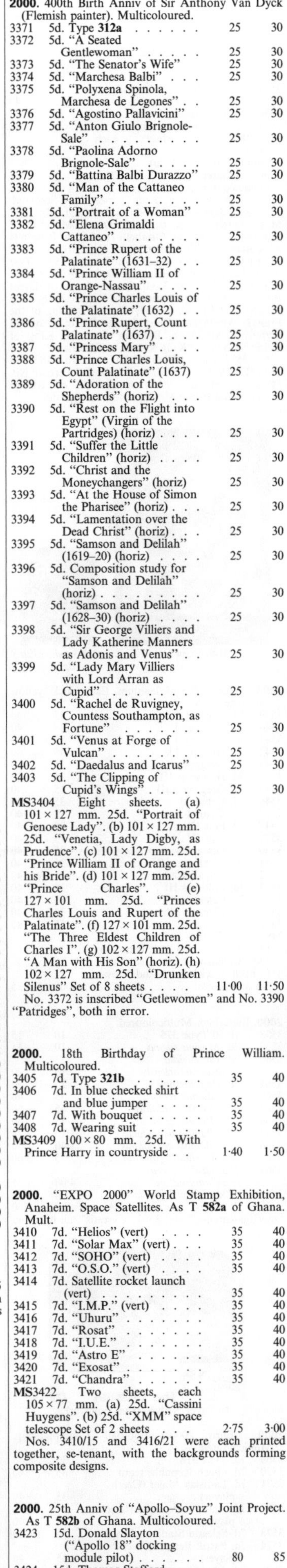

312a "A Genoese Senator"

312b Prince William as Young Boy with Hands Clasped

2000. 400th Birth Anniv of Sir Anthony Van Dyck (Flemish painter). Multicoloured.
3371 5d. Type **312a** 25 30
3372 5d. "A Seated Gentlewoman" 25 30
3373 5d. "The Senator's Wife" 25 30
3374 5d. "Marchesa Balbi" 25 30
3375 5d. "Polyxena Spinola, Marchesa de Legones" 25 30
3376 5d. "Agostino Pallavicini" 25 30
3377 5d. "Anton Giulo Brignole-Sale" 25 30
3378 5d. "Paolina Adorno Brignole-Sale" 25 30
3379 5d. "Battina Balbi Durazzo" 25 30
3380 5d. "Man of the Cattaneo Family" 25 30
3381 5d. "Portrait of a Woman" 25 30
3382 5d. "Elena Grimaldi Cattaneo" 25 30
3383 5d. "Prince Rupert of the Palatinate" (1631–32) 25 30
3384 5d. "Prince William II of Orange-Nassau" 25 30
3385 5d. "Prince Charles Louis of the Palatinate" (1632) 25 30
3386 5d. "Prince Rupert, Count Palatinate" (1637) 25 30
3387 5d. "Princess Mary" 25 30
3388 5d. "Prince Charles Louis, Count Palatinate" (1637) 25 30
3389 5d. "Adoration of the Shepherds" (horiz) 25 30
3390 5d. "Rest on the Flight into Egypt" (Virgin of the Partridges) (horiz) 25 30
3391 5d. "Suffer the Little Children" (horiz) 25 30
3392 5d. "Christ and the Moneychangers" (horiz) 25 30
3393 5d. "At the House of Simon the Pharisee" (horiz) 25 30
3394 5d. "Lamentation over the Dead Christ" (horiz) 25 30
3395 5d. "Samson and Delilah" (1619–20) (horiz) 25 30
3396 5d. Composition study for "Samson and Delilah" (horiz) 25 30
3397 5d. "Samson and Delilah" (1628–30) (horiz) 25 30
3398 5d. "Sir George Villiers and Lady Katherine Manners as Adonis and Venus" 25 30
3399 5d. "Lady Mary Villiers with Lord Arran as Cupid" 25 30
3400 5d. "Rachel de Ruvigney, Countess Southampton, as Fortune" 25 30
3401 5d. "Venus at Forge of Vulcan" 25 30
3402 5d. "Daedalus and Icarus" 25 30
3403 5d. "The Clipping of Cupid's Wings" 25 30
MS3404 Eight sheets. (a) 101×127 mm. 25d. "Portrait of Genoese Lady". (b) 101×127 mm. 25d. "Venetia, Lady Digby, as Prudence". (c) 101×127 mm. 25d. "Prince William II of Orange and his Bride". (d) 101×127 mm. 25d. "Prince Charles". (e) 127×101 mm. 25d. "Princes Charles Louis and Rupert of the Palatinate". (f) 127×101 mm. 25d. "The Three Eldest Children of Charles I". (g) 102×127 mm. 25d. "A Man with His Son" (horiz). (h) 102×127 mm. 25d. "Drunken Silenus" Set of 8 sheets 11·00 11·50

No. 3372 is inscribed "Getlewomen" and No. 3390 "Patridges", both in error.

2000. 18th Birthday of Prince William. Multicoloured.
3405 7d. Type **321b** 35 40
3406 7d. In blue checked shirt and blue jumper 35 40
3407 7d. With bouquet 35 40
3408 7d. Wearing suit 35 40
MS3409 100×80 mm. 25d. With Prince Harry in countryside 1·40 1·50

2000. "EXPO 2000" World Stamp Exhibition, Anaheim. Space Satellites. As T **582a** of Ghana. Mult.
3410 7d. "Helios" (vert) 35 40
3411 7d. "Solar Max" (vert) 35 40
3412 7d. "SOHO" (vert) 35 40
3413 7d. "O.S.O." (vert) 35 40
3414 7d. Satellite rocket launch (vert) 35 40
3415 7d. "I.M.P." (vert) 35 40
3416 7d. "Uhuru" 35 40
3417 7d. "Rosat" 35 40
3418 7d. "I.U.E." 35 40
3419 7d. "Astro E" 35 40
3420 7d. "Exosat" 35 40
3421 7d. "Chandra" 35 40
MS3422 Two sheets, each 105×77 mm. (a) 25d. "Cassini Huygens". (b) 25d. "XMM" space telescope Set of 2 sheets 2·75 3·00

Nos. 3410/15 and 3416/21 were each printed together, se-tenant, with the backgrounds forming composite designs.

2000. 25th Anniv of "Apollo–Soyuz" Joint Project. As T **582b** of Ghana. Multicoloured.
3423 15d. Donald Slayton ("Apollo 18" docking module pilot) 80 85
3424 15d. Thomas Stafford ("Apollo 18" Commander) 80 85
3425 15d. Vance Brand ("Apollo 18" command module pilot) 80 85
MS3426 70×87 mm. 25d. Diagram of docking tunnel (horiz) 1·40 1·50

2000. 50th Anniv of Berlin Film Festival. As T **582c** of Ghana. Multicoloured.
3427 7d. Pane, *Amore e Fantasia*, 1954 35 40
3428 7d. Lord Olivier in *Richard III*, 1956 35 40
3429 7d. *Smultronstallet*, 1958 35 40
3430 7d. Sidney Poitier in *The Defiant Ones*, 1958 35 40
3431 7d. *The Living Desert*, 1954 35 40
3432 7d. *A Bout de Souffle*, 1960 35 40
MS3433 90×103 mm. 25d. Henry Fonda in "Twelve Angry Men", 1957 1·40 1·50

2000. 175th Anniv of Stockton and Darlington Line (first public railway). As T **582d** of Ghana. Multicoloured.
3434 15d. As Type **582d** of Ghana 80 85
3435 15d. Septimus Norris' locomotive *Chesapeake*, 1846 80 85

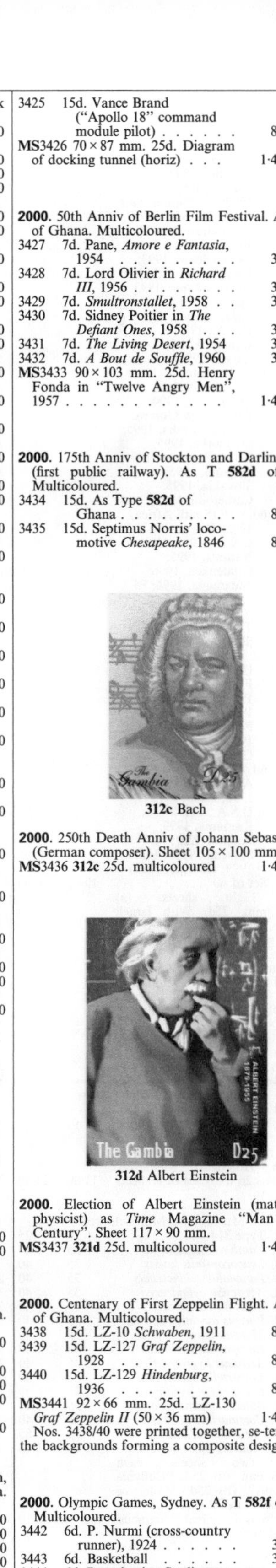

312c Bach

2000. 250th Death Anniv of Johann Sebastian Bach (German composer). Sheet 105×100 mm.
MS3436 **312c** 25d. multicoloured 1·40 1·50

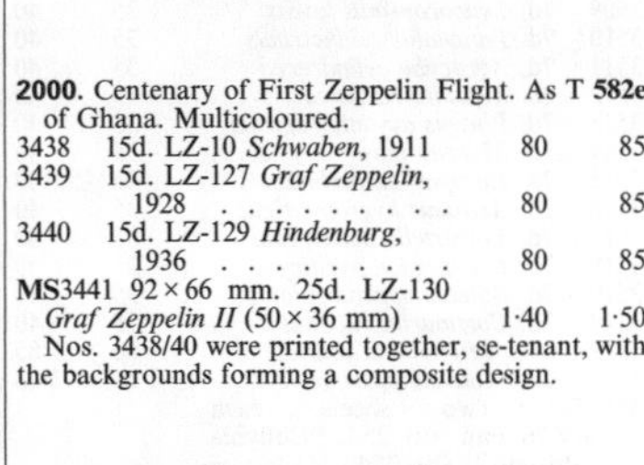

312d Albert Einstein

2000. Election of Albert Einstein (mathematical physicist) as *Time* Magazine "Man of The Century". Sheet 117×90 mm.
MS3437 **321d** 25d. multicoloured 1·40 1·50

2000. Centenary of First Zeppelin Flight. As T **582e** of Ghana. Multicoloured.
3438 15d. LZ-10 *Schwaben*, 1911 80 85
3439 15d. LZ-127 *Graf Zeppelin*, 1928 80 85
3440 15d. LZ-129 *Hindenburg*, 1936 80 85
MS3441 92×66 mm. 25d. LZ-130 *Graf Zeppelin II* (50×36 mm) 1·40 1·50

Nos. 3438/40 were printed together, se-tenant, with the backgrounds forming a composite design.

2000. Olympic Games, Sydney. As T **582f** of Ghana. Multicoloured.
3442 6d. P. Nurmi (cross-country runner), 1924 30 35
3443 6d. Basketball 30 35
3444 6d. Panathenian Stadium, Greece (1890) and Greek flag 30 35
3445 6d. Ancient Greek chariot racing 30 35

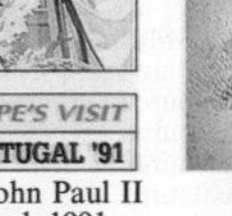

313 Pope John Paul II in Portugal, 1991

314 Morchella esculenta

2000. Travels of Pope John Paul II.
3446/55 6d. × 10 (Type **313**: Poland, 1991; Hungary, 1991; Brazil, 1991; Senegal, 1992; Gambia, 1992; Guinea, 1992; Angola, 1992; St. Thomas and Prince Islands, 1992; Dominican Republic, 1992)
3456/65 6d. × 10 (Benin, 1993; Uganda, 1993; Sudan, 1993; Albania, 1993; Spain, 1993; Jamaica, 1993; Mexico, 1993; U.S.A., 1993; Lithuania, 1993; Latvia, 1993)
3466/75 6d. × 10 (Estonia, 1993; Croatia, 1994; Philippines, 1994; Papua New Guinea, 1995; Australia, 1995; Sri Lanka, 1995; Czech Republic, 1995; Belgium, 1995; Slovakia, 1995; Cameroon, 1995)
3476/85 6d. × 10 (South Africa, 1995; Kenya, 1995; U.S.A., 1995; United Nations, 1995; Guatemala, 1996; Nicaragua, 1996; El Salvador, 1996; Venezuela, 1996; Tunisia, 1996; Slovenia, 1996)
3486/95 6d. × 10 (Germany, 1996; Hungary, 1996; France, 1996; Bosnia, 1996; Czech Republic, 1997; Lebanon, 1997; Poland, 1997; France, 1997; Brazil, 1997; Cuba, 1998)
3496/505 6d. × 10 (Nigeria, 1998; Austria, 1998; Croatia, 1998; Mexico, 1999; U.S.A., 1999; Romania, 1999; Poland, 1999; Slovenia, 1999; India, 1999; Georgia, 1999)
3446/505 Set of 60 . . . . . . 19·00 20·00
MS3506 Eight sheets. (a) 80 × 75 mm. 25d. With Israeli children, 2000 (26 × 34 mm). (b) 75 × 80 mm. 25d. Rekindling "The Eternal Flame" at Yad Vashem Holocaust Museum, 2000 (26 × 34 mm). (c) 80 × 75 mm. 25d. Giving blessing from Mount Nebo, Jordan, 2000 (26 × 34 mm). (d) 80 × 75 mm. 25d. Looking down, Israel, 2000 (26 × 34 mm). (e) 80 × 75 mm. 25d. Praying at Western Wall, Jerusalem, 2000 (26 × 34 mm). (f) 80 × 75 mm. 25d. With Jewish bible, 2000 (26 × 34 mm). (g) 80 × 75 mm. 25d. Placing prayer in Western Wall, 2000 (26 × 34 mm). (h) 75 × 80 mm. 25d. Speaking at Yad Vashem Holocaust Memorial, 2000 (34 × 26 mm) Set of 8 sheets 11·00 11·50

2000. African Mushrooms. Multicoloured.

3507	4d. Type **314**	20	25
3508	5d. *Cantharellus cibarius*	25	30
3509	7d. *Leucocoprinus luteus*	35	40
3510	7d. *Panaeolus sphinctrinus*	35	40
3511	7d. *Agrocybe cylindracea*	35	40
3512	7d. *Amanita caesarea*	35	40
3513	7d. *Pluteus aurantiorugosus*	35	40
3514	7d. *Mycena pura*	35	40
3515	7d. *Lycoperdon perlatum*	35	40
3516	7d. *Astraeus hygrometricus*	35	40
3517	7d. *Volvariella bombycina*	35	40
3518	7d. *Lycoperdon pyriforme*	35	40
3519	7d. *Boletus appendiculatus*	35	40
3520	7d. *Cortinarius rubellus*	35	40
3521	15d. *Tricholoma ustale*	80	85
3522	20d. *Clavulinopsis helvola*	1·10	1·25

MS3523 Two sheets, each 106 × 76 mm. (a) 25d. "Collybia erythropus". (b) 25d. "Calocybe gambosa" Set of 2 sheets . . . 2·75 3·00
No. 3516 is inscribed "Astracus" and No. 3519 "apendiculatus", both in error.

314a King James IV of Scotland

2000. Monarchs of the Millennium.

3524	**314a**	7d. multicoloured	35	40
3525	–	7d. multicoloured	35	40
3526	–	7d. multicoloured	35	40
3527	–	7d. multicoloured	35	40
3528	–	7d. multicoloured	35	40
3529	–	7d. multicoloured	35	40
3530	–	7d. black, stone and brown	35	40
3531	–	7d. multicoloured	35	40
3532	–	7d. multicoloured	35	40
3533	–	7d. black, stone and brown	35	40
3534	–	7d. multicoloured	35	40
3535	–	7d. black, stone and brown	35	40
3536	–	7d. multicoloured	35	40
3537	–	7d. multicoloured	35	40

MS3538 Three sheets, each 117 × 137 mm. (a) 25d. multicoloured. (b) 25d. multicoloured. (c) 25d. multicoloured Set of 3 sheets 4·00 4·25
DESIGNS: No. 3525, King James V of Scotland; 3526, King James VI of Scotland (I of England); 3527, Mary, Queen of Scots; 3528, Queen Mary II of England; 3529, Queen Elizabeth II of Great Britain (I of Scotland); 3530, King Charles II of France; 3531, Queen Catherine de Medici of France; 3532, Tsar Boris Godunov of Muscovy; 3533, Vasily III, Grand Prince of Moscow; 3534, Queen Anne of Great Britain; 3535, King Charles IX of France; 3536, King Charles I of England; 3537, Clovis IV, King of the Franks; **MS**3538a, King James IV of Scotland (*different*); **MS**3538b, Bahadur Shah II, King of Delhi; **MS**3538c, "King Robert I of Scotland".
No. 3537 is inscr "CLOVIS III", and No. **MS**3538a "JAMES IV OF ENGLAND"; both in error. No. **MS**3538c actually shows a portrait of Robert Walpole, first Prime Minister of Great Britain.

314b Felix IV

315 *Amphicallia tigris*

2000. Popes of the Millennium. Each black, yellow and olive.

3539	7d. Type **314b**	35	40
3540	7d. Gelasius I	35	40
3541	7d. Gregory I	35	40
3542	7d. Gregory IX	35	40
3543	7d. Gregory XII	35	40
3544	7d. Honorius III	35	40
3545	7d. Gregory XIII	35	40
3546	7d. Urban II	35	40
3547	7d. Sixtus I	35	40
3548	7d. Pius IX	35	40
3549	7d. Pius IV	35	40
3550	7d. Pascal I	35	40
3551	7d. Alexander VII	35	40
3552	7d. Benedict XI	35	40
3553	7d. Callistus III	35	40
3554	7d. Celestine V	35	40
3555	7d. Clement IX	35	40
3556	7d. Fabian	35	40

MS3557 Three sheets, each 115 × 135 mm. (a) 25d. Peter. (b) 25d. Damasus I. (c) 25d. John I. Each black, stone and brown Set of 3 sheets . . . . 4·00 4·25

2000. Butterflies. Multicoloured.

3558	1d.50 Type **315**	10	15
3559	2d. *Myrina silenus*	10	15
3560	3d. *Chrysiridia madagascariensis*	15	20
3561	5d. *Papilionidae*	25	30
3562	7d. *Salamis temora*	35	40
3563	8d. *Cryestis camillus*	45	50
3564	10d. *Dasiothia medea*	55	60
3565	20d. *Papilio demodocus*	1·10	1·25
3566	25d. *Danaus chrysippus*	1·40	1·50
3567	50d. *Coeliades forestan*	2·75	3·00
3568	75d. *Ornithoptera alexandrae*	4·00	4·25
3568a	100d. *Morpho cypris*	5·00	5·75

No. 3558 is inscribed "Amphicalia", 3560 "madagascarensis" and 3563 "Cyrestis", all in error.

316 Pavel Nedved (Czech player)

2000. "Euro 2000" Football Championship. Multicoloured.

3569	7d. Type **316**	35	40
3570	7d. Czech Republic team	35	40
3571	7d. Ladislav Maier (Czech player)	35	40
3572	7d. Antonin Panenka (Czech player)	35	40
3573	7d. Selessin Stadium, Liege	35	40
3574	7d. Patrik Berger (Czech player)	35	40
3575	7d. Alan Shearer (English player)	35	40
3576	7d. English team	35	40
3577	7d. David Seaman (English player)	35	40
3578	7d. Sol Campbell (English player)	35	40
3579	7d. Philips Stadium, Eindhoven	35	40
3580	7d. Gareth Southgate (English player)	35	40
3581	7d. Oyvind Leonhardsen (Norwegian player)	35	40
3582	7d. Norwegian team	35	40
3583	7d. Erik Mykland (Norwegian player)	35	40
3584	7d. Stale Solbakken (Norwegian player)	35	40
3585	7d. Kjetil Rekdal (Norwegian player)	35	40
3586	7d. Sergen Yalcin (Turkish player)	35	40
3587	7d. Turkish team	35	40
3588	7d. Okan Buruk (Turkish player)	35	40
3589	7d. Arif Erdem (Turkish player)	35	40
3590	7d. Koning Boudewijn Stadium	35	40
3591	7d. Tayfun Korkut (Turkish player)	35	40
3592	7d. Fredrik Ljungberg (Swedish player)	35	40
3593	7d. Swedish team	35	40
3594	7d. Andersson (Swedish player)	35	40
3595	7d. Roland Nilsson (Swedish player)	35	40
3596	7d. Stefan Schwarz (Swedish player)	35	40
3597	7d. Aleksander Knavs (Slovene player)	35	40
3598	7d. Slovenian team	35	40
3599	7d. Alatko Zahovic (Slovene player)	35	40
3600	7d. Ales Ceh (Slovene player)	35	40
3601	7d. Stade Communal, Charleroi	35	40
3602	7d. Miran Pavlin (Slovene player)	35	40

MS3603 Six sheets, each 145 × 95 mm. (a) 25d. Jozef Chovanec (Czech trainer) (vert). (b) 25d. Kevin Keegan (English trainer) (vert). (c) 25d. Nils-Johan Semb (Norwegian trainer) (vert). (d) 25d. Mustafa Denizli (Turkish trainer) (vert). (e) 25d. Tommy Soderberg and Lars Lagerback (Swedish trainers) (vert). (f) 25d. Srecko Katanec (Slovene trainer) (vert) Set of 6 sheets . . . . 8·00 8·25
No. 3581 is inscribed "LEONARDSEN" in error.

317 West Highland White Terrier Puppy

318 Queen Elizabeth the Queen Mother

2000. "The Stamp Show 2000" International Stamp Exhibition, London. Cats and Dogs of the World.
(a) Dogs. Multicoloured.

3604	1d. Type **317**	10	10
3605	1d.50 Bernese mountain dog puppy	10	15
3606	3d. Yorkshire terrier puppy	15	20
3607	4d. Labrador (inscr "West Highland White Terrier Puppy")	20	25
3608	7d. Border collie puppy (brown)	35	40
3609	7d. Border collie puppy (black)	35	40
3610	7d. Yorkshire terrier puppies	35	40
3611	7d. German shepherd puppy	35	40
3612	7d. Beagle puppy	35	40
3613	7d. Spaniel puppy	35	40
3614	10d. Chow Chow puppy	55	60
3615	15d. Poodle puppy	80	85

MS3616 106 × 75 mm. 25d. Boxer puppy . . . . 1·40 1·50

(b) Cats. Designs as T **317**, but horiz.

3617	4d. black, green and grey	20	25
3618	4d. black, green and grey	20	25
3619	4d. black, brown and grey	20	25
3620	4d. black, yellow and grey	20	25
3621	4d. black, blue and grey	20	25
3622	4d. black, orange and grey	20	25
3623	4d. black, blue and grey	20	25
3624	4d. black, yellow and grey	20	25
3625	5d. black, blue and grey	25	30
3626	5d. black, yellow and grey	25	30
3627	5d. black, green and grey	25	30
3628	5d. black, yellow and grey	25	30
3629	5d. black, yellow and grey	25	30
3630	5d. black, green and grey	25	30
3631	5d. black, yellow and grey	25	30
3632	5d. black, yellow and grey	25	30

MS3633 Two sheets, each 106 × 77 mm. (a) 25d. multicoloured. (b) 25d. multicoloured Set of 2 sheets 2·75 3·00
DESIGNS: No. 3617, Egyptian mau; 3618, Singapura; 3619, American shorthair; 3620, Cornish rex; 3621, Birman; 3622, Scottish fold; 3623, Turkish angora; 3624, Turkish van; 3625, Ragdoll; 3626, Bombay; 3627, Koral; 3628, Somali; 3629, British shorthair; 3630, American curl; 3631, Maine coon; 3632, Turkish van; **MS**3633a, Mother cat with kitten; **MS**3633b, Egyptian mau.

2000. Queen Elizabeth the Queen Mother's 100th Birthday.
3634 **318** 7d. multicoloured . . . 35 40

2000. Faces of the Millennium: Queen Elizabeth the Queen Mother's 100th Birthday. As T **307a** showing collage of miniature flower photographs. Multicoloured.

3635	5d. Top of head (face value at left)	25	30
3636	5d. Top of head (face value at right)	25	30
3637	5d. Eye and temple (face value at left)	25	30
3638	5d. Temple (face value at right)	25	30
3639	5d. Cheek (face value at left)	25	30
3640	5d. Cheek (face value at right)	25	30
3641	5d. Chin (face value at left)	25	30
3642	5d. Neck (face value at right)	25	30

Nos. 3635/42 were printed together, se-tenant, in sheetlets of 8 with the stamps arranged in two vertical columns separated by a gutter also containing miniature photographs. When viewed as a whole, the sheetlet forms a portrait of the Queen Mother.

2000. Faces of the Millennium: 80th Birthday of Pope John Paul II. As T **307a** showing collage of miniature religious photographs. Multicoloured.

3643	6d. Top of head (face value at left)	30	35
3644	6d. Top of head (face value at right)	30	35
3645	6d. Ear (face value at left)	30	35
3646	6d. Forehead (face value at right)	30	35
3647	6d. Neck (face value at left)	30	35
3648	6d. Cheek (face value at right)	30	35
3649	6d. Shoulder (face value at left)	30	35
3650	6d. Hands (face value at right)	30	35

Nos. 3643/50 were printed together, se-tenant, in sheetlets of 8 with the stamps arranged in two vertical columns separated by a gutter also containing miniature photographs. When viewed as a whole, the sheetlet forms a portrait of Pope John Paul II.

319 "A White Pheasant and other Fowl in a Classical Landscape" (Abraham Bisschop)

321 Antonio Vivaldi

320 Allard on Peking–Paris Rally

2000. Bird Paintings. Multicoloured.

3651	1d.50 Type **319**	10	15
3652	3d. "Salmon-crested Cockatoo" (Bartolomeo Bimbi)	15	20
3653	4d. "Great Bustard Cock and Other Birds" (Ludger Tom Ring)	20	25
3654	5d. "Still Life of Birds" (Caravaggio) (horiz)	25	30
3655	5d. "Turkeys with Young and Rock Doves" (Johan Wenzel Peter) (horiz)	25	30
3656	5d. "The Threatened Swan" (Jan Asselyn) (horiz)	25	30
3657	5d. "Still Life of Fruit and Birds in a Landscape" (Jokob Bogdani) (horiz)	25	30
3658	5d. "Mobbing the Owl" (Tobias Stranover) (horiz)	25	30
3659	5d. "Concert of Birds" (Melchior de Hondecoeter) (horiz)	25	30
3660	5d. "Owls and Young Ones" (William Tomkins) (horiz)	25	30
3661	5d. "Birds by a Stream" (Jean Baptiste Oudry) (horiz)	25	30
3662	5d. "Peacocks Hens and Mouse" (Tobias Stranover)	25	30
3663	5d. "Lady in a Red Jacket feeding a Parrot" (Frans van Mieris)	25	30

No.	Description	Unused	Used
3664	5d. "Birds by a Pool" (Melchior de Hondecoeter)	25	30
3665	5d. "Ganymede and the Eagle" (Rubens)	25	30
3666	5d. "Leda and the Swan" (Cesare da Sesto)	25	30
3667	5d. "Ducks and Ducklings at the Foot of a Tree in a Mediterranean Landscape" (Adriaen van Oolen)	25	30
3668	5d. "Portrait of the Falconer Robert Cheseman carrying a Hooded Falcon" (Holbein)	25	30
3669	5d. "Golden Pheasant on a Stone Plinth, with other Birds" (Jacobus Vonck)	25	30
3670	15d. "Great Black-backed Gull and other Birds" (Jokob Bogdani)	80	85
MS3671	Two sheets, each 76 × 63 mm. (a) 25d. "Still Life of Birds" (Georg Flegel) (horiz). (b) 25d. "King Eagle pursued to the Sun" (Philip Reinagle) Set of 2 sheets	2·75	3·00

2000. 12th Classic Car Marathon. Showing cars from Himalayan Rally (No. **MS**3688a) or Peking–Paris Rally (others). Multicoloured.

No.	Description	Unused	Used
3672	5d. Type **320**	25	30
3673	5d. Ford Coupe	25	30
3674	5d. Citroen Pilot	25	30
3675	5d. Packard (white)	25	30
3676	5d. Austin A90	25	30
3677	5d. Bentley	25	30
3678	5d. Packard (red)	25	30
3679	5d. Aston Martin	25	30
3680	5d. Morgan	25	30
3681	5d. Rover	25	30
3682	5d. Marmon	25	30
3683	5d. Rolls Royce Silver Cloud	25	30
3684	5d. Rolls Royce Phantom	25	30
3685	5d. Mercedes 680S	25	30
3686	5d. Mercedes saloon	25	30
3687	5d. Invicta	25	30
MS3688	Two sheets, each 86 × 59 mm. (a) 25d. Morris Minor. (b) 25d. Cadillac Set of 2 sheets	2·75	3·00

2000. Classical Opera and Oratorio Composers. Multicoloured.

No.	Description	Unused	Used
3689	7d. Type **321**	35	40
3690	7d. Giacomo Puccini	35	40
3691	7d. Franz Joseph Haydn	35	40
3692	7d. Leopold Stokowski	35	40
3693	7d. Felix Mendelssohn	35	40
3694	7d. Gaetano Donizetti	35	40
3695	7d. Witold Lutoslawski	35	40
3696	7d. Sir William Sterndale Bennett	35	40
3697	7d. Wolfgang Amadeus Mozart	35	40
3698	7d. Ludwig van Beethoven	35	40
3699	7d. Sergei Rachmaninov	35	40
3700	7d. Pyotr Tchaikovsky	35	40
MS3701	Two sheets. (a) 95 × 72 mm. 25d. Frederic Chopin. (b) 67 × 95 mm. 25d. Manuel de Falla Set of 2 sheets	2·75	3·00

322 Mazda RX-Evolv

2000. Transport in the Next Millennium. Mult.

No.	Description	Unused	Used
3702	7d. Type **322**	35	40
3703	7d. Isuzu Kai	35	40
3704	7d. Ford 021C	35	40
3705	7d. Pontiac GTO	35	40
3706	7d. Chevrolet Cerv III	35	40
3707	7d. Toyota Will VI	35	40
3708	7d. Blended-wing body BWB-1 aircraft	35	40
3709	7d. Boeing's 767-400ERX	35	40
3710	7d. New Lockheed concept fighter	35	40
3711	7d. Boeing "X" bomber	35	40
3712	7d. American National Aerospaceplane X30 concept	35	40
3713	7d. Hotol space plane separating from Antonov AN-225	35	40
3714	8d. Pendolare concept speedboat	45	50
3715	8d. Plansail catamaran	45	50
3716	8d. New Airfoil concept	45	50
3717	8d. Ferry Sea Coaster hydrofoil concept	45	50
3718	8d. *Shinaitoku Matu*(tanker) showing new sail technology	45	50
3719	8d. Supersport luxury yacht concept	45	50
3720	8d. Maglev MLU-002 train	45	50
3721	8d. Airport magnetic rail car system	45	50
3722	8d. Modern monorail train	45	50
3723	8d. Two-car monorail, Seattle	45	50
3724	8d. New "above cabin" monorail concept	45	50
3725	8d. Streamlined monorail concept	45	50
MS3726	Four sheets, each 110 × 85 mm. (a) 25d. Honda Sproket concept. (b) 25d. Nautic Air 400 flying boat concept. (c) 25d. Triton U.S. Coast Guard patrol vessel concept (58 × 43 mm). (d) 25d. Maglev train (58 × 43 mm) Set of 4 sheets	5·50	5·75

No. 3722 is inscribed "MONRAIL" in error.

323 Ships of the Spanish Armada, 1588

2000. Historic Ships of the World. Multicoloured.

No.	Description	Unused	Used
3727	5d. Type **323**	25	30
3728	7d. 18th-century Chinese junks	35	40
3729	7d. 15th-century cog	35	40
3730	7d. *Henri Grace a Dieu* (galleon) at anchor	35	40
3731	7d. Tapestry of St. Brendan at sea	35	40
3732	7d. Figurehead by Grinling Gibbons	35	40
3733	7d. 16th-century British carrack	35	40
3734	7d. 18th-century British first-rate ship of the line	35	40
3735	7d. 16th-century Spanish galleon	35	40
3736	7d. Russian four-masted barque	35	40
3737	7d. *Henri Grace a Dieu* (galleon) at sea	35	40
3738	7d. Frontispiece from John Dee's *Arte of Navigation*	35	40
3739	7d. 19th-century British ironclad	35	40
3740	10d. *Colombo* (Brazilian river gunboat)	55	60
3741	15d. *Jenissel* (Russian minelayer)	80	85
3742	20d. *Yamato* (Japanese ironclad)	1·10	1·25
MS3743	Two sheets, each 102 × 115 mm. (a) 25d. H.M.S. *Challenger* (survey ship). (b) 25d. *Golden Hind* (Drake) Set of 2 sheets	2·75	3·00

Nos. 3728/33 and 3734/9 were each printed together, se-tenant, with the backgrounds forming composite designs.

324 Yellow-rumped Tinkerbird

326 Head of Akhal-Teke Horse

325 "At Full Stretch" (John Skeaping)

2000. Tropical Birds. Multicoloured.

No.	Description	Unused	Used
3744	7d. Type **324**	35	40
3745	7d. Black-throated honeyguide ("Greater Honeyguide")	35	40
3746	7d. Hoopoe	35	40
3747	7d. European roller	35	40
3748	7d. Carmine bee eater	35	40
3749	7d. White-throated bee eater	35	40
3750	7d. Grey parrot	35	40
3751	7d. Great spotted cuckoo	35	40
3752	7d. Bar-tailed trogon	35	40
3753	7d. African hobby	35	40
3754	7d. Green turaco	35	40
3755	7d. Trumpeter hornbill	35	40
3756	7d. Pied flycatcher	35	40
3757	7d. Blackcap	35	40
3758	7d. Common stonechat	35	40
3759	7d. Nightingale	35	40
3760	7d. Black-headed tchagra	35	40
3761	7d. Yellow wagtail	35	40
MS3762	Three sheets, each 85 × 110 mm. (a) 25d. European bee eater (horiz). (b) 25d. Bateleur (horiz). (c) 25d. Secretary bird (horiz) Set of 3 sheets	4·00	4·25

Nos. 3744/9, 3750/5 and 3756/61 were each printed together, se-tenant, with the backgrounds forming composite designs.

2000. Horse Paintings. Multicoloured.

No.	Description	Unused	Used
3763	4d. Type **325**	20	25
3764	5d. "The Burton" (Lionel Edwards)	25	30
3765	7d. "Horses emerging from the Sea" (Delacroix)	35	40
3766	7d. "The 9th Duke of Marlborough on a Grey Hunter" (Sir Alfred Munnings)	35	40
3767	7d. "Ovid in Exile amongst the Scythians" (Delacroix)	35	40
3768	7d. "Early Morning Gallop" (John Skeaping)	35	40
3769	7d. "Mare and Foal" (Sir Alfred Munnings)	35	40
3770	7d. "Three-a-side Polo at Simla" (Lionel Edwards)	35	40
3771	7d. "A Lady hawking" (E. Vernet) (vert)	35	40
3772	7d. "Captain Robert Orme" (Reynolds) (vert)	35	40
3773	7d. "Napoleon crossing the Alps" (David) (vert)	35	40
3774	7d. "Nobby Grey" (Sir Alfred Munnings) (vert)	35	40
3775	7d. "Amateur Jockeys near a Carriage" (Degas) (vert)	35	40
3776	7d. "Three-a-side Polo at Simla" (Lionel Edwards) (vert)	35	40
3777	10d. "Game of Polo" (Li-Lin)	55	60
3778	15d. "St. George and the Dragon" (Raphael)	80	85
MS3779	Two sheets, each 90 × 70 mm. (a) 25d. "The Reckoning" (George Morland). (b) 25d. "One of the Family" (Frederick Cotman) Set of 2 sheets	2·75	3·00

2000. Horses of the World. Multicoloured.

No.	Description	Unused	Used
3780	7d. Type **326**	35	40
3781	7d. Palomino	35	40
3782	7d. Kladuber	35	40
3783	7d. Paint horse	35	40
3784	7d. Pinto	35	40
3785	7d. Kabaroin	35	40
3786	7d. Akhal-Teke (horiz)	35	40
3787	7d. Kladruber (horiz)	35	40
3788	7d. Palomino (horiz)	35	40
3789	7d. Pinto (horiz)	35	40
3790	7d. Paint horse (horiz)	35	40
3791	7d. Kabaroin (horiz)	35	40
MS3792	87 × 70 mm. 25d. Palomino	1·40	1·50

326a "The Madonna of the Fish" (Raphael)

2000. "Espana 2000". International Stamp Exhibition, Madrid. Paintings from the Prado Museum. Multicoloured.

No.	Description	Unused	Used
3793	6d. Type **326a**	30	35
3794	6d. "The Holy Family with a Lamb" (Raphael)	30	35
3795	6d. "The Madonna of the Stair" (Andrea del Sarto)	30	35
3796	6d. Moneychanger from "The Moneychanger and his Wife" (Marinus van Reymerswaele)	30	35
3797	6d. "Madonna and Child" (Jan Gossaert)	30	35
3798	6d. Wife from "The Moneychanger and his Wife" (Van Reymerswaele)	30	35
3799	6d. "St. Andrew" (Francisco Rizi)	30	35
3800	6d. "Christ Crucified" (Velazquez)	30	35
3801	6d. "St. Onuphrius" (Francisco Collantes)	30	35
3802	6d. "Charles II of Spain" (Juan de Miranda)	30	35
3803	6d. "St. Sebastian" (De Miranda)	30	35
3804	6d. "Peter Ivanovich Potemkin" (De Miranda)	30	35
3805	6d. St. Benedict from "St. Benedict's Supper" (Juan Ricci)	30	35
3806	6d. "Our Lady of the Immaculate Conception" (Zurbaran)	30	35
3807	6d. Monk with candle from "St. Benedict's Supper" (Ricci)	30	35
3808	6d. "The Penitent Magdalen" (Jose de Ribera)	30	35
3809	6d. "Christ as Man of Sorrows" (Antonio de Pereda)	30	35
3810	6d. "St. Jerome" (De Pereda)	30	35
3811	6d. "Children with a Shell" (Murillo)	30	35
3812	6d. "Our Lady of the Immaculate Conception" (Murillo)	30	35
3813	6d. "The Good Shepherd" (Murillo)	30	35
3814	6d. Young woman from "The Parasol" (Goya)	30	35
3815	6d. "A Rural Gift" (Ramon Bayeu)	30	35
3816	6d. Young man from "The Parasol" (Goya)	30	35
3817	6d. "Portrait of a Young Woman" (Velazquez)	30	35
3818	6d. "The Painter Francisco Goya" (Vicente Portana)	30	35
3819	6d. "Portrait of a Girl" (Raphael Diaz)	30	35
3820	6d. Virgin Mary from "The Nativity" (Frederico Barocci)	30	35
3821	6d. "Madonna and Child with St. John" (Correggio)	30	35
3822	6d. Holy Child from "The Nativity" (Barocci)	30	35
3823	6d. "Queen Isabelle Farnese" (Jean Ranc)	30	35
3824	6d. "Young Woman from Back" (Jean-Baptiste Greuze)	30	35
3825	6d. "Charles III of Spain as a Child" (Ranc)	30	35
3826	6d. "James Bordieu" (Reynolds)	30	35
3827	6d. "Dr. Isaac Henrique Sequeria" (Reynolds)	30	35
3828	6d. "Portrait of a Clergyman" (Reynolds)	30	35
MS3829	Six sheets, each 110 × 90 mm. (a) 25d. "The Defence of Cádiz against the English" (Zubarán). (b) 25d. "The Surrender of Juliers" (Jusepe Leonardo). (c) 25d. "The Holy Family with a Little Bird" (Murillo). (d) 25d. "Jacob's Dream" (De Ribera) (horiz). (e) 25d. "Venus and Adonis" (Veronese) (horiz). (f) 25d. "Dane" (Titian) (horiz) Set of 6 sheets	8·00	8·25

327 Bristol Blenheim of 29 Squadron

2000. 60th Anniv of Battle of Britain. Mult.

No.	Description	Unused	Used
3830	5d. Type **327**	25	30
3831	5d. Helmut Wick shooting down Hurricane	25	30
3832	5d. Spitfire of 65 Squadron attacking Dornier 217	25	30
3833	5d. Bristol Beaufighter IIF of 604 Squadron	25	30
3834	5d. Boulton Paul Defiants of 264 Squadron	25	30
3835	5d. Spitfire in dogfight with Stuka JU-87	25	30
3836	5d. British fighters over Tower Bridge	25	30
3837	5d. Gloster Gladiator of 615 Squadron	25	30
3838	5d. Hurricane attacking Messerschmitt Bf 109	25	30
3839	5d. Spitfire attacking two Messerschmitt Bf 109s	25	30
3840	5d. Flt.-Lt. Gilliam attacking Dornier 217s	25	30
3841	5d. Two Hurricanes of 610 Squadron	25	30
3842	5d. Hurricanes of 85 Squadron	25	30
3843	5d. G. A. Langley attacking Messerschmitt 109	25	30
3844	5d. Bristol Blenheim IV of 23 Squadron	25	30
3845	5d. Spitfires of 222 Squadron taking off	25	30
MS3846	Two sheets, each 110 × 85 mm. (a) 25d. Adolf Galland (commander of Group III of JG26). (b) 25d. Group Captain Frank Carey Set of 2 sheets	2·75	3·00

No. 3834 is inscribed "Bolton-Paul" in error.

328 Moshe Weinberg (wrestling referee)

2000. Victims of Munich Olympics Massacre (1972) Commemoration. Showing Israeli athletes and officials. Multicoloured.

No.	Description	Unused	Used
3847	4d. Type **328**	20	25
3848	4d. Eliezer Halffin (wrestler)	20	25
3849	4d. Mark Slavin (wrestler)	20	25
3850	4d. Ze'ev Friedman (weightlifter)	20	25
3851	4d. Joseph Romano (weightlifter)	20	25
3852	4d. Kahat Shor (shooting coach)	20	25

3853 4d. David Berger (weightlifter) 20 25
3854 4d. Joseph Gottfreund (wrestling referee) 20 25
3855 4d. Andrei Schpitzer (fencing referee) 20 25
3856 4d. Amitsur Shapira (athletics coach) 20 25
3857 4d. Yaakov Springer (weightlifting referee) . . 20 25
3858 4d. Munich Olympics emblem 20 25
MS3859 96×130 mm. 25d. Israeli athlete with Olympic torch (vert) 1·40 1·50

329 Ferrari 333SP Racing Car

2000. Ferrari Racing Cars. Multicoloured.
3860 4d. Type **329** 20 25
3861 5d. Ferrari 512S 25 30
3862 10d. Ferrari 312P 55 60
3863 25d. Ferrari 330P4 . . . . 1·40 1·50

330 Symbolic Snake and Chinese Characters

2001. Chinese New Year ("Year of the Snake"). Showing different snakes. Multicoloured.
3864 4d. Type **330** 20 25
3865 4d. Orange and mauve snake 20 25
3866 4d. Blue and violet snake . . 20 25
3867 4d. Green and yellow snake 20 25
MS3868 71×100 mm. 15d. Snake in grass 80 85

330a "Vessels in a Strong Wind" (Jan Porcellis)

2001. Bicentenary of Rijksmuseum, Amsterdam. Dutch Paintings. Multicoloured.
3869 7d. Type **330a** 35 40
3870 7d. "Seascape in the Morning" (Simon de Vlieger) 35 40
3871 7d. "Travellers at a Country Inn" (Issack van Ostade) 35 40
3872 7d. "Orpheus with Animals in a Landscape" (Aelbert Cuyp) 35 40
3873 7d. "Italian with a Mountain Plateau" (Cornelis van Poelenburch) 35 40
3874 7d. Loading boat from "Boatman Moored on a Lake Shore" (Adam Pynacker) 35 40
3875 7d. Woman playing viol from "Gallant Company" (Pieter Codde) 35 40
3876 7d. Returning hunters from "Gallant Company" (Codde) 35 40
3877 7d. Kneeling man from "The Marriage of Willem van Loon and Margaretha Bas" (Jan Molenaer) 35 40
3878 7d. Bride's party from "The Marriage of Willem van Loon and Margaretha Bas" (Molenaer) 35 40
3879 7d. Man and two women from "The Marriage of Willem van Loon and Margaretha Bas" (Molenaer) 35 40
3880 7d. "Johanna Le Maire" (Nicolaes Pickenoy) . . . 35 40
3881 7d. "The Meagre Company" (Hals and Codde) . . . 35 40
3882 7d. "The Twins Clara and Aelbert de Bray" (Salomon de Bray) . . . 35 40
3883 7d. "Self-portrait" (Ferdinand Bol) 35 40
3884 7d. "Ambulatory of the New Church in Delft" (Gerard Houckgeest) . . 35 40
3885 7d. "Tomb of Willem the Silent in New Church of Delft" (Emanuel de Witte) 35 40
3886 7d. "Mountainous Landscape" (Hercules Segers) 35 40
3887 7d. Pie and glass of wine from "Still Life with Turkey Pie" (Pieter Claesz) 35 40
3888 7d. "Still Life with Gilt Goblet" (Willem Heda) 35 40
3889 7d. "Still Life with Lobster and Nautilus Cup" (Jan de Heem) 35 40
3890 7d. "Bacchanal" (detail) (Moses van Uyttenbroeck) 35 40
3891 7d. "The Anatomy Lesson of Dr. Nicolaes Tulp" (Rembrandt) 35 40
3892 7d. "Johannes Lutma" (Jacob Backer) 35 40
3893 7d. Decanter from "Still Life with Turkey Pie" (Claesz) 35 40
3894 7d. "Bouquet of Flowers in a Vase" (Ambrosius Bosschaert) 35 40
3895 7d. Vase of flowers from "Still Life with Flowers, Fruit and Shells" (Balthasar van der Ast) 35 40
3896 7d. Basket of flowers and building from "Still Life with Flowers, Fruit and Shells" (Van der Ast) . . 35 40
3897 7d. "Tulips in a Vase" (Hans Boulenger) 35 40
3898 7d. "Laid Table with Cheese and Fruit" (Floris van Dijck) 35 40
3899 7d. "Cows from "Boatman Moored on a Lake Shore" (Pynacker) 35 40
3900 7d. "The Ford in the River" (Jan Weenix) 35 40
3901 7d. "Two Horses near a Gate in a Meadow" (Paulus Potter) 35 40
3902 7d. "Cows and Sheep at a Stream" (Karel Dujardin) 35 40
3903 7d. Fiddler from "The Duet" (Cornelis Saftleven) 35 40
3904 7d. Viol player from "The Duet" (Saftleven) 35 40
MS3905 Six sheets. (a) 118×69 mm. 25d. "Meadow Landscape with Cattle" (Willem Roelofs) (horiz). (b) 118×69 mm. 25d. "Morning Ride on the Beach" (Anton Mauve) (horiz). (c) 118×96 mm. 25d. "The Spendthrift" (Cornelis Troost) (horiz). (d) 118×92 mm. 25d "View of New Church and Town Hall in Amsterdam" (Issak Outwater) (horiz). (e) 118×88 mm. 25d. "The Art Gallery of Jan Gildemeester Jansz" (Jan Ekels) (horiz). (f) 88×118 mm. 25d. "The Fall of Man" (Cornelis van Haarlem) (horiz) Set of 6 sheets . . . . 8·00 8·25

No. 3881 is inscribed "Frans Hal" and No. **MS**3905c "The Spendthrif", both in error.

331 Cowardly Lion

2001. Centenary of Publication of *The Wizard of Oz* (children's story by L. Frank Baum). Mult.
3906 7d. Type **331** 35 40
3907 7d. Land of Oz 35 40
3908 7d. Tin Man 35 40
3909 7d. Scarecrow 35 40
3910 7d. Toto 35 40
3911 7d. Munchkins 35 40
3912 7d. Witch of the North . . 35 40
3913 7d. Poppies of Oz 35 40
3914 7d. Dorothy's house 35 40
3915 7d. Witch of the East . . . 35 40
3916 7d. Dorothy 35 40
3917 7d. Wizard of Oz 35 40
3918 7d. Witch's wolf 35 40
3919 7d. Witch's forest 35 40
3920 7d. Witch's monkey 35 40
3921 7d. Dorothy asleep in poppies 35 40
3922 7d. Queen Mouse 35 40
3923 7d. Witch and evil bees . . 35 40
MS3924 Three sheets. (a) 77×106 mm. 27d. Gatekeeper. (b) 106×77 mm. 27d. Dorothy at crossroads (horiz). (c) 77×106 mm. 27d. Green Maiden Set of 3 sheets . . . . 4·25 4·50

332 Head of Melpomene (Muse of Tragedy)

2001. The History of Drama. Multicoloured.
3925 6d. Type **332** 30 35
3926 6d. Ancient Greek masks . . 30 35
3927 6d. Bust of Euripides (Greek tragedian) 30 35
3928 6d. Figures of two actors playing drunks 30 35
3929 6d. Scene from a play by Tang Hsien-Tsu (Chinese dramatist) 30 35
3930 6d. Uday and Amala Shankar (Indian actors) 30 35
3931 6d. Scene from a Japanese Noh play 30 35
3932 6d. Scene from *Clytemnestra* (Alexandros Mastas) . . . 30 35
3933 6d. William Shakespeare (English dramatist) . . . 30 35
3934 6d. Johann von Goethe (German philosopher and author) 30 35
3935 6d. Moliere (French dramatist) 30 35
3936 6d. Henrik Ibsen (Norwegian playwright) 30 35
3937 6d. George Bernard Shaw (Irish playwright) 30 35
3938 6d. Anton Chekhov (Russian dramatist) . . . 30 35
3939 6d. Sholom Aleichem (Jewish writer) 30 35
3940 6d. Tennessee Williams (American playwright) . . 30 35
MS3941 Two sheets, each 67×109 mm. (a) 25d. Sarah Bernhardt (French actress) as Phadera (vert). (b) 25d. John Barrymore (American actor) as Hamlet (vert) Set of 2 sheets 2·75 3·00

332a "Beedrill No. 15"

2001. Characters from "Pokemon" (children's cartoon series). Multicoloured.
3942 7d. Type **332a** 35 40
3943 7d. "Arbok No. 24" 35 40
3944 7d. "Machop No. 66" . . . 35 40
3945 7d. "Vileplume No. 45" . . . 35 40
3946 7d. "Clefairy No. 35" . . . 35 40
3947 7d. "Poliwirl No. 61" . . . 35 40
MS3948 74×115 mm. 25d. "Articuno No. 144" . . . . . 1·40 1·50

333 Succory **334** *Encyclia alata*

2001. Medicinal Plants. Multicoloured.
3949 3d. Pokeweed (horiz) . . . 15 20
3950 5d. Bay laurel (horiz) . . . 25 30
3951 8d. Type **333** 45 50
3952 8d. Dandelion 45 50
3953 8d. Garlic 45 50
3954 8d. Hemp agrimony 45 50
3955 8d. Star thistle 45 50
3956 8d. Cypress 45 50
3957 8d. Restharrow 45 50
3958 8d. White willow 45 50
3959 8d. Sweet serge 45 50
3960 8d. Passion flower 45 50
3961 8d. Rosemary 45 50
3962 8d. Pepper 45 50
3963 10d. Coltsfoot (horiz) . . . 55 60
3964 15d. Marsh mallow (horiz) 80 85
MS3965 Two sheets, each 83×108 mm. (a) 25d. Arbutus. (b) 25d. Olive Set of 2 sheets . . . 2·75 3·00

2001. "Hong Kong 2001" Stamp Exhibition. Orchids. Multicoloured.
3966 1d.50 Type **334** 10 15
3967 2d. *Dendrobium lasianthera* 10 15
3968 3d. *Cymbidiella pardalina* 15 20
3969 4d. *Cymbidium lowianum* 20 25
3970 4d. *Epidendrum pseudepidendrum* 20 25
3971 4d. *Eriopsis biloba* 20 25
3972 4d. *Masdevallia coccinea* . . 20 25
3973 4d. *Odontoglossum lindleyanum* 20 25
3974 4d. *Oerstedella wallisii* . . . 20 25
3975 4d. *Paphiopedilum acmodontum* 20 25
3976 4d. *Laelia rubescens* 20 25
3977 4d. *Huntleya wallisii* . . . 20 25
3978 4d. *Lycaste longiscapia* . . . 20 25
3979 4d. *Maxillaria variabilis* . . 20 25
3980 4d. *Mexicoa ghiesbrechtiana* 20 25
3981 4d. *Miltoniopsis phalaenopsis* 20 25
3982 5d. *Cypripedium irapeanum* 25 30
3983 7d. *Sobralia candida* . . . 35 40
3984 7d. *Phragmipedium besseae* 35 40
3985 7d. *Phaius tankervilleae* . . 35 40
3986 7d. *Vanda rothchildiana* . . 35 40
3987 7d. *Telipogon pulcher* . . . 35 40
3988 7d. *Rossioglossum insleayi* 35 40
3989 15d. *Doritis pulcherrima* . . 80 85
MS3990 Three sheets, each 72×98 mm. (a) 25d. *Cycnoches loddigesii*. (b) 25d. *Cattleya dowiana*. (c) 25d. *Chaubardia heteroclita* Set of 3 sheets . . . 4·00 4·25

No. 3984 is inscribed "BASSEAE" and No. 3389 "DORITAS", both in error.

335 *Seutieama Steelei* **336** *Disa uniflora*

2001. Orchids of Africa. Multicoloured.
3991 7d. Type **335** 25 20
3992 7d. *Dendrobium inaequale* 25 30
3993 7d. *Dendrobium lasiothera* "sepik blue" 25 30
3994 7d. *Calypso bulbosa* 25 30
3995 7d. *Vanda hindsi* 25 30
3996 7d. *Dendrobium violaceflavens* (d.Comber) 25 30
3997 8d. *Phaleonpis rosenstomii* (horiz) 30 35
3998 8d. *Cypripedium guttatum* (horiz) 30 35
3999 8d. *Cypripedium reginae* (horiz) 30 35
4000 8d. *Dendrobium engae* (horiz) 30 35
4001 8d. *Diploculobium hydrophilum* (horiz) . . . 30 35
4002 8d. *Dendrobium cuthbertsonii* (horiz) 30 35
4003 10d. *Eriopsis sceptrum* . . . 35 40
4004 10d. *Sarcan thopis meullum* 35 40
4005 10d. *Dendrobium lineale* "Bougainville White" . . 35 40
4006 10d. *Telipogon klotzchianus* 35 40
MS4007 Two sheets, each 91×64 mm. (a) 25d. *Dendrobium spectabile*. (b) 25d. *Menadenium labiosum* Set of 2 sheets . . . 1·80 1·80

Nos. 3991/6 printed together, se-tenant, with the background forming a composite design.

2001. African Flowers. Multicoloured.
4008 1d. Type **336** 10 10
4009 4d. *Monodora myristica* . . 20 25
4010 6d. *Clappertonia ficifolia* . . 30 35
4011 7d. *Canarina abyssinica* and european roller 35 40
4012 7d. *Amorphophallus abyssinicus* 35 40
4013 7d. *Calanthe rosea* and hoopoe 35 40
4014 7d. *Gloriosa simplex* 35 40
4015 7d. *Clappertonia ficifolia* (different) 35 40
4016 7d. *Ansellia gigantea* 35 40
4017 7d. *Vanilla planifolia* and antelope 35 40
4018 7d. *Strelitzia reginae* and antelope 35 40
4019 7d. *Spathiphyllum* ("Gladiolus cardinalis") 35 40
4020 7d. *Arctotis venusta* and antelope 35 40
4021 7d. *Protea obtusifolia* and antelope 35 40
4022 7d. *Geissorhiza rochensis* . . 35 40
4023 20d. *Calanthe rosea* (different) . . . . 1·10 1·25
MS4024 Two sheets. (a) 77×106 mm. 25d. *Arctotis venusta* (different). (b) 106×77 mm. 25d. *Geissorhiza rochensis* (horiz) Set of 2 sheets . . . . 2·75 3·00

Nos. 4011/16 and 4017/22 were each printed together, se-tenant, with the backgrounds forming composite designs.

Nos. 4008 and 4014 are inscribed "unifloria" or "Glorosa", both in error.

Mount Fuji and Tea Fields
by Matsuoka Eikyu (1881-1938)
THE GAMBIA D1

337 "Mount Fuji and Tea Fields" (Matsuoka Eikyu)

2001. "Philanippon '01" Internationl Stamp Exhibition, Tokyo. Japanese Art. Multicoloured.

No.	Description		
4025	1d. Type **337**	10	10
4026	2d. "Herons and Flowers" (one heron) (Okamo Shuki)	10	15
4027	3d. "Herons and Flowers" (two herons) (Shuki) . . .	15	20
4028	3d. "The Realm of the Gods in Yinzhou" (Timioka Tessai)	15	20
4029	4d. "Egret" (Takeuchi Seiho)	20	25
4030	4d. "Peach Blossom Spring in Wuling" (Tessai) . . .	20	25
4031	5d. "Sparrows" (Seiho) . .	25	30
4032	5d. "Spring Colours of the Lake and Mountains" (Shoda Gyokan)	25	30
4033	5d. Peonies	25	30
4034	5d. Iris	25	30
4035	5d. Hollyhocks and hydrangea	25	30
4036	5d. Fruit and Japanese white-eye on branch . . .	25	30
4037	5d. Little egret	25	30
4038	5d. Woodpecker in tree . .	25	30
4039	5d. Blossom and japonica flowers	25	30
4040	5d. Yellow flowers	25	30
4041	5d. Blossom and green pheasant in tree	25	30
4042	5d. Morning Glory	25	30
4043	5d. Blue and white flowers	25	30
4044	5d. White and red flowers	25	30
4045	7d. Workshop and man carrying pole (27 × 33 mm)	35	40
4046	7d. Two women and tree (27 × 33 mm)	35	40
4047	7d. Rocks and river (27 × 33 mm)	35	40
4048	7d. Two women on riverbank (27 × 33 mm)	35	40
4049	7d. Rocky landscape (27 × 33 mm)	35	40
4050	7d. Man by rocks (27 × 33 mm)	35	40
4051	7d. Couple by rocks (27 × 33 mm)	35	40
4052	7d. Women with scroll (27 × 33 mm)	35	40
4053	7d. White flowers and tree (27 × 33 mm)	35	40
4054	7d. Speckled cockerel by tree (27 × 33 mm)	35	40
4055	7d. Brown cockerel and red flowers (27 × 33 mm) . . .	35	40
4056	7d. Cockerel and white flowers (27 × 33 mm) . . .	35	40
4057	7d. Trees in stream (27 × 33 mm)	35	40
4058	7d. White cockerel and flowers (27 × 33 mm) . . .	35	40
4059	7d. Cockerel and chicken (27 × 33 mm)	35	40
4060	7d. Black and white cockerel by tree (27 × 33 mm) . . .	35	40
4061	10d. Branch with flower (27 × 33 mm)	55	60
4062	10d. European tree sparrows (27 × 33 mm)	55	60
4063	10d. Butterfly on blossom (27 × 33 mm)	55	60
4064	10d. Crayfish (27x33 mm)	55	60
4065	10d. "Ushiwakamaru" (Kano Osanobu)	55	60
4066	10d. "Red Lotus and White Goose" (Goun Saku) . .	55	60
4067	15d. "Woman selling Flowers" (Ito Shoha) . .	80	85
4068	20d. "The Sound of the Ocean" (Matsumoto Ichiyo)	1·10	1·25
MS4069	Five sheets, each 119 × 89 mm. (a) 30d. "Puppies and Morning Glories" (Yamaguchi Soken). (b) 30d. "Deep Pool" (Nishimura Goun). (c) 30d. "Poppies" (Tsuchida Bakusen). (d) 30d. "Spring Farming near a Riverside Village" (Mori Getsuj). (e) 30d. "Untitled" (couple and dogs by lake) (Utagawa Kuniyoshi). Imperf Set of 5 sheets	8·00	8·25

Nos. 4033/8 and 4039/44 ("Birds and Flowers of the Twelve Months" (Sakai Hoitsu)), 4045/52 (composite designs from "The Four Accomplishments" (Kaiho Yusho)), 4053/60 (composite designs from "Birds and Flowers" (Soga Chokuan)) and 4061/64 ("Book of Lacquer Paintings" (Shiban Zeshin)) were each printed together, se-tenant, in sheetlets of 4, 6 or 8.

338 Queen Victoria reading Speech from the Throne

2001. Death Centenary of Queen Victoria. Multicoloured.

No.	Description		
4070	15d. Type **338**	80	85
4071	15d. Prime Minister Benjamin Disraeli	80	85
4072	15d. Procession for State Opening of Parliament . .	80	85
MS4073	90 × 68 mm. 25d. Queen Victoria (vert)	1·40	1·50

339 Mao Tse-tung in 1935

341 Queen Elizabeth in Guards Uniform

340 "Madame Monet on the Sofa", 1871

2001. 25th Death Anniv of Mao Tse-tung (Chinese leader).

No.	Description		
4074	**339** 15d. black, blue and light blue	80	85
4075	– 15d. multicoloured . . .	80	85
4076	– 15d. black, deep blue and blue	80	85
MS4077	132 × 108 mm. 25d. multicoloured	1·40	1·50

DESIGNS: No. 4074, Type **339**; 4075, Mao in 1949; 4076, Mao in 1951; **MS**4077, Mao addressing meeting in 1928.

2001. 75th Death Anniv of Claude-Oscar Monet (French painter). Multicoloured .

No.	Description		
4078	10d. Type **340**	55	60
4079	10d. "The Picnic", 1865 . .	55	60
4080	10d. "The Luncheon", 1868	55	60
4081	10d. "Jean Monet on his Mechanical Horse", 1879	55	60
MS4082	137 × 110 mm. 25d. "La Japonaise", 1875 (vert)	1·40	1·50

2001. 75th Birthday of Queen Elizabeth II. Multicoloured.

No.	Description		
4083	15d. Type **341**	80	85
4084	15d. Queen Elizabeth in pink suit and hat	80	85
4085	15d. Queen Elizabeth wearing ruby tiara	80	85
4086	15d. Queen Elizabeth wearing sapphire necklace	80	85
MS4087	80 × 110 mm. 25d. Princess Elizabeth on her wedding day (38 × 50 mm)	1·40	1·50

342 Queen Elizabeth II

343 Verdi as an Old Man

2001. Golden Jubilee (1st issue).

No.	Description		
4088	**342** 8d. multicoloured . . .	45	50

No. 4088 was printed in sheetlets of 8, containing two vertical rows of four, separated by a large illustrated central gutter. Both the stamp and the illustration on the central gutter are made up of a collage of miniature flower photographs.

2001. Death Centenary of Giuseppe Verdi (Italian composer). Multicoloured.

No.	Description		
4089	10d. Type **343**	55	60
4090	10d. Singers and score for *La Traviata* (opera) . . .	55	60
4091	10d. Singer and score for *Aida* (opera)	55	60
4092	10d. Verdi as a young man	55	60
MS4093	76 × 106 mm. 25d. Verdi as an old man	1·40	1·50

Nos. 4089/92 were printed together, se-tenant, with the backgrounds forming a composite design.

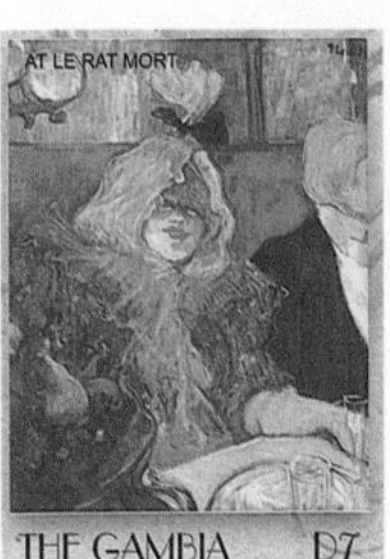

344 "At Le Rat Mort"

2001. Death Centenary of Henri de Toulouse-Lautrec (French painter). Multicoloured.

No.	Description		
4094	7d. Type **344**	35	40
4095	7d. "The Milliner"	35	40
4096	7d. "Messaline"	35	40
MS4097	66 × 85 mm. 25d. "Napoleon"	1·40	1·50

345 Marlene Dietrich in Evening Dress

2001. Birth Centenary of Marlene Dietrich (actress and singer).

No.	Description		
4098	**345** 10d. black, purple and claret	55	60
4099	– 10d. multicoloured . . .	55	60
4100	– 10d. multicoloured . . .	55	60
4101	– 10d. black, purple and claret	55	60

DESIGNS: No. 4099, Marlene Dietrich with roses; 4100, Marlene Dietrich with arms crossed; 4101, Marlene Dietrich wearing feathered hat.

346 *Orchis morio*

2001. "Belgica 2001" International Stamp Exhibition, Brussels. African Orchids. Multicoloured.

No.	Description		
4102	3d. Type **346**	15	20
4103	4d. *Fulophia speciosa* . . .	20	25
4104	5d. *Angraecum leonis* . . .	25	30
4105	8d. *Ceratostylis retisquama*	45	50
4106	8d. *Rangaeris rhipsalisocia*	45	50
4107	8d. *Phaius hybrid* and baby chimpanzee	45	50
4108	8d. *Disa hybrid*	45	50
4109	8d. *Disa uniflora*	45	50
4110	8d. *Angraecum leonis* and chimpanzee	45	50
4111	8d. *Satyrium erectum* (horiz)	45	50
4112	8d. *Aeranthes grandiose* (horiz)	45	50
4113	8d. *Aerangis somasticta* (horiz)	45	50
4114	8d. *Polystachya bella* (horiz)	45	50
4115	8d. *Eulophia guineensis* (horiz)	45	50
4116	8d. *Disa blacki* (horiz) . . .	45	50
4117	15d. *Oeceoclades maculata*	80	85
MS4118	78 × 97 mm. 25d. *Disa kirstenbosch Pride*	1·40	1·50

Nos. 4105/4110 and 4111/16 were each printed together, se-tenant, with the backgrounds forming composite designs.

347 Children with Balloons

2001. S.O.S. Children's Villages (Kinderdorf International).

No.	Description		
4119	**347** 10d. multicoloured . . .	55	60

348 Hoopoe

2001. Animals of Africa. Multicoloured.

No.	Description		
4120	2d. Type **348**	10	10
4121	3d. Great spotted cuckoo . .	10	15
4122	4d. Plain tiger (butterfly) . .	15	20
4123	5d. Zebra duiker	20	25
4124	10d. Sooty mangabey . . .	35	40
4125	20d. Greater kudu	75	80
MS4126	145 × 82 mm. 8d. Grey parrot; 8d. Rachel's malimbe ("RACHEL'S WEAVER"); 8d. European bee-eater; 8d. River kingfisher; 8d. Red river hog; 8d. Bush buck	1·80	1·80
MS4127	145 × 82 mm. 8d. Blue diadem (butterfly); 8d. Fire-footed rope squirrel; 8d. *Clappertonia ficifolia* (flower); 8d. *Costus spectabilis* (flower); 8d. African migrant (butterfly); 8d. Giant African snail	1·80	1·80
MS4128	145 × 82 mm. 8d. Hippopotamus; 8d. Elephant; 8d. Parusta simplex (butterfly); 8d. Grey heron; 8d. *Charaxes imperialis* (butterfly); 8d. *Gloriosa simplex* (flower)	1·80	1·80
MS4129	145 × 82 mm. 8d. Alpine swift; 8d. Blotched genet; 8d. Thomas' galago; 8d. Carmine bee eater; 8d. Tree pangolin; 8d. Campbell's monkey	1·80	1·80
MS4130	Two sheets, each 85 × 110 mm. (a) 25d. Long-tailed pangolin (vert). (b) 25d. Common pestrel ("EURASIAN KESTREL") (vert) Set of 2 sheets	1·80	1·80

349 Blue-winged Teal

2001. Ducks of the World. Multicoloured.

No.	Description		
4131	2d. Type **349**	10	10
4132	3d. Red-crested pochard . .	10	15
4133	3d. Wood duck (vert) . . .	10	15
4134	4d. Mallard (vert)	15	20
4135	4d. Falcated teal	15	20
4136	5d. Mandarin duck	20	25
4137	5d. Barrow's goldeneye (head) (vert)	20	25
4138	10d. Bufflehead (head) (vert)	35	40
4139	10d. King eider	35	40
4140	15d. Hooded merganser . .	55	60
MS4141	116 × 131 mm. 7d. Barrow's goldeneye in flight; 7d. Harlequin duck; 7d. Northern pintail; 7d. Red-billed whistling duck ("Black-bellied Whistling Duck"); 7d. Cinnamon teal; 7d. Surf scoter	1·50	1·50
MS4142	116 × 131 mm. 7d. Black scoter; 7d. North American black duck; 7d. Green-winged teal; 7d. Bufflehead; 7d. Red-breasted merganser; 7d. Fulvous whistling duck	1·50	1·50
MS4143	123 × 123 mm. 8d. European wigeon; 8d. Mallard; 8d. Garganey; 8d. Northern pintail; 8d. Northern shoveler; 8d. Green-winged teal	1·80	1·80
MS4144	123 × 123 mm. 8d. North American black duck; 8d. Bufflehead; 8d. Cinnamon teal; 8d. Common goldeneye; 8d. Ruddy shelduck; 8d. Ferruginous duck	1·80	1·80
MS4145	123 × 123 mm. 8d. Masked duck; 8d. Long-tailed duck ("OLD SQUAW"); 8d. Ring-necked duck; 8d. Harlequin duck; 8d. Redhead; 8d. Canvasback	1·80	1·80
MS4146	Four sheets. (a) 70 × 98 mm. 25d. Wood duck. (b) 70 × 98 mm. 25d. American wigeon. (c) 70 × 98 mm. 25d. Baikal teal. (d) 105 × 76 mm. Green-winged teal Set of 4 sheets	3·50	3·50

350 Martial Eagle

2001. "The Gambia—A Wildlife Paradise". Multicoloured.

4147	2d. Type **350**	10	10
4148	4d. Lion	10	15
4149	5d. Aardvark	20	25
4150	10d. Lion cub	35	40

MS4151 149 × 96 mm. 7d. Lion cub; 7d. Water buffalo; 7d. Topi; 7d. Hyena; 7d. Secretary bird; 7d. Genet . . . 1·50 1·50

MS4152 149 × 96 mm. 7d. Reedbuck; 7d. Hippopotamus; 7d. Waterbuck; 7d. Hoopoe; 7d. Eastern white pelican; 7d. Waterbuck . . . 1·50 1·50

MS4153 Two sheets, each 92 × 66 mm. (a) 25d. Crocodile. (b) 25d. Hippopotamus Set of 2 sheets 1·80 1·80

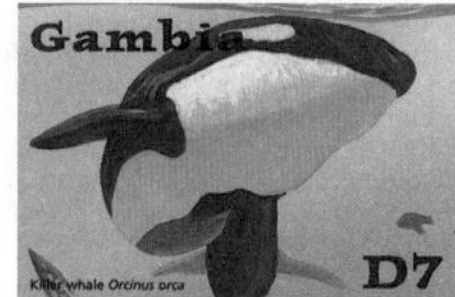

351 Killer Whale

2001. Whales. Multicoloured.

MS4154 149 × 96 mm. 7d. Type **351**; 7d. Two sperm whales; 7d. Narwhal; 7d. Grey whale; 7d. Blue whale; 7d. Northern right whale 1·50 1·50

MS4155 149 × 96 mm. 7d. Killer whale and tail fin of whale; 7d. Sperm whale; 7d. Strap-toothed whale; 7d. Humpback whale; 7d. Southern right whale; 7d. Beluga 1·50 1·50

MS4156 Two sheets, each 92 × 66 mm. (a) 25d. Killer whale. (b) 25d. Humpback whale . . 1·90 1·90

GAZA Pt. 19

EGYPTIAN OCCUPATION

A strip of territory along the coast from Gaza to the Egyptian frontier, seized by Egypt when the British Mandate for Palestine ended in May 1948.

In 1967 Israeli troops seized the Gaza Strip and from that date Israeli stamps were used.

In May 1994 the area became autonomous under the Palestinian National Authority.

1000 milliemes = £1 (Egyptian).

1948. Various stamps of Egypt optd **PALESTINE** in English and Arabic.
1 **91** 1m. brown (postage) 20 20
2 2m. red 20 20
3 **78** 3m. brown 20 20
4 **91** 4m. green 20 20
5 5m. brown 20 20
6 **78** 6m. green 20 20
7 **91** 10m. violet 20 20
8 **78** 13m. red 25 25
9 **91** 15m. purple 25 25
10 17m. green 25 25
11 20m. violet 25 25
12 22m. blue 35 35
13 – 30m. green (No. 340) 40 35
14 **106** 40m. brown 60 50
15 – 50m. blue (No. 342) 65 60
16 – 100m. purple (No. 280) 2·30 2·00
17 – 200m. violet (No. 281) 6·75 6·75
18 **86** 50p. brown and green 18·00 18·00
19 **87** £E1 brown and blue 32·00 32·00

20 **101** 2m. red (air) 25 25
21 3m. brown 25 25
22 5m. red 25 25
23 7m. brown 45 45
24 8m. green 45 45
25 10m. violet 55 55
26 20m. blue 90 90
27 30m. purple 1·80 1·80
28 40m. red 1·40 1·40
29 50m. blue 1·80 1·80
30 100m. green 3·50 3·50
31 200m. grey 9·00 9·00

1953. As above but with portrait obliterated by three horiz bars. (a) Postage.
32 **91** 1m. brown 20 20
33 2m. red 20 20
34 **78** 3m. brown 20 20
35 **91** 4m. green 20 20
36 5m. brown 20 20
37 **78** 6m. green 20 20
38 **91** 10m. violet 25 25
39 **78** 13m. red 35 35
40 **91** 15m. purple 35 35
41 17m. green 40 40
42 20m. violet 45 45
43 22m. blue 60 60
44 – 30m. green 60 60
45 **106** 40m. brown 85 85
46 – 50m. blue 3·50 3·25
47 – 100m. purple 6·00 7·25
48 – 200m. violet 13·50 16·00
49 **86** 50p. brown and green 27·00 34·00
50 **87** £E1 brown and blue 80·00 85·00

(b) Air.
51 **101** 2m. red 45 45
52 3m. brown 45 45
53 5m. red 8·50 9·50
54 7m. brown 45 65
55 8m. green 1·40 1·10
56 10m. violet 1·40 1·10
57 20m. blue 1·40 1·10
58 30m. purple 1·40 1·10
59 40m. red 4·00 4·00
60 50m. blue 13·50 13·50
61 100m. green 49·00 55·00
62 200m. grey 5·50 5·50

1953. Air. Nos. 480/2, 485 and 489/90 of Egypt optd **PALESTINE** in English and Arabic.
63 **101** 2m. red 45 45
64 3m. brown 9·00 9·00
65 5m. red 1·70 1·90
66 10m. violet 16·00 17·00
67 50m. blue 4·50 6·00
68 100m. olive 32·00 32·00

1955. Stamps of Egypt, 1953/4, optd **PALESTINE** in English and Arabic.
69 **137** 1m. brown 20 20
70 2m. purple 20 20
71 3m. blue 20 20
72 4m. green 20 20
73 5m. red 20 20
74 **130** 10m. sepia (B) 20 20
75 15m. grey 20 20
76 17m. turquoise 20 20
77 20m. violet 25 25
78 **131** 30m. green 25 25
79 32m. blue 45 45
80 35m. violet 35 35
81 40m. brown 60 60
82 50m. purple 60 60
83 **132** 100m. brown 1·10 1·10
84 200m. turquoise 8·25 8·50
85 500m. violet 34·00 34·00
86 £E1 red and green 60·00 60·00

1955. Air. Nos. 433/4 of Egypt optd **PALESTINE** in English and Arabic.
86a **133** 5m. brown 3·25 4·25
86b 15m. green 4·00 5·00

Types of Egypt (sometimes with colours changed) overprinted **PALESTINE** in English and Arabic.

1957. Re-occupation of Gaza Strip.
87 **152** 10m. green 3·75 4·00

1957. Stamps of 1957.
88 – 1m. turquoise (No. 538) 20 20
89 – 5m. sepia (No. 541) 20 20
90 **160** 10m. violet 20 20

UNITED ARAB REPUBLIC

1958. Stamps of 1958 (inscr "U A R EGYPT").
91 – 1m. red (No. 553) 20 20
92 – 2m. blue (No. 554) 20 20
93 **168** 3m. brown 20 20
94 – 4m. green (No. 556) 20 20
95 – 5m. sepia (No. 557) 20 20
96 **160** 10m. violet (No. 558) 25 20
96a – 35m. blue (No. 559) 1·50 1·40

1958. 5th Anniv of Republic.
97 **172** 10m. brown 1·40 1·40

1958. 10th Anniv of Declaration of Human Rights.
98 **178** 10m. purple 1·90 2·75
99 35m. brown 4·75 5·25

1959. No. 588.
100 **132** 55m. on 100m. red 2·75 4·00

Types of Egypt with some colours changed and additionally inscribed "PALESTINE" in English and Arabic.

1960. As Nos. 603, etc.
101 **160** 1m. orange 20 20
104 – 4m. brown 20 20
105 – 5m. violet 20 20
106 – 10m. green 20 20

1960. World Refugee Year.
109 **205** 10m. brown 25 25
110 35m. black 1·30 90

1961. World Health Day.
111 **213** 10m. blue 80 65

1961. Palestine Day.
112 **215** 10m. violet 20 20

1961. U.N. Technical Co-operation Programme and 16th Anniv of UNO.
113 – 10m. blue and orange 20 20
114 **220** 35m. purple and red 40 40

1961. Education Day.
115 **223** 10m. brown 20 20

1961. Victory Day.
116 **224** 10m. brown and chestnut 20 20

1962. 5th Anniv of Egyptian Occupation of Gaza.
117 **229** 10m. brown 20 20

1962. Arab League Week.
118 **231** 10m. purple 20 20

1962. Malaria Eradication.
119 **235** 10m. red and brown 20 20
120 – 35m. yellow and black 85 60

1962. 17th Anniv of UNO and Hammarskjold Commemoration.
121 **245** 5m. blue and pink 20 20
122 10m. blue and brown 20 20
123 35m. indigo and blue 40 40

1963. As No. 739.
124 4m. blue, orange and black 20 20

1963. Freedom from Hunger.
125 **252** 5m. brown and green 20 20
126 – 10m. yellow and green 20 20
127 – 35m. yellow and purple 40 40

1963. Centenary of Red Cross.
128 **253** 10m. red, purple and blue 20 20
129 – 35m. ultram, blue & red 35 35

1963. UNESCO Campaign for Preservation of Nubian Monuments (4th issue).
130 **256** 5m. yellow and purple 20 20
131 – 10m. yellow and black 20 20
132 – 35m. yellow and violet 80 35

1963. Air. As Nos. 758, 760 and 761/2.
133 50m. purple and blue 70 70
134 80m. indigo and blue 1·10 1·10
135 115m. yellow and black 1·80 1·80
136 140m. red and blue 2·30 2·30

1963. 15th Anniv of Declaration of Human Rights.
137 **259a** 5m. yellow and sepia 20 20
138 – 10m. black, grey & pur 20 20
139 – 35m. black, green & turq 40 40

1964. As No. 769, etc.
140 – 1m. violet and green 25 25
141 – 2m. blue and orange 25 25
142 – 3m. blue, brown & lt blue 25 25
143 – 4m. green, brown & pink 25 25
144 – 5m. red, blue and pink 25 25
145 – 10m. red, brown and green 25 25
146 – 15m. yellow, violet & lilac 25 25
147 – 20m. green and violet 55 55
148 **261** 30m. blue and orange 1·20 1·20
149 – 35m. brown, green & orge 90 90
150 – 40m. blue and green 1·20 1·20
151 – 60m. brown and blue 1·80 1·80
152 **263** 100m. brown and blue 2·75 2·75

1964. Arab League Heads of State Congress, Cairo.
153 **266** 10m. black and olive 20 20

1964. Ramadan Festival.
154 **267** 4m. olive, red and lake 20 20

1964. 10th Anniv of Arab Postal Union's Permanent Office.
155 **271** 10m. blue and green 20 20

1964. World Health Day.
156 **272** 10m. purple and red 20 20

1965. Ramadan Festival. As No. 834.
157 – 4m. brown and green 20 20

1965. 20th Anniv of Arab League.
158 **289** 10m. green and red 20 20
159 – 20m. brown and green 20 20

1965. Air. World Meteorological Day.
160 **290** 80m. orange and blue 2·30 2·30

1965. World Health Day.
161 **291** 10m. red and green 20 20

1965. Deir Yassin Massacre.
162 **292** 10m. red and blue 20 20

1965. Centenary of I.T.U.
163 **293** 5m. blue, yellow and green 20 20
164 10m. rose, blue and red 20 20
165 35m. blue, yell & ultram 80 30

1965. Air. Re-establishment of Egyptian Civil Airlines "MISRAIR".
166 **295** 10m. green and orange 35 35

1966. U.N. Day.
167 **321** 5m. violet and red 20 20
168 – 10m. violet and brown 20 20
169 – 35m. violet and green 25 25

1966. Victory Day.
170 **324** 10m. red and olive 20 20

1967. Arab Publicity Week.
171 **328** 10m. brown and blue 20 20

1967. Labour Day.
172 **331** 10m. sepia and olive 20 20

EXPRESS LETTER STAMP

1948. Express Letter stamp of Egypt optd **PALESTINE** in English and Arabic.
E32 **E 52** 40m. black and brown 6·00 5·50

POSTAGE DUE STAMPS

1948. Postage Due stamps of Egypt optd **PALESTINE** in English and Arabic.
D32 **D 59** 2m. orange 1·00 1·10
D33 4m. green 75 90
D34 6m. green 75 90
D35 8m. purple 75 90
D36 10m. lake 75 90
D37 12m. red 75 90
D38 30m. violet 2·40 4·75

This area was occupied by Israel on 6 June 1967. Post Offices were opened in July 1967 and Israeli stamps are now used.

GEORGIA Pt. 10

Formerly part of Russia, Georgia declared its independence after the Russian Revolution. In 1921 it became a Soviet Republic and in 1922 joined with Armenia and Azerbaijan to form the Transcaucasian Federation, whose stamps were used from September 1923. After absorption into the U.S.S.R. Russian stamps were used from 1924.

With the dissolution of the Soviet Union in 1991 Georgia again became an independent state.

1919. 100 kopeks = 1 rouble.
1993. kupon.
1995. 100 tetri = 1 lari.

1 St. George

3 Queen Tamara (A.D. 1184–1212)

1919. Imperf or perf.
10 **1** 10k. blue 20 1·00
1 40k. red 20 1·00
12 50k. green 20 1·00
2 60k. red 20 1·00
3 70k. mauve 20 1·00
15 – 1r. brown (20 × 25 mm) 20 1·00
16 **3** 2r. brown 30 75
17a 3r. blue 20 1·00
18 5r. yellow 50 1·00

4 Soldier

6 Industry and agriculture

1922. Perf.
28a **4** 500r. red 2·00 4·00
29 – 1000r. brown (Sower) 2·75 3·50
30 **6** 2000r. grey 3·25 3·50
31 3000r. brown 3·00 3·50
32 5000r. green 3·00 3·50

7

1922. Famine Relief. Designs as T **7**. Surch.
33 – 100r. on 50r. violet 50 2·00
34 – 3000r. on 100r. red 50 2·00
35 – 5000r. on 250r. green 50 2·00
36 **7** 10,000r. on 25r. blue 50 3·00

1923. Surch.
37 – 10,000r. on 1000r. (No. 29) 2·75 1·00
38 **6** 15,000r. on 2000r. grey 3·00 1·25
44 **4** 20,000r. on 500r. red 75 1·25
40a **6** 40,000r. on 5000r. green 1·25 1·00
46 80,000r. on 3000r. brown 1·75 2·00

1923. Surch. (a) On Arms types of Russia.
47 **22** 10,000r. on 7k. blue 32·00 32·00
48 **10** 15,000r. on 15k. blue & brn 3·00 3·50

(b) On No. 75B of Armenia.
49 **10** 1,5000r. on 5r. on 15k. blue and brown 22·00 20·00

1923. Arms types of Russia surch with hammer and sickle and value. Imperf or perf.
50 **22** 75,000r. on 1k. orange 4·00 4·50
52 20,000r. on 5k. red 3·00 4·00
53 **14** 30,000r. on 20k. red & blue 2·75 3·00
54 **22** 35,000r. on 3k. red 3·50 4·25
57 700,000r. on 2k. green 5·00 5·00

12 Map, National Flag and U.N. Emblem

13 Arms and Flag

1993. 1st Anniv of Admission to U.N.O.
58 **12** 25r. multicoloured 20 20
59 50r. multicoloured 30 30
60 100r. multicoloured 50 50
MS61 122 × 101 mm. Nos. 58/60 1·25 1·25

1993.
62 **13** 0.50k. multicoloured 15 15

14 18th-century Fresco in gold

15 "Apostle Simon" (icon)

1993. Treasures of the National Museum.
63 **14** 0.50k. multicoloured 15 15

1993. Ancient Art.
64 **15** 1k. multicoloured 15 15

16 "Three Women" (Lado Gudiashvili)

17 Juari Monastery, Mtskheta

1993. National Paintings.
65 **16** 1k. multicoloured 15 15

1993. Places of Worship.
66 **17** 30k. blue 10 10
67 – 40k. brown 15 15
68 – 50k. brown 20 20
69 – 60k. red 20 20
70 – 70k. lilac 25 25
71 – 80k. green 30 30
72 – 90k. black 35 35
DESIGNS: 40k. Gelati Church; 50k. Nikortsminda Church; 60k. Ikorta Church; 70k. Samtavisi Church; 80k. Bolnisi Zion Synagogue; 90k. Gremi Citadel Church.

18 Emblem

1994. 2nd Anniv of International Olympic Committee Recognition of Georgian National Olympic Committee.
73 **18** 100k.+50k. multicoloured 25 25

19 Emblem

1994. Admission (1993) of Georgia to U.P.U.
74 **19** 200k. multicoloured 40 40

20 Window and Nikoladze

1994. 150th Birth Anniv (1993) of Niko Nikoladze (journalist).
75 **20** 150k. multicoloured 30 30

1994. Nos. 62/5 surch.
76 **13** 5000k. on 0.50k. mult . . . 10 10
77 **14** 5000k. on 0.50k. mult . . . 10 10
78 **15** 10000k. on 1k. mult 20 20
79 **16** 10000k. on 1k. mult 30 30

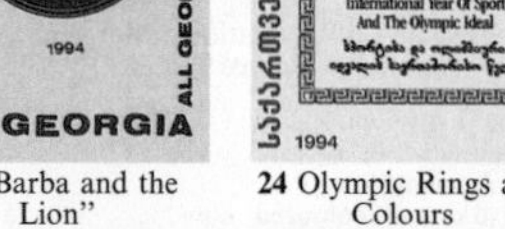

22 "Barba and the Lion"

24 Olympic Rings and Colours

1994. All-Georgian Congress.
80 **22** 100k. brown and pink . . . 70 70
81 – 200k. deep blue and blue . . 70 70
DESIGN: 200k. Equestrian statue

1994. Nos. 63/5 surch **Georgia** and new value.
82 **14** 200k. on 0.50k. mult 25 25
83 **15** 300k. on 1k. multicoloured 45 45
84 **16** 500k. on 1k. multicoloured 70 70

1995. Centenary of International Olympic Committee. Multicoloured.
85 10k. Type **24** (International Year of Sport) 20 20
86 15k. Emblem symbolizing founding congress 30 30
87 20k. Anniversary emblem . . 40 40
88 25k. Olympic rings and peace dove ("Olympic Truce") . . 50 50

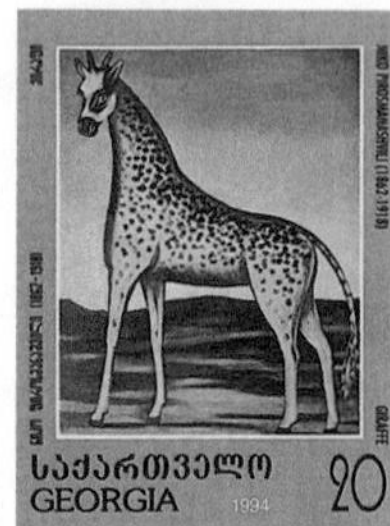

25 "Giraffe"

1995. 77th Death Anniv of Niko Pirosmanashvili (painter). Multicoloured.
89 20k. Type **25** 50 50
90 20k. "Three Princes Carousing on the Grass" (horiz) . . . 50 50
91 20k. "Brooder with Chicks" (horiz) 50 50
92 20k. "Boy on a Donkey" . . . 50 50
93 20k. "Fisherman" 50 50
94 20k. "Woman with a Tankard of Beer" 50 50
95 20k. "Bear on a Moonlit Night" 50 50
96 20k. "Georgian woman with a Tambourine" 50 50
97 20k. "Still Life" (horiz) . . . 50 50
98 20k. "Deer" 50 50
MS99 113 × 86 mm. 100k. "Family Picnicking" (horiz) . . . . . . 2·00 2·00

26 Alaverdi

27 Sveti-Zchoveli Cathedral, Mtskheta

28 Bitschvinta

1995. Monasteries. Value expressed by letter.
100 **26** A blue and black 60 60
101 – A green and black 60 60
102 **27** I lilac and black 60 60
103 – I brown and black 60 60
104 – I green and black 60 60
105 **28** U brown and black 60 60
106 – U brown and black 60 60
DESIGNS: No. 101, Ananuri; 103, Kumurdo; 104, Dranda; 106, Metechi.
The stamps are inscribed with letters of the Georgian alphabet.

1995. Monasteries. As Nos. 106, 100 and 104 but with value expressed by figure.
107 1 purple and black 60 60
108 2 brown and black 60 60
109 3 brown and black 60 60
DESIGNS: No. 107, Metechi; 108, Alaverdi; 109, Dranda.
The numbers on Nos. 107/9 represent classes of postage rather than the face value of the stamps.

29 Iashvili and Family

1995. Birth Centenary (1994) of Paolo Iashvili (writer).
110 **29** 300k. brown and black . . 60 60

30 Brontosaurus

1995. Prehistoric Animals. Multicoloured.
111 15k. Type **30** 30 30
112 15k. Ceratosaurus 30 30
113 15k. Deinonichus 30 30
114 15k. Parasaurolophus 30 30
115 15k. Saurolophus 30 30
116 15k. Scolosaurus 30 30
117 15k. Stegosaurus 30 30
118 15k. Triceratops 30 30
119 15k. Tyrannosaurus 30 30
MS120 106 × 76 mm. 100k. Deinonychus . . . . 3·00 3·00

31 White-headed Stork, Bar-tailed Godwit, Mandarin Duck, Hyacinth Macaw and Deer

1995. Wildlife. Multicoloured.
121 15k. Heads of horse, monkey, eagle, deer, bird, lynx and elephant 20 20
122 15k. Dragonfly and butterfly at left, mosquitoes and fishes among heads of woolly-necked stork and greater flamingo 20 20
123 15k. Fishes and butterfly with heads of lioness, cow, parrot, monkey and owl with egret at right 20 20
124 15k. Fox's face at left, northern lapwing, skunk and fish 20 20
125 15k. Butterfly, scorpion, bluethroat, fishes and elephant's trunk at right 20 20
126 15k. Type **31** 20 20
127 15k. Fishes, shells, antelope, dogs, dolphin and silver pheasant 20 20
128 15k. Body of pipefish, Indian peacock and king eider, fox and fly 20 20
129 15k. Rhinoceros, seahorse and dolphin 20 20
130 15k. Zebra, hippopotamus, deer, fishes, spur-winged goose, northern bullfinch, common pheasant and moth 20 20
131 15k. Dog's head, Abyssinian ground hornbill, lobster, fishes and other mammals 20 20
132 15k. Seal, warthog, rabbits, fishes, beetle and red-breasted goose 20 20
133 15k. Ostrich, other birds, fish and lion's face 20 20
134 15k. Snake's head, fishes, slavonian grebe, beetle, giraffe's head and frog . . 20 20
135 15k. Sheep, antelope, fishes, ant and birds, including dove 20 20
136 15k. Whale, stoat, great crested grebe, killdeer plover, parrot, butterfly and lizard 20 20
Nos. 121/36 were issued together, se-tenant, forming a composite design.

32 Bagrati Cathedral

1995. UNESCO World Heritage Sites.
137 **32** 100k. multicoloured . . . 60 60
MS138 75 × 105 mm. 500k. Jvari Monastery, Mtskhetha (28 × 42 mm) . . . . 3·00 3·00

33 Pterodactylus

1995. Prehistoric Animals. Multicoloured.
139 15t. Type **33** 35 35
140 15t. Rhamphorhynchus (inscr "Rhamphorhynghus") . . 35 35
141 15t. Pteranodon 35 35
142 15t. Spinosaurus 35 35
143 15t. Tyrannosaurus 35 35
144 15t. Velociraptor 35 35
145 15t. Monoklonius 35 35
146 15t. Ornithomimus 35 35
147 15t. Mastodon 35 35
Nos. 139/47 were issued together, se-tenant, forming a composite design.

34 Barn Swallows

1996. Birds. Multicoloured.
148 15t. Type **34** 20 20
149 15t. Redwing (spotted breast) 20 20
150 15t. Common starling (black with greenish wing) 20 20
151 15t. Hawfinch (brown with black patch on neck) . . . 20 20
152 15t. Barred warbler (black and white bird on twig) . . 20 20
153 15t. Golden oriole (yellow with black wing) 20 20
154 15t. Collared flycatcher (black and white bird on trunk of tree) 20 20
155 15t. Chaffinch (chestnut front and back and small crest) 20 20
156 15t. Crested tit (brown body, black and white head and crest) 20 20
157 15t. Yellowhammer (speckled black and yellow) 20 20
158 15t. White wagtail (white with black chest, nape and wings) 20 20
159 15t. Blackbird (black with yellow beak) 20 20
160 15t. Common redstart (grey and black head, chestnut patch on front) 20 20
161 15t. European robin (red face and chest) 20 20
162 15t. Eurasian nuthatch (bird with black stripe across eye, on tree trunk) 20 20
163 15t. Blue tit (blue head, wings and tail and green back) 20 20
164 15t. White-tailed sea eagle (white tail) 20 20
165 15t. Osprey (black and white bird in flight) 20 20
166 15t. Short-toed eagle (speckled brown and white on tip of branch) 20 20
167 15t. Long-legged buzzard (chestnut) 20 20
168 15t. Red kite (red tail, in flight) 20 20
169 15t. Western marsh harrier (white tail and white wings tipped with brown, in flight) 20 20
170 15t. Northern goshawk (grey bird with black eye stripe, on branch) 20 20
171 15t. Tawny owl (on branch, tips of fir trees) 20 20
172 15t. Northern hobby (black and white bird on branch overhanging water) 20 20
173 15t. Common kestrel (black head and tail and brown body, valley in background) 20 20
174 15t. Long-eared owl (with large ears, sitting upright) 20 20
175 15t. Great grey owl (on top of tree stump, fir trees behind) 20 20
176 15t. Imperial eagle (both wings raised above body and flying over water) . . 20 20
177 15t. Imperial eagle (brown bird with white wing-tips, on branch overhanging water) 20 20

178 15t. Little owl (white owl on thick branch at water's edge) 20 20
179 15t. Northern eagle owl (brown bird with ears, spreading wings) 20 20
MS180 Two sheets, each 100 × 70 mm. (a) 100t. Screech Owl; (b) 100t. Barn Swallow at nest . . . . 5·00 5·00
Nos. 148/63 and 164/79 were issued respectively together, se-tenant, forming composite designs.

35 Head of Common Crane

1996. Animals. Multicoloured.
181 10t. Type **35** 20 20
182 10t. Body of common crane 20 20
183 10t. Head of snake 20 20
184 10t. Body of snake and moth 20 20
185 10t. Lizard 20 20
186 10t. Common crane and bearded reedling 20 20
187 10t. Dragonfly 20 20
188 10t. Bees on clover and body of snake 20 20
189 10t. Butterfly 20 20
190 10t. Frog 20 20
191 10t. Snail 20 20
192 10t. Turtle 20 20
193 10t. Crayfish 20 20
194 10t. Water plant and head of salamander 20 20
195 10t. Crested salamander and body of salamander . . . 20 20
196 10t. Speckled salamander on trunk 20 20
Nos. 181/96 were issued together, se-tenant, forming a composite design of a pond.

36 Apatosaurus

1996. Prehistoric Animals. Multicoloured.
197 10t. Type **36** 25 25
198 10t. Archaeopteryx (bird) . . 25 25
199 10t. Leptoceratops (on rocks at entrance to cave) . . . 25 25
200 10t. Parasaurolophus (pair) and body of apatosaurus 25 25
201 10t. Pentaceratops (with horns and neck flap) . . . 25 25
202 10t. Hererasaurus (with mouth gaping, fronds in background) 25 25
203 10t. Hadrosaurus and nest with eggs 25 25
204 10t. Montanoceratops (green dinosaur with different dinosaur in background) 25 25
205 10t. Fulgoloterium (red dinosaur) 25 25
Nos. 197/205 were issued together, se-tenant, forming a composite design.

37 "Citizens of Paris" (Lado Gudiashvili)

1996. Paintings. Multicoloured.
206 10t. Type **37** 15 15
207 20t. "Abstract" (Wassily Kandinsky) 30 30
208 30t. "Still-life" (David Kakabadze) 45 45
209 50t. "Three Painters" (Shalva Kikodze) 80 80
MS210 83 × 100 mm. 80t. "Portrait of Niko Pirosmani" (Pablo Picasso) (black and gold). Imperf 1·25 1·25

38 Helsinki, 1952

1996. Cent of Modern Olympic Games. Mult.
211 1t. Type **38** 10 10
212 2t. Melbourne, 1956 . . . . 10 10
213 3t. Rome, 1960 . . . . . . 10 10
214 4t. Tokyo, 1964 . . . . . . 15 15
215 5t. Mexico, 1968 . . . . . . 20 20
216 6t. Munich, 1972 . . . . . . 25 25
217 7t. Montreal, 1976 . . . . . 30 30
218 8t. Moscow, 1980 . . . . . 35 35
219 9t. Seoul, 1988 . . . . . . 35 35
220 10t. Barcelona, 1992 . . . . 40 40
MS221 Two sheets, each 99 × 70 mm. Each black and scarlet. (a) 50t. Wrestling; (b) 70t. Athletics . . . . 4·75 4·75
Each stamp is also inscribed with the names of Georgian gold medal winners at the relevant games.

39 Anniversary Emblem

1997. 50th Anniv of U.N.O.
222 **39** 30t. blue and purple . . . 40 40
223 125t. blue and red . . . . 1·60 1·60

40 Javakhishvili and University

1997. 120th Birth Anniv (1996) of Ivane Javakhishvili (first director of Tbilisi University).
224 **40** 50t. multicoloured . . . . 1·00 1·00

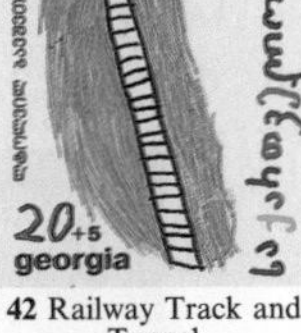

41 Anton I **42** Railway Track and Tunnel

1997. 210th Death Anniv (1998) of Anton I (head of Georgian Orthodox Church).
225 **41** 30t. brown 75 75

1997. 50th Anniv (1996) of UNICEF. Children's Paintings. Multicoloured.
226 20t.+5r. Type **42** 50 50
227 30t.+10r. Creature (horiz) . . 75 75

43 Rottweiler

1997. Dogs. Multicoloured.
228 10t. Type **43** 15 15
229 30t. Gordon setter 45 45
230 50t. St. Bernard 75 75
231 60t. English bulldog 90 90
232 70t. Caucasian sheepdog . . 1·00 1·00
233 125t. Caucasian sheepdog (different) . . . . 1·75 1·75
MS234 99 × 75 mm. No. 233 . . 1·75 1·75

44 Two Mice

1997. Animated Cartoon Characters. Mult.
235 20t. Type **44** 30 30
236 30t. Man in bed 45 45
237 40t. Girl and rabbit on cloud with balloons 60 60
238 50t. Dancing animals 75 75
239 60t. Duck wearing dress . . . 90 90

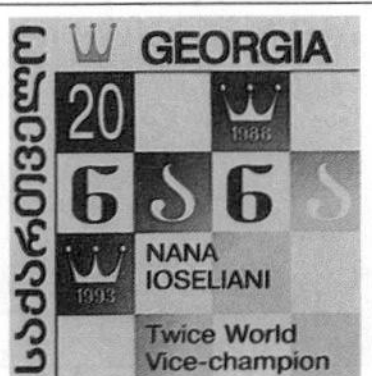

45 Nana Ioseliani (World Vice-Champion, 1988, 1993)

1997. Georgian Women Chess Players. Two sheets, each 90 × 90 mm, containing square design as T **45**.
MS240 Two sheets (a) 20t. ochre, brown and silver (T **45**); 20t. ochre, brown and silver (Nana Alexandria (world vice-champion, 1975, 1981)); 40t. ochre, brown and gold (Maia Chiburdanidze (world champion, 1978, 1981, 1984, 1986, 1988)); 50t. ochre, brown and gold (Nona Gaprindashvili (world champion, 1962, 1965, 1969, 1972, 1975)). (b) Each ochre, brown and gold. Winning teams at chess Olympiads; 30t. Manila, 1992; 30t. Moscow, 1994; 30t. Yerevan, 1996 4·75 4·75
The dates for Maia Chiburdanidze are inaccurate.

46 Map of Caucasus, 1745

1997. 300th Birth Anniv (1996) of Prince Vakhushti Bagration. Multicoloured.
241 40t. Type **46** 60 60
242 80t. Prince Vakhushti Bagration (vert) . . . . . 1·25 1·25

47 Tiflis Town Post **48** Congress and Cultural Emblems

1997. "Moscow '97" Int Stamp Exn.
243 **47** 80t. multicoloured . . . . 1·25 1·25
MS244 115 × 88 mm. 1l. As Type **47** but additionally dated "1857 1997". Imperf . . . . 1·50 1·50

1997. 1st World Junior (40t.) and Second World (80t.) Delphic Congresses, Tbilisi. Multicoloured.
245 40t. Type **48** 60 60
246 80t. Emblem and church, Mzcheta . . . . 1·25 1·25

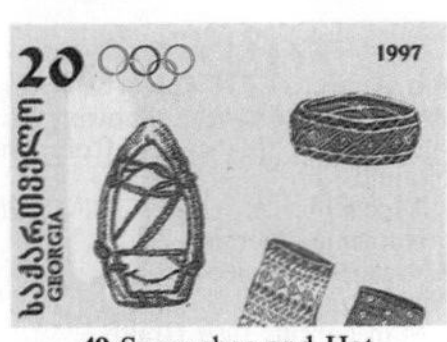

49 Snow-shoe and Hat

1998. Winter Olympic Games, Nagano, Japan. Mult.
(a) Clothes and accessories.
247 20t. Type **49** 35 35
248 30t. Glove and snow-shoe . . 50 50
249 40t. Sledge and gloves . . . 70 70
250 50t. Scarf and skates . . . . 1·50 1·50

(b) Ski Jumping.
251 20t. Ski jumper 35 35
252 30t. As No. 251 . . . . . . 50 50
253 40t. As No. 251 . . . . . . 70 70
254 50t. As No. 251 . . . . . . 1·50 1·50
MS255 Two sheets (a) 76 × 106 mm. 70t. Georgian wearing snow-shoes; (b) 99 × 70 mm. 70t. Upper body of ski jumper . . . . 2·50 2·50

50 Greek Galley (terracotta plate)

1998. Voyage of the Argonauts (ancient Greek legend). Multicoloured.
256 30t. Type **50** 45 45
257 40t. Preparation for battle . . 60 60
258 50t. Boreads, Phineus (blind seer) and Harpy 75 75
259 60t. Punishment of King Amicus 90 90
260 70t. Argonauts in Colchis . . 1·00 1·00
261 80t. The dragon vomiting Jason . . . . 1·25 1·25
Nos. 257/61 show vase paintings.

51 Brown Horse

1998. Horses. Multicoloured.
262 10t. Type **51** 15 15
263 40t. Black horse 75 75
264 70t. Chestnut . . . . 1·00 1·00
265 80t. White horse . . . . . . 2·75 2·75
MS266 110 × 90 mm. 100t. Grey. Imperf . . . . 1·75 1·75

52 Pteranodon

1998. Prehistoric Animals. Multicoloured.
267 15t. Type **52** (inscr "Pterodactylus") 30 30
268 15t. Rhamphorhynchus facing right 30 30
269 15t. Pterodactyl (inscr "Pteranodon") 30 30
270 15t. Velociraptor (inscr "Spinosaurus") 30 30
271 15t. Tyrannosaurus facing right 30 30
272 15t. Spinosaurus (inscr "Velociraptor") 30 30
273 15t. Mastodon (inscr "Monoklonius") 30 30
274 15t. Ornithomimus facing left 30 30
275 15t. Monoklonius (inscr "Mastodon") 30 30
Nos. 267/75 were issued together, se-tenant, forming a composite design.

53 Class VL8 No. 888

1998. Electric Railway Locomotives built at Tbilisi. Multicoloured.
276 10t. Type **53** 15 15
277 30t. Class VL10 No. 580 . . 45 45
278 40t. Class VL11 No. 500A . . 60 60
279 50t. Class VL11 No. 001B . . 75 75
280 80t. Class VL10u No. 591 . . 1·25 1·25
MS281 107 × 73 mm. 100t. Class E13 No. 008. Imperf . . . . 1·75 1·75

54 Flag and "26 May"

1998. 80th Anniv of Declaration of National Republic.
282 **54** 80t. multicoloured . . . . 1·25 1·25

55 Berikaoba

1998. Europa. National Festivals. Value expressed by letter of Georgian alphabet.
283 A(80t.) Type **55** . . . . . . 1·25 1·25
284 B(100t.) Chiakokononba . . 1·75 1·75

56 Marbled Polecat

1999. Mammals. Multicoloured.
285 10t. Type **56** 15 15
286 40t. Striped hyena 60 60
287 80t. Brown bear . . . . . . 1·25 1·25
MS287 90 × 110 mm. 100t. Wild goat (*Capra aegagrus*). Imperf . . . 1·75 1·75

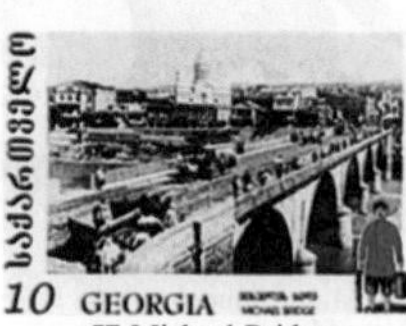

57 Michael Bridge

1999. Bridges in Tbilisi. Multicoloured.
289 10t. Type **57** 15 15
290 40t. Saarbruken 60 60
291 50t. N. Baratashvili Bridge 75 75
292 60t. Mukhrani railway bridge 90 90
293 70t. Avlabari Bridge . . . . 1·00 1·00
294 80t. Metekhi Bridge . . . . 1·25 1·25

58 Mink

1999. The European Mink. Values expressed by letter of Georgian alphabet. Multicoloured.
295 A(10t.) Type **58** 25 25
296 B(20t.) Mink with fish . . . 45 45
297 G(30t.) Two mink 65 65
298 D(60t.) Mink emerging from burrow . . . . 1·40 1·40

59 Batsara-Babaneury Reserve

61 Writing Letter

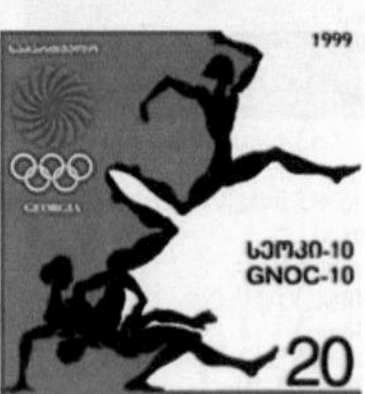

60 Emblem and Athletes

1999. Europa. Parks and Gardens. Value indicated by letter of Georgian alphabet. Multicoloured.
299 A(80t.) Type **59** . . . . . 1·25 1·25
300 B(100t.) Lagodekhy Reserve 1·75 1·75

1999. 10th Anniv of Georgian National Olympic Committee.
301 **60** 20t. red, black and gold . . 35 35
302 50t. red, black and gold . . 1·00 1·00

1999. 125th Anniv of Universal Postal Union. Illustrations by Sergo Kobuladze from *The Knight in the Tiger's Skin* (poem). Multicoloured.
303 20t. Type **61** 35 35
304 80t. Woman writing letter . . 1·50 1·50

62 Georgian Script and Emblem

1999. Admission of Georgia to European Council. Multicoloured.
305 50t. Type **62** . . . . 1·00 1·00
306 80t. "EUROPA" and emblem 1·00 1·50

63 KAZ-585 Tipper Truck

1999. Kutaisi Automobile Factory. Trucks. Multicoloured.
307 20t. Type **63** 35 35
308 40t. KAZ-608-717 . . . . . 80 80
309 50t. KAZ-608-3 . . . . . . 1·00 1·00
310 80t. KAZ-4530 . . . . . . 1·50 1·50

64 Scarce Swallowtail (*Iphiclides podalirius*)

1999. Butterflies. Multicoloured.
312 10t. Type **64** 20 20
313 20t. Apollo (*Parnassius apollo*) 35 35
314 50t. Dawn clouded yellow (*Colias aurorina* Herrich-Schaffer) . . . . 1·00 1·00
315 80t. *Tomares romanovi* . . . 1·50 1·50

65 Svanetia

1999. World Heritage Sites. Sheet 110 × 69 mm.
MS316 **65** 100t. multicoloured . . 1·75 1·75

66 "Building Europe"

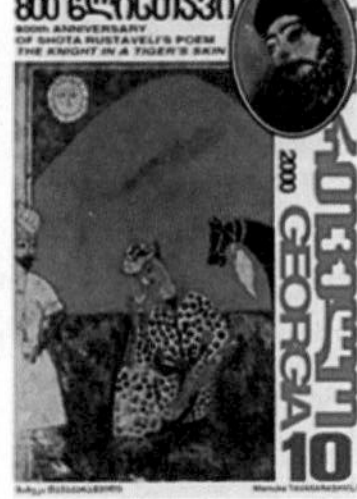

67 Man kneeling (Mamuka Tavakarashvili)

2000. Europa.
317 **66** 80t. multicoloured . . . . 1·50 1·50
318 100t. multicoloured . . . . 1·60 1·60

2000. 800th Anniv of *The Knight in a Tiger's Skin* (poem by Shota Rustaveli). Showing illustrations by named artists of scenes from the poem. Multicoloured.
319 10t. Type **67** 20 20
320 20t. Horsemen (Sergio Kobuladze and Jacob Nikoladze) 35 35
321 30t. Man fighting tiger (Irakli Toidze and Ucha Japaridze) 60 60
322 50t. Man and horse (Levan Tsutskiridze and Teimuraz Gotsadze) . . . . 1·00 1·00
323 60t. Woman's head (Natela Iankoshvili and Temo Natsvlishvili) . . . . . 1·50 1·50
MS324 85 × 110 mm. 80t. Man wearing headdress (Rusudan Petviashvili) . . . . 1·50 1·50

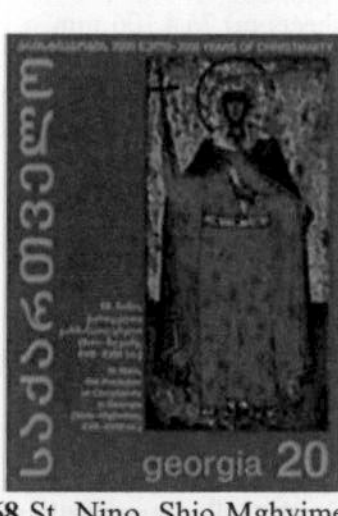

68 St. Nino, Shio Mghvime

2000. 2000th Birth Anniv of Jesus Christ. Icons. Multicoloured.
325 20t. Type **68** 35 35
326 50t. The Saviour, Alaverdi 1·00 1·00
327 80t. The Virgin Hodigitria, Tsilkani . . . . 1·50 1·50

69 Coins

2000. 3000th Anniv of Georgia. Sheet 123 × 95 mm.
MS328 **69** 100t. multicoloured . . 1·75 1·75

70 Fish

2000. Fishes.
329 **70** 10t. multicoloured 20 20
330 – 20t. multicoloured 35 35
331 – 30t. multicoloured 60 60
332 – 50t. multicoloured . . . . 1·00 1·00
333 – 80t. multicoloured . . . . 1·50 1·50
DESIGNS: 20t. to 80t. Depicting fishes.

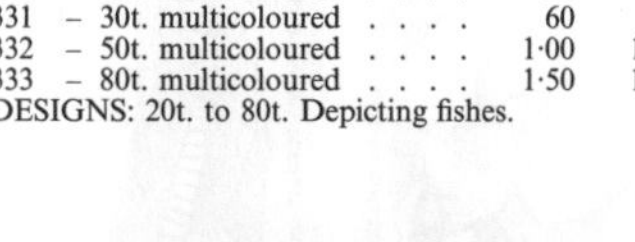

71 "1999"

2000. New Millennium. Each red and yellow.
334 20t. Type **71** 35 35
335 50t. "2000" . . . . 1·00 1·00
336 80t. "2001" . . . . 1·50 1·50

72 Athlete

2000. Olympic Games, Sydney. Multicoloured.
337 20t. Type **72** 35 35
338 50t. Athlete . . . . 1·00 1·00
339 80t. Athlete . . . . 1·50 1·50

73 Saradjishvili

2000. 89th Death Anniv of David Saradjishvili (first producer of brandy in Georgia).
340 **73** 80t. multicoloured . . . . 1·50 1·50

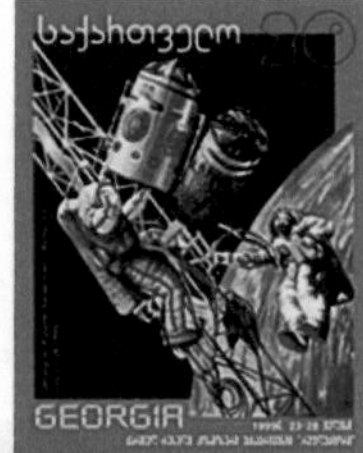

74 Cosmonauts working on Reflector

2000. Georgia–Russia Space Project. Multicoloured.
341 20t. Type **74** 35 35
342 80t. Antenna reflector in space . . . . 1·50 1·50

75 "hUMAN RighTS"

2000. Human Rights. Multicoloured.
343 50t. Type **75** . . . . 1·00 1·00
344 80t. "HuMAn RiGHtS" . . 1·50 1·50

76 Refugees

2000. 50th Anniv of United Nations High Commission for Refugees.
345 **76** 50t. multicoloured . . . . 1·00 1·00

77 Yellow Chanterelle (*Cantharellus cibarius*)

78 Church

2000. Fungi. Multicoloured.
346 10t. Type **77** 20 20
347 20t. Field mushroom (*Agaricus campestris*) . . . 35 35
348 30t. Boot-lace fungus (*Armillariella mella*) . . . 60 60
349 50t. *Russula adusta* . . . . 1·00 1·00
350 80t. Violet cort (*Cortinarius violaceus*) . . . . 1·50 1·50

2000. Churches.
351 **78** 10t. brown 20 20
352 – 50t. blue . . . . 1·00 1·00
DESIGN: 50t. Church.

79 Alexander Kazbegi

2000. Writers.
353 **79** 30t. black, red and pink . . 60 60
354 – 40t. black, brown and yellow 80 80
355 – 50t. black, deep green and green . . . . 1·00 1·00
356 – 70t. black, lavender and blue . . . . 1·40 1·40
357 – 80t. black, brown and chestnut . . . . 1·50 1·50
DESIGNS: 40t. Jakob Gogebashvili; 50t. Vadja Pshavela; 70t. Akaki Tsereteli; 80t. Ilia Chavchavadze.

80 Republic P-47 Thunderbolt

2000. 23rd Death Anniv of Alexander Kartveli (aircraft designer). Multicoloured.
358 10t. Type **80** 20 20
359 20t. Republic F-84 . . . . . . 35 35
360 80t. Republic F-105D Thunderchief . . . . . . 1·50 1·50
MS361 75 × 115 mm. 100t. Kartveli (vert) . . . . 1·75 1·75

81 Emblem and Horse-drawn Vehicle

2000. 175th Anniv of Fire Service.
362 **81** 50t. multicoloured . . . . 1·00 1·00

82 Ritsa Lake **83** Synagogue, Kutaisi

2001. Europa. Water Resources. Multicoloured.
363 40t. Type **82** 80 80
364 80t. Borjomi Spa . . . . . . 1·60 1·60

2001.
365 **83** 140t. multicoloured . . . . 1·90 1·90

84 Chess Pieces and Competition Emblem

2001. 1st Europe–Asia Intercontinental Chess Match, Batumi.
366 **84** 1l. multicoloured . . . . . 1·90 1·90

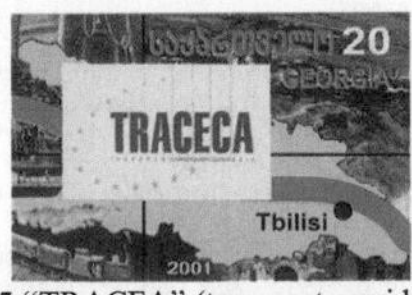
85 "TRACEA" (transport corridor Europe–Caucasus–Asia) and Route

2001. The Great Silk Route. Multicoloured.
367 20t. Type **85** 60 60
MS368 74 × 76 mm. 80t. Map and route . . . . 1·50 1·50

86 Georgian and American Flags

2001. Support for America after Attacks on World Trade Buildings, New York. Multicoloured.
369 30t.+10t. Type **86** . . . . . 1·00 1·00
MS370 135 × 77 mm. 120t.+10t. As No. 369 . . . . 3·60 3·60

87 Taras Chevtchenko

2002. Poets. Multicoloured.
371 50t. Type **87** . . . . 1·75 1·75
372 50t. Akakii Tsereteli . . . . 1·75 1·75
Stamps of the same design were issued by Ukraine.

88 Passenger Ship

2002. 140th Anniv of Poti Port. Sheet 104 × 57 mm containing T **88** and similar horiz designs. Multicoloured.
MS373 30t. Type **88**; 30t. Container suspended from hoist; 30t. Tug guiding ship; 30t. Crane and rowboat; 30t. Steam tug; 30t. Tanker ship . . . . 4·50 4·50

89 Scenes from *Mtiuluri* **90** Woman and Childrenn (statue)

2002. National Ballet. Scenes from ballets by Soliko Virsaladze. Multicoloured.
374 30t. Type **89** 85 85
375 50t. *Samaya* . . . . 1·00 1·00
376 80t. *Jeirani* . . . . 1·90 1·90

2002.
377 **90** 100t. blue . . . . 1·75 1·75

91 Man holding House (bas-relief) **92** Acrobat

2002.
378 **91** 5l. brown . . . . 7·50 7·50

2002. Europa. Circus. Multicoloured.
379 40t. Type **92** . . . . 1·50 1·50
380 80t. Tbilisi circus . . . . . . 2·75 2·75

93 Refugees

2002. 50th Anniv of United Nations' Convention on the Status of Refugees.
381 **93** 50t. multicoloured . . . . 1·50 1·50

94 Crucifixion (10th-century) **95** The Annunciation

2002. Pectoral Crosses. Multicoloured.
382 10t. Type **94** 30 30
383 20t. Virgin and Child (Martvili, 7–9th century) 60 60
384 50t. Saints surrounding central stone (Martvili, 10th-century) . . . . . . 1·50 1·50
385 80t. Stone encrusted (King Tamari, 12th-century) . . . 2·40 2·40

2002. Frescoes. Multicoloured.
386 10t. Type **95** 30 30
387 30t. Angel, Mary and Saints (horiz) 90 90
388 80t. Angel with upraised wings . . . . 2·40 2·40

96 Winning Football Team

2002. Dinamo Tbilisi. Winners of European Cup Winners Cup, 1981.
389 **96** 20t. multicoloured 65 65

97 Woman, House and Man holding Rifle

2002. Traditional Costumes. Multicoloured.
390 20t. Type **97** 65 65
391 30t. Woman, round tower and man holding dagger 95 95
392 50t. Woman, fortress and man holding sword and shield . . . . 1·50 1·50

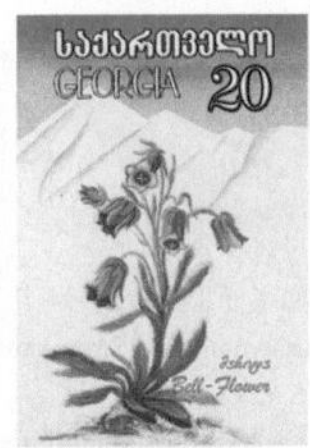
98 Bell Flower

2002. Flowers. Multicoloured.
393 20t. Type **98** 70 70
394 30t. Caucasia rhododendron 95 95
395 50t. Anemone . . . . 1·50 1·50
396 80t. Marsh marigold . . . . 2·40 2·40

99 SU 25 Scorpio

2002. Aircraft. Multicoloured.
397 30t. Type **99** 95 95
398 80t. MIG 21U . . . . 2·40 2·40

100 Children encircling Globe **101** First Georgian Stamp and Ifsda Emblem

2002. United Nations Year of Dialogue among Civilizations.
399 **100** 40t. multicoloured . . . . 1·20 1·20

2002. 50th Anniv of Ifsda (international federation of stamp dealers' association).
400 **101** 100t. multicoloured . . . 2·50 2·50

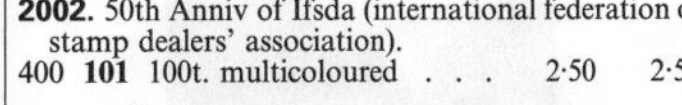

102 Alexandre Dumas **103** Three men, Donkey and Dog

2002. Birth Bicentenary of Alexandre Dumas (writer). Sheet 124 × 104 mm.
MS401 **102** 120t. multicoloured 3·75 3·75

2003. Europa. Poster Art. Multicoloured.
402 40t. Type **103** . . . . 1·50 1·50
403 80t. Boy and men . . . . . 2·75 2·75

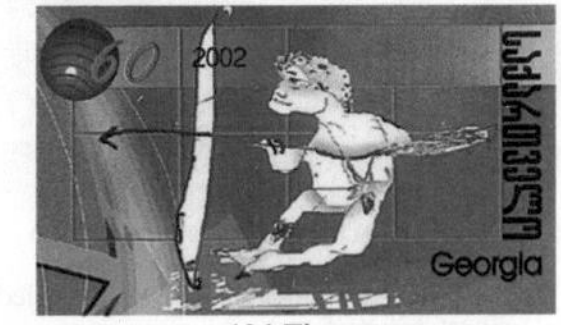
104 Figure

2003. Pre-historic Man. Sheet 130 × 76 mm containing T **104** and similar horiz design. Multicoloured.
MS404 60t. Type **104**; 60t. Skull 4·25 4·25

105 Players **106** Rainbow, Boy and Girl on Horseback

2003. World Cup Football Championship, Japan and South Korea. Sheet 82 × 105 mm.
MS405 **105** 1l. black, red and salmon 2·75 2·75

2003. Youth.
406 **106** 50t. multicoloured . . . . 1·20 1·20

107 Women holding Globe and Doves

2003. United Nations Development Fund for Women.
407 **107** 50t. multicoloured . . . . 1·20 1·20

108 Sloe (*Prunus spinosa*) **109** Elephant

2003. Fruits. Multicoloured.
408 10t. Type **108** 25 25
409 20t. Cherry laurel (*Laurocerasus officinalis*) 45 45
410 30t. Quince (*Cydonia oblonga*) 70 70
411 50t. Pomegranate (*Punica granatum*) . . . . 1·20 1·20
412 80t. Pear (*Pyrus caucasica*) 1·90 1·90

2003. Tbilisi Zoological Park. Multicoloured.
413 20t. Type **109** 45 45
414 30t. Wolf 70 70
415 40t. Ostrich 95 95
416 50t. Bear . . . . 1·20 1·20

110 Rock Crystal

2003. Minerals. Multicoloured.
417 10t. Type **110** 45 45
418 20t. Agate with amethyst . . 70 70
419 30t. Orpiment rose (*Arsenic Sulfide*) 95 95
420 50t. Realgar (*Arsenic Sulfide*) 1·20 1·20

111 "Old Tbilisi" and Elene Akhvlediani

2003. Birth Centenary (2001) of Elene Akhvlediani (artist). Sheet 170 × 75 mm.
MS421 **111** 80t. multicoloured . . 2·00 2·00

112 Self-portrait with Grey Felt Hat

2003. 150th Birth Anniv of Vincent Van Gogh (artist). Sheet 132 × 65 mm.
MS422 **112** 100t. multicoloured 2·75 2·75

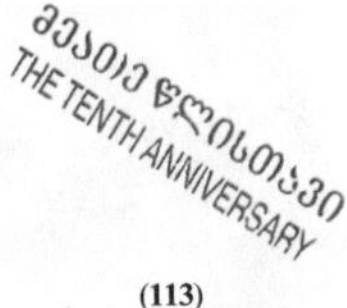

(113)

2003. 10th Anniv of Georgia. No. 58 and **MS**61 optd with T **113**.
423 25t. multicoloured . . . . .
MS424 122 × 101 mm. 25, 50, 100t. multicoloured . . . . 3·00 3·00

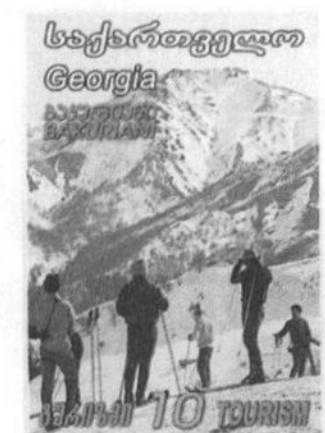

114 Snow Slopes, Bakuriani

2003. Tourism. Multicoloured.
425 10t. Type **114** 45 45
426 20t. Caves, Vardzia 70 70
427 30t. Coastline and ship, Batumi 95 95
428 50t. Mountains and Lake Ritsa . . . . 1·20 1·20

115 Aladasturi

2003. Grapes. Multicoloured.
429 10t. Type **115** 45 45
430 20t. Rkhatsiteli 70 70
431 30t. Ojaleshi 95 95
432 50t. Goruli Mtsvane . . . . 1·20 1·20
433 80t. Aleksandrouli (Khvanchkhara) . . . . . 1·90 1·90

116 Association Emblem

2003. 10th Anniv of International Association of Academies of Sciences.
434 **116** 30t. multicoloured 95 95

117 Map of Route

2003. Baku—Tbilisi—Ceyhan Oil Pipeline.
435 **117** 80t. multicoloured 95 95

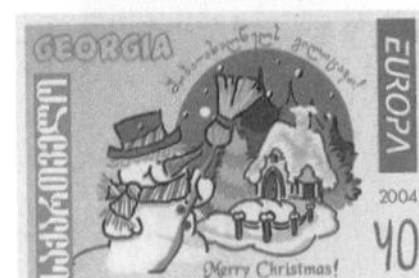

118 Snowman and Snow-covered House

2004. Europa. Holidays. Multicoloured.
436 40t. Type **118** ("Happy Christmas") 25 25
437 80t. Child carrying lantern and bowl of eggs ("Happy Easter") 45 45

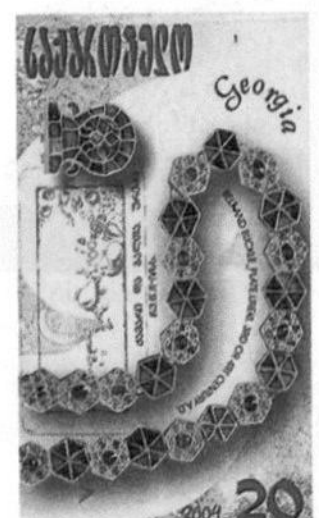

119 Belt and Buckle (Ureki) (3rd—4th century)

2004. Jewellery. Multicoloured.
438 20t. Type **119** . . . .
439 30t. Belt buckle and necklace (Aragvispri) (3rd—4th century) . . . .
440 40t. Necklace and pins (Trialeti) (2000—1500 BC) 25 25
441 80t. Necklace (Vani) (5th century) and pin (Urbnisi) (3000 BC) 45 45

120 Towers (Ushguli) (12th—13th century)

2004. World Heritage Sites. Multicoloured.
442 20t. Type **120** 10 10
443 30t. Bagrati Cathedral (11th century) 20 20
444 50t. Gelati Monastery (12th century) 30 30
445 60t. Samtavro Monastery (11th century) 35 35
446 70t. Svetitskhoveli Cathedral (11th century) 40 40
447 80t. Jvari Monastery (6th century) 45 45

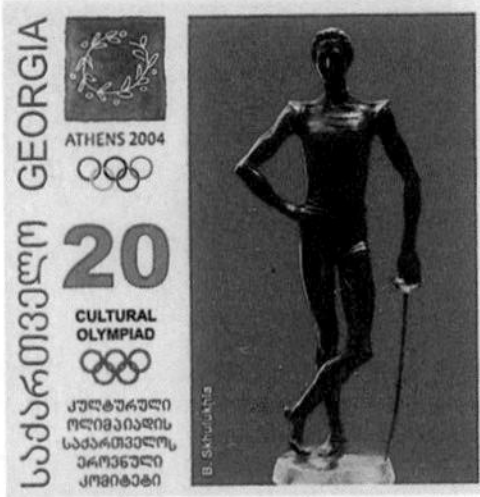

121 Fencer (sculpture) (B. Skhulukhia)

2004. Olympic Games, Athens. Multicoloured.
448 20t. Type **121** 10 10
449 30t. Athlete (sculpture) (V. Cherkezishvilli) 20 20
450 50t. Runners (sculpture) (N. Jikia) 30 30
451 80t. Judo competitor (painting) (L. Vardosanidze) 45 45

122 Boris Paichadze

2004. Centenary of FIFA (Federation Internationale de Football Association). Caricatures of players. Multicoloured.
452 20t. Type **122** 10 10
453 30t. Avtandil Gogoberidze . . 20 20
454 50t. Mikhail Meskhi 30 30
455 80t. David Kipiani 45 45

123 Giorgi Tsereteli

2004. Birth Centenary of Giorgi Tsereteli (linguist).
456 **123** 30t. multicoloured 20 20

124 Crowd waving New Flag, Tbilisi

2004. Rose Revolution. Sheet 91 × 77 mm containing T **124** and similar horiz designs. Multicoloured.
MS457 50t. × 2, Type **124**; Protestors, Batumi 60 60

GERMAN COMMANDS Pt. 7

EASTERN COMMAND

German occupation of Estonia, Latvia and Lithuania during the war of 1914–18.

100 pfennig = 1 mark.

1916. Stamps of Germany inscr "DEUTSCHES REICH" optd **Postgebiet Ob. Ost.**
1 **24** 2½pf. grey . . . . 70 1·80
2 **10** 3pf. brown 30 45
3 5pf. green . . . . 70 1·80
4 **24** 7½pf. orange . . . . 70 1·80
5 **10** 10pf. red . . . . 70 1·80
6 **24** 15pf. brown . . . . 3·50 3·50
7 15pf. violet . . . . 70 1·80
8 **10** 20pf. blue . . . . 1·20 1·80
9 25pf. black & red on yellow 45 90
10 40pf. black and red . . . . 1·30 6·75
11 50pf. black & pur on buff 1·40 2·75
12a **12** 1m. red . . . . 10·50 4·50

WESTERN COMMAND

For Forces in Belgium and Northern France.

100 centimes = 1 franc.

1916. Stamps of Germany surch with new values as **2 Cent., 1F.** or **1F.25 Cent.**
1 **10** 3c. on 3pf. brown 30 65
2 5c. on 5pf. green . . . . 65 1·60
3 **24** 8c. on 7½pf. orange . . . . 65 1·60
4 **10** 10c. on 10pf. red . . . . . 1·60 3·00
5 **24** 15c. on 15pf. brown . . . 35 65
6 **10** 25c. on 20pf. blue . . . . 90 2·75
7 40c. on 30pf. black and orange on buff . . . . . 65 1·80
8 50c. on 40pf. black and red 90 1·80
9 75c. on 60pf. purple . . . 5·00 1·80
10 1f. on 80pf. black and red on red . . . . 4·50 8·75
11a **12** 1f.25 on 1m. red . . . . . 22·00 28·00
12 **13** 2f.50 on 2m. blue . . . . 24·00 20·00

GERMAN EAST AFRICA Pt. 7

A German colony on the east coast of Africa. Placed under British mandate after the First World War.

1893. 64 pesa = 1 rupee.
1905. 100 heller = 1 rupee.

1893. Stamps of Germany surch with value in "PESA".
1 **8** 2p. on 3pf. brown . . . . . . 44·00 65·00
2 3p. on 5pf. green . . . . . . 55·00 65·00
4 **9** 5p. on 10pf. red . . . . 35·00 31·00
5 10p. on 20pf. blue . . . . . . 24·00 18·00
6 25p. on 50pf. brown . . . . . 40·00 35·00

1896. Stamps of Germany surch **Deutsch-Ostafrika** and value in "Pesa".
7 **8** 2p. on 3pf. brown . . . . . 11·00 11·00
10 3p. on 5pf. green . . . . . . 3·00 5·25
11 **9** 5p. on 10pf. red . . . . . . 3·00 5·25
13 10p. on 20pf. blue . . . . . 5·75 5·75
14 25p. on 50pf. brown . . . . 24·00 31·00

1901. "Yacht", key-type inscr "DEUTSCH-OSTAFRIKA". Currency in pesa and rupees.
15 N 2p. brown . . . . 3·00 2·00
16 3p. green . . . . 3·00 2·20
17 5p. red . . . . 3·50 3·00
18 10p. blue . . . . 5·75 5·75
19 15p. black and orange on buff . . . . 5·75 7·50
20 20p. black and red . . . . . 8·00 16·00
21 25p. black and purple on buff . . . . 8·00 16·00
22 40p. black and red on rose 10·00 24·00
23 O 1r. red . . . . 20·00 65·00
24 2r. green . . . . 11·00 £100
44 3r. black and red . . . . . 31·00 £225

1905. "Yacht" key-types inscr "DEUTSCH-OSTAFRIKA". Currency in heller.
34 N 2½h. brown . . . . 1·10 90
35 4h. green . . . . 1·10 65
36 7½h. red . . . . 1·30 65
37 15h. blue . . . . 2·40 1·30
38 20h. black and red on yellow 2·75 18·00
39 30h. black and red . . . . . 3·00 8·75
40 45h. black and mauve . . . 5·25 55·00
33 60h. black and red on rose 24·00 £100

For stamps issued for this territory under British auspices since 1915 see under Tanganyika in Volume 4.

GERMAN NEW GUINEA Pt. 7

A German colony, part of the island of New Guinea.

100 pfennig = 1 mark.

1897. Stamps of Germany optd **Deutsch-Neu-Guinea.**
1a **8** 3pf. brown . . . . 8·75 10·50
2 5pf. green . . . . 4·50 5·75
3 **9** 10pf. red . . . . 7·00 9·75
4 20pf. blue . . . . 9·75 15·00
5 25pf. orange . . . . 31·00 60·00
6 50pf. brown . . . . 31·00 49·00

1901. "Yacht" key-types inscr "DEUTSCH-NEU-GUINEA".
7 N 3pf. brown . . . . 1·10 1·30
8 5pf. green . . . . 8·75 1·30
9 10pf. red . . . . 27·00 3·00
10 20pf. blue . . . . 1·60 3·00
11 25pf. black and red on yellow . . . . 1·60 16·00
12 30pf. black & orange on buff 1·60 22·00
13 40pf. black and red . . . . 1·60 24·00
14 50pf. black & purple on buff 2·00 22·00
15 80pf. black and red on rose 4·00 31·00
16 O 1m. red . . . . 4·00 60·00
17 2m. blue . . . . 6·75 85·00
18 3m. black . . . . 8·75 £180
19 5m. red and black £160 £500

Australian forces occupied German New Guinea in 1914 and it was administered as a League of Nations mandate from 1920. For stamps issued since 1914 see under New Guinea.

GERMAN OCCUPATION OF ALSACE Pt. 7

100 pfennig = 1 mark.

1940. Stamps of Germany optd **Elsa**.
1 **94** 3pf. brown 45 45
2 4pf. slate 90 90
3 5pf. green 45 45
4 6pf. green 45 45
5 8pf. orange 45 45
6 10pf. brown 45 65
7 12pf. red 45 45
8 15pf. red 90 90
9 20pf. blue 90 90
10 25pf. blue . . . . 1·10 1·30
11 30pf. olive . . . . 1·30 1·30
12 40pf. mauve . . . . 1·30 1·30
13 50pf. black and green . . . 2·00 2·00
14 60pf. black and red . . . . 2·40 2·40
15 80pf. black and blue . . . . 4·00 4·00
16 100pf. black and yellow . . 6·75 4·50

GERMAN OCCUPATION OF BELGIUM Pt. 4

German occupation of E. Belgium during the war of 1914–18.

100 centimes = 1 franc.

Stamps of Germany inscr "DEUTSCHES REICH" surcharged.

1914. Surch **Belgien** and value thus: **3 Centimes**, **1Franc** or **1Fr.25C.**
1 **10** 3c. on 3pf. brown 40 35
2 5c. on 5pf. green 40 30
3 10c. on 10pf. red 45 30
4 25c. on 20pf. blue . . . . . 75 1·10
5 50c. on 40pf. black and red 2·75 1·40
6 75c. on 60pf. purple . . . . 1·00 1·40
7 1f. on 80pf. black and red on rose . . . . 2·10 1·60
8 **12** 1f.25 on 1m. red . . . . . 21·00 11·50
9 **13** 2f.50 on 2m. blue . . . . . 18·00 14·50

1916. Surch **Belgien** and value, thus: **2 Cent.,1F.**, or **1F.25Cent.**
10 **24** 2c. on 2pf. grey 30 80
11 **10** 3c. on 3pf. brown . . . . 40 1·40
12 5c. on 5pf. green . . . . . 40 1·40
13 **24** 8c. on 7½pf. orange . . . . 50 1·40
14 **10** 10c. on 10pf. red . . . . . 30 1·00
15 **24** 15c. on 15pf. brown 50 95
16 15c. on 15pf. violet . . . . 30 1·40
17 **10** 20c. on 25pf. black and red on yellow . . . . 35 1·40
18 25c. on 20pf. blue . . . . 35 1·40
19 40c. on 30pf. black and orange on buff 30 40
20 50c. on 40pf. black and red 30 1·40
21 75c. on 60pf. mauve . . . 1·50 19·00
22 1f. on 80f. black and red on rose . . . . 1·40 1·25
23a **12** 1f.25 on 1m. red . . . . . 2·50 2·50
24 **13** 2f.50 on 2m. blue . . . . 21·00 22·00
25 **15** 6f.25 on 5m. red and black 25·00 28·00

GERMAN OCCUPATION OF DALMATIA Pt. 3

Areas formerly under Italian control which were occupied by the Germans in 1943.

A. ZARA (Zadar)

100 centesimi = 1 lira.

1943. Imperial series of Italy, 1929, optd **Deutsche Besetzung Zara**.
1 **98** 5c. brown . . . . 60·00 £120
2 – 10c. brown . . . . 5·25 9·00
3 – 15c. green . . . . 8·25 17·00
4 **99** 20c. red . . . . 5·25 10·50
5 – 25c. green . . . . 5·25 10·50
6 **103** 30c. brown . . . . 5·25 10·50
7 – 35c. blue £200 £375
8 – 75c. red . . . . 17·00 26·00
9 **99** 1l. violet . . . . 5·25 10·50
10 1l.25 blue . . . . 9·00 17·00
11 1l.75 red . . . . 25·00 48·00
12 – 2l. red . . . . 48·00 75·00
13 **98** 2l.55 green £300 £500
14 3l.70 violet £1800 £3000
15 5l. red . . . . 50·00 75·00
16 – 10l. violet £900 £1300
17 **99** 20l. green £13000 £13000
18 – 25l. black £24000 £24000
19 – 50l. violet £21000 £14000

1943. War Propaganda stamps of Italy (Nos. 571/4) optd **Deutsche Besetzung Zara** on stamp and label.
20 **103** 50c. violet (Navy) . . . . 10·50 21·00
21 50c. violet (Army) . . . . 10·50 21·00
22 50c. violet (Air Force) . . . 10·50 21·00
23 50c. violet (Militia) . . . . 10·50 21·00

1943. Air. Nos. 270/7 of Italy optd **Deutsche Besetzung Zara**.
26 – 25c. green . . . . 9·00 17·00
27 **110** 50c. brown . . . . 8·25 17·00
28 – 75c. brown £325 £450
29 – 80c. red . . . . 38·00 65·00
30 – 1l. violet . . . . 10·50 17·00
31 **113** 2l. blue . . . . 24·00 38·00
32 **110** 5l. green £6500 £6500
33 10l. red £14000 £14000

1943. Imperial series of Italy, 1929, optd **ZARA** within pattern of bars.
46 **103** 50c. violet . . . . 5·75 15·00
47 – 75c. red . . . . 7·00 17·00
48 – 1l.25 blue . . . . 60·00 £110

1943. War Propaganda stamps of Italy (Nos. 563/70) optd **ZARA** within pattern of bars on stamp and label.
49 – 25c. green (Navy) . . . . 13·00 22·00
50 – 25c. green (Army) . . . . 13·00 22·00
51 – 25c. green (Air Force) . . 13·00 22·00
52 – 25c. green (Militia) . . . . 13·00 22·00
53 **103** 30c. brown (Navy) . . . . 11·00 18·00
54 30c. brown (Army) . . . . 11·00 18·00
55 30c. brown (Air Force) . . 11·00 18·00
56 30c. brown (Militia) . . . 11·00 18·00

EXPRESS LETTER STAMPS

1943. Nos. E350/1 of Italy optd **Deutsche Besetzung Zara**.
E24 **E 132** 1l.25 green . . . . . . 13·00 25·00
E25 2l.50 orange . . . . . 70·00 £100

1943. Air. No. E370 of Italy optd **Deutsche Besetzung Zara**.
E34 **E 133** 2l. black . . . . 25·00 38·00

1943. Nos. E350/1 of Italy optd **ZARA** within pattern of bars, twice.
E57 **E 132** 1l.25 green . . . . . . 20·00 27·00
E58 2l.50 orange £130 £180

POSTAGE DUE STAMPS

1943. Italian Postage Due stamps optd **Deutsche Besetzung Zara**.
D35 **D 141** 5c. brown . . . . . . 28·00 75·00
D36 10c. blue . . . . . . 28·00 75·00
D37 20c. red . . . . 25·00 75·00
D38 25c. green £700 £750
D39 30c. red . . . . 25·00 75·00
D40 40c. brown . . . . . . 25·00 75·00
D41 50c. violet . . . . . . 25·00 75·00
D42 60c. blue £700 £800
D43 **D 142** 1l. orange £650 £800
D44 2l. green £750 £1000
D45 5l. violet £650 £800

B. GULF OF KOTOR

Italian and German currency.

1944. Imperial series of Italy, 1929, surch **Deutsche Militar-verwaltung Kotor** and new value in lire.
1 – 0.50LIT. on 10c. brown . . 50·00 70·00
2 – 1LIT. on 25c. green . . . . 50·00 70·00
3 **103** 1.50LIT. on 50c. violet . . 50·00 70·00
4 3LIT. on 30c. brown . . . 50·00 70·00
5 **99** 4LIT. on 20c. red . . . . . 50·00 70·00
6 10LIT. on 20c. red . . . . 50·00 70·00

1944. Nos. 419/20 of Yugoslavia (King Petar II) surch **Boka Kotorska** and new value in Reichsmarks.
7 **99** 0,10R.M. on 3d. brown . . 4·50 4·50
8 0,15R.M. on 3d. brown . . 4·50 4·50
9 0,25R.M. on 4d. blue . . . 7·00 8·50
10 0,50R.M. on 4d. blue . . . 11·00 13·00

GERMAN OCCUPATION OF ESTONIA Pt. 10

100 kopeks = 1 rouble.

2

3 "Long Hermann" Tower, Reval (Tallinn)

1941. Tartu issue.
3A **2** 15(k.) brown . . . . 13·00 14·00
4A 20(k.) green . . . . 10·50 12·00
5A 30(k.) blue . . . . 10·50 12·00

Originally issued for local use, the above were made available for use throughout Estonia from 29.9.41 to 30.4.42. However, not many were used since the German **OSTLAND** stamps were used from 1 December 1941.

1941. Reconstruction Fund.
6 **3** 15+15(k.) sepia and brown 35 3·50
7 – 20+20(k.) purple and brown 35 3·50
8 – 30+30(k.) blue and brown . . 35 3·50
9 – 50+50(k.) green and brown 40 7·00
10 – 60+60(k.) red and brown . . 55 5·50
11 – 100+100(k.) slate and brown 95 8·75

DESIGNS—HORIZ: 20k. Stone Bridge, Tartu; 30k. Two Narva Castles; 50k. Reval of Tallinn. VERT: 60k. Tartu University; 100k. Hermann Castle, Narva.

German stamps optd **OSTLAND** (see German Occupation of Russia, Nos. 1/20) were used from 1 December 1941 until the Russian re-occupation of Estonia in 1944. Since then Russian stamps have been in use.

GERMAN OCCUPATION OF LATVIA Pt. 10

100 kopeks = 1 rouble.

1941. Russian stamps of 1936–39 optd **LATVIJA 1941. 1. VII.**
1 5k. red (No. 847a) . . . . . 90 4·00
2 10k. blue (No. 727f) . . . . 90 4·00
3 15k. green (No. 847c) . . . . 25·00 70·00
4 20k. green (No. 727h) . . . . 90 4·00
5 30k. blue (No. 847d) . . . . 90 4·00
6 50k. brown on buff (No. 727m) 1·90 8·50

German stamps optd **OSTLAND** (see German Occupation of Russia, Nos. 1/20) were used from 4th November, 1941, until the Russian re-occupation of Latvia in 1944–45. Since then Russian stamps have been in use.

GERMAN OCCUPATION OF LITHUANIA Pt. 10

100 kopeks = 1 rouble.

1941. Russian stamps of 1936–40 optd **NEPRIKLAUSOMA LIETUVA 1941-VI-23.**
1 2k. green (No. 542) . . . . . 32·00 £120
2 5k. red (No. 847a) . . . . . 1·60 7·50
3 10k. blue (No. 727f) . . . . 1·60 7·50
4 15k. green (No. 847c) . . . . 1·60 7·50
5 20k. green (No. 727h) . . . . 1·60 7·50
6 30k. blue (No. 847d) . . . . 1·60 7·50
7 50k. brown on buff (No. 727m) 5·50 18·00
8 60k. red (No. 847f) . . . . . 7·00 28·00
9 80k. blue (No. 905) . . . . . 14·00 40·00

1941. Issue for Vilnius and South Lithuania. Russian stamps of 1936–39 optd **VILNIUS**.
10 5k. red (No. 847a) . . . . . 1·90 3·00
11 10k. blue (No. 727f) . . . . 2·25 3·00
12 15k. green (No. 847c) . . . . 2·25 3·00
13 20k. green (No. 727h) . . . . 5·75 10·50
14 30k. blue (No. 847d) . . . . 5·00 7·50
15 50k. brown on buff (No. 727m) . . . . 5·75 7·50
16 60k. red (No. 847f) . . . . . 5·75 8·25
17 80k. red and deep red (No. 772) £250 £225
18 1r. black and red (No. 779) . . £700 £600

German stamps optd **OSTLAND** (see German Occupation of Russia, Nos. 1/20) were used from 4th November, 1941, till the Russian re-occupation of Lithuania in 1944. Since then Russian stamps have been in use.

GERMAN OCCUPATION OF LORRAINE Pt. 7

100 pfennig = 1 mark.

1940. Stamps of Germany optd **Lothringen**.
1 **94** 3pf. brown 65 90
2 4pf. slate 65 90
3 5pf. green 65 90
4 6pf. green 65 45
5 8pf. orange 65 90
6 10pf. brown 65 60
7 12pf. red 65 60
8 15pf. lake . . . . 65 1·50
9 20pf. blue . . . . 90 1·50
10 25pf. blue . . . . 1·10 1·30
11 30pf. olive . . . . 1·30 1·60
12 40pf. mauve . . . . 1·30 1·60
13 50pf. black and green . . . 2·75 2·75
14 60pf. black and red . . . . 3·00 3·00
15 80pf. black and blue . . . . 3·50 3·50
16 100pf. black and yellow . . 6·25 5·75

GERMAN OCCUPATION OF POLAND Pt. 5

German occupation of Poland, 1915–18.

100 pfennig = 1 mark.

1915. Stamps of Germany inscr "DEUTSCHES REICH" optd **Russisch-Polen.**
1 **10** 3pf. brown 40 40
2 5pf. green 75 35
3 10pf. red 80 35
4 20pf. blue . . . . 1·50 50
5 40pf. black and red . . . . . 4·25 2·40

1916. Stamps of Germany inscr "DEUTSCHES REICH" optd **Gen.-Gouv. Warschau.**
6 **24** 2½pf. grey . . . . 60 1·25
7 **10** 3pf. brown . . . . 70 1·40
8 5pf. green . . . . 70 1·10
9 **24** 7½pf. orange 70 95
10 **10** 10pf. red . . . . 70 1·25
11 **24** 15pf. brown . . . . 2·25 1·90
12 15pf. violet . . . . 55 1·10
13 **10** 20pf. blue . . . . 90 1·40
14 30pf. black & orange on buff . . . . 3·50 8·00
15 40pf. black and red . . . . 1·40 1·25
16 60pf. purple . . . . 1·25 1·60

GERMAN OCCUPATION OF RUMANIA Pt. 3

German occupation of Rumania, 1917–18.

100 bani = 1 leu.

Stamps of Germany inscr "DEUTSCHES REICH".

1917. Surch **M.V.i.R.** in frame and value in "Bani".
1 **24** 15b. on 15pf. violet . . . . . 1·10 1·25
2 **10** 25b. on 20pf. blue . . . . . 1·00 1·25
3 40b. on 30pf. black and orange on buff . . . . . . 23·00 29·00

1917. Surch **M.V.i.R.** (not in frame) and value in "Bani".
4 **10** 10b. on 10pf. red . . . . . . 60 1·25
5 **24** 15b. on 15pf. violet . . . . . 4·25 5·00
6 **10** 25b. on 20pf. blue . . . . . 60 2·25
7 40b. on 30pf. black and orange on buff . . . . . . 1·00 1·25

1918. Surch **Rumanien** and value in "Bani".
8 **10** 5b. on 5pf. green 20 50
9 10b. on 10pf. red 50 90
10 **24** 15b. on 15pf. violet 35 25
11 **10** 25b. on 20pf. blue . . . . . 1·25 1·25
12 40b. on 30pf. black and orange on buff 40 40

1918. Stamps of Germany inscr "DEUTSCHES REICH" optd **Gultig 9. Armee** in frame.
13 **10** 10pf. red . . . . 12·00 48·00
14 **24** 15pf. violet . . . . 18·00 40·00
15 **10** 20pf. blue . . . . 3·25 2·25
16 30pf. black & orange on buff . . . . 15·00 24·00

POSTAGE DUE STAMPS

1918. Postage Due stamps of Rumania optd **M.V.i.R.** in frame.
D1B **D 38** 5b. blue on green . . . 6·00 14·50
D2B 10b. blue on green . . . 6·00 12·50
D3B 20b. blue on green . . 6·00 5·00
D4B 30b. blue on green . . 6·00 5·00
D5B 50b. blue on green . . 6·00 5·00

GERMAN OCCUPATION OF RUSSIA Pt. 10

100 pfennig = 1 reichsmark.

1941. Issue for Ostland. Stamps of Germany of 1941 optd **OSTLAND**.
1 **173** 1pf. grey 15 20
2 3pf. brown 15 20
3 4pf. slate 15 20
4 5pf. green 15 20
5 6pf. violet 15 20
6 8pf. red 15 20
7 10pf. brown . . . . 1·40 1·25
10 12pf. red . . . . 55 2·50
11 15pf. lake 10 20
12 16pf. green 40 40
13 20pf. blue 10 10
14 24pf. brown 40 35
15 25pf. blue 25 20
16 30pf. olive 25 20
17 40pf. mauve 25 35
18 50pf. green 25 35
19 60pf. brown 25 35
20 80pf. blue 25 80

1941. Issue for Ukraine. Stamps of Germany of 1941 optd **UKRAINE**.
21 **173** 1pf. grey 10 10
22 3pf. brown 10 10
23 4pf. slate 10 10
24 5pf. green 10 10
25 6pf. violet 10 10
26 8pf. red 10 10
27 10pf. brown . . . . 1·00 1·50
29 12pf. red . . . . 1·00 1·50
31 15pf. lake 20 20
32 16pf. green 25 35
33 20pf. blue 20 15
34 24pf. brown 25 35
35 25pf. blue 25 20
36 30pf. olive 25 10
37 40pf. mauve 20 35
38 50pf. green 25 20
39 60pf. brown 25 30
40 80pf. blue 25 35

GERMAN OCCUPATION OF ZANTE Pt. 3

German occupation of Ionian Islands, 1943–44.

100 centesimi = 1 lira = 8 drachma.

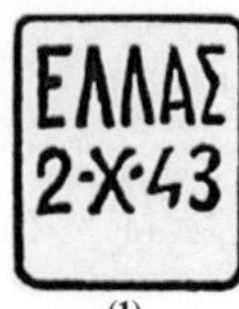

(1)

1943. Stamps of Italian Occupation of Ionian Islands further optd with T **1**.

1 – 25c. green (postage) . . . . 22·00 60·00
2 **103** 50c. violet . . . . 22·00 60·00
3 **110** 50c. brown (air) £110 £190

GERMAN POST OFFICES IN CHINA Pt. 7

German post offices in China, now closed.

1898. 100 pfennig = 1 mark.
1905. 100 cents = 1 dollar.

1898. Stamps of Germany optd **China**.

7 **8** 3pf. brown . . . . 6·75 6·25
8 5pf. green . . . . 2·75 2·75
9 **9** 10pf. red . . . . 5·75 6·25
4 20pf. blue . . . . 16·00 11·00
11 25pf. orange . . . . 31·00 35·00
12 50pf. brown . . . . 16·00 13·50

1901. Stamps of Germany inscr "REICHSPOST" optd **China**.

22 **10** 3pf. brown . . . . 1·60 1·60
23 5pf. green . . . . 1·60 1·20
24 10pf. red . . . . 2·75 1·20
25 20pf. blue . . . . 3·25 1·80
26 25pf. black & red on yellow . . . . 10·50 18·00
27 30pf. black & orge on pink 10·50 14·00
28 40pf. black and red . . . 10·50 9·75
29 50pf. black & pur on pink 10·50 9·75
30 80pf. black and red on pink . . . . 12·50 12·50
31 **12** 1m. red . . . . 30·00 37·00
32 **13** 2m. blue . . . . 30·00 32·00
33 **14** 3m. black . . . . 49·00 70·00
35b **15** 5m. red and black £225 £350

1905. Stamps of Germany inscr "DEUTSCHES REICH" surch **China** and new value.

46 **10** 1c. on 3pf. brown . . . . 45 1·10
47 2c. on 5pf. green . . . . 45 1·10
48 4c. on 10pf. red . . . . 45 1·10
39 10c. on 20pf. blue . . . . 3·00 2·00
50 20c. on 40pf. black and red 1·10 3·25
51 40c. on 80pf. black and red on rose . . . . . . 1·10 55·00
42 **12** ½d. on 1m. red . . . . . 16·00 22·00
43 **13** 1d. on 2m. blue . . . . 18·00 24·00
44a **14** 1½d. on 3m. black . . . . 18·00 55·00
55 **15** 2½d. on 5m. red and black 90·00 £120

GERMAN POST OFFICES IN MOROCCO Pt. 7

German Post Offices in Morocco, now closed.

100 centimos = 1 peseta.

Stamps of Germany surcharged **Marocco** (or **Marokko**) and new value.

1889. Spelt **Marocco**.

1 **8** 3c. on 3pf. brown . . . . . . 3·00 2·40
2 5c. on 5pf. green . . . . . 3·00 2·75
3 **9** 10c. on 10pf. red . . . . . 8·75 7·00
4 25c. on 20pf. blue . . . . . 18·00 18·00
5 30c. on 25pf. orange . . . . 27·00 35·00
6 60c. on 50pf. brown . . . . . 20·00 44·00

1900. Inscr "REICHSPOST" surch **Marocco** (3c. to 1p.) or **Marocco Marocco** (others).

7 **10** 3c. on 3pf. brown . . . . 1·30 2·00
8 5c. on 5pf. green . . . . 1·60 1·30
9 10c. on 10pf. red . . . . 2·20 1·30
10 25c. on 20pf. blue . . . . 3·00 3·00
11 30c. on 25pf. black and red on yellow . . . . . . 11·00 16·00
12 35c. on 30pf. black and orange on rose . . . . . 7·50 6·75
13 50c. on 40pf. black and red 7·50 6·75
14 60c. on 50pf. black and purple on rose . . . . . 18·00 33·00
15 1p. on 80pf. black and red on rose . . . . 13·50 13·50
16 **12** 1p.25 on 1m. red . . . . . 33·00 55·00
17 **13** 2p.50 on 2m. blue . . . . 38·00 60·00
18 **14** 3p.75 on 3m. black . . . . 44·00 75·00
19b **15** 6p.25 on 5m. red and black £200 £325

1905. Inscr "DEUTSCHES REICH" surch **Marocco** (3c. to 1p.) or **Marocco Marocco** (others).

26 **10** 3c. on 3pf. brown . . . . 3·00 3·00
27 5c. on 5pf. green . . . . 5·00 1·10
28 10c. on 10pf. red . . . . . 10·50 1·10
42 25c. on 20pf. blue . . . . 18·00 6·75
30 30c. on 25pf. black and red on yellow . . . . . . 6·75 5·25
31 35c. on 30pf. black and orange on buff . . . . 10·50 5·75
32 50c. on 40pf. black and red 10·50 8·75
33 60c. on 50pf. black and purple on buff . . . . 27·00 27·00
34 1p. on 80pf. black and red on rose . . . . 27·00 20·00
35a **12** 1p.25 on 1m. red . . . . . 60·00 40·00
36 **13** 2p.50 on 2m. blue . . . . 90·00 £160
37a **14** 3p.75 on 3m. black . . . . 49·00 60·00
38 **15** 6p.25 on 5m. red & black £160 £200

1911. Inscr "DEUTSCHES REICH". Spelt **Marokko**.

51 **10** 3c. on 3pf. brown 45 90
52 5c. on 5pf. green . . . . . 45 1·10
53 10c. on 10pf. red . . . . . 45 1·10
54 25c. on 20pf. blue . . . . . 65 1·60
55 30c. on 25pf. black and red on yellow . . . . . . 1·60 18·00
56 35c. on 30pf. black and orange on buff . . . . . 1·30 8·75
57 50c. on 40pf. black and red 1·30 5·25
58 60c. on 50pf. black and purple on buff . . . . . 1·60 40·00
59 1p. on 80pf. black and red on rose . . . . 2·00 29·00
60 **12** 1p.25 on 1m. red . . . . . 2·75 70·00
61 **13** 2p.50 on 2m. blue . . . . 5·75 60·00
62 **14** 3p.75 on 3m. black . . . . 7·50 £275
63 **15** 6p.25 on 5m. red & black 20·00 £375

GERMAN POST OFFICES IN THE TURKISH EMPIRE Pt. 7

German Post Offices in the Turkish Empire, now closed.

1884. 40 para = 1 piastre.
1908. 100 centimes = 1 franc.

1884. Stamps of Germany inscr "DEUTSCHE REICHS-POST" and "PFENNIG" without final "E" surch with new value.

1 **5** 10pa. on 5pf. mauve . . . . 35·00 33·00
2 **6** 20pa. on 10pf. red . . . . . 70·00 90·00
3 1pi. on 20pf. blue . . . . 70·00 5·25
4 1¼pi. on 25pf. brown £130 £275
6 2½pi. on 50pf. green . . . . £110 85·00

1889. Stamps of Germany inscr "REICHSPOST" surch.

10 **8** 10pa. on 5pf. green . . . . 4·00 4·00
11 **9** 20pa. on 10pf. red . . . . 8·75 2·50
12 1pi. on 20pf. blue . . . . 5·75 2·30
14 1¼pi. on 25pf. orange . . . 39·00 25·00
16 2½pi. on 50pf. brown . . . 40·00 25·00

1900. Stamps of Germany inscr "REICHSPOST" surch in **PARA** or **PIASTER**.

17 **10** 10pa. on 5pf. green . . . . 1·80 1·80
18 20pa. on 10pf. red . . . . 2·20 2·30
19 1pi. on 20pf. blue . . . . 5·00 2·20
20 1¼pi. on 25pf. black and red on yellow . . . . . 7·00 £400
21 1½pi. on 30pf. black and orange on buff . . . . . 7·00 £400
22 2pi. on 40pf. black and red 7·00 £400
23 2½pi. on 50pf. black and purple on buff . . . . . 13·50 13·50
24 4pi. on 80pf. black and red on rose . . . . 16·00 14·00
25 **12** 5pi. on 1m. red . . . . . 35·00 43·00
26 **13** 10pi. on 2m. blue . . . . 35·00 44·00
27 **14** 15pi. on 3m. black . . . . 49·00 £100
28a **15** 25pi. on 5m. red and black £170 £300

1905. Stamps of Germany inscr "DEUTSCHES REICH" surch in **Para** or **Piaster**.

47 **10** 10pa. on 5pf. green . . . . 2·20 65
48 20pa. on 10pf. red . . . . 2·75 65
49 1pi. on 20pf. blue . . . . 4·50 90
38 1¼pi. on 25pf. black and red on yellow . . . . . 11·00 7·50
51 1½pi. on 30pf. black and orange on buff . . . . . 13·50 11·00
52 2pi. on 40pf. black and red 5·25 1·80
53 2½pi. on 50pf. black and purple on buff . . . . . 11·00 16·00
54 4pi. on 80pf. black and red on pink . . . . 8·75 22·00
55 **12** 5pi. on 1m. red . . . . . 22·00 35·00
56 **13** 10pi. on 2m. blue . . . . 22·00 49·00
45 **14** 15pi. on 3m. black . . . . 55·00 50·00
58 **15** 25pi. on 5m. red and black 29·00 80·00

1908. Stamps of Germany inscr "DEUTSCHES REICH", surch in **Centimes**.

60 **10** 5c. on 5pf. green . . . . 1·30 2·40
61 10c. on 10pf. red . . . . 3·50 5·00
62 25c. on 20pf. blue . . . . 7·50 31·00
63 50c. on 40pf. black and red 37·00 65·00
64 100c. on 80pf. black and red on rose . . . . 75·00 80·00

GERMAN SOUTH WEST AFRICA Pt. 7

A German colony in S.W. Africa.

100 pfennig = 1 mark.

1897. Stamps of Germany optd. (a) **Deutsch-Sudwest-Afrika**.

1 **8** 3pf. brown . . . . 8·75 13·50
2 5pf. green . . . . 4·00 4·50
3 **9** 10pf. red . . . . 20·00 18·00
4 20pf. blue . . . . 5·00 5·25

(b) **Deutsch-Sudwestafrika**.

5 **8** 3pf. brown . . . . 4·50 22·00
6 5pf. green . . . . 3·50 3·00
7 **9** 10pf. red . . . . 3·50 3·25
8 20pf. blue . . . . 14·00 18·00
9 25pf. orange £325 £450
10 50pf. brown . . . . 18·00 11·00

1901. "Yacht" key-types inscr "DEUTSCH-SUDWESTAFRIKA".

24 N 3pf. brown . . . . 90 3·75
25 5pf. green . . . . 90 1·60
26 10pf. red . . . . 1·10 1·60
27 20pf. blue . . . . 1·10 4·00
15 25pf. black and red on yellow . . . . 1·80 5·25
16 30pf. black & orange on buff 21·00 3·00
17 40pf. black and red . . . . 2·00 3·50
18 50pf. black & purple on buff 2·20 2·40
19 80pf. black and red on rose 2·20 8·75
29 O 1m. red . . . . 13·50 80·00
30 2m. blue . . . . 13·50 35·00
22 3m. black . . . . 31·00 44·00
32 5m. red and black . . . . . 22·00 £300

South Africa occupied the colony in 1914 and administered the territory under a League of Nations mandate from 1920. For stamps issued from 1923 see under South West Africa in Volume 4.

GERMANY Pt. 7

A country in Northern Central Europe. A federation of states forming the German Reich. An empire till November 1918 and then a republic until the collapse of Germany in 1945. Until 1949 under Allied Military Control when the German Federal Republic was set up for W. Germany and the German Democratic Republic for E. Germany. See also notes before No. 899.

I. GERMANY 1871–1945

1872. Northern areas including Alsace and Lorraine: 30 groschen = 1 thaler. Southern areas: 90 kreuzer = 1 gulden.
1875. Throughout Germany: 100 pfennig = 1 mark.
1923. 100 renten-pfennig = 1 rentenmark (gold currency).
1928. 100 pfennig = 1 reichsmark

1

A

1872. Arms embossed as Type A.

1 **1** ¼g. violet . . . . £225 80·00
2 ⅓g. green . . . . £500 38·00
3 ½g. red . . . . £900 35·00
4 ½g. yellow . . . . £1300 39·00
5 1g. red . . . . £300 13·50
6 2g. blue . . . . £1700 10·50
7 5g. bistre . . . . £900 85·00
8 1k. green . . . . £700 55·00
9 2k. red £600 £300
10 2k. yellow . . . . 40·00 £160
11 3k. red . . . . £1800 14·00
12 7k. blue . . . . £2500 85·00
13 18k. bistre £550 £475

2

B

1872.

14 **2** 10g. grey . . . . 60·00 £1600
15 – 30g. blue £120 £3000
38d **2** 2m. purple . . . . 75·00 3·25

On the 30g. the figures are in a rectangular frame.

1872. Arms embossed as Type B.

16 **1** ¼g. purple . . . . 70·00 £110
17 ⅓g. green . . . . 40·00 13·00
18 ½g. orange . . . . 44·00 6·25
19 1g. red . . . . 65·00 2·20
20 2g. blue . . . . 24·00 4·75
21 2½g. brown . . . . £2250 50·00
22 5g. olive . . . . 26·00 23·00
23 1k. green . . . . 38·00 27·00
24 2k. orange £500 £2250
25 3k. red . . . . 22·00 3·75
26 7k. blue . . . . 38·00 55·00
27 9k. brown £450 £250
28 18k. olive . . . . 40·00 £1900

1874. Surch with bold figures over arms.

29 **1** "2½" on 2½g. brown . . . . 44·00 30·00
30 "9" on 9k. brown . . . . . 75·00 £850

5

6

1875. "PFENNIGE" with final "E".

31 **5** 3pf. green . . . . 70·00 4·50
32 5pf. mauve . . . . £120 2·75
33 **6** 10pf. red . . . . 44·00 95
34a 20pf. blue . . . . £550 1·50
35 25pf. brown . . . . £600 13·00
36a 50pf. grey . . . . £1800 10·50
37 50pf. green £2000 £170

1880. "PFENNIG" without final "E".

39a **5** 3pf. green . . . . 3·50 90
40a 5pf. purple . . . . 1·80 75
41b **6** 10pf. red . . . . 7·50 70
42a 20pf. blue . . . . 7·00 75
43b 25pf. brown . . . . 22·00 3·50
44a 50pf. green . . . . 8·75 1·00

8

9

1889.

45 **8** 2pf. grey 55 75
46 3pf. brown . . . . 2·00 70
47a 5pf. green . . . . 1·60 70
48b **9** 10pf. red . . . . 1·50 55
49 20pf. blue . . . . 10·50 55
50b 25pf. yellow . . . . 30·00 1·20
51b 50pf. brown . . . . 28·00 75

10 "Germania"

12 General Post Office, Berlin

13 Allegory of Union of N. and S. Germany (after Anton von Werner)

14 Unveiling of Kaiser Wilhelm I Memorial in Berlin (after W. Pape)

15 25th Anniv of German Empire Address by Wilhelm II (after W. Pape)

1899. Types **10** to **15** inscr "REICHSPOST".

52 **10** 2pf. grey 85 60
53 3pf. brown . . . . 1·10 55
54 5pf. green . . . . 1·30 55
55 10pf. red . . . . 2·20 55
56 20pf. blue . . . . 10·50 60
57B 25pf. black & red on yellow . . . . 15·00 3·00
58B 30pf. black & orge on rose 22·00 65
59B 40pf. black and red . . . 27·00 1·10
60B 50pf. black & pur on rose 27·00 85
61B 80pf. black and red on rose . . . . 49·00 1·80
62 **12** 1m. red . . . . 90·00 1·80
63 **13** 2m. blue . . . . 90·00 5·75
64 **14** 3m. black . . . . £120 60·00
65b **15** 5m. red and black £350 £400

1902. T **10** to **15** inscr "DEUTSCHES REICH".

67 **10** 2pf. grey . . . . 1·70 45
83a 3pf. brown 90 65
84a 5pf. green . . . . 1·60 65
85a 10pf. red . . . . 4·75 40
86d 20pf. blue 90 90
87 25pf. black & red on yellow 70 90
88a 30pf. black & orge on buff 70 90
89a 40pf. black and red . . . 1·20 90
90a 50pf. black & pur on buff 70 90
91a 60pf. purple . . . . 1·80 1·10
92a 80pf. black and red on rose . . . . 1·30 1·60
93B **12** 1m. red . . . . 2·20 1·30
94B **13** 2m. blue . . . . 5·75 4·00

95B 14 3m. black . . . . 2·50 3·50
96B 15 5m. red and black . . . . 2·20 3·25
No. 93 has three pedestrians in front of the carriage in the right foreground and has no tram in the background. See No. 113 for redrawn design.

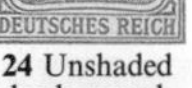
24 Unshaded background

26

27

28

1916. Inscr "DEUTSCHES REICH".
97 24 2pf. grey . . . . 20 3·50
98 2½pf. grey 15 85
140 10 5pf. brown 15 65
99a 24 7½pf. yellow 20 95
141 10 10pf. orange 15 55
100 24 15pf. brown . . . . . . 3·00 1·00
101 15pf. violet 15 95
102 15pf. purple . . . . . . 40 1·10
142 10 20pf. green . . . . . . 15 1·00
143a 30pf. blue . . . . . . 15 1·00
103 24 35pf. brown . . . . . . 15 1·10
144a 10 40pf. red . . . . 20 1·00
145a 50pf. purple . . . . . . 70 1·40
146 60pf. olive . . . . . . 20 1·20
104 75pf. black and green . . 20 95
147a 75pf. purple 20 90
148a 80pf. blue . . . . . . 10 1·20
149 1m. green and violet . . . 15 1·00
113 12 1m. red . . . . 2·20 1·40
150 10 1¼m. purple and red . . . 20 90
114 12 1m.25 green . . . . . . 1·80 1·20
115 1m.50 brown . . . . . . 25 1·20
151 10 2m. blue and red . . . . 70 1·00
116a 13 2m.50 red . . . . 1·00 1·50
152 10 4m. red and black . . . . 20 1·30
No. 113 has one pedestrian behind the carriage in the right foreground and a tram in the background.

1919. War Wounded Fund. Surch **5 Pf. fur Kriegs = beschadigte**.
105 10 10pf.+5pf. (No. 85a) . . . 55 4·75
106 24 15pf.+5pf. (No. 101) . . . 55 4·75

1919. National Assembly, Weimar.
107 26 10pf. red . . . . 15 1·30
108 27 15pf. blue and brown . . . 15 1·30
109 28 25pf. red and green . . . 15 1·40
110 30pf. red and purple . . . 20 1·40

29

30 L.V.G. Schneider Biplane

1919. Air.
111 29 10pf. orange . . . . 15 2·10
112 30 40pf. green . . . . 15 3·00

1920. Stamps of Bavaria optd **Deutsches Reich**.
117 26 5pf. green . . . . 20 1·20
118 10pf. orange . . . . 20 1·10
119 15pf. red . . . . 20 1·00
120 27 20pf. purple 20 95
121 30pf. blue 20 95
122 40pf. brown 20 95
123 28 50pf. red . . . . 20 1·50
124 60pf. green 20 95
125 75pf. purple . . . . 95 4·25
126 80pf. blue . . . . 25 1·90
127 29 1m. red and grey . . . . . 45 1·90
128 1¼m. blue and bistre . . . 45 1·90
129 1½m. green and grey . . . 45 3·00
130 2m. violet and bistre . . . 90 3·25
131 2½m. black and grey . . . 35 2·20
132 30 3m. blue . . . . 3·50 8·25
133 4m. red . . . . 3·50 8·75
134 5m. yellow . . . . 3·00 8·25
135 10m. green . . . . 2·75 9·25
136 20m. black . . . . 6·25 10·50

1920. Surch with new value and stars.
137 12 1m.25 on 1m. green . . . 35 5·75
138 1m.50 on 1m. brown . . . 35 6·50
139 13 2m.50 on 2m. purple . . . 8·75 £225

35

36 Blacksmiths

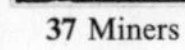
37 Miners

38 Reapers

40

41 Ploughman

39 Posthorn

1921.
153 35 5pf. red . . . . 10 1·50
154 10pf. olive . . . . 15 1·20
155 15pf. blue . . . . 10 1·00
156 25pf. brown 10 95
157 30pf. green 10 95
158 40pf. orange 10 95
182 50pf. purple . . . . 25 1·10
160 36 60pf. red 10 95
184 35 75pf. blue . . . . 10 2·50
161 36 80pf. red . . . . 30 26·00
186 37 100pf. green . . . . 25 1·70
163 120pf. blue . . . . 10 1·00
188 38 150pf. orange . . . . . . 20 1·10
165 160pf. green . . . . 10 6·75
193 40 5m. orange . . . . 25 1·10
170 10m. red . . . . 40 2·40
195 41 20m. blue and green . . . 15 4·50

1921. 1902 stamps surch.
172 10 1m.60 on 5pf. brown . . . 20 1·20
173 3m. on 1¼m. purple and red . . . . 15 1·30
174 5m. on 75pf. purple . . . 25 1·30
175 10m. on 75pf. purple . . . 40 1·60

1921.
190 39 2m. violet and pink . . . . 45 1·70
204 2m. purple . . . . 20 1·00
191 3m. red and yellow . . . . 40 5·75
205 3m. red 10 90
192 4m. green and light green 10 1·10
206 4m. green . . . . 20 1·10
207 5m. orange and yellow . . 15 1·20
208 5m. orange . . . . 20 1·10
209 6m. blue . . . . 20 1·10
210 8m. green . . . . 20 1·30
211 10m. red and pink . . . . 15 1·00
212 20m. violet and red . . . 25 1·00
213 20m. violet . . . . 20 1·10
214 30m. brown and yellow . . 20 1·00
215 30m. brown . . . . 75 25·00
216 40m. green . . . . 15 1·50
217 50m. green and purple . . 20 1·10

47 Arms of Munich

48

1922. Munich Exhibition.
198 47 1¼m. red . . . . 25 1·10
199 2m. violet . . . . 20 1·10
200 3m. red . . . . 20 1·20
201 4m. blue . . . . 20 1·30
202 10m. brown on buff . . . . 70 2·20
203 20m. red on rose . . . . . 4·00 8·00

1922. Air.
218 48 25pf. brown . . . . 50 16·00
219 40pf. orange . . . . 45 26·00
220 50pf. purple . . . . 30 8·25
221 60pf. red . . . . 60 19·00
222 80pf. green . . . . 35 17·00
223 – 1m. green . . . . 20 3·75
224 – 2m. red and grey . . . . 15 3·75
225 – 3m. blue and grey . . . . 25 4·00
226 – 5m. orange and yellow . . 15 3·50
227 – 10m. purple and red . . . 15 9·00
228 – 25m. brown and yellow . . 15 8·25
229 – 100m. olive and red . . . 15 6·00
The mark values are larger (21 × 27 mm).
See also Nos. 269/73 and 358/64.

1922. New values.
235 40 50m. black . . . . 25 1·10
230 100m. purple on buff . . . 15 1·10
231 200m. red on buff . . . . 20 1·20
238 300m. green on buff . . . . 10 1·10
239 400m. brown on buff . . . 10 1·10
240 500m. orange on buff . . . 10 1·10
241 1000m. grey . . . . 10 1·10
242 2000m. blue . . . . 25 1·10
243 3000m. brown . . . . . . 20 1·10
244 4000m. violet . . . . . . 10 1·30
245 5000m. green . . . . . . 25 1·30
246 100000m. red . . . . . . 15 1·20

50 Allegory of Charity

51 Miners

54

1922. Fund for the Old and for Children.
247 50 6m.+4m. blue and bistre 25 9·50
248 12m.+8m. red and lilac . . 25 11·00

1923.
249 51 5m. orange . . . . 10 11·00
250 38 10m. blue . . . . 10 1·00
251 12m. red . . . . 10 1·10
252 51 20m. purple . . . . 15 1·00
253 38 25m. bistre . . . . 10 1·10
254 51 30m. olive . . . . 15 1·80
255 38 40m. green . . . . 20 1·10
256 51 50m. blue . . . . 45 80·00

1923. Relief Fund for Sufferers in the Rhine and Ruhr Occupation Districts. Surch **Rhein = Ruhr = Hilfe** and premium.
257 51 5+100m. orange . . . . . 15 9·75
258 38 25+500m. bistre . . . . . 15 23·00
259 41 20+1000m. blue and green 2·10 90·00

1923. T = Tausend (thousand).
261 54 100m. purple . . . . . . 15 1·00
262 200m. red . . . . 15 1·20
263 300m. green . . . . . . 10 1·10
264 400m. brown . . . . . . 10 5·00
265 500m. red . . . . 10 7·50
266 1000m. grey . . . . . . 10 1·20
312 5T. blue . . . . 10 17·00
313 50T. brown 10 95
314 75T. purple . . . . 10 11·00

55 Wartburg Castle

62

1923.
267 55 5000m. blue . . . . 20 2·20
268 – 10,000m. olive . . . . . 30 3·25
DESIGN—VERT: 10,000m. Cologne Cathedral.

1923. Air. As T **48**, but larger (21 × 27 mm).
269 5m. orange . . . . 15 21·00
270 10m. purple . . . . 15 8·25
271 25m. brown . . . . 15 8·25
272 100m. green . . . . 15 9·50
273 200m. blue . . . . 15 32·00

1923. Surch with new value in **Tausend** or **Millionen** (marks). Perf or rouletted.
274 35 5T. on 40pf. orange . . . 10 1·20
275a 8T. on 30pf. green . . . 10 1·20
276 38 15T. on 40m. green . . . 20 1·40
277 20T. on 12m. red . . . . 10 1·20
278 20T. on 25m. brown . . . 10 2·00
279 54 20T. on 200m. red . . . 15 1·60
280 38 25T. on 25m. brown . . . 10 11·50
281 30T. on 10m. blue . . . . 10 1·20
282 54 30T. on 200m. blue . . . 10 1·20
283 75T. on 300m. green . . . 10 11·00
284 75T. on 400m. green . . . 15 1·20
285 75T. on 1000m. green . . 15 1·40
286 100T. on 100m. purple . . 15 1·50
287 100T. on 400m. green . . 10 1·20
288 125T. on 1000m. red . . 15 1·60
289 250T. on 200m. red . . . 10 4·75
290 250T. on 300m. green . . 10 14·00
291 250T. on 400m. brown . . 10 17·00
292 250T. on 500m. pink . . 10 1·00
293 250T. on 500m. orange . 10 16·00
306 35 400T. on 15pf. brown . . 10 4·75
307 400T. on 25pf. brown . . 10 4·75
308 400T. on 30pf. brown . . 10 4·00
309 400T. on 40pf. brown . . 10 4·00
294 800T. on 5pf. green . . . 10 3·50
295 800T. on 10pf. green . . 10 4·75
296 54 800T. on 200m. red . . . 20 70·00
297 800T. on 300m. green . . 10 4·00
298 800T. on 400m. green . . 10 3·50
299 800T. on 400m. brown . . 10 12·00
300 800T. on 500m. green . . 20 £1600
301 800T. on 1000m. green . . 15 1·10
302 2M. on 200m. red . . . . 20 1·00
303 2M. on 300m. green . . . 10 1·50
304 2M. on 500m. red . . . . 10 5·75
305 2M. on 5T. red . . . . . 25 1·10

1923. Perf or rouletted.
315 62 500T. brown . . . . . . 10 2·30
316 1M. blue . . . . 15 1·00
317 2M. purple . . . . 15 20·00
318 4M. green . . . . 15 1·30
319 5M. red 15 95
320 10M. red 15 95
321 20M. blue . . . . 10 1·10
322 30M. purple . . . . . . 10 9·25
323 50M. green . . . . 15 1·30
324 100M. grey . . . . 10 1·10
325 200M. brown . . . . . . 15 1·10
326 500M. olive . . . . . . 15 1·00

1923. As T **62**, but value in "Milliarden". Perf or roul.
327 62 1Md. brown . . . . 20 1·10
328 2Md. green and flesh . . . 15 1·30
329 5Md. brown and yellow . . 15 1·10
330 10Md. green & light green 15 1·20
331 20Md. brown and green . . 15 1·50
332 50Md. blue . . . . 35 30·00

1923. Surch in **Milliarden**. Perf or roul.
342 54 1Md. on 100m. purple . . 35 27·00
343 62 5Md. on 2M. purple . . . 25 £120
344 5Md. on 4M. green . . . . 40 21·00
345 5Md. on 10M. red . . . . 20 2·50
346 10Md. on 20M. blue . . . 25 3·25
347 10Md. on 50M. green . . . 20 2·75
348 10Md. on 100M. grey . . . 20 9·00

1923. As T **62**, but without value in words and tablet blank.
352 62 3pf. brown 50 25
353 5pf. green 70 20
354 10pf. red 70 20
355 20pf. blue . . . . 1·00 30
356 50pf. orange . . . . 3·50 80
357 100pf. purple . . . . . . 10·50 90
The values of this and the following issues are expressed on the basis of the gold mark.

1924. Air.
358 48 5pf. green . . . . 1·60 1·60
359 10pf. red . . . . 1·60 1·80
360 20pf. blue . . . . 6·75 5·50
361 50pf. orange . . . . 13·50 25·00
362 100pf. purple . . . . . . 35·00 55·00
363 200pf. blue . . . . 65·00 80·00
364 300pf. grey £100 £120

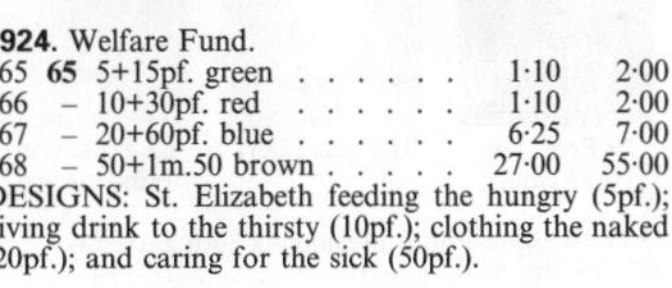
65 66

1924. Welfare Fund.
365 65 5+15pf. green . . . . . . 1·10 2·00
366 – 10+30pf. red . . . . . . 1·10 2·00
367 – 20+60pf. blue . . . . . . 6·25 7·00
368 – 50+1m.50 brown . . . . . 27·00 55·00
DESIGNS: St. Elizabeth feeding the hungry (5pf.); giving drink to the thirsty (10pf.); clothing the naked (20pf.); and caring for the sick (50pf.).

1924.
369 66 3pf. brown 40 15
370 5pf. green 45 15
371 10pf. red 65 15
372 20pf. blue . . . . 2·20 30
373 30pf. red . . . . 2·75 40
374 40pf. olive . . . . 17·00 75
375 50pf. orange . . . . 17·00 1·40

67 Rheinstein

71 Dr. von Stephan

1924.
376 67 1m. green . . . . 13·00 2·20
377 – 2m. blue (A) . . . . . . 19·00 1·90
458 – 2m. blue (B) . . . . . . 31·00 11·50
378 – 3m. red . . . . 23·00 5·00
379 – 5m. green . . . . 40·00 14·50
DESIGNS: 2m. Cologne. (A) inscr "Zwei Mark"; (B) inscr "ZWEI REICHSMARK"; 3m. Marienburg; 5m. Speyer Cathedral.

1924. 50th Anniv of U.P.U.
380 71 10pf. green 55 20
381 20pf. blue . . . . 1·20 60
382 – 60pf. brown . . . . 4·50 55
383 – 80pf. deep green . . . . 11·00 1·40
DESIGN: Nos. 382/3. Similar to Type **71** but with border changed.

73 German Eagle and Rhine

74

1925. Rhineland Millenary.
384 73 5pf. green 45 25
385 10pf. red 90 30
386 20pf. blue . . . . 5·50 1·10

1925. Munich Exhibition.
387 74 5pf. green . . . . 3·75 5·75
388 10pf. red . . . . 3·75 10·50

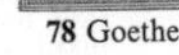

75 Arms of Prussia · 76 · 78 Goethe

1925. Welfare Fund. Arms dated "1925".
389 **75** 5pf.+5pf. yell, blk & grn . . 45 1·10
390 – 10pf.+10pf. brn, bl & red . . 1·10 1·40
391 – 20pf.+20pf. brn, grn & bl . . 6·25 13·50
ARMS: 10pf. Bavaria; 20pf. Saxony.
See also Nos. 413/16a, 446/50 and 451/5.

1926. Air.
392 **76** 5pf. green 65 80
393 10pf. red 90 80
394 15pf. purple . . . . 1·80 1·20
395 20pf. blue . . . . 1·80 1·60
396 50pf. orange . . . . 20·00 5·25
397 1m. red and black . . . . 18·00 6·00
398 2m. blue and black . . . . 20·00 21·00
399 3m. olive and black . . . 55·00 80·00

1926. Portraits.
400 **78** 3pf. brown 65 20
402 – 5pf. green (Schiller) . . . . 1·30 15
404 – 8pf. green (Beethoven) . . 1·30 15
405 – 10pf. red (Frederick the Great) . . . . 1·10 15
406 – 15pf. red (Kant) . . . . . 2·30 15
407 – 20pf. deep green (Beethoven) . . . . . . 11·50 90
408 **78** 25pf. blue . . . . 3·50 70
409 – 30pf. olive (Lessing) . . . 7·00 45
410 – 40pf. violet (Leibniz) . . . 11·50 55
411 – 50pf. brown (Bach) . . . . 14·00 6·25
412 – 80pf. brown (Durer) . . . 30·00 5·00

1926. Welfare Fund. As T **75**. Arms, dated "1926".
413 5pf.+5pf. multicoloured . . 1·00 1·30
414 10pf.+10pf. red, gold and rose . . . . 1·50 1·90
415 25pf.+25pf. blue, yell & red 11·50 18·00
416a 50pf.+50pf. multicoloured 41·00 70·00
ARMS: 5pf. Wurttemberg; 10pf. Baden; 25pf. Thuringia; 50pf. Hesse.

79 Pres. von Hindenburg · 81 Pres. Ebert · 82 Pres. von Hindenburg

1927. Welfare Fund. President's 80th Birthday.
417 **79** 8pf.+7pf. green . . . . . 90 1·30
418 15pf.+15pf. red . . . . . 1·10 2·30
419 25pf.+25pf. blue . . . . . 7·00 22·00
420 50pf.+50pf. brown . . . . 12·00 26·00

1927. International Labour Office Session, Berlin. Optd **I.A.A. 10.–15. 10. 1927.**
421 – 8pf. green (No. 404) . . . 18·00 60·00
422 – 15pf. red (No. 406) . . . . 18·00 60·00
423 **78** 25pf. blue . . . . 18·00 60·00

1928.
424 **81** 3pf. brown 25 25
425 **82** 4pf. blue 55 25
426 5pf. green 40 25
427 **81** 6pf. olive 75 20
428 8pf. green 25 25
429 10pf. red . . . . 1·30 1·10
430 10pf. purple . . . . 1·60 1·00
431 **82** 12pf. orange . . . . 1·30 20
432 15pf. red 65 20
433 **81** 20pf. deep green . . . . . 7·00 3·00
434 20pf. grey . . . . 6·25 35
435 **82** 25pf. blue . . . . 7·00 50
436 **81** 30pf. olive . . . . 4·75 45
437 **82** 40pf. violet . . . . 13·50 50
438 **81** 45pf. orange . . . . 9·00 2·30
439 **82** 50pf. brown . . . . 9·50 1·60
440 **81** 60pf. brown . . . . 11·50 2·20
441 **82** 80pf. brown . . . . 29·00 5·00
442 80pf. yellow . . . . 11·00 1·30

83 Airship "Graf Zeppelin"

1928. Air.
443 **83** 1m. red . . . . 26·00 32·00
444 2m. blue . . . . 55·00 47·00
445 4m. brown . . . . 31·00 32·00

1928. Welfare Fund. As T **75**, dated "1928".
446 5pf.+5pf. green, red & yellow 60 3·50
447 8pf.+7pf. multicoloured . . . 60 3·50
448 15pf.+15pf. red, bl & yellow 90 3·75
449 25pf.+25pf. blue, red & yellow . . . . 10·50 38·00
450 50pf.+50pf. multicoloured . . 55·00 95·00
ARMS: 5pf. Hamburg; 8pf. Mecklenburg-Schwerin; 15pf. Oldenburg; 25pf. Brunswick; 50pf. Anhalt.

1929. Welfare Fund. As T **75**, dated "1929".
451 5pf.+2pf. green, yellow & red 65 1·30
452 8pf.+4pf. yellow, red & green 65 1·30
453 15pf.+5pf. yellow, blk & red 90 1·40
454 25pf.+10pf. multicoloured . . 13·50 28·00
455 50pf.+40pf. yellow, red & brn 49·00 70·00
ARMS: 5pf. Bremen; 8pf. Lippe; 15pf. Lubeck; 25pf. Mecklenburg-Strelitz; 50pf. Schaumburg-Lippe.

1930. Air. "Graf Zeppelin" 1st S. American Flight. T **83** inscr "I. SUDAMERIKA FAHRT".
456 2m. blue £300 £275
457 4m. brown £300 £275

1930. Evacuation of Rhineland by Allied Forces. Optd **30. JUNI 1930.**
459 **81** 8pf. green . . . . 1·10 95
460 **82** 15pf. red . . . . 1·30 1·10

86 Aachen · 92 Heidelberg Castle

1930. International Philatelic Exhibition, Berlin.
461 **86** 8pf.+4pf. green . . . . . 25·00 65·00
462 – 15pf.+5pf. red . . . . . 25·00 65·00
463 – 25pf.+10pf. blue . . . . . 25·00 65·00
464 – 50pf.+40pf. brown . . . . 25·00 65·00
MS464a 195 × 148 mm. Nos. 461/4 (sold at 2m.70 in the exhibition) £350 £1600
DESIGNS: 15p. Berlin; 25pf. Marienwerder; 50pf. Wurzburg.

1930. Welfare Fund.
465 **86** 8pf.+4pf. green . . . . . 14·50 25·00
466 – 15pf.+5pf. red . . . . . 14·50 26·00
467 – 25pf.+10pf. blue . . . . . 18·00 37·00
468 – 50pf.+40pf. brown . . . . 23·00 65·00
DESIGNS: 15pf. Berlin; 25pf. Marienwerder; 50pf. Wurzburg.

1931. Air. "Graf Zeppelin" Polar Flight. Optd **POLAR-FAHRT 1931.**
469 **83** 1m. red £700 £350
470 2m. blue . . . . 75·00 £200
471 4m. brown . . . . 75·00 £200

1931. Welfare Fund.
472 – 8pf.+4pf. green 35 75
473 – 15pf.+5pf. red . . . . . . 40 1·00
474 **92** 25pf.+10pf. blue . . . . . 8·25 19·00
475 – 50pf.+40pf. brown . . . . 36·00 60·00
DESIGNS—VERT: 8pf. The Zwinger, Dresden; 15pf. Town Hall, Breslau; 50pf. The Holstentor, Lubeck.
See also Nos. 485/9.

1932. Welfare Fund. Nos. 472/3 surch.
476 6+4pf. on 8pf.+4pf. green . . 4·50 8·50
477 12+3pf. on 15pf.+5pf. red . . 5·75 11·50

94 President von Hindenburg · 96 Frederick the Great (after A. von Menzel)

1932. 85th Birthday of Pres. von Hindenburg.
478 **94** 4pf. blue 60 35
496B 5pf. green 90 40
480 12pf. orange . . . . 5·25 35
481 15pf. red . . . . 3·50 10·50
503B 25pf. blue . . . . 1·30 40
483 40pf. violet . . . . 17·00 1·50
484 50pf. brown . . . . 6·75 11·00
See also Nos. 493/509 and 545/50.

1932. Welfare Fund. As T **92**.
485 4pf.+2pf. blue 30 55
486 6pf.+4pf. olive 30 55
487 12pf.+3pf. red 45 90
488 25pf.+10pf. blue . . . . . . 7·75 16·00
489 40pf.+40pf. purple . . . . . 28·00 55·00
CASTLES: 4pf. Wartburg; 6pf. Stolzenfels; 12pf. Nuremberg; 25pf. Lichtenstein; 40pf. Marburg.

1933. Opening of Reichstag in Potsdam.
490 **96** 6pf. green 55 85
491 12pf. red 55 85
492 25pf. blue . . . . 37·00 19·00

1933.
493B **94** 1pf. black 10 15
494B 3pf. brown 10 15
495B 4pf. grey 10 15
497B 6pf. green 10 15
498B 8pf. orange 10 15
499B 10pf. brown 20 25
500B 12pf. red 15 25
501B 15pf. red 40 25
502B 20pf. blue 40 25
504B 30pf. green 75 25
505B 40pf. mauve 80 25
506B 50pf. black and green . . 2·40 35
507B 60pf. black and red . . . 75 35
508B 80pf. black and blue . . 2·20 1·20
509B 100pf. black and yellow 3·75 70

1933. Air. "Graf Zeppelin" Chicago World Exhibition Flight. Optd **Chicagofahrt Weltausstellung 1933.**
510 **83** 1m. red £700 £325
511 2m. blue . . . . 65·00 £170
512 4m. brown . . . . 65·00 £170

99 Tannhauser

1933. Welfare Fund. Wagner's Operas.
513 **99** 3pf.+2pf. brown . . . . 1·80 4·50
514 – 4pf.+2pf. blue . . . . . 1·30 1·80
515 – 5pf.+2pf. green . . . . . 7·75 5·00
516 – 6pf.+4pf. green . . . . . 1·30 1·20
517 – 8pf.+4pf. orange . . . . 2·20 3·00
518 – 12pf.+3pf. red . . . . . 2·20 1·60
519a – 20pf.+10pf. light blue . . £100 70·00
520 – 25pf.+15pf. blue . . . . 26·00 55·00
521 – 40pf.+35pf. mauve . . . £110 £110
OPERAS: 4pf. "The Flying Dutchman"; 5pf. "Rhinegold"; 6pf. "The Mastersingers"; 8pf. "The Valkyries"; 12pf. "Siegfried"; 20pf. "Tristan and Isolde"; 25pf. "Lohengrin"; 40pf. "Parsifal".

1933. Welfare Fund. Stamps as 1924, issued together in sheets of four, each stamp optd **1923–1933.**
522 **65** 5+15pf. green . . . . . . 70·00 £300
523 – 10+30pf. red . . . . . . 70·00 £300
524 – 20+60pf. blue . . . . . . 70·00 £300
525 – 50pf.+1.50m. brown . . . 70·00 £300
MS525a 210 × 148 mm. Nos. 522/5 £1200 £9500

100 Golden Eagle, Globe and Swastika · 101 Count Zeppelin and Airship LZ-127 "Graf Zeppelin"

1934. Air.
526 **100** 5pf. green 55 40
527 10pf. red 70 60
528 15pf. blue . . . . 1·30 80
529 20pf. blue . . . . 2·30 1·30
530 25pf. brown . . . . 3·75 1·20
531 40pf. mauve . . . . 6·25 90
532 50pf. green . . . . 10·50 65
533 80pf. yellow . . . . 6·50 3·50
534 100pf. black . . . . 6·50 2·30
535 – 2m. grey and green . . . 19·00 16·00
536 **101** 3m. grey and blue . . . . 39·00 35·00
DESIGN—As Type **101**: 2m. Otto Lilienthal and Lilienthal biplane glider.

103 Franz A. E. Luderitz · 104 "Saar Ownership" · 105 Nuremberg Castle

1934. German Colonizers' Jubilee.
537 **103** 3pf. brown and chocolate 3·50 4·75
538 – 6pf. brown and green . . 1·50 90
539 – 12pf. brown and red . . . 2·40 1·30
540 – 25pf. brown and blue . . 13·00 16·00
DESIGNS: 6pf. Gustav Nachtigal; 12pf. Karl Peters; 25pf. Hermann von Wissmann.

1934. Saar Plebiscite.
541 **104** 6pf. green . . . . 3·25 30
542 – 12pf. red . . . . 6·00 30
DESIGN: 12pf. Eagle inscribed "Saar" in rays from a swastika-eclipsed sun.

1934. Nuremberg Congress.
543 **105** 6pf. green . . . . 3·00 30
544 12pf. red . . . . 5·25 30

1934. Hindenburg Memorial. Portrait with black borders.
545 **94** 3pf. brown 85 35
546 5pf. green 85 50
547 6pf. green . . . . 1·40 30
548 8pf. orange . . . . 2·40 30
549 12pf. red . . . . 2·30 30
550 25pf. blue . . . . 7·25 6·50

106 Blacksmith · 107 Friedrich von Schiller · 108 "The Saar comes home"

1934. Welfare Fund.
551 – 3pf.+2pf. brown . . . . 90 1·10
552 **106** 4pf.+2pf. black . . . . 75 1·00
553 – 5pf.+2pf. green . . . . 5·25 6·25
554 – 6pf.+4pf. green 50 50
555 – 8pf.+4pf. red 80 95
556 – 12pf.+3pf. red 45 45
557 – 20pf.+10pf. green . . . 14·50 19·00
558 – 25pf.+15pf. blue . . . . 16·00 19·00
559 – 40pf.+35pf. lilac . . . . 42·00 55·00
DESIGNS: 3pf. Merchant; 5pf. Mason; 6pf. Miner; 8pf. Architect; 12pf. Farmer; 20pf. Scientist; 25pf. Sculptor; 40pf. Judge.

1934. 175th Birth Anniv of Schiller.
560 **107** 6pf. green . . . . 2·50 30
561 12pf. red . . . . 4·50 30

1935. Saar Restoration.
562 **108** 3pf. brown . . . . 65 1·20
563 6pf. green 65 40
564 12pf. red . . . . 2·20 40
565 25pf. blue . . . . 8·75 6·25

109 "Steel Helmet" · 110 "Victor's Crown"

1935. War Heroes' Day.
566 **109** 6pf. green . . . . 1·10 1·30
567 12pf. red . . . . 1·10 1·30

1935. Apprentices Vocational Contest.
568 **110** 6pf. green . . . . 90 1·10
569 12pf. red . . . . 1·10 1·10

111 Heinrich Schutz · 112 Allenstein Castle

1935. Musicians' Anniversaries.
570 **111** 6pf. green . . . . 1·00 25
571 – 12pf. red (Bach) . . . . 1·20 25
572 – 25pf. blue (Handel) . . . 2·30 85

1935. International Philatelic Exhibition, Konigsberg. In miniature sheets.
573 **112** 3pf. brown . . . . 33·00 36·00
574 – 6pf. green . . . . 33·00 36·00
575 – 12pf. red . . . . 33·00 36·00
576 – 25pf. blue . . . . 33·00 36·00
MS576a 148 × 105 mm. Nos. 573/6 £800 £650
DESIGNS: 6pf. Tannenberg Memorial; 12pf. Konigsberg Castle; 25pf. Heilsberg Castle.

113 Stephenson Locomotive "Adler", 1835 · 114 Trumpeter

1935. German Railway Centenary. Locomotive types inscr "1835–1935".
577 **113** 6pf. green . . . . 1·20 45
578 – 12pf. red . . . . 1·20 45
579 – 25pf. blue . . . . 9·00 1·90
580 – 40pf. purple . . . . . . 12·50 2·10
DESIGNS: 12pf. Class 03 steam train, 1930s; 25pf. Diesel train "Flying Hamburger"; 40pf. Class 05 streamlined steam locomotive No. 001, 1935.

1935. World Jamboree of "Hitler Youth".
581 **114** 6pf. green . . . . 1·30 2·20
582 15pf. red . . . . 1·80 2·50

115 Nuremberg · 116 East Prussia

1935. Nuremberg Congress.
583 **115** 6pf. green 80 30
584 12pf. red . . . . 1·60 30

1935. Welfare Fund. Provincial Costumes.
585 **116** 3pf.+2pf. brown 20 25
586 – 4pf.+3pf. blue . . . . . 75 1·20
587 – 5pf.+3pf. green 20 60
588 – 6pf.+4pf. green 15 25
589 – 8pf.+4pf. brown . . . . 1·20 1·20
590 – 12pf.+6pf. red 20 25
591 – 15pf.+10pf. brown . . . 3·00 5·00
592 – 25pf.+15pf. blue . . . . 4·75 5·00
593 – 30pf.+20pf. grey . . . . 12·50 18·00
594 – 40pf.+35pf. mauve . . . 9·50 13·00
COSTUMES: 4pf. Silesia; 5pf. Rhineland; 6pf. Lower Saxony; 8pf. Kurmark; 12pf. Black Forest; 15pf. Hesse; 25pf. Upper Bavaria; 30pf. Friesland; 40pf. Franconia.

117 S.A. Man and Feldherrnhalle, Munich

118 Skating

1935. 12th Anniv of 1st Hitler Putsch.
595 **117** 3pf. brown 35 50
596 12pf. red 90 45

1935. Winter Olympic Games, Garmisch-Partenkirchen.
597 **118** 6pf.+4pf. green 70 55
598 – 12pf.+6pf. red . . . . . 1·20 90
599 – 25pf.+15pf. blue . . . . 6·25 8·00
DESIGNS: 12pf. Ski jumping; 25pf. Bobsleighing.

119 Heinkel He 70 Blitz

120 Gottlieb Daimler

1936. 10th Anniv of Lufthansa Airways.
600 **119** 40pf. blue . . . . 6·75 2·30

1936. Berlin Motor Show. 50th Anniv of Invention of First Motor Car.
601 **120** 6pf. green 80 45
602 12pf. red (Carl Benz) . . 1·10 65

121 Airship LZ-129 "Hindenburg"

122 Otto von Guericke

1936. Air.
603 **121** 50pf. blue . . . . 22·00 60
604 75pf. green . . . . 27·00 70

1936. 250th Death Anniv of Otto von Guericke (scientist).
605 **122** 6pf. green 35 40

123 Gymnastics

124 Symbolical of Local Government

1936. Summer Olympic Games, Berlin.
606 **123** 3pf.+2pf. brown 35 30
607 – 4pf.+3pf. blue 25 60
608 – 6pf.+4pf. green 35 25
609 – 8pf.+4pf. red . . . . . . 3·50 1·30
610 – 12pf.+6pf. red 45 25
611 – 15pf.+10pf. red . . . . . 5·25 3·00
612 – 25pf.+15pf. blue . . . . 3·00 3·75
613 – 40pf.+35pf. violet . . . 7·00 7·50
MS613a Two sheets, each 148 × 105 mm. (a) Nos. 606/8 and 613; (b) Nos. 609/12 . . . . . 50·00 85·00
DESIGNS: 4pf. Diver; 6pf. Footballer; 8pf. Javelin thrower; 12pf. Olympic torchbearer; 15pf. Fencer; 25pf. Double scullers; 40pf. Show jumper.

1936. 6th Int Local Government Congress.
614 **124** 3pf. brown 30 25
615 5pf. green 30 25
616 12pf. red 65 45
617 25pf. blue . . . . 1·10 1·10

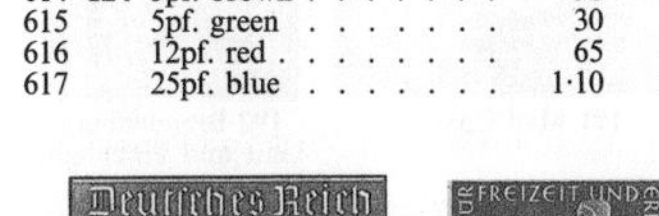

125 "Brown Ribbon" Race

126 "Leisure Time"

1936. "Brown Ribbon of Germany". Single stamp in miniature sheet.
MS618 **125** 42pf. brown . . . . 6·00 10·50

1936. Int Recreational Congress, Hamburg.
619 **126** 6pf. green 40 55
620 15pf. red 65 85

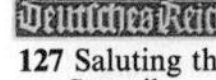
127 Saluting the Swastika

128 Luitpoldhain Heroes Memorial, Nuremberg

1936. Nuremberg Congress.
621 **127** 6pf. green 55 30
622 12pf. red 80 40

1936. Winter Relief Fund.
623 – 3pf.+2pf. brown 15 25
624 – 4pf.+3pf. black 20 50
625 **128** 5pf.+3pf. green 10 25
626 – 6pf.+4pf. green 15 25
627 – 8pf.+4pf. brown . . . . 80 1·40
628 – 12pf.+6pf. red 20 25
629 – 15pf.+10pf. brown . . . 2·00 3·50
630 – 25pf.+15pf. blue . . . . 1·80 3·25
631 – 40pf.+35pf. mauve . . . 2·75 5·25
DESIGNS: 3pf. Munich frontier road; 4pf. Air Ministry, Berlin; 6pf. Bridge over River Saale; 8pf. Deutschlandhalle, Berlin; 12pf. Alpine road; 15pf. Fuhrerhaus, Munich; 25pf. Bridge over River Mangfall; 40pf. German Art Museum, Munich.

129 R(eichs) L(uftschutz) B(und) = Civil Defence Union

1937. 4th Anniv of Civil Defence Union.
632 **129** 3pf. brown 35 30
633 6pf. green 40 25
634 12pf. red 80 50

130 Adolf Hitler

1937. Hitler's Culture Fund and 48th birthday. Four stamps in miniature sheet (148 × 105 mm). Perf or Imperf.
MS635 **130**6+19pf. green . . . . 11·50 13·50

1937. "Brown Ribbon of Germany". No. **MS**618 optd with German eagle and ornamental border surrounding, "1. AUGUST 1937 MUNCHEN-REIM" in red.
MS637a **125** 42pf. (+108pf.) brown 55·00 80·00

1937. Nuremberg Congress. Four stamps in miniature sheet, as No. **MS**637, but optd **REICHSPARTEITAG NURNBERG 1937** in panels of stamps.
MS638 **130**6+19pf. green . . . . 55·00 47·00

131 Fishing Smacks

132 Hitler Youth

1937. Winter Relief Fund.
639 – 3pf.+2pf. brown 20 35
640 – 4pf.+3pf. black . . . . 1·00 70
641 **131** 5pf.+3pf. green 20 35
642 – 6pf.+4pf. green 20 35
643 – 8pf.+4pf. orange . . . . 75 1·30
644 – 12pf.+6pf. red 20 35
645 – 15pf.+10pf. brown . . . 2·20 3·75
646 – 25pf.+15pf. blue . . . . 4·50 3·75
647 – 40pf.+35pf. purple . . . 6·25 7·25
DESIGNS: 3pf. "Bremen" (lifeboat), 1931; 4pf. "Burgemeister Oswald" (lightship); 6pf. "Wilhelm Gustloff" (liner); 8pf. "Padua" (barque); 12pf. "Tannenberg" (liner); 15pf. "Schwerin" (train ferry); 25pf. "Hamburg" (liner); 40pf. "Europa" (liner).

1938. Hitler Culture Fund. 5th Anniv of Hitler's Leadership.
648 **132** 6pf.+4pf. green . . . . . 90 1·30
649 12pf.+8pf. red . . . . . 1·40 1·70

133 "Unity"

134 Adolf Hitler

1938. Austrian Plebiscite.
650 **133** 6pf. green 25 35

1938. Hitler's Culture Fund and 49th Birthday.
652 **134** 12pf.+38pf. red . . . . . 1·60 2·00
See also No. 660.

135 Breslau Cathedral

136 Airship Gondola and Airship LZ-127 "Graf Zeppelin"

1938. 16th German Sports Tournament, Breslau. Inscr as in T **135**.
653 **135** 3pf. brown 30 30
654 – 6pf. green 40 30
655 – 12pf. red 65 30
656 – 15pf. brown . . . . . . 1·10 70
DESIGNS: 6pf. Hermann Goering Stadium; 12pf. Breslau Town Hall; 15pf. Centenary Hall.

1938. Air. Birth Cent of Count Zeppelin.
657 – 25pf. blue . . . . 2·75 85
658 **136** 50pf. green . . . . 3·50 95
DESIGN: 25pf. Count Zeppelin in primitive airship gondola and airship LZ-5.

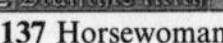
137 Horsewoman

138 Saarpfalz Gautheater, Saarbrucken

1938. "Brown Ribbon of Germany".
659 **137** 42pf.+108pf. brown . . . 25·00 40·00

1938. Nuremberg Congress and Hitler's Culture Fund. As No. 652, but inscr "Reichsparteitag 1938".
660 **134** 6pf.+19pf. green . . . . 3·00 3·25

1938. Opening of Gautheater and Hitler's Culture Fund.
661 **138** 6pf.+4pf. green . . . . . 1·20 1·50
662 12pf.+8pf. red . . . . . 2·00 2·50

139 Forchtenstein Castle, Burgenland

140 Sudeten Miner and Wife

1938. Winter Relief.
663 **139** 3pf.+2pf. brown 20 25
664 – 4pf.+3pf. blue . . . . . 1·70 1·20
665 – 5pf.+3pf. green 15 30
666 – 6pf.+4pf. green 15 20
667 – 8pf.+4pf. red . . . . . . 1·50 1·20
668 – 12pf.+6pf. red 25 30
669 – 15pf.+10pf. red . . . . . 3·50 4·25
670 – 25pf.+15pf. blue . . . . 3·25 4·25
671 – 40pf.+35pf. mauve . . . 7·00 7·25
DESIGNS: 4pf. Flexenstrasse; 5pf. Zell am See; 6pf. Grossglockner; 8pf. Augstein Castle, Wachau; 12pf. Wien (Prince Eugene Statue, Vienna); 15pf. Erzberg, Steiermark; 25pf. Hall-in-Tirol; 40pf. Braunau.

1938. Acquisition of Sudetenland and Hitler's Culture Fund.
672 **140** 6pf.+4pf. green . . . . . 1·20 2·10
673 12pf.+8pf. red . . . . . 2·30 3·25

141 Racing Cars

142 Eagle and Laurel Wreath

1939. Int Motor Show, Berlin, and Hitler's Culture Fund.
674 – 6pf.+4pf. green . . . . . 2·75 3·25
675 **141** 12pf.+8pf. red . . . . . 2·75 3·25
676 – 25pf.+10pf. blue . . . . 8·50 6·25
DESIGNS: 6pf. Early Benz and Daimler cars; 25pf. Volkswagen car.

1939. Apprentices' Vocational Contest.
677 **142** 6pf. green . . . . 1·40 2·75
678 12pf. red . . . . 1·90 2·75

143 Adolf Hitler in Braunau

144 Horticultural Exhibition Entrance and Arms of Stuttgart

1939. Hitler's 50th Birthday and Culture Fund.
679 **143** 12pf.+38pf. red . . . . . 1·80 3·75

1939. Stuttgart Horticultural Exhibition and Hitler's Culture Fund.
680 **144** 6pf.+4pf. green . . . . . 1·10 2·50
681 15pf.+5pf. red . . . . . 1·30 2·50

145 Adolf Hitler Speaking

147 "Investment" and Jockey

1939. National Labour Day and Hitler's Culture Fund.
682 **145** 6pf.+19pf. brown . . . . 3·75 4·25
See also No. 689.

1939. Nurburgring Races and Hitler's Culture Fund. Nos. 674/6 optd **Nurburgring-Rennen**.
683 – 6pf.+4pf. green . . . . . 32·00 27·00
684 **141** 12pf.+8pf. red . . . . . 32·00 27·00
685 – 25pf.+10pf. blue . . . . 32·00 27·00

1939. 70th Anniv of German Derby.
686 **147** 25pf.+50pf. blue . . . . 14·00 13·50

148 Training Thoroughbred Horses

149 "Young Venetian Woman" after Durer

1939. "Brown Ribbon of Germany" and Hitler's Culture Fund.
687 **148** 42pf.+108pf. brown . . . 14·00 23·00

1939. German Art Day.
688 **149** 6pf.+19pf. green . . . . 5·50 7·50

1939. Nuremberg Congress and Hitler's Culture Fund. As T **145**, but inscr "REICHS-PARTEITAG 1939".
689 6pf.+19pf. brown . . . . . 3·50 8·50

150 Mechanics at Work and Play

151 St. Mary's Church, Danzig

1939. Postal Employees' and Hitler's Culture Funds. Inscr "Kameradschaftsblock der Deutschen Reichspost".
690 – 3pf.+2pf. brown . . . . 2·20 4·75
691 – 4pf.+3pf. blue . . . . . 2·20 4·75
692 **150** 5pf.+3pf. green . . . . 75 1·30
693 – 6pf.+4pf. green . . . . . 75 1·20
694 – 8pf.+4pf. orange . . . . 75 1·50
695 – 10pf.+5pf. brown . . . . 75 1·90
696 – 12pf.+6pf. red . . . . . 90 1·90
697 – 15pf.+10pf. red . . . . . 80 1·90
698 – 16pf.+10pf. green . . . . 95 1·90
699 – 20pf.+10pf. blue . . . . 95 1·90
700 – 24pf.+10pf. olive . . . . 2·10 3·50
701 – 25pf.+15pf. blue . . . . 2·10 3·25
DESIGNS: 3pf. Postal employees' rally; 4pf. Review in Vienna; 6pf. Youths on parade; 8pf. Flag bearers; 10pf. Distributing prizes; 12pf. Motor race; 15pf. Women athletes; 16pf. Postal police; 20pf. Glider workshop; 24pf. Mail coach; 25pf. Sanatorium, Konigstein.
See also Nos. 761/6 and 876/81.

1939. Occupation of Danzig. Inscr "DANZIG IST DEUTSCH".
702 **151** 6pf. green 25 55
703 – 12pf. red (Crane Gate) . . 35 80

1939. Stamps of Danzig surch **Deutsches Reich** and new values.
704 **28** Rpf. on 3pf. brown . . . . 75 1·80
705 4Rpf. on 35pf. blue . . . . 75 1·80

706 Rpf. on 5pf. orange . . . 75 1·80
707 Rpf. on 8pf. green . . . . 1·20 3·00
708 Rpf. on 10pf. green . . . . 2·00 3·25
709 12Rpf. on 7pf. green . . . 1·20 1·90
710 Rpf. on 15pf. red . . . . 4·75 8·50
711 Rpf. on 20pf. grey . . . . 2·50 6·00
712 Rpf. on 25pf. red . . . . 3·75 8·75
713 Rpf. on 30pf. purple . . . 1·80 3·50
714 Rpf. on 40pf. blue . . . . 2·30 4·50
715 Rpf. on 50pf. red and blue 2·75 6·25
716 **42** 1Rm on 1g. black & orge 7·50 39·00
717 – 2Rm on 2g. black and red (No. 206) . . . . 11·00 36·00

155 Elbogen Castle

156 Leipzig Library and Gutenberg

1939. Winter Relief Fund.
718 **155** 3pf.+2pf. brown 15 35
719 – 4pf.+3pf. black . . . . . 1·40 1·70
720 – 5pf.+3pf. green 20 40
721 – 6pf.+4pf. green 20 25
722 – 8pf.+4pf. red . . . . . . 1·40 1·50
723 – 12pf.+6pf. red 25 30
724 – 15pf.+10pf. brown . . . 2·00 4·00
725 – 25pf.+15pf. blue . . . . 2·40 4·00
726 – 40pf.+35pf. purple . . . 3·50 5·50
DESIGNS: 4pf. Drachenfels; 5pf. Goslar Castle; 6pf. Clocktower, Graz; 8pf. The Romer, Frankfurt; 12pf. City Hall, Klagenfurt; 15pf. Ruins of Schreckenstein Castle; 25pf. Salzburg Fortress; 40pf. Hohentwiel Castle.

1940. Leipzig Fair.
727 **156** 3pf. brown 30 35
728 – 6pf. green 35 35
729 – 12pf. red 45 35
730 – 25pf. blue . . . . 80 1·00
DESIGNS: 6pf. Augustusplatz; 12pf. Old Town Hall; 25pf. View of Fair.

157 Courtyard of Chancellery, Berlin

158 Hitler and Child

1940. 2nd Berlin Philatelic Exhibition.
731 **157** 24pf.+76pf. green . . . . 6·75 13·50

1940. Hitler's 51st Birthday.
732 **158** 12pf.+38pf. red . . . . . 2·20 5·00

159 Wehrmacht Symbol

160 Horseman

1940. National Fete Day and Hitler's Culture Fund.
733 **159** 6pf.+4pf. green 40 95

1940. Hamburg Derby and Hitler's Culture Fund.
734 **160** 25pf.+100pf. blue . . . . 5·00 8·50

161 Chariot

162 Malmedy

1940. Hitler's Culture Fund and "Brown Ribbon" Race.
735 **161** 42pf.+108pf. brown . . . 21·00 26·00

1940. Eupen and Malmedy reincorporated in Germany, and Hitler's Culture Fund. Inscr "Eupen-Malmedy wieder Deutsch".
736 **162** 6pf.+4pf. green . . . . . 1·10 2·20
737 – 12pf.+8pf. red . . . . . 1·10 1·60
DESIGNS: 12pf. View of Eupen.

163 Heligoland

164 Artushof, Danzig

1940. 50th Anniv of Cession of Heligoland to Germany and Hitler's Culture Fund.
738 **163** 6pf.+94pf. red and green 6·00 8·00

1940. Winter Relief Fund.
739 **164** 3pf.+2pf. brown 10 25
740 – 4pf.+3pf. blue 55 75
741 – 5pf.+3pf. green 20 40
742 – 6pf.+4pf. green 20 25
743 – 8pf.+4pf. orange 80 85
744 – 12pf.+6pf. red 20 25
745 – 15pf.+10pf. brown . . . 80 2·50
746 – 25pf.+15pf. blue . . . . 1·40 2·50
747 – 40pf.+35pf. purple . . . 2·20 5·50
DESIGNS: 4pf. Town Hall, Thorn; 5pf. Kaub Castle; 6pf. City Theatre, Posen; 8pf. Heidelberg Castle; 12pf. Porta Nigra, Trier; 15pf. New Theatre, Prague; 25pf. Town Hall, Bremen; 40pf. Town Hall, Munster.

165 Emil von Behring (bacteriologist)

166 Postilion and Globe

1940. 50th Anniv of Development of Diphtheria Antitoxin.
748 **165** 6pf.+4pf. green . . . . . 70 1·40
749 25pf.+10pf. blue . . . . 1·10 2·50

1941. Stamp Day.
750 **166** 6pf.+24pf. green . . . . 80 1·80

167 Mussolini and Hitler

168 House of Nations, Leipzig

1941. Hitler's Culture Fund.
751 **167** 12pf.+38pf. red . . . . . 95 2·30

1941. Leipzig Fair. Buildings. Inscr "REICHSMESSE LEIPZIG 1941".
752 **168** 3pf. brown 25 65
753 – 6pf. green 25 65
754 – 12pf. red 35 90
755 – 25pf. blue . . . . 70 1·30
DESIGNS: 6pf. Cloth Hall; 12pf. Exhibition Building; 25pf. Railway Station.

169 Dancer

170 Adolf Hitler

1941. Vienna Fair.
756 **169** 3pf. brown 25 50
757 – 6pf. green 25 50
758 – 12pf. red 35 60
759 – 25pf. blue . . . . 75 1·60
DESIGNS: 6pf. Arms and Exhibition Building; 12pf. Allegory and Municipal Theatre; 25pf. Prince Eugene's Equestrian Monument.

1941. Hitler's 52nd Birthday and Culture Fund.
760 **170** 12pf.+38pf. red . . . . . 1·60 3·00

1941. Postal Employees' and Hitler's Culture Funds. Inscr "Kameradschaftsblock der Deutschen Reichspost" as Nos. 693/4, 696 and 698/700, but premium values and colours changed.
761 6pf.+9pf. green . . . . . . 65 1·30
762 8pf.+12pf. red . . . . . . 85 1·10
763 12pf.+18pf. red . . . . . . 85 1·10
764 16pf.+24pf. black . . . . . 1·30 3·25
765 20pf.+30pf. blue . . . . . 1·30 3·25
766 24pf.+36pf. violet . . . . . 4·75 11·00

171 Racehorse

172 Two Amazons

1941. 72nd Anniv of Hamburg Derby.
767 **171** 25pf.+100pf. blue . . . . 4·00 7·00

1941. "Brown Ribbon of Germany".
768 **172** 42pf.+108pf. brown . . . 2·40 4·75

173 Adolf Hitler

174 Brandenburg Gate, Berlin

1941.
769 **173** 1pf. grey 10 10
770 3pf. brown 10 10
771 4pf. slate 10 10
772 5pf. green 10 10
773 6pf. violet 10 10
774 8pf. red 10 10
777 10pf. brown 25 15
776 12pf. red 25 15
779 15pf. lake 10 15
780 16pf. green . . . . 10 1·10
781 20pf. blue 10 15
782 24pf. brown . . . . 10 1·20
783 25pf. blue 10 15
784 30pf. olive 10 15
785 40pf. mauve 10 15
786 50pf. green 10 15
787 60pf. brown 10 15
788 80pf. blue 10 30
Nos. 783/8 are larger ($21\frac{1}{2} \times 26$ mm).

1941. Berlin Grand Prix and Hitler's Culture Fund.
789 **174** 25pf.+50pf. blue . . . . 2·20 4·75

175 Belvedere Palace, Vienna

176 Belvedere Gardens, Vienna

1941. Vienna Fair and Hitler's Culture Fund.
790 **175** 12pf.+8pf. red . . . . . 60 2·50
791 **176** 15pf.+10pf. violet . . . . 80 3·00

177 Marburg

178 Veldes

1941. Annexation of Northern Slovenia, and Hitler's Culture Fund.
792 **177** 3pf.+7pf. brown . . . . 65 1·80
793 **178** 6pf.+9pf. violet . . . . . 60 1·90
794 – 12pf.+13pf. red . . . . . 80 2·20
795 – 25pf.+15pf. blue . . . . 1·40 2·30
DESIGNS: 12pf. Pettau; 25pf. Triglav.

179 Mozart

180 Philatelist

1941. 150th Death Anniv of Mozart and Hitler's Culture Fund.
796 **179** 6pf.+4pf. purple 20 50

1942. Stamp Day and Hitler's Culture Fund.
797 **180** 6pf.+24pf. violet . . . . 55 2·30

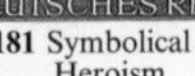

181 Symbolical of Heroism

182 Adolf Hitler

1942. Heroes' Remembrance Day and Hitler's Culture Fund.
798 **181** 12pf.+38pf. slate . . . . 40 1·50

1942.
799a **182** 1m. green . . . . 65 2·75
800 2m. violet . . . . 45 3·00
801 3m. red . . . . 45 9·00
802a 5m. blue . . . . 90 28·00

183 Adolf Hitler

184 Jockey and Three-year-old Horse

1942. Hitler's 53rd Birthday and Culture Fund.
803 **183** 12pf.+38pf. red . . . . . 1·90 5·25

1942. Hamburg Derby and Hitler's Culture Fund.
804 **184** 25pf.+100pf. blue . . . . 5·50 10·00

185 Equine Trio

186 Cream Jug and Loving Cup

1942. "Brown Ribbon of Germany" and Hitler's Culture Fund.
805 **185** 42pf.+108pf. brown . . . 1·80 4·75

1942. 10th Anniv of National Goldsmiths' Institution.
806 **186** 6pf.+4pf. red 25 85
807 12pf.+88pf. green . . . . 45 1·70

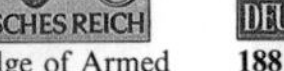

187 Badge of Armed S.A.

188 Peter Henlein

1942. S.A. Military Training Month.
808 **187** 6pf. violet 20 70

1942. 400th Death Anniv of Henlein (inventor of the watch).
809 **188** 6pf.+24pf. violet . . . . 45 1·20

189 Mounted Postilion

1942. European Postal Congress, Vienna.
810 – 3pf.+7pf. blue . . . . . 20 1·40
811 – 6pf.+14pf. brown & blue 25 1·40
812 **189** 12pf.+38pf. brown & red 50 2·10
DESIGNS—HORIZ: 3pf. Postilion and map of Europe. VERT: 6pf. Mounted postilion and globe.

1942. Signing of European Postal Union Agreement. Nos. 810/2 optd **19.Okt.1942.**
813 – 3pf.+7pf. blue . . . . . 75 2·00
814 – 6pf.+14pf. brown & blue 75 2·00
815 **189** 12pf.+38pf. brown & red 1·30 4·50

191 Mail Coach

192 Brandenburg Gate and Torchlight Parade

1943. Stamp Day and Hitler's Culture Fund.
816 **191** 6pf.+24pf. brn, yell & bl 30 90

1943. 10th Anniv of Third Reich.
817 **192** 54pf.+96pf. red . . . . . 40 1·80

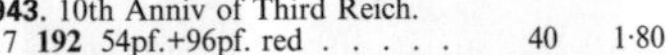

193

194 Machine Gunners

1943. Philatelic Cancellation Premium.

818	**193**	3pf.+2pf. bistre	20	60

1943. Armed Forces' and Heroes' Day.

819	–	3pf.+2pf. brown	35	1·10
820	**194**	4pf.+3pf. brown	30	1·10
821	–	5pf.+4pf. green	30	1·10
822	–	6pf.+9pf. violet	35	1·10
823	–	8pf.+7pf. red	35	1·10
824	–	12pf.+8pf. red	35	1·10
825	–	15pf.+10pf. purple	35	1·10
826	–	20pf.+14pf. blue	40	1·10
827	–	25pf.+15pf. blue	45	1·10
828	–	30pf.+30pf. green	55	1·80
829	–	40pf.+40pf. purple	55	1·90
830	–	50pf.+50pf. green	80	2·75

DESIGNS: 3pf. U-boat Type VIIA (submarine); 5pf. Armed motor cyclists; 6pf. Wireless operators; 8pf. Engineers making pontoon; 12pf. Grenade thrower; 15pf. Heavy artillery; 20pf. Anti-aircraft gunners; 25pf. Junkers Ju 87B "Stuka" dive bombers; 30pf. Parachutists; 40pf. Tank; 50pf. "S-22" (motor torpedo-boat).

195 Hitler Youth

1943. Youth Dedication Day.

831	**195**	6pf.+4pf. green	30	90

196 Adolf Hitler

1943. Hitler's 54th Birthday and Culture Fund.

832	**196**	3pf.+7pf. black	35	1·20
833		6pf.+14pf. green	35	1·20
834		8pf.+22pf. blue	35	1·20
835		12pf.+38pf. red	35	1·20
836		24pf.+76pf. purple	80	3·50
837		40pf.+160pf. olive	80	3·50

197 Attestation **198** Huntsman

1943. Labour Corps.

838	**197**	3pf.+7pf. brown	10	50
839	–	5pf.+10pf. green	10	45
840	–	6pf.+14pf. blue	10	45
841	–	12pf.+18pf. red	20	1·50

DESIGNS: 5pf. Harvester sharpening scythe; 6pf. Labourer wielding sledge-hammer; 12pf. "Pick and shovel fatigue".

1943. "Brown Ribbon of Germany".

842	**198**	42pf.+108pf. brown	25	1·00

199 Birthplace of Peter Rosegger **200** Peter Rosegger

1943. Birth Cent of Peter Rosegger (poet).

843	**199**	6pf.+4pf. green	15	60
844	**200**	12pf.+8pf. red	20	85

201 Racehorse **202** Mother and Children

1943. Grand Prix, Vienna.

845	**201**	6pf.+4pf. violet	20	1·00
846		12pf.+88pf. red	20	1·20

1943. 10th Anniv of Winter Relief Fund.

847	**202**	12pf.+38pf. red	25	95

203 St George and the Dragon **204** Lubeck

1943. 11th Anniv of National Goldsmiths' Institution.

848	**203**	6pf.+4pf. green	15	65
849		12pf.+88pf. purple	20	95

1943. 800th Anniv of Lubeck.

850	**204**	12pf.+8pf. red	20	85

205

1943. 20th Anniv of Munich Rising.

851	**205**	24pf.+26pf. red	30	95

206 Dr. Robert Koch **207** Adolf Hitler

1944. Birth Centenary of Dr. Robert Koch (bacteriologist).

852	**206**	12pf.+38pf. sepia	20	85

1944. 11th Anniv of Third Reich.

853	**207**	54pf.+96pf. brown	25	95

208 Focke Wulf Fw 200 Condor over Tempelhof Airport **209** Dornier Do-26 Flying Boat

1944. 25th Anniv of Air Mail Services.

854	**208**	6pf.+4pf. green	15	60
855	**209**	12pf.+8pf. purple	15	75
856	–	42pf.+108pf. blue	25	1·90

DESIGNS—VERT: 42pf. Junkers Ju 90B airplane seen from above.

210 Day Nursery **211** "Mothers' Help"

1944. 10th Anniv of "Mother and Child" Organization.

857	**210**	3pf.+2pf. brown	10	40
858	**211**	6pf.+4pf. green	10	40
859	–	12pf.+8pf. red	10	40
860	–	15pf.+10pf. purple	15	60

DESIGNS: 12pf. Child auscultation; 15pf. Mothers at convalescent home.

212 Landing Craft **213** Fulda Monument

1944. Armed Forces' and Heroes' Day.

861	**212**	3pf.+2pf. brown	25	1·00
862	–	4pf.+3pf. blue	15	60
863	–	5pf.+3pf. green	15	45
864	–	6pf.+4pf. violet	15	45
865	–	8pf.+4pf. red	15	55
866	–	10pf.+5pf. brown	15	45
867	–	12pf.+6pf. red	15	45
868	–	15pf.+10pf. purple	15	55
869	–	16pf.+10pf. green	25	1·00
870	–	20pf.+10pf. blue	25	1·10
871	–	24pf.+10pf. brown	35	1·10
872	–	25pf.+15pf. blue	65	3·00
873	–	30pf.+20pf. olive	65	3·00

DESIGNS: 4pf. Caterpillar tricar; 5pf. Parachutists; 6pf. Submarine officer; 8pf. Mortar-firing party; 10pf. Searchlight unit; 12pf. Machine gunners; 15pf. Tank; 16pf. "S-128" (motor torpedo-boat); 20pf. Arado Ar 196A seaplane; 24pf. Railway gun; 25pf. Rocket projectiles; 30pf. Alpine trooper.

1944. 1200th Anniv of Fulda.

874	**213**	12pf.+38pf. brown	15	85

214 Adolf Hitler **215** Postwoman

1944. Hitler's 55th Birthday.

875	**214**	54pf.+96pf. red	45	1·40

1944. Postal Employees' and Hitler's Culture Funds. Inscr "Kameradschaftsblock der Deutschen Reichspost".

876	**215**	6pf.+9pf. blue	10	45
877	–	8pf.+12pf. grey	10	45
878	–	12pf.+18pf. mauve	15	45
879	–	16pf.+24pf. green	15	50
880	–	20pf.+30pf. blue	20	1·20
881	–	24pf.+36pf. violet	35	1·30

DESIGNS—As Type **150**: 8pf. Mail coach; 16pf. Motor-car race; 20pf. Postal police march; 24pf. Glider workshop. As Type **215**: 12pf. The Field Post on Eastern Front.

216 Girl Worker **217** Labourer

1944. Labour Corps.

882	**216**	6pf.+4pf. green	10	45
883	**217**	12pf.+8pf. red	15	60

218 Riflemen **219** Duke Albrecht

1944. 7th Innsbruck Shooting Competition.

884	**218**	6pf.+4pf. green	10	50
885		12pf.+8pf. red	20	2·10

1944. 400th Anniv of Albert University, Konigsberg.

886	**219**	6pf.+4pf. green	25	90

220 Racehorse and Foal

1944. "Brown Ribbon of Germany".

887	**220**	42pf.+108pf. brown	30	1·10

221 Racehorse and Laurel Wreath **222** Chambered Nautilus Beaker

1944. Vienna Grand Prix.

888	**221**	6pf.+4pf. green	15	90
889		12pf.+88pf. red	20	1·10

1944. National Goldsmiths' Institution.

890	**222**	6pf.+4pf. green	10	80
891		12pf.+88pf. red	20	95

223 Posthorn **224** Eagle and Dragon

1944. Stamp Day.

892	**223**	6pf.+24pf. green	25	95

1944. 21st Anniv of Munich Rising.

893	**224**	12pf.+8pf. red	25	90

225 Adolf Hitler **226** Count Anton Gunther

1944.

894	**225**	42pf. green	10	1·20

1945. 600th Anniv of Oldenburg.

895	**226**	6pf.+14pf. purple	25	95

227 "Home Guard" **228** S.S. Troopers

1945. Mobilization of "Home Guard".

896	**227**	12pf.+8pf. red	45	1·60

1945. 12th Anniv of Third Reich.

897	**228**	12pf.+38pf. red	22·00	65·00
898	–	12pf.+38pf. red	31·00	65·00

DESIGN: No. 898, S.A. man with torch.

For Nos. 899 onwards see section B of Allied Occupation.

MILITARY FIELDPOST STAMPS

M 184 Junkers Ju 52/3m **M 185**

1942. Air. No value indicated. Perf. or roul.

M804	**M 184**	(–) blue	40	30

1942. Parcel Post. Size 28×23 mm. No value indicated. Perf or roul.

M805	**M 185**	(–) brown	40	45

Nos. M804/5 also exist overprinted **INSELPOST** in various types for use in Crete and the Aegean Islands and there are various other local fieldpost issues.

1944. Christmas Parcel Post. Size 22½×18 mm. No value indicated. Perf.

M895	**M 185**	(–) green	1·20	1·60

1944. For 2 kilo parcels. No value indicated. No. 785 optd **FELDPOST 2kg.**

M896	**173**	(–) on 40pf. mauve	1·20	2·10

NEWSPAPER STAMPS

N 156 Newspaper Messenger and Globe

1939.

N727	**N 156**	5pf. green	75	2·75
N728		10pf. brown	75	2·75

OFFICIAL STAMPS

O 23 **O 24**

1903.

O82	O 23	2pf. grey	85	3·75
O83		3pf. brown	85	4·50
O84		5pf. green	25	40
O85		10pf. red	25	40
O86		20pf. blue	25	40
O87		25pf. black and red on yellow	25	40
O88		40pf. black and red	45	1·70
O89		50pf. blk & pur on buff	60	1·40

1905.

O90	O 24	2pf. grey	60·00	65·00
O91		3pf. brown	8·00	10·50
O92		5pf. green	5·00	7·00
O93		10pf. red	75	2·20
O94		20pf. blue	2·00	2·75
O95		25pf. black and red on yellow	40·00	55·00

O 31 O 32

1920. Numeral designs as Types O 31 and O 32.

O117		5pf. green	25	3·00
O118		10pf. red	60	1·20
O119		15pf. brown	20	1·10
O120		20pf. blue	20	95
O121		30pf. orange on pink	10	95
O122		50pf. violet on pink	35	1·10
O123		1m. red on pink	7·75	4·00

1920. Similar designs but without figures "21".

O124		5pf. green	1·60	5·50
O125		10pf. red	80	1·10
O126		10pf. orange	70	£500
O127		15pf. purple	80	1·50
O128		20pf. blue	80	1·10
O129		30pf. orange on pink	80	1·80
O130		40pf. red	80	1·50
O131		50pf. violet on pink	80	1·70
O132		60pf. brown	15	1·10
O133		1m. red on pink	10	90
O134		1m.25 blue on yellow	10	1·10
O135a		2m. blue	2·00	1·50
O136		5m. brown on yellow	25	1·20

1920. Official stamps of Bavaria optd **Deutsches Reich.**

O137	O 31	5pf. green	10	3·25
O138		10pf. orange	10	1·80
O139		15pf. red	10	1·80
O140		20pf. purple	10	1·40
O141		30pf. blue	10	1·20
O142		40pf. brown	10	1·20
O143	O 32	50pf. red	10	1·20
O144		60pf. green	10	1·20
O145		70pf. violet	2·50	2·75
O146		75pf. red	50	1·40
O147		80pf. blue	10	1·20
O148		90pf. olive	1·70	2·20
O149	O 33	1m. brown	10	1·20
O150		1¼m. green	10	1·20
O151		1½m. red	10	1·20
O152		2½m. blue	20	1·30
O153		3m. red	20	1·30
O154		5m. black	12·00	29·00

1920. Municipal Service stamps of Wurttemberg optd **Deutsches Reich.**

O155	M 5	5pf. green	4·25	9·50
O156		10pf. red	2·30	4·50
O157		15pf. violet	2·50	5·25
O158		20pf. blue	5·00	8·50
O159		50pf. purple	4·50	20·00

1920. Official stamps of Wurttemberg optd **Deutsches Reich.**

O160	O 5	5pf. green	2·50	4·25
O161		10pf. red	1·50	3·00
O162		15pf. purple	1·50	3·00
O163		20pf. blue	1·50	1·60
O164		30pf. black and orange	1·50	3·75
O165		40pf. black and red	1·50	3·00
O166		50pf. purple	1·50	3·75
O167		1m. black and grey	2·50	7·75

O 48 O 50 O 81

1922. Figure designs.

O249	O 48	75pf. blue	20	6·75
O247	–	3m. brown on red	10	1·40
O248	O 50	10m. green on red	10	6·50
O251		20m. blue on red	10	1·30
O252		50m. violet on red	10	1·30
O253		100m. red on rose	10	1·30

1923. Postage stamps optd **Dienstmarke.**

O274	51	20m. purple	10	8·50
O275		30m. olive	10	25·00
O276	38	40m. green	20	3·25
O277	54	200m. red	10	1·20
O278		300m. green	10	1·20
O279		400m. brown	10	1·20
O280		500m. orange	20	1·20
O342	62	100M. grey	20	£170
O343		200M. brown	20	£170
O344		2Md. green and pink	30	£100
O345		5Md. brown and yellow	30	85·00
O346		10Md. green and light green	4·50	£160
O347		20Md. brown and green	5·00	£160
O348		50Md. blue	2·50	£200

1923. Official stamps of 1920 and 1922 surch **Tausend** or **Millionen** and figure.

O312	–	5T. on 5m. brown on yellow	10	3·25
O313	–	20T. on 30pf. orange on rose (No. O129)	10	2·75
O317	O 50	75T. on 50m. violet on rose	10	2·75
O314	–	100T. on 15pf. purple	10	2·75
O315	–	250T. on 10pf. red (No. O125)	10	2·75
O318	–	400T. on 15pf. purple	10	29·00
O319	–	800T. on 30pf. orge on rose (No. O129)	15	4·50
O320	O 48	1M. on 75pf. blue	10	46·00
O321	–	2M. on 10pf. red (No. O125)	15	3·75
O322	O 50	5M. on 100m. red on rose	10	6·50

1923. Nos. 352/7 optd **Dienstmarke.**

O358	64	3pf. brown	40	40
O359		5pf. green	40	40
O360		10pf. red	50	40
O361		20pf. blue	1·00	40
O362		50pf. orange	1·00	80
O363		100pf. purple	4·50	8·50

1924. Optd **Dienstmarke.**

O376	66	3pf. brown	50	1·30
O377		5pf. green	30	40
O378		10pf. red	30	40
O379		20pf. blue	40	40
O380		30pf. red	1·00	50
O381		40pf. olive	1·00	60
O382		50pf. orange	6·50	3·00
O384	72	60pf. brown	2·20	4·00
O385		80pf. grey	9·50	37·00

1927.

O424	O 81	3pf. brown	45	20
O425		4pf. blue	40	45
O427		5pf. green	20	20
O428		6pf. green	50	45
O429		8pf. green	40	20
O430		10pf. red	10·00	9·50
O432		10pf. mauve	40	45
O433		10pf. brown	3·75	7·25
O434		12pf. orange	40	45
O436		15pf. red	1·50	50
O437		20pf. green	6·00	2·40
O438		20pf. grey	1·50	70
O439		30pf. green	1·20	40
O440		40pf. violet	1·20	40
O441		60pf. brown	1·50	1·70

O 100

1934.

O809	O 100	3pf. brown	20	85
O810		4pf. blue	20	85
O528		5pf. green	20	65
O529		6pf. green	20	65
O812		6pf. violet	20	3·00
O813		8pf. red	30	85
O531		10pf. brown	35	1·30
O815		12pf. red	40	2·00
O533		15pf. red	1·20	6·75
O534		20pf. blue	40	1·20
O535		30pf. green	75	1·20
O536		40pf. mauve	75	1·20
O537		50pf. yellow	1·00	1·30
O820		50pf. green	2·20	41·00

SPECIAL STAMPS FOR USE BY OFFICIALS OF THE NATIONAL SOCIALIST GERMAN WORKERS' PARTY

P 132 Party Badge

1938.

O648	P 132	1pf. black	1·20	3·25
O799		3pf. brown	55	1·20
O800		4pf. blue	65	85
O651		5pf. green	75	1·30
O652		6pf. green	75	1·30
O802		6pf. violet	30	1·10
O803		8pf. red	2·20	95
O804		12pf. red	2·75	95
O655		16pf. grey	2·00	12·50
O805		16pf. blue	4·00	39·00
O656		24pf. green	3·00	5·75
O806		24pf. brown	60	2·50
O807		30pf. green	1·20	3·00
O808		40pf. mauve	1·40	2·75

II. ALLIED OCCUPATION

The defeat of Germany in May 1945 resulted in the division of the country into four zones of occupation (British, American, French and Russian), while Berlin was placed under joint allied control. Allied Military Post Stamps came into use in the British and American zones, the French issued special stamps in their zone and in the Russian zone the first issues were made by local administrations.

The territory occupied by the Anglo-American and French Zones subsequently became the German Federal Republic (West Germany) which was set up in September 1949. By the Nine Power Agreement of 3 October 1954, the occupation of West Germany was ended and full sovereignty was granted to the German Federal Government as from 5 May 1955 (see Section III).

The territory in the Russian Zone became the German Democratic Republic (East Germany) which was set up on 7 October 1949 (see Section V).

Separate issues for the Western Sectors of Berlin came into being in 1948 (see Section IV). The Russian Zone issues inscribed "STADT BERLIN" were for use in the Russian sector of the city and Brandenburg and these were superseded first by the General Issues of the Russian Zone and then by the stamps of East Germany.

100 pfennige = 1 Reichsmark.
21.6.48. 100 pfennige = 1 Deutsche Mark (West).
24.6.48. 100 pfennige = 1 Deutsche Mark (East).

A. Allied Military Post (British and American Zones)

A 1

1945.

A16	A 1	1pf. black	15	40
A 1		3pf. violet	15	35
A18		4pf. grey	15	35
A19a		5pf. green	65	70
A20		6pf. yellow	15	30
A 5		8pf. orange	15	35
A 6		10pf. brown	15	40
A23		12pf. purple	35	40
A24		15pf. red	15	45
A25		16pf. green	15	2·00
A26		20pf. blue	30	50
A27		24pf. brown	25	2·20
A28		25pf. blue	35	3·00
A29		30pf. olive	30	2·40
A30		40pf. mauve	30	1·10
A31		42pf. green	30	1·10
A32		50pf. slate	15	90
A33		60pf. plum	65	4·50
A34		80pf. blue	31·00	55·00
A35		1m. green	3·50	8·50

Values 30pf. to 80pf. are size 22 × 25 mm and 1m. is size 25 × 29½ mm.

Nos. A36 etc continue in Section C.

Used prices are for cancelled-to-order.

B. American, British and Russian Zones 1946–48

From February 1946 to June 1948 these zones used the same stamps (Nos. 899/956). It had been intended that they should be used throughout all four zones but until the creation of the German Federal Republic, in September 1949, the French Zone always had its own stamps, while after the revaluation of the currency in June 1948 separate stamps were again issued for the Russian Zone.

229 Numeral 231 1160: Leipzig obtains Charter

1946.

899	229	1pf. black	15	1·50
900		2pf. black	15	20
901		3pf. brown	15	2·50
902		4pf. blue	15	2·50
903		5pf. green	15	70
904		6pf. violet	15	20
905		8pf. red	15	20
906		10pf. brown	15	20
907		12pf. red	15	20
908		12pf. grey	15	20
909		15pf. red	15	3·75
910		15pf. green	15	20
911		16pf. green	15	20
912		20pf. blue	15	20
913		24pf. brown	15	20
914		25pf. blue	15	4·50
915		25pf. orange	15	1·00
916		30pf. green	15	20
917		40pf. purple	15	20
918		42pf. green	1·60	40·00
919		45pf. red	15	30
920		50pf. green	15	20
921		60pf. red	15	20
922		75pf. blue	15	20
923		80pf. blue	15	20
924		84pf. green	15	20
925		1m. green (24 × 30 mm)	15	20
MS925a		107 × 51 mm. Nos. 912/13 and 917 (sold at 5m.)	£110	£375

1947. Leipzig Spring Fair. Inscr "LEIPZIGER MESSE 1947".

926	231	24pf.+26pf. brown	1·00	2·50
927	–	60pf.+40pf. blue	1·00	2·50

DESIGN: 60pf. 1268: Foreign merchants at Leipzig Fair.

See also Nos. 951/4.

233 Gardener 237 "Dove of Peace"

1947.

928	233	2pf. black	20	50
929		6pf. violet	20	20
930	A	8pf. red	20	20
931		10pf. green	20	50
932	B	12pf. grey	20	20
933	233	15pf. brown	40	2·00
934	C	16pf. green	20	50
935	A	20pf. blue	20	50
936	C	24pf. brown	20	50
937	233	25pf. orange	20	50
938	B	30pf. red	40	1·20
939	A	40pf. mauve	20	50
940	C	50pf. blue	40	1·20
941	B	60pf. red	20	60
942		60pf. brown	20	80
943		80pf. blue	20	80
944	C	84pf. green	50	80
945	237	1m. green	20	80
946		2m. violet	20	1·00
947		3m. lake	20	14·00
948		5m. blue	2·50	60·00

DESIGNS: A, Sower; B, Labourer; C, Bricklayer and reaper.

238 Dr. von Stephan

1947. 50th Death Anniv of Von Stephan.

949	238	24pf. brown	20	60
950		75pf. blue	30	1·30

1947. Leipzig Autumn Fair. As T **231**.

951		12pf. red	25	1·20
952		75pf. blue	25	2·00

DESIGNS: 12pf. 1497: Maximilian I granting Charter; 75pf. 1365: Assessment and Collection of Ground Rents.

1948. Leipzig Spring Fair. As T **231** but dated "1948".

953		50pf. blue	25	1·00
954		84pf. green	25	1·70

DESIGNS: 50pf. 1388: At the customs barrier; 84pf. 1433: Bringing merchandise.

For similar types, dated "1948", "1949" or "1950", but with premium values, see Nos. R31/2, R51/2, R60/1 of Russian Zone and E7/8 of East Germany.

239 Weighing Goods

1948. Hanover Trade Fair.

955	239	24pf. red	25	1·10
956		50pf. blue	25	1·60

C. British and American Zones 1948–49

(A 2)

1948. Currency Reform. (a) On Pictorial issue of 1947, Nos. 928/44. (i) Optd with Type A **2**.

A36		2pf. black	15	20
A37		6pf. violet	15	20
A38		8pf. red	15	20
A39		10pf. green	20	30
A40		12pf. grey	20	15
A41		15pf. brown	7·75	18·00
A42		16pf. green	1·40	2·75
A43		20pf. blue	65	1·20
A44		24pf. brown	20	15
A45		25pf. orange	35	55
A46		30pf. red	2·75	6·50
A47		40pf. mauve	75	1·20
A48		50pf. blue	90	1·20
A49		60pf. brown	75	1·10
A50		60pf. red	55·00	£225

A51 80pf. blue . . . . 1·20 2·75
A52 84pf. green . . . . 3·75 7·50

(ii) Optd with multiple posthorns over whole stamp.
A53 2pf. black . . . . 90 1·60
A54 6pf. violet . . . . 90 1·60
A55 8pf. red . . . . 90 1·60
A56 10pf. green 20 30
A57 12pf. grey . . . . 1·00 1·80
A58 15pf. brown 20 75
A59 16pf. green 30 35
A60 20pf. blue 20 35
A61 24pf. brown . . . . 65 1·80
A62 25pf. orange . . . . 8·75 20
A63 30pf. red 30 75
A64 40pf. mauve 30 65
A65 50pf. blue 35 65
A66 60pf. brown . . . . 2·75 7·25
A67 60pf. red 35 75
A68 80pf. blue 45 75
A69 84pf. green . . . . 85 1·60

(b) On Numeral issue of 1946, Nos. 900 to 924. (i) Optd with Type A 2.
A70 **229** 2pf. black . . . . 5·50 32·00
A71 8pf. red . . . . 11·50 65·00
A72 10pf. brown . . . . 1·20 4·50
A73 12pf. red . . . . 7·75 50·00
A74 12pf. grey £150 £600
A75 15pf. red . . . . 7·75 60·00
A76 15pf. green . . . . 2·75 16·00
A77 16pf. green . . . . 46·00 £200
A78 24pf. brown . . . . 85·00 £225
A79 25pf. blue . . . . 16·00 65·00
A80 25pf. orange . . . . 1·80 7·75
A81 30pf. olive . . . . 1·80 7·75
A82 40pf. purple . . . . 65·00 £225
A83 45pf. red . . . . 2·75 7·75
A84 50pf. green . . . . 2·75 7·75
A85 75pf. blue . . . . 5·50 23·00
A86 84pf. green . . . . 5·50 23·00

(ii) Optd with multiple posthorns over whole stamp.
A 87 **229** 2pf. black . . . . . . 25·00 75·00
A 88 8pf. red . . . . . . 37·00 £130
A 89 10pf. brown . . . . . . 35·00 £130
A 90 12pf. red . . . . . . 12·50 65·00
A 91 12pf. grey £275 £1100
A 92 15pf. red . . . . . . 12·50 50·00
A 93 15pf. green . . . . . . 1·20 7·75
A 94 16pf. green . . . . . . 41·00 £160
A 95 24pf. brown . . . . . . 46·00 £225
A 96 25pf. blue . . . . . . 14·00 60·00
A 97 25pf. orange . . . . . . 41·00 £180
A 98 30pf. olive . . . . . . 2·10 6·50
A 99 40pf. purple . . . . . . 60·00 £250
A100 45pf. red . . . . . . 2·75 13·50
A101 50pf. green . . . . . . 2·75 13·50
A102 75pf. blue . . . . . . 2·75 14·00
A103 84pf. green . . . . . . 2·75 15·00

A 4 Crowned Head

A 7 Cologne Cathedral

1948. 700th Anniv of Cologne Cathedral and Restoration Fund.
A104 A 4 6pf.+4pf. brown 65 65
A105 – 12pf.+8pf. blue . . . . 1·60 2·10
A106 – 24pf.+16pf. red . . . . 2·50 3·50
A107 A 7 50pf.+50pf. blue . . . . 6·50 9·25
DESIGNS—As Type A 4: 12pf. The Three Wise Men; 24pf. Cologne Cathedral.

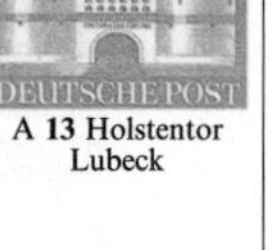

A 9 The Romer, Frankfurt am Main

A 10 Frauenkirche, Munich

A 13 Holstentor Lubeck

1948. Various designs.
A108 A 9 2pf. black 20 15
A109 A 10 4pf. brown 25 15
A110a A 5pf. blue 30 15
A111 A 10 6pf. brown 20 35
A112 6pf. orange 30 15
A113 A 9 8pf. yellow 30 35
A114 A 10 8pf. slate 30 15
A115a A 10pf. green 30 15
A116 A 10 15pf. orange . . . . . 2·10 5·50
A117 A 9 15pf. violet . . . . . 1·20 15
A118 16pf. green 60 55
A119 20pf. blue . . . . . 1·00 2·30
A120 B 20pf. red 70 15
A121 24pf. red 30 20
A122 A 25pf. red . . . . . 1·00 15
A123 B 30pf. blue . . . . . 1·20 20
A124 A 10 30pf. red . . . . . 2·75 5·50
A125 A 40pf. mauve . . . . . 1·60 30
A126 B 50pf. blue . . . . . 1·20 1·80
A127 A 10 50pf. green . . . . . 1·60 15
A128a A 60pf. purple . . . . . 80·00 15
A129 B 80pf. mauve . . . . . 3·00 15
A130 A 10 84pf. purple . . . . . 2·10 5·50
A131 A 90pf. mauve . . . . . 3·00 15
A132 A 13 1Dm. green . . . . . 32·00 65
A133 2Dm. violet . . . . . 28·00 65
A134 3Dm. mauve . . . . 32·00 3·25
A135 5Dm. blue . . . . 37·00 26·00
DESIGNS—As Type A 9/10: A, Cologne Cathedral; B, Brandenburg Gate.

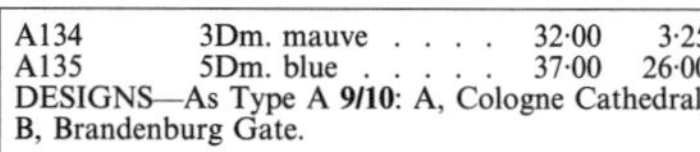

A 15 Brandenburg Gate, Berlin

1948. Aid to Berlin.
A140 A 15 10pf.+5pf. green . . . 7·00 7·75
A141 20pf.+10pf. red . . . 7·00 7·75

A 16 Herman Hillebrant Wedigh (after Holbein)

A 17 Racing Cyclists

1949. Hanover Trade Fair.
A142 A 16 10pf. green . . . . . 2·75 2·50
A143 20pf. red . . . . . 2·75 2·50
A144 30pf. blue . . . . . 3·75 3·25
MSA145 110 × 65 mm. Nos. A142/4 (sold at 1Dm.) . . . . 90·00 £225

1949. Trans-Germany Cycle Race.
A146 A 17 10pf.+5pf. green . . . 4·50 4·50
A147 20pf.+10pf. brown . . 12·50 17·00

A 18 Goethe in Italy

A 19 Goethe

1949. Birth Bicentenary of Goethe (poet).
A148 A 18 10pf.+5pf. green . . . 3·25 3·25
A149 A 19 20pf.+10pf. red . . . 5·50 5·50
A150 – 30pf.+15pf. blue . . . 25·00 25·00
DESIGN—VERT: 30pf. Profile portrait.

OBLIGATORY TAX STAMPS

AT 14

1948. Aid for Berlin. Perf or imperf.
AT136 AT 14 2pf. blue 40 20

The Anglo-American Zones, together with the French Zone, became the Federal German Republic (West Germany) in September 1949.

D. French Zone.

(a) General Issues, 1945–46.

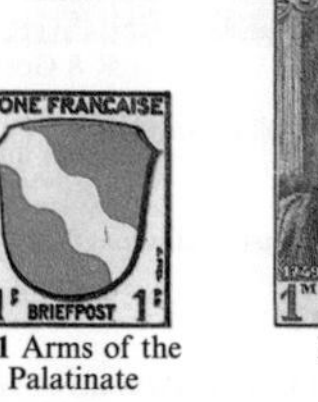

F 1 Arms of the Palatinate

F 2 Goethe

1945. (a) Arms.
F 1 F 1 1pf. green, black & yellow 20 25
F 2 – 3pf. yellow, black and red 30 20
F 3 – 5pf. black, yellow & brn 20 20
F 4 – 8pf. red, yellow and brown 20 20
F 5 F 1 10pf. green, brown & yell 7·75 45·00
F 6 – 12pf. yellow, black & red 20 20
F 7 – 15pf. blue, black and red 20 25
F 8 – 20pf. black, yellow & red 20 25
F 9 – 24pf. blue, black and red 20 35
F10 – 30pf. red, yellow & black 20 25
ARMS: 3, 12pf. Rhineland; 5, 20pf. Wurttemberg; 8, 30pf. Baden; 15, 24pf. Saar.

(b) Poets.
F11 2 1m. brown . . . . 1·80 19·00
F12 – 2m. blue (Schiller) . . . . 1·40 55·00
F13 – 5m. red (Heine) . . . . . 1·50 55·00

(b) Baden, 1947–49.

FB 1 J. P. Hebel

FB 2 Rastatt Castle

FB 3 Hollental Black Forest

FB 4 Freiburg Cathedral

1947. Inscr "BADEN".
FB 1 FB 1 2pf. grey 20 35
FB 2 – 3pf. brown 20 25
FB 3 – 10pf. blue 20 25
FB 4 FB 1 12pf. green 20 25
FB 5 – 15pf. violet 20 40
FB 6 FB 2 16pf. green . . . . . 25 1·40
FB 7 – 20pf. blue 20 50
FB 8 FB 2 24pf. red 20 20
FB 9 – 45pf. mauve 20 95
FB10 FB 1 60pf. orange 20 25
FB11 – 75pf. blue . . . . . 20 1·40
FB12 FB 3 84pf. green . . . . . 25 1·70
FB13 FB 4 1m. brown 25 95
DESIGNS—18 × 23 mm: 3, 15, 45pf. Badensian girl and yachts; 10, 20, 75pf. Hans Baldung Grien.

1948. Currency Reform. As 1947 issue. (a) Value in "PF."
FB14 FB 1 2pf. orange 25 40
FB15 – 6pf. brown 25 25
FB16 – 10pf. brown . . . . . 70 1·40
FB17 FB 1 12pf. red 40 25
FB18 – 15pf. blue 40 25
FB19 FB 2 24pf. green 50 70
FB20 – 30pf. mauve . . . . . 1·20 2·40
FB21 – 50pf. blue . . . . . 5·75 1·20

(b) New currency. Value in "D.PF" or "D.M." (= "Deutschpfennig" or "Deutschmark").
FB22 – 8dpf. green 70 25
FB23 FB 2 16dpf. violet . . . . . 1·40 1·40
FB24 – 20dpf. brown . . . . . 1·40 25
FB25 FB 1 60dpf. grey . . . . . 6·75 70
FB26 FB 3 84dpf. red . . . . . 7·75 5·75
FB27 FB 4 1dm. blue . . . . . 7·75 5·75
DESIGNS—As Types FB 1/2: 6, 15pf. Badensian girl and yachts; 10pf., 20dpf. Hans Baldung Grien; 8dpf., 30pf. Black Forest girl in festive headdress; 50pf. Grand-Duchess Stephanie of Baden.

Nos. FB14/21 were sold on the new currency basis though not inscribed "D.PF."

1948. As 1947 issue, but "PF" omitted.
FB28 FB 1 2pf. orange . . . . . 1·20 70
FB29 – 4pf. violet 95 60
FB30 – 5pf. blue . . . . . 1·40 85
FB31 – 6pf. brown . . . . . 34·00 19·00
FB32 – 8pf. brown . . . . . 1·40 1·40
FB33 – 10pf. green . . . . . 1·20 1·90
FB34 – 20pf. mauve . . . . . 1·90 50
FB35 – 40pf. brown . . . . . 70·00 £100
FB36 FB 1 80pf. red . . . . . 14·00 9·00
FB37 FB 3 90pf. red . . . . . 85·00 £100
DESIGNS—18 × 23 mm: 4pf., 40pf. Rastatt; 5pf., 6pf. Badensian girl and yachts; 8pf. Black Forest girl in festive headdress; 10pf., 20pf. Portrait of Hans Baldung Grien.

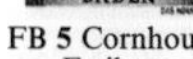

FB 5 Cornhouse, Freiburg

FB 6 Arms of Baden

1949. Freiburg Rebuilding Fund.
FB38 FB 5 4pf.+16pf. violet . . . 14·00 46·00
FB39 – 10pf.+20pf. green . . . 14·00 46·00
FB40 – 20pf.+30pf. red . . . 14·00 46·00
FB41 – 30pf.+50pf. blue . . . 19·00 60·00
MSFB41a 65 × 78 mm. Nos. FB38/41 . . . . £120 £450
MSFB41b Ditto but imperf . . . £120 £450
DESIGNS: 10pf. Freiburg Cathedral; 20pf. Trumpeting angel, Freiburg; 30pf. "Fischbrunnen," Freiburg.

1949. Red Cross Fund.
FB42 FB 6 10pf.+20pf. green . . 23·00 £100
FB43 20pf.+40pf. lilac . . . 23·00 £100
FB44 30pf.+60pf. blue . . . 23·00 £100
FB45 40pf.+80pf. grey . . . 23·00 £100
MSFB45a 90 × 100 mm. Nos. FB42/5 . . . . 95·00 £1300

FB 7 Seehof Hotel, Constance

1949. Engineers' Congress, Constance.
FB46 FB 7 30pf. blue . . . . . . 22·00 70·00

FB 8 Goethe

FB 9 Carl Schurz and Revolutionary Scene

FB 10 Conradin Kreutzer

1949. Birth Bicentenary of Goethe (poet).
FB47 FB 8 10pf.+5pf. green . . . 10·50 24·00
FB48 – 20pf.+10pf. red . . . 10·50 24·00
FB49 – 30pf.+15pf. blue . . . 14·00 60·00

1949. Cent of Rastatt Insurrection.
FB50 FB 9 10pf.+5pf. green . . . 12·00 36·00
FB51 20pf.+10pf. mauve . . 12·00 36·00
FB52 30pf.+15pf. blue . . . 14·00 36·00

1949. Death Centenary of Conradin Kreutzer (composer).
FB53 FB 10 10pf. green . . . . . 3·50 10·50

FB 11 1849 Mail Coach

FB 12 Posthorn and Globe

1949. German Stamp Centenary.
FB54 FB 11 10pf. green . . . . . 6·00 13·50
FB55 – 20pf. brown . . . . 6·00 13·50
DESIGN: 20pf. Postal motor-coach with trailer and Douglas DC-4 airliner.

1949. 75th Anniv of U.P.U.
FB56 FB 12 20pf. red . . . . . . 7·25 15·00
FB57 30pf. blue . . . . . 7·25 12·00

(c) Rhineland Palatinate, 1947–49.

FR 1 "Porta Nigra", Trier

FR 2 Karl Marx

FR 4 Statue of Charlemagne

FR 5 St. Martin

1947. Inscr "RHEINLAND-PFALZ".
FR 1 – 2pf. grey 20 25
FR 2 – 3pf. brown 20 20
FR 3 – 10pf. blue 20 20
FR 4 FR 1 12pf. green 20 20
FR 5 FR 2 15pf. violet 20 20
FR 6 – 16pf. green 20 80
FR 7 – 20pf. blue 20 30
FR 8 – 24pf. red 20 20
FR 9 – 30pf. mauve . . . . . 40 2·40
FR10 – 45pf. mauve 20 55
FR11 – 50pf. blue . . . . . 20 1·80
FR12 – 60pf. orange 20 25
FR13 – 75pf. blue 20 60
FR14 – 84pf. green . . . . . 25 1·20
FR15 FR 4 1m. brown 25 80
DESIGNS—SMALL SIZE: 2pf., 60pf. Beethoven's death mask; 3pf. Baron von Ketteler, Bishop of Mainz; 10pf. Girl vintager; 16pf. Rocks at Arnweiler; 20pf. Palatinate village house; 24pf. Worms Cathedral; 30pf., 75pf. Gutenberg (printer); 45pf., 50pf. Mainz Cathedral. LARGE SIZE—HORIZ: 84pf. Gutenfels Castle and Rhine.

1948. Currency Reform. As 1947 issue. (a) Value in "PF."
FR16 – 2pf. orange 25 30
FR17 – 6pf. brown 25 30

FR18 – 10pf. brown 45 90
FR19 FR **1** 12pf. red 45 20
FR20 FR **2** 15pf. blue 95 35
FR21 – 24pf. green 95 55
FR22 – 30pf. mauve . . . . . 65 1·10
FR23 – 50pf. blue . . . . . . 2·40 65

(b) New currency. Value in "D.PF." or "D.M." (= "Deutschpfennig" or "Deutschmark").

FR24 FR **1** 8dpf. green 45 60
FR25 – 16dpf. violet 85 75
FR26 – 20dpf. brown . . . . 1·20 50
FR27 – 60dpf. grey . . . . . 8·25 45
FR28 – 84dpf. red . . . . . 4·25 5·75
FR29 FR **4** 1dm. blue . . . . . . 5·00 5·75

DESIGNS—SMALL SIZE: 6pf. Baron von Ketteler; 30pf. Mainz Cathedral; 50pf. Gutenberg (printer). Others as 1947 issue.

Nos. FR16/23 were sold on the new currency basis though not inscribed "D.PF.".

1948. Ludwigshafen Explosion Relief Fund.
FR30 FR **5** 20pf.+30pf. mauve . . 1·20 28·00
FR31 – 30pf.+50pf. blue . . . 1·20 28·00
DESIGN: 30pf. St. Christopher.

1948. Inscr "RHEINLAND-PFALZ". As 1947 issue, but "PF" omitted.
FR32 – 2pf. orange 65 45
FR33 – 4pf. violet 65 40
FR34 FR **2** 5pf. blue 80 65
FR35 – 6pf. brown . . . . . 25·00 16·00
FR36 FR **1** 8pf. red . . . . . . 85·00 £300
FR37 – 10pf. green 75 40
FR38 – 20pf. mauve 85 40
FR39 – 40pf. brown . . . . . 2·75 4·00
FR40 FR **1** 80pf. red . . . . . . 3·00 5·00
FR41 – 90pf. red . . . . . . 5·00 18·00
DESIGNS—SMALL SIZE: 4pf. Rocks at Arnweiler; 40pf. Worms Cathedral. LARGE SIZE—HORIZ: 90pf. Gutenfels Castle and Rhine. Others as 1947–48 issues.

1949. Red Cross Fund. As Type FB **6** of Baden, but Arms of Rhineland and inscr "RHEINLANDPFALZ".
FR42 10pf.+20pf. green . . . . 18·00 95·00
FR43 20pf.+40pf. lilac . . . . . 18·00 95·00
FR44 30pf.+60pf. blue . . . . . 18·00 95·00
FR45 40pf.+80pf. grey . . . . . 18·00 95·00
MSFR45a 90×100 mm. Nos. FR42/5 . . . . 85·00 £1100

1949. Birth Bicentenary of Goethe. As Nos. FB47/9 of Baden.
FR46 10pf.+5pf. green . . . . . 5·50 21·00
FR47 20pf.+10pf. mauve . . . . 5·50 21·00
FR48 30pf.+15pf. blue . . . . . 12·50 46·00

1949. Centenary of German Postage Stamp. As Nos. FB54/5 of Baden.
FR49 10pf. green . . . . 9·00 21·00
FR50 20pf. brown . . . . 9·00 21·00

1949. 75th Anniv of U.P.U. As Nos. FB56/7 of Baden.
FR51 20pf. red . . . . 5·50 12·50
FR52 30pf. blue . . . . 5·50 10·00

(d) Saar, 1945–47.

The Saar District, from 1945 to 1947 part of the French Zone, also had its own stamps, but as it was in a different political category, we list its stamps for convenience of reference all together under **SAAR**.

(e) Wurttemberg, 1947–49.

FW **1** Fr. von Schiller FW **2** Bebenhausen Monastery FW **3** Lichtenstein Castle

1947. Inscr "WURTTEMBERG".
FW 1 FW **1** 2pf. grey 20 55
FW 2 – 3pf. brown 20 25
FW 3 – 10pf. blue 20 35
FW 4 FW **1** 12pf. green 20 20
FW 5 – 15pf. violet 20 35
FW 6 FW **2** 16pf. green 20 85
FW 7 – 20pf. blue 20 85
FW 8 FW **2** 24pf. red 20 20
FW 9 – 45pf. mauve 20 85
FW10 FW **1** 60pf. orange 20 70
FW11 – 75pf. blue . . . . . 25 1·30
FW12 FW **3** 84pf. green . . . . 25 1·40
FW13 – 1m. brown . . . . . 35 1·20
DESIGNS—SMALL SIZE: 3pf., 15pf., 45pf. Holderlin (poet); 10pf., 20pf., 75pf. Wangen Gate. LARGE SIZE—VERT: 1m. Zwiefalten Monastery Church.

1948. Currency Reform. As 1947 issue. (a) Value in "PF."
FW14 FW **1** 2pf. orange 30 45
FW15 – 6pf. brown 30 35
FW16 – 10pf. brown . . . . 1·20 1·30
FW17 FW **1** 12pf. red 30 40
FW18 – 15pf. blue 30 40
FW19 FW **2** 24pf. green 80 55
FW20 – 30pf. mauve . . . . 1·00 1·50
FW21 – 50pf. blue . . . . . 2·50 80

(b) Value in "D.PF" (= Deutsch Pfennig) or "D.M." (= Deutsch Mark).

FW22 – 8dpf. green . . . . . 1·00 1·20
FW23 FW **2** 16dpf. violet . . . . 1·50 1·30
FW24 – 20dpf. brown . . . . 3·00 75
FW25 FW **1** 60dpf. grey . . . . 14·50 70
FW26 FW **3** 84dpf. red . . . . . 5·00 4·75
FW27 – 1dm. blue . . . . . 5·00 4·75
DESIGNS—SMALL SIZE: 6pf., 15pf. Fr. Holderlin (poet); 8 dpf., 30pf. Waldsee Castle; 50pf. Ludwig Uhland (poet). Others as 1947 issue.

Nos. FW14/21 were sold on the new currency basis though not inscribed "D.PF."

1948. Inscr "WURTTEMBERG". As 1947 issue, but "PF" omitted.
FW28 FW **1** 2pf. orange . . . . 1·60 70
FW29 FW **2** 4pf. violet . . . . 3·50 45
FW30 – 5pf. blue . . . . . 8·50 2·50
FW31 – 6pf. brown . . . . 10·50 6·00
FW32 – 8pf. red . . . . . 10·50 2·50
FW33 – 10pf. green . . . . 10·50 30
FW34 – 20pf. mauve . . . . 10·50 30
FW35 FW **2** 40pf. brown . . . . 25·00 48·00
FW36 FW **1** 80pf. red . . . . . 55·00 48·00
FW37 FW **3** 90pf. red . . . . . 90·00 £110
DESIGNS—SMALL SIZE: 5pf., 6pf. Holderlin. Others as 1947 and 1948 issues.

FW **4** Isny and Coat of Arms FW **5** Gustav Werner

1949. Ski Championships (Northern Combination) at Isny/Allgau.
FW38 FW **4** 10pf.+4pf. green . . 9·00 23·00
FW39 – 20pf.+6pf. lake . . . 9·00 23·00
DESIGN: 20pf. Skier and view of Isny.

1949. Red Cross Fund. As Type FB **6** of Baden, but Arms of Wurttemberg and inscr "WURTTEMBERG".
FW40 10pf.+20pf. green . . . . 38·00 £130
FW41 20pf.+40pf. lilac . . . . . 38·00 £130
FW42 30pf.+60pf. blue . . . . . 38·00 £130
FW43 40pf.+80pf. grey . . . . . 38·00 £130
MSFW43a 90×100 mm. Nos. FW40/3 . . . . £130 £1400

1949. Birth Bicentenary of Goethe. As Nos. FB47/9 of Baden.
FW44 10pf.+5pf. green . . . . . 9·50 21·00
FW45 20pf.+10pf. mauve . . . . 14·00 30·00
FW46 30pf.+15pf. blue . . . . . 14·00 42·00

1949. Centenary of Christian Institution "Zum Bruderhaus".
FW47 FW **5** 10pf.+5pf. green . . 6·50 15·00
FW48 20pf.+10pf. purple 6·50 15·00

1949. German Stamp Centenary. As Nos. FB54/5 of Baden.
FW49 10pf. green . . . . 8·00 31·00
FW50 20pf. brown . . . . 8·00 31·00

1949. 75th Anniv of U.P.U. As Nos. FB56/7 of Baden.
FW51 20pf. red . . . . 7·00 29·00
FW52 30pf. blue . . . . 7·00 23·00

The French Zone was incorporated in West Germany in September 1949.

E. Russian Zone.

For a list of the stamps issued by the Russian Zone Provincial Administrations of Berlin (Brandenburg), Mecklenburg-Vorpommern, Saxony (Halle, Leipzig and Dresden) and Thuringia, see Stanley Gibbons Part 7 (Germany) Catalogue.

General Issues.

In February 1946, the Provincial Issues were replaced by the General Issues, Nos. 899/956 until the revaluation of the currency in June 1948, when Nos. 928/44 were brought into use handstamped with District names and numbers as a control measure pending the introduction of the following overprinted stamps on 3rd July. There are over 1,900 different types of district handstamp.

Sowjetische Besatzungs Zone
(R **1**)

R **3** Kathe Kollwitz

1948. Optd **Sowjetische Besatzungs Zone.** (a) On Pictorial issue of 1947, Nos. 928/44.
R 1 2pf. black 20 35
R 2 6pf. violet 20 20
R 3 8pf. red 20 20
R 4 10pf. green 20 20
R 5 12pf. grey 20 30
R 6 15pf. brown 20 35
R 7 16pf. green 20 45
R 8 20pf. blue 20 20
R 9 24pf. brown 20 20
R10 25pf. orange 20 45
R11 30pf. red 50 45
R12 40pf. mauve 50 45
R13 50pf. blue 80 95
R14 60pf. brown . . . . 1·00 95
R15 60pf. red . . . . 60·00 £110
R16 80pf. blue . . . . 1·30 1·10
R17 84pf. green . . . . 1·30 1·60

(b) On Numerical issue of 1946, Nos. 903, etc.

R18 **229** 5pf. green . . . . . . 40 1·10
R19 30pf. olive . . . . . . 1·10 3·25
R20 45pf. red . . . . 50 1·40
R21 75pf. blue . . . . . . 50 1·40
R22 84pf. green . . . . . . 1·50 1·90

(c) On stamps inscr "STADT BERLIN".

R23 R **1** 5pf. green 40 95
R25 – 6pf. violet 40 95
R26 – 8pf. orange 40 95
R27 – 10pf. brown 40 95
R28 – 12pf. red . . . . . . 70 1·60
R29 – 20pf. blue . . . . . . 60 1·40
R30 – 30pf. olive . . . . . . 60 2·00
DESIGNS: 6pf. Bear with spade; 8pf. Bear on shield; 10pf. Bear holding brick; 12pf. Bear carrying plank; 20pf. Bear on small shield; 30pf. Oak sapling amid ruins.

1948. Leipzig Autumn Fair. As T **231** but dated "1948".
R31 16pf.+9pf. purple 50 65
R32 50pf.+25pf. blue 50 65
DESIGNS: 16pf. 1459: The first Spring Fair; 50pf. 1469: Foreign merchants displaying cloth.

1948. Politicians, Artists and Scientists.
R33 R **3** 2pf. grey . . . . 1·20 25
R34 – 6pf. violet . . . . . . 1·20 25
R35 – 8pf. red . . . . 1·20 40
R36 – 10pf. green 40 40
R37 – 12pf. blue . . . . . . 5·50 40
R38 – 15pf. brown . . . . . . 1·00 1·70
R39 – 16pf. blue 90 60
R40 R **3** 20pf. purple 90 95
R41 – 24pf. red . . . . . . 6·00 40
R42 – 25pf. olive . . . . . . 1·30 2·20
R43 – 30pf. red . . . . . . 4·50 1·70
R44 – 40pf. purple . . . . . 1·00 95
R45 – 50pf. blue . . . . . . 1·00 65
R46 – 60pf. green . . . . . 3·50 65
R47 – 80pf. blue . . . . . . 2·00 65
E95 – 80pf. red . . . . . . 16·00 25·00
R48 – 84pf. brown . . . . . 3·50 3·25
PORTRAITS: 6, 40pf. Gerhart Hauptmann; 8, 50pf. Karl Marx; 10, 84pf. August Bebel; 12, 30pf. Friedrich Engels; 15, 60pf. G. F. W. Hegel; 16, 25pf. Rudolf Virchow; 24, 80pf. Ernst Thalmann.

R **4** R **5** Liebknecht and Rosa Luxemburg

1948. Stamp Day.
R49 R **4** 12pf.+3pf. red 40 65

1949. 30th Death Anniv of Karl Liebknecht and Rosa Luxemburg (revolutionaries).
R50 R **5** 24pf. red 45 85

1949. Leipzig Spring Fair. As T **231** but dated "1949".
R51 30pf.+15pf. red . . . . . . 4·00 4·50
R52 50pf.+25pf. blue . . . . . . 4·25 5·25
DESIGNS: 30pf. 1st Neubau Town Hall bazaar, 1556; 50pf. Italian merchants at Leipzig, 1536.

R **6** Dove R **8** Goethe

1949. 3rd German Peoples' Congress.
R53 R **6** 24pf. red . . . . 1·40 2·30

1949. Optd **3. Deutscher Volkskongre 29.-30 Mai 1949.**
R54 R **6** 24pf. red . . . . 1·60 2·75

1949. Birth Bicent of Goethe. Portraits of Goethe.
R55 R **8** 6pf.+4pf. violet . . . . 3·00 3·50
R56 – 12pf.+8pf. brown . . . 3·00 3·50
R57 – 24pf.+16pf. lake . . . 2·50 3·00
R58 – 50pf.+25pf. blue . . . 2·50 3·00
R59 – 84pf.+36pf. grey . . . 4·50 5·50

1949. Goethe Festival Week, Weimar. Sheet 106×104 mm.
MSR59a R **9** 50pf. (+Dm. 4.50) blue £200 £275

1949. Leipzig Autumn Fair. As T **231** but dated "1949".
R60 12pf.+8pf. slate . . . . . 4·75 6·50
R61 24pf.+16pf. lake . . . . . 6·50 8·25
DESIGNS: 12pf. Russian merchants, 1650; 24pf. Goethe at Fair, 1765.

The Russian Zone was incorporated in East Germany in October 1949.

III. GERMAN FEDERAL REPUBLIC

The Federal Republic was set up on 23 May 1949. Until October 1990 it comprised the territory which formerly came under the British, American and French Zones. On 3 October 1990 the former territory of East Germany (German Democratic Republic) was absorbed into the Federal Republic.

1949. 100 pfennig = 1 Deutsche Mark (West).
2002. 100 cents = 1 euro.

257 Constructing Parliament Building **258** Reproduction of T **1** of Bavaria

1949. Opening of West German Parliament, Bonn.
1033 **257** 10pf. green . . . . . . 50·00 25·00
1034 20pf. red . . . . 60·00 28·00

1949. Centenary of 1st German Stamps.
1035 **258** 10pf.+2pf. black & grn 15·00 22·00
1036 – 20pf. blue and red . . . 44·00 43·00
1037 – 30pf. brown and blue . . 60·00 75·00
DESIGN: 20pf., 30pf. Reproductions of T **2** of Bavaria.

259 Dr. von Stephan, Old G.P.O., Berlin and Standehaus, Berne

1949. 75th Anniv of U.P.U.
1038 **259** 30pf. blue . . . . 65·00 44·00

260 St. Elisabeth of Thuringia

1949. Refugees' Relief Fund. Inscr as in T **260**.
1039 **260** 8pf.+2pf. purple . . . . 21·00 25·00
1040 – 10pf.+5pf. green . . . . 21·00 16·00
1041 – 20pf.+10pf. red . . . . 21·00 16·00
1042 – 30pf.+15pf. blue £100 £120
PORTRAITS: 10pf. Paracelsus von Hohenheim; 20pf. F. W. A. Froebel; 30pf. J. H. Wichern.

261 J. S. Bach's Seal **262** Numeral and Posthorn

1950. Death Bicent of Bach (composer).
1043 **261** 10pf.+2pf. green . . . . 70·00 50·00
1044 20pf.+3pf. red . . . . . 80·00 60·00

1951.

1045 **262** 2pf. green . . . . 5·25 95
1046 4pf. brown . . . . . . 3·00 20
1047 5pf. purple . . . . . . 10·50 20
1048 6pf. orange . . . . . . 23·00 3·50
1049 8pf. grey . . . . 25·00 10·00
1050 10pf. green . . . . . . 6·00 15
1051 15pf. violet . . . . . . 46·00 1·10
1052 20pf. red . . . . 4·50 15
1053 25pf. plum . . . . . . £110 5·50
1054 30pf. blue . . . . 60·00 35
1055 40pf. purple £180 35
1056 50pf. grey £200 35
1057 60pf. brown £140 35
1058 70pf. yellow . . . . . . £475 16·00
1059 80pf. red . . . . £550 2·20
1060 90pf. green . . . . . . £600 2·50
The 30pf. to 90pf. are 20×24½ mm.

264 Figures **265** Stamps under Magnifier

1951. 700th Anniv of St. Mary's Church, Lubeck.
1065 **264** 10pf.+5pf. black & grn 95·00 33·00
1066 20pf.+5pf. black & red £120 95·00

1951. National Philatelic Exn, Wuppertal.
1067 **265** 10pf.+2pf. yellow, black and green . . . . . . 50·00 55·00
1068 20pf.+3pf. yellow, black and red . . . . 50·00 50·00

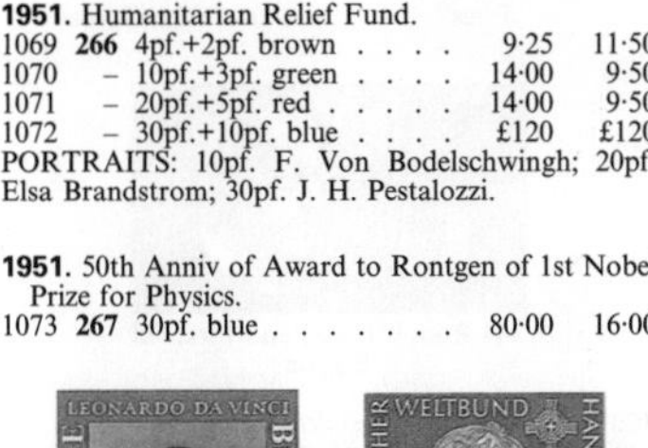

266 St. Vincent de Paul **267** W. C. Rontgen (physicist)

1951. Humanitarian Relief Fund.
1069 **266** 4pf.+2pf. brown . . . . 9·25 11·50
1070 – 10pf.+3pf. green . . . . 14·00 9·50
1071 – 20pf.+5pf. red . . . . . 14·00 9·50
1072 – 30pf.+10pf. blue £120 £120
PORTRAITS: 10pf. F. Von Bodelschwingh; 20pf. Elsa Brandstrom; 30pf. J. H. Pestalozzi.

1951. 50th Anniv of Award to Rontgen of 1st Nobel Prize for Physics.
1073 **267** 30pf. blue . . . . 80·00 16·00

268 Mona Lisa **269** Martin Luther

1952. 500th Birth Anniv of Leonardo da Vinci.
1074 **268** 5pf. multicoloured . . . 1·30 1·00

1952. Lutheran World Federation Assembly, Hanover.
1075 **269** 10pf. green . . . . . . 14·50 4·75

270 A. N. Otto and Diagram **271** Nuremberg Madonna

1952. 75th Anniv of Otto Gas Engine.
1076 **270** 30pf. blue . . . . 30·00 16·00

1952. Centenary of German National Museum, Nuremberg.
1077 **271** 10pf.+5pf. green . . . . 16·00 18·00

272 Trawler "Senator Schaffer" off Heligoland **273** Carl Schurz

1952. Rehabilitation of Heligoland.
1078 **272** 20pf. red . . . . 15·00 5·75

1952. Centenary of Arrival of Schurz in America.
1079 **273** 20pf. pink, black and blue . . . . 20·00 7·75

274 Boy Hikers **275** Elizabeth Fry

1952. Youth Hostels Fund. Inscr "JUGENDMARKE 1952".
1080 **274** 10pf.+2pf. green . . . . 23·00 22·00
1081 – 20pf.+3pf. red . . . . . 23·00 22·00
DESIGN: 20pf. Girl hikers.

1952. Humanitarian Relief Fund.
1082 **275** 4pf.+2pf. brown . . . . 9·25 7·00
1083 – 10pf.+5pf. green . . . . 9·25 6·50
1084 – 20pf.+10pf. lake . . . . 18·00 12·50
1085 – 30pf.+10pf. blue . . . . 90·00 £100
PORTRAITS: 10pf. Dr. C. Sonnenschein; 20pf. T. Fliedner; 30pf. H. Dunant.

276 Postman, 1852 **277** P. Reis

1952. Thurn and Taxis Stamp Centenary.
1086 **276** 10pf. multicoloured . . . 7·50 2·30

1952. 75th Anniv of German Telephone Service.
1087 **277** 30pf. blue . . . . 46·00 16·00

278 Road Accident Victim **279**

1953. Road Safety Campaign.
1088 **278** 20pf. multicoloured . . . 17·00 4·25

1953. 50th Anniv of Science Museum, Munich.
1089 **279** 10pf.+5pf. green . . . . 28·00 27·00

280 Red Cross and Compass **281** Prisoner of War

1953. 125th Birth Anniv of Henri Dunant (founder of Red Cross).
1090 **280** 10pf. red and green . . . 22·00 6·50

1953. Commemorating Prisoners of War.
1091 **281** 10pf. black and grey . . 6·50 30

282 J. von Liebig **283** "Rail Transport"

1953. 150th Birth Anniv of Liebig (chemist).
1092 **282** 30pf. blue . . . . 46·00 21·00

1953. Transport Exn, Munich. Inscr as in T **283**.
1093 **283** 4pf. brown . . . . . . 7·00 4·50
1094 – 10pf. green . . . . . . 13·50 7·00
1095 – 20pf. red . . . . 18·00 10·00
1096 – 30pf. blue . . . . . . 55·00 24·00
DESIGNS: 10pf. "Air" (dove and aeroplanes); 20pf. "Road" (traffic lights and cars); 30pf. "Sea" (buoy and ships).

284 Gateway, Thurn and Taxis Palace **285** A. H. Francke

1953. International Philatelic Exhibition, Frankfurt am Main. Inscr "IFRABA 1953".
1097 **284** 10pf.+2pf. brown, black and green . . . . . . 28·00 29·00
1098 – 20pf.+3pf. grey, blue and red . . . . 28·00 29·00
DESIGN: 20pf. Telecommunications Buildings, Frankfurt am Main.

1953. Humanitarian Relief Fund.
1099 **285** 4pf.+2pf. brown . . . . 4·50 7·75
1100 – 10pf.+5pf. green . . . . 9·25 7·75
1101 – 20pf.+10pf. red . . . . 14·00 10·50
1102 – 30pf.+10pf. blue . . . . 65·00 70·00
PORTRAITS: 10pf. S. Kneipp; 20pf. J. C. Senckenberg; 30pf. F. Nansen.

286 Pres. Heuss

1954.

(a) Size 18½ × 22½ mm or 18 × 22 mm.
1103 **286** 2pf. green 25 20
1104 4pf. brown 25 20
1105 5pf. mauve 25 20
1106 6pf. brown 25 80
1107 7pf. green 25 20
1108 8pf. grey 25 55
1109 10pf. green 25 20
1110 15pf. blue 70 30
1111 20pf. red 25 20
1112 25pf. purple 90 55
1122a 30pf. green 45 70
1122c 40pf. blue . . . . . . 2·75 15
1122e 50pf. olive . . . . . . 1·20 15
1122f 60pf. brown . . . . . 4·25 55
1122g 70pf. violet . . . . . 14·50 55
1122h 80pf. orange . . . . . 7·50 2·00
1122i 90pf. green . . . . . 23·00 1·00

(b) Size 20 × 24 mm.
1113 **286** 30pf. blue . . . . . . 18·00 4·75
1114 40pf. purple . . . . . . 7·00 20
1115 50pf. slate £225 50
1116 60pf. brown . . . . . . 46·00 55
1117 70pf. olive . . . . . . 18·00 1·80
1118 80pf. red . . . . 3·50 5·25
1119 90pf. green . . . . . . 18·00 2·75

(c) Size 25 × 30 mm.
1120 **286** 1Dm. olive . . . . . . 1·80 30
1121 2Dm. lavender . . . . . 3·50 1·30
1122 3Dm. purple . . . . . . 8·75 2·00

287 P. Ehrlich and E. von Behring **288** Gutenburg and Printing-press

1954. Birth Centenaries of Ehrlich and Von Behring (bacteriologists).
1123 **287** 10pf. green . . . . . . 10·50 3·75

1954. 500th Anniv of Gutenberg Bible.
1124 **288** 4pf. brown . . . . . . 1·30 50

289 Sword-pierced Mitre **290** Kathe Kollwitz

1954. 1,200th Anniv of Martyrdom of St. Boniface.
1125 **289** 20pf. red and brown . . 7·50 4·75

1954. Humanitarian Relief Fund.
1126 **290** 7pf.+3pf. brown . . . . 3·75 3·75
1127 – 10pf.+5pf. green . . . . 1·80 1·90
1128 – 20pf.+10pf. red . . . . 10·50 5·25
1129 – 40pf.+10pf. blue . . . . 37·00 45·00
PORTRAITS: 10pf. L. Werthmann; 20pf. J. F. Oberlin; 40pf. Bertha Pappenheim.

291 C. F. Gauss **292** "Flight"

1955. Death Cent of Gauss (mathematician).
1130 **291** 10pf. green . . . . . . 5·50 55

1955. Re-establishment of "Lufthansa" Airways.
1131 **292** 5pf. mauve and black . . 90 85
1132 10pf. green and black . . 1·40 1·20
1133 15pf. blue and black . . 8·75 6·00
1134 20pf. red and black . . . 25·00 7·75

293 O. von Miller **295** Schiller

1955. Birth Centenary of Von Miller (electrical engineer).
1135 **293** 10f. green . . . . 5·50 1·70

1955. 150th Death Anniv of Schiller (poet).
1136 **295** 40pf. blue . . . . 15·00 5·00

296 Motor-coach, 1906 **297** Arms of Baden-Wurttemburg

1955. 50th Anniv of Postal Motor Transport.
1137 **296** 20pf. black and red . . . 12·00 4·50

1955. Baden-Wurttemberg Agricultural Exhibition, Stuttgart.
1138 **297** 7pf. black, brn & bistre 4·25 4·25
1139 10pf. black, grn & bistre 7·50 2·50

298 "Earth and Atom" **299** Refugees

1955. Cosmic Research.
1140 **298** 20pf. lake . . . . 10·00 1·20

1955. 10th Anniv of Expulsion of Germans from beyond the Oder–Neisse Line.
1141 **299** 20pf. red . . . . 4·00 60
See also No. 1400.

300 Orb, Arrows and Waves **301** Magnifying Glass and Carrier Pigeon

1955. Millenary of Battle of Lechfeld.
1142 **300** 20pf. purple . . . . . . 8·75 4·50

1955. West European Postage Stamp Exn.
1143 **301** 10pf.+2pf. green . . . . 5·25 6·00
1144 – 20pf.+3pf. red . . . . . 11·50 14·50
DESIGN: 20pf. Tweezers and posthorn.

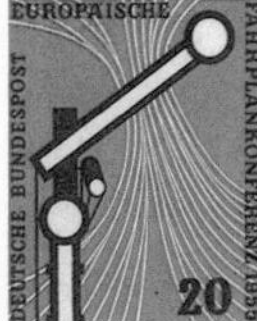

302 Railway Signal **303** Stifter Monument

1955. Railway Timetable Conference.
1145 **302** 20pf. black and red . . . 9·25 2·50

1955. 150th Birth Anniv of Stifter (Austrian poet).
1146 **303** 10pf. green . . . . . . 3·75 2·10

304 U.N. Emblem **305** Amalie Sieveking

1955. U.N. Day.
1147 **304** 10pf. green and brown 3·75 4·25

1955. Humanitarian Relief Fund.
1148 **305** 7pf.+3pf. brown . . . . 3·75 3·75
1149 – 10pf.+5pf. green . . . . 2·30 1·90
1150 – 20pf.+10pf. red . . . . 2·30 1·90
1151 – 40pf.+10pf. blue . . . . 36·00 39·00
PORTRAITS: 10pf. A. Kolping; 20pf. Dr. S. Hahnemann; 40pf. Florence Nightingale.

306 **307** Von Stephan's Signature

1955.
1152 **306** 1pf. grey 30 20

1955. 125th Birth Anniv of H. von Stephan.
1153 **307** 20pf. red 7·50 2·50

308 Spinet and Opening Bars of Minuet
309 Heinrich Heine

1956. Birth Bicent of Mozart (composer).
1154 **308** 10pf. black and lilac 90 30

1956. Death Centenary of Heine (poet).
1155 **309** 10pf. green and black 3·25 3·25

310 Old Houses and Crane
311

1956. Millenary of Luneburg.
1156 **310** 20pf. red 8·75 7·50

1956. Olympic Year.
1157 **311** 10pf. green 90 60

312 Boy and Dove
313 Robert Schumann

1956. Youth Hostels' Fund. Inscr "JUGEND".
1158 **312** 7pf.+3pf. grey, black and brown 2·50 3·75
1159 – 10pf.+5pf. grey black and green 8·50 9·75
DESIGN: 10pf. Girl playing flute and flowers.

1956. Death Centenary of Schumann (composer).
1160 **313** 10pf. black, red & bistre 75 25

314
315 T. Mann (author)

1956. Evangelical Church Convention, Frankfurt am Main.
1161 **314** 10pf. green 4·50 4·00
1162 20pf. red 5·50 5·25

1956. Thomas Mann Commemoration.
1163 **315** 20pf. red 3·50 2·20

316
317 Ground Plan of Cologne Cathedral and Hand

1956. 800th Anniv of Maria Laach Abbey.
1164 **316** 20pf. grey and red 2·75 2·10

1956. 77th Meeting of German Catholics, Cologne.
1165 **317** 10pf. green and brown 3·00 2·50

318
320 Nurse and Baby

1956. International Police Exhibition, Essen.
1166 **318** 20pf. green, orange & blk 3·25 2·75

1956. Europa. As Nos. 1582/3 of Belgium.
1167 10pf. green 1·60 20
1168 40pf. blue 8·75 1·40

1956. Humanitarian Relief Fund. Centres in black.
1169 **320** 7pf.+3pf. brown 1·60 2·50
1170 – 10pf.+5pf. green 90 80
1171 – 20pf.+10pf. red 90 80
1172 – 40pf.+10pf. blue 20·00 19·00
DESIGNS: 10pf. I. P. Semmelweis and cot; 20pf. Mother, and baby in cradle; 40f. Nurse maid and children.

321 Carrier Pigeon
322 "Military Graves"

1956. Stamp Day.
1173 **321** 10pf. green 1·80 75

1956. War Graves Commission.
1174 **322** 10pf. green 1·80 70

323 Arms
324 Children with Luggage

1957. Return of the Saar to West Germany.
1175 **323** 10pf. brown and green 60 50

1957. Berlin Children's Holiday Fund.
1176 **324** 10pf.+5pf. orange and green 1·60 2·30
1177 – 20pf.+10pf. blue and orange 3·75 4·50
DESIGN: 20pf. Girl returning from holiday.

325 Heinrich Hertz
326 Paul Gerhardt

1957. Birth Cent of Hertz (physicist).
1178 **325** 10pf. black and green 1·40 65

1957. 350th Birth Anniv of Paul Gerhardt (hymn-writer).
1179 **326** 20pf. red 65 50

327 "Flora and Philately"
328 Emblem of Aschaffenburg

1957. Exhibition and 8th Congress of Int Federation of "Constructive Philately".
1180 **327** 20pf. orange 65 50

1957. Millenary of Aschaffenburg.
1181 **328** 20pf. red and black 65 60

329 University Class

1957. 500th Anniv of Freiburg University.
1182 **329** 10pf. black, red & green 35 25

330 "Bayernstein" (freighter)

1957. German Merchant Shipping Day.
1183 **330** 15pf. black, red and blue 1·20 1·10

331 Justus Liebig University
332 Albert Ballin

1957. 350th Anniv of Justus Liebig University, Giessen.
1184 **331** 10pf. green 50 30

1957. Birth Centenary of Albert Ballin (director of Hamburg-America Shipping Line).
1185 **332** 20pf. black and red 1·40 40

333 Television Screen
334 "Europa" Tree

1957. Publicizing West German Television Service.
1186 **333** 10pf. green and blue 45 30

1957. Europa.
1187 **334** 10pf. green and blue 55 20
1188 40pf. blue 4·75 45

335 Young Miner
336 Water Lily

1957. Humanitarian Relief Fund.
1189 **335** 7pf.+3pf. black & brn 1·60 1·80
1190 – 10pf.+5pf. black & grn 1·20 95
1191 – 20pf.+10pf. black & red 1·60 95
1192 – 40pf.+10pf. black & bl 20·00 20·00
DESIGNS: 10pf. Miner drilling coal-face; 20pf. Miner with coal-cutting machine; 40pf. Operator at mine lift-shaft.

1957. Nature Protection Day.
1193 **336** 10pf. orange, yell & grn 50 45
1194 – 20pf. multicoloured 70 55
DESIGN—VERT: 20pf. European robin.

337 Carrier Pigeons
338 Baron von Stein

1957. International Correspondence Week.
1195 **337** 20pf. black and red 95 50

1957. Birth Bicentenary of Baron von Stein (statesman).
1196 **338** 20pf. red 1·60 75

339 Dr Leo Baeck (philosopher)
340 Wurttemberg Parliament House

1957. 1st Death Anniv of Dr. Leo Baeck.
1197 **339** 20pf. red 1·60 70

1957. 500th Anniv of First Wurttemberg Parliament.
1198 **340** 10pf. olive and green 90 50

341 Stage Coach
342 "Max and Moritz" (cartoon characters)

1957. Death Centenary of Joseph von Eichendorff (novelist).
1199 **341** 10pf. green 85 50

1958. 50th Death Anniv of Wilhelm Busch (writer and illustrator).
1200 **342** 10pf. olive and black 30 15
1201 – 20pf. red and black 1·00 50
DESIGN: 20pf. Wilhelm Busch.

343 "Prevent Forest Fires"
345 "The Fox who stole the Goose"

344 Rudolf Diesel and First Oil Engine

1958. Forest Fires Prevention Campaign.
1202 **343** 20pf. black and red 75 50

1958. Birth Centenary of Rudolf Diesel (engineer).
1203 **344** 10pf. myrtle 35 30

1958. Berlin Students' Fund. Inscr "Fur die Jugend".
1204 **345** 10pf.+5pf. red, black and green 2·10 2·75
1205 – 20pf.+10pf. brown, green and red 4·25 4·25
DESIGN: 20pf. "A hunter from the Palatinate" (horseman).

346 Giraffe and Lion
347 Old Munich

1958. Centenary of Frankfurt am Main Zoo.
1206 **346** 10pf. black and green 60 40

1958. 800th Anniv of Munich.
1207 **347** 20pf. red 60 45

348 Trier and Market Cross
349 Deutsche Mark (coin)

1958. Millenary of Trier Market.
1208 **348** 20pf. red and black 65 40

1958. 10th Anniv of Currency Reform.
1209 **349** 20pf. black and orange 65 50

350 Emblem of Gymnastics
351 H. Schulze-Delitzsch

1958. 150th Anniv of German Gymnastics.
1210 **350** 10pf. black, green & grey 35 40

1958. 150th Birth Anniv of Schulze-Delitzsch (pioneer of German co-operative movement).
1211 **351** 10pf. green 45 30

1958. Europa. As No. 643 of Luxembourg, size 24½ × 30 mm.
1212 10pf. blue and green 45 20
1213 40pf. red and blue 3·25 45

352 Friedrich Raiffeisen (philanthropist) **353** Dairymaid

1958. Humanitarian Relief and Welfare Funds.
1214 **352** 7pf.+3pf. brown, deep brown and chestnut . . . 50 65
1215 **353** 10pf.+5pf. red, yellow and green 50 45
1216 – 20pf.+10pf. blue, green and red 50 45
1217 – 40pf.+10pf. yellow, orange and blue . . . 7·50 7·75
DESIGNS— As Type **353**: 20pf. Vine-dresser; 40pf. Farm labourer.

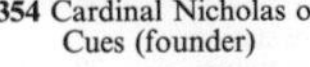

354 Cardinal Nicholas of Cues (founder) **355** Jakob Fugger (merchant prince)

1958. 500th Anniv of Hospice of St. Nicholas.
1218 **354** 20pf. black and mauve 50 25

1959. As Type B **53** of West Berlin but without "BERLIN".
1219 7pf. green 30 20
1220 10pf. green 50 20
1221 20pf. red 50 20
1222 40pf. blue . . . . 17·00 1·00
1223 70pf. violet . . . . 5·00 70

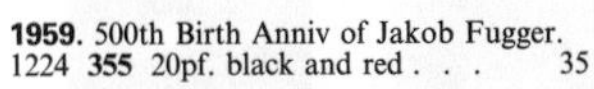

1959. 500th Birth Anniv of Jakob Fugger.
1224 **355** 20pf. black and red . . . 35 30

356 Adam Riese (mathematician) **357** A. von Humboldt (naturalist)

1959. 400th Death Anniv of Adam Riese.
1225 **356** 10pf. black and green . . 35 30

1959. Death Cent of Alexander von Humboldt.
1226 **357** 40pf. blue . . . . 1·80 1·40

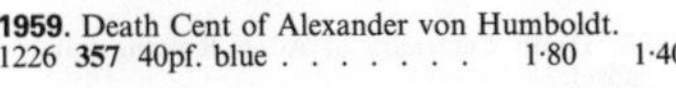

358 First Hamburg Stamp of 1859 **359** Buxtehude

1959. International Stamp Exhibition, Hamburg, and Centenary of First Stamps of Hamburg and Lubeck.
1228 **358** 10pf.+5pf. brown & grn 30 50
1230 – 20pf.+10pf. brn & red 30 70
DESIGN: 20pf. First Lubeck stamp of 1859.

1959. Millenary of Buxtehude.
1231 **359** 20pf. red, black and blue 35 30

360 Holy Tunic of Trier **361** Congress Emblem

1959. Holy Tunic of Trier Exhibition.
1232 **360** 20pf. black, buff & purple 35 30

1959. German Evangelical Church Day and Congress, Munich.
1233 **361** 10pf. violet, green & blk 30 30

1959. Inauguration of Beethoven Hall, Bonn. T **361a** and similar horiz designs in sheet 148 × 104 mm with extract from Beethoven's music notebooks.
MS1233a 10pf. green (Handell); 15pf. blue (Spohr); 20pf. red (T **361a**); 25pf. brown (Haydn); 40pf. blue (Mendelssohn) . . . 26·00 55·00

1959. Europa. As Nos. 659/60 of Luxembourg, but size 24½ × 30 mm.
1234 10pf. green 20 20
1235 40pf. blue . . . . 1·30 45

362 "Feeding the Poor" **363** "Uprooted Tree"

1959. Humanitarian Relief and Welfare Funds.
1236 **362** 7pf.+3pf. sepia & yellow 30 45
1237 – 10pf.+5pf. green & yell 30 35
1238 – 20pf.+10pf. red & yell 35 45
1239 – 40pf.+10pf. mult . . . . 3·75 4·75
DESIGNS: 10pf. "Clothing the Naked"; 20pf. "Bounty from Heaven" (scenes from the Brothers Grimm story "The Star Thaler"); 40pf. The Brothers Grimm.

1960. World Refugee Year.
1240 **363** 10pf. black, purple & grn 25 20
1241 40pf. black, red and blue 2·40 2·00

364 P. Melanchthon **365** Cross and Symbols of the Crucifixion

1960. 400th Death Anniv of Philip Melanchthon (Protestant reformer).
1242 **364** 20pf. black and red . . . 1·40 1·20

1960. Oberammergau Passion Play.
1243 **365** 10pf. grey, ochre and blue 30 25

366 **367** Wrestling

1960. 37th World Eucharistic Congress, Munich.
1244 **366** 10pf. green 70 50
1245 20pf. red 90 70

1960. Olympic Year. Inscr as in T **367**.
1246 **367** 7pf. brown 20 20
1247 – 10pf. green 45 20
1248 – 20pf. red 45 20
1249 – 40pf. blue . . . . . . 1·40 1·40
DESIGNS: 10pf. Running; 20pf. Javelin and discus-throwing; 40pf. Chariot-racing.

368 Hildesheim Cathedral **368a** Conference Emblem

1960. Birth Millenary of Bishops St. Bernward and St. Godehard.
1250 **368** 20pf. purple 85 60

1960. Europa.
1251 **368a** 10pf. green and olive 20 15
1252 20pf. vermilion and red 70 30
1253 40pf. light blue and blue . . . . . . 1·40 1·20

369 Little Red Riding Hood meeting Wolf

1960. Humanitarian Relief and Welfare Funds.
1254 **369** 7pf.+3pf. black, red and bistre 45 60
1255 – 10pf.+5pf. black, red and green 45 25
1256 – 20pf.+10pf. black, green and red 45 25
1257 – 40pf.+20pf. black, red and blue . . . . . 4·50 4·25
DESIGNS: 10pf. Red Riding Hood and wolf disguised as grandmother; 20pf. Woodcutter and dead wolf; 40pf. Red Riding Hood with grandmother.

1960. 1st Death Anniv of Gen. George C. Marshall. Portrait as T **364**.
1258 40pf. black and blue . . . . 2·75 1·60

371 "Adler", 1835 **372** St. George and the Dragon

1960. 125th Anniv of German Railway.
1259 **371** 10pf. black and bistre . . 30 30

1961. Pathfinders (German Boy Scouts) Commemoration.
1260 **372** 10pf. green 30 20

1961. Famous Germans. As Nos. B194, etc of West Berlin but without "BERLIN".
1261 5pf. olive 20 20
1262 7pf. brown 20 20
1263 8pf. violet 20 25
1264 10pf. green 20 20
1265 15pf. blue 45 90
1266 20pf. red 45 25
1267 25pf. brown 20 25
1268 30pf. sepia 20 15
1269 40pf. blue 30 15
1270 50pf. brown 45 25
1271 60pf. red 45 30
1272 70pf. green 20 30
1273 80pf. brown 55 50
1274 90pf. bistre 45 30
1275 1Dm. violet 55 40
1276 2Dm. green . . . . 3·75 55
PORTRAIT: 90pf. Franz Oppenheimer (economist).

373 Early Daimler Motor Car **374** Nuremberg Messenger of 1700

1961. 75th Anniv of Daimler-Benz Patent.
1277 **373** 10pf. green and black . . 20 15
1278 – 20pf. red and black . . . 45 35
DESIGN: 20pf. Early Benz motor car.

1961. "The Letter during Five Centuries" Exhibition, Nuremberg.
1279 **374** 7pf. black and red . . . 30 20

375 Speyer Cathedral **376** Doves

1961. 900th Anniv of Speyer Cathedral.
1280 **375** 20pf. red 30 30

1961. Europa.
1281 **376** 10pf. green 30 25
1282 40pf. blue 35 45

377 Hansel and Gretel in the Wood **378** Telephone Apparatus

1961. Humanitarian Relief and Welfare Funds. Multicoloured.
1283 7pf.+3pf. Type **377** 15 25
1284 10pf.+5pf. Hansel, Gretel and the Witch 15 15
1285 20pf.+10pf. Hansel in the Witch's cage 15 15
1286 40pf.+20pf. Hansel and Gretel reunited with their father . . . . 1·40 2·10

1961. Centenary of Philipp Reis's Telephone.
1287 **378** 10pf. green 30 25

379 Baron W. E. von Ketteler **380** Drusus Stone

1961. 150th Birth Anniv of Baron W. E. von Ketteler (Catholic leader).
1288 **379** 10pf. black and green . . 30 25

1962. Bimillenary of Mainz.
1289 **380** 20pf. purple 30 25

381 Apollo **382** Part of "In Dulci Jubilo", from "Musae Sioniae" (M. Praetorius)

1962. Child Welfare. Butterflies. Mult.
1290 7pf.+3pf. Type **381** 45 55
1291 10pf.+5pf. Camberwell beauty 45 55
1292 20pf.+10pf. Small tortoiseshell . . . . . . 90 1·20
1293 40pf.+20pf. Scarce swallowtail . . . . 1·40 2·10

1962. "Song and Choir" (Summer Music Festivals).
1294 **382** 20pf. red and black . . . 30 30

383 "Belief, Thanksgiving and Service" **384** Open Bible

1962. Catholics' Day.
1295 **383** 20pf. mauve 30 30

1962. 150th Anniv of Wurttembergische Bibelanstalt (Bible publishers).
1296 **384** 20pf. black and red . . . 30 30

385 Europa "Tree" **386** Snow White and the Seven Dwarfs

1962. Europa.
1297 **385** 10pf. green 25 20
1298 40pf. blue 55 45

1962. Humanitarian Relief and Welfare Funds. Scenes from "Snow White and the Seven Dwarfs" (Brothers Grimm). Multicoloured.
1299 7pf.+3pf. The "Magic Mirror" 15 20
1300 10pf.+5pf. Type **386** . . . 15 15
1301 20pf.+10pf. "The Poisoned Apple" 20 15
1302 40pf.+20pf. Snow White and Prince Charming . . . . 1·10 1·50

387 "Bread for the World" **388** Relief Distribution

1963. Freedom from Hunger.
1303 **387** 20pf. brown and black 30 30

1963. CRALOG and CARE Relief Organizations.
1304 **388** 20pf. red 30 25

389 Ears of Wheat, Cross and Globe

390 Snake's Head Lily

1963. Freedom from Hunger.
1305 **389** 20pf. black, red and grey . . . 30 30

1963. "Flora and Philately" Exhibition, Hamburg. Multicoloured.
1306 10pf. Type **390** 25 15
1307 15pf. Lady's slipper orchid . . 25 15
1308 20pf. Columbine 25 20
1309 40pf. Sea holly 45 40

391 "Heidelberger Catechismus"

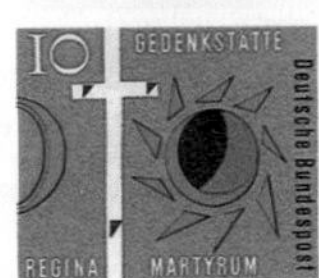
392 Cross, Sun and Moon

1963. 400th Anniv of Heidelberg Catechism.
1310 **391** 20pf. black, red and orange 30 30

1963. Consecration of Regina Martyrum Church, Berlin.
1311 **392** 10pf. multicoloured . . . 30 20

393 Emblems of Conference Participating Countries

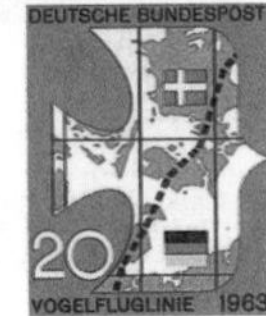
394 Map and Flags

1963. Centenary of Paris Postal Conference.
1312 **393** 40pf. blue 50 40

1963. Opening of Denmark–Germany Railway ("Vogelfluglinie").
1313 **394** 20pf. multicoloured . . . 35 25

395 Red Cross Emblem

396 Hoopoe

1963. Red Cross Centenary.
1314 **395** 20pf. red, purple & yell 30 25

1963. Child Welfare. Bird designs inscr "FUR DIE JUGEND 1963". Multicoloured.
1315 10pf.+5pf. Type **396** . . . 55 65
1316 15pf.+5pf. Golden oriole . . 45 70
1317 20pf.+10pf. Northern bullfinch 45 70
1318 40pf.+20pf. River kingfisher 2·00 2·75

397 Congress Emblem

398 "Co-operation"

1963. German Evangelical Church Day and Congress, Dortmund.
1319 **397** 20pf. black and brown 35 30

1963. Europa.
1320 **398** 15pf. green 25 25
1321 20pf. red 25 15

399 Mother Goat warning kids

400 Atlantic Herring

1963. Humanitarian Relief and Welfare Funds.
1322 **399** 10pf.+5pf. mult 20 25
1323 – 15pf.+5pf. mult 20 20
1324 – 20pf.+10pf. mult . . . 20 20
1325 – 40pf.+20pf. mult . . . . 80 1·10
DESIGNS: 15pf. Wolf entering house; 20pf. Wolf in house, threatening kids; 40pf. Mother Goat and Kids dancing round wolf in well. From Grimm's "Wolf and the Seven Kids".

1964. Child Welfare. Fish designs inscr "Fur die Jugend 1964". Multicoloured.
1326 10pf.+5pf. Type **400** . . . 25 45
1327 15pf.+5pf. Redfish 25 30
1328 20pf.+10pf. Mirror carp . . 45 45
1329 40pf.+20pf. Atlantic cod . . 1·20 1·90

401 Old Town Hall, Hanover

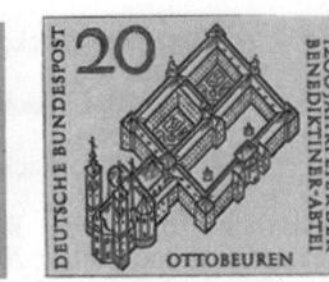
402 Ottobeuren Abbey

1964. Capitals of the Federal Lands. Mult.
1330 20pf. Type **401** 30 20
1331 20pf. Hamburg 30 20
1332 20pf. Kiel 30 20
1333 20pf. Munich 30 20
1334 20pf. Wiesbaden 30 20
1335 20pf. Berlin 30 20
1336 20pf. Mainz 30 20
1337 20pf. Dusseldorf 30 20
1338 20pf. Bonn 30 20
1339 20pf. Bremen 30 20
1340 20pf. Stuttgart 30 20
1340a 20pf. Saarbrucken 30 25
DESIGNS: No. 1331, Liner "Lichtenfels" and St. Michael's Church (775th anniv); 1332, Ferry "Kronprinz Harald"; 1333, National Theatre; 1334, Kurhaus; 1335, Reichstag; 1336, Gutenberg Museum; 1337, Jan Wellen's Monument and Town Hall; 1338, Town Hall; 1339, Market Hall; 1340, Town view; 1340a, Ludwig's Church.

1964. 1200th Anniv of Benedictine Abbey, Ottobeuren.
1341 **402** 20pf. black, red and pink 30 25

1964. Re-election of Pres. Lubke. As Type B **67** of West Berlin, inscr "DEUTSCHE BUNDESPOST" only.
1342 20pf. red 20 15
1343 40pf. blue 30 20

402b Sophie Scholl

1964. 20th Anniv of Attempt on Hitler's Life. Anti-Hitlerite Martyrs. Each black and grey.
1343a 20pf. Type **402b** . . . . . 65 1·50
1343b 20pf. Ludwig Beck . . . . 65 1·50
1343c 20pf. Dietrich Bonhoeffer 65 1·50
1343d 20pf. Alfred Delp . . . . 65 1·50
1343e 20pf. Karl Friedrich Goerdeler . . . . 65 1·50
1343f 20pf. Wilhelm Leuschner 65 1·50
1343g 20pf. Helmuth James (Von Moltke) . . . . 65 1·50
1343h 20pf. Claus Schenk (Von Stauffenberg) . . . . . 65 1·50

403 Calvin

404 Diagran of Benzene Formula

1964. World Council of Reformed Churches.
1344 **403** 20pf. black and red . . . 30 25

1964. Scientific Anniversaries (1st series).
1345 10pf. green, black and brown 20 20
1346 15pf. multicoloured 20 20
1347 20pf. green, black and red 20 20
DESIGNS: 10pf. Type **404** (centenary of publication of Kekule's benzene formula); 15pf. Diagram of nuclear reaction (25th anniv of publication of Hahn-Strassman treatise on splitting the nucleus of the atom); 20pf. Gas engine (centenary of Otto-Langen internal-combustion engine).
See also Nos. 1426/7 and 1451/3.

405 F. Lassalle

406 "The Sun"

1964. Death Centenary of Ferdinand Lassalle (Socialist founder and leader).
1348 **405** 20pf. black and blue . . 30 20

1964. 80th Catholics' Day.
1349 **406** 20pf. red and blue . . . 30 20

407 Europa "Flower"

408 "The Sleeping Beauty"

1964. Europa.
1350 **407** 15pf. violet and green . . 20 25
1351 20pf. violet and red . . . 20 20

1964. Humanitarian Relief and Welfare Funds.
1352 **408** 10pf.+5pf. mult 20 25
1353 – 15pf.+5pf. mult 20 20
1354 – 20pf.+10pf. mult 20 15
1355 – 40pf.+20pf. mult . . . . 55 1·10
DESIGNS: 15pf., 20pf., 40pf. Various scenes from Grimm's "The Sleeping Beauty".

409 Judo

410 Prussian Eagle

1964. "Olympic Year".
1356 **409** 20pf. multicoloured . . . 30 25

1964. 250th Anniv of German Court of Accounts.
1357 **410** 20pf. orange and black 30 25

411 Pres. Kennedy

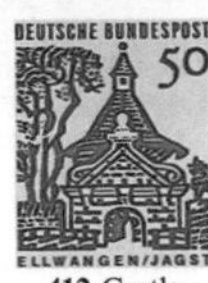
412 Castle Gateway, Ellwangen (Jagst)

1964. Pres. Kennedy Commemoration.
1358 **411** 40pf. blue 30 25

1964. Twelve Centuries of German Architecture.
(a) Size $18\frac{1}{2}\times22$ mm. Plain background.
1359 – 10pf. brown 25 15
1360 – 15pf. green 25 15
1361 – 20pf. brown 30 15
1362 – 40pf. blue 25 15
1363 **412** 50pf. brown 45 20
1364 – 60pf. red . . . . . . 1·20 45
1365 – 70pf. green . . . . . . 1·40 45
1366 – 80pf. brown . . . . . . 1·20 30
(b) Size $19\frac{1}{2}\times24$ mm. Coloured background.
1367 – 5pf. brown 20 15
1368 – 10pf. brown 20 15
1369 – 20pf. green 25 15
1370 – 30pf. green 30 15
1371 – 30pf. red 30 15
1372 – 40pf. brown 45 25
1373 – 50pf. blue 55 20
1374 – 60pf. orange . . . . . . 3·00 1·70
1375 – 70pf. green . . . . . . 1·40 20
1376 – 80pf. brown . . . . . . 2·50 1·50
1377 – 90pf. black . . . . . . 1·10 35
1378 – 1Dm. blue 90 20
1379 – 1Dm.10 brown . . . . . 1·10 45
1380 – 1Dm.30 green . . . . . 2·30 80
1381 – 2Dm. purple . . . . . . 2·30 50
BUILDINGS: 5pf. Berlin Gate, Stettin; 10pf. Zwinger pavilion, Dresden; 15pf. Tegel Castle, Berlin; 20pf. Monastery Gate, Lorsch; 30pf. North Gate, Flensburg; 40pf. Trifels Castle (Palatinate); 60pf. Treptow Portal, Neubrandenburg; 70pf. Osthofen Gate, Soest; 80pf. Ellingen Portal, Weissenburg (Bavaria); 90pf. Zschokk's Convent, Konigsberg; 1Dm. Melanchthon House, Wittenberg; 1Dm.10, Trinity Hospital, Hildesheim; 1Dm.30, Tegel Castle, Berlin (diff); 2Dm. Burghers' Hall, Lowenberg Town Hall (Silesia).

413 Owl, Hat, Walking-stick and Satchel

414 Eurasian Woodcock

1965. 150th Death Anniv of Matthias Claudius (poet).
1383 **413** 20pf. black and red on grey 30 25

1965. Child Welfare. Inscr "FUR DIE JUGEND 1965". Multicoloured.
1384 10pf.+5pf. Type **414** . . . 25 25
1385 15pf.+5pf. Common pheasant 25 25
1386 20pf.+10pf. Black grouse . . 25 30
1387 40pf.+20pf. Western capercaillie 35 95

415 Bismarck (statesman)

416 Boeing 727-100 Airliner and Space Capsule

1965. 150th Birth Anniv of Otto von Bismarck.
1388 **415** 20pf. black and red . . . 30 25

1965. Int Transport Exn, Munich. Mult.
1389 5pf. Traffic lights and road signs 20 20
1390 10pf. "Syncom" satellite and tracking station 20 20
1391 15pf. Old and modern postal buses 20 20
1392 20pf. Old semaphore station and modern signal tower 20 20
1393 40pf. Locomotive "Adler" (1835) and Class E.10.12 electric locomotive (1960s) 20 20
1394 60pf. Type **416** 35 40
1395 70pf. "Bremen" (liner) and "Hammonia" (19th-century steamship) 45 45
No. 1394 was also issued to mark the 10th anniv of Lufthansa's renewed air services.

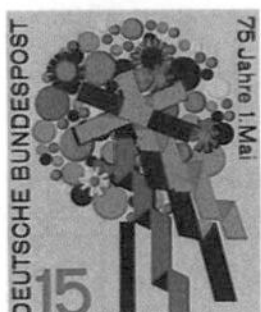
417 Bouquet

418 I.T.U. Emblem

1965. 75th Anniv of "May 1st" (Labour Day).
1396 **417** 15pf. multicoloured . . . 25 25

1965. Centenary of I.T.U.
1397 **418** 40pf. black and blue . . 35 35

419 A. Kopling

420 Rescue Vessel "Theodor Heuss"

1965. Death Centenary of Adolf Kolping (miners' padre).
1398 **419** 20pf. black, red and grey 30 25

1965. Cent of German Sea-rescue Service.
1399 **420** 20pf. violet, black & red 30 25

1965. 20th Anniv of Influx of East German Refugees. As T **299** but inscr "ZWANZIG JAHRE VERTREIBUNG 1945 1965".
1400 20pf. purple 30 25

421 Evangelical Church Emblem

422 Radio Tower

1965. German Evangelical Church Day and Synod, Cologne.
1401 **421** 20pf. black, turq & bl . . 30 25

1965. Radio Exhibition, Stuttgart.
1402 **422** 20pf. black, blue & mve 30 25

423 Thurn and Taxis 1, 2 and 5sgr. Stamps of 1852

1965. 125th Anniv of 1st Postage Stamp.
1403 **423** 20pf. multicoloured . . . 30 25

424 Europa "Sprig"

1965. Europa.
1404 **424** 15pf. green 20 20
1405 20pf. red 20 20

425 Cinderella with Birds 426 N. Soderblom

1965. Humanitarian Relief Funds. Mult.
1406 10pf.+5pf. Type **425** . . . 20 20
1407 15pf.+5pf. Cinderella and birds with dress 20 20
1408 20pf.+10pf. Prince offering slipper to Cinderella . . . 20 20
1409 40pf.+20pf. Cinderella and Prince on horse 65 85

1966. Birth Centenary of Nathan Soderblom (Archbishop of Uppsala).
1410 **426** 20pf. black and lilac . . 30 25

427 Cardinal von Galen 428 Brandenburg Gate, Berlin

1966. 20th Death Anniv of Cardinal Clemens von Galen.
1411 **427** 20pf. red, mauve & black 30 25

1966.
1412 **428** 10pf. brown 25 15
1413 20pf. green 45 15
1414 30pf. red 45 20
1415 50pf. blue . . . . . . 1·80 25
1415a 100pf. blue . . . . . . 10·50 45

429 Roe deer 430 Christ and Fishermen (Miracle of the Fishes)

1966. Child Welfare. Multicoloured.
1416 10pf.+5pf. Type **429** . . . 25 25
1417 20pf.+10pf. Chamois . . . 25 25
1418 30pf.+15pf. Fallow deer . . 25 25
1419 50pf.+25pf. Red deer . . . 75 1·10

1966. Catholics' Day.
1420 **430** 30pf. black and salmon 30 25

431 19th-cent Postman 432 G. W. Leibniz

1966. F.I.P. Meeting, Munich. Multicoloured.
1421 30pf.+15pf. Bavarian mail coach 45 80
1422 50pf.+25pf. Type **431** . . . 70 80

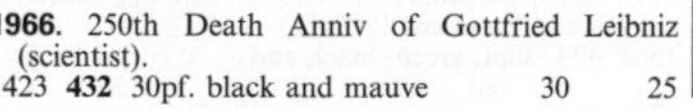

1966. 250th Death Anniv of Gottfried Leibniz (scientist).
1423 **432** 30pf. black and mauve 30 25

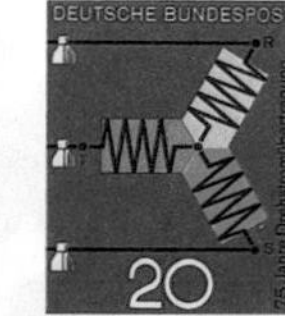

433 Europa "Ship" 434 Diagram of A.C. Transmission (75th Anniv)

1966. Europa.
1424 **433** 20pf. multicoloured . . . 25 25
1425 30pf. multicoloured . . . 25 15

1966. Scientific Annivs (2nd series). Mult.
1426 20pf. Type **434** 20 20
1427 30pf. Diagram of electric dynamo (cent) 25 20

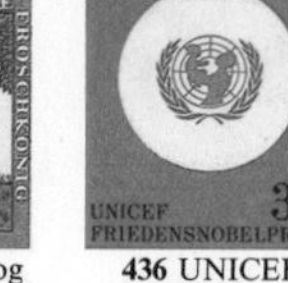

435 Princess and Frog 436 UNICEF Emblem

1966. Humanitarian Relief Funds. Mult.
1428 10pf.+5pf. Type **435** 20 25
1429 20pf.+10pf. Frog dining with Princess 20 20
1430 30pf.+15pf. Prince and Princess 20 25
1431 50pf.+25pf. In coach . . . 55 1·00
Designs from Grimm's "The Frog Prince".

1966. Award of Nobel Peace Prize to United Nations Children's Fund.
1432 **436** 30pf. sepia, black and red 30 25

437 W. von Siemens (electrical engineer) 438 Common Rabbit

1966. 150th Birth Anniv of Werner von Siemens (electrical engineer).
1433 **437** 30pf. red 30 25

1967. Child Welfare. Multicoloured.
1434 10pf.+5pf. Type **438** . . . 20 30
1435 20pf.+10pf. Stoat 30 35
1436 30pf.+15pf. Common hamster 55 60
1437 50pf.+25pf. Red fox . . . . 1·20 1·70
See also Nos. 1454/7.

439 Cogwheels 440 Francis of Taxis

1967. Europa.
1438 **439** 20pf. multicoloured . . . 30 25
1439 30pf. multicoloured . . . 25 15

1967. 450th Death Anniv of Francis of Taxis.
1440 **440** 30pf. black and orange 35 25

441 Evangelical Symbols 442 Friedrich von Bodelschwingh (Head of Hospital 1910–46)

1967. 13th German Evangelical Churches Day.
1441 **441** 30pf. black and mauve 30 25

1967. Cent of Bethel Hospital, Bielefeld.
1442 **442** 30pf. black and brown 30 25

443 Frau Holle at Spinning-wheel 444 Wartburg (castle), Eisenach

1967. Humanitarian Relief Funds. Mult.
1443 10pf.+5pf. Type **443** . . . 25 25
1444 20pf.+10pf. In the clouds . . 25 25
1445 30pf.+15pf. With shopping-basket and cockerel . . . 25 25
1446 50pf.+25pf. Covered with soot . . . . 65 1·30
Designs from Grimm's "Frau Holle" ("Mother Carey").

1967. Re-election of Pres. Lubke. As Type B **67** of West Berlin, but inscr "DEUTSCHE BUNDESPOST".
1447 30pf. red 25 25
1448 50pf. blue 45 35

1967. 450th Anniv of Luther's "Theses" and the Reformation.
1449 **444** 30pf. red 30 30

445 Cross on South American Map 446 Koenig's Printing Machine

1967. "Adveniat" (Aid for Catholic Church in Latin America).
1450 **445** 30pf. multicoloured . . . 30 25

1968. Scientific Anniv (3rd series). Mult.
1451 10pf. Type **446** 15 15
1452 20pf. Ore Crystals 15 15
1453 30pf. Lens Refraction . . . 25 20
ANNIVS: 10pf. 150th anniv; 20pf. Millenary of ore mining in Harz Mountains; 30pf. Centenary of Abbe-Zeiss Scientific Microscope.

1968. Child Welfare. As T **438** but inscr "1968". Multicoloured.
1454 10pf.+5pf. Wildcat 30 45
1455 20pf.+10pf. European otter 45 80
1456 30pf.+15pf. Eurasian badger 70 1·00
1457 50pf.+25pf. Eurasian beaver 2·10 3·00

447 Trade Symbols

1968. German Crafts and Trades.
1458 **447** 30pf. multicoloured . . . 25 20

448 Dr. Adenauer

1968. Adenauer Commemoration (1st issue). T **448** and similar horiz designs in sheet 149 × 106 mm.
MS1459 10pf. brown and black; 20pf. green and black; 30pf. red and black; 50pf. blue and black 2·50 2·75
DESIGNS: 10pf. Sir Winston Churchill; 20pf. Alcide de Gasperi; 30pf. Robert Schuman.
See also No. 1469.

449 Europa "Key" 450 Karl Marx

1968. Europa.
1460 **449** 20pf. yellow, brn & grn 25 20
1461 30pf. yellow, brn & red 25 15

1968. 150th Birth Anniv of Karl Marx.
1462 **450** 30pf. red, black & grey 30 25

451 F. von Langen (horseman) 453 Dr. Adenauer

452 Opening Bars of "The Mastersingers"

1968. Olympic Games (1972) Promotion Fund (1st series).
1463 **451** 10pf.+5pf. black & grn 30 25
1464 – 20pf.+10pf. black & grn 30 25
1465 – 30pf. black and lilac . . 30 20
1466 – 30pf.+15pf. black & red 70 50
1467 – 50pf.+25pf. black & bl 1·20 95
DESIGN: 20pf. R. Harbig (runner); 30pf. (No. 1465) Pierre de Coubertin (founder of Olympics); 30pf. (No. 1466) Helene Mayer (fencer); 50pf. Carl Diem (sports organiser).
See also Nos. 1493/6, 1524/7, 1589/92, 1621/4, **MS**1625 and 1629/32.

1968. Centenary of 1st Performance of Richard Wagner's Opera "The Mastersingers".
1468 **452** 30pf. multicoloured . . . 35 20

1968. Adenauer Commemoration (2nd issue).
1469 **453** 30pf. black and orange 30 20

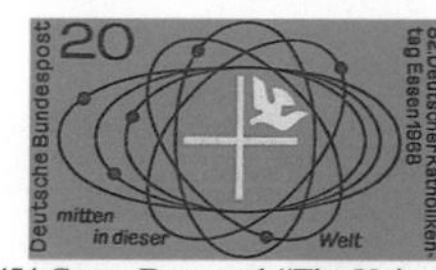

454 Cross, Dove and "The Universe"

1968. Catholics' Day.
1470 **454** 20pf. violet, yellow & grn 30 25

455 Northern District 1g. and Southern District 7k. stamps of 1868

1968. Cent of North German Postal Confederation and First Stamps.
1471 **455** 30pf. red, blue and black 30 25

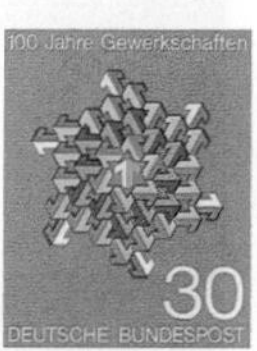

456 Arrows 457 Doll of 1878

1968. Cent of German Trade Unions.
1472 **456** 30pf. multicoloured . . . 30 25

1968. Humanitarian Relief Funds. Mult.
1473 10pf.+5pf. Type **457** . . . 25 25
1474 20pf.+10pf. Doll of 1850 . . 25 20
1475 30pf.+15pf. Doll of 1870 . . 30 25
1476 50pf.+25pf. Doll of 1885 . . 75 1·00

458 Human Rights Emblem 459 Pony

1968. Human Rights Year.
1477 **458** 30pf. multicoloured . . . 30 25

1969. Child Welfare.
1478 **459** 10pf.+5pf. brown, black and yellow 35 30
1479 – 20pf.+10pf. brown, black and buff 35 30
1480 – 30pf.+15pf. brown, black and red 80 65
1481 – 50pf.+25pf. mult . . . . 1·80 1·70
HORSES: 20pf. Draught-horse; 30pf. Saddle-horse; 50pf. Thoroughbred.

460 Junkers Ju 52/3m "Boelke"

1969. 50th Anniv of German Airmail Services. Multicoloured.
1482 20pf. Type **460** 45 20
1483 30pf. Boeing 707 airliner 75 20

461 Colonnade

462 "The Five Continents"

1969. Europa.
1484 **461** 20pf. yellow, grn & bl 35 20
1485 30pf. yellow, red & violet 45 20

1969. 50th Anniv of I.L.O.
1486 **462** 30pf. multicoloured 50 20

463 Eagle Emblems of Weimar and Federal Republics

464 "War Graves"

1969. 20th Anniv of German Federal Republic.
1487 **463** 30pf. black, gold and red 1·20 30

1969. 50th Anniv of German War Graves Commission.
1488 **464** 30pf. blue and yellow 35 20

465 Lakeside Landscape

466 "Running Track"

1969. Nature Protection. Multicoloured.
1489 10pf. Type **465** 25 20
1490 20pf. Highland landscape 75 35
1491 30pf. Alpine landscape 35 20
1492 50pf. River landscape 1·00 50

1969. Olympic Games (1972). Promotion Fund (2nd series). Multicoloured.
1493 10pf.+5pf. Type **466** 20 20
1494 20pf.+10pf. "Hockey" 35 30
1495 30pf.+15pf. "Shooting target" 55 55
1496 50pf.+25pf. "Sailing" 1·20 1·10

467 "Longing for Justice"

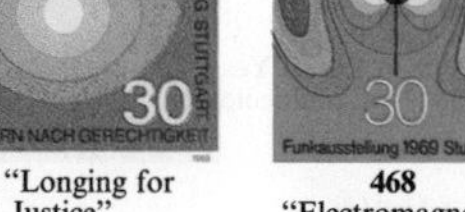
468 "Electromagnetic Field"

1969. 14th German Protestant Congress, Stuttgart.
1497 **467** 30pf. multicoloured 35 20

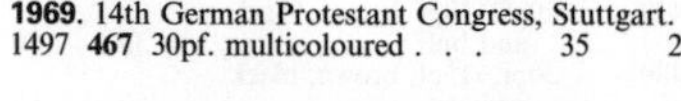
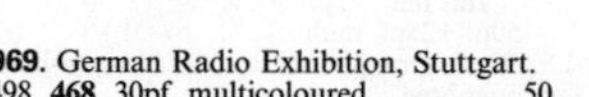

1969. German Radio Exhibition, Stuttgart.
1498 **468** 30pf. multicoloured 50 20

469 Marie Juchacz

1969. "Fifty Years of German Women's Suffrage". Sheet 102 × 61 mm containing T **469** and similar vert portraits of women politicians.
MS1499 10pf. olive; 20pf. green; 30pf. red 85 75
DESIGNS: 20pf. Marie-Elizabeth Luders; 30pf. Helene Weber.

470 Maltese Cross Symbol

471 Bavaria 3k. Stamp of 1867

1969. "Malteser Hilfsdienst" (welfare organization).
1500 **470** 30pf. red and black 50 20

1969. German Philatelic Federation Congress and Exn, Garmisch-Partenkirchen.
1501 **471** 30pf. red and slate 50 20

472 Map of Pipeline

1969. 350th Anniv of Bad Reichenhall–Traunstein Brine Pipeline.
1502 **472** 20pf. multicoloured 35 20

473 Rothenburg ob der Tauber

1969. Tourism.
1503 **473** 30pf. black and red 35 20
See also Nos. 1523, 1558, 1564, 1587, 1606, 1641/2, 1655/6 and 1680/2.

474 Mahatma Gandhi

475 Pope John XXIII

1969. Birth Centenary of Mahatma Gandhi.
1504 **474** 20pf. black and green 35 20

1969. Pope John XXIII Commemoration.
1505 **475** 30pf. red 35 20

476 "Adler" (1835)

477 E. M. Arndt

1969. Humanitarian Relief Funds. Pewter Figurines. Mult. (a) Inscr. "WOHLFAHRTSMARKE".
1506 10pf.+5pf. Type **476** 20 15
1507 20pf.+10pf. Woman watering flowers (1780) 30 25
1508 30pf.+15pf. Bird salesman (1850) 40 35
1509 50pf.+25pf. Mounted dignitary (1840) 1·10 95
(b) Christmas. Inscr "WEIHNACHTSMARKE".
1510 10pf.+5pf. "Child Jesus in crib" (1850) 30 25

1969. Birth Bicent of Ernst Arndt (writer).
1511 **477** 30pf. lake and bistre 35 20

478 "H. von Rugge"

1970. Child Welfare. Minnesinger Themes. Multicoloured.
1512 10pf.+5pf. Type **478** 45 40
1513 20pf.+10pf. "W. von Eschenbach" 70 45
1514 30pf.+15pf. "W. von Metz" 90 70
1515 50pf.+25pf. "W. von der Vogelweide" 2·10 1·60

479 Beethoven

480 Saar 1m. Stamp of 1947

1970. Birth Bicentenaries.
1516 **479** 10pf. black and blue 90 20
1517 – 20pf. black and olive 45 20
1518 – 30pf. black and pink 45 20
DESIGNS: 20pf. G. W. Hegel (philosopher); 30pf. F. Holderlin (poet).

1970. "Sabria 70" Stamp Exn, Saarbrucken.
1519 **480** 30pf. green, black and red 35 20

481 "Flaming Sun"

482 Von Munchhausen on Severed Horse

1970. Europa.
1520 **481** 20pf. green 35 15
1521 30pf. red 45 15

1970. 250th Birth Anniv of Baron H. von Munchhausen.
1522 **482** 20pf. multicoloured 35 20

1970. Tourism. As T **473**, but with view of Oberammergau.
1523 30pf. black and orange 35 20

483 Royal Palace

1970. Olympic Games (1972). Promotion Fund (3rd series).
1524 **483** 10pf.+5pf. brown 20 20
1525 – 20pf.+10pf. turquoise 45 40
1526 – 30pf.+15pf. red 65 55
1527 – 50pf.+25pf. blue 1·50 95
DESIGNS (Munich buildings): 20pf. Propylaea; 30pf. Glyptothek; 50pf. "Bavaria" (statue and colonnade).

484 Liner "Kungsholm IV" and Road-tunnel

485 Nurse with Invalid

1970. 75th Anniv of Kiel Canal.
1528 **484** 20pf. multicoloured 35 20

1970. Voluntary Relief Services. Mult.
1529 5pf. Oxygen-lance operator 20 20
1530 10pf. Mountain rescue 30 20
1531 20pf. Type **485** 30 20
1532 30pf. Fireman with hose 90 20
1533 50pf. Road-accident casualty 90 45
1534 70pf. Rescue from drowning 1·10 70

486 President Heinemann

487 Illuminated Cross

1970.
1535 **486** 5pf. black 25 20
1536 10pf. brown 25 20
1537 20pf. green 25 20
1538 25pf. green 35 15
1539 30pf. brown 45 20
1540 40pf. orange 45 20
1541 50pf. blue 1·80 20
1542 60pf. blue 70 20
1543 70pf. brown 90 25
1544 80pf. green 90 30
1545 90pf. red 1·70 1·40
1546 1Dm. green 1·10 30
1547 110pf. grey 1·30 60
1548 120pf. brown 1·60 75
1549 130pf. brown 1·60 80
1550 140pf. green 1·60 1·20
1551 150pf. red 1·60 55
1552 160pf. orange 2·50 85
1553 170pf. orange 1·80 55
1554 190pf. purple 2·75 70
1555 2Dm. violet 2·30 35

1970. Catholic Church World Mission.
1556 **487** 20pf. yellow and green 35 20

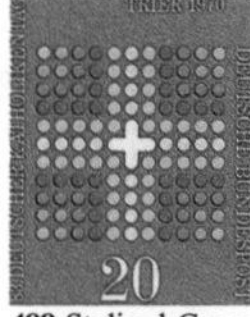
488 Stylized Cross

489 "Jester"

1970. Catholics Day and 83rd German Catholic Congress, Trier.
1557 **488** 20pf. multicoloured 35 20

1970. Tourism. As T **473**.
1558 20pf. black and green 35 20
DESIGN: 20pf. View of Cochem.

1970. Humanitarian Relief Funds. Puppets. Multicoloured. (a) Relief Funds
1559 10pf.+5pf. Type **489** 25 25
1560 20pf.+10pf. "Buffoon" 30 30
1561 30pf.+15pf. "Clown" 45 45
1562 50pf.+25pf. "Harlequin" 1·20 95
(b) Christmas.
1563 10pf.+5pf. "Angel" 30 25

1970. Tourism. As T **473**, but with view of Freiburg im Breisgau.
1564 20pf. brown and green 35 20

490 A. J. Comenius (scholar)

491 Engels as Young Man

1970. Int Education Year and 300th Death Anniv of Comenius (Jan Komensky).
1565 **490** 30pf. red and black 35 20

1970. 150th Birth Anniv of Friedrich Engels.
1566 **491** 50pf. blue and red 1·40 70

492 German Eagle

493 "Ebert" Stamp of 1928 and inscr "To the German People"

1971. Centenary of German Unification.
1567 **492** 30pf. black, red & orange 1·30 20

1971. Birth Centenary of Friedrich Ebert (Chancellor 1918 and President 1919–25).
1568 **493** 30pf. green, black and red 1·50 20

494 "King of Blackamoors" **495** Molecular Chain

1971. Child Welfare. Children's Drawings. Multicoloured.
1569 10pf.+5pf. Type **494** . . . 35 30
1570 20pf.+10pf. "Flea" 45 45
1571 30pf.+15pf. "Puss-in-Boots" 65 60
1572 50pf.+25pf. "Serpent" . . . 1·20 95

1971. 125 Years of Chemical Fibre Research.
1573 **495** 20pf. black, red & green 30 20

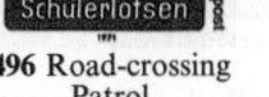

496 Road-crossing Patrol **497** Luther before Charles V

1971. New Road Traffic Regulations (1st series).
1574 **496** 10pf. black, blue and red 20 15
1575 – 20pf. black, red & green 40 20
1576 – 30pf. red, black and grey 55 20
1577 – 50pf. black, blue and red 90 55
ROAD SIGNS: 20pf. "Right-of-way across junction"; 30pf. "STOP"; 50pf. "Pedestrian Crossing".
See also Nos. 1579/82.

1971. 450th Anniv of Diet of Worms.
1578 **497** 30pf. black and red . . . 65 20

1971. New Traffic Regulations (2nd series). Horiz designs similar to T **496**.
1579 5pf. red, black and blue . . 20 15
1580 10pf. multicoloured 25 15
1581 20pf. red, black and green 45 20
1582 30pf. yellow, black and red 65 20
NEW HIGHWAY CODE: 5pf. Overtaking; 10pf. Warning of obstruction; 20pf. Lane discipline; 30pf. Pedestrian Crossing.

498 Europa Chain **499** Thomas a Kempis writing "The Imitation of Christ"

1971. Europa.
1583 **498** 20pf. gold, green & black 25 15
1584 30pf. gold, red and black 45 20

1971. 500th Death Anniv of Thomas a Kempis (devotional writer).
1585 **499** 30pf. black and red . . . 50 20

500 Durer's Monogram **501** Meeting Emblem

1971. 500th Birth Anniv of Albrecht Durer.
1586 **500** 30pf. brown & red . . . 1·20 20

1971. Tourism. As T **473**, but with view of Nuremburg.
1587 30pf. black and red 50 20

1971. Whitsun Ecumenical Meeting, Augsburg.
1588 **501** 30pf. black, orange & red 50 20

502 Ski Jumping **503** Astronomical Calculus

1971. Olympic Games (1972). Promotion Fund (4th series). Winter Games, Sapporo.
1589 **502** 10pf.+5pf. black & brn 25 20
1590 – 20pf.+10pf. black & grn 45 40
1591 – 30pf.+15pf. black & red 90 80
1592 – 50pf.+25pf. black & bl 1·70 1·30
MS1593 112 × 66 mm. Nos. 1589/92 3·00 2·50
DESIGNS: 20pf. Ice dancing; 30pf. Skiing start; 50pf. Ice hockey.

1971. 400th Birth Anniv of Johann Kepler (astronomer).
1594 **503** 30pf. gold, red and black 45 20

504 Dante **505** Alcohol and front of Car ("Don't Drink and Drive")

1971. 650th Death Anniv of Dante Alighieri.
1595 **504** 10pf. black 25 20

1971. Accident Prevention.
1596 – 5pf. orange 25 15
1597 – 10pf. brown 25 15
1598 – 20pf. violet 35 15
1599 **505** 25pf. green 45 15
1600 – 30pf. red 45 15
1601 – 40pf. mauve 45 15
1602 – 50pf. blue . . . . . 2·50 15
1603 – 60pf. blue . . . . . 1·80 40
1603a – 70pf. blue and green . . 1·20 30
1604 – 1Dm. green . . . . . 2·30 20
1605 – 1Dm.50 brown . . . . 6·50 1·00
DESIGNS: 5pf. Man within flame, and spent match ("Fire Prevention"); 10pf. Fall from ladder; 20pf. Unguarded machinery ("Factory Safety"); 30pf. Falling brick and protective helmet; 40pf. Faulty electric plug; 50pf. Protruding nail in plank; 60pf., 70pf. Ball in front of car ("Child Road Safety"); 1Dm. Crate on hoist; 1Dm.50, Open manhole.

1971. Tourism. As T **473** but with view of Goslar.
1606 20pf. black and green . . . 35 25

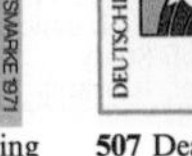

506 Women churning Butter **507** Deaconess and Nurse

1971. Humanitarian Relief Funds. Wooden Toys. Mult. (a) Inscr. "WOHLFAHRTSMARKE".
1607 20pf.+10pf. Type **506** . . . 25 20
1608 25pf.+10pf. Horseman on wheels 25 20
1609 30pf.+15pf. Nutcracker man 45 45
1610 60pf.+30pf. Dovecote . . . 1·30 1·10

(b) Christmas. Inscr "WEIHNACHTSMARKE".
1611 20pf.+10pf. Angel with three candles 35 40

1972. Death Cent of Johann Wilhelm Lohe (founder of Deaconesses Mission, Neuendettelsau).
1612 **507** 25pf. slate, black & green 35 20

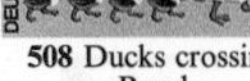

508 Ducks crossing Road **509** Senefelder's Press

1972. Child Welfare. Annimal Protection. Multicoloured.
1613 20pf.+10pf. Type **508** . . . 70 55
1614 25pf.+10pf. Hunter scaring deer 45 40
1615 30pf.+15pf. Child protecting bird from cat 90 80
1616 60pf.+30pf. Boy annoying mute swans . . . . . . 1·80 1·50

1972. "175 Years of Offset Lithography".
1617 **509** 25pf. multicoloured . . . 35 20

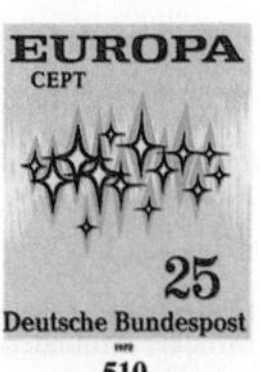

510 "Communications" **511** Lucas Cranach

1972. Europa.
1618 **510** 25pf. multicoloured . . . 45 20
1619 30pf. multicoloured . . . 55 20

1972. 500th Birth Anniv of Lucas Cranach the Elder (painter).
1620 **511** 25pf. black, stone & grn 60 20

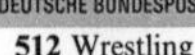

512 Wrestling **514** Invalid Archer

513 Gymnastics Stadium

1972. Olympic Games, Munich (5th series). Multicoloured.
1621 20pf.+10pf. Type **512** . . . 45 40
1622 25pf.+10pf. Sailing 45 40
1623 30pf.+15pf. Gymnastics . . 45 40
1624 60pf.+30pf. Swimming . . . 1·80 1·50
See also Nos. 1629/32.

1972. Olympic Games, Munich (6th series). Sheet 148 × 105 mm containing T **513** and similar multicoloured designs.
MS1625 25pf.+10pf. Type **513**; 30pf.+15pf. Athletics stadium; 40pf.+20pf. Tented area; 70pf.+35pf. TV tower . . . . 4·50 4·50

1972. 21st Int Games for the Paralysed, Heidelberg.
1626 **514** 40pf. red, black & yellow 75 25

515 Posthorn and Decree **516** K. Schumacher

1972. Cent of German Postal Museum.
1627 **515** 40pf. multicoloured . . . 75 20

1972. 20th Death Anniv of Kurt Schumacher (politician).
1628 **516** 40pf. black and red . . . 1·40 20

1972. Olympic Games, Munich (7th series). As Type **512**. Multicoloured.
1629 25pf.+5pf. Long jumping . . 90 80
1630 30pf.+10pf. Basketball . . . 90 1·10
1631 40pf.+10pf. Throwing the discus . . . . 90 1·10
1632 70pf.+10pf. Canoeing . . . 90 85
MS1633 111 × 66 mm. Nos. 1629/32 4·25 4·25

517 Open Book **518** Music and Signature

1972. International Book Year.
1634 **517** 40pf. multicoloured . . . 75 20

1972. 300th Death Anniv of Heinrich Schutz (composer).
1635 **518** 40pf. multicoloured . . . 75 20

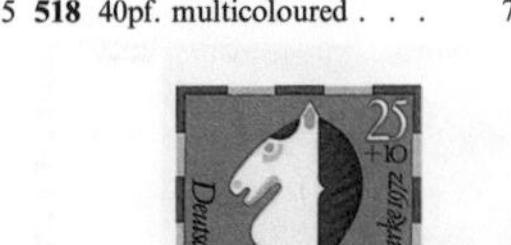

519 Knight

1972. Humanitarian Relief Funds. Mult. (a) 19th-century Faience Chessmen. Inscr "WOHLFAHRTSMARKE".
1636 25pf.+10pf. Type **519** . . . 30 35
1637 30pf.+15pf. Rook 30 35
1638 40pf.+20pf. Queen 65 35
1639 70pf.+35pf. King . . . . . 2·30 1·90

(b) Christmas. Inscr "WEIHNACHTSMARKE".
1640 30pf.+15pf. "The Three Wise Men" (horiz) . . . 70 55

1972. Tourism. As T **473**.
1641 30pf. black and green . . . 55 20
1642 40pf. black and orange . . . 65 20
VIEWS: 30pf. Heligoland; 40pf. Heidelberg.

520 Revellers

1972. 150th Anniv of Cologne Carnival.
1643 **520** 40pf. multicoloured . . . 1·00 20

521 H. Heine

1972. 175th Birth Anniv of Heinrich Heine (poet).
1644 **521** 40pf. black, red and pink 1·00 20

522 "Brot fur die Welt" **523** Wurzburg Cathedral (seal)

1972. Freedom from Hunger Campaign.
1645 **522** 30pf. red and green . . . 50 45

1972. Catholic Synod '72.
1646 **523** 40pf. black, purple & red 60 20

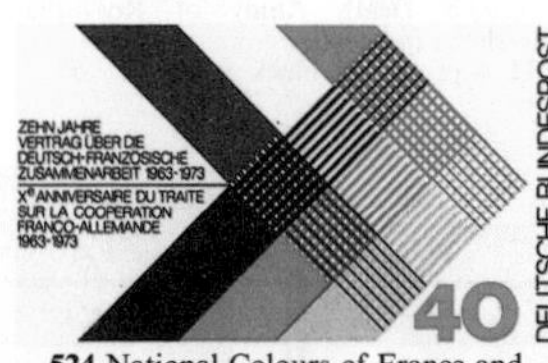

524 National Colours of France and Germany

1973. 10th Anniv of Franco-German Treaty.
1647 **524** 40pf. multicoloured . . . 1·20 30

525 Osprey **527** Radio Mast and Transmission

526 Copernicus

1973. Youth Welfare. Birds of Prey. Multicoloured.
1648 25pf.+10pf. Type **525** . . . 1·10 90
1649 30pf.+15pf. Common buzzard . . . . 1·40 1·20
1650 40pf.+20pf. Red kite . . . . 2·00 1·70
1651 70pf.+35pf. Montagu's harrier . . . . 4·50 3·75

1973. 500th Birth Anniv of Copernicus.
1652 **526** 40pf. black and red . . . 1·20 20

1973. 50th Anniv of Interpol.
1653 **527** 40pf. black, red and grey 60 20

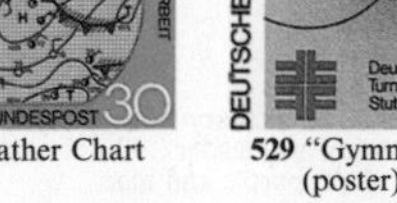

528 Weather Chart **529** "Gymnast" (poster)

1973. Cent of Int Meteorological Organization.
1654 **528** 30pf. multicoloured . . . 50 20

1973. Tourism. As T **473**.
1655 40pf. black and red . . . . 1·10 20
1656 40pf. black and orange . . . 90 20
VIEWS: No. 1655, Hamburg; 1656, Rudesheim.

1973. Gymnastics Festival, Stuttgart.
1657 **529** 40pf. multicoloured . . . 50 20

530 Kassel (Hesse) Sign

532 "R" Motif

531 Europa "Posthorn"

1973. "I.B.R.A. Munchen 73" International Stamp Exhibition, Munich. F.I.P. Congress. Post-house Signs. Multicoloured.
1658 40pf.+20pf. Type **530** . . . 90 80
1659 70pf.+35pf. Prussia . . . . 1·60 1·50
MS1660 74 × 105 mm. 40pf.+20pf. Wurttemberg; 70pf.+35pf. Kurpfalz (Bavaria) (sold at 2.20Dm.) . . . . 4·00 4·00

1973. Europa.
1661 **531** 30pf. yell, myrtle & grn 50 20
1662 40pf. yellow, lake & pink 70 20

1973. 1000th Death Anniv of Roswitha von Gandersheim (poetess).
1663 **532** 40pf. yellow, black & red 55 20

533 M. Kolbe

534 "Profile" (from poster)

1973. Father Maximilian Kolbe (Concentration camp victim) Commemoration.
1664 **533** 40pf. red, brown & black 50 20

1973. 15th German Protestant Church Conference.
1665 **534** 30pf. multicoloured . . . 35 20

535 Environmental Conference Emblem and Waste

1973. "Protection of the Environment". Multicoloured.
1666 25pf. Type **535** 45 20
1667 30pf. Emblem and "Water" 45 20
1668 40pf. Emblem and "Noise" 90 25
1669 70pf. Emblem and "Air" . . 1·60 75

536 Schickard's Calculating Machine

537 Otto Wels

1973. 350th Anniv of Schickard's Calculating Machine.
1670 **536** 40pf. black, red and orange 50 45

1973. Birth Centenary of Otto Wels (Social Democratic Party leader).
1671 **537** 40pf. purple and lilac . . 65 20

538 Lubeck Cathedral

1973. 800th Anniv of Lubeck Cathedral.
1672 **538** 40pf. multicoloured . . . 1·10 20

539 U.N. and German Eagle Emblems

1973. Admission of German Federal Republic to U.N. Organization.
1673 **539** 40pf. multicoloured . . . 1·60 20

540 French Horn

1973. Humanitarian Relief Funds. Multicoloured. (a) Musical Instruments. Inscr "WOHLFAHRTSMARKE".
1674 25pf.+10pf. Type **540** . . . 70 40
1675 30pf.+15pf. Grand piano . . 70 40
1676 40pf.+20pf. Violin 90 60
1677 70pf.+70pf. Harp . . . . . 2·30 1·50

(b) Christmas. Inscr "WEIHNACHTSMARKE".
1678 30pf.+15pf. Christmas star 70 55

541 Radio set of 1923

1973. "50 Years of German Broadcasting".
1679 **541** 30pf. multicoloured . . . 35 20

1974. Tourism. As Type **473**.
1680 30pf. black and green . . . 70 20
1681 40pf. black and red 70 20
1682 40pf. black and red 70 20
VIEWS: No. 1680, Saarbrucken; 1681, Aachen; 1682, Bremen.

542 Louise Otto-Peters

1974. Women in German Politics. Each black and orange.
1683 40pf. Type **542** 70 45
1684 40pf. Helene Lange 70 45
1685 40pf. Rosa Luxemburg . . . 70 45
1686 40pf. Gertrud Baumer . . . 70 45

543 Drop of Blood and Emergency Light

1974. Blood Donor and Accident/Rescue Services.
1687 **543** 40pf. red and blue . . . 85 20

544 "Deer in Red" (Franz Marc)

1974. German Expressionist Paintings. Mult.
1688 30pf. Type **544** 50 20
1689 30pf. "Girls under Trees" (A. Macke) 70 25
1690 40pf. "Portrait in Blue" (A. von Jawiensky) (vert) . . 70 20
1691 50pf. "Pechstein asleep" (E. Heckel) (vert) . . . . 1·20 30
1692 70pf. "Still Life with Telescope" (Max Beckmann) . . . . 1·00 85
1693 120pf. "Old Peasant" (L. Kirchner) (vert) . . . 2·10 1·60

545 St. Thomas teaching Pupils

1974. 700th Death Anniv of St. Thomas Aquinas.
1694 **545** 40pf. black and red . . . 55 20

546 Disabled Persons in Outline

1974. Rehabilitation of the Handicapped.
1695 **546** 40pf. red and black . . . 85 20

547 Construction (Bricklayer)

548 "Ascending Youth" (W. Lehmbruck)

1974. Youth Welfare. Youth Activities. Multicoloured.
1696 25pf.+10pf. Type **547** . . . 65 55
1697 30pf.+15pf. Folk dancing 1·10 90
1698 40pf.+20pf. Study . . . . . 1·80 1·60
1699 70pf.+35pf. Research . . . 3·25 2·75

1974. Europa.
1700 **548** 30pf. black, green & sil 50 15
1701 – 40pf. black, red and lilac 70 20
DESIGN: 40pf. "Kneeling Woman" (W. Lehmbruck).

549 Immanuel Kant

551 Country Road

550 Ferderal Arms and National Colours

1974. 250th Birth Anniv of Immanuel Kant (philosopher).
1702 **549** 90pf. red . . . . 1·90 30

1974. 25th Anniv of Formation of Federal Republic. Sheet 94 × 64 mm.
MS1703 **550** 40pf. multicoloured 1·30 1·40

1974. Rambling, and Birth Centenaries of Richard Schirrman and Wilhelm Munker (founders of Youth Hostelling Assn).
1704 **551** 30pf. multicoloured . . . 50 20

552 Friedrich Klopstock

553 "Crowned Cross" Symbol

1974. 250th Birth Anniv of Friedrich Gottlieb Klopstock (poet).
1705 **552** 40pf. black and red . . . 65 20

1974. 125th Anniv of German Protestant Church Diaconal Association (charitable organization).
1706 **553** 40p. multicoloured . . . 60 20

554 Goalkeeper saving Goal

1974. World Cup Football Championship. Multicoloured.
1707 30pf. Type **554** 90 20
1708 40pf. Mid-field melee . . . 1·80 20

555 Hans Holbein (self-portrait)

556 Broken Bars of Prison Window

1974. 450th Death Anniv of Hans Holbein the Elder (painter).
1709 **555** 50pf. black and red . . . 85 25

1974. Amnesty International Commemoration.
1710 **556** 70pf. black and blue . . 1·20 40

557 "Man and Woman looking at the Moon"

1974. Birth Bicentenary of Caspar David Friedrich (artist).
1711 **557** 50pf. multicoloured . . . 1·20 30

558 Campion

559 Early German Post-boxes

1974. Humanitarian Relief Funds. Flowers. Multicoloured. (a) 25th Anniv of Welfare Stamps. Inscr "25 JAHRE WOHLFAHRTSMARKE".
1712 30pf.+15pf. Type **558** . . . 35 25
1713 40pf.+20pf. Foxglove . . . 45 40
1714 50pf.+25pf. Mallow 55 45
1715 70pf.+35pf. Campanula . . 1·60 1·30

(b) Christmas. Inscr "WEIHNACHTSMARKE".
1716 40pf.+20pf. Poinsettia . . . 75 70

1974. Cent of Universal Postal Union.
1717 **559** 50pf. multicoloured . . . 1·20 35

560 Annette Kolb

562 Mother and Child and Emblem

561 Hans Bockler (Trade Union leader)

1975. International Women's Year. Women Writers.
1718 30pf. Type **560** 65 30
1719 40pf. Ricarda Huch 65 30
1720 50pf. Else Lasker-Schuler . . 65 30
1721 70pf. Gertrud von le Fort 1·10 85

1975. Birth Centenaries.
1722 **561** 40pf. black and green . . 70 20
1723 – 50pf. black and red . . . 75 20
1724 – 70pf. black and blue . . 1·90 50
DESIGNS: 50pf. Matthias Erzberger (statesman); 70pf. Albert Schweitzer (medical missionary).

1975. 25th Anniv of Organization for the Rest and Recuperation of Mothers.
1725 **562** 50pf. multicoloured . . . 75 20

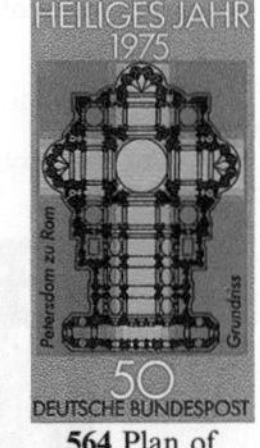

563 Detail of Ceiling Painting, Sistine Chapel
564 Plan of St. Peter's, Rome within a cross

1975. 500th Birth Anniv of Michelangelo.
1726 **563** 70pf. black and blue . . 1·80 1·10

1975. "Holy Year (Year of Reconcillation)".
1727 **564** 50pf. multicoloured . . . 70 20

565 Ice Hockey

1975. World Ice Hockey Championships, Munich and Dusseldorf.
1728 **565** 50pf. multicoloured . . . 1·20 20

566 Class 218 Diesel Locomotive

1975. Youth Welfare. Railway Locomotives. Multicoloured.
1729 30pf.+15pf. Type **566** . . . 55 55
1730 40pf.+20pf. Class 103 electric locomotive 85 80
1731 50pf.+25pf. Class 403 electric railcar . . . . . 1·20 1·10
1732 70pf.+35pf. Transrapid Maglev train (model) . . 2·10 1·70

567 "Concentric Group"
569 "Nuis" (woodcarving)

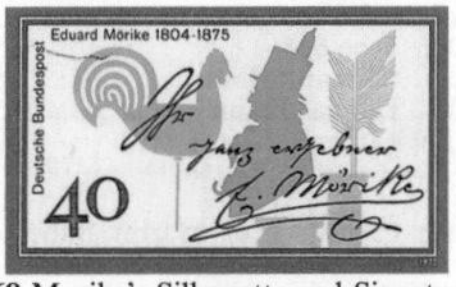

568 Morike's Silhouette and Signature

1975. Europa. Paintings by Oskar Schlemmer. Multicoloured.
1733 40pf. Type **567** 60 20
1734 50pf. "Bauhaus Staircase" 80 20

1975. Death Cent of Eduard Morike (writer).
1735 **568** 40pf. multicoloured . . . 60 20

1975. 500th Anniv of Siege of Neuss.
1736 **569** 50pf. multicoloured . . . 90 20

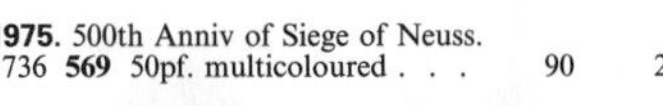

570 Jousting Contest

1975. 500th Anniv of "Landshut Wedding" (festival).
1737 **570** 50pf. multicoloured . . . 1·10 20

571 Mainz Cathedral
572 Telecommunication Satellite

1975. Millenary of Mainz Cathedral.
1738 **571** 40pf. multicoloured . . . 1·10 20

1975. Industry and Technology.
1739 **572** 5pf. green 15 15
1740 – 10pf. mauve 15 15
1741 – 20pf. red 20 15
1742 – 30pf. lilac 30 15
1743 – 40pf. green 35 15
1744 – 50pf. mauve 45 15
1745 – 60pf. red 65 15
1746 – 70pf. blue 85 20
1747 – 80pf. green 90 15
1748 – 100pf. brown . . . . . 1·00 20
1748a – 110pf. purple . . . . 1·60 55
1749 – 120pf. blue . . . . . 1·30 35
1749a – 130pf. red . . . . . 2·10 50
1750 – 140pf. red . . . . . 1·40 45
1751 – 150pf. red . . . . . 2·75 65
1752 – 160pf. green . . . . . 2·00 70
1753 – 180pf. brown . . . . . 2·30 70
1753a – 190pf. brown . . . . . 2·30 55
1754 – 200pf. purple . . . . . 2·00 30
1754a – 230pf. purple . . . . 3·25 70
1754b – 250pf. green . . . . . 4·50 1·30
1754c – 300pf. green . . . . . 4·50 1·30
1755 – 500pf. black . . . . . 5·50 85
DESIGNS: 10pf. Electric train; 20pf. Modern lighthouse; 30pf. MBB-Bolkow Bo 105C rescue helicopter; 40pf. Space laboratory; 50pf. Dish aerial; 60pf. X-ray apparatus; 70pf. Ship-building; 80pf. Farm tractor; 100pf. Lignite excavator; 110pf. Colour television camera; 120pf. Chemical plant; 130pf. Brewery plant; 140pf. Power station; 150, 190pf. Mechanical shovel; 160pf. Blast furnace; 180pf. Wheel loader; 200pf. Marine drilling platform; 230, 250pf. Frankfurt Airport; 300pf. Electromagnetic monorail; 500pf. Radio telescope.

573 Town Hall and Market, Alsfeld

1975. European Architectural Heritage Year. German Buildings. Multicoloured.
1756 50pf. Type **573** 90 55
1757 50pf. Plonlein corner, Siebers tower and Kobelzeller gate, Rothenburg-on-Tauber . . 90 55
1758 50pf. Town Hall ("The Steipe") Trier 90 55
1759 50pf. View of Xanten . . . 1·20 55

574 Effects of Drug-taking

1975. Campaign to Fight the Abuse of Drugs and Intoxicants.
1760 **574** 40pf. multicoloured . . . 50 20

575 Posthouse Sign, Royal Prussian Establishment for Transport 1776
576 Edelweiss

1975. Stamp Day.
1761 **575** 10pf. multicoloured . . . 35 20

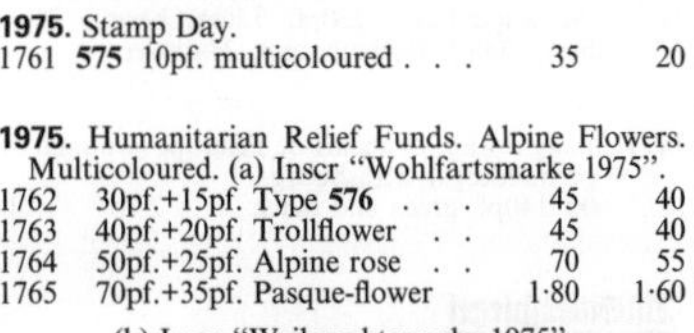

1975. Humanitarian Relief Funds. Alpine Flowers. Multicoloured. (a) Inscr "Wohlfartsmarke 1975".
1762 30pf.+15pf. Type **576** . . . 45 40
1763 40pf.+20pf. Trollflower . . 45 40
1764 50pf.+25pf. Alpine rose . . 70 55
1765 70pf.+35pf. Pasque-flower 1·80 1·60

(b) Inscr "Weihnachtsmarke 1975".
1766 40pf.+20pf. Christmas rose 1·10 85
See also Nos. 1796/9, 1839/42, 1873/6 and 1905/8.

577 Gustav Stresemann (statesman)

1975. German Nobel Peace Prize Winners. Sheet 100 × 70 mm containing T **577** and similar vert designs in black.
MS1767 50pf. Type **577**; 50pf. Ludwig Quidde (Reichstag deputy); 50pf. Carl von Ossietzky (journalist) . . . . 2·30 1·70

578 Stylized Ski-runners
579 Konrad Adenauer

1975. Winter Olympic Games, Innsbruck.
1768 **578** 50pf. multicoloured . . . 75 20

1976. Birth Centenary of Konrad Adenauer (Chancellor 1949–63).
1769 **579** 50pf. green . . . . . . 1·60 20

580 Cover Pages from Hans Sachs' Books
581 Junkers F-13 "Herta"

1976. 400th Death Anniv of Hans Sachs (poet and composer).
1770 **580** 40pf. multicoloured . . . 70 20

1976. 50th Anniv of Lufthansa (German civil airline).
1771 **581** 50pf. multicoloured . . . 1·20 20

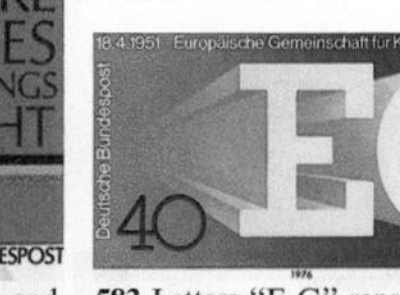

582 Emblem and Commemorative Inscription
583 Letters "E G" representing Steel Girders

1976. 25th Anniv of Federal Constitutional Court.
1772 **582** 50pf. multicoloured . . . 90 20

1976. 25th Anniv of European Coal and Steel Community.
1773 **583** 40pf. multicoloured . . . 85 20

584 Monorail Train
585 Basketball

1976. 75th Anniv of Wuppertal Monorailway.
1774 **584** 50pf. multicoloured . . . 90 20

1976. Youth Welfare. Training for the Olympics. Multicoloured.
1775 30pf.+15pf. Type **585** . . . 45 40
1776 40pf.+20pf. Rowing 85 75
1777 50pf.+25pf. Gymnastics . . 1·10 1·00
1778 70pf.+35pf. Volleyball . . . 1·60 1·40

586 Swimming

1976. Olympic Games, Montreal. Mult.
1779 40pf.+25pf. Type **586** . . . 70 60
1780 50pf.+25pf. High jumping 1·00 90
MS1781 110 × 70 mm. 30pf.+15pf. black, orange-red and pale yellow; 70pf. + 35pf. black, new blue and pale blue . . . . 1·60 1·60
DESIGNS: 30pf. Hockey; 50pf. High jumping; 70pf. Rowing four.

587 Girl selling Trinkets and Copperplate Prints
588 Carl Sonnenschein

1976. Europa. Ludwigsburg China Figures. Multicoloured.
1782 40pf. Type **587** 55 15
1783 50pf. Boy selling copperplate prints 70 15

1976. Birthday Centenary of Dr. Carl Sonnenschein (clergyman).
1784 **588** 50pf. multicoloured . . . 70 20

589 Opening bars of Hymn "Entrust Yourself to God"

1976. 300th Birth Anniv of Paul Gerhardt (composer).
1785 **589** 40pf. multicoloured . . . 50 20

590 Carl Maria von Weber conducting

1976. 150th Death Anniv of Carl Maria von Weber (composer).
1786 **590** 50pf. black and brown 90 20

591 Carl Schurz

1976. Bicent of American Revolution.
1787 **591** 70pf. multicoloured . . . 1·10 40

592 Wagnerian Stage

1976. Centenary of Bayreuth Festival.
1788 **592** 50pf. multicoloured . . . 1·20 20

593 Bronze Ritual Chariot

1976. Archaeological Heritage. Mult.
1789 30pf. Type **593** 45 30
1790 40pf. Gold-ornamental bowl 65 30
1791 50pf. Silver necklet 90 35
1792 120pf. Roman gold goblet 2·10 1·60

594 Golden Plover **595** Mythical Creature

1976. Bird Protection.
1793 **594** 50pf. multicoloured . . . 1·20 20

1976. 300th Death Anniv of J. J. C. von Grimmelshausen (writer).
1794 **595** 40pf. multicoloured . . . 1·30 20

596 18th-century Posthouse Sign, Hochst-am-Main **597** Sophie Schroder ("Sappho")

1976. Stamp Day.
1795 **596** 10pf. multicoloured . . . 35 20

1976. Humanitarian Relief Funds. Garden Flowers. Designs similar to T **576**. Multicoloured.
1796 30pf.+15pf. Phlox 55 45
1797 40pf.+20pf. Marigolds . . . 70 60
1798 50pf.+25pf. Dahlias 80 70
1799 70pf.+35pf. Pansies . . . . 1·40 1·20

1976. Famous German Actresses. Mult.
1800 30pf. Carolin Neuber ("Medea") 55 20
1801 40pf. Type **597** 55 25
1802 50pf. Louise Dumont ("Hedda Gabler") 80 35
1803 70pf. Hermine Korner ("Macbeth") . . . . . . 1·40 90

598 "Madonna and Child" ("Marienfenster" window, Frauenkirche, Esslingen)

1976. Christmas. Sheet 71 × 101 mm.
MS1804 **598** 50pf.+25pf. multicoloured 90 80

599 Eltz Castle **600** Palais de l'Europe

1977. German Castles.
1805 – 10pf. blue 20 15
1805c – 20pf. orange 20 15
1805d – 25pf. red 45 20
1806 – 30pf. bistre 45 15
1806c – 35pf. red 65 30
1807 **599** 40pf. green 55 15
1807a – 40pf. brown 65 15
1808 – 50pf. red 70 15
1808b – 50pf. green 85 15

1809 – 60pf. brown . . . . . 1·20 15
1809a – 60pf. red 80 20
1810 – 70pf. blue . . . . . 1·20 25
1810a – 80pf. green . . . . . 1·20 20
1810c – 90pf. blue . . . . . 1·40 35
1810d – 120pf. violet . . . . 1·80 70
1811 – 190pf. red . . . . . 2·30 85
1812 – 200pf. green . . . . 3·00 75
1812a – 210pf. brown . . . . 3·75 85
1812b – 230pf. green . . . . 3·75 85
1812c – 280pf. blue . . . . 4·25 75
1812d – 300pf. orange . . . . 4·75 65
DESIGNS: 10pf. Glucksburg; 20, 190pf. Pfaueninsel, Berlin; 25pf. Gemen; 30pf. Ludwigstein, Werratal; 35pf. Lichtenstein; 40pf. (1807a) Wolfsburg; 50pf. (1808) Neuschwanstein; 50pf. (1808b) Inzlingen; 60pf. (1809) Marksburg; 60pf. (1809a) Rheydt; 70pf. Mespelbrunn; 80pf. Wilhelmsthal; 90pf. Vischering; 120pf. Charlottenburg, Berlin; 200pf. Burresheim; 210pf. Schwanenburg; 230pf. Lichtenberg; 280pf. Ahrensburg; 300pf. Herrenhausen, Hanover.

1977. Inauguration of Palais de l'Europe (Council of Europe buildings), Strasbourg.
1813 **600** 140pf. green and black 2·10 60

601 Book Illustrations **603** Jean Monnet

1977. "Till Eulenspiegel" (popular fable).
1814 **601** 50pf. multicoloured . . . 70 20

1977. Award of "Citizen of Europe" honour to Jean Monnet (French statesman).
1816 **603** 50pf. black, grey & yell 75 20

604 "Flower" **605** Plane of Complex Numbers

1977. 25th Anniv of Federal Horticultural Show.
1817 **604** 50pf. multicoloured . . . 85 20

1977. Birth Bicentenary of Carl Friedrich Gauss (mathematician).
1818 **605** 40pf. multicoloured . . . 1·20 20

606 "Wappen von Hamburg" (warship) **607** Head of Barbarossa

1977. Youth Welfare. Ships. Multicoloured.
1819 30pf.+15pf. Type **606** . . . 65 55
1820 40pf.+20pf. "Preussen" (full-rigged sailing ship) . . . 85 75
1821 50pf.+25pf. "Bremen" (liner) 1·10 95
1822 70pf.+35pf. "Sturmfels" (container ship) . . . . . 1·60 1·30

1977. Staufer Year, Baden-Wurttemberg.
1823 **607** 40pf. multicoloured . . . 1·20 25

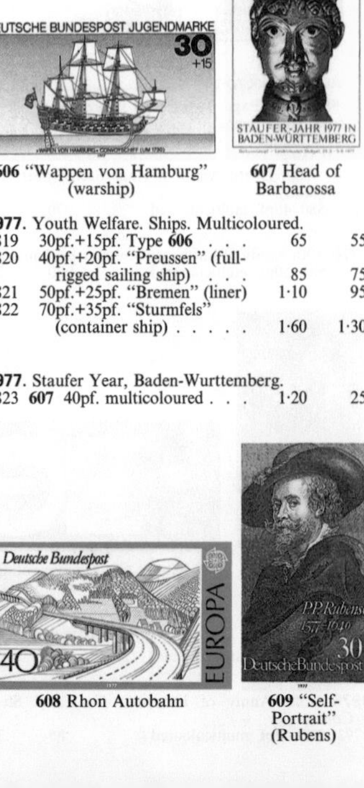

608 Rhon Autobahn **609** "Self-Portrait" (Rubens)

1977. Europa.
1824 **608** 40pf. black and green . . 70 20
1825 – 50pf. black and red . . . 80 20
DESIGN: 50pf. Rhine landscape.

1977. 400th Birth Anniv of Peter Paul Rubens.
1826 **609** 30pf. black . . . . . . 1·10 20

610 Ulm Cathedral **611** Rector's Seal, Mainz University (500th Anniv)

1977. 600th Anniv of Ulm Cathedral.
1827 **610** 40pf. brown, green & bl 80 20

1977. University Anniversaries.
1828 **611** 50pf. black and red . . . 85 25
1829 – 50pf. black and red . . . 1·10 25
1830 – 50pf. black and red . . . 1·20 30
DESIGNS: No. 1829, Great Seal, Marburg University (450th anniv); No. 1830, Great Seal, Tubingen University (500th anniv).

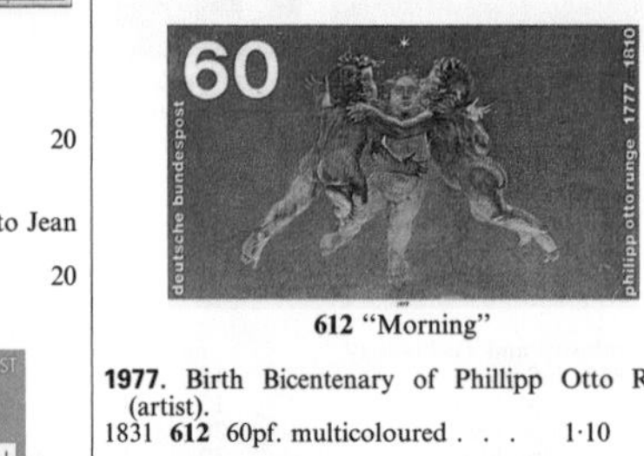

612 "Morning"

1977. Birth Bicentenary of Phillipp Otto Runge (artist).
1831 **612** 60pf. multicoloured . . . 1·10 35

613 Ketteler's Coat of Arms **614** Fritz von Bodelschwingh

1977. Death Centenary of Bishop Wilhelm Emmanuel von Ketteler.
1832 **613** 50pf. multicoloured . . . 80 25

1977. Birth Centenary of Pastor Fritz von Bodelschwingh (pioneer of welfare work for the disabled).
1833 **614** 50pf. multicoloured . . . 85 20

615 Golden Hat

1977. Archaeological Heritage. Multicoloured.
1834 30pf. Type **615** 45 25
1835 120pf. Gilt helmet . . . . . 1·80 1·10
1836 200pf. Bronze centaur head 2·50 2·00

616 Operator and Switchboard **617** 19th-century Posthouse Sign, Hamburg

1977. Centenary of Telephone in Germany.
1837 **616** 50pf. multicoloured . . . 1·20 25

1977. Stamp Day.
1838 **617** 10pf. multicoloured . . . 50 15

1977. Humanitarian Relief Funds. Meadow Flowers. As T **576**. Multicoloured.
1839 30pf.+15pf. Caraway . . . 45 40
1840 40pf.+20pf. Dandelion . . . 55 45
1841 50pf.+25pf. Red clover . . . 70 60
1842 70pf.+35pf. Meadow sage 1·40 1·20

618 Travelling Surgeon **619** Wilhelm Hauff

1977. 250th Death Anniv of Dr. Johann Andreas Eisenbarth.
1843 **618** 50pf. multicoloured . . . 85 20

1977. 150th Death Anniv of Wilhelm Hauff (poet and novelist).
1844 **619** 40pf. multicoloured . . . 55 20

620 "King presenting Gift" (stained glass window, Basilica of St. Gereon, Cologne)

1977. Christmas. Sheet 70 × 105 mm.
MS1845 **620** 50pf.+25pf. multicoloured . . . . 1·00 90

621 Book Cover Designs **622** Refugees

1978. Birth Centenary of Rudolph Alexander Schroder (writer).
1846 **621** 50pf. multicoloured . . . 75 20

1978. 20th Anniv of Friedland Aid Society.
1847 **622** 50pf. multicoloured . . . 75 20

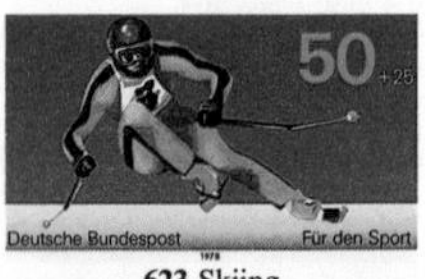

623 Skiing

1978. Sport Promotion Fund. Multicoloured.
1848 50pf.+25pf. Type **623** . . . 1·50 1·30
1849 70pf.+35pf. Show jumping 3·00 2·75

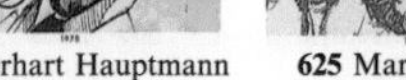

624 Gerhart Hauptmann **625** Martin Buber

1978. German Winners of Nobel Prize for Literature. Multicoloured.
1850 30pf. Type **624** 35 20
1851 50pf. Hermann Hesse . . . 55 40
1852 70pf. Thomas Mann 85 60
MS1853 120 × 70 mm. Nos. 1850/2 2·20 1·40

1978. Birth Centenary of Martin Buber (religious philosopher).
1854 **625** 50pf. multicoloured . . . 75 20

626 Museum Tower and Cupola

627 Wilhelmine Reichart's Balloon, Munich October Festival, 1820

1978. 75th Anniv of German Scientific and Technical Museum, Munich.
1855 **626** 50pf. black, yellow & red . . . 75 20

1978. Youth Welfare. Aviation History (1st series). Multicoloured.
1856 30pf.+15pf. Type **627** . . . 65 60
1857 40pf.+20pf. Airship LZ-1, 1900 . . . . 85 75
1858 50pf.+25pf. Bleriot XI monoplane, 1909 . . . . 1·10 90
1859 70pf.+35pf. Hans Grade's monoplane, 1909 . . . . 1·40 1·20
See also Nos. 1886/9 and 1918/21.

628 Old Town Hall, Bamberg

1978. Europa. Multicoloured.
1860 40pf. Type **628** 65 20
1861 50pf. Old Town Hall, Regensburg 25 20
1862 70pf. Old Town Hall, Esslingen am Neckar . . 1·40 75

629 Piper and Children

1978. Pied Piper of Hamelin.
1863 **629** 50pf. multicoloured . . . 1·00 20

630 Janusz Korczak

631 Fossil Bat

1978. Birth Centenary of Janusz Korczak (educational reformer).
1864 **630** 90pf. multicoloured . . . 1·20 50

1978. Archaeological Heritage, Fossils. Mult.
1865 80pf. Type **631** . . . . . . 1·80 1·50
1866 200pf. Horse ("eohippus") skeleton . . . . 2·10 1·70

632 Parliament Building, Bonn

1978. 65th Interparliamentary Union Conference, Bonn.
1867 **632** 70pf. multicoloured . . . 1·20 30

633 Rose Window, Freiburg Minster

634 Silhouette

1978. 85th Conference of German Catholics, Freiburg.
1868 **633** 40pf. multicoloured . . . 50 20

1978. Birth Bicent of Clemens Brentano (poet).
1869 **634** 30pf. multicoloured . . . 45 20

635 Text

1978. 25th Anniv of European Convention for the Protection of Human Rights.
1870 **635** 50pf. multicoloured . . . 1·00 20

636 Baden Post-house Sign

638 "Christ Child" (stained glass window, Frauenkirche, Munich)

637 "Easter at the Walchensee" (Lovis Corinth)

1978. Stamp Day and World Philatelic Movement. Multicoloured.
1871 40pf. Type **636** 50 25
1872 50pf. 1850 3pf. stamp of Saxony 50 25

1978. Humanitarian Relief Funds. Woodland Flowers. As T **576**. Multicoloured.
1873 30pf.+15pf. Arum 45 40
1874 40pf.+20pf. Weasel-snout . . 65 45
1875 50pf.+25pf. Turk's-cap lily 90 80
1876 70pf.+35pf. Liverwort . . . 1·20 1·10

1978. Impressionist Paintings. Multicoloured.
1877 50pf. Type **637** 70 45
1878 70pf. "Horseman on the Shore turning Left" (Max Liebermann) (vert) . . . 1·20 70
1879 120pf. "Lady with a Cat" (Max Slevogt) (vert) . . . 1·80 1·50

1978. Christmas. Sheet 65 × 93 mm.
MS1880 **638** 50pf.+25pf. multicoloured 90 85

639 Child

1979. International Year of the Child.
1881 **639** 60pf. multicoloured . . . 70 40

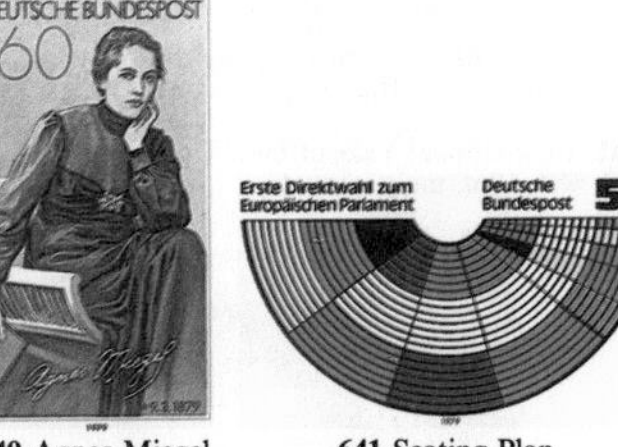

640 Agnes Miegel

641 Seating Plan

1979. Birth Cent of Agnes Miegel (poet).
1882 **640** 60pf. multicoloured . . . 80 20

1979. First Direct Elections to European Parliament.
1883 **641** 50pf. multicoloured . . . 1·10 20

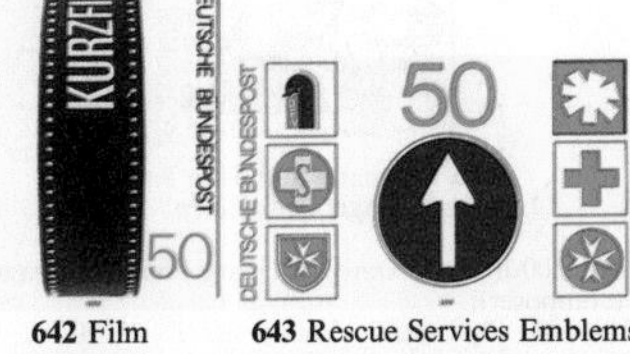

642 Film

643 Rescue Services Emblems

1979. 25th West German Short Film Festival.
1884 **642** 50pf. black and turquoise . . . . . . 1·00 20

1979. Rescue Services on the Road.
1885 **643** 50pf. multicoloured . . . 1·00 20

1979. Youth Welfare. History of Aviation (2nd series). As T **627**. Multicoloured.
1886 40pf.+20pf. Dornier Do-J Wal flying boat, 1922 . . 65 55
1887 50pf.+25pf. Heinkel He 70 Blitz, 1932 . . . . 90 75
1888 60pf.+30pf. Junkers W.33 "Bremen", 1928 . . . . . 1·10 85
1889 90pf.+45pf. Focke Achgelis Fa 61 helicopter, 1936 . . 1·60 1·30

644 Handball

1979. Sport Promotion Fund. Multicoloured.
1890 60pf.+30pf. Type **644** . . . 1·10 95
1891 90pf.+45pf. Canoeing . . . 1·60 1·30

645 Telegraph Office, 1863

646 Anne Frank

1979. Europa. Multicoloured.
1892 50pf. Type **645** 70 20
1893 60pf. Post Office counter, 1854 . . . . 1·00 20

1979. 50th Birth Anniv of Anne Frank (concentration camp victim and diary writer).
1894 **646** 60pf. black, grey and red 1·00 20

647 Werner von Siemens's Electric Railway, 1879

1979. International Transport Exhibition. Hamburg.
1895 **647** 60pf. multicoloured . . . 1·00 20

648 Hand operating Radio Dial

1979. World Administrative Radio Conference, Geneva.
1896 **648** 60f. multicoloured . . . 1·00 20

649 "Moses receiving the Tablets of the Law" (woodcut, Cranach the Elder)

650 Cross and Orb

1979. 450th Anniv of Publication of Martin Luther's Catechisms.
1897 **649** 50pf. black and green . . 1·20 20

1979. Pilgrimage to Aachen.
1898 **650** 50pf. multicoloured . . . 75 20

651 Hildegard von Bingen

1979. 800th Death Anniv of Hildegard von Bingen (writer and mystic).
1899 **651** 110pf. multicoloured . . 1·20 60

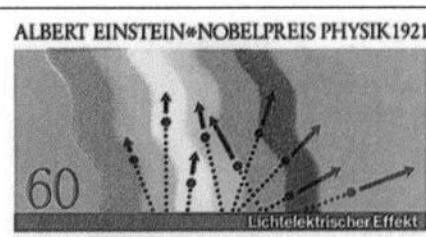

652 Photo-electric Effect

1979. Birth Centenaries of Nobel Prize Winners. Multicoloured.
1900 60pf. Type **652** (Albert Einstein, Physics, 1921) 1·00 35
1901 60pf. Splitting of uranium nucleus (Otto Hahn, Chemistry, 1944) . . . . 1·80 35
1902 60pf. Diffraction pattern of X-rays passed through crystal (Max von Laue, Physics, 1914) . . . . . 1·00 35

653 Pilot and Helmsman

654 Posthouse Sign, Altheim, Saar (German side), 1754

1979. 300th Anniv of 1st Pilotage Regulations.
1903 **653** 60pf. brown and claret 75 20

1979. Stamp Day.
1904 **654** 60pf.+30pf. mult . . . . 1·20 1·10

1979. Humanitarian Relief Funds. Woodland Flowers and Fruit. As T **576**. Multicoloured.
1905 40pf.+20pf. Red beech (horiz) 55 45
1906 50pf.+25pf. English oak (horiz) 75 60
1907 60pf.+30pf. Hawthorn (horiz) 85 70
1908 90pf.+45pf. Mountain pine (horiz) . . . . 1·40 1·30

656 "Bird Garden"

1979. Birth Cent of Paul Klee (artist).
1909 **656** 90pf. multicoloured . . . 1·20 60

657 Faust and Mephistopheles

658 Lightbulb

1979. Doctor Johannes Faust.
1910 **657** 60pf. multicoloured . . . 1·20 20

1979. "Save Energy".
1911 **658** 40pf. multicoloured . . . 65 20

659 "Nativity" (Altenberg medieval manuscript)

1979. Christmas.
1912 **659** 60pf.+30pf. mult . . . . 1·20 1·00

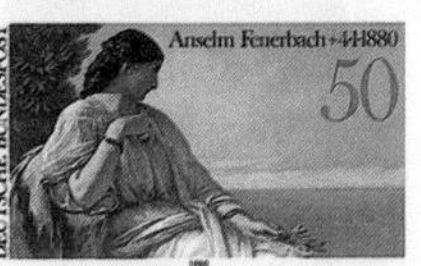

660 "Iphigenia"

1980. Death Centenary of Anselm Feuerbach (artist).
1913 **660** 50pf. multicoloured . . . 1·00 20

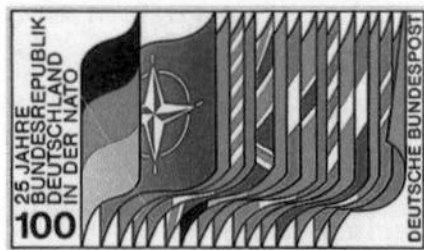

661 Flags of NATO Members

1980. 25th Anniv of NATO Membership.
1914 **661** 100pf. multicoloured . . . 1·80 70

662 Town Hall, St. Mary's Church, and St Peter's Cathedral

1980. 1200th Anniv of Osnabruck Town and Bishopric.
1915 **662** 60pf. multicoloured . . . 1·00 20

663 "Gotz von Berlichingen" (glass picture)

1980. 500th Birth Anniv of Gotz von Berlichingen (Frankish knight).
1916 **663** 60pf. multicoloured . . . 1·00 20

664 Texts from 1880 and 1980 Duden Dictionaries

1980. Centenary of Konrad Duden's 1st Dictionary.
1917 **664** 60pf. multicoloured . . . 90 20

1980. Youth Welfare. Aviation History (3rd series). As T **627**. Multicoloured.
1918 40pf.+20pf. Phoenix FS 24 glider, 1957 . . . . . . 45 40
1919 50pf.+25pf. Lockheed L.1049G Super Constellation 75 60
1920 60pf.+30pf. Airbus Industrie A300B2, 1972 . . . . . 1·10 85
1921 90pf.+45pf. Boeing 747-100, 1969 . . . . 1·70 1·30
No. 1919 is incorrectly dated "1950".

665 Emblems of Association Members

1980. Centenary of German Association of Welfare Societies.
1922 **665** 60pf. blue, red and black 1·00 20

666 "Frederick I with his sons" (Welf Chronicle)

1980. 800th Anniv of Imperial Diet of Gelnhausen.
1923 **666** 60pf. multicoloured . . . 1·20 20

667 Football

1980. Sport Promotion Fund. Multicoloured.
1924 50pf.+25pf. Type **667** . . . 65 50
1925 60pf.+30pf. Dressage . . . 85 65
1926 90pf.+45pf. Skiing . . . . . 1·60 1·40

668 Albertus Magnus (scholar)

669 Reading the Augsburg Confession (engraving, G Kohler)

1980. Europa. Multicoloured.
1927 50pf. Type **668** . . . . . . 1·00 20
1928 60pf. Gottfried Leibniz (philosopher) . . . . . . 1·10 20

1980. 450th Anniv of Augsburg Confession.
1929 **669** 50pf. black, yellow & grn 75 20

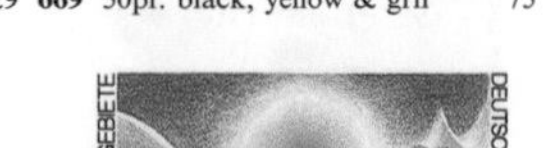

670 Nature Reserve

1980. Nature Conservation.
1930 **670** 40pf. multicoloured . . . 1·20 20

671 Ear and Oscillogram Pulses

1980. International Congress for the Training and Education of the Hard of Hearing, Hamburg.
1931 **671** 90pf. multicoloured . . . 1·20 35

672 First Book of Daily Bible Readings, 1731

673 St. Benedict

1980. 250th Anniv of Moravian Brethren's Book of Daily Bible Readings.
1932 **672** 50pf. multicoloured . . . 90 20

1980. 1500th Birth Anniv of St. Benedict of Nursia (founder of Benedictine Order).
1933 **673** 50pf. multicoloured . . . 75 20

674 Helping Hand

675 Marie von Ebner-Eschenbach

1980. Birth Bicentenary of Friedrich Joseph Haass (philanthropist).
1934 **674** 60pf. multicoloured . . . 90 20

1980. 150th Birth Anniv of Marie von Ebner-Eschenbach (novelist).
1935 **675** 60pf. buff, black & orge 90 20

676 Rigging

1980. Birth Centenary of Johan Kinau ("Gorch Fock") (poet).
1936 **676** 60pf. multicoloured . . . 1·80 20

677 Positioning Keystone of South Tower Finial (engraving)

678 "Ceratocephalus falcatus"

1980. Centenary of Completion of Cologne Cathedral.
1937 **677** 60pf. multicoloured . . . 1·80 25

1980. Humanitarian Relief Funds. Endangered Wildflowers. Multicoloured.
1938 40pf.+20pf. Type **678** . . . 65 60
1939 50pf.+25pf. Yellow Vetchling 85 75
1940 60pf.+30pf. Corn Cockle . . 90 90
1941 90pf.+45pf. Tassel Hyacinth 1·60 1·40
See also Nos. 1972/5.

679 Wine-making (woodcuts)

1980. Bimillenary of Vine Growing in Central Europe.
1942 **679** 50pf. multicoloured . . . 90 20

680 Posthouse Sign, Altheim, Saar, 1754 (French side)

681 "Nativity" (Altomunster manuscript)

1980. 49th International Philatelic Federation Congress, Essen.
1943 **680** 60pf.+30pf. mult 85 75

1980. Christmas.
1944 **681** 60pf.+30pf. mult . . . . 1·20 95

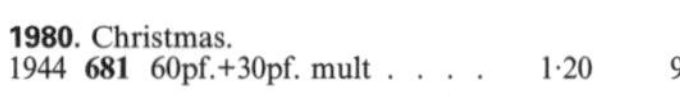

682 "Landscape with Two Fir Trees" (etching)

1980. 500th Birth Anniv of Albrecht Altdorfer (painter, engraver and architect).
1945 **682** 40pf. lt brown, blk & brn 65 20

683 Elly Heuss-Knapp

1981. Birth Centenary of Elly Heuss-Knapp (social reformer).
1946 **683** 60pf. multicoloured . . . 90 20

684 Society accepting the Handicapped

1981. International Year of Disabled Persons.
1947 **684** 60pf. multicoloured . . . 1·00 20

685 Old Town Houses

1981. European Campaign for Urban Renaissance.
1948 **685** 60pf. multicoloured . . . 1·00 20

686 Telemann and Title Page of "Singet dem Herrn"

1981. 300th Birth Anniv of Georg Philipp Telemann (composer).
1949 **686** 60pf. multicoloured . . . 90 25

687 Visiting a Foreign Family

1981. Integration of Guest Worker Families.
1950 **687** 50pf. multicoloured . . . 90 20

688 Polluted Butterfly, Fish and Plant

1981. Preservation of the Environment.
1951 **688** 60pf. multicoloured . . . 1·20 25

689 Patent Office Emblem and Scientific Signs

1981. Establishment of European Patent Office, Munich.
1952 **689** 60pf. grey, red and black 90 20

690 Scintigram showing Distribution of Radioactive Isotope

691 Borda Circle, 1800

1981. Cancer Prevention through Medical Check-ups.
1953 **690** 40pf. multicoloured . . . 75 20

1981. Youth Welfare. Optical Instruments. Multicoloured.
1954 40pf.+20pf. Type **691** . . . 65 50
1955 50pf.+25pf. Reflecting telescope, 1770 . . . . . 1·10 85
1956 60pf.+30pf. Binocular microscope, 1860 . . . . 1·10 85
1957 90pf.+45pf. Octant, 1775 . . 1·60 1·30

692 Rowing

1981. Sport Promotion Fund. Multicoloured.
1958 60pf.+30pf. Type **692** . . . 1·10 80
1959 90pf.+45pf. Gliding . . . . 1·70 1·40

693 South German Dancers

1981. Europa. Multicoloured.
1960 50pf. Type **693** 75 20
1961 60pf. North German dancers 90 20

694 Convention Cross

1981. 19th German Protestant Convention, Hamburg.
1962 **694** 50pf. multicoloured . . . 90 20

695 Group from Crucifixion Altar

696 Georg von Neumayer Antarctic Research Station

1981. 450th Death Anniv of Tilman Riemenschneider (woodcarver).
1963 **695** 60pf. multicoloured . . . 90 25

1981. Polar Research.
1964 **696** 110pf. multicoloured . . 1·90 50

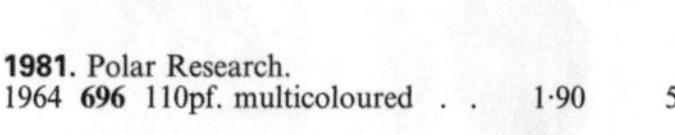
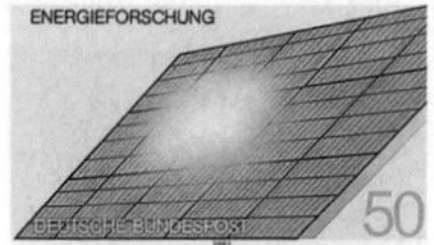
697 Solar Generator

1981. Energy Research.
1965 **697** 50pf. multicoloured . . . 1·00 20

698 Hand holding Baby Black Coot

700 Wilhelm Raabe

699 Arms of different Races forming Square

1981. Animal Protection.
1966 **698** 60pf. multicoloured . . . 1·20 20

1981. Co-operation with Developing Countries.
1967 **699** 90pf. multicoloured . . . 1·30 50

1981. 150th Birth Anniv of Wilhelm Raabe (poet).
1968 **700** 50pf. light green & green 90 20

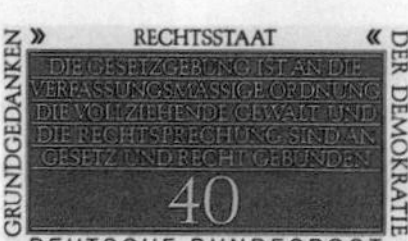
701 Constitutional Freedom

1981. Fundamental Concepts of Democracy. Article 20 of the Basic Law. Multicoloured.
1969 40pf. Type **701** 90 20
1970 50pf. Separation of Powers 90 20
1971 60pf. Sovereignty of the People . . . . 1·40 25

1981. Humanitarian Relief Funds. Endangered Wildflowers. As T **678**. Multicoloured.
1972 40pf.+20pf. Water nut . . . 55 45
1973 50pf.+25pf. Floating Heart 75 60
1974 60pf.+30pf. Water gilly-flower 90 85
1975 90pf.+45pf. Water lobelia 1·80 1·50

702 Posthouse Scene c. 1855

703 "Nativity" (glass painting)

1981. Stamp Day.
1976 **702** 60pf. multicoloured . . . 1·20 25

1981. Christmas.
1977 **703** 60pf.+30pf. mult . . . . 1·00 90

704 St. Elisabeth

705 Clausewitz (after W. Wach)

1981. 750th Death Anniv of St. Elisabeth of Thuringia.
1978 **704** 50pf. multicoloured . . . 1·00 20

1981. 150th Death Anniv of General Carl von Clausewitz (military writer).
1979 **705** 60pf. multicoloured . . . 1·00 25

706 People forming Figure "100"

707 Map of Antarctica

1981. Cent of Social Insurance.
1980 **706** 60pf. multicoloured . . . 90 20

1981. 20th Anniv of Antarctic Treaty.
1981 **707** 100pf. blue, lt blue & blk 1·50 45

708 Pot with Lid

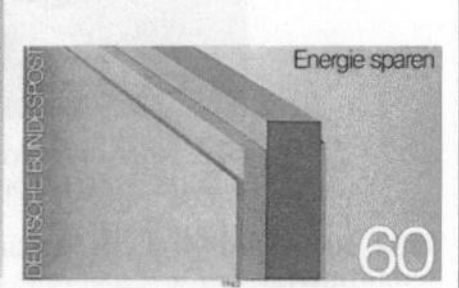
709 Insulated Wall

1982. 300th Birth Anniv of Johann Friedrich Bottger (founder of Meissen China Works).
1982 **708** 60pf. multicoloured . . . 90 20

1982. Energy Conservation.
1983 **709** 60pf. multicoloured . . . 90 20

710 Silhouette (Dora Brandenburg-Polster)

711 Goethe (after Georg Melchior Kraus)

1982. "The Town Band of Bremen" (German fairy tale).
1984 **710** 40pf. black and red . . . 75 20

1982. 150th Death Anniv of Johann Wolfgang von Goethe (writer).
1985 **711** 60pf. multicoloured . . . 2·40 25

712 Robert Koch

1982. Centenary of Discovery of Tubercle Bacillus.
1986 **712** 50pf. multicoloured . . . 2·75 25

713 Benz Patent "Motorwagen", 1886

1982. Youth Welfare. Motor Cars. Mult.
1987 40pf.+20pf. Type **713** . . . 65 60
1988 50pf.+25pf. Mercedes "Tourenwagen", 1913 . . 90 55
1989 60pf.+30pf. Hannomag "Kommissbrot", 1925 . . 1·20 85
1990 90pf.+45pf. Opel "Olympia", 1937 . . . . 1·80 1·50

714 Jogging

1982. Sport Promotion Fund. Multicoloured.
1991 60pf.+30pf. Type **714** . . . 1·10 90
1992 90pf.+45pf. Disabled archers 1·70 1·40

715 "Good Helene"

1982. 150th Birth Anniv of Wilhelm Busch (writer and illustrator).
1993 **715** 50pf. black, green & yell 1·20 20

716 "Procession to Hambach Castle, 1832" (wood engraving)

1982. Europa.
1994 **716** 50pf. black, yellow & red 1·20 20
1995 – 60pf. multicoloured . . . 1·80 25
DESIGN: 60pf. Excerpt from Treaty of Rome (instituting European Economic Community), 1957, and flags.

717 Racing Yachts

1982. Centenary of Kiel Regatta Week.
1996 **717** 60pf. multicoloured . . . 1·20 25

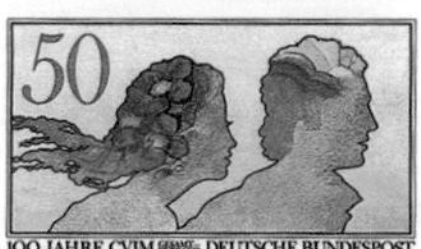
718 Young Couple

1982. Centenary of Young Men's Christian Association in Germany.
1997 **718** 50pf. multicoloured . . . 85 20

719 Polluted Sea

1982. "Prevent the Pollution of the Sea".
1998 **719** 120pf. multicoloured . . 2·50 45

720 Battered Licence Plate

1982. "Don't Drink and Drive".
1999 **720** 80pf. multicoloured . . . 1·20 30

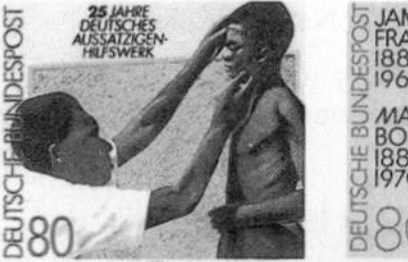
721 Doctor examining Leper

722 Franck and Born

1982. 25th Anniv of German Lepers' Welfare Organization.
2000 **721** 80pf. multicoloured . . . 1·20 30

1982. Birth Centenaries of James Franck and Max Born (physicists and Nobel Prize Winners).
2001 **722** 80pf. grey, black and red 1·30 30

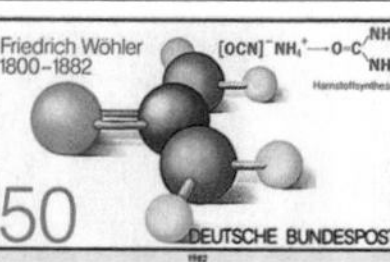
723 Atomic Model of Urea

1982. Death Centenary of Friedrich Wohler (chemist).
2002 **723** 50pf. multicoloured . . . 90 25

724 "St. Francis preaching to the Birds" (fresco by Giotto)

725 Hybrid Tea Rose

1982. 87th German Catholics' Congress, Dusseldorf and 800th Birth Anniv of St. Francis of Assisi.
2003 **724** 60pf. multicoloured . . . 85 25

1982. Humanitarian Relief Funds. Roses. Multicoloured.
2004 50pf.+20pf. Type **725** . . . 65 55
2005 60pf.+30pf. Floribunda . . 90 70
2006 80pf.+40pf. Bourbon . . . 1·30 1·20
2007 120pf.+60pf. Polyantha hybrid . . . . 1·70 1·60

726 Letters on Desk

1982. Stamp Day.
2008 **726** 80pf. multicoloured . . . 1·40 30

727 Gregorian Calendar by Johannes Rasch, 1586

728 Theodor Heuss

1982. 400th Anniv of Gregorian Calendar.
2009 **727** 60pf. multicoloured . . . 90 25

1982. Presidents of the Federal Republic. Sheet 130 × 100 mm containing T **728** and similar horiz designs. Multicoloured.
MS2010 80pf. Type **728**; 80pf. Heinrich Lubke; 80pf. Gustav Heinemann; 80pf. Walter Scheel; 80pf. Karl Carstens . . . . . 5·50 4·75

729 "Nativity" (detail from St. Peter Altar by Master Bertram)

730 Edith Stein

1982. Christmas.
2011 **729** 80pf.+40pf. mult . . . . 1·40 1·00

1983. 40th Death Anniv (1982) of Edith Stein (philosopher).
2012 **730** 80pf. lt grey, grey & blk 1·80 30

731 White Rose and Barbed Wire

1983. Persecution and Resistance 1933–45.
2013 **731** 80pf. multicoloured . . . 1·80 30

732 "Light Space Modulator" (Laszlo Moholy-Nagy)

1983. Birth Cent of Walter Gropius (founder of Bauhaus School of Art, Weimar). Bauhaus Art. Multicoloured.
2014 50pf. Type **732** 90 20
2015 60pf. "Sanctuary" (lithograph by Josef Albers) . . . . 1·10 30
2016 80pf. Skylights from Bauhaus Archives, Berlin (Walter Gropius) . . . . 1·40 35

733 Federahannes (Rottweil carnival figure)

1983. Carnival.
2017 **733** 60pf. multicoloured . . . 1·20 25

734 Daimler-Maybach, 1885

1983. Youth Welfare. Motor Cycles. Mult.
2018 50pf.+20pf. Type **734** . . . 65 60
2019 60pf.+30pf. N.S.U., 1901 . . 90 75
2020 80pf.+40pf. Megola "Sport", 1922 . . . . . 1·40 1·30
2021 120pf.+60pf. B.M.W. world record holder, 1936 . . . 2·30 1·90

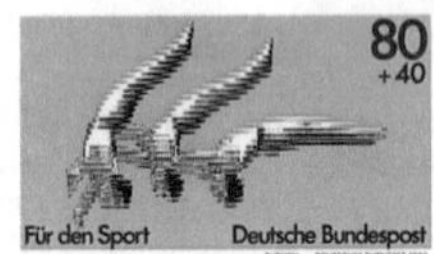
735 Gymnastics (German Festival, Frankfurt am Main)

1983. Sports Promotion Fund. Multicoloured.
2022 80pf.+40pf. Type **735** . . . 1·30 1·10
2023 120pf.+60pf. Modern pentathlon (world championships, Warendorf) . . . . 2·10 1·70

736 Stylized Flower

1983. 4th International Horticultural Show. Munich.
2024 **736** 60pf. multicoloured . . . 1·00 30

737 Modern Type and Gutenberg Letters

1983. Europa. Multicoloured.
2025 60pf. Type **737** . . . . . . 2·50 30
2026 80pf. Resonant circuit and electric flux lines . . . . 1·70 25

738 Johannes Brahms

1983. 150th Birth Anniv of Johannes Brahms (composer).
2027 **738** 80pf. multicoloured . . . 1·80 25

739 Kafka's Signature and Teyn Church, Prague

1983. Birth Cent of Franz Kafka (writer).
2028 **739** 80pf. multicoloured . . . 1·50 25

740 Brewing (frontispiece of 1677 treatise)

1983. 450th Anniv of Beer Purity Law.
2029 **740** 80pf. multicoloured . . . 1·80 25

741 "Concord"

1983. 300th Anniv of First German Settlers in America.
2030 **741** 80pf. multicoloured . . . 1·60 25

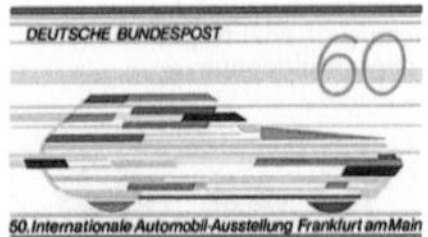
742 Children crossing Road

1983. Children and Road Traffic.
2031 **742** 80pf. multicoloured . . . 1·50 25

743 Flags forming Car

1983. 50th International Motor Show, Frankfurt-on-Main.
2032 **743** 60pf. multicoloured . . . 90 20

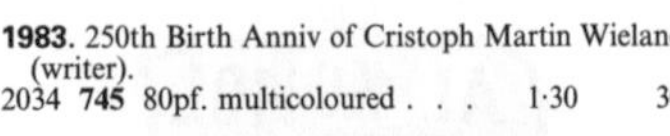
744 Warburg (after Oberland) 745 Wieland (after G. B. Bosio)

1983. Birth Centenary of Otto Warburg. (physiologist and chemist).
2033 **744** 50pf. multicoloured . . . 90 20

1983. 250th Birth Anniv of Cristoph Martin Wieland (writer).
2034 **745** 80pf. multicoloured . . . 1·30 30

746 Rosette in National Colours

1983. 10th Anniv of U.N. Membership.
2035 **746** 80pf. multicoloured . . . 1·90 30

747 "Das Rauhe Haus" and Children

1983. 150th Anniv of "Das Rauhe Haus" (children's home, Hamburg).
2036 **747** 80pf. multicoloured . . . 1·30 25

748 Surveying Maps

1983. International Geodesy and Geophysics Union General Assembly, Hamburg.
2037 **748** 120pf. multicoloured . . 1·80 60

749 Swiss Androsace 750 Horseman with Posthorn

1983. Humanitarian Relief Funds. Endangered Alpine Flowers. Multicoloured.
2038 50pf.+20pf. Type **749** . . . 75 60
2039 60pf.+30pf. Krain groundsel 1·00 80
2040 80pf.+40pf. Fleischer's willow herb . . . . . . 1·40 1·20
2041 120pf.+60pf. Alpine sow-thistle . . . . 2·30 1·90

1983. Stamp Day.
2042 **750** 80pf. multicoloured . . . 1·50 30

751 Luther (engraving by G. Konig after Cranach)

1983. 500th Birth Anniv of Martin Luther (Protestant reformer).
2043 **751** 80pf. multicoloured . . . 2·75 25

752 Interwoven National Colours

1983. Federation, Lander and Communities Co-operation.
2044 **752** 80pf. multicoloured . . . 1·80 25

753 Customs Stamps

1983. 150th Anniv of German Customs Union.
2045 **753** 60pf. multicoloured . . . 1·90 20

754 Epiphany Carol Singers 756 Reis and Telephone Apparatus

755 Black Gate, Trier

1983. Christmas.
2046 **754** 80pf.+40pf. mult . . . . . 1·80 1·30

1984. 2000th Anniv of Trier.
2047 **755** 80pf. multicoloured . . . 2·10 30

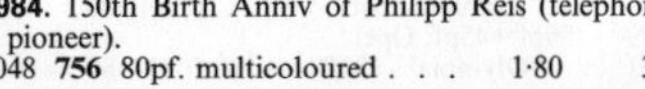

1984. 150th Birth Anniv of Philipp Reis (telephone pioneer).
2048 **756** 80pf. multicoloured . . . 1·80 30

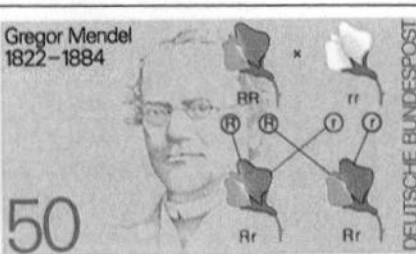
757 Mendel and Genetic Diagram

1984. Death Cent of Gregor Mendel (geneticist).
2049 **757** 50pf. multicoloured . . . 1·20 25

758 Town Hall 760 Bee-eating Beetle

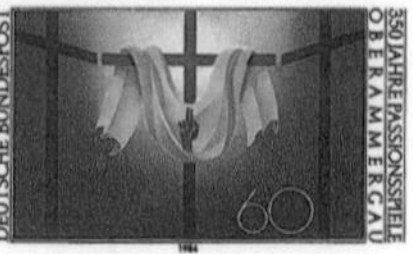
759 Cloth draped on Cross

1984. 500th Anniv of Michelstadt Town Hall.
2050 **758** 60pf. multicoloured . . . 1·00 25

1984. 350th Anniv of Oberammergau Passion Play.
2051 **759** 60pf. multicoloured . . . 1·00 25

1984. Youth Welfare. Pollinating Insects. Multicoloured.
2052 50pf.+20pf. Type **760** . . . 65 60
2053 60pf.+30pf. Red admiral . . 1·30 1·20
2054 80pf.+40pf. Honey bee . . . 1·60 1·30
2055 120pf.+60pf. "Chrysotoxum festivium" (hover fly) . . 2·40 2·10

761 Throwing the Discus

1984. Sport Promotion Fund. Multicoloured.
2056 60pf.+30pf. Type **761** . . . 1·10 90
2057 80pf.+40pf. Rhythmic gymnastics . . . . 1·50 1·30
2058 120pf.+60pf. Windsurfing 3·00 2·50

762 Parliament Emblem 763 Bridge

1984. 2nd Direct Elections to European Parliament.
2059 **762** 80pf. yellow, blue and light blue . . . . . . 1·90 30

1984. Europa. 25th Anniv of European Post and Telecommunications Conference.
2060 **763** 60pf. blue, lt blue & blk 1·30 30
2061 80pf. purple, red & black 1·40 30

764 St. Norbert (sculpture) 765 Nursery Rhyme Illustration

1984. 850th Death Anniv of St. Norbert von Xanten.
2062 **764** 80pf. green & deep green 1·30 30

1984. Death Centenary of Ludwig Richter (illustrator).
2063 **765** 60pf. black and brown 90 25

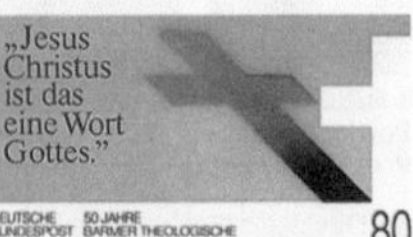
766 Cross and Shadow

1984. 50th Anniv of Protestant Churches' Barmen Theological Declaration.
2064 **766** 80pf. multicoloured . . . 1·40 30

767 Letter sorting, 1800s

1984. 19th Universal Postal Union Congress, Hamburg. Sheet 138 × 104 mm containing T **767** and similar square designs.
MS2065 60pf. brown and black; 80pf. multicoloured; 120pf. green, black and grey . . . . 3·75 3·25
DESIGNS: 80pf. Modern automatic letter sorting machine scanning device; 120pf. Heinrich von Stephan (founder of U.P.U.).

768 Groom leading Horse (detail from tomb of Oclatius) **769** Bessel

1984. 2000th Anniv of Neuss.
2066 **768** 80pf. multicoloured . . . 1·30 30

1984. Birth Bicentenary of Friedrich Wilhelm Bessel (astronomer and mathematician).
2067 **769** 80pf. grey, black and red 1·30 30

770 Eugenio Pacelli (Pope Pius XII)

1984. 88th German Catholics' Congress, Munich.
2068 **770** 60pf. multicoloured . . . 1·20 30

771 Town Hall **772** Medieval Document and Visual Display Unit

1984. 750th Anniv of Duderstadt Town Hall.
2069 **771** 60pf. multicoloured . . . 1·00 25

1984. 10th International Archives Congress, Bonn.
2070 **772** 70pf. multicoloured . . . 1·40 30

773 Knoop Lock

1984. Bicent of Schleswig-Holstein Canal.
2071 **773** 80pf. multicoloured . . . 1·40 30

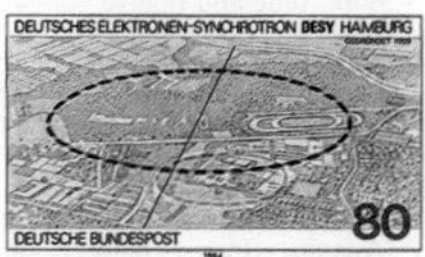
774 Research Centre and Storage Rings

1984. 25th Anniv of German Electron Synchrotron (physics research centre), Hamburg–Bahrenfeld.
2072 **774** 80pf. multicoloured . . . 1·80 30

775 "Aceras anthropophorum"

1984. Humanitarian Relief Funds. Orchids. Multicoloured.
2073 50pf.+20pf. Type **775** . . 85 65
2074 60pf.+30pf. "Orchis ustulata" 85 65
2075 80pf.+40pf. "Limodorum abortivum" . . . . 1·30 1·20
2076 120pf.+60pf. "Dactylorhiza sambucina" . . . . . . 2·50 2·30

776 Taxis Posthouse, Augsburg

1984. Stamp Day.
2077 **776** 80pf. multicoloured . . . 2·10 30

777 Burning Match

1984. Anti-smoking Campaign.
2078 **777** 60pf. multicoloured . . . 1·00 25

778 Male and Female Symbols

1984. Equal Rights for Men and Women.
2079 **778** 80pf. black, mauve & bl 1·50 30

779 Ballot Slip

1984. For Peace and Understanding.
2080 **779** 80pf. grey, black & blue 1·30 30

780 St. Martin giving Cloak to Beggar

1984. Christmas.
2081 **780** 80pf.+40pf. mult . . . . 1·50 1·30

781 Emperor Augustus (bust), Buildings and Arms

1985. 2000th Anniv of Augsburg.
2082 **781** 80pf. multicoloured . . . 1·70 30

782 Spener (engraving by Bartholome Kilian after Johann Georg Wagner)

1985. 350th Birth Anniv of Philipp Jakob Spener (church reformer).
2083 **782** 80pf. black and green . . 1·30 30

783 Grimm Brothers (engraving by Lazarus Sichling)

1985. Birth Bicentenaries of Grimm Brothers (folklorists) and 7th International Union for German Linguistics and Literature Congress, Gottingen.
2084 **783** 80pf. black, grey and red 1·90 30

784 Romano Guardini

1985. Birth Centenary of Romano Guardini (theologian).
2085 **784** 80pf. multicoloured . . . 1·30 30

785 Verden

1985. Millenary of Market and Coinage Rights in Verden.
2086 **785** 60pf. multicoloured . . . 1·80 30

786 Flags and German–Danish Border

1985. 30th Anniv of Bonn–Copenhagen Declarations.
2087 **786** 80pf. multicoloured . . . 1·80 30

787 Bowling

1985. Sport Promotion Fund. Multicoloured.
2088 80pf.+40pf. Type **787** (cent. of German Nine-pin Bowling Association) . . 1·70 1·40
2089 120pf.+60pf. Kayak (world rapid-river and slalom canoeing championships) 2·10 2·00

788 Kisch **789** "Hebel and the Margravine"

1985. Birth Centenary of Egon Erwin Kisch (journalist).
2090 **788** 60pf. multicoloured . . . 1·20 30

1985. 225th Birth Anniv of Johann Peter Hebel (poet).
2091 **789** 80pf. multicoloured . . . 1·30 30

790 Draisienne Bicycle, 1817 **791** Handel

1985. Youth Welfare International Youth Year. Cycles. Multicoloured.
2092 50pf.+20pf. Type **790** . . . 90 80
2093 60pf.+30pf. NSU Germania "ordinary", 1866 . . . . 1·10 1·00
2094 80pf.+40pf. Cross-frame low bicycle, 1887 . . . . 1·50 1·30
2095 120pf.+60pf. Adler tricycle, 1888 . . . . 3·00 2·50

1985. Europa. Composers' 300th Birth Anniversaries. Multicoloured.
2096 60pf. Type **791** . . . . . . 2·10 35
2097 80pf. Bach . . . . 2·30 35

792 Saint George's Cathedral **793** Capital (presbytery, "Wies" Church)

1985. 750th Anniv of Limburg Cathedral.
2098 **792** 60pf. multicoloured . . . 1·20 30

1985. 300th Birth Anniv of Dominikus Zimmermann (architect).
2099 **793** 70pf. multicoloured . . . 1·20 30

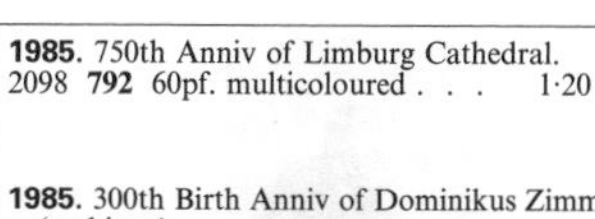
794 Josef Kentenich

1985. Birth Centenary of Father Josef Kentenich (founder of International Schonstatt (Catholic laymen's) Movement).
2100 **794** 80pf. multicoloured . . . 1·30 30

795 Clock and Forest

1985. Save the Forests.
2101 **795** 80pf. multicoloured . . . 1·80 30

796 Tug of War and Scouting Emblem

1985. 30th World Scouts Conference, Munich.
2102 **796** 60pf. multicoloured . . . 1·00 30

797 "Sunday Walk"

1985. Death Cent of Carl Spitzweg (artist).
2103 **797** 60pf. multicoloured . . . 1·60 30

798 Horses and Postilion

1985. "Mophila 1985" Stamp Exhibition, Hamburg. Multicoloured.
2104 60pf.+20pf. Type **798** . . . 2·30 2·00
2105 80pf.+20pf. Mail coach . . 2·30 2·00
Nos. 2104/5 were printed se-tenant, forming a composite design.

799 Stock Exchange

1985. 400th Anniv of Frankfurt Stock Exchange.
2106 **799** 80pf. black, red and grey 1·60 30

800 Flowers and Butterfly

1985. Humanitarian Relief Funds. Designs depict motifs from borders of medieval prayer book. Multicoloured.
2107 50pf.+20pf. Type **800** . . . 75 65
2108 60pf.+30pf. Flowers, bird and butterfly . . . . . 1·00 90
2109 80pf.+40pf. Flowers, berries and snail . . . . 1·40 1·10
2110 120pf.+60pf. Flowers, snail and butterfly . . . . . 2·30 2·10

801 Fritz Reuter

1985. 175th Death Anniv of Fritz Reuter (writer).
2111 **801** 80pf. black, grey and blue . . . . 2·00 30

802 "Inauguration of First German Railway" (Heim)

1985. 150th Anniv of German Railways and Birth Bicent. of Johannes Scharrer (joint founder).
2112 **802** 80pf. multicoloured . . . 2·00 30

803 Carpentry Joint in National Colours

805 "Nativity" (detail, High Altar, Freiburg)

804 Iron Cross and National Colours

1985. 40th Anniv of Integration of Refugees.
2113 **803** 80pf. multicoloured . . . 2·20 30

1985. 30th Anniv of Federal Armed Forces.
2114 **804** 80pf. red, black & yellow 2·50 30

1985. Christmas. 500th Birth Anniversary of Hans Baldung Grien (artist).
2115 **805** 80pf.+40pf. mult . . . . 1·60 1·40

806 Early and Modern Cars

1986. Centenary of Motor Car.
2116 **806** 80pf. multicoloured . . . 1·90 30

807 Town Buildings

1986. 1250th Anniv of Bad Hersfeld.
2117 **807** 60pf. multicoloured . . . 1·20 30

808 "Self-portrait"

1986. Birth Centenary of Oskar Kokoschka (artist and writer).
2118 **808** 80pf. black, grey and red 1·20 30

809 Comet and "Giotto" Space Probe

1986. Appearance of Halley's Comet.
2119 **809** 80pf. multicoloured . . . 1·90 30

810 Running

1986. Sport Promotion Fund. Multicoloured.
2120 80pf.+40pf. Type **810** (European Athletics Championships, Stuttgart) 1·80 1·50
2121 120pf.+55pf. Bobsleigh (World Championships, Konigsee) . . . . 2·75 2·40

811 Optician

1986. Youth Welfare. Trades (1st series). Multicoloured.
2122 50pf.+25pf. Type **811** . . . 1·10 95
2123 60pf.+30pf. Bricklayer . . . 1·30 1·10
2124 70pf.+35pf. Hairdresser . . 1·50 1·30
2125 80pf.+40pf. Baker . . . . . 2·30 1·90
See also Nos. 2179/82.

812 Walsrode Monastery

1986. Millenary of Walsrode.
2126 **812** 60pf. multicoloured . . . 1·20 30

813 Ludwig and Neuschwanstein Castle

1986. Death Centenary of King Ludwig II of Bavaria.
2127 **813** 60pf. multicoloured . . . 2·30 30

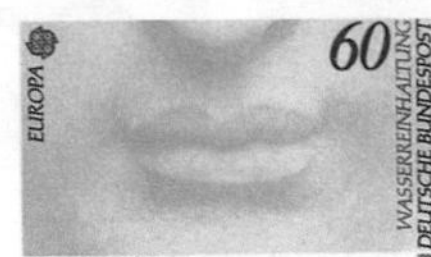

814 Mouth

1986. Europa. Details of "David" (sculpture) by Michelangelo. Multicoloured.
2128 60pf. Type **814** . . . . . . 1·50 30
2129 80pf. Nose . . . . 1·60 30

815 Karl Barth

817 Weber and Score of "Gloria"

816 Ribbons

1986. Birth Centenary of Karl Barth (theologian).
2130 **815** 80pf. black, red & purple 1·50 30

1986. Union of German Catholic Students' Societies 100th Assembly, Frankfurt am Main.
2131 **816** 80pf. multicoloured . . . 1·50 30

1986. Birth Bicentenary of Carl Maria von Weber (composer).
2132 **817** 80pf. brown, black & red 1·90 30

818 "TV-Sat" and Earth

1986. Launch of German "TV-Sat" and French "TDF-1" Broadcasting Satellites.
2133 **818** 80pf. multicoloured . . . 2·20 35

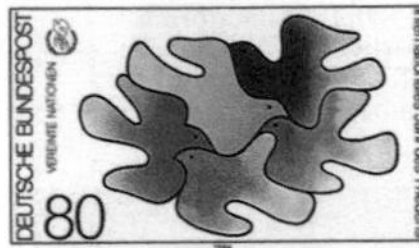

819 Doves

1986. International Peace Year.
2134 **819** 80pf. multicoloured . . . 1·80 30

820 Liszt

1986. Death Centenary of Franz Liszt (composer).
2135 **820** 80pf. blue and orange . . 1·60 30

821 Reichstag, Berlin

1986. Important Buildings in West German History. Sheet 100 × 130 mm containing T **821** and similar horiz designs. Multicoloured.
MS2136 80pf. Type **821**; 80pf. Koenig Museum, Bonn (venue of 1948–49 Parliamentary Council); 80pf. Bundeshaus, Bonn (parliamentary building) . . . 4·00 3·75

822 Pollution Damage of Stained Glass Window

1986. Protection of Monuments.
2137 **822** 80pf. multicoloured . . . 2·20 30

823 Frederick the Great (after Anton Graff)

824 Congress Card

1986. Death Bicentenary of Frederick the Great.
2138 **823** 80pf. multicoloured . . . 2·50 30

1986. Centenary of First German Skat Congress and 24th Congress, Cologne.
2139 **824** 80pf. multicoloured . . . 1·50 30

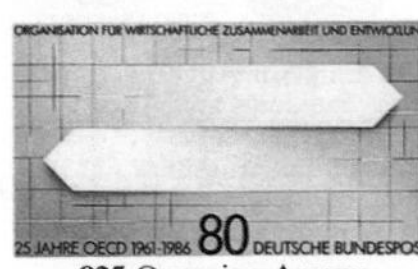

825 Opposing Arrows

1986. 25th Anniv of Organization for Economic Co-operation and Development.
2140 **825** 80pf. multicoloured . . . 1·60 30

826 Old University

1986. 600th Anniv of Heidelberg University.
2141 **826** 80pf. multicoloured . . . 1·80 30

827 Fan of Stamps behind Stagecoach

1986. 50th Anniv of Stamp Day.
2142 **827** 80pf. multicoloured . . . 1·60 30

828 Ornamental Flask, 300 A.D.

829 "Dance in Silence" from "Autumnal Dances"

1986. Humanitarian Relief Funds. Glassware. Multicoloured.
2143 50pf.+25pf. Type **828** . . . 85 75
2144 60pf.+30pf. Goblet with decorated stem, 1650 . . 1·10 95
2145 70pf.+35pf. Imperial Eagle tankard, 1662 . . . . . 1·30 1·20
2146 80pf.+40pf. Engraved goblet, 1720 . . . . . . 1·50 1·30

1986. Birth Centenary of Mary Wigman (dancer).
2147 **829** 70pf. multicoloured . . . 1·20 30

830 Cross over Map

1986. 25th Anniv of Adveniat (Advent collection for Latin America).
2148 **830** 80pf. green, blue & blk 1·00 45

831 "Adoration of the Infant Jesus" (Ortenberg altarpiece)

832 Christine Teusch (politician)

1986. Christmas.
2149 **831** 80pf.+40pf. mult . . . . 1·40 1·30

1986. Famous German Women. Inscr "Deutsche Bundespost".
2150 – 5pf. brown and grey . . 30 20
2151 – 10pf. brown and violet 30 15
2152 – 20pf. blue and red . . . 25 20
2152a – 30pf. bistre and purple 45 30
2153 – 40pf. red and blue . . 70 25
2154 **832** 50pf. green and brown 90 20
2155 – 60pf. lilac and green . . 90 25
2155a – 70pf. green and red . . 1·50 65
2156 – 80pf. brown and green 1·10 20
2156a – 80pf. brown and blue 90 45
2157 – 100pf. grey and red . . 1·40 20
2157a – 100pf. bistre and lilac 1·10 45
2158 – 120pf. green and brown 1·60 1·00
2159 – 130pf. violet and blue 2·75 70
2160 – 140pf. ochre and blue 3·25 1·20
2161 – 150pf. blue and red . . 3·75 1·50
2162 – 170pf. purple and green 2·30 65
2163 – 180pf. purple and blue 2·30 1·10
2164 – 200pf. red and brown 2·10 90
2165 – 240pf. brown and green 3·25 1·20
2166 – 250pf. blue and mauve 4·25 1·60
2167 – 300pf. green and purple 2·75 1·10
2168 – 350pf. brown and black 4·50 1·90
2168a – 400pf. black and red . . 5·50 2·00
2168b – 450pf. ultramarine & bl 5·00 2·50
2169 – 500pf. red and green . . 5·75 2·00

DESIGNS: 5pf. Emma Ihrer (politician and trade unionist); 10pf. Paula Modersohn-Becker (painter); 20pf. Cilly Aussem (tennis player); 30pf. Kathe Kollwitz (artist); 40pf. Maria Sibylla Merian (artist and naturalist); 60pf. Dorothea Erxleben (first German woman Doctor of Medicine); 70pf. Elisabet Boehm (founder of Agricultural Association of Housewives); 80pf. (2156), Clara Schumann (pianist and composer); 80pf. (2156a), Rahel Varnhagen von Ense (humanist) (after Wilhelm Hensel); 100pf. (2157), Therese Giehse (actress); 100pf. (2157a), Luise Henriette of Orange (mother of King Friedrich I of Prussia) (after Gerhard von Honthorst); 120pf. Elisabeth Selbert (politician); 130pf. Lise Meitner (physicist); 140pf. Cecile Vogt (medical researcher); 150pf. Sophie Scholl (resistance member); 170pf. Hannah Arendt (sociologist); 180pf. Lotte Lehmann (opera singer); 200pf. Bertha von Suttner (novelist and pacifist); 240pf. Mathilda Franziska Anneke (women's rights activist); 250pf. Queen Louise of Prussia; 300pf. Fanny Hensel (composer) (after Eduard Magnus); 350pf. Hedwig Dransfeld (politician); 400pf. Charlotte von Stein (friend of Goethe); 450pf. Hedwig Courths-Mahler (novelist); 500pf. Alice Salomon (women's rights activist).

For similar designs inscribed "Deutschland", see Nos. 2785/95.

833 Berlin Landmarks

1987. 750th Anniv of Berlin.
2170 **833** 80pf. multicoloured . . . 2·30 50

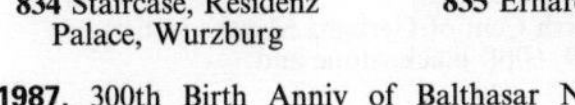
834 Staircase, Residenz Palace, Wurzburg
835 Erhard

1987. 300th Birth Anniv of Balthasar Neumann (architect).
2171 **834** 80pf. grey, black and red 1·60 30

1987. 90th Birth Anniv of Ludwig Erhard (former Chancellor).
2172 **835** 80pf. multicoloured . . . 1·80 30

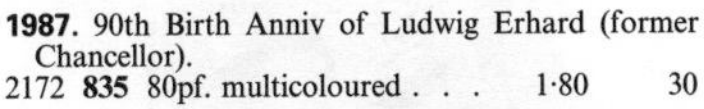
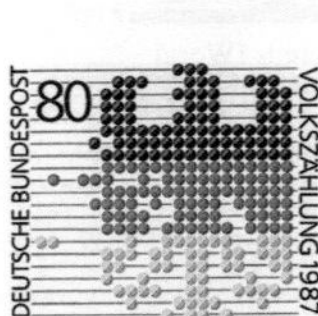

836 Abacus Beads forming Eagle
838 Chief Winnetou (from book cover)

837 Clemenswerth Castle

1987. Census.
2173 **836** 80pf. multicoloured . . . 1·90 30

1987. 250th Anniv of Clemenswerth Castle.
2174 **837** 60pf. multicoloured . . . 1·30 30

1987. 75th Death Anniv of Karl May (writer).
2175 **838** 80pf. multicoloured . . . 1·40 30

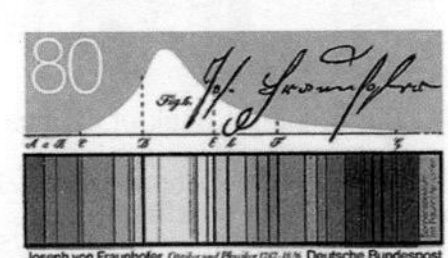
839 Solar Spectrum

1987. Birth Bicentenary of Joseph von Fraunhofer (optician and physicist).
2176 **839** 80pf. multicoloured . . . 1·30 30

840 World Sailing Championships, Kiel

1987. Sport Promotion Fund. Multicoloured.
2177 80pf.+40pf. Type **840** . . . 1·60 1·50
2178 120pf.+55pf. World Nordic Skiing Championships, Oberstdorf . . . . 2·10 2·10

1987. Youth Welfare. Trades (2nd series). As T **811**. Multicoloured.
2179 50pf.+25pf. Plumber . . . . 1·30 1·10
2180 60pf.+30pf. Dental technician . . . . 1·50 1·30
2181 70pf.+35pf. Butcher . . . . 1·70 1·50
2182 80pf.+40pf. Bookbinder . . 2·40 2·20

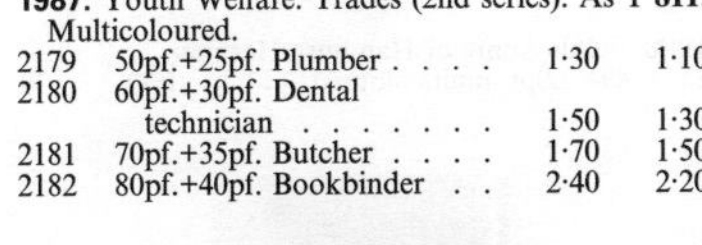

841 Clefs, Notes and Leaves

1987. 125th Anniv of German Choir Association.
2183 **841** 80pf. multicoloured . . . 1·50 30

842 Pope's Arms, Madonna and Child and Kevelaer

1987. Visit of Pope John Paul II to Kevelaer (venue for 17th Marian and 10th Mariological Congresses).
2184 **842** 80pf. multicoloured . . . 1·60 30

843 Dulmen's Wild Horses

1987. European Environment Year.
2185 **843** 60pf. multicoloured . . . 1·90 30

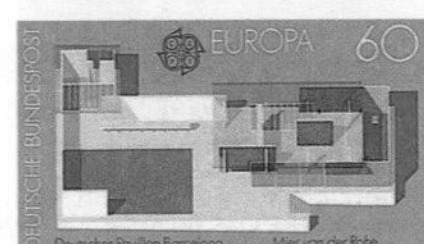
844 German Pavilion, International Exhibition, Barcelona, 1929 (Ludwig Mies van der Rohe)

1987. Europa. Architecture. Multicoloured.
2186 60pf. Type **844** . . . . . . 1·40 35
2187 80pf. Kohlbrand Bridge, Hamburg (Thyssen Engineering) . . . . . . 1·80 35

845 Emblem and Globe

1987. Rotary International Convention, Munich.
2188 **845** 70pf. ultram, yell & bl 1·50 30

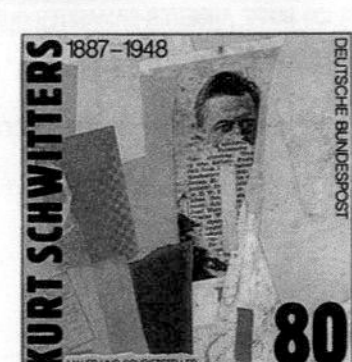
846 "Without Title (With an Early Portrait)"

1987. Birth Centenary of Kurt Schwitters (artist and writer).
2189 **846** 80pf. multicoloured . . . 1·20 30

847 Organ Pipes and Signature
848 Bengal

1987. 350th Birth Anniv of Dietrich Buxtehude (composer).
2190 **847** 80pf. black, stone and red . . . . 1·00 30

1987. 300th Birth Anniv of Johann Albrecht Bengel (theologian).
2191 **848** 80pf. brown, ochre & blk 1·20 30

849 Wilhelm Kaisen

1987. Birth Centenary of Wilhelm Kaisen (Senate president and Mayor of Bremen).
2192 **849** 80pf. multicoloured . . . 1·40 30

850 Charlemagne, Bishop Willehad, Bremen Cathedral and City Arms (after mural)

1987. 1200th Anniv of Bremen Bishopric.
2193 **850** 80pf. multicoloured . . . 1·20 30

851 Target, Crossed Rifles and Wreath

1987. 7th European Riflemen's Festival, Lippstadt.
2194 **851** 80pf. multicoloured . . . 1·20 30

852 4th-century Roman Bracelet

1987. Humanitarian Relief Funds. Precious Metal Work. Multicoloured.
2195 50pf.+25pf. Type **852** . . . 1·10 85
2196 60pf.+30pf. 6th-century East Gothic buckle . . . . . 1·30 1·20
2197 70pf.+35pf. 7th-century Merovingian disc fibula 1·40 1·20
2198 80pf.+40pf. 8th-century reliquary . . . . 1·80 1·50

853 Loading and Unloading Mail Train, 1897
854 Corner Tower, Celle Castle

1987. Stamp Day.
2199 **853** 80pf. multicoloured . . . 1·30 65

1987. Tourist Sights. Inscr "DEUTSCHE BUNDESPOST".

2200	–	5pf. blue and grey . . .	75	50
2201	–	10pf. blue and indigo	30	15
2202	–	20pf. pink and blue . .	65	40
2203	**854**	30pf. brown and green	1·40	95
2204	–	33pf. green and red . .	1·10	75
2205	–	38pf. grey and blue . .	1·50	1·10
2206	–	40pf. brown, red & blue	1·60	1·10
2206a	–	41pf. grey and yellow	55	50
2207	–	45pf. pink and blue . .	1·10	80
2208	–	50pf. brown and blue	1·80	1·10
2209	–	60pf. green and black	2·30	1·30
2210	–	70pf. pink and blue . .	2·00	1·20
2210a	–	70pf. brown and blue	1·70	1·10
2211	–	80pf. grey and green . .	1·20	65
2212	–	90pf. bistre and yellow	3·50	2·50
2213	–	100pf. green and orange	3·25	1·80
2214	–	120pf. green and red . .	4·00	2·40
2215	–	140pf. bistre and yellow	4·50	2·50
2216	–	170pf. grey and yellow	3·25	2·75
2216a	–	200pf. blue and brown	2·40	2·20
2217	–	280pf. grey and blue . .	4·75	1·70
2218	–	300pf. pink and brown	3·25	4·75
2219	–	350pf. grey and blue . .	4·25	60
2220	–	400pf. red and brown	4·50	60
2220a	–	450pf. blue and brown	5·00	55
2220b	–	500pf. stone and purple	4·75	1·50
2220c	–	550pf. brown and blue	5·25	1·80
2220d	–	700pf. green and yellow	7·00	1·80

DESIGNS: 5pf. Brunswick Lion; 10pf. Frankfurt airport; 20, 70 (2210) pf. Head of Nefertiti, Berlin Museum; 33, 120pf. Schleswig Cathedral; 38, 280pf. Statue of Roland, Bremen; 40pf. Chile House, Hamburg; 41, 170pf. Russian Church, Wiesbaden; 45pf. Rastatt Castle; 50pf. Freiburg Cathedral; 60pf. "Bavaria" (bronze statue), Munich; 70pf. (2210a) Heligoland; 80pf. Zollern II Dortmund Mine Industrial Museum, Westphalia; 90, 140pf. Bronze flagon, Reinheim; 100pf. Pilgrimage Chapel, Altotting; 200pf. Magdeburg Cathedral; 300pf. Hambach Castle; 350pf. Externsteine (rock formation), Horn-Bad Meinberg; 400pf. Dresden Opera House; 450pf. New Gate, Neubrandenburg; 500pf. Cottbus State Theatre; 550pf. Suhl-Heinrichs Town Hall, Thuringia; 700pf. National Theatre, Berlin.

The 10, 60, 80 and 100pf. also exist imperforate and self-adhesive from booklets.

For similar designs inscribed "DEUTSCHLAND", see Nos. 2654/66.

855 Gluck and Score of "Armide"

1987. Death Bicentenary of Christoph Willibald Gluck (composer).
2221 **855** 60pf. black, grey and red 1·00 25

856 Poster by Emil Orlik for "The Weavers"

1987. 125th Birth Anniv of Gerhart Hauptmann (playwright).
2222 **856** 80pf. lt red, black & red 1·50 30

857 Paddy Field

1987. 25th Anniv of German Famine Aid.
2223 **857** 80pf. multicoloured . . . 1·50 30

858 "Birth of Christ" (13th-century Book of Psalms)

1987. Christmas.
2224 **858** 80pf.+40pf. mult . . . . 1·40 1·30

859 Jester
860 Kaiser

1988. 150th Anniv of Mainz Carnival.
2225 **859** 60pf. multicoloured . . . 1·00 30

1988. Birth Centenary of Jakob Kaiser (trade unionist and politician).
2226 **860** 80pf. black and grey . . 1·00 30

861 Stein and Mayer

1988. Beatification of Edith Stein and Father Rupert Mayer.
2227 **861** 80pf. multicoloured . . . 1·30 30

862 Dr Konrad Adenauer (West German Chancellor) and Charles de Gaulle (French President)

1988. 25th Anniv of Franco-German Co-operation Treaty.
2228 **862** 80pf. purple and black 1·70 3·25

863 "Solitude of the Green Woods" (woodcut of poem, Ludwig Richter)

865 Schopenhauer

864 Raiffeisen and Ploughed Field

1988. Birth Bicentenary of Joseph von Eichendorff (writer).
2229 **863** 60pf. multicoloured . . . 1·20 30

1988. Death Centenary of Friedrich Wilhelm Raiffeisen (philanthropist and agricultural co-operative founder).
2230 **864** 80pf. green and black . . 2·00 30

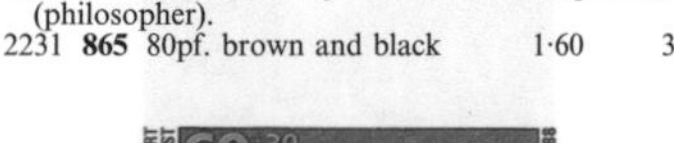

1988. Birth Bicentenary of Arthur Schopenhauer (philosopher).
2231 **865** 80pf. brown and black 1·60 30

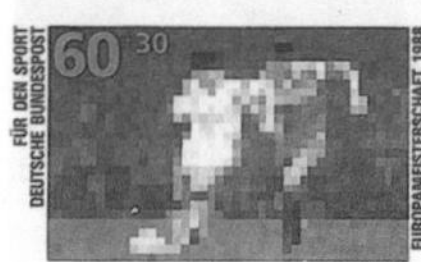

866 Football (European Championship)

1988. Sport Promotion Fund. Multicoloured.
2232 60pf.+30pf. Type **866** . . . 1·00 85
2233 80pf.+40pf. Tennis (Olympic Games) . . . . 1·50 1·30
2234 120pf.+55pf. Diving (Olympic Games) . . . . 2·30 2·10

867 Buddy Holly

1988. Youth Welfare. Pop Music. Mult.
2235 50pf.+25pf. Type **867** . . . 1·30 1·30
2236 60pf.+30pf. Elvis Presley . . 2·00 1·80
2237 70pf.+35pf. Jim Morrison 1·80 1·80
2238 80pf.+40pf. John Lennon 2·75 2·30

868 Hutten (wood engraving from "Conquestiones")

1988. 500th Birth Anniv of Ulrich von Hutten (writer).
2239 **868** 80pf. multicoloured . . . 1·30 45

869 City Buildings and Jan Wellem Monument

1988. 700th Anniv of Dusseldorf.
2240 **869** 60pf. multicoloured . . . 1·00 30

870 Airbus Industrie A320 and Manufacturing Nations' Flag

1988. Europa. Transport and Communications. Multicoloured.
2241 60pf. Type **870** . . . . . . 1·20 35
2242 80pf. Diagram of Integrated Services Digital Network 1·10 35

871 University Buildings and City Landmarks

872 Monnet

1988. 600th Anniv of Cologne University.
2243 **871** 80pf. multicoloured . . . 1·40 30

1988. Birth Centenary of Jean Monnet (statesman).
2244 **872** 80pf. multicoloured . . . 1·20 30

873 Storm

1988. Death Centenary of Theodor Storm (writer).
2245 **873** 80pf. multicoloured . . . 1·30 30

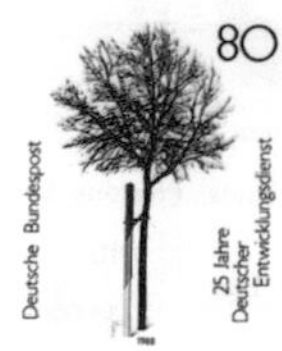

874 Tree supported by Stake in National Colours

876 Gmelin

875 Meersburg

1988. 25th Anniv of German Volunteer Service.
2246 **874** 80pf. multicoloured . . . 1·20 35

1988. Millenary of Meersburg.
2247 **875** 60pf. multicoloured . . . 1·00 30

1988. Birth Bicentenary of Leopold Gmelin (chemist).
2248 **876** 80pf. multicoloured . . . 1·00 30

877 Vernier Caliper Rule in National Colours

1988. "Made in Germany".
2249 **877** 140pf. multicoloured . . 2·40 75

878 Bebel

1988. 75th Death Anniv of August Bebel (Social Democratic Labour Party co-founder).
2250 **878** 80pf. mauve, blue & sil 1·50 30

879 Carrier Pigeon

1988. Stamp Day.
2251 **879** 20pf. multicoloured . . . 65 20

880 13th-century Rock Crystal Reliquary

881 Red Cross

1988. Humanitarian Relief Funds. Precious Metal Work. Multicoloured.
2252 50pf.+25pf. Type **880** . . . 65 60
2253 60pf.+30pf. 14th-century bust of Charlemagne . . 1·10 1·10
2254 70pf.+35pf. 10th-cent. crown of Otto III . . . . 1·20 1·20
2255 80pf.+40pf. 17th-cent. jewelled flowers . . . . . 1·60 1·40

1988. 125th Anniv of Red Cross.
2256 **881** 80pf. red and black . . . 1·40 30

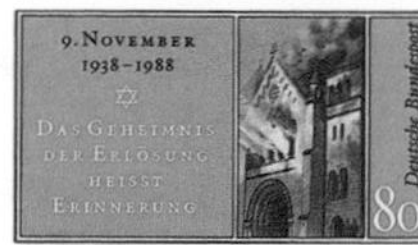

882 Burning Synagogue, Baden-Baden

1988. 50th Anniv of "Kristallnacht" (Nazi pogrom).
2257 **882** 80pf. purple and black 1·20 30

883 Cancelled Postage Stamps

1988. Centenary of Collection of Used Stamps for the Bethel Charity.
2258 **883** 60pf. multicoloured . . . 1·30 30

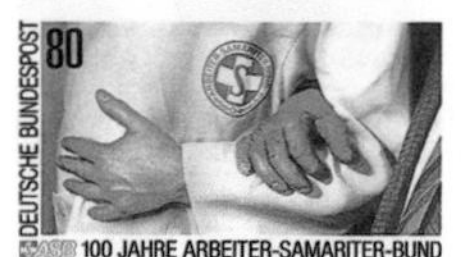

884 Linked Arms

1988. Centenary of Samaritan Workers' (first aid) Association.
2259 **884** 80pf. multicoloured . . . 1·30 30

885 "Adoration of the Magi" (illus from Henry the Lion's Gospel Book)

1988. Christmas.
2260 **885** 80pf.+40pf. mult . . . . 1·50 1·30

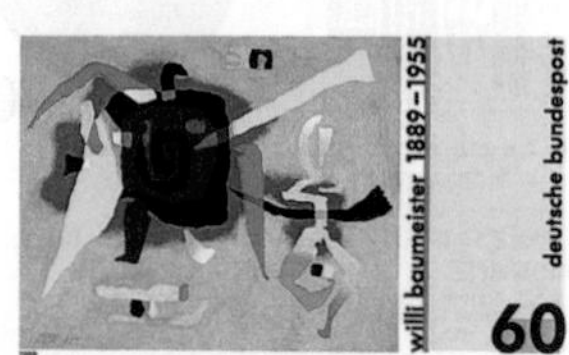

886 "Bluxao I"

1989. Birth Centenary of Willi Baumeister (painter).
2261 **886** 60pf. multicoloured . . . 1·20 30

887 Bonn

1988. 2000th Anniv of Bonn.
2262 **887** 80pf. multicoloured . . . 1·80 45

888 Grass growing from Dry, Cracked Earth

1989. 30th Anniversaries of Misereor and Bread for the World (Third World relief organizations).
2263 **888** 80pf. multicoloured . . . 1·30 30

889 "Cats in the Attic" (woodcut)

1989. Birth Cent of Gerhard Marcks (artist).
2264 **889** 60pf. black, stone and red . . . . 1·20 30

890 Table Tennis (World Championships)

1989. Sport Promotion Fund. Multicoloured.
2265 100pf.+50pf. Type **890** . . 2·30 2·10
2266 140pf.+60pf. Gymnastics (World Championships) 3·25 2·75

891 Elephants

1989. Youth Welfare. Circus. Multicoloured.
2267 60pf.+30pf. Type **891** . . . 1·80 1·60
2268 70pf.+30pf. Acrobat on horseback . . . . 2·30 2·30
2269 80pf.+35pf. Clown . . . . 3·25 2·30
2270 100pf.+50pf. Caravans and Big Top . . . . 4·50 2·75

892 Posthorn and Book of Stamps

1989. "IPHLA '89" International Philatelic Literature Exhibition, Frankfurt.
2271 **892** 100pf.+50pf. mult . . . 2·75 2·40

893 European and Members' Flags

1989. 3rd Direct Elections to European Parliament.
2272 **893** 100pf. multicoloured . . 2·30 75

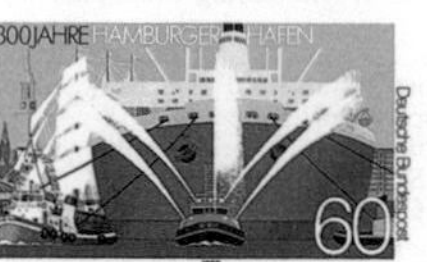

894 Shipping

1989. 800th Anniv of Hamburg Harbour.
2273 **894** 60pf. multicoloured . . . 1·30 30

895 Asam (detail of fresco, Weltenburg Abbey)

1989. 250th Death Anniv of Cosmas Damian Asam (painter and architect).
2274 **895** 60pf. multicoloured . . . 90 30

896 Kites

1989. Europa. Children's Toys. Multicoloured.
2275 60pf. Type **896** . . . . . . 1·20 35
2276 100pf. Puppet show . . . . 1·80 35

897 Emblem, National Colours and Presidents' Signatures

1989. 40th Anniv of German Federal Republic.
2277 **897** 100pf. multicoloured . . 1·80 50

898 Council Assembly and Stars

1989. 40th Anniv of Council of Europe.
2278 **898** 100pf. blue and gold . . 1·70 50

899 Gabelsberger and Shorthand

1989. Birth Bicentenary of Franz Xaver Gabelsberger (shorthand pioneer).
2279 **899** 100pf. multicoloured . . 1·60 45

900 Score of "Lorelei" and Silhouette of Silcher

1989. Birth Bicentenary of Friedrich Silcher (composer).
2280 **900** 80pf. multicoloured . . . 1·20 30

901 Saints Kilian, Totnan and Colman (from 12th-century German manuscript)

1989. 1300th Death Anniversaries of Saints Kilian, Colman and Totnan (Irish missionaries to Franconia).
2281 **901** 100pf. multicoloured . . 1·50 45

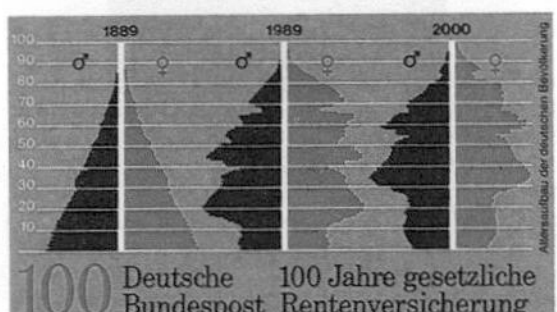

902 Age Graphs of Men and Women

1989. Centenary of National Insurance.
2282 **902** 100p. blue, red & lt blue 1·50 45

903 "Summer Evening" (Heinrich Vogler)

1989. Cent of Worpswede Artists' Village.
2283 **903** 60pf. multicoloured . . . 1·00 30

904 Schneider

906 Cathedral

905 List (after Kriehuber) and Train

1989. 50th Death Anniv of Reverend Paul Schneider (concentration camp victim).
2284 **904** 100pf. blk, lt grey & grey 1·30 45

1989. Birth Bicentenary of Friedrich List (economist).
2285 **905** 170pf. black and red . . 2·50 85

1989. 750th Anniv of Frankfurt Cathedral.
2286 **906** 60pf. multicoloured . . . 1·30 30

907 Children building House

1989. "Don't Forget the Children".
2287 **907** 100pf. multicoloured . . 1·50 45

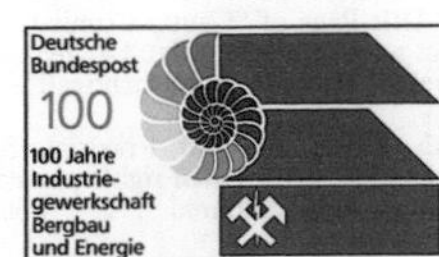

908 Ammonite and Union Emblem

1989. Centenary of Mining and Power Industries Trade Union.
2288 **908** 100pf. multicoloured . . 1·20 45

909 18th-century Mounted Courier, Thurn and Taxis

1989. Humanitarian Relief Funds. Postal Deliveries. Multicoloured.
2289 60pf.+30pf. Type **909** . . . 1·40 1·00
2290 80pf.+35pf. Hamburg postal messenger, 1808 . . . . . 1·80 1·50
2291 100pf.+50pf. Bavarian mail coach, 1900 . . . . . . 2·75 2·20

910 Maier

1989. Birth Centenary of Reinhold Maier (politician).
2292 **910** 100pf. multicoloured . . 1·50 45

911 Organ Pipes

1989. 300th Anniv of Arp Schnitger Organ, St. James's Church, Hamburg.
2293 **911** 60pf. multicoloured . . . 1·20 30

912 Angel

1989. Christmas. 16th-century Carvings by Veit Stoss, St. Lawrence's Church, Nuremberg. Multicoloured.
2294 60pf.+30pf. Type **912** . . . 1·40 1·20
2295 100pf.+50pf. "Nativity" . . 1·80 1·70

913 Speyer

1990. 2000th Anniv of Speyer.
2296 **913** 60pf. multicoloured . . . 1·40 40

914 "Courier" (Albrecht Durer) **915** Vine forming Initial "R"

1990. 500th Anniv of Regular European Postal Services.
2297 **914** 100pf. deep brown, light brown and brown . . 1·90 45

1990. 500 Years of Riesling Grape Cultivation.
2298 **915** 100pf. multicoloured . . 1·20 45

916 Old Lubeck

1990. UNESCO World Heritage Site, Old Lubeck.
2299 **916** 100pf. multicoloured . . 1·20 45

917 15th-century Seal and Grand Master's Arms

1990. 800th Anniv of Teutonic Order.
2300 **917** 100pf. multicoloured . . 1·60 45

918 Frederick II's Seal and Fair Entrance Hall

1990. 750th Anniv of Granting of Fair Privileges to Frankfurt.
2301 **918** 100pf. multicoloured . . 1·80 45

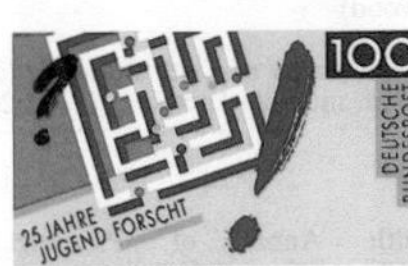

919 Maze

1990. 25th Anniv of Youth Research Science Competition.
2302 **919** 100pf. multicoloured . . 1·60 45

920 Wildlife

1990. North Sea Protection.
2303 **920** 100pf. multicoloured . . 1·80 45

921 Handball

1990. Sport Promotion Fund. Multicoloured.
2304 100pf.+50pf. Type **921** . . 2·50 1·80
2305 140pf.+60pf. Keep-fit . . . 3·50 2·75

922 Widow Bolte

1990. Youth Welfare. 125th Anniv of Max and Moritz (characters from books by Wilhelm Busch). Multicoloured.
2306 60pf.+30pf. Type **922** . . . 90 80
2307 70pf.+30pf. Max asleep . . 1·30 1·20
2308 80pf.+35pf. Moritz watching Max sawing through bridge . . . . 1·80 1·60
2309 100pf.+50pf. Max and Moritz . . . . 2·30 2·10

923 "1.MAI" and Factory Silhouette

1990. Centenary of Labour Day.
2310 **923** 100pf. red and black . . 1·40 45

924 Woman's Face

1990. 75th Anniv of German Association of Housewives.
2311 **924** 100pf. multicoloured . . 1·40 45

925 Collection Box

1990. 125th Anniv of German Lifeboat Institution.
2312 **925** 60pf. multicoloured . . . 1·20 40

926 Thurn and Taxis Palace, Frankfurt

1990. Europa. Post Office Buildings. Mult.
2313 60pf. Type **926** . . . . . . 1·40 45
2314 100pf. Postal Giro Office, Frankfurt . . . . 2·10 45

927 St Philip's Church, Protestant Church Flag and Candle Flames

1990. Centenary of Rummelsberg Diaconal Institution.
2315 **927** 100pf. multicoloured . . 1·30 45

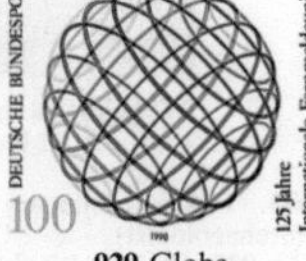

928 Leuschner **929** Globe

1990. Birth Centenary of Wilhelm Leuschner (trade unionist and member of anti-Hitler Resistance).
2316 **928** 100pf. black and lilac . . 1·70 45

1990. 125th Anniv of I.T.U.
2317 **929** 100pf. multicoloured . . 1·40 45

930 National Colours and Students

1990. 175th Anniv of German Students' Fraternity and of their Colours (now national colours).
2318 **930** 100pf. multicoloured . . 1·70 45

931 Hands exchanging Money and Goods

1990. 30th World Congress of International Chamber of Commerce, Hamburg.
2319 **931** 80pf. multicoloured . . . 1·20 50

932 Closing Sentence of Charter

1990. 40th Anniv of Expelled Germans Charter.
2320 **932** 100pf. multicoloured . . 1·60 45

933 Children of Different Races

1990. 10th International Youth Philatelic Exhibition, Dusseldorf. Sheet 165 × 101 mm.
MS2321 **933** 6 × 100pf.+50pf. multicoloured . . . . 16·00 16·00

934 Claudius
935 Mail Motor Wagon, 1900

1990. 250th Birth Anniv of Matthias Claudius (writer).
2322 **934** 100pf. blue, black and red . . . . 1·50 45

1990. Humanitarian Relief Funds. Posts and Telecommunications. Multicoloured.
2323 60pf.+30pf. Type **935** . . . 1·10 1·10
2324 80pf.+35pf. Telephone exchange, 1890 . . . . . 1·80 1·60
2325 100pf.+50pf. Parcel sorting office, 1900 . . . . 2·10 2·00

936 "German Unity" and National Colours

1990. Reunification of Germany.
2326 **936** 50pf. black, red & yellow 1·10 40
2327 100pf. black, red & yell 1·80 50

937 Schliemann and Lion Gate, Mycenae

1990. Death Centenary of Heinrich Schliemann (archaeologist).
2328 **937** 60pf. multicoloured . . . 1·40 40

938 Penny Black, Bavaria 1k. and West Germany 1989 100pf. Stamps

1990. Stamp Day. 150th Anniv of the Penny Black.
2329 **938** 100pf. multicoloured . . 1·70 45

939 National Colours spanning Breach in Wall
940 Angel with Candles

1990. 1st Anniv of Opening of Berlin Wall.
2330 50pf. Type **939** . . . . . . 1·20 50
2331 100pf. Brandenburg Gate and crowd . . . . 1·70 50
MS2332 146 × 100 mm. As Nos. 2330/1 . . . . 2·75 2·75

1990. Christmas. Multicoloured.
2333 50pf.+20pf. Type **940** . . . 90 90
2334 60pf.+30pf. Figure of man smoking . . . . 1·10 1·10
2335 70pf.+30pf. "Soldier" nutcrackers . . . . 1·50 1·50
2336 100pf.+50pf. Tinsel angel . . 2·30 1·80

941 Kathe Dorsch in "Mrs Warren's Profession"

1990. Birth Centenary of Kathe Dorsch (actress).
2337 **941** 100pf. violet and red . . 1·50 45

942 View of City

1991. 750th Anniv of Hanover.
2338 **942** 60pf. multicoloured . . . 1·20 45

943 "Three Golden Circles with a Full Circle in Blue" (relief in wood)
944 Miniature from 13th-century French Code

1991. Birth Centenary of Erich Buchholz (artist).
2339 **943** 60pf. multicoloured . . . 1·20 45

1991. 750th Anniv of Promulgation of Pharmaceutical Ethics in Germany.
2340 **944** 100pf. multicoloured . . 1·70 45

945 Brandenburg Gate (from "Old Engravings of Berlin")

1991. Bicentenary of Brandenburg Gate.
2341 **945** 100pf. black, red and grey . . . . 1·90 45

946 Eucken
947 Globe and "25" (poster)

1991. Birth Centenary of Walter Eucken (economist).
2342 **946** 100pf. multicoloured . . 1·50 40

1991. 25th International Tourism Fair, Berlin.
2343 **947** 100pf. multicoloured . . 1·50 40

948 Two-man Bobsleigh
949 Weightlifting (World Championships)

1991. World Bobsleigh Championships, Altenberg. Sheet 55 × 80 mm.
MS2344 **948** 100pf. multicoloured 1·80 2·00

1991. Sport Promotion Fund. Multicoloured.
2345 70pf.+30pf. Type **949** . . . 1·40 1·30
2346 100pf.+50pf. Cycling (world championships) . . . . . 1·80 1·60
2347 140pf.+60pf. Basketball (centenary) . . . . 2·30 2·10
2348 170pf.+80pf. Wrestling (European championships) 2·75 2·40

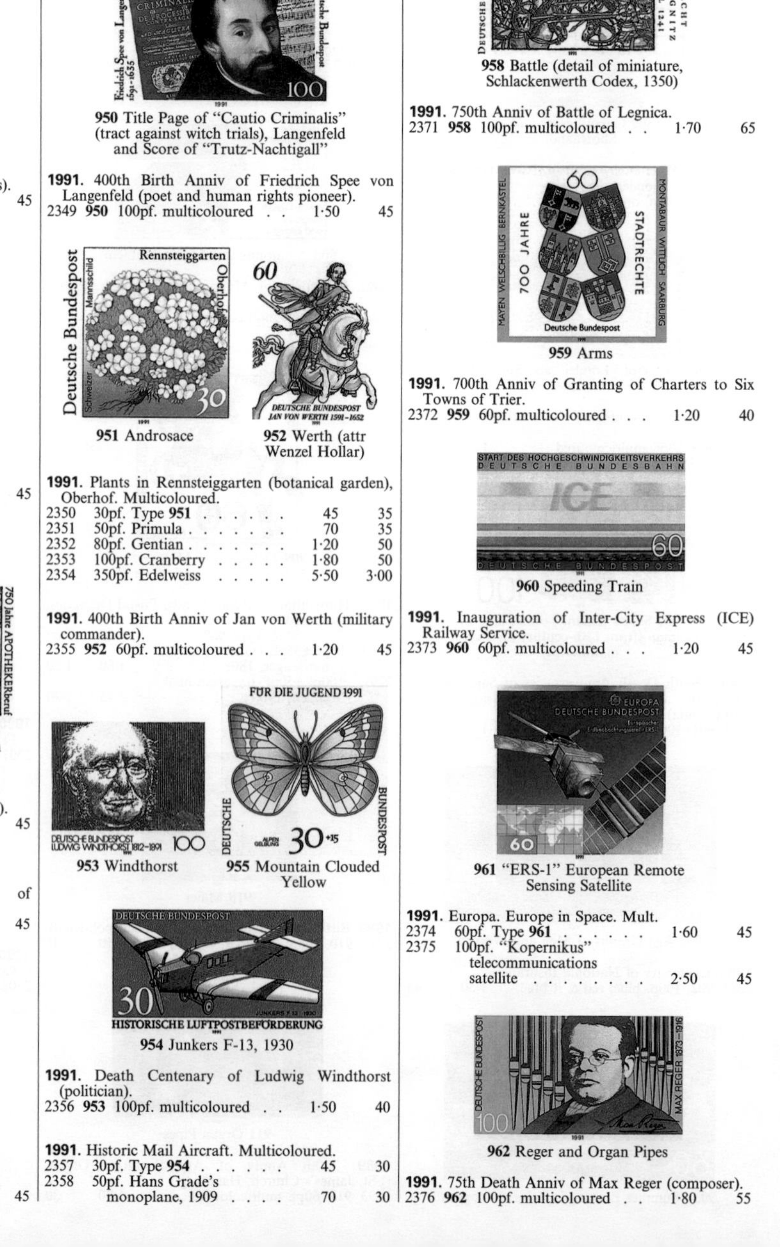

950 Title Page of "Cautio Criminalis" (tract against witch trials), Langenfeld and Score of "Trutz-Nachtigall"

1991. 400th Birth Anniv of Friedrich Spee von Langenfeld (poet and human rights pioneer).
2349 **950** 100pf. multicoloured . . 1·50 45

951 Androsace
952 Werth (attr Wenzel Hollar)

1991. Plants in Rennsteiggarten (botanical garden), Oberhof. Multicoloured.
2350 30pf. Type **951** 45 35
2351 50pf. Primula 70 35
2352 80pf. Gentian . . . . 1·20 50
2353 100pf. Cranberry . . . . . . 1·80 50
2354 350pf. Edelweiss . . . . . 5·50 3·00

1991. 400th Birth Anniv of Jan von Werth (military commander).
2355 **952** 60pf. multicoloured . . . 1·20 45

953 Windthorst
955 Mountain Clouded Yellow

954 Junkers F-13, 1930

1991. Death Centenary of Ludwig Windthorst (politician).
2356 **953** 100pf. multicoloured . . 1·50 40

1991. Historic Mail Aircraft. Multicoloured.
2357 30pf. Type **954** 45 30
2358 50pf. Hans Grade's monoplane, 1909 . . . . 70 30
2359 100pf. Fokker F.III, 1922 1·80 35
2360 165pf. Airship "Graf Zeppelin", 1928 . . . . . 3·00 2·40

1991. Youth Welfare. Endangered Butterflies. Multicoloured.
2361 30pf.+15pf. Type **955** . . . 45 55
2362 50pf.+25pf. Poplar admiral 60 60
2363 60pf.+30pf. Purple emperor 1·10 1·10
2364 70pf.+30pf. Violet copper 1·20 1·20
2365 80pf.+35pf. Swallowtail . . 1·40 1·50
2366 90pf.+45pf. Small apollo . . 1·80 1·90
2367 100pf.+50pf. Moorland clouded yellow . . . . . 2·30 2·20
2368 140pf.+60pf. Large copper 2·75 2·75
See also Nos. 2449/53.

956 Academy Building, 1830

1991. Bicentenary of Choral Academy, Berlin.
2369 **956** 100pf. multicoloured . . 1·70 50

957 Typesetting School, 1875

1991. 125th Anniv of Lette Foundation (institute for professional training of women).
2370 **957** 100pf. multicoloured . . 1·50 40

958 Battle (detail of miniature, Schlackenwerth Codex, 1350)

1991. 750th Anniv of Battle of Legnica.
2371 **958** 100pf. multicoloured . . 1·70 65

959 Arms

1991. 700th Anniv of Granting of Charters to Six Towns of Trier.
2372 **959** 60pf. multicoloured . . . 1·20 40

960 Speeding Train

1991. Inauguration of Inter-City Express (ICE) Railway Service.
2373 **960** 60pf. multicoloured . . . 1·20 45

961 "ERS-1" European Remote Sensing Satellite

1991. Europa. Europe in Space. Mult.
2374 60pf. Type **961** . . . . . . 1·60 45
2375 100pf. "Kopernikus" telecommunications satellite . . . . 2·50 45

962 Reger and Organ Pipes

1991. 75th Death Anniv of Max Reger (composer).
2376 **962** 100pf. multicoloured . . 1·80 55

963 Ruffs

1991. Seabirds. Multicoloured.
2390 60pf. Type **963** 90 40
2391 80pf. Little terns . . . . . 1·40 80
2392 100pf. Brent geese . . . . . 1·40 60
2393 140pf. White-tailed sea eagles . . . . 2·30 1·70

964 Wilhelm August Lampadius (gas pioneer)

1991. 18th World Gas Congress, Berlin. Each black and blue.
2394 60pf. Type **964** 90 30
2395 100pf. Gas street lamp, Berlin . . . . 1·20 45

965 Wallot (after Franz Wurbel) and Reichstag Building, Berlin

1991. 150th Birth Anniv of Paul Wallot (architect).
2396 **965** 100pf. multicoloured . . 1·90 40

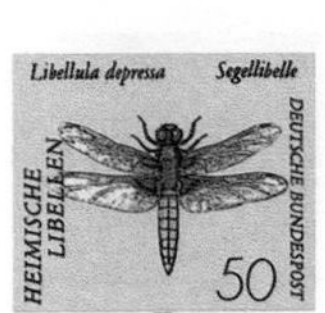

966 "Libellula depressa"

967 Hand clutching Cloak

1991. Dragonflies. Multicoloured.
2397 50pf. Type **966** 70 50
2398 60pf. Type **966** . . . . . . 1·40 75
2399 60pf. "Sympetrum sanguineum" . . . . . . 1·40 75
2400 60pf. "Cordulegaster boltonii" . . . . 1·40 75
2401 60pf. "Aeshna viridis" . . . 1·40 75
2402 70pf. As No. 2399 . . . . . 1·40 75
2403 80pf. As No. 2400 . . . . . 1·40 70
2404 100pf. As No. 2401 . . . . 1·40 70

1991. 40th Anniv of Geneva Convention on Refugees.
2405 **967** 100pf. lilac and black . . 1·70 40

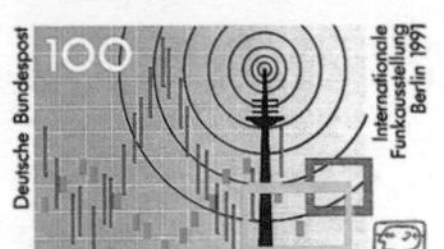

968 Radio Waves and Mast

1991. International Radio Exhibition, Berlin.
2406 **968** 100pf. multicoloured . . 1·70 40

969 Pedestrians and Traffic

1991. Road Safety Campaign.
2407 **969** 100pf. multicoloured . . 1·80 50

970 Lilienthal

1991. Centenary of First Heavier-than-Air Manned Flight by Otto Lilienthal and "Lilienthal '91" European Airmail Exhibition, Dresden. Sheet 57 × 82 mm.
MS2408 **970** 100pf.+50pf. brown, blue and red . . . . 3·75 3·50

971 August Heinrich Hoffmann von Fallersleben (lyricist) and Third Verse

1991. 150th Anniv of "Song of the Germans" (national anthem).
2409 **971** 100pf. red, black & green 1·60 40

972 Thadden-Trieglaff

1991. Birth Cent of Reinold von Thadden-Trieglaff (founder of German Protestant Convention).
2410 **972** 100pf. multicoloured . . 1·40 40

973 Transmission Test between Lauffen am Neckar and Frankfurt am Main

1991. Centenary of Three-phase Energy Transmission.
2411 **973** 170pf. multicoloured . . 2·50 1·10

974 Quill, Pen and Sword

975 Albers in "The Winner"

1991. Birth Bicentenary of Theodor Korner (poet). Sheet 55 × 80 mm containing T **974** and similar vert designs. Multicoloured.
MS2412 60pf. Type **974**; 100pf. Korner . . . . 2·50 2·40

1991. Birth Centenary of Hans Albers (actor).
2413 **975** 100pf. multicoloured . . 2·40 40

976 Harbour

1991. 275th Anniv of Rhine-Ruhr Port, Duisburg.
2414 **976** 100pf. multicoloured . . 1·70 40

977 Bethel Post Office

1991. Humanitarian Relief Funds. Postal Buildings. Multicoloured.
2415 30pf.+15pf. Type **977** . . . 55 60
2416 60pf.+30pf. Budingen post station . . . . 1·10 1·00
2417 70pf.+30pf. Stralsund post office . . . . 1·40 1·30
2418 80pf.+35pf. Lauscha post office . . . . 1·70 1·70
2419 100pf.+50pf. Bonn post office . . . . 2·20 1·90
2420 140pf.+60pf. Weilburg post office . . . . 2·75 2·40

978 Postal Delivery in Spreewald Region

1991. Stamp Day.
2421 **978** 100pf. multicoloured . . 1·50 40

979 "Bird Monument" (detail)

980 "Portrait of the Dancer Anita Berber"

1991. Birth Centenary of Max Ernst (painter).
2422 **979** 100pf. multicoloured . . 1·50 40

1991. Birth Cent of Otto Dix (painter). Mult.
2423 60pf. Type **980** 90 40
2424 100pf. "Self-portrait in Right Profile" . . . . . 1·80 45

981 "The Violinist and the Water Sprite"

1991. Sorbian Legends. Multicoloured.
2425 60pf. Type **981** . . . . . . 1·10 40
2426 100pf. "The Midday Woman and the Woman from Nochten" . . . . . 1·70 45

982 Angel (detail of "The Annunciation")

1991. Christmas. Works by Martin Schongauer. Multicoloured.
2427 60pf.+30pf. Type **982** . . . 1·20 1·20
2428 70pf.+30pf. Virgin Mary (detail of "The Annunciation") . . . . . 1·40 1·50
2429 80pf.+35pf. Angel (detail of "Madonna in a Rose Garden") . . . . 2·30 2·30
2430 100pf.+50pf. "Nativity" . . 3·25 2·50

983 Leber

984 Nelly Sachs

1991. Birth Cent of Julius Leber (politician).
2431 **983** 100pf. multicoloured . . 1·40 40

1991. Birth Centenary of Nelly Sachs (writer).
2432 **984** 100pf. dp violet & violet 1·50 45

985 Mozart

1991. Death Bicentenary of Wolfgang Amadeus Mozart (composer). Sheet 82 × 56 mm.
MS2433 **985** 100pf. lilac and brown 2·50 2·75

986 Base of William I Monument and City Silhouette

1992. 2000th Anniv of Koblenz.
2434 **986** 60pf. multicoloured . . . 1·50 40

987 Niemoller

988 Child's Eyes

1992. Birth Centenary of Martin Niemoller (theologian).
2435 **987** 100pf. multicoloured . . 1·30 45

1992. 25th Anniv of Terre des Hommes (child welfare organization) in Germany.
2436 **988** 100pf. multicoloured . . 1·80 50

989 Arms of Baden-Wurttemberg

1992. Lander of the Federal Republic.
2437 **989** 100pf. multicoloured . . 1·50 60
See also Nos. 2448, 2465, 2470, 2474, 2479, 2506, 2526, 2527, 2534, 2539, 2556, 2567, 2580, 2584 and 2597.

990 Fencing

991 Honegger and Score of Ballet "Semiramis"

1992. Sport Promotion Fund. Olympic Games, Albertville and Barcelona. Multicoloured.
2438 60pf.+30pf. Type **990** . . . 90 1·00
2439 80pf.+40pf. Rowing eight 1·10 1·20
2440 100pf.+50pf. Dressage . . . 2·30 2·10
2441 170pf.+80pf. Skiing (slalom) 3·75 3·50

1992. Birth Centenary of Arthur Honegger (composer).
2442 **991** 100pf. black and brown 1·60 50

992 Zeppelin and "Graf Zeppelin"

1992. 75th Death Anniv of Ferdinand von Zeppelin (airship manufacturer).
2443 **992** 165pf. multicoloured . . 2·40 95

993 Kiel City and Harbour

1992. 750th Anniv of Kiel.
2444 **993** 60pf. multicoloured . . . 1·00 40

994 Andreas Marggraf, Beet, Franz Achard and Carl Scheibler

1992. 125th Anniv of Berlin Sugar Institute.
2445 **994** 100pf. multicoloured . . 1·40 45
The stamp depicts the discoverer of beet sugar, the founder of the beet sugar industry and the founder of the Institute respectively.

995 Horses and Renz

996 Adenauer

1992. Death Centenary of Ernst Jakob Renz (circus director).
2446 **995** 100pf. multicoloured . . 1·40 45

1992. 25th Death Anniv of Konrad Adenauer (Chancellor, 1949–63).
2447 **996** 100pf. brn & cinnamon 1·90 45

1992. Lander of the Federal Republic. As T **989**. Multicoloured.
2448 100pf. Bavaria . . . . . . 1·50 60

1992. Youth Welfare. Endangered Moths. As T **955**. Multicoloured.
2449 60pf.+30pf. Purple tiger moth . . . . 1·50 1·50
2450 70pf.+30pf. Hawk moth . . 1·70 1·70
2451 80pf.+40pf. "Noctuidae sp." 2·10 2·00
2452 100pf.+50pf. Tiger moth . . 2·30 2·10
2453 170pf.+80pf. "Arichanna melanaria" . . . . 2·75 2·75

997 Schall

1992. 400th Birth Anniv of Adam Schall (missionary astronomer).
2454 **997** 140pf. black, yellow & bl 2·10 85

998 Cathedral and St. Severus's Church
999 Woodcut from 1493 Edition of Columbus's Letters

1992. 1250th Anniv of Erfurt.
2455 **998** 60pf. multicoloured . . . 1·00 40

1992. Europa. 500th Anniv of Discovery of America by Columbus. Multicoloured.
2456 60pf. Type **999** . . . . . . 1·00 40
2457 100pf. "Rene de Laudonniere and Chief Athore" (Jacques le Moyne de Morgues, 1564) 1·80 45

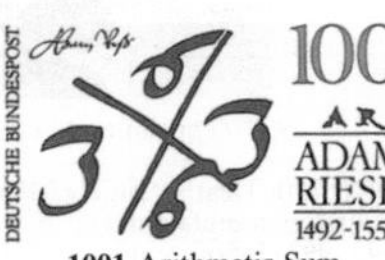

1000 "Consecration of St. Ludgerus" (from "Vita Liudgeri" by Altfridus)
1001 Arithmetic Sum

1992. 1250th Birth Anniv of St. Ludgerus (first Bishop of Munster).
2458 **1000** 100pf. multicoloured . . 1·70 45

1992. 500th Birth Anniv of Adam Riese (mathematician).
2459 **1001** 100pf. multicoloured . . 1·70 40

1002 Order of Merit

1992. 150th Anniv of Civil Class of Order of Merit (for scientific or artistic achievement).
2460 **1002** 100pf. multicoloured . . 1·70 40

1003 "Landscape with Horse" (Franz Marc)

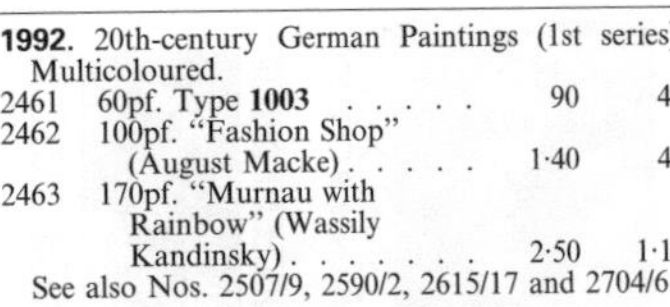

1992. 20th-century German Paintings (1st series). Multicoloured.
2461 60pf. Type **1003** 90 45
2462 100pf. "Fashion Shop" (August Macke) . . . . . 1·40 45
2463 170pf. "Murnau with Rainbow" (Wassily Kandinsky) . . . . 2·50 1·10
See also Nos. 2507/9, 2590/2, 2615/17 and 2704/6.

1004 Lichtenberg

1992. 250th Birth Anniv of Georg Christoph Lichtenberg (physicist and essayist).
2464 **1004** 100pf. multicoloured . . 1·50 50

1992. Lander of the Federal Republic. As T **989**. Multicoloured.
2465 100pf. Berlin . . . . 1·50 60

1005 Rainforest

1992. "Save the Tropical Rain Forest".
2466 **1005** 100pf.+50pf. mult . . . 1·90 1·70
The premium was for the benefit of environmental projects.

1006 Garden

1992. Leipzig Botanical Garden.
2467 **1006** 60pf. multicoloured . . 95 40

1007 Stylized House and Globe

1992. 17th International Home Economics Congress, Hanover.
2468 **1007** 100pf. multicoloured . . 1·70 50

1008 Family
1009 "Assumption of the Virgin Mary" (Rohr Monastery Church)

1992. Family Life.
2469 **1008** 100pf. multicoloured . . 1·70 40

1992. Lander of the Federal Republic. As T **989**. Multicoloured.
2470 100pf. Brandenburg . . . . 1·50 60

1992. 300th Birth Anniv of Egid Quirin Asam (sculptor).
2471 **1009** 60pf. multicoloured . . 1·00 40

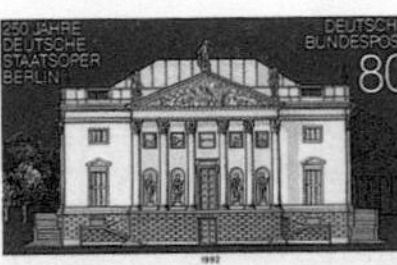

1010 Opera House (Georg von Knobelsdorff)

1992. 250th Anniv of German State Opera House, Berlin.
2472 **1010** 80pf. multicoloured . . 1·30 45

1011 Masked Actors

1992. Centenary of German Amateur Theatres Federation.
2473 **1011** 100pf. multicoloured . . 1·70 45

1992. Lander of the Federal Republic. As T **989**. Multicoloured.
2474 100pf. Bremen . . . . . . 1·50 60

1012 Globe

1992. 500th Anniv of Martin Behaim's Terrestrial Globe.
2475 **1012** 60pf. multicoloured . . 1·20 45

1013 1890 Pendant and 1990 Clock
1014 Bergengruen (after Hanni Fries)

1992. 225th Anniv of Jewellery and Watch-making in Pforzheim.
2476 **1013** 100pf. multicoloured . . 1·70 40

1992. Birth Centenary of Werner Bergengruen (writer).
2477 **1014** 100pf. grey, blue & blk 1·70 40

1015 Neue Holzbrucke Bridge, nr Essing

1992. Inauguration of Main–Donau Canal.
2478 **1015** 100pf. multicoloured . . 1·70 40

1992. Lander of the Federal Republic. As T **989**. Multicoloured.
2479 100pf. Hamburg . . . . . 1·50 60

1016 Turret Clock, 1400

1992. Humanitarian Relief Funds. Clocks. Multicoloured.
2480 60pf.+30pf. Type **1016** . . 1·10 1·10
2481 70pf.+30pf. Astronomical mantel clock, 1738 . . . 1·40 1·30
2482 80pf.+40pf. Flute clock, 1790 . . . . 1·60 1·60
2483 100pf.+50pf. Figurine clock, 1580 . . . . 2·00 1·80
2484 170pf.+80pf. Table clock, 1550 . . . . 3·00 2·75

1017 Distler and Score of "We Praise Our Lord Jesus Christ"
1018 Balloon Post

1992. 50th Death Anniv of Hugo Distler (composer).
2485 **1017** 100pf. black and violet 1·50 45

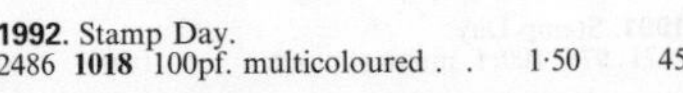

1992. Stamp Day.
2486 **1018** 100pf. multicoloured . . 1·50 45

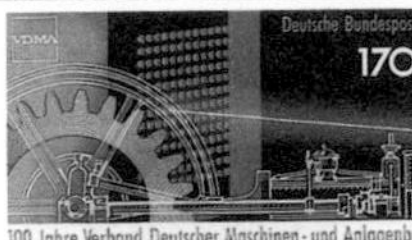

1019 Otto Engine, 1892, Cogwheel and Laser Beam

1992. Centenary of German Plant and Machine Builders Association.
2487 **1019** 170pf. multicoloured . . 2·00 85

1020 "Adoration of the Magi"

1992. Christmas. Carvings by Franz Maidburg, St. Anne's Church, Annaberg-Buchholz. Mult.
2488 60pf.+30pf. Type **1020** . . 1·10 1·30
2489 100pf.+50pf. "Birth of Christ" . . . . 1·80 1·70

1021 Blucher (after Simon Meister)

1992. 250th Birth Anniv of Field Marshal Gebhard Leberecht von Blucher.
2490 **1021** 100pf. multicoloured . . 1·70 45

1022 Werner von Siemens
1023 Klepper

1992. Death Centenary of Werner von Siemens (electrical engineer).
2491 **1022** 100pf. brown & dp brn 1·40 45

1992. 50th Death Anniv of Jochen Klepper (writer).
2492 **1023** 100pf. multicoloured . . 1·30 45

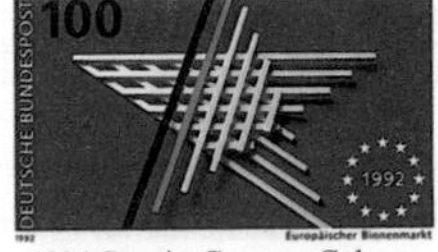

1024 Star in German Colours

1992. European Single Market.
2493 **1024** 100pf. multicoloured . . 2·00 45

1025 Cathedral and Uberwasser Church

1993. 1200th Anniv of Munster.
2494 **1025** 60pf. multicoloured . . 1·00 45

1026 Newton, Sketch of Refraction of Light and Formula

1993. 350th Birth Anniv of Sir Isaac Newton (scientist).
2495 **1026** 100pf. multicoloured . . 1·20 45

1027 Route Map and Compass Rose

1993. 125th Anniv of North German Naval Observatory, Hamburg.
2496 **1027** 100pf. multicoloured . . 1·20 45

1028 Emblem and Safety Stripes

1993. European Year of Health, Hygiene and Safety in the Workplace.
2497 **1028** 100pf. blue, yell & blk 1·40 45

1029 Wires and Wall Socket forming House
1030 Ski-jumping Hill, Garmisch-Partenkirchen

1993. Centenary of German Association of Electrical Engineers.
2498 **1029** 170pf. multicoloured . . 2·30 90

1993. Sport Promotion Fund. German Olympic Venues. Multicoloured.
2499 60pf.+30pf. Type **1030** . . 1·40 1·30
2500 80pf.+40pf. Olympia-park, Munich . . . . 1·80 1·70
2501 100pf.+50pf. Olympic Stadium, Berlin . . . . . 2·75 2·20
2502 170pf.+80pf. Olympic Harbour, Kiel . . . . . 3·50 3·00

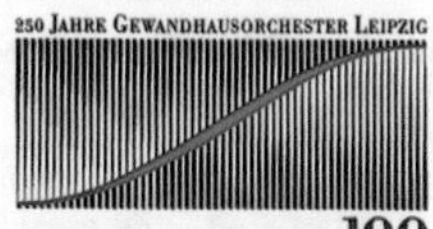

1031 Stylised Sound Vibration

1993. 250th Anniv of Leipzig Gewandhaus Orchestra.
2503 **1031** 100pf. gold and black 1·20 45

1032 Statue of St. John and Charles Bridge, Prague

1993. 600th Death Anniv of St. John of Nepomuk.
2504 **1032** 100pf. multicoloured . . 1·20 45

1033 Diagram explaining New Postcodes

1993. Introduction of Five-digit Postcode System.
2505 **1033** 100pf. multicoloured . . 1·80 45

1993. Lander of the Federal Republic. As T **989**. Multicoloured.
2506 100pf. Hesse . . . . 1·40 50

1993. 20th-century German Paintings (2nd series). As T **1003**. Multicoloured.
2507 100pf. multicoloured . . . . 1·50 55
2508 100pf. black, grey and mauve . . . . 1·50 55
2509 100pf. multicoloured . . . . 1·50 55
DESIGNS: No. 2507, "Cafe" (George Grosz); 2508. "Sea and Sun" (Otto Pankok); 2509, "Audience" (Andreas Paul Weber).

1034 Abbeys

1993. 900th Anniversaries of Maria Laach and Bursfelde Benedictine Abbeys.
2510 **1034** 80pf. multicoloured . . 1·20 40

1035 Alpine Longhorn Beetle

1993. Youth Welfare. Endangered Beetles. Multicoloured.
2511 80pf.+40f. Type **1035** . . . 1·70 1·60
2512 80pf.+40pf. Rose chafer . . 1·70 1·60
2513 100pf.+50pf. Stag beetle . . 2·10 1·80
2514 100pf.+50pf. Tiger beetle . . 2·10 1·80
2515 200pf.+50pf. Cockchafer . . 3·50 3·50

1036 Plants

1993. 5th International Horticultural Show, Stuttgart.
2516 **1036** 100pf. multicoloured . . 1·20 45

1037 Horse Race

1993. 125th Anniv of Hoppegarten Racecourse.
2517 **1037** 80pf. multicoloured . . 1·20 45

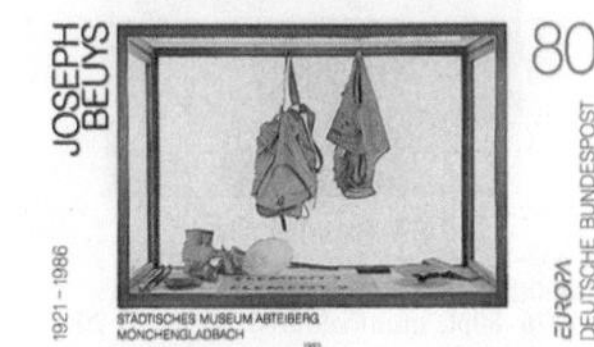

1038 "Storage Place" (Joseph Beuys)

1993. Europa. Contemporary Art. Mult.
2518 80pf. Type **1038** . . . . . 1·50 55
2519 100pf. "Homage to the Square" (Josef Albers) . . 1·50 55

1039 Church and Pupils

1993. 450th Anniv of Pforta School.
2520 **1039** 100pf. multicoloured . . 1·20 45

1040 Students, Flag, City Hall and Castle

1993. 125th Anniv of Coburg Association of University Student Unions.
2521 **1040** 100pf. black, grn & red 1·20 45

1041 "Hohentwiel" (lake steamer) and Flags

1993. Lake Constance European Region.
2522 **1041** 100pf. multicoloured . . 1·20 45

1042 "Old Market—View of St. Nicholas's Church" (detail, Ferdinand von Arnim)

1993. Millenary of Potsdam.
2523 **1042** 80pf. multicoloured . . 1·50 40

1043 Holderlin (after Franz Hiemer)

1993. 150th Death Anniv of Friedrich Holderlin (poet).
2524 **1043** 100pf. multicoloured . . 1·30 40

1044 "If People can fly to the Moon, why can't they do anything about so many Children dying?"

1993. 40th Anniv of German United Nations Children's Fund Committee.
2525 **1044** 100pf. multicoloured . . 1·30 40

1993. Lander of the Federal Republic. As T **989**. Multicoloured.
2526 100pf. Mecklenburg-Vorpommern . . . . . . 1·40 50

1993. Lander of the Federal Republic. As T **989**. Multicoloured.
2527 100pf. Lower Saxony . . . 1·40 50

1045 Fallada (after E. O. Plauen)

1993. Birth Centenary of Hans Fallada (writer).
2528 **1045** 100pf. green, brn & red 1·30 40

1046 Harz Mountain Range

1993. Landscapes (1st series). Multicoloured.
2529 100pf. Type **1046** . . . . . 1·40 50
2530 100pf. Rugen . . . . 1·40 50
2531 100pf. Hohe Rhon . . . . 1·40 50
See also Nos. 2585/8, 2646/9, 2709/12 and 2806/8.

1047 Stages of Manufacture

1993. 250th Death Anniv of Mathias Klotz (violin maker).
2532 **1047** 80pf. multicoloured . . 1·10 40

1048 George as Gotz von Berlichingen in Goethe's "Urgotz"
1050 Swedish Flag, Heart and Cross

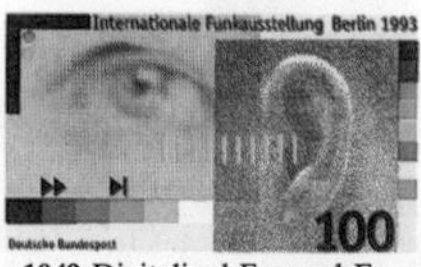

1049 Digitalised Eye and Ear

1993. Birth Centenary of Heinrich George (actor).
2533 **1048** 100pf. multicoloured . . 1·30 45

1993. Lander of the Federal Republic. As T **989**. Multicoloured.
2534 100pf. Nordrhein-Westfalen 1·40 50

1993. International Radio Exhibition, Berlin.
2535 **1049** 100pf. multicoloured . . 1·30 45

1993. Birth Centenary of Birger Forell (founder of Espelkamp (town for war refugees)).
2536 **1050** 100pf. yell, ultram & bl 1·80 45

1051 "Tuledu Bridge" (engraving)
1052 Singing Clown

1993. Birth Centenary of Hans Leip (writer and artist).
2537 **1051** 100pf. black, red & blue 1·80 45

1993. "For Us Children". Sheet 49 × 83 mm.
MS2538 **1052** 100pf. multicoloured 1·70 1·60

1993. Lander of the Federal Republic. As T **989**. Multicoloured.
2539 100pf. Rheinland-Pfalz . . . 1·40 50

1053 Postman delivering Letter

1993. Stamp Day.
2540 **1053** 100pf.+50pf. mult . . . 1·70 1·70

1054 "Swan Lake"

1993. Death Centenary of Pyotr Tchaikovsky (composer).
2541 **1054** 80pf. multicoloured . . 1·30 40

1055 Fohr, Schleswig-Holstein

1993. Humanitarian Relief Funds. Traditional Costumes (1st series). Multicoloured.
2542 80pf.+40pf. Type **1055** . . 1·40 1·30
2543 80pf.+40pf. Rugen, Mecklenburg-Vorpommern . . . . . . 1·40 1·30
2544 100pf.+50pf. Oberndorf, Bavaria . . . . 1·80 1·70
2545 100pf.+50pf. Schwalm, Hesse . . . . 1·80 1·70
2546 200pf.+40pf. Ernstroda, Thuringia . . . . . . 3·50 3·00
See also Nos. 2598/2602.

1056 St. Jadwiga (miniature, Schlackenwerther Codex)

1993. 750th Death Anniv of St. Jadwiga of Silesia.
2547 **1056** 100pf. multicoloured . . 1·80 45

1057 Reinhardt on Stage
1058 Brandt

1993. 50th Death Anniv of Max Reinhardt (theatrical producer).
2548 **1057** 100pf. black, brn & red 1·70 45

1993. 80th Birth Anniv of Willy Brandt (statesman).
2549 **1058** 100pf. multicoloured . . 1·90 45

1059 Monteverdi

1993. 350th Death Anniv of Claudio Monteverdi (composer).
2550 **1059** 100pf. multicoloured . . 1·70 45

1060 Paracelsus (after Augustin Hirschvogel)
1061 "Adoration of the Magi"

1993. 500th Birth Anniv of Paracelsus (physician and philosopher).
2551 **1060** 100pf. ochre, brown and green . . . . . 1·70 45

1993. Christmas. Carvings from Altar Triptych, Blaubeuren Minster. Multicoloured.
2552 80pf.+40pf. Type **1061** . . 1·10 1·20
2553 100pf.+50pf. "Birth of Christ" . . . . 2·00 1·80

1062 Quayside Buildings, Town Hall and St. Cosmas's Church

1994. Millenary of Stade.
2554 **1062** 80pf. red, brown & blue 1·20 45

1063 "FAMILIE"

1994. International Year of the Family.
2555 **1063** 100pf. multicoloured . . 1·20 45

1994. Lander of the Federal Republic. As T **989**. Multicoloured.
2556 100pf. Saarland . . . . . . 1·50 60

1064 Hertz and Electromagnetic Waves

1994. Death Centenary of Heinrich Hertz (physicist).
2557 **1064** 200pf. black, red and drab . . . . 2·40 1·10

1065 Frankfurt am Main

1994. 1200th Anniv of Frankfurt am Main.
2558 **1065** 80pf. multicoloured . . 1·20 45

1066 Ice Skating

1994. Sport Promotion Fund. Sporting Events and Anniversaries. Multicoloured.
2559 80pf.+40pf. Type **1066** (Winter Olympic Games, Lillehammer, Norway) . . 1·40 1·30
2560 100pf.+50pf. Football and trophy (World Cup Football Championship, U.S.A.) . . . . 1·80 1·60
2561 100pf.+50pf. Flame (cent of International Olympic Committee) . . . . . . 1·80 1·60
2562 200pf.+80pf. Skier (Winter Paralympic Games, Lillehammer) . . . . . . 3·25 3·00

1067 Cathedral, St. Michael's Church and Castle

1994. 1250th Anniv of Fulda.
2563 **1067** 80pf. multicoloured . . 1·00 40

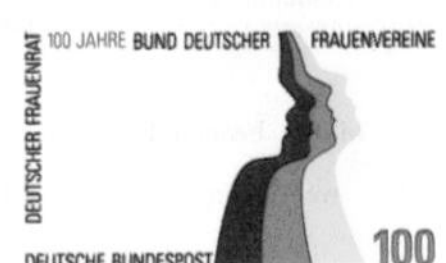

1068 Council Emblem

1994. Cent of Federation of German Women's Associations—German Women's Council.
2564 **1068** 100pf. black, red & yell 1·20 45

1069 Members' Flags as Stars

1994. 4th Direct Elections to European Parliament.
2565 **1069** 100pf. multicoloured . . 1·70 45

1070 People holding Banner

1994. "Living Together" (integration of foreign workers in Germany).
2566 **1070** 100pf. multicoloured . . 1·20 45

1994. Lander of the Federal Republic. As T **989**. Multicoloured.
2567 100pf. Saxony . . . . . . 1·50 60

1071 Johnny Head-in-the-Air

1994. Youth Welfare. Death Centenary of Heinrich Hoffmann (writer). Designs illustrating characters from "Slovenly Peter". Multicoloured.
2568 80pf.+40pf. Type **1071** . . 1·40 1·50
2569 80pf.+40pf. Little Pauline 1·40 1·50
2570 100pf.+50pf. Naughty Friederich . . . . 1·70 1·80
2571 100pf.+50pf. Slovenly Peter 1·70 1·80
2572 200pf.+80pf. Fidget-Philipp 3·25 3·25

1072 Frauenkirche

1994. 500th Anniv of Frauenkirche, Munich.
2573 **1072** 100pf. multicoloured . . 1·70 45

1073 Resistor and Formula
1074 Pfitzner (after Emil Orlik)

1994. Europa. Discoveries. Multicoloured.
2574 80pf. Type **1073** (Ohm's Law) . . . . 1·20 50
2575 100pf. Radiation from black body and formula (Max Planck's Quantum Theory) 90 45

1994. 125th Birth Anniv of Hans Pfitzner (composer).
2576 **1074** 100pf. deep blue, blue and red . . . . . . 1·20 45

1075 Hegenbeck and Animals

1994. 150th Anniversaries. Sheet 77 × 108 mm containing T **1075** and similar horiz design. Multicoloured.
MS2577 100pf. Type **1075** (birth anniv of Carl Hagenbeck (circus owner and founder of first zoo without bars)); 200pf. Animals and entrance to Berlin Zoo . . 3·50 3·75

1076 Spandau Castle

1994. 400th Anniv of Spandau Castle.
2578 **1076** 80pf. multicoloured . . 1·20 45

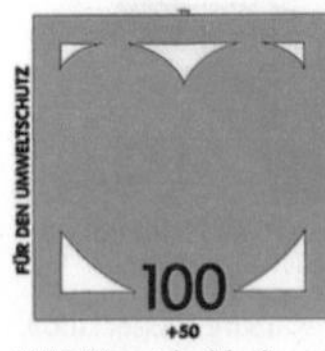

1077 Village Sign showing Society Emblem

1994. Centenary of Herzogsagmuhle (Society for the Domestic Missions welfare village).
2579 **1077** 100pf. multicoloured . . 1·30 45

1994. Lander of the Federal Republic. As T **989**. Multicoloured.
2580 100pf. Saxony-Anhalt . . . 1·50 60

1078 Heart inside Square
1079 Friedrich II (13th-century miniature, "Book of Falcons")

1994. Environmental Protection.
2581 **1078** 100pf.+50pf. green and black . . . . 1·70 1·60

1994. 800th Birth Anniv of Emperor Friedrich II.
2582 **1079** 400pf. multicoloured . . 4·25 3·25

1080 "20 JULY 1944" behind Bars

1994. 50th Anniv of Attempt to Assassinate Hitler. Sheet 105 × 70 mm.
MS2583 **1080** 100pf. black, yellow and red . . . . 1·70 1·50

1994. Lander of the Federal Republic. As T **989**. Multicoloured.
2584 100pf. Schleswig-Holstein . . 1·50 60

1994. Landscapes (2nd series). As T **1046**. Multicoloured.
2585 100pf. The Alps . . . . . . 1·30 65
2586 100pf. Erzgebirge . . . . . 1·30 65
2587 100pf. Main valley . . . . 1·30 65
2588 100pf. Mecklenburg lakes . . 1·30 65

1081 Herder (after Anton Graff)

1994. 250th Birth Anniv of Johann Gottfried Herder (philosopher).
2589 **1081** 80pf. multicoloured . . 1·20 45

1994. 20th-century German Paintings (3rd series). As T **1003**. Multicoloured.
2590 100pf. "Maika" (Christian Schad) 90 55
2591 200pf. "Dresden Landscape" (Erich Heckel) . . . . . 2·10 1·90
2592 300pf. "Aleksei Javlensky and Marianne Werefkin" (Gabriele Munter) . . . . 3·25 2·30

1082 Early 20th-century Makonde Mask (Tanzania)

1994. 125th Anniv of Leipzig Ethnology Museum.
2593 **1082** 80pf. multicoloured . . 1·20 45

1083 Helmholtz, Eye and Colour Triangle

1994. Death Centenary of Hermann von Helmholtz (physicist).
2594 **1083** 100pf. multicoloured . . 1·30 45

1084 Richter
1086 St. Wolfgang with Church Model (woodcut)

1085 "Flying on Dragon"

1994. Birth Cent of Willi Richter (President of Confederation of German Trade Unions).
2595 **1084** 100pf. brown, purple and black . . . . . 1·30 45

1994. "For Us Children". Sheet 106 × 61 mm.
MS2596 **1085** 100pf. multicoloured 1·50 1·50

1994. Lander of the Federal Republic. As T **989**. Multicoloured.
2597 100pf. Thuringia . . . . . 1·50 60

1994. Humanitarian Relief Funds. Traditional Costumes (2nd series). As T **1055**. Multicoloured.
2598 80pf.+40pf. Buckeburg . . . 1·40 1·30
2599 80pf.+40pf. Halle an der Saale . . . . 1·40 1·40
2600 100pf.+50pf. Minden . . . 1·80 1·70
2601 100pf.+50pf. Hoyerswerda . 1·80 1·70
2602 200pf.+70pf. Betzingen . . . 2·75 2·75

1994. Death Millenary of St. Wolfgang, Bishop of Regensburg.
2603 **1086** 100pf. gold, cream and black . . . . 1·30 45

1087 Sachs

1088 Spreewald Postman, 1900

1994. 500th Birth Anniv of Hans Sachs (mastersinger and poet).
2604 **1087** 100pf. purple and green on greyish . . . . . 1·30 45

1994. Stamp Day.
2605 **1088** 100pf. multicoloured . . 1·30 45

1089 Quedlinburg

1090 "Adoration of the Magi"

1994. Millenary of Quedlinburg.
2606 **1089** 80pf. multicoloured . . 1·20 45

1994. Christmas. 500th Death Anniv of Hans Memling (painter). Details of his triptych in St. John's Hospice, Bruges. Multicoloured.
2607 80pf.+40pf. Type **1090** . . 1·40 1·30
2608 100pf.+50pf. "Nativity" . . 1·80 1·70

1091 Steuben and "Surrender of Cornwallis at Yorktown" (detail, John Trumbull)

1994. Death Bicentenary of Gen. Friedrich Wilhelm von Steuben (Inspector General of Washington's Army).
2609 **1091** 100pf. multicoloured . . 1·30 45

1092 Cemetery

1994. 75th Anniv of National Assn for the Preservation of German Graves Abroad.
2610 **1092** 100pf. black and red . . 1·30 45

1093 Obersuhl Checkpoint, 11 November 1989

1994. 5th Anniv of Opening of Borders between East and West Germany.
2611 **1093** 100pf. multicoloured . . 1·30 45

1094 Fontane (after Max Liebermann) and Lines from "Prussian Song"

1095 Simson Fountain, Town Hall and St. Mary's and St Salvator's Churches

1994. 175th Birth Anniv of Theodor Fontane (writer).
2612 **1094** 100pf. green, black and mauve . . . . 1·30 45

1995. Millenary of Gera.
2613 **1095** 80pf. multicoloured . . 1·00 45

1096 Emperor Friedrich III, First Page of "Libellus" and Zur Munze (venue)

1995. 500th Anniv of Diet of Worms.
2614 **1096** 100pf. black and red . . 1·20 60

1995. 20th-century German Paintings (4th series). As T **1003**. Multicoloured.
2615 100pf. "The Water Tower, Bremen" (Franz Radziwill) . . . . 1·10 70
2616 200pf. "Still Life with Cat" (Georg Schrimpf) . . . . 2·30 2·10
2617 300pf. "Estate in Dangast" (Karl Schmidt-Rottluff) 3·00 2·40

1097 Canoeing

1098 Friedrich Wilhelm (after A. Romandon)

1995. Sport Promotion Fund. Multicoloured.
2618 80pf.+40pf. Type **1097** (27th World Canoeing Championships, Duisburg) . . . . 1·20 1·20
2619 100pf.+50pf. Hoop exercises (10th Int Gymnastics Festival, Berlin) . . . . . 1·40 1·50
2620 100pf.+50pf. Boxing (8th World Amateur Boxing Championships, Berlin) 1·40 1·50
2621 200pf.+80pf. Volleyball (centenary) . . . . 3·25 3·00

1995. 375th Birth Anniv of Friedrich Wilhelm of Brandenburg, The Great Elector.
2622 **1098** 300pf. multicoloured . . 3·50 2·75

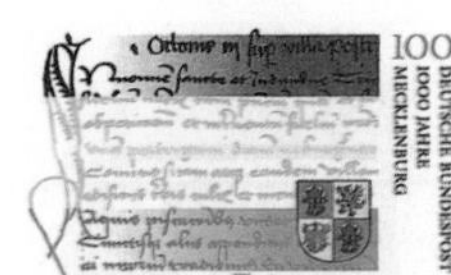

1099 Deed of Donation (995) and Arms of Mecklenburg-Vorpommern

1995. Millenary of Mecklenburg.
2623 **1099** 100pf. multicoloured . . 1·20 60

1100 Computer Image of Terminal and Lion

1995. 250th Anniv of Carolo-Wilhelmina Technical University, Braunschweig.
2624 **1100** 100pf. multicoloured . . 1·20 60

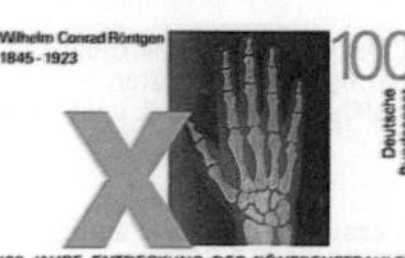

1101 X-ray of Hand

1995. 150th Birth Anniv of Wilhelm Rontgen and Centenary of his Discovery of X-rays.
2625 **1101** 100pf. multicoloured . . 1·20 60

1102 Globe and Rainbow

1995. 1st Conference of Signatories to General Convention on Climate, Berlin.
2626 **1102** 100pf. multicoloured . . 1·20 60

1103 Old Town Hall Reliefs

1995. 750th Anniv of Regensburg.
2627 **1103** 80pf. multicoloured . . 90 50

1104 Bonhoeffer

1995. 50th Death Anniv of Dietrich Bonhoeffer (theologian).
2628 **1104** 100pf. black, bl & grey 1·20 60

1105 Symbols of Speech, Writing and Pictures

1995. Freedom of Expression.
2629 **1105** 100pf. multicoloured . . 1·20 60

1106 St. Clement's Church, Munster

1995. 300th Birth Anniv of Johann Conrad Schlaun (architect).
2630 **1106** 200pf. multicoloured . . 2·20 1·70

1107 Friedrich Schiller, Signature and Schiller Museum, Marbach

1108 St. Vincent de Paul

1995. Centenary of German Schiller Society.
2631 **1107** 100pf. multicoloured . . 1·20 60

1995. 150th Anniv of Vincent Conferences (charitable organization) in Germany.
2632 **1108** 100pf. multicoloured . . 1·20 60

1109 Number on Cloth and Barbed Wire

1995. 50th Anniv of Liberation of Concentration Camps. Sheet 105 × 70 mm.
MS2633 **1109** 100pf. grey, blue and black . . . . 1·40 1·30

1110 City Ruins

1995. 50th Anniv of End of Second World War. Sheet 104 × 70 mm containing T **1110** and similar square design. Multicoloured.
MS2634 100pf. Type **1110**; 100pf. Refugees . . . . 2·50 2·50

1111 Returning Soldiers ("End of War")

1112 Shipping Routes before and after 1895

1995. Europa. Peace and Freedom.
2635 **1111** 100pf. black and red . . 1·10 60
2636 – 200pf. blue, yell & blk 2·20 1·70
DESIGN: 200pf. Emblem of European Community ("Moving towards Europe").

1995. Centenary of Kiel Canal.
2637 **1112** 80pf. multicoloured . . 1·00 55

1113 Guglielmo Marconi and Wireless Equipment

1995. 100 Years of Radio.
2638 **1113** 100pf. multicoloured . . 1·20 60

1114 U.N. Emblem

1995. 50th Anniv of U.N.O.
2639 **1114** 100pf. lilac, gold and grey . . . . 1·20 60

1115 Munsterlander

1116 Opening Bars of "Carmina Burana" and Characters

1995. Youth Welfare. Dogs (1st series). Mult.
2640 80pf.+40pf. Type **1115** . . 1·20 1·20
2641 80pf.+40pf. Giant schnauzer 1·20 1·20
2642 100pf.+50pf. Wire-haired dachshund . . . . 1·60 1·70
2643 100pf.+50pf. German shepherd . . . . 1·60 1·70
2644 200pf.+80pf. Keeshund . . 3·00 3·00
See also Nos. 2696/2700.

1995. Birth Centenary of Carl Orff (composer).
2645 **1116** 100pf. multicoloured . . 1·20 60

1995. Landscapes (3rd series). As T **1046**. Multicoloured.
2646 100pf. Franconian Switzerland . . . . 1·10 75
2647 100pf. River Havel, Berlin 1·10 75
2648 100pf. Oberlausitz . . . . . 1·10 75
2649 100pf. Sauerland . . . . . 1·10 75

1117 Lion (from 12th-century coin)

1118 Kaiser Wilhelm Memorial Church

1995. 800th Death Anniv of Henry the Lion, Duke of Saxony and Bavaria.
2650 **1117** 400pf. multicoloured . . 4·00 3·25

1995. Centenary of Kaiser Wilhelm Memorial Church, Berlin.
2651 **1118** 100pf. multicoloured . . 1·20 60

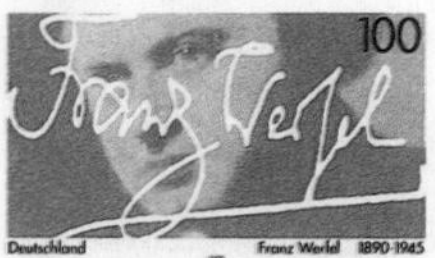

1119 Werfel and Signature

1995. 50th Death Anniv of Franz Werfel (writer).
2652 **1119** 100pf. mauve, bl & blk 1·20 60

1995. Tourist Sights. As T **854** but inscr "DEUTSCHLAND".
2654 47pf. green and black . . . 55 60
2656 100pf. blue and black . . . 90 80
2657 110pf. cinnamon and brown 1·10 60
2658 110pf. orange and blue . . . 1·20 70
2659 220pf. green and black . . . 2·10 1·10
2661 440pf. orange and blue . . . 4·50 3·50
2663 510pf. red and blue . . . . 5·50 4·00
2665 640pf. blue and brown . . . 6·25 4·00
2666 690pf. black and green . . . 6·75 4·75
DESIGNS: 47pf. Berus Monument, Uberherrn; 100pf. Goethe-Schiller Monument, Weimar; 110pf. (2657) Bellevue Castle, Berlin; 110pf. (2658) Emblem of "Expo 2000" World's Fair, Hanover; 220pf. Bruhl's Terrace, Dresden; 440pf. Town Hall, Bremen; 510pf. Holsten Gate, Lubeck; 640pf. Speyer Cathedral; 690pf. St. Michael's Church, Hamburg.

1120 Strauss

1995. 80th Birth Anniv of Franz Josef Strauss (politician).
2675 **1120** 100pf. multicoloured . . 1·20 60

1121 Postwoman

1995. Stamp Day.
2676 **1121** 200pf.+100pf. mult . . 3·00 2·75

1122 "Metropolis" (dir. Fritz Lang)

1995. Centenary of Motion Pictures. Sheet 100 × 130 mm containing T **1122** and similar horiz designs showing frames from films. Multicoloured.
MS2677 80pf. Type **1122**; 100pf. "Little Superman" (dir. Wolfgang Staudte); 200pf. "The Sky over Berlin" (dir. Wim Wenders) . . 4·00 4·50

1123 Eifel

1995. Humanitarian Relief Funds. Farmhouses (1st series). Multicoloured.
2678 80pf.+40pf. Type **1123** . . 1·20 1·20
2679 80pf.+40pf. Saxony . . . . 1·20 1·20
2680 100pf.+50pf. Lower Germany . . . . 1·60 1·70
2681 100pf.+50pf. Upper Bavaria 1·60 1·70
2682 200pf.+70pf. Mecklenburg 3·00 3·00
See also Nos. 2742/6.

1124 Schumacher

1126 Ranke

1125 Animals gathered on Hill

1995. Birth Centenary of Kurt Schumacher (politician).
2683 **1124** 100pf. multicoloured . . 1·20 60

1995. "For Us Children". Sheet 110 × 60 mm.
MS2684 **1125** 80pf. multicoloured 1·30 1·30

1995. Birth Bicentenary of Leopold von Ranke (historian).
2685 **1126** 80pf. multicoloured . . 90 55

1127 Hindemith

1995. Birth Centenary of Paul Hindemith (composer).
2686 **1127** 100pf. multicoloured . . 1·20 60

1128 Alfred Nobel and Will

1995. Centenary of Nobel Prize Trust Fund.
2687 **1128** 100pf. multicoloured . . 1·20 60

1129 "CARE" in American Colours

1995. 50th Anniv of CARE (Co-operative for Assistance and Remittances Overseas).
2688 **1129** 100pf. multicoloured . . 1·20 60

1130 Berlin Wall

1995. Commemorating Victims of Political Oppression, 1945–89.
2689 **1130** 100pf. multicoloured . . 1·20 60

1131 "The Annunciation"

1995. Christmas. Stained Glass Windows in Augsburg Cathedral. Multicoloured.
2690 80pf.+40pf. Type **1131** . . 1·30 1·30
2691 100pf.+50pf. "Nativity" . . 1·70 1·70

1132 Dribbling

1995. Borussia Dortmund, German Football Champions.
2692 **1132** 100pf. multicoloured . . 1·20 60

1133 Auguste von Sartorius (founder)

1996. 150th Anniv of German Institute for Children's Missionary Work.
2693 **1133** 100pf. multicoloured . . 1·00 60

1134 Bodelschwingh

1996. 50th Death Anniv of Friedrich von Bodelschwingh (theologian).
2694 **1134** 100pf. black and red . . 1·00 60

1135 Luther (after Lucas Cranach)

1996. 450th Death Anniv of Martin Luther (Protestant reformer).
2695 **1135** 100pf. multicoloured . . 1·00 60

1996. Youth Welfare. Dogs (2nd series). As T **1115**. Multicoloured.
2696 80pf.+40pf. Borzoi . . . . 1·30 1·30
2697 80pf.+40pf. Chow chow . . 1·30 1·30
2698 100pf.+50pf. St. Bernard . . 1·70 1·70
2699 100pf.+50pf. Rough collie 1·70 1·70
2700 200pf.+80pf. Briard . . . . 2·75 3·00

1136 Siebold

1996. Birth Bicentenary of Philipp Franz von Siebold (physician and Japanologist).
2701 **1136** 100pf. multicoloured . . 1·00 60

1137 Cathedral Square

1996. Millenary of Cathedral Square, Halberstadt.
2702 **1137** 80pf. multicoloured . . 85 50

1138 Galen

1996. 50th Death Anniv of Cardinal Count Clemens von Galen, Bishop of Munster.
2703 **1138** 100pf. grey, blue & gold 1·00 60

1996. 20th-century German Paintings (5th series). As T **1003**. Multicoloured.
2704 100pf. "Seated Female Nude" (Max Pechstein) 1·10 70
2705 200pf. "For Wilhelm Runge" (Georg Muche) 2·00 1·80
2706 300pf. "Still Life with Guitar, Book and Vase" (Helmut Kolle) . . . . . 3·00 2·20

1139 Detail of Ceiling Fresco, Prince-bishop's Residence, Wurzburg

1996. 300th Birth Anniv of Giovanni Battista Tiepolo (artist).
2707 **1139** 200pf. multicoloured . . 1·90 1·60

1140 Post Runner

1141 Paula Modersohn-Becker (self-portrait)

1996. "For Us Children". Sheet 83 × 67 mm.
MS2708 **1140** 100pf. multicoloured 1·00 1·20

1996. Landscapes (4th series). As T **1046**. Multicoloured.
2709 100pf. Eifel . . . . 1·00 70
2710 100pf. Holstein Switzerland 1·00 70
2711 100pf. Saale . . . . 1·00 70
2712 100pf. Spreewald . . . . . 1·00 70

1996. Europa. Famous Women.
2713 **1141** 80pf. multicoloured . . 85 55
2714 – 100pf. black, grey and mauve . . . . 1·10 70
DESIGN: 100pf. Kathe Kollwitz (self-portrait).

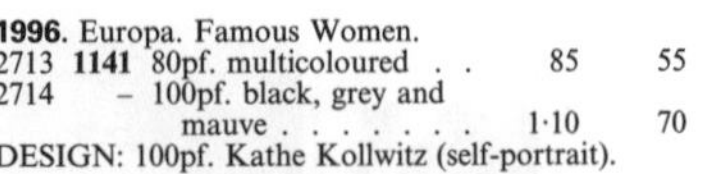

1142 Opening Lines of Document and Town (1642 engraving, Matthaeus Merian)

1996. Millenary of Granting to Freising the Right to hold Markets.
2715 **1142** 100pf. multicoloured . . 1·00 60

1143 Borchert

1996. 75th Birth Anniv of Wolfgang Borchert (writer).
2716 **1143** 100pf. multicoloured . . 1·00 60

1144 Emblem

1996. 50th Anniv of Ruhr Festival, Recklinghausen.
2717 **1144** 100pf. multicoloured . . 1·00 60

1145 Ticket and Stage Curtain

1996. 150th Anniv of German Theatre Assn.
2718 **1145** 200pf. multicoloured . . 1·90 1·50

1146 Leibniz and Mathematical Diagram

1996. 350th Birth Anniv of Gottfried Leibniz.
2719 **1146** 100pf. red and black . . 1·00 60

1147 Kneeling Figure and Motto forming "A"

1996. 300th Anniv of Berlin Academy of Arts.
2720 **1147** 100pf. multicoloured . . 1·00 60

1148 Carl Schuhmann (wrestling, equestrian sports and gymnastics, 1896)

1996. Sport Promotion Fund. Centenary of Modern Olympic Games. German Olympic Champions. Multicoloured.
2721 80pf.+40pf. Type **1148** . . 1·20 1·30
2722 100pf.+50pf. Josef Neckermann (dressage, 1964 and 1968) . . . . . 1·60 1·70
2723 100pf.+50pf. Annie Hubler-Horn (ice skating, 1908) 1·60 1·70
2724 200pf.+80pf. Alfred and Gustav Flatow (gymnastics, 1896) . . . . 3·00 3·00

1149 Townscape

1996. 800th Anniv of Heidelberg.
2725 **1149** 100pf. multicoloured . . 1·00 60

1150 Children's Handprints

1996. 50th Anniv of UNICEF.
2726 **1150** 100pf. multicoloured . . 1·00 60

1151 "Wedding" (illustration by Bruno Paul)

1996. 75th Death Anniv of Ludwig Thoma (satirist).
2727 **1151** 100pf. multicoloured . . 1·00 60

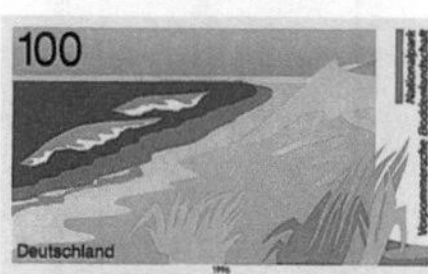

1152 Beach

1996. Western Pomerania National Park. Sheet 166 × 111 mm containing T **1152** and similar horiz designs showing Park landscapes. Multicoloured.
MS2728 100pf. Type **1152**; 200pf. Mudflat; 300pf. Sea inlet . . . 6·25 5·75

1153 Map and Tropical Wildlife

1996. Environmental Protection. Preservation of Tropical Habitats.
2729 **1153** 100pf.+50pf. mult . . . 1·50 1·50

1154 Volklingen Blast Furnace

1996. UNESCO World Heritage Sites.
2730 **1154** 100pf. multicoloured . . 1·00 60

1155 Lincke

1996. 50th Death Anniv of Paul Lincke (composer and conductor).
2731 **1155** 100pf. multicoloured . . 1·00 60

1156 Gendarmenmarkt, Berlin

1996. Images of Germany.
2732 **1156** 100pf. multicoloured . . 1·00 60

1157 "50" comprising Stamp under Magnifying Glass

1996. Stamp Day. 50th Anniv of Association of German Philatelists.
2733 **1157** 100pf. multicoloured . . 1·00 60

1158 Book

1996. Centenary of German Civil Code.
2734 **1158** 300pf. multicoloured . . 3·00 2·20

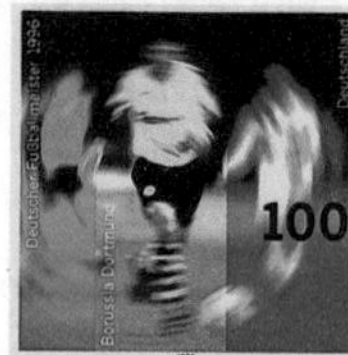

1159 Players

1996. Borussia Dortmund, German Football Champions.
2735 **1159** 100pf. multicoloured . . 1·00 60

1160 Bamburg Old Town

1996. UNESCO World Heritage Sites.
2736 **1160** 100pf. multicoloured . . 1·00 60

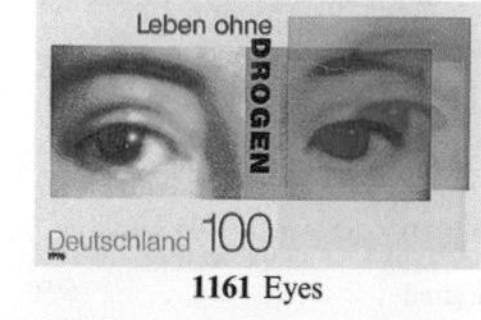

1161 Eyes

1996. "Life without Drugs".
2737 **1161** 100pf. multicoloured . . 1·00 60

1162 "Like will Cure Like" and Samuel Hahnemann (developer of principle)

1163 Bruckner and Symphony No. III

1996. Bicentenary of Homeopathy.
2738 **1162** 400pf. multicoloured . . 3·75 3·50

1996. Death Centenary of Anton Bruckner (composer).
2739 **1163** 100pf. multicoloured . . 1·00 60

1164 Mueller, Map and Plants

1996. Death Centenary of Ferdinand von Mueller (botanist).
2740 **1164** 100pf. multicoloured . . 1·00 60

1165 Score by John Cage

1996. 75th Anniv of Donaueschingen Music Festival.
2741 **1165** 100pf. blue, blk & mve 1·00 60

1996. Humanitarian Relief Funds. Farmhouses (2nd series). As T **1123**. Multicoloured.
2742 80pf.+40pf. Spree Forest . . 1·10 1·20
2743 80pf.+40pf. Thuringia . . . 1·10 1·20
2744 100pf.+50pf. Black Forest 1·50 1·60
2745 100pf.+50pf. Westphalia . . 1·50 1·60
2746 200pf.+70pf. Schleswig-Holstein . . . . 3·00 3·25

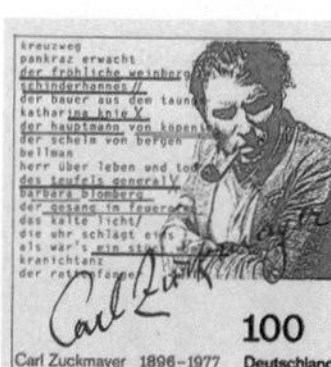

1166 Titles of Plays and Zuckmayer

1996. Birth Centenary of Carl Zuckmayer (dramatist).
2747 **1166** 100pf. multicoloured . . 1·00 60

1167 "Adoration of the Magi"

1996. Christmas. Illustrations from Henry II's "Book of Pericopes" (illuminated manuscript of readings from the Gospels). Multicoloured.
2748 80pf.+40pf. Type **1167** . . 1·30 1·30
2749 100pf.+50pf. "Nativity" . . 1·70 1·70

1168 Schmid

1996. Birth Centenary of Carlo Schmid (politician and writer).
2750 **1168** 100pf. multicoloured . . 1·00 60

1169 "Friends of Schubert in Afzenbrugg" (detail, L. Kupelwieser)

1170 Pitch, Player and Herberger

1997. Birth Bicentenary of Franz Schubert (composer).
2751 **1169** 100pf. multicoloured . . 1·00 60

1997. Birth Centenary of Sepp Herberger (national football team coach, 1936–64).
2752 **1170** 100pf. green, red & blk 1·00 60

1171 Motor Cars

1997. "More Safety for Children" (road safety campaign).
2752a **1171** 10pf. multicoloured . . 30 25
2753 100pf. multicoloured 1·00 60

1172 Melanchthon (after Lucas Cranach the younger)

1173 Revellers "Wiggling"

1997. 500th Birth Anniv of Philipp Melanchthon (religious reformer).
2754 **1172** 100pf. multicoloured . . 1·00 60

1997. 175th Anniv of Cologne Carnival.
2755 **1173** 100pf. multicoloured . . 1·00 60

1174 Erhard

1997. Birth Centenary of Ludwig Erhard (Chancellor, 1963–66).
2756 **1174** 100pf. black and red . . 1·00 60

1175 Aerobics

1997. Sport Promotion Fund. Fun Sports. Multicoloured.
2757 80pf.+40pf. Type **1175** . . 1·20 1·20
2758 100pf.+50pf. Inline skating 1·60 1·60
2759 100pf.+50pf. Streetball . . . 1·60 1·60
2760 200pf.+80pf. Freeclimbing 3·00 2·50

1176 New Pavilion

1997. 500th Anniv of Granting of Imperial Fair Rights to Leipzig.
2761 **1176** 100pf. silver, red & blue 1·00 60

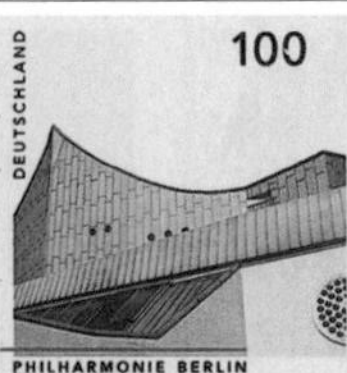
1177 Philharmonic, Berlin (Hans Scharoun)

1997. Post-1945 German Architecture. Sheet 137 × 101 mm containing T **1177** and similar square designs. Multicoloured.
MS2762 100pf. Type **1177**; 100pf. National Gallery, Berlin (Ludwig Miles van der Rohe); 100pf. St. Mary, Queen of Peace Pilgrimage Church, Neviges (Gottfried Bohm); 100pf. German Pavilion, 1967 World's Trade Fair, Montreal (Frei Otto) . . 3·75 4·00

1178 Straubing

1997. 1100th Anniv of Straubing.
2763 **1178** 100pf. multicoloured . . 1·00 60

1179 Stephan, Telephone and Postcards

1997. Death Centenary of Heinrich von Stephan (founder of U.P.U.).
2764 **1179** 100pf. multicoloured . . 1·00 60

1180 Augustusburg and Falkenlust Castles

1997. UNESCO World Heritage Sites.
2765 **1180** 100pf. multicoloured . . 1·00 60

1181 Diamonds 1182 St. Adalbert

1997. 500th Anniv of Idar-Oberstein Region Gem Industry.
2766 **1181** 300pf. multicoloured . . 3·00 2·30

1997. Death Millenary of St. Adalbert (Bishop of Prague).
2767 **1182** 100pf. lilac . . . . . . 1·00 60

1183 "The Fisherman and His Wife" (Brothers Grimm)

1997. Europa. Tales and Legends. Mult.
2768 80pf. Type **1183** 90 60
2769 100pf. "Rubezahl" . . . . 1·10 70

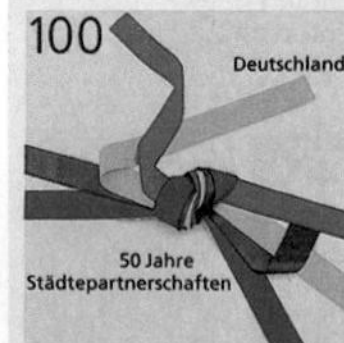
1184 Knotted Ribbons

1997. 50th Anniv of Town Twinning Movement.
2770 **1184** 100pf. multicoloured . . 1·00 60

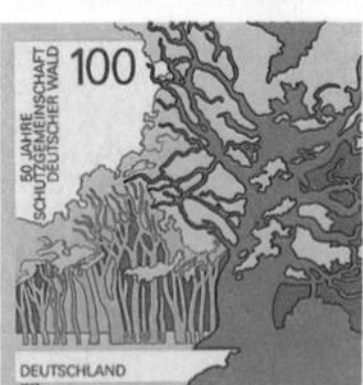
1185 Deciduous Trees

1997. 50th Anniv of Society for the Protection of the German Forest. Sheet 105 × 70 mm containing T **1185** and similar square design. Multicoloured.
MS2771 100pf. Type **1185**; 200pf. Evergreen trees . . . . 3·00 2·75

1186 Kneipp

1997. Death Cent of Father Sebastian Kneipp (developer of naturopathic treatments).
2772 **1186** 100pf. multicoloured . . 1·00 60

1187 United States Flag, George Marshall and Bomb Site

1997. 50th Anniv of Marshall Plan (European Recovery Program).
2773 **1187** 100pf. multicoloured . . 1·00 60

1188 Rheno-German Heavy Horse

1997. Youth Welfare. Horses. Multicoloured.
2774 80pf.+40pf. Type **1188** . . . 1·20 1·20
2775 80pf.+40pf. Shetland ponies 1·20 1·20
2776 100pf.+50pf. Frisian . . . . 1·60 1·50
2777 100pf.+50pf. Haflinger . . . 1·60 1·50
2778 200pf.+80pf. Hanoverian with foal . . . . 3·00 2·75

1189 Train on Bridge

1997. Centenary of Mungsten Railway Bridge.
2779 **1189** 100pf. multicoloured . . 1·00 60

1997. Famous Women. As T **832** but inscr "Deutschland".
2785 100pf. brown and green . . 1·10 65
2786 110pf. drab and violet . . . 1·00 65
2790 220pf. ultramarine and blue 2·30 1·50
2792 300pf. brown and blue . . . 3·00 2·00
2795 440pf. brown and violet . . 4·50 3·25
DESIGNS: 100pf. Elisabeth Schwarzhaupt (politician); 110pf. Marlene Dietrich (actress); 220pf. Marie-Elisabeth Luders (politician); 300pf. Maria Probst (social reformer and politician); 440pf. Gret Palucca (dancer).

1190 "Composition" (Fritz Winter)

1997. 10th "Documenta" Modern Art Exhibition, Kassel. Sheet 137 × 97 mm containing T **1190** and similar horiz designs. Multicoloured.
MS2780 100pf. Type **1190**; 100pf. "Mouth No. 15" (Tom Wesselmann); 100pf. "Quathlamba" (Frank Stella); 100pf. "Beuys/Bois" (Nam June Paik) . . . . 4·00 4·00

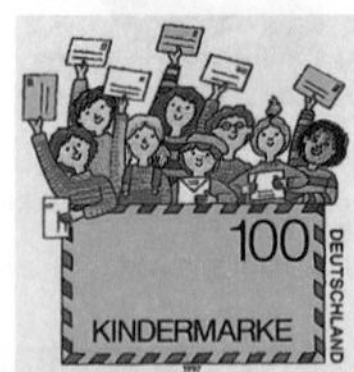
1191 Children holding Envelopes

1997. "For Us Children". Sheet 70 × 105 mm.
MS2781 **1191** 100pf. multicoloured 1·20 1·10

1192 Arms of Brandenburg

1997. Flood Relief Funds.
2805 **1192** 110pf.+90pf. mult . . . 1·90 1·60

1997. Landscapes (5th series). As T **1046**. Multicoloured.
2806 110pf. Bavarian Forest . . . 1·20 80
2807 110pf. North German Moors . . . . 1·20 80
2808 110pf. Luneburg Heath . . 1·20 80

1193 Rudolf Diesel and First Oil Engine

1997. Centenary of Diesel Engine.
2809 **1193** 300pf. black and blue 3·00 2·30

1194 Potato Plant and Cultivation

1997. 350th Anniv of Introduction of the Potato to Germany.
2810 **1194** 300pf. multicoloured . . 3·00 2·30

1195 Biplane and Motorized Tricycle

1997. Stamp Day. Sheet 70 × 105 mm.
MS2811 **1195** 440pf.+220pf. multicoloured . . . . 6·50 5·75

1196 Mendelssohn-Bartholdy and Music Score

1997. 150th Death Anniv of Felix Mendelssohn-Bartholdy (composer).
2813 **1196** 110pf. green, olive & yell . . . . 1·20 70

1197 Watermill, Black Forest

1997. Humanitarian Relief Funds. Mills. Multicoloured.
2814 100pf.+50pf. Type **1197** . . 1·80 1·10
2815 110pf.+50pf. Watermill, Hesse . . . . 2·10 1·80
2816 110pf.+50pf. Post mill, Lower Rhine . . . . . . 2·10 1·80
2817 110pf.+50pf. Scoop windmill, Schleswig-Holstein . . . . 2·10 1·80
2818 220pf.+80pf. Dutch windmill 3·25 2·30

1198 Emblem

1997. Saar–Lor–Lux European Region.
2819 **1198** 110pf. multicoloured . . 1·20 1·90

1199 Team celebrating

1997. Bayern Munchen, German Football Champions.
2820 **1199** 110pf. multicoloured . . 1·20 70

1200 Dehler

1997. Birth Centenary of Thomas Dehler (politician).
2821 **1200** 110pf. multicoloured . . 1·20 70

1201 Heine (after Wilhelm Hensel)

1997. Birth Bicentenary of Heinrich Heine (journalist and poet).
2822 **1201** 110pf. multicoloured . . 1·20 70

1202 Tree and Title of Hymn

1997. 300th Birth Anniv of Gerhard Tersteegen (religious reformer).
2823 **1202** 110pf. brown, grey and black . . . . 1·20 75

1203 Emblem

1997. Cent of Deutscher Caritas Verband (Catholic charitable association).
2824 **1203** 110pf. multicoloured . . 1·20 70

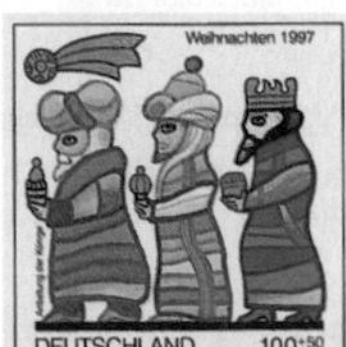
1204 Three Kings

1997. Christmas. Multicoloured.
2825 100pf.+50pf. Type **1204** . . 1·50 85
2826 110pf.+50pf. Nativity . . . 1·80 1·70
The premium was for the benefit of the Federal Association of Free Welfare Work, Bonn.

1205 Monastery Plan and Church

1998. UNESCO World Heritage Site. Maulbronn Monastery.
2827 **1205** 100pf. multicoloured . . 1·00 1·30

1206 Walled City

1998. 1100th Anniv of Nordlingen.
2828 **1206** 110pf. multicoloured . . 1·20 70

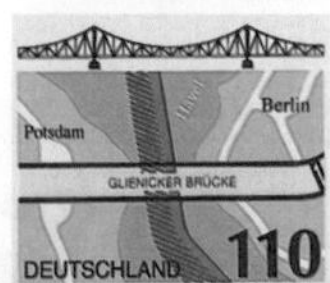
1207 Glienicke Bridge, Potsdam–Berlin

1998. Bridges. (1st series).
2829 **1207** 110pf. multicoloured . . 1·20 70
See also Nos. 2931, 2956 and 3046.

1208 Football

1998. Sport Promotion Fund. International Championships. Multicoloured.
2830 100pf.+50pf. Type **1208** (World Cup Football Championship, France) 1·50 85
2831 110pf.+50pf. Ski jumping (Winter Olympic Games, Nagano, Japan) . . . . . 1·70 1·60
2832 110pf.+50pf. Rowing (World Rowing Championships, Cologne) . . . . 1·70 1·60
2833 300pf.+100pf. Disabled skier (Winter Paralympic Games, Nagano) . . . . 4·25 2·75

1209 Characters in Brecht's Head

1998. Birth Centenary of Bertolt Brecht (dramatist).
2834 **1209** 110pf. multicoloured . . 1·20 2·20

1210 X-ray Photographs of Moon, Ionic Lattice Structure and Nerve of Goldfish and Founding Assembly

1998. 50th Anniv of Max Planck Society for the Advancement of Science.
2835 **1210** 110pf. multicoloured . . 1·20 70

1211 Bad Frankenhausen

1998. Millenary of First Documentary Mention of Bad Frankenhausen.
2836 **1211** 110pf. multicoloured . . 1·20 65

1212 Signatories

1998. 350th Anniv of Peace of Westphalia (settlements ending Thirty Years' War).
2837 **1212** 110pf. blk, grey & mve 1·20 70

1213 Baden-Wurttemberg (Kurt Viertel)

1998. Federal State Parliament Buildings (1st series). Multicoloured.
2838 110pf. Type **1213** . . . . . 1·10 70
2839 110pf. Bavaria (designed Friedrich Burklein) . . . 1·10 75
2840 110pf. Chamber of Deputies, Berlin (Friedrich Schulze) 1·10 75
2841 110pf. Brandenburg (Franz Schwechten) . . . . . . 1·10 75
See also Nos. 2885, 2893/4, 2897, 2953, 2957, 2978, 3025, 3043, 3052, 3064 and 3071.

1214 Hildegard's Vision of Life Cycle

1998. 900th Birth Anniv of Hildegard of Bingen (writer and mystic).
2842 **1214** 100pf. multicoloured . . 1·00 65

1215 Marine Life

1998. "For Us Children". Sheet 110 × 66 mm.
MS2843 **1215** 110pf. multicoloured 1·20 1·20

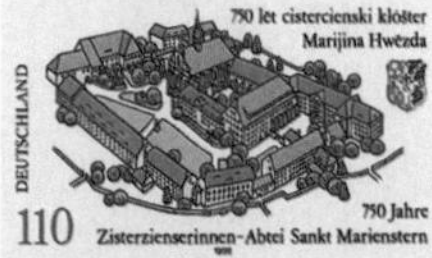
1216 St. Marienstern Abbey

1998. 750th Anniv of St. Marienstern Abbey, Panschwitz-Kuckau.
2844 **1216** 110pf. multicoloured . . 1·20 70

1217 Auditorium

1998. 250th Anniv of Bayreuth Opera House.
2845 **1217** 300pf. multicoloured . . 3·00 2·30

1218 Junger

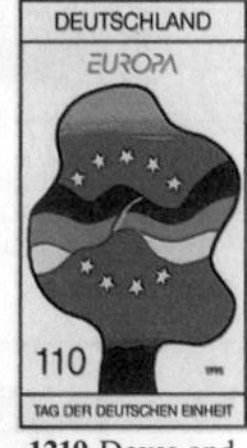
1219 Doves and Tree (German Unification Day)

1998. Ernst Junger (writer) Commemoration.
2846 **1218** 110pf. multicoloured . . 1·20 70

1998. Europa. National Festivals.
2847 **1219** 110pf. multicoloured . . 1·20 70

1220 Association Manifesto

1998. 50th Anniv of German Rural Women's Association.
2848 **1220** 110pf. grn, emer & blk 1·40 80

1221 Opening Session of Parliamentary Council, 1948

1998. Parliamentary Anniversaries. Sheet 105 × 70 mm containing T **1221** and similar square design. Multicoloured.
MS2849 110pf. Type **1221**; 220pf. First German National Assembly, St. Paul's Church, Frankfurt, 1848 3·25 3·25

1222 Coast and Ocean

1998. Environmental Protection.
2850 **1222** 110pf.+50pf. mult . . . 1·70 1·70

1223 "The Mouse"

1224 Crowds of People and Cross

1998. Youth Welfare. Children's Cartoons. Multicoloured.
2851 100pf.+50pf. Type **1223** . . 1·40 1·50
2852 100pf.+50pf. "The Sandman" . . . . 1·40 1·50
2853 110pf.+50pf. "Maja the Bee" . . . . 1·70 1·60
2854 110pf.+50pf. "Captain Bluebear" . . . . 1·70 1·60
2855 220pf.+80pf. "Pumuckl" . . 3·50 3·00

1998. 150th Anniv of First Congress of German Catholics.
2856 **1224** 110pf. multicoloured . . 1·20 70

1225 One Deutschmark Coin

1998. 50th Anniv of the Deutschmark.
2857 **1225** 110pf. multicoloured . . 1·20 70

1226 Harvesting Hops

1998. 1100 Years of Hop Cultivation in Germany.
2858 **1226** 110pf. multicoloured . . 1·20 70

1227 Euro Banknotes forming "EZB"

1998. Inauguration of European Central Bank, Frankfurt am Main.
2859 **1227** 110pf. multicoloured . . 1·20 70

1228 Rock Face, Elbe Sandstone Mountains

1998. Saxon Switzerland National Park. Sheet 105 × 70 mm containing T **1228** and similar square design. Multicoloured.
MS2860 110pf. Type **1228**; 220pf. Elbe Sandstone Mountains . . 2·10 2·75

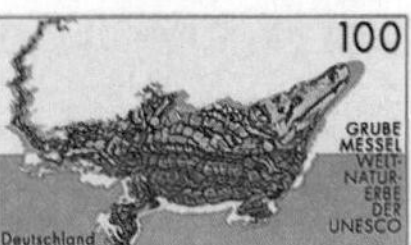
1229 Skeleton of Crocodile

1998. UNESCO World Heritage Sites. Grube Messel Fossil Deposits.
2861 **1229** 100pf. multicoloured . . 1·20 65

1230 Coloured Squares and Ludolphian Number **1231** Wurzburg Palace

1998. 23rd International Congress of Mathematicians, Berlin.
2862 **1230** 110pf. multicoloured . . 1·20 70

1998. UNESCO World Heritage Sites. Multicoloured.
2863 110pf. Type **1231** . . . . . 1·10 70
2864 110pf. Puning Temple, Chengde, China . . . . . 1·10 70

1232 Glasses (Peter Behrens)

1998. Contemporary Design (1st series). Sheet 138 × 97 mm containing T **1232** and similar horiz designs. Multicoloured.
MS2865 110pf. Type **1232**; 110pf. Teapot (Marianne Brandt); 110pf. Table lamp (Wilhelm Wagenfeld); 110pf. "Wassily" chair (Marcel Breuer) . . . . 4·50 4·50
See also No. **MS**2922.

1233 Players, Ball and Pitch

1998. 1st FC Kaiserslautern, National Football Champions, 1998.
2866 **1233** 110pf. multicoloured . . 1·20 70

1234 Main Building **1235** Hausmann and Book Cover

1998. 300th Anniv of Francke Charitable Institutions, Halle.
2867 **1234** 110pf. multicoloured . . 1·20 70

1998. Birth Centenary of Manfred Hausmann (writer).
2868 **1235** 100pf. multicoloured . . 1·20 70

1236 Hands on T-shirt **1237** Hen Harriers and Chicks

1998. Child Protection.
2869 **1236** 110pf. red and black . . 1·20 70

1998. Humanitarian Relief Funds. Birds. Multicoloured.
2870 100pf.+50pf. Type **1237** . . 1·40 1·50
2871 110pf.+50pf. Great bustards 1·70 1·60
2872 110pf.+50pf. Ferruginous ducks . . . . 1·70 1·60
2873 110pf.+50pf. Aquatic warblers on reeds . . . . 1·70 1·60
2874 220pf.+80pf. Woodchat shrike . . . . 3·25 3·00

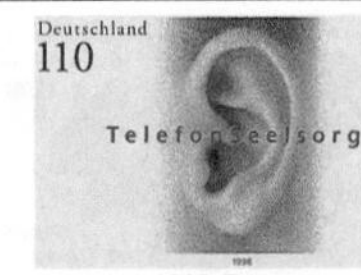

1238 Ear

1998. Telephone Help Lines.
2875 **1238** 110pf. black and orange 1·20 70

1239 "Hiorten" (sailing packet), 1692

1998. Stamp Day.
2876 **1239** 110pf. multicoloured . . 1·20 70

1240 Ramin

1998. Birth Centenary of Gunther Ramin (choir leader and organist).
2877 **1240** 300pf. multicoloured . . 3·00 2·30

1241 Shepherds following Star

1998. Christmas. Multicoloured.
2878 100pf.+50pf. Type **1241** . . 1·50 1·50
2879 110pf.+50pf. Baby Jesus . . 1·70 1·70

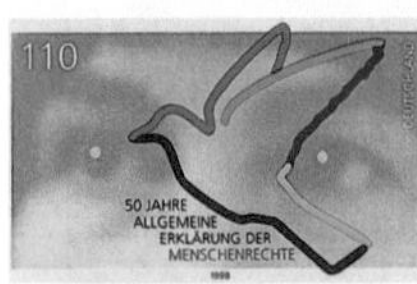

1242 Dove

1998. 50th Anniv of Declaration of Human Rights.
2880 **1242** 110pf. multicoloured . . 1·20 70
For charity stamp for Kosovo Relief Fund in similar design see No. 2899.

1243 Conductor's Hands and Baton

1998. 450th Anniv of Saxony State Orchestra, Dresden.
2881 **1243** 300pf. multicoloured . . 3·00 2·30

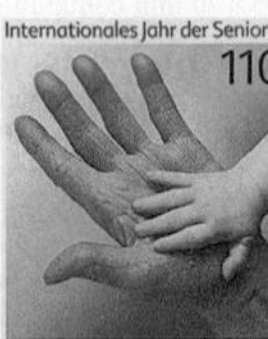

1244 National Theatre, Schiller, Goethe, Wieland and Herder **1245** Hands of Elderly Person and Child

1999. 1100th Anniv of Weimar, European City of Culture.
2882 **1244** 100pf. multicoloured . . 1·00 65

1999. International Year of the Elderly.
2883 **1245** 110pf. multicoloured . . 1·20 70

1246 Katharina von Bora

1999. 500th Birth Anniv of Katharina von Bora (wife of Martin Luther).
2884 **1246** 110pf. multicoloured . . 1·20 70

1999. Federal State Parliament Buildings (2nd series). As T **1213**.
2885 110pf. Hesse (Richard Goerz) (former palace of Dukes of Hesse) . . . . 1·20 75

1247 Cycle Racing

1999. Sport Promotion Fund. Multicoloured.
2886 100pf.+50pf. Type **1247** . . 1·50 1·40
2887 110pf.+50pf. Horse racing 1·70 1·70
2888 110pf.+50pf. Motor racing 1·70 1·60
2889 300pf.+100pf. Motor cycle racing . . . . 4·25 4·25

1248 Cover Illustration (by Walter Trier) of "Emil and the Detectives" (novel)

1999. Birth Centenary of Erich Kastner (writer).
2890 **1248** 300pf. multicoloured . . 3·00 2·20

1249 Coloured Diodes

1999. 50th Anniv of Fraunhofer Society (for applied research).
2891 **1249** 110pf. multicoloured . . 1·20 70

1250 Emblem and Initials

1999. 50th Anniv of North Atlantic Treaty Organization.
2892 **1250** 110pf. multicoloured . . 1·20 70

1999. Federal State Parliament Buildings (3rd series). As T **1213**. Multicoloured.
2893 110pf. City Parliament of Hamburg . . . . 1·20 85
2894 110pf. Mecklenburg-Western Pomerania (Schwerin Castle, rebuilt by Georg Demmler and Friedrich Stuler) . . . . 1·20 75

1251 Maybach Cabriolet of 1936 and Club Emblem

1999. Centenary of German Automobile Club.
2895 **1251** 110pf. multicoloured . . 1·20 70

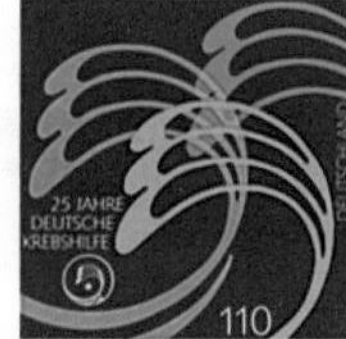

1252 Emblem

1999. 25th Anniv of German Cancer Relief.
2896 **1252** 110pf. multicoloured . . 1·20 70

1999. Federal State Parliament Buildings (4th series). As T **1213**.
2897 110pf. Bremen (Wassili Luckhardt) . . . . 1·20 75

1253 "Man, Nature, Technology"

1999. "EXPO 2000" World's Fair, Hanover (1st issue).
2898 **1253** 110pf. multicoloured . . 1·20 70
See also Nos. 2936, 2959 and 2979.

1999. Kosovo Relief Fund. As T **1242** but with inscription changed to "KOSOVO–HILFE 1999".
2899 110pf.+100pf. multicoloured 2·10 1·80

1254 Bavaria 1849 1k. and Saxony 1850 3pf. Stamps

1999. "iBRA'99" International Stamp Exhibition, Nuremberg. Sheet 140 × 100 mm.
MS2900 **1254** 300pf.+110pf. black, red and gold/cream . . . . . 4·00 4·00

1255 Berchtesgaden National Park

1999. Europa. Parks and Gardens. Sheet 110 × 66 mm.
MS2901 **1255** 110pf. multicoloured 1·40 1·20

1256 Cross of St. John

1999. 900th Anniv of Order of Knights of St. John of Jerusalem.
2902 **1256** 110pf. multicoloured . . 1·20 70

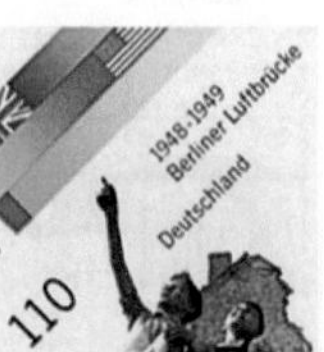

1257 Flags and Children

1999. 50th Anniv of Berlin Airlift of 1948–49.
2903 **1257** 110pf. multicoloured . . 1·20 70

1258 Emblem

1999. 50th Anniv of Council of Europe.
2904 **1258** 110pf. multicoloured . . 1·20 70

1259 State Arms and Article 1

1999. 50th Anniv of German Basic Law. Sheet 110 × 66 mm.
MS2905 **1259** 110pf. multicoloured 1·20 1·10

1260 Politicians and New Parliament Chamber, Berlin

1999. 50th Anniv of Federal Republic of Germany. Sheet 138 × 97 mm containing T **1260** and similar horiz designs. Multicoloured.
MS2906 110pf. Type **1260**; 110pf. Child playing in rubble and child among flowers; 110pf. Berlin Wall and its fall; 110pf. Soldiers confronting civilians and debating chamber . . . . 4·50 4·25

1261 Lars, the Little Polar Bear

1999. Youth Welfare. Cartoon Characters. Mult.
2907 100pf.+50pf. Type **1261** . . 1·60 1·40
2908 100pf.+50pf. Rudi the Crow 1·60 1·40
2909 110pf.+50pf. Twipsy (mascot of "Expo 2000" World's Fair, Hanover) . . . . . 1·70 1·60
2910 110pf.+50pf. Mecki (hedgehog) . . . . 1·70 1·60
2911 220pf.+80pf. Tabaluga (dragon) . . . . 3·25 3·00

1262 Cross Clasp, Altar, Cathedral Spire and Time-line

1999. 1200th Anniv of Paderborn Diocese.
2912 **1262** 110pf. multicoloured . . 1·20 70

1263 House (child's painting)

1264 "Ball at the Viennese Hofburg" and Score

1999. 50th Anniv of S.O.S. Children's Villages.
2913 **1263** 110pf. multicoloured . . 1·20 70

1999. Death Centenary of Johann Strauss the younger (composer).
2914 **1264** 300pf. multicoloured . . 3·00 2·20

1265 Children at Desks (tapestry)

1999. 115th Anniv of Dominikus-Ringeisen Institute for Disabled People, Ursberg.
2915 **1265** 110pf. multicoloured . . 1·20 70

1266 Heinemann

1999. Birth Centenary of Gustav Heinemann (President 1969–74).
2916 **1266** 110pf. grey and red . . 1·20 70

1267 "Old Woman laughing" (Ernst Barlach)

1999. Cultural Foundation of the Federal States (1st series). Sculptures. Multicoloured.
2917 110pf. Type **1267** . . . . . 1·20 75
2918 220pf. "Bust of a Thinker" (Wilhelm Lehmbruck) . . 2·10 1·60
See also Nos. 2960/1.

1268 Participating Countries and Dove

1999. Centenary of First Peace Conference, The Hague.
2919 **1268** 300pf. grey, red and blue . . . . 3·00 2·20

1269 Goethe (after J. K. Stieler)

1999. 250th Birth Anniv of Johann Wolfgang von Goethe (poet and playwright).
2920 **1269** 110pf. multicoloured . . 1·20 75

1270 Mouse carrying Letter

1999. "For Us Children". Sheet 105 × 71 mm.
MS2921 **1270** 110pf. multicoloured 1·20 2·50

1271 HF1 Television Set (Herbert Hirche)

1999. Contemporary Design (2nd series). Sheet 138 × 97 mm containing T **1271** and similar horiz designs. Multicoloured.
MS2922 110pf. Type **1271**; 110pf. "Mono-a" cutlery (Peter Raacke); 110pf. Pearl bottles (Gunter Kupetz); 110pf. Transrapid Maglev train (Alexander Neumeister) . . . . 4·50 2·75

1272 Player

1999. FC Bayern Munich, National Football Champions.
2923 **1272** 110pf. multicoloured . . 1·20 75

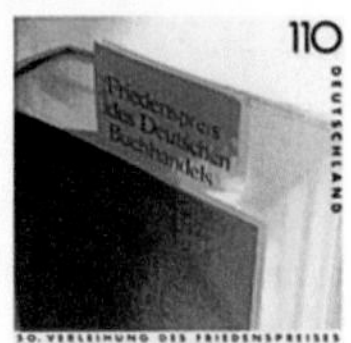
1273 Book and Bookmark

1999. 50th Anniv of Federal Association of German Book Traders' Peace Prize.
2924 **1273** 110pf. multicoloured . . 1·20 70

1274 Strauss and Poster from "Salome" (opera)

1999. 50th Death Anniv of Richard Strauss (composer).
2925 **1274** 300pf. multicoloured . . 3·00 2·20

1275 Andromeda Galaxy

1999. Humanitarian Relief Funds. Outer Space. Multicoloured.
2926 100pf.+50pf. Type **1275** . . 1·50 1·40
2927 100pf.+50pf. Swan constellation . . . . . . 1·50 1·40
2928 110pf.+50pf. X-ray image of exploding star . . . . . 1·70 1·60
2929 110pf.+50pf. Comet colliding with Jupiter . . 1·70 1·60
2930 300pf.+100pf. Gamma ray image of sky . . . . . . 4·25 4·00

1276 Goltzsch Valley Railway Bridge

1999. Bridges (2nd series).
2931 **1276** 110pf. multicoloured . . 1·20 70

1277 "DGB"

1999. 50th Anniv of German Federation of Trade Unions.
2932 **1277** 110pf. black and bright red . . . . 1·20 70

1278 Greater Horseshoe Bats

1999. Endangered Species.
2933 **1278** 100pf. multicoloured . . 1·00 65

1279 The Annunciation

1999. Christmas. Multicoloured.
2934 100pf.+50pf. Type **1279** . . 1·50 1·40
2935 110pf.+50pf. Nativity . . . 1·70 1·70

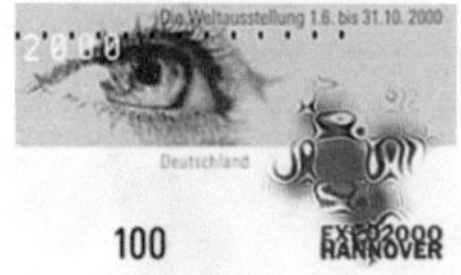
1280 Emblem and Eye

2000. "EXPO 2000" World's Fair, Hanover (2nd issue).
2936 **1280** 100pf. multicoloured . . 1·00 65

1281 Emblem

2000. Holy Year 2000.
2937 **1281** 110pf. multicoloured . . 1·20 70

1282 Charlemagne and Plan of Palace Chapel

2000. 1200th Anniv of Aachen Cathedral.
2938 **1282** 110pf. multicoloured . . 1·20 70

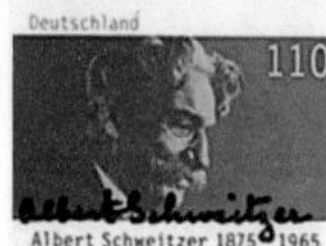
1283 Schweitzer and Signature

2000. 125th Birth Anniv of Albert Schweitzer (missionary doctor).
2939 **1283** 110pf. multicoloured . . 1·20 70

1284 Football

2000. Centenary of German Football Association.
2940 **1284** 110pf. multicoloured . . 1·20 70

1285 Wehner

2000. 10th Death Anniv of Herbert Wehner (politician).
2941 **1285** 110pf. multicoloured . . 1·20 70

1286 Woman

2000. Prevention of Violence Against Women.
2942 **1286** 110pf. red, grey and black . . . . 1·20 70

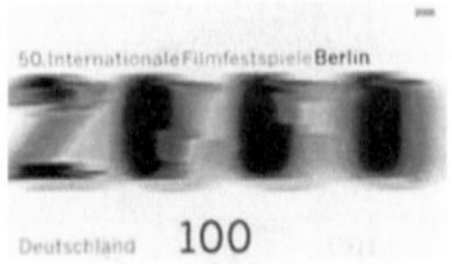

1287 "2000" in Moving Film Sequence

2000. 50th Berlin International Film Festival.
2943 **1287** 100pf. multicoloured . . 1·00 65

1288 Boxing

2000. Sport Promotion Fund. Multicoloured.
2944 100pf.+50pf. Type **1288** (fair play) . . . . 1·40 1·30
2945 110pf.+50pf. Rhythmic gymnastics (beauty) . . . 1·70 1·50
2946 110pf.+50pf. Running (competition) . . . . . . 1·70 1·50
2947 300pf.+100pf. Raised hands (culture of interaction) . . 4·25 4·25

1289 Gutenberg (after engraving by A. Thevet) and Letters from Gutenberg Bible

1290 Jester

2000. 600th Birth Anniv of Johannes Gutenberg (inventor of printing press).
2948 **1289** 110pf. black and red . . 1·20 70

2000. 175th Anniv of First Dusseldorf Carnival.
2949 **1290** 110pf. multicoloured . . 1·20 70

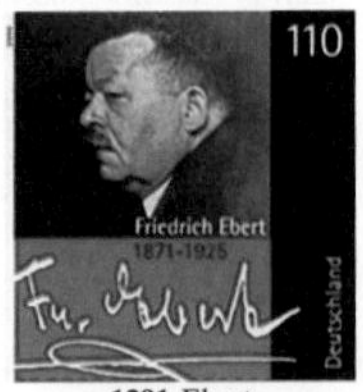

1291 Ebert

2000. 75th Death Anniv of Friedrich Ebert (President, 1919–25).
2950 **1291** 110pf. multicoloured . . 1·20 70

1292 Weill at Rehearsal of "One Touch of Venus" (musical), 1943

2000. Birth Centenary of Kurt Weill (composer).
2951 **1292** 300pf. blk, stone & red 3·00 2·40

1293 Passau

2000. Images of Germany.
2952 **1293** 110pf. multicoloured . . 1·20 75

2000. Federal State Parliament Buildings (5th series). As T **1213**. Multicoloured.
2953 110pf. Leine Palace, Lower Saxony . . . . 1·20 75

1294 Trees

2000. Hainich National Park. Sheet 105 × 70 mm.
MS2954 **1294** 110pf. multicoloured 1·20 1·10

1295 Toy Windmill and "Post!"

2000.
2955 **1295** 110pf. multicoloured . . 1·20 70

1296 "Blue Wonder" Bridge, Dresden

2000. Bridges (3rd series).
2956 **1296** 100pf. multicoloured . . 1·10 65

2000. Federal State Parliament Buildings (6th series). As T **1213**. Multicoloured.
2957 110pf. North-Rhine/ Westphalia (Fritz Eller) 1·20 75

1297 City Buildings

2000. 750th Anniv of Greifswald.
2958 **1297** 110pf. multicoloured . . 1·20 70

2000. "EXPO 2000" World's Fair, Hanover (3rd issue). As No. 2898 but self-adhesive.
2959 **1253** 110pf. multicoloured . . 4·50 2·40

1298 "Expulsion from Paradise" (Leonhard Kern)

2000. Cultural Foundation of the Federal States. Sculptures. Multicoloured.
2960 110pf. Type **1298** . . . . . 1·20 70
2961 220pf. Silver table fountain (Melchior Gelb) . . . . . 2·20 1·70

1299 "Building Europe"

2000. Europa. Ordinary or self-adhesive gum.
2962 **1299** 110pf. multicoloured . . 1·20 75

1300 Von Zinzendorf and Natives

2000. 300th Birth Anniv of Nikolaus Ludwig von Zinzendorf (leader of Moravian Brethren).
2964 **1300** 110pf. multicoloured . . 1·20 70

1301 Countryside

2000. Environmental Protection.
2965 **1301** 110pf.+50pf. mult . . . 1·60 1·40

1302 Crowd at Music Festival

2000. Youth Welfare. "EXPO 2000" World's Fair, Hanover (4th issue). Multicoloured.
2966 100pf.+50pf. Type **1302** . . 1·70 1·70
2967 100pf.+50pf. Back-packers 1·70 1·70
2968 110pf.+50pf. Map of Africa and text . . . . 1·80 1·60
2969 110pf.+50pf. Eye of Buddha 1·80 1·60
2970 110pf.+50pf. Chinese calligraphy . . . . . . 1·80 1·60
2971 300pf.+100pf. Psychedelic swirl . . . . 3·75 3·50

1303 Front Page of Issue 17, 1650, and Modern Pages of Newspaper

2000. 350th Anniv of Einkommende Zeitungen (first German daily newspaper).
2972 **1303** 110pf. multicoloured . . 1·20 70

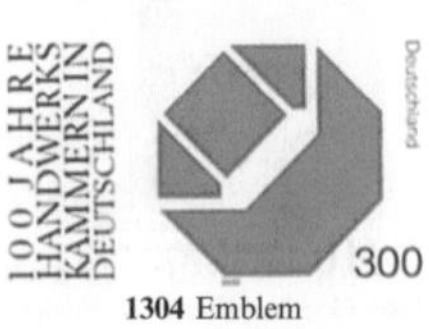

1304 Emblem

2000. Centenary of Chambers of Handicrafts.
2973 **1304** 300pf. orange and black 3·00 2·40

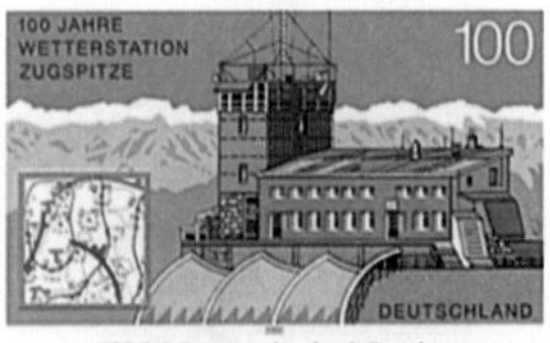

1305 Meteorological Station

2000. Centenary of the Zugspitze Meteorological Station.
2974 **1305** 100pf. multicoloured . . 1·10 65

1306 Road Sign and Flashing Light

2000. 50th Anniv of Technisches Hilfwerk (Federal disaster relief organization).
2975 **1306** 110pf. multicoloured . . 1·20 70

1307 Bach

2000. 250th Death Anniv of Johann Sebastian Bach (composer).
2976 **1307** 110pf. multicoloured . . 1·20 70

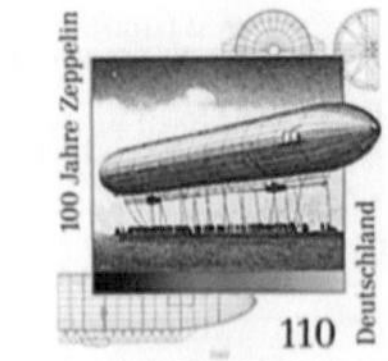

1308 LZ-1

2000. Centenary of Inaugural Flight of LZ-1 (Zeppelin airship), 1900.
2977 **1308** 110pf. multicoloured . . 1·20 70

2000. Federal State Parliament Buildings (7th series). As T **1213**. Multicoloured.
2978 110pf. Rhineland-Palatinate, Mainz . . . . 1·20 75

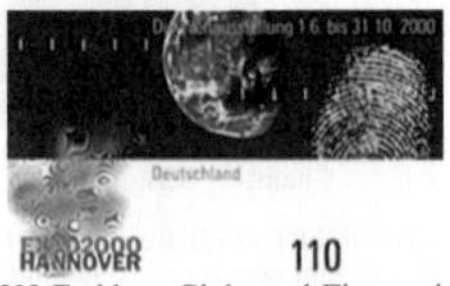

1309 Emblem, Globe and Fingerprint

2000. "EXPO 2000" World's Fair, Hanover (5th issue).
2979 **1309** 110pf. multicoloured . . 1·20 70

1310 Wiechert

2000. 50th Death Anniv of Ernst Wiechert (writer).
2980 **1310** 110pf. multicoloured . . 1·20 70

1311 Nietzsche (Edvard Munch)

2000. Death Centenary of Friedrich Nietzsche (philosopher).
2981 **1311** 110pf. multicoloured . . 1·20 70

1312 "For You"

2000. Greetings Stamp.
2982 **1312** 100pf. multicoloured . . 1·10 65

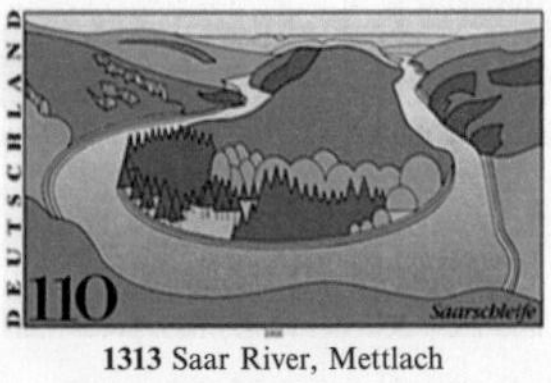

1313 Saar River, Mettlach

2000. Images of Germany.
2983 **1313** 110pf. multicoloured . . 1·20 75

1314 Adolph Kopling

2000. 150th Anniv of Kopling Society (voluntary organization).
2984 **1314** 110pf. multicoloured . . 1·20 70

1315 Building

2000. 50th Anniv of Federal Court of Justice.
2985 **1315** 110pf. multicoloured . . 1·20 70

1316 Clown's Face

2000. "For Us Children". Sheet 55 × 82 mm.
MS2986 **1316** 110pf. multicoloured 1·20 1·10

1317 Nocht (founder), World Map and Microscope Images of Pathogens

2000. Centenary of Bernard Nocht Institute for Tropical Medicine.
2987 **1317** 300pf. multicoloured . . 3·00 2·40

1318 Town Hall, Wernigerode
1319 National Colours

2000. Tourist Sights. Showing face values in German currency and euros.
2988 **1318** 10pf. grey, orge & slate 30 20
2989 – 20pf. orange and black 20 15
2990 – 47pf. mauve and green 55 40
2991 – 50pf. brown and red . . 65 45
2992 – 80pf. green and brown 80 70
2993 – 100pf. blue and brown 1·10 80
2994 – 110pf. pur, brn & orge 1·10 60
2997 – 220pf. blue and brown 2·30 1·50
3000 – 300pf. brown and blue 2·75 2·00
3001 – 400pf. brown and red 4·00 3·00
3002 – 440pf. black and grey 4·50 2·75
3003 – 510pf. pink and red . . 5·25 3·75
3004 – 720pf. purple & mauve 7·25 4·75
DESIGNS: 20pf. Bottcherstrasse, Bremen; 47pf. Wilhelmshohe Park, Kassel; 50pf. Ceiling decoration, Kircheim Castle; 80pf. St. Reinoldi Church, Dortmund; 100pf. Schwerin Castle, Mecklenberg; 110pf. Stone bridge, Regensburg; 220pf. St. Nikolai Cathedral, Greifswald; 300pf. Town Hall Grimma; 400pf. Wartburg Castle, Eisenach; 440pf. Cologne Cathedral; 510pf. Heidelberg Castle; 720pf. Town Hall, Hildesheim.
Nos. 2988, 2993/4 also come self-adhesive.

2000. 10th Anniv of Reunification of Germany.
3010 **1319** 110pf. black, red & yell 1·20 70

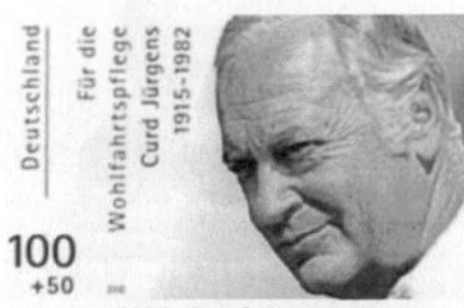

1320 Curd Jurgens

2000. Humanitarian Relief Funds. Actors. Mult.
3011 100pf.+50pf. Type **1320** . . 1·70 1·50
3012 100pf.+50pf. Lilli Palmer . . 1·70 1·50
3013 110pf.+50pf. Heinz Ruhmann . . . . 1·80 1·60
3014 110pf.+50pf. Romy Schneider . . . . 1·80 1·60
3015 300pf.+100pf. Gert Frobe 3·75 3·75

1321 Pens, Envelope and 1999 110pf. Stamp
1322 Grethe Weiser (actress and singer)

2000. Stamp Day.
3016 **1321** 110pf. multicoloured . . 1·20 70

2000. Famous German Women.
3017 **1322** 100pf. green and brown 1·10 85
3018 – 110pf. red and green . . 1·20 80
3019 – 220pf. brown and green 2·20 1·50
3020 – 300pf. purple and brown . . . . 3·00 2·10
DESIGNS: 110pf. Kate Strobel (politician); 200pf. Marieluise Fleisser (writer); 300pf. Nelly Sachs (writer).

2000. Federal State Parliament Buildings (8th series). As T **1213**. Multicoloured.
3025 110pf. Saarland . . . . . . 1·10 75

1323 Book Cover
1324 Bode

2000. 125th Birth Anniv of Rainer Maria Rilke (poet).
3026 **1323** 110pf. multicoloured . . 1·10 70

2000. Birth Centenary of Arnold Bode (artist).
3027 **1324** 110pf. black and red . . 1·10 70

1325 "Birth of Christ" (Conrad von Soest)

2000. Christmas. Multicoloured.
3028 100pf.+50pf. Type **1325** . . 1·70 1·50
3029 110pf.+50pf. Nativity . . . 1·80 1·60

1326 Indian Pepper (illustration from *New Book of Herbs*)

2001. 500th Birth Anniv of Leonhart Fuchs (physician and botanist).
3030 **1326** 100pf. multicoloured . . 1·00 65

1327 "VdK"

2001. 50th Anniv (2000) of Disabled War Veterans' Association.
3031 **1327** 110pf. multicoloured . . 1·10 70

1328 Prussian Eagle

2001. 300th Anniv of the Kingdom of Prussia.
3032 **1328** 110pf. multicoloured . . 1·10 70

1329 Lortzing and Music Score

2001. Birth Bicent of Albert Lortzing (composer).
3033 **1329** 110pf. multicoloured . . 1·10 70

1330 Telephone Handset and Number

2001. National Federation of Child and Youth Telephone Helplines.
3034 **1330** 110pf. yellow, red & blk 1·10 75

1331 Bucer

2001. 450th Death Anniv of Martin Bucer (teacher and Protestant reformer).
3035 **1331** 110pf. multicoloured . . 1·10 65

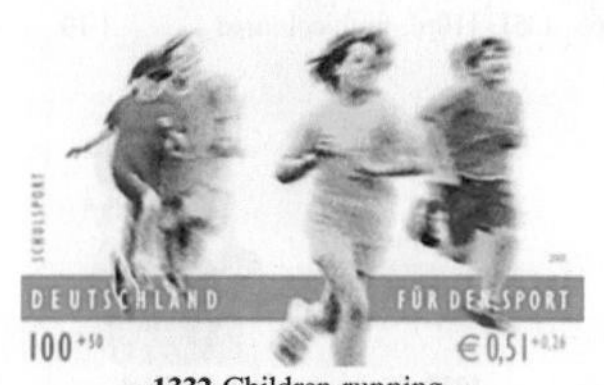

1332 Children running

2001. Sport Promotion Fund. Multicoloured.
3036 100pf.+50pf. Type **1332** . . 1·50 1·40
3037 110pf.+50pf. Disabled and able-bodied athletes . . . 1·70 1·50
3038 110pf.+50pf. Adult and children skating . . . . . 1·70 1·50
3039 300pf.+100pf. Men playing basketball . . . . 4·00 3·50

1333 Hand holding Quill

2001. 250th Birth Anniv of Johann Heinrich Voss (writer and translator). (a) Ordinary gum.
3040 **1333** 300pf. multicoloured . . 3·00 2·40

(b) Self-adhesive gum.
3040a €1.53 multicoloured . . . 2·50 1·90

1334 Ollenhauer

2001. Birth Centenary of Erich Ollenhauer (politician).
3041 **1334** 110pf. red, black & sil 1·10 70

1335 Arnold

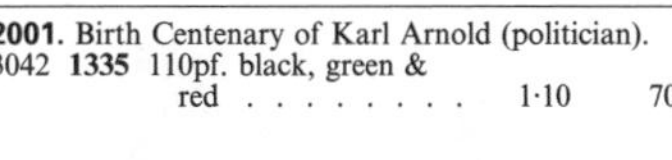
2001. Birth Centenary of Karl Arnold (politician).
3042 **1335** 110pf. black, green & red . . . . 1·10 70

2001. Federal State Parliament Buildings (9th series). As T **1213**. Multicoloured.
3043 110pf. Saxony . . . . . . 1·10 75

1336 Badge

2001. 50th Anniv of Federal Border Police.
3044 **1336** 110pf. multicoloured . . 1·10 70

1337 Suspension Railway

2001. Centenary of Suspension Railway, Wuppertal.
3045 **1338** 110pf.+50pf. mult . . . 1·60 1·50

1338 Rendsberg Railway Viaduct

2001. Bridges (4th series).
3046 **1338** 100pf. multicoloured . . 1·00 70

1339 "Post!"

2001.
3047 **1339** 110pf. multicoloured . . 1·10 70

1340 Accordion

2001. Folk Music.
3048 **1340** 110pf. multicoloured . . 1·10 70

1341 World Map

2001. 50th Anniv of Goethe Institute.
3049 **1341** 300pf. multicoloured 3·00 2·40

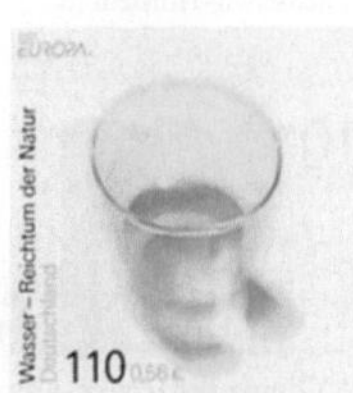

1342 Glass of Water

2001. Europa. Water Resources.
3050 **1342** 110pf. multicoloured . . 1·10 65

1343 Egk

2001. Birth Centenary of Werner Egk (composer and conductor).
3051 **1343** 110pf. multicoloured . . 1·10 65

2001. Federal State Parliament Buildings (10th series). As T **1213**. Multicoloured.
3052 110pf. Saxony-Anhalt . . . 1·10 70

1344 Mountain Gorilla with Young

2001. Endangered Species. Multicoloured. Ordinary or self-adhesive gum.
3053 110pf. Type **1344** . . . . . 1·90 1·10
3054 110pf. Indian rhinoceros with young . . . . 1·90 1·10

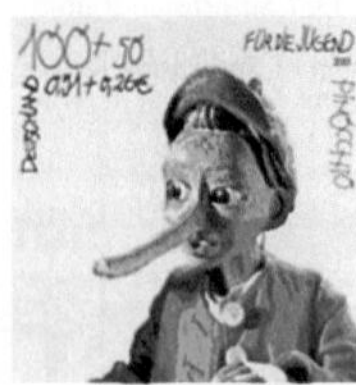

1345 Pinocchio

2001. Youth Welfare. Characters from Children's Stories. Multicoloured.
3057 100pf.+50pf. Type **1345** . . 1·50 1·50
3058 100pf.+50pf. Pippi Longstocking . . . . . . 1·50 1·50
3059 110pf.+50pf. Heidi and Peter . . . . 1·60 1·60
3060 110pf.+50pf. Jim Knopf . . 1·60 1·60
3061 300pf.+100pf. Tom Sawyer and Huckleberry Finn . . 3·75 3·75

1346 St. Catherine's Monastery and Oceanographic Chart

2001. 750th Anniv of St. Catherine's Monastery and 50th Anniv of German Oceanographic Museum, Stralsund.
3062 **1346** 110pf. multicoloured . . 1·10 75

1347 Church Exterior and Plan

2001. 250th Anniv of Catholic Court Church, Dresden.
3063 **1347** 110pf. multicoloured . . 1·10 70

2001. Federal State Parliament Buildings (11th series). As T **1213**. Multicoloured.
3064 110pf. Schleswig-Holstein . . 1·10 75

1348 Church Bell Tower, Canzow

2001.
3065 **1348** 110pf. black, blue and mauve . . . . 1·10 70

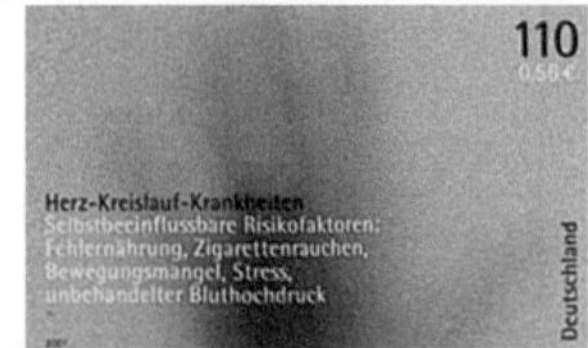

1349 Hand (circulatory disease)

2001. Health Awareness Campaign. Sheet 138 × 110 mm containing T **1349** and similar horiz designs. Multicoloured.
MS3066 110pf. Type **1349**; 110pf. Torso (cancer); 110pf. Lower body (infectious diseases); 110pf. Man holding head (depression) . . . 4·50 4·25

1350 Emblem

2001. Dragon Lancing Festival, Furth im Wald.
3067 **1350** 100pf. multicoloured . . 1·00 65

1351 Lime Tree, Himmelsberg

2001. Natural Heritage. Ordinary or self-adhesive gum.
3068 **1351** 110pf. multicoloured . . 1·10 70

1352 "Schoolmaster Lampel" (Wilhelm Busch) and Text

2001. Lifelong Learning.
3070 **1352** 110pf. multicoloured . . 1·10 70

1353 Felix standing on Cat

2001. "For Us Children". Sheet 110 × 66 mm.
MS3071 **1353** 110pf. multicoloured 1·20 1·10

2001. Federal State Parliament Buildings (12th series). As T **1213**. Multicoloured.
3072 110pf. Thuringia . . . . . 1·10 70

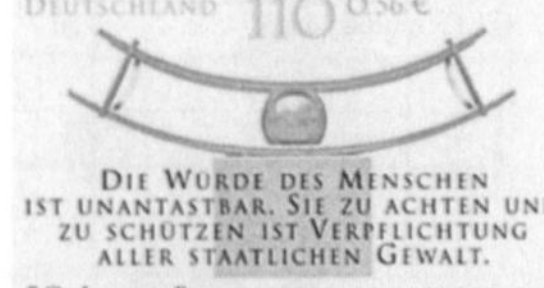

1354 "Justice" (sculpture)

2001. 50th Anniv of Federal Constitutional Court.
3073 **1354** 110pf. multicoloured . . 1·10 75

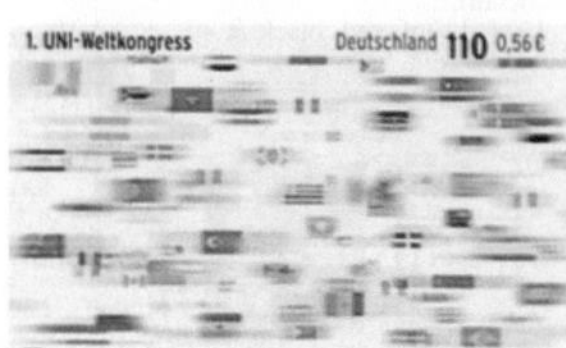

1355 Members' Flags

2001. 1st Union Network International World Congress, Berlin.
3074 **1355** 110pf. multicoloured . . 1·10 70

1356 Museum Floor Plan

2001. Jewish Museum, Berlin.
3075 **1356** 110pf. multicoloured . . 1·10 70

1357 Marilyn Monroe

2001. Humanitarian Relief Funds. Film Industry. Multicoloured.
3076 100pf.+50pf. Type **1357** . . 1·60 1·40
3077 100pf.+50pf. Charlie Chaplin . . . . 1·60 1·40
3078 110pf.+50pf. Greta Garbo . . 1·80 1·50
3079 110pf.+50pf. Film reel . . . 1·80 1·50
3080 300pf.+100pf. Jean Gabin 4·00 4·00
MS3080a 205 × 156 mm. As Nos. 3076/80 . . . . 10·00 10·00

1358 Ribbon and "fur Dich"

2001. Greetings Stamp.
3081 **1358** 110pf. red and black . . 1·10 1·10

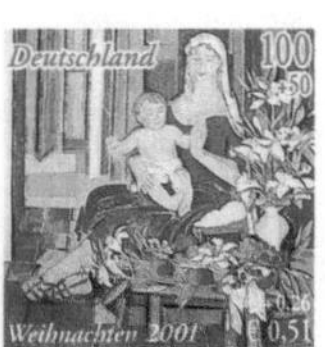

1359 "Virgin and Child" (Alfredo Roldan)

2001. Christmas. Religious Paintings. Mult.
3082 100pf.+50pf. Type **1359** . . 1·10 70
3083 110pf.+50pf. "The Shepherd's Adoration" (Jusepe de Ribera) . . . . 1·50 1·20

1360 *Gauss* (survey barquentine)

2001. Centenary of German Antarctic Research. Sheet 135 × 105 mm containing T **1360** and similar horiz design. Multicoloured.
MS3084 110pf. Type **1360**; 220pf. *Polarstern* (exploration ship) 3·25 3·25

1361 Heisenberg

2001. Birth Centenary of Werner Heisenberg (physicist).
3085 **1361** 300pf. black and blue 2·75 2·75

New Currency. 100 cents = 1 euro

1362 Bautzen

2002. Millenary of Bautzen. Ordinary or self-adhesive gum.
3086 **1362** 56c. multicoloured . . . 3·00 1·60

1363 Von Dohnanyi

2002. Birth Centenary of Hans von Dohnanyi (German resistance co-ordinator).
3087 **1363** 56c. multicoloured . . . 1·20 70

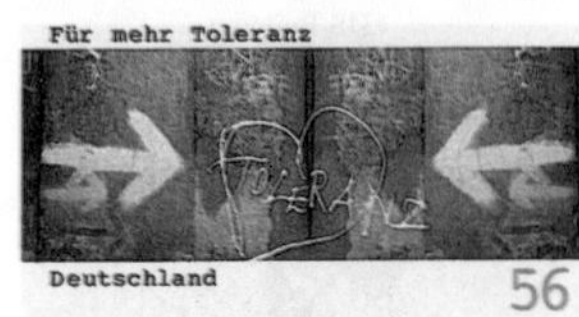

1364 Graffiti

2002. "Tolerance".
3088 **1364** 56c. multicoloured . . . 1·20 75

1365 " € "

2002. New Currency. Ordinary or self-adhesive gum.
3089 **1365** 56c. yellow and blue . . 1·20 70

1366 Mountains

2002. International Year of Mountains.
3091 **1366** 56c.+26c. multicoloured 2·10 2·10
No. 3091 was sold with a premium towards environmental protection.

1367 Cross-country Skier (biathlon)

2002. Winter Olympic Games, Salt Lake City, U.S.A. Multicoloured.
3092 51c.+26c. Type **1367** . . . . 1·50 1·50
3093 56c.+26c. Ice skater (speed skating) . . . . 1·60 1·50
3094 56c.+26c. Skier (ski jumping) . . . . 1·60 1·60
3095 153c.+51c. Man in helmet (luge) . . . . 4·00 2·75
MS3096 142 × 98 mm. As Nos. 3092/5 . . . . 9·50 9·50
Nos. 3092/MS3096 were sold with a premium towards "Foundation for the Promotion of Sport in Germany".

1368 Knigge and Books

2002. 250th Birth Anniv of Adolf Freiherr Knigge (author of *Uber den Umgang mit Menschen* (book on etiquette)).
3097 **1368** 56c. multicoloured . . . 1·20 70

1369 Front of Train Carriage

2002. Centenary of Berlin Subway.
3098 **1369** 56c. multicoloured . . . 1·20 70

1370 Deggendorf

2002. Millenary of Deggendorf.
3099 **1370** 56c. multicoloured . . . 1·20 70

1371 Mechanical Calculator (Johann Christoph Schuster)

2002. Cultural Foundation of the Federal States.
3100 **1371** 56c. multicoloured . . . 1·20 70

1372 Ecksberg Pilgrimage Church

2002. 150th Anniv of Ecksberg Foundation (for people with disabilities).
3101 **1372** 56c. multicoloured . . . 1·10 70

1373 Exhibits and Building

2002. Centenary of Freemason's Museum, Bayreuth.
3102 **1373** 56c. multicoloured . . . 1·20 75

1374 Armorial Lions

2002. 50th Anniv of Baden-Württenberg State.
3103 **1374** 56c. black, gold and yellow . . . . 1·20 70

1375 "post"

2002.
3104 **1375** 56c. multicoloured . . . 1·20 70

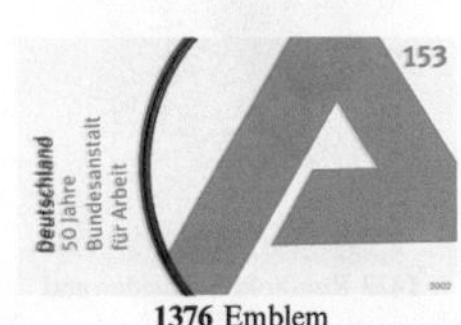
1376 Emblem

2002. 50th Anniv of Federal Employment Services.
3105 **1376** €1.53 red and black 3·00 2·30

1377 Modern Student and Elector Friedrich the Wise (founder of Wittenberg University

2002. 500th Anniv of Martin Luther University, Halle-Wittenberg.
3106 **1377** 56c. grey, blue and mauve . . . . 1·20 70

1378 "KINDERGOTTESDIENST!"

2002. 150th Anniv of Children's Church Services.
3107 **1378** 56c. multicoloured . . . 1·20 70

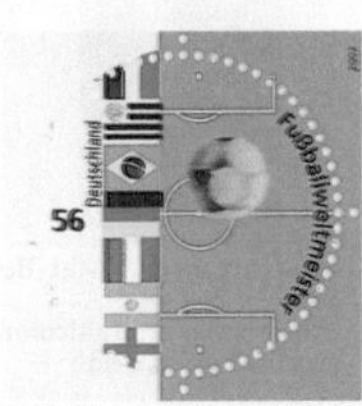
1379 "Documenta11"

2002. 11th "Documenta" Modern Art Exhibition, Kassel. Sheet 100 × 70 mm.
MS3108 **1379** 56c. ultramarine, lilac and blue . . . . 1·20 1·10

1380 Flags of Championship Winners and Football

2002. 20th-century World Cup Football Champions. Multicoloured.
3109 56c. Type **1380** . . . . . . 1·20 70
3110 56c. German Footballer . . 1·20 70

1381 Clown

2002. Europa. Circus. Ordinary or self-adhesive gum.
3111 **1381** 56c. black, red and green . . . . 1·20 70

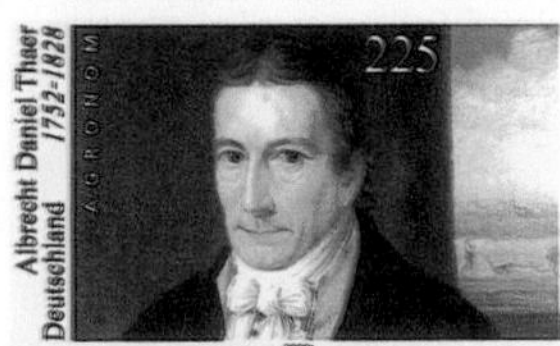
1382 Dessau-Worlitz

2002. UNESCO World Heritage Site. Dessau-Worlitz Gardens. Ordinary or self-adhesive gum.
3113 **1382** 56c. multicoloured . . . 1·20 75

1383 Thaer

2002. 250th Birth Anniv of Albrecht Daniel Thaer (agronomist).
3115 **1383** €2.25 multicoloured 4·50 4·50

1384 Desmoulin's Whorl Snail

2002. Endangered Species. Molluscs. Multicoloured.
3116 51c. Type **1384** . . . . . . 1·00 65
3117 56c. Freshwater pearl mussel 1·10 70

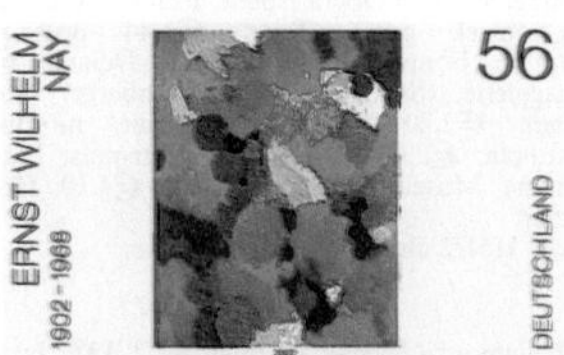
1385 Chess Pieces

2002. Youth Welfare. Toys. Multicoloured.
3118 51c.+26c. Type **1385** . . . . 1·50 1·40
3119 51c.+26c. Wooden crane . . 1·50 1·40
3120 56c.+26c. Doll . . . . . . 1·70 1·60
3121 56c.+26c. Teddy bear . . . 1·70 1·60
3122 153c.+51c. Electric train . . 4·00 4·00

1386 "Yellow Feather in Red"

2002. Birth Centenary of Ernst Wilhelm Nay (artist).
3123 **1386** 56c. multicoloured . . . 1·20 70

1387 Leaves and Silhouettes

2002. 40th Anniv of "Deutsche Welthungerhilfe" (humanitarian aid organization).
3124 **1387** 51c. multicoloured . . . 1·10 70

1388 "Way of Human Rights" (sculpture, Danni Karavan)

2002. 150th Anniv of National Museum of German Art and Culture, Nuremberg.
3125 **1388** 56c. multicoloured . . . 1·20 75

1389 Hesse

2002. 125th Birth Anniv of Hermann Hesse (writer).
3126 **1389** 56c. blue and yellow . . 1·20 70

1390 Trees and Rocks

2002. Hochharz National Park. Sheet 110 × 66 mm.
MS3127 **1390** 56c. multicoloured 1·20 1·10

1391 Felder

2002. 2nd Death Anniv of Josef Felder (politician and journalist).
3128 **1391** 56c. multicoloured . . . 1·20 70

1392 Museum Buildings

2002. UNESCO World Heritage Site. Museum Island, Berlin.
3129 **1392** 56c. black and green . . 1·20 70

1393 Firemen fighting Fire

2002. Voluntary Fire Brigades.
3130 **1393** 56c. multicoloured . . . 1·20 70

1394 Building Facade

2002. 130th Anniv of Communications Museum, Berlin.
3131 **1394** 153c. multicoloured . . 3·00 2·50

2002. Flood Relief. As T **1222** but with "HOCHWASSERHILFE 2002" inscribed at left and new face value.
3132 56c.+44c. multicoloured . . 1·90 1·90

1395 Walls of Roman Bathhouse, Wurmlingen (illustration from *Die Alammannen* by Konrad Theiss)

2002. Archaeology.
3133 **1395** 51c. multicoloured . . . 1·00 1·00

1396 Face painted on Child's Toe

2002. "For Us Children". Sheet 110 × 66 mm.
MS3134 **1396** 56c. multicoloured 1·20 1·10

1397 "Rotes Elisabeth-Ufer" (painting, Ernst Ludwig Kirchner)

2002.
3135 **1397** 112c. multicoloured . . 2·00 1·70

1398 Von Kleist (miniature, Peter Friedel)

2002. 225th Birth Anniv of Heinrich von Kleist (writer).
3136 **1398** 56c. multicoloured . . . 1·20 70

1399 Jochum rehearsing

2002. Birth Centenary of Eugen Jochum (conductor).
3137 **1399** 56c. multicoloured . . . 1·20 70

1400 Diagram of Planets (Copernicus), Horsemen and Sphere

2002. 400th Birth Anniv of Otto von Guericke (engineer and physicist).
3138 **1400** 153c. multicoloured . . 3·00 2·40

1401 Angel (detail, "The Annunciation")

2002. Christmas. Paintings by Rogier van der Weyden. Multicoloured.
3139 51c.+26c. Type **1401** . . . . 1·50 1·50
3140 56c.+26c. The Holy Family (detail, Miraflores alterpiece) . . . . 1·70 1·60

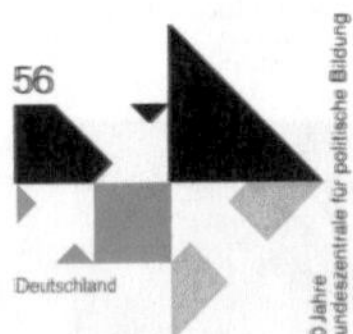

1402 Arrows

2002. 50th Anniv of Federal Agency for Civic Education.
3141 **1402** 56c. black, red and yellow . . . . 1·20 70

1403 Clock and Eye

2002. 50th Anniv of German Television.
3142 **1403** 56c. multicoloured . . . 1·20 70

1404 BMW Isetta 300

2002. Cars. Multicoloured.
3144 45c.+20c. Type **1404** . . . . 1·20 75
3145 55c.+25c. Volkswagen Beetle 1·60 1·60
3146 55c.+25c. Mercedes Benz 300 SL . . . . 1·60 1·60
3147 55c.+25c. VEB Sachsenring Trabant P50 . . . . . . 1·60 1·60
3148 144c.+56c. Borgward Isabella Coupe . . . . . 4·00 4·00
See also Nos. 3238/42.

1405 "Halle Market Church" (Lyonel Feininger)

3149 **1405** 55c. multicoloured . . . 1·20 1·20

2002. Tourist Sights. As T **1318** but with face value in new currency.
3150 5c. brown and green 90 90
3151 25c. olive and violet 90 90
3153 40c. multicoloured . . . . . 1·90 1·90
3154 44c. yellow and black . . . 2·75 2·75
3155 45c. pink and black . . . . 3·00 3·00
3156 55c. yellow and black . . . 3·50 3·50
3157 €1 grey and black . . . . 3·75 3·75
3158 €1.44 pink and green . . . 4·25 4·25
3159 €1.60 grey, black and orange . . . . 5·00 5·00
3160 €1.80 green and chestnut 7·75 7·75
3161 €2 red and green . . . . . 2·60 1·30
3162 €2.20 blue and black . . . 3·00 1·50
3163 €2.60 blue and red . . . . 3·50 1·75
3164 €4.10 purple and blue . . . 5·50 2·20
DESIGNS: 5c. Erfuster Cathedral; 25c. J.S. Bach (statue), Leipzig; 40c. Schloss Arolsen; 44c. Philharmonic Hall, Berlin; 45c. Canal warehouse, Tonning; 55c. Old Opera House, Frankfurt; €1 Porta Niga (black gate), Trier; €1.44 Beethoven's birthplace, Bonn; €1.60 Bauhaus, Dessau; €1.80 Staatsgalerie, Stuttgart; €2 Bamberger Reister (statue); €2.20 Theodor Fontane monument, Neuruppin; €2.60 *Seute Dern* (four-mast barque), Maritime Museum, Bremerhaven; €4.10 Houses, Wismar.
Nos. 3151/2 also come self-adhesive.

2002. Famous German Women. As T **1322** but with face value in new currency.
3190 45c. green and blue 90 90
3191 55c. red and black . . . . 1·10 1·10
3192 €1 purple and blue . . . . 1·90 1·90
3193 €1.44 brown and blue . . . 2·75 2·75
DESIGNS: 45c. Annette von Droste-Hulshoff (writer); 55c. Hildegard Knef (actress); €1 Marie Juchacz (politician); €1.44 Esther von Kirchbach (writer).

1406 Town Buildings

2003. Millenary of Kronach.
3194 **1406** 45c. multicoloured . . . 90 90

1407 Georg Elser

2003. Birth Centenary of Georg Elser (attempted assassination of Adolf Hitler).
3195 **1407** 55c. multicoloured . . . 1·10 1·10

1408 Bridge joined by Heart

2003. 40th Anniv of German–French Co-operation Treaty.
3196 **1408** 55c. multicoloured . . . 1·10 1·10

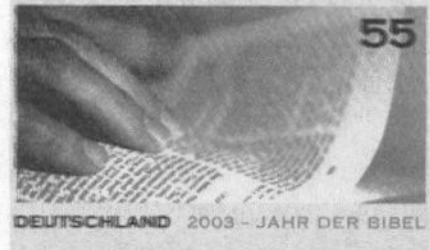

1409 Hand and Page

2003. Year of the Bible.
3197 **1409** 55c. multicoloured . . . 1·10 1·10

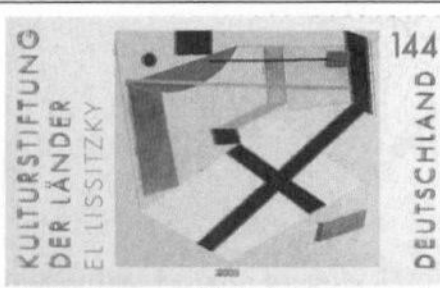

1410 "Proun 30t" (El Lissitzky)

2003. Cultural Foundation of the Federal States.
3198 **1410** €1.44 multicoloured 2·75 2·75

1411 St. Thomas Church Choir, Leipzig

2003. Boys' Choirs. Sheet 172 × 77 mm containing T **1411** and similar horiz designs. Multicoloured.
MS3199 45c. Type **1411**; 55c. Dresden Church choir; 100c. St. Peter's Cathedral choir, Regensburg . . . . 4·00 4·00

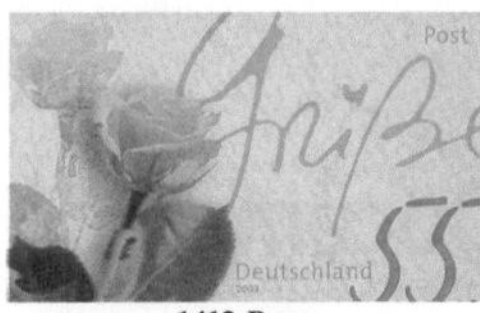

1412 Rose

2003. Greetings Stamp. Ordinary or self-adhesive gum.
3200 **1412** 55c. multicoloured . . . 1·10 1·10

1413 "Junger Argentier" (Max Beckman)

2003. Artists' Anniversaries. Multicoloured.
3202 55c. Type **1413** (53rd death anniv) . . . . 1·10 1·10
3203 €1 "Komposition" (Adolf Holzel) (150th birth anniv) . . . . 1·90 1·90

1414 Footballer

2003. Sports Promotion Fund. World Cup Football Championship (2006), Germany. Multicoloured.
3204 45c.+20c. Type **1414** . . . . 1·30 1·30
3205 55c.+25c. Boys playing football . . . . 1·60 1·60
3206 55c.+25c. Fan with arms raised . . . . 1·60 1·60
3207 55c.+25c. Young player heading ball . . . . . . 1·60 1·60
3208 €1.44+56c. Boy kicking ball to older man . . . . 4·00 4·00

1415 Building Facade

2003. UNESCO World Heritage Sites. Cologne Cathedral. Ordinary or self-adhesive gum.
3209 **1415** 55c. grey, red and black 1·10 1·10

1416 Flower

2003. International Horticultural Exhibition, Rostock.
3211 **1416** 45c. multicoloured . . . 90 90

1417 Oskar von Miller (founder) and Technological Symbols

2003. Centenary of Deutsches Museum, Munich.
3212 **1417** 55c. multicoloured . . . 1·10 1·10

1418 Cut-out Figures

2003. 50th Anniv of Deutscher Kinderschutzbund (children's organization).
3213 **1418** 55c. multicoloured . . . 1·10 1·10

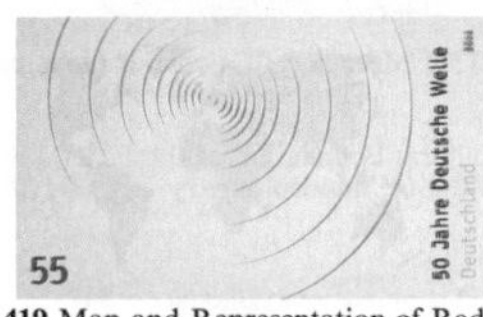

1419 Map and Representation of Radio Waves

2003. 50th Anniv of Deutsche Welle (radio station).
3214 **1419** 55c. multicoloured . . . 1·10 1·10

1420 Aviators and Junkers W 33 Bremen

2003. 75th Anniv East–West North Atlantic Flight.
3215 **1420** 144c.+56c. multicoloured . . . . 3·75 3·75

1421 1960s Posters

2003. Europa. Poster Art.
3216 **1421** 55c. multicoloured . . . 1·10 1·10

1422 Justus von Liebig

2003. Birth Bicentenary of Justus von Liebig (chemist).
3217 **1422** 55c. multicoloured . . . 1·10 1·10

1423 Reinhold Schneider and Text

2003. Birth Centenary of Reinhold Schneider (writer).
3218 **1423** 55c. multicoloured . . . 1·10 1·10

1424 Helicopter and Patrol Vehicle

2003. Centenary of ADAC (automobile association).
3219 **1424** 55c. multicoloured . . . 1·10 1·10

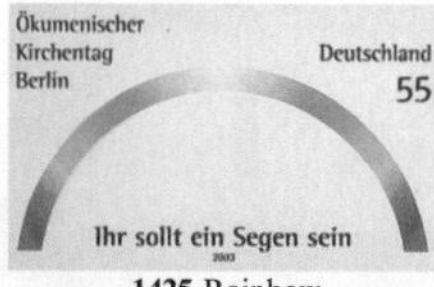

1425 Rainbow

2003. Ecumenical Church Conference, Berlin.
3220 **1425** 55c. multicoloured . . . 1·10 1·10

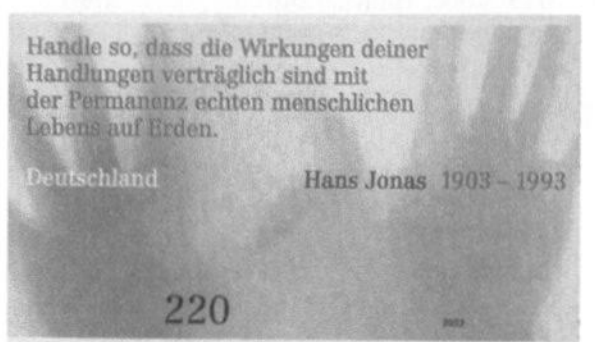

1426 Hands and Text

2003. Birth Centenary of Hans Jonas (philosopher).
3221 **1426** 220c. multicoloured . . 4·25 4·25

1427 Hand with Face and Feet

2003. 10th Anniv of Postal Codes.
3222 **1427** 55c. multicoloured . . . 1·10 1·10

1428 Bridge over Salzach River

2003. Centenary of Oberndorf–Laufen Bridge. Ordinary or self-adhesive gum.
3223 **1428** 55c. multicoloured . . . 1·10 1·10
A stamp of the same design was issued by Austria.

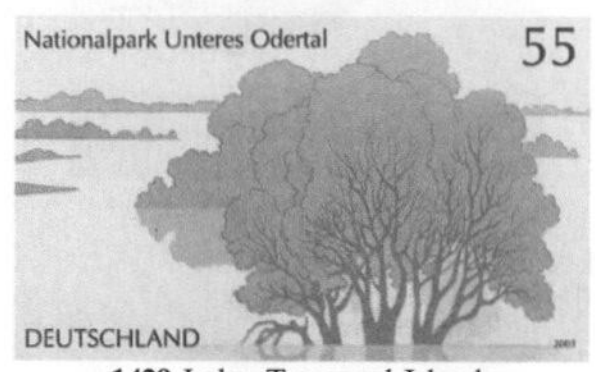

1429 Lake, Trees and Islands

2003. Unteres Odertal National Park. Sheet 111 × 66 mm.
MS3225 **1429** 55c. multicoloured 1·10 1·10

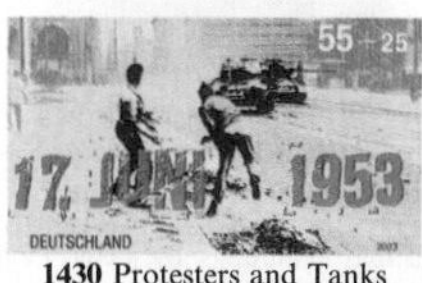

1430 Protesters and Tanks

2003. 50th Anniv of Uprising in East Berlin.
3226 **1430** 55c.+25c. multicoloured 1·60 1·60

1431 Musical Notations

2003. 50th Anniv of Deutscher Musikrat (music association).
3227 **1431** €1.44 silver and blue 2·75 2·75

1432 Father chasing Son

2003. "For Us Children". "Father and Son" (cartoon by E.O. Plauen (Erich Ohser)). Sheet 111 × 191 mm containing T **1432** and similar horiz designs. Multicoloured.
MS3228 45c.+20c. Type **1432**; 55c.+25c. Father and son falling; 55c.+25c. Father looking over shoulder at son running away; 55c.+25c. Father chasing son in a circle; €1.44+56c. Father and son sliding . . . . 10·00 10·00

1433 Winding Gear and Trees

2003. Ruhr District Industrial Landscape.
3229 **1433** 55c. multicoloured . . . 1·10 1·10

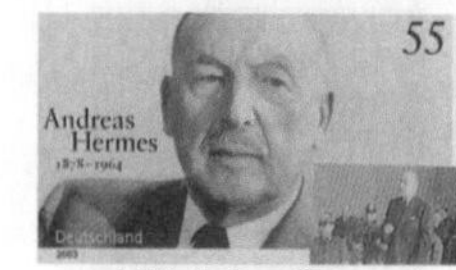

1434 Andres Hermes

2003. 125th Birth Anniv of Andreas Hermes (politician).
3230 **1434** 55c. multicoloured . . . 1·10 1·10

1435 Market Stalls, Munich

2003. German Cities. Multicoloured. Ordinary or self-adhesive gum.
3231 45c. Type **1435** 90 90
3232 55c. Building facades, Altstadt Gorlitz 70 30

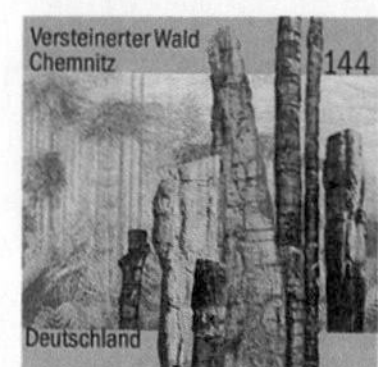

1436 Petrified Forest, Chemnitz

2003.
3234 **1436** 144c. multicoloured . . 2·75 2·75

1437 Viaduct and Enz River

2003. 150th Anniv of Enztal Viaduct (railway).
3235 **1437** 55c. multicoloured . . . 1·10 1·10

1438 Theodor Adorno and Manuscript

2003. Birth Centenary of Theodor Adorno (philosopher and sociologist).
3236 **1438** 55c. multicoloured . . . 1·10 1·10

1439 Elephant and Bird

2003. "For Us Children". Sheet 111 × 65 mm.
MS3237 **1439** 55c. multicoloured 1·10 1·10

2003. Cars. As T **1404**. Multicoloured.
3238 45c.+20c. Wartburg 311 Coupe . . . . 1·30 1·30
3239 55c.+25c. Ford Taunus 17 M P3 . . . . 1·60 1·60
3240 55c.+25c. Porsche 356 B Coupe . . . . 1·60 1·70
3241 55c.+25c. Opel Olympia Rekord P1 . . . . 1·60 1·60
3242 144c.+56c. Auto Union 1000 S . . . . 4·00 4·00

1440 Letter Box

2003. Post.
3243 **1440** 55c. multicoloured . . . 1·10 1·10

1441 Lifeguards

2003. 90th Anniv of DLRG (safety organization).
3244 **1441** 144c. multicoloured . . 2·75 2·75

1442 Nativity Figures (19th-century)

2003. Christmas. Multicoloured.
3245 45c.+20c. Type **1442** . . . . 1·30 1·30
3246 55c.+25c. Holy Family . . . 1·60 1·60

1443 Dresden Opera House

2003. Birth Bicentenary of Gottfried Semper (architect).
3247 **1443** 55c. multicoloured . . . 1·10 1·10

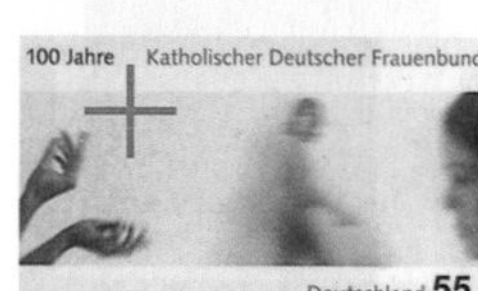

1444 Hands and Women

2003. Centenary of German Catholic Women's Federation.
3248 **1444** 55c. multicoloured . . . 1·10 1·10

1445 Stars

2003. 10th Anniv of Maastricht Treaty.
3249 **1445** 55c. blue and yellow . . 1·10 1·10

1446 St. Martin's Church

2004. 800th Anniv of Landshut.
3250 **1446** 45c. multicoloured . . . 90 90

1447 Cathedral and Images of Schleswig

2004. 1200th Anniv of Schleswig.
3251 **1447** 55c. multicoloured . . . 1·10 1·10

1448 Clouds, Sun and Trees

2004. Environmental Protection and Renewable Energy.
3252 **1448** 55c.+25c. multicoloured 1·60 1·60

1449 Football Players

2004. Sport Promotion Fund. Multicoloured.
3253 45c.+20c. Type **1449** (European Football Championship) . . . . . 1·30 1·30
3254 55c.+25c. Wheelchair athlete (Paralympics) . . . . . . 1·60 1·60
3255 55c.+25c. Runner (Olympic Games, Greece) . . . . . 1·60 1·60
3256 55c.+25c. Footballer (50th anniv of Germany winning World Cup) . . . 1·60 1·60
3257 144c.+56c. Hands holding trophy (Centenary of FIFA) . . . . 4·00 4·00

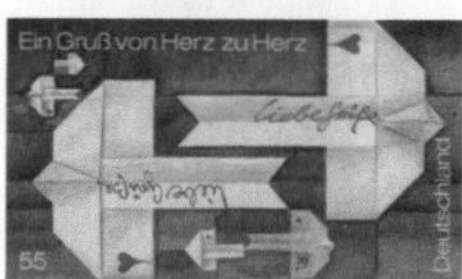

1450 Paper Airplanes

2004. Post.
3258 **1450** 55c. multicoloured . . . 1·10 1·10

1451 Buildings

2004. 1300th Anniv of Arnstadt.
3259 **1451** 55c. multicoloured . . . 1·10 1·10

1452 Shadow of Boy, Apple and Arrow

2004. Classic Theatre. Sheet 102 × 73 mm containing T **1452** and similar square design. Multicoloured.
MS3260 45c. Type **1452** (William Tell (Friedrich von Schiller) (200th anniv)); 100c. Faust and the devil (Faust II (Johann Wolfgang von Goethe) (150th anniv)) . . . . 2·75 2·75

1453 Joseph Schmidt

2004. Birth Centenary of Joseph Schmidt (singer).
3261 **1453** 55c. brown . . . . . . 1·10 1·10

1454 Paul Ehrlich (chemistry) and Emil von Behring (medicine)

2004. 150th Birth Anniv of Nobel Prize Winners.
3262 **1454** 144c. multicoloured . . 2·75 2·75

1455 White Stork in Flight

2004. Endangered Species. White Stork (*Circona circona*).
3263 **1455** 55c. black, blue and red 1·10 1·10

1456 Master House, Dessau

2004. Bauhaus (design group).
3264 **1456** 55c. multicoloured . . . 1·10 1·10

1457 Kurt Kiesinger

2004. Birth Centenary of Kurt Georg Kiesinger (politician).
3265 **1457** 55c. multicoloured . . . 1·10 1·10

1458 Early and Modern Light Bulbs

2004. 150th Anniv of Electric Light Bulb.
3266 **1458** 220c. multicoloured . . 4·25 4·25

1459 Sunflower and Holiday Symbols

2004. Europa. Holidays.
3267 **1459** 45c. multicoloured . . . 90 90

1460 New Members' Flags as Cones

2004. Enlargement of European Union.
3268 **1460** 55c. multicoloured . . . 1·10 1·10

1461 Reinhard Schwarz-Schilling

2004. Birth Centenary of Reinhard Schwarz-Schilling (composer).
3269 **1461** 55c. sepia . . . . . . 1·10 1·10

1462 St. Boniface under Attack

2004. 350th Anniv of Martyrdom of St. Boniface (papal envoy to Germany).
3270 **1462** 55c. multicoloured . . . 1·10 1·10

1463 Schloss Ludwigsburg

2004. 300th Anniv of Schloss Ludwigsburg.
3271 **1463** €1.44 multicoloured 2·75 2·75

1464 Two Kittens playing with String

2004. "For Us Children". Cats. Multicoloured.
3272 45c.+20c. Type **1464** . . . 1·30 1·30
3273 55c.+25c. Three kittens playing with ball . . . . 1·60 1·60
3274 55c.+25c. Mother and kitten 1·60 1·60
3275 55c.+25c. Cat washing paw 1·60 1·60
3276 €1.44+56c. Two kittens asleep . . . . 4·00 4·00

1465 Sea and Sand

2004. Wattenmeer National Park.
3277 **1465** 55c. multicoloured . . . 1·10 1·10

1466 National Flags as Heart-shaped Kite

2004. 21st-century German—Russian Youth Forum.
3278 **1466** 55c. multicoloured . . . 1·10 1·10

1467 Greifswalder Oie, Baltic Sea

2004. Lighthouses. Multicoloured. (a) Ordinary gum.
3279 45c. Type **1467** 90 90
3280 55c. Roter Sands . . . . . 1·10 1·10

(b) Self-adhesive gum.
3281 55c. As No. 3280 (35 × 35 mm) 75 30

1468 *Bremen* (passenger ship) and New York Harbour

2004. *Bremen*—1929 Winner of Blue Ribbon (Europe to America speed record). (a) Ordinary gum.
3282 **1468** 55c. multicoloured . . . 1·10 1·10

(b) Self-adhesive gum.
3283 **1468** 55c. multicoloured . . . 1·10 1·10

1469 Ludwig Fuerbach

2004. Birth Bicentenary of Ludwig Fuerbach (philosopher).
3284 **1469** 144c. rosine and black 2·75 2·75

1470 Camellia

2004. Greetings Stamp. Ordinary or Self-adhesive gum.
3285 **1470** 55c. multicoloured . . . 1·10 1·10

1471 Church Facade

2004. Centenary of Protestant Regional Church, Speyer.
3287 **1471** 55c. multicoloured . . . 1·10 1·10

1472 Scene from "Hansel and Gretel" and Engelbert Humperdinck

2004. 150th Birth Anniv of Engelbert Humperdinck (composer).
3288 **1472** 45c. multicoloured . . . 90 90

1473 Ink Pot, Quill Pen, Manuscript and Glasses

2004. Birth Bicentenary of Eduard Morike (writer).
3289 **1473** 55c. multicoloured . . . 1·10 1·10

1474 Feet and Hand Prints forming Face

2004. "For Us Children".
3290 **1474** 55c. multicoloured . . . 1·10 1·10

1475 Kaiser Wilhelm Cathedral church, Berlin and Egon Eiermann

2004. Birth Centenary of Egon Eiermann (architect).
3291 **1475** 100c. multicoloured . . 1·90 1·90

1476 Court Seal

2004. 50th Anniv of Federal Social Court.
3292 **1476** 144c. multicoloured . . 2·75 2·75

1477 Iceberg, Greenland

2004. Climate Zones. Multicoloured.
3293 45c.+20c. Type **1477** (arctic) 90 90
3294 55c.+25c. Mountains, Tibet (alpine) . . . . 1·10 1·10
3295 55c.+25c. River and grazing animals, Mecklenburg-Vorpommern (temperate)
3296 55c.+25c. Dunes, Sahara (desert) . . . . 1·10 1·10
3297 144c.+56c. Rainforest, Galapagos Islands (tropics) . . . . 1·75 1·75

1478 Flying Boat Do X (1930)

2004. Stamp Day.
3298 **1478** 55c. ultramarine and vermilion 75 30

1479 "Flight into Egypt"

2004. Christmas. Paintings by Peter Paul Rubens. Multicoloured.
3299 45c.+20c. Type **1479** . . . 90 90
3300 55c.+25c. "Adoration of the Magi" . . . . 1·10 1·10

Stamps of the same design were issued by Belgium.

1480 Snow-covered Avenue

2004. Post.
3301 **1480** 55c. multicoloured . . . 75 30

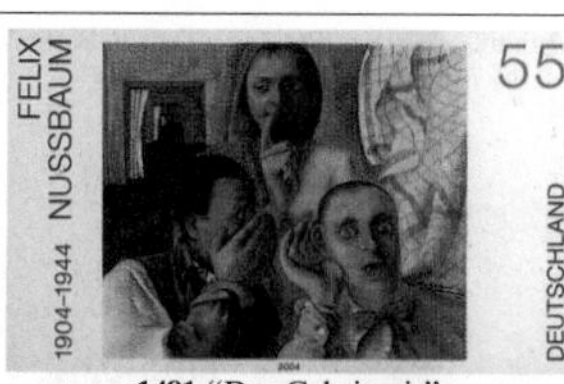

1481 "Das Geheimnis"

2004. Birth Centenary of Felix Nussbaum (artist).
3302 **1481** 55c. multicoloured . . . 75 30

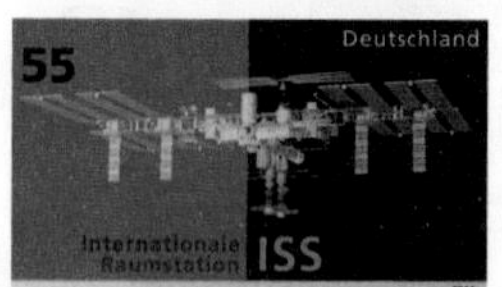

1482 International Space Station

2004.
3303 **1482** 55c. multicoloured . . . 75 30

1483 City Hall

2005. 1200th Anniv of Forchheim.
3304 **1483** 45c. multicoloured . . . 60 30

1484 Three Kings (board painting, Cologne (c. 1350)) **1485** Sunflower

2005. Art.
3305 **1484** 55c. multicoloured . . . 75 30

2005. Flowers. Multicoloured.
3306 45c. Daisy 60 30
3320 95c. Type **1485** . . . . . . 1·30 65
3321 €4.30 Larkspur . . . . . 6·00 3·00

1486 Celtic Statue, Glauberg

2005. Archaeology.
3335 **1486** €1.44 multicoloured 2·00 1·00

1487 Championship Mascot (⅗-size illustration)

2005. Sport Promotion Fund. Multicoloured.
3336 45c.+20c. Type **1487** (World Cup Football Championship, Germany 2006) 85 85
3337 55c.+25c. Footballers (World Cup Football Championships, Germany 2006) . . . . 1·10 1·10
3338 55c.+25c. Skier (Nordic World Ski Championships, Oberstdorf) . . . . 1·10 1·10
3339 55c.+25c. Gymnasts (International German Gymnastics Festival, Berlin) . . . . 1·10 1·10
3340 144c.+56c. Fencers (Fencing World Championships, Leipzig) . . . . 2·75 2·75

1488 Pillar

2005. 150th Anniv of Advertisement Pillars.
3341 **1488** 55c. multicoloured . . . 75 30

1489 Cathedral Facade

2005. 150th Anniv of Berlin Cathedral. Ordinary or self adhesive gum.
1489 95c. multicoloured . . . . . 1·30 65

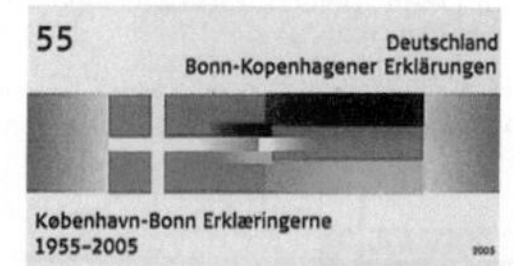

1490 Postman walking in Mountains

2005. Postal Service. Multicoloured.
3344 55c. Type **1490** 75 30
3345 55c. Postman cycling . . . 75 30

1491 Danish and German Flags

2005. 50th Anniv of Germany—Denmark Relations.
3346 **1491** 55c. multicoloured . . . 75 30
A stamp of the same design was issued by Denmark.

1492 Airliner

2005. 50th Anniv of Resumption of German Air Traffic.
3347 **1492** 155c. multicoloured . . 75 30

1493 Aquaduct

2005. Centenary of Mittelland Canal.
3348 **1493** 45c. multicoloured . . . 60 30

1494 Rock, Ferns and Tree

2005. National Parks. Bavarian Forest.
3349 **1494** 55c. multicoloured . . . 75 30

1495 Silhouettes of Characters

2005. Birth Bicentenary of Hans Christian Andersen (writer).
3350 **1495** 144c. light orange, orange and black . . 2·00 1·00

IV. WEST BERLIN

The Russian Government withdrew from the four-power control of Berlin on 1 July 1948, with the Western Sectors remaining under American, British and French control. West Berlin was constituted a "Land" of the Federal Republic on 1 September 1950. The Russian Zone issues inscribed "STADT BERLIN" (which we do not list unoverprinted in this Catalogue), were not intended for use throughout Berlin, but were for the Russian sector of the city and for Brandenburg.

The first stamps to be used in the Western Sectors were Nos. A4/5 and A7 of the Anglo-American Zones, followed by Nos. A36/52, which were on sale from 24 June to 31 August 1948, and remained valid until 19 September 1948.

1948. 100 pfennig = 1 Deutsche Mark (East).
1949. 100 pfennig = 1 Deutsche Mark (West).

1948. Pictorial issue of 1947 (Nos. 928/48) optd **BERLIN**.
B21 2pf. black . . . . 2·75 2·00
B 2 6pf. violet . . . . 1·20 5·25
B 3 8pf. red . . . . 1·20 5·50
B 4 10pf. green . . . . 1·20 1·40
B 5 12pf. grey . . . . 1·20 90
B25 15pf. brown . . . . 10·50 2·10
B 7 16pf. green . . . . 4·50 1·90
B26 20pf. blue . . . . 3·00 80
B 9 24pf. brown . . . . 1·20 55
B10 25pf. orange . . . . 23·00 60·00
B11 30pf. red . . . . 4·50 9·00
B12 40pf. mauve . . . . 7·00 9·00
B13 50pf. blue . . . . 10·00 37·00
B14 60pf. brown . . . . 2·75 50
B15 80pf. blue . . . . 10·50 29·00
B16 84pf. green . . . . 18·00 £110
B17 1m. olive . . . . 65·00 £170
B18 2m. violet . . . . 70·00 £650
B19 3m. red . . . . 90·00 £900
B20 5m. blue £120 £900

B 2 Schoneberg **B 3** Douglas C-54 Skymaster Transport over Tempelhof Airport

1949. Inscr "DEUTSCHE POST". Berlin Views.
(a) Small size.
B35 – 1pf. grey 30 20
B36 **B 2** 4pf. brown 90 20
B36c – 4pf. brown . . . . . . 7·50 5·00
B37 – 5pf. green . . . . . . 1·20 20
B38 – 6pf. purple . . . . . . 2·10 1·20
B39 **B 2** 8pf. orange . . . . . . 2·10 1·60
B40 – 10pf. green 90 20
B41 **B 3** 15pf. brown . . . . . . 18·00 90
B42 – 20pf. red . . . . . . 5·50 20
B42b – 20pf. red . . . . . . 85·00 1·00
B43 – 25pf. yellow . . . . . . 32·00 1·20
B44 – 30pf. blue . . . . . . 16·00 1·30
B45 **B 2** 40pf. lake . . . . . . 23·00 1·10
B46 – 50pf. olive . . . . . . 25·00 25
B47 – 60pf. red . . . . . . 90·00 25
B48 – 80pf. blue . . . . . . 21·00 1·40
B49 – 90pf. green . . . . . . 23·00 1·40

(b) Large size.
B50 **B 3** 1Dm. olive . . . . 32·00 1·30
B51 – 2Dm. purple . . . . . . 90·00 1·70
B52 – 3Dm. red . . . . £375 17·00
B53 – 5Dm. blue . . . . £180 17·00

DESIGNS—As Type **B 2**: 1pf. Brandenburg Gate; 4pf. (B36c) Exhibition Building; 5, 25pf. "Tegel Schloss". 6, 50pf. Reichstag Building. 10, 30pf. "Kleistpark". 20 (B42), 80, 90pf. Technical High School; 20pf. (B42b) Olympia Stadium; 60pf. National Gallery. As Type **B 3**: 2Dm. "Gendarmenmarkt"; 3Dm. Brandenburg Gate; 5Dm. "Tegel Schloss".

For similar views inscribed "DEUTSCHE POST BERLIN" see Nos. B118/19.

B 4 Stephan Monument and Globe **B 5** Heinrich von Stephan Monument

1949. 75th Anniv of U.P.U.
B54 **B 4** 12pf. grey . . . . 35·00 8·50
B55 16pf. green . . . . 50·00 19·00
B56 24pf. orange . . . . . . 35·00 80
B57 50pf. olive . . . . £200 47·00
B58 60pf. brown . . . . . . £250 42·00
B59 **B 5** 1Dm. olive £160 £140
B60 2Dm. purple . . . . . . £160 90·00

B 6 Goethe and Scene from "Iphigenie" **B 9** Alms Bowl and Bear

1949. Birth Bicent of Goethe (poet). Portraits of Goethe and scenes from his works.
B61 **B 6** 10pf. green . . . . £180 80·00
B62 – 20pf. red . . . . £180 90·00
B63 – 30pf. blue . . . . 35·00 60·00
DESIGNS—Scenes from: 20pf. "Reineke Fuchs"; 30pf. "Faust".

1949. Numeral and pictorial issues of 1946/7 surch **BERLIN** and bold figures.
B64 **229** 5pf. on 45pf. red . . . . 4·50 25
B65 **C** 10pf. on 24pf. brown . . . 18·00 25
B66 **B** 20pf. on 80pf. blue . . . 85·00 19·00
B67 **237** 1m. on 3m. lake . . . . £225 20·00

1949. Berlin Relief Fund.
B68 **B 9** 10pf.+5pf. green £120 £190
B69 20pf.+5pf. red £140 £190
B70 30pf.+5pf. blue £140 £300
MSB70a 111 × 65 mm. Nos. B68/70 (sold at 1Dm.) £900 £2750

B 10 **B 11** Harp

1950. European Recovery Programme.
B71 **B 10** 20pf. red . . . . 95·00 43·00

1950. Restablishment of Berlin Philharmonic Orchestra.
B72 **B 11** 10pf.+5pf. green . . . . 60·00 41·00
B73 – 30pf.+5pf. blue £120 £110
DESIGN: 30pf. "Singing Angels" (after H. and J. van Eyck).

B 13 G. A. Lortzing **B 14** Freedom Bell

1951. Death Cent of Lortzing (composer).
B74 **B 13** 20pf. brown . . . . . . 60·00 55·00

1951. (a) Clapper at left.
B75 **B 14** 5pf. brown . . . . . . 2·30 8·50
B76 10pf. green . . . . . . 21·00 27·00
B77 20pf. red . . . . . . 10·50 24·00
B78 30pf. blue . . . . . . 75·00 85·00
B79 40pf. purple . . . . . . 14·00 44·00

(b) Clapper at right.
B82 **B 14** 5pf. green . . . . 2·30 1·90
B83 10pf. green . . . . . . 7·50 4·25
B84 20pf. red . . . . 28·00 21·00
B85 30pf. blue . . . . 75·00 55·00
B86 40pf. red . . . . 28·00 18·00

(c) Clapper in centre.
B101 **B 14** 5pf. brown . . . . . . 1·00 95
B102 10pf. green . . . . . . 2·10 1·50
B103 20pf. red . . . . . . 8·75 3·75
B104 30pf. blue . . . . . . 16·00 15·00
B105 40pf. violet . . . . . 75·00 42·00

B 15 Boy Stamp Collectors **B 16** Mask of Beethoven (taken from life, 1812)

1951. Stamp Day.
B80 **B 15** 10pf.+3pf. green . . . . 32·00 31·00
B81 20pf.+2pf. red . . . . . 37·00 41·00

1952. 125th Death Anniv of Beethoven (composer).
B87 **B 16** 30pf. blue . . . . 48·00 35·00

B 17 Olympic Torch B 18 W. von Siemens (electrical engineer)

1952. Olympic Games Festival, Berlin.
B88 **B 17** 4pf. brown . . . . . . 90 2·00
B89 10pf. green . . . . . . 14·00 19·00
B90 20pf. red . . . . 21·00 27·00

1952. Famous Berliners.
B 91 – 4pf. brown 45 45
B 92 – 5pf. blue . . . . 1·40 45
B 93 – 6pf. purple . . . . . . 7·50 12·00
B 94 – 8pf. brown . . . . . . 2·30 2·50
B 95 – 10pf. green . . . . . . 3·50 50
B 96 – 15pf. lilac . . . . . . 21·00 19·00
B 97 **B 18** 20pf. red . . . . . . 2·75 85
B 98 – 25pf. green . . . . . . 65·00 6·25
B 99 – 30pf. purple . . . . . 21·00 10·00
B100 – 40pf. black . . . . . . 37·00 3·25
PORTRAITS: 4pf. Zelter (musician); 5pf. Lilienthal (aviator); 6pf. Rathenau (statesman); 8pf. Fontane (writer); 10pf. Von Menzel (artist); 15pf. Virchow (pathologist); 25pf. Schinkel (architect); 30pf. Planck (physicist); 40pf. W. von Humboldt (philologist).

B 19 Church before Bombing B 20 Chainbreaker

1953. Kaiser Wilhelm Memorial Church Reconstruction Fund.
B106 **B 19** 4pf.+1pf. brown . . . 45 15·00
B107 10pf.+5pf. green . . . 1·40 50·00
B108 – 20pf.+10pf. red . . . . 4·25 50·00
B109 – 30pf.+15pf. blue . . . 21·00 £100
DESIGN: 20pf., 30pf. Church after bombing.

1953. East German Uprising. Inscr "17. JUNI 1953".
B110 **B 20** 20pf. black . . . . . 4·50 1·70
B111 – 30pf. red . . . . . . 37·00 30·00
DESIGN: 30pf. Brandenburg Gate.

B 21 Ernst Reuter B 22 Conference Buildings

1954. Death of Ernst Reuter (Mayor of West Berlin).
B112 **B 21** 20pf. brown . . . . . 8·75 2·20

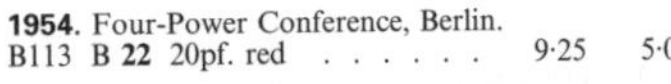

1954. Four-Power Conference, Berlin.
B113 **B 22** 20pf. red . . . . . . 9·25 5·00

B 23 O. Mergenthaler and Linotype Machine B 25 "Germany in Bondage"

1954. Birth Cent of Mergenthaler (inventor).
B114 **B 23** 10pf. green . . . . . . 3·25 3·00

1954. West German Presidential Election. No. B103 optd **Wahl des Bundesprasidenten in Berlin 17. Juli 1954.**
B115 **B 14** 20pf. red . . . . . . 4·50 5·75

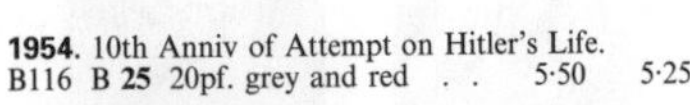

1954. 10th Anniv of Attempt on Hitler's Life.
B116 **B 25** 20pf. grey and red . . 5·50 5·25

B 26 Prussian Postilion, 1827 B 27 Memorial Library

1954. National Stamp Exhibition.
B117 **B 26** 20pf.+10pf. mult . . . 15·00 35·00

1954. Berlin Views. As Type **B 2** but inscr "DEUTSCHE POST BERLIN".
B118 7pf. green . . . . 7·50 80
B119 70pf. olive . . . . £130 23·00
DESIGNS: 7pf. Exhibition building; 70pf. Grunewald hunting lodge.

1954.
B120 **B 27** 40pf. purple . . . . . 12·00 3·25

B 28 Richard Strauss B 29 Blacksmiths forging Rail

1954. 5th Death Anniv of Strauss (composer).
B121 **B 28** 40pf. blue . . . . . . 12·50 4·25

1954. Death Cent of A. Borsig (industrialist).
B122 **B 29** 20pf. brown . . . . . 9·25 2·20

B 30 "Berlin" (liner) B 31 Wilhelm Furtwangler (conductor)

1955.
B123 **B 30** 10pf. green . . . . . . 1·60 35
B124 25pf. blue . . . . . . 8·75 4·25

1955. 1st Death Anniv of Furtwangler.
B125 **B 31** 40pf. blue . . . . . . 23·00 21·00

B 32 B 33 Prussian Rural Postilion, 1760

1955. Federal Parliament Session, Berlin.
B126 **B 32** 10pf. black, yell & red 45 50
B127 20pf. black, yell & red 6·00 9·75

1955. Stamp Day and Philatelic Fund.
B128 **B 33** 25pf.+10pf. mult . . . 7·50 16·00

B 34 St. Otto B 35 Radio Tower and Exhibition Hall

1955. 25th Anniv of Berlin Bishopric.
B129 **B 34** 7pf.+3pf. brown . . . 90 3·25
B130 – 10pf.+5pf. green . . . 1·40 3·75
B131 – 20pf.+10pf. mauve . . . 2·50 5·00
DESIGNS: 10pf. St. Hedwig; 20pf. St. Peter.

1956. Berlin Buildings and Monuments.
B133 – 1pf. grey 20 15
B133b – 3pf. violet 30 20
B134 – 5pf. mauve 20 15
B132 **B 35** 7pf. turquoise (A) . . 9·25 2·75
B135 – 7pf. turquoise (B) . . 20 15
B136 – 8pf. grey 55 45
B136a – 8pf. red 30 35
B137 – 10pf. green 20 15
B138 – 15pf. blue 45 25
B139 – 20pf. red 45 15
B140 – 25pf. brown 55 50
B141 – 30pf. green 90 95
B142 – 40pf. blue . . . . . 13·50 7·75
B143 – 50pf. green 90 95
B144 – 60pf. brown . . . . . 1·20 1·10
B145 – 70pf. violet . . . . . 35·00 14·50
B146 – 1Dm. green . . . . . 2·50 2·40
B146a – 3Dm. red . . . . . . 7·00 12·50
7pf. (A) Type **B 35**. (B) As Type **B 35** but with inscription at top.

DESIGNS—As Type **B 35** (B)—HORIZ: 1pf., 3pf. Brandenburg Gate; 5pf. P.O. Headquarters; 20pf. Free University; 40pf. Charlottenburg Castle; 60pf. Chamber of Commerce and Bourse; 70pf. Schiller Theatre. VERT: 8pf. Town Hall, Neukollin; 10pf. Kaiser Wilhelm Memorial Church; 15pf. Airlift Monument; 25pf. Lilienthal Monument; 30pf. Pfaueninsel Castle; 50pf. Reuter Power-station. LARGER (24 × 30 mm): 1Dm. "The Great Elector" (statue, after Schluter). (29½ × 25 mm): 3Dm. Congress Hall, Berlin.

B 37 Eagle and Arms of Berlin B 38

1956. Federal Council Meeting.
B147 **B 37** 10pf. black, yell & red 1·40 45
B148 25pf. black, yell & red 5·50 5·00

1956. Centenary of German Engineers' Union.
B149 **B 38** 10pf. green . . . . . . 2·50 1·60
B150 20pf. red . . . . . . 6·00 5·75

1956. Flood Relief Fund. As No. B 77 (colour changed) surch **+10 Berlinhilfe fur die Hochwassergeschadigten DEUTSCHE BUNDESPOST-BERLIN** and bar.
B151 **B 14** 20pf.+10pf. bistre . . . 3·00 3·25

B 40 P. Lincke B 41 Wireless Transmitter

1956. 10th Death Anniv of Lincke (composer).
B152 **B 40** 20pf. red . . . . . . 2·75 3·25

1956. Industrial Exhibition.
B153 **B 41** 25pf. brown . . . . . 6·75 9·50

B 42 Brandenburg Postilion, 1700 B 43 Spandau

1956. Stamp Day and Philatelic Fund.
B154 **B 42** 25pf.+10pf. mult . . . 3·00 3·75

1957. 725th Anniv of Spandau.
B155 **B 43** 20pf. olive and brown 60 75

B 44 Model of Hansa District B 45 Friedrich K. von Savigny (jurist)

1957. International Building Exn, Berlin.
B156 **B 44** 7pf. brown 20 20
B157 – 20pf. red . . . . . . 1·00 90
B158 – 40pf. blue . . . . . . 2·50 2·50
DESIGNS—HORIZ: 20pf. Aerial view of Exhibition; 40pf. Exhibition Congress Hall.

1957. Portraits as Type **B 45**.
B159 – 7pf. brown and green 20 15
B160 – 8pf. brown and grey 20 20
B161 – 10pf. brown and green 30 20
B162 – 15pf. sepia and blue . . 45 80
B163 – 20pf.+10pf. sepia and red 20 50
B164 – 20pf. brown and red 90 65
B165 – 25pf. sepia and lake . . 1·20 1·00
B166 **B 45** 30pf. sepia and green 2·75 2·75
B167 – 40pf. sepia and blue . . 1·20 95
B168 – 50pf. sepia and olive 5·00 7·75
PORTRAITS—VERT: 7pf. T. Mommsen (historian); 8pf. H. Zille (painter); 10pf. E. Reuter (Mayor of Berlin); 15pf. F. Haber (chemist); 20pf. (No. B164), F. Schleiermacher (theologian); 20pf. (B163), L. Heck (zoologist); 25pf. Max Reinhardt (theatrical producer); 40pf. A. von Humboldt (naturalist); 50pf. C. D. Rauch (sculptor).

The premium on No. B163 was for the Berlin Zoo. No. B167 commemorates Humboldt's death centenary.

B 46 Uta von Naumburg (statue) B 47 "Unity Justice and Freedom"

1957. German Cultural Congress.
B169 **B 46** 25pf. brown . . . . . 1·00 1·00

1957. 3rd Federal Parliament Assembly.
B170 **B 47** 10pf. black, ochre & red 35 85
B171 20pf. black, ochre & red . . . . 2·50 3·25

B 48 Postilion, 1897–1925 B 49 Torch of Remembrance

1957. Stamp Day.
B172 **B 48** 20pf. multicoloured . . 85 85

1957. 7th World War Veterans Congress.
B173 **B 49** 20pf. myrtle, yell & grn 90 80

B 50 Elly Heuss-Knapp (social worker) B 51 Christ and Symbols of the Cosmos

1957. Mothers' Convalescence Fund.
B174 **B 50** 20pf.+10pf. red . . . . 1·60 2·50

1958. German Catholics' Day.
B175 **B 51** 10pf. black and green 50 50
B176 20pf. black and mauve 1·30 1·60

B 52 Otto Suhr B 53 Pres. Heuss

1958. 1st Death Anniv of Burgomaster Otto Suhr.
B177 **B 52** 20pf. red . . . . . . 1·20 1·50
See also Nos. B187 and B193.

1959.
B178 **B 53** 7pf. green 20 35
B179 10pf. green 30 30
B180 20pf. red 70 30
B181 40pf. blue . . . . . . 3·25 5·00
B182 70pf. violet . . . . . 11·50 12·50

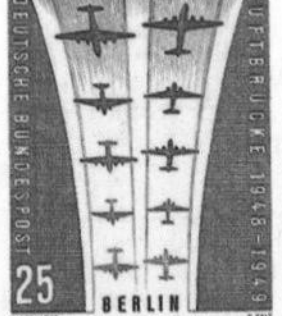

B 54 Symbolic Airlift B 55 Brandenburg Gate, Berlin

1959. 10th Anniv of Berlin Airlift.
B183 **B 54** 25pf. black and red . . 45 40

1959. 14th World Communities Congress, Berlin.
B184 **B 55** 20pf. blue, red & lt blue 90 40

B 56 Schiller — B 57 Robert Koch

1959. Birth Bicentenary of Schiller (poet).
B185 B 56 20pf. brown and red 40 40

1960. 50th Death Anniv of Robert Koch (bacteriologist).
B186 B 57 20pf. purple 40 45

1960. 4th Death Anniv of Walther Schreiber (Mayor of Berlin, 1951–53). As Type B **52**.
B187 20pf. red 60 70
DESIGN: Portrait of Schreiber.

B 58 Boy at Window — B 59 Hans Boeckler

1960. Berlin Children's Holiday Fund. Inscr "FERIENPLATZE FUR BERLINER KINDER".
B188 B 58 7pf.+3pf. dp brown, brown & light brown 30 45
B189 – 10pf.+5pf. deep green, olive and green . . . 30 45
B190 – 20pf.+10pf. brown, red and pink 55 80
B191 – 40pf.+20pf. deep blue, blue & light blue . . 1·40 4·00
DESIGNS: 10pf. Girl in street; 20pf. Girl blowing on Alpine flower; 40pf. Boy on beach.

1961. 10th Anniv of Hans Boeckler (politician).
B192 B 59 20pf. black and red . . 35 25

1961. Louise Schroeder Commemoration. As Type B **52**.
B193 20pf. brown 35 25
DESIGN: Portrait of Schroeder.

B 60 Durer — B 61 "Five Crosses" Symbol and St. Mary's Church

1961. Famous Germans.
B194 5pf. olive (Magnus) 20 20
B195 7pf. brown (St. Elizabeth of Thuringia) 20 45
B196 8pf. violet (Gutenberg) . . 20 35
B197 10pf. green (Type B **60**) . . 20 20
B198 15pf. blue (Luther) 20 45
B199 20pf. red (Bach) 20 20
B200 25pf. brown (Neumann) . . 20 40
B201 30pf. brown (Kant) 20 55
B202 40pf. blue (Lessing) 70 85
B203 50pf. brown (Goethe) . . . 45 1·10
B204 60pf. red (Schiller) . . . . 45 1·20
B205 70pf. green (Beethoven) . . 70 1·10
B206 80pf. brown (Kleist) . . . . 4·25 9·50
B207 1Dm. violet (Annette von Droste-Hulshoff) . . . . 1·60 3·25
B208 2Dm. green (Hauptmann) 2·30 5·25

1961. 10th Evangelical Churches' Day. Crosses in violet.
B210 B 61 10pf. green 25 20
B211 – 20pf. purple 30 25
DESIGN: 20pf. "Five Crosses" and Kaiser Wilhelm Memorial Church.

B 62 Exhibition Emblem

1961. West Berlin Radio and Television Exn.
B212 B 62 20pf. brown and red 30 25

B 63 "Die Linden" (1650) — B 64 Euler Gelberhund Biplane, 1912, and Boeing 707 Airliner

1962. "Old Berlin" series.
B213 B 63 7pf. sepia and brown 20 15
B214 – 10pf. sepia and green 20 15
B215 – 15pf. black and blue 20 15
B216 – 20pf. sepia and brown 20 15
B217 – 25pf. sepia and olive 20 30
B218 – 40pf. black and blue 35 35
B219 – 50pf. sepia and purple 35 45
B220 – 60pf. sepia and mauve 55 60
B221 – 70pf. black and purple 55 60
B222 – 80pf. sepia and red . . 75 80
B223 – 90pf. sepia and brown 85 90
B224 – 1Dm. sepia and green 90 1·20
DESIGNS: 10pf. "Waisenbrucke" (Orphans' Bridge), 1783; 15pf. Mauerstrasse, 1780; 20pf. Berlin Castle, 1703; 25pf. Potsdamer Platz, 1825; 40pf. Bellevue Castle, c. 1800; 50pf. Fischer Bridge, 1830; 60pf. Halle Gate, 1880; 70pf. Parochial Church, 1780; 80pf. University, 1825; 90pf. Opera House, 1780; 1Dm. Grunewald Lake, c. 1790.

1962. 50th Anniv of German Airmail Transport.
B225 B 64 60pf. black and blue 60 50

B 65 Exhibition Emblem — B 66 Town Hall Schoneberg

1963. West Berlin Broadcasting Exn.
B226 B 65 20pf. ultram, grey & bl 30 25

1964. 700th Anniv of Schoneberg.
B227 B 66 20pf. brown 30 25

B 67 Pres. Lubke — B 68 Kaiser Wilhelm Memorial Church

1964. Re-election of Pres. Lubke.
B228 B 67 20pf. red 20 15
B229 40pf. blue 45 30
See also Nos. B308/9.

WEST BERLIN DESIGNS. Except where illustrated the following are the same or similar designs to German Federal Republic additonally inscr "BERLIN".

1964. Capitals of the Federal Lands. As No. 1335.
B230 20pf. multicoloured 35 30

1964. Humanitarian Relief and Welfare Funds. As Nos. 1352/5.
B231 10pf.+5pf. multicoloured . . 20 20
B232 15pf.+5pf. multicoloured . . 20 15
B233 20pf.+10pf. multicoloured 40 15
B234 40pf.+20pf. multicoloured 70 1·10

1964. Pres. Kennedy Commem. As Type **411**.
B235 40pf. blue 45 45

1964. Twelve Centuries of German Architecture. (a) Size 18½×22½ mm. As Nos. 1359/66. Plain backgrounds.
B236 10pf. brown 20 15
B237 15pf. green 20 25
B238 20pf. red 20 20
B239 40pf. blue . . . . 85 1·10
B240 50pf. bistre . . . . . . 1·80 1·60
B241 60pf. red . . . . 1·30 1·30
B242 70pf. green . . . . . . 2·50 3·25
B243 80pf. brown . . . . . . 2·50 1·80

(b) Size 19½×24 mm. As Nos. 1367/81. Coloured backgrounds.
B244 5pf. bistre 20 15
B245 8pf. red 20 15
B246 10pf. purple 20 15
B247 20pf. green 25 15
B248 30pf. olive 30 25
B249 30pf. red 30 20
B250 40pf. bistre 70 85
B251 50pf. blue 55 50
B252 60pf. red . . . . 1·80 2·10
B253 70pf. bronze . . . . . . 1·10 85
B254 80pf. brown . . . . . . 1·20 2·00
B255 90pf. black 70 85
B256 1Dm. blue 70 80
B257 1Dm.10 brown . . . . . 1·60 1·50
B258 1Dm.30 green . . . . . 2·75 2·40
B259 2Dm. purple . . . . . . 2·75 2·10

BUILDINGS: 8pf. Palatine Castle, Kaub. Others as Nos. 1359/81 of German Federal Republic.

1965. Child Welfare. As Nos. 1384/7.
B261 10pf.+5pf. Eurasian woodcock 20 15
B262 15pf.+5pf. Common pheasant 20 25
B263 20pf.+10pf. Black grouse 20 25
B264 40pf.+20pf. Western capercaillie 65 90

1965. "New Berlin". Multicoloured.
B265 10pf. Type B **68** 10 10
B266 15pf. Opera House (horiz) 10 10
B267 20pf. Philharmonic Hall (horiz) 20 10
B268 30pf. Jewish Community Centre (horiz) 30 15
B269 40pf. Regina Martyrum Memorial Church (horiz) 30 25
B270 50pf. Ernst-Reuter Square (horiz) 30 30
B271 60pf. Europa Centre . . . 35 35
B272 70pf. Technical University, Charlottenburg (horiz) . . 45 45
B273 80pf. City Motorway . . . 55 45
B274 90pf. Planetarium (horiz) 75 70
B275 1Dm. Telecommunications, Tower 85 80
B276 1Dm.10 University Clinic, Steglitz (horiz) . . . . . 90 1·00

1965. Humanitarian Relief Funds. As Nos. 1406/9.
B277 10pf.+5pf. Type **425** . . . 20 20
B278 15pf.+5pf. Cinderella and birds with dress 20 20
B279 20pf.+10pf. Prince offering slipper to Cinderella . . . 30 20
B280 40pf.+20pf. Cinderella and Prince on horse 55 90

1966. As Nos. 1412/15a.
B281 10pf. brown 25 15
B282 20pf. green 25 15
B283 30pf. red 25 15
B284 50pf. blue 70 50
B284a 100pf. blue . . . . 5·50 4·50

1966. Child Welfare. As Nos. 1416/19.
B285 10pf.+5pf. Type **429** . . . 20 25
B286 20pf.+10pf. Chamois . . . 20 25
B287 30pf.+15pf. Fallow deer . . 30 25
B288 50pf.+25pf. Red deer . . . 75 85

1966. Humanitarian Relief Funds. As Nos. 1428/31.
B289 10pf.+5pf. Type **435** . . . 20 20
B290 20pf.+10pf. Frog dining with Princess 20 20
B291 30pf.+15pf. Frog Prince and Princess 35 25
B292 50pf.+25pf. In coach . . . 55 85
Designs from Grimm's "The Frog Prince".

1967. Child Welfare. As Nos. 1434/7.
B293 10pf.+5pf. Common rabbit 20 30
B294 20pf.+10pf. Stoat 20 30
B295 30pf.+15pf. Common hamster 35 30
B296 50pf.+25pf. Red fox . . . . 1·10 1·50

B 69 "Bust of a Young Man" (after C. Meit) — B 70 Broadcasting Tower and T.V. Screen

1967. Berlin Art Treasures.
B297 B 69 10pf. sepia and bistre 20 15
B298 – 20pf. olive and blue . . 20 15
B299 – 30pf. brown and olive 30 25
B300 – 50pf. sepia and grey . . 35 40
B301 – 1Dm. black and blue 85 85
B302 – 1Dm.10 brn & chest . . 1·20 1·50
DESIGNS: 20pf. Head of "The Elector of Brandenburg" (statue by Schluter); 30pf. "St. Mark" (statue by Riemenschneider); 50pf. Head from Quadriga, Brandenburg Gate. 1Dm. "Madonna" (carving by Feuchtmayer). (22½×39 mm) 1Dm.10, "Christ and St. John" (after carving from Upper Swabia, c. 1320).

1967. West Berlin Broadcasting Exn.
B303 B 70 30pf. multicoloured . . 30 30

1967. Humanitarian Relief Funds. As Nos. 1443/6.
B304 10pf.+5pf. multicoloured . . 20 30
B305 20pf.+10pf. multicoloured 20 30
B306 30pf.+15pf. multicoloured 30 45
B307 50pf.+25pf. multicoloured 65 85

1967. Re-election of President Lubke. As Type B **67**.
B308 B 67 30pf. red 20 20
B309 50pf. blue 45 35

1968. Child Welfare. As Nos. 1454/7.
B310 10pf.+5pf. Wild cat 30 45
B311 20pf.+10pf. European otter 45 45
B312 30pf.+15pf. Eurasian badger 70 85
B313 50pf.+25pf. Eurasian beaver 2·10 2·20

B 71 Former Court-house — B 72 Festival Emblems

1968. 500th Anniv of Berlin Magistrates' Court.
B314 B 71 30pf. black 30 25

1968. Athletics Festival, Berlin.
B315 B 72 20f. red, black and grey 30 20

1968. Humanitarian Relief Funds. As Nos. 1473/6.
B316 10pf.+5pf. Doll of 1878 . . 20 25
B317 20pf.+10pf. Doll of 1850 . . 20 20
B318 30pf.+15pf. Doll of 1870 . . 20 25
B319 50pf.+25pf. Doll of 1885 . . 70 85

B 74 "The Newspaper Seller" (C. W. Allers, 1889) — B 75 Orang-Utan Family

1969. 19th-cent Berliners. Contemporary Art.
B320 – 5pf. black 20 15
B321 B 74 10pf. purple 20 15
B322 – 10pf. brown 20 15
B323 – 20pf. green 25 25
B324 – 20pf. turquoise 25 25
B325 – 30pf. brown 80 50
B326 – 30pf. brown 80 50
B327 – 50pf. blue . . . . . . 2·10 1·80
DESIGNS—HORIZ: 5pf. "The Cab-driver" (H. Zille, 1875). VERT: 10pf. "The Bus-driver" (C. W. Allers, 1890); 20pf. (No. B323) "The Cobblers Boy" (F. Kruger, 1839); 20pf. (No. B324) "The Cobbler" (A. von Menzel, 1833); 30pf. (No. B325) "The Borsig Forge" (P. Meyerheim, 1878); 30pf. (No. B326) "Three Berlin Ladies" (F. Kurger, 1839); 50pf. "At the Brandenburg Gate" (C. W. Allers, 1889).

1969. Child Welfare. As Nos. 1478/81.
B328 10pf.+5pf. brn, blk & yell 20 20
B329 20pf.+10pf. brown, black and buff 20 30
B330 30pf.+15pf. brn, blk & red 35 50
B331 50pf.+25pf. grey, yellow, black and blue . . . . . 1·30 1·30

1969. 125th Anniv of Berlin Zoo. Sheet 99×74 mm containing Type B **75** and similar horiz designs.
MSB332 10pf. black and brown; 20pf. black and green; 30pf. black and purple; 50pf. black and blue (sold for 1Dm.30) . . . . . . 2·00 2·00
DESIGNS: 20pf. Dalmatian pelican family; 30pf. Gaur and calf; 50pf. Common zebra and foal.

B 76 Postman — B 77 J. Joachim (violinist and director, after A. von Menzel)

1969. 20th Congress of Post Office Trade Union Federation (I.P.T.T.), Berlin.
B333 B 76 10pf. olive 20 25
B334 – 20pf. brown and buff 30 25
B335 – 30pf. violet and ochre 55 55
B336 – 50pf. blue and light blue . . . . 1·20 1·00
DESIGNS: 20pf. Telephonist; 30pf. Technician; 50pf. Airmail handlers.

1969. Anniversaries. Multicoloured.
B337 30pf. Type B **77** 55 45
B338 50pf. Alexander von Humboldt (after J. Stieler) . . . . 90 1·30
ANNIVERSARIES: 30pf. Centenary of Berlin Academy of Music; 50pf. Birth bicentenary of Humboldt.

B 78 Railway Carriage (1835) — B 79 T. Fontane

1969. Humanitarian Relief Funds. Pewter Models. Multicoloured. (a) Inscr "WOHLFAHRTSMARKE".
B339 10pf.+5pf. Type B **78** . . . 20 20
B340 20pf.+10pf. Woman feeding chicken (1850) 20 20
B341 30pf.+15pf. Market stall (1850) 35 40
B342 50pf.+25pf. Mounted postilion (1860) . . . . . 1·30 1·10

(b) Christmas. Inscr "WEIHNACHTSMARKE".
B343 10pf.+5pf. "The Three Kings" 35 30

1970. 150th Birth Anniv of Theodor Fontane (writer).
B344 B **79** 20pf. multicoloured . . 35 30

B **80** Heinrich von Stretlingen

B **81** Film "Title"

1970. Miniatures of Minnesingers. Mult.
B345 10pf.+5pf. Type B **80** . . . 20 20
B346 20pf.+10pf. Meinloh von Sevelingen 45 45
B347 30pf.+15pf. Burkhart von Hohenfels 65 60
B348 50pf.+25pf. Albrecht von Johannsdorf . . . . . . 1·50 1·50

1970. 20th International Film Festival, Berlin.
B349 B **81** 30pf. multicoloured . . 45 45

1970. Pres. Heinemann. As Nos. 1535/55.
B350 **486** 5pf. black 25 15
B351 8pf. brown 90 95
B352 10pf. brown 25 15
B353 15pf. bistre 30 25
B354 20pf. green 25 15
B355 25pf. green . . . . . . 1·20 60
B356 30pf. brown . . . . . . 1·40 45
B357 40pf. orange 70 30
B358 50pf. blue 35 20
B359 60pf. blue 90 70
B360 70pf. brown . . . . . . 1·00 70
B361 80pf. green . . . . . . 1·20 1·00
B362 90pf. red . . . . 2·30 2·50
B363 1Dm. green . . . . . . 1·20 80
B364 110pf. grey . . . . . . 1·40 1·30
B365 120pf. brown . . . . . 1·40 1·10
B366 130pf. brown . . . . . 1·80 1·60
B367 140pf. green . . . . . 2·10 1·90
B368 150pf. red . . . . . . 2·10 1·60
B369 160pf. orange . . . . . 2·75 2·20
B370 170pf. orange . . . . . 2·10 1·80
B371 190pf. purple . . . . . 2·30 1·90
B372 2Dm. violet . . . . . . 2·50 1·60

B **82** Allegory of Folklore

B **83** "Caspar"

1970. 20th Berlin Folklore Week.
B373 B **82** 30pf. multicoloured . . 60 45

1970. Humanitarian Relief Funds. Puppets. Multicoloured. (a) Relief Funds.
B374 10pf.+5pf. Type B **83** . . . 20 20
B375 20pf.+10pf. "Polichinelle" . . 35 30
B376 30pf.+15pf. "Punch" . . . 55 45
B377 50pf.+25pf. "Pulcinella" . . 1·20 1·20

(b) Christmas.
B378 10pf.+5pf. "Angel" 30 25

B **84** L. von Ranke (after painting by J. Schrader)

1970. 175th Birth Anniv of Leopold von Ranke (historian).
B379 B **84** 30pf. multicoloured . . 45 40

1971. Centenary of German Unification.
B380 **492** 30pf. black, red & orange 65 60

B **85** Class ET 165.8 Electric Train, 1933

1971. Berlin Rail Transport. Multicoloured.
B381 5pf. Class T.12 steam train, 1925 . . . . 30 25
B382 10pf. Electric tram, 1890 . . 30 20
B383 20pf. Horse tram, 1880 . . 35 30
B384 30pf. Type B **85** 55 45
B385 50pf. Electric tram, 1950 . . 2·10 1·40
B386 1Dm. Underground train No. 2431, 1971 . . . . . 2·30 2·00

B **86** "Fly"

B **87** "The Bagpiper" (copper engraving, Durer, c. 1514)

1971. Child Welfare. Children's Drawings. Multicoloured.
B387 10pf.+5pf. Type B **86** . . . 35 40
B388 20pf.+10pf. "Fish" 30 25
B389 30pf.+15pf. "Porcupine" . . 45 45
B390 50pf.+25pf. "Cockerel" . . 1·70 1·50

1971. 500th Birth Anniv of Albrecht Durer.
B391 B **87** 10pf. black and brown 45 30

B **88** Communications Tower and Dish Aerials

B **90** H. von Helmholtz (from painting by K. Morell-Kramer)

B **89** Bach and part of 2nd Brandenburg Concerto

1971. West Berlin Broadcasting Exhibition.
B392 B **88** 30pf. indigo, blue & red 85 60

1971. 250th Anniv of Bach's Brandenburg Concertos.
B393 B **89** 30pf. multicoloured . . 75 50

1971. 150th Anniv of Hermann von Helmholtz (scientist).
B394 B **90** 25pf. multicoloured . . 60 30

B **91** "Opel" Racing-car (1921)

B **92** Dancing Men

1971. 50th Anniv of Avus Motor-racing Track. Sheet 100 × 75 mm containing horiz designs as Type B **91**. Multicoloured.
MSB395 10pf. Type B **91**; 25pf. "Auto-Union" (1936); 30pf. "Mercedes-Benz SSKL" (1931); 60pf. "Mercedes" racing with "Auto-Union" (1937) . . . . 1·60 1·50

1971. Accident Prevention. As Nos. 1596/1605.
B396 5pf. orange 30 30
B397 10pf. brown 30 15
B398 20pf. violet 25 20
B399 25pf. green 30 45
B400 30pf. red 45 55
B401 40pf. mauve 45 40
B402 50pf. blue 45 90
B403 60pf. blue . . . . 2·30 1·70
B404 70pf. blue and green . . . 2·30 1·90
B405 100pf. green . . . . . . 1·50 1·40
B406 150pf. brown . . . . . . 5·50 8·00

1971. Humanitarian Relief Funds. Wooden Toys. Mult. (a) Inscr "WOHLFAHRTSMARKE".
B407 10pf.+5pf. Type B **92** . . . 20 20
B408 25pf.+10pf. Horseman on wheels 35 40
B409 30pf.+15pf. Acrobat 65 65
B410 60pf.+30pf. Nurse and babies . . . . 1·20 1·20

(b) Christmas. Inscr "WEIHNACHTSMARKE".
B411 10pf.+5pf. Angel with two candles 35 30

B **93** Microscope

B **94** F. Gilly (after bust by Schadow)

1971. Birth Centenary of Material-testing Laboratory, Berlin.
B412 B **93** 30pf. multicoloured . . 45 40

1972. Birth Bicentenary of Friedrich Gilly (architect).
B413 B **94** 30pf. black and blue 60 40

B **95** Boy raiding Bird's-nest

B **97** E. T. A. Hoffman

B **96** "Grunewaldsee" (A. von Riesen)

1972. Child Welfare. Animal Protection. Multicoloured.
B414 10pf.+5pf. Type B **95** . . . 30 25
B415 25pf.+10pf. Care of kittens 35 40
B416 30pf.+15pf. Man beating watch-dog 70 60
B417 60pf.+30pf. Animals crossing road at night . . 1·60 1·40

1972. Paintings of Berlin Lakes. Multicoloured.
B418 10pf. Type B **96** 30 25
B419 25pf. "Wannsee" (Max Liebermann) 60 55
B420 30pf. "Schlachtensee" (W. Leistikow) . . . . . 1·20 75

1972. 150th Death Anniv of E. T. A. Hoffman (poet and musician).
B421 B **97** 60pf. black and violet 1·20 95

B **98** Max Liebermann (self-portrait)

B **99** Stamp Printing-press

1972. 125th Birth Anniv of Max Liebermann (painter).
B422 B **98** 40pf. multicoloured . . 75 45

1972. Stamp Day.
B423 B **99** 20pf. blue, black & red 45 30

1972. Humanitarian Relief Funds. Multicoloured. (a) 19th-century Faience Chessmen. As Nos. 1636/40 of West Germany. Inscr "WOLHFAHRTSMARKE".
B424 20pf.+10pf. Knight 35 40
B425 30pf.+15pf. Rook 65 60
B426 40pf.+20pf. Queen . . . . 1·50 1·40
B427 70pf.+35pf. King . . . . . 2·10 1·90

(b) Christmas. Inscr "WEIHNACHTSMARKE".
B428 20pf.+10pf. "The Holy Family" 65 50

B **100** Prince von Hardenberg (after Tischbein)

B **101** Northern Goshawk

1972. 150th Death Anniv of Karl August von Hardenberg (statesman).
B429 B **100** 40pf. multicoloured 75 45

1973. Youth Welfare. Birds of Prey. Mult.
B430 20pf.+10pf. Type B **101** . . 70 60
B431 30pf.+15pf. Peregrine falcon 90 80
B432 40pf.+20pf. Northern sparrow hawk . . . . . 1·20 1·00
B433 70pf.+35pf. Golden eagle 2·10 1·80

B **102** Horse-bus, 1907

1973. Berlin Buses. Multicoloured.
B434 20pf. Type B **102** 35 30
B435 20pf. Trolley bus, 1933 . . 35 30
B436 30pf. Motor bus, 1919 . . . 85 45
B437 30pf. Double-decker, 1970 1·20 45
B438 40pf. Double-decker, 1925 1·70 90
B439 40pf. "Standard" bus, 1973 1·70 90

B **103** L. Tieck

B **104** J. J. Quantz

1973. Birth Bicentenary of Ludwig Tieck (poet and writer).
B440 B **103** 40pf. multicoloured 75 45

1973. Death Bicentenary of Johann Quantz (composer).
B441 B **104** 40pf. black 90 60

B **105** Radio Set, 1926

1973. "50 Years of German Broadcasting". Sheet 148 × 105 mm containing horiz designs as Type B **105**.
MSB442 20pf. black and yellow; 30pf. black and green; 40pf. black and red; 70pf. black and blue (sold at 1.80Dm) . . . . 4·00 4·00
DESIGNS: 30pf. Hans Bredow and microphone of 1924; 40pf. Girl with TV and video tape-recorder; 70pf. TV camera

B **106** 17th-century Hurdy-Gurdy

B **107** G. W. Knobelsdorff

1973. Humanitarian Relief Funds. Mult. (a) Musical Instruments. Inscr "WOHLFAHRTSMARKE".
B443 20pf.+10pf. Type B **106** . . 35 40
B444 30pf.+15pf. 16th century drum 85 75
B445 40pf.+20pf. 18th century lute . . . . 1·00 90
B446 70pf.+35pf. 16th century organ . . . . 1·70 1·40

(b) Christmas. Inscr "WEIHNACHTSMARKE".
B447 20pf.+10pf. Christmas star 65 60

1974. 275th Birth Anniv of Georg W. von Knobelsdorff (architect).
B448 B **107** 20pf. brown 35 30

B **108** G. R. Kirchoff

B **109** A. Slaby

1974. 150th Birth Anniv of Gustav R. Kirchhoff (physicist).
B449 B **108** 30pf. green and grey 35 40

1974. 125th Birth Anniv of Adolf Slaby (radio pioneer).
B450 B **109** 40pf. black and red 65 45

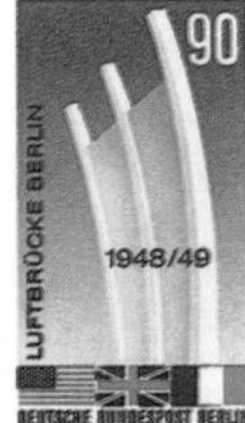

B **110** Airlift Memorial — B **111** Photography

1974. 25th Anniv of Berlin Airlift.

B451	B **110** 90pf. multicoloured	1·90	1·60

1974. Youth Welfare. Youth Activities. Multicoloured.

B452	20pf.+10pf. Type B **111**	35	40
B453	30pf.+15pf. Athletics	55	45
B454	40pf.+20pf. Music	1·00	95
B455	70pf.+35pf. Voluntary service (Nurse)	1·50	1·30

B **112** School Seal — B **113** Spring Bouquet

1974. 400th Anniv of Evangelical Grammar School, Berlin.

B456	B **112** 50pf. grey, brn & gold	90	50

1974. Humanitarian Relief Funds. Flowers. Multicoloured. (a) 25th Anniv of Humanitarian Relief Stamps. Inscr "25 JAHRE WOHLFAHRTSMARKE".

B457	30pf.+15pf. Type B **113**	35	40
B458	40pf.+20pf. Autumn bouquet	65	65
B459	50pf.+25pf. Bouquet of roses	90	80
B460	70pf.+35pf. Winter bouquet	1·70	1·40

(b) Christmas. Inscr "WEIHNACHTSMARKE."

B461	30pf.+15pf. Christmas bouquet	85	80

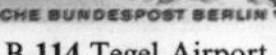

B **114** Tegel Airport — B **115** "Venus" (F. E. Meyer)

1974. Opening of Tegel Airport. Berlin.

B462	B **114** 50pf. violet, bl & grn	1·10	70

1974. Berlin Porcelain Figures. Mult.

B463	30pf. Type B **115**	65	40
B464	40pf. "Astronomy" (W. C. Meyer)	75	60
B465	50pf. "Justice" (J. G. Muller)	85	75

B **116** Gottfried Schadow

1975. 125th Death Anniv of Gottfried Schadow (sculptor).

B466	B **116** 50pf. brown	90	60

B **117** "Prinzess Charlotte"

1975. Berlin Pleasure Boats. Multicoloured.

B467	30pf. Type B **117**	85	45
B468	40pf. "Siegfried"	85	45
B469	50pf. "Sperber"	1·50	80
B470	60pf. "Vaterland"	1·50	80
B471	70pf. "Moby Dick"	1·80	1·60

B **118** Steam Locomotive "Drache", 1848

1975. Youth Welfare. Railway Locomotives. Multicoloured.

B472	30pf.+15pf. Type B **118**	90	75
B473	40pf.+20pf. Class 89 tank locomotive	90	90
B474	50pf.+25pf. Class 050 steam locomotive	1·80	1·30
B475	70pf.+35pf. Class 010 steam locomotive	2·75	2·40

B **119** Ferdinand Sauerbruch (surgeon) — B **120** Gymnastics Emblem

1975. Birth Cent of Ferdinand Sauerbruch.

B476	B **119** 50pf. dp brn, brn & pk	85	60

1975. Gymnaestrada (Gymnastic Games), Berlin.

B477	B **120** 40pf. black, gold and green	65	45

1975. Industry and Technology. As Nos. 1742/55.

B478	–	5pf. green	20	15
B479	–	10pf. purple	20	15
B480	–	20pf. red	30	15
B481	–	30pf. violet	35	20
B482	**572**	40pf. green	75	25
B483	–	50pf. red	75	20
B483a	–	60pf. red	1·20	35
B484	–	70pf. blue	1·20	50
B485	–	80pf. green	1·20	30
B486	–	100pf. brown	1·20	50
B486a	–	110pf. purple	1·60	1·20
B487	–	120pf. blue	1·60	1·00
B487a	–	130pf. red	2·30	1·50
B488	–	140pf. red	1·60	1·50
B488a	–	150pf. red	3·50	1·50
B489	–	160pf. green	3·25	1·50
B489a	–	180pf. brown	3·50	2·20
B489b	–	190pf. brown	3·50	2·40
B490	–	200pf. purple	2·10	55
B490a	–	230pf. purple	2·75	2·20
B490b	–	250pf. green	4·50	2·40
B490c	–	300pf. green	4·50	2·40
B491	–	500pf. black	7·00	4·25

B **121** "Lovis Corinth" (self-portrait) — B **122** Buildings in Naunynstrasse, Berlin-Kreuzberg

1975. 50th Death Anniv of Lovis Corinth (painter).

B492	B **121** 50pf. multicoloured	90	60

1975. European Architectural Heritage Year.

B493	B **122** 50pf. multicoloured	1·00	60

B **123** Yellow Gentian

1975. Humanitarian Relief Funds. Alpine Flowers. Multicoloured.

B494	30pf.+15pf. Type B **123**	65	50
B495	40pf.+20pf. Arnica	65	60
B496	50pf.+25pf. Cyclamen	85	75
B497	70pf.+35pf. Blue gentian	1·30	1·20

1975. Christmas. As Type B **123**, inscr "WEIHNACHTSMARKE". Mult.

B498	30pf.+15pf. Snow heather	85	75

See also Nos. B508/11, B540/3 and B557/60.

B **124** Paul Lobe

1975. Birth Cent of Paul Lobe (politician).

B499	B **124** 50pf. red	85	60

B **125** Ears of Wheat, with inscription "Grune Woche" — B **126** Putting the Shot

1976. "International Agriculture Week", Berlin.

B500	B **125** 70pf. yellow and green	1·00	70

1976. Youth Welfare. Training for the Olympics. Multicoloured.

B501	30pf.+15pf. Type B **126**	70	60
B502	40pf.+20pf. Hockey	70	60
B503	50pf.+25pf. Handball	90	80
B504	70pf.+35pf. Swimming	1·80	1·60

B **127** Hockey

1976. Women's World Hockey Championships.

B505	B **127** 30pf. green	75	45

B **128** Treble Clef

1976. German Choristers' Festival.

B506	B **128** 40pf. multicoloured	85	60

B **129** Fire Service Emblem — B **130** Julius Tower, Spandau

1976. 125th Anniv of Berlin Fire Service.

B507	B **129** 50pf. multicoloured	1·30	85

1976. Humanitarian Relief Funds. Garden Flowers. As Type B **123**. Multicoloured.

B508	30pf.+15pf. Iris	35	40
B509	40pf.+20pf. Wallflower	45	45
B510	50pf.+25pf. Dahlia	85	75
B511	70pf.+35pf. Larkspur	1·30	1·20

1976. Berlin Views (1st series).

B512	–	30pf. black and blue	60	45
B513	B **130**	40pf. black and brown	90	45
B514	–	50pf. black and green	1·00	60

DESIGNS: 30pf. Yacht on the Havel; 50pf. Lake and Victory Column, Tiergarten park.

See also Nos. B562/4, B605/7 and B647/9.

B **131** "Annunciation to the Shepherds" (window, Frauenkirche, Esslingen)

1976. Christmas. Sheet 71 × 101 mm.

MSB515	B **131** 30pf.+15pf. multicoloured	85	70

1977. Coil Stamps. German Castles. As Nos. 1805/12d.

B516	10pf. blue	20	15
B517	20pf. orange	20	15
B517a	25pf. red	45	40
B518	30pf. brown	30	20
B518c	35pf. red	45	40
B519	40pf. green	35	20
B519a	40pf. brown	65	35
B520	50pf. red	60	20
B520b	50pf. green	65	35
B521	60pf. brown	1·00	55
B521a	60pf. red	90	50
B522	70pf. blue	1·20	60
B522a	80pf. green	90	30
B522b	90pf. blue	1·20	80
B522c	120pf. violet	1·40	1·00
B523	190pf. red	1·60	1·50
B524	200pf. green	1·60	1·50
B524a	210pf. brown	2·50	1·60
B524b	230pf. green	2·50	1·60
B524c	280pf. blue	4·50	2·50
B524d	300pf. orange	4·50	2·20

B **132** "Eugenie d'Alton" (Cristian Rauch) — B **133** "Eduard Gaertner" (self-portrait)

1977. Birth Bicentenary of Christian Daniel Rauch (sculptor).

B525	B **132** 50pf. black	85	60

1977. Death Cent of Eduard Gaertner (artist).

B526	B **133** 40pf. black, green and deep green	65	45

B **134** Bremen Kogge, 1380 — B **135** Female Figure

1977. Youth Welfare. Ships. Multicoloured.

B527	30pf.+15pf. Type B **134**	50	50
B528	40pf.+20pf. "Helena Sloman" (steamship), 1850	60	60
B529	50pf.+25pf. "Cap Polonio" (liner), 1914	1·00	1·00
B530	70pf.+35pf. "Widar" (bulk carrier), 1971	1·40	1·30

1977. Birth Cent of Georg Kolbe (sculptor).

B531	B **135** 30pf. green and black	65	45

B **136** Crosses and Text — B **137** Telephones of 1905 and 1977

1977. 17th Evangelical Churches Day.

B532	B **136** 40pf. yellow, blk & grn	65	45

1977. International Telecommunications Exhibition and Centenary of German Telephone Service.

B533	B **137** 50pf. buff, black & red	2·10	1·10

B **138** Imperial German Patent Office, Berlin-Kreuzberg

1977. Centenary of German Patent Office.

B534	B **138** 60pf. black, red & grey	1·60	70

B 139 Untitled Painting (G. Grosz)

B 141 "Madonna and Child" (stained glass window, Basilica of St. Gereon, Cologne)

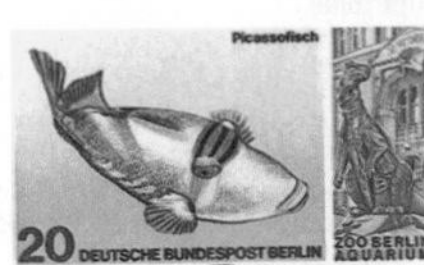

B 140 Picasso Triggerfish

1977. 15th European Art Exhibition.
B535 **B 139** 70pf. multicoloured . . . 1·40 80

1977. 25th Anniv of Reopening of Berlin Aquarium. Multicoloured.
B536 20pf. Type **B 140** 65 45
B537 30pf. Paddlefish 75 65
B538 40pf. Radiated tortoise . . 1·20 80
B539 50pf. Rhinoceros iguana . . 1·70 1·10

1977. Humanitarian Relief Funds. Meadow Flowers. As Type **B 123**. Multicoloured.
B540 30pf.+15pf. Daisy 35 40
B541 40pf.+20pf. Marsh marigold 65 60
B542 50pf.+25pf. Sainfoin . . . 90 80
B543 70pf.+35pf. Forget-me-not 1·40 1·30

1977. Christmas. Sheet 70 × 105 mm.
MSB544 **B 141** 30pf.+15pf. multicoloured 85 80

B 142 Walter Kollo

1978. Birth Cent of Walter Kollo (composer).
B545 **B 142** 50pf. brown and red 1·20 65

B 143 Emblem of U.S. Chamber of Commerce

1978. 75th Anniv of U.S. Chamber of Commerce in Germany.
B546 **B 143** 90pf. blue and red . . 1·50 1·00

1978. Youth Welfare. Aviation History (1st series). As T **627**. Multicoloured.
B547 30pf.+15pf. Montgolfier balloon, 1783 . . . . 45 45
B548 40pf.+20pf. Lilienthal glider, 1891 . . . . . 75 70
B549 50pf.+25pf. Wright Type A biplane 90 85
B550 70pf.+35pf. Etrich/Rumpler Taube, 1910 . . . . . 1·40 1·30
See also Nos. B567/70 and B589/92.

1978. Sport Promotion Fund. As T **623**. Multicoloured.
B551 50pf.+25pf. Cycling 90 75
B552 70pf.+35pf. Fencing . . . . 1·40 1·20

B 146 Albrecht von Graefe

B 147 Friedrich Ludwig Jahn

1978. 150th Birth Anniv of Albrecht von Graefe (pioneer of medical eye services).
B553 **B 146** 30pf. black and brown 75 40

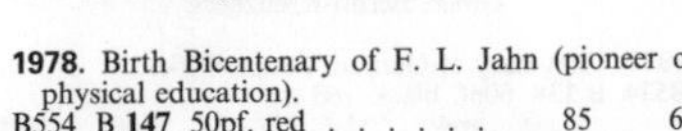
1978. Birth Bicentenary of F. L. Jahn (pioneer of physical education).
B554 **B 147** 50pf. red 85 60

B 148 Swimming

1978. 3rd World Swimming Championships.
B555 **B 148** 40pf. multicoloured 1·20 85

B 149 "The Boat" (Karl Hofer)

1978. Birth Centenary of Karl Hofer (Impressionist painter).
B556 **B 149** 50pf. multicoloured 85 60

1978. Humanitarian Relief Funds. Woodland Flowers. As Type **B 123**. Multicoloured.
B557 30pf.+15pf. Solomon's seal 55 45
B558 40pf.+20pf. Wood primrose 70 60
B559 50pf.+25pf. Red helle-borine 90 80
B560 70pf.+35pf. Bugle . . . . . 1·40 1·30

B 150 Prussian State Library

1978. Opening of New Prussian State Library Building.
B561 **B 150** 90pf. olive and red . . 1·50 1·20

1978. Berlin Views (2nd series). As Type **B 130**.
B562 40pf. black and green . . . 75 45
B563 50pf. black and purple . . 85 65
B564 60pf. black and brown . . 1·20 75
DESIGNS: 40pf. Belvedere; 50pf. Landwehr Canal; 60pf. Village church, Lichtenrade.

B 151 "Madonna" (stained glass window, Frauenkirche, Munich)

1978. Christmas. Sheet 65 × 92 mm.
MSB565 **B 151** 30pf.+15pf. multicoloured 85 75

B 152 Congress Centre

B 154 Old and New Arms

B 153 Relay Runners

1979. Opening of International Congress Centre, Berlin.
B566 **B 152** 60pf. black, blue & red . . . . 1·10 80

1979. Youth Welfare. History of Aviation (2nd series). As T **627**. Multicoloured.
B567 40pf.+20pf. Vampyr glider, 1921 . . . . 55 60
B568 50pf.+25pf. Junkers Ju 52/3m D-2202 "Richthofen", 1932 . . . 80 80
B569 60pf.+30pf. Messerschmitt Bf 108 D-1010, 1934 . . 1·20 1·10
B570 90pf.+45pf. Douglas DC-3 NC-14988, 1935 . . . . 1·80 1·60

1979. Sport Promotion Fund. Multicoloured.
B571 60pf.+30pf. Type **B 153** . . 1·10 95
B572 90pf.+45pf. Archers . . . . 1·40 1·30

1979. Centenary of State Printing Works, Berlin.
B573 **B 154** 60pf. multicoloured 1·60 1·10

B 155 Arrows and Target

1979. World Archery Championships.
B574 **B 155** 50pf. multicoloured 90 60

B 156 Television Screen

B 157 Moses Mendelssohn

1979. International Telecommunications Exhibition, Berlin.
B575 **B 156** 60pf. black, grey & red . . . . 1·20 85

1979. 250th Birth Anniv of Moses Mendelssohn (philosopher).
B576 **B 157** 90pf. black . . . . . 1·30 85

B 158 Venus Slipper Orchid and Great Tropical House

1979. 300th Anniv of Berlin Botanical Gardens.
B577 **B 158** 50pf. multicoloured 85 60

B 159 Gas Lamp, Kreuzberg District

1979. 300th Anniv of Street Lighting.
B578 **B 159** 10pf. green, bl & grey 45 20
B579 – 40pf. green, bis & grey 90 70
B580 – 50pf. green, brn & grey . . . . 1·30 80
B581 – 60pf. green, red & grey . . . . 1·40 1·20
DESIGNS: 40pf. Electric carbon-arc lamp, Hardenbergstrasse; 50pf. Gas Lamps, Wittenbergplatz; 60pf. Five-armed chandelier, Charlottenburg.

1979. Humanitarian Relief Funds. Woodland Flowers and Fruit. As Type **B 123**, but horiz. Multicoloured.
B582 40pf.+20pf. Larch 75 50
B583 50pf.+25pf. Hazelnut . . . 90 70
B584 60pf.+30pf. Horse chestnut 1·30 1·00
B585 90pf.+45pf. Blackthorn . . 1·60 1·60

B 161 Advertisement Pillar

B 162 "Nativity" (Altenberg medieval manuscript)

1979. 125th Anniv of Advertisement Pillars.
B586 **B 161** 50pf. red and lilac . . 1·60 85

1979. Christmas.
B587 **B 162** 40pf.+20pf. mult . . . 1·00 90

B 163 Map showing Wegener's Theory of Continental Drift

1980. Birth Centenary of Alfred Wegener (explorer and geophysicist).
B588 **B 163** 60pf. black, orange and blue . . . . . 1·30 1·10

1980. Youth Welfare. Aviation History (3rd series). As T **627**. Multicoloured.
B589 40pf.+20pf. Vickers Viscount 810 . . . . . . 85 75
B590 50pf.+25pf. Fokker Friendship "Condor" . . 90 85
B591 60pf.+30pf. Sud Aviation Caravelle F-BKSZ, 1955 1·20 1·00
B592 90pf.+45pf. Sikorsky S-55 helicopter OO-SHB, 1949 1·70 1·50
Nos. B589/90 are incorrectly dated.

B 164 Throwing the Javelin

1980. Sport Promotion Fund. Multicoloured.
B593 50pf.+25pf. Type **B 164** . . 75 75
B594 60pf.+30pf. Weightlifting . . 90 85
B595 90pf.+45pf. Water polo . . 1·40 1·20

B 165 Cardinal Preysing

B 166 "Operatio" (enamel medallion)

1980. 86th German Catholics Congress.
B596 **B 165** 50pf. red and black 85 65

1980. 150th Anniv of Prussian Museums. Multicoloured.
B597 40pf. Type **B 166** 90 45
B598 60pf. "Monks Reading" (oak sculpture, Ernst Barlach) . . . . 1·20 75

B 167 Robert Stolz

B 168 Von Steuben

1980. Birth Centenary of Robert Stolz (composer).
B599 **B 167** 60pf. multicoloured 1·20 90

1980. 250th Birth Anniv of Friedrich Wilhelm von Steuben (American general).
B600 **B 168** 40pf. multicoloured 1·10 60

B 169 Orlaya grandiflora

1980. Humanitarian Relief Funds. Endangered Wild Flowers. Multicoloured.
B601 40pf.+20pf. Type **B 169** . . 85 75
B602 50pf.+25pf. Yellow gagae 1·00 90
B603 60pf.+30pf. Summer pheasant's-eye . . . . . 1·00 90
B604 90p.+45pf. Venus's looking-glass . . . . 1·80 1·70
See also Nos. B622/5

1980. Berlin Views (3rd series). As Type **B 130**.
B605 40pf. black and green . . . 90 45
B606 50pf. black and brown . . 1·10 70
B607 60pf. black and blue . . . 1·60 95
DESIGNS: 40pf. Lilienthal Monument; 50pf. "Grosse Neugierde"; 60pf. Grunewald Tower.

B 170 "Message to the Shepherds" (Altomunster manuscript)

B 171 Von Arnim (after Strohling)

1980. Christmas.
B608 B **170** 40pf.+20pf. mult . . . 1·00 90

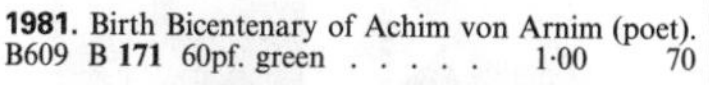

1981. Birth Bicentenary of Achim von Arnim (poet).
B609 B **171** 60pf. green . . . . . 1·00 70

B 172 Von Chamisso (bronze medallion, David d'Angers)

1981. Birth Bicentenary of Adelbert von Chamisso (poet and naturalist).
B610 B **172** 60pf. brown, deep brown and ochre 1·00 75

B 173 Von Gontard

1981. 250th Birth Anniv of Karl Phillipp von Gontard (architect).
B611 B **173** 50pf. red, black & grey . . . . 1·00 75

B 174 Kreuzberg War Memorial

B 175 Theodolite, c. 1810

1981. Birth Bicentenary of Karl Friedrich Schinkel (architect).
B612 B **174** 40pf. green and brown 1·20 70

1981. Youth Welfare. Optical Instruments. Multicoloured.
B613 40pf.+20pf. Type B **175** . . 55 60
B614 50pf.+25pf. Equatorial telescope, 1820 . . . . . 85 80
B615 60pf.+30pf. Microscope, 1790 . . . . 1·10 1·00
B616 90pf.+45pf. Sextant, 1830 1·80 1·70

B 176 Group Gymnastics

1981. Sport Promotion Fund. Multicoloured.
B617 60pf.+30pf. Type B **176** . . 1·20 80
B618 90pf.+45pf. Cross-country race . . . . 1·80 1·30

B 177 "Cupid and Psyche"

B 178 Badge of Order "Pour le Merite"

1981. 150th Birth Anniv of Reinhold Begas (sculptor).
B619 B **177** 50pf. black and blue 85 60

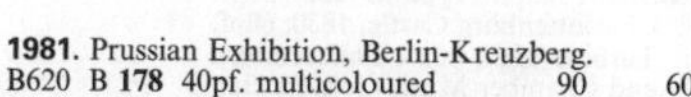

1981. Prussian Exhibition, Berlin-Kreuzberg.
B620 B **178** 40pf. multicoloured 90 60

B 179 Broadcasting House, Charlottenburg

B 180 "Three Kings" (glass painting)

1981. International Telecommunications Exhibition, Berlin.
B621 B **179** 60pf. multicoloured 1·30 90

1981. Humanitarian Relief Funds. Endangered Wild Flowers. As Type B **169**. Multicoloured.
B622 40pf.+20pf. Common bistort 90 70
B623 50pf.+25pf. Moor-king . . 1·00 85
B624 60pf.+30pf. "Gladiolus palustris" . . . . 1·20 90
B625 90pf.+45pf. Siberian iris . . 2·00 1·70

1981. Christmas.
B626 B **180** 40pf.+20pf. mult . . . 90 70

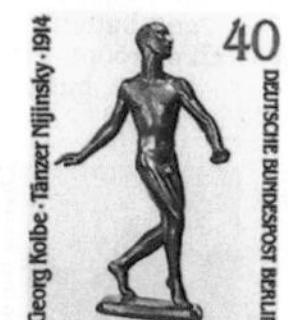

B 181 Peter Beuth

B 182 "Dancer Nijinsky" (Georg Kolbe)

1981. Birth Bicentenary of Peter Beuth (constitutional lawyer).
B627 B **181** 60pf. black and brown 90 80

1981. 20th Century Sculptures. Mult.
B628 40pf. Type B **182** 55 45
B629 60pf. "Mother Earth II" (Ernst Barlach) 90 60
B630 90pf. "Flora Kneeling" (Richard Scheibe) . . . . 1·50 1·20

B 183 Arms and View of Spandau, c. 1700

1982. 750th Anniv of Spandau.
B631 B **183** 60pf. multicoloured 1·40 1·10

B 184 Daimler Steel-wheeled Car, 1889

1982. Youth Welfare Fund. Motor Cars. Multicoloured.
B632 40pf.+20pf. Type B **184** . . 90 85
B633 50pf.+25pf. Wanderer "Puppchen", 1911 . . . 90 85
B634 60pf.+30p. Adler limousine, 1913 . . . . 1·20 1·00
B635 90pf.+45pf. DKW "F 1", 1913 . . . . 1·80 1·70

B 185 Sprinting

1982. Sport Promotion Fund. Multicoloured.
B636 60pf.+30pf. Type B **185** . . 1·20 85
B637 90pf.+45pf. Volleyball . . . 1·70 1·20

B 186 Harp

B 187 "Emigrants reaching Prussian Frontier" (woodcut after drawing by Adolph von Menzel)

1982. Centenary of Berlin Philharmonic Orchestra.
B638 B **186** 60pf. grey, red & green . . . . 1·10 80

1982. 250th Anniv of Salzburg Emigrants' Arrival in Prussia.
B639 B **187** 50pf. stone, deep brown and brown 1·00 65

B 188 "Italian Stone Carriers" (Max Pechstein)

1982. Paintings. Multicoloured.
B640 50pf. Type B **188** . . . . 1·20 75
B641 80pf. "Two Girls Bathing" (Otto Mueller) . . . . . 1·60 1·30

B 189 Floribunda-Grandiflora

B 191 "Adoration of the Kings" (detail from St. Peter altar by Master Bertram)

B 190 Castle Theatre, Charlottenburg

1982. Humanitarian Relief Funds. Roses. Multicoloured.
B642 50pf.+20pf. Type B **189** . . 1·20 80
B643 60pf.+30pf. Hybrid tea . . 1·30 1·10
B644 80pf.+40pf. Floribunda . . 1·70 1·50
B645 120pf.+60pf. Miniature rose 2·75 2·75

1982. 250th Birth Anniv of Carl Gotthard Langhans (architect).
B646 B **190** 80pf. red, grey and black . . . . 1·80 1·30

1982. Berlin Views (4th series). As Type B **130**.
B647 50pf. black and blue . . . 1·20 65
B648 60pf. black and red . . . . 1·40 80
B649 80pf. black and brown . . 1·70 95
DESIGNS: 50pf. Villa Borsig; 60pf. Sts. Peter and Paul Church; 80pf. Villa von der Heydt.

1982. Christmas.
B650 B **191** 50pf.+20pf. mult . . . 1·20 85

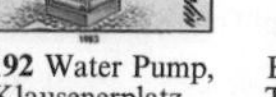

B 192 Water Pump, Klausenerplatz

B 193 Royal Prussian Telegraphy Inspectors at St. Anne's Church

1983. Street Water Pumps. Multicoloured.
B651 50pf. Type B **192** . . . . 1·20 65
B652 60pf. Chamissoplatz . . . . 1·60 80
B653 80pf. Schloss-strasse . . . . 1·80 1·30
B654 120pf. Kuerfurstendamm . . 2·50 2·10

1983. 150th Anniv of Berlin–Coblenz Optical-Mechanical Telegraph.
B655 B **193** 80pf. brown . . . . . 2·20 1·50

B 194 Hildebrand & Wolfmuller, 1894

1983. Youth Welfare. Motor Cycles. Mult.
B656 50pf.+20pf. Type B **194** . . 90 65
B657 60pf.+30pf. Wanderer, 1908 1·40 90
B658 80pf.+40pf. D.K.W.-Lomos, 1922 . . . . 1·60 1·20
B659 120pf.+60pf. Mars, 1925 . . 3·50 2·20

B 195 Latin-American Dancing

1983. Sport Promotion Fund. Multicoloured.
B660 80pf.+40pf. Type B **195** . . 1·70 1·20
B661 120pf.+60pf. Ice hockey . . 2·75 2·00

B 196 "La Barbarina" (painting of Barbara Campanini)

B 197 Ringelnatz (silhouette by E. M. Engert)

1983. 300th Birth Anniv of Antoine Pesne (artist).
B662 B **196** 50pf. multicoloured 1·20 65

1983. Birth Centenary of Joachim Ringelnatz (poet and painter).
B663 B **197** 50pf. green, brn & red 1·10 80

B 198 Paul Nipkow's Picture Transmission System, 1884

1983. International Broadcasting Exn, Berlin.
B664 B **198** 80pf. multicoloured 1·80 1·20

B 199 Mountain Windflower

B 200 Nigerian Yoruba Crib

1983. Humanitarian Relief Funds. Endangered Alpine Flowers. Multicoloured.
B665 50pf.+20pf. Type B **199** . . 70 65
B666 60pf.+30pf. Alpine auricula 1·20 1·10
B667 80pf.+40pf. Little primrose 2·10 1·80
B668 120pf.+60pf. Einsele's aquilegia . . . . 2·75 2·75

1983. Christmas.
B669 B **200** 50pf.+20pf. mult . . . 1·00 90

B 201 Queen Cleopatra VII (Antikenmuseum)

B 202 "Trichius Fasciatus"

1984. Art Objects in Berlin Museums. Multicoloured.
B670 30pf. Type B **201** . . . . 1·10 80
B671 50pf. Statue of seated couple from Giza Necropolis (Egyptian Museum) . . . . 1·60 1·20
B672 60pf. Goddess with pearl turban (Ethnology Museum) . . . . 1·90 1·50
B673 80pf. Majolica dish (Applied Arts Museum) 2·30 2·00

1984. Youth Welfare. Pollinating Insects. Multicoloured.
B674 50pf.+20pf. Type B **202** . . 1·30 95
B675 60pf.+30pf. "Agrumenia carniolica" . . . . 1·30 95
B676 80pf.+40pf. "Bombus terrestris" . . . . 1·80 1·30
B677 120pf.+60pf. "Eristalis tenax" . . . . 2·75 2·40

B 203 Hurdling

1984. Sport Promotion Fund. Multicoloured.
B678 60pf.+30pf. Type B **203** . . 1·40 1·10
B679 80pf.+40pf. Cycling . . . . 2·30 1·30
B680 120pf.+60pf. Four-seater kayaks . . . . 3·75 2·75

B **204** Klausener B **205** "Electric Power" (K. Sutterlin)

1984. 50th Death Anniv of Dr. Erich Klausener (chairman of Catholic Action).
B681 B **204** 80pf. green & dp green . . . . 1·20 85

1984. Centenary of Berlin Electricity Supply.
B682 B **205** 50pf. yell, orge & blk 90 75

B **206** Conference Emblem

1984. 4th European Ministers of Culture Conference, Berlin.
B683 B **206** 60pf. multicoloured 1·10 70

B **207** Brehm and White Stork

1984. Death Centenary of Alfred Brehm (zoologist).
B684 B **207** 80pf. multicoloured 1·90 1·30

B **208** Heim (bust, Freidrich Tieck) B **209** "Listera cordata"

1984. 150th Death Anniv of Ernst Ludwig Heim (medical pioneer).
B685 B **208** 50pf. black and red 1·10 85

1984. Humanitarian Relief Funds. Orchids. Multicoloured.
B686 50pf.+20pf. Type B **209** . . 1·80 1·30
B687 60pf.+30pf. "Ophrys insectifera" . . . . 2·10 1·30
B688 80pf.+40pf. "Epipactis palustris" . . . . 2·75 2·40
B689 120pf.+60pf. "Ophrys coriophora" . . . . . . 4·50 4·25

B **210** "Sunflowers on Grey Background" B **211** St. Nicholas

1984. Birth Centenary of Karl Schmidt-Rottluff (artist).
B690 B **210** 60pf. multicoloured 1·10 85

1984. Christmas.
B691 B **211** 50pf.+20pf. mult . . . 1·20 1·10

B **212** Bettina von Arnim B **213** Humboldt (statue, Paul Otto)

1985. Birth Bicentenary of Bettina von Arnim (writer).
B692 B **212** 50pf. black, brn & red 1·00 90

1985. 50th Death Anniv of Wilhelm von Humboldt (philologist).
B693 B **213** 80pf. black, blue & red . . . . 1·60 1·30

B **214** Ball in Net

1985. Sport Promotion Fund. Multicoloured.
B694 80pf.+40pf. Type B **214** (50th anniv of basketball in Germany and European championships, Stuttgart) . . . . 1·60 1·50
B695 120pf.+60pf. Table tennis (60th anniv of German Table Tennis Association) 2·75 2·40

B **215** Stylized Flower

1985. Federal Horticultural Show, Berlin.
B696 B **215** 80pf. multicoloured 1·50 1·20

B **216** Bussing Bicycle, 1868

1985. Youth Welfare. International Youth Year. Bicycles. Multicoloured.
B697 50pf.+20pf. Type B **216** . . 1·40 1·30
B698 60pf.+30pf. Child's tricycle, 1885 . . . . 1·40 1·20
B699 80pf.+40pf. Jaray bicycle, 1925 . . . . 1·80 1·80
B700 120pf.+60pf. Opel racing bicycle, 1925 . . . . . . 4·00 3·50

B **217** Stock Exchange, 1863–1945

1985. 300th Anniv of Berlin Stock Exchange.
B701 B **217** 50pf. multicoloured 1·10 90

B **218** Otto Klemperer

1985. Birth Centenary of Otto Klemperer (orchestral conductor).
B702 B **218** 60pf. blue . . . . . . 1·50 1·20

B **219** Association Emblem

1985. 11th International Gynaecology and Obstetrics Association Congress, Berlin.
B703 B **219** 60pf. multicoloured 1·10 90

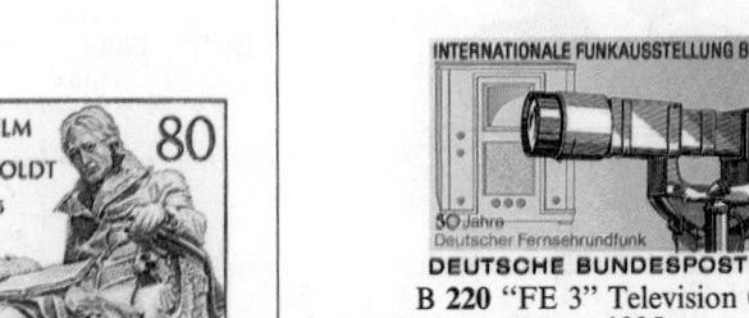

B **220** "FE 3" Television Camera, 1935

1985. International Broadcasting Exn, Berlin.
B704 B **220** 80pf. multicoloured 2·00 1·60

B **221** Seal of Brandenburg-Prussia and Preamble of Edict

1985. 300th Anniv of Edict of Potsdam (admitting Huguenots to Prussia).
B705 B **221** 50pf. lilac and black 1·00 70

B **222** Flowers, Strawberries and Ladybirds

1985. Humanitarian Relief Funds. Motifs from borders of medieval prayer book. Multicoloured.
B706 50pf.+20pf. Type B **222** . . 1·40 1·30
B707 60pf.+30pf. Flowers, bird and butterfly . . . . . . 1·60 1·60
B708 80pf.+40pf. Flowers, bee and butterfly . . . . . . 1·80 1·70
B709 120pf.+60pf. Flowers, berries, butterfly and snail 2·75 2·75

B **223** "Adoration of the Kings" (detail, Epiphany Altar) B **224** Kurt Tucholsky

1985. Christmas. 500th Birth Anniv of Hans Baldung Grien (artist).
B710 B **223** 50pf.+20pf. mult . . . 1·40 1·10

1985. 50th Death Anniv of Kurt Tucholsky (writer and journalist).
B711 B **224** 80pf. multicoloured 1·80 1·20

B **225** Furtwangler and Score

1986. Birth Centenary of Wilhelm Furtwangler (composer and conductor).
B712 B **225** 80pf. multicoloured 1·90 1·60

B **226** Rohe and National Gallery

1986. Birth Centenary of Ludwig Mies van der Rohe (architect).
B713 B **226** 50pf. multicoloured 1·40 1·10

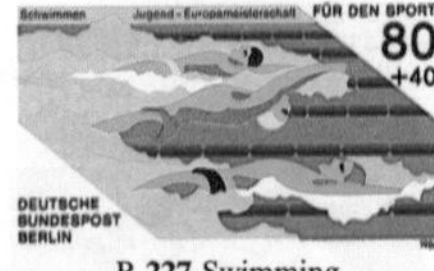

B **227** Swimming

1986. Sport Promotion Fund. Multicoloured.
B714 80pf.+40pf. Type B **227** (European Youth Championships, Berlin) 2·00 1·80
B715 120pf.+55pf. Show-jumping (World Championships, Aachen) . . . . 2·50 2·20

B **228** Glazier

1986. Youth Charity. Trades (1st series). Multicoloured.
B716 50pf.+25pf. Type B **228** . . 1·20 1·20
B717 60pf.+30pf. Locksmith . . . 1·60 1·50
B718 70pf.+35pf. Tailor . . . . 1·80 1·70
B719 80pf.+40pf. Carpenter . . . 2·30 2·10
See also Nos. B765/8.

B **229** Flags

1986. 16th European Communities Day.
B720 B **229** 60pf. multicoloured 1·20 1·00

B **230** Ranke B **231** Benn

1986. Death Centenary of Leopold von Ranke (historian).
B721 B **230** 80pf. brown and grey 2·00 1·30

1986. Birth Centenary of Gottfried Benn (poet).
B722 B **231** 80pf. blue . . . . . . 1·80 1·30

B **232** Charlottenburg Gate B **233** "The Flute Concert" (detail, Adolph von Menzel)

1986. Gateways. Multicoloured.
B723 50pf. Type B **232** . . . . 1·40 1·20
B724 60pf. Griffin Gate, Glienicke Palace . . . . 1·60 1·30
B725 80pf. Elephant Gate, Berlin Zoo . . . . 2·10 1·60

1986. Death Bicentenary of Frederick the Great.
B726 B **233** 80pf. multicoloured 1·80 1·20

B **234** Cantharus, 1st century A.D. B **235** "Adoration of the Three Kings" (Ortenberg altarpiece)

1986. Humanitarian Relief Funds. Glassware. Multicoloured.
B727 50pf.+25pf. Type B **234** . . 1·30 1·20
B728 60pf.+30pf. Beaker, 200 A.D. . . . . 1·60 1·50
B729 70pf.+35pf. Jug, 3rd century A.D. . . . . 1·80 1·60
B730 80pf.+40pf. Diatreta 4th century A.D. . . . . . . 2·50 2·20

1986. Christmas.
B731 B **235** 50pf.+25pf. mult . . . 1·00 90

1986. Famous German Women. As Nos. 2149a/54, 2158, 2161, 2166/9a.
B732 5pf. brown and grey . . . 35 1·90
B733 10pf. brown and violet . . 50 1·60
B734 20pf. blue and red . . . 1·80 3·50
B735 40pf. red and blue . . . . 1·40 3·75
B736 50pf. green and brown . . 1·80 3·00
B737 60pf. lilac and green . . . . 90 3·75
B738 80pf. brown and green . . 1·70 2·40
B739 100pf. grey and red . . . 1·80 1·60
B740 130pf. violet and blue . . . 4·50 11·50
B741 140pf. brown and blue . . 4·50 12·00
B742 170pf. purple and green . . 3·00 9·50
B743 180pf. purple and blue . . . 4·50 12·00
B744 240pf. brown and blue . . 4·00 13·00
B745 250pf. blue and mauve . . 8·25 21·00
B746 300pf. green and plum . . . 8·75 21·00
B747 350pf. brown and black . . 7·00 16·00
B748 500pf. red and green . . . 9·25 33·00

B **236** Berlin, 1650

1987. 750th Anniv of Berlin. (a) As No. 2170.
B760 **833** 80pf. multicoloured . . 1·90 1·60

(b) Sheet 130 × 100 mm containing Type B **236** and similar horiz designs. Multicoloured.
MSB761 40pf. Type B **236**; 50pf. Charlottenburg Castle, 1830; 60pf. Turbine Hall; 80pf. Philharmonic and Chamber Music Concert Hall 4·25 4·00

B 237 Louise Schroeder

B 239 "Bohemian Refugees" (detail of relief, King Friedrich Wilhelm Monument, Berlin-Neukolln)

B 238 German Gymnastics Festival, Berlin

1987. Birth Centenary of Louise Schroeder (Mayor of Berlin).
B762 B **237** 50pf. brown and orange on light brown . . . . . . 1·20 1·10

1987. Sport Promotion Fund. Multicoloured.
B763 80pf.+40pf. Type B **238** . . 1·80 1·70
B764 120pf.+55pf. World Judo Championships, Essen . . 2·75 2·50

1987. Youth Welfare. Trades (2nd series). As Type B **228**. Multicoloured.
B765 50pf.+25pf. Cooper . . . . 1·30 1·30
B766 60pf.+30pf. Stonemason . . 1·40 1·30
B767 70pf.+35pf. Furrier . . . . 1·70 1·70
B768 80pf.+40pf. Painter/lacquerer . . . . 1·80 1·80

1987. 250th Anniv of Bohemian Settlement, Rixdorf.
B769 B **239** 50pf. brown and green 1·00 85

B **240** New Buildings

1987. International Building Exhibition, Berlin.
B770 B **240** 80pf. silver, black & bl . . . . 1·40 1·10

B **241** Tree in Arrow Circle

1987. 14th International Botanical Congress, Berlin.
B771 B **241** 60pf. multicoloured 1·00 85

B **242** Compact Disc and Gramophone

1987. International Broadcasting Exhibition, Berlin. Centenary of Gramophone Record.
B772 B **242** 80pf. multicoloured 1·40 1·10

B **243** 5th-century Bonnet Ornament

1987. Humanitarian Relief Funds. Precious Metal Work. Multicoloured.
B773 50pf.+25pf. Type B **243** . . 90 85
B774 60pf.+30pf. Athene plate, 1st-century B.C. . . . . 1·40 1·30
B775 70pf.+35pf. "Armilla" armlet, 1180 . . . . . . 1·60 1·50
B776 80pf.+40pf. Snake bracelet, 300 B.C. . . . . 2·10 1·80

1987. Tourist Sights. As Nos. 2200/19.
B777 5pf. blue and grey 30 45
B778 10pf. blue and indigo . . . 45 35
B779 20pf. flesh and blue . . . 45 80
B780 30pf. brown and green . . 1·20 95
B781 40pf. brown, red and blue 1·20 1·90
B782 50pf. ochre and blue . . . 1·60 90
B783 60pf. green and black . . 1·20 1·00
B784 70pf. flesh and blue . . . 1·70 2·20
B785 70pf. brown and blue . . . 2·30 4·25
B786 80pf. grey and green . . . 1·60 90
B787 100pf. green and orange . . 1·40 1·20
B788 120pf. green and red . . . 2·50 3·25
B789 140pf. bistre and yellow . . 2·75 3·50
B790 300pf. flesh and brown . . 5·50 4·00
B791 350pf. brown and blue . . 5·50 6·50

B **244** "Adoration of the Magi" (13th-century Book of Psalms)

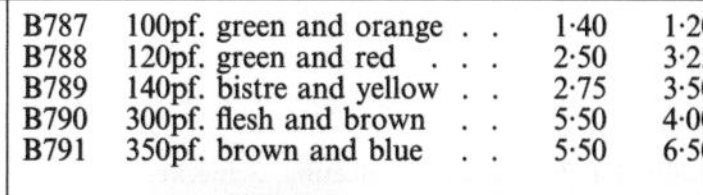

B **245** Heraldic Bear

1987. Christmas.
B797 B **244** 50pf.+25pf. mult . . . 1·00 90

1988. Berlin, European City of Culture.
B798 B **245** 80pf. multicoloured 1·90 1·60

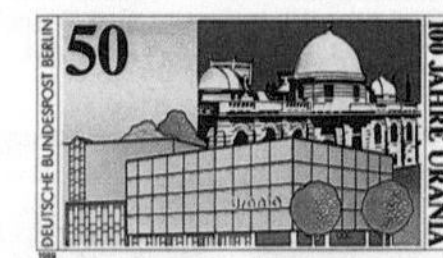

B **246** Old and New Buildings

1988. Centenary of Urania Science Museum.
B799 B **246** 50pf. multicoloured 1·40 1·30

B **247** "Large Pure-bred Foal" (bronze)

1988. Birth Centenary of Rene Sintenis (sculptor).
B800 B **247** 60pf. multicoloured 90 80

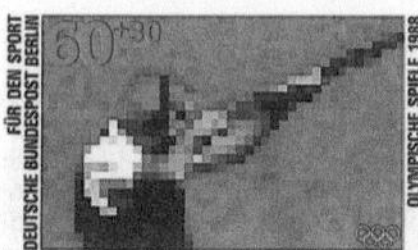

B **248** Clay-pigeon Shooting

1988. Sport Promotion Fund. Olympic Games. Multicoloured.
B801 60pf.+30pf. Type B **248** . . 1·60 1·30
B802 80pf.+40pf. Figure skating (pairs) . . . . 1·80 1·20
B803 120pf.+55pf. Throwing the hammer . . . . 2·30 2·10

B **249** Piano, Violin and Cello

1988. Youth Welfare. Music. Multicoloured.
B804 50pf.+25pf. Type B **249** . . 1·40 1·30
B805 60pf.+30pf. Wind quintet 1·80 1·60
B806 70pf.+35pf. Guitar, recorder and mandolin . . . . . 1·80 1·80
B807 80pf.+40pf. Children's choir 2·30 2·10

B **250** Great Elector and Family in Berlin Castle Gardens

B **251** Globe

1988. 300th Death Anniv of Friedrich Wilhelm, Great Elector of Brandenburg.
B808 B **250** 50pf. multicoloured 1·20 1·10

1988. International Monetary Fund and World Bank Boards of Governors Annual Meetings, Berlin.
B809 B **251** 70pf. multicoloured 1·10 1·00

B **252** First Train leaving Potsdam Station

1988. 150th Anniv of Berlin–Potsdam Railway.
B810 B **252** 10pf. multicoloured 60 50

B **253** "The Collector" (bronze statue)

1988. 50th Death Anniv of Ernst Barlach (artist).
B811 B **253** 40pf. multicoloured 75 60

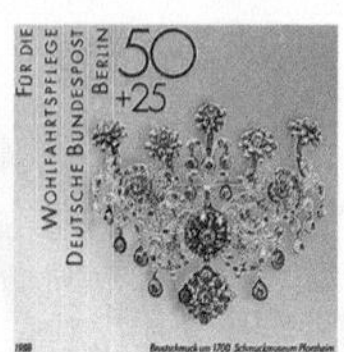

B **254** 18th-century Breast Ornament

1988. Humanitarian Relief Funds. Precious Metal Work. Multicoloured.
B812 50pf.+25pf. Type B **254** . . 1·20 1·20
B813 60pf.+30pf. 16th-century lion-shaped jug . . . . . 1·40 1·50
B814 70pf.+35pf. 16th-century goblet . . . . 1·60 1·60
B815 80pf.+40pf. 15th-century cope clasp . . . . 1·80 1·80

B **255** "Annunciation to the Shepherds" (illus from Henry the Lion's Gospel Book)

1988. Christmas.
B816 B **255** 50pf.+25pf. mult . . . 1·40 1·20

B **256** Volleyball (European Championships)

1989. Sport Promotion Fund. Multicoloured.
B817 100pf.+50pf. Type B **256** 2·75 2·40
B818 140pf.+60pf. Hockey (Champions Trophy) . . 3·75 3·25

B **257** Tigers and Tamer

1989. Youth Welfare. Circus. Multicoloured.
B819 60pf.+30pf. Type B **257** . . 1·80 1·90
B820 70pf.+30pf. Trapeze artistes 2·30 2·30
B821 80pf.+35pf. Sealions . . . . 2·75 2·75
B822 100pf.+50pf. Jugglers . . . 3·75 3·25

B **258** U.S. and U.K. Flags forming Airplane

1989. 40th Anniv of Berlin Airlift.
B823 B **258** 60pf. multicoloured 1·40 1·10

B **259** Emblem

1989. 13th International Organization of Chief Accountants Congress.
B824 B **259** 80pf. multicoloured 1·50 1·30

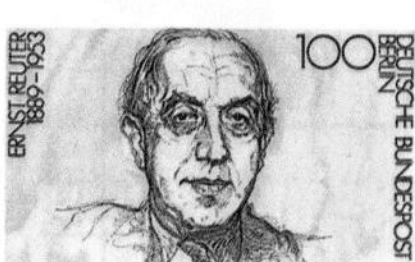

B **260** Reuter

1989. Birth Centenary of Ernst Reuter (politician and Mayor of Berlin).
B825 B **260** 100pf. multicoloured 2·00 1·70

B **261** Satellite Radio Waves and T.V. Screen

1989. International Broadcasting Exn, Berlin.
B826 B **261** 100pf. multicoloured 1·80 1·30

B **262** Plan of Berlin Zoo and Lenne

1989. Birth Bicentenary of Peter Joseph Lenne (landscape designer).
B827 B **262** 60pf. multicoloured 1·80 1·20

B **263** Ossietzky and Masthead of "Die Weltbühne"

1989. Birth Centenary of Carl von Ossietzky (journalist and peace activist).
B828 B **263** 100pf. multicoloured 1·90 1·70

B **264** Former School Building

1989. 300th Anniv of Berlin Lycee Francais.
B829 B **264** 40pf. multicoloured 1·00 90

B **265** St. Nicholas's Church, Berlin-Spandau

1989. 450th Anniv of Reformation.
B830 B **265** 60pf. multicoloured 1·00 90

B **266** 15th-century Letter Messenger

B **267** "Journalists"

1989. Humanitarian Relief Funds. Postal Deliveries. Multicoloured.
B831 60pf.+30pf. Type B **266** . . 2·50 2·30
B832 80pf.+35pf. Brandenburg mail coach, 1700 . . . . 3·75 3·00
B833 100pf.+50pf. 19th-century Prussian postal messengers . . . . 4·50 4·00

1989. Birth Centenary of Hannah Hoch (painter).
B834 B **267** 100pf. multicoloured 1·90 1·50

B 268 Angel

1989. Christmas. 16th-century Carvings by Veit Stoss, St. Lawrence's Church, Nuremberg. Multicoloured.
B835 40pf.+20pf. Type B 268 . . 1·20 1·20
B836 60pf.+30pf. "Adoration of the Magi" . . . . 2·30 2·10

B 269 Horse-drawn Passenger Vehicle

1990. 250th Anniv of Public Transport in Berlin.
B837 B 269 60pf. multicoloured 2·30 1·40

B 270 Rudorff

1990. 150th Birth Anniv of Ernst Rudorff (founder of conservation movement).
B838 B 270 60pf. multicoloured 2·10 1·40

1990. 500th Anniv of Regular European Postal Services. As No. 2297.
B839 914 100pf. deep brown, light brown and brown . . 2·50 2·00

B 271 Curtain and Theatre

1990. Cent of National Free Theatre, Berlin.
B840 B 271 100pf. multicoloured 2·10 1·90

B 272 Facade

1990. 40th Anniv of Bundeshaus, Berlin.
B841 B 272 100pf. multicoloured 3·00 2·10

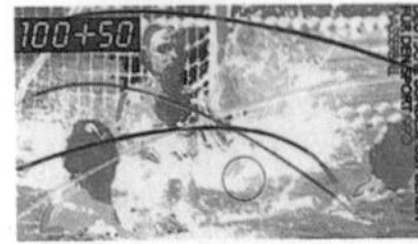

B 273 Water Polo

1990. Sport Promotion Fund. Multicoloured.
B842 100pf.+50pf. Type B 273 3·75 3·50
B843 140pf.+60pf. Wheelchair basketball . . . . 5·50 5·75

B 274 Moritz filling Pipe with Gunpowder

1990. Youth Welfare. 125th Anniv of Max and Moritz (characters from books by Wilhelm Busch). Multicoloured.
B844 60pf.+30pf. Type B 274 . . 1·60 1·70
B845 70pf.+30pf. Max and Moritz running off . . . 2·30 2·10
B846 80pf.+35pf. Moritz slashing sack open . . . . 2·75 2·50
B847 100pf.+50pf. Insect on Uncle Fritz's nose . . . 3·25 2·75

B 275 Poster B 276 "Street Singer" (etching, Ludwig Knaus)

1990. 90th German Catholic Day.
B848 B 275 60pf. multicoloured 1·90 1·50

1990. Bicentenary of Barrel-organ.
B849 B 276 100pf. multicoloured 2·10 1·80

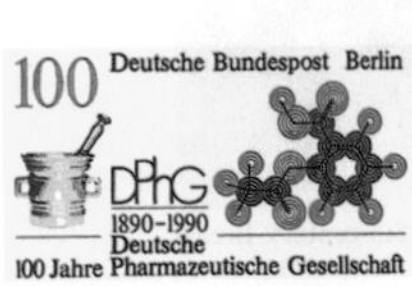

B 277 Pestle and Mortar and Diagram of Aspirin Molecule B 278 Diesterweg

1990. Centenary of German Pharmaceutical Society.
B850 B 277 100pf. multicoloured 4·25 3·00

1990. Birth Bicentenary of Adolph Diesterweg (educationist).
B851 B 278 60pf. multicoloured 2·75 2·50

B 279 Travelling Post Office, 1900

1990. Humanitarian Relief Funds. Posts and Telecommunications. Multicoloured.
B852 60pf.+30pf. Type B 279 . . 2·50 2·20
B853 80pf.+35pf. Installing telephone lines, 1900 . . 3·25 3·00
B854 100pf.+50pf. Electric parcels van, 1930 . . . . 4·50 4·00

With the absorption of East Germany into the Federal Republic of Germany on 3 October 1990, separate issues for West Berlin ceased.

V. GERMAN DEMOCRATIC REPUBLIC (East Germany)

The German Democratic Republic was set up in October 1949 and comprised the former Russian Zone. Its stamps were used in East Berlin.

On 3 October 1990 the territory was absorbed into the German Federal Republic.

1949. 100 pfennig = 1 Deutsche mark (East).
1990. 100 pfennig = 1 Deutsche mark (West).

E 1 Pigeon and Globe E 2 Postal Workers and Globe

1949. 75th Anniv of U.P.U.
E1 E 1 50pf. blue and deep blue 10·50 10·00

1949. Postal Workers' Congress.
E2 E 2 12pf. blue . . . . 10·50 8·75
E3 30pf. red . . . . 17·00 18·00

E 3 Type 1 of Bavaria and Magnifying Glass E 4 Skier

1949. Stamp Day.
E4 E 3 12pf.+3pf. black . . . . . 8·25 5·75

1950. 1st Winter Sports Meeting, Schierke.
E5 E 4 12pf. violet . . . . 8·25 4·75
E6 – 24pf. blue . . . . 10·50 8·00
DESIGN: 24pf. Girl skater.

1950. Leipzig Spring Fair. As T 231 but dated "1950".
E7 24pf.+12pf. purple . . . . . 12·50 8·75
E8 30pf.+14pf. red . . . . 15·00 11·50
DESIGNS: 24pf. First Dresden China Fair, 1710; 30pf. First Sample Fair, 1894.

E 5 Globe and Sun E 6 Wilhelm Pieck

E 7 Wilhelm Pieck E 8 Shepherd Playing Pipes

1950. 60th Anniv of Labour Day.
E9 E 5 30pf. red . . . . 22·00 19·00

1950.
E68 E 6 5pf. green . . . . 13·50 4·50
E69 12pf. blue . . . . 32·00 1·70
E70 24pf. brown . . . . . . 30·00 1·60
E12 E 7 1Dm. green . . . . . . 39·00 4·75
E13 2Dm. red . . . . 24·00 4·25
E14 5Dm. blue . . . . 10·00 1·80

For 1 and 2Dm. with different portrait of president, see Nos. E320/1 (1953).

1950. Death Bicentenary of J. S. Bach (composer).
E15 E 8 12pf.+4pf. green . . . . 8·25 5·50
E16 – 24pf.+6pf. olive . . . . . 8·25 5·50
E17 – 30pf.+8pf. red . . . . . 16·00 12·50
E18 – 50pf.+16pf. blue . . . . 25·00 16·00
DESIGNS: 24pf. Girl playing hand-organ; 30pf. Bach; 50pf. Three singers.

E 9 Dove, Globe and Stamp E 10 L. Euler

1950. Philatelic Exhibition (DEBRIA), Leipzig.
E19 E 9 84pf.+41pf. red . . . . . 55·00 11·50

1950. 250th Anniv of Academy of Science, Berlin.
E20 E 10 1pf. grey . . . . 5·00 1·70
E21 – 5pf. green . . . . 7·50 5·25
E22 – 6pf. violet . . . . . . 14·50 5·25
E23 – 8pf. brown . . . . . . 23·00 11·50
E24 – 10pf. green . . . . . . 21·00 11·50
E25 – 12pf. blue . . . . . . 18·00 3·75
E26 – 16pf. blue . . . . . . 25·00 18·00
E27 – 20pf. purple . . . . . 23·00 16·00
E28 – 24pf. red . . . . . . 24·00 3·75
E29 – 50pf. blue . . . . . . 37·00 21·00
PORTRAITS: 5pf. A. von Humboldt; 6pf. T. Mommsen; 8pf. W. von Humboldt; 10pf. H. von Helmholtz; 12pf. M. Planck; 16pf. J. Grimm; 20pf. W. Nernst; 24pf. G. W. Leibniz; 50pf. A. von Harnack.

1950. German Stamp Exhibition, "DEBRIA". Sheet 92 × 52 mm.
MSE29a Nos. E4 and E19 . . . £160 75·00

E 11 Miner E 12 Ballot Box

1950. 750th Anniv of Mansfeld Copper Mines.
E30 E 11 12pf. blue . . . . 7·50 8·75
E31 – 24pf. red . . . . 11·50 8·75
DESIGN: 24pf. Copper smelting.

1950. East German Elections.
E32 E 12 24pf. brown . . . . . . 18·00 4·25

E 13 Hand, Dove and Burning Buildings E 14 Tobogganing

1950. Peace Propaganda. Inscr "ERKAMPFT DEN FRIEDEN".
E33 – 6pf. blue . . . . 5·00 3·75
E34 E 13 8pf. brown . . . . . . 5·00 1·80
E35 – 12pf. blue . . . . 7·50 3·75
E36 – 24pf. red . . . . 7·50 2·00
DESIGNS (all include hand and dove): 6pf. Tank; 12pf. Atom bomb explosion; 24pf. Rows of gravestones.

1951. 2nd Winter Sports Meeting, Oberhof.
E37 E 14 12pf. blue . . . . 30·00 8·25
E38 – 24f. red (ski jumper) . . 14·50 10·00

E 15

1951. Leipzig Spring Fair.
E39 E 15 24pf. red . . . . 23·00 18·00
E40 50pf. blue . . . . 23·00 18·00

E 16 Presidents Pieck and Bierut

1951. Visit of Polish President to Berlin.
E41 E 16 24pf. red . . . . 26·00 21·00
E42 50pf. blue . . . . 26·00 20·00

E 17 Mao Tse-tung

E 18 Chinese Land Reform

1951. Friendship with China.
E43 E 17 12pf. green . . . . . . £120 27·00
E44 E 18 24pf. red . . . . £140 35·00
E45 E 17 50pf. blue . . . . £120 31·00

E 19 Youth Hoisting Flag E 20 Symbols of Agriculture & Industry

1951. 3rd World Youth Festival. Inscr as in Type E 19. On coloured papers.
E46 E 19 12pf. brown . . . . . . 15·00 6·50
E47 – 24pf. green and red . . 15·00 4·50
E48 E 19 30pf. buff and green . . 18·00 8·50
E49 – 50pf. red and blue . . . 18·00 8·25
DESIGN: 24pf., 50pf. Three girls dancing.

1951. Five Year Plan.
E50 E 20 24pf. multicoloured . . 5·75 2·40

E 21 K. Liebknecht E 22 Instructing Young Collectors

1951. 80th Birth Anniv of Liebknecht (revolutionary).
E51 E 21 24pf. slate and red . . . 5·75 2·40

1951. Stamp Day.
E52 E 22 12pf. blue . . . . 5·25 2·50

E 23 P. Bykow and E. Wirth

1951. German–Soviet Friendship.
E53 E 23 12pf. blue . . . . 5·00 4·00
E54 – 24pf. red . . . . 6·50 5·75
DESIGN: 24pf. Stalin and Pres. Pieck.

E 24 Skier E 25 Beethoven

1952. 3rd Winter Sports Meeting. Oberhof.
E55 E 24 12pf. green . . . . . . 7·50 4·25
E56 – 24pf. blue . . . . 7·50 4·25
DESIGN: 24pf. Ski jumper.

1952. 125th Death Anniv of Beethoven (composer).
E57 – 12pf. blue and light blue 2·50 65
E58 E 25 24pf. brown and grey 3·75 1·00
DESIGN: 12pf. Full face portrait.

E 26 President Gottwald E 27 Bricklayers

1952. Czechoslovak–German Friendship.
E59 E 26 24pf. blue . . . . 3·25 2·10

1952. National Reconstruction Fund.
E60 – 12pf.+3pf. violet . . . . 2·10 55
E61 E 27 24pf.+6pf. red . . . . . 1·80 70
E62 – 30pf.+10pf. green . . . 2·30 90
E63 – 50pf.+10pf. blue . . . . 3·00 1·70
DESIGNS: 12pf. Workers clearing debris; 30pf. Carpenters; 50pf. Architect and workmen.

E 28 Cyclists E 29 Handel

1952. 5th Warsaw–Berlin–Prague Cycle Race.
E64 E 28 12pf. blue . . . . 4·00 1·70

1952. Handel Festival, Halle.
E65 E 29 6pf. brown . . . . . . 2·30 1·70
E66 – 8pf. red . . . . 3·50 2·50
E67 – 50pf. blue . . . . 4·25 3·25
COMPOSERS: 8pf. Lortzing; 50pf. Weber.

E 31 Victor Hugo E 32 Machinery, Dove and Globe

1952. Cultural Anniversaries.
E73 E 31 12pf. brown . . . . . . 3·75 5·50
E74 – 20pf. green . . . . . . 3·75 5·50
E75 – 24pf. red . . . . 3·75 5·00
E76 – 35pf. blue . . . . 6·00 7·50
PORTRAITS: 20pf. Leonardo da Vinci; 24pf. N. Gogol; 35pf. Avicenna.

1952. Leipzig Autumn Fair.
E77 E 32 24pf. red . . . . 3·00 1·80
E78 35pf. blue . . . . 3·00 2·50

E 33 F. L. Jahn E 34 University Building

1952. Death Centenary of Jahn (patriot).
E79 E 33 12pf. blue . . . . 2·50 1·40

1952. 450th Anniv of Halle-Wittenberg University.
E80 E 34 24pf. green . . . . . . 2·50 1·30

E 35 Dove, Stamp and Flags E 36 Dove, Globe and St. Stephen's Cathedral, Vienna

1952. Stamp Day.
E81 E 35 24pf. brown . . . . . . 2·50 1·40

1952. Vienna Peace Congress.
E97 E 36 24pf. red . . . . 2·10 3·25
E98 35pf. blue . . . . 2·10 4·75

E 37 President Pieck E 38 Karl Marx

1953. President's Birthday.
E320 E 37 1Dm. olive . . . . . . 18·00 90
E321 2Dm. brown . . . . . 3·25 1·30

1953. 70th Death Anniv of Marx.
E102 – 6pf. red and green . . 5·25 80
E103 – 10pf. brown and green 5·50 1·10
E104 – 12pf. red and green . . 90 1·10
E105 – 16pf. blue and red . . 3·75 2·20
E106 – 20pf. brown and yellow 1·40 1·50
E107 E 38 24pf. brown and red 3·75 1·10
E108 – 35pf. yellow and purple 3·75 3·75
E109 – 48pf. brown and green 2·50 1·10
E110 – 60pf. red and brown 5·00 3·25
E111 – 84pf. brown and blue 4·50 2·00
MSE111a Two sheets, each 148 × 104 mm. (a) the six vert, and (b) the four horiz designs Set of 2 sheets £425 £325
DESIGNS—VERT: 6pf. Flag and foundry; 12pf. Flag and Spassky Tower, Kremlin; 20pf. Marx reading from "Das Kapital"; 35pf. Marx addressing meeting; 48pf. Marx and Engels. HORIZ: 10pf. Marx, Engels and "Communist Manifesto"; 16pf. Marching crowd; 60pf. Flag and workers; 84pf. Marx in medallion and Stalin Avenue, Berlin.
In each case the flag shows heads of Marx, Engels, Lenin and Stalin.

E 39 Gorky E 40 Cyclists

1953. 85th Birth Anniv of Maksim Gorky (writer).
E112 E 39 35pf. brown 45 55

1953. 6th International Cycle Race.
E113 E 40 24pf. green . . . . . . 3·75 2·75
E114 – 35pf. blue . . . . . . 1·60 1·40
E115 – 60pf. brown . . . . . 2·10 2·75
DESIGNS—VERT: 35pf. Cyclists and countryside; 60pf. Cyclists in town.

E 41 H. Von Kleist E 42 Miner

1953. 700th Anniv of Frankfurt-on-Oder.
E116 E 41 16pf. brown . . . . . 1·80 2·50
E117 – 20pf. green . . . . . . 1·20 2·00
E118 – 24pf. red . . . . . . 1·80 2·75
E119 – 35pf. blue . . . . . . 1·80 2·75
DESIGNS—HORIZ: 20pf. St. Mary's Church; 24pf. Frankfurt from R. Oder; 35pf. Frankfurt Town Hall and coat of arms.

1953. Five Year Plan. (a) Design in minute dots.
E120 E 42 1pf. black . . . . . . 2·10 45
E121 – 5pf. green . . . . . . 2·50 1·00
E122 – 6pf. violet . . . . . . 2·50 90
E123 – 8pf. brown . . . . . . 3·75 1·00
E124 – 10pf. green . . . . . . 2·50 85
E125 – 12pf. blue . . . . . . 2·50 90
E126 – 15pf. violet . . . . . . 3·50 1·70
E127 – 16pf. violet . . . . . . 4·25 2·20
E128 – 20pf. green . . . . . . 4·50 2·20
E129 – 24pf. red . . . . 8·00 85
E130 – 25pf. green . . . . . . 6·00 3·50
E131 – 30pf. red . . . . 6·00 3·50
E132 – 35pf. blue . . . . . . 12·00 3·50
E133 – 40pf. red . . . . 12·00 3·25
E134 – 48pf. mauve . . . . . 12·00 3·50
E135 – 60pf. blue . . . . . . 12·00 5·50
E136 – 80pf. turquoise . . . . 12·00 5·50
E137 – 84pf. brown . . . . . 12·00 14·50

(b) Design in lines.
E153 E 42 1pf. black 85 30
E310 – 5pf. green . . . . . . 1·60 35
E155 – 6pf. violet . . . . . . 3·00 40
E156 – 8pf. brown . . . . . . 3·25 40
E312 – 10pf. green . . . . . . 2·10 35
E311 – 10pf. blue 15 30
E159 – 12pf. turquoise . . . . 3·00 40
E160 – 15pf. lilac . . . . . . 14·00 50
E313 – 15pf. violet . . . . . . 1·60 35
E162 – 16pf. violet . . . . . . 3·75 2·30
E163 – 20pf. green . . . . . . 47·00 90
E314 – 20pf. red . . . . 1·00 20
E165 – 24pf. red . . . . 7·00 50
E315 – 25pf. green . . . . . . 1·60 20
E316 – 30pf. red . . . . 1·10 20
E168 – 35pf. blue . . . . . . 11·00 3·75
E169 – 40pf. red . . . . 8·25 70
E317 – 40pf. mauve 85 20
E171 – 48pf. mauve . . . . . 12·00 1·20
E318 – 50pf. blue 90 20
E173 – 60pf. blue . . . . . . 14·00 55
E319 – 70pf. brown 90 20
E175 – 80pf. turquoise . . . . 3·75 2·00
E176 – 84pf. brown . . . . . 16·00 1·40
DESIGNS—VERT: 5pf. Woman turning wheel; 6pf. Workmen shaking hands; 8pf. Students; 10pf. grn Engineers; 10pf. bl and 12pf. Agricultural and industrial workers; 15pf. mve Tele-typist; 15pf. vio and 16pf. Foundry worker; 20pf. grn Workers' health centre, Elster; 20pf. red and 24pf. Stalin Avenue, Berlin; 25pf. Locomotive construction workers; 30pf. Folk dancers; 35pf. Stadium; 40pf. red, Scientist; 40pf. mve, 48pf. Zwinger, Dresden; 50pf., 60pf. Launching ship; 80pf. Farm workers; 70pf., 84pf. Workman and family.

E 43 Mechanical Grab

1953. Leipzig Autumn Fair.
E138 E 43 24pf. brown . . . . . 1·80 2·75
E139 – 35pf. green . . . . . . 2·75 2·20
DESIGN: 35pf. Potato-harvester.

E 44 G. W. von Knobelsdorff and Opera House, Berlin

1953. German Architects.
E140 E 44 24pf. mauve . . . . . 1·50 1·60
E141 – 35pf. slate . . . . . . 2·25 1·90
DESIGN: 35pf. B. Neumann and Wurzburg Palace.

E 45 Lucas Cranach E 46 Nurse and Patient

1953. 400th Death Anniv of Cranach (painter).
E142 E 45 24pf. brown . . . . . 3·00 1·90

1953. Red Cross.
E143 E 46 24pf. red and brown 2·75 2·20

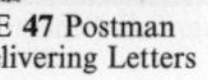

E 47 Postman delivering Letters E 48 Lion

1953. Stamp Day.
E144 E 47 24pf. blue . . . . . . 2·10 85

1953. 75th Anniv of Leipzig Zoo.
E145 E 48 24pf. brown . . . . . 2·30 90

E 49 Muntzer and Peasants E 50 Franz Schubert

1953. German Patriots.
E146 E 49 12pf. brown . . . . . 1·40 1·40
E147 – 16pf. brown . . . . . 1·40 1·40
E148 – 20pf. red . . . . . . 1·20 60
E149 – 24pf. blue . . . . . . 1·20 60
E150 – 35pf. green . . . . . . 2·40 2·75
E151 – 48pf. sepia . . . . . 2·50 2·30
DESIGNS: 16pf. Baron vom Stein and scroll; 20pf. Von Schill and cavalry; 24pf. Blucher and infantry; 35pf. Students marching; 48pf. Barricade, 1848 Revolution.

1953. 125th Death Anniv of Schubert.
E152 E 50 48pf. brown . . . . . 3·00 1·90

E 52 G. E. Lessing (writer) E 53 Conference Table and Crowd

1954. 225th Birth Anniv of Lessing.
E177 E 52 20pf. green . . . . . . 1·80 1·10

1954. Four-Power Conference, Berlin.
E178 E 53 12pf. blue . . . . . . 1·70 2·10

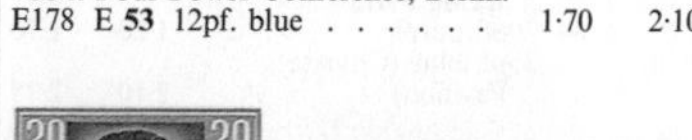

E 54 Stalin E 55 Racing Cyclists

1954. 1st Death Anniv of Stalin.
E179 E 54 20pf. brown, orange and grey . . . . . 3·00 1·10

1954. 7th International Cycle Race.
E180 E 55 12pf. brown . . . . . 1·60 1·10
E181 – 24pf. green . . . . . . 2·50 3·00
DESIGN: 24pf. Cyclists racing through countryside.

E 56 Folk Dancing E 57 F. Reuter

1954. 2nd German Youth Assembly.
E182 E 56 12pf. green . . . . . . 1·40 2·30
E183 – 24pf. red . . . . . . 1·50 1·20
DESIGN: 24pf. Young people and flag.

1954. 80th Death Anniv of Reuter (author).
E184 E 57 24pf. brown . . . . . 2·10 2·75

E 58 Dam and Forest E 59 E. Thalmann

1954. Flood Relief Fund.
E185 E 58 24pf.+6pf. green . . . 90 1·20

1954. 10th Death Anniv of Thalmann (politician).
E186 E 59 24pf. brown, bl & orge 1·20 2·00

E 60 Exhibition Buildings

1954. Leipzig Autumn Fair.
E187 E **60** 24pf. red 80 65
E188 35pf. blue . . . . . . 90 1·80

1954. (a) Nos. E155, etc surch in figures.
E189 5pf. on 6pf. violet . . . . . 1·20 40
E190 5pf. on 8pf. brown . . . . 1·20 40
E191 10pf. on 12pf. turquoise . . 1·20 40
E192 15pf. on 16pf. lilac . . . . 1·20 40
E194 20pf. on 24pf. red . . . . 1·40 55
E195 40pf. on 48pf. mauve . . . 3·75 2·75
E196 50pf. on 60pf. blue . . . . 4·25 1·10
E197 70pf. on 84pf. brown . . . 15·00 1·30
(b) No. E129 similarly surch.
E193a 20pf. on 24pf. red . . . . 1·20 80

E 62 President Pieck

1954. 5th Anniv of German Democratic Republic.
E198 E **62** 20pf. brown . . . . . 2·75 2·50
E199 35pf. blue . . . . . . 2·75 3·25

E 63 Stamp of 1953 E 64 Russian Pavilion

1954. Stamp Day.
E200 E **63** 20pf. mauve . . . . . 1·60 2·00
MSE200b 60×80 mm. No. E200 imperf (sold at Dm.30) . . . . 55·00 60·00

1955. Leipzig Spring Fair.
E201 E **64** 20pf. purple . . . . . 1·20 1·70
E202 – 35pf. blue (Chinese Pavilion) . . . . . 2·10 2·75

1955. Flood Relief Fund. Surch in figures.
E203 E **58** 20+5pf. on 24pf.+6pf. green . . . . 90 1·60

E 66 "Women of All Nations"

1955. 45th Anniv of International Women's Day.
E204 E **66** 10pf. green . . . . . . 1·40 1·30
E205 20pf. red . . . . . . 1·40 1·30

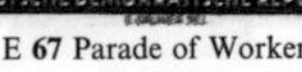
E 67 Parade of Workers E 68 Monument to Fascist Victims, Brandenburg

1955. International Conference of Municipal Workers, Vienna.
E206 E **67** 10pf. black and red . . 1·20 2·30

1955. International Liberation Day.
E207 E **68** 10pf. blue . . . . . . 1·30 2·50
E208 20pf. mauve . . . . . 1·50 3·00
MSE208a 73×99 mm. Nos. E207/8 21·00 31·00

E 69 Monument to Russian Soldiers, Treptow E 70 Schiller (poet)

1955. 10th Anniv of Liberation.
E209 E **69** 20pf. mauve . . . . . 1·80 1·80

1955. 150th Death Anniv of Schiller.
E210 E **70** 5pf. green . . . . . . 3·25 5·75
E211 – 10pf. blue 40 45
E212 – 20pf. brown 40 50
MSE212a 73×100 mm. Nos. E210/12 (+15pf.) . . . . . . 25·00 35·00
PORTRAITS OF SCHILLER: 10pf. Full-face; 20pf. Facing left.

E 71 Cyclists E 72 Karl Liebknecht

1955. 8th International Cycle Race.
E213 E **71** 10pf. turquoise . . . . 70 1·30
E214 20pf. red . . . . . . 90 1·50

1955. German Labour Leaders.
E215 E **72** 5pf. green 35 60
E216 – 10pf. blue 50 60
E217 – 15pf. violet . . . . . 7·75 12·50
E218 – 20pf. red 50 60
E219 – 25pf. blue 50 60
E220 – 40pf. red . . . . . . 2·75 60
E221 – 60pf. brown 50 60
PORTRAITS: 10pf. A. Bebel; 15pf. F. Mehring; 20pf. E. Thalmann; 25pf. Clara Zetkin; 40pf. Wilhelm Liebknecht; 60pf. Rosa Luxemburg.

E 73 Pottery E 74 Workers and Charter

1955. Leipzig Autumn Fair.
E222 – 10pf. blue 80 90
E223 E **73** 20pf. green 80 90
DESIGN: 10pf. Camera and microscope.

1955. 10th Anniv of Land Reform.
E224 E **74** 5pf. green . . . . . . 6·00 10·00
E225 – 10pf. blue 80 70
E226 – 20pf. red 65 80
DESIGNS—VERT: 10pf. Bricklayers at work. HORIZ: 20pf. Combine-harvesters.

E 75 "Solidarity" E 76 Engels Speaking

1955. 10th Anniv of People's Solidarity Movement.
E227 E **75** 10pf. blue 80 90

1955. 135th Birth Anniv of Engels.
E228 E **76** 5pf. blue and yellow . . 35 35
E229 – 10pf. violet and yellow 80 35
E230 – 15pf. green and yellow 80 35
E231 – 20pf. brown and orange . . . . . . 1·60 35
E232 – 30pf. brown and grey 10·00 20·00
E233 – 70pf. green and red . . 3·00 65
MSE233a 148×105 mm. Nos. E228/33 . . . . 70·00 90·00
DESIGNS: 10pf. Engels and Marx; 15pf. Engels and newspaper; 20pf. Portrait facing right; 30pf. Portrait facing left; 70pf. 1848 Revolution scene.

E 77 Magdeburg Cathedral E 78 Georg Agricola

1955. Historic Buildings.
E234 E **77** 5pf. sepia 65 95
E235 – 10pf. green 65 95
E236 – 15pf. purple 65 95
E237 – 20pf. red . . . . . . 65 1·60
E238 – 30pf. brown . . . . . 14·50 29·00
E239 – 40pf. blue . . . . . . 1·80 1·70
DESIGNS: 10pf. State Opera House, Berlin; 15pf. Old Town Hall, Leipzig; 20pf. Town Hall, Berlin; 30pf. Erfurt Cathedral; 40pf. Zwinger, Dresden.

1955. 400th Death Anniv of Agricola (scholar).
E240 E **78** 10pf. brown . . . . . 80 1·00

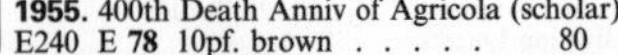

E 79 "Portrait of a Young Man" (Durer) E 80 Mozart

1955. Dresden Gallery Paintings. (1st series).
E241 E **79** 5pf. brown 70 35
E242 – 10pf. brown 70 35
E243 – 15pf. purple . . . . . 35·00 50·00
E244 – 20pf. sepia 70 35
E245 – 40pf. green 70 70
E246 – 70pf. blue . . . . . . 1·80 1·90
PAINTINGS: 10pf. "The Chocolate Girl" (Liotard); 15pf. "Portrait of a Boy" (Pinturicchio); 20pf. "Self-portrait with Saskia" (Rembrandt); 40pf. "Maiden with Letter" (Vermeer); 70pf. "Sistine Madonna" (Raphael).
See also Nos. E325/30 and E427/31.

1956. Birth Bicent of Mozart (composer).
E247 E **80** 10pf. green . . . . . . 13·50 21·00
E248 – 20pf. brown . . . . . 3·75 3·50
PORTRAIT: 20pf. Facing left.

E 81 Ilyushin Il-14P DDR-ABA E 82 Heinrich Heine (poet)

1956. Establishment of East German Lufthansa Airways.
E249 – 5pf. multicoloured . . 14·50 22·00
E250 E **81** 10pf. green 90 35
E251 – 15pf. blue 90 35
E252 – 20pf. red 90 35
DESIGNS: 5pf. Lufthansa flag; 15pf. View of Ilyushin Il-14P DDR-ABF airplane from below; 20pf. Ilyushin Il-14P DDR-ABA airplane facing left.

1956. Death Centenary of Heine.
E253 E **82** 10pf. green . . . . . . 15·00 13·00
E254 – 20pf. red . . . . . . 3·00 1·40
PORTRAIT: 20pf. Full-face.

E 83 Mobile Cranes E 84 E Thalmann

1956. Leipzig Spring Fair.
E255 E **83** 20pf. red 80 65
E256 35pf. blue . . . . . . 1·40 1·70

1956. 70th Birth Anniv of Thalmann (communist leader).
E257 E **84** 20pf. black, brn & red 55 65
MSE257a 73×100 mm. No. E257 10·00 28·00

E 85 Hand, Laurels and Cycle Wheel E 86 New Buildings, Old Market-place

1956. 9th International Cycle Race.
E258 E **85** 10pf. green 80 70
E259 – 20pf. red 80 70
DESIGN: 20pf. Arms of Warsaw, Berlin and Prague and cycle wheel.

1956. 750th Anniv of Dresden.
E260 E **86** 10pf. green 30 45
E261 – 20pf. red 30 30
E262 – 40pf. violet . . . . . 2·20 4·50
DESIGNS: 20pf. Elbe Bridge; 40pf. Technical High School.

E 87 Workman

1956. 10th Anniv of Industrial Reforms.
E263 E **87** 20pf. red 50 55

E 88 Robert Schumann E 88a Robert Schumann

1956. Death Centenary of Schumann (composer). (a) Type E 88 (wrong music).
E264 E **88** 10pf. green . . . . . . 2·75 3·75
E265 20pf. red 85 30
(b) Type E **88a** (correct music).
E266 E **88a** 10pf. green . . . . . 7·00 4·50
E267 20pf. red . . . . . . 3·75 70

E 89 Footballers E 90 T. Mann (author)

1956. 2nd Sports Festival, Leipzig.
E268 E **89** 5pf. green 25 25
E269 – 10pf. blue 25 25
E270 – 15pf. purple . . . . . 2·75 2·75
E271 – 20pf. red 25 25
DESIGNS: 10pf. Javelin thrower; 15pf. Hurdlers; 20pf. Gymnast.

1956. 1st Death Anniv of Thomas Mann.
E272 E **90** 20pf. black . . . . . . 1·20 1·20

E 91 J. B. Cisinski E 92 Lace

1956. Birth Centenary of Cisinski (poet).
E273 E **91** 50pf. brown . . . . . 1·20 1·20

1956. Leipzig Autumn Fair.
E274 E **92** 10pf. green and black 40 65
E275 – 20pf. pink and black (Sailing dinghy) . . . 40 65

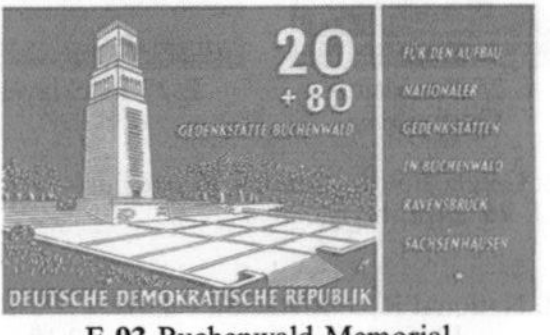
E 93 Buchenwald Memorial

1956. Concentration Camp Memorials Fund.
E276 E **93** 20pf.+80pf. red . . . . 1·40 6·25
For similar stamp see No. E390.

E 94 Torch and Olympic Rings E 95

1956. Olympic Games.
E277 E **94** 20pf. brown 45 30
E278 – 35pf. slate 90 75
DESIGN: 35pf. Greek athlete.

1956. 500th Anniv of Greifswald University.
E279 E **95** 20pf. red 55 60

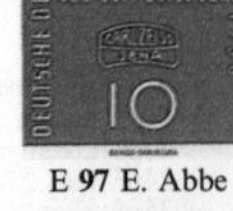
E 96 Postal Carrier, 1450 E 97 E. Abbe

1956. Stamp Day.
E280 E **96** 20pf. red 60 75

1956. 110th Anniv of Zeiss Factory, Jena.
E281 E **97** 10pf. green 15 25
E282 – 20pf. brown 25 25
E283 – 25pf. blue 50 65
DESIGNS—HORIZ: 20pf. Factory buildings; 25pf. Carl Zeiss.

E **98** "Negro" E **99** Indian Elephants

1956. Human Rights Day.
E284 – 5pf. green on olive . . 1·80 2·75
E285 E **98** 10pf. brown on pink 25 35
E286 – 25pf. blue on lavender 25 35
DESIGNS: 5pf. "Chinese"; 25pf. "European".

1956. Berlin Zoological Gardens. Centres in grey.
E287 E **99** 5pf. black 25 25
E288 – 10pf. green 25 25
E289 – 15pf. purple . . . . . 5·50 7·00
E290 – 20pf. red 30 30
E291 – 25pf. brown 35 30
E292 – 30pf. blue 45 35
DESIGNS: 10pf. Greater flamingos; 15pf. Black rhinoceros; 20pf. Mouflon; 25pf. European bison; 30pf. Polar bear.

1956. Egyptian Relief Fund. No. E237 surch **HELFT AGYPTEN +10**.
E293 20pf.+10pf. red 60 65

1956. Hungarian Socialists' Relief Fund. No. E237 surch **HELFT DEM SOZIALISTISCHEN UNGARN +10**.
E294 20pf.+10pf. red 60 65

E **103** "Frieden" (freighter)

1957. Leipzig Spring Fair.
E295 E **103** 20pf. red 30 35
E296 – 25pf. blue 30 50
DESIGN: 25pf. Class E251 electric locomotive.

E **104** Silver Thistle

1957. Nature Protection Week.
E297 E **104** 5pf. brown 25 25
E298 – 10pf. green . . . . . 2·75 5·00
E299 – 20pf. brown 30 25
DESIGNS: 10pf. Green lizard; 20pf. Lady's slipper orchid.

E **105** Friedrich Froebel and Children

1957. 175th Birth Anniv of Froebel (educator).
E300 – 10pf. black and green 1·60 2·30
E301 E **105** 20pf. black and brown 25 25
DESIGN: 10pf. Children at play.

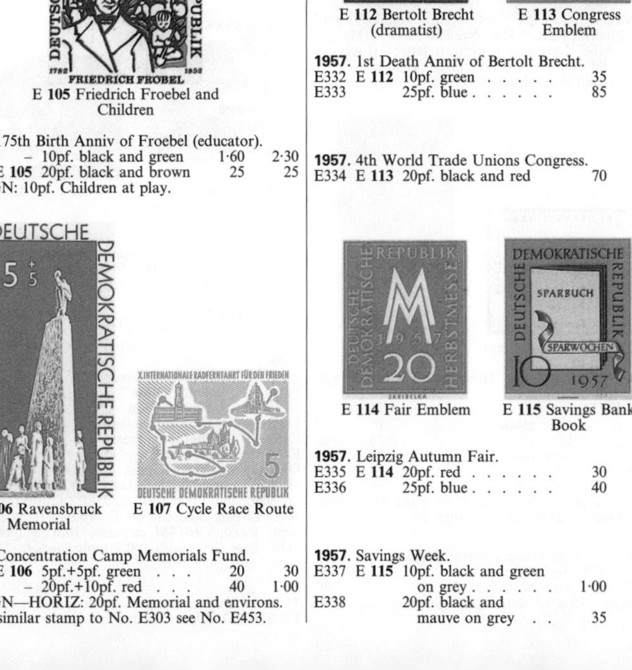

E **106** Ravensbruck Memorial E **107** Cycle Race Route

1957. Concentration Camp Memorials Fund.
E302 E **106** 5pf.+5pf. green . . . 20 30
E303 – 20pf.+10pf. red . . . 40 1·00
DESIGN—HORIZ: 20pf. Memorial and environs.
For similar stamp to No. E303 see No. E453.

1957. 10th International Cycle Race.
E304 E **107** 5pf. orange 40 65

E **108** Miner E **109** Henri Dunant and Globe

1957. Coal Mining Industry.
E305 – 10pf. green 15 25
E306 – 20pf. brown 30 25
E307 E **108** 25pf. blue . . . . . . 3·00 2·10
DESIGNS (39 × 21 mm): 10pf. Mechanical shovel and coal trucks; 20pf. Gantry.

1957. Int Red Cross Day. Cross in red.
E308 E **109** 10pf. brown and green 25 55
E309 – 25pf. brown and blue 25 55
DESIGN: 25pf. H. Dunant wearing hat, and globe.

E **110** Joachim Jungius (botanist) E **111** Clara Zetkin and Flower

1957. Scientists' Anniversaries.
E322 E **110** 5pf. brown . . . . . 1·80 1·80
E323 – 10pf. green 25 25
E324 – 20pf. brown 25 25
PORTRAITS: 10pf. L. Euler (mathematician); 20pf. H. Hertz (physicist).

1957. Dresden Gallery Paintings (2nd series). As Type E **79**.
E325 5pf. sepia 20 25
E326 10pf. green 20 25
E327 15pf. brown 20 25
E328 20pf. red 20 25
E329 25pf. purple 35 30
E330 40pf. grey . . . . 5·75 5·00
PAINTINGS—VERT: 5pf. "The Holy Family" (Mantegna); 10pf. "The Dancer, Barbarina Campani" (Carriera); 15pf. "Portrait of Morette" (Holbein the Younger); 20pf. "The Tribute Money" (Titian); 25pf. "Saskia with a Red Flower" (Rembrandt); 40pf. "A Young Standard-bearer" (Piazetta).

1957. Birth Cent of Clara Zetkin (patriot).
E331 E **111** 10pf. green and red 70 60

E **112** Bertolt Brecht (dramatist) E **113** Congress Emblem

1957. 1st Death Anniv of Bertolt Brecht.
E332 E **112** 10pf. green 35 55
E333 25pf. blue 85 55

1957. 4th World Trade Unions Congress.
E334 E **113** 20pf. black and red 70 65

E **114** Fair Emblem E **115** Savings Bank Book

1957. Leipzig Autumn Fair.
E335 E **114** 20pf. red 30 35
E336 25pf. blue 40 35

1957. Savings Week.
E337 E **115** 10pf. black and green on grey . . . . . . 1·00 1·50
E338 20pf. black and mauve on grey . . 35 65

E **116** Postrider of 1563

E **117** Revolutionary's Rifle and Red Flag

1957. Stamp Day.
E339 E **116** 5pf. blue on brown 70 55

1957. 40th Anniv of Russian Revolution.
E340 E **117** 10pf. green and red 30 35
E341 25pf. blue and red . . 30 60

E **118** Artificial Satellite

E **119** Professor Ramin

1957. International Geophysical Year.
E342 E **118** 10pf. blue 50 65
E343 – 20pf. red 65 35
E344 – 25pf. blue . . . . . . 2·50 3·25
DESIGNS: 20pf. Stratosphere balloon; 25pf. Ship using echo-sounder.

1957. "National Prize" Composers.
E345 E **119** 10pf. black and green 1·20 2·20
E346 – 20pf. black and orange 25 25
PORTRAIT: 20pf. Professor Abendroth.

E **120** Ernst Thalmann

1957. National Memorials Fund. East German War Victims. Portraits in grey.
E347 E **120** 20pf.+10pf. mauve . . 20 30
E348 – 25pf.+15pf. blue . . . 20 30
E349 – 40pf.+20pf. violet . . 45 95
MSE349a 140 × 95 mm. Nos. E347/9 (+20pf.) . . . . 55·00 95·00
PORTRAITS: 25pf. R. Breitscheid; 40pf. Father P. Schneider.
For other stamps as Type E **120** see Nos. E374/8, E448/52, E485/7, E496/500, E540/4 and E588/92.

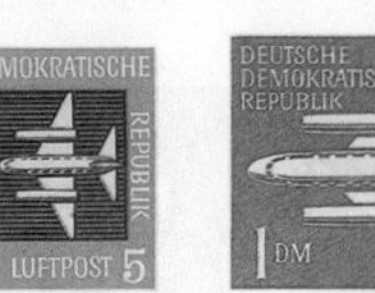

E **121**

E **122**

1957. Air.
E350 E **121** 5pf. black and grey 1·80 30
E351 20pf. black and red 25 30
E352 35pf. black and violet 25 30
E353 50pf. black and brown 45 30
E354 E **122** 1Dm. olive and yellow 1·40 30
E355 3Dm. brown & yellow 2·30 60
E356 5Dm. blue and yellow 5·50 3·50

E **123** Fair Emblem

1958. Leipzig Spring Fair.
E357 E **123** 20pf. red 30 30
E358 25pf. blue 45 35

E **124** Transmitting Aerial and Posthorn

1958. Communist Postal Conf, Moscow.
E359 E **124** 5pf. black and grey 1·10 1·60
E360 – 20pf. red 40 35
DESIGN—HORIZ: 20pf. Aerial as in 5pf. but posthorn above figures of value.

E **125** "Zille at play"

1958. Birth Cent of Heinrich Zille (painter).
E361 E **125** 10pf. drab and green 3·25 3·50
E362 – 20pf. drab and red . . 80 35
DESIGN—VERT: 20pf. Self-portrait of Zille.

E **126** Max Planck

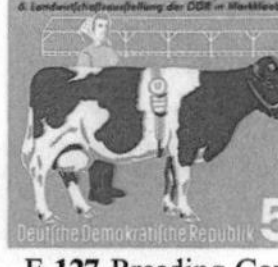

E **127** Breeding Cow

1958. Birth Cent of Max Planck (physicist).
E363 – 10pf. olive . . . . . . 1·80 2·75
E364 E **126** 20pf. mauve 40 35
DESIGN—VERT: 10pf. "h" (symbol of Planck's Constant).

1958. 6th Markkleeberg Agricultural Exn. Inscr "6 Landwirtschaftsausstellung der DDR in Markkleeberg".
E365 E **127** 5pf. grey . . . . . . 2·75 3·50
E366 – 10pf. green 30 35
E367 – 20pf. red 30 35
DESIGNS (39 × 22½ mm): 10pf. Chaff-cutter; 20pf. Beet-harvester.

E **128** Charles Darwin

E **129** Congress Emblem

1958. Centenary of Darwin's Theory of Evolution and Bicentenary of Linnaeus's Plant Classification System. Portraits in black.
E368 E **128** 10pf. green . . . . . 1·70 2·75
E369 – 20pf. red 25 25
PORTRAIT—HORIZ: 20pf. Linnaeus (Carl von Linne) inscr "200 JAHRE SYSTEMA NATURAE".

1958. 5th German Socialist Unity Party Congress.
E370 E **129** 10pf. red 35 65

E **130** "The Seven Towers of Rostock", Liner and Freighters

E **131** Mare and Foal

1958. Rostock Port Reconstruction.
E371 – 10pf. green 25 25
E372 E **130** 20pf. orange 35 65
E373 – 25pf. blue . . . . . 1·40 2·50
DESIGNS: 10pf. "Freundschaft" (freighter) at quayside; 25pf. "Frieden" (freighter) in Rostock harbour.

1958. "Resistance Fighters". As Type E **120**. Portraits in grey.
E374 5pf.+5pf. brown . . . . . 30 1·50
E375 10pf.+5pf. green . . . . . 20 1·50
E376 15pf.+10pf. violet . . . . 20 6·00
E377 20pf.+10pf. brown . . . . 20 1·40
E378 25pf.+15pf. black . . . . 80 24·00
PORTRAITS—VERT: 5pf. A. Kuntz; 10pf. R. Arndt; 15pf. Dr. K. Adams; 20pf. R. Renner; 25pf. W. Stoecker.

1958. "Grand Prix of the D.D.R." Horse Show.
E379 E **131** 5pf. sepia . . . . . . 2·75 5·50
E380 – 10pf. green 25 35
E381 – 20pf. brown 25 35
DESIGNS: 10pf. Horse-trotting; 20pf. Racing horses.

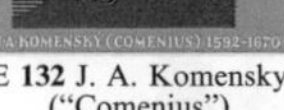

E **132** J. A. Komensky ("Comenius") E **133** Camp Bugler

1958. Komensky Commem. Centres in black.

E382	E **132**	10pf. green	1·90	2·75
E383	–	20pf. brown	25	35

DESIGN: 20pf. Komensky with pupils (from an old engraving).

1958. 10th Anniv of East German "Pioneer" Organization.

E384	E **133**	10pf.+5pf. green	30	60
E385	–	20pf.+10pf. red	45	60

DESIGN—VERT: 20pf. Young Pioneer saluting.

E **134** University Seal

1958. 400th Anniv of Friedrich Schiller University, Jena.

E386	E **134**	5pf. black and grey	1·80	2·50
E387	–	20pf. grey and red	30	35

DESIGN: 20pf. University building.

E **135** Model with Hamster-lined Coat, and Leipzig Central Railway Station E **136** Soldier climbing Wall

1958. Leipzig Autumn Fair.

E388	E **135**	10pf. brown and green	25	35
E389	–	25pf. black and blue	25	50

DESIGN: 25pf. Model with Karakul fur coat, and Leipzig Old Town Hall.

1958. Concentration Camp Memorials Fund. As Type E **93** but additionally inscr "14. SEPTEMBER 1958" in black.

E390	20pf.+20pf. red	60	1·10

1958. 1st Summer Military Games, Leipzig.

E391	E **136**	10pf. brown and green	1·90	2·50
E392	–	20pf. yellow and brown	15	25
E393	–	25pf. red and blue	15	25

DESIGNS: 20pf. Games emblem; 25pf. Marching athletes with banner.

E **137** Warding off the Atomic Bomb

1958. Campaign Against Atomic Warfare.

E394	E **137**	20pf. red	20	25
E395		25pf. blue	60	55

E **138** 17th-century Mail Cart

1958. Stamp Day.

E396	E **138**	10pf. green	2·75	2·75
E397	–	20pf. red	45	30

DESIGN: 20pf. Modern postal sorting train and Baade-Bonin 152 jetliner.

E **139** Revolutionary and Soldier E **140** Brandenburg Gate, Berlin

1958. 40th Anniv of November Revolution.

E398	E **139**	20pf. purple and red	12·00	85·00

1958. Brandenburg Gate Commemoration.

E399	E **140**	20pf. red	60	35
E400		25pf. blue	3·25	3·50

E **141** "Girl's Head" (bas-relief) E **142** Negro and European Youths

1958. Antique Art Treasures.

E401	E **141**	10pf. black and green	1·80	2·75
E402	–	20pf. black and red	25	30

DESIGN: 20pf. "Large Head" (from Pergamon frieze).

See also Nos. E475/8.

1958. 10th Anniv of Declaration of Human Rights.

E403	E **142**	10pf. black and green	25	25
E404	–	25pf. black and blue	2·20	2·50

DESIGN: 25pf. Chinese and European girls.

E **143** O. Nuschke E **144** "The Red Flag" (Party Newspaper)

1958. 1st Death Anniv of Vice-Premier Otto Nuschke.

E405	E **143**	20pf. red	35	60

1958. 40th Anniv of German Communist Party.

E406	E **144**	20pf. red	50	40

E **145** Pres. Pieck E **146** Rosa Luxemburg (revolutionary)

1959. Pres. Pieck's 83rd Birthday.

E407	E **145**	20pf. red	50	35

For 20pf. black see No. E517.

1959. 40th Death Anniv of Rosa Luxemburg and Karl Liebknecht. Centres in black.

E408	E **146**	10pf. green	2·40	3·00
E409	–	20pf. red	25	35

DESIGN—HORIZ: 20pf. Liebknecht-(revolutionary).

E **147** Concert Hall, Leipzig

1959. 150th Birth Anniv of Felix Mendelssohn-Bartholdy (composer).

E410	E **147**	10pf. green on green	45	95
E411	–	25pf. blue on blue	2·10	5·75

DESIGN—HORIZ: 25pf. Opening theme of Symphony in A Major ("The Italian").

E **148** "Schwarze Pumpe" plant E **149** Boy holding Book for Girl

1959. Leipzig Spring Fair. Inscr as in Type E **148**.

E412	E **148**	20pf. red	15	30
E413	–	25pf. blue	50	40

DESIGN—HORIZ: 25pf. Various cameras.

1959. 5th Anniv of "Youth Consecration".

E414	E **149**	10pf. black on green	2·10	2·30
E415	–	20pf. black on salmon	25	30

DESIGN: 20pf. Girl holding book for boy.

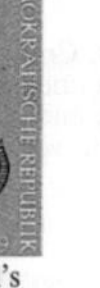

E **150** Handel's Statue, Oboe and Arms of Halle E **151** A. von Humboldt and Jungle Scene

1959. Death Bicentenary of Handel. Centre in black.

E416	E **150**	10pf. green	2·10	2·50
E417	–	20pf. red	25	35

DESIGN: 20pf. Portrait of Handel (after oil painting by Thomas Hudson).

1959. Death Centenary of Alexander von Humboldt (naturalist).

E418	E **151**	10pf. green	2·00	2·75
E419	–	20pf. red	30	35

DESIGN: 20pf. As Type E **151** but with view of sleigh in forest.

E **152** Posthorn E **153** Grey Heron

1959. Socialist Countries' Postal Ministers Conference, Berlin.

E420	E **152**	20pf. black, yell & red	25	35
E421		25pf. black, yell & bl	1·10	1·80

1959. Nature Preservation.

E422	E **153**	5pf. lilac, black & blue	25	25
E423	–	10pf. brn, sep & turq	25	25
E424	–	20pf. multicoloured	25	25
E425	–	25pf. multicoloured	45	35
E426	–	40pf. yell, blk & grey	7·50	7·00

DESIGNS: 10pf. Eurasian bittern; 20pf. Lily of the valley and "Inachis io" (butterfly); 25pf. Eurasian beaver; 40pf. "Apis mellifera" (bee) and willow catkin.

1959. Dresden Gallery Paintings as Type E **79** (3rd series).

E427	5pf. olive	25	25
E428	10pf. green	25	25
E429	20pf. orange	25	25
E430	25pf. brown	45	35
E431	40pf. red	7·00	7·00

PAINTINGS—VERT: 5pf. "The Vestal Virgin" (Kauffman); 10pf. "The Needlewoman" (Metsu); 20pf. "Mlle. Lavergne reading a letter" (Liotard); 25pf. "Old woman with a brazier" (Rubens); 40pf. "Young man in black coat" (Hals).

E **154** Great Cormorant E **155**

1959. "Birds of the Homeland". Centres and inscriptions in black.

E432	E **154**	5pf. yellow	15	35
E433	–	10pf. green	15	35
E434	–	15pf. violet	6·25	7·00
E435	–	20pf. pink	25	35
E436	–	25pf. blue	25	35
E437	–	40pf. red	30	35

BIRDS: 10pf. Black Stork; 15pf. Eagle Owl; 20pf. Black Grouse; 25pf. Hoopoe; 40pf. Peregrine Falcon.

1959. 7th World Youth Festival, Vienna.

E438	E **155**	20pf. red	15	25
E439	–	25pf. blue	90	1·30

DESIGN—HORIZ: 25pf. White girl embracing negro girl.

E **156** Hoop Exercises

1959. 3rd German Gymnastic and Sports Festival, Leipzig.

E440	E **156**	5pf.+5pf. brown	15	30
E441	–	10pf.+5pf. green	15	30
E442	–	20pf.+10pf. red	15	30
E443	–	25pf.+10pf. blue	25	30
E444	–	40pf.+20pf. purple	2·50	1·90

DESIGNS: 10pf. High jumping; 20pf. Vaulting; 25pf. Club exercises; 40pf. Fireworks over Leipzig Stadium.

E **157** Modern Leipzig Building

1959. Leipzig Autumn Fair.

E445	E **157**	20pf. grey and red	40	55

See also Nos. E483/4.

E **158** Glass Tea-set

1959. 75 Years of Jena Glassware.

E446	E **158**	10pf. turquoise	20	25
E447	–	25pf. blue	2·50	2·50

DESIGN—VERT: 25pf. Laboratory retorts.

1959. Ravensbruck Concentration Camp Victims. As Type E **120**. Portraits in black.

E448	5pf.+5pf. brown	15	25
E449	10pf.+5pf. green	15	25
E450	15pf.+10pf. violet	15	25
E451	20pf.+10pf. mauve	15	25
E452	25pf.+15pf. blue	75	2·75

PORTRAITS: 5pf. T. Klose; 10pf. K. Niederkirchner; 15pf. C. Eisenblatter; 20pf. O. Benario-Prestes; 25pf. M. Grollmuss.

1959. Concentration Camp Memorials Fund. As No. E303 but inscr "12. SEPTEMBER 1959" in black.

E453	20pf.+10pf. red	65	55

E **159** "Russian Pennant on the Moon"

1959. Landing of Russian Rocket on the Moon.

E454	E **159**	20pf. red	85	65

E **160** E. German Flag and Combine-harvester E **161** J. R. Becher

1959. 10th Anniv of German Democratic Republic. Designs as Type E **160** showing E. German flag in black, red and yellow. Inscriptions in black and red on coloured paper.

E455	E **160**	5pf. buff	20	30
E456	–	10pf. grey	20	30
E457	–	15pf. pale yellow	20	30
E458	–	20pf. lilac	20	30
E459	–	25pf. pale olive	20	30
E460	–	40pf. yellow	20	30
E461	–	50pf. salmon	20	30
E462	–	60pf. turquoise	20	45
E463	–	70pf. pale green	20	45
E464	–	1Dm. brown	55	70

DESIGNS—East German flag and: 10pf. "Fritz Heckert" convalescent home; 15pf. Zwinger Palace, Dresden; 20pf. Steel worker; 25pf. Industrial chemist; 40pf. Leipzig Stadium; 50pf. Woman tractor-driver; 60pf. Ilyushin Il-14M airplane; 70pf. Shipbuilding; 1Dm. East Germany's first atomic reactor.

1959. 1st Death Anniv of Becher (poet).

E465	E **161**	20pf. slate and red	1·70	50

E 162 Schiller

E 163 18th-century Courier and Milestone

1959. Birth Bicentenary of Schiller (poet).
E466 – 10pf. green on green 1·90 2·75
E467 E **162** 20pf. lake on pink . . 70 30
DESIGN: 10pf. Schiller's house, Weimar.

1959. Stamp Day.
E468 E **163** 10pf. green . . . . . 1·50 2·50
E469 – 20pf. lake 20 30
DESIGN: 20pf. Postwoman on motor cycle.

E **164** Eurasian Red Squirrels

1959. Forest Animals.
E470 E **164** 5pf. red, brown & grey 45 20
E471 – 10pf. lt brn, brn & grn 55 20
E472 – 20pf. multicoloured 55 20
E473 – 25pf. multicoloured 70 30
E474 – 40pf. yellow, brown and blue . . . . 10·50 7·00
ANIMALS: 10pf. Brown hares; 20pf. Roe deer; 25pf. Red deer; 40pf. Lynx.

1959. Antique Art Treasures (2nd series). As Type E **141**.
E475 5pf. black and yellow . . . 15 25
E476 10pf. black and green . . . 15 25
E477 20pf. black and red . . . 15 25
E478 25pf. black and blue . . . 1·30 1·80
DESIGNS: 5pf. Attic goddess (about 580 B.C.); 10pf. Princess of Tell el-Amarna (about 1360 B.C.); 20pf. Bronze horse of Toprak-Kale, Armenia (7th-century B.C.). HORIZ: (49 × 28 mm): 25pf. Altar of Zeus, Pergamon (about 160 B.C.).

E **165** Boxing

1960. Olympic Games. As Type E **165** inscr "OLYMPISCHE SOMMERSPIELE 1960" or "WINTERSPIELE" etc (20pf.). Centres and inscriptions in bistre.
E479 E **165** 5pf. brown . . . . . 5·50 5·75
E480 – 10pf. green 15 25
E481 – 20pf. red 15 25
E482 – 25pf. blue 25 25
DESIGNS: 10pf. Running; 20pf. Ski jumping; 25pf. Sailing.

1960. Leipzig Spring Fair. As Type E **157** but inscr "LEIPZIGER FRUHJAHRSMESSE 1960".
E483 20pf. grey and red 25 30
E484 25pf. grey and blue 35 30
DESIGNS: 20pf. Northern Entrance, Technical Fair; 25pf. Ring Fair Building.

1960. Sachsenhausen Concentration Camp Victims (1st issue). As Type E **120**. Portraits in black.
E485 5pf.+5pf. drab 15 25
E486 10pf.+5pf. myrtle 15 25
E487 20pf.+10pf. purple 25 35
PORTRAITS: 5pf. L. Erdmann; 10pf. E. Schneller; 20pf. L. Horn.
See also Nos. E496/500.

E **166** Purple Foxglove

E **167** Lenin

1960. Medicinal Flowers. Background in pale drab.
E488 E **166** 5pf. red and green . . 30 25
E489 – 10pf. olive and green 30 25
E490 – 15pf. red and green 30 25
E491 – 20pf. violet & turq . . 30 25
E492 – 40pf. red, green & brn 7·00 5·50
FLOWERS: 10pf. Camomile; 15pf. Peppermint; 20pf. Poppy; 40pf. Wild Rose.

1960. 90th Birth Anniv of Lenin.
E493 E **167** 20pf. red 35 40

1960. Re-opening of Rostock Port. No. E371 optd **Inbetriebnahme des Hochsee-hafens 1. Mai 1960**.
E494 10pf. green 35 60

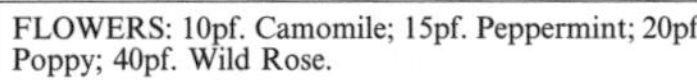

E **169** Russian Soldier and Liberated Prisoner

1960. 15th Anniv of Liberation.
E495 E **169** 20pf. red 35 60

1960. Sachsenhausen Concentration Camp Victims (2nd issue). As Type E **120**. Portraits in black.
E496 10pf.+5pf. green 20 25
E497 15pf.+5pf. violet . . . . . 1·30 1·70
E498 20pf.+10pf. lake 20 25
E499 25pf.+10pf. blue 25 50
E500 40pf.+20pf. brown . . . . 2·50 4·00
PORTRAITS: 10pf. M. Lademann; 15pf. L. Breunig; 20pf. M. Thesen; 25pf. G. Sandtner; 40pf. H. Rothbarth.

E **170** Model and Plan of "Fritz Heckert" (Liner)

1960. Launching of Cruise Liner "Fritz Heckert".
E501 E **170** 5pf. slate, red & yell 15 25
E502 – 10pf.+5pf. black, red and yellow 15 25
E503 – 20pf.+10pf. black, red and blue 25 25
E504 – 25pf. black, yellow and blue . . . . . 5·50 9·75
DESIGNS: 10pf. Liner under construction at Wismar; 20pf. Liner off Stubbenkammer; 25pf. Liner and Russian cruiser "Aurora" at Leningrad.

E **171** Lenin Statue, Eisleben

E **172** Masked Dancer (statuette)

1960. Lenin-Thalmann Statues.
E505 E **171** 10pf. green 30 45
E506 – 20pf. red 30 60
DESIGN: 20pf. Thalmann statue, Pushkin, U.S.S.R.

1960. 250th Anniv of Porcelain Industry, Meissen. Centres and inscriptions in blue. Figures in colours given.
E507 E **172** 5pf. orange 15 25
E508 – 10pf. green 15 25
E509 – 15pf. purple . . . . . 4·50 7·00
E510 – 20pf. red 25 35
E511 – 25pf. olive 25 35
DESIGNS: 10pf. Dish inscr with swords and years "1710 1960"; 15pf. Otter; 20pf. Potter; 25pf. Coffee-pot.

E **173** Racing Cyclist

1960. World Cycling Championships.
E512 E **173** 20pf.+10pf. mult . . . 25 40
E513 – 25pf.+10pf. brown, drab and blue . . . 1·80 5·50
DESIGN (38½ × 21 mm): 25pf. Racing cyclists on track.

E **174** Opera House, Leipzig

1960. Leipzig Autumn Fair.
E514 E **174** 20pf. grey and red . . 30 25
E515 – 25pf. brown and blue 45 55
DESIGN: 25pf. Export goods.

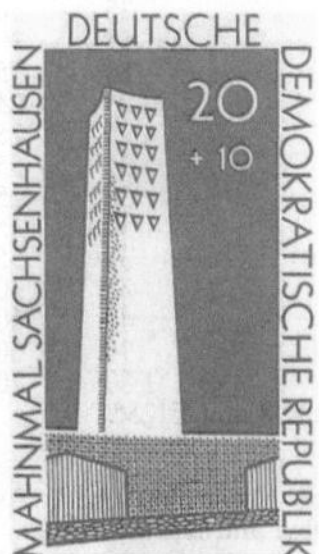

E **175** Sachsenhausen Memorial

E **176** 18th-century Rook

1960. Concentration Camp Memorials Fund.
E516 E **175** 20pf.+10pf. red . . . 35 65

1960. President Pieck Mourning issue.
E517 E **145** 20pf. black 55 65
MSE517a 88 × 108 mm. No. E517. Imperf . . . . 1·70 2·30

1960. 14th Chess Olympiad, Leipzig. German Chessmen.
E518 E **176** 10pf.+5pf. green . . . 15 25
E519 – 20pf.+10pf. purple . . 15 25
E520 – 25pf.+10pf. blue . . . 1·30 5·75
DESIGNS: 20pf. 18th-century knight; 25pf. 14th-century knight.

E **177** Mail Vans

1960. Stamp Day.
E521 E **177** 20pf. yell, blk & mve 25 35
E522 – 25pf. mauve, blk & bl 3·00 3·75
DESIGN: 25pf. 19th-century railway mail coach.

E **178** Medal of 1518 showing Hans Burgkmair (painter)

E **179** Count N. von Gneisenau

1960. 400th Anniv of Dresden Art Collections.
E523 E **178** 20pf. ochre, green and buff 25 35
E524 – 25pf. black and blue 1·80 4·25
DESIGN: 25pf. "Dancing Peasants" (after Durer).

1960. Birth Bicent of Count N. von Gneisenau.
E525 E **179** 20pf. black and red 25 35
E526 – 25pf. blue . . . . . . 1·70 3·00
DESIGN: 25pf. Similar portrait but vert.

E **180** R. Virchow

1960. 250th Anniv of Berlin Charity and 150th Anniv of Humboldt University, Berlin. Centres in black.
E527 E **180** 5pf. ochre 20 25
E528 – 10pf. green 20 25
E529 – 20pf. brown 20 25
E530 – 25pf. blue 20 25
E531 – 40pf. red . . . . . . 3·00 3·75
DESIGNS—As Type E **180** (Berlin Charity); 10pf. Robert Koch; 40pf. W. Griesinger. (Humboldt University); 20pf. University building and statues of William and Alexander von Humboldt; 25pf. Plaque with profiles of Von Humboldt brothers.

E **181** Scientist with Notebook

1960. Chemical Workers' Day.
E532 E **181** 5pf. grey and red . . 25 25
E533 – 10pf. green and orange 25 25
E534 – 20pf. red and blue . . 25 25
E535 – 25pf. blue and yellow 2·30 5·00
DESIGNS: 10pf. Chemical worker with fertiliser; 20pf. Girl worker with jar, and Trabant car; 25pf. Laboratory assistant and synthetic dress.

E **182** "Young Socialists' Express" (double-deck train)

E **183** President Pieck

1960. 125th Anniv of German Railways.
E536 E **182** 10pf. black and green 15 25
E537 – 20pf. black and red 15 25
E538 – 25pf. black and blue 5·50 10·00
DESIGNS—As Type E **182**: 25pf. Stephenson locomotive "Adler" (1835) and Class V180 diesel locomotive. (43 × 25½ mm): 20pf. Sassnitz Harbour station and train ferry "Sassnitz".

1961. 85th Birth Anniv of President Pieck.
E539 E **183** 20pf. red and black 35 60

1961. Concentration Camp Victims. As Type E **120**. Portraits in black.
E540 5pf.+5pf. green 15 25
E541 10pf.+5pf. green 15 25
E542 15pf.+5pf. violet . . . . . 1·80 5·50
E543 20pf.+10pf. red 15 25
E544 25pf.+10pf. blue 15 25
PORTRAITS: 5pf. W. Kube; 10pf. H. Gunther; 15pf. Elvira Eisenschneider; 20pf. Hertha Lindner; 25pf. H. Tschape.

E **184** High-voltage Switchgear

E **185** Lilienstein Saxony

1961. Leipzig Spring Fair. Inscr as in Type E **184**.
E545 E **184** 10pf. slate and green 35 35
E546 – 25pf. slate and blue 55 60
DESIGN: 25pf. Fair Press Centre.

1961. Landscapes and Historical Buildings.
E547 – 5pf. grey 25 25
E548 – 10pf. green 25 25
E549 E **185** 20pf. brown 25 55
E550 – 20pf. red 25 25
E551 – 25pf. blue 25 40
DESIGNS—VERT: 5pf. Ruins of Rudelsburg; 10pf. Wartburg; 20pf. (No. E550), Town Hall, Wernigerode. HORIZ: 25pf. Brocken, Oberharz.

E **186** "Ros" (Trawler)

1961. Deep Sea Fishing Industry.
E552 E **186** 10pf. green 15 25
E553 – 20pf. purple 15 25
E554 – 25pf. blue 15 25
E555 – 40pf. violet . . . . . 3·00 4·00
DESIGNS: 20pf. Hauling nets; 25pf. "Robert Koch" (trawler); 40pf. Processing Atlantic cod.

E **187** Cosmonaut in Capsule

1961. 1st Manned Space Flight. Inscr "12.4.1961".
E556 – 10pf. red and green . . 70 95
E557 E **187** 20pf. red 70 95
E558 – 25pf. blue . . . . . . 5·50 11·00
DESIGNS: 10pf. Space rocket leaving globe; 25pf. Capsule's parachute descent.

E 188 Marx, Engels, Lenin and Demonstrators

1961. 15th Anniv of German Socialist Unity Party.

E559 E 188 20pf. red 55 60

E 189 Common Zebra

1961. Centenary of Dresden Zoo.

E560 E 189 10pf. black and green 6·00 9·75

E561 – 20pf. black and mauve 45 70

DESIGN: 20pf. Eastern black-and-white colobus.

E 190 Pioneers playing Volleyball

1961. Pioneers Meeting, Erfurt. Mult.

E562 10pf.+5pf. Type E 190 . . 15 25

E563 20pf.+10pf. Folk dancing 15 25

E564 25pf.+10pf. Model airplane construction . . . . . . 3·50 5·75

E 191 High Jump E 192 Salt Miners and Castle

1961. 3rd European Women's Gymnastic Championships, Leipzig.

E565 E 191 10pf. green 25 25

E566 – 20pf. mauve 25 25

E567 – 25pf. blue . . . . . 6·00 10·50

DESIGNS—VERT: 20pf. Gymnast. HORIZ: 25pf. Exercise on parallel bars.

1961. Halle (Saale) Millenary.

E568 E 192 10pf. black, yell & grn 3·25 3·50

E569 – 20pf. black, yell & red 25 35

DESIGN: 20pf. Scientist and Five Towers of Halle.

E 193 Canadian Canoe

1961. World Canoeing Championships.

E570 – 5pf. blue and grey . . 3·50 6·00

E571 E 193 10pf. green and grey 25 25

E572 – 20pf. purple and grey 25 25

DESIGNS: 5pf. Folding canoe; 20pf. Canadian two-seater canoe.

E 194 Line-casting E 195 Old Weigh-house, Leipzig

1961. World Angling Championships.

E573 E 194 10pf. green and blue 3·50 4·75

E574 – 20pf. lake and blue . . 25 35

DESIGN: 20pf. River-fishing.

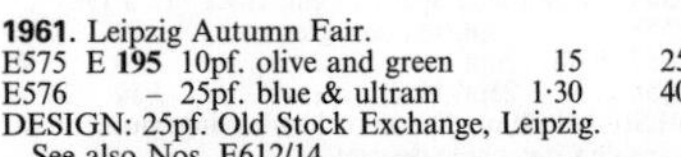

1961. Leipzig Autumn Fair.

E575 E 195 10pf. olive and green 15 25

E576 – 25pf. blue & ultram 1·30 40

DESIGN: 25pf. Old Stock Exchange, Leipzig.

See also Nos. E612/14.

E 196 Walter Ulbricht E 197 Dahlia

1961. Type E 196 or larger, 24 × 29 mm (Dm. values).

E577 5pf. blue 30 30

E578 10pf. green 35 30

E579 15pf. purple 55 30

E580 20pf. red 80 75

E581 25pf. turquoise 25 25

E582 30pf. red 25 25

E582a 35pf. green 35 65

E583 40pf. violet 30 25

E584 50pf. blue 30 25

E584a 60pf. green 35 55

E585 70pf. brown 35 30

E585a 80pf. blue 40 60

E586 1Dm. green 90 60

E587 2Dm. brown . . . . . . 1·80 70

See also Nos. E805/6, E1197/8 and E1255.

1961. Concentration Camps Memorials Fund. As Type E 120. Portraits in grey and black.

E588 5pf.+5pf. green 15 35

E589 10pf.+5pf. green 15 35

E590 20pf.+10pf. mauve 25 35

E591 25pf.+10pf. blue 25 35

E592 40pf.+20pf. lake . . . . 2·40 13·00

PORTRAITS: 5pf. C. Schonhaar; 10pf. H. Baum; 20pf. Liselotte Herrmann. HORIZ: (41 × 32½ mm): 25pf. Sophie and Hans Scholl; 40pf. Hilde and Hans Coppi.

1961. International Horticultural Exn.

E593 – 10pf. red, yellow & grn 25 35

E594 E 197 20pf. red, yellow & brn 25 35

E595 – 40pf. red, yellow & bl 8·00 17·00

FLOWERS: 10pf. Tulip. 40pf. Rose.

E 198 Liszt and Berlioz (after Von Kaulbach and Prinzhofer) E 199 TV Camera and Screen

1961. 150th Birth Anniv of Liszt (composer).

E596 E 198 5pf. black 30 25

E597 – 10pf. green . . . . . 2·75 4·50

E598 – 20pf. red 30 25

E599 – 25pf. blue . . . . . 3·25 5·50

DESIGNS: 10pf. Young hand of Liszt (from French sculpture, Liszt Museum, Budapest); 20pf. Liszt (after Rietschel); 25pf. Liszt and Chopin (after Bartolini and Bovy).

1961. Stamp Day.

E600 E 199 10pf. black and green 2·00 5·75

E601 – 20pf. black and red 15 35

DESIGNS: 20pf. Studio microphone and radio tuning-scale.

E 200 G. S. Titov with Young Pioneers

1961. 2nd Russian Manned Space Flight.

E602 E 200 5pf. violet and red . . 15 25

E603 – 10pf. green and red 15 25

E604 – 15pf. mauve and blue 8·00 16·00

E605 – 20pf. red and blue . . 25 35

E606 – 25pf. blue and red . . 25 35

E607 – 40pf. blue and red . . 1·40 1·60

DESIGNS—HORIZ: 15pf. Titov in space-suit; 20pf. Titov receiving Karl Marx Order from Ulbricht; 25pf. "Vostok 2" rocket in flight; 40pf. Titov and Ulbricht in Berlin. VERT: 10pf. Titov in Leipzig.

E 201 "Formica ruta" (Ant)

1962. Fauna Protection Campaign (1st series).

E608 E 201 5pf. yellow, brn & blk 4·00 13·50

E609 – 10pf. brown and green 15 25

E610 – 20pf. brown and red 15 25

E611 – 40pf. yellow, blk & vio 70 70

DESIGNS: 10pf. Weasels; 20pf. Eurasian common shrews; 40pf. Common long-eared bat.

See also Nos. E699/703.

1962. Leipzig Spring Fair. As Type E 195.

E612 10pf. sepia and green . . . 20 25

E613 20pf. black and red 35 25

E614 25pf. purple and blue . . . 1·10 2·10

BUILDINGS: 10pf. Zum Kaffeebaum; 20pf. Gobliser Schlosschen; 25pf. Romanus-Haus.

E 203 Pilot and Mikoyan Gurevich MiG-17 Jet Fighters

1962. 6th Anniv of East German People's Army.

E615 E 203 5pf. blue 15 25

E616 – 10pf. green 15 25

E617 – 20pf. red 15 25

E618 – 25pf. blue 30 70

E619 – 40pf. brown . . . . . 2·10 3·50

DESIGNS: 10pf. Soldier and armoured car; 20pf. Factory guard; 25pf. Sailor and Habich I class minesweeper; 40pf. Tank and driver.

E 204 Danielle Casanova

1962. Concentration Camps Memorial Fund. Camp Victims.

E620 E 204 5pf.+5pf. black . . . 15 25

E621 – 10pf.+5pf. green . . . 15 25

E622 – 20pf.+10pf. purple . . 25 25

E623 – 25pf.+10pf. blue . . . 30 30

E624 – 40pf.+20pf. purple . . 2·10 5·25

PORTRAITS: 10pf. Julius Fucik; 20pf. Johanna J. Schaft; 25pf. Pawel Finder; 40pf. Soja A. Kosmodemjanskaja.

E 205 Racing Cyclists and Prague Castle

1962. 15th Int Peace Cycle Race. Mult.

E625 10pf. Type E 205 . . . . 15 25

E626 20pf.+10pf. Cyclists and Palace of Culture and Science, Warsaw 25 50

E627 25pf. Cyclist and Town Hall, East Berlin . . . . 1·80 3·50

E 206 Johann Fichte

1962. Birth Bicent of Fichte (philosopher).

E628 – 10pf. green and black 1·80 4·25

E629 E 206 20pf. red and black 35 35

DESIGN: 10pf. Fichte's birthplace, Ramenau.

E 207 Cross of Lidice E 208 Dimitrov at Leipzig

1962. 20th Anniv of Destruction of Lidice.

E630 E 207 20pf. red and black 20 30

E631 25pf. blue and black 1·20 2·50

1962. 80th Birth Anniv of G. Dimitrov (Bulgarian statesman).

E632 E 208 5pf. black & turquoise 70 1·20

E633 – 20pf. black and red 25 35

DESIGN: 20pf. Dimitrov as Premier of Bulgaria.

E 209 Maize-planting machine

1962. 10th D.D.R. Agricultural Exhibition, Markkleeberg. Multicoloured.

E634 10pf. Type E 209 . . . . . 15 25

E635 20pf. Milking shed 15 25

E636 40pf. Combine-harvester . . 2·10 3·75

E 210 "Frieden" (freighter)

1962. 5th Baltic Sea Week, Rostock.

E637 – 10pf. turquoise & blue 15 25

E638 – 20pf. red and yellow 15 25

E639 E 210 25pf. bistre and blue 2·20 4·50

DESIGNS—HORIZ: 10pf. Map of Baltic Sea inscr "Meer des Friedens" ("Sea of Peace"). VERT: 20pf. Hochhaus, Rostock.

E 211 Brandenburg Gate, Berlin E 212 Youth of Three Races

E 213 Folk Dancers E 214 Youth of Three Nations

1962. World Youth Festival Games, Helsinki. Multicoloured.

E640 5pf. Type E 211 . . . . . 2·30 4·75

E641 5pf. Type E 212 . . . . . 2·30 4·75

E642 10pf.+5pf. Type E 213 . . . 45 35

E643 15pf.+5pf. Type E 214 . . . 45 35

E644 20pf. Dove . . . . 2·30 4·75

E645 20pf. National Theatre, Helsinki . . . . 2·30 4·75

Nos. 640/11 and 644/5 were issued together as a se-tenant block of four and Nos. 642/3 in horizontal pairs, both forming composite designs.

E 217 Free-style Swimming E 218 Municipal Store, Leipzig

1962. 10th European Swimming Championships, Leipzig. Design in blue: value colours given.

E646 E 217 5pf. orange 15 25

E647 – 10pf. blue 15 25

E648 – 20pf.+10pf. mauve . . 15 25

E649 – 25pf. blue 15 25

E650 – 40pf. violet . . . . . 1·40 2·75

E651 – 70pf. brown 15 25

DESIGNS: 10pf. Back stroke; 20pf. High diving; 25pf. Butterfly stroke; 40pf. Breast stroke; 70pf. Water-polo.

On Nos. E649/51 the value, etc, appears at the foot of the design.

1962. Leipzig Autumn Fair.

E652 E 218 10pf. black and green 20 30

E653 – 20pf. black and red 30 35

E654 – 25pf. black and blue 1·20 1·60

DESIGNS: 20pf. Madler Arcade, Leipzig; 25pf. Leipzig Airport and Ilyushin Il-14M airplane.

E **219** "Transport and Communications"   E **220** Rene Blieck

E **219a**P. Popovich and A. Nikolaev

1962. 10th Anniv of "Friedrich List" Transport High School, Dresden.
E655 E **219** 5pf. black and blue . . . 45 35

1962. "Vostok 3" and "Vostok 4" Space Flights. Sheet 89 × 108 mm.
MSE655a E **219a** 70pf. green, blue and yellow . . . . 2·50 2·75

1962. Concentration Camp Victims. Memorials Fund.
E656 E **220** 5pf.+5pf. blue 15 25
E657 – 10pf.+5pf. green . . . 15 25
E658 – 15pf.+5pf. violet . . . 15 25
E659 – 20pf.+10pf. purple . . 25 35
E660 – 70pf.+30pf. brown . . 2·30 5·75
PORTRAITS—As Type E **220**: 10pf. Dr. A. Klahr; 15pf. J. Diaz; 20pf. J. Alpari. HORIZ: (39 × 21 mm): 70pf. Seven Cervi brothers.

E **221** Television Screen and Call-sign   E **222** G. Hauptmann

1962. Stamp Day and 10th Anniv of German Television.
E661 E **221** 20pf. purple and green 20 30
E662 – 40pf. purple & mauve 2·00 4·25
DESIGN: 40pf. Children with stamp album (inscr "TAG DER BRIEFMARKE 1962").

1962. Birth Centenary of Gerhart Hauptmann (author).
E663 E **222** 20pf. black and red 60 35

E **222a** Gagarin and "Vostok 1"

1962. Five Years of Russian Space Flights. Sheet 127 × 108 mm. Multicoloured.
MSE663a 5pf. Dogs "Belka" and "Strelka" , 10pf. Type E**222a**; 15pf. "Sputniks 1, 2 and 3"; 20pf. Titov and "Vostok 2"; 25pf. "Luniks 1 and 2"; 30pf. Nikolaev and Popovich; 40pf. Interplanetary station and spacecraft; 50pf. "Lunik 3" . . 29·00 42·00

E **223** Pierre de Coubertin   E **224** Party Flag

1963. Birth Centenary of Pierre de Coubertin (reviver of Olympic Games).
E664 E **223** 20pf. red and grey . . 20 30
E665 – 25pf. blue and ochre 2·00 5·50
DESIGN: 25pf. Stadium.

1963. 6th Socialists Unity Party Day.
E666 E **224** 10pf. red, black & yell 35 35

E **225** Insecticide Sprayer

1963. Malaria Eradication.
E667 E **225** 20pf. black, red & orge 15 25
E668 – 25pf. multicoloured 15 25
E669 – 50pf. multicoloured 1·50 3·50
DESIGNS: 25pf. Rod of Aesculapius; 50pf. Mosquito. Map is common to all values.

E **226** Red Fox (Silver Fox race)   E **227** Barthels Hof, Leipzig (1748–1872)

1963. International Fur Auctions, Leipzig.
E670 E **226** 20pf. blue and red . . 25 35
E671 – 25pf. indigo and blue 1·80 4·75
DESIGN: 25pf. Karakul lamb.

1963. Leipzig Spring Fair.
E672 E **227** 10pf. black and yellow 25 30
E673 – 20pf. black and brown 30 60
E674 – 25pf. black and blue 1·40 2·50
LEIPZIG BUILDINGS: 20pf. New Town Hall; 25pf. Clock-tower, Karl-Marx Square.

E **227a** Laboratory Worker and Apparatus

1963. "Chemistry for Freedom and Socialism". Sheet 105 × 74 mm with Type E **227a** and similar horiz design. Imperf. No gum.
MSE674a 50pf. blue and black (E **227a**); 70pf. blue and grey (oil refinery) . . . . 4·50 18·00

E **228** J. G. Seume (poet) and Scene from "Syracuse Walk" (Birth Bicent)

1963. Cultural Anniversaries. Design and portrait in black.
E675 E **228** 5pf. yellow 15 25
E676 – 10pf. turquoise . . . 15 25
E677 – 20pf. orange 15 25
E678 – 25pf. blue . . . . . 2·20 4·00
DESIGNS: 10pf. F. Hebbel (poet) and scene from "Mary Magdalene" (150th birth anniv); 20pf. G. Buchner (poet) and scene from "Woyzeck" (150th birth anniv); 25pf. R. Wagner (composer) and scene from "The Flying Dutchman" (150th birth anniv).

E **229** Nurse bandaging Patient   E **230** W. Bohne (runner)

1963. Centenary of Red Cross.
E679 E **229** 10pf. multicoloured 1·40 2·50
E680 – 20pf. black, grey and red 20 30
DESIGN: 20pf. Barkas type "B 1000" ambulance.

1963. Concentration Camps Memorial Fund. Sportsmen Victims (1st series). Designs in black.
E681 E **230** 5pf.+5pf. yellow . . . 15 40
E682 – 10pf.+5pf. green . . 15 40
E683 – 15pf.+5pf. mauve . . 15 55
E684 – 20pf.+10pf. pink . . . 25 60
E685 – 25pf.+10pf. blue . . . 2·50 20·00
SPORTSMEN: 10pf. W. Seelenbinder (wrestler); 15pf. A. Richter (cyclist); 20pf. H. Steyer (footballer); 25pf. K. Schlosser (mountaineer).
See also Nos. E704/8.

E **231** Gymnastics   E **232** E. Pottier (lyricist) and Opening Bars of the "Internationale"

1963. 4th East German Gymnastics and Sports Festival, Leipzig. Inscr in black.
E686 E **231** 10pf.+5pf. yellow and green 25 25
E687 – 20pf.+10pf. violet and red 25 25
E688 – 25pf.+10pf. green and blue . . . . 4·25 7·00
DESIGNS: 20pf. Dederon kerchief exercises; 25pf. Relay-racing.

1963. 75th Anniv of "Internationale" (song).
E689 E **232** 20pf. black and red 20 30
E690 – 25pf. black and blue 1·30 3·00
DESIGN: 25pf. As 20pf. but portrait of P.-C. Degeyter.

E **233** V. Tereshkova   E **234** V. Bykovsky and "Vostok 6" and "Vostok 5"

1963. 2nd "Team" Manned Space Flights.
E691 E **233** 20pf. black, grey & bl 90 25
E692 E **234** 20pf. black, grey & bl 90 25
Nos. E691/2 were printed together, se-tenant, forming a composite design.

E **235** Motor Cyclist competing in "Motocross", Apolda   E **236** Treblinka Memorial

1963. World Motor Cycle Racing Championships.
E693 E **235** 10pf. emerald & green 4·00 8·25
E694 – 20pf. red and pink . . 25 35
E695 – 25pf. blue & light blue 25 35
DESIGNS—HORIZ (39 × 22 mm): 20pf. Motor cyclist; 25pf. Two motor cyclists cornering.

1963. Erection of Treblinka Memorial, Poland.
E696 E **236** 20pf. blue and red . . 35 35

E **237** Transport   E **238** Transport

1963. Leipzig Autumn Fair.
E697 E **237** 10pf. multicoloured 90 25
E698 E **238** 10pf. multicoloured 90 25
Nos. E697/8 were printed together, se-tenant, forming a composite design.

1963. Fauna Protection Campaign (2nd series). As Type E **201**. Fauna in natural colours, background colours given.
E699 10pf. green 15 25
E700 20pf. red 15 25
E701 30pf. red 25 35
E702 50pf. blue . . . . 4·00 7·75
E703 70pf. brown . . . . 45 1·20
DESIGNS: 10pf. Stag-beetle; 20pf. Salamander; 30pf. European pond tortoise; 50pf. Green toad; 70pf. West European hedgehogs.

1963. Concentration Camps Memorial Fund. Sportsmen Victims (2nd series). As Type E **230**. Designs in black.
E704 5pf.+5pf. yellow 15 40
E705 10pf.+5pf. green 15 40
E706 15pf.+5pf. violet 15 40
E707 20pf. 10pf. red 15 40
E708 40pf.+20pf. blue . . . . . 3·75 12·50
SPORTSMEN: 5pf. H. Tops (Gymnast); 10pf. Kate Tucholla (hockey-player); 15pf. R. Seiffert (swimmer); 20pf. E. Grube (athlete); 40pf. K. Biedermann (canoeist).

E **239** N. von Gneisenau and G. L. von Blucher

1963. 150th Anniv of German War of Liberation.
E709 E **239** 5pf. black, buff & yell 15 25
E710 – 10pf. black, buff & grn 15 25
E711 – 20pf. blk, buff & orge 25 25
E712 – 25pf. black, buff & bl 25 25
E713 – 40pf. black, buff & red . . . . 2·75 2·40
DESIGNS: 10pf. "Cossacks and (German) Soldiers in Berlin" (Ludwig Wolf); 20pf. E. M. Arndt and Baron vom Stein; 25pf. Lutzow corps in battle order (detail from painting by Hans Kohlschein); 40pf. G. von Scharnhorst and Prince Kutuzov.

E **240** V. Tereshkova   E **241** Synagogue aflame

1963. Visit of Soviet Cosmonauts to East Berlin.
E714 E **240** 10pf. green and blue 15 25
E715 – 20pf. black, red & buff 25 25
E716 – 20pf. green, red & buff 25 25
E717 – 25pf. orange and blue 4·50 5·25
DESIGNS—SQUARE: No. E717, Tereshkova in capsule. VERT: (24 × 32 mm). No. E715, Tereshkova with bouquet; No. E716, Gagarin (visit to Berlin).

1963. 25th Anniv of "Kristallnacht" (Nazi pogrom).
E718 E **241** 10pf. multicoloured 35 65

E **242** Letter-sorting Machine

1963. Stamp Day. Multicoloured.
E719 10pf. Type E **242** . . . . 1·90 5·00
E720 20pf. Fork-lift truck loading mail train 25 35

E **243** Ski Jumper commencing Run   E **244** "Vanessa atlanta"

1963. Winter Olympic Games, Innsbruck, 1964. Rings in different colours; skier in black.
E721 E **243** 5pf. yellow 15 25
E722 – 10pf. green 15 25
E723 – 20pf.+10pf. red . . . 20 25
E724 – 25pf. blue . . . . . . 2·30 5·00
DESIGNS: Ski jumper—10pf. Taking-off; 20pf. In mid-air; 25pf. Landing.

1964. Butterflies. Butterflies in natural colours; inscr in black.
E725 E **244** 10pf. olive 45 25
E726 – 15pf. lilac 45 25
E727 – 20pf. orange 45 25
E728 – 25pf. blue 45 25
E729 – 40pf. blue . . . . . 5·75 5·25
BUTTERFLIES: 15pf. "Parnassius phoebus"; 20pf. "Papilio machaon"; 25pf. "Colius croceus"; 40pf. "Nymphalis polychloros".

E **245** Shakespeare (b. 1564)

1964. Cultural Anniversaries.
E730 – 20pf. blue and pink 15 25
E731 – 25pf. purple and blue 15 25
E732 E **245** 40pf. blue and lilac . . 1·60 2·50
DESIGNS: 20pf. Quadriga, Brandenburg Gate (J. G. Schadow, sculptor, b. 1764); 25pf. Portal keystone, German Historical Museum (A. Schluter, sculptor, b. 1664).

E **246** "Elektrotecknik" Hall

1964. Leipzig Spring Fair.
E733 E **246** 10pf. black and green 3·25 50
E734 – 20pf. black and red 3·25 50
DESIGN: 20pf. Braunigkes Hof, c. 1700.

E **247** A. Saefkow

1964. Concentration Camp Victims. Memorials Fund.
E735 E **247** 5pf.+5pf. brown & bl 20 25
E736 – 10pf.+5pf. brn & ol 20 25
E737 – 15pf.+5pf. brn & vio 20 25
E738 – 20pf.+5pf. olive and red 30 30
E739 – 25pf.+10pf. blue & ol 40 55
E740 – 40pf.+10pf. ol & brn 1·60 3·75
PORTRAITS—As Type E **247**: 10pf. F. Jacob; 15pf. B. Bastlein; 20pf. H. Schulze-Boysen; 25pf. Dr. A. Kuckhoff. (49 × 27½ mm): 40pf. Dr. A. and Mildred Harnack.

E **248** Mr. Khrushchev with East German Officials

E **249** Boys and Girls

1964. Mr. Khrushchev's 70th Birthday.
E741 E **248** 25pf. blue 25 25
E742 – 40pf. black and purple 2·75 5·00
DESIGN: 40pf. Mr. Khrushchev with cosmonauts Tereshkova and Gagarin.

1964. German Youth Meeting, Berlin. Multicoloured.
E743 10pf. Type E **249** 15 25
E744 20pf. Young gymnasts . . . 15 25
E745 25pf. Youth with accordion and girl with flowers . . 1·90 2·20

E **250** Flax, Krumel and Struppi, the dog

1964. Children's Day. Multicoloured.
E746 5pf. Type E **250** 15 25
E747 10pf. Master Nadelohr . . 15 25
E748 15pf. Pittiplatsch 15 25
E749 20pf. Sandmannschen (sandman) 15 25
E750 40pf. Bummi (teddy bear) and Schnatterinchen (duckling) . . . . 2·20 3·50
The designs show characters from children's T.V. programmes.

E **251** Governess and Child (with portrait of Jenny Marx)

1964. East German Women's Congress. Mult.
E751 20pf. Type E **251** 15 25
E752 25pf. Switchboard technicians . . . . 1·40 2·10
E753 70pf. Farm girls 30 25

E **252** Cycling

E **253** Diving

1964. Olympic Games, Tokyo. Multicoloured. (a) 1st Series. As Type E **252**.
E754 5pf. Type E **252** 15 25
E755 10pf. Volleyball 15 25
E756 20pf. Judo 15 25
E757 25pf. Diving 15 25
E758 40pf.+20pf. Running . . . 35 50
E759 70pf. Horse-jumping . . . 2·30 3·75

(b) 2nd Series. As Type E **253**.
E760 10pf. Type E **253** . . . . 3·25 6·25
E761 10pf.+5pf. Horse-jumping 3·25 6·25
E762 10pf. Volleyball . . . . . . 3·25 6·25
E763 10pf. Cycling . . . . 3·25 6·25
E764 10pf.+5pf. Running . . . . 3·25 6·25
E765 10pf. Judo . . . . 3·25 6·25
Nos. E760/5 were printed together in se-tenant blocks of six (3 × 2) within sheets of 60 (6 × 10), and with an overall pattern of the five Olympic "rings" in each block.

E **254** Young Artists

1964. 5th Young Pioneers' Meeting, East Berlin. Multicoloured.
E766 10pf.+5pf. Type E **254** . . 1·20 35
E767 20pf.+10pf. Planting tree . . 1·20 35
E768 25pf.+10pf. Playing with ball . . . . 3·75 6·00

E **255** Leningrad Memorial

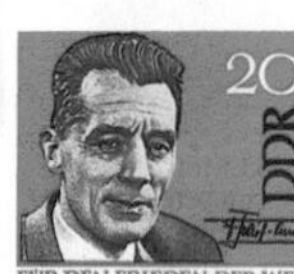

E **256** F. Joliot-Curie

1964. Victims of Leningrad Siege Commem.
E769 E **255** 25pf. black, yellow and blue . . . . . 1·20 40

1964. "World Peace".
E770 E **256** 20pf. sepia and red . . 25 30
E771 – 25pf. black and blue 25 30
E772 – 50pf. black and lilac 1·80 2·00
PORTRAITS (Campaigners for "World Peace"): 25pf. B. von Suttner; 50pf. C. von Ossietzky.

E **257** Ancient Glazier's Shop

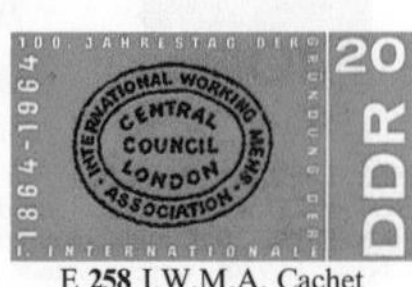

E **258** I.W.M.A. Cachet

1964. Leipzig Autumn Fair. Multicoloured.
E773 10pf. Type E **257** 80 25
E774 15pf. Jena glass factory . . 80 25

1964. Centenary of "First International".
E775 E **258** 20pf. black and red 20 25
E776 25pf. black and blue 80 1·40

E **259** "Rostock Port" Stamp of 1958

E **260** Modern Buildings and Flag ("Reconstruction")

1964. National Stamp Exn, East Berlin.
E777 E **259** 10pf.+5pf. green and orange 25 25
E778 – 20pf.+10pf. blue and purple 30 35
E779 – 50pf. brown and grey 2·50 3·50
DESIGNS: 20pf., 12pf. "Peace" stamp of 1950; 50pf., 5pf. "Dresden Paintings" stamp of 1955.

1964. 15th Anniv of German Democratic Republic. Multicoloured.
E780 10pf. Type E **260** 30 35
E781 10pf. Surveyor and conveyor ("Coal") . . . 30 35
E782 10pf. Scientist and chemical works ("Chemical Industry") 30 35
E783 10pf. Guard and chemical works ("Chemical Industry") 30 35
E784 10pf. Milkmaid and dairy pen ("Agriculture") . . . 30 35
E785 10pf. Furnaceman and mills ("Steel") 30 35
E786 10pf. Student with microscope, and lecture hall ("Education") . . . 30 35
E787 10pf. Operator and lathe ("Engineering") 30 35
E788 10pf. Scientist and planetarium ("Optics") 30 35
E789 10pf. Girl with cloth, and loom ("Textiles") 30 35
E790 10pf. Docker and ship at quayside ("Shipping") . . 30 35
E791 10pf. Leipzig buildings and "businessmen" formed of Fair emblem ("Exports") 30 35
E792 10pf. Building worker and flats ("New Construction") 30 35
E793 10pf. Sculptor modelling and Dresden gateway ("Culture") 30 35
E794 10pf. Girl skier and holiday resort ("Recreation") . . 30 35
MSE794a 210 × 285 mm. Nos. E780/94 . . . . 55·00 75·00

E **261** Monchgut (Rugen) Costume

E **262** Dr. Schweitzer and Lambarene River

1964. Provincial Costumes (1st series). Mult.
E795 5pf. Type E **261** . . . . 14·00 16·00
E796 5pf. Monchgut (male) . . . 14·00 16·00
E797 10pf. Spreewald (female) . . 45 35
E798 10pf. Spreewald (male) . . . 45 35
E799 20pf. Thuringen (female) . . 45 50
E800 20pf. Thuringen (male) . . 45 50
See Nos. E932/7 and E1073/6.

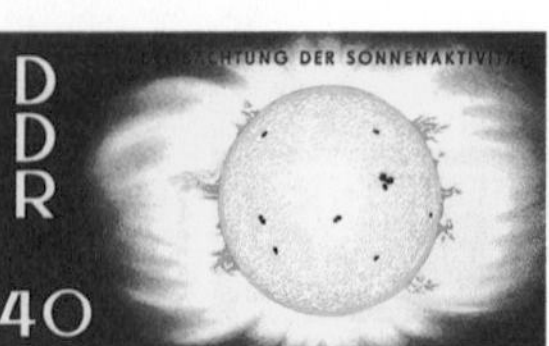

E **261a** Observation of Sun's Activity

1964. Quiet Sun Year. Three sheets, each 108 × 90 mm incorporating stamp as Type E **261a**. Multicoloured.
MSE801 (a) 25pf. Rocket over part of Earth. (b) 40pf. Type E **261a**. (c) 70pf. Earth and rocket routes 10·00 14·00

1965. 90th Birthday of Dr. Albert Schweitzer.
E802 E **262** 10pf. yellow, blk & grn 25 25
E803 – 20pf. yellow, blk & red 30 25
E804 – 25pf. yellow, blk & bl 3·50 5·00
DESIGNS: 20pf. Schweitzer and "nuclear disarmament" marchers; 25pf. Schweitzer and part of a Bach organ prelude.

1965. As Nos. E586/7 but values expressed in "MDN" (Deutschen Notenbank Marks) instead of "DM".
E805 1MDN. green 65 75
E806 2MDN. brown . . . . . . 75 1·00

E **263** A. Bebel

E **264** Fair Medal (obverse)

1965. 125th Birth Anniv of August Bebel (founder of Social Democratic Party).
E807 E **263** 20pf. yellow, brn & red 50 35
See also Nos. E814/15, E839, E842 and E871.

1965. Leipzig Spring Fair and 800th Anniv of Leipzig Fair.
E808 E **264** 10pf. gold and mauve 25 25
E809 – 15pf. gold and mauve 25 25
E810 – 25pf. multicoloured 70 55
DESIGNS: 15pf. Fair medal (reverse); 25pf. Chemical Works.

E **265** Giraffe

E **266** Belyaev and Leonov

1965. 10th Anniv of East Berlin Zoo.
E811 E **265** 10pf. grey and green 15 25
E812 – 25pf. grey and blue 30 30
E813 – 30pf. grey and sepia 2·75 3·50
ANIMALS—HORIZ: 25pf. Iguana; 30pf. Black wildebeest.

1965. 120th Birth Anniv of W. C. Rontgen (physicist). As Type E **263** but portrait of Rontgen.
E814 10pf. yellow, brown and green 60 35

1985. 700th Birth Anniv of Dante. As Type E **263** but portrait of Dante.
E815 50pf. yellow, brown & lemon . . . . 1·60 35

1965. Space Flight of "Voskhod 2".
E816 E **266** 10pf. red 35 35
E817 – 25pf. blue . . . . . . 2·50 3·75
DESIGN: 25pf. Leonov in space.

E **267** Boxing Gloves

E **269** Transmitter Aerial and Globe

E **268** Dimitrov denouncing Fascism

1965. European Boxing Championships, Berlin.
E818 E **267** 10pf.+5pf. mult . . . 25 25
E819 – 20pf. gold, black and red . . . . 90 1·60
DESIGN: 20pf. Boxing glove.

1965. 20th Anniv of Liberation. Multicoloured.
E820 5pf.+5pf. Type E **268** . . . 15 25
E821 10pf.+5pf. Distributing "Communist Manifesto" 15 25
E822 15pf.+5pf. Soldiers of International Brigade fighting in Spain 15 25
E823 20pf.+10pf. "Freedom for Ernst Thalmann" demonstration 15 25

E824 25pf.+10pf. Founding of "Free Germany" National Committee (Moscow) 20 25
E825 40pf. Ulbricht and Weinert distributing "Manifesto" on Eastern Front 20 25
E826 50pf. Liberation of concentration camps . . 25 25
E827 60pf. Hoisting Red Flag on Reichstag . . . . 2·75 4·75
E828 70pf. Bilateral demonstration of Communist and Socialist parties 30 30

1965. 20th Anniv of East German Broadcasting Service.
E829 E **269** 20pf. black, red and cerise 25 25
E830 – 40pf. black and blue 1·80 1·10
DESIGN: 40pf. Radio workers.

E **270** I.T.U. Emblem and Radio Circuit Diagram
E **271** F.D.G.B. Emblem

1965. Centenary of I.T.U.
E831 E **270** 20pf. black, yell & ol 45 25
E832 – 25pf. black, mve & vio . . . . 2·75 1·10
DESIGN: 25pf. I.T.U. emblem and switch diagram.

1965. 20th Anniv of Free German (F.D.G.B.) and World Trade Unions.
E833 E **271** 20pf. gold and red . . 25 25
E834 – 25pf. black, bl & gold 1·40 90
DESIGN—HORIZ (39×21½ mm): 25pf. Workers of "two hemispheres" (inscr "20 JAHRE WELTGEWERKSCHAFTSBUND").

E **272** Industrial Machine
E **273** Marx and Lenin

1965. 800th Anniv of Karl-Marx-Stadt (formerly Chemnitz).
E835 E **272** 10pf. green and gold 25 25
E836 – 20pf. red and gold . . 25 25
E837 – 25pf. blue and gold 1·60 1·10
DESIGNS: 20pf. Red Tower, Chemnitz; 25pf. Town Hall, Chemnitz.

1965. Socialist Countries' Postal Ministers Conference, Peking.
E838 E **273** 20pf. black, yell & red 35 35

1965. 90th Birth Anniv of Dr. Wilhelm Kulz (politician). As Type E **263** but portrait of Kulz.
E839 25pf. yellow, brown and blue . . . . 1·20 35

E **274** Congress Emblem

1965. World Peace Congress, Helsinki.
E840 E **274** 10pf.+5pf. green and blue 15 25
E841 20pf.+5pf. blue and red 65 80

1965. 75th Birth Anniv of Erich Weinert (poet). As Type E **263**, but portrait of Weinert.
E842 40pf. yellow, brown and red 60 35

1965. "Help for Vietnam". Surch **Hilfe fur VIETNAM +10**.
E843 E **260** 10pf.+10pf. mult . . . 50 35

E **276** Rebuilt Weigh-house and Modern Buildings, Katharinenstrasse

1965. 800th Anniv of Leipzig.
E844 E **276** 10pf. purple, bl & gold 15 25
E845 – 25pf. orge, sep & gold 25 25
E846 – 40pf. multicoloured 30 25
E847 – 70pf. blue and gold 2·40 1·90
DESIGNS: 25pf. Old Town Hall; 40pf. Opera House and new G.P.O.; 70pf. "Stadt Leipzig" Hotel.

E **277** "Praktica" and "Praktisix" Cameras
E **278** Show Jumping

1965. Leipzig Autumn Fair.
E848 E **277** 10pf. blk, gold & grn 15 25
E849 – 15pf. multicoloured 15 25
E850 – 25pf. multicoloured 85 50
DESIGNS: 15pf. Clavichord and electric guitar; 25pf. "Zeiss" microscope.

1965. Leipzig Philatelic Exhibition, "INTERMESS III". Nos. E844/7 in two miniature sheets each 137×99 mm.
MSE851 (a) Nos. E844 and E847. (b) Nos. E845/6 (sold for 1 MDN.75) . . . . 5·75 5·75

1965. World Modern Pentathlon Championships, Leipzig. Multicoloured.
E852 10pf. Type E **278** 25 25
E853 10pf. Swimming 25 25
E854 10pf. Running . . . . . . 3·25 5·50
E855 10pf.+5pf. Fencing 25 25
E856 10pf.+5pf. Pistol-shooting 25 25

E **279** E. Leonov
E **280** Memorial at Putten, Netherlands

1965. Soviet Cosmonauts Visit to East Germany.
E857 E **279** 20pf. blue, silver & red . . . . 70 1·40
E858 – 20pf. blue, silver & red . . . . 70 1·40
E859 – 25pf. multicoloured 70 1·40
DESIGNS—As Type E **275**. No. E858, Belyaev. HORIZ (48×29 mm): No. E859, "Voskhod 2" and Leonov in space.

1965. Putten War Victims Commem.
E860 E **280** 25pf. black, yell & bl 80 35

E **281** Stoking Furnace (from old engraving)
E **282** Red Kite

1965. Bicent of Mining School, Freiberg. Multicoloured.
E861 10pf. Type E **281** 20 25
E862 15pf. Mining ore (old engraving) . . . . 85 1·60
E863 20pf. Ore 20 25
E864 25pf. Sulphur 20 30

1965. Birds of Prey. Multicoloured.
E865 5pf. Type E **282** 20 25
E866 10pf. Lammergeier 20 25
E867 20pf. Common Buzzard . . 30 25
E868 25pf. Common Kestrel . . 30 25
E869 40pf. Northern Goshawk 45 50
E870 70pf. Golden Eagle . . . . 5·00 6·50

1965. 150th Birth Anniv of A. von Menzel (painter). As Type E **263** but portrait of Menzel.
E871 10pf. yellow, brown and red 80 35

E **283** Otto Grotewohl
E **285** Ladies' Single-seater
E **284** Extract from Newsletter

1965. Grotewohl Commemoration.
E872 E **283** 20f. black 80 35

1966. 50th Anniv of Spartacus Group Conference. Miniature sheet 138×98 mm. Type E **284** and similar horiz design.
MSE873 20pf. black and red (Type E **284**); 50pf. black and red (Karl Liebknecht and Rosa Luxemburg) . . . . 2·10 6·25

1966. World Tobogganing Championships, Friedrichroda.
E874 E **285** 10pf. green and olive 20 25
E875 – 20pf. blue and red . . 20 25
E876 – 25pf. indigo and blue 1·60 1·80
DESIGNS: 20pf. Men's double-seater; 25pf. Men's single seater.

E **286** Electronic Punch-card Computer

1966. Leipzig Spring Fair. Multicoloured.
E877 10pf. Type E **286** 25 25
E878 15pf. Drilling and milling plant . . . . 1·20 40

E **287** Soldier and National Gallery, Berlin
E **288** J. A. Smoler (Sorb patriot and savant)

1966. 10th Anniv of National People's Army.
E879 E **287** 5pf. black, olive & yell 15 25
E880 – 10pf. black, ol & yell 15 25
E881 – 20pf. black, ol & yell 25 25
E882 – 25pf. black, ol & yell 1·60 2·10
DESIGNS: Soldier and—10pf. Brandenburg Gate; 20pf. Industrial plant; 25pf. Combine-harvester.

1966. 150th Birth Anniv of Jan Smoler.
E883 E **288** 20pf. black, red & blue 20 25
E884 – 25pf. black, red & blue . . . . 70 1·10
DESIGN: 25pf. House of the Sorbs, Bautzen.

E **289** "Good Knowledge" Badge
E **290** "Luna 9" on Moon

1966. 20th Anniv of "Freie Deutsche Jugend" (Socialist Youth Movement).
E885 E **289** 20pf. multicoloured 70 35

1966. Moon Landing of "Luna 9".
E886 E **290** 20pf. multicoloured 2·75 65

E **291** Road Signs

1966. Road Safety.
E887 E **291** 10pf. red, bl & ultram 20 25
E888 – 15pf. black, yell & grn 20 25

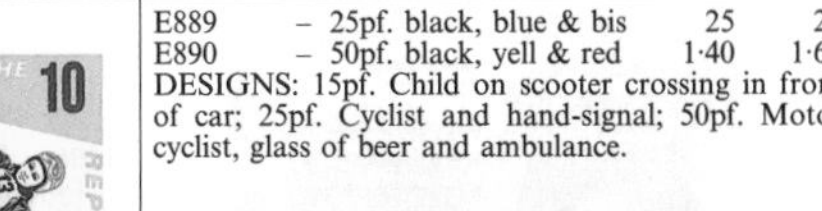

E889 – 25pf. black, blue & bis 25 25
E890 – 50pf. black, yell & red 1·40 1·60
DESIGNS: 15pf. Child on scooter crossing in front of car; 25pf. Cyclist and hand-signal; 50pf. Motor cyclist, glass of beer and ambulance.

E **292** Marx and Lenin Banner

1966. 20th Anniv of Socialist Unity Party (S.E.D.).
E891 – 5pf. multicoloured . . 15 25
E892 E **292** 10pf. yellow, blk & red 15 25
E893 – 15pf. black and green 20 25
E894 – 20pf. black and red 25 25
E895 – 25pf. black, yell & red 2·10 2·50
DESIGNS—VERT: 5pf. Party badge and demonstrators; 15pf. Marx, Engels and manifesto; 20pf. Pieck and Grotewohl. HORIZ: 25pf. Workers greeting Ulbricht.

E **293** W.H.O. Building

1966. Inaug of W.H.O. Headquarters, Geneva.
E896 E **293** 20pf. multicoloured 35 55

E **294** Spreewald

1966. National Parks. Multicoloured.
E897 10pf. Type E **294** 15 25
E898 15pf. Konigsstuhl (Isle of Rugen) 15 25
E899 20pf. Sachsische Schweiz . . 15 25
E900 25pf. Westdarss 25 25
E901 30pf. Teufelsmauer 25 35
E902 50pf. Feldberg Lakes . . . 2·30 2·30

E **295** Lace "Flower"
E **296** Lily of the Valley

1966. Plauen Lace. Floral Patterns as Type E **295**.
E903 E **295** 10pf. myrtle and green 15 25
E904 – 20pf. indigo and blue 15 25
E905 – 25pf. red and rose . . 25 25
E906 – 50pf. violet and lilac 2·75 2·75

1966. Int Horticultural Show, Erfurt. Mult.
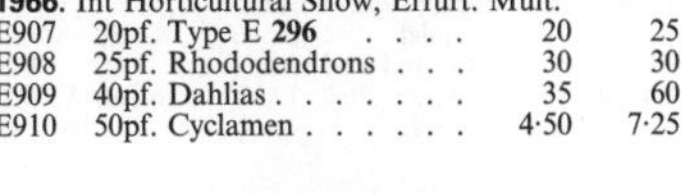
E907 20pf. Type E **296** 20 25
E908 25pf. Rhododendrons . . . 30 30
E909 40pf. Dahlias 35 60
E910 50pf. Cyclamen . . . . . . 4·50 7·25

E **297** Parachutist on Target

1966. 8th World Parachute Jumping Championships, Leipzig.
E911 E **297** 10pf. blue, black & bis 20 25
E912 – 15pf. multicoloured 80 1·40
E913 – 20pf. black, bistre & bl 25 25
DESIGNS: 15pf. Group descent; 20pf. Free fall.

E **298** Hans Kahle and Music of "The Thalmann Column"

1966. 30th Anniv of International Brigade in Spain. Multicoloured.

E914 5pf. Type E **298** 25 25
E915 10pf.+5pf. W. Bredel and open-air class 25 25
E916 15pf. H. Beimler and Madrid street-fighting . . 25 25
E917 20pf.+10pf. H. Rau and march-past after Battle of Brunete 25 25
E918 25pf.+10pf. H. Marchwitza and soldiers 25 25
E919 40pf.+10pf. A. Becker and Ebro battle . . . . . . 1·80 2·20

E **299** Canoeing

1966. World Canoeing Championships, Berlin. Multicoloured.

E920 10pf.+5pf. Type E **299** . . 25 25
E921 15pf. Kayak doubles . . . 1·50 2·30

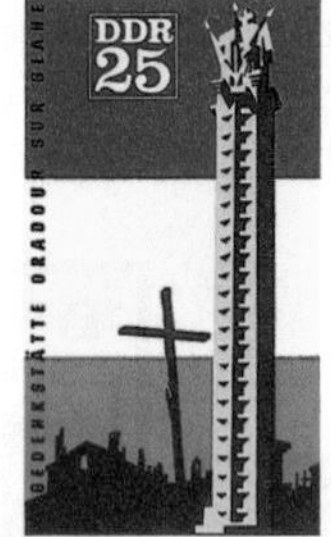

E **300** Television Set

1966. Leipzig Autumn Fair. Multicoloured.

E922 10pf. Type E **300** 55 25
E923 15pf. Electric typewriter . . 1·30 55

E **301** Oradour Memorial

1966. Oradour-sur-Glane War Victims Commem.

E924 E **301** 25pf. black, blue & red 35 30

E **302** "Blood Donors"

1966. International Health Co-operation.

E925 E **302** 5pf. red and green . . 15 25
E926 – 20pf.+10pf. red and violet 30 25
E927 – 40pf. red and blue . . 1·80 1·20

DESIGNS—HORIZ: 20pf. I.C.Y. emblem. VERT: 40pf. Health symbol.

E **303** Weightlifting ("snatch")

E **304** Congress Hall

1966. World and European Weightlifting Championships, Berlin.

E928 E **303** 15pf. black and brown 1·80 3·00
E929 – 20pf.+5pf. black and blue 35 35

DESIGN: 20pf. Weightlifting ("jerk").

1966. 6th Int Journalists' Congress, Berlin.

E930 E **304** 10pf. multicoloured 55 75
E931 – 20pf. yellow and blue 25 25

DESIGN—VERT: 20pf. Emblem of Int Organization of journalists.

1966. Provincial Costumes (2nd series). As Type E **261**. Multicoloured.

E932 5pf. Altenburg (female) . . 35 35
E933 10pf. Altenburg (male) . . . 35 35
E934 10pf. Mecklenburg (female) 35 35
E935 15pf. Mecklenburg (male) 35 35
E936 20pf. Magdeburger Borde (female) . . . . 2·30 4·75
E937 30pf. Magdeburger Borde (male) . . . . 2·30 4·75

E **305** "Vietnam is Invincible"

1966. Aid for Vietnam.

E938 E **305** 20pf.+5pf. black and pink 40 50

E **306** Oil Rigs and Pipeline Map

1966. Inaug of Int "Friendship" Oil Pipeline.

E939 E **306** 20pf. black and red 25 25
E940 – 25pf. black and blue 1·10 80

DESIGN: 25pf. "Walter Ulbricht" Oil Works, Leuna and pipeline map.

E **307** Black Phantom Tetra

1966. Aquarium Fishes. Multicoloured.

E941 5pf. Type E **307** 15 25
E942 10pf. Cardinal tetra 15 25
E943 15pf. Rio Grande cichlid . . 3·00 4·50
E944 20pf. Blue gularis 20 25
E945 25pf. Ramirez's dwarf cichlid 25 25
E946 40pf. Honey gourami . . . 30 50

E **308** "Horse" (detail from Ishtar Gate)

1966. Babylonian Art Treasures, Vorderasiatisches Museum, Berlin. Multicoloured.

E947 10pf. Type E **308** 15 25
E948 20pf. Mythological animal, Ishtar Gate 15 25
E949 25pf. Lion facing right (vert) 25 30
E950 50pf. Lion facing left (vert) 85 2·40

E **309** The Wartburg from the East

E **310** "Gentiana pneumonanthe"

1966. 900th Anniv of Wartburg Castle.

E951 E **309** 10pf.+5pf. slate . . . 15 25
E952 – 20pf. green 20 25
E953 – 25pf. purple 75 90

DESIGNS: 20pf. Castle bailiwick; 25pf. Residence.

1966. Protected Plants (1st series). Mult.

E954 10pf. Type E **310** 15 25
E955 20pf. "Cephalanthera rubra" 25 25
E956 25pf. "Arnica montana" . . . 1·80 2·10

See also Nos. E1177/82 and E1284/9.

E **311** Son leaves Home

E **312** Worlitz Castle

1966. Fairy Tales (1st series). "The Wishing Table". Multicoloured.

E957 5pf. Type E **311** 25 75
E958 10pf. Setting the table . . . 25 75
E959 20pf. The thieving inn-keeper . . . . 70 1·50
E960 25pf. The magic donkey . . 70 1·50
E961 30pf. The cudgel in the sack 25 75
E962 50pf. Return of the son . . 25 75

See also Nos. E1045/50, E1147/52, E1171/6, E1266/71, E1437/42, E1525/30, E1623/8, E1711/16, E1811/13, E1902/7, E1996/2001 and E2092/7.

1967. Principal East German Buildings. (1st series). Multicoloured.

E964 5pf. Type E **312** 15 25
E965 10pf. Stralsund Town Hall (vert) 15 25
E966 15pf. Chorin Monastery (vert) 25 25
E967 20pf. Ribbeck House, Berlin 25 25
E968 25pf. Moritzburg, Zeitz (vert) 25 25
E969 40pf. Old Town Hall, Potsdam (vert) . . . . . 1·80 2·10

See also Nos. E1100/3 and E1155/60.

E **313** Rifle-shooting

1967. World Biathlon Championships, Altenburg.

E970 E **313** 10pf. blue, drab & mve 15 25
E971 – 20pf. olive, blue & grn 20 25
E972 – 25pf. green, blue & ol 1·10 1·20

DESIGNS: 20pf. Shooting on skis; 25pf. Riflemen racing on skis.

E **314** "Multilock" Loom

1967. Leipzig Spring Fair.

E973 E **314** 10pf. green, grey & pur 25 25
E974 – 15pf. bistre & blue . . 1·10 30

DESIGN: 15pf. Zeiss tracking telescope.

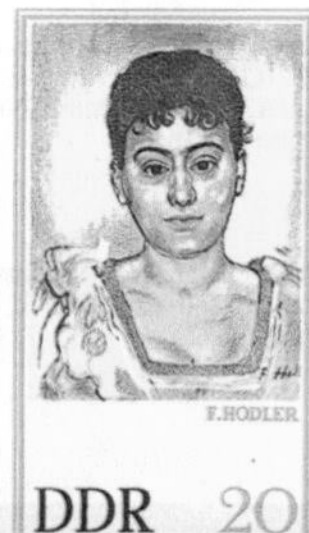

E **315** Mother and Child

E **317** "Portrait of a Girl" (after F Hodler)

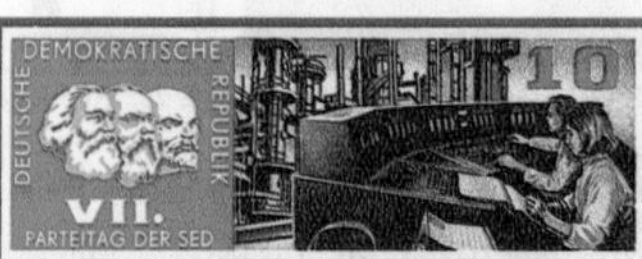

E **316** Industrial Control Desk

1967. 20th Anniv of German Democratic Women's Federation.

E975 E **315** 20pf. grey, red and purple 25 35
E976 – 25pf. brown, turquoise and brown . . . . 90 1·70

DESIGN: 25pf. Professional woman.

1967. Socialist Party Rally. Multicoloured.(a) 1st series.

E977 10pf. Type E **316** 15 25
E978 20pf. Ulbricht meeting workers 15 25
E979 25pf. Servicemen guarding industrial plants 20 30
E980 40pf. Agricultural workers and harvesters . . . . . 85 1·50

Each with inset portraits of Marx, Engels and Lenin.

(b) 2nd series. As Type E **316** but vert.

E981 5pf. Agricultural worker . . 15 25
E982 10pf. Teacher and pupil . . 15 25
E983 15pf. Socialist family . . . 45 85
E984 20pf. Servicemen 20 30

Each with inset portraits as above.

1967. Dresden Gallery Paintings (1st series). Multicoloured.

E985 20pf. Type E **317** 15 25
E986 25pf. "Peter at the Zoo" (H. Hakenbeck) 15 25
E987 30pf. "Venetian Episode" (R. Bergander) 25 25
E988 40pf. "Tahitian Women" (Gauguin) (horiz) 25 30
E989 50pf. "The Grandchild" (J. Scholtz) . . . . 2·50 4·00
E990 70pf. "Cairn in the Snow" (C. D. Friedrich) (horiz) 30 35

See also Nos. E1114/19 and E1249/54.

E **318** Barn Owl

E **319** Cycle Wheels

1967. Protected Birds. Multicoloured.

E991 5pf. Type E **318** 15 25
E992 10pf. Common Crane . . . 15 25
E993 20pf. Peregrine Falcon . . . 25 25
E994 25pf. Northern bullfinches 25 25
E995 30pf. River kingfisher . . . 4·50 5·75
E996 40pf. European roller . . . 45 30

1967. 20th Warsaw–Berlin–Prague Cycle Race.

E997 E **319** 10pf. violet, black and yellow 15 25
E998 – 25pf. red and blue . . 50 85

DESIGN: 25pf. Racing cyclists.

E **320** "Tom Cat"

1967. Int Children's Day. Multicoloured.

E 999 5pf. Type E **320** 15 25
E1000 10pf. "Snow White" . . . 15 25
E1001 15pf. "Fire Brigade" . . . 25 25
E1002 20pf. "Cockerel" 25 25
E1003 25pf. "Vase of Flowers" 25 45
E1004 30pf. "Children Playing with Ball" . . . . . . 1·30 1·70

E **321** "Girl with Grapes" (Gerard Dou)

E **322** Exhibition Emblem

1967. Paintings Missing from German National Galleries (after World War II).

E1005 E **321** 5pf. blue 15 25
E1006 – 10pf. brown 15 25
E1007 – 20pf. green 20 30
E1008 – 25pf. purple 25 30
E1009 – 40pf. olive 25 30
E1010 – 50pf. sepia . . . . 2·10 3·00

DESIGNS—VERT: 25pf. "Portrait of W Schroeder-Devrient" (after K. Begas); 40pf. "Young Girl in Straw Hat" (after S. Bray); 50pf. "The Four Evangelists" (after Jordaens). HORIZ: 5pf. "Three Horsemen" (after Rubens); 20pf. "Spring Idyll" (after H. Thoma).

1967. 15th Agricultural Exn, Markkleeberg.

E1011 E **322** 20pf. red, green and yellow 30 35

E 323 Marie Curie (Birth Cent) E 324 Jack of Diamonds

1967. Birth Anniversaries.
E1012 – 5pf. brown 15 25
E1013 E 323 10pf. blue 15 25
E1014 – 20pf. red 20 25
E1015 – 25pf. sepia 25 25
E1016 – 40pf. green . . . . . 1·20 1·40
PORTRAITS: 5pf. G. Herwegh (poet—150th); 20pf. Kathe Kollwitz (artist—cent); 25pf. J. J. Winckelmann (archaeologist—250th); 40pf. T. Storm (poet—150th).

1967. German Playing-cards. Multicoloured.
E1017 5pf. Type E **324** 15 25
E1018 10pf. Jack of Hearts . . . 15 25
E1019 20pf. Jack of Spades . . . 25 25
E1020 25pf. Jack of Clubs . . . 6·50 6·75

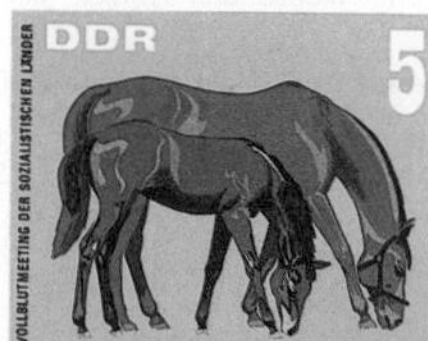

E 325 Mare and Filly

1967. Thoroughbred Horse Meeting, Berlin. Multicoloured.
E1021 5pf. Type E **325** 25 25
E1022 10pf. Stallion 25 25
E1023 20pf. Horse-racing 30 25
E1024 50pf. Two fillies (vert) . . 3·75 4·75

E 326 Kitchen Equipment E 328 Kragujevac Memorial

E 327 Max Reichpietsch and "Friedrich der Grosse" (battleship), 1914–18

1967. Leipzig Autumn Fair. Multicoloured.
E1025 10pf. Type E **326** 45 30
E1026 15pf. Fur coat and "Interpelz" brand-mark 1·30 75

1967. 50th Anniv of Revolutionary Sailors' Movement. Multicoloured.
E1027 10pf. Type E **327** 25 25
E1028 15pf. Albin Kobis and "Prinzregent Luitpold" (battleship), 1914–18 . . 1·60 1·20
E1029 20pf. Sailors' demonstration and "Seydlitz" (battle cruiser), 1914–18 . . . . 45 25

1967. Victims of Kragujevac (Yugoslavia) Massacre.
E1030 E **328** 25pf. black, yellow and red 95 55

E 329 Worker and Dam ("Electrification") E 330 Martin Luther (from engraving by Lucas Cranach the Elder)

1967. 50th Anniv of October Revolution.
E1031 – 5pf. black, orange and red 20 25
E1032 E **329** 10pf. black, red and bistre 20 25
E1033 – 15pf. black, red and grey 20 25
E1034 – 20pf. black, red and orange 30 25
E1035 – 40pf. black, red and orange . . . . . 3·50 4·50
MSE1036 127×83 mm. Nos. E1034/5. Imperf (sold for 85pf.) 1·40 4·50
DESIGNS: 5pf. Worker and newspaper headline "Hands off Soviet Russia!"; 15pf. Treptow Memorial ("Victory over Fascism"); 20pf. German and Soviet soldiers ("Friendship"); 40pf. Lenin and "Aurora" (Russian cruiser) . Each with hammer and sickle.

1967. 450th Anniv of Reformation.
E1037 E **330** 20pf. black & mauve 25 25
E1038 – 25pf. black and blue 25 25
E1039 – 40pf. black and bistre . . . . . 2·50 2·20
DESIGNS—HORIZ: 25pf. Luther's house, Wittenberg. VERT: 40pf. Castle church, Wittenberg.

E 331 Young Workers E 332 Goethe's House, Weimar

1967. 10th "Masters of Tomorrow" Fair, Leipzig.
E1040 E **331** 20pf. black, gold and blue . . . . . . 55 1·20
E1041 – 20pf. black, gold and blue . . . . . . 55 1·20
E1042 – 25pf. multicoloured 55 1·20
DESIGNS—VERT: No. E1041, Young man and woman. HORIZ: (51×29 mm): No. E1042, Presentation of awards.

1967. Cultural Places.
E1043 E **332** 20pf. blk, brn & grey 30 25
E1044 – 25pf. olive, brn & yell . . . . . . 2·10 1·40
DESIGN: 25pf. Schiller's House, Weimar.

E 333 Queen and Courtiers E 335 Nutcracker and Two "Smokers"

E 334 Peasants and Modern Farm Buildings

1967. Fairy Tales (2nd series). "King Thrushbeard". Designs showing different scenes.
E1045 E **333** 5pf. multicoloured 25 75
E1046 – 10pf. multicoloured 25 75
E1047 – 15pf. multicoloured 90 1·70
E1048 – 20pf. multicoloured 90 1·70
E1049 – 25pf. multicoloured 25 75
E1050 – 30pf. multicoloured 25 75

1967. 15th Anniv of Agricultural Co-operatives.
E1052 E **334** 10pf. sepia, green and olive 35 35

1967. Popular Art of the Erzgebirge. Multicoloured.
E1053 10pf. Type E **335** 90 95
E1054 20pf. "Angel" and miner with candles (carved figures) 25 25

E 336 Ice Skating E 337 Actinometer

1968. Winter Olympic Games, Grenoble.
E1055 E **336** 5pf. blue, red and light blue 25 25
E1056 – 10pf.+5pf. blue, red and turquoise . . 25 25
E1057 – 15pf. multicoloured 25 25
E1058 – 20pf. ultramarine, red and blue . . . 25 25
E1059 – 25pf. multicoloured 25 35
E1060 – 30pf. ultramarine, red and blue . . . 4·00 3·00
DESIGNS: 10pf. Tobogganing; 15pf. Slalom; 20pf. Ice hockey; 25pf. Figure skating (pairs); 30pf. Cross-country skiing.

1968. 75th Anniv of Potsdam Meteorological Observatory and World Meteorological Day (23 March).
E1061 E **337** 10pf. blk, red & pur 45 1·00
E1062 – 20pf. multicoloured 45 1·00
E1063 – 25pf. blk, yell & grn 45 1·00
DESIGNS—VERT: 25pf. Cornfield by day and night. HORIZ—(50×28 mm): 20pf. Satellite picture of clouds.

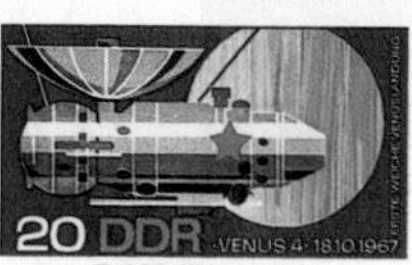

E 338 "Venus 4"

1968. Soviet Space Achievements. Mult.
E1064 20pf. Type E **338** 25 25
E1065 25pf. Coupled satellites "Cosmos 186" and "188" . . . . 1·30 1·20

E 339 "Illegal Struggle" (man, wife and child) E 341 Gorky

E 340 Type DE1 Diesel-electric Locomotive (built for Brazil)

1968. Stained-glass Windows, Sachsenhausen National Memorial Museum. Multicoloured.
E1066 10pf. Type E **339** 20 25
E1067 20pf. "Liberation" 20 25
E1068 25pf. "Partisans' Struggle" 65 80

1968. Leipzig Spring Fair. Multicoloured.
E1069 10pf. Type E **340** 45 35
E1070 15pf. Deep sea trawler . . 1·30 85

1968. Birth Cent of Maxim Gorky (writer).
E1071 E **341** 20pf. purple and red 25 35
E1072 – 25pf. purple and red 90 85
DESIGN: 25pf. Fulmar (from "Song of the Stormy Petrel"—poem).

1968. Provincial Costumes (3rd series). As Type E **261**. Multicoloured.
E1073 10pf. Hoyerswerda (female) 20 25
E1074 20pf. Schleife (female) . . 25 25
E1075 40pf. Crostwitz (female) 30 35
E1076 50pf. Spreewald (female) 3·25 2·40

E 342 Common Pheasants E 343 Karl Marx

1968. Small Game. Multicoloured.
E1077 10pf. Type E **342** 20 25
E1078 15pf. Grey Partridges . . . 25 25
E1079 20pf. Mallards 25 25
E1080 25pf. Greylag Geese . . . 25 25
E1081 30pf. Wood Pigeon . . . 25 35
E1082 40pf. Brown hares . . . . 4·00 12·50

1968. 150th Birth Anniv of Karl Marx.
E1083 – 10pf. black and green 30 85
E1084 E **343** 20pf. black, yell & red 30 85
E1085 – 25pf. blk, brn & yell 30 85
MSE1086 126×86 mm. Nos. E1083/5. Imperf . . . . 1·20 3·00
DESIGNS: 10pf. Title-page of "Communist Manifesto"; 25pf. Title-page of "Das Kapital".

E 344 "Fritz Heckert" (after E. Hering) E 345 Hammer and Anvil ("The right to work")

1968. 7th Confederation of Free German Trade Unions Congress. Multicoloured.
E1087 10pf. Type E **344** 20 25
E1088 20pf. Young workers and new tenements 35 65

1968. Human Rights Year.
E1089 E **345** 5pf. mauve & purple 15 25
E1090 – 10pf. bistre & brown 15 25
E1091 – 25pf. blue & turq . . 90 1·20
DESIGNS: 10pf. Tree and Globe ("The right to live"); 25pf. Dove and Sun ("The right to peace").

E 346 Vietnamese Mother and Child

1968. Aid for Vietnam.
E1092 E **346** 10pf.+5pf. mult . . . 30 25

E 347 Angling (World Angling Championships, Gustrow)

1968. Sporting Events.
E1093 E **347** 20pf. blue, grn & red 25 30
E1094 – 20pf. blue, turq & grn 25 30
E1095 – 20pf. purple, red & bl . . . . 90 1·10
DESIGNS: No. E1094, Sculling (European Women's Rowing Championships, Berlin); No. E1095, High jumping (2nd European Youth Athletic Competitions).

E 348 Brandenburg Gate and Torch E 349 Festival Emblem

1968. German Youth Sports Day. Mult.
E1096 10pf. Type E **348** 25 25
E1097 25pf. Stadium plan and torch . . . . 1·10 85

1968. Peace Festival, Sofia.
E1098 E **349** 20pf.+5pf. mult . . . 35 20
E1099 25pf. multicoloured 90 1·10

1968. Principal East German Buildings (2nd series). As Type E **312**. Multicoloured.
E1100 10pf. Town Hall, Wernigerode 15 25
E1101 20pf. Moritzburg Castle, Dresden 15 25
E1102 25pf. Town Hall, Greifswald 15 25
E1103 30pf. New Palace, Potsdam 95 2·10
DESIGN SIZES—VERT: 10pf., 25pf. (24×29 mm). HORIZ: 20pf., 30pf. (51½×29½ mm).

E 350 Walter Ulbricht

1968. 75th Birthday of Walter Ulbricht (Chairman of Council of State).
E1104 E **350** 20pf. black, red and orange 35 35

E 351 Ancient Rostock

1968. 750th Anniv of Rostock. Mult.

E1105 20pf. Type E **351** 20 25
E1106 25pf. Rostock, 1968 . . . 70 1·10

E **352** Dr K. Landsteiner (physician and pathologist, birth cent)

1968. Celebrities' Annivs. (1st series).

E1107 E **352** 10pf. grey 15 25
E1108 – 15pf. black 15 25
E1109 – 20pf. brown 25 25
E1110 – 25pf. blue 25 25
E1111 – 40pf. red . . . . . 1·20 1·40

DESIGNS: 15pf. Dr. E. Lasker (chess master, birth cent); 20pf. Hans Eisler (composer, 70th birth anniv); 25pf. Ignaz Semmelweis (physician, 150th birth anniv); 40pf. Max von Pettenkofer (hygienist, 150th birth anniv).

See also Nos. E1161/4 and E1256/61.

E **353** Zlin Z-226 Trener 6 DM-WKM looping

E **354** "At the Seaside" (Womacka)

1968. Aerobatics World Championships, Magdeburg. Multicoloured.

E1112 10pf. Type E **353** 15 25
E1113 25pf. Stunt flying . . . . 75 1·10

1968. Dresden Gallery Paintings (2nd series). Multicoloured.

E1114 10pf. Type E **354** 25 25
E1115 15pf. "Peasants Mowing Mountain Meadow" (Egger-Lienz) 25 25
E1116 20pf. "Portrait of a Farmer's Wife" (Liebl) (vert) 25 25
E1117 40pf. "Portrait of my Daughter" (Venturelli) (vert) 45 35
E1118 50pf. "High-School Girl" (Michaelis) (vert) . . . 45 60
E1119 70pf. "Girl with Guitar" (Castelli) (vert) . . . . 2·75 3·00

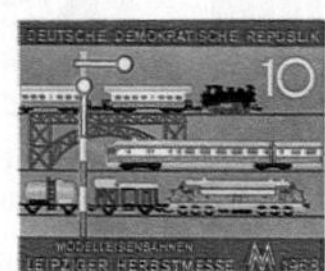

E **355** Model Trains

1968. Leipzig Autumn Fair.

E1120 E **355** 10pf. multicoloured 30 50

E **356** Spremberg Dam

1968. East German Post-War Dams. Multicoloured.

E1121 5pf. Type E **356** 15 25
E1122 10pf. Pohl Dam (vert) . . 15 25
E1123 15pf. Ohra Valley Dam (vert) . . . . 65 1·30
E1124 20pf. Rappbode Dam . . 30 35

E **357** Sprinting

1968. Olympic Games, Mexico. Multicoloured.

E1125 5pf. Type E **357** 15 25
E1126 10pf.+5pf. Pole-vaulting (vert) 15 25
E1127 20pf.+10pf. Football (vert) 25 25
E1128 25pf. Gymnastics (vert) . . 25 25
E1129 40pf. Water-polo (vert) . . 30 35
E1130 70pf. Sculling . . . . . . 1·80 3·00

E **358** Breendonk Memorial, Belgium

E **359** "Cicindela campestris"

1968. Breendonk War Victims Commem.

E1131 E **358** 25pf. multicoloured 35 30

1968. "Useful Beetles". Multicoloured.

E1132 10pf. Type E **359** 20 25
E1133 15pf. "Cychrus caraboides" 20 25
E1134 20pf. "Adalia bipunctata" 20 25
E1135 25pf. "Carabus arvensis" ("arcensis") . . . . . . 2·75 3·75
E1136 30pf. "Hister bipustulatus" 30 30
E1137 40pf. "Clerus mutillarius" ("Pseudoclerops mutillarius") 30 50

E **360** Lenin and Letter to Spartacus Group

1968. 50th Anniv of German November Revolution.

E1138 E **360** 10pf. black, red and yellow 15 25
E1139 – 20pf. black, red and yellow 15 25
E1140 – 25pf. black, red and yellow 55 80

DESIGNS: 20pf. Revolutionaries and title of Spartacus newspaper "Die Rote Fahne"; 25pf. Karl Liebknecht and Rose Luxemburg.

E **361** "Lailio-cattleya alba rubra" ("Maggie Raphaela")

1968. Orchids. Multicoloured.

E1141 5pf. Type E **361** 15 25
E1142 10pf. "Paphiopedilum albertianum" 15 25
E1143 15pf. "Cattleya fabia" . . 15 25
E1144 20pf. "Cattleya aclaniae" 20 25
E1145 40pf. "Sobralia macrantha" 30 50
E1146 50pf. "Dendrobium alpha" 2·75 3·50

E **362** Trying on the Boots

1968. Fairy Tales (3rd series). "Puss in Boots". As Type E **362**. Designs showing different scenes.

E1147 5pf. multicoloured . . . . 25 1·00
E1148 10pf. multicoloured . . . 25 1·00
E1149 15pf. multicoloured . . . 1·20 2·50
E1150 20pf. multicoloured . . . 1·20 2·50
E1151 25pf. multicoloured . . . 25 1·00
E1152 30pf. multicoloured . . . 25 1·00

E **363** Young Pioneers

1968. 20th Anniv of Ernst Thalmann's "Young Pioneers." Multicoloured.

E1153 10pf. Type E **363** 25 25
E1154 15pf. Young pioneers (diff) 90 65

1969. Principal East German Buildings (3rd series). As Type E **312**. Multicoloured.

E1155 5pf. Town Hall, Tangermunde (vert) . . 15 25
E1156 10pf. State Opera House, Berlin 15 25
E1157 20pf. Rampart Pavilion, Dresden Castle (vert) . . 15 25
E1158 25pf. Patrician's House, Luckau (vert) . . . . . 1·40 1·50
E1159 30pf. Dornburg Castle . . 25 30
E1160 40pf. "Zum Stockfisch" Inn, Erfurt (vert) . . . 30 30

1969. Celebrities' Annivs. (2nd series). As Type E **352**.

E1161 10pf. olive 15 25
E1162 20pf. brown 15 25
E1163 25pf. blue . . . . 1·10 85
E1164 40pf. brown 25 25

DESIGNS: 10pf. M. A. Nexo (Danish poet—birth cent.); 20pf. O. Nagel (painter—75th birth anniv); 25pf. A. von Humboldt (naturalist—bicent. of birth); 40pf. T. Fontane (writer—150th birth anniv).

E **364** Pedestrian Crossing

1969. Road Safety. Multicoloured.

E1165 5pf. Type E **364** 15 25
E1166 10pf. Traffic lights 15 25
E1167 20pf. Class 103 electric locomotive and railway crossing sign 25 25
E1168 25pf. Motor-vehicle overtaking 70 80

E **365** "E-512" Combine- harvester

1969. Leipzig Spring Fair. Multicoloured.

E1169 10pf. Type E **365** 15 25
E1170 15pf. "Planeta-Varianii" lithograph printing-press 30 50

E **366** Jorinde and Joringel

E **367** Spring Snowflake

1969. Fairy Tales (4th series). "Jorinde and Joringel". As Type E **366**, showing different scenes.

E1171 5pf. multicoloured 25 60
E1172 10pf. multicoloured . . . 25 60
E1173 15pf. multicoloured . . . 60 1·10
E1174 20pf. multicoloured . . . 60 1·10
E1175 25pf. multicoloured . . . 25 60
E1176 30pf. multicoloured . . . 25 60

1969. Protected Plants (2nd series). Mult.

E1177 5pf. Type E **367** 15 25
E1178 10pf. Yellow pheasant's-eye ("Adonis vernalis") 15 25
E1179 15pf. Globe flower ("Trollius europaeus") 15 25
E1180 20pf. Martagon lily ("Lilium martagon") . . 25 25
E1181 25pf. Sea holly ("Eryngium maritmum") . . . . . . 3·50 4·00
E1182 30pf. "Dactylorchis latifolia" 35 25

See also Nos. E1284/9.

E **368** Plantation of Young Conifers

E **369** Symbols of the Societies

1969. Forest Fires Prevention. Mult.

E1183 5pf. Type E **368** 15 25
E1184 10pf. Lumber, and resin extraction 25 25
E1185 20pf. Forest stream . . . 25 25
E1186 25pf. Woodland camp . . 2·10 1·40

1969. 50th Anniv of League of Red Cross Societies. Multicoloured.

E1187 10pf. Type E **369** 25 25
E1188 15pf. Similar design with symbols in oblong . . . 1·60 85

E **370** Erythrite (Schneeberg)

E **371** Women and Symbols

1969. East German Minerals. Multicoloured.

E1189 5pf. Type E **370** 15 25
E1190 10pf. Fluorite (Halsbrucke) 15 25
E1191 15pf. Galena (Neudorf) . . 15 25
E1192 20pf. Smoky Quartz (Lichtenberg) 20 25
E1193 25pf. Calcite (Niederrabenstein) . . . 1·20 1·80
E1194 50pf. Silver (Freiberg) . . 30 45

1969. 2nd D.D.R. Women's Congress.

E1195 E **371** 20pf. red and blue 25 25
E1196 – 25pf. blue and red 1·10 80

DESIGN: 25pf. Woman and Symbols (different).

1969. As Nos. E586/7 (Ulbricht), but with face values expressed in "M" (Mark).

E1197 1M. green . . . . 35 1·20
E1198 2M. brown . . . . 55 1·80

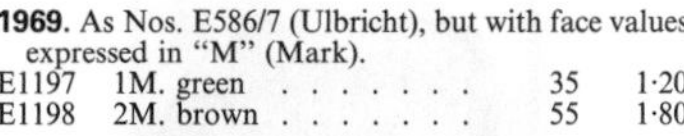

E **372** Badge of D.D.R. Philatelists' Association

E **373** Armed Volunteers

1969. 20th Anniv of D.D.R. Stamp Exhibition, Magdeburg (1st issue).

E1199 E **372** 10pf. gold, blue and red 30 35

See also Nos. E1233/4.

1969. Aid for Vietnam.

E1200 E **373** 10pf.+5pf. mult . . . 30 35

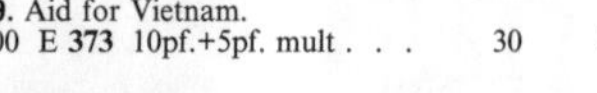

E **374** "Development of Youth"

E **375** Inaugural Ceremony

1969. Int Peace Meeting, East Berlin. Mult.

E1201 10pf. Type E **374** . . . . 85 1·90
E1202 20pf.+5pf. Berlin landmarks (50 × 28 mm) 85 1·90
E1203 25pf. "Workers of the World" . . . . 85 1·90

1969. 5th Gymnastics and Athletic Meeting, Leipzig. Multicoloured.

E1204 5pf. Type E **375** 15 25
E1205 10pf.+5pf. Gymnastics . . 15 25
E1206 15pf. Athletes' parade . . 25 25
E1207 20pf.+5pf. "Sport" Art Exhibition 25 25
E1208 25pf. Athletic events . . . 2·10 95
E1209 30pf. Presentation of colours 25 25

E **376** Pierre de Coubertin (from bust by W. Forster)

E **377** Knight

1969. 75th Anniv of Pierre de Coubertin's Revival of Olympic Games' Movement.

E1210 E **376** 10pf. sepia, black & bl 15 25
E1211 – 25pf. sepia, blk & red . . . . 1·20 90

DESIGN: 25pf. Coubertin monument, Olympia.

1969. World Sports Championships. Mult.

E1212 E **377** 20pf. gold, red & pur 25 30
E1213 – 20pf. multicoloured 25 30
E1214 – 20pf. multicoloured 25 30

DESIGNS AND EVENTS: No. E1212, 16th World Students' Team Chess Championship, Dresden; No. E1213, Cycle Wheel (World Covered Court Cycling Championships, Erfurt); No. E1214, Ball and net (2nd World Volleyball Cup).

E **378** Fair Display Samples

E **380** Flags and Rejoicing Crowd (½-size illustration)

E **379** Rostock

1969. Leipzig Autumn Fair.

E1215 E **378** 10pf. multicoloured 25 35

1969. 20th Anniv of German Democratic Republic. (1st issue). Multicoloured.

E1216 10pf. Type E **379** 20 25
E1217 10pf. Neubrandenburg . . 20 25
E1218 10pf. Potsdam 20 25
E1219 10pf. Eisenhuttenstadt . . 20 25
E1220 10pf. Hoyerswerda 20 25
E1221 10pf. Magdeburg 20 25
E1222 10pf. Halle-Neustadt . . . 20 25
E1223 10pf. Suhl 20 25
E1224 10pf. Dresden 20 25
E1225 10pf. Leipzig 20 25
E1226 10pf. Karl-Marx Stadt . . 20 25
E1227 10pf. East Berlin 20 25
MSE1228 88 × 110 mm. 1m. East Berlin and D.D.R. emblem (30 × 52 mm) . . . . 2·30 3·50

1969. 20th Anniv of German Democratic Republic (2nd issue). Sheet 110 × 154 mm.

MSE1229 E **380** 1m. multicoloured 1·80 2·10

E **381** T.V. Tower, East Berlin

1969. 20th Anniv of German Democratic Republic (3rd issue). Completion of East Berlin T.V. Tower. Type E **381** and similar vert designs. Multicoloured.

E1230 10pf. Type E **381** 20 25
E1231 20pf. "Globe" of Tower on T.V. screen 30 30
MSE1232 96 × 115 mm. 1m. T.V. Tower and receiver . . . . . 75 1·40

The design of No. **MS**E1232 is larger, 21½ × 60½ mm.

E **382** O. von Guericke Memorial, Cathedral and Hotel International, Magdeburg

1969. 20th Anniv of D.D.R. Stamp Exhibition, Magdeburg (2nd issue). Multicoloured.

E1233 20pf. Type E **382** 25 25
E1234 40pf.+10pf. Von Guericke's vacuum experiment . . . . . . 1·30 1·20

E **383** Ryvangen Memorial

E **384** U.F.I. Emblem

1969. War Victims' Memorial, Ryvangen (Copenhagen).

E1235 E **383** 25pf. multicoloured 75 35

1969. 36th Int Fairs Union (U.F.I.) Congress, Leipzig.

E1236 E **384** 10pf. multicoloured 25 25
E1237 15pf. multicoloured 2·10 80

E **385** I.L.O. Emblem

E **386** University Seal and Building

1969. 50th Anniv of I.L.O.

E1238 E **385** 20pf. silver and green 25 25
E1239 25pf. silver & mauve 1·60 80

1969. 550th Anniv of Rostock University. Multicoloured.

E1240 10pf. Type E **386** 25 25
E1241 15pf. Steam-turbine rotor and curve (University emblem) . . . . 1·40 60

E **387** "Horseman" Pastry-mould

E **388** Antonov An-24B

1969. Lausitz Folk Art.

E1242 E **387** 10pf. brn, blk & flesh 1·40 2·30
E1243 – 20pf.+5pf. mult . . . 45 70
E1244 – 50pf. multicoloured 2·30 3·75

DESIGNS: 20pf. Plate; 50pf. Pastry in form of Negro couple.

1969. Interflug Aircraft. Multicoloured.

E1245 20pf. Type E **388** 15 25
E1246 25pf. Ilyushin Il-18 . . . . 1·60 2·20
E1247 30pf. Tupolev Tu-134 . . 20 25
E1248 50pf. Mil Mi-8 helicopter DM-SPA 30 30

E **389** "Siberian Teacher" (Svechnikov)

1969. Dresden Gallery Paintings (3rd series). Multicoloured.

E1249 5pf. Type E **389** 15 25
E1250 10pf. "Steel-worker" (Serov) 15 25
E1251 20pf. "Still Life" (Aslamasjan) 15 25
E1252 25pf. "A Warm Day" (Romas) . . . . 1·40 2·30
E1253 40pf. "Springtime Again" (Kabatchek) 25 25
E1254 50pf. "Man by the River" (Makovsky) 30 50

1970. Coil Stamp. As Nos. E577 etc, but value expressed in "M".

E1255 E **196** 1m. olive . . . . . 70 6·00

1970. Celebrities Annivs. (3rd series). As Type E **352**.

E1256 5pf. blue 25 25
E1257 10pf. brown 25 25
E1258 15pf. blue 25 25
E1259 20pf. purple 45 25
E1260 25pf. blue . . . . 3·00 1·30
E1261 40pf. red 60 35

DESIGNS: 5pf. E. Barlach (sculptor and playwright; birth cent); 10pf. J. Gutenberg (printer; 500th death anniv) (1968); 15pf. K. Tucholsky (author; 80th birth anniv); 20pf. Beethoven (birth bicent); 25pf. F. Holderlin (poet; birth bicent); 40 pf G. W. F. Hegel (philosopher; birth bicent).

E **390** Red fox

1970. Int Fur Auction, Leipzig. Mult.

E1262 10pf. Rabbit 15 25
E1263 20pf. Type E **390** 25 25
E1264 25pf. European mink . . . 3·75 5·00
E1265 40pf. Common hamster . . 45 50

E **391** "Little Brother and Little Sister"

1970. Fairy Tales (5th series). "Little Brother and Little Sister".

E1266 E **391** 5pf. multicoloured 25 75
E1267 – 10pf. multicoloured 25 75
E1268 – 15pf. multicoloured 70 1·30
E1269 – 20pf. multicoloured 70 1·30
E1270 – 25pf. multicoloured 25 75
E1271 – 30pf. multicoloured 25 75

DESIGNS: 10pf. to 30pf. showing different scenes.

E **392** Telephone and Electrical Switchgear

1970. Leipzig Spring Fair. Multicoloured.

E1272 10pf. Type E **392** 20 25
E1273 15pf. High-voltage transformer (vert) . . . 75 30

E **393** Horseman's Gravestone (A.D. 700)

1970. Archaeological Discoveries.

E1274 E **393** 10pf. olive, blk & grn 15 25
E1275 – 20pf. black, yell & red 15 25
E1276 – 25pf. grn, blk & yell 1·20 2·50
E1277 – 40pf. chestnut, black and brown 25 25

DESIGNS: 20pf. Helmet (A.D. 500); 25pf. Bronze basin (1000 B.C.); 40pf. Clay drum (2500 B.C.).

E **394** Lenin and "Iskra" (= the Spark) press

1970. Birth Centenary of Lenin. Multicoloured.

E1278 10pf. Type E **394** 15 25
E1279 20pf. Lenin and Clara Zetkin 15 25
E1280 25pf. Lenin and "State and Revolution" (book) . . 2·50 2·30
E1281 40pf. Lenin Monument, Eisleben 20 25
E1282 70pf. Lenin Square, East Berlin 30 50
MSE1283 118 × 84 mm. 1m. Lenin (vert) . . . . 2·10 3·75

1970. Protected Plants (3rd series). Vert designs as Type E **367**. Multicoloured.

E1284 10pf. Sea kale ("Crambe maritima") 15 25
E1285 20pf. Pasque flower ("Pulsatilla vulgaris") . . 15 25
E1286 25pf. Fringed gentian ("Gentiana ciliata") . . 2·30 4·25
E1287 30pf. Military orchid ("Orchis militaris") . . . 20 30
E1288 40pf. Labrador tea ("Ledum palustre") . . 30 40
E1289 70pf. Round-leaved wintergreen ("Pyrola rotundifolia") 35 65

E **395** Capture of the Reichstag, 1945

E **396** Shortwave Aerial

1970. 25th Anniv of "Liberation from Fascism". Multicoloured.

E1290 10pf. Type E **395** 30 25
E1291 20pf. Newspaper headline, Kremlin and State Building, East Berlin . . 30 25
E1292 25pf. C.M.E.A. Building, Moscow and flags . . . 1·50 1·20
MSE1293 135 × 105 mm. 70pf. Buchenwald Monument (horiz) 2·10 3·00

1970. 25th Anniv of D.D.R. Broadcasting Service. Multicoloured.

E1294 10pf. Type E **396** . . . . 70 1·60
E1295 15pf. Radio Station, East Berlin (horiz) (50 × 28 mm) . . . . . 1·20 2·30

E **397** Globe and Ear of Corn

E **398** Fritz Heckert Medal

1970. 5th World Corn and Bread Congress, Dresden. Multicoloured.

E1296 20pf. Type E **397** . . . . 1·20 1·90
E1297 25pf. Palace of Culture and ear of corn . . . . 1·20 1·90

1970. 25th Annivs of German Confederation of Trade Unions and World Trade Union Federation ("Federation Syndicale Mondiale"). Mult.

E1298 20pf. Type E **398** 15 25
E1299 25pf. F.S.M. Emblem . . 70 1·10

E **399** Gods Amon, Shu and Tefnut

1970. Sudanese Archaeological Excavations by Humboldt University Expedition. Multicoloured.

E1300 10pf. Type E **399** 15 25
E1301 15pf. King Arnekhamani 15 25
E1302 20pf. Cattle frieze 15 25
E1303 25pf. Prince Arka . . . . 1·50 2·00
E1304 30pf. God Arensnuphis (vert) 15 25
E1305 40pf. War elephants and prisoners 20 25
E1306 50pf. God Apedemak . . 20 25

The above designs reproduce carvings unearthed at the Lions' Temple, Musawwarat, Sudan.

E **400** Road Patrol

E **401** D.K.B. Emblem

1970. 25th Anniv of "Deutsche Volkspolizei" (police force). Multicoloured.

E1307 5pf. Type E **400** 25 25
E1308 10pf. Policewoman with children 25 25
E1309 15pf. Radio patrol car . . 25 25

E1310 20pf. Railway policeman and Class SVT18.16 diesel-hydraulic locomotive 25 25
E1311 25pf. River police in patrol boat . . . . 1·70 85

1970. 25th Anniv of "Deutscher Kulturbund" (cultural assn).
E1312 E **401** 10pf. brown, silver and blue . . . . . 2·75 5·25
E1313 – 25pf. brown, gold and blue . . . . . 2·75 5·25
DESIGN: 25pf. Johannes Becher medal.

E **402** Arms of D.D.R. and Poland

1970. 20th Anniv of Gorlitz Agreement on Oder–Neisse Border.
E1314 E **402** 20pf. multicoloured 35 35

E **403** Vaulting

E **405** Cecilienhof Castle

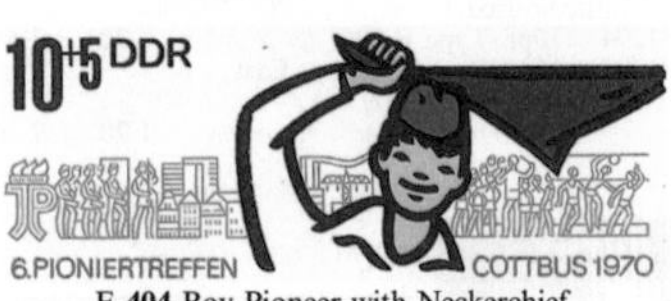

E **404** Boy Pioneer with Neckerchief

1970. 3rd Children and Young People's Sports Days. Multicoloured.
E1315 10pf. Type E **403** 20 25
E1316 20pf.+5pf. Hurdling . . . 60 30

1970. 6th Young Pioneers Meeting. Cottbus. Multicoloured.
E1317 10pf.+5pf. Type E **404** . . 30 70
E1318 25pf.+5pf. Girl pioneer with neckerchief 30 70
Nos. E1317/18 were issued together, se-tenant, forming a composite design.

1970. 25th Anniv of Potsdam Agreement.
E1319 E **405** 10pf. yellow, red and black . . . . . . 25 1·00
E1320 – 20pf. black, red and yellow . . . . . . 25 1·00
E1321 – 25pf. black and red 25 1·00
DESIGNS—VERT: 20pf. "Potsdam Agreement" in four languages. HORIZ (77 × 28 mm): 25pf. Conference delegates around the table.

E **406** Pocket-watch and Wristwatch

1970. Leipzig Autumn Fair.
E1322 E **406** 10pf. multicoloured 35 35

E **407** T. Neubauer and M. Poser

1970. "Anti-Fascist Resistance".
E1323 E **407** 20pf. purple, red & bl 25 35
E1324 – 25pf. olive and red 30 60
DESIGN—VERT: 25pf. "Motherland"—detail from Soviet War Memorial, Treptow, Berlin.

E **408** Pres. Ho-Chi-Minh

1970. Aid for Vietnam and Ho-Chi-Minh. Commemoration.
E1325 E **408** 20pf.+5pf. black, red and pink 35 35

E **409** Compass and Map

1970. World "Orienteering" Championships. East Germany. Multicoloured.
E1326 10pf. Type E **409** 25 25
E1327 25pf. Runner and three map sections . . . . . 1·50 80

E **410** "Forester Scharf's Birthday" (Nagel)

1970. "The Art of Otto Nagel, Kathe Kollwitz and Ernst Barlach".
E1328 E **410** 10pf. multicoloured 15 25
E1329 – 20pf. multicoloured 15 25
E1330 – 25pf. brown & mauve . . . . . . 1·60 2·75
E1331 – 30pf. black and pink 15 25
E1332 – 40pf. black and yellow 20 25
E1333 – 50pf. black and yellow 25 30
DESIGNS: 20pf. "Portrait of a Young Girl" (Nagel); 25pf. "No More War" (Kollwitz); 30pf. "Mother and Child" (Kollwitz); 40pf. Sculptured head from Gustrow Cenotaph (Barlach); 50pf. "The Flute-player" (Barlach).

E **411** "The Little Trumpeter" (Weineck Memorial, Halle)

E **413** Musk Ox

E **412** Flags Emblem

1970. 2nd National Youth Stamp Exhibition, Karl-Marx-Stadt. Multicoloured.
E1334 10pf. Type E **411** 25 60
E1335 15pf.+5pf. East German 25pf. stamp of 1959 . . 25 60

1970. "Comrades-in-Arms". Warsaw Pact Military Manoeuvres.
E1336 E **412** 10pf. multicoloured 15 25
E1337 20pf. multicoloured 30 55

1970. Animals in East Berlin "Tierpark" (Zoo). Multicoloured.
E1338 10pf. Type E **413** 35 25
E1339 15pf. Whale-headed Stork 35 25
E1340 20pf. Addax 70 65
E1341 25pf. Sun bear . . . . 7·00 10·50

E **414** U.N. Emblem and Headquarters, New York

E **415** Engels

1970. 25th Anniv of United Nations.
E1342 E **414** 20pf. multicoloured 75 40

1970. 150th Birth Anniv of Friedrich Engels.
E1343 E **415** 10pf. black, grey and orange 25 25
E1344 – 20pf. blk, grn & orge 25 25
E1345 – 25pf. blk, red & orge 1·70 1·70
DESIGNS: 20pf. Engels, Marx and "Communist Manifesto"; 25pf. Engels and "Anti-Duhring".

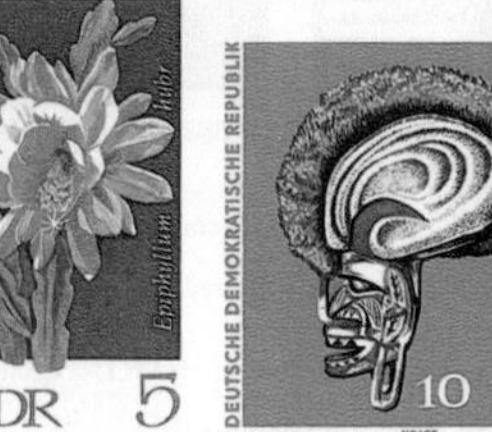

E **416** "Epiphyllum hybr"

E **417** Dancer's Mask, Bismarck Archipelago

1970. Cacti Cultivation in D.D.R. Mult.
E1346 5pf. Type E **416** 15 25
E1347 10pf. "Astrophytum myriostigma" 15 25
E1348 15pf. "Echinocereus salm-dyckianus" 15 25
E1349 20pf. "Selenicereus grandiflorus" 20 25
E1350 25pf. "Hamatoc setispinus" . . . . . . 2·40 3·75
E1351 30pf. "Mamillaria boolii" 30 25

1970. Birth Bicentenary of Beethoven. As No. E1259, but colour and face value changed, in sheet 81 × 55 mm.
MSE1352 1m. green . . . . . . 1·80 2·10

1971. Exhibits from the Ethnological Museum, Leipzig.
E1353 E **417** 10pf. multicoloured 15 25
E1354 – 20pf. brown & orange 15 25
E1355 – 25pf. multicoloured 1·20 1·50
E1356 – 40pf. brown and red 30 25
DESIGNS: 20pf. Bronze head, Benin; 25pf. Tea-pot, Thailand; 40pf. Zapotec earthenware Jaguar-god, Mexico.

E **418** "Venus 5"

1971. Soviet Space Research. Multicoloured.
E1357 20pf. Type E **418** 25 50
E1358 20pf. Orbital space station 25 50
E1359 20pf. "Luna 10" and "Luna 16" . . . . . . 45 1·00
E1360 20pf. Various "Soyuz" spacecraft . . . . . . 45 1·00
E1361 20pf. "Proton 1" satellite and "Vostok" rocket . . 45 1·00
E1362 20pf. "Molniya 1" communications satellite 45 1·00
E1363 20pf. Gagarin and "Vostok 1" 30 60
E1364 20pf. Leonov in space . . 30 60

E **419** K. Liebknecht

E **420** J. R. Becher (poet)

1971. Birth Centenaries of Karl Liebknecht and Rosa Luxemburg (revolutionaries).
E1365 E **419** 20pf. mauve, gold and black . . . . 60 1·10
E1366 – 25pf. mauve, gold and black . . . . 60 1·10
DESIGN: 25pf. Rosa Luxemburg.

1971. Celebrities' Birth Anniversaries.
E1367 E **420** 5pf. brown 15 25
E1368 – 10pf. blue 15 25
E1369 – 15pf. black 15 25
E1370 – 20pf. purple 20 25
E1371 – 25pf. green . . . . . 1·00 1·50
E1372 – 50pf. blue 30 30
DESIGNS: 5pf. (80th birth anniv); 10pf. H. Mann (writer—birth cent); 15pf. J. Heartfield (artist—80th birth anniv); 20pf. W. Bredel (70th birth anniv); 25pf. F. Mehring (politician—125th birth anniv); 50pf. J. Kepler (astronomer—400th birth anniv).
See also Nos. E1427 and E1451/5.

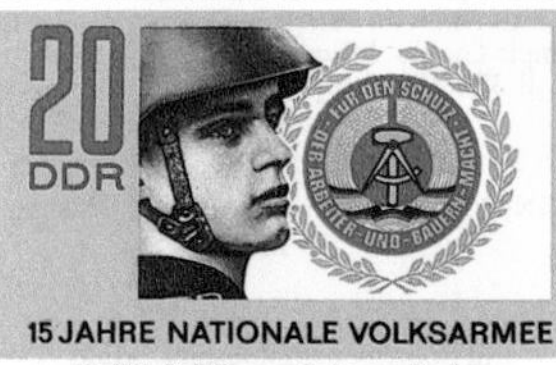

E **421** Soldier and Army Badge

1971. 15th Anniv of National People's Army.
E1373 E **421** 20pf. multicoloured 45 35

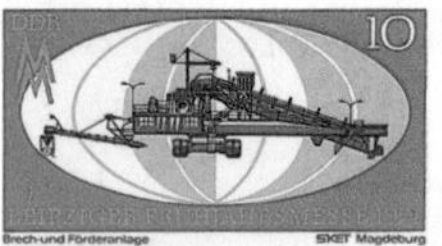

E **422** "Sket" Mobile Ore-crusher

1971. Leipzig Spring Fair. Multicoloured.
E1374 10pf. Type E **422** 20 25
E1375 15pf. Dredger "Takraf" . . 25 25

E **423** Proclamation of the Commune

E **425** St. Mary's Church

E **424** "Lunokhod 1" on Moon's Surface

1971. Centenary of Paris Commune.
E1376 E **423** 10pf. black, brown and red 20 25
E1377 – 20pf. black, brown and red 20 25
E1378 – 25pf. black, brown and red . . . . . 85 1·40
E1379 – 30pf. black, grey and red 20 25
DESIGNS: 20pf. Women at the Place Blanche barricade; 25pf. Cover of "L'Internationale"; 30pf. Title page of Karl Marx's "The Civil War in France".

1971. Moon Mission of "Lunokhod 1".
E1380 E **424** 20pf. turquoise, blue and red 65 65

1971. Berlin Buildings. Multicoloured.
E1381 10pf. Type E **425** 15 25
E1382 15pf. Kopenick Castle (horiz) 15 25
E1383 20pf. Old Library (horiz) 20 25
E1384 25pf. Ermeler House . . . 3·50 5·00
E1385 50pf. New Guardhouse (horiz) 30 30
E1386 70pf. National Gallery (horiz) 35 45

E **426** "The Discus-thrower"

1971. 20th Anniv of D.D.R. National Olympics Committee.
E1387 E **426** 20pf. multicoloured 80 40

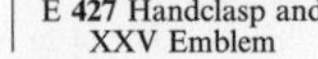

E **427** Handclasp and XXV Emblem

E **428** Schleife Costume

1971. 25th Anniv of Socialist Unity Party.
E1388 E **427** 20pf. black, red and gold 30 45

1971. Sorbian Dance Costumes. Mult.
E1389 10pf. Type E **428** 15 25
E1390 20pf. Hoyerswerda 15 25
E1391 25pf. Cottbus . . . . . . 90 1·70
E1392 40pf. Kamenz 25 35
For 10pf. and 20pf. in smaller size, see Nos. E1443/4.

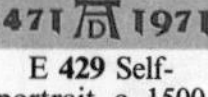
E **429** Self-portrait, c. 1500

E **432** "Internees"

E **430** Construction Worker

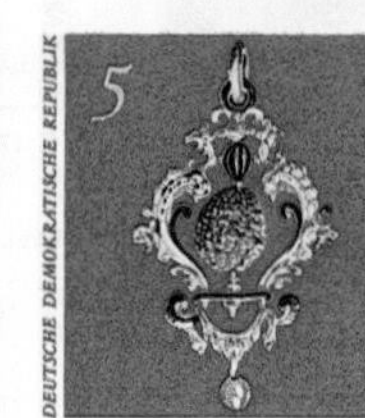
E **433** Cherry stone with 180 Carved Heads

1971. 500th Birth Anniv of Albrecht Durer. Paintings. Multicoloured.
E1393 10pf. Type E **429** 25 25
E1394 40pf. "The Three Peasants" 35 25
E1395 70pf. "Philipp Melanchthon" . . . . . 2·20 2·10

1971. 8th S.E.D. Party Conference.
E1396 E **430** 5pf. multicoloured 15 25
E1397 – 10pf. multicoloured 15 25
E1398 – 20pf. multicoloured 15 25
E1400 – 20pf. gold, red and mauve 35 35
E1399 – 25pf. multicoloured 55 95
DESIGNS: 10pf. Technician; 20pf. (No. E1398) Farm girl; 20pf. (No. E1400) Conference emblem (smaller, 23 × 29 mm); 25pf. Soldier.

1971. 20th Anniv of International Resistance Federation (F.I.R.). Lithographs from Fritz Cremer's "Buchenwaldzyklus".
E1401 E **432** 20pf. black & yellow 70 1·20
E1402 – 25pf. black and blue 70 1·20
DESIGN: 25pf. "Attack on Guard".

1971. Art Treasures of Dresden's Green Vaults. Multicoloured.
E1403 5pf. Type E **433** 15 25
E1404 10pf. Insignia of the Golden Fleece, c. 1730 15 25
E1405 15pf. Nuremberg jug, c. 1530 . . . . . . 15 25
E1406 20pf. Mounted Moorish drummer figurine, c. 1720 . . . . 20 25
E1407 25pf. Writing-case, 1562 1·20 2·20
E1408 30pf. St. George medallion, c. 1570 . . . 25 25

E **434** Mongolian Arms

E **435** Child's Face

1971. 50th Anniv of Mongolian People's Republic.
E1409 E **434** 20pf. multicoloured 30 50

1971. 25th Anniv of UNICEF.
E1410 E **435** 20pf. multicoloured 35 30

E **436** Servicemen

E **438** Vietnamese Woman and Child

E **437** "Ivan Franko" (liner)

1971. 10th Anniv of Berlin Wall. Mult.
E1411 20pf. Type E **436** . . . . 90 1·00
E1412 35pf. Brandenburg Gate 1·80 2·40

1971. East German Shipbuilding Industry.
E1413 E **437** 10pf. brown 15 25
E1414 – 15pf. blue and brown 15 25
E1415 – 20pf. green 15 25
E1416 – 25pf. blue . . . . . 1·50 2·75
E1417 – 40pf. brown 25 25
E1418 – 50pf. blue 30 25
DESIGNS: 15pf. "Irkutsk" (freighter); 20pf. "Rostock" freighter, 1966; 25pf. "Junge Welt" (fish-factory ship); 40pf. "Hansel" (container ship); 50pf. "Akademik Kurchatov" (research ship).

1971. Aid for Vietnam.
E1419 E **438** 10pf.+5pf. mult . . . 35 35

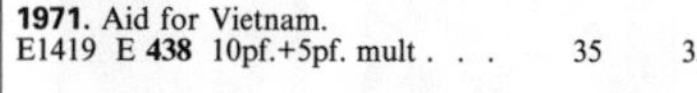

E **439** MAG-Butadien Plant

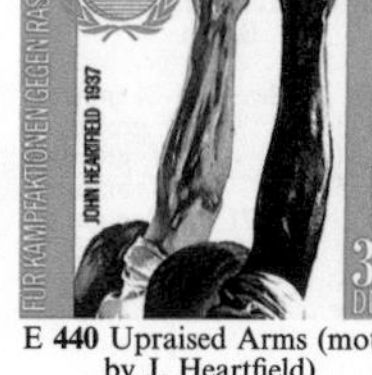
E **440** Upraised Arms (motif by J. Heartfield)

1971. Leipzig Autumn Fair.
E1420 E **439** 10pf. vio, mve & grn 20 25
E1421 – 25pf. violet, grn & bl 35 50
DESIGN: 25pf. SKL reactor plant.

1971. Racial Equality Year.
E1422 E **440** 35pf. black, sil & bl 35 30

E **441** Tupolev Tu-134 Mail Plane at Airport

1971. Philatelists' Day.
E1423 E **441** 10pf.+5pf. blue, red and green 20 25
E1424 – 25pf. red, green & bl 60 95
DESIGN: 25pf. Milestone and Zurner's measuring cart.

E **442** Wiltz Memorial, Luxembourg

E **443** German Violin

1971. Monuments. Multicoloured.
E1425 25pf. Type E **442** 30 30
E1426 35pf. Karl Marx monument, Karl-Marx-Stadt 35 30

1971. 150th Birth Anniv of R. Virchow (physician). As Type E **420**.
E1427 40pf. plum 45 45

1971. Musical Instruments in Markneukirchen Museum. Multicoloured.
E1428 10pf. North African "darbuka" 15 25
E1429 15pf. Mongolian "morin chuur" 15 25
E1430 20pf. Type E **443** 15 25
E1431 25pf. Italian mandolin . . 15 25
E1432 40pf. Bohemian bagpies . . 25 35
E1433 50pf. Sudanese "kasso" . . 1·50 2·20

E **444** "Dahlta O 10 A" Theodolite

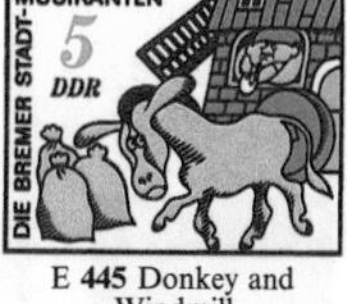
E **445** Donkey and Windmill

1971. 125th Anniv of Carl Zeiss Optical Works, Jena.
E1434 E **444** 10pf. black, red & bl 70 1·20
E1435 – 20pf. black, red & bl 70 1·20
E1436 – 25pf. blue, yellow and ultramarine 70 1·20
DESIGNS—VERT: 20pf. "Ergaval" microscope. HORIZ (52 × 29 mm) 25pf. Planetarium.

1971. Fairy Tales (6th series). As Type E **445**. "The Town Musicians of Bremen".
E1437 5pf. multicoloured . . . . 25 1·00
E1438 10pf. multicoloured . . . 25 1·00
E1439 15pf. multicoloured . . . 70 1·90
E1440 20pf. multicoloured . . . 70 1·90
E1441 25pf. multicoloured . . . 25 1·00
E1442 30pf. multicoloured . . . 25 1·00

1971. Sorbian Dance Costumes. As Nos. E1389/90 but smaller, size 23 × 28 mm.
E1443 E **428** 10pf. multicoloured 30 25
E1444 – 20pf. multicoloured 75 90

E **446** Tobogganing

1971. Winter Olympic Games, Sapporo, Japan (1972).
E1445 E **446** 5pf. black, green and mauve 15 25
E1446 – 10pf.+5pf. blk, bl & mve 15 25
E1447 – 15pf.+5pf. black, grn & bl 25 25
E1448 – 20pf. black, mauve & violet 25 25
E1449 – 25pf. black, violet & mauve . . . . . . 2·10 2·75
E1450 – 70pf. black, blue and violet 35 45
DESIGNS: 10pf. Figure skating; 15pf. Speed skating; 20pf. Cross-country skiing; 25pf. Biathlon; 70pf. Ski jumping.

1972. German Celebrities. As Type E **420**.
E1451 10pf. green 15 25
E1452 20pf. mauve 15 25
E1453 25pf. blue 15 25
E1454 35pf. brown 15 25
E1455 50pf. lilac . . . . 1·70 3·00
CELEBRITIES: 10pf. J. Tralow (writer); 20pf. L. Frank (writer); 25pf. K. A. Kocor (composer); 35pf. H. Schliemann (archaeologist); 50pf. Caroline Neuber (actress).

E **447** Gypsum from Eisleben

1972. Minerals. Multicoloured.
E1456 5pf. Type E **447** 15 25
E1457 10pf. Zinnwaldite, Zinnwald 15 25
E1458 20pf. Malachite, Ullersreuth 15 25
E1459 25pf. Amethyst, Wiesenbad 20 25
E1460 35pf. Halite, Merkers . . . 25 25
E1461 50pf. Proustite, Schneeberg 1·50 2·40

E **448** Vietnamese Woman

E **451** W.H.O. Emblem

E **449** Soviet Exhibition Hall

1972. Aid for Vietnam.
E1462 E **448** 10pf.+5pf. mult . . . 35 30

1972. Leipzig Spring Fair. Multicoloured.
E1463 10pf. Type E **449** 15 25
E1464 25pf. East German and Soviet flags 30 45

E **450** Anemometer of 1896 and Koppen's Chart of 1876

1972. International Meteorologists Meeting, Leipzig. Three sheets, each 85 × 57 mm. Multicoloured.
MSE1465 20pf. Type E **450**; 35pf. Weather station and clouds; 70pf. Satellite and weather map . . . 2·50 3·00

1972. World Health Day.
E1466 E **451** 35pf. ultramarine, silver and blue . . 35 50

E **452** Kamov Ka-26 Helicopter

1972. East German Aircraft. Multicoloured.
E1467 5pf. Type E **452** 15 25
E1468 10pf. Letov Z-37 Cmelak crop-sprayer DM-SMC 15 25
E1469 35pf. Ilyushin Il-62M . . . 30 25
E1470 1m. Ilyushin Il-62M . . . 1·80 2·75

E **453** Wrestling

1972. Olympic Games, Munich. Mult.
E1471 5pf. Type E **453** 15 25
E1472 10pf.+5pf. High-diving . . 20 25
E1473 20pf. Pole-vaulting 20 25
E1474 25pf.+10pf. Rowing . . . 20 30
E1475 35pf. Handball 30 50
E1476 70pf. Gymnastics . . . . 3·50 4·00

E **454** Soviet and East German Flags

1972. 25th Anniv of German–Soviet Friendship Society. Multicoloured.
E1477 10pf. Type E **454** 70 60
E1478 20pf. Brezhnev (U.S.S.R.) and Honecker (D.D.R.) 70 1·70

E **455** Steel Workers

E **456** "Karneol" Rose

1972. Trade Unions Federation Congress.
E1479 E **455** 10pf. pur, orge & brn 25 60
E1480 – 35pf. blue and brown 25 60
DESIGN: 35pf. Students.

1972. International Rose Exhibition. German Species. Multicoloured.
E1481 5pf. Type E **456** 20 25
E1482 10pf. "Berger's Rose" . . 20 25
E1497 10pf. "Berger's Rose" . . 25 35
E1483 15pf. "Charme" . . . . . 2·20 3·75
E1484 20pf. "Izetka Spreeathen" 15 25
E1485 25pf. "Kopernicker Sommer" 20 25
E1498 25pf. "Kopernicker Sommer" . . . . 1·60 1·10
E1486 35pf. "Professor Knoll" . . 30 25
E1499 35pf. "Professor Knoll" . . 1·60 1·10
Nos. E1497/9 are smaller, size 24 × 28 mm.

E **457** "Portrait of Young Man"

1972. 500th Birth Anniv of Lucas Cranach the Elder. Multicoloured.
E1487 5pf. Type E **457** 20 25
E1488 20pf. "Mother and Child" 20 30
E1489 25pf. "Margarete Luther" 30 70
E1490 70pf. "Nymph" (horiz) . . 2·50 6·25

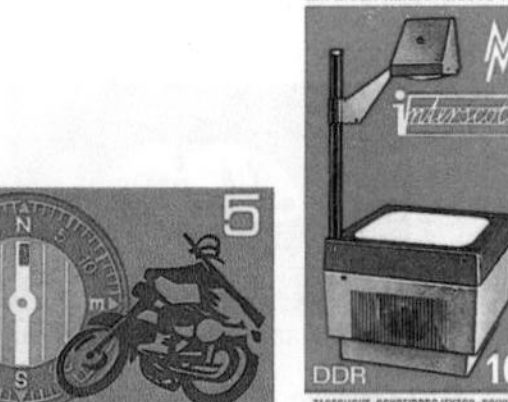

E **458** Compass and Motor Cyclist

E **460** Overhead Projector

E **459** "Young Worker Reading" (J. Damme)

1972. Sports and Technical Sciences Association. Multicoloured.
E1491 5pf. Type E **458** 20 30
E1492 10pf. Light airplane and parachute 20 30
E1493 20pf. Target and obstacle race 20 30
E1494 25pf. Radio set and Morse key . . . . 1·00 1·80
E1495 35pf. "Wilhelm Pieck" (brigantine) and propeller 20 25

1972. Int Book Year.
E1496 E **459** 50pf. multicoloured 75 60

1972. Leipzig Autumn Fair.
E1500 E **460** 10pf. black and red 15 25
E1501 – 25pf. black and green 30 55
DESIGN—HORIZ: 25pf. Slide projector.

E **461** G. Dimitrov

E **462** "Catching Birds" (Egyptian relief painting, c. 2400 B.C.)

1972. 90th Birth Anniv of Georgi Dimitrov (Bulgarian statesman).
E1502 E **461** 20pf. black and red 35 30

1972. "Interartes" Stamp Exhibition, East Berlin. Multicoloured.
E1503 10pf. Type E **462** 15 25
E1504 15pf.+5pf. "Persian Spearman" (glazed tile, c. 500 B.C.) . . . . 1·00 1·90
E1505 20pf. Anatolian tapestry c. 1400 B.C . . 15 25
E1506 35pf.+5pf. "The Grapesellers" (Max Lingner, 1949) (horiz) 25 25

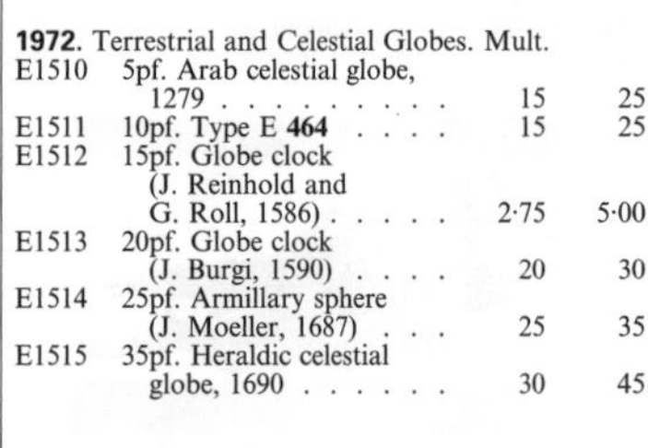

E **463** Red Cross Team and Patient
E **464** Terrestrial Globe (J. Praetorius, 1568)

1972. East German Red Cross.
E1507 E **463** 10pf. ultramarine, blue and red . . . 30 65
E1508 – 15pf. ultramarine, blue and red . . . 30 65
E1509 – 35pf. red, blue and ultramarine . . . 30 65
DESIGNS—VERT: 15pf. Sea-rescue launch. HORIZ (50½ × 28 mm): 35pf. World map on cross, and transport.

1972. Terrestrial and Celestial Globes. Mult.
E1510 5pf. Arab celestial globe, 1279 . . . . 15 25
E1511 10pf. Type E **464** 15 25
E1512 15pf. Globe clock (J. Reinhold and G. Roll, 1586) . . . . . 2·75 5·00
E1513 20pf. Globe clock (J. Burgi, 1590) 20 30
E1514 25pf. Armillary sphere (J. Moeller, 1687) . . . 25 35
E1515 35pf. Heraldic celestial globe, 1690 . . . . . . 30 45

E **465** Monument

E **467** "Mauz and Hoppel" (Cat and Hare)

E **466** Educating Juveniles

1972. German–Polish Resistance Memorial, Berlin, Inauguration.
E1516 E **465** 25pf. multicoloured 45 50

1972. Juvenile Inventions Exhibition. Mult.
E1517 10pf. Type E **466** 25 75
E1518 25pf. Youths with welding machine 25 75

1972. Children's T.V. Characters. Mult.
E1519 5pf. Type E **467** 25 60
E1520 10pf. "Fuchs and Elster" (Fox and Magpie) . . . 25 60
E1521 15pf. "Herr Uhn" (Eagle Owl) . . . . 90 1·60
E1522 20pf. "Frau Igel and Borstel" (Hedgehogs) . . 90 1·60
E1523 25pf. "Schuffel and Pieps" (Dog and Mouse) . . . 25 60
E1524 35pf. "Paulchen" (Paul from the children's library) 25 60

E **468** "The Snow Queen"

E **469** H. Heine

1972. Fairy Tales (7th series). As Type E **468**. "The Snow Queen" (Hans Christian Andersen).
E1525 5pf. multicoloured . . . 25 1·50
E1526 10pf. multicoloured . . . 70 2·75
E1527 15pf. multicoloured . . . 25 1·50
E1528 20pf. multicoloured . . . 25 1·50
E1529 25pf. multicoloured . . . 70 2·75
E1530 35pf. multicoloured . . . 25 1·50

1972. 175th Birth Anniv of Heinrich Heine (poet). Sheet 60 × 86 mm.
MSE1531 E **469** 1m. black, red and green . . . . 2·10 2·10

E **470** Arms of U.S.S.R.

1972. 50th Anniv of U.S.S.R.
E1532 E **470** 20pf. multicoloured 45 35

E **471** Leninplatz, East Berlin

E **472** M. da Caravaggio

1973. (a) Size 29 × 24 mm.
E1533 – 5pf. green 30 35
E1534 – 10pf. green 55 35
E1535 – 15pf. mauve 55 35
E1536 E **471** 20pf. mauve . . . . 1·00 30
E1537 – 25pf. green . . . . 1·20 30
E1538 – 30pf. orange . . . 30 30
E1539 – 35pf. blue . . . . . 1·00 50
E1540 – 40pf. violet 70 35
E1541 – 50pf. blue 70 35
E1542 – 60pf. purple . . . . 1·00 35
E1543 – 70pf. brown 70 35
E1544 – 80pf. blue . . . . . 1·20 30
E1545 – 1m. green . . . . . 1·60 35
E1546 – 2m. red . . . . . . 2·50 35
E1546a – 3m. mauve . . . . 2·75 1·00

(b) Size 22 × 18 mm.
E2197 – 5pf. green 25 30
E1548 – 10pf. green 50 45
E2198 – 10pf. green 35 35
E2199 – 15pf. mauve 50 40
E2200 E **471** 20pf. mauve 50 45
E1549a – 25pf. green 50 50
E2202 – 30pf. orange . . . 50 55
E2203 – 35pf. blue 25 40
E2204 – 40pf. violet . . . . 1·10 55
E2205 – 50pf. blue 60 60
E2206 – 60pf. purple 90 50
E2207 – 70pf. brown 75 65
E2208 – 80pf. blue . . . . . 1·10 60
E2209 – 1m. green . . . . . 1·40 1·50
E2210 – 2m. red . . . . . . 2·30 1·70
E2211 – 3m. mauve . . . . 3·00 1·70
DESIGNS: 5pf. Eastern white pelican and Alfred Brehm House, Tierpark, Berlin; 10pf. (Nos. E1534, E1548) Neptune Fountain and Rathausstrasse, Berlin; 10pf. (No. E2198) Palace of the Republic, Berlin; 15pf. Apartment Blocks, Fishers' Island, Berlin; 25pf. TV Tower, Alexander Square, Berlin; 30 pf, Workers' Memorial, Halle; 35pf. Karl-Marx-Stadt; 40pf. Brandenburg Gate Berlin; 50pf. New Guardhouse, Berlin; 60pf. Crown Gate and Zwinger, Dresden; 70pf. Old Town Hall, Leipzig; 80pf. Rostock-Warnemunde; 1m. Soviet War Memorial, Treptow; 2, 3m. Arms of East Germany.

1973. Cultural Anniversaries.
E1551 E **472** 5pf. brown . . . . . 1·20 1·80
E1552 – 10pf. green 15 25
E1553 – 20pf. purple 15 25
E1554 – 25pf. blue 15 25
E1555 – 35pf. red 15 25
PORTRAITS AND ANNIVERSARIES: 5pf. (painter, 400th birth anniv); 10pf. Friedrich Wolf (dramatist, 85th birth anniv); 20pf. Max Reger (composer, birth cent.); 25pf. Max Reinhardt (impressario, birth cent.); 35pf. Johannes Dieckmann (politician, 80th birth anniv).

E **473** "Lebachia speciosa"

1973. Fossils in Palaeontological Collection, Berlin Natural History Museum. Multicoloured.
E1556 10pf. Type E **473** 15 25
E1557 15pf. "Spheronopteris hollandica" 15 25
E1558 20pf. "Pterodactylus kochi" 15 25
E1559 25pf. "Botryopteris" . . . 15 25
E1560 35pf. "Archaeopteryx lithographica" 15 25
E1561 70pf. "Odontopleura ovata" . . . . 2·20 3·50

E **474** Copernicus (½-size illustration)

1973. 500th Birth Anniv of Copernicus.
E1562 E **474** 70pf. multicoloured 90 65

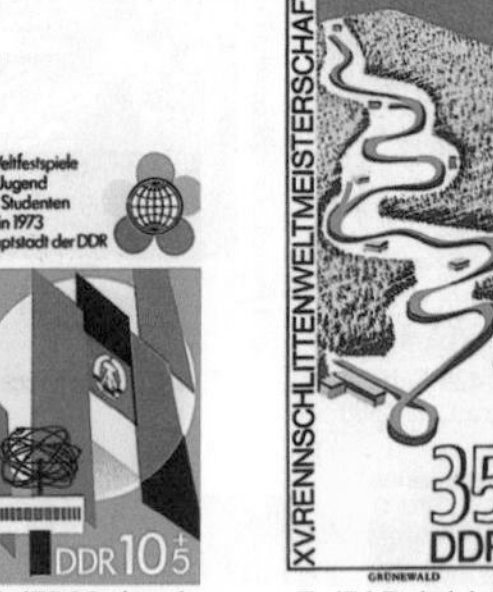

E **475** National Flags
E **476** Bobsleigh Course

1973. 10th World Youth Festival, Berlin (1st issue). Multicoloured.
E1563 10pf.+5pf. Type E **475** . . 20 25
E1564 25pf.+5pf. Youths and peace dove 30 55
See also Nos. E1592/6.

1973. 15th World Bobsleigh Championships, Oberhof.
E1565 E **476** 35pf. multicoloured 35 65

E **477** Combine Harvester

1973. Leipzig Spring Fair. Multicoloured.
E1566 10pf. Type E **477** 15 25
E1567 25pf. Automatic lathe . . 30 55

E **478** Firecrests

1973. Songbirds. Multicoloured.
E1568 5pf. Type E **478** 15 25
E1569 10pf. White-winged crossbill 15 25
E1570 15pf. Bohemian waxwing 15 25
E1571 20pf. Bluethroats 15 25
E1572 25pf. Eurasian goldfinch 20 30
E1573 35pf. Golden oriole . . . 25 30
E1574 40pf. Grey wagtail 30 35
E1575 60pf. Wallcreeper . . . . 3·25 5·75

E **479** Class 211 Electric Locomotive No. 200-3

1973. Railway Rolling Stock. Multicoloured.
E1576 5pf. Type E **479** 15 25
E1577 10pf. Refrigerator wagon 15 25
E1578 20pf. Long-distance passenger carriage . . . 15 25
E1579 25pf. Tank wagon 15 25
E1580 35pf. Double-deck carriage 20 30
E1581 85pf. Passenger carriage 2·75 4·75

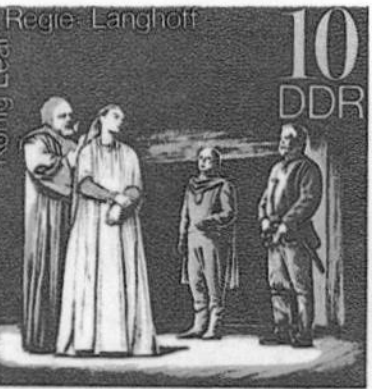

E **480** "King Lear" (directed by W. Langhoff)

E **481** H. Matern

1973. Famous Theatrical Productions. Mult.
E1582 10pf. Type E **480** 15 25
E1583 25pf. "A Midsummer Night's Dream" (opera) (Benjamin Britten) (directed by Walter Felsenstein) 15 25
E1584 35pf. "Mother Courage" (directed by Berthold Brecht) . . . . 1·00 1·70

1973. 80th Birth Anniv of Hermann Matern (politician).
E1585 E **481** 40pf. red 60 40

E **482** Goethe and House

E **483** Firework Display

1973. Cultural Celebrities and Houses in Weimar. Multicoloured.
E1586 10pf. Type E **482** 20 25
E1587 15pf. C. M. Wieland (writer) 20 25
E1588 20pf. F. Schiller (writer) 20 25
E1589 25pf. J. G. Herder (writer) 20 25
E1590 35pf. Lucas Cranach the Elder (painter) 20 25
E1591 50pf. Franz Liszt (composer) . . . . . . 2·40 3·00

1973. World Festival of Youth and Students, East Berlin (2nd issue). Multicoloured.
E1592 5pf. Type E **483** 20 25
E1593 15pf. Students ("Int Solidarity") 20 25
E1594 20pf. Young workers ("Economic Integration") 20 25
E1595 30pf. Students ("Aid for Young Nations") . . . 1·50 1·20
E1596 35pf. Youth and Students' Emblems 20 25
MSE1597 86×107 mm. 50pf. Emblem and Brandenburg Gate (26.7) . . . . 1·00 1·00

E **484** W. Ulbricht

E **485** Power Network

1973. Death of Walter Ulbricht.
E1598 E **484** 20pf. black 60 50

1973. 10th Anniv of "Peace" United Energy Supply System.
E1599 E **485** 35pf. orge, pur & bl 35 60

E **486** "Leisure Activities"

1973. Leipzig Autumn Fair. Multicoloured.
E1600 10pf. Type E **486** 25 15
E1601 25pf. Yacht, guitar and power drill 40 25

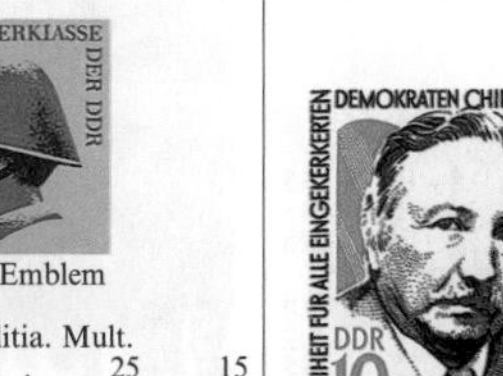

E **487** Militiaman and Emblem

1973. 20th Anniv of Workers Militia. Mult.
E1602 10pf. Type E **487** 25 15
E1603 20pf. Militia guard 40 25
MSE1604 61×87 mm. 50pf. Militiamen (vert) 90 90

E **488** Red Flag encircling Globe

E **489** Langenstein-Zwieberge Memorial

1973. 15th Anniv of "Problems of Peace and Socialism".
E1605 E **488** 20pf. red and gold 50 25

1973. Langenstein-Zwieberge Monument.
E1606 E **489** 25pf. multicoloured 50 25

E **490** U.N. H.Q. and Emblems

E **491** "Young Couple" (G. Glombitza)

1973. Admission of German Democratic Republic to United Nations Organization.
E1607 E **490** 35pf. multicoloured 60 20

1973. Philatelists' Day and 3rd Young Philatelists' Stamp Exhibition, Halle.
E1608 E **491** 20pf.+5pf. mult . . . 35 20

E **492** Congress Emblem

E **493** Vietnamese Child

1973. 8th World Trade Union Congress, Varna, Bulgaria.
E1609 E **492** 35pf. multicoloured 35 30

1973. "Solidarity with Vietnam".
E1610 E **493** 10pf.+5pf. mult . . . 35 25

E **494** Launching Rocket

1973. Soviet Science and Technology Days. Multicoloured.
E1611 10pf. Type E **494** 15 15
E1612 20pf. Soviet map and emblem (horiz) 15 15
E1613 25pf. Oil refinery . . . . 1·20 90

E **495** L. Corvalan

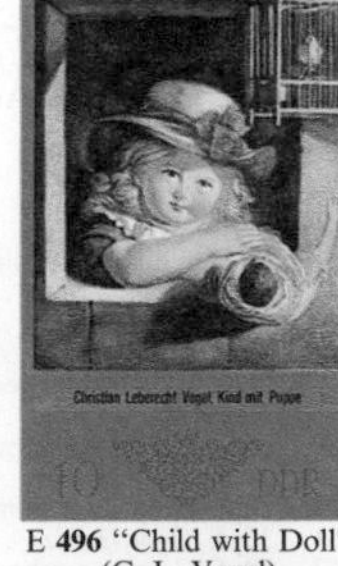

E **496** "Child with Doll" (C. L. Vogel)

1973. Solidarity with the Chilean People. Multicoloured.
E1614 10pf.+5pf. Type E **495** . . 30 25
E1615 25pf.+5pf. Pres. Allende 55 45

1973. Paintings by Old Masters. Mult.
E1616 10pf. Type E **496** 20 15
E1617 15pf. "Madonna with Rose" (Parmigianino) 20 15
E1618 20pf. "Woman with Fair Hair" (Rubens) 20 15
E1619 25pf. "Lady in White" (Titian) 20 15
E1620 35pf. "Archimedes" (D. Fetti) 25 15
E1621 70pf. "Flower Arrangement" (Jan D. de Heem) . . . . 3·00 1·90

E **497** Flame Emblem

E **498** "Catching the Pike"

1973. 25th Anniv of Declaration of Human Rights.
E1622 E **497** 35pf. multicoloured 50 30

1973. Fairy Tales (8th series). As Type E **498**. "At the Bidding of the Pike".
E1623 5pf. multicoloured 25 50
E1624 10pf. multicoloured . . . 90 1·30
E1625 15pf. multicoloured . . . 25 50
E1626 20pf. multicoloured . . . 25 50
E1627 25pf. multicoloured . . . 90 1·30
E1628 35pf. multicoloured . . . 25 50

E **499** E. Hoernle

E **500** Pablo Neruda

1974. Socialist Personalities.
E1629 E **499** 10pf. grey 25 15
E1630 – 10pf. lilac 25 15
E1631 – 10pf. blue 25 15
E1632 – 10pf. brown 25 15
E1633 – 10pf. green 25 15
E1634 – 10pf. brown 25 15
E1635 – 10pf. blue 25 15
E1636 – 10pf. brown 25 15
PERSONALITIES: No. E1630, Etkar Andre; E1631, Paul Merker; E1632, Hermann Duncker; E1633, Fritz Heckert; E1634, Otto Grotewohl; E1635, Wilhelm Florin; E1636, Georg Handke.
See also Nos. E1682/4.

1974. Pablo Neruda (Chilean poet) Commem.
E1637 E **500** 20pf. multicoloured 35 25

E **501** "Comecon" Emblem

E **502** "Echinopsis multiplex"

1974. 25th Anniv of Council for Mutual Economic Aid.
E1638 E **501** 20pf. multicoloured 35 20

1974. Cacti. Multicoloured.
E1639 5pf. Type E **502** 15 15
E1640 10pf. "Lobivia haageana" 15 15
E1641 15pf. "Parodia sanguiniflora" . . . . . 2·75 2·40
E1642 20pf. "Gymnocal monvillei" 20 15
E1643 25pf. "Neoporteria rapifera" 25 20
E1644 35pf. "Notocactus concinnus" 30 30

E **503** Handball Players

E **504** High-tension Testing Plant

1974. 8th Men's World Indoor Handball Championships.
E1645 E **503** 5pf. multicoloured 40 40
E1646 – 10pf. multicoloured 40 40
E1647 – 35pf. multicoloured 40 40
Nos. E1645/7 were issued together, se-tenant, forming a composite design of a handball match.

1974. Leipzig Spring Fair. Multicoloured.
E1648 10pf. Type E **504** 25 15
E1649 25pf. "Robotron" computer (horiz) 35 20

E **505** "Rhodophyllus sinuatus"

E **506** Gustav Kirchhoff

1974. Poisonous Fungi. Multicoloured.
E1650 5pf. Type E **505** 20 15
E1651 10pf. "Boletus satanas" . . 20 15
E1652 15pf. "Amanita pantherina" 20 15
E1653 20pf. "Amanita muscaria" 20 15
E1654 25pf. "Gyromitra esculenta" 25 15
E1655 30pf. "Inocybe patouillardii" 30 25
E1656 35pf. "Amanita phalloides" 30 25
E1657 40pf. "Clitocybe dealbata" 2·30 1·70

1974. Celebrities' Birth Anniversaries.
E1658 E **506** 5pf. black and grey 15 15
E1659 – 10pf. ultram & bl . . 15 15
E1660 – 20pf. red and pink 20 15
E1661 – 25pf. green & turq 25 15
E1662 – 35pf. choc & brn . . 90 80
PORTRAITS AND ANNIVERSARIES: 5pf. (physicist, 150th); 10pf. Immanuel Kant (philosopher, 250th); 20pf. Elm Welk (writer, 90th); 25pf. Johann Herder (author, 230th); 35pf. Lion Feuchtwanger (novelist, 90th).

E **507** Globe and "PEACE"

1974. 25th Anniv of 1st World Peace Congress.
E1663 E **507** 35pf. multicoloured 50 30

E **508** Tractor Driver

E **509** Buk Lighthouse, 1878

1974. 25th Anniv of German Democratic Republic. Multicoloured.
E1664 10pf. Type E **508** 20 15
E1665 20pf. Students 20 15
E1666 25pf. Woman worker . . . 20 15
E1667 35pf. East German family 1·20 95

1974. Lighthouses (1st series). Multicoloured.
E1668 10pf. Type E **509** 15 15
E1669 15pf. Warnemunde lighthouse, 1898 . . . . 15 15
E1670 20pf. Darsser Ort lighthouse, 1848 . . . . 15 15
E1671 35pf. Arkona lighthouse in 1827 and 1902 . . . . 20 15
E1672 40pf. Greifswalder Oie lighthouse, 1855 . . . . 1·70 1·20
See also Nos. E1760/4.

E **510** "Man and Woman looking at the Moon"

1974. Birth Bicentenary of Caspar Friedrich (painter). Multicoloured.
E1673 10pf. Type E **510** 15 15
E1674 20pf. "The Stages of Life" (seaside scene) 15 15
E1675 25pf. "Heath near Dresden" . . . . 2·20 2·00
E1676 35pf. "Trees in the Elbe Valley" 30 15
MSE1677 80 × 55 mm. E **511** 70pf. sepia . . . . 1·70 1·80

E **512** Lace Pattern E **513** Show Jumping

1974. Plauen Lace.
E1678 E **512** 10pf. black and violet 15 15
E1679 – 20pf. brown, black and bistre 15 15
E1680 – 25pf. black, blue and turquoise . . . . 1·60 1·40
E1681 – 35pf. black, mauve and pink 25 15
DESIGNS: Nos. E1679/81, Lace patterns similar to Type E **512**.

1974. Socialist Personalities. As Type E **499**.
E1682 10pf. blue 25 15
E1683 10pf. violet 25 15
E1684 10pf. brown 25 15
DESIGNS: No. E1682, R. Breitscheid; No. E1683, K. Burger; No. E1684, C. Moltmann.

1974. International Horse-breeders' Congress, Berlin. Multicoloured.
E1685 10pf. Type E **513** 15 15
E1686 20pf. Horse & trap (horiz) 15 15
E1687 25pf. Haflinger draught horses (horiz) . . . . . 1·80 2·00
E1688 35pf. Horse-racing (horiz) 30 20

E **514** Crane lifting Diesel Locomotive

1974. Leipzig Autumn Fair. Multicoloured.
E1689 10pf. Type E **514** 20 15
E1690 25pf. Agricultural machine 35 25

E **515** "The Porcelain Shop" E **517** Arms of East Germany and Family

E **516** Ardeatine Caves Memorial, Rome

1974. "Mon Plaisir". Exhibits in Dolls' Village, Castle Museum, Arnstadt. Mult.
E1691 5pf. Type E **515** 15 15
E1692 10pf. "Fairground Crier" 15 15
E1693 15pf. "Wine-tasting in Cellar" 15 15
E1694 20pf. "Cooper and Apprentice" 15 15
E1695 25pf. "Bagpiper playing for Dancing Bear" . . . 1·90 1·60
E1696 35pf. "Butcher's Wife and Crone" 25 20

1974. International War Memorials.
E1697 E **516** 35pf. black, grn & red 45 30
E1698 – 35pf. black, bl & red 45 30
DESIGN: No. E1698, Resistance Memorial, Chateaubriant, France.

1974. 25th Anniv of German Democratic Republic. Sheet 90 × 108 mm.
MSE1699 E **517** 1m. multicoloured 2·40 2·40

E **518** "James Watt" (paddle-steamer) and Modern Freighter

1974. Centenary of U.P.U. Multicoloured.
E1700 10pf. Type E **518** 15 15
E1701 20pf. Steam and diesel railway locomotives . . 15 15
E1702 25pf. Early airliner and Tupolev Tu-134 . . . . 15 15
E1703 35pf. Early mail coach and modern truck . . . . . 1·40 90

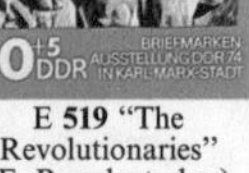

E **519** "The Revolutionaries" (E. Rossdeutscher) E **520** "The Sun shines for all" (G. Milosch)

1974. "DDR 74" Stamp Exhibition. Sculptures in Karl-Marx-Stadt. Each black, bistre and green.
E1704 10pf.+5pf. Type E **519** . . 25 25
E1705 20pf. "The Dialectics" . . 25 25
E1706 25pf. "The Party" 25 25

1974. Children's Paintings. Multicoloured.
E1707 20pf. Type E **520** 40 40
E1708 20pf. "My Friend Sascha" (B. Ozminski) 40 40
E1709 20pf. "Carsten the Best Swimmer" (M. Kluge) 40 40
E1710 20pf. "Me and the Blackboard" (P. Westphal) 40 40

E **521** "The Woodchopper" E **523** Banded Jasper

E **522** "Still Life" (R. Paris)

1974. Fairy Tales (9th series). "Twittering To and Fro" by A. Tolstoi.
E1711 E **521** 10pf. multicoloured 25 40
E1712 – 15pf. multicoloured 1·20 95
E1713 – 20pf. multicoloured 25 40
E1714 – 30pf. multicoloured 25 40
E1715 – 35pf. multicoloured 1·20 95
E1716 – 40pf. multicoloured 25 40
DESIGNS: Nos. E1712/16, Scenes from "Twittering To and Fro" fairy tale, similar to Type E **521**.

1974. Paintings from Berlin Museums. Mult.
E1717 10pf. Type E **522** 15 15
E1718 15pf. "Girl in Meditation" (W. Lachnit) (vert) . . . 15 15
E1719 20pf. "Fisherman's House" (H. Hakenbeck) (vert) 15 15
E1720 35pf. "Girl in Red" (R. Bergander) 30 15
E1721 70pf. "Parents" (W. Sitte) (vert) . . . . 1·90 1·90

1974. Gem-stones in Freiberg Mining Academy Collection. Multicoloured.
E1722 10pf. Type E **523** 15 15
E1723 15pf. Smoky quartz . . . 15 15
E1724 20pf. Topaz 15 15
E1725 25pf. Amethyst 20 15
E1726 35pf. Aquamarine 35 15
E1727 70pf. Agate . . . . 2·20 2·00

E **524** Martha Arendsee E **525** Peasants doing Forced Labour

1975. 90th Birth Anniv of Martha Arendsee (Socialist).
E1728 E **524** 10pf. red 35 20

1975. 450th Anniv of Peasants' War.
E1729 E **525** 5pf. black, green and grey 45 45
E1730 – 10pf. black, brown and grey 45 45
E1731 – 20pf. black, blue and grey 45 45
E1732 – 25pf. black, yellow and grey 60 55
E1733 – 35pf. black, lilac and grey 60 55
E1734 – 50pf. black, grey and light grey 45 45
DESIGNS: 10pf. "Paying Tithe"; 20pf. Thomas Muntzer (leader); 25pf. "Armed Peasants"; 35pf. "Liberty" flag; 50pf. Peasants on trial.

E **526** Women and Emblem E **527** Pentakta "A-100" (microfilm camera)

1975. International Women's Year.
E1735 E **526** 10pf. multicoloured 30 25
E1736 – 20pf. multicoloured 30 25
E1737 – 25pf. multicoloured 30 25
DESIGNS: 20pf., 25pf. Similar to Type E **526**.

1975. Leipzig Spring Fair. Multicoloured.
E1738 10pf. Type E **527** 15 15
E1739 25pf. "SKET" (cement works) 35 20

E **528** Hans Otto (actor) (1900–33) E **529** Blue and Yellow Macaws

1975. Celebrities' Birth Anniversaries.
E1740 E **528** 5pf. blue 15 15
E1741 – 10pf. red 15 15
E1742 – 20pf. green 15 15
E1743 – 25pf. brown 20 15
E1744 – 35pf. blue . . . . . 1·20 85
PORTRAITS AND ANNIVERSARIES: 10pf. Thomas Mann, author (1875–1955); 20pf. Dr. A. Schweitzer (1875–1965); 25pf. Michelangelo (1475–1564); 35pf. Andre-Marie Ampere, scientist (1775–1836).

1975. Zoo Animals. Multicoloured.
E1745 5pf. Type E **529** 15 15
E1746 10pf. Orang-utan 15 15
E1747 15pf. Ibex 15 15
E1748 20pf. Indian rhinoceros (horiz) 15 15
E1749 25pf. Pygmy hippopotamus (horiz) 15 15
E1750 30pf. Grey seals (horiz) . . 20 15
E1751 35pf. Tiger (horiz) 25 15
E1752 50pf. Common zebra . . . 2·30 1·90

E **530** Soldiers, "Industry" and "Agriculture"

1975. 20th Anniv of Warsaw Treaty.
E1753 E **530** 20pf. multicoloured 1·20 20

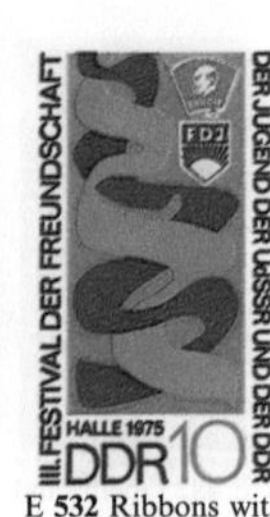

E **531** Soviet Memorial, Berlin-Treptow E **532** Ribbons with "Komsomol" and "F.D.J." Badges

1975. 30th Anniv of Liberation. Mult.
E1754 10pf. Type E **531** 20 15
E1755 20pf. Detail of Buchenwald memorial 20 15
E1756 25pf. Woman voluntary worker 20 15
E1757 55pf. "Socialist economic integration" 90 80
MSE1758 109 × 90 mm. 50pf. Soldier planting Red flag on Reichstag. Imperf 90 90

1975. 3rd Youth Friendship Festival, Halle.
E1759 E **532** 10pf. mult 50 20

1975. Lighthouses (2nd series). As Type E **509**. Multicoloured.
E1760 5pf. Trimmendorf lighthouse 15 15
E1761 10pf. Gellen lighthouse . . 15 15
E1762 20pf. Sassnitz lighthouse 15 15
E1763 25pf. Dornbusch lighthouse 20 15
E1764 35pf. Peenemunde lighthouse . . . . . . 1·30 1·10

E **533** Wilhelm Leibknecht and August Bebel E **534** Dove and "Scientific Co-operation between Socialist Countries"

1975. Centenary of Marx's "Programmkritik" and Gotha Unity Congress.
E1765 E **533** 10pf. deep brown, brown and red . . 25 25
E1766 – 20pf. multicoloured 25 25
E1767 – 25pf. deep brown, brown and red . . 25 25
DESIGNS: 20pf. Tivoli (meeting place at Gotha) and title-page of Minutes of Unity Congress; 25pf. Karl Marx and Friedrich Engels.

1975. 25th Anniv of Eisenhuettenstadt.
E1768 E **534** 20pf. multicoloured 35 20

E **535** Construction Workers E **536** Automatic Clock, 1585

1975. 30th Anniv of Free-German Trade Union Association.
E1769 E **535** 20pf. multicoloured 35 20

1975. Ancient Clocks. Multicoloured.
E1770 5pf. Type E **536** 15 15
E1771 10pf. Astronomical Mantlepiece clock, 1560 15 15
E1772 15pf. Automatic clock, 1600 . . . . 2·10 1·80
E1773 20pf. Mantlepiece Clock, 1720 . . . . 15 15
E1774 25pf. Mantlepiece Clock, 1700 . . . . 20 15
E1775 35pf. Astronomical Clock, 1738 . . . . 30 20

E **537** Jacob and Wilhelm Grimm's German Dictionary

1975. 275th Anniv of Academy of Science.
E1776 E **537** 10pf. black, grn & red 20 15
E1777 – 20pf. black and blue 20 15
E1778 – 25pf. blk, yell & grn 20 15
E1779 – 35pf. multicoloured 1·20 1·10
DESIGNS: 20pf. Karl Schwarzschildt observatory, Tautenberg; 25pf. Electron microscope and chemical plant; 35pf. Intercosmic satellite.

E **538** Runner with Torch
E **539** Map of Europe

1975. 5th National Youth Sports Day.
E1780 E **538** 10pf. black and pink 20 15
E1781 – 20pf. black and yellow 20 15
E1782 – 25pf. black and blue 20 15
E1783 – 35pf. black and green . . . . . . 1·20 1·10
DESIGNS: 20pf. Hurdling; 25pf. Swimming; 35pf. Gymnastics.

1975. European Security and Co-operation Conference, Helsinki.
E1784 E **539** 20pf. multicoloured 35 25

E **540** Asters
E **541** "Medimorph" (Anaesthetizing machine)

1975. Flowers. Multicoloured.
E1785 5pf. Type E **540** 20 15
E1786 10pf. Pelargoniums 20 15
E1787 20pf. Gerberas 20 15
E1788 25pf. Carnation 20 15
E1789 35pf. Chrysanthemum . . 30 15
E1790 70pf. Pansies . . . . . . 3·00 2·30

1975. Leipzig Autumn Fair. Multicoloured.
E1791 10pf. Type E **541** 25 15
E1792 25pf. Zschopau "TS-250" motor-cycle (horiz) . . . 45 25

E **542** School Crossing

1975. Road Safety. Multicoloured.
E1793 10pf. Type E **542** 20 15
E1794 15pf. Policewoman controlling traffic . . . 1·80 1·10
E1795 20pf. Policeman assisting motorist 20 15
E1796 25pf. Car having check-up 25 15
E1797 35pf. Road safety instruction 25 15

E **543** Launch of "Soyuz"
E **544** Clenched Fist and Red Star

1975. "Apollo"–"Soyuz" Space Link. Mult.
E1798 10pf. Type E **543** 20 15
E1799 20pf. Spaceships in linking manoeuvre 20 15
E1800 70pf. The completed link (88 × 33 mm) . . . . . 2·10 1·80

1975. "International Solidarity".
E1801 E **544** 10pf.+5pf. black, red and olive 35 20

E **545** "Weimar in 1650" (Merian)

1975. Millenary of Weimar.
E1802 E **545** 10pf. brown, light green and green 20 15
E1803 – 20pf. multicoloured 20 15
E1804 – 35pf. multicoloured 70 60
DESIGNS:—VERT: 20pf. Buchenwald memorial. HORIZ: 35pf. Weimar buildings (975–1975).

E **546** Vienna Memorial (F. Cremer)
E **547** Louis Braille

1975. Austrian Patriots Monument, Vienna.
E1805 E **546** 35pf. multicoloured 35 20

1975. International Braille Year. Mult.
E1806 20pf. Type E **547** 20 15
E1807 35pf. Hands reading braille 20 15
E1808 50pf. An eye-ball, eye shade and safety goggles 1·60 1·40

E **548** Post Office Gate, Wurzen

1975. National Philatelists' Day. Mult.
E1809 10pf.+5pf. Type E **548** . . 60 55
E1810 20pf. Post Office, Barenfels 20 15

E **549** Hans Christian Andersen and scene from "The Emperor's New Clothes" (½-size illustration)

1975. Fairy Tales (10th series). "The Emperor's New Clothes".
E1811 E **549** 20pf. multicoloured 55 55
E1812 – 35pf. multicoloured 90 90
E1813 – 50pf. multicoloured 55 55
DESIGNS: 35, 50pf. Different scenes.

E **550** Tobogganing

1975. Winter Olympic Games, Innsbruck (1976). Multicoloured.
E1814 5pf. Type E **550** 15 15
E1815 10pf.+5pf. Bobsleigh track 20 15
E1816 20pf. Speed-skating rink 20 15
E1817 25pf.+5pf. Ski-jump . . . 30 15
E1818 35pf. Skating-rink 30 15
E1819 70pf. Skiing . . . . . . 2·75 1·90
MSE1820 80 × 55 mm. 1m. Innsbruk (33 × 28 mm) . . . . 2·50 2·10

E **551** W. Pieck
E **552** Organ, Rotha

1975. Birth Cent of President Pieck (statesman).
E1821 E **551** 10pf. brown & blue 25 15

1976. Members of German Workers' Movement. As Type E **551**.
E1822 10pf. brown and red . . . 25 15
E1823 10pf. brown and green . . 25 15
E1824 10pf. brown and orange 25 15
E1825 10pf. brown and violet . . 25 15
PORTRAITS: No. E1822, Ernst Thalmann; E1823, Georg Schumann; E1824, Wilhelm Koenen; E1825, John Schehr.

1976. Gottfried Silbermann (organ builder) Commemoration. Multicoloured.
E1826 10pf. Type E **552** 20 15
E1827 20pf. Organ, Freiberg . . 20 15
E1828 35pf. Organ, Fraureuth . . 25 15
E1829 50pf. Organ, Dresden . . 1·50 1·00

E **553** Richard Sorge

1976. Dr. Richard Sorge (Soviet agent) Commemoration. Sheet 82 × 65 mm.
MSE1830 E **553** 1m. black and pale olive-grey . . . . 2·10 2·10

E **554** Servicemen and Emblem

1976. 20th Anniv of National Forces (N.V.A.). Multicoloured.
E1831 10pf. Type E **554** 25 15
E1832 20pf. N.V.A. equipment 30 25

E **555** Telephone and Inscription
E **556** Block of Flats, Leipzig

1976. Centenary of Telephone.
E1833 E **555** 20pf. blue 35 20

1976. Leipzig Spring Fair. Multicoloured.
E1834 10pf. Type E **556** 25 15
E1835 25pf. "Prometey" (deep sea trawler) (horiz) . . . 45 25

E **557** Palace of the Republic, Berlin

1976. Opening of Palace of Republic, Berlin.
E1836 E **557** 10pf. multicoloured 85 20

E **558** Telecommunications Satellite Tracking Radar
E **559** Marx, Engels, Lenin and Socialist Party Emblem

1976. "Intersputnik".
E1837 E **558** 20pf. multicoloured 30 20

1976. 9th East German Socialist Party Congress.
E1838 E **559** 10pf. red, gold and deep red 25 15
E1839 – 20pf. multicoloured 35 20
MSE1840 110 × 91 mm. E **557** 1m. multicoloured . . . . 1·70 1·50
DESIGN—HORIZ: 20pf. Industrial site, housing complex and emblem.

E **560** Cycling

1976. Olympic Games, Montreal. Mult.
E1841 5pf. Type E **560** 20 15
E1842 10pf.+5pf. Modern swimming pool 20 15
E1843 20pf. Modern sports hall 20 15
E1844 25pf. Regatta course . . . 30 15
E1845 35pf.+10pf. Rifle-range . . 30 15
E1846 70pf. Athletics . . . . . . 3·00 2·20
MSE1847 81 × 55 mm. 1m. Modern sports stadium (33 × 28 mm) 1·80 1·80

E **561** Intertwined Ribbon and Emblem

1976. 10th Youth Parliament Conference, Berlin. Multicoloured.
E1848 10pf. Type E **561** 15 15
E1849 20pf. Members of Youth Parliament and stylised industrial plant 30 25

E **562** "Himantoglossum hircinum"
E **564** Marx, Engels, Lenin and Red Flag

E **563** "Shetland Pony" (H. Drake)

1976. Flowers. Multicoloured.
E1850 10pf. Type E **562** 15 15
E1851 20pf. "Dactylorhiza incarnata" 15 15
E1852 25pf. "Anacamptis pyramidalis" 25 15
E1853 35pf. "Dactylorhiza sambucina" 30 15
E1854 40pf. "Orchis coriophora" 30 15
E1855 50pf. "Cypripedium calceolus" . . . . . . 3·00 2·10

1976. Statuettes from Berlin Museums.
E1856 E **563** 10pf. black and blue 20 15
E1857 – 20pf. black & brown 25 15
E1858 – 25pf. black & orange 25 15
E1859 – 35pf. black and green 25 15
E1860 – 50pf. black and pink 2·30 1·80
STATUETTES—VERT: 20pf. "Tanzpause" (W. Arnold); 25pf. "Am Strand" (L. Englehardt); 35pf. "Herman Duncker" (W. Howard); 50pf. "Das Gesprach" (G. Weidanz).

1976. European Communist Parties' Conference.
E1861 E **564** 20pf. blue, deep red and red 35 20

E **565** State Carriage, 1790

1976. 19th-century Horse-drawn Vehicles. Multicoloured.
E1862 10pf. Type E **565** 15 15
E1863 20pf. Russian trap, 1800 15 15
E1864 25pf. Carriage, 1840 . . . 20 15
E1865 35pf. State carriage, 1860 25 15
E1866 40pf. Stagecoach, 1850 . . 30 25
E1867 50pf. Carriage, 1889 . . . 2·75 2·50

E **566** Gera, c. 1652

1976. National Philatelists' Day, Gera. Mult.
E1868 10pf.+5pf. Type E **566** . . 25 25
E1869 20pf. Gera buildings . . . 25 30

E **567** Boxer

1976. Domestic Dogs. Multicoloured.
E1870 5pf. Type E **567** 15 15
E1871 10pf. Airedale Terrier . . 15 15
E1872 20pf. Alsatian 15 15
E1873 25pf. Collie 20 15
E1874 35pf. Schnauzer 25 25
E1875 70pf. Great Dane . . . . 3·00 2·75

E **568** Oil Refinery

1976. Autumn Fair, Leipzig. Multicoloured.
E1876 10pf. Type E **568** 20 15
E1877 25pf. Library, Leipzig . . 45 20

E **569** Templin Lake Railway Bridge

1976. East German Bridges. Multicoloured.
E1878 10pf. Type E **569** 20 15
E1879 15pf. Adlergestell Railway Bridge, Berlin 20 15
E1880 20pf. River Elbe Railway Bridge, Rosslau 20 15
E1881 25pf. Goltzschtal Viaduct 25 15
E1882 35pf. Elbe River Bridge, Magdeburg 25 15
E1883 50pf. Grosser Dreesch Bridge, Schwerin . . . . 2·30 2·10

E **570** Memorial Figures

1976. Patriots' Memorial, Budapest.
E1884 E **570** 35pf. multicoloured 50 20

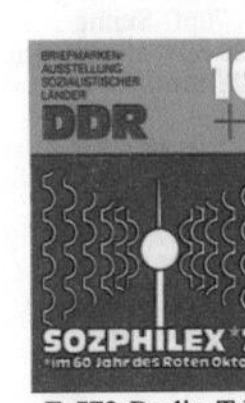

E **571** Brass Jug, c. 1500
E **572** Berlin T.V. Tower

1976. Exhibits from Applied Arts Museum, Kopenick Castle, Berlin. Multicoloured.
E1885 10pf. Type E **571** 20 15
E1886 20pf. Faience covered vase, c. 1710 . . . . . 20 15
E1887 25pf. Porcelain "fruit-seller" table centre, c. 1768 . . . . . 25 15
E1888 35pf. Silver "basket-carrier" statuette, c. 1700 . . . . 25 15
E1889 70pf. Coloured glass vase, c. 1900 . . . . . 2·30 2·10

1976. "Sozphilex 77" Stamp Exhibition. East Berlin (1st issue).
E1890 E **572** 10pf.+5pf. blue, black and red . . 35 20
See also Nos. E1962/3.

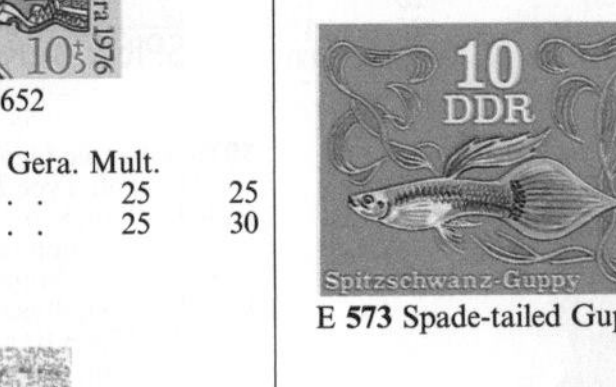

E **573** Spade-tailed Guppy

E **575** The Miller and the King

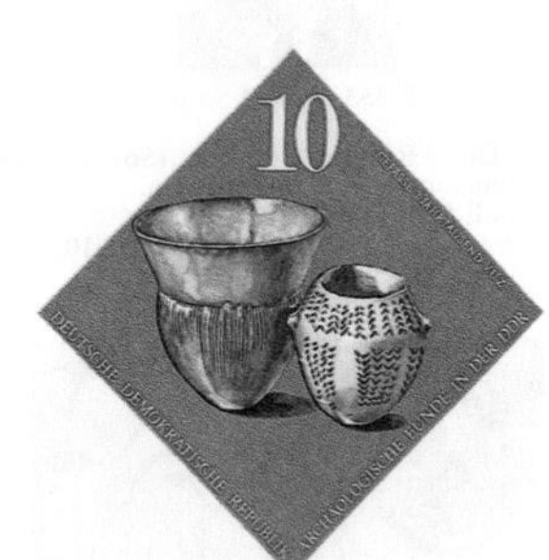

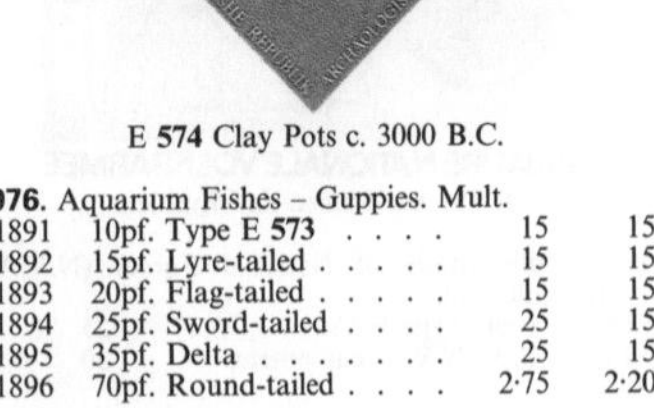
E **574** Clay Pots c. 3000 B.C.

1976. Aquarium Fishes – Guppies. Mult.
E1891 10pf. Type E **573** 15 15
E1892 15pf. Lyre-tailed 15 15
E1893 20pf. Flag-tailed 15 15
E1894 25pf. Sword-tailed 25 15
E1895 35pf. Delta 25 15
E1896 70pf. Round-tailed . . . . 2·75 2·20

1976. Archaeological Discoveries in D.D.R. Multicoloured.
E1897 10pf. Type E **574** 15 15
E1898 20pf. Bronze cult vessel on wheels, c. 1300 B.C. . . 15 15
E1899 25pf. Roman gold aureus of Tetricus I, A.D. 270–273 . . . . 25 15
E1900 35pf. Viking cross-shaped pendant, 10th century A.D. 25 15
E1901 70pf. Roman glass beaker, 3rd century A.D. . . . 2·75 2·10

1976. Fairy Tales (11th series). "Rumpelstiltskin".
E1902 E **575** 5pf. multicoloured 25 30
E1903 – 10pf. multicoloured 70 60
E1904 – 15pf. multicoloured 25 30
E1905 – 20pf. multicoloured 25 30
E1906 – 25pf. multicoloured 70 60
E1907 – 30pf. multicoloured 25 30
DESIGNS: 10pf. to 30pf. Scenes from the fairy tale.

E **576** "The Air" (R. Carriera)
E **577** Arnold Zweig (author)

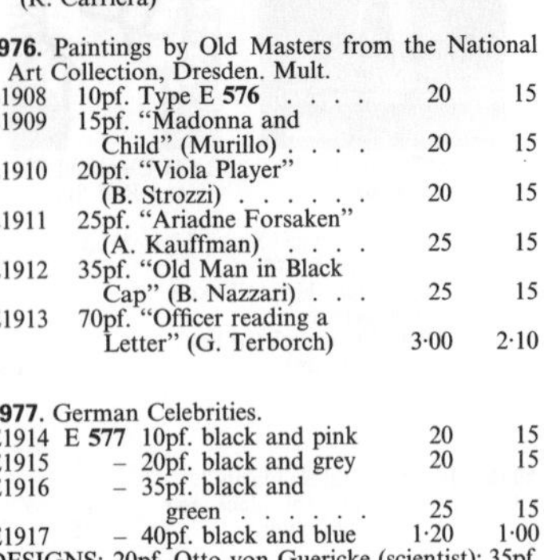

1976. Paintings by Old Masters from the National Art Collection, Dresden. Mult.
E1908 10pf. Type E **576** 20 15
E1909 15pf. "Madonna and Child" (Murillo) 20 15
E1910 20pf. "Viola Player" (B. Strozzi) 20 15
E1911 25pf. "Ariadne Forsaken" (A. Kauffman) 25 15
E1912 35pf. "Old Man in Black Cap" (B. Nazzari) . . . 25 15
E1913 70pf. "Officer reading a Letter" (G. Terborch) 3·00 2·10

1977. German Celebrities.
E1914 E **577** 10pf. black and pink 20 15
E1915 – 20pf. black and grey 20 15
E1916 – 35pf. black and green 25 15
E1917 – 40pf. black and blue 1·20 1·00
DESIGNS: 20pf. Otto von Guericke (scientist); 35pf. Albrecht D. Thaer (agriculturalist); 40pf. Gustav Hertz (physicist).

E **578** Spring near Plaue, Thuringia
E **579** Book Fair Building

1977. Natural Phenomena. Multicoloured.
E1918 10pf. Type E **578** 20 15
E1919 20pf. Rock face near Jonsdorf 20 15
E1920 25pf. Oaks near Reuterstadt Stavenhagen 20 15
E1921 35pf. Rocky ledge near Saalburg 25 15
E1922 50pf. Erratic boulder near Furstenwalde/Spree . . 1·80 1·60

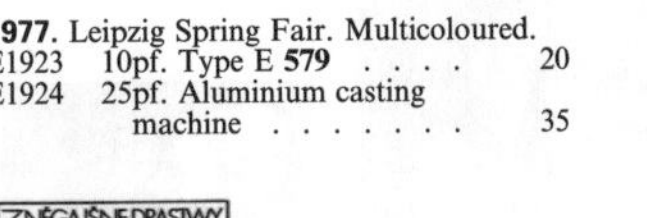

1977. Leipzig Spring Fair. Multicoloured.
E1923 10pf. Type E **579** 20 15
E1924 25pf. Aluminium casting machine 35 20

E **580** Senftenberg Costume, Zly Komorrow
E **581** Carl Friedrich Gauss

1977. Sorbian Historical Costumes. Mult.
E1925 10pf. Type E **580** 15 15
E1926 20pf. Bautzen, Budysin . . 15 15
E1927 25pf. Klitten, Kletno . . . 25 15
E1928 35pf. Nochten, Wochozy 25 15
E1929 70pf. Muskau, Muzakow 2·75 2·00

1977. Birth Bicentenary of Carl Friedrich Gauss (mathematician).
E1930 E **581** 20pf. black and blue 75 20

E **582** Start of Race
E **583** Three Flags

1977. 30th International Peace Cycle Race. Multicoloured.
E1931 10pf. Type E **582** 30 35
E1932 20pf. Spurt 30 35
E1933 35pf. Race finish 30 35

1977. 9th Congress of Free German Trade Unions Association.
E1934 E **583** 20pf. multicoloured 35 20

E **584** VKM Channel Converter and Filters
E **585** Shooting

1977. World Telecommunications Day.
E1935 E **584** 20pf. black, blue and red 35 20

1977. 25th Anniv of Sports and Technical Sciences Association.
E1936 E **585** 10pf. black, grn & red 20 15
E1937 – 20pf. black, bl & mve 20 15
E1938 – 35pf. black, pk & grn . . . . 1·10 95
DESIGNS: 20pf. Skin diving; 25pf. Radio-controlled model boat.

E **586** Accordion, 1900
E **587** "Bathsheba at the Fountain"

1977. Old Musical Instruments from Vogtland. Multicoloured.
E1939 10pf. Type E **586** 15 15
E1940 20pf. Treble viola da gamba, 1747 . . . . . . 15 15
E1941 25pf. Oboe, 1785, Clarinet, 1830, Flute, 1817 . . . 15 15
E1942 35pf. Concert zither, 1891 20 15
E1943 70pf. Trumpet, 1860 . . . 2·75 2·40

1977. 400th Birth Anniv of Peter Paul Rubens. Dresden Gallery Paintings. Multicoloured.
E1944 10pf. Type E **587** 15 15
E1945 15pf. "Mercury and Argus" (horiz) 25 15
E1946 20pf. "The Drunk Hercules" 25 15
E1947 25pf. "Diana's Return from Hunting" (horiz) 25 15
E1948 35pf. "The Old Woman with the Brazier" . . . 30 15
E1949 50pf. "Leda with the Swan" (horiz) . . . . . 3·25 2·30

E **588** Soviet and East German Flags

1977. 30th Anniv of German-Soviet Friendship Society. Sheet 80 × 55 mm.
MSE1950 E **588** 50pf. multicoloured 1·30 1·20

E **589** Tractor and Plough

1977. Modern Agricultural Techniques. Multicoloured.
E1951 10pf. Type E **589** 15 15
E1952 20pf. Fertilizer spreader on truck 15 15
E1953 25pf. Potato digger and loader 20 15
E1954 35pf. High pressure collecting press 25 15
E1955 50pf. Milking machine . . 2·40 2·10

E **590** High Jump

E **591** "Bread for Everybody" (Wolfram Schubert)

1977. 6th Gymnastics and Athletic Meeting and 6th Children and Young People's Sports Days, Leipzig. Multicoloured.

E1956 5pf. Type E **590** 20 15
E1957 10pf.+5pf. Running . . . 20 15
E1958 20pf. Hurdling 20 15
E1959 25pf.+5pf. Gymnastics . . 20 15
E1960 35pf. Dancing 25 15
E1961 40pf. Torch bearer and flags . . . . 2·30 2·10

1977. "Sozphilex 77" Stamp Exhibition, East Berlin (2nd issue). Multicoloured.

E1962 10pf. Type E **591** 25 20
E1963 25pf. "... when Communists are Dreaming" (Walter Womacka) 55 45
MSE1964 Two sheets, each 77 × 110 mm. (a) No. E1962 × 4; (b) No. E1963 × 4 Set of 2 sheets 1·60 1·60
MSE1965 85 × 54 mm. 50pf.+20pf. "World Youth Song" (Lothar Zitzmann) (horiz) . . . . . . 1·30 1·30

E **592** "Konsument" Department Store, Leipzig

E **593** Bust of Dzerzhinsky and Young Pioneers

1977. Leipzig Autumn Fair. Multicoloured.

E1966 10pf. Type E **592** 25 15
E1967 25pf. Carved bowl and Thuringian blown-glass vases 40 25

1977. Birth Centenary of Feliks E. Dzerzhinsky (founder of Soviet Cheka). Sheet 127 × 69 mm containing Type E **593** and similar vert design. Multicoloured.

MSE1968 20pf. Type E **593**; 35pf. Portrait . . . . 1·40 1·40

E **594** Steam Locomotive "Muldenthal", 1861

1977. Transport Museum, Dresden. Mult.

E1969 5pf. Type E **594** 15 15
E1970 10pf. Dresden tram, 1896 15 15
E1971 20pf. Hans Grade's monoplane, 1909 . . . 25 15
E1972 25pf. Phanomobil tricar, 1924 . . . . 25 15
E1973 35pf. River Elbe passenger steamer, 1837 . . . . . 2·40 1·80

E **595** "Aurora" (cruiser)

1977. 60th Anniv of October Revolution. Multicoloured.

E1974 10pf. Type E **595** 25 20
E1975 25pf. Assault on Winter Palace 55 45
MSE1976 55 × 86 mm. 1m. Lenin (vert) . . . . 2·50 2·10

E **596** Soviet Memorial

E **597** Flaming Torch

1977. Soviet Memorial, Berlin-Schoenholz.

E1977 E **596** 35pf. multicoloured 50 20

1977. "Solidarity".

E1978 E **597** 10pf.+5pf. mult . . . 35 20

E **598** Ernst Meyer

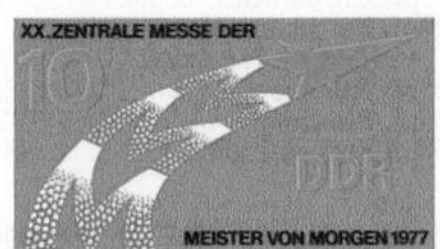

E **599** H. von Kleist

1977. Socialist Personalities.

E1979 E **598** 10pf. brown 25 15
E1980 – 10pf. red 25 15
E1981 – 10pf. blue 25 15

PERSONALITIES: No. E1980, A. Frolich; No. E1981, G. Eisler.

1977. Birth Bicentenary of Heinrich von Kleist (poet). Sheet 82 × 54 mm.

MSE1982 E **599** 1m. black and red 3·00 2·10

E **600** Rocket pointing Right

1977. 20th "Masters of Tomorrow" Fair, Leipzig.

E1983 E **600** 10pf. red, silver and black 20 30
E1984 – 20pf. blue, gold and black 20 30

DESIGN: 20pf. Rocket pointing left.

E **601** Mouflon

E **602** Firemen with Scaling Ladders

1977. Hunting. Multicoloured.

E1985 10pf. Type E **601** 15 15
E1986 15pf. Red deer . . . . . 2·50 2·20
E1987 20pf. Shooting common pheasant 15 15
E1988 25pf. Red fox and mallard 20 15
E1989 35pf. Tractor driver with roe deer fawn 30 15
E1990 70pf. Wild boars 35 25

1977. Fire Brigade. Multicoloured.

E1991 10pf. Type E **602** 20 15
E1992 20pf. Children visiting fire brigade (vert) 20 15
E1993 25pf. Fire engines in countryside 20 15
E1994 35pf. Artificial respiration (vert) 20 15
E1995 50pf. Fire-fighting tug . . 2·50 2·10

E **603** Traveller and King

E **605** Amilcar Cabral

E **604** Rosehips

1977. Fairy Tales (12th series). "Six World Travellers" (Brothers Grimm).

E1996 E **603** 5pf. multicoloured 25 40
E1997 – 10pf. multicoloured 1·20 85
E1998 – 20pf. multicoloured 25 40
E1999 – 25pf. multicoloured 25 40
E2000 – 35pf. multicoloured 1·20 85
E2001 – 60pf. multicoloured 25 40

DESIGNS: 10pf. to 60pf. Scenes from the fairy tale.

1978. Medicinal Plants. Multicoloured.

E2002 10pf. Type E **604** 15 15
E2003 15pf. Birch leaves 15 15
E2004 20pf. Camomile flowers . . 15 15
E2005 25pf. Coltsfoot 25 15
E2006 35pf. Lime flowers 25 15
E2007 50pf. Elder flowers . . . . 2·75 2·10

1978. Amilcar Cabral (nationalist leader of Guinea-Bissau) Commemoration.

E2008 E **605** 20pf. multicoloured 35 20

E **606** Town Hall, Suhl-Heinrichs

E **608** Ear-pendant, 11th century

E **607** Post Office Van, 1921

1978. Half-timbered Buildings. Multicoloured.

E2009 10pf. Type E **606** 15 15
E2010 20pf. Farmhouse, Niederoderwitz 15 15
E2011 25pf. Farmhouse, Strassen 15 15
E2012 35pf. House, Quedlinburg 25 15
E2013 40pf. House, Eisenach . . 2·40 2·00

1978. Postal Transport. Multicoloured.

E2014 10pf. Type E **607** 25 25
E2015 20pf. Postal truck, 1978 . . 45 45
E2016 25pf. Railway mail coach, 1896 . . . . 60 55
E2017 35pf. Railway mail coach, 1978 . . . . 70 75

1978. Slavonic Treasures. Multicoloured.

E2018 10pf. Type E **608** 15 15
E2019 20pf. Ear-ring, 10th century 15 15
E2020 25pf. Bronze tag, 10th century 20 15
E2021 35pf. Bronze horse, 12th century 20 15
E2022 70pf. Arabian coin, 8th century . . . . 2·20 1·80

E **609** "Royal House" Market Square, Leipzig

E **610** "M-100" Meteorological Rocket

1978. Leipzig Spring Fair.

E2023 E **609** 10pf. yell, blk & red 25 15
E2024 – 25pf. green, blk & red 45 25

DESIGN: 25pf. Universal measuring instrument, UMK 10/1318.

1978. "Interkosmos" Space Programme. Mult.

E2025 10pf. Type E **610** 15 15
E2026 20pf. "Interkosmos 1" satellite 15 15
E2027 35pf. "Meteor" satellite with Fourier spectrometer . . . . 1·10 1·10
MSE2028 90 × 109 mm. 1m. "MKF-6" multispectral camera 3·00 2·50

E **611** Samuel Heinicke (founder)

1978. Bicentenary of First National Deaf and Dumb Educational Institution.

E2029 20pf. Type E **611** 20 15
E2030 25pf. Child learning alphabet 80 70

E **612** Radio-range Tower, Dequede, and Television Transmission Van

E **613** Saxon miner in Gala Uniform

1978. World Telecommunications Day. Mult.

E2031 10pf. Type E **612** 15 15
E2032 20pf. Equipment in Berlin television tower and Dresden television tower 40 40

1978. 19th-Century Gala Uniforms of Mining and Metallurgical Industries. Multicoloured.

E2033 10pf. Type E **613** 15 15
E2034 20pf. Freiberg foundry worker 25 15
E2035 25pf. School of Mining academician 25 15
E2036 35pf. Chief Inspector of Mines . . . . 1·60 1·30

E **614** Lion Cub

E **615** Loading Container

1978. Centenary of Leipzig Zoo. Multicoloured.

E2037 10pf. Type E **614** 15 15
E2038 20pf. Leopard cub 15 15
E2039 35pf. Tiger cub 20 15
E2040 50pf. Snow leopard cub . . 1·70 1·30

1978. Container Goods Traffic. Multicoloured.

E2041 10pf. Type E **615** 15 15
E2042 20pf. Placing container on truck 15 15
E2043 35pf. Diesel locomotive and container wagons 25 25
E2044 70pf. Placing containers on "Boltenhagen" . . . . 2·30 1·70

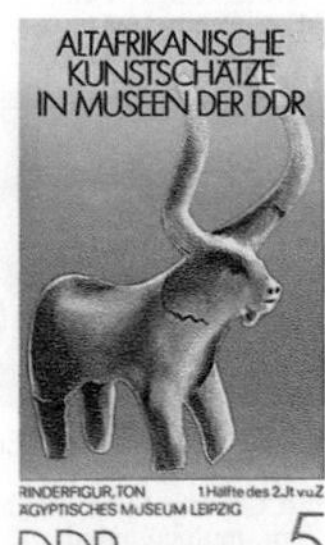

E **616** Clay Ox (Egyptian Museum, Leipzig)

1978. Ancient African Works of Art in Egyptian Museums at Leipzig and Berlin. Multicoloured.

E2045 5pf. Type E **616** 15 15
E2046 10pf. Clay head of woman (Leipzig) 15 15
E2047 20pf. Gold bangle (Berlin) (horiz) 15 15
E2048 25pf. Gold ring plate (Berlin) 20 15
E2049 35pf. Gold signet-ring plate (Berlin) 25 15
E2050 40pf. Necklace (Berlin) (horiz) . . . . 1·80 1·50

E **617** Justus von Liebig (agricultural chemist, 175th birth anniv)

1978. Celebrities' Birth Anniversaries.
E2051 E **617** 5pf. black and ochre 15 15
E2052 – 10pf. black and blue 15 15
E2053 – 15pf. black and green 15 15
E2054 – 20pf. black and blue 15 15
E2055 – 25pf. black and red 20 15
E2056 – 35pf. black and green 20 15
E2057 – 70pf. black and drab 2·10 1·60
DESIGNS: 10pf. Joseph Dietzgen (writer, 150th); 15pf. Alfred Doblin (novelist, 100th); 20pf. Hans Loch (politician, 80th); 25pf. Theodor Brugsch (scientist, 100th); 35pf. Freidrich Ludwig Jahn (gymnast, 200th); 70pf. Albrecht von Graefe (ophthalmatician, 150th).

E **618** Cottbus, 1730

1978. 5th National Youth Stamp Exhibition, Cottbus. Multicoloured.
E2058 10pf.+5pf. Type E **618** . . 30 35
E2059 20pf. Modern Cottbus . . 30 35

E **619** Havana Buildings and Festival Emblem

1978. 11th World Youth and Students' Festival, Havana. Multicoloured.
E2060 20pf. Type E **619** 45 50
E2061 35pf. Festival emblem and East Berlin buildings . . 45 50

E **620** "Trooper with Halberd" (Hans Schaufelein)

E **621** "Multicar 25" Truck

1978. Drawings in Berlin State Museum. Sheet 110 × 98 mm containing Type E **620** and similar vert designs, each brownish black and stone.
MSE2062 10pf. Type E **620**; 20pf. "Woman reading a Letter" (Jean Antoine Watteau); 25pf. "Seated Boy" (Gabriel Metsu); 30pf. "Young Man cutting a Loaf" (Cornelis Saftleven); 35pf. "St. Anthony in a Landscape" (Matthias Grunewald); 50pf. "Man seated in an Armchair" (Abraham van Diepenbeeck) 4·00 4·00

1978. Leipzig Autumn Fair. Multicoloured.
E2063 10pf. Type E **621** 25 15
E2064 25pf. "Three Kings" Fair building, Petersstrasse 50 25

E **622** "Soyuz" Spaceship and Emblems

1978. Soviet–East German Space Flight (1st issue).
E2065 E **622** 20pf. multicoloured 35 25
See also Nos. E2069/**MS**2073.

E **623** Mauthausen Memorial

1978. War Victims' Memorial, Mauthausen, Austria.
E2066 E **623** 35pf. multicoloured 35 30

E **624** W.M.S. Unit on the March

1978. 25th Anniv of Workers' Militia Squads.
E2067 20pf. Type E **624** 40 45
E2068 35pf. Members of Red Army, National People's Army and W.M.S. . . . 40 45

E **625** "Soyuz", "MKF 6M" Camera and Space Station

E **626** Human Pyramid

1978. Soviet–East German Space Flight (2nd issue). Multicoloured.
E2069 5pf. Type E **625** 15 15
E2070 10pf. Albert Einstein and "Soyuz" 15 15
E2071 20pf. Sigmund Jahn (first East German cosmonaut) (vert) . . . 15 15
E2072 35pf. "Salyut", "Soyuz" and Lilienthal monoplane glider . . . 1·40 1·10
MSE2073 110 × 90 mm. 1m. Space station and cosmonauts Valeri Bykovski and Jahn (54 × 32 mm) 2·20 2·20

1978. The Circus. Multicoloured.
E2074 5pf. Type E **626** 35 65
E2075 10pf. Elephant on tricycle 70 1·20
E2076 20pf. Performing horse . . 1·20 1·90
E2077 35pf. Polar bear kissing girl . . . . 2·30 3·75

E **627** African behind Barbed Wire

E **628** Construction of Natural Gas Pipe Line

1978. International Anti-Apartheid Year.
E2078 E **627** 20pf. multicoloured 35 20

1978. Construction of "Friendship Line" (Drushba-Trasse) by East German Youth.
E2079 E **628** 20pf. multicoloured 35 20

E **629** "Parides hahneli" ("Papilio hahneli")

E **631** Old Woman and Youth

E **630** Wheel-lock Gun, 1630

1978. 250th Anniv of Dresden Scientific Museums. Multicoloured.
E2080 10pf. Type E **629** 20 15
E2081 20pf. "Agama lehmanni" 20 15
E2082 25pf. Agate 20 15
E2083 35pf. "Palaeobatrachus diluvianus" 20 15
E2084 40pf. Mantlepiece clock, c. 1720 . . . . . 30 15
E2085 50pf. Table telescope, c. 1750 . . . 3·00 2·30

1978. Sporting Guns from Suhl. Multicoloured.
E2086 5pf. Type E **630** 15 20
E2087 10pf. Double-barrelled gun, 1978 . . . . 20 20
E2088 20pf. Spring-cock gun, 1780 . . . . 30 35
E2089 25pf. Superimposed double-barrelled gun, 1978 . . . . 35 40
E2090 35pf. Percussion gun, 1850 55 60
E2091 70pf. Three-barrelled gun, 1978 . . . . 1·20 1·10

1978. Fairy Tales. "Rapunzel". Multicoloured.
E2092 10pf. Type E **631** 25 40
E2093 15pf. Old Woman climbing tower on Rapunzel's hair . . . . 1·20 90
E2094 20pf. Prince calling to Rapunzel 25 40
E2095 25pf. Prince climbing through window 25 40
E2096 35pf. Old woman about to cut Rapunzel's hair . . 1·20 90
E2097 50pf. "Happy ever after" 25 40

E **632** Chaffinches

E **633** Chabo

1979. Songbirds. Multicoloured.
E2098 5pf. Type E **632** 15 15
E2099 10pf. Eurasian nuthatch 15 15
E2100 20pf. European robin . . . 15 15
E2101 25pf. Common rosefinch 20 15
E2102 35pf. Blue tit 25 20
E2103 50pf. Linnet . . . . 3·00 2·00

1979. Poultry. Multicoloured.
E2104 10pf. Type E **633** 15 15
E2105 15pf. Crows head 15 15
E2106 20pf. Porcelain-colour Feather-footed dwarf . . 15 15
E2107 25pf. Saxonian 20 15
E2108 35pf. Phoenix 25 15
E2109 50pf. Striped Italian . . . 3·00 2·10

E **634** Telephone Exchanges in 1900 and 1979

1979. Telephone and Telegraphs Communications. Multicoloured.
E2110 20pf. Type E **634** 20 15
E2111 35pf. Transmitting telegrams in 1800 and 1979 . . . . 1·20 75

E **635** Albert Einstein

E **636** Max Klinger Exhibition House, Leipzig

1979. Birth Centenary of Albert Einstein (physicist). Sheet 55 × 86 mm.
MSE2112 E **635** 1m. light brown, deep brown and brown . . . . 2·50 2·30

1979. Leipzig Spring Fair. Multicoloured.
E2113 10pf. Type E **636** 25 15
E2114 25pf. Horizontal drill and milling machine 45 25

E **637** Otto Hahn (physicist, centenary)

1979. Celebrities' Birth Anniversaries.
E2115 E **637** 5pf. black and pink 20 15
E2116 – 10pf. black and blue 20 15
E2117 – 20pf. black and yellow 20 15
E2118 – 25pf. black and green 25 15
E2119 – 35pf. black and blue 25 15
E2120 – 70pf. black and pink 2·50 1·90
DESIGNS: 10pf. Max von Laue (physicist, centenary); 20pf. Arthur Scheunert (physiologist, centenary); 25pf. Friedrich August Kekule (chemist, 150th); 35pf. Georg Forster (explorer and writer, 225th); 70pf. Gotth Ephraim Lessing (playwright and essayist, 250th).

E **638** "Radebeul" (container ship), "Sturmvogel" (tug) and Shipping Route Map

1979. World Navigation Day.
E2121 E **638** 20pf. multicoloured 35 20

E **639** Horch "8", 1911

1979. Zwickau Motor Industry. Multicoloured.
E2122 20pf. Type E **639** 45 55
E2123 35pf. Trabant "601 S de luxe", 1978 . . . . . . 80 70

E **640** MXA Electric Train

1979. East German Locomotives and Wagons. Multicoloured.
E2124 5pf. Type E **640** 20 15
E2125 10pf. Self-discharging wagon 20 15
E2126 20pf. Diesel locomotive No. 110836.4 . . . . . 20 15
E2127 35pf. Railway car transporter . . . . . . 1·20 95

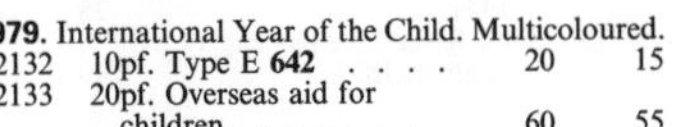

E **641** Durga (18th century)

E **642** Children Playing

1979. Indian Miniatures. Multicoloured.
E2128 20pf. Type E **641** 15 15
E2129 35pf. Mahavira (15th/16th century) 25 15
E2130 50pf. Todi Ragini (17th century) 30 15
E2131 70pf. Asavari Ragini (17th century) . . . . 2·75 2·40

1979. International Year of the Child. Multicoloured.
E2132 10pf. Type E **642** 20 15
E2133 20pf. Overseas aid for children 60 55

E **643** Construction Work on Leipziger Strasse Complex

1979. "Berlin Project" of Free German Youth Organization. Multicoloured.
E2134 10pf. Type E **643** 15 15
E2135 20pf. Berlin-Marzahn building site 50 40

E **644** Torchlight Procession of Free German Youth, 1949

1979. National Youth Festival. Mult.

E2136	10pf.+5pf. Type E **644** . .	30	35
E2137	20pf. Youth rally	30	35

E **645** Exhibition Symbol

1979. "agra 79" Agricultural Exhibition, Markkleeberg.

E2138	E **645** 10pf. multicoloured	35	20

E **646** "Rostock" (train ferry), 1977

1979. 70th Anniv of Sassnitz–Trelleborg Railway Ferry. Multicoloured.

E2139	20pf. Type E **646**	45	50
E2140	35pf. "Rugen" (train ferry)	45	50

E **647** Hospital Classroom

1979. Rehabilitation. Multicoloured.

E2141	10pf. Type E **647**	15	15
E2142	35pf. Wheelchair-bound factory worker	65	60

E **648** Cycling

1979. 7th Children's and Young People's Sports Day, Berlin. Multicoloured.

E2143	10pf. Type E **648**	20	15
E2144	20pf. Roller-skating . . .	60	45

E **649** Dahlia "Rubens"

E **650** Goose-thief Fountain, Dresden

1979. "iga" International Garden Exhibition, Erfurt. Dahlias. Multicoloured.

E2145	10pf. Type E **649**	15	15
E2146	20pf. "Rosalie"	15	15
E2147	25pf. "Corinna"	20	15
E2148	35pf. "Enzett-Dolli" . . .	25	15
E2149	50pf. "Enzett-Carola" . .	30	25
E2150	70pf. "Don Lorenzo" . .	3·25	2·75

1979. National Stamp Exhibition, Dresden. Multicoloured.

E2151	10pf.+5pf. Type E **650** . .	60	45
E2152	20pf. Dandelion fountain, Dresden	20	15
MSE2153	86 × 55 mm. 1m. Dresden buildings (horiz)	2·50	2·10

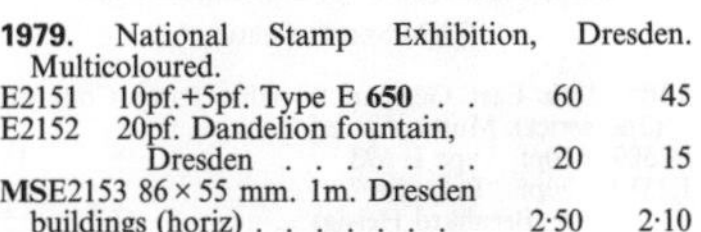

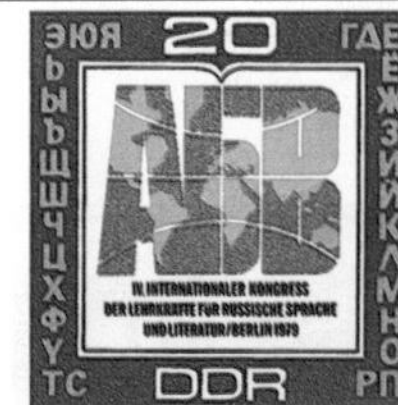

E **651** World Map and Russian Alphabet

1979. 4th International Congress of Russian Language and Literature Teachers, Berlin.

E2154	E **651** 20pf. multicoloured	35	20

E **652** Italian Lira de Gamba, 1592

1979. Musical Instruments in Leipzig Museum. Multicoloured.

E2155	20pf. Type E **652**	20	15
E2156	25pf. French serpent, 17th/18th century	25	15
E2157	40pf. French barrel-lyre, 1750	30	15
E2158	85pf. German tenor flugelhorn, 1850	2·75	2·10

E **653** Horseracing

1979. 30th International Congress on Horse-breeding in Socialist Countries, Berlin. Multicoloured.

E2159	10pf. Type E **653**	20	15
E2160	25pf. Dressage (pas de deux)	95	80

E **654** Mittelbau-Dora Memorial

E **655** Teddy Bear

1979. Mittelbau-Dora Memorial, Nordhausen.

E2161	E **654** 35pf. black and violet	60	30

1979. Leipzig Autumn Fair. Multicoloured.

E2162	10pf. Type E **655**	15	15
E2163	25pf. Grosser Blumenberg building, Richard Wagner Square	40	20

E **656** Philipp Dengel

E **657** Building Worker and Flats

1979. Socialist Personalities.

E2164	E **656** 10pf. black, green and deep green . .	25	15
E2165	– 10pf. black, bl & ind	25	15
E2166	– 10pf. blk, stone & bis	25	15
E2167	– 10pf. black, red & brn	25	15

DESIGNS: No. E2165, Otto Buchwitz; No. E2166, Bernard Koenen; No. E2167, Heinrich Rau.

1979. 30th Anniv of German Democratic Republic. Multicoloured.

E2168	5pf. Type E **657**	20	15
E2169	10pf. Boy and girl	20	15
E2170	15pf. Soldiers	75	50
E2171	20pf. Miner and Soviet soldier	20	15
MSE2172	90 × 110 mm. 1m. Family and flats (29 × 51 mm)	2·10	1·50

E **658** Girl applying Lipstick (1966/7)

E **659** Vietnamese Soldier, Mother and Child

1979. Meissen Porcelain. Multicoloured.

E2173	5pf. Type E **658**	15	20
E2174	10pf. "Altozier" coffee pot (18th cent)	25	25
E2175	15pf. "Gosser Ausschnitt" coffee pot (1973/4) . . .	30	35
E2176	20pf. Vase with lid (18th century)	45	50
E2177	25pf. Parrot with cherry (18th century)	55	60
E2178	35pf. Harlequin with tankard (18th century)	80	90
E2179	50pf. Flower girl (18th century)	1·20	1·20
E2180	70pf. Sake bottle (18th century)	1·60	1·80

1979. "Invincible Vietnam".

E2181	E **659** 10pf.+5pf. black and red	35	30

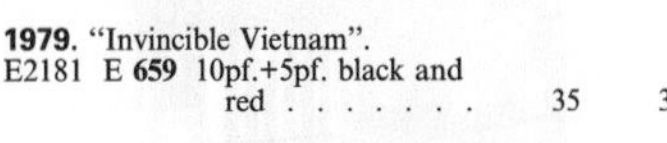

E **660** Rag-doll, 1800

E **661** "Balance on Ice" (Johanna Starke)

1979. Dolls. Multicoloured.

E2182	10pf. Type E **660**	25	40
E2183	15pf. Ceramic doll, 1960	1·20	90
E2184	20pf. Wooden doll, 1780	25	40
E2185	35pf. Straw puppet, 1900	25	40
E2186	50pf. Jointed doll, 1800 . .	1·20	90
E2187	70pf. Tumbler-doll, 1820	25	40

1980. Winter Olympic Games, Lake Placid. Multicoloured.

E2188	10pf. "Bobsleigh Start" (Gunter Rechn) (horiz)	15	15
E2189	20pf. Type E **661**	15	15
E2190	25pf.+10pf. "Ski jumpers" (plastic sculpture, Gunter Schultz)	20	15
E2191	35pf. "Speed Skaters at the Start" (Axel Wunsch)	1·60	1·50
MSE2192	79 × 55 mm. 1m. "Skiing Girls" (Lothar Zitmann) (29 × 24 mm)	2·50	2·10

E **662** Stille Musik Rock Garden, Grosssedlitz

1980. Baroque Gardens. Multicoloured.

E2193	10pf. Type E **662**	20	15
E2194	20pf. Belvedere Orangery, Weimar	20	15
E2195	50pf. Flower garden, Dornburg Castle	30	20
E2196	70pf. Park, Rheinsberg Castle	2·10	1·90

E **663** Cable-laying Machine and Dish Aerial

1980. Post Office Activities. Multicoloured.

E2212	10pf. Type E **663**	15	15
E2213	20pf. T.V. Tower, Berlin, and television	30	25

E **664** Johann Wolfgang Dobereiner (chemist, bicent)

1980. Celebrities' Birth Anniversaries.

E2214	E **664** 5pf. black and bistre	15	15
E2215	– 10pf. black and red	15	15
E2216	– 20pf. black and green	15	15
E2217	– 25pf. black and blue	15	15
E2218	– 35pf. black and blue	20	15
E2219	– 70pf. black and red	1·90	1·20

DESIGNS: 10pf. Frederic Joliot-Curie (physicist, and chemist, 80th anniv); 20pf. Johann Friedrich Naumann (zoologist, bicent); 25pf. Alfred Wegener (explorer and geophysicist, cent); 35pf. Carl von Clausewitz (Prussian general, bicent); 70pf. Helene Weigel (actress, 80th anniv).

E **665** Karl Marx University, Leipzig

E **666** Werner Eggerath

1980. Leipzig Spring Fair. Multicoloured.

E2220	10pf. Type E **665** . . .	25	15
E2221	25pf. "ZT 303" tractor . .	30	25

1980. 80th Birth Anniv of Werner Eggerath (socialist).

E2222	E **666** 10pf. brown and red	50	25

E **667** Cosmonauts and "Interkosmos" Emblem

1980. "Interkosmos" Programme. Sheet 109 × 89 mm.

MSE2223	E **667** 1m. multicoloured	2·50	2·10

E **668** "On the Horizontal Beam" (sculpture, Erich Wurzer)

1980. Olympic Games, Moscow (1st issue). Multicoloured.

E2224	10pf. Type E **668**	15	15
E2225	20pf.+5pf. "Runners before the Winning Post" (Lothar Zitmann)	15	15
E2226	50pf. "Coxless Four" (Wilfred Falkenthal) . .	1·50	1·30

See also Nos. E2247/9.

E 669 Flags of Member States

E 670 Co-operative Society Building (W. Gropius)

1980. 25th Anniv of Warsaw Pact.
E2227 E **669** 20pf. multicoloured . . . 50 25

1980. Bauhaus Architecture. Multicoloured.
E2228 5pf. Type E **670** 20 15
E2229 10pf. Socialists' Memorial Place (M. v. d. Rhode) (horiz) 20 15
E2230 15pf. Monument to the Fallen of March 1922 (W. Gropius) 20 15
E2231 20pf. Steel Building 1926 (G. Muche and R. Paulick) (horiz) . . . 20 15
E2232 50pf. Trade Union school (H. Meyer) 30 15
E2233 70pf. Bauhaus building (W. Gropius) (horiz) . . 3·00 2·00

E **671** Rostock Buildings

1980. 18th Workers' Festival, Rostock. Mult.
E2234 10pf. Type E **671** 25 15
E2235 20pf. Costumed dancers . . 45 25

E **672** Radar Complex, Berlin-Schoenefeld Airport

1980. "Aerosozphilex 1980" International Airmail Exhibition, Berlin. Multicoloured.
E2236 20pf. Type E **672** 45 50
E2237 25pf. Ilyushin Il-62M at Schonefeld Airport . . . 45 50
E2238 35pf. PZL-106A Kruk crop-spraying airplane . . 70 60
E2239 70pf. Antonov An-2 aerial photography biplane and multispectrum camera . . . . 1·40 1·20
MSE2240 64 × 95 mm. 1m.+10pf. Ilyushin Il-62M jetliner and globe . . 3·50 3·25

E **673** Okapi

E **675** Huntley Microscope

E **674** Suhl, 1700

1980. Endangered Animals. Multicoloured.
E2241 5pf. Type E **673** 15 15
E2242 10pf. Lesser pandas . . . 15 15
E2243 15pf. Maned wolf 20 15
E2244 20pf. Arabian oryx 20 15
E2245 25pf. White-eared pheasant 25 15
E2246 35pf. Musk oxen . . . . . 2·30 1·60

1980. Olympic Games, Moscow (2nd issue). As Type E **668**. Multicoloured.
E2247 10pf. "Judo" (Erhard Schmidt) 15 15
E2248 20pf.+10pf. "Swimmer" (Willi Sitte) (vert) . . 25 15
E2249 50pf. "Spurt" (sculpture, Siegfried Schreiber) . . 1·60 1·30
MSE2250 79 × 55 mm. 1m. "Spinnakers" (Karl Raetsch) (29 × 24 mm) . . . . 2·50 2·10

1980. 6th National Youth Stamp Exhibition, Suhl. Multicoloured.
E2251 10pf.+5pf. Type E **674** . . 40 40
E2252 20pf. Modern Suhl 40 40

1980. Carl Zeiss Optical Museum, Jena. Mult.
E2253 20pf. Type E **675** 35 40
E2254 25pf. Magny microscope, 1751 . . . . 45 50
E2255 35pf. Amici microscope, 1845 . . . . 65 65
E2256 70pf. Zeiss microscope, 1873 . . . . 1·40 1·20

E **676** Majdanek Memorial

1980. War Victims' Memorial, Majdanek, Poland.
E2257 E **676** 35pf. multicoloured . . 65 30

E **677** Information Centre, Leipzig

1980. Leipzig Autumn Fair. Multicoloured.
E2258 10pf. Type E **677** 25 15
E2259 25pf. Carpet-knitting machine 55 25

E **678** Palace of Republic, Berlin

1980. 67th Interparliamentary Conference, Berlin.
E2260 E **678** 20pf. multicoloured . . 90 20

E **679** "Laughing Boy with Flute"

E **680** Clenched Fist and Star

1980. 400th Anniv of Frans Hals (artist). Multicoloured.
E2261 10pf. Type E **679** 20 15
E2262 20pf. "Portrait of Young Man in Drab Coat" . . 20 15
E2263 25pf. "The Mulatto" . . . 25 15
E2264 35pf. "Portrait of Young Man in Black Coat" . . 1·40 1·10
MSE2265 80 × 55 mm. 1m. brown (Self-portrait) (29 × 23 mm) . . 2·75 2·10

1980. "Solidarity".
E2266 E **680** 10pf.+5pf. turq & red 35 25

E **681** "Leccinum versipelle" ("Leccinum testaceo scabrum")

1980. Edible Mushrooms. Multicoloured.
E2267 5pf. Type E **681** 15 15
E2268 10pf. "Boletus miniatoporus" ("Boletus erythropus") 15 15
E2269 15pf. "Agaricus campestris" ("Agaricus campester") 20 15
E2270 20pf. "Xerocomus badius" 25 15
E2271 35pf. "Boletus edulis" . . 30 20
E2272 70pf. "Cantharellus cibarius" . . . . 2·40 2·10

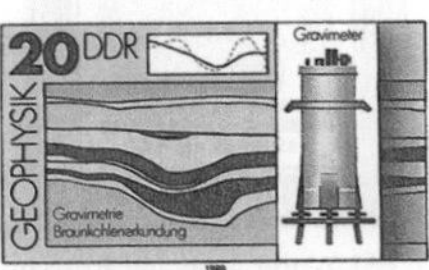

E **682** Gravimetry

1980. Geophysics. Multicoloured.
E2273 20pf. Type E **682** 35 30
E2274 25pf. Bore-hole measuring 45 45
E2275 35pf. Seismic prospecting 70 65
E2276 50pf. Seismology . . . . . 1·00 90

E **683** Radebeul–Radeburg Steam Locomotive

1980. Narrow-gauge Railways (1st series). Multicoloured.
E2277 20pf. Type E **683** 45 50
E2278 20pf. Bad Doberan–Ostseebad Kuhlungsborn steam locomotive . . . 45 50
E2279 25pf. Radebeul–Radeburg passenger carriage . . . 45 50
E2280 35pf. Bad Doberan–Ostseebad Kuhlungsborn passenger carriage . . . 45 50
See also Nos. E2342/5, E2509/12 and E2576/9.

E **684** Toy Steam Locomotive, 1850

E **685** Mozart

1980. Historical Toys. Multicoloured.
E2281 10pf. Type E **684** 25 50
E2282 20pf. Aeroplane, 1914 . . 1·00 90
E2283 25pf. Steam-roller, 1920 . . 25 30
E2284 35pf. Sailing ship, 1825 . . 25 30
E2285 40pf. Car, 1900 . . . . . 1·00 90
E2286 50pf. Balloon, 1920 . . . 25 30

1981. 225th Birth Anniv of Wolfgang Amadeus Mozart (composer). Sheet 55 × 80 mm.
MSE2287 E **685** 1m. black, carmine-rose and stone . . . . 1·40 1·20

E **686** "Malus pumila"

E **687** Heinrich von Stephan

1981. Rare Plants in Berlin Arboretum. Mult.
E2288 5pf. Type E **686** 20 15
E2289 10pf. "Halesia carolina" (horiz) 20 15
E2290 20pf. "Colutea arborescens" 20 15
E2291 25pf. "Paulownia tomentosa" 30 15
E2292 35pf. "Lonicera periclymenum" (horiz) . . 30 15
E2293 50pf. "Calycanthus floridus" . . . . 2·75 2·40

1981. 150th Birth Anniv of Heinrich von Stephan (founder of U.P.U.).
E2294 E **687** 10pf. black and yellow 35 20

E **688** Soldiers on Parade

1981. 25th Anniv of National People's Army. Multicoloured.
E2295 10pf. Type E **688** 25 15
E2296 20pf. Marching soldiers . . 30 15

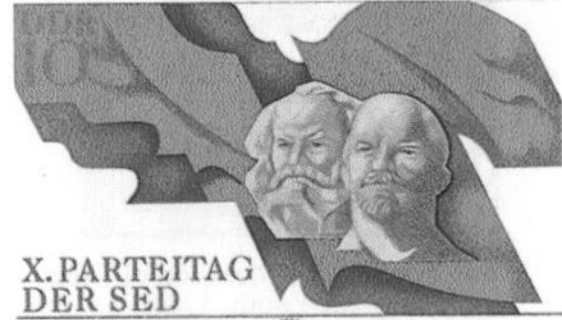

E **689** Marx and Lenin

1981. 10th East German Socialist Party Congress (1st series).
E2297 E **689** 10pf. multicoloured 35 20
See Nos. E2309/**MS**2313.

E **690** Counter Clerks

1981. Post Office Training. Multicoloured.
E2298 5pf. Type E **690** 20 15
E2299 10pf. Telephone engineers 20 15
E2300 15pf. Radio communications 20 15
E2301 20pf. Rosa Luxemburg Engineering School, Leipzig 30 15
E2302 25pf. Friedrich List Communications School, Dresden . . . . 1·50 1·10

E **691** Erich Baron

E **692** Hotel Merkur Leipzig

1981. Socialist Personalities.
E2303 E **691** 10pf. black and green 25 15
E2304 – 10pf. black and yellow 25 15
E2305 – 10pf. black and blue 25 15
E2306 – 10pf. black and brown 25 15
DESIGNS: No. E2304, Conrad Blenkle; E2305, Arthur Ewert; E2306, Walter Stoecker.

1981. Leipzig Spring Fair. Multicoloured.
E2307 10pf. Type E **692** 25 15
E2308 25pf. Open-cast mining machine 45 25

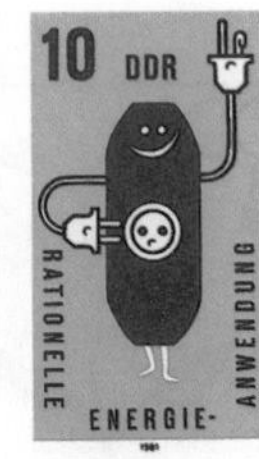

E **693** "Ernst Thalmann" (Willi Sitte)

E **695** Plugs and Socket

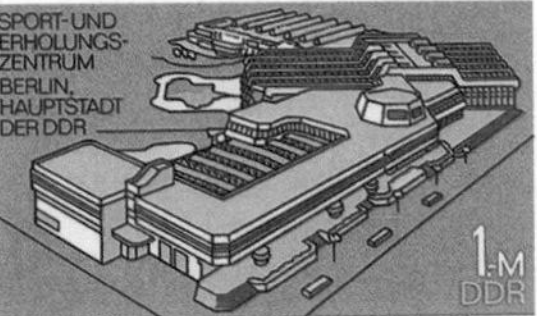

E **694** Sports Centre

1981. 10th East German Socialist Party Congress (2nd series). Multicoloured.
E2309 10pf. Type E **693** 15 15
E2310 20pf. "Brigadier" (Bernhard Heisig) . . . 15 15

E2311 25pf. "Festival Day" (Rudolf Bergander) . . 1·10 95
E2312 35pf. "Comrades in Arms" (Paul Michaelis) 25 15
MSE2313 108 × 82 mm. 1m. "When Communists are Dreaming" (Walter Womacka) . . . . . . 2·10 1·40

1981. Sports Centre, Berlin. Sheet 110 × 90 mm.
MSE2314 E **694** 1m. multicoloured 2·75 2·20

1981. Conservation of Energy.
E2315 E **695** 10pf. black & orange 30 20

E **696** Heinrich Barkhausen

1981. Celebrities' Birth Anniversaries.
E2316 E **696** 10pf. black and blue 15 15
E2317 – 20pf. black and red 20 15
E2318 – 25pf. black and brown . . . . . . 2·75 1·90
E2319 – 35pf. black and violet 30 15
E2320 – 50pf. black and green 35 15
E2321 – 70pf. black and brown 55 25
DESIGNS: 10pf. Type E **696** (physicist, birth centenary); 20pf. Johannes R. Becher (writer, 90th birth anniv); 25pf. Richard Dedekind (mathematician, 150th birth anniv); 35pf. Georg Philipp Telemann (composer, 300th anniv); 50pf. Adelbert V. Chamisso (poet and naturalist, bicentenary); 70pf. Wilhelm Raabe (novelist, 150th birth anniv).

E **697** Free German Youth Members and Banner

1981. 11th Free German Youth Parliament. Multicoloured.
E2322 10pf. Type E **697** 30 35
E2323 20pf. Free German Youth members instructing foreign students 30 35

E **698** Worlitz Park

1981. Landscaped Parks. Multicoloured.
E2324 5pf. Type E **698** 15 15
E2325 10pf. Tiefurt Park, Weimar 15 15
E2326 15pf. Marxwalde 15 15
E2327 20pf. Branitz Park 20 15
E2328 25pf. Treptow Park, Berlin 2·00 1·50
E2329 35pf. Wiesenburg Park . . 30 25

E **699** Children at Play and Sport

1981. 8th Children's and Young People's Sports Days, Berlin. Multicoloured.
E2330 10pf.+5pf. Type E **699** . . 75 45
E2331 20pf. Artistic gymnastics 30 20

E **700** Berlin Theatre

1981. Birth Bicentenary of Karl Friedrich Schinkel (architect).
E2332 E **700** 10pf. stone and black 1·00 15
E2333 – 25pf. stone and black 2·50 85
DESIGN: 25pf. Old Museum, Berlin.

E **701** Throwing the Javelin from a Wheel chair

E **702** House, Zaulsdorf

1981. International Year of Disabled Persons. Multicoloured.
E2334 5pf. Type E **701** 30 20
E2335 15pf. Disabled people in art gallery 30 20

1981. Half-timbered Buildings. Multicoloured.
E2336 10pf. Type E **702** 15 15
E2337 20pf. "Sugar-loaf" cottage, Gross Zicker (horiz) . . 15 15
E2338 25pf. Farmhouse, Weckersdorf 25 15
E2339 35pf. House, Pillgram (horiz) 30 15
E2340 50pf. House, Eschenbach 35 25
E2341 70pf. House, Ludersdorf (horiz) . . . . 3·75 2·40

1981. Narrow-Gauge Railways (2nd series). As Type E **683**. Multicoloured.
E2342 5pf. black and red 25 30
E2343 5pf. black and red 25 30
E2344 15pf. multicoloured . . . 25 30
E2345 20pf. multicoloured . . . 25 30
DESIGNS: Nos. E2342, Freital–Kurort Kipsdorf steam locomotive; E2343, Putbus–Gohren steam locomotive; E2344, Freital–Kurort Kipsdorf luggage van; E2345, Putbus–Gohren passenger carriage.

E **703** Chemical Works

E **704** Ebers Papyrus (Leipzig University Library)

1981. Leipzig Autumn Fair. Multicoloured.
E2346 10pf. Type E **703** 25 15
E2347 25pf. New Draper's Hall (horiz) 45 35

1981. Precious Books from East German Libraries. Multicoloured.
E2348 20pf. Type E **704** 15 15
E2349 35pf. Maya manuscript (Dresden Library) . . . 25 15
E2350 50pf. Miniature from "Les six visions Messire Francoys Petrarque" (Berlin State Library) . . 1·80 1·50

E **705** Sassnitz Memorial

E **706** Henbane and Incense Burner

1981. Resistance Fighters' Memorial, Sassnitz.
E2351 E **705** 35pf. multicoloured 60 30

1981. Early Medical Equipment in the Karl-Sudhoff Institute, Leipzig. Multicoloured.
E2352 10pf. Type E **706** 15 15
E2353 20pf. Dental instruments 15 15
E2354 25pf. Forceps 20 15
E2355 35pf. Bladder knife and hernia shears 30 15
E2356 50pf. Speculum and gynaecological forceps (vert) . . . . 3·25 2·75
E2357 85pf. Triploid elevators (vert) 60 30

E **707** Letter from Friedrich Engels, 1840

E **708** African breaking Chains

1981. Stamp Day. Multicoloured.
E2358 10pf.+5pf. Type E **707** . . 1·10 40
E2359 20pf. Postcard from Karl Marx, 1878 . . . . . . 30 15

1981. "Solidarity".
E2360 E **708** 10pf.+5pf. mult . . . 30 15

E **709** Tug

E **710** Windmill, Dabel

1981. Inland Shipping. Multicoloured.
E2361 10pf. Type E **709** 20 15
E2362 20pf. Tug and barges . . . 20 15
E2363 25pf. Diesel-electric paddle-ferry, River Elbe 25 15
E2364 35pf. Ice-breaker in the Oder estuary 30 15
E2365 50pf. "Schonewalde" (motor barge) 35 25
E2366 85pf. Dredger . . . . . . 3·00 2·75

1981. Windmills. Multicoloured.
E2367 10pf. Type E **710** 20 15
E2368 20pf. Pahrenz 20 15
E2369 25pf. Dresden-Gohlis . . . 25 15
E2370 70pf. Ballstadt . . . . . . 2·20 1·60

E **711** Snake, 1850

E **712** Coffee Pot, 1715

1981. Historical Toys. Multicoloured.
E2371 10pf. Type E **711** 25 40
E2372 20pf. Teddy bear, 1910 . . 25 40
E2373 25pf. Goldfish, 1935 . . . 1·40 1·10
E2374 35pf. Hobby-horse, 1850 1·40 1·10
E2375 40pf. Pull-along duck, 1800 . . . . 25 40
E2376 70pf. Clockwork frog, 1930 . . . . 25 40

1982. 300th Birth Anniv of Johann Friedrich Bottger (founder of Meissen China Works). Multicoloured.
E2377 10pf. Type E **712** 25 20
E2378 20pf. Vase decorated with flowers, 1715 . . . . . 45 45
E2379 25pf. "Oberon" (figurine), 1969 . . . . 60 55
E2380 35pf. Vase "Day and Night", 1979 . . . . . 85 70
MSE2381 89 × 110 mm. 50pf. Portrait medal; 50pf. Bottger's seal 2·75 2·30

E **713** Post Office, Bad Liebenstein

1982. Post Office Building. Multicoloured.
E2382 20pf. Type E **713** 20 15
E2383 25pf. Telecommunications Centre, Berlin 20 15
E2384 35pf. Head Post Office, Erfurt 30 15
E2385 50pf. Head Post Office, Dresden 6 . . . . . . 2·10 1·80

E **714** Alpine Marmot

E **715** Silhouette of Goethe

1982. International Fur Auction, Leipzig. Multicoloured.
E2386 10pf. Type E **714** 15 15
E2387 20pf. Polecat 20 15
E2388 25pf. European mink . . . 25 15
E2389 35pf. Beech marten . . . 1·60 1·30

1982. Johann Wolfgang von Goethe and Friedrich von Schiller (writers) Commemoration. Sheet 110 × 90 mm containing Type E **715** and similar vert design. Multicoloured.
MSE2390 50pf. Type E **715** (150th death anniv); 50pf. Silhouette of Schiller (175th death (1980) and 225th birth (1984) annivs) . . . 2·50 2·50

E **716** West Entrance to Fairground

1982. Leipzig Spring Fair. Multicoloured.
E2391 10pf. Type E **716** 20 15
E2392 25pf. Seamless steel tube plant, Riesa Zeithain . . 40 25

E **717** Dr. Robert Koch

E **718** Max Fechner

1982. Centenary of Discovery of Tubercle Bacillus. Sheet 80 × 55 mm.
MSE2393 E **717** 1m. multicoloured 2·50 2·20

1982. Socialist Personalities.
E2394 E **718** 10pf. brown 20 10
E2395 – 10pf. green 20 10
E2396 – 10pf. lilac 20 10
E2397 – 10pf. blue 20 10
E2398 – 10pf. green 20 10
DESIGNS: No. E2395, Ottomar Geschke; E2396, Helmut Lehmann; E2397, Herbert Warnke; E2398, Otto Winzer.

E **719** Meadow Saffron

E **720** Decorative Initial "I"

1982. Poisonous Plants. Multicoloured.
E2399 10pf. Type E **719** 20 15
E2400 15pf. Bog arum 20 15
E2401 20pf. Labrador tea 20 15
E2402 25pf. Bryony 20 15
E2403 35pf. Monkshood 30 20
E2404 50pf. Henbane . . . . . . 1·80 1·50

1982. International "Art of the Book" Exhibition, Leipzig.
E2405 E **720** 15pf. multicoloured 55 60
E2406 – 35pf. brn, red & blk 55 60
DESIGN: 35pf. Exhibition emblem.

E **721** "Mother with Child" (W. Womacka)

E **722** Osprey

1982. 10th Free German Trade Unions Association Congress, Berlin.

E2407	E **721** 10pf. black, red and yellow	15	15
E2408	– 20pf. multicoloured	25	15
E2409	– 25pf. multicoloured	90	70

DESIGNS—HORIZ: 20pf. "Discussion by Collective of Innovators" (Willi Neubert). VERT: 25pf. "Young Couple" (Karl-Heinz Jakob).

1982. Protected Birds. Multicoloured.

E2410	10pf. Type E **722**	25	15
E2411	20pf. White-tailed sea eagle (horiz)	25	15
E2412	25pf. Little owl	25	15
E2413	35pf. Eagle owl	2·10	1·50

E **723** Old and Modern Buildings

1982. 19th Workers' Festival, Neubrandenburg. Multicoloured.

E2414	10pf. Type E **723**	30	20
E2415	20pf. Couple in traditional costume	55	40

E **724** Memorial Medal

1982. Birth Centenary of Georgi Dimitrov (Bulgarian statesman). Sheet 80 × 55 mm.

MSE2416	E **724** 1m. multicoloured	3·00	2·10

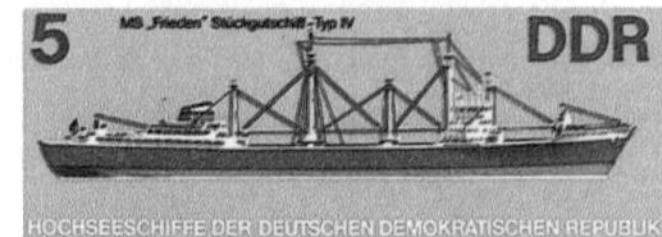

E **725** "Frieden" (freighter)

1982. Ocean-going Ships. Multicoloured.

E2417	5pf. Type E **725**	20	15
E2418	10pf. "Fichtelberg" (roll on roll off freighter)	20	15
E2419	15pf. "Brocken" (heavy cargo carrier)	20	15
E2420	20pf. "Weimar" (container ship)	20	15
E2421	25pf. "Vorwarts" (freighter)	20	15
E2422	35pf. "Berlin" (container ship)	2·10	1·60

E **726** Members' Activities

1982. 30th Anniv of Sports and Science Association.

E2423	E **726** 20pf. multicoloured	50	20

E **727** Bird Wedding

1982. Sorbian Folk Customs. Multicoloured.

E2424	10pf. Type E **727**	25	20
E2425	20pf. Shrove Tuesday procession	30	30
E2426	25pf. Egg rolling	45	45
E2427	35pf. Painted Easter eggs	70	60
E2428	40pf. St. John's Day riders	80	80
E2429	50pf. Distribution of Christmas gifts to hard-working children	1·00	95

E **728** Schwerin, 1640

1982. 7th National Youth Stamp Exhibition, Schwerin. Multicoloured.

E2430	10pf.+5pf. Type E **728**	30	40
E2431	20pf. Modern Schwerin	30	40

E **729** Flag and Pioneers

1982. 7th Pioneers Meeting, Dresden. Mult.

E2432	10pf.+5pf. Type E **729**	60	55
E2433	20pf. Trumpet and drum	25	15

E **730** "Stormy Sea" (Ludolf Backhuysen)

1982. Paintings in Schwerin State Museum. Multicoloured.

E2434	5pf. Type E **730**	15	15
E2435	10pf. "Music making at Home" (Frans van Mieris) (vert)	15	15
E2436	20pf. "The Watchman" (Carel Fabritius) (vert)	20	15
E2437	25pf. "Company of Peasants" (Adriaen Brouwer)	30	15
E2438	35pf. "Breakfast Table with Ham" (Willem Claesz Heda)	30	15
E2439	70pf. "River Landscape" (Jan van Goyen)	2·40	2·10

E **731** Karl-Marx-Stadt

1982. 13th Socialist Countries' Postal Ministers Conference, Karl-Marx-Stadt.

E2440	E **731** 10pf. multicoloured	35	30

E **732** Stentzlers Hof

1982. Leipzig Autumn Fair. Multicoloured.

E2441	10pf. Type E **732**	15	15
E2442	25pf. Amber box, ring and pendant	40	25

E **733** Auschwitz-Birkenau Memorial

E **734** Federation Badge

1982. War Victims' Memorial, Auschwitz-Birkenau.

E2443	E **733** 35pf. blue, blk & red	35	25

1982. 9th International Federation of Resistance Fighters Congress, Berlin.

E2444	E **734** 10pf. multicoloured	35	25

E **735** "Anemone hupehensis"

E **736** Palestinian Family

1982. Autumn Flowers. Multicoloured.

E2445	5pf. Type E **735**	15	15
E2446	10pf. French marigolds	15	15
E2447	15pf. Gazania	15	15
E2448	20pf. Sunflower	25	15
E2449	25pf. Annual chrysanthemum	30	15
E2450	35pf. Cosmea	2·75	1·80

1982. Solidarity with Palestinian People.

E2451	E **736** 10pf.+5pf. mult	45	20

E **737** "B 1000" Ambulance

E **738** Fair Emblem

1982. IFA Vehicles. Multicoloured.

E2452	5pf. Type E **737**	20	15
E2453	10pf. Road cleaner	20	15
E2454	20pf. "LD 3000" omnibus	20	15
E2455	25pf. "LD 3000" lorry	30	15
E2456	35pf. "W 50" lorry	30	15
E2457	85pf. "W 50" milk tanker	3·00	2·20

1982. 25th "Masters of Tomorrow" Fair, Leipzig.

E2458	E **738** 20pf. multicoloured	35	25

E **739** Aircraft and Envelope

E **740** Seal of Eisleben, 1500

1982. Air.

E2459	E **739** 5pf. black and blue	15	15
E2460	15pf. black and mauve	25	20
E2461	20pf. black and orange	35	15
E2462	25pf. black and bistre	45	20
E2463	30pf. black and green	30	15
E2464	40pf. black and green	35	15
E2465	1m. black and blue	1·30	35
E2466	3m. black and brown	3·00	1·40
E2467	5m. black and red	4·50	1·20

1982. 500th Birth Anniv of Martin Luther (Protestant reformer).

E2471	10pf. Type E **740**	15	15
E2472	20pf. Luther as Junker Jog, 1521	30	15
E2473	35pf. Seal of Wittenberg, 1500	55	15
E2474	85pf. Luther (after Cranach)	3·50	2·10

See also No. **MS**2548.

E **741** Carpenter

E **742** Johannes Brahms

1982. Mechanical Toys. Multicoloured.

E2475	10pf. Type E **741**	25	40
E2476	20pf. Shoemaker	1·40	1·00
E2477	25pf. Baker	25	40
E2478	35pf. Cooper	25	40
E2479	40pf. Tanner	1·40	1·00
E2480	70pf. Wheelwright	25	40

1983. 150th Birth Anniv of Johannes Brahms (composer). Sheet 55 × 80 mm.

MSE2481	E **742** 1m.15, green, brown and sepia	4·00	2·75

E **743** Franz Dahlem

E **744** Telephone Handset and Push-buttons

1983. Socialist Personalities.

E2482	E **743** 10pf. brown	20	15
E2483	– 10pf. green	20	15
E2484	– 10pf. green	20	15
E2485	– 10pf. lilac	20	15
E2486	– 10pf. blue	20	15

DESIGN: No. E2483, Karl Maron; E2484, Josef Miller; E2485, Fred Oelssner; E2486, Siegfried Radel.

1983. World Communications Year.

E2487	E **744** 5pf. brown, black and deep brown	20	15
E2488	– 10pf. blue, turquoise and deep blue	20	15
E2489	– 20pf. green, deep green and black	20	15
E2490	– 35pf. multicoloured	1·60	1·10

DESIGNS: 10pf. Aerials and tankers (Rugen Radio); 20pf. Aircraft, container ship, letter and parcel; 35pf. Optical fibre cables.

E **745** Otto Nuschke

E **746** Stolberg Town Hall

1983. Birth Cent of Otto Nuschke (politician).

E2491	E **745** 20pf. light brown, black and brown	35	25

1983. Historic Town Halls. Multicoloured.

E2492	10pf. Type E **746**	15	15
E2493	20pf. Gera (vert)	20	15
E2494	25pf. Possneck (vert)	25	15
E2495	35pf. Berlin	1·70	1·40

E **747** Petershof

1983. Leipzig Spring Fair. Multicoloured.

E2496	10pf. Type E **747**	25	15
E2497	25pf. Robotron micro-electronic calculator	40	25

E **748** Paul Robeson

1983. 85th Birth Anniv of Paul Robeson (singer).

E2498	E **748** 20pf. multicoloured	35	25

E **749** Harnack, Schulze-Boysen and Sieg

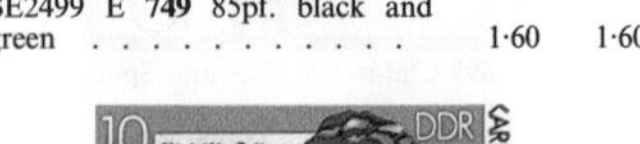

1983. 40th Death Annivs of Arvid Harnack, Harro Schulze-Boysen and John Sieg (Resistance workers). Sheet 80 × 55 mm.

MSE2499	E **749** 85pf. black and green	1·60	1·60

E **750** Karl Marx and Newspaper Mastheads

1983. Death Cent of Karl Marx. Multicoloured.

E2500	10pf. Type E **750**	15	15
E2501	20pf. Marx, Lyons silk weavers and title page of "Deutsche-Franzosische Jahrbucher"	20	15
E2502	35pf. Marx, Engels and "Communist Manifesto"	30	15
E2503	50pf. Marx and German, Russian and French versions of "Das Kapital"	30	25

E2504 70pf. Marx and part of letter to Wilhelm Bracke containing commentary on German Workers' Party Programme . . . 35 25
E2505 85pf. Globe and banner portraying Marx, Engels, Lenin . . . . . 3·25 3·00
MSE2506 81 × 56 mm. 1m.15 Karl Marx (26 × 32 mm) . . . . . 2·75 2·75

E **751** "Athene"

E **752** Chancery Hourglass with Wallmount, 1674

1983. Sculptures in State Museum, Berlin.
E2507 E **751** 10pf. brown, light brown and blue 25 15
E2508 – 20pf. brown, light brown and green 55 25
DESIGN: 20pf. "Amazon".

1983. Narrow-gauge Railways (3rd series). As Type E **683**.
E2509 15pf. grey, black and red 55 55
E2510 20pf. multicoloured . . . 55 55
E2511 20pf. grey, black and red 55 55
E2512 50pf. brown, black and grey 55 55
DESIGNS: No. E2509, Wernigerode–Nordhausen steam locomotive; E2510, Wernigerode–Nordhausen passenger carriage; E2511, Zittau–Kurort Oybin/Kurort Jonsdorf steam locomotive; E2512, Zittau–Kurort Oybin/Kurort Jonsdorf luggage van.

1983. Hourglasses and Sundials. Multicoloured.
E2513 5pf. Type E **752** 15 15
E2514 10pf. Chancery hour-glass, 1700 . . . . 15 15
E2515 20pf. Horizontal table sundial, 1611 . . . . . 25 15
E2516 30pf. Equatorial sundial, 1750 . . . . 30 20
E2517 50pf. Equatorial sundial, 1760 . . . . 45 30
E2518 85pf. "Noon Gun" table sundial, 1800 . . . . . 3·25 2·20

E **753** "Coryphantha elephantidens"

E **755** "Glasewaldt and Zinna defending the Barricade, Berlin, 1848" (Theodor Hosemann)

E **754** Thimo and Wilhelm

1983. Cultivated Cacti. Multicoloured.
E2519 5pf. Type E **753** 20 15
E2520 10pf. "Thelocactus schwarzii" 20 15
E2521 20pf. "Leuchtenbergia principis" 20 15
E2522 25pf. "Submatucana madisoniorum" 30 15
E2523 35pf. "Oroya peruviana" 30 20
E2524 50pf. "Copiapoa cinerea" 2·20 1·80

1983. Founders of Naumberg Cathedral. Statues in the West Choir. Multicoloured.
E2525 20pf. Type E **754** 45 40
E2526 25pf. Gepa and Gerburg 55 45
E2527 35pf. Hermann and Reglindis 65 55
E2528 85pf. Eckehard and Uta 1·70 1·40

1983. "Junior Sozphilex 1983" Stamp Exhibition, Berlin.
E2529 E **755** 10pf.+5pf. brown, black and red . . 90 60
E2530 – 20pf. multicoloured 30 15
DESIGN—HORIZ: 20pf. "Instruction at Polytechnic" (Harald Metzkes).

E **756** Simon Bolivar and Alexander von Humboldt

1983. Birth Bicentenary of Simon Bolivar.
E2531 E **756** 35pf. black, brown and deep brown 75 30

E **757** Exercise with Balls

E **758** Arms of Cottbus

1983. 7th Gymnastics and Sports Festival and 9th Children and Young People's Sports Days, Leipzig. Multicoloured.
E2532 10pf.+5pf. Type E **757** . . 65 45
E2533 20pf. Volleyball 25 25

1983. Town Arms (1st series).
E2534 E **758** 50pf. multicoloured 95 85
E2535 – 50pf. multicoloured 95 85
E2536 – 50pf. red, black and silver 95 85
E2537 – 50pf. multicoloured 95 85
E2538 – 50pf. black, red and silver 95 85
DESIGNS: No. E2535, Dresden; E2536, Erfurt; E2537, Frankfurt-on-Oder. (21 × 39 mm); No. E2538, Berlin.

See also Nos. E2569/73 and E2644/8.

E **759** Central Fair Palace

E **760** Militiaman

1983. Leipzig Autumn Fair. Multicoloured.
E2539 10pf. Type E **759** 25 15
E2540 25pf. Microchip 55 25

1983. 30th Anniv of Workers' Militia. Sheet 63 × 86 mm.
MSE2541 E **760** 1m. multicoloured 2·30 2·00

E **761** Euler, Formula and Model

1983. Death Bicentenary of Leonhard Euler (mathematician).
E2542 E **761** 20pf. blue and black 50 30

E **762** Sanssouci Castle

1983. Public Palaces and Gardens of Potsdam-Sanssouci. Multicoloured.
E2543 10pf. Type E **762** 15 15
E2544 20pf. Chinese tea house . . 30 15
E2545 40pf. Charlottenhof Palace 55 25
E2546 50pf. Film museum (former stables) . . . . 3·25 2·30

E **763** "Mother Homeland" (Yevgeni Vuzhetich)

E **765** Learning to Read and Write

E **764** "D.M.L." (Dr. Martin Luther)

1983. Volograd War Memorial.
E2547 E **763** 35pf. blue, blk & grn 75 30

1983. 500th Birth Anniv of Martin Luther (Protestant reformer) (2nd issue). Sheet 108 × 83 mm.
MSE2548 E **764** 1m. multicoloured 3·75 3·00

1983. "Solidarity with Nicaragua".
E2549 E **765** 10pf.+5pf. mult . . . 45 25

E **766** Cockerel

1983. Thuringian Glass. Multicoloured.
E2550 10pf. Type E **766** 20 15
E2551 20pf. Beaker 20 15
E2552 25pf. Vase 25 15
E2553 70pf. Goblet . . . . . . 2·40 1·90

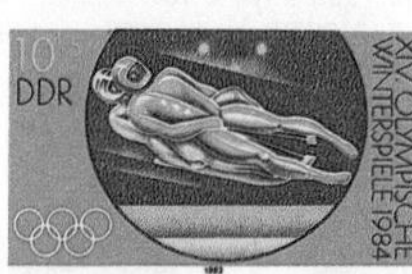

E **767** Luge

1983. Winter Olmpic Games, Sarajevo (1984).
E2554 E **767** 10pf.+5pf. multicoloured . .
E2555 – 20pf.+10pf. multicoloured . .
E2556 – 25pf. multicoloured
E2557 – 35pf. multicoloured
MSE2558 83 × 57 mm. 85pf. blue and silver . . . . 2·10 1·70
DESIGNS: 20pf. Cross-country skiing and ski jumping; 25pf. Cross-country skiing; 35pf. Biathlion; 85pf. Olympic Centre, Sarajevo.

E **768** Dove and Greeting in German and English

1983. New Year. Sheet 93 × 83 mm containing Type E **768** and similar horiz designs, each showing dove and greeting in named languages. Multicoloured.
MSE2559 10pf. Type E **768**; 20pf. German and Russian; 25pf. French and German; 35pf. Spanish and German . . . . . 2·10 1·70

E **769** Dr. Otto Schott (chemist)

E **770** Friedrich Ebert

1984. Centenary of Jena Glass.
E2560 E **769** 20pf. multicoloured 35 25

1984. Socialist Personalities.
E2561 E **770** 10pf. black 25 15
E2562 – 10pf. green 25 15
E2563 – 10pf. black 25 15
DESIGNS: No. E2562, Fritz Grosse; E2563, Albert Norden.

E **771** Mendelssohn

1984. 175th Birth Anniv of Felix Mendelssohn Bartholdy (composer). Sheet 82 × 57 mm.
MSE2564 E **771** 85pf. multicoloured 1·20 1·20

E **772** Milestones, Muhlau and Oederan

E **773** Old Town Hall, Leipzig

1984. Postal Milestones. Multicoloured.
E2565 10pf. Type E **772** 15 15
E2566 20pf. Milestones, Johanngeorgenstadt and Schonbrunn 25 20
E2567 35pf. Distance column, Freiberg 55 45
E2568 85pf. Distance column, Pegau . . . . 1·20 95

1984. Town Arms (2nd series). As Type E **758**.
E2569 50pf. multicoloured . . . 70 60
E2570 50pf. red, black and silver 70 60
E2571 50pf. multicoloured . . . 70 60
E2572 50pf. multicoloured . . . 70 60
E2573 50pf. multicoloured . . . 70 60
DESIGNS: No. E2569, Gera; E2570, Halle; E2571, Karl-Marx-Stadt; E2572, Leipzig; E2573, Magdeburg.

1984. Leipzig Spring Fair. Multicoloured.
E2574 10pf. Type E **773** 25 15
E2575 25pf. Body stamping press 30 25

1984. Narrow-gauge Railways (4th series). As Type E **683**.
E2576 30pf. grey, black and red 30 30
E2577 40pf. grey, black and red 40 40
E2578 60pf. multicoloured . . . 55 60
E2579 80pf. multicoloured . . . 85 80
DESIGNS: 30pf. Cranzahl–Kurort Oberwiesenthal steam locomotive; 40pf. Selketalbahn steam locomotive; 60pf. Selketalbahn passenger carriage; 80pf. Cranzahl–Kurort Oberwiesenthal passenger carriage.

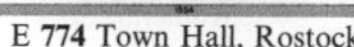

E **774** Town Hall, Rostock

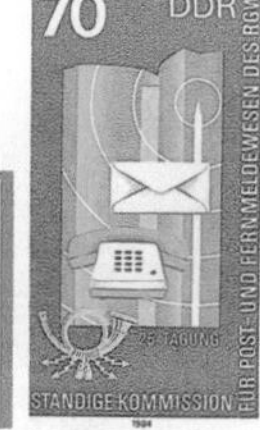

E **775** Telephone, Letter, Pencil and Headquarters

1984. 7th International Society for Preservation of Monuments General Assembly, Rostock and Dresden. Multicoloured.
E2580 10pf. Type E **774** 15 15
E2581 15pf. Albrecht Castle, Meissen 25 15
E2582 40pf. Gateway, Rostock (vert) 65 45
E2583 85pf. Stables, Dresden . . 1·20 1·10

1984. 25th Meeting of Posts and Telecommunications Commission of Council of Mutual Economic Aid, Cracow.
E2584 E **775** 70pf. multicoloured 75 40

E **776** Cast Iron Bowl

E **777** String Puppet

1984. Cast Iron from Lauchhammer. Multicoloured.
E2585 20pf. Type E **776** 30 25
E2586 85pf. "Climber" (Fritz Cremer) . . . . 1·10 1·10

1984. Puppets. Multicoloured.
E2587 50pf. Type E **777** 70 60
E2588 80pf. Hand puppet . . . . 1·20 1·00

E **778** Marchers with Flags

1984. National Youth Festival, Berlin. Multicoloured.
E2589 10pf.+5pf. Type E **778** . . 20 20
E2590 20pf. Young construction workers 30 30

E **779** Gera Buildings

1984. 20th Workers' Festival, Gera. Multicoloured.
E2591 10pf. Type E **779** 20 20
E2592 20pf. Couple in traditional costume 35 25

E **780** Salt Carrier
E **781** Bakers' Seal, Berlin

1984. National Stamp Exhibition, Halle. Mult.
E2593 10pf.+5pf. Type E **780** . . 25 15
E2594 20pf. Citizen of Halle with his bride 30 25

1984. Historical Seals of 1442. Multicoloured.
E2595 5pf. Type E **781** 35 20
E2596 10pf. Wool weavers, Berlin 70 40
E2597 20pf. Wool weavers, Colln on Spree . . . . 1·40 50
E2598 35pf. Shoemakers, Colln on Spree . . . . 2·30 1·80

E **782** New Flats and Restored Terrace
E **783** Frege House, Katherine Street

1984. 35th Anniv of German Democratic Republic (1st issue). Multicoloured.
E2599 10pf. Type E **782** 25 15
E2600 20pf. Surface mining . . . 40 30
MSE2601 80 × 55 mm. 1m. Privy Council building . . . . 1·40 1·40
See also Nos. E2604/**MS**E2607 and E2069/**MS**E2613.

1984. Leipzig Autumn Fair. Multicoloured.
E2602 10pf. Type E **783** 25 15
E2603 25pf. Crystal jar from Olbernhau 35 25

E **784** East Ironworks

1984. 35th Anniv of German Democratic Republic (2nd issue). Multicoloured.
E2604 10pf. Type E **784** 15 15
E2605 20pf. Soldiers, Mil Mi-8 helicopter, tank and warship 30 25
E2606 25pf. Petro-chemical complex, Schwedt . . . 50 40
MSE2607 110 × 90 mm. 1m. bright carmine (Family and new flats) (51 × 29 mm) . . . . 1·40 1·40

E **785** "Members of the Resistance" (Arno Wittig)

1984. Resistance Memorial, Georg-Schumann Building, Technical University of Dresden.
E2608 E **785** 35pf. multicoloured 75 30

E **786** Construction Workers

1984. 35th Anniv of German Democratic Republic (3rd issue). Multicoloured.
E2609 10pf. Type E **786** 15 15
E2610 20pf. Soldiers 30 20
E2611 25pf. Industrial workers 45 30
E2612 35pf. Agricultural workers 55 45
MSE2613 108 × 88 mm. 1m. Dove and national arms (vert) . . . 1·40 1·40

E **787** Magdeburg, 1551

1984. 8th National Youth Exhibition, Magdeburg. Multicoloured.
E2614 10pf.+5pf. Type E **787** . . 25 25
E2615 20pf. Modern Magdeburg 25 25

E **788** "Spring"
E **789** Entwined Cable and Red Star

1984. Statuettes by Balthasar Permoser in Green Vault, Dresden. Multicoloured.
E2616 10pf. Type E **788** 15 15
E2617 20pf. "Summer" 30 30
E2618 35pf. "Autumn" 55 45
E2619 70pf. "Winter" . . . . . 1·20 95
MSE2620 144 × 115 mm. No. E 2617 × 8 . . . . 1·80 1·80

1984. "Solidarity".
E2621 E **789** 10pf.+5pf. mult . . . 35 20

E **790** Falkenstein Castle

1984. Castles (1st series). Multicoloured.
E2622 10pf. Type E **790** 15 15
E2623 20pf. Kriebstein Castle . . 30 30
E2624 35pf. Ranis Castle 70 55
E2625 80pf. Neuenburg . . . . 1·40 1·10
See also Nos. E2686/9 and E2742/5.

E **791** Queen and Princess

1984. Fairy Tales. "Dead Tsar's Daughter and the Seven Warriors" by Pushkin. Multicoloured.
E2626 5pf. Type E **791** 25 30
E2627 10pf. Princess and dog outside cottage 25 30
E2628 15pf. Princess and seven warriors . . . . 3·75 2·50
E2629 20pf. Princess holding poisoned apple . . . . 3·75 2·50
E2630 35pf. Princess awakened by Prince 25 30
E2631 50pf. Prince and Princess on horse 25 30

E **792** Anton Ackermann
E **794** Letter-box, 1850

E **793** Luge

1985. Socialist Personalities.
E2632 E **792** 10pf. black 25 15
E2633 – 10pf. brown 25 15
E2634 – 10pf. purple 25 15
DESIGNS: No. E2633, Alfred Kurella; E2634, Otto Schon.

1985. 24th World Luge Championships, Oberhof.
E2635 E **793** 10pf. multicoloured 35 20

1984. Letter-boxes.
E2636 E **794** 10pf. brown and black 15 15
E2637 – 20pf. black, brown and red 20 20
E2638 – 35pf. multicoloured 45 45
E2639 – 50pf. brown, black and grey 65 60
DESIGNS: 20pf. Letter-box, 1860; 35pf. Letter-box, 1900; 50pf. Letter-box, 1920.

E **795** Semper Opera House, 1985

1985. Re-opening of Semper Opera House, Dresden. Sheet 57 × 80 mm.
MSE2640 E **795** 85pf. brown, grey and red . . . . 1·20 1·20

E **796** Bach Statue, Leipzig
E **797** Johann Sebastian Bach

1985. Leipzig Spring Fair. Multicoloured.
E2641 10pf. Type E **796** 25 15
E2642 25pf. Meissen porcelain pot 30 25

1985. 300th Birth Annivs of Bach and Handel and 400th Birth Anniv of Schutz (composers). Sheet 90 × 114 mm containing Type E **797** and similar vert designs, together with se-tenant horiz labels.
MSE2643 10pf. blue and bistre; 20pf. purple and bistre; 85pf. green and bistre . . . . 2·10 2·10
DESIGNS: 20pf. Georg Friedrich Handel; 85pf. Heinrich Schutz.

1985. Town Arms (3rd series). As Type E **758**. Multicoloured.
E2644 50pf. Neubrandenburg . . 70 60
E2645 50pf. Potsdam 70 60
E2646 50pf. Rostock 70 60
E2647 50pf. Schwerin 70 60
E2648 50pf. Suhl 70 65

E **798** Liberation Monument
E **800** Sigmund Jahn and Valeri Bykovski

E **799** Egon Erwin Kisch

1985. Liberation Monument, Seelow Heights.
E2649 E **798** 35pf. multicoloured 50 30

1985. Birth Centenary of Egon Erwin Kisch (journalist).
E2650 E **799** 35pf. multicoloured 50 45

1985. 40th Anniv of Defeat of Fascism. Multicoloured.
E2651 10pf. Type E **800** 15 15
E2652 20pf. Adolf Hennecke as miner 30 20
E2653 25pf. Agricultural workers reading paper 35 30
E2654 50pf. Laboratory technicians 85 80
MSE2655 55 × 81 mm. 1m. Soviet war memorial, Berlin-Treptow (22 × 40 mm) . . . . 1·50 1·40

E **801** Flags forming "Frieden" (Peace)

1985. 30th Anniv of Warsaw Pact.
E2656 E **801** 20pf. multicoloured 40 25

E **802** Emblem and Berlin Buildings

1985. 12th Free German Youth Parliament, Berlin. Multicoloured.
E2657 10pf.+5pf. Type E **802** . . 20 20
E2658 20pf. Flags, Ernst Thalmann and emblem 20 20

E **803** "Solidarity" and Dove on Globe
E **804** Olympic Flag

1985. "Solidarity".
E2659 E **803** 10pf.+5pf. mult . . . 35 25

1985. 90th International Olympic Committee Meeting, Berlin.
E2660 E **804** 35pf. multicoloured 75 50

E **805** "40" and Emblem
E **806** Harpy Eagle

1985. 40th Anniv of Free German Trade Unions Federation.
E2661 E **805** 20pf. multicoloured 30 25

1985. Protected Animals. Multicoloured.
E2662 5pf. Type E **806** 15 15
E2663 10pf. Red-breasted geese (horiz) 15 15
E2664 20pf. Spectacled bear (horiz) 30 25
E2665 50pf. Bantengs (horiz) . . 70 55
E2666 85pf. Sunda gavial (horiz) 1·60 1·20

E **807** Support Steam-engine, Gera, 1833

E **808** Students reading

1985. Steam Engines. Multicoloured.
E2667 10pf. Type E **807** 25 15
E2668 85pf. Balance steam-engine, Frieberg, 1848 1·40 1·00

1985. 12th World Youth and Students' Festival, Moscow. Multicoloured.
E2669 20pf.+5pf. Type E **808** . . 30 35
E2670 50pf. Students with raised arms 55 60

E **809** Diver at Turning Post

1985. Second World Orienteering Diving Championship, Neuglobsow. Multicoloured.
E2671 10pf. Type E **809** 20 15
E2672 70pf. Divers . . . . 1·10 90

E **810** Bose House, Saint Thomas Churchyard

E **811** Passenger Mail Coach (relief, Hermann Steinemann)

1985. Leipzig Autumn Fair. Multicoloured.
E2673 10pf. Type E **810** 25 15
E2674 25pf. J. Scherzer Bach-trumpet 45 25

1985. "Sozphilex '85" Stamp Exhibition, Berlin. Multicoloured.
E2675 5pf. Type E **811** 15 20
E2676 20pf.+5pf. Team of horses 30 25
Nos. E2675/6 were printed together, se-tenant, forming a composite design.

E **812** Electrification of Railway

E **813** Gertrauden Bridge

1985. Railways. Multicoloured.
E2677 20pf. Signal box 30 20
E2678 25pf. Andreas Schubert (engineer), his steam locomotive "Saxonia", 1838, and electric locomotive Type BR250 45 25
E2679 50pf. Type E **812** 70 50
E2680 85pf. Leipzig Central Station . . . . 1·60 1·30

1985. Berlin Bridges. Multicoloured.
E2681 10pf. Type E **813** 20 15
E2682 20pf. Jungfern Bridge . . 30 25
E2683 35pf. Weidendammer Bridge 55 45
E2684 70pf. Marx-Engels Bridge 1·10 85
MSE2685 107 × 128 mm. No. E2673 × 8 . . . . 3·25 3·25

1985. Castles (2nd series). As Type E **790**. Mult.
E2686 10pf. Hohnstein Castle . . 15 15
E2687 20pf. Rochsburg 25 25
E2688 35pf. Schwarzenberg Castle 45 45
E2689 80pf. Stein Castle . . . . 1·40 1·10

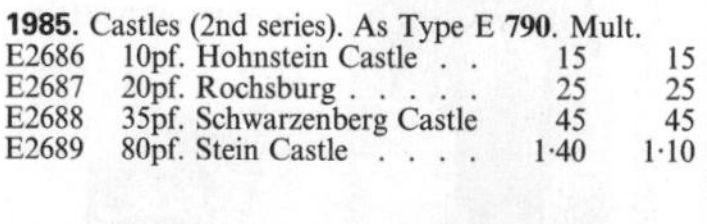

E **814** Humboldt University

E **815** Cecilienhof Castle and U.N. Emblem

1985. Anniversaries. Multicoloured.
E2690 20pf. Type E **814** (175th anniv of Humboldt University, Berlin) . . . 30 30
E2691 85pf. New and old Charite buildings (275th anniv of Berlin Charite (training clinic)) . . . . 1·30 1·10

1985. 40th Anniv of U.N.O.
E2692 E **815** 85pf. multicoloured 1·20 50

E **816** Elephants on Balls

E **817** Grimm Brothers

1985. Circus. Multicoloured.
E2693 10pf. Type E **816** 30 30
E2694 20pf. Trapeze artiste . . . 35 45
E2695 35pf. Acrobats on monocycles . . . . 1·20 1·00
E2696 50pf. Tigers and trainer . . 1·60 1·50

1985. Birth Bicentenaries of Jacob and Wilhelm Grimm (folklorists). Multicoloured.
E2697 5pf. Type E **817** 25 40
E2698 10pf. "The Valiant Tailor" 25 40
E2699 20pf. "Lucky John" . . . 70 95
E2700 25pf. "Puss in Boots" . . . 70 95
E2701 35pf. "The Seven Ravens" 25 40
E2702 85pf. "The Sweet Pap" . . 25 40

E **818** Water Pump, Berlin, 1900

E **819** Saxon Postilion

1986. Water Supply.
E2703 E **818** 10pf. green and red 20 15
E2704 – 35pf. deep brown, brown and green 45 35
E2705 – 50pf. purple & green 70 60
E2706 – 70pf. blue and brown 1·20 85
DESIGNS: 35pf. Water tower, Berlin-Altglienicke, 1906; 50pf. Waterworks, Berlin-Friedrichshagen, 1893; 70pf. Rappbode dam, 1959.

1986. Postal Uniforms of 1850. Multicoloured.
E2707A 10pf. Type E **819** . . . 25 15
E2708A 20pf. Prussian postman 30 25
E2709A 85pf. Prussian postal official . . . . 1·50 1·00
E2710A 1m. Postal official from Mecklenburg region 2·10 1·70

E **820** Flag

1986. 40th Anniv of Free German Youth.
E2711 E **820** 20pf. yellow, bl & blk 35 30

E **821** Flag

1986. 30th Anniv of National People's Army.
E2712 E **821** 20pf. multicoloured 65 30

E **822** Exhibition Hall

1986. Leipzig Spring Fair. Multicoloured.
E2713 35pf. Type E **822** 45 30
E2714 50pf. "Atlantik 488" (factory trawler) 80 45

E **823** Yuri Gagarin and "Vostok"

1986. 25th Anniv of Manned Space Flight. Multicoloured.
E2715 40pf. Type E **823** (first man in space) 45 50
E2716 50pf. Cosmonauts Valeri Bykovski and Sigmund Jahn, space station and "Interkosmos" emblem 55 65
E2717 70pf. Space probe "Venera", orbit around Venus and spectrometer 75 80
E2718 85pf. Reconnaissance camera MKF-6, photo, "Soyuz 22" spaceship, airplane and research ship . . . . 90 1·00

E **824** Marx, Engels and Lenin

E **825** Memorial

1986. 11th Socialist Unity Party of Germany Day.
E2719 E **824** 10pf. black, red and silver 15 15
E2720 – 20pf. red, black and silver 20 20
E2721 – 50pf. multicoloured 70 60
E2722 – 85pf. black, red and silver . . . . . . 1·40 1·10
MSE2723 80 × 55 mm. 1m. multicoloured . . . . 1·40 1·40
DESIGNS: 20pf. Ernst Thalmann (birth centenary); 50pf. Wilhelm Pieck and Otto Grotewohl, April 1946; 85pf. Family; 1m. Construction worker holding symbolic key.

1986. Opening of Ernst Thalmann Park, Berlin.
E2724 E **825** 20pf. multicoloured 40 30

E **826** Horse Tram, Dresden, 1886

1986. Trams. Multicoloured.
E2725 10pf. Type E **826** 20 15
E2726 20pf. Leipzig, 1896 . . . . 25 25
E2727 40pf. Berlin, 1919 . . . . 70 60
E2728 70pf. Halle, 1928 . . . . 1·40 1·10

E **827** Orang-utan

E **828** City Seal, 1253

1986. 125th Anniv of Dresden Zoo. Multicoloured.
E2729 10pf. Type E **827** 25 15
E2730 20pf. Eastern black-and-white colobus 30 20
E2731 50pf. Mandrill 90 80
E2732 70pf. Ring-tailed lemurs 1·60 1·30

1986. 750th Anniv of Berlin (1st issue).
E2733 E **828** 10pf. deep brown, bistre and brown 25 15
E2734 – 20pf. olive, grn & brn 30 20
E2735 – 50pf. blk, brn & red 1·40 65
E2736 – 70pf. green & brown 2·50 1·40
MSE2737 54 × 80 mm. 1m. green 1·80 1·60
DESIGNS—HORIZ: 20pf. City map, 1648; 50pf. Oldest City arms. VERT: 70pf. St. Nicolas's Church, 1832; 1m. Cabinet building tower.
See also Nos. E2780/MSE2784 and MSE2828.

E **829** Couple, Tractor and House

1986. 21st Workers' Festival, Magdeburg. Mult.
E2738 20pf. Type E **829** 20 35
E2739 50pf. Port and town of Magdeburg 45 50

E **830** Berlin, 1652

1986. 9th Youth Stamp Exhibition, Berlin. Multicoloured.
E2740 10pf.+5pf. Type E **830** . . 20 30
E2741 20pf. Historic and modern Berlin buildings 25 30

E **831** Schwerin Castle

1986. Castles (3rd series). Multicoloured.
E2742 10pf. Type E **831** 15 15
E2743 20pf. Gustrow castle . . . 30 20
E2744 85pf. Rheinsberg castle . . 1·20 95
E2745 1m. Ludwigslust castle . . 1·60 1·40

E **832** Soldiers and Girl before Brandenburg Gate

1986. 25th Anniv of Berlin Wall.
E2746 E **832** 20pf. multicoloured 50 40

E **833** Doves flying from Emblem

E **834** Ring-Messehaus

1986. International Peace Year.
E2747 E **833** 35pf. multicoloured 50 30

1986. Leipzig Autumn Fair. Sheet 82 × 57 mm containing Type E **834** and similar vert design.
MSE2748 25pf. Type E **834**; 85pf. Merchants displaying cloth . . 1·60 1·60

E **835** Rostock, 1637

E **836** Man with Rifle

1986. Coins.
E2749 E **835** 10pf. black, silver and red 20 15
E2750 – 35pf. black, silver and blue 45 45
E2751 – 50pf. multicoloured 70 55
E2752 – 85pf. black, silver and blue . . . . . 1·20 1·00
E2753 – 1m. black, silver and green . . . . . 1·40 1·20
DESIGNS: 35pf. Nordhausen, 1660; 50pf. Erfurt, 1633; 85pf. Magdeburg, 1638; 1m. Stralsund, 1622;

1986. 44th World Sports Shooting Championships, Suhl.
E2754 E **836** 20pf. black, green and grey 20 20
E2755 – 70pf. black, red and grey 90 80
E2756 – 85pf. black, blue and grey . . . . . . 1·20 1·10
DESIGNS: 70pf. Woman with pistol; 85pf. Man with double-barrelled shotgun.

E **837** Guard and Boundary Post

E **838** Hemispheres and Red Banner

1986. 40th Anniv of Border Guards.
E2757 E **837** 20pf. multicoloured 40 40

1986. 11th World Trade Unions Congress, Berlin.
E2758 E **838** 70pf. multicoloured 1·20 85

E **839** German Members Memorial, Friedrichshain

E **840** Memorial

1986. 50th Anniv of Formation of International Brigades in Spain.
E2759 E **839** 20pf. brown, black and red 35 30

1986. 25th Anniv of Sachsenhausen Memorial.
E2760 E **840** 35pf. black, grn & bl 60 30

E **841** Double-deck Train Ferry Loading Ramps

1986. Opening of Mukran–Klaipeda Railway Ferry Service. Multicoloured.
E2761 50pf. Type E **841** 55 55
E2762 50pf. "Mukran" (train ferry) 55 55
Nos. E2761/2 were printed together, se-tenant, forming a composite design.

E **842** "Help for Developing Countries"

1986. "Solidarity".
E2763 E **842** 10pf.+5pf. mult . . . 35 30

E **843** Weber (after F. Jugel)

1986. Birth Bicentenary of Carl Maria von Weber (composer). Sheet 82 × 57 mm.
MSE2764 E **843** 85pf. multicoloured 1·40 1·20

E **844** Indira Gandhi

E **845** Candle Holder, 1778

1986. 2nd Death Anniv of Indira Gandhi (Indian Prime Minister).
E2765 E **844** 10pf. stone & brown 30 25

1986. Candle Holders from the Erzgebirge. Multicoloured.
E2766 10pf. Type E **845** 25 25
E2767 20pf. Candle holder, 1796 25 25
E2768 25pf. Candle holder, 1810 70 65
E2769 35pf. Candle holder, 1821 70 65
E2770 40pf. Candle holder, 1830 25 25
E2771 85pf. Candle holder, 1925 25 25

E **846** Roland Statue, Stendal

E **847** Post Office, Freiberg

1987. Statues of Roland (1st series).
E2772 10pf. lt brown, brown & yell 15 15
E2773 20pf. lt brown, brown & bl 20 20
E2774 35pf. lt brown, brown & orge 60 50
E2775 50pf. lt brown, brown & grn 90 70
DESIGNS: Statues at—10pf. Type E **846**; 20pf. Halle; 35pf. Brandenburg; 50pf. Quedlinburg.
See also Nos. E2984/7.

1987. Post Offices.
E2776 E **847** 10pf. black, red and blue 20 15
E2777 – 20pf. multicoloured 30 25
E2778 – 70pf. multicoloured 75 70
E2779 – 1m.20 mult . . . . 1·70 1·40
DESIGNS: 20pf. Perleberg; 70pf. Weimar; 1m.20, Kirschau.

1987. 750th Anniv of Berlin (2nd issue). As Type E **828**.
E2780 20pf. brown and green . . 25 25
E2781 35pf. green and red . . . 55 45
E2782 70pf. blue and red . . . 85 75
E2783 85pf. olive and green . . . 1·40 1·10
MSE2784 Four sheets, 75 × 108 mm (a) or 107 × 75 mm (others). (a) 10pf. As No. E2780; (b) 10pf. × 4, As No. E2781; (c) 20pf. × 4, As No. E2782; (d) 20pf. × 4, As No. E2783 . . . . 4·00 4·00
DESIGNS—VERT: 20pf. Ephraim Palace. HORIZ: 35pf. New buildings, Alt Marzahn; 70pf. Marx-Engels Forum; 85pf. Friedrichstadtpalast.

E **848** Woman with Flower in Hair

E **850** Clara Zetkin

E **849** Fair Hall 20

1987. 40th Anniv and 12th Congress (Berlin) of German Democratic Women's Federation.
E2785 E **848** 10pf. blue, red & sil 35 30

1987. Leipzig Spring Fair. Multicoloured.
E2786 35pf. Type E **849** 45 45
E2787 50pf. "Traders at Weighbridge, 1804" (Christian Geissler) . . . 80 65

1987. Socialist Personalities. Multicoloured.
E2788 E **850** 10pf. purple 25 15
E2789 – 10pf. black 25 15
E2790 – 10pf. black 25 15
E2791 – 10pf. green 25 15
DESIGNS: No. E2789, Fritz Gabler; E2790, Walter Vesper; E2791, Robert Siewert.

E **851** Construction Industry

1987. 11th Federation of Free German Trade Unions Congress, Berlin. Multicoloured.
E2792 20pf. Type E **851** 25 30
E2793 50pf. Communications industry 55 55

E **852** Flag, World Map and Doves

1987. 10th German Red Cross Congress, Dresden.
E2794 E **852** 35pf. multicoloured 60 25

E **853** Museum and Karl August Lingner (founder) (after Robert Sterl)

1987. 75th Anniv of German Hygiene Museum, Dresden.
E2795 E **853** 85pf. multicoloured 1·20 75

E **854** Old and New Farming Methods

1987. 35th Anniv of Agricultural Co-operatives.
E2796 E **854** 20pf. multicoloured 35 25

E **855** Ludwig Uhland (poet)

1987. Birth Anniversaries. Multicoloured.
E2797 10pf. Type E **855** (bicent) 15 15
E2798 20pf. Arnold Zweig (writer, centenary) . . . 25 20
E2799 35pf. Gerhart Hauptmann (writer, 125th anniv) . . 55 45
E2800 50pf. Gustav Hertz (physicist, centenary) . . 90 80

E **856** Bream

1987. Freshwater Fishes. Multicoloured.
E2801 5pf. Type E **856** 15 15
E2802 10pf. Brown trout 20 20
E2803 20pf. Wels 30 25
E2804 35pf. European grayling 45 40
E2805 50pf. Barbel 70 50
E2806 70pf. Northern pike . . . 1·20 90

E **857** Woman holding Baby

E **859** Ludwig Lazarus Zamenhof (inventor)

E **858** Horse-drawn Hand-pumped Fire Engine, 1756

1987. "Solidarity" Anti-Apartheid Campaign.
E2807 E **857** 10pf.+5pf. mult . . . 35 25

1987. Fire Engines. Multicoloured.
E2808 10pf. Type E **858** 20 15
E2809 25pf. Steam engine, 1903 25 20
E2810 40pf. Model "LF 15", 1919 . . . . 60 55
E2811 70pf. Model "LF 16-TS 8", 1971 . . . . 90 85

1987. Centenary of Esperanto (invented language). Sheet 55 × 80 mm.
MSE2812 E **859** 85pf. multicoloured 1·20 1·60

E **860** Otters

1987. Endangered Animals. European Otter. Multicoloured.
E2813 10pf. Type E **860** 20 15
E2814 25pf. Otter swimming . . 35 30
E2815 35pf. Otter 60 45
E2816 60pf. Otter's head . . . . 1·50 1·00

E **861** Tug-of-War

1987. 8th Gymnastics and Sports Festival and 11th Children and Young People's Sports Days, Leipzig. Multicoloured.
E2817 5pf. Type E **861** 15 15
E2818 10pf. Handball 15 15
E2819 20pf.+5pf. Long jumping 30 25
E2820 35pf. Table tennis 45 40
E2821 40pf. Bowling 65 55
E2822 70pf. Running . . . . . . 1·50 1·20

E **862** Association Activities

1987. 35th Anniv of Association of Sports and Technical Sciences.
E2823 E **862** 10pf. multicoloured 30 20

E **863** Head Post Office, Berlin, 1760

1987. Stamp Day. Multicoloured.
E2824 10pf.+5pf. Type E **863** . . 25 30
E2825 20pf. Wartenberg Palace 25 30

E **864** Market Scene

1987. Leipzig Autumn Fair. Sheet 80 × 58 mm containing Type E **864** and similar vert design showing "Market Scene" by Christian Geissler.
MSE2826 40pf. multicoloured; 50pf. multicoloured . . . . 1·70 1·70

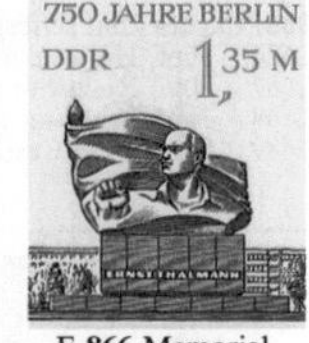

E **865** Memorial Statue (Jozsef Somogyi)

E **866** Memorial, Ernst Thalmann Park

1987. War Victims' Memorial, Budapest.
E2827 E **865** 35pf. multicoloured 50 25

1987. 750th Anniv of Berlin (3rd issue). Sheet 80 × 55 mm.
MSE2828 E **866** 1m.35 black, stone and red . . . . 2·10 2·10

E 867 "Weidendamm Bridge" (Arno Mohr)

1987. 10th Art Exhibition, Dresden. Mult.

E2829	10pf. Type E **867**	15	15
E2830	50pf. "They only wanted to learn Reading and Writing (Nicaragua)" (Willi Sitte)	65	60
E2831	70pf. "Big Mourning Man" (Wieland Forster)	85	75
E2832	1m. Vase (Gerd Lucke) (horiz)	1·80	1·40

E **868** Red Flag, Smolny Building (Leningrad), "Aurora" and Lenin

1987. 70th Anniv of Russian Revolution. Multicoloured.

E2833	10pf. Type E **868**	15	15
E2834	20pf. Moscow Kremlin towers	30	15

E **869** Youth using Personal Computer

E **870** Annaberg, 1810

1987. 39th "Masters of Tomorrow" Fair, Leipzig. Multicoloured.

E2835	10pf. Type E **869**	15	15
E2836	20pf. "ZIM 10-S" robot-welder	30	15

1987. Christmas Pyramids from Erzgebirge. Multicoloured.

E2837	10pf. Type E **870**	25	25
E2838	20pf. Freiberg, 1830	70	50
E2839	25pf. Neustadtel, 1870	25	25
E2840	35pf. Schneeberg, 1870	25	30
E2841	40pf. Lossnitz, 1880	70	60
E2842	85pf. Seiffen, 1910	25	50

E **871** Ski Jumping

1988. Winter Olympic Games, Calgary. Mult.

E2843	5pf. Type E **871**	15	15
E2844	10pf. Speed skating	20	15
E2845	20pf.+10pf. Four-man bobsleigh	35	35
E2846	35pf. Biathlon	70	55
MSE2847	80 × 55 mm. 1m.20 Two-man and single luge (horiz)	2·10	1·60

E **872** Berlin-Buch Post Office

1988. Postal Buildings. Multicoloured.

E2848	15pf. Type E **872**	35	25
E2849	20pf. Postal museum	35	25
E2850	50pf. Berlin-Marzahn general post office	1·20	65

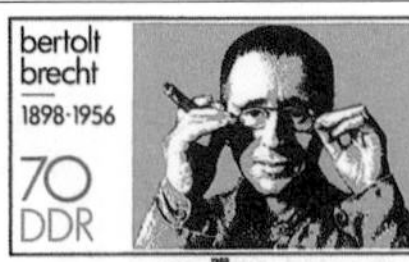

E **873** Brecht

1988. 90th Birth Anniv of Bertholt Brecht (writer). Sheet 58 × 82 mm.

MSE2851	E **873** 70pf. grey, black and red	1·20	1·00

E **874** "Tillandsia macrochlamys"

E **875** Madler-passage Entrance

1988. Bromeliads. Multicoloured.

E2852	10pf. Type E **874**	20	15
E2853	25pf. "Tillandsia bulbosa"	30	25
E2854	40pf. "Tillandsia kalmbacheri"	55	45
E2855	70pf. "Guzmania blassii"	1·20	95

1988. Leipzig Spring Fair. 75th Anniv of Madler-passage (fair building). Each brown, orange and pink.

E2856	20pf. Type E **875**	25	20
E2857	70pf. "Faust and Mephistopheles" (bronze statue, Matthieu Molitor)	1·20	90

E **876** Eichendorff

E **877** Saddler, Muhlhausen, 1565

1988. Birth Bicentenary of Joseph von Eichendorff (writer). Sheet 82 × 55 mm.

MSE2858	E **876** 70pf. olive, drab and blue	1·50	1·20

1988. Historic Seals. Multicoloured.

E2859	10pf. Type E **877**	15	15
E2860	25pf. Butcher, Dresden, 1564	30	25
E2861	35pf. Smith, Nauen, 16th-century	40	40
E2862	50pf. Clothier, Frankfurt on Oder, 16th-century	65	60

E **878** Georg Forster Antarctic Research Station

1988. 12th Anniv of Georg Forster Antarctic Research Station.

E2863	E **878** 35pf. multicoloured	55	25

E **879** Wismar

1988. Northern Towns of the Democratic Republic.

E2864	5pf. black, green & turquoise	15	15
E2865	10pf. black, ochre and brown	15	15
E2866	25pf. black, lightt blue & blue	35	25
E2867	60pf. black, pink and red	75	60
E2868	90pf. black, lt green & green	1·00	80
E2869	1m.20 black, brown and red	1·60	1·30

DESIGNS: 5pf. Type E **879**.; 10pf. Anklam; 25pf. Ribnitz-Damgarten; 60pf. Stralsund; 90pf. Bergen; 1m.20, Greifswald.

E **880** Hutten

1988. 500th Birth Anniv of Ulrich von Hutten (humanist). Sheet 54 × 80 mm.

MSE2870	E **880** 70pf. black, yellow and ochre	1·20	1·20

E **881** Chorin and Neuzelle Monasteries, Industrial and Agricultural Symbols

1988. 22nd Workers' Arts Festival, Frankfurt-on-Oder. Multicoloured.

E2871	20pf. Type E **881**	25	25
E2872	50pf. Buildings of Frankfurt	55	55

E **882** Cosmonauts Sigmund Jahn and Valery Bykovski

1988. 10th Anniv of U.S.S.R.–East German Manned Space Flight (1st issue). Multicoloured.

E2873	5pf. Type E **882**	25	15
E2874	10pf. "MKS-M" multi-channel spectrometer	25	15
E2875	20pf. "Mir"–"Soyuz" space complex	25	25

See also Nos. E2894/6.

E **883** Erfurt, 1520

1988. 10th Youth Stamp Exhibition, Erfurt and Karl-Marx-Stadt. Multicoloured.

E2876	10pf.+5pf. Type E **883**	15	20
E2877	20pf.+5pf. Chemnitz, 1620	30	25
E2878	25pf. Modern view of Erfurt	30	20
E2879	50pf. Modern view of Karl-Marx-Stadt (formerly Chemnitz)	70	55

E **884** Swearing-in Ceremony

1988. 35th Anniv of Workers' Militia Squads. Multicoloured.

E2880	5pf. Type E **884**	20	15
E2881	10pf. Tribute to Ernst Thalmann	20	15
E2882	15pf. Parade	35	30
E2883	20pf. Arms distribution	25	25

E **885** Balloons and Doves over Karl-Marx-Stadt

1988. 8th Pioneers Meeting, Karl-Marx-Stadt. Multicoloured.

E2884	10pf. Type E **885**	15	20
E2885	10pf.+5pf. Doves, balloons and Pioneers	25	25

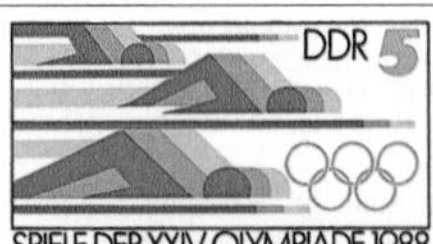

E **886** Swimming

1988. Olympic Games, Seoul. Multicoloured.

E2886	5pf. Type E **886**	15	15
E2887	10pf. Handball	20	15
E2888	20pf.+10pf. Hurdling	45	45
E2889	25pf. Rowing	35	30
E2890	35pf. Boxing	70	55
E2891	50pf.+20pf. Cycling	70	75
MSE2892	55 × 80 mm. 85pf. Relay race	2·50	2·20

E **887** Examining Fair Goods, 1810

E **889** "'Adolph Friedrich' at Stralsund: Captain C. Leplow" (E. Laschke)

E **888** Buchenwald Memorial (Fritz Cremer)

1988. Leipzig Autumn Fair and 175th Anniv of Battle of Leipzig. Sheet 110 × 90 mm containing Type E **887** and similar vert designs. Multicoloured.

MSE2893	5pf. Type E **887**; 15pf. Battle of Leipzig Monument; 100pf. Fair, 1820	1·60	1·60

1988. 10th Anniv of U.S.S.R.–East German Manned space Flight (2nd issue). As Nos. E2873/5 but values changed. Multicoloured.

E2894	10pf. Type E **882**	25	25
E2895	20pf. As No. E2874	25	25
E2896	35pf. As No. E2875	60	50

1988. War Memorials.

E2897	E **888** 10pf. green, black and brown	30	20
E2898	– 35pf. multicoloured	50	25

DESIGN: 35pf. Resistance Monument, Lake Como, Italy

1988. 500th Anniv of Stralsund Shipping Company. Captains' Paintings. Multicoloured.

E2899	5pf. Type E **889**	15	15
E2900	10pf. "'Gartenlaube' of Stralsund: Captain J. F. Kruger" (A. Luschky)	20	15
E2901	70pf. "Brigantina 'Auguste Mathilde' of Stralsund: Captain I. C. Grunwaldt" (Johnsen-Seby Bergen)	1·10	90
E2902	1m.20 "Brig 'Hoffnung' of Cologne-on-Rhine: Captain G. A. Luther" (anon)	1·50	1·30

E **890** Medical Scene and African Child

1988. "Solidarity".

E2903	E **890** 10pf.+5pf. mult	70	55

E **891** Magdeburg Drawbridge

E **892** Menorah

1988. Drawbridges and Ship Lifts. Mult.

E2904	5pf. Type E **891**	15	15
E2905	10pf. Lift, Magdeburg–Rothensee Canal	20	15
E2906	35pf. Lift, Niederfinow	55	40

E2907 70pf. Bridge and lock, Altfriesack 85 75
E2908 90pf. Drawbridge, Rugendamm . . . . . 1·20 95

1988. 50th Anniv of "Kristallnacht" (Nazi pogrom).
E2909 E **892** 35pf. purple, yellow and black 50 25

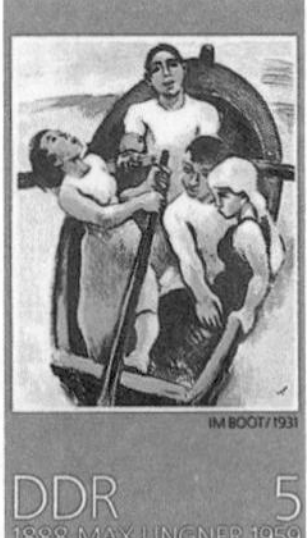

E **893** "In the Boat" E **894** Lace (Regine Wengler)

1988. Birth Centenary of Max Lingner (artist). Multicoloured.
E2910 5pf. Type E **893** 20 15
E2911 10pf. "Mademoiselle Yvonne" 20 15
E2912 20pf. "Free, Strong and Happy" 20 20
E2913 85pf. "New Harvest" . . . 1·20 1·00

1988. Bobbin Lace from Erzgebirge. Pieces by lacemakers named. Each black, brown and yellow.
E2914 20pf. Type E **894** 25 25
E2915 25pf. Wally Tilp 70 50
E2916 35pf. Elisabeth Mehnert-Pfabe 25 30
E2917 40pf. Ute Siewert 25 30
E2918 50pf. Regine Siebdraht . . 70 60
E2919 85pf. Elise Schubert . . . 25 50

E **895** W.H.O. Emblem E **896** Dr. Wolf

1988. 40th Anniv of W.H.O.
E2920 E **895** 85pf. silver, bl & grey . . . . . . 1·20 45

1988. Birth Centenary of Dr. Friedrich Wolf (writer). Sheet 87 × 59 mm.
MSE2921 E**896** 110pf. grey, black and vermilion . . . . 1·50 1·50

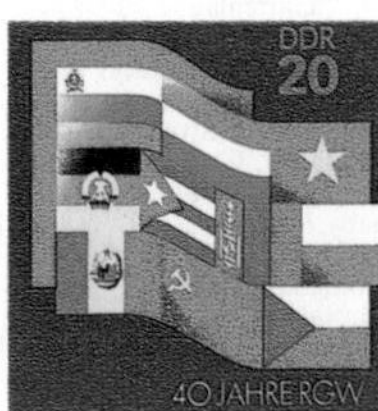

E **897** Members' Flags

1989. 40th Anniv of Council of Mutual Economic Aid.
E2922 E **897** 20pf. multicoloured 35 25

E **898** Edith Baumann E **899** Philipp Reis Telephone, 1861

1989. Socialist Personalities.
E2923 E **898** 10pf. brown 25 15
E2924 – 10pf. green 25 15
E2925 – 10pf. brown 25 15
E2926 – 10pf. blue 25 15
DESIGNS: No. E2924, Otto Meier; E2925, Alfred Oelssner; E2926, Fritz Selbmann.

1989. Telephones. Multicoloured.
E2927 10pf. Type E **899** 20 15
E2928 20pf. Siemens & Halske wall telephone, 1882 . . 25 20
E2929 50pf. "OB 03" wall telephone, 1903 . . . . 70 60
E2930 85pf. "OB 05" desk telephone, 1905 . . . . 1·20 95

E **900** Johann Beckmann (technologist, 250th anniv)

1989. Birth Anniversaries. Multicoloured.
E2931 10pf. Type E **900** 25 15
E2932 10pf. Rudolf Mauersberger and church choir (musician, cent) 25 15
E2933 10pf. Carl von Ossietzky and masthead of "Die Weltbuhne" (journalist and peace activist, centenary) 25 15
E2934 10pf. Ludwig Renn and International Brigades flag (writer, centenary) 25 15
E2935 10pf. Adam Scharrer and cover of "Stateless People" (novelist, centenary) 25 15

E **901** Handelshof Fair Building E **902** Muntzer (after Christoph van Stichen and Romeyn de Hooghe)

1989. Leipzig Spring Fair. Multicoloured.
E2936 70pf. Type E **901** (80th anniv) . . . . 1·20 80
E2937 85pf. Naschmarkt bake-house and bread shop, 1690 . . . . 1·40 1·00

1989. 500th Birth Anniv of Thomas Muntzer (religious reformer) (1st issue). Sheet 86 × 66 mm.
MSE2938 E **902** 110pf. black and buff . . . . 1·40 1·60
See also Nos. E2967/**MS**2972.

E **903** Friedrich List (economist and promoter of railway system)

1989. 150th Anniv of Leipzig–Dresden Railway (first German long-distance service).
E2939 E **903** 15pf. brown, pale brown and green 25 25
E2940 – 20pf. black, green and red 25 20
E2941 – 50pf. black, brown and deep brown 90 70
DESIGNS: 20pf. Dresdner Station, Leipzig, 1839; 50pf. Leipziger Station, Dresden, 1839.

E **904** Tea Caddy E **905** Renaissance Initial "I"

1989. Meissen Porcelain. 250th Anniv of Onion Design. Each brown, blue and ultramarine.
E2942A 10pf. Type E **904** . . . 25 15
E2943A 20pf. Vase 25 20
E2944A 35pf. Bread board . . . 75 50
E2945A 70pf. Coffee pot . . . . 1·30 95

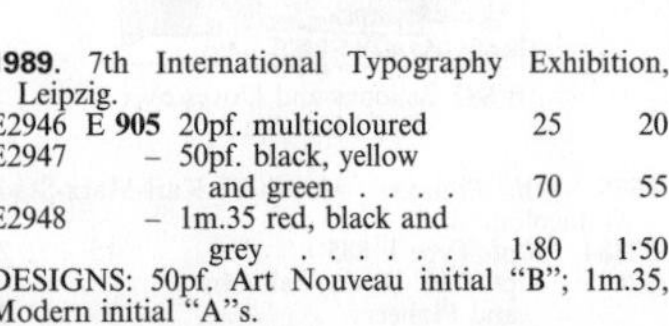

1989. 7th International Typography Exhibition, Leipzig.
E2946 E **905** 20pf. multicoloured 25 20
E2947 – 50pf. black, yellow and green 70 55
E2948 – 1m.35 red, black and grey . . . . . . 1·80 1·50
DESIGNS: 50pf. Art Nouveau initial "B"; 1m.35, Modern initial "A"s.

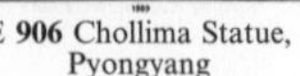

E **906** Chollima Statue, Pyongyang E **907** "Princess Louise"

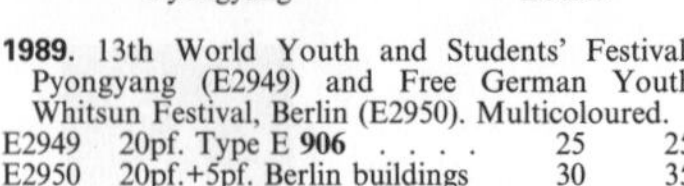

1989. 13th World Youth and Students' Festival, Pyongyang (E2949) and Free German Youth Whitsun Festival, Berlin (E2950). Multicoloured.
E2949 20pf. Type E **906** 25 25
E2950 20pf.+5pf. Berlin buildings 30 35

1989. 225th Birth Anniv of Johann Gottfried Schadow (sculptor). Details of "Princesses". Multicoloured.
E2951 50pf. Type E **907** 85 45
E2952 85pf. "Princess Friederike" 1·50 1·10

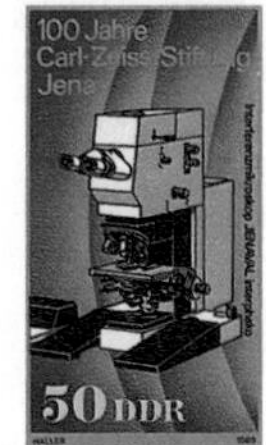

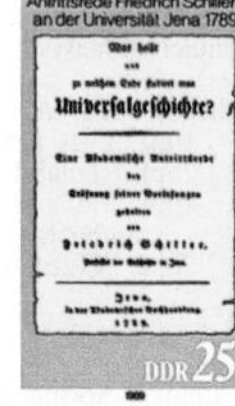

E **908** JENEVAL Interference Microscope E **909** Front Page of Address

1989. Centenary of Carl Zeiss Foundation, Jena. Multicoloured.
E2953 50pf. Type E **908** 60 55
E2954 85pf. "ZKM 01-250 C" bi-coordinate measuring instrument . . . . . . 1·10 1·00

1989. Bicentenary of Inaugural Address to Jena University by Friedrich Schiller (writer and philosopher). Each brown, black & grey.
E2955 25pf. Type E **909** 30 35
E2956 85pf. Part of address . . . 1·00 90

E **910**A. E. Berhm

1989. 160th Birth Anniv of Alfred Edmund Brehm and 125th Death Anniv of Christian Ludwig Brehm (naturalists). Sheet 110 × 80 mm containing Type E **910** and similar vert design. Multicoloured.
MSE2957 50pf. Type E **910**; 85pf. C. L. Brehm . . . . 2·10 11·50

E **911** Storming the Bastille

1989. Bicent of French Revolution. Mult.
E2958 5pf. Type E **911** 20 15
E2959 20pf. Sans-culottes 25 20
E2960 90pf. Invading the Tuileries . . . . 1·20 95

E **912** Haflingers

1989. 40th International Horse Breeding in Socialist States Congress, Berlin. Multicoloured.
E2961 10pf. Type E **912** 15 15
E2962 20pf. English thoroughbreds (racehorses) 20 20
E2963 70pf. Heavy horses (plough team) 85 80
E2964 110pf. Thoroughbreds (dressage) . . . . 1·50 1·30

E **913** Till Eulenspiegel Fountain

1989. National Stamp Exn, Magdeburg. Fountains by Heinrich Apel. Multicoloured.
E2965 20pf. Type E **913** 25 20
E2966 70pf.+5pf. Devil's fountain 1·00 90

E **914** "Annunciation to the Peasants" E **916** African Children

E **915** New Fair Building

1989. 500th Birth Anniv of Thomas Muntzer (Protestant reformer) (2nd issue). Details of "Early Bourgeois Revolution in Germany" by Werner Tubke. Multicoloured.
E2967 5pf. Type E **914** 15 15
E2968 10pf. "Fountain of Life" 20 15
E2969 20pf. "Muntzer in the Battle" 25 20
E2970 50pf. "Lutheran Cat Battle" 85 60
E2971 85pf. "Justice, Jester" . . 1·40 1·10

1989. Leipzig Autumn Fair. Sheet 105 × 75 mm containing Type E **915** and similar horiz design. Multicoloured.
MSE2973 50pf. Type E **915**; 85pf. New fair building (different) . . 2·10 2·10

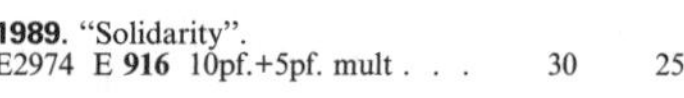

1989. "Solidarity".
E2974 E **916** 10pf.+5pf. mult . . . 30 25

E **917** "Mother Group" (Fritz Cremer) E **918** "Adriana"

1989. 30th Anniv of Ravensbruck War Victims' Memorial.
E2975 E **917** 35pf. multicoloured 50 25

1989. Epiphyllums. Multicoloured.
E2976 10pf. Type E **918** 20 15
E2977 35pf. "Fire Magic" 35 30
E2978 50pf. "Franzisko" 90 80

E **919** Dove, Flag and Schoolchildren

1989. 40th Anniv of German Democratic Republic. Multicoloured.
E2979 5pf. Type E **919** 15 15
E2980 10pf. Combine harvester and agricultural workers 15 15

E2981 20pf. Political activists working together . . . 20 20
E2982 25pf. Industrial workers 75 50
MSE2983 113 × 93 mm. 135pf. Construction workers (54 × 32 mm) . . . . 4·50 2·10

1989. Statues of Roland (2nd series). As Type E **846**. Multicoloured.
E2984 5pf. Zerbst 15 15
E2985 10pf. Halberstadt 20 15
E2986 20pf. Buch-Altmark . . . 30 20
E2987 50pf. Perleberg 85 65

E **920** Nehru
E **921** Schneeberg, 1860

1989. Birth Centenary of Jawaharlal Nehru (Indian statesman).
E2988 E **920** 35pf. brown and black 50 45

1989. Chandeliers from the Erzgebirge. Mult.
E2989 10pf. Type E **921** 25 25
E2990 20pf. Schwarzenberg, 1850 70 50
E2991 25pf. Annaberg, 1880 . . . 25 25
E2992 35pf. Seiffen, 1900 . . . . 25 40
E2993 50pf. Seiffen, 1930 . . . . 70 60
E2994 70pf. Annaberg, 1925 . . . 25 50

E **922** Bee on Apple Blossom
E **923** "Courier" (Albrecht Durer)

1990. The Honey Bee. Multicoloured.
E2995 5pf. Type E **922** 15 15
E2996 10pf. Bee on heather . . . 15 15
E2997 20pf. Bee on rape 25 25
E2998 50pf. Bee on clover . . . 1·20 85

1990. 500th Anniv of Regular European Postal Services.
E2999 E **923** 35pf. chocolate, light brown and brown 50 50

E **924** Erich Weinert
E **925** 19th-century Sign, Blankenburg

1990. Socialist Personalities.
E3000 E **924** 10pf. blue 30 25
E3001 – 10pf. brown 30 25
DESIGN: No. E3001, Bruno Leuschner.

1990. Posthouse Signs. Multicoloured.
E3002B 10pf. Type E **925** . . . 15 20
E3003A 20pf. Royal Saxony sign (19th century) 30 25
E3004A 50pf. German Empire sign (1870s) 90 80
E3005A 110pf. German Empire auxiliary station sign (1900s) . . . . 1·80 1·60

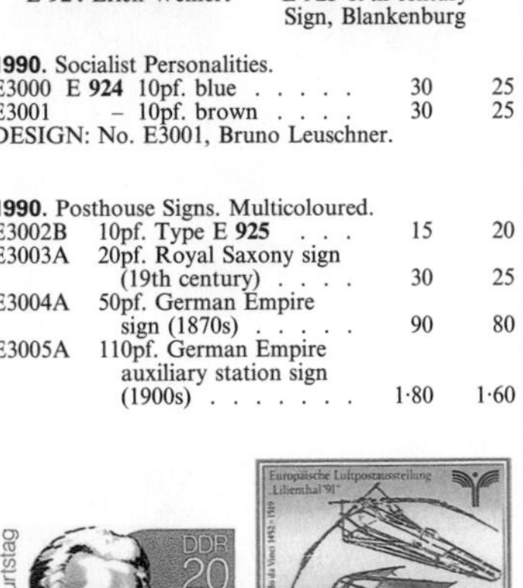

E **926** Bebel
E **927** Drawings by Leonardo da Vinci

1990. 150th Birth Anniv of August Bebel (politician).
E3006 E **926** 20pf. black, grey and red 50 40

1990. "Lilienthal '91" European Airmail Exhibition. Historic Flying Machine Designs. Multicoloured.
E3007 20pf. Type E **927** 30 20
E3008 35pf.+5pf. Melchior Bauer's man-powered airplane design, 1764 . . 70 65
E3009 50pf. Albrecht Berblinger's man-powered flying machine, 1811 . . . . . 80 75
E3010 90pf. Otto Lilienthal's design for a monoplane glider . . . . 1·50 1·40

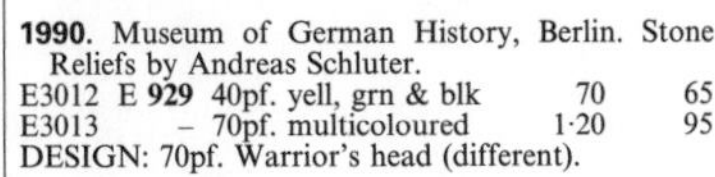

E **928** St. Nicholas's Church, Leipzig, and Demonstrators
E **929** Warrior's Head

1990. "We Are The People".
E3011 E **928** 35pf.+15pf. mult . . 75 70

1990. Museum of German History, Berlin. Stone Reliefs by Andreas Schluter.
E3012 E **929** 40pf. yell, grn & blk 70 65
E3013 – 70pf. multicoloured 1·20 95
DESIGN: 70pf. Warrior's head (different).

E **930** Fair Seal, 1268
E **931** Kurt Tucholsky (writer, centenary)

1990. Leipzig Spring Fair and 825th Anniv of Leipzig. Multicoloured.
E3014 70pf. Type E **930** . . . . 1·30 85
E3015 85pf. Fair seal, 1497 . . . 1·80 1·10

1990. Birth Anniversaries.
E3016 E **931** 10pf. black, green and deep green . . 35 30
E3017 – 10pf. black, brown and red 35 30
DESIGN: No. E3017, Friedrich Adolph Wilhelm Diesterweg (educationist, bicent).

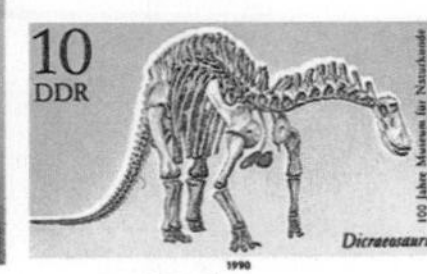

E **932** "Solidarity of Labour" (Walter Crane)
E **933** Dicraeosaurus

1990. Centenary of Labour Day.
E3018 E **932** 10pf. grey, black and red 45 25
E3019 – 20pf. red, grey and black 90 60
DESIGN: 20pf. Red carnation.

1990. Centenary of Natural Science Museum, Berlin. Dinosaur Skeletons. Multicoloured.
E3020 10pf. Type E **933** 15 15
E3021 25pf. Kentrurosaurus . . . 35 40
E3022 35pf. Dysalotosaurus . . . 50 50
E3023 50pf. Brachiosaurus (vert) 70 75
E3024 85pf. Skull of brachiosaurus (vert) . . 1·30 1·20

E **934** Penny Black
E **935** Edward Hughes and 1855 Printing Telegraph

1990. 150th Anniv of the Penny Black.
E3025 E **934** 20pf. black, mauve and magenta . . . 45 50
E3026 – 35pf.+15pf. red, lilac and black 90 90
E3027 – 110pf. multicoloured 2·50 2·20
DESIGNS: 35pf. Saxony 1850 3pf. stamp; 110pf. First East Germany stamp, 1949.

1990. 125th Anniv of I.T.U. Multicoloured.
E3028 10pf. Type E **935** 20 20
E3029 20pf. Distribution rods from Berlin-Kopenick post office 30 35
E3030 25pf. Transmitting tower and radio control desk 55 55
E3031 50pf. "Molniya" communications satellite and globe . . . . 1·20 1·00
MSE3032 82 × 56 mm. 70pf. Philipp Reis (telephone pioneer) . . . 2·40 2·20

E **936** Pope John Paul II

1990. Pope's 70th Birthday.
E3033 E **936** 35pf. multicoloured 65 50

E **937** Halle (18th-century)

1990. 11th National Youth Stamp Exhibition, Halle. Multicoloured.
E3034 10pf.+5pf. Type E **937** . . 30 35
E3035 20pf. Modern Halle . . . 35 35

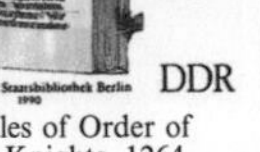

E **938** Rules of Order of Teutonic Knights, 1264
E **939** Albrechts Castle and Cathedral, Meissen

1990. Exhibits in German State Library, Berlin. Multicoloured.
E3036 20pf. Type E **938** 35 25
E3037 25pf. World map from "Rudimentum Novitiorum", 1475 . . . 85 35
E3038 50pf. "Chosrou and Schirin" by Nizami (18th century Persian manuscript) . . . . . . 1·20 85
E3039 110pf. Book cover from Amalia musical library 3·25 2·10

WEST GERMAN CURRENCY

On 1 July 1990 the Ostmark was abolished and replaced by the West German Deutsche Mark.

1990. Tourist Sights.
E3040 E **939** 10pf. blue 25 15
E3041 – 30pf. green 35 25
E3042 – 50pf. green 55 35
E3043 – 60pf. brown 70 55
E3044 – 70pf. brown 75 65
E3045 – 80pf. red 90 75
E3046 – 100pf. red . . . . . 1·20 85
E3047 – 200pf. violet . . . . 2·10 1·80
E3048 – 500pf. green . . . . 5·50 4·00
DESIGNS: 30pf. Goethe-Schiller Monument, Weimar; 50pf. Brandenburg Gate, Berlin; 60pf. Kyffhauser Monument; 70pf. Semper Opera House, Dresden; 80pf. Sanssouci Palace, Potsdam; 100pf. Wartburg Castle, Eisenach; 200pf. Magdeburg Cathedral; 500pf. Schwerin Castle.

E **940** Different Alphabets
E **942** Louis Lewandowski (choir conductor)

E **941** Letter-carrier (from playing card) and Messenger, 1486

1990. International Literacy Year.
E3049 E **940** 30pf.+5pf. on 10pf.+5pf. mult . . 1·20 1·30
No. E3049 was not issued without surcharge.

1990. 500th Anniv of Regular European Postal Services.
E3050 E **941** 30pf. blk, brn & grn 45 40
E3051 – 50pf. black, red and blue 70 60
E3052 – 70pf. black, brown and red 85 75
E3053 – 100pf. black, grn & bl . . . . 1·60 1·40
DESIGNS: 50pf. "Courier" (Albrecht Durer) and post rider, 1590; 70pf. Open wagon, 1595, and mail carriage, 1750; 100pf. Travelling post office vans, 1842 and 1900.

1990. Reconstruction of New Synagogue, Berlin. Multicoloured.
E3054 30pf. Type E **942** 35 30
E3055 50pf.+15pf. New Synagogue . . . . . . 1·00 90

E **943** Schliemann and Two-handled Vessel
E **944** Dresden

1990. Death Cent of Heinrich Schliemann (archaeologist). Multicoloured.
E3056 30pf. Type E **943** 40 45
E3057 50pf. Schliemann and double pot (horiz) . . . 90 80

1990. 41st International Astronautics Federation Congress, Dresden.
E3058 E **944** 30pf. black and grey 30 30
E3059 – 50pf. multicoloured 70 60
E3060 – 70pf. dp bl, grn & bl 90 80
E3061 – 100pf. multicoloured 1·50 1·40
DESIGNS: 50pf. Earth; 70pf. Moon; 100pf. Mars.

On 3 October 1990 the territory of the Democratic Republic was absorbed into the Federal Republic of Germany, whose stamps have been used since then.

OFFICIAL STAMPS

EO **58** (Cross-piece projects to left)
EO **59** (Cross-piece projects to right)
EO **84**

1954. (a) Design in minute dots.
EO185 EO **58** 5pf. green . . . . . — 1·40
EO186 6pf. violet . . . . — 11·00
EO187 8pf. brown . . . . — 1·80
EO188 10pf. turquoise . . — 1·40
EO189 12pf. blue . . . . — 1·70
EO190 15pf. violet . . . — 1·40
EO191 16pf. violet . . . — 2·75
EO192 20pf. olive . . . . — 90
EO193 24pf. red . . . . — 2·75
EO194 25pf. turquoise . . — 11·00
EO195 30pf. red . . . . — 1·80
EO196 40pf. red . . . . — 1·30
EO197 48pf. lilac . . . . — 18·00
EO198 50pf. lilac . . . . — 4·50
EO199 60pf. blue . . . . — 18·00
EO200 70pf. brown . . . — 2·30
EO201 84pf. brown . . . — 90·00

(b) Design in lines.
EO202 EO **59** 5pf. green . . . . . — 3·25
EO203 10pf. turquoise . . — 90
EO204 12pf. turquoise . . — 90
EO205 15pf. violet . . . . — 90
EO298 20pf. olive . . . . — 40
EO212 20pf. olive . . . . — 1·40
EO207 25pf. green . . . . — 5·50
EO299 30pf. red . . . . . — 40
EO300 40pf. red . . . . . — 40
EO210 50pf. lilac . . . . — 1·40
EO211 70pf. brown . . . . — 1·80

1956. For internal use.
EO257 EO **84** 5pf. black . . . . . — 45
EO258 10pf. black . . . . — 45
EO259 20pf. black . . . . — 45
EO260 40pf. black . . . . — 45
EO261 70pf. black . . . . — 65
Nos. EO257/61 were not on sale to the public in unused condition, although specimens of all values are available on the market. The used prices are for cancelled-to-order, with segments across the corners of the stamps. Postally used are worth more.

OFFICIAL CENTRAL COURIER SERVICE STAMPS

These were for use on special postal services for confidential mail between Government officials and state-owned enterprises.

EO **95**

1956. With or without control figures.
EO303 EO **95** 10pf. black & purple . . . . . 75 1·60
EO304 20pf. black & purple . . . . . 2·20 95

EO305	40pf. black & purple	80	2·75
EO306	70pf. black & purple	3·00	43·00

EO 123

1958. With various control figures. (a) With one bar (thick or thin) each side of figure.

EO357	EO **123**	(10pf.) red & yell	37·00	4·75
EO373		(10pf.) brown & bl	22·00	4·75
EO375		(10pf.) violet and orange	42·00	6·75
EO377		(10pf.) red and green	8·50	8·50

(b) With two bars (thick or thin) each side of figure.

EO358	EO **123**	(20pf.) red & yell	37·00	3·25
EO374		(20pf.) brown & bl	45·00	3·50
EO376		(20pf.) violet and orange	49·00	4·75
EO378		(20pf.) red and green	16·00	4·25

Used prices for Nos. EO357/EO378 are for postally used copies.

EO 149

1959. With various control figures. (a) With one bar each side of figure.

EO414	EO **149**	(10pf.) red, violet and green	8·50	6·75
EO416		(10pf.) black & bl	11·00	55·00
EO418		(10pf.) black, brown and blue	44·00	70·00

(b) With two bars each side of figure.

EO415	EO **149**	(20pf.) blue, brown and yellow	12·50	4·25
EO417		(20pf.) green, blue and red	19·00	7·00
EO419		(20pf.) violet, black and brown	29·00	4·75

REGISTRATION STAMPS

SELF-SERVICE POST OFFICE

These registration labels embody a face value to cover the registration fee and have franking value to this extent. They are issued in pairs from automatic machines together with a certificate of posting against a 50pf. coin. The stamps are serially numbered in pairs and inscribed with the name of the town of issue.

The procedure is to affix one label to the letter (already franked with stamps for carriage of the letter) and complete page 1 of the certificate of posting which is then placed in the box provided together with the letter. The duplicate label is affixed to the second page of the certificate and retained for production as evidence in the event of a claim. They are not obtainable over the post office counter.

Unused prices are for pairs.

ER 318

1967.

ER992	ER **318**	50pf. red and black	4·75

ER 319

1968.

ER993	ER **319**	50pf. red	2·10

ER 345

1968. For Parcel Post.

ER1089	ER **345**	50pf. black	8·00

GHADAMES Pt. 6

A caravan halting place in the Libyan desert, under French administration from 1943 until 1951 when the area reverted to Libya. From 1943 to 1948 stamps of Fezzan were used.

100 centimes = 1 franc.

1 Cross of Agadem

1949.

1 **1** 4f. chestnut & brn (postage) 3·00 7·50
2 5f. green and blue 3·00 7·50
3 8f. chestnut and brown 4·25 10·00
4 10f. blue and black 4·25 10·00
5 12f. mauve and purple 6·25 20·00
6 15f. chestnut and brown 5·75 18·00
7 20f. green and brown 6·75 18·00
8 25f. blue and brown 6·00 18·00

9 50f. cerise and purple (air) 5·50 18·00
10 100f. purple and brown 6·00 18·00

GHANA Pt. 1

Formerly the British Colony of Gold Coast. Attained Dominion status on 6 March 1957, and became a republic within the British Commonwealth in 1960.

1957. 12 pence = 1 shilling;
20 shillings = 1 pound.
1965. 100 pesewas = 1 cedi.
1967. 100 new pesewas = 1 new cedi.
1972. 100 pesewas = 1 cedi = 0.8 (1967) new cedi.

CANCELLED REMAINDERS. In 1961 remainders of some issues of 1957 to 1960 were put on the market cancelled-to-order in such a way as to be indistinguishable from genuine postally used copies. Our used quotations which are indicated by an asterisk are, therefore, for cancelled-to-order copies.

29 Dr. Kwame Nkrumah, Palm-nut Vulture and Map of Africa

1957. Independence Commemoration.
166 **29** 2d. red 10 10*
167 2½d. green 10 15*
168 4d. brown 10 15*
169 1s.3d. blue 15 15*

1957. Queen Elizabeth stamps of 1952 of Gold Coast optd **GHANA INDEPENDENCE 6TH.. MARCH, 1957.**
170 ½d. brown and red 10 10*
171 1d. blue 10 10*
172 1½d. green 10 10*
173 2d. brown 30 30
174 2½d. red 1·00 1·25
175 3d. mauve 30 10*
176 4d. blue 6·00 7·00
177 6d. black and orange 10 10*
178 1s. black and red 10 10*
179 2s. olive and red 60 10*
180 5s. purple and black 75 10*
181 10s. black and olive 75 70*

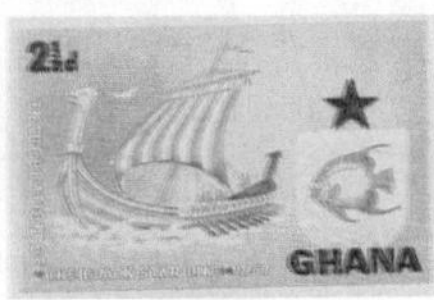

31 Viking Ship

1957. Inauguration of Black Star Shipping Line.
182 **31** 2½d. green 30 20
183 – 1s.3d. blue 35 1·25
184 – 5s. purple 45 3·00
DESIGNS—HORIZ: 1s.3d. Galleon; 5s. M.V. "Volta River".

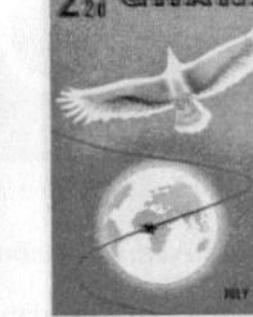

34 Ambassador Hotel, Accra

1958. 1st Anniv of Independence. Flag and Coat of Arms in national colours.
185 **34** ½d. black and red 10 10
186 – 2½d. black, red and yellow 10 10
187 – 1s.3d. black and blue 30 10
188 – 2s. yellow and black 45 35
DESIGNS—HORIZ: 2½d. State Opening of Parliament; 1s.3d. National Monument. VERT: 2s. Ghana Coat of Arms.

38 Map showing the Independent African States **40** Palm-nut Vulture over Globe

41 Bristol Britannia

1958. 1st Conference of Independent African States, Accra. Star in black and yellow.
189 **38** 2½d. red and yellow 10 10
190 3d. green and brown 10 10
191 – 1s. blue, yellow and orange 20 10
192 – 2s.6d. red and purple 40 65
DESIGN—VERT: 1s., 2s.6d. Map of Africa and flaming torch.

1958. Inauguration of Ghana Airways. Inscr as in T **40/41**.
193 **40** 2½d. black, bistre and red 45 10
194 **41** 1s.3d. multicoloured 90 20
195 – 2s. multicoloured 1·00 55
196 – 2s.6d. black and bistre 1·00 95
DESIGNS—(As Type **41**): 2s. Boeing Stratocruiser and yellow-nosed albatross. (As Type **40**): 2s.6d. Palm-nut vulture and Vickers VC-10 aircraft.

1958. Prime Minister's Visit to United States and Canada. Optd **PRIME MINISTER'S VISIT, U.S.A. AND CANADA.**
197 **29** 2d. red 10 40
198 2½d. green 10 30
199 4d. brown 10 50
200 1s.3d. blue 15 25

45 **46** Dr. Nkrumah and Lincoln Statue, Washington

1958. United Nations Day.
201 **45** 2½d. brown, green and black 10 10
202 1s.3d. brown, blue and black 15 10
203 2s.6d. brown, violet black 15 35

1959. 150th Birth Anniv of Abraham Lincoln.
204 **46** 2½d. pink and purple 10 10
205 1s.3d. light blue and blue 10 10
206 2s.6d. yellow and olive 15 35
MS206a 102×77 mm. Nos. 204/6. Imperf 55 2·25

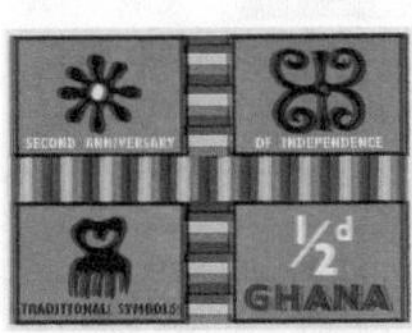

48 Kente Cloth and Traditional Symbols

1959. Independence. Inscr "SECOND ANNIVERSARY OF INDEPENDENCE".
207 **48** ½d. multicoloured 10 10
208 – 2½d. multicoloured 10 10
209 – 1s.3d. multicoloured 15 10
210 – 2s. multicoloured 30 1·25
DESIGNS—HORIZ: 2½d. Talking drums and elephant-horn blower; 2s. Map of Africa, Ghana flag and palms. VERT: 1s.3d. "Symbols of Greeting".

52 Globe and Flags

1959. Africa Freedom Day.
211 **52** 2½d. multicoloured 15 10
212 8½d. multicoloured 15 20

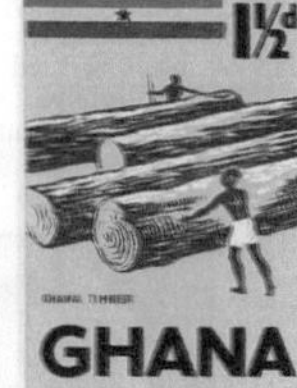

54 Nkrumah Statue, Accra **55** Ghana Timber

65a Red-fronted Gazelle

1959. Multicoloured.
213 ½d. "God's Omnipotence" (postage) 10 10
213a ½d. "Gye Nyame" 30 10
214 1d. Type **54** 10 10
215 1½d. Type **55** 10 10
216 2d. Volta river 10 10
217 2½d. Cocoa bean 10 10
218 3d. "God's Omnipotence" 10 10
218a 3d. "Gye Nyame" 30 10
219 4d. Diamond and mine 4·50 65
220 6d. Red-crowned bishop (bird) 50 10
221 11d. Golden-spider lily 25 10
222 1s. Shell ginger 25 10
223 2s.6d. Giant blue turaco 2·25 15
224 5s. Tiger orchid 3·25 65
225 10s. Jewel cichlid 75 70
225a £1 Type **65a** 3·75 4·75

226 1s.3d. Pennant-winged nightjar (air) 2·50 10
227 2s. Crowned cranes 1·75 10
SIZES—HORIZ (As Type **54**): ½d. (As Type **55**): 2d., 2½d., 3d., 4d., 6d., 1s.3d., 2s.6d. (As Type **65a**): 10s. VERT (As Type **55**): 11d., 1s., 2s., 5s.
The 3d. is a different symbolic design from the ½d.

68 Gold Cup and West African Map

1959. West African Football Competition, 1959. Multicoloured.
228 ½d. Type **68** 10 10*
229 1d. Footballers (vert) 10 10*
230 3d. Goalkeeper saving ball 10 10*
231 8d. Forward attacking goal 40 15*
232 2s.6d. "Kwame Nkrumah" Gold Cup (vert) 50 15*

73 Duke of Edinburgh and Arms of Ghana

1959. Visit of the Duke of Edinburgh.
233 **73** 3d. black and mauve 30 10*

74 Ghana Flag and Talking Drums

1959. U.N. Trusteeship Council. Multicoloured.
234 3d. Type **74** 10 10*
235 6d. Ghana flag and U.N. emblem (vert) 10 10*
236 1s.3d. As 6d. but emblem above flag (vert) 20 15*
237 2s.6d. "Totem pole" (vert) 25 15*

78 Eagles in Flight **85** Dr. Nkrumah

82 Flags and Map forming letter "A"

1960. 3rd Anniv of Independence. Mult.
238 ½d. Type **78** 10 10*
239 3d. Fireworks 10 10*
240 1s.3d. "Third Anniversary" 30 10*
241 2s. "Ship of State" 30 15*

1960. African Freedom Day. Multicoloured.
242 3d. Type **82** 10 10*
243 6d. Letter "f" 20 10*
244 1s. Letter "d" 20 10*

1960. Republic Day. Inscr "REPUBLIC DAY 1ST JULY 1960". Multicoloured.
245 3d. Type **85** 10 10
246 1s.3d. Ghana flag 20 10
247 2s. Torch of Freedom 20 15
248 10s. Ghana arms (horiz) 50 80
MS248a 102×77 mm. Nos. 245/8. Imperf 40 1·50

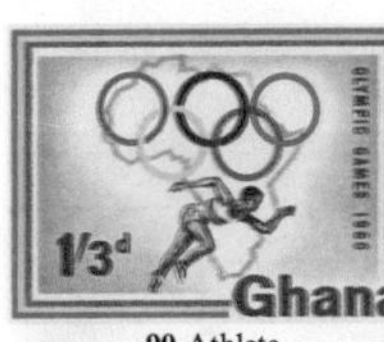

90 Athlete

1960. Olympic Games.
249 – 3d. multicoloured 10 10
250 – 6d. multicoloured 15 10
251 **90** 1s.3d. multicoloured 25 10
252 2s.6d. multicoloured 35 60
DESIGN—VERT: 3d., 6d. Olympic torch.

91 President Nkrumah

1960. Founder's Day. Inscribed as in T **91**.
253 **91** 3d. multicoloured 10 10
254 – 6d. multicoloured 10 10
255 – 1s.3d. multicoloured 20 20
DESIGNS—VERT: 6d. President Nkrumah within star; 1s.3d. Map of Africa and column.

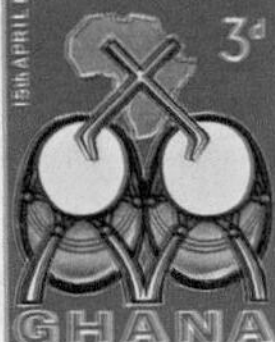

94 U.N. Emblem and Ghana Flag **97** Talking Drums

1960. Human Rights Day.
256 **94** 3d. multicoloured 10 10
257 – 6d. yellow, black and blue 15 15
258 – 1s.3d. multicoloured 25 55
DESIGNS: U.N. Emblem with torch (6d.) or within laurel (1s.3d.).

1961. Africa Freedom Day. Inscr "15th APRIL 1961".
259 **97** 3d. multicoloured 10 10
260 – 6d. red, black and green 20 10
261 – 2s. multicoloured 50 45
DESIGNS—VERT: 6d. Map of Africa. HORIZ: 2s. Flags and map.

100 Eagle on Column

103 Dove with Olive Branch

1961. 1st Anniv of Republic. Multicoloured.
262 3d. Type **100** 10 10
263 1s.3d. "Flower" 10 10
264 2s. Ghana flags 20 90

1961. Belgrade Conference.
265 **103** 3d. green 10 10
266 – 1s.3d. blue 15 10
267 – 5s. purple . . . . 40 1·00
DESIGNS—HORIZ: 1s.3d. World map, chain and olive branch; 5s. Rostrum, Conference room.

106 President Nkrumah and Globe

1961. Founder's Day. Multicoloured.
268 3d. Type **106** 10 10
269 1s.3d. President in Kente cloth (vert) 20 10
270 5s. President in national costume (vert) . . . . . . 65 2·50
MS270a Three sheets, 106 × 86 mm (3d.) or 86 × 106 mm (others), each with Nos. 268/70 in block of four. Imperf Set of three sheets . . . 3·25 14·00

109 Queen Elizabeth II and African Map

1961. Royal Visit.
271 **109** 3d. multicoloured 15 10
272 1s.3d. multicoloured . . . 30 20
273 5s. multicoloured . . . . 65 3·75
MS273a 106 × 84 mm. No. 273 in block of 4. Imperf . . . . . . 2·25 7·50

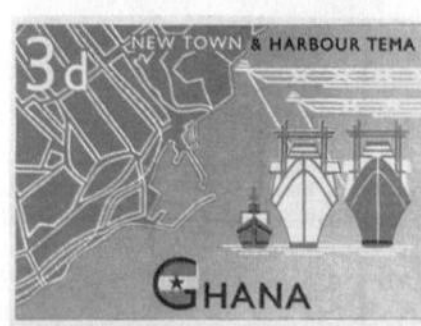

110 Ships in Tema Harbour

1962. Opening of Tema Harbour. Multicoloured.
274 3d. Type **110** (postage) . . . 15 10
275 1s.3d. Douglas DC-8 aircraft and ships at Tema (air) . . 65 15
276 2s.6d. As No. 275 . . . . . 80 2·50

112 Africa and Peace Dove

1962. 1st Anniv of Casablanca Conference.
277 **112** 3d. multicoloured (postage) 10 10
278 1s.3d. multicoloured (air) 20 15
279 2s.6d. multicoloured . . . 30 2·00

113 Compass over Africa

115 Atomic Bomb-burst "Skull"

1962. Africa Freedom Day.
280 **113** 3d. sepia, turquoise & pur 10 10
281 6d. sepia, turquoise & brn 10 15
282 1s.3d. sepia, turq & red 15 15

1962. The Accra Assembly.
283 – 3d. black and lake 10 10
284 **115** 6d. black and red 25 45
285 – 1s.3d. turquoise 30 60
DESIGNS: 3d. Ghana Star over "five continents"; 1s.3d. Dove of Peace.

117 Patrice Lumumba

1962. 1st Death Anniv of Lumumba.
286 **117** 3d. black and yellow . . . 10 10
287 6d. black, green and slate 10 30
288 1s.3d. black, pink and green 15 35

118 Star over Two Columns

121 President Nkrumah

1962. 2nd Anniv of Republic. Inscribed "1st JULY 1962". Multicoloured.
289 3d. Type **118** 10 10
290 6d. Flaming torch 20 20
291 1s.3d. Eagle trailing flag (horiz) 40 40

1962. Founder's Day.
292 **121** 1d. multicoloured 10 10
293 – 3d. multicoloured 10 10
294 – 1s.3d. black and blue . . . 30 15
295 – 2s. multicoloured . . . . 30 1·25
DESIGNS: 3d. Nkrumah medallion; 1s.3d. President and Ghana Star; 2s. Laying "Ghana" brick.

125 Campaign Emblem

126 Campaign Emblem

1962. Malaria Eradication.
296 **125** 1d. red 10 10
297 4d. green . . . . 20 1·25
298 6d. bistre 20 30
299 1s.3d. violet 25 90
MS299a 90 × 115 mm. Nos. 296/9. Imperf . . . . 75 1·50

1963. Freedom from Hunger.
300 **126** 1d. multicoloured 15 25
301 – 4d. sepia, yellow and orange . . . . 75 1·25
302 – 1s.3d. ochre, black grn . . 1·60 1·25
DESIGNS—HORIZ: 4d. Emblem in hands; 1s.3d. World map and emblem.

129 Map of Africa

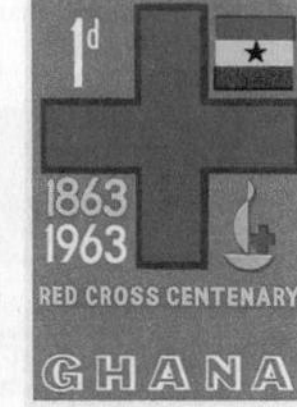

133 Red Cross

1963. Africa Freedom Day.
303 **129** 1d. gold and red 10 10
304 – 4d. red, black and yellow 10 10
305 – 1s.3d. multicoloured . . . 20 10
306 – 2s.6d. multicoloured . . . 35 1·25
DESIGNS—HORIZ: 4d. Carved stool. VERT: 1s.3d. Map and bowl of fire; 2s.6d. Topi (antelope) and flag.

1963. Centenary of Red Cross. Multicoloured.
307 1d. Type **133** 40 15
308 1½d. Centenary emblem (horiz) . . . . 55 2·25
309 4d. Nurses and child (horiz) 75 20
310 1s.3d. Emblem, globe and laurel . . . . 1·75 2·00
MS310a 102 × 127 mm. Nos. 307/10. Imperf . . . . 2·75 12·00

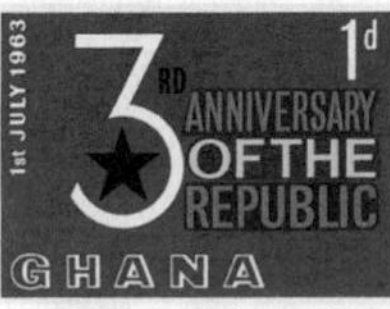

137 "3rd Anniversary"

1963. 3rd Anniv of Republic. Multicoloured.
311 1d. Type **137** 10 10
312 4d. Three Ghanian flags . . . 10 10
313 1s.3d. Map, flag and star (vert) 20 15
314 2s.6d. Flag and torch (vert) 35 2·25

141 President Nkrumah and Ghana Flag

145 Rameses II, Abu Simbel

1963. Founder's Day.
315 **141** 1d. multicoloured 10 10
316 – 4d. multicoloured 15 10
317 – 1s.3d. multicoloured . . . 30 10
318 – 5s. yellow and mauve . . 65 75
DESIGNS—VERT: 4d. Type **141** but with larger flag behind President Nkrumah. HORIZ: 1s.3d. President Nkrumah and fireworks; 5s. Native symbol of wisdom.

1963. Preservation of Nubian Monuments. Multicoloured.
319 1d. Type **145** 15 10
320 1½d. Rock paintings (horiz) 20 65
321 2d. Queen Nefertari (horiz) 20 10
322 4d. Sphinx, Sebua 35 15
323 1s.3d. Rock Temple, Abu Simbel (horiz) 80 90

150 Class 248 Steam Locomotive and Diesel-electric Locomotive No. 1401

1963. 60th Anniv of Ghana Railway.
324 **150** 1d. multicoloured 10 10
325 6d. multicoloured 50 10
326 1s.3d. multicoloured . . . 60 60
327 2s.6d. multicoloured . . . 1·00 2·25

151 Eleanor Roosevelt and "Flame of Freedom"

154 Sun and Globe Emblem

1963. 5th Anniv of Declaration of Human Rights. Multicoloured.
328 1d. Type **151** 10 10
329 4d. Type **151** 10 30
330 6d. Eleanor Roosevelt . . . 10 10
331 1s.3d. Eleanor Roosevelt and emblems (horiz) 15 15

1964. International Quiet Sun Years.
332 **154** 3d. multicoloured 15 10
333 6d. multicoloured 25 10
334 1s.3d. multicoloured . . . 25 15
MS334a 90 × 90 mm. No. 334 in block of 4. Imperf . . . . . . 75 2·50

155 Harvesting Corn on State Farm

1964. 4th Anniv of Republic.
335 **155** 3d. olive, brown and yellow 10 10
336 – 6d. green, brown turq . . 10 10
337 – 1s.3d. red, brn salmon . . 10 10
338 – 5s. multicoloured . . . . 40 1·25
MS338a 126 × 100 mm. Nos. 335/8. Imperf . . . . 85 2·00
DESIGNS: 6d. Oil refinery, Tema; 1s.3d. "Communal Labour"; 5s. Procession headed by flag.

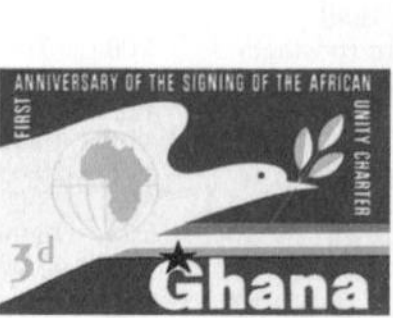

159 Globe and Dove

163 President Nkrumah and Hibiscus Flowers

1964. 1st Anniv of African Unity Charter.
339 **159** 3d. multicoloured 10 10
340 – 6d. green and red 10 10
341 – 1s.3d. multicoloured . . . 15 10
342 – 5s. multicoloured 45 70
DESIGNS—VERT: 6d. Map of Africa and quill pen; 5s. Planting flower. HORIZ: 1s.3d. Hitched rope on map of Africa.

1964. Founder's Day.
343 **163** 3d. multicoloured 10 10
344 6d. multicoloured 15 10
345 1s.3d. multicoloured . . . 25 10
346 2s.6d. multicoloured . . . 40 1·00
MS346a 90 × 122 mm. No. 346 in block of 4. Imperf . . . . . . 70 2·50

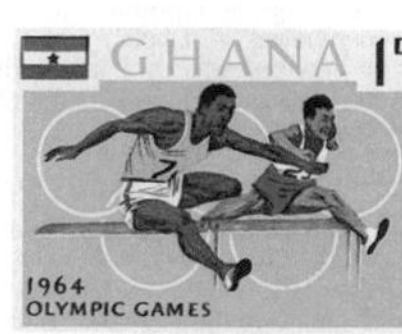

164 Hurdling

1964. Olympic Games, Tokyo. Multicoloured.
347 1d. Type **164** 10 10
348 2½d. Running . . . . 10 1·50
349 3d. Boxing (vert) 10 10
350 4d. Long-jumping (vert) . . . 10 10
351 6d. Football (vert) 15 10
352 1s.3d. Athlete holding Olympic Torch (vert) . . . 20 10
353 5s. Olympic "Rings" and flags . . . . 55 3·50
MS353a 128 × 102 mm. Nos. 351/3. Imperf . . . . 75 2·50

171 G. Washington Carver (botanist) and Plant

1964. UNESCO Week.
354 **171** 6d. blue and green . . . 10 10
355 – 1s.3d. purple and blue . . 30 10
356 **171** 5s. sepia and red . . . . 50 4·25
MS356a 127 × 77 mm. Nos. 354/6. Imperf . . . . 75 2·00
DESIGN: 1s.3d. Albert Einstein (scientist) and Atomic symbol.

173 African Elephant

181 I.C.Y. Emblem

1964. Multicoloured.
357 1d. Type **173** 50 50
358 1½d. Secretary bird (horiz) . . 75 2·50
359 2½d. Purple wreath (flower) 30 2·50
360 3d. Grey parrot 75 50
361 4d. Blue-naped mousebird (horiz) 75 70
362 6d. African tulip tree (horiz) 30 30

363 1s.3d. Violet starling (horiz) 1·00 1·25
364 2s.6d. Hippopotamus (horiz) 1·00 5·50
MS364a Two sheets. (a) 150×86 mm. Nos. 357/9. (b) 150×110 mm. Nos. 360/4. Imperf
Set of 2 sheets 4·75 14·00

1965. International Co-operation Year.
365 **181** 1d. multicoloured 35 70
366 4d. multicoloured 1·00 1·60
367 6d. multicoloured 1·00 70
368 1s.3d. multicoloured 1·25 2·75
MS368a 100×100 mm. No. 368 in block of 4. Imperf 2·75 5·00

182 I.T.U. Emblem and Symbols

1965. Centenary of I.T.U.
369 **182** 1d. multicoloured 15 15
370 6d. multicoloured 30 15
371 1s.3d. multicoloured 55 25
372 5s. multicoloured 1·25 3·25
MS372a 132×115 mm. Nos. 369/72. Imperf 7·50 10·00

183 Lincoln's Home

1965. Death Centenary of Abraham Lincoln.
373 **183** 6d. multicoloured 10 10
374 – 1s.3d. black, red and blue 15 15
375 – 2s. black, brown and yellow 15 35
376 – 5s. black and red 30 1·75
MS376a 115×115 mm. Nos. 373/6. Imperf 75 3·50
DESIGNS: 1s.3d. Lincoln's inaugural address; 2s. Abraham Lincoln; 5s. Adaption of U.S. 90c. Lincoln stamp of 1869.

187 Obverse (President Nkrumah) and Reverse of 5p. Coin

1965. Introduction of Decimal Currency. Multicoloured designs showing coins expressed in the same denominations as on the stamps.
377 5p. Type **187** 20 10
378 10p. As Type **187** 25 10
379 25p. Size 63×39 mm 55 1·00
380 50p. Size 71×43½ mm 1·00 2·50

1965. Nos. 214/27 surch **Ghana New Currency 19th July. 1965.** and value. Multicoloured.
381 **54** 1p. on 1d. (postage) 10 10
382 – 2p. on 2d. 10 10
383 – 3p. on 3d. (No. 218a) 1·00 5·50
384 – 4p. on 4d. 5·00 45
385 – 6p. on 6d. 50 10
386 – 11p. on 11d. 25 10
387 – 12p. on 1s. 25 10
388 – 30p. on 2s.6d. 4·50 8·00
389 – 60p. on 5s. 4·50 70
390 – 1c.20 on 10s. 75 2·25
391 **65a** 2c.40 on £1 1·00 6·50
392 – 15p. on 1s.3d. (air) 2·50 70
393 – 24p. on 2s. 2·50 30

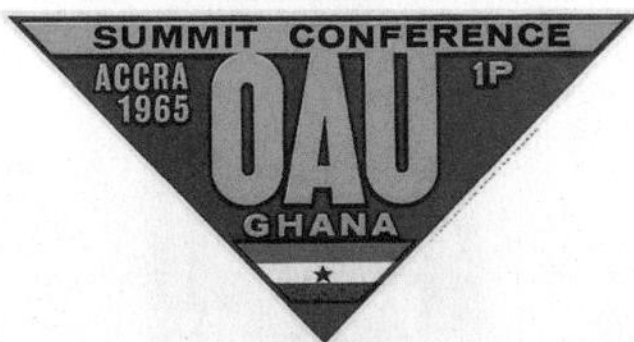

189 "OAU" and Flag

1965. O.A.U. Summit Conf, Accra. Mult.
394 1p. Type **189** 10 10
395 2p. "OAU" heads and flag 10 10
396 5p. OAU emblem and flag 10 10
397 6p. African map and flag (horiz) (37½×27½ mm) 10 10
398 15p. "Sunburst" and flag (horiz) (37½×27½ mm) 20 30
399 24p. "O.A.U." on map, and flag (horiz) (37½×27½ mm) 35 60

195 Goalkeeper saving Ball

1965. African Soccer Cup Competition. Mult.
400 6p. Type **195** 25 10
401 15p. Player with ball (vert) 40 30
402 24p. Player, ball and Soccer Cup 45 70

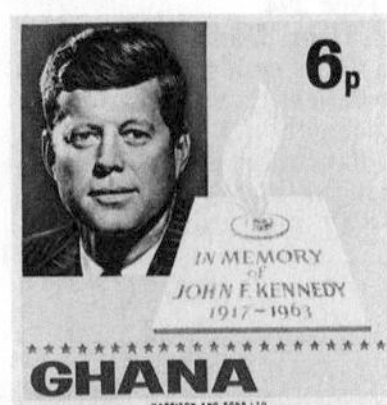

198 President Kennedy and Grave Memorial

1965. 2nd Death Anniv of President Kennedy.
403 **198** 6p. multicoloured 15 10
404 – 15p. violet, red and green 20 35
405 – 24p. black and purple 20 60
406 – 30p. purple and black 25 1·25
MS407 114½×114 mm. Nos. 403/6. Imperf 3·00 6·50
DESIGNS: 15p. President Kennedy and Eternal Flame; 24p. President Kennedy and Memorial Inscription; 30p. President Kennedy.

202 Section of Dam and Generators

1966. Volta River Project.
408 **202** 6p. multicoloured 15 10
409 – 15p. multicoloured 20 15
410 – 24p. multicoloured 25 20
411 – 30p. black and blue 35 50
DESIGNS: 15p. Dam and Lake Volta; 24p. Word "GHANA" as Dam; 30p. "Fertility".

1965. "Black Stars" Victory in African Soccer Cup Competition. Optd **Black Stars Retain Africa Cup 21st Nov. 1966.**
412 **195** 6p. multicoloured 30 15
413 – 15p. multicoloured 50 30
414 – 24p. multicoloured 55 70

207 W.H.O. Building and Ghana Flag

1966. Inaug of W.H.O. Headquarters, Geneva. Mult.
415 6p. Type **207** 50 10
416 15p. Type **207** 1·25 65
417 24p. W.H.O. Building and emblem 1·40 1·60
418 30p. W.H.O. Building and emblem 1·60 3·75
MS419 120×101 mm. Nos. 415/18. Imperf 20·00 21·00

209 Atlantic Herring

1966. Freedom from Hunger. Multicoloured.
420 6p. Type **209** 25 10
421 15p. Turbot 45 15
422 24p. Spadefish 50 35
423 30p. Red snapper 50 1·25
424 60p. Blue-finned tuna 80 4·75
MS425 126×109 mm. No. 423 in block of 4. Imperf 10·00 13·00

214 African "Links" and Ghana Flag

1966. 3rd Anniv of African Charter. Multicoloured.
426 6p. Type **214** 15 10
427 15p. Flags as "quill" and diamond (horiz) 35 55
428 24p. Ship's wheel, map and cocoa bean (horiz) 40 70

217 Player heading Ball, and Jules Rimet Cup

1966. World Cup Football Championship. Multicoloured.
429 5p. Type **217** 30 10
430 15p. Goalkeeper clearing ball 70 20
431 24p. Player and Jules Rimet Cup (replica) 85 35
432 30p. Players and Jules Rimet Cup (replica) 1·10 1·25
433 60p. Players with ball 1·75 7·00
MS434 120×102 mm. No. 433 in block of 4. Imperf 24·00 26·00

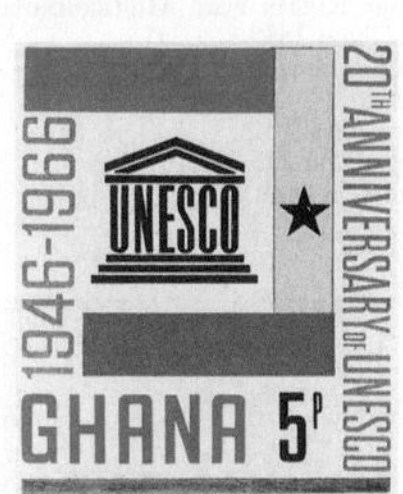

222 UNESCO Emblem

1966. 20th Anniv of UNESCO.
435 **222** 5p. multicoloured 60 15
436 15p. multicoloured 1·40 50
437 24p. multicoloured 1·75 1·00
438 30p. multicoloured 2·00 2·75
439 60p. multicoloured 2·75 8·00
MS440 140×115 mm. Nos. 435/9. Imperf 25·00 26·00

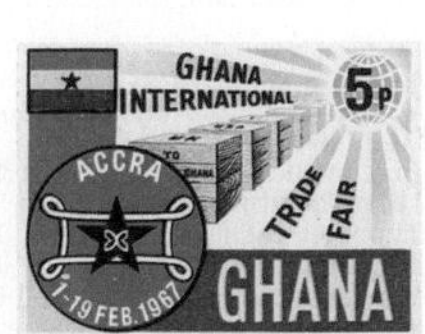

223 Fair Emblem and Crates

1967. Ghana Trade Fair, Accra. Multicoloured.
441 5p. Type **223** 10 10
442 15p. Fair emblem and world map 15 20
443 24p. Shipping and flags 25 30
444 36p. Fair emblem and hand-held hoist 40 2·50

1967. New Currency. Nos. 216/26 and 393 surch with new value.
445 1½n.p. on 2d. (postage) 2·00 6·00
446 3½n.p. on 4d. 7·00 4·00
447 5n.p. on 6d. 2·50 2·25
448 9n.p. on 11d. 30 30
449 10n.p. on 1s. 30 1·00
450 25n.p. on 2s.6d. 3·50 6·00
451 1n.c. on 10s. 3·00 15·00
452 2n.c. on £1 6·00 24·00
453 12½n.p. on 1s.3d. (air) 4·00 3·75
454 20n.p. on 24p. on 2s. 6·50 6·50

229 Ghana Eagle and Flag

1967. 1st Anniv of 24 February Revolution.
455 **229** 1n.p. multicoloured 10 90
456 4n.p. multicoloured 10 10
457 12½n.p. multicoloured 35 60
458 25n.p. multicoloured 65 3·50
MS459 89×108 mm. Nos. 455/8. Perf or imperf 5·00 12·00

230 Maize

232 The Ghana Mace

1967. Multicoloured.
460 1n.p. Type **230** 10 10
461 1½n.p. Forest kingfisher 1·00 2·75
462 2n.p. Type **232** 10 10
463 2½n.p. Commelina 35 10
464 3n.p. West African lungfish 20 40
465 4n.p. Rufous-crowned roller 1·50 10
466 6n.p. Akosombo Dam 15 2·25
467 8n.p. Adomi Bridge 15 65
468 9n.p. Chameleon 75 10
469 10n.p. Tema Harbour 15 10
470 20n.p. Bush hare (blue) 20 10
471 50n.p. Black-winged stilt 8·50 2·50
472 1n.c. Wooden stool 2·00 1·00
473 2n.c. Frangipani 2·00 3·50
474 2n.c.50 Seat of State 1·75 8·00
SIZES—VERT (As Type **230**): 4n.p. (As Type **232**): 1½n.p:, 2½n.p., 20n.p., 2n.c., 2n.c.50. HORIZ (as Type **230**): 8n.p. (As Type **232**): 3n.p., 6n.p., 9n.p., 10n.p., 50n.p., 1n.c.

245 Kumasi Fort

1967. Castles and Forts.
475 **245** 4n.p. multicoloured 25 10
476 – 12½n.p. multicoloured 75 1·00
477 – 20n.p. multicoloured 1·00 2·75
478 – 25n.p. multicoloured 1·00 3·50
DESIGNS: 12½n.p. Christiansborg Castle and British galleon; 20n.p. Elmina Castle and Portuguese galleon; 25n.p. Cape Coast Castle and Spanish galleon.

249 "Luna 10"

255 U.N. Headquarters Building

252 Scouts and Campfire

1967. "Peaceful Use of Outer Space". Multicoloured.
479 4n.p. Type **249** 10 10
480 10n.p. "Orbiter 1" 10 45
481 12½n.p. Man in Space 20 80
MS482 140×90 mm. Nos. 479/81. Imperf 1·75 4·00

1967. 50th Anniv of Ghanaian Scout Movement. Multicoloured.
483 4n.p. Type **252** 20 10
484 10n.p. Scout on march 40 50
485 12½n.p. Lord Baden-Powell 50 1·75
MS486 167×95 mm. Nos. 483/5. Imperf 6·00 10·00

1967. United Nations Day (24 October).
487 **255** 4n.p. multicoloured 10 10
488 10n.p. multicoloured 10 15
489 – 50n.p. multicoloured 20 70
490 – 2n.c.50 multicoloured 55 4·00
MS491 76×75 mm. No. 490. Imperf 2·25 9·50
DESIGN: 50n.p., 2n.c.50, General view of U.N. H.Q., Manhattan.

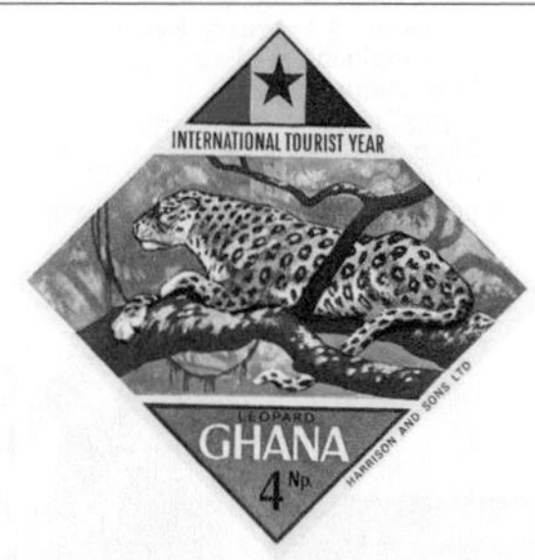

257 Leopard

1967. International Tourist Year. Multicoloured.
492 4n.p. Type **257** . . . . . . 1·00 20
493 12½n.p. "Papilio demodocus" (butterfly) . . . . 2·50 1·50
494 20n.p. Carmine bee eater . . 3·00 3·75
495 50n.p. Waterbuck . . . . . 3·00 9·00
MS496 126×126mm. Nos. 492/5. Imperf . . . . 18·00 21·00

261 Revolutionaries entering Accra

1968. 2nd Anniv of February Revolution. Mult.
497 4n.p. Type **261** 10 10
498 12½n.p. Marching troops . . 20 20
499 20n.p. Cheering people . . . 30 40
500 40n.p. Victory celebrations 50 2·25

265 Microscope and Cocoa Beans

1968. Cocoa Research.
501 **265** 2½n.p. multicoloured . . . 10 1·00
502 – 4n.p. multicoloured . . . 10 10
503 **265** 10n.p. multicoloured . . . 15 20
504 – 25n.p. multicoloured . . . 60 1·50
MS505 102×102 mm. Nos. 501/4. Imperf . . . . 2·25 5·00
DESIGNS: 4n.p. and 25n.p. Microscope and cocoa tree, beans and pods.

267 Kotoka and Flowers

1968. 1st Death Anniv of Lt.-Gen. E. K. Kotoka. Multicoloured.
506 4n.p. Type **267** 10 10
507 12½n.p. Kotoka and wreath 20 30
508 20n.p. Kotoka in civilian clothes 35 75
509 40n.p. Lt.-Gen. Kotoka . . . 50 2·25

271 Tobacco **277** Hurdling

276 Surgeons, Flag and W.H.O. Emblem

1968. Flora and Fauna. Multicoloured.
510 4n.p. Type **271** 15 10
511 5n.p. North African crested porcupine . . . . 15 1·25
512 12½n.p. Rubber 20 75
513 20n.p. "Cymothoe sangaris" (butterfly) . . . . 1·50 2·75
514 40n.p. "Charaxes ameliae" (butterfly) . . . . 1·75 5·00
MS515 88×114 mm. Nos. 510 and 512/14. Imperf . . . . 3·75 9·00

1968. 20th Anniv of W.H.O.
516 **276** 4n.p. multicoloured . . . 20 10
517 12½n.p. multicoloured . . 40 40
518 20n.p. multicoloured . . . 60 1·25
519 40n.p. multicoloured . . . 1·00 4·50
MS520 132×110 mm. Nos. 516/19. Imperf . . . . 2·75 7·00

1969. Olympic Games, Mexico (1968). Multicoloured.
521 4n.p. Type **277** 10 10
522 12½n.p. Boxing 20 30
523 20n.p. Torch, Olympic Rings and flags 40 75
524 40n.p. Football . . . . . . 70 3·25
MS525 89×114 mm. Nos. 521/4. Imperf . . . . 3·50 8·00

281 U.N. Building **285** Dr. J. B. Danquah

1969. United Nations Day. Multicoloured.
526 4n.p. Type **281** 10 10
527 12½n.p. Native stool, staff and U.N. emblem 15 25
528 20n.p. U.N. building and emblem over Ghanian Flag 20 40
529 40n.p. U.N. emblem encircled by flags . . . . 40 2·50
MS530 127×117 mm. Nos. 526/9. Imperf . . . . 75 3·50

1969. Human Rights Year. Multicoloured.
531 4n.p. Type **285** 10 10
532 12½n.p. Dr. Martin Luther King 20 35
533 20n.p. As 12½n.p. 35 75
534 40n.p. Type **285** . . . . . . 50 2·75
MS535 116×50 mm. Nos. 531/4. Imperf . . . . 80 3·75

287 Constituent Assembly Building

1969. 3rd Anniv of Revolution. Multicoloured.
536 4n.p. Type **287** 10 10
537 12½n.p. Arms of Ghana . . . 10 15
538 20n.p. Type **287** 15 20
539 40n.p. As 12½n.p. 20 75
MS540 114×89 mm. Nos. 536/9. Imperf . . . . 70 2·75

1969. New Constitution. Nos. 460/74 optd **NEW CONSTITUTION 1969**.
541 **230** 1n.p. multicoloured . . . 10 2·00
542 – 1½n.p. multicoloured . . . 1·75 4·00
543 **232** 2n.p. multicoloured . . . 10 3·50
544 – 2½n.p. multicoloured . . . 10 2·00
545 – 3n.p. multicoloured . . . 1·00 2·25
546 – 4n.p. multicoloured . . . 3·50 50
547 – 6n.p. multicoloured . . . 15 2·75
548 – 8n.p. multicoloured . . . 15 3·00
549 – 9n.p. multicoloured . . . 15 3·25
550 – 10n.p. multicoloured . . . 20 3·00
551 – 20n.p. multicoloured . . . 35 2·25
552 – 50n.p. multicoloured . . . 7·00 6·00
553 – 1n.c. multicoloured . . . 1·50 7·00
554 – 2n.c. multicoloured . . . 1·50 8·50
555 – 2n.c.50 multicoloured . . 1·50 9·50
On Nos. 541, 545, 547/50 and 552/3 the opt is horiz. The rest are vert.

290 Map of Africa and Flags **294** Red Cross and Globe

293 I.L.O. Emblem and Cogwheels

1969. Inauguration of 2nd Republic. Multicoloured.
556 4n.p. Type **290** 10 10
557 12½n.p. Figure "2", branch and Ghanaian colours . . 20 15
558 20n.p. Hands receiving egg 35 35
559 40n.p. Type **290** . . . . . . 60 1·50

1970. 50th Anniv of I.L.O.
560 **293** 4n.p. multicoloured . . . 10 10
561 12½n.p. multicoloured . . 20 55
562 20n.p. multicoloured . . . 30 1·25
MS563 117×89 mm. Nos. 560/2. Imperf . . . . 70 3·00

1970. 50th Anniv of League of Red Cross Societies. Multicoloured.
564 4n.p. Type **294** 20 10
565 12½n.p. Henri Dunant and Red Cross emblem (horiz) 25 25
566 20n.p. Patient receiving medicine (horiz) 30 75
567 40n.p. Patient having arm bandaged (horiz) . . . . . 35 2·25
MS568 114×89 mm. Nos. 564/7. Imperf . . . . 1·50 6·00

298 General Kotoka, Vickers VC-10 and Airport **302** Lunar Module landing on Moon

1970. Inauguration of Kotoka Airport. Mult.
569 4n.p. Type **298** 15 10
570 12½n.p. Control tower and tail of Vickers VC-10 . . . 25 15
571 20n.p. Aerial view of airport 40 30
572 40n.p. Airport and flags . . . 75 80

1970. Moon Landing. Multicoloured.
573 4n.p. Type **302** 30 10
574 12½n.p. Astronaut's first step onto the Moon 50 60
575 20n.p. Astronaut with equipment on Moon (horiz) . . . . 60 1·40
576 40n.p. Astronauts (horiz) . . 75 3·25
MS577 142×142 mm. Nos. 573/6. Imperf . . . . 2·25 12·00

306 Adult Education

1970. International Education Year. Multicoloured.
578 4n.p. Type **306** 10 10
579 12½n.p. International education 20 20
580 20n.p. "Ntesie" and I.E.Y. symbols 35 30
581 40n.p. Nursery schools . . . 60 1·00

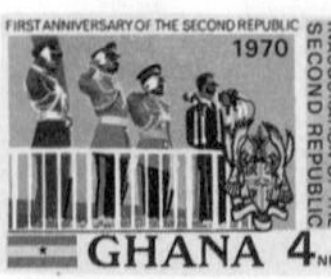

310 Saluting March-Past

1970. 1st Anniv of Second Republic. Multicoloured.
582 4n.p. Type **310** 20 10
583 12½n.p. Busia Declaration . . 15 15
584 20n.p. Doves symbol 25 30
585 40n.p. Opening of Parliament 50 1·00

314 "Crinum ornatum"

1970. Flora and Fauna. Multicoloured.
586 4n.p. Type **314** . . . . . . 1·75 25
587 12½n.p. Lioness . . . . . . 1·25 85
588 20n.p. "Ansellia africana" (flower) . . . . 1·25 1·50
589 40n.p. African elephant . . . 2·00 6·00

315 Kuduo Brass Casket

1970. Monuments and Archaeological Sites in Ghana. Multicoloured.
590 4n.p. Type **315** 15 10
591 12½n.p. Akan traditional house 30 20
592 20n.p. Larabanga Mosque . . 35 50
593 40n.p. Funerary clay head . . 50 1·40
MS594 89×71 mm. Nos. 590, 592 and 12½n.p. Basilica of Pompeii, 40n.p. Pistrinum of Pompeii. Imperf . . . . 6·50 9·50

316 Trade Fair Building

1971. International Trade Fair, Accra. Multicoloured.
595 4n.p. Type **316** 10 10
596 12½n.p. Cosmetic and pharmaceutical goods . . . 60 20
597 20n.p. Vehicles 65 25
598 40n.p. Construction equipment 95 95
599 50n.p. Transport and packing case (vert) . . . . 1·10 1·10

317 Christ on the Cross **318** Corn Cob

1971. Easter. Multicoloured.
600 4n.p. Type **317** 20 10
601 12½n.p. Christ and Disciples 40 70
602 20n.p. Christ blessing Disciples . . . . 50 1·40

1971. Freedom from Hunger Campaign.
603 **318** 4n.p. multicoloured . . . 10 10
604 12½n.p. multicoloured . . 30 90
605 20n.p. multicoloured . . . 40 2·00
Remainder stocks of the above stamps were optd on the occasion of the death of Lord Boyd Orr and further surch 12½, 20 and 60n.p.
It is understood that 8070 sets from the agency were overprinted locally and returned to New York. Limited remainders of these stamps (only 330 of 60n.p.) were sold at the G.P.O. We do not list these as they were not freely on sale in Ghana.

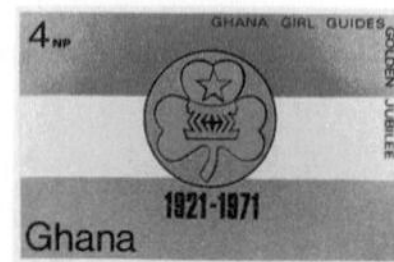

319 Guides Emblem and Ghana Flag

1971. Golden Jubilee of Ghana Girl Guides. Each design includes Guides emblem. Mult.
606 4n.p. Type **319** 20 10
607 12½n.p. Mrs E. Ofuatey-Kodjoe (founder) and guides with flags 50 50
608 20n.p. Guides laying stones 70 90
609 40n.p. Camp-fire and tent . . 1·25 1·75
610 50n.p. Signallers . . . . . . 1·50 2·00

320 Child-care Centre

1971. Y.W.C.A. World Council Meeting, Accra. Multicoloured.
612 4n.p. Type **320** 10 10
613 12½n.p. Council meeting . . . 10 15
614 20n.p. School typing class . . 15 30
615 40n.p. Building Fund Day . . 30 1·00
MS616 84×83 mm. Nos. 612/15. Imperf . . . . 70 2·00

321 Firework Display

322 Weighing Baby

1971. Christmas. Multicoloured.
617 1n.p. Type **321** 10 70
618 3n.p. African Nativity . . . 15 80
619 6n.p. The Flight into Egypt 15 80

1971. 25th Anniv of UNICEF. Multicoloured.
620 5n.p. Type **322** 10 10
621 15n.p. Mother and child (horiz) 20 30
622 30n.p. Nurse 30 70
623 50n.p. Young boy (horiz) . . 50 2·25
MS624 111 × 120 mm. Nos. 620/3. Imperf . . . . 1·75 6·50

323 Unity Symbol and Trade Fair Emblem

1972. All African Trade Fair. Multicoloured.
625 5n.p. Type **323** 10 10
626 15n.p. Horn of Plenty . . . 15 30
627 30n.p. Fireworks on map of Africa 20 70
628 60n.p. "Participating Nations" . . . . 25 2·00
629 1n.c. As No. 628 . . . . . . 40 2·50

On 24 June 1972, on the occasion of the Belgian International Philatelic Exhibition, Nos. 625/9 were issued optd **BELGICA 72**. Only very limited supplies were sent to Ghana (we understand not more than 900 sets), and for this reason we do not list them.

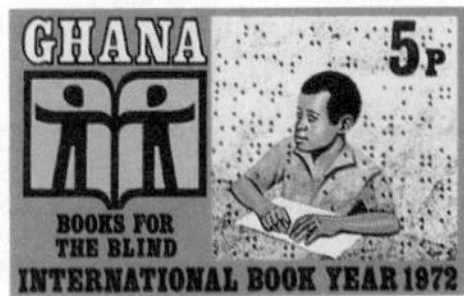

324 Books for the Blind

1972. International Book Year. Multicoloured.
630 5p. Type **324** 30 10
631 15p. Children's books 65 50
632 30p. Books for recreation . . 1·25 1·25
633 50p. Books for students . . . 1·75 3·00
634 1c. Book and flame of knowledge (vert) . . . . . 2·25 5·00
MS635 99 × 106 mm. Nos. 630/4. Imperf . . . . 7·00 11·00

325 "Hypoxis urceolata"

1972. Flora and Fauna. Multicoloured.
636 5p. Type **325** 30 10
637 15p. Mona monkey 65 65
638 30p. "Crinum ornatum" . . 3·00 4·00
639 1c. De Winton's tree squirrel 2·00 8·00

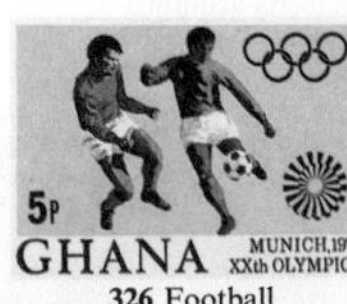

326 Football

1972. Olympic Games, Munich. Multicoloured.
640 5p. Type **326** 20 10
641 15p. Running 30 20
642 30p. Boxing 50 65
643 50p. Long-jumping . . . . . 65 2·25
644 1c. High-jumping . . . . . . 1·10 3·50
MS645 86 × 43 mm. 40p. as No. 642 se-tenant with 60p. as No. 640 2·50 7·00

327 Senior Scout and Cub

1972. 65th Anniv of Boy Scouts. Multicoloured.
646 5p. Type **327** 30 10
647 15p. Scout and tent 55 45
648 30p. Sea scouts . . . . . . 80 1·25
649 50p. Leader with cubs . . . 90 2·00
650 1c. Training school . . . . . 1·25 3·50
MS651 110 × 110 mm. 40p. as 30p.; 60p. as 1c. . . . . 3·25 5·50

328 "The Holy Night" (Correggio)

330 Under 5's Clinic

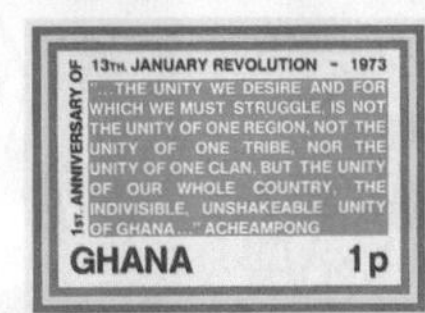

329 Extract from Speech

1972. Christmas. Multicoloured.
652 1p. Type **328** 10 50
653 3p. "Adoration of the Kings" (Holbein the Elder) 10 50
654 15p. "Madonna of the Passion" (School of Ricco) 30 30
655 30p. "King Melchior" . . . 60 70
656 60p. "King Gaspar, Mary and Jesus" . . . . 80 2·00
657 1c. "King Balthasar" . . . . 1·00 3·25
MS658 139 × 90 mm. Nos. 655/7. Imperf . . . . 5·00 9·00

1973. 1st Anniv of 13 January Revolution. Multicoloured.
659 1p. Type **329** 10 40
660 3p. Market scene 10 40
661 5p. Selling bananas (vert) . . 10 10
662 15p. Farmer with hoe and produce (vert) 20 25
663 30p. Market traders 30 40
664 1c. Farmer cutting palm-nuts 70 1·40
MS665 90 × 55 mm. 40p. as 1c. and 60p. Miners . . . . 70 2·25

1973. 25th Anniv of W.H.O. Multicoloured.
666 5p. Type **330** 10 10
667 15p. Radiography 15 25
668 30p. Immunisation 25 40
669 50p. Starving child 25 80
670 1c. W.H.O. H.Q., Geneva . . 25 1·75

1973. World Scouting Conference, Nairobi/Addis Ababa. Nos. 646/50 optd **1st WORLD SCOUTING CONFERENCE IN AFRICA.**
671 **327** 5p. multicoloured 10 15
672 – 15p. multicoloured . . . 30 60
673 – 30p. multicoloured . . . 40 1·40
674 – 50p. multicoloured . . . 55 2·00
675 – 1c. multicoloured . . . . 70 3·00
MS676 110 × 110 mm. 40p. as 30p.; 60p. as 1c. . . . . 1·75 6·50

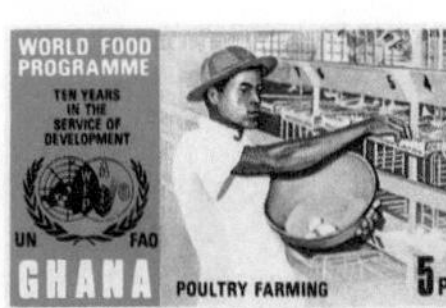

332 Poultry Farming

1973. 10th Anniv of World Food Programme. Multicoloured.
677 5p. Type **332** 10 10
678 15p. Mechanisation 15 15
679 50p. Cocoa harvest 40 90
680 1c. F.A.O. H.Q., Rome . . . 60 1·90
MS681 92 × 104 mm. 40p. as 15p.; 60p. as 1c. . . . . 60 2·25

333 "Green Alert"

1973. 50th Anniv of Interpol. Multicoloured.
682 5p. Type **333** 15 10
683 30p. "Red Alert" 75 80
684 50p. "Blue Alert" . . . . . 1·00 1·75
685 1c. "Black Alert" . . . . . 1·75 4·00

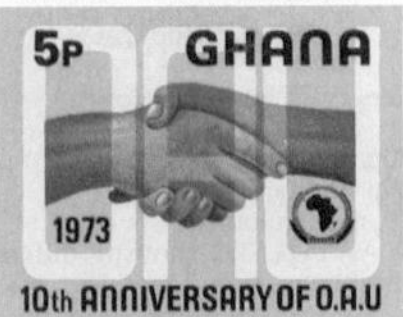

334 Handshake

1973. 10th Anniv of O.A.U. Multicoloured.
686 5p. Type **334** 10 10
687 30p. Africa Hall, Addis Ababa 15 30
688 50p. O.A.U. emblem . . . . 20 1·00
689 1c. "X" in colours of Ghana flag . . . . 35 1·50

335 Weather Balloon

1973. Centenary of I.M.O./W.M.O. Multicoloured.
690 5p. Type **335** 10 10
691 15p. Satellite "Tiros" 15 20
692 30p. Computer weather map 30 65
693 1c. Radar screen . . . . . . 60 2·25
MS694 120 × 95 mm. 40p. as 15p.; 60p. as 30p. . . . . 1·25 3·25

336 Epiphany Scene

337 "Christ carrying the Cross" (Thomas de Kolozsvar)

1973. Christmas. Multicoloured.
695 1p. Type **336** 10 50
696 3p. Madonna and Child . . . 10 50
697 30p. "Madonna and Child" (Murillo) 30 75
698 50p. "Adoration of the Magi" (Tiepolo) . . . . . 45 1·25
MS699 77 × 103 mm. Nos. 695/8. Imperf . . . . 1·25 3·00

1974. Easter.
700 **337** 5p. multicoloured 10 10
701 – 30p. blue, silver and brown 15 35
702 – 50p. red, silver and brown 25 60
703 – 1c. green, silver and brown . . . . 35 1·25
MS704 111 × 106 mm. 15p. as No. 700; 20p. as No. 701; 25p. as No. 702. Imperf . . . . 80 1·75

DESIGNS (from 15th-century English carved alabaster): 30p. "The Betrayal"; 50p. "The Deposition"; 1c. "The Risen Christ and Mary Magdalene".

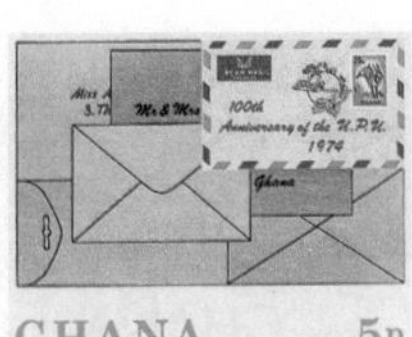

338 Letters

1974. Centenary of U.P.U. Multicoloured.
705 5p. Type **338** 10 10
706 9p. U.P.U. Monument and H.Q. 10 15
707 50p. Airmail letter . . . . . 35 1·10
708 1c. U.P.U. Monument and Ghana stamp . . . . . . 60 2·00
MS709 108 × 90 mm. 20p. as No. 705; 30p. as No. 706; 40p. as No. 707; 60p. as No. 708 . . . 75 1·60

1974. "Internaba 1974" Stamp Exhibition. As Nos. 705/8 additionally inscr "INTERNABA 1974".
710 5p. multicoloured 10 10
711 9p. multicoloured 10 15
712 50p. multicoloured . . . . . 30 1·00
713 1c. multicoloured . . . . . . 45 1·75
MS714 108 × 90 mm. 20p. as No. 710; 30p. as No. 711; 40p. as No. 712; 60p. as No. 713 . . . 1·50 4·00

339 Footballers

1974. World Cup Football Championship.
715 **339** 5p. multicoloured 10 10
716 – 30p. multicoloured . . . 20 60
717 – 50p. multicoloured . . . 25 85
718 – 1c. multicoloured . . . . 30 1·50
MS719 148 × 94 mm. 25, 40, 55 and 60p. as Nos. 715/18 . . . . . 1·00 3·25

DESIGNS: As Type **339** showing footballers in action.

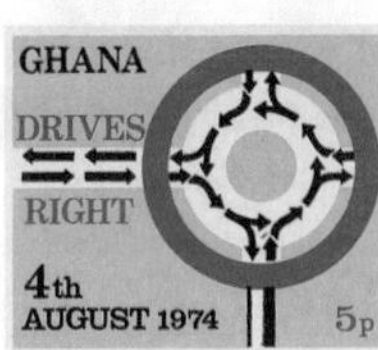

340 Roundabout

1974. Change to Driving on the Right.
720 **340** 5p. green, red and black 10 10
721 – 15p. purple, red and black 20 35
722 – 30p. multicoloured . . . 30 40
723 – 50p. multicoloured . . . 40 85
724 – 1c. multicoloured . . . . 75 1·75

DESIGNS—HORIZ: 15p. Warning triangle sign. VERT: 30p. Highway arrow and slogan; 50p. Warning hands; 1c. Car on symbolic hands.

1974. West Germany's Victory in World Cup. Nos. 715/18 optd **WEST GERMANY WINNERS.**
725 5p. multicoloured 10 10
726 30p. multicoloured 20 40
727 50p. multicoloured 30 55
728 1c. multicoloured . . . . . . 45 1·25
MS729 148 × 94 mm. 25, 40, 55 and 60p. as Nos. 725/8 . . . . . . 1·40 2·50

342 "Planned Family"

1974. World Population Year. Multicoloured.
730 5p. Type **342** 10 10
731 30p. Family planning clinic 25 35
732 50p. Immunization 35 60
733 1c. Population census enumeration . . . . 60 1·40

343 Angel

346 Angel

GHANA
WOMAN TRACTOR DRIVER
7p
International Women's Year 1975
345 Tractor Driver

1974. Christmas. Multicoloured.
734 5p. Type **343** 10 10
735 7p. The Magi (diamond 47 × 47 mm) 10 10

736 9p. The Nativity 10 10
737 1c. The Annunciation 60 1·40
MS738 128 × 128 mm. 15p. Type **343**; 30p. as 7p.; 45p. as 9p.; 60p. as 1c. Imperf 80 2·50

1975. "Apollo"–"Soyuz" Space Link. Nos. 715/18 optd **APOLLO SOYUZ JULY 15, 1975**.
739 **339** 5p. multicoloured 10 10
740 – 30p. multicoloured 20 25
741 – 50p. multicoloured 30 55
742 – 1c. multicoloured 55 80
MS743 148 × 94 mm. 25, 40, 55 and 60p. as Nos. 739/42 1·00 2·00

1975. International Women's Year. Multicoloured.
744 7p. Type **345** 45 10
745 30p. Motor mechanic 1·00 35
746 60p. Factory workers 1·10 80
747 1c. Cocoa research 1·40 1·40
MS748 136 × 110 mm. 15, 40, 65 and 80p. as Nos. 744/7. Imperf 2·00 6·00

1975. Christmas.
749 **346** 2p. multicoloured 10 10
750 – 5p. yellow and green 10 10
751 – 7p. yellow and green 10 10
752 – 30p. yellow and green 20 20
753 – 1c. yellow and green 50 1·00
MS754 98 × 87 mm. 15, 40, 65 and 80p. as Nos. 750/3. Imperf 90 3·00
DESIGNS: 5p. Angle with harp; 7p. Angel with lute; 30p. Angel with violin; 1c. Angel with trumpet.

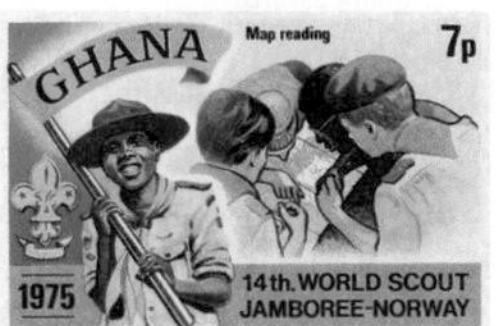

347 Map Reading

1976. 14th World Scout Jamboree, Norway. Multicoloured.
755 7p. Type **347** 20 10
756 30p. Sailing 55 90
757 60p. Hiking 70 2·25
758 1c. Life-saving 80 2·50
MS759 133 × 99 mm. 15, 40, 65 and 80p. as Nos. 755/8 2·25 6·50

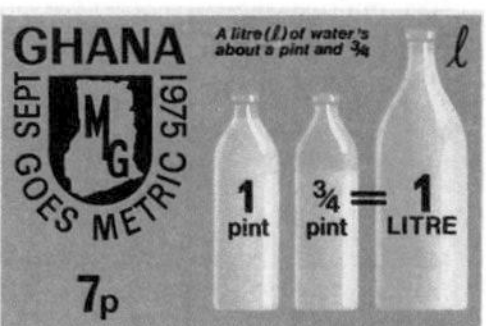

348 Bottles (litre)

1976. Metrication Publicity. Multicoloured.
760 7p. Type **348** 15 10
761 30p. Scales (kilogramme) 20 40
762 60p. Tape measure and bale of cloth (metre) 40 1·00
763 1c. Ice, thermometer and kettle (temperature) 60 1·75

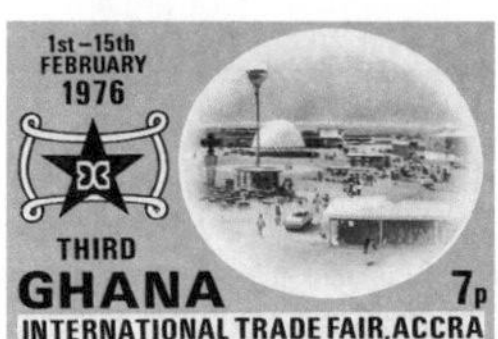

349 Fair Site

1976. International Trade Fair, Accra.
764 **349** 7p. multicoloured 10 10
765 – 30p. multicoloured 15 20
766 – 60p. multicoloured 25 60
767 – 1c. multicoloured 40 1·00
DESIGNS: As Type **349** showing different views of the Fair.

1976. Interphil Stamp Exhibition. Nos. 755/8 optd **'INTERPHIL' 76 BICENTENNIAL EXHIBITION**.
768 **347** 7p. multicoloured 15 15
769 – 30p. multicoloured 35 50
770 – 60p. multicoloured 55 75
771 – 1c. multicoloured 80 1·25
MS772 133 × 99 mm. 15, 40, 65 and 80p. as Nos. 768/71 1·25 2·50

351 Shot-put

1976. Olympic Games, Montreal. Multicoloured.
773 7p. Type **351** 15 10
774 30p. Football 30 25
775 60p. Women's 1500 m 45 50
776 1c. Boxing 60 80
MS777 103 × 135 mm. 15, 40, 65 and 80p. as Nos. 773/6 1·50 1·50

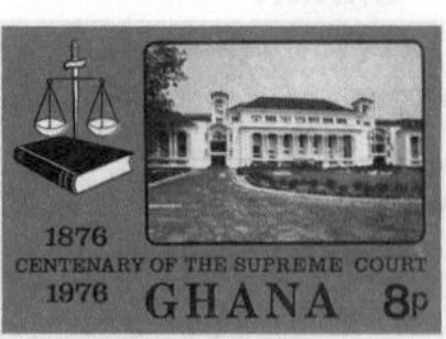

352 Supreme Court

1976. Centenary of Supreme Court.
778 **352** 8p. multicoloured 10 10
779 – 30p. multicoloured 20 25
780 – 60p. multicoloured 35 50
781 – 1c. multicoloured 60 1·00
DESIGNS: As Type **352** showing different views of the Court Buildings.

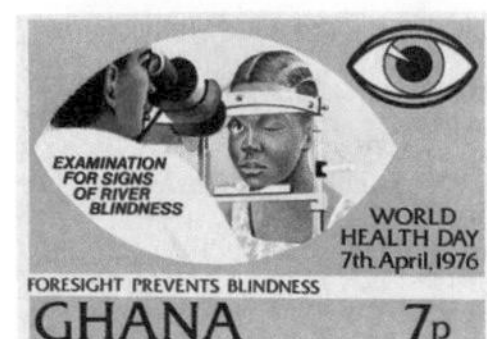

353 Examination for River Blindness

1976. Prevention of Blindness. Multicoloured.
782 7p. Type **353** 65 10
783 30p. Entomologist 1·75 1·40
784 60p. Normal vision 2·75 2·75
785 1c. Blackfly eradication 4·25 5·00

354 Fireworks Party, Christmas Eve

1976. Christmas. Multicoloured.
786 6p. Type **354** 15 10
787 8p. Children and gifts 15 10
788 30p. Christmas feast 35 30
789 1c. As 8p. 75 1·75
MS790 122 × 98 mm. 15, 40, 65 and 80p. as Nos. 786/9. Imperf 1·10 4·00

355 "Gallows Frame" Telephone and Alexander Graham Bell

1976. Centenary of Telephone. Multicoloured.
791 8p. Type **355** 15 10
792 30p. Bell and 1895 telephone 30 30
793 60p. Bell and 1929 telephone 45 70
794 1c. Bell and 1976 telephone 1·00 1·25
MS795 125 × 92 mm. 15, 40, 65 and 80p. as Nos. 791/4 1·00 1·40

1977. Olympic Winners. Nos. 773/6 optd **WINNERS** and country name.
796 **351** 7p. multicoloured 15 15
797 – 30p. multicoloured 20 40
798 – 60p. multicoloured 35 85
799 – 1c. multicoloured 40 1·50
MS800 103 × 135 mm. 15, 40, 65 and 80p. as Nos. 796/9 2·25 2·50
OPTD: 7p., 30p. **EAST GERMANY**; 60p. **U.S.S.R.**; 1c. **U.S.A.**

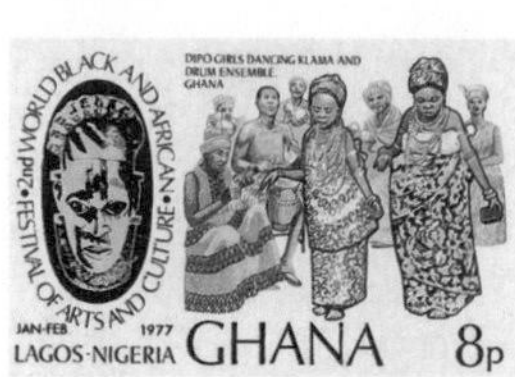

357 Dipo Dancers and Drum Ensemble

1977. 2nd World Black and African Festival of Arts and Culture, Nigeria. Multicoloured.
801 8p. Type **357** 15 15
802 30p. Arts and crafts 25 60
803 60p. Acon music and dancing priests 35 1·25
804 1c. African huts 40 2·00
MS805 164 × 120 mm. 15, 40, 65 and 80p. as Nos. 801/4 1·00 1·50

1977. Prince Charles's Visit to Ghana. Nos. 791/94 optd **PRINCE CHARLES VISITS GHANA 17th TO 25th MARCH, 1977**.
806 8p. Type **355** 50 55
807 30p. 1895 telephone 1·25 1·00
808 60p. 1929 telephone 1·50 2·00
809 1c. 1976 telephone 2·00 2·50
MS810 125 × 92 mm. 15, 40, 65 and 80p. as Nos. 806/9 6·50 9·00

359 Olive Colobus Monkey

1977. Wildlife. Multicoloured.
811 8p. Type **359** 45 15
812 20p. Temminck's giant squirrel 1·25 80
813 30p. Hunting dog 1·50 1·25
814 60p. African manatee (sea cow) 2·50 2·75
MS815 140 × 101 mm. 15, 40, 65 and 80p. as Nos. 811/14 4·00 4·50

360 "Le Chapeau de Paille" (Rubens—400th Birth Anniv)

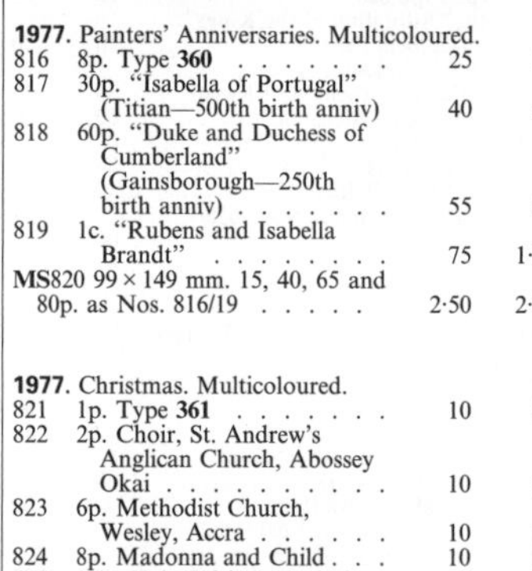

361 The Magi, Madonna and Child

1977. Painters' Anniversaries. Multicoloured.
816 8p. Type **360** 25 10
817 30p. "Isabella of Portugal" (Titian—500th birth anniv) 40 40
818 60p. "Duke and Duchess of Cumberland" (Gainsborough—250th birth anniv) 55 65
819 1c. "Rubens and Isabella Brandt" 75 1·25
MS820 99 × 149 mm. 15, 40, 65 and 80p. as Nos. 816/19 2·50 2·25

1977. Christmas. Multicoloured.
821 1p. Type **361** 10 10
822 2p. Choir, St. Andrew's Anglican Church, Abossey Okai 10 10
823 6p. Methodist Church, Wesley, Accra 10 10
824 8p. Madonna and Child 10 10
825 30p. Holy Spirit Cathedral, Accra 30 50
826 1c. Ebenezer Presbyterian Church, Accra 1·00 1·60
MS827 122 × 97 mm. 15, 40, 65 and 80p. as Nos. 822/3 and 825/6. Imperf 1·25 3·75

1978. Referendum. Nos. 821/26 optd **REFERENDUM 1978 VOTE EARLY**.
828 1p. Type **361** 10 10
829 2p. Choir, St. Andrew's Anglican Church, Abossey Okai 10 10
830 6p. Methodist Church, Wesley, Accra 10 10
831 8p. Madonna and Child 10 10
832 30p. Holy Spirit Cathedral, Accra 30 50
833 1c. Ebenezer Presbyterian Church, Accra 1·00 1·50
MS834 122 × 97 mm. 15, 40, 65 and 80p. as Nos. 829/30 and 832/3 27·00 17·00

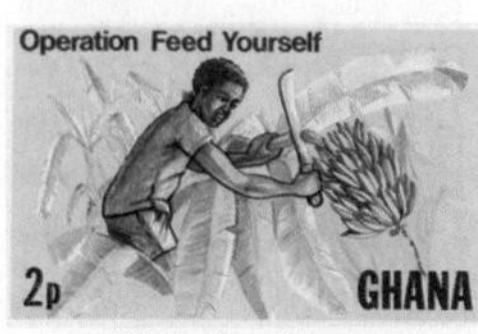

363 Cutting Bananas

1978. Operation "Feed Yourself". Multicoloured.
835 2p. Type **363** 10 10
836 8p. Home produce 15 10
837 30p. Market 35 35
838 60p. Fishing 70 60
839 1c. Mechanisation 1·25 1·25

364 Wright Flyer III

367 "The Betrayal"

366 Players and African Cup Emblem

1978. 75th Anniv of Powered Flight.
840 **364** 8p. black, brown and ochre 20 10
841 – 30p. black, brown and green 30 30
842 – 60p. black, brown and red 40 60
843 – 1c. black, brown and blue 2·75 1·10
MS844 167 × 100 mm. 15, 40, 65 and 80p. as Nos. 840/3 2·00 1·40
DESIGNS: 30p. Handley Page H.P.42; 60p. De Havilland Comet 1; 1c. Concorde.

1978. "CAPEX 1978" International Stamp Exhibition, Toronto. Nos. 840/3 optd **"CAPEX 78 JUNE 9-18 1978"**.
845 **364** 8p. black, brown and ochre 15 15
846 – 30p. black, brown and green 25 25
847 – 60p. black, brown and red 50 50
848 – 1c. black, brown and blue 1·10 80
MS849 167 × 100 mm. 15, 40, 65 and 80p. as Nos. 845/8 1·25 1·60

1978. Football Championships. Multicoloured.
850 8p. Type **366** 20 15
851 30p. Players and African Cup emblem (different) 25 30
852 60p. Players and World Cup emblem 40 60
853 1c. Goalkeeper and World Cup emblem 55 1·00
MS854 111 × 105 mm. 15, 40, 65 and 80p. as Nos. 850/3 1·10 1·25

1978. Easter. Drawings by Durer.
855 **367** 11p. black and mauve 10 10
856 – 39p. black and flesh 25 30
857 – 60p. black and yellow 35 45
858 – 1c. black and green 40 65
DESIGNS: 39p. "The Crucifixion"; 60p. "The Deposition"; 1c. "The Resurrection".

1978. Football Victories of Ghana and Argentina. Nos. 850/3 and **MS**854 optd **"GHANA WINNERS"** (8, 30p.) or **"ARGENTINA WINS"** (others).
859 **366** 8p. multicoloured 45 15
860 – 30p. multicoloured 45 30
861 – 60p. multicoloured 70 45
862 – 1c. multicoloured 80 75
MS863 111 × 105 mm. 15, 40, 65 and 80p. as Nos. 859/62 but all optd 1·00 1·10

369 "Bauhinia purpurea"

1978. Flowers. Multicoloured.
864 11p. Type **369** 15 10
865 39p. "Cassia fistula" 20 55
866 60p. "Plumeria acutifolia" 20 70
867 1c. "Jacaranda mimosifolia" 20 1·00

370 Mail Van

1978. 75th Anniv of Ghana Railways. Multicoloured.
868 11p. Type **370** 15 10
869 39p. Pay and bank car 20 65

870 60p. Steam locomotive No. 1 "Amanful", 1922 . . . . . 20 1·00
871 1c. Diesel-electric locomotive No. 1651, 1960 . . . . . 20 1·40

371 "Orbiter" Spacecraft

1979. "Pioneer" Venus Space Project. Multicoloured.
872 11p. Type **371** 15 10
873 39p. "Multiprobe" space craft 15 30
874 60p. "Orbiter" and "Multiprobe" spacecraft in Venus orbit 20 45
875 3c. Radar chart of Venus . . 30 1·40
MS876 135 × 94 mm. 15, 40, 65p. and 2c. as Nos. 872/5. Imperf 1·10 1·25

372 "O Come All Ye Faithful"

1979. Christmas. Lines and Scenes from Christmas Carols. Multicoloured.
877 8p. Type **372** 10 10
878 10p. "O Little Town of Bethlehem" 10 10
879 15p. "We Three Kings of Orient Are" 10 10
880 20p. "I Saw Three Ships come Sailing By" 10 10
881 2c. "Away In a Manger" . . 30 80
882 4c. "Ding Dong Merrily on High" . . . . 50 1·40
MS883 110 × 95 mm. 25, 65p., 1 and 2c. as Nos. 877, 879 and 881/2 75 1·00

373 Dr. J. B. Danquah (lawyer and nationalist)

375 Children in Classroom

374 Tribesman ringing Clack Bells

1980. Famous Ghanaians. Multicoloured.
884 20p. Type **373** 10 10
885 65p. John Mensah Sarbah (nationalist) 10 10
886 80p. Dr J. E. K. Aggrey (educationalist) 15 20
887 2c. Dr. Kwame Nkrumah (nationalist) 20 30
888 4c. G. E. (Paa) Grant (lawyer) 40 80

1980. Death Centenary of Sir Rowland Hill (1979). Multicoloured.
889 20p. Type **374** 15 15
893 25p. Type **374** 15 40
894 50p. Chieftain with Golden Elephant staff 15 40
890 65p. As 50p. 15 20
895 1c. Signalling with drums . . 20 85
891 2c. As 1c. 25 75
892 4c. Chieftain with ivory and gold staff . . . . 30 1·50
896 5c. As 4c. . . . . 35 3·00
MS897 115 × 86 mm. Nos. 893/6 75 1·00

1980. International Year of the Child (1979). Multicoloured.
898 20p. Type **375** 15 15
899 65p. Playing football 25 45
900 2c. Playing in a boat . . . . 40 1·00
901 4c. Mother and child . . . . 60 1·75
MS902 156 × 94 mm. 25, 50p., 1 and 3c. as Nos. 898/901 . . . . . 75 1·75

1980. "London 1980" International Stamp Exhibition. Nos. 889/96 optd **"LONDON 1980" 6th - 14th May 1980.**
903 **374** 20p. multicoloured . . . 15 15
907 – 25p. multicoloured . . . 1·25 2·75
908 – 50p. multicoloured . . . 1·50 3·00
904 – 65p. multicoloured . . . 15 50
909 – 1c. multicoloured . . . . 2·25 3·50
905 – 2c. multicoloured . . . . 25 1·25
906 – 4c. multicoloured . . . . 35 2·25
910 – 5c. multicoloured . . . . 4·00 6·00
MS911 115 × 86 mm. Nos. 907/10 1·00 2·00

1980. Papal Visit. Nos. 898/901 optd **"PAPAL VISIT" 8th - 9th May 1980.**
912 **375** 20p. multicoloured . . . 55 35
913 – 65p. multicoloured . . . 1·00 60
914 – 2c. multicoloured . . . . 1·75 1·40
915 – 4c. multicoloured . . . . 2·50 2·50
MS916 156 × 94 mm. 25, 50p., 1 and 3c. as Nos. 912/15 . . . . . . 9·00 7·50

378 Parliament House

1980. 3rd Republic Commemoration. Multicoloured.
917 20p. Type **378** 10 10
918 65p. Supreme Court 20 25
919 2c. The Castle 40 70
MS920 72 × 113 mm. 25p., 1 and 3c. as Nos. 917/19 . . . . 60 1·10

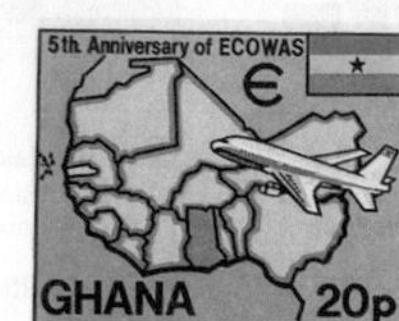

379 Boeing 737 Airliner and Map of West Africa

1980. 5th Anniv of Economic Community of West African States. Multicoloured.
921 20p. Type **379** 10 10
922 65p. Antenna and map . . . 15 20
923 80p. Cog-wheels and map . . 20 25
924 2c. Corn and map 35 50

380 "O.A.U." 381 "The Adoration of the Magi"

1980. 1st Organization of African Unity Economic Summit Conference, Nigeria.
925 **380** 20p. multicoloured . . . 10 10
926 – 65p. multicoloured . . . 15 20
927 – 80p. deep red, red and black 15 25
928 – 2c. multicoloured 20 65
DESIGNS: 65p. Maps of Africa and Ghana and banner; 80p. Map of Africa; 2c. Map of Africa, banner and Ghanaian flag.

1980. Christmas. Paintings by Fra Angelico. Multicoloured.
929 15p. Type **381** 10 10
930 20p. "The Virgin and Child, enthroned with Four Angels" 10 10
931 2c. "The Virgin and Child enthroned with Eight Angels" 35 80
932 4c. "The Annunciation" . . . 60 1·60
MS933 77 × 112 mm. 25, 50p., 1 and 3c. as Nos. 929/32 . . . . . . 75 1·25

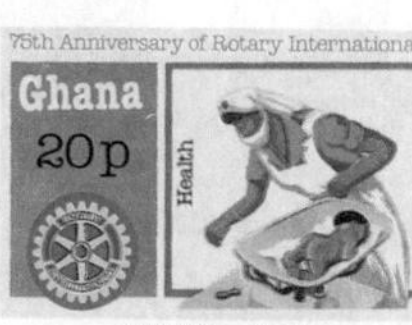

382 "Health"

1980. 75th Anniv of Rotary International. Multicoloured.
934 20p. Type **382** 10 10
935 65p. Rotary emblem and motto with maps of World and Ghana 15 30
936 2c. Rotary emblem, globe and outstretched hands . . 35 85
937 4c. "Eradication of Hunger" 60 1·50
MS938 121 × 93 mm. 25, 50p., 1 and 3c. as Nos. 934/7 . . . . . 1·10 2·00

383 Narina's Trogon ("Narina Trogon")

385 Royal Yacht "Britannia"

384 Pope John Paul II, Archbishop of Canterbury and President Limann during Papal Visit

1981. Birds. Multicoloured.
939 20p. Type **383** . . . . . . 1·00 15
940 65p. White-crowned robin chat . . . . 1·50 50
941 2c. Swallow-tailed bee eater 2·00 1·75
942 4c. Rose-ringed parakeet . . 2·50 3·25
MS943 89 × 121 mm. 25, 50p., 1 and 3c. as Nos. 939/42 . . . . . . 5·00 4·00

1981. 1st Anniv of Papal Visit.
944 **384** 20p. multicoloured . . . 25 15
945 65p. multicoloured . . . 45 55
946 80p. multicoloured . . . 60 70
947 2c. multicoloured . . . . 1·10 2·00

1981. Royal Wedding. Multicoloured.
948 20p. Prince Charles and Lady Diana Spencer 10 10
952 65p. As 20p. 15 25
949 80p. Prince Charles on visit to Ghana 15 20
953 1c. As 80p. 25 35
955 2c. Type **385** . . . . 1·00 1·50
954 3c. Type **385** . . . . 70 1·10
950 4c. Type **385** 50 80
956 5c. As 20p. . . . . 1·00 2·75
MS951 95 × 85 mm. 7c. St. Paul's Cathedral . . . . 70 1·25

386 Earth Satellite Station 388 "The Betrothal of St. Catherine of Alexandria" (Lucas Cranach)

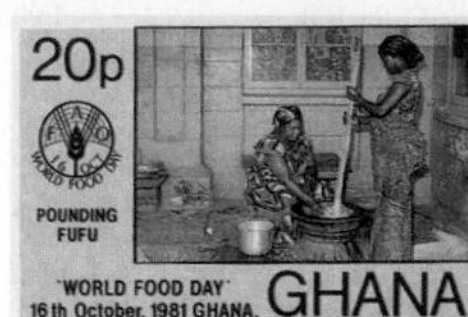

387 Pounding Fufu

1981. Commissioning of Earth Satellite Station. Mult.
957 20p. Type **386** 10 10
958 65p. Satellites beaming signals to Earth 15 15
959 80p. Satellite 15 20
960 4c. Satellite orbiting Earth . . 1·00 1·50
MS961 112 × 100 mm. 25p., 50p., 1c. and 3c. as Nos. 957/60 . . . . 70 1·40

1981. World Food Day. Multicoloured.
962 20p. Type **387** 10 10
963 65p. Plucking cocoa 25 35
964 80p. Preparing banku 35 40
965 2c. Garri processing . . . . 75 2·25
MS966 131 × 99 mm. 25p., 50p., 1c. and 3c. as Nos. 962/5 . . . . . 1·00 1·50

1981. Christmas. Details from Paintings. Multicoloured.
967 15p. Type **388** 15 10
968 20p. "Angelic Musicians play for Mary and Child" (Aachener Altares) 15 10
969 65p. "Child Jesus embracing his Mother" (Gabriel Metsu) 20 15
970 80p. "Madonna and Child" (Fra Filippo Lippi) 20 20
971 2c. "The Madonna with Infant Jesus" (Barnaba da Modena) 40 70
972 4c. "The Immaculate Conception" (Murillo) . . 45 1·10
MS973 82 × 102 mm. 6c. "Madonna and Child with Angels" (Hans Memling) . . . . 1·00 2·25

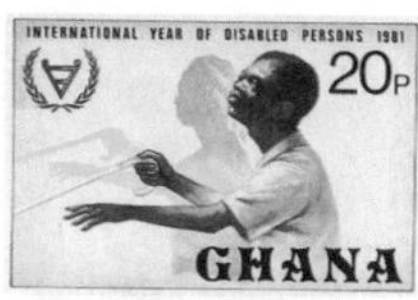

389 Blind Person

1982. International Year for Disabled Persons. Multicoloured.
974 20p. Type **389** 10 10
975 65p. Disabled person with crutches 30 35
976 80p. Blind child reading braille 40 45
977 4c. Disabled people helping one another . . . . 1·75 2·25
MS978 109 × 85 mm. 6c. Group of disabled people . . . . 2·75 3·00

390 African Clawless Otter 391 "Precis westermanni"

1982. Flora and Fauna. Multicoloured.
979 20p. Type **390** 25 15
980 65p. Bushbuck 40 40
981 80p. Aardvark 40 50
982 1c. Scarlet bell tree 40 60
983 2c. Glory-lilies . . . . 60 1·25
984 4c. Blue-pea . . . . 1·00 2·25
MS985 76 × 100 mm. 5c. Chimpanzee . . . . 1·25 5·00

1982. Butterflies. Multicoloured.
986 20p. Type **391** 70 15
987 65p. "Papilio menestheus" . . 1·25 1·00
988 2c. "Antanartia delius" . . . 2·00 3·50
989 4c. "Charaxes castor" . . . 2·75 4·75
MS990 98 × 123 mm. 25p., 50p., 1c. and 3c. as Nos. 986/9 . . . . 7·00 12·00

392 Scouts planting Tree

1982. 75th Anniv of Boy Scout Movement. Multicoloured.
991 20p. Type **392** 25 15
992 65p. Scouts cooking on campfire 70 65
993 80p. Sea Scouts sailing . . . 90 85
994 3c. Scouts observing African elephant . . . . 2·25 3·25
MS995 101 × 71 mm. 5c. Lord Baden-Powell (vert) . . . . . 2·25 6·50

393 Initial Stages of Construction

1982. Kpong Hydro-Electric Project. Multicoloured.
996 20p. Type **393** 65 10
997 65p. Truck removing rubble 1·25 45
998 80p. Hydro-electric turbines 2·00 65
999 2c. Aerial view of completed plant . . . . 2·75 1·60

394 Footballers

1982. World Cup Football Championship, Spain.
1000 **394** 20p. multicoloured . . . 60 10
1005 30p. multicoloured . . . 65 20
1001 – 65p. multicoloured . . . 80 35
1002 – 80p. multicoloured (Heading) . . . . . . 1·00 45

1006 – 80p. multicoloured (Three footballers) . . 85 45
1007 – 1c. multicoloured 90 55
1008 – 3c. multicoloured . . . . 1·40 1·60
1003 – 4c. multicoloured . . . . 1·90 2·00
MS1004 110 × 90 mm. 6c. multicoloured . . . . 3·75 2·75
DESIGNS: 65p. to 6c. Scenes showing footballers.

395 The Fight against Tuberculosis

1982. Centenary of Robert Koch's Discovery of Tubercle Bacillus. Multicoloured.
1009 20p. Type **395** 70 20
1010 65p. Robert Koch . . . . . 1·60 1·25
1011 80p. Robert Koch in Africa 2·00 1·75
1012 1c. Centenary of discovery of Tuberculosis . . . . . . 2·25 2·75
1013 2c. Robert Koch and Nobel Prize, 1905 . . . . 3·25 4·00

396 The Shepherds worship Jesus

397 Ghana and Commonwealth Flags with Coat of Arms

1982. Christmas. Multicoloured.
1014 15p. Type **396** 10 10
1015 20p. Mary, Joseph and baby Jesus 10 10
1016 65p. The Three Kings sight star 20 30
1017 4c. Winged Angel . . . . . 70 1·75
MS1018 90 × 110 mm. 6c. The Three Kings with Jesus . . . . . . 1·00 1·75

1983. Commonwealth Day. Multicoloured.
1019 20p. Type **397** 25 15
1020 55p. Satellite view of Ghana 45 65
1021 80p. Minerals of Ghana . . 1·00 1·25
1022 3c. African fish eagle . . . 1·50 4·25

1983. Italy's Victory in World Cup Football Championships (1982). Nos. 1000/8 optd **WINNER ITALY 3–1**.
1023 20p. multicoloured 15 10
1028 30p. multicoloured 75 90
1024 65p. multicoloured 25 15
1025 80p. multicoloured 25 20
1029 80p. multicoloured . . . . 1·25 1·50
1030 1c. multicoloured . . . . . 1·50 1·75
1031 3c. multicoloured . . . . . 2·00 3·75
1026 4c. multicoloured . . . . . 1·40 1·75
MS1027 110 × 90 mm. 6c. multicoloured . . . . 1·75 1·50

1983. No. 470 surch **C1**.
1031a 1c. on 20n.p. Bush hare (blue) 40 40

399 Short-finned Pilot Whale

1983. Coastal Marine Mammals. Multicoloured.
1032 1c. Type **399** . . . . 45 1·00
1033 1c.40 Risso's dolphin . . . 50 1·10
1034 2c. False killer whale . . . 55 1·25
1035 3c. Spinner dolphin . . . . 60 1·60
1036 4c. Atlantic hump-backed dolphin . . . . 60 2·00
MS1037 117 × 76 mm. 6c. As 4c. 1·25 1·00

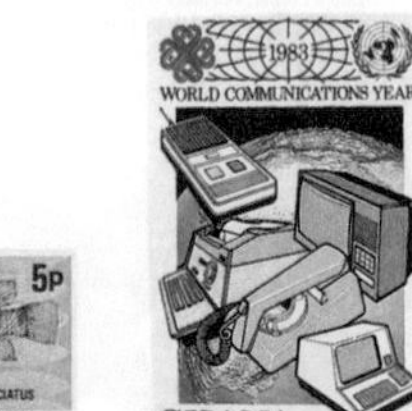

400 Banded Jewelfish

401 Communication Devices

1983.
1038 **400** 5p. multicoloured . . . 30 20
1039 – 10p. multicoloured . . . 30 20
1040 – 20p. multicoloured . . . 40 20
1041 – 50p. green, orange blk 40 30
1042 – 1c. orange, blue and black 50 20
1043 – 2c. multicoloured 50 30
1044 – 3c. multicoloured . . . . 1·25 30
1045 – 4c. multicoloured 40 40
1046 – 5c. multicoloured 50 40
1047 – 10c. multicoloured . . . 65 1·00
DESIGNS—HORIZ: 10p. Banded jewelfish (different); 2c. Jet airliner. VERT: 20p. "Haemanthus rupestris"; 50p. Mounted warrior; 1c. Scorpion; 3c. White-collared mangabey; 4c. Demidoff's galago; 5c. "Kaemferia nigerica"; 10c. Grey-backed camaroptera.

1983. World Communications Year. Multicoloured.
1048 1c. Type **401** 15 25
1049 1c.40 Satellite dish aerial . . 20 30
1050 2c.30 Cable and "Long Lines" (cable ship) . . . 35 55
1051 3c. Switchboard operators 40 65
1052 5c. Aircraft cockpit and air traffic controllers 55 85
MS1053 95 × 70 mm. 6c. Space satellite 30 50

402 Children receiving Presents

1983. Christmas. Multicoloured.
1054 70p. Type **402** 15 10
1055 1c. Nativity and Star of Bethlehem (vert) 15 10
1056 1c.40 Children celebrating (vert) 20 55
1057 2c.30 Family praying together (vert) . . . . . 25 1·00
1058 3c. Dancing to bongo drum 35 1·25
MS1059 70 × 90 mm. 6c. As 2c.30 30 1·50

403 Soldiers with Rifles

407 Cross and Crown of Thorns

1983. Namibia Day.
1060 **403** 50p. green and black . . 10 10
1061 – 1c. multicoloured . . . 10 10
1062 – 1c.40 blue, lt blue blk . . 15 15
1063 – 2c.30 multicoloured . . . 20 25
1064 – 3c. multicoloured 25 30
DESIGNS: 1c. Soldiers supported by tank; 1c.40, Machete cutting chains; 2c.30, Peasant woman; 3c. Soldiers and artillery support.

1984. (a) Nos. 948/50, 952 and 954 surch.
1065 1c. on 20p. Prince Charles and Lady Diana Spencer 2·50 3·00
1066 9c. on 65p. Prince Charles and Lady Diana Spencer 3·00 4·00
1067 9c. on 80p. Prince Charles on visit to Ghana . . . . 3·00 4·00
1068 20c. on 3c. Type **385** . . . 3·50 6·00
1069 20c. on 4c. Type **385** . . . 3·50 6·00
MS1070 95 × 85 mm. 60c on 7c. St. Paul's Cathedral . . . . . 1·00 3·00

(b) Nos. 991/2 and 994 surch.
1071 10c. on 20p. Type **392** . . . 40 45
1072 19c. on 65p. Scouts cooking on campfire 80 85
1073 30c. on 3c. Scouts observing African elephant . . . . 2·00 2·00
MS1074 101 × 71 mm. 60c. on 5c. Lord Baden-Powell . . . . . 1·00 3·50

(c) Nos. 1000/3, 1005/6 and 1008 surch.
1075 **394** 1c. on 20p. multicoloured 30 50
1076 – 9c. on 65p. multicoloured 70 70
1077 – 9c. on 3c. multicoloured 70 70
1078 **394** 10c. on 30p. multicoloured 70 70
1079 – 10c. on 80p. multicoloured 70 70
1080 – 20c. on 80p. multicoloured . . . . 1·75 1·75
1081 – 20c. on 4c. multicoloured 1·75 1·75
MS1082 110 × 90 mm. 60c. on 6c. multicoloured . . . . 1·00 2·25

(d) Nos. 1019/22 surch.
1083 1c. on 20p. Type **397** . . . 10 10
1084 9c. on 55p. Satellite view of Ghana 50 45
1085 30c. on 80p. Minerals of Ghana . . . . 2·00 1·75
1086 50c. on 3c. African fish eagle . . . . 3·00 3·50

(e) Nos. 1023/6, 1028/9 and 1031 surch.
1087 **394** 1c. on 20p. multicoloured 20 50
1088 – 9c. on 65p. multicoloured 55 60
1089 – 9c. on 3c. multicoloured 55 60
1090 **394** 10c. on 30p. multicoloured 55 60
1091 – 10c. on 80p. multicoloured 55 60
1092 – 20c. on 80p. multicoloured . . . . 90 1·00
1093 – 20c. on 4c. multicoloured 90 1·00
MS1094 110 × 90 mm. 60c. on 6c. multicoloured . . . . 1·00 2·00

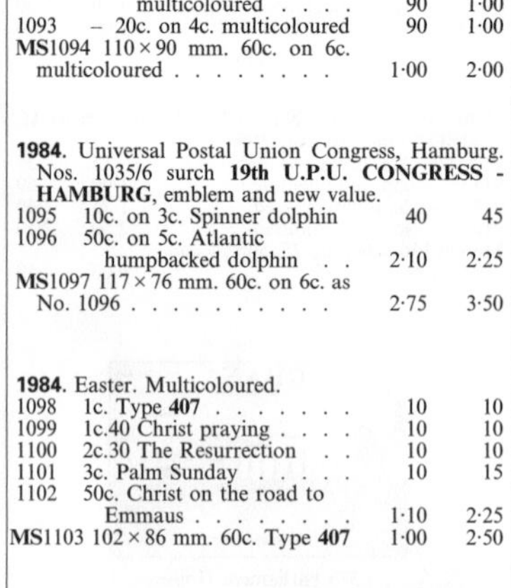

1984. Universal Postal Union Congress, Hamburg. Nos. 1035/6 surch **19th U.P.U. CONGRESS - HAMBURG**, emblem and new value.
1095 10c. on 3c. Spinner dolphin 40 45
1096 50c. on 5c. Atlantic humpbacked dolphin . . 2·10 2·25
MS1097 117 × 76 mm. 60c. on 6c. as No. 1096 . . . . 2·75 3·50

1984. Easter. Multicoloured.
1098 1c. Type **407** 10 10
1099 1c.40 Christ praying 10 10
1100 2c.30 The Resurrection . . 10 10
1101 3c. Palm Sunday 10 15
1102 50c. Christ on the road to Emmaus . . . . 1·10 2·25
MS1103 102 × 86 mm. 60c. Type **407** 1·00 2·50

408 Women's 400 Metre Race

409 "Amorphophallus johnsonii"

1984. Olympic Games, Los Angeles. Multicoloured.
1104 1c. Type **408** 10 10
1105 1c.40 Boxing 15 10
1106 2c.30 Hockey 20 15
1107 3c. Men's 400 metre hurdles race 20 15
1108 50c. Rhythmic gymnastics 1·75 3·50
MS1109 103 × 78 mm. 70c. Football 2·00 3·50
No. 1108 is inscribed "RYTHMIC" in error.

1984. Flowers. Multicoloured.
1110 1c. Type **409** 10 10
1111 1c.40 "Pancratium trianthum" 10 10
1112 2c.30 "Eulophia cucullata" 10 15
1113 3c. "Amorphophallus abyssinicus" 10 15
1114 50c. "Chlorophytum togoense" . . . . 1·10 5·00
MS1115 70 × 96 mm. 60c. Type **409** 1·25 3·50

410 Young Bongo

1984. Endangered Antelopes. Multicoloured.
1116 1c. Type **410** 30 20
1117 2c.30 Bongo bucks fighting 55 55
1118 3c. Bongo family 70 70
1119 20c. Bongo herd in high grass . . . . 1·75 3·50
MS1120 Two sheets, each 100 × 71 mm. (a) 70c. Head of Kob; (b) 70c. Head of Bush buck Set of 2 sheets . . . . 10·00 13·00

411 Dipo Girl

412 The Three Wise Men bringing Gifts

1984. Ghanaian Culture. Multicoloured.
1121 1c. Type **411** 10 25
1122 1c.40 Adowa dancer 10 25
1123 2c.30 Agbadza dancer . . . 10 25
1124 3c. Damba dancer 10 25
1125 50c. Dipo dancer . . . . . 90 3·50
MS1126 70 × 84 mm. 70c. Mandolin player . . . . 1·50 3·00

1984. Christmas. Multicoloured.
1127 70p. Type **412** 10 10
1128 1c. Choir of angels 10 10
1129 1c.40 Mary and shepherds at manger 10 10
1130 2c.30 The flight into Egypt 10 10
1131 3c. Simeon blessing Jesus . . 10 15
1132 50c. Holy Family and angels 90 3·00
MS1133 70 × 90 mm. 70c. Type **412** 1·50 2·75

1984. Olympic Winners. Nos. 1104/8 optd.
1134 1c. Type **408** (optd **VALERIE BRISCO-HOOKS U.S.A.**) 10 10
1135 1c.40 Boxing (optd **U.S. WINNERS**) 10 10
1136 2c.30 Hockey (optd **PAKISTAN (FIELD HOCKEY)**) 10 10
1137 3c. Men's 400 metre hurdles race (optd **EDWIN MOSES U.S.A.**) 10 10
1138 50c. Rhythmic gymnastics (optd **LAURI FUNG CANADA**) . . . . 1·10 1·60
MS1139 103 × 78 mm. 70c. Football (optd **FRANCE**) . . . . 1·75 2·50

414 The Queen Mother attending Church Service

415 Moslems going to Mosque

1985. Life and Times of Queen Elizabeth the Queen Mother. Multicoloured.
1140 5c. Type **414** 10 15
1141 12c. At Ascot Races 25 30
1142 100c. At Clarence House on her 84th birthday . . . . 1·75 2·50
MS1143 56 × 84 mm. 110c. With Prince Charles at Garter ceremony 1·75 3·00
Stamps as Nos. 1140/2 but with face values of 8c., 20c. and 70c. exist from additional sheetlets with changed background colours.

1985. Islamic Festival of Id-el-Fitr. Multicoloured.
1144 5c. Type **415** 25 20
1145 8c. Moslems at prayer . . . 35 30
1146 12c. Pilgrims visiting the Dome of the Rock . . . 55 45
1147 18c. Preaching the Koran 70 60
1148 50c. Banda Nkwanta Mosque, Accra, and map of Ghana . . . . 1·75 1·60

416 Youths clearing Refuse ("Make Ghana Clean")

418 Fork-tailed Flycatcher

417 Honda "Interceptor", 1984

1985. International Youth Year. Multicoloured.
1149 5c. Type **416** 10 10
1150 8c. Planting sapling ("Make Ghana Green") 15 15
1151 12c. Youth carrying bananas ("Feed Ghana") 20 25
1152 100c. Open-air class ("Educate Ghana") . . . 65 2·25
MS1153 103 × 78 mm. 110c. as 8c. 1·25 3·00

1985. Centenary of the Motorcycle. Multicoloured.
1154 5c. Type **417** 40 30
1155 8c. DKW, 1938 . . . . . . 50 40
1156 12c. BMW "R 32", 1923 . . 75 70
1157 100c. NSU, 1900 . . . . . 3·00 7·00
MS1158 78 × 108 mm. 110c. Zündapp, 1973 (vert) . . . . . 3·50 4·25

1985. Birth Bicentenary of John J. Audubon (ornithologist). Designs showing original paintings. Multicoloured.
1159 5c. Type **418** . . . . 1·25 50
1160 8c. Barred owl . . . . . . 2·25 2·00
1161 12c. Black-throated mango 2·25 2·00
1162 100c. White-crowned pigeon 6·50 9·50
MS1163 85 × 115 mm. 110c. Downy Woodpecker . . . . 6·50 3·50
No. 1159 is inscribed "York-tailed fly catcher" in error.

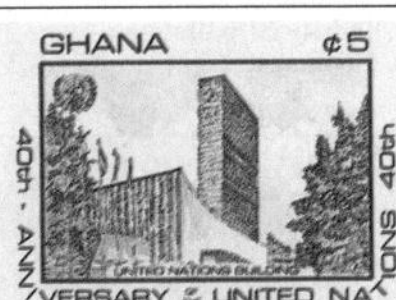

419 United Nations Building, New York

1985. 40th Anniv of U.N.O. Multicoloured.
1164 5c. Type **419** 10 10
1165 8c. Flags of member nations and U.N. Building . . . 10 15
1166 12c. Dove with olive branch 10 25
1167 18c. General Assembly . . . 15 35
1168 100c. Flags of Ghana and United Nations . . . . . 90 1·75
MS1169 90 × 70 mm. 110c. United Nations (New York) 1955 4c. 10th anniv stamp . . . . 75 1·75

420 Coffee

1985. 20th Anniv of United Nations Conference on Trade and Development. Designs showing export products. Multicoloured.
1170 5c. Type **420** 10 10
1171 8c. Cocoa 15 15
1172 12c. Timber 25 25
1173 18c. Bauxite . . . . 1·25 90
1174 100c. Gold . . . . 6·50 8·50
MS1175 104 × 74 mm. 110c. Agricultural produce and plate of food . . . . 1·25 2·50

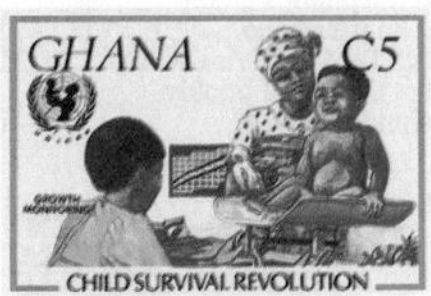

421 Growth Monitoring

1985. UNICEF Child Survival Campaign. Multicoloured.
1176 5c. Type **421** 30 10
1177 8c. Oral rehydration therapy 50 30
1178 12c. Breast-feeding 70 40
1179 100c. Immunization . . . . 2·50 4·50
MS1180 99 × 69 mm. 110c. Campaign logo . . . . 1·75 2·25

422 Airline Stewardess and Boys with Stamp Album

1986. "Ameripex" International Stamp Exhibition, Chicago. Multicoloured.
1181 5c. Type **422** 15 15
1182 25c. Globe and Douglas DC-10 airplane 60 45
1183 100c. Ghana Airways stewardess (vert) . . . . 2·25 3·00
MS1184 90 × 70 mm. 150c. Stamp collecting class . . . . 1·50 2·50

423 Kejetia Roundabout, Kumasi

1986. "Inter-Tourism '86" Conference. Mult.
1185 5c. Type **423** 10 10
1186 15c. Fort St. Jago, Elmina 30 30
1187 25c. Tribal warriors 45 45
1188 100c. Chief holding audience 1·75 3·25
MS1189 110 × 70 mm. 150c. African elephants . . . . 3·75 6·00

424 Tackling

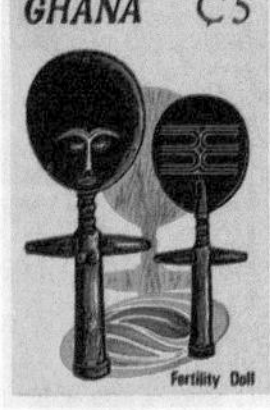

425 Fertility Doll

1987. World Cup Football Championship, Mexico (1986). Multicoloured.
1190 5c. Type **424** 20 10
1191 15c. Player taking control of ball 30 15
1192 25c. Player kicking ball . . 50 25
1193 100c. Player with ball . . . 1·50 2·25
MS1194 90 × 70 mm. 150c. Player kicking ball (different) . . . . 1·50 2·00

1987. Ghanaian Fertility Dolls. Designs showing different dolls.
1195 **425** 5c. multicoloured 10 10
1196 – 15c. multicoloured . . . 15 15
1197 – 25c. multicoloured . . . 25 25
1198 – 100c. multicoloured . . . 90 2·00
MS1199 90 × 70 mm. **425** 150c. multicoloured . . . . 1·50 2·00

426 Children of Different Races, Peace Doves and Sun

1987. International Peace Year (1986). Multicoloured.
1200 5c. Type **426** 15 10
1201 25c. Plough, peace dove and rising sun 75 25
1202 100c. Peace dove, olive branch and globe (vert) 2·50 3·00
MS1203 90 × 70 mm. 150c. Dove perched on plough (vert) . . . 1·75 2·25

427 Lumber and House under Construction

1987. "Gifex '87" International Forestry Exposition, Accra. Multicoloured.
1204 5c. Type **427** 10 10
1205 15c. Planks and furniture . . 15 15
1206 25c. Felled trees 25 25
1207 200c. Logs and wood carvings . . . . 1·60 2·25

1987. Appearance of Halley's Comet (1986). As T **151a** of Gambia. Multicoloured.
1208 5c. Mikhail Lomonosov (scientist) and Chamber of Curiosities, St. Petersburg 20 10
1209 25c. Lunar probe "Surveyor 3", 1966 . . . . 70 30
1210 200c. Wedgwood plaques for Isaac Newton, 1790 and "Apollo 11" Moon landing, 1968 . . . . . . 3·25 2·25
MS1211 100 × 70 mm. 250c. Halley's Comet . . . . 4·25 2·75

428 Demonstrator and Arms breaking Shackles

1987. Solidarity with the People of Southern Africa. Multicoloured.
1212 5c. Type **428** 10 10
1213 15c. Miner and gold bars . . 40 15
1214 25c. Xhosa warriors 30 25
1215 100c. Nelson Mandela and shackles . . . . 1·25 3·00
MS1216 70 × 90 mm. 150c. Nelson Mandela . . . . 1·50 2·00

429 Aerophones

1987. Musical Instruments. Multicoloured.
1217 5c. Type **429** 10 10
1218 15c. Xylophone 15 15
1219 25c. Chordophones 30 25
1220 100c. Membranophones . . 1·00 1·25
MS1221 90 × 70 mm. 200c. Idiophones . . . . 1·90 2·25

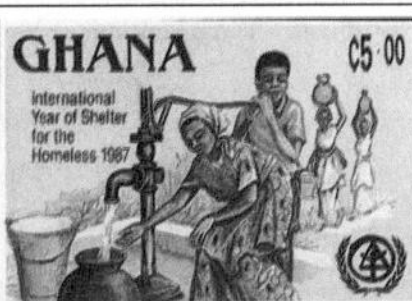

430 Woman filling Water Pot at Pump

1987. Int Year of Shelter for the Homeless. Mult.
1222 5c. Type **430** 10 10
1223 15c. Building house from breeze blocks 15 15
1224 25c. Modern village with stream 20 25
1225 100c. Modern houses with verandahs . . . . 75 1·25

431 Ga Women preparing Kpokpoi for Homowo Festival

1988. Ghana Festivals. Multicoloured.
1226 5c. Type **431** 10 10
1227 15c. Efute hunters with deer, Aboakyir festival 15 15
1228 25c. Fanti chief dancing at Odwira festival 25 25
1229 100c. Chief in palanquin, Yam festival . . . . . . 65 1·25

432 Port Installation

1988. 5th Anniv (1987) of 31 December Revolution. Multicoloured.
1230 5c. Type **432** . . . . 1·25 40
1231 15c. Repairing railway line 12·00 2·50
1232 25c. Planting cocoa . . . . 1·75 55
1233 100c. Miners with ore truck 13·00 14·00

433 Nurse giving Injection

435 Akwadjan Men

434 Fishing

1988. UNICEF Global Immunization Campaign. Multicoloured.
1234 5c. Type **433** 20 10
1235 15c. Girl receiving injection 25 20
1236 25c. Schoolgirl crippled by polio 35 50
1237 100c. Nurse giving oral vaccine to baby . . . . . 60 2·25

1988. 10th Anniv of International Fund for Agricultural Development. Multicoloured.
1238 5c. Type **434** 85 30
1239 15c. Women harvesting crops . . . . 1·40 40
1240 25c. Cattle . . . . 1·75 50
1241 100c. Village granaries . . . 4·00 8·50

1988. Tribal Costumes. Multicoloured.
1242 5c. Type **435** 15 10
1243 25c. Banaa man 35 20
1244 250c. Agwasen woman . . . 1·50 2·00

1988. Nos. 460, 464/6, 469/70, 1031a, 1038/42, 1044 and 1046 surch.
1245 – 20c. on 50p. green, orange and black (No. 1041) 30 30
1246 – 20c. on 1c. orange, blue and black (No. 1042) 30 30

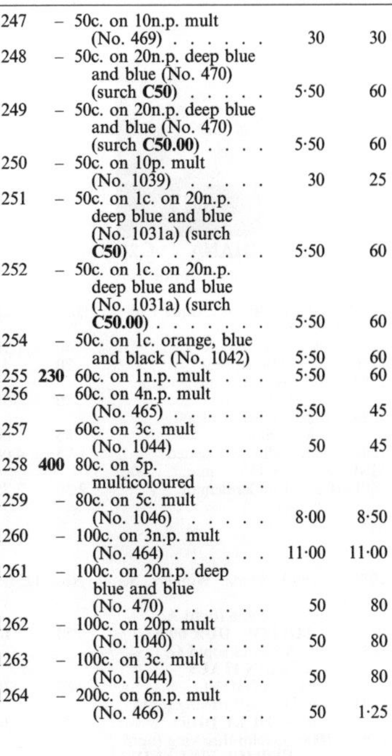
1247 – 50c. on 10n.p. mult (No. 469) 30 30
1248 – 50c. on 20n.p. deep blue and blue (No. 470) (surch **C50**) . . . . . 5·50 60
1249 – 50c. on 20n.p. deep blue and blue (No. 470) (surch **C50.00**) . . . . 5·50 60
1250 – 50c. on 10p. mult (No. 1039) 30 25
1251 – 50c. on 1c. on 20n.p. deep blue and blue (No. 1031a) (surch **C50**) . . . . 5·50 60
1252 – 50c. on 1c. on 20n.p. deep blue and blue (No. 1031a) (surch **C50.00**) . . . . 5·50 60
1254 – 50c. on 1c. orange, blue and black (No. 1042) 5·50 60
1255 **230** 60c. on 1n.p. mult . . . 5·50 60
1256 – 60c. on 4n.p. mult (No. 465) . . . . . . 5·50 45
1257 – 60c. on 3c. mult (No. 1044) 50 45
1258 **400** 80c. on 5p. multicoloured . . . .
1259 – 80c. on 5c. mult (No. 1046) . . . . . 8·00 8·50
1260 – 100c. on 3n.p. mult (No. 464) . . . . . . 11·00 11·00
1261 – 100c. on 20n.p. deep blue and blue (No. 470) 50 80
1262 – 100c. on 20p. mult (No. 1040) 50 80
1263 – 100c. on 3c. mult (No. 1044) 50 80
1264 – 200c. on 6n.p. mult (No. 466) . . . . . . 50 1·25

440 Boxing

1988. Olympic Games, Seoul. Multicoloured.
1265 20c. Type **440** 20 15
1266 60c. Athletics 45 55
1267 80c. Discus-throwing . . . 50 80
1268 100c. Javelin-throwing . . . 60 1·10
1269 350c. Weightlifting . . . . 1·40 3·00
MS1270 75 × 105 mm. As 80c. 4·00 3·00

441 Nutrition Lecture

443 "African Solidarity"

442 Tropical Forest

1988. 125th Anniv of Int Red Cross. Mult.
1271 20c. Type **441** 40 15
1272 50c. Red Cross volunteer with blind woman 90 90
1273 60c. Distributing flood relief supplies . . . . 1·00 1·00
1274 200c. Giving first aid . . . 2·50 3·25

1988. Christmas. Multicoloured.
1275 20c. Type **442** 15 10
1276 60c. Christ Child (vert) . . 35 35
1277 80c. Virgin and Child with Star (vert) 50 50
1278 100c. Three Wise Men following Star 60 70
1279 350c. Symbolic Crucifixion (vert) . . . . 2·00 2·50
MS1280 100 × 70 mm. 500c. Virgin and Child (vert) . . . . 2·00 2·75

1989. 25th Anniv (1988) of Organization of African Unity. Multicoloured.
1281 20c. Type **443** 10 10
1282 50c. O.A.U. Headquarters Addis Ababa 15 20
1283 60c. Emperor Haile Selassie and Ethiopian flag (horiz) 30 25
1284 200c. Kwame Nkrumah (former Ghanaian President) and flag (horiz) 60 85

444 "Amor"

1989. 500th Birth Anniv of Titian (artist). Multicoloured.
1285 20c. Type **444** 40 15
1286 60c. "The Appeal" 70 45
1287 80c. "Bacchus and Ariadne" (detail) 80 55
1288 100c. "Portrait of a Musician" . . . . 85 1·00
1289 350c. "Philip II seated" . . 1·75 4·00
MS1290 77 × 115 mm. 500c. "Portrait of a Gentleman" . . 2·50 2·75

1989. Olympic Medal Winners, Seoul. Nos. 1251/5 optd.
1291 20c. Type **436** (optd **A. ZUELOW DDR 60 KG**) 50 10
1292 60c. Athletics (optd **G. BORDIN ITALY MARATHON**) 65 25
1293 80c. Discus-throwing (optd **J. SCHULT DDR**) . . . 70 30
1294 100c. Javelin-throwing (optd **T. KORJUS FINLAND**) 75 35
1295 350c. Weightlifting (optd **B. GUIDIKOV BULGARIA 75 KG**) . . . . 1·75 1·10
MS1296 75 × 105 mm. 500c. As 80c. (optd **GOLD J. SCHULT DDR SILVER R. OUBARTAS USSR BRONZE R. DANNEBERG W. GERMANY** on sheet margin 2·40 2·10

1989. Various stamps surch. (a) Nos. 949/50 and 952/4.
1297 80c. on 65p. Prince Charles and Lady Diana Spencer 70 70
1298 100c. on 80p. Prince Charles on visit to Ghana 80 90
1299 100c. on 1c. Prince Charles on visit to Ghana . . . 80 90
1300 300c. on 3c. Type **385** . . . 2·00 2·50
1301 500c. on 4c. Type **385** . . . 3·25 4·25

(b) Nos. 1048/51 and **MS**1053.
1302 60c. on 1c. Type **401** . . . 1·10 50
1303 80c. on 1c.40 Satellite dish aerial . . . . 1·25 65
1304 200c. on 2c.30 Cable and cable-laying ship . . . . 3·00 3·00
1305 300c. on 3c. Switchboard operators . . . . 3·25 4·00
MS1306 95 × 70 mm. 500c. on 6c. Space satellite . . . . 7·00 8·00

(c) Nos. 1104/7 and **MS**1109.
1307 60c. on 1c. Type **408** . . . 30 30
1308 80c. on 1c.40 Boxing . . . 40 40
1309 200c. on 2c.30 Hockey . . . 1·25 1·60
1310 300c. on 3c. Men's 400 metre hurdles race . . . . 1·40 1·75
MS1311 103 × 78 mm. 600c. on 70c. Football . . . . 3·00 4·50

(d) Nos. 1134/7 and **MS**1139.
1312 60c. on 1c. Type **408** (optd **VALERIE BRISCO-HOOKS U.S.A.**) . . . . 1·25 1·00
1313 80c. on 1c.40 Boxing (optd **U.S. WINNERS**) . . . . 1·50 1·25
1314 200c. on 2c.30 Field hockey (optd **PAKISTAN (FIELD HOCKEY)**) . . . 4·25 4·25
1315 300c. on 3c. Men's 400 metre hurdles race (optd **EDWIN MOSES U.S.A.**) 4·25 4·75
MS1316 103 × 78 mm. 600c. on 70c. Football (optd **FRANCE**) . . . 5·00 5·50

(e) Nos. 1140/2. and **MS**1143.
1317 80c. on 5c. Type **414** . . . 35 40
1318 250c. on 12c. At Ascot Races . . . . 1·10 1·75
1319 300c. on 100c. At Clarence House on her 84th birthday . . . . 1·25 1·75
MS1320 56 × 84 mm. 500c. on 110c. With Prince Charles at Garter Ceremony . . . . 3·25 4·50

(f) Nos. 1159/61 and **MS**1163.
1321 80c. on 5c. Type **418** . . . 2·50 1·00
1322 100c. on 8c. Barred owl . . 3·75 2·50
1323 300c. on 12c. Black-throated mango . . . . 4·25 4·75
MS1324 85 × 115 mm. 500c. on 110c. Downy Woodpecker . . . . . 9·00 9·00

(g) Nos. 1190/2 and **MS**1194.
1325 60c. on 5c. Type **424** . . . 45 45
1326 200c. on 15c. Player taking control of ball . . . . . 1·50 2·00
1327 300c. on 25c. Player kicking ball . . . . 2·00 2·75
MS1328 90 × 70 mm. 600c. on 150c. Player kicking ball (different) 7·00 8·00

(h) As Nos. 1190/2 and **MS**1194 but with unissued opt **WINNERS Argentina 3 W.Germany 2**.
1329 60c. on 5c. Type **424** . . . 1·00 40
1330 200c. on 15c. Player taking control of ball . . . . . 2·00 2·50
1331 300c. on 25c. Player kicking ball . . . . 2·50 3·00
MS1332 90 × 70 mm. 600c. on 150c. Player kicking ball (different) 3·75 4·50

(i) Nos. 1208/10.
1333 60c. on 5c. Mikhail Lomonosov (scientist) and Chamber of Curiosities, St. Petersburg . . . . . 1·10 60
1334 80c. on 25c. Lunar probe "Surveyor 3", 1966 . . . 1·50 85
1335 500c. on 200c. Wedgwood plaques for Isaac Newton, 1790, and "Apollo 11" Moon landing, 1968 . . . 4·25 6·00
MS1336 100 × 70 mm. 750c. on 250c. Halley's Comet . . . . 4·00 5·00

(j) As Nos. 1208/10 and **MS**1211 optd **HALLEYS COMET 1985 - OFFICIAL - 1996** and emblem.
1337 60c. on 5c. Mikhail Lomonosov (scientist) and Chamber of Curiosities, St. Petersburg 50 40
1338 80c. on 25c. Lunar probe "Surveyor 3", 1966 . . . 60 50
1339 500c. on 200c. Wedgwood plaques for Isaac Newton, 1790, and "Apollo 11" Moon landing, 1968 . . . 2·75 4·75
MS1340 100 × 70 mm. 750c. on 250c. Halley's Comet . . . . 6·00 7·00

448 French Royal Standard and Field Gun

449 Storming the Bastille

1989. "Philexfrance 89" International Stamp Exhibition, Paris. Multicoloured.
1341 20c. Type **448** 60 25
1342 60c. Regimental standard, 1789, and French infantry- man . . . . . . 1·25 90
1343 80c. Revolutionary standard, 1789, and pistol . . . . . 1·50 1·00
1344 350c. Tricolour, 1794, and musket . . . . 3·75 5·50
MS1345 77 × 106 mm. 600c. Street plan of Paris, 1789 (horiz) . . 3·00 3·50

1989. Japanese Art. Portraits. As T **177a** of Gambia. Multicoloured.
1346 20c. "Minamoto-no-Yoritomo" (Fujiwara-no-Takanobu) (vert) 35 20
1347 50c. "Takami Senseki" (Watanabe Kazan) (vert) 50 30
1348 60c. "Ikkyu Sojun" (study) (Bokusai) (vert) 55 35
1349 75c. "Nakamura Kuranosuka" (Ogata Korin) (vert) 60 40
1350 125c. "Portrait of a Lady" (Kyoto branch, Kano School) (vert) 85 75
1351 150c. "Portrait of Zemmui" (anon, 12th-century) (vert) 85 80
1352 200c. "Ono no Komachi the Poetess" (Hokusai) (vert) 1·00 1·25
1353 500c. "Kobo Daisi as a Child" (anon) (vert) . . . 2·50 3·50
MS1354 Two sheets, each 102 × 77 mm. (a) 500c. "Kodai-no-Kimi" (attr Fujiwara-no-Nobuzane) (vert). (b) 500c. "Emperor Hanazono" (Fujiwara-no-Goshin) Set of 2 sheets . . 8·50 8·50

1989. Bicentenary of French Revolution. Mult.
1355 20c. Type **449** 55 20
1356 60c. Declaration of Human Rights . . . . 1·00 50
1357 80c. Storming the Bastille (horiz) . . . . 1·25 75
1358 200c. Revolution monument (horiz) . . . . 2·25 2·50
1359 350c. Tree of Liberty (horiz) 3·00 4·00

450 "Collybia fusipes"

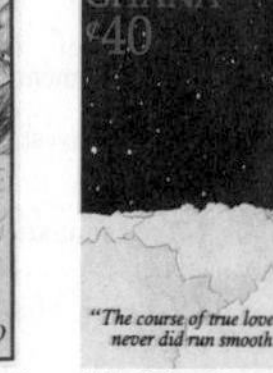

451 "The Course of True Love ..."

1989. Fungi (1st series). Multicoloured.
1360 20c. Type **450** 35 25
1361 50c. "Coprinus comatus" . . 50 40
1362 60c. "Xerocomus subtomentosus" 55 45
1363 80c. "Lepista nuda" 65 55
1364 150c. "Suillus placidus" . . 1·10 95
1365 200c. "Lepista nuda" (different) . . . . 1·40 1·25
1366 300c. "Marasmius oreades" 2·00 2·00
1367 500c. "Agaricus campestris" 3·25 3·25
MS1368 Two sheets, each 110 × 80 mm. (a) 600c. "*Boletus rhodoxanthus*". (b) 600c. "*Amanita rubescens*" Set of 2 sheets . . . 7·50 8·00
See also Nos. 1489/96.

1989. 425th Birth Anniv of Shakespeare. Verses and scenes from "A Midsummer Night's Dream". Multicoloured.
1369 40c. Type **451** 75 65
1370 40c. "Love looks not with the eye but with the mind" 75 65
1371 40c. "Nature here shows art" 75 65
1372 40c. "Things growing are not ripe till their season" 75 65
1373 40c. "He is defiled that draws a sword on thee" 75 65
1374 40c. "It is not enough to speak, but to speak true" 75 65
1375 40c. "Thou art as wise as thou are beautiful" . . . 75 65
1376 40c. Wildcat in wood (face value at left) 75 65
1377 40c. Man 75 65
1378 40c. Woman with flower . . 75 65
1379 40c. King and queen 75 65
1380 40c. Bottom 75 65
1381 40c. Wildcat in wood (face value at right) 75 65
1382 40c. Woman 75 65
1383 40c. Leopard 75 65
1384 40c. Tree trunk and man . . 75 65
1385 40c. Meadow flowers . . . 75 65
1386 40c. Mauve flowers 75 65
1387 40c. Plants 75 65
1388 40c. Lion 75 65
1389 40c. Fern and flowers . . . 75 65
Nos. 1369/89 were printed together, forming a composite design.

451a Bronze Mannikin

1989. Birds. Multicoloured.
1390 20c. Type **451a** 30 10
1391 50c. African pied wagtail 45 30
1392 60c. African pygmy kingfisher (inscr "Halcyon malimbicus") 1·25 1·75
1392a 60c. African pygmy kingfisher (inscr "Ispidina picta") . . . . 2·00 2·00
1393 80c. Blue-breasted kingfisher (inscr "Ispidina picta") . . . . 1·75 2·25
1393a 80c. Blue-breasted kingfisher (inscr "Halcyon malimbicus") 2·00 2·50
1394 150c. Striped kingfisher (vert) . . . . 1·10 1·25
1395 200c. Shikra (vert) . . . . 1·25 1·40
1396 300c. Grey parrot (vert) . . 1·50 1·75
1397 500c. Black kite (vert) . . 2·50 3·25
MS1398 Two sheets. (a) 128 × 83 mm. 600c. Cinnamon-breasted rock bunting and barn swallow (horiz). (b) 83 × 128 mm. 600c. Senegal puff-back flycatcher Set of 2 sheets . . . . 14·00 14·00

452 Command Module "Columbia" orbiting Moon

1989. 20th Anniv of First Manned Landing on Moon. Multicoloured.
1399 20c. Type **452** 30 15
1400 80c. Neil Armstrong's footprint on Moon . . . 50 60
1401 200c. Edwin Aldrin on Moon . . . . 1·25 1·75
1402 300c. "Apollo 11" capsule on parachutes . . . . . 1·60 2·00
MS1403 Two sheets, each 100 × 72 mm. (a) 500c. Launch of "Apollo 11". (b) 500c. Earth seen from Moon Set of 2 sheets . . 5·50 7·00

453 Desertification of Pasture

1989. World Environment Day. Multicoloured.
1404 20c. Type **453** 50 15
1405 60c. Wildlife fleeing bush fire 90 80
1406 400c. Industrial pollution . . 2·75 3·50
1407 500c. Erosion . . . . 3·00 3·75

454 "Bebearia arcadius"

1990. Butterflies. Multicoloured.
1408 20c. Type **454** 35 20
1409 60c. "Charaxes laodice" . . 50 40
1410 80c. "Euryphura porphyrion" 60 45
1411 100c. "Neptis nicomedes" 70 50
1412 150c. "Citrinophila erastus" 90 90
1413 200c. "Aethiopana honorius 1·25 1·25
1414 300c. "Precis westermanni" 1·50 1·75
1415 500c. "Cymothoe hypatha" 2·00 2·50
MS1416 Two sheets, each 104 × 72 mm. (a) 600c. "Telipna acraea". (b) 600c. "Pentila abraxas" Set of 2 sheets . . . 9·00 10·00

455 Great Ribbed Cockle

1990. Seashells. Multicoloured.
1417 20c. Type **455** 60 25
1418 60c. Elephant's snout . . . 75 40
1419 80c. Garter cone 85 80
1420 200c. Tankerville's ancilla 2·25 2·50
1421 350c. Coronate prickly-winkle . . . . 3·00 4·00

456 Nehru welcoming President Nkrumah of Ghana

1990. Birth Centenary of Jawaharlal Nehru (Indian statesman). Multicoloured.
1422 20c. Type **456** 60 25
1423 60c. Nehru addressing Bandung Conference, 1955 . . . . 75 30
1424 80c. Nehru with garland and flowers (vert) 80 55
1425 200c. Nehru releasing pigeon (vert) . . . . 1·25 1·50
1426 350c. Nehru (vert) . . . . . 1·75 2·75

457 Wyon Medal, 1838

1990. 150th Anniv of the Penny Black.
1427 **457** 20c. black and violet . . 40 20
1428 – 60c. black and green . . 80 30
1429 – 80c. black and violet . . 1·00 35
1430 – 200c. black and green . . 1·50 1·25
1431 – 350c. black and green . . 2·00 2·50
1432 – 400c. black and red . . . 2·50 3·00
MS1433 Two sheets, each 112 × 83 mm. (a) 600c. brown and black; (b) 600c. brown, buff and black Set of 2 sheets . . . . 6·00 7·00
DESIGNS: 60, 600c. (**MS**1433b) Bath mail coach, 1840; 80c. Leeds mail coach, 1840; 200c. Proof of Queen's head engraved by Heath, 1840; 350c. Master die, 1840; 400c. London mail coach, 1840; 600c. (**MS**1433a) Printing the Penny Black.

458 Anniversary Emblem

1990. 10th Anniv (1989) of 4 June Revolution. Multicoloured.
1434 20c. Type **458** 15 15
1435 60c. Foodstuffs 20 20

1436 80c. Cocoa 25 30
1437 200c. Mining . . . . 1·50 1·75
1438 350c. Scales of Justice and sword . . . . 1·75 2·25

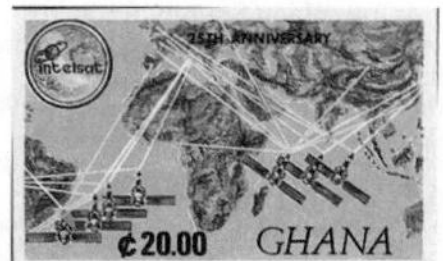

459 Map of Africa and Satellite Network

1990. 25th Anniv of Intelsat Satellite System. Multicoloured.
1439 20c. Type **459** 20 20
1440 60c. Map of Americas . . . 30 30
1441 80c. Map of Asia and Pacific 35 35
1442 200c. Map of South America and Africa . . . 90 1·00
1443 350c. Map of Indian Ocean and Pacific . . . . 1·50 2·00

460 Housewife using Telephone

1990. 2nd Anniv of Introduction of International Direct Dialling Service. Multicoloured.
1444 20c. Type **460** 25 20
1445 60c. Businessman using telephone 35 35
1446 80c. Man using phonecard telephone 40 40
1447 200c. Public telephones for internal and IDD services 90 1·00
1448 350c. Satellite station . . . 1·50 2·00

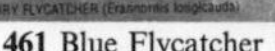

461 Blue Flycatcher

463 "Eulophia guineensis"

462 Jupiter

1990. African Tropical Rain Forest. Multicoloured.
1449 40c. Type **461** 90 90
1450 40c. Boomslang (snake) . . 90 90
1451 40c. Superb sunbird 90 90
1452 40c. Bateleur 90 90
1453 40c. Yellow-casqued hornbill 90 90
1454 40c. "Salamis temora" (butterfly) 90 90
1455 40c. Potto 90 90
1456 40c. Leopard 90 90
1457 40c. Bongo 90 90
1458 40c. Grey parrot 90 90
1459 40c. Okapi 90 90
1460 40c. Gorilla 90 90
1461 40c. Flap-necked chameleon 90 90
1462 40c. West African dwarf crocodile 90 90
1463 40c. Python 90 90
1464 40c. Giant ground pangolin 90 90
1465 40c. "Pseudacraea boisduvali" (butterfly) . . 90 90
1466 40c. North African crested porcupine 90 90
1467 40c. Rosy-columned aerangis (orchid) 90 90
1468 40c. "Cymothoe sangaris" (butterfly) 90 90
MS1469 100 × 75 mm. 600c. Head of leopard (vert) . . . . 4·50 5·00

Nos. 1449/68 were printed together, se-tenant, forming a composite design.

1990. Space Flight of "Voyager 2". Multicoloured.
1470 100c. Type **462** 85 85
1471 100c. Neptune and Triton 85 85
1472 100c. Ariel, moon of Uranus 85 85
1473 100c. Saturn from Mimas 85 85
1474 100c. Saturn 85 85
1475 100c. Rings of Saturn . . . 85 85
1476 100c. Neptune 85 85
1477 100c. Uranus from Miranda 85 85
1478 100c. Volcano on Io 85 85
MS1479 Two sheets. (a) 111 × 81 mm. 600c. "Voyager 2" spacecraft (vert). (b) 80 × 111 mm. 600c. Lift off of "Voyager 2" (vert) Set of 2 sheets . . . . 4·50 5·00

1990. Orchids. Multicoloured.
1480 20c. Type **463** 45 45
1481 40c. "Eurychone rothschildiana" 60 60
1482 60c. "Bulbophyllum barbigerum" 80 80
1483 80c. "Polystachya galeata" 1·10 1·10
1484 200c. "Diaphananthe kamerunensis" . . . . . 2·00 1·75
1485 300c. "Podangis dactyloceras" . . . . . . 2·25 2·00
1486 400c. "Ancistrochilus rothschildianus" . . . . 2·50 2·00
1487 500c. "Rangaeris muscicola" 2·75 2·00
MS1488 Two sheets, each 101 × 70mm. (a) 600c. "Bolusiella imbricata". (b) "Diaphananthe rotila" Set of 2 sheets . . . . 13·00 14·00

464 "Coprinus atramentarius"

1990. Fungi (2nd series). Multicoloured.
1489 20c. Type **464** 70 45
1490 50c. "Marasmius oreades" 90 65
1491 60c. "Oudemansiella radicata" . . . . 1·00 70
1492 80c. "Boletus edulis" (Cep) 1·25 90
1493 150c. "Hebeloma crustuliniforme" . . . . 2·00 1·50
1494 200c. "Coprinus micaceus" 2·25 2·00
1495 300c. "Macrolepiota procera" ("Lepiota procera") . . . . 2·50 2·50
1496 500c. "Amanita phalloides" 2·75 3·00
MS1497 Two sheets, each 104 × 82 mm. (a) Nos. 1489, 1491/2 and 1496. (b) Nos. 1490 and 1493/5 Set of 2 sheets . . 8·00 9·00

465 Italian and Swedish Players chasing Ball

1990. World Cup Football Championship, Italy. Multicoloured.
1498 20c. Type **465** 45 20
1499 50c. Egyptian player penetrating Irish defence 55 30
1500 60c. Cameroon players celebrating 60 30
1501 80c. Rumanian player beating challenge 70 40
1502 100c. Russian goalkeeper Dassayev 85 65
1503 150c. Roger Milla of Cameroon (vert) . . . . 1·40 1·10
1504 400c. South Korean player challenging opponent . . 2·25 2·75
1505 600c. Klinsman of West Germany celebrating . . . 2·75 3·75
MS1506 Two sheets, each 88 × 98 mm. (a) 800c. United Arab Emirates player watching ball. (b) 800c. Colombian player Set of 2 sheets . . . . 5·50 6·50

1990. 350th Death Anniv of Rubens. As T **195c** of Gambia, but vert. Multicoloured.
1507 20c. "Duke of Mantua" . . 55 20
1508 50c. "Jan Brant" 75 30
1509 60c. "Portraits of a Young Man" 75 30
1510 80c. "Michel Ophovius" . . 90 40
1511 100c. "Caspar Gevaerts" . . 1·25 65
1512 200c. "Head of Warrior" (detail) . . . . 1·75 1·75
1513 300c. "Study of a Bearded Man" . . . . 2·25 2·75
1514 400c. "Paracelsus" . . . . 2·50 3·75
MS1515 Two sheets, each 71 × 100 mm. (a) 600c. "Warrior with two Pages" (detail). (b) 600c. "Archduke Ferdinand" (detail) Set of 2 sheets . . . . 8·00 9·00

466 Manganese Ore

467 Dance Drums

1991. Minerals. Multicoloured.
1516 20c. Type **466** 55 30
1517 60c. Iron ore 70 60
1518 80c. Bauxite ore 90 75
1519 200c. Gold ore . . . . . . 2·00 2·00
1520 350c. Diamond . . . . . . 3·00 4·00
MS1521 70 × 90 mm. 600c. Uncut and cut diamonds . . . . . . 9·50 10·00

1991. Tribal Drums. Multicoloured.
1522 20c. Type **467** 50 20
1523 60c. Message drums . . . . 1·00 40
1524 80c. War drums . . . . . . 1·25 50
1525 200c. Dance drums (different) . . . . 2·25 2·50
1526 350c. Ceremonial drums . . 2·75 4·50
MS1527 70 × 90 mm. 600c. Drum with carrying strap . . . . . . 7·50 8·50

468 "Amorphophallus dracontioides"

469 Transport and Telecommunication Symbols

1991. Flowers (1st series). Multicoloured.
1528 20c. Type **468** 80 25
1529 60c. "Anchomanes difformis" . . . . 1·25 50
1530 80c. "Kaemferia nigerica" 1·50 70
1531 200c. "Aframomum sceptrum" . . . . 2·50 2·75
1532 350c. "Amorphophallus flavovirens" . . . . . . 2·75 3·75
MS1533 70 × 90 mm. 600c. "Amorphophallus flavovirens" (different) . . . . 5·50 6·00

1991. Flowers (2nd series). As T **468** but inscr "GHANA" in capitals. Multicoloured.
1534 20c. "Urginea indica" . . . 45 25
1535 60c. "Hymencallis littoralis" 85 50
1536 80c. "Crinum jagus" . . . . 1·50 70
1537 200c. "Dipcadi tacazzeanum" . . . . . 2·00 2·75
1538 350c. "Haemanthus rupestris" . . . . 2·50 3·75
MS1539 70 × 90mm. 600c. "Urginea indica" (different) . . . . . . 5·50 6·00

1991. 40th Anniv of United Nations Development Programme. Multicoloured.
1540 20c. Type **469** 55 20
1541 60c. Agricultural research 80 40
1542 80c. Literacy 90 55
1543 200c. Advances in agricultural crop growth 1·75 2·00
1544 350c. Industrial symbols . . 2·75 4·00

470 Drawing of Scout from First Handbook

471 Women sorting Fish

1991. 50th Death Anniv of Lord Baden-Powell.
1545 **470** 20c. black and buff . . . 90 20
1546 – 50c. grey, blue and black 1·10 40
1547 – 60c. multicoloured . . . 1·10 45
1548 – 80c. black and buff . . . 1·40 55
1549 – 100c. multicoloured . . . 2·00 75
1550 – 200c. multicoloured . . . 2·50 2·00
1551 – 500c. multicoloured . . . 3·50 4·00
1552 – 600c. multicoloured . . . 3·75 5·50
MS1553 Two sheets. (a) 104 × 75 mm. 800c. multicoloured. (b) 74 × 105 mm. 800c. multicoloured Set of 2 sheets 9·00 10·00

DESIGNS—VERT: 50c. Lord Baden-Powell; 80c. Handbook illustrations by Norman Rockwell; 500c. Scout at prayer. HORIZ: 60c. Hands holding Boy Scout emblem; 100c. Mafeking Siege 1d. Goodyear stamp and African runner; 200c. Scouts with Blitz victim, London, 1944; 600c. Mafeking Siege 1d. Goodyear stamp; 800c. (MS1553a) Scout camp; 800c. (MS1553b) Envelope from Mafeking Siege.

1991. Chorkor Smoker (fish smoking process). Multicoloured.
1554 20c. Type **471** 30 20
1555 60c. Cleaning the ovens . . 55 40
1556 80c. Washing fish 65 55
1557 200c. Laying fish on pallets 1·25 1·50
1558 350c. Stacking pallets over ovens . . . . 1·75 2·50

472 African Hind

1991. Fishes. Multicoloured.
1559 20c. Type **472** 25 25
1560 50c. Shrew squeaker 40 40
1561 80c. West African triggerfish 55 55
1562 100c. Stonehead 70 70
1563 200c. Lesser pipefish . . . . 1·50 1·50
1564 300c. Aba . . . . 1·60 1·60
1565 400c. Jewel cichlid . . . . . 1·75 1·75
1566 500c. Smooth hammerhead 1·90 1·90
MS1567 Two sheets, each 108 × 81 mm. (a) 800c. Bayad. (b) 800c. Eastern flying gurnard Set of 2 sheets . . . . 6·00 7·00

1991. Death Centenary (1990) of Vincent van Gogh (artist). As T **200b** of Gambia. Multicoloured.
1568 20c. "Reaper with Sickle" 35 25
1569 50c. "The Thresher" 55 40
1570 60c. "The Sheaf-Binder" . . 60 50
1571 80c. "The Sheep-Shearers" 70 65
1572 100c. "Peasant Woman cutting Straw" 85 80
1573 200c. "The Sower" . . . . 1·60 1·75
1574 500c. "The Plough and the Harrow" (horiz) . . . . 2·25 2·50
1575 600c. "The Woodcutter" . . 2·25 2·50
MS1576 Two sheets, each 117 × 80 mm. (a) 800c. "Evening: The Watch" (horiz). (b) 800c. "Evening: The End of the Day" (horiz). Imperf Set of 2 sheets 8·50 9·00

473 Gamal Nasser (Egypt) and Conference Hall

1991. 10th Non-Aligned Ministers' Conference, Accra. Statesmen. Multicoloured.
1577 20c. Type **473** 50 30
1578 60c. Josip Tito (Yugoslavia) 55 45
1579 80c. Pandit Nehru (India) 3·50 1·25
1580 200c. Kwame Nkrumah (Ghana) . . . . 1·75 2·25
1581 350c. Achmad Sukarno (Indonesia) . . . . 1·90 3·00

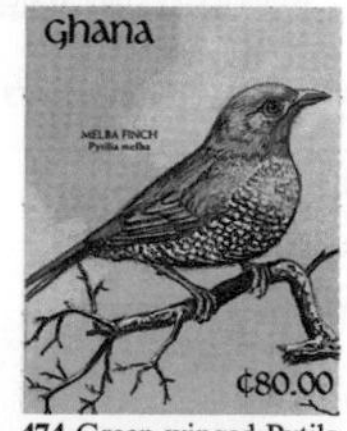

474 Green-winged Pytila

1991. Birds. As T **474**. Multicoloured.
1582/1629 80c. × 16, 100c. × 32 . . Set of 48 . . . . 22·00 25·00
MS1630 Three sheets, each 107 × 86 mm. (a) 800c. Marabou stork. (b) 800c. African fish eagle. (c) 800c. Saddle-bill stork Set of 3 sheets . . . . 11·00 12·00

Nos. 1582/1629 were issued together, se-tenant, as three sheetlets of 16 forming composite designs. The 80c. values show Green-winged pytilia, Orange-cheeked waxbill, African paradise flycatcher, Great blue turaco ("Blue plantain-eater"), Red bishop, Splendid glossy starling, Red-faced lovebird, African palm swift, Narina's trogon ("Narina Trogon"), Tawny eagle, Bateleur, Hoopoe, Secretary bird, African white-backed vulture, White-necked bald crow ("Bare-headed rockfowl"), Abyssinian ground hornbill, and the 100c. African open-bill stork, African spoonbill, Pink-backed pelican, Little bittern, Purple swamphen ("King reed-hen"), Saddle-bill stork, Glossy ibis, White-faced whistling duck, Black-headed heron, Hammerkop, African darter, Woolly-necked stork, Yellow-billed stork, Black-winged stilt, Goliath heron, African jacana ("Lily trotter"), Shikra, Abyssinian roller, Carmine bee eater, Pin-tailed whydah, Purple glossy starling, Yellow-mantled whydah, Pel's fishing owl, Crested touraco, Red-cheeked cordon-bleu, Olive-bellied sunbird, Red-billed hornbill, Red-billed quelea, South African crowned crane, Indian blue quail ("Blue Quail"), Egyptian vulture and Helmeted guineafowl.

475 "Nularda" (beetle)

476 Boti Falls

1991. Insects. Multicoloured.

- 1631 20c. Type **475** 70 20
- 1632 50c. "Zonocrus" (grasshopper) 85 30
- 1633 60c. "Gryllotalpa africana" (mole cricket) 95 30
- 1634 80c. Weevil 1·10 60
- 1635 100c. "Coenagrion" (dragonfly) 1·40 70
- 1636 150c. "Sahlbergella" (fly) 1·75 2·25
- 1637 200c. "Anthia" (ant) 2·00 2·50
- 1638 350c. "Megacephala" (beetle) 2·50 3·75
- **MS**1639 106×79 mm. 600c. "Lacetus" (lacewing) 9·50 10·00

1991. Multicoloured.

- 1639a 20c. Oil palm fruit 10 10
- 1640 50c. Type **476** 20 10
- 1641 60c. Larabanga Mosque (horiz) 20 10
- 1642 80c. Fort Sebastian, Shama (horiz) 20 10
- 1643 100c. Cape Coast Castle (horiz) 1·40 20
- 1644 200c. White-toothed cowrie (horiz) 2·00 45
- 1645 400c. True achatina (horiz) 3·00 90

1991. Christmas. Religious Paintings. As T **200c** of Gambia. Multicoloured.

- 1646 20c. "Adoration of the Magi" (Bosch) 55 20
- 1647 50c. "The Annunciation" (Campin) 75 30
- 1648 60c. "Virgin and Child" (detail) (Bouts) 80 30
- 1649 80c. "Presentation in the Temple" (Memling) 1·00 50
- 1650 100c. "Virgin and Child enthroned with Angel and Donor" (Memling) 1·25 65
- 1651 200c. "Virgin and Child with Saints and Donor" (Van Eyck) 2·00 2·00
- 1652 400c. "St. Luke painting the Virgin" (Van der Weyden) 3·00 3·75
- 1653 700c. "Virgin and Child" (Bouts) 4·25 6·00
- **MS**1654 Two sheets, each 103×128 mm. (a) 800c. "Virgin and Child standing in a Niche" (Van der Weyden). (b) 800c. "The Annunciation" (Memling) Set of 2 sheets 7·00 8·50

477 Women collecting Water from Bore Hole

1992. Decade of Revolutionary Progress. Multicoloured.

- 1655 20c. Type **477** 15 10
- 1656 50c. Miners 40 15
- 1657 60c. Wood carver 30 15
- 1658 80c. Forestry 30 20
- 1659 200c. Cacao tree 60 75
- 1660 350c. Village electrification 1·00 1·50

478 Mount Fuji and Flying Fish

1992. "Phila Nippon '91" International Stamp Exhibition, Tokyo. Multicoloured.

- 1661 20c. Type **478** 65 30
- 1662 60c. Itsukushima Jingu Shrine 80 40
- 1663 80c. Geisha 1·00 50
- 1664 100c. Samurai house 1·40 70
- 1665 200c. Bonsai tree 2·25 1·75
- 1666 400c. Olympic Sports Hall 2·75 3·00
- 1667 500c. Great Buddha (statue) 2·75 3·25
- 1668 600c. Nagoya Castle 3·00 3·50
- **MS**1669 Two sheets, each 109×80 mm. (a) 800c. Takamatsu Castle. (b) 800c. Heian Shrine Set of 2 sheets 12·00 13·00

479 East and West Germans celebrating

1992. Reunification of Germany. Multicoloured.

- 1670 20c. Type **479** 30 20
- 1671 60c. Signing Reunification Treaty 40 40
- 1672 80c. Chariot on Brandenburg Gate and fireworks 45 45
- 1673 1000c. Germans with unified currency 7·50 9·50
- **MS**1674 Three sheets. (a) 109×78 mm. 400c. Doves and Brandenburg Gate; 400c. Chancellor Kohl and Prime Minister De Maizire. (b) 125×87 mm. 800c. Chancellor Kohl and members of last German Democratic Republic administration. (c) 130×92 mm. 300c. President Gorbachev (vert); 300c. Chancellor Kohl (vert); 300c. Map of Western Germany (face value in black) (vert); 300c. Map of Eastern Germany (face value in white) (vert) Set of 3 sheets 13·00 13·00

480 Steam Side-tank Locomotive, 1903

1992. Ghanaian Railways. Multicoloured.

- 1675 20c. Type **480** 40 30
- 1676 50c. AIA-AIA diesel locomotive 60 40
- 1677 60c. First class coach, 1931 60 45
- 1678 80c. Railway inspection coach No. 2212 70 70
- 1679 100c. Steam locomotive No. 401 on Kumasi turntable 90 90
- 1680 200c. Cocoa wagon, 1921 1·40 1·50
- 1681 500c. Steam locomotive No. 223 "Prince of Wales" 2·25 2·75
- 1682 600c. Cattle wagon 2·25 2·75
- **MS**1683 Two sheets. (a) 106×76 mm. 800c. Beyer-Garratt steam locomotive No. 301, 1943. (b) 76×106 mm. 800c. German-built steam locomotive Set of 2 sheets 8·50 9·00

1992. Olympic Games, Albertville and Barcelona. Past Medal Winners. As T **203** of Gambia. Mutlcoloured.

- 1684 20c. E. Blay (Ghana) (boxing) and windmill 50 20
- 1685 60c. M. Ahey (Ghana) (athletics) and Catalan coat of arms 70 35
- 1686 80c. T. Wilson (U.S.A.) (70 m ski jump) and grapes 90 50
- 1687 100c. Four-man bobsleighing (East Germany) and passport 1·25 75
- 1688 200c. G. Louganis (U.S.A.) (platform diving) and decorative vase 2·00 1·50
- 1689 300c. L. Visser (Netherlands) (5000 m speed skating) and wine bottle cork 2·25 2·25
- 1690 350c. J. Passler (Italy) (biathlon) and lily 2·25 2·50
- 1691 400c. M. Retton (U.S.A.) (gymnastics) and silhouette of castle 2·50 2·75
- 1692 500c. J. Hingsen (West Germany) (decathlon) and gold and silver coins 2·50 2·75
- 1693 600c. R. Neubert (West Germany) (heptathlon) and leather work 2·50 2·75
- **MS**1694 Two sheets. (a) 112×82 mm. 800c. Silhouette of windmill. (b) 82×112 mm. 800c. Silhouette of folk dancer (vert) Set of 2 sheets 12·00 13·00

481 "Angides lugubris"

1992. Reptiles. Multicoloured.

- 1695 20c. Type **481** 20 20
- 1696 50c. "Kinixys erosa" (tortoise) 30 30
- 1697 60c. "Agama agama" (lizard) 30 30
- 1698 80c. "Chameleo gracilis" (chameleon) 40 40
- 1699 100c. "Naja melanleuca" (snake) 50 50
- 1700 200c. "Crocodylus niloticus" (crocodile) 90 1·10
- 1701 400c. "Chelonia mydas" (turtle) 1·75 2·25
- 1702 500c. "Varanus exanthematicus" (lizard) 1·90 2·50
- **MS**1703 94×66 mm. 600c. Tortoise and snake 2·75 3·50

1992. Easter. Religious Paintings. As T **204a** of Gambia but vert designs. Multicoloured.

- 1704 20c. "The Four Apostles" (detail) (Durer) 40 20
- 1705 50c. "The Last Judgement" (detail) (Rubens) 60 30
- 1706 60c. "The Four Apostles" (different detail) (Durer) 60 30
- 1707 80c. "The Last Judgement" (different detail) (Rubens) 75 40
- 1708 100c. "Crucifixion" (Rubens) 90 50
- 1709 200c. "The Last Judgement" (different detail) (Rubens) 1·75 1·50
- 1710 500c. "Christum Videre" (Rubens) 2·75 3·50
- 1711 600c. "The Last Judgement" (different detail) (Rubens) 3·00 4·00
- **MS**1712 Two sheets. (a) 69×100 mm. 800c. "Last Communion of St. Francis of Assisi" (detail) (Rubens) (vert). (b) 100×69 mm. 800c. "Scourging the Money Changers from the Temple" (detail) (El Greco) Set of 2 sheets 7·50 8·50

481a "Two Men at Table" (Velazquez)

1992. "Granada '92" International Stamp Exhibition, Spain. Spanish Paintings. Mult.

- 1713 20c. Type **481a** 40 20
- 1714 60c. "Christ in the House of Mary and Martha" (detail) (Velazquez) 55 30
- 1715 80c. "The Supper at Emmaus" (Velazquez) 65 40
- 1716 100c. "Three Musicians" (Velazquez) 75 50
- 1717 200c. "Old Woman cooking Eggs" (Velazquez) (vert) 1·50 1·25
- 1718 400c. "Old Woman cooking Eggs" (detail) (Velazquez) (vert) 2·50 2·75
- 1719 500c. "The Surrender of Breda" (detail) (Velazquez) (vert) 2·75 3·00
- 1720 700c. "The Surrender of Breda" (different detail) (Velazquez) (vert) 3·00 3·75
- **MS**1721 Two sheets. (a) 95×120 mm. 900c. "The Waterseller of Seville" (Velazquez) (86×111 mm). (b) 120×95 mm. 900c. "They still Say that Fish is Expensive" (Joaquín Sorolla y Bastida) (111×86 mm). Imperf Set of 2 sheets 9·00 9·50

482 "Danaus chrysippus"

483 Martin Pinzon and "Pinta"

1992. "Genova '92" International Thematic Stamp Exhibition. Butterflies. Mult.

- 1722 20c. Type **482** 50 30
- 1723 60c. "Papilio dardanus" 80 45
- 1724 80c. "Cynthia cardui" 90 60
- 1725 100c. "Meneris tulbaghia" 1·00 75
- 1726 200c. "Salamis temora" 1·50 1·60
- 1727 400c. "Charaxes jasius" 2·00 2·50
- 1728 500c. "Precis oenone" 2·25 2·50
- 1729 700c. "Precis sophia" 2·50 2·75
- **MS**1730 Two sheets, each 100×70 mm. (a) 900c. "Papilio demodocus". (b) 900c. "Precis octavia" Set of 2 sheets 7·50 8·50

1992. Prehistoric Animals. As T **207a** of Gambia. Multicoloured.

- 1731 20c. Iguanodon 35 25
- 1732 50c. Anchisaurus 50 35
- 1733 60c. Heterodontosaurus 55 35
- 1734 80c. Ouranosaurus 60 45
- 1735 100c. Anatosaurus 75 55
- 1736 200c. Elaphrosaurus 1·25 1·50
- 1737 500c. Coelophysis 2·25 2·75
- 1738 600c. Rhamphorynchus 2·50 3·00
- **MS**1739 Two sheets, each 100×70 mm. (a) 1500c. As 200c. (b) 1500c. As 500c. Set of 2 sheets 9·00 10·00

1992. World Columbian Stamp "Expo '92", Chicago. 500th Anniv of Discovery of America by Columbus. Multicoloured.

- 1740 200c. Type **483** 90 1·00
- 1741 200c. Vicente Pinzon and "Nina" 90 1·00
- 1742 200c. Columbus and Father Marchena at La Rabida 90 1·00
- 1743 200c. Columbus in his cabin 90 1·00
- 1744 200c. Fleet sights land 90 1·00
- 1745 200c. Columbus on Samana Cay 90 1·00
- 1746 200c. Wreck of "Santa Maria" 90 1·00
- 1747 200c. Amerindians at Spanish Court 90 1·00
- **MS**1748 122×86 mm. 500c. Columbus and "Santa Maria" 3·50 4·00

484 Olive-grey Ancilla

485 "Presentation in the Temple" (Master of the Braunschweiti)

1992. Shells. Multicoloured.

- 1749 20c. Type **484** 20 20
- 1750 20c. Radula cerith 20 20
- 1751 60c. Rugose donex 30 30
- 1752 60c. Horned murex 30 30
- 1753 80c. Concave ear moon 40 40
- 1754 80c. Triple twella 40 40
- 1755 200c. "Pila africana" 90 1·00
- 1756 200c. Rat cowrie 90 1·00
- 1757 350c. "Thais hiatula" 1·60 1·90
- 1758 350c. West African helmet 1·60 1·90
- **MS**1759 Two sheets, each 87×117 mm. (a) 600c. Fanel moon ("Natica fanel"). (b) 600c. Giant hairy melongena ("Pugilina moria") Set of 2 sheets 6·00 7·00

1992. Christmas. Religious Paintings. Mult.

- 1760 20c. Type **485** 40 20
- 1761 50c. "Presentation in the Temple" (detail) (Master of St. Severin) 60 30
- 1762 60c. "The Visitation" (Sebastiano del Piombo) 70 30
- 1763 80c. "The Visitation" (detail) (Giotto) 80 40
- 1764 100c. "The Circumcision" (detail) (Studio of Bellini) 95 50
- 1765 200c. "The Circumcision" (Studio of Garofalo) 1·75 1·60
- 1766 500c. "The Visitation" (Studio of Van der Weyden) 2·75 3·00
- 1767 800c. "The Visitation" (detail) (Studio of Van der Weyden) 3·25 4·25
- **MS**1768 Two sheets, each 77×102 mm. (a) 900c. "Presentation in the Temple" (Bartolo di Fredi). (b) 900c. "The Visitation" (larger detail) (Giotto) Set of 2 sheets 7·50 9·00

486 "Calappa rubroguttata"

1993. Crabs. Multicoloured.

- 1769 20c. Type **486** 40 20
- 1770 60c. "Cardisoma amatum" 70 25
- 1771 80c. "Maia squinado" 80 30
- 1772 400c. "Ocypoda cursor" 1·75 2·00
- 1773 800c. "Grapus grapus" 2·50 3·25
- **MS**1774 127×97 mm. Nos. 1769/73 6·00 6·00

487 "Clerodendrum thomsoniae"

1993. Flowers. Multicoloured.

1775 20c. Type **487** 20 15
1776 20c. "Lagerstroemia flos-reginae" 20 15
1777 60c. "Cassia fistula" 35 25
1778 60c. "Spathodea campanulata" 35 25
1779 80c. "Hildegardia barteri" 40 25
1780 80c. "Mellitea ferrugenea" 40 25
1781 200c. "Petrea volubilis" 60 85
1782 200c. "Ipomoea asarifolia" 60 85
1783 350c. "Bryphyllum pinnatum" 90 1·25
1784 350c. "Ritchiea reflexa" 90 1·25
MS1785 Two sheets, each 86 × 125 mm. (a) 50c. As No. 1777; 100c. As No. 1783; 150c. As No. 1782; 300c. As No. 1779. (b) 50c. As No. 1778; 100c. As No. 1776; 150c. As No. 1780; 300c. As No. 1784 Set of 2 sheets 4·50 5·00

488 Zeppelin LZ-3 entering Floating Hangar, Lake Constance

1993. Anniversaries and Events. Multicoloured.

1786 20c. Type **488** 85 30
1787 100c. Launch of European "Ariane 4" rocket (vert) 1·25 75
1788 200c. Leopard 2·00 1·75
1789 300c. Colosseum and fruit 2·25 2·50
1790 400c. Mozart (vert) 3·75 3·25
1791 600c. Launch of Japanese "H-1" rocket (vert) 3·75 4·25
1792 800c. Zeppelin LZ-10 "Schwaben" 3·75 4·50
MS1793 Four sheets. (a) 106 × 76 mm. 900c. Count Ferdinand von Zeppelin (vert). (b) 76 × 106 mm. 900c. Launch of American space shuttle (vert). (c) 106 × 76 mm. 900c. Bongo. (d) 99 × 69 mm. 900c. Cherubino from "The Marriage of Figaro" (vert) Set of 4 sheets 16·00 16·00

ANNIVERSARIES AND EVENTS: Nos. 1786, 1792, **MS**1793a, 75th death anniv of Count Ferdinand von Zeppelin; 1787, 1791, **MS**1793b, International Space Year; 1788, **MS**1793c, Earth Summit '92, Rio; 1789, International Conference on Nutrition, Rome; 1790, **MS**1793d, Death bicentenary of Mozart.

1993. Bicentenary of the Louvre, Paris. As T **209b** of Gambia. Multicoloured.

1794 200c. "Carnival Minuet" (left detail) (Giovanni Domenico Tiepolo) 85 1·00
1795 200c. "Carnival Minuet" (centre detail) (Giovanni Domenico Tiepolo) 85 1·00
1796 200c. "Carnival Minuet" (right detail) (Giovanni Domenico Tiepolo) 85 1·00
1797 200c. "The Tooth Puller" (left detail) (Giovanni Domenico Tiepolo) 85 1·00
1798 200c. "The Tooth Puller" (right detail) (Giovanni Domenico Tiepolo) 85 1·00
1799 200c. "Rebecca at the Well" (Giovanni Battista Tiepolo) 85 1·00
1800 200c. "Presenting Christ to the People" (left detail) (Giovanni Battista Tiepolo) 85 1·00
1801 200c. "Presenting Christ to the People" (right detail) (Giovanni Battista Tiepolo) 85 1·00
MS1802 100 × 70 mm. 700c. "Chancellor Seguier" (Charles le Brun) (85 × 52 mm) 2·75 3·25

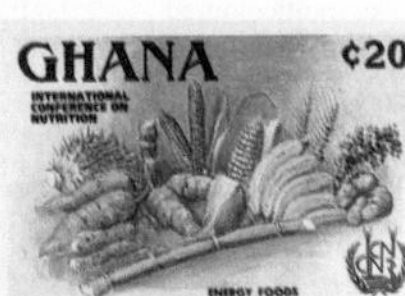

489 Energy Foods

1993. Int Conference on Nutrition, Rome. Mult.

1803 20c. Type **489** 30 15
1804 60c. Body-building foods 50 20
1805 80c. Protective foods 55 25
1806 200c. Disease prevention equipment 1·75 1·25
1807 400c. Quality control and preservation of fish products 2·25 3·00

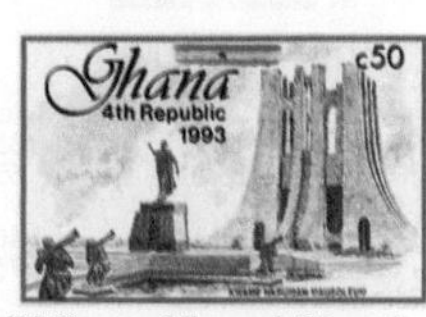

490 Kwame Nkrumah Mausoleum

1993. Proclamation of 4th Republic. Mult.

1808 50c. Type **490** 20 15
1809 100c. Kwame Nkrumah Conference Centre 35 25
1810 200c. Book of Constitution (vert) 80 80
1811 350c. Independence Square (vert) 1·60 2·00
1812 400c. Christiansborg Castle (vert) 1·75 2·00

491 Resurrection Egg

491b Airship "Graf Zeppelin" over Alps

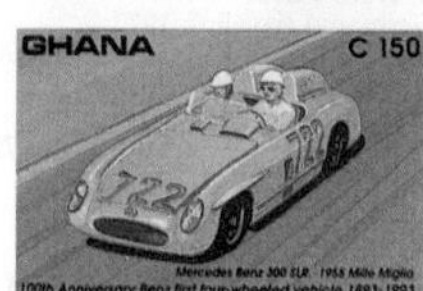

491a Mercedes Benz "300 SLR", Mille Migla, 1955

1993. Easter. Faberge Eggs. Multicoloured.

1813 50c. Type **491** 40 15
1814 80c. Imperial Red Cross egg with Resurrection triptych 65 25
1815 100c. Imperial Uspensky Cathedral egg 75 25
1816 150c. Imperial Red Cross egg with portraits 1·10 65
1817 200c. Orange Tree egg 1·25 1·25
1818 250c. Rabbit egg 1·25 1·50
1819 400c. Imperial Coronation egg 2·00 2·50
1820 900c. Silver-gilt enamel Easter egg 3·25 5·00
MS1821 Two sheet. (a) 73 × 100 mm. 1000c. Renaissance egg. (b) 100 × 73 mm. 1000c. Egg charms (horiz) Set of 2 sheets 8·00 9·00

1993. Centenaries of Henry Ford's First Petrol Engine (Nos. 1823/4) and Karl Benz's First Four-wheeled Car (others). Multicoloured.

1822 150c. Type **491a** 75 50
1823 400c. Ford "Depot Wagon", 1920 1·75 1·75
1824 600c. Ford "Mach 1 Mustang", 1970 2·25 2·75
1825 800c. Mercedes Benz racing car, Monaco Grand Prix, 1937 3·50 4·50
MS1826 Two sheets, each 110 × 80 mm. (a) 1000c. Mercedes Benz "Type 196" racing car, 1955 (85½ × 28½ mm). (b) 1000c. Ford "Super T", 1910 (85½ × 28½ mm) Set of 2 sheets 7·75 8·25

1993. Aviation Anniversaries. Multicoloured.

1827 50c. Type **491b** 50 30
1828 150c. Airship LZ-7 "Deutschland" (horiz) 85 55
1829 400c. Avro Vulcan jet bomber (horiz) 1·75 1·75
1830 400c. U.S. Mail Ford Trimotor (horiz) 1·75 1·75
1831 600c. Nieuport 27 biplane 2·25 2·25
1832 600c. Loading mail on "Graf Zeppelin" 2·25 2·25
1833 800c. Airship LZ-10 "Schwaben" (horiz) 3·50 4·00
MS1834 Three sheets, each 111 × 80 mm. (a) 1000c. LZ-127 "Graf Zeppelin". (b) 1000c. S.E.5A, 1918. (c) 1000c. Early airmail flight by Walter Edwards between Portland and Vancouver (57 × 42½ mm) Set of 3 sheets 14·00 14·00

ANNIVERSARIES: Nos. 1827/28, 1833, **MS**1834a, 125th birth anniv of Hugo Eckener (airship commander); 1829, 1831, **MS**1834b, 75th anniv of Royal Air Force; 1830, 1832, **MS**1834c, Bicentenary of first airmail flight.

492 African Buffalo

1993. Wild Animals. Multicoloured.

1835 20c. Type **492** 30 15
1836 50c. Giant forest hog 40 20
1837 60c. Potto 45 25
1838 80c. Bay duiker 60 30
1839 100c. Royal antelope 70 35
1840 200c. Serval 1·25 90
1841 500c. Golden cat 2·00 2·75
1842 800c. "Megaloglossus woermanni" (bat) 3·25 4·00
MS1843 Two sheets, each 68 × 98 mm. (a) 900c. Dormouse. (b) 900c. White-collared mangabey Set of 2 sheets 7·50 8·50

1993. 40th Anniv of Coronation. Nos. 1549/53 optd **40TH ANNIVERSARY OF CORONATION H.M. ELIZABETH II.**

1844 100c. multicoloured 1·25 30
1845 200c. multicoloured 2·00 1·00
1846 500c. multicoloured 4·00 4·00
1847 600c. multicoloured 4·00 4·50
MS1848 Two sheets. (a) 104 × 75 mm. 800c. multicoloured. (b) 74 × 105 mm. 800c. multicoloured Set of 2 sheets 12·00 12·00

1993. 35th Anniv of Rotary International and 60th Anniv of Ghana Red Cross Society (1992). Nos. 1562 and 1564/6 optd **35 YEARS OF ROTARY INTERNATIONAL GHANA 1958** (Nos. 1849, 1852, **MS**1853a) or **GHANA RED CROSS SOCIETY FOUNDED 1932** and cross (others).

1849 100c. Stonehead 1·25 30
1850 300c. Aba 3·00 3·00
1851 400c. Jewel cichlid 3·25 3·50
1852 500c. Smooth hammerhead 3·75 4·00
MS1853 Two sheets, each 108 × 81 mm. (a) 800c. Bayad. (b) 800c. Eastern flying gurnard Set of 2 sheets 9·50 10·00

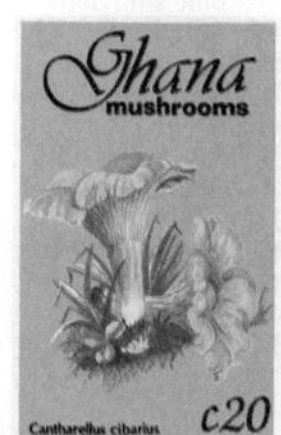

496 "Cantharellus cibarius"

1993. Mushrooms. Multicoloured.

1854 20c. Type **496** 40 25
1855 50c. "Russula cyanoxantha" 50 30
1856 60c. "Clitocybe rivulosa" 55 30
1857 80c. "Cortinarius elatior" 60 35
1858 80c. "Mycena galericulata" 60 35
1859 200c. "Tricholoma gambosum" 1·00 1·00
1860 200c. "Boletus edulis" 1·00 1·00
1861 200c. "Lepista saeva" 1·00 1·00
1862 250c. "Gyroporus castaneus" 1·10 1·10
1863 300c. "Boletus chrysenteron" 1·25 1·25
1864 350c. "Nolanea sericea" 1·40 1·40
1865 350c. "Hygrophorus punicea" ("Hygrophorus puiceus") 1·40 1·40
1866 500c. "Gomphidius glutinosus" 1·60 1·75
1867 600c. "Russula olivacea" 1·75 2·00
1868 1000c. "Russula aurata" 2·25 2·75
MS1869 Two sheets, each 85 × 130 mm. (a) 50c. As No. 1856; 100c. As No. 1858; 150c. As No. 1860; 1000c. As No. 1864. (b) 100c. As Type **496**; 150c. As No. 1857; 300c. As No. 1859; 600c. As No. 1865 Set of 2 sheets 9·50 11·00

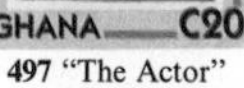

497 "The Actor" (Picasso)

498 Abedi Pele (Ghana)

1993. Anniversaries and Events. Multicoloured.

1870 20c. Type **497** 75 50
1871 20c. Early astronomical equipment 75 50
1872 80c. "Portrait of Allan Stein" (Picasso) 85 50
1873 200c. Modern telescope 1·50 1·50
1874 200c. "Tattoo" (Lesek Sobocki) 1·50 1·50
1875 600c. "Prison" (Sasza Blonder) 2·75 3·50
1876 800c. "Seated Male Nude" (Picasso) 3·50 4·00
MS1877 Four sheets. (a) 75 × 105 mm. 900c. "Guernica" (Picasso). (b) 75 × 105 mm. 1000c. "Bajika o Czlowieku Szczesliwym" (detail) (Antoni Mickalak) (horiz). (c) 105 × 75 mm. 1000c. Copernicus (face value at top left). (d) 105 × 75 mm. 1000c. Copernicus (face value at centre top) Set of 4 sheets 14·00 15·00

ANNIVERSARIES AND EVENTS: Nos. 1870, 1872, 1876, **MS**1877a, 20th death anniv of Picasso (artist); 1871, 1873, **MS**1877c/d, 450th death anniv of Copernicus (astronomer); 1874/5, **MS**1877b, "Polska '93" International Stamp Exhibition, Poznan.

1993. World Cup Football Championship, U.S.A. (1st issue). Multicoloured.

1878 50c. Type **498** 80 35
1879 80c. Pedro Troglio (Argentina) 90 40
1880 100c. Fernando Alvez (Uruguay) 1·00 40
1881 200c. Franco Baresi (Italy) 2·00 1·25
1882 250c. Gomez (Colombia) and Katanec (Yugoslavia) 2·00 1·75
1883 600c. Diego Maradona (Argentina) 3·50 3·50
1884 800c. Hasek (Czechoslovakia) and Wynalda (U.S.A.) 3·50 4·00
1885 1000c. Lothar Matthaeus (Germany) 4·25 4·75
MS1886 Two sheets, each 70 × 100 mm. (a) 1200c. Rabie Yassein (Egypt) and Ruud Gullit (Netherlands). (b) 1200c. Giuseppe Giannini (Italy) Set of 2 sheets 12·00 13·00

See also Nos. 2037/43.

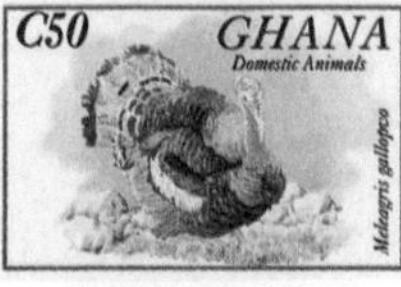

499 Common Turkey

1993. Domestic Animals. Multicoloured.

1887 50c. Type **499** 60 25
1888 100c. Goats 80 40
1889 150c. Muscovy ducks 1·25 75
1890 200c. Donkeys 1·50 1·00
1891 250c. Red junglefowl cock 1·50 1·25
1892 300c. Pigs 1·60 1·40
1893 400c. Helmeted guineafowl 1·90 1·75
1894 600c. Dog 2·75 3·00
1895 800c. Red junglefowl hen 3·25 3·75
1896 1000c. Sheep 3·75 4·25
MS1897 Two sheets, each 133 × 106 mm. (a) 100c. As No. 1888; 250c. No. 1894; 350c. No. 1892; 500c. No. 1896. (b) 100c. No. 1893; 250c. As No. 1891; 350c. No. 1895; 500c. Type **499** Set of 2 sheets 15·00 15·00

1993. Christmas. Religious Paintings. As T **221b** of Gambia. Black, yellow and red (Nos. 1898, 1900/1, 1905 and **MS**1906a) or multicoloured (others).

1898 50c. "Adoration of the Magi" (Durer) 60 20
1899 100c. "The Virgin and Child with St. John and an Angel" (Botticelli) 80 25
1900 150c. "Mary as Queen of Heaven" (Durer) 1·00 45
1901 200c. "Saint Anne" (Durer) 1·25 65
1902 250c. "The Madonna of the Magnificat" (Botticelli) 1·40 75
1903 400c. "The Madonna of the Goldfinch" (Botticelli) 2·25 2·50
1904 600c. "The Virgin and Child with the young St. John the Baptist" (Botticelli) 3·00 3·75
1905 1000c. "Adoration of the Shepherds" (Durer) 4·25 6·50
MS1906 Two sheets, each 102 × 128 mm. (a) 1000c. "Madonna in a Circle" (detail) (Dürer). (b) 1000c. "Mystic Nativity" (detail) (Botticelli) (horiz) Set of 2 sheets 9·00 11·00

500 Doll

501 Mickey Mouse in "Steamboat Willie", 1928

1994. Traditional Crafts. Multicoloured.

1907 50c. Type **500** 40 30
1908 50c. Pot with "head" lid 40 30
1909 200c. Bead necklace 1·00 1·00
1910 200c. Snake charmers (statuette) 1·00 1·00
1911 250c. Hoe 1·00 1·00
1912 250c. Scabbard 1·00 1·00
1913 600c. Pipe 2·25 2·75
1914 600c. Deer (carving) 2·25 2·75

1915 1000c. Mask . . . . 3·50 4·00
1916 1000c. Doll (different) . . . 3·50 4·00
MS1917 Two sheets, each 95×128 mm. (a) 100c. As Type **500**; 250c. As No. 1909; 350c. As No. 1911; 500c. As No. 1913. (b) 100c. As No. 1908; 250c. As No. 1910; 350c. As No. 1912; 500c. As No. 1914 Set of 2 sheets . . . . 5·50 7·00

1994. "Hong Kong '94" International Stamp Exhibition (1st issue). As T **222a** of Gambia. Multicoloured.
1918 200c. Hong Kong 1986 50c. "Expo '86" stamp and tram . . . . 1·00 1·25
1919 200c. Ghana 1992 20c. Railways stamp and tram 1·00 1·25
Nos. 1918/19 were printed together, se-tenant, forming a complete design. See also Nos. 1920/25.

1994. "Hong Kong '94" International Stamp Exhibition (2nd issue). Imperial Palace Clocks. As T **222b** of Gambia. Multicoloured.
1920 100c. Windmill clock . . . 1·10 1·10
1921 100c. Horse clock . . . . . 1·10 1·10
1922 100c. Balloon clock . . . . 1·10 1·10
1923 100c. Zodiac clock . . . . 1·10 1·10
1924 100c. Shar-pei dog clock . . 1·10 1·10
1925 100c. Cat clock . . . . . . 1·10 1·10

1994. 65th Anniv (1993) of Mickey Mouse (Walt Disney cartoon character) (1993). Scenes from various cartoon films.
1926 50c. Type **501** 60 15
1927 100c. "The Band Concert", 1935 . . . . 80 20
1928 150c. "Moose Hunters", 1937 . . . . 1·10 45
1929 200c. "Brave Little Tailor", 1938 . . . . 1·25 60
1930 250c. "Fantasia", 1940 . . . 1·40 80
1931 400c. "The Nifty Nineties", 1941 . . . . 2·25 2·75
1932 600c. "Canine Caddy", 1941 2·75 3·25
1933 1000c. "Mickey's Christmas Carol", 1983 . . . . . . 3·50 4·25
MS1934 Two sheets, each 127×102 mm. (a) 1200c. "Mickey's Elephant", 1936. (b) 1200c. "Mickey's Amateurs", 1937 Set of 2 sheets . . . . 7·50 9·00
No. 1929 is inscribed "TAYLOR" in error. The dates on Nos. 1927 and 1932 are incorrectly shown as "1937" and "1944".

501a Boy Hiker

1994. Easter. Hummel Figurines. Multicoloured.
1935 50c. Type **501a** 35 15
1936 100c. Girl with basket behind back 45 20
1937 150c. Boy with rabbits . . . 65 35
1938 200c. Boy holding basket . . 75 50
1939 250c. Girl with chicks . . . 80 70
1940 400c. Girl with lamb . . . . 1·75 2·00
1941 600c. Girl waving red handkerchief with lamb 2·00 2·25
1942 1000c. Girl with basket and posy . . . . 2·75 3·25
MS1943 Two sheets, each 93×126 mm. (a) 50c. As No. 1935; 150c. As No. 1942; 500c. As No. 1936; 1200c. As No. 1938. (b) 200c. As No. 1940; 300c. As No. 1939; 500c. As No. 1941; 1000c. As No. 1937 Set of 2 sheets 7·50 8·00

502 Diana Monkey with Young

1994. Wildlife. Multicoloured.
1944 50c. Type **502** 40 15
1945 100c. Bushbuck (horiz) . . . 40 20
1946 150c. Spotted hyena (horiz) 55 35
1947 200c. Diana monkey on branch facing left 75 50
1948 500c. Diana monkey on branch facing right . . . 1·25 1·50
1949 800c. Head of Diana monkey . . . . 1·75 2·00
1950 1000c. Aardvark (horiz) . . 2·00 2·50
MS1951 Two sheets, each 106×76 mm. (a) 2000c. Leopard. (b) 2000c. Waterbuck Set of 2 sheets . . . . 10·00 11·00

Designs of Nos. 1944 and 1947/9 include the W.W.F. Panda emblem.

503 Norwegian Forest Cat

1994. Cats. Multicoloured.
1952 200c. Type **503** 50 50
1953 200c. Blue longhair 50 50
1954 200c. Red self longhair . . . 50 50
1955 200c. Black longhair 50 50
1956 200c. Chinchilla 50 50
1957 200c. Dilute calico longhair 50 50
1958 200c. Blue tabby and white longhair 50 50
1959 200c. Ruby Somali 50 50
1960 200c. Blue smoke longhair 50 50
1961 200c. Calico longhair . . . 50 50
1962 200c. Brown tabby longhair 50 50
1963 200c. Balinese 50 50
1964 200c. Sorrel Abyssinian . . 50 50
1965 200c. Silver classic tabby . . 50 50
1966 200c. Chocolate-point Siamese 50 50
1967 200c. Brown tortie Burmese 50 50
1968 200c. Exotic shorthair . . . 50 50
1969 200c. Havana brown 50 50
1970 200c. Devon rex 50 50
1971 200c. Black Manx 50 50
1972 200c. British blue shorthair 50 50
1973 200c. Calico American wirehair 50 50
1974 200c. Spotted oriental Siamese 50 50
1975 200c. Red classic tabby . . 50 50
MS1976 Two sheets, each 102×89 mm. (a) 2000c. Brown mackerel tabby Scottish fold. (b) 2000c. Seal-point colourpoint Set of 2 sheets . . . . . . 8·50 9·00
No. 1957 is inscribed "Dilut" in error.

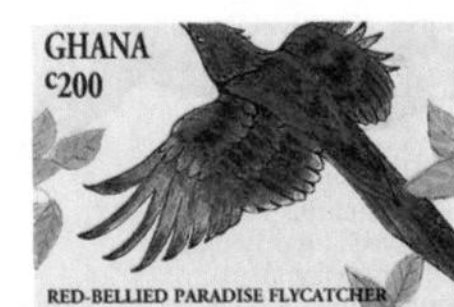

504 Red-bellied Paradise Flycatcher

1994. Birds. Multicoloured.
1977 200c. Type **504** 60 60
1978 200c. Many-coloured bush shrike 60 60
1979 200c. Broad-tailed paradise whydah 60 60
1980 200c. White-crowned robin chat 60 60
1981 200c. Violet turaco ("Violet plantain-eater") 60 60
1982 200c. Village weaver 60 60
1983 200c. Red-crowned bishop . 60 60
1984 200c. Common shoveler . . 60 60
1985 200c. Spur-winged goose . . 60 60
1986 200c. African crake 60 60
1987 200c. Purple swamphen ("King reed-hen") 60 60
1988 200c. White-crested tiger bittern 60 60
1989 200c. Oriole warbler ("Moho") 60 60
1990 200c. Superb sunbird . . . 60 60
1991 200c. Blue-breasted kingfisher 60 60
1992 200c. African blue cuckoo shrike 60 60
1993 200c. Great blue turaco ("Blue plantain-eater") . . 60 60
1994 200c. Greater flamingo . . . 60 60
1995 200c. African jacana ("Lily-trotter") 60 60
1996 200c. Black-crowned night heron 60 60
1997 200c. Black-winged stilt . . 60 60
1998 200c. White-spotted crake . . 60 60
1999 200c. African pygmy goose 60 60
2000 200c. African pitta 60 60
MS2001 Two sheets, each 113×83 mm. (a) 2000c. African spoonbill. (b) 2000c. Goliath heron Set of 2 sheets . . . . . 9·00 10·00

505 Women at Stand-pipe

1994. 1st Anniv of Fourth Republic. Multicoloured.
2002 50c. Type **505** 25 15
2003 100c. Presenting certificate to farmers 35 20
2004 200c. Village electricity supply 50 35
2005 600c. Bridge . . . . 1·25 1·75
2006 800c. National Theatre . . . 1·50 2·00
2007 1000c. Lighting perpetual flame . . . . 1·75 2·25

1994. 25th Anniv of First Manned Moon Landing. As T **326** of Antigua showing scientists. Mult.
2008 300c. Sigmund Jahn . . . . 1·00 1·00
2009 300c. Ulf Merbold . . . . . 1·00 1·00
2010 300c. Hans Wilhelm Schegal 1·00 1·00
2011 300c. Ulrich Walter . . . . 1·00 1·00
2012 300c. Reinhard Furrer . . . 1·00 1·00
2013 300c. Ernst Messerschmid 1·00 1·00
2014 300c. Mamoru Mohri . . . 1·00 1·00
2015 300c. Klaus-Dietrich Flade 1·00 1·00
2016 300c. Chaiki Naito-Mukai 1·00 1·00
MS2017 130×118 mm. 2000c. Poster for "Frau im Mond" (film) by Fritz Lang . . . . 5·50 6·00

1994. Centenary of International Olympic Committee. Gold Medal Winners. As T **227b** of Gambia, but vert. Multicoloured.
2018 300c. Dieter Modenburg (Germany) (high jump), 1984 . . . . 70 75
2019 400c. Ruth Fuchs (Germany) (javelin), 1972 and 1976 . . . . 90 1·00
MS2020 77×106 mm. 1500c. Jans Weissflog (Germany) (ski jump), 1994 . . . . 3·75 4·00

1994. 50th Anniv of D-Day. As T **331** of Antigua. Multicoloured.
2021 60c. H.M.S. "Roberts" (monitor) . . . . 1·50 60
2022 100c. H.M.S. "Warspite" (battleship) . . . . 1·75 1·10
2023 200c. U.S.S. "Augusta" (cruiser) . . . . 2·25 2·50
MS2024 107×76 mm. 1500c. U.S.S. "Nevada" (battleship) firing salvo 6·00 6·00

1994. "Philakorea '94" International Stamp Exn, Seoul. As T **227d** of Gambia. Mult.
2025 20c. Ch'unghak-dong village elder in traditional costume, ($24\frac{1}{2}\times38$ mm) 15 15
2026 150c. Stone Pagoda, Punhwangsa ($24\frac{1}{2}\times38$ mm) 40 40
2027 250c. Character with eggs 45 50
2028 250c. Character with pair of birds on house 45 50
2029 250c. Character with cock 45 50
2030 250c. Character with dragon and pagoda 45 50
2031 250c. Character with orange flowers 45 50
2032 250c. Character with parrot and pagoda 45 50
2033 250c. Character with plant 45 50
2034 250c. Character with fish . . 45 50
2035 300c. Traditional country house, Andong ($24\frac{1}{2}\times34$ mm) 50 55
MS2036 100×70 mm. 1500c. Temple judges deliberating ($42\frac{1}{2}\times28\frac{1}{2}$ mm) . . . . 4·00 4·50

506 Dennis Bergkamp (Netherlands)

1994. World Cup Football Championship, U.S.A. (2nd issue). Multicoloured.
2037 200c. Type **506** 75 80
2038 200c. Lothar Matthaus (Germany) 75 80
2039 200c. Giuseppe Signori (Italy) 75 80
2040 200c. Carlos Valderama (Colombia) 75 80
2041 200c. Jorge Campos (Mexico) 75 80
2042 200c. Tony Meola (U.S.A.) 75 80
MS2043 Two sheets, each 100×70 mm. (a) 1200c. Giants' Stadium, New Jersey (vert). (b) 1200c. Citrus Bowl, Orlando (vert) Set of 2 sheets . . . . 6·50 7·50

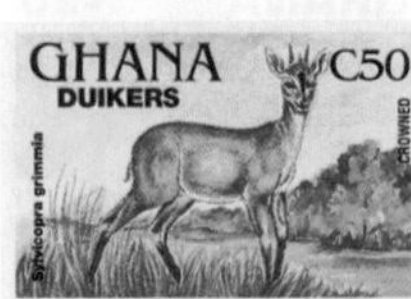

507 Common ("Crowned") Duiker

1994. Duikers (antelopes). Multicoloured.
2044 50c. Type **507** 30 15
2045 100c. Red-flanked duiker . . 40 25
2046 200c. Yellow-backed duiker 60 40
2047 400c. Ogilby's duiker . . . 1·00 1·25
2048 600c. Bay duiker . . . . . 1·25 1·75
2049 800c. Jentink's duiker . . . 1·50 2·00
MS2050 Two sheets, each 106×76 mm. (a) 2000c. Red forest duiker. (b) 2000c. Black duiker Set of 2 sheets . . . . 8·00 9·00

1994. Christmas. Religious Paintings. As T **231a** of Gambia. Multicoloured.
2051 100c. "Madonna of the Annunciation" (Simone Martini) 60 15
2052 200c. "Madonna and Child" (Niccolo di Pietro Gerini) 90 20
2053 250c. "Virgin and Child on the Throne with Angels and Saints" (Raffaello Botticini) . . . . 1·10 60
2054 300c. "Madonna and Child with Saints" (Antonio Fiorentino) . . . . 1·40 1·10
2055 400c. "Adoration of the Magi" (Bartolo di Fredi) 1·50 1·50
2056 500c. "The Annunciation" (Cima da Congeliano) . . 1·75 2·00
2057 600c. "Virgin and Child with the Young St. John the Baptist" (workshop of Botticelli) . . . . 2·25 2·75
2058 1000c. "The Holy Family" (Giorgione) . . . . . . 2·75 3·75
MS2059 Two sheets, each 135×95 mm. (a) 2000c. "Adoration of the Kings" (detail showing Holy Family) (Giorgione). (b) 2000c. "Adoration of the Kings" (detail showing King and attendants) (Giorgione) Set of 2 sheets . . 8·50 9·00

508 Northern Region Dancer

510 Fertility Doll

509 Red Cross Stretcher-bearers

1994. Panafest '94 (2nd Pan-African Historical Theatre Festival). Multicoloured.
2060 50c. Type **508** 20 15
2061 100c. Traditional artefacts 35 25
2062 200c. Chief with courtiers 65 60
2063 400c. Woman in ceremonial costume . . . . 1·25 1·25
2064 600c. Cape Coast Castle . . 1·75 2·50
2065 800c. Clay figurines . . . . 2·25 3·25

1994. 75th Anniv of Red Cross. Multicoloured.
2066 50c. Type **509** 70 15
2067 200c. Worker with children 1·50 50
2068 600c. Workers erecting tents 2·50 3·50
MS2069 147×99 mm. Nos. 2066/7 and 1000c. As 600c. . . . . . 4·50 5·50

1994. Fertility Dolls.
2070 **510** 50c. multicoloured . . . 40 10
2071 – 100c. multicoloured . . . 60 15
2072 – 150c. multicoloured . . . 80 30
2073 – 200c. multicoloured . . . 90 30
2074 – 400c. multicoloured . . . 1·50 1·50
2075 – 600c. multicoloured . . . 1·75 2·00
2076 – 800c. multicoloured . . . 2·00 2·50
2077 – 1000c. multicoloured . . 2·25 2·75
MS2078 147×99 mm. Nos. 2071, 2074/5 and 250c. As 1000c. . . 4·50 5·00
DESIGNS: 100c. to 1000c. Different dolls.

511 Ghanaian Family

1994. International Year of the Family. Mult.
2079 50c. Type **511** 35 15
2080 100c. Teaching carpentry . . 55 15
2081 200c. Child care 90 25
2082 400c. Care for the elderly 1·40 1·40
2083 600c. Learning pottery . . . 1·75 2·00
2084 1000c. Adult education students . . . . 2·25 2·75

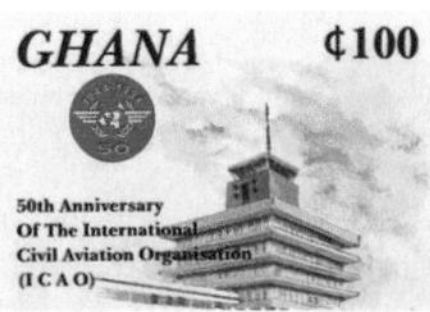

512 Control Tower and Emblem

1995. 50th Anniv of I.C.A.O. Mult. (a) Inscr "50th Anniversary Of Ghana Civil Aviation Authority".

No.	Description		
2085	100c. Type **512**	1·50	
2086	400c. Communications equipment	2·75	
2087	1000c. Airliner taking off	4·00	

(b) Inscr "50th Anniversary Of The International Civil Aviation Organisation (I.C.A.O.)."

No.	Description		
2088	100c. Type **512**	40	20
2089	400c. Communications equipment	90	90
2090	1000c. Airliner taking off	2·00	2·50

513 Pluto, Donald Duck and Chip n' Dale around Table

1995. 60th Anniv of Donald Duck. Walt Disney Cartoon Characters at Birthday Party. Mult.

No.	Description		
2091	40c. Type **513**	25	15
2092	50c. Mickey Mouse and pup with banner	25	15
2093	60c. Daisy Duck with balloons	25	20
2094	100c. Goofy making cake	35	25
2095	150c. Goofy on roller blades delivering cake	45	40
2096	250c. Donald pinning donkey tail on Goofy	60	60
2097	400c. Ludwig von Drake singing to Pluto	90	90
2098	500c. Grandma Duck giving cake to puppies	1·00	1·00
2099	1000c. Mickey and Minnie Mouse at piano	1·75	2·00
2100	1500c. Pluto with bone and ball	2·50	3·25
MS2101	Two sheets. (a) 117×95 mm. 2000c. Donald blowing out birthday candles (vert). (b) 95×117 mm. 2000c. Donald wearing party hat (vert) Set of 2 sheets	9·00	9·00

514 Fort Appolonia, Beyin

1995. Forts and Castles of Ghana. Multicoloured.

No.	Description		
2102	50c. Type **514**	30	10
2103	200c. Fort Patience, Apam	60	25
2104	250c. Fort Amsterdam, Kormantin	65	45
2105	300c. Fort St. Jago, Elmina	75	70
2106	400c. Fort William, Anomabo	90	90
2107	600c. Kumasi Fort	1·50	2·00
MS2108	Two sheets, each 102×72 mm. (a) 800c. Elmina Castle (vert). (b) 1000c. Fort St. Antonio, Axim Set of 2 sheets	4·00	4·50

515 Cochem Castle, Germany

1995. Castles of the World. Multicoloured.

No.	Description		
2109	150c. Type **515**	40	30
2110	500c. Windsor Castle, England	70	70
2111	500c. Osaka Castle, Japan	70	70
2112	500c. Vaj Dahunyad Castle, Hungary	70	70
2113	500c. Karlstejn Castle, Czech Republic	70	70
2114	500c. Kronborg Castle, Denmark	70	70
2115	500c. Alcazar of Segovia, Spain	70	70
2116	500c. Chambourd Castle, France	70	70
2117	500c. Linderhof Castle, Germany	70	70
2118	500c. Red Fort, Delhi, India	70	70
2119	600c. Hohenzollern Castle, Germany	80	80
2120	800c. Uwajima Castle, Japan	1·00	1·00
2121	1000c. Hohenschwangau Castle, Germany	1·10	1·10
MS2122	Two sheets, each 102×72 mm. (a) 2500c. Neuschwanstein Castle, Germany. (b) 2500c. Himeji Castle, Japan Set of 2 sheets	9·00	9·00

516 European Pochard ("Eurasian Pochard")

1995. Ducks. Multicoloured.

No.	Description		
2123	200c. Type **516**	80	35
2124	400c. African pygmy goose	90	90
2125	400c. Southern pochard	90	90
2126	400c. Cape teal	90	90
2127	400c. Ruddy shelduck	90	90
2128	400c. Fulvous whistling duck	90	90
2129	400c. White-faced whistling duck	90	90
2130	400c. Ferruginous duck ("Ferruginous White-eye")	90	90
2131	400c. Hottentot teal	90	90
2132	400c. African black duck	90	90
2133	400c. African yellow-bill ("Yellow-billed Duck")	90	90
2134	400c. Bahama pintail ("White-checked Pintail Duck")	90	90
2135	400c. Hartlaub's duck	90	90
2136	500c. Maccoa duck	1·10	1·10
2137	800c. Cape shoveler	1·50	1·75
2138	1000c. Red-crested pochard	1·90	2·25
MS2139	Two sheets, each 104×74 mm. (a) 2500c. Roseate tern. (b) 2500c. Northern shoveler Set of 2 sheets	8·50	9·00

Nos. 2124/35 were printed together, se-tenant, forming a composite design.

No. 2128 is inscribed "Wistling" in error.

517 Cycling

518 "Cymothoe beckeri" (butterfly)

1995. Olympic Games, Atlanta (1996) (1st issue). Multicoloured.

No.	Description		
2140	300c. Type **517**	1·10	1·00
2141	300c. Archery	1·10	1·00
2142	300c. Diving	1·10	1·00
2143	300c. Swimming	1·10	1·00
2144	300c. Women's gymnastics	1·10	1·00
2145	300c. Fencing	1·10	1·00
2146	300c. Boxing	1·10	1·00
2147	300c. Men's gymnastics	1·10	1·00
2148	300c. Javelin	1·10	1·00
2149	300c. Tennis	1·10	1·00
2150	300c. Football	1·10	1·00
2151	300c. Equestrian	1·10	1·00
2152	500c. Carl Lewis (U.S.A.)	1·10	1·10
2153	800c. Eric Liddell (Great Britain)	1·40	1·60
2154	900c. Jesse Owens (U.S.A.)	1·40	1·60
2155	1000c. Jim Thorpe (U.S.A.)	1·40	1·60
MS2156	Two sheets, each 70×100 mm. (a) 1200c. Pierre de Coubertin (founder of International Olympic Committee). (b) 1200c. John Akii Bua (Uganda) Set of 2 sheets	3·50	4·00

Nos. 2140/51 were printed together, se-tenant, forming a composite design.

See also Nos. 2334/55.

1995. Multicoloured.

No.	Description		
2156c	300c. European goldfinch (vert)	30	20
2157	400c. Type **518**	40	20
2158	500c. "Graphium policenes" (butterfly)	50	20
2159	1000c. African long-tailed hawk (vert)	1·00	60
2159a	1100c. Kente cloth	1·00	70
2160	2000c. Swordfish	2·00	1·50
2161	3000c. Guinean fingerfish	2·75	2·75
2162	5000c. Purple heron (vert)	4·00	4·00

519 Ghanaian Scouts

520 Trygve Lie (1946–52) and United Nations Building

1995. 18th World Scout Jamboree, Netherlands.

No.	Description		
2163	**519** 400c. multicoloured	90	1·00
2164	– 800c. multicoloured	1·25	1·40
2165	– 1000c. multicoloured	1·25	1·40
MS2166	70×100 mm. 1200c. multicoloured	1·90	2·25

DESIGNS: 800c. to 1200c. Ghanaian scouts (different).

1995. 50th Anniv of End of Second World War in Europe. As T **237a** of Gambia. Multicoloured.

No.	Description		
2167	400c. Winston Churchill	75	75
2168	400c. Gen. Dwight D. Eisenhower	75	75
2169	400c. Air Marshal Sir Arthur Tedder	75	75
2170	400c. Field-Marshal Sir Bernard Montgomery	75	75
2171	400c. Gen. Omar Bradley	75	75
2172	400c. Gen. Charles de Gaulle	75	75
2173	400c. French resistance fighters	75	75
2174	400c. Gen. George S. Patton	75	75
MS2175	104×74 mm. 1200c. "GIVE ME FIVE YEARS & YOU WILL NOT RECOGNISE GERMANY AGAIN" quote by Adolf Hitler in English and German (42×57 mm)	2·40	2·75

1995. 50th Anniv of United Nations. Secretary-Generals. Multicoloured.

No.	Description		
2176	200c. Type **520**	30	40
2177	300c. Dag Hammarskjold (1953–61)	40	50
2178	400c. U. Thant (1961–71)	50	60
2179	500c. Kurt Waldheim (1972–81)	60	70
2180	600c. Javier Perez de Cuellar (1982–91)	70	90
2181	800c. Boutrous Boutrous-Ghali (1992)	80	1·00
MS2182	104×74 mm. 1200c. U.N. flag (horiz)	1·90	2·50

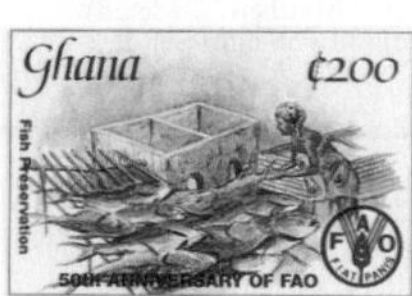

521 Preserving Fish

1995. 50th Anniv of F.A.O. Multicoloured.

No.	Description		
2183	200c. Type **521**	70	15
2184	300c. Fishermen with fish traps	85	40
2185	400c. Ox-drawn plough	95	80
2186	600c. Harvesting bananas	1·25	1·40
2187	800c. Planting saplings	1·50	2·00
MS2188	100×70 mm. 2000c. Canoe and cattle	3·00	3·50

522 National Flag and Rotary Emblem

1995. 90th Anniv of Rotary International. Multicoloured.

No.	Description		
2189	600c. Type **522**	1·00	1·25
MS2190	94×65 mm. 1200c. Ghanaian Rotary banner (vert)	1·90	2·25

1995. 95th Birthday of Queen Elizabeth the Queen Mother. As T **239a** of Gambia. Multicoloured.

No.	Description		
2191	600c. brown, light brown and black	2·25	2·25
2192	600c. multicoloured	2·25	2·25
2193	600c. multicoloured	2·25	2·25
2194	600c. multicoloured	2·25	2·25
MS2195	102×127 mm. 2500c. multicoloured	4·75	4·25

DESIGNS: No. 2191, Queen Elizabeth the Queen Mother (pastel drawing); 2192, Wearing light blue hat and floral dress; 2193, At desk (oil painting); 2194, Wearing red hat and dress; **MS**2195, Wearing pale blue hat and jacket.

1995. 50th Anniv of End of Second World War in the Pacific. Medals. As T **229b** of Gambia. Mult.

No.	Description		
2196	500c. Navy Cross and Purple Heart, U.S.A.	85	85
2197	500c. Air Force Cross and Distinguished Flying Cross, Great Britain	85	85
2198	500c. Navy and Marine Corps Medal and Distinguished Service Cross, U.S.A.	85	85
2199	500c. Distinguished Service Medal and Distinguished Conduct Medal, Great Britain	85	85
2200	500c. Military Medal and Military Cross, Great Britain	85	85
2201	500c. Distinguished Service Cross and Distinguished Service Order, Great Britain	85	85
MS2202	108×76 mm. 1200c. Congressional Medal of Honor, U.S.A.	2·50	2·50

523 Seismosaurus

524 Arms of Otumfuo Opoku Ware II

1995. "Singapore '95" International Stamp Exhibition. Prehistoric Animals. Multicoloured.

No.	Description		
2203	400c. Type **523**	65	65
2204	400c. Supersaurus	65	65
2205	400c. Ultrasaurus	65	65
2206	400c. Saurolophus	65	65
2207	400c. Lambeosaurus	65	65
2208	400c. Parasaurolophus	65	65
2209	400c. Triceratops	65	65
2210	400c. Styracosaurus	65	65
2211	400c. Pachyrhinosaurus	65	65
2212	400c. Peteinosaurus	65	65
2213	400c. Quetzalcoatlus	65	65
2214	400c. Eudimorphodon	65	65
2215	400c. Allosaurus	65	65
2216	400c. Daspletosaurus	65	65
2217	400c. Tarbosaurus bataar	65	65
2218	400c. Velociraptor mongoliensis	65	65
2219	400c. Herrerasaurus	65	65
2220	400c. Coelophysis	65	65
MS2221	Two sheets, each 106×76 mm. (a) 2500c. Tyrannosaurus rex (horiz). (b) 2500c. Albertosaurus (horiz) Set of 2 sheets	8·00	8·50

Nos. 2203/11 and 2212/20 respectively were printed together, se-tenant, forming composite designs.

1995. Silver Jubilee of Otumfuo Opoku Ware II (King of Ashanti). Multicoloured.

No.	Description		
2222	50c. Type **524**	30	10
2223	100c. Silver casket	45	10
2224	200c. Golden stool	70	20
2225	400c. Busummuru sword bearer	1·10	75
2226	600c. Otumfuo Opoku Ware II	1·75	1·75
2227	800c. Otumfuo Opoku Ware II under umbrella	2·00	2·25
2228	1000c. Mponponsuo sword bearer	2·25	2·75

525 Nelson Mandela (1993 Peace)

1995. Centenary of Nobel Prize Trust Fund. Past Prize Winners. Multicoloured.

No.	Description		
2229	400c. Type **525**	80	80
2230	400c. Albert Schweitzer (1952 Peace)	80	80
2231	400c. Wole Soyinka (1986 Literature)	80	80
2232	400c. Emil Fischer (1902 Chemistry)	80	80
2233	400c. Rudolf Mossbauer (1961 Physics)	80	80
2234	400c. Archbishop Desmond Tutu (1984 Peace)	80	80
2235	400c. Max Born (1954 Physics)	80	80
2236	400c. Max Planck (1918 Physics)	80	80
2237	400c. Hermann Hesse (1946 Literature)	80	80
MS2238	104×75 mm. 1200c. Paul Ehrlich (1908 Medicine) and medal	1·75	2·00

1995. Christmas. Religious Paintings. As T **245a** of Gambia. Multicoloured.

No.	Description		
2239	50c. "The Child Jesus and the Young St. John" (Murillo)	25	10
2240	80c. "Rest on the Flight into Egypt" (Memling)	30	10

2241 300c. "Holy Family" (Van Dyck) 70 45
2242 600c. "Enthroned Madonna and Child" (Uccello) . . 1·10 1·40
2243 800c. "Madonna and Child" (Van Eyck) . . . . 1·25 1·75
2244 1000c. "Head of Christ" (Rembrandt) . . . . . . 1·40 2·00
MS2245 Two sheets, each 101 × 127 mm. (a) 2500c. "The Holy Family" (Pulzone). (b) 2500c. "Madonna and Child with Two Saints" (Montagna) Set of 2 sheets . . . . 7·75 8·00

526 Ernemann Camera (1903)

1995. Centenary of Cinema. Multicoloured.
2246 400c. Type **526** . . . . . . 1·25 1·00
2247 400c. Charlie Chaplin . . . 1·25 1·00
2248 400c. Rudolph Valentino . . 1·25 1·00
2249 400c. Will Rogers . . . . . 1·25 1·00
2250 400c. Greta Garbo . . . . 1·25 1·00
2251 400c. Jackie Cooper . . . . 1·25 1·00
2252 400c. Bette Davis . . . . . 1·25 1·00
2253 400c. John Barrymore . . . 1·25 1·00
2254 400c. Shirley Temple . . . . 1·25 1·00
MS2255 106 × 76 mm. 2500c. Laurel and Hardy . . . . 5·50 5·50
No. 2246 is inscribed "ERNMANN" in error.

527 John Lennon

1995. John Lennon (musician) Commemoration. Multicoloured.
2256 400c. Type **527** . . . . . . 1·10 1·10
2257 400c. Full face portrait (green background) . . . 1·10 1·10
2258 400c. With guitar . . . . . 1·10 1·10
2259 400c. Wearing glasses and caftan . . . . 1·10 1·10
2260 400c. Full face portrait (red background) . . . . . . 1·10 1·10
2261 400c. Wearing headphones 1·10 1·10
2262 400c. Wearing purple T-shirt 1·10 1·10
2263 400c. Full face portrait (blue background) . . . . . . 1·10 1·10
2264 400c. Facing right . . . . . 1·10 1·10
2265 400c. As No. 2263, but smaller (24 × 39 mm) . . 1·10 1·10
MS2266 102 × 73 mm. 2000c. John Lennon playing guitar . . . . 6·00 6·50

528 Louis Pasteur in Laboratory

529 Rat Musicians

1995. Death Centenary of Louis Pasteur (scientist). Multicoloured.
2267 600c. Type **528** . . . . . . 1·60 1·60
2268 600c. Pasteur injecting rabid dog . . . . 1·60 1·60
2269 600c. Pasteur and microscope slide . . . . 1·60 1·60
2270 600c. Laboratory equipment and birds . . . . 1·60 1·60
2271 600c. Yeast vats . . . . . 1·60 1·60

1996. Chinese New Year ("Year of the Rat").
2272 **529** 250c. brown, violet and red 60 60
2273 – 250c. brown, violet and red 60 60
2274 – 250c. brown, violet and red 60 60
2275 – 250c. brown, violet and red 60 60
MS2276 142 × 60 mm. As Nos. 2272/5, but face values and "GHANA" in red instead of white 2·00 2·00
MS2277 106 × 75 mm. 1000c. red and orange . . . . 2·00 2·00
DESIGNS:—VERT: No. 2273, Rats carrying banners; 2274, Rats carrying palanquin; 2275, Rats with offerings. HORIZ: No. **MS**2277, Four rats carrying palanquin.

1996. 125th Anniv of Metropolitan Museum of Art, New York. As T **251** of Gambia. Multicoloured.
2278 400c. "Portrait of a Man" (Van der Goes) 80 80
2279 400c. "Paradise" (detail) (Di Paolo) 80 80
2280 400c. "Portrait of a Young Man" (Messina) 80 80
2281 400c. "Tommaso Portinari" (detail) (Memling) 80 80
2282 400c. "Maria Portinari" (detail) (Memling) 80 80
2283 400c. "Portrait of a Lady" (detail) (Ghirlandaio) . . 80 80
2284 400c. "St. Christopher and the Infant Christ" (Ghirlandaio) 80 80
2285 400c. "Francesco D'Este" (detail) (Weyden) 80 80
2286 400c. "The Interrupted Sleep" (Boucher) 80 80
2287 400c. "Diana and Cupid" (detail) (Batoni) 80 80
2288 400c. "Boy blowing Bubbles" (Chardin) 80 80
2289 400c. "Ancient Rome" (detail) (Pannini) 80 80
2290 400c. "Modern Rome" (detail) (Pannini) 80 80
2291 400c. "The Calmady Children" (Lawrence) . . 80 80
2292 400c. "The Triumph of Marius" (detail) (Tiepolo) 80 80
2293 400c. "Garden at Vaucression" (detail) (Vuillard) 80 80
MS2294 Two sheets, each 95 × 70 mm. (a) 2500c. "The Epiphany" (detail) (Giotto) (80 × 56 mm). (b) 2500c. "The Calling of Matthew" (detail) (Hemessen) (80 × 56 mm) Set of 2 sheets . . . . 11·00 12·00

530 Toco Toucan

1996. Wildlife of the Rainforest. Multicoloured.
2295 400c. Type **530** 90 80
2296 400c. Two-toed sloth . . . 90 80
2297 400c. Orang-utan 90 80
2298 400c. Crested hawk eagle . . 90 80
2299 400c. Tiger 90 80
2300 400c. Painted stork 90 80
2301 400c. Green-winged macaw 90 80
2302 400c. Common squirrel-monkey 90 80
2303 400c. Crab-eating macaque 90 80
2304 400c. "Cithaerias menander" and "Ithomiidae" (butterflies) 90 80
2305 400c. "Coryptophanes cristatus" and "Gekkonidae" (lizards) 90 80
2306 400c. Boa constrictor . . . 90 80
2307 400c. Hoatzin 90 80
2308 400c. Western tarsier . . . 90 80
2309 400c. Golden Lion tamarin 90 80
2310 400c. "Pteropus gouldii" (bat) 90 80
2311 400c. Guianan cock of the rock 90 80
2312 400c. Resplendent quetzal 90 80
2313 400c. Tree frog and poison-arrow frog 90 80
2314 400c. Ring-tailed lemur . . 90 80
2315 400c. Iguana 90 80
2316 400c. "Heliconius burneyi" (butterfly) 90 80
2317 400c. Vervain hummingbird 90 80
2318 400c. Verreauv's sifaka . . . 90 80
MS2319 Two sheets, each 74 × 104 mm. (a) 3000c. Raggiana bird of paradise. (b) 3000c. King vulture Set of 2 sheets . . . . 12·00 12·00

531 Pagoda of Kaiyan Si Temple, Fujian

532 Serafim Todorow (Bulgaria)

1996. "CHINA '96" 9th Asian International Stamp Exhibition. Pagodas. Multicoloured.
2320 400c. Type **531** . . . . . . 1·10 1·10
2321 400c. Kaiyuan Si Temple, Hebei . . . . 1·10 1·10
2322 400c. Fogong Si Temple, Shanxi . . . . 1·10 1·10
2323 400c. Xiangshan, Beijing . . 1·10 1·10
MS2324 Two sheets. (a) 100 × 70 mm. 1000c. Baima Si Temple, Henan. (b) 143 × 98 mm. 1000c. Gold statue (38 × 50 mm) Set of 2 sheets . . . . 4·00 4·00

1996. 70th Birthday of Queen Elizabeth II. As T **255a** of Gambia showing different photographs. Multicoloured.
2325 1000c. Queen Elizabeth II 2·00 2·00
2326 1000c. In blue hat and coat 2·00 2·00
2327 1000c. Wearing straw hat and carrying bouquet . . 2·00 2·00
MS2328 125 × 103 mm. 2500c. In open carriage at Trooping the Colour (horiz) . . . . 4·75 4·75

1996. 50th Anniv of International Amateur Boxing Association. Multicoloured.
2329 300c. Type **532** 65 55
2330 400c. Oscar de la Hoya (U.S.A.) 80 70
2331 800c. Ariel Hernandez (Cuba) . . . . 1·50 1·75
2332 1500c. Arnoldo Mesa (Cuba) . . . . 2·50 3·00
MS2333 80 × 110 mm. 3000c. Tadahiro Sasaki (Japan) . . . 4·75 5·50

533 Ancient Greek Wrestlers

1996. Olympic Games, Atlanta (2nd issue). Previous Medal Winners. Multicoloured.
2334 300c. Type **533** 75 55
2335 400c. Aileen Riggin, 1920 (U.S.A.) 85 85
2336 400c. Pat McCormick, 1952 (U.S.A.) 85 85
2337 400c. Dawn Fraser, 1956 (Australia) 85 85
2338 400c. Chris von Saltza, 1960 (U.S.A.) 85 85
2339 400c. Anita Lonsbrough, 1960 (Great Britain) . . . 85 85
2340 400c. Debbie Meyer, 1968 (U.S.A.) 85 85
2341 400c. Shane Gould, 1972 (Australia) 85 85
2342 400c. Petra Thuemer, 1976 (Germany) 85 85
2343 400c. Marjorie Gestring, 1936 (U.S.A.) 85 85
2344 400c. Abedi Pele (Ghana) (vert) 85 85
2345 400c. Quico Navarez (Spain) (vert) 85 85
2346 400c. Heino Hanson (Denmark) (vert) 85 85
2347 400c. Mostafa Ismail (Egypt) (vert) 85 85
2348 400c. Anthony Yeboah (Ghana) (vert) 85 85
2349 400c. Jurgen Klinsmann (Germany) (vert) 85 85
2350 400c. Cobi Jones (U.S.A.) (vert) 85 85
2351 400c. Franco Baresi (Italy) (vert) 85 85
2352 400c. Igor Dobrovolski (Russia) (vert) 85 85
2353 500c. Wilma Rudolph (U.S.A.) (track and field, 1960) . . . . 1·00 1·00
2354 600c. Olympic Stadium, 1960, and Roman landmarks . . . . 1·25 1·40
2355 800c. Ladies Kayak pairs, 1960 (Soviet Union) . . . 1·50 1·75
MS2356 Two sheets, each 110 × 80 mm. (a) 2000c. Tracy Caulkins (U.S.A.) (200m freestyle, 1984). (b) 2000c. Kornelia Ender (Germany) (200m freestyle, 1976) Set of 2 sheets . . . . 8·50 8·50
Nos. 2335/43 (swimming and diving), and 2344/52 (football) respectively were printed together, se-tenant, with the backgrounds forming composite designs.

534 E. W. Agyare (35 years service with Ghana Broadcasting)

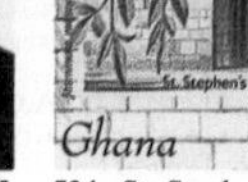

534a St. Stephen's Gate and "Jasminum mesyni"

1996. Local Broadcasting.
2357 **534** 100c. multicoloured . . . 40 40

1996. 50th Anniv of UNICEF. As T **258a** of Gambia. Multicoloured.
2358 400c. Ghanaian child . . . 35 35
2359 500c. Mother and child . . 45 45
2360 600c. Mother and child drinking 55 65
MS2361 74 × 104 mm. 1000c. Young child . . . . 1·10 1·25

1996. 3000th Anniv of Jerusalem. Multicoloured.
2362 400c. Type **534a** 60 40
2363 600c. The Citadel, Tower of David and "Nerium oleander" 80 80
2364 800c. Chapel of the Ascension and "Romulea bulbocodium" . . . . . 1·00 1·10
MS2365 65 × 80 mm. 2000c. Russian Orthodox Church of St. Mary Magdalene (48 × 30 mm) . . . 2·75 3·00

1996. Centenary of Radio. Entertainers. As T **259a** of Gambia. Multicoloured.
2366 500c. Frank Sinatra 45 35
2367 600c. Judy Garland 60 70
2368 600c. Bing Crosby 60 70
2369 800c. Martin and Lewis . . 80 90
MS2370 81 × 110 mm. 2000c. Edgar Bergen and Charlie McCarthy 2·25 2·75

1996. 50th Anniv of UNESCO. As T **273a** of Gambia. Multicoloured.
2371 400c. The Citadel, Haiti (vert) 50 25
2372 800c. Ait-Ben-Hadou (fortified village), Morocco (vert) . . . . . 90 1·00
2373 1000c. Spissky Hrad, Slovakia . . . . 1·25 1·40
MS2374 106 × 76mm. 2000c. Cape Coast Castle, Ghana . . . . . 2·25 2·75

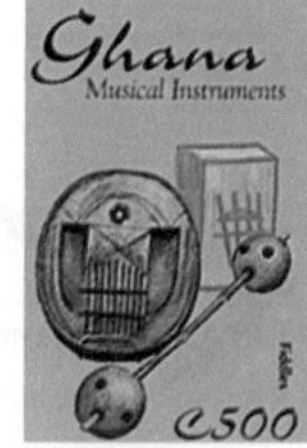

535 Fiddles

1996. Musical Insruments. Multicoloured.
2375 500c. Type **535** 75 75
2376 500c. Proverbial drum . . . 75 75
2377 500c. Double clapless bell and castanet 75 75
2378 500c. Gourd rattle 75 75
2379 500c. Horns 75 75

536 Ariel, Flounder and Sebastian

1996. Disney Friends. Disney Cartoon Characters. Multicoloured.
2380 60c. Type **536** 30 30
2381 60c. Pinocchio and Jiminy Cricket 30 30
2382 60c. Cogsworth and Lumiere 30 30
2383 60c. Copper and Tod . . . 30 30
2384 60c. Pocahontas, Meeko and Flit 30 30
2385 60c. Bambi, Flower and Thumper 30 30
2386 150c. As No. 2381 . . . . . 50 50
2387 200c. Type **536** 50 50
2388 200c. As No. 2383 . . . . . 50 50
2389 300c. As No. 2385 . . . . . 60 60
2390 350c. As No. 2382 . . . . . 60 60
2391 450c. As No. 2384 . . . . . 65 65
2392 600c. Aladdin and Abu . . 70 70

2393 700c. Penny and Rufus . . 75 75
2394 800c. Mowgli and Baloo . . 80 80
MS2395 Two sheets. (a) 98 × 124 mm. 3000c. Winnie the Pooh (vert). (b) 133 × 108 mm. 3000c. Simba and Timon Set of 2 sheets . . . . 6·00 6·50

1996. 20th Anniv of Rocky (film). Sheet 143 × 182 mm, containing vert design as T **266** of Gambia. Multicoloured.
MS2396 2000c. × 3 Sylvester Stallone in "Rocky II" . . . . 5·50 6·00

537 Herd Boy and Ox

1997. Chinese New Year ("Year of the Ox"). "The Herd Boy and Weaver". Each brown, silver and black.
2397 500c. Type **537** 70 70
2398 500c. Ox and weaver in lake 70 70
2399 500c. Weaver at work . . . 70 70
2400 500c. Herd boy with dying Ox 70 70
2401 500c. Weaver flying out of window 70 70
2402 500c. Herd boy carrying children 70 70
2403 500c. Family separated by "river" 70 70
2404 500c. Petitioning the emperor 70 70
2405 500c. Family reunited . . . 70 70

538 The Tomb of Dr. Hideyo Noguchi

539 Dipo Hairstyle

1997. 120th Birth Anniv of Dr. Hideyo Noguchi (bacteriologist). Multicoloured.
2406 1000c. Type **538** . . . . . . 1·25 1·40
2407 1000c. Dr. Hideyo Noguchi 1·25 1·40
2408 1000c. Birthplace of Dr. Noguchi at Sanjogarta . . . . 1·25 1·40
2409 1000c. Noguchi Institute, Legon . . . . 1·25 1·40
2410 1000c. Noguchi Gardens, Accra . . . . 1·25 1·40
MS2411 Two sheets, each 67 × 97 mm. (a) 3000c. Dr. Noguchi in his laboratory. (b) 3000c. Statue of Dr. Noguchi Set of 2 sheets . . . . 6·00 7·00

1997. Ghanaian Women's Hairstyle. Multicoloured.
2412 1000c. Type **539** 75 75
2413 1000c. Oduku with flowers 75 75
2414 1000c. Dansinkran 75 75
2415 1000c. Mbobom 75 75
2416 1000c. Oduku with hair pins 75 75
2417 1000c. African corn row . . 75 75
2418 1000c. Chinese raster . . . 75 75
2419 1000c. Chinese raster with top knot 75 75
2420 1000c. Corn row 75 75
2421 1000c. Mbakaa 75 75

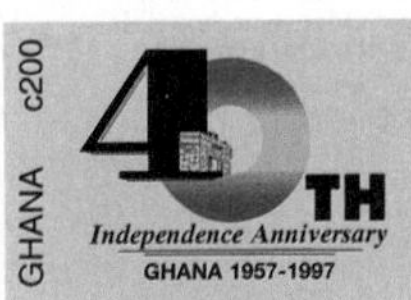

540 Independence Anniversary Emblem

1997. 40th Anniv of Independence. Multicoloured.
2422 200c. Type **540** 35 25
2423 200c. President J. J. Rawlings (vert) . . . . . 1·75 1·50
2424 550c. Dr. Kwane Nkrumah (first President) (vert) . . 75 80
2425 800c. Children in class . . . 1·25 1·50
2426 1100c. Akosombo Dam . . 1·75 2·00
MS2427 Two sheets. (a) 70 × 100 mm. 2000c. Dr. Nkrumah proclaiming independence (vert). (b) 101 × 141 mm. 3000c. United Nations Secretary-General Kofi Annan (37 × 50 mm) Set of 2 sheets . . . . 5·50 6·50
No. 2425 is inscribed "Acheivement" in error.

1997. 10th Anniv of Chernobyl Nuclear Disaster. As T **276b** of Gambia. Multicoloured.
2428 800c. Child's face and UNESCO emblem . . . . 1·25 1·40
2429 1000c. As No. 2428, but inscribed "CHABAD'S CHILDREN OF CHERNOBYL" at foot 1·40 1·60

541 Deng Xiaoping

1997. Deng Xiaoping (Chinese statesman) Commemoration. Different portraits. Multicoloured.
2430 300c. Type **541** 45 30
2431 500c. Looking thoughtful . . 60 55
2432 600c. Wearing glasses . . . 70 70
2433 600c. Delivering speech . . 70 70
2434 800c. As No. 2432 . . . . 90 1·00
2435 800c. As No. 2433 . . . . 90 1·00
2436 1000c. Type **541** . . . . . 1·10 1·25
2437 1000c. As No. 2431 . . . . 1·10 1·25
MS2438 Two sheets, each 101 × 70 mm. (a) 3000c. Deng Xiaoping making speech (47 × 34 mm). (b) 4000c. Deng Xiaoping with hand raised (47 × 34 mm) Set of 2 sheets . . 6·00 7·00

1997. 50th Death Anniv of Paul Harris (founder of Rotary International). As T **276c** of Gambia. Multicoloured.
2439 2000c. Paul Harris and Egyptian patient receiving polio vaccination . . . . 2·00 2·50
MS2440 78 × 107 mm. 3000c. Paul Harris with Rotary and PolioPlus emblems . . . . 2·25 2·75

1997. Golden Wedding of Queen Elizabeth and Prince Philip. As T **276d** of Gambia. Multicoloured.
2441 800c. Queen Elizabeth II . . 90 90
2442 800c. Royal coat of arms . . 90 90
2443 800c. Queen Elizabeth and Prince Philip waving . . . 90 90
2444 800c. Queen Elizabeth and Prince Philip on official visit 90 90
2445 800c. Queen in Irish State Coach 90 90
2446 800c. Prince Philip in 1947 90 90
MS2447 100 × 71 mm. 3000c. Princess Elizabeth in 1947 . . 2·25 2·50

1997. "Pacific '97" International Stamp Exhibition, San Francisco. Death Centenary of Heinrich von Stephan (founder of the U.P.U.). As T **276e** of Gambia.
2448 1000c. blue . . . . 1·00 1·10
2449 1000c. brown . . . . 1·00 1·10
2450 1000c. red . . . . 1·00 1·10
MS2451 82 × 119 mm. 3000c. green 2·50 3·00
DESIGNS: No. 2448, Early motor car; 2449, Von Stephan and Mercury; 2450, Blanchard's balloon flight, 1784; MS2451, African messenger.

541a "Nihonbashi Bridge and Edobashi Bridge"

542a *"Amorphophallus flavovirens"*

1997. Birth Bicentenary of Hiroshige (Japanese painter). "One Hundred Famous Views of Edo". Multicoloured.
2452 600c. Type **541a** 70 70
2453 600c. "View of Nihonbashi Tori 1-chome" 70 70
2454 600c. "Open Garden at Fukagawa Hachiman Shrine" 70 70
2455 600c. "Inari Bridge and Minato Shrine, Teppozu" 70 70
2456 600c. "Bamboo Yards, Kyobashi Bridge" 70 70
2457 600c. "Hall of Thirty-Three Bays, Fukagawa" 70 70
MS2458 Two sheets, each 102 × 127 mm. (a) 3000c. "Sumiyoshi Festival, Tsukudajima". (b) 3000c. "Teppozu and Tsukiji Honganji Temple" Set of 2 sheets . . . 5·00 6·00

1997.
2458c 200c. Type **542a** 15 10
2458d 550c. Atumpan drums . . 10 40
2458e 800c. *Cyrestis camillus* (butterfly) 60 15

542 Jackie Gleason

1997. Famous Comedians. Multicoloured.
2459 600c. Type **542** 75 75
2460 600c. Danny Kaye 75 75
2461 600c. John Cleese 75 75
2462 600c. Lucille Ball 75 75
2463 600c. Jerry Lewis 75 75
2464 600c. Sidney James 75 75
2465 600c. Louis Defuenes . . . 75 75
2466 600c. Mae West 75 75
2467 600c. Bob Hope 75 75
MS2468 Two sheets. (a) 83 × 113 mm. 3000c. Groucho Marx. (b) 76 × 106 mm. 2000c. Professor Ajax Bukana in front of curtain; 2000c. Professor Ajax Bukana (different) (both 28 × 42 mm) Set of 2 sheets . . 4·50 5·00

543 "Gelerina calyptrata"

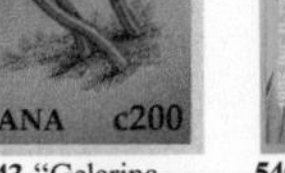

545 Ghanaian Players holding Trophy

544 African Pygmy Angelfish

1997. Fungi of the World. Multicoloured.
2469 200c. Type **543** 30 30
2470 300c. "Lepiota ignivolvata" 40 40
2471 400c. "Omphalotus olearius" 50 50
2472 550c. "Amanita phalloides" 60 60
2473 600c. "Entoloma conferendum" 60 60
2474 800c. "Entoloma nitidum" 70 70
2475 800c. "Coprinus picaceus" 70 70
2476 800c. "Stropharia aurantiaca" 70 70
2477 800c. "Cortinarius splendens" 70 70
2478 800c. "Gomphidius roseus" 70 70
2479 800c. "Russula sardonia" 70 70
2480 800c. "Geastrum schmidelia" 70 70
MS2481 Two sheets, each 73 × 103 mm. (a) 3000c. "Craterellus cornucopioides". (b) 3000c. "Mycena crocata" Set of 2 sheets . . . . 5·50 6·00

1997. World Football Championship, France (1998). As T **283a** of Gambia. Multicoloured.
2482 200c. Azteca Stadium, Mexico 35 30
2483 300c. The Rose Bowl, U.S.A. 45 40
2484 400c. Stadio Giuseppe Meazza, Italy 60 50
2485 500c. Olympiastadion, Germany 65 55
2486 600c. Patrick Kluivert, Netherlands 70 70
2487 600c. Roy Keane, Republic of Ireland 70 70
2488 600c. Abedi Ayew Pele, Ghana 70 70
2489 600c. Peter Schmeichel, Denmark 70 70
2490 600c. Roberto di Matteo, Italy 70 70
2491 600c. Bebeto, Brazil 70 70
2492 600c. Steve McManaman, England 70 70
2493 600c. George Oppon Weah, Liberia 70 70
2494 1000c. Maracana Stadium, Brazil . . . . 1·10 1·25
2495 2000c. Bernabeu Stadium, Spain . . . . 1·75 2·00
MS2496 Two sheets. (a) 127 × 102 mm. 3000c. David Seaman, England. (b) 102 × 127 mm. 3000c. Juninho, Brazil Set of 2 sheets . . . . . 6·00 7·00

1997. Marine Life. Multicoloured.
2497 400c. Type **544** 50 50
2498 500c. Violet-crested turaco 55 55
2499 500c. Pied avocet 55 55
2500 500c. Bottle-nosed dolphin 55 55
2501 500c. Bottle-nosed dolphin and long-toed lapwing . . 55 55
2502 500c. Longfinned spadefish 55 55
2503 500c. Imperial angelfish and manta 55 55
2504 500c. Racoon butterflyfish and African pompano . . 55 55
2505 500c. Silvertip shark 55 55
2506 500c. Longfin banner fish 55 55
2507 500c. Longfin banner fish and manta 55 55
2508 500c. Rust parrotfish . . . 55 55
2509 500c. Coral trout 55 55
2510 600c. Angelfish 60 60
2511 800c. Broomtail wrasse . . 70 75
2512 1000c. Indian butterflyfish 85 95
MS2513 Two sheets, each 106 × 76 mm. (a) 3000c. King angelfish. (b) 3000c. Crown butterflyfish Set of 2 sheets . . 6·00 7·00
Nos. 2498/2509 were printed together, se-tenant, with the backgrounds forming a composite design.

1997. J.V.C. Under-17 World Soccer Champions (1995). Multicoloured.
2514 200c.+50c. Type **545** . . . 40 40
2515 550c.+50c. Ghana football team (horiz) 75 75
2516 800c.+50c. Abu Iddrisu . . 90 90
2517 1000c.+50c. Emmanuel Bentil (captain) . . . . . 1·10 1·25
2518 1500c.+50c. Basiru Gambo 1·60 1·75

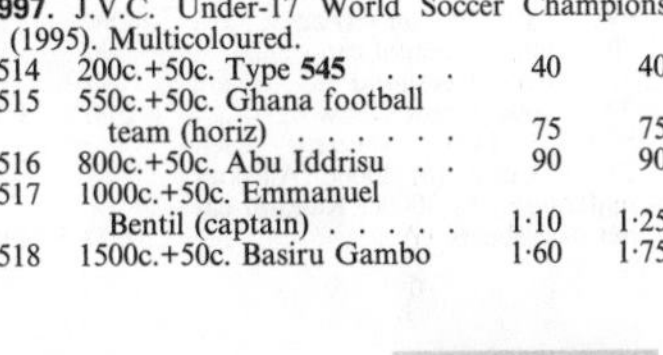

546 "Eurychone rothschildiana"

547 Eurasian Goldfinch

1997. Flowers of the World. Multicoloured.
2519 200c. Type **546** 40 30
2520 550c. "Bulbophyllum lepidum" 70 60
2521 800c. "Ansellia africana" . . 80 80
2522 800c. "Strophanthus preusii" (vert) 80 80
2523 800c. "Ancistrochilus rothschildlanus" (vert) . . 80 80
2524 800c. "Mussaendra arcuata" (vert) 80 80
2525 800c. "Microcoelia guyoniane" (vert) 80 80
2526 800c. "Gloriosa simplex" (vert) 80 80
2527 800c. "Brachycorythis kalbreyeri" (vert) 80 80
2528 800c. "Aframomum sceptrum" (vert) 80 80
2529 800c. "Thunbergia alata" (vert) 80 80
2530 800c. "Clerodendrum thomsoniae" (vert) 80 80
2531 1100c. "Combbretum grandiflorum" . . . . . 1·25 1·50
MS2532 Two sheets, each 82 × 77 mm. (a) 3000c. "Kigelia africana" (vert). (b) 3000c. "Spathodea campanulata" (vert) Set of 2 sheets . . . . 5·50 5·50
Nos. 2522/30 were printed together, se-tenant, with the backgrounds forming a composite design.

1997. Birds of Africa. Multicoloured.
2533 200c. Type **547** 40 30
2534 300c. Cape puff-back flycatcher ("Cape Batis") 55 40
2535 400c. Double-toothed barbet ("Bearded Barbet") . . . 65 50
2536 500c. African white-necked raven ("White-necked Raven") 70 60
2537 600c. Purple grenadier . . . 80 75
2538 800c. Black bustard 80 80
2539 800c. Northern lapwing . . 80 80
2540 800c. Lichtenstein's sandgrouse ("Sandgrouse") 80 80
2541 800c. Red-crested turaco . . 80 80
2542 800c. White-browed coucal 80 80
2543 800c. Lilac-breasted roller 80 80
2544 800c. Golden pipit 80 80
2545 800c. Burchell's gonolek ("Crimson-breasted Gonolek") 80 80

2546 800c. Blackcap 80 80
2547 1000c. Zebra waxbill 1·10 1·40
MS2548 Two sheets, each 106×75 mm. (a) 3000c. Shaft-tailed whydah. (b) 3000c. Yellow-tufted malachite sunbird Set of 2 sheets 6·00 6·00

548 Havana Cat

1997. Cats and Dogs. Multicoloured.
2549 20c. Type **548** 25 25
2550 50c. Singapura cat 25 25
2551 80c. Papillon 30 30
2552 100c. Sphinx cat 30 30
2553 150c. British white cat 30 30
2554 200c. Bulldog 30 30
2555 300c. Snowshoe cat 40 40
2556 400c. Shetland sheepdog 50 50
2557 500c. Schnauzer 55 55
2558 600c. Persian cat 60 60
2559 800c. Shih tzu 70 70
2560 1000c. Russian wolfhound 90 90
2561 1000c. Birman cat 90 90
2562 1000c. Basset hound 90 90
2563 1000c. Silver tabby cat 90 90
2564 1000c. Afghan 90 90
2565 1000c. Burmilla cat 90 90
2566 1000c. Abyssinian cat 90 90
2567 1000c. Border terrier 90 90
2568 1000c. Scottish fold cat 90 90
2569 1000c. Boston terrier 90 90
2570 1000c. Oriental cat 90 90
2571 1000c. Keeshond 90 90
2572 2000c. Chow Chow 1·60 1·75
MS2573 Two sheets, each 73×100 mm. (a) 3000c. Alaskan malamute. (b) 3000c. Ragdoll cat Set of 2 sheets 7·00 7·00

549 "Landscape" (Huang Binhong)

550 Diana, Princess of Wales

1997. Return of Hong Kong to China.
2574 **549** 200c. multicoloured 30 30
2575 – 300c. multicoloured 35 35
2576 – 400c. multicoloured 40 40
2577 – 500c. multicoloured 50 50
2578 – 600c. multicoloured 60 60
2579 – 800c. multicoloured 70 70
2580 – 1000c. multicoloured 90 95
2581 – 2000c. multicoloured 1·60 1·75
MS2582 138×105 mm. (a) 2000c. multicoloured (farm). (b) 2000c. multicoloured (mountains) (each 50×37 mm). P 14×13½ 2·50 2·75
MS2583 150×125 mm. (a) 1000c.×2 multicoloured (Lin Tse-Hue). (b) 1000c.×2 multicoloured (Gwen Tian-Pei) (each 63×31 mm) 2·50 2·75
DESIGNS: Nos. 2575/81 and MS2582, Landscape paintings by Huang Binhong; MS2583, Historical scenes.

1997. Christmas. Paintings. As T **284a** of Gambia. Multicoloured.
2584 200c. "Cupid" (Botticelli) 25 10
2585 550c. "Zephyr and Chloris" (Botticelli) 50 25
2586 800c. "Triumphant Cupid" (Caravaggio) 75 65
2587 1100c. "The Seven Works of Mercy" (Caravaggio) 1·25 1·40
2588 1500c. "The Toilet of Venus" (Diego Velazquez) 1·40 1·60
2589 2000c. "Freeing of St. Peter" (Raphael) 1·60 1·75
MS2590 Two sheets. (a) 95×105 mm. 5000c. "The Cavalcanti Annunciation" (Donatello). (b) 105×95 mm. 5000c. Ancient Egyptian painting of Isis and Nephthys Set of 2 sheets 8·00 8·50

1997. Diana, Princess of Wales Commemoration. Multicoloured (except Nos. 2591, 2596, 2602).
2591 1200c. Type **550** (red) 80 90
2592 1200c. Wearing blue suit and holding flowers 80 90
2593 1200c. Looking right 80 90
2594 1200c. Sitting crossed-legged 80 90
2595 1200c. With Prince William 80 90
2596 1200c. Wearing spotted scarf (blue and black) 80 90
2597 1200c. Wearing pink shirt 80 90
2598 1200c. Wearing red dress 80 90
2599 1200c. Carrying bouquet 80 90
2600 1200c. Wearing sunglasses 80 90
2601 1200c. With children 80 90
2602 1200c. Wearing hat (brown and black) 80 90
MS2603 Two sheets. (a) 100×70 mm. 3000c. Diana, Princess of Wales. (b) 70×100 mm. 3000c. Diana, Princess of Wales (violet and black) Set of 2 sheets 5·50 6·00

551 Horse

1998. Animals of the Chinese Lunar Calendar. Multicoloured.
2604 400c. Type **551** 30 30
2605 400c. Monkey 30 30
2606 400c. Ram 30 30
2607 400c. Cock 30 30
2608 400c. Dog 30 30
2609 400c. Ox 30 30
2610 400c. Rabbit 30 30
2611 400c. Pig 30 30
2612 400c. Snake 30 30
2613 400c. Dragon 30 30
2614 400c. Tiger 30 30
2615 400c. Rat 30 30

552 Mortie and Ferdie (January)

554 Maya Angelou

553 Union Pacific SD60M diesel Locomotive No. 6331, U.S.A.

1998. A Year in the Life of Mickey Mouse and Friends. Walt Disney cartoon characters. Multicoloured.
2616 1000c. Type **552** 1·40 1·40
2617 1000c. Minnie on Valentine's Day (February) 1·40 1·40
2618 1000c. Goofy with kite (March) 1·40 1·40
2619 1000c. Mickey, Minnie and Pluto in rain (April) 1·40 1·40
2620 1000c. Minnie with flowers (May) 1·40 1·40
2621 1000c. Daisy watering garden (June) 1·40 1·40
2622 1000c. Donald at Independance Day celebrations (July) 1·40 1·40
2623 1000c. Donald and Daisy on the beach (August) 1·40 1·40
2624 1000c. Morty and Ferdie returning to school (September) 1·40 1·40
2625 1000c. Hewey, Dewey and Louie at Hallowe'en (October) 1·40 1·40
2626 1000c. Mickey on Thanksgiving Day (November) 1·40 1·40
2627 1000c. Mickey and Minnie at Christmas (December) 1·40 1·40
MS2628 Four sheets, each 132×107 mm. (a) 5000c. Mickey bottle feeding calf (Spring) (horiz). (b) 5000c. Minnie camping (Summer). (c) 5000c. Goofy sweeping leaves (Autumn). (d) 5000c. Daisy and Nephews on ice (Winter) (horiz) Set of 4 sheets 19·00 19·00

1998. Trains of the World. Multicoloured.
2629 300c. Type **553** 20 15
2630 500c. ETR 450 high-speed train, Italy 40 25
2631 800c. X200 high-speed train, Sweden 60 60
2632 800c. SPS steam locomotive, Pakistan 60 60
2633 800c. Class WP steam locomotive, India 60 60
2634 800c. Class QJ steam locomotive, China 60 60
2635 800c. Type 12 steam locomotive, Belgium 60 60
2636 800c. Class P8 steam locomotive, Germany 60 60
2637 800c. Class "Castle" steam locomotive, Great Britain 60 60
2638 800c. Tank locomotive, Austria 60 60
2639 800c. Class P36 steam locomotive, Russia 60 60
2640 800c. Steam locomotive "William Mason", U.S.A. 60 60
2641 800c. AVE high-speed train, Spain 60 60
2642 800c. Diesel locomotive No. 1602, Luxembourg 60 60
2643 800c. "Hikari" express train, Japan 60 60
2644 800c. Santa Fe Railroad GM F7 "Warbonnet" diesel locomotive, U.S.A. 60 60
2645 800c. Class E1500 diesel locomotive, Morocco 60 60
2646 800c. Class "Deltic" diesel locomotive, Great Britain 60 60
2647 800c. XPT high-speed train, Australia 60 60
2648 800c. Channel Tunnel shuttle train, France and Great Britain 60 60
2649 800c. Class 201 diesel locomotive, Ireland 60 60
2650 1000c. TGV Duplex high-speed train, France 70 70
2651 2000c. Class EL diesel locomotive, Australia 1·40 1·60
2652 3000c. Eurostar high-speed train, Great Britain 1·60 1·70
MS2653 Two sheets, each 106×76 mm. (a) 5500c. Class "Duchess" steam locomotive heading the "Irish Mail", Great Britain (56×42 mm). (b) 5500c. TGV express train, France (56×42 mm) Set of 2 sheets 6·00 6·50

1998. Great Writers of the 20th Century. Mult.
2654 350c. Type **554** 30 30
2655 350c. Alex Haley 30 30
2656 350c. Charles Johnson 30 30
2657 350c. Richard Wright 30 30
2658 350c. Toni Cade Bambara 30 30
2659 350c. Henri Louis Gates Jr 30 30

555 Breguet Br 14 B2, France

1998. History of Aviation. Multicoloured.
2660 800c. Type **555** 60 60
2661 800c. Curtiss BF2C-1 Goshawk, U.S.A. 60 60
2662 800c. Supermarine Spitfire Mk IX, Great Britain 60 60
2663 800c. Fiat G.50, Italy 60 60
2664 800c. Douglas B-18A, U.S.A. 60 60
2665 800c. Boeing FB-5, U.S.A. 60 60
2666 800c. Bristol F2B "Brisfit", Great Britain 60 60
2667 800c. Hawker Fury 1, Great Britain 60 60
2668 800c. Fiat CR-42, Italy 60 60
2669 800c. Messerschmitt Bf 109 E-7, Germany 60 60
2670 800c. Lockheed PV-2 Harpoon, U.S.A. 60 60
2671 800c. Airspeed Oxford Mk 1, Great Britain 60 60
2672 800c. Junkers Ju 87D-1, Germany 60 65
2673 800c. Yakovlev Yak-9D, U.S.S.R. 60 60
2674 800c. North American P-51D Mustang, U.S.A. 60 60
2675 800c. Douglas A-206 Havoc, U.S.A. 60 60
2676 800c. Supermarine Attacker F1, Great Britain 60 60
2677 800c. Mikoyan Gurevich MiG-15, U.S.S.R. 60 60
MS2678 Two sheets, each 106×76 mm. (a) 3000c. Supermarine Spitfires Mk 1 and Mk XIV, Great Britain (58×43 mm). (b) 3000c. Mitsubishi AGM8 Reisen, Japan (58×43 mm) Set of 2 sheets 3·25 3·50

556 "Empress of Ireland" (liner)

1998. Famous Ships. Multicoloured.
2679 800c. Type **556** 60 60
2680 800c. "Transylvania" (liner) 60 60
2681 800c. "Mauretania I" (liner) 60 60
2682 800c. "Reliance" (liner) 60 60
2683 800c. "Aquitania" (liner) 60 60
2684 800c. "Lapland" (liner) 60 60
2685 800c. "Cap Polonio" (liner) 60 60
2686 800c. "France I", 1910 (liner) 60 60
2687 800c. "Imperator" (liner) 60 60
2688 800c. H.M.S. "Rodney" (battleship) 60 60
2689 800c. U.S.S. "Alabama" (battleship) 60 60
2690 800c. H.M.S. "Nelson" (battleship) 60 60
2691 800c. "Ormonde" (camouflaged liner) 60 60
2692 800c. U.S.S. "Radford" (destroyer) 60 60
2693 800c. "Empress of Russia" (camouflaged liner) 60 60
2694 800c. Type XIV U-boat 60 60
2695 800c. Japanese Type A midget submarine 60 60
2696 800c. "Brin" (Italian submarine) 60 60
MS2697 Two sheets, each 100×75 mm. (a) 5500c. "Titanic" (liner) (43×57 mm). (b) 5500c. "Amistad" (slave schooner) (43×57 mm) Set of 2 sheets 7·00 7·00
No. 2681 is inscribed "MAURITANIA" in error.

1998. "Israel 98" International Stamp Exhibition, Tel-Aviv. Nos. 2362/4 optd with Emblem.
2698 400c. St. Stephen's Gate and "Jasminum mesnyi" 50 40
2699 600c. The Citadel, Tower of David and "Nerium oleander" 60 60
2700 800c. Chapel of the Ascension and "Romulea bulbocodium" 80 80
MS2701 65×80 mm. 2000c. Russian Orthodox Church of St. Mary Magdalene (48×30 mm) 2·00 2·00
No. **MS**2701 is additionally overprinted **ISRAEL 98 – WORLD STAMP EXHIBITION TEL-AVIV 13–21 MAY 1998** on the sheet margin.

558 "Renanthera imschootiana"

559 Elvis Presley

1998. Orchids of the World. Multicoloured.
2702 800c. Type **558** 60 60
2703 800c. "Arachnis flos-aeris" 60 60
2704 800c. "Restrepia lansbergi" 60 60
2705 800c. "Paphiopedilum tonsum" 60 60
2706 800c. "Phalaenopsis ebauche" 60 60
2707 800c. "Pleione limprichti" 60 60
2708 800c. "Phragmipedium schroderae" 60 60
2709 800c. "Zygopetalum clayii" 60 60
2710 800c. "Vanda coerulea" 60 60
2711 800c. "Odontonia boussole" 60 60
2712 800c. "Disa uniflora" 60 60
2713 800c. "Dendrobium bigibbum" 60 60
MS2714 Two sheets, each 98×68 mm. (a) 5500c. "Cypripedium calceolus". (b) 5500c. "Sobralia candida" Set of 2 sheets 6·00 6·50

1998. 30th Anniv of Elvis Presley's "68 Special" Television Programme. Multicoloured.
2715 800c. Type **559** 60 60
2716 800c. Elvis in white suit 60 60
2717 800c. In leather jacket, holding microphone 60 60
2718 800c. Wearing light blue jacket 60 60

2719 800c. Elvis with silhouetted figures in background . . 60 60
2720 800c. Elvis with guitar and microphone 60 60

560 Crest of Accra Metropolitan Assembly and Surf Boats

1998. Centenary of Accra Metropolitan Assembly. Multicoloured.
2721 200c. Type **560** 20 10
2722 550c. King Tackie Tawiah I 40 20
2723 800c. Achimota School . . 55 30
2724 1100c. Korle Bu Hospital 70 80
2725 1500c. Christianborg Castle 90 1·00

561 Tetteh Quarshie (cocoa industry pioneer)

1998. 50th Anniv of Ghana Cocoa Board. Multicoloured.
2726 200c. Type **561** 20 10
2727 550c. Ripe hybrid cocoa pods 50 20
2728 800c. Opening cocoa pods 60 50
2729 1100c. Fermenting cocoa beans 70 80
2730 1500c. Loading freighter with cocoa . . . . 90 1·00

562 Bamboo

1998. Oriental Flowers. Multicoloured.
2731 2000c. Type **562** . . . . . 1·00 1·00
2732 2000c. Cherry blossom . . . 1·00 1·00
2733 2000c. Yellow chrysanthemum . . . . . 1·00 1·00
2734 2000c. Orchid . . . . 1·00 1·00
2735 2000c. Green peony . . . . 1·00 1·00
2736 2000c. Red peony . . . . . 1·00 1·00
2737 2000c. Pink peony . . . . . 1·00 1·00
2738 2000c. White peony . . . . 1·00 1·00
MS2739 Two sheets, each 109 × 85 mm. (a) 5500c. Cherry blossom (horiz). (b) 5500c. Peonies (horiz) Set of 2 sheets . . . . 6·50 7·00

563 Two Dolphins

1998. International Year of the Ocean. Multicoloured.
2740 500c. Type **563** 40 40
2741 500c. Dolphin 40 40
2742 500c. Seagull 40 40
2743 500c. Least tern 40 40
2744 500c. Emperor angelfish . . 40 40
2745 500c. White ear (juvenile) 40 40
2746 500c. Blue shark and diver 40 40
2747 500c. Parrotfish 40 40
2748 500c. Dottyback 40 40
2749 500c. Blue-spotted stingray 40 40
2750 500c. Masked butterflyfish 40 40
2751 500c. Jackknife-fish 40 40
2752 500c. Octopus 40 40
2753 500c. Lionfish 40 40
2754 500c. Seadragon 40 40
2755 500c. Rock cod 40 40
MS2756 Two sheets. (a) 63 × 98 mm. 3000c. Great white shark. (b) 98 × 63 mm. 3000c. Devil ray Set of 2 sheets . . . . 4·25 4·50

Nos. 2740/55 were printed together, se-tenant, with the backgrounds forming a composite design.

No. 2745 is inscribed "Whit Ear" in error.

1998. Millennium Series. Famous People of the Twentieth Century. Inventors. As T **289a** of Gambia. Multicoloured.
2757 1000c. Thomas Edison . . . 60 60
2758 1000c. Peephole kinetoscope (Edison) (53 × 38 mm) . . 60 60
2759 1000c. Tesla coil (53 × 38 mm) 60 60
2760 1000c. Nikola Tesla 60 60
2761 1000c. Gottlieb Daimler . . 60 60
2762 1000c. Motorcycle (Daimler) (53 × 38 mm) 60 60
2763 1000c. Early transmitter circuit (Marconi) and dish aerial (53 × 38 mm) . . . 60 60
2764 1000c. Guglielmo Marconi 60 60
2765 1000c. Orville and Wilbur Wright 60 60
2766 1000c. "Flyer I" (Wright Brothers) (53 × 38 mm) . . 60 60
2767 1000c. Neon lights and signs (Claude) (53 × 38 mm) . . 60 60
2768 1000c. Georges Claude . . . 60 60
2769 1000c. Alexander Graham Bell 60 60
2770 1000c. Early telephone transmitter (Bell) (53 × 38 mm) 60 60
2771 1000c. Uses of lasers (Townes) (53 × 38 mm) . . 60 60
2772 1000c. Charles Townes . . . 60 60
MS2773 Two sheets, each 76 × 106 mm. (a) 5500c. Paul Ehrlich. (b) 5500c. Robert Goddard Set of 2 sheets . . . 5·50 6·50

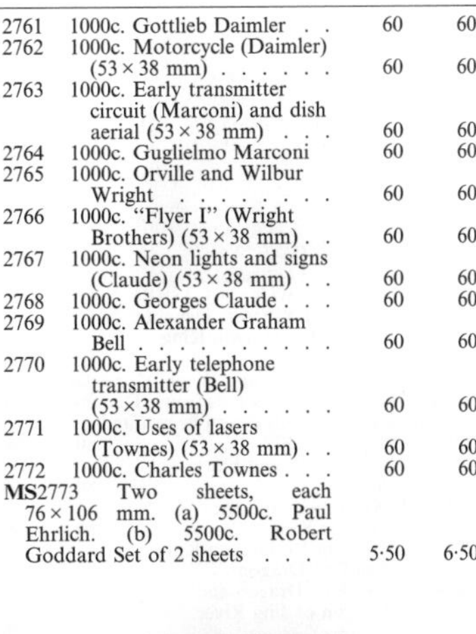
564 British Colourpoint with Tree Decoration

1998. Christmas. Cats and Dogs. Multicoloured.
2774 500c. Type **564** 45 15
2775 600c. American shorthair kitten with basket 50 20
2776 800c. Peke-faced Persian on piano keys 65 30
2777 1000c. German spitz dog in box 80 40
2778 2000c. British shorthair Blue with antlers . . . . . . 1·40 1·60
2779 3000c. Persian in sleigh . . 1·60 1·75
MS2780 Two sheets, each 76 × 106 mm. (a) 5500c. English pointer puppy. (b) 5500c. Manx cat with decoration Set of 2 sheets 7·00 7·50

1999. 25th Death Anniv of Pablo Picasso (painter). As T **293a** of Gambia. Multicoloured.
2781 1000c. "Composition with Butterfly" 75 80
2782 1000c. "Mandolin and Clarinet" (vert) 75 80
2783 2000c. "Woman throwing a Stone" . . . . 1·40 1·60
MS2784 101 × 127 mm. 5500c. "Tomato Plant" (vert) . . . . 4·00 4·50

564a Lampredi

1999. Birth Centenary of Enzo Ferrari (car manufacturer). Multicoloured.
2785 2000c. Type **564a** . . . . . 1·40 1·40
2786 2000c. 250 GT Cabriolet . . 1·40 1·40
2787 2000c. 121 LM . . . . . . 1·40 1·40
MS2788 100 × 70 mm. 3000c. 365 GTS/4 Spyder (91 × 34 mm) . . 3·00 3·50

1999. 19th World Scout Jamboree, Chile. As T **291b** of Gambia. Multicoloured (except No. **MS**2792).
2789 2000c. Scout salute . . . . 1·25 1·50
2790 2000c. Scout with backpack 1·25 1·50
2791 2000c. Bowline knot . . . . 1·25 1·50
MS2792 55 × 70 mm. 5000c. Lord Baden-Powell (bistre and black) 2·75 3·00

1999. 50th Death Anniv of Mahatma Gandhi. As T **292** of Gambia. Multicoloured.
2793 2000c. Gandhi, 1931 . . . . 1·25 1·40
2794 2000c. On Salt March, 1930 (53 × 38 mm) . . . . . . 1·25 1·40
2795 2000c. Collecting natural salt, 1930 (53 × 38 mm) 1·25 1·40
2796 2000c. After graduating from high school, 1887 . . 1·25 1·40
MS2797 60 × 79 mm. 5500c. Mahatma Gandhi seated, 1931 4·25 4·50

1999. 80th Anniv of Royal Air Force. As T **292** of Gambia. Multicoloured.
2798 2000c. C-130 Hercules on tarmac . . . . 1·50 1·50
2799 2000c. HC2 Chinook helicopter . . . . 1·50 1·50
2800 2000c. C-130 Hercules W2 taking off . . . . 1·50 1·50
2801 2000c. Panavia Tornado F3 1·50 1·50
MS2802 Two sheets, each 90 × 70 mm. (a) 5500c. Chipmunk and EF-2000 Euro-fighter. (b) 5500c. Bristol F2B fighter and merlin (bird) Set of 2 sheets . . 7·00 7·50

1999. 1st Death Anniv of Diana, Princess of Wales. As T **293a** of Gambia.
2803 1000c. multicoloured . . . . 1·00 1·00

565 Farmer working

1999. Chinese New Year ("Year of the Rabbit"). "Farmer and the Hare" (Han Fei Tzu). Mult.
2804 1400c. Type **565** . . . . . 1·00 1·10
2805 1400c. Farmer watching hare hit tree . . . . 1·00 1·10
2806 1400c. Farmer with dead hare . . . . 1·00 1·10
2807 1400c. Farmer asleep under tree . . . . 1·00 1·10

566 Shirley Temple praying

1999. 70th Birthday of Shirley Temple (actress). Showing film scenes from "Curly Top". Multicoloured.
2808 1000c. Type **566** 60 70
2809 1000c. Man looking at painting 60 70
2810 1000c. With butler 60 70
2811 1000c. As old woman in rocking chair 60 70
2812 1000c. With mother (horiz) 60 70
2813 1000c. Wearing brown coat and bowler hat (horiz) . . 60 70
2814 1000c. With cuddly toys (horiz) 60 70
2815 1000c. Pulling father's tie (horiz) 60 70
2816 1000c. With family (horiz) 60 70
2817 1000c. Watching parents (horiz) 60 70
MS2818 106 × 76 mm. 5000c. Shirley Temple on piano . . . . . . 3·75 4·25

567 Corythosaurus

1999. Prehistoric Animals. Multicoloured.
2819 400c. Type **567** 60 30
2820 600c. Struthiomimus 70 40
2821 800c. Pterodactylus 75 80
2822 800c. Scelidosaurus 75 80
2823 800c. Pteranodon 75 80
2824 800c. Plateosaurus 75 80
2825 800c. Ornithosuchus 75 80
2826 800c. Kentrosaurus 75 80
2827 800c. Hypsognathus 75 80
2828 800c. Erythrosuchus 75 80
2829 800c. Stegoceras 75 80
2830 800c. Ankylosaurus 75 80
2831 800c. Anatosaurus 75 80
2832 800c. Diplodocus 75 80
2833 800c. Monoclonius 75 80
2834 800c. Tyrannosaurus 75 80
2835 800c. Camptosaurus 75 80
2836 800c. Ornitholestes 75 80
2837 800c. Archaeopteryx 75 80
2838 800c. Allosaurus 75 80
2839 1000c. Lambeosaurus . . . 80 85
2840 2000c. Hesperasuchus . . . 1·25 1·50
MS2841 Two sheets, each 85 × 110 mm. (a) 5000c. Dimorphodon (vert). (b) 5000c. Apatosaurus Set of 2 sheets . . . 7·00 7·50

Nos. 2821/9 and 2830/8 respectively were printed together, se-tenant, with the backgrounds forming composite designs.

568 Badgers

1999. Endangered Species. Multicoloured.
2842 200c. Type **568** 20 15
2843 400c. Azure-winged magpie 40 20
2844 600c. White stork 55 25
2845 800c. Red fox 60 30
2846 1000c. European bee eater ("Merops apiaster") . . . 70 75
2847 1000c. Hoopoe ("Upupa epops") 70 75
2848 1000c. Red deer 70 75
2849 1000c. Short-toed eagle ("Cycaetus gallicus") . . 70 75
2850 1000c. Lacerta oceliata (lizard) 70 75
2851 1000c. Lynx 70 75
2852 1000c. Pine martin 70 75
2853 1000c. Tawny owl ("Strix aluco") 70 75
2854 1000c. Wild boar 70 75
2855 1000c. Northern goshawk ("Accipiter gentilis") . . . 70 75
2856 1000c. Garden dormouse . . 70 75
2857 1000c. Stag beetles 70 75
2858 2000c. Cinereous vulture (vert) . . . . 1·25 1·50
2859 3000c. Jay (vert) . . . . . 1·50 2·00
MS2860 Two sheets, each 85 × 110 mm. (a) 5000c. Imperial eagle ("Iberian Imperial Eagle"). (b) 5000c. Wolf cub (vert) Set of 2 sheets . . . . 7·00 7·00

Nos. 2846/51 and 2852/7 respectively were printed together, se-tenant, with the backgrounds forming composite designs.

569 California Sister Butterfly

1999. "Australia '99" International Stamp Exhibition, Melbourne. Butterflies. Multicoloured.
2861 300c. Type **569** 30 15
2862 500c. Red-splashed sulphur 40 20
2863 600c. Checked white 50 25
2864 800c. Blue emperor 60 30
2865 1000c. Red admiral (vert) 70 75
2866 1000c. Buckeye (vert) . . . 70 75
2867 1000c. Desert chequered skipper (vert) 70 75
2868 1000c. Orange sulphur (vert) 70 75
2869 1000c. Tiger swallowtail (vert) 70 75
2870 1000c. Orange-bordered blue (vert) 70 75
2871 1000c. Gulf fritillary "vanillae") (vert) 70 75
2872 1000c. Monarch (vert) . . . 70 75
2873 1000c. Small tortoiseshell (vert) 70 75
2874 1000c. Brimstone (vert) . . 70 75
2875 1000c. Camberwell beauty (vert) 70 75
2876 1000c. Marbled white (vert) 70 75
2877 1000c. Purple Emperor (vert) 70 75
2878 1000c. Clouded yellow (vert) 70 75
2879 1000c. Ladoga camilla (vert) 70 75
2880 1000c. Marsh fritillary (vert) 70 75
MS2881 Two sheets, each 106 × 76 mm. (a) 5000c. Homerus swallowtail (vert). (b) 5000c. Blue copper Set of 2 sheets . . . . 7·00 7·00

Nos. 2865/72 and 2873/80 respectively were printed together, se-tenant, with the backgrounds forming composite designs.

No. 2862 is inscribed "Red-splashed Sulfer" and No. 2864 "Blue Emperorl", both in error.

571 ICE 2 (Germany), 1966

1999. Railways of the World. Multicoloured.
2883 400c. Type **571** 30 20
2884 500c. M41 No. 2112 (Hungary), 1982 . . . . 40 20
2885 600c. DVR No. 2526 (Finland), 1963 . . . . . 50 30
2886 1000c. Class AVE 100 (Spain), 1992 . . . . . . 70 40
2887 1300c. Conrail EMD SD80 No. 4110 (U.S.A.), 1993 80 85
2888 1300c. Columbus and Greenville EMD SDP35 No. 701 (U.S.A.), 1964–6 80 85
2889 1300c. Providence and Worcester MLW M420 (U.S.A.), 1973–77 . . . . 80 85
2890 1300c. Missouri Pacific C36-7 No. 9044 (U.S.A.), 1978–85 . . . . 80 85

2891 1300c. Virginia and Maryland ALCO C-420 No. 203 (U.S.A.), 1963–68 . . 80 85
2892 1300c. Reading EMD GP30 No. 3615 (U.S.A.), 1961–63 . . . . 80 85
2893 1300c. Illinois Terminal EMD GP7 No. 1506 (U.S.A.), 1949/54 . . . . 80 85
2894 1300c. Canadian Pacific EMD SD 38-2 (Canada), 1972–79 . . . . 80 85
2895 1300c. EMD SD 60M 500 No. 6058 (U.S.A.), 1989–96 . . . . 80 85
2896 1300c. GE U25C No. 2808 (U.S.A.), 1963–65 . . . . 80 85
2897 1300c. EMD GP 28 (U.S.A.), 1961–63 . . . . 80 85
2898 1300c. EMD SD 9 No. 162 (U.S.A.), 1954–59 . . . . 80 85
MS2899 Two sheets. (a) 85 × 110 mm. 5000c. Swiss Federal Class RE 6/6 No. 11630, 1972. (b) 110 × 85 mm. 5000c. AGP44 (U.S.A), 1990–91 Set of 2 sheets 7·00 7·50

1999. "iBRA '99" International Stamp Exhibition, Nuremberg. Multicoloured. As T **298a** of Gambia.
2900 500c. "Schomberg" (sailing ship) and Hanover 1850 1 ggr. stamp 40 20
2901 800c. Class P8 railway locomotive and Hamburg 1859 ½s. 60 30
2902 1000c. "Schomberg" (sailing ship) and Lubeck 1859 ½s. 70 60
2903 2000c. Class P8 railway locomotive and Heligoland 1867 ½s. . . . 1·25 1·50
MS2904 134 × 106 mm. 5000c. Germany 3pf. stamp on 1912 Bork-Bruck flown cover (vert) 3·00 3·25

1999. 150th Death Anniv of Katsushika Hokusai (Japanese artist). Multicoloured as T **298b** of Gambia, but horiz.
2905 1300c. "Girl picking Plum Blossoms" 80 85
2906 1300c. "Surveying a Region" 80 85
2907 1300c. "Sumo Wrestler" (bending down) 80 85
2908 1300c. "Sumo Wrestler" (dancing) 80 85
2909 1300c. "Landscape with Seaside Village" 80 85
2910 1300c. "Courtiers crossing a Bridge" 80 85
2911 1300c. "Climbing the Mountain" 80 85
2912 1300c. "Nakahara in Sagami Province" 80 85
2913 1300c. "Sumo Wrestlers" . . 80 85
2914 1300c. "An Oiran and Maid by a Fence" 80 85
2915 1300c. "Fujiwara Yoshitaka" 80 85
MS2916 Two sheets, each 100 × 70 mm. (a) 5000c. "Palanquin Bearers on a Steep Hill" (vert). (b) 5000c. "Three Ladies by a Well" (vert) Set of 2 sheets . . . . 6·50 7·00

1999. 10th Anniv of United Nations Rights of the Child Convention. Vert designs as T **298c** of Gambia. Multicoloured.
2917 3000c. Boy smiling and U.N. Headquarters Building . . . . 1·60 1·90
2918 3000c. Dove and Earth . . 1·60 1·90
2919 3000c. Mother and baby . . 1·60 1·90
MS2920 110 × 85 mm. 5000c. Boy and UNICEF emblem . . . . 3·25 3·75
Nos. 2917/19 were printed together, se-tenant, forming a composite design.

1999. "PhilexFrance '99" International Stamp Exhibition, Paris. Railway Locomotives. Two sheets, each 106 × 76 mm, containing horiz designs as T **299d** of Gambia. Multicoloured.
MS2921 Two sheets. (a) 5000c. Western Railway suburban tank locomotive. (b) 5000c. National Railways Class 232-U1 Set of 2 sheets . . . . 6·50 7·00

1999. 250th Birth Anniv of Johann von Goethe (German writer). As T **298d** of Gambia. Multicoloured.
2922 2000c. Wagner entreats Faust in his study . . . . 1·25 1·50
2923 2000c. Von Goethe and Von Schiller . . . . 1·25 1·50
2924 2000c. Mephistopheles disguised as the Fool . . 1·25 1·50
MS2925 106 × 71 mm. 5000c. Faust attended by Spirits . . . . . . 3·25 3·75

1999. 30th Anniv of First Manned Landing on Moon. T **298e** of Gambia. Multicoloured.
2926 1300c. Command module 1·25 1·40
2927 1300c. Lunar module ascending . . . . 1·25 1·40
2928 1300c. Giant moon rock . . 1·25 1·40
2929 1300c. Lunar module's aerials and Earth from Moon . . . . 1·25 1·40
2930 1300c. Neil Armstrong . . . 1·25 1·40
2931 1300c. "One small step" (alighting on lunar surface) . . . . 1·25 1·40
MS2932 71 × 106 mm. 5000c. Earth from Moon . . . . 3·50 4·00

Nos. 2926/31 were printed together, se-tenant, forming a composite design. No. 2927 is inscribed "LUNAR MODULE ASCENSION" in error.

572 Gate of Understanding, Macao

1999. "China '99" World Philatelic Exhibition, Beijing. Return of Macao to China.
2933 **572** 1000c. multicoloured . . 1·25 1·50

1999. "Queen Elizabeth the Queen Mother's Century". As T **304a** of Gambia.
2934 2000c. black and gold . . . 1·50 1·60
2935 2000c. black and gold . . . 1·50 1·60
2936 2000c. multicoloured . . . . 1·50 1·60
2937 2000c. multicoloured . . . . 1·50 1·60
MS2938 153 × 157 mm. 5000c. multicoloured . . . . 4·50 4·75
DESIGNS: No. 2934, Lady Elizabeth Bowes-Lyon with her brother, David, 1904; 2935, Queen Mother in Rhodesia, 1957; 2936, Queen Mother seated, 1970; 2937, Queen Mother holding bouquet, 1992. (37 × 50 mm)—**MS**2938, Queen Mother in garden, 1970.

573 Dr. Ephraim Apu

1999. Birth Centenary of Dr. Ephraim Apu (traditional musicologist). Multicoloured.
2939 200c. Type **573** 20 15
2940 800c. Playing Odurugya flute 70 70
2941 1100c. Indigenious flutes . . 90 1·10

574 Grandma Alice and Village

1999. 25th Anniv of S.O.S. in Ghana (200, 1100c.) and 50th Anniv of S.O.S. Kinderdorf International (children's villages) (others). Multicoloured.
2942 200c. Type **574** 25 15
2943 550c. Kindergarten 55 30
2944 800c. Hermann Gneiner (founder) and Asiakwa S.O.S. building 75 75
2945 1100c. Preparing food . . . 1·00 1·25

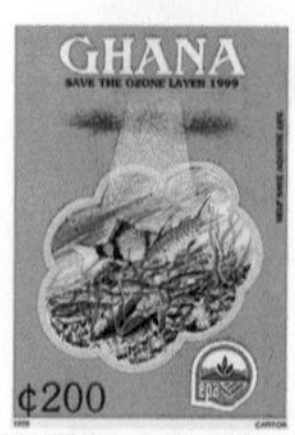

575 Fishes inside Cloud

576 Peace Doves flying from Ghana

1999. Save the Ozone Layer Campaign. Mult.
2946 200c. Type **575** 25 15
2947 550c. African looking at diagram of ozone layer 55 30
2948 800c. Earth weeping 75 65
2949 1100c. Africans shielding Earth . . . . 1·00 1·25
2950 1500c. CFC and no-CFC appliances . . . . 1·25 1·50

1999. New Millennium. Multicoloured.
2951 300c. Type **576** 30 20
2952 700c. Kwame Nkrumah (first President) speaking (horiz) 70 70
2953 1200c. Clock tower, University of Ghana . . . 1·10 1·40

577 Liu-Yi meets Daughter of the Dragon King

2000. Chinese New Year ("Year of the Dragon"). Vert designs showing scenes from "Daughter of the Dragon King". Each design brown and silver.
2954 1600c. Type **577** 80 90
2955 1600c. Liu-Yi and Fairy Soldier 80 90
2956 1600c. Liu-Yi and the Dragon King 80 90
2957 1600c. Liu-Yi, Dragon King and Red Dragon 80 90
2958 1600c. Red Dragon and Dragon of Jing River fighting 80 90
2959 1600c. Dragon King with his daughter and brother 80 90
2960 1700c. Dragon King's brother inviting Liu-Yi to marry his niece 80 90
2961 1700c. Liu-Yi bidding farewell to Dragon King 80 90
2962 1700c. Liu-Yi with gifts from Dragon King . . . 80 90
2963 1700c. Liu-Yi with third wife 80 90
2964 1700c. Liu-Yi with third wife and son 80 90
2965 1700c. Liu-Yi realises that third wife is Daughter of the Dragon King 80 90

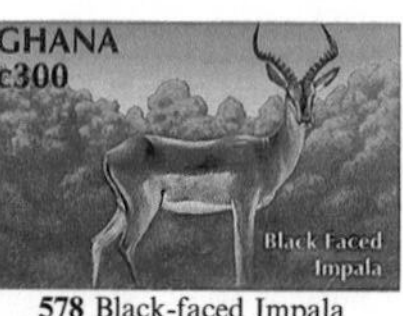

578 Black-faced Impala

2000. African Wildlife. Multicoloured.
2966 300c. Type **578** 30 10
2967 500c. Cheetah 45 15
2968 1000c. Wildebeest 60 30
2969 1100c. Chimpanzee (vert) . . 70 75
2970 1100c. Boomslang tree snake (vert) 70 75
2971 1100c. Ruppell's griffon ("Vulture") (vert) 70 75
2972 1100c. Leopard (vert) . . . 70 75
2973 1100c. African rhinoceros (vert) 70 75
2974 1100c. Zebra (vert) 70 75
2975 1100c. South African crowned crane ("Crowned Crane") (vert) 70 75
2976 1100c. Female lesser Kudu (vert) 70 75
2977 1200c. Rufous-crowned roller ("Purple Roller") (vert) 70 75
2978 1200c. Eastern white pelican ("Pelicans") (vert) 70 75
2979 1200c. Cattle egret ("Egrets") (vert) 70 75
2980 1200c. Zebra waxbill ("Orange-breasted Waxbill") (vert) 70 75
2981 1200c. Giraffe (vert) 70 75
2982 1200c. African buffalo (vert) 70 75
2983 1200c. Elephant (vert) . . . 70 75
2984 1200c. African lion (vert) . . 70 75
2985 3000c. Hippopotamus . . . 1·50 2·00
MS2986 Two sheets, each 76 × 106 mm. (a) 7000c. Ostrich. (b) 7000c. Young waterbuck Set of 2 sheets . . . . . . 6·50 7·00
Nos. 2969/76 and 2977/84 were each printed together, se-tenant, with the backgrounds forming composite designs.

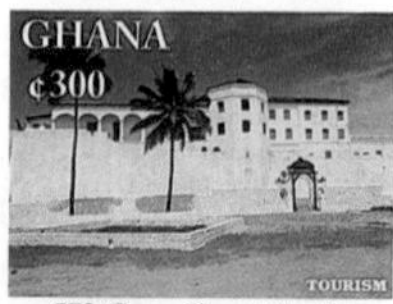

579 Cape Coast Castle

2000. Tourism. Multicoloured.
2987 300c. Type **579** 30 20
2988 300c. Banda Nkwanta Mosque, Accra 30 20
2989 300c. Elephants 70 35
2990 1100c. Tribal chief . . . . 90 1·00
2991 1200c. Ghanaians with antelope . . . . 90 1·00
2992 1800c. Tribal chiefs . . . . 1·40 1·75

580 Banded ("Zebra") Duiker

2000. Fauna and Flora. Multicoloured.
2993 500c. Type **580** 40 15
2994 600c. Leopard 50 20
2995 1600c. Large spotted genet 80 85
2996 1600c. Tree pangolin . . . 80 85
2997 1600c. Bongo 80 85
2998 1600c. Elephant 80 85
2999 1600c. Flap-necked chameleon 80 85
3000 1600c. West African dwarf crocodile 80 85
3001 1600c. Lowe's monkey . . . 80 85
3002 1600c. Diana monkey . . . 80 85
3003 1600c. Potto 80 85
3004 1600c. Moustached monkey 80 85
3005 1600c. Thomas's galago . . 80 85
3006 1600c. Chimpanzee 80 85
3007 1600c. Grey parrot 80 85
3008 1600c. Hoopoe 80 85
3009 1600c. European roller . . . 80 85
3010 1600c. European bee-eater 80 85
3011 1600c. Blue-breasted kingfisher 80 85
3012 1600c. White-throated bee eater 80 85
3013 2000c. Bushbuck . . . . . 1·00 1·10
3014 3000c. African wood owl . . 1·50 1·60
MS3015 Two sheets. (a) 100 × 70 mm. 6000c. Hippopotamus (vert). (b) 70 × 100 mm. 6000c. Great blue turaco (vert) Set of 2 sheets . . 6·50 7·00
Nos. 2995/3000, 3001/6 and 3007/12 were each printed together, se-tenant, with the backgrounds forming composite designs.
No. 2995 is inscribed "BLOTHED GENET" in error.

581 *Suillus luteus*

2000. African Mushrooms. Multicoloured.
3016 1500c. Type **581** . . . . . 90 1·00
3017 1500c. *Laccaria amethystina* 90 1·00
3018 1500c. *Coriolus versicolor* 90 1·00
3019 1500c. *Armillaria mellea* . 90 1·00
3020 1500c. *Lepiota rhacodes* . . 90 1·00
3021 1500c. *Russula queletil* . . 90 1·00
3022 2000c. *Amanita vaginata* . . 1·10 1·25
3023 2000c. *Lycoperdon perlatum* 1·10 1·25
3024 2000c. *Schizophyllum commune* . . . . . . 1·10 1·25
3025 2000c. *Cantharellus cinereus* 1·10 1·25
3026 2000c. *Coprinus disseminatus* . . . . 1·10 1·25
3027 2000c. *Russula cyanoxantaha* . . . . 1·10 1·25
MS3028 Two sheets, each 53 × 81 mm. (a) 5000c. *Aleuria aurantia* (vert). (b) 5000c. *Tylopilus felleus* (vert) Set of 2 sheets . . 7·00 7·00

582 Cooking Demonstration

2000. 19th International Home Economics Congress, Accra. Multicoloured.
3029 300c. Type **582** 20 15
3030 700c. Student with home economics text book (vert) 55 30
3031 1200c. Mrs. Alberta Ollennu, Ms. Patience Adow and Association logo 80 90
3032 1800c. Congress logo (vert) 1·25 1·50

2000. 18th Birthday of Prince William. At T **312b** of Gambia. Multicoloured.
3033 2000c. In skiing gear . . . . 1·50 1·60
3034 2000c. In Eton uniform . . 1·50 1·60
3035 2000c. With Prince Harry 1·50 1·60
3036 2000c. Prince William (Royal Artillery cap in background) . . . . . . 1·50 1·60
MS3037 100 × 80 mm. 8000c. Prince William in blue jumper (37 × 50 mm) . . . . 6·00 6·25

582a "Mercury"

2000. "EXPO 2000" World Stamp Exhibition, Anaheim. Manned Spacecraft. Multicoloured.
3038 2000c. Type **582a** . . . . . 1·40 1·50
3039 2000c. "Gemini" . . . . . 1·40 1·50
3040 2000c. "Apollo" . . . . . 1·40 1·50
3041 2000c. "Vostok" . . . . . 1·40 1·50
3042 2000c. "Voskhod 2" . . . . 1·40 1·50
3043 2000c. "Soyuz" . . . . . 1·40 1·50
MS3044 75 × 115 mm. 2000c. Space Shuttle *Challenger* mission emblem (vert) . . . . 1·50 1·75
Nos. 3038/43 were printed together, se-tenant, with the backgrounds forming a composite design.

582b "Apollo 18"

582c *Wetherby*, 1985

2000. 25th Anniv of "Apollo"–"Soyuz" Joint Project. Multicoloured.
3045 4000c. Type **582b** . . . . . 2·25 2·50
3046 4000c. "Apollo 18" and "Soyuz 19" docking . . . 2·25 2·50
3047 4000c. "Soyuz 19" . . . . 2·25 2·50
MS3048 105 × 75 mm. 8000c. "Soyuz 19" and Earth . . . . 4·50 5·00
Nos. 3045/7 were printed together, se-tenant, with the backgrounds forming a composite design.

2000. 50th Anniv of Berlin Film Festival. Mult.
3049 2000c. Type **582c** . . . . . 1·25 1·40
3050 2000c. *Die Frau und der Fremde*, 1985 . . . . . . 1·25 1·40
3051 2000c. *Hong Gaoliang*, 1988 1·25 1·40
3052 2000c. *Skrivanci na Nitich*, 1990 . . . . 1·25 1·40
3053 2000c. *Music Box*, 1990 . . 1·25 1·40
3054 2000c. *Terma*, 1987 . . . . 1·25 1·40
MS3055 95 × 103 mm. 6000c. *Justice est Faite*, 1951 . . . . 5·50 6·00

582d Marc Seguin

2000. 175th Anniv of Stockton and Darlington Line (first public railway). Multicoloured.
3056 4000c. Type **582d** . . . . . 2·25 2·50
3057 4000c. Blenkinsop's locomotive . . . . 2·25 2·50
3058 4000c. Pumping station at Dawlish . . . . 2·25 2·50

2000. Election of Albert Einstein (mathematical physicist) as *Time Magazine* "Man of the Century". Sheet 120 × 90 mm, containing vert portrait as T **312d** of Gambia.
MS3059 8000c. multicoloured . . 4·25 4·50

582e LZ-129 *Hindenburg*, 1936

2000. Centenary of First Zeppelin Flight. Mult.
3060 1600c. Type **582e** . . . . . 1·25 1·40
3061 1600c. LZ-9 *Ersatz Deutschland*, 1911 . . . . 1·25 1·40
3062 1600c. LZ-4, 1908 . . . . . 1·25 1·40
MS3063 96 × 65 mm. 5000c. LZ-11 *Viktoria Luise*, 1912 . . . . . 3·75 4·00
Nos. 3060/2 were printed together, se-tenant, with the backgrounds forming a composite design.

582f Gymnast on Parallel Bars, Athens (1896)

2000. Olympic Games, Sydney. Multicoloured.
3064 1300c. Type **582f** . . . . . 95 1·00
3065 1300c. Long jumping . . . 95 1·00
3066 1300c. Olympic Stadium, Los Angeles (1984) . . . 95 1·00
3067 1300c. Ancient Greek chariot racing . . . . . . 95 1·00

583 African Shorthair Cat

584 Xu Xian, White Lady and Xiao Qing

2000. Domestic Cats and Dogs. Multicoloured.
3068 1100c. Type **583** 60 60
3069 1200c. Russian blue cat . . 60 60
3070 1600c. Weimaraner (horiz) 70 70
3071 1800c. Keeshond (horiz) . . 80 90
3072 1800c. Fox terrier (horiz) . . 80 90
3073 1800c. Saluki (horiz) 80 90
3074 1800c. Dalmatian (horiz) . . 80 90
3075 1800c. English setter (horiz) 80 90
3076 1800c. Basenji 80 90
3077 1800c. Silver Persian (horiz) 80 90
3078 1800c. Creampoint Himalayan (horiz) 80 90
3079 1800c. British tortoiseshell shorthair (horiz) 80 90
3080 1800c. American shorthair tabby (horiz) 80 90
3081 1800c. Black Persian (horiz) 80 90
3082 1800c. Turkish van (horiz) 80 90
3083 2000c. Basset hound . . . . 1·00 1·25
MS3084 Two sheets, each 110 × 85 mm. (a) 8000c. Lilac Persian cat. (b) 8000c. Cocker spaniel Set of 2 sheets . . . . 7·50 8·00

2001. Chinese New Year ("Year of the Snake"). Showing scenes from *Tale of the White Snake* (traditional Chinese story). Each red and silver.
3085 2500c. Type **584** . . . . . 1·00 1·10
3086 2500c. White Lady and Xu Xian in pharmacy . . . . 1·00 1·10
3087 2500c. Xu Xian with monk Fa Hai . . . . 1·00 1·10
3088 2500c. Xu Xian and White Lady drinking wine . . . 1·00 1·10
3089 2500c. Xu Xian having heart attack . . . . 1·00 1·10
3090 2500c. White Lady attacked by stork . . . . 1·00 1·10
3091 2500c. White Lady, Xiao Qing with swords confront Fa Hai . . . . 1·00 1·10
3092 2500c. Xiao Qing and Xu Xian on staircase . . . . 1·00 1·10
3093 2500c. Fa Hai entrapping White Lady beneath pagoda . . . . 1·00 1·10
3094 2500c. Xiao Qing, Xu Xian praying at pagoda . . . . 1·00 1·10
3095 2500c. Xiao Qing attacking Fa Hai . . . . 1·00 1·10
3096 2500c. Fa Hai turned into crab . . . . 1·00 1·10

585 Walter Gropius (architect)

2001. Twentieth Century Achievements in Architecture, Art and Medicine. Multicoloured.
3097 2500c. Type **585** . . . . . 90 1·00
3098 2500c. Aldo Rossi . . . . . 90 1·00
3099 2500c. Le Corbusier . . . . 90 1·00
3100 2500c. Antonio Gaudi . . . . 90 1·00
3101 2500c. Paolo Soleri . . . . 90 1·00
3102 2500c. Mies van der Rohe 90 1·00
3103 2500c. Wassily Kandinsky 90 1·00
3104 2500c. Henry Moore . . . . 90 1·00
3105 2500c. Marc Chagall . . . . 90 1·00
3106 2500c. Norman Rockwell . . 90 1·00
3107 2500c. Antonio Lopez Garcia . . . . 90 1·00
3108 2500c. Frida Kahlo . . . . 90 1·00
MS3109 Three sheets, each 93 × 64 mm. (a) 14000c. "FRANK LLOYD WRIGHT". (b) 14000c. "Picasso". (c) 14000c. Double helix structure of DNA molecule Set of 3 sheets . . . . 14·00 15·00

586 James Cagney

586a Margie Hendrix (shoulder at bottom right)

2001. Hollywood Legends. James Cagney and Edward G. Robinson. Designs showing different portraits.
3110 **586** 4000c. green and black 1·25 1·40
3111 – 4000c. green and black 1·25 1·40
3112 – 4000c. blue and black . . 1·25 1·40
3113 – 4000c. brown and black 1·25 1·40
3114 – 4000c. mauve and black 1·25 1·40
3115 – 4000c. orange and black 1·25 1·40
3116 – 4000c. green and black 1·25 1·40
3117 – 4000c. lilac, purple and black . . . . 1·25 1·40
3118 – 4000c. purple and black 1·25 1·40
3119 – 4000c. brown and black 1·25 1·40
3120 – 4000c. brown and black 1·25 1·40
3121 – 4000c. blue and black . . 1·25 1·40
Nos. 3110/15 (Cagney) and 3116/21 (Robinson) were each printed together, se-tenant, showing a photograph of the actor.

2001. Famous Girl Pop Groups. The Cookies (Nos. 3122/4), The Ronettes (Nos. 3125/7) and The Supremes (Nos. 3128/30). Multicoloured.
3122 2700c. Type **586a** . . . . . 1·25 1·40
3123 2700c. Ethel McCrea (with straight hair) . . . . . . 1·25 1·40
3124 2700c. Pat Lyles's head (background at bottom right) . . . . 1·25 1·40
3125 2700c. Estelle Bennett (inscr and value clear of portrait) . . . . 1·25 1·40
3126 2700c. Veronica Bennett (inscr and value touch portrait) . . . . 1·25 1·40
3127 2700c. Nedra Talley (inscr touches, value clear of portrait) . . . . 1·25 1·40
3128 2700c. Florence Ballard (left earring) . . . . 1·25 1·40
3129 2700c. Mary Wilson (two earrings) . . . . 1·25 1·40
3130 2700c. Diana Ross (right earring) . . . . 1·25 1·40
Each group forms a horizontal strip with different background colour: The Cookies cobalt, The Ronettes blue and The Supremes yellow and red.

587 Edward "Kid" Ory (trombonist)

2001. Famous American Jazz Musicians. Multicoloured.
3131 4000c. Type **587** . . . . . 1·25 1·40
3132 4000c. Earl "Fatha" Hines (pianist) . . . . 1·25 1·40
3133 4000c. Lil Hardin-Armstrong (pianist) . . . 1·25 1·40
3134 4000c. John Philip Sousa (composer) . . . . 1·25 1·40
3135 4000c. James P. Johnson (pianist) . . . . 1·25 1·40
3136 4000c. Johnny St. Cyr (banjo/guitar player) . . . 1·25 1·40
3137 4000c. Scott Joplin (composer) . . . . 1·25 1·40
3138 4000c. Clarence Williams (pianist) . . . . 1·25 1·40
3139 4000c. Sidney Bechet (clarinetist/saxophonist) 1·25 1·40
3140 4000c. Willie "The Lion" Smith (pianist) . . . . . 1·25 1·40
3141 4000c. Ferdinand "Jelly Roll" Morton (composer) 1·25 1·40
3142 4000c. Coleman "Bean" Hawkins (saxophonist) . . 1·25 1·40
MS3143 Two sheets, each 60 × 77 mm. (a) 14000c. Louis "Satchmo" Armstrong (cornet player). (b) 14000c. Joe "King" Oliver (cornet player) Set of 2 sheets . . . . 7·50 8·50

588 "Cranes" (Kano Eisen'in Michinobu)

2001. "Philanippon '01" International Stamp Exhibition, Tokyo. Japanese Paintings. Multicoloured.
3144 500c. Type **588** 20 15
3145 800c. "Flowers and Trees in Chen Chun's Style" (Tsubaki Chinzan) . . . 25 15
3146 1200c. "Poetry Contest of 42 Matches" (unsigned) 35 25
3147 2000c. "Cranes" (different detail) (Kano Eisen'in Michinobu) 65 35
3148 3000c. "Coming-of-Age Rite" (vert) 80 90
3149 3000c. "West Wing" (vert) 80 90
3150 3000c. "Akuta River" (vert) 80 90
3151 3000c. "Eastbound Trip: Mt. Utsu" (vert) 80 90
3152 3000c. "Eastbound Trip: Mt. Fuji" (vert) 80 90
3153 3000c. "Eastbound Trip: Black-headed Gulls" (vert) 80 90
3154 3000c. "Crossing Kawachi" (vert) 80 90
3155 3000c. "By Well Wall" (vert) 80 90
3156 4000c. "Excursion through South Gate" (vert) . . . 1·00 1·10
3157 4000c. "Excursion through East Gate" (vert) . . . . 1·00 1·10
3158 4000c. "Excursion through North Gate" (vert) . . . 1·00 1·10
3159 4000c. "Excursion through West Gate" (vert) . . . . 1·00 1·10
3160 4000c. "Sakyamuni entering Nirvana" (vert) . . . . . 1·00 1·10
3161 4000c. "Animals" (vert) . . 1·00 1·10
3162 5000c. "Poetry Contest of 42 Matches" (different detail) (unsigned) . . . . 1·25 1·40
3163 12000c. "Plum Trees" (Tani Buncho) . . . . 3·00 3·50
MS3164 Four sheets, each 100 × 76 mm. (a) 14000c. "Cranes" (Kano Eisen'in Michinobu) ("GHANA" and value in red). (b) 14000c. "Cranes" (Kano Eisen'in Michinobu) ("GHANA" in yellow). (c) 14000c. "Coming-of-Age Rite" (Sumiyoshi Jokei). (d) 14000c. "Musashino Plain" (unknown artist) Set of 4 sheets 16·00 17·00
Nos. 3148/55 ("The Tales of Ise" (Sumiyoshi Jokei)) and 3156/63 ("The Story of Sakyamuni").

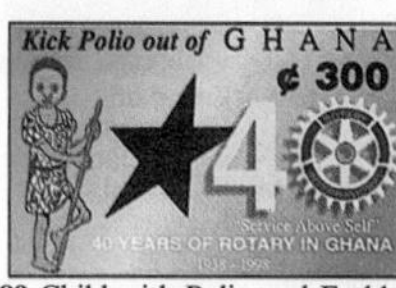

589 Child with Polio and Emblem

2001. 40th Anniv of Rotary in Ghana. Each including the Rotary International symbol. Multicoloured.
3165 300c. Type **589** 20 15
3166 1100c. Boy getting clean water from tap 50 60
3167 1200c. Paul Harris (founder of Rotary International) 50 60
3168 1800c. Man giving blood . . 75 90

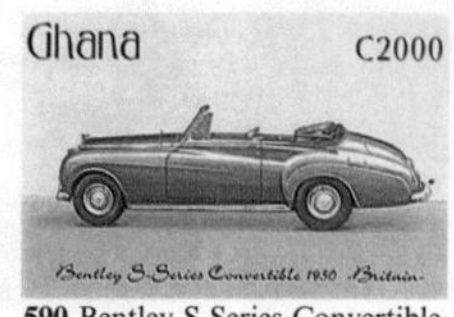

590 Bentley S-Series Convertible (1950)

2001. "Belgica 2001" International Stamp Exhibition, Brussels. Twentieth-century classic Cars. Multicoloured.
3169 2000c. Type **590** 50 35
3170 3000c. Chrysler Town and Country (1948) 75 50
3171 4000c. B.M.W. 507 (1956–59) . . . . 90 1·00
3172 4000c. Bentley English Tourer (1934) . . . . . . 90 1·00
3173 4000c. Morris Minor (1948) 90 1·00
3174 4000c. Daimler SP-250 Dart (1954) . . . . 90 1·00
3175 4000c. DeSoto Custom Convertible (1950) . . . . 90 1·00
3176 4000c. Ford Thunderbird (1955–60) . . . . 90 1·00
3177 4000c. Porsche 356B (1959–63) . . . . 90 1·00
3178 4000c. Rolls-Royce Silver Cloud (1962) . . . . . . 90 1·00
3179 4000c. Austin Healey Sprite Mk 1 (1958) . . . . . . 90 1·00
3180 4000c. Mercedes 300SL (1954–57) . . . . 90 1·00
3181 4000c. Citroen 2cv (1949) 90 1·00
3182 4000c. Cadillac Series-62 (1949) . . . . 90 1·00
3183 5000c. Lotus Elite (1957) . . 1·25 1·40
3184 6000c. Corvette Sting Ray (1966) . . . . 1·40 1·50
MS3185 Two sheets, each 102 × 74 mm. (a) 14000c. Mercedes-Benz (1933) (85 × 28 mm). (b) 14000c. Triumph TR2 (1953–55) (85 × 28 mm) Set of 2 sheets . . . . . . 7·00 7·50
No. 3172 is inscribed "Bentler" and No. 3181 "Citreon", both in error.

590a Princess Victoria as a Young Girl

590b Mao in Uniform acknowledging Crowd

2001. Death Centenary of Queen Victoria. Multicoloured.
3186 5000c. Type **590a** . . . . . 1·40 1·50
3187 5000c. Albert Edward, Prince of Wales . . . . . 1·40 1·50
3188 5000c. Queen Victoria and Prince of Wales . . . . . 1·40 1·50
3189 5000c. Queen Victoria and Prince Albert on Wedding Day . . . . 1·40 1·50
MS3190 66 × 96 mm. 12000c. Princess Victoria (The Princess Royal) . . . . 3·50 3·75
MS3190 is inscr Princess Victoria in error.

2001. 25th Death Anniv of Mao Tse-tung (Chinese leader). Multicoloured.
3191 7000c. Type **590b** . . . . . 1·50 1·75
3192 7000c. Head and shoulders portrait . . . . 1·50 1·75
3193 7000c. Mao in overcoat acknowledging crowd . . 1·50 1·75
MS3194 116 × 102 mm. 12000c. Mao as a young man . . . . 3·00 3·50

590c "Zaandam"

2001. 75th Death Anniv Claude-Oscar Monet. (French painter). Multicoloured.
3195 5000c. Type **590c** . . . . . 1·25 1·50
3196 5000c. "On the Seine at Bennecourt" . . . . . . 1·25 1·50
3197 5000c. "The Studio-boat" 1·25 1·50
3198 5000c. "Houses on the Waterfront, Zaandam" . . 1·25 1·50
MS3199 139 × 110 mm. 15000c. "Madame Gaudibert" (vert) . . 3·75 4·25

590d Queen Elizabeth in pink hat

590e Giuseppe Verdi

2001. 75th Birthday of Queen Elizabeth II. Multicoloured.
3200 4000c. Type **590d** . . . . . 1·10 1·25
3201 4000c. Queen Elizabeth in white hat with flowers . . 1·10 1·25
3202 4000c. In red "trilby" . . . 1·10 1·25
3203 4000c. Wearing tiara . . . . 1·10 1·25
3204 4000c. In matching blue and pink hat and coat . . . . 1·10 1·25
3205 4000c. Queen Elizabeth in uniform for Trooping the Colour . . . . 1·10 1·25
MS3206 85 × 135 mm. 15000c. Queen Elizabeth with Duke of Edinburgh (horiz) . . . . . . 4·00 4·25

2001. Death Centenary of Giuseppe Verdi (Italian composer). Multicoloured.
3207 5000c. Type **590e** . . . . . 1·50 1·60
3208 5000c. Musical scores for *Aida* and *Rigoletto* . . . 1·50 1·60
3209 5000c. Inn at Le Roncole (Verdi's birthplace) . . . 1·50 1·60
3210 5000c. Map of Italy . . . . 1·50 1·60
MS3211 76 × 106 mm. 13000c. Giuseppe Verdi . . . . 4·00 4·25
Nos. 3207/11 were printed together, se-tenant, with the backgrounds forming a composite design.

590f "Jane Avril leaving the Moulin Rouge"

Death Centenary of Henri de Toulouse-Lautrec ...ch painter). Multicoloured.
...00c. Type **590f** . . . . . 1·40 1·60
...00c. "Jane Avril dancing" 1·40 1·60
...700c. "Jane Avril entering the Moulin Rouge" . . . 1·40 1·60

591 Killer Whale

2001. Whales and Dolphins. Multicoloured.
3215 1000c. Type **591** 50 25
3216 3000c. Narwhal 85 65
3217 4000c. Humpback whale . . 1·10 1·25
3218 4000c. Fin whale . . . . . 1·10 1·25
3219 4000c. Bowhead whale . . . 1·10 1·25
3220 4000c. Grey whale . . . . . 1·10 1·25
3221 4000c. Narwhal . . . . . . 1·10 1·25
3222 4000c. White whale ("Beluga") . . . . 1·10 1·25
3223 4000c. Head of blue whale 1·10 1·25
3224 4000c. Killer whale . . . . 1·10 1·25
3225 4000c. Northern bottlenose dolphin . . . . 1·10 1·25
3226 4000c. Sperm whale . . . . 1·10 1·25
3227 4000c. Southern right whale 1·10 1·25
3228 4000c. Pygmy right whale 1·10 1·25
3229 5000c. White whale ("Beluga") . . . . 1·40 1·50
3230 6000c. Bowhead whale . . . 1·50 1·60
MS3231 Two sheets, each 100 × 85 mm. (a) 14000c. Blue whale adult and calf. (b) 14000c. Head of sperm whale Set of 2 sheets . . . . 8·00 8·00
Nos. 3217/22 and 3223/8 were each printed together, se-tenant, the backgrounds forming composite designs.

592 *Paphiopedilum hennisianum*

2001. African Orchids. Multicoloured.
3232 1100c. Type **592** 45 30
3233 1200c. *Vuylstekeara cambria Plush* 45 30
3234 1800c. *Cymbidium Ormoulu* 60 50
3235 2000c. *Phalaenopsis Barbara Moler* 65 50
3236 4500c. *Odontocidium Tigersun* . . . . 1·25 1·40
3237 4500c. *Miltonia Emotion* . . 1·25 1·40
3238 4500c. *Odontonia sappho Excul* . . . . 1·25 1·40
3239 4500c. *Cymbidium Bulbarrow* 1·25 1·40
3240 4500c. *Dendrobium nobile* . . 1·25 1·40
3241 4500c. *Paphiopedilum insigne* 1·25 1·40
3242 4500c. *Cattleya capra* . . . 1·25 1·40
3243 4500c. *Odontoglossum rossii* 1·25 1·40
3244 4500c. *Epidendrum pseudepidendrum* . . . . 1·25 1·40
3245 4500c. *Encyclia cochleata* . . 1·25 1·40
3246 4500c. *Cymbidium Baldoyle Melbury* . . . . 1·25 1·40
3247 4500c. *Phalaenopsis asean* 1·25 1·40
MS3248 Two sheets, each 68 × 98 mm. (a) 15000c. *Calanthe vestita*. (b) 15000c. *Angraecum eburneum* Set of 2 sheets . . . 8·00 8·50

593 50th Anniversary Logo

2001. 50th Anniv of Kwame Nkrumah University of Science and Technology, Kumasi. Multicoloured.
3249 300c. Type **593** 20 10
3250 700c. Main entrance 35 25
3251 1100c. Milking cows 50 55
3252 1200c. Students in pharmacy department 50 55
3253 1800c. Halls of residence . . 70 80
MS3254 120 × 100 mm. As Nos. 3250/3, but each with a face value of 4000c. . . . . 4·00 4·50

594 Bamboo Orchestra

2001. Musical Instruments. Multicoloured.
3255 4000c. Type **594** . . . . . 1·00 1·10
3256 4000c. Women playing mensuon (wind instruments) . . . . 1·00 1·10
3257 4000c. Fontomfrom (drums) 1·00 1·10
3258 4000c. Pati . . . . 1·00 1·10

595 George Olah (Chemistry Prize, 1994)

2002. Centenary of Nobel Prizes. Chemistry Prize Winners (except Nos. **MS**3277d/e). Multicoloured.
3259 4000c. Type **595** . . . . . 1·00 1·10
3260 4000c. Kary Mullis (1993) 1·00 1·10
3261 4000c. Sir Harold Kroto (1996) . . . . 1·00 1·10
3262 4000c. Richard Ernst (1991) 1·00 1·10
3263 4000c. Ahmed Zewail (1999) 1·00 1·10
3264 4000c. Paul Crutzen (1995) 1·00 1·10
3265 4000c. John Walker (1997) 1·00 1·10
3266 4000c. Jens Skou (1997) . . 1·00 1·10
3267 4000c. Alan MacDiarmid (2000) . . . . 1·00 1·10
3268 4000c. Thomas Cech (1989) 1·00 1·10
3269 4000c. John Pople (1998) . . 1·00 1·10
3270 4000c. Rudolph Marcus (1992) . . . . 1·00 1·10
3271 4000c. Walter Kohn (1998) 1·00 1·10
3272 4000c. Frank Rowland (1995) . . . . 1·00 1·10
3273 4000c. Mario Molina (1995) 1·00 1·10
3274 4000c. Hideki Shirakawa (2000) . . . . 1·00 1·10
3275 4000c. Paul Boyer (1997) . . 1·00 1·10
3276 4000c. Richard Smalley (1996) . . . . 1·00 1·10
MS3277 Five sheets, each 106 × 77 mm. (a) 15000c. Svante Arrhenius (1903). (b) 15000c. Alfred Werner (1913). (c) 15000c. Peter Debye (1936). (d) 15000c. Wole Soyinka (Literature, 1986). (e) 15000c. Nelson Mandela (Peace, 1993) Set of 5 sheets . . 17·00 18·00

596 Queen Elizabeth at the Races

2002. Golden Jubilee. Multicoloured.
3278 6500c. Type **596** . . . . . 1·75 1·90
3279 6500c. Queen Elizabeth on horseback . . . . 1·75 1·90
3280 6500c. Queen Elizabeth inspecting horses . . . . 1·75 1·90
3281 6500c. Queen Elizabeth in carriage with Duke of Edinburgh, Ascot races 1·75 1·90
MS3282 76 × 108 mm. 15000c. Princess Elizabeth with Duke of Edinburgh . . . . 4·25 4·50

597 Conference Logo

598 Jay Jay Okacha (Nigeria)

2002. 5th International Copyright Conference, Accra. Multicoloured.
3283 300c. Type **597** 20 10
3284 700c. Girl reading (horiz) . . 35 25
3285 1100c. Spider on web (horiz) 50 55
3286 1200c. Woven cloth in shape of Ghana (horiz) 50 55
3287 1800c. Woman playing drum (horiz) 70 80

2002. World Cup Football Championship, Japan and Korea. Multicoloured.
3288 100c. Type **598** 10 15
3289 150c. South African player 15 15
3290 300c. Pele (Brazil) 20 20
3291 400c. Roger Milla (Cameroun) 20 20
3292 500c. Bobby Charlton (England) 25 20
3293 800c. Michel Platini (France) 30 25
3294 1000c. Franz Beckenbauer (West Germany) 40 35
3295 1500c. Ulsan Munsu Stadium, Korea (horiz) 60 60
3296 2000c. German player . . . 65 65
3297 3000c. Brazilian player . . . 90 1·00
3298 4000c. South Korean player 1·00 1·10
3299 5000c. Yokohama International Stadium, Japan (horiz) . . . . . . 1·25 1·40
3300 6000c. Italian player . . . . 1·50 1·60
3301 11000c. Publicity poster, Brazil, 1950 . . . . . . 2·75 3·25
3302 12000c. Publicity poster, Italy, 1934 . . . . 3·00 3·50
MS3303 Two sheets. (a) 77 × 107 mm. 15000c. Geoff Hurst (England), 1966 (43 × 58 mm). (b) 107 × 77 mm. 15000c. Gordon Banks (England), 1970 (58 × 43 mm) Set of 2 sheets . . 8·00 8·50

599 Girl on Pony

2002. Chinese New Year ("Year of the Horse"). Multicoloured.
3304 4000c. Type **599** . . . . . 1·00 1·10
3305 4000c. Girl and caparisoned pony . . . . 1·00 1·10
3306 4000c. Girl with whip and pony . . . . 1·00 1·10
3307 4000c. Girl on hobby horse 1·00 1·10

2002. No. 2159a surch **c 1000**.
3308 1000c. on 1100c. Kente cloth . . . . 3·50 3·50

2002. No. 2458e surch **c2,500**.
3309 2500c. on 800c. *Cyrestis camillus* (butterfly) . . . . 6·00 6·50

602 Crown Prince Willem-Alexander and Princess Maxima of the Netherlands

2002. "Amphilex 2002" International Stamp Exhibition, Amsterdam. Visit of Crown Prince and Princess of the Netherlands. Multicoloured.
3310 6000c. Type **602** . . . . . 1·25 1·40
3311 6000c. Royal couple on wedding day . . . . . . 1·25 1·40
3312 6000c. Standing by windmill 1·25 1·40
3313 6000c. Serenaded by accordionist on wedding day . . . . 1·25 1·40
3314 6000c. Meeting crowds . . . 1·25 1·40
3315 6000c. Kissing on wedding day . . . . 1·25 1·40

603 "Trying to retrieve a Ball caught in a Tree"

2002. Japanese Paintings by Katsukawa Shunsho. Multicoloured.
MS3316 170 × 123 mm. 9000c. Type **603**; 9000c. "Listening to a Cuckoo in the Bedroom"; 9000c. "Holding a Cage filled with Fireflies for a Woman to read a Book" . . . . 6·50 7·50
MS3317 170 × 123 mm. 9000c. "Mother and Child taking a Tub-bath while Woman holds a Revolving Lantern"; 9000c. "Strips of Paper with Wishes and Poems are Tied on a Bamboo"; 9000c. "Women enjoying the Cool Air on a Boat" . . . . 6·50 7·50
MS3318 170 × 123 mm. 9000c. "Celebrating Feast of the Chrysanthemum"; 9000c. "Looking out for Coloured Leaves"; 9000c. "Mother reading Picture Book while sitting at a Foot-warmer" . . . . 6·50 7·50
MS3319 Four sheets, each 95 × 105 mm. (a) 15000c. "Three Women decorating a Gate with Twigs of Holly on the Day before the Setting-in of the Spring". (b) 15000c. Woman looking at flowering plant in pot. (c) 15000c. Woman at writing desk. (d) 15000c. Woman pulling down blind Set of 4 sheets . . . . . 14·00 16·00

Nos. **MS**3316/19a show details of paintings on silk "Activities of Women in the Twelve Months".
Nos. **MS**3319b/d show details from triptych "Snow, Moonlight and Flowers".

604 Scout hiking

2002. 20th World Scout Jamboree, Thailand. Multicoloured.
MS3320 109 × 90 mm. 6500c. Type **604**; 6500c. Scout hiking (standing on horizon); 6500c. Campfire and tent; 6500c. Scout tying knot . . . . 7·00 7·50
MS3321 99 × 71 mm. 15000c. Ghanian scout (vert) . . . . . 4·00 4·25

605 Mt. Tateyama, Japan

2002. International Year of Mountains. Multicoloured.
MS3322 105 × 90 mm. 6000c. Type **605**; 6000c. Mt. Shivling, India; 6000c. Wong Leng, Hong Kong; 6000c. Mt. Blanc, France 5·50 6·00
MS3323 100 × 72 mm. 15000c. Mt. Fuji, Japan . . . . 4·25 4·50

606 Lindbergh and Ryan NYP Special *Spirit of St. Louis*

2002. 75th Anniv of First Solo Trans-Atlantic Flight. Multicoloured.
MS3324 171 × 129 mm. 8500c. Type **606**; 8500c. Charles and Anne Lindbergh in *Spirit of St. Louis* . . . . 5·50 6·00
MS3325 114 × 81 mm. 15000c. Charles Lindbergh (vert) . . . 4·25 4·50

607 Variable Sunbird

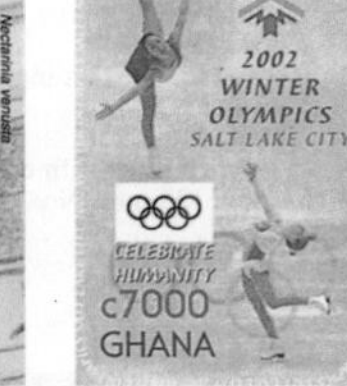

609 Ice Skaters

2002. Year of Eco Tourism. Multicoloured.
MS3326 116 × 125 mm. 4000c. Type **607**; 4000c. Leopard; 4000c. Kob (antelope); 4000c. African buffalo; 4000c. Chimpanzee; 4000c. Lesser bushbaby . . . . 6·50 7·00
MS3327 81 × 97 mm. 12000c. African elephant . . . . 4·25 4·25

2002. Queen Elizabeth the Queen Mother Commemoration. Nos. 2191/5 (95th Birthday) surch **C3000**.
3328 3000c. on 600c. brown, light brown and black . . . . 1·00 1·10
3329 3000c. on 600c. multicoloured . . . . . . 1·00 1·10
3330 3000c. on 600c. multicoloured . . . . . . 1·00 1·10
3331 3000c. on 600c. multicoloured . . . . . . 1·00 1·10
MS3332 102 × 127 mm. 20000c. on 2500c. multicoloured . . . . . . 7·00 7·00
The sheetlet and miniature sheet margins have black borders and are overprinted **IN MEMORIAM 1900–2002**.

2002. Winter Olympic Games, Salt Lake City. Multicoloured.
3333 7000c. Type **609** . . . . . 2·25 2·50
3334 7000c. Skier in aerials competition . . . . . . 2·25 2·50
MS3335 88 × 119 mm. Nos. 3333/4 4·50 5·00

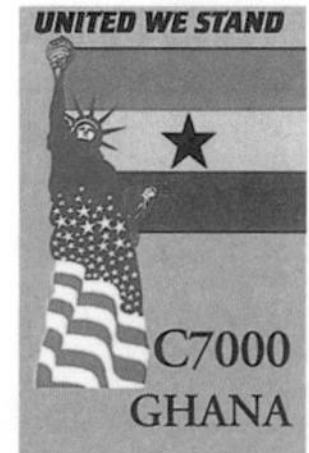

610 US Flag as Statue of Liberty with Ghana Flag

2002. "United We Stand". Support for Victims of 11 September 2001 Terrorist Attacks.
3336 **610** 7000c. multicoloured . . 2·25 2·50

611 Malachite Kingfisher

2002. Birds, Butterflies, Insects and Moths. Multicoloured.
MS3337 160 × 93 mm. 4500c. Type **611**; 4500c. Brown snake eagle ("Brown Harrier-eagle"); 4500c. Heuglin's masked weaver; 4500c. Egyptian plover; 4500c. Swallow-tailed bee eater; 4500c. Black-faced fire-finch . . . . . 7·00 7·50
MS3338 160 × 93 mm. 4500c. *Iolaus menas*; 4500c. *Neptis melicerta*; 4500c. *Cymothoe lucas*; 4500c. *Euphaedra francina*; 4500c. Lilac nymph; 4500c. Mocker swallowtail 7·00 7·50
MS3339 160 × 93 mm. 4500c. *Phymateus viridipes* (bush-hopper); 4500c. *Tomatares citrinus* (ant-lion); 4500c. *Amegilla acraensis* (digger-bee); 4500c. *Mesotopus tarandus* (stag-beetle); 4500c. *Pseudocreobotra wahlbergi* (mantis); 4500c. *Phosphorus jansoni* (longhorn beetle) . . . 7·00 7·50
MS3340 160 × 93 mm. 4500c. *Phiala cunina*; 4500c. *Mazuca strigicincta*; 4500c. Steindachner's emperor moth; 4500c. *Amphicallia pactolicus*; 4500c. Verdant sphinx moth; 4500c. Oleander hawk-moth 7·00 7·50
MS3341 Four sheets, each 83 × 86 mm. (a) 15000c. Rufous fishing owl. (b) 15000c. Giant blue swallowtail. (c) 15000c. *Pseudocreobotra wahlbergi* (mantis nymph). (d) 15000c. African moon-moth Set of 4 sheets . . 14·00 16·00

612 Casting of Net

2002. Edina Bakatue Festival. Multicoloured.
3342 1000c. Type **612** 40 25
3343 2000c. Chief in palanquin 70 70
3344 2500c. Canoe in regatta . . 80 90
3345 3000c. Fishermen in festival boat . . . . 90 1·00
3346 4000c. Opening ritual . . . 1·00 1·10
3347 5000c. Parade of priestesses 1·25 1·40
MS3348 160 × 90 mm. 4000c. As No. 3347; 4000c. As No. 3343; 4000c. As No. 3344; 4000c. As No. 3345; 4000c. As No. 3346; 4000c. Type **612** . . . . 6·00 7·00

613 Home Economics

614 Kofi Annan with Pres. Kufuor at Nobel Prize Award Ceremony

2002. 25th Anniv of Japan Overseas Co-operation Volunteers in Ghana. Multicoloured.
3349 1000c. Type **613** 40 25
3350 1000c. Public health administration 40 25
3351 2000c. Education in science and mathematics 70 70
3352 2500c. Computer technology 80 80
3353 3000c. Judo coaching . . . 90 90
MS3354 172 × 120 mm. 4000c. As No. 3351; 4000c. As No. 3350; 4000c. As No. 3353; 4000c. As No. 3352; 4000c. Type **613** . . 6·00 7·00
Stamps from No. **MS**3354 have the white descriptive inscriptions omitted.

2002. Kofi Annan (United Nations Secretary-General). Multicoloured.
3355 1000c. Type **614** 40 25
3356 2000c. Kofi Annan holding Citation and Nobel Peace Medal 70 70
3357 2500c. Kofi Annan 80 80
3358 3000c. In academic procession, Kwame Nkrumah University, Kumasi 90 90

615 Charlie Chaplin

616 Marlene Dietrich

2003. 25th Death Anniv of Charlie Chaplin (actor and director). Multicoloured.
MS3359 151 × 126 mm. 6500c. Type **615**; 6500c. Wearing dark jacket; 6500c. Wearing pinstriped dungarees; 6500c. Holding Honorary Academy Award, 1972 8·00 8·00

2003. 10th Death Anniv (2002) of Marlene Dietrich (actress and singer). Sheets containing T **616** and similar vert designs showing different portraits.
MS3360 127 × 178 mm. 4500c. × 6 multicoloured . . . . 7·00 7·50
MS3361 76 × 101 mm. 15000c. Holding cigarette . . . . . . 4·00 4·25

617 Popeye alongside Canal

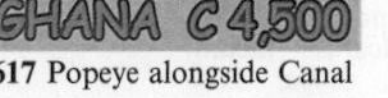

618 "Under the Pagoda Tree"

2003. "Popeye the Sailorman tours Amsterdam". Multicoloured.
MS3362 173 × 202 mm. 4500c. Type **617**; 4500c. Outside Anne Frank's House; 4500c. At Restaurant Row; 4500c. Downtown, carrying Olive Oyl; 4500c. At Central Station; 4500c. With telescope, by windmill . . 6·50 7·00
MS3363 136 × 93 mm. 15000c. Eating spinach (50 × 75 mm) 3·75 4·25

2003. Chinese New Year ("Year of the Ram").
MS3364 **618** 141 × 115 mm. 5000c. × 4 multicoloured . . . 6·00 6·50

619 Nana Yaa Asantewaa (Asante warrior)

620 Children holding Drawings ("tomorrow's leaders")

2003. Women Achievers. Multicoloured.
3365 1000c. Type **619** 35 20
3366 2000c. Justice Annie Jiagge (judge) 65 40
3367 2500c. Dr. Esther Ocloo (industrialist) 75 70
3368 3000c. Dr. Efua T. Sutherland (playwright) 80 80
3369 5000c. Rebecca Dedei Aryeetay (womens rights activist) . . . . 1·25 1·50

2003. 60th Anniv of British Council in Ghana. Multicoloured.
3370 1000c. Type **620** 35 20
3371 2000c. Women holding Africawoman newspapers 65 40
3372 2500c. Singers on stage ("partners in culture") . . 75 70
3373 3000c. People reading in library ("window on the world") 80 80
3374 5000c. Footballers and coach ("leadership through sport") . . . . . 1·25 1·50

621 Queen Elizabeth II wearing Diadem

623 Romain Maes (1935)

622 Ryan NYP Special *Spirit of St. Louis*

2003. 50th Anniv of Coronation. Multicoloured.
MS3375 156 × 94 mm. 10000c. Type **621**; 10000c. Queen wearing blue dress and hat; 10000c. Wearing Garter robes . . . . 7·00 7·50
MS3376 76 × 106 mm. 20000c. Wearing Garter robes (different) 4·00 4·25

2003. Centenary of Powered Flight. Multicoloured.
MS3377 185 × 116 mm. 7000c. Type **622**; 7000c. Lockheed Vega V *Winnie Mae* (first solo round-the-world flight, 1933); 7000c. Heinkel He 178 (first turbo-jet aircraft, 1939); 7000c. Bell XS-1 rocket airplane (first manned supersonic flight, 1947) . . . . 7·00 7·50
MS3378 106 × 76 mm. 20000c. Dr. Robert Goddard and first liquid-fuelled rocket . . . . . 4·00 4·25

2003. Centenary of Tour de France Cycle Race. Designs showing past winners. Multicoloured.
MS3379 7000c. Type **623**; 7000c. Sylvere Maes (1936); 7000c. Roger Lapebie (1937); 7000c. Gino Bartali (1938) . . . . 6·00 6·50
MS3380 107 × 75 mm. 20000c. Henri Pelissier (1923) . . . . 4·00 4·25

624 Cadillac Sixty Special (1941)

2003. Centenary of General Motors Cadillac. Multicoloured.
MS3381 126 × 176 mm. 7000c. Type **624**; 7000c. Eldorado (1953); 7000c. Eldorado Brougham (1957); 7000c. Eldorado Convertible (1959) . . . . . . 7·00 7·50
MS3382 90 × 125 mm. 20000c. Early Cadillac . . . . 4·00 4·25

625 Corvette (1962)

2003. 50th Anniv of General Motors Chevrolet Corvette. Multicoloured.

MS3383 126×152 mm. 7000c. Type **625**; 7000c. Corvette Stingray (1963); 7000c. Corvette Stingray (1964); 7000c. Corvette (1968) . . . . 7·00 7·50

MS3384 126×89 mm. 20000c. Corvette Stingray (1966) . . . 4·00 4·25

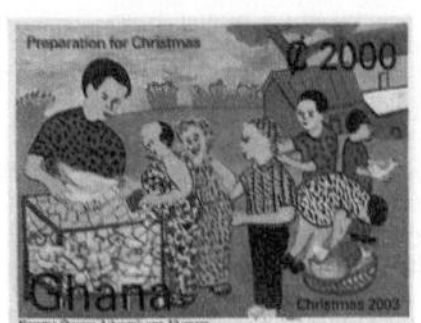

626 "Preparation for Christmas" (Kwame Owusu Aduomi)

2003. Christmas. Children's Paintings. Multicoloured.

3385	2000c. Type **626**	25	30
3386	4000c. "Typical Christmas Present" (Thomas Kyeremateng) (vert) . . .	50	55
3387	4500c. "Making Merry at Christmas" (Samuel Baffoe Maison)	55	60
3388	5000c. "Christmas is Here" (Patrick Annan)	60	65

627 Female Mandrill **628** Richie Jen

2004. Chinese New Year ("Year of the Monkey"). Multicoloured.

MS3389 137×172 mm. 5000c. Type **627**; 5000c. Mueller's gibbon; 5000c. Red howler monkey . . . . 1·80 1·80

2004. Chinese Actors and Singers. Multicoloured.

MS3390 176×126 mm. 5000c. Type **628**; 5000c. Richie Jen wearing black; 5000c.Wearing gold helmet; 5000c. With moustache; 5000c. In Elixir of Love (wearing brown hat); 5000c. Wearing red jacket . . . . . . 3·00 3·00

MS3391 176×126 mm. 5000c. Ray Lui (wearing jacket and tie); 5000c. With shaven head; 5000c. Wearing hood; 5000c. Wearing spotted shirt; 5000c. Wearing pigtail; 5000c. As Xiang Yu in The Great Emperor's Concubine . . 3·00 3·00

MS3392 176×126 mm. 5000c. Jiang Wen (with head tilted left); 5000c. With copper pot on head; 5000c. Looking to left; 5000c. Wearing brown jacket; 5000c. Wearing black T-shirt; 5000c. Wearing blue T-shirt . . . . 3·00 3·00

No. **MS**3390 shows Richie Jen (singer and actor), **MS**3391 Ray Lui (actor) and **MS**3392 Jiang Wen (actor).

629 Edwene Asa

2004. Kente Designs. Multicoloured.

3393	2000c. Type **629**	25	30
3394	4000c. Fatia Fata Nkruma	50	55
3395	4500c. Asam Takra	55	60
3396	5000c. Toku Akra Ntoma	60	65
3397	6000c. Sika Futuro	75	80

630 Exodus from Notsie

...stival of Hogbetsotso. Multicoloured.

	...0c. Type **630**	25	30
	...0c. Misego Dance . . .	50	55
	...00c. Royal stools carried in procession	55	60
3401	5000c. Man pouring libation	60	65
3402	6000c. King carried aloft . .	75	80

MS3403 190×145 mm. 3000c. Two men pouring libation; 3000c. Togbe Adeladza II, Paramount Chief of Anlo; 3000c. Display of traditional symbols of wealth; 3000c. Exodus from Notsie; 3000c. Procession of the royalty; 3000c. Royalty at Durbar; 3000c. Ewe cultural dance; 3000c. Woman with symbols of bountiful harvest; 3000c. Royal stools carried in procession (different) . . . . . 3·25 3·25

631 Girl Scout

2004. 25th Death Anniv of Norman Rockwell (artist). Multicoloured.

MS3404 180×116 mm. 7000c. Type **631**; 7000c. Cub scout (with tartan neckerchief); 7000c. Boy scout; 7000c. Cub scout (with yellow and mauve neckerchief) 3·50 3·50

MS3405 87×94 mm. 20000c. "Good Friends" . . . . 2·10 2·10

No. **MS**3404 shows details from Boy Scout calendar of 1971.

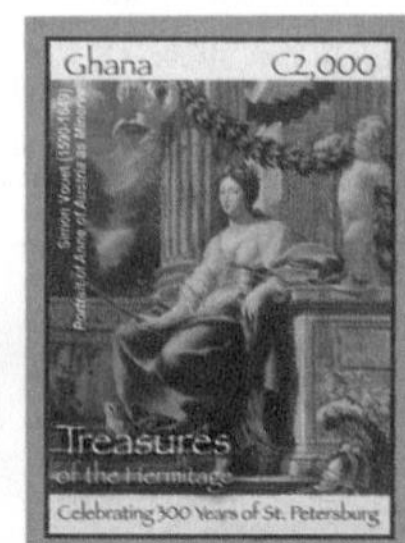

632 "Portrait of Anne of Austria as Minerva" (Simon Vouet)

2004. 300th Anniv of St. Petersburg. "Treasures of the Hermitage". Multicoloured.

3406	2000c. Type **632**	25	30
3407	3000c. "Lasciviousness" (Pompeo Girolamo Batoni)	35	40
3408	10000c. "Allegory of Faith" (Moretto da Brescia) . . .	1·20	1·30

MS3409 162×142 mm. 6500c. "Allegory of the Arts" (Bernardo Strozzi); 6500c. "Vulcan's Forge" (Luca Giordano); 6500c. "Daedalus and Icarus" (detail) (Charles Lebrun); 6500c. "The Infant Hercules Strangling Serpents in His Cradle" (Sir Joshua Reynolds) . . . . 3·25 3·25

MS3410 Two sheets. (a) 55×78 mm. 20000c. "Cupid Undoing Venus's Belt" (Sir Joshua Reynolds). (b) 78×55 mm. 20000c. "Perseus Liberating Andromeda" (Rubens). Both Imperf. Set of 2 sheets . . 4·25 4·25

633 "Jacqueline in a Black Scarf"

2004. 30th Death Anniv of Pablo Picasso (artist) (2003). Multicoloured.

MS3411 154×154 mm. 6500c. Type **633**; 6500c. "Portrait of Olga"; 6500c. "Woman in White (Sara Murphy)"; 6500c. "Portrait of Dora Maar" . . . .

MS3412 45×68 mm. 16000c. "Portrait of the Artist's Sister, Lola". Imperf . . . . 3·20 3·20

634 "Head of a Peasant Woman"

2004. Death Centenary of James Whistler (artist) (2003). Multicoloured.

3413	2000c. Type **634**	25	30
3414	4000c. "The Master Smith of Lyme Regis"	50	55
3415	5000c. "The Little Rose of Lyme Regis"	60	65
3416	6000c. "Arrangement in Grey: Portrait of a Painter (Self-portrait)"	75	80

MS3417 128×130 mm. 7500c. "Rose and Silver: La Princesse du pays de la porcelaine"; 7500c. "Variations in Flesh Colour and Green, The Balcony"; 7500c. "Caprice in Purple and Gold: The Golden Screen" (detail); 7500c. "Purple and Rose: The Lange Lijzen of the Six Marks" . . . 3·50 3·50

MS3418 82×102 mm. 20000c. "Harmony in Green and Rose: The Music Room" (horiz) . . 2·10 2·10

635 Jacques Rogge and Olympic Flame

2004. Olympic Games, Athens. Multicoloured.

3419	500c. Type **635**	10	10
3420	800c. Abedi Ayew Pele (footballer)	10	10
3421	7000c. Margaret Simpson	85	90
3422	10000c. Athletes in ancient Greek art – 384 meter diaulos (horiz)	1·20	1·30

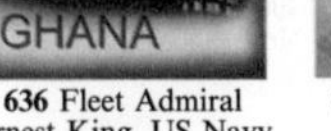

636 Fleet Admiral Ernest King, US Navy **638** Deng Xiaoping

637 Martin Luther King

2004. 60th Anniv of D-Day Landings. Multicoloured.

MS3423 155×108 mm. 8000c. Type **636**; 8000c. General William Lee, US Airborne; 8000c. Lt Commander John Bulkeley, US Naval Reserve; 8000c. Admiral Sir Bertram Ramsey, Royal Navy 4·25 4·50

MS424 105×77 mm. 20000c. Rear Admiral Alan Kirk, US Navy (horiz) . . . . 2·40 2·50

2004. European Football Championship 2004, Portugal. Multicoloured designs as T **407** of Dominica.

MS3425 147×85 mm. 7500c. Gerd Müller; 7500c. Presentation of the European Cup; 7500c. Franz Beckenbauer; 7500c. Heysel Stadium, Brussels . . . . . . 3·75 4·00

MS3426 97×85 mm. 20000c. Germany, 1972 (50×38 mm) 2·40 2·50

2004. 25th Anniv of the Pontificate of Pope John Paul II. Sheet 163×152 mm containing horiz designs as T **408** of Dominica. Multicoloured.

MS3427 6000c. Pope in Ghana, 1980; 6000c. Pope receiving gift, Ghana, 1982; 6000c. Pope in 1991; 6000c. Pope giving blessing, 2000; 6000c. Pope giving blessing to children, 2001 . . . . 3·75 4·00

2004. United Nations International Year of Peace. Sheet 137×77 mm containing T **637** and similar horiz designs showing Martin Luther King. Multicoloured.

MS3428 10000c. Type **637**; 10000c. Making speech; 10000c. Martin Luther King (looking to left) 3·50 3·75

2004. Birth Centenary of Deng Xiaoping (Chinese leader). Sheet 98×68 mm.

MS3429 **638** 20000c. multicoloured 2·40 2·50

639 Zebra Bullhead Shark

2004. Sharks. Multicoloured.

MS3430 137×108 mm. 7500c. Type **639**; 7500c. Swellshark; 7500c. Port Jackson shark; 7500c. Leopard shark . . . . 3·75 4·00

MS3431 95×65 mm. 20000c. California horn shark . . . . 2·40 2·50

640 Lion Cubs

2004. Lions. Multicoloured.

3432	5000c. Type **640**	60	65
3433	5000c. Lions standing in water	60	65
3434	5000c. Male lion	60	65
3435	5000c. Lioness with cubs . .	60	65

MS3436 155×125 mm. Nos. 3432/5, each×2 . . . . 4·75 5·00

641 *Boletus badius*

2004. Mushrooms. Multicoloured.

3437	500c. Type **641**	10	10
3438	3000c. *Clitocybe nebularis*	35	40
3439	5000c. *Amanita muscaria* . .	60	65
3440	8000c. *Russula vesca*	95	1·00

MS3441 115×135 mm. 7500c. *Boletus parasiticus* (vert); 7500c. *Cortinarius armillatus* (vert); 7500c. *Gymnopilus spectabilis* (vert); 7500c. *Cortinarius flexipes* (vert) . . . . 3·75 4·00

MS3442 67×95 mm. 20000c. *Chlorosplenium aeruginosum* (vert) 2·40 2·10

POSTAGE DUE STAMPS

1958. Postage Due stamps of Gold Coast optd **GHANA** and bar.

D 9	D 1	1d. black	10	30
D10		2d. black	10	30
D11		3d. black	10	30
D12		6d. black	15	65
D13		1s. black	20	1·50

D 3

1958.
D14 D 3 1d. red 10 30
D15 2d. green 10 30
D16 3d. orange 10 30
D17 6d. blue 10 50
D18 1s. violet . . . . 15 2·00

1965. Surch **Ghana New Currency 19th July. 1965.** and value.
D19 D 3 1p. on 1d. 10 60
D20 2p. on 2d. 10 80
D21 3p. on 3d. 10 80
D22 6p. on 6d. . . . . . . 10 1·75
D23 12p. on 1s. . . . . . . 15 2·25

1968. Nos. D20/2 additionally surch.
D24 D 3 1½n.p. on 2p. on 2d. . . 5·50 4·25
D25 2½n.p. on 3p. on 3d. . . 1·00 5·00
D26 5n.p. on 6p. on 6d. . . 1·25

1970. Inscr in new currency.
D27 D 3 1n.p. red . . . . 1·25 4·50
D28 1½n.p. green . . . . . . 1·50 5·00
D29 2½n.p. orange . . . . . 1·75 6·50
D30 5n.p. blue . . . . 2·50 6·50
D31 10n.p. violet . . . . . . 3·25 8·00

1980. Currency described as "p".
D32 D 3 2p. orange . . . . . . 1·25 4·25
D33 3p. brown . . . . 1·25 4·25

GIBRALTAR Pt. 1

A British colony at the W. entrance to the Mediterranean.

1886. 12 pence = 1 shilling;
20 shillings = 1 pound.
1971. 100 (new) pence = 1 pound.

1886. Stamps of Bermuda (Queen Victoria) optd **GIBRALTAR**.
1 9 ½d. green . . . . 14·00 7·50
2 1d. red . . . . 55·00 4·25
3 2d. purple . . . . £100 75·00
4 2½d. blue . . . . £140 3·25
5 4d. orange . . . . £140 90·00
6 6d. lilac £225 £190
7 1s. brown £425 £350

2 7

1886. Various frames.
39 2 ½d. green . . . . 6·00 1·75
40 1d. red . . . . 6·50 50
10 2d. purple . . . . 30·00 20·00
42 2½d. blue . . . . 30·00 50
12 4d. orange . . . . 75·00 75·00
13 6d. lilac £100 £100
14 1s. brown £200 £180

1889. Surch with new value in **CENTIMOS**.
15 2 5c. on ½d. green . . . . . . 6·00 20·00
16 10c. on 1d. red . . . . . . 12·00 10·00
17 25c. on 2d. purple . . . . . 4·75 7·50
18 25c. on 2½d. blue . . . . . 20·00 2·25
19 40c. on 4d. orange . . . . . 50·00 70·00
20 50c. on 6d. lilac . . . . . 55·00 70·00
21 75c. on 1s. brown . . . . . 55·00 65·00

1889.
22 7 5c. green . . . . 4·50 80
23 10c. red . . . . 4·50 50
24 20c. green and brown . . . . 42·00 18·00
25 20c. green . . . . 12·00 70·00
26 25c. blue . . . . 19·00 70
27 40c. orange . . . . 3·75 2·75
28 50c. lilac . . . . 3·25 2·00
29 75c. green . . . . 32·00 32·00
30 1p. brown . . . . 75·00 20·00
31 1p. brown and blue . . . . . 4·75 5·50
32 2p. black and red . . . . . 11·00 30·00
33 5p. grey . . . . 42·00 £100

1898. As 1886.
41 2 2d. purple and blue . . . . . 22·00 1·75
43 4d. brown and green . . . . 18·00 5·50
44 6d. violet and red . . . . . 42·00 21·00
45 1s. brown and red . . . . . 38·00 16·00

8 9

1903.
66 8 ½d. green . . . . 4·50 1·75
57c 1d. purple on red . . . . . 5·00 85
58a 2d. green and red . . . . . 8·50 6·00
49 2½d. purple and black on blue . . . . 4·75 60
60a 6d. purple and violet . . . 30·00 12·00
61 1s. black and red . . . . . 50·00 40·00
62 9 2s. green and blue . . . . . 80·00 £100
53 4s. purple and green . . . . 85·00 £150
54 8s. purple and black on blue £120 £150
55 £1 purple and black on red £500 £600

1907.
67 8 1d. red . . . . 5·50 60
68 2d. grey . . . . 8·00 11·00
69 2½d. blue . . . . 5·50 1·60
70 6d. purple £130 £375
71 1s. black on green . . . . . 23·00 21·00
72 9 2s. purple and blue on blue 50·00 48·00
73 4s. black and red £110 £150
74 8s. purple and green £190 £200

1912. As T **8/9**, but portrait of King George V. (3d. A. Inscr "3 PENCE". B. Inscr "THREE PENCE").
89 ½d. green . . . . 1·50 1·50
90 1d. red . . . . 1·75 1·00
91a 1½d. brown . . . . 1·75 30
93 2d. grey . . . . 1·25 1·25
79 2½d. blue . . . . 7·00 2·00
95a 3d. blue (A) . . . . 2·50 1·50
109 3d. blue (B) . . . . 7·50 2·00
97a 6d. purple . . . . 1·60 3·50
81 1s. black on green . . . . . 9·00 3·25
102a 1s. olive and black . . . . 14·00 12·00
82 2s. purple and blue on blue 26·00 3·50
103 2s. brown and black . . . . 9·50 30·00
104 2s.6d. green and black . . . 9·50 18·00
83 4s. black and red . . . . . 32·00 55·00
105 5s. red and black . . . . . 15·00 50·00
84 8s. purple and green . . . . 80·00 95·00
106 10s. blue and black . . . . 32·00 70·00
85 £1 purple and black on red £130 £200
107 £1 orange and black £140 £190
108 £5 violet and black £1300 £4250

1918. Optd **WAR TAX**.
86 ½d. green (No. 89) . . . . . . 1·00 1·75

13 The Rock of Gibraltar

1931.
110 13 1d. red . . . . 2·50 2·50
111 1½d. brown . . . . 1·75 2·25
112 2d. grey . . . . 6·50 1·75
113 3d. blue . . . . 5·50 3·00

1935. Silver Jubilee. As T **10a** of Gambia.
114 2d. blue and black . . . . . 1·60 2·50
115 3d. brown and blue . . . . 3·25 3·50
116 6d. green and blue . . . . . 9·50 12·00
117 1s. grey and purple . . . . 10·00 12·00

1937. Coronation. As T **10b** of Gambia.
118 ½d. green 25 50
119 2d. grey . . . . 1·50 3·25
120 3d. blue . . . . 2·75 3·25

14 King George VI
15 Rock of Gibraltar

1938. King George VI.
121 14 ½d. green 10 40
122b 15 1d. brown 50 60
123 1½d. red . . . . 35·00 75
123b – 1½d. violet . . . . 75 1·50
124a – 2d. grey . . . . 2·50 35
124c – 2d. red 50 60
125b – 3d. blue 50 30
125c – 5d. orange . . . . 1·00 1·25
126b – 6d. red and violet . . . . 4·75 1·75
127b – 1s. black and green . . . 3·25 4·25
128b – 2s. black and brown . . . 5·00 6·50
129b – 5s. black and red . . . . 18·00 17·00
130a – 10s. black and blue . . . 38·00 25·00
131 14 £1 orange . . . . 38·00 45·00

DESIGNS—HORIZ: 2d. The Rock (North side); 3d., 5d. Europa Point; 6d. Moorish Castle; 1s. South-port Gate; 2s. Eliott Memorial; 5s. Government House; 10s. Catalan Bay.

1946. Victory. As T **11a** of Gambia.
132 ½d. green . . . . 10 1·00
133 3d. blue . . . . 50 1·25

1948. Silver Wedding. As T **11b/11c** of Gambia.
134 ½d. green . . . . 80 2·00
135 £1 orange . . . . 55·00 70·00

1949. U.P.U. As T **11d/11g** of Gambia.
136 2d. red . . . . 1·00 1·25
137 3d. blue . . . . 2·00 1·50
138 6d. purple . . . . 1·25 2·00
139 1s. green . . . . 1·00 3·25

1950. Inauguration of Legislative Council. Optd **NEW CONSTITUTION 1950.**
140 2d. red (No. 124c) . . . . . . 30 1·50
141 3d. blue (No. 125b) . . . . . 65 1·00
142 6d. red and violet (No. 126b) 75 2·00
143 1s. black and green (No. 127b) . . . . 75 1·75

1953. Coronation. As T **11h** of Gambia.
144 ½d. black and green . . . . 50 1·50

24 Cargo and Passenger Wharves

1953.
145 24 ½d. blue and green . . . 15 30
146 – 1d. green . . . . 1·50 40
147 – 1½d. black . . . . 1·00 1·25
148 – 2d. brown . . . . 1·75 60
149a – 2½d. red . . . . 4·00 1·00
150 – 3d. blue . . . . 4·00 10
151 – 4d. blue . . . . 4·25 3·50
152 – 5d. purple . . . . . . 1·00 1·00
153 – 6d. black and blue . . . 1·50 1·00
154a – 1s. blue and brown . . . 40 80
155a – 2s. orange and violet . . 23·00 4·50
156 – 5s. brown . . . . 28·00 12·00
157 – 10s. brown and blue . . . 45·00 35·00
158 – £1 red and yellow . . . . 45·00 40·00

DESIGNS—HORIZ: 1d. South view from Straits; 1½d. Gibraltar Fish Canneries; 2d. Southport Gate; 2½d. Sailing in the Bay; 3d. Liner; 4d. Coaling wharf; 5d. Airport; 6d. Europa Point; 1s. Straits from Buena Vista; 2s. Rosia Bay and Straits; 5s. Main entrance, Government House. VERT: 10s. Tower of Homage, Moorish Castle; £1 Arms of Gibraltar.

1954. Royal Visit. As No. 150, but inscr "ROYAL VISIT 1954".
159 3d. blue 20 20

38 Gibraltar Candytuft
40 Rock and Badge of Gibraltar Regiment

1960.
160 38 ½d. purple and green . . . 15 50
161 – 1d. black and green . . . 20 10
162 – 2d. blue and brown . . . 70 20
163a – 2½d. black and blue . . . 65 30
164 – 3d. blue and orange . . . 30 10
199 – 4d. brown and turquoise . . 30 1·75
166 – 6d. brown and green . . . 70 70
167 – 7d. blue and red . . . . 1·75 1·75
168 – 9d. blue and turquoise . . 1·00 1·00
169 – 1s. brown and green . . . 1·50 70
170 – 2s. brown and blue . . . 16·00 2·75
171 – 5s. blue and green . . . . 8·00 6·00
172 – 10s. yellow and blue . . . 20·00 13·00
173 40 £1 black and brown . . . 15·00 12·00

DESIGNS (As Type **38**):—HORIZ: 1d. Moorish Castle; 2d. St George's Hall; 3d. The Rock by moonlight; 4d. Catalan Bay; 1s. Barbary ape; 2s. Barbary Partridge; 5s. Blue Rock Thrush. VERT: 2½d. The keys; 6d. Map of Gibraltar; 7d. Air terminal; 9d. American War Memorial; 10s. Rock lily.

1963. Freedom from Hunger. As T **20a** of Gambia.
174 9d. sepia . . . . 3·75 1·50

1963. Centenary of Red Cross. As T **20b** of Gambia.
175 1d. red and black . . . . . 1·00 1·75
176 9d. red and blue . . . . . . 5·00 3·75

1964. 400th Birth Anniv of Shakespeare. As T **22a** of Gambia.
177 7d. bistre 50 20

1964. New Constitution. Nos. 164 and 166 optd **NEW CONSTITUTION 1964.**
178 3d. blue and orange 20 10
179 6d. sepia and green 20 60

NEW CONSTITUTION 1964.

44 I.T.U. Emblem

1965. Centenary of I.T.U.
180 44 4d. green and yellow . . . 2·00 50
181 2s. green and blue . . . . 5·50 3·25

45 I.C.Y. Emblem

1965. I.C.Y.
182 45 ½d. green and lavender . . 20 2·25
183 4d. purple and turquoise 70 50
The value of the ½d. stamp is shown as "1/2".

46 Winston Churchill and St. Paul's Cathedral in Wartime

1966. Churchill Commemoration.
184 46 ½d. blue . . . . 20 2·25
185 1d. green 30 10
186 4d. brown . . . . 1·25 10
187 9d. violet . . . . 1·25 2·50

47 Footballer's Legs, Ball and Jules Rimet Cup

1966. World Cup Football Championships.
188 47 2½d. multicoloured . . . . 75 1·00
189 6d. multicoloured . . . . 1·00 50

53 Red Seabream

1966. European Sea Angling Championships. Gibraltar.
190 53 4d. red, blue and black . . 30 10
191 – 7d. red, green and black 30 70
192 – 1s. brown, green and black 50 30

DESIGNS—HORIZ: 7d. Red scorpionfish. VERT: 1s. Stone bass.

54 W.H.O. Building

1966. Inauguration of W.H.O. Headquarters, Geneva.
193 54 6d. black, green and blue 2·75 1·75
194 9d. black, purple and ochre 3·25 1·75

56 "Our Lady of Europa"

1966. Centenary of Re-enthronement of "Our Lady of Europa".
195 56 2s. blue and black 30 80

56a "Education"

56b "Science"

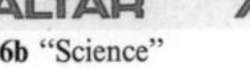
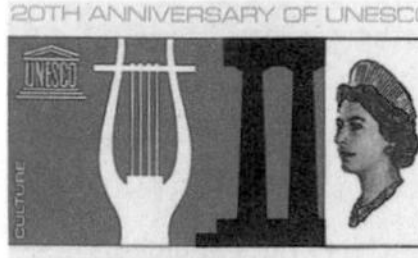

56c "Culture"

1966. 20th Anniv of UNESCO.

No.	Type	Description	Unused	Used
196	**56a**	2d. multicoloured	35	10
197	**56b**	7d. yellow, violet and olive	1·50	10
198	**56c**	5s. black, purple & orge	3·50	3·00

57 H.M.S. "Victory"

1967. Multicoloured.

No.	Type	Description	Unused	Used
200		½d. Type **57**	10	20
201		1d. "Arab" (early steamer)	10	10
202		2d. H.M.S. "Carmania" (merchant cruiser)	15	10
203		2½d. "Mons Calpe" (ferry)	40	30
204		3d. "Canberra" (liner)	20	10
205		4d. H.M.S. "Hood" (battle cruiser)	30	10
205a		5d. "Mirror" (cable ship)	2·00	55
206		6d. Xebec (sailing vessel)	30	50
207		7d. "Amerigo Vespucci" (Italian cadet ship)	30	60
208		9d. "Raffaello" (liner)	30	1·00
209		1s. "Royal Katherine" (galleon)	30	35
210		2s. H.M.S. "Ark Royal" (aircraft carrier, 1937)	3·50	2·50
211		5s. H.M.S. "Dreadnought" (nuclear submarine)	3·50	7·00
212		10s. "Neuralia" (liner)	14·00	23·00
213		£1 "Mary Celeste" (sailing vessel)	14·00	23·00

58 Aerial Ropeway

1967. International Tourist Year. Multicoloured.

No.	Type	Description	Unused	Used
214		7d. Type **58**	15	10
215		9d. Shark fishing (horiz)	15	10
216		1s. Skin-diving (horiz)	20	15

59 Mary, Joseph and Child Jesus

1967. Christmas. Multicoloured.

No.	Type	Description	Unused	Used
217		2d. Type **59**	15	10
218		6d. Church window (vert)	15	10

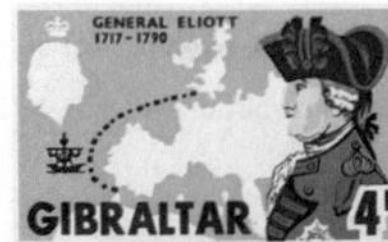

61 General Eliott and Route Map

1967. 250th Birth Anniv of General Eliott. Mult.

No.	Type	Description	Unused	Used
[illegible]		4d. Type **61**	15	10
		9d. Heathfield Tower and Monument, Sussex	15	10
		General Eliott (vert)	15	10
		s. Eliott directing rescue operations (55×21 mm)	25	50

65 Lord Baden-Powell

1968. 60th Anniv of Gibraltar Scout Association.

No.	Type	Description	Unused	Used
223	**65**	4d. buff and violet	15	10
224	–	7d. ochre and green	15	20
225	–	9d. blue, orange and black	15	30
226	–	1s. yellow and green	15	30

DESIGNS: 7d. Scout flag over the Rock; 9d. Tent, Scouts and salute; 1s. Scout badges.

66 Nurse and W.H.O. Emblem

1968. 20th Anniv of W.H.O. Multicoloured.

No.	Type	Description	Unused	Used
227		2d. Type **66**	10	15
228		4d. Doctor and W.H.O. emblem	10	10

68 King John signing Magna Carta

70 Shepherd, Lamb and Star

1968. Human Rights Year.

No.	Type	Description	Unused	Used
229	**68**	1s. orange, brown and gold	15	10
230	–	2s. myrtle and gold	15	20

DESIGN: 2s. "Freedom" and Rock of Gibraltar.

1968. Christmas. Multicoloured.

No.	Type	Description	Unused	Used
231		4d. Type **70**	10	10
232		9d. Mary holding Holy Child	15	20

72 Parliament Houses

1969. Commonwealth Parliamentary Association Conference.

No.	Type	Description	Unused	Used
233	**72**	4d. green and gold	10	10
234	–	9d. violet and gold	10	10
235	–	2s. red, gold and blue	15	20

DESIGNS—HORIZ: 9d. Parliamentary emblem and outline of "The Rock". VERT: 2s. Clock Tower, Westminster (Big Ben) and Arms of Gibraltar.

75 Silhouette of Rock and Queen Elizabeth II

1969. New Constitution.

No.	Type	Description	Unused	Used
236	**75**	½d. gold and orange	10	10
237		5d. silver and green	20	10
238		7d. silver and purple	20	10
239		5s. silver and blue	65	1·10

77 Soldier and Cap Badge, Royal Anglian Regiment, 1969

80 "Madonna of the Chair" (detail, Raphael)

1969. Military Uniforms (1st series). Multicoloured.

No.	Type	Description	Unused	Used
240		1d. Royal Artillery Officer, 1758, and modern cap badge	15	10
241		6d. Type **77**	20	15
242		9d. Royal Engineers' Artificer, 1786, and modern cap badge	30	15
243		2s. Private, Fox's Marines, 1704, and modern Royal Marines' cap badge	75	70

See also Nos. 248/51, 290/3, 300/303, 313/16, 331/4, 340/3 and 363/6.

1969. Christmas. Multicoloured.

No.	Type	Description	Unused	Used
244		5d. Type **80**	10	35
245		7d. "Virgin and Child" (detail, Morales)	20	35
246		1s. "The Virgin of the Rocks" (detail, Leonardo da Vinci)	20	40

83 Europa Point

88 Stamp and Rock of Gibraltar

1970. Europa Point.

No.	Type	Description	Unused	Used
247	**83**	2s. multicoloured	45	30

1970. Military Uniforms (2nd series). As T **77**. Multicoloured.

No.	Type	Description	Unused	Used
248		2d. Royal Scots Officer (1839) and cap badge	25	10
249		5d. South Wales Borderers Private (1763) and cap badge	35	10
250		7d. Queen's Royal Regiment Private (1742) and cap badge	35	10
251		2s. Royal Irish Rangers piper (1969) and cap badge	1·00	90

1970. "Philympia 70" Stamp Exhibition, London.

No.	Type	Description	Unused	Used
252	**88**	1s. red and green	15	10
253	–	2s. blue and mauve	25	65

DESIGN: 2s. Stamp and Moorish Castle.

The stamps shown in the designs are well-known varieties with values omitted.

90 "The Virgin and Mary" (stained-glass window, Gabriel Loire)

1970. Christmas.

No.	Type	Description	Unused	Used
254	**90**	2s. multicoloured	30	40

91 Saluting Battery, Rosia

92 Saluting Battery, Rosia, Modern View

1971. Decimal Currency.

No.	Type	Description	Unused	Used
255	**91**	½p. multicoloured	20	30
256	**92**	½p. multicoloured	20	30
257	–	1p. multicoloured	80	30
258	–	1p. multicoloured	80	30
259	–	1½p. multicoloured	20	50
260	–	1½p. multicoloured	20	50
317	–	2p. multicoloured	1·25	2·00
318	–	2p. multicoloured	1·25	2·00
263a	–	2½p. multicoloured	20	50
264	–	2½p. multicoloured	20	50
265	–	3p. multicoloured	20	20
266	–	3p. multicoloured	20	20
319	–	4p. multicoloured	1·40	2·25
320	–	4p. multicoloured	1·40	2·25
269	–	5p. multicoloured	35	35
270	–	5p. multicoloured	35	35
271	–	7p. multicoloured	65	65
272	–	7p. multicoloured	65	65
273	–	8p. multicoloured	70	80
274	–	8p. multicoloured	70	80
275	–	9p. multicoloured	70	80
276	–	9p. multicoloured	70	80
277	–	10p. multicoloured	80	80
278	–	10p. multicoloured	80	80
279	–	12½p. multicoloured	1·00	1·75
280	–	12½p. multicoloured	1·00	1·75
281	–	25p. multicoloured	1·10	1·75
282	–	25p. multicoloured	1·10	1·75
283	–	50p. multicoloured	1·25	2·50
284	–	50p. multicoloured	1·25	2·50
285	–	£1 multicoloured	2·00	4·00
286	–	£1 multicoloured	2·00	4·00

DESIGNS: The two versions of each value show the same Gibraltar view taken from an early 19th-century print (first design) or modern photograph (second design): HORIZ: 1p. Prince George of Cambridge Quarters and Trinity Church; 1½p. The Wellington Bust, Alameda Gardens; 2p. Gibraltar from the North Bastion; 2½p. Catalan Bay; 3p. Convent Garden; 4p. The Exchange and Spanish Chapel; 5p. Commercial Square and Library; 7p. South Barracks and Rosia Magazine; 8p. Moorish Mosque and Castle; 9p. Europa Pass Road; 10p. South Barracks from Rosia Bay; 12½p. Southport Gates; 25p. Trooping the Colour, The Alameda. VERT: 50p. Europa Pass Gorge; £1 Prince Edward's Gate.

93

94 Regimental Arms

1971. Coil Stamps.

No.	Type	Description	Unused	Used
287	**93**	½p. orange	15	30
288		1p. blue	15	30
289		2p. green	50	1·10

1971. Military Uniforms (3rd series). As T **77**. Multicoloured.

No.	Type	Description	Unused	Used
290		1p. The Black Watch (1845)	35	30
291		2p. Royal Regimental of Fusiliers (1971)	55	30
292		4p. King's Own Royal Border Regiment (1704)	75	50
293		10p. Devonshire and Dorset Regiment (1801)	2·75	3·00

1971. Presentation of Colours to the Gibraltar Regiment.

No.	Type	Description	Unused	Used
294	**94**	3p. black, gold and red	55	30

95 Nativity Scene

1971. Christmas. Multicoloured.

No.	Type	Description	Unused	Used
295		3p. Type **95**	40	60
296		5p. Mary and Joseph going to Bethlehem	40	65

96 Soldier Artificer, 1773

97 "Our Lady of Europa"

1972. Bicentenary of Royal Engineers in Gibraltar. Multicoloured.

No.	Type	Description	Unused	Used
297		1p. Type **96**	40	60
298		3p. Modern tunneller	50	80
299		5p. Old and new uniforms and badge (horiz)	60	90

1972. Military Uniforms (4th series). As T **77**. Multicoloured.

No.	Type	Description	Unused	Used
300		1p. The Duke of Cornwall's Light Infantry, 1704	50	20
301		3p. King's Royal Rifle Corps, 1830	1·25	40
302		7p. 37th North Hampshire, Officer, 1825	2·00	70
303		10p. Royal Navy, 1972	2·25	1·50

1972. Christmas.

No.	Type	Description	Unused	Used
304	**97**	3p. multicoloured	10	20
305		5p. multicoloured	10	35

98 Keys of Gibraltar and "Narcissus niveus"

1972. Royal Silver Wedding.
306 **98** 5p. red 25 20
307 7p. green 25 20

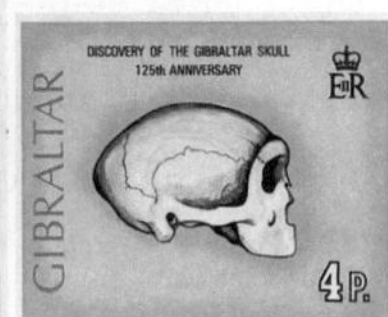

99 Flags of Member Nations and E.E.C. Symbol
100 Skull

1973. Britain's Entry into E.E.C.
308 **99** 5p. multicoloured 40 50
309 10p. multicoloured . . . . 60 1·00

1973. 125th Anniv of Gibraltar Skull Discovery. Multicoloured.
310 4p. Type **100** . . . . 1·25 50
311 6p. Prehistoric man . . . . . 1·50 70
312 10p. Prehistoric family . . . 2·00 1·25
No. 312 is size 40 × 26 mm.

1973. Military Uniforms (5th series). As T **77**. Multicoloured.
313 1p. King's Own Scottish Borderers, 1770 . . . . . 50 50
314 4p. Royal Welsh Fusiliers, 1800 . . . . 1·50 1·10
315 6p. Royal Northumberland Fusiliers, 1736 . . . . . . 2·25 2·25
316 10p. Grenadier Guards, 1898 3·00 4·50

101 "Nativity" (Danckerts)

1973. Christmas.
321 **101** 4p. violet and red 30 15
322 6p. mauve and blue . . . 40 1·10

101a Princess Anne and Captain Mark Phillips

1973. Royal Wedding.
323 **101a** 6p. multicoloured . . . 10 10
324 14p. multicoloured . . . 20 20

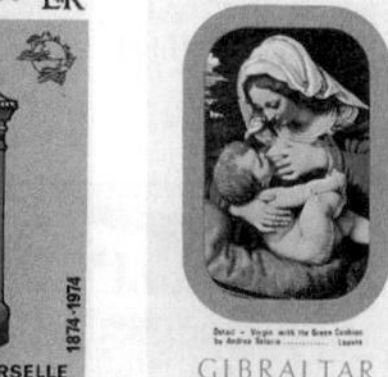

102 Victorian Pillar-box
103 "Madonna with the Green Cushion" (Solario)

1974. Centenary of U.P.U. Multicoloured.
325 2p. Type **102** 15 30
326 6p. Pillar-box of George VI 20 35
327 14p. Pillar-box of Elizabeth II 30 80

Nos. 325/7 also come self-adhesive from booklet panes.

1974. Military Uniforms (6th series). As T **77**. Multicoloured.
331 4p. East Lancashire Regiment, 1742 . . . . . 50 50
332 6p. Somerset Light Infantry, 1833 . . . . 70 70
333 10p. Royal Sussex Regiment, 1790 . . . . 1·00 1·40
334 16p. R.A.F. officer, 1974 . . 2·25 4·00

1974. Christmas. Multicoloured.
335 4p. Type **103** 40 30
336 6p. "Madonna of the Meadow" (Bellini) 60 95

104 Churchill and Houses of Parliament

1974. Birth Centenary of Sir Winston Churchill. Multicoloured.
337 **104** 6p. black, purple and lavender 25 15
338 – 20p. black, brown and red 35 45
MS339 114 × 93 mm. Nos. 337/8 4·50 6·50
DESIGN: 20p. Churchill and "King George V" (battleship).

1975. Military Uniforms (7th series). As T **77**. Multicoloured.
340 4p. East Surrey Regiment, 1846 . . . . 30 20
341 6p. Highland Light Infantry, 1777 . . . . 45 40
342 10p. Coldstream Guards, 1704 . . . . 60 70
343 20p. Gibraltar Regiment, 1974 . . . . 1·10 2·50

105 Girl Guides' Badge

1975. 50th Anniversary of Gibraltar Girl Guides.
346 **105** 5p. gold, blue and violet 25 55
347 7p. gold, brown and light brown 35 60
348 – 15p. silver, black and brown . . . . 50 1·25
No. 348 is as Type **105** but shows a different badge.

106 Child at Prayer
107 Bruges Madonna

1975. Christmas. Multicoloured.
349 6p. Type **106** 40 60
350 6p. Angel with lute 40 60
351 6p. Child singing carols . . . 40 60
352 6p. Three children 40 60
353 6p. Girl at prayer 40 60
354 6p. Boy and lamb 40 60

1975. 500th Birth Anniv of Michelangelo. Multicoloured.
355 6p. Type **107** 20 25
356 9p. Taddei Madonna 20 40
357 15p. Pieta . . . . 30 1·10
Nos. 355/7 also come self-adhesive from booklet panes.

108 Bicentennial Emblem and Arms of Gibraltar
109 The Holy Family

1976. Bicentenary of American Revolution.
361 **108** 25p. multicoloured . . . 50 50
MS362 85 × 133 mm. No. 361 × 4 4·50 7·00

1976. Military Uniforms (8th series). As T **24**. Multicoloured.
363 1p. Suffolk Regiment, 1795 15 20
364 6p. Northamptonshire Regiment, 1779 . . . . . 30 30
365 12p. Lancashire Fusiliers, 1793 . . . . 40 60
366 25p. Ordnance Corps, 1896 55 1·40

1976. Christmas. Multicoloured.
367 6p. Type **109** 25 15
368 9p. Madonna and Child . . . 35 25
369 12p. St. Bernard 50 60
370 20p. Archangel Michael . . . 85 1·40
Nos. 367/70 show different stained-glass windows from St. Joseph's Church, Gibraltar.

110 Queen Elizabeth II, Royal Arms and Gibraltar Arms
111 Toothed Orchid

1977. Silver Jubilee. Multicoloured.
371 **110** 6p. red 15 20
372 £1 blue . . . . 1·10 2·25
MS373 124 × 115 mm. Nos. 371/2 1·25 2·25

1977. Birds, Flowers, Fish and Butterflies. Multicoloured.
374 ½p. Type **111** . . . . . . 60 2·25
375 1p. Red mullet (horiz) . . . 15 70
376 2p. "Maculinea arion" (butterfly) (horiz) . . . . 30 1·75
377 2½p. Sardinian warbler . . . 1·75 2·50
378 3p. Giant squill 20 10
379 4p. Grey wrasse (horiz) . . 30 10
380 5p. "Vanessa atalanta" (butterfly) (horiz) . . . . 50 1·00
381 6p. Black kite . . . . . . 2·25 55
382 9p. Shrubby scorpion-vetch 70 70
383 10p. John dory (fish) (horiz) 40 20
384 12p. "Colias crocea" (butterfly) (horiz) . . . . 1·00 35
384b 15p. Winged asparagus pea 1·50 55
385 20p. Audouin's gull . . . . 2·00 3·00
386 25p. Barbary nut (iris) . . . 1·25 2·00
387 50p. Swordfish (horiz) . . . 2·00 1·50
388 £1 "Papilio machaon" (butterfly) (horiz) . . . . 4·25 5·00
389 £2 Hoopoe . . . . 9·00 11·00
389a £5 Arms of Gibraltar . . . 10·00 11·00

112 "Our Lady of Europa" Stamp

1977. "Amphilex '77" Stamp Exhibition, Amsterdam. Multicoloured.
390 6p. Type **112** 10 20
391 12p. "Europa Point" stamp 15 30
392 25p. "E.E.C. Entry" stamp 20 50

113 "The Annunciation" (Rubens)

1977. Christmas and 400th Birth Anniv of Rubens. Multicoloured.
393 3p. Type **113** 10 10
394 9p. "The Adoration of the Magi" 25 25
395 12p. "The Adoration of the Magi" (horiz) 30 50
396 15p. "The Holy Family under the Apple Tree" 30 55
MS397 110 × 200 mm. Nos. 393/6 2·75 4·00

114 Aerial View of Gibraltar

1978. Gibraltar from Space. Multicoloured.
398 12p. Type **114** 25 50
MS399 148 × 108 mm. 25p. Aerial view of Straits of Gibraltar . . 80 80

115 Holyroodhouse

1978. 25th Anniv of Coronation. Multicoloured.
400 6p. Type **115** 20 15
401 9p. St. James's Palace 25 15
402 12p. Sandringham 30 30
403 18p. Balmoral 40 85
406 25p. Windsor Castle . . . . 90 2·00
Nos. 402/3 also exist as self-adhesive stamps from booklet panes, No. 406 only coming in this form.

116 Short S.25 Sunderland, 1938–58

1978. 60th Anniv of Royal Air Force. Multicoloured.
407 3p. Type **116** 15 10
408 9p. Caudron G-3, 1918 . . . 35 40
409 12p. Avro Shackleton M.R.2, 1953–66 . . . . 40 55
410 16p. Hawker Hunter F.6, 1954–77 . . . . 45 1·00
411 18p. Hawker Siddeley Nimrod M.R.1, 1969–78 50 1·10

117 "Madonna with Animals"

1978. Christmas. Paintings by Durer. Multicoloured.
412 5p. Type **117** 20 10
413 9p. "The Nativity" 25 15
414 12p. "Madonna of the Goldfinch" 30 40
415 15p. "Adoration of the Magi" . . . . 35 1·00

118 Sir Rowland Hill and 1d. Stamp of 1886

1979. Death Centenary of Sir Rowland Hill.
416 **118** 3p. multicoloured 10 10
417 – 9p. multicoloured 15 15
418 – 12p. multicoloured . . . 15 20
419 – 25p. black, purple yellow 25 50
DESIGNS: 9p. 1971 1p. coil stamp; 12p. 1840 Post Office Regulations; 25p. "G" cancellation.

119 Posthorn, Dish Antenna and Early Telephone

1979. Europa. Communications.
420 **119** 3p. green and pale green 15 10
421 9p. brown and ochre . . 30 90
422 12p. blue and violet . . . 35 1·25

120 African Child **121** Early Policeman

1979. Christmas. International Year of the Child. Multicoloured.
423 12p. Type **120** 25 30
424 12p. Asian child 25 30
425 12p. Polynesian child 25 30
426 12p. American Indian child 25 30
427 12p. Nativity and children of different races 25 30
428 12p. European child 25 30

1980. 150th Anniv of Gibraltar Police Force. Multicoloured.
429 3p. Type **121** 20 10
430 6p. Policemen of 1895, early 1900s and 1980 . . . . . 20 15
431 12p. Police officer and police ambulance 25 20
432 37p. Policewoman and police motor-cyclist . . . . . . 55 1·25

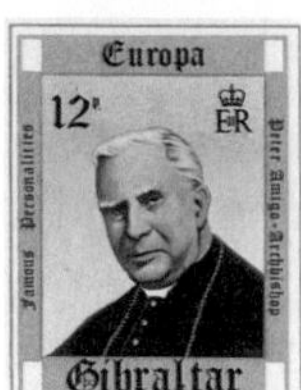

122 Peter Amigo (Archbishop) **124** "Horatio Nelson" (J. F. Rigaud)

123 Queen Elizabeth the Queen Mother

1980. Europa. Personalities. Multicoloured.
433 12p. Type **122** 20 30
434 12p. Gustavo Bacarisas (artist) 20 30
435 12p. John Mackintosh (philanthropist) 20 30

1980. 80th Birthday of The Queen Mother.
436 **123** 15p. multicoloured . . . 30 30

1980. 175th Death Anniv of Nelson. Paintings. Multicoloured.
437 3p. Type **124** 15 10
438 9p. "H.M.S. Victory' (horiz) 25 25
439 15p. "Horatio Nelson" (Sir William Beechey) 35 35
440 40p. "'H.M.S. Victory' being towed into Gibraltar" (Clarkson Stanfield) (horiz) 80 1·00
MS441 159 × 99 mm. No. 439 . . 75 1·75

125 Three Kings

1980. Christmas.
442 **125** 15p. brown and yellow . . 25 35
443 – 15p. brown and yellow . . 25 35
DESIGN: No. 443, Nativity scene.

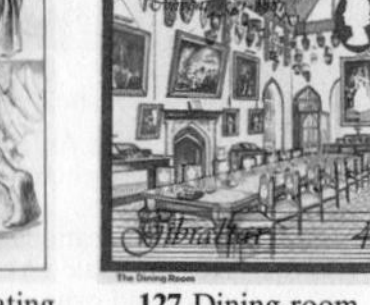

[Her]cules creating [the] Mediterranean **127** Dining-room

1981. Europa. Multicoloured.
444 9p. Type **126** 20 15
445 15p. Hercules and Pillars of Hercules 25 35

1981. 450th Anniv of The Convent (Governor's Residence). Multicoloured.
446 4p. Type **127** 10 10
447 14p. King's Chapel 15 15
448 15p. The Convent 15 15
449 55p. Cloister 60 80

128 Prince Charles and Lady Diana Spencer **129**

1981. Royal Wedding.
450 **128** £1 multicoloured . . . . 1·25 1·25

1981.
451 **129** 1p. black 30 30
452 4p. blue 30 30
453 15p. green 30 30

130 Paper Airplane

1981. 50th Anniv of Gibraltar Airmail Service. Multicoloured.
454 14p. Type **130** 15 15
455 15p. Airmail letters, post box and aircraft tail fin 15 15
456 55p. Jet airliner circling globe 60 80

131 Carol Singers

1981. Christmas. Children's Drawings. Multicoloured.
457 15p. Type **131** 30 15
458 55p. Postbox (vert) . . . . . 1·00 85

132 I.Y.D.P. Emblem and Stylized Faces

1981. International Year for Disabled Persons.
459 **132** 14p. multicoloured . . . 30 30

133 Douglas DC-3

1982. Aircraft. Multicoloured.
460 1p. Type **133** . . . . 25 2·00
461 2p. Vickers Viking 1B . . . 30 1·75
462 3p. Airspeed Ambassador AS.57 . . . . 30 1·75
463 4p. Vickers Viscount 800 . . 40 20
464 5p. Boeing 727-100 . . . . . 90 60
465 10p. Vickers Vanguard . . . 1·75 50
466 14p. Short Solent 2 . . . . . 1·75 3·50
467 15p. Fokker F.27 Friendship 2·75 3·50
468 17p. Boeing 737 . . . . . . 1·00 55
469 20p. B.A.C. One Eleven . . . 1·00 50
470 25p. Lockheed Constellation 4·00 4·50
471 50p. Hawker Siddeley Comet 4B . . . . 4·00 2·25
472 £1 Saro Windhover . . . . . 5·50 2·25
473 £2 Hawker Siddeley Trident 2E . . . . 6·50 5·00
474 £5 De Havilland D.H.89A Dragon Rapide . . . . . 8·00 14·00

134 Crest, H.M.S. "Opossum" **136** Gibraltar Chamber of Commerce Centenary

135 Hawker Hurricane Mk I and Supermarine Spitfires at Gibraltar

1982. Naval Crests (1st series). Multicoloured.
475 ½p. Type **134** 10 30
476 15½p. H.M.S. "Norfolk" . . 30 55
477 17p. H.M.S. "Fearless" . . . 30 60
478 60p. H.M.S. "Rooke" . . . 75 2·75
See also Nos. 493/6, 510/13, 522/5, 541/4, 565/8, 592/5, 616/19 and 651/4.

1982. Europa. Operation Torch. Multicoloured.
479 14p. Type **135** 25 70
480 17p. General Giraud, General Eisenhower and Gibraltar 35 80

1982. Anniversaries. Multicoloured.
481 ½p. Type **136** 10 65
482 15½p. British Forces Postal Service centenary 45 30
483 60p. 75th anniv of Gibraltar Scout Association . . . . 1·25 2·00

137 Printed Circuit forming Map of World

1982. International Direct Dialling.
484 **137** 17p. black, blue and orange 35 35

138 Gibraltar illuminated at Night and Holly

1982. Christmas. Multicoloured.
485 14p. Type **138** 50 30
486 17p. Gibraltar illuminated at night and mistletoe 50 35

139 Yacht Marina

1983. Commonwealth Day. Multicoloured.
487 4p. Type **139** 10 10
488 14p. Scouts and Guides Commonwealth Day Parade 20 15
489 17p. Flag of Gibraltar (vert) 25 20
490 60p. Queen Elizabeth II (from photo by Tim Graham) (vert) . . . . . 70 1·00

140 St. George's Hall Gallery

1983. Europa.
491 **140** 16p. black and brown . . 35 50
492 – 19p. black and blue . . . 40 75
DESIGN: 19p. Water catchment slope.

1983. Naval Crests (2nd series). As T **134**. Multicoloured.
493 4p. H.M.S. "Faulknor" . . . 30 10
494 14p. H.M.S. "Renown" . . . 70 35
495 17p. H.M.S. "Ark Royal" . . 75 40
496 60p. H.M.S. "Sheffield" . . . 1·75 1·50

141 Landport Gate, 1729

1983. Fortress Gibraltar in the 18th Century. Multicoloured.
497 4p. Type **141** 15 10
498 17p. Koehler Gun, 1782 . . . 35 30
499 77p. King's Bastion, 1779 . . 1·00 1·25
MS500 97 × 145 mm. Nos. 497/9 2·25 1·50

142 "Adoration of the Magi" (Raphael)

1983. Christmas. 500th Birth Anniv of Raphael. Multicoloured.
501 4p. Type **142** 25 10
502 17p. "Madonna of Foligno" (vert) 70 35
503 60p. "Sistine Madonna" (vert) . . . . 1·75 1·40

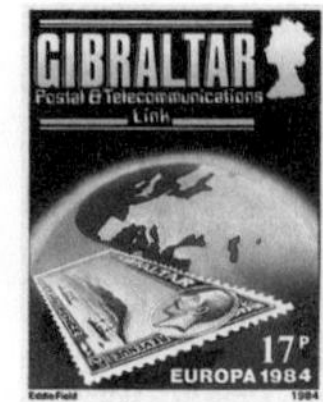

143 1932 2d. Stamp and Globe

1984. Europa, Posts and Telecommunications. Multicoloured.
504 17p. Type **143** 35 50
505 23p. Circuit board and globe 45 1·00

144 Hockey

1984. Sports. Multicoloured.
506 20p. Type **144** 70 80
507 21p. Basketball 70 80
508 26p. Rowing . . . . 70 1·25
509 29p. Football . . . . 70 1·50

1984. Naval Crests (3rd series). As T **134**. Multicoloured.
510 20p. H.M.S. "Active" . . . . 1·60 2·00
511 21p. H.M.S. "Foxhound" . . 1·60 2·25
512 26p. H.M.S. "Valiant" . . . 1·75 2·25
513 29p. H.M.S. "Hood" . . . . 1·90 2·50

145 Mississippi River Boat Float

1984. Christmas. Epiphany Floats. Multicoloured.
514 20p. Type **145** 30 30
515 80p. Roman Temple float . . 1·40 2·75

146 Musical Symbols, and Score from Beethoven's 9th (Choral) Symphony

1985. Europa. European Music Year. Multicoloured.
516 **146** 20p. multicoloured . . . 30 30
517 – 29p. multicoloured . . . 40 1·50
DESIGN: The 29p. is as T **146**, but shows different symbols.

147 Globe and Stop Polio Campaign Logo

1985. Stop Polio Campaign.
518 26p. multicoloured (Type **147**) . . . . 90 1·40
519 26p. multicoloured ("ST" visible) . . . . 90 1·40
520 26p. multicoloured ("STO" visible) . . . . 90 1·40
521 26p. multicoloured ("STOP" visible) . . . . 90 1·40
Each design differs in the position of the logo across the centre of the globe. On No. 518 only the letter "S" is fully visible, on No. 519 "ST", on No. 520 "STO" and on No. 521 "STOP". Other features of the design also differ, so that the word "Year" moves towards the top of the stamp and on No. 521 the upper logo is omitted.

1985. Naval Crests (4th series). As T **134**. Multicoloured.
522 4p. H.M.S. "Duncan" . . . 60 10
523 9p. H.M.S. "Fury" 90 50
524 21p. H.M.S. "Firedrake" . . 2·00 2·00
525 80p. H.M.S. "Malaya" . . . 4·00 6·00

148 I.Y.Y. Logo **149** St. Joseph

1985. International Youth Year. Multicoloured.
526 4p. Type **148** 35 10
527 20p. Hands passing diamond 1·40 1·10
528 80p. 75th anniv logo of Girl Guide Movement . . . . 3·25 3·75

1985. Christmas. Centenary of St. Joseph's Parish Church. Multicoloured.
529 4p. Type **149** 65 90
530 4p. St. Joseph's Parish Church 65 90
531 80p. Nativity crib . . . . . 4·00 4·75

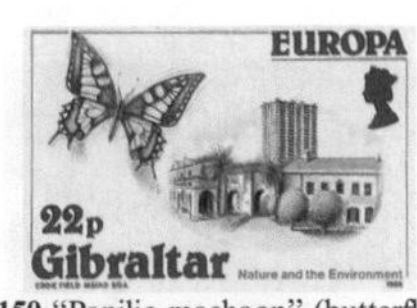

150 "Papilio machaon" (butterfly) and The Convent

1986. Europa. Nature and the Environment. Multicoloured.
532 22p. Type **150** . . . . 1·00 50
533 29p. Herring gull and Europa Point . . . . 1·50 4·25

151 1887 Queen Victoria 6d. Stamp **152** Queen Elizabeth II in Robes of Order of the Bath

1986. Centenary of First Gibraltar Postage Stamps. Designs showing stamps. Multicoloured.
534 4p. Type **151** 30 10
535 22p. 1903 Edward VII 2½d. 1·00 1·00
536 32p. 1912 George V 1d. . . . 1·50 2·00
537 36p. 1938 George VI £1 . . . 1·60 2·50
538 44p. 1953 Coronation ½d. (29 × 46 mm) . . . . . . 2·00 3·00
MS539 102 × 73 mm. 29p. 1886 "GIBRALTAR" overprinted on Bermuda 1d. . . . . 2·50 2·75

1986. 60th Birthday of Queen Elizabeth II.
540 **152** £1 multicoloured . . . . . 1·75 3·00

1986. Naval Crests (5th series). As T **134**. Multicoloured.
541 22p. H.M.S. "Lightning" . . 1·75 1·00
542 29p. H.M.S. "Hermione" . . 2·00 1·75
543 32p. H.M.S. "Laforey" . . . 2·25 3·25
544 44p. H.M.S. "Nelson" . . . 2·75 4·50

153 Prince Andrew and Miss Sarah Ferguson

1986. Royal Wedding. Sheet 115 × 85 mm.
MS545 **153 153** 44p. multicoloured 1·40 2·25

154 Three Kings and Cathedral of St. Mary the Crowned **155** Neptune House

1986. Christmas. International Peace Year. Multicoloured.
546 18p. Type **154** . . . . . . 1·00 50
547 32p. St. Andrew's Church . . 1·50 3·00

1987. Europa. Architecture. Multicoloured.
563 22p. Type **155** . . . . . . 1·50 50
564 29p. Ocean Heights . . . . . 2·50 4·25

1987. Naval Crests (6th series). As T **134**. Multicoloured.
565 18p. H.M.S. "Wishart" . . . 1·25 75
566 22p. H.M.S. "Charybdis" . . 1·40 1·10
567 32p. H.M.S. "Antelope" . . 1·90 3·50
568 44p. H.M.S. "Eagle" . . . . 2·50 4·50

156 13-inch Mortar, 1783 **157** Victoria Stadium

1987. Guns. Multicoloured.
569 1p. Type **156** 20 70
570 2p. 6-inch coastal gun, 1909 30 70
571 3p. 8-inch howitzer, 1783 . . 30 70
572 4p. Bofors "L40/70" AA gun, 1951 . . . . 40 10
573 5p. 100 ton rifled muzzle-loader, 1882 . . . . 40 70
574 10p. 5.25 inch heavy AA gun, 1953 . . . . 40 70
575 18p. 25-pounder gun-how, 1943 . . . . 65 1·00
576 19p. 64-pounder rifled muzzle-loader, 1873 . . . 70 1·25
577 22p. 12-pounder gun, 1758 70 50
578 50p. 10-inch rifled muzzle-loader, 1870 . . . . 1·40 3·00
579 £1 Russian 24-pounder gun, 1854 . . . . 2·50 2·50
580 £3 9.2 inch "Mk 10" coastal gun, 1935 . . . . 3·50 14·00
581 £5 24-pounder gun, 1779 . . 6·00 16·00

1987. Bicentenary of Royal Engineers' Royal Warrant. Multicoloured.
582 18p. Type **157** . . . . . . 1·25 65
583 32p. Freedom of Gibraltar scroll and casket . . . . . 1·75 3·00
584 44p. Royal Engineers' badge 2·50 4·00

158 The Three Kings

1987. Christmas. Multicoloured.
585 4p. Type **158** 20 10
586 22p. The Holy Family . . . 1·00 1·00
587 44p. The Shepherds . . . . 1·90 3·50

159 "Canberra" (liner) passing Gibraltar

1988. Europa. Transport and Communications. Multicoloured.
588 22p. Type **159** . . . . . . 1·50 2·25
589 22p. "Gibline I" (ferry), dish aerial and Boeing 737 airliner . . . . 1·50 2·25
590 32p. Horse-drawn carriage and modern coach . . . . 2·00 2·75
591 32p. Car, telephone and Rock of Gibraltar . . . . 2·00 2·75

1988. Naval Crests (7th series). As T **134**.
592 18p. multicoloured . . . . . 1·50 65
593 22p. black, brown and gold 2·00 1·25
594 32p. multicoloured . . . . . 2·25 3·50
595 44p. multicoloured . . . . . 3·00 4·75
DESIGNS: 18p. H.M.S. "Clyde"; 22p. H.M.S. "Foresight"; 32p. H.M.S. "Severn"; 44p. H.M.S. "Rodney".

160 European Bee Eater

1988. Birds. Multicoloured.
596 4p. Type **160** 75 20
597 22p. Atlantic puffin . . . . . 1·75 90
598 32p. Western honey buzzard ("Honey Buzzard") . . . . 2·25 2·50
599 44p. Blue rock thrush . . . . 2·75 3·50

161 "Zebu" (brigantine)

1989. Operation Raleigh. Multicoloured.
600 19p. Type **161** 65 60
601 22p. Miniature of Sir Walter Raleigh and logo 75 70
602 32p. "Sir Walter Raleigh" (expedition ship) and world map . . . . 1·10 2·00
MS603 135 × 86 mm. 22p. As No. 601; 44p. "Sir Walter Raleigh" (expedition ship) passing Gibraltar . . . . 4·00 4·75

162 "Snowman" (Rebecca Falero)

1988. Christmas. Children's Paintings. Multicoloured.
604 4p. Type **162** 15 10
605 22p. "The Nativity" (Dennis Penalver) 55 60
606 44p. "Father Christmas" (Gavin Key) (23 × 31 mm) 1·00 2·00

163 Soft Toys and Toy Train

1989. Europa. Children's Toys. Multicoloured.
607 25p. Type **163** . . . . . . 1·25 75
608 32p. Soft toys, toy boat and doll's house . . . . 1·75 2·75

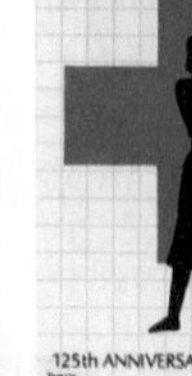

164 Port Sergeant with Keys **165** Nurse and Baby

1989. 50th Anniv of Gibraltar Regiment. Mult.
609 4p. Type **164** 40 10
610 22p. Regimental badge and colours . . . . 1·25 1·10
611 32p. Drum major . . . . . . 1·75 3·00
MS612 124 × 83 mm. 22p. As No. 610; 44p. Former Gibraltar Defence Force badge . . . . . 4·50 4·75

1989. 125th Anniv of International Red Cross.
613 **165** 25p. black, red and brown 1·00 60
614 – 32p. black, red and brown 1·25 1·75
615 – 44p. black, red and brown 1·50 3·50
DESIGNS: 32p. Famine victims; 44p. Accident victims.

1989. Naval Crests (8th series). As T **134**.
616 22p. multicoloured . . . . . 1·50 75
617 25p. black and gold . . . . 1·50 1·50
618 32p. gold, black and red . . 2·00 3·25
619 44p. multicoloured . . . . . 3·00 5·00
DESIGNS: 22p. H.M.S. "Blankney"; 25p. H.M.S. "Deptford"; 32p. H.M.S. "Exmoor"; 44p. H.M.S. "Stork".

166 One Penny Coin **167** Father Christmas in Sleigh

1989. New Coinage. T **166** and similar vert designs in two miniature sheets.
MS620 72 × 94 mm. 4p. bronze, black and red (Type **166**); 4p. bronze, black and brown (two pence); 4p. silver, black and yellow (ten pence); 4p. silver, black and green (five pence) . . . . . . 1·25 1·75
MS621 100 × 95 mm. 22p. silver, black and green (fifty pence); 22p. gold, black and blue (five pounds); 22p. gold, black and brown (two pounds); 22p. gold, black and green (one pound); 22p. gold, black and violet (obverse of coin series); 22p. silver, black and blue (twenty pence) . . . . 4·75 6·50

1989. Christmas. Multicoloured.
622 4p. Type **167** 20 10
623 22p. Shepherds and sheep . . 90 70
624 32p. The Nativity . . . . . 1·40 1·75
625 44p. The Three Wise Men . . 2·25 4·00

168 General Post Office Entrance **169** 19th-century Firemen

1990. Europa. Post Office Buildings. Multicoloured.
626 22p. Type **168** . . . . . . 1·00 1·50
627 22p. Interior of General Post Office . . . . 1·00 1·50

628 32p. Interior of South District Post Office . . . . 1·50 2·50
629 32p. South District Post Office . . . . 1·50 2·50

1990. 125th Anniv of Gibraltar Fire Service. Multicoloured.
630 4p. Type **169** 85 15
631 20p. Early fire engine (horiz) 2·00 1·10
632 42p. Modern fire engine (horiz) . . . . 2·50 3·75
633 44p. Modern fireman in breathing apparatus . . . 2·75 3·75

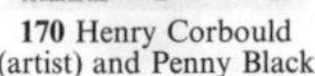
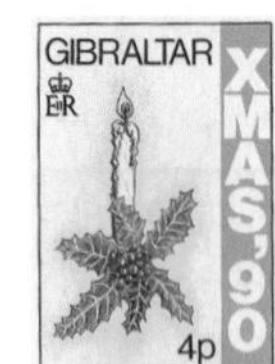

170 Henry Corbould (artist) and Penny Black

172 Candle and Holly

171 Model of Europort Development

1990. 150th Anniv of the Penny Black. Multicoloured.
634 19p. Type **170** 95 80
635 22p. Bath Royal Mail coach 1·00 90
636 32p. Sir Rowland Hill and Penny Black . . . . 2·25 4·00
MS637 145 × 95 mm. 44p. Penny Black with Maltese Cross cancellation . . . . 4·25 5·50

1990. Naval Crests (9th series). As T **134**. Multicoloured.
638 22p. H.M.S. "Calpe" . . . . 1·50 70
639 25p. H.M.S. "Gallant" . . . 1·60 1·75
640 32p. H.M.S. "Wrestler" . . . 2·00 3·25
641 44p. H.M.S. "Greyhound" 2·50 5·50

1990. Development Projects. Multicoloured.
642 22p. Type **171** 75 80
643 23p. Construction of building material factory . . . . . 75 1·50
644 25p. Land reclamation . . . 95 1·50

1990. Christmas. Multicoloured.
645 4p. Type **172** 15 10
646 22p. Father Christmas . . . 75 65
647 42p. Christmas tree . . . . . 1·50 2·50
648 44p. Nativity crib . . . . . 1·50 2·50

173 Space Laboratory and Spaceplane (Columbus Development Programme)

1991. Europa. Europe in Space. Multicoloured.
649 25p. Type **173** 75 75
650 32p. "ERS-1" earth resources remote sensing satellite . . 1·00 2·25

1991. Naval Crests (10th series). As T **134**.
651 4p. black, blue and gold . . 35 10
652 21p. multicoloured . . . . . 1·25 1·25
653 22p. multicoloured . . . . . 1·25 1·25
654 62p. multicoloured . . . . . 3·25 6·00
DESIGNS: 4p. H.M.S. "Hesperus"; 21p. H.M.S. "Forester"; 22p. H.M.S. "Furious"; 62p. H.M.S. "Scylla".

174 Shag

1991. Endangered Species. Birds. Multicoloured.
655 13p. Type **174** . . . . . . 85 1·25
656 13p. Barbary partridge . . . 85 1·25
657 13p. Egyptian vulture . . . . 85 1·25
658 13p. Black stork . . . . . . 85 1·25

1991. No. 580 surch **£1.05**.
659 £1.05 on £3 9.2-inch "Mk.10" coastal gun, 1935 . . . . 3·50 1·60

176 "North View of Gibraltar" (Gustavo Bacarisas)

1991. Local Paintings. Multicoloured.
660 22p. Type **176** 85 50
661 26p. "Parson's Lodge" (Elena Mifsud) . . . . 1·00 1·00
662 32p. "Governor's Parade" (Jacobo Azagury) . . . . 1·50 2·25
663 42p. "Waterport Wharf" (Rudesindo Mannia) (vert) 2·25 4·50

177 "Once in Royal David's City"

1991. Christmas. Carols. Multicoloured.
664 4p. Type **177** 30 10
665 24p. "Silent Night" . . . . . 1·50 70
666 25p. "Angels We Have Heard on High" . . . . 1·50 1·25
667 49p. "O Come All Ye Faithful" . . . . 2·25 5·00

178 "Danaus chrysippus"

1991. "Phila Nippon '91" International Stamp Exhibition, Tokyo. Sheet 116 × 91 mm.
MS668 **178** £1.05, multicoloured 3·50 4·50

179 Columbus and "Santa Maria"

1992. Europa. 500th Anniv of Discovery of America by Columbus. Multicoloured.
669 24p. Type **179** . . . . . . 1·25 2·00
670 24p. Map of Old World and "Nina" . . . . 1·25 2·00
671 34p. Map of New World and "Pinta" . . . . 1·50 2·50
672 34p. Map of Old World and look-out . . . . 1·50 2·50
Nos. 669/70 and 671/2 were issued together, se-tenant, each pair forming a composite design.

179a Gibraltar from North

1992. 40th Anniv of Queen Elizabeth II's Accession. Multicoloured.
673 4p. Type **179a** 15 10
674 20p. H.M.S. "Arrow" (frigate) and Gibraltar from south 60 60
675 24p. Southport Gates 75 80
676 44p. Three portraits of Queen Elizabeth . . . . 1·25 1·60
677 54p. Queen Elizabeth II . . . 1·60 1·90

180 Compass Rose, Sail, and Atlantic Map

181 Holy Trinity Cathedral

1992. Round the World Yacht Rally. Multicoloured designs, each incorporating compass rose and sail.
678 21p. Type **180** 75 80
679 24p. Map of Indonesian Archipelago (horiz) . . . . 95 1·40
680 25p. Map of India Ocean (horiz) . . . . 95 1·75
MS681 108 × 72 mm. 21p. Type **180**; 49p. Map of Mediterranean and Red Sea . . . . 2·50 3·50

1992. 150th Anniv of Anglican Diocese of Gibraltar-in-Europe. Multicoloured.
682 4p. Type **181** 20 10
683 24p. Diocesan crest and map (horiz) . . . . 1·00 65
684 44p. Construction of Cathedral and Sir George Don (horiz) . . . . 1·75 3·00
685 54p. Bishop Tomlinson . . . 2·00 3·50

182 Sacred Heart of Jesus Church

183 "Drama and Music"

1992. Christmas. Churches. Multicoloured.
686 4p. Type **182** 35 10
687 24p. Cathedral of St. Mary the Crowned . . . . . . 1·50 55
688 34p. St. Andrew's Church of Scotland . . . . 2·00 2·50
689 49p. St. Joseph's Church . . 2·50 5·50

1993. Europa. Contemporary Art. Multicoloured.
690 24p. Type **183** . . . . . . 1·50 2·00
691 24p. "Sculpture, Art and Pottery" . . . . 1·50 2·00
692 34p. "Architecture" . . . . 2·00 2·75
693 34p. "Printing and Photography" . . . . . . 2·00 2·75

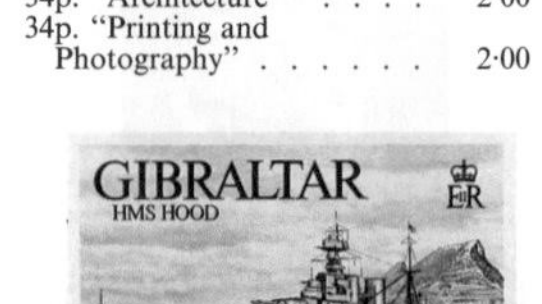

184 H.M.S. "Hood" (battle cruiser)

1993. Second World War Warships (1st series). Sheet 120 × 79 mm, containing T **184** and similar horiz designs. Multicoloured.
MS694 24p. Type **184**; 24p. H.M.S. "Ark Royal" (aircraft carrier, 1937); 24p. H.M.A.S. "Waterhen" (destroyer); 24p. U.S.S. "Gleaves" (destroyer) . . . . 8·50 8·50
See also Nos. **MS**724, **MS**748, **MS**779 and **MS**809.

185 Landport Gate

186 £sd and Decimal British Coins (25th anniv of decimal currency)

1993. Architectural Heritage. Multicoloured.
695 1p. Type **185** . . . . 20 1·00
696 2p. St. Mary the Crowned Church (horiz) . . . . . 40 1·00
697 3p. Parsons Lodge Battery (horiz) . . . . 40 1·00
698 4p. Moorish Castle (horiz) 40 1·00
699 5p. General Post Office . . 40 30
699a 6p. House of Assembly . . 1·25 75
699b 7p. Bleak House (horiz) . . 1·25 75
699c 8p. General Eliott Memorial 1·25 75
699d 9p. Supreme Court Building (horiz) . . . . 1·25 75
700 10p. South Barracks (horiz) 40 60
700a 20p. The Convent (horiz) 2·00 75
701 21p. American War Memorial 60 80
702 24p. Garrison Library (horiz) 70 80
703 25p. Southport Gates . . . 70 80
704 26p. Casemates Gate (horiz) 70 80
704a 30p. St. Bernard's Hospital 3·00 80
704b 40p. City Hall (horiz) . . . 3·00 1·50
705 50p. Central Police Station (horiz) . . . . 1·50 2·25
706 £1 Prince Edward's Gate . . 2·00 2·75
706a £2 Church of the Sacred Heart of Jesus . . . . . 7·00 5·50
707 £3 Lighthouse, Europa Point . . . . 7·00 10·00
708 £5 Coat of Arms and fortress keys . . . . . . 10·00 14·00

1993. Anniversaries. Multicoloured.
709 21p. Type **186** 75 65
710 24p. R.A.F. crest with Handley Page 0/400 and Panavia Tornado F Mk 3 (75th anniv) . . . . 1·25 75
711 34p. Garrison Library badge and building (bicent) . . . 1·40 2·25
712 49p. Sir Winston Churchill and air raid (50th anniv of visit) . . . . 2·25 4·50

187 Mice decorating Christmas Tree

1993. Christmas. Multicoloured.
713 5p. Type **187** 20 10
714 24p. Mice pulling cracker . . 90 70
715 44p. Mice singing carols . . 1·75 2·50
716 49p. Mice building snowman 1·90 3·00

188 Exploding Atom (Lord Penney)

1994. Europa. Scientific Discoveries. Mult.
717 24p. Type **188** . . . . . . 1·00 1·50
718 24p. Polonium and radium experiment (Marie Curie) 1·00 1·50
719 34p. First oil engine (Rudolph Diesel) . . . . . 1·25 2·00
720 34p. Early telescope (Galileo) 1·25 2·00

189 World Cup and Map of U.S.A.

1994. World Cup Football Championship, U.S.A. Multicoloured.
721 26p. Type **189** 80 55
722 39p. Players and pitch in shape of U.S.A . . . . . 1·25 2·00
723 49p. Player's legs (vert) . . . 1·60 2·75

1994. Second World War Warships (2nd series). Sheet 112 × 72 mm, containing horiz designs as T **184**. Multicoloured.
MS724 5p. H.M.S. "Penelope" (cruiser); 25p. H.M.S. "Warspite" (battleship); 44p. U.S.S. "McLanahan" (destroyer); 49p. "Isaac Sweers" (Dutch destroyer) 7·00 8·50

190 Pekingese

1994. "Philakorea '94" International Stamp Exhibition, Seoul. Sheet 102 × 76 mm.
MS725 **190** £1.05, multicoloured 3·00 4·00

191 Golden Star Coral

193 Great Tit

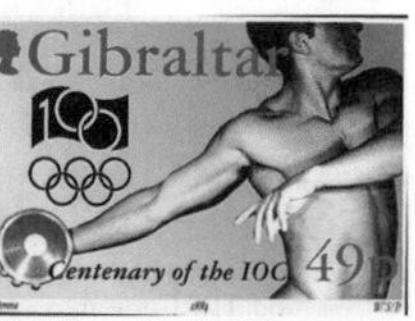

192 Throwing the Discus and Centenary Emblem

1994. Marine Life. Multicoloured.
726 21p. Type **191** 75 45
727 24p. Star fish 90 55

728 34p. Gorgonian sea-fan . . . 1·50 2·25
729 49p. Peacock wrasse ("Turkish wrasse") . . . . 2·00 3·50

1994. Centenary of Int Olympic Committee. Mult.
730 49p. Type **192** . . . . . . 1·75 2·25
731 54p. Javelin throwing and emblem . . . . 1·75 2·50

1994. Christmas. Songbirds. Multicoloured.
732 5p. Type **193** 60 10
733 24p. European robin (horiz) 1·75 70
734 34p. Blue tit (horiz) . . . . 2·00 1·50
735 54p. Eurasian goldfinch ("Goldfinch") . . . . . . 2·75 4·50

194 Austrian Flag, Hand and Star

1995. Expansion of European Union. Multicoloured.
736 24p. Type **194** 60 55
737 26p. Finnish flag, hand and star 60 60
738 34p. Swedish flag, hand and star . . . . 90 1·50
739 49p. Flags of new members and European Union emblem . . . . 1·60 3·25

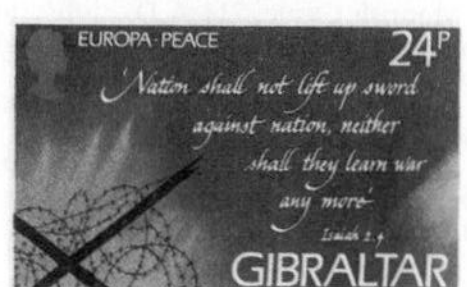

195 Barbed Wire and Quote from Isaiah Ch 2.4

1995. Europa. Peace and Freedom. Multicoloured.
740 24p. Type **195** . . . . . . 1·10 1·50
741 24p. Rainbow and hands releasing peace dove . . . 1·10 1·50
742 34p. Shackles on wall and quote from Isaiah ch 61.1 1·40 2·00
743 34p. Hands and sea birds . . 1·40 2·00

196 Fairey Swordfish, I Class Destroyer and Rock of Gibraltar

1995. 50th Anniv of End of Second World War. Sheet 101 × 66 mm.
MS744 **196** £1.05, multicoloured 3·25 4·00

197 Yachting **198** Bee Orchid

1995. Island Games '95. Multicoloured.
745 24p. Type **197** 70 60
746 44p. Athlete on starting blocks . . . . 1·60 2·50
747 49p. Swimmer at start of race 1·60 2·50

1995. Second World War Warships (3rd series). Sheet 133 × 85 mm, containing horiz designs as T **184**. Multicoloured.
MS748 5p. H.M.S. "Calpe" (destroyer); 24p. H.M.S. "Victorious" (aircraft carrier); 44p. U.S.S. "Weehawken" (attack transport); 49p. "Savorgan de Brazza" (French destroyer) . . 7·50 8·00

1995. "Singapore '95" International Stamp Exhibition. Orchids. Multicoloured.
749 22p. Type **198** . . . . . . 1·10 1·40
750 23p. Brown bee orchid . . . 1·10 1·40
751 24p. Pyramidal orchid . . . 1·10 1·40
752 25p. Mirror orchid . . . . . 1·10 1·40
753 26p. Sawfly orchid . . . . . 1·10 1·40

199 Handshake and United Nations Emblem

1995. 50th Anniv of United Nations. Multicoloured.
754 34p. Type **199** . . . . . . 1·25 1·10
755 49p. Peace dove and U.N. emblem . . . . 1·50 2·50

200 Marilyn Monroe

1995. Centenary of Cinema. T **200** and similar horiz designs showing film stars. Multicoloured.
MS756 Two sheets, each 116 × 80 mm. (a) 5p. Type **200**; 25p. Romy Schneider; 28p. Yves Montand; 38p. Audrey Hepburn. (b) 24p. Ingrid Bergman; 24p. Vittorio de Sica; 24p. Marlene Dietrich; 24p. Laurence Olivier Set of 2 sheets . . . . 4·50 5·50

201 Father Christmas

1995. Christmas. Multicoloured.
757 5p. Type **201** 30 10
758 24p. Toys in sack . . . . . . 1·00 55
759 34p. Reindeer . . . . 1·50 1·25
760 54p. Sleigh over houses . . . 2·50 4·00

202 Shih Tzu

1996. Puppies. Multicoloured.
761 5p. Type **202** 40 85
762 21p. Dalmatians 75 95
763 24p. Cocker spaniels . . . . 80 1·10
764 25p. West Highland white terriers . . . . 80 1·10
765 34p. Labrador . . . . 90 1·25
766 35p. Boxer . . . . 90 1·25
No. 762 is inscr "Dalmation" in error.

203 Princess Anne

1996. Europa. Famous Women.
767 **203** 24p. black and yellow . . 1·40 1·50
768 – 24p. black and green . . 1·40 1·50
769 – 34p. black and red . . . 1·75 2·25
770 – 34p. black and purple . . 1·75 2·25
DETAILS: Nos. 768, Princess Diana; 769, Queen Elizabeth II; 770, Queen Elizabeth the Queen Mother.

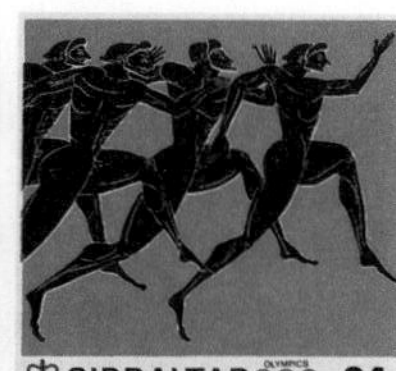

204 West German Player, 1980 **205** Ancient Greek Athletes

1996. European Football Championship, England. Players from previous winning teams. Multicoloured.
771 21p. Type **204** 55 45
772 24p. French player, 1984 . . 65 55
773 34p. Dutch player, 1988 . . . 95 1·10
774 £1.20 Danish player, 1992 . . 3·00 4·75
MS775 135 × 91 mm. As Nos. 771/4 6·50 7·50

1996. Centenary of Modern Olympic Games.
776 **205** 34p. black, purple & orge 95 90
777 – 49p. black and brown . . 1·40 1·75
778 – £1.05 multicoloured . . . 3·00 4·50
DESIGNS: 49p. Start of early race; £1.05, Start of modern race

1996. Second World War Warships (4th series). Sheet 118 × 84 mm, containing horiz designs as T **184**. Multicoloured.
MS779 5p. H.M.S. "Starling" (sloop); 25p. H.M.S. "Royalist" (cruiser); 49p. U.S.S. "Philadelphia" (cruiser); 54p. H.M.C.S. "Prescott" (corvette) 5·00 6·00

206 Asian Children

1996. 50th Anniv of UNICEF.
780 **206** 21p. multicoloured . . . 60 80
781 – 24p. multicoloured . . . 70 90
782 – 49p. multicoloured . . . 1·25 2·00
783 – 54p. multicoloured . . . 1·40 2·25
DESIGNS: 24p. to 54p. Children from different continents.

207 Red Kites in Flight

1996. Endangered Species. Red Kite. Multicoloured.
784 34p. Type **207** . . . . . . 1·10 1·50
785 34p. Red kite on ground . . 1·10 1·50
786 34p. On rock . . . . 1·10 1·50
787 34p. Pair at nest . . . . . . 1·10 1·50

208 Christmas Pudding

1996. Christmas. Designs created from "Lego" Blocks. Multicoloured.
788 5p. Type **208** 15 15
789 21p. Snowman face 70 45
790 24p. Present 80 55
791 34p. Father Christmas face . 1·10 1·25
792 54p. Candle . . . . 1·50 2·75

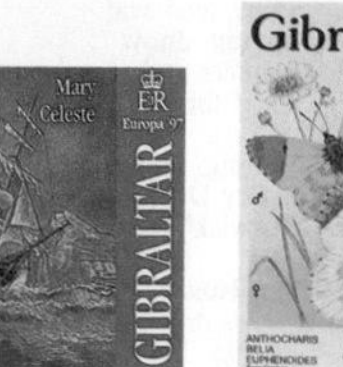

209 "Mary Celeste" passing Gibraltar **211** "Anthocharis belia euphenoides"

210 American Shorthair Silver Tabby

1997. Europa. Tales and Legends. "The Mary Celeste". Multicoloured.
793 28p. Type **209** . . . . . . 1·25 1·25
794 28p. Boarding the "Mary Celeste" . . . . 1·25 1·25
795 30p. Crew leaving "Mary Celeste" . . . . 1·25 1·50
796 30p. "Mary Celeste" found by "Dei Gratia" . . . . . 1·25 1·50

1997. Kittens. Multicoloured.
797 5p. Type **210** . . . . 40 1·00
798 24p. Rumpy Manx red tabby 75 1·25
799 26p. Blue point birmans . . . 75 1·25
800 28p. Red self longhair . . . 80 1·25
801 30p. British shorthair tortoiseshell and white . . 80 1·25
802 35p. British bicolour shorthairs . . . . 90 1·40
MS803 132 × 80 mm. Nos. 797/802 with "HONG KONG '97" International Stamp Exhibition logo at bottom left . . . . . . 7·00 8·00

1997. Butterflies. Multicoloured.
804 23p. Type **211** 70 50
805 26p. "Charaxes jasius" . . . 85 60
806 30p. "Vanessa cardui" . . . 95 90
807 £1.20 "Iphiclides podalirius" 3·25 5·00
MS808 135 × 90 mm. Nos. 804/7 5·25 6·50

1997. Second World War Warships (5th series). Sheet 117 × 82 mm, containing horiz designs as T **184**. Multicoloured.
MS809 24p. H.M.S. "Enterprise" (cruiser); 26p. H.M.S. "Cleopatra" (cruiser); 38p. U.S.S. "Iowa" (battleship); 50p. "Orkan" (Polish destroyer) . . . . 3·50 4·00

212 Queen Elizabeth and Prince Philip at Carriage-driving Trials

1997. Golden Wedding of Queen Elizabeth and Prince Philip. Multicoloured.
810 £1.20 Type **212** . . . . . . 4·00 4·25
811 £1.40 Queen Elizabeth in Trooping the Colour uniform . . . . 4·00 4·25

213 Christian Dior Evening Dress **214** "Our Lady and St. Bernard" (St. Joseph's Parish Church)

1997. Christian Dior Spring/Summer '97 Collection. Multicoloured.
812 30p. Type **213** . . . . . . 80 1·25
813 35p. Tunic top and skirt . . 1·10 1·60
814 50p. Ballgown . . . . 1·25 1·75
815 62p. Two-piece suit . . . . 1·60 2·25
MS816 110 × 90 mm. £1.20, Ballgown (different) . . . . . 2·75 3·50

1997. Christmas. Stained Glass Windows. Mult.
817 5p. Type **214** 25 10
818 26p. "The Epiphany" (Our Lady of Sorrows Church) 1·00 60
819 38p. "St. Joseph" (Our Lady of Sorrows Church) . . . 1·25 95
820 50p. "The Holy Family" (St. Joseph's Parish Church) . . . . 1·50 2·25
821 62p. "The Miraculous Medal" (St. Joseph's Parish Church) . . . . 1·75 3·25

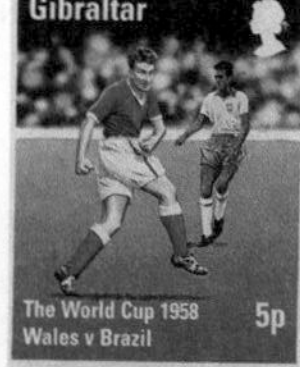

215 Sir Joshua Hassan **216** Wales v Brazil (1958)

1997. Sir Joshua Hassan (former Chief Minister) Commemoration.
822 **215** 26p. black 75 60

1998. World Football Championship, France (1998). Multicoloured.
823 5p. Type **216** 25 10
824 26p. Northern Ireland v France (1958) . . . . . . 1·00 60

825 38p. Scotland v Holland (1978) . . . . 1·25 90
826 £1.20 England v West Germany (1966) . . . . . 2·75 4·75
MS827 153 × 96 mm. Nos. 823/6 4·75 5·50

1998. Diana, Princess of Wales Commemoration. Sheet 145 × 70 mm, containing vert designs as T **177** of Ascension. Multicoloured.
MS828 26p. Wearing jacket with white fur collar, 1988; 26p. Wearing pink checked suit and hat; 38p. Wearing black jacket, 1995; 38p. Wearing blue jacket with gold embroidery, 1987 (sold at £1.28+20p. charity premium) 3·25 3·75

216a Saro London (flying boat)

1998. 80th Anniv of Royal Air Force. Multicoloured.
829 24p. Type **216a** 70 55
830 26p. Fairey Fox 75 60
831 38p. Handley Page Halifax GR.VI . . . . 95 1·25
832 50p. Hawker Siddeley Buccaneer S.2B . . . . . 1·25 2·50
MS833 110 × 77 mm. 24p. Sopwith 1½ Strutter; 26p. Bristol M.IB; 38p. Supermarine Spitfire XII; 50p. Avro York . . . . 3·50 4·50

217 Miss Gibraltar saluting

219 Nileus (dog) with Hat and Telescope

218 Striped Dolphin

1998. Europa. Festivals. National Day. Mult.
834 26p. Type **217** . . . . . . 1·10 1·25
835 26p. In black bodice and long red skirt . . . . 1·10 1·25
836 38p. In black bodice and short red skirt, with Gibraltar flag . . . . . . 1·40 1·60
837 38p. In Genoese-style costume . . . . 1·40 1·60

1998. International Year of the Ocean. Sheet 155 × 64 mm, containing T **218** and similar multicoloured designs.
MS838 5p. Type **218**; 5p. Common dolphin (vert); 26p. Killer whale (vert); £1.20, Blue whale . . . 4·75 5·50

1998. Bicentenary of Battle of the Nile. Multicoloured.
839 12p. Type **219** 50 30
840 26p. Rear-Admiral Sir Horatio Nelson 95 55
841 28p. Frances Nisbet, Lady Nelson . . . . 1·25 75
842 35p. H.M.S. "Vanguard" (ship of the line) . . . . . 1·50 1·75
843 50p. Battle of the Nile (47 × 29 mm) . . . . . . 1·75 3·25

220 "Love comforts like Sunshine after Rain" (William Shakespeare)

221 The Nativity

1998. Famous Quotations. Multicoloured.
844 26p. Type **220** . . . . . . 90 1·00
845 26p. "The price of greatness is responsibility" (Sir Winston Churchill) . . . . 90 1·00
846 38p. "Hate the sin, love the sinner" (Mahatma Gandhi) 1·10 1·50
847 38p. "Imagination is more important than knowledge" (Albert Einstein) . . . . . 1·10 1·50

1998. Christmas. Multicoloured.
848 5p. Type **221** 35 10
849 26p. Star and stable . . . . 1·25 70
850 30p. King with gold . . . . 1·40 75
851 35p. King with myrrh . . . . 1·40 1·25
852 50p. King with frankincense 1·75 2·75

222 Barbary Macaque

223 Queen Elizabeth II

1999. Europa. Parks and Gardens. Upper Rock Nature Reserve. Multicoloured.
853 30p. Type **222** . . . . . . 1·25 1·40
854 30p. Dartford warbler . . . 1·25 1·40
855 42p. Dusky grouper . . . . 1·50 2·00
856 42p. River kingfisher ("Common Kingfisher") . . 1·50 2·00

1999. (a) Ordinary gum.
857 **223** 1p. purple 10 10
858 2p. brown 10 10
859 4p. blue 10 10
860 5p. green 15 10
861 10p. orange 25 25
862 12p. red 30 30
863 20p. green 55 45
864 28p. mauve 75 60
865 30p. orange 80 65
866 40p. grey . . . . 1·00 85
867 42p. green . . . . . . 1·00 90
868 50p. bistre . . . . . . 1·25 1·10
869 £1 black . . . . 2·50 2·10
869a £1.20 red . . . . 2·75 2·75
869b £1.40 blue . . . . . . 3·00 3·00
870 £3 blue . . . . 6·00 6·25

(b) Self-adhesive.
871 **223** (1st) orange 70 60

Nos. 868/71 are larger, 22 × 28 mm.
No. 871 was initially sold at 26p.

224 Roman Marine and Galley

225 John Lennon (musician)

1999. Maritime Heritage. Multicoloured.
872 5p. Type **224** 25 10
873 30p. Arab sailor, medieval galley house and dhow . . 95 65
874 42p. Marine officer and British ship of the line (1779–83) . . . . 1·50 1·50
875 £1.20 Naval rating, Queen Alexandra Dry Dock and H.M.S. "Berwick" (cruiser) (1904) . . . . 3·25 4·25
MS876 116 × 76 mm. Nos. 872/5 4·50 5·50

1999. 30th Wedding Anniv of John Lennon and Yoko Ono. Designs showing John Lennon.
877 – 20p. multicoloured . . . 75 55
878 **225** 30p. black and blue . . . 1·10 90
879 – 40p. multicoloured . . . 1·40 1·60
MS880 Two sheets, each 62 × 100 mm. (a) £1 black and blue. (b) £1 multicoloured Set of 2 sheets . . . . 7·00 7·00
DESIGNS: 20p. With flower over left eye; 40p. Wearing orange glasses; £1 (No. **MS**880a), Holding marriage certificate; £1 (No. **MS**880b), Standing on aircraft steps.

226 Postal Van at Dockside, 1930s

1999. 125th Anniv of U.P.U. Multicoloured.
881 5p. Type **226** 25 20
882 30p. Space shuttle and station 75 1·25

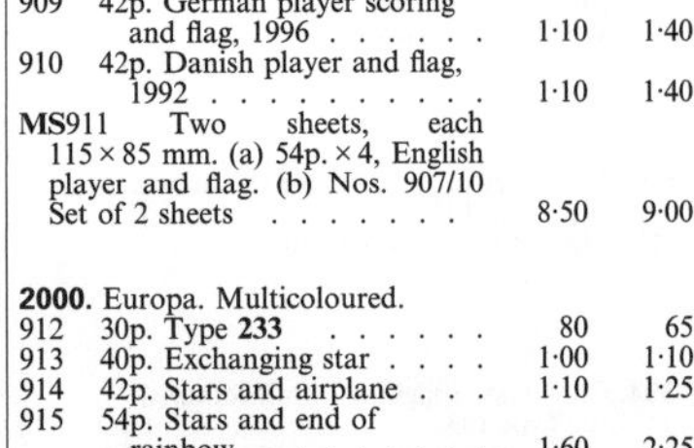

227 EF-2000 Eurofighter

1999. "Wings of Prey" (1st series). Birds of Prey and R.A.F. Fighter Aircraft. Multicoloured.
883 30p. Type **227** . . . . . . 1·00 1·25
884 30p. Panavia Tornado F3 . . 1·00 1·25
885 30p. BAe Harrier II GR7 . . 1·00 1·25
886 42p. Lesser kestrel . . . . . 1·00 1·25
887 42p. Peregrine falcon . . . . 1·00 1·25
888 42p. Common kestrel ("Kestrel") . . . . 1·00 1·25
MS889 Two sheets, each 105 × 86 mm. (a) Nos. 883/5. (b) Nos. 886/8 Set of 2 sheets . . . 5·50 6·00
See also Nos. 943/8 and 982/7.

228 Prince Edward and Sophie Rhys-Jones

1999. Royal Wedding. Multicoloured.
890 30p. Type **228** 70 65
891 42p. Prince Edward and Sophie Rhys-Jones holding hands (vert) . . . . 1·00 90
892 54p. In carriage on wedding day . . . . 1·40 2·00
893 66p. On Chapel steps after wedding (vert) . . . . . . 1·50 2·25

229 Football

230 "Seasons Greetings"

1999. Local Sporting Centenaries. Multicoloured.
894 30p. Type **229** 75 65
895 42p. Rowing . . . . 1·00 90
896 £1.20 Cricket . . . . 3·25 4·25

1999. Christmas. Multicoloured.
897 5p. Type **230** 15 10
898 5p. "Happy Christmas" . . . 15 10
899 30p. "Happy Millennium" . . 80 80
900 30p. "Happy Christmas" and Santa with reindeer 80 80
901 42p. Santa Claus in chimney 1·25 1·75
902 54p. Santa Claus leaving presents . . . . 1·40 2·50

231 "People travelling with Environmentally-friendly Jet-packs" (Colin Grech)

2000. "Stampin' the Future" (children's stamp design competition). Multicoloured.
903 30p. Type **231** . . . . . . 1·50 1·60
904 42p. "Robotic Postman" (Kim Barea) . . . . 1·50 1·60
905 54p. "Living on the Moon" (Stephan Williamson-Fa) 1·50 1·60
906 66p. "Jet-powered Cars" (Michael Podesta) . . . . 1·50 1·60

232 Dutch Football Player and Flag, 1988

233 Fountain of Stars

2000. European Football Championship, Belgium and Netherlands. Multicoloured.
907 30p. Type **232** 85 90
908 30p. French player and flag, 1984 . . . . 85 90
909 42p. German player scoring and flag, 1996 . . . . . . 1·10 1·40
910 42p. Danish player and flag, 1992 . . . . 1·10 1·40
MS911 Two sheets, each 115 × 85 mm. (a) 54p. × 4, English player and flag. (b) Nos. 907/10 Set of 2 sheets . . . . 8·50 9·00

2000. Europa. Multicoloured.
912 30p. Type **233** 80 65
913 40p. Exchanging star . . . . 1·00 1·10
914 42p. Stars and airplane . . . 1·10 1·25
915 54p. Stars and end of rainbow . . . . 1·60 2·25

234 3000 m Waterfall between Gibraltar and North African Coast, 5 Million B.C.

235 Princess Diana holding Prince William, 1982

2000. New Millennium. History of Gibraltar. Multicoloured (except Nos. 926/30).
916 5p. Type **234** 30 50
917 5p. Sabre-tooth tiger, 2 million B.C. 30 50
918 5p. Neanderthal hunting goat, and skull, 30,000 B.C. 30 50
919 5p. Phoenician traders and galley, 700 B.C. 30 50
920 5p. Roman warship, 100 B.C. 30 50
921 5p. Tarik-Ibn-Zayad, ape and Moorish Castle, 711 A.D. 30 50
922 5p. Coat of arms, 1502 . . . 30 50
923 5p. Admiral George Rooke and Union Jack, 1704 . . 30 50
924 30p. General Eliott at The Great Siege, 1779–83 . . . 80 90
925 30p. H.M.S. *Victory*, 1805 . . 80 90
926 30p. Queen Alexandra in horse-drawn carriage, 1903 (brown, silver and black) 80 90
927 30p. 100 ton gun, 1870s (grey, silver and black) . . 80 90
928 30p. Evacuees, 1940 (purple, silver and black) 80 90
929 30p. Tank and anti-aircraft gun, 1940s (brown, silver and black) 80 90
930 30p. Queen Elizabeth II in Gibraltar, 1954 (grey, silver and black) 80 90
931 30p. Aerial view of office district, 2000 . . . . . 80 90

2000. 18th Birthday of Prince William. Multicoloured.
932 30p. Type **235** 90 65
933 42p. Prince William as a toddler . . . . 1·25 90
934 54p. Prince William with Prince Charles . . . . . . 1·50 2·00
935 66p. Prince William at 18 . . 1·75 2·75
MS936 115 × 75 mm. Nos. 932/5 5·00 5·50

236 Lady Elizabeth Bowes-Lyon signing Book

2000. Queen Elizabeth the Queen Mother's 100th Birthday.
937 **236** 30p. black and blue . . . 90 65
938 – 42p. black and brown . . 1·25 90
939 – 54p. multicoloured . . . 1·50 2·00
940 – 66p. multicoloured . . . 1·75 2·75
MS941 115 × 75 mm. Nos. 937/40 4·75 5·50
DESIGNS: 42p. Duke and Duchess of York; 54p. Queen Mother with bouquet; 66p. Queen Mother in orange coat and hat.

237 Moorish Castle

2000.
942 **237** £5 black, silver and gold 10·00 11·00
The Queen's head on this stamp is printed in optically variable ink, which changes colour from gold to green when viewed from different angles.

2000. "Wings of Prey" (2nd series). Birds of Prey and R.A.F. Second World War Aircraft. As T **227**. Multicoloured.
943 30p. Supermarine Spitfire Mk IIA *Gibraltar* . . . . 1·40 1·50
944 30p. Hawker Hurricane Mk IIC . . . . 1·40 1·50

945 30p. Avro Lancaster BI-III *City of Lincoln* 1·40 1·50
946 42p. Merlin (male) 1·60 1·75
947 42p. Merlin (female) 1·60 1·75
948 42p. Bonelli's eagle 1·60 1·75
MS949 Two sheets, each 105×85 mm. (a) Nos. 943/5. (b) Nos. 946/8 Set of 2 sheets 7·50 8·50

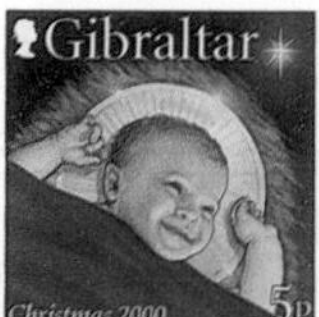

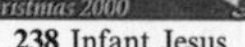

238 Infant Jesus

239 Wedding of Queen Victoria and Prince Albert

2000. Christmas. Multicoloured.
950 5p. Type **238** 25 15
951 30p. Virgin Mary with infant Jesus 85 65
952 30p. Journey to Bethlehem 85 65
953 40p. Mary and Joseph with innkeeper 1·10 1·00
954 42p. The Nativity 1·10 1·25
955 54p. Visit of the Wise Men 1·60 2·25

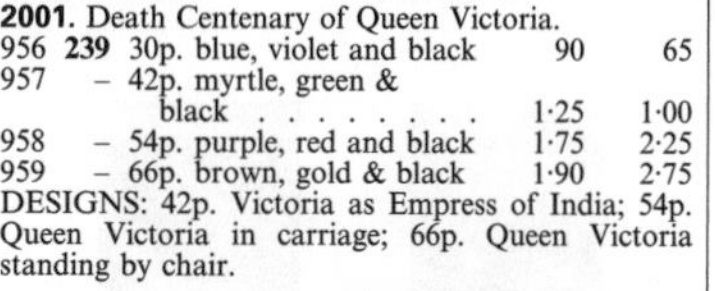

2001. Death Centenary of Queen Victoria.
956 **239** 30p. blue, violet and black 90 65
957 – 42p. myrtle, green & black 1·25 1·00
958 – 54p. purple, red and black 1·75 2·25
959 – 66p. brown, gold & black 1·90 2·75
DESIGNS: 42p. Victoria as Empress of India; 54p. Queen Victoria in carriage; 66p. Queen Victoria standing by chair.

240 Grass Snake

241 Long-snouted Seahorse

2001. Snakes. Multicoloured.
960 5p. Type **240** 25 40
961 5p. Ladder snake 25 40
962 5p. Montpellier snake 25 40
963 30p. Viperine snake 85 1·00
964 30p. Southern smooth snake 85 1·00
965 30p. False smooth snake 85 1·00
966 66p. Horseshoe whip snake (30×62 mm) 1·75 2·50
MS967 155×87 mm. Nos. 960/6 5·50 6·00
No. **MS**967 also commemorates the Chinese New Year "Year of the Snake".
No. 962 and **MS**967 are inscribed "MONTPELIER" in error.

2001. Europa. Water and Nature. Multicoloured.
968 30p. Type **241** 1·25 65
969 40p. Snapdragon 1·50 1·00
970 42p. Herring gull ("Yellow-legged Gull") 2·00 1·50
971 54p. Goldfish 2·00 2·75

242 Queen Elizabeth II as a Baby   **243** Battle of Trafalgar, 1805

2001. 75th Birthday of Queen Elizabeth II.
972 **242** 30p. black and mauve 85 75
973 – 30p. black and violet 85 75
974 – 42p. black and red 1·25 1·50
975 – 42p. black and violet 1·25 1·50
976 – 54p. multicoloured 1·60 2·25
MS977 101×89 mm. £2 multicoloured 4·75 5·50
DESIGNS—HORIZ: No. 973, Queen Elizabeth as teenager; 974, On wedding day, 1947; 975, After Coronation, 1953; 976, Queen Elizabeth in blue hat. VERT: (35×49 mm)—No. **MS**977, Queen Elizabeth II, 2001 (photo by Fiona Hanson).
No. **MS**977 marks a successful attempt on the record for the fastest produced stamp issue. The miniature sheet was on sale in Gibraltar 10 hours and 24 minutes after the artwork was approved at Buckingham Palace.

2001. Bicentenary of *The Gibraltar Chronicle* (newspaper). Each black.
978 30p. Type **243** 1·25 65
979 42p. Invention of the telephone, 1876 1·25 90
980 54p. Winston Churchill (Victory in Second World War, 1945) 2·00 2·25
981 66p. Footprint on Moon (Moon landing, 1969) 2·25 3·00

2001. "Wings of Prey" (3rd series). Birds of Prey and Modern Military Aircraft. As T **227**. Multicoloured.
982 40p. Royal Navy Sea Harrier FA MK.2 1·00 1·25
983 40p. Western marsh harrier ("Marsh Harrier") 1·00 1·25
984 40p. R.A.F. Hawk T MK.1 1·00 1·25
985 40p. Northern sparrowhawk ("Sparrowhawk") 1·00 1·25
986 40p. R.A.F. Jaguar GR1B 1·00 1·25
987 40p. Northern hobby ("Hobby") 1·00 1·25
MS988 Two sheets, each 103×84 mm. (a) Nos. 982, 984 and 986. (b) Nos 983, 985 and 987 Set of 2 sheets 5·50 6·00

244 Snoopy as Father Christmas with Woodstock

246 Joshua Grimaldi

245 One Cent Coin

2001. Christmas. Peanuts (cartoon characters by Charles Schulz). Multicoloured.
989 5p. Type **244** 25 15
990 30p. Charlie Brown and Snoopy with Christmas tree 85 65
991 40p. Snoopy asleep in wreath 1·10 1·00
992 42p. Snoopy with plate of biscuits 1·25 1·25
993 54p. Snoopy asleep on kennel 1·75 2·50
MS994 140×85 mm. Nos. 989/93 4·75 5·50

2002. Introduction of Euro Currency by European Union. Coins. Sheet 165×105 mm, containing T **245** and similar square designs showing coins. Multicoloured.
MS995 5p. Type **245**; 12p. 2 cents; 30p. 5 cents; 35p. 10 cents; 40p. 20 cents; 42p. 50 cents; 54p. 1 Euro; 66p. 2 Euros. 7·00 7·50

2002. Golden Jubilee. As T **219** of Falkland Islands.
996 30p. black, red and gold 1·00 1·10
997 30p. agate, red and gold 1·00 1·10
998 30p. multicoloured 1·00 1·10
999 30p. multicoloured 1·00 1·10
1000 75p. multicoloured 2·00 2·50
MS1001 162×95 mm. Nos. 996/1000 5·50 6·00
DESIGNS—HORIZ: No. 996, Princess Elizabeth and Princess Margaret making radio broadcast, 1940; 997, Princess Elizabeth in Girl Guide uniform, 1942; 998, Queen Elizabeth in evening dress, 1961; 999, Queen Elizabeth in Chelsea, 1993. VERT (38×51 mm): No 1000, Queen Elizabeth after Annigoni.

2002. Europa. Circus. Famous Clowns. Multicoloured.
1002 30p. Type **246** 90 65
1003 40p. Karl Wettach ("Grock") 1·25 1·25
1004 42p. Nicolai Polakovs ("Coco") 1·25 1·25
1005 54p. Charlie Cairoli 1·75 2·50

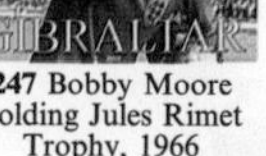

247 Bobby Moore holding Jules Rimet Trophy, 1966

248 Barbary Macaque

2002. World Cup Football Championship, Japan and Korea (2002). England's Victory, 1966. Multicoloured.
1006 30p. Type **247** 1·00 65
1007 42p. Kissing Trophy 1·40 90
1008 54p. Bobby Moore with Queen Elizabeth II 1·75 2·00
1009 66p. Bobby Moore in action 2·00 2·50
MS1010 135×90 mm. Nos. 1006/9 5·50 6·00

2002. Wildlife. Multicoloured.
1011 30p. Type **248** 90 80
1012 30p. Red fox (horiz) 90 80
1013 40p. White-toothed shrew (horiz) 1·25 85
1014 £1 Rabbit 2·75 3·25
MS1015 125×100 mm. Nos. 1011/14 5·50 6·00

249 Gibraltar from the North

250 Princess Diana holding Prince Harry

2002. Views of the Rock of Gibraltar. Multicoloured.
1016 30p. Type **249** 90 75
1017 30p. View from the south 90 75
1018 £1 View from the east (50×40 mm) 2·75 3·25
1019 £1 View from the west (50×40 mm) 2·75 3·25
Nos. 1016/19 were printed together, se-tenant, with powdered particles of the Rock sintered to their surface using thermography.

2002. 18th Birthday of Prince Harry. Multicoloured.
1020 30p. Type **250** 90 65
1021 42p. Prince Harry waving 1·25 90
1022 54p. Prince Harry skiing 1·50 1·60
1023 66p. Wearing dark suit 1·90 2·50
MS1024 115×75 mm. Nos. 1020/3 5·00 5·50

251 Crib, Cathedral of St. Mary the Crowned

2002. Christmas. Cribs from Gibraltar Cathedrals and Churches. Multicoloured.
1025 5p. Type **251** 25 10
1026 30p. St. Joseph's Parish Church 90 65
1027 40p. St. Theresa's Parish Church 1·25 85
1028 42p. Our Lady of Sorrows Church 1·25 90
1029 52p. St. Bernard's Church 1·50 2·00
1030 54p. Cathedral of the Holy Trinity 1·50 2·00

252 Archbishop of Canterbury crowning Queen Elizabeth II

254 Drama Festival Poster

253 Young Prince William with Princess Diana

2003. 50th Anniv of the Coronation. Each black, grey and purple.
1031 30p. Type **252** 90 80
1032 30p. Queen Elizabeth II in Coronation robes 90 80
1033 40p. Queen Elizabeth holding the Orb and Sceptre 1·25 85
1034 £1 Queen Elizabeth in Coronation Coach 2·75 3·25
MS1035 116×76 mm. Nos. 1031/4 5·50 6·00

2003. 21st Birthday of Prince William of Wales. Each black, grey and violet.
1036 30p. Type **253** 90 80
1037 30p. Prince William at Eton College 90 80
1038 40p. Prince William 1·25 85
1039 £1 Prince William in Operation Raleigh sweatshirt 2·75 3·25
MS1040 115×75mm. Nos. 1036/9 5·50 6·00

2003. Europa. Poster Art. Multicoloured.
1041 30p. Type **254** 90 65
1042 40p. Spring Festival poster 1·25 1·00
1043 42p. Art Festival poster 1·25 1·00
1044 54p. Dance festival poster 1·75 2·00

255 Wright Brothers' *Flyer I*, 1903

2003. Centenary of Powered Flight. Aircraft.
1045 **255** 30p. multicoloured 90 65
1046 – 40p. black and brown 1·25 1·25
1047 – 40p. black and blue 1·25 1·25
1048 – 42p. black and blue 1·25 1·25
1049 – 44p. multicoloured 1·40 1·40
1050 – 66p. multicoloured 2·00 2·25
MS1051 140×110 mm. Nos. 1045/50 7·25 7·50
DESIGNS—HORIZ: (37×28 mm) 40p. (No. 1046) Charles Lindbergh and *Spirit of St. Louis* (first Transatlantic solo flight, 1927); 40p. (No. 1047) Boeing 314 Yankee Clipper flying boat (first Transatlantic scheduled air service, 1939). (77×28 mm)—42p. Saunders Roe Saro A 21 Windhover amphibian (first scheduled air service between Gibraltar and Tangier, 1931); 44p. British Airways Concorde (first supersonic airliner, 1976). VERT (37×58 mm)—66p. Space shuttle *Columbia* (first shuttle flight in Space orbit, 1981).

256 Flag of St. George

2003. 1700th Death Anniv of St. George. Multicoloured.
1052 30p. Type **256** 80 65
1053 40p. Cross of Military Constantinian Order of St. George 1·10 95
1054 £1.20 "St. George and the Dragon" (stained glass window, St. Joseph's Church, Gibraltar) (32×63 mm) 3·00 3·25
MS1055 150×100 mm. Nos. 1052/4 4·50 5·00

257 Big Ben, Swift and Rock of Gibraltar

2003.
1056 **257** (£3) multicoloured† 6·00 6·25
No. 1056 is inscribed "UK express" and was initially sold at £3.
†The Queen's head on this stamp is printed in optically variable ink which changes colour from gold to green when viewed from different angles.

258 Wood Blewit (*Lepista nuda*)

2003. Mushrooms of Gibraltar. Multicoloured.
1057 30p. Type **258** 80 80
1058 30p. Blue-green funnel-cap (*Clitocybe odora*) 80 80
1059 30p. Sulphur tuft (*Hypholoma fasciculare*) 80 80
1060 £1.20 Field mushrooms (*Agaricus campestris*) 3·00 3·25
MS1061 105×90mm. Nos. 1057/60 4·75 5·50

259 Daisy (Latvia), Cornflower (Estonia) and Rue (Lithuania)

2003. Enlargement of the European Union (2004). Designs showing the national flowers of new member countries. Multicoloured.
1062 30p. Type **259** 90 65
1063 40p. Rose (Cyprus) and Maltese Centaury (Malta) 1·25 1·00
1064 42p. Tulip (Hungary), Carnation (Slovenia) and Dog Rose (Slovakia) . . 1·25 1·00
1065 54p. Corn Poppy (Poland) and Scented Thyme (Czech Republic) . . . . 1·75 2·00

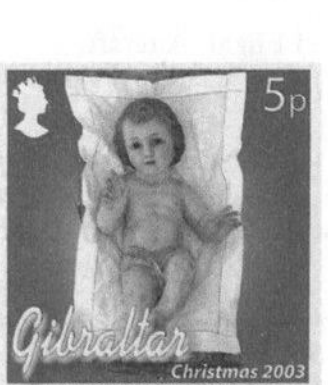

260 Baby Jesus Crib Figure, Our Lady of Sorrows Church **261** Street Cafe

2003. Christmas. Multicoloured.
1066 5p. Type **260** 20 10
1067 30p. Children making Crib 90 65
1068 40p. Three Kings Cavalcade 1·25 1·00
1069 42p. Children's provisions for Santa and reindeer . . 1·25 1·00
1070 54p. Cathedral of St. Mary the Crowned lit for Christmas Eve Midnight Mass . . . . 1·75 2·00
MS1071 100 × 80mm. £1 Cartoon characters from Peanuts carol singing around Christmas tree (50 × 40mm) . . . . 3·25 3·75

2004. Europa. Holidays. Multicoloured.
1072 40p. Type **261** . . . . . 1·25 1·25
1073 40p. St. Michael's Cave . . 1·25 1·25
1074 54p. Dolphins . . . . . . 1·75 2·00
1075 54p. Harbourside restaurant 1·75 2·00

262 Arms

2004. 300th Anniv of British Gibraltar (1st series). Multicoloured.
1076 8p. Type **262** 40 50
MS1077 144 × 114 mm. 30p. Royal Katarine flying Red Ensign, 1704; 30p. Landing party, 1704; 30p. Soldiers of 1704; 30p. Arms of Gibraltar on military uniform; 30p. Royal Gibraltar police helmet and red phone box; 30p. Post Office arms and red pillar box; 30p. Graduates and University of Cambridge examination certificate; 30p. Crowd waving Union Jacks and Gibraltar flags; £1.20 Union Jack . . . . . . 9·00 10·00
See also **MS**1095.

263 Queen Elizabeth holding Bouquet

2004. 50th Anniv of Visit of Queen Elizabeth II.
1078 **263** 38p. multicoloured . . . 80 85
1079 – 40p. black and yellow . . 80 85
1080 – 47p. multicoloured . . . 95 1·00
1081 – £1 black . . . . 2·00 2·00
MS1082 95 × 110 mm. £1.50 black 3·00 3·00
DESIGNS: 38p. Type **263**; 40p.Queen Elizabeth holding out keys; 47p. Queen and Duke of Edinburgh in car; £1 Queen, Prince Charles and Princess Anne with members of British armed forces; £1.50 Queen waving with Duke of Edinburgh.

264 Scoring a Goal

2004. European Football Championships 2004, Portugal. Multicoloured.
1083 30p. Type **264** 60 65
1084 40p. Two defenders blocking a goal attempt 80 85
1085 40p. Overhead kick 80 85
1086 £1 Player performing header 2·00 2·10
MS1087 Two sheets. (a) 102 × 77 mm. £1.50 Player celebrating with arms in air (51 × 39 mm) (b) 105 × 105 mm (circular). Nos. 1083/6 . . . . 7·25 7·25

265 Landing at St. Aubin, 1944

2004. 60th Anniv of D-Day Landings. Each black, brown and red.
1088 38p. Type **265** 80 85
1089 40p. Cruiser tank Mk VIII Cromwell 80 85
1090 47p. Handley Page Halifax plane . . . . 95 1·00
1091 £1 HMS *Belfast* . . . . . . 2·00 2·10
MS1092 170 × 100 mm. Nos. 1089/92 . . . . 4·50 4·50

266 Union Jack Flag **267** Mallow-leaved Bindweed

2004. 300th Anniv of British Gibraltar (2nd series). Elton John Tercentenary Concert. Circular sheet 105 × 105 mm.
MS1093 266 £1.20 multicoloured 2·40 2·40
Stamp in No. **MS**1093 is similar in design to the £1.20 stamp in No. **MS**1077.

2004. Wild Flowers. Multicoloured.
1094 1p. Type **267** 10 10
1095 2p. Gibraltar sea lavender 10 10
1096 5p. Gibraltar chickweed . . 10 10
1097 (G) Romulea 15 10
1098 10p. Common centaury . . 20 25
1099 (G1) Pyramidal orchid . . . 60 65
1100 (S) Friars cowl 55 60
1101 (UK) Corn poppy 80 85
1102 (E) Giant tangier fennel . . 60 65
1103 (U) Snapdragon . . . . . . 1·00 1·10
1104 50p. Common gladiolus . . 1·00 1·10
1105 £1 Yellow horned poppy . . 2·00 2·10
1106 £3 Gibraltar candytuft . . . 6·00 6·25

268 Father Christmas

2004. Christmas. Decorations. Multicoloured.
1107 7p. Type **268** 15 20
1108 28p. Cherub 55 60
1109 38p. Red star 75 80
1110 40p. Gold conical tree . . . 80 85
1111 47p. Red bauble . . . . . . 95 1·00
1112 53p. Gold star . . . . . . 1·10 1·20

269 Ferrari F2003 GA

2004. Ferrari. Multioloured.
1113 5p. Type **269** 10 10
1114 5p. F2004 . . . . 10 10
1115 30p. F2001 . . . . 60 65
1116 30p. F2002 . . . . 60 65
1117 75p. F399 . . . . 1·50 1·60
1118 75p. F1-2000 . . . . 1·50 1·60
MS1119 161 × 116 mm. Nos. 1113/18 . . . . 4·50 4·75

270 Soldier guarding Nelson's Body

2005. Bicentenary of the Battle of Trafalgar. Multicoloured.
1120 38p. Type **270** 70 75
1121 40p. HMS *Entreprenante* . . 80 85
1122 47p. Admiral Nelson (vert) 95 1·00
1123 £1.60 HMS *Victory* . . . . 3·25 3·40
MS1124 120 × 80 mm. £2 HMS *Victory* (44 × 44 mm) . . . . . 4·00 4·25
Nos. 1120/4 contain traces of powdered wood from HMS *Victory*.

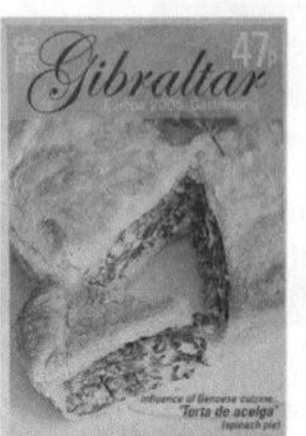

271 Spinach Pie

2005. Europa. Gastronomy. Multicoloured.
1125 47p. Type **271** . . . . . . 95 1·00
1126 47p. Grilled sea-bass . . . . 95 1·00
1127 47p. Veal "Birds" . . . . . 95 1·00
1128 47p. Sherry trifle . . . . . 95 1·00

POSTAGE DUE STAMPS

D 1 D 2

1956.
D1 D **1** 1d. green . . . . 1·50 4·25
D2 2d. brown . . . . 1·50 2·75
D3 4d. blue . . . . 1·75 5·00

1971. As Nos. D1/3, but inscr in decimal currency.
D4 ½p. green 25 80
D5 1p. brown 25 70
D6 2p. blue . . . . 25 1·00

1976.
D 7 D **2** 1p. orange 15 60
D 8 3p. blue 15 75
D 9 5p. red 20 75
D10 7p. violet 20 75
D11 10p. green 25 75
D12 20p. green . . . . . . 45 1·00

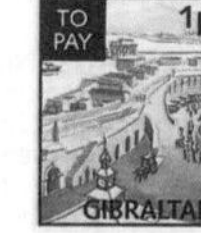

D **3** Gibraltar Coat of Arms D **4** Water Port Gates

1984.
D13 D **3** 1p. black 25 50
D14 3p. red 35 50
D15 5p. blue 40 50
D16 10p. blue 50 50
D17 25p. mauve . . . . . . 90 1·00
D18 50p. orange . . . . . . 1·40 1·75
D19 £1 green . . . . 2·25 3·00

1996. Gibraltar Landmarks.
D20 D **4** 1p. black, emerald and green 15 50
D21 – 10p. black and grey . . 50 60
D22 – 25p. black, brown and chestnut 80 80
D23 – 50p. black and lilac . . . 1·25 1·40
D24 – £1 black, brown and chestnut . . . . . . 2·75 3·00
D25 – £2 black and blue . . . 4·25 4·75
DESIGNS: 10p. Naval Dockyard; 25p. Military Hospital; 50p. Governor's Cottage; £1 Swans on the Laguna; £2 Catalan Bay.

D **5** Greenfinch

2002. Gibraltar Finches. Type D **5** Multicoloured.
D26 5p. Type D **5** 10 10
D27 10p. Serin 20 15
D28 20p. Siskin 40 45
D29 50p. Linnet . . . . 1·00 1·10
D30 £1 Chaffinch . . . . 2·00 2·10
D31 £2 Goldfinch . . . . 4·00 4·25

GILBERT AND ELLICE ISLANDS

Pt. 1

A British colony in the South Pacific.

1911. 12 pence = 1 shilling;
20 shillings = 1 pound.
1966. 100 cents = $1 Australian.

1911. Stamps of Fiji (King Edward VII) optd **GILBERT & ELLICE PROTECTORATE.**
1 **23** ½d. green . . . . 4·75 45·00
2 1d. red . . . . 45·00 28·00
3 2d. grey . . . . 9·00 15·00
4 2½d. blue . . . . 12·00 30·00
5 5d. purple and green . . . . 45·00 75·00
6 6d. purple . . . . 20·00 45·00
7 1s. black on green . . . . . 20·00 60·00

2 Pandanus Pine **3**

1911.
8 **2** ½d. green . . . . 4·25 15·00
9 1d. red . . . . 2·00 7·00
10 2d. grey . . . . 1·50 7·00
11 2½d. blue . . . . 5·00 11·00

1912.
27 **3** ½d. green . . . . 3·25 3·25
13 1d. red . . . . 2·25 5·00
28 1d. violet . . . . 4·50 5·50
29 1½d. red . . . . 4·50 2·00
30 2d. grey . . . . 7·00 27·00
15 2½d. blue . . . . 1·75 11·00
16 3d. purple on yellow . . . . 2·50 8·50
17 4d. black and red on yellow 75 7·00
18 5d. purple and green . . . . 1·75 7·00
19 6d. purple . . . . 1·25 7·50
20 1s. black on green . . . . . 1·25 5·50
21 2s. purple and blue on blue 14·00 30·00
22 2s.6d. black and red on blue 16·00 25·00
23 5s. green and red on yellow 32·00 60·00
35 10s. green and red on green £150 £350
24 £1 purple and black on red £550 £1400

1918. Optd **WAR TAX.**
26 **3** 1d. red . . . . 50 6·50

1935. Silver Jubilee. As T **10a** of Gambia.
36 1d. blue and black . . . . . 2·25 9·00
37 1½d. blue and red . . . . . 1·75 3·75
38 3d. brown and blue . . . . . 5·50 12·00
39 1s. grey and purple . . . . . 20·00 20·00

1937. Coronation. As T**10b** of Gambia.
40 1d. violet 35 65
41 1½d. red 35 65
42 3d. blue 40 70

6 Great Frigate Bird

7 Pandanus Pine

1939.
43 **6** ½d. blue and green . . . . 60 1·00
44 **7** 1d. green and purple . . . . 30 1·50
45 – 1½d. black and red . . . . 30 1·25
46 – 2d. brown and black . . . . 75 1·00
47 – 2½d. black and green . . . 40 70
48 – 3d. black and blue . . . . 45 1·00
49 – 5d. blue and brown . . . . 4·25 1·50
50 – 6d. green and violet 50 60
51a – 1s. black and turquoise . . 6·00 3·25
52 – 2s. blue and red . . . . . 10·00 10·00
53 – 2s.6d. blue and green . . . 10·00 11·00
54 – 5s. red and blue . . . . . . 13·00 14·00

DESIGNS: 1½d. Canoe crossing reef; 2d. Canoe and boat-house; 2½d. Native house; 3d. Seascape; 5d. Ellice Is. canoe; 6d. Coconut palms; 1s. Jetty, Ocean Is.; 2s. H.M.C.S. "Nimanoa"; 2s.6d. Gilbert Is. canoe; 5s. Coat of arms.

1946. Victory. As T **11a** of Gambia.
55 1d. purple 15 50
56 3d. blue 15 50

1949. Silver Wedding. As T **11b/c** of Gambia.
57 1d. violet 40 50
58 £1 red . . . . 12·00 20·00

1949. U.P.U. As T **11d/g** of Gambia.
59 1d. purple . . . . 40 1·25
60 2d. black . . . . 2·00 2·75
61 3d. blue . . . . 50 2·50
62 1s. blue . . . . 50 2·00

1953. Coronation. As T **11h** of Gambia.
63 2d. black and grey . . . . . 55 2·25

18 Great Frigate Bird

1956. As 1939 issue but with portrait of Queen Elizabeth II as in T **18** and colours changed.
64 **18** ½d. black and blue . . . . 65 1·25
65 **7** 1d. olive and violet . . . . 60 1·25
85 – 2d. green and purple . . . . 75 2·00
67 – 2½d. black and green . . . 50 60
68 – 3d. black and red 50 60
69 – 5d. blue and orange . . . . 8·50 1·75
70 – 6d. brown and black . . . . 55 2·75
71 – 1s. black and olive . . . . 2·25 60
72 – 2s. blue and sepia . . . . . 7·00 4·00
73 – 2s.6d. red and blue . . . . 8·00 4·00
74 – 5s. blue and green . . . . . 8·50 7·00
75 – 10s. black & turq (as 1½d.) 28·00 13·00

19 Loading Phosphate from Cantilever

1960. Diamond Jubilee of Phosphate Discovery at Ocean Is. Inscr "1900 1960".
76 **19** 2d. green and red 70 85
77 – 2½d. black and olive 70 85
78 – 1s. black and turquoise . . 70 85
DESIGNS: 2½d. Phosphate rock; 1s. Phosphate mining.

1963. Freedom from Hunger. As T **20a** of Gambia.
79 10d. blue 75 30

1963. Red Cross Cent. As T **20b** of Gambia.
80 2d. red and black 50 50
81 10d. red and blue . . . . . . 75 2·50

23 Reef Heron in Flight

1964. First Air Service.
82 – 3d. blue, black and light blue 70 30
83 **23** 1s. light blue, black and blue 90 30
84 – 3s.7d. green, black & emerald . . . . 1·40 1·50
DESIGNS—VERT: 3d. De Havilland Heron 2 and route map; 3s.7d. De Havilland Heron 2 over Tarawa lagoon.

1965. Cent of I.T.U. As T **44** of Gibraltar.
87 3d. orange and green 15 10
88 2s.6d. turquoise and purple . . 45 20

26 Gilbertese Women's Dance

1965. Multicoloured.
89 ½d. Maneaba and Gilbertese man blowing Bu shell (vert) 10 10
90 1d. Ellice Islanders Reef fishing by flare (vert) . . . 10 10
91 2d. Gilbertese girl weaving head-garland (vert) 10 10
92 3d. Gilbertese woman performing Ruoia (vert) . . 10 10
93 4d. Gilbertese man performing Kamei (vert) 15 10
94 5d. Gilbertese girl drawing water (vert) 20 10
95 6d. Ellice Islander performing a Fatele (vert) 20 10
96 7d. Ellice youths performing spear dance (vert) 25 10
97 1s. Gilbertese girl tending Ikaroa Babai plant (vert) 50 10
98 1s.6d. Ellice Islanders dancing a Fatele (vert) . . . . . . 1·00 65
99 2s. Ellice Islanders pounding Pulaka (vert) . . . . . . 1·00 1·40
100 3s.7d. Type **26** . . . . . . 1·75 65
101 5s. Gilbertese boys playing a stick game . . . . 1·75 80
102 10s. Ellice youths beating the box for the Fatele . . . . 2·50 1·00
103 £1 Coat of arms . . . . . . 3·00 1·75

1965. I.C.Y. As T **45** of Gibraltar.
104 ½d. purple and turquoise . . 10 10
105 3s.7d. green and lavender . . 50 20

1966. Churchill Commem. As T **46** of Gibraltar.
106 ½d. blue 10 10
107 3d. green 20 10
108 3s. brown 40 35
109 3s.7d. violet 45 35

1966. Decimal Currency. Nos. 89/103 surch.
110 1c. on 1d. 10 10
111 2c. on 2d. 10 10
112 3c. on 3d. 10 10
113 4c. on ½d. 10 10
114 5c. on 6d. 15 10
115 6c. on 4d. 15 10
116 8c. on 5d. 15 10
117 10c. on 1s. 15 10
118 15c. on 7d. 60 40
119 20c. on 1s.6d. 30 25
120 25c. on 2s. 30 20
121 35c. on 3s.7d. . . . . 1·00 20
122 50c. on 5s. 55 35
123 $1 on 10s. 55 40
124 $2 on £1 . . . . 1·25 2·50

1966. World Cup Football Championship. As T **47** of Gibraltar.
125 3c. multicoloured 20 10
126 35c. multicoloured 55 20

1966. Inauguration of W.H.O. Headquarters, Geneva. As T **54** of Gibraltar.
127 3c. black, green and blue . . 20 10
128 12c. black, purple and ochre 45 40

1966. 20th Anniv of UNESCO. As T **56a/c** of Gibraltar.
129 5c. multicoloured 25 35
130 10c. yellow, violet and olive 35 10
131 20c. black, purple and orange 60 45

41 H.M.S. "Royalist"

1967. 75th Anniv of Protectorate.
132 **41** 3c. red, blue and green . . 30 50
133 – 10c. multicoloured 15 15
134 – 35c. sepia, yellow and green 30 50
DESIGNS: 10c. Trading post; 35c. Island family.

1968. Decimal Currency. As Nos. 89/103, but with values inscr in decimal currency.
135 – 1c. multicoloured (as 1d.) 10 15
136 – 2c. multicoloured (as 2d.) 15 10
137 – 3c. multicoloured (as 3d.) 15 10
138 – 4c. multicoloured (as ½d.) 15 10
139 – 5c. multicoloured (as 6d.) 15 10
140 – 6c. multicoloured (as 4d.) 20 10
141 – 8c. multicoloured (as 5d.) 20 10
142 – 10c. multicoloured (as 1s.) 20 10
143 – 15c. multicoloured (as 7d.) 50 20
144 – 20c. multicoloured (as 1s.6d.) 65 15
145 – 25c. multicoloured (as 2s.) 1·25 20
146 **26** 35c. multicoloured . . . . 1·50 20
147 – 50c. multicoloured (as 5s.) 1·50 2·50
148 – $1 multicoloured (as 10s.) 1·50 3·75
149 – $2 multicoloured (as £1) 4·00 3·75

45 Map of Tarawa Atoll

1968. 25th Anniversary of Battle of Tarawa.
150 3c. Type **45** 20 30
151 10c. Marines landing 20 20
152 15c. Beach-head assault . . . 20 35
153 35c. Raising U.S. and British flags 25 50

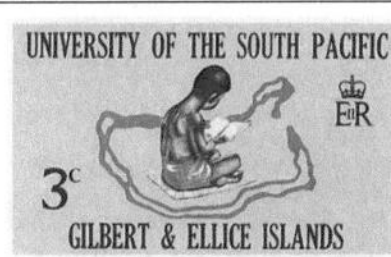

46 Young Pupil against Outline of Abemama Island

1969. End of Inaugural Year of South Pacific University.
154 **46** 3c. multicoloured 10 25
155 – 10c. multicoloured 10 10
156 – 35c. black, brown and green 15 30
DESIGNS: 10c. Boy and girl students and Tarawa atoll; 35c. University graduate and South Pacific islands.

47 "Virgin and Child" in Pacific Setting

1969. Christmas.
157 – 2c. multicoloured 15 20
158 **47** 10c. multicoloured 15 10
DESIGN: 2c. as Type **47**. but with grass foreground instead of sand.

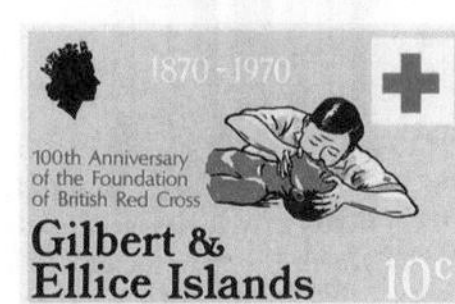

48 "Kiss of Life"

1970. Centenary of British Red Cross.
159 **48** 10c. multicoloured 20 10
160 – 15c. multicoloured 30 45
161 – 35c. multicoloured 60 90
Nos. 160/1 are as Type **48**, but arranged differently.

49 Foetus and Patients

1970. 25th Anniversary of U.N.
162 **49** 5c. multicoloured 15 30
163 – 10c. black, grey and red . . 15 15
164 – 15c. multicoloured 20 30
165 – 35c. blue, green and black 30 45
DESIGNS: 10c. Nurse and surgical instruments; 15c. X-ray plate and technician; 35c. U.N. emblem and map.

53 Map of Gilbert Islands

1970. Centenary of Landing in Gilbert islands by London Missionary Society.
166 **53** 2c. multicoloured 15 90
167 – 10c. black and green . . . 25 15
168 – 25c. brown and blue . . . 20 20
169 – 35c. blue, black and red . . 50 70
DESIGNS—VERT: 10c. Sailing-ship "John Williams III"; 25c. Rev. S. J. Whitmee. HORIZ: 35c. M.V. "John Williams VII".

57 "Child with Halo" (T. Collis)

1970. Christmas. Sketches. Multicoloured.
170 2c. Type **57** 10 30
171 10c. "Sanctuary, Tarawa Cathedral" (Mrs A. Burroughs) 10 10
172 35c. "Three Ships inside Star" (Mrs. C. Barnett) . . 20 20

60 Casting Nets

1971. Multicoloured.
173 1c. Cutting toddy (vert) . . . 10 10
174 2c. Lagoon fishing 15 30
175 3c. Cleaning pandanus leaves 15 15
176 4c. Type **60** 20 25
177 5c. Gilbertese canoe 45 15
178 6c. De-husking coconuts (vert) 30 45
179 8c. Weaving pandanus fronds (vert) 35 15
180 10c. Weaving a basket (vert) 40 15
181 15c. Tiger shark and fishermen (vert) . . . . . 2·75 1·50
182 20c. Beating rolled pandanus leaf . . . . 1·50 90
183 25c. Loading copra . . . . . 2·00 1·00
184 35c. Fishing at night . . . . 2·25 50
185 50c. Local handicrafts (vert) 1·00 1·50
186 $1 Weaving coconut screens (vert) . . . . 1·40 1·25
187 $2 Coat of arms (vert) . . . 2·50 8·00

61 House of Representatives

1971. New Constitution. Multicoloured.
188 3c. Type **61** 10 20
189 10c. Maneaba Betio (Assembly hut) 20 10

62 Pacific Nativity Scene

1971. Christmas.
190 **62** 3c. black, yellow and blue 10 20
191 – 10c. black, gold and blue 10 10
192 – 35c. black, gold and red . . 25 35
DESIGNS: 10c. Star and palm leaves; 35c. Outrigger canoe and star.

63 Emblem and Young Boys

1971. 25th Anniv of UNICEF. Multicoloured.
193 3c. Type **63** 10 90
194 10c. Young boy 15 25
195 35c. Young boy's face . . . 45 90
Nos. 193/5 include the UNICEF emblem within each design.

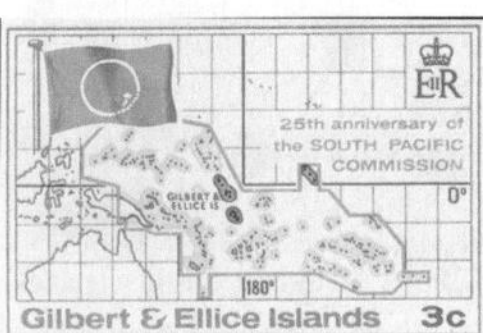

64 Flag and Map of South Pacific

1972. 25th Anniv of South Pacific Commission. Multicoloured.
196 3c. Type **64** 10 80
197 10c. Flag and native boats . . 15 20
198 35c. Flags of member nations 15 95

65 "Alveopora"

1972. Coral. Multicoloured.
199 3c. Type **65** 25 45
200 10c. "Euphyllia" 30 15
201 15c. "Melithea" 40 35
202 35c. "Spongodes" 80 60

66 Star of Peace   69 Dancer

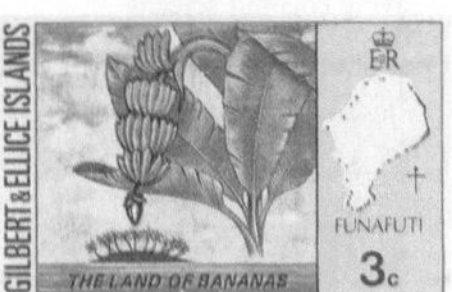

68 Funafuti ("The Land of Bananas")

1972. Christmas. Multicoloured.
208 3c. Type **66** 10 10
209 10c. "The Nativity" 10 10
210 35c. Baby in "manger" (horiz) 30 30

1972. Royal Silver Wedding. As T **98** of Gibraltar, but with Floral Headdresses in background.
211 3c. brown 10 15
212 35c. brown 25 15

1973. Legends of Island Names (1st series). Mult.
213 3c. Type **68** 15 60
214 10c. Butaritari ("The Smell of the Sea") 15 20
215 25c. Tarawa ("The Centre of the World") 25 55
216 35c. Abemama ("The Land of the Moon") 30 65
See also Nos. 252/5.

1973. Christmas. Multicoloured.
217 3c. Type **69** 10 25
218 10c. Canoe and lagoon . . . 10 10
219 35c. Lagoon at evening . . . 30 15
220 50c. Map of Christmas Island 40 1·60

1973. Royal Wedding. As T **101a** of Gibraltar. Multicoloured, background colours given.
221 3c. green 10 15
222 35c. blue 20 15

70 Meteorological Observation

1973. Centenary of I.M.O./W.M.O. Mult.
223 3c. Type **70** 30 30
224 10c. Island observing-station 30 20
225 35c. Wind-finding radar . . . 40 25
226 50c. World weather watch stations . . . . 50 1·25

71 Te Mataaua Crest

1974. Canoe Crests. Multicoloured.
227 3c. Type **71** 10 25
228 10c. "Te Nimta-wawa" . . . 15 10
229 35c. "Tara-tara-venei-na" . . 25 10
230 50c. "Te Bou-uoua" . . . . 35 1·60
MS231 154 × 130 mm. Nos. 227/30 2·00 5·50

72 £1 Stamp of 1924 and Te Koroba (canoe)

1974. Centenary of U.P.U.
232 **72** 4c. multicoloured 20 40
233 – 10c. multicoloured 20 15
234 – 25c. multicoloured 25 30
235 – 35c. multicoloured 30 50
DESIGNS: 10c. 5s. stamp of 1939 and sailing vessel "Kiakia"; 25c. $2 stamp of 1971 and B.A.C. One Eleven airplane; 35c. U.P.U. emblem.

73 Toy Canoe

1974. Christmas. Multicoloured.
236 4c. Type **73** 10 30
237 10c. Toy windmill 15 15
238 25c. Coconut "ball" 20 40
239 35c. Canoes and constellation Pleiades 25 55

74 North Front Entrance, Blenheim Palace

1974. Birth Cent of Sir Winston Churchill. Mult.
240 4c. Type **74** 10 40
241 10c. Churchill painting . . . 10 15
242 35c. Churchill's statue, London 25 50

75 Barometer Crab

1975. Crabs. Multicoloured.
243 4c. Type **75** . . . . 40 1·25
244 10c. "Ranina ranina" 40 25
245 25c. Pelagic swimmming crab 65 90
246 35c. Ghost crab . . . . . . 75 1·75

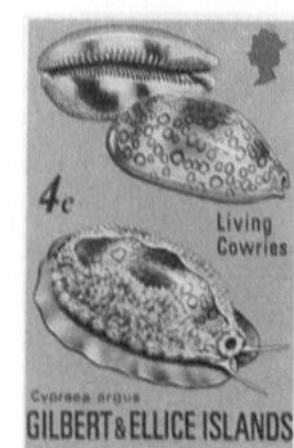

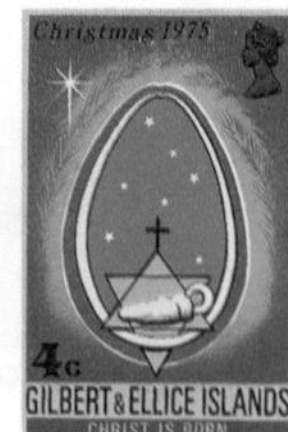

76 Eyed Cowrie   77 "Christ is Born"

1975. Cowrie Shells. Multicoloured.
247 4c. Type **76** . . . . 55 1·25
248 10c. Sieve cowrie 70 30
249 25c. Mole cowrie . . . . . . 1·10 1·50
250 35c. All-red map cowrie . . . 1·25 2·50
MS251 146 × 137 mm. Nos. 247/50 14·00 17·00

1975. Legends of Island Names (2nd series). As T **68**. Multicoloured.
252 4c. Beru ("The Bud") 10 50
253 10c. Onotoa ("Six Giants") 10 15
254 25c. Abaiang ("Land to the North") 20 40
255 35c. Marakei ("Fish-trap floating on eaves") 30 55

1975. Christmas. Multicoloured.
256 4c. Type **77** 15 80
257 10c. Protestant Chapel, Tarawa 15 35
258 25c. Catholic Church, Ocean Island . . . . 1·25 1·00
259 35c. Fishermen and star . . . 30 1·75

POSTAGE DUE STAMPS

D 1

1940.
D1 D 1 1d. green . . . . 9·00 23·00
D2 2d. red . . . . 9·50 23·00
D3 3d. brown . . . . 14·00 24·00
D4 4d. blue . . . . 16·00 30·00
D5 4d. olive . . . . 21·00 30·00
D6 6d. purple . . . . 21·00 30·00
D7 1s. violet . . . . 23·00 42·00
D8 1s.6d. green . . . . . . 45·00 85·00

GILBERT ISLANDS Pt. 1

On 1 January 1976 the Gilbert Islands and Tuvalu (Ellice) Islands became separate Crown Colonies. The Gilbert Islands became independent on 12 July 1979, under the name of Kiribati.

100 cents = $1.

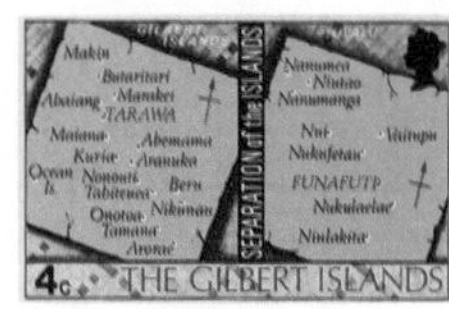

1 Charts of Gilbert Islands and Tuvalu (formerly Ellice) Islands

1976. Separation of the Islands. Multicoloured.
1 4c. Type **1** 40 75
2 35c. Maps of Tarawa and Funafuti . . . . 70 1·50

1976. Nos. 173/87 of Gilbert and Ellice Islands optd **THE GILBERT ISLANDS**.
3 1c. Cutting toddy 25 30
5 2c. Lagoon fishing 50 30
12 3c. Cleaning pandanus leaves 40 1·75
7 4c. Type **60** . . . . 30 1·00
13 5c. Gilbertese canoe . . . . . 50 1·00
14 6c. De-husking coconuts . . . 50 1·00
15 8c. Weaving pandanus fronds 50 1·00
16 10c. Weaving a basket . . . . 50 1·00
17 15c. Tiger shark . . . . . . 2·50 1·25
18 20c. Beating a pandanus leaf 75 2·00
19 25c. Loading copra . . . . . 1·25 1·25
20 35c. Fishing at night . . . . 1·75 1·75
21 50c. Local handicrafts . . . . 1·25 2·25
22 $1 Weaving coconut screens 2·25 8·00

3 "Teraaka" (training ship)

1978. Multicoloured.
23 1c. Type **3** 40 80
24 3c. "Tautunu" (inter-island freighter) 60 90
25 4c. Moorish idol (fish) 60 80
26 5c. Hibiscus 30 40
27 6c. Reef heron . . . . 1·50 1·00
28 7c. Catholic Cathedral, Tarawa 20 30
29 8c. Frangipani 20 30
30 10c. Maneaba, Bikenibeu . . . 20 30
31 12c. Betio Harbour 35 45
32 15c. Evening scene 40 45
33 20c. Marakei Atoll 25 35
34 35c. G.I.P.C. Chapel, Tangintebu 25 40
35 40c. Flamboyant tree 40 45
36 50c. "Hypolimnas bolina", (butterfly) . . . . 1·25 1·75
37 $1 "Tabakea" (Tarawa Lagoon ferry) . . . . . . 75 2·50
38 $2 National flag . . . . . . 75 2·50

4 Church

1976. Christmas. Children's Drawings. Mult.
39 5c. Type **4** 20 15
40 15c. Feasting (vert) 30 15
41 20c. Maneaba (vert) 30 35
42 35c. Dancing 30 45

5 Porcupine Fish Helmet   6 The Queen in Coronation Robes

1976. Artefacts. Multicoloured.
43 5c. Type **5** 20 15
44 15c. Shark's teeth dagger . . . 30 35
45 20c. Fighting gauntlet 30 40
46 35c. Coconut body armour . . 45 55
MS47 140 × 130 mm. Nos. 43/6 4·50 13·00

1977. Silver Jubilee. Multicoloured.
48 8c. Prince Charles' visit, 1970 10 10
49 20c. Prince Philip's visit, 1959 15 15
50 40c. Type **6** 20 35

7 Commodore Bryon and H.M.S. "Dolphin"

1977. Explorers. Multicoloured.
51 5c. Type **7** . . . . 45 1·50
52 15c. Capt. Fanning and "Betsey" . . . . 55 2·75
53 20c. Admiral Bellingshausen and "Vostok" . . . . . . 55 2·75
54 35c. Capt. Wilkes and U.S.S. "Vincennes" . . . . 65 4·00

8 H.M.S. "Resolution" and H.M.S. "Discovery"   9 Scout Emblem and Island Scene

1977. Christmas and Bicentenary of Capt. Cook's Discovery of Christmas Is. Mult.
55 8c. Type **8** 30 15
56 15c. Logbook entry (horiz) . . 30 15
57 20c. Captain Cook 40 20
58 40c. Landing party (horiz) . . 40 60
MS59 140 × 140 mm. Nos. 55/8 2·75 9·00

1977. 50th Anniv of Scouting in the Gilbert Is. Multicoloured.
60 8c. Type **9** 40 15
61 15c. Patrol meeting (horiz) . . 45 20
62 20c. Scout making mat (horiz) 50 20
63 40c. Canoeing 65 55

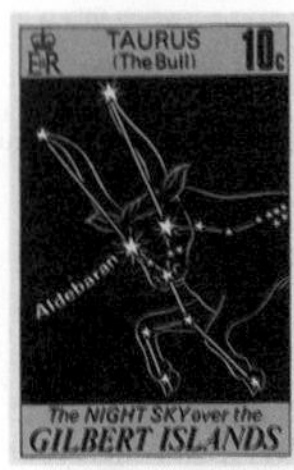

10 Taurus (The Bull)   11 Unicorn of Scotland

1978. The Night Sky over the Gilbert Islands.
64 **10** 10c. black and blue 45 35
65 – 20c. black and red 50 50
66 – 25c. black and green 50 55
67 – 45c. black and orange . . . 75 90
DESIGNS: 20c. Canis Major (the Great Dog); 25c. Scorpio (the Scorpion); 45c. Orion (the Giant Warrior).

1978. 25th Anniv of Coronation.
68 **11** 45c. green, violet and silver 25 40
69 – 45c. multicoloured 25 40
70 – 45c. green, violet and silver 25 40
DESIGNS: No. 69, Queen Elizabeth II. No. 70, Great Frigate Bird.

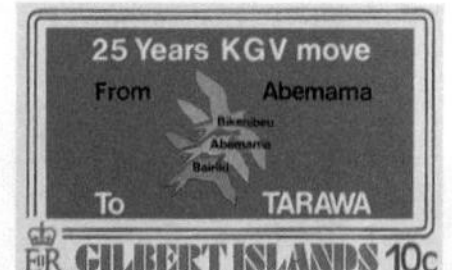

12 Birds in Flight to Tarawa

1978. 25th Anniv of Return of George V School to Tarawa. Multicoloured.

No.	Type	Description	Unused	Used
71		10c. Type **12**	10	10
72		20c. Tarawa, Abemama and school badge	20	20
73		25c. Rejoicing islanders	20	20
74		45c. King George V School on Tarawa and Abemama	35	35

13 "Te Kaue ni Maie"

1978. Christmas. Kaue (traditional head decorations). Multicoloured.

No.	Type	Description	Unused	Used
75		10c. Type **13**	10	10
76		20c. "Te Itera"	15	15
77		25c. "Te Bau"	20	20
78		45c. "Te Tai"	25	30
MS79		149 × 99 mm. Nos. 75/8	90	4·50

14 H.M.S. "Endeavour"

1979. Bicent of Captain Cook's Voyages, 1768–79.

No.	Type	Description	Unused	Used
80	**14**	10c. multicoloured	20	15
81	–	20c. multicoloured	25	30
82	–	25c. black, lilac and green	25	45
83	–	45c. multicoloured	25	80

DESIGNS: 20c. Green Turtle; 25c. Quadrant; 45c. Flaxman/Wedgwood medallion.

For later issues see **KIRIBATI.**

GOLD COAST Pt. 1

A British colony on the W. coast of Africa. For later issues after independence in 1957 see under Ghana.

12 pence = 1 shilling;
20 shillings = 1 pound.

1

4

1875.

No.	Type	Description	Unused	Used
4	**1**	½d. yellow	70·00	24·00
11a		½d. green	3·25	1·00
5		1d. blue	22·00	6·50
12		1d. red	4·00	50
6		2d. green	90·00	9·00
13b		2d. grey	4·00	50
14		2½d. blue and orange	4·50	70
15		3d. olive	11·00	4·50
16		4d. mauve	11·00	1·50
17		6d. orange	11·00	5·00
18a		1s. mauve	6·50	1·25
19a		2s. brown	45·00	15·00

1889. Surch **ONE PENNY.** and bar.

No.	Type	Description	Unused	Used
20	**1**	1d. on 6d. orange	£110	48·00

1889.

No.	Type	Description	Unused	Used
26	**4**	½d. mauve and green	3·00	1·00
27		1d. mauve and red	3·25	50
27b		2d. mauve and red	50·00	£150
28		2½d. mauve and blue	6·00	5·50
29		3d. mauve and orange	5·00	1·50
30		6d. mauve and violet	5·50	1·50
31		1s. green and black	10·00	17·00
32		2s. green and red	14·00	19·00
22		5s. mauve and blue	65·00	16·00
33		5s. green and mauve	50·00	30·00
23		10s. mauve and red	75·00	15·00
34		10s. green and brown	£140	50·00
24		20s. green and red	£3250	
25		20s. mauve and black on red	£160	35·00

1901. Surch **ONE PENNY.** and bar.

No.	Type	Description	Unused	Used
35	**4**	1d. on 2½d. mauve and blue	3·50	4·25
36		1d. on 6d. mauve and violet	3·50	3·50

1902. As T **4**, but with portrait of King Edward VII.

No.	Type	Description	Unused	Used
38		½d. purple and green	1·50	40
39		1d. purple and red	1·50	15
51		2d. purple and red	5·00	50
41		2½d. purple and blue	4·50	9·00
42		3d. purple and orange	3·00	1·50
43		6d. purple and violet	3·75	1·50
44		1s. green and black	14·00	3·25
45		2s. green and red	15·00	19·00
57		2s.6d. green and yellow	28·00	£110
46		5s. green and mauve	42·00	90·00
47		10s. green and brown	60·00	£130
48		20s. purple and black on red	£140	£180

1907. As last.

No.	Type	Description	Unused	Used
59		½d. green	4·00	30
60		1d. red	8·00	40
61		2d. grey	2·25	40
62		2½d. blue	8·50	2·00
63		3d. purple on yellow	8·00	55
64a		6d. purple	3·75	3·50
65		1s. black and green	13·00	50
66		2s. purple and blue on blue	8·00	16·00
67		2s.6d. black and red on blue	28·00	90·00
68		5s. green and red on yellow	55·00	£180

8

13 King George V and Christiansborg Castle

1908.

No.	Type	Description	Unused	Used
69	**8**	1d. red	3·50	10

1913. As T **4** and **8** (1d.) but portraits of King George V.

No.	Type	Description	Unused	Used
86		½d. green	80	50
72		1d. red	1·25	10
87		1d. brown	70	10
88		1½d. red	1·75	10
89		2d. grey	1·75	30
76		2½d. blue	6·00	1·00
90		2½d. orange	75	9·00
77b		3d. purple on yellow	1·50	40
91		3d. blue	1·75	60
78		6d. purple	3·25	2·25
79e		1s. black on green	1·50	50
96		2s. purple and blue on blue	3·00	3·25
81		2s.6d. black and red on blue	5·00	13·00
98		5s. green and red on yellow	12·00	55·00
83a		10s. green and red on green	19·00	65·00
100a		15s. purple and green	£110	£300
84		20s. purple and black on red	£130	85·00
102		£2 green and orange	£375	£950

1918. Surch **WAR TAX ONE PENNY.**

No.	Type	Description	Unused	Used
85		1d. on red (No. 72)	2·00	50

1928.

No.	Type	Description	Unused	Used
103	**13**	½d. green	85	40
104		1d. brown	85	10
105		1½d. red	1·50	1·50
106		2d. grey	1·50	20
107		2½d. orange	1·75	3·50
108		3d. blue	1·75	40
109		6d. black and purple	1·50	40
110		1s. black and orange	3·25	75
111		2s. black and violet	22·00	4·75
112		3s. red and olive	55·00	45·00

1935. Silver Jubilee. As T **10a** of Gambia.

No.	Type	Description	Unused	Used
113		1d. blue and black	60	50
114		3d. brown and blue	3·00	6·00
115		6d. green and blue	8·00	14·00
116		1s. grey and purple	5·00	21·00

1937. Coronation. As T **10b** of Gambia.

No.	Type	Description	Unused	Used
117		1d. brown	1·50	2·50
118		2d. grey	1·50	4·50
119		3d. blue	1·75	2·25

14

15 King George VI and Christiansborg Castle, Accra

1938.

No.	Type	Description	Unused	Used
120a	**14**	½d. green	40	50
121a		1d. brown	40	10
122a		1½d. red	40	50
123a		2d. slate	40	10
124a		3d. blue	40	35
125a		4d. mauve	80	1·25
126a		6d. purple	80	20
127a		9d. orange	1·25	55
128a	**15**	1s. black and olive	1·50	65
129		1s.3d. brown and blue	2·00	50
130a		2s. blue and violet	5·00	13·00
131a		5s. olive and red	10·00	16·00
132		10s. black and violet	7·00	24·00

1946. Victory. As T **11a** of Gambia.

No.	Type	Description	Unused	Used
133a		2d. violet	10	10
134a		4d. mauve	1·50	3·00

16 Northern Territories Mounted Constabulary

1948.

No.	Type	Description	Unused	Used
135	**16**	½d. green	20	30
136	–	1d. blue	15	15
137	–	1½d. red	1·25	80
138	–	2d. brown	55	10
139	–	2½d. brown and red	2·00	4·00
140	–	3d. blue	4·00	50
141	–	4d. mauve	3·50	2·50
142	–	6d. black and orange	30	30
143	–	1s. black and red	60	30
144	–	2s. olive and red	3·25	2·25
145	–	5s. purple and black	26·00	6·50
146	–	10s. black and olive	8·00	6·50

DESIGNS—HORIZ: 1d. Christiansborg Castle; 1½d. Emblem of Joint Provincial Council; 2½d. Map showing position of Gold Coast; 3d. Nsuba manganese mine; 4d. Lake Bosumtwi; 1s. Breaking cocoa pods; 2s. Gold Coast Regt. trooping the Colour; 5s. Surfboats. VERT: 2d. Talking drums; 6d. Cocoa farmer; 10s. Forest.

1948. Silver Wedding. As T **11b/c** of Gambia.

No.	Type	Description	Unused	Used
147		1½d. red	30	40
148		10s. olive	18·00	24·00

1949. U.P.U. As T **11d/g** of Gambia.

No.	Type	Description	Unused	Used
149		2d. brown	25	20
150		2½d. orange	1·50	4·00
151		3d. blue	25	1·75
152		1s. green	25	30

1952. As 1948 but portrait of Queen Elizabeth II. Designs as for corresponding values except where stated.

No.	Type	Description	Unused	Used
153		½d. brown and red (as 2½d.)	10	20
154		1d. blue	30	10
155		1½d. green	30	1·25
156		2d. brown	30	10
157		2½d. red (as ½d.)	35	1·25
158		3d. mauve	75	10
159		4d. blue	35	30
160		6d. black and orange	40	15
161		1s. black and red	50	15
162		2s. olive and red	11·00	85
163		5s. purple and black	17·00	5·50
164		10s. black and olive	16·00	12·00

1953. Coronation. As T **11h** of Gambia.

No.	Type	Description	Unused	Used
165		2d. black and brown	1·00	10

POSTAGE DUE STAMPS

D 1

1923.

No.	Type	Description	Unused	Used
D1	**D 1**	½d. black	15·00	£120
D2		1d. black	75	1·25
D3		2d. black	13·00	4·50
D6		3d. black	3·00	21·00
D7		6d. black	1·75	8·00
D8		1s. black	1·75	65·00

For later issues see **GHANA.**

GREAT BRITAIN Pt. 1

Consisting of England, Wales, Scotland and Northern Ireland, lying to the N.W. of the European continent.

1840. 12 pence = 1 shilling;
20 shillings = 1 pound sterling.
1971. 100 (new) pence = 1 pound sterling.

1

3

1840. Letters in lower corners. Imperf.

No.	Type	Description	Unused	Used
2	**1**	1d. black	£5500	£250
5		2d. blue	£12000	£600

1841. Imperf.

No.	Type	Description	Unused	Used
8	**1**	1d. brown	£300	15·00
14	**3**	2d. blue	£2500	75·00

In T **3** there are white lines below "POSTAGE" and above "TWO PENCE".

12

10

1847. Imperf.

No.	Type	Description	Unused	Used
59	**12**	6d. purple	£6000	£750
57	**10**	10d. brown	£5000	£950
54		1s. green	£7500	£700

1854. Perf.

No.	Type	Description	Unused	Used
29	**1**	1d. brown	£180	15·00
40		1d. red	40·00	9·00
34	**3**	2d. blue	£1750	50·00

14 18 19

1855. No letters in corners.

No.	Type	Description	Unused	Used
66a	**14**	4d. red	£1000	90·00
70	**18**	6d. lilac	£800	85·00
72	**19**	1s. green	£1100	£250

7 5 8 6

1858. Letters in four corners.

No.	Type	Description	Unused	Used
48	**7**	½d. red	90·00	15·00
43	**5**	1d. red	15·00	2·00
52	**8**	1½d. red	£350	45·00
45	**6**	2d. blue	£300	10·00

21

22

23 24 25

1862. Small white letters in corners.

No.	Type	Description	Unused	Used
76	**21**	3d. red	£1400	£225
82	**22**	4d. red	£1200	80·00
84	**23**	6d. lilac	£1250	80·00
87	**24**	9d. bistre	£2500	£300
90	**25**	1s. green	£1500	£150

30

32

1865. Designs as 1862 and T **30** and **32**, but large white letters in corners.

No.	Type	Description	Unused	Used
103	**21**	3d. red	£400	50·00
94	**22**	4d. red	£425	50·00
97	**23**	6d. lilac (with hyphen)	£650	75·00
109		6d. lilac (without hyphen)	£450	75·00
111	**24**	9d. straw	£1400	£225
112	**30**	10d. brown	£2100	£275
117	**25**	1s. green	£550	32·00
118	**32**	2s. blue	£2000	£140
121		2s. brown	£14000	£2500

35

38

1867.

126 **35** 5s. red £4500 £550
128 – 10s. green £35000 £2200
129 – £1 brown £45000 £3250
137 **38** £5 orange £8000 £3800

The 10s. and £1 are as Type **35**, but have different frames.

34

1872. Large white letters in corners.
122b **34** 6d. brown . . . . £500 45·00
125 6d. grey £1250 £200

41

46

1873. Large coloured letters in corners.
141 **41** 2½d. mauve . . . . £380 45·00
157 2½d. blue . . . . £325 25·00
143 **21** 3d. red . . . . £325 35·00
152 **22** 4d. red £1600 £400
153 4d. green £800 £225
160 4d. brown . . . . £325 55·00
161 **34** 6d. grey . . . . £325 55·00
156 **46** 8d. orange £1000 £275
150 **25** 1s. green . . . . £475 80·00
163 1s. brown £425 £120

The 3d, 4d. and 1s. are as 1862, and the 6d. as Type **34**, but all with large coloured letters.

52

53

1880. Various frames.
164 **52** ½d. green . . . . 40·00 10·00
187 ½d. blue . . . . 20·00 7·00
166 **53** 1d. brown . . . . 20·00 10·00
167 – 1½d. red . . . . £150 40·00
168 – 2d. red . . . . £200 80·00
169 – 5d. blue £575 £100

57

58

61

1881.
174 **57** 1d. lilac . . . . 2·50 1·50

1883. Types, as 1873, surch **3d.** or **6d.**
159 **21** 3d. on 3d. lilac £425 £110
162 **34** 6d. on 6d. lilac £475 £125

1883.
178 **58** 2s.6d. lilac £400 £125
180 – 5s. red £800 £180
183 – 10s. blue £1500 £450
185 **61** £1 brown £20000 £2000
212 £1 green £2700 £600

The 5s. and 10s. are similar to Type **58**, but have different frames.

62

63

1883. Various frames.
188 **62** 1½d. purple . . . . 90·00 35·00
189 **63** 2d. purple . . . . £150 65·00
190 2½d. purple . . . . 70·00 12·00
191 **62** 3d. purple . . . . £180 85·00
192 4d. green £400 £175
193 5d. green £400 £175
194 **63** 6d. green £425 £200
195 9d. green £800 £375
196 **62** 1s. green £850 £200

71

72

73

74

75

76

77

78

79

80

81

82

1887.
197 **71** ½d. red . . . . 1·50 1·00
213 ½d. green* . . . . 1·75 2·00
198 **72** 1½d. purple and green . . 15·00 7·00
200 **73** 2d. green and red . . . . 28·00 12·00
201 **74** 2½d. purple on blue . . . 22·00 3·00
202 **75** 3d. purple on yellow . . . 22·00 3·25
205 **76** 4d. green and brown . . . 30·00 13·00
206 **77** 4½d. green and red . . . 10·00 40·00
207a **78** 5d. purple and blue . . . 35·00 11·00
208 **79** 6d. purple on red . . . . 30·00 10·00
209 **80** 9d. purple and blue . . . 60·00 40·00
210 **81** 10d. purple and red . . . 45·00 38·00
211 **82** 1s. green . . . . £200 60·00
214 1s. green and red . . . . 50·00 £125

*No. 213, in blue, has had the colour changed after issue.

83

90

1902. Designs not shown are as 1887 (2s.6d. to £1 as 1883) but with portrait of King Edward VII.
217 **83** ½d. green . . . . 2·00 1·50
219 1d. red . . . . 2·00 1·50
221 – 1½d. purple and green . . . 35·00 18·00
291 – 2d. green and red . . . . 25·00 20·00
231 **83** 2½d. blue . . . . 20·00 10·00
234 – 3d. purple on yellow . . . 35·00 15·00
238 – 4d. green and brown . . . 40·00 18·00
240 – 4d. orange . . . . 20·00 15·00
294 – 5d. purple and blue . . . 30·00 20·00
245 **83** 6d. purple . . . . 35·00 18·00
249 **90** 7d. grey . . . . 10·00 18·00
307 – 9d. purple and blue . . . 60·00 60·00
311 – 10d. purple and red . . . 60·00 60·00
314 – 1s. green and red . . . . 55·00 35·00
260 – 2s.6d. purple £220 £120
263 – 5s. red £350 £200
265 – 10s. blue £600 £450
266 – £1 green £1500 £650

98 (Hair heavy)

99 (Lion unshaded)

1911.
325 **98** ½d. green . . . . 4·50 1·50
327 **99** 1d. red . . . . 8·00 2·50

101 (Hair light)

102 (Lion shaded)

1912.
344 **101** ½d. green . . . . 7·00 3·00
341 **102** 1d. red . . . . 5·00 2·00

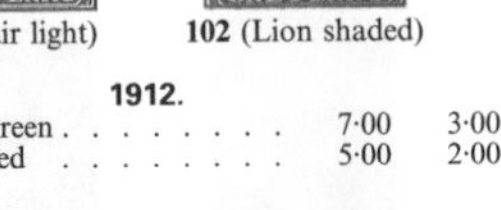

104

105

106

107

108

109

1912. Lined background.
418 **105** ½d. green . . . . 1·00 1·00
419 **104** 1d. red . . . . 1·00 1·00
420 **105** 1½d. brown . . . . . . 1·00 1·00
421 **106** 2d. orange . . . . . . 2·50 2·50
422 **104** 2½d. blue . . . . 5·00 3·00
376 **106** 3d. violet . . . . 9·00 2·50
424 4d. green . . . . 12·00 2·50
381 **107** 5d. brown . . . . 15·00 5·00
426a 6d. purple . . . . 3·00 1·50
387 7d. green . . . . 20·00 10·00
390 8d. black on yellow . . . 32·00 11·00
392 **108** 9d. black . . . . 25·00 6·00
427 9d. green . . . . 12·00 3·50
394 10d. blue . . . . 22·00 20·00
395 1s. brown . . . . 20·00 4·00
450 **109** 2s.6d. brown . . . . . . 70·00 40·00
451 5s. red . . . . £160 85·00
452 10s. blue . . . . £340 80·00
403 £1 green £1800 £1100

112

1924. British Empire Exhibition. Dated "1924".
430 **112** 1d. red . . . . 10·00 11·00
431 1½d. brown . . . . 15·00 15·00

1925. Dated "1925".
432 **112** 1d. red . . . . 15·00 30·00
433 1½d. brown . . . . 40·00 70·00

113

114

115

116 St. George and the Dragon

1929. 9th U.P.U. Congress, London.
434 **113** ½d. green . . . . 2·25 2·25
435 **114** 1d. red . . . . 2·25 2·25
436 1½d. brown . . . . 2·25 1·75
437 **115** 2½d. blue . . . . 10·00 10·00
438 **116** £1 black £750 £550

118

119

120

121

122

123

1934. Solid background.
439 **118** ½d. green 50 50
440 **119** 1d. red 50 50
441 **118** 1½d. brown 50 50
442 **120** 2d. orange 75 75
443 **119** 2½d. blue . . . . 1·50 1·25
444 **120** 3d. violet . . . . 1·50 1·25
445 4d. green . . . . 2·00 1·25
446 **121** 5d. brown . . . . 6·50 2·75
447 **122** 9d. olive . . . . 12·00 2·25
448 10d. blue . . . . 15·00 10·00
449 1s. brown . . . . 15·00 1·25

1935. Silver Jubilee.
453 **123** ½d. green . . . . 1·00 1·00
454 1d. red . . . . 1·50 2·00
455 1½d. brown . . . . 1·00 1·25
456 2½d. blue . . . . 6·00 6·50

Emblems at right differ.

124 King Edward VIII

126 King George VI and Queen Elizabeth

1936.
457 **124** ½d. green 30 30
458 1d. red 60 50
459 1½d. brown 30 30
460 2½d. blue 30 85

1937. Coronation.
461 **126** 1½d. brown 30 30

128

129

130

131 King George VI

1937.
462 **128** ½d. green 30 25
503 ½d. orange 30 30
463 1d. red 30 25
504 1d. blue 30 30
464 1½d. brown 30 25
505 1½d. green 65 60
465 2d. orange . . . . 1·20 50
506 2d. brown 75 40
466 2½d. blue 40 25

507 2½d. red 60 40
490 3d. violet 2·00 1·00
468 **129** 4d. green 60 75
508 4d. blue 2·00 1·75
469 5d. brown 3·50 85
470 6d. purple 1·50 60
471 **130** 7d. green 5·00 60
472 8d. red 7·50 80
473 9d. green 6·50 80
474 10d. blue 7·00 80
474a 11d. purple 3·00 2·75
475 1s. brown 9·00 75

1939.

476 **131** 2s.6d. brown 35·00 6·00
476a 2s.6d. green 11·50 1·50
477 5s. red 20·00 2·00
478a – 10s. blue 20·00 5·00
478b – £1 brown 20·00 26·00

The 10s. and £1 values have the portrait in the centre in an ornamental frame.

134 Queen Victoria and King George VI

1940. Centenary of First Adhesive Postage Stamps.
479 **134** ½d. green 30 75
480 1d. red 1·00 75
481 1½d. brown 50 1·50
482 2d. orange 1·00 75
483 2½d. blue 2·25 1·00
484 3d. violet 3·00 4·50

135

1946. Victory Commemoration.
491 **135** 2½d. blue 20 20
492 – 3d. violet 20 50
DESIGN—HORIZ: 3d. Symbols of Peace and Reconstruction.

137

138 King George VI and Queen Elizabeth

1948. Royal Silver Wedding.
493 **137** 2½d. blue 35 20
494 **138** £1 blue 40·00 40·00

139 Globe and Laurel Wreath

140 "Speed"

1948. Olympic Games. Inscr "OLYMPIC GAMES 1948".
495 **139** 2½d. blue 35 10
496 **140** 3d. violet 35 50
497 – 6d. purple 75 40
498 – 1s. brown 1·50 1·50
DESIGNS: 6d. Olympic symbol; 1s. Winged Victory.

143 Two Hemispheres

144 U.P.U. Monument, Berne

1949. 75th Anniv of U.P.U. Inscr as in T **143/4**.
499 **143** 2½d. blue 25 10
500 **144** 3d. violet 25 50
501 – 6d. purple 50 75
502 – 1s. brown 1·00 1·25
DESIGNS: 6d. Goddess Concordia, globe and points of compass; 1s. Posthorn and globe.

147 H.M.S. "Victory"

1951.

509 **147** 2s.6d. green 2·00 1·00
510 – 5s. red 40·00 1·00
511 – 10s. blue 10·00 7·50
512 – £1 brown 48·00 18·00
DESIGNS: 5s. White Cliffs of Dover; 10s. St. George and dragon; £1 Royal Coat of Arms.

152 Festival Symbol

1951. Festival of Britain.
513 – 2½d. red 20 15
514 **152** 4d. blue 30 35
DESIGN: 2½d. Britannia, cornucopia and Mercury.

154

155

157

158

159 Queen Elizabeth II and National Emblems

1952.

570 **154** ½d. orange 10 10
571 1d. blue 10 10
517 1½d. green 10 20
573 2d. brown 10 10
519 **155** 2½d. red 15 15
575 3d. lilac 10 20
576a 4d. blue 15 15
577 4½d. brown 10 25
616c **157** 5d. brown 25 35
617 6d. purple 30 30
617a 7d. green 55 50
617b **158** 8d. mauve 40 45
582 9d. green 60 40
617d 10d. blue 70 60
553 11d. plum 50 1·10
617e **159** 1s. brown 40 35
585 1s.3d. green 45 30
618a 1s.6d. blue 2·00 2·00

The 4d., 4½d. and 1s.3d. values are printed with colour tones reversed.

Stamps with either one or two vertical black lines on the back were issued in 1957 in connection with the Post Office automatic facing machine experiments in the Southampton area. Later the lines were replaced by almost invisible phosphor bands on the face, in the above and later issues. They are listed in the Stanley Gibbons British Commonwealth Catalogue.

For stamps as T **157**, but with face values in decimal currency, see Nos. 2031/3.

161

163

1953. Coronation. Portraits of Queen Elizabeth II.
532 **161** 2½d. red 20 25
533 – 4d. blue 1·10 1·90
534 **163** 1s.3d. green 5·00 10·00
535 – 1s.6d. blue 8·00 4·75
DESIGNS: 4d. Coronation and National Emblems; 1s.6d. Crowns and Sceptres dated "2 JUNE 1953".

166 Carrickfergus Castle

1955.

595a **166** 2s.6d. brown 35 40
596a – 5s. red 1·20 4·50
597a – 10s. blue 4·00 4·50
762 – £1 black 4·50 6·00
CASTLES: 5s. Caernarvon; 10s. Edinburgh; £1 Windsor.

170 Scout Badge and "Rolling Hitch"

171 "Scouts coming to Britain"

1957. World Scout Jubilee Jamboree.
557 **170** 2½d. red 50 50
558 **171** 4d. blue 75 1·50
559 – 1s.3d. green 4·50 4·50
DESIGN: 1s.3d. Globe within a compass.

1957. Inter-Parliamentary Union Conference. As No. 576a but inscr "46th PARLIAMENTARY CONFERENCE".
560 4d. blue 1·00 1·00

176 Welsh Dragon

1958. 6th British Empire and Commonwealth Games, Cardiff. Inscr as in T **176**.
567 **176** 3d. lilac 20 20
568 – 6d. mauve 40 45
569 – 1s.3d. green 2·25 2·40
DESIGNS: 6d. Flag and Games emblem; 1s.3d. Welsh Dragon.

180 Postboy of 1660

181 Posthorn of 1660

1960. Tercentenary of Establishment of General Letter Office.
619 **180** 3d. lilac 50 50
620 **181** 1s.3d. green 3·75 4·25

182 Conference Emblem

1960. 1st Anniv of European Postal and Telecommunications Conference.
621 **182** 6d. green and purple 1·50 50
622 1s.6d. brown and blue 8·50 5·00

184 "Growth of Savings"

1961. Centenary of Post Office Savings Bank. Inscr "POST OFFICE SAVINGS BANK".
623A – 2½d. black and red 25 25
624A **184** 3d. brown and violet 20 20
625A – 1s.6d. red and blue 2·50 2·25
DESIGNS—VERT: 2½d. Thrift plant. HORIZ: 1s.6d. Thrift plant.

186 C.E.P.T. Emblem

187 Doves and Emblem

1961. Europa.
626 **186** 2d. orange, pink and brown 15 20
627 **187** 4d. buff, mauve and blue 15 25
628 – 10d. turquoise, green bl 15 80
DESIGN: 10d. As 4d. but arranged differently.

189 Hammer Beam Roof, Westminster Hall

1961. 7th Commonwealth Parliamentary Conference.
629 **189** 6d. purple and gold 25 25
630 – 1s.3d. green and blue 2·75 3·00
DESIGN—VERT: 1s.3d. Palace of Westminster.

191 "Units of Productivity"

1962. National Productivity Year.
631 **191** 2½d. green and red 20 20
632 – 3d. blue and violet 25 25
633 – 1s.3d. red, blue and green 1·50 2·00
DESIGNS: 3d. Arrows over map; 1s.3d. Arrows in formation.

194 Campaign Emblem and Family

1963. Freedom from Hunger.
634 **194** 2½d. red and pink 25 10
635 – 1s.3d. brown and yellow 1·75 1·90
DESIGN: 1s.3d. Children of three races.

196 "Paris Conference"

1963. Centenary of Paris Postal Conference.
636 **196** 6d. green and mauve 30 50

197 Posy of Flowers

1963. National Nature Week. Multicoloured.
637 3d. Type **197** 15 15
638 4½d. Woodland life 25 35

199 Rescue at Sea

1963. 9th International Lifeboat Conference, Edinburgh. Multicoloured.
639 2$\frac{1}{2}$d. Type **199** 25 25
640 4d. 19th-century lifeboat . . 50 50
641 1s.6d. Lifeboatmen . . . . . 3·00 3·25

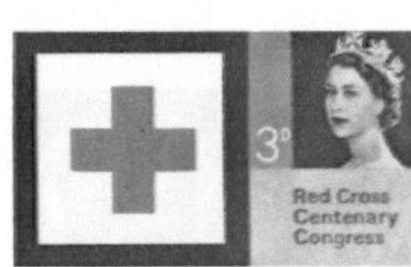

202 Red Cross

1963. Red Cross Centenary Congress.
642 **202** 3d. red and lilac 25 25
643 – 1s.3d. red, blue and grey 3·00 3·00
644 – 1s.6d. red, blue and bistre 3·00 3·00
DESIGNS: Nos. 643/4 are as Type **202** but differently arranged.

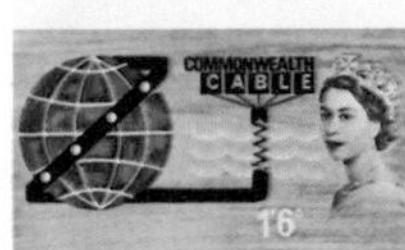

205 Commonwealth Cable

1963. COMPAC (Trans-Pacific Telephone Cable) Opening.
645 **205** 1s.6d. blue and black . . 2·75 2·50

206 Puck and Bottom ("A Midsummer Night's Dream")

210 Hamlet contemplating Yorick's Skull ("Hamlet") and Queen Elizabeth II

1964. Shakespeare Festival.
646 **206** 3d. multicoloured 15 15
647 – 6d. multicoloured 30 30
648 – 1s.3d. multicoloured . . . 75 1·00
649 – 1s.6d. multicoloured . . . 1·00 85
650 **210** 2s.6d. slate-purple . . . . 2·75 2·75
DESIGNS—As Type **206**: 6d. Feste ("Twelfth Night"); 1s.3d. Balcony scene ("Romeo and Juliet"); 1s.6d. "Eve of Agincourt" ("Henry V").

211 Flats near Richmond Park

1964. 20th Int Geographical Congress, London. Multicoloured.
651 2$\frac{1}{2}$d. Type **211** 10 10
652 4d. Shipbuilding yards, Belfast 30 30
653 8d. Beddgelert Forest Park, Snowdonia 75 85
654 1s.6d. Nuclear reactor, Dounreay . . . . 3·50 3·60
The designs represent "Urban development", "Industrial activity", "Forestry" and "Technological development" respectively.

215 Spring Gentian

1964. 10th Int Botanical Congress, Edinburgh. Multicoloured.
655 3d. Type **215** 25 25
656 6d. Dog rose 50 50
657 9d. Honeysuckle . . . . . . 1·75 2·25
658 1s.3d. Fringed water lily . . 2·25 2·50

219 Forth Road Bridge

1964. Opening of Forth Road Bridge.
659 **219** 3d. black, blue and violet 10 10
660 – 6d. lilac, blue and red . . 40 40
DESIGN: 6d. Forth Road and Railway Bridges.

221 Sir Winston Churchill

1965. Churchill Commemoration.
661 **221** 4d. black and drab . . . 10 10
662 – 1s.3d. black and grey . . 30 40
The 1s.3d. shows a closer view of Churchill's head.

222 Simon de Montfort's Seal

1965. 700th Anniv of Simon de Montfort's Parliament.
663 **222** 6d. olive 20 20
664 – 2s.6d. black, grey and drab . . . . 80 1·50
DESIGN—(58$\frac{1}{2}$ × 21$\frac{1}{2}$ mm): 2s.6d. Parliament buildings (after engraving by Hollar, 1647).

224 Bandsmen and Banner

1965. Centenary of Salvation Army. Mult.
665 3d. Type **224** 25 25
666 1s.6d. Three Salvationists . . 1·00 1·50

226 Lister's Carbolic Spray

1965. Centenary of Joseph Lister's Discovery of Antiseptic Surgery.
667 **226** 4d. blue, brown and grey 25 15
668 – 1s. black, purple and blue 1·00 1·10
DESIGN: 1s. Lister and chemical symbols.

228 Trinidad Carnival Dancers

1965. Commonwealth Arts Festival.
669 **228** 6d. black and orange . . 20 20
670 – 1s.6d. black and violet . . 80 1·10
DESIGN: 1s.6d. Canadian folk-dancers.

230 Flight of Supermarine Spitfires

234 Supermarine Spitfire attacking Junkers Ju 87B "Stuka"

1965. 25th Anniv of Battle of Britain. Inscr "Battle of Britain 1940".
671 **230** 4d. olive and black . . . 1·00 1·00
672 – 4d. olive and black . . . 1·00 1·00
673 – 4d. multicoloured . . . 1·00 1·00
674 – 4d. olive and black . . . 1·00 1·00
675 **234** 4d. olive and black . . . 1·00 1·00
676 – 4d. multicoloured . . . 1·00 1·00
677p – 9d. violet, orange and purple . . . . 1·75 2·00
678p – 1s.3d. grey, black and blue . . . . 1·75 2·00
DESIGNS: No. 672, Pilot in Hawker Hurricane Mk I; 673, Wing-tips of Supermarine Spitfire and Messerschmitt BF 109; 674, Supermarine Spitfires attacking Heinkel HE 111H bomber; 676, Hawker Hurricanes Mk 1 over wreck of Dornier DO-17Z bomber; 9d. Anti-aircraft artillery in action; 1s.3d. Air battle over St. Paul's Cathedral.

239 Tower and "Nash" Terrace, Regent's Park

1965. Opening of Post Office Tower.
679 – 3d. yellow, blue and green 10 15
680p **239** 1s.3d. green and blue . . 30 45
DESIGN—VERT: 3d. Tower and Georgian buildings.

240 U.N. Emblem

1965. 20th Anniv of U.N.O. and International Co-operation Year.
681 **240** 3d. black, orange and blue 25 20
682 – 1s.6d. black, purple blue 1·00 80
DESIGN: 1s.6d. I.C.Y. Emblem.

242 Telecommunications Network

1965. Centenary of I.T.U. Multicoloured.
683 9d. Type **242** 50 40
684 1s.6d. Radio waves and switchboard . . . . 1·50 1·25

244 Robert Burns (after Skirving chalk drawing)

1966. Burns Commemoration.
685 **244** 4d. black, indigo and blue 15 15
686 – 1s.3d. black, blue orange 40 70
DESIGN: 1s.3d. Robert Burns (after Nasmyth portrait).

246 Westminster Abbey

1966. 900th Anniv of Westminster Abbey.
687 **246** 3d. black, brown and blue 15 20
688 – 2s.6d. black 55 80
DESIGN: 2s.6d. Fan vaulting, Henry VII Chapel.

248 View near Hassocks, Sussex

1966. Landscapes.
689 **248** 4d. black, green and blue 10 15
690 – 6d. black, green and blue 15 20
691 – 1s.3d. black, yellow & bl 25 35
692 – 1s.6d. black, orange & blue 40 35
VIEWS: 6d. Antrim, Northern Ireland; 1s.3d. Harlech Castle, Wales; 1s.6d. Cairngorm Mountains, Scotland.

253 Goalmouth Melee

1966. World Cup Football Championship. Multicoloured.
693 4d. Players with ball (vert) 10 25
694 6d. Type **253** 15 25
695 1s.3d. Goalkeeper saving goal 50 1·00

255 Black-headed Gull

1966. British Birds. Multicoloured.
696 4d. Type **255** 20 20
697 4d. Blue tit 20 20
698 4d. European robin 20 20
699 4d. Blackbird 20 20

1966. England's World Cup Football Victory. As No. 693 but inscr "ENGLAND WINNERS".
700 4d. multicoloured 30 30

260 Jodrell Bank Radio Telescope

1966. British Technology.
701p **260** 4d. black and lemon . . 10 10
702p – 6d. red, blue and orange 15 20
703p – 1s.3d. multicoloured . . 25 40
704 – 1s.6d. multicoloured . . 50 60
DESIGN: 6d. British motor-cars; 1s.3d. SRN 6 hovercraft; 1s.6d. Windscale reactor.

264

265

1966. 900th Anniv of Battle of Hastings. Mult.
705 4d. Type **264** 10 30
706 4d. Type **265** 10 30
707 4d. "Yellow" horse 10 30
708 4d. "Blue" horse 10 30
709 4d. "Purple" horse 10 30
710 4d. "Grey" horse 10 30
711 6d. Norman horsemen . . . 10 30
712 1s.3d. Norman horsemen attacking Harold's troops (59 × 22$\frac{1}{2}$ mm) 20 75

272 King of the Orient

274 Sea Freight

1966. Christmas. Multicoloured.
713 3d. Type **272** 10 25
714 1s.6d. Snowman 30 50

1967. European Free Trade Assn (EFTA).
715 9d. Type **274** 25 20
716p 1s.6d. Air freight 25 40

276 Hawthorn and Bramble

282

1967. British Wild Flowers. Multicoloured.
717p 4d. Type **276** 10 15
718p 4d. Larger bindweed and viper's bugloss 10 15
719p 4d. Ox-eye daisy, coltsfoot and buttercup 10 15
720p 4d. Bluebell, red campion and wood anemone . . . 15 10
721p 9d. Dog violet 15 25
722p 1s.9d. Primroses 20 30

1967.
723 **282** $\frac{1}{2}$d. brown 10 20
724 1d. olive 10 10
726 2d. brown 10 15
729 3d. violet 10 10
731 4d. sepia 10 10
733 4d. red 10 10
735 5d. blue 10 10
736 6d. purple 20 25
737 7d. green 40 35

738 8d. red 20 45
739 8d. turquoise 50 60
740 9d. green 40 25
741 10d. drab 50 50
742 1s. violet 45 25
743 1s.6d. blue and indigo . . 45 35
744 1s.9d. orange and black 50 45
For decimal issue, see Nos. X841 etc.

284 "Mares and Foals in a Landscape" (George Stubbs)

1967. British Paintings.
748 – 4d. multicoloured 10 10
749 **284** 9d. multicoloured 15 15
750 – 1s.6d. multicoloured . . . 25 35
PAINTINGS—VERT: 4d. "Master Lambton" (Sir Thomas Lawrence). HORIZ: 1s.6d. "Children Coming Out of School" (L. S. Lowry).

286 "Gipsy Moth IV"

1967. Sir Francis Chichester's World Voyage.
751 **286** 1s.9d. multicoloured . . . 20 20

287 Radar Screen

1967. British Discovery and Invention. Mult.
752 4d. Type **287** 10 10
753 1s. "Penicillium notatum" . . 10 20
754 1s.6d. Vickers VC-10 jet engines 20 25
755 1s.9d. Television equipment 20 30

292 "Madonna and Child" (Murillo)

1967. Christmas.
756 – 3d. multicoloured 10 15
757 **292** 4d. multicoloured 10 15
758 – 1s.6d. multicoloured . . . 15 50
PAINTINGS—VERT: 3d. "The Adoration of the Shepherds" (School of Seville). HORIZ: 1s.6d. "The Adoration of the Shepherds" (Louis le Nain).

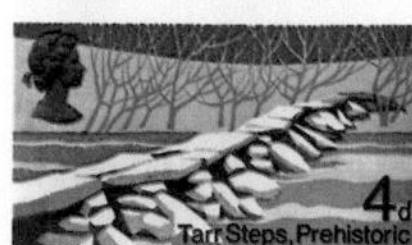

294 Tarr Steps, Exmoor

1968. British Bridges. Multicoloured.
763 4d. Type **294** 10 10
764 9d. Aberfeldy Bridge 10 15
765 1s.6d. Menai Bridge 15 25
766 1s.9d. M4 viaduct 20 30

298 "T U C" and Trades Unionists

1968. British Annivs. Events described on stamps.
767 **298** 4d. multicoloured 10 10
768 – 9d. violet, grey and black 10 15
769 – 1s. multicoloured 15 15
770 – 1s.9d. ochre and brown 35 35
DESIGNS: 9d. Mrs. Emmeline Pankhurst (statue); 1s. Sopwith Camel and English Electric Lightning fighters; 1s.9d. Captain Cook's "Endeavour" and signature.

302 "Queen Elizabeth I" (unknown artist)

1968. British Paintings.
771 **302** 4d. multicoloured 10 10
772 – 1s. multicoloured 10 20
773 – 1s.6d. multicoloured . . . 20 25
774 – 1s.9d. multicoloured . . . 25 40
PAINTINGS—VERT: 1s. "Pinkie" (Lawrence); 1s.6d. "Ruins of St. Mary Le Port" (Piper). HORIZ: 1s.9d. "The Hay Wain" (Constable).

306 Boy and Girl with Rocking Horse

1968. Christmas. Multicoloured.
775 4d. Type **306** 10 15
776 9d. Girl with doll's house (vert) 15 25
777 1s.6d. Boy with train set (vert) 15 50

310 Elizabethan Galleon

1969. British Ships. Multicoloured.
778 5d. "Queen Elizabeth 2" . . 10 15
779 9d. Type **310** 10 25
780 9d. East Indiaman 10 25
781 9d. "Cutty Sark" 10 25
782 1s. "Great Britain" 40 35
783 1s. "Mauretania I" 40 35
Nos. 778 and 782/3 are 58 × 23 mm.

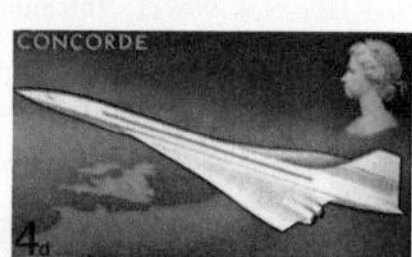

315 Concorde in Flight

1969. 1st Flight of Concorde.
784 **315** 4d. multicoloured 25 25
785 – 9d. multicoloured 55 75
786 – 1s.6d. indigo, grey and blue . . . . 75 1·00
DESIGNS: 9d. Plan and elevation views; 1s.6d. Concorde's nose and tail.

318 Queen Elizabeth II

1969.
787 **318** 2s.6d. brown 35 30
788 5s. lake . . . . 1·75 60
789 10s. blue . . . . 6·00 7·00
790 £1 black . . . . 3·25 1·50
For decimal issues see Nos. 829/31b.
No. 790 has an italic "£". For larger version with roman "£" see No. 831b.

319 Page from "Daily Mail", and Vickers Vimy Biplane

1969. Anniversary Events described on stamps.
791 **319** 5d. multicoloured 10 15
792 – 9d. multicoloured 15 25
793 – 1s. claret, red and blue . . 15 25
794 – 1s.6d. multicoloured . . . 15 30
795 – 1s.9d. turquoise, yell & sepia 20 40
DESIGNS: 9d. Europa and C.E.P.T. emblems; 1s. I.L.O. emblem; 1s.6d. Flags of N.A.T.O. countries; 1s.9d. Vickers Vimy biplane and globe showing flight route.

324 Durham Cathedral

1969. British Architecture (Cathedrals). Mult.
796 5d. Type **324** 10 20
797 5d. York Minster 10 20
798 5d. St. Giles' Cathedral, Edinburgh 10 20
799 5d. Canterbury Cathedral . . 10 20
800 9d. St. Paul's Cathedral . . . 25 50
801 1s.6d. Liverpool Metropolitan Cathedral 25 50

332 Queen Eleanor's Gate, Caernarvon Castle

1969. Investiture of H.R.H. The Prince of Wales.
802 – 5d. multicoloured 10 15
803 – 5d. multicoloured 10 15
804 **332** 5d. multicoloured 10 15
805 – 9d. multicoloured 15 30
806 – 1s. black and gold 15 30
DESIGNS: No. 802, The King's Gate, Caernarvon Castle; No. 803, The Eagle Tower, Caernarvon Castle; No. 805, Celtic Cross, Margam Abbey; No. 806, H.R.H. The Prince of Wales.

335 Mahatma Gandhi

1969. Gandhi Centenary Year.
807 **335** 1s.6d. multicoloured . . . 30 30

336 National Giro "G" Symbol

1969. Post Office Technology Commemoration.
808 **336** 5d. multicoloured 10 10
809 – 9d. green, blue and black 15 20
810 – 1s. green, lavender & black 15 20
811 – 1s.6d. purple, blue & black 15 35
DESIGNS: 9d. International subscriber dialling (Telecommunications); 1s. Pulse code modulations (Telecommunications); 1s 6d. Automatic sorting (Postal Mechanisation).

340 Herald Angel

1969. Christmas. Multicoloured.
812 4d. Type **340** 10 10
813 5d. The Three Shepherds . . 15 15
814 1s.6d. The Three Kings . . . 20 20

343 Fife Harling

1970. British Rural Architecture. Multicoloured.
815 5d. Type **343** 10 10
816 9d. Cotswold limestone . . . 10 25
817 1s. Welsh stucco 15 25
818 1s.6d. Ulster thatch 20 40
The 1s. and 1s.6d. are larger (38 × 27 mm).

347 Signing the Declaration of Arbroath

1970. Anniversaries. Events described on stamps. Multicoloured.
819 5d. Type **347** 10 10
820 9d. Florence Nightingale attending patients 15 15
821 1s. Signing of International Co-operative Alliance . . . 20 25
822 1s.6d. Pilgrims and "Mayflower" 20 30
823 1s.9d. Sir William and Sir John Herschel, Francis Baily and Telescope . . . 25 30

352 Mr Pickwick and Sam ("Pickwick Papers")

357 Queen Elizabeth II

1970. Literary Annivs. Death Cent of Charles Dickens (novelist) (824/7) and Birth Bicent of William Wordsworth (poet) (828). Mult.
824 5d. Type **352** 10 25
825 5d. Mr. and Mrs. Micawber ("David Copperfield") . . 10 25
826 5d. David Copperfield and Betsy Trotwood ("David Copperfield") 10 25
827 5d. "Oliver asking for more" ("Oliver Twist") 10 25
828 1s.6d. "Grasmere" (from engraving by J. Farrington, R.A.) 25 50

1970. Decimal Currency. Designs as T **318** but inscr in decimal currency as T **357**.
829 **357** 10p. red 50 75
830 20p. green 60 25
831 50p. blue . . . . 1·25 40
831b £1 black . . . . 3·50 80
On No. 831b the "£" is in roman type.

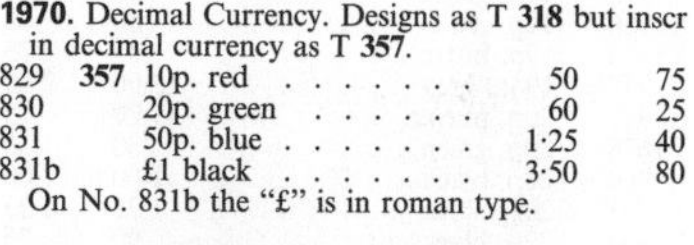

360 Cyclists

1970. 9th British Commonwealth Games. Mult.
832 5d. Runners 25 15
833 1s.6d. Swimmers 50 50
834 1s.9d. Type **360** 50 50

361 1d. Black (1840)

364 Shepherds and Apparition of the Angel

1970. "Philympia 70" Stamp Exhibition. Mult.
835 5d. Type **361** 25 10
836 9d.1s. green (1847) 25 30
837 1s.6d. 4d. red (1855) 25 45

1970. Christmas. Multicoloured.
838 4d. Type **364** 15 10
839 5d. Mary, Joseph, and Christ in the manger 15 15
840 1s.6d. The Wise Men bearing gifts 25 30

367

1971. Decimal currency. As Nos. 723, etc. but new colours and with decimal figures of value as in T **367**.
X 841 ½p. blue 10 10
Y1667 1p. red 25 25
X 848 1½p. black 15 25
Y1668 2p. green 10 10

X1001	2p. light green and green	75	50
X 851	2½p. mauve	20	15
X 929	2½p. red	15	20
X 856	3p. blue	15	20
X 930	3p. mauve	20	25
X 859	3½p. grey	30	35
X 931	3½p. brown	50	60
X 861	4p. brown	20	25
Y1669	4p. blue	25	25
X 865	4½p. blue	25	30
X 866	5p. violet	20	20
Y1670	5p. brown	25	25
X 869	5½p. violet	25	30
X 870	6p. green	25	20
X 872	6½p. blue	25	20
X 875	7p. brown	25	30
X 937	7p. red	1·10	1·25
Y1672	7p. grey	35	35
Y1672a	7p. mauve	25	25
X 877	7½p. brown	25	35
X 879	8p. red	25	30
Y1673	8p. yellow	35	35
X 881	8½p. green	30	25
X 882	9p. yellow and black	45	55
X 883	9p. violet	35	25
X 883	9p. violet	35	25
Y1673a	9p. yellow	20	25
X 885	10p. brown and light brown	35	30
X 888	10p. brown	35	25
Y1674	10p. orange	30	30
X 890	10½p. yellow	40	45
X 891	10½p. blue	45	50
X 892	11p. red	40	30
X 893	11½p. drab	40	35
X 942	11½p. brown	55	55
X 896	12p. green	45	45
X 898	12½p. green	45	50
X 900	13p. brown	40	40
X 944	13p. grey	45	50
X 945	13½p. brown	60	60
X 946	14p. blue	50	50
X 947	15p. blue	50	50
X 948	15½p. violet	60	50
X 949	16p. drab	55	55
X 950	16½p. brown	80	75
X 951	17p. green	60	60
X 952	17p. blue	60	60
X 953	17½p. brown	70	75
X 954	18p. violet	70	70
X 955	18p. grey	75	60
X 913	18p. green	60	50
X 956	19p. red	80	60
Y1675	19p. bistre	75	75
X 957	19½p. grey	2·00	2·00
X 958	20p. purple	1·00	75
Y1678	20p. green	30	35
X 960	20p. black	1·00	1·00
X 961	20½p. blue	1·25	1·25
X 962	22p. blue	90	75
X 963	22p. green	90	80
X1016	22p. orange	1·00	90
X 965	23p. red	1·25	1·00
X 966	23p. green	1·10	1·10
X 967	24p. violet	1·60	1·50
X 968	24p. red	2·00	1·60
X 969	24p. brown	80	80
X 970	25p. purple	1·00	1·00
Y1752	25p. red	1·10	1·10
X 971	26p. red	1·10	60
Y1683	26p. brown	1·10	1·10
Y1683b	26p. gold	1·00	90
X 973	27p. brown	1·25	1·25
X 974	27p. violet	1·50	1·25
X 975	28p. violet	1·25	1·25
X 976	28p. ochre	1·40	1·25
X 977	28p. grey	1·40	1·25
X 978	29p. brown	1·75	1·75
X 979	29p. mauve	1·75	1·75
Y1684	29p. grey	1·25	1·25
Y1685	30p. grey	1·10	1·10
X 981	31p. purple	1·25	1·50
X 982	31p. blue	1·60	1·50
Y1686	31p. mauve	1·20	1·20
X 983	32p. blue	1·90	1·75
Y1687	33p. green	1·50	1·50
Y1687a	34p. green	1·25	1·00
X 985	34p. brown	1·75	1·75
X 986	34p. grey	2·00	1·90
X 987	34p. mauve	1·75	1·75
X 988	35p. brown	1·60	1·60
X 989	35p. yellow	1·75	1·60
Y1689b	35p. olive	70	75
Y1690	36p. blue	1·50	1·50
X 990	37p. red	2·00	1·75
Y1691	37p. mauve	1·40	1·40
Y1691a	37p. black	1·40	1·40
Y1692	38p. red	1·50	1·50
Y1693	38p. blue	2·00	2·00
Y1694	39p. mauve	1·50	1·50
Y1694b	39p. grey	1·20	1·20
Y1695	40p. blue	1·40	1·40
Y1757	41p. drab	1·75	1·75
Y1698a	42p. grey	1·40	1·40
Y1700	43p. brown	2·50	2·50
Y1700b	43p. green	1·40	1·40
Y1701	44p. brown	4·25	4·25
Y1702	45p. mauve	1·50	1·50
Y1702a	46p. yellow	95	1·00
Y1702b	47p. green	1·75	1·75
Y1703	50p. brown	1·75	1·20
Y1758	60p. grey	2·50	2·50
Y1704	63p. green	2·00	2·00
Y1705	64p. green	2·25	2·25
Y1706	65p. blue	2·10	2·10
Y1706a	68p. brown	2·10	2·10
X 993	75p. black	2·50	1·50
X1024	75p. grey and black	9·00	8·50
Y1707	£1 violet	3·25	3·00
Y1708	£1.50 red	3·60	3·60
Y1709	£2 green	5·00	5·00
Y1801	£2 blue	6·00	2·25
Y1710	£3 mauve	7·50	5·00
Y1802	£3 violet	9·00	3·00
Y1711	£5 blue	11·75	6·00
Y1803	£5 brown	15·00	5·00

For 26p. in gold see No. 1978.

For stamps in this design but with face values expressed as 2nd, 1st or E see Nos. 1663a etc. (1989) and 1979.

368 "A Mountain Road" (T. P. Flanagan)

1971. "Ulster '71" Festival. Paintings. Mult.

881	3p. Type **368**	25	25
882	7½p. "Deer's Meadow" (Tom Carr)	50	50
883	9p. "Slieve na brock" (Colin Middleton)	50	50

371 John Keats (150th Death Anniv)

1971. Literary Anniversaries.

884	**371**	3p. black, gold and blue	25	10
885	–	5p. black, gold and green	40	50
886	–	7½p. black, gold and brown	40	45

DESIGNS AND ANNIVERSARIES: 5p. Thomas Gray (death bicentenary); 7½p. Sir Walter Scott (birth bicentenary).

374 Servicemen and Nurse of 1921

1971. British Anniversaries Events described on stamps. Multicoloured.

887	3p. Type **374**	25	25
888	7½p. Roman centurion	50	50
889	9p. Rugby football, 1871	50	50

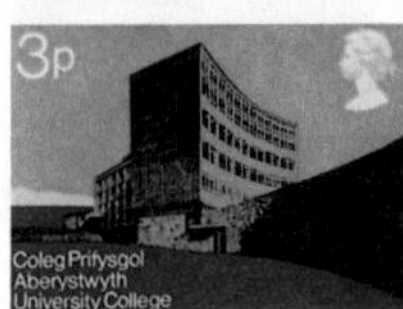

377 Physical Sciences Building, University College of Wales, Aberystwyth

1971. British Architecture. Modern University Buildings.

890	**377**	3p. multicoloured	10	10
891	–	5p. multicoloured	25	20
892	–	7½p. ochre, black and brown	25	55
893	–	9p. multicoloured	75	80

DESIGNS: 5p. Faraday Building, Southampton University; 7½p. Engineering Department, Leicester University; 9p. Hexagon Restaurant, Essex University.

381 "Dream of the Wise Men"

1971. Christmas. Multicoloured.

894	2½p. Type **381**	10	10
895	3p. "Adoration of the Magi"	10	10
896	7½p. "Ride of the Magi"	55	75

384 Sir James Clark Ross

391 St. Andrew's Greensted-juxta-Ongar, Essex

388 Statuette of Tutankhamun

1972. British Polar Explorers. Multicoloured.

897	3p. Type **384**	10	10
898	5p. Sir Martin Frobisher	15	15
899	7½p. Henry Hudson	45	40
900	9p. Capt. Robert Scott	70	75

See also Nos. 923/7.

1972. General Anniveraries. Multicoloured.

901	3p. Type **388**	25	25
902	7½p. 19th-century Coastguard	50	50
903	9p. Ralph Vaughan Williams (composer) and score	50	50

ANNIVERSARIES: 3p. 50th anniversary of discovery of Tutankhamun's tomb; 7½p. 150th anniversary of Formation of H.M. Coastguard: 9p. Birth centenary.

1972. British Architecture. Village Churches. Multicoloured.

904	3p. Type **391**	10	10
905	4p. All Saints, Earls Barton, Northants	10	20
906	5p. St. Andrew's, Letheringsett, Norfolk	15	20
907	7½p. St. Andrew's, Helpringham, Lincs	50	50
908	9p. St. Mary the Virgin, Huish Episcopi, Somerset	60	80

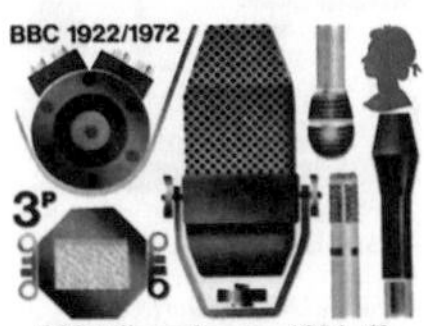

396 Microphones, 1924–69

1972. Broadcasting Anniversaries Multicoloured.

909	3p. Type **396**	10	10
910	5p. Horn loudspeaker	10	20
911	7½p. T.V. camera, 1972	45	50
912	9p. Oscillator and spark transmitter, 1897	50	50

ANNIVERSARIES: Nos. 909/11, 50th anniversary of daily broadcasting by the B.B.C.; No. 912, 75th anniversary of Marconi and Kemp's radio experiments.

400 Angel holding Trumpet

403 Queen Elizabeth and Duke of Edinburgh

1972. Christmas. Multicoloured.

913	2½p. Type **400**	10	10
914	3p. Angel playing lute	10	10
915	7½p. Angel playing harp	50	70

1972. Royal Silver Wedding.

916	**403**	3p. black, blue and silver	25	25
917		20p. black, purple & silver	1·00	1·00

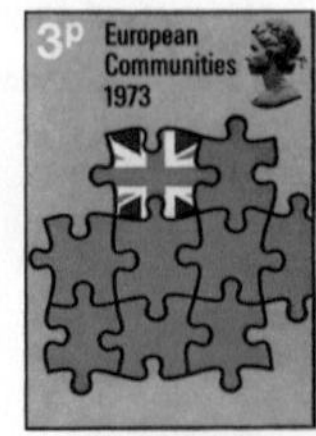

404 "Europe"

411 W. G. Grace

405 Oak Tree

1973. Britain's Entry into European Communities.

919	**404**	3p. multicoloured	25	25
920		5p. mult (blue jigsaw)	25	50
921		5p. mult (green jigsaw)	25	50

1973. Tree Planting Year. British Trees (1st issue).

922	**405**	9p. multicoloured	35	40

See also No. 949.

1973. British Explorers. As T **384**. Mult.

923	3p. David Livingstone	40	25
924	3p. H. M. Stanley	40	25
925	5p. Sir Francis Drake	40	50
926	7½p. Sir Walter Raleigh	40	50
927	9p. Charles Sturt	40	75

1973. County Cricket 1873–1973. Designs as T **411** showing caricatures of W. G. Grace by Harry Furniss.

928	**411**	3p. black, brown and gold	25	25
929	–	7½p. black, green and gold	75	75
930	–	9p. black, blue and gold	1·25	1·00

414 "Self-portrait" (Reynolds)

422 Palace of Westminster, seen from Whitehall

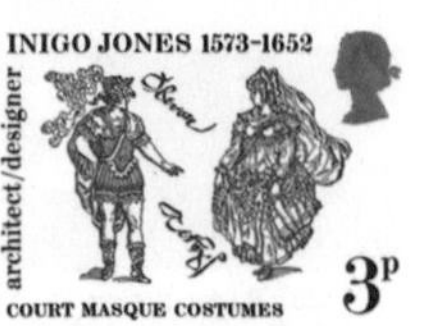

418 Court Masque Costumes

1973. British Paintings. 250th Birth Anniv of Sir Joshua Reynolds, and 150th Death Anniv of Sir Henry Raeburn. Multicoloured.

931	3p. Type **414**	10	10
932	5p. "Self-portrait" (Raeburn)	25	25
933	7½p. "Nelly O' Brien" (Reynolds)	25	25
934	9p. "Rev. R. Walker (The Skater)" (Raeburn)	50	50

1973. 400th Birth Anniv of Inigo Jones (architect and designer). Multicoloured.

935	3p. Type **418**	10	25
936	3p. St. Paul's Church, Covent Garden	10	25
937	5p. Prince's Lodging, Newmarket	35	50
938	5p. Court Masque stage scene	35	50

1973. 19th Commonwealth Parliamentary Conf.

939	**422**	8p. black, grey and stone	45	50
940	–	10p. gold and black	45	50

DESIGN: 10p. Palace of Westminster, seen from Millbank.

424 Princess Anne and Capt. Mark Phillips

1973. Royal Wedding.

941	**424**	3½p. violet and silver	25	25
942		20p. brown and silver	1·00	75

425 "Good King Wenceslas looked out."

1973. Christmas. Multicoloured.

943	3p. Type **425**	20	25
944	3p. King and page at window	20	25
945	3p. Leaving the palace	20	25
946	3p. Struggling against the wind	20	25
947	3p. Delivering gifts	20	25
948	3½p. King, page and peasant	20	25

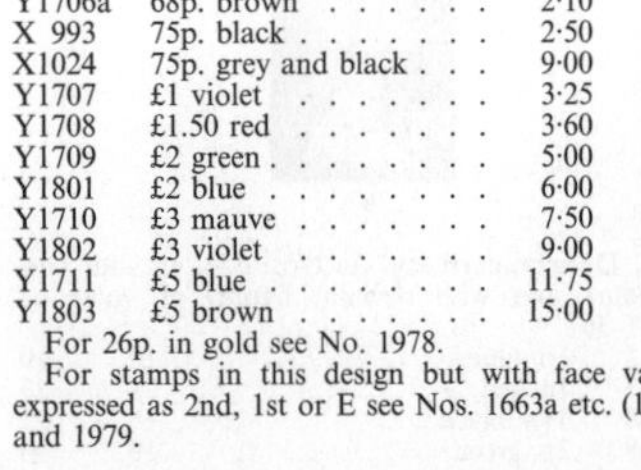

431 Horse Chestnut

1974. British Trees (2nd issue).
949 **431** 10p. multicoloured . . . 40 35

432 First Motor Fire-engine, 1904

1974. Bicentenary of Fire Prevention (Metropolis) Act. Multicoloured.
950 3½p. Type **432** 25 10
951 5½p. Prize-winning fire-engine, 1863 . . . . 25 30
952 8p. First steam fire-engine, 1830 . . . . 50 50
953 10p. Fire-engine. 1766 . . . 50 50

436 P.&O. Packet "Peninsular", 1888

1974. Cent of Universal Postal Union. Mult.
954 3½p. Type **436** 25 10
955 5½p. Farman H.F.III biplane, 1911 . . . . 25 30
956 8p. Airmail—blue van and postbox, 1930 . . . . . 25 35
957 10p. Imperial Airways Short S.21 flying boat "Maia", 1937 . . . . 50 40

440 Robert the Bruce

1974. Medieval Warriors. Multicoloured.
958 4½p. Type **440** 25 10
959 5½p. Owain Glyndwr 25 35
960 8p. Henry the Fifth 50 50
961 10p. The Black Prince . . . 50 50

444 Churchill in Royal Yacht Squadron Uniform

1974. Birth Centenary of Sir Winston Churchill.
962 **444** 4½p. silver, blue and green 20 15
963 – 5½p. silver, brown and grey 35 35
964 – 8p. silver, red and pink 60 50
965 – 10p. silver, brown and stone 60 50
DESIGNS: 5½p. Prime Minister, 1940; 8p. Secretary for War and Air, 1919; 10p. War correspondent, South Africa, 1899.

448 "Adoration of the Magi" (York Minster, c. 1355)

1974. Christmas. Church Roof Bosses. Multicoloured.
966 3½p. Type **448** 10 10
967 4½p. "The Nativity" (St. Helen's Church, Norwich, c. 1480) 10 10
968 8p. "Virgin and Child" (Ottery St. Mary Church, c. 1350) 25 50
969 10p. "Virgin and Child" (Worcester Cathedral, c. 1224) 50 50

452 Invalid in Wheelchair

1975. Health and Handicap Funds.
970 **452** 4½p.+1½p. blue and azure 25 25

453 "Peace—Burial at Sea"

1975. Birth Bicentenary of J. M. W. Turner (painter). Multicoloured.
971 4½p. Type **453** 25 25
972 5½p. "Snowstorm—Steamer off a Harbour's Mouth" 25 25
973 8p. "The Arsenal, Venice" . . 25 50
974 10p. "St. Laurent" 50 50

457 Charlotte Square, Edinburgh

1975. European Architectural Heritage Year. Multicoloured.
975 7p. Type **457** 25 25
976 7p. The Rows, Chester . . . 25 25
977 8p. Royal Observatory, Greenwich 40 30
978 10p. St. George's Chapel, Windsor 40 30
979 12p. National Theatre, London 40 40

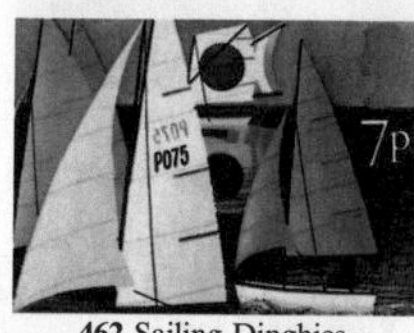

462 Sailing Dinghies

1975. Sailing. Multicoloured.
980 7p. Type **462** 25 20
981 8p. Racing keel yachts . . . 35 40
982 10p. Cruising yachts 35 45
983 12p. Multihulls 50 50

466 Stephenson's "Locomotion", 1825

1975. 150th Anniv of Public Railways. Mult.
984 7p. Type **466** 25 25
985 8p. "Abbotsford", 1876 . . . 50 50
986 10p. "Caerphilly Castle", 1923 . . . . 50 50
987 12p. High Speed Train, 1975 40 75

470 Palace of Westminster

1975. 62nd Inter-Parliamentary Union Conference.
988 **470** 12p. multicoloured . . . 50 40

471 Emma and Mr. Woodhouse ("Emma")

1975. Birth Bicentenary of Jane Austen (novelist). Multicoloured.
989 8½p. Type **471** 25 20
990 10p. Catherine Morland ("Northanger Abbey") . . 45 45
991 11p. Mr. Darcy ("Pride and Prejudice") 45 45
992 13p. Mary and Henry Crawford ("Mansfield Park") 50 50

475 Angels with Harp and Lute

1975. Christmas. Multicoloured.
993 6½p. Type **475** 25 25
994 8½p. Angel with mandolin . . 25 40
995 11p. Angel with horn 50 45
996 13p. Angel with trumpet . . 50 45

479 Housewife

1976. Centenary of Telephone. Multicoloured.
997 8½p. Type **479** 25 20
998 10p. Policeman 40 40
999 11p. District nurse 45 45
1000 13p. Industrialist 50 50

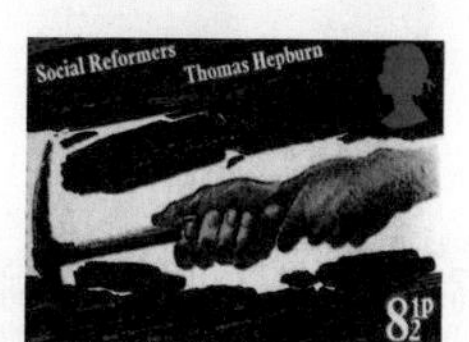

483 Hewing Coal (Thomas Hepburn)

1976. Social Reformers. Multicoloured.
1001 8½p. Type **483** 25 20
1002 10p. Machinery (Robert Owen) 40 40
1003 11p. Chimney cleaning (Lord Shaftesbury) . . . 45 45
1004 13p. Hands clutching prison bars (Elizabeth Fry) . . . 45 45

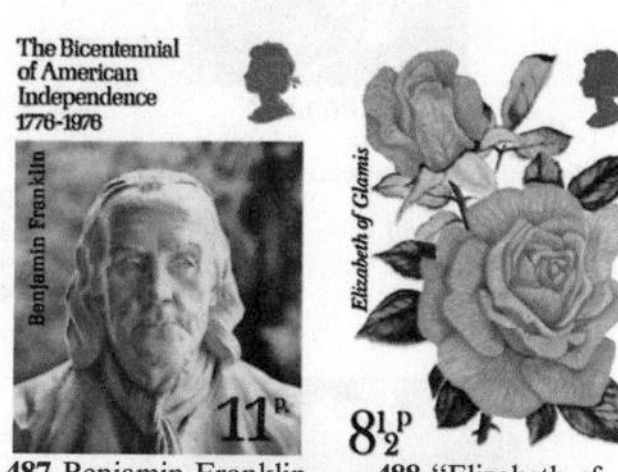

487 Benjamin Franklin (bust by Jean-Jacques Caffieri) **488** "Elizabeth of Glamis"

1976. Bicentenary of American Revolution.
1005 **487** 11p. multicoloured . . . 35 35

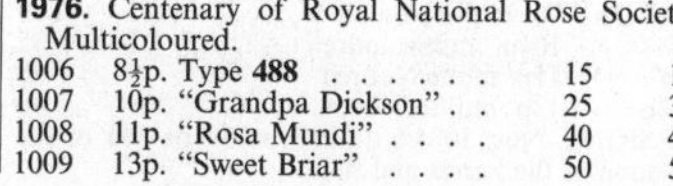

1976. Centenary of Royal National Rose Society. Multicoloured.
1006 8½p. Type **488** 15 10
1007 10p. "Grandpa Dickson" . . 25 30
1008 11p. "Rosa Mundi" 40 40
1009 13p. "Sweet Briar" 50 50

492 Archdruid **496** Woodcut from "The Canterbury Tales"

1976. British Cultural Traditions. Multicoloured.
1010 8½p. Type **492** 25 20
1011 10p. Morris dancing 40 40
1012 11p. Scots piper 45 45
1013 13p. Welsh harpist 50 50
The 8½p. and 13p. commemorate the 800th Anniv of the Royal National Eisteddfod.

1976. 500th Anniv of British Printing. Multicoloured.
1014 8½p. Type **496** 25 20
1015 10p. Extract from "The Tretyse of Love" 40 40
1016 11p. Woodcut from "The Game and Playe of Chesse" by William Caxton 45 45
1017 13p. Early printing press . . 45 50

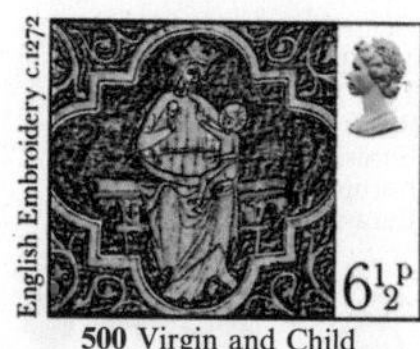

500 Virgin and Child

1976. Christmas. English Medieval Embroidery. Multicoloured.
1018 6½p. Type **500** 25 25
1019 8½p. Angel with crown . . . 35 25
1020 11p. Angel appearing to Shepherds 40 45
1021 13p. The Three Kings . . . 45 50

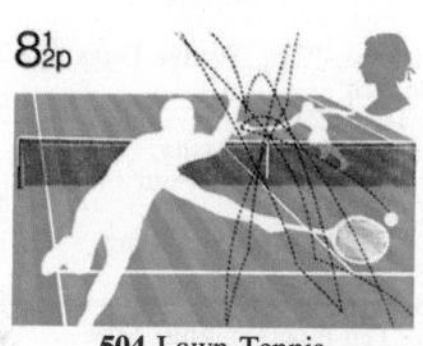

504 Lawn Tennis

1977. Racket Sports. Multicoloured.
1022 8½p. Type **504** 25 20
1023 10p. Table tennis 40 40
1024 11p. Squash 45 40
1025 13p. Badminton 45 50

508

1977.
1026 **508** £1 green and olive . . 3·00 25
1026b £1.30 brown and blue . . 5·50 6·00
1026c £1.33 mauve and black 7·50 7·00
1026d £1.41 brown and blue 8·50 8·50
1026e £1.50 olive and black 6·00 5·00
1026f £1.60 brown and blue 6·50 7·00
1027 £2 green and brown . . 12·00 50
1028 £5 pink and blue . . . 22·00 3·00

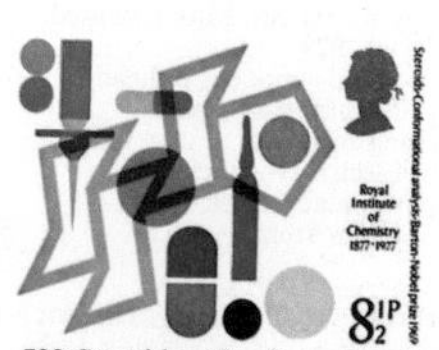

509 Steroids—Conformational Analysis

1977. Centenary of Royal Insitute of Chemistry. Multicoloured.
1029 8½p. Type **509** 25 20
1030 10p. Vitamin C—synthesis 45 45
1031 11p. Starch—chromatography 45 45
1032 13p. Salt—crystallography 45 45

513

1977. Silver Jubilee. Multicoloured.
1033 8½p. Type **513** 25 25
1034 9p. Type **513** 25 25
1035 10p. "Leaf" initials 25 25
1036 11p. "Star" initials 50 50
1037 13p. "Oak" initials 50 50

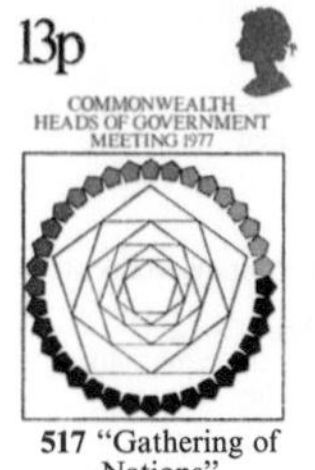

517 "Gathering of Nations" **518** West European Hedgehog

1977. Commonwealth Heads of Government Meeting, London.
1038 **517** 13p. multicoloured . . . 35 50

1977. British Wildlife. Multicoloured.
1039 9p. Type **518** 40 40
1040 9p. Brown hare 25 40
1041 9p. Eurasian red squirrel . . 25 40
1042 9p. European otter 25 40
1043 9p. Eurasian badger 25 40

523 "Three French Hens, Two Turtle Doves and a Partridge in a Pear Tree"

1977. Christmas. "The Twelve Days of Christmas". Multicoloured.
1044 7p. Type **523** 20 15
1045 7p. "Six Geese a-laying, Five Gold Rings, Four Colly Birds" 20 15
1046 7p. "Eight Maids a-milking, Seven Swans a-Swimming" 20 15
1047 7p. "Ten Pipers piping, Nine Drummers drumming" . . 20 10
1048 7p. "Twelve Lords a-leaping, Eleven Ladies dancing" 20 15
1049 9p. "A Partridge in a Pear Tree" 20 15

529 Oil—North Sea Production Platform **537** State Coach

533 The Tower of London

1978. Energy Resources. Multicoloured.
1050 9p. Type **529** 25 25
1051 10½p. Coal—modern pithead 25 25
1052 11p. Natural gas—flame rising from sea 50 50
1053 13p. Electricity—nuclear power station and uranium atom 50 50

1978. British Architecture. Historic Buildings. Multicoloured.
1054 9p. Type **533** 25 20
1055 10½p. Holyroodhouse . . . 25 40
1056 11p. Caernarvon Castle . . 50 40
1057 13p. Hampton Court Palace 50 40
MS1058 121 × 90mm. Nos. 1054/7 1·25 1·75

1978. 25th Anniv of Queen's Coronation.
1059 **537** 9p. gold and blue . . . 35 25
1060 – 10½p. gold and red . . . 40 45
1061 – 11p. gold and green . . 40 45
1062 – 13p. gold and violet . . 50 50
DESIGNS: 10½p. St. Edward's Crown; 11p. The Sovereign's Orb; 13p. Imperial State Crown.

541 Shire Horse

1978. Horses. Multicoloured.
1063 9p. Type **541** 20 10
1064 10½p. Shetland pony 35 40
1065 11p. Welsh pony 35 45
1066 13p. Thoroughbred 45 50

545 "Penny-farthing" and 1884 Safety Bicycle

1978. Centenaries of Cyclists' Touring Club and British Cycling Federation. Multicoloured.
1067 9p. Type **545** 25 20
1068 10½p. 1920 Touring bicycles 35 40
1069 11p. Modern small-wheeled bicycles 40 40
1070 13p. 1978 Road-racers . . . 50 50

549 Singing Carols round the Christmas Tree

1978. Christmas. Carol-singing. Mult.
1071 7p. Type **549** 25 25
1072 9p. The Waits 25 25
1073 11p. 18th-century carol singers 50 50
1074 13p. "The Boar's Head Carol" 50 50

553 Old English Sheepdog

1979. Dogs. Multicoloured.
1075 9p. Type **553** 25 20
1076 10½p. Welsh springer spaniel 40 40
1077 11p. West Highland terrier 40 40
1078 13p. Irish setter 40 50

557 Primrose

1979. Spring Wild Flowers. Multicoloured.
1079 9p. Type **557** 25 20
1080 10½p. Daffodil 25 45
1081 11p. Bluebell 50 45
1082 13p. Snowdrop 50 40

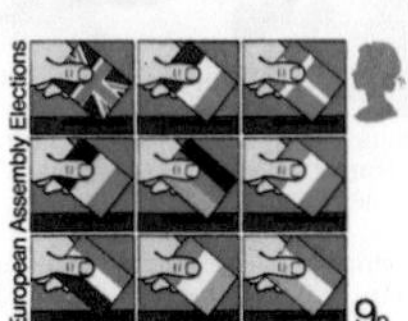

561 Hands placing National Flags into Ballot Boxes

1979. First Direct Elections to European Assembly.
1083 **561** 9p. multicoloured . . . 25 20
1084 – 10½p. multicoloured . . 35 35
1085 – 11p. multicoloured . . . 40 40
1086 – 13p. multicoloured . . . 45 40
DESIGNS: Nos. 1084/6 differ from Type **561** in the position of the hands and flags.

565 "Saddling 'Mahmoud' for the Derby, 1936" (Sir Alfred Munnings)

1979. Horse-racing Paintings. Bicentenary of the Derby (9p). Multicoloured.
1087 9p. Type **565** 25 25
1088 10½p. "The Liverpool Great National Steeple Chase, 1839" (aquatint, F. C. Turner) 25 25
1089 11p. "The First Spring Meeting, Newmarket, 1793" (J. N. Sartorius) . . 50 50
1090 13p. "Racing at Dorsett Ferry, Windsor, 1684" (Francis Barlow) 50 50

569 "The Tale of Peter Rabbit" (Beatrix Potter) **573** Sir Rowland Hill

1979. International Year of the Child. Multicoloured.
1091 9p. Type **569** 30 35
1092 10½p. "The Wind in the Willows" (Kenneth Grahame) 35 35
1093 11p. "Winnie-the-Pooh" (A. A. Milne) 40 40
1094 13p. "Alice's Adventures in Wonderland" (Lewis Carroll) 60 60

1979. Death Cent of Sir Rowland Hill. Mult.
1095 10p. Type **573** 25 20
1096 11½p. Postman, c. 1839 . . 25 35
1097 13p. London postman, c. 1839 . . . . 50 45
1098 15p. Woman and young girl with letters, 1840 . . . . 75 50
MS1099 82 × 121mm. Nos. 1095/8 1·25 1·50

577 Policeman on the Beat

1979. 150th Anniv of Metropolitan Police. Mult.
1100 10p. Type **577** 30 20
1101 11½p. Policeman directing traffic 35 35
1102 13p. Mounted policewoman 40 50
1103 15p. River patrol boat . . . 60 50

581 The Three Kings

1979. Christmas. Multicoloured.
1104 8p. Type **581** 25 20
1105 10p. Angel appearing to the Shepherds 25 25
1106 11½p. The Nativity 25 35
1107 13p. Mary and Joseph travelling to Bethlehem 50 50
1108 15p. The Annunciation . . 55 55

586 River Kingfisher ("Kingfisher")

1980. Cent of Wild Bird Protection Act. Mult.
1109 10p. Type **586** 20 10
1110 11½p. White-throated dipper ("Dipper") 40 35
1111 13p. Moorhen 50 45
1112 15p. Yellow wagtails 50 45

590 "Rocket" approaching Moorish Arch, Liverpool

1980. 150th Anniv of Liverpool and Manchester Railway. Multicoloured.
1113 12p. Type **590** 40 40
1114 12p. First and Second Class carriages passing through Olive Mount cutting . . . 40 40
1115 12p. Third Class carriage and sheep truck crosssing Chat Moss 40 40
1116 12p. Horsebox and carriage truck near Bridgewater Canal 40 40
1117 12p. Truck and mail coach at Manchester 40 40

595 Montage of London Buildings

1980. "London 1980" International Stamp Exn.
1118 **595** 50p. brown . . . . . . 1·25 1·25
MS1119 90 × 123 mm. No. 1118 (sold at 75p.) . . . . 1·50 1·75

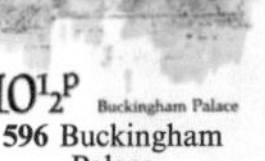

596 Buckingham Palace **605** Queen Elizabeth the Queen Mother

601 Charlotte Bronte ("Jane Eyre")

1980. London Landmarks. Multicoloured.
1120 10½p. Type **596** 25 10
1121 12p. The Albert Memorial 25 15
1122 13½p. Royal Opera House 35 40
1123 15p. Hampton Court . . . 45 50
1124 17½p. Kensington Palace . . 60 50

1980. Famous Authoresses. Multicoloured.
1125 12p. Type **601** 35 20
1126 13½p. George Eliot ("The Mill on the Floss") . . . 40 45
1127 15p. Emily Bronte ("Wuthering Heights") . . 50 45
1128 17½p. Elizabeth Gaskell ("North and South") . . 50 50

1980. 80th Birthday of The Queen Mother.
1129 **605** 12p. multicoloured . . . 75 75

606 Sir Henry Wood **610** Running

1980. British Conductors. Multicoloured.
1130 12p. Type **606** 30 10
1131 13½p. Sir Thomas Beecham 45 45
1132 15p. Sir Malcolm Sargent 50 50
1133 17½p. Sir John Barbirolli . . 50 50

1980. Sport Centenaries. Multicoloured.
1134 12p. Type **610** 25 20
1135 13½p. Rugby 50 50

1136	15p. Boxing	50	50
1137	17½p. Cricket	50	50

CENTENARIES: 12p. Amateur Athletics Association; 13½p. Welsh Rugby Union; 15p. Amateur Boxing Association; 17½p. First England–Australia Test Match.

614 Christmas Tree

1980. Christmas. Multicoloured.

1138	10p. Type **614**	20	10
1139	12p. Candles	20	20
1140	13½p. Mistletoe and apples	40	40
1141	15p. Crown, chains and bell	55	50
1142	17½p. Holly wreath	55	50

619 St. Valentine's Day

1981. Folklore. Multicoloured.

1143	14p. Type **619**	25	25
1144	18p. Morris dancers	50	50
1145	22p. Lammastide	75	75
1146	25p. Medieval mummers	1·00	1·00

623 Blind Man with Guide Dog

1981. Int Year of Disabled Persons. Mult.

1147	14p. Type **623**	50	25
1148	18p. Hands spelling "Deaf" in sign language	50	50
1149	22p. Disabled man in wheelchair	75	75
1150	25p. Disabled artist painting with foot	1·00	75

627 "Aglais urticae"

636 Prince Charles and Lady Diana Spencer

631 Glenfinnan, Scotland

1981. Butterflies. Multicoloured.

1151	14p. Type **627**	25	20
1152	18p. "Maculinea arion"	75	65
1153	22p. "Inachis io"	70	70
1154	25p. "Carterocephalus palaemon"	75	75

1981. 50th Anniv of National Trust for Scotland. British Landscapes. Multicoloured.

1155	14p. Type **631**	15	25
1156	18p. Derwentwater, England	45	50
1157	20p. Stackpole Head, Wales	70	75
1158	22p. Giant's Causeway, Northern Ireland	75	1·00
1159	25p. St. Kilda, Scotland	90	1·25

1981. Royal Wedding.

1160 **636**	14p. multicoloured	65	25
1161	25p. multicoloured	1·25	1·50

637 "Expeditions"

1981. 25th Anniv of Duke of Edinburgh Award Scheme. Multicoloured.

1162	14p. Type **637**	25	20
1163	18p. "Skills"	45	50
1164	22p. "Service"	70	70
1165	25p. "Recreation"	80	80

641 Cockle-dredging from "Linsey II"

1981. Fishing Industry. Multicoloured.

1166	14p. Type **641**	25	25
1167	18p. Hauling in trawl net	50	50
1168	22p. Lobster potting	75	75
1169	25p. Hoisting seine net	75	75

645 Father Christmas

1981. Christmas. Children's Pictures. Mult.

1170	11½p. Type **645**	25	20
1171	14p. Jesus Christ	35	20
1172	18p. Flying angel	50	60
1173	22p. Joseph and Mary arriving at Bethlehem	75	70
1174	25p. Three Kings approaching Bethlehem	85	75

650 Charles Darwin and Giant Tortoises

1982. Death Cent of Charles Darwin. Mult.

1175	15½p. Type **650**	50	20
1176	19½p. Darwin and Marine iguanas	50	60
1177	26p. Darwin and cactus ground finch and large ground finch	75	85
1178	29p. Darwin and prehistoric skulls	75	90

654 Boys' Brigade

658 Ballerina

1982. Youth Organizations. Multicoloured.

1179	15½p. Type **654**	25	15
1180	19½p. Girls' Brigade	50	55
1181	26p. Boy Scout Movement	75	75
1182	29p. Girl Guides Movement	1·00	80

1982. Europa. British Theatre. Multicoloured.

1183	15½p. Type **658**	25	15
1184	19½p. Harlequin	50	50
1185	26p. Hamlet	1·00	1·00
1186	29p. Opera singer	1·00	90

662 Henry VIII and "Mary Rose"

1982. Maritime Heritage. Multicoloured.

1187	15½p. Type **662**	35	25
1188	19½p. Admiral Blake and "Triumph"	50	50
1189	24p. Lord Nelson and H.M.S. "Victory"	75	75
1190	26p. Lord Fisher and H.M.S. "Dreadnought"	75	75
1191	29p. Viscount Cunningham and H.M.S. "Warspite"	1·00	1·00

667 "Strawberry Thief" (William Morris)

1982. British Textiles. Multicoloured.

1192	15½p. Type **667**	25	25
1193	19½p. Untitled (Steiner and Co.)	75	75
1194	26p. "Cherry Orchard" (Paul Nash)	75	1·00
1195	29p. "Chevron" (Andrew Foster)	1·00	1·25

671 Development of Communications (⅔-size illustration)

1982. Information Technology. Multicoloured.

1196	15½p. Type **671**	75	25
1197	26p. Modern technological aids	1·25	1·25

673 Austin "Seven" and "Metro"

1982. British Motor Industry. Multicoloured.

1198	15½p. Type **673**	50	25
1199	19½p. Ford "Model T" and "Escort"	75	75
1200	26p. Jaguar "SS1" and "XJ6"	75	75
1201	29p. Rolls-Royce "Silver Ghost" and "Silver Spirit"	1·00	1·00

677 "While Shepherds Watched"

1982. Christmas. Carols. Multicoloured.

1202	12½p. Type **677**	25	20
1203	15½p. "The Holly and the Ivy"	50	20
1204	19½p. "I saw Three Ships"	65	75
1205	26p. "We Three Kings"	75	80
1206	29p. "Good King Wenceslas"	1·00	90

682 Atlantic Salmon

1983. British River Fishes. Multicoloured.

1207	15½p. Type **682**	30	10
1208	19½p. Northern pike	60	60
1209	26p. Brown trout	75	75
1210	29p. Eurasian perch	90	90

686 Tropical Island

1983. Commonwealth Day. Geographical Regions. Multicoloured.

1211	15½p. Type **686**	40	25
1212	19½p. Desert	75	75
1213	26p. Temperate farmland	75	75
1214	29p. Mountain range	1·00	1·00

690 Humber Bridge

1983. Europa. Engineering Achievements. Multicoloured.

1215	16p. Type **690**	50	25
1216	20½p. Thames Flood Barrier	1·00	1·00
1217	28p. "Iolair" (oilfield emergency support vessel)	1·00	1·00

693 Musketeer and Pikeman, The Royal Scots (1633)

698 20th-century Garden, Sissinghurst

1983. British Army Uniforms. Multicoloured.

1218	16p. Type **693**	50	10
1219	20½p. Fusilier and Ensign, The Royal Welsh Fusiliers (mid-18th century)	50	60
1220	26p. Riflemen, 95th Rifles (The Royal Green Jackets) (1805)	75	90
1221	28p. Sergeant (khaki service uniform) and Guardsman (full dress), The Irish Guards (1900)	75	90
1222	31p. Paratroopers, The Parachute Regiment (1983)	75	80

1983. British Gardens. Multicoloured.

1223	16p. Type **698**	50	10
1224	20½p. 19th-century garden, Biddulph Grange	50	55
1225	28p. 18th-century garden, Blenheim	75	90
1226	31p. 17th-century garden. Pitmedden	1·00	90

702 Merry-go-round

1983. British Fairs. Multicoloured.

1227	16p. Type **702**	35	25
1228	20½p. Big wheel, helter-skelter and performing animals	75	75
1229	28p. Side shows	75	1·00
1230	31p. Early produce fair	1·00	1·00

706 "Christmas Post" (pillar-box)

1983. Christmas. Multicoloured.

1231	12½p. Type **706**	25	25
1232	16p. "The Three Kings" (chimney pots)	50	25
1233	20½p. "World at Peace" (dove and blackbird)	75	1·00
1234	28p. "Light of Christmas" (street lamp)	75	1·00
1235	31p. "Christmas Dove" (hedge sculpture)	1·00	1·25

711 Arms of College of Arms

1984. 500th Anniv of College of Arms. Mult.

1236	16p. Type **711**	50	15
1237	20½p. Arms of King Richard III (founder)	50	65
1238	28p. Arms of Earl Marshal of England	1·00	90
1239	31p. Arms of City of London	1·25	1·00

715 Highland Cow

1984. Cattle. Multicoloured.
1240 16p. Type **715** 35 15
1241 20½p. Chillingham wild bull 55 60
1242 26p. Hereford bull 75 75
1243 28p. Welsh black bull . . . 75 85
1244 31p. Irish moiled cow . . . 1·00 90

720 Garden Festival Hall, Liverpool

1984. Urban Renewal. Multicoloured.
1245 16p. Type **720** 30 10
1246 20½p. Milburngate Centre, Durham 50 60
1247 28p. Bush House, Bristol . . 1·00 1·00
1248 31p. Commercial Street development, Perth . . . 1·00 1·00

725 Abduction of Europa

1984. 25th Anniv of C.E.P.T. (Europa) (Nos. 1249, 1251), and Second Election to European Parliament (others).
1249 – 16p. grey, blue and gold 50 25
1250 **725** 16p. grey, black, and gold 50 25
1251 – 20½p. red, purple and gold . . . . 1·25 1·25
1252 **725** 20½p. red, pur, blk gold 1·25 1·25
DESIGN: Nos. 1249 and 1251, Bridge (C.E.P.T. 25th anniv logo).

726 Lancaster House **727** View of Earth from "Apollo 11"

1984. London Economic Summit Conference.
1253 **726** 31p. multicoloured . . . 1·00 1·00

1984. Centenary of Greenwich Meridian. Mult.
1254 16p. Type **727** 50 25
1255 20½p. Navigational chart of the English Channel . . . 75 75
1256 28p. Greenwich Observatory 1·00 75
1257 31p. Sir George Airey's Transit Telescope . . . . 1·00 1·00

731 Bath Mail Coach leaving London, 1784

1984. Bicentenary of First Mail Coach Run, Bath and Bristol to London. Multicoloured.
1258 16p. Type **731** 40 35
1259 16p. Attack on Exeter Mail, 1816 . . . . 40 35
1260 16p. Norwich Mail in thunderstorm, 1827 . . . 40 35
1261 16p. Holyhead and Liverpool Mails leaving London, 1828 . . . . . 40 35
1262 16p. Edinburgh Mail snowbound, 1831 . . . . 40 35

736 Nigerian Clinic

1984. 50th Anniv of British Council. Mult.
1263 17p. Type **736** 50 25
1264 22p. Violinist and Acropolis, Athens . . . . 75 1·00
1265 31p. Building project, Sri Lanka . . . . 75 1·00
1266 34p. British Council library, Middle East . . . . . . 75 1·00

740 The Holy Family

1984. Christmas. Multicoloured.
1267 13p. Type **740** 25 25
1268 17p. Arrival in Bethlehem 50 25
1269 22p. Shepherd and Lamb . . 75 75
1270 31p. Virgin and Child . . . 1·00 90
1271 34p. Offering of Frankincense . . . . . . 1·00 1·00

745 "Flying Scotsman"

1985. Famous Trains. Multicoloured.
1272 17p. Type **745** 75 25
1273 22p. "Golden Arrow" . . . 75 1·00
1274 29p. "Cheltenham Flyer" . . 1·00 1·25
1275 31p. "Royal Scot" . . . . 1·25 1·50
1276 34p. "Cornish Riviera" . . 1·50 1·50

750 "Bombus terrestris" (bee) **755** "Water Music" (George Frideric Handel)

1985. Insects. Multicoloured.
1277 17p. Type **750** 40 10
1278 22p. "Coccinella septempunctata" (ladybird) 65 55
1279 29p. "Decticus verrucivorus" (bush-cricket) 85 90
1280 31p. "Lucanus cervus" (stag beetle) . . . . 1·10 1·00
1281 34p. "Anax imperator" (dragonfly) . . . . 1·10 90

1985. Europa. European Music Year. British Composers. Mutlicoloured.
1282 17p. Type **755** 55 10
1283 22p. "The Planets" Suite (Gustav Holst) 75 90
1284 31p. "The First Cuckoo" (Frederick Delius) . . . . 1·50 1·25
1285 34p. "Sea Pictures" (Edward Elgar) . . . . 1·50 1·25

759 R.N.L.I. Lifeboat and Signal Flags

1985. Safety at Sea. Multicoloured.
1286 17p. Type **759** 40 25
1287 22p. Beachy Head Lighthouse and chart . . 60 75
1288 31p. "Marecs A" communications satellite and dish aerials . . . . . 90 1·00
1289 34p. Buoys . . . . 1·00 1·25

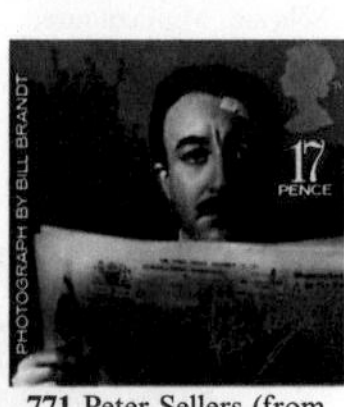

763 Datapost Motorcyclist, City of London **771** Peter Sellers (from photo by Bill Brandt)

767 King Arthur and Merlin

1985. 350 Years of Royal Mail Public Postal Service. Multicoloured.
1290 17p. Type **763** 50 10
1291 22p. Rural postbus 75 70
1292 31p. Parcel delivery in winter . . . . 1·00 1·00
1293 34p. Town letter delivery . . 1·00 1·00

1985. Arthurian Legends. Multicoloured.
1294 17p. Type **767** 50 25
1295 22p. Lady of the Lake . . . 75 75
1296 31p. Queen Guinevere and Sir Lancelot . . . . . . 1·00 1·25
1297 34p. Sir Galahad . . . . . 1·00 1·25

1985. British Film Year. Multicoloured.
1298 17p. Type **771** 45 25
1299 22p. David Niven (from photo by Cornell Lucas) 60 75
1300 29p. Charlie Chaplin (from photo by Lord Snowdon) 1·00 1·25
1301 31p. Vivien Leigh (from photo by Angus McBean) 1·10 1·50
1302 34p. Alfred Hitchcock (from photo by Howard Coster) 1·40 1·50

776 Principal Boy

1985. Christmas. Pantomime Characters. Mult.
1303 12p. Type **776** 50 15
1304 17p. Genie 50 25
1305 22p. Dame 75 90
1306 31p. Good fairy . . . . . . 1·25 1·10
1307 34p. Pantomime cat . . . . 1·25 1·25

781 Light Bulb and North Sea Oil Drilling Rig (Energy)

1986. Industry Year. Multicoloured.
1308 17p. Type **781** 75 25
1309 22p. Thermometer and pharmaceutical laboratory (Health) 50 75
1310 31p. Garden hoe and steelworks (Steel) . . . . 1·00 1·25
1311 34p. Loaf of bread and cornfield (Agriculture) . . 1·25 1·25

785 Dr. Edmond Halley as Comet

1986. Appearance of Halley's Comet. Multicoloured.
1312 17p. Type **785** 50 25
1313 22p. "Giotto" spacecraft approaching comet . . . 75 75
1314 31p. "Twice in a lifetime" 1·00 1·00
1315 34p. Comet orbiting sun and planets . . . . 1·25 1·25

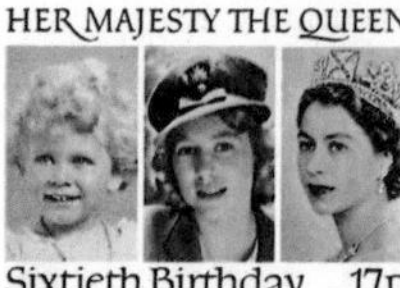

789 Queen Elizabeth II in 1928, 1942 and 1952

1986. 60th Birthday of Queen Elizabeth II. Multicoloured.
1316 17p. Type **789** 60 50
1317 17p. Queen Elizabeth II in 1958, 1973 and 1982 . . . 60 50
1318 34p. Type **789** . . . . . . 1·40 1·75
1319 34p. As No. 1317 . . . . . 1·40 1·75

791 Barn Owl

1986. Europa. Nature Conservation. Endangered Species. Multicoloured.
1320 17p. Type **791** 40 10
1321 22p. Pine marten . . . . . 80 1·00
1322 31p. Wild cat . . . . 1·25 1·25
1323 34p. Natterjack toad . . . . 1·40 1·40

795 Peasants working in Fields

1986. 900th Anniv of Domesday Book. Mult.
1324 17p. Type **795** 40 10
1325 22p. Freemen working at town trades 70 35
1326 31p. Knights and retainers 1·10 1·40
1327 34p. Lord at banquet . . . 1·25 1·40

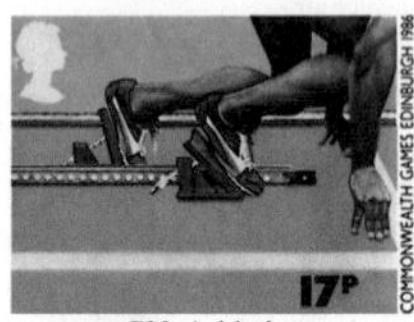

799 Athletics

1986. 13th Commonwealth Games. Edinburgh, and World Hockey Cup for Men, London. Multicoloured.
1328 17p. Type **799** 40 25
1329 22p. Rowing 55 75
1330 29p. Weightlifting . . . . . 75 1·00
1331 31p. Rifle shooting . . . . 1·00 1·25
1332 34p. Hockey . . . . 1·25 1·25

804 Prince Andrew and Miss Sarah Ferguson (from photo by Gene Nocon) **806** Stylized Cross on Ballot Paper

1986. Royal Wedding.
1333 **804** 12p. multicoloured . . . 50 30
1334 – 17p. multicoloured . . . 1·00 95
DESIGN: 17p. As Type **804** but with naval motif at foot.

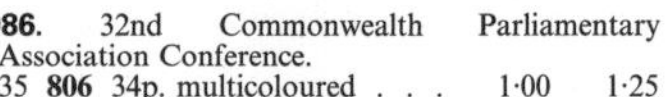
1986. 32nd Commonwealth Parliamentary Association Conference.
1335 **806** 34p. multicoloured . . . 1·00 1·25

807 Lord Dowding and Hawker Hurricane Mk I

1986. History of Royal Air Force. Multicoloured.
1336 17p. Type **807** 50 10
1337 22p. Lord Tedder and Hawker Typhoon IB . . 75 95
1338 29p. Lord Trenchard and De Havilland D.H.9A . . 1·00 1·10
1339 31p. Sir Arthur Harris and Avro Type 683 Lancaster 1·50 1·40
1340 34p. Lord Portal and De Havilland D.H.98 Mosquito . . . . 1·75 1·50
Nos. 1336/40 were issued to celebrate 50th anniv of the first R.A.F. Commands.

812 The Glastonbury Thorn

1986. Christmas. Folk Customs. Multicoloured.
1341 12p. Type **812** 50 50
1342 13p. Type **812** 25 15
1343 18p. The Tanad Valley Plygain 50 15
1344 22p. The Hebrides Tribute 1·00 1·00
1345 31p. The Dewsbury Church Knell . . . . 1·25 1·00
1346 34p. The Hereford Boy Bishop . . . . 1·25 1·10

817 North American Blanket Flower

821 "Principia Mathematica"

1987. Flower Photographs by Alfred Lammer. Multicoloured.
1347 18p. Type **817** 40 10
1348 22p. Globe thistle 70 85
1349 31p. "Echeveria" . . . . . 1·00 1·25
1350 34p. Autumn crocus . . . . 1·10 1·25

1987. 300th Anniv of "Principia Mathematica" by Sir Isaac Newton. Multicoloured.
1351 18p. Type **821** 50 15
1352 22p. "Motion of Bodies in Ellipses" 75 75
1353 31p. "Optick Treatise" . . . 1·25 1·50
1354 34p. "The System of the World" . . . . 1·25 1·25

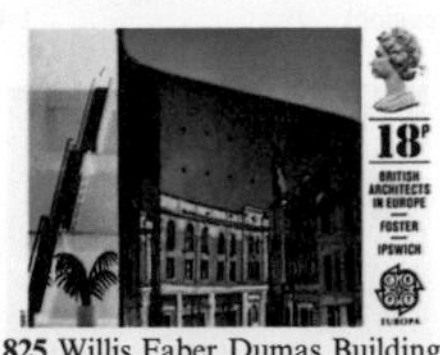
825 Willis Faber Dumas Building, Ipswich

1987. Europa. British Architects in Europe.
1355 18p. Type **825** 50 15
1356 22p. Pompidou Centre, Paris 75 75
1357 31p. Staatsgalerie, Stuttgart 1·25 1·25
1358 34p. European Investment Bank, Luxembourg . . . 1·25 1·25

829 Brigade Members with Ashford Litter, 1887

833 Arms of the Lord Lyon, King of Arms

1987. Centenary of St. John Ambulance Brigade. Multicoloured.
1359 18p. Type **829** 40 25
1360 22p. Bandaging blitz victim, 1940 . . . . 60 75
1361 31p. Volunteer with fainting girl, 1965 . . . . 1·00 1·25
1362 34p. Transport of transplant organ by Air Wing, 1987 1·25 1·25

1987. 300th Anniv of Revival of Order of the Thistle. Multicoloured.
1363 18p. Type **833** 50 10
1364 22p. Scottish heraldic banner of Prince Charles 75 90
1365 31p. Arms of Royal Scottish Academy of Painting, Sculpture and Architecture . . . . . . 1·40 1·40
1366 34p. Arms of Royal Society of Edinburgh . . . . . . 1·50 1·40

837 Crystal Palace, "Monarch of the Glen" (Landseer) and Grace Darling

1987. 150th Anniv of Queen Victoria's Accession. Multicoloured.
1367 18p. Type **837** 50 10
1368 22p. "Great Eastern", "Beeton's Book of Household Management" and Prince Albert 80 75
1369 31p. Albert Memorial, ballot box and Disraeli . . . . 1·50 1·50
1370 34p. Diamond Jubilee emblem, newspaper placard for Relief of Mafeking and morse key 1·60 1·60

841 Pot by Bernard Leach

1987. Studio Pottery. Multicoloured.
1371 18p. Type **841** 50 25
1372 26p. Pot by Elizabeth Fritsch 70 75
1373 31p. Pot by Lucie Rie . . . 1·25 1·25
1374 34p. Pot by Hans Coper . . 1·40 1·50

845 Decorating the Christmas Tree

1987. Christmas. Multicoloured.
1375 13p. Type **845** 30 10
1376 18p. Waiting for Father Christmas 40 20
1377 26p. Sleeping child and Father Christmas in sleigh 80 1·00
1378 31p. Child reading . . . . 1·10 1·25
1379 34p. Child playing recorder and snowman . . . . . . 1·25 1·50

850 Short-spined Seascorpion ("Bull-rout") (Jonathan Couch)

1988. Bicentenary of Linnean Society. Archive Illustrations. Multicoloured.
1380 18p. Type **850** 55 10
1381 26p. Yellow Waterlily (Major Joshua Swatkin) 85 1·00
1382 31p. Tundra swan ("Bewick's Swan") (Edward Lear) . . . . . 1·10 1·25
1383 34p. "Morchella esculenta" (James Sowerby) . . . . 1·25 1·40

854 Revd. William Morgan (Bible translator, 1588)

1988. 400th Anniversary of Welsh Bible. Mult.
1384 18p. Type **854** 40 10
1385 26p. William Salesbury (New Testament translator, 1567) 70 95
1386 31p. Bishop Richard Davies (New Testament translator, 1567) . . . . 1·25 1·25
1387 34p. Bishop Richard Parry (editor of Revised Welsh Bible, 1620) . . . . . . 1·40 1·25

858 Gymnastics (Cent of British Amateur Gymnastics Association)

1988. Sports Organizations. Multicoloured.
1388 18p. Type **858** 40 15
1389 26p. Downhill skiing (Ski Club of Great Britain) . . 70 80
1390 31p. Tennis (centenary of Lawn Tennis Association) 1·10 1·25
1391 34p. Football (centenary of Football League) . . . . 1·25 1·25

862 "Mallard" and Mailbags on Pick-up Arms

1988. Europa. Transport and Mail Services in 1930s. Multicoloured.
1392 18p. Type **862** 50 15
1393 26p. Loading transatlantic mail on liner "Queen Elizabeth" . . . . 1·00 1·00
1394 31p. Glasgow tram No. 1173 and pillar box 1·25 1·25
1395 34p. Imperial Airways Handley Page "Horatius" and airmail van . . . . . 1·60 1·50

866 Early Settler and Sailing Clipper

1988. Bicentenary of Australian Settlement. Mult.
1396 18p. Type **866** 60 50
1397 18p. Queen Elizabeth II with British and Australian Parliament Buildings . . . 60 50
1398 34p. W. G. Grace (cricketer) and tennis racquet . . . . 1·25 1·25
1399 34p. Shakespeare, John Lennon (entertainer) and Sydney Opera House . . 1·25 1·25
Stamps in similar designs were also issued by Australia.

870 Spanish Galeasse off The Lizard

1988. 400th Anniv of Spanish Armada. Mult.
1400 18p. Type **870** 70 40
1401 18p. English Fleet leaving Plymouth 70 65
1402 18p. Engagement off Isle of Wight 70 65
1403 18p. Attack of English fire-ships, Calais 70 65
1404 18p. Armada in storm, North Sea 70 65
Nos. 1400/4 were printed together, se-tenant, forming a composite design.

875 "The Owl and the Pussy-cat"

1988. Death Centenary of Edward Lear (artist and author).
1405 **875** 19p. black, cream and red 65 20
1406 – 27p. black, cream yellow 1·00 1·00
1407 – 32p. black, cream green 1·25 1·40
1408 – 35p. black, cream and blue . . . . 1·40 1·40
MS1409 122 × 90 mm. Nos. 1405/8 (sold at £1.35) . . . . 7·00 8·50
DESIGNS: 27p. "Edward Lear as a Bird" (self-portrait); 32p. "Cat" (from alphabet book); 35p. "There was a Young Lady whose Bonnet ..." (limerick).
The premium on No. **MS**1409 was used to support the "Stamp World London 90" International Stamp Exhibition.

CARRICKFERGUS CASTLE
879 Carrickfergus Castle

1988.
1410 **879** £1 green . . . . 4·25 60
1411 – £1.50 red . . . . 4·50 1·25
1412 – £2 blue . . . . 8·00 1·50
1413 – £5 brown . . . . 21·00 5·50
DESIGNS: £1.50, Caernarfon Castle; £2, Edinburgh Castle; £5, Windsor Castle.
For similar designs, but with silhouette of Queen's head, see Nos. 1611/14.

883 Journey to Bethlehem

1988. Christmas. Christmas Cards. Multicoloured.
1414 14p. Type **883** 45 25
1415 19p. Shepherds and Star . . 50 25
1416 27p. Three Wise Men . . . 90 1·00
1417 32p. Nativity . . . . 1·10 1·25
1418 35p. The Annunciation . . 1·40 1·25

888 Atlantic Puffin

1989. Centenary of Royal Society for the Protection of Birds. Multicoloured.
1419 19p. Type **888** 25 20
1420 27p. Pied avocet ("Avocet") 1·25 1·25
1421 32p. Oystercatcher . . . . 1·25 1·25
1422 35p. Northern gannet ("Gannet") . . . . 1·25 1·25

892 Rose

1989. Greetings Stamps. Multicoloured.
1423 19p. Type **892** . . . . . . 3·50 3·00
1424 19p. Cupid . . . . 3·50 3·00
1425 19p. Yachts . . . . 3·50 3·00
1426 19p. Fruit . . . . 3·50 3·00
1427 19p. Teddy bear . . . . . . 3·50 3·00

897 Fruit and Vegetables

1989. Food and Farming Year. Multicoloured.
1428 19p. Type **897** 45 15
1429 27p. Meat products 90 85
1430 32p. Dairy produce . . . . 1·25 1·40
1431 35p. Cereal products . . . . 1·40 1·50

901 Mortar Board

905 Toy Train and Airplane

1989. Anniversaries. Multicoloured.

1432	19p. Type **901** (150th anniv of Public Education in England)	1·00	50
1433	19p. Cross on Ballot paper (3rd Direct Elections to European Parliament)	1·00	50
1434	35p. Posthorn (26th Postal, Telegraph and Telephone International Congress, Brighton)	1·50	1·75
1435	35p. Globe (Inter-Parliamentary Union Centenary Conference, London)	1·50	1·50

1989. Europa. Games and Toys. Multicoloured.

1436	19p. Type **905**	65	25
1437	27p. Building bricks	95	1·00
1438	32p. Dice and board games	1·40	1·25
1439	35p. Toy robot, boat and doll's house	1·50	1·25

909 Ironbridge, Shropshire

913

1989. Industrial Archaeology. Multicoloured.

1440	19p. Type **909**	60	15
1441	27p. Tin Mine, St. Agnes Head, Cornwall	1·00	1·10
1442	32p. Cotton Mills, New Lanark, Strathclyde	1·10	1·25
1443	35p. Pontcysylte Aqueduct, Clwyd	1·25	1·50
MS1444	122×90 mm. 19p., 27p., 32p. and 35p. each multicoloured (horiz) (sold at £1.40)	6·00	6·50

The premium on **MS**1444 was used to support "Stamp World London 90" International Stamp Exhibition.

1989.

1663a	**913** (2nd) blue	1·00	1·00
1447	(1st) black	1·75	1·00
1664a	(1st) red	1·10	1·10
1664b	(1st) gold	1·00	1·00
1664c	(E) blue	1·25	1·25

The above were sold at the current rate for the day.

No. 1664c was valid for the basic European airmail rate.

The 2nd blue and 1st red exist with ordinary or self-adhesive gum.

For 1st class in gold see No. 1979.

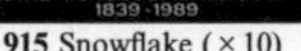

915 Snowflake (×10)

919 Royal Mail Coach

1989. 150th Anniv of Royal Microscopical Society. Multicoloured.

1453	19p. Type **915**	45	15
1454	27p. "Calliphora erythrocephala" (fly) (×5)	95	1·10
1455	32p. Blood cells (×500)	1·10	1·40
1456	35p. Microchip (×600)	1·25	1·40

1989. Lord Mayor's Show, London. Multicoloured.

1457	20p. Type **919**	70	40
1458	20p. Escort of Blues and Royals	70	40
1459	20p. Lord Mayor's Coach	70	40
1460	20p. Coach team passing St. Paul's	70	40
1461	20p. Blues and Royals drum horse	70	40

This issue commemorates the 800th anniv of the installation of the first Lord Mayor of London.

924 14th-century Peasants from Stained-glass Window

1989. Christmas. 800th Anniv of Ely Cathedral.

1462	**924** 15p. gold, silver and blue	40	15
1463	– 15p.+1p. gold, silver and blue	50	40
1464	– 20p.+1p. gold, silver and red	65	80
1465	– 34p.+1p. gold, silver and green	1·25	1·75
1466	– 37p.+1p. gold, silver and green	1·40	1·90

DESIGNS: 15p.+1p. Arches and roundels, West Front; 20p.+1p. Octagon Tower; 34p.+1p. Arcade from West Transept; 37p.+1p. Triple arch from West Front.

929 Queen Victoria and Queen Elizabeth II

930 Kitten

1990. 150th Anniv of the Penny Black.

1467	**929** 15p. blue	80	80
1469	20p. black and cream	1·00	1·00
1471	29p. mauve	1·75	1·75
1473	34p. grey	2·00	2·00
1474	37p. red	2·25	2·25

For this design with "1st" face value see No. 2133.

1990. 150th Anniv of Royal Society for Prevention of Cruelty to Animals. Multicoloured.

1479	20p. Type **930**	75	50
1480	29p. Rabbit	1·25	1·25
1481	34p. Duckling	1·25	1·50
1482	37p. Puppy	1·50	1·50

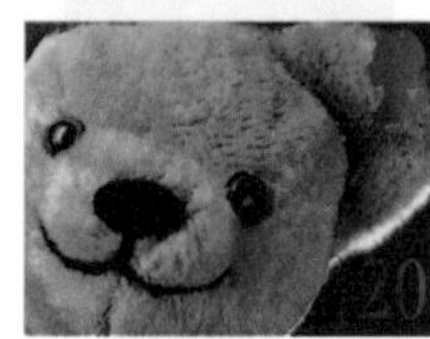

934 Teddy Bear

1990. Greetings Stamps. "Smiles". Multicoloured (except No. 1492).

1483	20p. Type **934**	3·50	2·50
1484	20p. Dennis the Menace	3·50	2·50
1485	20p. Punch	3·50	2·50
1486	20p. Cheshire Cat	3·50	2·50
1487	20p. The Man in the Moon	3·50	2·50
1488	20p. The Laughing Policeman	3·50	2·50
1489	20p. Clown	3·50	2·50
1490	20p. Mona Lisa	3·50	2·50
1491	20p. Queen of Hearts	3·50	2·50
1492	20p. Stan Laurel (comedian) (gold and black)	3·50	2·50

See also Nos. 1550/9.

944 Alexandra Palace ("Stamp World London 90" Exhibition)

948 Export Achievement Award

1990. Europa (Nos. 1493 and 1495) and "Glasgow 1990 European City of Culture" (Nos. 1494 and 1496). Multicoloured.

1493	20p. Type **944**	50	25
1494	20p. Glasgow School of Art	50	25
1495	29p. British Philatelic Bureau, Edinburgh	1·25	1·75
1496	37p. Templeton Carpet Factory, Glasgow	1·50	1·75

1990. 25th Anniv of Queen's Awards for Export and Technology. Multicoloured.

1497	20p. Type **948**	70	50
1498	20p. Technological Achievement Award	70	50
1499	37p. Type **948**	1·25	1·50
1500	37p. As No. 1498	1·25	1·50

1990. "Stamp World London 90" International Stamp Exhibition, London. Sheet 122×90 mm, containing No. 1469.

MS1501	**929** 20p. black and cream (sold at £1)	5·00	5·00

The premium on No. **MS**1501 was used to support the "Stamp World London 90" International Stamp Exhibition.

950 Cycad and Sir Joseph Banks Building

954 Thomas Hardy and Clyffe Clump, Dorset

1990. 150th Anniv of Kew Gardens. Mult.

1502	20p. Type **950**	55	15
1503	29p. Stone pine and Princess of Wales Conservatory	75	1·00
1504	34p. Willow tree and Palm House	1·25	1·60
1505	37p. Cedar tree and Pagoda	1·50	1·50

1990. 150th Anniv of Thomas Hardy (author).

1506	**954** 20p. multicoloured	80	75

955 Queen Elizabeth the Queen Mother

959 Victoria Cross

1990. 90th Birthday of Queen Elizabeth the Queen Mother. Multicoloured.

1507	20p. Type **955**	95	25
1508	29p. Queen Elizabeth	1·40	1·50
1509	34p. Elizabeth, Duchess of York	2·00	2·50
1510	37p. Lady Elizabeth Bowes-Lyon	2·25	2·50

1990. Gallantry Awards. Multicoloured.

1517	20p. Type **959**	80	75
1518	20p. George Cross	80	75
1519	20p. Distinguished Service Cross and Distinguished Service Medal (horiz)	80	75
1520	20p. Military Cross and Military Medal (horiz)	80	75
1521	20p. Distinguished Flying Cross and Distinguished Flying Medal (horiz)	80	75

964 Armagh Observatory, Jodrell Bank Radio Telescope and La Palma Telescope

1990. Astronomy. Multicoloured.

1522	22p. Type **964**	65	15
1523	26p. Newton's moon and tides diagram with early telescopes	1·00	1·10
1524	31p. Greenwich Old Observatory and early astronomical equipment	1·25	1·40
1525	37p. Stonehenge, gyroscope and navigating by stars	1·50	1·40

Nos. 1522/5 commemorate the Centenary of the British Astronomical Association and the Bicentenary of the Armagh Observatory.

968 Building a Snowman

1990. Christmas. Multicoloured.

1526	17p. Type **968**	50	15
1527	22p. Fetching the Christmas tree	70	20
1528	26p. Carol singing	70	1·10
1529	31p. Tobogganing	1·25	1·50
1530	37p. Ice-skating	1·25	1·50

973 "King Charles Spaniel"

988 Michael Faraday. (inventor of electric motor) (birth bicentenary)

978 Song Thrush's Nest

1991. Dogs. Paintings by George Stubbs. Mult.

1531	22p. Type **973**	50	15
1532	26p. "A Pointer"	75	1·25
1533	31p. "Two Hounds in a Landscape"	1·00	1·25
1534	33p. "A Rough Dog"	1·25	1·25
1535	37p. "Fino and Tiny"	1·25	1·25

1991. Greetings Stamps. "Good Luck". Mult.

1536	(1st) Type **978**	1·75	1·90
1537	(1st) Shooting star and rainbow	1·75	1·90
1538	(1st) Black-billed magpies and charm bracelet	1·75	1·90
1539	(1st) Black cat	1·75	1·90
1540	(1st) River kingfisher with key	1·75	1·90
1541	(1st) Mallard and frog	1·75	1·90
1542	(1st) Four-leaf clover in boot and match box	1·75	1·90
1543	(1st) Pot of gold at end of rainbow	1·75	1·90
1544	(1st) Heart-shaped butterflies	1·75	1·90
1545	(1st) Wishing well and sixpence	1·75	1·90

The background of the stamps forms a composite design.

Nos. 1536/45 were sold at the current rate.

1991. Scientific Achievements. Multicoloured.

1546	22p. Type **988**	60	50
1547	22p. Charles Babbage (computer science pioneer) (birth bicentenary)	60	50
1548	31p. Radar sweep of East Anglia (50th anniv of operational radar network)	1·20	1·50
1549	37p. Gloster Whittle E28/39 airplane over East Anglia (50th anniv of first flight of Sir Frank Whittle's jet engine)	1·40	1·75

992 Teddy Bear

1991. Greetings Stamps. "Smiles". As Nos. 1483/92, but inscr "1st" as in T **992**. Multicoloured (except No. 1559).

1550	(1st) Type **992**	1·50	1·50
1551	(1st) Dennis the Menace	1·50	1·50
1552	(1st) Punch	1·50	1·50
1553	(1st) Cheshire Cat	1·50	1·50
1554	(1st) The Man in the Moon	1·50	1·50
1555	(1st) The Laughing Policeman	1·50	1·50
1556	(1st) Clown	1·50	1·50
1557	(1st) Mona Lisa	1·50	1·50
1558	(1st) Queen of Hearts	1·50	1·50
1559	(1st) Stan Laurel (comedian) (gold and black)	1·50	1·50

Nos. 1550/9 were sold at the current rate.

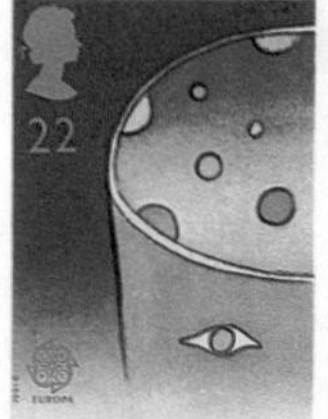

993/4 Man looking at Space

1991. Europa. Europe in Space. Multicoloured.

1560	22p. Type **993**	75	50
1561	22p. Type **994**	75	50
1562	37p. Space looking at Man (Queen's head on left)	2·00	1·50
1563	37p. Similar to No. 1562 (Queen's head on right)	2·00	1·50

Stamps of the same value were printed together in horizontal pairs, each pair forming a composite design.

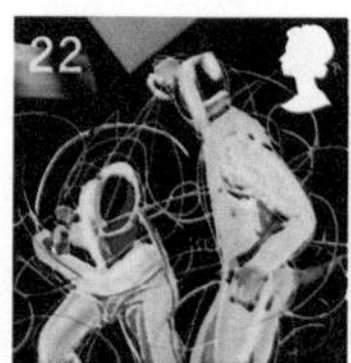

997 Fencing **1001** "Silver Jubilee"

1991. World Student Games, Sheffield (Nos. 1564/6) and World Cup Rugby Championship (No. 1567).
1564 22p. Type **997** 60 20
1565 26p. Hurdling . . . . . . 1·00 1·00
1566 31p. Diving . . . . . . 1·25 1·25
1567 37p. Rugby . . . . . . 1·50 1·50

1991. 9th World Congress of Roses, Belfast. Multicoloured.
1568 22p. Type **1001** 50 20
1569 26p. "Mme Alfred Carriere" 75 1·25
1570 31p. "Rosa moyesii" . . . . 1·00 1·25
1571 33p. "Harvest Fayre" . . . 1·25 1·50
1572 37p. "Mutabilis" . . . . 1·50 1·50

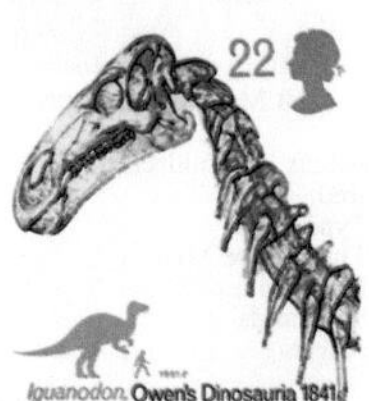

1006 Iguanodon

1991. 150th Anniv of Dinosaurs' Identification by Owen. Multicoloured.
1573 22p. Type **1006** 60 20
1574 26p. Stegosaurus . . . . . 1·10 1·25
1575 31p. Tyrannosaurus . . . . 1·25 1·25
1576 33p. Protoceratops . . . . 1·50 1·50
1577 37p. Triceratops . . . . . 1·60 1·50

1011 Map of 1816

1991. Bicentenary of Ordnance Survey. Maps of Hamstreet, Kent.
1578 **1011** 24p. black, mauve and cream 60 20
1579 – 28p. multicoloured . . 1·00 95
1580 – 33p. multicoloured . . 1·25 1·40
1581 – 39p. multicoloured . . 1·50 1·40
DESIGNS: 28p. Map of 1906; 33p. Map of 1959; 39p. Map of 1991.

1015 Adoration of the Magi

1991. Christmas. Illuminated Letters from "Acts of Mary and Jesus" Manuscript in Bodleian Library, Oxford. Multicoloured.
1582 18p. Type **1015** 75 10
1583 24p. Mary and Baby Jesus in the Stable 90 10
1584 28p. The Holy Family and Angel . . . . 95 1·25
1585 33p. The Annunciation . . 1·10 1·40
1586 39p. The Flight into Egypt 1·25 1·60

1020 Fallow Deer in Scottish Forest

1992. The Four Seasons. Wintertime. Multicoloured.
1587 18p. Type **1020** 55 25
1588 24p. Hare on North Yorkshire moors 75 25
1589 28p. Fox in the Fens . . . 1·00 1·25
1590 33p. Redwing and Home Counties village . . . . . 1·25 1·50
1591 39p. Welsh mountain sheep in Snowdonia . . . . . . 1·40 1·75

1025 Flower Spray

1992. Greetings Stamps. "Memories". Multicoloured.
1592 (1st) Type **1025** . . . . . 1·50 1·50
1593 (1st) Double locket . . . . 1·50 1·50
1594 (1st) Key . . . . 1·50 1·50
1595 (1st) Model car and cigarette cards . . . . 1·50 1·50
1596 (1st) Compass and map . . 1·50 1·50
1597 (1st) Pocket watch . . . . . 1·50 1·50
1598 (1st) 1854 1d. Red stamp and pen . . . . 1·50 1·50
1599 (1st) Pearl necklace . . . . 1·50 1·50
1600 (1st) Marbles . . . . 1·50 1·50
1601 (1st) Bucket, spade and starfish . . . . 1·50 1·50
Nos. 1592/1601 were issued together, se-tenant, the backgrounds forming a composite design.

1035 Queen Elizabeth in Coronation Robes and Parliamentary Emblem

1992. 40th Anniv of Accession. Multicoloured.
1602 24p. Type **1035** . . . . . 1·10 1·10
1603 24p. Queen Elizabeth in Garter robes and archiepiscopal arms . . . 1·10 1·10
1604 24p. Queen Elizabeth with baby Prince Andrew and Royal Arms . . . . . . 1·10 1·10
1605 24p. Queen Elizabeth at Trooping the Colour . . 1·10 1·10
1606 24p. Queen Elizabeth and Commonwealth emblem 1·10 1·10

1040 Tennyson in 1888 and "The Beguiling of Merlin" (Sir Edward Burne-Jones)

1992. Death Centenary of Alfred, Lord Tennyson (poet). Multicoloured.
1607 24p. Type **1040** 60 20
1608 28p. Tennyson in 1856 and "April Love" (Arthur Hughes) 85 85
1609 33p. Tennyson in 1864 and "I am Sick of the Shadows" (John Waterhouse) . . . . . . 1·40 1·60
1610 39p. Tennyson as a young man and "Mariana" (Dante Gabriel Rossetti) 1·50 1·60

1044 Carrickfergus Castle

1992. Designs as Nos. 1410/13, but showing Queen's head in silhouette as T **1044**.
1611 **1044** £1 green and gold . . . 5·50 1·00
1612 – £1.50 purple and gold 5·50 1·00
1613 – £2 blue and gold . . . 7·50 1·00
1995 **1044** £3 violet and gold . . . 26·00 3·50
1614 – £5 brown and gold . . 17·00 3·00
The Queen's head on these stamps is printed in optically variable ink which changes colour from gold to green when viewed from different angles.

1045 British Olympic Association Logo (Olympic Games, Barcelona)

1992. Europa. International Events. Mult.
1615 24p. Type **1045** . . . . . 1·00 75
1616 24p. British Paralympic Association symbol (Paralympics 92, Barcelona) . . . . . . 1·00 75
1617 24p. "Santa Maria" (500th anniv of discovery of America by Columbus) 1·00 75
1618 39p. "Kaisei" (Japanese cadet brigantine) (Grand Regatta Columbus, 1992) 1·25 1·50
1619 39p. British Pavilion, "EXPO '92", Seville . . . 1·40 1·50

1050 Pikeman

1992. 350th Anniv of the Civil War. Multicoloured.
1620 24p. Type **1050** 60 20
1621 28p. Drummer 85 85
1622 33p. Musketeer . . . . . . 1·40 1·40
1623 39p. Standard Bearer . . . 1·50 1·50

1054 "The Yeomen of the Guard"

1992. 150th Birth Anniv of Sir Arthur Sullivan (composer). Gilbert and Sullivan Operas. Multicoloured.
1624 18p. Type **1054** 50 20
1625 24p. "The Gondoliers" . . . 80 20
1626 28p. "The Mikado" . . . . 95 1·00
1627 33p. "The Pirates of Penzance" . . . . 1·50 1·60
1628 39p. "Iolanthe" . . . . . . 1·60 1·60

1059 "Acid Rain Kills"

1992. Protection of the Environment. Children's Paintings. Multicoloured.
1629 24p. Type **1059** 70 25
1630 28p. "Ozone Layer" . . . . 1·10 1·25
1631 33p. "Greenhouse Effect" . . 1·25 1·50
1632 39p. "Bird of Hope" . . . 1·40 1·50

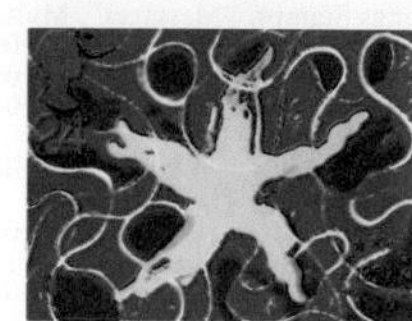

1063 European Star

1992. Single European Market.
1633 **1063** 24p. multicoloured . . 1·00 1·00

1064 "Angel Gabriel", St. James's, Pangbourne

1992. Christmas. Stained Glass Windows. Multicoloured.
1634 18p. Type **1064** 50 15
1635 24p. "Madonna and Child", St. Mary's, Bibury . . . 75 15
1636 28p. "King with Gold", Our Lady and St. Peter, Leatherhead . . . . . . 1·00 1·10
1637 33p. "Shepherds", All Saints, Porthcawl . . . . 1·25 1·40
1638 39p. "Kings with Frankincense and Myrrh", Our Lady and St. Peter, Leatherhead . . 1·25 1·50

1069 Mute Swan Cob and St. Catherine's Chapel, Abbotsbury

1993. 600th Anniv of Abbotsbury Swannery. Multicoloured.
1639 18p. Type **1069** . . . . . 1·25 25
1640 24p. Cygnet and decoy . . . 1·10 25
1641 28p. Swans and cygnet . . . 1·40 2·00
1642 33p. Eggs in nest and tithe barn, Abbotsbury . . . . 1·75 2·50
1643 39p. Young swan and the Fleet . . . . 1·90 2·50

1074 Long John Silver and Parrot ("Treasure Island")

1993. Greetings Stamps. "Gift Giving". Gold, cream and black (No. 1645) or multicoloured (others).
1644 (1st) Type **1074** . . . . . 1·25 1·25
1645 (1st) Tweedledum and Tweedledee ("Alice Through the Looking Glass") . . . . 1·25 1·25
1646 (1st) William ("William" books) . . . . 1·25 1·25
1647 (1st) Mole and Toad ("The Wind in the Willows") . . 1·25 1·25
1648 (1st) Teacher and Wilfrid ("The Bash Street Kids") 1·25 1·25
1649 (1st) Peter Rabbit and Mrs. Rabbit ("The Tale of Peter Rabbit") . . . . . 1·25 1·25
1650 (1st) Snowman ("The Snowman") and Father Christmas ("Father Christmas") . . . . . . 1·25 1·25
1651 (1st) The Big Friendly Giant and Sophie ("The BFG") 1·25 1·25
1652 (1st) Bill Badger and Rupert Bear . . . . 1·25 1·25
1653 (1st) Aladdin and the Genie 1·25 1·25

1084 Decorated Enamel Dial

1993. 300th Birth Anniv of John Harrison (inventor of the marine chronometer). Details of "H4" Clock. Multicoloured.
1654 24p. Type **1084** 60 25
1655 28p. Escapement, remontoire and fusee . . . . . . 1·00 1·25
1656 33p. Balance, spring and temperature compensator 1·40 1·25
1657 39p. Back of movement . . 1·50 1·50

1088 "Britannia"

1993.
1658 **1088** £10 multicoloured . . . 30·00 12·00

1089 "Dendrobium hellwigianum"

1993. 14th World Orchid Conference, Glasgow. Multicoloured.
1659 18p. Type **1089** 45 25
1660 24p. "Paphiopedilum" Maudiae "Magnificum" 75 25

1661 28p. "Cymbidium lowianum" . . . . 1·00 1·25
1662 33p. "Vanda" Rothschildiana . . . . . 1·25 1·50
1663 39p. "Dendrobium vexillarius var albiviride" 1·60 1·40

1094 "Family Group" (bronze sculpture) (Henry Moore)

1993. Europa. Contemporary Art. Multicoloured.
1767 24p. Type **1094** 60 20
1768 28p. "Kew Gardens" (lithograph) (Edward Bawden) . . . . 90 1·00
1769 33p. "St. Francis and the Birds" (Stanley Spencer) 1·25 1·40
1770 39p. "Still Life: Odyssey I" (Ben Nicholson) . . . . 1·40 1·50

1098 Emperor Claudius (from gold coin)

1993. Roman Britain. Multicoloured.
1771 24p. Type **1098** 60 20
1772 28p. Emperor Hadrian (bronze head) . . . . . . 90 1·00
1773 33p. Goddess Roma (from gemstone) . . . . 1·25 1·40
1774 39p. Christ (Hinton St. Mary mosaic) . . . . 1·40 1·50

1102 "Midland Maid" and other Narrow Boats, Grand Junction Canal

1993. Inland Waterways. Multicoloured.
1775 24p. Type **1102** 50 20
1776 28p. "Yorkshire Lass" and other Humber keels, Stainforth and Keadby Canal . . . . 1·00 1·00
1777 35p. "Valley Princess" and other horse-drawn barges, Brecknock and Abergavenny Canal . . . 1·25 1·25
1778 39p. Steam barges, including "Pride of Scotland", and fishing boats, Crinan Canal . . . . 1·50 1·40
Nos. 1775/8 commemorate the bicentenary of the Acts of Parliament authorizing the canals depicted.

1106 Horse Chestnut

1993. The Four Seasons. Autumn. Fruits and Leaves. Multicoloured.
1779 18p. Type **1106** 50 20
1780 24p. Blackberry 75 20
1781 28p. Hazel . . . . 1·10 1·25
1782 33p. Rowan . . . . 1·40 1·50
1783 39p. Pear . . . . 1·50 1·50

1111 "The Reigate Squire"

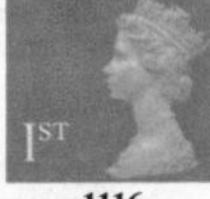

1116

1993. Sherlock Holmes. Centenary of the Publication of "The Final Problem". Multicoloured.
1784 24p. Type **1111** . . . . . 1·10 1·10
1785 24p. "The Hound of the Baskervilles" . . . . . . 1·10 1·10
1786 24p. "The Six Napoleons" 1·10 1·10
1787 24p. "The Greek Interpreter" . . . . . . 1·10 1·10
1788 24p. "The Final Problem" 1·10 1·10

1993. Self-adhesive.
1976 **1116** (2nd) blue . . . . . . 2·00 2·50
1789 (1st) red . . . . 1·25 1·40
Nos. 1976/7 were sold at the current rates.

1117 Bob Cratchit and Tiny Tim

1993. Christmas. 150th Anniv of Publication of "A Christmas Carol" by Charles Dickens. Multicoloured.
1790 19p. Type **1117** 60 15
1791 25p. Mr. and Mrs. Fezziwig 90 15
1792 30p. Scrooge . . . . 1·25 1·50
1793 35p. The prize turkey . . . 1·40 1·60
1794 41p. Mr. Scrooge's nephew 1·50 1·60

1122 Class 5 No. 44957 and Class B1 No. 61342 on West Highland Line

1994. The Age of Steam. Railway Photographs by Colin Gifford.
1795 **1122** 19p. green, grey black 55 25
1796 – 25p. lilac, grey and black 90 95
1797 – 30p. brown, grey & black . . . . 1·40 1·40
1798 – 35p. purple, grey & black . . . . 1·50 1·60
1799 – 41p. blue, grey and black . . . . 1·50 1·50
DESIGNS: 25p. Class A1 No. 60149 "Amadis" at Kings Cross; 30p. Class 4 No. 43000 on turntable at Blyth North; 35p. Class No. 42455 near Wigan Central; 41p. Class "Castle" No. 7002 "Devizes Castle" on bridge crossing Worcester and Birmingham Canal.

1127 Dan Dare and the Mekon

1994. Greetings Stamps. "Messages". Mult.
1800 (1st) Type **1127** . . . . . 1·00 90
1801 (1st) The Three Bears . . . 1·00 90
1802 (1st) Rupert Bear . . . . . 1·00 90
1803 (1st) Alice ("Alice in Wonderland") . . . . . 1·00 90
1804 (1st) Noggin and The Ice Dragon . . . . 1·00 90
1805 (1st) Peter Rabbit posting a letter . . . . 1·00 90
1806 (1st) Red Riding Hood and wolf . . . . 1·00 90
1807 (1st) Orlando the Marmalade Cat . . . . . 1·00 90
1808 (1st) Biggles . . . . 1·00 90
1809 (1st) Paddington Bear on station . . . . 1·00 90

1137 Castell Y Waun (Chirk Castle), Clwyd, Wales

1994. 25th Anniv of Investiture of the Prince of Wales. Paintings by Prince Charles. Multicoloured.
1810 19p. Type **1137** 55 20
1811 25p. Ben Arkle, Sutherland, Scotland . . . . 1·00 20
1812 30p. Mourne Mountains, County Down, Northern Ireland . . . . 1·10 1·40
1813 35p. Dersingham, Norfolk, England . . . . 1·40 1·50
1814 41p. Dolwyddelan, Gwynedd, Wales . . . . 1·50 1·50

1142 Bather at Blackpool

1994. Centenary of Picture Postcards. Mult.
1815 19p. Type **1142** 60 20
1816 25p. "Where's my Little Lad?" 90 20
1817 30p. "Wish You were Here!" . . . . 1·10 1·25
1818 35p. Punch and Judy show 1·40 1·50
1819 41p. "The Tower Crane" machine . . . . 1·50 1·50

1147 British Lion and French Cockerel over Tunnel

1994. Opening of Channel Tunnel. Multicoloured.
1820 25p. Type **1147** 80 70
1821 25p. Symbolic hands over train 80 70
1822 41p. Type **1147** . . . . . . 1·50 1·50
1823 41p. As No. 1821 . . . . . 1·50 1·50

1149 Groundcrew replacing Smoke Canisters on Douglas Boston of 88 Sqn

1994. 50th Anniv of D-Day. Multicoloured.
1824 25p. Type **1149** . . . . . 1·00 1·10
1825 25p. H.M.S. "Warspite" (battleship) shelling enemy positions . . . . 1·00 1·10
1826 25p. Commandos landing on Gold Beach . . . . . 1·00 1·10
1827 25p. Infantry regrouping on Sword Beach . . . . . . 1·00 1·10
1828 25p. Tank and infantry advancing, Ouistreham . . 1·00 1·10

1154 The Old Course, St. Andrews

1994. Scottish Golf Courses. Multicoloured.
1829 19p. Type **1154** 50 20
1830 25p. The 18th Hole, Muirfield 75 20
1831 30p. The 15th Hole ("Luckyslap"), Carnoustie 1·10 1·40
1832 35p. The 8th Hole ("The Postage Stamp"), Royal Troon . . . . 1·25 1·40
1833 41p. The 9th Hole, Turnberry . . . . 1·40 1·40
Nos. 1829/33 commemorate the 250th anniversary of golf's first set of rules produced by the Honourable Company of Edinburgh Golfers.

1159 Royal Welsh Show, Llanelwedd

1994. The Four Seasons. Summertime. Multicoloured.
1834 19p. Type **1159** 50 20
1835 25p. All England Tennis Championships, Wimbledon 75 20
1836 30p. Cowes Week . . . . . 1·10 1·25
1837 35p. Test Match, Lord's . . 1·25 1·60
1838 41p. Braemar Gathering . . 1·40 1·60

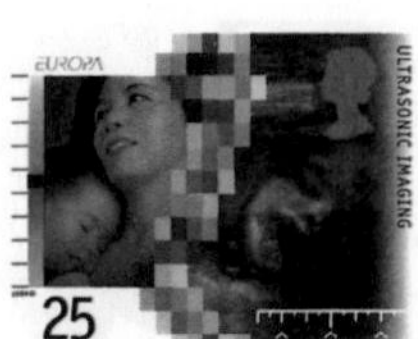

1164 Ultrasonic Imaging

1994. Europa. Medical Discoveries. Multicoloured.
1839 25p. Type **1164** 75 25
1840 30p. Scanning electron microscopy . . . . 1·00 1·25
1841 35p. Magnetic resonance imaging . . . . 1·25 1·50
1842 41p. Computed tomography 1·50 1·50

1168 Mary and Joseph

1994. Christmas. Children's Nativity Plays. Multicoloured.
1843 19p. Type **1168** 50 15
1844 25p. Three Wise Men . . . 75 15
1845 30p. Mary with doll . . . . 1·00 1·50
1846 35p. Shepherds . . . . . . 1·25 1·50
1847 41p. Angels . . . . 1·50 1·75

1173 Sophie (black cat)

1995. Cats. Multicoloured.
1848 19p. Type **1173** 75 20
1849 25p. Puskas (Siamese) and Tigger (tabby) 75 25
1850 30p. Chloe (ginger cat) . . . 1·00 1·50
1851 35p. Kikko (tortoiseshell) and Rosie (Abyssinian) 1·25 1·50
1852 41p. Fred (black and white cat) . . . . 1·50 1·50

1178 Dandelions

1995. The Four Seasons. Springtime. Plant Sculptures by Andy Goldsworthy. Multicoloured.
1853 19p. Type **1178** 80 15
1854 25p. Sweet chestnut leaves 95 15
1855 30p. Garlic leaves . . . . . 1·00 1·50
1856 35p. Hazel leaves . . . . . 1·25 1·50
1857 41p. Spring grass . . . . . 1·50 1·75

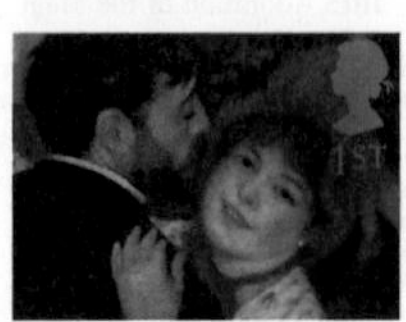

1183 "La Danse a la Campagne" (Renoir)

1995. Greetings Stamps. "Greetings in Art".
1858 **1183** (1st) multicoloured . . 1·00 80
1859 – (1st) multicoloured . . 1·00 80
1860 – (1st) multicoloured . . 1·00 80
1861 – (1st) multicoloured . . 1·00 80
1862 – (1st) multicoloured . . 1·00 80
1863 – (1st) multicoloured . . 1·00 80
1864 – (1st) brown and silver 1·00 80
1865 – (1st) multicoloured . . 1·00 80
1866 – (1st) multicoloured . . 1·00 80
1867 – (1st) black, yellow and silver . . . . 1·00 80
DESIGNS: No. 1859, "Troilus and Criseyde" (Peter Brookes); 1860, "The Kiss" (Rodin); 1861, "Girls on the Town" (Beryl Cook); 1862, "Jazz" (Andrew Mockett); 1863, "Girls performing a Kathak Dance" (Aurangzeb period); 1864, "Alice Keppel with her Daughter" (Alice Hughes); 1865, "Children Playing" (L. S. Lowry); 1866, "Circus Clowns" (Emily Firmin and Justin Mitchell); 1867, Decoration from "All the Love Poems of Shakespeare" (Eric Gill).

1193 Fireplace Decoration, Attingham Park, Shropshire

1198 British Troops and French Civilians celebrating

1995. Centenary of The National Trust. Multicoloured.

1868	19p. Type **1193**	60	20
1869	25p. Oak seedling	80	20
1870	30p. Carved table leg, Attingham Park	1·00	1·50
1871	35p. St. David's Head, Dyfed, Wales	1·25	1·50
1872	41p. Elizabethan window, Little Moreton Hall, Cheshire	1·40	1·75

1995. Europa. Peace and Freedom.

1873 **1198**	19p. silver, brown and black	70	40
1874 –	19p. multicoloured	70	40
1875 –	25p. silver, blue and black	1·00	1·00
1876 –	25p. multicoloured	1·00	1·00
1877 –	30p. multicoloured	1·25	2·25

DESIGNS: No. 1874, Symbolic hands and Red Cross; 1875, St. Paul's Cathedral and searchlights; 1876, Symbolic hand releasing peace dove; 1877, Symbolic hands.

Nos. 1873 and 1875 commemorate the 50th anniversary of the end of the Second World War, No. 1874 the 125th anniversary of the British Red Cross Society and Nos. 1876/7 the 50th anniversary of the United Nations.

Nos. 1876/7 include the "EUROPA" emblem.

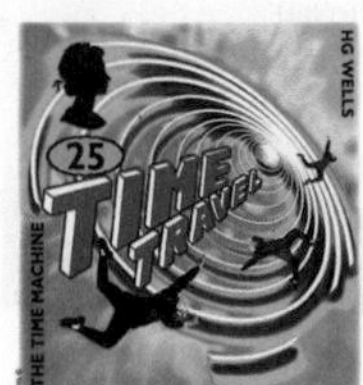

1203 "The Time Machine"

1995. Science Fiction. Novels by H. G. Wells. Multicoloured.

1878	25p. Type **1203**	75	25
1879	30p. "The First Men in the Moon"	1·25	1·50
1880	35p. "The War of the Worlds"	1·25	1·60
1881	41p. "The Shape of Things to Come"	1·50	1·60

Nos. 1878/81 commemorate the centenary of publication of Wells's "The Time Machine".

1207 The Swan, 1595

1995. Reconstruction of Shakespeare's Globe Theatre. Multicoloured.

1882	25p. Type **1207**	90	90
1883	25p. The Rose, 1592	90	90
1884	25p. The Globe, 1599	90	90
1885	25p. The Hope, 1613	90	90
1886	25p. The Globe, 1614	90	90

Nos. 1882/6 were printed together, se-tenant, forming a composite design.

1212 Sir Rowland Hill and Uniform Penny Postage Petition

1995. Pioneers of Communications.

1887 **1212**	19p. silver, red and black	75	30
1888 –	25p. silver, brown and black	1·00	50
1889 –	41p. silver, green and black	1·50	1·75
1890 –	60p. silver, blue and black	1·75	2·25

DESIGNS: 25p. Hill and Penny Black; 41p. Guglielmo Marconi and early wireless; 60p. Marconi and sinking of "Titanic" (liner).

Nos. 1887/8 mark the birth bicentenary of Sir Rowland Hill and Nos. 1889/90 the centenary of the first radio transmissions.

1216 Harold Wagstaff

1995. Centenary of Rugby League. Multicoloured.

1891	19p. Type **1216**	75	25
1892	25p. Gus Risman	75	30
1893	30p. Jim Sullivan	1·00	1·50
1894	35p. Billy Batten	1·00	1·60
1895	41p. Brian Bevan	1·50	1·75

1221 European Robin in Mouth of Pillar Box

1995. Christmas. Christmas Robins. Multicoloured.

1896	19p. Type **1221**	60	20
1897	25p. European robin on railings and holly	85	30
1898	30p. European robin on snow-covered milk bottles	1·25	1·40
1899	41p. European robin on road sign	1·60	1·60
1900	60p. European robin on door knob and Christmas wreath	1·75	1·90

19
WEE,
fleeket,
cowran,
tim'rous
beaſtie,
ROBERT BURNS 1759-1796

1226 Opening Lines of "To a Mouse" and Fieldmouse

1996. Death Bicent of Robert Burns (Scottish poet).

1901 **1226**	19p. cream, brown and black	75	25
1902 –	25p. multicoloured	1·00	30
1903 –	41p. multicoloured	1·50	2·00
1904 –	60p. multicoloured	1·75	2·50

DESIGNS: 25p. "O my Luve's like a red, red rose" and wild rose; 41p. "Scots, wha hae wi Wallace bled" and Sir William Wallace; 60p. "Auld Lang Syne" and highland dancers.

1230 "MORE! LOVE" (Mel Calman)

1996. Greetings Stamps. Cartoons.

1905 **1230**	(1st) black and mauve	80	75
1906 –	(1st) black and green	80	75
1907 –	(1st) black and blue	80	75
1908 –	(1st) black and violet	80	75
1909 –	(1st) black and red	80	75
1910 –	(1st) black and blue	80	75
1911 –	(1st) black and red	80	75
1912 –	(1st) black and violet	80	75
1913 –	(1st) black and green	80	75
1914 –	(1st) black and mauve	80	75

DESIGNS: No. 1906, "Sincerely" (Charles Barsotti); 1907, "Do you have something for the HUMAN CONDITION?" (Mel Calman); 1908, "MENTAL FLOSS" (Leo Cullum); 1909, "4.55 P.M." (Charles Barsotti); 1910, "Dear lottery prize winner" (Larry); 1911, "I'm writing to you because ..." (Mel Calman); 1912, "FETCH THIS, FETCH THAT" (Charles Barsotti); 1913, "My day starts before I'm ready for it" (Mel Calman); 1914, "THE CHEQUE IN THE POST" (Jack Ziegler).

Nos. 1905/14 were sold at the current rate.

1240 "Muscovy Duck"

1996. 50th Anniv of the Wildfowl and Wetlands Trust. Bird paintings by C. F. Tunnicliffe. Multicoloured.

1915	19p. Type **1240**	70	25
1916	25p. "Lapwing"	90	30
1917	30p. "White-fronted Goose"	1·00	1·25
1918	35p. "Bittern"	1·10	1·25
1919	41p. "Whooper Swan"	1·50	1·60

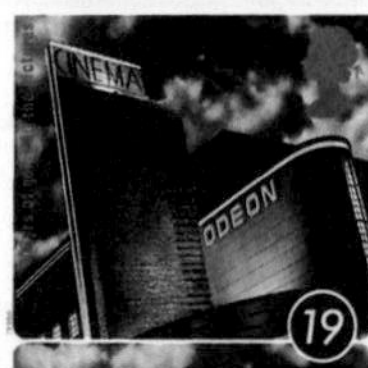

1245 The Odeon, Harrogate

1996. Centenary of Cinema.

1920 **1245**	19p. multicoloured	50	25
1921 –	25p. multicoloured	70	30
1922 –	30p. multicoloured	1·00	1·75
1923 –	35p. black, red and silver	1·25	2·00
1924 –	41p. multicoloured	1·50	2·25

DESIGNS: 25p. Laurence Olivier and Vivien Leigh in "Lady Hamilton" (film); 30p. Old cinema ticket; 35p. Pathe News still; 41p. Cinema sign, The Odeon, Manchester.

1250 Dixie Dean

1996. European Football Championship. Multicoloured.

1925	19p. Type **1250**	50	20
1926	25p. Bobby Moore	75	20
1927	35p. Duncan Edwards	1·25	1·75
1928	41p. Billy Wright	1·50	1·75
1929	60p. Danny Blanchflower	1·75	2·00

1255 Athlete on Starting Blocks

1996. Olympic and Paralympic Games, Atlanta. Multicoloured.

1930	26p. Type **1255**	1·10	1·00
1931	26p. Throwing the javelin	1·10	1·00
1932	26p. Basketball	1·10	1·00
1933	26p. Swimming	1·10	1·00
1934	26p. Athlete celebrating and Olympic Rings	1·10	1·00

1260 Prof. Dorothy Hodgkin (scientist)

1996. Europa. Famous Women.

1935 **1260**	20p. green, grey and black	60	25
1936 –	26p. mauve, grey & black	75	75
1937 –	31p. bronze, grey and black	1·10	1·10
1938 –	37p. silver, grey and black	1·25	1·40
1939 –	43p. gold, grey and black	1·50	1·50

DESIGNS: 26p. Dame Margot Fonteyn (ballerina); 31p. Dame Elisabeth Frink (sculptress); 37p. Dame Daphne du Maurier (novelist); 43p. Dame Marea Hartman (sports administrator).

Nos. 1936/7 include the "EUROPA" emblem.

1265 "Muffin the Mule"

1996. 50th Anniv of Children's Television. Multicoloured.

1940	20p. Type **1265**	55	20
1941	26p. "Sooty"	80	20
1942	31p. "Stingray"	1·00	1·50
1943	37p. "The Clangers"	1·40	1·75
1944	43p. "Dangermouse"	1·60	2·00

1270 Triumph TR3

1996. Classic Sports Cars. Multicoloured.

1945	20p. Type **1270**	55	20
1946	26p. MG TD	1·10	20
1947	37p. Austin-Healey 100	1·40	1·75
1948	43p. Jaguar XK120	1·60	1·75
1949	63p. Morgan Plus 4	1·75	1·75

1275 The Three Kings

1996. Christmas. Multicoloured.

1950	(2nd.) Type **1275**	75	20
1951	(1st) The Annunciation	1·00	35
1952	31p. The Journey to Bethlehem	1·25	1·75
1953	43p. The Nativity	1·25	1·75
1954	63p. The Shepherds	1·50	2·00

1280 "Gentiana acaulis" (Georg Ehret)

1997. Greeting Stamps. 19th-century Flower Paintings. Multicoloured.

1955	(1st) Type **1280**	85	90
1956	(1st) "Magnolia grandiflora" (Ehret)	85	90
1957	(1st) "Camellia japonica" (Alfred Chandler)	85	90
1958	(1st) "Tulipa" (Ehret)	85	90
1959	(1st) "Fuchsia" "Princess of Wales" (Augusta Withers)	85	90
1960	(1st) "Tulipa gesneriana" (Ehret)	85	90
1961	(1st) "Guzmania splendens" (Charlotte Sowerby)	85	90
1962	(1st) "Iris latifolia" (Ehret)	85	90
1963	(1st) "Hippeastrum rutilum" (Pierre-Joseph Redoute)	85	90
1964	(1st) "Passiflora coerulea" (Ehret)	85	90

1290 "King Henry VIII"

1997. 450th Death Anniv of King Henry VIII. Multicoloured.

1965	26p. Type **1290**	1·00	90
1966	26p. "Catherine of Aragon"	1·25	1·00
1967	26p. "Anne Boleyn"	1·25	1·00
1968	26p. "Jane Seymour"	1·25	1·00
1969	26p. "Anne of Cleves"	1·25	1·00
1970	26p. "Catherine Howard"	1·25	1·00
1971	26p. "Catherine Parr"	1·25	1·00

1297 St. Columba in Boat

1303 "Dracula"

1997. Religious Anniversaries. Multicoloured.

1972	26p. Type **1297**	75	35
1973	37p. St. Columba on Iona	1·10	1·50
1974	43p. St. Augustine with King Ethelbert	1·50	1·50
1975	63p. St. Augustine with Model of Cathedral	2·00	2·10

Nos. 1972/3 commemorate the 1400th death anniversary of St. Columba and Nos. 1974/5 the 1400th anniversary of the arrival of St. Augustine of Canterbury in Kent.

1997. Europa. Tales and Legends. Horror Stories. Multicoloured.

1980 26p. Type **1303** . . . . . 1·00 40
1981 31p. "Frankenstein" . . . . 1·10 1·40
1982 37p. "Dr. Jekyll and Mr. Hyde" . . . . 1·30 1·60
1983 43p. "The Hound of the Baskervilles" . . . . . . 1·75 1·75

Nos. 1980/3 commemorate the birth bicentenary of Mary Shelley (creator of Frankenstein) with the 26p. and 31p. values incorporating the "EUROPA" emblem.

1307 Reginald Mitchell and Supermarine Spitfire Mk IIA

1997. British Aircraft Designers. Multicoloured.

1984 20p. Type **1307** 75 40
1985 26p. Roy Chadwick and Avro Lancaster Mk I . . 1·10 1·25
1986 37p. Ronald Bishop and De Havilland Mosquito B Mk XVI . . . . 1·40 1·25
1987 43p. George Carter and Gloster Meteor T Mk 7 1·50 1·60
1988 63p. Sir Sidney Camm and Hawker Hunter FGA Mk 9 . . . . 2·00 2·00

1312 Carriage Horse and Coachman

1997. "All the Queen's Horses". 50th Anniv of the British Horse Society. Multicoloured.

1989 20p. Type **1312** 80 45
1990 26p. Lifeguards horse and trooper . . . . 1·10 1·50
1991 43p. Blues and Royals drum horse and drummer . . . 1·50 1·50
1992 63p. Duke of Edinburgh's horse and groom . . . . 2·00 2·00

1316 Haroldswick, Shetland

1997. Sub-Post Offices. Multicoloured.

1997 20p. Type **1316** 75 50
1998 26p. Painswick, Gloucestershire . . . . . 1·00 1·00
1999 43p. Beddgelert, Gwynedd 1·50 1·50
2000 63p. Ballyroney, County Down . . . . 2·25 2·25

Nos. 1997/2000 were issued on the occasion of the Centenary of The National Federation of Sub-Postmasters.

1320 "Noddy"

1997. Birth Centenary of Enid Blyton (children's author). Multicoloured.

2001 20p. Type **1320** 50 45
2002 26p. "Famous Five" . . . . 1·00 1·25
2003 37p. "Secret Seven" . . . . 1·25 1·25
2004 43p. "Faraway Tree" . . . 1·50 2·00
2005 63p. "Malory Towers" . . . 1·50 2·00

1325 Children and Father Christmas pulling Cracker

1997. Christmas. 150th Anniv of the Christmas Cracker. Multicoloured.

2006 (2nd.) Type **1325** 75 20
2007 (1st) Father Christmas with traditional cracker 90 30
2008 31p. Father Christmas riding cracker . . . . 1·00 1·50
2009 43p. Father Christmas on snowball . . . . 1·25 1·75
2010 63p. Father Christmas and chimney . . . . 1·60 2·00

1330 Wedding Photograph, 1947

1997. Royal Golden Wedding.

2011 **1330** 20p. gold, brown and black 85 45
2012 – 26p. multicoloured . . 1·10 70
2013 **1330** 43p. gold, green and black . . . . 1·90 2·25
2014 – 63p. multicoloured . . 2·50 3·00

DESIGNS: 26p. and 63p. Queen Elizabeth II and Prince Philip, 1997.

1332 Common Dormouse

1338 Diana, Princess of Wales (photo by Lord Snowdon)

1998. Endangered Species. Multicoloured.

2015 20p. Type **1332** 60 40
2016 26p. Lady's slipper orchid 70 40
2017 31p. Song thrush . . . . . 1·00 2·00
2018 37p. Shining ram's-horn snail . . . . 1·25 1·25
2019 43p. Mole cricket . . . . . 1·40 1·75
2020 63p. Devil's bolete . . . . 1·90 2·25

1998. Diana, Princess of Wales Commemoration. Multicoloured.

2021 26p. Type **1338** 90 90
2022 26p. At British Lung Foundation Function, April 1997 (photo by John Stillwell) 90 90
2023 26p. Wearing tiara, 1991 (photo by Lord Snowdon) 90 90
2024 26p. On visit to Birmingham, October 1995 (photo by Tim Graham) (checked suit) 90 90
2025 26p. In evening dress, 1987 (photo by Terence Donovan) 90 90

1343 Lion of England and Griffin of Edward III

1348

1998. 650th Anniv of the Order of the Garter. The Queen's Beasts. Multicoloured.

2026 26p. Type **1343** 90 90
2027 26p. Falcon of Plantagenet and Bull of Clarence . . . 90 90
2028 26p. Lion of Mortimer and Yale of Beaufort 90 90
2029 26p. Greyhound of Richmond and Dragon of Wales 90 90
2030 26p. Unicorn of Scotland and Horse of Hanover . . 90 90

1998. As Type **157** (Wilding definitive of 1952–54) but with face values in decimal currency as Type **1348**.

2031 **1348** 20p. green 70 75
2032 26p. brown 90 95
2033 37p. purple . . . . . . 2·75 2·75

See also Nos. 2295/8.

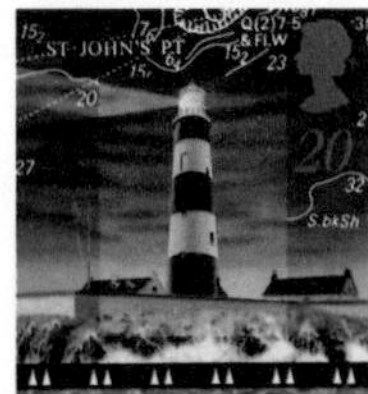

1349 St. John's Point Lighthouse, County Down

1998. 300th Anniv of the 1st Lighthouse and Final Year of Manned Lighthouses. Multicoloured.

2034 20p. Type **1349** 50 40
2035 26p. Smalls Lighthouse, Pembrokeshire 75 50
2036 37p. Needles Rock Lighthouse, Isle of Wight, c. 1900 . . . . . 1·10 1·50
2037 43p. Bell Rock Lighthouse, Arbroath, mid-19th century . . . . 1·50 1·75
2038 63p. Eddystone Lighthouse, Plymouth, 1698 . . . . . 2·10 2·50

1354 Tommy Cooper

1998. Comedians. Multicoloured.

2041 20p. Type **1354** 50 50
2042 26p. Eric Morecambe . . . 75 90
2043 37p. Joyce Grenfell . . . . 1·25 1·25
2044 43p. Les Dawson . . . . . 1·50 1·50
2045 63p. Peter Cook . . . . . 1·75 2·10

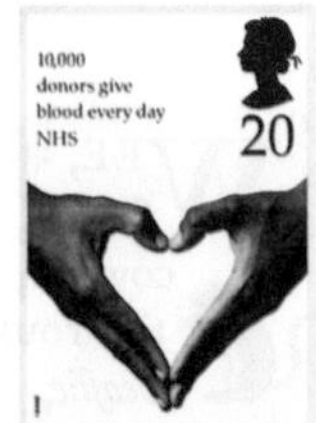

1359 Hands forming Heart

1998. 50th Anniv of the National Health Service. Multicoloured.

2046 20p. Type **1359** 50 50
2047 26p. Adult and child holding hands 90 90
2048 43p. Hands forming cradle 1·50 1·50
2049 63p. Hand taking pulse . . 2·10 2·10

1363 "The Hobbit" (J. R. R. Tolkien)

1998. Famous Children's Fantasy Novels. Multicoloured.

2050 20p. Type **1363** 50 45
2051 26p. "The Lion, The Witch and the Wardrobe" (C. S. Lewis) 75 55
2052 37p. "The Phoenix and the Carpet" (E. Nesbit) . . . 1·25 1·50
2053 43p. "The Borrowers" (Mary Norton) . . . . . 1·50 1·50
2054 63p. "Through the Looking Glass" (Lewis Carroll) . . 2·10 2·00

Nos. 2050/4 commemorate the birth centenary of C. S. Lewis and the death centenary of Lewis Carroll.

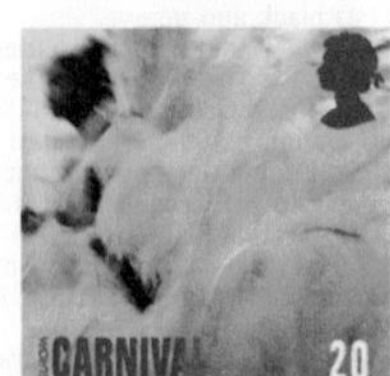

1368 Woman in Yellow Feathered Costume

1998. Europa. Festivals. Notting Hill Carnival. Multicoloured.

2055 20p. Type **1368** 75 45
2056 26p. Woman in blue costume and headdress . . 95 55
2057 43p. Group of children in white and gold robes . . 1·50 2·00
2058 63p. Child in "Tree" costume . . . . 2·00 2·75

The 20p. and 26p. incorporate the "EUROPA" emblem.

1372 Sir Malcolm Campbell's "Bluebird", 1925

1998. British Land Speed Record Holders. Multicoloured.

2059 20p. Type **1372** 50 25
2060 26p. Sir Henry Segrave's "Sunbeam", 1926 . . . . 75 30
2061 30p. John G. Parry Thomas's "Babs", 1926 1·25 1·50
2062 43p. John R. Cobb's "Railton Mobil Special", 1947 . . . . 1·50 1·60
2063 63p. Donald Campbell's "Bluebird CN7", 1964 . . 2·25 2·40

Nos. 2059/63 commemorate the 50th death anniversary of Sir Malcolm Campbell.

1377 Angel with Hands raised in Blessing

1998. Christmas. Angels. Multicoloured.

2064 20p. Type **1377** 50 50
2065 26p. Angel praying 75 60
2066 30p. Angel plaing flute . . . 1·25 1·50
2067 43p. Angel playing lute . . 1·50 1·60
2068 63p. Angel praying (different) . . . . 2·00 2·25

1382 Greenwich Meridian and Clock (John Harrison's chronometer)

1999. Millennium Series. The Inventors' Tale. Multicoloured.

2069 20p. Type **1382** 70 70
2070 26p. Industrial worker and blast furnace (James Watt's discovery of steam power) . . . . 95 1·00
2071 43p. Early photos of leaves (Henry Fox-Talbot's photographic experiments) 1·50 1·60
2072 63p. Computer inside human head (Alan Turing's work on computers) . . . . 2·25 2·40

1386 Airliner hugging Globe (International air travel)

1999. Millennium Series. The Travellers' Tale.

2073 **1386** 20p. multicoloured . . 75 70
2074 – 26p. multicoloured . . 95 1·00
2075 – 43p. black, stone and bronze . . . . 1·50 1·60
2076 – 63p. multicoloured . . 2·25 2·40

DESIGNS: 26p. Women on bicycle (development of the bicycle); 43p. Victorian railway station (growth of public transport); 63p. Captain Cook and Maori (Captain James Cook's voyages).

1390

1999. (a) Self-adhesive.

2077 **1390** (1st) grey (face value) (Queen's head in colourless relief) . . . 3·00 2·25

(b) Ordinary gum.

2078 **1390** (1st) black . . . . . . 3·00 2·25

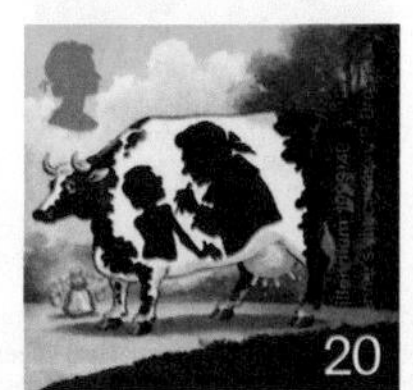

1391 Vaccinating Child (pattern in cow markings) (Jenner's development of smallpox vaccine)

1999. Millennium Series. The Patients' Tale. Multicoloured.

2080 20p. Type **1391** 75 70

2081 26p. Patient on trolley (nursing care) . . . . . . 95 1·00

2082 43p. Penicillin mould (Fleming's discovery of penicillin) . . . . 1·50 1·60

2083 63p. Sculpture of test-tube baby (development of in-vitro fertilization) . . . . 2·25 2·40

1395 Dove and Norman Settler (medieval migration to Scotland)

1999. Millennium Series. The Settlers' Tale. Multicoloured.

2084 20p. Type **1395** 75 70

2085 26p. Pilgrim Fathers and Red Indian (17th-century migration to America) . . 95 1·00

2086 43p. Sailing ship and aspects of settlement (19th-century migration to Australia) . . 2·00 1·75

2087 63p. Hummingbird and superimposed stylized face (20th-century migration to Great Britain) . . . . . 3·00 3·00

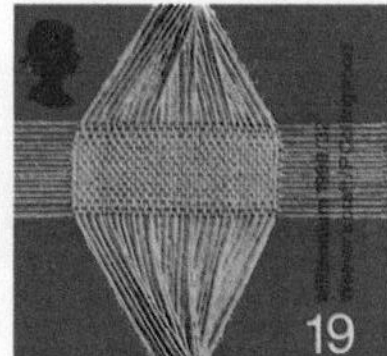

1399 Woven Threads (woollen industry)

1999. Millennium Series. The Workers' Tale. Multicoloured.

2088 19p. Type **1399** 75 70

2089 26p. Salts Mill, Saltaire (cotton industry) . . . . 95 1·00

2090 44p. Hull on slipway (shipbuilding) . . . . . . 1·75 1·60

2091 64p. Lloyd's Building (City of London finance centre) 2·25 2·40

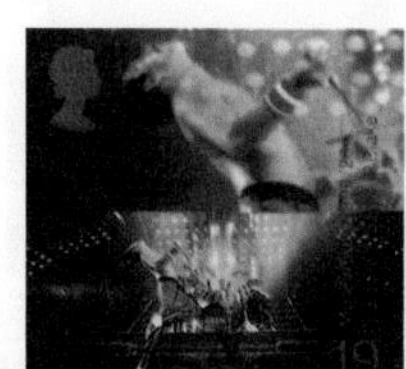

1403 Freddie Mercury (lead singer of pop group Queen) ("Popular Music")

1999. Millennium Series. The Entertainers' Tale. Multicoloured.

2092 19p. Type **1403** 75 70

2093 26p. Bobby Moore with World Cup, 1966 ("Sport") . . . . 95 1·00

2094 44p. Dalek from "Dr. Who" (science-fiction series) ("Television") . . . . 1·50 1·60

2095 64p. Charlie Chaplin (film star) ("Cinema") . . . . 2·25 2·40

1407 Prince Edward and Miss Sophie Rhys-Jones (from photo by John Swannell)

1999. Royal Wedding. Multicoloured.

2096 26p. Type **1407** 85 85

2097 64p. Couple in profile . . . 1·90 1·90

1409 Suffragette behind Prison Window (Equal Rights for Women)

1999. Millennium Series. The Citizens' Tale. Multicoloured.

2098 19p. Type **1409** 75 70

2099 26p. Water tap (Right to Health) . . . . 95 1·00

2100 44p. Generations of school children (Right to Education) . . . . 1·75 1·60

2101 64p. "MAGNA CARTA" (Human Rights) . . . . 2·50 2·40

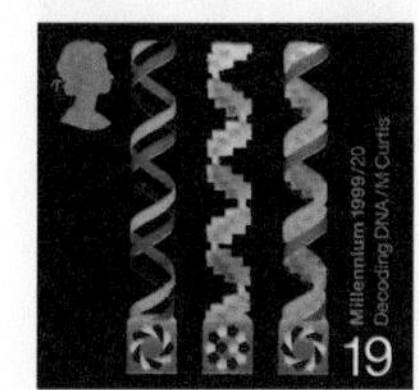

1413 Molecular Structures (DNA Decoding)

1999. Millennium Series. The Scientists' Tale. Multicoloured.

2102 19p. Type **1413** 75 70

2103 26p. Large ground finch and fossilized skeleton (Darwin's Theory of Evolution) . . . . 1·50 1·00

2104 44p. Rotation of polarized light by magnetism (Faraday's work on electricity) . . . . 1·50 1·60

2105 64p. Saturn (development of astronomical telescopes) 2·25 2·50

1999. Solar Eclipse. Sheet 89 × 101 mm.

MS2106 No. 2105 × 4 (sold at £2.56) 21·00 21·00

1417 Upland Landscape (Strip Farming)

1999. Millennium Series. The Farmers' Tale. Multicoloured.

2107 19p. Type **1417** 75 70

2108 26p. Horse-drawn plough (Mechanical Farming) . . 95 1·00

2109 44p. Man peeling potato (food imports) . . . . . 1·50 1·60

2110 64p. Aerial view of combine harvester (Satellite Agriculture) . . . . . . 2·25 2·40

1421 Robert the Bruce (Battle of Bannockburn, 1314)

1999. The Millennium Series. The Soldiers' Tale.

2111 **1421** 19p. black, stone and silver 75 70

2112 – 26p. multicoloured . . 95 1·00

2113 – 44p. grey, black and silver . . . . 2·00 1·60

2114 – 64p. multicoloured . . 2·50 2·40

DESIGNS: 26p. Cavalier and horse (English Civil War); 44p. War Graves Cemetery, The Somme (World Wars); 64p. Soldiers with boy (Peace-keeping).

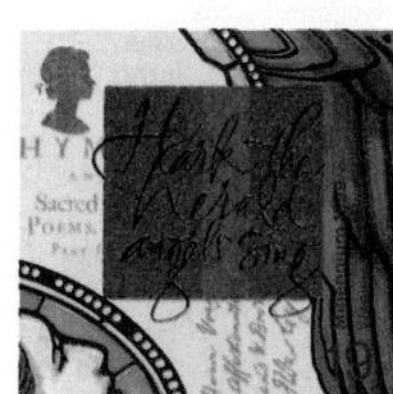

1425 "Hark the herald angels sing" and Hymnbook (John Wesley)

1999. Millennium Series. The Christians' Tale. Multicoloured.

2115 19p. Type **1425** 75 70

2116 26p. King James I and Bible (Authorised version of Bible) . . . . 95 1·00

2117 44p. St. Andrews Cathedral, Fife ("Pilgrimage") . . . 1·50 1·60

2118 64p. Nativity ("First Christmas") . . . . . . 2·25 2·40

1429 "World of the Stage" (Allen Jones)

1999. The Millennium Series. The Artists' Tale. Multicoloured.

2119 19p. Type **1429** 70 75

2120 26p. "World of Music" (Bridget Riley) . . . . . 90 1·00

2121 44p. "World of Literature" (Lisa Milroy) . . . . . . 1·50 1·60

2122 64p. "New Worlds" (Sir Howard Hodgkin) . . . . 2·25 2·50

1433 Clock Face and Map of North America

1434 Clock Face and Map of Asia

1435 Clock Face and Map of Middle East

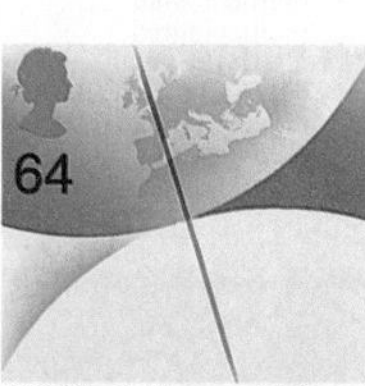

1436 Clock Face and Map of Europe

1999. Millennium Series. "Millennium Timekeeper". Sheet 120 × 89 mm. Multicoloured.

MS2123 64p. Type **1433**; 64p. Type **1434**; 64p. Type **1435**; 64p. Type **1436** . . . . 24·00 20·00

No. **MS**2123 also exists overprinted **EARLS COURT, LONDON 22–28 MAY 2000 THE STAMP SHOW 2000** from Exhibition Premium Passes, costing £10, available from 1 March 2000.

1437 Queen Elizabeth II

1438 Barn Owl (World Owl Trust, Muncaster)

2000. New Millennium.

2124 **1437** (1st) brown . . . . . . 1·00 1·00

2000. Millennium Projects (1st series). "Above and Bend".

2125 19p. Type **1438** . . . . . 1·25 70

2126 26p. Night sky (National Space Science Centre, Leicester) . . . . 95 1·00

2126a (1st) As No. 2126 . . . . 5·25 3·50

2127 44p. River Goyt and textile mills (Torrs Walkway, New Mills) . . . . . . 1·50 1·75

2128 64p. Cape gannets (Seabird Centre, North Berwick) 2·50 2·50

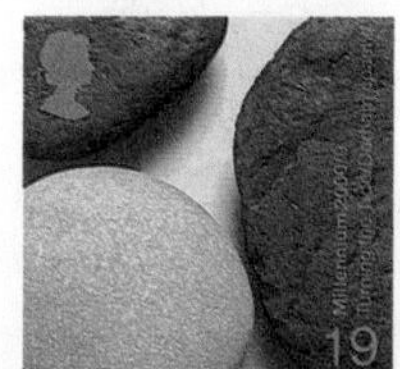

1442 Millennium Beacon (Beacons across The Land)

2000. Millennium Projects (2nd series). "Fire and Light". Multicoloured.

2129 19p. Type **1442** 70 75

2130 26p. Garratt steam locomotive No. 143 pulling train (Rheilffordd Eryri, Welsh Highland Railway) . . . . 1·25 1·00

2131 44p. Lightning (Dynamic Earth Centre, Edinburgh) 1·50 1·50

2132 64p. Multicoloured lights (Lighting Croydon's Skyline) . . . . 2·25 2·50

2000. As T **929** but with "1st" face value.

2133 (1st) black and cream . . . 1·50 1·25

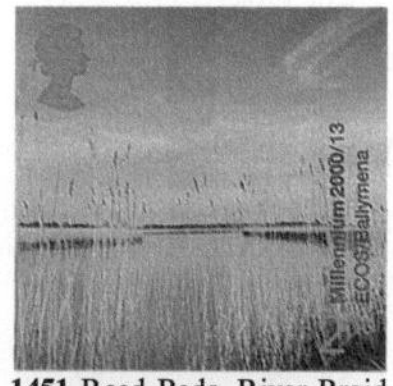

1447 Beach Pebbles (Turning the Tide, Durham Coast)

2000. Millennium Projects (3rd series). "Water and Coast".

2134 19p. Type **1447** 70 75

2135 26p. Frog's legs and water lilies (National Pondlife Centre, Merseyside) . . . 1·25 1·00

2136 44p. Cliff Boardwalk (Parc Arfordirol, Llanelli Coast) 1·50 1·50

2137 64p. Reflections in water (Portsmouth Harbour Development) . . . . . . 2·25 2·50

1451 Reed Beds, River Braid (ECOS, Ballymena)

2000. Millennium Projects (4th series). "Life and Earth".

2138 (2nd.) Type **1451** 70 75

2139 (1st) South American leaf-cutter ants ("Web of Life" Exhibition, London Zoo) 1·25 1·00

2140 44p. Solar sensors (Earth Centre, Doncaster) . . . 1·50 1·50

2141 64p. Hydroponic leaves (Project SUZY, Teesside) 2·25 1·50

1455 Pottery Glaze (Ceramica Museum, Stoke-on-Trent)

2000. Millennium Projects (5th series). "Art and Craft".
2142 (2nd.) Type **1455** 70 75
2143 (1st) Bankside Galleries (Tate Modern, London) 1·25 1·00
2144 45p. Road marking (Cycle Network Artworks) . . . 1·50 1·50
2145 65p. People of Salford (Lowry Centre, Salford) 2·25 2·50

2000. "Stamp Show 2000" International Stamp Exhibition, London. Jeffrey Matthews Colour Palette. Sheet 124 × 70 mm, containing stamps as T **367**.
MS2146 4p. blue; 5p. brown; 6p. green; 10p. orange; 31p. mauve; 39p. mauve; 64p. green; £1 violet 18·00 18·00

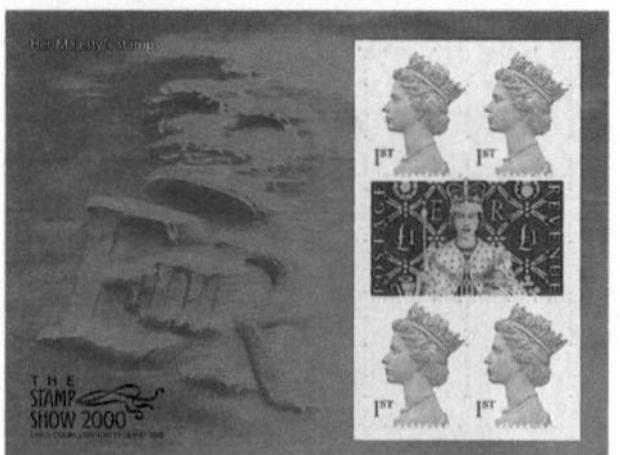

1459 (½-size illustration)

2000. "Stamp Show 2000" International Stamp Exhibition, London. "Her Majesty's Stamps". Sheet 121 × 89 mm.
MS2147 **1459** (1st) brown (Type **1437**) × 4; £1 green (as Type **163**) . . . . 21·00 21·00
The £1 value is an adaptation of the 1953 Coronation 1s.3d. stamp originally designed by Edmund Dulac.

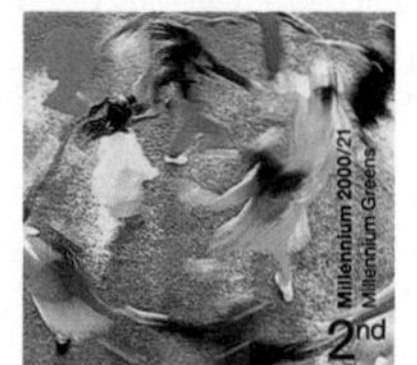

1460 Children playing (Millennium Greens Project)

2000. Millennium Projects (6th series). "People and Places". Multicoloured.
2148 (2nd.) Type **1460** 75 70
2149 (1st) Millennium Bridge, Gateshead . . . . 1·25 1·00
2150 45p. Daisies (Mile End Park, London) . . . . . 1·50 1·50
2151 65p. African Hut and Thatched Cottage ("On the Meridian Line" Project) . . . . 2·25 2·50

1464 Raising the Stone (Strangford Stone, Killyleagh)

2000. Millennium Projects (7th series). "Stone and Soil".
2152 **1464** (2nd.) blk, grey & silver 75 70
2153 – (1st) multicoloured . . 1·25 1·00
2154 – 45p. multicoloured . . 1·50 1·75
2155 – 65p. multicoloured . . 2·50 2·50
DESIGNS: No. 2153, Horse's Hooves (Trans Pennine Trail, Derbyshire); 2154 Cyclist (Kingdom of Fife Cycle Ways, Scotland); 2155, Bluebell Wood (Groundwork's "Changing Places" Project).

1468 Tree Roots ("Yews for the Millennium" Project)

2000. Millennium Projects (8th series). "Tree and Leaf". Multicoloured.
2156 (2nd.) Type **1468** 75 70
2157 (1st) Sunflower ("Eden" Project, St. Austell) . . . 1·25 1·00
2158 45p. Sycamore seeds (Millennium Seed Bank, Wakehurst Place, Surrey) 1·50 1·60
2159 65p. Forest, Doire Dach ("Forest for Scotland") 2·50 2·50

1472 Queen Elizabeth the Queen Mother

1472a Royal Family on Queen Mother's 99th Birthday (½-size illustration)

2000. Queen Elizabeth the Queen Mother's 100th Birthday. Multicoloured.
2160 27p. Type **1472** . . . . . . 2·50 2·75
MS2161 121 × 89 mm. **1427a** multicoloured . . . . 11·00 11·00

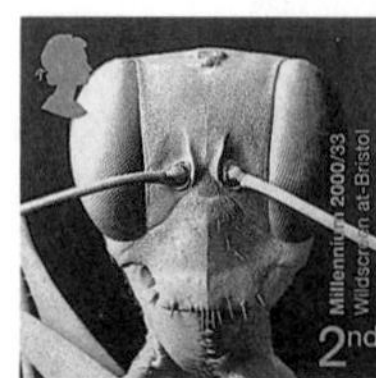

1473 Head of *Gigantiops destructor* (Ant) (Wildscreen at Bristol)

2000. Millennium Projects (9th series). "Mind and Matter". Multicoloured.
2162 (2nd.) Type **1473** 75 70
2163 (1st) Gathering water lilies on Broads (Norfolk and Norwich Project) . . . . 1·25 1·00
2164 45p. X-ray of hand holding computer mouse (Millennium Point, Birmingham) . . . . . . 1·50 1·75
2165 65p. Tartan wool holder (Scottish Cultural Resources Access Network) . . . . 2·25 2·50

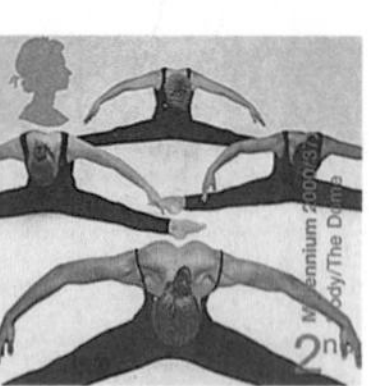

1477 Acrobatic Performers (Millennium Dome)

2000. Millennium Projects (10th series). "Body and Bone".
2166 **1477** (2nd.) black, blue & silver 75 70
2167 – (1st) multicoloured . . 1·25 1·00
2168 – 45p. multicoloured . . 1·50 1·50
2169 – 65p. multicoloured . . 2·25 2·50
DESIGNS: No. 2167, Football players (Hampden Park, Glasgow); 2168, Bather (Bath Spa Project); 2169, Hen's egg under magnification (Centre for Life, Newcastle).

1481 Virgin and Child Stained Glass Window, St. Edmundsbury Cathedral (Suffolk Cathedral Millennium Project)

2000. Millennium Projects (11th series). "Spirit and Faith". Multicoloured.
2170 (2nd.) Type **1481** 75 70
2171 (1st) Floodlit church of St. Peter and St. Paul, Overstowey (Church Floodlighting Trust) . . . 1·25 1·00
2172 45p. 12th-cent Latin Gradual (St. Patrick Centre, Downpatrick) . . 1·50 1·50
2173 65p. Chapter House ceiling, York Minster (York Millennium Mystery Plays) . . . . 2·25 2·50

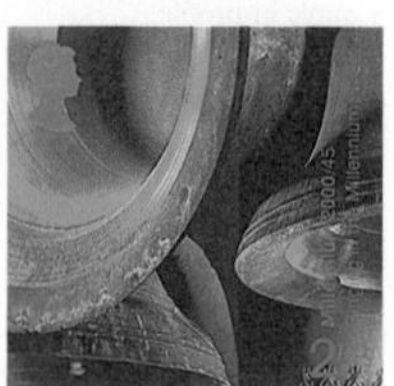

1485 Church Bells (Ringing in the Millennium)

2000. Millennium Projects (12th series). "Sound and Vision". Multicoloured.
2174 (2nd.) Type **1485** 75 70
2175 (1st) Eye (Year of the Artist) . . . . 1·25 1·00
2176 45p. Top of harp (Canolfan Mileniwm, Cardiff) . . . 1·50 1·50
2177 65p. Silhouetted figure within latticework (TS2K Creative Enterprise Centres, London) . . . . 2·25 2·50

1489 "Flower" ("Nurture Children")

2001. New Millennium. Rights of the Child, Face Paintings. Multicoloured.
2178 (2nd.) Type **1489** 75 75
2179 (1st) "Tiger" ("Listen to Children") . . . . 1·00 1·10
2180 45p. "Owl" ("Teach Children") . . . . 1·60 1·75
2181 65p. "Butterfly" ("Ensure Children's Freedom") . . 2·40 2·50

1493 "Love"

2001. "Occasions" Greetings Stamps. Multicoloured.
2182 (1st) Type **1493** . . . . . 1·10 1·00
2183 (1st) "THANKS" . . . . . 1·10 1·00
2184 (1st) "abc" "New Baby" . . 1·10 1·00
2185 (1st) "WELCOME" . . . . 1·10 1·00
2186 (1st) "Cheers" . . . . . . 1·10 1·00
The silver-grey backgrounds are printed in Iriodin ink which gives a shiny effect.

1498 Dog and Owner on Bench

2001. Cats and Dogs. Self-adhesive.
2187 **1498** (1st) black, grey & silver . . . . 1·25 1·00
2188 – (1st) black, grey & silver . . . . 1·25 1·00
2189 – (1st) black, grey & silver . . . . 1·25 1·00
2190 – (1st) black, grey & silver . . . . 1·25 1·00
2191 – (1st) black, grey & silver . . . . 1·25 1·00
2192 – (1st) black, grey & silver . . . . 1·25 1·00
2193 – (1st) black, grey & silver . . . . 1·25 1·00
2194 – (1st) black, grey & silver . . . . 1·25 1·00
2195 – (1st) black, grey & silver . . . . 1·25 1·00
2196 – (1st) black, grey & silver . . . . 1·25 1·00
DESIGNS: No. 2188 Dog in bath; 2189, Boxer at dog show; 2190, Cat in handbag; 3192, Dog in car; 2193, Cat at window; 2194, Dog behind fence; 2195, Cat watching bird; 2196, Cat in washbasin.

1508 "RAIN"

2001. The Weather. Multicoloured.
2197 19p. Type **1508** 70 75
2198 27p. "FAIR" . . . . 85 1·00
2199 45p. "STORMY" . . . . . 1·50 1·50
2200 65p. "VERY DRY" . . . . 2·40 2·50
MS2201 105 × 105 mm. Nos. 2197/2200 . . . . 13·00 13·00
The violet on the 27p. and miniature sheet is printed in thermochromic ink, which changes from violet to blue when exposed to heat.

1512 *Vanguard* Class Submarine, 1992

2001. Centenary of Royal Navy Submarine Service. Multicoloured. (a) Ordinary gum.
2202 (2nd) Type **1512** 70 75
2203 (1st) *Swiftsure* Class Submarine, 1973 . . . . 85 90
2204 45p. *Unity* Class Submarine, 1939 . . . . 1·50 1·60
2205 65p. "Holland" Type Submarine, 1901 . . 2·40 2·50
MS2206 92 × 97 mm. (a) (1st) White Ensign; (b) (1st) Union Jack; (c) (1st) Jolly Roger flown by H.M.S. *Proteus* (submarine); (d) (1st) Flag of Chief of Defence Staff . . . 9·00 9·00

(b) Self-adhesive.
2207 (1st) *Swiftsure* Class Submarine, 1973 . . . . 38·00 37·00
2208 (1st) White Ensign . . . . 10·00 10·00
2209 (1st) Jolly Roger Flown by H.M.S. *Proteus* (submarine) . . . . . . 10·00 10·00

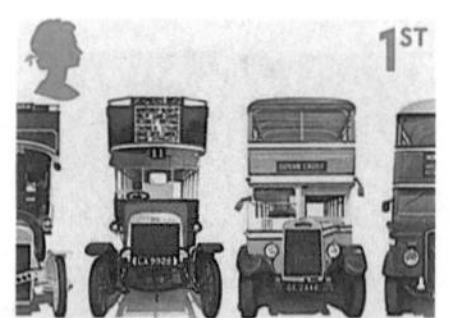

1520 Leyland X2 Open-top, London General B Type, Leyland Titan TD1 and AEC Regent 1

1521 AEC Regent 1, Daimler COG5, Utility Guy Arab Mk II and AEC Regent III RT Type

1522 AEC Regent III RT Type, Bristol KSW5G Open-top, AEC Routemaster and Bristol Lodekka FSF6G

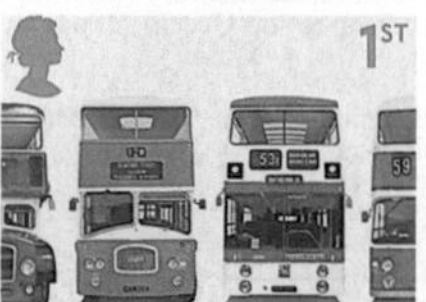

1523 Bristol Lodekka FSF6G, Leyland Titan PD3/4, Leyland Atlantean PDR1/1 and Daimler Fleetline CRG6LX-33

1524 Daimler Fleetline CRG6LX-33, MCW Metrobus DR102/43, Leyland Olympian ONLXB/1R and Dennis Trident

2001. 150th Anniv of First Double-decker Bus.

2210	**1520** (1st) multicoloured . .	1·10	1·10
2211	**1521** (1st) multicoloured . .	1·10	1·10
2212	**1522** (1st) multicoloured . .	1·10	1·10
2213	**1523** (1st) multicoloured . .	1·10	1·10
2214	**1524** (1st) multicoloured . .	1·10	1·10
MS2215	120 × 105 mm. Nos. 2210/14	8·25	8·25

In No. **MS**2215 the illustrations of the AEC Regent III RT Type and the Daimler Fleetline CRG6LX-33 appear twice.

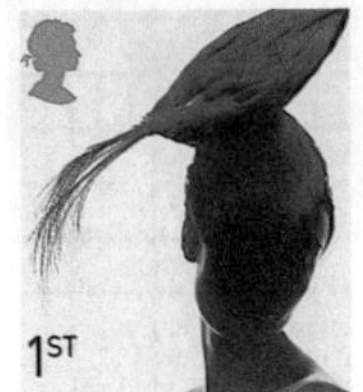

1525 Toque Hat by Pip Hackett

2001. Fashion Hats. Multicoloured.

2216	(1st) Type **1525**	85	90
2217	(E) Butterfly hat by Dai Rees	1·10	1·25
2218	45p. Top hat by Stephen Jones	1·50	1·60
2219	65p. Spiral hat by Philip Treacy	2·40	2·50

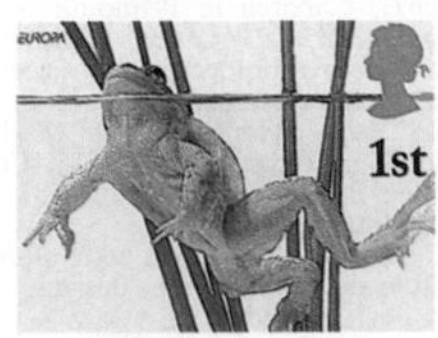

1529 Common Frog

2001. Europa. Pond Life. Multicoloured.

2220	(1st) Type **1529**	1·00	1·00
2221	(E) Great diving beetle . . .	1·25	1·25
2222	45p. Three-spined stickleback	1·50	1·50
2223	65p. Southern hawker dragonfly	2·00	2·25

The 1st and E values incorporate the "EUROPA" emblem.

1533 Policeman

2001. Punch and Judy Show Puppets. Multicoloured.

(a) Ordinary Gum.

2224	(1st) Type **1533**	80	75
2225	(1st) Clown	80	75
2226	(1st) Mr. Punch	80	75
2227	(1st) Judy	80	75
2228	(1st) Beadle	80	75
2229	(1st) Crocodile	80	75

(b) Self-adhesive.

2230	(1st) Mr. Punch	8·00	8·00
2231	(1st) Judy	8·00	8·00

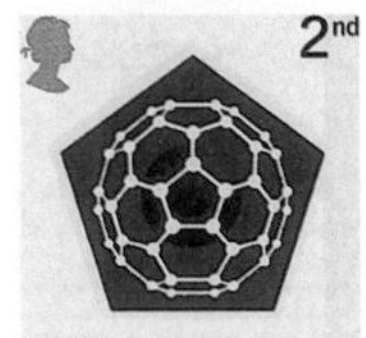

1539 Carbon 60 Molecule (Chemistry)

2001. Centenary of Nobel Prizes.

2232	**1539** (2nd) black, silver and grey	75	65
2233	– (1st) multicoloured . .	1·00	90
2234	– (E) black, silver and green	1·00	1·25
2235	– 40p. multicoloured . .	1·25	1·25
2236	– 45p. multicoloured . .	1·50	1·75
2237	– 65p. black and silver . .	2·25	2·50

DESIGNS: No. 2233, Globe (Economic Sciences); 2234, Embossed Dove (Peace); 2235, Crosses (Physiology or Medicine); 2236, Poem "The Addressing of Cats" by T. S. Eliot in Open Book (Literature); 2237, Hologram of Boron Molecule (Physics).

The grey on No. 2232 is printed in thermochromic ink which temporarily changes to pale grey when exposed to heat.

The centre of No. 2235 is coated with a eucalyptus scent.

1545 Robins with Snowman

2001. Christmas. Robins. Self-adhesive. Multicoloured.

2238	(2nd) Type **1545**	75	70
2239	(1st) Robins on bird table	1·00	1·00
2240	(E) Robins skating on bird bath	1·00	1·10
2241	45p. Robins with Christmas pudding	1·50	1·50
2242	65p. Robins in paper chain nest	2·00	2·25

1550 "How the Whale got his Throat"

2002. Centenary of Publication of Rudyard Kipling's *Just So Stories*. Multicoloured. Self-adhesive.

2243	(1st) Type **1550**	95	85
2244	(1st) "How the Camel got his Hump"	95	85
2245	(1st) "How the Rhinoceros got his Skin"	95	85
2246	(1st) "How the Leopard got his Spots"	95	85
2247	(1st) "The Elephant's Child"	95	85
2248	(1st) "The Sing-Song of Old Man Kangaroo"	95	85
2249	(1st) "The Beginning of the Armadillos"	95	85
2250	(1st) "The Crab that played with the Sea"	95	85
2251	(1st) "The Cat that walked by Himself"	95	85
2252	(1st) "The Butterfly that stamped"	95	85

1560 Queen Elizabeth II, 1952 (Dorothy Wilding)

1566

2002. Golden Jubilee. Studio portraits of Queen Elizabeth II by photographers named. Multicoloured.

2253	(2nd) Type **1560**	75	55
2254	(1st) Queen Elizabeth II, 1968 (Cecil Beaton) . . .	1·00	80
2255	(E) Queen Elizabeth II, 1978 (Lord Snowdon)	1·25	1·25
2256	45p. Queen Elizabeth II, 1984 (Yousef Karsh) . . .	1·50	1·50
2257	65p. Queen Elizabeth II, 1996 (Tim Graham) . . .	2·25	2·25

2002. As T **154/5** (Wilding definitive of 1952–54), but with service indicator as T **1566**.

2258	**1566** (2nd) red	1·20	1·00
2259	– (1st) green	1·25	1·25

1567 Rabbits ("a new baby")

2002. "Occasions". Greetings Stamps. Mult.

2260	(1st) Type **1567**	1·00	1·00
2261	(1st) "LOVE"	1·00	1·00
2262	(1st) Aircraft sky-writing "hello"	1·00	1·00
2263	(1st) Bear pulling potted topiary tree (Moving Home)	1·00	1·00
2264	(1st) Flowers ("best wishes")	1·00	1·00

No. 2262 also comes self-adhesive.

1572 Studland Bay, Dorset

2002. British Coastlines. Multicoloured.

2265	27p. Type **1572**	75	80
2266	27p. Luskentyre, South Harris	75	80
2267	27p. Cliffs, Dover, Kent . .	75	80
2268	27p. Padstow Harbour, Cornwall	75	80
2269	27p. Broadstairs, Kent . . .	75	80
2270	27p. St. Abbs Head, Scottish Borders	75	80
2271	27p. Dunster Beach, Somerset	75	80
2272	27p. Newquay Beach, Cornwall	75	80
2273	27p. Portrush, County Antrim	75	80
2274	27p. Sand-spit, Conwy . . .	75	80

1582 Slack Wire Act

2002. Circus. Multicoloured.

2275	(2nd) Type **1582**	50	60
2276	(1st) Lion tamer	75	85
2277	(E) Trick tri-cyclists	1·00	1·25
2278	45p. Krazy kar	1·50	1·50
2279	65p. Equestrienne	2·00	2·25

1587 Queen Elizabeth the Queen Mother

2002. Queen Elizabeth the Queen Mother Commemoration. As Nos. 1507/10 with changed face values and showing both the Queen's head and frame in black.

2280	**1587** (1st) multicoloured . .	1·00	85
2281	(E) black and blue . .	1·25	1·10
2282	45p. multicoloured . .	1·50	1·50
2283	65p. black, stone and brown	2·00	2·25

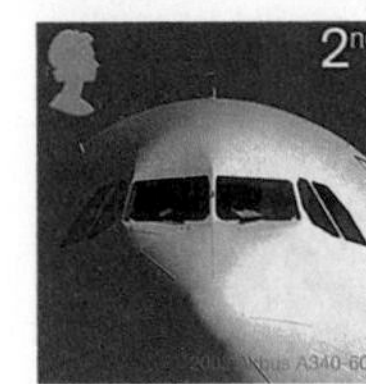

1588 Airbus A340-600 (2002)

2002. 50th Anniv of Passenger Jet Aviation. Airliners. Multicoloured.

2284	(2nd) Type **1588**	75	55
2285	(1st) Concorde (1976) . . .	1·00	80
2286	(E) Trident (1964)	1·25	1·25
2287	45p. VC 10 (1964)	1·50	1·50
2288	65p. Comet (1952)	2·00	2·25
MS2289	120 × 105mm. Nos. 2284/8	8·25	8·25

No. 2285 also comes self-adhesive.

1593 Crowned Lion with Shield of St. George

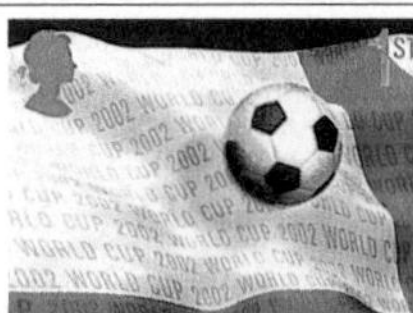
1594 Top Left Quarter of English Flag, and Football

1595 Top Right Quarter of English Flag, and Football

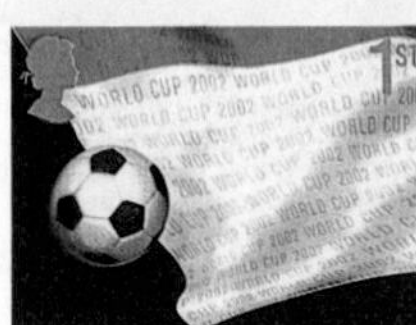
1596 Bottom Left Quarter of English Flag, and Football

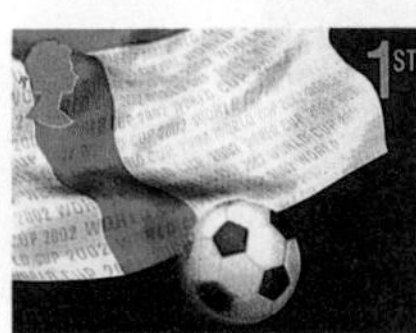

1597 Bottom Right Quarter of English Flag, and Football

2002. World Cup Football Championship, Japan and Korea (2002).

2291	**1593** (1st) blue, red and silver	1·50	1·25
MS2292	145 × 74 mm. No. 2291; **1594** (1st) multicoloured; **1595** (1st) multicoloured, **1596** (1st) multicoloured; **1597** (1st) multicoloured	5·00	5·75

(b) Self-adhesive.

2293	**1594** (1st) multicoloured . .	2·00	2·25
2294	**1595** (1st) multicoloured . .	2·00	2·25

2002. Self-adhesive.

2295	**914** (1st) gold	1·00	1·00
2296	**1093a** (E) blue	1·25	1·25
2297	**367a** 42p. grey	1·25	1·25
2298	68p. brown	2·00	2·00

No. 2295 was initially sold for 27p.

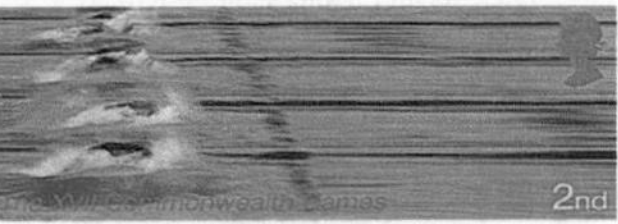

1598 Swimming

2002. 17th Commonwealth Games, Manchester. Multicoloured.

2299	(2nd) Type **1598**	75	55
2300	(1st) Running	1·00	80
2301	(E) Cycling	1·25	1·25
2302	47p. Long jumping	1·50	1·50
2303	68p. Wheelchair racing . . .	2·00	2·25

1603 Tinkerbell

2002. 150th Anniv of Great Ormond Street Children's Hospital. *Peter Pan* by Sir James Barrie. Multicoloured.

2304	(2nd) Type **1063**	50	55
2305	(1st) Wendy, John and Michael Darling in front of Big Ben	70	80
2306	(E) Crocodile and alarm clock	90	1·00
2307	47p. Captain Hook	1·25	1·40
2308	68p. Peter Pan	1·90	2·00

1608 Millennium Bridge, 2001

2002. Bridges of London. Multicoloured.
2309 (2nd) Type **1608** 75 55
2310 (1st) Tower Bridge, 1894 . . 1·00 80
2311 (E) Westminster Bridge, 1864 . . . . 1·25 1·25
2312 47p. "Blackfriars Bridge, c 1800" (William Marlow) 1·50 1·40
2313 68p. "London Bridge, c 1670" (Wenceslaus Hollar) . . . . 2·00 2·25
No. 2310 also comes self-adhesive.

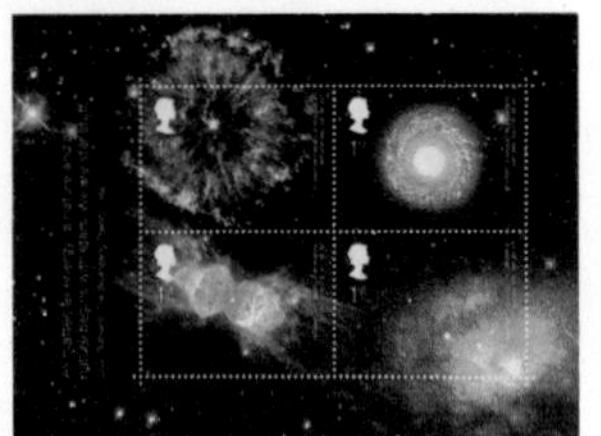

1613 Galaxies and Nebula (½-size illustration)

2002. Astronomy. Sheet 120 × 89 mm. Multicoloured.
MS2315 **1613** (1st) Planetary nebula in Aquila; (1st) Seyfert 2 galaxy in Pegasus; (1st) Planetary nebula in Norma; (1st) Seyfert 2 galaxy in Circinus . . . . 5·25 5·25

1614 Green Pillar Box, 1857 **1619** Blue Spruce Star

2002. 150th Anniv of the First Pillar Box.
2316 (2nd) Type **1614** 75 55
2317 (1st) Horizontal Aperture Box, 1874 . . . . 1·00 1·25
2318 (E) Air Mail Box, 1934 . . 1·25 1·25
2319 47p. Double Aperture Box, 1939 . . . . 1·50 1·50
2320 68p. Modern Style Box, 1980 . . . . 2·00 2·25

2002. Christmas. Self-adhesive.
2321 (2nd) Type **1619** 75 55
2322 (1st) Holly . . . . 1·00 80
2323 (E) Ivy . . . . 1·25 1·25
2324 47p. Mistletoe . . . . . . 1·50 1·50
2325 68p. Pine cone . . . . . . 2·00 2·25

2002. 50th Anniv of Wilding Definitives (1st issue). Sheet 124 × 70 mm, containing designs as T **154/5** and **157/60** (1952–54 issue), but with values in decimal currency as T **1348** or with service indicator as T **1566**, printed on cream.
MS2326 1p. red; 2p. blue; 5p. brown; (2nd) red; (1st) green; 33p. brown; 37p. mauve; 47p. brown; 50p. green . . . . 7·00 7·00
See also No. **MS**2367.

1624 Barn Owl landing

1625 Barn Owl with folded Wings and Legs down

1626 Barn Owl with extended Wings and Legs down

1627 Barn Owl in Flight with Wings lowered

1628 Barn Owl in Flight with Wings raised

1629 Kestrel with Wings folded

1630 Kestrel with Wings fully extended upwards

1631 Kestrel with Wings horizontal

1632 Kestrel with Wings partly extended downwards

1633 Kestrel with Wings fully extended downwards

2003. Birds of Prey.
2327 **1624** (1st) multicoloured . . 70 80
2328 **1625** (1st) multicoloured . . 70 80
2329 **1626** (1st) multicoloured . . 70 80
2330 **1627** (1st) multicoloured . . 70 80
2331 **1628** (1st) multicoloured . . 70 80
2332 **1629** (1st) multicoloured . . 70 80
2333 **1630** (1st) multicoloured . . 70 80
2334 **1631** (1st) multicoloured . . 70 80
2335 **1632** (1st) multicoloured . . 70 80
2336 **1633** (1st) multicoloured . . 70 80

1634 "Gold star, See me, Playtime"

2003. "Occasions" Greetings Stamps.
2337 **1634** (1st) yellow and blue 70 80
2338 – (1st) red and blue . . . 70 80
2339 – (1st) purple and green 70 80
2340 – (1st) green and red . . 70 80
2341 – (1st) blue and yellow 70 80
2342 – (1st) blue and purple 70 80
DESIGNS: No. 2338, "I U, XXXX, S.W.A.L.K."; 2239, "Angel, Poppet, Little terror"; 2340, "Yes, No, Maybe"; 2341, "Oops!, Sorry, Will try harder"; 2342, "I did it!, You did it!, We did it!".

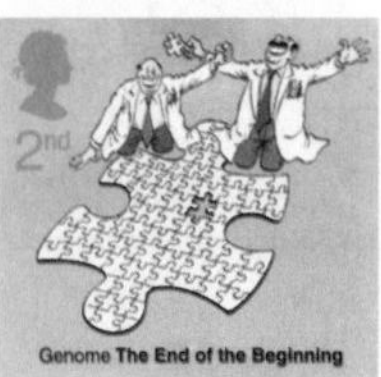

1640 Completing the Genome Jigsaw

2003. 50th Anniv of Discovery of DNA. Multicoloured.
2343 (2nd) Type **1640** . . . . . 1·00 55
2344 (1st) Ape with Moustache and Scientist . . . . . . 1·00 80
2345 (E) DNA Snakes and Ladders . . . . 1·25 1·25
2346 47p. "Animal Scientists" . . 1·50 1·50
2347 68p. Genome Crystal Ball 2·00 2·25

1645 Strawberry

2003. Fruit and Vegetables. Self-adhesive.
2348 (1st) Type **1645** 70 80
2349 (1st) Potato 70 80
2350 (1st) Apple 70 80
2351 (1st) Red pepper 70 80
2352 (1st) Pear 70 80
2353 (1st) Orange 70 80
2354 (1st) Tomato 70 80
2355 (1st) Lemon 70 80
2356 (1st) Cabbage 70 80
2357 (1st) Aubergine 70 80
Nos. 2348/57 are accompanied by a similar-sized pane of self-adhesive labels showing ears, eyes, mouths, hats etc which are intended for the adornment of fruit and vegetables depicted.

1655

2003. Overseas Stamps. Self-adhesive.
2358 **1655** (Europe) blue and red 80 85
2359 (Worldwide) red and blue . . . . 1·60 1·75
2359a (Worldwide postcard) black, red and blue 65 70
Nos. 2358/9 were intended to pay postage on mail up to 40 grams to either Europe (52p.) or foreign destinations outside Europe (£1.12). No. 2359a was intended to pay postcard rate to foreign destination (43p.)

1656 Amy Johnson (pilot) and Bi-plane

2003. Extreme Endeavours. (British Explorers).
2360 (2nd) Type **1656** 50 50
2361 (1st) Members of 1953 Everest team 75 75
2362 (E) Freya Stark (traveller and writer) and desert . . 1·25 1·50
2363 42p. Ernest Shackleton (Antarctic explorer) and wreck of *Endurance* . . . 1·25 1·75
2364 47p. Francis Chichester (yachtsman) and *Gipsy Moth IV* . . . . 1·50 2·00
2365 68p. Robert Falcon Scott (Antarctic explorer) and Norwegian Expedition at the Pole . . . . 2·00 2·50
No. 2361 also comes self-adhesive.

2003. 50th Anniv of Wilding Definitives (2nd issue). Sheet 124 × 70 mm, containing designs as Nos. 519, 575, 617b and 585 (1952–54 issue), but with values in decimal currency as T **1348** or with service indicator as T **1566**, printed on cream.
MS2367 4p. lilac; 8p. blue; (1st) purple; 20p. green; 28p. green; 34p. purple; (1st) chestnut; 42p. blue; 68p. blue . . . . 10·50 11·25

1662 Guardsmen in Coronation Procession

2003. 50th Anniv of Coronation.
2368 **1662** (1st) multicoloured . . 45 50
2369 – (1st) black and gold . . 45 50
2370 – (1st) multicoloured . . 45 50
2371 – (1st) black and gold . . 45 50
2372 – (1st) multicoloured . . 45 50
2373 – (1st) black and gold . . 45 50
2374 – (1st) multicoloured . . 45 50
2375 – (1st) black and gold . . 45 50
2376 – (1st) multicoloured . . 45 50
2377 – (1st) black and gold . . 45 50
DESIGNS: No. 2369, East End children reading Coronation party poster; 2670, Queen Elizabeth II in Coronation Chair with Bishops of Durham and Bath & Wells; 2671, Children in Plymouth working on Royal Montage; 2672, Queen Elizabeth II in Coronation Robes (photograph by Cecil Beaton); 2673, Childrens Race at East End Street Party; 2674, Coronation Coach passing through Marble Arch; 2675, Children in Fancy Dress; 2676, Coronation Coach outside Buckingham Palace; 2677, Children eating at London street party.
No. 2372 does not show a silhouette of the Queens head in gold as do the other nine designs.

2003. 50th Anniv of Coronation. Designs as Nos. 585, 534 (Wilding definitive of 1952) and **163** (Coronation commemorative of 1953), but with values in decimal currency as T **1348**.
2378 47p. brown . . . . 5·00 2·50
2379 68p. blue . . . . 5·00 2·50
2380 £1 green . . . . 40·00 45·00

1672 Prince William in September 2001 (Brendan Beirne)

2003. 21st Birthday of Prince William of Wales.
2381 **1672** 28p. multicoloured . . 1·00 50
2382 – (E) mauve, black and green . . . . 1·25 1·50
2383 – 47p. multicoloured . . 1·25 2·00
2384 – 68p. deep green, black and green . . . . . 1·75 2·00
DESIGNS: No. 2382, Prince William in September 2000 (Tim Graham); 2383, Prince William in September 2001 (Camera Press); 2384, Prince William in September 2001 (Tim Graham).

1676 Loch Assynt, Sutherland

2003. A British Journey: Scotland. Multicoloured.
2385 (2nd) Type **1676** 50 35
2386 (1st) Ben More, Isle of Mull 75 50
2387 (E) Rothiemurchus, Cairngorms . . . . . . 1·25 1·25
2388 42p. Dalveen Pass, Lowther Hills . . . . 1·25 1·25
2389 47p. Glenfinnan Viaduct, Lochaber . . . . 1·50 2·00
2390 68p. Papa Little, Shetland Islands . . . . 2·00 2·50
No. 2386 also comes self-adhesive.

1682 "The Station" (Andrew Davidson)

2003. British Pub Signs. Multicoloured.
2392 (1st) Type **1682** 75 50
2393 (E) "Black Swan" (Stanley Chew) . . . . 2·00 2·00
2394 42p. "The Cross Keys" (George Mackenney) . . 1·50 1·50
2395 47p. "The Mayflower" (Ralph Ellis) . . . . . . 1·75 2·00
2396 68p. "The Barley Sheaf" (Joy Cooper) . . . . . . 2·00 2·25

1687 Meccano Constructor Biplane, c. 1931

2003. Classic Transport Toys. Multicoloured.
2397 (1st) Type **1687** 75 50
2398 (E) Wells-Brimtoy Clockwork Double-decker Omnibus, c. 1938 . . . . 1·25 1·25
2399 42p. Hornby M1 Clockwork Locomotive and Tender, c. 1948 . . . . . 1·50 1·50
2400 47p. Dinky Toys Ford Zephyr, c. 1956 . . . . . 1·75 1·75
2401 68p. Mettoy Friction Drive Space Ship Eagle, c. 1960 2·00 2·00
MS2402 115 × 105 mm. Nos. 2397/401 . . . . 7·00 8·25
No. 2397 also comes self-adhesive.

1692 Coffin of Denytenamun, Egyptian, c. 900BC

2003. 250th Anniv of the British Museum. Multicoloured.
2404 (2nd) Type **1692** 50 35
2405 (1st) Alexander the Great, Greek, c. 200BC 75 50
2406 (E) Sutton Hoo Helmet, Anglo-Saxon, c. AD600 1·25 1·25
2407 42p. Sculpture of Parvati, South Indian, c. AD1550 1·50 1·50
2408 47p. Mask of Xiuhtecuhtli, Mixtec-Aztec, c. AD1500 1·50 2·00
2409 68p. Hoa Hakananai'a, Easter Island, c. AD1000 2·00 2·75

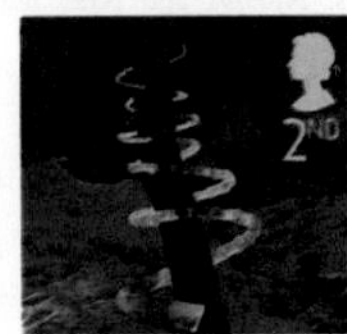

1698 Ice Spiral

2003. Christmas. Ice Sculptures by Andy Goldsworthy. Multicoloured.
2410 (2nd) Type **1698** 75 35
2411 (1st) Icicle Star . . . . . . 1·25 50
2412 (E) Wall of Ice Blocks . . . 1·50 1·50
2413 53p. Ice Ball . . . . 1·75 1·75
2414 68p. Ice Hole . . . . 2·00 2·00
2415 £1.12 Snow Pyramids . . . 2·00 2·00

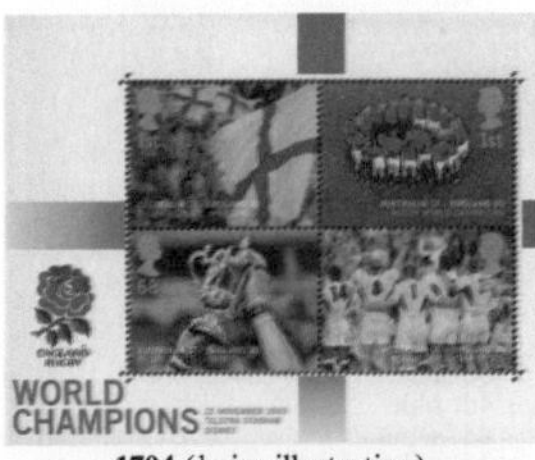

1704 (½-size illustration)

2003. England's Victory in Rugby World Cup Championship, Australia. Sheet 115 × 85 mm. Multicoloured.
MS2416 **1704** (1st) England flags and fans; (1st) England team standing in circle before match; 68p. World Cup trophy; 68p. Victorious England players after match . . . . 5·00 5·00

1705 Dolgoch, Rheilffordd Talyllyn Railway, Gwynedd

2004. Classic Locomotives. Multicoloured.
2417 20p. Type **1705** 65 65
2418 28p. CR Class 439, Bo'ness and Kinneil Railway, West Lothian 90 90
2419 (E) GCR Class 8K, Leicestershire . . . . . . 1·20 1·20
2420 42p. GWR Manor Class *Bradley Manor*, Severn Valley Railway, Worcestershire 65 70
2421 47p. SR West Country class *Blackmoor Vale*, Bluebell Railway, East Sussex . . 1·50 1·50
2422 68p. (1710 BR Standard class, Keighley & Worth Valley Railway, Yorkshire) . . . . 2·20 2·20
MS2423 190 × 67 mm. Nos. 2417/22 5·75 12·00

1711 Postman

2004. Occasions.
2424 **1711** (1st) mauve and black 90 90
2425 – (1st) magenta and black 90 90
2426 – (1st) lemon and black 90 90
2427 – (1st) green and black 90 90
2428 – (1st) blue and black . . 90 90
DESIGNS: No. 2425, Face; 2426, Duck; 2427, Baby; 2428, Aircraft.

1716 Map showing Middle Earth

2004. 50th Anniv of Publication of *The Fellowship of the Ring* and *The Two Towers* by J. R. R. Tolkien. Multicoloured.
2429 (1st) Type **1716** 90 90
2430 (1st) Forest of Lothlorien in Spring 90 90
2431 (1st) Dust-jacket for *The Fellowship of the Ring* . . 90 90
2432 (1st) Rivendell 90 90
2433 (1st) The Hall at Bag End 90 90
2434 (1st) Orthanc 90 90
2435 (1st) Doors of Durin . . . 90 90
2436 (1st) Barad-dur 90 90
2437 (1st) Minas Tirth 90 90
2438 (1st) Fangorn Forest 90 90

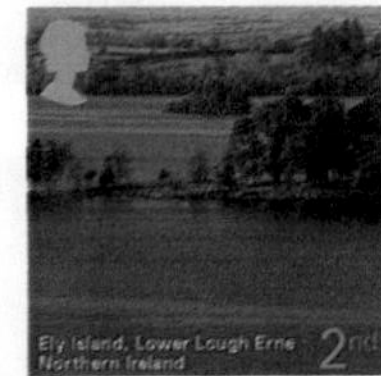

1726 Ely Island, Lower Lough Erne

2004. A British Journey: Northern Ireland. Multicoloured.
2439 (2nd) Type **1726** 65 65
2440 (1st) Giant's Causeway, Antrim Coast 90 90
2441 (E) Slemish, Antrim Mountains . . . . 1·20 1·20
2442 42p. Banns Road, Mourne Mountains . . . . 1·30 1·30
2443 47p. Glenelly Valley, Sperrins . . . . 1·50 1·50
2444 68p. Islandmore, Strangford Lough . . . . 2·20 2·20
No. 2440 also comes self-adhesive.

1732 "Lace 1 (trial proof) 1968" (Sir Terry Frost)

2004. Centenary of the Entente Cordiale. Contemporary Paintings.
2446 **1732** 28p. grey, black and red 90 90
2447 – 57p. multicoloured . . 1·90 1·90
DESIGN: No. 1733, "Coccinelle" (Sonia Delaunay)
Stamps in similar designs were issued by France.

1734 "RMS Queen Mary 2, 2004" (Edward D. Walker)

2004. Ocean Liners. Multicoloured.
2448 (1st) Type **1734** 90 90
2449 (E) "SS Canberra 1961" (David Cobb) . . . . . . 1·30 1·30
2450 42p. "RMS Queen Mary 1936" (Charles Pears) . . 1·30 1·30
2451 47p. "RMS Mauretania, 1907" (Thomas Henry) 1·50 1·50
2452 57p. "SS City of New York, 1888" (Raphael Monleaon y Torres) . . . . 1·80 1·80
2453 68p. "PS Great Western, 1838" (Joseph Walter) . . 2·20 2·20
MS2454 114 × 104 mm. Nos. 2448/53 . . . . 18·00 18·00
No.2448 also comes self-adhesive.
Nos. 2448/55 commemorate the introduction to service of the *Queen Mary 2*.

1740 Dianthus Allwoodii Group

2004. Bicentenary of the Royal Horticultural Society (1st issue). Multicoloured.
2456 (2nd) Type **1740** 70 70
2457 (1st) Dahlia "Garden Princess" 90 90
2458 (E) Clematis "Arabella" . . 1·30 1·30
2459 42p. Miltonia "French Lake" . . . . 1·40 1·40
2460 47p. Lilium "Lemon Pixie" 1·50 1·50
2461 68p. Delphinium "Clifford Sky" . . . . 2·20 2·20
MS2462 115 × 105 mm. Nos. 2456/61 . . . . 8·00 8·00

2004. Bicentenary of the Royal Horticultural Society (2nd issue). Designs as Nos. 1955, 1958 and 1962 (1997 Greeting Stamps 19th-century Flower Paintings). Multicoloured.
2463 (1st) Type **1280** . . . . . . 1·50 1·50
2464 (1st) "Tulipa" (Ehret) . . . 50 50
2465 (1st) "Iris latifolia" (Ehret) 1·50 1·50

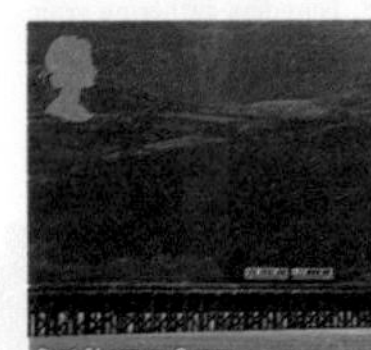

1746 Barmouth Bridge

2004. A British Journey: Wales. Multicoloured. (a) Ordinary gum.
2466 (2nd) Type **1746** 70 70
2467 (1st) Hyddgen, Plynlimon 90
2468 40p. Brecon Beacons . . . 1·30 1·30
2469 43p. Pen-pych, Rhondda Valley . . . . 1·40 1·40
2470 47p. Rhewl, Dee Valley . . 1·50 1·50
2471 68p. Marloes Sands . . . . 2·20 2·20

(b) Self-adhesive.
2472 (1st) Hyddgen, Plynlimon 2·50 2·50
The (1st) and 40p. values include the "EUROPA" emblem.

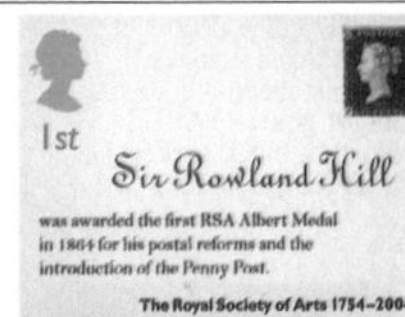

1752 Sir Rowland Hill Award

2004. 250th Anniv of the Royal Society of Arts.
2473 **1752** (1st) multicoloured . . 95 95
2474 – 40p. multicoloured . . 1·30 1·30
2475 – 43p. multicoloured . . 1·40 1·40
2476 – 47p. multicoloured . . 1·50 1·50
2477 – 57p. silver, vermilion and black . . . . . 1·90 1·90
2478 – 68p. silver, vermilion and black . . . . . 2·20 2·20
DESIGNS: No. 2474, William Shipley (Founder of Royal Society of Arts); 2475, "RSA" as Typewriter Keys and Shorthand; 2476 Chimney Sweep; 2477, "Gill Typeface"; 2478, "Zero Waste".

1758 Pine Martin

2004. Woodland Animals. Multicoloured.
2479 (1st) Type **1758** 90 90
2480 (1st) Roe deer 90 90
2481 (1st) Badger 90 90
2482 (1st) Yellow-necked mouse 90 90
2483 (1st) Wild cat 90 90
2484 (1st) Red squirrel 90 90
2485 (1st) Stoat 90 90
2486 (1st) Natterer's bat 90 90
2487 (1st) Mole 90 90
2488 (1st) Fox 90 90

1768 Pte. McNamara, 5th Dragoon Guards, Heavy Brigade Charge, Battle of Balaklava

1774 Father Christmas on Snowy Roof

2004. 150th Anniv of the Crimean War. Multicoloured.
2489 (2nd) Type **1768** 70 70
2490 (1st) Piper Muir, 42nd Regt of Foot, Amphibious Assault on Kerch 90 90
2491 40p. Sgt. Maj. Edwards, Scots Fusilier Guards, Gallant Action, Battle of Inkerman . . . . 1·30 1·30
2492 57p. Sgt. Powell, 1st Regt of Foot Guards, Battles of Alma and Inkerman . . . 1·80 1·80
2493 68p. Sgt. Maj. Poole, Royal Sappers and Miners, Defensive Line, Battle of Inkerman . . . . 2·20 2·20
2494 £1.12 Sgt. Glasgow, Royal Artillery, Gun Battery besieged Sevastopol . . . 3·75 3·75
Nos. 2489/94 show "Crimean Heroes" photographs taken in 1856.

2004. Christmas. Multicoloured. (a) Self-adhesive.
2495 (2nd) Type **1774** 70 70
2496 (1st) Celebrating the sunrise 90 90
2497 40p. On roof in gale . . . . 1·30 1·30
2498 57p. With umbrella in rain 1·80 1·80
2499 68p. On edge of roof with torch . . . . 2·20 2·20
2500 £1.12 Sheltering behind chimney . . . . 3·75 3·75

(b) Ordinary gum.
MS2501 115 × 105 mm. As Nos. 2495/500 . . . . 10·50 10·50

1780 British Saddleback Pigs

2005. Farm Animals. Multicoloured.
2502 (1st) Type **1780** . . . . . . 65 1·00
2503 (1st) Khaki Campbell ducks 65 1·00
2504 (1st) Suffolk horses . . . . 65 1·00
2505 (1st) Dairy Shorthorn cattle 65 1·00

2506 (1st) Border collie dog . . . 65 1·00
2507 (1st) Light Sussex chicks . . 65 1·00
2508 (1st) Suffolk sheep . . . . 65 1·00
2509 (1st) Bagot goat . . . . . . 65 1·00
2510 (1st) Norfolk black turkeys 65 1·00
2511 (1st) Embden geese . . . . 65 1·00

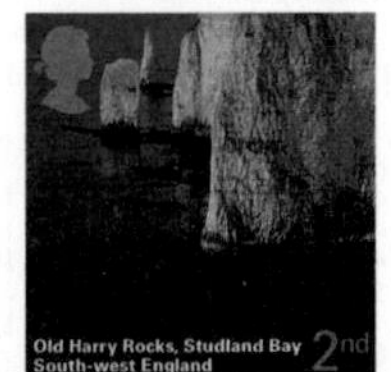

1790 Old Harry Rocks, Studland Bay

2005. A British Journey: South West England. Multicoloured.
2512 (2nd) Type **1790** 50 50
2513 (1st) Wheal Coates, St. Agnes 50 75
2514 40p. Start Point, Start Bay 1·00 1·75
2515 43p. Horton Down, Wiltshire . . . . 1·25 2·00
2516 57p. Chiselcombe, Exmoor 1·50 2·50
2517 68p. St. James's Stone, Lundy . . . . 2·00 3·00

1796 "Mr Rochester"

2004. 150th Death Anniv of Charlotte Bronte. Illustrations of scenes from "Jane Eyre" by Paula Rego.
2518 **1796** (2nd) multicoloured . . 30 35
2519 – (1st) multicoloured . . 40 45
2520 – 40p. multicoloured . . 60 65
2521 – 57p. silver, grey and black 85 90
2522 – 68p. multicoloured . . 1·00 1·10
2523 – £1.12 silver, grey and black . . . . . . 1·70 1·80
MS2524 114 × 105 mm. Nos. 2518/23 . . . . 4·75 5·25
DESIGNS: No. 1797, "Come to Me"; 1798, "In the Comfort of her Bonnet"; 1799, "La Ligne des Rats"; 1800, "Refectory"; 1801, "Inspection".

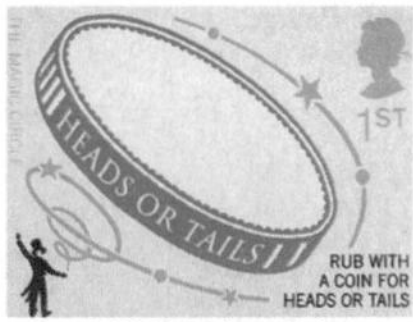

1802 Spinning Coin

2005. Centenary of the Magic Circle. Multicolored.
2525 (1st) Type **1802** 40 45
2526 40p. Rabbit out of Hat Trick 60 65
2527 47p. Knotted Scarf Trick . . 95 1·00
2528 68p. Card Trick . . . . . 1·00 1·10
2529 £1.12 Pyramid under Fez Trick . . . . 1·70 1·80

2005. 50th Anniv of First Castles Definitives. Sheet 127 × 73 mm, containing horiz designs as Nos. 595a/597a and 762 (Castles definitive of 1955–58) but with values in decimal currency.
MS2530 **166** 50p. black; 50p. black; £1 vermilion; 168 £1 blue . . . 4·50 4·75

1807 (½-size illustration)

2005. Royal Wedding. Sheet 85 × 115 mm. Multicoloured.
MS2531 1807 30p. × 2 Prince Charles and Mrs Camilla Parker Bowles laughing; 68p. × 2 Prince Charles and Mrs Camilla Parker Bowles smiling into camera . . . . . 3·20 3·50

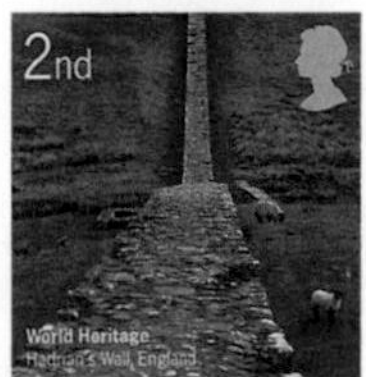

1808 Hadrian's Wall, England

2005. World Heritage Sites. Multicoloured.
2532 (2nd) Type **1808** 35 40
2533 (2nd) silver, Uluru-Kata Tjuta National Park, Australia 35 40
2534 (1st) Stonehenge, England 50 55
2535 (1st) Wet Tropics of Queensland, Australia . . 50 55
2536 47p. Blenheim Palace, England 75 80
2537 47p. Greater Blue Mountains Area, Australia 75 80
2538 68p. Heart of Neolithic Orkney, Scotland . . . . 1·10 1·20
2539 68p. Purnululu National Park, Australia . . . . 1·10 1·20
Stamps in these designs were issued by Australia.

1816 Ensign of the Scots Guards, 2002

2005. Trooping the Colour. Multicoloured.
2540 (2nd) Type **1816** 35 40
2541 (1st) Queen taking the salute as Colonel-in-Chief of the Grenadier Guards, 1983 50 55
2542 42p. Trumpeter of the Household Cavalry, 2004 65 70
2543 60p. Welsh Guardsman, 1990s 90 95
2544 68p. Queen riding side-saddle, 1972 . . . . . 1·10 1·20
2545 £1.12 Queen and Duke of Edinburgh in carriage, 2004 . . . . 1·60 1·70
MS2546 115 × 105 mm. Nos. 2540/5 5·00 5·25

REGIONAL ISSUES

I. CHANNEL ISLANDS.

Islands in the English Channel off N.W. coast of France. Occupied by German forces from June 1940 to May 1945, when separate issues for both islands were made.

C **1** Gathering Vraic (seaweed)

1948. 3rd Anniversary of Liberation.
C1 C **1** 1d. red 25 30
C2 – 2½d. blue 25 30
DESIGN: 2½d. Islanders gathering vraic.

II. GUERNSEY.

2

3

1958.
6 **2** 2½d. red 35 40
7p **3** 3d. lilac 15 20
9 4d. blue 10 20
10 4d. sepia 10 15
11 4d. red 20 25
12 5d. blue 20 30

For War Occupation issues and issues of independent postal administration from 1967 see **GUERNSEY**.

III. ISLE OF MAN.

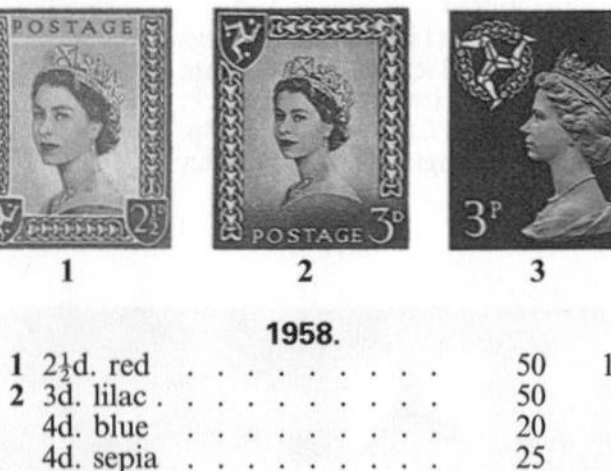

1 2 3

1958.
1 **1** 2½d. red . . . . 50 1·25
2 **2** 3d. lilac 50 20
3p 4d. blue 20 30
5 4d. sepia 25 40
6 4d. red 45 75
7 5d. blue 45 75

1971. Decimal Currency.
8 **3** 2½p. red 20 15
9 3p. blue 20 15
10 5p. violet 40 60
11 7½p. brown 40 75

For issues of independent postal administration from 1973 see **ISLE OF MAN**.

IV. JERSEY.

8

9

1958.
9 **8** 2½d. red 30 45
10p **9** 3d. lilac 15 15
11p 4d. blue 15 25
12 4d. sepia 15 25
13 4d. red 15 25
14 5d. blue 15 50

For War Occupation issues and issues of independent postal administration from 1969 see **JERSEY**.

V. ENGLAND

EN **1** Three Lions

2001.
EN1 EN **1** (2nd) green and silver 60 40
EN2 – (1st) brown and silver 75 60
EN3 – (E) green and silver . . 1·00 75
EN4 – 65p. lilac and silver . . 2·50 2·25
EN5 68p. lilac and silver . . 2·00 1·75
DESIGNS: No. EN2, Crowned Lion with Shield of St. George; EN3, Oak Tree; EN4/5, Tudor Rose.
Nos EN1/3 were initially sold at 19p., 27p. and 36p., the latter representing the basic European airmail rate.

2003. As Nos. EN1/3 and EN5 but with white borders.
EN 6 EN **1** (2nd) green and silver 65 50
EN 7 – (1st) brown and silver 75 90
EN 8 – (E) green and silver 1·00 90
EN 9 – 40p. green and silver 1·25 1·25
EN 10 – 68p. lilac and silver 2·00 1·75

VI. NORTHERN IRELAND.

N 1 N 2

N 3 N 4

1958.
NI 1 N **1** 3d. lilac 15 10
NI 2 4d. blue 15 15
NI 8 4d. sepia 15 15
NI 9 4d. red 20 20
NI10 5d. blue 20 20
NI 3 N **2** 6d. purple 20 25
NI 4 9d. green 30 70
NI 5 N **3** 1s.3d. green 30 70
NI 6 1s.6d. blue 30 70

1971.
NI12 N **4** 2½p. mauve 70 45
NI14 3p. blue 20 15
NI15 3½p. grey 20 25
NI17 4½p. blue 30 25
NI18 5p. violet . . . . . 1·00 1·00
NI19 5½p. violet 20 20
NI21 6½p. blue 20 20
NI22 7p. brown 35 25
NI23 7½p. brown . . . . . 1·25 1·25
NI24 8p. red 35 40
NI25 8½p. green 35 40
NI26 9p. violet 40 40
NI27 10p. brown 40 50
NI29 10½p. blue 40 50
NI30 11p. red 50 50
NI34 11½p. drab 85 85
NI31 12p. green 50 50
NI36 12½p. green 60 60
NI37Ea 13p. brown . . . . . 1·00 30
NI32 13½p. brown 60 70
NI38 14p. blue 75 75
NI33 15p. blue 60 70
NI41 15½p. violet 80 80
NI42 16p. brown . . . . . 1·00 1·00
NI43 17p. blue 90 95
NI45 18p. violet . . . . . 1·00 1·00
NI46 18p. grey . . . . . . 1·00 90
NI47 18p. green . . . . . 1·00 95
NI49 19p. red . . . . . . 1·00 1·00
NI69 19p. bistre 90 80
NI50 19½p. grey . . . . . 1·50 1·75
NI51 20p. black . . . . . 1·00 80
NI79 20p. green 75 70
NI52 20½p. blue . . . . . 4·50 3·50
NI53 22p. blue . . . . . . 4·25 1·10
NI54 22p. green . . . . . 1·10 1·10
NI55 22p. red . . . . . . 1·25 90
NI56 23p. green . . . . . 1·25 1·10
NI57 24p. red . . . . . . 1·25 1·25
NI58 24p. brown . . . . . 1·10 90
NI72 25p. red 75 75
NI60 26p. red . . . . . . 1·25 1·25
NI61 26p. drab . . . . . 1·75 1·75
NI81 26p. brown . . . . . 1·25 1·00
NI62 28p. blue . . . . . . 1·50 1·50
NI63 28p. grey . . . . . . 1·50 1·50
NI74 30p. grey . . . . . . 1·25 1·25
NI64 31p. purple . . . . . 1·75 2·00
NI65 32p. blue . . . . . . 1·75 1·75
NI66 34p. grey . . . . . . 1·75 1·75
NI67 37p. red . . . . . . 2·00 2·50
NI82 37p. mauve . . . . . 2·25 2·25
NI83 38p. blue . . . . . . 4·25 4·00
NI68 39p. mauve . . . . . 2·00 2·25
NI84 40p. blue . . . . . . 2·00 2·00
NI76 41p. brown . . . . . 2·25 1·75
NI85 63p. green . . . . . 4·75 5·00
NI86 64p. green . . . . . 6·00 6·00
NI87 65p. blue . . . . . . 2·75 3·00

2000. As Type N **4** but with "1st" face value.
NI88 (1st) bright red . . . . . . 1·90 1·90

N **6** Basalt Columns, Giant's Causeway

2001.
NI89 N **6** (2nd) multicoloured . . 50 35
NI90 – (1st) black, blue & yellow . . . . 1·00 50
NI91 – (E) black, blue & orange . . . . 1·25 1·25
NI92 – 65p. black, mauve & yell . . . . 2·75 2·75
NI93 68p. black, mauve and yellow . . . . 2·75 2·75
DESIGNS: NI90, Aerial view of patchwork fields; NI91, Linen pattern; NI92/3, Vase pattern from Belleck.
Nos. NI89, NI90 and NI91 were initially sold at 19p., 27p. and 36p., the latter representing the basic European airmail rate.

2003. As Nos. NI89/91 and NI93 but with white borders.
NI94 N **6** (2nd) multicoloured . . 50 35
NI95 – (1st) black, blue and yellow 60 50
NI96 – (E) black and blue . . . 75 65
NI97 – 40p. 40p black and blue 1·25 1·25
NI98 – 68p. black, mauve and yellow . . . . 2·75 2·75

VII. SCOTLAND.

S 1

S 2

S 3

S 4

1958.
S 7 S **1** 3d. lilac 10 15
S 8 4d. blue 10 15
S 9 4d. sepia 10 10
S10 4d. red 10 10

S11		5d. blue	20	10
S 3	S 2	6d. purple	20	15
S 4		9d. green	35	40
S 5	S 3	1s.3d. green	40	40
S 6		1s.6d. blue	45	50

1971. Decimal Currency.

S14	S 4	2½p. mauve	20	20
S16		3p. blue	15	15
S17		3½p. grey	20	25
S19		4½p. blue	30	25
S20		5p. violet	1·00	1·25
S21		5½p. violet	20	20
S23		6½p. blue	20	20
S24		7p. brown	30	30
S25		7½p. brown	1·25	1·25
S26		8p. red	45	40
S27		8½p. green	40	40
S28		9p. violet	40	40
S30		10p. brown	40	50
S31		10½p. blue	45	50
S32		11p. red	50	50
S36		11½p. drab	80	80
S33		12p. green	55	50
S38		12½p. green	60	70
S39		13p. brown	75	75
S34		13½p. brown	70	80
S54		14p. blue	60	70
S35		15p. blue	60	70
S41		15½p. violet	80	80
S42		16p. drab	80	85
S58		17p. blue	1·00	1·10
S44		18p. violet	80	80
S59		18p. grey	1·10	85
S60		18p. green	1·25	90
S62		19p. red	70	70
S81		19p. bistre	80	70
S45		19½p. grey	1·75	1·75
S64		20p. black	95	95
S90		20p. green	60	60
S46		20½p. blue	3·50	3·50
S47		22p. blue	1·00	1·00
S65		22p. green	1·25	1·50
S66		22p. red	1·25	90
S67		23p. green	1·25	1·10
S69		24p. red	1·25	1·25
S70		24p. brown	1·40	1·25
S84		25p. red	1·25	1·00
S49		26p. red	1·25	1·25
S73		26p. drab	1·25	1·25
S91		26p. brown	1·00	1·00
S74		28p. blue	1·25	1·25
S75		28p. grey	1·25	1·50
S86		30p. grey	1·25	1·25
S76		31p. purple	2·25	2·25
S77		32p. blue	1·75	2·25
S78		34p. grey	1·75	1·75
S79		37p. red	2·00	2·25
S92		37p. mauve	1·50	1·50
S80		39p. mauve	2·00	2·25
S88		41p. brown	1·75	2·00
S93		63p. green	4·00	4·00

S 5 Scottish Flag

1999.

S94	S 5	(2nd) blue, deep blue and silver	30	35
S95	–	(1st) multicoloured	40	45
S96	–	(E) lilac, deep lilac and silver	1·75	1·75
S97	–	64p. multicoloured	9·00	7·75
S98		65p. multicoloured	3·00	3·25
S99		68p. multicoloured	3·25	3·25

DESIGNS: No. S95, Scottish Lion; S96, Thistle; S97/9, Tartan.

Nos. S94, S95 and S96 were initially sold at 19p., 26p. and 30p., the latter representing the basic European airmail rate.

2000. As Type S **4** but with "1st" face value.

S108		(1st) bright red	3·00	3·25

2003. As Nos. S94/6 and S99 but with white borders.

S109	S 5	(2nd) blue, deep blue and silver	30	35
S110	–	(1st) multicoloured	45	50
S111	–	(E) lilac, deep lilac and silver	60	65
S112	–	40p. lilac, deep lilac and silver	1·25	1·25
S113	–	68p. multicoloured	1·10	1·20

2004. Scottish Parliament. Sheet 123×70 mm containing Nos. S109, S110×2 and S112×2.

MSS120	(2nd) deep blue; blue and silver; (1st)×2 yellow; deep red, red and silver; 40p.×2 lilac, deep lilac and silver	5·00	5·00

VIII. WALES.

W 1

W 2

W 3

W 4

1958.

W 1	W 1	3d. lilac	15	15
W 8		4d. blue	10	15
W 9		4d. sepia	15	15
W10		4d. red	15	15
W11		5d. blue	15	15
W 3	W 2	6d. purple	35	30
W 4		9d. green	40	35
W 5	W 3	1s.3d. green	40	40
W 6		1s.6d. blue	50	40

1971. Decimal Currency.

W13	W 4	2½p. mauve	20	20
W14		3p. blue	25	20
W16		3½p. grey	20	30
W18		4½p. blue	30	30
W19		5p. violet	1·25	1·25
W20		5½p. violet	25	30
W22		6½p. blue	20	20
W23		7p. brown	25	25
W24		7½p. brown	1·75	1·75
W25		8p. red	30	35
W26		8½p. green	30	35
W27		9p. violet	40	40
W29		10p. brown	40	40
W30		10½p. blue	45	45
W31		11p. red	45	45
W35		11½p. drab	90	80
W32		12p. green	50	50
W37		12½p. green	70	70
W38		13p. brown	60	60
W33		13½p. brown	60	70
W40		14p. blue	70	70
W34		15p. blue	60	70
W42		15½p. violet	75	75
W43		16p. drab	1·75	1·75
W44		17p. blue	70	80
W46		18p. violet	1·00	95
W47		18p. grey	95	90
W48		18p. green	75	75
W50		19p. red	1·00	80
W70		19p. bistre	80	70
W51		19½p. grey	1·75	2·00
W52		20p. black	90	90
W72		20p. green	1·75	2·00
W53		20½p. blue	3·50	3·50
W54		22p. blue	1·10	1·10
W55		22p. green	95	1·10
W56		22p. red	1·00	1·10
W57		23p. green	1·00	1·25
W58		24p. red	1·25	1·25
W59		24p. brown	75	75
W73		25p. red	1·25	1·00
W61		26p. red	1·10	1·10
W62		26p. drab	1·75	1·75
W74		26p. brown	2·00	2·25
W63		28p. blue	1·50	1·50
W64		28p. grey	1·50	1·50
W75		30p. grey	1·25	1·25
W65		31p. purple	1·75	1·75
W66		32p. blue	1·75	1·75
W67		34p. grey	1·75	1·75
W68		37p. red	2·25	2·25
W76		37p. mauve	2·75	3·00
W69		39p. mauve	2·25	2·25
W77		41p. brown	2·00	2·00
W78		63p. green	4·50	4·75

W 5 Without "p"

1997.

W79	W 5	20p. green	80	80
W80		26p. brown	1·00	1·00
W81		37p. mauve	2·75	2·75
W82		63p. green	4·00	4·50

W 6 Leek

1999.

W83	W 6	(2nd) brown, orange and black	60	50
W84	–	(1st) multicoloured	1·00	60
W85	–	(E) multicoloured	1·50	1·50
W86	–	64p. multicoloured	7·00	7·75
W87		65p. multicoloured	3·00	3·25
W88		68p. multicoloured	2·75	2·75

DESIGNS: No. W84, Welsh Dragon; W85, Daffodil; W86/8, Prince of Wales Feathers.

Nos. W83, W84 and W85 were initially sold at 19p., 26p. and 30p., the latter representing the basic European airmail rate.

2000. As Type W **5** but with "1af/st" face value.

W97		(1st) bright red	3·00	2·75

2003. As Nos. W83, W84/5 and W88, but with white borders.

W 98	W 6	(2nd) orange, brown and black	30	35
W 99	–	(1st) multicoloured	45	50
W100	–	(E) blue, deep blue and black	60	65
W101	–	40p. blue, deep blue and black	1·25	1·25
W102	–	68p. multicoloured	1·10	1·20

OFFICIAL STAMPS
(for Government Departments)

ADMIRALTY

Overprinted **ADMIRALTY OFFICIAL**.

1903. Stamps of King Edward VII.

O101	83	½d. turquoise	15·00	12·00
O102	–	1d. red	10·00	6·00
O103	–	1½d. purple and green	£110	70·00
O104	–	2d. green and red	£185	85·00
O105	83	2½d. blue	£200	70·00
O106	–	3d. purple on yellow	£185	70·00

ARMY
Overprinted **ARMY OFFICIAL**.

1896. Stamps of Queen Victoria.

O41	71	½d. red	3·50	1·50
O42		½d. green	4·00	7·00
O43	57	1d. lilac	3·50	2·50
O44	74	2½d. purple on blue	30·00	20·00
O45	79	6d. purple on red	50·00	30·00

1902. Stamps of King Edward VII.

O48	83	½d. turquoise	5·00	2·00
O49		1d. red	5·00	2·00
O50		6d. purple	£150	70·00

BOARD OF EDUCATION
Overprinted **BOARD OF EDUCATION**.

1902. Stamps of Queen Victoria.

O81	78	5d. purple on blue	£1000	£225
O82	82	1s. green and red	£3000	£1800

1902. Stamps of King Edward VII.

O83	83	½d. turquoise	£100	35·00
O84		1d. red	£100	35·00
O85		2½d. blue	£1500	£110
O86	–	5d. purple and blue	£6000	£2000
O87	–	1s. green and red	£60000	

GOVERNMENT PARCELS
Overprinted **GOVT. PARCELS**.

1883. Stamps of Queen Victoria.

O61	62	1½d. purple	£300	60·00
O62	–	6d. green (No. 194)	£1500	£600
O63	–	9d. green (No. 195)	£1250	£500
O64	25	1s. brown (No. 163)	£700	£175

1887. Stamps of Queen Victoria.

O69	57	1d. lilac	70·00	15·00
O65	72	1½d. purple and green	70·00	7·00
O70	73	2d. green and red	£140	20·00
O71	77	4½d. green and red	£225	£175
O66	79	6d. purple on red	£140	25·00
O67	80	9d. purple and blue	£200	35·00
O68	82	1s. green	£350	£140
O72		1s. green and red	£350	£125

1902. Stamps of King Edward VII.

O74	83	1d. red	30·00	12·00
O75	–	2d. green and red	£125	30·00
O76	83	6d. purple	£225	60·00
O77	–	9d. purple and blue	£450	£100
O78	–	1s. green and red	£750	£175

INLAND REVENUE
Overprinted **I.R. OFFICIAL**.

1882. Stamps of Queen Victoria.

O 1	52	½d. green	60·00	20·00
O 5		½d. blue	60·00	22·00
O 3	57	1d. lilac	4·00	2·00
O 6	–	2½d. purple (No.3 190)	£300	£100
O 4	34	6d. grey (No. 161)	£325	80·00
O 7	–	1s. green (No. 196)	£3500	£900
O 9	–	5s. red (No. 181)	£3000	£1000
O10	–	10s. blue (No. 183)	£4250	£1250
O11	61	£1 brown	£32000	£16000

1888.

O13	71	½d. red	8·00	3·00
O17		½d. green	10·00	6·00
O14	74	2½d. purple on blue	£100	10·00
O18	79	6d. purple on red	£300	80·00
O15	89	1s. green	£450	£175
O19		1s. green and red	£2000	£550
O16	61	£1 green	£6500	£1500

1902. Stamps of King Edward VII.

O20	83	½d. turquoise	22·00	3·00
O21		1d. red	15·00	2·00
O22		2½d. blue	£650	£175
O23		6d. purple	£120000	£70000
O24	–	1s. green and red	£1900	£450
O25	–	5s. red	£9000	£5000
O26	–	10s. blue	£45000	£22000
O27	–	£1 green	£35000	£16000

OFFICE OF WORKS
Overprinted **O.W. OFFICIAL**.

1896. Stamps of Queen Victoria.

O31	71	½d. red	£200	£100
O32		½d. green	£300	£150
O33	57	1d. lilac	£350	£100
O34	78	5d. purple and blue	£1800	£600
O35	81	10d. purple and red	£2800	£850

1902. Stamps of King Edward VII.

O36	83	½d. turquoise	£500	£150
O37	–	1d. red	£500	£150
O38	–	2d. green and red	£1300	£350
O39	83	2½d. blue	£1600	£500
O40	–	10d. purple and red	£20000	£4750

ROYAL HOUSEHOLD
Overprinted **R.H. OFFICIAL**.

1902. Stamps of King Edward VII.

O91	83	½d. turquoise	£300	£180
O92		1d. red	£250	£150

POSTAGE DUE STAMPS

D 1

D 4

1914.

D 1	D 1	½d. green	50	25
D56		½d. orange	15	1·25
D 2		1d. red	50	25
D57		1d. blue	15	50
D 3		1½d. brown	48·00	20·00
D58		1½d. green	90	3·50
D69		2d. black	75	1·00
D60		3d. violet	30	30
D15		4d. green	15·00	4·25
D61		4d. blue	30	30
D62		5d. brown	45	60
D63		6d. purple	50	30
D76		8d. red	1·25	1·00
D17		1s. blue	8·50	50
D64		1s. brown	90	30
D65		2s.6d. purple on yellow	3·00	50
D66		5s. red on yellow	8·25	1·00
D67		10s. blue on yellow	11·50	5·75
D68		£1 black on yellow	45·00	8·25

On the 2s.6d. to £1 the inscription reads "TO PAY".

1970. Decimal Currency.

D77	–	½p. blue	15	2·50
D78	–	1p. purple	15	15
D79	–	2p. green	20	15
D80	–	3p. blue	20	15
D81	–	4p. brown	25	15
D82	–	5p. violet	25	15
D83	–	7p. brown	35	1·00
D84	D 4	10p. red	30	30
D85		11p. green	50	1·00
D86		20p. brown	60	25
D87		50p. blue	2·00	1·25
D88		£1 black	4·00	1·00
D89		£5 yellow and black	36·00	1·50

DESIGN: ½p. to 7p. similar to Type D **4**, but with "TO PAY" reading vertically upwards at the left.

D 5

D 7

1982.

D 90	D 5	1p. red	10	30
D 91		2p. blue	30	30
D 92		3p. mauve	15	30
D 93		4p. blue	15	25
D 94		5p. brown	20	25
D 95	–	10p. brown	30	40
D 96	–	20p. green	50	60
D 97	–	25p. blue	80	90
D 98	–	50p. black	1·75	1·75
D 99	–	£1 red	3·25	1·25
D100	–	£2 blue	7·00	4·25
D101	–	£5 orange	14·00	2·25

DESIGNS: 10p. to £5, as Type D **5** but with "TO PAY" horizontal.

1994.

D102	D 7	1p. red, yellow and black	10	75
D103		2p. mauve, purple blk	10	75
D104		5p. yellow, brown blk	15	50
D105		10p. yellow, green blk	30	75
D106		20p. green, violet blk	75	1·50
D107		25p. mauve, red black	1·50	2·00
D108		£1 violet, mauve black	7·00	10·00
D109		£1.20 blue, green blk	8·00	12·00
D110		£5 dp green, green blk	30·00	20·00

GREAT COMORO Pt. 6

A French island north west of Madagascar. From 1914 to 1950 the stamps of Madagascar were used. In 1950 it became part of the Comoro Islands.

100 centimes = 1 franc.

1897. "Tablet" key-type inscr "GRANDE COMORE" in red or blue.

1	D	1c. black on blue	1·00	1·25
2		2c. brown on buff	75	1·40
3		4c. brown on grey	1·75	2·25
4		5c. green on light green	2·75	1·40
5		10c. black on lilac	3·25	4·00
14		10c. red	10·50	13·00
6		15c. blue	19·00	7·25
15		15c. grey	11·50	15·00
7		20c. red on green	8·00	13·00
8		25c. black on pink	4·00	6·00
16		25c. blue	12·00	13·00
9		30c. brown on drab	10·00	13·50

17 35c. black on yellow 17·00 19·00
10 40c. red on yellow 15·00 15·00
18 45c. black on green 60·00 60·00
11 50c. red on pink 18·00 19·00
19 50c. brown on blue 32·00 35·00
12 75c. brown on blue 35·00 38·00
13 1f. green 15·00 22·00

1912. Surch.
20 D 05 on 2c. brown on buff 45 35
21 05 on 4c. brown on grey 40 35
22 05 on 15c. blue 1·00 85
23 05 on 20c. red on green 15 2·50
24 05 on 25c. black on pink 60 85
25 05 on 30c. brown on drab 50 85
26 10 on 40c. red on yellow 95 1·75
27 10 on 45c. black on green 1·25 1·75
28 10 on 50c. red on pink 20 85
29 10 on 75c. brown on orange 1·75 3·25

GREECE Pt. 3

A country in the S.E. of Europe, under Turkish rule till 1830, when it became a kingdom. A republic was established from 1924 to 1935 when the monarchy was restored. The country was under German occupation from April 1941 to October 1944. The monarchy was once again abolished during 1973 and a republic set up.

1861. 100 lepta = 1 drachma.
2002. 100 cents = 1 euro.

1 Hermes **2**

1861. Imperf or perf.
62 1 1l. brown 4·00 3·25
17 2l. buff 8·75 20·00
55 5l. green 12·50 2·75
19b 10l. orange on blue £190 14·00
56 10l. orange 12·50 2·75
20 20l. blue £170 4·75
59a 20l. red 2·50 2·20
53 30l. brown 37·00 4·75
60 30l. blue £120 7·50
28 40l. mauve on blue £250 13·00
37 40l. orange on green £425 37·00
43d 40l. bistre on blue 14·00 27·00
43f 40l. green on blue 14·00 27·00
50 40l. buff 14·00 35·00
61 40l. mauve 35·00 9·75
52 60l. green on green 17·00 50·00
54 60l. green £300 30·00
22 80l. red 50·00 15·00

1886. Imperf.
73 2 1l. brown 85 1·10
86 2l. buff 1·60 1·60
87b 5l. green 3·50 1·60
76 10l. orange 5·75 2·50
89c 20l. red 3·75 75
90d 25l. blue 47·00 1·60
91 25l. purple 4·25 1·50
79 40l. purple 50·00 21·00
93 40l. blue 6·00 1·70
80 50l. green 2·50 1·70
81 1d. grey 44·00 1·80

1886. Perf.
100 2 1l. brown 1·70 1·20
96 2l. buff 1·10 1·10
102 5l. green 4·75 1·50
103b 10l. orange 9·00 1·40
104 20l. red 2·50 45
105d 25l. blue 44·00 1·80
106a 25l. purple 4·25 1·30
107 40l. purple 60·00 25·00
108 40l. blue 10·00 2·50
83 50l. green 10·00 3·75
84 1d. grey 85·00 5·25

3 Wrestlers **4** Discus thrower

5 Vase depicting Pallas Athene **6** Quadriga of Chariot driving

1896. 1st International Olympic Games. Perf.
110 3 1l. yellow 1·20 50
111 2l. red 1·30 50
112 4 5l. mauve 3·25 90
113 10l. grey 3·50 1·00
114 5 20l. brown 13·50 45
115 6 25l. red 18·00 80
116 5 40l. violet 9·00 3·50
117 6 60l. black 25·00 15·00
118 – 1d. blue 60·00 11·00
119 – 2d. olive £150 41·00
120 – 5d. green £375 £180
121 – 10d. brown £400 £225
DESIGNS—As Type 6—HORIZ: 1d. Acropolis and Stadium; 10d. Acropolis with Parthenon. VERT: 2d. "Hermes" (after statue by Praxiteles); 5d. "Victory" (after statue by Paeonius).

1900. Surch. Imperf.
122 2 20l. on 25l. blue 2·50 1·00
130 1 30l. on 40l. purple 5·00 4·00
131 40l. on 2l. buff 6·50 5·50
132 50l. on 40l. buff 5·00 5·00
123 2 1d. on 40l. purple 12·50 7·25
124 2d. on 40l. purple £170
133 1 3d. on 10l. orange 44·00 34·00
134 5d. on 40l. purple on blue £110 £120

1900. Surch. Perf.
125 2 20l. on 25l. blue 2·50 2·75
135 1 30l. on 40l. purple 7·50 6·50
136 40l. on 2l. buff 9·25 4·75
137 50l. on 40l. buff 8·00 5·75
126 2 1d. on 40l. purple 17·00 8·50
127a 2d. on 40l. purple 8·50 10·00
138 1 3d. on 10l. orange 47·00 47·00
139 5d. on 40l. purple on blue £120 £120

1900. Surch **AM** and value.
140 2 25l. on 40l. purple (No. 79) 4·25 7·25
142 25l. on 40l. purple (No. 107) 8·50 9·50
141 50l. on 25l. blue (No. 90d) 20·00 20·00
143 50l. on 25l. blue (No. 105) 44·00 25·00
144 1 1d. on 40l. brown on blue (No. 43d) 85·00 £100
146 1d. on 40l. brown on blue (Perf) £120 £140
145 2d. on 5l. green (No. 55) 12·50 16·00
147 2d. on 5l. green (No. 102) 16·00 15·00

1900. Olympic Games stamps surch **AM** and value.
148 – 5l. on 1d. blue 8·25 8·00
149 5 25l. on 40l. violet 65·00 55·00
150 – 50l. on 2d. olive 75·00 55·00
151 – 1d. on 5d. green £275 £150
152 – 2d. on 10d. brown 70·00 70·00

15 **16** Hermes after the "Mercury" of Giovanni da Bologna **17**

1901.
167 15 1l. brown 60 25
168 2l. grey 60 25
169 3l. orange 70 35
170 16 5l. green 70 25
171 10l. red 2·10 30
172 15 20l. mauve 4·25 25
173 16 25l. blue 5·00 30
160 15 30l. purple 8·75 1·50
175 40l. brown 24·00 2·50
176 50l. lake 17·00 1·70
163 17 1d. black 44·00 2·00
164 2d. bronze 9·25 7·50
165 3d. silver 8·50 8·00
166 5d. gold 8·50 10·50

19 Head of Hermes **20** Athlete throwing Discus **21** Jumper

23 Atlas offering the Apples of Hesperides to Hercules

1902.
178 19 5l. orange 2·10 1·20
179 25l. green 25·00 4·00
180 50l. blue 25·00 4·00
181 1d. red 25·00 10·00
182 2d. brown 44·00 30·00

1906. Olympic Games. Dated "1906".
183 20 1l. brown 1·10 60
184 2l. black 1·10 60
185 21 3l. orange 1·50 60
186 5l. green 2·20 50
187 – 10l. red 3·00 60
188 23 20l. red 9·50 65
189 – 25l. blue 18·00 1·10
190 – 30l. purple 15·00 4·25
191 – 40l. brown 7·25 3·50
192 23 50l. purple 18·00 4·25
193 – 1d. black 50·00 12·00
194 – 2d. red 75·00 25·00
195 – 3d. yellow £110 95·00
196 – 5d. blue £110 95·00
DESIGNS—As Type **20**: 10l. Victory; 20l. Wrestlers; 40l. "Daemon" or God of the Games. As Type **23**: 25l. Hercules and Antaeus; 1d., 2d., 3d. Race, Ancient Greeks; 5d. Olympic Offerings.

29 Head of Hermes **30** Iris **31** Hermes

32 Hermes and Arcas (**34**) "Greek Administration"

1911. Roul.
213 29 1l. green 20 20
214 30 2l. red 20 20
215 29 3l. red 30 20
216 31 5l. green 55 15
217 29 10l. red 35 15
218 30 15l. blue 35 20
219 20l. lilac 25 40
220 25l. blue 2·50 40
221 31 30l. red 1·00 55
222 30 40l. blue 3·25 1·60
223 31 50l. purple 3·50 90
224 80l. purple 5·50 70
225 32 1d. blue 4·75 25
226 2d. red 5·50 40
227 3d. red (20 × 26½ mm) 10·00 50
209 3d. red (20¾ × 25½ mm) 22·00 90
228 5d. blue (20 × 26½ mm) 16·00 50
210 5d. blue (20¾ × 25½ mm) 27·00 4·25
229 10b. blue (20 × 26½ mm) 11·50 75
211b 10d. blue (20¾ × 25½ mm) 34·00 25·00
212 – 25d. blue 50·00 33·00
230 – 25d. slate 14·50 2·75
The 25d. is as Type 29 but larger (24 × 31 mm).

1912. Optd with T **34**.
232A 29 1l. green 80 80
233 30 2l. red 80 70
234 29 3l. red 70 80
249B 31 5l. green 80 80
236A 29 10l. red 1·70 1·30
237A 30 20l. lilac 2·50 2·20
231 15 20l. mauve 2·20 2·50
238A 30 25l. blue 2·50 2·50
239A 31 30l. red 2·50 2·50
240B 30 40l. blue 2·75 4·00
241A 31 50l. purple 4·00 4·00
242A 32 1d. blue 10·00 2·50
243A 2d. red 38·00 21·00
244B 3d. red 30·00 21·00
245A 5d. blue 20·00 18·00
246B 10d. blue 34·00 22·00
247d – 25d. blue (No. 212) 41·00 42·00

35 Vision of Constantine over Athens and Salamis **36** Victorious Eagle over Mt. Olympus

1913. Occupation of Macedonia, Epirus and the Aegean Islands. Rouletted.
252 35 1l. brown 45 35
253 36 2l. red 45 35
254 3l. orange 35 40
255 35 5l. green 1·00 35
256 10l. red 7·50 25
257 20l. violet 20·00 2·75
258 36 25l. blue 2·50 60
259 35 30l. green 44·00 1·90
260 36 40l. blue 11·50 4·25
261 35 50l. blue 4·25 2·50
262 36 1d. purple 6·75 2·75
263 35 2d. brown 41·00 6·50
264 36 3d. blue £150 21·00
265 35 5d. grey £120 29·00
266 36 10d. red £120 £170
267 35 25d. black £120 £170

37 Hoisting the Greek Flag at Suda Bay, 1 May 1913 (**38**)

1913. Union of Crete with Greece.
268 37 25l. black and blue 6·50 3·25

1916. Stamps of 1911 optd with T **38**.
269 29 1l. green 20 20
270 30 2l. red 30 25
271 29 3l. red 35 35
272 31 5l. green 40 30
273 29 10l. red 85 25
274 30 20l. lilac 1·20 25
275 25l. blue 1·20 25
280 31 30l. red 1·50 85
277 30 40l. blue 10·00 2·75
278 31 50l. purple 31·00 1·30
281 32 1d. blue 29·00 1·70
282 2d. red 19·00 2·30
283 3d. red 12·00 2·50
284 5d. blue 40·00 6·00
285 10d. blue 17·00 15·00

39 Iris (**46**) "Revolution, 1922"

1917. Perf or imperf.
286 39 1l. green 30 35
287 5l. green 30 30
288 10l. red 60 25
289 25l. blue 70 45
290 50l. purple 5·50 1·70
291 1d. blue 2·50 75
292 2d. red 4·00 1·20
293 3d. red 4·25 3·50
294 5d. blue 8·00 3·25
295 10d. blue 48·00 15·00
296 25d. grey 80·00 75·00

1923. Revolution of 1922. Stamps of 1913, surch as T **46**.
340 36 5l. on 3l. orange 20 25
341 35 10l. on 20l. violet 1·00 1·10
342 36 10l. on 25l. blue 80 1·20
343 35 10l. on 30l. green 85 1·20
344 36 10l. on 40l. blue 1·10 1·70
345 35 50l. on 50l. blue 55 60
346 2d. on 2d. brown 45·00 60·00
347 36 3d. on 3d. blue 5·00 5·00
348 35 5d. on 5d. grey 5·00 5·00
349 36 10d. on 1d. purple 10·00 10·00
350 10d. on 10d. red £1400

1923. Stamps of 1916 surch as T **46**.
351 39 5l. on 10l. red 20 20
352 50l. on 50l. purple 25 30
353 1d. on 1d. blue 30 35
354 2d. on 2d. red 45 55
355 3d. on 3d. red 1·70 1·70
356 5d. on 5d. blue 2·50 25
357 25d. on 25d. blue 25·00 25·00

1923. Cretan stamps of 1900 surch as T **46**.
358 1 5l. on 1l. brown 32·00
359 3 10l. on 10l. red 20 20
361 10l. on 25l. blue 25 25
362 1 50l. on 50l. lilac 35 85
363 50l. on 50l. blue 7·00 8·25
364 4 50l. on 1d. violet 2·50 2·75
365 – 50l. on 5d. (No. 19) 25·00

1923. Cretan stamps of 1905 surch as T **46**.
366 – 10l. on 20l. (No. 24) 90·00 85·00
367 – 10l. on 25l. (No. 25) 25 25
368 – 50l. on 50l. (No. 26) 35 60
369 16 50l. on 1d. (No. 27) 3·00 5·00
370 – 3d. on 3d. (No. 28) 14·00 16·00
371 – 5d. on 5d. (No. 29) 9·25 12·00

1923. Cretan stamps of 1907/8 surch as T **46**.
372 21 10l. on 10l. red 25 25
373 19 10l. on 25l. black and blue 1·10 1·00
374 50l. on 1d. (No. 31) 4·00 6·00
No. 372 is as Crete No. 36 but without "HELLAS" optd. No. 377 is the optd stamp.

1923. Optd stamps of Crete surch as T **46**.
375 1 5l. on 1l. brown (No. 32) 20 20
376 – 5l. on 5l. green (No. 34) 25 25
377 21 10l. on 10l. red (No. 36) 25 25
378 – 10l. on 20l. (No. 37) 25 25
379 – 10l. on 25l. (No. 30) 30 35
381 – 50l. on 50l. (No. 39) 45 45
382 16 50l. on 1d. (No. 40) 5·00 6·75
384 – 3d. on 3d. (No. 42) 10·00 16·00
385 – 5d. on 5d. (No. 43) £200 £250

1923. Postage Due stamps of Crete of 1900 surch as T **38**.
386 D 8 5l. on 5l. red 20 25
387 5l. on 10l. red 20 25
388 10l. on 20l. red 10·50 10·00
389 10l. on 40l. red 30 85
390 50l. on 50l. red 35 80
391 50l. on 1d. red 50 1·20
392 50l. on 1d. on 1d. red 8·50 9·50
393 2d. on 2d. red 85 1·10

1923. Postage Due stamps of Crete of 1908 with opt, surch as T **46**.
397 D 8 5l. on 5l. red 20 20
398 5l. on 10l. red 20 20
399 10l. on 20l. red 35 30
400 50l. on 50l. red 60 60
401 50l. on 1d. red 2·40 2·75
402 2d. on 2d. red 5·50 5·50

47 Lord Byron

49 Grave of Marco Botzaris

1924. Byron Centenary.
403 **47** 80l. blue 70 25
404 – 2d. black and violet . . . 1·80 80
DESIGN—HORIZ: (45 × 30 mm): 2d. Byron at Missolonghi.

1926. Centenary of Fall of Missolonghi. Roul.
405 **49** 25l. mauve 80 35

50 Savoia Marchetti S-55C Flying Boat over Fortress

1926. Air. Each showing Savoia Marchetti S-55C flying boat. Multicoloured.
406 2d. Type **50** . . . . 2·00 1·10
407 3d. Acropolis . . . . 12·50 8·25
408 5d. Map of Greece and Mediterranean . . . . . . 2·50 1·10
409 10d. Colonnade . . . . . . 13·50 8·75

51 Corinth Canal

52 Dodecanese Costume

53 Temple of Theseus, Athens

54 Acropolis

1927.
410 **51** 5l. green 20 10
411 **52** 10l. red 35 10
412 – 20l. violet 40 10
413 – 25l. green 45 10
414 – 40l. green 60 10
415 **51** 50l. violet . . . . 1·60 10
416 80l. black and blue . . . 1·30 25
417 **53** 1d. brown and blue . . . 1·60 10
418b – 2d. black and green . . . 4·75 25
419d – 3d. black and violet . . . 5·25 20
419e – 4d. brown . . . . 17·00 75
420 – 5d. black and orange . . 13·50 90
421 – 10d. black and red . . . 32·00 5·00
422 – 15d. black and green . . 47·00 8·00
423a **54** 25d. black and green . . 31·00 9·75
DESIGNS—As Type **52**: 20l. Macedonian costume; 25l. Monastery of Simon Peter, Athos; 40l. White Tower, Salonika. As Type **53**: 2d. Acropolis; 3d. Cruiser "Averoff"; 4d. Mistra Cathedral. As Type **54**: 5, 15d. The Academy of Sciences, Athens; 10d. Temple of Theseus.

55 General Favier and Acropolis

1927. Centenary of Liberation of Athens.
424 **55** 1d. red 55 20
425 3d. blue . . . . 3·00 50
426 6d. green . . . . 15·00 8·50

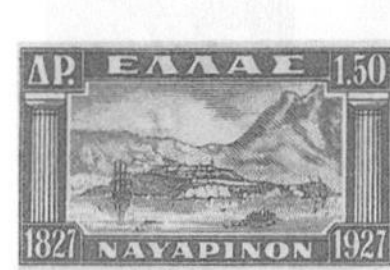
56 Navarino Bay and Pylos

58 Sir Edward Codrington

1927. Centenary of Battle of Navarino.
427 **56** 1d.50 green . . . . 1·75 30
428 – 4d. blue . . . . 11·50 1·10
429 **58** 5d. black and brown (A) 7·00 3·50
430 – 5d. black and brown (B) 37·00 7·75
431 – 5d. black and blue . . . . 36·00 6·25
432 – 5d. black and red . . . . 17·50 6·75
DESIGNS: 4d. Battle of Navarino; 5d. (No. 429) "Sir Codrington" (A); 5d. (No. 430) "Sir Edward Codrington" (B); 5d. (No. 431) De Rigny; 5d. (No. 432) Van der Heyden.

59 Righas Ferreo

64 Monastery of Arkadi, Crete, and Abbott Gabriel

1930. Centenary of Independence.
433 **59** 10l. brown 20 10
434 – 20l. black 20 15
435 – 40l. green 25 20
436 – 50l. red 30 25
437 – 50l. blue 30 25
438 – 1d. red 30 25
439 – 1d. orange 30 25
440 – 1d.50 blue 65 15
441 – 1d.50 red 60 20
442 – 2d. orange 70 25
443 – 3d. brown . . . . 1·30 45
444 – 4d. blue . . . . 5·50 45
445 – 5d. purple . . . . 2·20 95
446 – 10d. black . . . . 12·00 4·50
447 – 15d. green . . . . 16·00 7·25
448 – 20d. blue . . . . 17·00 10·00
449 – 25d. black . . . . 15·00 12·00
450 – 50d. brown . . . . 30·00 42·00
DESIGNS as Type **59**: 20l. Patriarch Gregory V; 40l. A. Ypsilanti; 50l. (No. 436) L. Bouboulina; 50l. (437), Ath. Diakos; 1d. (438), Th. Colocotroni; 1d. (439), C. Kanaris; 1d.50, (440), Karaiskakes; 1d.50 (441), M. Botzaris; 2d. A. Miaoulis; 3d. L. Kondouriotis; 5d. Capo d'Istria; 10d. P. Mavromichalis; 15d. Solomos; 20d. Corais. (27½ × 40 mm): 4d. Map of Greece. (27 × 44 mm): 50d. Sortie from Missolonghi. (43 × 28½ mm): 25d. Declaration of Independence.

1930.
451 **64** 8d. violet . . . . 26·00 65

1932. Stamps of 1927 surch.
452 – 1d.50l. on 5d. black and blue (No. 431) . . . . . 2·75 20
453 – 1d.50l. on 5d. black and red (No. 432) . . . . . 2·75 20
454 **55** 2d. on 3d. blue . . . . . 3·25 35
455 **58** 2d. on 5d. black and brown (No. 429) . . . . 2·75 95
456 – 2d. on 5d. black and brown (No. 430) . . . . 8·25 25
457 **55** 4d. on 6d. green . . . . . 3·25 80

66 "Graf Zeppelin" and Acropolis

1933. Air.
458 **66** 30d. red . . . . 19·00 9·75
459 100d. blue . . . . 85·00 41·00
460 120d. brown . . . . 80·00 65·00

67 Swinging the Propeller

68 "Flight"

1933. Air. Aeroespresso Company issue.
461 **67** 50l. orange and green . . . 50 40
462 – 1d. orange and blue . . . 80 50
463 – 3d. brown and purple . . . 1·10 85
464 **68** 5d. blue and orange . . . 8·50 7·50
465 – 10d. black and red . . . . 1·80 2·20
466 – 20d. green and black . . . 12·00 7·75
467 – 50d. blue and brown . . . 80·00 60·00
DESIGNS—HORIZ: 1d. Temple of Neptune, Corinth; 3d. Marina Fiat MF.5 flying boat over Hermoupolis; 10d. Map of Italy–Greece–Rhodes–Turkey air routes. VERT: 20d. Hermes and Marina Fiat MF.5 flying boat; 50d. Woman and Marina Fiat MF.5 flying boat.

71 Greece

1933. Air. Government issue.
468 **71** 50l. green 55 45
469 1d. red . . . . 1·40 60
470 – 2d. violet . . . . 1·60 1·10
471 – 5d. blue . . . . 6·75 4·75
472 – 10d. red . . . . 19·00 11·50
473 **71** 25d. blue . . . . 35·00 19·00
474 – 50d. brown . . . . 50·00 45·00
DESIGNS—VERT: 2, 10d. Ikarian Islands. HORIZ: 5, 50d. Junkers G.24 airplane and Acropolis.

74 Admiral Kondouriotis and Cruiser "Averoff"

75 "Greece"

1933.
475 **74** 50d. blue and black . . . 80·00 3·00
476 **75** 75d. purple and black . . . £120 £120
477 – 100d. green and brown . . £475 30·00
DESIGN—VERT: 100d. Statue (Youth of Marathon).

78 Athens Stadium, Entrance

1934.
479 **78** 8d. blue . . . . 85·00 90

79 Sun Chariot

83 King Constantine

1935. Air. Mythological designs.
488a **79** 1d. red . . . . 1·00 3·00
488b – 2d. blue . . . . 2·00 55
488c – 5d. mauve . . . . 20·00 4·25
488d – 7d. blue . . . . 30·00 10·00
484 – 10d. brown . . . . 8·25 2·50
488e – 10d. orange . . . . . . 4·00 3·75
485 – 25d. red . . . . 9·00 10·50
486 – 30d. green . . . . 1·40 2·75
487 – 50d. mauve . . . . 5·50 9·25
488 – 100d. brown . . . . . . 3·00 3·75
DESIGNS—HORIZ: 2d. Iris; 30d. Triptolemus; 100d. Phrixus and Helle. VERT: 5d. Daedalus and Icarus; 7d. Minerva; 10d. Hermes; 25d. Zeus and Ganymede; 50d. Bellerophon on Pegasus.

(81)

(82)

1935. Restoration of Greek Monarchy. Surch with T **81** (489/91) or **82** (492/3).
489 D **20** 50l. on 40l. blue 35 25
490 3d. on 3d. red 85 80
492 – 5d. on 100d. green and brown (No. 477) . . . 2·00 1·00
493 **75** 15d. on 75d. pur & blk 8·75 5·50

1936. Re-interment of King Constantine and Queen Sophia.
494 **83** 3d. brown and black . . . 50 20
495 8d. blue and black . . . . 1·70 1·30

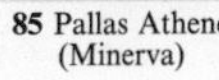
85 Pallas Athene (Minerva)

86 Bull-leaping

89 King George II

89a Statue of King Constantine

1937. Cent of Athens University.
496 **85** 3d. brown 75 35

1937.
497 **86** 5l. blue and brown . . . 10 15
498 – 10l. brown and blue . . . 10 10
499 – 20l. green and black . . . 10 10
500 – 40l. black and green . . . 10 10
501 – 50l. black and brown . . 10 10
502 – 80l. brown and violet . . 10 10
503 **89** 1d. green 20 10
515 **89a** 1d.50 green 55 15
504 – 2d. blue 20 15
505 **89** 3d. brown 35 10
506 – 5d. red 20 15
507 – 6d. olive 20 20
508 – 7d. brown 80 65
509 **89** 8d. blue . . . . 1·20 35
510 – 10d. brown 20 15
511 – 15d. green 25 25
512 – 25d. blue 20 30
516 **89a** 30d. red . . . . 3·50 3·50
513 **89** 100d. red . . . . 13·50 11·00
DESIGNS—(Size as Type **89a**). VERT: 10l. Court Lady of Tiryns; 20l. Zeus and Thunderbolt; 80l. Venus of Milo; 25d. "Glory" of Psara. HORIZ: 40l. Amphictyonic Coin; 50l. Chairing Diagoras of Rhodes; 2d. Battle of Salamis; 5d. Panathenaic chariot; 6d. Alexander the Great at Battle of Issus; 7d. St. Paul on Mt. Areopagus; 10d. Temple of St. Demetrius, Salonica; 15d. Leo III (the Isaurian) destroying Saracens.

93 Prince Paul and Princess Frederika Louise

1938. Royal Wedding.
517 **93** 1d. green 20 20
518 3d. brown 60 20
519 8d. blue . . . . 75 1·10

94 Arms of Greece, Rumania, Turkey and Yugoslavia

1938. Balkan Entente.
520 **94** 6d. blue . . . . 6·25 2·20

1938. Air. Postage Due stamp optd with Junkers G.24 airplane. Perf or rouletted.
521 D **20** 50l. brown 20 25

96 Arms of Ionian Islands

97 Corfu Bay and Citadel

1939. 75th Anniv of Cession of Ionian Islands.
523 **96** 1d. blue . . . . 2·10 45
524 **97** 4d. green . . . . 5·25 1·60
525 – 20d. orange . . . . 25·00 20·00
526 – 20d. blue . . . . 25·00 20·00
527 – 20d. red . . . . 25·00 20·00
DESIGN—HORIZ: 20d. As Type **1** of Ionian Is. but with portraits of George I of Greece and Queen Victoria.

99 Javelin Thrower

100 Arms of Greece, Rumania, Turkey and Yugoslavia

1939. 10th Pan-Balkan Games, Athens.
528 – 50l. green 30 35
529 **99** 3d. red 60 35
530 – 6d. brown on orange . . . 4·00 2·75
531 – 8d. blue on grey . . . . . 4·00 4·00

DESIGNS: 50l. Runner; 6d. Discus-thrower; 8d. Jumper.

1940. Balkan Entente.
532 **100** 6d. blue . . . . 7·25 1·40
533 8d. slate . . . . 6·50 1·50

101 Greek Youth Badge **103** Meteora Monasteries

1940. 4th Anniv of Greek Youth Organization. (a) Postage.
534 **101** 3d. blue, red and silver . . 85 1·10
535 – 5d. black and blue . . . 4·75 2·75
536 – 10d. black and orange . . 6·00 4·50
537 – 15d. black and green . . 44·00 48·00
538 – 20d. black and red . . . 35·00 30·00
539 – 25d. black and blue . . . 40·00 33·00
540 – 30d. black and purple . . 40·00 33·00
541 – 50d. black and red . . . 50·00 39·00
542 – 75d. gold, brown and blue 50·00 38·00
543 **101** 100d. blue, red and silver 65·00 47·00
DESIGNS—VERT: 5d. Boy member; 10d. Girl member; 15d. Javelin thrower; 20d. Youths in column formation; 25d. Standard bearer and buglers; 30d. Three youths in uniform; 50d. Youths on parade; 75d. Coat of arms.

(b) Air.
544 **103** 2d. black and orange . . 80 75
545 – 4d. black and green . . . 3·25 2·50
546 – 6d. black and red . . . . 6·00 5·00
547 – 8d. black and blue . . . 9·25 9·25
548 – 16d. black and violet . . 22·00 18·00
549 – 32d. black and orange . . 41·00 42·00
550 – 45d. black and green . . 41·00 42·00
551 – 55d. black and red . . . 50·00 47·00
552 – 65d. black and blue . . . 47·00 46·00
553 – 100d. black and violet . . 60·00 46·00
DESIGNS (views and aircraft): 4d. Simon Peter Monastery, Mt. Athos; 6, 16d. Isle of Santorin; 8d. Church at Pantanassa; 32d. Ponticonissi, Corfu; 45d. Acropolis; 55d. Erechtheum; 65d. Temple of Nike; 100d. Temple of Zeus.

1941. Postage Due stamps optd with Junkers G.24 airplane, No. 556 also surch. Perf (558/60), perf or rouletted (556/7).
556 D **20** 1d. on 2d. red 25 25
557 5d. blue . . . . 1·60 25
558 10d. green 10 35
559 25d. red . . . . 70 1·60
560 50d. orange . . . . . . 95 2·00

105 "Boreas" (North Wind)

1942. Air. Winds. (Symbolic designs).
561 **105** 2d. emerald and green . . 15 30
562 – 5d. orange and red . . . 20 30
563 – 10d. red and brown . . . 25 35
567 – 10d. red and orange . . . 20 55
564 – 20d. ultramarine and blue 45 55
565 – 25d. orange & light orange 30 90
568 – 25d. green and grey . . . 15 20
566 – 50d. black and grey . . . 95 1·60
569 – 50d. violet and blue . . . 15 20
570 **105** 100d. black and grey . . 15 20
571 – 200d. red and pink . . . 15 20
572 – 400d. green and blue . . 15 25
DESIGNS: 5d. "Notos" (South); 10d. "Apiliotis" (East); 20d. "Lips" (South-west); 25d. "Zephyr" (West); 50d. "Kekias" (North-east); 200d. "Evros" (South-east); 400d. "Skiron" (North-west).

106 Windmills on Mykonos Is.

1942.
573 **106** 2d. brown 10 20
574 – 5d. green 10 15
575 – 10d. blue 10 15
576 – 15d. purple 10 15
577 – 25d. orange 10 15
578 – 50d. blue 10 15
579 – 75d. red 10 15
580 – 100d. black 10 15
581 – 200d. blue 10 15
582 – 500d. brown 10 15
583 – 1000d. brown 10 15
584 – 2000d. blue 10 15
585 – 5000d. red 10 15
586 – 15,000d. purple 10 15
587 – 25,000d. green 10 15
588 – 500,000d. blue 20 30
589 **106** 2,000,000d. green . . . 20 30
590 – 5,000,000d. red 20 30

DESIGNS: 5d., 5,000,000d. Burzi Fortress, Nauplion; 10d., 500,000d. Katokhi on Aspropotamos River; 15d. Heraklion, Crete; 25d. Houses on Hydra Is; 50d., Meteora Monastery; 75d. Edessa; 100d., 200d. Monastery on Mt. Athos; 500d., 5000d. Konitza Bridge; 1000d., 15,000d. Ekatontapiliani Church; 2000d., 25,000d. Kerkyra (Corfu) Is.

110 Child

1943. Children's Welfare Fund.
592 **110** 25d.+25d. green 10 15
593 – 100d.+50d. purple 10 15
594 – 200d.+100d. brown . . . 10 20
DESIGN: 100d. Mother and child; 200d. Madonna and child.

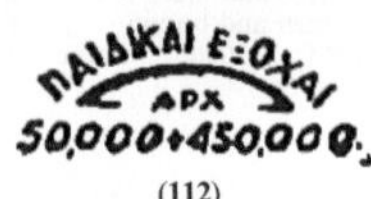

(**112**)

1944. Children's Convalescent Camp Fund. Surch as T **112**.(a) Postage.
595 **106** 50,000d.+450,000d. on 2d. brown 55 75
596 – 50,000d.+450,000d. on 5d. green (No. 574) 55 75
597 – 50,000d.+450,000d. on 10d. blue (No. 575) . . 55 75
598 – 50,000d.+450,000d. on 15d. purple (No. 576) 55 75
599 – 50,000d.+450,000d. on 25d. orange (No. 577) 55 75

(b) Air.
600 – 50,000d.+450,000d. on 10d. red (No. 567) . . . 55 75
601 – 50,000d.+450,000d. on 25d. green (No. 568) . . 55 75
602 – 50,000d.+450,000d. on 50d. blue (No. 569) . . 55 75
603 **106** 50,000d.+450,000d. on 100d. black 55 75
604 – 50,000d.+450,000d. on 200d. claret (No. 571) 55 75

ΔΡΑΧΜΑΙ ΝΕΑΙ
(**113**) (Trans "New drachmas")

1944. Optd as T **113**.
605 – 50l. black and brown (No. 501) 10 20
606 – 2d. blue (No. 504) 10 10
607 – 5d. red (No. 506) 10 15
608 – 6d. olive (No. 507) 10 20

92 "Glory" of Psara **114** "OXI" = No

1945.
609 **92** 1d. purple 10 20
610 3d. red 20 15
611 5d. blue 20 15
612 10d. brown 25 15
613 20d. violet 35 15
614 50d. green 80 30
615 100d. blue . . . . 6·50 6·75
616 200d. green . . . . . . 5·00 1·60
For 25d. in Type **92** but larger, see No. 512.

1945. Resistance to Italian Ultimatum.
617 **114** 20d. orange 25 20
618 40d. blue 25 20

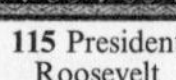

115 President Roosevelt (**116**)

1945. Roosevelt Mourning Issue. Black borders.
619 **115** 30d. purple 25 15
620 60d. grey 25 20
621 200d. violet 25 20

1946. Surch as T **116**.
622 – 10d. on 10d. (No. 567) . . 25 20
623 – 10d. on 2000d. (No. 584) 25 20
624 – 20d. on 50d. (No. 569) . . 25 20
625 – 20d. on 500d. (No. 582) 25 20
626 – 20d. on 1000d. (No. 583) 25 20
627 – 30d. on 5d. (No. 574) . . 25 20
628 – 50d. on 50d. (No. 578) . . 25 20
629 – 50d. on 25,000d. (No. 587) 45 20
630 – 100d. on 10d. (No. 575) 1·50 20
631 **106** 100d. on 2,000,000d. . . 85 20
632 – 130d. on 20l. (No. 499) 85 20
633 – 250d. on 20l. (No. 499) 85 20
634 – 300d. on 80l. (No. 502) 50 30
635 – 450d. on 75d. (No. 579) 1·70 35
636 – 500d. on 5,000,000d. (No. 590) . . . . . 2·50 40
637 – 1000d. on 500,000d. (No. 588) . . . . . . 10·00 1·10
638 – 2000d. on 5,000d. (No. 585) . . . . . . 32·00 3·50
639 – 5000d. on 15,000d. (No. 586) . . . . . . £120 24·00

117 E. Venizelos

1946. 10th Anniv of Death of Venizelos (statesman).
640 **117** 130d. green 25 20
641 300d. brown 25 20

1946. Restoration of Monarchy. Surch with value in circle and date **1-9-1946**.
642 **89** 50d. on 1d. green 50 15
643 250d. on 3d. brown . . . 85 15
644 600d. on 8d. blue . . . . 6·75 85
645 3000d. on 100d. red . . . 17·00 1·00

119 Women carrying Munitions, Pindos Mountains **121** Panayiotis Tsaldaris

1946. Victory. War Scenes.
646 – 50d. green 25 45
647 – 100d. blue 35 20
648 **119** 250d. green 50 15
649 – 500d. brown 85 15
650 – 600d. brown . . . . . . 1·40 70
651 – 1000d. violet . . . . . . 3·50 35
682 – 1000d. green . . . . . . 5·00 55
652 – 2000d. blue . . . . . . 14·00 1·90
653 – 5000d. red . . . . 26·00 1·40
DESIGNS—HORIZ: 50d. Convoy; 500d. Infantry column; 1000d. (No. 651) Supermarine Spitfire Mk IIB and pilot; 1000d. (No. 682) Battle of Crete; 2000d. Torpedo boat "Hyacinth" towing submarine "Perla". VERT: 100d. Torpedoing of Cruiser "Helle"; 600d. Badge, Alpine troops and map of Italy; 5000d. War Memorial at El Alamein.

1946. 10th Death Anniv of P. Tsaldaris (statesman).
654 **121** 250d. brown and pink . . 3·00 75
655 600d. blue . . . . 3·00 1·20

1947. King George II Mourning issue. Surch with value in circle in corner and black border.
656 **89** 50d. on 1d. green 45 20
657 250d. on 3d. brown . . . 1·20 20
658 600d. on 8d. blue . . . . 3·00 65

124 Castelrosso Fortress **126** Apollo (T **1** of Dodecanese Is.)

1947. Restoration of Dodecanese Is. to Greece.
659 **124** 20d. blue 25 15
660 – 30d. pink and black . . . 25 15
661 – 50d. blue 25 10
662 – 100d. green and olive . . 25 10
663 – 200d. orange 85 10
664 – 250d. grey 85 10
665 – 300d. orange 70 10
666 – 400d. blue . . . . 1·70 10
667 **126** 450d. blue . . . . 2·20 10
668 – 450d. blue . . . . 1·70 10
669 **126** 500d. red . . . . 1·20 10
670 – 600d. purple . . . . . . 1·20 20
671 – 700d. mauve . . . . . . 2·20 20
672 – 700d. green . . . . . . 17·00 15
673 – 800d. green and violet . . 3·50 15
674 – 1000d. olive 85 15
675 **126** 1300d. red . . . . 13·00 15
676 **124** 1500d. brown . . . . . . 55·00 30
677 – 1600d. blue . . . . 6·50 30
678 – 2000d. red and brown . . 37·00 20
679 – 2600d. green . . . . . . 8·50 50
680 – 5000d. violet . . . . . . 50·00 60
681 – 10,000d. blue . . . . . . 65·00 55
DESIGNS—HORIZ: 100, 400d. St. John's Convent, Patmos. VERT: 30, 1600, 2000d. Dodecanese vase; 50, 300d. Woman in national costume; 200, 250d. E. Xanthos; 450 (No. 668), 800d. Casos Is. and 19th-century frigate; 600, 700 (2), 5000d. Statue of Hippocrates; 1000, 2600, 10,000d. Colossus of Rhodes.

129 Column of Women and Children

1949. Abduction of Greek Children to neighbouring Countries.
683 **129** 450d. violet . . . . . . 3·00 19·00
684 – 1000d. brown . . . . . . 5·50 1·50
685 – 1800d. red . . . . 5·75 1·50
DESIGNS—VERT: 1000d. Captive children and map of Greece; 1800d. Hand menacing woman and child.

130 Maps and Flags

1950. Battle of Crete.
686 **130** 1000d. blue . . . . 6·75 25

131 "Youth of Marathon"

1950. 75th Anniv of U.P.U. Inscr "1874–1949" in white figures at top.
687 **131** 1000d. green on buff . . . 85 30

133 St. Paul **134** St. Paul

1951. 19th Cent of St. Paul's Travels in Greece.
688 – 700d. purple . . . . . . 2·00 70
689 **133** 1600d. blue . . . . 7·25 2·00
690 **134** 2600d. brown . . . . . . 11·00 2·40
691 – 10,000d. brown . . . . . 95·00 55·00
DESIGNS—As Type **134**: 700d. Sword and altar (horiz); 10,000d. St. Paul preaching to Athenians (vert).

135 "Industry" **136** Blessing before Battle

1951. Reconstruction Issue.
692 **135** 700d. orange . . . . . . 1·90 20
693 – 800d. green . . . . 4·50 25
694 – 1300d. blue . . . . 6·00 25
695 – 1600d. olive . . . . . . 18·00 25
696 – 2600d. violet . . . . . . 47·00 1·20
697 – 5000d. purple . . . . . . 47·00 35

DESIGNS—VERT: 800d. Fish and trident; 1300d. Workmen and column; 1600d. Ceres and tractors; 2600d. Women and loom; 5000d. Map and stars ("Electrification").

1952. Air. Anti-Communist Campaign.
698 **136** 1,000d. blue . . . . . . 1·00 25
699 – 1,700d. turquoise . . . . 4·25 70
700 – 2,700d. brown . . . . . 10·50 2·75
701 – 7,000d. green . . . . . . 30·00 12·50
DESIGNS—VERT: 1,700d. "Victory" over mountains; 2,700d. Infantry attack; 7,000d. "Victory" and soldiers.

137 King Paul **138** "Spirit of Greece"

1952. 50th Birthday of King Paul.
702 **137** 200d. green 85 25
703 1,000d. red . . . . 2·00 25
704 **138** 1,400d. blue . . . . . . 9·00 85
705 **137** 10,000d. purple . . . . . 31·00 7·75

139 "Oranges"

1953. National Products.
706 **139** 500d. orange and red . . 1·10 15
707 – 700d. yellow and brown 1·10 15
708 – 1,000d. green and blue . . 1·80 15
709 – 1,300d. buff and purple 3·00 25
710 – 2,000d. green and brown 9·25 25
711 – 2,600d. bistre and violet 17·00 60
712 – 5,000d. green and brown 20·00 45
DESIGNS—VERT: 700d. "Tobacco" (tobacco plant); 1,300d. "Wine" (wineglass and vase); 2,000d. "Figs" (basket of figs); 2,600d. "Dried Fruit" (grapes and currant bread); 5,000d. "Grapes" (male figure holding grapes). HORIZ: 1,000d. "Olive Oil" (Pallas Athene and olive branch).

140 Bust of Pericles **141** Alexander the Great

1954. Ancient Greek Art. Sculptures, etc.
713 **140** 100d. brown 25 10
714 – 200d. black 25 10
715 – 300d. violet 40 15
716 – 500d. green 60 10
717 – 600d. red . . . . 1·10 10
718 **141** 1,000d. black and blue . 1·80 10
719 – 1,200d. olive . . . . . . 1·70 10
720 – 2,000d. brown . . . . . . 5·25 20
721 – 2,400d. blue . . . . . . 5·50 35
722 – 2,500d. green . . . . . . 6·25 25
723 – 4,000d. red . . . . 17·00 25
724 – 20,000d. purple . . . . . £110 1·00
DESIGNS—As Type **140**: VERT: 200d. Mycenaean oxhead vase; 1,200d. Head of charioteer of Delphi; 2,000d. Vase of Dipylon; 2,500d. Man carrying calf; 20,000d. Two pitcher bearers. HORIZ: 2,400d. Hunting wild boar. As Type **141**: VERT: 300d. Bust of Homer; 500d. Zeus of Istiaca; 600d. Youth's head; 4,000d. Dish depicting voyage of Dionysus.
See also Nos. 733a/41.

143 Athlete Bearing Torch

1954. Air. 5th Anniv of N.A.T.O. Inscr "NATO".
725 **143** 1,200d. orange . . . . . 3·25 20
726 – 2,400d. green . . . . . . 37·00 1·80
727 – 4,000d. blue . . . . . . 55·00 2·50
DESIGNS—VERT: 2,400d. Amphictyonic coin; 4,000d. Pallas Athene.

Currency revalued.
1000 old drachma = one new drachma.

144 Extracts from "Hansard" (Parliamentary Debates) **145** Samian Coin Depicting Pythagoras

1954. "Enosis" (Union of Cyprus with Greece).
728 **144** 1.20d. black and yellow 2·75 30
729 2d. black and salmon . . 8·00 2·30
730 2d. black and blue . . . 8·00 2·30
731 2.40d. black and lavender 8·00 1·60
732 2.50d. black and pink . . 8·50 1·40
733 4d. black and lemon . . . 28·00 2·30
On No. 728 the text is in Greek, on Nos. 730/1 in French and on the remainder in English.

1955. As Nos. 713/24 but new colours and values.
733a **140** 10l. green 20 10
734 – 20l. myrtle (No. 714) . . 25 15
734a – 20l. purple (No. 714) . . 20 15
735 **140** 30l. brown 35 10
736 – 50l. lake (No. 716) . . . 70 15
736a – 50l. green (No. 716) . . 45 10
736b – 70l. orange (No. 719) . . 20 15
737 – 1d. green (No. 717) . . . 1·20 10
737a – 1d. brown (No. 717) . . 1·70 10
737b – 1d.50 blue (No. 724) . . 10·00 20
738 **141** 2d. black and brown . . 8·00 10
738a 2d.50 black and mauve 10·00 10
739 – 3d. orange (No. 721) . . 6·50 20
739a – 3d. blue (No. 722) . . . 1·70 20
740 – 3d.50 red (No. 715) . . 7·50 45
741 – 4d. blue (No. 723) . . . 50·00 25

1955. Pythagorean Congress.
742 **145** 2d. green . . . . 1·80 30
743 – 3d.50 black . . . . 4·25 1·90
744 **145** 5d. purple . . . . 32·00 1·40
745 – 6d. blue . . . . 26·00 23·00
DESIGNS—VERT: 3d.50, Representation of Pythagoras theorem. HORIZ: 6d. Map of Samos.

146 Rotary Emblem and Globe **147** King George I

1956. 50th Anniv of Rotary International.
746 **146** 2d. blue . . . . 7·50 40

1956. Royal Family.
747 – 10l. violet 20 10
748 – 20l. purple 15 10
749 **147** 30l. brown 25 10
750 – 50l. brown 25 10
751 – 70l. blue 35 15
752 – 1d. blue 50 15
753 – 1d.50 grey . . . . 1·30 25
754 – 2d. black . . . . 1·40 15
755 – 3d. brown . . . . 1·60 10
756 – 3d.50 brown . . . . . . 6·00 20
757 – 4d. green . . . . 6·00 15
758 – 5d. red . . . . 4·00 15
759 – 7d.50 blue . . . . 5·25 1·20
760 – 10d. blue . . . . 19·00 50
PORTRAITS—HORIZ: 10l. King Alexander; 5d. King Paul and Queen Frederika; 10d. King and Queen and Crown Prince Constantine. VERT: 20l. Crown Prince Constantine; 50l. Queen Olga; 70l. King Otto; 1d. Queen Amalia; 1d.50, King Constantine; 2d. King Paul; 3d. King George II; 3d.50, Queen Sophia; 4d. Queen Frederika; 7d.50, King Paul.
See also Nos. 764/77.

148 Dionysios Solomos **149** "Argo" (5th Century B.C.)

1957. Death Centenary of D. Solomos (national poet).
761 – 2d. yellow and brown . . 3·50 30
762 **148** 3d.50 grey and blue . . . 3·50 1·80
763 – 5d. bistre and green . . . 4·25 5·00
DESIGNS—HORIZ: 2d. Solomos and K. Mantzaros (composer); 5d. Zante landscape and Solomos.

1957. As Nos. 747/60. Colours changed.
764 – 10l. red 10 40
765 – 20l. orange 10 40
766 **147** 30l. black 15 40
767 – 50l. green 20 40
768 – 70l. purple 45 35
769 – 1d. red 65 10
770 – 1d.50 green . . . . 1·60 10
771 – 2d. red . . . . 2·00 10
772 – 3d. blue . . . . 2·10 15
773 – 3d.50 purple . . . . . . 5·50 20
774 – 4d. brown . . . . 7·50 15
775 – 5d. blue . . . . 6·00 20
776 – 7d.50 yellow . . . . . . 1·60 1·00
777 – 10d. green . . . . 34·00 60

1958. Greek Merchant Marine Commemoration. Ship designs.
778 – 50l. multicoloured 10 10
779 – 1d. ochre, black and blue 20 15
780 – 1d.50 red, black and blue 90 1·00
781 – 2d. multicoloured 35 30
782 – 3d.50 black, red and blue 1·10 1·30
783 **149** 5d. multicoloured . . . . 7·50 7·75
SHIPS: 50l. "Michael Carras" (tanker); 1d. "Queen Frederika" (liner); 1d.50, Full-rigged sailing ship, 1821; 2d. Byzantine galley; 3d.50, 6th-century B.C. galley.

150 The Piraeus (Port of Athens) **151** "Narcissus" and Flower

1958. Air. Greek Ports.
784 **150** 10d. multicoloured . . . 11·00 15
785 – 15d. multicoloured . . . 1·80 20
786 – 20d. multicoloured . . . 11·00 15
787 – 25d. multicoloured . . . 1·80 40
788 – 30d. multicoloured . . . 1·80 40
789 – 50d. blue, black and brown . . . . 5·00 40
790 – 100d. blue, black & brown . . . . 30·00 2·00
PORTS: 15d. Salonika; 20d. Patras; 25d. Hermoupolis (Syra); 30d. Volos (Thessaly); 50d. Kavalla; 100d. Heraklion (Crete).

1958. International Congress for Protection of Nature, Athens. Mythological and Floral designs. Multicoloured.
791 20l. Type **151** 10 15
792 30l. "Daphne and Apollo" 10 45
793 50l. "Venus and Adonis" (Venus and hibiscus) . . . 10 45
794 70l. "Pan and the Nymph" (Pan and pine cones) . . . 25 45
795 1d. Crocus (21½ × 26 mm) . . 45 50
796 2d. Iris (22 × 32 mm) 55 30
797 3d.50 Tulip (22 × 32 mm) . . 25 35
798 5d. Cyclamen (22 × 32 mm) 2·10 2·50

152 Jupiter's Head and Eagle (Olympia 4th-century B.C. coin)

1959. Ancient Greek Coins. Designs as T **152** showing both sides of each coin. Inscriptions in black.
799 **152** 10l. green and brown . . 10 15
800 – 20l. grey and blue . . . 20 10
801 – 50l. grey and purple . . . 25 10
802 – 70l. grey and blue 35 20
803 – 1d. drab and red 65 10
804 – 1d.50 grey and ochre . . 1·00 10
805 – 2d.50 drab and mauve . 1·50 10
806 – 4d.50 grey and green . . 5·50 35
807 – 6d. blue and olive . . . 15·00 25
808 – 8d.50 drab and red . . . 2·30 1·40
COINS—HORIZ: 20l. Athene's head and owl (Athens 5th cent. B.C.); 50l. Nymph Arethusa and chariot (Syracuse 5th cent. B.C.); 70l. Hercules and Jupiter (Alexander the Great 4th cent. B.C.); 1d.50, Griffin and squares (Abdera, Thrace 5th cent. B.C.); 2d.50, Apollo and lyre (Chalcidice, Macedonia 4th cent. B.C.). VERT: 1d. Helios and rose (Rhodes 4th cent. B.C.); 4d.50, Apollo and labyrinth (Crete 3rd cent. B.C.); 6d. Venus and Apollo (Paphos, Cyprus 4th cent. B.C.); 8d.50, Ram's heads and incised squares (Delphi 5th cent. B.C.).
See also Nos. 909/17.

153 Amphitheatre, Delphi **154** "Victory" and Greek Soldiers through the Ages

1959. Ancient Greek Theatre.
809 – 20l. multicoloured 20 20
810 – 50l. brown and olive . . . 25 20
811 – 1d. multicoloured 30 25
812 – 2d.50 brown and blue . . 45 20
813 **153** 3d.50 multicoloured . . . 8·75 8·75
814 – 4d.50 brown and black . . 1·30 60
815 – 6d. brown, grey and black 1·20 90
DESIGNS—VERT: 20l. Ancient theatre audience (after a Pharsala Thessaly vase of 580 B.C.); 50l. Clay mask of 3rd century B.C.; 1d. Flute, drum and lyre; 2d.50, Actor (3rd century statuette); 6d. Performance of a satirical play (after a mixing-bowl of 410 B.C.). HORIZ: 4d.50, Performance of Euripides' "Andromeda" (after a vase of 4th century B.C.).

1959. 10th Anniv of Greek Anti-Communist Victory.
816 **154** 2d.50 blue, black & brn 2·10 30

155 "The Good Samaritan" **156** Imre Nagy (formerly Prime Minister of Hungary)

1959. Red Cross Commem. Cross in red.
817 – 20l. multicoloured 20 20
818 – 50l. grey, red and blue . . 30 25
819 – 70l. black, brown, bis & bl 40 35
820 – 2d.50 blk, brn, grey & red 60 25
821 – 3d. multicoloured . . . . 5·00 5·75
822 – 4d.50 orange and red . . 95 95
823 **155** 6d. multicoloured 90 70
DESIGNS—HORIZ: 20l. Hippocrates Tree, Cos. VERT: 50l. Bust of Aesculapius; 70l. St. Basil (after mosaic in Hosios Loukas Monastery, Boeotia); 2d.50, Achilles and Patroclus (from vase of 6th cent B.C.); 3d. (32 × 47½ mm) Red Cross, globe, infirm people and nurses; 4d.50, J. H. Dunant.

1959. 3rd Anniv of Hungarian Revolt.
824 **156** 4d.50 sepia, brown & red 1·10 95
825 6d. black, blue & ultram 1·10 95

157 Kostes Palamas **158** Brig in Storm

1960. Birth Cent of Palamas (poet).
826 **157** 2d.50 multicoloured . . . 1·90 35

1960. World Refugee Year. Multicoloured.
827 2d.50 Type **158** 30 20
828 4d.50 Brig in calm waters . . 55 75

159 Scout emulating St. George **160** Sprinting

1960. 50th Anniv of Greek Boy Scout Movement. Multicoloured.
829 20l. Type **159** 10 20
830 30l. Ephebi Oath and Scout Promise 10 20
831 40l. Fire rescue work (horiz) 10 20
832 50l. Planting tree (horiz) . . 25 20
833 70l. Map reading (horiz) . . 10 20
834 1d. Scouts on beach (horiz) 30 25
835 2d.50 Crown Prince Constantine in uniform . . 85 45
836 6d. Greek Scout Flag and Medal (horiz) . . . . . . 1·00 1·10

1960. Olympic Games.
837 – 20l. brown, black and blue 10 20
838 – 50l. brown and black . . 10 20
839 – 70l. brown, black & green 10 20
840 – 80l. multicoloured 15 20
841 – 1d. multicoloured 30 25
842 – 1d.50 brown, blk & orge 30 30
843 – 2d.50 brown, black & bl 75 35
844 **160** 4d.50 multicoloured . . . 70 65
845 – 5d. multicoloured . . . . 1·60 1·00
846 – 6d. brown, black & violet 1·80 1·00
847 – 12d.50 multicoloured . . 6·75 6·75

DESIGNS—VERT: 20l. "Armistice" (official holding plaque); 70l. Athlete taking oath; 2d.50, Discus-throwing; 5d. Javelin-throwing. HORIZ: 50l. Olympic flame; 80l. Cutting branches from crown-bearing olive tree; 1d. Entrance of chief judges; 1d.50 Long jumping; 6d. Crowning the victor; 12d.50, Quadriga or chariot-driving (entrance of the victor).

1960. 1st Anniv of European Postal and Telecommunications Conf. As T **371a** of Italy.
848 4d.50 blue 2·50 1·40

162 Crown Prince Constantine and "Nirefs"

1961. Victory of Crown Prince Constantine in Dragon-class Yacht Race, Olympic Games.
849 **162** 2d.50 multicoloured 40 25

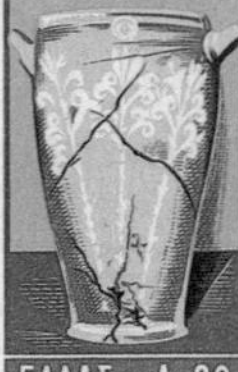

163 Kastoria **164** Lilies Vase of Knossos

1961. Tourist Publicity Issue.
850 **163** 10l. blue 10 10
851 – 20l. plum 10 10
852 – 50l. blue 15 10
853 – 70l. purple 20 10
854 – 80l. blue 30 25
855 – 1d. brown 55 10
856 – 1d.50 green 60 10
857 – 2d.50 red 1·90 10
858 – 3d.50 violet 70 30
859 – 4d. green 4·50 15
860 – 4d.50 blue 80 10
861 – 5d. lake 4·00 10
862 – 6d. myrtle 1·50 10
863 – 7d.50 black 65 20
864 – 8d. blue 2·50 30
865 – 8d.50 orange 2·75 40
866 – 12d.50 sepia 1·20 50
DESIGNS—HORIZ: 20l. The Meteora (Monasteries); 50l. Hydra; 70l. Acropolis, Athens; 80l. Mykonos. 1d. Salonika; 1d.50, Olympia; 2d.50, Knossos; 3d.50, Rhodes; 4d. Epidavros; 4d.50, Sounion; 5d. Temple of Zeus, Athens; 7d.50, Yannina; 12d.50, Delos, VERT: 6d. Delphi; 8d. Mount Athos; 8d.50, Santorini (Thira).

1961. Minoan Art.
867 **164** 20l. multicoloured 15 20
868 – 50l. multicoloured 25 20
869 – 1d. multicoloured 30 20
870 – 1d.50 multicoloured 60 25
871 – 2d.50 multicoloured 3·25 20
872 – 4d.50 multicoloured 1·60 1·50
873 – 6d. multicoloured 5·50 1·10
874 – 10d. multicoloured 5·00 6·25
DESIGNS—VERT: 1d.50, Knossos rhyton-bearer; 4d.50, Part of Hagia trias sarcophagus. HORIZ: 50l. Partridges and fig-pecker (Knossos frieze); 1d. Kamares fruit dish; 2d.50, Ladies of Knossos Palace (painting); 6d. Knossos dancer (painting); 10d. Kamares prochus and pithos with spout.

165 Reactor Building

1961. Inauguration of "Democritus" Nuclear Research Centre, Aghia Paraskevi.
875 **165** 2d.50 purple and mauve 30 25
876 – 4d.50 blue and grey 60 60
DESIGN: 4d.50, Democritus and atomic symbol.

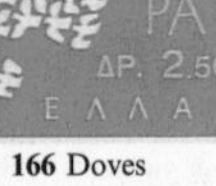

166 Doves **167** Emperor Nicephorus Phocas

1961. Europa.
877 **166** 2d.50 red and pink 10 20
878 4d.50 ultramarine & blue 15 25

1961. Millenary of Liberation of Crete from the Saracens.
879 **167** 2d.50 multicoloured 35 35

168 "Hermes" 1l. Stamp of 1861

1961. Centenary of First Greek Postage Stamps. "Hermes" stamps of 1861. Multicoloured.
880 20l. Type **168** 10 15
881 50l. "2l." 10 10
882 1d.50 "5l." 15 10
883 2d.50 "10l." 20 20
884 4d.50 "20l." 35 25
885 6d. "40l." 45 45
886 10d. "80l." 95 1·00

169 Ptolemais Steam Plant

1962. Electrification Project. Multicoloured.
887 20l. Tauropos dam (vert) 10 20
888 50l. Ladhon River hydro-electric plant (vert) 20 20
889 1d. Type **169** 20 25
890 1d.50 Louros River dam 20 20
891 2d.50 Aliverion steam plant 70 20
892 4d.50 Salonika hydro-electric sub-station 65 75
893 6d. Agra River power station 1·90 1·90

170 Zappion Building

1962. N.A.T.O. Ministers' Conference, Athens.
894 **170** 2d.50 multicoloured 20 10
895 – 3d. sepia, brown and buff 20 10
896 – 4d.50 black and blue 25 35
897 – 6d. black and red 25 30
DESIGNS—VERT: 3d. Ancient Greek warrior with shield; 4d.50, Soldier kneeling (after Marathon tomb); 6d. (21 × 37 mm), Soldier (statue in Temple of Aphea, Aegina).

171 Europa "Tree"

1962. Europa.
898 **171** 2d.50 red and black 35 20
899 4d.50 blue and black 1·00 60

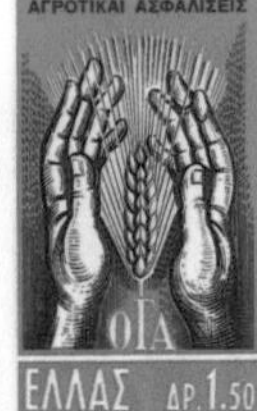

172 "Protection" **173** Demeter, Goddess of Corn

1962. Greek Farmers' Social Insurance Scheme.
900 **172** 1d.50 black, brown & red 25 10
901 2d.50 black, brown & grn 35 20

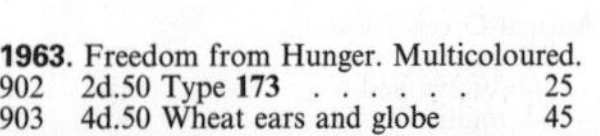

1963. Freedom from Hunger. Multicoloured.
902 2d.50 Type **173** 25 20
903 4d.50 Wheat ears and globe 45 45

174 Kings of the Greek Dynasty

1963. Cent of Greek Royal Dynasty.
904 **174** 50l. red 20 10
905 1d.50 green 30 15
906 2d.50 brown 60 15
907 4d.50 blue 1·10 75
908 6d. violet 1·50 25

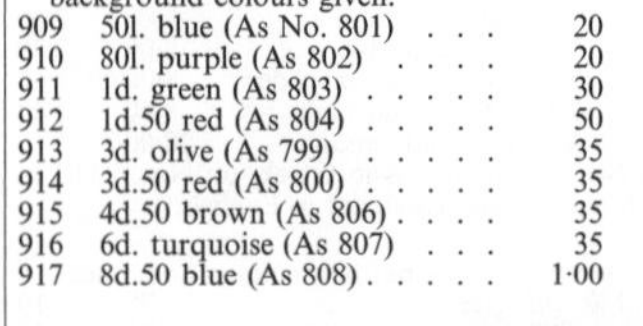

1963. Ancient Greek Coins. As Nos. 799/808 but colours changed and some designs rearranged. Inscr in black; coins in black and drab or grey; background colours given.
909 50l. blue (As No. 801) 20 10
910 80l. purple (As 802) 20 20
911 1d. green (As 803) 30 10
912 1d.50 red (As 804) 50 10
913 3d. olive (As 799) 35 10
914 3d.50 red (As 800) 35 25
915 4d.50 brown (As 806) 35 15
916 6d. turquoise (As 807) 35 20
917 8d.50 blue (As 808) 1·00 55

175 "Athens at Dawn" (after watercolour by Lord Baden-Powell) **176** Delphi

1963. 11th World Scout Jamboree, Marathon.
918 **175** 1d. multicoloured 10 20
919 – 1d.50 orange, black & bl 10 20
920 – 2d.50 multicoloured 50 25
921 – 3d. black, brown & green 30 25
922 – 4d.50 multicoloured 60 50
DESIGNS—HORIZ: 3d. A. Lefkadites (founder of Greek Scout Movement) and Lord Baden-Powell. VERT: 1d.50, Jamboree Badge; 2d.50, Crown Prince Constantine, Chief Scout of Greece; 4d.50, Scout bugling with Atlantic trumpet triton shell.

1963. Red Cross Centenary. Multicoloured.
923 1d. Type **176** 25 15
924 2d. Centenary emblem 15 10
925 2d.50 Queen Olga 15 20
926 4d.50 Henri Dunant 45 50

177 "Co-operation"

1963. Europa.
927 **177** 2d.50 green 1·70 20
928 4d.50 purple 2·75 2·00

178 Great Lavra Church **179** King Paul

1963. Millenary of Mt. Athos Monastic Community. Multicoloured.
929 30l. Vatopediou Monastery (horiz) 10 20
930 80l. Dionysion Monastery (horiz) 10 20
931 1d. Protaton Church, Karyae 10 20
932 2d. Stavronikita Monastery (horiz) 35 10
933 2d.50 Cover of Nicephorus Phocas Gospel, Great Lavra Church (horiz) 1·10 20
934 3d.50 St. Athanasius the Anthonite (fresco) (horiz) 45 60
935 4d.50 11th-century papyrus, Iviron Monastery (horiz) 40 40
936 6d. Type **178** 45 35

1964. Death of Paul I.
937 **179** 30l. brown 10 10
938 50l. violet 10 10
939 1d. green 65 10
940 1d.50 orange 20 10
941 2d. blue 50 10
942 2d.50 sepia 55 10
943 3d.50 purple 45 20
944 4d. blue 1·10 30
945 4d.50 blue 1·20 65
946 6d. red 2·10 35

180 Gold Coin **181** Trident of Paxi

1964. Byzantine Art Exn, Athens. Mult.
947 1d. Type **180** 15 10
948 1d.50 "Two Saints" 15 20
949 2d. "Archangel Michael" 15 10
950 2d.50 "Young Lady" 20 15
951 4d.50 "Angel" 50 60
DESIGN origins: 1d. reign of Emperor Basil II (976–1025); 1d.50, from Harbaville's 10th cent ivory triptych (Louvre); 2d. 14th cent Constantinople icon (Byzantine Museum, Athens); 2d.50, from 14th cent fresco "The Birth of the Holy Virgin" by Panselinos (Protaton Church, Mt. Athos); 4d.50, from 11th cent mosaic (Daphne Church, Athens).

1964. Centenary of Union of Ionian Islands with Greece. Inscr "1864–1964".
952 **181** 20l. grey, slate and green 10 15
953 – 30l. multicoloured 10 10
954 – 1d. lt brn, brn & red-brn 10 10
955 – 2d. multicoloured 10 10
956 – 2d.50 pale green, deep green and green 20 20
957 – 4d.50 multicoloured 55 65
958 – 6d. multicoloured 35 25
DESIGNS: 30l. Venus of Cythera; 1d. Ulysses of Ithaca; 2d. St. George of Levkas; 2d.50, Zakynthos of Zante; 4d.50, Cephalus of Cephalonia; 6d. War galley emblem of Corfu.

182 Greek Child **183** Europa "Flower"

1964. 50th Anniv of National Institution of Social Welfare (P.I.K.P.A.).
959 **182** 2d.50 multicoloured 40 20

1964. Europa.
960 **183** 2d.50 red and green 95 30
961 4d.50 brown and drab 1·40 85

184 King Constantine II and Queen Anne-Marie **185** Peleus and Atlanta (amphora)

1964. Royal Wedding.
962 **184** 1d.50 green 20 25
963 2d.50 red 10 10
964 4d.50 blue 20 30

1964. Olympic Games, Tokyo. Multicoloured.
965 10l. Type **185** 10 20
966 1d. Running (bowl) (horiz) 10 20
967 2d. Jumping (pot) (horiz) 10 20
968 2d.50 Throwing the discus 20 20
969 4d.50 Chariot-racing (sculpture) (horiz) 35 45
970 6d. Boxing (vase) (horiz) 20 25
971 10d. Apollo (part of frieze, Zeus Temple, Olympia) 30 30

186 "Christ stripping off His garments" **187** Aesculapius Theatre, Epidavros

1965. 350th Death Anniv of El Greco. Mult.
972 50l. Type **186** 10 10
973 1d. "Angels' Concert" 10 15
974 1d.50 El Greco's signature (horiz) 10 15

975 2d.50 Self-portrait 10 10
976 4d.50 "Storm-lashed Toledo" 35 35

1965. Greek Artistic Festivals. Mult.
977 1d.50 Type **187** 10 10
978 4d.50 Herod Atticus Theatre, Athens 30 25

188 ITU Emblem and Symbols

1965. Centenary of I.T.U.
979 **188** 2d.50 red, blue and grey 35 15

189 "New Member making Affirmation" (after Tsokos)

1965. 150th Anniv of "Philiki Hetaeria" ("Friends' Society"). Multicoloured.
980 1d.50 Type **189** 10 10
981 4d.50 Society flag 30 25

190 AHEPA Emblem

191 Venizelos as Revolutionary

1965. American Hellenic Educational Progressive Assn (AHEPA) Congress, Athens.
982 **190** 6d. black, olive and blue 35 25

1965. Birth Cent of E. Venizelos (statesman).
983 **191** 1d.50 green 20 20
984 – 2d. blue 25 40
985 – 2d.50 brown 20 20
DESIGNS: 2d. Venizelos signing Treaty of Sevres (1920); 2d.50, Venizelos.

192 Games' Flag

193 Symbols of the Planets

1965. Balkan Games, Athens. Multicoloured.
986 1d. Type **192** 10 20
987 2d. Victor's medal (vert) . . 10 20
988 6d. Karaiskakis Stadium, Athens 25 25

1965. Int Astronautic Conference Athens. Mult.
989 50l. Type **193** 10 20
990 2d.50 Astronaut in space . . 20 20
991 6d. Rocket and space-ship . . 25 25

194 Europa "Sprig"

1965. Europa.
992 **194** 2d.50 blue, black and grey 30 15
993 4d.50 green, black & olive 75 60

195 Hipparchus (astronomer) and Astrolabe

1965. Opening of Evghenides Planetarium, Athens.
994 **195** 2d.50 black, red and green 30 20

196 Carpenter Ants

197 St. Andrew's Church, Patras

1965. 50th Anniv of P.O. Savings Bank. Multicoloured.
995 10l. Type **196** 10 10
996 2d.50 Savings Bank and book 30 20

1965. Restoration of St. Andrew's Head to Greece. Multicoloured.
997 1d. Type **197** 10 10
998 5d. St. Andrew, after 11th-cent mosaic, Hosios Loukas Monastry, Boeotia 25 20

198 T. Brysakes

200 Geannares (revolutionary leader)

199 Greek 25d. Banknote of 1867

1966. Modern Greek Painters. Multicoloured.
999 80l. Type **198** 10 20
1000 1d. N. Lytras 10 10
1001 2d.50 C. Volonakes 10 10
1002 4d. N. Gyses 15 15
1003 5d. G. Jacobides 20 20

1966. 125th Anniv of Greek National Bank.
1004 – 1d.50 green 10 10
1005 – 2d.50 brown 10 20
1006 – 4d. blue 10 10
1007 **199** 6d. black 30 25
DESIGNS—VERT: (23 × 33½ mm): 1d.50, J.-G. Eynard; 2d.50, G. Stavros (founders). HORIZ: (As Type **199**): 4d. National Bank Headquarters, Athens.

1966. Centenary of Cretan Revolt. Mult.
1008 2d. Type **200** 10 10
1009 2d.50 Explosion of gunpowder machine, Arkadi Monastery (horiz) 10 20
1010 4d.50 Map of Crete (horiz) 20 25

201 "Movement of Water" (Decade of World Hydrology)

202 Tragedian's Mask of 4th Century, B.C.

1966. U.N.O. Events.
1011 **201** 1d. blue, brown and black 10 10
1012 – 3d. multicoloured . . . 10 10
1013 – 3d. black, blue and red 20 25
DESIGNS—VERT: 3d. U.N.E.S.C.O. emblem (20th anniv); 5d. W.H.O. Building (inauguration of H.Q., Geneva).

1966. 2,500th Anniv of Greek Theatre.
1014 **202** 1d. multicoloured . . . 10 20
1015 – 1d.50 black, red & brn 10 20
1016 – 2d.50 black, grn & lt grn 10 20
1017 – 4d.50 multicoloured . . 25 25
DESIGNS—HORIZ: 1d.50, Dionysus in a Thespian ship-chariot (vase painting, 500–480 B.C.); 2d.50, Theatre of Dionysus, Athens. VERT: 4d.50, Dionysus dancing (after vase painting by Kleophredes, c. 500 B.C.).

203 Boeing 707 Jetliner crossing Atlantic Ocean

1966. Inauguration of Greek Airways Transatlantic Flights.
1018 **203** 6d. indigo, blue & lt blue 35 30

204 Tending Plants

1966. Greek Tobacco. Multicoloured.
1019 1d. Type **204** 15 15
1020 5d. Sorting leaf 35 30

205 Europa "Ship"

206 Horseman (embroidery)

1966. Europa.
1021 **205** 1d.50 black, olive & grn 30 20
1022 4d.50 deep brown, brown and light brown 60 50

1966. Greek "Popular" Art. Multicoloured.
1023 10l. Knitting-needle boxes (vert) 10 10
1024 30l. Type **206** 10 10
1025 50l. Cretan lyre (vert) . . . 10 10
1026 1d. "Massa" (Musical instrument) (vert) 10 10
1027 1d.50 "Cross and Angels" (bas-relief after Melios) (vert) 10 10
1028 2d. "Sts. Constantine and Helen" (icon) (vert) . . . 70 10
1029 2d.50 Carved altar-screen, St. Nicholas' Church, Galaxidion (vert) 15 10
1030 3d. 19th-century ship of Skyros (embroidery) . . . 20 10
1031 4d. "Psiki" (wedding procession) (embroidery) 60 10
1032 4d.50 Distaff (vert) 25 15
1033 5d. Earrings and necklace (vert) 45 10
1034 20d. Detail of handwoven cloth 85 35

207 Princess Alexia

208 "Woodcutter" (after D. Filippotes)

1966. Princess Alexia's First Birthday.
1035 **207** 2d. green 10 10
1036 – 2d.50 brown 15 10
1037 – 3d.50 blue 25 25
PORTRAITS: 2d.50, Royal Family; 3d.50, Queen Anne-Marie with Princess Alexia.

1967. Greek Sculpture. Multicoloured.
1038 20l. "Night" (I. Cossos) (vert) 10 20
1039 50l. "Penelope" (L. Drossos) (vert) 10 20
1040 80l. "Shepherd" (G. Phitalis) (vert) . . . . 10 4·25
1041 2d. "Woman's Torso" (K. Demetriades) (vert) 20 20
1042 2d.50 "Kolokotronis" (L. Sochos) (vert) 10 20
1043 3d. "Girl Sleeping" (I. Halepas) 35 30
1044 10d. Type **208** 20 25

209 Olympic Rings ("Olympic Day")

210 Cogwheels

1967. Sports Events. Multicoloured.
1045 1d. Type **209** 10 15
1046 1d.50 Marathon Cup, first Olympics (1896) 10 20
1047 2d.50 Hurdling 15 10
1048 5d. "The Discus-thrower" after C. Demetriades . . . 30 25
1049 6d. Ancient Olympic stadium 35 15
The 2d.50, commemorates the European Athletics Cup, 1967. 5d. (vert), The European Highest Award Championships, 1968. 6d. The Inaug of "International Academy" buildings, Olympia.

1967. Europa.
1050 **210** 2d.50 multicoloured . . 45 25
1051 4d.50 multicoloured . . 90 60

211 "Lonchi" (destroyer) and Sailor

212 The Plaka, Athens

1967. Nautical Week. Multicoloured.
1052 20l. Type **211** 10 15
1053 1d. "Eugene Eugenides" (cadet ship) (vert) 10 10
1054 2d.50 Merchant Marine Academy, Aspropyrgos, Attica 10 10
1055 3d. "Averoff" (cruiser) and Naval School, Poros . . . 35 25
1056 6d. "Australis" (liner) and figurehead 35 25

1967. International Tourist Year. Multicoloured.
1057 2d.50 Island of Skopelos (horiz) 10 10
1058 4d.50 Apollo's Temple, Bassai, Peleponnese (horiz) 40 25
1059 6d. Type **212** 35 20

213 Soldier and Phoenix

214 Industrial Skyline

1967. National Revolution of April 21st (1967).
1060 **213** 2d.50 multicoloured . . 10 10
1061 3d. multicoloured . . . 10 10
1062 4d.50 multicoloured . . 30 25

1967. 1st Convention of U.N. Industrial Development Organisation, Athens.
1063 **214** 4d.50 ultramarine, black and blue 20 25

215 "Seaside Scene" (A. Pelaletos)

1967. Children's Drawings. Multicoloured.
1064 20l. Type **215** 10 10
1065 1d.50 "Steamer and Island" (L. Tsirikas) 10 10
1066 3d.50 "Country Cottage" (K. Ambeliotis) 20 25
1067 6d. "The Church on the Hill" (N. Frangos) . . . 20 20

216 Throwing the Javelin

217 F.I.A. and E.L.P.A. Emblems

1968. Sports Events, 1968. Multicoloured.
1068 50l. Type **216** 10 10
1069 1d. Long jumping 10 10
1070 1d.50 "Apollo's Head", Temple of Zeus (vert) . . 10 10
1071 2d.50 Olympic scene on Attic vase (vert) 15 10
1072 4d. Olympic rings (Olympic Day) 20 20
1073 4d.50 "Throwing the Discus", sculpture by Demetriades (European Athletic Championships, 1969) (vert) 35 35
1074 6d. Long-distance running (vert) 15 20
The 50l., 1d. and 6d. represent the Balkan Games, and the 1d.50 and 2d.50, the Olympic Academy Meeting.

1968. General Assembly of International Automobile Federation (F.I.A.), Athens.
1075 **217** 5d. blue and brown . . . 40 30

218 Europa "Key"

1968. Europa.
1076 **218** 2d.50 multicoloured . . 55 25
1077 4d.50 multicoloured . . 1·30 75

219 "Athene defeats Alkyoneus" (from frieze, Altar of Zeus, Pergamos)

1968. "Hellenic Fight for Civilization" Exhibition, Athens. Multicoloured.
1078 10l. Type **219** 10 10
1079 20l. Athene attired for battle (bronze from Piraeus) (vert) (24 × 37 mm) . . . 10 10
1080 50l. Alexander the Great (from sarcophagus of Alexander of Sidon) (vert) (24 × 37 mm) 10 10
1081 1d.50 Emperors Constantine and Justinian making offerings to the Holy Mother (Byzantine mosaic) 15 15
1082 2d.50 Emperor Constantine Paleologos (lithograph by D. Tsokos) (vert) (24 × 37 mm) 15 10
1083 3d. "Greece in Missolonghi" (painting by Delacroix) (vert) (28 × 40 mm) . . . 15 15
1084 4d.50 "Evzone" (Greek soldier, painting by G. B. Scott) (vert) (28 × 40 mm) 30 25
1085 6d. "Victory of Samothrace" (statue) (vert) (28 × 40 mm) 35 35

220 "The Unknown Priest and Teacher" (Rhodes monument)

221 Congress Emblem

1968. 20th Anniv of Dodecanese Union with Greece. Multicoloured.
1086 2d. Type **220** 20 10
1087 5d. Greek flag on map (vert) 70 60

1968. 19th Biennial Congress of Greek Orthodox Archdiocese of North and South America.
1088 **221** 6d. multicoloured . . . 35 30

222 GAPA Emblem

223 "Hand of Aesculapius" (fragment of bas-relief from Asclepios' Temple, Athens)

1968. Regional Congress of Greek-American Progressive Association (GAPA).
1089 **222** 6d. multicoloured . . . 35 30

1968. 5th European Cardiological Congress. Athens.
1090 **223** 4d.50 black, yell & lake 85 75

224 Panathenaic Stadium

226 Goddess "Hygeia"

225 Westland Lysander Mk 1 ramming Savoia Marchetti S.M.79–11 Sparviero Bomber

1968. Olympic Games, Mexico. Multicoloured.
1091 2d.50 Type **224** 15 10
1092 5d. Ancient Olympia . . . 45 15
1093 10d. One of Pindar's odes 75 65
The 10d. is 28 × 40 mm.

1968. Royal Hellenic Air Force. Mult.
1094 2d.50 Type **225** 70 50
1095 3d.50 Mediterranean Flight in Breguet 19 bomber, 1928 . . . . 20 25
1096 8d. Farman H.F.III biplane and Lockheed Super Starfighter (vert) 55 50

1968. 20th Anniv of World Health Organization.
1097 **226** 5d. multicoloured . . . 40 25

227 St. Zeno, the Letter-carrier

228 "Workers' Festival Parade" (detail from Minoan vase)

1969. Greek Post Office Festival.
1098 **227** 2d.50 multicoloured . . 35 20

1969. 50th Anniv of I.L.O. Multicoloured.
1099 1d.50 "Hephaestus and Cyclops" (detail from ancient bas-relief) 15 10
1100 10d. Type **228** 55 50

229 Yacht Harbour, Vouliagmeni

230 Ancient Coin of Kamarina

1969. Tourism. Multicoloured.
1101 1d. Type **229** 10 10
1102 5d. "Chorus of Elders" (Ancient drama) (vert) . . 40 40
1103 6d. View of Astypalia . . . 20 20

1969. 20th Anniv of N.A.T.O. Multicoloured.
1104 2d.50 Type **230** 20 10
1105 4d.50 "Going into Battle" (from Corinthian vase) (horiz) 55 50

231 Colonnade

232 Gold Medal

1969. Europa.
1106 **231** 2d.50 multicoloured . . 1·10 25
1107 4d.50 multicoloured . . 1·60 95

1969. 9th European Athletic Championships, Athens. Multicoloured.
1108 20l. Type **232** 10 10
1109 3d. Pole-vaulting, and ancient pentathlon contest 15 15
1110 5d. Relay-racing, and Olympic race c. 525 B.C. (horiz) 20 20
1111 8d. Throwing the discus, modern and c. 480 B.C. 55 60

233 "19th-century Brig and Steamship" (I. Poulakas)

234 Raising the Flag on Mt. Grammos

1969. Navy Week and Merchant Marine Year. Multicoloured.
1112 80l. Type **233** 20 20
1113 2d. "Olympic Garland" (tanker) (horiz) 10 10
1114 2d.50 "Themistodes and Karteria, War of Independence, 1821" (anon) (41 × 29 mm) . . . 20 10
1115 4d.50 "Velos" (modern destroyer) (horiz) 45 35
1116 6d. "The Battle of Salamis" (K. Volonakis) (41 × 29 mm) 70 60

1969. 20th Anniv of Communists' Defeat on Mounts Grammos and Vitsi.
1117 **234** 2d.50 multicoloured . . 50 25

235 Athena Promachos

236 Demetrius Karatasios (statue by G. Demetriades)

1969. 25th Anniv of Liberation. Multicoloured.
1118 4d. Type **235** 15 10
1119 5d. "Resistance" (21 × 37 mm) 60 55
1120 6d. Map of Eastern Mediterranean theatre . . 20 10

1969. Heroes of Macedonia's Fight for Freedom. Multicoloured.
1121 1d.50 Type **236** 10 10
1122 2d.50 Emmanuel Pappas (statue by N. Perantinos) 10 10
1123 3d.50 Pavlos Melas (from painting by P. Mathiopoulos) 20 20
1124 4d.50 Capetan Kotas . . . 55 55

237 Dolphin Mosaic, Delos (110 B.C.)

1970. Greek Mosaics. Multicoloured.
1125 20l. "Angel of the Annunciation", Daphne (11th-century) (vert) (23 × 34 mm) 10 10
1126 1d. Type **237** 10 10
1127 1d.50 "The Holy Ghost", Hosios Loukas Monastery (11th-century) (vert) (23 × 34 mm) 20 20
1128 2d. "Hunter", Pella (4th-century B.C.) (vert) (23 × 34 mm) 25 15
1129 5d. "Bird", St. George's Church, Salonika (5th-century) (vert) (23 × 34 mm) 30 25
1130 6d. "Christ", Nea Moni Church, Khios (5th-century) 55 65

238 Overwhelming the Cretan Bull (sculpture)

1970. "The Labours of Hercules".
1131 **238** 20l. multicoloured . . . 10 20
1132 – 30l. multicoloured . . . 10 20
1133 – 1d. black, blue and slate 15 10
1134 – 1d.50 brn, grn & ochre 15 10
1135 – 2d. multicoloured . . . 1·20 10
1136 – 2d.50 brown, red & buff 20 10
1137 – 3d. multicoloured . . . 1·20 10
1138 – 4d.50 multicoloured . . . 25 15
1139 – 5d. multicoloured . . . 25 10
1140 – 6d. multicoloured . . . 25 10
1141 – 20d. multicoloured . . . 1·10 50
DESIGNS—HORIZ: 30l. Hercules and Cerberus (from decorated pitcher); 1d.50, The Lernean Hydra (from stamnos); 2d. Hercules and Geryon (from amphora); 4d.50, Combat with the River-god Achelous (from pitcher); 5d. Overwhelming the Nemean Lion (from amphora); 6d. The Stymphalian Birds (from vase); 20d. Wrestling with Antaeus (from bowl). VERT: 1d. Golden Apples of the Hesperides (sculpture); 2d.50, The Erymanthine Boar (from amphora); 3d. The Centaur Nessus (from vase).

239 "Flaming Sun"

1970. Europa.
1142 **239** 2d.50 yellow and red . . 1·60 25
1143 – 3d. blue and light blue 90 35
1144 **239** 4d.50 yellow and blue . . 2·50 1·50
DESIGN—VERT: 3d. "Owl" and CEPT emblem.

240 Satellite and Dish Aerial

1970. Satellite Earth Telecommunications Station, Thermopylae.
1145 **240** 2d.50 multicoloured . . 20 20
1146 4d.50 multicoloured . . 70 70

241 Saints Cyril and Methodius with Emperor Michael III, (from 12th-cent wall-painting)

1970. Saints Cyril and Methodius Commemoration. Multicoloured.
1147 50l. Saints Demetrius, Cyril and Methodius (mosaic) (21 × 37 mm) 10 15
1148 2d. St. Cyril (Russian miniature) (25 × 32 mm) 35 50
1149 5d. Type **241** 35 20
1150 10d. St. Methodius (Russian miniature) (25 × 32 mm) 45 55
Nos. 1148 and 1150 were issued together, se-tenant, forming a composite design.

242 Cephalonian Fir

244 New U.P.U. Headquarters Building, Berne (Opening)

243 "Cultural Links"

1970. Nature Conservation Year. Mult.
1151 80l. Type **242** 25 25
1152 2d.50 "Jankaea heldreichii" (plant) (23 × 34 mm) . . . 85 15
1153 6d. Rock Partridge (horiz) 1·30 40
1154 8d. Wild goat . . . . 1·40 1·80

1970. American–Hellenic Education Progressive Association Congress, Athens.
1155 **243** 6d. multicoloured . . . 60 25

1970. Anniversaries. Multicoloured.
1156 50l. Type **244** 10 10
1157 2d.50 Emblem (Int Education Year) (vert) (28½ × 41 mm) 20 10
1158 3d.50 Mahatma Gandhi (birth cent) (vert) 20 20
1159 4d. "25" (25th Anniv of United Nations) (vert) . . 40 20
1160 4d.50 Beethoven (birth bicent) (vert) (28½ × 41 mm) . . . . . 1·00 1·00

245 "The Nativity"

1970. Christmas. Scenes from "The Mosaic of the Nativity", Hosios Loukas Monastery. Mult.
1161 2d. "The Shepherds" (vert) 15 20
1162 4d.50 "The Magi" (vert) . . 25 25
1163 6d. Type **245** 60 60

246 "Death of Bishop of Salona in Battle, Alamana" (lithograph)

1971. 150th Anniv of War of Independence (1st issue). The Church. Multicoloured.
1164 50l. Warriors taking the oath (medal) (vert) . . . 10 20
1165 2d. Patriarch Gregory V (statue by Phitalis) (vert) 10 20
1166 4d. Type **246** 20 20
1167 10d. "Bishop Germanos blessing the Standard" (Vryzakis) 65 50
See also Nos. 1168/73, 1178/80, 1181/6 and 1187/89.

1971. 150th Anniv of War of Independence (2nd issue). The War at Sea. As T **246**. Multicoloured.
1168 20l. "Leonidas" (warship) (37 × 24 mm) 10 20
1169 1d. "Pericles" (warship) (37 × 24 mm) 20 20
1170 1d.50 "Terpsichore" (warship) (from painting by Roux) (37 × 24 mm) 20 20
1171 2d.50 "Karteria" (warship) (from painting by Hastings) (37 × 24 mm) 20 20
1172 3d. "Battle of Samos" (contemporary painting) (40 × 28 mm) 50 35
1173 6d. "Turkish Frigate ablaze, Battle of Yeronda" (Michalis) (40 × 28 mm) 1·10 75

247 Spyridon Louis winning Marathon, Athens, 1896

1971. 75th Anniv of Olympic Games Revival. Multicoloured.
1174 3d. Type **247** 25 10
1175 8d. P. de Coubertin and Memorial, Olympia (vert) 80 65

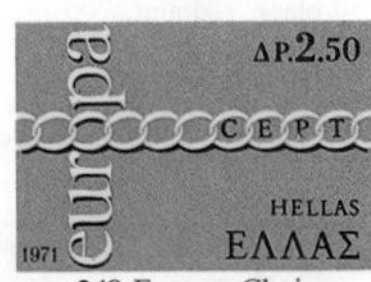

248 Europa Chain

1971. Europa.
1176 **248** 2d.50 yellow, grn & blk 1·20 25
1177 5d. yellow, orange & blk 3·00 1·40

1971. 150th Anniv of War of Independence (3rd issue). "Teaching the People". As T **246**. Multicoloured.
1178 50l. Eugenius Voulgaris (vert) 20 10
1179 2d.50 Dr. Adamantios Korais (vert) 20 20
1180 15d. "The Secret School" (N. Ghyzis) (horiz) . . . 70 70
SIZES: 50l., 2d.50, 23 × 34 mm. 15d. as Type **246**.

1971. 150th Anniv of War of Independence (4th issue). The War on Land. As T **246**. Mult.
1181 50l. "Battle of Corinth" (Krazeisen) (vert) 70 10
1182 1d. "Sacrifice of Kapsalia" (Vryzakis) (vert) 70 20
1183 2d. "Suliot Women in Battle" (Deneuville) (horiz) 20 10
1184 5d. "Battle of Athens" (Zographos) (vert) 25 20
1185 6d.50 "Battle of Maniaki" (lithograph) (horiz) . . . 30 20
1186 9d. "Death of Markos Botsaris at Karpenisi" (Vryzakis) (horiz) 55 70
SIZES: 50l., 1d., 5d. 25 × 40 mm. 2d. 40 × 25 mm. 6d.50, 9d. as Type **246**.

249 Kaltetsi Monastery and Seal of Peloponnesian Senate

1971. 150th Anniv of War of Independence (5th issue). Government.
1187 **249** 2d. black, green & brown 35 20
1188 – 2d.50 black, lt blue & bl 20 20
1189 – 20d. black, yellow & brn 1·20 1·10
DESIGNS: 2d.50, National Assembly Memorial, Epidavros, and Seal of Provincial Administration; 20d. Signature and seal of John Capodistria, first President of Greece.

250 Hosios Loukas Monastery, Boeotia

1972. Greek Monasteries and Churches. Mult.
1190 50l. Type **250** 10 15
1191 1d. Daphni Church, Attica 10 10
1192 2d. St. John the Divine, Patmos 15 15
1193 2d.50 Panaghia Koumbelidiki Church, Kastoria 20 15
1194 4d.50 Panaghia ton Chalkeon, Saloniki . . . 25 15
1195 6d.50 Panaghia Paregoritissa Church, Arta 30 20
1196 8d.50 St. Paul's Monastery, Mount Athos . . . . . . 85 1·00

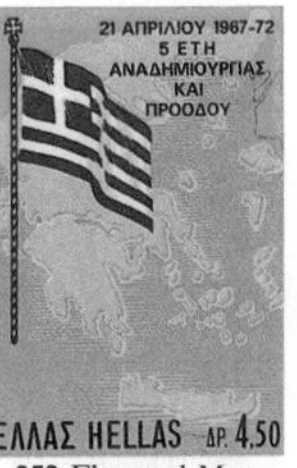

251 Cretan Costume

252 Flag and Map

1972. Greek Costumes (1st series). Mult.
1197 50l. Type **251** 10 10
1198 1d. Pindus bride 10 10
1199 2d. Warrior-chief Missolonghi 20 10
1200 2d.50 Sarakatsana woman, Attica 10 10
1201 3d. Nisiros woman 15 10
1202 4d.50 Megara woman . . . 15 15
1203 6d.50 Trikeri (rural) 25 20
1204 10d. Pylaia woman, Macedonia . . . . 1·60 95
See also Nos. 1232/48 and 1282/96.

1972. 5th Anniv of 1967 Revolution. Mult.
1205 2d.50 Commemorative medal (horiz) 15 10
1206 4d.50 Type **252** 20 20
1207 5d. Facets of modern development 30 30

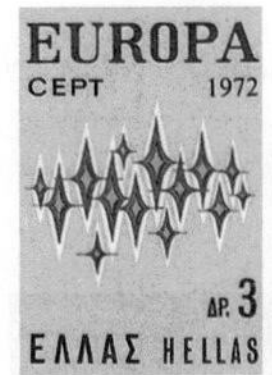

253 "Communications"

254 Acropolis, Athens

1972. Europa.
1208 **253** 3d. multicoloured . . . 55 25
1209 4d.50 multicoloured . . 1·80 1·10

1972. 20th Anniv of Acropolis Motor Rally. Multicoloured.
1210 4d.50 Type **254** 40 45
1211 5d. Emblem and map . . . 40 45

255 "Gaia delivering Erecthonius to Athene"

1972. Greek Mythology. Museum Pieces (1st series).
1212 **255** 1d.50 black and green 15 15
1213 – 2d. black and blue . . . 20 20
1214 – 2d.50 black and brown 20 25
1215 – 5d. black and brown . . . 45 35
DESIGNS: 2d. "Uranus" (altar piece); 2d.50, "The Gods repulsing the Giants"; 5d. "Zeus".
See also Nos. 1252/5 and 1271/4.

256 "Young Athlete" (statue)

1972. Olympic Games, Munich. Ancient Olympics. Multicoloured.
1216 50l. Type **256** 10 15
1217 1d.50 "Wrestlers" (bas-relief) (horiz) 10 10
1218 3d.50 "Female athlete" (statuette) 15 20
1219 4d.50 "Ballgame" (bas-relief) (horiz) 25 25
1220 10d. "Runners" (amphora) (horiz) 80 55

257 Young Stamp Collector

258 "The Birth of Christ"

1972. Stamp Day.
1221 **257** 2d.50 multicoloured . . 15 25

1972. Christmas. Multicoloured.
1222 2d.50 "Pilgrimage of the Magi" 15 20
1223 4d.50 Type **258** 20 20
Nos. 1222/3 were issued together, se-tenant, forming a composite design.

259 University Buildings

1973. Cent of Nat Polytechnic University, Athens.
1224 **259** 2d.50 multicoloured . . 15 20

260 "Spring" (wall fresco)

1973. Archaeological Discoveries, Island of Thera. Multicoloured.
1225 10l. Type **260** 10 20
1226 20l. "Barley" jug 10 10
1227 30l. "Blue Apes" fresco (horiz) 10 10
1228 1d.50 "Bird" (jug) 10 10
1229 2d.50 "Swallows" (detail, "Spring" fresco) (horiz) 20 20
1230 5d. "Wild Goats" fresco (horiz) 20 25
1231 6d.50 "Wrestlers" (detail, fresco) (horiz) 30 30

1973. Greek Regional Costumes (2nd series). As Type **251**. Multicoloured.
1232 10l. Peloponnese 10 20
1233 20l. Central Greece 10 20
1234 30l. Locris (Livanates) . . . 10 20
1235 50l. Skyros (male) 10 20
1236 1d. Spetsai 10 20
1237 1d.50 Almyros 10 20
1238 2d.50 Macedonia (Roumlouki) 10 10
1239 3d.50 Salamis 10 20
1240 4d.50 Epirus (Souli) 10 10
1241 5d. Lefkas (Santa Maura) 10 10
1242 6d.50 Skyros (female) . . . 20 10
1243 8d.50 Corinth 20 20
1244 10d. Corfu (Garitsa) 30 10
1245 15d. Epirus 40 10
1246 20d. Thessaly (Karagouniko) 65 10
1247 30p. Macedonia (Episkopi) 75 30
1248 50d. Thrace (Makra Gefyra) 1·75 65

261 Europa "Posthorn"

1973. Europa.
1249 **261** 2d.50 blue and light blue 25 25
1250 3d. red, orange and lake 30 25
1251 4d.50 brown, bronze and green 40 40

262 "Olympus" (from photograph by Boissonnas)

1973. Greek Mythology (2nd series).
1252 **262** 1d. black and grey . . . 10 20
1253 – 2d. multicoloured . . . 20 25

1254 – 2d.50 black, grey & brn 20 20
1255 – 4d.50 multicoloured . . 40 40
DESIGNS: 2d. "Zeus in combat with Typhoeus" (amphora); 2d.50, "Zeus at Battle of Giants" (altar relief); 4d.50, The "Punishment of Atlas and Prometheus" (vase).

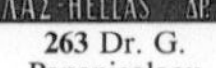
263 Dr. G. Papanicolaou

264 "Our Lady of the Annunciation"

1973. Honouring Dr. George Papanicolaou (cancer specialist).
1256 **263** 2d.50 multicoloured . . 10 10
1257 6d.50 multicoloured . . 20 25

1973. 150th Anniv of Discovery of Miraculous Icon of our Lady of the Annunciation, Tinos.
1258 **264** 2d.50 multicoloured . . 40 25

265 "Triptolemus in a Chariot" (vase)

267 G. Averof

266 Child examining Stamp

1973. European Transport Ministers Conference, Athens.
1259 **265** 4d.50 multicoloured . . 25 25

1973. Stamp Day.
1260 **266** 2d.50 multicoloured . . 25 25

1973. National Benefactors (1st series).
1261 **267** 1d.50 brown 10 20
1262 – 2d. red 10 20
1263 – 2d.50 green 10 20
1264 – 4d. lilac 10 20
1265 – 6d.50 black 20 25
DESIGNS: 2d. A. Arsakis; 2d.50, C. Zappas; 4d. A. Syngros; 6d.50, I. Varvakis.
See also Nos. 1315/18.

268 "Lord Byron in Suliot costume" (by Thomas Phillips)

269 "Harpist of Keros"

1974. 150th Death Anniv of Lord Byron. Multicoloured.
1266 2d.50 Type **268** 10 15
1267 4d.50 "Byron taking the Oath at Grave of Markos Botsaris" (lithograph) . . 10 15

1974. Europa. Ancient Greek Sculptures. Multicoloured.
1268 3d. Type **269** 15 10
1269 4d.50 "Athenian Maiden" 25 20
1270 6d.50 "Charioteer of Delphi" (bronze) 50 55

270 "Theocracy of Zeus" (vase)

271 U.P.U. Emblem within Mycenaean Vase Design

1974. Greek Mythology (3rd series).
1271 **270** 1d.50 black and orange 10 15
1272 – 2d. brown, red & orange 10 10
1273 – 2d.50 black, brn & orge 10 15
1274 – 10d. brown, red & orange 20 20
DESIGNS—HORIZ: 2d. "Athena's Birth" (vase); 2d.50, "Artemis, Apollo and Lito" (vase). VERT: 10d. "Hermes" (vase).

1974. Centenary of U.P.U. Multicoloured.
1275 2d. Type **271** 10 20
1276 4d.50 Hermes (horiz) . . . 10 30
1277 6d.50 Woman reading letter 15 60

272 Crete 1d. Stamp of 1905

1974. Stamp Day.
1278 **272** 2d.50 black, red & violet 15 20

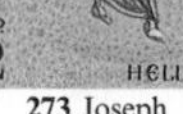
273 Joseph

274 Secret Assembly, Vostitsa

1974. Christmas. Multicoloured.
1279 2d. Type **273** 10 15
1280 4d.50 Virgin and Child on donkey 10 15
1281 8d.50 Jacob 10 15
Nos. 1279/81 were issued together, se-tenant, forming a composite design.

1974. Greek Costumes (3rd series). As T **251**. Multicoloured.
1282 20l. Megara 10 15
1283 30l. Salamis 10 15
1284 50l. Edipsos 10 15
1285 1d. Kymi 10 15
1286 1d.50 Sterea Hellas 10 15
1287 2d. Desfina 10 10
1288 3d. Epirus 10 10
1289 3d.50 Naousa 10 10
1290 4d. Hasia 10 15
1291 4d.50 Thasos 10 10
1292 5d. Skopelos 10 10
1293 6d.50 Epirus 10 10
1294 10d. Pelion 15 15
1295 25d. Kerkyra 25 20
1296 30d. Boeotia (Tanagra) . . 80 65

1975. 150th Death Anniv of Girgorios Dikeos Papaflessas (Soldier).
1297 **274** 4d. black, brown & stone 10 10
1298 – 7d. multicoloured . . . 10 10
1299 – 11d. multicoloured . . . 15 25
DESIGNS—VERT: 7d. Papaflessas in uniform. HORIZ: 11d. Aghioi Apostoli (chapel), Kalamala.

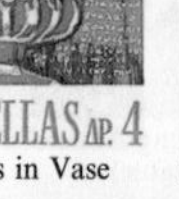
275 Roses in Vase

277 Neolithic Goddess

276 Mansion, Kastoria

1975. Europa. Multicoloured.
1300 4d. Type **275** 15 20
1301 7d. Erotokritos and Aretussa 25 30
1302 11d. Girl and sheep . . . . 1·10 60

1975. National Architecture.
1303 **276** 10l. black and blue . . . 10 15
1304 – 40l. black and red . . . 10 15
1305 – 4d. black and brown . . 10 15
1306 – 6d. black and blue . . . 10 15
1307 – 11d. black and orange 20 25
DESIGNS: 40l. House, Arnea, Halkidiki; 4d. House, Veria; 6d. Mansion, Siatista; 11d. Mansion, Amelakia, Thessaly.

1975. International Women's Year.
1308 **277** 1d.50 brown, deep mauve and mauve . . 10 15
1309 – 8d.50 black, red and ochre 10 15
1310 – 11d. black, dp blue & bl 15 20
DESIGNS: 8d.50, Confrontation between Antigone and Creon; 11d. Women "Looking to the Future".

278 Alexandros Papanastasiou (founder) and University Buildings

1975. 50th Anniv of Thessaloniki University.
1311 **278** 1d.50 sepia and brown 10 15
1312 – 4d. multicoloured . . . 10 15
1313 – 11d. multicoloured . . . 15 25
DESIGNS: 4d. Original University building; 11d. Plan of University city.

279 Greek 100d. Stamp of 1933

281 Pontos Lyre

280 Evangelos Zappas and Zappeion Building

1975. Stamp Day.
1314 **279** 11d. brown, cream & grn 15 20

1975. National Benefactors (2nd series).
1315 **280** 1d. black, grey and green 10 15
1316 – 4d. black, grey and brown 10 10
1317 – 6d. black, brown & orge 10 10
1318 – 11d. black, grey and red 20 25
DESIGNS: 4d. Georgios Rizaris and Rizarios Ecclesiastical School; 6d. Michael Tositsas and Metsovion Technical University; 11d. Nicolaos Zosimas and Zosimea Academy.

1975. Musical Instruments. Multicoloured.
1319 10l. Type **281** 10 10
1320 20l. Musicians (Byzantine mural) 10 15
1321 1d. Cretan lyre 10 10
1322 1d.50 Tambourine 10 10
1323 4d. Cithern-player (from amphora) (horiz) 10 10
1324 6d. Bagpipes 10 10
1325 7d. Lute 10 10
1326 10d. Barrel-organ 10 10
1327 11d. Pipes and zournades 10 10
1328 20d. "Praise God" (Byzantine mural) (horiz) 20 10
1329 25d. Drums 20 15
1330 30d. Kanonaki (horiz) . . . 55 35

282 Early telephone

1976. Telephone Centenary. Multicoloured.
1331 7d. Type **282** 15 20
1332 11d. Modern telephone and globe 20 20
Nos. 1331/2 were issued together, se-tenant, forming a composite design.

283 Battle of Missolonghi

1976. 150th Anniv of Fall of Missolonghi.
1333 **283** 4d. multicoloured . . . 10 20

284 Florina Jug

285 Lion attacking Bull

1976. Europa. Multicoloured.
1334 7d. Type **284** 20 20
1335 8d.50 Plate with birds design (25 × 30 mm) 20 20
1336 11d. Egina pitcher 45 40

1976. Ancient Sealing-stones. Multicoloured.
1337 2d. Type **285** 10 10
1338 4d.50 Water birds 10 10
1339 7d. Wounded bull 10 15
1340 8d.50 Head of Silenus (27 × 40 mm) 10 15
1341 11d. Cow feeding calf (40 × 27 mm) 15 25

286 Long-jumping **287** Lemnos

1976. Olympic Games, Montreal. Mult.
1342 50l. Type **286** 10 15
1343 2d. Handball 10 10
1344 3d.50 Wrestling 10 10
1345 4d. Swimming 15 15
1346 11d. Athens and Montreal stadiums (52 × 37 mm) . . 20 20
1347 25d. The Olympic flame . . 45 45

1976. Tourist Publicity. Multicoloured.
1348 30d. Type **287** 30 10
1349 50d. Lesbos (horiz) 55 25
1350 75d. Chios (horiz) 70 25
1351 100d. Samos (horiz) . . . . 95 1·00

288 "The Magi speaking to the Jews"

289 Lascaris Book of Grammar, 1476

1976. Christmas. Illustrations from manuscripts at Esfigmenou Monastery. Multicoloured.
1352 4d. Type **288** 10 15
1353 7d. "The Adoration of the Magi" 20 20

1976. 500th Anniv of Printing of First Greek Book.
1354 **289** 4d. multicoloured . . . 10 15

290 Heinrich Schliemann **291** "Patients visiting Aesculapius" (relief)

1976. Centenary of Schliemann's Excavation of the Royal Graves, Mycenae. Multicoloured.
1355 2d. Type **290** 10 10
1356 4d. Gold bracelet (horiz) . . 10 10
1357 5d. Silver and gold brooch 10 15
1358 7d. Gold diadem (horiz) . . 10 15
1359 11d. Gold mask 20 25

1977. International Rheumatism Year.
1360 **291** 50l. black, stone and red 10 15
1361 – 1d. black, orange and red 10 10
1362 – 1d.50 black, stone and red 10 10
1363 – 2d. black, orange and red 10 10
1364 – 20d. black, stone and red 15 25
DESIGNS—(22 × 27 mm): 1d. Ancient clinic; 1d.50, "Aseculapius curing a young man" (relief); 2d. Hercules and nurse. (23 × 34 mm): 20d. "Cured patient offering model of leg" (relief).

292 Fortresses of Mani

1977. Europa. Multicoloured.
1365 5d. Type **292** 15 15
1366 7d. Santorin (vert) 15 20
1367 15d. Lassithi Plain, Crete . . 60 50

293 Emblem and Transport

1977. 45th European Conference of Ministers of Transport.
1368 **293** 7d. multicoloured . . . 10 15

294 Alexandria Lighthouse (Roman coin)

1977. "The Civilizing Influence of Alexander the Great". Multicoloured.
1369 50l. Type **294** 10 20
1370 1d. "Placing the Works of Homer in Achilles' tomb" (fresco, Raphael) 10 10
1371 1d.50 Descending to sea bed in special ship (Flemish miniature) 10 10
1372 3d. In search of the water of life (Hindu plate) 10 15
1373 7d. Alexander the Great on horseback (Coptic carpet) 10 15
1374 11d. Listening to oracle (Byzantine manuscript) . . 20 25
1375 30d. Death of Alexander the Great (Persian miniature) 25 30

295 Wreath in Front of University **296** Archbishop Makarios

1977. Restoration of Democracy.
1376 **295** 4d. blue, green and black 10 10
1377 – 7d. multicoloured . . . 10 10
1378 – 20d. multicoloured . . . 20 25
DESIGNS—HORIZ: (26 × 22 mm) 7d. Demonstrators at University. VERT: (22 × 26 mm) 20d. Hand with olive branch, University and flags.

1977. Archbishop Makarios Commemoration.
1379 **296** 4d. black and grey . . . 10 15
1380 – 7d. black, brown & stone 10 15
DESIGN: 7d. Makarios and map of Cyprus.

297 Melas Building, Athens (former post office)

1977. 19th-century Hellenic Architecture.
1381 **297** 50l. black, stone and red 10 10
1382 – 1d. black, stone & green 10 10
1383 – 1d.50 black, stone & bl 10 10
1384 – 2d. black, stone & green 10 10
1385 – 5d. black, stone & yellow 10 10
1386 – 50d. black, stone & orge 25 45
DESIGNS: 1d. Institution for the Blind, Thessalonika; 1d.50, Town Hall of Hermoupolis, Syros; 2d. Branch Office of National Bank, Piraeus; 5d. Ilissia (Palace of Duchess of Plakentia), Athens; 50d. Municipal Theatre, Patras.

298 The Battle of Navarino

1977. 150th Anniv of Battle of Navarino.
1387 **298** 4d. yellow, black & brn 10 15
1388 – 7d. multicoloured . . . 15 20
DESIGN: 7d. Admirals Van der Heyden, Sir Edward Codrington and Comte de Rigny.

299 Parthenon and Industrial Complex

1977. Environmental Protection. Mult.
1389 3d. Type **299** 10 10
1390 4d. Birds and fish (horiz) . . 10 10
1391 7d. Living and dead trees (horiz) 10 15
1392 30d. Head of Erechtheum caryatid and chimneys . . 25 35

300 Map of Greece and Ships

1977. "Greeks Abroad". Multicoloured.
1393 4d. Type **300** 10 10
1394 5d. Globe and Greek flag 10 10
1395 7d. Globe and swallows . . 10 15
1396 11d. Envelope with flags . . 15 15
1397 13d. Map of the World . . 20 30

301 "The Port of Kalamata" (C. Parthenis)

1977. Greek Paintings. Multicoloured.
1398 1d.50 Type **301** 15 20
1399 2d.50 "Arsanas" (S. Papaloucas) (vert) . . 10 15
1400 4d. "Santorin" (C. Maleas) 10 10
1401 7d. "The Engagement" (N. Gyzis) 10 15
1402 11d. "The Straw Hat" (N. Lytras) (vert) 15 15
1403 15d. "Spring" (G. Iacovidis) 20 25

302 "Ebenus cretica" **303** Horse Postman and Pre-stamp Cancel

1978. Greek Flora. Multicoloured.
1404 1d.50 Type **302** 10 15
1405 2d.50 "Fritillaria rhodokanakis" 10 10
1406 3d. "Campanula oreadum" 10 10
1407 4d. "Lilium heldreichii" . . 15 15
1408 7d. "Viola delphinantha" . . 15 20
1409 25d. "Paeonia rhodia" . . . 25 30

1978. 150th Anniv of Postal Service. Mult.
1410 4d. Type **303** 10 10
1411 5d. "Maximilianos" (passenger steamer) and Greek "Hermes" stamp 15 10
1412 7d. Steam mail train and 1896 Olympic Games stamp 15 20
1413 30d. Postmen on motor cycles and 1972 "Stamp Day" commemorative . . 20 35
MS1414 101 × 92 mm. Nos. 1410/13 (sold at 60d.) 95 60

304 Lighting the Olympic Flame **305** St. Sophia, Salonika

1978. 80th International Olympic Committee Session, Athens. Multicoloured.
1415 7d. Type **304** 20 15
1416 13d. Start of 100 m race . . 45 40

1978. Europa. Multicoloured.
1417 4d. Type **305** 25 25
1418 7d. Lysicrates' Monument, Athens 35 35

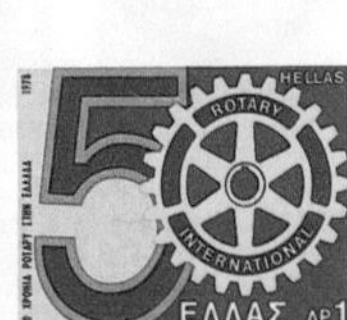

306 Bust of Aristotle **307** Rotary Emblem (50th anniv)

1978. 2300th Death Anniv of Aristotle. Multicoloured.
1419 2d. Type **306** 10 15
1420 4d. "The School of Athens" (detail Raphael) 10 15
1421 7d. Map of Chalkidiki and statue plinth 10 15
1422 20d. "Aristotle the Wise" (Byzantine fresco) (21 × 37 mm) 20 30

1978. Anniversaries and Events. Mult.
1423 1d. Type **307** 10 15
1424 1d.50 Surgery (11th Greek Surgery Congress) (vert) 10 15
1425 2d.50 Ugo Foscolo (poet, birth bicentenary) 10 15
1426 5d. Bronze head (25th anniv of European Convention on Human Rights) . . . 10 15
1427 7d. Hand with reins (Conference of Ministers of Culture of Council of Europe countries) (vert) 10 15
1428 13d. Wright Flyer I with Daedalus and Icarus (75th anniv of first powered flight) (vert) 20 30

308 The Poor Woman with Five Children

1978. "The Twelve Months" (Greek fairy tale). Multicoloured.
1429 2d. Type **308** 10 10
1430 3d. The poor woman and the twelve months 10 15
1431 4d. The poor woman and the gold coins 10 15
1432 20d. The poor woman with her children and the rich woman with the snakes 20 25

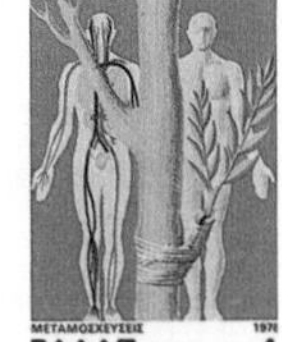

309 Grafted Plant and Circulation Diagram

1978. Transplants. Multicoloured.
1433 4d. Type **309** 10 10
1434 10d. "Miracle of Sts. Cosmas and Damian" (Alonso de Sedano) . . . 10 15

310 "Virgin and Child" **311** First Academy, Nauplion, and Cadet

1978. Christmas. Icons from Stavronikita Monastery, Mount Athos. Multicoloured.
1435 4d. Type **310** 10 10
1436 7d. "The Baptism of Christ" 10 15

1978. 150th Anniv of Military Academy. Multicoloured.
1437 1d.50 Type **311** 10 15
1438 2d. Academy coat of arms (vert) 10 10
1439 10d. Modern Academy, Athens, and cadet 20 25

312 "Antipliarchos Laskos" (destroyer)

1978. Greek Naval Ships. Multicoloured.
1440 50l. Type **312** 10 10
1441 1d. "Andromeda" (motor torpedo-boat) 10 10
1442 2d.50 "Papanicolis" (submarine) 10 10
1443 4d. "Psara" (cruiser) 10 10
1444 5d. "Madonna of Hydra" (armed sailing caique) . . 15 10
1445 7d. Byzantine dromon . . . 15 15
1446 50d. Athenian trireme . . . 70 45

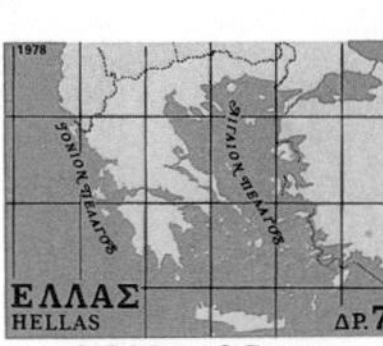

313 Map of Greece **314** Kitsos Tsavellas

1978. The Greek State.
1447 **313** 7d. multicoloured . . . 10 10
1448 11d. multicoloured . . . 15 10
1449 13d. multicoloured . . . 20 25

1979. "The Struggle of the Souliots".
1450 **314** 1d.50 lt brn, blk & brn 10 10
1451 – 3d. multicoloured . . . 10 10
1452 – 10d. multicoloured . . . 10 15
1453 – 20d. ochre, black and brown 15 20
DESIGNS—HORIZ: 3d. Souli Castle; 10d. Fighting Souliots. VERT: 20d. The dance of Zalongo.

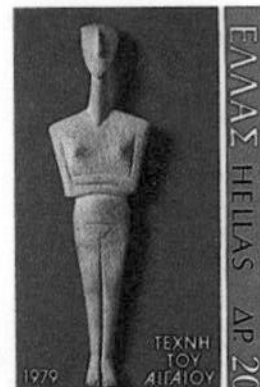

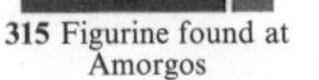

315 Figurine found at Amorgos — 316 Cretan Postmen

1979. Art of the Aegean.
1454 **315** 20d. multicoloured . . . 20 25

1979. Europa. Multicoloured.
1455 4d. Type **316** 10 15
1456 7d. Mounted postman . . . 15 1·60
Nos. 1454/5 were issued in se-tenant pairs, forming a composite design.

317 Nicolas Skoufas — 318 Flags of Member States forming Ear of Wheat

1979. Anniversaries and Events. Mult.
1457 1d.50 Type **317** (founder of Friendly Society, birth bicentenary) 10 25
1458 2d. Steam and diesel locomotives (75th anniv of railway) (horiz) 10 20
1459 3d. Basketball (European Basketball Championship) 10 20
1460 4d. Fossil moonfish "Mene psarianos" (7th International Congress of Mediterranaen Neogene) (horiz) 10 20
1461 10d. Greek church (Balkan Tourist Year) 10 20
1462 20d. Victory of Paeonius and flags (50th anniv of Balkan Sports) 20 30

1979. Signing of Treaty, Accession of Greece to European Community. Multicoloured.
1463 7d. Type **318** 10 10
1464 30d. European Parliament (horiz) 15 35

319 "Girl with Dove" (classic statue) — 320 Head of Philip of Macedonia

1979. International Year of the Child. Multicoloured.
1465 5d. Type **319** 10 10
1466 8d. Girl with doves 10 15
1467 20d. "Mother and Children" (detail, Iacovides) 20 25

1979. Archaeological Discoveries from Vergina. Multicoloured.
1468 6d. Type **320** 10 10
1469 8d. Gold Wreath 10 15
1470 10d. Copper vessel 10 10
1471 14d. Golden casket (horiz) 10 15
1472 18d. Silver ewer 10 25
1473 20d. Gold quiver 20 20
1474 30d. Iron cuirass 35 50

321 Purple Heron — 322 Agricultural Bank of Greece (50th anniv)

1979. Endangered Birds. Multicoloured.
1475 6d. Type **321** 15 20
1476 8d. Audouin's gull 30 20
1477 10d. Eleonora's falcon (horiz) 30 20
1478 14d. River kingfisher (horiz) 35 30
1479 20d. Eastern white pelican 85 80
1480 25d. White-tailed sea eagle 1·10 85

1979. Anniversaries and Events.
1481 **322** 3d. black, yellow & olive 10 15
1482 – 4d. multicoloured . . . 10 15
1483 – 6d. multicoloured . . . 10 15
1484 – 8d. multicoloured . . . 10 15
1485 – 10d. multicoloured . . . 15 20
1486 – 12d. multicoloured . . . 15 20
1487 – 14d. multicoloured . . . 20 20
1488 – 18d. multicoloured . . . 20 20
1489 – 25d. multicoloured . . . 40 45
DESIGNS—HORIZ: 10d. Ionic capital and map of Balkans ("Balkanfila '79" Stamp Exhibition); 25d. Parliamentary Meeting (104th anniv of Greek Parliament). VERT: 4d. Cosmas the Aetolian (monk and martyr) (death bicent.); 6d. Basil the Great (1600th death anniv); 8d. Magnifying glass and map of Balkan countries ("Balkanfila '79" Stamp Exhibition); 12d. Aristolelis Valaoritis (poet) (death centenary); 14d. Golfer (World Golfing Championship); 18d. Bust of Hippocrates (International Hippocratic Foundation, Kos).

323 Parnassos — 324 Gate of Galerius

1979. Landscapes. Multicoloured.
1490 50l. Type **323** 10 10
1491 1d. Tempi (horiz) 10 10
1492 2d. Milos 10 10
1493 4d. Vikos Gorge 10 10
1494 5d. Misolonghi (horiz) . . . 10 10
1495 6d. Louros Aqueduct . . . 10 10
1496 7d. Samothraki 10 10
1497 8d. Sithonia, Chalkidike (horiz) 10 10
1498 10d. Samaria Gorge 10 10
1499 12d. Sifnos 10 10
1500 14d. Kymi (horiz) 10 15
1501 18d. Ios 10 15
1502 20d. Thasos 15 15
1503 30d. Paros (horiz) 20 15
1504 50d. Cephalonia 55 60

1980. 1st Hellenic Nephrology Congress, Thessalonika.
1505 **324** 8d. blue, black and red 15 15

325 Aegosthena Castle — 326 Aristarchus' Theorem and Temple of Hera

1980. Castles, Caves and Bridges. Mult.
1506 4d. Type **325** 10 15
1507 6d. Byzantine castle, Thessalonika (horiz) . . . 10 15
1508 8d. Perama cave, Ioannina 10 10
1509 10d. Dyros cave, Mani . . . 10 10
1510 14d. Arta bridge (horiz) . . 10 10
1511 20d. Kalogiros bridge, Epirus (horiz) 25 30

1980. 2300th Birth Anniv of Aristarchus of Samos (astronomer).
1512 **326** 10d. pink, black & brown 15 15
1513 – 20d. multicoloured . . . 20 35
DESIGN: 20d. Heliocentric system.

327 George Seferis (writer)

1980. Europa.
1514 **327** 8d. brown, blue & black 15 15
1515 – 14d. brn, blk and cream 25 35
DESIGN: 14d. Maria Callas (opera singer).

328 Open Book

1980. Energy Conservation. Multicoloured.
1516 8d. Type **328** 10 15
1517 20d. Lightbulb and candle (vert) 10 25

329 Fire-fighting

1980. Anniversaries and Events. Mult.
1518 4d. Type **329** (50th anniv of fire brigade) 10 20
1519 6d. St. Demetrius (mosaic) (1700th birth anniv) (vert) 10 20
1520 8d. Revolutionaries (Theriso revolution, 75th anniv) . . 10 20
1521 10d. Ancient vase and olive branch (World Olive Oil Year) (vert) 10 20
1522 14d. International press emblem (15th International Journalists Federation Congress) (vert) 15 20
1523 20d. Constantinos Ikonomos (cleric and scholar), (birth bicent.) (vert) 15 25

330 Olympia and Coin of Elia

1980. Olympic Games, Moscow. Designs showing Greek stadia. Multicoloured.
1524 8d. Type **330** 10 10
1525 14d. Delphi and Delphic coin 20 30
1526 18d. Epidaurus and coin of Olympia 15 20
1527 20d. Rhodes and coin of Kos 15 15
1528 50d. Panathenaic stadium and First Olympic Games medal 50 55

331 Asbestos

1980. Minerals. Multicoloured.
1529 6d. Type **331** 10 10
1530 8d. Gypsum (vert) 10 10
1531 10d. Copper 10 10
1532 14d. Barite (vert) 20 30
1533 18d. Chromite 10 15
1534 20d. Mixed sulphides (vert) 10 15
1535 30d. Bauxite (vert) 30 30

332 Dassault Mirage III Jet Fighter — 333 Left Detail of Poulakis' Painting

1980. Anniversaries and Events. Mult.
1536 6d. Breakdown truck (20th anniv of Automobile and Touring Club of Greece road assistance service) (horiz) 10 20
1537 8d. Type **332** (50th anniv of Air Force) 10 20
1538 12d. Piper Super Cub light airplane outside hangar (50th anniv of Thessalonika Flying Club) (horiz) 15 20
1539 20d. Harbour scene (50th anniv of Piraeus Port Organization) 30 30
1540 25d. Association for Macedonian Studies Headquarters (40th anniv) 25 35

1980. Christmas. Details from "He is Happy Thanks to You" by T. Poulakis (in St. John's Monastery, Pataros). Multicoloured.
1541 6d. Type **333** 10 20
1542 14d. Virgin and Child (centre) 10 20
1543 20d. Right detail 20 30
Nos. 1541/3 were issued together, se-tenant, forming a composite design.

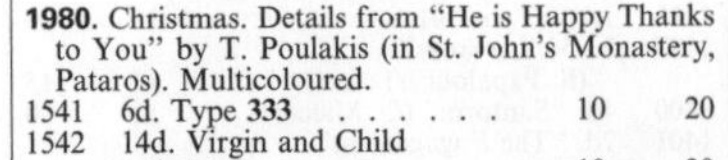

334 Fresh and Canned Vegetables

1981. Exports. Multicoloured.
1544 9d. Type **334** 10 10
1545 17d. Fruit 15 15
1546 20d. Cotton 15 15
1547 25d. Marble 20 30

335 "Kira Maria" (Alexandrian folk dance)

1981. Europa. Multicoloured.
1548 12d. Type **335** 15 15
1549 17d. "Sousta" (Cretan dance) 35 35

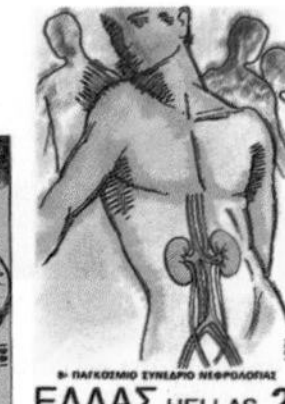

336 Olympic Stadium, Kalogreza — 337 Human Figure showing Kidneys

1981. European Athletic Championships, Athens (1982) (1st issue).
1550 **336** 12d. blue, black & lt blue 10 10
1551 – 17d. multicoloured . . . 20 30
DESIGN: 17d. Athletes converging on Greece.
See also Nos. 1586/8.

1981. Anniversaries and Events.
1552 **337** 2d. multicoloured . . . 10 20
1553 – 3d. multicoloured . . . 10 20
1554 – 6d. multicoloured . . . 10 20
1555 – 9d. yellow, black & brn 10 20
1556 – 12d. multicoloured . . . 25 20
1557 – 21d. multicoloured . . . 15 25
1558 – 40d. red, blue & dp blue 20 50
DESIGNS AND EVENTS—VERT: 2d. Type **337** (8th World Nephrology Conference, Athens); 3d. Parachutist, glider, Potez 25 biplane and boy with model glider (50th anniv of Greek National Air Club); 6d. Meteora Monasteries, Thessaly, and Konitsa Bridge, Epirus (International Historical Symposium, Volos, and centenary of incorporation of Thessaly and Epirus into Greece); 12d. Oil rig (first Greek oil production); 40d. Heart (15th World Cardiovascular Surgery Conference Athens). HORIZ: 9d. Bowl with "eye" decoration (50th anniv of Greek Ophthalmological Society); 21d. Globes, plant and coin (Foundation in Athens of World Association for International Relations).

338 Variable Scallops — 339 Aegean Island Bell Tower

1981. Shells, Fishes and Butterflies. Mult.
1559 4d. Type **338** 15 20
1560 5d. Painted comber (fish) . . 15 20
1561 12d. Mediterranean parrotfishes 15 20
1562 15d. Dentex (fish) 15 20
1563 17d. Apollo (butterfly) . . . 20 50
1564 50d. Pale clouded yellow (butterfly) 55 70

1981. Bell Towers and Altar Screens. Mult.
1565 4d. Type **339** 10 20
1566 6d. Altar gate, St. Paraskevi Church, Metsovo 10 20
1567 9d. Altar gate, Pelion (horiz) 10 10
1568 12d. Bell tower, Saints Constantine and Helen Church, Halkiades, Epirus 10 10
1569 17d. Altar screen, St. Nicholas Church, Velvendos (horiz) 15 20

1570 30d. Icon of St. Jacob and stand, Alexandroupolis Church Museum 20 20
1571 40d. Upper section of altar gate, St. Nicholas Church, Makrinitsa 40 50

340 Town Scene

1981. Anniversaries and Events. Mult.
1572 3d. Type **340** (Council of Europe Urban Renaissance campaign) . . 10 20
1573 9d. St. Simeon, Archbishop of Thessalonika (Canonization by Greek Orthodox Church) (vert) 10 20
1574 12d. Child Jesus (detail from Byzantine icon) (Breast feeding campaign) (vert) 10 20
1575 17d. Gina Bachauer (pianist, 5th death anniv) (vert) . . 15 20
1576 21d. Constantine Broumidis (artist, 175th birth anniv) (vert) 15 20
1577 50d. "Phoenix" banknotes 1831 (first banknotes, 150th anniv) 25 50

341 Old Parliament Building (museum)

342 "Flight from Missolonghi"

1982. Anniversaries and Events. Mult.
1578 2d. Type **341** (centenary of Historical and Ethnological Society) . . 10 20
1579 9d. Angelos Sikelianos (poet, 31st death anniv) (vert) 15 10
1580 15d. Harilaos Tricoupis (politician, 150th birth anniv) (vert) 10 20
1581 21d. Mermaid (History of Aegean Islands Exhibition) (vert) 10 20
1582 30d. Airbus Industrie A300 jetliner and emblem (25th anniv of Olympic Airways) 20 30
1583 50d. Skull of Petralona man and Petralona cave (3rd European Congress of Anthropology, Petralona) (vert) 35 55

1982. Europa. Multicoloured.
1584 21d. Bust of Miltiades and shield (Battle of Marathon) 45 20
1585 30d. Type **342** . . . . . . 1·00 70

343 Pole-vaulter and Wreath

1982. European Athletic Championships (2nd issue). Multicoloured.
1586 21d. Type **343** 15 20
1587 25d. Women runners (vert) 15 20
1588 40d. Athletes at start of race, shot putter, high jumper and hurdler . . . 45 40

344 Lectionary Heading

1982. Byzantine Book Illustrations. Mult.
1589 4d. Type **344** 10 10
1590 6d. Initial letter E (vert) . . 10 10
1591 12d. Initial letter T (vert) . . 10 10
1592 15d. Canon-table of Gospel readings (vert) 15 15
1593 80d. Heading from zoology book 40 60

345 "Karaiskakis' Camp in Piraeus" (detail, von Krazeisen)

346 Cypriot "Disappearances" Demonstration

1982. Birth Bicentenary of Georges Karaiskakis (revolutionary leader).
1594 **345** 12d. green, black & blue 15 10
1595 – 50d. multicoloured . . . 50 60
DESIGN: 50d. Karaiskakis meditating.

1982. Amnesty International Year of the "Disappearances". Multicoloured.
1596 15d. Type **346** 10 15
1597 75d. Victims, barbed wire and candle 50 75

347 "Demonstration in Athens, 25 March 1942–44" (P. Zachariou.)

1982. National Resistance, 1941–44. Mult.
1598 1d. Type **347** 10 10
1599 2d. "Kalavryta's Sacrifice" (S. Vasillou) 10 10
1600 5d. "Resistance in Thrace" (A. Tassos) (vert) 10 10
1601 9d. "The Onset of the Struggle in Crete" (P. Gravalos) (vert) . . . 10 10
1602 12d. Resistance Fighters (vert) 15 10
1603 21d. "Gorgopotamos" (A. Tassos) (vert) 30 25
1604 30d. "Kaisariani, Athens" (G. Sikeliotis) 25 25
1605 50d. "The Struggle in Northern Greece" (V. Katraki) 55 40
MS1606 Two sheets (a) 90 × 81 mm. Nos. 1598/9 and 1604/5; (b) 81 × 90 mm. Nos. 1600/3 . . . 3·00 2·25

348 Mary and Jesus

1982. Christmas. Early Christian Bas-reliefs. Multicoloured.
1607 9d. Type **348** 10 20
1608 21d. Jesus in manger . . . 20 50

349 Figurehead from Tsamados's "Ares" (brig)

1983. 25th Anniv of International Maritime Organization. Ships' Figureheads. Mult.
1609 11d. Type **349** 15 30
1610 15d. Miaoulis's "Ares" (full-rigged ship) (vert) 15 10
1611 18d. Topsail schooner from Sphakia (vert) 20 10
1612 25d. Bouboulina's "Spetses" (full-rigged ship) (vert) . . 25 20
1613 40d. Babas's "Epameinondas" (brig) (vert) 40 30
1614 50d. "Carteria" (steamer) 70 55

350 Letter and Map of Greece showing Postcode Districts

351 Archimedes

1983. Inauguration of Postcode. Multicoloured.
1615 15d. Type **350** 15 10
1616 25d. Hermes' head within posthorn 30 25

1983. Europa. Multicoloured.
1617 25d. Acropolis, Athens (49 × 34 mm) 50 35
1618 80d. Type **351** . . . . . . 1·10 1·10

352 Rowing

353 Marinos Antypas (farmers' leader)

1983. Sports. Multicoloured.
1619 15d. Type **352** 10 20
1620 18d. Water skiing (vert) . . 30 20
1621 27d. Windsurfing (vert) . . 50 40
1622 50d. Ski lift (vert) 30 30
1623 80d. Skiing 70 95

1983. Personalities. Multicoloured.
1624 **353** 6d. multicoloured . . . 10 10
1625 – 9d. multicoloured . . . 10 10
1626 – 15d. multicoloured . . . 10 10
1627 – 20d. multicoloured . . . 15 10
1628 – 27d. multicoloured . . . 20 15
1629 – 32d. multicoloured . . . 30 30
1630 – 40d. yellow, brown & blk 35 30
1631 – 50d. multicoloured . . . 55 55
DESIGNS: 9d. Nicholas Plastiras (soldier and statesman); 15d. George Papandreou (statesman); 20d. Constantin Cavafy (poet); 27d. Nikos Kazantzakis (writer); 32d. Manolis Calomiris (composer); 40d. George Papanicolaou (medical researcher); 50d. Despina Achladioti, "Matron of Rho" (patriot).

354 Democritus

355 Poster by V. Katraki

1983. 1st Int Democritus Congress, Xanthe.
1632 **354** 50d. multicoloured . . . 35 35

1983. 10th Anniv of Polytechnic School Uprising. Multicoloured.
1633 15d. Type **355** 10 10
1634 30d. Students leaving Polytechnic 25 30

356 The Deification of Homer

357 Horse's Head, Chariot of Seline

1983. Homeric Odes. Multicoloured.
1635 **356** 2d. sepia and brown . . 10 10
1636 – 3d. brown, lt orge & orge 10 10
1637 – 4d. yellow, brn & dp brn 10 10
1638 – 5d. multicoloured . . . 10 10
1639 – 6d. orange and brown 10 10
1640 – 10d. lt orge, brn & orge 10 10
1641 – 14d. orge, lt orge & brn 10 10
1642 – 15d. lt orge, orge & brn 10 10
1643 – 20d. bistre, black & brn 20 10
1644 – 27d. brown, pale orange and orange 20 10
1645 – 30d. brown, pale orange and orange 20 10
1646 – 32d. orge, brn & lt orge 35 20
1647 – 50d. brn, lt orge & orge 35 20
1648 – 75d. brown, orange & red 45 20
1649 – 100d. sepia, green & brn 1·00 65
DESIGN—HORIZ: 3d. Abduction of Helen by Paris (pot); 4d. Wooden horse; 5d. Achilles throwing dice with Ajax (jar); 14d. Battle between Ajax and Hector (dish); 15d. Priam requesting body of Hector (pot); 27d. Ulysses escaping from Polyphemus's cave; 32d. Ulysses and Sirens; 50d. Ulysses slaying suitors; 75d. Heroes of Iliad (cup). VERT: 6d. Achilles; 10d. Hector receiving arms from his parents (vase); 20d. Binding of Polyphemus; 30d. Ulysses meeting Nausica; 100d. Homer (bust).

1984. Parthenon Marbles. Multicoloured.
1650 14d. Type **357** 20 20
1651 15d. Dionysus 20 20
1652 20d. Hestia, Dione and Aphrodite 30 30
1653 27d. Ilissus 35 30
1654 32d. Lapith and Centaur . . 75 80
MS1655 105 × 81 mm. 15d. Horseman (left); 21d. Horeman (right); 27d. Heroes (left); 32d. Heroes (right) . . . . 3·50 2·25

358 Bridge

359 Ancient Stadium, Olympia

1984. Europa. 25th Anniv of C.E.P.T.
1656 **358** 15d. multicoloured . . . 30 25
1657 27d. multicoloured . . . 95 1·00

1984. Olympic Games, Los Angeles. Multicoloured.
1658 14d. Type **359** 20 20
1659 15d. Athletes preparing for training 20 20
1660 20d. Flute player, discus thrower and long jumper 35 20
1661 32d. Athletes training . . . 50 45
1662 80d. K. Vikelas and Panathenaic Stadium . . 1·20 1·10

360 Tank on Map of Cyprus

361 Pelion Steam Train

1984. 10th Anniv of Turkish Invasion of Cyprus. Multicoloured.
1663 20d. Type **360** 30 20
1664 32d. Hand grasping barbed wire and map of Cyprus 45 40

1984. Railway Centenary. Multicoloured.
1665 15d. Type **361** 35 25
1666 20d. Steam goods train on Papadia Bridge (vert) . . 80 70
1667 30d. Piraeus-Peloponnese steam train 55 35
1668 50d. Cogwheel railway, Kalavryta (vert) . . . . . 1·40 95

362 Athens 5th Cent B.C. Silver Coin on Plan of City

363 "10" enclosing Arms

1984. 150th Anniv of Athens as Capital. Multicoloured.
1669 15d. Type **362** 35 20
1670 100d. Symbols of ancient Athens and skyline of modern Athens 40 85

1984. 10th Anniv of Revolution.
1671 **363** 95d. multicoloured . . . 85 35

364 "Annunciation"

365 Running

1984. Christmas. Multicoloured.
1672 14d. Type **364** 40 25
1673 20d. "Nativity" 45 25
1674 25d. "Presentation in the Temple" 50 45
1675 32d. "Baptism of Christ" . . 60 60
Nos. 1672/5 show scenes from Hagion Panton icon by Athanasios Tountas.

1985. 16th European Indoor Athletics Championships, New Phaleron. Multicoloured.
1676 12d. Type **365** 20 20
1677 15d. Putting the shot . . . 20 15
1678 20d. Sports stadium (37 × 24 mm) 35 20
1679 25d. Hurdling 35 20
1680 80d. High jumping 85 70

366 Catacomb Niche

1985. Catacombs of Melos. Multicoloured.
1681 15d. Type **366** 20 10
1682 20d. Martyrs' altars and niches central passageway 30 15
1683 100d. Niches 70 60

367 Apollo and Marsyas

1985. Europa. Multicoloured.
1684 27d. Type **367** 55 45
1685 80d. Dimitris Mitropoulos and Nikos Skalkotas (composers) 80 60

368 Coin (315 B.C.) and "Salonika" (relief)

1985. 2300th Anniv of Salonika. Mult.
1686 1d. Type **368** 10 20
1687 5d. Saints Demetrius and Methodius (mosaics) (49 × 34 mm) 15 20
1688 15d. Galerius's Arch (detail) (Roman period) 10 10
1689 20d. Salonika's eastern walls (Byzantine period) 25 10
1690 32d. Upper City, Salonika 25 20
1691 50d. Greek army liberating Salonika, 1912 . . . . . 70 20
1692 80d. Soldier's legs and Salonika (German occupation 1941–44) . . . 70 30
1693 95d. Contemporary views of Salonika (60th anniv of Aristotelian University and International Trade Fair) (49 × 34 mm) . . . 1·10 1·00

369 Urn on Map of Cyprus

370 "Democracy crowning the City" (relief)

1985. 25th Anniv of Republic of Cyprus.
1694 **369** 32d. multicoloured . . . 35 35

1985. Athens, "Cultural Capital of Europe".
1695 **370** 15d. multicoloured . . . 15 10
1696 – 20d. black, grey and blue 20 20
1697 – 32d. multicoloured . . . 55 30
1698 – 80d. multicoloured . . . 80 85
DESIGNS—HORIZ: 20d. Tritons and dolphins (mosaic floor, Roman baths, Hieratis); 80d. Capodistrian University, Athens. VERT: 32d. Angel (fresco, Pentelis Cave).

371 Children of different Races

373 Folk Dance

372 Girl with Flower Crown

1985. International Youth Year (1st issue) (15, 25d.) and 40th Anniv of United Nations Organization (27, 100d.). Multicoloured.
1699 15d. Type **371** 10 10
1700 25d. Doves and youths . . . 25 20
1701 27d. Interior of U.N. General Assembly 55 20
1702 100d. U.N. Building, New York, and U.N. emblem 75 90
See also No. **MS**1703.

1985. International Youth Year (2nd issue). "Piraeus '85" Stamp Exhibition. Sheet 87 × 62 mm.
MS1703 **372** 100d. multicoloured 1·10 1·10

1985. Pontic Culture. Multicoloured.
1704 12d. Type **373** 20 20
1705 15d. Monastery of Our Lady of Soumela 30 20
1706 27d. Women's costumes (vert) 45 25
1707 32d. Trapezus High School 50 25
1708 80d. Sinope Castle 75 75

374 Hestia

375 "Ephebos of Antikythera"

1986. Gods of Olympus.
1709 **374** 5d. orange, black & brn 10 15
1710 – 18d. orange, black & brn 20 15
1711 – 27d. orange, black & bl 35 15
1712 – 32d. orange, black & red 45 25
1713 – 35d. orange, black & brn 45 25
1714 – 40d. orange, black & red 60 20
1715 – 50d. orange, black & grey 75 25
1716 – 110d. orange, blk & brn 95 25
1717 – 150d. orange, blk & grey 1·40 25
1718 – 200d. orange, black & bl 1·60 35
1719 – 300d. orange, black & bl 2·20 90
1720 – 500d. orange, black & bl 5·50 2·50
DESIGNS: 18d. Hermes; 27d. Aphrodite; 32d. Ares; 35d. Athene; 40d. Hephaestus; 50d. Artemis; 110d. Apollo; 150d. Demeter; 200d. Poseidon; 300d. Hera; 500d. Zeus.

1986. Sports Events and Anniversaries.
1721 **375** 18d. green, black & grey 20 20
1722 – 27d. yellow, black & red 40 30
1723 – 32d. multicoloured . . . 60 45
1724 – 35d. green, black & bis 90 70
1725 – 40d. multicoloured . . . 75 60
1726 – 50d. multicoloured . . . 75 40
1727 – 110d. multicoloured . . 2·10 1·50
DESIGNS—VERT: 18d. Type **375** (1st World Junior Athletics Championships); 32d. Footballers (Pan-European Junior Football Finals); 35d. "Wrestlers" (sculpture) (Pan-European Freestyle and Greco-Roman Wrestling Championships); 50d. Cyclists (6th International Round Europe Cycling Meet.). HORIZ: 27d. "Diadoumenos" (sculpture by Polycleitus) (1st World Junior Athletics Championships); 40d. Volleyball players (Men's World Volleyball Championships); 110d. "Victory" (unadopted design by Nikephoros Lytras for first Olympic Games commemoratives, 1896) (90th anniv of modern Olympic Games).

376 Fastening Seat Belt

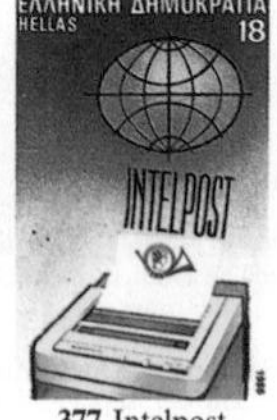

377 Intelpost

1986. European Road Safety Year. Mult.
1728 18d. Type **376** 30 10
1729 27d. Motorcyclist in traffic 70 45
1730 110d. Child strapped in back seat of car and speed limit signs . . . . 1·40 80

1986. New Postal Services. Multicoloured.
1731 18d. Type **377** 25 20
1732 110d. "Express Mail" banner around globe . . 85 95

378 Sapling between Hands and burning Forest

1986. Europa.
1733 **378** 35d. green, black & orge 1·80 1·70
1734 – 110d. blue, black & grn 2·10 2·20
DESIGN: 110d. Dalmatian pelicans on Prespa Lake.

379 Victims' Memorial and Workers

1986. Centenary of Chicago May Day Strike.
1735 **379** 40d. multicoloured . . . 45 35

380 Swearing-in of Venizelos Government **381** Dove and Sun

1986. 50th Death Anniv of Eleftherios Venizelos (politician) (18d.) and 6th International Crete Conference, Hania (110d.). Multicoloured.
1736 18d. Type **380** 25 20
1737 110d. Hania harbour . . . 1·00 85

1986. International Peace Year. Multicoloured.
1738 18d. Type **381** 20 20
1739 35d. Dove holding olive branch with flags as leaves 45 35
1740 110d. Dove with olive branch flying out of globe (horiz) 80 95

382 "Madonna and Child"

383 "The Fox and the Grapes"

1986. Christmas. Designs showing icons. Multicoloured.
1741 22d. Type **382** 20 10
1742 46d. "Adoration of the Magi" (24 × 32 mm) . . . 50 55
1743 130d. "Christ enthroned with St. John the Evangelist" 90 65

1987. Aesop's Fables. Multicoloured.
1744A 2d. Type **383** 15 20
1745A 5d. "The North Wind and the Sun" 15 20
1746A 10d. "The Stag at the Spring and the Lion" 30 20
1747A 22d. "Zeus and the Snake" 50 20
1748A 32d. "The Crow and the Fox" 60 25
1749A 40d. "The Woodcutter and Hermes" 95 65
1750A 46d. "The Ass in a Lion's Skin and the Fox" . . . 1·40 75
1751A 130d. "The Hare and the Tortoise" . . . . 2·50 90

384 "Composition" (Archilleas Apergis)

385 Player shooting Goal and Indoor Court

1987. Europa. Sculptures. Multicoloured.
1752b 40d. Type **384** . . . . . 1·50 1·50
1753a 130d. "Delphic Light" (Gerassimos Sklavos) . . 1·70 1·80

1987. 25th European Men's Basketball Championships, Athens. Multicoloured.
1754 22d. Type **385** 35 50
1755 25d. Emblem and spectators (32 × 24 mm) 25 10
1756 130d. Players . . . . 1·00 1·20
MS1757 113 × 63 mm. 40d. Players; 60d. Players around goal; 100d. Player shooting goal (each 28 × 40 mm) . . . . 2·00 1·60

386 Banner and Students

1987. 150th Annivs. of Athens University (3, 23d.) and National Metsovio Polytechnic Institute (others). Multicoloured.
1758 3d. Type **386** 15 15
1759 23d. Medal and owl 25 15
1760 40d. Building facade, measuring instruments and computer terminal (vert) 35 35
1761 60d. Students outside building (vert) 80 85

387 Ionic and Corinthian Capitals, Temple of Apollo, Phigaleia-Bassae

1987. Classical Architecture Capitals. Mult.
1762 2d. Type **387** 10 10
1763 26d. Doric capital, Parthenon 20 20
1764 40d. Ionic capital, The Erechtheum 30 25
1765 60d. Corinthian capital, The Tholos, Epidaurus . . . . 1·10 1·00

388 Hands holding Cup Aloft

389 Diploma Engraving (Yiannis Kephalinos)

1987. Greek Victory in European Basketball Championship.
1766 **388** 40d. multicoloured . . . 60 60

1987. 150th Anniv of Fine Arts High School (1767) and 60th Anniv of Panteios Political Science High School (1768). Multicoloured.
1767 26d. Type **389** 20 10
1768 60d. School campus (horiz) 65 65

390 Angel and Christmas Tree (left half)

391 Eleni Papadaki in "Hecuba" (Euripides) and Philippi Amphitheatre

1987. Christmas.
1769 26d. Type **390** 35 30
1770 26d. Angel and Christmas tree (right half) 35 30
Nos. 1769/70 were printed together, se-tenant, forming a composite design.

1987. Greek Theatre. Multicoloured.
1771 2d. Type **391** 10 20
1772 4d. Christopher Nezer in "The Wasps" (Aristophanes) and Dodona amphitheatre . . 10 20
1773 7d. Emilios Veakis in "Oedipus Rex" (Sophocles) and Delphi amphitheatre 15 20
1774 26d. Marika Kotopouli in "The Shepherdess's Love" (Dimitris Koromilas) . . 25 25
1775 40d. Katina Paxinou in "Abraham's Sacrifice" (Vitzentzos Cornaros) . . 40 20
1776 50d. Kyveli in "Countess Valeraina's Secret" (Gregory Xenopoulos) . . 50 20
1777 60d. Karolos Koun and stage set 60 60
1778 100d. Dimitris Rontiris teaching National Theatre dancers an ancient dance 1·30 40

392 "Codonellina sp." (polyzoan)

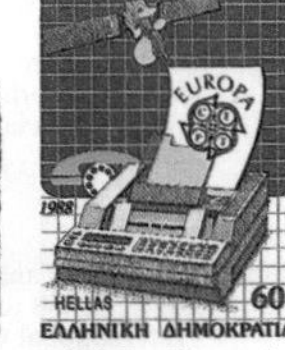

394 Satellite and Fax Machine

393 Ancient Olympia

1988. Marine Life. Multicoloured.

1779A	30d. Type **392**	55	40
1780A	40d. "Diaperoecia major" (polyzoan (clump-forming animals)) . . .	60	40
1781A	50d. "Artemia" (marine animal)	85	55
1782A	60d. "Posidonia oceanica" (plant) and Marmora sea-bream	1·60	1·20
1783A	100d. "Padina pavonica" (plant)	2·75	1·20

1988. Olympic Games, Seoul. Multicoloured.

1784A	4d. Type **393**	30	25
1785A	20d. Ancient athletes in Gymnasium	70	40
1786A	30d. Modern Olympics centenary emblem . . .	1·20	65
1787A	60d. Ancient athletes training	3·00	2·20
1788A	170d. Runner with Olympic flame	4·75	1·70

1988. Europa. Transport and Communications. Multicoloured.

1789B	60d. Type **394**	4·00	1·30
1790B	150d. Modern express and commuter trains	5·00	1·90

395 Katarraktis Falls

396 Emblems

1988. European Campaign for Rural Areas. Waterfalls. Multicoloured.

1791A	10d. Type **395**	1·10	45
1792A	60d. Edessa waterfalls . .	3·00	1·60
1793A	100d. River Edessaios cascades	4·75	1·50

1988. 20th European Postal Workers Trade Unions Congress.

1794A	**396** 60d. multicoloured . .	4·00	2·10

397 Mytilene Harbour, Lebos (painting by Theophilos)

398 Eleftherios Venizelos, Map and Flag

1988. Prefecture Capitals (1st series). Mult.

1795B	2d. Type **397**	10	10
1796B	3d. Alexandroupolis lighthouse, Evros (vert)	10	10
1797B	4d. St. Nicholas's bell-tower, Kozani (vert) . .	10	10
1798B	5d. Workmen's centre, Hermoupolis, Cyclades (vert)	10	10
1799B	7d. Sparta Town Hall, Lakonia	10	10
1800B	8d. Pegasus, Leukas . . .	15	10
1801B	10d. Castle of the Knights, Rhodes, Dodecanese (vert)	15	10
1802B	20d. Acropolis, Athens (vert)	15	10
1803B	25d. Aqueduct, Kavala . .	20	15
1804B	30d. Castle and statue of Athanasios Diakos, Lamia, Phthiotis (vert)	20	15
1805B	50d. Preveza Cathedral bell-tower and clock (vert)	35	15
1806B	60d. Esplanade, Corfu . .	50	35
1807B	70d. Aghios Nicholaos, Lassithi	55	30
1808B	100d. Six Springheads, Poligiros, Khalkidiki . .	1·20	25
1809B	200d. Church of Paul the Apostle, Corinth, Corinthia	2·75	40

See also Nos. 1848/62, 1911/22 and 1955/64.

1988. 75th Annivs. of Union of Crete and Greece (30d.) and Liberation of Epirus and Macedonia (70d.). Multicoloured.

1810A	30d. Type **398**	60	30
1811A	70d. Flags, map and "Liberty"	1·50	80

399 "Adoration of the Magi" (El Greco)

400 Map of E.E.C. and Castle of Knights, Rhodes

1988. Christmas. Multicoloured.

1812	30d. Type **399**	55	35
1813	70d. "The Annunciation" (Kostas Parthenis) (horiz)	1·00	75

1988. European Economic Community. Meeting of Heads of State, Rhodes. Multicoloured.

1814A	60d. Type **400**	1·20	1·00
1815A	100d. Members' flags and coin	1·10	85

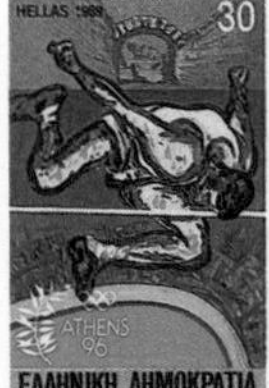

401 Ancient Olympia and High Jumper

402 Flags

1989. Centenary (1996) of Modern Olympic Games (1st issue). Multicoloured.

1816A	30d. Type **401**	25	30
1817A	60d. Wrestlers and Delphi	1·00	80
1818A	70d. Acropolis, Athens, and swimmers	1·10	1·00
1819A	170d. Stadium and Golden Olympics emblem . . .	2·20	1·50

See also Nos. 1863/7, **MS**1995 and 1998/2001.

1989. International Anniversaries. Mult.

1820A	30d. Type **402** (5th anniv of Six-nation Initiative for Peace and Disarmament)	50	40
1821A	50d. Flag and "Liberty" (bicentenary of French Revolution)	55	45
1822A	60d. Flag and ballot box (third direct European Parliament elections) . .	1·70	1·40
1823A	70d. Coins (cent of Interparliamentary Union)	1·70	1·50
1824A	200d. Flag (40th anniv of Council of Europe) . .	3·25	1·10

403 Whistling Bird

404 Magnifying Glass and Bird

1989. Europa. Children's Toys. Multicoloured.

1825B	60d. Type **403**	2·20	1·50
1826B	170d. Butterfly	2·50	1·20

1989. "Balkanfila XII" International Stamp Exhibition, Salonica. Multicoloured.

1827	60d. Type **404**	55	40
1828	70d. Eye looking through magnifying glass	55	55
MS1829	86 × 61 mm. 200d. Stamp collectors (42 × 30 mm)	1·75	1·75

405 Dog Roses

1989. Wild Flowers. Multicoloured.

1830	8d. Type **405**	15	10
1831	10d. Common myrtle . . .	15	10
1832	20d. Common poppies . . .	20	20
1833	30d. Anemones	30	25
1834	60d. Dandelions and chicory	45	35
1835	70d. Mallow	60	50
1836	200d. Thistles	1·10	1·20

406 Brown Bear

407 Gregoris Lambrakis

1990. Endangered Animals. Multicoloured.

1837	40d. Type **406**	35	20
1838	70d. Loggerhead turtle . . .	60	35
1839	90d. Mediterranean monk seal	75	50
1840	100d. Lynx	90	90

1990. Politicians' Death Anniversaries. Mult.

1841	40d. Type **407** (27th anniv)	40	35
1842	40d. Pavlos Bakoyiannis (first anniv)	40	35

408 Clasped Hands, Roses and Flag

409 Old Central Post Office Interior

1990. National Reconciliation. Multicoloured.

1843	40d. Type **408**	30	20
1844	70d. Dove with banner . . .	50	40
1845	100d. Map and hands holding roses	95	95

1990. Europa. Post Offices Buildings. Mult.

1846	70d. Type **409**	1·30	1·20
1847	210d. Exterior of modern post office	1·90	1·70

410 "Animal Fair" (D. Gioldassi) (Karditsa)

411 Yachting

1990. Prefecture Capitals (2nd series). Mult.

1848B	2d. Type **410**	10	10
1849B	5d. Fort, Trikala (horiz)	10	10
1850B	8d. Street, Veroia (Imathia)	10	10
1851B	10d. Monument to Fallen Heroes, Missolonghi (Aetolia) (horiz)	10	10
1852B	15d. Harbour, Chios (horiz)	10	15
1853B	20d. Street, Tripolis (Arcadia) (horiz)	10	10
1854B	25d. "City and Town Hall" (woodcut, A. Tassos) (Volos, Magnesia) (horiz) . . .	30	20
1855B	40d. Town Hall, Kalamata (Messenia) (horiz) . . .	20	20
1856B	50d. Market, Pyrgos (Elia) (horiz)	30	25
1857B	70d. Lake and island, Yannina (horiz)	35	30
1858B	80d. Harhour sculpture, Rethymnon	55	25
1859B	90d. Argostolion (Cephalonia) (horiz) . .	55	50
1860B	100d. Citadel and islet, Nauplion (Argolis) (horiz)	75	40
1861B	200d. Lighthouse, Patras (Akhaia)	1·50	55
1862B	250d. Street, Florina (horiz)	2·30	1·10

1990. Centenary (1996) of Modern Olympic Games (2nd issue). Multicoloured.

1863	20d. Type **411**	20	20
1864	50d. Wrestling	45	35
1865	80d. Running	85	80
1866	100d. Handball	90	60
1867	250d. Football	2·75	95

412 Schliemann and Lion Gate, Mycenae

413 "Woman knitting" (lithograph, Vasso Katraki)

1990. Death Cent of Heinrich Schliemann (archaeologist).

1868	**412** 80d. multicoloured . . .	2·40	1·20

1990. 50th Anniv of Greek–Italian War. Mult.

1869	50d. Type **413**	30	20
1870	80d. "Virgin Mary protecting Army" (lithograph, George Gounaropoulou)	50	50
1871	100d. "Women's War Work" (lithograph, Kosta Grammatopoulou) . . .	75	60

414 Hermes

1990. Stamp Day. Sheet 87 × 62 mm.

MS1872	**414** 300d. multicoloured	7·50	7·50

415 Calliope, Euterpe and Erato

1991. The Nine Muses. Multicoloured.

1873	50d. Type **415**	45	25
1874	80d. Terpsichore, Polyhymnia and Melpomene	85	45
1875	250d. Thalia, Clio and Urania	2·10	95

416 Battle Scene (Ioannis Anousakis)

1991. 50th Anniv of Battle for Crete. Mult.

1876	60d. Type **416**	90	50
1877	300d. Map and flags of allied nations (32 × 24 mm)	1·90	1·10

417 Icarus pushing Satellite

418 Swimming

1991. Europa. Europe in Space. Mult.

1878	80d. Type **417**	1·40	95
1879	300d. Chariot of the Sun . .	2·75	1·90

1991. 11th Mediterranean Games, Athens. Multicoloured.

1880	10d. Type **418**	20	15
1881	60d. Basketball	40	25
1882	90d. Gymnastics	60	25
1883	130d. Weightlifting	80	50
1884	300d. Throwing the hammer	2·10	1·60

419 Pillar of Democracy

421 Pres Konstantinos Karamanlis signing Treaty of Athens

420 Europa and Zeus as Bull (from Attic vase)

1991. 2500th Anniv of Birth of Democracy.

1885 **419** 100d. black, stone & blue 95 55

1991. Greek Presidency of European Postal and Telecommunications Conference. Sheet 81 × 62 mm.

MS1886 **420** 300d. multicoloured 8·50 7·50

1991. 10th Anniv of Greek Admission to European Community. Multicoloured.

1887 50d. Type **421** 35 30

1888 80d. Map of Europe and Pres. Karamanlis 55 45

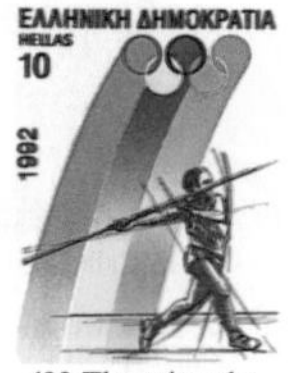

422 Emblem and Speed Skaters

423 Throwing the Javelin

1991. Winter Olympic Games, Albertville. Multicoloured.

1889 80d. Type **422** 90 80

1890 300d. Slalom skier . . . . . 2·00 1·30

1992. Olympic Games, Barcelona. Mult.

1891 10d. Type **423** 20 15

1892 60d. Show jumping 65 30

1893 90d. Runner (37 × 24 mm) 1·00 65

1894 120d. Gymnastics . . . . . 1·30 50

1895 340d. Runners' heads forming Olympic rings (37 × 24 mm) . . . . . . 2·75 1·30

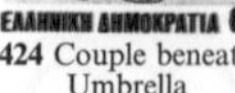

424 Couple beneath Umbrella

425 "Santa Maria", Map and Columbus

1992. Health. Multicoloured.

1896 60d. Type **424** (anti-AIDS campaign) 20 25

1897 80d. Doctor examining child (1st European Gastroenterology Week) 65 30

1898 90d. Crab killing flower on healthy plant (anti-cancer campaign) 75 35

1899 120d. Hephaestus's forge (from 6th-century B.C. urn) (European Year of Social Security, Hygiene and Health in the Workplace) 85 55

1900 280d. Alexandros Onassis Cardiosurgical Centre . . 2·75 1·20

1992. Europa. 500th Anniv of Discovery of America by Columbus. Multicoloured.

1901 90d. Type **425** . . . . . . 1·30 1·30

1902 340d. Chios in late 15th century . . . . 3·25 1·80

426 Proetus, Bellerophon and Pegasus

1992. European Transport Ministers' Conference, Athens. Sheet 85 × 59 mm.

MS1903 **426** 300d. multicoloured 4·00 4·00

427 Head of Hercules with Lion Skin (relief)

428 Piraeus

1992. Macedonia. Multicoloured.

1904 10d. Type **427** 20 15

1905 20d. Map of Macedonia and bust of Aristotle (horiz) 25 15

1906 60d. Alexander the Great at Battle of Issus (mural) (horiz) 55 20

1907 80d. Tomb of Philip II at Vergina, and Manolis Andronikos (archaeologist) 95 35

1908 90d. Deer hunt (mosaic, Pella) . . . . 1·00 35

1909 120d. Macedonian coin . . 1·40 70

1910 340d. 4th-century Church, Philippi, and Apostle Paul 4·00 1·70

1992. Prefecture Capitals (3rd series). Mult.

1911B 10d. Type **428** 10 10

1912B 20d. Amphissa (Phocis) . . 10 10

1913B 30d. The Heraion, Samos 20 15

1914B 40d. Canea 25 15

1915B 50d. Zakynthos 35 25

1916B 60d. Karpenisi (Evrytania) 35 25

1917B 70d. Cave, Kilkis (vert) . . 50 35

1918B 80d. Door of Town Hall Xanthi (vert) 55 35

1919B 90d. Macedonian Struggle Museum, Thessaloniki 75 40

1920B 120d. Tsanakleous School, Komotini (Rhodope) . . 1·00 50

1921B 340d. Spring, Drama . . . 2·50 95

1922B 400d. Pinios Bridge, Larissa . . . . 2·40 1·30

429 Column, Map, Flags and European Community Emblem

1992. Single European Market.

1923 **429** 90d. multicoloured . . . 70 1·50

430 Headstone (4th century B.C.)

431 Georgakis Olympios at Sekkou Monastery, 1821

1993. 2400th Anniv of Rhodes. Multicoloured.

1924 60d. Type **430** 50 25

1925 90d. "Aphrodite bathing" (statue) . . . . 1·10 40

1926 120d. "St. Irene" (from St. Catherine's church) . . 1·00 60

1927 250d. St. Paul's Gate, Naillac Mole . . . . . . 2·75 1·70

1993. Historical Events. Multicoloured.

1928 10d. Type **431** (War of Independence) 20 15

1929 30d. Theodore Kolokotronis (War of Independence) . . 25 20

1930 60d. Pavlos Melas (military hero) 50 25

1931 90d. "Glory crowns the Casualties" (Balkan Wars, 1912–13) . . . . 1·20 65

1932 120d. Soldiers of Sacred Company, El Alamein, 1942 (horiz) . . . . . . 1·90 80

1933 150d. Sacred Company on Aegean Islands, 1943–45 (horiz) . . . . 1·90 95

1934 200d. Victims' Monument, Kalavryta (destruction of village, 1943) . . . . . . 2·75 1·60

432 "The Benefits of Transportation" (Konstantinus Parthenis) (left half)

1993. Europa. Contemporary Art. Mult.

1935 90d. Type **432** . . . . . . 1·30 1·20

1936 350d. "The Benefits of Transportation" (right half) . . . . 3·50 3·25

Nos. 1935/6 were issued together, se-tenant, forming a composite design.

433 Athens Concert Hall

1993. Modern Athens. Multicoloured.

1937 30d. Type **433** 30 20

1938 60d. Iliou Melathron (former house of Heinrich Schliemann (archaeologist), now Numismatic Museum) . . 55 35

1939 90d. National Library . . . 90 50

1940 200d. Athens Eye Hospital 1·90 1·20

434 Presidency Emblem and Map

1993. Greek Presidency (1994) of European Union (1st issue). Sheet 84 × 60 mm.

MS1941 **434** 400d. multicoloured 4·00 4·00

See also Nos. 1953/4.

435 "Hermes leading Selene's Chariot" (Boeotian vase)

436 "Last Supper" (icon by Michael Damaskinou, St. Catherine's Church, Heraklion, Crete)

1994. 2nd Pan-European Transport Conf.

1942 **435** 200d. multicoloured . . 1·50 80

1994. Easter. Multicoloured.

1943 30d. Type **436** 20 15

1944 60d. "Crucifixion" (detail of wall painting, Great Meteoron) 35 10

1945 90d. "Burial of Christ" (icon, Church of the Presentation of the Lord, Patmos) (horiz) 60 35

1946 150d. "Resurrection" (detail, illuminated manuscript from Mt. Athos) (horiz) 1·30 85

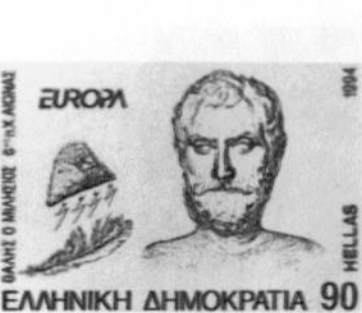

437 Thales of Miletus (philosopher)

438 Demetrios Vikelas (first president, after G. Roilos)

1994. Europa. Discoveries. Multicoloured.

1947 90d. Type **437** . . . . . . 1·00 80

1948 350d. Konstantinos Karatheodoris (mathematician) and equations . . . . 2·75 1·70

1994. Sports Events and Anniversary. Mult.

1949 60d. Type **438** (centenary of International Olympic Committee) 40 25

1950 90d. Modern footballer and ancient relief (World Cup Football Championship, U.S.A.) (horiz) 60 50

1951 120d. Ball, net and laurel (World Volleyball Championship, Piraeus and Salonika) . . . . . 1·00 45

MS1952 68 × 70 mm. 400d. Modern footballers, Statue of Liberty and ancient relief (World Cup) (41 × 51 mm) . . . . 3·00 3·00

439 "Greece" driving E.U. Chariot

1994. Greek Presidency of European Union. Multicoloured.

1953 90d. Type **439** 75 55

1954 120d. Doric columns and E.U. flag . . . . 1·10 65

440 Parigoritissas Byzantine Church, Arta

441 "Declaration of Constitution" (detail, Carl Haupt)

1994. Prefecture Capitals (4th series). Mult.

1955B 10d. Tsalopoulou mansion house, Katerini (Pieria) (vert) 10 10

1956B 20d. Type **440** 10 10

1957B 30d. Bridge and tower, Levadia (Boeotia) (vert) 20 15

1958B 40d. Koumbelidikis church Kastoria 20 20

1959B 50d. Outdoor theatre, Grevena 20 20

1960B 60d. Waterfall, Edessa (Pella) 30 20

1961B 80d. Red House, Chalkida (Euboea) 55 35

1962B 90d. Government House, Serres 70 35

1963B 120d. Town Hall, Heraklion 75 45

1964B 150d. Church of our Lady of the Annunciation, Igoumenitsa (Thesprotia) (vert) . . . . 1·00 55

1994. 150th Anniv of Constitution. Mult.

1965 60d. Type **441** 35 20

1966 150d. Ioannis Makrygiannis, Andreas Metaxas and Dimitrios Kallergis (from "Neos Aristophanes" (magazine)) 25 40

1967 200d. "The Night of 3rd September 1843" (anon) (horiz) . . . . 1·70 95

1968 340d. Article 107 of 1844 Constitution and Parliament Seal (horiz) . . 2·75 2·00

442 Mercouri and Demonstrators (fighter for Democracy)

1995. Melina Mercouri (actress and Minister of Culture) Commemoration. Multicoloured.

1969 60d. Type **442** 65 20

1970 90d. Mercouri and Acropolis (politician) . . 75 35

1971 100d. Mercouri in three roles (actress) . . . . . . 1·40 55

1972 340d. Mercouri with flowers (vert) . . . . 4·00 1·10

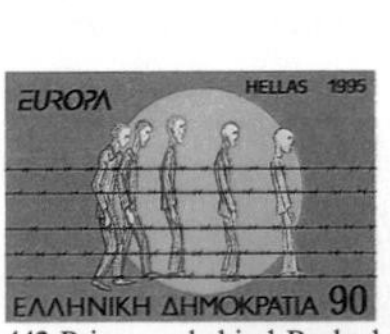

443 Prisoners behind Barbed Wire

444 Emblem

1995. Europa. Peace and Freedom. Mult.

1973	90d. Type **443**	1·30	1·60
1974	340d. Doves flying from crushed barbed wire . . .	3·50	2·00

Nos. 1973/4 were issued together, se-tenant, forming a composite design.

1995. Anniversaries and Events. Mult.

1975	10d. Type **444** (5th World Junior Basketball Championship)	25	10
1976	70d. Agriculture University, Athens (75th anniv) (horiz)	60	25
1977	90d. Delphi (50th anniv of U.N.O.)	85	25
1978	100d. Greek flag and returning soldier (50th anniv of end of Second World War)	1·10	45
1979	120d. "Peace" (statue by Kifissodotos) (50th anniv of U.N.O.)	1·20	65
1980	150d. Dolphins (European Nature Conservation Year) (horiz)	1·60	65
1981	200d. Old telephone and modern key-pad (cent of telephone in Greece) . . .	2·10	95
1982	300d. Owl sitting on ball (29th European Basketball Championship)	3·75	1·20

445 "The First Vision of the Apocalypse" (icon, Thomas Bathas)

1995. 1900th Anniv of the Apocalypse of St. John. Multicoloured.

1983	80d. Type **445**	95	65
1984	110d. St. John dictating to Prochoros in front of the Cave of the Apocalypse (miniature from the Four Gospels, Codex 81 of library of Patmos Monastery)	1·00	70
1985	300d. Trumpet of the First Angel (gilded Gospel cover) (horiz)	2·50	1·50

446 Goddess Athene with Argonauts

447 Psyttaleia

1995. Jason and the Argonauts. Mult.

1986	80d. Type **446**	45	40
1987	120d. Phineas (blind seer), god Hermes and the Voreadae pursuing Harpies	95	80
1988	150d. Medea, Nike and Jason taming bull	1·10	90
1989	200d. Jason and Medea killing snake and taking the Golden Fleece	1·50	1·20
1990	300d. Jason presenting Golden Fleece to Pelias	2·50	1·50

1995. Lighthouses. Multicoloured.

1991	80d. Type **447**	65	45
1992	120d. Sapienza	95	65
1993	150d. Kastri, Othonoi . . .	1·40	85
1994	500d. Zourva, Hydra . . .	4·00	2·00

448 1l. Stamp

1996. Centenary of Modern Olympic Games (3rd issue). Reproduction of Olympic Games issue of 1896. Three sheets each 88 × 88 mm, containing designs as T **448**. Inscriptions in brown, backgrounds flesh; colour of reproductions listed below.

MS1995	3 sheets (a) 80d. ochre (Type **448**); 120d. pink (2l.); 150d. brown (5l.); 650d. olive (10d.). (b) 80d. red (25l.); 120d. black (60l.); 150d. blue (1d.); 650d. reddish brown (10d.). (c) 80d. brown (20l.); 120d. lilac (40l.); 150l. brown (2d.); 650d. green (5d.) Set of 3 sheets	16·00	16·00

449 Sappho (poet)

450 Running

1996. Europa. Famous women.

1996	**449** 120d. multicoloured . .	1·10	1·20
1997	– 430d. brown, black & bl	4·25	3·25

DESIGN: 430d. Amalia Fleming.

1996. Centenary of Modern Olympic Games (3rd issue). Mult.

1998	10d. Type **450**	45	10
1999	80d. Throwing the discus . .	70	45
2000	120d. Weightlifting	1·20	60
2001	200d. Wrestling (horiz) . . .	1·70	1·30

451 Hippocrates

452 Mytilene

1996. 1st Int Medical Olympiad, Athens.

2002	**451** 80d. brown, pink & black	85	70
2003	– 120d. brown, green & blk	1·40	1·10

DESIGN: 120d. Galen.

1996. Castles (1st series). Multicoloured.

2004B	10d. Type **452**	15	10
2005B	20d. Lindos	20	10
2006B	30d. Rethymnon	25	15
2007B	70d. Assos Cephalonia . .	35	40
2008B	80d. Castle of the Serbs . .	60	50
2009B	120d. Monemvasia	1·10	55
2010B	200d. Didimotihon	1·50	70
2011B	430d. Vonitsas	3·00	1·50
2012B	1000d. Nikopolis	8·25	4·00

See also Nos. 2069/78.

453 Puppets

1996. Shadow Puppets. Multicoloured.

2013	80d. Type **453**	60	35
2014	100d. Men courting woman	65	55
2015	120d. Soldiers	1·10	65
2016	200d. Men fighting dragon	1·90	1·20

454 Inscription on Wine Jug (720 B.C.)

456 St Dimitrios (patron saint) (fresco, Aghios Nikolaos Orphanos Church)

455 Papandreou, Cap, Degree and Books

1996. The Greek Language. Multicoloured.

2017	80d. Type **454**	60	25
2018	120d. Homer's "Iliad" (papyrus scroll, 436–45)	95	50
2019	150d. Psalm (6th century)	1·00	65
2020	350d. Dionysios Solomos (writer) and verse of poem (1824)	3·25	1·60

1997. Andreas Papandreou (Prime Minister, 1981–89 and 1993–96) Commemoration. Multicoloured.

2021	80d. Type **455** (Doctorate in Economics, Harvard University, 1943)	55	35
2022	120d. Return from exile, 1974, and smoking pipe	80	45
2023	150d. Parliament building and Papandreou	1·20	70
2024	500d. State flag, dove and Papandreou wearing glasses	3·25	2·50

1997. Thessaloniki, Cultural Capital of Europe. Multicoloured.

2025	80d. Type **456**	55	35
2026	100d. Hippocratic Hospital (horiz)	85	40
2027	120d. Marble statue pedestal (2nd century) and circular relief of woman's head . .	1·00	60
2028	150d. Mosaic (detail) in cupola of Rotunda . . .	1·30	80
2029	300d. 14th-century chalice (horiz)	3·00	1·20

457 Trikomo

1997. Macedonian Bridges. Multicoloured.

2030	80d. Type **457**	55	35
2031	120d. Portitsa	1·00	60
2032	150d. Ziakas	1·20	75
2033	350d. Kastro	3·00	1·40

458 Prometheus the Fire-stealer

1997. Europa. Tales and Legends. Mult.

2034	120d. Type **458**	1·10	85
2035	430d. Knights (Digenes Akritas)	3·50	2·20

459 Running

1997. 6th World Athletics Championships, Athens. Multicoloured.

2036	20d. Type **459**	20	15
2037	100d. "Nike" (statue) . . .	50	35
2038	140d. High jumping	95	55
2039	170d. Hurdling	1·20	90
2040	500d. Stadium, Athens . . .	4·25	2·10

460 Alexandros Panagoulis (resistance leader)

461 Vassilis Avlonitis

1997. Anniversaries. Multicoloured.

2041	20d. Type **460** (20th death anniv (1996))	20	10
2042	30d. Grigorios Xenopoulos (writer, 130th birth anniv)	20	10
2043	40d. Odysseas Elytis (poet, first death anniv) (horiz)	25	25
2044	50d. Panayiotis Kanellopoulos (Prime Minister, 1945 and 1967, tenth death anniv (1996))	30	20
2045	100d. Harilaos Trikoupis (Prime Minister 1881–85, death centenary (1996)) (horiz)	95	40
2046	170d. Maria Callas (opera singer, 20th death anniv) (horiz)	1·40	80
2047	200d. Rigas Velestinlis-Feraios (revolutionary writer, death bicent (1998))	1·90	1·30

1997. Greek Actors. Multicoloured.

2048	20d. Type **461**	20	10
2049	30d. Vassilis Argyropoulos	20	10
2050	50d. Georgia Vassileiadou	45	20
2051	70d. Lambros Constantaras	55	30
2052	100d. Vassilis Logothetidis	85	35
2053	140d. Dionysis Papagiannopoulos	1·20	55
2054	170d. Nikos Stavrides . . .	1·30	65
2055	200d. Mimis Fotopoulos . .	1·90	70

462 "Greece", Greek Flag and Colossus of Rhodes

463 Aghia Sofia Hospital, Athens

1998. 50th Anniv of Incorporation of Dodecanese Islands into Greece. Multicoloured.

2056	100d. German commander signing surrender to British and Greek military authorities at Simi, 1945	60	45
2057	140d. Type **462**	1·10	85
2058	170d. Greek and British military representatives at transfer ceremony, Rhodes, 1947	1·50	90
2059	500d. Raising Greek flag, Kasos, 1947	3·50	95

1998. Anniversaries and Events. Mult.

2060	20d. Type **463** (cent of Aghia Sofia Children's Hospital)	20	15
2061	100d. St. Xenophon's Monastery (millenary) (vert)	65	40
2062	140d. Woman in traditional costume (4th International Thracian Congress, Nea Orestiada) (vert)	1·20	70
2063	150d. Parthenon and congress emblem (International Cardiography Research Congress, Rhodes) . . .	1·30	85
2064	170d. Sculpture of man and young boy (Cardiography Congress) (vert)	1·50	80
2065	500d. Emblem (50th anniv of Council of Europe) (vert)	3·50	1·60

464 Ancient Theatre, Epidavros

1998. Europa. National Festivals. Mult.

2066	140d. Type **464**	1·10	80
2067	500d. Festival in Herod Atticus Theatre, Athens	4·25	3·00

465 Players

1998. World Basketball Championship, Athens. Sheet 70 × 68 mm. containing T **465**.
MS2068 **465** 300d. multicoloured . . 2·75 2·75

466 Ierapetra, Crete

1998. Castles (2nd series). Multicoloured.
2069 30d. Type **466** 20 10
2070 50d. Corfu 30 15
2071 70d. Limnos 35 25
2072 100d. Argolis 70 30
2073 150d. Iraklion, Crete . . . 95 55
2074 170d. Naupaktos (vert) . . 1·10 70
2075 200d. Ioannina (vert) . . . 1·40 90
2076 400d. Platamona . . . . . 3·00 1·70
2077 550d. Karitainas (vert) . . . 4·00 2·30
2078 600d. Fragkokastello, Crete 4·75 2·50

467 "Church of St. George of the Greeks" (18th-century copperplate)

1998. 500th Anniv of Greek Orthodox Community in Venice. Multicoloured.
2079 30d. Type **467** 20 20
2080 40d. "Christ Pantocrator" (icon) (vert) 25 20
2081 140d. Illuminated script of hymn "Epi Soi hairei" by Georgios Klontzas (vert) 80 65
2082 230d. "St. George of the Greeks" (illuminated manuscript, 1640) . . . . 2·20 75·00

468 Homer (poet)

1998. Ancient Greek Writers.
2083 **468** 20d. brown and gold . . 20 20
2084 – 100d. brown and gold 75 50
2085 – 140d. red and gold . . . 95 85
2086 – 200d. black and gold . . 1·20 95
2087 – 250d. brown and gold 2·10 1·40
DESIGNS: No. 2084, Sophocles (poet); 2085, Thucydides (historian); 2086, Plato (philosopher); 2087, Demosthenes (orator).

469 Ancient Trireme and Circulation of Mediterranean Sea Currents

1999. International Year of the Ocean. Multicoloured.
2088 40d. Type **469** 20 20
2089 100d. Galleon (detail of icon "Thou art Great, O Lord" by I. Kornaros) . . 45 45
2090 200d. "Aigaio" (oceanographic vessel), astrolabe and seismic sounding of seabed . . . 1·30 95
2091 500d. Apollo on ship (3rd-century B.C. silver tetradrachmon coin of Antigonus Dosonos) . . . 2·10 2·50

470 Karamanlis

1999. 1st Death Anniv of Konstantinos Karamanlis (Prime Minister 1955–63 and 1974; President 1980–85 and 1990–95). Multicoloured.
2092 100d. Type **470** 55 40
2093 170d. Karamanlis and jubilant crowd, 1974 . . . 1·00 70
2094 200d. Karamanlis and Council of Europe emblem, 1979 . . . . . . 1·30 80
2095 500d. Karamanlis and Greek flag (vert) . . . . 2·10 2·10

471 Mt. Olympus and Flowers

1999. Europa. Parks and Gardens. Multicoloured.
2096 170d. Type **471** . . . . . 1·10 55
2097 550d. Mt. Olympus and flowers (different) . . . . 2·10 1·70
Nos. 2096/7 were issued together, se-tenant, forming a composite design.

472 Ancient Greek and Japanese Noh Theatre Masks

1999. Centenary of Diplomatic Relations between Greece and Japan.
2098 **472** 120d. multicoloured . . 55 40

473 Temple of Hylates Apollo, Kourion

1999. Cyprus–Greece Joint Issue. 4000 Years of Greek Culture. Multicoloured.
2099 120d. Type **473** 55 40
2100 120d. Mycenaean pot depicting warriors (Athens) 55 40
2101 120d. Mycenaean crater depicting horse (Nicosia) 55 40
2102 120d. Temple of Apollo, Delphi 55 30

474 Trains

1999. Fifth Anniv of Community Support Programme. Multicoloured.
2103 20d. Type **474** (modernization of railways) 10 30
2104 120d. Bridge over River Antirrio 50 60
2105 140d. Compact disk, delivery lorries and conveyor belt (modernization of Post Office) 70 75
2106 250d. Athens underground train . . . . 1·40 2·00
2107 500d. Control tower, Eleftherios Venizelos airport, Athens . . . . . 2·20 2·40

475 Helicopter and Commandos in Inflatable Boat

1999. Armed Forces. Multicoloured.
2108 20d. Type **475** 10 15
2109 30d. Missile corvette 15 20
2110 40d. Two F-16 aircraft . . . 20 25
2111 50d. CL-215 aircraft dispersing water on forest fire 20 20
2112 70d. Destroyer 30 30
2113 120d. Forces distributing aid in Bosnia 60 55
2114 170d. Dassault Mirage 2000 jet fighter above Aegean 85 85
2115 250d. Helicopters, tanks and soldiers on joint exercise 1·30 1·30
2116 600d. Submarine "Okeanos" 2·40 3·00

476 Birth of Christ

2000. Birth Bimillenary of Jesus Christ. Icons. Mult.
2117 20d. Type **476** 10 20
2118 50d. Discussion between men of different denominations 25 25
2119 120d. Angels praising God 60 60
2120 170d. Epiphany (horiz) . . . 85 85
2121 200d. Communion (35 × 35 mm) . . . . . . 1·00 1·00
2122 500d. Heavenly beings above priests and worshippers (27 × 57 mm) 2·50 2·50

477 "Building Europe"

478 *Ilissos* (steamship)

2000. Europa.
2123 **477** 170d. multicoloured . . 85 1·00

2000. Ships. Multicoloured.
2124 10d. Type **478** 10 10
2125 120d. *Adrias* (destroyer) . . 60 60
2126 170d. *Ia II* (steamship) . . . 85 85
2127 400d. *Vas Olga* (destroyer) 2·10 1·50

479 Rainbow over Village (Spyros Dalakos)

2000. "Stampin' the Future". Winning Entries in Children's International Painting Competition. Mult.
2128 130d. Type **479** 75 50
2129 180d. Robots (Moshovaki-Chaiger Ornella) 90 90
2130 200d. Cars and house (Zisis Zariotis) . . . . . . 1·00 1·00
2131 620d. Children astride rocket (Athina Limioudi) 3·00 2·50

480 Torch and Flag

481 Emblem and Olympic Rings

2000. Olympic Games, Sydney. Multicoloured.
2132 200d. Type **480** 90 95
2133 650d. Torch, flag and Sydney Opera House . . 2·75 2·20

2000. Olympic Games, Athens (2004) (1st issue).
2134 **481** 10d. multicoloured . . . 10 10
2135 50d. multicoloured . . . 40 35
2136 130d. multicoloured . . 65 65
2137 180d. multicoloured . . 90 90
2138 200d. multicoloured . . 1·20 1·10
2139 650d. multicoloured . . 3·25 2·75

See also Nos. **MS**2169, 2191/**MS**2196, 2207/10, **MS**2211, 2216/21, **MS**2222, 2234/8, **MS**2239, 2246/51, 2252/**MS**2258, 2259/63, 2264/**MS**2270, **MS**2271, **MS**2272, 2275/**MS**2279, **MS**2285 and 2286/**MS**2288.

482 Create 1901 1d. Stamp

2000. Centenary of First Create Stamp. Sheet 104 × 73 mm containing T **482** and similar vert designs. Multicoloured.
MS2140 200d. Type **482**; 650d. Create 1901 6d. stamp . . . . 3·25 3·25

483 Orpheus Christ (sculpture)

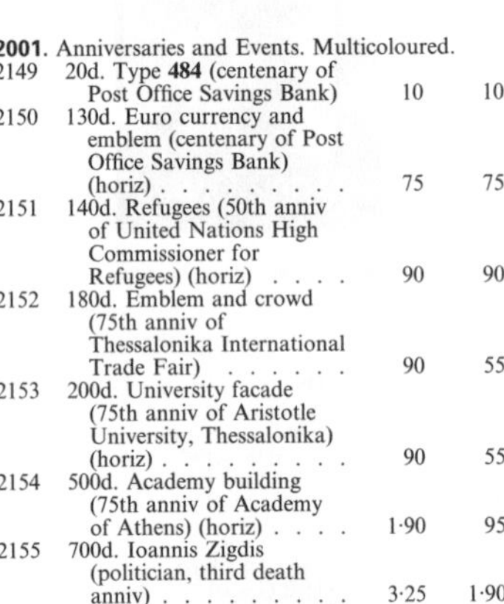

484 Mother and Child holding Money Box

2000. Birth Bimillenary of Jesus Christ. Mult.
2141 20d. Type **483** 10 10
2142 30d. The Good Shepherd (sculpture) 15 20
2143 40d. Christ Pantocrator (mosaic, Holy Monastery of Sina) 25 25
2144 100d. Anapeson in the Protato of Mount Athos (fresco, Manuel Panselinos) (horiz) 65 60
2145 130d. Christ (icon) 90 90
2146 150d. Christ (icon) . . . . 1·20 1·20
2147 180d. Christ Pantocrator (Encaustic icon) . . . . . 1·50 1·50
2148 1000d. Christ Pantocrator (Byzantine coin) (horiz) 6·75 6·75

2001. Anniversaries and Events. Multicoloured.
2149 20d. Type **484** (centenary of Post Office Savings Bank) 10 10
2150 130d. Euro currency and emblem (centenary of Post Office Savings Bank) (horiz) 75 75
2151 140d. Refugees (50th anniv of United Nations High Commissioner for Refugees) (horiz) 90 90
2152 180d. Emblem and crowd (75th anniv of Thessalonika International Trade Fair) 90 55
2153 200d. University facade (75th anniv of Aristotle University, Thessalonika) (horiz) 90 55
2154 500d. Academy building (75th anniv of Academy of Athens) (horiz) . . . . 1·90 95
2155 700d. Ioannis Zigdis (politician, third death anniv) . . . . 3·25 1·90

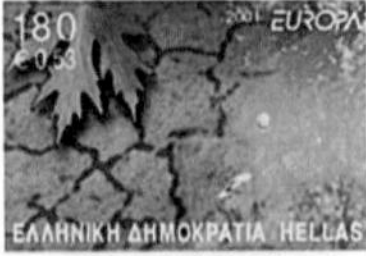

485 Dried Earth

2001. Europa. Water Resources. Multicoloured.
2156 180d. Type **485** 95 45
2157 650d. Pool of water and droplet . . . . 2·75 1·10

486 Little Egret

2001. Flora and Fauna. Multicoloured.
2158 20d. Type **486** 10 20
2159 50d. White storks 30 25
2160 100d. Bearded vulture . . . 60 35
2161 140d. Orchid (vert) 85 45
2162 150d. Dalmatian pelican (vert) . . . . 1·00 45
2163 200d. Lily, Plastina Lake, Karditsa . . . . 1·20 55
2164 700d. Egyptian vulture . . . 2·40 1·90
2165 850d. Black vulture . . . . 3·75 2·50

487 Emblem

2001. New Name of Hellenic Post.
2166 **487** 140d. blue and yellow . . 85 85
2167 200d. blue . . . . 1·20 1·20

488 "The Annuciation" (13th century muniture Athens)

2001. 1700th Anniv of Christianity in Armenia.
MS2168 **488** 850d. multicoloured 4·50 4·50

489 Figures of Swimmers from Amphora

2001. Olympic Games, Athens (2004). Sheet 80 × 70 mm.
MS2169 **489** 1200d. multicoloured 7·50 7·50

490 Kamakaki, Salamina

2002. Traditional Dances. Multicoloured.
2170 2c. Type **490** 10 10
2171 3c. Prikia (bride's dowry) . . 10 10
2172 5c. Zagorissios, Epirus (vert) 10 10
2173 10c. Balos, Aegean Islands 15 10
2174 15c. Synkathistos, Thrace 20 10
2175 20c. Tsakonikos, Peloponnese (vert) 30 15
2176 30c. Pyrrichios (Sera) (Pontian Greek) 40 20
2177 35c. Fourles, Kythnos (vert) 50 25
2178 40c. Apokriatos, Skyros . . 55 30
2179 45c. Kotsari (Pontian Greek) 50 30
2180 50c. Pentozalis, Crete (vert) 70 35
2181 55c. Karagouna, Thessaly 75 40
2182 60c. Hassapiko, Smyrneikos 85 40
2183 65c. Zalistos, Naoussa . . . 90 45
2184 85c. Pogonissios, Epirus . . 1·20 60
2185 €1 Kalamtianos, Peloponnese . . . . . . 1·40 70
2186 €2 Maleviziotis, Crete . . . 2·75 1·40
2187 €2.15 Tsamikos, Roumeli 3·00 1·50
2188 €2.60 Zeibekikos (vert) . . 3·50 1·80
2189 €3 Nyfiatikos, Corfou . . . 4·25 2·10
2190 €4 Paschaliatikos . . . . . 5·50 2·75

491 Runners (vase painting)

2002. Olympics Games, Athens (2004) (3rd issue). Multicoloured.
2191 41c. Type **491** 55 30
2192 59c. Charioteer (8th-century bronze statuette) (vert) . . 80 40
2193 80c. Javelin thrower (vase painting) . . . . 1·10 55
2194 €2.05 Doryphoros ("Spear Bearer") (statue, Polycleitos) (vert) . . . . 2·75 1·40
2195 €2.35 Weightlifter (vase painting) . . . . 3·25 1·60
MS2196 121 × 80 mm. €5 "Crypt of the ancient Olympic stadium, Olympia" (49 × 29 mm) . . . . 7·00 7·00

492 Performing Elephant

2002. Europa. Circus. Multicoloured.
2197 60c. Type **492** 85 40
2198 €2.60 Equestrian acrobat 3·75 1·80

493 Navy Scout

2002. Scouts. Multicoloured.
2199 45c. Type **493** 60 30
2200 60c. Scout and World Conference emblem . . . 85 40
2201 70c. Air scout and Cub scouts planting tree . . . 1·00 50
2202 €2.15 Scouts, mountains and map . . . . 3·00 1·50

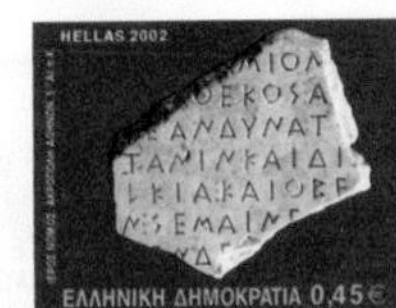

494 Fragment of 5th-century B.C. Tablet, Acropolis, Athens

2002. The Greek Language. Multicoloured.
2203 45c. Type **494** 60 30
2204 60c. 13th-century B.C. Linear B script tablet, Glay 85 40
2205 90c. Manuscript and General Makrygiannis (writer) . . . . 1·30 65
2206 €2.15 Manuscript and page from 11th-century Byzantine manuscript, Mount Athos . . . . . . 3·00 1·50

495 Man wearing Olive Wreath holding Two Ears of Corn

2002. Olympics Games, Athens (2004) (4th issue). Multicoloured.
2207 45c. Type **495** 60 30
2208 60c. Man wearing wreath and chewing ear of corn 85 40
2209 €2.15 Man beside column wearing wreath and chewing ear of corn . . . 3·00 1·50
2210 €2.60 Man beside tilted column holding wreath . . 3·50 1·80

496 Facade

2002. Olympics Games, Athens (2004) (5th issue). Early Stadia. Sheet 120 × 75 mm.
MS2211 **496** €6 multicoloured 8·50 5·50

497 Chrysostomos Papadopoulos (1923–38)

2002. Archbishops of Athens. Multicoloured.
2212 10c. Type **497** 15 10
2213 45c. Chrysanthos Philippides (1938–41) 60 30
2214 €2.15 Damaskinos Papandreou (1941–49) . . 3·00 1·50
2215 €2.60 Seraphem Tikas (1974–98) . . . . 3·50 1·80

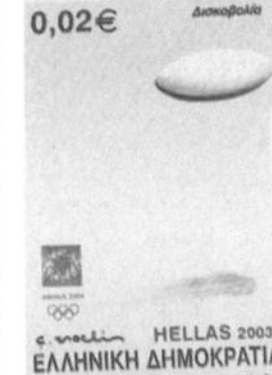

498 Discus

499 Athena (Girl Mascot)

2003. Olympic Games, Athens (2004) (6th issue). Multicoloured.
2216 2c. Type **498** 10 10
2217 5c. Shot put 10 10
2218 47c. Javelin 60 30
2219 65c. High jump 85 40
2220 €2.17 Hurdles . . . . . . 3·00 1·50
2221 €2.85 Dumbbells . . . . . 4·00 2·00

2003. Olympic Games, Athens (2004) (7th issue). Sheet 128 × 82 mm containing T **499** and similar horiz design. Multicoloured.
MS2222 €2.50 Type **499**; €2.85 Phevos (boy mascot) . . . . . 7·50 3·75

500 Globe

501 Swallow and European Stars

2003. Greetings Stamps. Sheet 123 × 124 containing T **500** and similar square designs. Multicoloured.
MS2223 47c. (a) Type **500** (corporate); 47c. (b) 2004 Olympics emblem (sponsor); 47c. (c) Man wearing wreath (Greece); 47c. (d) Roses (wedding); 47c. (e) Grid and skyline (corporate); 47c. (f) Stylized train (children); 47c. (g) Couple (social occasion); 65c. (h) Statue head (Greece); 65c. (i) Acropolis (Greece) . . . . . . 6·25 6·50

2003. Greek Presidency of the European Union. Multicoloured.
2224 47c. Type **501** 60 30
2225 65c. White Tower, Thessaloniki formed from letters 85 40
2226 €2.17 Swallows (fresco, Thera) . . . . 2·00 1·00
2227 €2.85 Stars and flags of member countries as jigsaw puzzle . . . . . . 4·00 2·00

502 Stylized Figure

2003. Europa. Poster Art. Multicoloured.
2228 65c. Type **502** 85 40
2229 €2.85 House with flag pole and veranda . . . . . . 4·00 2·00

503 Apple floating in Space and Trees

2003. Environmental Protection. Multicoloured.
2230 15c. Type **503** 20 10
2231 47c. Apple floating in water 60 30
2232 65c. Wreath above waves . . 85 40
2233 €2.85 Planet above apple tree . . . . 4·00 2·00

504 High Jump

2003. Olympic Games, Athens (2004) (8th issue). Multicoloured.
2234 5c. Type **504** 10 10
2235 47c. Wrestlers 60 30
2236 65c. Runners 85 40
2237 80c. Cyclists (vert) . . . . . 1·10 55
2238 €4 Windsurfer (vert) . . . 5·75 2·75

505 Athena (Girl Mascot)

2003. Olympic Games, Athens (2004) (9th issue). Sheet 128 × 80 mm containing T **505** and similar horiz design. Multicoloured.
MS2239 €2.50 Type **505**; €2.85 Phevos (boy mascot) . . . . . 7·50 3·75

506 Stair Maker

2003. Traditional Trades and Crafts. Multicoloured.
2240 3c. Type **506** 10 10
2241 10c. Shoemaker 15 10
2242 50c. Smith 65 30
2243 €1 Type setter . . . . . . 1·40 70
2244 €1.40 Sponge diver . . . . 1·90 95
2245 €4 Hand weaver . . . . . 5·75 2·75
MS2245a 115 × 149 mm. Nos. 2240/5 . . . . 10·00 5·00

507 Weightlifting

2003. Olympic Games 2004, Athens (10th issue). Athletes. Multicoloured.
2246 20c. Type **507** 25 10
2247 30c. Throwing javelin . . . 40 20
2248 40c. Charioteers 55 25
2249 47c. Soldier carrying spear and shield 60 30
2250 €2 Running . . . . 2·75 1·30
2251 €2.85 Throwing discus . . 4·00 2·00

508 Volos

2004. Olympic Games 2004, Athens (11th issue). Cities. Multicoloured.
2252 1c. Type **508** 10 10
2253 2c. Patra 10 10
2254 5c. Herakleio, Crete 10 10
2255 47c. Athens 60 30
2256 €1.40 Thessalonika . . . . 1·90 95
2257 €4 Athens . . . . 5·75 2·75
MS2258 120 × 135 mm. Nos. 2252/7 8·50 4·25

509 Spiros Louis

2004. Olympic Games 2004, Athens (12th issue). Greek Olympic Champions. Multicoloured.
2259 3c. Type **509** (marathon, 1896) 10 10
2260 10c. Aristides Konstantinides (cycling, 1896) 15 10
2261 €2 Ioannis Fokianos (modern Olympic pioneer) 2·75 1·30

2262 €2.17 Ioannis Mitropoulos (gymnast, 1896) . . . . . 3·00 1·40
2263 €3.60 Konstantinos Tsiklitiras (long jump, 1912) . . . . 5·00 5·25

510 Swimming

2004. Olympic Games 2004, Athens (13th issue). Sport Disciplines. Multicoloured.
2264 5c. Type **510** 10 10
2265 10c. Hands applying rosin 15 10
2266 20c. Canoeing 25 10
2267 47c. Relay race 60 30
2268 €2 Gymnastics floor exercise (vert) . . . . . . 2·75 1·30
2269 €5 Gymnastics ring exercise (vert) . . . . 3·25 1·60
MS2270 162 × 140 mm. Nos. 2264/9 7·00 3·50

511 Woman holding Torch **513** Yacht

512 Dove and Olympic Rings

2004. Olympic Games 2004, Athens (14th issue). Greetings Stamps. Sheet 90 × 75 mm containing T **511** and similar square design.
MS2271 47c. multicoloured . . . 4·00 4·00

2004. Olympic Games 2004, Athens (15th issue). Sheet 128 × 81 mm containing T **512** and similar horiz design. Multicoloured.
MS2272 47c. Type **512**; €2.50 Dove and children . . . . 4·50 4·50

2004. Europa. Holidays. Multicoloured.
2273 65c. Type **513** 85 40
2274 €2.85 Hot air balloon . . . 4·00 2·00

514 Obverse and Reverse of 3 Drachma Coin (480—450 BC)

2004. Olympic Games, Athens 2004 (16th issue). Ancient Coins. Multicoloured.
2275 47c. Type **514** 80 50
2276 65c. Philip of Macedonia gold stater . . . . . . 1·10 70
2277 €2 Obverse and reverse of 2 drachma coin (460 BC) 3·50 3·50
2278 €2.17 Obverse and reverse of 4 drachma coin . . . . 4·00 4·00
MS2279 140 × 120 mm. Nos. 2275/8 11·00 11·00

515 Championship Trophy

2004. Greece—European Football Champions, 2004. Multicoloured.
2280 47c. Type **515** 80 50
2281 65c. Team members . . . . 1·10 70
2282 €1 Team members with raised arms . . . . 1·80 1·00
2283 €2.88 Outstretched hands and trophy . . . . 6·25 6·25
MS2284 160 × 135 mm. Nos. 2280/3 11·00 11·00

516 Sea

2004. Olympic Games, Athens 2004 (17th issue). Modern Art. Three sheets containing T **516** and similar multicoloured designs.
MS2285 (a) 120 × 80 mm. 50c. Type **516**; €2.50 Rainbow. (b) 120 × 80 mm. €1 Multicoloured paint brush and glass; €2 Roller making Greek flag. (c) 135 × 163 mm. As Nos. **MS**2285a/b . . . . 24·00 24·00

517 Temple of Heaven, Beijing **518** Athena and Phevos holding Athens 2004 Emblem

2004. Olympic Games, Athens 2004 (18th issue). Athens 2004—Beijing 2008. Multicoloured.
2286 50c. Type **517** 85 50
2287 65c. Parthenon, Athens . . 1·10 70
MS2288 90 × 120 mm. Nos. 2286/7 10 1·90

2004. Olymphilex 2004, International Olympic Stamp and Memorabilia Exhibition. Sheet 81 × 70 mm.
MS2289 **518** €6 multicoloured 13·00 13·00

519 Thomas Bimis and Nikos Siranidis

2004. Greek Olympic Medal Winners. Multicoloured.
2290 65c. Type **519** (gold) (synchronised diving) . . 1·10 70
2292 65c. Ilias Iliadis (gold) (judo) . . . . 1·10 70
2293 65c. Emilia Tsoulfa and Sofia Bekatorou (gold) (women's sailing) . . . . 1·10 70
2294 65c. Pyrros Dimas (bronze) (weight lifting) . . . . . 1·10 70
2295 65c. Dimosthenis Tabacos (gold) (gymnastics) . . . 1·10 70
2296 65c. Anastasia Kelesidou (silver) (discus) . . . . . 1·10 70
2297 65c. Vasilis Polymeros and Nikos Skiathitis (bronze) (rowing) . . . . 1·10 70
2298 65c. Athanasia Tzoumeleka (gold) (20km.walk) . . . 1·10 70
2299 65c. Chrysopigi Devezi (silver) (triple jump) . . . 1·10 70
2300 65c. Fani Chalkia (gold) (400m. hurdles) . . . . . 1·10 70
2301 65c. Nikos Kaklamanakis (silver) (sailing) . . . . .
2302 65c. Artiom Kiourgian (bronze) (Greco-roman wrestling) . . . . 1·10 70
2303 65c. Women's water polo team (silver) . . . . . . 1·10 70
2304 65c. Mirela Maniani (bronze) (women's javelin) 1·10 70
2305 65c. Elisavet Mystakidou (silver) (women's Taekwondo) . . . . 1·10 70
2306 65c. Alexandros Nikolaidis (silver) (men's Taekwondo) . . . . . . 1·10 70

No. 2291 was later withdrawn from circulation when the athlete, Leonidas Sampanis, was stripped of his medal after failing a drug test.

520 Horse Riders

2004. Paralympics. Multicoloured.
2307 20c. Type **520** 30 20
2308 49c. Disabled runner . . . 80 50
2309 €2 Wheelchair basket ball players . . . . 3·50 3·50
2310 €2.24 Wheelchair archer . . 4·25 4·25

521 Santorini

2004. Tourism. Greek Islands. Multicoloured.
2311 2c. Type **521** 10 10
2312 3c. Karpathos 10 10
2313 5c. Crete – Vai 10 10
2314 10c. Mykonos 15 10
2315 49c. Chania 80 50
2316 50c. Kastelorizo 85 55
2317 €1 Astypalaia . . . . . . 1·80 1·00
2318 €2 Serifos . . . . 3·50 3·50
2319 €2.24 Milos . . . . 4·25 4·25
2320 €4 Skiathos . . . . 9·00 9·00

522 Necklace (730 BC)

2005. Jewellery. Multicoloured.
2321 1c. Type **522** 10 10
2322 15c. Snake-shaped bracelet (2nd—3rd century BC) (vert) 20 10
2323 30c. Necklace with bulls head pendant (5th century) 40 20
2324 49c. Central part of crown (2nd century) 85 55
2325 €4 Earring (8th century BC) (vert) . . . . 9·00 9·00

CHARITY TAX STAMPS

C **38** Dying Soldier, Widow and Child C **39** Red Cross, Nurses, Wounded and Bearers

1914. Roul.
C269 C **38** 2l. red 40 30
C270 5l. blue 55 45

1915. Red Cross. Roul.
C271 C **39** (5l.) red and blue . . . 13·50 1·60

C **40** Greek Women's Patriotic League Badge

1915. Greek Women's Patriotic League.
C272 C **40** (5l.) red and blue . . . 90 80

Κ. Π.
λεπτοῦ
1
(C **42**)

C **43**

Κ. Π.
λεπτοῦ
1
(C **44**)

Κ.Π.
10 ΛΕΠΤΑ 10
(C **46**)

1917. Surch as Type C **42**.
C297 **15** 1 on 1l. brown . . . . . 1·50 1·60
C303 1 on 3l. orange 30 30
C299 5 on 1l. brown . . . . . 1·40 1·50
C300 5 on 20l. mauve 55 55
C307 **36** 5 on 25l. blue 60 60
C304 **15** 5 on 40l. brown 55 55
C308 **36** 5 on 40l. blue 30 30
C305 **15** 5 on 50l. lake 55 60
C309 **35** 5 on 50l. blue 30 30
C306 **17** 5 on 1d. black . . . . . 1·40 1·40
C301 **15** 10 on 30l. purple 80 80
C302 30 on 30l. purple . . . . 1·40 1·10

1917. Fiscal stamps surch as Type C **44**. Roul.
C310 C **43** 1l. on 10l. blue 70 70
C328 1l. on 50l. purple . . . 70 70
C311 1l. on 80l. blue 60 60
C330 5l. on 10l. purple . . . 70 60
C329 5l. on 10l. blue 80 60
C312 5l. on 60l. blue . . . . 4·00 2·75
C313 5l. on 80l. blue . . . . 2·75 2·20
C331 10l. on 50l. purple . . 6·50 7·50
C326 10l. on 70l. blue . . . 6·50 5·50
C315 10l. on 90l. blue . . . 9·75 7·75
C316 20l. on 20l. blue . . . £1500 £700
C317 20l. on 30l. blue . . . 3·25 3·25
C318 20l. on 40l. blue . . . 12·00 12·00
C319 20l. on 50l. blue . . . 5·50 5·00
C320 20l. on 60l. blue . . . £275 £180
C321 20l. on 80l. blue . . . 55·00 33·00
C322 20l. on 90l. blue . . . 3·00 2·40
C333 20l. on 2d. blue . . . 7·25 5·50

1917. Fiscal stamps surch as Type C **46**. Roul.
C334 C **43** 1l. on 10l. blue . . . . 1·10 1·00
C341 5l. on 10l. purple & red 6·75 2·75
C335 5l. on 50l. blue . . . . 31·00 31·00
C338 10l. on 50l. blue . . . 7·25 6·25
C339 20l. on 50l. blue . . . 15·00 15·00
C340 30l. on 50l. blue . . . 10·50 9·25

C **48** Wounded Soldier C **77** St. Demetrius

C **49**

1918. Red Cross. Roul.
C342 C **48** 5l. red, blue and yellow 5·25 2·00

1918. Optd **P.I.P.** in Greek.
C343 C **48** 5l. red, blue and yellow 6·25 1·50

1922. Greek Women's Patriotic League. Surch as in Type C **49**.
C344 C **49** 5l. on 10l. red and blue £190 7·00
C345 5l. on 20l. red and blue 31·00 28·00
C346 5l. on 50l. red and blue £160 80·00
C347 5l. on 1d. red and blue 2·75 32·00
Nos. C344/7 were not issued without surcharge.

1924. Red Cross. As Type C **48** but wounded soldier and family.
C406 10l. red, blue and yellow . . 1·10 60

1934. Salonika Int Exn Fund.
C478 C **77** 20l. brown 20 10

C **78** Allegory of Health

+
ΠΡΟΝΟΙΑ
(C **85**)

1934. Postal Staff Anti-tuberculosis Fund.
C480 C **78** 10l. orange and green 10 10
C481 20l. orange and blue 30 30
C482 50l. orange and green 1·40 45

1935. As Type C **78** but with country inscription at top.
C494 10l. orange and green . . . 35 10
C495 20l. orange and blue . . . 35 20
C496 50l. orange and green . . . 55 20
C497 50l. orange and brown . . 90 25

1937. Nos. D273 and 415 optd with Type C **85**.
C498 D **20** 10l. red 35 25
C500 **51** 50l. violet 45 15

+
Λ.50
ΠΡΟΝΟΙΑ
(C **95**)

C **96** Queens Olga and Sophia

1938. Surch with Type C **95**.
C521 D **20** 50l. on 5l. green . . . 80 45
C522 50l. on 20l. slate . . . 5·50 1·10
C523 **52** 50l. on 20l. violet . . . 55 10

1939.
C524 C **96** 10l. red 10 10
C525 50l. green 10 10
C526 1d. blue 20 20

(C 104)

1940. Postal staff Anti-tuberculosis Fund. Optd with Type C **104**.
C554 C **96** 50l. green 25 30

K.Π. λεπτῶν 50
(C 105)

ΔΡ.1
(C 107)

1941. Social Funds. No. 410 surch with Type C **105**.
C561 **51** 50l. on 5l. green 20 10

1941. Postal Staff Anti-tuberculosis Fund. Surch **50** and bars.
C562 C **78** 50l. on 10l. 75 95
C563 – 50l. on 10l. (No. C494) 30 10

1942. Sample Fair, Salonika. No. C478 surch with Type C **107**.
C573 C **77** 1d. on 20l. brown . . 30 10

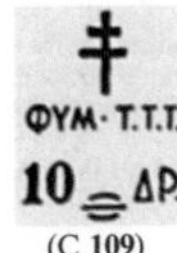

(C 109)

(C 111)

1942. Postal Staff Anti-tuberculosis Fund. Nos. 410 and 413 surch with Type C **109**.
C591 **51** 10d. on 5l. green 10 10
C592 10l. on 25l. green 20 10

1944. Postal Staff Anti-tuberculosis Fund. No. 580 optd with Type C **111**.
C599 100d. black 10 10

(C 112)

1944. Postal Staff Anti-tuberculosis Fund. No. 579 surch with Type C **112**.
C600 5000d. on 75d. red 10 10

(C 113)

1944. Postal Staff Anti-tuberculosis Fund. Surch as Type C **113**.
C619 – 1d. on 40l. (No. 500) . . 10 10
C620 – 2d. on 40l. (No. 500) . . 10 10
C605 **106** 25,000d. on 2d. 30 30

(C 117)

C 127 St. Demetrius

ΔΡ. — 50
(C 123)

1946. Postal Staff Anti-tuberculosis Fund. Surch as Type C **117**.
C640 C **117** 20d. on 5l. . . . . . 1·40 30
C641 20d. on 40l. (No. 500) 60 10

1946. Red Cross. Surch as Type C **117**.
C642 C **96** 50d. on 50l. (No. C525) 60 10

1946. Social Funds. Surch as Type C **117**.
C643 C **96** 50d. on 1d. (No. C526) 30 10

1947. Postal Staff Anti-tuberculosis Fund. Additionally surch with T C **123**.
C659 C **96** 50d. on 50l. (C525) . . 38·00
C660 50l. on 50d. (C554) . . 1·25 10

1948. Church Restoration Fund.
C682 C **127** 50d. brown 45 20

1950. Postal Staff Anti-tuberculosis Fund. Surch with Type C **117**.
C686 50d. on 10l. (No. 498) . . . 95 10

ΠΡΟΝΟΙΑ ΤΑΧ. ΥΠΑΛΛΗΛΩΝ ΔΡΑΧΜΑΙ 50
(C 136)

ΠΡΟΣΘΕΤΟΝ ΔΡ. 100
(C 139)

1951. Postal Staff Welfare Fund. Surch with Type C **136**.
C698 **86** 50d. on 5l. blue & brown 1·60 10

1951. Postal Staff Anti-tuberculosis Fund. Surch with Cross of Lorraine and **50**.
C699 **89** 50d. on 3d. brown . . . 1·40 10

1952. State Welfare Fund. No. 509 surch with Type C **139**.
C706 **89** 100d. on 8d. blue 80 10

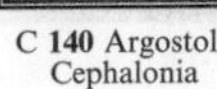

C **140** Argostoli, Cephalonia

C **148** Zeus (Macedonian Coin of Philip II)

1953. Ionian Is. Earthquake Fund.
C713 – 300d. slate 90 10
C714 C **140** 500d. brown & yellow 2·75 75
DESIGN: 300d. Church of Faneromeni, Zante.

1956. Macedonian Cultural Fund.
C761 C **148** 50l. red 95 25
C762 – 1d. blue (Aristotle) . . 4·25 1·20

POSTAGE DUE STAMPS

D 2

D 20

1875.
D73 D **2** 1l. green and black . . . 75 75
D74 2l. green and black . . . 75 75
D75 5l. green and black . . . 90 1·00
D88 10l. green and black . . 90 1·00
D89 20l. green and black . . 90 1·00
D78 40l. green and black . . 5·75 5·50
D91 60l. green and black . . 5·75 5·50
D80 70l. green and black . . 6·25 6·00
D81 80l. green and black . . 9·00 8·25
D82 90l. green and black . . 7·50 6·75
D95 100l. green and black . . 7·25 6·75
D96 200l. green and black . . 9·75 6·75
D83 1d. green and black . . 9·75 6·75
D84 2d. green and black . . 10·00 8·00

1902.
D183 D **20** 1l. brown 35 25
D184 2l. grey 35 25
D185 3l. orange 35 25
D186 5l. green 35 25
D273 10l. red 25 25
D188 20l. mauve 25 25
D275 25l. blue 15 10
D190 30l. purple 45 30
D191 40l. brown 20 35
D451 50l. brown 10 10
D193 1d. black . . . . . . 1·10 85
D194 2d. bronze . . . . . . 2·20 1·20
D195 3d. silver . . . . . . 2·75 1·70
D196 5d. gold . . . . 6·25 4·25

1912. Optd with T **34**.
D252A D **20** 1l. brown 50 50
D253A 2l. grey 50 50
D254A 3l. orange 35 35
D255A 5l. green 45 45
D256A 10l. red 80 80
D257D 20l. mauve 65 65
D258 30l. purple . . . . . 2·75 2·50
D259D 40l. brown 75 75
D260 50l. brown 60 60
D261D 1d. black . . . . . 6·25 6·00
D262D 2d. bronze . . . . . 7·50 7·25
D263D 3d. silver . . . . . 11·50 11·50
D264D 5d. gold . . . . . . 22·00 21·00

1913. Perf or roul.
D269 D **20** 1l. green 10 10
D270 2l. red 10 10
D271 3l. red 10 10
D274 20l. slate 20 15
D276 30l. red 10 15
D277 40l. blue 20 20
D279 80l. purple 45 40
D452 1d. blue 35 25
D453 2d. red 10 10
D282 3d. red . . . . 4·25 2·25
D455 5d. blue 10 10
D456 10d. green 10 10
D595 10d. orange 15 15
D457 15d. brown 20 20
D458 25d. red 45 70
D596 25d. blue 10 20
D480 50d. orange 20 40
D481 100d. green 25 40
D597 100d. brown 10 10
D598 200d. violet 10 10

1942. Surch **50**.
D564 D **20** 50l. on 30l. red . . . 45 60

GREEK WAR ISSUES, 1912–1913

For provisional issues used in territories occupied by Greece during the Balkan War, see Stanley Gibbons Part 3 (Balkans) Catalogue.

GREEK OCCUPATION OF ALBANIA Pt. 3

100 lepta = 1 drachma.

Stamps of Greece optd with T 1.

ΕΛΛΗΝΙΚΗ ΔΙΟΙΚΗΣΙΣ
(1)

1940. Stamps of 1937.
1 **86** 5l. blue and brown 15 15
2 – 10l. brown & blue (No. 498) 15 15
3 – 20l. green & blk (No. 499) 15 15
4 – 40l. black & grn (No. 500) 15 15
5 – 50l. black & brn (No. 501) 15 15
6 – 80l. brown & vio (No. 502) 15 15
7 **89** 1d. green 25 25
8 – 2d. blue (No. 504) . . . 25 25
9 **89** 3d. brown 25 25
10 – 5d. red (No. 506) . . . 40 40
11 – 6d. olive (No. 507) . . . 40 40
12 – 7d. brown (No. 508) . . 50 50
13 **89** 8d. blue 50 50
14 – 10d. brown (No. 510) . . 1·00 1·00
15 – 15d. green (No. 511) . . 75 75
16 – 25d. blue (No. 512) . . . 2·50 2·50
17 **89a** 30d. red . . . . 5·00 5·00

1940. Charity Tax Stamps of 1939.
18 C **96** 10l. red on rose 15 15
19 50l. green on green . . 15 15
20 1d. blue on blue . . . 25 25

1940. Nos. 534/53 (Youth Organization).
26 **101** 3d. blue, red & sil (postage) 75 75
27 – 5d. black and blue . . . 3·50 3·50
28 – 10d. black and orange . . 5·75 5·75
29 – 15d. black and green . . 12·50 12·50
30 – 20d. black and red . . . 7·75 7·75
31 – 25d. black and blue . . 7·75 7·75
32 – 30d. black and violet . . 9·50 9·50
33 – 50d. black and red . . . 12·00 12·00
34 – 75d. gold, blue and brown 12·50 12·50
35 **101** 100d. blue, red and silver 16·00 16·00
36 **103** 2d. black and orange (air) 25 25
37 – 4d. black and green . . 1·30 1·00
38 – 6d. black and red . . . 2·00 1·80
39 – 8d. black and blue . . . 3·75 3·50
40 – 16d. black and violet . . 6·50 6·25
41 – 32d. black and orange . . 11·50 11·00
42 – 45d. black and green . . 11·50 11·50
43 – 55d. black and red . . . 12·00 11·00
44 – 65d. black and blue . . 12·50 11·00
45 – 100d. black and violet . . 17·00 13·50

POSTAGE DUE STAMPS

1940. Postage Due stamps of 1913.
D21 D **20** 2d. red 25 25
D22 5d. blue 65 65
D23 10d. green 90 90
D24 15d. brown . . . . . . 1·00 1·00

1940. Postage Due stamp surch also.
D25 D **20** 50l. on 25d. red . . . . 1·00 1·00

GREENLAND Pt. 11

A Danish possession N.E. of Canada. On 5 June 1963, Greenland became an integral part of the Danish Kingdom.

100 ore = 1 krone.

1 Christian X

2 Polar Bear

1938.
1 **1** 1ore green 15 25
2 5ore red . . . . 1·40 1·00
3 7ore green . . . . 1·90 2·30
4 10ore violet 85 45
5 15ore red 85 60
5a 20ore red . . . . 1·30 90
6 **2** 30ore blue . . . . 7·00 5·75
6a 40ore blue . . . . 23·00 5·25
7 1k. brown . . . . 8·50 6·75

3 Harp Seal

4 King Christian X

5 Eskimo Kayak

1945.
8 **3** 1ore violet and black . . . . 24·00 22·00
9 5ore buff and violet . . . . 24·00 22·00
10 7ore black and green . . . . 24·00 22·00
11 **4** 10ore olive and purple . . . 22·00 22·00
12 15ore blue and red . . . . . 22·00 22·00
13 – 30ore brown and blue . . . 22·00 22·00
14 – 1k. grey and brown . . . . 22·00 22·00
15 **5** 2k. green and brown . . . . 23·00 22·00
16 – 5k. brown and purple . . . . 28·00 22·00
DESIGNS—HORIZ: As Type **5**: 30ore Dog team; 1k. Polar bear; 5k. Eider.

1945. Liberation of Denmark. Nos. 8/16 optd **DANMARK BEFRIET 5 MAJ 1945**.
17 **3** 1ore violet and black . . . . 65·00 41·00
18 5ore buff and violet . . . . 65·00 41·00
19 7ore black and green . . . . 65·00 41·00
20 **4** 10ore olive and purple . . . 65·00 75·00
21 15ore blue and red . . . . . 65·00 75·00
22 – 30ore brown and blue . . . 65·00 75·00
23 – 1k. grey and brown . . . . 65·00 75·00
24 **5** 2k. green and brown . . . . 65·00 75·00
25 – 5k. brown and purple . . . . 65·00 75·00

7 King Frederik IX

8 Polar Ship "Gustav Holm"

1950.
26 **7** 1ore green 25 15
27 5ore red 35 20
28 10ore green 40 20
29a 15ore violet 55 40
30 25ore red . . . . 1·90 85
31 30ore blue . . . . 23·00 1·40
32 30ore red 65 30
33 **8** 50ore blue . . . . 42·00 11·00
34 1k. brown . . . . 14·50 1·80
35 2k. red . . . . 6·25 1·70
36 5k. grey . . . . 3·50 1·20

1956. Nos. 6a and 7 surch **60 ore**.
37 **2** 60ore on 40ore blue . . . . 6·25 90
38 60ore on 1k. brown . . . . 45·00 5·50

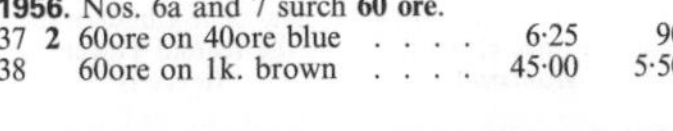

10 "The Boy and the Fox"

12 Hans Egede (after J. Horner)

14 Knud Rasmussen (founder of Thule)

1957. Greenland Legends.
39 **10** 50ore red . . . . 1·80 70
40 – 60ore blue . . . . 1·80 75
41 – 80ore brown . . . . 1·90 90
42 – 90ore blue . . . . 2·50 2·20

DESIGNS: 60ore "Mother of the Sea"; 80ore "The Girl and the Eagle"; 90ore "Great Northern Diver and Raven".

1958. Royal Tuberculosis Relief Fund. No. 33 surch with Cross of Lorraine and **30+10**.
43 **8** 30ore+10ore on 50ore blue . . . 2·10 90

1958. Death Bicent of Hans Egede (missionary).
44 **12** 30ore red . . . . 6·50 95

1959. Greenland Fund. Surch **Gronlandsfonden 30+10** and bars.
45 **7** 30ore+10ore on 25ore red . . 4·50 3·25

The note below No. 413 of Denmark also applies here.

1960. 50th Anniv of Thule Settlement.
46 **14** 30ore red . . . . 1·20 85

15 Drum Dance

16 Northern Lights

17 Frederik IX

18 Polar Bear

1961.

47 **15** 35ore green 90 50

1963.

48	**16**	1ore green	20	15
49		5ore red	25	20
50		10ore green	45	30
51		12ore green	35	35
52		15ore purple	80	60
53	**17**	20ore blue	2·50	2·20
54		25ore brown	40	30
54a		30ore green	35	30
55		35ore red	35	30
56		40ore grey	40	30
57		50ore blue	7·00	5·25
57a		50ore red	45	30
57b		60ore red	50	25
58		80ore orange	65	60
59	**18**	1k. brown	70	25
60		2k. red	2·30	55
61		5k. blue	2·30	95
62		10k. green	3·00	55

18a Prof. Niels Bohr

19 S. Kleinschmidt

1963. 50th Anniv of Bohr's Atomic Theory.
63 **18a** 35ore red 30 30
64 60ore blue . . . . 2·50 2·40

1964. 150th Birth Anniv of S. Kleinschmidt (philologist).
65 **19** 35ore brown 60 60

20a Princess Margrethe and Prince Henri de Monpezat

21a "The Children in the Round Tower" (legend)

1967. Royal Wedding.
66 **20a** 50ore red . . . . 2·40 2·10

1968. Child Welfare.
67 **21a** 60ore+10ore red 65 65

22 King Frederik IX and Map of Greenland

1969. King Frederik's 70th Birthday.
68 **22** 60ore red . . . . 1·10 95

24 Musk Ox

25 Celebrations at Jakobshavn

1969.

69	–	1k. blue	55	45
70	–	2k. green	75	40
71	–	5k. blue	1·50	60
72	–	10k. brown	2·75	1·20
73	**24**	25k. olive	6·50	1·90

DESIGN—HORIZ: 1k. Bowhead whale and coastline; 2k. Narwhal; 5k. Polar bear; 10k. Walruses.

1970. 25th Anniv of Denmark's Liberation.
74 **25** 60ore red . . . . 1·60 1·50

26 Egede and Gertrud Rask aboard the "Haabet"

27 Mail Kayaks

1971. 250th Anniv of Hans Egede's Arrival in Greenland.
75 **26** 60ore red . . . . 1·00 1·00
76 – 60ore+10ore red . . . . . 1·20 1·30

DESIGN: No. 76, Hans Egede and Gertrud Rask meeting Greenlanders.

The premium on No. 76 was for the Greenland Church Building Fund.

1971. Greenland Mail Transport.

77	**27**	50ore green	25	25
78	–	70ore red	35	25
79	–	80ore black	40	40
80	–	90ore blue	35	30
81	–	1k. red	55	50
82	–	1k.30 blue	55	45
83	–	1k.50 green	80	45
84	–	2k. blue	75	50

DESIGNS: 70 ore Umiak (women's boat); 80 ore Consolidated Catalina amphibian; 90 ore Mail dog-sledge; 1k. "Kununhuak" (coaster) and "Dlik" (tug); 1k.30 "Sokongen" (schooner); 1k.50 "Karen" (sailing longboat); 2k. Sikorsky S-61N helicopter.

28 King Frederik IX and Royal Yacht "Dannebrog"

29 Queen Margrethe

1972. King Frederik IX's and Queen Ingrid's Fund.
85 **28** 60ore+10ore red 75 65

1973.

86	**29**	10ore green	25	20
87		60ore brown	30	35
88		90ore brown	50	45
88a		100ore red	40	25
89		120ore blue	65	60
89a		130ore blue	50	50

For values inscribed "KALAALLIT NUNAAT" at top, see Nos. 99/104.

30 Heimaey Eruption

1973. Aid for Victims of Heimaey (Iceland) Eruption.
90 **30** 70ore+20ore blue and red . . 90 85

31 "Carl Egede" (trawler) and Kayaks

32 Gyr Falcon and Radio Aerial

1974. Bicentenary of Royal Greenland Trade Department.
91 **31** 1k. brown 65 50
92 – 2k. brown 65 45

DESIGN—VERT: 2k. Trade Department Headquarters, Trangraven, Copenhagen.

1975. 50th Anniv of Greenland's Telecommunications Service.
93 **32** 90ore red 45 45

33 Sirius Sledge Patrol

1975. 25th Anniv of Sirius Sledge Patrol.
94 **33** 1k.20 brown 45 45

34 Arm-wrestling (after H. Egede)

35 Inuit Carved Mask

1976. Greenland Sports Publicity.
95 **34** 100ore+20ore brown and green on stone 45 45

1977. Eskimo Mask.
96 **35** 9k. grey . . . . 2·30 2·00

36 Bronlund and Disko Bay, Jakobshavn

37 Cape York Meteorite and "Ulo" (woman's knife)

1977. Birth Cent of Jorgen Bronlund (explorer).
97 **36** 1k. brown 35 30

1978. Centenary of Commission for Scientific Researches in Greenland.
98 **37** 1k.20 brown 45 35

38 Queen Margrethe

1978.

99	**38**	5ore red	25	15
100		80ore brown	30	25
101		120ore brown	45	40
102		130ore red	45	30
103		160ore blue	50	50
104		180ore green	60	50

39 Sun rising over Mountains

1978. 25th Anniv of Constitution.
105 **39** 1k.50 blue 40 40

40 Foundation Ceremony

41 Tupilak (imaginary animal)

1978. 250th Anniv of Godthab.
106 **40** 2k.50 brown 70 45

1978. Folk Art.
107 **41** 6k. red . . . . 1·50 1·30
108 – 7k. green . . . . 1·70 1·30
109 – 8k. blue . . . . 1·90 1·50

DESIGNS: 7k. Soapstone figure (Simon Kristoffersen); 8k. "Eskimo Family" (driftwood sculpture by Johannas Kreutzamann).

42 Helmsman

43 Rasmussen with Eskimos

1979. Internal Autonomy.
110 **42** 1k.10 brown 45 30

1979. Birth Centenary of Knud Rasmussen (polar explorer).
111 **43** 1k.30+20ore red 45 40

45 Eskimo Child

47 Queen Margrethe and Map of Greenland

1979. International Year of the Child.
112 **45** 2k. green 65 45

1980.

113	**47**	50ore violet	30	25
114		80ore brown	45	35
115		1k.30 red	50	45
116		1k.50 blue	60	55
117		1k.60 blue	65	50
118		1k.80 red	75	70
119		2k.30 green	65	65
120		2k.50 red	75	50
121		2k.80 brown	1·10	70
122		3k. red	1·20	75
122a		3k.20 red	1·20	65
123		3k.80 black	1·20	1·20
124		4k.10 blue	1·50	1·40
124a		4k.40 blue	1·70	1·40

48 Eskimos and Rasmus Berthelsen in Library

49 "Reindeer Sledge and the Larva" (drawing, Jens Kreutzmann)

1980. 150th Anniv of Greenland Public Libraries.
125 **48** 2k. brown on yellow . . . 60 45

1980. Greenland Art.
126 **49** 1k.60 red 45 45
127 – 2k.70 violet 75 80
128 – 3k. black 80 65

DESIGNS: 2k.70 "Harpooning Walrus" (printing by Jakob Danielsen); 3k. "Foot Race between Quloqutsuk and Aqigssia (woodcut by Aron from Kangeq).

50 Mikkelsen and Eskimo

52 Atlantic Cod

1980. Birth Centenary of Ejnar Mikkelsen (Inspector of East Greenland).
129 **50** 4k. green . . . . 1·00 85

1981.

130 **52** 25k. brown and blue . . . 5·75 3·75

53 Stone Tent Ring, Wolf and King Eiders

54 Reindeer and Hunter (Saqqaq culture, 2000 B.C.)

1981. Peary Land Expeditions.
131 **53** 1k.60+20ore brown 65 65

1981. Greenland Prehistory.
132 **54** 3k.50 blue 90 90
133 – 5k. brown . . . . 1·30 1·20

DESIGN: 5k. Hunters dragging walrus (Tunit-Dorset culture, 50 B.C.).

55 Shrimps

57 Eric the Red discovering Greenland, 982

1982.

134 **55** 10k. blue and red . . . . 2·50 1·50

1982. Millenary of Greenland (1st issue).
135 **57** 2k.+40ore brown 85 80

See also Nos. 136/7, 140/2, 145/7 and 152/3.

58 Eskimos hunting Bowhead Whale (1000–1100)

1982. Millennary of Greenland (2nd issue).
136 **58** 2k. red 55 50
137 – 2k.70 blue 80 75
DESIGN: 2k.70, Bishop Joen Smyrill's staff and house at Gardar (1100–1200).

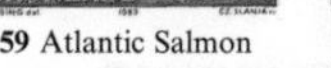

59 Atlantic Salmon

60 Blind Person, Armband, Cassette and White Stick

1983.
138 **59** 50k. black and blue . . . 11·00 5·50

1983. Welfare of the Blind.
139 **60** 2k.50+40ore red 85 95

61 Eskimos and Northerners bartering (1200–1300)

62 Herrnhut Bandsmen

1983. Millennary of Greenland (3rd issue).
140 **61** 2k.50 brown 70 65
141 – 3k.50 brown 75 90
142 – 4k.50 blue . . . . 1·20 1·20
DESIGNS: 3k.50, Mummy of Eskimo boy (1300–1400); 4k.50, Hans Pothorst's expedition to America (1400–1500).

1983. 250th Anniv of Herrnhut Moravian Brethren Settlement.
143 **62** 2k.50 brown 70 75

63 "Polar Bear killing Seal Hunter"

64 Bowhead Whales and Glass Beads (trading goods) (1500–1600)

1984. 50th Death Anniv of Karale Andreassen (writer and artist).
144 **63** 3k.70 black . . . . 1·10 1·00

1984. Millenary of Greenland (4th issue).
145 **64** 2k.70 brown 85 90
146 – 3k.70 blue 95 95
147 – 5k.50 brown . . . . 1·40 1·30
DESIGNS: 3k.70 Greenlanders in European dress and apostle spoons (1600–1700); 5k.50, Hans Egede's mission station, Godthab, and key (1700–1800).

65 Prince Henrik of Denmark

66 Danish Grenadier, 1734

1984. Prince Henrik's 50th Birthday.
148 **65** 2k.70 brown . . . . 1·10 1·10

1984. 250th Anniv of Christianshab.
149 **66** 3k.70 brown . . . . 1·00 90

67 Lund

68 Spotted Wolffish

1984. 36th Death Anniv of Henrik Lund (composer).
150 **67** 5k. green . . . . 1·70 1·50

1984.
151 **68** 10k. black and blue . . . 3·00 2·75

69 "Hvalfisken" (brig) (1800–1900)

70 Queen Ingrid and "Chrysanthemum frutescens" "Sofiero"

1985. Millenary of Greenland (5th issue).
152 **69** 2k.80 purple . . . . 1·10 1·00
153 – 6k. black . . . . 1·30 1·40
DESIGN: 6k. Communications satellite and globe (1900–2000).

1985. 50th Anniv of Queen Ingrid's Arrival in Denmark.
154 **70** 2k.80 multicoloured . . . 70 75

71 Nesting Birds and I.Y.Y. Emblem

72 "Hare Hunt"

1985. International Youth Year.
155 **71** 3k.80 multicoloured . . . 90 90

1985. 130th Birth Anniv of Gerhard Kleist (artist).
156 **72** 9k. green . . . . 2·20 2·00

73 Greenland Halibut

74 Post Office Flags

1985.
157 **73** 10k. brown and blue . . . 2·40 2·40

1986. Postal Independence.
158 **74** 2k.80 red 70 65

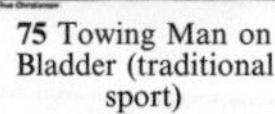

75 Towing Man on Bladder (traditional sport)

76 Needle Case and Combs

1986. Greenland Athletic Federation.
159 **75** 2k.80+50ore mult . . . . 1·20 1·10

1986. Local Craft Artefacts.
160 **76** 2k.80 brown and red . . . 90 80
161 – 3k. violet and red 90 65
162 – 3k.80 black and blue . . . 1·00 95
163 – 3k.80 purple and blue . . . 1·40 1·20
164 – 5k. brown and green . . . 1·50 1·30
165 – 6k.50 brown and green . . 1·90 1·70
166 – 10k. brown and purple . . 3·00 2·40
DESIGNS: 3k. Tubs; 3k.80, (No. 162) Ulos (knives for working sealskins); 3k.80, (No. 163) Eye masks; 5k. Harpoon heads; 6k.50, Lard lamps; 10k. Masks.

77 "Daily Life in Thule" (collage by Aninaaq)

78 Capelin

1986. Art from Thule.
167 **77** 2k.80 brown 80 85

1986.
168 **78** 10k. brown and green . . . 2·75 2·30

79 Fulmar and Iceberg

1987. "Hafnia 87" International Stamp Exhibition, Copenhagen (1st issue). Sheet 95 × 70 mm containing T **79** and similar vert designs showing coastal view of Greenland from sketch by Jens Lorentzen. Multicoloured.
MS169 2k.80 Type **79**; 3k.80 Uummannaq Mountain and ice floes; 6k.50 Fulmars swimming and steamer in bay (sold at 19k.50) 6·25 7·25
See also No. **MS**193.

80 "Ammassalik Fjord" (Peter Rosing)

81 Father and Son on Ice-floe

1987. Greenland Art.
170 **80** 2k.80 brown 80 75

1987. Fishing, Sealing and Whaling Industries Year.
171 **81** 3k.80 multicoloured . . . 1·00 1·00

83 Rock Ptarmigans

84 Uummannaq Mountain

1987. Birds. Multicoloured.
172 3k. Gyr falcons . . . . . . 1·50 85
173 3k.20 Long-tailed ducks . . . 1·10 80
174 4k. Snow geese . . . . . . 1·60 85
175 4k.10 Common ravens . . . 1·40 1·20
176 4k.40 Snow buntings . . . . 1·60 1·30
177 5k. Type **83** . . . . 1·60 1·20
178 5k.50 White-tailed sea eagles 2·10 1·80
179 5k.50 Black guillemots . . . 1·70 1·50
180 6k.50 Brunnich's guillemots 2·30 1·80
181 7k. Great northern divers . . 2·40 1·90
182 7k.50 Long-tailed skuas . . . 2·30 1·90
183 10k. Snowy owl . . . . . . 2·75 2·00

1987. "Hafnia 87" International Stamp Exhibition, Copenhagen (2nd issue). Sheet 94 × 68 mm.
MS193 **84** 2k.80 blue and red (sold at 4k.) . . . . 2·30 2·50

85 Telefax, Sledge and De Havilland Dash Seven

1988. 50 Years of Greenland Postal Administration.
194 **85** 3k.+50ore multicoloured 1·30 1·50

87 National Flag

1989. 10th Anniv of Internal Autonomy. Mult.
195 3k.20 Type **87** 85 70
196 4k.40 National arms . . . . 1·30 1·20

88 Cotton Grass

89 Queen Margrethe

1989. Flowers. Multicoloured.
197 4k. Bellflower (vert) . . . . 1·20 90
198 4k. Hairy lousewort (vert) . . 1·30 1·20
199 5k. Type **88** . . . . 1·50 1·20
200 5k.50 Labrador tea . . . . . 1·60 1·30
201 6k.50 Arctic white heather . . 2·20 1·80
202 7k.25 Purple saxifrage . . . 2·75 2·20
203 10k. Arctic poppy (vert) . . . 2·75 2·20

1990.
210 **89** 25ore green 25 15
213 1k. brown 40 35
218 4k. red . . . . 1·10 80
219 4k.25 red . . . . 1·30 1·00
221 6k.50 blue . . . . 1·90 1·70
222 7k. violet . . . . 2·10 1·80

90 Chained Sledge Dog and nesting Eiders

91 Frederik Lynge

1990. Greenland Environmental Foundation.
225 **90** 400ore+50ore mult . . . . 2·20 2·00

1990. Augo and Frederik Lynge (Greenland Members of Danish Folketing).
226 **91** 10k. red and blue . . . . 3·00 2·10
227 – 25k. purple and blue . . . 6·75 3·75
DESIGN: 25k. Augo Lynge.

92 Ringed Seal ("Phoca hispida")

93 Dogs and Fisherman

1991. Marine Mammals. Multicoloured.
228 4k. Type **92** . . . . 1·30 1·20
229 4k. Harp seals ("Pagophilus groenlandicus") . . . . . 1·30 1·20
230 7k.25 Hooded seals ("Cystophora cristata") . . 1·90 1·70
231 7k.25 Walrus ("Odobenus rosmarus") . . . . 1·90 1·70
232 8k.50 Bearded seal ("Erignatus barbatus") . . 2·20 1·90
233 8k.50 Common seal ("Phoca vitulina") . . . . 2·20 1·90
MS234 142 × 86 mm. Nos. 228/33 12·00 13·00

1991. 250th Anniv of Ilulissat (Jakobshavn).
235 **93** 4k. multicoloured . . . . 1·30 1·20

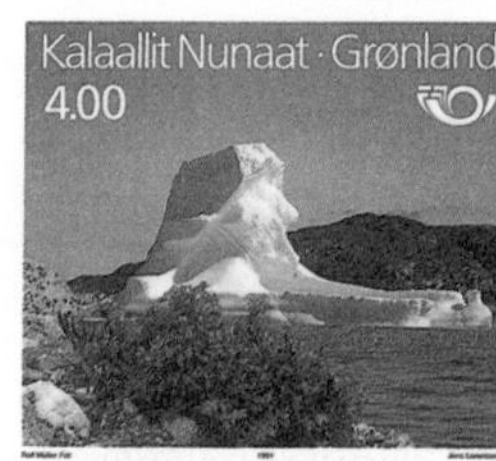

94 Iceberg and Summer Flowers

1991. Nordic Countries' Postal Co-operation. Tourism. Multicoloured.
236 4k. Type **94** . . . . 1·10 1·00
237 8k.50 Ski party and dog sled in winter . . . . 2·30 2·30

95 Birds

96 Jonathan Petersen (composer, 110th anniv)

1991. 75th Anniv of Blue Cross (health education organization).
238 **95** 4k.+50ore multicoloured 4·25 6·50

1991. Birth Anniversaries.
239 **96** 10k. black and blue . . . 3·00 2·00
240 – 50k. brown and blue . . . 11·50 11·50
DESIGN: 50k. Hans Lynge (writer and artist, 85th anniv).

97 Arms and Paamiut

1992. Bicentenary of Paamiut (Fredrikshaab).
241 **97** 7k.25 brown and blue . . . 2·10 2·00

98 Royal Couple in 1992 and in Official Wedding Photograph

1992. Silver Wedding of Queen Margrethe and Prince Henrik.
242 **98** 4k. multicoloured . . . . 1·70 1·40

99 Moller and Drawing of Godthab Church

100 Rainbow and Landscape

1992. 150th Birth Anniv of Lars Moller (editor and printer).
243 **99** 100k. red and blue . . . . 22·00 19·00

1992. Neriuffik Cancer Research Organization.
244 **100** 4k.+50ore multicoloured 3·00 2·50

101 Mother and Child with Father Christmas

102 Flame and Laurel Wreath framed by Dance Drum

1992. Christmas.
245 **101** 4k. multicoloured . . . . 1·70 1·20

1993. Int Year of Indigenous Peoples.
246 **102** 4k. multicoloured . . . . 1·30 1·10

103 Flat Crab

1993. Crabs.
247 **103** 4k. red, yellow and green 1·20 90
248 – 7k.25 brown and blue . . 2·40 2·30
249 – 8k.50 multicoloured . . . 2·40 2·40
DESIGNS: 7k.25, Sand crab; 8k.50, Stone crabs.

104 Ummannaq Church

1993. Nordic Countries' Postal Co-operation. Churches. Multicoloured.
250 4k. Type **104** . . . . 1·00 1·20
251 8k.50 Hvalso church ruins . . 2·30 4·50

105 Children in Tent

1993. Anniversaries.
252 **105** 4k.+50ore multicoloured 1·60 1·80
253 – 4k.+50ore red and violet 1·60 1·80
MS254 140 × 80 mm. Nos. 252/3 each × 2 . . . . 14·50 16·00
DESIGNS: No. 252 Type **105** (50th anniv of scouts in Greenland); 253, Birds, crosses and landscape (70th anniv of Red Cross in Greenland).

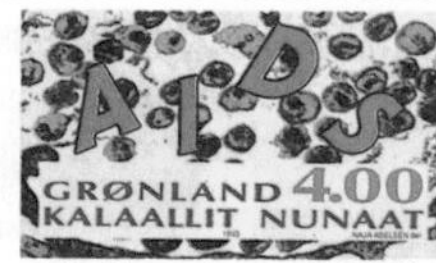

106 Corpuscles and "AIDS"

1993. Anti-AIDS Campaign.
255 **106** 4k. multicoloured . . . . 1·20 1·10

107 Wolf

108 Dog Sled

1993. Animals. Multicoloured.
256 4k. Polar bear . . . . 1·40 1·30
257 5k. Type **107** . . . . 1·50 1·50
258 5k.50 Ermine . . . . 1·60 1·60
259 7k.25 Arctic lemmings . . . 1·70 1·90
260 7k.25 Wolverine . . . . . . 2·30 2·30
261 7k.50 Musk ox . . . . . . 2·50 2·75
262 8k.50 Arctic fox . . . . . . 2·40 2·50
263 9k. Mountain hare . . . . . 2·50 2·75
264 10k. Reindeer . . . . 2·75 3·00

1993. Christmas.
265 **108** 4k. multicoloured . . . . 1·40 1·30

109 Skiers

111 First Church

110 Transmission Line

1994. Winter Olympic Games, Lillehammer, Norway.
266 **109** 4k.+50ore multicoloured 1·90 1·40
MS267 140 × 80 mm. No. 266 × 4 13·00 10·50

1994. Inauguration of Buksefjorden Hydroelectric Power Station.
268 **110** 4k. multicoloured . . . . 1·20 1·10

1994. Centenary of Ammassalik.
269 **111** 7k.25 blue, brown & grn 2·10 1·90

112 "Danmark" (sail/steam barque)

1994. Europa. Discoveries. "Danmark" Expedition to North-east Coast, 1906–08. Multicoloured.
270 4k. Type **112** . . . . 1·20 1·10
271 7k.25 "Danmark" and dogs following ELG Mobil car 2·10 2·00

113 "Ceres" (William Moen)

1994. Figureheads from Greenlandic Ships (1st series). Multicoloured.
272 4k. Type **113** . . . . 1·10 1·10
273 8k.50 "Nordlyset" (Johan Heldt) . . . . 2·20 2·30
See also Nos. 287/8 and 306/7.

114 Christmas Visiting

1994. Christmas. Multicoloured.
274 4k. Type **114** . . . . 1·10 1·10
275 5k. Santa Claus outside igloo 1·40 1·30

115 "Listera cordata"

116 Teacher and Student

1995. Arctic Orchids (1st series). Multicoloured.
276 4k. Type **115** . . . . 1·10 1·00
277 7k.25 "Leucorchis albida" . . 2·00 1·90
See also Nos. 293/5.

1995. 150th Anniv of Nuuk Training College.
278 **116** 4k. multicoloured . . . . 1·20 1·10

116a U.N. Emblem and "50"

1995. 50th Anniv of United Nations.
279 **116a** blue, green and red . . . 2·10 2·00

117 Iceberg and Meadow

1995. Nordic Countries' Postal Co-operation. Tourism.
280 4k. Type **117** . . . . 1·20 1·20
281 8k.50 Mountains and valleys 2·20 2·30

118 Airmail Envelope

1995. Europa. Peace and Freedom. Multicoloured.
282 4k. Type **118** . . . . 1·50 1·10
283 8k.50 Doves and seascape . . 2·75 2·30

119 King Christian X

1995. 50th Anniv of Liberation. Three sheets each 140 × 80 mm, containing reproductions of 1945 "American Series", surcharged in red. Multicoloured.
MS284 (a) 5k. on 10ore Type **119**; 5k. on 15ore Type **119**; (b) 1k. on 1ore Seal; 5k. on 5ore Seal; 7k. on 7ore Seal; (c) 4k. on 30ore Dog team; 4k. on 1k. Polar bear; 4k. on 2k. Eskimo kayak; 4k. on 5k. Eider Set of 3 sheets . . . . . 22·00 21·00

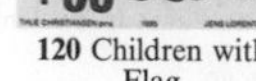

120 Children with Flag

121 Boy running with Lamps

1995. 10th Anniv of National Flag.
285 **120** 4k.+50ore multicoloured 2·10 1·60
MS286 80 × 140 m. No. 285 × 4 13·50 10·50

The premium was for the benefit of the Greenland Flag Society.

1995. Figureheads from Greenlandic Ships (2nd series). As T **113**. Multicoloured.
287 4k. "Hvalfisken" (H. J. Moen) (vert) . . . . 1·50 1·10
288 8k.50 "Tjalfe" . . . . 2·50 2·40

1995. Christmas. Multicoloured.
289 4k. Type **121** . . . . 1·50 1·00
290 5k. Boy running with lamp and moon . . . . 1·80 1·20

1995. Nos. 210 and 213 surch.
291 **89** 4k.25 on 25ore green . . . 2·50 1·80
292 4k.50 on 1k. brown . . . 3·00 2·10

1996. Arctic Orchids (2nd series). As T **115**. Multicoloured.
293 4k.25 Early coral-root . . . 1·30 1·00
294 4k.50 Round-leaved orchid 1·50 1·20
295 7k.50 Northern green orchid 2·30 2·20

124 Killer Whale

1996. Whales (1st series). Each black, red and blue.
296 25ore Type **124** 45 40
297 50ore Humpback whale . . . 45 45
298 1k. Beluga 60 50
299 4k.50 Sperm whale . . . . . 1·20 1·30
300 6k.50 Bowhead whale . . . . 1·90 1·70
301 9k.50 Minke whale . . . . . 1·80 2·30
MS302 140 × 80 mm. Nos.296/301 6·50 6·75
See also Nos. 318/22.

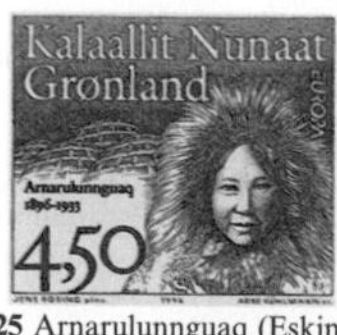

125 Arnarulunnguaq (Eskimo traveller)

1996. Europa. Famous Women.
303 **125** 4k.50 blue . . . . 2·10 1·20

126 Man in Wheelchair at Sea Shore

1996. Greenland Society of Handicapped and Disabled.
304 **126** 4k.25+50ore mult . . . . 1·50 1·40
MS305 140 × 81 mm. No. 304 × 4 7·25 5·50

1996. Figureheads from Greenlandic Ships (3rd series). As T **113**. Multicoloured.
306 15k. "Blaa Hejren" . . . . . 4·00 3·75
307 20k. "Gertrud Rask" (horiz) 5·00 5·50

127 Child and Angels

1996. Christmas. Multicoloured.
308 4k.25 Type **127** . . . . . . 1·20 1·20
309 4k.50 Star and children . . . 1·20 1·30

128 Arctic Fritillary

129 Queen Margrethe in Greenlandic Costume

1997. Butterflies. Multicoloured.
310 2k. Type **128** 65 55
311 3k. Northern clouded yellow 95 85
312 4k.75 Arctic blue . . . . . . 1·40 1·20
313 8k. Small copper . . . . . . 2·10 2·00

1997. Silver Jubilee of Queen Margrethe.
314 **129** 4k.50 multicoloured . . . 1·20 95

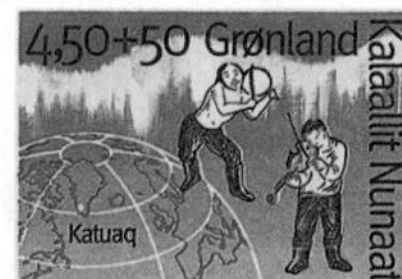

130 Globe and Musicians

1997. Opening of Katuaq Cultural Centre, Nuuk.
315 **130** 4k.50+50ore mult . . . . 1·40 1·50
MS316 140 × 82 mm. No. 315 × 4 6·50 7·00

131 Bear of the Sea inhaling Umiak (boat)

1997. Europa. Tales and Legends.
317 **131** 4k.75 blue . . . . 1·90 1·70

1997. Whales (2nd series). As T **124**. Mult.
318 5k. Blue whale . . . . 1·40 1·40
319 5k.75 Fin whale . . . . . . 1·50 1·60
320 6k. Sei whale . . . . 1·50 1·50
321 8k. Narwhal . . . . 1·80 1·90
MS322 140 × 81 mm. Nos. 318/21 6·00 7·00

132 Dancing Children and Church

1997. Bicentenary of Nanortalik.
323 **132** 4k.50 multicoloured . . . 1·30 1·20

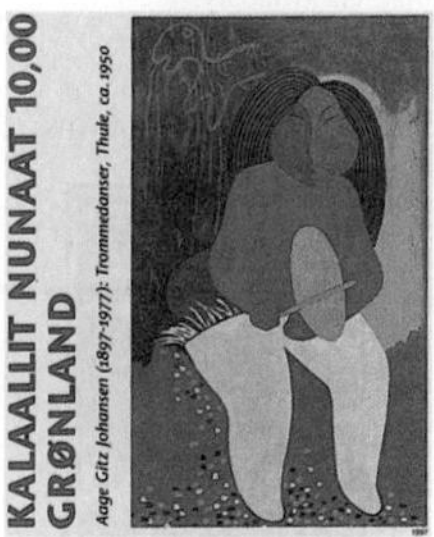

133 "Drum Dancer"

1997. Greenland Art (1st series). 20th Death Anniv of Aage Gitz-Johansen. Multicoloured.
324 10k. Type **133** . . . . . . 2·40 2·50
325 16k. "Ammassalik Woman" 3·75 3·75
See also Nos. 342/3 and 353/4.

134 Boy with Huskies

1997. Christmas. Multicoloured.
326 4k.50 Type **134** . . . . . . 1·50 1·50
327 4k.75 Family on sledge and father disentangling traces 1·50 1·30

135 Common Porpoise

1998. International Year of the Ocean. Cetaceans. Multicoloured.
328 2k. Type **135** 75 65
329 3k. White-beaked dolphin . . 85 85
330 4k.50 Long-finned pilot whale ("Globicephala melaena") 1·10 1·10
331 4k.50 Northern bottle-nosed whale ("Hyperoodon ampullatus") . . . . 1·10 1·10
332 4k.75 Atlantic white-sided dolphin ("Lagenorhynchus acutus") . . . . 1·10 1·10
333 4k.75 Black right whale ("Eubalaena glacialis") . . 1·10 1·10
MS334 141 × 81 mm. Nos. 328/33 6·50 6·00

136 Augo and Frederik Lynge (first Greenland members of Danish Parliament)

137 Kathrine Chemnitz

1998. New Order, 1950 (redefinition of Greenland's status).
335 **136** 4k.50 blue, lilac and red 1·10 1·20

1998. 20th Death Anniv of Kathrine Chemnitz (founder) and 50th Anniv of Women's Society of Greenland.
336 **137** 4k.50+50ore mult . . . . 1·20 1·30
MS337 80 × 140 mm. No. 336 × 4 5·25 5·25

138 "Children's Faces" (Class 4B, Atuarfik Ukaliusaq School)

139 "Gertrud Rask" (sailing coaster)

1998. Europa. National Festivals. Children's Day. Multicoloured.
338 4k.75 Type **138** . . . . . . 1·50 1·50
339 10k. "Children playing" (Class 5A, Edvard Kruse-p Atuarfia School) . . . . . 2·40 2·30

1998. Nordic Countries' Postal Co-operation. Sailing Ships. Multicoloured.
340 4k.50 Type **139** . . . . . . 1·90 1·20
341 4k.75 "Hans Egede" (sailing coaster) . . . . 1·50 1·30

140 "Breastfeeding Older Brother"

1998. Greenland Art (2nd series). 10th Death Anniv of Hans Lynge (artist). Multicoloured.
342 11k. Type **140** . . . . . . 2·50 2·75
343 25k. "Refuelling" . . . . . 5·75 6·00

141 Jacket and Slippers on Line

142 Owl with Chicks

1998. Christmas. Multicoloured.
344 4k.50 Type **141** . . . . . . 1·30 1·20
345 4k.75 Hat and slippers on line . . . . 1·30 1·30

1999. Endangered Species. The Snowy Owl Multicoloured.
346 1k. Type **142** 60 55
347 4k.75 Owl in flight . . . . 1·00 1·20
348 5k.50 Male and female owls 1·00 1·30
349 5k.75 Owl on rock . . . . . 2·10 1·70

143 Ammassalik Pincushion

144 Polar Bear

1999. Greenland National Museum and Archives.
350 **143** 4k.50+50ore black, blue and red . . . . 1·40 1·40
MS351 80 × 141 mm. No. 350 × 4 5·75 5·75

1999. Europa. Parks and Gardens.
352 **144** 6k. multicoloured . . . . 2·00 1·90

145 "The Man from Aluk"

1999. Greenland Art (3rd series). Paintings by Peter Rosing. Multicoloured.
353 7k. Type **145** . . . . 1·90 1·90
354 20k. "Homecoming" . . . . 5·00 5·00

146 Viking Longship

1999. Greenland Vikings (1st series).
355 **146** 4k.50 green and blue . . 1·20 1·20
356 – 4k.75 green and blue . . 1·20 1·30
357 – 5k.75 brown and blue . . 1·50 1·50
358 – 8k. brown and blue . . . 1·80 1·90
MS359 140 × 80 mm. Nos. 355/8 5·50 5·75
DESIGNS: 4k.75, Man collecting driftwood; 5k.75, Arrowhead and coins; 8k. Tjodhilde's Church, Brottal.
See also Nos. 363/7 and 390/4.

147 Writing Letter

1999. Christmas. Multicoloured.
360 4k.50 Type **147** . . . . . . 1·20 1·10
361 4k.75 Candles and clasped hands . . . . 1·20 1·20

148 Ice Cap

1999. New Millennium.
362 **148** 5k.75 multicoloured . . . 1·60 1·60

2000. Greenland Vikings (2nd series). As T **146**.
363 25ore brown and blue . . . 80 60
364 3k. brown and blue . . . . 1·20 1·10
365 5k.50 blue . . . . 1·60 1·60
366 21k. blue . . . . 3·50 4·25
MS367 140 × 81 mm. Nos. 363/6 7·00 7·25
DESIGNS: 25ore Walruses; 3k. Story teller and model of great northern diver; 5k.50, Dog chasing reindeer; 21k. Viking with gyr falcon, polar bear, walrus tusks and straps and bag of ship's tar (trading goods).

149 Huskies pulling Sledge

2000. 50th Anniv of "Sirius" (naval sledge patrol).
368 **149** 10k. multicoloured . . . 2·50 2·50

150 Queen Margrethe II (from photograph by Rigmor Mydtskov)

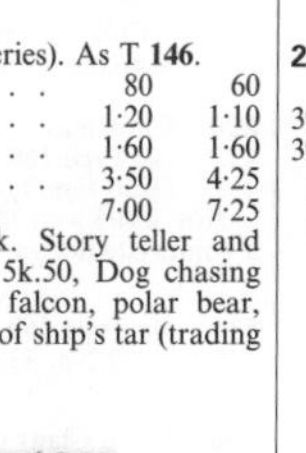

151 "Building Europe"

2000.
372 **150** 25ore blue and black . . 25 15
373 50ore blue and brown . . 75 55
374 4k.50 blue and red . . . 1·20 1·10
375 4k.75 blue & ultramarine 1·20 1·20
378 8k. blue and bistre . . . 2·00 1·90
379 10k. blue and green . . . 2·00 2·00
380 12k. blue and purple . . . 2·75 2·75

2000. Europa.
381 **151** 4k.75 multicoloured . . . 1·80 1·60

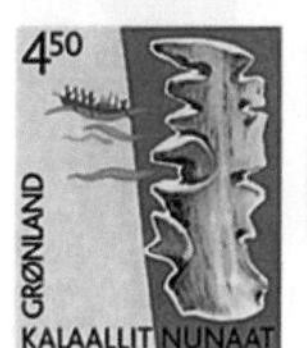

152 Wooden Map

153 Drum Dance

2000. Cultural Heritage (1st series). Multicoloured.
382 4k.50 Type **152** . . . . . . 1·10 1·20
383 4k.75 Sealskin . . . . 1·40 1·40
See also Nos. 395/6, 408/9 and 428/9.

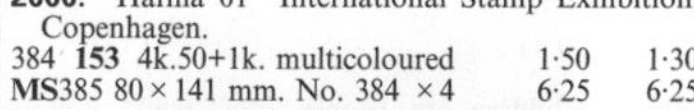

2000. "Hafnia 01" International Stamp Exhibition, Copenhagen.
384 **153** 4k.50+1k. multicoloured 1·50 1·30
MS385 80 × 141 mm. No. 384 × 4 6·25 6·25

154 Candles and Stars

2000. Christmas. Multicoloured.
386 4k.50 Type **154** . . . . . . 1·30 1·40
387 4k.75 Winter landscape and star . . . . 1·60 1·40

155 Gymnast and Map

2001. Arctic Winter Games, Nunavut.
388 **155** 4k. 50+50 multicoloured 1·60 1·40
MS389 81 × 140 mm. No. 388 × 4 5·75 5·75

2001. Greenland Vikings (3rd series). As T **146**.
390 1k. red and blue 95 80
391 4k.50 ultramarine and blue 1·40 1·10
392 5k. ultramarine and blue . . 1·40 1·40
393 10k. red and blue . . . . . 2·50 2·10
MS394 141 × 81 mm. Nos. 390/3 5·00 5·00
DESIGNS: 1k. Fisherman and seals; 4k.50, Mouse sitting on food; 5k. Man with packhorses; 10k. Stone wall and common raven.

2001. Cultural Heritage (2nd series). As T **152**. Multicoloured.
395 4k.50 Preserving trout . . . 1·20 1·10
396 4k.75 Fishing spear . . . . . 1·10 2·50

156 Krill

2001. Europa. Water Resources.
397 **156** 15k. multicoloured . . . 3·00 3·25

157 Rock Ptarmigan and Berries

2001. Christmas. Multicoloured.
398 4k.50 Type **157** . . . . . . 1·10 1·10
399 4k.75 Doves flying . . . . . 1·30 1·30

158 Northern Lights

2001. Essays by Harry Nielsen for First Greenland Stamps. Each black and brown.
400 5k.75 Type **158** . . . . . . 1·80 1·70
401 8k. Seal . . . . 3·50 3·50

402 21k. Polar bear . . . . . . 6·25 5·75
MS403 142 × 80 mm. Nos. 400/2 6·25 7·00

159 Detail of "Stone and Man"

160 Banner, Igloo Builders and Polar Bears

2002. Nordic Countries' Postal Co-operation. Modern Art. Multicoloured.
404 1k. Type **159** (sculpture project, Aka Hoegh and others) 25 25
405 31k. Snow Sculpture (Nuuk Snow Festival, 2001) . . . 6·25 6·75

2002. "Children are People Too" (child welfare project).
406 **160** 4k.50+50ore multicoloured . . . . . 1·20 1·20
MS407 81 × 140 mm. No. 406 × 4 4·50 3·50

2002. Cultural Heritage (3rd series). As T **152**. Multicoloured.
408 4k.50 Drum, Thule 65 95
409 4k.75 Inuit carved mask . . . 1·30 1·30

161 *Nordlyset* (sailing barque)

2002. Ships (1st series). Multicoloured.
410 2k. Type **161** 65 55
411 4k. *Hvidbjornen* (steam/sailing barque) . . . . 1·60 90
412 6k. *Staerkodder* (sloop) . . . 1·30 1·30
413 16k. *Haabet* (crayer) . . . . 3·75 4·00
See also Nos. 438/41 and 462/5.

162 Clown, Child and Snow Scene

2002. Europa. Circus.
414 **162** 11k. multicoloured . . . 2·75 2·75

163 Man carrying Gifts and Children on Sledge

2002. Christmas. (a) Ordinary gum.
415 4k.50 Type **163** . . . . . . 1·00 1·00
416 4k.75 Mother with child and carol singers . . . . 1·10 1·10

(b) Self-adhesive gum.
417 4k.50 No. 414 . . . . 1·00 1·10
418 4k.75 No. 416 . . . . 1·10 1·10
Nos. 417/18 form a composite design.

164 Cliffs and Greenland Shark (*Somniosus microcephalus*)

2002. Centenary of International Council for the Exploration of the Sea. Multicoloured.
419 7k. Type **164** . . . . 1·60 1·60
420 19k. Deepwater redfish (*Sebates mentella*) . . . . 4·25 4·50
MS421 185 × 60 mm. Nos. 419/20 5·75 6·00
Stamps of a similar design were issued by Denmark and Faroe Islands.

165 Puppies

2003. Sled Dogs. Each black.
422 4k.50 Type **165** 85 80
423 4k.75 Adult . . . . 95 1·00
424 6k. Adult wearing harness . . 2·50 2·40

166 Tents and mountains

2003. Centenary of the Danish Literary Expedition to Greenland.
425 **166** 15k. agate, green and blue 4·00 4·00
426 – 21k. blue (28 × 22 mm) . . 3·75 3·75
MS427 166 × 61 mm Nos. 424/5 plus label . . . . 6·25 6·25
DESIGN: 21k. Knud Ramussen Stamps of a similar design were issued by Denmark.

2003. Cultural Heritage (4th series). As T **152**. Multicoloured.
428 25ore Comb, East Greenland 20 20
429 1k. Water bucket, East Greenland 25 25

167 Silamiut Theatre Poster

168 Narwhals and Cliffs

2003. Europa. Poster Art.
430 **167** 5k.50 multicoloured . . . 1·60 1·40

2003. 50th Anniv of Qaanaaq (settlement).
431 **168** 15k. multicoloured . . . 1·90 2·75

169 Children around Christmas Tree

170 Santa Claus inside Bauble

2003. Christmas. (a) Ordinary gum.
432 5k. Type **169** 90 90
433 5k.50 Family entering church 1·00 1·00
Nos. 434/5 were issued togethert, se-tenant, forming a composite design.

(b) Self adhesive gum.
434 5k. Type **169** 90 90
435 5k.50 No. 433 . . . . 4·00 4·00

2003. Santa Claus of Greenland.
436 **170** 5k.+50ore multicoloured 1·00 1·00
MS437 81 × 140 mm. No. 436 × 4 4·00 4·00

2003. Ships (2nd series). As T **161**. Multicoloured.
438 6k.75 *Emma* (galleass) . . . 1·25 1·25
439 7k.75 *Gamle Fox* (screw-propelled schooner) . . . . 1·40 1·40
440 8k.75 *Godthaab* (screw-propelled barquentine) . . 1·60 1·60
441 26k. *Sonja* (whaling steamer) 4·75 4·75

171 Moon Man

172 Route Map

2004. Nordic Mythology. Multicoloured.
442 5k.50 Type **171** . . . . . . 1·00 1·00
443 6k.50 Northern lights . . . . 1·10 1·10
MS444 106 × 70 mm. Nos. 442/3 2·10 2·10
Stamps of a similar theme were issued by Aland Island, Denmark, Faeroe Islands, Finland, Iceland, Norway and Sweden.

2004. 50th Anniv of First Scheduled Flight from Denmark to Greenland.
445 **172** 8k.75 multicoloured . . . 1·60 1·60

173 National Arms

174 Rowing Boat attempting Landing on Island

2004. 50th Anniv of Home Rule.
446 **173** 11k. multicoloured . . . 2·00 2·00

2004. 150th Birth Anniv of Otto Sverdrup (polar explorer).
447 **174** 17k.50 purple and buff . . 2·75 2·75
MS448 165 × 60 mm. No. 447 plus 2 labels . . . . 2·75 2·75
No. **MS**448 was issued with two stamp-sized labels showing designs of Canada and Norway stamps. Stamps of similar designs were issued by Norway and Canada.

175 Children

176 Prince Frederik and Mary Donaldson

2004. 80th Anniv of Society of Greenlandic Children.
449 **175** 5k.+50ore. Multicoloured 1·00 1·00
MS450 140 × 80 mm. No. 449 × 4 4·00 4·00

2004. Marriage of Crown Prince Frederik and Mary Elizabeth Donaldson. Multicoloured.
451 5k. Type **176** 95 95
452 5k.50 As No. 451 but with design reversed . . . . . 1·00 1·00
MS453 130 × 65 mm. Nos. 451/2 2·00 2·00
Stamps of similar design were issued by Denmark and Faroe Islands.

177 *Angelica archangelica*

2004. Edible Plants (1st series). Multicoloured.
454 5k. Type **177** 95 95
455 5k.50 *Thymus praecox* . . . 1·00 1·00
456 17k. *Empetrum hermaphroditum* . . . . . 3·00 3·00

178 Family and Decorated Tree

179 Girls wearing Traditional Dress

2004. Christmas. (a) Ordinary gum.
457 5k. Type **178** 95 95
458 5k.50 Family entering church 1·10 1·10

(b) Self-adhesive gum.
459 5k. Type **178** 95 95
460 5k.50 No. 458 . . . . 1·10 1·10

2004. Europa. Holidays.
461 **179** 6k.50 multicoloured . . . 1·20 1·20

2004. Ships (3rd series). As T **161**. Multicoloured.
462 6k.50 *Constance* (brig) . . . 1·20 1·20
463 8k.75 *Disko* (passenger ship) 1·60 1·60
464 14k. *Julius Thomsen* (polar ship) . . . . 2·50 2·50
465 21k.75 *Misigssut* (tuberculosis hospital ship) . . . . . . 4·00 4·00

180 *Leccinum*

2005. Fungi. Multicoloured. (a) Ordinary or self-adhesive gum.
466 5k.25 Type **180** 95 95
467 6k. *Russula subrubens* . . . . 1·10 1·10
468 7k. *Amanita groenlandica* . . 1·30 1·30

181 Child's Face

183 Mountains and Church Steeple

182 Ilulissat Fiord

2005. 60th Anniv of Save the Children Fund (charitable organization).
472 **181** 5k.25+50ore multicoloured . . . . . 1·10 1·10
MS473 140 × 80 mm. No. 472 × 4 multicoloured . . . . 4·50 4·50

2005. World Heritage Site. Ilulissat Fiord.
474 **182** 6k. multicoloured . . . . 1·10 1·10

2005. Centenary of Church Law.
475 **183** 9k.25 multicoloured . . . 1·70 1·70

184 Musk Ox Meat

2005. Europa. Gastronomy.
475 **184** 11k.75 multicoloured . . 2·20 2·20

PARCEL POST STAMPS

P **1** Arms of Greenland

1905.
P 4A P **1** 1ore green . . . . . . 50·00 39·00
P 5A 2ore yellow . . . . . . £375 80·00
P 6A 5ore brown . . . . . . £130 90·00
P 7A 10ore blue . . . . . . 44·00 41·00
P 8A 15ore violet £200 £130
P 9A 20ore red . . . . 8·75 6·25
P13 70ore violet £120 £120
P14 1k. yellow . . . . . . 42·00 60·00
P12A 3k. brown £100 £140
Prices for used stamps are for rubber stamp cancellations applied in Copenhagen, the various Greenland cancellations being worth much more. Stamps with numeral cancellations have been used as saving stamps.

GRENADA Pt. 1

One of the Windward Is., Br. W. Indies. Ministerial Government was introduced on 1 January 1960. Achieved Associated Statehood on 3 March 1967 and Independence on 7 February 1974.

1861. 12 pence = 1 shilling;
20 shillings = 1 pound.
1949. 100 cents = 1 West Indian dollar.

1

5

1861.
14 **1** 1d. green . . . . 75·00 7·50
6 6d. red . . . . £600 13·00

1875. Surch **POSTAGE** and value in words.
21 **5** ½d. mauve . . . . 12·00 5·50
22 2½d. lake . . . . 60·00 7·00

23 4d. blue . . . . £100 8·00
13 1s. mauve . . . . £700 11·00

1883. Revenue stamp surch crown and value (in green) optd **POSTAGE.**
27 **5** 1d. orange . . . . £350 60·00

1883. Revenue stamp as last but optd **POSTAGE** diagonally on each half.
29 **5** Half of 1d. orange £275 £110

13 **21**

1883.
30 **13** ½d. green . . . . 1·25 1·00
31 1d. red . . . . 70·00 3·25
32 2½d. blue . . . . 7·00 1·00
33 4d. grey . . . . 6·00 1·75
34 6d. mauve . . . . 3·25 4·00
35 8d. brown . . . . 9·50 12·00
36 1s. violet . . . . £120 55·00

1886. Revenue stamps as No. 27 but surch **POSTAGE.** and value in words or figures.
43 **5** ½d. on 2s. orange . . . . . 12·00 21·00
37 1d. on 1½d. orange . . . . . 45·00 30·00
39 1d. on 4d. orange . . . . . £160 90·00
38 1d. on 1s. orange . . . . . 40·00 30·00
41 4d. on 2s. orange . . . . . 38·00 19·00

1887. As T **13**, but inscr "GRENADA POSTAGE & REVENUE" at top.
40 **13** 1d. red . . . . 1·75 1·50

1890. Revenue stamp as No. 27 but surch **POSTAGE AND REVENUE 1d.**
45 **5** 1d. on 2s. orange . . . . . 60·00 55·00

1891. Surch **POSTAGE AND REVENUE 1d.**
46 **13** 1d. on 8d. brown . . . . . 10·00 13·00

1891. Surch **2½d.**
47 **13** 2½d. on 8d. brown . . . . 8·00 11·00

1895.
48 **21** ½d. mauve and green . . . 2·50 1·75
49 1d. mauve and red . . . 4·50 75
50 2d. mauve and brown . . . 40·00 32·00
51 2½d. mauve and blue . . . 5·50 1·50
52 3d. mauve and orange . . . 6·50 16·00
53 6d. mauve and green . . . 12·00 35·00
54 8d. mauve and black . . . 12·00 45·00
55 1s. green and orange . . . . 19·00 42·00

23 Flagship of Columbus (Columbus named Grenada "La Concepcion")

1898. 400th Anniv of Discovery of Grenada by Columbus.
56 **23** 2½d. blue . . . . 14·00 6·00

1902. As T **21**, but portrait of King Edward VII.
57 ½d. purple and green . . . . . 3·25 1·25
58 1d. purple and red . . . . . 4·50 30
59 2d. purple and brown . . . . 3·00 10·00
60 2½d. purple and blue . . . . 3·50 2·75
61 3d. purple and orange . . . . 3·75 9·00
72 6d. purple and green . . . . 5·50 13·00
63 1s. green and orange . . . . 4·50 28·00
64 2s. green and blue . . . . . 22·00 55·00
65 5s. green and red . . . . . 42·00 60·00
66 10s. green and purple £120 £250

26 Badge of the Colony **28**

1906.
77 **26** ½d. green . . . . 4·50 30
78 1d. red . . . . 6·50 10
79 2d. orange . . . . 3·00 3·00
80 2½d. blue . . . . 6·00 1·75
84 3d. purple on yellow . . . . 4·75 1·75
85 6d. purple . . . . 20·00 23·00
86 1s. black on green . . . . . 7·00 4·50
87 2s. blue and purple on blue . . 20·00 12·00
88 5s. green and red on yellow . . 60·00 70·00
83 10s. green and red on green . . 95·00 £190

1913.
112 **28** ½d. green . . . . 1·25 30
113 1d. red 80 75
114 1d. brown . . . . 1·50 30
115 1½d. red . . . . 1·50 1·50
116 2d. orange . . . . 1·25 30
117 2d. grey . . . . 2·50 2·75
94 2½d. blue . . . . 1·75 3·50
118 2½d. grey . . . . 1·00 9·00
96 3d. purple on yellow . . . 65 85
121 3d. blue . . . . 1·25 11·00
123 4d. black and red on yellow . . . . 1·00 3·75
124 5d. purple and green . . . 1·50 4·25
97 6d. purple . . . . 1·50 9·00
126 6d. black and red . . . . 2·25 2·50
127 9d. purple and black . . . 2·25 9·50
98a 1s. black on green . . . . 1·25 7·50
129 1s. brown . . . . 3·00 10·00
99 2s. purple and blue on blue . . . . 6·50 12·00
131 2s.6d. black & red on blue 7·00 21·00
132 3s. green and violet . . . 6·50 27·00
133 5s. green and red on yellow . . . . 12·00 35·00
101 10s. green and red on green . . . . 55·00 95·00

1916. Optd **WAR TAX.**
111 **28** 1d. red 30 20

31 Grand Anse Beach **32** Badge of the Colony

1934.
135 **31** ½d. green . . . . 15 1·25
136a **32** 1d. black and brown . . . 65 35
137a – 1½d. black and red . . . 1·25 40
138 **32** 2d. black and orange . . 1·00 75
139 – 2½d. blue 50 50
140 **32** 3d. black and olive . . . 1·00 2·75
141 6d. black and purple . . 2·00 1·75
142 1s. black and brown . . . 2·00 4·00
143 2s.6d. black and blue . . 8·00 28·00
144 5s. black and violet . . . 38·00 50·00
DESIGNS—VERT: 1½d. Grand Etang; 2½d. St. George's.

1935. Silver Jubilee. As T **10a** of Gambia.
145 ½d. black and green . . . 80 1·25
146 1d. blue and grey . . . . 80 1·75
147 1½d. blue and red . . . . 80 2·75
148 1s. grey and purple . . . . 6·50 20·00

1937. Coronation. As T **10b** of Gambia.
149 1d. violet . . . . 40 1·25
150 1½d. red 40 50
151 2½d. blue . . . . 80 1·25

35 King George VI **40** Badge of the Colony

1937.
152b **35** ¼d. brown 20 80

1938. As 1934, but with portrait of King George VI.
153a **31** ½d. green . . . . 60 1·25
154a **32** 1d. black and brown . . 50 50
155 – 1½d. black and red . . . 50 85
156 **32** 2d. black and orange . . 30 50
157 – 2½d. blue 30 30
158ab **32** 3d. black and olive . . . 30 80
159 6d. black and purple . . 1·25 40
160 1s. black and brown . . . 2·25 40
161 2s. black and blue . . . 21·00 1·75
162 5s. black and violet . . . 3·75 2·00
163e **40** 10s. blue and red . . . 27·00 8·50

1946. Victory. As T **11a** of Gambia.
164 1½d. red 10 50
165 3½d. blue . . . . 10 1·00

1948. Silver Wedding. As T **11b/c** of Gambia.
166 1½d. red 15 10
167 10s. grey . . . . 12·00 17·00

1949. U.P.U. As T **11d/g** of Gambia.
168 5c. blue 15 10
169 6c. olive . . . . 1·50 2·50
170 12c. mauve 15 30
171 24c. brown 15 40

41 King George VI **42** Badge of the Colony

1951.
172 **41** ½c. black and brown . . . 15 1·60
173 1c. black and green . . . 15 25
174 2c. black and brown . . . 15 50
175 3c. black and red 15 10
176 4c. black and orange . . . 35 40
177 5c. black and violet 20 10
178 6c. black and olive 30 60
179 7c. black and blue . . . . 1·75 10
180 12c. black and purple . . . 2·25 30
181 **42** 25c. black and brown . . . 2·25 80
182 50c. black and blue . . . 6·50 40
183 $1.50 black and orange . . 7·50 7·00
184 $2.50 slate and red . . . 5·50 5·50
No. 184 is larger, 24½ × 30½ mm.

43a Arms of University **43b** Princess Alice

1951. Inauguration of B.W.I. University College.
185 **43a** 3c. black and red . . . . 45 1·25
186 **43b** 6c. black and olive . . . 45 50

1951. New Constitution. Nos. 175/7 and 180 optd **NEW CONSTITUTION 1951.**
187 **41** 3c. black and red 20 60
188 4c. black and orange . . . 20 60
189 5c. black and violet . . . 20 80
190 12c. black and purple . . . 20 1·00

1953. Coronation. As T **11h** of Gambia.
191 3c. black and red 20 10

1953. As T **41**, but with portrait of Queen Elizabeth II, and T **42**, but Royal Cypher changed.
192 **41** ½c. black and brown . . . 10 10
193 1c. black and green . . . 10 10
214 2c. black and brown . . . 10 10
195 3c. black and red 10 10
196 4c. black and orange . . . 10 10
197 5c. black and violet . . . 10 10
198 6c. black and olive . . . 45 1·25
199 7c. black and blue . . . 1·25 10
219 12c. black and purple . . 20 10
201 **42** 25c. black and brown . . 1·25 20
202 50c. black and blue . . . 5·50 40
203 $1.50 black and orange . . 11·00 14·00
204 $2.50 slate and red . . . 18·00 10·00
No. 204 is larger, 24½ × 30½ mm.

47a Federation Map

1958. British Caribbean Federation.
205 **47a** 3c. green 35 10
206 6c. blue 45 60
207 12c. red 55 10

48 Queen Victoria, Queen Elizabeth II, Mail Van and Post Office, St. George's

1961. Grenada Stamp Centenary.
208 **48** 3c. red and black 25 10
209 – 8c. blue and orange . . . 55 25
210 – 25c. lake and blue 55 25
DESIGNS (incorporating Queen Victoria and Queen Elizabeth II): 8c. Flagship of Columbus; 25c. "Solent I" (paddle-steamer) and Douglas DC-3 aircraft.

1963. Freedom from Hunger. As T **20a** of Gambia.
211 8c. green 30 15

1963. Centenary of Red Cross. As T **20b** of Gambia.
212 3c. red and black 20 15
213 25c. red and blue 40 15

1965. Centenary of I.T.U. As T **44** of Gibraltar.
221 2c. orange and olive 10 10
222 50c. yellow and red 25 20

1965. I.C.Y. As T **45** of Gibraltar.
223 1c. purple and turquoise . . 10 15
224 25c. green and lavender . . . 20 15

1966. Churchill Commem. As T **46** of Gibraltar.
225 1c. blue 10 15
226 3c. green 10 15
227 25c. brown 15 10
228 35c. violet 25 15

49 Queen Elizabeth II and Duke of Edinburgh

1966. Royal Visit.
229 **49** 3c. black and blue 25 15
230 35c. black and mauve . . . 65 15

52 Hillsborough, Carriacou

1966. Multicoloured.
231 1c. Type **52** . . . . 20 1·25
232 2c. Bougainvillea 20 10
233 3c. Flamboyant plant . . . . 1·00 1·00
234 5c. Levera Beach . . . . . . 1·25 10
235 6c. Carenage, St. George's . . 1·00 10
236 8c. Annandale Falls . . . . 1·00 10
237 10c. Cocoa pods 50 10
238 12c. Inner Harbour . . . . . 30 1·25
239 15c. Nutmeg . . . . 30 1·25
240 25c. St. George's 30 10
241 35c. Grand Anse beach . . . 30 10
242 50c. Bananas . . . . 1·25 1·75
243 $1 Badge of the Colony (vert) (25 × 39 mm) . . . . . . 7·00 3·75
244 $2 Queen Elizabeth II (vert) (25 × 39 mm) . . . . . . 5·00 7·50
245 $3 Map of Grenada (vert) (25 × 39 mm) . . . . . . 4·50 14·00

1966. World Cup Football Championship. As T **47** of Gibraltar.
246 5c. multicoloured 10 10
247 50c. multicoloured 40 90

1966. Inauguration of W.H.O. Headquarters, Geneva. As T **54** of Gibraltar.
248 8c. black, green and blue . . 20 10
249 25c. black, purple and ochre 45 20

1966. 20th Anniv of UNESCO. As T **56a/c** of Gibraltar.
250 2c. multicoloured 10 10
251 15c. yellow, violet and orange 15 10
252 50c. black, purple and orange 30 90

1967. Statehood. Nos. 232/3, 236 and 240 optd **ASSOCIATED STATEHOOD 1967.**
253 2c. multicoloured 10 15
254 3c. multicoloured 10 15
255 8c. multicoloured 15 10
256 25c. multicoloured 15 15

1967. World Fair, Montreal. Nos. 232, 237, 239 and 243/4 surch or optd **expo67 MONTREAL CANADA** and emblem.
257 1c. on 15c. multicoloured . . 10 20
258 2c. multicoloured 10 20
259 3c. on 10c. multicoloured . . 10 20
260 $1 multicoloured 30 25
261 $2 multicoloured 45 30

1967. Nos. 231/45 optd **ASSOCIATED STATEHOOD.**
262 **52** 1c. multicoloured 10 10
263 – 2c. multicoloured 10 10
264 – 3c. multicoloured 10 10
265 – 5c. multicoloured 10 10
266 – 6c. multicoloured 10 10
267 – 8c. multicoloured 10 10
268 – 10c. multicoloured 10 10
269 – 12c. multicoloured 10 10
270 – 15c. multicoloured 10 10
271 – 25c. multicoloured 20 10
272 – 35c. multicoloured 55 10
273 – 50c. multicoloured . . . . 1·00 20
274 – $1 multicoloured . . . . . 1·50 60
275 – $2 multicoloured . . . . . 1·25 3·75
276 – $3 multicoloured . . . . . 2·25 5·50

70 Kennedy and Local Flower

1968. 50th Birth Anniv of Pres. Kennedy. Multicoloured.
277 1c. Type **70** 10 15
278 15c. Type **70** 10 10
279 25c. Kennedy and strelitzia . . 10 10
280 35c. Kennedy and roses . . . 10 10
281 50c. As 25c. 15 20
282 $1 As 35c. 25 60

73 Scout Bugler

1968. World Scout Jamboree, Idaho. Mult.
283 1c. Type **73** 10 10
284 2c. Scouts camping 10 10
285 3c. Lord Baden-Powell . . . 10 10
286 35c. Type **73** 25 10
287 50c. As 2c. 35 20
288 $1 As 3c. 50 55

76 "Near Antibes"

1968. Paintings by Sir Winston Churchill. Multicoloured.
289 10c. Type **76** 10 10
290 12c. "The Mediterranean" . . 15 10
291 15c. "St. Jean, Cap Ferratt" 15 10
292 25c. Type **76** 20 10
293 35c. As No. 291 . . . . . . 25 10
294 50c. Sir Winston painting . . 35 25

1968. No. 275 surch **$5**.
295 $5 on $2 multicoloured . . . 1·50 2·25

1968. "Children Need Milk". Surch **CHILDREN NEED MILK** and value. (a) Nos. 244/5.
296 2c.+3c. on $2 multicoloured 10 10
297 3c.+3c. on $3 multicoloured 10 10

(b) Nos. 243/4.
298 1c.+3c. on $1 multicoloured 10 40
299 2c.+3c. on $2 multicoloured 13·00 55·00

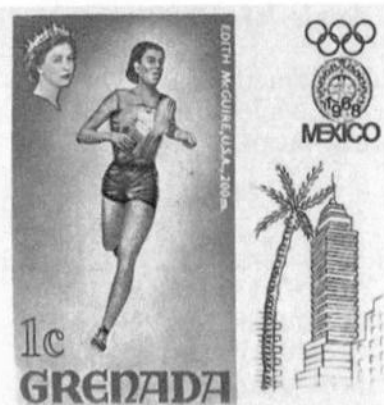

83 Edith McGuire (U.S.A.)

1968. Olympic Games, Mexico.
300 **83** 1c. brown, black and blue 10 30
301 – 2c. multicoloured 10 30
302 – 3c. scarlet, brown and green 10 30
303 **83** 10c. multicoloured 15 30
304 – 50c. multicoloured 55 75
305 – 60c. red, brown and orange 60 80
DESIGNS: 2c., 50c. Arthur Wint (Jamaica); 3c., 60c. Ferreira da Silva (Brazil).

86 Hibiscus

102 Kidney Transplant

1968. Multicoloured.
306 1c. Type **86** 10 10
307 2c. Strelitzia 10 10
308 3c. Bougainvillea 10 10
309 5c. Rock hind (horiz) . . . 10 10
310 6c. Sailfish 10 10
311 8c. Red snapper (horiz) . . 10 30
312 10c. Marine toad (horiz) . . 10 10
313 12c. Turtle 15 10
314 15c. Tree boa (horiz) . . . 1·00 60
314a 15c. Thunbergia . . . . . . 2·75 2·50
315 25c. Greater Trinidadian murine opossum 30 10
316 35c. Nine-banded armadillo (horiz) 35 10
317 50c. Mona monkey 45 25
317a 75c. Yacht in St. George's Harbour (horiz) . . . . . 14·00 8·50
318 $1 Bananaquit . . . . . . 3·00 1·50
319 $2 Brown pelican . . . . . 8·00 11·00
320 $3 Magnificent frigate bird 4·50 5·00
321 $5 Bare-eyed thrush . . . . 10·00 22·00
Nos. 318/21 are larger, 25½ × 48 mm.

1968. 20th Anniv of W.H.O. Multicoloured.
322 5c. Type **102** 20 10
323 25c. Heart transplant 30 10
324 35c. Lung transplant 30 10
325 50c. Eye transplant 35 50

106 "The Adoration of the Kings" (Veronese)

114 Dame Hylda Bynoe

111 Dame Hylda Bynoe (Governor) and Island Scene

1968. Christmas.
326 **106** 5c. multicoloured 10 10
327 – 15c. multicoloured 10 10
328 – 35c. multicoloured 10 10
329 – $1 multicoloured 30 40
DESIGNS: 15c. "Madonna and Child with Saints John and Catherine" (Titian); 35c. "The Adoration of the Kings" (Botticelli); $1 "A Warrior Adoring" (Catena).

1969. Caribbean Free Trade Area Exhibition. Nos. 300/5 surch **VISIT CARIFTA EXPO '69 April 5-30** and value.
330 **83** 5c. on 1c. 10 10
331 – 8c. on 2c. 10 10
332 – 25c. on 3c. 10 10
333 **83** 35c. on 10c. 10 10
334 – $1 on 50c. 20 30
335 – $2 on 60c. 35 60

1969. Carifta Expo '69. Multicoloured.
336 5c. Type **111** 10 10
337 15c. Premier E. M. Gairy and island scene 10 10
338 50c. Type **111** 10 30
339 60c. Emblems of 1958 and 1967 World's Fairs 10 65

1969. Human Rights Year. Multicoloured.
340 5c. Type **114** 10 10
341 25c. Dr. Martin Luther King 15 10
342 35c. As 5c. 15 10
343 $1 "Balshazzar's Feast" (Rembrandt) (horiz) . . . 30 45

117 Batsman and Wicket-keeper

1969. Cricket.
344 **117** 3c. yellow, brown and blue . . . . 25 1·00
345 – 10c. multicoloured 25 40
346 – 25c. brown, ochre & green 45 85
347 – 35c. multicoloured 65 90
DESIGNS: 10c. Batsman playing defensive stroke; 25c. Batsman sweeping ball; 35c. Batsman playing on-drive.

129 Astronaut handling Moon Rock

1969. First Man on the Moon. Multicoloured.
348 ½c. As Type **129** but larger (56 × 35 mm) 10 10
349 1c. Moon rocket and moon 10 10
350 2c. Module landing 10 10
351 3c. Declaration left on the moon 10 10
352 8c. Module leaving rocket . . 10 10
353 25c. Rocket lifting-off (vert) 25 10
354 35c. Spacecraft in orbit (vert) 25 10
355 50c. Capsule with parachutes (vert) 35 30
356 $1 Type **129** . . . . 50 1·25
MS357 115 × 90 mm. Nos. 351 and 356. Imperf . . . . 1·00 2·75

130 Gandhi

1969. Birth Cent of Mahatma Gandhi. Mult.
358 6c. Type **130** 15 20
359 15c. Gandhi standing 20 10
360 25c. Gandhi walking 25 10
361 $1 Head of Gandhi 50 75
MS362 155 × 122 mm. Nos. 358/61. Imperf . . . . 1·75 3·50

1969. Christmas. Nos. 326/9 optd **1969** and surch (No. 363).
363 – 2c. on 15c. multicoloured 10 90
364 **106** 5c. multicoloured 10 10
365 – 35c. multicoloured 20 10
366 – $1 multicoloured . . . . 80 1·90

135 "Blackbeard" (Edward Teach)

1970. Pirates.
367 **135** 15c. black 35 10
368 – 25c. green 50 10
369 – 50c. lilac 90 20
370 – $1 carmine . . . . 1·50 75
DESIGNS: 25c. Anne Bonney; 50c. Jean Lafitte; $1 Mary Read.

1970. No. 348 surch **5c**.
371 5c. on ½c. multicoloured . . . 10 10

141/2 "The Last Supper" (detail, Del Sarto)

1970. Easter. Paintings.
372 **141** 5c. multicoloured 10 30
373 **142** 5c. multicoloured 10 30
374 – 15c. multicoloured 15 35
375 – 15c. multicoloured 15 35
376 – 25c. multicoloured 15 35
377 – 25c. multicoloured 15 35
378 – 60c. multicoloured 20 60
379 – 60c. multicoloured 20 60
MS380 120 × 140 mm. Nos. 376/9 75 1·75
DESIGNS: 15c. "Christ crowned with Thorns" (detail, Van Dyck); 25c. "The Passion of Christ" (detail, Memling); 60c. "Christ in the Tomb" (detail, Rubens).

Each value was issued in sheets containing the two stamps se-tenant. Each design is spread over two stamps as in Types **141/2**.

149 Girl with Kittens in Pram

1970. Birth Bicentenary of Wordsworth. "Children and Pets". Multicoloured.
381 5c. Type **149** 15 15
382 15c. Girl with puppy and kitten 25 15
383 30c. Boy with fishing-rod and cat 30 30
384 60c. Boys and girls with cats and dogs . . . . 40 1·50
MS385 Two sheets, each 114 × 126 mm. Nos. 381, 383 and Nos. 382, 384. Imperf . . . . 1·00 2·00

153 Parliament of India

1970. 7th Regional Conference of Commonwealth Parliamentary Association. Parliament Buildings. Multicoloured.
386 5c. Type **153** 10 10
387 25c. Great Britain 10 10
388 50c. Canada 20 15
389 60c. Grenada 20 15
MS390 126 × 90 mm. Nos. 386/9 50 90

157 Tower of the Sun

1970. World Fair, Osaka. Multicoloured.
391 1c. Type **157** 10 35
392 2c. Livelihood and Industry Pavilion (horiz) 10 35
393 3c. Flower painting, 1634 . . 10 35
394 10c. "Adam and Eve" (Tintoretto) (horiz) 10 10
395 25c. Organization For Economic Co-operation and Development (O.E.C.D.) Pavilion (horiz) 15 10
396 50c. San Francisco Pavilion 30 1·60
MS397 121 × 91 mm. $1 Japanese Pavilion (56 × 34 mm) . . . . 55 1·50

164 Roosevelt and "Raising U.S. Flag on Iwo Jima"

1970. 25th Anniv of Ending of World War II. Multicoloured.
398 ½c. Type **164** 10 80
399 5c. Zhukov and "Fall of Berlin" 70 30
400 15c. Churchill and "Evacuation at Dunkirk" 1·50 45
401 25c. De Gaulle and "Liberation of Paris" . . . 1·25 45
402 50c. Eisenhower and "D-Day Landing" . . . . 1·50 1·50
403 60c. Montgomery and "Battle of Alamein" . . . . . . 1·50 3·25
MS404 163 × 113 mm. Nos. 398, 400, 402/3 . . . . 2·75 7·00

1970. "Philympia 1970" Stamp Exhibition, London. Nos. 353/6 optd **PHILYMPIA LONDON 1970**.
405 – 25c. multicoloured 10 10
406 – 35c. multicoloured 10 10
407 – 50c. multicoloured 15 15
408 **129** $1 multicoloured 20 30

170 U.P.U. Headquarters Building and Transport

1970. New U.P.U. Headquarters Building. Multicoloured.
409 15c. Type **170** 60 20
410 25c. As Type **170**, but modern transport 60 20
411 50c. Sir Rowland Hill and U.P.U. Building (vert) . . 35 35
412 $1 Abraham Lincoln and U.P.U. Building (vert) . . 40 1·75
MS413 79 × 85 mm. Nos. 411/12 1·00 3·50

171 "The Madonna of the Goldfinch" (Tiepolo)

1970. Christmas. Multicoloured.

414 ½c. Type **171** 10 35
415 ½c. "The Virgin and Child with St. Peter and St. Paul" (Bouts) 10 35
416 ½c. "The Virgin and Child" (Bellini) 10 35
417 2c. "The Madonna of the Basket" (Correggio) 10 35
418 3c. Type **171** 10 35
419 35c. As No. 415 20 10
420 50c. As 2c. 30 40
421 $1 As No. 416 50 1·60
MS422 102 × 87 mm. Nos. 420/1 1·00 3·00

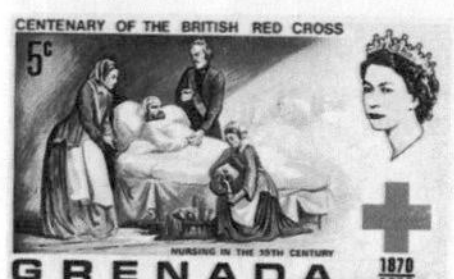

172 19th-Century Nursing

1970. Cent of British Red Cross. Multicoloured.

423 5c. Type **172** 20 10
424 15c. Military ambulance, 1918 25 10
425 25c. First-aid post, 1941 35 10
426 60c. Red Cross transport, 1970 90 1·25
MS427 113 × 82 mm. Nos. 423/6 2·00 1·60

173 John Dewey and Art Lesson

1971. Int Education Year. Multicoloured.

428 5c. Type **173** 10 10
429 10c. Jean-Jacques Rousseau and "Alphabetization" 15 10
430 50c. Maimonides and laboratory 50 15
431 $1 Bertrand Russell and mathematics class 95 40
MS432 90 × 98 mm. Nos. 430/1 1·00 2·00

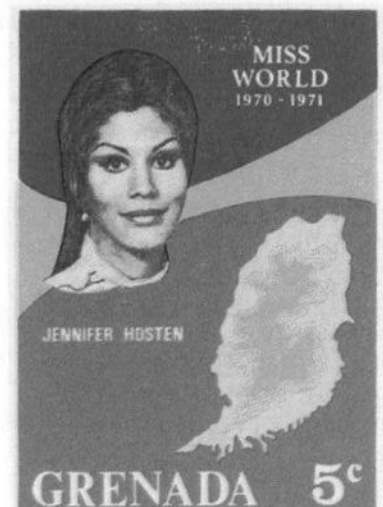

174 Jennifer Hosten and Outline of Grenada

1971. Winner of "Miss World" Competition (1970).

433 **174** 5c. multicoloured 10 10
434 10c. multicoloured 10 10
435 15c. multicoloured 15 10
436 25c. multicoloured 15 10
437 35c. multicoloured 15 10
438 50c. multicoloured 35 55
MS439 92 × 89 mm. **174** 50c. multicoloured. Printed on silk. Imperf 75 1·75

175 French and Canadian Scouts

1971. 13th World Scout Jamboree, Asagiri, Japan. Multicoloured.

440 5c. Type **175** 10 10
441 35c. German and American scouts 25 25
442 50c. Australian and Japanese scouts 30 50
443 75c. Grenada and British scouts 35 1·00
MS444 101 × 114 mm. Nos. 442/3 1·25 2·50

176 "Napoleon reviewing the Guard" (E. Detaille)

1971. 150th Death Anniv of Napoleon Bonaparte. Paintings. Multicoloured.

445 5c. Type **176** 15 15
446 15c. "Napoleon before Madrid" (Vernet) 20 15
447 35c. "Napoleon crossing Mt. St. Bernard" (David) 25 15
448 $2 "Napoleon in his Study" (David) 50 1·50
MS449 101 × 76 mm. No. 447. Imperf 1·25 1·60

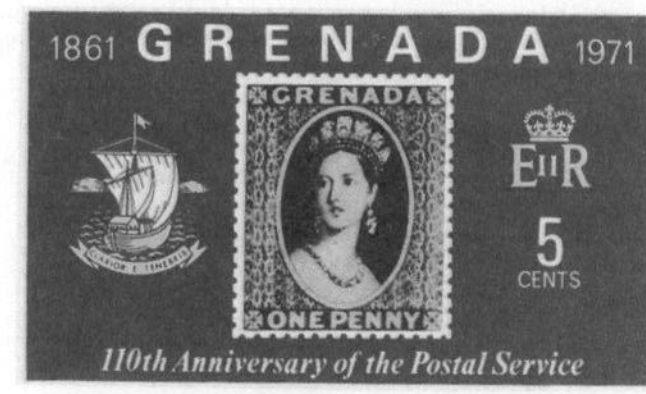

177 1d. Stamp of 1861 and Badge of Grenada

1971. 110th Anniv of the Postal Service. Mult.

450 5c. Type **177** 20 20
451 15c. 6d. stamp of 1861 and Queen Elizabeth II 25 15
452 35c. 1d. and 6d. stamps of 1861 and badge of Grenada 40 20
453 50c. Scroll and 1d. stamp of 1861 50 2·00
MS454 96 × 114 mm. Nos. 452/3 1·00 1·00

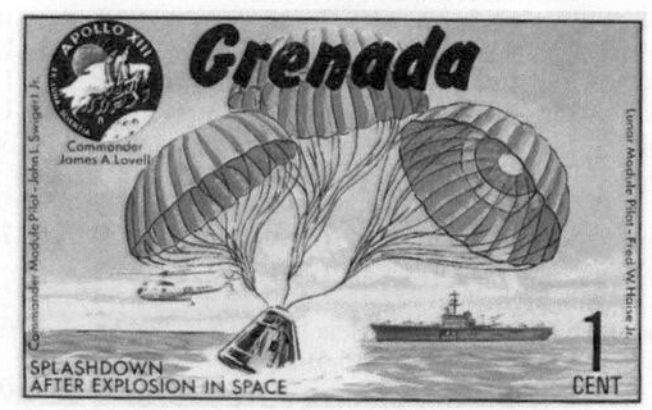

178 Apollo Splashdown

1971. Apollo Moon Exploration Series. Mult.

455 1c. Type **178** 10 35
456 2c. Recovery of "Apollo 13" 10 35
457 3c. Separation of Lunar Module from "Apollo 14" 10 35
458 10c. Shepard and Mitchell taking samples of moon rock 25 10
459 25c. Moon Buggy 75 20
460 $1 "Apollo 15" blast-off (vert) 2·00 3·50
MS461 77 × 108 mm. 50c. as $1 1·40 1·50

179 67th Regt. of Foot, 1787

1971. Military Uniforms. Multicoloured.

462 ½c. Type **179** 10 10
463 1c. 45th Regt. of Foot, 1792 10 10
464 2c. 29th Regt. of Foot, 1794 10 10
465 10c. 9th Regt. of Foot, 1801 45 10
466 25c. 2nd Regt. of Foot, 1815 85 20
467 $1 70th Regt. of Foot, 1764 2·50 2·00
MS468 108 × 99 mm. Nos. 466/7 2·25 2·75

180 "The Adoration of the Kings" (Memling)

1972. Christmas (1971). Multicoloured.

469 15c. Type **180** 15 10
470 25c. "Madonna and Child" (Michelangelo) 20 10
471 35c. "Madonna and Child" (Murillo) 25 10
472 50c. "The Virgin with the Apple" (Memling) 30 2·00
MS473 105 × 80 mm. $1 "The Adoration of the Kings" (Mostaert) 75 1·25

1972. Winter Olympic Games, Sapporo, Japan. Nos. 462/4 surch **WINTER OLYMPICS FEB. 3-13, 1972 SAPPORO, JAPAN,** Olympic rings and premium. Nos. 476/7 additionally optd **AIR MAIL.**

474 $2 on 2c. mult (postage) 50 90
476 35c. on ½c. multicoloured (air) 15 25
477 50c. on 1c. multicoloured 15 35
MS475 108 × 99 mm. Nos. 466/7 1·00 1·25

1972. General Election. Nos. 307/8, 310 and 315 optd **VOTE FEB. 28 1972.**

478 2c. multicoloured 20 50
479 3c. multicoloured 20 50
480 6c. multicoloured 30 50
481 25c. multicoloured 50 30

183 King Arthur

1972. UNICEF. Multicoloured.

482 ½c. Type **183** 10 20
483 1c. Robin Hood 10 20
484 2c. Robinson Crusoe (vert) 10 20
485 25c. Type **183** 10 10
486 50c. As 1c. 25 40
487 75c. As 2c. 30 1·10
488 $1 Mary and her little lamb (vert) 45 1·25
MS489 65 × 98 mm. No. 488 55 80

1972. "Interpex" Stamp Exbn, New York. Nos. 433/8 optd **INTERPEX 1972.**

490 **174** 5c. multicoloured 10 10
491 10c. multicoloured 10 10
492 15c. multicoloured 10 10
493 25c. multicoloured 10 10
494 35c. multicoloured 15 15
495 50c. multicoloured 25 30
MS496 92 × 89 mm. **174** 50c. multicoloured. Printed on silk. Imperf 6·00 11·00

1972. Nos. 306/8 and 433 surch **12c.**

497 – 12c. on 1c. multicoloured 40 70
498 – 12c. on 2c. multicoloured 40 70
499 – 12c. on 3c. multicoloured 40 70
500 **174** 12c. on 5c. multicoloured 40 70

1972. Air. Optd **AIR MAIL** or surch in addition.

501 – 5c. mult (No. 309) 10 10
518 **175** 5c. multicoloured 1·10 10
502 – 8c. mult (No. 311) 15 10
503 – 10c. mult (No. 312) 15 10
504 – 15c. mult (No. 314a) 30 10
505 – 25c. mult (No. 315) 35 20
506 – 30c. on 1c. mult (No. 306) 40 25
507 – 35c. mult (No. 316) 40 25
519 – 35c. mult (No. 441) 2·50 30
508 – 40c. on 2c. mult (No. 307) 50 25
509 – 45c. on 3c. mult (No. 308) 55 35
510 – 50c. mult (No. 317) 55 35
520 – 50c. mult (No. 442) 2·50 45
511 – 60c. on 5c. mult (No. 309) 60 40
512 – 70c. on 6c. mult (No. 310) 70 50
521 – 75c. mult (No. 443) 3·50 1·50
513 – $1 multicoloured (No. 318) 7·00 1·00
514 – $1.35 on 8c. mult (No. 311) 3·50 2·25
515 – $2 multicoloured (No. 319) 9·50 9·50
516 – $3 multicoloured (No. 320) 10·00 9·50
517 – $5 multicoloured (No. 321) 12·00 17·00

187 Yachting

1972. Olympic Games, Munich. Multicoloured.

522 ½c. Type **187** (postage) 10 10
523 1c. Show-jumping 10 10
524 2c. Running (vert) 10 10
525 35c. As 2c. 30 10
526 50c. As 1c. 40 40
527 25c. Boxing (air) 25 10
528 $1 As 25c. 65 85
MS529 82 × 85 mm. 60c. as 25c. and 70c. as 1c. 1·00 1·40

1972. Royal Silver Wedding. As T **98** of Gibraltar, but with Badge of Grenada and Nutmegs in background.

530 8c. brown 10 10
531 $1 blue 45 55

189 Boy Scout Saluting

1972. 65th Anniv of Boy Scouts. Multicoloured.

532 ½c. Type **189** (postage) 10 10
533 1c. Scouts knotting ropes 10 10
534 2c. Scouts shaking hands 10 10
535 3c. Lord Baden-Powell 10 10
536 75c. As 2c. 70 2·75
537 $1 As 3c. 75 2·75
538 25c. Type **189** (air) 40 20
539 35c. As 1c. 50 20
MS540 87 × 88 mm. 60c. as 3c. and 70c. as 2c. 1·50 1·50

190 Madonna and Child

1972. Christmas. Multicoloured.

541 1c. Type **190** 10 25
542 3c. The Three Kings 10 25
543 5c. The Nativity 10 10
544 25c. Type **190** 15 10
545 35c. As 3c. 15 10
546 $1 As 5c. 40 1·00
MS547 102 × 76 mm. 60c. Type **190** and 70c. as 3c. 60 80

191 Greater Flamingos

1973. National Zoo. Multicoloured.

548 25c. Type **191** 70 35
549 35c. Brazilian tapir 40 35
550 60c. Blue and yellow macaws 1·25 1·75
551 70c. Ocelot 70 2·00

192 Class II Racing Yacht

1973. Yachting. Multicoloured.

552 25c. Type **192** 25 10
553 35c. Harbour, St. George's 30 10
554 60c. Yacht "Bloodhound" 45 65
555 70c. St. George's 50 75

193 Helios (Greek god) and Earth orbiting the Sun

1973. Centenary of I.M.O./W.M.O. Greek Gods. Multicoloured.
556 ½c. Type **193** 10 10
557 1c. Poseidon and "Normad" storm detector 10 10
558 2c. Zeus and radarscope . . 10 10
559 3c. Iris and weather ballon 10 10
560 35c. Hermes and "ATS-3" satellite 25 10
561 50c. Zephyrus and diagram of pressure zones 30 30
562 75c. Demeter and space photo 30 60
563 $1 Selene and rainfall diagram . . . . 30 1·00
MS564 123 × 92 mm. $2 Computer weather map (42 × 31 mm.) . . 1·00 1·25

194 Racing Class Yachts

1973. Carriacou Regatta. Multicoloured.
565 ½c. Type **194** 10 10
566 1c. Cruising Class yacht . . . 10 10
567 2c. Open-decked sloops . . . 10 10
568 35c. "Mermaid" (sloop) . . . 30 10
569 50c. St. George's Harbour . . 35 25
570 75c. Map of Carriacou . . . 40 55
571 $1 Boat-building 55 70
MS572 109 × 88 mm. $2 End of race 1·00 1·75

195 Ignatius Semmelweis (obstetrician)

197 "Virgin and Child" (Maratti)

196 Princess Anne and Capt. Mark Phillips

1973. 25th Anniv of W.H.O. Multicoloured.
573 ½c. Type **195** 10 35
574 1c. Louis Pasteur 10 35
575 2c. Edward Jenner 10 35
576 3c. Sigmund Freud 10 35
577 25c. Emil von Behring (bacteriologist) 65 10
578 35c. Carl Jung 75 20
579 50c. Charles Calmette (bacteriologist) . . . . . . 1·10 1·00
580 $1 William Harvey . . . . . 1·40 2·50
MS581 105 × 80 mm. $2 Marie Curie 1·25 1·60

1973. Royal Wedding.
582 **196** 25c. multicoloured 10 10
583 $2 multicoloured 30 45
MS584 79 × 100 mm. 75c. and $1 as Nos. 582/3 . . . . 40 30

1973. Christmas. Multicoloured.
585 ½c. Type **197** 10 10
586 1c. "Madonna and Child" (Crivelli) 10 10
587 2c. "Virgin and Child with two Angels" (Verrocchio) 10 10
588 3c. "Adoration of the Shepherds" (Roberti) . . . 10 10
589 25c. "The Holy Family with the Infant Baptist" (Baroccio) 15 10
590 35c. "The Holy Family" (Bronzino) 15 10
591 75c. "Mystic Nativity" (Botticelli) 20 20
592 $1 "Adoration of the Kings" (Geertgen) 25 30
MS593 89 × 89 mm. $2 "Adoration of the Kings" (Mostaert) (30 × 45 mm) . . . . 1·00 1·10

1974. Independence. Nos. 306/9, 311/13, 315/16 and 317a/21 optd **INDEPENDENCE 7TH FEB. 1974.**
594 **86** 1c. multicoloured 10 50
595 – 2c. multicoloured 10 50
596 – 3c. multicoloured 10 50
597 – 5c. multicoloured 10 10
598 – 8c. multicoloured 15 10
599 – 10c. multicoloured 20 15
600 – 12c. multicoloured 20 15
601 – 25c. multicoloured 45 25
602 – 35c. multicoloured 75 25
603 – 75c. multicoloured . . . . 2·00 1·50
604 – $1 multicoloured . . . . . 3·75 1·75
605 – $2 multicoloured . . . . . 6·00 6·50
606 – $3 multicoloured . . . . . 8·00 8·50
607 – $5 multicoloured . . . . . 12·00 17·00

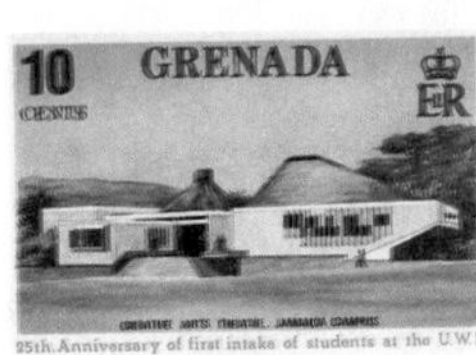

199 Creative Arts Theatre, Jamaica Campus

1974. 25th Anniv of University of West Indies. Multicoloured.
608 10c. Type **199** 10 10
609 25c. Marryshow House . . . 10 10
610 50c. Chapel, Jamaica Campus (vert) 20 10
611 $1 University arms (vert) . . 30 30
MS612 69 × 86 mm. $2 as No. 611 50 1·00

200 Nutmeg Pods and Scarlet Mace

201 Footballers (West Germany v. Chile)

1974. Independence. Multicoloured.
613 3c. Type **200** 10 10
614 8c. Map of Grenada 10 10
615 25c. Prime Minister Eric Gairy 15 10
616 35c. Grand Anse Beach and flag 15 10
617 $1 Coat of arms 35 40
MS618 91 × 125 mm. $2 as $1 . . 55 1·00

1974. World Cup Football Championship, West Germany. Multicoloured.
619 ½c. Type **201** 10 10
620 1c. East Germany v. Australia 10 10
621 2c. Yugoslavia v. Brazil . . . 10 10
622 10c. Scotland v. Zaire 10 10
623 25c. Netherlands v. Uruguay 15 10
624 50c. Sweden v. Bulgaria . . . 20 10
625 75c. Italy v. Haiti 35 15
626 $1 Poland v. Argentina . . . 50 25
MS627 114 × 76 mm. $2 Country flags . . . . 1·00 1·75

202 Early U.S. Mail-trains and Concorde

1974. Centenary of U.P.U. Multicoloured.
628 ½c. Type **202** 10 10
629 1c. "Caesar" (snow) (1839) and Westland Wessex HU Mk 5 helicopter 10 10
630 2c. Airmail transport 10 10
631 8c. Pigeon post (1480) and telephone dial 15 10
632 15c. 18th-century bellman and tracking antenna . . . 30 10
633 25c. Messenger (1450) and satellite 35 10
634 35c. French pillar-box (1850) and mail-boat 50 10
635 $1 18th-century German postman and British Advanced Passenger Train 1·50 85
MS636 105 × 66 mm. $2 St. Gotthard mail-coach (1735) 1·00 1·75

203 Sir Winston Churchill

1974. Birth Centenary of Sir Winston Churchill.
637 **203** 35c. multicoloured 15 10
638 $2 multicoloured . . . . 45 1·00
MS639 126 × 96 mm. 75c. as 35c. and $1 as $2 . . . . 75 75

204 "Madonna and Child of the Eucharist" (Botticelli)

1974. Christmas. "Madonna and Child" paintings by named artists. Multicoloured.
640 ½c. Type **204** 10 10
641 1c. Niccolo di Pietro 10 10
642 2c. Van der Weyden 10 10
643 3c. Bastiani 10 10
644 10c. Giovanni 10 10
645 25c. Van der Weyden 20 10
646 50c. Botticelli 25 20
647 $1 Mantegna 35 50
MS648 117 × 96 mm. $2 as 1c. 60 1·00

205 Yachts, Point Saline

1975. Multicoloured.
649 ½c. Type **205** 10 85
650 1c. Yacht Club race 10 10
651 2c. Carenage taxi 10 10
652 3c. Large working boats . . 10 10
653a 5c. Deep-water dock 10 15
654 6c. Cocoa beans in drying trays 10 10
655 8c. Nutmegs . . . . 1·25 10
656 10c. Rum distillery, River Antoine Estate, c. 1785 10 10
657 12c. Cocoa tree 30 10
658 15c. Fishermen at Fontenoy 10 10
659 20c. Parliament Building . . 15 15
660 25c. Fort George cannons 20 15
661 35c. Pearls Airport 20 15
662 50c. General Post Office . . 15 30
663 75c. Carib's Leap, Sauteurs Bay 45 50
664 $1 Carenage, St. George's 50 70
665 $2 St. George's Harbour by night . . . . 50 1·50
666 $3 Grand Anse Beach . . . 55 2·00
667 $5 Canoe Bay and Black Bay . . . . 65 3·00
668 $10 Sugar-loaf Island . . . 1·25 6·50
Nos. 663/8 are size 45 × 28 mm.

206 Sailfish

1975. Big Game Fishing. Multicoloured.
669 ½c. Type **206** 10 10
670 1c. Blue marlin 10 10
671 2c. White marlin 10 10
672 10c. Yellow-finned tuna . . . 10 10
673 25c. Wahoo 25 10
674 50c. Dolphin (fish) 40 15
675 70c. Giant grouper 60 20
676 $1 Great barracuda 80 35
MS677 107 × 80 mm. $2 Short-finned mako . . . . 1·25 1·25

207 Granadilla Barbadine

1975. Flowers. Multicoloured.
678 ½c. Type **207** 10 10
679 1c. Bleeding Heart (Easter Lily) 10 10
680 2c. Poinsettia 10 10
681 3c. Cocoa flower 10 10
682 10c. Gladioli 10 10
683 25c. Redhead/Yellowhead . . 20 10
684 50c. Plumbago 30 15
685 $1 Orange flower 50 25
MS686 102 × 82 mm. $2 Barbados gooseberry . . . . 1·10 1·25

208 Dove, Grenada Flag and U.N. Emblem

210 "Blood of the Redeemer" (G. Bellini)

209 Paul Revere's Midnight Ride

1975. Grenada's Admission to the U.N. (1974). Multicoloured.
687 ½c. Type **208** 10 10
688 1c. Grenada and U.N. flags 10 10
689 2c. Grenada coat of arms . . 10 10
690 35c. U.N. emblem over map of Grenada 15 10
691 50c. U.N. buildings and flags 20 15
692 $2 U.N. emblem and scroll 45 45
MS693 122 × 91 mm. 75c. Type **208** and $1 as 2c. 65 90

CANCELLED REMAINDERS*. Some of the following issues have been remaindered, cancelled to order, at a fraction of their face value. For all practical purposes these are indistinguishable from genuine postally used copies. Our used quotations, which are indicated by an asterisk, are the same for cancelled-to-order or postally used copies.

1975. Bicentenary of American Revolution (1st issue). Multicoloured.
694 ½c. Type **209** (postage) . . . 10 10*
695 1c. Crispus Attucks 10 10*
696 2c. Patrick Henry 10 10*
697 3c. Franklin visits Washington 10 10*
698 5c. Rebel troops 10 10*
699 10c. John Paul Jones 10 10*
700 40c. "John Hancock" (Copley) (vert) (air) 25 10*
701 50c. "Benjamin Franklin" (Roslin) (vert) 40 15*
702 75c. "John Adams" (Copley) (vert) 55 15*
703 $1 "Lafayette" (Casanova) (vert) 60 20*
MS704 Two sheets, each 131 × 102 mm: $2 Grenada arms and U.S. seal; $2 Grenada and U.S. flags . . . . 1·00 60*
Stamps from No. **MS**704 are horiz and larger: 47½ × 35 mm.
See also Nos. 785/92.

1975. Easter. Multicoloured.
705 ½c. Type **210** 10 10*
706 1c. "Pieta" (Bellini) 10 10*
707 2c. "The Entombment" (Van der Weyden) 10 10*
708 3c. "Pieta" (Bellini) 10 10*
709 35c. "Pieta" (Bellini) 20 10*
710 75c. "The Dead Christ" (Bellini) 25 10*
711 $1 "The Dead Christ supported by Angels" (Procaccini) 30 10*
MS712 117 × 100 mm. $2 "Pieta" (Botticelli) 75 30*

211 Wildlife Study

1975. 14th World Scout Jamboree, Norway. Multicoloured.
713 ½c. Type **211** 10 10*
714 1c. Sailing 10 10*
715 2c. Map-reading 10 10*
716 35c. First-aid 40 10*
717 40c. Physical training 40 10*
718 75c. Mountaineering 50 10*
719 $2 Sing-song 85 20*
MS720 106 × 80 mm. $1 Boat-building . . . . 1·00 30*

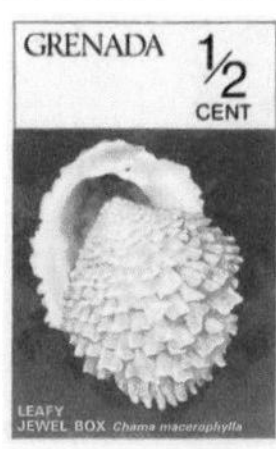

212 Leafy Jewel Box

213 "Lycorea ceres"

1975. Sea Shells. Multicoloured.
721 ½c. Type **212** 10 10*
722 1c. Emerald nerite 10 10*
723 2c. Yellow American cockle 10 10*
724 25c. Common purple janthina 85 10*
725 50c. Atlantic turkey wing . . 1·75 15*
726 75c. West Indian fighting conch . . . . 2·25 20*
727 $1 Noble wentletrap . . . . 2·25 20*
MS728 102 × 76 mm. $2 Music volute . . . . 2·00 80*

1975. Butterflies. Multicoloured.
729 ½c. Type **213** 10 10*
730 1c. "Adelpha cytherea" . . . 10 10*
731 2c. "Atlides polybe" 10 10*
732 35c. "Anteos maerula" . . . 80 10*
733 45c. "Parides neophilus" . . 85 10*
734 75c. "Nymula orestes" . . . 1·25 15*
735 $2 "Euptychia cephus" . . . 1·75 20*
MS736 108 × 83 mm. $1 "Papilio astyalus" (sub-species "lycophron") . . . . 1·25 40*

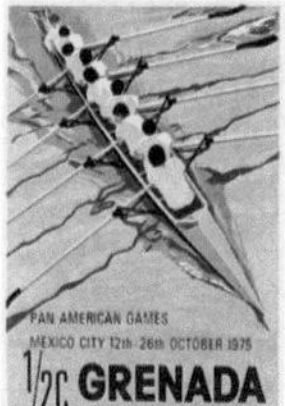

214 Rowing

215 "The Boy David" (Michelangelo)

1975. Pan-American Games, Mexico City. Mult.
737 ½c. Type **214** 10 10*
738 1c. Swimming 10 10*
739 2c. Show-jumping 10 10*
740 35c. Gymnastics 15 10*
741 45c. Football 15 10*
742 75c. Boxing 25 15*
743 $2 Cycling 65 20*
MS744 106 × 81 mm. $1 Yachting 1·00 40*

1975. 500th Birth Anniv of Michelangelo. Multicoloured.
745 ½c. Type **215** 10 10*
746 1c. "Young Man" (detail) . . 10 10*
747 2c. "Moses" 10 10*
748 40c. "Prophet Zachariah" . . 30 10*
749 50c. "St. John the Baptist" 30 15*
750 75c. "Judith and Holofernes" 40 20*
751 $2 "Doni Madonna" (detail from "Holy Family") . . . 70 25*
MS752 104 × 89 mm. $1 "Madonna" (head from Pieta) . . . . . . 1·00 30*

216 "Madonna and Child" (Filippino Lippi)

217 Bananaquit

1975. Christmas. "Virgin and Child" paintings by artists named. Multicoloured.
753 ½c. Type **216** 10 10*
754 1c. Mantegna 10 10*
755 2c. Luis de Morales 10 10*
756 35c. G. M. Morandi 15 10*
757 50c. Antonello da Messina 15 10*
758 75c. Durer 20 10*
759 $1 Velasquez 25 10*
MS760 125 × 95 mm. $2 Bellini 1·00 30*

1976. Flora and Fauna. Multicoloured.
761 ½c. Type **217** 10 10*
762 1c. Brazilian agouti 10 10*
763 2c. Hawksbill turtle (horiz) 10 10*
764 5c. Dwarf poinciana 10 10*
765 35c. Black-finned tuna ("Albacore") (horiz) . . . 90 10*
766 40c. Cardinal's guard 95 10*
767 $2 Nine-banded armadillo (horiz) . . . . 2·50 30*
MS768 82 × 89 mm. $1 Belted kingfisher . . . . 7·50 90*

218 Carnival Time

1976. Tourism. Multicoloured.
769 ½c. Type **218** 10 10*
770 1c. Scuba diving 10 10*
771 2c. Liner "Southward" at St. George's 10 10*
772 35c. Game fishing 65 10*
773 50c. St. George's Golf Course 2·25 20*
774 75c. Tennis . . . . 2·50 25*
775 $1 Ancient rock carvings at Mount Rich . . . . . . 2·75 25*
MS776 100 × 73 mm. $2 Small boat sailing . . . . 1·75 60*

219 "Pieta" (Master of Okolicsno)

220 Sharpshooters

1976. Easter. Paintings by artists named. Multicoloured.
777 ½c. Type **219** 10 10*
778 1c. Correggio 10 10*
779 2c. Van der Weyden 10 10*
780 3c. Durer 10 10*
781 35c. Master of the Holy Spirit 15 10*
782 75c. Raphael 30 15*
783 $1 Raphael 35 20*
MS784 108 × 86 mm. $2 Crespi 1·00 60*

1976. Bicentenary of American Revolution (2nd issue). Multicoloured.
785 ½c. Type **220** 10 10*
786 1c. Defending the Liberty Pole 10 10*
787 2c. Loading muskets 10 10*
788 35c. The Fight for Liberty . . 30 10*
789 50c. Peace Treaty, 1783 . . 35 10*
790 $1 Drummers 50 20*
791 $3 Gunboat 90 30*
MS792 93 × 79 mm. 75c. as 35c. and $2 as 50c. 75 60*

221 Nature Study

222 Volleyball

1976. 50th Anniv of Girl Guides in Grenada. Multicoloured.
793 ½c. Type **221** 10 10*
794 1c. Campfire cooking 10 10*
795 2c. First aid 10 10*
796 50c. Camping 50 10*
797 75c. Home economics 65 15*
798 $2 First aid 90 25*
MS799 111 × 85 mm. $1 Painting 1·00 70*

1976. Olympic Games, Montreal. Multicoloured.
800 ½c. Type **222** 10 10*
801 1c. Cycling 10 10*
802 2c. Rowing 10 10*
803 35c. Judo 30 10*
804 45c. Hockey 60 10*
805 75c. Gymnastics 60 20*
806 $1 High jump 60 20*
MS807 106 × 81 mm. $3 Equestrian event . . . . 1·00 80*

223 "Cha-U-Kao at the Moulin Rouge"

225 Satellite Assembly

224 Piper Apache 235

1976. 75th Death Anniv of Toulouse-Lautrec. Multicoloured.
808 ½c. Type **223** 10 10*
809 1c. "Quadrille of the Moulin Rouge" 10 10*
810 2c. "Profile of a Woman" . . 10 10*
811 3c. "Salon in the Rue des Moulins" 10 10*
812 40c. "The Laundryman" . . 55 10*
813 50c. "Marcelle Lender dancing the Bolero" . . . 65 10*
814 $2 "Signor Boileau at the Cafe" . . . . 1·75 25*
MS815 152 × 125 mm. $1 "Woman with Boa" . . . . 2·25 70*

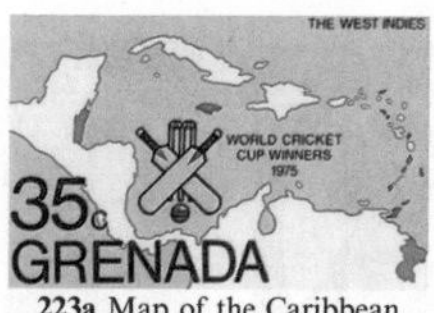

223a Map of the Caribbean

1976. West Indian Victory in World Cricket Cup.
816 35c. Type **223a** . . . . . . 1·00 35
817 $1 The Prudential Cup . . . 1·50 5·00

1976. Airplanes. Multicoloured.
818 ½c. Type **224** 10 10*
819 1c. Beech 50 Twin Bonanza 10 10*
820 2c. De Havilland Twin Otter 100 . . . . 10 10*
821 40c. Britten Norman Islander 60 10*
822 50c. De Havilland Heron 2 65 10*
823 $2 Hawker Siddeley H.S.748 2·00 50*
MS824 75 × 83 mm. $3 B.A.C. One Eleven 500 . . . . 1·50 80*

1976. Viking and Helios Space Missions. Multicoloured.
825 ½c. Type **225** 10 10*
826 1c. Helios satellite 10 10*
827 2c. Helios encapsulation . . . 10 10*
828 15c. Systems test 10 10*
829 45c. Viking lander (horiz) . . 20 10*
830 75c. Lander on Mars 30 15*
831 $2 Viking encapsulation . . . 60 25*
MS832 110 × 85 mm. $3 Orbiter and lander . . . . 1·00 75*

226 S.S. "Geestland"

1976. Ships. Multicoloured.
833 ½c. Type **226** 10 10*
834 1c. M.V. "Federal Palm" . . 10 10*
835 2c. H.M.S "Blake" 10 10*
836 25c. M.V. "Vistafjord" . . . 45 10*
837 75c. S.S. "Canberra" 80 15*
838 $1 S.S. "Regina" 90 20*
839 $5 S.S. "Arandora Star" . . 1·75 40*
MS840 91 × 78 mm. $2 "Santa Maria" . . . . 1·60 4·00

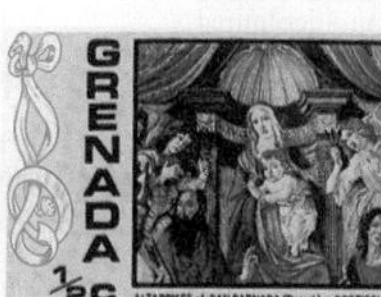

227 "San Barnaba Altarpiece" (Botticelli)

1976. Christmas. Multicoloured.
841 ½c. Type **227** 10 10*
842 1c. "Annunciation" (Botticelli) 10 10*
843 2c. "Madonna of Chancellor Rolin" (Jan van Eyck) . . 10 10*
844 35c. "Annunciation" (Fra Filippo Lippi) 15 10*
845 50c. "Madonna of the Magnificat" (Botticelli) . . 20 10*
846 75c. "Madonna of the Pomegranate" (Botticelli) 30 15*
847 $3 "Madonna with St. Cosmas and other Saints" (Botticelli) 70 25*
MS848 71 × 57 mm. $2 "Gypsy Madonna" (Titian) . . . . . 1·00 60*

228 Alexander Graham Bell and Telephones

1976. Centenary of First Telephone. Multicoloured.
849 ½c. Type **228** 10 10*
850 1c. Telephone users within globe 10 10*
851 2c. Telephone satellite . . . 10 10*
852 18c. Telephone viewer and console 20 10*
853 40c. Satellite and tracking stations 25 10*
854 $1 Satellite transmitting to ships 35 15*
855 $2 Dish aerial and modern telephone 55 25*
MS856 107 × 80 mm. $5 Globe encircled by flags . . . . . 1·25 75*

229 Coronation Scene

1977. Silver Jubilee. Multicoloured.(a) Perf.
857 ½c. Type **229** 10 10*
858 1c. Sceptre and orb 10 10*
859 35c. The Queen on horseback 10 10*
860 $2 Spoon and ampulla . . . 25 15*
861 $2.50 The Queen and Prince Philip 25 15*
MS862 103 × 79 mm. $5 Royal Visit to Grenada 75 60*

(b) Roul. Self-adhesive.
863 35c. As $2.50 . . . . 50 15
864 50c. As $2 . . . . 25 1·00
865 $1 As 1c. . . . . 50 1·40
866 $3 As 35c. . . . . 1·25 2·75

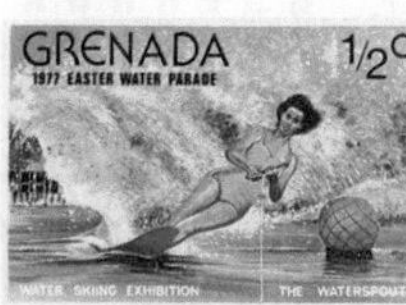

230 Water Skiing

1977. Easter Water Parade. Multicoloured.
867 ½c. Type **230** 10 10*
868 1c. Speedboat race 10 10*
869 2c. Row boat race 10 10*
870 22c. Swimming 20 10*
871 35c. Work boat race 30 10*
872 75c. Water polo 50 15*
873 $2 Game fishing . . . . . . 1·00 25*
MS874 115 × 85 mm. $3 Yacht race 1·25 75*

231 Meeting Place, Grand Anse Beach

1977. 7th Meeting of Organization of American States.
875 **231** 35c. multicoloured 10 10
876 $1 multicoloured 25 60
877 $2 multicoloured . . . . 40 1·75

232 Rafting

1977. Caribbean Scout Jamboree, Jamaica. Multicoloured.
878 ½c. Type **232** 10 10*
879 1c. Tug-of-war 10 10*
880 2c. Sea Scouts regatta 10 10*
881 18c. Camp fire 20 10*
882 40c. Field kitchen 25 10*
883 $1 Scouts and sea scouts . . 55 15*
884 $2 Hiking and map reading 75 25*
MS885 107 × 85 mm. $3 Semaphore 2·00 80*

233 Angel and Shepherd

1977. Christmas. Ceiling Panels from Church of St. Martin, Zillis. Multicoloured.
886 ½c. Type **233** 10 10*
887 1c. St. Joseph 10 10*
888 2c. Virgin and Child fleeing to Egypt 10 10*
889 22c. Angel 10 10*
890 35c. Magus on horseback 10 10*
891 75c. Three horses 15 15*
892 $2 Virgin and Child 40 25*
MS893 85 × 112 mm. $3 Magus offering gift 1·00 70*

1977. Royal Visit. Nos. 857/61 optd **Royal Visit W.I. 1977.**
894 ½c. Type **229** 10 10
895 1c. Sceptre and Orb 10 10
896 35c. Queen on horseback 10 10
897 $2 Spoon and ampulla 30 40
898 $2.50 The Queen and Prince Philip 35 45
MS899 103 × 79 mm. $5 Royal visit to Grenada 70 80

235 Christjaan Eijkman (Medicine)

237 Rocket Launching

236 Count von Zeppelin and First Zeppelin Airship LZ-1

1978. Nobel Prize Winners. Multicoloured.
900 ½c. Type **235** 10 10*
901 1c. Sir Winston Churchill (Literature) 30 10*
902 2c. Woodrow Wilson (Peace) 10 10*
903 35c. Frederic Passy (Peace) 15 10*
904 $1 Albert Einstein (Physics) 1·00 20*
905 $3 Carl Bosch (Chemistry) 1·75 35*
MS906 114 × 99 mm. $2 Alfred Nobel 70 60*

1978. 75th Anniv of First Zeppelin Flight and 50th Anniv of Lindbergh's Transatlantic Flight. Multicoloured.
907 ½c. Type **236** 10 10*
908 1c. Lindbergh with "Spirit of St. Louis" 10 10*
909 2c. Airship "Deutschland" 10 10*
910 22c. Lindbergh's arrival in France 30 10*
911 75c. Lindbergh and "Spirit of St. Louis" in flight 60 10*
912 $1 "Graf Zeppelin" over Alps 65 15*
913 $3 "Graf Zeppelin" over White House 1·40 25*
MS914 103 × 85 mm. Lindbergh in cockpit; $2 Count von Zeppelin and airship LZ-5 1·00 60*

1978. Space Shuttle. Multicoloured.
915 ½c. Type **237** 10 10*
916 1c. Booster jettison 10 10*
917 2c. External tank jettison 10 10*
918 18c. Space Shuttle in orbit 30 10*
919 75c. Satellite placement 65 10*
920 $2 Landing approach 1·40 20*
MS921 103 × 85 mm. $3 Shuttle after landing 1·40 60*

238 Black-headed Gull

239 "The Landing of Marie de Medici at Marseilles"

1978. Wild Birds of Grenada. Multicoloured.
922 ½c. Type **238** 10 10*
923 1c. Wilson's storm petrel ("Wilsons Petrel") 10 10*
924 2c. Killdeer plover ("Killdeer") 10 10*
925 50c. White-necked jacobin 1·50 10*
926 75c. Blue-faced booby 1·75 15*
927 $1 Broad-winged hawk 2·50 20*
928 $2 Red-necked pigeon 3·00 30*
MS929 103 × 94 mm. $3 Scarlet ibis 6·00 1·00*

1978. 400th Birth Anniv of Peter Paul Rubens. Multicoloured.
930 5c. Type **239** 10 10*
931 15c. "Rubens and Isabella Brandt" 10 10*
932 18c. "Marchesa Brigida Spindola-Doria" 10 10*
933 25c. "Ludovicus Nonninus" 10 10*
934 45c. "Helene Fourment and her Children" 15 10*
935 75c. "Clara Serena Rubens" 25 10*
936 $3 "Le Chapeau de Paille" 60 20*
MS937 65 × 100 mm. $5 "Self Portrait" 1·00 60*

240 Ludwig van Beethoven

241 King Edward's Chair

1978. 150th Death Anniv of Beethoven. Mult.
938 5c. Type **240** 10 10*
939 15c. Woman violinist (horiz) 15 10*
940 18c. Musical instruments (horiz) 20 10*
941 22c. Piano (horiz) 20 10*
942 50c. Violins 40 10*
943 75c. Piano and sonata score 50 15*
944 $3 Beethoven's portrait and home (horiz) 1·25 25*
MS945 83 × 62 mm. $2 Beethoven and score 1·10 60*

1978. 25th Anniv of Coronation. Mult. (a) Perf.
946 35c. Type **241** 10 10
947 $2 Queen with regalia 30 35
948 $2.50 St. Edward's Crown 30 40
MS949 102 × 76 mm. $5 Queen and Prince Philip 80 80

(b) Roul × imperf. Self-adhesive.
950 25c. Queen Elizabeth II taking salute, Trooping the Colour 15 15
951 35c. Queen at Maundy Thursday ceremony 15 25
952 $5 Queen and Prince Philip at Opening of Parliament 1·50 2·50

243 Goalkeeper reaching for Ball

1978. World Cup Football Championship, Argentina.
953 **243** 40c. multicoloured 10 10
954 – 60c. multicoloured 15 20
955 – 90c. multicoloured 25 30
956 – $2 multicoloured 60 60
MS957 130 × 97 mm. $2.70, multicoloured 1·10 1·10
DESIGNS: 60c. to $2.70, Designs similar to Type **243** with goalkeeper reaching for ball.

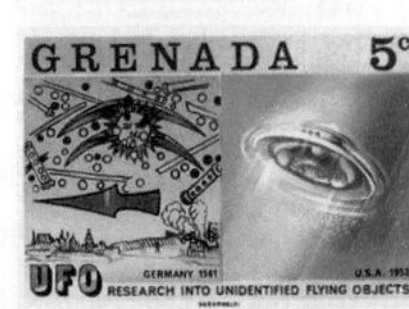

244 Aerial Phenomena, Germany, 1561 and U.S.A., 1952

1978. U.F.O. Research. Multicoloured.
958 5c. Type **244** 15 10
959 35c. Various aerial phenomena, 1950 35 25
960 $3 U.F.O.s, 1965 2·00 1·75
MS961 112 × 89 mm. $2 Sir Eric Gairy and U.F.O. research laboratory 1·25 1·25

245 Wright Flyer III, 1902

1978. 75th Anniv of Powered Flight. Mult.
962 5c. Type **245** 10 10
963 15c. Wright Flyer I, 1903 10 10
964 18c. Wright Type A 10 10
965 22c. Wright Flyer I from above 15 10
966 50c. Orville Wright and Wright Type A 20 20
967 75c. Wright Type A, Pau, France, 1908 25 25
968 $3 Wilbur Wright and Wright glider No. IV 80 70
MS969 114 × 85 mm. $2 Wright glider No. III 1·00 75

246 Cook and Hawaiian Feast

1978. 250th Birth Anniv of Captain James Cook and Bicentenary of Discovery of Hawaii. Multicoloured.
970 18c. Type **246** 60 20
971 35c. Cook and Hawaiian dance 75 25
972 75c. Cook and Honolulu harbour 1·25 1·00
973 $3 Cook's statue and H.M.S. "Resolution" 1·75 5·50
MS974 116 × 88 mm. $4 Cook and death scene 3·00 1·50

247 "Paumgartner Altarpiece" (detail)

248 National Convention and Cultural Centre (interior)

1978. Christmas. Paintings by Durer. Multicoloured.
975 40c. Type **247** 20 15
976 60c. "The Adoration of the Magi" 25 20
977 90c. "Virgin and Child" 30 20
978 $2 "Virgin and Child with St. Anne" (detail) 55 55
MS979 113 × 83 mm. $4 "Madonna and Child" 1·10 1·50

1979. 5th Anniv of Independence.
980 5c. Type **248** 10 10
981 18c. National Convention and Cultural Centre (exterior) 10 10
982 22c. Easter Water Parade, 1978 10 10
983 35c. Sir Eric M. Gairy (Prime Minister) 10 10
984 $3 The Cross, Fort Frederick 45 60

249 "Acalypha hispida"

250 Birds in Flight

1979. Flowers. Multicoloured.
985 18c. Type **249** 10 10
986 50c. "Hibiscus rosa sinensis" 20 15
987 $1 "Thunbergia grandiflora" 30 25
988 $3 "Nerium oleander" 80 1·10
MS989 115 × 90 mm. $2 "Lagerstroemia speciosa" 75 1·00

1979. 30th Anniv of Declaration of Human Rights. Multicoloured.
990 15c. Type **250** 10 10
991 $2 Bird in Flight 55 65

251 Children playing Cricket

1979. Int Year of the Child (1st issue). Mult.
992 18c. Type **251** 1·00 50
993 22c. Children playing baseball 40 30
994 $5 Children playing in a tree 3·25 7·00
MS995 114 × 92 mm. $4 Children with model spaceship 1·25 2·25
See also Nos. 1006/7 and 1025/34.

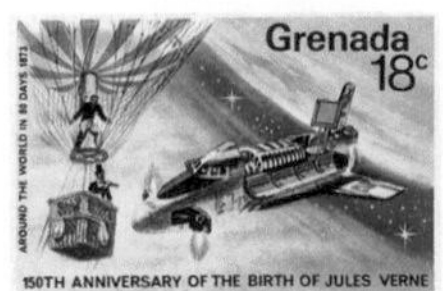

252 "Around the World in 80 Days"

1979. 150th Birth Anniv of Jules Verne. Mult.
996 18c. Type **252** 35 20
997 35c. "20,000 Leagues under the Sea" 50 20
998 75c. "From the Earth to the Moon" 60 50
999 $3 "Master of the World" 1·40 2·00
MS1000 110 × 85 mm. $4 "Clipper of the Clouds" 1·25 1·25

253 Mail Runner, Africa (early 19th-century)

1979. Death Cent of Sir Rowland Hill. Mult.
1001 20c. Type **253** 10 10
1002 40c. Pony Express, America (mid 19th-century) 10 10
1003 $1 Pigeon post 15 25
1004 $3 Mail coach, Europe (18–19th century) 40 80
MS1005 127 × 100 mm. $5 Sir Rowland Hill and 1891 1d. on 8d. × 4 75 1·10

254 "The Pistol of Peace" (vaccination gun), Map of Grenada and Children

1979. International Year of the Child (2nd issue). "Grenada—First Nation 100% Immunized".
1006 **254** 5c. multicoloured 25 75
1007 $1 multicoloured 75 2·50

255 Reef Shark

1979. Marine Wildlife. Multicoloured.
1008 40c. Type **255** 40 30
1009 45c. Spotted eagle ray 40 30
1010 50c. Many-toothed conger 45 40
1011 60c. Golden olive (shell) 70 85
1012 70c. West Indian murex (shell) 85 1·00
1013 75c. Giant tun (shell) 90 1·10
1014 90c. Brown booby 2·25 2·25
1015 $1 Magnificent frigate bird 2·25 2·25
MS1016 109 × 78 mm. $2.50, Sooty tern 2·50 2·00

256 The Flight into Egypt

1979. Christmas. Tapestries. Multicoloured.
1017 6c. Type **256** 10 10
1018 25c. The Flight into Egypt (detail) 10 10
1019 30c. Angel (vert) 10 10
1020 40c. (Doge Marino Grimani) (detail) (vert) 10 10
1021 90c. The Annunciation to the Shepherds (vert) . . . 15 15
1022 $1 The Flight into Egypt (Rome) (vert) 15 15
1023 $2 The Virgin in Glory (vert) 25 40
MS1024 111 × 148 mm. $4 Doge Marino Grimani (vert) . . . . 70 1·00

257 Mickey Mouse playing Baseball
258 Paul Harris (founder)

1979. International Year of the Child (3rd issue). Disney cartoon characters. Multicoloured.
1025 ½c. Type **257** 10 10
1026 1c. Donald Duck high-jumping 10 10
1027 2c. Goofy playing basketbal . . . 10 10
1028 3c. Goofy hurdling 10 10
1029 4c. Donald Duck playing golf 10 10
1030 5c. Mickey Mouse playing cricket 10 10
1031 10c. Mickey Mouse playing football 10 10
1032 $2 Mickey Mouse playing tennis . . . . 1·75 3·50
1033 $2.50 Minnie Mouse riding horse . . . . 1·75 3·50
MS1034 125 × 100 mm. $3 Goofy in riding gear . . . . 1·25 1·50

1980. 75th Anniv of Rotary International. Mult.
1035 6c. Type **258** 10 10
1036 30c. "Health" 10 15
1037 90c. "Hunger" 15 30
1038 $2 "Humanity" 40 80
MS1039 104 × 89 mm. $4 Rotary International emblem . . . . 1·00 1·60

1980. 1st Anniv of Revolution (1st issue). Nos. 651/2, 654/7, 659/60 and 662/8 optd **PEOPLE'S REVOLUTION 13 MARCH 1979.**
1040 2c. Carenage taxi 10 40
1041 3c. Large working boats . . 10 40
1042 6c. Cocoa beans in drying trays 10 10
1043 8c. Nutmegs 10 10
1044 10c. Rum distillery, River Antoine Estate, c. 1785 10 10
1045 12c. Cocoa tree 10 10
1046 20c. Parliament Building . . 10 15
1047 25c. Fort George cannons 30 30
1048 50c. General Post Office . . 30 30
1049 75c. Carib's Leap, Sauteurs Bay 50 40
1050 $1 Carenage, St. George's 60 60
1051 $2 St. George's Harbour by night . . . . 1·25 2·00
1052 $3 Grand Anse Beach . . 1·50 3·25
1053 $5 Canoe Bay and Black Bay . . . . 2·00 5·50
1054 $10 Sugar-loaf Island . . . 3·25 8·00
See also Nos. 1069/72.

260 Boxing

1980. Olympic Games, Moscow. Multicoloured.
1055 25c. Type **260** 10 10
1056 40c. Cycling 15 10
1057 90c. Show-jumping 20 30
1058 $2 Running . . . . 40 1·00
MS1059 128 × 95 mm. $4 Sailing 1·00 1·40

261 Tropical Kingbird

1980. Wild Birds. Multicoloured.
1060 20c. Type **261** 85 20
1061 40c. Rufous-breasted hermit 1·25 25
1062 $1 Troupial . . . . 1·75 1·75
1063 $2 Ruddy quail dove . . . 2·25 4·00
MS1064 85 × 114 mm. $3 Prarie warbler . . . . 3·75 1·75

1980. "London 1980" International Stamp Exhibition. Nos. 1001/4 optd **LONDON 1980.**
1065 20c. Type **253** 15 15
1066 40c. Pony Express, America 20 15
1067 $1 Pigeon post 30 30
1068 $3 Mail coach, Europe . . . 85 90

263 Free Hot Lunch at Schools

1980. 1st Anniv of Revolution (2nd issue). Multicoloured.
1069 10c. Type **263** 10 10
1070 40c. "From tree to can" (agro-industry) 15 15
1071 $1 National Health care . . 30 30
1072 $2 New housing projects . . 50 70
MS1073 110 × 85 mm. $5 Prime Minister Maurice Bishop (vert) 75 85

264 Jamb Statues, West Portal, Chartres Cathedral

1980. Famous Works of Art. Multicoloured.
1074 8c. Type **264** 10 10
1075 10c. "Les Demoiselles d' Avignon" (painting, Picasso) 10 10
1076 40c. Winged Victory of Samothrace (statue) . . . 15 15
1077 50c. "The Night Watch" (painting, Rembrandt) . . 15 15
1078 $1 "Portrait of Edward VI as a Child" (painting, Holbein the Younger) . . 25 25
1079 $3 Portrait head of Queen Nefertiti (carving) 70 70
MS1080 101 × 101 mm. $4 "Weier Haws" (detail of painting by Durer) (vert) 75 75

265 Carib Canoes

1980. Shipping. Multicoloured.
1081A ½c. Type **265** 10 40
1082A 1c. Boat building 10 40
1083A 2c. Small working boat . . 15 40
1084A 4c. Columbus's "Santa Maria" 40 40
1085A 5c. West Indiaman barque, c. 1840 . . . . 40 30
1086A 6c. "Orinoco" (paddle-steamer), c. 1851 . . . 40 40
1087A 10c. Working schooner . . 50 10
1088A 12c. Trimaran at Grand Anse anchorage . . . . 1·00 55
1089A 15c. Spice Island cruising yacht "Petite Amie" . . . 50 10
1090A 20c. Fishing pirogue . . . 1·00 20
1091A 25c. Harbour police launch . . . . 2·00 30
1092A 30c. Grand Anse speedboat . . . . 1·50 30
1093A 40c. "Seimstrand" (freighter) . . . . 2·00 35
1094B 50c. "Ariadne" (cadet schooner) 50 50
1095A 90c. "Geestide" (freighter) 1·75 50
1096A $1 "Cunard Countess" (liner) . . . . 3·00 80
1097A $3 Rum-runner . . . . . 2·50 4·25
1098A $5 "Statendam" (liner) off St. George's . . . . . 3·50 7·50
1099B $10 Coastguard patrol boat . . . . 3·75 8·50
Nos. 1081/99 come with and without date imprint.

1980. Christmas. Scenes from Walt Disney's "Snow White and the Seven Dwarfs". As T **257**. Multicoloured.
1100 ½c. Snow White at well . . 10 10
1101 1c. The Wicked Queen . . . 10 10
1102 2c. Snow White singing to animals 10 10
1103 3c. Snow White doing housework for Dwarfs . . 10 10
1104 4c. The Seven Dwarfs . . . 10 10
1105 5c. Snow White with Dwarfs 10 10
1106 10c. Witch offering Snow White apple 10 10
1107 $2.50 Snow White with Prince and Dwarfs . . . 3·25 1·75
1108 $3 Snow White and Prince 3·75 2·00
MS1109 127 × 102 mm. $4 Snow White sleeping (vert) . . . . . 4·25 1·50

1981. 50th Anniv of Walt Disney's Pluto (cartoon character). As T **257**. Multicoloured.
1110 $2 Pluto with birthday cake 1·00 1·00
MS1111 127 × 102 mm. $4 Pluto in scene from film "Pueblo Pluto" 1·25 1·00

266 Revolution and Grenada Flags

1981. Festival of the Revolution. Multicoloured.
1112 5c. Type **266** 10 10
1113 10c. Teacher, pupil, book and pencil ("education") 10 10
1114 15c. Food processing plant ("industry") 10 10
1115 25c. Selection of fruits and farm scene ("agriculture") 15 10
1116 40c. Crawfish and boat ("fishing") 20 15
1117 90c. "Cunard Countess" arriving at St. George's Harbour ("shipping") . . 50 30
1118 $1 Straw-work ("native handicrafts") 60 40
1119 $3 Map of Caribbean with expanded view of Grenada . . . . 1·75 1·75

1981. Easter. Walt Disney cartoon characters. As T **257**. Multicoloured.
1120 35c. Mickey Mouse and Goofy 30 15
1121 40c. Donald Duck, Chip and Daisy Duck 30 15
1122 $2 Minnie Mouse . . . . . 75 1·00
1123 $2.50 Pluto and Mickey Mouse . . . . 75 1·10
MS1124 127 × 101 mm. $4 Goofy 1·75 1·50

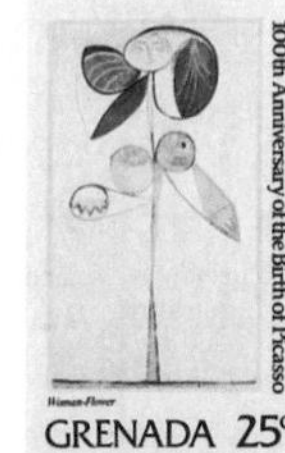

267 "Woman-Flower"
268 Prince Charles playing Polo

1981. Birth Centenary of Picasso. Multicoloured.
1125 25c. Type **267** 15 10
1126 30c. "Portrait of Madame" 15 10
1127 90c. "Cavalier with Pipe" 25 30
1128 $4 "Large Heads" . . . . . 70 1·00
MS1129 128 × 103 mm. $5 "Woman on the Banks of the Seine" (after Courbet). Imperf . . . . . . 2·50 1·40

1981. Royal Wedding (1st issue). Multicoloured.
1134 30c. Prince Charles and Lady Diana Spencer . . . 20 20
1135 40c. Holyrood House 30 30
1130 50c. As 30c. 10 10
1131 $2 As 40c. 35 50
1132 $4 Type **268** 50 75
MS1133 98 × 94 mm. $5 Glass Coach 75 75

269 Lady Diana Spencer
270 "The Bath" (Mary Cassatt)

1981. Royal Wedding (2nd issue). Multicoloured. Self-adhesive.
1136 $1 Type **269** 30 65
1137 $2 Prince Charles 30 65
1138 $5 Prince Charles and Lady Diana Spencer . . . . . 1·00 1·75

1981. "Decade for Women". Paintings. Mult.
1139 15c. Type **270** 10 10
1140 40c. "Mademoiselle Charlotte du Val d'Ognes" (Constance Marie Charpentier) . . . 20 10
1141 60c. "Self-portrait" (Mary Beale) 30 20
1142 $3 "Woman in White Stockings" (Suzanne Valadon) . . . . 1·25 1·00
MS1143 101 × 77 mm. $5 "The Artist hesitating between the Arts of Music and Painting" (Angelica Kauffman) (horiz) . . . . . . 1·75 2·00

1981. Christmas. As T **257** showing scenes from Walt Disney's cartoon film "Cinderella".
1144 ½c. multicoloured 10 10
1145 1c. multicoloured 10 10
1146 2c. multicoloured 10 10
1147 3c. multicoloured 10 10
1148 4c. multicoloured 10 10
1149 5c. multicoloured 10 10
1150 10c. multicoloured 15 10
1151 $2.50 multicoloured . . . . 3·50 2·50
1152 $3 multicoloured . . . . . 3·50 2·75
MS1153 127 × 103 mm. $5 multicoloured . . . . 5·50 3·25

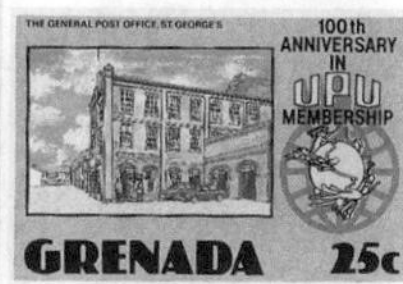

271 Landing
273 General Post Office, St. George's

272 West German Footballer and Flag

1981. Space Shuttle Project. Multicoloured.
1154 30c. Type **271** 20 15
1155 60c. Working in space . . . 40 30
1156 70c. Lift off 45 35
1157 $3 Separation . . . . 1·10 1·25
MS1158 117 × 89 mm. $5 In orbit 1·75 1·25

1981. World Cup Football Championship, Spain (1982). Multicoloured.
1159 25c.+10c. Type **272** 75 30
1160 40c.+20c. Argentinian footballer and flag 90 40
1161 50c.+25c. Brazilian footballer and flag . . . . 1·00 50
1162 $1+50c. English footballer and flag . . . . 1·50 95
MS1163 141 × 128 mm. $5+50c. Spanish orange mascot and Jules Rimet Trophy (vert) . . . . . 3·50 2·00

1981. Cent of U.P.U. Membership. Mult.
1164 25c. Type **273** 25 15
1165 30c. 1861 1d. stamp 30 20
1166 90c. New U.P.U. Headquarters Building 25c. commemorative . . . 70 50
1167 $4 1961 Stamp Centenary 25c. commemorative . . . 1·25 2·00
MS1168 137 × 87 mm. $5 1974 Centenary of U.P.U. ½c. commemorative . . . . 3·25 3·75

274 Artist without Hands

276 "Dryas julia"

275 Tending Vegetable Patch

1982. International Year for the Disabled (1981). Multicoloured.
1169 30c. Type **274** 20 10
1170 40c. Computer operator without hands 20 10
1171 70c. Blind schoolteacher teaching braille 50 15
1172 $3 Midget playing drums . . 1·10 80
MS1173 101 × 72 mm. $4 Auto mechanic confined to wheelchair 3·00 3·25

1982. 75th Anniv of Boy Scout Movement and 125th Birth Anniv of Lord Baden-Powell. Multicoloured.
1174 70c. Type **275** 50 45
1175 90c. Map-reading 55 55
1176 $1 Bee-keeping 65 65
1177 $4 Hospital reading . . . . 2·25 2·75
MS1178 100 × 71 mm. $5 Presentation of trophies . . . 1·25 1·00

1982. Butterflies. Multicoloured.
1179 10c. Type **276** 75 30
1180 60c. "Phoebis agarithe" . . 2·50 1·50
1181 $1 "Anartia amathea" . . . 3·00 2·00
1182 $3 "Battus polydamas" . . . 4·25 7·00
MS1183 111 × 85 mm. $5 "Junonia evarete" . . . . 6·00 2·25

277 "Saying Grace"

278 Kensington Palace

1982. Norman Rockwell (painter) Commemoration. Multicoloured.
1184 15c. Type **277** 40 10
1185 30c. "Nothing Up His Sleeve" (inscr "Card Tricks") 65 15
1186 60c. "Pharmacist" 85 25
1187 70c. "Hobo" (inscr "Pals") . . 90 35

1982. 21st Birthday of Princess of Wales. Multicoloured.
1188 50c. Type **278** . . . . . . 90 1·00
1189 60c. Type **278** . . . . . . 1·50 50
1190 $1 Prince and Princess of Wales . . . . 1·50 1·75
1191 $2 As $1 . . . . 2·75 1·50
1192 $3 Princess of Wales . . . . 2·75 2·75
1193 $4 As $3 . . . . 3·00 2·50
MS1194 103 × 75 mm. $5 Princess Diana (different) . . . . 3·00 1·50

279 Mary McLeod Bethune appointed Director of Negro Affairs, 1942

1982. Birth Centenary of Franklin D. Roosevelt. Multicoloured.
1195 10c. Type **279** 10 10
1196 60c. Huddie Ledbetter "Leadbelly" in concert (Works Progress administration) 30 20
1197 $1.10 Signing bill No. 8802, 1941 (Fair Employment committee) 40 25
1198 $3 Farm Security administration 55 60
MS1199 100 × 70 mm. $5 William Hastie, first Negro Judicial appointee . . . . 1·25 1·25

1982. Birth of Prince William of Wales. Nos. 1188/93 optd **ROYAL BABY 21.6.82.**
1200 50c. Type **278** . . . . . . 30 1·00
1201 60c. Type **278** 35 35
1202 $1 Prince and Princess of Wales . . . . 55 1·25
1203 $2 As $1 . . . . 1·00 1·00
1204 $3 Princess of Wales . . . . 1·75 2·25
1205 $4 As $3 . . . . 1·90 1·90
MS1206 103 × 75 mm. $5 Princess Diana (different) . . . . 2·00 1·25

280 Apostle and Tormentor

1982. Easter. Details from Painting "The Way to Calvary" by Raphael. Multicoloured.
1207 40c. Type **280** 25 10
1208 70c. Captain of the guards (vert) 30 15
1209 $1.10 Christ and apostle (vert) 35 25
1210 $4 Mourners (vert) . . . . 70 1·25
MS1211 102 × 126 mm. $5 Christ falls beneath the cross (vert) . . 1·50 1·50

281 "Orient Express"

1982. Famous Trains of the World. Mult.
1212 30c. Type **281** 50 35
1213 60c. "Trans-Siberian Express" 60 70
1214 70c. "Fleche d'Or" 70 80
1215 90c. "Flying Scotsman" . . 85 1·00
1216 $1 German Federal Railways steam locomotive . . . . 1·00 1·25
1217 $3 German National Railways Class 05 steam locomotive . . . . 2·25 4·00
MS1218 109 × 81 mm. $5 "20th Century Limited" . . . . . . 2·00 2·00

282 Footballers

1982. World Cup Football Championship Winners.
1219 **282** 60c. multicoloured . . . 35 35
1220 $4 multicoloured . . . 2·00 2·00
MS1221 93 × 119 mm. $5 multicoloured . . . . 2·50 2·25

1982. Christmas. Scenes from Walt Disney's cartoon film "Robin Hood". As T **257**, but horiz.
1222 ½c. multicoloured 10 10
1223 1c. multicoloured 10 10
1224 2c. multicoloured 10 10
1225 3c. multicoloured 10 10
1226 4c. multicoloured 10 10
1227 5c. multicoloured 10 10
1228 10c. multicoloured 10 10
1229 $2.50 multicoloured . . . . 3·00 3·50
1230 $3 multicoloured . . . . . 3·00 3·50
MS1231 121 × 96 mm. $5 multicoloured . . . . 6·50 4·00

283 Killer Whale

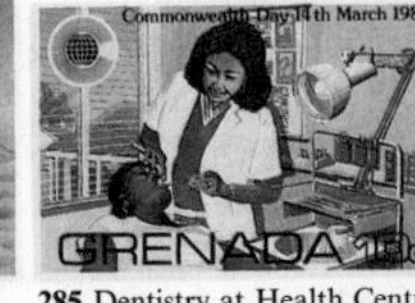

285 Dentistry at Health Centre

284 "Construction of Ark"

1983. Save the Whales. Multicoloured.
1232 15c. Type **283** . . . . . . 1·00 30
1233 40c. Sperm whale . . . . . 2·25 90
1234 70c. Blue whale . . . . . . 2·75 2·75
1235 $3 Common dolphin . . . . 3·50 6·50
MS1236 84 × 74 mm. $5 Humpback whales . . . . 6·50 4·00

1983. 500th Birth Anniv of Raphael. Mult.
1237 25c. Type **284** 20 10
1238 30c. "Jacob's Vision" . . . 20 10
1239 90c. "Joseph interprets the Dreams of his Brothers" 40 30
1240 $4 "Joseph interprets Pharaoh's dreams" . . . 1·10 1·40
MS1241 128 × 100 mm. $5 "Creation of the Animals" . . . . 1·25 1·75

1983. Commonwealth Day. Multicoloured.
1242 10c. Type **285** 10 10
1243 70c. Airport runway construction 35 35
1244 $1.10 Tourism 40 55
1245 $3 Boat-building . . . . . 80 1·40

286 Maritime Communications via Satellite

1983. World Communications Year. Multicoloured.
1246 30c. Type **286** 15 15
1247 40c. Rural telephone installation 20 15
1248 $2.50 Satellite weather map 60 1·00
1249 $4 Airport control room . . 60 1·10
MS1250 111 × 85 mm. $5 Communications satellite . . . 1·25 1·25

287 Franklin Sport Sedan, 1928

1983. 75th Anniv of Model "T" Ford Car. Multicoloured.
1251 6c. Type **287** 15 20
1252 10c. Delage "D8", 1933 . . 20 10
1253 40c. Alvis, 1938 . . . . . . 35 25
1254 60c. Invicta "S-type" tourer, 1931 . . . . 45 45
1255 70c. Alfa-Romeo "1750 Gran Sport", 1930 . . . 55 55
1256 90c. Isotta Fraschini, 1930 60 75
1257 $1 Bugatti "Royale Type 41" 70 75
1258 $2 BMW "328", 1938 . . . 1·40 1·75
1259 $3 Marmon "V16", 1931 . . 1·60 2·50
1260 $4 Lincoln "K8" saloon, 1932 . . . . 1·90 3·00
MS1261 114 × 90 mm. $5 Cougar "TR 7", 1972 . . . . 1·50 2·00

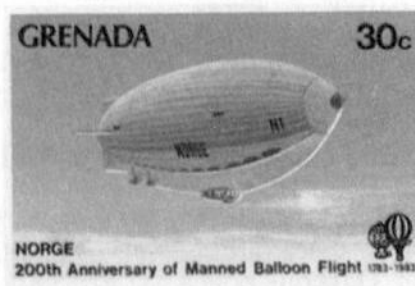

288 Airship N.1 "Norge"

1983. Bicentenary of Manned Flight. Multicoloured.
1262 30c. Type **288** 60 30
1263 60c. Gloster VI seaplane . . 1·00 1·00
1264 $1.10 Curtiss NC-4 flying boat . . . . 1·60 1·75
1265 $4 Dornier Do 18 flying boat "Aeolus" . . . . . 3·50 4·50
MS1266 114 × 85 mm. $5 Modern hot-air balloon (vert) . . . . . 1·50 1·50

289 Morty

291 William I

290 Daisy Duck on Pommel Horse

1983. Christmas. Multicoloured.
1267 ½c. Type **289** 10 10
1268 1c. Ludwig von Drake . . . 10 10
1269 2c. Gyro Gearloose 10 10
1270 3c. Pluto and Figaro 10 10
1271 4c. Morty and Ferdie . . . 10 10
1272 5c. Mickey Mouse and Goofy 10 10
1273 10c. Chip n'Dale 10 10
1274 $2.50 Mickey and Minnie Mouse . . . . 2·25 3·50
1275 $3 Donald and Grandma Duck . . . . 2·25 3·50
MS1276 127 × 102 mm. $5 Goofy with Christmas tree . . . . . 4·50 4·50

Nos. 1267/75 show Disney cartoon characters in scenes from "It's beginning to look a lot like Christmas" (song).

1984. Olympic Games. Los Angeles. Multicoloured.

A. Inscr "1984 LOS ANGELES"
1277A ½c. Type **290** 10 10
1278A 1c. Mickey Mouse boxing 10 10
1279A 2c. Daisy Duck in archery event 10 10
1280A 3c. Clarabelle Cow on uneven bars 10 10
1281A 4c. Mickey and Minnie Mouse in hurdles race 10 10
1282A 5c. Donald Duck with Chip'n'Dale weightlifting 10 10
1283A $1 Little Hiawatha in single kayak . . . . . 2·50 2·25
1284A $2 The Tortoise and the Hare in marathon . . . 3·00 3·75
1285A $3 Mickey Mouse polevaulting . . . . . 3·50 4·00
MS1286A 127 × 101 mm. $5 Donald Duck in medley relay (vert) . . 5·50 3·50

B. Inscr "1984 OLYMPICS LOS ANGELES" and Olympic Emblem.
1227B ½c. Type **290** 10 10
1278B 1c. Mickey Mouse boxing 10 10
1279B 2c. Daisy Duck in archery event 10 10
1280B 3c. Clarabelle Cow on uneven bars 10 10
1281B 4c. Mickey and Minnie Mouse in hurdles race 10 10
1282B 5c. Donald Duck with Chip'n'Dale weightlifting 10 10
1283B $1 Little Hiawatha in single kayak . . . . . 2·50 2·25
1284B $2 The Tortoise and the Hare in marathon . . . 3·00 3·75
1285B $3 Mickey Mouse polevaulting . . . . . . 3·50 4·00
MS1286B 127 × 100 mm. $5 Donald Duck in medley relay (vert) . . 6·50 5·50

1984. English Monarchs. Multicoloured.
1287 $4 Type **291** . . . . 2·00 2·75
1288 $4 William II . . . . 2·00 2·75
1289 $4 Henry I . . . . 2·00 2·75
1290 $4 Stephen . . . . 2·00 2·75
1291 $4 Henry II . . . . 2·00 2·75
1292 $4 Richard I . . . . 2·00 2·75
1293 $4 John . . . . 2·00 2·75
1294 $4 "Henry III" . . . . . . 2·00 2·75
1295 $4 Edward I . . . . 2·00 2·75
1296 $4 Edward II . . . . 2·00 2·75
1297 $4 Edward III . . . . . . 2·00 2·75
1298 $4 Richard II . . . . 2·00 2·75
1299 $4 Henry IV . . . . 2·00 2·75
1300 $4 Henry V . . . . 2·00 2·75
1301 $4 Henry VI . . . . 2·00 2·75
1302 $4 Edward IV . . . . . . 2·00 2·75
1303 $4 Edward V . . . . 2·00 2·75
1304 $4 Richard III . . . . . . 2·00 2·75
1305 $4 Henry VII . . . . 2·00 2·75
1306 $4 Henry VIII . . . . . . 2·00 2·75
1307 $4 Edward VI . . . . . . 2·00 2·75
1308 $4 Jane Grey . . . . 2·00 2·75
1309 $4 Mary I . . . . 2·00 2·75
1310 $4 Elizabeth I . . . . . . 2·00 2·75
1311 $4 James I . . . . 2·00 2·75
1312 $4 Charles I . . . . 2·00 2·75
1313 $4 Charles II . . . . 2·00 2·75
1314 $4 James II . . . . 2·00 2·75
1315 $4 William III . . . . . . 2·00 2·75
1316 $4 Mary II . . . . 2·00 2·75
1317 $4 Anne . . . . 2·00 2·75
1318 $4 George I . . . . 2·00 2·75

1319 $4 George II 2·00 2·75
1320 $4 George III 2·00 2·75
1321 $4 George IV 2·00 2·75
1322 $4 William IV 2·00 2·75
1323 $4 Victoria 2·00 2·75
1324 $4 Edward VII 2·00 2·75
1325 $4 George V 2·00 2·75
1326 $4 Edward VIII 2·00 2·75
1327 $4 George VI 2·00 2·75
1328 $4 Elizabeth II 2·00 2·75
Although inscribed "Henry III" the portrait on No. 1294 is actually of Edward II.

292 Lantana

1984. Flowers. Multicoloured.
1329 25c. Type **292** 20 15
1330 30c. Plumbago 25 15
1331 90c. Spider lily 60 35
1332 $4 Giant alocasia 1·50 2·75
MS1333 108 × 90 mm. $5 Orange trumpet vine 1·00 1·50

293 Blue Parrotfish

1984. Coral Reef Fishes. Multicoloured.
1334 10c. Type **293** 1·40 45
1335 30c. Flame-backed angelfish 2·75 1·10
1336 70c. Painted wrasse 4·00 3·25
1337 90c. Rosy razorfish 4·75 3·50
MS1338 81 × 85 mm. $5 Spanish hogfish 6·50 4·75

1984. Universal Postal Union Congress, Hamburg. Nos. 1331/2 optd **19TH U.P.U CONGRESS HAMBURG**.
1339 90c. Spider lily 60 65
1340 $4 Giant alocasia 2·00 2·50
MS1341 108 × 90 mm. $5 Orange trumpet vine 1·50 2·50

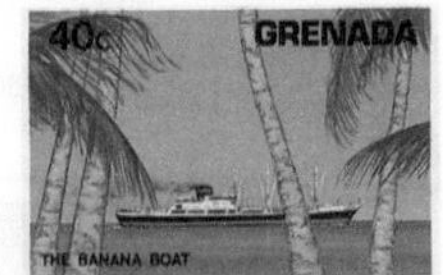

295 Freighter

1984. Ships. Multicoloured.
1342 40c. Type **295** 1·25 55
1343 70c. "Queen Elizabeth 2" 1·50 1·50
1344 90c. Sailing boats 1·60 2·00
1345 $4 "Amerikanis" 3·50 8·00
MS1346 107 × 80 mm. $5 Spanish galleon 5·00 7·00

296 "The Night" (detail) (Correggio)

1984. 450th Death Anniv of Correggio (painter). Multicoloured.
1347 10c. Type **296** 45 15
1348 30c. "The Virgin adoring the Child" 80 50
1349 40c. "The Mystical Marriage of St. Catherine with St. Sebastian" 2·00 1·75
1350 $4 "The Madonna and the Fruit Basket" 4·50 5·50
MS1351 54 × 73 mm. $5 "The Madonna at the Spring" 4·25 3·00

297 "L'Absinthe" (Degas)

298 Train on Puffing Billy Line, Victoria

1984. 150th Birth Anniv of Edgar Degas (painter). Multicoloured.
1352 25c. Type **297** 80 30
1353 70c. "Pouting" (horiz) 1·50 1·25
1354 $1.10 "The Millinery Shop" 2·00 2·00
1355 $3 "The Bellelli Family" (horiz) 3·75 4·25
MS1356 84 × 54 mm. $5 "The Cotton Market" 4·25 3·00

1984. "Ausipex" International Stamp Exhibition, Melbourne. Multicoloured.
1357 $1.10 Type **298** 2·25 1·75
1358 $4 Yacht "Australia II" (winner of America's Cup) 4·75 5·25
MS1359 107 × 76 mm. $5 Melbourne tram 4·25 4·00

299 George Stephenson's "Locomotion" (1825)

1984. Railway Locomotives. Multicoloured.
1360 30c. Type **299** 80 35
1361 40c. Braithwaite and Ericsson's "Novelty" (1829) 95 40
1362 60c. William Norris's "Washington Farmer" (1836) 1·00 75
1363 70c. French Crampton type (1859) 1·00 1·00
1364 90c. Dutch State Railways (1873) 1·10 1·50
1365 $1.10 "Champion", U.S.A. (1882) 1·25 2·00
1366 $2 Webb Compound type (1893) 1·75 3·25
1367 $4 Berlin "No. 74" (1900) 2·75 5·50
MS1368 Two sheets, each 100 × 70 mm. (a) $5 Crampton "Phoenix" (1863); (b) $5 Mikado type, Japan (1897) Set of 2 sheets 6·00 6·50

1984. Opening of Point Saline International Airport (1st issue). Nos. 1247 and 1249 optd **OPENING OF POINT SALINE INT'L AIRPORT**.
1369 40c. Rural telephone installation 30 30
1370 $3 Airport control room 2·00 2·00
MS1371 111 × 85 mm. $5 Communications satellite 3·50 3·25
See also Nos. 1399/6.

301 Donald Duck as Father Christmas looking into Mirror

1984. Christmas. Walt Disney cartoon characters. Multicoloured.
1372 45c. Type **301** 1·25 40
1373 60c. Donald Duck filling stocking with presents 1·50 55
1374 90c. As Father Christmas pulling a sleigh 2·00 1·10
1375 $2 As Father Christmas decorating Christmas tree 3·50 3·75
1376 $4 Donald Duck and nephews singing carols 5·00 6·00
MS1377 127 × 102 mm. $5 Father Christmas in sleigh 7·00 8·00

1985. Birth Bicentenary of John J. Audubon (ornithologist) (1st issue). As T **418** of Ghana. Multicoloured.
1378 50c. Clapper rail (vert) 2·00 75
1379 70c. Hooded warbler (vert) 2·25 1·50
1380 90c. Common flicker (vert) 2·75 1·75
1381 $4 Bohemian waxwing (vert) 5·50 8·00
MS1382 82 × 112 mm. $5 Merlin ("Pigeon Hawk") 9·00 4·50
See also Nos. 1480/4.

302 Honda "XL500R"

1985. Centenary of the Motor Cycle. Multicoloured.
1383 25c. Type **302** 1·00 50
1384 50c. Suzuki "GS1100ES" 1·50 1·00
1385 90c. Kawasaki "KZ700" 2·00 2·25
1386 $4 BMW "K100" 6·00 6·50
MS1387 109 × 81 mm. $5 Yamaha "500CC V Four" 7·50 5·00

303 "Explorer"

1985. 75th Anniv of Girl Guide Movement. Designs showing work for Guide badges. Multicoloured.
1388 25c. Type **303** 55 30
1389 60c. "Cook" 90 65
1390 90c. "Musician" 1·50 1·10
1391 $3 "Home nurse" 3·00 4·50
MS1392 97 × 70 mm. $5 Flags of Girl Guides and Grenada 2·50 2·50

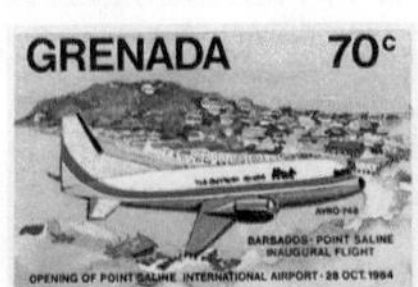

304 Hawker Siddeley H.S.748 on Inaugural Flight from Barbados

1985. Opening of Point Saline International Airport (1984) (2nd issue). Multicoloured.
1393 70c. Type **304** 2·50 1·00
1394 $1 Lockheed TriStar 500 on inaugural flight from New York 3·25 1·50
1395 $4 Lockheed TriStar 500 on inaugural flight to Miami 6·50 8·50
MS1396 101 × 72 mm. $5 Point Saline Airport terminal and Hawker Siddeley H.S.748 on tarmac 5·50 3·75

305 Douglas DC-8-61

1985. 40th Anniv of International Civil Aviation Organization. Multicoloured.
1397 10c. Type **305** 40 20
1398 50c. Lockheed Starliner (inscr "Super Constellation") 1·00 75
1399 60c. Vickers 952 Cargoliner 1·25 85
1400 $4 De Havilland Twin Otter 200/300 4·50 7·00
MS1401 102 × 64 mm. $5 Hawker Siddeley H.S.748 turboprop 3·00 3·00

306 Model Boat Racing

1985. Water Sports. Multicoloured.
1402 10c. Type **306** 25 10
1403 50c. Scuba diving, Carriacou 55 35
1404 $1.10 Windsurfers on Grand Anse Beach 85 1·25
1405 $4 Windsurfing 2·00 6·00
MS1406 107 × 77 mm. $5 Beach scene 2·25 2·75

307 Bird of Paradise (flower)

1985. Native Flowers. Multicoloured.
1407 ½c. Type **307** 50 60
1408 1c. Passion flower 50 60
1409 2c. Oleander 50 60
1410a 4c. Bromeliad 80 40
1411a 5c. Anthurium 80 40
1412a 6c. Bougainvillea 80 50
1413a 10c. Hibiscus 80 30
1414a 15c. Ginger 1·25 30
1415a 25c. Poinsettia 1·25 30
1425d 30c. Mexican creeper 30 60
1417a 40c. Angel's trumpet 1·00 50
1425e 50c. Amaryllis 40 75
1425f 60c. Prickly pear 50 1·25
1420a 70c. Chenille plant 1·50 1·50
1420b 75c. Cordia 1·50 2·00
1425g $1 Periwinkle 50 1·25
1422a $1.10 Ixora 2·50 2·75
1423a $3 Shrimp plant 3·00 6·50
1424a $5 Plumbago 2·50 7·00
1425a $10 "Lantana camara" 4·00 10·00
1425b $20 Peregrina 8·50 16·00

308 The Queen Mother at Royal Opera House, London

309 Youth Gardening (Horticulture)

1985. Life and Times of Queen Elizabeth the Queen Mother. Multicoloured.
1426 $1 Type **308** 40 60
1427 $1.50 The Queen Mother playing snooker at London Press Club (horiz) 55 85
1428 $2.50 At Epsom Races, 1960 95 1·50
MS1429 56 × 85 mm. $5 With Prince of Wales on 80th Birthday 1·75 3·00
Stamps as Nos. 1426/8 but with face values of 90c., $1 and $3 exist from additional sheetlets with changed background colours.

1985. International Youth Year. Multicoloured.
1430 25c. Type **309** 25 20
1431 50c. Young people on beach (Leisure) 35 40
1432 $1.10 Girls in classroom (Education) 60 1·10
1433 $3 Nurse and young patient (Health Care) 1·50 2·50
MS1434 111 × 80 mm. $5 Children of different races 1·50 3·00

309a Crumhorn

1985. 300th Birth Anniv of Johann Sebastian Bach (composer).
1435 **309a** 25c. multicoloured 80 20
1436 – 70c. multicoloured 1·50 85
1437 – $1 multicoloured 2·00 1·25
1438 – $3 multicoloured 3·00 5·00
MS1439 104 × 74 mm. $5 black, grey and cinnamon 3·50 3·75
DESIGNS: 70c. Oboe d'amore; $1 Violin; $3 Harpsichord; $5 Johann Sebastian Bach.

310 Cub Scouts Camping

1985. 4th Caribbean Cuboree. Multicoloured.
1440 10c. Type **310** 30 15
1441 50c. Cub scouts swimming ("Physical Fitness") 65 40
1442 $1 Stamp collecting 1·50 80
1443 $4 Birdwatching 3·50 3·00
MS1444 103 × 75 mm. $5 Cub scouts saluting leader (vert) 3·25 3·75

310a Flags of Great Britain and Grenada

1985. Royal Visit. Multicoloured.
1445 50c. Type **310a** 1·00 40
1446 $1 Queen Elizabeth II (vert) 1·00 1·25
1447 $4 Royal Yacht "Britannia" 2·75 5·00
MS1448 111 × 85 mm. $5 Map of Grenada 1·75 3·25

1985. 150th Birth Anniv of Mark Twain (author). As T **145a** of Gambia. Designs showing Walt Disney cartoon characters in scenes from "The Prince and the Pauper". Multicoloured.
1449 25c. Mortie as Tom meeting the Prince (Ferdie) 60 20
1450 50c. Tom and the Prince exchanging clothes 80 50
1451 $1.10 The Prince with John Cantry 1·75 1·75

1452 $1.50 The Prince knights Mike Hendon (Goofy) . . 2·25 2·75
1453 $2 Tom and the Whipping Boy . . . . 2·50 3·00
MS1454 124 × 100 mm. $5 The Prince, Tom and Mike Hendon 6·00 6·00

1985. Birth Bicentenaries of Grimm Brothers (folklorists). As T **145b** of Gambia, showing Walt Disney cartoon characters in scenes from "The Fisherman and his Wife". Multicoloured.
1455 30c. The Fisherman (Goofy) catching enchanted fish 85 30
1456 60c. The Fisherman scolded by his Wife (Clarabelle) 1·25 80
1457 70c. The Fisherman's Wife with dream cottage . . . 1·40 95
1458 $1 The Fisherman's Wife as King . . . . 2·25 1·50
1459 $3 The Fisherman and Wife in their original shack . . 3·75 4·50
MS1460 126 × 100 mm. $5 The Fisherman in boat . . . . . . 6·00 6·00

311 Red-spotted Hawkfish

1985. Marine Life. Multicoloured.
1461 25c. Type **311** . . . . . . 1·50 55
1462 50c. Spot-finned butterflyfish 2·25 1·10
1463 $1.10 Fire coral and orange sponges . . . . 3·75 3·25
1464 $3 Pillar coral . . . . . . 6·00 7·50
MS1465 127 × 100 mm. $5 Bigeye 3·75 4·50

311a Mary McLeod Bethune (educationist) and 1975 International Women's Year 10c.

1985. 40th Anniv of U.N.O. Designs showing United Nations (New York) stamps. Mult.
1466 50c. Type **311a** 30 30
1467 $2 Maimonides (physician) and 1966 W.H.O. 5c. . . 2·50 3·50
1468 $2.50 Alexander Graham Bell (telephone inventor) and 1956 I.T.U. 3c. . . . 2·00 4·00
MS1469 110 × 85 mm. $5 Dag Hammarskjold (Secretary-General) (vert) . . . . 1·25 2·00

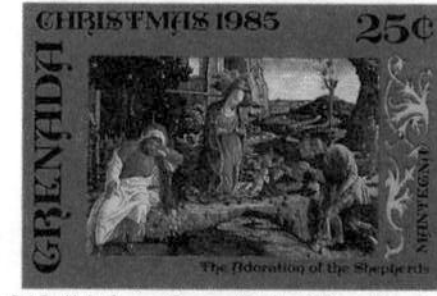

312 "Adoration of the Shepherds" (Mantegna)

1985. Christmas. Religious Paintings. Multicoloured.
1470 25c. Type **312** 20 15
1471 60c. "Journey of the Magi" (Sassetta) 30 40
1472 90c. "Madonna and Child enthroned with Saints" (Raphael) 35 70
1473 $4 "Nativity" (Monaco) . . 1·00 4·25
MS1474 107 × 81 mm. $5 "Madonna and Child enthroned with Saints" (Gaddi) . . . . 1·50 2·50

312a Columbus Monument, 1893 **312b** Snowy Egret

1986. Centenary of Statue of Liberty (1st issue). Multicoloured.
1475 5c. Type **312a** 15 20
1476 25c. Columbus Monument, 1986 . . . . 30 20
1477 40c. Mounted police, Central Park, 1895 (horiz) 1·75 1·10
1478 $4 Mounted police, 1986 (horiz) . . . . 5·00 8·00
MS1479 104 × 76 mm. $5 Statue of Liberty (vert) . . . . 2·75 2·75
See also Nos. 1644/52.

1986. Birth Bicentenary of John J. Audubon (ornithologist) (2nd issue). Multicoloured.
1480 50c. Type **312b** . . . . . . 2·00 80
1481 90c. Greater flamingo . . . 2·75 2·00
1482 $1.10 Canada goose . . . . 2·75 2·50
1483 $3 Smew . . . . 4·50 6·00
MS1484 103 × 72 mm. $5 Brent goose (horiz) . . . . 13·00 13·00

1986. Visit of President Reagan. Nos. 1418 and 1424 optd **VISIT OF PRES REAGAN 20 FEB. 1986.**
1485 50c. Amaryllis 50 50
1486 $5 Plumbago . . . . 3·00 5·00

314 Methodist Church, St. George's

1986. Bicentenary of Methodist Church in Grenada. Multicoloured.
1487 60c. Type **314** . . . . . . 70 1·00
MS1488 102 × 73 mm. $5 St. Georges . . . . 1·00 3·00

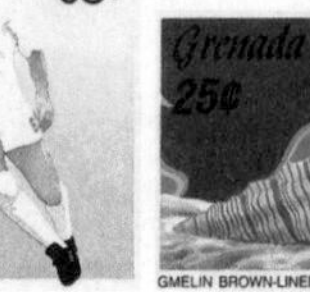

315 Player with Ball **316** Brown-lined Latirus

1986. World Cup Football Championship, Mexico. Multicoloured.
1489 50c. Type **315** 80 55
1490 70c. Player heading ball . . 1·00 1·00
1491 90c. Player controlling ball 1·50 1·50
1492 $4 Player controlling ball with right foot . . . . . 5·50 7·00
MS1493 103 × 71 mm. $5 Player tackling . . . . 4·25 5·00

1986. Appearance of Halley's Comet (1st issue). As T **151a** of Gambia. Multicoloured.
1494 5c. Clyde Tombaugh (astronomer) and Dudley Observatory, New York 40 40
1495 20c. N.A.S.A. – U.S.A.F. "X-24B" Space Shuttle prototype, 1973 . . . . . 50 30
1496 40c. German comet medal, 1618 . . . . 70 45
1497 $4 Destruction of Sodom and Gomorrah, 1949 B.C. 3·50 4·50
MS1498 102 × 70 mm. $5 Halley's Comet over Grenada . . . . . 6·50 7·00
See also Nos. 1533/7 and 1980/4.

1986. 60th Birthday of Queen Elizabeth II. As T **151b** of Gambia.
1499 2c. black and yellow 10 15
1500 $1.50 multicoloured 80 80
1501 $4 multicoloured . . . . . 1·60 2·50
MS1502 120 × 85 mm. $5 black and brown . . . . 1·75 3·25
DESIGNS: 2c. Princess Elizabeth in 1951; $1.50, Queen presenting trophy at polo match, Windsor, 1965; $4 at Epsom, Derby Day, 1977; $5 King George VI and family, 1939.

315a Goofy as Pitcher

1986. "Ameripex" International Stamp Exhibition, Chicago. Designs showing Walt Disney cartoon characters playing baseball. Multicoloured.
1503 1c. Type **315a** 10 10
1504 2c. Goofy as catcher 10 10
1505 3c. Mickey Mouse striking ball and Donald Duck as catcher 10 10
1506 4c. Huey forcing out Dewey 10 10
1507 5c. Chip n'Dale chasing flyball 10 10
1508 6c. Mickey Mouse, Donald Duck and Clarabelle in argument 10 10
1509 $2 Minnie Mouse and Donald Duck reading baseball rules . . . . . . 1·75 2·75
1510 $3 Ludwig von Drake as umpire with Goofy and Pete colliding . . . . . . 2·25 3·25
MS1511 Two sheets, each 126 × 101 mm. (a) $5 Donald Duck striking ball. (b) $5 Minnie and Mickey Mouse running between bases Set of 2 sheets 11·00 13·00

1986. Royal Wedding. As T **153b** of Gambia. Multicoloured.
1512 2c. Prince Andrew and Miss Sarah Ferguson 10 30
1513 $1.10 Prince Andrew . . . 70 80
1514 $4 Prince Andrew with H.M.S. "Brazen's" Westland Lynx helicopter 3·50 3·50
MS1515 88 × 88 mm. $5 Prince Andrew and Miss Sarah Ferguson (different) . . . . 4·50 5·00

1986. Sea Shells. Multicoloured.
1516 25c. Type **316** 45 25
1517 60c. Lamellose wentletrap 75 90
1518 70c. Turkey wing . . . . . 85 1·00
1519 $4 Rooster tail conch . . . 2·00 5·00
MS1520 110 × 75 mm. $5 Angular triton . . . . 2·75 6·00

317 "Lepiota roseolamellata" **318** Dove on Rifles and Mahatma Gandhi (Disarmament Week)

1986. Mushrooms. Multicoloured.
1521 10c. Type **317** 60 40
1522 60c. "Lentinus bertieri" . . 1·75 1·75
1523 $1 "Lentinus retinervis" . . 2·50 2·50
1524 $4 "Eccilia cystiophorus" 5·75 7·50
MS1525 127 × 100 mm. $5 "Cystolepiota eriophora" . . . 10·00 13·00

1986. World Cup Football Championship Winners, Mexico. Nos. 1489/92 optd **WINNERS Argentina 3 W. Germany 2.**
1526 50c. Type **315** 85 85
1527 70c. Player heading ball . . 1·00 1·00
1528 90c. Player controlling ball 1·40 1·60
1529 $4 Player controlling ball with right foot . . . . . 4·50 5·00
MS1530 101 × 71 mm. $5 Player tackling . . . . 3·50 4·50

1986. International Events. Multicoloured.
1531 60c. Type **318** 50 50
1532 $4 Hands passing olive branch and Martin Luther King (International Peace Year) (horiz) . . . . . . 1·50 3·00

1986. Appearance of Halley's Comet (2nd issue). Nos. 1494/7 optd with T **447a** of Ghana.
1533 5c. Clyde Tombaugh (astronomer) and Dudley Observatory, New York 60 60
1534 20c. N.A.S.A. – U.S.A.F. "X-24B" Space Shuttle prototype, 1973 . . . . . 85 60
1535 40c. German comet medal, 1618 . . . . 1·25 70
1536 $4 Destruction of Sodom and Gomorrah, 1949 B.C. 5·00 7·00
MS1537 102 × 70 mm. $5 Halley's Comet over Grenada . . . . . 3·50 4·25

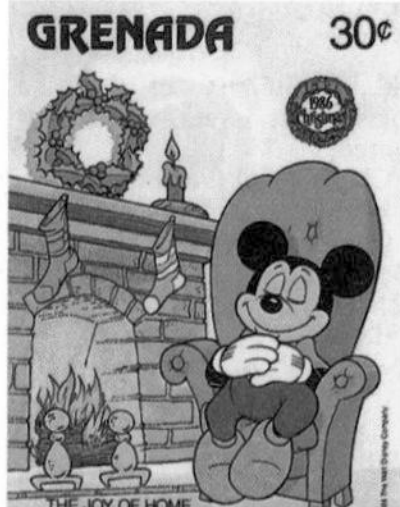

318a Mickey Mouse asleep in Armchair

1986. Christmas. Multicoloured.
1538 30c. Type **318a** 35 25
1539 45c. Young Mickey Mouse with Father Christmas . . 45 30
1540 60c. Donald Duck with toy telephone (horiz) 60 50
1541 70c. Pluto with pushcart (horiz) 70 70
1542 $1.10 Daisy Duck with doll (horiz) . . . . 1·00 1·25
1543 $2 Goofy as Father Christmas . . . . 1·75 2·00
1544 $2.50 Goofy singing carols at piano . . . . 2·00 2·50
1545 $3 Mickey Mouse, Donald Duck and nephew riding toy train (horiz) . . . . . 2·25 3·00
MS1546 Two sheets, each 127 × 101 mm. (a) $5 Donald Duck, Goofy and Mickey Mouse delivering presents (vert). (b) $5 Father Christmas playing toy piano Set of 2 sheets . . . . . 7·00 11·00

319 Cockerel and Hen

1986. Fauna and Flora. Multicoloured.
1547 10c. Type **319** 20 10
1548 30c. Fish-eating bat 35 20
1549 60c. Goat 55 45
1550 70c. Cow 60 50
1551 $1 Anthurium . . . . . . 1·50 1·25
1552 $1.10 Royal poinciana . . . 1·50 1·25
1553 $2 Frangipani . . . . . . 2·50 3·25
1554 $4 Orchid . . . . 8·50 9·50
MS1555 Two sheets, each 104 × 73 mm. (a) $5 Grenada landscape. (b) $5 Horse Set of 2 sheets . . . . 12·00 13·00

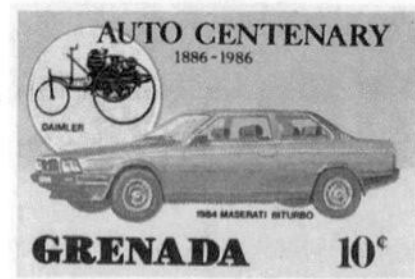

320 Maserati "Biturbo" (1984)

1986. Centenary of Motoring. Multicoloured.
1556 10c. Type **320** 25 25
1557 30c. AC "Cobra" (1960) . . 40 40
1558 60c. Corvette (1963) 60 60
1559 70c. Dusenberg "SJ7" (1932) 70 70
1560 90c. Porsche (1957) . . . . 85 1·00
1561 $1 Stoewer (1930) . . . . . 1·00 1·25
1562 $2 Volkswagen "Beetle" (1957) . . . . 1·60 2·00
1563 $3 Mercedes "600 Limo" (1963) . . . . 1·90 2·50
MS1564 Two sheets, each 106 × 77 mm. (a) $5 Stutz (1914). (b) $5 Packard (1941) Set of 2 sheets . . . . 5·50 7·00

321 Pole Vaulting **321a** Painting by Chagall

1986. Olympic Games, Seoul, South Korea (1988). Multicoloured.
1565 10c.+5c. Type **321** 10 30
1566 50c.+20c. Gymnastics . . . 35 60
1567 70c.+30c. Putting the shot 50 85
1568 $2+$1 High jumping . . . . 1·00 2·25
MS1569 80 × 100 mm. $3+$1 Swimming . . . . 1·50 3·25
The premiums on Nos. 1565/9 were to support the participation of the Grenada team.

1986. Birth Centenary of Marc Chagall (artist). Designs showing various paintings.
1570/1609 $1 × 40 multicoloured Set of 40 . . . . . . 24·00 26·00

MS1610 Ten sheets, each 110 × 95 mm. $5 × 10 multicoloured (each 104 × 89 mm). Imperf Set of 10 sheets . . . . 24·00 26·00

321b "Columbia", 1958

1987. America's Cup Yachting Championship. Multicoloured.
1611 10c. Type **321b** 25 20
1612 60c. "Resolute", 1920 . . . 55 60

1613 $1.10 "Endeavor", 1934 . . 85 1·25
1614 $4 "Rainbow", 1934 . . . . 1·75 3·50
MS1615 113×84 mm. $5 "Weatherly", 1962 . . . . . . 2·25 4·00

322 Virgin Mary and Outline Map of Grenada **323** Black Grouper

1987. 500th Anniv (1992) of Discovery of America by Christopher Columbus (1st issue). Multicoloured.
1616 10c. Type **322** 30 20
1617 30c. "Santa Maria", "Pinta" and "Nina" (horiz) . . . 80 35
1618 50c. Columbus and outline map of Grenada 90 45
1619 60c. Christopher Columbus 90 55
1620 90c. King Ferdinand and Queen Isabella of Spain (horiz) 90 80
1621 $1.10 Map of Antilles by Columbus . . . . 1·25 1·00
1622 $2 Caribs with sailing raft (horiz) . . . . 1·40 2·50
1623 $3 Columbus in the New World, 1493 (contemporary drawing) 1·60 2·50
MS1624 Two sheets, each 104×72 mm. (a) $5 Route map and Colombus' signature. (b) $5 Columbus carrying Christ Child Set of 2 sheets . . . . 5·00 7·50
See also Nos. 2051/5, 2091/9, 2222/30, 2389/95 and 2423/4.

322a Cornu's First Helicopter, 1907

1987. Milestones of Transportation. Multicoloured.
1625 10c. Type **322a** . . . . . . 1·25 65
1626 15c. "Monitor" and "Merrimack" (first battle between ironclad warships), 1862 . . . . . 1·25 65
1627 30c. LZ1 (first Zeppelin), 1900 . . . . 1·40 80
1628 50c. "Sirius" (first transatlantic paddle-steamer crossing), 1838 1·50 85
1629 60c. Steam locomotive on Trans-Siberian Railway (longest line) . . . . . 1·75 1·00
1630 70c. U.S.S "Enterprise" (largest aircraft carrier), 1960 . . . . 1·75 1·25
1631 90c. Blanchard and Jeffries' balloon (first balloon across English Channel), 1785 . . . . 1·75 1·40
1632 $1.50 U.S.S. "Holland I" (first steam-powered submarine), 1900 . . . . 2·50 2·50
1633 $2 "Oceanic I" (first luxury liner), 1871 . . . . . . 3·00 3·00
1634 $3 Lamborghini "Countach" (fastest commercial car), 1984 . . . . 3·25 3·50

1987. "Capex '87" International Stamp Exhibition, Toronto. Game Fishes. Multicoloured.
1635 10c. Type **323** 35 15
1636 30c. Blue marlin (horiz) . . 50 15
1637 60c. White marlin 70 55
1638 70c. Bigeye threshershark (horiz) 80 70
1639 $1 Bonefish (horiz) . . . . 1·10 1·00
1640 $1.10 Wahoo (horiz) . . . . 1·25 1·25
1641 $2 Sailfish (horiz) . . . . . 2·00 2·50
1642 $4 Albacore (horiz) . . . . 3·00 3·75
MS1643 Two sheets, each 100×70 mm. (a) $5 Yellow-finned tuna. (b) $5 Great barracuda (horiz) Set of 2 sheets . . . . 8·00 11·00

323a Computer Projections on Statue and Base

1987. Centenary of Statue of Liberty (2nd issue). Multicoloured.
1644 10c. Type **323a** 15 15
1645 25c. Statue and fireworks . . 20 15
1646 50c. Statue and fireworks (different) 35 35
1647 60c. Statue and boats (vert) 45 45
1648 70c. Computer projection of top of Statue 50 50
1649 $1 Rear view of Statue and fireworks (vert) 80 80
1650 $1.10 Aerial view of Statue (vert) . . . . 95 1·25
1651 $2 Statue and flotilla (vert) 2·00 2·25
1652 $4 "Queen Elizabeth 2" in New York Harbour (vert) 3·50 4·00

324 Alice and the Rabbit Hole

1987. 50th Anniv of First Full-Length Disney Cartoon Film. Nos. 1653/1706 show scenes from various films and No. **MS**1707 depict scenes from "Alice in Wonderland", "Cinderella", "Peter Pan", "Pinocchio", "Sleeping Beauty" and "Snow White and the Seven Dwarfs".
1653/1706 30c. × 54 multicoloured Set of 54 . . . . . 17·00 18·00
MS1707 Six sheets, each 127×102 mm. $5×6 multicoloured Set of 6 sheets 30·00 30·00

325 Isaac Newton holding Apple (Law of Gravity)

1987. Great Scientific Discoveries. Multicoloured.
1708 50c. Type **325** 85 85
1709 $1.10 John Jacob Berzelius and symbols of chemical elements . . . . 1·75 1·75
1710 $2 Robert Boyle (law of Pressure and Volume) . . 2·50 3·25
1711 $3 James Watt and drawing of steam engine . . . . 4·75 5·00
MS1712 105×75 mm. $5 "Voyager" (experimental aircraft) and Wright glider No. IV . . . . 3·00 4·00
No. 1711 is inscribed "RUDOLF DIESEL" and No. **MS**1712 "Flyer I", both in error.

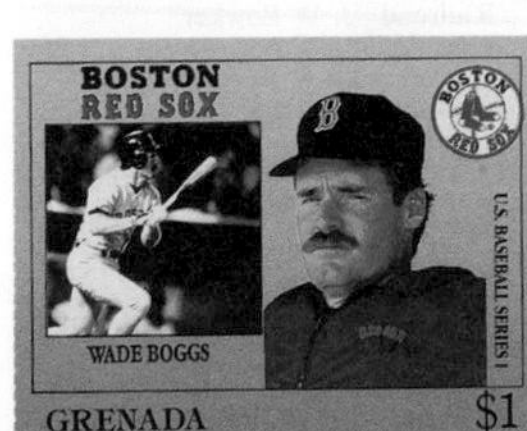

326 Wade Boggs (Boston Red Sox)

1987. All-star Baseball Game, Oakland, California. Sheet 114×82 mm, containing T **326** and similar horiz design. Multicoloured.
MS1713 $1 Type **326**; $1 Eric Davis (Cincinnati Reds) . . . . . . 75 1·50

1987. 60th Anniv of International Social Security Association. Nos. 1413, 1418 and 1423 optd **INTERNATIONAL SOCIAL SECURITY ASSOCIATION** and emblem.
1714 10c. Hibiscus 10 15
1715 50c. Amaryllis 25 35
1716 $3 Shrimp plant . . . . . . 1·40 2·25

327a Independance Hall, Philadelphia

1987. Bicentenary of U.S. Constitution. Mult.
1717 15c. Type **327a** 10 10
1718 50c. Benjamin Franklin (Pennsylvania delegate) 25 35
1719 60c. State Seal, Massachusetts (horiz) . . 25 35
1720 $4 Robert Morris (Pennsylvania delegate) 1·75 2·75
MS1721 105×75 mm. $5 James Madison (Virginia delegate) (vert) 1·50 3·50

GRENADA 15c

328 Goofy in "The Shadow" **329** "The Annunciation" (Fra Angelico)

1987. "Hafnia '87" International Stamp Exhibition. Walt Disney cartoon characters in scenes from Hans Christian Andersen's fairy tales. Multicoloured.
1722 25c. Type **328** 50 30
1723 30c. Mother Stork and brood in "The Storks" . . 50 30
1724 50c. King Richard, Robin Hood and Little John (from Robin Hood) in "The Emperor's New Clothes" 75 55
1725 60c. Goofy and Pluto in "The Tinderbox" 75 55
1726 70c. Daisy and Donald Duck in "The Shepherdess and the Chimney Sweep" 80 70
1727 $1.50 Mickey and Minnie Mouse in "The Little Mermaid" . . . . 1·60 1·75
1728 $3 Clarabelle and Goofy in "The Princess and the Pea" . . . . 2·50 3·50
1729 $4 Minnie Mouse and Pegleg Pete in "The Marsh King's Daughter" 2·50 3·50
MS1730 Two sheets, each 127×102 mm. (a) $5 Goofy in "The Flying Trunk". (b) $5 Goofy as "The Sandman" Set of 2 sheets 12·00 14·00

1987. Christmas. Religious Paintings. Multicoloured.
1731 15c. Type **329** 55 10
1732 30c. "The Annunciation" (attr. Hubert van Eyck) 90 30
1733 60c. "The Adoration of the Magi" (Januarius Zick) 1·75 1·40
1734 $4 "The Flight into Egypt" (Gerard David) . . . . . 5·50 7·00
MS1735 99×75 mm. $5 "The Circumcision" (Giovanni Bellini studio) . . . . 7·00 8·00

330 T. Albert Marryshow

1988. Birth Centenary of T. Albert Marryshow (nationalist).
1736 **330** 25c. brown, lt brn & red 30 30

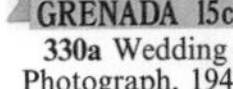

330a Wedding Photograph, 1947 **332** Scout fishing from Boat

331 Goofy and Daisy Duck lighting Olympic Torch, Olympia

1988. Royal Ruby Wedding. Multicoloured.
1737 **330a** 15c. brown, black & bl 45 10
1738 – 50c. multicoloured . . . 80 50
1739 – $1 brown and black . . 1·40 1·00
1740 – $4 multicoloured . . . 3·25 4·00
MS1741 76×100 mm. $5 multicoloured . . . . 2·25 3·25

DESIGNS: 50c. Queen Elizabeth II with Prince Charles and Princess Anne, c. 1955; $1 Queen with Princess Anne, c. 1957; $4 Queen Elizabeth (from photo by Tim Graham), 1980; $5 Princess Elizabeth in wedding dress, 1947.

1988. Olympic Games, Seoul. Designs showing Walt Disney cartoon characters. Multicoloured.
1742 1c. Type **331** 10 10
1743 2c. Donald and Daisy Duck carrying Olympic torch 10 10
1744 3c. Donald Duck, Goofy and Mickey Mouse carrying flags of U.S., Korea and Spain 10 10
1745 4c. Donald Duck releasing doves 10 10
1746 5c. Mickey Mouse flying with rocket belt 10 10
1747 10c. Morty and Ferdie carrying banner with Olympic motto 10 10
1748 $6 Donald Duck, Minnie Mouse and Hodori the Tiger (mascot of Seoul Games) . . . . 6·00 5·50
1749 $7 Pluto. Hodori and old post office, Seoul . . . . 6·00 5·50
MS1750 Two sheets, each 127×101 mm. (a) $5 Mickey Mouse taking athlete's oath. (b) $5 Donald and Daisy Duck as athletes at Closing Ceremony Set of 2 sheets . . . . 8·50 10·00

1988. Stamp Exhibitions. Nos. 1631/4 optd.
1751 90c. Blanchard and Jeffries' balloon, 1785 (optd **OLYMPHILEX '88**, Seoul) . . . . 1·25 90
1752 $1.50 U.S.S "Holland I", 1900 (optd **INDEPENDENCE 40**, Israel) . . . . 1·75 1·50
1753 $2 "Oceanic I", 1871 (optd **FINLANDIA 88**, Helsinki) . . . . 2·25 2·25
1754 $3 Lamborghini "Countach", 1984 (optd **PRAGA 88**, Prague) . . . 2·75 2·75

1988. World Scout Jamboree, Australia. Mult.
1755 20c. Type **332** 40 15
1756 70c. Scouts hiking through forest (horiz) . . . . . . 1·00 1·00
1757 90c. Practising first aid (horiz) . . . . 1·40 1·40
1758 $3 Shooting rapids in inflatable canoe . . . . . 3·00 3·75
MS1759 114×80 mm. $5 Scout with koala . . . . 2·10 3·00

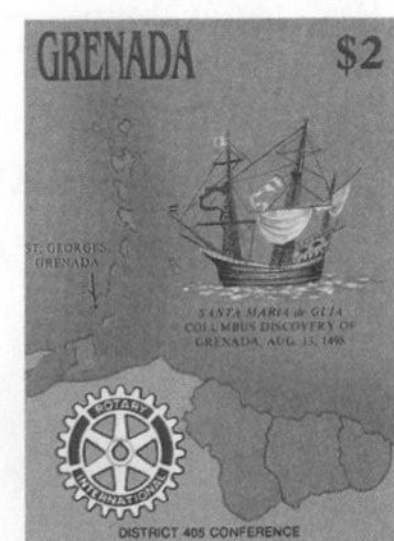

333 "Santa Maria de Guia" (Columbus), 1498 and Map of Rotary District

1988. Rotary District 405 Conference, St. George's. Multicoloured.
1760 $2 Type **333** . . . . . . 80 1·00
MS1761 133×90 mm. $10 Rotary emblem (horiz) . . . . 4·25 6·00

GRENADA $2

334 Roseate Tern **335** Vauxhall Type "OE 30/98", 1925

1988. Birds. Multicoloured.
1762 10c. Type **334** 80 30
1763 25c. Laughing gull . . . . 1·00 30
1764 50c. Osprey . . . . 1·60 70
1765 60c. Rose-breasted grosbeak 1·60 70
1766 90c. American purple gallinule ("Purple Gallinule") . . . . 1·60 90
1767 $1.10 White-tailed tropic bird . . . . 1·60 1·00

1768 $3 Blue-faced booby . . . . 2·25 2·75
1769 $4 Common shoveler . . . 2·25 3·00
MS1770 Two sheets, each 100×71 mm. (a) $5 Belted kingfisher. (b) $5 Grenada flycatcher ("Rusty-tailed Flycatcher") Set of 2 sheets . . 7·00 9·00

1988. Cars. Multicoloured.
1771 $2 Type **335** . . . . . . 1·25 1·25
1772 $2 Wills "Sainte Claire", 1926 . . . . 1·25 1·25
1773 $2 Bucciali, 1928 . . . . . 1·25 1·25
1774 $2 Irving Napier "Golden Arrow", 1929 . . . . . 1·25 1·25
1775 $2 Studebaker "President", 1930 . . . . 1·25 1·25
1776 $2 Thomas "Flyer", 1907 1·25 1·25
1777 $2 Isotta-Franschini "Tipo J", 1908 . . . . . . 1·25 1·25
1778 $2 Fiat 10/14HP, 1910 . . 1·25 1·25
1779 $2 Mercer "Type 35 Raceabout", 1911 . . . . 1·25 1·25
1780 $2 Marmon "Model 34 Cloverleaf", 1917 . . . . 1·25 1·25
1781 $2 Tatra "Type 77", 1934 1·25 1·25
1782 $2 Rolls-Royce "Phantom III", 1938 . . . . 1·25 1·25
1783 $2 Studebaker "Champion Starlight", 1947 . . . . . 1·25 1·25
1784 $2 Porsche "Gmund", 1948 1·25 1·25
1785 $2 Tucker, 1948 . . . . . . 1·25 1·25
1786 $2 Peerless "V-16", 1931 . . 1·25 1·25
1787 $2 Minerva "AL", 1931 . . 1·25 1·25
1788 $2 Reo "Royale", 1953 . . 1·25 1·25
1789 $2 Pierce Arrow "Silver Arrow", 1933 . . . . . 1·25 1·25
1790 $2 Hupmobile "Aerodynamic", 1934 . . 1·25 1·25
1791 $2 Peugeot "404", 1965 . . 1·25 1·25
1792 $2 Ford "Capri", 1969 . . 1·25 1·25
1793 $2 Ferrari "312T", 1975 . . 1·25 1·25
1794 $2 Lotus "T-79", 1978 . . 1·25 1·25
1795 $2 Williams-Cosworth "FW07", 1979 . . . . . 1·25 1·25
1796 $2 H.R.G. "1500 Sports", 1948 . . . . 1·25 1·25
1797 $2 Crosley "Hotshot", 1949 1·25 1·25
1798 $2 Volvo "PV444", 1955 . . 1·25 1·25
1799 $2 Maserati "Tipo 61", 1960 1·25 1·25
1800 $2 Saab "96", 1963 . . . . 1·25 1·25

1988. 500th Birth Anniv of Titian (artist). As T **166a** of Gambia. Multicoloured.
1801 10c. "Lavinia Vecellio" . . 10 10
1802 20c. "Portrait of a Man" . . 10 10
1803 25c. "Andrea de Franceschi" 10 15
1804 90c. "Head of a Soldier" . . 40 45
1805 $1 "Man with a Flute" . . 45 50
1806 $2 "Lucrezia and Tarquinius" . . . . . . 80 1·00
1807 $3 "Duke of Mantua with Dog" . . . . 1·25 1·60
1808 $4 "La Bella di Tiziano" . . 1·60 2·00
MS1809 Two sheets, each 110×95 mm. (a) $5 "Allegory of Alfonso D'Avalos (detail). (b) $5 "Fall of Man" (detail) (horiz) Set of 2 sheets . . . . 4·25 5·50

336 "Graf Zeppelin" over Chicago World's Fair, 1933

338 Pineapple

337 Tasmanian Wolf, Mickey Mouse and Pluto

1988. Airships. Multicoloured.
1810 10c. Type **336** 50 20
1811 15c. LZ-1 over Lake Constance, 1901 (horiz) 60 25
1812 25c. "Washington" (balloon) and "George Washington Curtis" (balloon barge), 1862 . . . . 70 30
1813 45c. "Hindenburg" and Maybach "Zeppelin" car (horiz) 80 40
1814 50c. Goodyear Aerospace airship in Statue of Liberty Centenary Race, 1986 . . . . 80 40
1815 60c. "Hindenburg" over Statue of Liberty, 1937 (horiz) 90 50
1816 90c. Heinkel biplane docking experiment with "Hindenburg", 1936 (horiz) . . . . 1·40 80
1817 $2 "Hindenburg" over Olympic Stadium, Berlin, 1936 . . . . 2·00 2·00
1818 $3 "Hindenburg" over Christ of the Andes Monument, 1937 . . . . 2·50 2·50
1819 $4 "Hindenburg" and "Bremen" (liner), 1936 (horiz) . . . . 2·75 2·75
MS1820 Two sheets. (a) 75×95 mm. $5 LZ-127 "Graf Zeppelin", 1930 (horiz). (b) 95×75 mm. $5 LZ-129 "Hindenburg", 1935 (horiz) Set of 2 sheets . . . . 4·75 5·50

1988. "Sydpex '88". National Stamp Exhibition, Sydney and 60th Birthday of Mickey Mouse. Multicoloured.
1821 1c. Type **337** 10 10
1822 2c. Mickey Mouse feeding wallabies 10 10
1823 3c. Mickey Mouse and Goofy with kangaroo . . 10 10
1824 4c. Mickey and Minnie Mouse riding emus . . . 10 10
1825 5c. Mickey and Minnie Mouse with wombat . . . 10 10
1826 10c. Mickey Mouse and Donald Duck watching platypus 10 10
1827 $5 Mickey Mouse and Goofy photographing blue-winged kookaburra 5·50 5·50
1828 $6 Mickey Mouse and Koala on map of Australia . . . . 5·50 5·50
MS1829 Two sheets, each 127×102 mm. (a) $5 Mickey Mouse with birthday cake. (b) $5 Mickey and Minnie Mouse with rainbow lories Set of 2 sheets 12·00 13·00

1988. 10th Anniv of International Fund for Agricultural Development. Multicoloured.
1830 25c. Type **338** 35 15
1831 75c. Bananas 70 60
1832 $3 Mace and nutmeg (horiz) 2·50 2·75

339 Lignum Vitae

1988. Flowering Trees and Shrubs. Mult.
1833 15c. Type **339** 15 15
1834 25c. Saman 20 15
1835 35c. Red frangipani 25 20
1836 45c. Flowering maple . . . 30 25
1837 60c. Yellow poui 40 40
1838 $1 Wild chestnut 60 70
1839 $3 Mountain immortelle . . 1·50 2·25
1840 $4 Queen of flowers . . . . 1·75 2·50
MS1841 Two sheets, each 117×88 mm. (a) $5 Flamboyant. (b) $5 Orchid tree Set of 2 sheets 4·25 5·50

340 Mickey Mantle (New York Yankees)

1988. Major League Baseball Players (1st series). Designs showing portraits or league emblems.
1842/1922 30c.×81 multicoloured Set of 81 . . . . . . 12·00 14·00

340a Donald Duck's Nephew on Mantelpiece

1988. Christmas. "Mickey's Christmas Eve". Designs showing Walt Disney cartoon characters. Multicoloured.
1923 $1 Type **340a** 65 65
1924 $1 Goofy with string of popcorn 65 65
1925 $1 Chip'n'Dale decorating Christmas tree 65 65
1926 $1 Father Christmas in sleigh 65 65
1927 $1 Donald's nephew with stocking 65 65
1928 $1 Donald's nephew unpacking decorations . . 65 65
1929 $1 Donald Duck with present 65 65
1930 $1 Mickey Mouse with present 65 65
MS1931 Two sheets, each 127×102 mm. (a) $5 Ferdie leaving drink for Father Christmas. (b) $5 Mordie and Ferdie asleep Set of 2 sheets . . 7·00 8·50

341 Tina Turner

1988. Entertainers. Multicoloured.
1932 10c. Type **341** 30 20
1933 25c. Lionel Ritchie 30 20
1934 45c. Whitney Houston . . . 45 30
1935 60c. Joan Armatrading . . . 60 45
1936 75c. Madonna 90 60
1937 $1 Elton John . . . . . . 1·00 80
1938 $3 Bruce Springsteen . . . 2·00 2·75
1939 $4 Bob Marley . . . . . . 4·00 4·00
MS1940 115×155 mm. 55c.×2 Yoko Minamino; $1×2 Yoko Minamino (different) . . . . . 1·90 2·75
No. 1935 is incorrectly inscribed "JOAN AMMERTRADING".

342 Atlantic Railway No. 2, 1889, Canada

343 Women's Long Jump (Jackie Joyner-Kersee, U.S.A.)

1989. North American Railway Locomotives. Mult.
1941 $2 Type **342** . . . . . . 1·25 1·25
1942 $2 Virginia & Truckee Railroad "J. W Bowker" type, 1875, U.S.A. . . . . 1·25 1·25
1943 $2 Philadelphia & Reading Railway "Ariel", 1872, U.S.A. . . . . 1·25 1·25
1944 $2 Chicago & Rock Island Railroad "America" type, 1867, U.S.A. . . . . . . 1·25 1·25
1945 $2 Lehigh Valley Railroad Consolidation No. 63, 1866, U.S.A. . . . . . . 1·25 1·25
1946 $2 Great Western Railway "Scotia", 1860, Canada 1·25 1·25
1947 $2 Grand Trunk Railway Class "Birkenhead", 1854, Canada . . . . 1·25 1·25
1948 $2 Camden & Amboy Railroad "Monster", 1837, U.S.A. . . . . . . 1·25 1·25
1949 $2 Baltimore & Ohio Railroad Class "Grasshopper", 1834, U.S.A. . . . . 1·25 1·25
1950 $2 Peter Cooper's "Tom Thumb", 1829, Baltimore & Ohio Railroad, U.S.A. 1·25 1·25
1951 $2 United Railways of Yucatan "Yucatan", 1925, Mexico . . . . 1·25 1·25
1952 $2 Canadian National Railways Class T2, 1924 1·25 1·25
1953 $2 St. Louis–San Francisco Railroad Class "Light Mikado", 1919, U.S.A. 1·25 1·25
1954 $2 Atlantic Coast Line Railroad Class "Light Pacific", 1919, U.S.A. . . 1·25 1·25

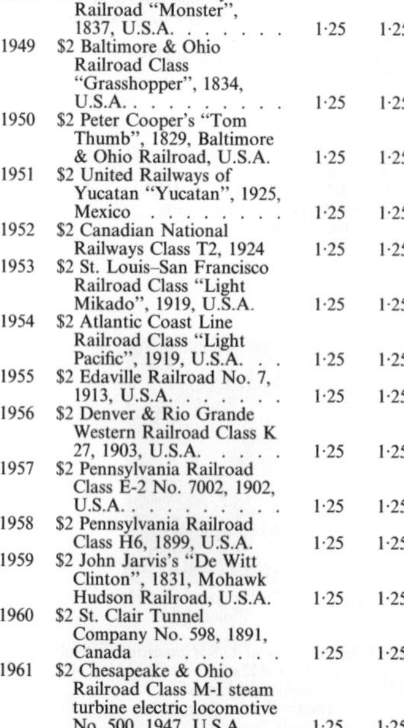

1955 $2 Edaville Railroad No. 7, 1913, U.S.A. . . . . . 1·25 1·25
1956 $2 Denver & Rio Grande Western Railroad Class K 27, 1903, U.S.A. . . . . 1·25 1·25
1957 $2 Pennsylvania Railroad Class E-2 No. 7002, 1902, U.S.A. . . . . 1·25 1·25
1958 $2 Pennsylvania Railroad Class H6, 1899, U.S.A. 1·25 1·25
1959 $2 John Jarvis's "De Witt Clinton", 1831, Mohawk Hudson Railroad, U.S.A. 1·25 1·25
1960 $2 St. Clair Tunnel Company No. 598, 1891, Canada . . . . 1·25 1·25
1961 $2 Chesapeake & Ohio Railroad Class M-I steam turbine electric locomotive No. 500, 1947, U.S.A. . . 1·25 1·25
1962 $2 Rutland Railroad steam locomotive No. 93, 1946, U.S.A. . . . . 1·25 1·25
1963 $2 Pennsylvania Railroad Class T1, 1942, U.S.A. . . 1·25 1·25
1964 $2 Chesapeake & Ohio Railroad Class H-8, 1942, U.S.A. . . . . 1·25 1·25
1965 $2 Atchison, Topeka & Santa Fe Railway Model FT diesel, 1941, U.S.A. 1·25 1·25
1966 $2 Gulf, Mobile & Ohio Railroad Models S-I and S-2 diesels, 1940, U.S.A. 1·25 1·25
1967 $2 New York, New Haven & Hartford Railroad Class 15, 1937, U.S.A. . . 1·25 1·25
1968 $2 Seaboard Air Line Railroad Class R, 1936, U.S.A. . . . . 1·25 1·25
1969 $2 Newfoundland Railway Class R-2, 1930 . . . . . 1·25 1·25
1970 $2 Canadian National Railway diesel No. 9000, 1928 . . . . 1·25 1·25

1989. Olympic Gold Medal Winners, Seoul (1988). Multicoloured.
1971 10c. Type **343** 30 20
1972 25c. Women's Singles Tennis (Steffi Graf, West Germany) 70 35
1973 45c. Men's 1500 m (Peter Rono, Kenya) 80 40
1974 75c. Men's 1000 m single kayak (Greg Barton, U.S.A.) 90 60
1975 $1 Women's team foil (Italy) 1·10 75
1976 $2 Women's 100 m freestyle swimming (Kristin Otto, East Germany) . . . . . 2·25 2·25
1977 $3 Men's still rings gymnastics (Holger Behrendt, East Germany) 2·50 2·75
1978 $4 Synchronized swimming pair (Japan) . . . . . . 2·75 3·00
MS1979 Two sheets, each 76×100 mm. (a) $6 Olympic flame. (b) $6 Runner with Olympic torch Set of 2 sheets . . . . . 8·50 9·50

344 Nebulae

1989. Appearance of Halley's Comet (1986) (3rd issue).
1980 **344** 25c.+5c. multicoloured 70 80
1981 – 75c.+5c. black & green 1·10 1·40
1982 – 90c.+5c. multicoloured 1·25 1·60
1983 – $2+5c. multicoloured . . 1·75 2·50
MS1984 111×78 mm. $5+5c. multicoloured. Imperf . . . . 4·00 5·00
DESIGNS: 75c.+5c. Marine astronomical experiments; 90c.+5c. Moon's surface; $2+5c. Edmond Halley, Sir Isaac Newton and his book "Principia". (102×69 mm)—$5+5c. 17th-century warships and astrological signs.

1989. Japanese Art. Paintings by Hiroshige. As T **177a** of Gambia. Multicoloured.
1985 10c. "Shinagawa on Edo Bay" 30 20
1986 25c. "Pine Trees on the Road to Totsuka" 40 30
1987 60c. "Kanagawa on Edo Bay" 60 50
1988 75c. "Crossing Banyu River to Hiratsuka" 65 55
1989 $1 "Windy Shore at Odawara" 80 70
1990 $2 "Snow-Covered Post Station of Mishima" . . . 1·40 1·75
1991 $3 "Full Moon at Fuchu" 1·60 2·00
1992 $4 "Crossing the Stream at Okitsu" . . . . 2·25 2·50
MS1993 Two sheets, each 102×76 mm. (a) $5 "Mountain Pass at Nissaka". (b) $5 "Mt Uzu at Okabe" Set of 2 sheets . . . 4·25 5·50

345 Great Blue Heron

1989. Birds. Multicoloured.
1994 5c. Type **345** . . . . . . 90 1·00
1995a 10c. Green-backed heron ("Green Heron") 90 70
1996a 15c. Ruddy turnstone . . . 1·00 75
1997a 25c. Blue-winged teal . . . 1·10 30
1998a 35c. Little ringed plover ("Ring-necked Plover") (vert) . . . . 1·25 30
1999a 45c. Green-throated carib ("Emerald-throated Hummingbird") (vert) 1·25 40
2000a 50c. Rufous-breasted hermit ("Hairy Hermit") (vert) . . . . 1·40 45
2001a 60c. Lesser Antillean bullfinch (vert) . . . . . 1·50 65
2002a 75c. Brown pelican (vert) 1·75 75
2003a $1 Black-crowned night heron (vert) . . . . . . 2·00 1·00
2004a $3 American kestrel ("Sparrow Hawk") (vert) 3·00 3·25

2005a $5 Barn swallow (vert) 4·00 4·75
2006 $10 Red-billed tropic bird (vert) 6·00 8·50
2007 $20 Barn owl (vert) 12·00 15·00

345a Scotland Player

1989. World Cup Football Championship, Italy (1990) (1st issue). Multicoloured.
2008 10c. Type **345a** 40 20
2009 25c. England and Brazil players 50 30
2010 60c. Paolo Rossi (Italy) 75 55
2011 75c. Jairzinho (Brazil) 90 70
2012 $1 Sweden striker 1·10 90
2013 $2 Pele (Brazil) 2·25 2·00
2014 $3 Mario Kempes (Argentina) 3·00 2·75
2015 $4 Pat Jennings (Northern Ireland) 3·25 3·00
MS2016 Two sheets. (a) 70 × 93 mm. $6 Players jumping for ball. (b) 82 × 71 mm. $6 Goalkeeper Set of 2 sheets 8·50 10·00
See also Nos. 2174/8 and **MS**2179.

346 Xebec and Sugar Cane

1989. "Philexfrance '89" International Stamp Exhibition, Paris. Designs showing French sailing vessels and plantation crops. Mult.
2017 25c. Type **346** 1·00 30
2018 75c. Lugger and cotton 1·60 85
2019 $1 Full-rigged ship and cocoa 1·75 1·10
2020 $4 Ketch and coffee 3·50 5·50
MS2021 114 × 70 mm. $6 "View of Fort and Town of St. George, 1779" (105 × 63 mm). Imperf 5·50 7·00

347 Alan Shepard and "Freedom 7" Spacecraft, 1961 (first American in Space)

1989. 20th Anniv of First Manned Landing on Moon. Multicoloured.
2022 15c. Type **347** 70 40
2023 35c. "Friendship 7" spacecraft, 1962 (first manned earth orbit) 90 55
2024 45c. "Apollo 8" orbiting Moon, 1968 (first manned lunar orbit) 1·00 65
2025 70c. "Apollo 15" lunar rover, 1972 1·50 85
2026 $1 "Apollo 11" emblem and lunar module "Eagle" on Moon, 1969 1·75 1·10
2027 $2 "Gemini 8" and "Agena" rocket, 1966 (first space docking) 3·00 2·25
2028 $3 Edward White in space, 1965 (first U.S. space walk) 3·25 3·00
2029 $4 "Apollo 7" emblem 3·75 3·50
MS2030 Two sheets, each 101 × 71 mm. (a) $5 Moon and track of "Apollo 11", 1969. (b) $5 Armstrong and Aldrin raising U.S. flag on Moon, 1969 Set of 2 sheets 12·00 10·00

348 "Hygrocybe occidentalis" **349** Y.W.C.A. Logo and Grenada Scenery

1989. Fungi. Multicoloured.
2031 15c. Type **348** 50 40
2032 40c. "Marasmius haematocephalus" 65 55
2033 50c. "Hygrocybe hypohaemacta" 75 65
2034 70c. "Lepiota pseudoignicolor" 1·00 90
2035 90c. "Cookeina tricholoma" 1·25 1·25
2036 $1.10 "Leucopaxillus gracillimus" 1·50 1·50
2037 $2.25 "Hygrocybe nigrescens" 2·75 3·00
2038 $4 "Clathrus crispus" 3·75 4·00
MS2039 Two sheets, each 57 × 70 mm. (a) $6 "Mycena holoporphyra". (b) $6 "Xeromphalina tenuipes" Set of 2 sheets 12·00 13·00

1989. Centenary of Young Women's Christian Association. Multicoloured.
2040 50c. Type **349** 45 45
2041 75c. Y.W.C.A. logo and town (horiz) 80 80

350 "Historis odius"

1989. Butterflies. Multicoloured.
2042 6c. Type **350** 30 30
2043 30c. "Marpesia petreus" 55 55
2044 40c. "Danaus gilippus" 60 60
2045 60c. "Dione juno" 80 80
2046 $1.10 "Agraulis vanillae" 1·25 1·25
2047 $1.25 "Danaus plexippus" 1·50 1·50
2048 $4 "Papilio androgeus" 3·25 3·25
2049 $5 "Dryas julia" 3·25 3·25
MS2050 Two sheets, each 87 × 115 mm. (a) $6 "Anartia jatrophae". (b) $6 "Strymon simaethis" Set of 2 sheets 9·50 11·00

351 Amerindian Hieroglyph

1989. 500th Anniv (1992) of Discovery of America by Columbus (2nd issue). Designs showing different hieroglyphs.
2051 **351** 45c. brown, black & blue 80 50
2052 – 60c. brown, black & grn 90 60
2053 – $1 brown, black and violet 1·60 1·00
2054 – $4 dp brown, black & brn 4·25 4·75
MS2055 74 × 86 mm. $6 brown, black and red 4·00 5·50

352 Amos leaving Home

1989. "World Stamp Expo '89" International Stamp Exhibition, Washington. Designs showing Walt Disney cartoon characters in scenes from "Ben and Me". Multicoloured.
2056 1c. Type **352** 10 10
2057 2c. Meeting of Benjamin Franklin and Amos 10 10
2058 3c. The Franklin stove 10 10
2059 4c. Ben and Amos with bi-focals 10 10
2060 5c. Amos on page of "Pennsylvania Gazette" 10 10
2061 6c. Ben working printing press 10 10
2062 10c. Conducting experiment with electricity 10 10
2063 $5 Ben disembarking in England 5·00 5·50
2064 $6 Ben with Document of Agreement 5·50 6·00
MS2065 Two sheets, each 127 × 101 mm. (a) $6 Benjamin Franklin teaching (vert). (b) $6 Signatories of Declaration of Independence Set of 2 sheets 8·00 10·00

352a "Christ in the House of Mary and Martha"

1990. Christmas. Paintings by Rubens. Multicoloured.
2066 20c. Type **352a** 50 25
2067 35c. "The Circumcision" 65 40
2068 60c. "Trinity adored by Duke of Mantua and Family" 1·00 65
2069 $2 "Holy Family with St. Francis" 2·75 2·75
2070 $3 "The Ildefonso Altarpiece" 3·25 3·50
2071 $4 "Madonna and Child with Garland and Putti" 3·75 4·00
MS2072 Two sheets, each 70 × 95 mm. (a) $5 "Adoration of the Magi". (b) $5 "Virgin and Child adored by Angels" Set of 2 sheets 7·50 9·00

353 Alexander Graham Bell and Early Telephone System (150th anniv of invention)

1990. Anniversaries. Multicoloured.
2073 10c. Type **353** 30 20
2074 25c. George Washington and Capitol (bicentenary of presidential inauguration) 30 20
2075 35c. Shakespeare and birthplace, Stratford (425th birth anniv) 1·50 35
2076 75c. Nehru and Gandhi (birth cent of Nehru) 3·50 1·50
2077 $1 Dr. Hugo Eckener, Ferdinand von Zeppelin and airship "Graf Zeppelin" (80th anniv of first passenger Zeppelin) 2·00 1·25
2078 $2 Charlie Chaplin (birth cent) 5·00 3·00
2079 $3 Container ship in Hamburg Harbour (800th anniv) 2·75 3·50
2080 $4 Friedrich Ebert (first President) and Heidelberg gate (70th anniv of German Republic) 2·75 3·50
MS2081 Two sheets, each 100 × 72 mm. (a) $6 13th-century ships in Hamburg Harbour (vert) (800th anniv). (b) $6 Concorde (20th anniv of first test flight) Set of 2 sheets 8·50 10·00
No. 2080 is inscribed "40th Anniversary of German Republic" in error.

354 "Odontoglossum triumphans" **354a** "Marpesia petreus"

1990. "EXPO '90" International Garden and Greenery Exhibition, Osaka. Caribbean Orchids. Multicoloured.
2082 1c. Type **354** 10 10
2083 25c. "Oncidium splendidum" 30 20
2084 60c. "Laelia anceps" 60 60
2085 75c. "Cattleya trianaei" 75 75
2086 $1 "Odontoglossum rossii" 1·00 1·00
2087 $2 "Brassia gireoudiana" 1·75 1·75
2088 $3 "Cattleya dowiana" 2·25 2·25
2089 $4 "Sobralia macrantha" 2·50 2·50
MS2090 Two sheets, each 97 × 68 mm. (a) $6 "Oncidium lanceanum". (b) $6 "Laelia rubescens" Set of 2 sheets 8·50 9·50

1990. 500th Anniv (1992) of Discovery of America by Columbus (3rd issue). New World Natural History—Butterflies. Multicoloured.
2091 15c. Type **354a** 65 20
2092 25c. "Junonia evarete" 80 25
2093 75c. "Siproeta stelenes" 1·40 70
2094 90c. "Historis odius" 1·60 85
2095 $1 "Mestra cana" 1·60 90
2096 $2 "Biblis hyperia" 2·50 2·75
2097 $3 "Dryas julia" 3·00 3·50
2098 $4 "Anartia amathea" 3·00 3·75
MS2099 Two sheets, each 101 × 69 mm. (a) $6 "Pseudolycaena marsyas". (b) $6 "Phoebis philea" Set of 2 sheets 12·00 13·00

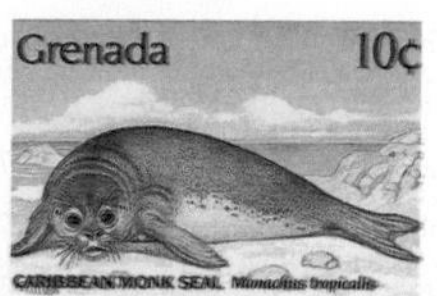

354b Caribbean Monk Seal

1990. Local Fauna. Multicoloured.
2100 10c. Type **354b** 50 30
2101 15c. Little brown bat 60 30
2102 45c. Brown rat 70 50
2103 60c. Common rabbit 80 60
2104 $1 Water opossum 1·25 95
2105 $2 White-nosed ichneumon 1·75 1·75
2106 $3 Little big-eared bat (vert) 2·25 2·50
2107 $4 Mouse opossum 2·25 2·50
MS2108 Two sheets, each 107 × 80 mm. (a) $6 Common rabbit (different). (b) $6 Water opossum (different) Set of 2 sheets 8·50 10·00

354c British Tanks during Operation Battleaxe, 1941

1990. 50th Anniv of Second World War. Mult.
2109 25c. Type **354c** 30 30
2110 35c. Allied tank in southern France, 1944 40 40
2111 45c. U.S. forces landing on Guadalcanal, 1942 45 45
2112 50c. U.S. attack in New Guinea, 1943 50 50
2113 60c. Hoisting U.S. flag on Leyte, Phillippines, 1944 60 60
2114 75c. U.S. tanks entering Cologne, 1945 75 75
2115 $1 Anzio offensive, 1944 95 95
2116 $2 Battle of the Bismarck Sea, 1943 1·75 1·75
2117 $3 U.S.S. "Langley" and U.S.S. "Ticonderoga" (aircraft carriers), 1944 2·25 2·25
2118 $4 Focke Wulf Fw 190A fighter attacking Salerno landing, 1943 2·50 2·50
MS2119 111 × 83 mm. $6 German "U-30" submarine, 1939 3·50 4·00

1990. "Stamp World London '90" International Stamp Exhibition (1st issue). As T **193** of Gambia, but horiz showing Walt Disney cartoon characters and British trains.
2120 5c. Mickey Mouse driving S.R. "King Arthur" class locomotive, 1925 30 10
2121 10c. Mickey and Minnie Mouse with "Puffing Billy", 1813 30 10
2122 20c. Mickey Mouse with Pluto pulling Durham colliery wagon, 1765 50 15
2123 45c. Mickey Mouse timing L.N.E.R. locomotive No. 2509 "Silver Link", 1935 80 25
2124 $1 Mickey Mouse and Donald Duck with locomotive No. 60149 "Amadis", 1948 1·75 1·00
2125 $2 Goofy and Mickey Mouse with Liverpool & Manchester Railway locomotive, 1830 2·50 2·75
2126 $4 Goofy and Donald Duck with Great Northern locomotive No. 1, 1870 3·25 4·00
2127 $5 Mickey Mouse and Gyro the Mechanic with Advanced Passenger Train, 1972 3·25 4·00
MS2128 Two sheets, each 127 × 101 mm. (a) $6 Minnie Mouse, Donald and Daisy Duck in Trevithick's Catch-Me-Who-Can, 1808 (horiz). (b) $6 Donald Duck and Locomotion, 1825 Set of 2 sheets 12·00 13·00
No. 2126 is inscribed "Flying Scotsman" in error.
See also No. **MS**2146.

355 U.S. Paratroop Drop over Grenada

1990. 50th Anniv of United States Airborne Forces.

2129 75c. Type **355** . . . . . . 1·25 1·25
MS2130 Two sheets, each 115×87 mm. (a) $2.50, Paratrooper landing. (b) $6 Paratroop uniforms of 1940 and 1990 Set of 2 sheets . . . . . 5·50 6·50

1990. 90th Birthday of Queen Elizabeth the Queen Mother. As T **194** of Gambia showing photographs from the 1960s. Multicoloured.

2131 $2 Queen Mother in coat and hat . . . . 1·75 1·75
2132 $2 Queen Mother in evening dress . . . . 1·75 1·75
2133 $2 Queen Mother in Garter robes . . . . 1·75 1·75
MS2134 90×75 mm. $6 Queen Mother (as No. 2131) . . . . 3·50 4·00

1990. Olympic Games, Barcelona (1992) (1st issue). As T **195a** of Gambia. Multicoloured.

2135 10c. Men's steeplechase . . 30 20
2136 15c. Dressage 45 30
2137 45c. Men's 200 m. butterfly swimming 50 45
2138 50c. Men's hockey . . . . 1·50 60
2139 65c. Women's beam gymnastics 60 60
2140 75c. "Flying Dutchman" class sailing . . . . . . 1·00 80
2141 $2 Freestyle wrestling . . . 1·75 1·75
2142 $3 Men's springboard diving 2·25 2·75
2143 $4 Women's 1000 m. sprint cycling . . . . 3·75 3·75
2144 $5 Men's basketball . . . . 4·50 4·50
MS2145 Two sheets, each 101×70 mm. (a) $8 Equestrian three-day event. (b) $8 Men's 10000 metres Set of 2 sheets . . 9·50 11·00
See also Nos. 2414/22.

356 Map of North America and Logo

1990. "Stamp World London 90" International Stamp Exhibition (2nd issue). Sheet 97×75 mm.

MS2146 **356** $6 mauve . . . . . 4·25 5·50

357 Yellow Goatfish

1990. Coral Reef Fishes. Multicoloured.

2147 10c. Type **357** 30 30
2148 25c. Black margate 45 35
2149 65c. Blue-headed wrasse . . 85 75
2150 75c. Puddingwife 95 85
2151 $1 Four-eyed butterflyfish 1·10 95
2152 $2 Honey damselfish . . . . 2·00 2·00
2153 $3 Queen angelfish . . . . 2·50 2·50
2154 $5 Cherub angelfish . . . . 3·00 3·50
MS2155 Two sheets, each 103×72 mm. (a) $6 Smooth trunkfish. (b) $6 Sergeant major Set of 2 sheets . . . . 8·00 9·00

358 Tropical Mockingbird

1990. Birds. Multicoloured.

2156 15c. Type **358** 30 30
2157 25c. Grey kingbird 35 35
2158 65c. Bare-eyed thrush . . . 75 75
2159 75c. Antillean crested hummingbird 85 85
2160 $1 House wren . . . . 1·00 1·00
2161 $2 Purple martin . . . . . . 1·75 1·75
2162 $4 Lesser Antillian tanager ("Hooded Tanager") . . 2·50 2·50
2163 $5 Scaly-breasted ground dove . . . . 3·00 3·00
MS2164 Two sheets, each 101×72 mm. (a) $6 Fork-tailed flycatcher. (b) $6 Smooth-billed ani Set of 2 sheets . . . . . . 12·00 13·00

359 Coral Crab

1990. Crustaceans. Multicoloured.

2165 5c. Type **359** 20 30
2166 10c. Smoothtail spiny lobster 20 30
2167 15c. Flamestreaked box crab 20 30
2168 25c. Spotted swimming crab 30 25
2169 75c. Sally lightfoot rock crab 70 60
2170 $1 Spotted spiny lobster . . 90 80
2171 $3 Longarm spiny lobster 2·00 2·50
2172 $20 Caribbean spiny lobster 13·00 18·00
MS2173 Two sheets, 106×75 mm. (a) $6 Copper lobster. (b) $6 Spanish lobster Set of 2 sheets 8·00 9·00

360 Cameroon Player

1990. World Cup Football Championship, Italy (2nd issue). Multicoloured.

2174 10c. Type **360** 20 15
2175 25c. Michel (Spain) 25 15
2176 $1 Brehme (West Germany) 85 85
2177 $5 Nevin (Scotland) . . . . 3·00 4·00
MS2178 Two sheets, each 95×90 mm. (a) $6 Giannini (Italy). (b) $6 Perdomo (Uruguay) Set of 2 sheets . . . . 9·50 11·00

1990. World Cup Football Championship, Italy (1990) (3rd issue). No. **MS**2016a optd **1990 W GERMANY 1 ARGENTINA 0.**

MS2179 70×93 mm. $6 Players jumping for ball . . . . 6·50 7·50

1990. Christmas. Paintings by Raphael. As T **195b** of Gambia. Multicoloured.

2180 10c. "The Ansidei Madonna" 20 10
2181 15c. "The Sistine Madonna" 20 10
2182 $1 "The Madonna of the Baldacchino" . . . . . . 1·50 70
2183 $2 "The Large Holy Family" (detail) . . . . . 2·50 2·75
2184 $5 "Madonna in the Meadow" . . . . 4·00 6·00
MS2185 Two sheets, each 71×101 mm. (a) $6 "Madonna of the Diadem" (detail). (b) $6 "The Madonna of the Veil" (detail) Set of 2 sheets . . . . 13·00 14·00

1991. 350th Death Anniv of Rubens. As T **195c** of Gambia. Multicoloured.

2186 5c. "The Brazen Serpent" (detail) 20 10
2187 10c. "The Garden of Love" 20 10
2188 25c. "Head of Cyrus" (detail) 40 20
2189 75c. "Tournament in Front of a Castle" . . . . 1·00 60
2190 $1 "The Brazen Serpent" (different detail) . . . . . 1·10 75
2191 $2 "Judgement of Paris" (detail) . . . . 1·75 2·00
2192 $4 "The Brazen Serpent" . . 2·50 3·50
2193 $5 "The Karmesse" (detail) 3·00 3·50
MS2194 Two sheets, each 101×70 mm. (a) $6 "Anger of Neptune" (detail). (b) $6 "The Prodigal son" (detail) Set of 2 sheets . . . . 12·00 13·00

362 "The Sorcerer's Apprentice"

1991. 50th Anniv of "Fantasia" (cartoon film). Multicoloured.

2195 5c. Type **362** 50 20
2196 10c. Dancing mushrooms ("The Nutcracker Suite") 50 20
2197 20c. Pterodactyls ("The Rite of Spring") 90 20
2198 45c. Centaurs ("The Pastoral Symphony") . . 1·50 40
2199 $1 Bacchus and Jacchus ("The Pastoral Symphony") . . . . . 2·50 1·25
2200 $2 Dancing ostrich ("Dance of the Hours") . . . . . 3·25 3·25
2201 $4 Elephant ballet ("Dance of the Hours") . . . . . 4·25 4·75
2202 $5 Diana ("The Pastoral Symphony") . . . . . . 4·25 4·75
MS2203 Two sheets, each 122×102 mm. (a) $6 Mickey Mouse as the Sorcerer's Apprentice. (b) $6 Mickey Mouse with Leopold Stokowski (conductor) Set of 2 sheets . . 13·00 14·00
MS2204 176×213 mm. $12 Mickey Mouse as the Sorcerer's Apprentice (vert) . . . . . . 13·00 14·00

363 "Adelpha iphicla"

1991. Butterflies. Multicoloured.

2205 5c. Type **363** 50 50
2206 10c. "Nymphalidae claudina" 50 40
2207 15c. "Brassolidae polyxena" 60 30
2208 20c. "Zebra Longwing" . . 70 30
2209 25c. "Marpesia corinna" . . 70 25
2210 30c. "Morpho hecuba" . . 70 30
2211 45c. "Morpho rhetenor" . . 90 45
2212 50c. "Dismorphia spio" . . 95 55
2213 60c. "Prepona omphale" . . 1·00 65
2214 70c. "Morpho anaxibia" . . 1·25 75
2215 75c. "Marpesia iole" . . . . 1·25 80
2216 $1 "Amarynthis meneria" 1·40 1·00
2217 $2 "Morpho cisseis" . . . . 2·25 2·50
2218 $3 "Danaidae plexippus" . . 2·75 3·00
2219 $4 "Morpho achilleana" . . 3·25 4·00
2220 $5 "Calliona argenissa" . . 3·75 4·25
MS2221 Four sheets, each 118×80 mm. (a) $6 "Anteos clorinde". (b) $6 "Haetera piera". (c) $6 "Papilio cresphontes". (d) $6 "Prepona pheridames" Set of 4 sheets . . . . 17·00 19·00

363a Vitus Bering in Bering Sea, 1728–9

1991. 500th Anniv (1992) of Discovery of America by Columbus. History of Exploration. Mult.

2222 5c. Type **363a** 60 50
2223 10c. De Bougainville off Pacific island, 1766–69 . . 60 40
2224 25c. Polynesian canoe . . . 45 30
2225 50c. De Mendana off Solomon Islands, 1567–69 1·25 50
2226 $1 Darwin's H.M.S. "Beagle". 1831–35 . . . . 2·25 1·25
2227 $2 Cook's H.M.S. "Endeavour", 1768–71 . . 3·75 3·25
2228 $4 William Schouten in LeMaire Strait, 1615–17 3·75 4·25
2229 $5 Tasman off New Zealand, 1642–44 . . . . 3·75 4·25
MS2230 Two sheets, each 116×77 mm. (a) $6 "Santa Maria" sinking. (b) $6 Bow of "Santa Maria" (vert) Set of 2 sheets . . . . 8·50 9·50

1991. "Phila Nippon '91" International Stamp Exhibition, Tokyo. Horiz designs as T **198c** of Gambia showing Walt Disney cartoon characters at Japanese festivals. Multicoloured.

2231 5c. Minnie Mouse and Daisy Duck at Dolls festival 35 20
2232 10c. Morty and Ferdie with Boys' Day display 35 20
2233 20c. Mickey and Minnie Mouse at Star festival . . 60 20
2234 45c. Minnie and Daisy folk-dancing . . . . 1·00 35
2235 $1 Huey, Dewey and Louie wearing Eboshi headdresses . . . . 1·75 85
2236 $2 Mickey and Goofy pulling decorated car at Gion festival . . . . . . 3·25 3·25
2237 $4 Minnie and Daisy preparing rice broth, Seven Plants festival . . . 4·00 4·25
2238 $5 Huey and Dewey with straw boat at Lanterns festival . . . . 4·00 4·25
MS2239 Three sheets, each 127×101 mm. (a) $6 Minnie Mouse in kimono. (b) $6 Mickey taking photo (horiz). (c) $6 Goofy behind fair stall (horiz) Set of 3 sheets . . . . 14·00 15·00

1991. Death Centenary (1990) of Vincent van Gogh (artist). As T **200b** of Gambia. Multicoloured.

2240 20c. "Blossoming Almond Branch in Glass" (vert) 50 25
2241 25c. "La Mousme sitting" (vert) 50 25
2242 30c. "Still Life with Red Cabbages and Onions" 55 30
2243 40c. "Japonaiserie: Flowering Plum Tree" (vert) 70 40
2244 45c. "Japonaiserie: Bridge in the Rain" (vert) 70 40
2245 60c. "Still Life with Basket of Apples" . . . . 1·00 60
2246 75c. "Italian Woman" (vert) 1·10 70
2247 $1 "The Painter on his Way to Work" (vert) . . . . 1·60 1·00
2248 $2 "Portrait of Pere Tanguy" (vert) . . . . . 2·50 2·25
2249 $3 "Still Life with Plaster Statuette, a Rose and Two Novels" (vert) . . . 3·25 3·25
2250 $4 "Still Life: Bottle, Lemons and Oranges" . . 3·50 3·75
2251 $5 "Orchard with Blossoming Apricot Trees" . . . . 3·50 3·75
MS2252 Five sheets. (a) 76×102 mm. $6 "Roubine du Roi Canal with Washerwoman" (73×99 mm). (b) 102×76 mm. $6 "Farmhouse in a Wheatfield" (99×73 mm). (c) 102×76 mm. $6 "The Gleize Bridge over the Vigueirat Canal" (99×73 mm). (d) 102×76 mm. $6 "Rocks with Oak Tree" (99×73 mm). (e) 76×102 mm. $6 "Japonaiserie: Oiran" (73×99 mm). Imperf. Set of 5 sheets . . . . 22·00 24·00

364 "Psilocybe cubensis"

1991. Fungi. Multicoloured.

2253 15c. Type **364** 70 30
2254 25c. "Leptonia caeruleocapitata" 80 30
2255 65c. "Cystolepiota eriophora" . . . . 1·40 85
2256 75c. "Chlorophyllum molybdites" . . . . 1·40 1·00
2257 $1 "Xerocomus hypoxanthus" . . . . . . 1·60 1·25
2258 $2 "Volvariella cubensis" . . 2·50 2·75
2259 $4 "Xerocomus coccolobae" 3·25 4·00
2260 $5 "Pluteus chrysophlebius" 3·25 4·00
MS2261 Two sheets, each 100×70 mm. (a) $6 "Psathyrella tuberculata". (b) $6 "Hygrocybe miniata" Set of 2 sheets . . . 14·00 14·00

365 Johannes Kepler (astronomer)

1991. Exploration of Mars. Designs showing astronomers, spacecraft and Martian landscapes. Multicoloured.

2262/97 75c.×9, $1.25×9, $2×9, $7×9 . . . . Set of 36 . . . . 48·00 48·00
MS2298 Three sheets, each 112×92 mm. (a) $6 Projected spacecraft. (b) $6 Mars and part of spacecraft. (c) $6 Phobos satellite over Mars Set of 3 sheets . . . 11·00 12·00

1991. 65th Birthday of Queen Elizabeth II. As T **198a** of Gambia. Multicoloured.

2299 15c. Royal Family on balcony after Trooping the Colour, 1985 . . . . 50 15
2300 40c. Queen and Prince Philip at Peterborough, 1988 . . . . 75 35
2301 $2 Queen and Queen Mother at Windsor, 1986 2·50 1·75
2302 $4 Queen and Prince Philip on visit to United Arab Emirates . . . . 3·00 3·00
MS2303 68×90 mm. $5 Separate photographs of the Queen and Prince Philip . . . . 3·50 4·25

1991. 10th Wedding Anniv of the Prince and Princess of Wales. As T **198b** of Gambia. Multicoloured.

2304 10c. Prince and Princess in July 1985 . . . . 60 10
2305 50c. Separate photographs of Prince, Princess and sons . . . . 1·25 45
2306 $1 Prince Henry at Trooping the Colour and Prince William in Majorca 1·50 1·00
2307 $5 Separate photographs of Prince Charles and Princess Diana . . . . . . 4·25 4·50
MS2308 68×90 mm. $5 Prince, Princess and sons on holiday in Majorca . . . . 6·00 5·50

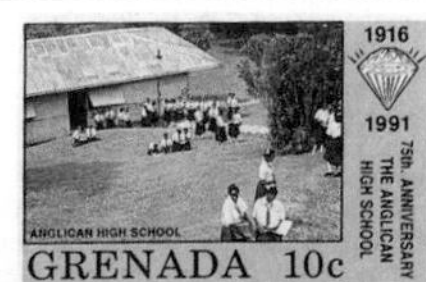

366 Anglican High School Pupils

1991. 75th Anniv of Anglican High School (10, 25c.) and 40th Anniv of University of the West Indies (45, 50c.). Multicoloured.

2309 10c. Type **366** 35 20
2310 25c. Artist's impression of new Anglican High School 60 20
2311 45c. Marryshow House, Grenada 85 55
2312 50c. University Administrative Building, Barbados . . . . 90 1·00

367 George Stephenson's First Locomotive, 1814 (Great Britain)

1991. Great Railways of the World. Mult.

2313 75c. Type **367** 60 60
2314 75c. George Stephenson . . 60 60
2315 75c. Killingworth locomotive, 1816 (Great Britain) 60 60
2316 75c. George Stephenson's "Locomotion", 1825 (Great Britain) 60 60
2317 75c. "Locomotion" in Darlington, 1825 (Great Britain) 60 60
2318 75c. Opening of Stockton & Darlington Railway, 1825 60 60
2319 75c. Timothy Hackworth's "Royal George", 1827 (Great Britain) 60 60
2320 75c. Northumbrian T831 (Great Britain) 60 60
2321 75c. "Planet", 1830 (Great Britain) 60 60
2322 $1 "Old Ironsides", 1832 (U.S.A.) 80 80
2323 $1 "Wilberforce", 1832 (Great Britain) 80 80
2324 $1 "Adler", 1835 (Germany) 80 80
2325 $1 "North Star", 1837 (Great Britain) 80 80
2326 $1 London & Birmingham Railway No. 1, 1838 (Great Britain) 80 80
2327 $1 Stephenson's "Austria", 1838 (Austria) 80 80
2328 $1 Baltimore & Ohio Railroad No. 378 "Muddigger", 1840 (U.S.A.) 80 80
2329 $1 Baltimore & Ohio Railroad Norris, 1840 (U.S.A.) 80 80
2330 $1 "Centaur", 1840 (Great Britain) 80 80
2331 $2 "Lion", 1841 (Great Britain) . . . . 1·50 1·50
2332 $2 "Beuth", 1843 (Germany) 1·50 1·50
2333 $2 "Derwent", 1845 (Great Britain) . . . . 1·50 1·50
2334 $2 "Bets", 1846 (Hungary) 1·50 1·50
2335 $2 Opening of Budapest to Vac railway, 1846 (Hungary) . . . . 1·50 1·50
2336 $2 Carriages, Stockton & Darlington Railway, 1846 (Great Britain) . . . . . 1·50 1·50
2337 $2 "Long Boiler" type, 1847 (France) . . . . 1·50 1·50
2338 $2 Baldwin locomotive, 1850 (U.S.A.) . . . . 1·50 1·50
2339 $2 Steam locomotive, 1850 (Germany) . . . . 1·50 1·50
MS2340 Two sheets, each 116 × 86 mm. (a) $6 Part of Stephenson's "Locomotion", 1825 (Great Britain). (b) $6 Train on Liverpool & Manchester Railway, 1833 (Great Britain) Set of 2 sheets 14·00 15·00

368 Barbu

1991. Marine Life of the Sandflats. Mult.

2341 50c. Type **368** 80 80
2342 50c. Beau Gregory 80 80
2343 50c. Porcupinefish 80 80
2344 50c. Queen or pink conch and conchfish 80 80
2345 50c. Hermit crab 80 80
2346 50c. Bluestripe lizardfish . . 80 80
2347 50c. Spot-finned mojarra . . 80 80
2348 50c. Southern stingray . . . 80 80
2349 50c. Long-spined sea urchin and slippery dick 80 80
2350 50c. Peacock flounder . . . 80 80
2351 50c. West Indian sea star . . 80 80
2352 50c. Spotted goatfish . . . 80 80
2353 50c. Netted olive and West Indian sea egg 80 80
2354 50c. Pearly razorfish 80 80
2355 50c. Spotted jawfish and yellow-headed jawfish . . 80 80
MS2356 105 × 76 mm. $6 Short-nosed batfish . . . . 11·00 12·00

Nos. 2341/55 were printed together, se-tenant, forming a composite design.

1991. Christmas. Religious Paintings by Albrecht Durer. As T **200c** of Gambia. Mult.

2357 10c. "Adoration of the Magi" (detail) 60 10
2358 35c. "Madonna with the Siskin" (detail) 90 25
2359 50c. "Feast of the Rose Garlands" (detail) . . . . 1·25 45
2360 75c. "Virgin with the Pear" (detail) . . . . 1·75 80
2361 $1 "Virgin in Half-length" (detail) . . . . 2·25 1·00
2362 $2 "Madonna and Child" (detail) . . . . 3·25 3·25
2363 $4 "Virgin and Child with St. Anne" (detail) . . . . 3·75 5·00
2364 $5 "Virgin and Child" (detail) . . . . 3·75 5·00
MS2365 Two sheets, each 102 × 127 mm. (a) $6 "Virgin with a Multitude of Animals" (detail). (b) $6 "The Nativity" (detail).Set of 2 sheets . . . . 13·00 14·00

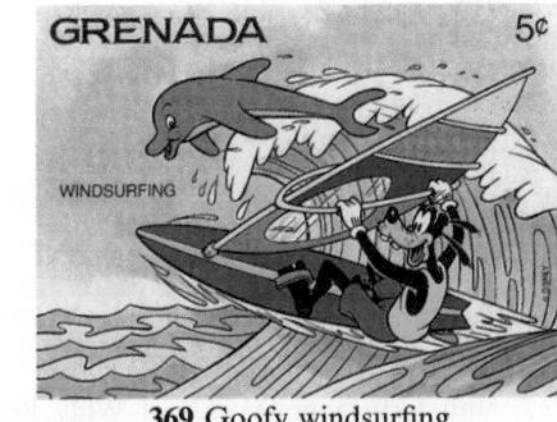

369 Goofy windsurfing

1992. Thrill Sports. Walt Disney cartoon characters. Multicoloured.

2366 5c. Type **369** 40 30
2367 10c. Mickey Mouse skateboarding 50 30
2368 20c. Daisy Duck gliding . . . 80 30
2369 45c. Mickey's nephews stunt kite flying . . . . 1·25 30
2370 $1 Donald Duck mountain biking . . . . 2·00 1·10
2371 $2 Donald and Chipmunk parachuting . . . . . 2·75 2·75
2372 $4 Mickey go-karting . . . 4·00 4·75
2373 $5 Minnie water skiing . . . 4·00 4·75
MS2374 Four sheets, each 128 × 102 mm. (a) $6 Mickey bungee jumping (vert). (b) $6 Mickey and Minnie river rafting. (c) $6 Donald's nephews playing roller hockey. (d) $6 Mickey hang-gliding Set of 4 sheets . . . . 16·00 17·00

1992. 40th Anniv of Queen Elizabeth II's Accession. As T **202a** of Gambia. Mult.

2375 10c. Waterfall 65 20
2376 50c. Street in St. George's 75 40
2377 $1 Colonial-style houses, St. George's . . . . . 1·40 80
2378 $5 St. George's from the sea 4·25 4·50
MS2379 Two sheets, each 75 × 96 mm. (a) $6 Village on hillside. (b) $6 Yacht at anchor off village Set of 2 sheets . . . . 11·00 11·00

1992. "Granada '92" International Stamp Exhibition, Spain. Spanish Paintings. As T **481a** of Ghana. Multicoloured.

2380 10c. "The Corpus Christi Procession in Seville" (Manuel Cabral y Aguado) (horiz) 40 20
2381 35c. "The Mancorbo Channel" (Carlos de Haes) 55 20
2382 50c. "Amalia de Llano y Dotres, Countess of Vilches" (Federico de Madrazo y Kuntz) . . . 75 40
2383 75c. "Conchita Serrano y Dominguez, Countess of Santovenia" (Eduardo Rosales Gallina) . . . . 1·00 70
2384 $1 "Queen Maria Isabel de Braganza" (Bernardo Lopez Piquer) . . . . . 1·40 85
2385 $2 "The Presentation of Don John of Austria to Charles V" (detail) (Gallina) . . . . 2·25 2·25
2386 $4 "The Presentation of Don John of Austria to Charles V" (different detail) (Gallina) . . . . . 3·50 4·25
2387 $5 "The Testament of Isabella the Catholic" (Gallina) (horiz) . . . . . 3·50 4·25
MS2388 Two sheets, each 120 × 95 mm. (a) $6 "The Horse Corral in the Old Madrid Bullring" (Manuel Castellano) (111 × 85 mm). (b) $6 "Meeting of Poets in Antonio Mariá Esquivel's Studio" (Antonia Mariá Esquivel y Suárez de Urbina) (111 × 85 mm). Imperf Set of 2 sheets . . . . 8·00 9·00

370 Green-winged Macaw

370a Ruby-throated Hummingbird

1992. 500th Anniv of Discovery of America by Columbus (5th issue). World Columbian Stamp "Expo '92", Chicago. Multicoloured.

2389 10c. Type **370** 85 40
2390 25c. "Santa Maria" 90 40
2391 35c. Christopher Columbus 95 40
2392 50c. 15th-century sandglass 95 55
2393 75c. Queen Isabella . . . . 1·00 80
2394 $4 Cantino map of 1502 (detail) . . . . 5·00 7·00
MS2395 Two sheets, each 80 × 108 mm. (a) $6 Map of Genoa (detail). (b) $6 Detail of 15th-century map by Thomas Bly Set of 2 sheets . . . . 9·00 10·00

1992. "Genova '92" International Thematic Stamp Exhibition. Hummingbirds. Multicoloured.

2396 10c. Type **370a** 70 25
2397 25c. Vervain hummingbird 90 25
2398 35c. Blue-headed hummingbird 95 25
2399 50c. Cuban emerald . . . . 1·25 60
2400 75c. Antillean mango . . . 1·60 75
2401 $2 Purple-throated carib . . 2·50 2·50
2402 $4 Puerto Rican emerald . . 3·50 4·25
2403 $5 Green-throated carib . . 3·50 4·25
MS2404 Two sheets, each 109 × 80 mm. (a) $6 Young Antillean Crested Hummingbird. (b) $6 Rufous-breasted Hermit Set of 2 sheets . . . . 13·00 13·00

371 Gracie Fields

372 Badminton

1992. 50th Anniv of United Service Organization (forces' entertainment programme). Multicoloured.

2405 15c. Type **371** 30 20
2406 25c. Jack Benny 30 20
2407 35c. Jinx Falkenburg . . . 30 25
2408 50c. Francis Langford . . . 45 40
2409 75c. Joe E. Brown 80 70
2410 $1 Phil Silvers . . . . . . 1·25 80
2411 $2 Danny Kaye . . . . . . 2·25 2·25
2412 $5 Frank Sinatra . . . . . 6·50 6·50
MS2413 Two sheets, each 107 × 80 mm. (a) $6 Bob Hope. (b) $6 Anna May Wong Set of 2 sheets . . . . 8·00 9·00

1992. Olympic Games, Barcelona (2nd issue). Multicoloured.

2414 10c. Type **372** 50 30
2415 25c. Women's long jump . . 50 20
2416 35c. Women's 100 m . . . 50 30
2417 50c. 1000 m cycling sprint 1·00 50
2418 75c. Decathlon (horiz) . . . 1·00 80
2419 $2 Judo (horiz) . . . . . . 2·00 2·25
2420 $4 Women's gymnastics—asymmetrical bars . . . . 3·25 3·75
2421 $5 Men's javelin . . . . . 3·25 3·75
MS2422 Two sheets, each 100 × 70 mm. (a) $6 Men's gymnastics – vault. (b) $6 Men's gymnastics – floor exercise Set of 2 sheets . . . . 8·00 9·00

372a Columbus meeting Amerindians

1992. 500th Anniv of Discovery of America by Columbus (6th issue). Organization of East Caribbean States. Multicoloured.

2423 $1 Type **372a** 70 70
2424 $2 Ships approaching island 1·40 1·60

372b "The Blue Comet" Locomotive, Boucher (1933)

1992. Toy Trains from American Manufacturers. Multicoloured.

2425 10c. Type **372b** 40 20
2426 35c. No. 2220 switching locomotive, Voltamp (1906) 50 25
2427 40c. No. 221 tunnel locomotive, Knapp (1905) 50 30
2428 75c. "Grand Canyon" locomotive, American Flyer (1931) 80 55
2429 $1 "Streamliner" tin locomotive, Hafner (1930s) . . . . 1·10 80
2430 $2 No. 237 switching locomotive, Elektoy (1911) . . . . 2·00 2·25
2431 $4 Parlor car, Ives (1928) 3·50 4·00
2432 $5 "Improved President's Special" locomotive, American Flyer (1927) . . 3·50 4·00
MS2433 Two sheets, each 133 × 103 mm. (a) $6 No. 1122 locomotive, Ives (1921) (38½ × 50 mm). (b) $6 No. 3239 locomotive, Ives (1912) (50 × 38½ mm) Set of 2 sheets 8·00 9·00

1992. Postage Stamp Mega Event, New York. Sheet 100 × 70 mm, containing multicoloured design as T **207a** of Gambia.

MS2434 $6 Guggenheim Museum 3·50 4·25

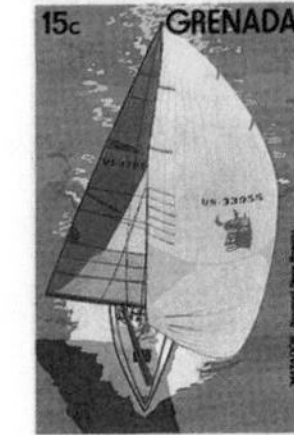

373 "Matador" (yacht), Newport News Regatta

1992. World Regattas. Multicoloured.

2435 15c. Type **373** 20 20
2436 25c. "Awesome", Antigua 25 25
2437 35c. "Mistress Quickly", Bermuda 30 30
2438 50c. "Emeraude", St. Tropez 50 50
2439 $1 "Diva G", German Admirals Cup 80 80
2440 $2 "Lady Be", French Admirals Cup . . . . . 1·50 1·75
2441 $4 "Midnight Sun", Admirals Cup . . . . . 2·75 3·50
2442 $5 "CARAT", Sardinia Cup 2·75 3·50
MS2443 Two sheets, each 113 × 85 mm. (a) $6 Yachts, Grenada Regatta (horiz). (b) $6 Fastnet Race, 1979 (horiz) Set of 2 sheets . . . . 9·00 11·00

1992. Christmas. Religious Paintings. As T **207b** of Gambia. Multicoloured.

2444 10c. "Adoration of the Magi" (detail) (Fra Filippo Lippi) 45 15
2445 15c. "Madonna adoring Child in a Wood" (Lippi) 55 20
2446 25c. "Adoration of the Magi" (detail) (Botticelli) 70 20
2447 35c. "The Epiphany—Adoration of the Magi" (detail) (Hieronymus Bosch) 75 20
2448 50c. "Adoration of the Magi" (detail) (Giovanni de Paolo) . . . . 1·00 45
2449 75c. "Adoration of the Magi" (Gentile da Fabriano) . . . . 1·50 60
2450 90c. "Adoration of the Magi" (detail) (Juan Batista Maino) . . . . . 1·75 70
2451 $1 "Adoration of the Child" (Master of Liesborn) . . . 1·75 90
2452 $2 "Adoration of the Kings" (Master of Liesborn) . . . . 2·75 2·75
2453 $3 "Adoration of the Three Wise Men" (Pedro Berruguete) . . . . 3·00 3·50
2454 $4 "Adoration of the Child" (Lippi) . . . . 3·75 4·50
2455 $5 "Adoration of the Child" (Correggio) . . . . . . 3·75 4·50
MS2456 Three sheets, each 72 × 97 mm. (a) $6 "Adoration of the Magi" (detail) (Andrea Mantegna). (b) $6 "Adoration of the Magi" (detail) (Hans Memling). (c) $6 "Adoration of the Shepherds" (La Tour) Set of 3 sheets . . . . 15·00 16·00

No. 2447 is inscribed "Hieronymous" in error.

374 Cher

375 Grenada Dove

1992. Gold Record Award Winners. Mult.
2457 90c. Type **374** . . . . . . 1·25 1·25
2458 90c. Michael Jackson . . . 1·25 1·25
2459 90c. Elvis Presley . . . . . 1·25 1·25
2460 90c. Dolly Parton . . . . . 1·25 1·25
2461 90c. Johnny Mathis . . . . 1·25 1·25
2462 90c. Madonna . . . . . . 1·25 1·25
2463 90c. Nat King Cole . . . . 1·25 1·25
2464 90c. Janice Joplin . . . . . 1·25 1·25
MS2465 Two sheets, each 100 × 70 mm. (a) $3 Chuck Berry; $3 James Brown. (b) $3 Frank Sinatra; $3 Perry Como Set of 2 sheets . . . . 12·00 12·00
Nos. 2457/64 were printed together, se-tenant, with a composite background design.

1992. Anniversaries and Events. Mult.
2466 10c. Type **375** . . . . . . 1·00 65
2467 25c. Airship LZ-1 on maiden flight, 1900 (horiz) 1·00 30
2468 50c. ENDOSAT (robot plane) project (horiz) . . 1·25 55
2469 75c. Konrad Adenauer (German statesman) and industrial skyline (horiz) 1·25 70
2470 $1.50 Golden lion tamarin (horiz) . . . . 2·75 2·00
2471 $2 Mountain gorilla (horiz) 3·50 2·75
2472 $2 Outline of man and heart (horiz) . . . . 3·25 2·75
2473 $3 Wolfgang Amadeus Mozart . . . . 4·50 3·75
2474 $4 "Voyager 2" and Neptune (horiz) . . . . . 4·50 4·50
2475 $4 Adenauer with flag and map of West Germany (horiz) . . . . 4·50 4·50
2476 $5 Count von Zeppelin and "Graf Zeppelin" (horiz) 4·50 4·75
2477 $6 Admiral Richard Byrd (polar explorer) (horiz) . . 4·50 4·75
MS2478 Five sheets. (a) 110 × 80 mm. $6 Count von Zeppelin (horiz). (b) 110 × 80 mm. $6 Space shuttle recovering "Intelsat 6" satellite. (c) 110 × 80 mm. $6 Konrad Adenauer (horiz). (d) 95 × 70 mm. $6 Spotted Little Owl (horiz). (e) 100 × 70 mm. $6 Papageno costume from "The Magic Flute" Set of 5 sheets . . . . 24·00 25·00
ANNIVERSARIES AND EVENTS: No. 2466, National bird; 2467, 2476, **MS**2478a, 75th death anniv of Count Ferdinand von Zeppelin; 2468, 2475, **MS**2478b, International Space Year; 2469, 2475, **MS**2478c, 25th death anniv of Konrad Adenauer; 2470/1, **MS**2478d, Earth Summit '92, Rio; 2472, United Nations World Health Organization Projects; 2473, **MS**2478e, Death bicentenary of Mozart; 2477, 75th anniv of International Association of Lions Clubs.

376 Care Bear on Beach

1992. Ecology.
2479 75c. Type **376** . . . . . . 1·00 60
MS2480 71 × 101 mm. $2 Care Bear and butterfly (vert) . . . . . . 2·25 2·25

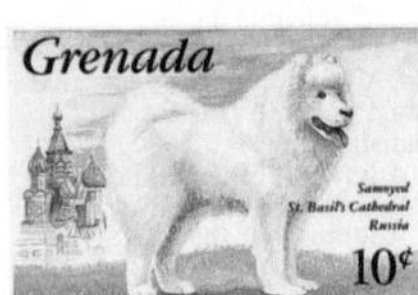

377 Samoyed and St. Basil's Cathedral, Moscow

1993. Dogs of the World. Multicoloured.
2481 10c. Type **377** 70 40
2482 15c. Chow and Ling Yin Monastery, China 85 40
2483 25c. Boxer and Tower of London 90 30
2484 90c. Basenji and Yamma Mosque, Niger . . . . . 1·60 75
2485 $1 Golden labrador and Parliament Building, Ottawa . . . . 1·60 80
2486 $3 St. Bernard and Parsenn, Switzerland . . . . 2·75 3·00
2487 $4 Rhodesian ridgeback and Melrose House, South Africa . . . . 3·00 3·50
2488 $5 Afghan hound and Mazar-i-Sharif, Afghanistan . . . . . . 3·00 3·50
MS2489 Two sheets, each 100 × 70 mm. (a) $6 Australian cattle dog. (b) $6 Alaskan malamute Set of 2 sheets . . . 10·00 10·00
No. **MS**2489a is inscribed "Austrailian" in error.

1993. Bicentenary of the Louvre, Paris. Paintings by Jean-Antoine Watteau. As T **209b** of Gambia. Multicoloured.
2490 $1 "The Faux-pas" 95 95
2491 $1 "Portrait of a Gentleman" 95 95
2492 $1 "Young Lady with Archlute" 95 95
2493 $1 "Young Man Dancing" 95 95
2494 $1 "Autumn, Pamona and a Cherub" 95 95
2495 $1 "Judgement of Paris" . . 95 95
2496 $1 "Pierrot" (detail) . . . 95 95
2497 $1 "Pierrot" (different detail) 95 95
MS2498 100 × 70 mm. $6 "The Embarkation for Cythére" (85 × 52 mm). . . . . 4·25 5·00

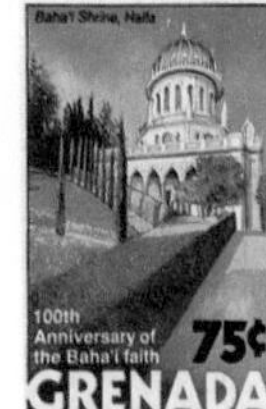

378 Baha'i Shrine, Haifa

1993. Centenary of Baha'i Faith.
2499 **378** 75c. multicoloured . . . 1·50 1·00

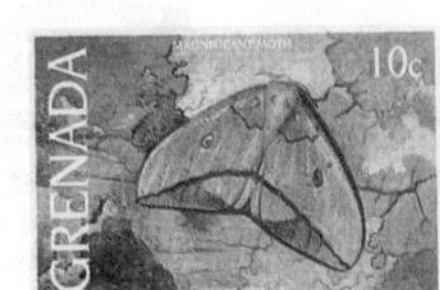

379 "Citheronia magnifica"

1993. Moths. Multicoloured.
2500 10c. Type **379** 25 25
2501 35c. "Automeris metali" . . 40 25
2502 45c. "Thysania zenobia" . . 50 30
2503 75c. "Agrius cingulatus" . . 70 55
2504 $1 "Composia fidelissima" 80 65
2505 $2 "Synchlora xysteraria" 1·50 1·75
2506 $4 "Eumorpha labruscae" 2·50 2·75
2507 $5 "Ascalapha odorata" . . 2·50 2·75
MS2508 Two sheets, each 100 × 70 mm. (a) $6 "Epimecis detexta" (vert). (b) $6 "Xylophanes titana" (vert) Set of 2 sheets . . . . 7·50 8·50

380 Heliconia

381 "Woman with Loaves" (Picasso)

1993. Flowers. Multicoloured.
2509 10c. Type **380** 25 25
2510 35c. Pansy 40 25
2511 45c. Water lily 50 30
2512 75c. Bougainvillea 70 55
2513 $1 Calla lily 80 65
2514 $2 California poppy . . . . 1·50 1·75
2515 $4 Red ginger . . . . . . 2·50 3·00
2516 $5 Anthurium . . . . . . 2·50 3·00
MS2517 Two sheets, each 70 × 100 mm. (a) $6 Christmas rose (horiz). (b) $6 Moth orchid (horiz) Set of 2 sheets . . . . 7·50 8·50

1993. 40th Anniv of Coronation. As T **215a** of Gambia.
2518 35c. multicoloured 70 75
2519 70c. multicoloured 80 85
2520 $1 brown and black 85 90
2521 $5 multicoloured . . . . . 2·25 2·50
MS2522 70 × 100 mm. $6 multicoloured . . . . 5·50 6·00
DESIGNS: 35c. Queen Elizabeth II at Coronation (photograph by Cecil Beaton); 70c. Sceptres; $1 Queen Elizabeth receiving sceptre from Archbishop of Canterbury; $5 Queen and Prince Philip with their children, 1960s. (28½ × 42½ mm)—$6 "Queen Elizabeth II, 1965" (detail) (Peter Greenham).

1993. Anniversaries and Events. Each brown, deep brown and black (Nos. 2527, 2535, **MS**2536d) or multicoloured (others).
2523 25c. Type **381** 30 20
2524 35c. 16th-century telescope 35 20
2525 35c. Public Library building 35 20
2526 35c. Gaetan Boucher (speed skating, 1984) 35 20
2527 50c. Willy Brandt with Senator Edward Kennedy (horiz) 40 30
2528 75c. Carnival float (horiz) 50 40
2529 90c. "Weeping Woman" (Picasso) 65 45
2530 $1 "Marii Prohaska" (Tyrus Czyzewski) 70 50
2531 $3 "Marysia et Burek a Geylan" (S. Wirkiewicz) 2·25 2·25
2532 $4 "Woman seated in Airchair" (Picasso) . . . 2·75 2·75
2533 $4 Astronaut on Moon . . 2·75 2·75
2534 $5 Norbert Schramm (figure skating, 1984) . . . . . 2·75 2·75
2535 $5 Willy Brandt and Kurt Waldheim (horiz) . . . . 2·75 2·75
MS2536 Five sheets. (a) 76 × 107 mm. $5 Copernicus. (b) 75 × 105 mm. $6 "Three Women at the Spring" (detail) (Picasso). (c) 76 × 105 mm. $6 Women's Super G skiing medal winners, 1988 (horiz). (d) 105 × 75 mm. $6 Newspaper headline, 1974. (e) 105 × 76 mm. $6 "Parting" (detail) (Witold Wojtkiewicz) Set of 5 sheets . . . . 17·00 18·00
ANNIVERSARIES AND EVENTS: Nos. 2523, 2529, 2532, **MS**2536b, 20th death anniv of Picasso (artist); 2524, 2533, **MS**2536a, 450th death anniv of Copernicus (astronomer); 2525, Centenary (1992) of Grenada Public Library; 2526, 2534, **MS**2536c, Winter Olympic Games '94, Lillehammer; 2527, 2535, **MS**2536d, 80th birth anniv (1992) of Willy Brandt (German politician); 2528, Grenada Carnival; 2530/1, **MS**2536e, "Polska '93" International Stamp Exhibition, Poznan.

382 Yellow-green Vireo ("Red-eyed Vireo")

1993. Songbirds. Multicoloured.
2537 15c. Type **382** 60 60
2538 25c. Fork-tailed flycatcher ("Scissor-tailed Flycatcher") 65 65
2539 35c. Palm chat 75 75
2540 35c. Chaffinch 75 75
2541 45c. Yellow wagtail 80 80
2542 45c. Painted bunting 80 80
2543 50c. Short-tailed pygmy tyrant ("Short-tailed Pygmy Flycatcher") . . . 80 80
2544 65c. Orange-breasted bunting ("Rainbow Bunting") 90 90
2545 75c. Red crossbill 90 90
2546 75c. Kauai akialoa 90 90
2547 $1 Yellow-throated longclaw ("Yellow-throated Wagtail") . . . . 1·00 1·00
2548 $4 Barn swallow . . . . . 2·50 2·75
MS2549 Two sheets, each 105 × 86 mm. (a) $6 Song thrush. (b) $6 White-crested laughing thrush Set of 2 sheets . . . . 7·00 8·00
Nos. 2537/48 were printed together, se-tenant, with the backgrounds forming a composite design.

383 Atlantic Grey Cowrie and Atlantic Yellow Cowrie

1993. Seashells. Multicoloured.
2550 15c. Type **383** 55 55
2551 15c. Candy-stick tellin and sunrise tellin 55 55
2552 25c. Caribbean vase 60 60
2553 35c. Lightning venus and royal comb venus 70 70
2554 35c. Crown cone 70 70
2555 45c. Reticulated cowrie-helmet 80 80
2556 50c. Barbados mitre and variegated turret shell . . 80 80
2557 50c. Common egg cockle and Atlantic strawberry cockle 80 80
2558 75c. Measled cowrie 90 90
2559 75c. Rooster-tail conch . . . 90 90
2560 $1 Lion's-paw scallop and Antillean scallop . . . . 1·00 1·00
2561 $4 Dog-head triton . . . . 2·25 2·75
MS2562 Two sheets, each 76 × 106 mm. (a) $6 Dyson's keyhole limpet. (b) $6 Virgin nerite and Emerald nerite Set of 2 sheets 11·00 11·00
Nos. 2550/61 were printed together, se-tenant, with the backgrounds forming a composite design.

1993. Asian International Stamp Exhibitions. As T **219a** of Gambia. Mult. (a) "Indopex '93", Surabaya, Indonesia.
2563 35c. Megalithic carving, Sumba Island 35 25
2564 45c. Entrance to Gao Gajah, Bali 45 30
2565 $1.50 Statue of kris holder 1·00 1·00
2566 $1.50 Hanuman protecting Sita . . . . 1·00 1·00
2567 $1.50 Sendi of Visu mounted on Garuda . . . 1·00 1·00
2568 $1.50 Wahana (votif figure) 1·00 1·00
2569 $1.50 Hanuman (different) 1·00 1·00
2570 $1.50 Singa (symbolic lion) 1·00 1·00
2571 $2 Loving-mother Bridge, Taroko Gorge National Park . . . . 1·40 1·50
2572 $4 Head of Kala over temple gateway, Northern Bali . . . . 2·50 3·00
MS2573 104 × 134 mm. $6 Slow loris 3·75 4·25

(b) "Taipei '93", Taiwan.
2574 35c. Fire-breathing dragon, New Year's Fair, Chongqing 35 25
2575 45c. Stone elephant, Ming Tomb, Nanjing 45 30
2576 $1.50 "Ornamental Cock" (Han Meilin) . . . . . . 1·00 1·00
2577 $1.50 "He's even afraid of Cows" (Meilin) . . . . . 1·00 1·00
2578 $1.50 "On a Moonlit Night" (Meilin) . . . . 1·00 1·00
2579 $1.50 "Eyes that see in the Dark" (Meilin) . . . . . 1·00 1·00
2580 $1.50 "He's well behaved" (Meilin) . . . . 1·00 1·00
2581 $1.50 "He doesn't Bite" (Meilin) . . . . 1·00 1·00
2582 $2 Marble peifang, Ming 13 Tombs, Beijing . . . . . 1·40 1·50
2583 $4 Stone pillar, Nanjing . . 2·50 3·00
MS2584 104 × 134 mm. $6 Orang-utan, Mt. Lesuser National Park 3·75 4·25

(c) "Bangkok 1993", Thailand.
2585 35c. Nora Nair, Prasad Phra Thepidon, Wat Phra Kaew 35 25
2586 45c. Stucco deities at Library of Wat Phra Singh 45 30
2587 $1.50 Wooden carved horses 1·00 1·00
2588 $1.50 Wheel of the law . . . 1·00 1·00
2589 $1.50 Lanna bronze elephant . . . . 1·00 1·00
2590 $1.50 Kendi in the form of elephant . . . . 1·00 1·00
2591 $1.50 Bronze duck . . . . 1·00 1·00
2592 $1.50 Horseman . . . . . 1·00 1·00
2593 $2 Naga snake, Chiang Mai's Temple . . . . . . 1·40 1·50
2594 $4 Stucco figures, Wat Chang Lom . . . . 2·50 3·00
MS2595 134 × 104 mm. $6 Elephant calf (horiz) . . . . 3·75 4·25
No. 2590 is incorrectly inscribed "Kendi in the form of an Elphant".

1993. World Cup Football Championship, U.S.A. (1994) (1st issue). As T **221a** of Gambia. Mult.
2596 10c. Nikolai Larionov (Russia) 35 30
2597 25c. Andrea Carnevale (Italy) 60 25
2598 35c. Enzo Schifo (Belgium) and Soon-Ho Choi (South Korea) 70 25
2599 45c. Gary Lineker (England) 1·00 30
2600 $1 Diego Maradona (Argentina) . . . . 1·50 80
2601 $2 Lothar Mattaeus (Germany) . . . . 1·75 2·00
2602 $4 Jan Karas (Poland) and Julio Cesar Silva (Brazil) 2·50 3·25
2603 $5 Claudio Caniggia (Argentina) . . . . 2·50 3·25
MS2604 Two sheets, each 75 × 104 mm. (a) $6 Wlodzimierz (Poland). (b) $6 José Basualdo (Argentina) Set of 2 sheets . . 7·00 8·00
See also Nos. 2743/9.

384 James K. Spensley

1993. Centenary of Italian Football. Past and present Genoa players. Each blue, red and black.
2605 $3 Type **384** . . . . 2·50 2·50
2606 $3 Renzo de Vecchi . . . . 2·50 2·50
2607 $3 Giovanni de Pra' . . . . 2·50 2·50
2608 $3 Luigi Burlando . . . . . 2·50 2·50
2609 $3 Felice Levratto . . . . . 2·50 2·50
2610 $3 Guglielmo Stabile . . . . 2·50 2·50

2611 $3 Vittorio Sardelli . . . . 2·50 2·50
2612 $3 Juan Carlos Verdeal . . 2·50 2·50
2613 $3 Fosco Becattini . . . . 2·50 2·50
2614 $3 Julio Cesar Abadie . . . 2·50 2·50
2615 $3 Luigi Meroni . . . . . 2·50 2·50
2616 $3 Roberto Pruzzo . . . . 2·50 2·50
MS2617 Two sheets. (a) 100 × 75 mm. $15 Genoa Football Club badge (29 × 45 mm). (b) 129 × 106 mm. $15 Genoa team of 1991–92 (48 × 35 mm) Set of 2 sheets . . . . 22·00 22·00

385 "The Band Concert", 1935

1993. 65th Anniv of Mickey Mouse. Scenes from Walt Disney cartoon films. Multicoloured.
2618 25c. Type **385** 90 20
2619 35c. "Mickey's Circus", 1936 . . . . 1·00 20
2620 50c. "Magician Mickey", 1937 . . . . 1·25 35
2621 75c. "Moose Hunters", 1937 1·60 60
2622 $1 "Mickey's Amateurs", 1937 . . . . 1·75 80
2623 $2 "Tugboat Mickey", 1940 2·50 2·50
2624 $4 "Orphan's Benefit", 1941 3·50 4·25
2625 $5 "Mickey's Christmas Carol", 1983 . . . . . . 3·50 4·25
MS2626 Two sheets, each 127 × 102 mm. (a) $6 "Mickey's Birthday Party", 1942. (b) $6 "Mickey's Trailer", 1938 (vert) Set of 2 sheets . . . . 11·00 11·00
No. 2624 is inscribed "Oprhan's Benefit" in error.

1993. Christmas. Religious Paintings. As T **221b** of Gambia. Black, yellow and red (Nos. 2627/8, 2632 and 2634, **MS**2635a) or multicoloured (others).
2627 10c. "The Nativity" (Durer) 25 15
2628 25c. "The Annunciation" (Durer) 35 15
2629 35c. "The Litta Madonna" (Da Vinci) 40 20
2630 60c. "The Virgin and Child with St. John the Baptist and St. Anne" (Da Vinci) 50 40
2631 90c. "The Madonna with the Carnation" (Da Vinci) 65 65
2632 $1 "Adoration of the Magi" (Durer) 75 75
2633 $4 "The Benois Madonna" (Da Vinci) . . . . 2·50 3·25
2634 $5 "The Virgin Mary in the Sun" (Durer) . . . . . 2·50 3·25
MS2635 Two sheets, each 102 × 128 mm. (a) $6 "The Holy Family with Three Hares" (detail) (Dürer). (b) $6 "Adoration of the Magi" (detail) (Da Vinci) Set of 2 sheets . . . . 8·00 9·00
Nos. 2629/31, 2633 and **MS**2635b are inscribed "LEONARDO DI VINCI" in error.

386 Blanchard's Balloon over Walnut St. Prison

1993. Aviation Anniversaries. Multicoloured.
2636 35c. Airship "Graf Zeppelin" over Vienna at night 35 20
2637 45c. Type **386** 20 25
2638 50c. Lysander 50 35
2639 75c. "Graf Zeppelin" over Pyramids 75 55
2640 $2 Blanchard waving hat from balloon (vert) . . . 90 95
2641 $3 Hawker Typhoon . . . . 2·00 2·50
2642 $5 "Graf Zeppelin" over Rio de Janeiro . . . . . 3·25 3·75
MS2643 Three sheets, each 106 × 77 mm. (a) $6 "Graf Zeppelin". (b) Blanchard's balloon (vert). (c) $6 Hawker Hurricane Set of 3 sheets . . . . . . 10·50 11·00
ANNIVERSARIES: Nos. 2636, 2639, 2642, **MS**2643a, 125th birth anniv of Hugo Eckener (airship commander); 2637, 2640, **MS**2643b, Bicentenary of first airmail flight; 2638, 2641, **MS**2643c, 75th anniv of Royal Air Force.

387 Mercedes Benz "370 S" Cabriolet, 1932

1993. Centenaries of Henry Ford's First Petrol Engine (Nos. 2645/6, **MS**2648b) and Karl Benz's First Four-wheeled Car (others). Multicoloured.
2644 35c. Type **387** 55 20
2645 45c. Ford "Mustang", 1966 65 30
2646 $3 Ford "Model A" Phaeton, 1930 . . . . . 3·25 3·75
2647 $4 Mercedes Benz "300 Sl" Gullwing . . . . 3·50 4·00
MS2648 Two sheets, each 76 × 106 mm. (a) $6 Mercedes Benz "290", 1934. (b) $6 Ford "Model A", 1903 Set of 2 sheets 8·00 9·00

1993. Famous Paintings by Rembrandt and Matisse. As T **221c** of Gambia. Multicoloured.
2649 15c. "Self-portrait", 1900 (Matisse) 30 20
2650 35c. "Self-portrait", 1629 (Rembrandt) 35 20
2651 45c. "Self-portrait", 1918 (Matisse) 40 25
2652 50c. "Self-portrait", 1640 (Rembrandt) 50 35
2653 75c. "Self-portrait", 1652 (Rembrandt) 65 55
2654 $2 "Self-portrait", 1906 (Matisse) . . . . 1·40 1·75
2655 $4 "Self-portrait", 1900 (different) (Matisse) . . . 2·50 3·50
2656 $5 "Self-portrait", 1625–31 (Rembrandt) . . . . . 2·75 3·50
MS2657 Two sheets. (a) 100 × 125 mm. $6 "The Painter in his Studio" (detail) (Matisse). P 13½ × 14. (b) 125 × 100 mm. $6 "The Sampling Officials of the Drapers' Guild" (detail) (Rembrandt) (horiz).Set of 2 sheets . . . . 7·00 8·00

388 Fishermen with Blue Marlin

389 National Flag and Ketch in Bay

1994. 25th Anniv of Spice Island Billfish Tournament. Multicoloured.
2658 15c. Type **388** 50 30
2659 25c. Sailfish with angler . . 55 30
2660 35c. Yellow-finned tuna with angler 65 30
2661 50c. White marlin with angler 75 60
2662 75c. Catching a sailfish . . . 85 1·00

1994. 25th Anniv of Independence.
2663 35c. Type **389** 75 40
MS2664 76 × 106 mm. $6 Map of Grenada . . . . 4·00 5·00

1994. "Hong Kong '94" International Stamp Exhibition (1st issue). As T **222a** of Gambia. Multicoloured.
2665 40c. Hong Kong 1971 Scouting 50c. stamp and "Hong Kong Post Office, 1846" (left detail) (M. Bruce) 50 65
2666 40c. Grenada 1988 Rotary $2 and "Hong Kong Post Office, 1846" (right detail) (M. Bruce) 50 65
Nos. 2665/6 were printed together, se-tenant, with the centre part of each pair forming the complete painting.
See also Nos. 2667/72.

1994. "Hong Kong '94" International Stamp Exhibition (2nd issue). Qing Dynasty Porcelain. As T **222b** of Gambia. Multicoloured.
2667 45c. Vase with dragon decoration 60 60
2668 45c. Hat stand with brown base 60 60
2669 45c. Gourd-shaped vase . . 60 60
2670 45c. Rotating vase with openwork 60 60
2671 45c. Candlestick with dogs 60 60
2672 45c. Hat stand with orange base 60 60

390 "Hygrocybe acutoconica"

1994. Fungi. Multicoloured.
2673 35c. Type **390** 50 30
2674 45c. "Leucopaxillus gracillimus" 55 30
2675 50c. "Leptonia caeruleocapitata" 55 30
2676 75c. "Leucocoprinus birnbaumii" 70 50
2677 $1 "Marasmius atrorubens" 85 75
2678 $2 "Boletellus cubensis" . . 1·40 1·50
2679 $4 "Chlorophyllum molybdites" . . . . . . 2·25 2·75
2680 $5 "Psilocybe cubensis" . . 2·25 2·75
MS2681 Two sheets, each 100 × 70 mm. (a) $6 "Mycena pura". (b) $6 "Pyrrhoglossum lilaceipes" Set of 2 sheets . . . 9·00 9·00

391 Quetzalcoatlus

1994. Prehistoric Animals. Multicoloured.
2682 75c. Type **391** 70 65
2683 75c. Pteranodon ingens . . 70 65
2684 75c. Tropeognathus 70 65
2685 75c. Phobetor 70 65
2686 75c. Alamosaurus 70 65
2687 75c. Triceratops 70 65
2688 75c. Tyrannosaurus rex . . 70 65
2689 75c. Head of Tyrannosaurus rex 70 65
2690 75c. Lambeosaurus 70 65
2691 75c. Spinosaurus 70 65
2692 75c. Parasaurolophus . . . 70 65
2693 75c. Hadrosaurus 70 65
2694 75c. Germanodactylus . . . 70 65
2695 75c. Dimorphodon 70 65
2696 75c. Ramphorynchus . . . 70 65
2697 75c. Apatosaurus 70 65
2698 75c. Pterodactylus 70 65
2699 75c. Stegosaurus 70 65
2700 75c. Brathiosaurus 70 65
2701 75c. Allosaurus 70 65
2702 75c. Plesiosaurus 70 65
2703 75c. Ceratosaurus 70 65
2704 75c. Compsognathus 70 65
2705 75c. Elaphosaurus 70 65
MS2706 Two sheets. (a) 100 × 70 mm. $6 Pteranodon ingens (different). (b) 70 × 100 mm. $6 Head of Plateosaurus (vert) Set of 2 sheets . . . . . . 8·50 9·00
Nos. 2682/93 and 2694/2705 respectively were printed together, se-tenant, forming composite designs.

1994. 25th Anniv of First Manned Moon Landing. Space Shuttle "Challenger". As T **227a** of Gambia. Multicoloured.
2707 $2 Space shuttle "Challenger" . . . . . . 1·25 1·40
2708 $2 Judith Resnick (astronaut) . . . . 1·25 1·40
2709 $2 Aircraft in memorial fly past . . . . 1·25 1·40
2710 $2 Dick Scobee (astronaut) 1·25 1·40
2711 $2 Mission logo . . . . . . 1·25 1·40
2712 $2 Michael Smith (astronaut) . . . . 1·25 1·40
MS2713 107 × 76 mm. $6 "Challenger" crew . . . . . . 3·75 4·50

1994. Centenary of International Olympic Committee. Gold Medal Winners. As T **227b** of Gambia. Multicoloured.
2714 50c. Heike Dreschler (Germany) (long jump), 1992 . . . . 50 30
2715 $1.50 Nadia Comaneci (Rumania) (gymnastics), 1976 and 1980 . . . . . 1·90 1·90
MS2716 107 × 76 mm. $6 Dan Jansen (U.S.A.) (1000 metre speed skating), 1994 . . . . 3·75 4·25

391a Grenadian Family

1994. International Year of the Family.
2717 **391a** $1 multicoloured . . . 80 80

1994. 50th Anniv of D-Day. As T **227c** of Gambia. Multicoloured.
2718 40c. Sherman amphibious tank leaving landing craft 75 30
2719 $2 Tank on Churchill "Ark" bridging vehicle . . . . . 2·25 2·00
2720 $3 Churchill "Bobbin" tank laying roadway . . . . . 2·50 2·50
MS2721 107 × 76 mm. $6 Churchill AVRE with fascine . . . . . 3·50 4·00

1994. "Philakorea '94" International Stamp Exhibition, Seoul. As T **227d** of Gambia. Multicoloured.
2722 40c. Wonson Park (horiz) 30 25
2723 $1 Pusan (horiz) 55 60
2724 $1 "Lady in a Hooded Cloak" (left detail) (Sin Yunbok) 55 60
2725 $1 "Lady in a Hooded Cloak" (right detail) . . . 55 60
2726 $1 "Kiaseng House" (left detail) (Sin Yunbok) . . . 55 60

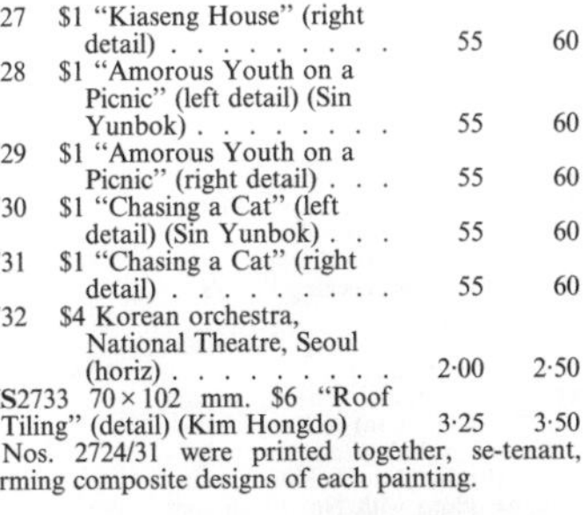

2727 $1 "Kiaseng House" (right detail) 55 60
2728 $1 "Amorous Youth on a Picnic" (left detail) (Sin Yunbok) 55 60
2729 $1 "Amorous Youth on a Picnic" (right detail) . . . 55 60
2730 $1 "Chasing a Cat" (left detail) (Sin Yunbok) . . . 55 60
2731 $1 "Chasing a Cat" (right detail) 55 60
2732 $4 Korean orchestra, National Theatre, Seoul (horiz) . . . . 2·00 2·50
MS2733 70 × 102 mm. $6 "Roof Tiling" (detail) (Kim Hongdo) 3·25 3·50
Nos. 2724/31 were printed together, se-tenant, forming composite designs of each painting.

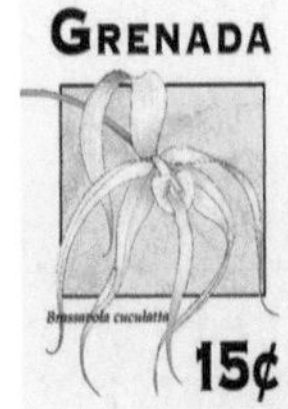

392 "Brassavola cuculatta"

393 Tony Meola (U.S.A.)

1994. Orchids. Multicoloured.
2734 15c. Type **392** 30 20
2735 25c. "Comparettia falcata" 40 20
2736 45c. "Epidendrum ciliare" 50 30
2737 75c. "Epidendrum cochleatum" 70 50
2738 $1 "Ionopsis utricularioides" 80 70
2739 $2 "Onicidium cebolletta" 1·25 1·40
2740 $4 "Onicidium luridium" . . 2·25 2·50
2741 $5 "Rodriquezia secunda" 2·25 2·50
MS2742 Two sheets, each 100 × 70 mm. (a) $6 "Ionopsis utricariodes" (different). (b) $6 "Onicidium luridium" (different) Set of 2 sheets . . . . . . 8·00 8·50
No. **MS**2742b is inscribed "Onicium luridum" in error.

1994. World Cup Football Championship, U.S.A. (2nd issue). Multicoloured.
2743 75c. Type **393** 80 80
2744 75c. Steve Mark (Grenada) 80 80
2745 75c. Gianluigi Lentini (Italy) 80 80
2746 75c. Belloumi (Algeria) . . . 80 80
2747 75c. Nunoz (Spain) 80 80
2748 75c. Lothar Matthaus (Germany) 80 80
MS2749 Two sheets. (a) 99 × 70 mm. $6 World Cup Championship poster, 1930. (b) 70 × 114 mm. $6 Steve Mark (Grenada) (different) Set of 2 sheets . . . . 7·50 8·00

393a Sir Shridath Ramphal

1994. 1st Recipients of Order of the Caribbean Community. Multicoloured.
2750 15c. Type **393a** 10 10
2751 65c. William Demas 40 40
2752 $2 Derek Walcott . . . . . 1·75 1·75

394 Yellow-tailed Snapper

1994. Fishes. Multicoloured.
2753 15c. Type **394** 40 20
2754 20c. Blue tang 40 20
2755 25c. Porkfish (vert) 40 20
2756 75c. Four-eyed butterflyfish 75 50
2757 $1 Reid's seahorse (vert) . . 85 70
2758 $2 Spotted moray (vert) . . 1·50 1·60
2759 $4 Royal gramma ("Fairy basslet") . . . . 2·50 2·75
2760 $5 Queen triggerfish (vert) 2·50 2·75
MS2761 Two sheets, each 106 × 76 mm. (a) $6 Queen angelfish. (b) $6 Long-spined squirrelfish Set of 2 sheets . . 7·50 8·00

395 Mickey Mouse bathing Pluto

1994. Chinese New Year ("Year of the Dog"). Walt Disney cartoon characters. Multicoloured.
2762 2c. Type **395** 15 10
2763 3c. Dog taking mouthwash 15 10
2764 4c. Dog with curlers in tail 15 10
2765 5c. Brushing dog's eyelashes 15 10
2766 10c. Giving dog manicure 25 10
2767 15c. Mickey spraying Pluto with flea powder 40 15
2768 20c. Dogs on display . . . 40 20
2769 $4 Judge checking Pluto's teeth . . . . 4·50 4·75
2770 $5 Pluto wearing "1st Prize" rosette . . . . 4·50 4·75
MS2771 Three sheets, each 127 × 102 mm. (a) $6 King Charles Spaniel rubbing against judge's leg. (b) $6 Pluto holding rosette. (c) $6 Pluto with No. 13 on coat Set of 3 sheets . . . . 11·00 12·00

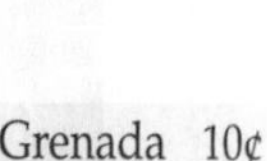

396 "Anartia amathea"

1994. Butterflies. Multicoloured.
2772A 10c. Type **396** 30 20
2773A 15c. "Marpesia petreus" 30 20
2774B 25c. "Hylephila phylaeus" 40 20
2775B 35c. "Junonia evarete" . . 45 25
2776A 45c. "Pseudolycaena marsyas" 50 30
2777A 50c. "Heliconius charitonius" 50 30
2778A 75c. "Hypolimnas misippus" 70 45
2778cB 90c. "Purgus oilcus" . . . 45 50
2779A $1 "Cepheuptychia cephus" 75 55
2779cB $1.50 "Allosmaitia piplea" 80 85
2780A $2 "Historis odius" . . . 1·75 1·50
2781A $3 "Phoebis philea" . . . 2·50 2·75
2782A $4 "Urbanus proteus" . . 3·25 3·75
2783A $5 "Battus polydamas" 3·50 4·00
2784A $10 "Philaethria dido" . . 6·00 7·50
2785A $20 "Hamadryas arethusa" . . . . . . 10·00 13·00

1994. Christmas. Religious Paintings by Francisco de Zurbaran. As T **231a** of Gambia. Multicoloured.
2786 10c. "The Virgin and Child with St. John" (1658) . . 20 15
2787 15c. "The Circumcision" . . 30 20
2788 25c. "Adoration of St. Joseph" 30 20
2789 35c. "Adoration of the Magi" 30 20
2790 75c. "The Portiuncula" . . 60 45
2791 $1 "The Virgin and Child with St. John" (1662) . . 75 60
2792 $2 "The Virgin and Child with St. John" (1658/64) 1·25 1·75
2793 $4 "The Flight into Egypt" 2·25 3·25
MS2794 Two sheets. (a) 74 × 86 mm. $6 "Our Lady of Ransom and Two Mercedarians" (detail). (b) 114 × 100 mm. $6 "Adoration of the Shepherds" (detail) (horiz) Set of 2 sheets . . . . 7·50 8·00

397 Grenada Dove on Nest

1995. Birds. Multicoloured.
2795 25c. Type **397** . . . . . . 1·10 50
2796 35c. Pair of Grenada doves at nest . . . . 1·10 50
2797 45c. Cuban tody (vert) . . . 1·25 50
2798 75c. Grenada dove on branch (vert) . . . . . . 1·50 1·50
2799 75c. Painted bunting . . . . 1·50 1·50
2800 $1 Grenada dove in flight (vert) . . . . 1·60 1·60
2801 $1 Red-legged honeycreeper 1·60 1·60
2802 $5 Green jay . . . . 3·50 4·25
MS2803 Two sheets, each 101 × 71 mm. (a) $6 Chaffinch. (b) $6 Chestnut-sided shrike vireo Set of 2 sheets . . . . 7·50 8·00
Nos. 2795/6, 2798 and 2800 also show the W.W.F. Panda emblem.

397a Junior Murray (West Indies)

1995. Centenary of First English Cricket Tour to the West Indies. Multicoloured.
2804 25c. Type **397a** 40 30
2805 35c. Richie Richardson (West Indies) 45 30
2806 $2 Alec Stewart (England) and Wisden Trophy (horiz) . . . . 1·60 1·75
MS2807 75 × 95 mm. $3 West Indian team, 1994 . . . . 2·25 2·25

398 Hooded Merganser

1995. Water Birds of the World. Multicoloured.
2808 25c. Type **398** 30 30
2809 35c. Green-winged teal . . . 35 30
2810 75c. King eider 70 75
2811 75c. Common shoveler . . . 70 75
2812 75c. Long-tailed duck . . . 70 75
2813 75c. Chiloe wigeon 70 75
2814 75c. Red-breasted merganser 70 75
2815 75c. Falcated teal 70 75
2816 75c. Vericolor teal 70 75
2817 75c. Smew 70 75
2818 75c. Red-crested pochard . . 70 75
2819 75c. Pintail 70 75
2820 75c. Barrow's goldeneye . . 70 75
2821 75c. Stellar's eider 70 75
2822 $1 Harlequin duck 75 75
2823 $3 European wigeon . . . . 1·75 2·00
MS2824 Two sheets, each 74 × 104 mm. (a) $5 Common shelduck ("European Wigeon"). (b) $6 Egyptian goose Set of 2 sheets . . . . 6·50 7·50
Nos. 2810/21 were printed together, se-tenant, forming a composite design.
No. 2811 is inscribed "Shobeler" in error.

399 Pig Priest, China

1995. Chinese New Year ("Year of the Pig"). Ornaments. Multicoloured.
2825 50c. Type **399** 45 55
2826 75c. Porcelain pig, Scotland 55 65
2827 $1 Seated porcelain pig, Italy 60 75
MS2828 107 × 77 mm. $2 Jade pig, China . . . . 1·25 1·40

400 Yellow-tailed Damselfish

1995. Marine Life. Multicoloured.
2829 $1 Type **400** 75 75
2830 $1 Blue-headed wrasse . . . 75 75
2831 $1 Balloonfish 75 75
2832 $1 Shy hamlet 75 75
2833 $1 Orange tube coral . . . 75 75
2834 $1 Rock beauty 75 75
2835 $1 Creole wrasse 75 75
2836 $1 Queen angelfish 75 75
2837 $1 Trumpetfish 75 75
2838 $1 Barred hamlet 75 75
2839 $1 Tube sponge 75 75
2840 $1 Porcupine fish 75 75
2841 $1 Firecoral 75 75
2842 $1 Royal gramma ("Fairy basslet") 75 75
2843 $1 Sea anemone 75 75
MS2844 Two sheets, each 106 × 76 mm. (a) $5 Seahorse. (b) $6 Elkhorn coral Set of 2 sheets 6·00 7·00
Nos. 2829/34 and 2835/43 respectively were printed together, se-tenant, forming composite designs.

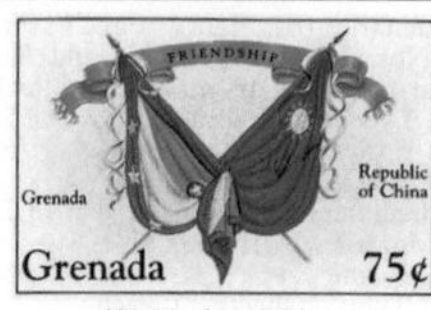

401 National Flags

1995. Grenada–Taiwan (Republic of China) Friendship. Multicoloured.
2845 75c. Type **401** . . . . . . 1·00 75
2846 $1 Prime Minister Brathwaite and President Lee Teng-hui . . . . . . 1·00 80
MS2847 76 × 106 mm. Nos. 2845/6 2·00 1·75

402 Cocker Spaniel

404 "Swords into Ploughshares"

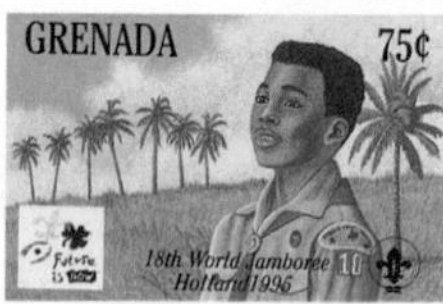

403 Grenadian Scout

1995. Domestic Animals. Multicoloured.
2848 10c. Type **402** 50 30
2849 15c. Pinto (horse) 60 30
2850 25c. Rottweiler 70 20
2851 35c. German shepherd . . . 75 20
2852 45c. Persian (cat) 80 25
2853 50c. Snowshoe (cat) 80 30
2854 75c. Percheron (horse) . . . 1·25 60
2855 $1 Scottish fold (cat) . . . 1·25 70
2856 $2 Arabian (horse) . . . . 2·00 2·00
2857 $3 Andalusian (horse) . . . 2·25 2·50
2858 $4 C.P. Shorthair (cat) . . . 2·50 3·00
2859 $5 Chihuahua . . . . . . 3·00 3·25
MS2860 Three sheets, each 100 × 71 mm. (a) $5 Manx (cat). (b) $5 Donkey. (c) $6 Shar Pei Set of 3 sheets . . . . 8·00 9·00

1995. Centenary (1992) of Sierra Club (environmental protection society). Endangered Species. As T **224a** of Gambia. Multicoloured.
2861 $1 Head of margay at night 70 70
2862 $1 Margay sitting 70 70
2863 $1 Head of margay in daylight 70 70
2864 $1 Head of Andean condor 70 70
2865 $1 Andean condor facing right 70 70
2866 $1 Andean condor facing left 70 70
2867 $1 White-faced saki on branch 70 70
2868 $1 White-faced saki showing mane 70 70
2869 $1 Patagonia landscape . . 70 70
2870 $1 Lesser rheas feeding (horiz) 70 70
2871 $1 Pair of lesser rheas (horiz) 70 70
2872 $1 Lesser rhea (horiz) . . . 70 70
2873 $1 Sunset over snow-covered mountains, Patagonia (horiz) 70 70
2874 $1 Volcanic eruption, Patagonia (horiz) 70 70
2875 $1 White-faced Saki (horiz) 70 70
2876 $1 Common caracara on branch (horiz) 70 70
2877 $1 Pair of common caracaras at nest (horiz) 70 70
2878 $1 Common caracara facing left (horiz) 70 70

1995. 18th World Scout Jamboree, Netherlands. Multicoloured.
2879 75c. Type **403** 45 50
2880 $1 Scout abseiling 55 60
2881 $2 Scout saluting and national flag . . . . . . 85 1·00
MS2882 107 × 77 mm. $6 Scout in canoe . . . . 3·00 3·50

1995. 50th Anniv of End of Second World War in Europe. Fighter Aircraft. As T **237a** of Gambia. Multicoloured.
2883 $2 Lavochkin La-7 (fighter) 1·50 1·40
2884 $2 Hawker Hurricane . . . 1·50 1·40
2885 $2 North American P-51D Mustang . . . . 1·50 1·40
2886 $2 Messerschmitt Bf 109 . . 1·50 1·40
2887 $2 Bristol Type 152 Beaufighter . . . . 1·50 1·40
2888 $2 Messerschmitt Me 262 1·50 1·40
2889 $2 Republic P-47 Thunderbolt . . . . . . 1·50 1·40
2890 $2 Hawker Tempest . . . . 1·50 1·40
MS2891 106 × 76 mm. $6 Nose of Republic P-47 Thunderbolt . . 3·50 3·75

1995. 50th Anniv of United Nations. Multicoloured.
2892 75c. Type **404** 40 50
2893 $1 Globe and dove 50 60
2894 $2 U.N. Building, New York . . . . 85 1·10
MS2895 101 × 71 mm. $6 Anniversary logo (horiz) . . . 2·50 3·00

405 Woman with Baskets

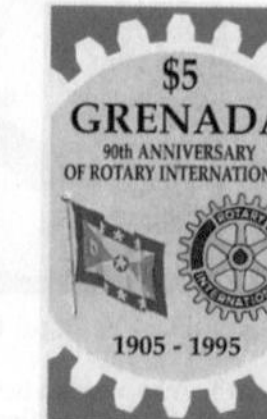

406 National Flag and Rotary Logo

1995. 50th Anniv of F.A.O. Multicoloured.
2896 75c. Type **405** 40 50
2897 $1 Boy with basket on head 50 60
2898 $2 Men harvesting bananas 85 1·10
MS2899 72 × 102 mm. $6 F.A.O. logo . . . . 2·50 3·00

1995. 90th Anniv of Rotary International. Multicoloured.
2900 $5 Type **406** . . . . 2·10 2·40
MS2901 76 × 106 mm. $6 Paul Harris (founder) and logo . . 2·75 3·25

1995. 95th Birthday of Queen Elizabeth the Queen Mother. As T **239a** of Gambia.
2902 $1.50 brown, lt brown & blk 1·60 1·60
2903 $1.50 multicoloured . . . . 1·60 1·60
2904 $1.50 multicoloured . . . . 1·60 1·60
2905 $1.50 multicoloured . . . . 1·60 1·60
MS2906 127 × 102 mm. $6 multicoloured . . . . 6·00 6·00
DESIGNS: No. 2902, Queen Elizabeth the Queen Mother (pastel drawing); 2903, Holding rose; 2904, At desk (oil painting); 2905, In blue hat and white coat; **MS**2906, Wearing floral hat.

1995. 50th Anniv of End of Second World War in the Pacific. As T **239b** of Gambia. Multicoloured.
2907 $2 Dogfight over the Marianas . . . . 1·40 1·40
2908 $2 U.S. dive-bomber and burning aircraft carrier, Battle of Midway . . . . 1·40 1·40
2909 $2 U.S. aircraft attacking Japanese transport, Battle of the Bismarck Sea . . . 1·40 1·40
2910 $2 "Mushashi" (Japanese battleship) on fire in Leyte Gulf . . . . 1·40 1·40
2911 $2 U.S. aircraft taking off from Henderson Field . . 1·40 1·40
2912 $2 Battleships at Guadalcanal . . . . . . 1·40 1·40
MS2913 108 × 77 mm. $6 U.S. bomber . . . . 3·50 3·75

407 Tian Bingyi (China) (badminton)

408 Junior Murray (West Indies)

1995. Olympic Games, Atlanta (1996) (1st issue). Multicoloured.
2914 75c. Type **407** 80 80
2915 75c. Waldemar Leigien (Poland) and Frank Wieneke (West Germany) (judo) 80 80
2916 75c. Nelli Kim (U.S.S.R.) (gymnastics) 80 80
2917 75c. Alessandro Andri (Italy) (shot put) 80 80
2918 $2 Jackie Joyner (U.S.A.) (heptathlon) . . . . . . 1·75 1·75
2919 $2 Mitsuo Tsukahara (Japan) (gymnastics) . . . 1·75 1·75
2920 $2 Flo Hyman (U.S.A.) and Zhang Rung Fang (China) (volleyball) . . . 1·75 1·75
2921 $2 Steffi Graf (West Germany) (tennis) . . . . 1·75 1·75
MS2922 Two sheets, each 72 × 102 mm. (a) $6 Wilma Rudolph (U.S.A.) (athletics). (b) $6 Soling class yacht Set of 2 sheets . . . . 7·00 8·00
No. **MS**2922b is inscribed "Sailing" in error.
See also Nos. 3102/24.

1995. Anniversaries and Events. Multicoloured.
2923 25c. Type **408** (centenary of first English cricket tour to the West Indies) . . . 1·25 50
2924 75c. Nutmeg (opening of Grenada Spice Factory) 90 75
2925 $1 Sendall Tunnel (centenary (1994)) . . . . 95 1·10
2926 $1 Caribbean Development Bank building (25th anniv) . . . . 95 1·10

409 Ajamu

410 Elvis Presley and Signature

1995. Local Entertainers. Multicoloured.
2927 35c. Type **409** 50 50
2928 35c. Mighty Sparrow . . . 50 50
2929 50c. Mighty Sparrow in evening dress 60 60
2930 75c. Ajamu (different) . . . 75 75

1995. Entertainment Legends. Multicoloured.
2931 75c. Type **410** 65 65
2932 75c. Marilyn Monroe . . . 65 65

411 Elvis Presley

1995. 60th Birth Anniv of Elvis Presley (singer). Multicoloured.
2933 $1 Type **411** 70 70
2934 $1 With beard 70 70
2935 $1 With long hair and microphone 70 70
2936 $1 Wearing white shirt . . . 70 70
2937 $1 Wearing pink shirt and purple jacket 70 70
2938 $1 With short hair and microphone 70 70
2939 $1 Wearing magenta shirt 70 70
2940 $1 Wearing orange shirt . . 70 70
2941 $1 Wearing purple shirt . . 70 70

412 Film Reel and Oscar Statuette

1995. Centenary of Cinema. Multicoloured.
2942 $1 Type **412** 90 85
2943 $1 "HOLLYWOOD" sign 90 85
2944 $1 Charlie Chaplin 90 85
2945 $1 Shirley Temple 90 85
2946 $1 Spencer Tracy and Katherine Hepburn . . . 90 85
2947 $1 Marilyn Monroe 90 85
2948 $1 John Wayne 90 85
2949 $1 Marlon Brando 90 85
2950 $1 Tom Cruise 90 85
MS2951 107 × 77 mm. $5 Orson Welles (horiz) . . . . 7·00 7·00
Nos. 2942/50 were printed together, se-tenant, forming a composite design.

413 "B1 Level Vista Dome" Electric Locomotive, Japan

1995. Trains of the World (1st series). Multicoloured.
2952 $1 Type **413** . . . . 1·00 90
2953 $1 Rolios Rail Class 25NC steam locomotive, South Africa . . . . 1·00 90
2954 $1 Class 460 electric locomotive, Switzerland 1·00 90
2955 $1 Central Railway diesel locomotive No. 605, Peru 1·00 90
2956 $1 X2000 tilt body train, Sweden . . . . 1·00 90
2957 $1 Via Rail Toronto to Vancouver observation car, Canada . . . . . . 1·00 90
2958 $1 Intercity 125 diesel locomotive, Great Britain 1·00 90
2959 $1 "The Flying Scotsman" steam locomotive, Great Britain . . . . 1·00 90
2960 $1 "Indian Pacific" diesel locomotive, Australia . . 1·00 90
2961 $1 ETR 450 electric train, Italy . . . . 1·00 90
2962 $1 Isparta to Bozanonu Line steam locomotive, Turkey 1·00 90
2963 $1 TGV train, France . . . 1·00 90
2964 $1 ICE train, Germany . . 1·00 90
2965 $1 Nishi Line electric locomotive, Japan . . . . 1·00 90
2966 $1 "Hikari" train, Japan . . 1·00 90
2967 $1 Central Pacific Jupiter steam locomotive, U.S.A. 1·00 90
2968 $1 Amtrak Type 900 electric locomotive, U.S.A. . . . 1·00 90
2969 $1 "Sir Nigel Gresley" steam locomotive, Great Britain . . . . 1·00 90
MS2970 Two sheets, each 106 × 76 mm. (a) $5 Diesel hydraulic train, Korea. (b) $6 Peking–Ulan Bator express, Mongolia Set of 2 sheets . . . 7·00 8·00
See also Nos. 3167/83.

414 Teresa Teng

1995. Teresa Teng (Chinese actress) Commem. Different portraits. Multicoloured unless otherwise indicated.
2971 35c. Type **414** 50 50
2972 35c. As a child (brown, ochre and yellow) 50 50
2973 35c. Wearing feather boa (black, grey and yellow) 50 50
2974 35c. With motor scooter . . 50 50
2975 35c. Holding microphone . . 50 50
2976 35c. In white sweater . . . 50 50
2977 35c. Playing flute 50 50
2978 35c. With hand to hair (black, grey and yellow) 50 50
2979 35c. Wearing gold decorated dress 50 50
2980 35c. With fan 50 50
2981 35c. As South-sea islander 50 50
2982 35c. With hands clasped . . 50 50
2983 35c. In kimono 50 50
2984 35c. Holding bow tie . . . 50 50
2985 35c. Wearing black blouse 50 50
2986 35c. Resting on chair arm 50 50
2987 75c. In army uniform . . . 65 65
2988 75c. In navy uniform . . . 65 65
2989 75c. In air force uniform . . 65 65
2990 75c. Singing with hand out stretched (black, grey and yellow) 65 65
2991 75c. Singing with flowers in hair 65 65
2992 75c. Singing in blue floral dress 65 65
2993 75c. With pink scarf 65 65
2994 75c. In fringed dress 65 65
2995 75c. In pale green sweater 65 65
2996 75c. With hands to face . . 65 65
Nos. 2987/96 are larger, 34 × 46 mm.

415 Mickey Mouse fighting Big Pete

1995. Mickey's Pirate Adventure. Walt Disney cartoon characters. Multicoloured.
2997 15c. Type **415** 30 20
2998 25c. Mickey with treasure chest 30 20
2999 35c. Minnie Mouse trying on plunder 30 20
3000 75c. Goofy with telescope and Mickey swimming with barrel 55 40
3001 $3 Big Pete . . . . 2·00 2·25
3002 $5 Mickey with monkey, seagull and handkerchief 2·50 3·00
MS3003 Two sheets, each 108 × 103 mm. (a) $6 Sea rat pirate. (b) $6 Minnie being thrown overboard by pirates Set of 2 sheets . . . . 8·00 8·50

416 Albert Michelson (1907 Physics)

1995. Centenary of Nobel Trust Fund. Multicoloured.
3004 $1 Type **416** 95 85
3005 $1 Ralph Bunche (1950 Peace) 95 85
3006 $1 Edwin Neher (1991 Medicine) 95 85
3007 $1 Klaus Vonklitzing (1985 Physics) 95 85
3008 $1 Johann Deisenhofer (1988 Chemistry) 95 85
3009 $1 Max Delbruck (1969 Medicine) 95 85
3010 $1 J. Georg Bednorz (1987 Physics) 95 85
3011 $1 Feodor Lynen (1964 Medicine) 95 85
3012 $1 Walther Bothe (1954 Physics) 95 85
3013 $1 James Franck (1925 Physics) 95 85
3014 $1 Gustav Hertz (1925 Physics) 95 85
3015 $1 Friedrich Bergius (1931 Chemistry) 95 85
3016 $1 Otto Loewi (1936 Medicine) 95 85
3017 $1 Fritz Lipmann (1953 Medicine) 95 85
3018 $1 Otto Meyerhof (1922 Medicine) 95 85
3019 $1 Paul Heyse (1910 Literature) 95 85
3020 $1 Jane Addams (1931 Peace) 95 85
3021 $1 Carl Braun (1909 Physics) 95 85
3022 $1 Hans Dehmelt (1989 Physics) 95 85
3023 $1 Heinrich Boll (1972 Literature) 95 85
3024 $1 Georges Kohler (1984 Medicine) 95 85
3025 $1 Wolfgang Pauli (1945 Physics) 95 85
3026 $1 Sir Bernard Katz (1970 Medicine) 95 85
3027 $1 Ernest Ruska (1986 Physics) 95 85
3028 $1 William Golding (1983 Literature) 95 85
3029 $1 Hartmut Michel (1988 Chemistry) 95 85
3030 $1 Hans Bethe (1967 Physics) 95 85
MS3031 Three sheets, each 105 × 76 mm. (a) $6 Theodore Roosevelt (1906 Peace). (b) $6 Woodrow Wilson (1919 Peace). (c) $6 Sir Winston Churchill (1953 Literature) Set of 3 sheets . . . 11·00 12·00
Nos. 3004/12, 3013/21 and 3022/30 respectively were printed together, se-tenant, forming composite designs.
No. 3015 is inscribed "Friedrich" in error.

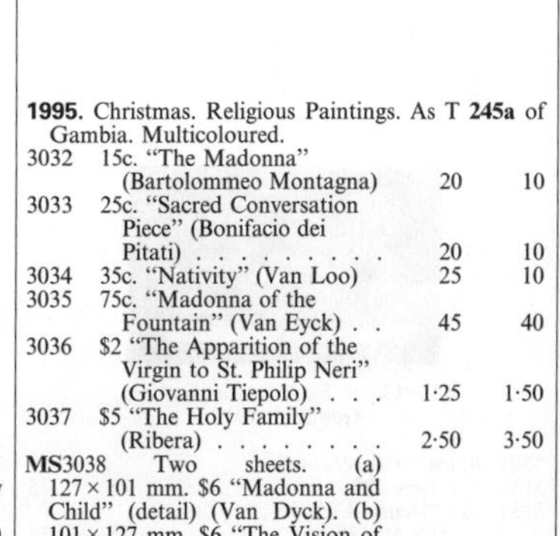

1995. Christmas. Religious Paintings. As T **245a** of Gambia. Multicoloured.
3032 15c. "The Madonna" (Bartolommeo Montagna) 20 10
3033 25c. "Sacred Conversation Piece" (Bonifacio dei Pitati) 20 10
3034 35c. "Nativity" (Van Loo) 25 10
3035 75c. "Madonna of the Fountain" (Van Eyck) . . 45 40
3036 $2 "The Apparition of the Virgin to St. Philip Neri" (Giovanni Tiepolo) . . . 1·25 1·50
3037 $5 "The Holy Family" (Ribera) . . . . 2·50 3·50
MS3038 Two sheets. (a) 127 × 101 mm. $6 "Madonna and Child" (detail) (Van Dyck). (b) 101 × 127 mm. $6 "The Vision of St. Anthony" (detail) (Van Dyck) Set of 2 sheets . . . . 7·50 8·50

417 Pres. Ronald Reagan at Fort George

1995. 12th Anniv of Liberation of Grenada (1st issue). Multicoloured.
3039 75c. Type **417** 60 70
3040 75c. Pres. Reagan with U.S. and Grenadian flags . . . 60 70
3041 75c. St. George's 60 70
MS3042 Two sheets, each 70 × 100 mm. (a) $5 Pres. Reagan and beach. (b) $6 Pres. Reagan and waterfall Set of 2 sheets . . 6·00 7·00
Nos. 3039/41 were printed together, se-tenant, forming a composite design.
See also Nos. 3043/51.

418 Pres. Ronald Reagan

419 Pope John Paul II and Statue of Liberty

1995. 12th Anniv of Liberation of Grenada (2nd issue). Designs showing Pres. Ronald Reagan. Multicoloured.
3043 $1 With wife 95 85
3044 $1 Type **418** 95 85
3045 $1 With microphones . . . 95 85
3046 $1 Wearing stetson 95 85
3047 $1 In front of U.S. flag . . . 95 85
3048 $1 In front of Brandenburg Gate, Berlin 95 85
3049 $1 Saluting by helicopter . . 95 85
3050 $1 On horseback 95 85
3051 $1 Addressing troops . . . 95 85

1995. Papal Visit to New York. Multicoloured.
3052 $1 Type **419** 80 80
3053 $1 Pope John Paul II and cathedral 80 80
MS3054 105 × 76 mm. $6 Pope John Paul II . . . . 3·50 3·75

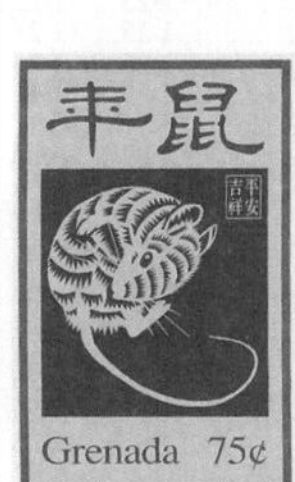

420 Rat asleep

421 "Young Woman" (Durer)

1996. Chinese New Year ("Year of the Rat").
3055 **420** 75c. buff, green and brown 60 60
3056 – 75c. orange, red and violet 60 60
3057 – 75c. buff, red and green 60 60
MS3058 95 × 58 mm. Nos. 3055/7 1·50 1·75
MS3059 76 × 106 mm. $1 multicoloured 75 85
DESIGNS—VERT: No. 3056, Rat eating; 3057, Rat asleep (T **420** reversed). HORIZ: No. **MS**3059, Two rats.

1996. Famous Drawings and Paintings by Durer and Rubens. Multicoloured.
3060 15c. Type **421** 40 20
3061 25c. "Four Horsemen of the Apocalypse" (Durer) . . 45 20
3062 35c. "Assumption and Coronation of the Virgin" (Durer) 50 20
3063 75c. "Mulay Ahmed" (Rubens) 80 50
3064 $1 "Anthony van Dyck aged 15" (Rubens) 90 60
3065 $2 "Head of a Young Monk" (Rubens) . . . . 1·75 1·75
3066 $3 "A Scholar inspired by Nature" (Rubens) . . . . 2·00 2·25
3067 $5 "Hanns Durer" (Durer) 3·00 3·50
MS3068 Two sheets, each 102 × 127 mm. (a) $5 "Martyrdom of St. Ursula" (detail) (Rubens). (b) $6 "The Death of the Virgin" (detail) (Durer) Set of 2 sheets 10·00 10·00

422 Goofy Tap-dancing

1996. Famous Dances. Walt Disney cartoon characters Dancing. Multicoloured.

3069 35c. Type **422** 70 20
3070 45c. Donald Duck doing Mexican hat dance (horiz) 80 25
3071 75c. Daisy Duck as hula dancer . . . . 1·25 55
3072 90c. Mickey and Minnie Mouse doing the tango (horiz) . . . . 1·25 70
3073 $1 Donald and Daisy doing the jitterbug . . . . . . 1·40 85
3074 $2 Mickey and Minnie performing Ukrainian folk dance (horiz) . . . . . . 2·25 2·50
3075 $3 Goofy and Pluto as ballet dancers (horiz) . . 2·50 2·75
3076 $4 Mickey and Minnie line-dancing . . . . 2·50 2·75
MS3077 Two sheets, each 133 × 109 mm. (a) $5 Minnie doing the can-can (horiz). (b) $6 Scrooge McDuck doing the Scottish sword dance Set of 2 sheets . . . . . 6·50 7·50

1996. 70th Birthday of Queen Elizabeth II. As T **255a** of Gambia showing different photographs. Multicoloured.

3078 35c. As Type **255a** of Gambia 50 25
3079 75c. Wearing white hat . . 85 55
3080 $4 With bouquet . . . . . 3·00 3·50
MS3081 103 × 125 mm. $6 Queen and Prince Philip . . . . . . 5·00 5·50

423 Ferrari "125 F1"

1996. Ferrari Racing Cars. Multicoloured.

3082 $1.50 Type **423** . . . . . 1·25 1·25
3083 $1.50 "Tipo 625" . . . . . 1·25 1·25
3084 $1.50 "P4" . . . . 1·25 1·25
3085 $1.50 "312P" . . . . . . 1·25 1·25
3086 $1.50 "312" Formula 1 . . 1·25 1·25
3087 $1.50 "312B" . . . . . . 1·25 1·25
MS3088 100 × 71 mm. $6 "F333 SP" (84 × 28 mm) . . . . 4·00 4·00

1996. 50th Anniv of UNICEF. As T **258a** of Gambia. Multicoloured.

3089 35c. Child writing in book (horiz) 20 25
3090 $2 Child planting seedling (horiz) . . . . 1·00 1·25
3091 $3 Children and UNICEF emblem (horiz) . . . . . 1·50 2·00
MS3092 75 × 106 mm. $5 Young boy . . . . 2·50 3·00

424 Lions' Gate, Jerusalem

1996. 3000th Anniv of Jerusalem. Multicoloured.

3093 75c. Type **424** 60 45
3094 $2 New Gate . . . . 1·40 1·40
3095 $3 Dung Gate . . . . . . 1·75 2·00
MS3096 114 × 74 mm. $5 The Old City (horiz) . . . . 3·25 3·25

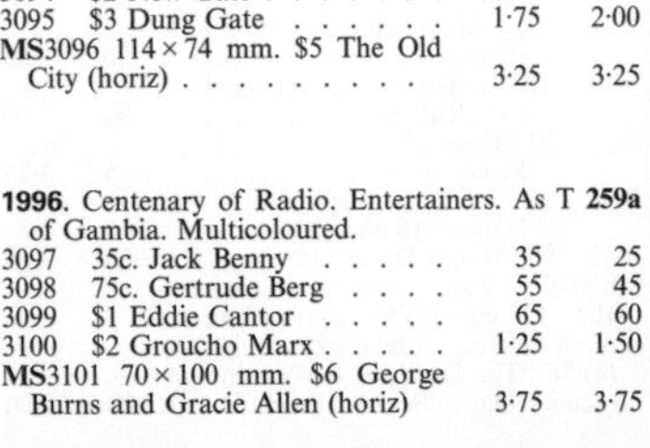

1996. Centenary of Radio. Entertainers. As T **259a** of Gambia. Multicoloured.

3097 35c. Jack Benny 35 25
3098 75c. Gertrude Berg 55 45
3099 $1 Eddie Cantor 65 60
3100 $2 Groucho Marx . . . . . 1·25 1·50
MS3101 70 × 100 mm. $6 George Burns and Gracie Allen (horiz) 3·75 3·75

425 Olympic Stadium, Athens, 1896

1996. Olympic Games, Atlanta (2nd issue). Previous Medal Winners. Multicoloured.

3102 35c. Gold medal of 1896 (vert) 40 25
3103 75c. Type **425** 65 45
3104 $1 Boughera el Quafi (France) (Gold, 1928) . . 70 70
3105 $1 Gustav Jansson (Sweden) (Bronze, 1952) 70 70
3106 $1 Spiridon Louis (Greece) (Gold, 1896) 70 70
3107 $1 Basil Heatley (Great Britain) (Silver, 1964) . . 70 70
3108 $1 Emil Zatopek (Czechoslovakia) (Gold, 1952) 70 70
3109 $1 Frank Shorter (U.S.A.) (Gold, 1972) 70 70
3110 $1 Alain Minoun O'Kacha (France) (Gold, 1956) . . 70 70
3111 $1 Kokichi Tsu Uraya (Japan) (Bronze, 1964) . . 70 70
3112 $1 Delfo Cabrera (Argentina) (Gold, 1948) 70 70
3113 $1 Harald Sakata (U.S.A.) (Silver—light heavyweight, 1948) 70 70
3114 $1 Tom Kono (U.S.A.) (Gold—middleweight, 1952 and 1956) 70 70
3115 $1 Naim Suleymanoglu (Turkey) (Gold—featherweight, 1988) . . . 70 70
3116 $1 Lee Hyung Kun (South Korea) (Gold—light heavyweight, 1988) . . . 70 70
3117 $1 Vassily Alexeyev (U.S.S.R.) (Gold—super heavyweight, 1972 and 1976) 70 70
3118 $1 Chen Weiqiang (China) (Gold—featherweight, 1984) 70 70
3119 $1 Ye Huanming (China) (Gold—featherweight, 1988) 70 70
3120 $1 Manfred Nerlinger (Germany) (Silver—super heavyweight, 1988) . . . 70 70
3121 $1 Joseph Depietro (U.S.A.) (Gold—bantamweight, 1948) 70 70
3122 $2 Ancient Greek runners 1·50 1·60
3123 $3 Spiridon Louis (Greece) (Gold—marathon, 1896) 2·00 2·25
MS3124 Two sheets, each 75 × 105 mm. (a) $5 Manfred Nerlinger (Germany) (Silver – super heavyweight weightlifting, 1988) (vert). (b) $6 Thomas Hicks (U.S.A.) (Gold – marathon, 1904) (vert) Set of 2 sheets . . . . . 7·00 8·00

Nos. 3104/12 (marathon runners) and 3113/21 (weightlifters) respectively were printed together, se-tenant, with the backgrounds forming composite designs.

426 Mercedes-Benz, 1929

1996. Classic Cars. Multicoloured.

3125 35c. Type **426** 35 25
3126 50c. Bugatti Type 35, 1927 45 30
3127 75c. J. Dusenberg, 1935 . . 65 45
3128 $1 Mercer, 1914 . . . . . 70 70
3129 $1 Type 57C Atalante, 1939 70 70
3130 $1 Cannstatt-Daimler, 1900 70 70
3131 $1 Delage, 1925 . . . . . . 70 70
3132 $1 Coventry Daimler, 1899 70 70
3133 $1 Vauxhall, 1900 . . . . . 70 70
3134 $1 T-15 Hispano-Suza, 1912 70 70
3135 $2 Alfa Romeo, 1929 . . . 1·50 1·60
3136 $3 Rolls Royce, 1910 . . . 1·90 2·25
MS3137 Two sheets, each 66 × 96 mm. (a) $6 L-Head Mercer, 1915 (56 × 42 mm). (b) $6 Mercedes, 1937 (56 × 42 mm) Set of 2 sheets . . . . 8·00 9·00

427 "Gorch Fock" (cadet barque), Germany, 1916

1996. Ships. Multicoloured.

3138 $1 Type **427** 75 75
3139 $1 "Henry B. Hyde", U.S.A., 1886 . . . . . . 75 75
3140 $1 "Resolution" (galleon), Great Britain, 1652 . . . 75 75
3141 $1 U.S.S. "Constitution" (frigate), U.S.A., 1797 . . 75 75
3142 $1 "Nippon Maru" (cadet ship), Japan, 1930 . . . . 75 75
3143 $1 "Preussen" (full-rigged sailing ship), Germany, 1902 . . . . 75 75
3144 $1 "Taeping" (clipper), Great Britain, 1852 . . . 75 75
3145 $1 "Chariot of Fame" (clipper), U.S.A., 1853 . . 75 75
3146 $1 "Star of India" (clipper), U.S.A., 1861 . . . . . . 75 75
3147 $1 H.M.S. "Bounty" . . . 75 75
3148 $1 "Bismark" (German battleship) 75 75
3149 $1 "Chuii Apoo" and two junks 75 75
3150 $1 "Lubeck" (German frigate) 75 75
3151 $1 Dutch galleon 75 75
3152 $1 "Augsburg" (German frigate) 75 75
3153 $1 "Henri Grace a Dieu" (British galleon) 75 75
3154 $1 H.M.S. "Prince of Wales" (battleship) . . . 75 75
3155 $1 "Santa Anna" (Spanish carrack) 75 75
MS3156 Two sheets, each 104 × 74 mm. (a) $5 H.M.S. "Victory" (ship of the line), Great Britain, 1805. (b) $6 "Cutty Sark" (clipper), Great Britain, 1869 Set of 2 sheets . . . . 7·50 8·00

No. 3151 is inscribed "BARBARY CORSAIR" and No. 3153 is stated to be French, both in error.

428 Jacqueline Kennedy

1996. Jacqueline Kennedy Onassis Commemoration. Multicoloured.

3157 $1 Type **428** 70 70
3158 $1 Wearing mauve blouse 70 70
3159 $1 In evening dress (inscr at right) 70 70
3160 $1 In evening dress (inscr at left) 70 70
3161 $1 Wearing pink dress . . . 70 70
3162 $1 Wearing blue dress with collar embroidered . . . 70 70
3163 $1 Wearing white jacket and brooch 70 70
3164 $1 In yellow jacket and green shirt 70 70
3165 $1 Wearing black jacket . . 70 70
MS3166 76 × 106 mm. $6 Jacqueline Kennedy Onassis (different) . . 3·50 4·25

429 Class C51 Locomotive of Imperial Train, Japan

1996. Trains of the World (2nd series). Multicoloured.

3167 35c. Type **429** 50 25
3168 75c. "Rheingold" express, Germany 75 45
3169 $1 Atlantic Coast Line locomotive No. 153, 1894, U.S.A. 75 75
3170 $1 Smith Compound No. 1619, Great Britain 75 75
3171 $1 Trans-Siberian Soviet Railways 75 75
3172 $1 Palatinate Railway Krauss locomotive, 1898, Germany 75 75
3173 $1 Paris, Lyons and Mediterranean line, France 75 75
3174 $1 Diesel-electric 0341 locomotive, Italy 75 75
3175 $1 Class C62 locomotive, Japan 75 75
3176 $1 Shantung Railways locomotive, China 75 75
3177 $1 Class C57 locomotive, Japan 75 75
3178 $1 Diesel express train, Japan 75 75
3179 $1 Shanghai–Nanking Railway locomotive, China 75 75
3180 $1 Class D51 locomotive, Japan 75 75
3181 $2 "Pioneer", 1851, U.S.A. 1·50 1·60
3182 $3 "France", France . . . . 1·90 2·25
MS3183 Two sheets, each 105 × 73 mm. (a) $5 Baden State Railways locomotive, Germany. (b) $6 Class C11 locomotive, Japan Set of 2 sheets . . . . . 8·00 9·00

430 Winter Jasmine

1996. Flowers. Multicoloured.

3184 $1 Type **430** 70 70
3185 $1 Chrysanthemum 70 70
3186 $1 Lilac 70 70
3187 $1 Japanese iris 70 70
3188 $1 Hibiscus 70 70
3189 $1 Sacred lotus 70 70
3190 $1 Apple blossom 70 70
3191 $1 Gladiolus 70 70
3192 $1 Japanese quince 70 70
3193 $1 Canterbury bell (vert) . . 70 70
3194 $1 Rose (vert) 70 70
3195 $1 Nasturtium (vert) 70 70
3196 $1 Daffodil (vert) 70 70
3197 $1 Tulip (vert) 70 70
3198 $1 Snapdragon (vert) . . . 70 70
3199 $1 Zinnia (vert) 70 70
3200 $1 Sweetpea (vert) 70 70
3201 $1 Pansy (vert) 70 70
MS3202 Two sheets. (a) 104 × 74 mm. $5 Aster. (b) 74 × 104 mm. $6 Peony (vert) Set of 2 sheets . . . . 8·00 9·00

Nos. 3184/92 and 3193/3201 respectively were printed together, se-tenant, with the backgrounds forming a composite design.

431 Zeppelin L-31 (Germany)

1996. Airships. Multicoloured.

3203 30c. Type **431** 40 40
3204 30c. Zeppelin L-35 (Germany) 40 40
3205 50c. Zeppelin L-30 (Germany) 55 45
3206 75c. Zeppelin L-2 10 (Germany) 75 55
3207 $1.50 Zeppelin L-21 (Germany) . . . . 1·25 1·40
3208 $1.50 Zodiac Type 13 Spiess (France) . . . . 1·25 1·40
3209 $1.50 N1 "Norge" (Roald Amundsen) . . . . 1·25 1·40
3210 $1.50 LZ-127 "Graf Zeppelin" (Germany) . . 1·25 1·40
3211 $1.50 LZ-129 "Hindenburg" (Germany) . . . . 1·25 1·40
3212 $1.50 Zeppelin NT (Germany) . . . . 1·25 1·40
3213 $3 Zeppelin L-3 (Germany) 2·00 2·25
3214 $3 Beardmore No. 24 (Great Britain) . . . . 2·00 2·25
MS3215 Two sheets, each 104 × 74 mm. (a) $6 Zeppelin ZT (Germany). (b) $6 Zeppelin L-13 (Germany) Set of 2 sheets . . . 8·00 8·00

432 Horned Guan

1996. West Indian Birds. Multicoloured.

3216 $1.50 Type **432** . . . . . . 1·40 1·40
3217 $1.50 St. Lucia amazon ("St. Lucia Parrot") . . . 1·40 1·40
3218 $1.50 Highland guan ("Black Penelopina") . . 1·40 1·40
3219 $1.50 Grenada dove . . . . 1·40 1·40
3220 $1.50 St. Vincent amazon ("St. Vincent Parrot") . . 1·40 1·40
3221 $1.50 White-breasted trembler . . . . 1·40 1·40
MS3222 Two sheets, each 100 × 70 mm. (a) $5 Semper's warbler. (b) $6 Yellow warbler ("Barbados Yellow Warbler") Set of 2 sheets . . . . 8·00 9·00

The inscriptions on Nos. **MS**3222a and **MS**3222b are transposed in error.

Nos. 3216/21 were printed together, se-tenant, with the backgrounds forming a composite design.

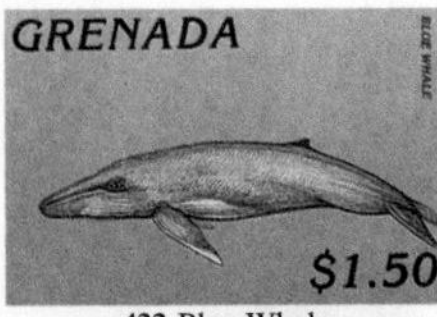

433 Blue Whale

1996. Whales and Turtles. Multicoloured.

3223 $1.50 Type **433** . . . . . . 1·40 1·40
3224 $1.50 Humpback whale . . 1·40 1·40
3225 $1.50 Right whale . . . . . 1·40 1·40
3226 $1.50 Hawksbill turtle . . . 1·40 1·40

3227 $1.50 Leatherback turtle . . 1·40 1·40
3228 $1.50 Green turtle . . . . . 1·40 1·40

434 Killer Whale

1996. Marine Life. Multicoloured.
3229 $1 Type **434** 75 75
3230 $1 Dolphin 75 75
3231 $1 Two dolphins 75 75
3232 $1 Sea lion and regal angelfish 75 75
3233 $1 Dolphins and hawksbill turtle 75 75
3234 $1 Three hawksbill turtles 75 75
3235 $1 Regal angelfish and pennant coralfish 75 75
3236 $1 Pennant coralfish 75 75
3237 $1 Sea lion and squirrelfish 75 75
3238 $1 Brown pelican 75 75
3239 $1 Killer whale (different) 75 75
3240 $1 Whale 75 75
3241 $1 Dolphins and sea lion . . 75 75
3242 $1 Shortfin pilot whale, blue-ringed octopus and sea lion 75 75
3243 $1 Hammerhead sharks and sea lion 75 75
3244 $1 Blue-striped grunts . . . 75 75
3245 $1 Stingray and Van Gogh fusilier 75 75
3246 $1 Van Gogh fusilier, ribbon moray and percoid fish 75 75
MS3247 Two sheets, each 106 × 76 mm. (a) $6 Pair of sea lions (horiz). (b) $6 Pair of dolphins (horiz) Set of 2 sheets 8·00 9·00
Nos. 3229/37 and 3238/46 respectively were printed together, se-tenant, with the backgrounds forming a composite design.

1996. Christmas. Religious Paintings. As T **245a** of Gambia. Multicoloured.
3248 25c. "The Visitation" (Tintoretto) 40 20
3249 35c. "Virgin with the Child" (Palma Vecchio) 45 25
3250 50c. "The Adoration of the Magi" (Botticelli) 55 30
3251 75c. "The Annunciation" (Titian) 75 45
3252 $1 "The Flight into Egypt" (Tintoretto) 90 65
3253 $3 "The Holy Family with the Infant Saint John" (Andrea del Sarto) . . . 2·00 2·50
MS3254 Two sheets, each 106 × 76 mm. (a) $6 "Adoration of the Magi" (Paolo Schiavo). (b) $6 "Madonna and Child with Saints" (Vincenzo Ponna) Set of 2 sheets 8·00 8·50
No. 3250 is inscr "Botticceli" in error.

1996. 20th Anniv of Rocky (film). Sheet 143 × 182 mm, containing vert design as T **266** of Gambia. Multicoloured.
MS3255 $2 × 3, Sylvester Stallone in "Rocky V" . . . . 3·50 4·00

435 Ox

1997. Chinese New Year ("Year of the Ox"). Sheet 150 × 75 mm, containing T **435** and similar triangular designs. Multicoloured. Self-adhesive on silver foil.
MS3256 $2 Type **435** ("GRENADA" in black); $2 Ox ("GRENADA" in pink); $2 Ox ("GRENADA" in blue) . . . 4·00 4·00

436 Mickey at Tram Stop

1997. "HONG KONG '97" International Stamp Exhibition. Mickey in Hong Kong. Disney cartoon characters. Multicoloured.
3257 35c. Type **436** 80 90
3258 50c. Mickey and Donald fishing at Victoria Harbour 80 90
3259 75c. Donald and Mickey parachuting . . . . . . 1·00 1·10
3260 90c. Mickey and Minnie visiting Bank of China . . 1·00 1·10
3261 $1 Mickey with pet parrot 1·10 1·25
3262 $1 Mickey drinking Kung-fu Tea . . . . 1·10 1·25
3263 $1 Mickey, Minnie and Goofy shopping at Chinese Wet Market . . . 1·10 1·25
3264 $1 Mickey, Minnie and Goofy with grasshoppers 1·10 1·25
3265 $1 Mickey and Goofy with lanterns . . . . 1·10 1·25
3266 $1 Mickey and Minnie practising Tai-chi . . . . 1·10 1·25
3267 $2 Goofy delivering bottled gas . . . . 1·25 1·40
3268 $3 Mickey, Minnie and Donald at "Jumbo" floating restaurant . . . . 1·40 1·50
MS3269 Four sheets, each 132 × 108 mm. (a) $3 Mickey and skyscrapers (vert). (b) $4 Mickey and Minnie dancing (vert). (c) $5 Mickey pulling rickshaw (vert). (d) $6 Mickey with noodles (vert) Set of 4 sheets . . . . . . 13·00 14·00

1997. 50th Anniv of UNESCO. As T **273a** of Gambia. Multicoloured.
3270 35c. Temple, Kyoto, Japan 40 25
3271 75c. Timbered houses, Quedlinburg, Germany . . 60 45
3272 90c. View from walls, Dubrovnik, Croatia . . . 70 55
3273 $1 Ruins at Delphi, Greece 75 75
3274 $1 Bryggen Wharf, Bergen, Norway (vert) 75 75
3275 $1 Old city, Berne, Switzerland (vert) 75 75
3276 $1 Warsaw, Poland (vert) 75 75
3277 $1 Fortress walls, Luxembourg (vert) . . . 75 75
3278 $1 Interior of Drottningholm Palace, Sweden (vert) 75 75
3279 $1 Petajavesi Church, Finland (vert) 75 75
3280 $1 Vilnius, Lithuania (vert) 75 75
3281 $1 Jelling Church, Denmark (vert) 75 75
3282 $1 Entrance to caves, Desert of Taklamakan, China (vert) 75 75
3283 $1 House, Desert of Taklamakan, China (vert) 75 75
3284 $1 Monument, Desert of Taklamakan, China (vert) 75 75
3285 $1 Palace of Cielos Purpuras, Wudang, China (vert) 75 75
3286 $1 House, Wudang, China (vert) 75 75
3287 $1 Stone Guardian, The Great Wall, China (vert) 75 75
3288 $1 Ming Dynasty statue, Wudang, China (vert) . . 75 75
3289 $1 The Great Wall, China (vert) 75 75
3290 $1.50 Segovia Cathedral, Spain . . . . 1·10 1·25
3291 $1.50 Wurtzburg, Germany 1·10 1·25
3292 $1.50 Plitvice Lakes, Croatia 1·10 1·25
3293 $1.50 Batalha Monastery, Portugal . . . . 1·10 1·25
3294 $1.50 River Seine, Paris, France . . . . 1·10 1·25
3295 $2 Tomar, Portugal . . . . 1·40 1·60
3296 $3 Palace of Chaillot, Paris, France . . . . 1·90 2·25
MS3297 Three sheets, each 127 × 102 mm. (a) $6 Popocatepetl Monastery, Mexico. (b) $6 Woodland path, Shirakami-Sanchi, Japan. (c) $6 Interior of the Hieronymites' Monastery, Portugal Set of 3 sheets . . . 12·00 14·00

437 Devon Rex

1997. Cats and Dogs. Multicoloured.
3298 35c. Type **437** 50 25
3299 75c. King Charles spaniel 70 45
3300 90c. Japanese bobtail . . . 75 50
3301 $1 Afghan hound 75 75
3302 $1 Turkish van 75 75
3303 $1 Ragdoll 75 75
3304 $1 Siberian 75 75
3305 $1 Egyptian mau 75 75
3306 $1 American shorthair . . . 75 75
3307 $1 Benegal 75 75
3308 $1 Asian longhair 75 75
3309 $1 Somali 75 75
3310 $1 Turkish angora 75 75
3311 $1 Lhasa apso 75 75
3312 $1 Rough collie 75 75
3313 $1 Norwich terrier 75 75
3314 $1 American cocker spaniel 75 75
3315 $1 Chinese crested dog . . . 75 75
3316 $1 Old English sheepdog . . 75 75
3317 $1 Standard poodle 75 75
3318 $1 German shepherd 75 75
3319 $1 German shorthair pointer 75 75
3320 $2 Cornish rex . . . . . . 1·40 1·60
3321 $3 Pekingese . . . . 1·90 2·25
MS3322 Two sheets, each 106 × 76 mm. (a) $6 Singapura. (b) $6 Bernese mountain dog Set of 2 sheets . . . . 8·50 9·00

438 Dunkleosteus

1997. Dinosaurs. Multicoloured.
3323 35c. Type **438** 60 30
3324 75c. Tyrannosaurus rex . . 1·00 55
3325 $1.50 Sordes . . . . 1·25 1·40
3326 $1.50 Dimorphodon . . . . 1·25 1·40
3327 $1.50 Diplodocus . . . . . 1·25 1·40
3328 $1.50 Allosaurus . . . . . 1·25 1·40
3329 $1.50 Pentaceratops . . . . 1·25 1·40
3330 $1.50 Protoceratops . . . . 1·25 1·40
3331 $2 Askeptosaurus (vert) . . 1·40 1·60
3332 $3 Triceratops (vert) . . . . 1·90 2·25
MS3333 Two sheets, each 103 × 74 mm. (a) $6 Tristychius (vert). (b) $6 Maiasaura (vert) Set of 2 sheets . . . . 9·00 9·50
Nos. 3325/30 were printed together, se-tenant, with the backgrounds forming a composite design.

439 Porcelain Crab

1997. Marine Life. Multicoloured.
3334 45c. Type **439** 45 30
3335 75c. Humpback whale . . . 90 45
3336 90c. Hermit crab 75 50
3337 $1 Great white shark . . . 1·00 70
3338 $1.50 Octopus (vert) . . . . 1·25 1·40
3339 $1.50 Lei triggerfish (vert) 1·25 1·40
3340 $1.50 Lionfish (vert) . . . . 1·25 1·40
3341 $1.50 Harlequin wrasse (vert) . . . . 1·25 1·40
3342 $1.50 Clown fish (vert) . . . 1·25 1·40
3343 $1.50 Moray eel (vert) . . . 1·25 1·40
3344 $3 Green sea turtle . . . . 1·90 2·25
3345 $4 Whale shark . . . . . . 2·50 2·75
MS3346 Two sheets, each 106 × 76 mm. (a) $6 Pacific barracudas. (b) $6 Scalloped hammerhead shark Set of 2 sheets 8·50 9·00
Nos. 3338/43 were printed together, se-tenant, with the backgrounds forming a composite design.

1997. 300th Anniv of Mother Goose Nursery Rhymes. Sheet 72 × 102 mm, containing multicoloured design as T **276a** of Gambia.
MS3347 $5 Boy holding umbrella ("Rain") (vert) . . . . 3·50 4·00

1997. 10th Anniv of Chernobyl Nuclear Disaster. As T **276a** of Gambia. Multicoloured.
3348 $2 As Type **276b** of Gambia 1·40 1·60
3349 $2 As No. 3348, but inscribed "CHABAD'S CHILDREN OF CHERNOBYL" at foot 1·40 1·60

1997. 50th Death Anniv of Paul Harris (founder of Rotary International). As T **276c** of Gambia. Multicoloured.
3350 $3 Paul Harris and vocational training programme, Philippines 1·75 2·00
MS3351 78 × 107 mm. $6 Hands holding globe and doves . . . 3·25 3·75

1997. Golden Wedding of Queen Elizabeth and Prince Philip. As T **276d** of Gambia. Multicoloured.
3352 $1 Queen Elizabeth and Prince Philip waving . . . 75 75
3353 $1 Royal coat of arms . . . 75 75
3354 $1 Queen Elizabeth with Prince Philip in naval uniform 75 75
3355 $1 Queen Elizabeth and Prince Philip at Buckingham Palace . . . 75 75
3356 $1 Windsor Castle 75 75
3357 $1 Prince Philip 75 75
MS3358 100 × 70 mm. $6 Queen Elizabeth with Prince Philip in naval uniform (different) . . . 4·25 4·50

1997. "Pacific '97" International Stamp Exhibition, San Francisco (1st issue). Death Centenary of Heinrich von Stephan (founder of the U.P.U.). As T **276e** of Gambia.
3359 $2 green and black . . . . 1·25 1·40
3360 $2 brown . . . . 1·25 1·40
3361 $2 blue . . . . 1·25 1·40
MS3362 82 × 119 mm. $6 violet and black . . . . 3·50 4·25
DESIGNS: No. 3359, Postman on motorcycle; 3360, Von Stephan and Mercury; 3361, Postman on skis, Rocky Mountains, 1900s; **MS**3362, Von Stephan and Chinese letter carrier.
See also Nos. 3392/3409.

1997. Birth Bicentenary of Hiroshige (Japanese painter). As T **541a** of Ghana. Multicoloured.
3363 $1.50 "Nihon Embankment, Yoshiwara" . . . . 1·25 1·25
3364 $1.50 "Asakusa Ricefields and Torinomachi Festival" . . . . 1·25 1·25
3365 $1.50 "Senju Great Bridge" 1·25 1·25
3366 $1.50 "Dawn inside the Yoshiwara" . . . . 1·25 1·25
3367 $1.50 "Tile Kilns and Hasiba Ferry, Sumida River" . . . . 1·25 1·25
3368 $1.50 "View from Massaki of Suijin Shrine, Uchigawa Inlet and Sekiya" . . . . 1·25 1·25
MS3369 Two sheets, each 102 × 127 mm. (a) $6 "Kinryuzan Temple, Asakusa". (b) $6 "Night view of Saruwaka-machi" Set of 2 sheets . . . . 8·50 9·00

1997. 175th Anniv of Brothers Grimm's Third Collection of Fairy Tales. Snow White. As T **277a** of Gambia. Multicoloured.
3370 $2 Queen looking in mirror 1·50 1·50
3371 $2 Snow White and the Seven Dwarfs . . . . . . 1·50 1·50
3372 $2 Snow White and Prince 1·50 1·50
MS3373 124 × 96 mm. $6 Witch with apple . . . . 4·00 4·25

440 One-man Luge

1997. Winter Olympic Games, Nagano, Japan. Multicoloured.
3374 45c. Type **440** 45 30
3375 75c. Men's speed skating . . 65 45
3376 $1 One-man luge (different) 75 75
3377 $1 Ski jumping (blue ski suit) 75 75
3378 $1 Downhill skiing 75 75
3379 $1 Speed skating 75 75
3380 $1 Two-man bobsleigh . . . 75 75
3381 $1 Women's figure skating 75 75
3382 $1 Alpine combined 75 75
3383 $1 Ice hockey 75 75
3384 $1 Ski jumping (yellow ski suit) 75 75
3385 $2 Men's figure skating . . 1·40 1·60
3386 $3 Slalom . . . . 1·90 2·25
MS3387 Two sheets, each 96 × 69 mm. (a) $6 Four-man bobsleigh. (b) $6 Downhill skiing (vert) Set of 2 sheets . . . . . 8·50 9·00

441 Bank of China

1997. Return of Hong Kong to China. Multicoloured.
3388 90c. Type **441** 65 50
3389 $1 Skyscrapers 75 55
3390 $1.75 "Hong Kong '97" on modern buildings (63 × 32 mm) . . . . . . 1·40 1·60
3391 $2 Deng Xiaoping and Hong Kong (63 × 32 mm) 1·60 1·75

442 Minnie Mouse dancing the Hula

1997. "Pacific '97" International Stamp Exhibition, San Francisco (2nd issue). Centenary of the Cinema. Minnie Mouse in "Hawaiian Holiday". Multicoloured.
3392 50c. Type **442** (Frame 1) . . 60 60
3393 50c. Frame 2 . . . . 60 60
3394 50c. Frame 3 . . . . 60 60
3395 50c. Frame 4 . . . . 60 60
3396 50c. Frame 5 . . . . 60 60
3397 50c. Frame 6 . . . . 60 60
3398 50c. Frame 7 . . . . 60 60
3399 50c. Frame 8 . . . . 60 60

3400 50c. Frame 9 . . . . 60 60
3401 50c. Frame 10 . . . . . . 60 60
3402 50c. Frame 11 . . . . . . 60 60
3403 50c. Frame 12 . . . . . . 60 60
3404 50c. Frame 13 . . . . . . 60 60
3405 50c. Frame 14 . . . . . . 60 60
3406 50c. Frame 15 . . . . . . 60 60
3407 50c. Frame 16 . . . . . . 60 60
3408 50c. Frame 17 . . . . . . 60 60
MS3409 110 × 130 mm. $6 Frame 18 6·50 7·00

443 Hercules lifting Rock

1997. "Hercules" (cartoon film) (1st series). Multicoloured.
3410 $1 Type **443** 90 90
3411 $1 Pegasus 90 90
3412 $1 Megara 90 90
3413 $1 Philoktetes 90 90
3414 $1 Nessus 90 90
3415 $1 Hydra 90 90
3416 $1 Pain and Panic 90 90
3417 $1 Hades 90 90
MS3418 Two sheets. (a) 131 × 104 mm. $6 Hercules as a boy. (b) 104 × 131 mm. $6 The Muses Set of 2 sheets . . . . 9·00 10·00
See also Nos. 3561/85.

1997. World Cup Football Championship, France (1998). As T **283a** of Gambia. Multicoloured (except Nos. 3422/3 and 3428).
3419 15c. West German and Italian Players, 1982 (vert) 35 20
3420 75c. Italian player holding World Cup, 1982 (vert) 70 45
3421 90c. West German and Italian players wearing "20" shirts, 1982 (vert) . . 75 50
3422 $1 Uruguay team, 1950 (brown) 75 75
3423 $1 Brazilian team, 1958 (brown) 75 75
3424 $1 West German team, 1974 75 75
3425 $1 Argentine team, 1986 . . 75 75
3426 $1 Italian team, 1982 . . . 75 75
3427 $1 West German team, 1990 75 75
3428 $1 Italian team, 1934 (brown) 75 75
3429 $1 Brazilian team, 1970 . . 75 75
3430 $1 Seaman, England 75 75
3431 $1 Klinsmann, Germany . . 75 75
3432 $1 Berger, Czech Republic 75 75
3433 $1 McCoist, Scotland . . . 75 75
3434 $1 Gascoigne, England . . . 75 75
3435 $1 Djorkaeff, France . . . 75 75
3436 $1 Sammer, Germany . . . 75 75
3437 $1 Futre, Portugal 75 75
3438 $2 Italian player beating goal keeper, 1982 (vert) 1·40 1·60
3439 $3 Goal-mouth melee, 1982 (vert) . . . . 1·90 2·25
3440 $4 Two West German players tackling Italian player (vert) . . . . . . 2·50 2·75
MS3441 Two sheets. (a) 102 × 127 mm. $6 Beckenbaur holding World Cup, Germany (vert). (b) 127 × 102 mm. $6 Moore, England Set of 2 sheets 9·00 10·00

444 Peacock

1997. Butterflies and Moths. Multicoloured.
3442 45c. Type **444** 50 30
3443 75c. Orange flambeau . . . 70 45
3444 90c. Eastern tailed blue . . 75 50
3445 $1 Brimstone 75 75
3446 $1 Mocker swallowtail . . . 75 75
3447 $1 American painted lady 75 75
3448 $1 Tiger swallowtail 75 75
3449 $1 Long wing 75 75
3450 $1 Sunset moth 75 75
3451 $1 Australian Blue Mountain swallowtail . . 75 75
3452 $1 Bird wing 75 75
3453 $2 Black and red . . . . . 1·40 1·60
3454 $3 Large white . . . . . . 1·90 2·25
3455 $4 Oriental swallowtail . . . 2·50 2·75
MS3456 Two sheets, each 76 × 106 mm. (a) $5 Monarch. (b) $5 Blue morpho Set of 2 sheets 8·00 9·00

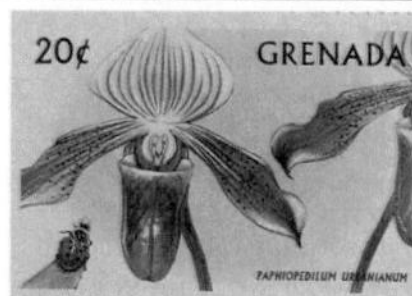

445 "Paphiopedilum urbanianum"

1997. Orchids of the World. Multicoloured.
3457 20c. Type **445** 45 20
3458 35c. "Trichoceros parviflorus" 60 25
3459 45c. "Euanthe sanderiana" (vert) 65 30
3460 75c. "Oncidium macranthum" (vert) . . . 75 45
3461 90c. "Psychopsis kramerianum" (vert) . . . 80 55
3462 $1 "Oncidium hastatum" (vert) 85 60
3463 $2 "Broughtonia sanguinea" (vert) . . . . 1·40 1·50
3464 $2 "Anguloa virginalis" (vert) . . . . 1·40 1·50
3465 $2 "Dendrobium bigibbum" (vert) . . . . 1·40 1·50
3466 $2 "Lucasiana" (vert) . . . 1·40 1·50
3467 $2 "Cymbidium" (vert) . . 1·40 1·50
3468 $2 "Cymbidium" and vase (vert) . . . . 1·40 1·50
3469 $2 "Odontoglossum crispum" (vert) . . . . . 1·40 1·50
3470 $2 "Cattleya brabantiae" (vert) . . . . 1·40 1·50
3471 $2 "Cattleya bicolor" (vert) 1·40 1·50
3472 $2 "Trichopilia suavia" (vert) . . . . 1·40 1·50
3473 $2 "Encyclia mariae" (vert) 1·40 1·50
3474 $2 "Angraecum leonis" (vert) . . . . 1·40 1·50
3475 $3 "Masdevallia saltatix" (vert) . . . . 1·90 2·25
3476 $4 "Cattleya luteola" . . . 2·50 2·75
MS3477 Two sheets. (a) 76 × 106 mm. $6 "Laelia milleri". (b) 106 × 76 mm. $6 "Oncidium onustum" Set of 2 sheets . . . 9·00 10·00
Nos. 3463/8 and 3469/74 respectively were printed together, se-tenant, with the backgrounds forming composite designs.

446 "Boletus erythropus"

1997. Fungi of the World. Multicoloured.
3478 35c. Type **446** 60 25
3479 75c. "Armillariella mellea" 70 45
3480 90c. "Amanita flavorubens" 80 50
3481 $1 Indigo milky 85 55
3482 $1.50 "Agaricus solidipes" 1·25 1·40
3483 $1.50 Salmon waxy cap . . 1·25 1·40
3484 $1.50 Fused maramius . . . 1·25 1·40
3485 $1.50 Shellfish-scented russula . . . . 1·25 1·40
3486 $1.50 Red-capped scaber stalk . . . . 1·25 1·40
3487 $1.50 "Calocybe gambosum" . . . . . . 1·25 1·40
3488 $1.50 "Boletus parasiticus" 1·25 1·40
3489 $1.50 "Frostis bolete" . . . 1·25 1·40
3490 $1.50 "Amanita myscara flavilolvata" . . . . . . 1·25 1·40
3491 $1.50 "Volvariella volvacea" 1·25 1·40
3492 $1.50 Stuntz's blue legs . . 1·25 1·40
3493 $1.50 Orange-latex milky . . 1·25 1·40
3494 $2 "Tylopilus balloui" . . . 1·40 1·90
3495 $4 "Boletus parasiticus" . . 2·50 2·75
MS3496 Two sheets, each 97 × 67 mm. (a) $6 "Agaricus argenteus". (b) $6 "Omphalotus illudens" Set of 2 sheets . . . 8·50 9·50

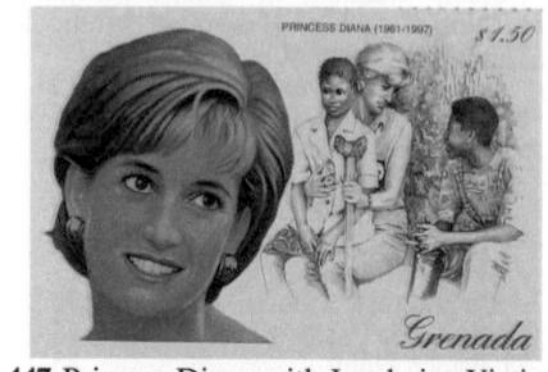

447 Princess Diana with Landmine Victims

1997. Diana, Princess of Wales Commemoration. Multicoloured.
3497 $1.50 Type **447** . . . . . . 1·25 1·25
3498 $1.50 With sick child . . . 1·25 1·25
3499 $1.50 With young boy on crutches . . . . 1·25 1·25
3500 $1.50 With leper . . . . . 1·25 1·25
3501 $1.50 Holding baby . . . . 1·25 1·25
3502 $1.50 Walking through minefield . . . . 1·25 1·25
MS3503 76 × 106 mm. $5 With Mother Teresa . . . . 3·75 3·75

448 "Angel" (Matthias Grunewald)

1997. Christmas. Religious Paintings. Multicoloured.
3504 35c. Type **448** 45 25
3505 50c. "St. Demetrius" (icon) 60 30
3506 75c. Three-panelled reliquary 75 45
3507 $1 "Angel of the Annunciation" (Jan van Eyck) 85 55
3508 $3 "The Annunciation" (Simone Martini) . . . . 2·25 2·50
3509 $4 "St. Michael" (icon) . . 2·50 3·00
MS3510 Two sheets. (a) 104 × 114 mm. $6 "The Coronation of the Virgin" (Fra Angelico). (b) 114 × 104 mm. $6 "The Annunciation" (Titian) (horiz) Set of 2 sheets . . . . 9·00 10·00

1998. Chinese New Year ("Year of the Tiger"). Sheet 150 × 75 mm, containing triangular designs as T **435** showing tigers. Multicoloured. Self-adhesive on silver foil.
MS3511 $1.50, "GRENADA" in pink; $1.50, "GRENADA" in gold; $1.50, "GRENADA" in bronze . . . . 1·80 1·90
No. MS3511 also exists on gold foil.

449 Black-tailed Damselfish

1998. Fishes. Multicoloured.
3512 65c. Type **449** 55 40
3513 90c. Yellow sweetlips . . . 75 50
3514 $1 Common squirrelfish . . 80 55
3515 $1.50 Blue tang . . . . . . 1·00 1·10
3516 $1.50 Porkfish . . . . . . 1·00 1·10
3517 $1.50 Banded butterflyfish 1·00 1·10
3518 $1.50 Thread-finned butterflyfish . . . . . . 1·00 1·10
3519 $1.50 Hooded butterflyfish ("Red-headed") . . . . . 1·00 1·10
3520 $1.50 Emperor angelfish . . 1·00 1·10
3521 $1.50 Duboulay's angelfish ("Scribbled Anglefish") 1·00 1·10
3522 $1.50 Lemon-peel angelfish 1·00 1·10
3523 $1.50 Bandit angelfish . . . 1·00 1·10
3524 $1.50 Bicoloured angelfish ("Biclor Cherub") . . . . 1·00 1·10
3525 $1.50 Palette surgeonfish ("Regal Tang") . . . . . 1·00 1·10
3526 $1.50 Yellow tang . . . . . 1·00 1·10
3527 $2 Powder-blue surgeonfish 1·25 1·40
MS3528 Two sheets, each 110 × 80 mm. (a) $6 Two-banded anemonefish. (b) $6 Forceps butterflyfish ("Long-nosed Butterflyfish") . . . . 9·00 10·00
Nos. 3515/20 and 3521/6 respectively were printed together, se-tenant, with the backgrounds forming composite designs.

450 "Sophronitis grandiflora"

1998. Flowers of the World. Multicoloured.
3529 $1.50 Type **450** 60 65
3530 $1.50 "Phalaenopsis amboinensis" 60 65
3531 $1.50 "Zygopetalum intermedium" 60 65
3532 $1.50 "Paphiopedilum purpuratum" 60 65
3533 $1.50 "Miltonia regnellii" 60 65
3534 $1.50 "Dendrobium parishii" 60 65
3535 $1.50 "Arachnis clarkei" . . 60 65
3536 $1.50 "Cymbidium eburneum" 60 65
3537 $1.50 "Dendrobium chrysotoxum" 60 65
3538 $1.50 "Paphiopedilum insigne" 60 65
3539 $1.50 "Paphiopedilum venustum" 60 65
3540 $1.50 "Renanthera imschootiana" 60 65
MS3541 Two sheets, each 104 × 72 mm. (a) $6 "Pleione maculata". (b) $6 "Lycaste aromatica" Set of 2 sheets . . 4·75 5·00

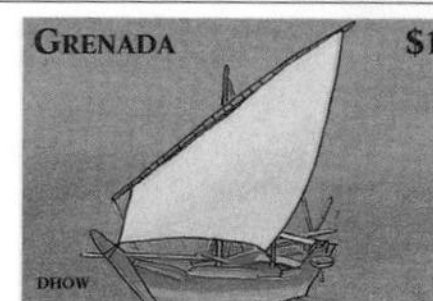

451 Dhow

1998. Famous Ships. Multicoloured.
3542 $1 Type **451** 40 45
3543 $1 Galleon 40 45
3544 $1 Felucca 40 45
3545 $1 Schooner 40 45
3546 $1 Aircraft carrier 40 45
3547 $1 Knau 40 45
3548 $1 Destroyer 40 45
3549 $1 Viking longship 40 45
3550 $1 "Queen Elizabeth 2" (liner) 40 45
3551 $1 Brig 40 45
3552 $1 Clipper 40 45
3553 $1 Caique 40 45
3554 $1 Mississippi riverboat . . 40 45
3555 $1 Luxury liner 40 45
3556 $1 "Mayflower" (Pilgrim Fathers) 40 45
3557 $1 Frigate 40 45
3558 $1 Janggolan 40 45
3559 $1 Junk 40 45
MS3560 Two sheets, each 100 × 75 mm. (a) $6 Nuclear submarine (58 × 43 mm). (b) $6 "Lusitania" (liner) (86 × 29 mm) Set of 2 sheets . . . . 4·75 5·00
Nos. 3542/50 and 3551/9 respectively were printed together, se-tenant, forming composite background designs.

1998. "Hercules" (cartoon film) (2nd series). As T **443** showing Disney cartoon characters. Multicoloured.
3561/8 10c. × 8 Hercules and giant statue; Hercules, Pegasus and Philoktetes; Hercules and Philoktetes with shield and arrows; Hercules swinging from blades; Nessus carrying off Megara; Hercules fighting Nessus; Hercules fighting giant lion; Hercules and Pegasus leaving prints on pavement . . . . .
3569/76 $1 × 8 Baby Hercules with Zeus and Alcmene; Baby Hercules with Hades; Hades in the Underworld; Baby Hercules and young Pegasus; Baby Hercules with Pain and Panic; Baby Hercules with mortal parents; Hercules towing hay waggon; Hercules receiving gold medallion . . . . . .
3577/84 $1 × 8 Hercules and Megara; Megara and Hades; Hercules training with Philoktetes; Hercules confronting Hades; Giant destroying city; Zeus; Hercules saving Megara by lifting pillar; Hercules diving into sea
3561/84 Set of 24 . . . . 18·00 20·00
MS3585 Six sheets, each 127 × 102 mm. (a) $6 Hades. (b) $6 Baby Pegasus. (c) $6 Hercules with sword. (d) $6 Hades on fire. (e) $6 Zeus and Hercules (horiz). (f) $6 Hercules and Megara riding Pegasus (horiz) Set of 6 sheets 27·00 30·00

452 Arctic Skua

1998. Seabirds. Multicoloured.
3586 90c. Type **452** 35 40
3587 $1 Fulmar ("Northern Fulmar") (horiz) 40 45
3588 $1 Black-legged kittiwake (horiz) 40 45
3589 $1 Pintado petrel ("Cape Petrel") (horiz) 40 45
3590 $1 Mediterranean gull (horiz) 40 45
3591 $1 Brandt's cormorant (horiz) 40 45
3592 $1 Greater shearwater (horiz) 40 45
3593 $1 Black-footed albatross (horiz) 40 45
3594 $1 Red-necked phalarope (horiz) 40 45
3595 $1 Black skimmer (horiz) . . 40 45
3596 $1.10 Humboldt penguin . . 45 50

3597 $2 Herring gull 80 85
3598 $3 Red knot . . . . 1·20 1·30
MS3599 Two sheets, each 100×70 mm. (a) $5 Black-browed albatross. (b) $5 King penguin Set of 2 sheets . . . . 4·00 4·25

Nos. 3587/95 were printed together, se-tenant, with the backgrounds forming a composite design.

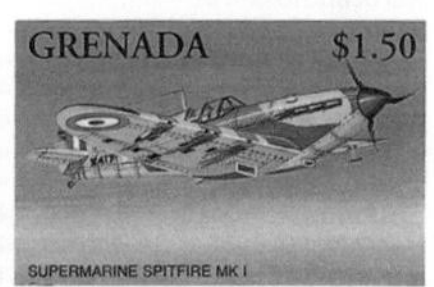

453 Supermarine Spitfire Mk I

1998. History of the Supermarine Spitfire (aircraft). Designs showing different versions. Multicoloured.
3600 $1.50 Type **453** 60 65
3601 $1.50 Mark VIII 60 65
3602 $1.50 Mark III 60 65
3603 $1.50 Mark XVI 60 65
3604 $1.50 Mark V 60 65
3605 $1.50 Mark XIX 60 65
3606 $1.50 Mark IX 60 65
3607 $1.50 Mark XIV 60 65
3608 $1.50 Mark XII 60 65
3609 $1.50 Mark XI 60 65
3610 $1.50 H.F. Mark VIII . . . 60 65
3611 $1.50 Mark VB 60 65
MS3612 Two sheets, each 80×106 mm. (a) $6 Mark IA. (b) $6 Mark IX (different) (both 56×41 mm) Set of 2 sheets . . 4·75 5·00

454 Walrus

1998. International Year of the Ocean. Multicoloured.
3613 75c. Type **454** 30 35
3614 75c. Jackass penguins ("African Black-footed Penguin") 30 35
3615 75c. Jackass penguin ("African Black-footed Penguin") 30 35
3616 75c. California sealion . . . 30 35
3617 75c. Green turtle 30 35
3618 75c. Redfin anthias 30 35
3619 75c. Sperm whale 30 35
3620 75c. French angelfish and Australian sealion 30 35
3621 75c. Jellyfish 30 35
3622 75c. Sawfish 30 35
3623 75c. Cuckoo wrasse 30 35
3624 75c. Garibaldi 30 35
3625 75c. Spinecheek anemonefish 30 35
3626 75c. Leafy seadragon . . . 30 35
3627 75c. Blue-spotted goatfish 30 35
3628 75c. Two-spot gobies . . . 30 35
MS3629 Two sheets, each 98×68 mm. (a) $5 Atlantic spotted dolphins. (b) $6 Octopus Set of 2 sheets . . . . 4·50 4·75

Nos. 3613/28 were printed together, se-tenant, with the backgrounds forming a composite design.

454a Flags of Grenada and CARICOM

1998. 25th Anniv of Caribbean Community.
3630 **454a** $1 multicoloured . . . 40 45

454b Stylized Americas

1998. 50th Anniv of Organization of American States.
3631 **454b** $1 multicoloured . . . 40 45

1998. 25th Death Anniv of Pablo Picasso (painter). As T **291a** of Gambia. Multicoloured.
3632 45c. "The Bathers" (vert) . . 20 25
3633 $2 "Luncheon on the Grass" 80 85
3634 $3 "The Swimmer" . . . . 1·20 1·30
MS3635 102×127 mm. $5 "Tomato Plant" (vert) . . . . 2·00 2·10

1998. Birth Centenary of Enzo Ferrari (car manufacturer). As T **564a** of Ghana. Multicoloured.
3636 $2 250 GT Berlinetta Lusso 1·50 1·50
3637 $2 250 GTO . . . . 1·50 1·50
3638 $2 250 GT Boano/Ellena cabriolet . . . . 1·50 1·50
MS3639 104×70 mm. $5 246 GTS Dino (91×34 mm) . . . . . . 4·00 4·50

454c Scout Saluting

454d Mahatma Gandhi

1998. 19th World Scout Jamboree, Chile. Multicoloured.
3640 $2 Type **454c** 80 85
3641 $3 International scout flag 1·20 1·30
3642 $4 Applying first aid . . . 1·60 1·70
MS3643 106×76 mm. $6 International scout flag . . . . 2·40 2·50

1998. 50th Death Anniv of Mahatma Gandhi.
3644 **454d** $1 black, grey and mauve 40 45
MS3645 70×100 mm. $6 multicoloured . . . . 2·40 2·50
DESIGN: $6, Gandhi and spinning wheel.

1998. 80th Anniv of Royal Air Force. As T **292a** of Gambia. Multicoloured.
3646 $2 Supermarine Spitfire Mk IIa 80 85
3647 $2 Supermarine Spitfire Mk IXb from above . . . 80 85
3648 $2 Supermarine Spitfire Mk IXb from side 80 85
3649 $2 Hawker Hurricane Mk IIC of Battle of Britain Memorial Flight 80 85
3650 $2 EF-2000 Eurofighter above clouds 80 85
3651 $2 Nimrod MR2P (maritime reconnaissance) 80 85
3652 $2 EF-2000 Eurofighter at low level 80 85
3653 $2 C-47 Dakota (transport) 80 85
MS3654 Four sheets, each 93×70 mm. (a) $6 Bristol F2B fighter and head of falcon. (b) $6 Bristol F2B fighter and northern goshawk (bird). (c) $6 Jet Provost (trainer) and EF-2000 Eurofighter. (d) $6 VC10 (transport) and EF-2000 Eurofighter Set of 4 sheets . . . . 9·75 10·00

455 "Knights in Combat"

1998. Birth Bicentenary of Eugene Delacroix (painter). Multicoloured.
3655 $1 Type **455** 40 45
3656 $1 "Murder of Bishop of Liege" 40 45
3657 $1 "Still Life" 40 45
3658 $1 "Battle of Nancy" . . . 40 45
3659 $1 "Shipwreck of Don Juan" 40 45
3660 $1 "The Death of Ophelia" 40 45
3661 $1 "Attila the Hun" 40 45
3662 $1 "Arab Entertainers" . . 40 45
MS3663 100×92 mm. $5 "The Capture of Constantinople" . . 2·00 2·10

1998. 1st Death Anniv of Diana, Princess of Wales. As T **293a** of Gambia. Multicoloured.
3664 $1 Diana, Princess of Wales 40 45

456 Arthur Ashe

1998. Famous Tennis Players. Multicoloured.
3665 45c. Type **456** 20 25
3666 75c. Martina Hingis 30 35
3667 90c. Chris Evert 35 40
3668 $1 Steffi Graf 40 45
3669 $1.50 A. Sanchez Vicario . . 60 65
3670 $2 Monica Seles 80 85
3671 $3 Martina Navratilova . . 1·20 1·30
MS3672 81×108 mm. $6 Martina Hingis (different) . . . . . . 2·40 2·50

457 Dove of Peace with Stars and Streamers

458 "The Angel's parting from Tobias" (Jean Bilevelt)

1998. Grenada's Participation in U.N. Peacekeeping Operations, Beirut, 1982–4.
3673 **457** $1 multicoloured 40 45

1998. Christmas. Religious Paintings. Multicoloured.
3674 35c. Type **458** 15 20
3675 45c. "Allegory of Faith" (Moretto Da Brescia) . . 20 25
3676 90c. "Crucifixion" (Ugolino Di Tedice) 35 40
3677 $1 "The Triumphal Entry into Jerusalem" (Master of the Thuison Altarpiece) 40 45

459 Antillean Euphonia ("Blue-hooded Euphonia")

1998. Christmas. Birds. Multicoloured.
3678 45c. Type **459** 20 25
3679 75c. Red-billed whistling duck ("Black-bellied Whistling Duck") 30 35
3680 90c. Caribbean martin ("Purple Martin") 35 40
3681 $1 Imperial amazon ("Imperial Parrot") . . . 40 45
3682 $2 Adelaide's warbler . . . 80 85
3683 $3 Greater flamingo ("Roseate Flamingo") . . 1·20 1·30
MS3684 Two sheets, each 97×84 mm. (a) $5 Green-throated carib. (b) $6 Purple-throated carib and Canada 1898 Imperial Penny Postage 2c. stamp (37×60 mm) Set of 2 sheets . . . . 4·50 4·75

1999. Chinese New Year ("Year of the Rabbit"). Sheet 150×75 mm, containing triangular designs as T **435** showing rabbits. Multicoloured. Self-adhesive on silver foil.
MS3685 $1 "GRENADA" in green; $1 "GRENADA" in orange; $1 "GRENADA" in pink . . . . 1·20 1·30

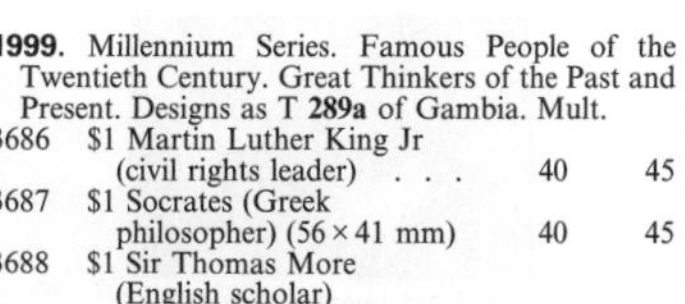

1999. Millennium Series. Famous People of the Twentieth Century. Great Thinkers of the Past and Present. Designs as T **289a** of Gambia. Mult.
3686 $1 Martin Luther King Jr (civil rights leader) . . . 40 45
3687 $1 Socrates (Greek philosopher) (56×41 mm) 40 45
3688 $1 Sir Thomas More (English scholar) (56×41 mm) 40 45
3689 $1 Chaim Weizmann (first President of Israel) . . . 40 45
3690 $1 Alexander Solzhenitsyn (Russian writer) 40 45
3691 $1 Galileo Galilei (Italian astronomer) (56×41 mm) 40 45
3692 $1 Michael Servetus (Spanish theologian) (56×41 mm) 40 45
3693 $1 Salman Rushdie (British novelist) 40 45
MS3694 106×76 mm. $6 Mother Teresa (founder of Missionaries of Charity) . . . . 2·40 2·50

No. 3692 is inscribed "MICHAEL SERVENTUS" in error.

460 Robert H. Goddard (rocket scientist)

1999. Space Exploration. Multicoloured.
3695 $1.50 Type **460** 60 65
3696 $1.50 Wernher von Braun (rocket scientist) 60 65
3697 $1.50 Yuri A. Gagarin (first cosmonaut to orbit Earth, 1961) 60 65
3698 $1.50 "Freedom 7" (first American manned Space flight, 1961) 60 65
3699 $1.50 Aleksei Leonov (first Russian to walk in Space, 1965) 60 65
3700 $1.50 Neil Armstrong and Edwin Aldrin (first astronauts on Moon, 1969) 60 65
3701 $1.50 "Mariner 9" (first spacecraft to orbit Mars, 1971) 60 65
3702 $1.50 "Voyager 1" (Jupiter probe, 1979) 60 65
3703 $1.50 Bruce McCandless (first astronaut to work in Space unattached, 1984) 60 65
3704 $1.50 "Giotto" probe (study of Halley's Comet, 1986) 60 65
3705 $1.50 Space Shuttle "Atlantis" (launch of "Galileo" probe, 1989) . . 60 65
3706 $1.50 "Magellan" (Venus probe, 1990) 60 65
MS3707 Two sheets, each 60×76 mm. (a) $6 John Glenn (first American to orbit Earth, 1962). (b) $6 Neil Armstrong (first astronaut to walk on Moon, 1969) Set of 2 sheets . . . . 4·75 5·00

Nos. 3695/3700 and 3701/6 were respectively printed together, se-tenant, with the backgrounds forming composite designs.

461 Goofy as Best Man

1999. 70th Birthday of Mickey Mouse. Mickey's Dream Wedding. Walt Disney cartoon characters. Multicoloured.
3708 $1 Type **461** 80 80
3709 $1 Mickey as groom 80 80
3710 $1 Minnie as bride 80 80
3711 $1 Daisy Duck as bridesmaid 80 80
3712 $1 Donald Duck 80 80
3713 $1 Pluto in love 80 80
3714 $1 Huey, Duey and Louie 80 80
3715 $1 Lady (Pekingese) 80 80
MS3716 Two sheets. (a) 102×127 mm. $6 Mickey's nephew eating cake. (b) 127×102 mm. $6 Mickey and Minnie in carriage (horiz) Set of 2 sheets . . . . 9·00 9·50

Nos. 3708/15 were printed together, se-tenant, with the backgrounds forming a composite design.

462 Grand Trunk Western, U.S.A.

1999. Trains of the World. Multicoloured.
3717 25c. Type **462** 10 15
3718 35c. Louisville & Nashville, U.S.A. 15 20
3719 45c. Gulf, Mobile and Ohio, U.S.A. 20 25
3720 75c. Missouri Pacific, U.S.A. 30 35
3721 90c. "RTG" National Railway, France 35 40
3722 $1 Florida East Coast, U.S.A. 40 45
3723 $1.50 Rio Grande, U.S.A. 60 65
3724 $1.50 Erie Lackawanna, U.S.A. 60 65
3725 $1.50 New York Central, U.S.A. 60 65
3726 $1.50 Pennsylvania, U.S.A. 60 65
3727 $1.50 Milwaukee Road, U.S.A. 60 65
3728 $1.50 Illinois Central, U.S.A. 60 65
3729 $1.50 Burlington Route, U.S.A. 60 65
3730 $1.50 "Texas Special", Missouri, Kansas and Texas, U.S.A. 60 65
3731 $1.50 City of Los Angeles, U.S.A. 60 65
3732 $1.50 Northwestern, U.S.A. 60 65
3733 $1.50 Canadian National . . 60 65
3734 $1.50 Rock Island, U.S.A. 60 65
3735 $1.50 TGV, French National Railways . . . 60 65
3736 $1.50 HST, British Railways 60 65
3737 $1.50 TEE, Trans Europe Express 60 65
3738 $1.50 Ancona Express, Italy 60 65
3739 $1.50 XPT, Australia . . . 60 65
3740 $1.50 APT-P, British Railways 60 65
3741 $1.50 Western Pacific, U.S.A. 60 65

3742 $1.50 Union Pacific, U.S.A. 60 65
3743 $1.50 Chesapeake and Ohio, U.S.A. 60 65
3744 $1.50 Southern Pacific, U.S.A. 60 65
3745 $1.50 Baltimore and Ohio, U.S.A. 60 65
3746 $1.50 Wabash, U.S.A. 60 65
3747 $3 Kansas City Southern, U.S.A. 1·20 1·30
3748 $4 New Haven, U.S.A. 1·60 1·70
MS3749 Four sheets, each 98×68 mm. (a) $6 Eld 4, Netherlands. (b) $6 "Hikari" express train, Japan. (c) $6 Santa Fe, U.S.A. (d) $6 Inter City express, Germany Set of 4 sheets 9·75 10·00

Nos. 3723/8, 3729/34, 3735/40 and 3741/6 respectively were printed together, se-tenant, with the backgrounds forming composite designs.

463 "Papilio blumei" (butterfly)

1999. "Australia '99" World Stamp Exhibition, Melbourne. Wildlife. Multicoloured.

3750 75c. Type **463** 30 35
3751 75c. Great egret ("Egret") 30 35
3752 75c. Kumarahou (flower) 30 35
3753 75c. Javan rhinoceros 30 35
3754 75c. Grey-backed white-eye ("Silver-eye") (bird) 30 35
3755 75c. Kiore (rodent) 30 35
3756 75c. "Cyclorana novaehollandiae" (frog) 30 35
3757 75c. Caterpillar 30 35
3758 75c. Pacific black duck ("Grey Duck") 30 35
3759 75c. Honey blue-eye (fish) 30 35
3760 75c. Krefft's turtle 30 35
3761 75c. Archer fish 30 35
3762 75c. Binturong (vert) 30 35
3763 75c. Two Indian elephants (vert) 30 35
3764 75c. Indian elephant (vert) 30 35
3765 75c. Chestnut-capped laughing thrush ("Garkulax mitratus") (vert) 30 35
3766 75c. "Vanda hookeriana" (orchid) (vert) 30 35
3767 75c. Grey heron ("Heron") (vert) 30 35
3768 75c. Fur seal (vert) 30 35
3769 75c. Black-faced cormorant ("Shag") (bird) (vert) 30 35
3770 75c. Round batfish (vert) 30 35
3771 75c. Loggerhead turtle (vert) 30 35
3772 75c. Three harlequin sweetlips (vert) 30 35
3773 75c. Two harlequin sweetlips (vert) 30 35
3774 $1 Orang-utan 40 45
3775 $2 Dourouculi (monkey) 80 85
3776 $3 Black caiman (alligator) 1·20 1·30
3777 $4 Panther ("Black Leopard") (vert) 1·60 1·70
MS3778 Two sheets. (a) 110×85 mm. $6 Impala. (b) 85×110 mm. $6 Ring-tailed lemur Set of 2 sheets 4·75 5·00

Nos. 3750/61 and 3762/73 respectively were printed together, se-tenant, with the backgrounds forming composite designs.

Nos. 3753 and 3775 were inscribed "JAUAN RHINOCEROS" and "DOUROCOULI" in error.

1999. "iBRA '99" International Stamp Exhibition, Nuremberg. Horiz designs as T **298a** of Gambia. Multicoloured.

3779 75c. Railway locomotive, 1893, and Prussia 1860 ⅓sgr. stamp 30 35
3780 90c. "Humboldt" (sailing ship) and Mecklenburg-Schwerin 1856 4×¼s. 35 40
3781 $1 Railway locomotive, 1893, and Saxony 1850 3pf. 40 45
3782 $2 "Humboldt" (sailing ship) and Mecklenburg-Strelitz 1864 ⅓sgr. 80 85
MS3783 121×104 mm. $6 Saxony 1850 3pf. with Leipzig postmark 2·40 2·50

1999. 150th Death Anniv of Katsushika Hokusai (Japanese artist). As T **298b** of Gambia. Multicoloured.

3784 $1.50 "The Actor Ichikawa Danjuro Danjuro as Tomoe Gozen" 60 65
3785 $1.50 "Washing Clothes" (drawing) 60 65
3786 $1.50 "The Prostitute of Eguchi" 60 65
3787 $1.50 "Sudden Shower from a Fine Sky" 60 65
3788 $1.50 "Hanging Clothes out to dry" (drawing) 60 65
3789 $1.50 "Shimada" 60 65
3790 $1.50 "Head of Old Man" 60 65
3791 $1.50 "Piebald Horse" (drawing) 60 65
3792 $1.50 "Girl making Cord for binding Hats" 60 65
3793 $1.50 "Li Po admiring Waterfall of Lo-shan" 60 65
3794 $1.50 "Bay Horse" (drawing) 60 65
3795 $1.50 "Potted Dwarf Pine with Basin" 60 65
MS3796 Two sheets, each 72×102 mm. (a) $6 "The Guardian God Fudo Myoo and his Attendants". (b) $6 "Women on the Beach at Enoshima" Set of 2 sheets 4·75 5·00

No. 3788 is inscribed "DRAWINFS" in error.

1999. 10th Anniv of United Nations Rights of the Child Convention. As T **298c** of Gambia. Multicoloured.

3797 $3 Eskimo girl and Russian boy 1·20 1·30
3798 $3 American girl 1·20 1·30
3799 $3 African boy and Indian girl 1·20 1·30
MS3800 110×85 mm. $6 Young boy 2·40 2·50

Nos. 3797/9 were printed together, se-tenant, forming a composite design.

1999. "PhilexFrance '99" International Stamp Exhibition, Paris. Railway Locomotives. Two sheets containing horiz designs as T **299d** of Gambia. Multicoloured.

MS3801 (a) 106×76 mm. $6 Paris, Lyons and Mediterranean Railway Compound Pacific. (b) 106×81 mm. $6 French heavy freight locomotive Set of 2 sheets 4·75 5·00

1999. 250th Birth Anniv of Johann von Goethe (German poet and dramatist). Multicoloured designs as T **298d** of Gambia.

3802 $3 mauve, purple and black 1·20 1·30
3803 $3 blue, lilac and black 1·20 1·30
3804 $3 violet, deep violet and black 1·20 1·30
MS3805 76×106 mm. $6 orange, brown and black 2·40 2·50

DESIGNS—HORIZ: No. 3802, Faust contemplating Moon; 3803, Goethe and Friedrich von Schiller (dramatist); 3804, Faust talking with Wagner. VERT: No. MS3805, Margaret (from "Faust").

1999. 30th Anniv of First Manned Landing on Moon. Horiz designs as T **298e** of Gambia. Multicoloured.

3806 $1.50 The Moon 60 65
3807 $1.50 Edward White on first space walk 60 65
3808 $1.50 Edwin "Buzz" Aldrin 60 65
3809 $1.50 The Earth 60 65
3810 $1.50 Michael Collins 60 65
3811 $1.50 Neil Armstrong 60 65
3812 $1.50 Footprint on the Moon 60 65
3813 $1.50 V2 rocket 60 65
3814 $1.50 Command module "Columbia" 60 65
3815 $1.50 Lunar Rover 60 65
3816 $1.50 Lunar module "Eagle" 60 65
3817 $1.50 Command module re-entering Earth's atmosphere 60 65
MS3818 Two sheets. (a) 110×85 mm. $6 Neil Armstrong with American flag. (b) 85×111 mm. $6 Launch of "Apollo 11" (vert) Set of 2 sheets 4·75 5·00

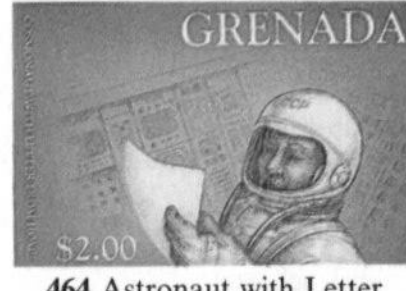

464 Astronaut with Letter

1999. 125th Anniv of Universal Postal Union. Space Mail. Multicoloured.

3819 $2 Type **464** 80 85
3820 $2 Supply spaceship "Progress" 80 85
3821 $2 Postmark of space station "MIR" 80 85
3822 $2 Buran shuttle and "MIR" 80 85
MS3823 104×75 mm. $6 Space station "MIR" 2·40 2·50

465 "Carry On Doctor"

1999. 50th Anniv of the Variety Club of Great Britain. Scenes from "Carry On" Films. Multicoloured.

3824 $1 "Carry On Dick" 40 45
3825 $1 Type **465** 40 45
3826 $1 "Carry On England" 40 45
3827 $1 "Carry On Matron" 40 45
3828 $1 "Carry On Round The Bend" 40 45
3829 $1 "Carry On Up The Jungle" 40 45
3830 $1 "Carry On Loving" 40 45
3831 $1 "Carry On Up The Khyber" 40 45
MS3832 110×86 mm. $6 Actors from "Carry On" films 2·40 2·50

1999. Royal Wedding. As T **298** of Gambia. Multicoloured.

3833 $3 Prince Edward 1·20 1·30
3834 $3 Sophie and Prince Edward 1·20 1·30
3835 $3 Sophie Rhys-Jones 1·20 1·30
MS3836 78×108 mm. $6 Prince Edward and Sophie Rhys-Jones 2·40 2·50

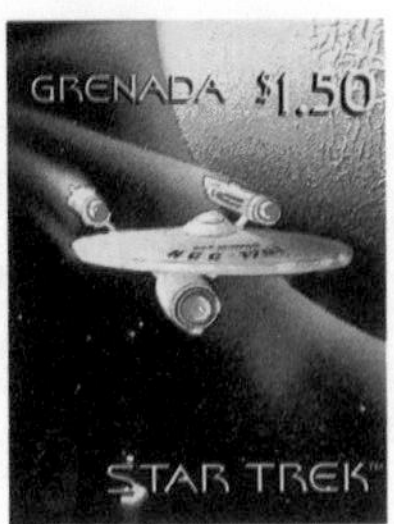

466 "U.S.S. Enterprise NCC-1701" (from original series)

1999. Spacecraft of "Star Trek". Multicoloured.

3837 $1.50 Type **466** 60 65
3838 $1.50 Klingon battle cruiser (blue and orange planets in background) (Voyager series) 60 65
3839 $1.50 "U.S.S. Enterprise" 1701 (green planet in background) (Next Generation series) 60 65
3840 $1.50 Warbird "Voyager" (below blue planet) 60 65
3841 $1.50 U.S.S. "Romulan" (in front of orange planet) (original series) 60 65
3842 $1.50 "U.S.S. Enterprise" 1701 (pink planet in background) (original series) 60 65
3843 $1.50 "Borg Cube" (Next Generation series) 60 65
3844 $1.50 "U.S.S. Enterprise NCC" 1701 (in front of multicoloured flames) 60 65
3845 $1.50 Klingon "Bird of Prey" (original series) 60 65

1999. "Queen Elizabeth the Queen Mother's Century". As T **304a** of Gambia.

3846 $2 black and gold 80 85
3847 $2 multicoloured 80 85
3848 $2 black and gold 80 85
3849 $2 multicoloured 80 85
MS3850 154×157 mm. $6 multicoloured 2·40 2·50

DESIGNS: No. 3846, Queen Mother with Prince Charles, 1948; 3847, Queen Mother in pink outfit, 1970; 3848, Queen Mother in Australia, 1958; 3849, Queen Mother waving. (37×50 mm)—MS3850, Queen Mother in Coronation robes, 1953.

No. **MS**3850 also shows the Royal Arms embossed in gold, and inscr "Good Health and Happiness to Her Majesty The Queen Mother on her 101st Birthday".

467 George Gershwin

1999. American Entertainers. Multicoloured.

3851 $1 Type **467** 40 45
3852 $1 Florence Mills 40 45
3853 $1 Sam Beckett 40 45
3854 $1 Bessie Smith 40 45
3855 $1 Billie Holiday 40 45
3856 $1 Bert Williams 40 45
3857 $1 Cole Porter 40 45
3858 $1 Sofie Tucker 40 45
3859 $1 Lon Chaney 40 45
3860 $1 Buster Keaton 40 45
3861 $1 Norma Shearer 40 45
3862 $1 James Cagney 40 45
3863 $1 Hedda Hopper 40 45
3864 $1 Jean Harlow 40 45
3865 $1 Marlene Dietrich 40 45
3866 $1 Ramon Novarro 40 45
MS3867 Two sheets, each 76×86 mm. (a) $6 Clark Gable. (b) $6 Louis Armstrong Set of 2 sheets 4·75 5·00

Nos. 3885/8 and 3859/66 respectively were printed together, se-tenant, with the backgrounds forming composite designs.

468 Ouranosaurus

1999. Prehistoric Animals. Multicoloured.

3868 35c. Type **468** 15 20
3869 45c. Struthiomimus (vert) 20 25
3870 75c. Parasaurolophus (vert) 30 35
3871 $1 Archaeopteryx 40 45
3872 $1 Brachiosaurus 40 45
3873 $1 Dilophosaurus 40 45
3874 $1 Dimetrodon 40 45
3875 $1 Psittacosaurus 40 45
3876 $1 Acrocanthosaurus 40 45
3877 $1 Stenonychosaurus 40 45
3878 $1 Dryosaurus 40 45
3879 $1 Campsognathus 40 45
3880 $1 Agathaumus 40 45
3881 $1 Camarosaurus 40 45
3882 $1 Quetzalcoatlus 40 45
3883 $1 Alioramus 40 45
3884 $1 Camptosaurus 40 45
3885 $1 Albertosaurus 40 45
3886 $1 Anatosaurus 40 45
3887 $1 Spinosaurus 40 45
3888 $1 Centrosaurus 40 45
3889 $2 Triceratops 80 85
3890 $3 Stegoceras 1·20 1·30
3891 $4 Stegosaurus 1·60 1·70
MS3892 Two sheets, each 85×110 mm. (a) $6 Velociraptor (vert). (b) $6 Tyrannosaurus (vert) Set of 2 sheets 4·75 5·00

Nos. 3871/9 and 3880/8 were printed together, se-tenant, with the backgrounds forming a composite design.

No. 3871 is inscribed "ARCHEOPTERYX" in error.

469 Christmas Rose

1999. Christmas. Multicoloured.

3893 20c. Type **469** 10 15
3894 75c. Tulip 30 35
3895 90c. Pear 35 40
3896 $1 Hibiscus 40 45
3897 $4 Lily 1·60 1·70
MS3898 106×91 mm. $6 "The Nativity" (Botticelli) (horiz) 2·40 2·50

1999. Faces of the Millennium: Diana, Princess of Wales. Vert designs as T **307** of Gambia showing collage of miniature flower photographs. Multicoloured.

3899 $1 Top of head (face value at left) 40 45
3900 $1 Top of head (face value at right) 40 45
3901 $1 Ear (face value at left) 40 45
3902 $1 Eye and temple (face value at right) 40 45
3903 $1 Cheek (face value at left) 40 45
3904 $1 Cheek (face value at right) 40 45
3905 $1 Blue background (face value at left) 40 45
3906 $1 Chin (face value at right) 40 45

Nos. 3899/906 were printed together, se-tenant, and when viewed as a whole, form a portrait of Diana, Princess of Wales.

470 Green Dragon

2000. Chinese New Year ("Year of the Dragon"). Multicoloured.

3907 $2 Type **470** 80 85
3908 $2 Dragon ("GRENADA" in red) 80 85
3909 $2 Dragon ("GRENADA" in violet) 80 85

471 Roseate Spoonbill

2000. Birds of Grenada. Multicoloured.

3910 75c. Type **471** 30 35
3911 90c. Scarlet ibis 35 40
3912 $1 Adelaide's warbler 40 45
3913 $1 Hispaniolan trogon 40 45
3914 $1 Sun conure ("Sun Parakeet") 40 45
3915 $1 Black-necked stilt 40 45
3916 $1 Sora crake ("Sora") 40 45
3917 $1 Fulvous whistling duck ("Fulvous Tree Duck") 40 45
3918 $1 Blue-headed parrot 40 45
3919 $1 Tropical mockingbird 40 45

3920 $1 Antillean euphonia ("Blue-hooded Euphonia") 40 45
3921 $1 Troupial 40 45
3922 $1 Brown-throated conure ("Caribbean Parakeet") 40 45
3923 $1 Forest thrush 40 45
3924 $1 Lesser Antillean tanager ("Hooded Tanager") . . 40 45
3925 $1 Stripe-headed tanager . . 40 45
3926 $1 Ringed kingfisher 40 45
3927 $1 Zenaida dove 40 45
3928 $1.50 Sparkling violetear . . 60 65
3929 $2 Northern jacana 80 85
MS3930 Two sheets, each 70 × 97 mm. (a) $6 Cedar waxwing (37 × 50 mm). (b) $6 Antillean siskin (50 × 37 mm) Set of 2 sheets 4·75 5·00

Nos. 3912/19 and 3920/7 were each printed together, se-tenant, with the backgrounds forming composite designs.

No. 3912 is inscribed "Ade; aode's Warbler" and No. 3919 "Tropical Mockinbird", both in error.

471a Jan Vermeer (Dutch painter) (died 1675)

472 *Clitcybe geotropa*

2000. New Millennium. People and Events of Seventeenth Century (1650–1700). Multicoloured.

3931 50c. Type **471a** 20 25
3932 50c. Antoni van Leeuwenhoek (discovered micro-organisms, 1674) 20 25
3933 50c. Salem Witch Trials, Massachusetts, 1692 . . . 20 25
3934 50c. Sir Isaac Newton and reflecting telescope, 1668 20 25
3935 50c. Voltaire (French writer and historian) (born 1694) 20 25
3936 50c. Ivan V and Peter I (joint rulers of Russia, 1682) 20 25
3937 50c. Shun Zhi, first Chinese Emperor of Qing Dynasty (died 1662) 20 25
3938 50c. Christian Huggens and Saturn, 1655 . . . . . . 20 25
3939 50c. Microscopic mite (Robert Hooke's experiments in cytology, 1665) 20 25
3940 50c. "Verdant Peaks" (Wang Shih-rnin), 1672 20 25
3941 50c. Rene Descartes (French philosopher) (died 1650) 20 25
3942 50c. Completion of Canal du Midi, 1681 . . . . . 20 25
3943 50c. William of Orange and Bill of Rights, 1688 . . . 20 25
3944 50c. William III on horseback (end of King William's War), 1697) . . 20 25
3945 50c. Cassini (French astronomer) and images of Mars, 1666 . . . . . 20 25
3946 50c. Sir Isaac Newton and apples (law of gravity, 1666) (59 × 39 mm) . . . 20 25
3947 50c. Jupiter's Moons (Olaus Roemer) (Danish astronomer) (discovered finite speed of light, 1676) 20 25

No. 3936 is dated "1694" in error.

2000. 400th Birth Anniv of Sir Anthony Van Dyck (Flemish painter). As T **312a** of Gambia. Mult.

3948 $1 "King Charles I on Horseback" 40 45
3949 $1 "St. Martin dividing his Cloak" 40 45
3950 $1 "Gio. Paolo Babli on Horseback" 40 45
3951 $1 "Marchese Anton Giulio Brignole-Sale on Horseback" 40 45
3952 $1 "Study of a Horse" . . . 40 45
3953 $1 "Oriental on Horseback" 40 45
3954 $1 "Young Woman resting Head on Hand" 40 45
3955 $1 "Self-portrait", 1613–14 40 45
3956 $1 "Woman looking Upwards" 40 45
3957 $1 "Head of an Old Man", c. 1621 . . . . . 40 45
3958 $1 "Head of a Boy" 40 45
3959 $1 "Head of an Old Man", 1616–18 . . . . 40 45
3960 $1.50 "Portrait of a Man" 60 65
3961 $1.50 "Portrait of a Man aged Seventy" 60 65
3962 $1.50 "Portrait of a Woman" 60 65
3963 $1.50 "Elderly Man" . . . 60 65
3964 $1.50 "Portrait of a Young Man" 60 65
3965 $1.50 "Man with a Glove" 60 65
3966 $1.50 "St. John the Baptist" 60 65
3967 $1.50 "St. Anthony of Padua and the Ass of Rimini" 60 65
3968 $1.50 "The Stoning of St. Stephen" 60 65
3969 $1.50 "The Martyrdom of St. Sebastian" 60 65
3970 $1.50 "St. Sebastian bound for Martyrdom" 60 65
3971 $1.50 "St. Jerome" 60 65
3972 $1.50 "Portrait of Anthony Van Dyck", 1614–15 . . 60 65
3973 $1.50 "Self-portrait" (after Rubens) 60 65
3974 $1.50 "Isabella Brant" . . . 60 65
3975 $1.50 "The Penitent Apostle Peter" 60 65
3976 $1.50 "Head of a Robber" (used by Rubens in his "Coup de Lance") . . . 60 65
3977 $1.50 "Heads of the Apostles" (detail from Ruben's "Feast at the House of Simon the Pharisee") 60 65
MS3978 Six sheets. (a) 103 × 127 mm. $5 "Prince Thomas-Francis of Savoy on Horseback". (b) 102 × 127 mm. $5 "Emperor Theodosius refused Entry in Milan Cathedral" (horiz). (c) 102 × 127 mm. $5 "King Charles I on Horseback". (d) 127 × 102 mm, $6 "St. Jerome in the Wilderness". (e) 102 × 127 mm. $6 "St. Martin" (horiz). (f) 127 × 102 mm. $6 Detail of "Portrait of a Man and His Wife" (horiz) Set of 6 sheets . . . . 13·50 14·00

No. **MS**3978b is inscribed "Emperor Theoddosius" in error.

2000. Fungi. Multicoloured.

3979 35c. Type **472** 15 20
3980 45c. *Psalliota augusta* . . . 20 25
3981 $1 *Amanita rubescens* . . . 40 45
3982 $1.50 *Pholiota spectabilis* . . 60 65
3983 $1.50 *Mycena polygramma* 60 65
3984 $1.50 *Collybia iocephala* . . 60 65
3985 $1.50 *Corinus comatus* . . . 60 65
3986 $1.50 *Amanita muscaria sp.* 60 65
3987 $1.50 *Boletus aereus* 60 65
3988 $1.50 *Ungulina marginata* . . 60 65
3989 $1.50 *Pleurotus ostreatus* . . 60 65
3990 $1.50 *Flammula penetrans* 60 65
3991 $1.50 *Morchella crassipes* . . 60 65
3992 $1.50 *Lepiota procera* . . . 60 65
3993 $1.50 *Tricholoma aurantium* 60 65
3994 $4 *Boletus satanas* . . . . . 1·60 1·70
MS3995 Two sheets. (a) 82 × 112 mm. $6 *Daedala quercina*. (b) 112 × 82 mm. $6 *Lepiota acutesquamosa* Set of 2 sheets 4·75 5·00

Nos. 3982/7 and 3988/93 were each printed together, se-tenant, with the backgrounds forming composite designs.

No. 3986 is inscribed "Aminita muscaria" in error.

2000. 18th Birthday of Prince William. As T **312b** of Gambia. Multicoloured.

3996 $1.50 Prince William wearing blue and white tie 60 65
3997 $1.50 With Prince of Wales 60 65
3998 $1.50 Prince William waving 60 65
3999 $1.50 In skiing gear 60 65
MS4000 100 × 80 mm. $6 Prince William (37 × 50 mm) . . . . 2·40 2·50

2000. "EXPO 2000" World Stamp Exhibition, Anaheim, U.S.A. Spacecraft. As T **582a** of Ghana. Multicoloured.

4001 $1.50 "Lunik 4" 60 65
4002 $1.50 "Clemintine" 60 65
4003 $1.50 "Luna 12" 60 65
4004 $1.50 "Luna 16" 60 65
4005 $1.50 Lunar Module *Eagle* from "Apollo 11" 60 65
4006 $1.50 "Ranger 7" 60 65
MS4007 117 × 84 mm. $6 "Apollo 13" . . . . 2·40 2·50

Nos. 4001/6 were printed together, se-tenant, with the backgrounds forming a composite design.

2000. 25th Anniv of "Apollo–Soyuz" Joint Project. As T **582b** of Ghana. Multicoloured.

4008 $3 Russian "A-2" rocket . . 1·20 1·30
4009 $3 "Soyuz 19" . . . . . . 1·20 1·30
4010 $3 "Apollo 18" command module docked with "Soyuz 19" . . . . 1·20 1·30
MS4011 88 × 70 mm. $6 Valeri Kubasov ("Soyuz" engineer) and Thomas Stafford ("Apollo" commander) (horiz) . . . . . 2·40 2·50

2000. 50th Anniv of Berlin Film Festival. As T **582c** of Ghana. Multicoloured.

4012 $1.50 *Alphaville*, 1965 . . . 60 65
4013 $1.50 Rod Steiger, 1964 . . 60 65
4014 $1.50 *Os Fuzis*, 1964 . . . . 60 65
4015 $1.50 Jean-Pierre Leaud, 1966 . . . . 60 65
4016 $1.50 *Cul-de-sac*, 1966 . . . 60 65
4017 $1.50 *Ikiru*, 1961 . . . . . 60 65
MS4018 97 × 103 mm. $6 *His Yen*, 1993 . . . . 2·40 2·50

No. 4012 is inscribed "ALPHAVILE" and No. 4016 "CUL-DELSAC", both in error.

2000. 175th Anniv of Stockton and Darlington Line (first public railway). As T **582d** of Ghana. Multicoloured.

4019 $3 As Type **582d** of Ghana 1·20 1·30
4020 $3 Robert Stephenson's John Bull locomotive, 1831 . . . . 1·20 1·30

2000. 250th Death Anniv of Johann Sebastian Bach (German composer). Sheet 77 × 89 mm, containing vert portrait (24 × 40 mm) as T **312c** of Gambia.

MS4021 $6 multicoloured . . . . 2·40 2·50

2000. Election of Albert Einstein (mathematical physicist) as *Time Magazine* "Man of the Century". Sheet 117 × 91 mm, containing vert portrait as T **312d** of Gambia.

MS4022 $6 multicoloured . . . . 2·40 2·50

2000. Centenary of First Zeppelin Flight. As T **582e** of Ghana, each incorporating a different portrait of Count Ferdinand von Zeppelin. Multicoloured.

4023 $3 LZ-130 *Graf Zeppelin II* 1·20 1·30
4024 $3 LZ-2, 1906 . . . . . . 1·20 1·30
4025 $3 LZ-127 *Graf Zeppelin*, 1928 . . . . 1·20 1·30
MS4026 119 × 76 mm. $6 LZ-129 *Hindenburg*, 1936 (50 × 37 mm) 2·40 2·50

2000. Olympic Games, Sydney. As T **582f** of Ghana. Multicoloured.

4027 $2 Archibald Hahn (athletics), St. Louis (1904) 80 85
4028 $2 Showjumping 80 85
4029 $2 Sports Palace, Rome (1960) and Italian flag . . 80 85
4030 $2 Ancient Greek chariot racing 80 85

472a Junior Murray

473 *Brassolaelio cattleya*

2000. West Indies Cricket Tour and 100th Test Match at Lord's. Multicoloured.

4031 90c. Type **472a** 35 40
4032 $5 Rawl Lewis . . . . . . 2·00 2·10
MS4033 120 × 105 mm. $6 Lord's Cricket Ground (horiz) . . . . 2·40 2·50

2000. Orchids. Multicoloured.

4034 75c. Type **473** 30 35
4035 90c. *Maxilbera* 35 40
4036 $1 *Isochilius* 40 45
4037 $1.50 *Lycaste* 60 65
4038 $1.50 *Cochleanthes* 60 65
4039 $1.50 *Brassocattleya* . . . 60 65
4040 $1.50 *Brassolaelio cattleya* 60 65
4041 $1.50 *Iwanagaara* 60 65
4042 $1.50 *Sophrocattleya* . . . 60 65
4043 $1.50 *Laeliocattleya* . . . 60 65
4044 $1.50 *Saphrocattleya* . . . 60 65
4045 $1.50 *Epidendrum* 60 65
4046 $1.50 *Cattleya* 60 65
4047 $1.50 *Ionopsis* 60 65
4048 $1.50 *Brassoepidendrum* . . 60 65
4049 $2 *Oncidium* 80 85
MS4050 Two sheets, each 73 × 103 mm. (a) $6 *Brassocattleya*. (b) $6 *Vanilla* Set of 2 sheets . . . . 4·75 5·00

474 Sir Donald Bradman playing a Stroke

475 Maine Coon

2000. Famous Cricketers. Six sheets, each 290 × 165 mm, containing T **474** and similar vert designs. Multicoloured.

MS4051 (a) $1 × 8, Type **474** and similar shots in sequence. (b) $1 × 8, Sequence of Shane Warne bowling. (c) $2 × 4, Sir Garfield Sobers bowling (two different) or batting (two different). (d) $2 × 4, Different shots of Sir Jack Hobbs batting. (e) $2 × 4, Different shots of Sir Viv Richards batting. (f) $2 × 5, Bradman, Sobers, Hobbs, Warne and Richards Set of 6 sheets . . . . 20·00 21·00

2000. Cats and Dogs. Multicoloured.

4052 75c. Type **475** 30 35
4053 90c. Selkirk rex cat 35 40
4054 $1.50 Spotted tabby British shorthair (horiz) 60 65
4055 $1.50 Burmilla (horiz) . . . 60 65
4056 $1.50 British blue shorthair (horiz) 60 65
4057 $1.50 Siamese (horiz) . . . 60 65
4058 $1.50 Japanese bobtail (horiz) 60 65
4059 $1.50 Oriental shorthair (horiz) 60 65
4060 $1.50 Labrador retriever (horiz) 60 65
4061 $1.50 Standard poodle (horiz) 60 65
4062 $1.50 Boxer (horiz) 60 65
4063 $1.50 Rough-coated jack russell terrier (horiz) . . . 60 65
4064 $1.50 Tibetan terrier (horiz) 60 65
4065 $1.50 Welsh corgi (horiz) . . 60 65
4066 $2 Shetland sheepdog . . . 80 85
4067 $3 Central Asian sheepdog 1·20 1·30
MS4068 Two sheets, each 106 × 76 mm. (a) $6 Scottish fold cat. (b) $6 Irish red and white setter (horiz) Set of 2 sheets . . 4·75 5·00

Nos. 4054/9 (cats) and 4060/5 (dogs) were each printed together, se-tenant, with the backgrounds forming composite designs.

476 *Marpesia eleuchea bahamaensis*

2000. Butterflies. Multicoloured.

4069 45c. Type **476** 20 25
4070 75c. *Pterourus palamedes* . . 30 35
4071 90c. *Dryas julia framptonii* 35 40
4072 $1 *Hypna clytemnestra iphegenia* 40 45
4073 $1.50 *Danaus plexippus* . . . 60 65
4074 $1.50 *Anartia amathea* . . . 60 65
4075 $1.50 *Colobura dirce* 60 65
4076 $1.50 *Parides gundiachianus* 60 65
4077 $1.50 *Spiroeta stelenes* . . . 60 65
4078 $1.50 *Hammadryas feronia* 60 65
4079 $1.50 *Merchantis isthmia* . . 60 65
4080 $1.50 *Colias eurytheme* . . . 60 65
4081 $1.50 *Papilio troilus* 60 65
4082 $1.50 *Junonia coenia* 60 65
4083 $1.50 *Doxocopa laure* . . . 60 65
4084 $1.50 *Pierella hyalinus* . . . 60 65
MS4085 Two sheets, each 95 × 68 mm. (a) $6 *Danaus gilippus*. (b) $6 *Agraulis vanilae insularis* Set of 2 sheets . . . . 4·75 5·00

Nos. 4073/8 and 4079/84 were each printed together, se-tenant, with the backgrounds forming composite designs.

477 Grenada National Cricket Stadium

2000. New National Cricket Stadium. Multicoloured.

4086 $2 Type **477** 80 85
MS4087 102 × 79 mm. $1 West Indies and New Zealand Test teams; $1 Cricket match in progress 80 85

478 Vanderhaeghe (Belgian player)

2000. "Euro 2000" Football Championship. Multicoloured.

4088 $1.50 Type **478** 60 65
4089 $1.50 Belgian team 60 65
4090 $1.50 Ronny Gaspercic (Belgian player) 60 65

4091 $1.50 Lorenzo Staelens (Belgian player) 60 65
4092 $1.50 Koning Boudewijn Stadium 60 65
4093 $1.50 Strupar and Mpenza (Belgian player and coach) 60 65
4094 $1.50 Sergi Barjuan (Spanish player) 60 65
4095 $1.50 Spanish team 60 65
4096 $1.50 Luis Enrique (Spanish player) 60 65
4097 $1.50 Hierro (Spanish player) 60 65
4098 $1.50 De Kuip Stadium, Rotterdam 60 65
4099 $1.50 Raul Gonzales (Spanish player) 60 65
4100 $1.50 Dejan Savicevic (Yugoslav player) 60 65
4101 $1.50 Yugoslav team . . . 60 65
4102 $1.50 Predrag Migatovic (Yugoslav player) 60 65
4103 $1.50 Savo Milosevic (Yugoslav player) 60 65
4104 $1.50 Jan Breydel Stadium, Bruges 60 65
4105 $1.50 Darko Kovacevic (Yugoslav player) 60 65
MS4106 Three sheets, each 145×95 mm. (a) $6 Robert Waseige (Belgian trainer) (vert). (b) $6 José Antonio Camacho (Spanish trainer) (vert). (c) $6 Vujadin Boskov (Yugoslav trainer) (vert) Set of 3 sheets 7·25 7·50

479 Porkfish

2000. Tropical Fish. Multicoloured.
4107 45c. Type **479** 20 25
4108 75c. Short bigeye 30 35
4109 90c. Red snapper 35 40
4110 $1 Creole wrasse 40 45
4111 $1 Hawksbill turtle 40 45
4112 $1 Foureye butterflyfish . . 40 45
4113 $1 Porcupinefish 40 45
4114 $1 Yellowtail damselfish . . 40 45
4115 $1 Adult French angelfish 40 45
4116 $1 Yellow goatfish 40 45
4117 $1 Blue-striped grunt . . . 40 45
4118 $1 Spanish grunt 40 45
4119 $1 Queen triggerfish . . . 40 45
4120 $1 Juvenile French angelfish 40 45
4121 $1 Beaugregory 40 45
4122 $1 Queen angelfish 40 45
4123 $1 Sergeant major 40 45
4124 $1 Bank butterflyfish . . . 40 45
4125 $1 Spanish hogfish 40 45
4126 $1 Porkfish (different) . . . 40 45
4127 $1 Banded butterflyfish . . 40 45
4128 $1 Longsnout seahorse . . . 40 45
4129 $2 Indigo hamlet 80 85
4130 $3 Blue tang . . . . 1·20 1·30
MS4131 Two sheets, each 102×73 mm. (a) $6 Blue tang (different). (b) $6 Queen angelfish (different) Set of 2 sheets . . . 4·75 5·00

Nos. 4111/19 and 4120/8 were each printed together, se-tenant, with the backgrounds forming composite designs.

No. 4126 is inscribed "Poskfish" in error.

2000. Monarchs of the Millenium. As T **314a** of Gambia.
4132 $1.50 multicoloured 60 65
4133 $1.50 multicoloured 60 65
4134 $1.50 lilac, stone and brown 60 65
4135 $1.50 lilac, stone and brown 60 65
MS4136 116×136 mm. $6 multicoloured . . . . 2·40 2·50

DESIGNS: No. 4132, King George III of Great Britain; 4133, King George IV of Great Britain; 4134, Duchess Charlotte of Luxembourg; 4135, Duke Jean of Luxembourg; **MS**4136 King Charles VIII of France.

2000. Popes of the Millennium. As T **314b** of Gambia. Multicoloured (except **MS**4143).
4137 $1.50 Stephen VIII 60 65
4138 $1.50 Theodore 60 65
4139 $1.50 Theodore II 60 65
4140 $1.50 Valentine 60 65
4141 $1.50 Vitalian 60 65
4142 $1.50 Zacharias 60 65
MS4143 116×136 mm. $6 Sylvester II (grey, black and stone) . . . 2·40 2·50

480 500 Mondial Sports Car, 1953

2000. Ferrari Cars. Multicoloured.
4144 20c. Type **480** 10 15
4145 45c. 166 Inter saloon, 1948 20 25
4146 75c. 340 MM sports car, 1953 . . . . 30 35
4147 90c. 500 Superfast saloon, 1964 . . . . 35 40
4148 $1 166 MM sports car, 1948 40 45
4149 $1.50 250 S saloon, 1952 . . 60 65
4150 $2 250 California convertible, 1957 . . . . 80 85
4151 $3 365 California convertible, 1966 . . . . 1·20 1·30

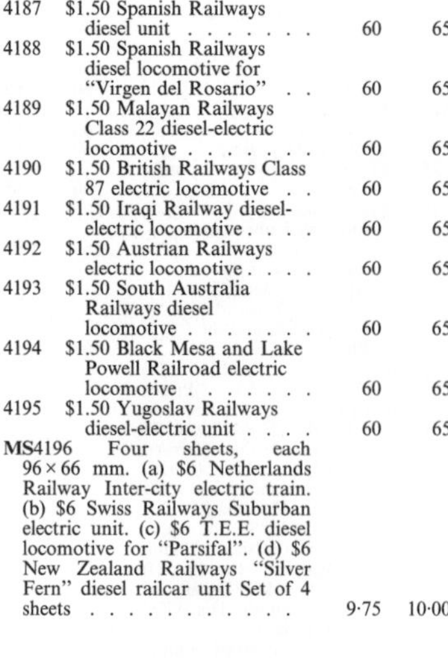

481 Marmon Model 34, 1921

2000. Classic Cars. Multicoloured.
4152 45c. Type **481** 20 25
4153 75c. Buick D44, 1917 . . . 30 35
4154 90c. Hudson Runabout Landau, 1918 . . . . . . 35 40
4155 $1 Chevrolet Royal Mail, 1915 . . . . 40 45
4156 $1.50 Rolls Royce, 1929 . . 60 65
4157 $1.50 Graham Convertible, 1932 . . . . 60 65
4158 $1.50 Mercedes-Benz 540K, 1937 . . . . 60 65
4159 $1.50 Jaguar Mk V, 1948 60 65
4160 $1.50 Lagonda Drophead Coupe, 1939 . . . . . . 60 65
4161 $1.50 Alfa Romeo Gran Sport, 1930 . . . . 60 65
4162 $1.50 Cadillac V63, 1925 . . 60 65
4163 $1.50 Plymouth, 1939 . . . 60 65
4164 $1.50 Franklin Club Sedan, 1934 . . . . 60 65
4165 $1.50 Fiat Ardita, 1933 . . 60 65
4166 $1.50 Essex Speedabout, 1929 . . . . 60 65
4167 $1.50 Stutz Bearcat, 1932 . . 60 65
4168 $2 Kissel Speedster, 1925 . . 80 85
4169 $3 Ford Model T, 1915 . . 1·20 1·30
MS4170 Two sheets, each 94×67 mm. (a) $6 Dodge Tourer, 1915. (b) $6 Chrysler, 1924 Set of 2 sheets . . . . 4·75 5·00

482 Borsig Standard Locomotive, 1863

2000. German Railway Locomotives. Mult.
4171 $1.50 Type **482** 60 65
4172 $1.50 German Federal Railway Austerity Class 52, 1940s 60 65
4173 $1.50 Stephenson locomotive *Adler* without tender, 1835 . . . . 60 65
4174 $1.50 Crampton locomotive *Bardenia*, 1863 . . . . . 60 65
4175 $1.50 Drache, 1848 . . . . 60 65
4176 $1.50 Stephenson locomotive *Adler* with tender, 1835 60 65
4177 $1.50 German Federal Railway Class 10, 1956 60 65
4178 $1.50 German Federal Railway Class E10 electric locomotive, 1957 . . . . 60 65
4179 $1.50 German Federal Railway Class 23, 1953 60 65
4180 $1.50 German Federal Railway tank locomotive, 1950s 60 65
4181 $1.50 East German State Railway rebuilt Class 01 Pacific, 1950s 60 65
4182 $1.50 East German State Railway diesel railcar on Berlin–Schonefeld service, 1950s 60 65
MS4183 Two sheets, each 80×72 mm. (a) $6 Borsig locomotive of Berlin and Anhalt Railway, 1841. (b) $6 German Federal Railway V.200 diesel-hydraulic locomotive, 1952 Set of 2 sheets . . . . 4·75 5·00

483 Thai State Railway Diesel-electric Locomotive

2000. Modern Railway Locomotives of the World. Multicoloured.
4184 $1.50 Type **483** 60 65
4185 $1.50 Danish diesel-electric express locomotive . . . 60 65
4186 $1.50 French-built Turbo train 60 65
4187 $1.50 Spanish Railways diesel unit 60 65
4188 $1.50 Spanish Railways diesel locomotive for "Virgen del Rosario" . . 60 65
4189 $1.50 Malayan Railways Class 22 diesel-electric locomotive 60 65
4190 $1.50 British Railways Class 87 electric locomotive . . 60 65
4191 $1.50 Iraqi Railway diesel-electric locomotive 60 65
4192 $1.50 Austrian Railways electric locomotive 60 65
4193 $1.50 South Australia Railways diesel locomotive 60 65
4194 $1.50 Black Mesa and Lake Powell Railroad electric locomotive 60 65
4195 $1.50 Yugoslav Railways diesel-electric unit 60 65
MS4196 Four sheets, each 96×66 mm. (a) $6 Netherlands Railway Inter-city electric train. (b) $6 Swiss Railways Suburban electric unit. (c) $6 T.E.E. diesel locomotive for "Parsifal". (d) $6 New Zealand Railways "Silver Fern" diesel railcar unit Set of 4 sheets . . . . 9·75 10·00

484 Girl at Skylight

2000. Nursery Rhymes. Multicoloured.
4197 $1.50 Type **484** 60 65
4198 $1.50 Woman and rainbow 60 65
4199 $1.50 Cow and rainbow . . 60 65
4200 $1.50 Boy in nightshirt . . . 60 65
4201 $1.50 Old Woman with baby 60 65
4202 $1.50 Boy on show 60 65
4203 $1.50 Bird in tree and crook 60 65
4204 $1.50 Little Bo-Peep 60 65
4205 $1.50 Sheep 60 65
4206 $1.50 Goose and fence . . . 60 65
4207 $1.50 Goose and Little Bo-Peep 60 65
4208 $1.50 Dog 60 65
4209 $1.50 Sheep and cottage . . 60 65
4210 $1.50 Sun and lane 60 65
4211 $1.50 Cow and haystack . . 60 65
4212 $1.50 Two geese 60 65
4213 $1.50 Dog and Boy Blue's leg 60 65
4214 $1.50 Little Boy Blue asleep 60 65
4215 $1.50 Dove and tower . . . 60 65
4216 $1.50 Cow jumping over moon 60 65
4217 $1.50 Spoon 60 65
4218 $1.50 Dog laughing 60 65
4219 $1.50 Cat playing fiddle . . 60 65
4220 $1.50 Dish 60 65
MS4221 Four sheets, each 106×77 mm. (a) $6 Old Woman and shoe (horiz). (b) $6 Little Bo-Peep (horiz). (c) $6 Little Boy Blue asleep (horiz). (d) $6 Cow jumping over moon (horiz) Set of 4 sheets 9·75 10·00

Nos. 4197/202 (Old Woman that lived in a Shoe), 4203/8 (Little Bo-Peep), 4209/14 (Little Boy Blue) and 4215/20 (The Cat and the Fiddle) were each printed together, se-tenant, with the backgrounds forming composite designs.

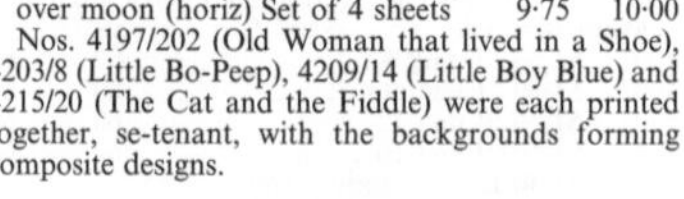

· a Shirley Temple film (1937) ·

485 Heidi walking with Governess

2000. Shirley Temple in *Heidi*. Showing scenes from the film. Multicoloured.
4222 $1.50 Type **485** 60 65
4223 $1.50 Heidi with grandfather 60 65
4224 $1.50 Heidi with Peter the Goat Boy 60 65
4225 $1.50 Heidi with doves . . . 60 65
4226 $1.50 Heidi with grandfather tying knot 60 65
4227 $1.50 Heidi and governess sitting on bench 60 65
4228 $1.50 Heidi in bed 60 65
4229 $1.50 Heidi with Klara Sesemann 60 65
4230 $1.50 Heidi with Andrews the butler 60 65
4231 $1.50 Heidi unwrapping Christmas presents with the Sesemanns 60 65
MS4232 105×75 mm. $6 Heidi sitting on log . . . . 2·40 2·50

486 Betty Boop sitting in Sports Car, Hollywood

2000. Betty Boop (cartoon character). Twelve sheets containing vert designs as T **486** showing geographical locations. Multicoloured.
MS4233 (a) 110×90 mm. $6 Type **486**. (b) 110×90 mm. $6 Riding horse, Argentina. (c) 110×90 mm. $6 Sitting on camel, Turkey. (d) 110×90 mm. $6 As flamenco dancer, Spain. (e) 110×90 mm. $6 Drinking champagne, France. (f) 110×90 mm. $6 Fishing, South Pacific. (g) 110×90 mm. $6 As belly dancer, Eygpt. (h) 90×110 mm. $6 With guardsman outside Buckingham Palace, London. (i) 90×110 mm. $6 In floral hat, Switzerland. (j) 90×110 mm. $6 In kimono, Japan. (k) 90×110 mm. $6 As Statue of Liberty, New York. (l) 90×110 mm. $6 Wearing lei, Hawaii Set of 12 sheets . . . . 29·00 30·00

2000. Scenes from *The Three Stooges* (American T.V. comedy series). As T **310** of Gambia. Multicoloured.
4234 $1 Moe pointing bottle at Curly Joe 40 45
4235 $1 Eating straw with horse 40 45
4236 $1 Larry holding flowers . . 40 45
4237 $1 Reading letter 40 45
4238 $1 Looking in saucepan . . 40 45
4239 $1 Holding wads of notes 40 45
4240 $1 Moe in breastplate (guard behind in purple and green) 40 45
4241 $1 Indoors with horse . . . 40 45
4242 $1 Larry in breastplate (guard behind in lilac and yellow) 40 45
4243 $1 Western bar brawl . . . 40 45
4244 $1 As "DELIGATES" . . . 40 45
4245 $1 In Victorian dress (two as women) 40 45
4246 $1 Moe pointing gun . . . 40 45
4247 $1 Holding certificate . . . 40 45
4248 $1 Moe using secateurs near Curly's nose 40 45
4249 $1 Larry (picture at right) 40 45
4250 $1 Moe in front of picture 40 45
4251 $1 Curly 40 45
MS4252 Twelve sheets. (a) 108×87 mm. $5 Curly in green shirt holding Moe's arm (vert). (b) 108×87 mm. $5 In evening dress with girl. (c) 108×87 mm. $5 Moe with Larry holding woman's hand (vert). (d) 91×137 mm. $5 With secretary from *He Cooked His Goose* (vert). (e) 108×87 mm. $5 As No. 4243. (f) 108×89 mm. $5 Having heads banged together by cowboy. (g) 97×118 mm. $5 Putting Larry in a jet engine (vert). (h) 98×125 mm. $5 Curly Joe with cigar (vert). (i) 107×88 mm. $5 Listening to jet engine. (j) 107×88 mm. $5 Swinging propeller. (k) 130×100 mm. $6 Larry and Moe in breastplates. (l) 130×100 mm. $6 Curly with hand in mangle Set of 12 sheets . . 25·00 26·00

487 Kane jumping over Opponent

488 American Purple Gallinule

2000. World Wrestling Federation. Kane. Multicoloured.
4253 $1 Type **487** 40 45
4254 $1 Kneeling by injured opponent 40 45
4255 $1 Jumping 40 45
4256 $1 Kane (red background) 40 45
4257 $1 Kane (blue and yellow background) 40 45
4258 $1 Holding lifting opponent in black tunic 40 45
4259 $1 With arms folded 40 45

4260 $1 Lifting opponent in black and white trousers 40 45
4261 $1 Lifting opponent No. 59 40 45
MS4262 Two sheets, each 77×118 mm. (a) $5 With black glove on right hand. (b) $5 Lifting opponent Set of 2 sheets . . . 4·00 4·25

2000. "Espana 2000" International Stamp Exhibition, Madrid. Paintings from the Prado Museum. As T **326a** of Gambia. Multicoloured.

4263 $1.50 King Ferdinand and priest from "The Virgin of the Catholic Monarchs" (anon) 60 65
4264 $1.50 Virgin and Child from "The Virgin of the Catholic Monarchs" . . . 60 65
4265 $1.50 Queen Isabella and priest from "The Virgin of the Catholic Monarchs" 60 65
4266 $1.50 "The Flagellation" (Alejo Fernandez) 60 65
4267 $1.50 "The Virgin and Souls in Purgatory" (Pedro Machuca) 60 65
4268 $1.50 "The Holy Trinity" (El Greco) 60 65
4269 $1.50 "The Saviour's Blessing" (Francisco de Zurbaran) 60 65
4270 $1.50 "St. John the Baptist" (Francesco Solimena) . . 60 65
4271 $1.50 "Noli Me Tangere" (Correggio) 60 65
4272 $1.50 "St. Casilda" (Francisco de Zurbaran) 60 65
4273 $1.50 "Nicolas Omazur" (Murillo) 60 65
4274 $1.50 "Juan Martinez Montanes" (Velazquez) 60 65
4275 $1.50 "Playing at Giants" (Goya) 60 65
4276 $1.50 "The Holy Family with Oak Tree" (Raphael and Giulio Romano) . . 60 65
4277 $1.50 "Don Gaspar Melchor de Jovellanos" (Goya) . . 60 65
4278 $1.50 Courtier from "Joseph in Pharaoh's Palace" (Jacopo Amiconi) 60 65
4279 $1.50 Pharaoh and Joseph from "Joseph in Pharaoh's Palace" 60 65
4280 $1.50 Servant with hat from "Joseph in Pharaoh's Palace" 60 65
MS4281 Three sheets. (a) 90×110 mm. $6 "The Virgin of the Catholic Monarchs" (anon). (b) 90×110 mm. $6 "St. Anne, the Virgin, St. Elizabeth, St. John and the Christ Child" (Fernando Yanez de la Almedina). (c) 110×90 mm. $6 "Joseph in Pharoah's Palace" (Jacopo Amiconi) (horiz) Set of 3 sheets 7·25 7·50

2000. Birds of the Caribbean. Multicoloured.

4282 25c. Type **488** 10 15
4283 40c. Limpkin 15 20
4284 50c. Black-necked stilt . . . 20 25
4285 60c. Painted bunting 25 30
4286 75c. Yellow-breasted flycatcher warbler ("Yellow-breasted Warbler") 30 35
4287 $1 Blackburnian warbler . . 40 45
4288 $1.25 Blue grosbeak 50 55
4289 $1.50 Black and white warbler 60 65
4290 $1.60 Himalayan whistling thrush ("Blue Whistling Thrush") 65 70
4291 $3 Common yellowthroat 1·20 1·30
4292 $4 Indigo bunting . . . . . 1·60 1·70
4293 $5 Catbird . . . . 2·00 2·25
4294 $10 Bananaquit . . . . . . 4·00 4·25
4295 $20 Blue-grey gnatcatcher 8·00 8·25

489 Messerschmitt Bf 109E under Attack

2000. 60th Anniv of Battle of Britain. Multicoloured.

4296 $1.50 Type **489** 60 65
4297 $1.50 Supermarine Spitfire Mk XI 60 65
4298 $1.50 V1 flying bomb . . . 60 65
4299 $1.50 U-Boat under attack 60 65
4300 $1.50 Anti-aircraft gun . . . 60 65
4301 $1.50 Bedford army ambulance 60 65
4302 $1.50 Messerschmitt Bf 109E 60 65
4303 $1.50 German pilot parachuting 60 65
4304 $1.50 Hawker Hurricane MkI 60 65
4305 $1.50 British airfield under attack 60 65
4306 $1.50 Heinkel He 111H on fire 60 65
4307 $1.50 R.A.F. emblem on Supermarine Spitfire Mk XI 60 65
MS4308 Two sheets, each 99×71 mm. (a) $6 Supermarine Spitfire Mk IX. (b) $6 Hawker Hurricane Mk 1s on tarmac Set of 2 sheets . . . . . . 4·75 5·00

No. 4304 is inscribed "Hanker Hurricane HK1" and No. **MS**4308 "HK1", both in error.

2000. Queen Elizabeth the Queen Mother's 100th Birthday. As T **318** of Gambia. Multicoloured.

4309 $1.50 Queen Mother in grey hat 60 65

2000. Faces of the Millennium: Queen Elizabeth the Queen Mother's 100th Birthday. As T **307a** of Gambia showing collage of miniature flower photographs. Multicoloured.

4310 $1 Top of head (face value at left) 40 45
4311 $1 Top of head (face value at right) 40 45
4312 $1 Eye and temple (face value at left) 40 45
4313 $1 Temple (face value at right) 40 45
4314 $1 Cheek (face value at left) 40 45
4315 $1 Cheek (face value at right) 40 45
4316 $1 Chin (face value at left) 40 45
4317 $1 Neck (face value at right) 40 45

Nos. 4310/17 were printed together, se-tenant, in sheetlets of 8 with the stamps arranged in two vertical columns separated by a gutter also containing miniature photographs. When viewed as a whole the sheetlet forms a portrait of the Queen Mother.

490 *Brassavola nodosa* **491** Angel in Red

2000. Caribbean Flowers. Multicoloured.

4318 25c. Type **490** 10 15
4319 35c. *Laelia anceps* (horiz) . . 15 20
4320 75c. *Plumeria rubra* (horiz) 30 35
4321 $1 *Bougainvillea glabra* (horiz) 40 45
4322 $1 *Allamanda catharticia* . . 40 45
4323 $1.50 *Cassia alata* 60 65
4324 $1.50 *Anthurium andreanum* 60 65
4325 $1.50 *Ipomea crassicaulis* . . 60 65
4326 $1.50 *Laelia anceps* 60 65
4327 $1.50 *Galeandra baueri* . . . 60 65
4328 $1.50 *Hibiscus rosa-sinensis* 60 65
4329 $1.50 *Alpinia purpurata* . . 60 65
4330 $1.50 *Strelitzia reginae* . . . 60 65
4331 $1.50 *Psychlis atropurpurea* 60 65
4332 $1.50 *Cattleya velutina* . . . 60 65
4333 $1.50 *Caularthron bicornutum* 60 65
4334 $1.50 *Cattleya warneri* . . . 60 65
4335 $1.50 *Mandevilla splendens* 60 65
4336 $1.50 *Tithonia rotundifolia* 60 65
4337 $1.50 *Lagerstromia speciosa* 60 65
4338 $1.50 *Columnea argentea* . . 60 65
4339 $1.50 *Brunfelsia calycina* . . 60 65
4340 $1.50 *Portlandia albiflora* . . 60 65
4341 $1.50 *Pachira insignis* . . . 60 65
4342 $1.50 *Jatropha integerrima* 60 65
4343 £1.50 *Jacaranda filicifolia* . . 60 65
4344 $1.50 *Cordia sebestena* . . . 60 65
4345 $1.50 *Allamanda cathartica* 60 65
4346 $1.50 *Samanea saman* . . . 60 65
4347 $2 *Lisianthius nigrescens* (horiz) 80 85
4348 $2 *Aspasia epidendroides* . . 80 85
4349 $3 *Oncidium splendidum* . . 1·20 1·30
MS4350 Four sheets. (a) 68×97 mm. $6 *Anthurium scherzerianum* (horiz). (b) 68×97 mm. $6 *Ipomea learii* (horiz). (c) 94×61 mm. $6 *Fuchsia* (horiz). (d) 94×61 mm. $6 *Heliconia psittaconia* Set of 4 sheets . . . . 9·75 10·00

Nos. 4323/8, 4329/34, 4335/40 and 4341/6 were each printed together, se-tenant, each forming a composite floral design.

No. 4320 is inscribed "Plumieria", 4341 "Pachira insigis", 4343 "Jacarancla filicifolia" and 4345 "Corclia filicifolia", all in error.

2000. Christmas. Holy Year. Multicoloured.

4351 15c. Type **491** 10 10
4352 25c. Angel praying 10 15
4353 50c. Type **491** 20 25
4354 $2 As 25c 80 85
4355 $2 Type **491** 80 85
4356 $5 As 25c . . . . 2·00 2·10
MS4357 110×120 mm. $6 Holy Child (horiz) . . . . 2·40 2·50

2001. Chinese New Year. ("Year of the Snake"). As T **470**. Multicoloured.

4358 $2 Blue and yellow snake 80 85
4359 $2 Green snake (inverted triangle) 80 85
4360 $2 Red snake 80 85

491a Lucy and Desi with Friends

2001. Scenes from *I Love Lucy* (American T.V. comedy series). Eight sheets, each containing multicoloured design as T **491a**.

MS4361 (a) 80×112 mm. $6 Type **491a**. (b) 80×110 mm. $6 Lucy and Desi dancing. (c) 88×127 mm. $6 Lucy in checked jacket. (d) 92×124 mm. $6 Lucy in checked jacket dancing with Desi. (e) 98×120 mm. $6 Desi laughing with William Frawley. (f) 118×92 mm. $6 Lucy leaning on mantelpiece. (g) 118×100 mm. $6 Lucy sitting at desk. (h) 92×124 mm. $6 William Frawley and Desi at desk (horiz) Set of 8 sheets . . . . 19·00 20·00

2001. Bicentenary of Rijksmuseum, Amsterdam. Dutch Paintings. As T **330a** of Gambia. Multicoloured.

4362 $1.50 "Syndics of Amsterdam Goldsmiths' Guild" (Thomas de Keyser) 60 65
4363 $1.50 "Gentleman" (De Keyser) 60 65
4364 $1.50 "Eva Wtewael" (Joachim Wtewael) . . . 60 65
4365 $1.50 "Ferry Boat" (Esaias van de Velde) 60 65
4366 $1.50 "Tares among the Wheat" (Abraham Bloemaert) 60 65
4367 $1.50 "Princess Henrietta Marie Stuart" (Bartholomeus van der Heist) 60 65
4368 $1.50 "William I, Prince of Orange" (Adriaen Key) 60 65
4369 $1.50 "Schimmelpenninck Family" (Pierre-Paul Prud'hon) 60 65
4370 $1.50 "Johan Rudolf Thorbecke" (Jan Neuman) 60 65
4371 $1.50 "St. Sebastian" (Wtewael) 60 65
4372 $1.50 "St. Sebastian" (Hendrick ter Brugghen) 60 65
4373 $1.50 "Man with a Ring" (Werner van der Valckert) 60 65
4374 $1.50 "Abraham Casteleyn and his Wife, Margarieta van Bancken" (Jan de Bray) 60 65
4375 $1.50 Piper and singer from "Concert" (Ter Brugghen) 60 65
4376 $1.50 "Procuress" (Dirck van Baburen) 60 65
4377 $1.50 "Woman seated at Virginal" (Vermeer) . . . 60 65
4378 $1.50 "Elegant Couples courting" (Willem Buytewech) 60 65
4379 $1.50 "Young Flute player" (Judith Leyster) 60 65
4380 $1.50 "Merry Fiddler" (Gerard van Honthorst) 60 65
4381 $1.50 "Merry Drinker" (Frans Hals) 60 65
4382 $1.50 "Granida and Daifilo" (Van Honthorst) 60 65
4383 $1.50 "Vertumnus and Pomona" (Paulus Moreelse) 60 65
4384 $1.50 Piper from "Concert" (Ter Brugghen) 60 65
4385 $1.50 "Young Student at his Desk" (Pieter Codde) . . 60 65
MS4386 Four sheets. (a) 119×88 mm. $6 "Winter Landscape with Skaters" (Hendrick Avercamp) (horiz). (b) 119×88 mm. $6 "Denial of St. Peter" (Rembrandt) (horiz). (c) 98×118 mm. $6 "Portuguese Synagogue, Amsterdam" (Emanuel de Witte). (d) 98×118 mm. $6 "The Raampoortje" (Wouter van Troostwijk) (horiz) Set of 4 sheets 9·75 10·00

No. 4381 is inscribed "Frans Hal" in error.

2001. Characters from "Pokemon" (children's cartoon series). As T **332a** of Gambia. Multicoloured.

4387 $1.50 "Rattata No. 19" . . 60 65
4388 $1.50 "Sandshrew No. 27" 60 65
4389 $1.50 "Wartortle No. 08" 60 65
4390 $1.50 "Primeape No. 57" . . 60 65
4391 $1.50 "Golduck No. 55" . . 60 65
4392 $1.50 "Persian No. 53" . . 60 65
MS4393 74×115 mm. $6 "Jolteon No. 135" . . . . 2·40 2·50

492 African Pygmy Goose

2001. "Hong Kong 2001" International Stamp Exhibition. Ducks of the World. Multicoloured.

4394 $1.25 Type **492** 50 55
4395 $1.25 Versicolor teal ("Silver Teal") 50 55
4396 $1.25 Marbled teal 50 55
4397 $1.25 Garganey 50 55
4398 $1.25 Wandering whistling duck 50 55
4399 $1.25 Northern shoveler . . 50 55
4400 $1.25 Flying steamer duck ("Flightless Steamer Duck") 50 55
4401 $1.25 Radjah shelduck . . . 50 55
4402 $1.25 Cape teal 50 55
4403 $1.25 Hartlaub's duck . . . 50 55
4404 $1.25 Ruddy shelduck . . . 50 55
4405 $1.25 Bahama pintail ("White-cheeked Pintail") 50 55
4406 $1.25 Fulvous whistling duck (vert) 50 55
4407 $1.25 African black duck (vert) 50 55
4408 $1.25 Madagascar pochard ("Madagascan White-eye") (vert) 50 55
4409 $1.25 African pygmy goose ("Pygmy Goose") (vert) 50 55
4410 $1.25 Wood duck (female) (vert) 50 55
4411 $1.25 Wood duck (male) (vert) 50 55
MS4412 Three sheets, each 100×70 mm. (a) $6 Flying steamer duck. (b) $6 Flightless steamer duck. (c) $6 Australian shelduck (vert) Set of 3 sheets 7·25 7·50

493 "Daily Life in Edo" (Miyagawa Choshum)

2001. "Philanippon '01" International Stamp Exhibition, Tokyo. Japanese Paintings. Multicoloured.

4413 75c. Type **493** 30 35
4414 90c. "Twelve Famous Places in Japan" (Kano Isen'in Naganobu) 35 40
4415 $1 "After the Rain" (Kawai Gyokudo) 40 45
4416 $1.25 "Ryogoku Bridge" (Kano Kyuei) 50 55
4417 $2 "Courtesan of Fukagawa" (Katsukawa Shun'ei) 80 85
4418 $2 "Yugao Chapter" (85×28 mm) 80 85
4419 $2 "Suetsumuhana Chapter" (85×28 mm) 80 85
4420 $2 "Wakamurasaki Chapter" (85×28 mm) . . 80 85
4421 $2 "Momiji-no-ga Chapter" (85×28 mm) 80 85
4422 $2 Praying in the woods (vert) 80 85
4423 $2 Lady with servants (vert) 80 85
4424 $2 Fire by river (vert) . . . 80 85
4425 $2 Pagoda by river (vert) . . 80 85
4426 $3 "Bear Killing" (unsigned) 1·20 1·30
MS4427 Two sheets. (a) 93×81 mm. $6 "Pomegranates and a Small Bird" (Onishi Keisai). (b) 97×76 mm. $6 from "Bodhisattva: Never Despise" (Enryaku-ji) (vert). Nos. 4418/21 depict "Tale of Genji" Set of 2 sheets . . . . 4·75 5·00

Nos. 4418/21 depict "Tale of Genji" (Kano Ryusetsu Hidenobu), and Nos. 4422/5 illustrates "The Lotus Sutra—Tactfulness" (Hompo-ji).

2001. Death Centenary of Queen Victoria. As T **590a** of Ghana. Multicoloured.

4428 $3 Princess Victoria as a young girl . . . . 1·20 1·30
4429 $3 Young Queen Victoria wearing crown . . . . . 1·20 1·30
4430 $3 In old age . . . . 1·20 1·30
MS4431 77×107 mm. $6 Queen Victoria on throne . . . . . . 2·40 2·50

2001. 25th Death Anniv of Mao Tse-tung (Chinese leader). As T **590b** of Ghana. Multicoloured.

4432 $2 Mao Tse-tung in 1936 . . 80 85
4433 $2 In 1919 . . . . 80 85
4434 $2 In 1945 . . . . 80 85
MS4435 133×126 mm. $3 Mao Tse-tung encouraging troops in 1938 1·20 1·30

2001. 75th Death Anniv of Claude-Oscar Monet (French painter). As T **590c** of Ghana. Multicoloured.

4436 $2 "Boats in Winter Quarters, Etretat" 80 85
4437 $2 "Regatta at Sainte Adresse" 80 85

4438 $2 "Bridge at Bougival" . . 80 85
4439 $2 "Beach at Sainte Adresse" 80 85
MS4440 136 × 111 mm. $6 "Monet's Garden at Vetheuil" (vert) . . 2·40 2·50

2001. 75th Birthday of Queen Elizabeth II. As T **590d** of Ghana. Multicoloured.
4441 $2 Queen in straw boater . . 80 85
4442 $2 Queen in red hat 80 85
4443 $2 Wearing multicoloured pastel hat 80 85
4444 $2 Wearing mauve turban-style hat 80 85
MS4445 76 × 100 mm. $6 Queen wearing mauve hat and coat (37 × 50 mm) . . . . 2·40 2·50

2001. Death Centenary of Giuseppe Verdi (Italian composer). As T **590e** of Ghana. Multicoloured.
4446 $2 Character from Ernani (opera) 80 85
4447 $2 Score from Ernani . . . 80 85
4448 $2 Verdi as a young man . . 80 85
4449 $2 La Scala Opera House, Milan 80 85
MS4450 76 × 106 mm. $6 Verdi in old age . . . . 2·40 2·50

2001. Death Centenary of Henri de Toulouse-Lautrec (French painter). As T **590f** of Ghana. Multicoloured.
4451 $2 "Alone" 80 85
4452 $2 "Two Half-naked Women" 80 85
4453 $2 "The Toilette" 80 85
4454 $2 "Justine Dieuhl" 80 85
MS4455 66 × 84 mm. $6 "Mademoiselle Dihau at the Piano" . . . . 2·40 2·50

494 Woman on Beach

2001. United Nations Women's Human Rights Campaign. Multicoloured.
4456 90c. Type **494** 35 40
4457 $1 "Caribbean Woman II" 40 45

495 Marlene Dietrich smoking

2001. Birth Centenary of Marlene Dietrich (actress and singer).
4458 **495** $2 multicoloured 80 85
4459 – $2 black, purple and red 80 85
4460 – $2 black, purple and red 80 85
4461 – $2 black, purple and red 80 85
DESIGNS No. 4459, Marlene Dietrich on stage with microphone; 4460, Wearing feather boa; 4461, Sitting in armchair.

496 Phoenician Merchant Ship

2001. "Belgica 2001" International Stamp Exhibition, Brussels. Sailing Ships. Mult.
4462 45c. Type **496** 20 25
4463 75c. Portuguese caravel . . 30 35
4464 90c. Marblehead schooner 35 40
4465 $1 Mala pansi 40 45
4466 $1 English cog 40 45
4467 $1 Roman merchantman . . 40 45
4468 $1 Greek war galley 40 45
4469 $1 Greek merchantman . . 40 45
4470 $1 Oseberg Viking longship 40 45
4471 $1 Egyptian sailing craft . . 40 45
4472 $1 Egyptian galley 40 45
4473 $1 16th-century galleass . . 40 45
4474 $1 Norman ship 40 45
4475 $1 English carrack 40 45
4476 $1 Mediterranean carrack . . 40 45
4477 $1 Spanish galleon 40 45
4478 $1 Elizabethan Grumster . . 40 45
4479 $1 British East Indiaman . . 40 45
4480 $1 Clipper 40 45
4481 $1 British ship of the line 40 45
4482 $1 British gun boat 40 45
4483 $1 English hoy 40 45
4484 $1 Gloucester fishing schooner 40 45
4485 $1 Sloop-rigged yacht . . . 40 45
4486 $1 Chinese junk 40 45
4487 $1 Sambuk 40 45
4488 $1 Baltimore clipper schooner 40 45
4489 $1 Schooner-rigged yacht . . 40 45
4490 $1 American clipper 40 45
4491 $1 American frigate 40 45
4492 $1 Sail/steam mail packet . . 40 45
4493 $1.50 American corvette . . 60 65
4494 $2 Racing schooner 80 85
MS4495 Two sheets, each 60 × 44 mm. (a) $6 *Suhaili* (yacht), 1968. (b) $6 *Gulf Streamer* (trimaran) and Polynesian outrigger Set of 2 sheets . . . 4·75 5·00
No. 4481 is inscribed "BRITISH GUN SHIP", 4482 "BRITISH FLAGSHIP" and 4484 "GLOUSTER", all in error.

497 Montauk Point Lighthouse, New York **497a** Anatoly Karpov

2001. Lighthouses. Multicoloured.
4496 25c. Type **497** 10 15
4497 50c. Alcatraz lighthouse, San Francisco 20 25
4498 $1 Barnegat lighthouse, New Jersey 40 45
4499 $1.50 Point Amour lighthouse, Canada . . . 60 65
4500 $1.50 Inubo-Saki lighthouse, Japan 60 65
4501 $1.50 Belle-Ile lighthouse, France 60 65
4502 $1.50 Faerder lighthouse, Norway 60 65
4503 $1.50 Cape Agulhas lighthouse, South Africa 60 65
4504 $1.50 Minicoy lighthouse, India 60 65
4505 $1.50 Admiralty lighthouse, Washington 60 65
4506 $1.50 Hooper's Strait lighthouse, Maryland . . 60 65
4507 $1.50 Hunting Island lighthouse, South Carolina 60 65
4508 $1.50 Key West Lighthouse Museum, Florida 60 65
4509 $1.50 Old Point Loma lighthouse, California . . 60 65
4510 $1.50 Old Makinac Point lighthouse, Michigan . . 60 65
4511 $1.50 Keri lighthouse, Estonia 60 65
4512 $1.50 Anholt lighthouse, Denmark 60 65
4513 $1.50 Porer lighthouse, Croatia 60 65
4514 $1.50 Laotieshan lighthouse, China 60 65
4515 $1.50 Sapienza Methoni lighthouse, Greece 60 65
4516 $1.50 Arkona lighthouse, Germany 60 65
4517 $2 St. Augustine lighthouse, Florida 80 85
MS4518 Four sheets, each 70 × 98 mm. (a) $6 Kvitsoy lighthouse, Norway. (b) $6 Mahota Pagoda lighthouse, China. (c) $6 Boston lighthouse, Massachusetts. (d) $6 Pellworm lighthouse, Germany. . . . . . 9·75 10·00
Nos. 4503 and 4515 are inscribed "Africca" or "Sapientza", both in error.

2001. First e-World Chess Championship. Sheet 88 × 103 mm.
MS4518a **497a** $20 multicoloured 8·00 8·25

498 Commerson's Dolphin

2001. Whales and Dolphins. Multicoloured.
4519 25c. Type **498** 10 15
4520 50c. Pacific white-sided dolphin 20 25
4521 $1.50 Risso's dolphin . . . 60 65
4522 $1.50 Fraser's dolphin . . . 60 65
4523 $1.50 Dall's porpoise . . . 60 65
4524 $1.50 Right whale 60 65
4525 $1.50 Grey whale 60 65
4526 $1.50 Minke whale 60 65
4527 $1.50 Common dolphin . . . 60 65
4528 $1.50 Antillean beaked whale 60 65
4529 $1.50 Killer whale's tail and divers 60 65
4530 $1.50 Bryde's whale 60 65
4531 $1.50 Cuvier's beaked whale 60 65
4532 $1.50 Sei whale 60 65
4533 $1.50 Harbour porpoise . . 60 65
4534 $1.50 Beluga 60 65
4535 $1.50 White-beaked dolphin 60 65
4536 $1.50 Narwhal 60 65
4537 $1.50 Bowhead whale . . . 60 65
4538 $1.50 Fin whale 60 65
4539 $2 Northern bottlenosed whale 80 85
4540 $3 Baird's beaked whale . . 1·20 1·30
MS4541 Four sheets, each 75 × 52 mm. (a) $6 Humpback whale and calf. (b) $6 Sperm whale calf. (c) $6 Blue whale with calf. (d) $6 Southern right whale . . 9·75 10·00
Nos. 4521/6, 4527/32 and 4533/8 were printed together, se-tenant, with the backgrounds forming composite designs.

499 World Cup Publicity Poster, Brazil, 1950

2001. World Cup Football Championship, Japan and Korea (2002). Multicoloured.
4542 $1.50 Type **499** 60 65
4543 $1.50 West German players, Switzerland, 1954 . . . . 60 65
4544 $1.50 Just Fontaine (France), Sweden, 1958 60 65
4545 $1.50 Garrincha (Brazil), Chile, 1962 . . . . 60 65
4546 $1.50 Bobby Moore (England), England, 1966 60 65
4547 $1.50 Pele (Brazil), Mexico, 1970 . . . . 60 65
4548 $1.50 Osvaldo Ardiles (Argentina), Argentina, 1978 . . . . 60 65
4549 $1.50 Lakhdar Belloumi (Algeria), Spain, 1982 . . 60 65
4550 $1.50 Diego Maradona (Argentina), Mexico, 1986 60 65
4551 $1.50 Lothar Matthaus and Rudi Voller (West Germany), Italy, 1990 . . 60 65
4552 $1.50 Seo Jung Won (South Korea), U.S.A., 1994 . . 60 65
4553 $1.50 Ronaldo (Brazil), France, 1998 . . . . . . 60 65
MS4554 Two sheets, each 88 × 75 mm. (a) $6 Detail of Jules Rimet Trophy, Uruguay, 1930. (b) $6 Detail of World Cup Trophy, Japan–Korea, 2002 . . . . . 4·75 5·00

500 Arsenal Football Stadium, Highbury

2001. British Football Clubs (1st series). Multicoloured.
4555 $1.50 Type **500** 60 65
4556 $1.50 Players celebrating European Cup Winners' Cup success, 1994 . . . . 60 65
4557 $1.50 Players celebrating Premiership success, 1998 60 65
4558 $1.50 Entrance to Highbury 60 65
4559 $1.50 Dressing room 60 65
4560 $1.50 Arsenal defenders with trophies and shield, 1998 60 65
4561 $1.50 Aston Villa emblem at Villa Park 60 65
4562 $1.50 Villa Park stands at night 60 65
4563 $1.50 Stands and boxes . . 60 65
4564 $1.50 Trinity Road Stand, Villa Park 60 65
4565 $1.50 Holte End Stand, Villa Park 60 65
4566 $1.50 Aston Villa supporters 60 65
4567 $1.50 Reebok Stadium, Bolton (empty) 60 65
4568 $1.50 Players celebrating Division 1 play-off success, 2001 . . . . . . 60 65
4569 $1.50 Fan holding banner 60 65
4570 $1.50 Fans celebrating promotion 60 65
4571 $1.50 Team with Division 1 Cup, 2001 . . . . 60 65
4572 $1.50 Reebok Stadium during match 60 65
4573 $1.50 Everton squad, 2001–02 . . . . 60 65
4574 $1.50 Manager Duncan Ferguson, 2000 . . . . . 60 65
4575 $1.50 Statue of Dixie Dean (former player) 60 65
4576 $1.50 Everton supporters watching match 60 65
4577 $1.50 Goodison Park Stadium 60 65
4578 $1.50 Everton squad, League champions, 1969–70 . . . . 60 65
4579 $1.50 Ipswich Town players and Division 1 Cup, 2000 60 65
4580 $1.50 Ipswich Town squad, 2001–02 . . . . 60 65
4581 $1.50 Manager George Burley shaking hands with David Sheepshanks (chairman) 60 65
4582 $1.50 Pablo Counago running 60 65
4583 $1.50 Matt Holland (captain), 2001 . . . . . 60 65
4584 $1.50 George Burley with Manager of the Year Award, 2001 . . . . 60 65
4585 $1.50 Anfield Stadium, Liverpool 60 65
4586 $1.50 Players celebrating Worthington Cup victory, 2000–01 . . . . 60 65
4587 $1.50 Players celebrating F.A. Cup victory, 2000–01 60 65
4588 $1.50 Supporters watching match 60 65
4589 $1.50 Victorious U.E.F.A. Cup Team, 2000–01 . . . 60 65
4590 $1.50 Players, manager and fans, Treble victory parade, 2001 . . . . . . 60 65
4591 $1.50 Billy Meredith, Denis Law and Bobby Charlton (former players) 60 65
4592 $1.50 Treble Trophies, 1998–9 . . . . 60 65
4593 $1.50 Different views of Old Trafford before 1950s . . 60 65
4594 $1.50 Different views of Old Trafford since 1974 . . . 60 65
4595 $1.50 Players celebrating third successive Premiership title, 2000–01 60 65
4596 $1.50 George Best, Bryan Robson and David Beckham (players) 60 65
4597 $1.50 Exterior of Ibrox Stadium, Glasgow 60 65
4598 $1.50 Rangers' European Cup winning team, 1972 60 65
4599 $1.50 Scottish F.A. and Premier League trophies, 2000 . . . . 60 65
4600 $1.50 Ibrox Stadium from the air 60 65
4601 $1.50 Match in progress at Ibrox Stadium 60 65
4602 $1.50 Scottish flag and emblem celebrating ninth consecutive league victory, 1997 . . . . 60 65

501 Father Christmas and House

2001. Christmas. Father Christmas. Multicoloured.
4603 15c. Type **501** 10 10
4604 50c. Father Christmas with snowman and fir trees . . 20 25
4605 $1 Father Christmas ice-skating 40 45
4606 $4 Father Christmas with children . . . . 1·60 1·70
MS4607 107 × 76 mm. $6 Father Christmas eating mince pie . . 2·40 2·50

502 Princess Diana wearing Blue Dress and Tiara

2001. 40th Birth Anniv of Diana, Princess of Wales. Multicoloured.
4608 $1.50 Type **502** 60 65
4609 $1.50 Wearing white evening dress 60 65
4610 $1.50 In red dress and tiara 60 65
MS4611 80 × 102 mm. $6 Wearing pearl choker . . . . 2·40 2·50

503 John F. Kennedy

2001. Presidents John F. Kennedy and Ronald Reagan Commemoration. Multicoloured.
4612 $1.50 Type **503** 60 65
4613 $1.50 John Kennedy and Empire State Building . . 60 65

4614 $1.50 John Kennedy with aircraft 60 65
4615 $1.50 Ronald Reagan in *Hellcats of the Navy* (film) 60 65
4616 $1.50 Wearing dark suit and red tie 60 65
4617 $1.50 Ronald Reagan with American flag 60 65
MS4618 Two sheets. (a) 67 × 83 mm. $6 John F. Kennedy. (b) 78 × 105 mm. $6 Ronald Reagan on telephone 4·75 5·00

2001. Centenary of Nobel Prizes. Prize Winners of 1901 (Nos. 4619/22 and 4629/30) and 1921 (others). As T **595** of Ghana. Multicoloured.

4619 75c. Emil von Behring (Medicine) 30 35
4620 90c. Wilhelm Rontgen (Physics) 35 40
4621 $1 Jacobus van't Hoff (Chemistry) 40 45
4622 $1.50 Frederic Passy (Peace) 60 65
4623 $1.50 Albert Einstein as a young man (horiz) 60 65
4624 $1.50 Smoking a pipe (horiz) 60 65
4625 $1.50 Wearing grey (horiz) 60 65
4626 $1.50 In pink jumper (horiz) 60 65
4627 $1.50 Wearing black jacket (horiz) 60 65
4628 $1.50 In blue jumper (horiz) 60 65
4629 $2 Jean-Henri Dunant (Peace) 80 85
4630 $3 Rene Sully-Prudhomme (Literature) 1·20 1·30
MS4631 65 × 87 mm. $6 Albert Einstein wearing Panama hat 2·40 2·50

504 Brown Horse with Pale Mane

2001. Chinese New Year ("Year of the Horse"). Tang Dynasty Ceramic Horses. Multicoloured.

4632 $1.50 Type **504** 60 65
4633 $1.50 Purple dappled horse 60 65
4634 $1.50 Blue horse 60 65
4635 $1.50 Brown horse with short mane 60 65
MS4636 100 × 70 mm. $4 Brown horse with flowers on bridle 1·60 1·70

505 Ruby

506 U.S. Flag as Statue of Liberty with Grenada Flag

2001. Precious Stones and Minerals. Multicoloured.

4637 $1.50 Type **505** 60 65
4638 $1.50 Sardonyx 60 65
4639 $1.50 Sapphire 60 65
4640 $1.50 Opal 60 65
4641 $1.50 Topaz 60 65
4642 $1.50 Turquoise 60 65
4643 $1.50 Garnet 60 65
4644 $1.50 Amethyst 60 65
4645 $1.50 Aquamarine 60 65
4646 $1.50 Diamond 60 65
4647 $1.50 Emerald 60 65
4648 $1.50 Pearl 60 65
4649 $1.50 Ruby (horiz) 60 65
4650 $1.50 Diamond (horiz) 60 65
4651 $1.50 Sapphire (horiz) 60 65
4652 $1.50 Opal (horiz) 60 65
4653 $1.50 Turquoise (horiz) 60 65
4654 $1.50 Jade (horiz) 60 65
MS4655 Three sheets. (a) 82 × 76 mm. $6 Uraninite (horiz). (b) 92 × 56 mm. $6 Calcite (horiz). (c) $6 68 × 78 mm. $6 Quartz 7·25 7·50

Nos. 4637/42 (polished gem stones), 4643/8 (polished gem stones) and 4649/54 (raw stones).

2002. "United We Stand". Support for Victims of 11 September 2001 Terrorist Attacks.

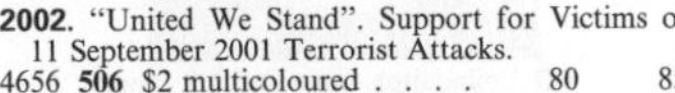

4656 **506** $2 multicoloured 80 85

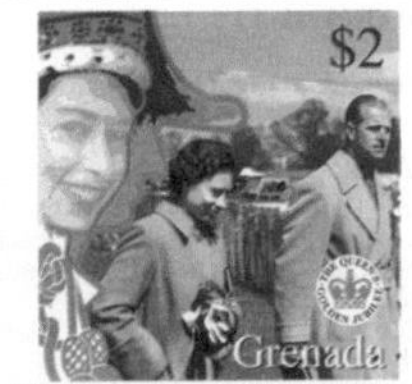

507 Queen Elizabeth with Prince Philip

2002. Golden Jubilee. Multicoloured.

4657 $2 Type **507** 80 85
4658 $2 Queen Elizabeth in open carriage 80 85
4659 $2 Queen Elizabeth in evening dress 80 85
4660 $2 Queen Elizabeth on bridge 80 85
MS4661 76 × 109 mm. $6 Queen Elizabeth in Grenadier uniform 2·40 2·50

508 Dale Earnhardt and Car, 1980, within "1"

2002. Dale Earnhardt (stock car driver) Commemoration. Designs each within figures commemorating his seven Winston Cup victories. Multicoloured.

4662 $2 Type **508** 80 85
4663 $2 With Winston Cup and car, 1986 80 85
4664 $2 With Winston Cup, 1987 80 85
4665 $2 With Winston Cup, 1990 80 85
4666 $2 With Winston Cup, 1991 80 85
4667 $2 With Winston Cup, 1993 80 85
4668 $2 With Winston Cup, 1994 80 85

509 Cannon on C.S.S. *Teaser* (gunboat)

2002. Naval Campaigns of the American Civil War.

4669 **509** $1 deep brown, brown and black 40 45
4670 – $1 deep brown, brown and black 40 45
4671 – $1 deep brown, brown and black 40 45
4672 – $1 deep brown, brown and black 40 45
4673 – $1 deep brown, brown and black 40 45
4674 – $1 deep brown, brown and black 40 45
4675 – $1.25 brown, ochre and black 50 55
4676 – $1.25 brown, ochre and black 50 55
4677 – $1.25 brown, ochre and black 50 55
4678 – $1.25 brown, ochre and black 50 55
4679 – $1.25 brown, ochre and black 50 55
4680 – $1.25 brown, ochre and black 50 55
4681 – $1.50 deep brown, brown and black 60 65
4682 – $1.50 deep brown, brown and black 60 65
4683 – $1.50 deep brown, brown and black 60 65
4684 – $1.50 deep brown, brown and black 60 65
4685 – $1.50 deep brown, brown and black 60 65
4686 – $1.50 deep brown, brown and black 60 65
4687 – $1.50 brown, yellow and black 60 65
4688 – $1.50 brown, yellow and black 60 65
4689 – $1.50 brown, yellow and black 60 65
4690 – $1.50 brown, yellow and black 60 65
4691 – $1.50 brown, yellow and black 60 65
4692 – $1.50 brown, yellow and black 60 65
MS4693 Four sheets, each 72 × 94 mm. (a) $6 blue, violet and black. (b) $6 violet, blue and black. (c) $6 deep blue, blue and black. (d) $6 deep blue, blue and black 9·75 10·00

DESIGNS: No. 4669, Type **509**; 4670, U.S. gunboats on James River, 1862; 4671, U.S.S. *Tyler* (river gunboat); 4672, U.S.S. *Maratanza* (steam gunboat); 4673, U.S.S. *Metacomet* (steam gunboat); 4674, U.S.S. *Rattler* (river gunboat); 4675, C.S.S. *Tennessee* (ironclad); 4676, U.S.S. *Hartford* (Federal flagship) engaging the *Tennessee*; 4677, U.S.S. *Chickasaw* (river monitor); 4678, U.S.S. *Ossipee* (steam sloop); 4679, Battle of Mobile Bay; 4680, U.S.S. *Chickasaw* in action at Mobile Bay; 4681, C.S.S. *Alabama* (commerce raider); 4682, U.S.S. *Kearsarge* engaging the *Alabama*; 4683, U.S.S. *Hatteras* (paddle gunboat); 4684, C.S.S. *Alabama* attacking merchant ships; 4685, C.S.S. *Sumte* (cruiser); 4686, U.S.S. *Kearsarge* (steam sloop); 4687, C.S.S. *H.L. Hunley* (submarine); 4688, U.S.S. *Cumberland* (frigate); 4689, C.S.S. *Old Dominion* (blockade runner); 4890, U.S.S. *Housatonic* (steam sloop); 4691, U.S.S. *Hartford*; 4692, U.S.S. *Essex* (river gunboat); **MS**4693a U.S.S. *Monitor* (monitor); **MS**4693b Captain Semmes of C.S.S. *Alabama*; **MS**4693c C.S.S. *Tennessee*; **MS**4693d C.S.S. *Florida* (steam corvette).

510 Mickey Mouse

2002. Birth Centenary (2001) of Walt Disney. Mickey Mouse. Multicoloured.

4694 $1 Type **510** 40 45
4695 $1 In "The Nifty Nineties", 1941 40 45
4696 $1 In "Magician Mickey", 1937 40 45
4697 $1 In "Steamboat Willie", 1928 40 45
4698 $1 In "Fantasia", 1940 40 45
4699 $1 In "Mickey Mouse Club", 1955 40 45
4700 $1 In "Cactus Kid", 1930 40 45
4701 $1 In "The Prince and the Pauper", 1990 40 45
4702 $1 In "Brave Little Tailor", 1938 40 45
4703 $1 In "Canine Caddy", 1941 40 45

511 Chiune Sugihara

2002. Chiune Sugihara (Japanese Consul-general in Lithuania who rescued Jews, 1939–40) Commemoration.

4704 **511** $2 multicoloured 80 85

512 Mawensi Peak, Kilimanjaro, Kenya

2002. International Year of Mountains. Multicoloured.

4705 $2 Type **512** 80 85
4706 $2 Mt. Stanley, Uganda 80 85
4707 $2 Mt. Taweche, Nepal 80 85
4708 $2 Mt. San Exupery, Argentina 80 85
MS4709 100 × 70 mm. $6 Mt. Aso, Japan 2·40 2·50

No. 4708 is inscribed "Exuprey" in error.

513 Church and Bunting

2002. Year of Eco Tourism. Multicoloured.

4710 $1 Type **513** 40 45
4711 $1 Little ringed plover 40 45
4712 $1 Relaxing on the patio 40 45
4713 $1 Scuba diver and grouper 40 45
4714 $1 Two red snappers 40 45
4715 $1 Four yachts 40 45
MS4716 75 × 75 mm. $6 Purple martin over Grenada 2·40 2·50

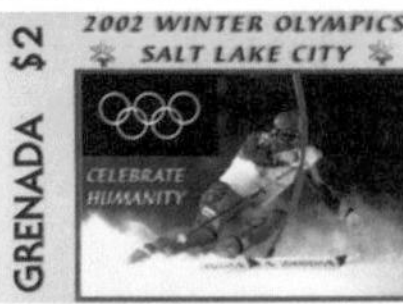

514 Downhill Skiing

2002. Winter Olympic Games, Salt Lake City. Multicoloured.

4717 $2 Type **514** 80 85
4718 $2 Slalom skiing 80 85
MS4719 82 × 102 mm. Nos. 4717/18 1·60 1·70

515 Scout in Canoe

2002. 20th World Scout Jamboree, Thailand. Multicoloured.

4720 $2 Type **515** 80 85
4721 $2 Paddling canoe 80 85
4722 $2 Scout blowing bugle 80 85
4723 $2 Scout saluting 80 85
MS4724 100 × 74 mm. $6 Thai scout saluting 2·40 2·50

Nos. 4720/3 were printed together, se-tenant, with the backgrounds forming a composite design.

516 Heidi Klum (model)

517 Army Bear

2002. APS Stampshow 2002, Atlantic City, U.S.A. Designs showing Heidi Klum. Multicoloured.

4725 $1.50 Type **516** 60 65
4726 $1.50 Wearing chain earrings 60 65
4727 $1.50 Close-up of face 60 65

2002. Centenary of the Teddy Bear (1st issue). Multicoloured.

4728 $2 Type **517** 80 85
4729 $2 Navy bear 80 85
4730 $2 Air Force bear 80 85
4731 $2 Marines bear 80 85
4732 $2 Basketball bear (38 × 50 mm) 80 85
4733 $2 Judo bear (38 × 50 mm) 80 85
4734 $2 Golf bear (38 × 50 mm) 80 85
4735 $2 Baseball bear (38 × 50 mm) 80 85
4736 $5 Bear with red hat and pink bow 2·00 2·10
4737 $5 Bear with clogs 2·00 2·10
4738 $5 Bear with black hat and scarf 2·00 2·10
4739 $5 Bear with cheeses 2·00 2·10

Nos. 4728/31 (armed forces bears), 4732/5 (sports bears) and 4736/9 (Dutch bears).

See also Nos. 4851/**MS**4852.

518 "Mareep No. 179"

2002. Pokémon (children's cartoon series). Multicoloured.

4740 $1.50 Type **518** 60 65
4741 $1.50 "Sunkern No. 191" 60 65
4742 $1.50 "Teddiursa No. 216" 60 65
4743 $1.50 "Swinub No. 220" 60 65
4744 $1.50 "Murkrow No. 198" 60 65
4745 $1.50 "Snubbull No. 209" 60 65
MS4746 66 × 91 mm. $6 "Togepi No. 175" 2·40 2·50

518a Elvis Presley wearing Stetson

2002. 25th Death Anniv of Elvis Presley.
4747 **518a** $1 multicoloured . . . 40 45

518b Axel, Zeeland

2002. "Amphilex '02" International Stamp Exhibition, Amsterdam (1st issue). Dutch Women's Traditional Costumes. Sheet, 120 × 140 mm, containing vert designs, each 37 × 51 mm. Multicoloured.
MS4748 $3 Type **518b**; $3 Eerde, Noord-Brabant; $3 Volendam, Noord-Holland . . . . 3·50 3·75

518c Jacobus van't Hoff (Chemistry, 1901)

2002. "Amphilex '02" International Stamp Exhibition, Amsterdam (2nd issue). (a) Dutch Nobel Prize Winners. Sheet 150 × 100 mm.
MS4749 $1.50 Type **518c** (black and green); $1.50 Peace Prize medal (black and blue); $1.50 Pieter Zeeman (Physics, 1902) (black and mauve); $1.50 Johannes van der Waals (Physics, 1910) (black and cinnamon); $1.50 Tobias Asser (Peace, 1911) (black and lilac); $1.50 Heike Kamerlingh Onnes (Physics, 1913) (black and green) 3·50 3·75

(b) Dutch Lighthouses. Sheet 128 × 148 mm. Multicoloured
MS4750 $1.50 Schiermonnikoog; $1.50 Texel; $1.50 Egmond; $1.50 Scheveningen; $1.50 Schouwen; $1.50 Hellevoetsluis . . . . . 3·50 3·75

519 Molly Middleton and Father

2002. Shirley Temple in *Our Little Girl*. Showing scenes from film. Multicoloured.

4751	$1.50 Type **519**	60	65
4752	$1.50 Family picnic	60	65
4753	$1.50 Molly with Sniff (dog), talking to park keeper	60	65
4754	$1.50 Molly with parents and another man	60	65
4755	$1.50 Molly and Sniff on see-saw	60	65
4756	$1.50 Molly with Sniff in pink bonnet	60	65
4757	$2 Molly with mother (vert)	80	85
4758	$2 Molly watching clown (vert)	80	85
4759	$2 Molly at prayer (vert) . .	80	85
4760	$2 Leaning on father's knee (vert)	80	85

MS4761 105 × 76 mm. $6 Molly wearing pink dress . . . . . . 2·40 2·50

520 World Trade Center

2002. 1st Anniv of 11 September 2001 Attacks. Sheet 140 × 98 mm.
MS4762 **520** $6 multicoloured . . 2·40 2·40

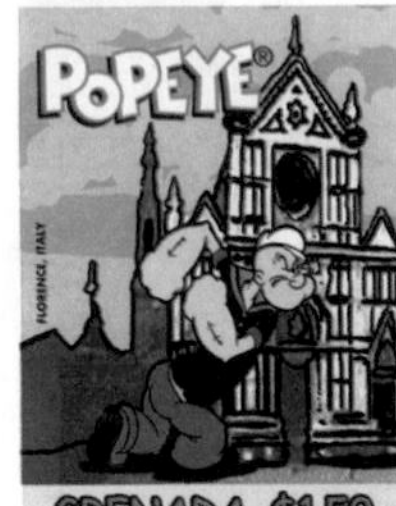
521 Popeye at Santa Croce Basilica, Florence

2002. "Popeye" (cartoon character). Multicoloured.

4763	$1.50 Type **521**	60	65
4764	$1.50 With Brutus at Eiffel Tower, Paris	60	65
4765	$1.50 On steps of Parthenon, Athens . . .	60	65
4766	$1.50 With Olive Oyl near Rialto Bridge, Venice . .	60	65
4767	$1.50 Near Big Ben, London	60	65
4768	$1.50 In front of traditional wooden building, Norway	65	65
4769	$2 Sweet Pea on footballer's back (29 × 44 mm) . . .	80	85
4770	$2 Jeep (dog) tugging footballer's shorts (29 × 44 mm)	80	85
4771	$2 Popeye in football kit (29 × 44 mm)	80	85
4772	$2 Brutus being kicked by Popeye (29 × 44 mm) . .	80	85

MS4773 Three sheets. (a) $6 Brutus heading ball (44 × 29 mm). (b) $6 Popeye celebrating with footballers (44 × 29 mm). (c) $6 Popeye and Leaning Tower of Pisa (50 × 78 mm) . . . . 7·25 7·50

Nos. 4769/72 were issued together, se-tenant, with the backgrounds forming a composite design.

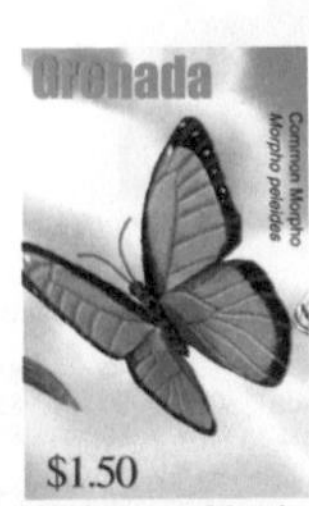
522 Common Morpho 523 Norman Wisdom

2002. Flora and Fauna. Multicoloured.

4774	$1.50 Type **522**	60	65
4775	$1.50 Blue night butterfly	60	65
4776	$1.50 Small flambeau . . .	60	65
4777	$1.50 Grecian shoemaker . .	60	65
4778	$1.50 Orange-barred sulphur	60	65
4779	$1.50 Cramer's mesene . . .	60	65
4780	$1.50 Honey bee	60	65
4781	$1.50 Dragonfly	60	65
4782	$1.50 Milkweed bug	60	65
4783	$1.50 Bumble bee	60	65
4784	$1.50 Migratory grasshopper	60	65
4785	$1.50 Monarch caterpillar	60	65
4786	$1.50 *Boletus crocipodius* . .	60	65
4787	$1.50 *Boletus edulis*	60	65
4788	$1.50 *Flammulina velutipes*	60	65
4789	$1.50 *Amanita phalloides* . .	60	65
4790	$1.50 *Tricholoma aurantium*	60	65
4791	$1.50 *Amanita muscaria* . .	60	65
4792	$1.50 Blue whale and calf	60	65
4793	$1.50 Pygmy sperm whale	60	65
4794	$1.50 Humpback whale . .	60	65
4795	$1.50 Killer whale	60	65
4796	$1.50 Bowhead whale . . .	60	65
4797	$1.50 Grey whale	60	65

MS4798 Four sheets, each 105 × 76 mm. (a) $6 Figure of eight butterfly. (b) $6 Hercules beetle. (c) $6 Sharp-scaled parasol (fungus). (d) $6 Blue whale . . 9·75 10·00

Nos. 4780/5 (butterflies), 4775/80 (insects), 4781/6 (fungi) and 4787/92 (whales) were each printed together, se-tenant, with the backgrounds forming composite designs.

Nos. 4792/7 and 4791 are inscribed "Flammula" or "Aminita", both in error.

2002. Sir Norman Wisdom (comedian and actor).
4799 **523** $1.50 multicoloured . . 60 65

523a Madonna and Child, Four Angels and St. Francis (Cimabue)

2002. Christmas. Religious Paintings. Multicoloured.

4800	15c. Type **523a**	10	10
4801	25c. "Madonna and Child and Two Angels" (Cimabue) (vert)	10	15
4802	50c. "Madonna Enthroned" (detail) (Cimabue) (vert)	20	25
4803	$1 "Madonna Enthroned" (Cimabue) (vert)	40	45
4804	$4 "Madonna and Child, Four Angels and St. Francis" (Cimabue) (vert)	1·60	1·75

MS4805 72 × 98 mm. $6 "Nativity" (Perugino) (vert) . . . . 2·40 2·50

524 Sextant

2002. 550th Birth Anniv of Amerigo Vespucci (explorer). Sheets containing T **524** and similar multicoloured designs.
MS4806 Two sheets. (a) 98 × 147 mm. $3 Type **524**; $3 Amerigo Vespucci; $3 Caravel (b) 138 × 90 mm. $3 Map of South America and caravel (horiz); $3 Compass and caravels (horiz); $3 Map of Africa and Europe (horiz) Set of 2 sheets . . . . 7·25 7·50
MS4807 Two sheets. (a) 78 × 85 mm. $6 Compass rose (28 × 42 mm). (b) 85 × 78 mm. $6 Globe and scroll (28 × 42 mm) Set of 2 sheets . . 4·75 5·00

525 Arsenal Stadium

2002. Arsenal Football Club -- FA Community Shield Winners. Sheet 125 × 125 mm containing T **525** and similar horiz designs. Multicoloured.
MS4808 $1.50 Type **525**; $1.50 Footballers celebrating after winning goal; $1.50 Winning team with FA Shield; $1.50 Arsenal 2002/3 squad with trophies; $1.50 Gilberto with FA Shield; $1.50 Arsenal FC, Stadium and new crest . . . . 3·50 3·75

2002. British Football Clubs. Eight sheets, each 125 × 125 mm, containing horiz designs as T **525**. Multicoloured.
MS4809 Arsenal 2001/2 $1.50 Team with FA Cup, Millennium Stadium, Cardiff; $1.50 Winning team with Championship banners; $1.50 Premiership Trophy winning team; $1.50 Winning team with Premiership trophy on rostrum; $1.50 Players celebrating FA Cup winning goal; $1.50 Arsene Wenger (Manager) and Tony Adams (captain) with trophies 4·00 4·25
MS4810 Celtic $1.50 Celtic Park Stadium; $1.50 Martin O'Neill with SPL Trophy; $1.50 Henrik Larsson; $1.50 Celtic squad of 2002/3; $1.50 Celtic scoring goal; $1.50 Celtic Park . . . . . . 4·00 4·25
MS4811 Chelsea $1.50 Crowd watching floodlit match; $1.50 Cup Winners' Cup winning team with trophy, 1988; $1.50 Chelsea supporters at match; $1.50 "The Shed End" at Stamford Bridge ground; $1.50 Stamford Bridge stadium; $1.50 Winning team with FA Cup, 2000 . . . . 4·00 4·25
MS4812 Liverpool $1.50 Anfield's Centenary stand seen from main stand; $1.50 First team squad, 2002/3; $1.50 Gerard Houllier and Phil Thompson; $1.50 Milan Baros; $1.50 Vladimir Smicer and Danny Murphy; $1.50 The Kop seen from Anfield Road end 4·00 4·25
MS4813 Manchester City $1.50 Maine Road stadium (from above); $1.50 Fans with Division One Champions flags; $1.50 Kevin Keegan (manager) with Division 1 trophy; $1.50 Winning Division 1 with trophy; $1.50 Winning team with medals; $1.50 Maine Road stadium (from stands) . . . . 4·00 4·25
MS4814 Manchester United $1.50 David Beckham; $1.50 First team squad, 2002/3; $1.50 Old Trafford stadium (aerial view); $1.50 Players after Ole Gunnar Solskjaer's 100th goal; $1.50 Manchester United fans; $1.50 North stand, Old Trafford . . 4·00 4·25
MS4815 Norwich City $1.50 Players at The Nest (NCFC ground 1908–35); $1.50 Norwich City players,1971/2; $1.50 With Milk Cup trophy, 1985; $1.50 Carrow Road stadium; $1.50 Winning UEFA Cup,1993; $1.50, Match of 1958/9 . . . . 4·00 4·25
MS4816 Tottenham Hotspur $1.50 Fans watching match; $1.50 Spurs v. Fulham match, 2001; $1.50 Spurs v. Liverpool match, 2002; $1.50 Winning UEFA Cup team, 1972; $1.50 Players celebrating win against Chelsea, 2002; $1.50 Club Shield and White Hart Lane stadium . . . . 4·00 4·25

526 Johan Mjallby (Sweden) 528 Princess Diana wearing Bow Tie

527 Foundation Logo and US Flag

2002. World Cup Football Championship, Japan and Korea. Miniature sheets containing T **526** and similar vert designs. Multicoloured.

MS4817	165 × 82 mm. $1.50 Type **526**; $1.50 Magnus Hedman (Sweden); $1.50 Fredrik Ljungberg (Sweden); $1.50 Khalilou Fadiga (Senegal); $1.50 El Hadji Diouf (Senegal); $1.50 Papa Bouba Diop (Senegal)	2·40	2·50
MS4818	165 × 82 mm. $1.50 Roberto Carlos (Brazil); $1.50 Juninho Paulista (Brazil); $1.50 Ronaldinho (Brazil); $1.50 Johan Walem (Belgium); $1.50 Marc Wilmots (Belgium); $1.50 Bart Goor (Belgium)	3·50	3·75
MS4819	Four sheets, each 82 × 82 mm. (a) $3 Henrik Larsson (Sweden); $3 Niclas Alexandersson (Sweden). (b) $3 Khalilou Fadiga (Senegal); $3 Bruno Metsou (coach, Senegal). (c) $3 Luiz Felipe Scolari (coach, Brazil); $3 Ronaldo (Brazil). (d) $3 Wesley Sonck (Belgium); $3 Robert Waseige (coach, Belgium) Set of 4 sheets	9·50	9·75

2002. National Law Enforcement and Firefighters Children's Foundation. Sheet 75 × 115 mm.

MS4820	**527** $6 multicoloured	2·40	2·50

2002. 5th Death Anniv of Diana, Princess of Wales. Two sheets containing T **528** and similar vert designs. Multicoloured.

MS4821	137 × 120 mm. $2 Type **528**; $2 Wearing blue dress; $2 Wearing red and white jacket and hat; $2 Wearing pink dress	2·40	2·50
MS4822	70 × 100 mm. $6 Wearing headset	2·40	2·50

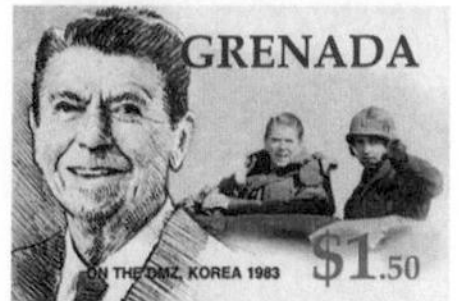

529 Pres Reagan on the DMZ in Korea, 1983

2002. Presidents Ronald Reagan and John F. Kennedy. Four sheets containing T **529** and similar multicoloured designs.

MS4823	175 × 117 mm. $1.50 Type **529**; $1.50 Pres Reagan with Prime Minister Margaret Thatcher; $1.50 Speaking at the Berlin Wall, 1987; $1.50 Signing INF Treaty with Soviet Secretary General Gorbachev; $1.50 With Egyptian President Sadat, 1981; $1.50 At home with horse Set of 4 sheets	4·25	4·50
MS4824	175 × 117 mm. $1.50 Pres Kennedy meeting with Cabinet; $1.50 Signing a bill into law; $1.50 Meeting Civil Rights leaders; $1.50 With astronaut John Glenn; $1.50 On the campaign trail; $1.50 With Jacqueline Kennedy arriving in Dallas, 1963	4·25	4·50
MS4825	Two sheets, each 82 × 115 mm. (a) $6 Pres. Reagan making speech. (b) Pres. Kennedy making speech (vert) Set of 2 sheets	4·75	5·00

530 Magnifying Glass and Globe

2002. 50th Anniv of International Federation of Stamp Dealers' Associations. P 14.

4826	**530** $2 multicoloured	80	85

531 Ram

2003. Chinese New Year ("Year of the Ram").

MS4827	130 × 123 mm. **531** $1.25 × 4, multicoloured	2·00	2·10

532 Toy Airplane

2003. Learning Resources (1st series). M Gears Childrens' Construction Sets. Sheet 222 × 152 mm containing T **532** and similar horiz designs showing toys. Multicoloured.

MS4828	$2 Type **532**; $2 Dune buggy; $2 Robot; $2 Racing car	3·25	3·50

See also **MS**4853.

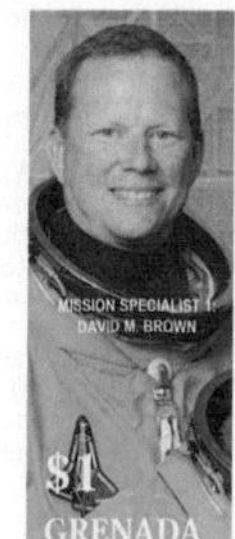

533 David Brown

2003. *Columbia* Space Shuttle Commemoration. Sheet 184 × 145 mm, containing T **533** and similar vert designs showing crew members. Multicoloured.

MS4829	$1 Type **533**; $1 Commander Rick Husband: $1 Laurel Clark; $1 Kalpana Chawla; $1 Payload Commander Michael Anderson; $1 Pilot William McCool; $1 Ilan Ramon	2·40	2·50

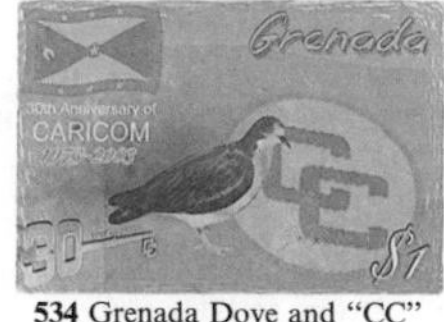

534 Grenada Dove and "CC" Emblem

2003. 30th Anniv of CARICOM.

4830	**534** $1 multicoloured	45	50

535 "A Harlot in Repose"

2003. Japanese Art. Paintings of Women by Taiso Yoshitoshi. Multicoloured.

4831	75c. Type **535**	30	35
4832	$1 "A 'Shakuni' or Geisha, who serves Wine or Sake"	45	50
4833	$1.25 "A 'Joro', or Low Ranking Prostitute, having a Snack"	50	55
4834	$3 "A Geisha known as a 'Geiko' or Entertainer relaxing"	1·20	1·40
MS4835	175 × 135 mm. $2 "Enjoying a Cool Evening Breeze in a Pleasure Boat"; $2 "A Fukagawa Waitress carrying a Wooden Table laden with Food"; $2 "A Spoiled Unmarried Woman pretending to be displeased with an Admirer"; $2 "A Coy Young Girl biting her Sleeve pretending to be Embarrassed"	3·25	3·50
MS4836	66 × 132 mm. $6 "A Geisha about to Board a Party-Boat" (detail)	2·40	2·50

536 "St. Catherine Altarpiece" (detail of St. Dorothy, St. Agnes and St. Cunigonde)

2003. 450th Death Anniv of Lucas Cranach the Elder (artist). Multicoloured.

4837	50c. Type **536**	20	25
4838	75c. "The St. Catherine Altarpiece" (detail of St. Margaret) (vert)	30	35
4839	$1.25 "The St. Catherine Altarpiece" (detail of St. Barbara) (vert)	50	55
4840	$3 "The St. Catherine Altarpiece" (detail of young girl) (vert)	1·20	1·40
MS4841	158 × 191 mm. $2 "Lot and his Daughters" (detail); $2 "David and Bathsheba" (detail); $2 "The Agony in the Garden" (detail); $2 "The Adoration of the Magi"	3·25	3·50
MS4842	120 × 100 mm. $6 "Samson and Delilah" (detail) (vert)	2·40	2·40

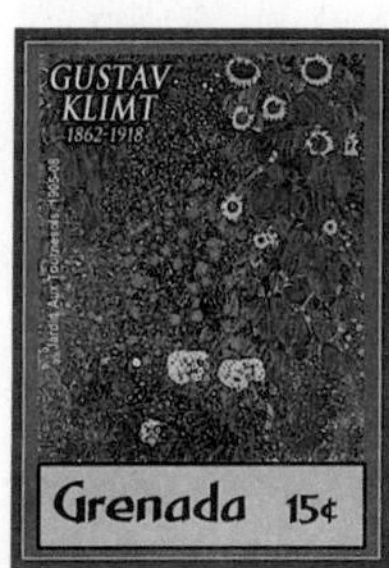

537 "Jardin Aux Tournesols"

2003. 85th Death Anniv of Gustav Klimt (artist). Multicoloured.

4843	15c. Type **537**	10	15
4844	25c. "L'allee Aux Poulets"	10	15
4845	75c. "Allee Dans Le Parc Du Schloss Kammer"	30	35
4846	$1 "Portrait de Johanna Staude"	40	45
4847	$1.25 "Portrait de Friederike Maria Beer"	50	55
4848	$3 "Portrait de Mada Primavesi"	1·20	1·40
MS4849	180 × 105 mm. $2 "La Jeune Fille"; $2 "Les Amies"; $2 "Le Berceau"; $2 "La Vie et la Mort"	3·25	3·50
MS4850	81 × 102 mm. $6 "Portrait de Margaret Stonborough-Wittgenstein". Imperf	2·40	2·50

538 Embroidery Teddy Bear

2003. Centenary of the Teddy Bear (2nd issue). Embroidered Fabric Teddy Bears. Self-adhesive. Imperf.

4851	**538** $15 ochre, silver and rose-red	6·00	6·00
MS4852	126 × 157 mm. No. 4850 × 4	25·00	24·00

539 Children reading Books

2003. Learning Resources (2nd series). Reading Rods. Sheet 222 × 156 mm containing T **539** and similar horiz designs. Multicoloured. .

MS4853	$2 Type **539**; $2 Girl playing with reading rods; $2 Children writing; $2 Teacher and children with book	3·25	3·50

540 Silvere Maes

2003. Centenary of Tour de France Cycle Race. Designs showing past winners. Multicoloured.

MS4854	160 × 100 mm. $2 Type **540**; $2 Jean Lazarides (1946); $2 Jean Robic (1947); $2 Gino Bartali (1948)	3·25	3·50
MS4855	160 × 100 mm. $2 Fausto Coppi (1949); $2 Ferdinand Kubler (1950); $2 Hugo Koblet (1951); $2 Fausto Coppi (1952)	3·25	3·50
MS4856	160 × 100 mm. $2 Roger Walkowiak (1956); $2 Jacques Anquetil (1957); $2 Charly Gaul (1958); $2 Federico Bahamontes (1959)	3·25	3·50
MS4857	Three sheets, each 100 × 70 mm. (a) $6 Fausto Coppi (1949). (b) $6 Ferdinand Kubler (1950). (c) $6 Jacques Anquetil (1964) Set of 3 sheets	7·25	7·50

541 Louis Bleriot and *Bleriot* XI (first powered flight across English Channel, 1909)

2003. Centenary of Powered Flight. Multicoloured.

MS4858	128 × 150 mm. $2 Type **541**; $2 Johnnie Johnson (World War II Ace pilot) and aircraft; $2 Wright Brothers and *Flyer I* (first powered flight, 1903); $2 Jacqueline Cochran and aircraft (first woman to break sound barrier)	3·25	3·50
MS4859	119 × 119 mm. $2 Alcock and Brown and Vickers FB-27 *Vimy* (first non-stop transatlantic flight, 1919); $2 Amelia Earhart and aircraft; $2 Chuck Yeager and Bell XS-1 rocket airplane (first manned supersonic flight, 1947); $2 Charles Lindbergh and Ryan NYP Special *Spirit of St. Louis* (first solo non-stop transatlantic flight, 1927)	3·25	3·50

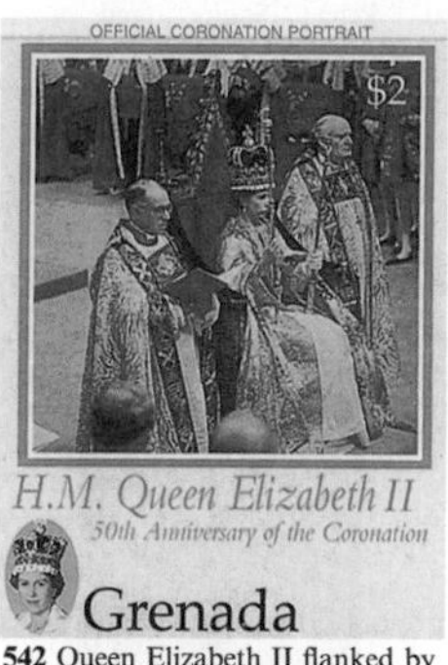

542 Queen Elizabeth II flanked by Bishops

2003. 50th Anniv of Coronation. Multicoloured.

4860	$2 Type **542**	80	85
4861	$2 Holy Communion	80	85
4863	$2 Enthronement of Queen	80	85
4864	$2 Queen and Duke of Edinburgh	80	85
4865	$2 Queen leaving Westminster Abbey in Coronation Coach	80	85
4866	$2 Queen and family on Palace balcony	80	85
4867	$2 Westminster Abbey	80	85
MS4868	106 × 76 mm. $6 Queen in Coronation Coach	2·40	2·50

No. 4867 is inscr "Floodlit Mall" in error.

543 Levera Pond **544** Clive Andrews

2003. International Year of Freshwater. Multicoloured.
MS4869 150 × 88 mm. $2 Type **543**; $2 Concord Falls; $2 Lake Antoine . . . . 2·40 2·50
MS4870 100 × 70 mm. $6 Lake Grand Etang . . . . 2·40 2·50

2003. Centenary of Circus Clowns. Multicoloured.
MS4871 119 × 194 mm. $2 Type **544**; $2 Bell Bozo; $2 Bumpsy; $2 Anne Fratellini . . . . 3·25 3·50
MS4872 146 × 218 mm. $2 Stag (acrobat); $2 Olga and Regina Kolpensky with white poodles; $2 Brad Byers; $2 Tiger . . . . . 3·25 3·50
No. **MS**4871 shows clowns and is cut in the shape of a clown. No. **MS**4872 shows other circus performers and is cut in the shape of a circus elephant.

545 Aerial View of Campus

2003. St. George's University School of Medicine. Multicoloured.
4873 75c. Type **545** 30 35
4874 $1 University buildings . . . 40 45

546 General Sir Mike Jackson and Tank

2003. Operation "Iraqi Freedom". Showing commanders of British armed forces in Iraq (**MS**4875) or British aircraft, tanks and ships (**MS**4876). Multicoloured.
MS4875 186 × 130 mm. $1 Type **546**; $1 Air Vice-Marshal Glenn Torpy and RAF Jaguar fighter; $1 Air Marshal Brian Burridge and RAF Harrier GR7 fighter; $1 Major General Tony Milton and warship; $1 Major General Peter Wall and soldiers; $1 Major General Barney White-Spunner ; $1 Admiral Sir Alan West and aircraft carrier; $1 Air Chief Marshal Peter Squire and surveillance aircraft . . . . . 3·25 3·50
MS4876 186 × 130 mm. $1 Royal Marine Gazelle helicopter; $1 Royal Marine hovercraft; $1 RAF Jaguar fighter; $1 HMS *Liverpool*; $1 RAF Harrier GR7; $1 Challenger 2 tank; $1 RAF Chinook helicopter; $1 RAF Tornado F3 . . . . 3·25 3·50

547 Prince William with Bouquet

2003. 21st Birthday of Prince William of Wales. Multicoloured.
MS4877 79 × 145 mm. $3 Type **547**; $3 Wearing blue T-shirt; $3 In close-up, looking down . . . . 4·25 4·50
MS4878 105 × 76 mm. $6 Prince William (horiz) . . . . 2·40 2·40

548 Yellow Allamanda

2003. Birds, Fish and Flowers of the Caribbean. Multicoloured.
4879 25c. Type **548** 10 15
4880 50c. Queen of the Night (flower) 20 15
4881 75c. Anthurium 30 35
4882 $1 Smallmouthed grunt (fish) 40 45
4883 $1 Spotfinned butterflyfish 40 45
4884 $1 Gold coney (fish) 40 45
4885 $1.25 Osprey 50 55
4886 $1.25 Red-eyed vireo (bird) 50 55
4887 $1.25 Northern oriole . . . 50 55
4888 $3 Oleander . . . . 1·20 1·40
4889 $3 Night sergeant (fish) . . 1·20 1·40
4890 $3 Bahama pintail (duck) 1·20 1·40
MS4891 105 × 85 mm. $2 Blue passion flower; $2 Chinese hibiscus; $2 Poinsettia; $2 Bird of Paradise (flower) . . . . . .
MS4892 105 × 85 mm. $2 Spot-finned hogfish ("Cuban Hogfish"); $2 Blueheaded wrasse; $2 Black-capped basslet ("Black Cap Gramma"); $2 Cherub angelfish ("Cherubfish") . . . . . .
MS4893 105 × 85 mm. $2 Slaty-capped shrike vireo; $2 Common flicker ("Northern Flicker"); $2 Blackburnian warbler; $2 Common tody flycatcher . . . 3·25 3·50
MS4894 Three sheets, each 96 × 66 mm. (a) $6 Shrimp plant. (b) $6 Banded butterflyfish. (c) $6 Blue grosbeak (vert) Set of 3 sheets 7·25 7·50

549 Spinosaurus

2003. Prehistoric Animals. Multicoloured.
MS4895 178 × 117 mm. $2 Type **549**; $2 Herrerasaurus; $2 Protarchaeopteryx; $2 Sinosauropteryx . . . . 3·25 3·50
MS4896 178 × 117 mm. $2 Allosaurus; $2 Crylophosaurus; $2 Eoraptor; $2 Caudipteryx . . . 3·25 3·50
MS4897 Two sheets, each 98 × 68 mm. (a) $6 Triceratops (vert). (b) $6 Archaeopteryx (vert) Set of 2 sheets . . . . 4·75 5·00

550 "Madonna and Child" (detail) (Giotto) from Church of Ognissanti

2003. Christmas. Multicoloured.
4898 35c. Type **550** 15 20
4899 75c. "The Ognissanti Madonna" (detail) (Giotto) 30 35
4900 $1 "Madonna of the Angels" (detail) (Giotto) 40 45
4901 $4 "Madonna and Child" (Giotto) from Florentine Church of San Giorgio alla Costa . . . . 1·60 1·75
MS4902 74 × 95 mm. $6 "Holy Family with John the Baptist and St. Elizabeth" (Nicolas Poussin) (horiz) . . . . 2·40 2·50

551 "At the Palmist's" (Jean-Baptiste Le Prince)

2003. 300th Anniv of St. Petersburg. "Treasures of the Hermitage". Multicoloured.
4903 45c. Type **551** 20 25
4904 $1 "A Visit to Grandmother" (Louis Le Nain) (horiz) 40 45
4905 $1.50 "Musicale" (Dirck Hals) (horiz) 60 65
4906 $3 "A Young Woman in the Morning" (Frans van Mieris the Elder) . . . . 1·20 1·40
MS4907 118 × 181 mm. $2 "Louis, Grand Dauphin de France" (Louis Tocqué); $2 "Count P. A. Stroganov as a Child" (Jean-Baptiste Greuze); $2 "A Boy with a Book" (Jean- Baptiste Perroneau); $2 "A Girl with a Doll" (Jean-Baptiste Greuze) 3·25 3·50
MS4908 (a) 78 × 65 mm. $6 "The Lute Player" (Caravaggio). Imperf. (b) 67 × 77 mm. $6 "The Spoiled Child" (Jean-Baptiste Greuze). Imperf . . . . 4·75 5·00

552 "The Spring Tonic"

2003. 25th Death Anniv of Norman Rockwell. Multicoloured.
MS4909 149 × 179 mm. $2 Type **552**; $2 "The Facts of Life"; $2 "The Proper Gratuity"; $2 "The Runaway" . . . . 3·25 3·50
MS4910 91 × 99 mm. $6 "Boy with Carriage" (detail) (horiz) . . . 2·40 2·50

553 "Claude Drawing"

2003. 30th Death Anniv of Pablo Picasso (artist). Multicoloured.
MS4911 132 × 168 mm. $2 Type **553**; $2 "Claude and Paloma at Play" (detail); $2 "Paloma at Three Years Old"; $2 "Paloma with an Orange" . . . . 3·25 3·50
MS4912 72 × 99 mm. $6 "Paloma in Blue". Imperf . . . . 2·40 2·50

554 Brown and White Monkey **556** Chinese Lady

555 *Lissy* (sail training ship) on River Weser

2004. Chinese New Year ("Year of the Monkey"). Multicoloured.
MS4913 116 × 141 mm. $1.50 Type **554**; $1.50 Proboscis monkey; $1.50 Light brown monkey; $1.50 Grey monkey 2·40 2·50

2004. Opening of Weser Tunnel, Germany. Sheet 113 × 82 mm.
MS4914 **555** $6 multicoloured . . 2·40 2·50

2004. Hong Kong 2004 International Stamp Exhibition. Paintings by Pu Hsin-yu. Multicoloured.
MS4915 156 × 112 mm. $1.50 Type **556**; $1.50 Two monkeys in tree; $1.50 Mountain landscape with temple and waterfall; $1.50 Bird in tree with red flower; $1.50 Man sat by gnarled tree; $1.50 Man in red . . . . 4·25 4·50
MS4916 107 × 105 mm. $3 Branch; $3 Bearded man . . . . 2·40 2·50

557 Muffy

2004. Arthur the Aardvark and Friends. Multicoloured.
MS4917 165 × 134 mm. $1.50 Type **557**; $1.50 Francine; $1.50 Brain with potted plants; $1.50 D.W. as astronaut in space; $1.50 Sue Ellen with insects in jam jars; $1.50 Arthur with model of solar system . . . . 2·40 2·50
MS4918 150 × 184 mm. $2 Arthur as Robin Hood; $2 Arthur as Rumpelstiltskin; $2 Arthur with sword; $2 Arthur as King Arthur 3·25 3·50
MS4919 150 × 184 mm. $1.50 Arthur holding bunch of flowers; $1.50 D.W. holding valentines card; $1.50 Binky holding box of chocolates; $1.50 Muffy holding out box of chocolates; $1.50 D.W. as Cupid; $1.50 Francine and hearts . . . . 3·00 3·00
MS4920 150 × 183 mm. $2 Arthur as Robinson Crusoe; $2 Arthur and map of Treasure Island; $2 Arthur as Tom Sawyer; $2 Arthur swinging on rope . . . . . . 3·25 3·25

558 Concorde, French Flag and Concorde at Take-off

2004. Last Flight of Concorde (2003). Multicoloured.
MS4921 88 × 129 mm. $3 Type **558**; $3 Concorde, French flag and spectators at perimeter fence; $3 Concorde, French flag and control panel (first flight, Toulouse, Fran, 1969) . . . . 4·25 4·00
MS4922 88 × 129 mm. $3 Concorde, Union Jack, Singapore flag and roof of building; $3 Concorde, Union Jack, Singapore flag and skyscraper; $3 Concorde, Union Jack, Singapore flag and street (London to Singapore flights, 1977) . . . . 4·25 4·00
MS4923 88 × 129 mm. $3 Concorde and dome of US Capitol; $3 Concorde, Capitol building and top of statue; $3 Concorde, Capitol and plinth of statue (last flight, Paris to Washington, 2003) 4·25 4·50

559 Lord Killanin (President of Olympic Committee, 1972—80)

2004. Olympic Games, Athens, Greece. Multicoloured.

4924	75c. Type **559**	30	35
4925	$1 Athletes running 10,000 metre race (horiz)	40	45
4926	$1.25 Commemorative plaque (detail)	50	55
4927	$3 "The Wreath of Olive" (Greek art)	1·20	1·30

560 Marilyn Monroe

561 Deng Xiaoping

2004. Marilyn Monroe Commemoration. Multicoloured.

4928	50c. Type **560**	20	25
MS4929	127 × 116 mm. $2 Wearing one-shoulder red top; $2 Wearing strapless orange top; $2 Wearing white top; $2 Wearing off-shoulder pink top	3·25	3·25

2004. Deng Xiaoping (Chinese politician) Commemoration. Sheet 99 × 68 mm.

MS4930	561 $6 multicoloured	2·40	2·40

562 Pres. George W. Bush

2004. Military Operations in Iraq. Sheet 127 × 118 mm containing T **562** and similar horiz designs. Multicoloured.

MS4931	$2 Type **562**; $2 Paul Bremer; $2 Col. James Hickey; $2 Soldier and Iraqi civilians	3·25	3·25

563 Jan Svehlik (Czech Republic footballer)

2004. European Football Championships 2004, Portugal. T **563** and similar multicoloured designs.

MS4932	147 × 84 mm. $2 Type **563**; $2 Franz Beckenbauer (German footballer); $2 Karol Dobias (Czech Republic footballer); $2 Crvena Zvezda football ground	3·25	3·25
MS4933	98 × 84 mm. $6 Czech Republic football team, 1976 (50 × 37 mm)	2·40	2·40

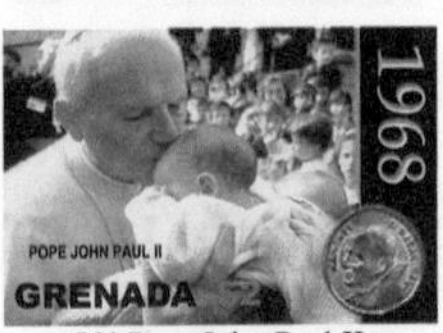

564 Pope John Paul II

2004. 25th Anniv of the Pontificate of Pope John Paul II. Sheet 163 × 154 mm containing T **564** and similar horiz designs. Multicoloured.

MS4934	$2 Type **564**; $2 With Mikhail Gorbachev; $2 With arms stretched overhead; $2 Meeting with Polish deportees; $2 With Patriarchate of the Russian Orthodox Church	4·00	4·00

OFFICIAL STAMPS

1982. Optd **P.R.G.** (a) Nos. 1085/97 and 1099.

O 1	5c. West Indiaman barque, c. 1840	30	40
O 2	6c. R.M.S.P. "Orinoco", c. 1851	30	40
O 3	10c. Working schooner	30	30
O 4	12c. Trimaran at Grand Anse anchorage	30	30
O 5	15c. Spice Island cruising yacht "Petite Amie"	30	30
O 6	20c. Fishing pirogue	35	30
O 7	25c. Harbour police launch	40	30
O 8	30c. Grand Anse speedboat	40	30
O 9	40c. M.V. "Seimstrand"	50	30
O10	50c. Three-masted schooner "Ariadne"	60	40
O11	90c. M.V. "Geestide"	90	1·00
O12	$1 M.V "Cunard Countess"	90	1·00
O13	$3 Rum-runner	2·25	4·25
O14	$10 Coast-guard patrol boat	6·00	12·00

(b) Nos. 1130/2 and 1134/5.

O15	30c. Prince Charles and Lady Diana Spencer	1·50	2·25
O16	40c. Holyrood House	2·25	2·75
O17	50c. Prince Charles and Lady Diana Spencer	1·25	2·00
O18	$2 Holyrood House	2·25	3·50
O19	$4 Type **268**	5·00	8·00

POSTAGE DUE STAMPS

D 1

1892.

D 8	D 1	1d. black	3·50	7·50
D 9		2d. black	11·00	1·75
D10		3d. black	13·00	6·00

1892. Surch **SURCHARGE POSTAGE** and value.

D4	13	1d. on 6d. mauve	85·00	1·25
D5		1d. on 8d. brown	£800	3·25
D6		2d. on 6d. mauve	£160	2·50
D7		2d. on 8d. brown	£1500	10·00

1921. As Type D **1** but inscr "POSTAGE DUE" instead of "SURCHARGE POSTAGE".

D11	D 1	1d. black	1·25	1·00
D12		1½d. black	8·50	21·00
D13		2d. black	2·00	1·75
D14		3d. black	2·00	4·50

1952. As last, but currency changed.

D15	D 1	3c. black	30	7·00
D16		4c. black	30	13·00
D17		6c. black	45	12·00
D18		8c. black	75	12·00

GRENADINES OF GRENADA (CARRIACOU AND PETITE MARTINIQUE) Pt. 1

The southern part of the group, attached to Grenada. Main islands Petit Martinique and Carriacou. From 1999 stamps were inscribed "Grenada Carriacou and Petite Martinique".

100 cents = 1 dollar.

1973. Royal Wedding. Nos. 582/3 of Grenada optd **GRENADINES**.
1 **196** 25c. multicoloured 15 10
2 $2 multicoloured 45 50

1974. Stamps of Grenada optd **GRENADINES**.
4 1c. multicoloured (No. 306) . . 10 10
5 2c. multicoloured (No. 307) . . 10 10
6 3c. multicoloured (No. 308) . . 10 10
7 5c. multicoloured (No. 309) . . 15 10
8 8c. multicoloured (No. 311) . . 15 10
9 10c. multicoloured (No. 312) 15 10
10 12c. multicoloured (No. 313) 20 10
11 25c. multicoloured (No. 315) 45 10
12 $1 multicoloured (No. 318) . . 2·50 60
13 $2 multicoloured (No. 319) . . 3·00 1·50
14 $3 multicoloured (No. 320) . . 3·00 1·75
15 $5 multicoloured (No. 321) . . 3·75 2·25

1974. World Cup Football Championship. As Nos. 619/27 of Grenada, but inscr "GRENADA GRENADINES".
16 ½c. multicoloured 10 10
17 1c. multicoloured 10 10
18 2c. multicoloured 10 10
19 10c. multicoloured 20 10
20 25c. multicoloured 25 10
21 50c. multicoloured 30 15
22 75c. multicoloured 30 20
23 $1 multicoloured 35 25
MS24 114 × 76 mm. $2 multicoloured 75 80

1974. Cent of U.P.U. As Nos. 628 etc of Grenada, but inscr "GRENADA GRENADINES".
25 8c. multicoloured 10 10
26 25c. multicoloured 15 10
27 35c. multicoloured 15 10
28 $1 multicoloured 70 40
MS29 172 × 109 mm. $1 as 15c. and $2 as $1 . . . . 1·00 1·00

1974. Birth Cent of Sir Winston Churchill. As Nos. 637/9 of Grenada, but inscr "GRENADA GRENADINES".
30 35c. multicoloured 15 10
31 $2 multicoloured 40 45
MS32 129 × 96 mm. 75c. as 35c. and $1 as $2 . . . . 35 80

1974. Christmas. As Nos. 640/8 of Grenada, but inscr "GRENADA GRENADINES" and background colours changed.
33 **204** ½c. multicoloured 10 10
34 – 1c. multicoloured 10 10
35 – 2c. multicoloured 10 10
36 – 3c. multicoloured 10 10
37 – 10c. multicoloured 10 10
38 – 25c. multicoloured 10 10
39 – 50c. multicoloured 15 15
40 – $1 multicoloured 30 25
MS41 117 × 96 mm. $2 as 1c. . . 45 60

1975. Big Game Fishing. As Nos. 669 etc of Grenada, but inscr "GRENADA GRENADINES" and background colours changed.
42 ½c. multicoloured 10 10
43 1c. multicoloured 10 10
44 2c. multicoloured 10 10
45 10c. multicoloured 15 10
46 25c. multicoloured 20 10
47 50c. multicoloured 20 15
48 70c. multicoloured 25 20
49 $1 multicoloured 35 35
MS50 107 × 80 mm. $2 multicoloured 60 90

1975. Flowers. As Nos. 678 etc of Grenada, but inscr "GRENADINES".
51 ½c. multicoloured 10 10
52 1c. multicoloured 10 10
53 2c. multicoloured 10 10
54 3c. multicoloured 10 10
55 10c. multicoloured 10 10
56 25c. multicoloured 10 10
57 50c. multicoloured 20 15
58 $1 multicoloured 30 20
MS59 102 × 82 mm. $2 multicoloured 60 70

CANCELLED REMAINDERS*. Some of the following issues have been remaindered, cancelled-to-order, at a fraction of their face value. For all practical purposes these are indistinguishable from genuine postally used copies. Our used quotations, which are indicated by an asterisk, are the same for cancelled-to-order or postally used copies.

3 "Christ Crowned with Thorns" (Titian)
4 "Dawn" (detail from Medici Tomb)

1975. Easter. Paintings showing Crucifixion and Deposition by artists listed. Multicoloured.
60 ½c. Type **3** 10 10*
61 1c. Giotto 10 10*
62 2c. Tintoretto 10 10*
63 3c. Cranach 10 10*
64 35c. Caravaggio 15 10*
65 75c. Tiepolo 20 10*
66 $2 Velasquez 40 15*
MS67 105 × 90 mm. $1 Titian . . 60 30

1975. 500th Anniv of Michelangelo. Multicoloured.
68 ½c. Type **4** 10 10*
69 1c. "Delphic Sibyl" 10 10*
70 2c. "Giuliano de Medici" . . . 10 10*
71 40c. "The Creation" (detail) 15 10*
72 50c. "Lorenzo de Medici" . . 15 10*
73 75c. "Persian Sibyl" 20 10*
74 $2 "Head of Christ" 30 15*
MS75 118 × 96 mm. $1 "The Prophet Jeremiah" 75 50

1975. Butterflies. As T **213** of Grenada, but inscr "GRENADINES". Multicoloured.
76 ½c. "Morpho peleides" 10 10*
77 1c. "Danaus eresimus" ("Danaus gilippus") 10 10*
78 2c. "Dismorphia amphione" 10 10*
79 35c. "Hamadryas feronia" . . 35 10*
80 45c. "Philaethria dido" . . . 45 10*
81 75c. "Phoebis argante" 70 15*
82 $2 "Prepona laertes" . . . . 1·40 30*
MS83 104 × 77 mm. $1 "Siproeta stelenes" . . . . 3·00 3·25

5 Progress "Standard" Badge

1975. 14th World Scout Jamboree, Norway. Multicoloured.
84 ½c. Type **5** 10 10*
85 1c. Boatman's badge 10 10*
86 2c. Coxswain's badge 10 10*
87 35c. Interpreter's badge . . . 15 10*
88 45c. Ambulance badge 20 10*
89 75c. Chief Scout's award . . . 25 10*
90 $2 Queen's Scout award . . . 35 15*
MS91 106 × 80 mm. $1 Venture award 55 30*

6 The Surrender of Lord Cornwallis

1975. Bicentenary of American Revolution (1976) (1st issue). Multicoloured.
92 ½c. Type **6** 10 10*
93 1c. Minute-men 10 10*
94 2c. Paul Revere's ride 10 10*
95 3c. Battle of Bunker Hill . . . 10 10*
96 5c. Fifer and drummers . . . 10 10*
97 45c. Backwoodsman 15 10*
98 75c. Boston Tea Party . . . 20 10*
99 $2 Naval engagement 45 10*
100 $2 George Washington . . . 45 35
101 $2 White House and flags . . 45 35
MS102 Two sheets 113 × 128 mm containing No. 100, and 128 × 113 mm containing No. 101. Imperf . . . . 1·10 1·40
Nos. 100/1 are larger, 35 × 60 mm.
See also Nos. 176/**MS**183

7 Fencing

1975. Pan-American Games, Mexico City. Multicoloured.
103 ½c. Type **7** 10 10*
104 1c. Hurdling 10 10*
105 2c. Pole-vaulting 10 10*
106 35c. Weightlifting 15 10*
107 45c. Throwing the javelin . . 15 10*
108 75c. Throwing the discus . . 15 10*
109 $2 Diving 35 15*
MS110 78 × 104 mm. $1 Sprinter 40 20*

1975. Nos. 649/68 of Grenada additionally inscr "GRENADINES".
111 ½c. Yachts, Point Saline . . . 10 30
112 1c. Yacht Club race, St. George's 10 15
113 2c. Carenage taxi 10 15
114 3c. Large working boats . . 10 15
115 5c. Deep-water dock, St. George's 10 15
116 6c. Cocoa beans in drying trays 10 15
117 8c. Nutmegs 10 15
118 10c. Rum distillery, River Antoine Estate, c. 1785 . . 10 15
119 12c. Cocoa tree 10 15
120 15c. Fishermen at Fontenoy 10 15
121 20c. Parliament Building . . 10 60
122 25c. Fort George cannons . . 10 15
123 35c. Pearls Airport 75 15
124 50c. General Post Office . . . 20 90
125 75c. Carib's Leap, Sauteurs Bay 40 60
126 $1 Carenage, St. George's . . 60 85
127 $2 St. George's Harbour by night . . . . 90 2·00
128 $3 Grand Anse beach . . . . 1·10 2·50
129 $5 Canoe Bay and Black Bay 1·25 5·00
130 $10 Sugar-loaf Island . . . . 2·25 5·50

8 Virgin and Child" (Durer)

1975. Christmas. "Virgin and Child" paintings by Artists named.
131 ½c. Type **8** 10 10*
132 1c. Durer 10 10*
133 2c. Correggio 10 10*
134 40c. Botticelli 15 10*
135 50c. Niccolo da Cremona . . 15 10*
136 75c. Correggio 15 10*
137 $2 Correggio 30 15*
MS138 114 × 120 mm. $1 Bellini 60 50*

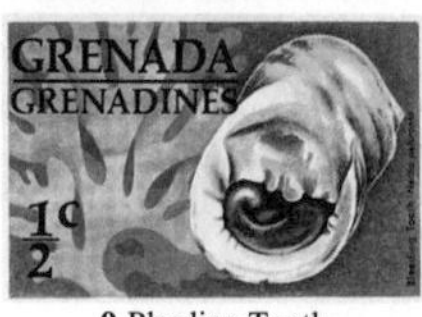
9 Bleeding Tooth

1976. Shells. Multicoloured.
139 ½c. Type **9** 10 10*
140 1c. Toothed donax 10 10*
141 2c. Hawk-wing conch 10 10*
142 3c. Atlantic distorsio 10 10*
143 25c. Scotch bonnet 40 10*
144 50c. King helmet 50 10*
145 75c. Queen or pink conch . . 75 15*
MS146 79 × 105 mm. $2 Atlantic trumpet triton . . . . 1·00 70*

10 Cocoa Thrush

1976. Flora and Fauna. Multicoloured.
147 ½c. "Lignum vitae" 10 10*
148 1c. Type **10** 10 10*
149 2c. "Eurypelma sp." (spider) 10 10*
150 35c. Lesser Antillean Tanager ("Hooded Tanager") . . . 1·25 10*
151 50c. "Nyctaginaceae" . . . . 1·00 15*
152 75c. Grenada dove . . . . . 2·50 25*
153 $1 Marine toad . . . . . . 2·50 25*
MS154 108 × 84 mm. $2 Blue-hooded euphonia . . . . . . 4·00 1·00*

11 Hooked Sailfish

1976. Tourism. Multicoloured.
155 ½c. Type **11** 10 10*
156 1c. Careened schooner, Carriacou 10 10*
157 2c. Carriacou Annual Regatta 10 10*
158 18c. Boat building on Carriacou 20 10*
159 22c. Workboat race, Carriacou Regatta 20 10*
160 75c. Cruising off Petit Martinique 30 20*
161 $1 Water skiing 40 20*
MS162 105 × 87 mm. $2 Yacht racing at Carriacou 70 75*

12 Making a Camp Fire

1976. 50th Anniv of Girl Guides in Grenada. Multicoloured.
163 ½c. Type **12** 10 10*
164 1c. First aid 10 10*
165 2c. Nature study 10 10*
166 50c. Cookery 50 15*
167 $1 Sketching 75 25*
MS168 85 × 110 mm. $2 Guide playing guitar . . . . 1·00 75*

13 "Christ Mocked" (Bosch)

1976. Easter. Multicoloured.
169 ½c. Type **13** 10 10*
170 1c. "Christ Crucified" (Antonello da Messina) . . 10 10*
171 2c. "Adoration of the Trinity" (Durer) 10 10*
172 3c. "Lamentation of Christ" (Durer) 10 10*
173 35c. "The Entombment" (Van der Weyden) 15 10*
174 $3 "The Entombment" (Raphael) 60 30*
MS175 57 × 72 mm. $2 "Blood of the Redeemer" (G. Bellini) 65 70*

14 "South Carolina" (frigate)

1976. Bicentenary of American Revolution (2nd issue). Multicoloured.
176 ½c. Type **14** 10 10*
177 1c. "Lee" (schooner) 10 10*
178 2c. H.M.S. "Roebuck" (frigate) 10 10*
179 35c. "Andrew Doria" (brig) 40 10*
180 50c. "Providence" (sloop) . . 50 15*
181 $1 "Alfred" (frigate) 75 20*
182 $2 "Confederacy" (frigate) . . 1·25 30*
MS183 72 × 85 mm. $3 "Revenge" (cutter) . . . . 1·00 1·00*

15 Piper Apache

1976. Aircraft. Multicoloured.
184 ½c. Type **15** 10 10*
185 1c. Beech 50 Twin Bonanza 10 10*
186 2c. De Havilland Twin Otter 10 10*
187 40c. Britten Norman Islander 30 10*
188 50c. De Havilland Heron 2 40 10*
189 $2 Hawker Siddeley H.S.748 1·25 25*
MS190 71 × 85 mm. $3 B.A.C. One-Eleven 500 . . . . 1·00 1·00*

16 Cycling

1976. Olympic Games, Montreal. Multicoloured.
191 ½c. Type **16** 10 10*
192 1c. Pommel horse 10 10*
193 2c. Hurdling 10 10*
194 35c. Shot putting 10 10*
195 45c. Diving 15 10*
196 75c. Sprinting 15 10*
197 $2 Rowing 35 25*
MS198 101 × 76 mm. $3 Sailing 80 75*

17 "Virgin and Child" (Cima)

1976. Christmas. Multicoloured.
199 ½c. Type **17** 10 10*
200 1c. "The Nativity" (Romanino) 10 10*
201 2c. "The Nativity" (Romanino) (different) 10 10*
202 35c. "Adoration of the Kings" (Bruegel) 15 10*
203 50c. "Madonna and Child" (Girolamo) 20 10*
204 75c. "Adoration of the Magi" (Giorgione) (horiz) 20 15*
205 $2 "Adoration of the Kings" (School of Fra Angelico) (horiz) 40 25*
MS206 120 × 100 mm. $3 "The Holy Family" (Garofalo) 60 2·25

18 Alexander Graham Bell and First Telephone

1977. Centenary of First Telephone Transmission. Designs showing Alexander Graham Bell and telephone. Multicoloured.
207 ½c. Type **18** 10 10*
208 1c. 1895 telephone 10 10*
209 2c. 1900 telephone 10 10*
210 35c. 1915 telephone 15 10*
211 75c. 1920 telephone 20 10*
212 $1 1929 telephone 25 15*
213 $2 1963 telephone 35 25*
MS214 107 × 78 mm. $3 Telephone, 1976 1·10 75*

19 Coronation Coach

1977. Silver Jubilee. Multicoloured. (a) Perf.
215 35c. Type **19** 10 10*
216 $2 Queen entering Abbey 20 10*
217 $4 Queen crowned 35 25*
MS218 100 × 70 mm. $5 The Mall on Coronation Night 60 1·25

(b) Imperf × roul. Self-adhesive.
219 35c. Royal visit 15 20
220 50c. Crown of St. Edward 30 80
221 $2 The Queen and Prince Charles 50 1·60
222 $5 Royal Standard 60 1·75
Nos. 219/22 come from booklets.

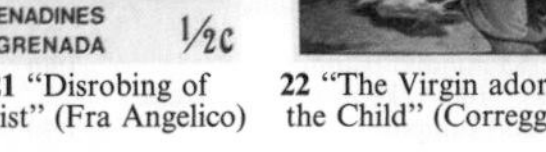

21 "Disrobing of Christ" (Fra Angelico)
22 "The Virgin adoring the Child" (Correggio)

1977. Easter. Paintings by artists named. Mult.
223 ½c. Type **21** 10 10*
224 1c. Fra Angelico 10 10*
225 2c. El Greco 10 10*
226 18c. El Greco 10 10*
227 35c. Fra Angelico 15 10*
228 50c. Giottino 15 10*
229 $2 Antonello da Messina 35 25*
MS230 121 × 94 mm. $3 Fra Angelico 65 65*

1977. Christmas. Multicoloured.
231 ½c. Type **22** 10 10*
232 1c. "Virgin and Child" (Giorgione) 10 10*
233 2c. "Virgin and Child" (Morales) 10 10*
234 18c. "Madonna della Tenda" (Raphael) 10 10*
235 35c. "Rest on the Flight into Egypt" (Van Dyck) 15 10*
236 50c. "Madonna and Child" (Lippi) 15 10*
237 $2 "Virgin and Child" (Lippi) (different) 35 25*
MS238 114 × 99 mm. $3 "Virgin and Child with Angels and Saints" (Ghirlandaio) 65 65*

1977. Royal Visit. Nos. 215/17 optd **ROYAL VISIT W.I. 1977.**
239 35c. Type **19** 10 10
240 $2 Queen entering Abbey 35 20
241 $4 Queen crowned 70 30
MS242 100 × 70 mm. $5 The Mall on Coronation Night 70 90

24 Life-saving

1977. Caribbean Scout Jamboree, Jamaica. Multicoloured.
243 ½c. Type **24** 10 10*
244 1c. Overnight hike 10 10*
245 2c. Cubs tying knots 10 10*
246 22c. Erecting a tent 15 10*
247 35c. Gang show limbo dance 25 10*
248 75c. Campfire cooking 40 15*
249 $3 Sea Scouts in "Mirror" dinghies 80 30*
MS250 109 × 85 mm. $2 Pioneering project—Spring bridge 1·10 90*

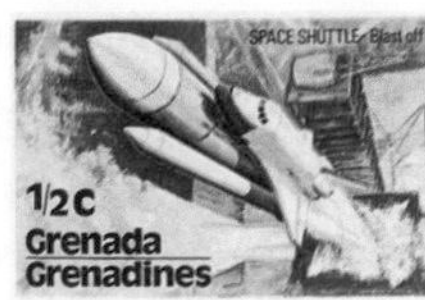

25 Blast-off

1977. Space Shuttle. Multicoloured.
251 ½c. Type **25** 10 10*
252 1c. Booster jettison 10 10*
253 2c. External tank jettison 10 10*
254 22c. Working in orbit 15 10*
255 50c. Shuttle re-entry 25 10*
256 $3 Shuttle landing 85 30*
MS257 85 × 103 mm. $2 Shuttle being towed 60 70*

26 Alfred Nobel and Physiology/ Medicine Medal

1978. Nobel Prize Awards. Multicoloured.
258 ½c. Type **26** 10 10*
259 1c. Physics and Chemistry medal 10 10*
260 2c. Peace medal (reverse) 10 10*
261 22c. Nobel Institute, Oslo 25 10*
262 75c. Peace Prize committee 50 15*
263 $3 Literature medal 1·50 30*
MS264 127 × 103 mm. $2 Peace medal and Nobel's will 50 60*

27 German Zeppelin Stamp, 1930

1978. 75th Anniv of First Zeppelin Flight and 50th Anniv of Lindbergh's Transatlantic Flight. Multicoloured.
265 5c. Type **27** 20 10*
266 15c. French Concorde stamp, 1970 60 10*
267 25c. Liechtenstein Zeppelin stamp, 1931 20 10*
268 35c. Panama Lindbergh stamp, 1928 20 10*
269 50c. Russia Airship stamp, 1931 25 10*
270 $3 Spanish Lindbergh stamp, 1930 75 30*
MS271 140 × 79 mm. 75c. U.S.A. Lindbergh stamp, 1927; $2 German LZ-129 *Hindenburg* stamp, 1936 1·10 90*

28 Coronation Ring

1978. 25th Anniv of Coronation. Multicoloured. (a) Horiz designs. Perf.
272 50c. Type **28** 10 10
273 $2 The Orb 25 30
274 $2.50 Imperial State Crown 30 35
MS275 97 × 67 mm. $5 Queen Elizabeth II 60 60

(b) Vert designs. Roul × imperf. Self-adhesive.
276 18c. Drummer, Royal Regiment of Fusiliers 15 35
277 50c. Drummer, Royal Anglian Regiment 15 45
278 $5 Drum Major, Queen's Regiment 1·00 3·00

30 "Le Chapeau de Paille"
32 Audubon's Shearwater

31 Wright Flyer I

1978. 400th Birth Anniv of Rubens. Mult.
279 5c. Type **30** 10 10
280 15c. "Archilles slaying Hector" 15 10
281 18c. "Helene Fourment and her Children" 15 10
282 22c. "Rubens and Isabella Brandt" 15 10
283 35c. "The Ildefonso Altarpiece" 20 10
284 $3 "Heads of Negroes" (detail) 75 1·00
MS285 85 × 127 mm. $2 "Self-portrait" 70 1·00

1978. 75th Anniv of Powered Flight.
286 **31** 5c. black, blue and brown 10 10
287 – 15c. black, brown and red 10 10
288 – 18c. black, brown and red 10 10
289 – 25c. black, yellow and green 10 10
290 – 35c. black, pink and purple 15 10
291 – 75c. black, lilac and yellow 25 25
292 – $3 black, violet and mauve 75 75
MS293 126 × 83 mm. $2 black, blue and green 75 1·00
DESIGNS—HORIZ: 25c. Wright Flyer III, 1905; 35c. Wright glider No. 1; 75c. Wright Flyer I (different); $2 Various Wright aircraft; $3 Wright Type A. VERT: 15c. Orville Wright; 18c. Wilbur Wright.

1978. Birds. Multicoloured.
294 5c. Type **32** 50 15
295 10c. Semi-palmated plover ("Northern Ring-necked Plover") 70 15
296 18c. Purple-throated carib ("Garnet-throated Hummingbird") (horiz) 1·00 15
297 22c. Red-billed whistling duck ("Black-bellied Tree Duck") (horiz) 1·00 20
298 40c. Caribbean martin (horiz) 1·50 35
299 $1 White-tailed tropic bird ("Yellow-tailed Tropicbird") 2·25 50
300 $2 Long-billed curlew 3·25 75
MS301 78 × 78 mm. $5 Snowy egret 5·00 2·75

33 Players with Ball

1978. World Cup Football Championship, Argentina. Multicoloured.
302 15c. Type **33** 10 10
303 35c. Running with ball 20 10
304 50c. Player with ball 25 20
305 $3 Heading 80 80
MS306 114 × 85 mm. $2 Player with ball (different) 80 1·25

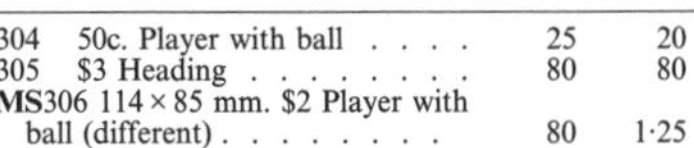

34 Captain Cook and Kalaniopu (King of Hawaii), 1778

1978. 250th Birth Anniv of Captain James Cook. Multicoloured.
307 18c. Type **34** 45 10
308 22c. Cook and native of Hawaii 60 15
309 50c. Cook and death scene, 1779 1·00 30
310 $3 Cook and offering ceremony 2·25 1·75
MS311 117 × 113 mm. $4 H.M.S. "Resolution" (vert) 1·50 1·00

35 "Virgin at Prayer"
36 "Strelitzia reginae"

1978. Christmas. Paintings by Durer. Multicoloured.
312 40c. Type **35** 15 10
313 60c. "The Dresden Altarpiece" 20 15
314 90c. "Madonna and Child with St. Anne" 20 15
315 $2 "Madonna and Child with Pear" 50 50
MS316 114 × 84 mm. $4 "Salvator Mundi" 1·00 1·40

1979. Flowers. Multicoloured.
317 22c. Type **36** 15 10
318 40c. "Euphorbia pulcherrima" 25 15
319 $1 "Heliconia humilis" 45 30
320 $3 "Thunbergia alata" 80 80
MS321 114 × 90 mm. $2 "Bougainvillaea glabra" 75 1·00

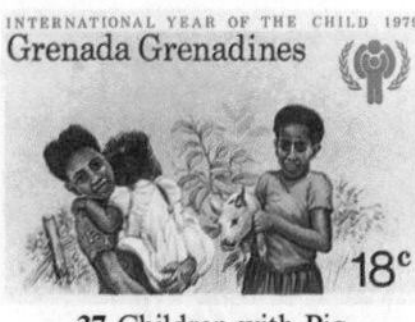

37 Children with Pig

1979. International Year of the Child. Multicoloured.
322 18c. Type **37** 10 10
323 50c. Children with donkey 20 25
324 $1 Children with goats 25 30
325 $3 Children fishing 65 80
MS326 104 × 86 mm. $4 Child with coconuts 1·00 1·90

38 "20,000 Leagues under the Sea"

1979. 150th Birth Anniv of Jules Verne (author). Multicoloured.
327 18c. Type **38** 40 10
328 38c. "From the Earth to the Moon" 45 20
329 75c. "From the Earth to the Moon" (different) 55 35
330 $3 "Five Weeks in a Balloon" 1·00 1·00
MS331 111 × 86 mm. $4 "Around the World in 80 Days" 1·00 1·60

39 Sir Rowland Hill and Mail Van

1979. Death Centenary of Sir Rowland Hill. Multicoloured.
332 15c. Type **39** 10 10
333 $1 "Britanis" (cargo liner) 20 20

334 $2 Diesel mail train 30 30
335 $3 Concorde 90 70
MS336 85 × 67 mm. $4 Sir Rowland Hill . . . . 75 1·00

40 "Virgin and Child Enthroned" (11th-century Byzantine)

1979. Christmas. Sculptures. Multicoloured.
337 6c. Type **40** 10 10
338 25c. "Presentation in the Temple" (Andre Beauneveu) 10 10
339 30c. "Flight to Egypt" (Utrecht, c. 1510) 10 10
340 40c. "Madonna and Child" (Jacopo della Quercia) . . 10 10
341 90c. "Madonna della Mela" (Luca della Robbia) . . . 15 15
342 $1 "Madonna and Child" (Antonio Rossellino) . . . 20 20
343 $2 "Madonna and Child" (Antwerp, 1700) 35 35
MS344 125 × 95 mm. $4 "Virgin", Krumau . . . . 65 1·00

41 Great Hammerhead

1979. Marine Wildlife. Multicoloured.
345 40c. Type **41** 40 30
346 45c. Spot-finned butterflyfish 45 30
347 50c. Permit (fish) 45 40
348 60c. Threaded turban (shell) 65 55
349 70c. Milk conch 75 75
350 75c. Great blue heron . . . 1·25 90
351 90c. Colourful Atlantic moon (shell) . . . . 95 1·00
352 $1 Red-footed booby . . . . 1·75 1·75
MS353 99 × 86 mm. $2.50 Collared plover . . . . 2·00 1·10

42 Doctor Goofy

1979. International Year of the Child. Walt Disney cartoon characters. Multicoloured.
354 ½c. Type **42** 10 10
355 1c. Admiral Mickey Mouse . 10 10
356 2c. Fireman Goofy 10 10
357 3c. Nurse Minnie Mouse . . 10 10
358 4c. Drum Major Mickey Mouse 10 10
359 5c. Policeman Donald Duck 10 10
360 10c. Pilot Donald Duck . . . 10 10
361 $2 Postman Goofy (horiz) . . 2·50 2·25
362 $2.50 Train driver Donald Duck (horiz) . . . . . . 2·50 2·25
MS363 128 × 102 mm. $3 Mickey Mouse as fireman . . . . . . 1·75 2·00

1980. 1st Anniv of Revolution. Nos. 116 and 119/30 optd **PEOPLE'S REVOLUTION 13 MARCH 1979**.
364 6c. Cocoa beans in drying trays 10 10
365 12c. Cocoa tree 10 10
366 15c. Fishermen at Fontenoy 10 10
367 20c. Parliament Building, St. George's 10 10
368 25c. Fort George cannons . . 15 10
369 35c. Pearls Airport 20 10
370 50c. General Post Office . . . 35 15
371 75c. Carib's Leap, Sauteurs Bay 40 20
372 $1 Carenage, St. George's . . 55 30
373 $2 St. George's Harbour by night 85 70
374 $3 Grand Anse Beach . . . 1·60 1·60
375 $5 Canoe Bay and Black Bay 2·25 2·50
376 $10 Sugar-loaf Island . . . . 3·75 4·25

43 Classroom

1980. 75th Anniv of Rotary International. Multicoloured.
377 6c. Type **43** 10 10
378 30c. Different races encircling Rotary emblem 20 10
379 60c. Rotary executive presenting doctor with cheque 35 20
380 $3 Nurses with young patients . . . . 1·25 75
MS381 85 × 72 mm. $4 Paul P. Harris (founder) . . . . . 1·00 1·60

44 Yellow-bellied Seedeater

1980. Wild Birds. Multicoloured.
382 25c. Type **44** 50 15
383 40c. Blue-hooded euphonia 55 20
384 90c. Yellow warbler . . . . 1·25 65
385 $2 Tropical mockingbird . . 1·75 1·25
MS386 83 × 110 mm. $3 Barn Owl 4·00 1·50

45 Running

1980. Olympic Games, Moscow. Multicoloured.
387 30c. Type **45** 20 15
388 40c. Football 15 20
389 90c. Boxing 35 35
390 $2 Wrestling 70 75
MS391 104 × 75 mm. $4 Athletes in silhouette . . . . 75 1·10

1980. "London 1980" International Stamp Exhibition. Nos. 332/5 optd **LONDON 1980**.
392 15c. Mail van 15 15
393 $1 "Britanis" (cargo liner) . . 75 35
394 $2 Diesel mail train . . . . 1·50 1·00
395 $3 Concorde . . . . 2·50 2·00

47 Long-jawed Squirrelfish

1980. Fishes. Multicoloured.
396A ½c. Type **47** 10 10
397A 1c. Blue chromis 10 10
398A 2c. Four-eyed butterflyfish 10 10
399A 4c. Sergeant major 10 10
400A 5c. Yellow-tailed snapper . 10 10
401A 6c. Mutton snapper 10 10
402A 10c. Cocoa damselfish . . . 10 10
403A 12c. Royal gramma 10 10
404A 15c. Cherub angelfish . . . 10 10
405A 20c. Black-barred soldierfish 15 10
406A 25c. Mottled grouper . . . 15 15
407A 30c. Caribbean long-nosed butterflyfish 15 20
408A 40c. Puddingwife 20 25
409A 50c. Midnight parrotfish . . 25 35
410A 90c. Red-spotted hawkfish 40 55
411A $1 Hogfish 45 60
412A $3 Beau Gregory . . . . . 1·25 1·50
413A $5 Rock beauty . . . . . 1·50 1·75
414A $10 Barred hamlet . . . . 2·25 2·75

1980. Christmas. Scenes from Walt Disney's "Bambi". As T **42**. Multicoloured.
415 ½c. Bambi with mother . . . 10 10
416 1c. Bambi with quails 10 10
417 2c. Bambi meets Thumper the rabbit 10 10
418 3c. Bambi meets Flower the skunk 10 10
419 4c. Bambi and Faline 10 10
420 5c. Bambi with his father . . 10 10
421 10c. Bambi on ice 10 10
422 $2.50 Faline with foals . . . 1·75 1·25
423 $3 Bambi and Faline . . . . 1·75 1·25
MS424 127 × 102 mm. $4 Bambi as Prince of the Forest (vert) . . 2·00 2·00

48 "The Unicorn in Captivity" (15th century unknown artist)

49 "Bust of a Woman"

1981. Art Masterpieces. Multicoloured.
425 6c. Type **48** 10 10
426 10c. "The Fighting 'Temeraire' " (Turner) (horiz) 10 10
427 25c. "Sunday Afternoon on the Ile de la Grande Jatte" (Seurat) (horiz) 15 15
428 90c. "Max Schmitt in a Single Scull" (Eakins) (horiz) 45 45
429 $2 "The Burial of the Count of Orgaz" (El Greco) . . . 85 85
430 $3 "Portrait of George Washington" (Stuart) . . . 1·10 1·10
MS431 66 × 101 mm. $5 "Kaiser Karl de Grosse" (detail Durer) 1·75 2·00

1981. 50th Anniv of Walt Disney's Pluto (cartoon character). As T **42**.
432 $2 Mickey Mouse serving birthday cake to Pluto . . 1·00 80
MS433 127 × 101 mm. $4 Pluto in scene from film "Pluto's Dream House" . . . . 1·50 1·50

1981. Easter. Walt Disney cartoon characters. As T **42**. Multicoloured.
434 35c. Chip 20 20
435 40c. Dewey 20 20
436 $2 Huey 60 60
437 $2.50 Mickey Mouse 75 75
MS438 126 × 102 mm. $4 Jimmy Cricket . . . . 1·50 1·50

1981. Birth Centenary of Picasso. Mult.
439 6c. Type **49** 10 10
440 40c. Woman (study for "Les Demoiselles d'Avignon") 20 15
441 90c. "Nude with raised Arms (The Dancer of Avignon)" 30 20
442 $4 "The Dryad" 75 75
MS443 103 × 128 mm. $5 "Les Demoiselles d'Avignon". Imperf 1·40 1·25

50 Balmoral Castle

51 Lady Diana Spencer

1981. Royal Wedding (1st issue). Multicoloured.
448 30c. Prince Charles and Lady Diana Spencer 35 20
444 40c. As 30c. 15 15
449 40c. Type **50** 45 35
445 $2 Type **50** 50 50
446 $4 Prince Charles as parachutist 90 90
MS447 97 × 84 mm. $5 Royal Coach 70 70

1981. Royal Wedding (2nd issue). Multicoloured. Self-adhesive.
450 $1 Type **51** 20 35
451 $2 Prince Charles 25 50
452 $5 Prince Charles and Lady Diana Spencer (horiz) . . . 1·25 2·00

52 Amy Johnson (1st solo flight, Britain to Australia by Woman, May 1930)

54 Footballer

53 Boeing 747 SCA Carrier

1981. "Decade for Women". Famous Female Aviators. Multicoloured.
453 30c. Type **52** 45 15
454 70c. Mme. La Baronne de Laroche (1st qualified woman pilot, March 1910) 70 30
455 $1.10 Ruth Nichols (solo Atlantic flight attempt, June 1931) 80 40
456 $3 Amelia Earhart (1st North Atlantic solo flight by woman, May 1932) . . . 1·75 1·10
MS457 90 × 85 mm. $5 Valentina Nikolayeva-Tereshkova (1st woman in space, June 1963) . . 1·25 1·40

1981. Christmas. Designs as T **42** showing scenes from Walt Disney's cartoon film "Lady and the Tramp".
458 ½c. multicoloured 10 10
459 1c. multicoloured 10 10
460 2c. multicoloured 10 10
461 3c. multicoloured 10 10
462 4c. multicoloured 10 10
463 5c. multicoloured 10 10
464 10c. multicoloured 10 10
465 $2.50 multicoloured . . . . 3·25 1·50
466 $3 multicoloured . . . . . . 3·25 1·50
MS467 128 × 103 mm. $5 multicoloured . . . . 5·00 3·00

1981. Space Shuttle Project. Multicoloured.
468 10c. Type **53** 30 10
469 40c. Re-entry 65 15
470 $1.10 External tank separation . . . . 1·25 45
471 $3 Touchdown . . . . 1·75 1·00
MS472 117 × 98 mm. $5 Launch . . 2·50 1·60

1981. World Cup Football Championship, Spain (1982).
473 **54** 20c. multicoloured 15 10
474 – 40c. multicoloured 20 15
475 – $1 multicoloured 35 30
476 – $2 multicoloured 65 55
MS477 106 × 128 mm. $4 multicoloured . . . . 1·40 1·60
DESIGNS: 40c. to $4 various designs showing footballers.

55 Mail Van and Stagecoach

1982. Cent of U.P.U. Membership. Multicoloured.
478 30c. Type **55** 30 15
479 40c. U.P.U. emblem 30 15
480 $2.50 "Queen Elizabeth 2" (liner) and sailing ship . . 1·50 70
481 $4 Concorde and De Havilland D.H.9 biplane . . 2·25 1·25
MS482 117 × 78 mm. $5 British Advanced Passenger Train and steam mail trains . . . . . . 3·00 2·25

56 National Sports Meeting

1982. 75th Anniv of Boy Scout Movement and 125th Birth Anniv of Lord Baden-Powell. Multicoloured.
483 6c. Type **56** 15 10
484 90c. Sea scouts sailing . . . 50 30
485 $1.10 Handicraft 65 60
486 $3 Animal tending . . . . . 1·40 1·40
MS487 100 × 71 mm. $5 Music around campfire . . . . 1·40 1·75

57 "Anartia jatrophae"

1982. Butterflies. Multicoloured.
488 30c. Type **57** 75 30
489 40c. "Chioides vintra" 80 35
490 $1.10 "Cynthia cardui" . . . 1·75 75
491 $3 "Historis odius" . . . . . 2·75 1·60
MS492 103 × 77 mm. $5 "Dione juno" . . . . 3·25 2·50

58 Prince and Princess of Wales

60 "Presentation of Christ in the Temple"

59 "New Deal"—Soil Conservation

1982. 21st Birthday of Princess of Wales. Multicoloured.
493 50c. Blenheim Palace . . . . 1·25 1·75
494 60c. As 50c. 75 75
495 $1 Type **58** . . . . 1·75 2·25
496 $2 Type **58** . . . . 1·75 2·00
497 $3 Princess of Wales . . . . 2·50 2·75
498 $4 As $3 . . . . 2·50 2·75
MS499 103 × 75 mm. $5 Princess Diana (different) . . . . 5·50 2·50

1982. Birth Centenary of Franklin D. Roosevelt. Multicoloured.
500 30c. Type **59** 25 10
501 40c. Roosevelt and George Washington Carver (scientist) 25 10
502 70c. Civilian conservation corps (reafforestation) . . 30 20
503 $3 Roosevelt with Pres. Barclay of Liberia, Casablanca Conference, 1943 . . . . 70 80
MS504 100 × 72 mm. $5 Roosevelt delivering address at Howard University . . . . 1·75 1·75

1982. Birth of Prince William of Wales. Nos. 493/8 optd **ROYAL BABY 21.6.82.**
505 50c. Blenheim Palace 50 75
506 60c. As 50c. 55 60
507 $1 Type **58** . . . . 70 1·00
508 $2 Type **58** . . . . 1·00 1·25
509 $3 Princess of Wales . . . . 1·25 1·75
510 $4 As $3 . . . . 1·50 1·75
MS511 103 × 75 mm. $5 Princess Diana (different) . . . . 2·10 2·25

1982. Easter. Easter Paintings by Rembrandt. Multicoloured.
512 30c. Type **60** 25 10
513 60c. "Descent from the Cross" 30 10
514 $2 "Raising of the Cross" . . 45 60
515 $4 "Resurrection of Christ" . . 80 1·25
MS516 101 × 126 mm. $5 "The Risen Christ" . . . . 2·40 2·00

61 "Santa Fe", U.S.A.

1982. Famous Trains of the World. Mult.
517 10c. Type **61** 50 15
518 40c. "Mistral", France . . . 70 20
519 70c. "Rheingold", Germany 80 45
520 $1 "ET 403", France . . . . 1·00 50
521 $1.10 Steam locomotive "Mallard", Great Britain 1·25 60
522 $2 Tokaido Shinkansen "Hikari", Japan . . . . . 1·40 90
MS523 121 × 95 mm. $5 "Settebello", Italy . . . . . . 1·50 2·00

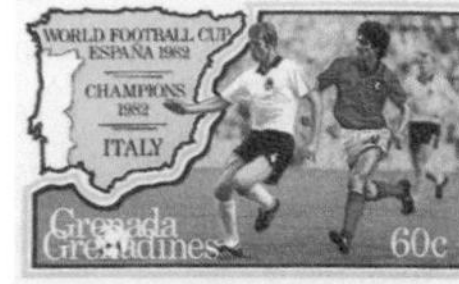

62 Footballers

1982. World Cup Football Championship Winners.
524 **62** 60c. multicoloured 75 35
525 $4 multicoloured . . . . 2·00 1·25
MS526 92 × 134 mm. $5 multicoloured . . . . 1·50 1·50

1982. Christmas. Scenes from Walt Disney's cartoon film "The Rescuers". As T **42**, but horiz.
527 ½c. multicoloured 10 10
528 1c. multicoloured 10 10
529 2c. multicoloured 10 10
530 3c. multicoloured 10 10
531 4c. multicoloured 10 10
532 5c. multicoloured 10 10
533 10c. multicoloured 10 10
534 $2.50 multicoloured . . . . 3·25 1·75
535 $3 multicoloured . . . . . . 3·25 1·75
MS536 120 × 96 mm. $5 multicoloured . . . . 5·00 2·75

63 Short-finned Pilot Whale

1982. Save the Whale. Multicoloured.
537 10c. Type **63** 85 55
538 60c. Dall's porpoise . . . . 2·00 1·75
539 $1.10 Humpback whale . . . 3·50 2·75
540 $3 Bowhead whale . . . . . 6·00 7·00
MS541 113 × 84 mm. $5 Spotted dolphin . . . . 4·50 4·00

64 "David and Goliath"

1983. 500th Anniv of Raphael. Multicoloured.
542 25c. Type **64** 15 15
543 30c. "David sees Bathsheba" 15 15
544 90c. "Triumph of David" . . 30 35
545 $4 "Anointing of Solomon" 70 90
MS546 126 × 101 mm. $5 "Anointing of David" . . . . 80 1·10

65 Voice and Visual Communication

1983. World Communications Year. Mult.
547 30c. Type **65** 10 10
548 60c. Ambulance 25 20
549 $1.10 Westland Whirlwind helicopters 45 45
550 $3 Satellite . . . . 1·00 1·00
MS551 127 × 85 mm. $5 Diver and bottle-nosed dolphin . . . . . 2·50 2·00

66 Chrysler "Imperial Roadster", 1931

1983. 75th Anniv of Model "T" Ford Car. Multicoloured.
552 10c. Type **66** 15 15
553 30c. Doble steam car, 1925 25 25
554 40c. Ford "Mustang", 1965 25 30
555 60c. Packard tourer, 1930 . . 35 40
556 70c. Mercer "Raceabout", 1913 . . . . 35 40
557 90c. Corvette "Stingray", 1963 . . . . 35 40
558 $1.10 Auburn "851 Supercharger Speedster", 1935 . . . . 40 45
559 $2.50 Pierce-Arrow "Silver Arrow", 1933 . . . . . . 65 95
560 $3 Duesenberg dual cowl phaeton, 1929 . . . . . . 75 1·25
561 $4 Mercedes-Benz "SSK", 1928 . . . . 75 1·50
MS562 119 × 90 mm. $5 McFarlan "Knickerbocker" cabriolet, 1923 1·50 2·50

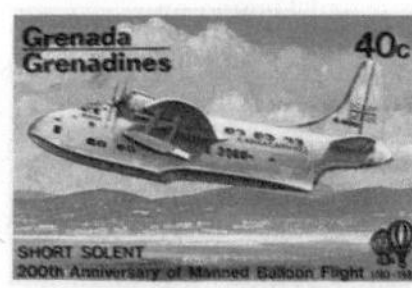

67 Short Solent 2 Flying Boat

1983. Bicentenary of Manned Flight. Mult.
563 40c. Type **67** 85 20
564 70c. Curtiss R3C-2 seaplane 1·00 35
565 90c. Hawker Nimrod biplane 1·25 40
566 $4 Montgolfier balloon . . . 3·25 2·75
MS567 112 × 85 mm. $5 LZ-11 "Viktoria Luise" (airship) . . . 1·75 2·00

68 Goofy

69 Weightlifting

1983. Christmas Disney cartoon characters in scenes from "Jingle Bells" (Christmas carol). Multicoloured.
568 ½c. Type **68** 10 10
569 1c. Clarabelle Cow 10 10
570 2c. Donald Duck 10 10
571 3c. Pluto 10 10
572 4c. Morty and Ferdie 10 10
573 5c. Huey, Dewey and Louie 10 10
574 10c. Daisy and Chip n'Dale 10 10
575 $2.50 Big Bad Wolf . . . . 4·75 5·00
576 $5 Mickey Mouse . . . . . 5·00 5·50
MS577 102 × 124 mm. $5 Donald Duck in sleigh . . . . 8·00 8·50

1984. Olympic Games, Los Angeles. Mult.
578 30c. Type **69** 20 15
579 60c. Gymnastics 45 35
580 70c. Archery 50 40
581 $4 Sailing . . . . 1·90 1·90
MS582 70 × 102 mm. $5 Basketball 2·25 2·25

70 Frangipani

71 Goofy

1984. Flowers. Multicoloured.
583 15c. Type **70** 15 10
584 40c. Dwarf poinciana 30 25
585 70c. Walking iris 55 45
586 $4 Lady's slipper . . . . . . 1·75 2·50
MS587 66 × 57 mm. $5 Brazilian glory vine . . . . 1·50 2·50

1984. Easter. Multicoloured.
588 ½c. Type **71** 10 10
589 1c. Chip and Dale 10 10
590 2c. Daisy Duck and Huey . . 10 10
591 3c. Daisy Duck 10 10
592 4c. Donald Duck 10 10
593 5c. Merlin and Madam Mim 10 10
594 10c. Flower 10 10
595 $2 Minnie and Mickey Mouse . . . . 1·25 2·00
596 $4 Minnie Mouse . . . . . 1·75 2·75
MS597 126 × 100 mm. $5 Minnie Mouse (different) . . . . . . 3·00 3·75

72 Bobolink

1984. Songbirds. Multicoloured.
598 40c. Type **72** . . . . 1·75 1·50
599 50c. Eastern kingbird . . . . 2·00 1·60
600 60c. Barn swallow . . . . . 2·25 2·00
601 70c. Yellow warbler . . . . 2·25 2·00
602 $1 Rose-breasted grosbeak 2·50 2·50
603 $1.10 Common yellowthroat ("Yellowthroat") . . . . . 2·75 2·75
604 $2 Catbird . . . . 3·50 4·50
MS605 71 × 65 mm. $5 Fork-tailed flycatcher . . . . 6·50 5·00

1984. Universal Postal Union Congress, Hamburg. Nos. 585/6 optd **19th U.P.U. CONGRESS HAMBURG.**
606 70c. Walking iris . . . . . . 1·00 1·00
607 $4 Lady's slipper . . . . . . 4·50 5·00
MS608 66 × 57 mm. $5 Brazilian glory vine . . . . 2·25 3·00

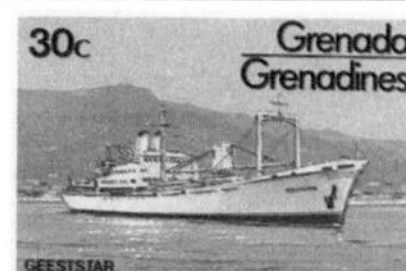

74 "Geeststar" (freighter)

1984. Ships. Multicoloured.
609 30c. Type **74** 75 75
610 60c. "Daphne" (liner) . . . . 1·00 1·25
611 $1.10 "Southwind" (schooner) . . . . 1·25 2·00
612 $4 "Oceanic" (liner) . . . . 2·00 5·50
MS613 108 × 80 mm. $5 Pirate ship 3·00 4·00

1984. 450th Death Anniv of Correggio (painter). As T **296** of Grenada. Multicoloured.
614 10c. "The Hunt—Blowing the Horn" 10 10
615 30c. "St. John the Evangelist" (horiz) 15 15
616 90c. "The Hunt—The Deer's Head" 50 50
617 $4 "The Virgin crowned by Christ" (horiz) . . . . . . 2·00 2·00
MS618 73 × 63 mm. $5 "Martyrdom of the Four Saints" . . . . . 2·40 3·00

1984. 150th Birth Anniv of Edgar Degas (painter). As T **297** of Grenada. Multicoloured.
619 25c. "The Song of the Dog" 40 15
620 70c. "Cafe-concert" 70 50
621 $1.10 "The Orchestra of the Opera" . . . . 1·50 1·25
622 $3 "The Dance Lesson" . . . 2·75 2·75
MS623 53 × 73 mm. $5 "Madame Camus at the Piano" . . . . . 2·40 3·00

1984. "Ausipex" International Stamp Exhibition, Melbourne. As T **298** of Grenada. Multicoloured.
624 $1.10 Queen Victoria Gardens, Melbourne . . . 50 50
625 $4 Ayers Rock . . . . 2·00 2·00
MS626 107 × 76 mm. $5 River Yarra, Melbourne . . . . . . 2·00 3·00

75 Col. Steven's Model (1825)

1984. Railway Locomotives. Multicoloured.
627 20c. Type **75** 55 25
628 50c. "Royal George" (1827) 70 50
629 60c. "Stourbridge Lion" (1829) 75 65
630 70c. "Liverpool" (1830) . . . 80 85
631 90c. "South Carolina" (1832) 90 1·25
632 $1.10 "Monster" (1836) . . . 90 1·50
633 $2 "Lafayette" (1837) . . . . 1·10 2·25
634 $4 "Lion" (1838) . . . . . . 1·40 3·75
MS635 Two sheets, each 100 × 70 mm. (a) $5 Sequin's locomotive (1829). (b) $5 "Adler" (1835). Set of 2 sheets . . . . 6·00 8·00

1984. Opening of Point Saline International Airport. Nos. 547, 549 and **MS**551 optd **OPENING OF POINT SALINE INT'L AIRPORT.**
636 30c. Type **65** 30 25
637 $1.10 Westland Whirlwind helicopters 95 75
MS638 127 × 85 mm. Diver and bottle-nosed dolphin . . . . . 4·25 3·50

1984. Christmas. Walt Disney cartoon characters. As T **301** of Grenada. Multicoloured.
639 45c. Donald Duck and nephews knitting Christmas stockings 70 40
640 60c. Donald Duck and nephews sitting on sofa . . 80 65
641 90c. Donald Duck getting out of bed . . . . 1·25 1·00
642 $2 Donald Duck putting presents in wardrobe . . . 2·00 2·50
643 $4 Nephews singing carols outside Donald Duck's window . . . . 3·25 4·25
MS644 126 × 102 mm. $5 Donald Duck filming nephews . . . . 4·25 4·00

1985. Birth Bicentenary of John J. Audubon (ornithologist). As T **418** of Ghana. Mult.
645 50c. Blue-winged teal . . . . 2·00 60
646 90c. White ibis . . . . 2·50 1·25
647 $1.10 Swallow-tailed kite . . 3·50 2·00
648 $3 Moorhen . . . . 4·50 4·75
MS649 82 × 111 mm. $5 Mangrove cuckoo (vert) . . . . 3·25 3·75
See also Nos. 736/40.

76 Kawasaki "750" (1972)

1985. Centenary of the Motor Cycle. Mult.
650 30c. Type **76** 65 45
651 60c. Honda "Goldwing GL1000" (1974) (horiz) 90 1·00
652 70c. Kawasaki "Z650" (1976) (horiz) 1·00 1·10
653 $4 Honda "CBX" (1977) 4·00 6·50
MS654 113 × 76 mm. $5 BMW "R100RS" (1978) 3·50 4·25

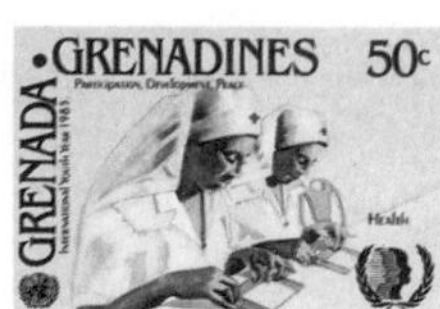

77 Nursing Cadets folding Bandages (Health)

1985. International Youth Year. Mult.
655 50c. Type **77** 70 45
656 70c. Scuba diver and turtle (Environment) 1·00 80
657 $1.10 Yachting (Leisure) 1·60 1·50
658 $3 Boys playing chess (Education) 10·00 9·00
MS659 98 × 70 mm. $5 Hands touching globe 2·75 3·00

1985. 40th Anniv of International Civil Aviation Organization. As T **305** of Grenada. Multicoloured.
660 5c. Lockheed Lodestar 40 20
661 70c. Hawker Siddeley H.S.748 1·75 55
662 $1.10 Boeing 727-200 2·25 90
663 $4 Boeing 707 3·50 2·50
MS664 87 × 68 mm. $4 Pilatus Britten Norman Islander 3·50 3·00

78 Lady Baden-Powell (founder) and Grenadian Guide Leaders

1985. 75th Anniv of Girl Guide Movement. Multicoloured.
665 30c. Type **78** 50 20
666 50c. Guide leader and guides on botany field trip 1·00 30
667 70c. Guide leader and guides camping (vert) 1·00 45
668 $4 Guides sailing (vert) 4·00 2·25
MS669 100 × 73 mm. $5 Lord and Lady Baden-Powell (vert) 3·75 4·25

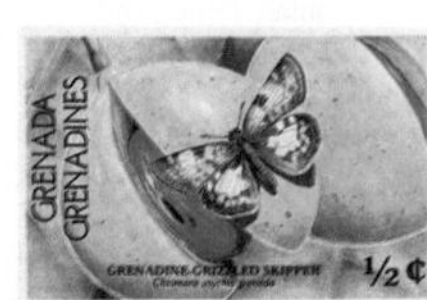

79 "Chiomara asychis"

1985. Butterflies. Multicoloured.
670 ½c. Type **79** 10 20
671 1c. "Anartia amathea" 10 20
672 2c. "Pseudolycaena marsyas" 10 20
673 4c. "Urbanus proteus" 10 20
674 5c. "Polygonus manueli" 15 20
675a 6c. "Battus polydamas" 20 15
676 10c. "Eurema daira" 30 15
677 12c. "Phoebis agarithe" 45 20
678 15c. "Aphrissa statira" 45 20
679 20c. "Strymon simaethis" 60 20
680 25c. "Mestra cana" 60 25
681 30c. "Agraulis vanillae" 60 30
682 40c. "Junonia evarete" 75 45
683 60c. "Dryas julia" 1·00 65
684 70c. "Philaethria dido" 1·10 75
685 $1.10 "Hamadryas feronia" 1·75 1·25
686 $2.50 "Strymon rufofusca" 3·25 3·00
687 $5 "Appias drusilla" 5·00 4·75
688 $10 "Polites dictynna" 8·00 9·00
688b $20 "Euptychia cephus" 12·00 17·00

80 The Queen Mother before Prince William's Christening **81** Scuba Diving

1985. Life and Times of Queen Elizabeth the Queen Mother. Multicoloured.
689 $1 Type **80** 45 60
690 $1.50 In winner's enclosure at Ascot (horiz) 60 75
691 $2.50 With Prince Charles at Garter ceremony, Windsor Castle 85 1·10
MS692 56 × 85 mm. $5 At opening of Royal York Hospice, London 1·75 3·00
Stamps as Nos. 689/91 but with face values of 70c., $1.10 and $3 exist from additional sheetlets with changed background colours.

1985. Water Sports. Multicoloured.
693 15c. Type **81** 30 10
694 70c. Boys playing in waterfall 60 45
695 90c. Water skiing 70 55
696 $4 Swimming 2·75 2·25
MS697 103 × 78 mm. $5 Scuba diver 2·75 3·25

82 Queen or Pink Conch

1985. Marine Life. Multicoloured.
698 60c. Type **82** 75 40
699 90c. Porcupinefish and fire coral 95 60
700 $1.10 Ghost crab 1·25 1·00
701 $4 West Indies spiny lobster 2·75 4·00
MS702 299 × 70 mm. $5 Long-spined urchin 5·00 4·00

1985. 300th Birth Anniv of Johann Sebastian Bach (composer). As T **309a** of Grenada. Multicoloured.
703 15c. Natural trumpet 50 10
704 60c. Bass viol 85 40
705 $1.10 Flute 1·50 70
706 $3 Double flageolet 2·25 1·75
MS707 110 × 75 mm. $5 Johann Sebastian Bach 3·25 3·50

1985. Royal Visit. As T **310a** of Grenada. Mult.
708 10c. Arms of Great Britain and Grenada 20 20
709 $1 Queen Elizabeth II (vert) 1·00 1·75
710 $4 Royal Yacht "Britannia" 3·00 4·75
MS711 111 × 83 mm. $5 Map of Grenada Grenadines 3·00 3·75

1985. 40th Anniv of United Nations Organization. Designs as T **311a** of Grenada showing United Nations (New York) stamps. Multicoloured.
712 $1 Neil Armstrong (first man on Moon) and 1982 Peaceful Uses of Outer Space 20c. 1·25 1·10
713 $2 Gandhi and 1971 Racial Equality Year 13c. 4·25 5·00
714 $2.50 Maimonides (physician) and 1956 World Health Organization 3c. 5·50 6·50
MS715 110 × 85 mm. $5 U.N. Under-Secretary 2·50 3·00

1985. 150th Birth Anniv of Mark Twain (author). As T **145a** of Gambia showing Walt Disney cartoon characters illustrating scenes from "Letters from Hawaii". Multicoloured.
716 25c. Minnie Mouse dancing the hula 60 30
717 50c. Donald Duck surfing 90 65
718 $1.50 Donald Duck roasting marshmallow in volcano 2·25 2·25
719 $3 Mickey Mouse and Chip n'Dale canoeing 3·75 4·00
MS720 127 × 120 mm. $5 Mickey Mouse with cat 4·75 3·75

1985. Birth Bicentenaries of Grimm Brothers (folklorists). As T **145b** of Gambia, but vert, showing Walt Disney cartoon characters in scenes from "The Elves and the Shoemaker". Multicoloured.
721 30c. Mickey Mouse as the unsuccessful Shoemaker 70 40
722 60c. Two elves making shoes 1·10 85
723 70c. The Shoemaker discovering the new shoes 1·40 1·00
724 $4 The Shoemaker's wife (Minnie Mouse) making clothes for the elves 4·25 5·00
MS725 126 × 101 mm. $5 The Shoemaker and his wife waving 5·50 5·00

83 "Madonna and Child" (Titian) **85** Two Footballers

1985. Christmas. Religious Paintings. Mult.
726 50c. Type **83** 45 35
727 70c. "Madonna and Child with St. Mary and John the Baptist" (Bugiardini) 55 50
728 $1.10 "Adoration of the Magi" (Di Fredi) 80 1·40
729 $3 "Madonna and Child with Young St. John the Baptist" (Bartolomeo) 1·25 3·75
MS730 112 × 81 mm. $5 "The Annunciation" (Botticelli) 2·75 6·00

1986. Centenary of Statue of Liberty (1st issue). As T **312a** of Grenada. Multicoloured.
731 5c. Croton Reservoir, New York (1875) 10 10
732 10c. New York Public Library (1986) 10 10
733 70c. Old Boathouse, Central Park (1894) 25 40
734 $4 Boating in Central Park (1986) 1·40 2·25
MS735 103 × 76 mm. $5 Statue of Liberty (vert) 3·75 4·25
See also Nos. 892/903.

1986. Birth Bicentenary of John J. Audubon (ornithologist) (2nd issue). As T **312b** of Grenada. Multicoloured.
736 50c. Louisiana heron 2·00 1·00
737 70c. Black-crowned night heron 2·50 1·50
738 90c. American bittern 2·75 2·00
739 $4 Glossy ibis 5·00 6·50
MS740 103 × 74 mm. $5 King eider 6·50 8·50

1986. Visit of President Reagan of U.S.A. Nos. 684 and 687, optd **VISIT OF PRES. REAGAN 20 FEBRUARY 1986.**
741 70c. "Philaethria dido" 1·50 1·25
742 $5 "Appias drusilla" 6·50 8·00

1986. World Cup Football Championship, Mexico. Designs showing footballers.
743 **85** 10c. multicoloured 60 40
744 – 70c. multicoloured 1·75 1·25
745 – $1 multicoloured 2·00 1·75
746 – $4 multicoloured 5·00 6·50
MS747 86 × 104 mm. $5 multicoloured 5·50 5·50

1986. Appearance of Halley's Comet (1st issue). As T **151a** of Gambia. Multicoloured.
748 5c. Nicholas Copernicus (astronomer) and Earl of Rosse's six foot reflector telescope 40 40
749 20c. "Sputnik I" (first satellite) orbiting Earth, 1957 60 40
750 40c. Tycho Brahe's notes and sketch of 1577 Comet 80 60
751 $4 Edmond Halley and 1682 Comet 3·75 4·50
MS752 101 × 70 mm. $5 Halley's Comet 3·00 3·50
See also Nos. 790/4.
The captions of Nos. 750/1 are transposed.

1986. 60th Birthday of Queen Elizabeth II. As T **151b** of Gambia.
753 2c. black and yellow 10 15
754 $1.50 multicoloured 80 1·00
755 $4 multicoloured 2·00 2·75
MS756 120 × 85 mm. $5 black and brown 2·00 3·50
DESIGNS: 2c. Princesses Elizabeth and Margaret, Windsor Park, 1933; $1.50, Queen Elizabeth; $4 In Sydney, Australia, 1970; $5 The Royal Family, Coronation Day, 1937.

1986. "Ameripex '86" International Stamp Exhibition, Chicago. As T **315a** of Grenada. Multicoloured.
757 30c. Donald Duck riding mule in Grand Canyon 60 45
758 60c. Daisy Duck, Timothy Mouse and Dumbo on Golden Gate Bridge, San Francisco 85 1·00
759 $1 Mickey Mouse and Goofy in fire engine and Chicago Watertower 1·50 1·75
760 $3 Mickey Mouse as airmail pilot and White House 3·00 4·00
MS761 126 × 101 mm. $5 Donald Duck and Mickey Mouse watching Halley's Comet over Statue of Liberty 3·75 7·50

1986. Royal Wedding. As T **153b** of Gambia. Multicoloured.
762 60c. Prince Andrew and Miss Sarah Ferguson 55 45
763 70c. Prince Andrew in car 75 55
764 $4 Prince Andrew with Westland Lynx naval helicopter 3·50 3·50
MS765 88 × 88 mm. $5 Prince Andrew and Miss Sarah Ferguson (different) 4·00 5·50

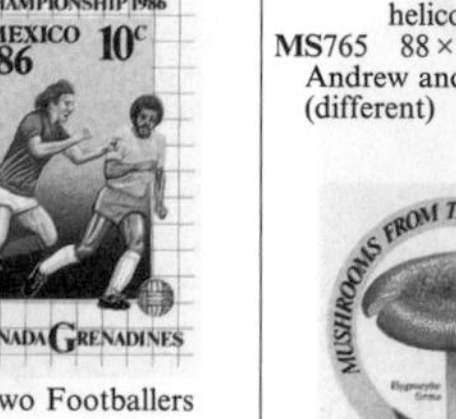
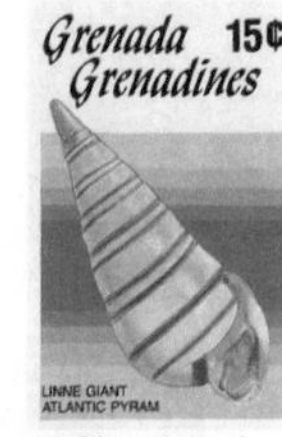

86 "Hygrocybe firma" **87** Giant Atlantic or Dolobrate Pyram

1986. Mushrooms of the Lesser Antilles. Mult.
766 15c. Type **86** 80 40
767 50c. "Xerocomus coccolobae" 1·75 1·25
768 $2 "Volvariella cubensis" 3·50 4·00
769 $3 "Lactarius putidus" 4·50 5·00
MS770 76 × 80 mm. $5 "Leptonia caeruleopitata" 9·00 12·00

1986. Sea Shells. Multicoloured.
771 15c. Type **87** 90 50
772 50c. Beau's murex 2·00 1·25
773 $1.10 West Indian fighting conch 2·25 2·75
774 $4 Alphabet conch 3·75 7·00
MS775 109 × 75 mm. $5 Brown-lined paper bubble 6·50 8·50

1986. World Cup Football Championship Winners, Mexico. Nos. 743/6 optd **WINNERS Argentina 3 W. Germany 2.**
776 **85** 10c. multicoloured 65 40
777 – 70c. multicoloured 1·40 1·10
778 – $1 multicoloured 1·75 1·40
779 – $4 multicoloured 4·00 5·50
MS780 86 × 104 mm. $5 multicoloured 8·00 10·00

88 Common Opossum **89** Cycling

1986. Wildlife. Multicoloured.
781 10c. Type **88** 20 20
782 30c. Giant toad 40 40
783 60c. Land tortoise 80 80
784 70c. Murine opossum (vert) 85 85
785 90c. Burmese mongoose (vert) 90 1·00
786 $1.10 Nine-banded armadillo 1·00 1·25
787 $2 Agouti 1·75 2·50
788 $3 Humpback whale 4·50 5·00
MS789 Two sheets, each 103 × 72 mm. (a) $5 Mona monkey (vert). (b) $5 Iguana. Set of 2 sheets 11·00 14·00

1986. Appearance of Halley's Comet (2nd issue). Nos. 748/51 optd with T **447a** of Ghana.
790 5c. Nicholas Copernicus (astronomer) and Earl of Rosse's six foot reflector telescope 60 60
791 20c. "Sputnik I" orbiting Earth, 1957 80 50
792 40c. Tycho Brahe's notes and sketch of 1577 Comet 1·00 60
793 $4 Edmond Halley and 1682 Comet 5·00 6·00
MS794 102 × 70 mm. $5 Halley's Comet 4·00 5·50

1986. Christmas. As T **318a** of Grenada showing Walt Disney cartoon characters. Multicoloured.
795 25c. Chip n'Dale with hummingbird 50 15
796 30c. Robin delivering card to Mickey Mouse (vert) 50 20
797 50c. Piglet, Pooh and Jose Carioca on beach 65 30
798 60c. Grandma Duck feeding birds (vert) 75 40
799 70c. Cinderella and birds with mistletoe (vert) 80 50
800 $1.50 Huey, Dewey and Louie windsurfing 1·50 2·25
801 $3 Mickey Mouse and Morty on beach with turtle 1·75 5·00
802 $4 Kittens playing on piano (vert) 2·25 4·00
MS803 Two sheets, each 127 × 102 mm. (a) $5 Mickey Mouse and Willie the Whale. (b) $5 Bambi, Thumper and Blossom in snow (vert). Set of 2 sheets 8·00 11·50

1986. Olympic Games, Seoul, South Korea (1988). Multicoloured.
804 10c.+5c. Type **89** 75 40
805 50c+20c. Sailing 75 90

806 70c.+30c. Gymnastics 75 1·10
807 $2+$1 Horse trials 2·00 3·00
MS808 80 × 100 mm. $3+$1 Marathon 2·50 4·50

90 Aston-Martin "Volante" (1984)

1986. Centenary of Motoring. Multicoloured.
809 10c. Type **90** 25 25
810 30c. Jaguar "MK V" (1948) 45 45
811 60c. Nash "Ambassador" (1956) 60 65
812 70c. Toyota "Supra" (1984) 60 70
813 90c. Ferrari "Testarosa" (1985) 70 90
814 $1 BMW "501B" (1955) 70 95
815 $2 Mercedes-Benz "280 SL" (1968) 1·00 2·00
816 $3 Austro-Daimler "ADR8" (1932) 1·25 2·50
MS817 Two sheets, each 116 × 85 mm. (a) $5 Morgan "+8" (1977). (b) $5 Checker taxi. Set of 2 sheets 5·50 11·00

1986. Birth Centenary of Marc Chagall (artist). As T **321a** of Grenada, showing various paintings.
818/57 $1.10 × 40 multicoloured. Set of 40 28·00 28·00
MS858 Two sheets, each 110 × 95 mm. $5 × 10 multicoloured (each 104 × 89 mm). Imperf. Set of 10 sheets 28·00 28·00

1987. America's Cup Yachting Championship. As T **321b** of Grenada. Multicoloured.
859 25c. "Defender", 1895 60 40
860 45c. "Galatea", 1886 80 60
861 70c. "Azzurra", 1981 1·00 1·00
862 $4 "Australia II", 1983 2·00 3·50
MS863 113 × 83 mm. $5 "Columbia" defeating "Shamrock", 1899 (horiz) 5·00 7·00

1987. 500th Anniv (1992) of Discovery of America by Christopher Columbus (1st issue). As T **322** of Grenada. Multicoloured.
864 15c. Christopher Columbus 35 25
865 30c. Queen Isabella of Castile 40 30
866 50c. "Santa Maria" 60 50
867 60c. Claiming the New World for Spain 60 60
868 90c. Early Spanish map of Lesser Antilles 80 75
869 $1 King Ferdinand of Aragon 80 80
870 $2 Fort La Navidad (drawing by Columbus) 1·50 2·00
871 $3 Galley and Caribs, Hispaniola (drawing by Columbus) 2·00 2·50
MS872 Two sheets, 104 × 72 mm. (a) $5 Caribs pearl fishing. (b) $5 "Santa Maria" at anchor. Set of 2 sheets 8·00 11·00
See also Nos. 1191/5, 1224/32, 1366/74, 1494/1500 and 1519/20.

1987. Milestones of Transportation. As T **322a** of Grenada. Multicoloured.
873 10c. Saunders Roe "SRNI" (first hovercraft), 1959 65 30
874 15c. Bugatti "Royale" (largest car), 1931 70 35
875 30c. Aleksei Leonov and "Voskhod II" (first spacewalk), 1965 90 55
876 50c. C.S.S "Hunley" (first submarine to sink enemy ship), 1864 1·25 75
877 60c. Rolls Royce "Flying Bedstead" (first VTOL aircraft), 1954 1·50 85
878 70c. "Jenny Lind" (first mass produced locomotive class), 1847 1·60 1·25
879 90c. Duryea "Buggyaut" (first U.S petrol-driven car), 1893 1·75 1·25
880 $1.50 Steam locomotive, Metropolitan Railway, London (first underground line), 1863 2·50 2·75
881 $2 S.S. "Great Britain" (first transatlantic crossing by screw-steamship), 1843 3·00 3·25
882 $3 "Budweiser Rocket" (fastest car), 1979 3·25 3·75

1987. "Capex '87" International Stamp Exhibition, Toronto. Game Fishes. As T **323** of Grenada but horiz. Multicoloured.
883 6c. Yellow chub 15 15
884 30c. King mackerel 40 30
885 50c. Short-finned mako 55 55
886 60c. Dolphin (fish) 60 60
887 90c. Skipjack tuna ("Bonito") 75 75
888 $1.10 Cobia 1·00 1·25
889 $3 Tarpon 2·25 2·75
890 $4 Swordfish 2·50 3·25
MS891 Two sheets, each 100 × 70 mm. (a) $5 Spotted jewfish. (b) $5 Amberjack. Set of 2 sheets 8·00 11·00

1987. Centenary of Statue of Liberty (1986) (2nd issue). As T **323a** of Grenada. Multicoloured.
892 10c. Cleaning face of statue 20 20
893 15c. Commemorative lapel badges 30 30
894 25c. Band playing and statue 40 40
895 30c. Band on parade and statue 45 45
896 45c. Face of statue 50 50
897 50c. Cleaning head of statue (horiz) 55 55
898 60c. Models of statue (horiz) 65 65
899 70c. Small boat flotilla (horiz) 75 85
900 $1 Unveiling ceremony 85 90
901 $1.10 Statue and Manhattan skyline 90 1·00
902 $2 Parade of warships 1·75 2·00
903 $3 Making commemorative flags 1·90 2·25

1987. Great Scientific Discoveries. As T **325** of Grenada. Multicoloured.
904 60c. Newton medal 1·00 80
905 $1 Louis Daguerre (inventor of daguerreotype) 1·25 1·00
906 $2 Antoine Lavoisier and apparatus 2·25 3·00
907 $3 Rudolf Diesel and first oil engine 7·00 5·50
MS908 105 × 75 mm. $5 Halley's Comet 6·00 7·50
No. 907 is inscribed "JAMES WATT" in error.

1987. Bicentenary of U.S. Constitution. As T **327a** of Grenada. Multicoloured.
909 10c. Washington addressing delegates, Constitutional Convention 25 20
910 50c. Flag and State Seal, Georgia 85 75
911 60c. Capitol, Washington (vert) 85 80
912 $4 Thomas Jefferson (statesman) (vert) 3·25 6·00
MS913 105 × 75 mm. $5 Alexander Hamilton (New York delegate) (vert) 2·25 4·00

1987. "Hafnia '87" International Stamp Exhibition, Copenhagen. Designs as T **328** of Grenada, but horiz, illustrating Hans Christian Andersen's fairy tales. Multicoloured.
914 25c. Donald and Daisy Duck in "The Swineherd" 50 30
915 30c. Mickey Mouse, Donald and Daisy Duck in "What the Good Man Does is Always Right" 55 35
916 50c. Mickey and Minnie Mouse in "Little Tuk" 75 75
917 60c. Minnie Mouse and Ferdie in "The World's Fairest Rose" 75 75
918 70c. Mickey Mouse in "The Garden of Paradise" 80 80
919 $1.50 Goofy and Mickey Mouse in "The Naughty Boy" 2·00 2·25
920 $3 Goofy in "What the Moon Saw" 2·75 3·00
921 $4 Alice as "Thumbelina" 3·25 3·50
MS922 Two sheets, each 127 × 101 mm. (a) $5 Daisy Duck in "Hans Clodhopper". (b) $5 Aunt Matilda and Mickey Mouse in "Elder-Tree Mother". Set of 2 sheets 11·00 12·00

91 "The Virgin and Child with Saints Martin and Agnes"

92 Scout signalling with Semaphore Flags

1987. Christmas. Religious Paintings by El Greco. Multicoloured.
923 10c. Type **91** 40 15
924 50c. "St. Agnes" (detail from "The Virgin and Child with Saints Martin and Agnes") 1·25 75
925 60c. "The Annunciation" 1·25 75
926 $4 "The Holy Family with St. Anne" 4·75 7·25
MS927 75 × 101 mm. $5 "The Adoration of the Shepherds" 7·50 8·50

1988. Royal Ruby Wedding. As T **330a** of Grenada. Multicoloured.
928 20c. brown, black and green 50 15
929 30c. brown and black 50 20
930 $2 multicoloured 2·25 2·50
931 $3 multicoloured 2·50 3·25
MS932 76 × 100 mm. $5 multicoloured 4·50 5·00
DESIGNS: 20c. Queen Elizabeth II with Princess Anne, c. 1957; 30c. Wedding photograph, 1947; $2 Queen with Prince Charles and Princess Anne, c. 1955; $3 Queen Elizabeth (from photo by Tim Graham), 1980; $5 Princess Elizabeth in wedding dress, 1947.

1988. Olympic Games, Seoul. As T **331** of Grenada showing Walt Disney cartoon characters as Olympic competitors. Multicoloured.
933 1c. Minnie Mouse as rhythmic gymnast (horiz) 10 10
934 2c. Pete and Goofy as pankration wrestlers (horiz) 10 10
935 3c. Huey and Dewey as synchronized swimmers (horiz) 10 10
936 4c. Huey, Dewey and Louie in hoplite race (horiz) 10 10
937 5c. Clarabelle and Daisy Duck playing baseball (horiz) 10 10
938 10c. Goofy and Donald Duck in horse race (horiz) 10 10
939 $6 Donald Duck and Uncle Scrooge McDuck windsurfing (horiz) 4·50 5·50
940 $7 Mickey Mouse in chariot race (horiz) 4·75 5·50
MS941 Two sheets, each 127 × 101 mm. (a) $5 Mickey Mouse throwing discus in pentathalon. (b) $5 Donald Duck playing tennis. Set of 2 sheets 7·50 9·00

1988. World Scout Jamboree, Australia. Mult.
942 50c. Type **92** 50 35
943 70c. Canoeing 60 50
944 $1 Cooking over campfire (horiz) 70 65
945 $3 Scouts around campfire (horiz) 2·00 3·00
MS946 110 × 77 mm. $5 Erecting tent (horiz) 4·00 4·50

1988. Birds. As T **334** of Grenada. Mult.
947 20c. Yellow-crowned night heron 30 25
948 25c. Brown pelican 30 25
949 45c. Audubon's shearwater 40 35
950 60c. Red-footed booby 50 45
951 70c. Bridled tern 55 50
952 90c. Red-billed tropic bird 70 70
953 $3 Blue-winged teal 1·75 2·25
954 $4 Sora crake ("Sora") 2·00 2·75
MS955 Two sheets, each 105 × 75 mm. (a) $5 Purple-throated carib. (b) $5 Little blue heron. Set of 2 sheets 6·00 6·50

1988. 500th Birth Anniv of Titian (artist). As T **166a** of Gambia. Multicoloured.
956 15c. "Man with Blue Eyes" 15 15
957 30c. "The Three Ages of Man" (detail) 20 20
958 60c. "Don Diego Mendoza" 35 35
959 75c. "Emperor Charles V seated" 50 50
960 $1 "A Young Man in a Fur" 60 60
961 $2 "Tobias and the Angel" 1·10 1·40
962 $3 "Pietro Bembo" 1·60 1·90
963 $4 "Pier Luigi Farnese" 1·75 2·25
MS964 110 × 95 mm. (a) $5 "Sacred and Profane Love" (detail). (b) $5 "Venus and Adonis" (detail). Set of 2 sheets 7·00 8·00

1988. Airships. As T **336** of Grenada. Multicoloured.
965 10c. "Hindenburg" over Sugarloaf Mountain, Rio de Janeiro, 1937 (horiz) 70 30
966 20c. "Hindenburg" over New York, 1937 (horiz) 85 30
967 30c. U.S. Navy "K" Class airships on Atlantic escort duty, 1944 (horiz) 95 35
968 40c. "Hindenburg" approaching Lakehurst, 1937 1·00 45
969 60c. "Graf Zeppelin" and "Hindenburg" over Germany, 1936 1·25 60
970 70c. "Hindenburg" and "Los Angeles" moored at Lakehurst, 1936 (horiz) 1·25 70
971 $1 "Graf Zeppelin II" over Dover, 1939 1·25 85
972 $2 "Ersatz Deutschland" on scheduled passenger flight, 1912 (horiz) 1·60 1·60
973 $3 "Graf Zeppelin" over Dome of the Rock, Jerusalem, 1931 (horiz) 2·50 2·25
974 $4 "Hindenburg" over Olympic stadium, Berlin, 1936 (horiz) 2·50 2·25
MS975 Two sheets (a) 76 × 95 mm. $5 LZ-127 "Graf Zeppelin", 1933. (b) 95 × 76 mm. $5 LZ-127 "Graf Zeppelin", 1931 (horiz). Set of 2 sheets 8·00 10·00

93 Bambi and his mother

1988. Disney Animal Cartoon Films.
976/1029 30c. × 54 multicoloured. Set of 54 17·00 15·00
MS1030 Six sheets, each 127 × 102 mm. $5 × 6 multicoloured. Set of 6 sheets 28·00 30·00
DESIGNS: Scenes from "Bambi", "Dumbo" $5 (vert), "Lady and the Tramp" $5 (vert), "The Aristocats", "The Fox and the Hound" and "101 Dalmatians".

1988. "Sydpex '88" National Stamp Exhibition, Sydney and 60th Birthday of Mickey Mouse. As T **337** of Grenada. Multicoloured.
1031 1c. Mickey Mouse conducting at Sydney Opera House 10 10
1032 2c. Mickey Mouse and Donald Duck at Ayers Rock 10 10
1033 3c. Goofy and Mickey Mouse on sheep station 10 10
1034 4c. Goofy and Mickey Mouse at Lone Pine Koala Sanctuary 10 10
1035 5c. Mickey Mouse, Donald Duck and Goofy playing Australian football 10 10
1036 10c. Mickey Mouse and Goofy camel racing 10 10
1037 $5 Donald Duck and his nephews bowling 4·50 5·00
1038 $6 Mickey Mouse with America's Cup trophy and "Australia II" (yacht) 5·50 6·00
MS1039 Two sheets, each 127 × 102 mm. (a) $5 Goofy diving on Great Barrier Reef. (b) $5 Donald Duck, Mickey and Minnie Mouse at beach barbecue. Set of 2 sheets 7·50 9·50

1988. Flowering Trees and Shrubs. As T **339** of Grenada. Multicoloured.
1040 10c. Potato tree (vert) 15 15
1041 20c. Wild cotton 15 15
1042 30c. Shower of gold (vert) 20 20
1043 60c. Napoleon's button (vert) 35 30
1044 90c. Geiger tree 60 70
1045 $1 Fern tree 70 80
1046 $2 French cashew 1·25 2·00
1047 $4 Amherstia (vert) 2·00 3·00
MS1048 Two sheets, each 117 × 88 mm. (a) $5 African tulip tree (vert). (b) $5 Swamp immortelle. Set of 2 sheets 4·25 5·50

1988. Cars. As T **335** of Grenada. Mult.
1049 $2 Doble "Series E", 1925 1·40 1·25
1050 $2 Alvis "12/50", 1926 1·40 1·25
1051 $2 Sunbeam 3-litre, 1927 1·40 1·25
1052 $2 Franklin "Airman", 1928 1·40 1·25
1053 $2 Delage "D8S", 1929 1·40 1·25
1054 $2 Mors, 1897 1·40 1·25
1055 $2 Peerless "Green Dragon", 1904 1·40 1·25
1056 $2 Pope-Hartford, 1909 1·40 1·25
1057 $2 Daniels "Submarine Speedstar", 1920 1·40 1·25
1058 $2 McFarlan 9.3 litre, 1922 1·40 1·25
1059 $2 Frazer Nash "Lemans" replica, 1949 1·40 1·25
1060 $2 Pegaso "Z102", 1953 1·40 1·25
1061 $2 Siata "Spyder V-8", 1953 1·40 1·25
1062 $2 Kurtis-Offenhauser, 1953 1·40 1·25
1063 $2 Kaiser-Darrin, 1954 1·40 1·25
1064 $2 Tracta, 1930 1·40 1·25
1065 $2 Maybach "Zeppelin", 1932 1·40 1·25
1066 $2 Railton "Light Sports", 1934 1·40 1·25
1067 $2 Hotchkiss, 1936 1·40 1·25
1068 $2 Mercedes-Benz "W163", 1939 1·40 1·25
1069 $2 Aston-Martin "Vantage V8", 1982 1·40 1·25
1070 $2 Porsche "956", 1982 1·40 1·25
1071 $2 Lotus "Esprit Turbo", 1983 1·40 1·25
1072 $2 McLaren "MP4/2", 1984 1·40 1·25
1073 $2 Mercedes-Benz "190E 2.3-16", 1985 1·40 1·25
1074 $2 Ferrari "250 GT Lusso", 1963 1·40 1·25
1075 $2 Porsche "904", 1964 1·40 1·25
1076 $2 Volvo "P1800", 1967 1·40 1·25
1077 $2 McLaren-Chevrolet "M8D", 1970 1·40 1·25
1078 $2 Jaguar "XJ6", 1981 1·40 1·25

1988. "Mickey's Christmas Parade". As T **340a** of Grenada showing Walt Disney cartoon characters. Multicoloured.
1079 $1 Dumbo 65 65
1080 $1 Goofy as Father Christmas 65 65
1081 $1 Minnie Mouse waving from window 65 65
1082 $1 Clarabelle, Mordie and Ferdie watching parade 65 65
1083 $1 Donald Duck's nephews 65 65
1084 $1 Donald Duck as drummer 65 65
1085 $1 Toy soldiers 65 65
1086 $1 Mickey Mouse on wooden horse 65 65
MS1087 Two sheets, each 127 × 102 mm. (a) $7 Peter Pan and Captain Hook on float (horiz). (b) $7 Mickey Mouse as Father Christmas and Donald Duck in carnival train (horiz). Set of 2 sheets 10·00 11·00

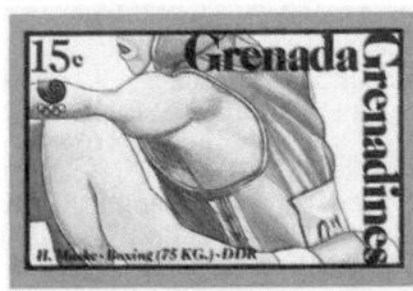

94 Middleweight Boxing (Gold, Henry Maske, East Germany)

1989. Olympic Medal Winners, Seoul (1988). Multicoloured.

1088 15c. Type **94** 40 20
1089 50c. Freestyle wrestling (130 kg) (Bronze, Andreas Schroeder, East Germany) 60 40
1090 60c. Women's team gymnastics (Bronze, East Germany) 70 50
1091 75c. Platform diving (Gold, Greg Louganis, U.S.A.) 80 60
1092 $1 Freestyle wrestling (52 kg) (Gold, Mitsuru Sato, Japan) 90 80
1093 $2 Men's freestyle 4 × 200 m relay swimming (Bronze, West Germany) 1·40 1·40
1094 $3 Men's 5000 m (Silver, Dieter Baumann, West Germany) 1·60 2·00
1095 $4 Women's heptathlon (Gold, Jackie Joyner-Kersee, U.S.A.) 2·00 2·50
MS1096 Two sheets, each 70 × 100 mm. (a) $6 Weightlifting (67.5 kg) (Gold, Joachim Kunz, East Germany). (b) $6 Team Three-Day Event (Gold, West Germany). Set of 2 sheets 6·50 8·50

1989. Japanese Art. Paintings by Hiroshige. As T **177a** of Gambia. Multicoloured.

1097 15c. "Crossing the Oi at Shimada by Ferry" 25 25
1098 20c. "Daimyo and Entourage at Arai" 30 30
1099 45c. "Cargo Portage through Goyu" 50 50
1100 75c. "Snowfall at Fujigawa" 75 75
1101 $1 "Horses for the Emperor at Chirifu" 85 85
1102 $2 "Rainfall at Tsuchiyama" 1·60 1·60
1103 $3 "An Inn at Ishibe" 2·25 2·25
1104 $4 "On the Shore of Lake Biwa at Otsu" 2·75 2·75
MS1105 Two sheets, each 102 × 78 mm. (a) $5 "Fishing Village of Yokkaichi on the Mie". (b) $5 "Pilgrimage to Atsuta Shrine at Miya". Set of 2 sheets 4·75 7·00

1989. World Cup Football Championship, Italy (1990) (1st issue). As T **345a** of Grenada. Mult.

1106 15c. World Cup trophy 50 20
1107 20c. Flags of Argentina (winners 1986) and International Federation of Football Associations (FIFA) (horiz) 1·00 20
1108 45c. Franz Beckenbauer (West Germany) with World Cup, 1974 1·00 35
1109 75c. Flags of Italy (winners 1982) and FIFA (horiz) 1·50 55
1110 $1 Pele (Brazil) with Jules Rimet trophy 1·50 85
1111 $2 Flags of West Germany (winners 1974) and FIFA (horiz) 2·00 2·00
1112 $3 Flags of Brazil (winners 1970) and FIFA (horiz) 2·00 2·75
1113 $4 Jules Rimet trophy and Brazil players 2·00 2·75
MS1114 (a) 100 × 81 mm. $6 Goalkeeper (horiz). (b) 66 × 95 mm. $6 Péle with Jules Rimet trophy. Set of 2 sheets 8·50 9·00

See also Nos. 1285/9.

1989. North American Railway Locomotives. As T **342** of Grenada. Multicoloured.

1115 $2 Morris & Essex Railroad "Dover", 1841, U.S.A. 1·50 1·50
1116 $2 Baltimore & Ohio Railroad No. 57 "Memnon", 1848, U.S.A. 1·50 1·50
1117 $2 Camden & Amboy Railroad "John Stevens", 1849, U.S.A. 1·50 1·50
1118 $2 Lawrence Machine Shop "Lawrence", 1853, U.S.A. 1·50 1·50
1119 $2 South Carolina Railroad "James S. Corry", 1859, U.S.A. 1·50 1·50
1120 $2 Mine Hill & Schuylkill Haven Railroad flexible beam No. 3, 1860, U.S.A. 1·50 1·50
1121 $2 Delaware, Lackawanna & Western Railroad "Montrose", 1861, U.S.A. 1·50 1·50
1122 $2 Central Pacific Railroad No. 68 "Pequop", 1868, U.S.A. 1·50 1·50
1123 $2 Boston & Providence Railroad "Daniel Nason", 1863, U.S.A. 1·50 1·50
1124 $2 Morris & Essex Railroad "Joe Scranton", 1870, U.S.A. 1·50 1·50
1125 $2 Central Railroad of New Jersey No. 124, 1871, U.S.A. 1·50 1·50
1126 $2 Baldwin tramway steam locomotive, 1876, U.S.A. 1·50 1·50

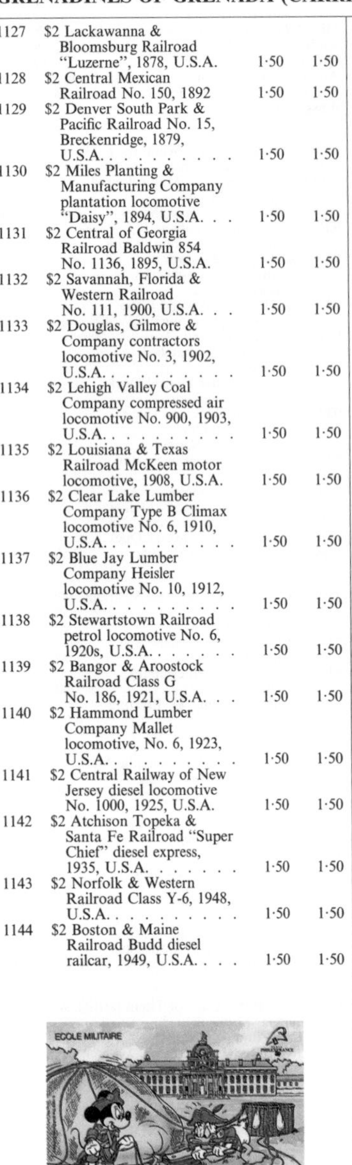

1127 $2 Lackawanna & Bloomsburg Railroad "Luzerne", 1878, U.S.A. 1·50 1·50
1128 $2 Central Mexican Railroad No. 150, 1892 1·50 1·50
1129 $2 Denver South Park & Pacific Railroad No. 15, Breckenridge, 1879, U.S.A. 1·50 1·50
1130 $2 Miles Planting & Manufacturing Company plantation locomotive "Daisy", 1894, U.S.A. 1·50 1·50
1131 $2 Central of Georgia Railroad Baldwin 854 No. 1136, 1895, U.S.A. 1·50 1·50
1132 $2 Savannah, Florida & Western Railroad No. 111, 1900, U.S.A. 1·50 1·50
1133 $2 Douglas, Gilmore & Company contractors locomotive No. 3, 1902, U.S.A. 1·50 1·50
1134 $2 Lehigh Valley Coal Company compressed air locomotive No. 900, 1903, U.S.A. 1·50 1·50
1135 $2 Louisiana & Texas Railroad McKeen motor locomotive, 1908, U.S.A. 1·50 1·50
1136 $2 Clear Lake Lumber Company Type B Climax locomotive No. 6, 1910, U.S.A. 1·50 1·50
1137 $2 Blue Jay Lumber Company Heisler locomotive No. 10, 1912, U.S.A. 1·50 1·50
1138 $2 Stewartstown Railroad petrol locomotive No. 6, 1920s, U.S.A. 1·50 1·50
1139 $2 Bangor & Aroostock Railroad Class G No. 186, 1921, U.S.A. 1·50 1·50
1140 $2 Hammond Lumber Company Mallet locomotive, No. 6, 1923, U.S.A. 1·50 1·50
1141 $2 Central Railway of New Jersey diesel locomotive No. 1000, 1925, U.S.A. 1·50 1·50
1142 $2 Atchison Topeka & Santa Fe Railroad "Super Chief" diesel express, 1935, U.S.A. 1·50 1·50
1143 $2 Norfolk & Western Railroad Class Y-6, 1948, U.S.A. 1·50 1·50
1144 $2 Boston & Maine Railroad Budd diesel railcar, 1949, U.S.A. 1·50 1·50

94a Mickey Mouse and Donald Duck at Ecole Militaire Inflating Balloon

1989. "Philexfrance '89" International Stamp Exn, Paris. Designs showing Walt Disney cartoon characters in Paris. Multicoloured.

1145 1c. Type **94a** 10 10
1146 2c. Mickey and Minnie Mouse on river boat passing Conciergerie 10 10
1147 3c. Mickey Mouse at Hotel de Ville (vert) 10 10
1148 4c. Mickey Mouse at Genie of the Bastille monument (vert) 10 10
1149 5c. Mickey and Minnie Mouse arriving at Opera House 10 10
1150 10c. Mickey and Minnie Mouse on tandem in Luxembourg Gardens 10 10
1151 $5 Mickey Mouse in aeroplane over L'Arch de La Defense (vert) 5·50 6·50
1152 $6 Mickey Mouse at Place Vendome (vert) 5·50 6·50
MS1153 Two sheets, each 127 × 102 mm. (a) $6 Mickey and Minnie Mouse on scooter in Place de la Concorde. (b) $6 Donald Duck, Mickey and Minnie Mouse in balloon over Versailles. Set of 2 sheets 11·00 13·00

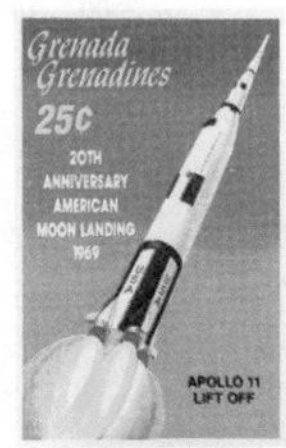

95 Launch of "Apollo 11"

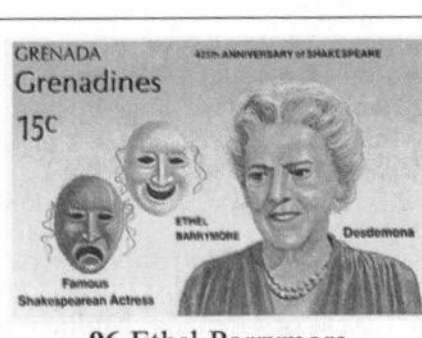

96 Ethel Barrymore

1989. 20th Anniv of First Manned Landing on Moon. Multicoloured.

1154 25c. Type **95** 30 30
1155 50c. Splashdown (horiz) 50 50
1156 60c. Modules in space 60 60
1157 75c. Aldrin setting up experiment (horiz) 70 70
1158 $1 "Apollo 11" leaving Earth orbit (horiz) 80 80
1159 $2 Moving "Apollo 11" to launch site 1·60 1·90
1160 $3 Lunar module "Eagle" leaving Moon (horiz) 2·00 2·50
1161 $4 "Eagle" landing on Moon 2·25 2·75
MS1162 (a) 71 × 100 mm. $5 Armstrong stepping onto Moon. (b) 101 × 72 mm. $5 Armstrong's footprint on Moon. Set of 2 sheets 6·50 8·00

1989. Fungi. As T **348** of Grenada. Mult.

1163 6c. "Agaricus purpurellus" (incorrectly inscr "Collybia aurea") 35 25
1164 10c. "Podaxis pistillaris" 35 25
1165 20c. "Hygrocybe firma" 55 45
1166 30c. "Agaricus rufoaurantiacus" 65 55
1167 75c. "Leptonia howellii" 1·40 1·40
1168 $2 "Marasmiellus purpureus" 2·50 2·75
1169 $3 "Marasmius trinitatis" 3·00 3·25
1170 $4 "Collybia aurea" (incorrectly inscr "Hygrocybe martinicensis") 3·25 3·50
MS1171 Two sheets, each 56 × 71 mm. (a) $6 "Lentinus crinitus" (incorrectly inscr "Agaricus purpurellus"). (b) $6 "Hygrocybe martinicensis" (incorrectly inscr "Lentinus crinitus"). Set of 2 sheets 12·00 13·00

1989. Butterflies. As T **350** of Grenada. Mult.

1172 25c. "Battus polydamas" (inscr "Papilio androgeus") 40 40
1173 35c. "Phoebis sennae" 45 45
1174 45c. "Hamadryas feronia" 55 55
1175 50c. "Cynthia cardui" 55 55
1176 75c. "Ascia monuste" 80 80
1177 90c. "Eurema lisa" 90 90
1178 $2 "Aphrissa statira" 2·00 2·00
1179 $3 "Hypolimnas misippus" 2·50 2·50
MS1180 Two sheets, each 87 × 115 mm. (a) $6 "Anartia amathea". (b) $6 "Pseudolycaena marsyas". Set of 2 sheets 9·00 11·00

1989. 425th Birth Anniv of Shakespeare. Shakespearean Actors. Multicoloured.

1181 15c. Type **96** 35 25
1182 $1.10 Richard Burton 1·50 1·25
1183 $2 John Barrymore 2·25 2·25
1184 $3 Paul Robeson 2·50 2·75
MS1185 103 × 77 mm. $6 Bando Tamasaburo and Nakamura Kanzaburo 4·50 5·50

1989. Musicians. Multicoloured.

1186 10c. Type **97** 35 25
1187 25c. Jimmy Hendrix 55 40
1188 75c. Mighty Sparrow 70 70
1189 $4 Katsutoji Kineya 3·00 4·00
MS1190 103 × 77 mm. $6 Kurt Weill 4·25 4·75

97a Arawaks canoeing

1989. 500th Anniv (1992) of Discovery of America by Columbus (2nd issue). Pre-Columbian Arawak Society. As T **247** of Antigua. Multicoloured.

1191 15c. Type **97a** 25 25
1192 75c. Family and campfire 75 75
1193 90c. Using stone tools 95 95
1194 $3 Eating and drinking 2·50 3·00
MS1195 84 × 87 mm. $6 Making fire 3·50 4·25

1989. "World Stamp Expo '89" International Stamp Exhibition, Washington. Designs showing Walt Disney cartoon characters illustrating proverbs from "Poor Richard's Almanack". As T **352** of Grenada. Multicoloured.

1196 1c. Uncle Scrooge McDuck with gold coins in sinking boat 10 10
1197 2c. Robin Hood shooting apple off Friar Tuck 10 10
1198 3c. Winnie the Pooh with honey 10 10
1199 4c. Goofy, Minnie Mouse and Donald Duck exercising 10 10
1200 5c. Pinnochio holding Jimminy Cricket 10 10
1201 6c. Huey and Dewey putting up wallpaper 10 10
1202 8c. Mickey Mouse asleep in storm 15 10
1203 10c. Mickey Mouse as Benjamin Franklin selling "Pennsylvania Gazette" 15 10
1204 $5 Mickey Mouse with chicken, recipe book and egg 4·00 5·00
1205 $6 Mickey Mouse missing carriage 4·50 5·00
MS1206 Two sheets, each 127 × 102 mm. (a) $6 Mickey Mouse bowing. (b) $6 Mickey Mouse delivering basket of food (vert). Set of 2 sheets 10·50 11·00

1990. Christmas. Paintings by Rubens. As T **352a** of Grenada. Multicoloured.

1207 10c. "The Annunciation" 35 15
1208 15c. "The Flight of the Holy Family into Egypt" 40 15
1209 25c. "The Presentation in the Temple" 55 15
1210 45c. "The Holy Family under the Apple Tree" 70 25
1211 $2 "Madonna and Child with Saints" 2·00 2·50
1212 $4 "The Virgin and Child enthroned with Saints" 3·00 4·00
1213 $5 "The Holy Family" 3·00 4·00
MS1214 Two sheets, each 70 × 95 mm. (a) $5 "The Adoration of the Magi" (sketch). (b) $5 "The Adoration of the Magi". Set of 2 sheets 12·00 14·00

1990. "EXPO '90" International Garden and Greenery Exhibition, Osaka. Caribbean Orchids. As T **354** of Grenada. Multicoloured.

1215 15c. "Brassocattleya" Thalie 30 30
1216 20c. "Odontocidium" Tigersun 35 35
1217 50c. "Odontioda" Hambuhren 55 55
1218 75c. "Paphiopedium" Delrosi 75 75
1219 $1 "Vuylstekeara" Yokara 95 95
1220 $2 "Paphiopedilum" Geelong 1·75 2·00
1221 $3 "Wilsonara" Tigerwood 2·00 2·25
1222 $4 "Cymbidium" Ormoulu 2·50 2·75
MS1223 Two sheets, each 98 × 68 mm. (a) $6 "Odontonia" Sappho. (b) $6 "Cymbidium" Vieux Rose. Set of 2 sheets 11·00 11·50

1990. 500th Anniv (1992) of Discovery of America by Columbus (3rd issue). New World Natural History—Insects. As T **354a** of Grenada. Mult.

1224 35c. "Dynastes hercules" (beetle) 35 35
1225 40c. "Chalcolepidius porcatus" (beetle) 35 35
1226 50c. "Acrocinus longimanus" (beetle) 40 40
1227 60c. "Battus polydamas" (butterfly) 75 75
1228 $1 "Orthemis ferruginea" (skimmer) 95 95
1229 $2 "Psiloptera variolosa" (beetle) 1·60 1·75
1230 $3 "Hypolimnas misippus" (butterfly) 2·50 2·75
1231 $4 Scarab beetle 2·50 2·75
MS1232 Two sheets, each 102 × 70 mm. (a) $6 "Calpodes ethlius" (butterfly). (b) "Danaus plexippus" (butterfly). Set of 2 sheets 8·50 9·50

1990. Wildlife. As T **254** of Antigua. Mult.

1233 5c. West Indies giant rice rat 20 20
1234 25c. Agouti 35 35
1235 30c. Humpback whale 70 65
1236 40c. Pilot whale 70 65
1237 $1 Spotted dolphin 95 95
1238 $2 Egyptian mongoose 1·75 2·00
1239 $3 Brazilian tree porcupine 2·25 2·75
1240 $4 American manatee 2·50 3·00
MS1241 Two sheets, each 107 × 80 mm. (a) $6 Caribbean monk seal. (b) $6 Egyptian mongoose (different). Set of 2 sheets 8·00 9·00

1990. 50th Anniv of Second World War. As T **354b** of Grenada. Multicoloured.

1242 6c. British tanks in France, 1939 30 30
1243 10c. Operation "Crusader", North Africa, 1941 30 30
1244 20c. Retreat of the Afrika Corps, 1942 40 40
1245 45c. American landing on Aleutian Islands, 1943 50 50
1246 50c. U.S marines landing on Tarawa, 1943 55 55
1247 60c. U.S army entering Rome, 1944 60 60
1248 75c. U.S tanks crossing River Seine, 1944 70 70
1249 $1 Battle of the Bulge, 1944 95 95

97 Buddy Holly

1250 $5 American infantry in Italy, 1945 . . . . 3·00 3·50
1251 $6 B-29 "Enola Gay" dropping atomic bomb on Hiroshima, 1945 . . . . 3·50 3·50
MS1252 112 × 84 mm. $6 St. Paul's Cathedral in London Blitz, 1940 4·00 5·00

1990. "Stamp World London '90" International Stamp Exhibition. As T **193** of Gambia showing Walt Disney cartoon characters at Shakespeare sites. Multicoloured.
1253 15c. Daisy Duck at Ann Hathaway's Cottage (horiz) 40 20
1254 30c. Minnie and Bill Mouse at Shakespeare's birthplace, Stratford . . . 55 35
1255 50c. Minnie Mouse in front of Mary Arden's house, Wilmcote 75 70
1256 60c. Mickey Mouse leaning on hedge in New Place gardens, Stratford (horiz) 90 90
1257 $1 Mickey Mouse walking in New Place gardens, Stratford (horiz) . . . . 1·25 1·25
1258 $2 Mickey Mouse carrying books in Scholars Lane, Stratford . . . . 2·25 2·50
1259 $4 Mickey Mouse and Royal Shakespeare Theatre, Stratford . . . . 3·25 4·00
1260 $5 Ludwig von Drake teaching Mickey Mouse at the Stratford Grammar School (horiz) . . . . . 3·25 4·00
MS1261 Two sheets, each 126 × 101 mm. (a) $6 Mickey Mouse as Shakespeare. (b) $6 Mickey and Minnie Mouse in rowing boat on River Avon, Stratford (horiz). Set of 2 sheets 11·00 12·00

1990. 90th Birthday of Queen Elizabeth the Queen Mother. As T **194** of Gambia, showing photographs 1970–79.
1262 $2 Queen Mother wearing pink hat and coat . . . . 1·10 1·40
1263 $2 Prince Charles and Queen Mother at Garter ceremony . . . . 1·10 1·40
1264 $2 Queen Mother in blue floral outfit . . . . 1·10 1·40
MS1265 90 × 75 mm. $6 Queen Mother in Garter robes . . . . 4·25 5·00

1990. Birds. As T **358** of Grenada, but vert. Multicoloured.
1267 25c. Yellow-bellied seedeater 30 30
1268 45c. Carib grackle 50 50
1269 50c. Black-whiskered vireo 55 55
1270 75c. Bananaquit 70 70
1271 $1 White-collared swift . . . 95 95
1272 $2 Yellow-bellied elaenia . . 1·50 1·50
1273 $3 Blue-hooded euphonia 2·00 2·00
1274 $5 Eared dove . . . . . . 3·25 3·25
MS1275 Two sheets, each 101 × 72 mm. (a) $6 Mangrove cuckoo. (b) $6 Scaly-breasted thrasher. Set of 2 sheets . . . 8·50 10·00

1990. Crustaceans. As T **359** of Grenada. Mult.
1276 10c. Slipper lobster 20 20
1277 25c. Green reef crab 30 30
1278 65c. Caribbean lobsterette 60 60
1279 75c. Blind deep sea lobster 70 70
1280 $1 Flattened crab 95 95
1281 $2 Ridged slipper lobster . . 1·75 2·00
1282 $3 Land crab . . . . 2·25 2·75
1283 $4 Mountain crab . . . . . 2·50 2·75
MS1284 Two sheets, each 108 × 76 mm. (a) $6 Caribbean king crab. (b) $6 Purse crab. Set of 2 sheets . . . . 8·00 10·00

15c WORLD CUP 1990 Grenada Grenadines

98 Lineker, England

1990. World Cup Football Championship, Italy (2nd issue). Multicoloured.
1285 15c. Type **98** 25 25
1286 45c. Burruchaga, Argentina 45 45
1287 $2 Hysen, Sweden . . . . . 1·75 2·25
1288 $4 Sang Ho, South Korea 2·75 3·75
MS1289 Two sheets, each 76 × 90 mm. (a) $6 Ramos, U.S.A. (b) $6 Stojkovic, Yugoslavia. Set of 2 sheets . . . . 8·50 9·50

1990. Olympic Games, Barcelona (1992). As T **195a** of Gambia. Multicoloured.
1290 10c. Boxing 10 10
1291 25c. Olympic flame 20 20
1292 50c. Football 40 40
1293 75c. Discus throwing . . . 60 60
1294 $1 Pole vaulting 85 85
1295 $2 Show jumping . . . . . 1·75 2·00
1296 $4 Women's basketball . . . 3·50 3·75
1297 $5 Men's gymnastics . . . . 3·00 3·75
MS1298 Two sheets. (a) 101 × 70 mm. $6 Sailboards. (b) 70 × 101 mm. $6 Decathlon. Set of 2 sheets . . . . 8·50 9·50

1991. 350th Death Anniv of Rubens. As T **195c** of Gambia. Multicoloured.
1299 5c. "Adam and Eve" (Eve detail) (vert) 30 20
1300 15c. "Esther before Ahasuerus" (detail) . . . 50 20
1301 25c. "Adam and Eve" (Adam detail) (vert) . . . 60 25
1302 50c. "Expulsion from Eden" 90 60
1303 $1 "Cain slaying Abel" (detail) (vert) . . . . . . 1·60 1·10
1304 $2 "Lot's Flight" . . . . . 2·25 2·25
1305 $4 "Samson and Delilah" (detail) . . . . 3·50 4·00
1306 $5 "Abraham and Melchizedek" . . . . . . 3·75 4·00
MS1307 Two sheets, each 101 × 71 mm. (a) $6 "The Meeting of David and Abigail" (detail). (b) $6 "Daniel in the Lions' Den" (detail). Set of 2 sheets . . . . 10·00 12·00

1991. Coral Reef Fishes. As T **357** of Grenada. Multicoloured.
1308 15c. Barred hamlet 50 25
1309 35c. Long-spined squirrelfish 80 50
1310 45c. Red-spotted hawkfish 85 60
1311 75c. Bigeye . . . . 1·25 1·00
1312 $1 Balloonfish ("Spiny puffer") . . . . 1·50 1·25
1313 $2 Small-mouth grunt . . . 2·25 2·50
1314 $3 Harlequin bass . . . . . 2·75 3·25
1315 $4 Creole fish . . . . 3·00 3·50
MS1316 Two sheets, each 103 × 72 mm. (a) $6 Copper sweeper. (b) $6 Royal gramma ("Fairy Basslet"). Set of 2 sheets 8·50 10·00

Christmas 1990 10c M.J. Hummel * GRENADA * GRENADINES

99 Angel with Star and Lantern

5c Brassia maculata GRENADA GRENADINES

100 "Brassia maculata"

1991. Christmas (1990). Hummel Figurines. Multicoloured.
1317 10c. Type **99** 30 10
1318 15c. Christ Child and Angel playing mandolin 40 15
1319 25c. Shepherd 55 25
1320 50c. Angel with trumpet and lantern . . . . 1·00 50
1321 $1 Nativity scene . . . . . 1·60 95
1322 $2 Christ Child and Angel holding candle . . . . . 2·50 2·50
1323 $4 Angel with baskets . . . 3·50 4·25
1324 $5 Angels singing . . . . . 3·75 4·25
MS1325 Two sheets, each 99 × 122 mm. (a) $6 As No. 1318; 40c. As No. 1320; 60c. As No. 1321; $3 As No. 1324. (b) 20c. As Type **99**; 30c. As No. 1319; 75c. As No. 1322; $6 As No. 1323. Set of 2 sheets . . . . 10·00 11·00

1991. Orchids. Multicoloured.
1326 5c. Type **100** 30 30
1327 10c. "Oncidium lanceanum" 30 30
1328 15c. "Broughtonia sanguinea" 35 20
1329 25c. "Diacrium bicornutum" 40 20
1330 35c. "Cattleya labiata" . . . 40 20
1331 45c. "Epidendrum fragrans" 50 25
1332 50c. "Oncidium papilio" . . 55 30
1333 75c. "Neocogniauxia monophylla" 70 50
1334 $1 "Epidendrum polybulbon" 80 70
1335 $2 "Spiranthes speciosa" . . 1·40 1·40
1336 $4 "Epidendrum ciliare" . . 2·25 2·75
1337 $5 "Phais tankervilliae" . . 2·50 3·00
1338 $10 "Brassia caudata" . . . 4·50 5·00
1339 $20 "Brassavola cordata" . . 9·25 11·00

1991. Butterflies. As T **363** of Grenada. Mult.
1340 5c. Crimson-patched longwing 40 30
1341 10c. "Morpho helena" . . . 40 30
1342 15c. "Morpho sulkowskyi" 55 35
1343 20c. "Dynastor napoleon" 60 40
1344 25c. "Pieridae callinira" . . 60 45
1345 30c. "Anartia amathea" . . 65 50
1346 35c. "Heliconiidae dido" . . 65 50
1347 45c. "Papilionidae columbus" 75 65
1348 50c. "Nymphalidae praeneste" 85 70
1349 60c. "Panacea prola" . . . 1·00 80
1350 75c. "Dryas julia" . . . . . 1·00 90
1351 $1 "Papilionidae orthosilaus" . . . . . . 1·25 1·10
1352 $2 "Pyrrhopyge cometes" 1·75 2·00
1353 $3 "Papilionidae paeon" . . 2·00 2·50
1354 $4 "Morpho cypris" . . . . 2·50 3·00
1355 $5 Choringa . . . . 3·00 3·25
MS1356 Four sheets, each 118 × 80 mm. (a) $6 "Danaus plexippus". (b) $6 "Caligo idomenides". (c) $6 "Nymphalidae amydon". (d) $6 "Papilio childrenae". Set of 4 sheets . . 15·00 15·00

Grenada GRENADINES 10c DEVELOP ALTERNATE TRANSPORTATION

101 Donald and Daisy Duck with Solar-powered Car

1991. Ecology Conservation. Walt Disney cartoon characters. Multicoloured.
1357 10c. Type **101** 60 20
1358 15c. Goofy saving water . . 70 20
1359 25c. Donald and Daisy on nature hike 90 35
1360 45c. Donald Duck returning chick to nest . . . . . . 1·25 55
1361 $1 Donald Duck and balloons . . . . 2·00 1·25
1362 $2 Minnie Mouse and Daisy Duck on hot day . . . . 3·00 2·75
1363 $4 Mickey's nephews cleaning beach . . . . . 3·75 4·25
1364 $5 Donald Duck on pedal generator . . . . 3·75 4·25
MS1365 Three sheets, each 127 × 102 mm. (a) $6 Hiawatha and felled forest. (b) $6 Donald Duck recycling (vert). (c) $6 Mickey Mouse with Arbor Day notice. Set of 3 sheets . . . . 14·00 15·00

1991. 500th Anniv (1992) of Discovery of America by Columbus (4th issue). History of Exploration. As T **363a** of Grenada. Multicoloured.
1366 15c. Magellan's "Vitoria" rounding Cape Horn, 1519–21 . . . . 1·00 50
1367 20c. Drake's Golden Hind, 1577–80 . . . . 1·40 50
1368 50c. Cook's H.M.S "Resolution", 1768–71 . . 2·00 90
1369 60c. Douglas World Cruiser seaplane, 1924 . . . . . 2·00 80
1370 $1 "Sputnik I" satellite, 1957 . . . . 2·00 1·00
1371 $2 Gagarin's space flight, 1961 . . . . 2·25 2·25
1372 $4 Glenn's space flight, 1962 2·50 3·50
1373 $5 Space shuttle, 1981 . . . 3·00 3·50
MS1374 Two sheets. (a) 105 × 78 mm. $6 Bow of "Pinta" (vert). (b) 78 × 105 mm. $6 Fleet of Columbus. Set of 2 sheets . . 8·00 10·00

1991. "Phila Nippon '91" International Stamp Exhibition, Tokyo. As T **198c** of Gambia but horiz showing Walt Disney cartoon characters in Japanese scenes. Multicoloured.
1375 15c. Minnie Mouse with silkworms 65 20
1376 30c. Mickey, Minnie, Morty and Ferdie at Torii Gate 85 35
1377 50c. Donald Duck and Mickey Mouse trying origami . . . . 1·25 60
1378 60c. Mickey and Minnie diving for pearls . . . . 1·40 70
1379 $1 Minnie Mouse in kimono 2·00 1·10
1380 $2 Mickey making masks 2·75 2·50
1381 $4 Donald and Mickey making paper . . . . . . 3·50 3·75
1382 $5 Minnie and Pluto making pottery . . . . 3·75 4·00
MS1383 Four sheets, each 122 × 102 mm. (a) $6 Mickey flower-arranging. (b) $6 Mickey carving a netsuke. (c) $6 Mickey at tea ceremony. (d) $6 Mickey making printing plate. Set of 4 sheets . . . . 16·00 16·00

1991. Fungi. As T **364** of Grenada. Multicoloured.
1384 5c. "Pyrrhoglossum pyrrhum" 35 25
1385 45c. "Agaricus purpurellus" 85 50
1386 50c. "Amanita craseoderma" 85 55
1387 90c. "Hygrocybe acutoconica" . . . . . . 1·50 1·25
1388 $1 "Limacella guttata" . . . 1·50 1·25
1389 $2 "Lactarius hygrophoroides" . . . . 2·00 2·00
1390 $4 "Boletellus cubensis" . . 3·25 3·50
1391 $5 "Psilocybe caerulescens" 3·25 3·50
MS1392 Two sheets, each 100 × 70 mm. (a) $6 "Marasmius haematocephalus". (b) $6 "Lepiota spiculata". Set of 2 sheets . . . . 12·00 13·00

1991. 65th Birthday of Queen Elizabeth II. As T **198a** of Gambia. Multicoloured.
1393 20c. Queen, Prince Philip, Prince Charles and Prince William at Trooping the Colour, 1990 . . . . 30 20
1394 25c. Queen and Prince Charles at polo match, 1985 . . . . 30 20
1395 $2 Queen and Prince Philip at Maundy service, 1989 2·00 2·50
1396 $4 Queen with Queen Mother on her 87th birthday, 1987 . . . . . 3·25 3·75
MS1397 68 × 90 mm. $5 The Queen at Caen Hill, 1990, and Prince Philip at R.A.F. Benson, 1989 3·75 4·50

1991. 10th Wedding Anniv of Prince and Princess of Wales. As T **198b** of Gambia. Multicoloured.
1398 5c. Prince and Princess of Wales kissing, 1987 . . . 65 25
1399 60c. Portraits of Prince, Princess and sons . . . . 1·50 70
1400 $1 Prince Harry in 1988 and Prince William in 1987 . . 1·50 1·10
1401 $5 Princess Diana in 1990 and Prince Charles in 1988 . . . . 5·50 4·75
MS1402 68 × 90 mm. $5 Princess with Prince Harry in Majorca, and Prince and Princess with Prince Harry at polo match . . . . . 5·50 5·00

1991. Death Centenary (1990) of Vincent van Gogh (artist). As T **200b** of Gambia. Multicoloured.
1403 5c. "Two Thistles" 50 30
1404 10c. "Baby Marcelle Roulin" 55 30
1405 15c. "Still Life: Basket with Six Oranges" (horiz) . . . 65 20
1406 25c. "Orchard in Blossom" 80 20
1407 45c. "Armand Roulin" . . . 1·00 35
1408 50c. "Wood Gatherers in Snow" (detail) (horiz) . . 1·00 50
1409 60c. "Almond Tree in Blossom" . . . . 1·25 50
1410 $1 "An Old Man" . . . . 1·75 1·25
1411 $2 "The Seine Bridge at Asnieres" (horiz) . . . . 2·50 2·50
1412 $3 "Vase with Lilacs, Daises and Anemones" . . . . . 2·75 3·00
1413 $4 "Self Portrait" . . . . . 3·00 3·50
1414 $5 "Patience Escalier" . . . 3·00 3·50
MS1415 Three sheets. (a) 127 × 102 mm. $6 "Quay with Men unloading Sand Barges" (horiz). (b) 127 × 102 mm. $6 "Sunset: Wheat Fields near Arles" (horiz). (c) 102 × 127 mm. "Les Alyscamps". Imperf. Set of 3 sheets . . . . 12·00 13·00

GRENADA GRENADINES SARGASSUM TRIGGERFISH Xanthichthys ringens 50¢

102 Sargassum Triggerfish

1991. Reef Fishes. Multicoloured.
1416 50c. Type **102** 90 90
1417 50c. Tobaccofish 90 90
1418 50c. Caribbean long-nosed butterflyfish 90 90
1419 50c. Cherub angelfish . . . 90 90
1420 50c. Black jack 90 90
1421 50c. Masked goby and black jack 90 90
1422 50c. Spot-finned hogfish . . 90 90
1423 50c. Royal gramma ("Fairy basslet") 90 90
1424 50c. Orange-backed bass . . 90 90
1425 50c. Candy basslet 90 90
1426 50c. Black-capped basslet . . 90 90
1427 50c. Long-jawed squirrelfish 90 90
1428 50c. Jackknife-fish 90 90
1429 50c. Bigeye 90 90
1430 50c. Short bigeye 90 90
MS1431 106 × 66 mm. $6 Caribbean flashlight fish . . . . 9·00 11·00
Nos. 1416/30 were printed together, se-tenant, forming a composite design.

1991. Christmas. Religious Paintings by Martin Schongauer. As T **200c** of Gambia.
1432 10c. black and brown . . . 60 15
1433 35c. multicoloured . . . . . 1·00 30
1434 50c. multicoloured . . . . . 1·40 50
1435 75c. multicoloured . . . . . 1·75 80
1436 $1 multicoloured . . . . . 1·90 1·25
1437 $2 multicoloured . . . . . 3·00 3·00
1438 $4 black and brown . . . . 3·75 4·25
1439 $5 black, grey and red . . . 3·75 4·50
MS1440 Two sheets, each 102 × 127 mm. (a) $6 multicoloured. (b) $6 multicoloured. Set of 2 sheets 9·50 11·00
DESIGNS: 10c. "Angel of the Annunciation"; 35c. "Madonna of the Rose Hedge" (detail); 50c. "Madonna of the Rose Hedge" (different detail); 75c. "Nativity" (detail); $1 "Adoration of the Shepherds" (detail); $2 "The Nativity"; $4 "Nativity" (different); $5 "Symbol of St. Matthew"; $6 (No. MS1440a) "Adoration of the Shepherds" (different detail); $6 (No. MS1440b) "Nativity".

1992. Great Railways of the World. As T **367** of Grenada. Multicoloured.
1441 75c. Medoc locomotive No. J-S 58, 1857 (Switzerland) 1·10 1·10
1442 75c. Stirling single locomotive No. 1, 1870 (Great Britain) . . . . . 1·10 1·10
1443 75c. Paris–Lyon–Mediterranee locomotive No. 90, 1877 (France) . . 1·10 1·10
1444 75c. Standard type, 1880 (U.S.A.) . . . . 1·10 1·10
1445 75c. Class 650 "Vittorio Emanuel II", 1884 (Italy) 1·10 1·10

1446 75c. Johnson single, 1887 (Great Britain) . . . . . 1·10 1·10
1447 75c. Locomotive No. 999, 1893 (U.S.A.) . . . . . . 1·10 1·10
1448 75c. Class Q1, 1896 (Great Britain) . . . . 1·10 1·10
1449 75c. "Claud Hamilton", 1900 (Great Britain) . . . 1·10 1·10
1450 $1 Class P8, 1906 (Germany) . . . . 1·10 1·10
1451 $1 Class P, 1910 (Denmark) 1·10 1·10
1452 $1 Southern Railway Ps4, 1926 (U.S.A.) . . . . . . 1·10 1·10
1453 $1 "Kestrel", 1932 (Ireland) 1·10 1·10
1454 $1 Southern Pacific Class GS2, 1937 (U.S.A.) . . . 1·10 1·10
1455 $1 Class 12, 1938 (Belgium) 1·10 1·10
1456 $1 Norfolk and Western Railroad Class J No. 600, 1941 (U.S.A.) . . . . . . 1·10 1·10
1457 $1 Alco PA series diesel, 1946 (U.S.A.) . . . . . . 1·10 1·10
1458 $1 Class 4E electric, 1954 (South Africa) . . . . . 1·10 1·10
1459 $2 Trans Europe Express train, 1957 . . . . 1·50 1·50
1460 $2 New Haven Railroad Type FL9 diesel, 1960 (U.S.A.) . . . . 1·50 1·50
1461 $2 "Hikari" train, 1964 (Japan) . . . . 1·50 1·50
1462 $2 Class 103.1 electric, 1970 (Germany) . . . . 1·50 1·50
1463 $2 RTG diesel, 1972 (France) . . . . 1·50 1·50
1464 $2 ETR 401 Pendolino train, 1976 (Italy) . . . . 1·50 1·50
1465 $2 Advanced Passenger Train Class 370, 1981 (Great Britain) . . . . . 1·50 1·50
1466 $2 Via Rail LRC diesel, 1982 (Canada) . . . . . 1·50 1·50
1467 $2 MAV BZMOT 601, 1983 (Hungary) . . . . 1·50 1·50
MS1468 Two sheets, each 120×80 mm. (a) $6 Werner von Siemens's electric locomotive, 1879 (Germany). (b) ETR 401 Pendolino train, 1976 (Italy). Set of 2 sheets . . . . 11·00 11·00

1992. 40th Anniv of Queen Elizabeth II's Accession. As T **202a** of Gambia. Multicoloured.
1469 60c. Swimming jetty on beach . . . . 1·10 40
1470 75c. View of Grenadines . . 1·25 45
1471 $2 Surf on beach . . . . . 2·50 1·75
1472 $4 Secluded bay . . . . . 3·75 3·25
MS1473 Two sheets, each 74×92 mm. (a) $6 Plantation house. (b) $6 St. George's. Set of 2 sheets . . . . 9·00 9·50

1992. Olympic Games, Barcelona. As T **372** of Grenada. Multicoloured.
1474 10c. Women's backstroke swimming 60 30
1475 15c. Women's handball . . 65 30
1476 25c. Men's 4×100 m relay 75 30
1477 35c. Men's hammer throw 80 35
1478 50c. Men's 110 m hurdles 90 60
1479 75c. Men's pole vault . . . 1·25 80
1480 $1 Men's volleyball . . . . 1·40 1·00
1481 $2 Men's weightlifting . . . 2·50 2·75
1482 $5 Men's gymnastics . . . 3·25 4·00
1483 $6 Football . . . . 3·75 4·25
MS1484 Two sheets, each 100×70 mm. (a) $15 Finn class single-handed dinghy sailing. (b) $15 Baseball. Set of 2 sheets 16·00 17·00

1992. Granada '92 Int Stamp Exn, Spain. Spanish Paintings. As T **481a** of Ghana. Mult.
1485 10c. "The Surrender of Seville" (Zurbaran) . . . 30 20
1486 35c. "The Liberation of St. Peter by an Angel" (Antonio de Pereda) . . . 50 35
1487 50c. "Joseph explains the Dreams of the Pharaoh" (Antonio del Castillo Saavedra) (horiz) 75 60
1488 75c. "The Flower Vase" (Juan de Arellano) . . . 1·00 70
1489 $1 "The Duke of Pastrana" (Juan Carreno de Miranda) . . . . 1·25 90
1490 $2 "The Annunciation" (detail) (Francisco Rizi) 2·00 2·00
1491 $4 "The Annunciation" (different detail) (Rizi) . . 3·00 3·50
1492 $5 "Old Women Seated" (attr Antonio Puga) . . . 3·00 3·50
MS1493 Two sheets. (a) 95×120 mm. $6 "The Triumph of Saint Hermenegildo" (Francisco de Herrera the younger) (86×111 mm). (b) 120×95 mm. $6 "Relief of Genoa" (De Pereda) (110×84 mm). Imperf. Set of 2 sheets . . . . 7·00 8·00

103 Don Isaac Abarbanel, Minister of Finance

1992. 500th Anniv of Discovery of America by Columbus (5th issue). World Columbian Stamp Expo '92, Chicago. Multicoloured.
1494 10c. Type **103** 15 15
1495 25c. Columbus on voyage 25 25
1496 35c. Look-out sighting land 30 30
1497 50c. King Ferdinand and Queen Isabella of Spain 50 50
1498 60c. Columbus showing map to Queen Isabella . . . 55 55
1499 $5 "Santa Maria" and bird 4·00 5·50
MS1500 Two sheets, each 100×71 mm. (a) $6 Christopher Columbus. (b) $6 Columbus with hand to face. Set of 2 sheets 7·00 8·00

1992. "Genova '92" International Thematic Stamp Exhibition. Hummingbirds. As T **370a** of Grenada. Multicoloured.
1501 5c. Male blue-headed hummingbird 25 30
1502 10c. Female rufous-breasted hermit 25 25
1503 20c. Female blue-headed hummingbird 30 25
1504 45c. Male green-throated carib 45 30
1505 90c. Male Antillean crested hummingbird 60 70
1506 $2 Male purple-throated carib . . . . 1·40 1·60
1507 $4 Female purple-throated carib . . . . 2·40 2·75
1508 $5 Female Antillean crested hummingbird . . . . . . 2·50 2·75
MS1509 Two sheets, each 104×75 mm. (a) $6 Male Rufous-breasted Hermit. (b) $6 Female Green-throated Carib. Set of 2 sheets . . . . 9·50 11·00

1992. 50th Anniv of United Service Organization (forces' entertainment programme). As T **371** of Grenada. Multicoloured.
1510 10c. James Cagney 60 25
1511 15c. Anne Sheridan 60 25
1512 35c. Jerry Colonna 60 25
1513 50c. Spike Jones 70 40
1514 75c. Edgar Bergen 90 55
1515 $1 The Andrews Sisters . . 1·40 80
1516 $2 Dinah Shore . . . . . . 2·00 2·00
1517 $5 Bing Crosby . . . . . . 4·50 4·50
MS1518 Two sheets, each 107×80 mm. (a) $6 Fred Astaire. (b) $6 Marlene Dietrich. Set of 2 sheets . . . . 7·00 7·50
No. 1515 is incorrectly inscribed "THE ANDREW SISTERS".

1992. 500th Anniv of Discovery of America by Columbus (6th issue). Organization of East Caribbean States. As Nos. 2423/4 of Grenada.
1519 $1 Columbus meeting Amerindians 65 65
1520 $2 Ships approaching island 1·25 1·50

1992. Toy Trains from American Manufacturers. As T **372b** of Grenada. Multicoloured.
1521 15c. No. 2220 switcher locomotive, Voltamp (1910) 25 15
1522 25c. Clockwork locomotive of Bridge Port Line, American Miniature Railroad (1907) 35 20
1523 50c. First electric toy locomotive, Ives (1910) . . 60 40
1524 75c. "J.C. Penney Special" locomotive, American Flyer (1920s) 80 60
1525 $1 Clockwork cast-metal locomotive, Hafner (1916) 90 80
1526 $2 Pull toy copper-plated locomotive, probably Hubley (1900) . . . . . 1·75 2·25
1527 $4 "Mayflower" locomotive, American Flyer (1928) . . 3·00 3·50
1528 $5 "Olympian" locomotive, Ives (1929) . . . . . . 3·00 3·50
MS1529 Two sheets. (a) 128×93 mm. $6 Clockwork locomotive, Ives (1910) (50×38½ mm). (b) 142×95 mm. $6 "Statesman" locomotive, American Flyer (50×38½ mm). P 13. Set of 2 sheets . . . . . . 7·50 8·50

1992. Postage Stamp Mega Event, New York. Sheet 100×70 mm containing multicoloured design as T **207a** of Gambia.
MS1530 $6 Brooklyn Bridge . . 3·50 4·25

1992. Christmas. Religious Paintings. "The Annunciation" by various artists. As T **207b** of Gambia. Multicoloured.
1531 5c. Robert Campin 15 10
1532 15c. Melchior Broederlam 25 10
1533 25c. Fra Filippo Lippi (two-panel diptych) 30 15
1534 35c. Simone Martini 40 20
1535 50c. Lippi (detail from left panel) 55 45
1536 75c. Lippi (detail from right panel) 70 60
1537 90c. Albert Bouts 80 80
1538 $1 D. di Michelino 90 90
1539 $2 Rogier van der Weyden 1·75 2·00
1540 $3 Sandro Botticelli (detail of angel) . . . . 2·25 2·75
1541 $4 Botticelli (detail of Virgin Mary) . . . . 2·75 3·50
1542 $5 Bernardo Daddi (horiz) 2·75 3·50
MS1543 Three sheets, each 72×97 mm. (a) $6 Van der Weyden (different). (b) $6 Botticelli (as $3). (c) $6 Hubert van Eyck. Set of 3 sheets . . . . . 10·50 12·00

1992. Gold Record Award Winners. As T **374** of Grenada. Multicoloured.
1544 90c. Leonard Bernstein . . 1·50 1·25
1545 90c. Ray Charles . . . . . 1·50 1·25
1546 90c. Bob Dylan . . . . . . 1·50 1·25
1547 90c. Barbra Streisand . . . 1·50 1·25
1548 90c. Frank Sinatra . . . . 1·50 1·25
1549 90c. Harry Belafonte . . . 1·50 1·25
1550 90c. Aretha Franklin . . . 1·50 1·25
1551 90c. Garth Brooks . . . . 1·50 1·25
MS1552 Two sheets, each 100×70 mm. (a) $3 Charlie Parker; $3 Miles Davis. (b) $3 Johnny Cash; $3 Willie Nelson. Set of 2 sheets . . . . . . 7·00 8·00
Nos. 1544/51 were printed together, se-tenant, with a composite background design.

1992. 60th Anniv of Goofy (Disney cartoon character). Scenes from various cartoon films. As T **207c** of Gambia. Multicoloured.
1553 5c. "Father's Day Off", 1953 . . . . 30 20
1554 10c. "Cold War", 1951 . . 35 20
1555 15c. "Home Made Home", 1951 . . . . 40 20
1556 25c. "Get Rich Quick", 1951 . . . . 50 25
1557 50c. "Man's Best Friend", 1952 . . . . 70 40
1558 75c. "Aquamania", 1961 . . 1·00 55
1559 90c. "Tomorrow We Diet", 1951 . . . . 1·10 65
1560 $1 "Teachers Are People", 1952 . . . . 1·25 75
1561 $2 "The Goofy Success Story", 1955 . . . . . . 2·00 1·75
1562 $3 "Double Dribble", 1946 2·50 3·00
1563 $4 "Hello Aloha", 1952 . . 2·75 3·25
1564 $5 "Father's Lion", 1952 . . 3·00 3·50
MS1565 Three sheets, each 128×102 mm. (a) $6 "Motor Mania", 1956. (b) $6 "Hold that Pose", 1950 (vert). (c) $6 "Father's Weekend", 1953 (vert). Set of 3 sheets . . . . 12·00 13·00

1992. Anniversaries and Events. As T **375** of Grenada. Multicoloured, except No. 1571.
1566 25c. Zeppelin "Viktoria Luise" over Kiel Harbour (horiz) 75 30
1567 50c. Space shuttle "Columbia" landing (horiz) 85 35
1568 75c. German Federal Republic flag and arms (horiz) 85 50
1569 $1.50 Giant anteater (horiz) 1·00 1·00
1570 $2 Scarlet macaw . . . . . 2·75 2·00
1571 $2 W.H.O. emblem (black and blue) (horiz) . . . . 1·50 1·50
1572 $3 Wolfgang Amadeus Mozart . . . . 4·00 3·00
1573 $4 The Berlin Airlift (horiz) 3·25 3·50
1574 $4 Repairing "Intelsat VI" satellite in space (horiz) 3·25 3·50
1575 $5 Zeppelin "Hindenburg" on fire (horiz) . . . . . . 3·25 3·50
1576 $5 Admiral Richard Byrd's Ford Trimotor aircraft (horiz) . . . . 3·25 3·50
MS1577 Five sheets. (a) 110×80 mm. $6 Zeppelin LZ-4, 1913 (51½×39½ mm). (b) 110×80 mm. $6 First flight of space shuttle "Endeavour" (51½×39½ mm). (c) 110×80 mm. $6 Map of West Germany (39½×51½ mm). (d) 110×80 mm. $6 Jaguar (51½×39½ mm). (e) 98×67 mm. $6 Figaro costume from "The Marriage of Figaro". Set of 5 sheets . . . . 18·00 20·00
ANNIVERSARIES AND EVENTS: Nos. 1566, 1575, **MS**1577a, 75th death anniv of Count Ferdinand von Zeppelin; 1567, 1574, **MS**1577b, International Space Year; 1568, 1573, **MS**1577c, 25th death anniv of Konrad Adenauer (German statesman); 1569/70, **MS**1577d, Earth Summit '92, Rio; 1571, United Nations World Health Organization Projects; 1572, **MS**1577e, Death bicentenary of Mozart; 1576, 75th anniv of International Association of Lions Clubs.

104 "Atalanta" and "Mischief" (yachts), 1881

105 "Battus polydamus"

1992. History of The Americas Cup Challenge Trophy. Multicoloured.
1578 15c. Type **104** 60 20
1579 25c. "Valkyrie III" and "Defender", 1895 . . . . 75 30
1580 35c. "Shamrock IV" and "Resolute", 1920 . . . . 90 45
1581 75c. "Endeavour II" and "Ranger", 1937 . . . . . 1·40 70
1582 $1 "Sceptre" and "Columbia", 1958 . . . . 1·60 85
1583 $2 "Australia II" and "Liberty", 1983 . . . . . 2·25 2·25
1584 $4 "Stars & Stripes" and "Kookaburra III", 1987 3·25 4·00
1585 $5 "New Zealand" and "Stars & Stripes", 1988 3·25 4·00
MS1586 Two sheets, each 114×85 mm. (a) $6 "America" (schooner), 1851 (57×43 mm). (b) $6 Americas Cup emblems (57×43 mm). Set of 2 sheets 10·00 11·00

1993. Dogs of the World. As T **377** of Grenada, but vert. Multicoloured.
1587 35c. Irish setter and Glendalough, Ireland . . 50 25
1588 50c. Boston terrier and Boston State House, U.S.A. 70 50
1589 75c. Beagle and Temple to Athena, Greece . . . . . 1·00 60
1590 $1 Weimaraner and Nesselwang, Germany . . 1·25 85
1591 $3 Norwegian elkhound and Urnes Stave Church, Norway . . . . 2·50 3·00
1592 $4 Mastiff and Sphinx, Egypt . . . . 2·75 3·00
1593 $5 Akita and Torii Temple, Kyoto, Japan . . . . . . 2·75 3·00
1594 $5 Saluki and Rub'al Khali, Saudi Arabia . . . . . . 2·75 3·00
MS1595 Two sheets, each 99×71 mm. (a) $6 Bull dog, Great Britain. (b) $6 Shar Pei, China. Set of 2 sheets . . . . 7·50 8·50

1993. Bicentenary of the Louvre, Paris. As T **209b** of Gambia. Multicoloured (except No. 1599).
1596 $1 "Madonna and Child with the young John the Baptist" (Botticelli) . . . 1·00 1·00
1597 $1 "The Buffet" (Chardin) 1·00 1·00
1598 $1 "Return from Market" (Chardin) . . . . 1·00 1·00
1599 $1 "Erasmus" (Durer) (black and grey) . . . . 1·00 1·00
1600 $1 "Self-portrait with Eryngium" (Durer) . . . 1·00 1·00
1601 $1 "Jeanne of Aragon" (Raphael) . . . . 1·00 1·00
1602 $1 "La Belle Jardiniere" (detail) (Raphael) . . . . 1·00 1·00
1603 $1 "La Belle Jardiniere" (different detail) (Raphael) 1·00 1·00
MS1604 70×100 mm. $6 "King Charles I Hunting" (Van Dyck) (52×85 mm) . . . . 3·75 4·50

1993. Butterflies. Multicoloured.
1605 15c. Type **105** 40 20
1606 35c. "Astraptes talus" . . . 55 20
1607 45c. "Pseudolycaena marsyas" 55 25
1608 75c. "Siproeta stelenes" . . 70 50
1609 $1 "Phoebis sennae" 80 60
1610 $2 "Dione juno" . . . . . 1·40 1·40
1611 $4 "Chlorostrymon simaethis" . . . . 2·25 2·75
1612 $5 "Urbanus proteus" . . . 2·50 2·75
MS1613 Two sheets, each 100×70 mm. (a) $6 "Historis odius" ("Orion"). (b) $6 "Heliconius charithonia" ("Zebra"). Set of 2 sheets . . . . 7·00 8·00

1993. Flowers. As T **380** of Grenada. Mult.
1614 35c. Hibiscus 50 20
1615 35c. Columbine 50 20
1616 45c. Red ginger 50 25
1617 75c. Bougainvillea 70 50
1618 $1 Crown imperial 80 60
1619 $2 Fairy orchid . . . . . . 1·40 1·40
1620 $4 Heliconia . . . . 2·25 2·75
1621 $5 Tulip . . . . 2·50 2·75

1993. 40th Anniv of Coronation. As T **215a** of Gambia.
1623 35c. multicoloured 30 55
1624 50c. multicoloured 40 60
1625 $2 green and black . . . . 1·10 1·40
1626 $4 multicoloured . . . . . 1·90 2·00
MS1627 70×100 mm. $6 multicoloured . . . . 6·00 6·50
DESIGNS—(38×27 mm): 35c. Queen Elizabeth II at Coronation (photograph by Cecil Beaton); 50c. Ampulla and spoon; $2 Queen Elizabeth II leaving for Coronation; $4 Prince Harry's christening. (28½×42½ mm)—$6 "Queen Elizabeth II, 1954" (detail) (Pietro Annigoni).

1993. Anniversaries and Events. As T **381** of Grenada. Multicoloured.
1628 15c. "Painter and Model" (Picasso) (horiz) 55 30
1629 35c. Keith Tkachuk and Dmitri Mironov (ice hockey, 1992) (horiz) . . . 1·00 40
1630 50c. Early telescope 85 50
1631 75c. "Gra w Gudziki" (Ludomir Slerdinski) (horiz) 90 90
1632 75c. Willy Brandt and Lyndon Johnson, 1961 (horiz) 90 90
1633 $1 "Artist and his Model" (Picasso) (horiz) . . . . . 1·00 1·00
1634 $2 "Pocalunek Mongolskiego Ksiecia" (S. Wirkiewicz) (horiz) . . 1·40 1·75

1635 $4 "The Drawing Lesson" (Picasso) (horiz) . . . . . 2·25 2·75
1636 $4 Radio telescope . . . . 2·25 2·75
1637 $5 Alberto Tomba (Giant Slalom, 1984) (horiz) . . 2·25 2·75
1638 $5 Willy Brandt and Eleanor Hulles, 1957 (horiz) . . . . 2·25 2·75
MS1639 Five sheets. (a) 105 × 75 mm. $5 Copernicus. (b) 105 × 75 mm. $6 Picasso (horiz). (c) 75 × 105 mm. $6 Emil Zogragski (70 metre ski jump, 1984). (d) 75 × 105 mm. $6 "Allegory" (detail) (Jan Wydra). (e) 105 × 75 mm. $6 Willy and Rut Brandt (grey and black) (horiz) Set of 5 sheets . . . . 17·00 19·00

ANNIVERSARIES AND EVENTS: Nos. 1628, 1633, 1635, **MS**1639b, 20th death anniv of Picasso (artist); 1629, 1637, **MS**1639c, Winter Olympic Games '94, Lillehammer; 1630, 1636, **MS**1639a, 450th death anniv of Copernicus (astronomer); 1631, 1634, **MS**1639d, Polska '93 International Stamp Exhibition, Poznan; 1632, 1638, **MS**1639e, 80th birth anniv of Willy Brandt (German politician).

1993. Songbirds. As T **382** of Grenada. Multicoloured.

1640 15c. Painted bunting 70 70
1641 15c. White-throated sparrow 70 70
1642 25c. Common grackle . . . 80 80
1643 25c. Royal flycatcher . . . 80 80
1644 35c. Swallow tanager . . . 85 85
1645 35c. Vermilion flycatcher . . 85 85
1646 45c. Black-headed bunting 90 90
1647 50c. Rose-breasted grosbeak 90 90
1648 75c. Corn bunting . . . . . 1·00 1·00
1649 75c. Rose-breasted thrush tanager . . . . 1·00 1·00
1650 $1 Buff-throated saltator . . 1·10 1·10
1651 $4 Plush-capped finch . . . 2·50 2·50
MS1652 Two sheets, each 115 × 86 mm. (a) $6 Pine grosbeak. (b) $6 Bohemian waxwing. Set of 2 sheets . . . . 12·00 12·00

Nos. 1640/51 were printed together, se-tenant, with the backgrounds forming a composite design.

Nos. 1645/6 show the scientific inscriptions transposed between the designs.

1993. Shells. As T **383** of Grenada. Mult.

1653 15c. Hawk-wing conch . . . 35 35
1654 15c. Music volute 35 35
1655 25c. Globe vase and deltoid rock shell 40 40
1656 35c. Spiny Caribbean vase 40 40
1657 35c. American common sundial and common purple janthina 40 40
1658 45c. Toothed donax and gaudy asaphis 40 40
1659 45c. Mouse cone 40 40
1660 50c. Gold-mouthed triton 50 50
1661 75c. Tulip mussel and trigonal tivela 60 60
1662 75c. Common dove shell and chestnut latirus . . . 60 60
1663 $1 Wide-mouthed purpura 70 70
1664 $4 American thorny oyster and Atlantic wing oyster 2·25 2·25
MS1665 Two sheets, each 70 × 106 mm. (a) $6 Atlantic turkey wing. (b) $6 Zebra or zigzag periwinkle. Set of 2 sheets 10·00 10·00

Nos. 1653/64 were printed together, se-tenant, with the backgrounds forming a composite design.

1993. Asian International Stamp Exhibitions. As T **219a** of Gambia. Multicoloured. (a) "Indopex '93", Surabaya, Indonesia.

1666 35c. National Museum, Central Jakarta (horiz) . . 40 20
1667 45c. Sacred wheel and deer (horiz) 45 25
1668 $1 Ramayana relief, Panataran Temple (horiz) 70 60
1669 $1.50 "Bullock Carts" (Batara Lubis) (horiz) . . 1·25 1·25
1670 $1.50 "Surat Irsa II" (A. D. Pirous) (horiz) . . . . . 1·25 1·25
1671 $1.50 "Self-portrait with Goat" (Kartika) (horiz) 1·25 1·25
1672 $1.50 "The Cow-est Cow" (Ivan Sagito) (horiz) . . . 1·25 1·25
1673 $1.50 "Rain Storm" (Sudjana Kerton) (horiz) 1·25 1·25
1674 $1.50 "Story of Pucuk Flower" (Effendi) (horiz) 1·25 1·25
1675 $5 Candi Tikus, Trawulan, East Java (horiz) . . . . 2·50 3·00
MS1676 134 × 105 mm. $6 Banteng cattle (horiz) . . . . 3·50 4·00

(b) "Taipei '93", Taiwan.

1677 35c. Macau Palace Casino, Hong Kong (horiz) . . . 40 20
1678 45c. Stone lion, Ming Tomb, Nanjing (horiz) 45 25
1679 $1 Stone camels, Ming Tomb, Nanjing (horiz) . . 70 60
1680 $1.50 Nesting quail incense burner (horiz) . . . . . 1·25 1·25
1681 $1.50 Standing quail incense burner (horiz) . . . . . 1·25 1·25
1682 $1.50 Seated qilin incense burner (horiz) . . . . . 1·25 1·25
1683 $1.50 Pottery horse, Han period (horiz) . . . . . 1·25 1·25
1684 $1.50 Seated caparisoned elephant (horiz) . . . . . 1·25 1·25
1685 $1.50 Cow in imitation of Delft faience (horiz) . . . 1·25 1·25
1686 $5 Stone lion and elephant, Ming Tomb, Nanjing (horiz) . . . . 2·50 3·00
MS1687 134 × 105 mm. $6 Sumatran tiger, Mt. Leuser National Park 3·50 4·00

(c) "Bangkok 1993", Thailand.

1688 35c. Three Naga snakes, Chiang Mai's Temple (horiz) 40 20
1689 45c. Sri Mariamman Temple, Singapore (horiz) 45 25
1690 $1 Topiary, Hua Hin Resort (horiz) 70 60
1691 $1.50 "Buddha's Victory over Mara" (horiz) . . . 1·25 1·25
1692 $1.50 "Mythological Elephant" (horiz) . . . . 1·25 1·25
1693 $1.50 "Battle with Mara" (Thon Buri) (horiz) . . 1·25 1·25
1694 $1.50 "Untitled" (Panya Wijinthanasarn) (horiz) 1·25 1·25
1695 $1.50 "Temple Mural" (horiz) . . . . 1·25 1·25
1696 $1.50 "Elephants in Pahcekha Buddha's Heaven" (horiz) . . . . . 1·25 1·25
1697 $5 Pak Tai Temple, Cheung Chau Island (horiz) . . . 2·50 3·00
MS1698 134 × 105 mm. $6 Monkey from Chiang Kong . . . . . 3·50 4·00

1993. World Cup Football Championship, U.S.A. (1994) (1st issue). As T **221a** of Gambia. Mult.

1699 15c. McCall (Scotland) and Verri (Brazil) (horiz) . . . 70 20
1700 25c. Verri (Brazil) and Maradona (Argentina) (horiz) 75 20
1701 35c. Schillaci (Italy) and Saldana (Uruguay) (horiz) 80 25
1702 45c. Gullit (Holland) and Wright (England) (horiz) 90 35
1703 $1 Verri (Brazil) and Maradona (Argentina) (different) (horiz) . . . . 1·25 80
1704 $2 Zubizarreta and Fernandez (Spain) with Albert (Belgium) (horiz) 1·75 1·75
1705 $4 Hagi (Rumania) and McGrath (Ireland) (horiz) 2·50 3·25
1706 $5 Gorriz (Spain) and Scifo (Belgium) (horiz) . . . 2·50 3·25
MS1707 Two sheets, each 104 × 75 mm. (a) $6 Foxboro Stadium, Massachusetts (horiz). (b) $6 Rudi Voeller (Germany). Set of 2 sheets . . . . 8·00 9·00

See also Nos. 1810/16.

1993. 65th Anniv of Mickey Mouse. Scenes from Walt Disney cartoon films. As T **385** of Grenada.

1708 15c. "Mickey's Rival", 1936 65 25
1709 35c. "The Worm Turns", 1937 . . . . 80 25
1710 50c. "The Pointer", 1939 . . 95 55
1711 75c. "Society Dog Show", 1939 . . . . 1·50 90
1712 $1 "A Gentleman's Gentleman", 1941 . . . . 1·60 1·00
1713 $2 "The Little Whirlwind", 1941 . . . . 2·25 2·50
1714 $4 "Mickey Down Under", 1948 . . . . 3·00 3·50
1715 $5 "R'coon Dawg", 1951 3·00 3·50
MS1716 Two sheets, each 127 × 102 mm. (a) $6 "Lonesome Ghosts", 1937. (b) $6 "Mickey's Garden", 1935 (vert). Set of 2 sheets . . . . 8·00 8·50

1993. Christmas. Religious Paintings. As T **211b** of Gambia. Black, yellow and red (Nos. 1717, 1721/3 and **MS**1725a) or multicoloured (others).

1717 10c. "Adoration of the Shepherds" (detail) (Durer) 30 20
1718 25c. "Adoration of the Magi" (detail) (Raphael) 40 20
1719 35c. "Presentation at the Temple" (detail) (Raphael) 45 20
1720 50c. "Adoration of the Magi" (different detail) (Raphael) 55 35
1721 75c. "Adoration of the Shepherds" (different detail) (Durer) 90 60
1722 $1 "Adoration of the Shepherds" (different detail) (Durer) . . . . . 1·00 85
1723 $4 "Adoration of the Shepherds" (different detail) (Durer) . . . . . 2·50 3·25
1724 $5 "Presentation at the Temple" (different detail) (Raphael) . . . . 2·50 3·25
MS1725 Two sheets. (a) 102 × 128 mm. $6 "Adoration of the Shepherds" (different detail) (Dürer) (horiz). (b) 128 × 102 mm. $6 "Annunciation" (detail) (Raphael). Set of 2 sheets . . . 7·00 8·00

1993. Aviation Anniversaries. As T **386** of Grenada. Multicoloured.

1726 15c. Avro Lancaster 30 25
1727 35c. Blanchard's balloon crossing the River Delaware 40 25
1728 50c. Airship "Graf Zeppelin" over Rio de Janeiro 50 35
1729 75c. Hugo Eckener 65 50
1730 $3 Pres. Washington handing passport to Blanchard . . . . 1·40 1·75
1731 $5 Short Sunderland flying boat . . . . 2·50 3·00
1732 $5 Eckener in "Graf Zeppelin" . . . . 2·50 3·00
MS1733 Three sheets. (a) 76 × 107 mm. $6 Supermarine Spitfire. (b) 107 × 76 mm. $6 Blanchard's balloon (vert). (c) 107 × 76 mm. $6 Eckener with Pres. Hoover. Set of 3 sheets 11·50 12·50

ANNIVERSARIES: Nos. 1726, 1731, **MS**1733a, 75th anniv of Royal Air Force; 1727, 1730, **MS**1733b. Bicentenary of first airmail flight; 1728/9, 1732, **MS**1733c, 125th birth anniv of Hugo Eckener (airship commander).

1993. Centenaries of Henry Ford's First Petrol Engine (Nos. 1735/6) and Karl Benz's First Four-wheeled Car (others). As T **387** of Grenada. Multicoloured.

1734 25c. Mercedes Benz "300 SLR", 1955 . . . . . . 85 25
1735 45c. Ford "Thunderbird", 1957 . . . . 1·00 25
1736 $4 Ford "150-A" station wagon, 1929 . . . . . . 3·50 3·75
1737 $5 Mercedes Benz "540 K" 3·50 3·75
MS1738 Two sheets, 76 × 107 mm. (a) $6 Mercedes Benz "SSK", 1929. (b) $6 Ford "Model T", 1924. Set of 2 sheets . . . . . 8·00 9·00

1993. Famous Paintings by Rembrandt and Matisse. As T **221c** of Gambia. Multicoloured.

1739 15c. "Hendrickje Stoffels as Flora" (Rembrandt) . . . 40 25
1740 35c. "Lady and Gentleman in Black" (Rembrandt) . . 50 25
1741 50c. "Aristotle with the Bust of Homer" (Rembrandt) 60 40
1742 75c. "Interior: Flowers and Parakeets" (Matisse) . . . 85 60
1743 $1 "Goldfish" (Matisse) . . 1·00 85
1744 $2 "The Girl with Green Eyes" (Matisse) . . . . 1·75 2·25
1745 $3 "Still Life with a Plaster Figure" (Matisse) . . . . 2·00 2·75
1746 $5 "Christ and the Woman of Samaria" (Rembrandt) 2·50 3·25
MS1747 Two sheets. (a) 100 × 125 mm. $6 "Anna accused of stealing the Kid" (detail) (Rembrandt). (b) 125 × 100 mm. $6 "Tea in the Garden" (detail) (Matisse) (horiz). Set of 2 sheets 8·00 9·00

1994. "Hong Kong '94" International Stamp Exhibition (1st issue). As T **222a** of Gambia. Multicoloured.

1748 40c. Hong Kong 1984 $5 aviation stamp and airliner at Kai Tak Airport 80 85
1749 40c. Grenada Grenadines 1988 20c. airships stamp and junk in Kowloon Bay 80 85

Nos. 1748/9 were printed together, se-tenant, forming a composite design.

See also Nos. 1750/5.

1994. "Hong Kong '94" International Stamp Exhibition (2nd issue). Jade Sculptures. As T **222b** of Gambia, but horiz. Multicoloured.

1750 45c. White jade brush washer 65 65
1751 45c. Archaic jade brush washer 65 65
1752 45c. Dark green jade brush washer 65 65
1753 45c. Green jade almsbowl 65 65
1754 45c. Archaic jade dog . . . 65 65
1755 45c. Yellow jade brush washer 65 65

1994. Fungi. As T **390** of Grenada, but with white backgrounds. Multicoloured.

1756 35c. "Hygrocybe hypohaemacta" 45 30
1757 45c. "Cantharellus cinnabarinus" 55 35
1758 50c. "Marasmius haematocephalus" 60 40
1759 75c. "Mycena pura" 80 60
1760 $1 "Gymnopilus russipes" 90 80
1761 $2 "Calocybe cyanocephala" 1·40 1·75
1762 $4 "Pluteus chrysophlebius" 2·50 3·00
1763 $5 "Chlorophyllum molybdites" . . . . . . 2·50 3·00
MS1764 Two sheets, each 100 × 70 mm. (a) $6 "Xeromphalina tenuipes". (b) "Collybia fibrosipes". Set of 2 sheets . . . . 7·50 8·00

No. 1757 is inscribed "Cantherellus cinnabarinus" and No. 1762 "Pleuteus chrysophlebius", both in error.

1994. Prehistoric Animals. As T **391** of Grenada. Multicoloured.

1765 15c. Spinosaurus 30 25
1766 35c. Apatosaurus (Brontosaurus) 45 30
1767 45c. Tyrannosaurus rex . . 50 35
1768 55c. Triceratops 50 40
1769 $1 Pachycephalosaurus . . . 85 75
1770 $2 Pteranodon . . . . . . 1·40 1·75
1771 $4 Parasaurolophus . . . . 2·50 3·00
1772 $5 Brachiosaurus . . . . . 2·50 3·00
MS1773 Two sheets, each 100 × 70 mm. (a) $6 Head of Brachiosaurus (vert). (b) $6 Spinosaurus and Tyrannosaurus rex fighting (vert). Set of 2 sheets 7·50 8·00

1994. 25th Anniv of First Manned Moon Landing. Space Shuttle "Challenger". As T **227a** of Gambia. Multicoloured.

1774 $1.10 "Challenger" crew in training . . . . 1·00 1·25
1775 $1.10 Christa McAuliffe (astronaut) . . . . 1·00 1·25
1776 $1.10 "Challenger" on launch pad . . . . 1·00 1·25
1777 $1.10 Gregory Jarvis (astronaut) . . . . 1·00 1·25
1778 $1.10 Ellison Onizuka (astronaut) . . . . 1·00 1·25
1779 $1.10 Ronald McNair (astronaut) . . . . 1·00 1·25
MS1780 107 × 76 mm. $6 Judith Resnick (astronaut) (vert) . . . 4·00 4·50

1994. Centenary of International Olympic Committee. Gold Medal Winners. As T **227b** of Gambia. Multicoloured.

1781 50c. Silke Renk (Germany) (javelin), 1992 . . . . . 35 35
1782 $1.50 Mark Spitz (U.S.A.) (swimming), 1972 . . . . 90 1·40
MS1783 106 × 77 mm. $6 Japanese team (Nordic skiing), 1994 . . 3·25 3·75

1994. International Year of the Family. As T **391a** of Grenada. Multicoloured.

1784 $1 Grenadines family . . . 60 60

1994. 50th Anniv of D-Day. As T **227c** of Gambia. Multicoloured.

1785 40c. Churchill bridge-laying tank 35 30
1786 $2 Sherman "Firefly" tank leaving landing craft . . . 1·00 1·50
1787 $3 Churchill "Crocodile" flame-thrower . . . . . . 1·60 2·00
MS1788 107 × 76 mm. $6 Sherman "Crab" flail tank . . . . . . 3·25 3·75

1994. "Philakorea '94" International Stamp Exhibition, Seoul (1st issue). As T **227d** of Gambia. Multicoloured.

1789 40c. Onung Tomb (horiz) 30 30
1790 $1 Stone pagoda, Mt. Namsam (horiz) 55 65
1791 $1 "Admiring Spring in the Country" (left detail) (Sin Yunbok) 55 65
1792 $1 "Admiring Spring in the Country" (right detail) . . 55 65
1793 $1 "Woman on Dano Day" (left detail) (Sin Yunbok) 55 65
1794 $1 "Woman on Dano Day" (right detail) 55 65
1795 $1 "Enjoying Lotuses while Listening to Music" (left detail) (Sin Yunbok) . . . 55 65
1796 $1 "Enjoying Lotuses while Listening to Music" (right detail) 55 65
1797 $1 "Women by a Crystal Stream" (left detail) (Sin Yunbok) 55 65
1798 $1 "Women by a Crystal Stream" (right detail) . . 55 65
1799 $4 Pusan (horiz) . . . . . . 2·25 2·75
MS1800 70 × 102 mm. $6 "Blacksmith Shop" (detail) (Kim Duksin) . . . . 3·25 3·75

The two details of each painting on Nos. 1791/8 were printed together, se-tenant, each pair forming a composite design.

See also Nos. 1817/31.

1994. Orchids. As T **392** of Grenada. Multicoloured.

1801 15c. "Cattleya aurantiaca" 35 25
1802 25c. "Blettia patula" 40 25
1803 45c. "Sobralia macrantha" 50 30
1804 75c. "Encyclia belizensis" 70 55
1805 $1 "Sophrolaeliocattleya" 85 75
1806 $2 "Encyclia fragrans" . . . 1·40 1·75
1807 $4 "Schombocattleya" . . . 2·50 3·00
1808 $5 "Brassolaeliocattleya" . . 2·50 3·00
MS1809 Two sheets, each 100 × 70 mm. (a) $6 "Ornithidium coccineum" (horiz). (b) $6 "Brassavola nodosa" (horiz). Set of 2 sheets . . . . 8·50 9·00

1994. World Cup Football Championship, U.S.A. (2nd issue). As T **393** of Grenada. Multicoloured.

1810 75c. Steve Mark (Grenada) 70 70
1811 75c. Jurgen Kohler (Germany) 70 70
1812 75c. Almir (Brazil) 70 70
1813 75c. Michael Windiscmann (U.S.A.) 70 70
1814 75c. Guiseppe Giannini (Italy) 70 70
1815 75c. Rashidi Yekini (Nigeria) 70 70
MS1816 Two sheets, each 90 × 70 mm. (a) $6 Kemari (ancient Japanese game). (b) Hand holding trophy. Set of 2 sheets 7·50 8·50

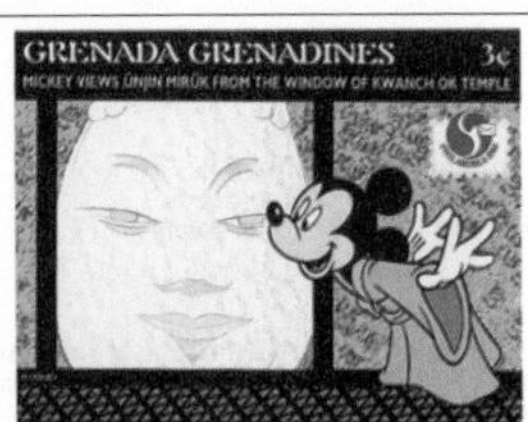

106 Mickey Mouse and Unjin Miruk Window from Kwanch Ok Temple

1994. "Philakorea '94" International Stamp Exhibition, Seoul (2nd issue). Walt Disney cartoon characters. Multicoloured.

1817 3c. Type **106** 30 40
1818 4c. Goofy imitating statue of Admiral Yi, Chonju 30 40
1819 5c. Cousin Gus and Donald Duck eating dinner 30 40
1820 10c. Mickey playing flute 45 35
1821 15c. Goofy with Tolharubang (statue) 60 20
1822 15c. Type **106** 60 20
1823 20c. Mickey and Minnie at Hyang-Wonjong 60 20
1824 35c. As 4c. 75 25
1825 50c. As 5c. 90 35
1826 75c. As 10c. 1·10 65
1827 $1 As 15c. 1·40 90
1828 $2 As 20c. 2·25 2·50
1829 $4 Mickey as Somori-Kut shaman 3·00 3·50
1830 $5 Minnie holding ceremonial fan 3·00 3·50
MS1831 Two sheets, each 130 × 103 mm. (a) $6 Minnie beating Buk drum (vert). (b) $6 Mickey in swimming pool at Pugok Hawaii (vert). Set of 2 sheets 8·00 9·00

1994. 1st Recipients of Order of the Caribbean Community. As Nos. 2750/2 of Grenada. Multicoloured.

1832 25c. Sir Shridath Ramphal 10 10
1833 50c. William Demas 25 30
1834 $2 Derek Walcott 2·75 2·50

1994. Fishes. As T **394** of Grenada. Multicoloured.

1835 75c. Porkfish 85 80
1836 75c. Blue chromis 85 80
1837 75c. Caribbean reef shark (facing left) 85 80
1838 75c. Long-spined squirrelfish 85 80
1839 75c. Four-eyed butterflyfish 85 80
1840 75c. Blue head 85 80
1841 75c. Royal gramma 85 80
1842 75c. Sharp-nosed puffer 85 80
1843 75c. Reid's seahorse 85 80
1844 75c. Black-barred soldierfish 85 80
1845 75c. Red-lipped blenny 85 80
1846 75c. Painted wrasse 85 80
1847 75c. Yellow-tailed snapper 85 80
1848 75c. Caribbean reef shark (facing right) 85 80
1849 75c. Great barracuda 85 80
1850 75c. Red-tailed parrotfish 85 80
1851 75c. Blue tang 85 80
1852 75c. Queen angelfish 85 80
1853 75c. Red hind 85 80
1854 75c. Rock beauty 85 80
1855 75c. Queen parrotfish 85 80
1856 75c. Spanish hogfish 85 80
1857 75c. Spotted moray 85 80
1858 75c. Queen triggerfish 85 80
MS1859 Two sheets, each 102 × 72 mm. (a) $6 Head of queen angelfish. (b) $6 Head of painted wrasse. Set of 2 sheets 8·00 9·00

Nos. 1835/46 and 1847/58 respectively were printed together, se-tenant, forming composite designs.

1994. Christmas. Religious Paintings by Bartolome Murillo. As T **231a** of Gambia. Multicoloured.

1860 15c. "The Annunciation" 30 20
1861 35c. "The Adoration of the Shepherds" 40 20
1862 50c. "Virgin and Child with St. Rose" 50 30
1863 50c. "Flight into Egypt" 50 30
1864 75c. "Virgin and Child" 70 45
1865 $1 "Virgin of the Rosary" 85 70
1866 $4 "The Holy Family" 2·50 3·25
MS1867 Two sheets. (a) 85 × 95 mm. $6 "Adoration of the Shepherds" (different) (detail). (b) 95 × 125 mm. $6 "The Holy Family with a Little Bird" (detail). Set of 2 sheets 7·50 8·00

1995. Birds. As T **397** of Grenada. Multicoloured.

1868 25c. Scaly-breasted ground dove ("Ground Dove") (vert) 1·00 40
1869 50c. White-winged dove 1·50 60
1870 $2 Inca dove (vert) 2·75 2·50
1871 $4 Mourning dove 3·75 5·50

1995. Centenary of First English Cricket Tour to the West Indies. As T **397a** of Grenada. Multicoloured.

1872 50c. Mike Atherton (England) and Wisden Trophy 1·10 65
1873 75c. Curtly Ambrose (West Indies) (vert) 1·40 1·10
1874 $1 Brian Lara (West Indies) (vert) 1·50 1·50
MS1875 75 × 95 mm. $3 West Indian team, 1994 3·00 3·00

107 Aspects of London, National Flag and Map

108 Pig

1995. Capitals of the World. Aspects of various cities, national flags and maps. Multicoloured.

1876 $1 Type **107** 65 70
1877 $1 Cairo 65 70
1878 $1 Vienna 65 70
1879 $1 Paris 65 70
1880 $1 Rome 65 70
1881 $1 Budapest 65 70
1882 $1 Moscow 65 70
1883 $1 Peking ("Beijing") 65 70
1884 $1 Tokyo 65 70
1885 $1 Washington 65 70

1995. Chinese New Year ("Year of the Pig"). Multicoloured designs showing "GRENADA GRENADINES" in colours indicated.

1886 75c. Type **108** (violet) 50 60
1887 75c. Pig (carmine) 50 60
1888 75c. Pig (brown) 50 60
1889 75c. Pig (vermilion) 50 60
MS1890 Two sheets. (a) 106 × 77 mm. $2 Two pigs (horiz). (b) 67 × 83 mm. Nos. 1886/9. Set of 2 sheets 3·25 3·50

109 Bull Shark and Diver

1995. Marine Life of the Caribbean. Multicoloured.

1891 $1 Type **109** 75 75
1892 $1 Great white shark 75 75
1893 $1 Octopus and shoal of fish 75 75
1894 $1 Great barracuda 75 75
1895 $1 Green moray 75 75
1896 $1 Spotted eagle ray 75 75
1897 $1 Sea snake 75 75
1898 $1 Stingray 75 75
1899 $1 Grouper 75 75
1900 $1 Dolphins 75 75
1901 $1 Lionfish 75 75
1902 $1 Sea turtle and rock beauty (fish) 75 75
1903 $1 Blue-cheeked butterflyfish and nurse shark 75 75
1904 $1 Queen angelfish 75 75
1905 $1 Grouper and coney 75 75
1906 $1 Rainbow eel and spotted moray 75 75
1907 $1 Sun flower-star and coral crab 75 75
1908 $1 Octopus on sea bed 75 75
MS1909 Two sheets each 107 × 77 mm. (a) $5 French angelfish. (b) $6 Smooth hammerhead. Set of 2 sheets 6·50 7·00

110 Suffolk Punch

1995. Domestic Animals. Multicoloured.

1910 15c. Type **110** 60 40
1911 25c. Shetland pony 60 40
1912 75c. Blue persian (cat) 60 65
1913 75c. Sorrel abyssinian (cat) 60 65
1914 75c. White angora (cat) 60 65
1915 75c. Brown Burmese (cat) 60 65
1916 75c. Red tabby exotic shorthair (cat) 60 65
1917 75c. Seal-point birman (cat) 60 65
1918 75c. Korat (cat) 60 65
1919 75c. Norwegian forest cat 60 65
1920 75c. Lilac-point Balinese (cat) 60 65
1921 75c. British shorthair (cat) 60 65
1922 75c. Red self longhair (cat) 60 65
1923 75c. Calico Manx (cat) 60 65
1924 75c. Shetland sheepdog 60 65
1925 75c. Bull terrier 60 65
1926 75c. Afghan hound 60 65
1927 75c. Scottish terrier 60 65
1928 75c. Labrador retriever 60 65
1929 75c. English springer spaniel 60 65
1930 75c. Samoyed (dog) 60 65
1931 75c. Irish setter 60 65
1932 75c. Border collie 60 65
1933 75c. Pekingese 60 65
1934 75c. Dachshund 60 65
1935 75c. Weimaraner (dog) 60 65
1936 $1 Arab 85 85
1937 $3 Shire horse 1·75 2·00
MS1938 Two sheets, each 105 × 75 mm. (a) $6 Seal-point colourpoint (cat). (b) $6 English setter. Set of 2 sheets 7·00 7·50

1995. Centenary (1992) of Sierra Club (environmental protection society). Endangered Species. As T **224a** of Gambia. Multicoloured.

1939 $1 Spotted owl ("Northern Spotted Owl") 90 80
1940 $1 Brown pelican on perch 90 80
1941 $1 Head of brown pelican 90 80
1942 $1 Head of jaguarundi 90 80
1943 $1 Jaguarundi looking over shoulder 90 80
1944 $1 Maned wolf in undergrowth 90 80
1945 $1 American wood stork ("Wood Stork") standing on two legs 90 80
1946 $1 American wood stork standing on one leg 90 80
1947 $1 Close-up of maned wolf 90 80
1948 $1 Brown pelican (horiz) 90 80
1949 $1 Close-up of spotted owl ("Northern Spotted Owl") (horiz) 90 80
1950 $1 Spotted owl ("Northern Spotted Owl") chick (horiz) 90 80
1951 $1 Jaguarundi (horiz) 90 80
1952 $1 Central American spider monkey sitting with young (horiz) 90 80
1953 $1 Central American spider monkey carrying young (horiz) 90 80
1954 $1 Central American spider monkey swinging from branch (horiz) 90 80
1955 $1 American wood stork ("Wood Stork") (horiz) 90 80
1956 $1 Pair of maned wolfs (horiz) 90 80

1995. 18th World Scout Jamboree, Netherlands. As T **403** of Grenada. Multicoloured.

1957 75c. Grenadian scout on beach 60 70
1958 $1 Scout with staff on hill 80 90
1959 $2 Scout saluting and national flag 1·10 1·50
MS1960 107 × 77 mm. $6 Scout snorkelling 3·50 4·00

1995. 50th Anniv of End of Second World War in Europe. Bombers. As T **237a** of Gambia. Mult.

1961 $2 Avro Type **683** Lancaster 1·50 1·50
1962 $2 Junkers Ju 88 1·50 1·50
1963 $2 North American B-25 Mitchell 1·50 1·50
1964 $2 Boeing B-17 Flying Fortress 1·50 1·50
1965 $2 Petlyakov Pe-2 1·50 1·50
1966 $2 Martin B-26 Marauder 1·50 1·50
1967 $2 Heinkel He 111H 1·50 1·50
1968 $2 Consolidated B-24 Liberator 1·50 1·50
MS1969 105 × 75 mm. $6 Pres. Truman and newspaper headline (57 × 43 mm) 3·00 3·50

1995. 50th Anniv of United Nations. As T **404** of Grenada. Multicoloured.

1970 75c. U.N. Headquarters, New York, and flag 60 90
1971 $1 Trygve Lie (first Secretary-General) 80 1·10
1972 $2 U.N. soldier 1·10 1·40
MS1973 101 × 76 mm. $6 Peace dove over emblem 2·50 3·00

Nos. 1970/2 were printed together, se-tenant, forming a composite design.

1995. 50th Anniv of F.A.O. As T **405** of Grenada. Multicoloured.

1974 75c. Man hoeing 60 90
1975 $1 Woman hoeing 80 1·10
1976 $2 Man and woman hoeing 1·10 1·40
MS1977 106 × 76 mm. $6 Child eating with chopsticks 2·50 3·00

Nos. 1974/6 were printed together, se-tenant, forming a composite design.

1995. 90th Anniv of Rotary International. As T **406** of Grenada. Multicoloured.

1978 $5 Paul Harris (founder) and logo (horiz) 2·50 3·00
MS1979 106 × 76 mm. $6 Rotary Club and International logos (horiz) 2·75 3·25

1995. 95th Birthday of Queen Elizabeth the Queen Mother. As T **239a** of Gambia.

1980 $1.50 brown, light brown and black 1·40 1·40
1981 $1.50 multicoloured 1·40 1·40
1982 $1.50 multicoloured 1·40 1·40
1983 $1.50 multicoloured 1·40 1·40
MS1984 102 × 127 mm. $6 multicoloured 6·00 5·50

DESIGNS: No. 1980, Queen Elizabeth the Queen Mother (pastel drawing); 1981, At Remembrance Day service; 1982, At desk (oil painting); 1983, Wearing green hat; **MS**1984, Unveiling memorial to Blitz victims.

1995. 50th Anniv of End of Second World War in the Pacific. As T **239b** of Gambia. Multicoloured.

1985 $2 Mitsubishi G4M1 "Betty" (bomber) 1·40 1·50
1986 $2 Japanese submarine "I 14" with seaplane on catapault 1·40 1·50
1987 $2 Mitsubishi GM31 "Nell" (bomber) 1·40 1·50
1988 $2 "Akizuki" (Japanese destroyer) 1·40 1·50
1989 $2 "Kirishima" (Japanese battleship) 1·40 1·50
1990 $2 "Asigari" (Japanese cruiser) 1·40 1·50
MS1991 108 × 76 mm. $6 Japanese Aichi D3A1 "Val" dive bomber 3·50 3·75

1995. Olympic Games, Atlanta (1996). As T **407** of Grenada. Multicoloured.

1992 15c. Rosemary Ackerman (East Germany) (high jump) (horiz) 50 60
1993 15c. Li Ning (China) (gymnastics) (horiz) 50 60
1994 15c. Denise Parker (U.S.A.) (archery) (horiz) 50 60
1995 $3 Terry Carlisle (U.S.A.) (skeet shooting) (horiz) 2·00 2·50
1996 $3 Kathleen Nord (East Germany) (swimming) (horiz) 2·00 2·50
1997 $3 Brigit Schmidt (East Germany) (canoeing) (horiz) 2·00 2·50
MS1998 Two sheets, each 102 × 72 mm. (a) $6 Dan Gable (U.S.A.) and Kikuo Wada (Japan) (wrestling). (b) $6 George Foreman (U.S.A.) (boxing). Set of 2 sheets 7·00 8·00

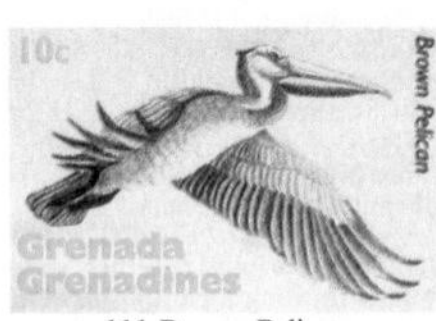

111 Brown Pelican

1995. Birds of the Caribbean. Multicoloured.

1999 10c. Type **111** 40 40
2000 15c. Black-necked stilt ("Common Stilt") 50 40
2001 25c. Cuban trogon ("Cuban Trogan") 55 30
2002 35c. Greater flamingo ("Flamingo") 60 30
2003 75c. Imperial amazon ("Parrot") 80 45
2004 $1 Pintail ("Pintail Duck") 90 1·00
2005 $1 Great blue heron 90 1·00
2006 $1 Jamaican tody 90 1·00
2007 $1 Laughing gull 90 1·00
2008 $1 Purple-throated carib 90 1·00
2009 $1 Red-legged thrush 90 1·00
2010 $1 Ruddy duck 90 1·00
2011 $1 Common shoveler ("Shoveler Duck") 90 1·00
2012 $1 Great red-bellied woodpecker ("West Indian Red-bellied Woodpecker") 90 1·00
2013 $2 Ringed kingfisher 1·40 1·75
2014 $3 Strip-headed tanager 1·75 2·25
MS2015 Two sheets, each 104 × 73 mm. (a) $5 Village weaver. (b) $5 Blue-hooded euphonia. Set of 2 sheets 7·00 7·50

No. 2001 is inscr "Cuban Trogan", No. 2008 "Purple-throated Carb" and No. 2013 "Ringed King Fisher", all in error.

No. **MS**2015, carry the "Singapore '95" exhibition logo.

1995. Mickey's Pirate Adventure. Walt Disney cartoon characters. As T **415** of Grenada. Multicoloured.

2016 10c. Goofy and Donald Duck with treasure chests (horiz) 35 25
2017 35c. Mickey and Minnie Mouse at ship's wheel (horiz) 55 25
2018 75c. Mickey, Donald and Goofy opening chest (horiz) 90 55
2019 $1 Big Pete and rats confronting Mickey (horiz) 1·00 75
2020 $2 Mickey, Goofy and Donald in boat (horiz) 1·75 2·00
2021 $5 Goofy fighting rat pirate with mop (horiz) 3·25 4·25
MS2022 Two sheets, each 108 × 130 mm. (a) $6 Goofy and cannon-balls. (b) $6 Monkey pinching Mickey's nose. Set of 2 sheets 8·00 8·50

1995. Centenary of Nobel Trust Fund. As T **416** of Gambia. Multicoloured.

2023/51 75c. × 2, $1 × 27 Set of 29 16·00 18·00
MS2052 Three sheets, each 105 × 76 mm. (a) $6 Sir Winston Churchill (1953 Literature). (b) $6 Willy Brandt (1971 Peace). (c) $6 Albert Schweitzer (1952 Peace). Set of 3 sheets 15·00 14·00

DESIGNS: 75c. W. Arthur Lewis (1979 Economics); Derek Walcott (1992 Literature); $1 Jules Border (1919 Medicine); Rene Cassin (1968 Peace); Verner von Heidenstam (1916 Literature); Jose Echegaray (1904 Literature); Otto Wallach (1910 Chemistry); Corneille Heymans (1938 Medicine); Ivar Giaever (1973 Physics); Sir William Cremer (1903 Peace); John Strutt (1904 Physics); James Franck (1925 Physics); Tobias Asser (1911 Peace); Carl Spitteler (1919 Literature); Christiaan Eijkman (1929 Medicine); Ragnar Granit (1967 Medicine); Frederic Passy (1901 Peace); Louis Neel (1970 Physics); Sir William Ramsay (1904 Chemistry); Philip Noel-Baker (1959 Peace); Heike Onnes (1913 Physics); Fridtjof Nansen (1922 Peace); Sir Ronald Ross (1902 Medicine); Paul Muller (1948 Medicine); Allvar Gullstrand (1911 Medicine); Gerhart Hauptmann (1912 Literature); Hans Spemann (1935 Medicine); Cecil Powell (1950 Physics); Walther Bothe (1954 Physics).

Nos. 2025/33, 2034/42 and 2043/51 respectively were printed together, se-tenant, forming composite designs.

No. 2027 (Von Heidenstam) is inscribed "1906" and No. 2044 "Fridtjof Nanser", both in error.

112 Nita Naldi and Rudolph Valentino

114 Symbolic Rat and Candle

113 Man on Donkey

1995. Centenary of Cinema. Multicoloured.
2053 $1 Type **112** 75 75
2054 $1 Ramon Novaro and Alice Terry 75 75
2055 $1 Frederic March and Joan Crawford 75 75
2056 $1 Clark Gable and Vivien Leigh 75 75
2057 $1 Barbara Stanwyck and Burt Lancaster 75 75
2058 $1 Warren Beatty and Natalie Wood 75 75
2059 $1 Spencer Tracy and Katharine Hepburn . . . 75 75
2060 $1 Humphrey Bogart and Lauren Bacall 75 75
2061 $1 Omar Sharif and Julie Christie 75 75
2062 $1 Marion Davies 75 75
2063 $1 Marlene Dietrich 75 75
2064 $1 Lillian Gish 75 75
2065 $1 Bette Davis 75 75
2066 $1 Elizabeth Taylor 75 75
2067 $1 Veronica Lake 75 75
2068 $1 Ava Gardner 75 75
2069 $1 Grace Kelly 75 75
2070 $1 Kim Novak 75 75
MS2071 Two sheets. (a) 72×102 mm. $6 Sophia Loren. (b) 102×72 mm. $6 Greta Garbo and John Gilbert (horiz). Set of 2 sheets . . . . 7·00 8·00

Nos. 2053/61 and 2062/70 respectively were printed together, se-tenant, forming composite designs.

1995. Racing Cars. As T **423** of Grenada. Multicoloured.
2072 10c. Williams-Renault Formula 1, 1990s 30 20
2073 25c. Porsche "956", Le Mans, 1980s 45 20
2074 35c. Lotus "John Player Special", 1970s 50 20
2075 75c. Ford "GT-40", 1960s 75 45
2076 $2 Mercedes-Benz "W196", 1950s . . . . 1·50 2·00
2077 $3 Mercedes "SSK", 1920s 2·00 2·50
MS2078 103×73 mm. $6 Jackie Stewart in Tyrell-Ford, 1971 (vert) 3·75 4·00

1995. Local Transport. Multicoloured.
2079 35c. Type **113** 50 25
2080 75c. Local bus . . . . . . 1·00 85

1995. Evolution of Sailing Ships. As T **427** of Grenada. Multicoloured.
2081 $1 "Preussen" (full-rigged ship) . . . . 90 1·00
2082 $1 Japanese junk . . . . . 90 1·00
2083 $1 Caribbean pirate ship . . 90 1·00
2084 $1 "Mayflower" (Pilgrim Fathers) . . . . 90 1·00
2085 $1 Chinese junk . . . . . . 90 1·00
2086 $1 "Santa Maria" (Columbus) . . . . . . 90 1·00
MS2087 103×73 mm. $5 Spanish galleon (56×41 mm) . . . . . . 3·25 3·50

1995. Christmas. Religious Paintings. As T **245a** of Gambia. Multicoloured.
2088 10c. "Immaculate Conception" (Piero di Cosimo) 30 20
2089 15c. "St. Michael dedicating Arms to the Madonna" (Le Nain) 35 20
2090 35c. "Annunciation" (Lorenzo di Credi) . . . 55 20
2091 50c. "The Holy Family" (Jacob Jordaens) 70 30
2092 $3 "Madonna and Child" (Lippi) . . . . 2·25 3·00
2093 $5 "Madonna and Child with Ten Saints" (Fiorentino) . . . . . . 3·25 4·00
MS2094 102×127 mm. (a) $6 "Adoration of the Shepherds" (detail) (Van Oost). (b) $6 "Holy Family" (detail) (Del Start). Set of 2 sheets . . . . 7·50 8·00

1996. Chinese New Year ("Year of the Rat"). Multicoloured, background colours given.
2095 **114** 75c. blue 55 60
2096 75c. lilac 55 60
2097 75c. brown 55 60
2098 75c. green 55 60
MS2099 69×84 mm. Nos. 2095/8 1·60 1·75
MS2100 76×106 mm. $2 Two rats (horiz) . . . . 1·40 1·50

The four designs show different Chinese characters.

1996. Works of Art by Durer and Rubens. As T **421** of Grenada. Multicoloured.
2101 15c. "The Centaur Family" (Durer) 30 20
2102 35c. "Oriental Ruler Seated" (Durer) 40 20
2103 50c. "The Entombment" (Durer) 55 30
2104 75c. "Man in Armour" (Rubens) 70 50
2105 $1 "Peace embracing Plenty" (Rubens) 85 75
2106 $2 "Departure of Lot" (Rubens) . . . . 1·50 1·75
2107 $3 "The Four Evangelists" (Rubens) . . . . 1·75 2·25
2108 $5 "Knight, Death and Devil" (Durer) . . . . . 3·00 3·75
MS2109 Two sheets, each 101×127 mm. (a) $5 "The Fathers of the Church" (detail) (Rubens). (b) $6 "St. Jerome" (detail) (Durer). Set of 2 sheets . . . . 6·50 7·50

115 Mickey and Minnie at New Year's Day "Hopping John" Tradition

1996. Traditional Holidays. Walt Disney cartoon characters. Multicoloured.
2110 25c. Type **115** 50 15
2111 50c. Disney characters dancing around maypole 70 30
2112 75c. Mickey, Minnie and Pluto watching Independence Day fireworks 95 40
2113 90c. Gyro Gearloose and Donald's nephews in Halloween costumes . . . 1·00 55
2114 $3 Donald Duck as Puritan and nephews as Indians on Thanksgiving Day . . 2·75 3·25
2115 $4 Huey and Dewey with Hanukkah dreidle . . . . 2·75 3·50
MS2116 Two sheets, each 124×98 mm. (a) $6 Mickey, Minnie and Donald taking part in Caribbean carnival. (b) $6 Traditional pot of gold in St. Patrick's Day parade (vert). Set of 2 sheets . . . . 9·50 10·00

116 Gateway in Imperial Palace, Peking (½-size illustration)

1996. "CHINA '96" 9th Asian International Stamp Exhibition, Peking. Multicoloured.
2117 $1 Type 116 . . . . 65 70
2118 $1 Eastern end of Great Wall at Shanhaiguan . . 65 70
2119 $1 Great Wall fortress, Shanhaiguan 65 70
2120 $1 Gate of Heavenly Peace, Peking 65 70
2121 $1 Sun Yat-sen's Mausoleum, Nanjing . . 65 70
2122 $1 Summer Palace, Peking 65 70
2123 $1 Temple of Heaven, Peking 65 70
2124 $1 Hall of Supreme Harmony, Forbidden City, Peking 65 70
MS2125 Three sheets. (a) 150×100 mm. $2 Traditional Chinese painting (39×50 mm). (b) 90×68 mm. $6 Great Wall of China from the air (39×50 mm). (c) 90×68 mm. $6 Marble Boat, Summer Palace, Peking (50×39 mm). Set of 3 sheets 7·00 7·50

1996. 70th Birthday of Queen Elizabeth II. As T **255a** of Gambia. Multicoloured.
2126 35c. As Type **255a** of Gambia 40 25
2127 $2 Queen wearing tiara and green dress . . . . . . 1·25 1·40
2128 $4 Windsor Castle . . . . 2·50 2·75
MS2129 103×125 mm. $6 Queen Elizabeth at Windsor . . . . . 3·75 4·00

1996. Flowers. As T **430** of Grenada. Multicoloured.
2130 35c. "Camellia" "Apple Blossom" 40 25
2131 75c. "Odontoglossum" . . . 60 60
2132 75c. "Cattleya" 60 60
2133 75c. "Paphiopedilum" "Venus's Slipper" 60 60
2134 75c. "Laeliocattleya" "Marysville" 60 60
2135 75c. Fuchsia "Citation" . . 60 60
2136 75c. Fuchsia "Amy Lye" . . 60 60
2137 75c. "Clysonimus" (butterfly) and temple . . 60 60
2138 75c. Foxglove ("Digitalis purpurea") 60 60
2139 75c. Martagon lily ("Lilium martagon") 60 60
2140 75c. "Tulipa" "Couleur Cardinal" 60 60
2141 75c. Snowdrop ("Galanthus nivalis") 60 60
2142 75c. "Rosa" "Superstar" . . 60 60
2143 75c. Crocus "Dutch Yellow Mammoth" 60 60
2144 75c. Japanese lily ("Lilium speciosum") 60 60
2145 75c. "Lilium" "Joan Evans" 60 60
2146 75c. "Rosa" "Rosemary Harkness" 60 60
2147 90c. "Camellia japonica" "Extravaganza" 65 65
2148 $1 Chrysanthemum "Primrose Dorothy Else" 75 75
2149 $2 Dahlia "Brandaris" . . . 1·25 1·40
MS2150 Two sheets, each 68×98 mm. (a) $5 Narcissus "Rembrandt". (b) $6 Gladiolus "Flowersong". Set of 2 sheets 6·50 7·50

Nos. 2135/46 were printed together, se-tenant, with the backgrounds forming a composite design.

No. 2135 is inscribed "Fuschcia", No. 2133 "Mammouth" and **MS**2150b "Gladiollus", all in error.

1996. 50th Anniv of UNICEF. As T **258a** of Gambia. Multicoloured.
2151 75c. Child's face (horiz) . . 55 45
2152 $2 Child with spoon (horiz) 1·10 1·40
2153 $3 Girl sewing (horiz) . . . 1·60 1·90
MS2154 105×75 mm. $6 Mother carrying child . . . . 3·00 3·50

1996. 3000th Anniv of Jerusalem. Multicoloured designs as T **424** of Grenada, but horiz.
MS2155 137×47 mm. $1 Pool of Bethesda and "Papaver rhoeas"; $2 Damascus Gate and "Chrysanthemum coronarium"; $3 Church of All Nations and "Myrtus communis". . . . . 4·00 3·75
MS2156 82×62 mm. $6 Church of the Holy Sepulchre . . . . . 4·00 3·75

1996. Centenary of Radio. Entertainers. As T **259a** of Gambia. Multicoloured.
2157 35c. Ed Wynn 35 25
2158 75c. Red Skelton 55 45
2159 $1 Joe Penner 65 55
2160 $3 Jerry Colonna . . . . . 1·75 2·00
MS2161 70×99 mm. $6 Bob Elliot and Ray Goulding (horiz) . . 3·25 3·75

1996. Olympic Games, Atlanta. Previous Medal Winners. As T **425** of Grenada. Multicoloured.
2162 35c. Los Angeles Memorial Coliseum 35 25
2163 75c. Connie Carpenter-Phinney (U.S.A.) (Cycling) 75 55
2164 $1 Josef Neckermann (Germany) (vert) 70 70
2165 $1 Harry Boldt (Germany) (vert) 70 70
2166 $1 Elena Petouchkova (Russia) (vert) 70 70
2167 $1 Alwin Schockemoehle (Germany) (vert) 70 70
2168 $1 Hans Winkler (Germany) (vert) 70 70
2169 $1 Joe Fargis (U.S.A.) (vert) 70 70
2170 $1 David Broome (Great Britain) (vert) 70 70
2171 $1 Reiner Klimke (Germany) (vert) 70 70
2172 $1 Richard Meade (Great Britain) (vert) 70 70
2173 $1 Julianne McNamara (U.S.A.) (vert) 70 70
2174 $1 Takuti Hayata (Japan) (vert) 70 70
2175 $1 Nikolai Adriana (Russia) (vert) 70 70
2176 $1 Mitch Gaylord (U.S.A.) (vert) 70 70
2177 $1 Ludmilla Tourischeva (Russia) (vert) 70 70
2178 $1 Karin Janz (Germany) (vert) 70 70
2179 $1 Peter Kormann (U.S.A.) (vert) 70 70
2180 $1 Sawoo Kato (Japan) (vert) 70 70
2181 $1 Nadia Comaneci (Rumania) (vert) 70 70
2182 $2 Mohamed Bouchighe (Algeria) (Boxing) (vert) 1·25 1·40
2183 $3 Jackie Joyner Kersee (U.S.A.) (Javelin) . . . . 1·75 1·90
MS2184 Two sheets, each 103×74 mm. (a) $5 Child waving flag (vert). (b) $6 William Steinkraus (U.S.A.) (Show jumping). Set of 2 sheets . . . 6·50 7·00

Nos. 2164/72 (equestrians) and 2173/81 (gymnasts) respectively were printed together, se-tenant, with the backgrounds forming composite designs.

1996. Classic Cars. As T **426** of Grenada. Multicoloured.
2185 35c. Chevrolet Belair convertible 40 25
2186 50c. V.I.P. car 55 30
2187 75c. Rolls-Royce Torpedo . . 65 45
2188 $1 Nissan "Cepric" type . . 70 70
2189 $1 Delaunay-Belleville HB6 70 70
2190 $1 Bugatti Type-15 . . . . 70 70
2191 $1 Mazda Type 800 . . . . 70 70
2192 $1 Mercedes 24/100/140 Sport 70 70
2193 $1 MG K3 Rover 70 70
2194 $1 Plymouth Fury 70 70
2195 $2 Mercedes-Benz 500K . . 1·25 1·40
2196 $3 Bugatti Type-13 . . . . 1·75 1·90
MS2197 Two sheets, each 106×76 mm. (a) $5 Bugatti "Roadster" Type-55. (b) $6 Lincoln Type-L. Set of 2 sheets 6·50 7·00

1996. Ships. As T **427** of Grenada. Multicoloured.
2198 35c. Grenada schooner . . . 50 25
2199 75c. Grenada schooner (different) 75 45
2200 $1 Athenian triremes, 1000 B.C. 80 80
2201 $1 Egyptian Nile galley, 30 B.C. 80 80
2202 $1 Bangladesh dinghi, 310 B.C. 80 80
2203 $1 Warship of Queen Hatshepsut, 476 B.C. . . 80 80
2204 $1 Chinese Junk, 200 B.C. 80 80
2205 $1 Polynesian ocean-going canoe, 600 B.C 80 80
2206 $1 "Europa" (liner), 1957 80 80
2207 $1 "Lusitania" (liner), 1906 80 80
2208 $1 "Queen Mary" (liner), 1936 . . . . 80 80
2209 $1 "Bianca C" (liner) . . . 80 80
2210 $1 "France" (liner), 1952 . . 80 80
2211 $1 "Orion" (liner), 1915 . . 80 80
MS2212 Two sheets, each 104×74 mm. (a) $5 "Queen Elizabeth 2" (liner), 1969 (56×42 mm). (b) $6 Viking longship, 610 (42×56 mm). Set of 2 sheets . . . . 6·50 7·00

117 Felix Mendelssohn

1996. Composers. Multicoloured.
2213 $1 Type **117** 80 70
2214 $1 Franz Schubert 80 70
2215 $1 Franz Joseph Haydn . . 80 70
2216 $1 Robert Schumann . . . 80 70
2217 $1 Ludwig van Beethoven 80 70
2218 $1 Gioacchino Rossini . . . 80 70
2219 $1 George Frederick Handel 80 70
2220 $1 Pyotr Tchaikovsky . . . 80 70
2221 $1 Frederic Chopin 80 70
2222 $1 Bela Bartok 80 70
2223 $1 Giacomo Puccini 80 70
2224 $1 George Gershwin 80 70
2225 $1 Leonard Bernstein . . . 80 70
2226 $1 Kurt Weill 80 70
2227 $1 John Cage 80 70
2228 $1 Aaron Copland 80 70
2229 $1 Sergei Prokofiev 80 70
2230 $1 Igor Stravinsky 80 70
MS2231 Two sheets, each 74×104 mm. (a) $5 Richard Strauss. (b) $6 Wolfgang Amadeus Mozart. Set of 2 sheets . . . . 8·50 7·50

Nos. 2213/21 and 2222/30 respectively were printed together, se-tenant, with the backgrounds forming composite designs.

1996. Railway Steam Locomotives. As T **429** of Grenada. Multicoloured.

2232 $1.50 Class 38 No. 382, Germany . . . . . . 1·10 1·10
2233 $1.50 "Duchess of Hamilton", Great Britain 1·10 1·10
2234 $1.50 Class W.P., India . . 1·10 1·10
2235 $1.50 Class 141R "Americaine", France . . 1·10 1·10
2236 $1.50 Class A4 "Mallard", Great Britain . . . . . . 1·10 1·10
2237 $1.50 Class 18 No. 201, Germany . . . . 1·10 1·10
2238 $1.50 Class A2 "Blue Peter", Great Britain . . 1·10 1·10
2239 $1.50 Class P36, Russia . . 1·10 1·10
2240 $1.50 Class QJ, China . . . 1·10 1·10
2241 $1.50 Class 12, Belgium . . 1·10 1·10
2242 $1.50 Class "Challenger", U.S.A. . . . . 1·10 1·10
2243 $1.50 Class 25, South Africa 1·10 1·10
MS2244 Two sheets, each 100 × 70 mm. (a) $5 Class "King", Great Britain. (b) $6 Class "Royal Scot", Great Britain. Set of 2 sheets . . . . 7·00 7·50

1996. Christmas. Religious Paintings. As T **245a** of Gambia. Showing different details from "Suffer Little Children to Come Unto Me" by Van Dyck.

2245 15c. multicoloured 40 20
2246 25c. multicoloured 40 20
2247 $1 multicoloured . . . . . 1·00 65
2248 $1.50 multicoloured . . . . 1·25 1·25
2249 $2 multicoloured . . . . . 1·60 1·60
2250 $4 multicoloured . . . . . 2·50 3·25
MS2251 Two sheets, each 106 × 76 mm. (a) $6 "Suffer Little Children to Come Unto Me" (detail) (Van Dyck) (horiz). (b) $6 "Adoration of the Magi" (Rembrandt) (horiz). Set of 2 sheets . . . . 7·50 8·50

118 Man Ho Temple, 1841

1997. "HONG KONG '97" International Stamp Exhibition. Hong Kong Past and Present. T **118** and similar horiz designs. Multicoloured. P 14.

MS2252 Five sheets, each 120 × 96 mm. (a) $3 Type **118**; $3 Man Ho Temple, 1983. (b) $3 St. John's Cathedral, Victoria 1886; $3 St. John's Cathedral, Victoria 1983. (c) $3 Victoria Harbour, 1858; $3 Victoria Harbour, 1983. (d) $3 Waterfront skyscraper; $3 Aerial view of central Victoria. (e) $3 Signing of Treaty of Nanking, 1852. $3 Margaret Thatcher signing The Joint Declaration, 1984. Set of 5 sheets . . . . 22·00 20·00

1997. 50th Anniv of UNESCO. As T **273a** of Gambia. Multicoloured.

2253 15c. Temple, Kyoto, Japan 40 20
2254 25c. Roman ruins, Trier, Germany 40 20
2255 $1 Gateway, Mount Taishan, China 80 80
2256 $1 Temple guardian, Kyoto, Japan (vert) 80 80
2257 $1 Temple deity, Kyoto, Japan (vert) 80 80
2258 $1 Temple lamp, Kyoto, Japan (vert) 80 80
2259 $1 Ayutthaya, Thailand (vert) 80 80
2260 $1 Statue, Borobudur Temple, Indonesia (vert) 80 80
2261 $1 Monuments at Pattadakal, India (vert) 80 80
2262 $1 Sleeping buddha, Polonnaruwa, Sri Lanka (vert) 80 80
2263 $1 Sagarmatha National Park, Nepal (vert) 80 80
2264 $1 Congonhas Sanctuary, Brazil (vert) 80 80
2265 $1 Cartagena, Colombia (vert) 80 80
2266 $1 Pueblo, Guatemala (vert) 80 80
2267 $1 Maya statue, Honduras (vert) 80 80
2268 $1 Popocatepetl Monastery, Mexico (vert) 80 80
2269 $1 Galapagos Islands, Ecuador (vert) 80 80
2270 $1 Waterfall, Costa Rica (vert) 80 80
2271 $1 Glaciares National Park, Argentina (vert) 80 80
2272 $1.50 Notre Dame Cathedral, Paris, France 1·10 1·10
2273 $1.50 Timbered house, Maulbronn, Germany . . 1·10 1·10
2274 $1.50 Gateway, Himeji-jo, Japan . . . . 1·10 1·10
2275 $1.50 Lion statues, Delphi, Greece . . . . 1·10 1·10
2276 $1.50 Palace of Fontainebleau, France . . 1·10 1·10
2277 $1.50 Scandola Nature Reserve, France . . . . . 1·10 1·10
2278 $2 Citadel, Dubrovnik, Croatia . . . . 1·50 1·60
2279 $4 Angra do Heroismo, Portugal . . . . 2·50 3·00
MS2280 Three sheets, each 127 × 102 mm. (a) $6 Mont St. Michel, France. (b) $6 Ruins of Teotihuacau, Mexico. (c) $6 Temple, Chengde, China. Set of 3 sheets . . . . 10·00 11·00

119 Springer Spaniel

1997. Cats and Dogs. Multicoloured.

2281 35c. Type **119** 50 25
2282 45c. Abyssinian blue 50 30
2283 50c. Burmese cream (vert) 50 30
2284 75c. Doberman pinscher . . 75 50
2285 90c. Persian tortoiseshell and white 75 50
2286 $1 Italian spinone (vert) . . 85 55
2287 $1.50 Siamese chocolate point . . . . 1·10 1·10
2288 $1.50 Oriental shorthair white . . . . 1·10 1·10
2289 $1.50 Burmese sable . . . . 1·10 1·10
2290 $1.50 Abyssinian tabby . . 1·10 1·10
2291 $1.50 Persian shaded silver 1·10 1·10
2292 $1.50 Tonkinese natural mink . . . . 1·10 1·10
2293 $1.50 Leonberger . . . . . 1·10 1·10
2294 $1.50 Newfoundland . . . . 1·10 1·10
2295 $1.50 Boxer . . . . 1·10 1·10
2296 $1.50 St. Bernard . . . . . 1·10 1·10
2297 $1.50 Silky terrier . . . . . 1·10 1·10
2298 $1.50 Miniature schnauzer 1·10 1·10
2299 $2 Cocker spaniel (vert) . . 1·50 1·60
2300 $3 Oriental shorthair agouti (vert) . . . . 2·00 2·25
MS2301 Two sheets. (a) 75 × 105 mm. $6 Sphynx (vert). (b) 105 × 75 mm. $6 Golden retriever puppy. Set of 2 sheets . . . . 7·50 8·00

Nos. 2287/92 (cats) and Nos. 2293/8 (dogs) respectively were printed together, se-tenant, with the backgrounds forming composite designs.

1997. Dinosaurs. As T **438** of Grenada. Mult.

2302 45c. Stegosaurus 60 30
2303 90c. Diplodocus 80 50
2304 $1 Pteranodon (vert) 80 55
2305 $1.50 Rhamphorhynchus and head of Brachiosaurus . . . . . 1·10 1·10
2306 $1.50 Archaeopteryx . . . . 1·10 1·10
2307 $1.50 Anurognathus and body of Brachiosaurus . . 1·10 1·10
2308 $1.50 Head of Albertosaurus 1·10 1·10
2309 $1.50 Herrerasaurus and legs of Brachiosaurus . . 1·10 1·10
2310 $1.50 Platyhystrix and body of Albertosaurus . . . . 1·10 1·10
2311 $2 Deinonychus and Ankylasaurus (vert) . . . 1·50 1·60
MS2312 Two sheets, each 103 × 74 mm. (a) $6 Allosaurus (vert). (b) $6 Hydacrosaurus. Set of 2 sheets . . . . 8·00 8·50

Nos. 2305/10 were printed together, se-tenant, with the backgrounds forming a composite design.

1997. 300th Anniv of Mother Goose Nursery Rhymes. Sheet 72 × 102 mm containing vert design as T **276a** of Gambia. Multicoloured.

MS2313 $6 Girl and sheep ("Baa, Baa, Black Sheep") . . . . . 3·50 4·00

1997. 50th Death Anniv of Paul Harris (founder of Rotary International). As T **276b** of Gambia. Multicoloured.

2314 $3 Paul Harris and village women with water pump, Burkina Faso . . . . . . 1·50 2·00
MS2315 78 × 108 mm. $6 Early Rotary parade float . . . . . . 3·00 3·50

1997. Golden Wedding of Queen Elizabeth and Prince Philip. As T **276c** of Gambia. Multicoloured (except Nos. 2318/19).

2316 $1 Engagement photograph, 1947 . . . . 80 80
2317 $1 Royal coat of arms . . . 80 80
2318 $1 Queen Elizabeth and Duke of Edinburgh, 1953 (brown) 80 80
2319 $1 Formal portrait of Queen Elizabeth with Prince Philip in uniform (brown) 80 80
2320 $1 Sandringham House . . 80 80
2321 $1 Queen Elizabeth and Prince Philip in carriage 80 80
MS2322 100 × 70 mm. $6 Wedding photograph, 1947 . . . . . . 3·50 3·75

1997. "Pacific '97" International Stamp Exhibition, San Francisco. Death Centenary of Heinrich von Stephan (founder of the U.P.U.). As T **276d** of Gambia.

2323 $1.50 green . . . . 1·10 1·10
2324 $1.50 brown . . . . 1·10 1·10
2325 $1.50 violet . . . . 1·10 1·10
MS2326 82 × 118 mm. $6 blue and black . . . . 3·25 3·75

DESIGNS: No. 2323, Pony Express, 1860; 2324, Von Stephan and Mercury; 2325, American steam locomotive; **MS**2326 Von Stephan and camel courier, Baghdad.

1997. Birth Bicentenary of Hiroshige (Japanese painter). "100 Famous Views of Edo". As T **541a** of Ghana but horiz. Multicoloured.

2327 $1.50 "Koume Embankment" . . . . . 1·00 1·00
2328 $1.50 "Azuma Shrine and the Entwined Camphor" 1·00 1·00
2329 $1.50 "Yanagishima" . . . 1·00 1·00
2330 $1.50 "Inside Akiba Shrine, Ukeji" . . . . 1·00 1·00
2331 $1.50 "Distant View of Kinryuzan Temple and Azuma Bridge" . . . . . 1·00 1·00
2332 $1.50 "Night View of Matsuchiyama and the San'ya Canal" . . . . . 1·00 1·00
MS2333 Two sheets, each 102 × 127 mm. (a) $6 "Five Pines, Onagi Canal". (b) $6 "Spiral Hall, Five Hundred Rakan Temple". Set of 2 sheets . . . . 7·00 7·50

1997. 175th Anniv of Brothers Grimm's Third Collection of Fairy Tales. "The Fox and the Geese". As T **277a** of Gambia. Multicoloured.

2334 $2 Fox and geese . . . . . 1·60 1·60
2335 $2 Fox with knife and fork and geese . . . . 1·60 1·60
2336 $2 Fox asleep and singing geese . . . . 1·60 1·60
MS2337 124 × 96 mm. $6 Fox (horiz) 3·75 4·00

1997. Winter Olympic Games, Nagano, Japan. As T**440** of Grenada. Multicoloured.

2338 90c. Slalom 65 50
2339 $1 Downhill skiing 70 70
2340 $1 Freestyle ski-jumping (blue and green ski suit) 70 70
2341 $1 Curling 70 70
2342 $1 Ski-jumping (pink ski suit) 70 70
2343 $1 Four-man bobsleigh . . 70 70
2344 $1 Nordic combined 70 70
2345 $1 Speed skating 70 70
2346 $1 Ice hockey 70 70
2347 $1 Cross-country skiing . . 70 70
2348 $2 One-man luge . . . . . 1·25 1·40
2349 $3 Men's figure-skating . . 1·75 1·90
2350 $5 Speed skating (different) 2·75 3·00
MS2351 Two sheets, each 97 × 67 mm. (a) $6 Figure skating. (b) $6 One-man luge (vert). Set of 2 sheets . . . . 7·00 7·50

120 Hong Kong

1997. Return of Hong Kong to China. Multicoloured.

2352 **120** $1 multicoloured 70 60
2353 – $1.25 multicoloured . . 80 80
2354 – $1.50 mult (63 × 32 mm) 95 1·00
2355 – $2 mult (63 × 32 mm) . . 1·25 1·40

DESIGNS: $1.25 to $2 Modern Hong Kong shown through inscriptions.

1997. Marine Life. As T **439** of Grenada. Mult.

2356 10c. Wimplefish 10 10
2357 15c. Clown triggerfish . . . 10 10
2358 25c. Ringed emperor angelfish 10 15
2359 35c. Hooded butterflyfish . . 15 20
2360 45c. Semicircle angelfish . . 20 25
2361 75c. Scribbled angelfish . . 30 35
2362 90c. Threadfin butterflyfish 35 40
2363 $1 Clown surgeonfish . . . 40 45
2364 $2 Bottle-nosed dolphin . . 80 85
2365 $5 Triggerfish . . . . 2·00 2·10
2366 $10 Lionfish . . . . 4·00 4·25
2367 $20 Jackknifefish . . . . . 8·00 8·25

121 Winnie the Pooh as Monday's Child

1997. "Monday's Child" (poem). Disney cartoon characters from Winnie the Pooh illustrating various verses. Multicoloured.

2368 $1 Type **121** . . . . 1·25 1·25
2369 $1 Kanga as Tuesday's child 1·25 1·25
2370 $1 Eeyore as Wednesday's child . . . . 1·25 1·25
2371 $1 Tigger as Thursday's child . . . . 1·25 1·25
2372 $1 Piglet as Friday's child 1·25 1·25
2373 $1 Rabbit as Saturday's child . . . . 1·25 1·25
MS2374 128 × 107 mm. $6 Christopher Robin as Sunday's child . . . . 5·50 5·50

122 Snow White kissing Grumpy

1997. Disney Sweethearts. Disney cartoon characters kissing. Multicoloured.

2375 $1 Type **122** . . . . 1·10 1·10
2376 $1 Figaro the Cat and Cleo the Fish . . . . 1·10 1·10
2377 $1 Peter Pan and Wendy . . 1·10 1·10
2378 $1 Cinderella and the Prince 1·10 1·10
2379 $1 Ariel and Eric . . . . . 1·10 1·10
2380 $1 Beauty and the Prince . . 1·10 1·10
2381 $1 Aladdin and Jasmine . . 1·10 1·10
2382 $1 Pocahontas and Captain John Smith . . . . 1·10 1·10
2383 $1 Phoebus and Esmeralda 1·10 1·10
MS2384 127 × 102 mm. $6 Georges Hautecourt kissing cats tail (vert) 6·00 6·00

1997. World Cup Football Championship, France (1998). As T **283a** of Gambia.

2385 10c. blue 25 25
2386 20c. multicoloured 30 30
2387 45c. brown 40 30
2388 $1 black 70 70
2389 $1 brown 70 70
2390 $1 black 70 70
2391 $1 brown 70 70
2392 $1 multicoloured 70 70
2393 $1 multicoloured 70 70
2394 $1 black 70 70
2395 $1 brown 70 70
2396 $1 multicoloured 70 70
2397 $1 black 70 70
2398 $1 black 70 70
2399 $1 black 70 70
2400 $1 black 70 70
2401 $1 black 70 70
2402 $1 black 70 70
2403 $1 black 70 70
2404 $1 black 70 70
2405 $1.50 multicoloured . . . . 95 1·00
2406 $5 black . . . . 2·75 3·00
MS2407 Two sheets. (a) 127 × 102 mm. $6 black. (b) 102 × 127 mm. $6 black. Set of 2 sheets . . . . 8·50 9·00

DESIGNS—HORIZ: No. 2385, Italian team, 1934; 2386, Angolan team; 2387, Brazilian team, 1958; 2388, Uruguay team, 1950; 2389, Winning England team, 1966; 2390, West German team, 1954; 2391, Uruguyan officials with Jules Rimet trophy, 1930; 2392, West German players celebrating, 1990; 2393, Maradona (Argentine player), 1986; 2394, Brazilian players, 1994; 2395, Argentine players, 1978; 2396, West German player holding World Cup, 1974; 2405, West German team, 1974; 2406, Italian team, 1938; **MS**2407b, Paulao, Angola. VERT: No. 2397, Ademir, Brazil; 2398, Kocsis, Hungary; 2399, Leonidas, Brazil; 2400, Nejedly, Czechoslavakia; 2401, Schiavio, Italy; 2402, Stabile, Uruguay; 2403, Pele, Brazil; 2404, Fritzwalter, West Germany; **MS**2407a, Shearer, England.

1997. Butterflies. As T **444** of Grenada. Mult.

2408 75c. "Polyura dehaani" . . 65 45
2409 90c. "Polyura dolon" . . . 70 50
2410 $1 "Charaxes candiope" . . 70 55
2411 $1.50 "Pantaporia punctata" 95 95
2412 $1.50 "Euthalia confucius" 95 95
2413 $1.50 "Euthalia kardama" 95 95
2414 $1.50 "Limenitis albomaculata" 95 95
2415 $1.50 "Hestina assimilis" . . 95 95
2416 $1.50 "Kallima inachus" . . 95 95
2417 $1.50 "Euthalia teutoides" 95 95
2418 $1.50 "Euphaedra francina" 95 95
2419 $1.50 "Euphaedra eleus" . . 95 95
2420 $1.50 "Euphaedra harpalyce" 95 95
2421 $1.50 "Euphaedra cyparissa" 95 95
2422 $1.50 "Euphaedra gausape" 95 95
2423 $1.50 "Euphaedra imperialis" 95 95
2424 $2 "Charaxes etesippe" . . 1·25 1·40
2425 $3 "Charaxes castor" . . . 1·75 1·90
MS2426 Two sheets, each 106 × 76 mm. (a) $5 "Charaxes nobilis" (vert). (b) $6 "Charaxes numenes" (vert). Set of 2 sheets 6·50 7·00

Nos. 2412/17 and 2418/23 respectively were printed together, se-tenant, with the backgrounds forming composite designs.

123 James Dean

1997. James Dean (actor) Commemoration. Different portaits. Multicoloured.
2427 $1 Type **123** 70 70
2428 $1 Wearing purple jumper 70 70
2429 $1 Wearing stetson and smoking 70 70
2430 $1 Wearing dinner jacket and tie 70 70
2431 $1 Full-face portrait 70 70
2432 $1 Grimacing 70 70
2433 $1 Wearing stetson 70 70
2434 $1 Leaning on arms 70 70
2435 $1 Smoking 70 70

124 "Symphyglossum sanguineum"

1997. Orchids of the World. Multicoloured.
2436 35c. Type **124** 40 25
2437 45c. "Doritaenopsis" "Mythic Beauty" . . . 50 30
2438 75c. "Odontoglossum cervantesii" 65 45
2439 90c. "Cattleya" "Pumpernickel" . . . 70 50
2440 $1 "Vanda" "Patricia Low" 70 55
2441/9 $1 × 9 ("Lycaste" "Aquila"; "Brassolaeliocattleya" "Dorothy Bertsch"; "Phalaenopsis" "Zuma Urchin"; "Promenaea xanthina"; "Amesiella philippinensis"; "Brassocattleya" "Angel Lace"; "Brassoepidendrum" "Peggy Ann"; "Miltonia seine"; "Sophralaeliocattleya" "Precious Stones") . . 5·50
2450/8 $1 × 9 ("Cymbidium" "Showgirl"; "Disa blackii"; "Phalaenopsis aphrodite"; "Iwanagaara" "Apple Blossom"; "Masdevallia" "Copper Angel"; "Paphiopedilum micranthum"; "Paphiopedilum" "Clare de Lune"; "Cattleya forbesii"; "Dendrobium" "Dawn Maree") . . . . 5·50
2459 $1.50 "Odontonia" "Debutante" . . . . . 1·00 1·00
2460/5 $1.50 × 6 ("Miltoniopsis" "Jean Sabourin"; "Cymbidium" "Red Beauty"; "Brassocattleya" "Green Dragon"; "Phalaenopsis" hybrid; "Laeliocattleya" "Mary Ellen Carter"; "Disa" hybrid) . . . . . . 5·50
2466/71 $1.50 × 6 ("Lycaste macrobulbon"; "Cochleanthes discolor"; "Cymbidium" "Nang Carpenter"; "Paphiopedilum" "Claire de Lune"; "Masdevallia caudata"; "Cymbidium" "Showgirl") . . . . . 5·50
2472 $2 "Laeliocattleya" "Mini Purple" . . . . 1·25 1·40
2473 $3 "Phragmipedium dominiarum" . . . . 1·75 1·90
MS2474 Two sheets, each 76 × 106 mm. (a) $5 "Phalenopsis" "Medford Star". (b) $6 "Brassolaelio-cattleya" "Dorothy Bertsch". Set of 2 sheets . . . 7·00 7·50
Nos. 2460/5 and 2466/71 respectively were printed together, se-tenant, with the backgrounds forming composite designs.

125 "Clitocybe metachroa"

1997. Fungi. Multicoloured.
2475 75c. Type **125** 60 45
2476 90c. "Clavulinopsis helvola" 70 50
2477 $1 "Lycoperdon pyriforme" 70 55
2478 $1.50 "Auricularia auricula-judae" 95 95
2479 $1.50 "Entoloma incanum" 95 95
2480 $1.50 "Coprinus atramentarius" 95 95
2481 $1.50 "Mycena polygramma" 95 95
2482 $1.50 "Lepista nuda" . . . 95 95
2483 $1.50 "Pleurotis cornucopiae" 95 95
2484 $1.50 "Laccaria amethystina" 95 95
2485 $2 "Clathrus archeri" . . . . 1·25 1·40
2486 $3 "Lactarius trivialis" . . . 1·75 1·90
MS2487 Two sheets, each 106 × 76 mm. (a) $6 "Morchella esculenta". (b) $6 "Amanita muscaria". Set of 2 sheets . . . 7·50 8·00

126 Ludwig van Beethoven

1997. Classical Composers. Multicoloured.
2488 $1 Type **126** 85 80
2489 $1 Pyotr Tchaikovsky . . . 85 80
2490 $1 Johann Christian Bach 85 80
2491 $1 Frederic Chopin 85 80
2492 $1 Igor Stravinsky 85 80
2493 $1 Franz Joseph Haydn . . 85 80
2494 $1 Gustav Mahler 85 80
2495 $1 Gioacchino Antonio Rossini 85 80
MS2496 Two sheets, each 106 × 76 mm. (a) $6 Wolfgang Amadeus Mozart. (b) $6 Franz Schubert. Set of 2 sheets . . . 9·50 9·50

127 Diana, Princess of Wales and Buckingham Palace

1997. Diana, Princess of Wales Commemoration. Multicoloured.
2497 $1.50 Type **127** . . . . . . 1·10 1·10
2498 $1.50 Princess Diana and lake at Althorp . . . . . 1·10 1·10
2499 $1.50 Princess Diana and Westminster Abbey . . . 1·10 1·10
2500 $1.50 Princess Diana and gates to Althorp . . . . 1·10 1·10
2501 $1.50 Princess Diana in pink hat and gates to Kensington Palace . . . . 1·10 1·10
2502 $1.50 Princess Diana and Althorp House . . . . . 1·10 1·10
MS2503 115 × 80 mm. $6 Holding bouquet (60 × 40 mm) . . . . 3·75 4·00

1997. Christmas. Religious Paintings. As T **448** of Grenada. Multicoloured.
2504 20c. "Choir of Angels (Simon Marmion) 30 15
2505 75c. "The Annunciation" (Giotto) 65 45
2506 90c. "Festival of the Rose Garlands" (Albrecht Durer) 70 50
2507 $1.50 "Madonna with Two Angels" (Hans Memling) 95 1·00
2508 $2 "The Ognissanti Madonna" (Giotto) . . . 1·25 1·40
2509 $3 "Angel with Candlestick" (Michelangelo) . . . . . 1·75 1·90
MS2510 Two sheets, each 114 × 104 mm. (a) $6 "The Rising of the Sun" (detail) (horiz) (Francois Boucher). (b) $6 "Cupid" (detail) (horiz) (Jean-Baptiste Huet). Set of 2 sheets 7·50 7·50
No. 2506 is inscribed "DUER" in error.

1998. Fishes. As T **449** of Grenada. Multicoloured.
2511 $1 Queen angelfish 75 75
2512 $1 Clown triggerfish 75 75
2513 $1 Four-spot butterflyfish 75 75
2514 $1 Yellow-tailed damselfish 75 75
2515 $1 Yellow-headed wrasse . . 75 75
2516 $1 Royal gramma 75 75
2517 $1 Candy basslet 75 75
2518 $1 Smooth trunkfish 75 75
2519 $1 Coral hind 75 75
MS2520 Two sheets. (a) 102 × 72 mm. $6 Black-finned reef shark. (b) 72 × 102 mm. $6 Yellow-headed jawfish (vert). Set of 2 sheets . . . . 8·50 8·50
Nos. 2511/19 were printed together, se-tenant , with the backgrounds forming a composite design.

128 Tiger (hologram)

1998. Chinese New Year ("Year of the Tiger").
2521 **128** $1.50 black on silver foil 1·25 1·25
MS2522 64 × 76 mm. 128 $3 black on silver foil (52 × 65 mm) . . 2·00 2·00

129 "Alabama" (Confederate warship)

1998. Famous Ships. Multicoloured. (a) Ships of the 1860s.
2523 75c. Type **129** 65 65
2524 75c. "Persia" (paddle-steamer) 65 65
2525 75c. "Ariel" (clipper) . . . 65 65
2526 75c. "Florida" (Confederate warship) 65 65
2527 75c. "Great Eastern" (paddle-steamer) 65 65
2528 75c. "Jacob Bell" on fire . . 65 65
2529 75c. "Star of India" (clipper) 65 65
2530 75c. "Robert E. Lee" (Mississippi paddle-steamer) 65 65
2531 75c. U.S.S. "Passaic" (monitor) 65 65
2532 75c. "Madagascar" (clipper) 65 65
2533 75c. H.M.S. "Devastation" (battleship) 65 65
2534 75c. "General Grant" (clipper) 65 65

(b) Ships of the American Civil War.
2535 $1 Clark Gable as Rhett Butler in "Gone with the Wind" (vert) 75 75
2536 $1 Crew abandoning blockade runner wrecked on Sullivan's Island (vert) 75 75
2537 $1 Margaret Mitchell (author of "Gone with the Wind") (vert) 75 75
2538 $1 George Alfred Trenholm (ship owner) (vert) . . . 75 75
2539 $1 Dock Street Theatre, Charleston (vert) 75 75
2540 $1 "Howlett" (paddle-steamer) sinking (vert) . . 75 75
2541 $1 U.S.S. "Tecumseh" on fire (vert) 75 75
2542 $1 City Jail, Charleston (vert) 75 75
MS2543 Two sheets, each 106 × 76 mm. (a) $6 "Nashville" sinking Union clipper "Harvey Birch" (57 × 42 mm). (b) $6 "Hatteras" (paddle-steamer) on fire (42 × 57 mm). Set of 2 sheets 8·00 8·50

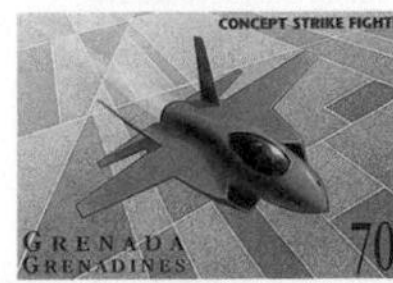

130 Concept Strike Fighter

1998. Aircraft Designs of the Future. Multicoloured.
2544 70c. Type **130** 50 40
2545 90c. Concept space shuttle 70 60
2546 $1 Velocity 173 RG Elite . . 75 75
2547 $1 Davis DA-9 . . . . . . 75 75
2548 $1 Concorde 75 75
2549 $1 Voyager 75 75
2550 $1 Factimobile 75 75
2551 $1 RAF 2000 . . . . 75 75
2552 $1 Boomerang 75 75
2553 $1 N1M Flying Wing 75 75
2554 $2 Concept air and space jet 1·40 1·40
2555 $3 V Jet II . . . . 1·75 1·75
MS2556 Two sheets, each 100 × 70 mm. (a) $6 Concept aeropod. (b) $6 Delmar. Set of 2 sheets . . . . 8·00 8·50

131 "Lycaste deppei"

1998. Orchids of the World. Multicoloured.
2557 $1 Type **131** 70 70
2558 $1 "Dendrobium victoriae" 70 70
2559 $1 "Dendrobium nobile" . . 70 70
2560 $1 "Cymbidium dayanum" 70 70
2561 $1 "Cymbidium" "Starbright" 70 70
2562 $1 "Cymbidium giganteum" 70 70
2563 $1 "Chysis aurea" 70 70
2564 $1 "Broughtonia sanguinea" 70 70
2565 $1 "Cattleya guttata" . . . 70 70
2566 $1 "Calanthe vestita" . . . 70 70
2567 $1 "Cattleya bicolor" . . . 70 70
2568 $1 "Laelia anceps" 70 70
2569 $1 "Epidendrum prismatocarpum" 70 70
2570 $1 "Coelogyne ochracea" 70 70
2571 $1 "Doritaenopsis eclantant" 70 70
2572 $1 "Laelia gouldiana" . . . 70 70
2573 $1 "Encyclia vitellina" . . . 70 70
2574 $1 "Maxillaria praestans" 70 70
2575 $1 "Laelia tenebrosa" . . . 70 70
2576 $1.50 "Phragmipedium besseae" . . . . 1·10 1·10
2577 $2 "Pschopsis papilio" . . . 1·40 1·40
2578 $3 "Masdevallia coccinea" 1·75 1·75
MS2579 Two sheets, each 29 × 43 mm. (a) $6 "Masdevallia ignea". (b) $6 "Encyclia brassavolae". Set of 2 sheets 8·00 8·50

1998. Seabirds. As T **452** of Grenada. Multicoloured.
2580 75c. Bonaparte's gull (horiz) 60 40
2581 90c. Western sandpiper (horiz) 70 50
2582 $1.50 Common tern (horiz) 1·00 1·00
2583 $1.50 Brown pelican (horiz) 1·00 1·00
2584 $1.50 Black-legged kittiwake and white tern (horiz) . . 1·00 1·00
2585 $1.50 Herring gull (horiz) 1·00 1·00
2586 $1.50 Lesser noddy (horiz) 1·00 1·00
2587 $1.50 Black-legged kittiwake (horiz) . . . . 1·00 1·00
2588 $1.50 Whimbrel (horiz) . . 1·00 1·00
2589 $1.50 Golden white-tailed tropic bird (horiz) . . . . 1·00 1·00
2590 $1.50 Arctic tern (horiz) . . 1·00 1·00
2591 $1.50 Ruddy turnstone (horiz) . . . . 1·00 1·00
2592 $1.50 Blue-eyed cormorant ("Imperial Shag") (horiz) 1·00 1·00
2593 $1.50 Magellan gull (horiz) 1·00 1·00
2594 $2 Great black-backed gull (horiz) . . . . 1·40 1·40
2595 $3 Dotterell (horiz) . . . . 1·75 1·75
MS2596 Two sheets, each 100 × 70 mm. (a) $5 Broad-billed prion (horiz). (b) $5 Yellow-nosed albatross. Set of 2 sheets . . . 7·50 8·00

1998. International Year of the Ocean. As T **454** of Grenada. Multicoloured.
2597 75c. Great black-backed gull 50 50
2598 75c. Common dolphin . . . 50 50
2599 75c. Seal 50 50
2600 75c. Amazonian catfish . . 50 50
2601 75c. Shark 50 50
2602 75c. Goldfish 50 50
2603 75c. Cyathopharynx 50 50
2604 75c. Killer whale 50 50
2605 75c. Telmatochromis 50 50
2606 75c. Crab 50 50
2607 75c. Octopus 50 50
2608 75c. Turtle 50 50
2609 90c. Two dolphins 55 55
2610 90c. Seal 55 55
2611 90c. Turtle on rock 55 55
2612 90c. Leopard shark 55 55
2613 90c. Flame angelfish 55 55
2614 90c. Syndontis 55 55
2615 90c. Lamprologus 55 55
2616 90c. "Krptopterus bicirrhus" 55 55
2617 90c. "Pterophyllum scalare" 55 55
2618 90c. Swimming pancake . . 55 55
2619 90c. Cowfish 55 55
2620 90c. Seahorse 55 55
MS2621 Two sheets, each 98 × 68 mm. (a) $6 "Tetraodon mbu". (b) $6 Goldfish. Set of 2 sheets . . . . 8·00 8·50
Nos. 2597/2608 and 2609/20 respectively were printed together, se-tenant, with the backgrounds forming composite designs.

1998. 50th Anniv of Organization of American States. As T **454a** of Grenada.
2622 $1 violet, orange and black 75 75

1998. 25th Death Anniv of Pablo Picasso (painter). As T **291a** of Gambia. Multicoloured.
2623 45c. "Bust of a Woman" (vert) 50 30
2624 $2 "Three Musicians" . . . 1·25 1·25

2625 $3 "Studio at La Californie" 1·75 1·75
MS2626 102×127 mm. $5 "Woman with a Blue Hat" 3·00 3·25

1998. Birth Centenary of Enzo Ferrari (car manufacturer). As T **454b** of Grenada. Multicoloured.
2627 $2 275 GTB 1·50 1·50
2628 $2 340 MM 1·50 1·50
2629 $2 250 GT SWB Berlinetta "Hot Rod" 1·50 1·50
MS2630 104×72 mm. $5 First Ferrari cabriolet (91×34 mm). P 14×14½ 3·50 3·75

1998. 19th World Scout Jamboree, Chile. As T **455** of Grenada. Multicoloured.
2631 90c. Scout greeting 60 40
2632 $1.50 Lord Baden-Powell 90 90
2633 $5 Scout salute 2·50 3·00
MS2634 76×106 mm. $6 Lord Baden-Powell (vert) 3·50 4·00

1998. 50th Death Anniv of Mahatma Gandhi. As T **455a** of Grenada.
2635 $1 grey, brown and black 1·00 80
MS2636 100×70 mm. $6 grey, brown and black 4·00 4·00

1998. 80th Anniv of Royal Air Force. As T **292a** of Gambia. Multicoloured.
2637 $2 Tornado GR1 1·40 1·40
2638 $2 BAe Hawk T1A 1·40 1·40
2639 $2 Sepecat Jaguar GR1 1·40 1·40
2640 $2 Harrier GR7 1·40 1·40
2641 $2 Chinook helicopter carrying three loads 1·40 1·40
2642 $2 Silhouette of BAe Harrier GR5 1·40 1·40
2643 $2 Panavia Tornado F3 ADV at sunset 1·40 1·40
2644 $2 Chinook HC2 carrying 105 mm light gun 1·40 1·40
MS2645 Four sheets, each 93×70 mm. (a) $6 Bristol F2B fighter and head of golden eagle (bird). (b) $6 Bristol F2B fighter and montagu's harrier in flight. (c) $6 Hawker Hunter and EF-2000 Eurofighter. (d) $6 Tornado and EF-2000 Eurofighter. Set of 4 sheets 15·00 16·00

1998. Birth Bicentenary of Eugene Delacroix (painter). As T **294** of Gambia. Multicoloured.
2646 $1 "The Natchez" 70 70
2647 $1 "Christ and His Disciples Crossing the Sea of Galilee" 70 70
2648 $1 "Sunset" 70 70
2649 $1 "Moroccans outside the Walls of Tangier" 70 70
2650 $1 "The Fireplace" 70 70
2651 $1 "Forest View with an Oak Tree" 70 70
2652 $1 "View of the Harbour at Dieppe" 70 70
2653 $1 "Arab Tax Collectors" 70 70
MS2654 85×105 mm. $5 "Young Orphan" 3·00 3·25

1998. 1st Death Anniv of Diana, Princess of Wales. As T **293a** of Gambia.
2655 $1.50 multicoloured 60 65

132 Father Christmas and Hare

1998. Disney's Christmas Trains. Walt Disney cartoon characters in train carriages. Multicoloured.
2656 $1 Type **132** 85 85
2657 $1 Giraffe, elephant and tiger 85 85
2658 $1 Three Pigs and Wolf 85 85
2659 $1 Pied Piper, Jiminy Cricket, penguins and children 85 85
2660 $1 Swans, Little Hiawatha and tortoise 85 85
2661 $1 Mickey Mouse as train driver 85 85
2662 $1 Pluto, Chip and Dale 85 85
2663 $1 Donald and Daisy Duck 85 85
2664 $1 Goofy, Huey, Dewey and Louie 85 85
2665 $1 Minnie Mouse and presents 85 85
2666 $1 Piglet as train driver 85 85
2667 $1 Winnie the Pooh and honey 85 85
2668 $1 Rabbit and Owl 85 85
2669 $1 Kanga, Roo and Christopher Robin 85 85
2670 $1 Eeyore and Tigger 85 85
MS2671 Three sheets, each 133×109 mm. (a) $6 Father Christmas and toy train. (b) $6 Mickey Mouse as train driver. (c) $6 Rabbit, Winnie the Pooh, Piglet and Eeyore. Set of 3 sheets 12·00 13·00

1999. Chinese New Year ("Year of the Rabbit"). Sheet 150×76 mm, containing triangular designs as T **435** of Grenada each showing rabbits. Multicoloured. Self-adhesive on gold foil.
MS2672 $1.50, "GRENADA GRENADINES" in green; $1.50 "GRENADA GRENADINES" in orange; $1.50 "GRENADA GRENADINES" in red 2·25 2·50

133 Troodon

1999. "Australia '99" World Stamp Exhibition, Melbourne. Prehistoric Animals. Multicoloured.
2673 $1 Type **133** 75 75
2674 $1 Camptosaurus 75 75
2675 $1 Parasaurolophus 75 75
2676 $1 Dryosaurus 75 75
2677 $1 Gallimimus 75 75
2678 $1 Camarasaurus 75 75
2679 $1.50 Duckbill (horiz) 1·00 1·00
2680 $1.50 Lambeosaurus (horiz) 1·00 1·00
2681 $1.50 Igaunodon (horiz) 1·00 1·00
2682 $1.50 Euoplocephalus (horiz) 1·00 1·00
2683 $1.50 Triceratops (horiz) 1·00 1·00
2684 $1.50 Brachiosaurus (horiz) 1·00 1·00
2685 $1.50 Ponoptosaurus (horiz) 1·00 1·00
2686 $1.50 Stegosaurus (horiz) 1·00 1·00
MS2687 Three sheets. (a) 106×76 mm. $6 Edmontosaurus (horiz). (b) 76×106 mm. $6 "Tyrannosaurus Rex". (c) 76×106 mm. $6 Halticosaurus. Set of 3 sheets 11·00 12·00

134 Great Indian Peninsula Passenger and Mail Locomotive

1999. Steam Trains of the World. Multicoloured.
2688 15c. Type **134** 50 25
2689 75c. Midland Great Western passenger locomotive (Ireland) 60 45
2690 90c. Canada Pacific express locomotive 70 55
2691 $1.50 East Indian Railway express locomotive 1·00 1·00
2692 $2 Victorian Railways suburban tank locomotive (Australia) 1·25 1·25
2693 $2 Eastern Railways compound locomotive (France) 1·25 1·25
2694 $2 Govt Railways Class WF tank locomotive (New Zealand) 1·25 1·25
2695 $2 Burma Railways oil-burning tank locomotive, 1899 1·25 1·25
2696 $2 Federated Malay States Railway Class G steam locomotive, 1899 1·25 1·25
2697 $2 Belfast and Northern Counties Railway narrow-gauge tank locomotive 1·25 1·25
2698 $2 Shunting tank locomotive (Russia) 1·25 1·25
2699 $2 G.N.R. Ivatt large-boilered "Atlantic" type 1·25 1·25
2700 $2 Palatine Railway "Atlantic" type express locomotive (Germany) 1·25 1·25
2701 $2 Belgian State Railways "Dunalastair" type locomotive 1·25 1·25
2702 $2 Swedish State Railways Class Cc locomotive 1·25 1·25
2703 $2 Antofagasta and Bolivian Railway tank locomotive (Chile) 1·25 1·25
2704 $2 Bolivian State Fairlie type locomotive 1·25 1·25
2705 $2 Belgian State Railways express locomotive 1·25 1·25
2706 $2 London and South Western Railway Drummond's mixed traffic locomotive 1·25 1·25
2707 $2 Belfast and Northern Counties Railways Compound locomotive 1·25 1·25
2708 $2 Dutch State Railway express passenger locomotive 1·25 1·25
2709 $2 Gothard Railway heavy freight locomotive (Switzerland) 1·25 1·25
2710 $2 Waterford, Limerick and Western railway goods locomotive (Ireland) 1·25 1·25
2711 $2 Atchison, Topeka and Santa Fe railway tandem compound express locomotive (U.S.A.) 1·25 1·25
2712 $2 Midland Railway Class "Princess of Wales" locomotive (Great Britain) 1·25 1·25
2713 $3 Glasgow and South Western Railway Stirling type locomotive 1·60 1·75
MS2714 Two sheets, each 100×70 mm. (a) $6 Paris, Lyons and Mediterranean compound locomotive (France). (b) $6 Italian Southern Railway compound locomotive. Set of 2 sheets 7·50 7·50
No. 2701 is inscribed "Dunalastiar" in error.

135 Porkfish

1999. Fauna and Flora. Multicoloured.
2715 75c. Type **135** 60 40
2716 90c. Leatherback turtle 70 55
2717 $1 Red-billed tropic bird ("White-tailed Tropicbird") (vert) 70 70
2718 $1 Laughing gull (vert) 70 70
2719 $1 Palm tree (vert) 70 70
2720 $1 Humpback whale (vert) 70 70
2721 $1 Painted bunting (vert) 70 70
2722 $1 Common grackle (vert) 70 70
2723 $1 Green anole (lizard) (vert) 70 70
2724 $1 "Morpho peleides" (butterfly) (vert) 70 70
2725 $1 "Prepona meander" (butterfly) (vert) 70 70
2726 $1 Common dolphin (vert) 70 70
2727 $1 "Catonephele numilia" (butterfly) (vert) 70 70
2728 $1 Sooty tern (vert) 70 70
2729 $1 Vermilion flycatcher (vert) 70 70
2730 $1 Blue grosbeak (vert) 70 70
2731 $1 Great egret (vert) 70 70
2732 $1 "Actinate pellenea" (butterfly) (vert) 70 70
2733 $1 "Anteos clorinde" (butterfly) (vert) 70 70
2734 $1 Common iguana (vert) 70 70
2735 $1.50 Ruby-throated hummingbird 90 90
2736 $2 "Theope eudocia" (butterfly) 1·40 1·40
MS2737 Two sheets, each 85×110 mm. (a) $6 Bananaquit. (b) $6 Beaugregory (fish). Set of 2 sheets 7·50 8·00
Nos. 2717/25 and 2726/34 respectively were printed together, se-tenant, with the backgrounds forming composite designs.
No. 2727 is inscribed "numili" in error.

136 John H. Glenn (astronaut), 1998

1999. John Glenn's (first American to orbit Earth) Return to Space. Multicoloured, except Nos. 2716, 2718 and 2720/1.
2738 $1 Type **136** 70 70
2739 $1 Glenn and Pres. John F. Kennedy (brown and red) 70 70
2740 $1 Inside "Discovery", 1998 70 70
2741 $1 Climbing from "Friendship 7" capsule, 1962 (brown and red) 70 70
2742 $1 Medical checkup 70 70
2743 $1 Climbing into space capsule, 1962 (brown and red) 70 70
2744 $1 As Democratic Senator for Ohio, 1974 (vert) (brown and red) 70 70
2745 $1 In space suit, 1962 (vert) 70 70
2746 $1 Smiling during suit up test, 1998 (vert) 70 70
2747 $1 Preparing for "Discovery" flight (vert) 70 70
2748 $1 At press conference (with microphone) (vert) 70 70
2749 $1 Smiling at camera (wearing glasses) (vert) 70 70
2750 $1 Participating in medical research (vert) 70 70
2751 $1 Posing in space suit, 1998 (vert) 70 70
No. 2744 was inscribed "Junior Senator form Ohio (1974)" in error.

1999. "iBRA '99" International Stamp Exhibition, Nuremberg. As T **298a** of Gambia. Multicoloured.
2752 35c. "Luckenbach" (full-rigged ship) and Thurn and Taxis Northern District 1852 ¼sgr. stamp 30 30
2753 45c. Leipzig–Dresden Railway carriage and Schleswig-Holstein 1850 1s. 30 30
2754 $1.50 Leipzig–Dresden Railway carriage and Oldenburg 1852 ⅓sgr. 1·00 1·00
2755 $3 "Luckenbach" (full-rigged ship) and North German Confederation 1868 ¼g. 1·75 2·00
MS2756 154×86 mm. $6 Thurn and Taxis Northern District 1865 ¼sgr. rouletted pair used on cover 3·50 3·75

1999. 150th Death Anniv of Katsushika Hokusai (Japanese artist). As T **298b** of Gambia. Multicoloured.
2757 $1.50 "Fuchu" 90 90
2758 $1.50 "Doll Fair at Fikkendana" 90 90
2759 $1.50 "Sumo Wrestlers" (in arm hold) 90 90
2760 $1.50 "Sumo Wrestlers" (in head lock) 90 90
2761 $1.50 "Sojo Henjo" 90 90
2762 $1.50 "Twin Gardens Gateway of Asakusa Kannon Temple" 90 90
2763 $1.50 "A Breeze on a Fine Day" 90 90
2764 $1.50 "Ejiri" 90 90
2765 $1.50 "Horse Drawings" (galloping) 90 90
2766 $1.50 "Horse Drawings" (stationary) 90 90
2767 $1.50 "View along Bank of Sumida River" 90 90
2768 $1.50 "Thunderstorm Below the Mountain" 90 90
MS2769 Two sheets, each 102×72 mm. (a) $6 "Stretching Cloth" (vert). (b) $6 "Kobo Daishi exorcising Demon that causes Sickness" (vert). Set of 2 sheets 7·00 8·00
No. 2762 is inscribed "TWIN GARDAINS GATEWAY" in error.

1999. 10th Anniv of United Nations Rights of the Child Convention. As T **298c** of Gambia. Multicoloured.
2770 $3 African boy 1·60 1·75
2771 $3 Liv Ullman (UNICEF's first female ambassador) 1·60 1·75
2772 $3 African woman in head scarf 1·60 1·75
MS2773 110×84 mm. $6 Maurice Pate (Founding Director of UNICEF) 2·75 3·25
Nos. 2770/2 were printed together, se-tenant, forming a composite design.

1999. "PhilexFrance '99" International Stamp Exhibition, Paris. Railway Locomotives. Two sheets containing horiz designs as T **299d** of Gambia. Multicoloured.
MS2774 (a) 106×81 mm. $6 Paris, Orleans and Mediterranean Railway Cha Pelon type steam locomotive. (b) 106×76 mm. $6 French National Railways Class 7000 high speed electric locomotive. Set of 2 sheets 7·50 8·00

1999. 250th Birth Anniv of Johann von Goethe (German writer). As T **298d** of Gambia.
2775 $3 multicoloured 1·60 1·75
2776 $3 blue and black 1·60 1·75
2777 $3 blue, violet and black 1·60 1·75
MS2778 71×106 mm. $6 brown, chestnut and black 2·75 3·25
DESIGNS—HORIZ: No. 2775, Peasants dancing under linden-tree; 2776, Goethe and Schiller; 2777, Faust dreams of soaring above the mortal. VERT: **MS**2778, Johann von Goethe.

1999. Royal Wedding. As T **298** of Gambia. Multicoloured.
2779 $3 Sophie Rhys-Jones 1·75 1·90
2780 $3 Sophie and Prince Edward 1·75 1·90
2781 $3 Prince Edward 1·75 1·90
MS2782 78×108 mm. $6 Sophie and Prince Edward on wedding day 3·25 3·50

1999. "Queen Elizabeth the Queen Mother's Century". As T **304a** of Gambia.
2783 $2 black and gold 1·40 1·40
2784 $2 multicoloured 1·40 1·40
2785 $2 black and gold 1·40 1·40
2786 $2 multicoloured 1·40 1·40
MS2787 153×157 mm. $6 multicoloured 3·50 3·50
DESIGNS: No. 2783, Lady Elizabeth Bowes-Lyon as a child; 2784, Queen Mother in Rhodesia, 1957; 2785, Queen Mother with Princesses Elizabeth and Anne, 1950; 2786, Queen Mother, 1988. (37×50 mm)—**MS**2787, Queen Mother reviewing Black Watch, Berlin.

138 George Raft   140 Kirk Douglas

139 "Sputnik I", 1957

1999. Early Cinema Actors. Multicoloured.
2788 **138** $1 multicoloured 70 70
2789 – $1 grey and black 70 70
2790 – $1 grey and black 70 70
2791 – $1 multicoloured 70 70
2792 – $1 multicoloured 70 70
2793 – $1 black and grey 70 70
2794 – $1 black, blue and grey 70 70
2795 – $1 multicoloured 1·10 1·10
2796 – $2 multicoloured 1·10 1·10
2797 – $2 black and grey 1·10 1·10
2798 – $2 multicoloured 1·10 1·10
2799 – $2 black and grey 1·10 1·10
MS2800 $6 multicoloured 3·50 3·50
DESIGNS: No. 2791, Fatty Arbuckle; 2792, Buster Keaton; 2795, Harold Lloyd; 2796, James Cagney; 2798, Edward G. Robinson; **MS**2800, Charlie Chaplin. (53 × 39 mm): No. 2789, George Raft in "Scarface"; 2790, Fatty Arbuckle with nurse; 2793, Buster Keaton on locomotive cow-catcher; 2794, Harold Lloyd hanging on clockface; 2797, James Cagney in "The Public Enemy"; 2799, Edward G. Robinson in "Little Caesar".

1999. Space Exploration. Multicoloured.
2801 $1.50 Type **139** 1·00 1·00
2802 $1.50 "Explorer I", 1958 1·00 1·00
2803 $1.50 "Telstar I" satellite, 1962 1·00 1·00
2804 $1.50 "Maristat I", 1976 1·00 1·00
2805 $1.50 Long Duration Exposure facility, 1984 1·00 1·00
2806 $1.50 Hubble Space Telescope, 1990 1·00 1·00
2807 $1.50 X-15 rocket plane, 1960 (vert) 1·00 1·00
2808 $1.50 "Freedom 7" rocket, 1961 (vert) 1·00 1·00
2809 $1.50 "Friendship 7", 1962 (vert) 1·00 1·00
2810 $1.50 "Gemini 4" rocket and Edward H. White, 1965 (vert) 1·00 1·00
2811 $1.50 Saturn V rocket and Edwin E. Aldrin stepping onto Moon, 1969 (vert) 1·00 1·00
2812 $1.50 Lunar Rover, "Apollo 15" mission, 1971 (vert) 1·00 1·00
MS2813 Two sheets, each 110 × 85 mm. (a) $6 "Mars Pathfinder", 1997 (55 × 42 mm); (b) $6 Space shuttle "Columbia", 1981 (55 × 42 mm). Set of 2 sheets 7·50 8·00
Nos. 2801/6 and 2807/12 were each printed together, se-tenant, with the backgrounds forming composite designs.

1999. Kirk Douglas (American actor). Multicoloured.
2814 $1.50 Type **140** 90 90
2815 $1.50 As a boxer in "Champion" 90 90
2816 $1.50 As Van Gogh in "Lust for Life" 90 90
2817 $1.50 With white hair and wearing black shirt 90 90
2818 $1.50 In French uniform for "Paths of Glory" 90 90
2819 $1.50 As a cowboy in "The Bad and the Beautiful" 90 90
MS2820 93 × 106 mm. $6 As Spartacus 3·00 3·25

141 Elvis Presley

1999. Elvis Presley Commemoration. Each grey, silver and black.
2821 $1.50 Type **141** 1·00 1·00
2822 $1.50 Resting chin on hand 1·00 1·00
2823 $1.50 Wearing roll-neck sweater 1·00 1·00
2824 $1.50 Leaning against brick wall 1·00 1·00
2825 $1.50 Singing into microphone 1·00 1·00
2826 $1.50 Singing with eyes closed 1·00 1·00

141a Howard Thurston (magician)   142 Poinsettia and Candle

1999. Famous Magicians. Multicoloured.
2826a $1.50 Type **141a** 90 90
2826b $1.50 Harry Houdini 90 90
2826c $1.50 Harry Kellar 90 90

1999. Christmas. Foliage and Candles. Mult.
2827 15c. Type **142** 15 10
2828 35c. Holly 25 20
2829 75c. Fir tree 60 35
2830 $1.50 Ivy 90 85
2831 $3 Geranium 1·60 2·00
MS2832 83 × 108 mm. $6 "The Adoration of the Magi" (horiz) 3·25 3·50
No. 2829 is inscribed "FUR TREE" in error.

2000. New Millennium. People and Events of Fourteenth Century (1300–30). As T **417a** of Grenada. Multicoloured.
2833 50c. Robert the Bruce, King of Scotland, 1306 40 40
2834 50c. Fresco by Giotto, 1306 40 40
2835 50c. Mansa Musa, ruler of Mali, 1307 40 40
2836 50c. Dante and *The Divine Comedy*, 1321 40 40
2837 50c. Noh Theatre masks, Japan, 1325 40 40
2838 50c. Staircase, Tenochtitlan (Aztec capital, founded 1325) 40 40
2839 50c. Ibn Batuta on camel (start of journey, 1325) 40 40
2840 50c. Great Munich Fire, 1327 40 40
2841 50c. Grand Duke Ivan I (transfer of capital to Moscow, 1328) 40 40
2842 50c. Archers and castle (beginning of Hundred Years War, 1337) 40 40
2843 50c. Cannon at siege of Calais, 1346 (first recorded use of cannon) 40 40
2844 50c. "Death" (Black Death in Europe, 1348) 40 40
2845 50c. Boccaccio composing *The Decameron*, 1348 40 40
2846 50c. Early Italian spectacles, 1350 40 40
2847 50c. Knight (introduction of plate armour, 1350) 40 40
2848 50c. Junks (completion of Grand Canal of China, 1326) (59 × 39 mm) 40 40
2849 50c. Maori canoe (Maori migration to New Zealand, 1350) 40 40

143 Dragon

2000. Chinese New Year ("Year of the Dragon"). Sheet 79 × 60 mm.
MS2850 **143** $4 multicoloured 2·25 2·40

144 Barn Swallow

2000. Birds. Multicoloured.
2851 75c. Type **144** 60 45
2852 90c. Caribbean coot 70 50
2853 $1 Turquoise parrot 70 70
2854 $1 Scarlet-chested parrot 70 70
2855 $1 Red-capped parrot 70 70
2856 $1 Eastern rosella 70 70
2857 $1 Budgerigar 70 70
2858 $1 Superb parrot ("Orange-Flanked Parakeet") 70 70
2859 $1 Mallee ringneck parrot 70 70
2860 $1 Red-rumped parrot 70 70
2861 $1 Yellow-fronted parakeet 70 70
2862 $1 Rainbow lory ("Red-collared Lorikeet") 70 70
2863 $1 Lesser sulphur-crested cockatoo ("Citron-crested Cockatoo") 70 70
2864 $1 Papuan lory ("Stella's Lorikeet") 70 70
2865 $1 Major Mitchell's cockatoo ("Leadbeator's Cockatoo") 70 70
2866 $1 Golden conure 70 70
2867 $1 Red-spotted lorikeet 70 70
2868 $1 Red-shouldered macaw ("Nobel macaw") 70 70
2869 $1 Goffin's cockatoo 70 70
2870 $1 Sun conure 70 70
2871 $1.50 Puerto Rican emerald 1·00 1·00
2872 $1.50 Green mango 1·00 1·00
2873 $1.50 Red-legged thrush 1·00 1·00
2874 $1.50 Green-cheeked amazon ("Red-crowned Parrot") 1·00 1·00
2875 $1.50 Hispaniolan amazon ("Hispaniolan Parrot") 1·00 1·00
2876 $1.50 Yellow-headed parrot ("Yellow-crowned Parrot") 1·00 1·00
2877 $1.50 Yellow-shouldered blackbird 1·00 1·00
2878 $1.50 Troupial 1·00 1·00
2879 $1.50 Green-throated carib 1·00 1·00
2880 $1.50 Nanday conure ("Black-hooded Parakeet") 1·00 1·00
2881 $1.50 Scarlet tanager 1·00 1·00
2882 $1.50 Golden bishop ("Yellow-crowned Bishop") 1·00 1·00
2883 $2 Moorhen ("Common Moorhen") 1·40 1·50
2884 $3 Orange-winged amazon ("Orange-winged Parrot") 1·75 1·90
MS2885 Four sheets. (a) 74 × 98 mm. $6 Crimson rosella ("Pennant's Parakeet"). (b) 74 × 98 mm. $6 Scarlet macaw (vert). (c) 75 × 107 mm. $6 Puerto Rican lizard cuckoo. (d) 75 × 107 mm. $6 Pin-tailed whydah (vert). Set of 4 sheets 14·00 15·00
Nos. 2853/61, 2862/70, 2871/6 and 2877/82 were each printed together, se-tenant, with the backgrounds forming composite designs.
No. 2859 is inscribed "Rigneck", No. 2863 "Cocatoo", No. 2865 "Cockatto" and No. 2869 "GoffinsCocatto", all in error.

145 *Cantharellus cinnabarinus*   146 Ferdinand Magellan (Spanish navigator)

2000. Fungi. Multicoloured.
2886 $2 Type **145** 1·25 1·25
2887 $2 *Hygrocybe conica* 1·25 1·25
2888 $2 *Cortinarius violaceus* 1·25 1·25
2889 $2 *Leccinum versipelle* 1·25 1·25
2890 $2 *Russula xerampelina* 1·25 1·25
2891 $2 *Entoloma nitidum* 1·25 1·25
2892 $2 *Lentinus tigrinus* 1·25 1·25
2893 $2 *Mycena flavoalba* 1·25 1·25
2894 $2 *Boletus legaliae* (horiz) 1·25 1·25
2895 $2 *Russula emetica* (horiz) 1·25 1·25
2896 $2 *Cortinarius alboviolaceus* (horiz) 1·25 1·25
2897 $2 *Volvariella bombycina* (horiz) 1·25 1·25
MS2898 Two sheets, each 103 × 81 mm. (a) $6 *Gomphus floccosus* (horiz). (b) $6 *Collybia dryophila* (horiz). Set of 2 sheets 7·50 8·00
No. 2886 is inscribed "Canharellus", No. 2889 "Lecinum", and No. **MS**2898 (a) "Comphus", all in error.

2000. New Millennium. Sea Exploration. Mult.
2899 50c. Type **146** 40 40
2900 50c. Ship in storm 40 40
2901 50c. Queen Elizabeth I's hand on globe 40 40
2902 50c. Two wandering albatrosses ("Albatrosses") 40 40
2903 50c. Emperor penguins 40 40
2904 50c. Tahitian woman 40 40
2905 50c. Breadfruit 40 40
2906 50c. Moai (carved statue) on Easter Island 40 40
2907 50c. Maori carving 40 40
2908 50c. Lobster 40 40
2909 50c. Orchid 40 40
2910 50c. Walrus 40 40
2911 50c. Kangaroo 40 40
2912 50c. H.M.S. *Beagle* (Charles Darwin) careened 40 40
2913 50c. Magnificent frigate bird ("Frigatebird") 40 40
2914 50c. Ship and boats in the Strait of Magellan (59 × 39 mm) 40 40
2915 50c. Captain James Cook (English navigator) 40 40

146a Salvador Allende elected President of Chile, 1970

2000. New Millennium. People and Events of Twentieth Century (1970–79). Multicoloured.
2916 20c. Type **146a** 25 25
2917 20c. Cartoon characters around globe (introduction of Earth Day holiday, 1970) 25 25
2918 20c. Computerized Axial Tomography (CAT) scanner, 1971 25 25
2919 20c. Pres. Richard Nixon in China (re-opening of U.S. relations with People's Republic, 1972) 25 25
2920 20c. Terrorist and flag (murder of Israeli athletes at Munich Olympics 1972) 25 25
2921 20c. Petrol ration sign (OPEC oil price rises, 1973) 25 25
2922 20c. Sydney Opera House, 1973 25 25
2923 20c. Pres. Richard Nixon leaving helicoptor (resignation 1974) 25 25
2924 20c. Stylized black hole (new theory, 1974) 25 25
2925 20c. U.S. Bicentennial celebrations, 1976 25 25
2926 20c. Louise Brown, first test tube baby, born (born 1978) 25 25
2927 20c. Pope John Paul II visiting Poland, 1978 25 25
2928 20c. Ayatollah Khomeini (Iran's Islamic Revolution, 1978) 25 25
2929 20c. Concorde (first flight, 1979) 25 25
2930 20c. Charles de Gaulle (died 1970) and Eiffel Tower 25 25
2931 20c. Pres. Sadat, Prime Minister Begin and Pres. Carter (Camp David Talks 1978/9) (59 × 39 mm) 25 25
2932 20c. Mother Teresa (Nobel Peace Prize, 1979) 25 25
No. 2932 is inscribed "Noble Peace Prize" in error.

147 Elongate Mbuna ("Slender Mbuna")

2000. Tropical Fish. Multicoloured.
2933 35c. Type **147** 30 25
2934 45c. *Pygoplites diacanthus* 30 25
2935 75c. *Pomacanthus semicirclatus* 60 60
2936 75c. Siamese fighting fish 60 60
2937 90c. *Zanclus canescens* 70 60
2938 $1 *Xiphophorus maculatus* 70 70
2939 $1 Dwarf pencilfish 70 70
2940 $1 Bumblebee goby 70 70
2941 $1 Black-headed blenny 70 70
2942 $1 Velvet boarfish 70 70
2943 $1 Red-tailed surgeonfish ("Achilles Tang") 70 70
2944 $1 Swordtail 70 70
2945 $1 Moorish idol 70 70
2946 $1 Banded pipefish 70 70
2947 $1 Striped catfish 70 70
2948 $1 Emperor angelfish 70 70
2949 $1 Magenta dottyback ("Strawberryfish") 70 70
2950 $1 Jackknife-fish 70 70
2951 $1 Flame angelfish 70 70
2952 $1 Yellow-tailed ("Clarke's") anemonefish 70 70
2953 $1 Flash-back dottyback 70 70
2954 $1 Coral trout 70 70
2955 $1 Foxface 70 70
2956 $1.65 *Bodianus rufus* 1·10 1·10
2957 $1.65 *Coris aygula* 1·10 1·10
2958 $1.65 *Centropyge bicolor* 1·10 1·10
2959 $1.65 *Balistoides conspicillum* 1·10 1·10
2960 $1.65 *Poecilia reticulata* 1·10 1·10
2961 $1.65 *Heniochus acuminatus* 1·10 1·10
2962 $1.65 *Plectorhinchus chaetodonoides* 1·10 1·10
2963 $1.65 *Bodianus pulchellus* 1·10 1·10
2964 $1.65 *Acanthurus leucosternon* 1·10 1·10
2965 $1.65 *Chromileptis altivelis* 1·10 1·10
2966 $1.65 *Pterophyllum scalare* 1·10 1·10
2967 $1.65 *Premnas biaculeatus* 1·10 1·10
2968 $2 Pennant coralfish ("Wimplefish") 1·40 1·60

2969 $2 *Gramma loreto* . . . . . 1·40 1·60
2970 $3 *Zebrasoma xanthurum* . . 1·60 1·75
MS2971 Four sheets. (a) 97 × 68 mm. $6 Harlequin Tuskfish. (b) 97 × 68 mm. $6 Purple Queen. (c) 93 × 65 mm. $6 *Equetus punctatus*. (d) 93 × 65 mm. $6 *Pomacanthus imperator* (vert). Set of 4 sheets . . . . 14·00 15·00

Nos. 2940/7, 2948/55, 2956/61 and 2962/7 were each printed together, se-tenant, with the backgrounds forming composite designs.

No. 2942 is inscribed "CCAPROS APER", No. 2949 "PSEUDOCHROMIS ORPHYREUS", No. 2954 "CEPHALOPHELIS MINIATUS", No. 2962 "PLECTORHYNCHUS CHAETODONOIDS" and No. 2963 "BODIANUS PUCHELLUS", all in error.

2000. 400th Birth Anniv of Sir Anthony Van Dyck (Flemish painter). As T **312a** of Gambia. Mult.
2972 $1.50 "Portrait of an Elderly Woman" 90 90
2973 $1.50 "Head of a Young Woman" 90 90
2974 $1.50 "Portrait of a Man" 90 90
2975 $1.50 "Jan van den Wouwer" 90 90
2976 $1.50 "Portrait of a Young Man" 90 90
2977 $1.50 "Everhard Jabach" . . 90 90
2978 $1.50 "Man in Armour" . . 90 90
2979 $1.50 "Portrait of a Young General" 90 90
2980 $1.50 "Emanuele Filiberto, Prince of Savoy" 90 90
2981 $1.50 "Donna Polixena Spinola Guzman de Leganes" 90 90
2982 $1.50 "Luigia Cattaneo Gentile" 90 90
2983 $1.50 "Giovanni Battista Cattaneo" 90 90
2984 $1.50 "Marchesa Paolina Adorno Brignole-Sale" (1623–25) 90 90
2985 $1.50 "Marchesa Geronima Spinola" 90 90
2986 $1.50 "Marchesa Paolina Adorna Brignole-Sale" (1627) 90 90
2987 $1.50 "Marcello Durazzo" 90 90
2988 $1.50 "Marchesa Grimaldi Cattaneo with a Black Page" 90 90
2989 $1.50 "Young Man of the House of Spinola" . . . 90 90
2990 $1.50 "Cardinal Bentivoglio" 90 90
2991 $1.50 "Cardinal Infante Ferdinand" 90 90
2992 $1.50 "Cesare Alessandro Scaglia, Abbe of Staffarda and Mandanici" 90 90
2993 $1.50 "A Roman Clergyman" 90 90
2994 $1.50 "Jean-Charles della Faille" 90 90
2995 $1.50 "Cardinal Domenico Rivarola" 90 90
MS2996 Six sheets. (a) 100 × 123 mm. $5 "Hendrick van der Bergh". (b) 100 × 123 mm. $5 "Jaques le Roy". (c) 100 × 123 mm. $6 "Justus van Meerstraeten". (d) 100 × 123 mm. $6 "Frederik Hendrik, Prince of Orange". (e) 100 × 123 mm. $6 "Maria Louisa de Tassis" (horiz). (f) 123 × 100 mm. $6 "Abbot Scaglia adoring the Virgin and Child" (horiz). Set of 6 sheets 19·00 21·00

Nos. 2972/3 are inscribed "Women", No. 2983 "Cattanaeo" and No. 2992 "Stafford", all in error.

2000. 18th Birthday of Prince William. As T **312b** of Gambia. Multicoloured.
2997 $1.50 Prince William with birthday gift . . . . . . 1·10 1·10
2998 $1.50 In Eton uniform . . . 1·10 1·10
2999 $1.50 Wearing checked shirt 1·10 1·10
3000 $1.50 Wearing grey suit . . 1·10 1·10
MS3001 100 × 80 mm. $6 Wearing blue jumper (37 × 50 mm) . . . 4·00 4·00

2000. "EXPO 2000" World Stamp Exhibition, Anaheim, U.S.A. Spacecraft. As T **582a** of Ghana. Multicoloured.
3002 $1.50 "Foton" and comet 1·00 1·00
3003 $1.50 "Sub-Satellite" and rock particle . . . . 1·00 1·00
3004 $1.50 Satellite near Eros . . 1·00 1·00
3005 $1.50 "Explorer 16" . . . . 1·00 1·00
3006 $1.50 Space Shuttle *Challenger* . . . . 1·00 1·00
3007 $1.50 Giotto facing right and Halley's Comet . . . 1·00 1·00
3008 $1.50 Circular satellite with aerial (inscr "Foton") . . 1·00 1·00
3009 $1.50 Giotto facing left (inscr "Sub-Satellite") . . 1·00 1·00
3010 $1.50 Satellite with solar panels extended (inscr "Near Eros") . . . . . . 1·00 1·00
3011 $1.50 Satellite over planet surface (inscr "Explorer XVI") . . . . 1·00 1·00
3012 $1.50 Satellite with folded solar panels (inscr "Astro Challenger") . . . . . . 1·00 1·00
3013 $1.50 Circular satellite with cones on base (inscr "Giotto Halley's Comet") 1·00 1·00
MS3014 Two sheets. (a) 76 × 106 mm. $6 "Pegasus" over Saturn. (b) 106 × 76 mm. $6 "Lunar Prospector". Set of 2 sheets . . . . 7·50 8·00

Nos. 3002/7 and 3008/13 were each printed together, se-tenant, with the backgrounds forming composite designs.

Inscriptions on Nos. 3008/13 repeat those of Nos. 3002/7 in error.

2000. 25th Anniv of "Apollo–Soyuz" Joint Project. As T **582b** of Ghana. Multicoloured.
3015 $3 Thomas P. Stafford (Commander of "Apollo 18") . . . . . . 1·75 1·90
3016 $3 Joint Mission Badge . . 1·75 1·90
3017 $3 Donald D. Slayton ("Apollo 18") . . . . . 1·75 1·90
MS3018 70 × 88 mm. $6 Alexei Leonov (Commander of "Soyuz 19") . . . . 3·50 3·75

2000. 50th Anniv of Berlin Film Festival. As T **582c** of Ghana. Multicoloured.
3019 $1.50 James Stewart in *Mr. Hobbs takes a Vacation*, 1962 . . . . 1·00 1·00
3020 $1.50 Sachiko Hidari in *Kanojo To Kare*, 1964 . . 1·00 1·00
3021 $1.50 Juliette Mayniel in *Kirmes*, 1960 . . . . . . 1·00 1·00
3022 $1.50 *Le Bonheur*, 1965 . . 1·00 1·00
3023 $1.50 *La Notte*, 1961 . . . 1·00 1·00
3024 $1.50 Lee Marvin in *Cat Ballou*, 1965 . . . . . . 1·00 1·00
MS3025 97 × 103 mm. $6 *The Thin Red Line*, 1999 . . . . 3·50 3·75

2000. 175th Anniv of Stockton and Darlington Line (first public railway). As T **582d** of Ghana. Multicoloured.
3026 $3 As Type **582d** of Ghana 2·00 2·00
3027 $3 George Stephenson's *Rocket* . . . . 2·00 2·00

2000. 250th Death Anniv of Johann Sebastian Bach (German composer). Sheet, 75 × 88 mm, containing vert design as T **312c** of Gambia. Multicoloured.
MS3028 $6 Statue of Johann Sebastian Bach . . . . 4·00 4·25

2000. Election of Albert Einstein (mathematical physicist) as *Time Magazine* "Man of the Century". Sheet, 117 × 90 mm, containing vert design as T **312d** of Gambia. Multicoloured.
MS3029 $6 Albert Einstein . . . 3·50 3·75

2000. Centenary of First Zeppelin Flight. As T **582e** of Ghana, each incorporating a portrait of Count Ferdinand von Zeppelin. Multicoloured.
3030 $3 LZ-3, 1906 . . . . . . 1·75 1·90
3031 $3 LZ-56, 1915 . . . . . . 1·75 1·90
3032 $3 LZ-88, 1917 . . . . . . 1·75 1·90
MS3033 118 × 75 mm. $6 LZ-1, 1900 (50 × 37 mm) . . . . 4·00 4·25

2000. Olympic Games, Sydney. As T **582f** of Ghana. Multicoloured.
3034 $2 Frantz Reichel (rugby), Paris (1900) . . . . . . 1·40 1·40
3035 $2 Modern discus-thrower 1·40 1·40
3036 $2 Seoul Sports Complex (1988) and South Korean flag . . . . 1·40 1·40
3037 $2 Ancient Greek wrestlers 1·40 1·40

148 *Euplagia quadripunctaria*

2000. Butterflies and Moths. Multicoloured.
3038 $1.50 Type **148** 90 90
3039 $1.50 *Oenosandra boisduvalii* 90 90
3040 $1.50 *Thinopteryx erocopterata* 90 90
3041 $1.50 *Euschemon rafflesia* . . 90 90
3042 $1.50 *Milionia isodoxa* . . . 90 90
3043 $1.50 *Oysphania euprina* . . 90 90
3044 $1.50 *Thaloina clara* 90 90
3045 $1.50 *Zerynthnia rumina* . . 90 90
3046 $1.50 *Attacus atlas* 90 90
3047 $1.50 *Lasiocampa quercus* 90 90
3048 $1.50 *Pararge schakra* . . . 90 90
3049 $1.50 *Arhopala amantes* . . 90 90
3050 $1.50 *Heliconius charithonia* 90 90
3051 $1.50 *Dismorphia amphione* 90 90
3052 $1.50 *Theela coronata* . . . 90 90
3053 $1.50 *Cithaerias esmeralda* 90 90
3054 $1.50 *Zerene eurydice* . . . 90 90
3055 $1.50 *Theela eudoela* 90 90
3056 $1.50 *Catonephele numilia* 90 90
3057 $1.50 *Diaethria clymena* . . 90 90
3058 $1.50 *Mesene phareus* . . . 90 90
3059 $1.50 *Estigmene aerea* . . . 90 90
3060 $1.50 *Marpesia petreus* . . . 90 90
3061 $1.50 *Cepheuptychia cephus* 90 90
MS3062 Six sheets. (a) 70 × 95 mm. $6 *Tajuria cippus*. (b) 78 × 97 mm. $6 *Ecpantheria serifonia*. (c) 75 × 105 mm. $6 *Ornithoptera alexandrae*. (d) 127 × 100 mm. $6 *Hyalophora cecropia* (vert). (e) 100 × 73 mm. $2 *Cyrestis thyodamos*; $2 *Papilionidae*; $2 *Apatura iris*; $2 *Crypsiphona ocyltaria*. (f) 100 × 73 mm. $2 *Hemaris thysbe*; $2 *Helicopis cupido*; $2 *Aretia eaja*; $2 *Erateina staudingeri*. Set of 6 sheets . . 21·00 23·00

Nos. 3038/43, 3044/9, 3050/5 and 3056/61 were each printed together, se-tenant, with the backgrounds forming composite designs.

No. 3038 is inscribed "quadripunctama", No. 3041 "Eusehemon zafflesia", No. 3045 "Zerynthia", No. 3048 "Parage", No. 3050 "charitonius", No. 3056 "numili", **MS**3062 (d) "Hyalophor", all in error.

150 Golsdorf Compound Tank Locomotive, Vienna Metropolitan Railway

2000. Railways of the World. Multicoloured.
3066 90c. Type **150** 75 50
3067 $1 Vauxhall, Dublin and Kingstown Railway . . . 75 55
3068 $1.50 Electric railcar, South Jersey Transit 90 90
3069 $1.50 "Metroliner", Amtrak 90 90
3070 $1.50 Maglev train, H.S.S.T. 90 90
3071 $1.50 Model E60C electric locomotive, Amtrak . . . 90 90
3072 $1.50 "Parsifal" diesel express, T.E.E. 90 90
3073 $1.50 Class G.G.I. electric locomotive, Pennsylvania 90 90
3074 $1.50 Electric locomotive, Norwegian State Railways 90 90
3075 $1.50 Diesel-electric locomotive, Jamaica Railway 90 90
3076 $1.50 Diesel-electric locomotive, China 90 90
3077 $1.50 Electric locomotive, Portuguese Railways . . . 90 90
3078 $1.50 "Re-6/6" electric locomotive, Swiss Federal Railways 90 90
3079 $1.50 Dual-purpose electric locomotive, Turkish State Railways 90 90
3080 $1.50 Passenger steam locomotive, Perak Govt Railway 90 90
3081 $1.50 Tank locomotive, Rhondda & Swansea Railway 90 90
3082 $1.50 Aspinal tank locomotive, Lancashire & Yorkshire Railway . . . 90 90
3083 $1.50 Tank locomotive, Northwestern Railway, India 90 90
3084 $1.50 Imperial Mail locomotive, Shanghai–Nanking Railway 90 90
3085 $1.50 Passenger tank locomotive, Danish State Railway 90 90
3086 $1.50 Braithwait steam locomotive, Eastern Counties Railway 90 90
3087 $1.50 *Philadelphia*, Austria 90 90
3088 $1.50 Stephenson locomotive of 1836 . . . . 90 90
3089 $1.50 *Aigle* locomotive, Western Railway, France 90 90
3090 $1.50 Borsig Standard steam locomotive, Germany . . 90 90
3091 $1.50 *Ajax*, Great Western Railway 90 90
3092 $2 Metro-Cammell diesel-electric locomotive, Nigerian Railways . . . . 1·25 1·25
3093 $3 T.G.V. 001 high-speed turbo train, French National Railways . . . 1·60 1·75
MS3094 Four sheets, each 81 × 57 mm. (a) $6 *The Experiment*, U.S.A. (b) $6 Freight steam locomotive, South African Railway. (c) $6 Diesel-electric locomotive, South African Railway. (d) $6 "Prospector" diesel railcar, Western Australia. Set of 4 sheets . . . . 14·00 15·00

151 Irish Setter

2000. Cats and Dogs. Multicoloured.
3095 45c. Type **151** 45 30
3096 75c. Blue point snowshoe 60 45
3097 90c. Dalmatian 70 55
3098 $1.50 California spangled cat 90 90
3099 $1.50 Russian blue 90 90
3100 $1.50 Seal point Siamese . . 90 90
3101 $1.50 Black Devon rex . . . 90 90
3102 $1.50 Silver tabby British shorthair 90 90
3103 $1.50 Tricolour Japanese bobtail 90 90
3104 $1.50 Great Dane 90 90
3105 $1.50 Newfoundland 90 90
3106 $1.50 Rottweiler 90 90
3107 $1.50 Bulldog 90 90
3108 $1.50 Japanese spitz 90 90
3109 $1.50 Bull terrier 90 90
3110 $1.50 British white shorthair 90 90
3111 $1.50 Blue-cream American shorthair 90 90
3112 $1.50 Bombay 90 90
3113 $1.50 Red Burmese 90 90
3114 $1.50 Sorrel Abyssinian . . 90 90
3115 $1.50 Ocicat 90 90
3116 $1.50 Alaskan malamute . . 90 90
3117 $1.50 Golden retriever . . . 90 90
3118 $1.50 Afghan hound 90 90
3119 $1.50 Long-haired dachshund 90 90
3120 $1.50 Irish terrier 90 90
3121 $1.50 Miniature poodle . . 90 90
3122 $2 German shepherd . . . 1·25 1·25
3123 $3 Black and white maine coon . . . . 1·60 1·75
3124 $4 Brown tabby British shorthair . . . . 1·90 2·00
MS3125 Four sheets. (a) 106 × 76 mm. $5 Silver Classic Tabby Persian (horiz). (b) 76 × 106 mm. $5 Red-white Bicolor British Shorthair. (c) 106 × 76 mm. $6 Basset Hound (horiz). (d) 76 × 106 mm. $6 Labrador Retriever. Set of 4 sheets 13·00 14·00

Nos. 3098/103 (cats), 3104/9 (dogs), 3110/15 (cats) and 3116/21 (dogs) were each printed together, se-tenant, with the backgrounds forming composite designs.

No. 3108 is inscribed "Sptz" and No. 3121 "Minature", both in error.

2000. "Euro 2000" Football Championship. As T **479** of Grenada. Multicoloured.
3126 $1.50 Tofting (Danish player) 90 90
3127 $1.50 Danish team 90 90
3128 $1.50 Michael Laudrup (Danish player) 90 90
3129 $1.50 Jorgensen (Danish player) 90 90
3130 $1.50 Philips Stadium, Eindhoven 90 90
3131 $1.50 Moller (Danish player) 90 90
3132 $1.50 Thuram (French player) 90 90
3133 $1.50 French team 90 90
3134 $1.50 Barthez (French player) 90 90
3135 $1.50 Zidane (French player) 90 90
3136 $1.50 Jan Breydel Stadium, Bruges 90 90
3137 $1.50 Michel Platini (French player) 90 90
3138 $1.50 Giovanni van Bronckhorst (Dutch player) 90 90
3139 $1.50 Dutch team 90 90
3140 $1.50 Patrick Kluivert (Dutch player) 90 90
3141 $1.50 Johan Cruyff (Dutch player) 90 90
3142 $1.50 Amsterdam Arena Stadium 90 90
3143 $1.50 Zenden (Dutch player) 90 90
MS3144 Three sheets, each 145 × 96 mm. (a) $6 Bo Johansson (Danish trainer) (vert). (b) $6 Roger Lemerre (French trainer) (vert). (c) $6 Frank Rijkaard (Dutch trainer) (vert). Set of 3 sheets . . . . 10·00 10·50

152 St. Lucia Amazon

2000. "The Stamp Show 2000" International Stamp Exhibition, London. South American Fauna. Multicoloured.
3145 75c. Type **152** 60 45
3146 90c. Three-toed sloth . . . 60 45
3147 $1 Hispaniolan solenodon 70 55
3148 $1.50 Red vakari . . . . . 1·00 1·00
3149 $1.50 St. Andrews virea ("San Andreas Vireo") . . 1·00 1·00
3150 $1.50 Golden lion tamarin 1·00 1·00
3151 $1.50 American crocodile . . 1·00 1·00
3152 $1.50 Spectacled caimen . . 1·00 1·00
3153 $1.50 Rhinoceros iguana . . 1·00 1·00
3154 $1.50 Jaguarundis . . . . . 1·00 1·00
3155 $1.50 Andean condor . . . 1·00 1·00
3156 $1.50 Lesser rhea ("Darwin's Rhea") . . . 1·00 1·00
3157 $1.50 Central American tapir . . . . 1·00 1·00
3158 $1.50 Jaguar . . . . 1·00 1·00
3159 $1.50 Jamaican hutia . . . 1·00 1·00
3160 $2 Thick-billed parrot . . . 1·40 1·50
MS3161 Two sheets, each 106 × 71 mm. (a) $6 Kemp Ridley Sea Turtle. (b) $6 Pronghorn. Set of 2 sheets . . . . 7·50 8·00

Nos. 3148/53 and 3154/9 were each printed together, se-tenant, with the backgrounds forming composite designs.

2000. Monarchs of the Millennium. As T **314a** of Gambia. Multicoloured (except Nos. 3162 and 3166).
3162 $1.50 King Louis XVI of France (lilac, green and brown) . . . . 1·00 1·00
3163 $1.50 King Louis XVIII of France . . . . 1·00 1·00

3164 $1.50 Kublai Khan's Empress, China . . . . . 1·00 1·00
3165 $1.50 Queen Mary I of England . . . . 1·00 1·00
3166 $1.50 Mohammed Ali, Shah of Iran (black, green and brown) . . . . 1·00 1·00
3167 $1.50 Emperor Qianlong of China . . . . 1·00 1·00
MS3168 116×136 mm. $6 Grand Duke Vladimir I of Kiev . . . 3·25 3·50

2000. Popes of the Millennium. As T **314b** of Gambia. Multicoloured (except No. **MS**3173).
3169 $1.50 Adrian VI . . . . . 1·10 1·10
3170 $1.50 Paul II . . . . 1·10 1·10
3171 $1.50 Callistus III . . . . . 1·10 1·10
3172 $1.50 Eugene IV . . . . . 1·10 1·10
MS3173 116×136 mm. $6 Gregory XI (grey, black and green) . . 3·50 3·50

153 "Wind"
154 David Copperfield (portrait at left with levitating legs at right)

2000. "The Storm Riders" (Chinese comic series by Ma Wing Sing). Multicoloured.
3174 $4 Type **153** . . . . 1·90 2·00
3175 $4 "Cloud" with sword . . 1·90 2·00
3176 $4 "Cloud" with dragon . . 1·90 2·00
3177 $4 "Wind" with waves . . . 1·90 2·00

2000. David Copperfield (conjurer). Multicoloured.
3178 $1.50 Type **154** 90 90
3179 $1.50 Portrait at right with levitating body at left . . 90 90
3180 $1.50 Portrait at right with levitating legs at left . . . 90 90
3181 $1.50 Portrait at left with levitating body at right . . 90 90

2000. "Espana 2000" International Stamp Exhibition, Madrid. Paintings from the Prado. As T **326a** of Gambia. Multicoloured.
3182 $1.50 "St. John the Baptist and the Franciscan Maestro, Henricus Werl" (Robert Campin) 90 90
3183 $1.50 "Justice and Peace" (Corrado Giaquinto) . . . 90 90
3184 $1.50 "St. Barbara" (Robert Campin) 90 90
3185 $1.50 "John Fane, 10th Earl of Westmoreland" (Thomas Lawrence) . . . 90 90
3186 $1.50 "The Marchioness of Manzanedo" (Jean-Louis-Ernest Meissonier) . . . 90 90
3187 $1.50 "Mr. Storer" (Martin Archer Shee) 90 90
3188 $1.50 "Isabella Carla Eugenia" (Alonso Sanchez Coello) 90 90
3189 $1.50 "Nobleman with his Hand on his Chest" (El Greco) 90 90
3190 $1.50 "King Philip III" (Juan Pantoja de la Cruz) 90 90
3191 $1.50 Madonna and Child from "The Holy Family with Sts. Ildefonsus and John the Evangelist, and the Master Alonso de Villegas" (Blas del Prado) 90 90
3192 $1.50 "The Last Supper" (Bartolme Carducci) . . . 90 90
3193 $1.50 St. John from "The Holy Family with Sts. Ildefonsus and John the Evangelist, and the Master Alonso de Villegas" 90 90
3194 $1.50 "St. Dominic of Silos" (Bartolome Bermejo) . . 90 90
3195 $1.50 "Head of a Prophet" (Jaume Huguet) 90 90
3196 $1.50 "Christ giving His Blessing" (Fernando Gallego) 90 90
3197 $1.50 "The Mystic Marriage of St. Catherine" (Alonso Sanchez Coello) 90 90
3198 $1.50 "St. Catherine of Alexandria" (Fernando Yanez de la Almedina) . . 90 90
3199 $1.50 "Virgin and Child" (Luis de Morales) 90 90
MS3200 Three sheets, each 110×90 mm. (a) $6 As No. 3192 (horiz). (b) $6 "The Coronation of the Virgin" (El Greco) (horiz). (c) $6 As No. 3191. Set of 3 sheets 9·50 10·00

155 Barbara Taylor Bradford

2000. Great Writers of the 20th Century: Barbara Taylor Bradford. Sheet 126×87 mm.
MS3201 **155** $6 multicoloured . . 3·00 3·50

2000. 60th Anniv of Battle of Britain. As T **327** of Gambia. Multicolourred.
3202 $1 R.A.F. Pilots running to their planes 80 80
3203 $1 Barrage balloons 80 80
3204 $1 Supermarine Spitfire B aircraft (fighter) 80 80
3205 $1 Princess Elizabeth broadcasting, 1940 . . . 80 80
3206 $1 Fire Watcher and auxilary fireman 80 80
3207 $1 Painting white bands round posts 80 80
3208 $1 Bombed building 80 80
3209 $1 Air Raid Wardens and auxilary policewoman . . 80 80
3210 $1 Women fire-fighters . . . 80 80
3211 $1 Family leaving bombed home 80 80
3212 $1 Searchlight 80 80
3213 $1 Winston Churchill inspecting bomb damage in Coventry 80 80
3214 $1 Rescue team evacuating casualty 80 80
3215 $1 Re-united family 80 80
3216 $1 After air raid on Buckingham Gate 80 80
3217 $1 Aftermath of air raid on Coventry 80 80
MS3218 Two sheets, each 106×76 mm. (a) $6 Hawker Hurricane (fighter). (b) $6 British family outside air raid shelter (vert). Set of 2 sheets . . . . . 8·00 8·00
No. 3215 is inscribed "RESCUSE" in error.

156 Queen Elizabeth, the Queen Mother

157 Rat Snake

2000. 100th Birthday of Queen Elizabeth, the Queen Mother.
3219 **156** $1.50 multicoloured . . 1·25 1·25

2000. Faces of the Millennium: Queen Elizabeth the Queen Mother. As T **307a** of Gambia showing collage of miniature flower photographs. Multicoloured.
3220 $1 Top of head (face value at left) 80 80
3221 $1 Top of head (face value at right) 80 80
3222 $1 Eye and temple (face value at left) 80 80
3223 $1 Temple (face value at right) 80 80
3224 $1 Cheek (face value at left) 80 80
3225 $1 Cheek (face value at right) 80 80
3226 $1 Chin (face value at left) 80 80
3227 $1 Neck (face value at right) 80 80
Nos. 3220/7 were printed together, se-tenant, in sheetlets of 8 with the stamps arranged in two vertical columns separated by a gutter also containing miniature photographs. When viewed as a whole the sheetlet forms a portrait of the Queen Mother.

2000. Faces of the Millennium: Pope John Paul II. As T **307a** of Gambia showing collage of miniature religious photographs. Multicoloured.
3228 $1 Top of head (face value at left) 80 80
3229 $1 Top of head (face value at right) 80 80
3230 $1 Ear (face value at left) 80 80
3231 $1 Temple and eye (face value at right) 80 80
3232 $1 Neck and collar (face value at left) 80 80
3233 $1 Cheek and fingertips (face value at right) . . . 80 80
3234 $1 Shoulder (face value at left) 80 80
3235 $1 Hands (face value at right) 80 80

Nos. 3228/35 were printed together, se-tenant, in sheetlets of 8 with the stamps arranged in two vertical columns separated by a gutter also containing miniature photographs. When viewed as a whole the sheetlet forms a portrait of Pope John Paul II.

2001. Chinese New Year. "Year of the Snake". Multicoloured.
3236 90c. Type **157** 60 70
3237 90c. Mangrove snake . . . 60 70
3238 90c. Boomslang 60 70
3239 90c. Emerald tree boa . . . 60 70
3240 90c. African egg-eating snake 60 70
3241 90c. Chinese green tree viper 60 70
MS3242 74×88 mm. $4 King Cobra 2·25 2·50

2001. Bicentenary of Rijksmuseum, Amsterdam. Dutch Paintings. As T **330a** of Gambia. Multicoloured.
3243 $1.50 Harpist from "A Music Party" (Rembrandt) 85 90
3244 $1.50 Woman singing from "A Music Party" 85 90
3245 $1.50 Boy and girl from "Rutger Jan Schimmelpenninck with his Wife and Children" (Pierre-Paul Prud'hon) . . 85 90
3246 $1.50 Girl from "Rutger Jan Schimmelpenninck with his Wife and Children" 85 90
3247 $1.50 "The Syndics" (Thomas de Keyser) . . . 85 90
3248 $1.50 "Marriage Portrait of Isaac Massa and Beatrix van der Laen" (Frans Hals) 85 90
3249 $1.50 Bride from "Marriage Portrait of Isaac Massa and Beatrix van der Laen" 85 90
3250 $1.50 "Winter Landscape with Ice Skaters" (Hendrick Avercamp) . . 85 90
3251 $1.50 Woman and clerk from "The Spendthrift" (Cornelis Troost) 85 90
3252 $1.50 Beggars from "The Spendthrift" 85 90
3253 $1.50 Two men and a Woman from "The Art Gallery of Jan Gildemeester Jansz" (Adriaan de Lelie) 85 90
3254 $1.50 Man examining painting from "The Art Gallery of Jan Gildemeester Jansz" . . . 85 90
3255 $1.50 Couple with musicians from "Garden Party" (Dirck Hals) 85 90
3256 $1.50 "Still Life with Gilt Goblet" (Willem Claesz Heda) 85 90
3257 $1.50 Two men arguing from "Orestes and Pylades disputing at the Altar" (Pieter Lastman) 85 90
3258 $1.50 Women at altar from "Orestes and Pylades disputing at the Altar" . . 85 90
3259 $1.50 "Self-portrait in a Yellow Robe" (Jan Lievens) 85 90
3260 $1.50 Couples with monkey from "Garden Party" . . 85 90
3261 $1.50 Goatherd and goats from "Dune Landscape" (Jan van Goyen) 85 90
3262 $1.50 "The Raampoortje" (Wouter Johannes van Troostwijk) 85 90
3263 $1.50 Houses from "The Ferryboat" (Esaias van de Velde) 85 90
3264 $1.50 "The Departure of a Dignitary from Middleburg" (Adriaen van de Venne) 85 90
3265 $1.50 Cart on ferry from "The Ferryboat" 85 90
3266 $1.50 Group of peasants by fence from "Dune Landscape" 85 90
MS3267 Four sheets. (a) 87×118 mm. $6 "Anna accused by Tobit of Stealing a Kid" (Rembrandt). (b) 118×87 mm. $6 "Cleopatra's Banquet" (Gerard Lairesse) (horiz). (c) 118×87 mm. $6 "View of Tivoli" (Isaac de Moucheron) (horiz). (d) 87×118 mm. $6 "A Music Party" (Rembrandt). Set of 4 sheets 14·00 15·00
No. 3248 is inscribed "Marraige" and "dr" in error.

158 Greater Flamingo

2001. Tropical Fauna. Multicoloured.
3268 75c. Type **158** 60 50
3269 90c. Cuban crocodile (horiz) 60 50
3270 $1 Jaguarundi 70 55

3271 $1.50 Red-breasted toucan 1·00 1·00
3272 $1.50 Mexican black howler monkey . . . . 1·00 1·00
3273 $1.50 Fieck's pygmy boa . . 1·00 1·00
3274 $1.50 Red-eyed tree frog . . 1·00 1·00
3275 $1.50 Caimen . . . . 1·00 1·00
3276 $1.50 Jaguar . . . . 1·00 1·00
3277 $1.50 Cuban pygmy owl . . 1·00 1·00
3278 $1.50 Woody spider monkey 1·00 1·00
3279 $1.50 Bee hummingbirds . . 1·00 1·00
3280 $1.50 Dragonfly, leaf frog and poison dart frog . . 1·00 1·00
3281 $1.50 Red brocket deer . . 1·00 1·00
3282 $1.50 Cuban stream anole 1·00 1·00
3283 $2 Wedge-capped capuchin monkey (horiz) . . . . . 1·25 1·40
MS3284 Two sheets. (a) 72×104 mm. $6 Ocelot. (b) 72×98 mm. $6 Western knight anole. Set of 2 sheets . . . . . 7·50 8·00
Nos. 3271/6 and 3277/82 were each printed together, se-tenant, with the backgrounds forming composite designs.
No. 3271 is inscribed "Red-Breated" in error.

2001. Characters from "Pokemon" (children's cartoon series). As T **332a** of Gambia. Multicoloured.
3285 $1.50 "Bellsprout No. 69" 85 90
3286 $1.50 "Vulpix No. 37" . . . 85 90
3287 $1.50 "Dewgong No. 87" 85 90
3288 $1.50 "Oddish No. 43" . . 85 90
3289 $1.50 "Dratini No. 147" . . 85 90
3290 $1.50 "Jigglypuff No. 39" 85 90
MS3291 74×114 mm. $6 "Pikachu No. 25" . . . . 3·00 3·25

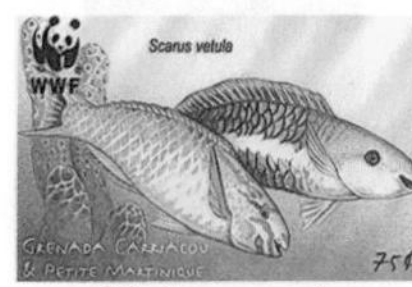

159 *Scarus vetula*

2001. Endangered Species. Fish. Multicoloured.
3292 75c. Type **159** 50 50
3293 75c. *Scarus taeniopterus* . . 50 50
3294 75c. *Sparisoma viride* . . . 50 50
3295 75c. *Sparisoma rubripinne* 50 50

160 Falkland Islands Flightless Streamer Duck ("Falklands Streamer Duck")

2001. Caribbean Ducks and Waterfowl. Mult.
3296 $1.50 Type **160** . . . . . . 1·00 1·00
3297 $1.50 Black-crowned night heron . . . . 1·00 1·00
3298 $1.50 Muscovy duck . . . . 1·00 1·00
3299 $1.50 Ruddy duck . . . . . 1·00 1·00
3300 $1.50 Northern screamer ("Black necked Screamer") . . . . 1·00 1·00
3301 $1.50 White-faced whistling duck . . . . 1·00 1·00
MS3302 60×93 mm. $6 Great egret (vert) . . . . 3·50 3·75
Nos. 3296/301 were printed together, se-tenant, with the backgrounds forming a composite design.

161 Virgie Cary (Shirley Temple) sitting on Chair

2001. Shirley Temple in *The Littlest Rebel*. Showing scenes from the film. Multicoloured.
3303 $2 Type **161** . . . . 1·10 1·25
3304 $2 Virgie with her mother (Karen Morley) . . . . . 1·10 1·25
3305 $2 Virgie with her father, Captain Cary (John Boles) . . . . 1·10 1·25
3306 $2 Virgie comforting her mother . . . . 1·10 1·25
3307 $2 Virgie with Uncle Billy (Bill Robinson) and Col. Morrison (Jack Holt) . . 1·10 1·25
3308 $2 Virgie hugging her father 1·10 1·25
3309 $2 Virgie being admonished by Col. Morrison (horiz) 1·10 1·25
3310 $2 Virgie disguised as a negro slave (horiz) . . . 1·10 1·25

3311 $2 Virgie escaping with her father in buggy (horiz) . . 1·10 1·25
3312 $2 Virgie with Abraham Lincoln (Frank McGlynn Sr.) (horiz) . . . . 1·10 1·25
MS3313 105×75 mm. $6 Virgie tap dancing with Uncle Billy . . . 3·00 3·50

2001. Betty Boop (cartoon character). As T **486** of Grenada showing Betty in various geographical locations. Multicoloured.
3314 $1 Flamenco dancing, Spain 65 70
3315 $1 In national dress, Turkey 65 70
3316 $1 Wearing lei, Hawaii . . . 65 70
3317 $1 As belly-dancer, Egypt 65 70
3318 $1 With flower in hair, South Pacific 65 70
3319 $1 Riding horse, Argentina 65 70
3320 $1 Drinking champagne, France 65 70
3321 $1 Sitting in sports car, Hollywood 65 70
3322 $1 As Statue of Liberty, New York 65 70
MS3323 Two sheets, each 90×110 mm. (a) $6 On a gondola, Venice. (b) $6 By river, India. Set of 2 sheets . . . . 7·50 8·00

162 Clark Gable smoking Cigar

2001. Birth Centenary of Clark Gable (American film star). Multicoloured.
3324 $1.50 Type **162** 85 90
3325 $1.50 In *Gone With the Wind* 85 90
3326 $1.50 Sitting in director's chair 85 90
3327 $1.50 Signing autograph . . 85 90
3328 $1.50 Wearing checked tie 85 90
3329 $1.50 In pin-stripe suit with legs crossed 85 90
3330 $1.50 Seated in car 85 90
3331 $1.50 In grey suit 85 90
3332 $1.50 In casual dress . . . 85 90
3333 $1.50 Arm resting on knee 85 90
3334 $1.50 On telephone 85 90
3335 $1.50 In evening dress . . . 85 90
MS3336 Two sheets. (a) 114×88 mm. $6 Wearing U.S. Air Force uniform. (b) 98×110 mm. $6 As Rhett Butler in *Gone With the Wind*. Set of 2 sheets . . . 7·50 8·00

2001. "Philanippon '01" International Stamp Exhibition, Tokyo. Japanese Paintings. As T **493** of Grenada. Multicoloured.
3337 75c. "Daily Life in Edo" (Miyagawa Choshun) . . 50 45
3338 90c. "Twelve Famous Places in Japan" (Kani Isen'in Naganobu) 60 50
3339 $1 "Along the Sumida River" (Kano Kyuei) . . 70 75
3340 $1.25 "Cranes" (Kano Eisen'in Michinobu) . . . 80 70
3341 $2 "Courtesan of Yoshiwara" (Katsukawa Shun'ei) . . . . 1·25 1·40
3342 $2 "Kiritsubo Chapter" (86×28 mm) . . . . . . 1·25 1·40
3343 $2 "Akahsi Chapter" (86×28 mm) . . . . . . 1·25 1·40
3344 $2 "Hatsune Chapter" (86×28 mm) . . . . . . 1·25 1·40
3345 $2 "E-Awase Chapter" (86×28 mm) . . . . . . 1·25 1·40
3346 $2 Buddha on golden elephant (vert) . . . . . 1·25 1·40
3347 $2 Buddha on white elephant (vert) . . . . . 1·25 1·40
3348 $2 Buddha on elephant and temple (vert) . . . . . 1·25 1·40
3349 $2 Buddha on elephant with crowd (vert) . . . . . 1·25 1·40
3350 $3 "Bear killing" (unsigned) 1·60 1·75
MS3351 Two sheets. (a) 86×74 mm. $6 "Sage pointing to the Moon" (Katagiri Ranseki). (b) 97×77 mm. $6 Frontispiece from "Devadatta" (Itsukushima-Jinja) (vert). Set of 2 sheets . . . . 7·50 8·00
Nos. 3342/5 depicts "Tale of Genji" (Kano Ryusetsu Hidenobu), and 3346/9 illustrates "The Lotus Sutra".

2001. Death Centenary of Queen Victoria. As **590a** of Ghana. Multicoloured.
3352 $3 Queen Victoria at her Coronation . . . . 1·75 1·90
3353 $3 Princess Victoria as a young girl, standing . . . 1·75 1·90
3354 $3 In old age . . . . 1·75 1·90
MS3355 107×77 mm. $6 Queen Victoria within royal arms . . 3·25 3·50

2001. 25th Death Anniv of Mao Tse-tung (Chinese leader). As T **590b** of Ghana. Multicoloured.
3356 $1.50 Young Mao Tse-tung on steps (horiz) 85 90
3357 $1.50 Mao talking with country people on the Long March (horiz) . . . 85 90
3358 $1.50 Visiting a rural market place (horiz) 85 90
3359 $1.50 Explaining doctrines to soldiers (horiz) 85 90
MS3360 93×134 mm. $3 Mao Tse-tung in 1939 proclaiming the People's Republic of China . . 1·60 1·90

2001. 75th Death Anniv of Claude-Oscar Monet (French painter). As T **590c** of Ghana. Mult.
3361 $1 "The Magpie" 70 75
3362 $1 "La Pointe de la Heve at Low Tide" 70 75
3363 $1 "Regatta at Argenteuil" 70 75
3364 $1 "La Grenouillere (the Frog Pond)" 70 75
MS3365 138×110 mm. $6 "J. F. Jacquemart with Parasol" (vert) 3·25 3·50

2001. 75th Birthday of Queen Elizabeth II. As T **590d** of Ghana. Multicoloured.
3366 $1.25 Princess Elizabeth wearing pearl necklace . . 85 85
3367 $1.25 Queen in blue coat with brooch 85 85
3368 $1.25 Wearing tiara 85 85
3369 $1.25 Queen Elizabeth in pink 85 85
3370 $1.25 Queen in Order of the Bath robes 85 85
3371 $1.25 Wearing blue hat and coat 85 85
3372 $2 Young Queen in red hat with feathers . . . . . . 1·40 1·40
3373 $2 Queen Elizabeth in evening dress with orders 1·40 1·40
3374 $2 Young Queen wearing tiara . . . . 1·40 1·40
MS3375 119×147 mm. $5 Queen Elizabeth at Coronation (38×51 mm) . . . . 3·00 3·25

2001. Death Centenary of Giuseppe Verdi (Italian composer). As T **590e** of Ghana. Showing various portraits of the composer.
3376 25c. multicoloured 50 55
3377 75c. multicoloured 75 80
3378 $2 multicoloured . . . . . 1·40 1·50
3379 $3 multicoloured . . . . . 1·60 1·75
MS3380 78×112 mm. $6 multicoloured . . . . 3·50 3·50
Nos. 3376/9 were printed together, se-tenant, with the backgrounds forming a composite design.

2001. Death Centenary of Henri de Toulouse-Lautrec (French painter). As T **590f** of Ghana. Multicoloured.
3381 $1 "Helene V" (horiz) . . . 70 75
3382 $1 "Clownesse" (horiz) . . . 70 75
3383 $1 "Madame Berthe Bady" (horiz) 70 75
3384 $1 "Woman with the Black Boa" (horiz) 70 75
MS3385 55×85 mm. $6 "Loie Fuller at the Folies Bergere" . . . . 3·25 3·50

2001. Birth Centenary of Marlene Dietrich (German actress). As T **495** of Grenada. Multicoloured.
3386 $2 Singing on stage . . . . 1·25 1·25
3387 $2 With feather boa . . . . 1·25 1·25
3388 $2 In floral dress . . . . . 1·25 1·25
3389 $2 Wearing hat, coat and gloves . . . . 1·25 1·25

163 *Creole* (racing schooner), 1927

2001. Ships. Multicoloured.
3390 90c. Type **163** 65 45
3391 $1 *Britannia* (steamer), 1887 70 55
3392 $1.25 *Santa Maria* and Christopher Columbus, 1492 . . . . 85 85
3393 $1.25 *Sao Gabriel* and Vasco da Gama, 1498 . . . . . 85 85
3394 $1.25 *Vitoria* and Ferdinand Magellan, 1519 . . . . . 85 85
3395 $1.25 *Golden Hind* and Sir Francis Drake, 1577 . . . 85 85
3396 $1.25 H.M.S. *Endeavour* and Captain James Cook, 1768 . . . . 85 85
3397 $1.25 H.M.S. *Erebus* and John Franklin 85 85
3398 $1.25 *William Fawcett* (paddle steamer), 1829 . . 85 85
3399 $1.25 *Sirius* (paddle steamer), 1838 . . . . . . 85 85
3400 $1.25 *Great Britain* (steam/sail vessel), 1843 . . . . 85 85
3401 $1.25 *Oriental* (American clipper), 1849 . . . . . . 85 85
3402 $1.25 *Lightning* (clipper), 1854 . . . . 85 85
3403 $1.25 *Great Eastern* (paddle steamer), 1858 . . . . . 85 85
3404 $1.25 *Mayflower* (Pilgrim Fathers), 1620 (vert) . . . 85 85
3405 $1.25 *Sv. Petr* (Bering), 1728 (vert) 85 85
3406 $1.25 H.M.S. *Beagle* (Darwin), 1825 (vert) . . 85 85
3407 $1.25 H.M.S. *Challenger* (survey ship), (vert) . . . 85 85
3408 $1.25 *Vega* (Nordenskjold), 1872 (vert) 85 85
3409 $1.25 *Fram* (Amundsen and Nansen), 1892 (vert) . . . 85 85
3410 $2 *Ariel* (clipper), 1865 . . . 1·40 1·50
3411 $3 *Sindia* (barque), 1887 . . 1·60 1·75
MS3412 Two sheets, each 60×45 mm. (a) $6 *Cutty Sark* (clipper), 1869. (b) $6 *Challenger* (American clipper), 1851. Set of 2 sheets . . . . 8·00 8·50
No. 3405 is inscribed "GABRIEL" in error. The same stamp shows two different incorrect spellings of Bering.
No. 3407 is inscribed "1852" in error.

164 *Vanda Singapore* (orchid)

2001. Orchids. Multicoloured.
3413 25c. Type **164** 30 20
3414 50c. *Vanda Joan Warne* . . 45 30
3415 75c. *Vanda lamellata* 60 45
3416 $1.50 *Papilionanthe teres* . . 90 90
3417 $1.50 *Vanda flabellata* . . . 90 90
3418 $1.50 *Vanda tessellata* (name bottom left) 90 90
3419 $1.50 *Vanda pumila* 90 90
3420 $1.50 *Rhynchostylis gigantea* 90 90
3421 $1.50 *Vandopsis gigantea* . . 90 90
3422 $1.50 *Vanda tessellata* (name centre left) 90 90
3423 $1.50 *Vanda helvola* 90 90
3424 $1.50 *Vanda brunnea* 90 90
3425 $1.50 *Vanda stageana* 90 90
3426 $1.50 *Vanda limbata* 90 90
3427 $1.50 *Vandopsis tricolor* . . 90 90
3428 $2 *Vanda merrillii* . . . . . 1·40 1·50
MS3429 Two sheets, each 68×97 mm. (a) $6 *Vanda insignis*. (b) $6 *Vandopsis lissochiloides*. Set of 2 sheets . . . . 8·00 8·50
No. 3425 is inscribed "STANGEANA" in error.

165 Richard Petty (stock car driver)

2001. Richard Petty (stock car driver). Two sheets each containing vert designs as T **165**. Multicoloured.
MS3430 (a) 92×130 mm. $6 Type **165**. (b) 92×135 mm. $6 Richard Petty being interviewed. Set of 2 sheets . . . . 7·50 8·00

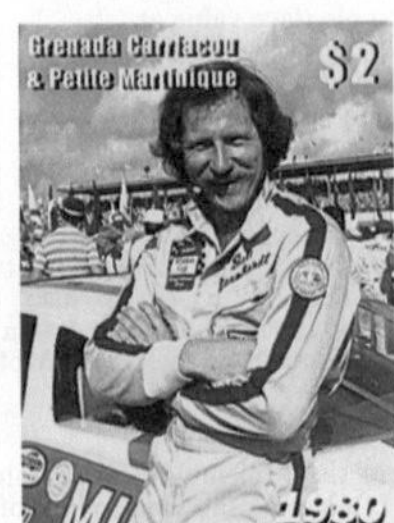

166 Dale Earnhardt in Yellow Overalls, 1980

2001. Dale Earnhardt (stock car driver) Commemoration. Multicoloured.
3431 $2 Type **166** . . . . 1·10 1·25
3432 $2 With Winston Cup, 1986 1·10 1·25
3433 $2 With Winston Cup, 1987 1·10 1·25
3434 $2 With Winston Cup, 1990 1·10 1·25
3435 $2 With Winston Cup, 1991 1·10 1·25
3436 $2 With Winston Cup, 1993 1·10 1·25
3437 $2 With Winston Cup, 1994 1·10 1·25
3438 $4 Dale Earnhardt's Chevrolet cars (76×52 mm) . . . . 1·75 1·90

167 Ferrari F1 86, 1986

2001. Ferrari Formula 1 Racing Cars. Multicoloured.
3439 $1.50 Type **167** . . . . . . 1·00 1·00
3440 $1.50 Ferrari F1 89, 1989 1·00 1·00
3441 $1.50 Ferrari F92A, 1992 1·00 1·00
3442 $1.50 Ferrari F1 93, 1993 1·00 1·00
3443 $1.50 Ferrari 412T1, 1994 1·00 1·00
3444 $1.50 Ferrari F310, 1996 . . 1·00 1·00

168 World Cup Publicity Poster, Brazil, 1950

169 "Coronation of the Virgin" (Filipo Lippi)

2001. World Cup Football Championship, Japan and Korea (2002). Designs showing publicity posters and badges from previous World Cups. Multicoloured.
3445 $1.50 Type **168** 90 90
3446 $1.50 Switzerland, 1954 . . 90 90
3447 $1.50 Sweden, 1958 . . . . 90 90
3448 $1.50 Chile, 1962 . . . . . 90 90
3449 $1.50 England, 1966 . . . . 90 90
3450 $1.50 Mexico, 1970 . . . . 90 90
3451 $1.50 Argentina, 1978 . . . 90 90
3452 $1.50 Spain, 1982 . . . . . 90 90
3453 $1.50 Mexico, 1986 . . . . 90 90
3454 $1.50 Italy, 1990 . . . . . 90 90
3455 $1.50 U.S.A., 1994 . . . . 90 90
3456 $1.50 France, 1998 . . . . 90 90
MS3457 Two sheets, 88×75 mm. (a) $6 Uruguay, 1930. (b) $6 Detail of World Cup trophy, Japan-Korea, 2002. Set of 2 sheets . . . . . 7·50 8·00

2001. Christmas. Italian Renaissance Religious Paintings. Multicoloured.
3458 25c. Type **169** 25 15
3459 75c. "Virgin and Child" (Andrea Mantegna) . . . 60 35
3460 $1.50 "Madonna and Child" (Tommaso Masaccio) . . 1·00 1·00
3461 $3 "Madonna and Child" (Raffaelo Sanzio) . . . . 1·75 2·25
MS3462 96×136 mm. $6 "Virgin and Child enthroned with Angels" (Mantegna) . . . . 3·25 3·50

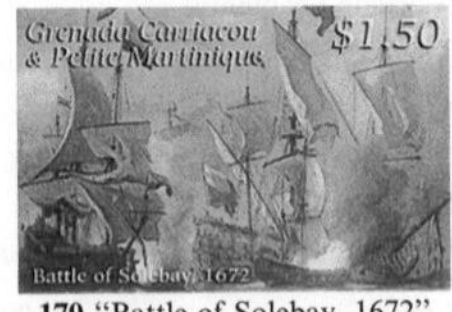

170 "Battle of Solebay, 1672"

2001. Royal Navy Commemoration. Marine Paintings. Multicoloured.
3463 75c. "H.M.S. Renown (battle cruiser), Portsmouth Harbour, 1922" (vert) 50 45
3464 90c. "Battle of the Saintes, 1782" (vert) 65 50
3465 $1.50 Type **170** 90 90
3466 $1.50 "Royal Prince, 1679" 90 90
3467 $1.50 "Battle of Texel, 1673" 90 90
3468 $1.50 "Battle of Scheveningen, 1653" . . . 90 90
3469 $1.50 "Battle against Barbary Pirates, 1600s" 90 90
3470 $1.50 "Capture of Royal Charles, 1667" 90 90
3471 $1.50 "The Glorious First of June, 1794" 90 90
3472 $1.50 "The Moonlight Battle, 1780" 90 90
3473 $1.50 "Great Ships of the Jacobean Navy, 1623" . . 90 90
3474 $1.50 "Battle of the Gulf of Genoa, 1795" 90 90
3475 $1.50 "Battle of the Nile, 1798" 90 90
3476 $1.50 "Battle of St. Lucia, 1778" 90 90
3477 $2 "Battle of Trafalgar, 1805" (vert) . . . . . . 1·25 1·40
3478 $3 "Henry VIII embarking at Dover, 1520" (vert) . . 1·75 1·90
MS3479 Two sheets, each 135×67 mm. (a) $6 "H.M.S. *Repulse* (battle cruiser), 1924". (b) $6 "Battle of Navarino, 1827". Set of 2 sheets . . . . 8·00 8·50
The date on No. 3466 is incorrect. The *Royal Prince* was sunk by the Dutch in 1666.

171 Lady Elizabeth Bowes-Lyon as a Young Child

2001. 101st Birthday of Queen Elizabeth, the Queen Mother.
3480 **171** $2 black and yellow . . 1·40 1·40
3481 – $2 multicoloured . . . . 1·40 1·40
3482 – $2 black and yellow . . 1·40 1·40
3483 – $2 multicoloured . . . . 1·40 1·40
MS3484 151 × 155 mm. $6 multicoloured . . . . 3·50 3·50
DESIGNS: No. 3481, Queen Mother in Rhodesia, 1957; 3482, Queen Elizabeth with Princess Elizabeth and Princess Anne, 1950; 3483, Queen Mother in blue hat, 1988. (37 × 50 mm); No. **MS**3484, Queen Mother inspecting Black Watch.

172 John F. Kennedy on *P.T. 109*

2001. John F. Kennedy (American President) Commemoration. Multicoloured.
3485 $1.50 Type **172** 90 90
3486 $1.50 John Kennedy in chair 90 90
3487 $1.50 Facing left 90 90
3488 $1.50 Facing forward, smiling 90 90
3489 $1.50 Wearing spotted tie 90 90
3490 $1.50 Wearing striped tie . . 90 90
MS3491 120 × 82 mm. $6 John Kennedy with Nikita Khrushchev (First Secretary of U.S.S.R.) (horiz) . . . . 3·25 3·50

173 Jacqueline Kennedy Onassis

175 Princess Diana in Evening Dress

174 General George Patton and Tank

2001. Jacqueline Kennedy Onassis (widow of American president) Commemoration. Multicoloured.
3492 $1.50 Type **173** 90 90
3493 $1.50 Wearing red coat . . 90 90
3494 $1.50 In green dress 90 90
3495 $1.50 Wearing evening cloak 90 90
3496 $1.50 In matching pink hat and coat 90 90
3497 $1.50 Jacqueline Kennedy Onassis and hot air balloon 90 90
MS3498 Two sheets. (a) 68 × 83 mm. $6 Portrait with face value at top right. (b) 83 × 68 mm. $6 Portrait with face value at top left . . . 7·50 8·00

2001. American Military Leaders. Multicoloured.
3499 75c. Type **174** 55 55
3500 75c. General Joseph Stilwell with President and Mrs. Chiang Kai-shek 55 55
3501 75c. Admiral Thomas Kinkaid and marine landing 55 55
3502 75c. General Jonathan Wainwright and Filipino troops 55 55
3503 75c. Lt.-General James Doolittle and aircraft carrier 55 55
3504 75c. General Matthew Ridgway and cheering crowd 55 55
3505 75c. General Maxwell Taylor and B-17s 55 55
3506 75c. Admiral Richmond Turner and island landing 55 55
3507 75c. General Curtis LeMay and heavy bombers . . . 55 55
3508 75c. General Hoyt Vandenberg and fighter aircraft 55 55
3509 75c. General Carl Spaatz and explosion of atomic bomb 55 55
3510 75c. Admiral Raymond Spruance and burning Japanese battleship . . . 55 55
3511 75c. General Omar Bradley and D-Day landings . . . 55 55
3512 75c. General George Marshall and Marine Corps memorial 55 55
3513 75c. General Douglas MacArthur and return to the Philippines 55 55
3514 75c. Admiral William Halsey and carrier landing . . . 55 55
3515 75c. General Dwight Eisenhower and reviewing troops 55 55
3516 75c. Admiral Chester Nimitz and beach landing 55 55
3517 75c. Admiral William Leahy and aircraft carriers . . . 55 55
3518 75c. General Henry Arnold and heavy bomber . . . 55 55
3519 75c. Admiral Ernest King and battleships 55 55
3520 75c. General George Washington and seated with his wife 55 55
3521 75c. General John Pershing and parade 55 55
MS3522 Two sheets, each 150 × 139 mm. (a) $6 General Dwight Eisenhower (38 × 49 mm). (b) $6 General Douglas MacArthur (38 × 49 mm) . . . 7·50 8·00

2001. 40th Birth Anniv of Diana, Princess of Wales. Multicoloured.
3523 $1.50 Type **175** . . . . . . 1·00 1·00
3524 $1.50 Wearing ski suit . . . 1·00 1·00
3525 $1.50 In pale blue hat . . . 1·00 1·00

176 *Nudaurelia cytheria* (moth)

2001. Moths. Multicoloured.
3526 75c. Type **176** 50 45
3527 90c. *Janomima westwoodi* . . 65 50
3528 $1.50 *Actias selene* 90 90
3529 $1.50 *Amphicallia bellatrix* 90 90
3530 $1.50 *Citheronia regalis* . . 90 90
3531 $1.50 *Arctica caja* 90 90
3532 $1.50 *Leto venus* 90 90
3533 $1.50 *Alcides zodiaca* . . . 90 90
3534 $1.50 *Graellsia isabellae* . . 90 90
3535 $1.50 *Dysphania cuprina* . . 90 90
3536 $1.50 *Automeris io* 90 90
3537 $1.50 *Agarista agricola* . . . 90 90
3538 $1.50 *Callioratis millari* . . 90 90
3539 $1.50 *Othreis fullonia* . . . 90 90
3540 $2 *Lasiocampa quercus* . . . 1·25 1·40
3541 $3 *Chrysiridia riphearia* . . 1·60 1·75
MS3542 Two sheets, each 77 × 106 mm. (a) $6 *Divana diva* (vert). (b) $6 *Argema mimosae* (vert) . . . . 7·50 8·00
No. 3539 is inscribed "Otthreis" in error.

177 Queen Elizabeth in Spotted Dress

178 Horse on Background of Chinese Characters

2002. Golden Jubilee. Multicoloured.
3543 $2 Type **177** . . . . 1·40 1·40
3544 $2 Queen Elizabeth wearing pink hat . . . . 1·40 1·40
3545 $2 Queen Elizabeth in evening dress . . . . . . 1·40 1·40
3546 $2 Queen Elizabeth wearing sunglasses . . . . 1·40 1·40
MS3547 76 × 109 mm. $6 Princess Elizabeth with family . . . . . 3·50 3·50

2002. Chinese New Year ("Year of the Horse"). Showing different horses.
3548 **178** 75c. multicoloured . . . 55 40
3549 – $1.25 multicoloured . . 80 85
3550 – $2 multicoloured . . . . 1·25 1·40
MS3551 **178** 70 × 102 mm. $6 black, light orange and orange . . . 3·00 3·50

179 US Flag on Twin Towers

180 Amerigo Vespucci

2002. "United We Stand". Support for Victims of 11 September 2001 Attacks.
3552 **179** 80c. multicoloured . . . 60 60

2002. 550th Birth Anniv of Amerigo Vespucci (explorer).
3553 **180** $1 multicoloured 70 55
3554 – $2 multicoloured . . . . 1·25 1·40
3555 – $3 multicoloured . . . . 1·60 1·75
MS3556 75 × 58 mm. $6 multicoloured . . . . 3·25 3·50
DESIGNS: $2 to $6 Various portraits.

181 F1 86, 1986

2002. Ferrari Racing Cars. Sheet 147 × 165 mm containing T **181** and similar horiz designs. Multicoloured.
MS3557 $1.50 Type **181**; $1.50 F1 89, 1989; $1.50 F 92 A, 1992; $1.50 F1 93, 1993; $1.50 412 T1, 1994; $1.50 F310, 1996 . . . . . . 4·50 4·75

2002. International Year of Mountains. Two sheets containing horiz designs as T **512** of Grenada. Multicoloured.
MS3558 143 × 93 mm. $2 Kilimanjaro, Tanzania; $2 Mount Kenya; $2 Mount Kea, Hawaii; $2 Mount Fuji, Japan . . . . . . 4·75 5·50
MS3559 115 × 65 mm. $6 Ko'olau Mountains, Hawaii . . . . . 3·25 3·50

182 Waterfall

2002. International Year of Ecotourism. Two sheets containing T **182** and similar horiz designs. Multicoloured.
MS3560 137 × 105 mm. $1.50 Type **182**; $1.50 Ringed kingfisher; $1.50 Butterfly; $1.50 Rock beauty (fish); $1.50 Cactus; $1.50 Orchid 3·50 3·50
MS3561 80 × 98 mm. $6 Blue-hooded euphonias . . . . . . 4·75 4·75

183 Olympic Rings and Skier (airborne)

184 *Bombus auricomus* (bumble bee)

2002. Winter Olympic Games, Salt Lake City. Multicoloured.
3562 $3 Type **183** . . . . 1·60 1·75
3563 $3 Olympic rings and skier (different) . . . . 1·60 1·75
MS3564 82 × 113 mm. Nos. 3562/3 3·25 3·50

2002. World Scout Jamboree, Thailand. Two sheets each containing multicoloured designs as T **515** of Grenada.
MS3565 107 × 90 mm. $2 Scout badge and campfire; $2 Scout hiking; $2 Boy scout feeding calf; $2 Girl saluting . . . . 4·50 4·75
MS3566 98 × 70 mm. $2 Scout at seashore (vert) . . . . 1·25 1·40

2002. Chiune Sugihara (Japanese Consul-general in Lithuania who rescued Jews, 1939–40) Commemoration. Two sheets each 60 × 90 mm containing vert designs as T **511** of Grenada.
MS3567 (a) $6 Sugihara and map showing route from Lithuania to Japan. (b) $6 Sugihara and wife Set of 2 sheets . . . . 7·50 8·00

2002. Flora and Fauna. Miniature sheets containing T **184** and similar multicoloured designs.
MS3568 135 × 170 mm. $1 Type **184**; $1 *Anax junius* (dragonfly); $1 *Dynastes tityus* (Hercules beetle); $1 *Coccinella novemrotata* (ladybug); $1 *Callicore maimuna* (figure-of-eight butterfly); $1 *Tenodera aridifolia sinensis* (praying mantis) . . . . 3·25 3·50
MS3569 135 × 170 mm. $1 Sperm whale; $1 Bottlenose whale; $1 Sei Whale; $1 Killer whale; $1 Humpback whale ("Humback Whale"); $1 Pygmy sperm whale 3·25 3·50
MS3570 135 × 170 mm. $2 *Anartia jatrophae*; $2 *Phoebis philea*; $2 *Cepheuptychia cephus*; $2 *Prepona meander*; $2 *Mesene phareus*; $2 *Morpho peleides* . . . . 6·50 7·00
MS3571 135 × 170 mm. $2 *Coprinus comatus*; $2 *Leucocoprinus rachodes*; $2 *Collybia iocephala*; $2 *Lepiota acutesquamosa*; $2 *Morchella crassipes*; $2 *Mycena galericulata* . . . . 6·50 7·00
MS3572 Four sheets, each 100 × 70 mm. (a) $6 *Anax junius* (dragonfly) (horiz). (b) $6 Blue whale (horiz). (c) $6 *Cepheuptychia cephus* (butterfly) (horiz). (d) $6 *Amanita phalloides* (mushroom) (horiz) Set of 4 sheets . . . . 13·00 14·00
No. **MS**3568 shows insects, **MS**3569 shows whales, **MS**3570 shows butterflies and **MS**3571 fungi.

2002. 25th Death Anniv of Elvis Presley. As T **518a** of Grenada. Multicoloured (No. 3573) or black and brown (No. **MS**3574).
3573 $1 Elvis Presley with guitar 70 70
MS3574 150 × 215 mm. $1 × 9 containing nine different portraits of Elvis Presley . . . . 5·50 5·50

2002. "Amphilex '02" International Stamp Exhibition, Amsterdam. As T **518b** of Grenada. (a) Dutch Nobel Prize Winners. Sheet 150 × 100 mm.
MS3575 $1.50 Paul J. Crutzen (Chemistry, 1995) (black and green); $1.50 Nobel medal (black and brown); $1.50 Martinus Veltman (Physics, 1999) (black and mauve); $1.50 Hendrik Lorentz (Physics, 1902) (black and blue); $1.50 Christiaan Eijkman (Medicine, 1929) (black and green); $1.50 Gerard 't Hooft (Physics, 1999) (black and brown) 5·50 5·50

(b) Dutch Lighthouses. Sheet 128 × 148 mm. Multicoloured.
MS3576 $1.50 Ameland; $1.50 Vlieland; $1.50 Julianadorp; $1.50 Noordwijk; $1.50 Hoek van Holland; $1.50 Goeree . . . . 5·50 5·50

(c) Dutch Women's Traditional Costumes. Sheet 120 × 140 mm containing multicoloured designs, each 36 × 50 mm.
MS3577 $3 Marken, Noord-Holland; $3 Staphorst, Overijsel; $3 Walchheren, Zeeland . . . 5·50 5·50

185 Teddy Bear holding "HAPPY BIRTHDAY" in Heart

2002. Centenary of the Teddy Bear (1st issue). T **185** and similar vert designs. Multicoloured.

MS3578 140 × 142 mm. 50c. Type **185**; $1 With waistcoat, briefcase and bowler hat; $2 Wearing raincoat, sunglasses and hat; $5 Wearing boxer shorts with heart pattern . . . . 5·00 5·00

MS3579 85 × 115 mm. 15c. Teddy Bear wearing Guardsmans plumed helmet; $2 Panda teddy bear wearing black hat; $3 Wearing beret and ruff; $4 White teddy bear wearing grey top hat . . . 5·50 5·50

No. **MS**3578 is heart-shaped.

See also Nos. 3611/12.

2002. World Cup Football Championship, Japan and Korea. Miniature sheets containing vert designs as T **524** of Grenada. Multicoloured.

MS3580 165 × 82 mm. $1.50 Oliver Neuville (Germany) and Eddie Pope (USA); $1.50 Claudio Reyna (USA) and Miroslav Klose (Germany); $1.50 Christian Ziege (Germany) and Frankie Hejduk (USA); $1.50 Nadal (Spain) and Jung Hwan Ahn (South Korea); $1.50 Luis Enrique (Spain) and Chong Gug Song (South Korea); $1.50 Park Ji Sung (South Korea) and Mendieta Gaizka (Spain) 5·50 5·50

MS3581 165 × 82 mm. $1.50 Danny Mills (England) and Ronaldo (Brazil); $1.50 Roque Junior (Brazil) and Emil Heskey (England); $1.50 Sol Campbell (England) and Rivaldo (Brazil); $1.50 Lamine Diatta (Senegal) and Hakan Sukur (Turkey); $1.50 Umit Davala (Turkey) and Khalilou Fadiga (Senegal); $1.50 El Hadji Diouf (Senegal) and Tugay Kerimoglu (Turkey) . . . 5·50 5·50

MS3582 Four sheets, each 82 × 82 mm. (a) $3 Oliver Kahn (Germany); $3 Brad Friedel (Germany). (b) $3 Chun Soo Lee (South Korea); $3 Juan Carlos Valeron (Spain). (c) $3 David Beckham (England) and Roberto Carlos (Brazil); $3 Ronaldinho (Brazil) and Nicky Butt (England). (d) $3 Alpay Ozalan (Turkey); $3 Khalilou Fadiga (Senegal) Set of 4 sheets . . . . 13·00 13·00

2002. Christmas. Religious Paintings. As T **523a** of Grenada. Multicoloured.

3583 15c. "The Redeemer and the Four Apostles" (Carpaccio) 20 10
3584 25c. "The Miracle of the Relic of the Cross" (Carpaccio) (vert) 25 15
3585 50c. "The Presentation in the Temple" (Carpaccio) 35 25
3586 $2 "The Visitation" (Carpaccio) . . . . 1·40 1·60
3587 $3 "The Birth of the Virgin" (Carpaccio) . . . . 1·60 1·90

MS3588 62 × 90 mm. $6 "Madonna and Child and Two Angels" (detail) (Cimabue) (vert) . . . 3·25 3·50

186 "Year of Ram" (Ren Yi)

2003. Chinese New Year ("Year of the Ram").

MS3589 **186** 179 × 108 mm. $1.25 × 4 multicoloured . . . . 3·00 3·25

2003. *Columbia* Space Shuttle Commemoration. Sheet 183 × 146 mm, containing vert designs as T **533** of Grenada showing crew members. Multicoloured.

MS3590 $1 David Brown; $1 Commander Rick Husband; $1 Laurel Clark; $1 Kalpana Chawla; $1 Michael Anderson; $1 William McCool; $1 Ilan Ramon . . . 4·50 4·75

2003. Japanese Art. Paintings by Toyohara Kunichika showing Famous Actors. As T **535** of Grenada. Multicoloured.

3591 50c. "Ichikawa Danjuro IX as the Beggar Akushichibyoe Kagekiyo" 35 25
3592 75c. "Ichikawa Danjuro IX as the Female Demon Ewanari" 55 40
3593 $1.25 "Sawamura Tossho II as Sutewakamaru" . . . 80 80
3594 $3 "Bando Hikosaburo V as Nikki Damjo" . . . . . 1·60 1·75

MS3595 175 × 137 mm. $2 "Nakamura Shikan IV as Keyamura Rokusuke"; $2 "Bando Hikosaburo V as Ichimisai no Musume Osono"; $2 "Ichikawa Sadanji I as Wada no Shimobe Busuke"; $2 "Ichikawa Sadanji I as Kiyomizu no Yoshitaka" . . 4·50 4·75

MS3596 122 × 82 mm. $6 "Onoe Kikugoro V as Torii Tsuneemon returning to Mikawa" (horiz) 3·25 3·50

2003. 450th Death Anniv of Lucas Cranach the Elder (artist). As T **536** of Grenada. Multicoloured.

3597 25c. "The St. Mary Altarpiece" (detail) (vert) 25 15
3598 $1 "The St. Mary Altarpiece" (different detail) (vert) 70 55
3599 $1.25 "Altar Piece of the Princes" (detail) (vert) . . 80 80
3600 $3 Frederick the Wise with St. Bartholomew (detail of altarpiece) (vert) . . . . 1·60 1·75

MS3601 150 × 160 mm. $2 "Judith at the Table of Holofernes" (detail); $2 "St. Catherine Altarpiece" (detail); $2 "Judith killing Holofernes" (detail); $2 "The Martyrdom of St. Catherine" (detail) . . . . 4·50 4·75

MS3602 102 × 123 mm. $6 "Cardinal Albrecht of Brandenbourg as St. Jerome in the Wilderness" (vert) . . . . 3·25 3·50

2003. 85th Death Anniv of Gustav Klimt (artist). As T **537** of Grenada. Multicoloured.

3603 15c. "Le Chapeau de Plumes Noires" 20 15
3604 25c. "Le Schloss Kammer am Attersee" 25 15
3605 50c. "Malcesine sur le Lac de Garde" 35 25
3606 75c. "Ferme en Haute-Autriche" 55 40
3607 $1.25 "Portrait d'une Dame" 80 75
3608 $4 "La Frise Beethoven" (detail) . . . . 1·90 2·00

MS3609 126 × 178 mm. $2 "Portrait de la Baronne Elisabeth Bachofen-Echt"; $2 "Portrait d'une Dame"; $2 "Portrait d'Emilie Floge"; $2 "Portrait d'Adele Bloch-Bauer" 4·50 4·75

MS3610 103 × 81 mm. $6 "Le Baiser" (detail). Imperf . . . . 3·25 3·50

2003. Centenary of the Teddy Bear (2nd issue). Embroidered Fabric Teddy Bears. As T **538** of Grenada. Self-adhesive. Imperf.

3611 $15 ochre, silver and red . . 8·00 8·50

MS3612 126 × 157 mm. No. 3611 × 4 28·00 29·00

2003. Centenary of Tour de France Cycle Race. As T **540** of Grenada showing past winners. Multicoloured.

MS3613 160 × 100 mm. $2 Ferdinand Kubler (1950); $2 Hugo Koblet (1951); $2 Fausto Coppi (1952); $2 Louison Bobet (1953) 5·50 5·50

MS3614 160 × 100 mm. $2 Louison Bobet (1954); $2 Louison Bobet (1955); $2 Roger Walkowiak (1956); $2 Jacques Anquetil (1957) 5·50 5·50

MS3615 160 × 100 mm. $2 Gastone Nencini (1960); $2 Jacques Anquetil (1961); $2 Jacques Anquetil (1962); $2 Jacques Anquetil (1963) . . . . 5·50 5·50

MS3616 Three sheets, each 100 × 70 mm. (a) $6 Louison Bobet (1953–1955). (b) $6 Jacques Anquetil (1957). (c) $6 Eddy Merckx (1969) Set of 3 sheets 10·00 10·00

187 John Kennedy, Choate Graduate, 1935

2003. 40th Death Anniv of President John F. Kennedy.

MS3617 144 × 131 mm. $2 Type **187** (agate, black and); $2 John Kennedy, 1946 (multicoloured); $2 With Jacqueline Kennedy on tennis court (multicoloured); $2 With young John F. Kennedy Jnr (multicoloured) . . . . 4·50 4·75

MS3618 144 × 131 mm. $2 With Jacqueline Kennedy (black, brown and grey); $2 Announcing Cuban blockade, 1962 (agate and mauve); $2 Sitting in chair, White House, 1962 (brown and black); $2 Jackie Kennedy with children at funeral, 1963 (black, mauve and purple) 4·50 4·75

188 Charles Lindbergh

2003. 75th Anniv of First Solo Trans-atlantic Flight. Multicoloured (No. **MS**3620).

MS3619 129 × 144 mm. $2 Type **188** (blue, grey and red); $2 Lindbergh and Ryan NYP Special *Spirit of St. Louis* (purple, blue and red); $2 Lindbergh and *Spirit of St. Louis* (black and red); $2 Lindbergh (purple, blue and red) . . . . 5·00 5·00

MS3620 129 × 144 mm. $2 Lindbergh (looking forward); $2 Lindbergh (looking left); $2 Lindbergh on arrival in Paris, 1927; $2 Lindbergh and *Spirit of St. Louis* . . . . 5·00 5·00

189 La Sagesse

2003. International Year of Freshwater. Multicoloured.

MS3621 150 × 88 mm. $2 Type **189**; $2 Annadale Falls; $2 Grand Etang . . . . 3·25 3·50

MS3622 100 × 70 mm. $6 St. George 3·25 3·50

2003. Centenary of Circus Clowns. As T **544** of Grenada. Multicoloured.

MS3623 119 × 194 mm. $2 Anton Pilossian; $2 Victor Vashnikov; $2 Dan Rice; $2 Tom Comet . . 3·25 3·25

MS3624 146 × 218 mm. $2 Boxer dog; $2 Macaw; $2 Monigue; $2 Vassily Trofimov . . . . . . 3·25 3·25

No. **MS**3623 shows clowns and is cut in the shape of a clown. No. **MS**3624 shows others circus performers and circus animals and is cut in the shape of an elephant.

190 Wright Flyer

2003. Centenary of Powered Flight. Multicoloured.

MS3625 176 × 97 mm. $2 Type 190; $2 NC-4; $2 Douglas World Cruiser; $2 Fokker Eindecker 3·25 3·25

MS3626 176 × 97 mm. $2 Hansa Brandenburg D.1; $2 B.E.2e; $2 Handley Page 0/400; $2 Avro 504 3·25 3·25

MS3627 176 × 97 mm. $2 Hawker Hart; $2 Martin B-10; $2 Armstrong Whitworth Siskin IIIA; $2 Loening OL-8 . . . . 3·25 3·25

MS3628 (a) 67 × 97 mm. $6 Wright Glider No. III. (b) 106 × 76 mm. $6 Wright *Flyer II*. (c) 106 × 76 mm. $6 Gloster Gamecock . . . . 7·00 7·00

191 Princess Elizabeth as Young Woman

2003. 50th Anniv of Coronation. Multicoloured.

MS3629 160 × 86 mm. $3 Type **191**; $3 Queen wearing azure blue; $3 Riding side saddle at Trooping the Colour . . . . 3·50 3·50

MS3630 76 × 106 mm. $6 Queen wearing tiara . . . . 2·40 2·40

2003. 21st Birthday of Prince William. As T **547** of Grenada. Multicoloured.

MS3631 160 × 86 mm. $3 Prince William (half-length photo); $3 Prince William (in close-up); $3 Prince William (looking left) 3·50 3·50

MS3632 106 × 76 mm. $6 Wearing hat and ski goggles . . . . . 2·40 2·40

192 Rose-breasted Grosbeak

2003. Birds, Tropical Fish and Flowers of the World. Multicoloured.

3633 25c. Type **192** 10 15
3634 25c. Three-spotted dascyllus ("Domino Damselfish") 10 15
3635 50c. Northern oriole ("Bullock's Oriole") . . . 20 25
3636 50c. Catbird ("Gray Catbird") 20 25
3637 75c. Porcupinefish 30 35
3638 75c. Wild rhododendron (vert) 30 35
3639 $1 Blue grosbeak 40 45
3640 $1 Peony (vert) 40 45
3641 $1.25 Black-tailed damselfish 50 55
3642 $1.25 Camellia (vert) . . . 50 55
3643 $2 Reticulate damselfish ("Clown Fish") 80 85
3644 $2 Laurel (vert) 80 85

MS3645 110 × 138 mm. $2 Lazuli bunting; $2 Indigo bunting; $2 Broad-tailed Hummingbird; $2 Scarlet tanager (all vert) . . . 3·25 3·25

MS3646 129 × 109 mm. $2 Halfmoon triggerfish; $2 Blackeye thicklip ("Half and Half Wrasser"); $2 Pennant coralfish ("Long-fin Banner Fish"); $2 Hump-headed bannerfish ("Butterfly Fish") . . . . . . 3·25 3·25

MS3647 110 × 130 mm. $2 Apple blossom; $2 Mock orange; $2 Wild rose; $2 Hibiscus (all vert) . . . 3·25 3·25

MS3648 98 × 68 mm. (a) $6 Barn swallow. (b) $6 Blue-girdled angelfish. (c) $6 Violets (vert) 7·00 7·00

No. **MS**3647 is inscribed "ASDA Postage Stamp Mega-Event" on the sheet margin.

193 "Madonna and Child" (detail), Carnesecchii Tabernacle (Domenico Veneziano)

2003. Christmas. Multicoloured.

3649 35c. Type **193** 15 20
3650 75c. "Madonna and Child" (detail), Magnoli Altarpiece (Domenico Veneziano) 30 35
3651 90c. "Crevole Madonna" (detail) (Duccio di Buoninsegna) 35 40
3652 $3 "Madonna and Child" (detail) (Domenico Veneziano) . . . . 1·20 1·20

MS3653 71 × 96 mm. $6 "Madonna and the Child by the Fireplace" (detail) (Robert Campin) . . . 2·40 2·40

2003. 300th Anniv of St. Petersburg. "Treasures of the Hermitage". As T **551** of Grenada. Multicoloured.

3654 75c. "Abraham and Isaac" (Rembrandt) 30 35
3655 $1 "David and Jonathan" (Rembrandt) 40 45

3656 $1.25 "Saint Onuphrus" (Juisepe de Ribera) . . . 50 55
3657 $2 "Pope Paul III" (Titian) 80 85
MS3658 115 × 145 mm. $2 "Rest on the Flight into Egypt" (Murillo); $2 "Esther before Ahasuerus" (Nicolas Poussin); $2 "Abraham's Servant and Rebecca" (Jacob Hogers); $2 "The Prophet Elisha and Naaman" (Lambert Jacobsz) (all horiz) . . . . 3·25 3·25
MS3659 (a) 66 × 78 mm. $6 "The Building of Noah's Ark" (Guido Reni). Imperf. (b) 78 × 66 mm. $6 "Hagar flees Abram's House" (Rubens). Imperf . . . . . . 4·75 4·75

2003. 25th Death Anniv of Norman Rockwell (artist). As T **552** of Grenada. Multicoloured.
MS3660 150 × 181 mm. $2 "The Trumpeter"; $2 "Waiting for the Vet"; $2 "The Diving Board"; $2 "The Discovery" . . . . . . 3·25 3·25
MS3661 $6 "Day in a Boy's Life" (detail) (horiz) . . . . 2·40 2·40

2003. 30th Death Anniv of Pablo Picasso (artist). As T **553** of Grenada. Multicoloured.
MS3662 128 × 168 mm. $2 "Jacqueline Sitting"; $2 "Jacqueline with Flower"; $2 "Seated Nude"; $2 "Woman in Armchair" . . . . 3·25 3·25
MS3663 74 × 98 mm. $6 "Head of a Woman". Imperf . . . . . . 2·40 2·40

2004. Chinese New Year ("Year of the Monkey"). As T **554** of Grenada. Multicoloured.
MS3664 118 × 144 mm. $1.50 Cotton-top tamarin; $1.50 Chimpanzee; $1.50 Baboon; $1.50 Bald uakari . . . . 2·40 2·40

194 "The Mind Landscape of Xie Youyu" (Zhao Mengfu)

2004. Hong Kong 2004 International Stamp Exhibition. Paintings by Zhao Mengfu (1254—1322). Multicoloured.
MS3665 120 × 119 mm. $2 Type **194**; $2 Mountains and trees; $2 "Twin Pines"; $2 Mountain range and plains . . . . 3·25 3·25
MS3666 87 × 81 mm. $6 "Autumn" 2·40 2·40

2004. Marilyn Monroe Commemoration. As T **560** of Grenada.
3670 50c. multicoloured . . . . .
MS3671 multicoloured 127 × 112 mm. $2 black, grey and red; $2 black, grey and red; $2 black, grey and red; $2 black, grey and red . . . . 3·25 3·25
DESIGNS: 50c. Wearing halter-neck dress and drop earrings; $2 Wearing white top and short hair; $2 Wearing beret; $2 Wearing white backless dress; $2 With long dark hair and black dress.

195 Deng Xiaoping

2004. Deng Xiaoping (Chinese politician) Commemoration. Sheet 98 × 68 mm.
MS3672 **195** $6 black, grey and red 2·40 2·40

2004. 25th Anniv of the Pontificate of Pope John Paul II. Sheet 163 × 153 mm containing horiz designs as T **564** of Grenada. Multicoloured.
MS3673 $2 Pope with Lech Walesa; $2 Pope with Chief Rabbi of Israel, Yisrael Meir Lau; $2 Pope with children; Pope using laptop; $2 Pope wearing mitre and gesturing . . . . 3·25 3·25

2004. Olympic Games, Athens, Greece. As T **559** of Grenada. Multicoloured.
3674 25c. Long jump 10 10
3675 50c. Avery Brundage 20 25
3676 $1 Commemorative medal 40 45
3677 $4 Greek vase showing "The Paidotribe" ("Paidotribai") . . . . . 1·60 1·70

OFFICIAL STAMPS

1982. Optd **P.R.G.** (a) Nos. 400/12 and 414.
O 1 5c. Yellow-tailed snapper . . 10 20
O 2 6c. Mutton snapper 10 20
O 3 10c. Cocoa damselfish . . . 10 20
O 4 12c. Royal gramma 10 20
O 5 15c. Cherub angelfish . . . 10 20
O 6 20c. Black-barred soldierfish 10 20
O 7 25c. Mottled grouper 10 20
O 8 30c. Long-snouted butterflyfish 15 20
O 9 40c. Puddingwife 15 25
O10 50c. Midnight parrotfish . . 20 30
O11 90c. Redspotted hawkfish . . 40 55
O12 $1 Hogfish 40 60
O13 $3 Beau Gregory . . . . . 1·25 2·50
O14 $10 Barred hamlet . . . . . 4·25 6·50

(b) Nos. 444/6 and 448/9.
O15 30c. Prince Charles and Lady Diana Spencer . . . 2·00 2·00
O16 40c. Prince Charles and Lady Diana Spencer . . . 1·60 1·60
O17 40c. Type **50** . . . . 2·00 2·75
O18 $2 Type **50** . . . . 2·50 3·50
O19 $4 Prince Charles as parachutist . . . . 6·50 8·50

(c) Nos. 473/6.
O20 **54** 20c. multicoloured 10 20
O21 – 40c. multicoloured 15 25
O22 – $1 multicoloured 35 70
O23 – $2 multicoloured . . . . 70 1·60

GRENADINES OF ST. VINCENT Pt. 1

Part of a group of Islands south of St. Vincent that include Bequia, Mustique, Canouan and Union.

100 cents = 1 dollar.

1973. Royal Wedding. As T **101a** of Gibraltar. Multicoloured. Background colours given.
1 25c. green 10 10
2 $1 brown 15 15

1974. Nos. 286/300 of St. Vincent optd **GRENADINES OF**.
3 1c. Green-backed heron ("Green Heron") 10 10
4 2c. Lesser Antillean bullfinches ("Bullfinch") 15 15
25 3c. St. Vincent amazon ("St. Vincent Parrot") . . . 25 30
6 4c. Rufous-throated solitaire ("Soufriere Bird") (vert) . . 10 10
7 5c. Red-necked pigeon ("Ramier") (vert) 10 10
8 6c. Bananaquits 10 10
9 8c. Purple-throated carib ("Humming Bird") 10 10
10 10c. Mangrove cuckoo (vert) 10 10
11 12c. Common black hawk ("Black Hawk") (vert) . . . 20 15
12 20c. Bare-eyed thrush 20 20
13 25c. Lesser Antillean tanager ("Prince") 20 20
14 50c. Blue hooded euphonia . . 40 40
15 $1 Barn owl (vert) 80 75
16 $2.50 Yellow-bellied elaenia ("Crested Elaenia") (vert) 80 1·00
17 $5 Ruddy quail dove . . . . 1·00 1·75

2 Map of Bequia

1974. Maps (1st series).
18 **2** 5c. black, green & deep green 10 10
19 – 15c. multicoloured 10 10
20 – 20c. multicoloured 10 10
21 – 30c. black, pink and red . . 10 10
22 – 40c. black, violet and purple 10 10
23 – $1 black, ultramarine and blue 20 20
MAPS: 15c. Prune Island; 20c. Mayreau Island and Tobago Cays; 30c. Mustique Island; 40c. Union Island; $1 Canouan Island.
See also Nos. 85/8.

3a U.P.U. Emblem

1974. Centenary of U.P.U. Multicoloured.
26 2c. Type **3a** 10 10
27 15c. Globe within posthorn . . 10 10
28 40c. Map of St. Vincent and hand-cancelling 10 10
29 $1 Map of the World 25 15

4 Boat-building

1974. Bequia Island (1st series). Multicoloured.
34 5c. Type **4** 10 15
31 30c. Careening at Port Elizabeth 10 15
32 35c. Admiralty Bay 10 15
33 $1 Fishing-boat race 15 25
See also Nos. 185/88.

5 Music Volute

1974. Shells and Molluscs. Multicoloured.
35A 1c. American thorny oyster 10 10
36A 2c. Zigzag scallop 10 10
37A 3c. Reticulated cowrie-helmet 10 10
38A 4c. Type **5** 10 10
39A 5c. Amber pen shell 10 10
40A 6c. Angular triton 10 10
41A 8c. Flame helmet 10 10
42A 10c. Caribbean olive . . . 10 10
43A 12c. American or common sundial 10 10
44A 15c. Glory of the Atlantic cone 25 20
45B 20c. Flame auger 30 20
46A 25c. King venus 50 20
47A 35c. Long-spined star shell 35 25
48A 45c. Speckled tellin 35 30
49A 50c. Rooster-tail conch . . 40 25
50B $1 Green star shell 60 60
51A $2.50 Antillean or incomparable cone . . . 60 75
52A $5 Rough file clam 75 80
52cA $10 Measled cowrie . . . . 3·50 1·00
Nos. 38/42, 45, 47 and 49/50 come with and without an imprint below the design.

1974. Birth Centenary of Sir Winston Churchill. As Nos. 403/6 of St. Vincent, but inscr "GRENADINES OF ST. VINCENT" and values (Nos. 53/5) and colours changed.
53 **75** 5c. multicoloured 10 15
54 – 40c. multicoloured 10 15
55 – 50c. multicoloured 10 15
56 – $1 multicoloured 20 50

6 Cotton House, Mustique

1975. Mustique Island. Multicoloured.
57 5c. Type **6** 10 10
58 35c. "Blue Waters", Endeavour Bay 10 10
59 45c. Endeavour Bay 10 10
60 $1 "Les Jolies Eaux", Gelliceaux Bay 25 20

7 "Danaus plexippus"

1975. Butterflies. Multicoloured.
61 3c. Type **7** 20 10
62 5c. "Agraulis vanillae" 25 10
63 35c. "Battus polydamas" . . . 50 10
64 45c. "Evenus dindymus" and "Junonia evarete" 50 10
65 $1 "Anartia jatrophae" . . . 75 45

8 Resort Pavilion

1975. Petit St. Vincent. Multicoloured.
66 5c. Type **8** 10 20
67 35c. The Harbour 10 20
68 45c. The Jetty 15 20
69 $1 Sailing in coral lagoon . . 50 1·10

9 Ecumenical Church, Mustique

1975. Christmas. Multicoloured.
70 5c. Type **9** 10 10
71 25c. Catholic Church, Union Island 10 10
72 50c. Catholic Church, Bequia 10 10
73 $1 Anglican Church, Bequia 25 15

10 Sunset Scene

1976. Union Island (1st series). Multicoloured.
74 5c. Type **10** 10 25
75 35c. Customs and Post Office, Clifton 10 20
76 45c. Anglican Church, Ashton 10 20
77 $1 Mail schooner, Clifton Harbour 25 80
See also Nos. 242/5.

11 Staghorn Coral

1976. Corals. Multicoloured.
78 5c. Type **11** 10 10
79 35c. Elkhorn coral 20 10
80 45c. Pillar coral 20 10
81 $1 Brain coral 40 20

12 25c. Bicentennial Coin

1976. Bicentenary of American Revolution.
82 **12** 25c. silver, black and blue 10 10
83 – 50c. silver, black and red . . 20 10
84 – $1 silver, black and mauve 25 20
DESIGNS: 50c. Half-dollar coin; $1 One dollar coin.

1976. Maps (2nd series). As T **2**.
85 5c. black, deep green and green 15 15
86 10c. black, green and blue . . 15 10
87 35c. black, brown and red . . 30 20
88 45c. black, red and orange . . 30 25
Nos. 85/8 exist in 7 different designs to each value as follows: A, Bequia, B, Canouan, C, Mayreau, D, Mustique, E, Petit St. Vincent, F, Prune, G, Union. To indicate any particular design use the appropriate catalogue No. together with the suffix for the island concerned.

13 Station Hill School and Post Office

1977. Mayreau Island. Multicoloured.
89 5c. Type **13** 10 10
90 35c. Church at Old Wall . . . 10 10
91 45c. La Sourciere Anchorage 20 10
92 $1 Saline Bay 35 15

14 Coronation Crown Coin

1977. Silver Jubilee. Multicoloured.
93 25c. Type **14** 15 10
94 50c. Silver Wedding crown . . 20 10
95 $1 Silver Jubilee crown . . . 20 15

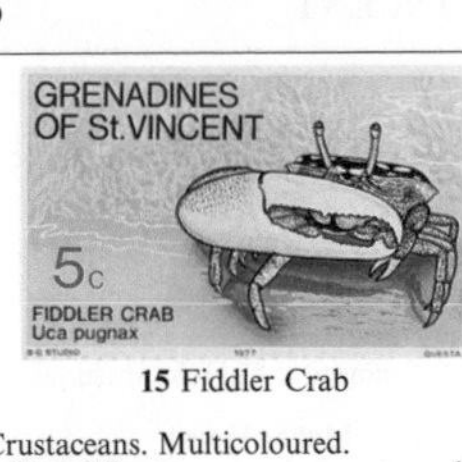

15 Fiddler Crab

1977. Crustaceans. Multicoloured.
96 5c. Type **15** 15 15
97 35c. Ghost crab 25 15
98 50c. Blue crab 30 20
99 $1.25 Spiny lobster 60 90

16 Snorkel Diving

1977. Prune Island. Multicoloured.
100 5c. Type **16** 15 15
101 35c. Palm Island Resort . . . 20 15
102 45c. Casuarina Beach 20 15
103 $1 Palm Island Beach Club 60 1·10

17 Mustique Island

1977. Royal Visit. Surch as in T **17**.
104 **17** 40c. turquoise and green 20 10
105 $2 ochre and brown . . . 45 25

18 The Clinic, Charlestown

1977. Canouan Island (1st series). Mult.
106 5c. Type **18** 10 15
107 35c. Town jetty, Charlestown 20 15
108 45c. Mail schooner arriving at Charlestown 20 15
109 $1 Grand Bay . . . . 40 1·00
See also Nos. 307/10.

19 Tropical Mockingbird

1978. Birds and their Eggs. Multicoloured.
110 1c. Type **19** 10 60
111 2c. Mangrove cuckoo 15 60
112 3c. Osprey 20 60
113 4c. Smooth-billed ani 20 60
114 5c. House wren 20 40
115 6c. Bananaquit 20 40
116 8c. Carib grackle 20 45
117 10c. Yellow-bellied elaenia . . 20 45
118 12c. Collared plover . . . . 30 1·25
119 15c. Cattle egret 30 45
120 20c. Red-footed booby . . . 30 45
121 25c. Red-billed tropic bird . . 30 45
122 40c. Royal tern . . . . . . 45 1·00
123 50c. Grenada flycatcher ("Rusty-tailed Flycatcher") 45 1·00
124 80c. American purple gallinule ("Purple Gallinule") . . . . 70 1·00
125 $1 Broad-winged hawk . . . 75 1·00
126 $2 Scaly-breasted ground dove ("Common Ground Dove") . . . . 75 1·60
127 $3 Laughing gull . . . . . 1·00 1·75
128 $5 Common noddy ("Brown Noddy") . . . . 1·25 1·75
129 $10 Grey kingbird . . . . . 2·00 2·25

19a Worcester Cathedral

1978. 25th Anniv of Coronation. British Cathedrals. Multicoloured.
130 5c. Type **19a** 10 10
131 40c. Coventry Cathedral . . 10 10
132 $1 Winchester Cathedral . . 15 20
133 $3 Chester Cathedral 25 45
MS134 130 × 102 mm. Nos. 130/3 45 80

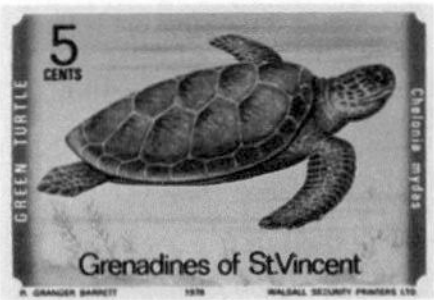

20 Green Turtle

1978. Turtles. Multicoloured.
135 5c. Type **20** 10 10
136 40c. Hawksbill turtle 15 10
137 50c. Leatherback turtle . . . 15 10
138 $1.25 Loggerhead turtle . . . 40 40

21 Three Kings following Star

22 Sailing Yachts

1978. Christmas. Scenes and Verses from the Carol "We Three Kings". Multicoloured.
139 5c. Type **21** 10 10
140 10c. King presenting gold . . 10 10
141 25c. King presenting frankincense 10 10
142 50c. King presenting myrrh 10 10
143 $2 Kings paying homage to infant Jesus 30 20
MS144 154 × 175 mm. Nos. 139/43 70 1·25

1979. National Regatta.
145 **22** 5c. multicoloured 10 10
146 – 40c. multicoloured 20 10
147 – 50c. multicoloured 25 10
148 – $2 multicoloured 75 60
DESIGNS: 40c. to $2, Various sailing yachts.

22a Green Iguana

1979. Wildlife. Multicoloured.
149 20c. Type **22a** 10 15
150 40c. Common opossum ("Manicou") 15 15
151 $2 Red-legged tortoise . . . 60 1·10

22b Sir Rowland Hill

1979. Death Centenary of Sir Rowland Hill. Multicoloured.
152 80c. Type **22b** 15 15
153 $1 Great Britain 1d. and 4d. stamps of 1858 with "A10" (Kingstown, St. Vincent) postmark 15 25
154 $2 St. Vincent ½d and 1d. stamps of 1894 with Bequia postmark 25 40
MS155 165 × 115 mm. Nos. 124/6 and 152/4 . . . . 1·40 2·50

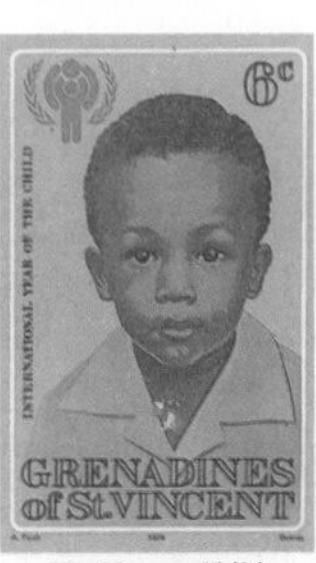

22c Young Child

1979. International Year of the Child. Designs showing portraits of young children.
156 **22c** 6c. black, silver and blue 10 10
157 – 40c. black, silver & salmon 10 10
158 – $1 black, silver and buff 20 10
159 – $3 black, silver and lilac 45 30

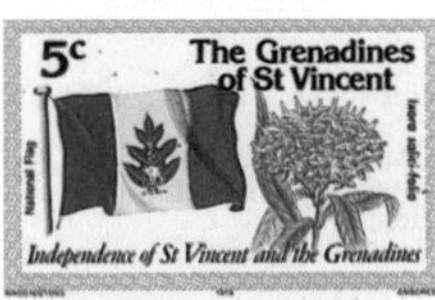

22d National Flag and "Ixora salicifolia" (flower)

1979. Independence. Multicoloured.
160 5c. Type **22d** 10 10
161 40c. House of Assembly and "Ixora odorata" (flower) 10 10
162 $1 Prime Minister R. Milton Cato and "Ixora javanica" (flower) 20 20

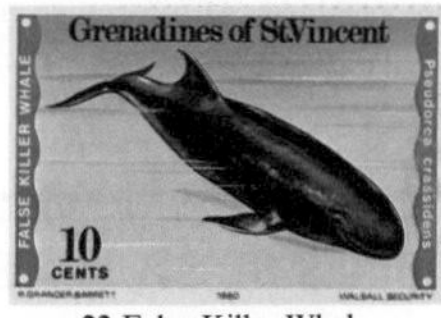

23 False Killer Whale

1980. Whales and Dolphins. Multicoloured.
163 10c. Type **23** 45 30
164 50c. Spinner dolphin 45 35
165 90c. Bottle-nosed dolphin . . 50 80
166 $2 Short-finned pilot whale ("Blackfish") . . . . . . 1·25 2·25

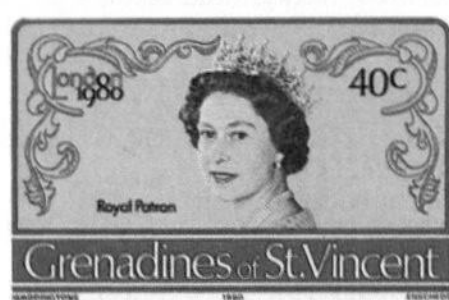

23a Queen Elizabeth II

1980. "London 1980" International Stamp Exhibition. Multicoloured.
167 40c. Type **23a** 10 15
168 50c. St. Vincent 2c. stamp of 1965 . . . . 15 15
169 $3 First Grenadines stamps 40 1·25
MS170 165 × 115 mm. Nos. 122/3, 127 and 167/9 . . . . 2·00 2·50

23b Running

24 Scene and Verse from the Carol "De Borning Day"

1980. Sport. Multicoloured.
171 25c. Type **23b** 10 10
172 50c. Sailing 10 10
173 $1 Long-jumping 20 20
174 $2 Swimming 30 30

1980. Hurricane Relief. Nos. 171/4 optd **HURRICANE RELIEF 50c**.
175 **22** 25c.+50c. multicoloured . . 10 30
176 – 50c.+50c. multicoloured . . 15 40
177 – $1+50c. multicoloured . . 20 50
178 – $2+50c. multicoloured . . 30 70

1980. Christmas. Multicoloured.
179 5c. Type **24** 10 10
180 50c. "Mary and de Baby lonely" 10 10
181 60c. "Mary and de Baby weary" 10 10
182 $1 "Mary and de Baby rest easy" 15 15
183 $2 "Star above shine in de sky" 25 25
MS184 159 × 178 mm. Nos. 179/83 50 1·40

25 Post Office, Port Elizabeth

1981. Bequia Island (2nd series). Mult.
185 50c. Type **25** 15 20
186 60c. Moonhole 15 20
187 $1.50 Fishing boats, Admiralty Bay 30 55
188 $2 "The Friendship Rose" (yacht) at jetty 50 70

26 Ins. Cannaouan (from map of Windward Islands by R. Ottens, c. 1765)

1981. Details from Early Maps. Multicoloured.
189 50c. Type **26** 30 30
190 50c. Cannouan Is. (from chart by J. Parsons, 1861) 30 30
191 60c. Ins. Moustiques (from map of Windward Islands by R. Ottens, c. 1765) . . 30 35
192 60c. Mustique Is. (from chart by J. Parsons, 1861) . . . 30 35
193 $2 Ins. Bequia (from map of Windward Islands by R. Ottens, c.1765) 50 75
194 $2 Bequia Is. (from map surveyed in 1763 by T. Jefferys) 50 75

26a "Mary"

1981. Royal Wedding. Royal Yachts. Multicoloured.
195 50c. Type **26a** 10 15
196 50c. Prince Charles and Lady Diana Spencer 35 40
197 $3 "Alexandra" 20 30
198 $3 As No. 196 . . . . 60 90
199 $3.50 "Britannia" 25 35
200 $3.50 As No. 196 . . . . . 65 90
MS201 120 × 109 mm. $5 As No. 196 . . . . 75 75

27 Bar Jack

1981. Game Fish. Multicoloured.
204 10c. Type **27** 15 10
205 50c. Tarpon 30 10
206 60c. Cobia 35 10
207 $2 Blue marlin . . . . 1·00 70

28 H.M.S. "Experiment" (frigate)

1982. Ships. Multicoloured.
208 1c. Type **28** 10 20
209 3c. "Lady Nelson" (cargo liner) 15 20
210 5c. "Daisy" (brig) 20 20
211 6c. Carib canoe 10 20
212 10c. "Hairoun Star" (freighter) 20 10
213 15c. "Jupiter" (liner) 40 10
214 20c. "Christina" (steam yacht) 40 10
215 25c. "Orinoco" (mail paddle-steamer) 40 15
216 30c. H.M.S. "Lively" (frigate) 40 15
217 50c. "Alabama" (Confederate warship) 50 30
218 60c. "Denmark" (freighter) 60 30
219 75c. "Santa Maria" . . . . 1·00 50
220 $1 "Baffin" (research vessel) 80 55
221 $2 "Queen Elizabeth 2" (liner) . . . . 1·00 1·25
222 $3 R.Y. "Britannia" . . . . 1·00 1·75
223 $5 "Geeststar" (freighter) . . 1·00 2·00
224 $10 "Grenadines Star" (ferry) 1·25 5·00

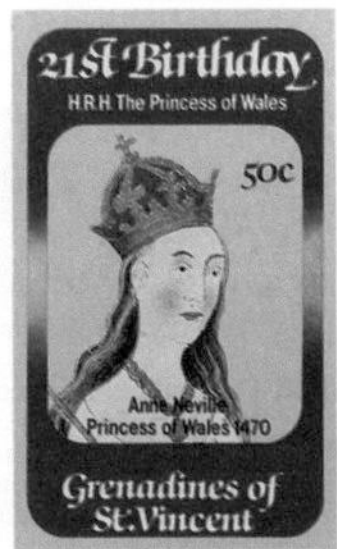

29 Prickly Pear Fruit **30** Anne Neville, Princess of Wales, 1470

1982. Prickly Pear Cactus. Multicoloured.
225 10c. Type **29** 15 15
226 50c. Prickly pear flower buds 35 35
227 $1 Flower of prickly pear cactus 60 60
228 $2 Prickly pear cactus . . . 1·25 1·25

1982. 21st Birthday of Princess of Wales. Multicoloured.
229 50c. Type **30** 10 15
230 60c. Coat of arms of Anne Neville 10 15
231 $6 Diana, Princess of Wales 60 80

31 Old and New Uniforms

1982. 75th Anniv of Boy Scout Movement. Multicoloured.
232 $1.50 Type **31** 50 75
233 $2.50 Lord Baden-Powell . . 60 1·00

1982. Birth of Prince William of Wales. Nos. 224/6 optd **ROYAL BABY** and Island name.
234 50c. Type **30** 10 15
235 60c. Coat of arms of Anne Neville 10 15
236 $6 Diana, Princess of Wales 60 80

Nos. 229/32 exist optd with 5 different island names as follows: A, Bequia, B, Canouan, C, Mayreau, D, Mustique, E, Union Island. To indicate any particular overprint use the appropriate catalogue No. together with the suffix for the island concerned.

33 Silhouette Figures of Mary and Joseph

1982. Christmas. Silhouette of figures. Multicoloured.
237 10c. Type **33** 10 10
238 $1.50 Animals in stable . . . 45 45
239 $2.50 Mary and Joseph with baby Jesus 60 60
MS240 168 × 99 mm. Nos. 237/9 1·00 2·00

1983. No. 123 surch **45c.**
241 45c. on 50c. Grenada flycatcher 45 30

35 Power Station, Clifton

1983. Union Island (2nd issue). Multicoloured.
242 50c. Type **35** 25 15
243 60c. Sunrise, Clifton harbour 25 15
244 $1.50 Junior Secondary School, Ashton 60 40
245 $2 Frigate Rock and Conch Shell Beach 85 55

36 British Man-of-war **37** Montgolfier Balloon, 1783

1983. Bicentenary of Treaty of Versailles. Mult.
246 45c. Type **36** 35 15
247 60c. American man-of-war 35 15
248 $1.50 Soldiers carrying U.S flags 75 45
249 $2 British troops in battle . . 80 55

1983. Bicentenary of Manned Flight. Mult.
250 45c. Type **37** 15 15
251 60c. Ayres Turbo Thrush Commander (horiz) 15 15
252 $1.50 Lebaudy-Juillot airship No. 1 "La Jaune" (horiz) 40 45
253 $2 Space shuttle "Columbia" (horiz) 40 55
MS254 110 × 145 mm. Nos. 250/3 1·00 1·50

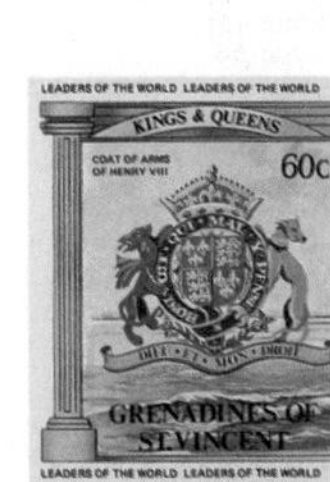

38 Coat of Arms of Henry VIII **39** Quarter Dollar and Half Dollar, 1797

1983. Leaders of the World. British Monarchs. Multicoloured.
255 60c. Type **38** 10 25
256 60c. Henry VIII 10 25
257 60c. Coat of Arms of James I 10 25
258 60c. James I 10 25
259 75c. Henry VIII at Hampton Court 10 25
260 75c. Hampton Court 10 25
261 75c. James I at Edinburgh Castle 10 25
262 75c. Edinburgh Castle . . . 10 25
263 $2.50 The "Mary Rose" . . 25 35
264 $2.50 Henry VIII and Portsmouth harbour . . . 25 35
265 $2.50 Gunpowder Plot . . . 25 35
266 $2.50 James I and Gunpowder Plot 25 35

1983. Old Coinage. Multicoloured.
267 20c. Type **39** 10 10
268 45c. Nine Bitts, 1811–14 . . 15 15
269 75c. Twelve Bitts and Six Bitts, 1811–14 . . . . . 25 25
270 $3 Sixty-six Shillings, 1798 80 80

40 Class D13

1984. Leaders of the World. Railway Locomotives (1st series). The first design in each pair shows technical drawings and the second the locomotive at work.
271 5c. multicoloured 10 10
272 5c. multicoloured 10 10
273 10c. multicoloured 10 10
274 10c. multicoloured 10 10
275 15c. multicoloured 10 15
276 15c. multicoloured 10 15
277 35c. multicoloured 10 20
278 35c. multicoloured 10 20
279 45c. multicoloured 10 20
280 45c. multicoloured 10 20
281 60c. multicoloured 15 20
282 60c. multicoloured 15 20
283 $1 multicoloured 15 25
284 $1 multicoloured 15 25
285 $2.50 multicoloured 25 35
286 $2.50 multicoloured 25 35
DESIGNS: Nos. 271/2, Class D13, U.S.A., 1892 (Type **40**); 273/4, High Speed Train 125, Great Britain (1980); 275/6, Class T9, Great Britain (1899); 277/8, "Claud Hamilton", Great Britain (1900); 279/80, Class J, U.S.A. (1941); 281/2, Class D16, U.S.A. (1895); 283/4, "Lode Star", Great Britain (1907); 285/6, "Blue Peter", Great Britain (1948).
See also Nos. 321/26, 351/8, 390/7, 412/9, 443/58, 504/19 and 520/35.

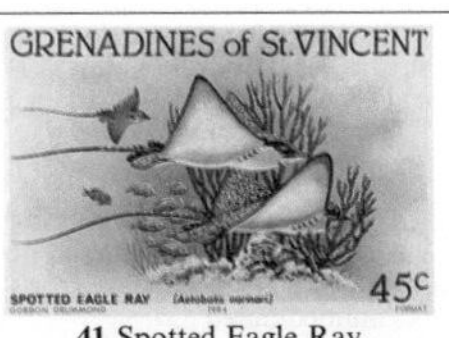

41 Spotted Eagle Ray

1984. Reef Fishes. Multicoloured.
287 45c. Type **41** 25 20
288 60c. Queen triggerfish 25 35
289 $1.50 White spotted filefish 40 1·25
290 $2 Schoolmaster . . . . . . 40 1·50

42 R. A. Woolmer **44** Lady of the Night

43 Junior Secondary School

1984. Leaders of the World. Cricketers (1st series). The first design in each pair shows a portrait and the second the cricketer in action.
291 1c. multicoloured 10 10
292 1c. multicoloured 10 10
293 3c. multicoloured 10 10
294 3c. multicoloured 10 10
295 5c. multicoloured 10 10
296 5c. multicoloured 10 10
297 30c. multicoloured 30 30
298 30c. multicoloured 30 30
299 60c. multicoloured 40 40
300 60c. multicoloured 40 40
301 $1 multicoloured 40 40
302 $1 multicoloured 40 40
303 $2 multicoloured 45 70
304 $2 multicoloured 45 70
305 $3 multicoloured 55 80
306 $3 multicoloured 55 80
DESIGNS: Nos. 291/2, R. A. Woolmer (Type **42**); K. S. Ranjitsinhji; 295/6, W. R. Hammond; 297/8, D. L. Underwood; 299/300, W. G. Grace; 301/2, E. A. E. Baptiste; 303/4, A. P. E. Knott; 305/6, L. E. G. Ames.
See also Nos. 331/8 and 364/9.

1984. Canouan Island (2nd series). Multicoloured.
307 35c. Type **43** 20 20
308 45c. Police Station 50 25
309 $1 Post Office 50 50
310 $3 Anglican Church . . . . 1·00 1·75

1984. Leaders of the World. Railway Locomotives (2nd issue). As T **40**. The first design in each pair shows technical drawings and the second the locomotive at work.
311 1c. multicoloured 10 10
312 1c. multicoloured 10 10
313 5c. multicoloured 10 10
314 5c. multicoloured 10 10
315 20c. multicoloured 15 15
316 20c. multicoloured 15 15
317 35c. multicoloured 15 15
318 35c. multicoloured 15 15
319 60c. multicoloured 25 25
320 60c. multicoloured 25 25
321 $1 multicoloured 25 30
322 $1 multicoloured 25 30
323 $1.50 multicoloured 30 40
324 $1.50 multicoloured 30 40
325 $3 multicoloured 35 55
326 $3 multicoloured 35 55
DESIGNS: Nos. 311/12, Class C62, Japan (1948); 313/14, Class V, Great Britain (1903); 315/16, Richard Trevithick's "Catch-Me-Who-Can", Great Britain (1808); 317/18, Class E10, Japan (1948); 319/20, "J. B. Earle", Great Britain (1904); 321/2, No. 762 "Lyn", Great Britain (1898); 323/4, "Talyllyn", Great Britain (1865); 325/6, "Cardean", Great Britain (1906).

1984. Night-blooming Flowers. Mult.
327 35c. Type **44** 30 30
328 45c. Four o'clock 35 35
329 75c. Mother-in-law's tongue 45 60
330 $3 Queen of the night . . . . 1·10 2·75

1984. Leaders of the World. Cricketers (2nd series). As T **42**. The first in each pair listed shows a head portrait and the second the cricketer in action.
331 5c. multicoloured 10 10
332 5c. multicoloured 10 10
333 30c. multicoloured 25 20
334 30c. multicoloured 25 20
335 $1 multicoloured 30 40
336 $1 multicoloured 30 40
337 $2.50 multicoloured 45 80
338 $2.50 multicoloured 45 80
DESIGNS: Nos. 331/2, S. F. Barnes; 333/4, R. Peel; 335/6, H. Larwood; 337/8, Sir John Hobbs.

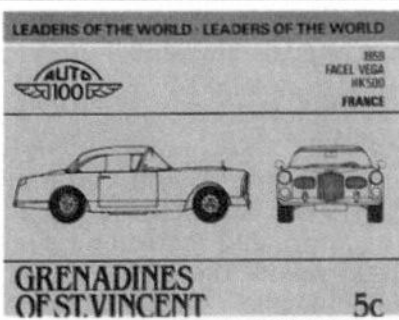

45 Facel "Vega HK500"

1984. Leaders of the World. Automobiles (1st series). The first design in each pair shows technical drawings and the second paintings.
339 5c. black, blue and green . . 10 10
340 5c. multicoloured 10 10
341 25c. black, lilac and pink . . 10 10
342 25c. multicoloured 10 10
343 50c. black, blue and orange 15 15
344 50c. multicoloured 15 15
345 $3 black, stone and brown 30 45
346 $3 multicoloured 30 45
DESIGNS: Nos. 339/40, Facel "Vega HK500" (Type **45**); 341/2, BMW "328"; 343/4, Frazer-Nash "TT Replica 1.5L"; 345/6, Buick "Roadmaster Riviera".
See also Nos. 378/85 and 431/42.

46 Three Wise Men and Star

1984. Christmas. Multicoloured.
347 20c. Type **46** 10 10
348 45c. Journeying to Bethlehem 15 25
349 $3 Presenting gifts . . . . . 70 1·40
MS350 177 × 107 mm. Nos. 347/9 1·00 2·00

1985. Leaders of the World. Railway Locomotives (3rd series). As T **40**. The first in each pair shows technical drawings and the second the locomotive at work.
351 1c. multicoloured 10 10
352 1c. multicoloured 10 10
353 15c. multicoloured 10 10
354 15c. multicoloured 10 10
355 75c. multicoloured 20 25
356 75c. multicoloured 20 25
357 $3 multicoloured 50 70
358 $3 multicoloured 50 70
MS359 142 × 122 mm. Nos. 355/8 1·75 6·50
DESIGNS: Nos. 351/2, P.L.M. "Grosse C", France (1898); 353/4, Class C12, Japan (1932); 355/6, Class D50, Japan (1923); 357/8, "Fire Fly", Great Britain (1840).

47 Caribbean King Crab

1985. Shell Fish. Multicoloured.
360 25c. Type **47** 20 15
361 60c. Queen or pink conch . . 30 35
362 $1 White sea urchin 35 60
363 $3 West Indian top shell or wilk . . . . 75 2·00

1985. Leaders of the World. Cricketers (3rd series). As T **42** (55, 60c.) the first in each pair showing a head portrait and the second the cricketer in action, or horiz designs showing teams ($2).
364 55c. multicoloured 25 35
365 55c. multicoloured 25 35
366 60c. multicoloured 25 40
367 60c. multicoloured 25 40
368 $2 multicoloured 40 85
369 $2 multicoloured 40 85
DESIGNS—VERT (As T **42**): Nos. 364/5 M. D. Moxon; 366/7, L. Potter. HORIZ (59 × 42 mm): No. 368, Kent team; 369, Yorkshire team.

48 "Cypripedium calceolus"

1985. Leaders of the World. Flowers. Multicoloured.
370 5c. Type **48** 10 10
371 5c. "Gentiana asclepiadea" 10 10
372 55c. "Clianthus formosus" . . 15 20
373 55c. "Clemisia coriacea" . . 15 20
374 60c. "Erythronium americanum" 15 20
375 60c. "Laelia anceps" 15 20

376 $2 "Leucadendron discolor" 35 50
377 $2 "Meconopsis horridula" 35 50

1985. Leaders of the World. Automobiles (2nd series). As T **45**. The first in each pair shows technical drawings and the second paintings.
378 5c. black, yellow and blue . . 10 10
379 5c. multicoloured 10 10
380 60c. black, yellow and orange 15 15
381 60c. multicoloured 15 15
382 $1 black, green and blue . . 15 20
383 $1 multicoloured 15 20
384 $1.50 black, blue and green 15 25
385 $1.50 multicoloured 15 25
DESIGNS: Nos. 378/9, Winton (1903); 380/1, Invicta 4½ litre (1932); 382/3, Daimler "SP250 Dart" (1959); 384/5, Brabham "Repco BT19" (1966).

49 Windsurfing

1985. Tourism. Watersports. Multicoloured.
386 35c. Type **49** 15 15
387 45c. Water-skiing 15 15
388 75c. Scuba-diving 15 25
389 $3 Deep-sea game fishing . . 30 1·40

1985. Leaders of the World. Railway Locomotives (4th series). As T **40**. The first design in each pair shows technical drawings and the second the locomotive at work.
390 10c. mutlicoloured 10 10
391 10c. multicoloured 10 10
392 40c. multicoloured 20 20
393 40c. multicoloured 20 20
394 50c. multicoloured 20 20
395 50c. multicoloured 20 20
396 $2.50 multicoloured 70 80
397 $2.50 multicoloured 70 80
DESIGNS: Nos. 390/1, Class 581 electric train, Japan (1968); 392/3, 231-132BT, Algeria (1936); 394/5, "Slieve Gullion", Ireland (1913); 396/7, Class "Beattie" well tank, Great Britain (1874).

50 Passion Fruits and Blossom

1985. Fruits and Blossoms. Multicoloured.
398 30c. Type **50** 15 20
399 75c. Guava 25 40
400 $1 Sapodilla 35 55
401 $2 Mango . . . . 50 1·10
MS402 145 × 120 mm. Nos. 398/401 2·00 2·25

51 Queen Elizabeth, the Queen Mother

1985. Leaders of the World. Life and Times of Queen Elizabeth, the Queen Mother. Various vertical portraits.
403 **51** 40c. multicoloured 10 20
404 – 40c. multicoloured 10 20
405 – 75c. multicoloured 15 20
406 – 75c. multicoloured 15 20
407 – $1.10 multicoloured . . . 15 20
408 – $1.10 multicoloured . . . 15 20
409 – $1.75 multicoloured . . . 15 30
410 – $1.75 multicoloured . . . 15 30
MS411 85 × 114 mm. $2 multicoloured; $2 multicoloured 50 1·50
Each value, issued in pairs, shows a floral pattern across the bottom of the portraits which stops short of the left-hand edge on the first stamp and of the right-hand edge on the second.

1985. Leaders of the World. Railway Locomotives (5th series). As T **40**. The first design in each pair shows technical drawings and the second the locomotive at work.
412 35c. multicoloured 15 20
413 35c. multicoloured 15 20
414 70c. multicoloured 20 30
415 70c. multicoloured 20 30
416 $1.20 multicoloured 30 40
417 $1.20 multicoloured 30 40
418 $2 multicoloured 40 65
419 $2 multicoloured 40 65
DESIGNS: Nos. 412/13, "Coronation", Great Britain (1937); 414/15, Class E18, Germany (1935); 416/17, Hayes type, U.S.A. (1854); 418/19, Class 2120, Japan (1890).

1985. Royal Visit. Nos. 199/200, 222, 287, 398 and 407/8 optd **CARIBBEAN ROYAL VISIT 1985** or surch also.
420 **50** 30c. multicoloured . . . . 80 1·50
421 **41** 45c. multicoloured . . . . 1·00 1·75
422 – $1.10 multicoloured (No. 407) . . . . 1·75 4·00
423 – $1.10 multicoloured (No. 408) . . . . 1·75 4·00
424 – $1.50 on $3.50 mult (No. 199) . . . . 2·00 2·25
425 – $1.50 on $3.50 mult (No. 200) . . . . 20·00 23·00
426 – $3 multicoloured (No. 222) 2·75 3·75

52 Donkey Man

1985. Traditional Dances. Multicoloured.
427 45c. Type **52** 10 30
428 75c. Cake dance (vert) . . . 15 40
429 $1 Bois-Bois man (vert) . . . 15 55
430 $2 Maypole dance . . . . . 25 1·10

1986. Leaders of the World. Automobiles (3rd series). As T **45**. The first in each pair shows technical drawings and the second paintings.
431 15c. black, lilac and mauve 10 10
432 15c. multicoloured 10 10
433 45c. black, yellow and brown 10 20
434 45c. multicoloured 10 20
435 60c. black, green and blue . . 10 25
436 60c. multicoloured 10 25
437 $1 black, brown and green 15 25
438 $1 multicoloured 15 25
439 $1.75 black, yellow and orange 15 35
440 $1.75 multicoloured 15 35
441 $3 multicoloured 25 45
442 $3 multicoloured 25 45
DESIGNS: Nos. 431/2, Mercedes-Benz 4.5 litre (1914); 433/4, Rolls Royce "Silver Wraith" (1954); 435/6, Lamborghini "Countach" (1974); 437/8, Marmon "V-16" (1932); 439/40, Lotus-Ford "49 B" (1968); 441/2, Delage 1.5 litre (1927).

1986. Leaders of the World. Railway Locomotives (6th series). As T **40**. The first in each pair shows technical drawings and the second the locomotive at work.
443 15c. multicoloured 15 10
444 15c. multicoloured 15 10
445 45c. multicoloured 20 20
446 45c. multicoloured 20 20
447 60c. multicoloured 20 30
448 60c. multicoloured 20 30
449 75c. multicoloured 20 35
450 75c. multicoloured 20 35
451 $1 multicoloured 25 40
452 $1 multicoloured 25 40
453 $1.50 multicoloured 25 50
454 $1.50 multicoloured 25 50
455 $2 multicoloured 30 65
456 $2 multicoloured 30 65
457 $3 multicoloured 30 80
458 $3 multicoloured 30 80
DESIGNS: Nos. 443/4, Class T15, Germany (1897); 445/6, Class 13, Great Britain (1900); 447/8, "Halesworth", Great Britain (1879); 449/50, Class "Problem", Great Britain (1859); 451/2, Class "Western" diesel, Great Britain (1961); 453/4, Drummond's "Bug", Great Britain (1899); 455/6, Class "Clan", Great Britain (1951); 457/8, Class 1800, Japan (1884).

52a Queen Elizabeth II

1986. 60th Birthday of Queen Elizabeth II. Mult.
459 5c. Type **52a** 15 15
460 $1 At Princess Anne's christening, 1950 . . . . . 30 40
461 $4 Princess Elizabeth . . . . 60 1·25
462 $6 In Canberra, 1982 (vert) 75 1·50
MS463 85 × 115 mm. $8 Queen Elizabeth II (different) . . . . 1·50 4·50

53 Handmade Dolls

1986. Handicrafts. Multicoloured.
464 10c. Type **53** 10 10
465 60c. Basketwork 20 35
466 $1 Scrimshaw work 30 50
467 $3 Model sailing dinghy . . . 80 2·25

54 Uruguayan Team

1986. World Cup Football Championship, Mexico. Multicoloured.
468 1c. Type **54** 10 10
469 10c. Polish team 10 10
470 45c. Bulgarian player (28 × 42 mm) 25 30
471 75c. Iraqi player (28 × 42 mm) 35 40
472 $1.50 South Korean player (28 × 42 mm) 60 90
473 $2 Northern Irish player (28 × 42 mm) . . . . . . 70 1·10
474 $4 Portuguese team . . . . . 1·00 1·50
475 $5 Canadian team . . . . . 1·00 1·50
MS476 Two sheets, 85 × 114 mm. (a) $1 As No. 474. (b) $3 Type **54**. Set of 2 sheets . . . . 1·50 2·75

55 "Marasmius pallescens"

1986. Fungi. Multicoloured.
477 45c. Type **55** . . . . 2·25 75
478 60c. "Leucocoprinus fragilissimus" . . . . . . 2·50 1·10
479 75c. "Hygrocybe occidentalis" . . . . 2·75 1·60
480 $3 "Xerocomus hypoxanthus" . . . . . . 8·00 7·00

55a Miss Sarah Ferguson and Princess Diana applauding

1986. Royal Wedding (1st issue). Multicoloured.
481 60c. Type **55a** 20 30
482 60c. Prince Andrew at shooting match 20 30
483 $2 Prince Andrew and Miss Sarah Ferguson (horiz) . . 60 90
484 $2 Prince Charles with Prince Andrew, Princess Anne and Princess Margaret on balcony (horiz) 60 90
MS485 115 × 85 mm. $8 Duke and Duchess of York in carriage after wedding (horiz) . . . . 2·75 4·50

1986. Royal Wedding (2nd issue). Nos. 481/4 optd **Congratulations to T.R.H. The Duke & Duchess of York**.
486 60c. Miss Sarah Ferguson and Princess Diana applauding 30 65
487 60c. Prince Andrew at shooting match 30 65
488 $2 Prince Andrew and Miss Sarah Ferguson (horiz) . . 1·00 1·25
489 $2 Prince Charles, Prince Andrew, Princess Anne and Princess Margaret on balcony (horiz) . . . . . 1·00 1·25

56 "Brachymesia furcata"

1986. Dragonflies. Multicoloured.
490 45c. Type **56** 25 20
491 60c. "Lepthemis vesiculosa" 30 40
492 75c. "Perithemis domitta" . . 30 45
493 $2.50 "Tramea abdominalis (vert) . . . . 45 1·40

1986. Centenary of Statue of Liberty. Vert views of Statue as T **323a** of Grenada in seperate miniature sheets. Multicoloured.
MS494 Nine sheets, each 85 × 115 mm. $1.50; $1.75; $2; $2.50; $3; $3.50; $5; $6; $8. Set of 9 sheets . . . . 3·00 12·00

57 American Kestrel ("Sparrow Hawk")

58 Santa playing Steel Band Drums

1986. Birds of Prey. Multicoloured.
495 10c. Type **57** 75 45
496 45c. Common black hawk ("Black Hawk") . . . . . 1·90 50
497 60c. Peregrine falcon ("Duck Hawk") . . . . 2·25 1·25
498 $4 Osprey ("Fish Hawk") . . 5·00 6·50

1986. Christmas. Multicoloured.
499 45c. Type **58** 30 30
500 60c. Santa windsurfing . . . 35 35
501 $1.25 Santa skiing 60 85
502 $2 Santa limbo dancing . . . 1·10 1·60
MS503 166 × 128 mm. Nos. 499/502 7·00 8·00

1987. Railway Locomotives (7th series). As T **40**. The first in each pair shows technical drawings and the second the locomotive at work.
504 10c. multicoloured 15 10
505 10c. multicoloured 15 10
506 40c. multicoloured 25 25
507 40c. multicoloured 25 25
508 50c. multicoloured 30 30
509 50c. multicoloured 30 30
510 60c. multicoloured 30 30
511 60c. multicoloured 30 30
512 75c. multicoloured 30 40
513 75c. multicoloured 30 40
514 $1 multicoloured 30 50
515 $1 multicoloured 30 50
516 $1.25 multicoloured 30 60
517 $1.25 multicoloured 30 60
518 $1.50 multicoloured 40 75
519 $1.50 multicoloured 40 75
DESIGNS: Nos. 504/5, Class 1001, No. 1275, Great Britain (1874); 506/7, Class 4P Garratt, Great Britain (1927); 508/9, "Papyrus", Great Britain (1929); 510/11, Class VI, Great Britain (1930); 512/13, Class 40 diesel, No. D200, Great Britain (1958); 514/15, Class 42 "Warship" diesel, Great Britain (1958); 516/17, Class P-69, U.S.A. (1902); 518/19, Class 60-3 Shay, No. 15, U.S.A. (1913).

1987. Railway Locomotives (8th series). As T **40**. The first in each pair shows technical drawings and the second the locomotive at work.
520 10c. multicoloured 15 15
521 10c. multicoloured 15 15
522 40c. multicoloured 25 30
523 40c. multicoloured 25 30
524 50c. multicoloured 30 35
525 50c. multicoloured 30 35
526 60c. multicoloured 30 40
527 60c. multicoloured 30 40
528 75c. multicoloured 30 45
529 75c. multicoloured 30 45
530 $1 multicoloured 30 45
531 $1 multicoloured 30 45
532 $1.50 multicoloured 40 55
533 $1.50 multicoloured 40 55
534 $2 multicoloured 45 70
535 $2 multicoloured 45 70
DESIGNS: Nos. 520/1, Class 142, East Germany (1977); 522/3, Class 120, West Germany (1979); 524/5, Class X, Australia (1954); 526/7, Class 59, Great Britain (1986); 528/9, New York Elevated Railroad "Spuyten Duyvel", U.S.A. (1875); 530/1, Camden & Amboy Railroad "Stevens" and rebuilt "John Bull", U.S.A. (1832); 532/3, Class HI-d, No. 2850, Canada (1938); 534/5, "Pioneer Zephyr" 3-car diesel set, U.S.A. (1934).

59 Queen Elizabeth with Prince Andrew

1987. Royal Ruby Wedding and 150th Anniv of Queen Victoria's Accession.
536 **59** 15c. multicoloured 20 15
537 – 45c. brown, black and yellow 25 20
538 – $1.50 multicoloured . . . 30 55
539 – $3 multicoloured . . . . 45 1·00
540 – $4 multicoloured . . . . 50 1·25
MS541 85 × 115 mm. $6 multicoloured . . . . 2·00 3·25
DESIGNS: 45c. Queen Victoria and Prince Albert, c. 1855; $1.50, Queen and Prince Philip after Trooping the Colour, 1977; $3 Queen and Duke of Edinburgh, 1953; $4 Queen in her study, c. 1980; Princess Elizabeth, 1947.

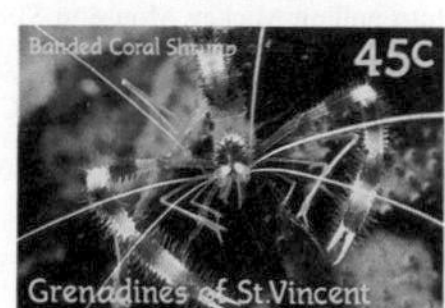

60 Banded Coral Shrimp

1987. Marine Life. Multicoloured.
542 45c. Type **60** 55 35
543 50c. Arrow crab and flamingo tongue 60 50
544 65c. Cardinal fish 70 90
545 $5 Moray eel . . . . 2·00 4·00
MS546 85 × 115 mm. $5 Porcupinefish ("Puffer Fish") 2·50 5·00

61 "Australia IV"

1988. Ocean Racing Yachts. Multicoloured.
547 50c. Type **61** 30 35
548 65c. "Crusader II" 35 50
549 75c. "New Zealand II" . . . 40 60
550 $2 "Italia" . . . . 60 1·25
551 $4 "White Crusader" . . . . 70 2·00
552 $5 "Stars and Stripes" . . . 70 2·25
MS553 100 × 140 mm. $1 "Champosa V" . . . . 1·25 2·00

62 Seine-fishing Boats racing

1988. Bequia Regatta. Multicoloured.
554 5c. Type **62** 10 15
555 50c. "Friendship Rose" (cruising yacht) 15 30
556 75c. Fishing boats racing . . 20 45
557 $3.50 Yachts racing . . . . 75 2·25
MS558 115 × 85 mm. $8 Port Elizabeth, Bequia (60 × 40 mm) 3·25 6·00

63 Britten Norman Islander making Night Approach

1988. Mustique Airways. Multicoloured.
559 15c. Type **63** 10 15
560 65c. Beech Baron aircraft in flight 15 35
561 75c. Britten Norman Islander over forest 15 35
562 $5 Beech Baron on airstrip 1·00 2·25
MS563 115 × 85 mm. $10 Baleine Falls (36 × 56 mm) . . . . . . 2·50 5·50

64 "Sv. Pyotr" in Arctic (Bering)

65 Asif Iqbal Razvi

1988. Explorers. Multicoloured.
564 15c. Type **64** 35 20
565 75c. Bering's ships in pack ice 40 30
566 $1 Livingstone's steam launch "Ma-Robert" on Zambesi 40 40
567 $2 Meeting of Livingstone and H. M. Stanley at Ujiji 50 75
568 $3 Speke and Burton at Tabori . . . . 50 1·00
569 $3.50 Speke and Burton in canoe on Lake Victoria . . 50 1·25
570 $4 Sighting the New World, 1492 . . . . 60 1·40
571 $4.50 Columbus trading with Indians . . . . 60 1·50
MS572 Two sheets, each 115 × 85 mm. (a) $5 Sextant and coastal scene. (b) $5 "Santa Maria" at anchor. Set of 2 sheets 2·50 5·50

1988. Cricketers of 1988 International Season. Multicoloured.
573 20c. Type **65** 40 30
574 45c. R. J. Hadlee 60 50
575 75c. M. D. Crowe 80 80
576 $1.25 C. H. Lloyd . . . . . 90 1·25
577 $1.50 A. R. Boarder . . . . 1·00 1·50
578 $2 M. D. Marshall . . . . . 1·25 2·00
579 $2.50 G. A. Hick . . . . . . 1·25 2·25
580 $3.50 C. G. Greenidge (horiz) 1·25 2·75
MS581 115 × 85 mm. $3 As $2 3·75 7·00

66 Pam Shriver

1988. International Tennis Players. Mult.
582 15c. Type **66** 20 20
583 50c. Kevin Curran (vert) . . 20 30
584 75c. Wendy Turnbull (vert) 25 35
585 $1 Evonne Cawley (vert) . . 35 50
586 $1.50 Ilie Nastase 40 65
587 $2 Billie Jean King (vert) . . 45 75
588 $3 Bjorn Borg (vert) . . . . 55 1·25
589 $3.50 Virginia Wade with Wimbledon trophy (vert) 60 1·50
MS590 115 × 85 mm. $2.25, Stefan Edberg with Wimbledon cup; $2.25, Steffi Graf with Wimbledon trophy . . . . 1·50 3·50
No. 584 is inscribed "WENDY TURNBALL" in error.

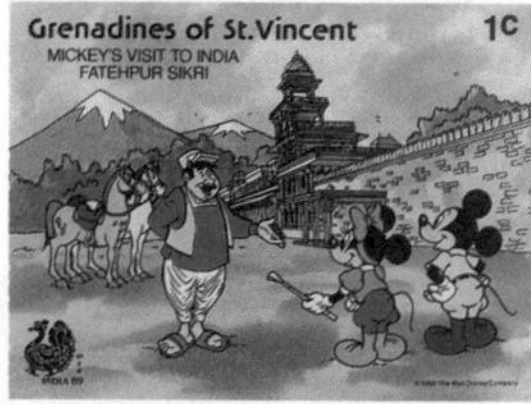

67 Mickey and Minnie Mouse visiting Fatehpur Sikri

1989. "India-89" International Stamp Exhibition. Designs showing Walt Disney cartoon characters in India. Multicoloured.
591 1c. Type **67** 10 10
592 2c. Mickey and Minnie Mouse aboard "Palace on Wheels" train 10 10
593 3c. Mickey and Minnie Mouse passing Old Fort, Delhi 10 10
594 5c. Mickey and Minnie Mouse on camel, Pinjore Gardens, Haryana 10 10
595 10c. Mickey and Minnie Mouse at Taj Mahal, Agra 15 10
596 25c. Mickey and Minnie Mouse in Chandni Chowk, Old Delhi 25 10
597 $4 Goofy on elephant with Mickey and Minnie Mouse at Agra Fort, Jaipur . . . 3·25 3·50
598 $5 Goofy, Mickey and Minnie Mouse at Gandhi Memorial Cape Comorin 3·25 3·50
MS599 Two sheets, each 127 × 102 mm. (a) $6 Mickey and Minnie Mouse in vegetable cart, Jaipur. (b) $6 Mickey and Minnie Mouse leaving carriage, Qutab Minar, New Delhi (vert). Set of 2 sheets . . . . 8·50 10·00

1989. Japanese Art. As T **177a** of Gambia but horiz. Multicoloured.
600 5c. "The View at Yotsuya" (Hokusai) 20 20
601 30c. "Landscape at Ochanomizu" (Hokuju) . . 50 50
602 45c. "Itabashi" (Eisen) . . . 60 60
603 65c. "Early Summer Rain" (Kunisada) 75 75
604 75c. "High Noon at Kasumigaseki" (Kuniyoshi) 80 80
605 $1 "The Yoshiwara Embankment by Moonlight" (Kuniyoshi) . . 1·00 1·00
606 $4 "The Bridge of Boats at Sano" (Hokusai) . . . . . 2·75 3·00
607 $5 "Lingering Snow on Mount Hira" (Kunitora) 2·75 3·00
MS608 Two sheets, each 103 × 76 mm. (a) $6 "Colossus of Rhodes" (Kunitora). (b) $6 "Shinobazu Pond" (Kokan). Set of 2 sheets . . . . 7·00 8·00

68 Player with Ball and Mt. Vesuvius

71 "Marpesia petreus"

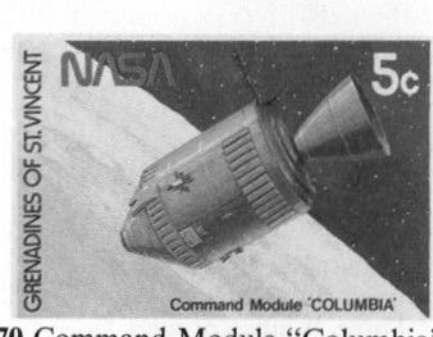

70 Command Module "Columbia"

1989. World Cup Football Championship, Italy (1st issue). Designs showing players and Italian landmarks. Multicoloured.
609 $1.50 Type **68** . . . . 1·40 1·40
610 $1.50 Fallen player, opponent kicking ball and Coliseum 1·40 1·40
611 $1.50 Player blocking ball and Venice . . . . 1·40 1·40
612 $1.50 Player tackling and Forum, Rome . . . . . . 1·40 1·40
613 $1.50 Two players competing for ball and Leaning Tower, Pisa . . . . 1·40 1·40
614 $1.50 Goalkeeper and Florence . . . . 1·40 1·40
615 $1.50 Two players competing for ball and St. Peter's, Vatican . . . . 1·40 1·40
616 $1.50 Player kicking ball and Pantheon . . . . 1·40 1·40
Nos 609/16 were printed together, se-tenant, forming a composite foreground design.
See also Nos. 680/3.

1989. 500th Anniv (1992) of Discovery of America by Columbus (1st issue). Pre-Columbian Arawak Society. As T **97a** of Grenadines of Grenada. Multicoloured.
617 25c. Arawak smoking tobacco 45 30
618 75c. Arawak rolling cigar . . 75 65
619 $1 Applying body paint . . . 90 80
620 $1.50 Making fire . . . . . 1·25 1·50
621 $1.50 Cassava production . . 1·25 1·50
622 $1.50 Woman baking bread 1·25 1·50
623 $1.50 Using stone implement 1·25 1·50
624 $4 Arawak priest . . . . . . 2·50 3·00
MS625 Two sheets, each 70 × 84 mm. (a) $6 Arawak chief. (b) $6 Men returning from fishing expedition. Set of 2 sheets . . 12·00 13·00
Nos. 620/3 were printed together, se-tenant, forming a composite design.
See also Nos. 818/23 and 864/5.

1989. 20th Anniv of First Manned Landing on Moon. Multicoloured.
626 5c. Type **70** 40 40
627 40c. Astronaut Neil Armstrong saluting U.S. flag . . . . 1·25 85
628 55c. "Columbia" above lunar surface . . . . 1·50 1·00
629 65c. Lunar module "Eagle" leaving moon . . . . . . 1·50 1·25
630 70c. "Eagle" on Moon . . . 1·50 1·25
631 $1 "Columbia" re-entering Earth's atmosphere . . . . 1·60 1·60
632 $3 "Apollo 11" emblem . . . 3·00 3·25
633 $5 Armstrong and Aldrin on Moon . . . . 3·25 3·75
MS634 Two sheets, each 110 × 82 mm. (a) $6 Launch of "Apollo 11" (vert). (b) $6 "Apollo 11" splashdown. Set of 2 sheets . . . . 11·00 12·00

1989. Butterflies. Multicoloured.
635 5c. Type **71** 50 50
636 30c. "Papilio androgeus" . . 1·25 60
637 45c. "Strymon maesites" . . 1·50 65
638 65c. "Junonia coenia" . . . 1·75 1·40
639 75c. "Eurema gratiosa" . . . 2·00 1·50
640 $1 "Hypolimnas misippus" 2·00 1·75
641 $4 "Urbanus proteus" . . . 4·25 4·50
642 $5 "Junonia evarete" . . . . 4·25 4·50
MS643 Two sheets. (a) 76 × 104 mm. $6 "Phoebis agarithe". (b) 104 × 76 mm. $6 "Dryas julia". Set of 2 sheets . . . . 15·00 13·00

72 "Solanum urens"

74 Exhibition Emblem

1989. Flowers from St. Vincent Botanical Gardens. Multicoloured.
644 80c. Type **72** . . . . 1·50 1·50
645 $1.25 "Passiflora andersonii" 2·00 2·00
646 $1.65 "Miconia andersonii" 2·25 2·25
647 $1.85 "Pitcairnia sulphurea" 2·50 2·50

1989. Christmas. As T **183** of Gambia. Mult.
648 5c. Goofy and Mickey Mouse in Rolls Royce "Silver Ghost", 1907 . . . . . . 20 15
649 10c. Daisy Duck driving first Stanley Steamer, 1897 . . 20 15
650 15c. Horace Horsecollar and Clarabelle Cow in Darracq "Genevieve", 1904 . . . . 25 20
651 45c. Donald Duck driving Detroit electric coupe, 1914 55 40
652 55c. Mickey and Minnie Mouse in first Ford, 1896 55 40
653 $2 Mickey Mouse driving Reo "Runabout", 1904 . . 2·00 2·00
654 $3 Goofy driving Winton mail truck, 1899 . . . . . 2·75 2·75
655 $5 Mickey and Minnie Mouse in Duryea car, 1893 3·50 4·00
MS656 Two sheets, each 127 × 102 mm. (a) $6 Mickey and Minnie Mouse in Pope-Hartford, 1912. (b) $6 Mickey and Minnie Mouse in Buick "Model 10", 1908. Set of 2 sheets . . . . . 10·00 12·00

1990. 50th Anniv of Second World War. As T **354c** of Grenada. Multicoloured.
657 10c. Destroyer in action, First Battle of Narvik, 1940 . . 35 25
658 15c. Allied tank at Anzio, 1944 . . . . 45 35
659 20c. U.S. carrier under attack, Battle of Midway, 1942 . . . . 50 40
660 45c. North American B-25 Mitchell bombers over Gustav Line, 1944 . . . . 80 70
661 55c. Map showing Allied zones of Berlin, 1945 . . . 85 75
662 65c. German U-boat pursuing convoy, Battle of the Atlantic, 1943 . . . . . . 90 80
663 90c. Allied tank, North Africa, 1943 . . . . 1·25 1·00
664 $3 U.S. forces landing on Guam, 1944 . . . . 2·75 2·75
665 $5 Crossing the Rhine, 1945 3·75 3·75
666 $6 Japanese battleships under attack, Lete Gulf, 1944 . . 4·25 4·25
MS667 100 × 70 mm. $6 Avro Type 683 Lancaster Mk III on "Dambusters" raid, 1943 . . . 5·00 6·00

1990. "Stamp World London 90" International Stamp Exhibition (1st issue). Mickey's Shakespeare Company. As T **193** of Gambia showing Walt Disney cartoon characters. Multicoloured.
668 20c. Goofy as Mark Anthony ("Julius Caesar") 30 20
669 30c. Clarabelle Cow as the Nurse ("Romeo and Juliet") 35 25
670 45c. Pete as Falstaff ("Henry IV") 50 40
671 50c. Minnie Mouse as Portia ("The Merchant of Venice") 55 40
672 $1 Donald Duck as Hamlet ("Hamlet") . . . . 1·00 85
673 $2 Daisy Duck as Ophelia ("Hamlet") . . . . 1·75 2·00

674 $4 Donald and Daisy Duck as Benedick and Beatrice ("Much Ado About Nothing") . . . . 3·00 3·25
675 $5 Minnie Mouse and Donald Duck as Katherine and Petruchio ("The Taming of the Shrew") . . 3·00 3·25
MS676 Two sheets, each 127 × 101 mm. (a) $6 Clarabelle as Titania ("A Midsummer Night's Dream") (vert). (b) $6 Mickey Mouse as Romeo ("Romeo and Juliet") (vert). Set of 2 sheets 11·00 12·00

1990. "Stamp World London 90" International Stamp Exhibition (2nd issue). 150th Anniv of the Penny Black.
677 **74** $1 black, pink and mauve 1·50 1·25
678 – $5 black, lilac and blue . . 3·75 4·25
MS679 130 × 100 mm. $6 black and pale blue . . . . 5·00 6·00
DESIGNS: $5 Negative image of Penny Black; $6 Penny Black.

74a McCleish, Scotland

1990. World Cup Football Championship, Italy (2nd issue). Multicoloured.
680 25c. Type **74a** 80 40
681 50c. Rasul, Egypt . . . . . 1·10 80
682 $2 Lindenberger, Austria . . 2·75 2·75
683 $4 Murray, U.S.A. . . . . . 3·75 4·25
MS684 Two sheets, each 102 × 77 mm. (a) $6 Robson, England. (b) $6 Gullit, Netherlands. Set of 2 sheets . . 16·00 12·00

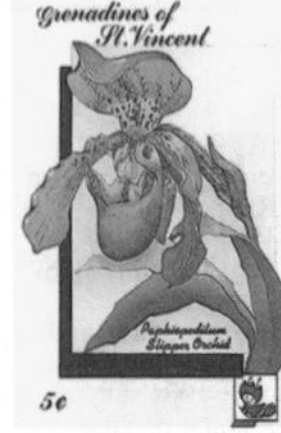

74b "Paphiopedilum"

1990. "EXPO 90" International Garden and Greenery Exposition, Osaka. Orchids. Mult.
685 5c. Type **74b** 80 50
686 25c. "Dendrobium phalaenopsis" and "Cymbidium hybrid" . . . 1·75 90
687 30c. "Miltonia candida hybrid" . . . . 1·75 90
688 50c. "Epidendrum ibaguense" and "Cymbidium" Elliot Rogers . . . . 2·25 1·25
689 $1 "Rossioglossum grande" 2·75 1·75
690 $2 "Phalaenopsis" Elisa Chang Lou and "Masdevallia coccinea" . . 3·25 2·50
691 $4 "Cypripedium acaule" and "Cypripedium calceolus" 3·75 4·00
692 $5 "Orchis spectabilis" . . . 3·75 4·00
MS693 Two sheets, each 108 × 78 mm. (a) $6 "Dendrobium anosmum". (b) $6 "Epidendrum ibaguense" and "Phalaenopsis". Set of 2 sheets . . . . 13·00 13·00

75 Scaly-breasted Ground Dove ("Common Ground Dove")

1990. Birds of the Caribbean. Multicoloured.
694 5c. Type **75** 20 20
695 25c. Purple martin 40 40
696 45c. Painted bunting 70 70
697 55c. Blue-hooded euphonia 80 80
698 75c. Blue-grey tanager . . . 1·00 1·00
699 $1 Red-eyed vireo . . . . . 1·25 1·25
700 $2 Palm chat . . . . 2·00 2·00
701 $3 Northern jacana ("North American Jacana") . . . . 2·50 2·50
702 $4 Green-throated carib . . . 2·75 2·75
703 $5 St. Vincent amazon ("St. Vincent Parrot") . . 3·00 3·00
MS704 Two sheets, each 117 × 87 mm. (a) $3 Magnificent frigate bird; $3 Bananaquit. (b) $6 Red-legged honeycreeper. Set of 2 sheets . . . . 9·50 10·00

1991. 90th Birthday of Queen Elizabeth the Queen Mother. As T **194** of Gambia.
705 $2 multicoloured . . . . . . 1·90 1·25
706 $2 multicoloured . . . . . . 1·90 1·25
707 $2 multicoloured . . . . . . 1·90 1·25
708 $2 multicoloured . . . . . . 1·90 1·25
709 $2 multicoloured . . . . . . 1·90 1·25
710 $2 multicoloured . . . . . . 1·90 1·25
711 $2 multicoloured . . . . . . 1·90 1·25
712 $2 multicoloured . . . . . . 1·90 1·25
713 $2 multicoloured . . . . . . 1·90 1·25
714 $2 multicoloured . . . . . . 1·90 1·25
715 $2 multicoloured . . . . . . 1·90 1·25
716 $2 multicoloured . . . . . . 1·90 1·25
717 $2 multicoloured . . . . . . 1·90 1·25
718 $2 multicoloured . . . . . . 1·90 1·25
719 $2 multicoloured . . . . . . 1·90 1·25
720 $2 multicoloured . . . . . . 1·90 1·25
721 $2 multicoloured . . . . . . 1·90 1·25
722 $2 multicoloured . . . . . . 1·90 1·25
723 $2 multicoloured . . . . . . 1·90 1·25
724 $2 multicoloured . . . . . . 1·90 1·25
725 $2 multicoloured . . . . . . 1·90 1·25
726 $2 multicoloured . . . . . . 1·90 1·25
727 $2 multicoloured . . . . . . 1·90 1·25
728 $2 multicoloured . . . . . . 1·90 1·25
729 $2 multicoloured . . . . . . 1·90 1·25
730 $2 multicoloured . . . . . . 1·90 1·25
731 $2 multicoloured . . . . . . 1·90 1·25
MS732 Nine sheets containing details of designs indicated. (a) 120 × 115 mm. $5 As No. 705. (b) 115 × 120 mm. $5 As No. 710. (c) 115 × 120 mm. $5 As No. 712. (d) 115 × 120 mm. $5 As No. 715. (e) 120 × 115 mm. $5 As No. 719. (f) 120 × 115 mm. $5 As No. 720. (g) 120 × 115 mm. $5 As No. 724. (h) 120 × 115 mm. $5 As No. 726. (i) 120 × 115 mm. $5 As No. 730. Set of 9 sheets . . . . 30·00 27·00
DESIGNS: No. 705, Lady Elizabeth Bowes-Lyon with sister; 706, Young Lady Elizabeth in long dress; 707, Young Lady Elizabeth wearing a hat; 708, Lady Elizabeth leaning on wall; 709, Lady Elizabeth on pony; 710, Studio portrait; 711, Lady Elizabeth in evening dress; 712, Duchess of York in fur-lined cloak; 713, Duchess of York holding rose; 714, Coronation, 1937; 715, King and Queen with Princess Elizabeth at Royal Lodge, Windsor; 716, Queen Elizabeth in blue hat; 717, King George VI and Queen Elizabeth; 718, Queen Elizabeth with Princess Elizabeth; 719, Queen Elizabeth watching sporting fixture; 720, Queen Elizabeth in white evening dress; 721, Princess Anne's christening, 1950; 722, Queen Mother with yellow bouquet; 723, Queen Mother and policewoman; 724, Queen Mother at ceremonial function; 725, Queen Mother in pink coat; 726, Queen Mother in academic robes; 727, Queen Mother in carriage with Princess Margaret; 728, Queen Mother in blue coat and hat; 729, Queen Mother with bouquet; 730, Queen Mother outside Clarence House on her birthday; 731, Queen Mother in turquoise coat and hat.

1991. Death Centenary (1990) of Vincent van Gogh (artist). As T **200b** of Gambia. Mult.
733 5c. "View of Arles with Irises" 40 30
734 10c. "Saintes-Maries" (vert) 40 30
735 15c. "Old Woman of Arles" (vert) 50 30
736 20c. "Orchard in Blossom, bordered by Cypresses" . . 55 30
737 25c. "Three White Cottages in Saintes-Maries" 55 30
738 35c. "Boats at Saintes-Maries" 70 40
739 40c. "Interior of a Restaurant in Arles" 75 45
740 45c. "Peasant Women" (vert) 80 50
741 55c. "Self-portrait" (vert) . . 90 60
742 60c. "Pork Butcher's Shop from a Window" (vert) . . 1·00 70
743 75c. "The Night Cafe in Arles" . . . . 1·10 80
744 $1 "2nd Lieut. Millet of the Zouaves" . . . . 1·40 95
745 $2 "The Cafe Terrace, Place du Forum, Arles at Night" (vert) . . . . 2·25 2·25
746 $3 "The Zouave" (vert) . . . 2·75 3·00
747 $4 "The Two Lovers" (detail) (vert) . . . . 3·50 3·75
748 $5 "Still Life" . . . . 3·75 4·00
MS749 Four sheets, each 112 × 76 mm. (a) $5 "Street in Saintes-Maries" (horiz). (b) $5 "Lane near Arles" (horiz). (c) $6 "Harvest at La Crau, with Montmajour in the Background" (horiz). (d) $6 "The Sower". Imperf. Set of 4 sheets . . . . 21·00 19·00

1991. 65th Birthday of Queen Elizabeth II. As T **198a** of Gambia. Multicoloured.
750 15c. Inspecting the Yeomen of the Guard 30 20
751 40c. Queen Elizabeth II with the Queen Mother at the Derby, 1988 . . . . 55 30
752 $2 The Queen and Prince Philip leaving Euston, 1986 2·00 2·00
753 $4 The Queen at the Commonwealth Institute, 1987 . . . . 2·75 3·00
MS754 68 × 90 mm. $5 Queen Elizabeth and Prince Philip with Prince Andrew in naval uniform 4·75 4·75

1991. 10th Wedding Anniv of Prince and Princess of Wales. As T **198b** of Gambia. Multicoloured.
755 10c. Prince and Princess at polo match, 1987 . . . . . 1·00 30
756 50c. Separate family portraits 1·75 55
757 $1 Prince William and Prince Henry at Kensington Palace, 1991 . . . . 1·75 1·00
758 $5 Portraits of Prince Charles and Princess Diana . . . 4·75 4·00
MS759 68 × 90 mm. $5 Separate portraits of Prince and Princess and sons . . . . 8·00 5·00

76 Class 150 Steam Locomotive and Map

1991. "Phila Nippon '91" International Stamp Exhibition, Toyko. Japanese Railway Locomotives. Each in black, red and green.
760 10c. Type **76** 80 50
761 25c. Class 7100 locomotive, "Benkei", 1880 . . . . . 1·10 80
762 35c. Class 8620 steam locomotive, 1914 . . . . . 1·40 90
763 50c. Class C53 steamlined steam locomotive, 1928 . . 1·90 1·25
764 $1 Class DD51 diesel-hydraulic locomotive, 1962 2·50 1·90
765 $2 Class KTR001 electric railcar Tango Explorer (inscr "RF 22327") . . . . 3·00 3·00
766 $4 Class EF55 electric locomotive, 1936 . . . . . 3·50 4·25
767 $5 Class EF58 electric locomotive, 1946 . . . . . 3·50 4·25
MS768 Four sheets, each 114 × 73 mm showing frontal views. (a) $6 Class 9600 steam locomotive (1913) (vert). (b) $6 Class C57 steam locomotive (1937) (vert). (c) $6 Class C62 steam locomotive (1948) (vert). (d) $6 Class 4100 tank locomotive (1912) (vert). Set of 4 sheets . . . . . 19·00 19·00

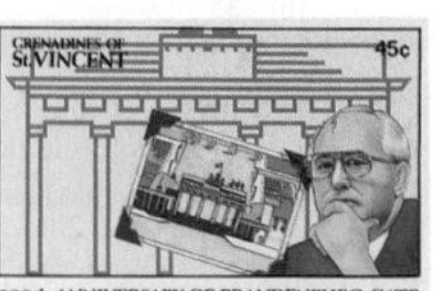

77 President Gorbachev and Brandenburg Gate

1991. Anniversaries and Events. Multicoloured.
769 45c. Type **77** 40 40
770 60c. General de Gaulle in Djibouti, 1959 . . . . . . 1·25 55
771 65c. "DIE MAUER MUSS WEG!" slogan 65 65
772 80c. East German border guard escaping to West . . 80 80
773 $1 "Abduction from the Seraglio" . . . . 3·75 1·75
774 $1.50 Lilienthal and glider . . 2·00 1·75
775 $1.75 Trans-Siberian identity plate . . . . 3·00 2·75
776 $1.75 Trans-Siberian steam locomotive (vert) . . . . . 3·00 2·75
777 $2 Czechoslovakia 1918 20h. stamp and scout delivering mail . . . . 3·00 3·00
778 $2 Zurich couple maypole dancing . . . . 3·00 3·00
779 $2 Man and woman in Vaud traditional costumes . . . 3·00 3·00
780 $2 Georg Laves (architect) and Hoftheater . . . . . 3·00 3·00
781 $3 Dresden, 1749 . . . . . 6·00 4·50
782 $4 Scouts and cog train on Snowdon (vert) . . . . . 4·50 5·00
MS783 Eleven sheets. (a) 100 × 71 mm. $5 Arms of Berlin. (b) 100 × 71 mm. $5 Berlin police badge. (c) 77 × 112 mm. $5 De Gaulle in civilian dress. (d) 69 × 101 mm. $5 General Charles de Gaulle (vert). (e) 75 × 101 mm. $5 Portrait of Mozart (vert). (f) 75 × 101 mm. $5 Bust of Mozart (vert). (g) 115 × 85 mm. $5 Trans-Siberian Class P36 No. 0250 steam locomotive leaving Moscow at night (43 × 56 mm). (h) 118 × 89 mm. $5 Jamboree emblem (buff background) (vert). (i) 118 × 89 mm. $5 Jamboree emblem (bluish violet background) (vert). (j) 101 × 72 mm. $5 Arms of Appenzell and Thurgau. (k) 101 × 72 mm. $5 Old Hanover Set of 11 sheets . . . . 35·00 38·00
Anniversaries and Events:—Nos. 769, 771/2, **MS**783a/b, Bicentenary of Brandenburg Gate; 770, **MS**783c/d, Birth centenary of Charles de Gaulle (French statesman); 773, 781, **MS**783e/f, Death bicentenary of Mozart; 774, Centenary of Otto Lilienthal's gliding experiments; 775/6, **MS**783g, Centenary of Trans-Siberian Railway; 777, 782, **MS**783h/i. 50th death anniv of Lord Baden-Powell and World Scout Jamboree, Korea; 778/9, **MS**783j, 700th anniv of Swiss Confederation; 780, **MS**783k, 750th anniv of Hanover.

78 Japanese Aircraft and Submarines leaving Truk

1991. 50th Anniv of Japanese Attack on Pearl Harbor. Multicoloured.
784 $1 Type **78** . . . . 1·90 1·60
785 $1 "Akagi" (Japanese aircraft carrier) . . . . 1·90 1·60
786 $1 Nakajima B5N2 "Kate" bombers . . . . 1·90 1·60
787 $1 Nakajima B5N2 "Kate" bombers attacking Battleship Row . . . . . 1·90 1·60
788 $1 Burning aircraft, Ford Island airfield . . . . . . 1·90 1·60
789 $1 Doris Miller winning Navy Cross . . . . 1·90 1·60
790 $1 U.S.S. "West Virginia" and "Tennessee" (battleships) ablaze . . . . 1·90 1·60
791 $1 U.S.S. "Arizona" (battleship) sinking . . . . 1·90 1·60
792 $1 U.S.S. "New Orleans" (cruiser) . . . . 1·90 1·60
793 $1 President Roosevelt declaring war . . . . . . 1·90 1·60

78a Pluto pulling Mickey Mouse in Sledge, 1974

1991. Christmas. Walt Disney Company Christmas Cards. Multicoloured.
794 10c. Type **78a** 60 30
795 55c. Mickey, Pluto and Donald Duck watching toy band, 1961 . . . . 1·25 70
796 65c. "The Same Old Wish", 1942 . . . . 1·40 85
797 75c. Mickey, Peter Pan, Donald and Nephews with Merlin the magician, 1963 1·50 95
798 $1.50 Mickey and Donald with leprechauns, 1958 . . 2·50 2·50
799 $2 Mickey and friends with book "Old Yeller", 1957 2·75 2·75
800 $4 Mickey controlling Pinocchio, 1953 . . . . . 4·00 4·25
801 $5 Cinderella and Prince dancing, 1987 . . . . . 4·00 4·25
MS802 Two sheets, each 128 × 102 mm. (a) $6 Santa Claus and American bomber, 1942. (b) $6 Snow White, 1957. Set of 2 sheets . . . . 13·00 14·00

1992. 40th Anniv of Queen Elizabeth II's Accession. As T **202a** of Gambia. Multicoloured.
803 15c. View across bay 75 20
804 45c. Schooner at anchor, Mayreau . . . . 1·25 25
805 $2 Hotel on hillside . . . . 1·75 1·75
806 $4 Tourist craft at anchor . . 3·75 3·75
MS807 Two sheets, each 74 × 97 mm. (a) $6 Beach and palms. (b) $6 Aerial view of hotel by beach. Set of 2 sheets . . . 9·50 10·00

78b Big Pete as Hernando Cortes in Mexico

1992. International Stamp Exhibitions. Walt Disney cartoon characters. Multicoloured. (a) "Grenada '92", Spain. Spanish Explorers.
808 15c. Type **78b** 30 15
809 40c. Mickey Mouse as Hernando de Soto at Mississippi River 50 30
810 $2 Goofy as Vasco Nunez de Balboa sights Pacific . . . 1·75 1·75
811 $4 Donald Duck as Francisco Coronado on Rio Grande 2·75 3·00
MS812 127 × 102 mm. $6 Mickey as Ponce de Leon . . . . 4·25 4·75

(b) "World Columbian Stamp Expo '92", Chicago. Local Personalities.
813 10c. Mickey Mouse and Pluto outside Walt Disney's birthplace 30 20
814 50c. Donald Duck and nephews in George Pullman's railway sleeping car . . . . 1·50 55
815 $1 Daisy Duck as Jane Addams (social reformer) and Hull House . . . . . 1·60 85
816 $5 Mickey as Carl Sandburg (novelist, poet and historian) . . . . 3·75 4·00
MS817 127 × 102 mm. $6 Daisy as Mrs O'Leary with her cow (source of Chicago fire of 1871) . . . 4·25 4·75

79 King Ferdinand and Queen Isabella of Spain

1992. 500th Anniv of Discovery of America by Columbus (2nd issue). Multicoloured.
818 10c. Type **79** 25 25
819 45c. "Santa Maria" and "Nina" in Acul Bay, Haiti 50 50
820 55c. "Santa Maria" (vert) . . 55 55
821 $1 Ships of Columbus (vert) 1·40 1·40
822 $4 Wreck of "Santa Maria" 2·50 2·50
823 $5 "Pinta" and "Nina" . . . 2·75 2·75
MS824 Two sheets, each 114 × 85 mm. (a) $6 Columbus landing on San Salvador. (b) $6 "Santa Maria" in storm. Set of 2 sheets . . . . 7·00 8·00

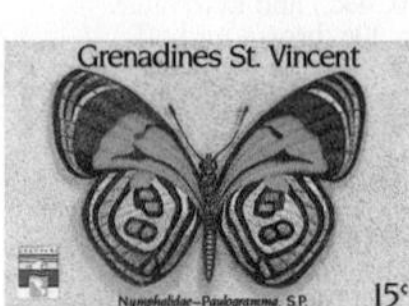

79a "Paulogramma sp."

1992. "Genova '92" International Thematic Stamp Exhibition (1st issue). Butterflies. Multicoloured.
825 15c. Type **79a** 75 65
826 20c. "Heliconius cydno" . . 80 70
827 30c. "Eutresis hypereia" . . . 85 75
828 45c. "Eurytides columbus" (vert) . . . . 1·40 1·25
829 55c. "Papilio ascolius" . . . 1·40 1·25
830 75c. "Anaea pasibula" . . . 1·40 1·25
831 80c. "Heliconius doris" . . . 1·40 1·25
832 $1 "Perisama pitheas" . . . 1·40 1·25
833 $2 "Batesia hypochlora" . . 2·00 2·00
834 $3 "Heliconius erato" . . . . 2·50 2·50
835 $4 "Elzunia cassandrina" . . 2·75 2·75
836 $5 "Sais ivcidice" . . . . . 2·75 2·75
MS837 Three sheets, each 109 × 79 mm. (a) $6 "Oleria tigilla" (horiz). (b) $6 "Dismorphia orise" (horiz). (c) $6 "Podotricha telesiphe" (horiz). Set of 3 sheets . . . . 11·00 12·00
See also Nos. 851/62.

79b "Entoloma bakeri"

1992. Fungi. Multicoloured.
838 10c. Type **79b** 50 50
839 15c. "Hydropus paraensis" 55 55
840 20c. "Leucopaxillus gracillimus" 60 60
841 45c. "Hygrotrama dennisianum" 80 80
842 50c. "Leucoagaricus hortensis" 80 80
843 65c. "Pyrrhoglossum pyrrhum" . . . . 1·00 1·00
844 75c. "Amanita craeoderma" 1·00 1·00
845 $1 "Lentinus bertieri" . . . 1·25 1·25
846 $2 "Dennisiomyces griseus" 2·00 2·00
847 $3 "Xerulina asprata" . . . 2·50 2·50
848 $4 "Hygrocybe acutoconica" 3·00 3·00
849 $5 "Lepiota spiculata" . . . 3·00 3·00
MS850 Three sheets, each 101 × 68 mm. (a) $6 "Pluteus crysophlebius". (b) $6 "Amanita lilloi". (c) $6 "Lepiota volvatua". Set of 3 sheets . . . . 12·00 13·00

1992. "Genova '92" International Thematic Stamp Exhibition (2nd issue). Hummingbirds. As T **370a** of Grenada. Multicoloured.
851 5c. Antillean crested hummingbird (female) (horiz) 40 30
852 10c. Blue-tailed emerald (female) 40 30
853 35c. Antillean mango (male) (horiz) 55 45
854 45c. Antillean mango (female) (horiz) 55 45
855 55c. Green-throated carib (horiz) 65 55
856 65c. Green violetear (male) 80 70
857 75c. Blue-tailed emerald (male) (horiz) 90 80
858 $1 Purple-throated carib . . 1·25 1·00
859 $2 Copper-rumped hummingbird (horiz) . . . 2·25 2·00
860 $3 Rufous-breasted hermit . . 3·25 2·75
861 $4 Antillean crested hummingbird (male) . . . 4·00 3·50
862 $5 Green-breasted mango (male) . . . . 4·25 3·75
MS863 Three sheets, each 105 × 74 mm. (a) $6 Blue-tailed emerald. (b) $6 Antillean mango. (c) $6 Antillean crested hummingbird. Set of 3 sheets 13·00 14·00

1992. 500th Anniv of Discovery of America by Columbus (3rd issue). Organization of East Caribbean States. As T **372a** of Grenada. Multicoloured.
864 $1 Columbus meeting Amerindians 75 75
865 $2 Ships approaching island 2·75 2·50

1992. Olympic Games, Albertville and Barcelona. As T **372** of Grenada. Multicoloured.
866 10c. Men's volleyball 70 40
867 15c. Men's gymnastics (horiz) 85 50
868 25c. Men's cross-country skiing . . . . 1·00 60
869 30c. Men's 110 m hurdles (horiz) . . . . 1·00 60
870 45c. Men's 120 m ski-jumping (horiz) . . . . 1·10 70
871 55c. Women's 4 × 100 m relay 1·25 80
872 75c. Men's triple jump . . . 1·60 1·00
873 80c. Men's mogul skiing . . 1·60 1·00
874 $1 Men's 110 m butterfly swimming (horiz) . . . . 1·60 1·25
875 $2 "Tornado" Class yachting (horiz) . . . . 2·25 1·75
876 $3 Men's decathlon (horiz) 2·50 2·75
877 $5 Show jumping (horiz) . . 3·75 3·75
MS878 Three sheets, each 101 × 70 mm. (a) $6 Ice hockey (horiz). (b) $6 Men's single luge (horiz). (c) $6 Football. Set of 3 sheets . . . . 14·00 14·00

1992. Christmas. Religious Paintings. As T **207b** of Gambia. Multicoloured.
879 10c. "Our Lady with St. Roch and St. Anthony of Padua" (Giorgione) . . 60 30
880 40c. "Anthony of Padua" (Master of the Embroidered Leaf) 80 55
881 45c. "Madonna and Child" (detail) (Orazio Gentileschi) 90 60
882 50c. "Madonna and Child with St. Anne (detail) (Da Vinci) 95 65
883 55c. "The Holy Family" (Crespi) . . . . 1·00 70
884 65c. "Madonna and Child" (Del Sarto) . . . . 1·10 80
885 75c. "Madonna and Child with Sts. Lawrence and Julian" (Gentile da Fabriano) . . . . 1·25 90
886 $1 "Virgin and Child" (detail) (School of Parma) 1·50 1·10
887 $2 "Madonna with the Iris" (detail) (style of Durer) . . 2·50 2·25
888 $3 "Virgin and Child with St. Jerome and St. Dominic" (Lippi) . . . 3·00 3·00
889 $4 "Rapolano Madonna" (Ambrogio Lorenzetti) . . 3·50 3·75
890 $5 "The Virgin and Child with Angels in a Garden with a Rose Hedge" (Stefano da Verona) . . . 3·50 3·75
MS891 Three sheets, each 73 × 98 mm. (a) $6 "Madonna and Child with Grapes" (detail) (Cranach the Elder). (b) $6 "Virgin and Child with St. John the Baptist" (detail) (Botticelli). (c) $6 "Madonna and Child with St. Anne" (different detail) (Da Vinci). Set of 3 sheets . . . . 15·00 15·00

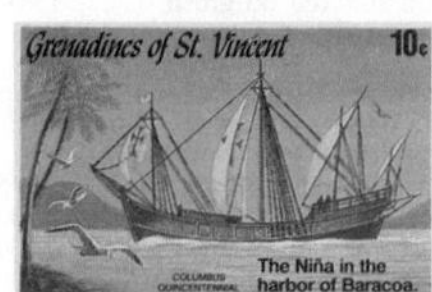

80 "Nina" in Baracoa Harbour

1992. Anniversaries and Events. Multicoloured.
892 10c. Type **80** . . . . . . 1·75 75
893 75c. Airship LZ-3 . . . . . 2·50 1·75
894 75c. Blind man with guide dog . . . . 2·75 1·75
895 75c. Training guide dog . . . 2·75 1·75
896 $1 Ships of Columbus . . . 2·75 1·75
897 $1 Adenauer, state arms and German flag . . . . . . 2·75 1·75
898 $1 "America III" and "Il Moro" (yachts) with trophy . . . . 1·50 1·50
899 $1 Hands breaking bread and emblem (vert) . . . . . . 1·50 1·50
900 $2 "Voyager 2" and planet 3·25 2·50
901 $3 Adenauer and children watching Berlin Airlift . . 2·75 3·00
902 $4 Airship LZ-37 in flames 3·25 3·75
903 $4 Adenauer and ruins in Cologne . . . . 3·00 3·75
904 $4 Mozart with his wife Constanze (vert) . . . . . 6·00 4·50
905 $5 Adenauer and modern office blocks . . . . 3·00 4·50
MS906 Seven sheets. (a) 100 × 70 mm. $6 Columbus sighting land. (b) 100 × 70 mm. $6 Count von Zeppelin facing left. (c) 110 × 70 mm. $6 Count von Zeppelin facing right. (d) 100 × 70 mm. $6 Konrad Adenauer (vert). (e) 100 × 70 mm. $6 Konrad Adenauer. (f) 100 × 70 mm. $6 "Mars Observer" spacecraft. (g) 100 × 70 mm. $6 Costume for "Don Giovanni" by Cassandre. Set of 7 sheets . . 35·00 38·00
ANNIVERSARIES AND EVENTS: Nos. 892, 896, **MS**906a, 500th anniv of discovery of America by Columbus; Nos. 893, 902, **MS**906b/c, 75th death anniv of Count Ferdinand von Zeppelin (airship pioneer); Nos. 894/5, 75th anniv of International Association of Lions Clubs; Nos. 897, 901, 903, 905, **MS**906d/e, 25th death anniv of Konrad Adenauer (German statesman); No. 898, Americas Cup yachting championship; No. 899, International Conference on Nutrition, Rome; No. 900, **MS**906f, International Space Year; No. 904, **MS**906g, Death bicentenary of Mozart.

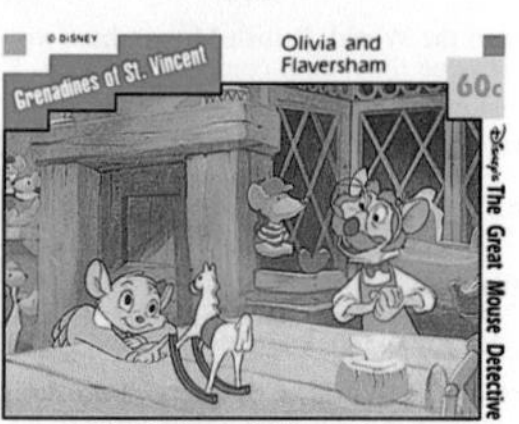

81 Olivia and Flaversham

1992. Walt Disney Cartoon Films.
907/50 60c. × 44 multicoloured. . . Set of 44 . . . . 23·00 24·00
MS951 Ten sheets, each 127 × 103 mm. $6 × 10 multicoloured. Set of 10 sheets 35·00 38·00
Nos. 907/50 were printed as five se-tenant sheetlets, each of nine different designs except that for "Darkwing Duck" which contains eight vertical designs (Nos. 943/50). The other four sheetlets depict scenes from "The Great Mouse Detective", "Oliver and Company", "The Legend of Sleepy Hollow" and "Ducktales the Movie".
No. **MS**951 contains two sheets for each film. On one sheet in the pairs for "The Legend of Sleepy Hollow", "Ducktales the Movie" and "Darkwing Duck" the stamp design is vertical.

1992. 15th Death Anniv of Elvis Presley (singer). As T **260** of Dominica. Mult.
952 $1 Elvis Presley . . . . . . 2·75 2·25
953 $1 Elvis with guitar . . . . 2·75 2·25
954 $1 Elvis with microphone . . 2·75 2·25

82 Prince Mickey searching for Bride

1992. "Tales of Uncle Scrooge" (fairy stories). Walt Disney cartoon characters.
955/1008 60c. × 54 multicoloured. Set of 54 . . . . 25·00 26·00
MS1009 Twelve sheets, each 128 × 102 mm or 102 × 128 mm. $6 × 12 multicoloured. Set of 12 sheets . . . . 45·00 48·00
Nos. 955/1008 (issued as six sheetlets each of nine different designs) depict scenes from "The Princess and the Pea", "Little Red Riding Hood", "Goldilocks and the Three Bears", "The Pied Piper of Hamelin", "Hop O'-My-Thumb" and "Puss in Boots".
No. **MS**1009 contains two sheets for each story, all being horizontal with the exception of the second sheet for "Puss in Boots". Of the stamp designs in these miniature sheets the two for "Little Red Riding Hood" and one of each for "Goldilocks and the Three Bears", "The Pied Piper of Hamelin" and "Puss in Boots" are vertical.

83 Oleander

1994. Medicinal Plants. Multicoloured.
1010 5c. Type **83** 55 50
1011 10c. Beach morning glory 60 30
1012 30c. Calabash 85 30
1013 45c. Portia tree 95 30
1014 55c. Cashew . . . . 1·00 40
1015 75c. Prickly pear . . . . . 1·40 70
1016 $1 Shell ginger . . . . . . 1·60 80
1017 $1.50 Avocado pear . . . . 2·25 2·00
1018 $2 Mango . . . . 2·50 2·50
1019 $3 Blood flower . . . . . . 3·00 3·25
1020 $4 Sugar apple . . . . . . 3·25 4·00
1021 $5 Barbados lily . . . . . 3·25 4·00

OFFICIAL STAMPS

1982. Nos. 195/200 optd **OFFICIAL**.
O1 50c. "Mary" 10 15
O2 50c. Prince Charles and Lady Diana Spencer 30 35
O3 $3 "Alexandra" 20 20
O4 $3 Prince Charles and Lady Diana Spencer 65 70
O5 $3.50 "Britannia" 20 20
O6 $3.50 Prince Charles and Lady Diana Spencer . . . 65 70

APPENDIX

The following stamps have either been issued in excess of postal needs, or have not been made available to the public in reasonable quantities at face value.

BEQUIA

1984.

Leaders of the World. Railway Locomotives (1st series). Two designs for each value, the first showing technical drawings and the second the locomotive at work. 1, 5, 10, 25, 35, 45c., $1.50, $2, each × 2.

Grenadines of St. Vincent 1982 Ships definitives (Nos. 208/24) optd **BEQUIA**. 1, 3, 5, 6, 10, 15, 20, 25, 30, 50, 60, 75c., $1, $2, $3, $5, $10.

Leaders of the World. Automobiles (1st series). Two designs for each value, the first showing technical drawings and the second the car in action. 5, 40c., $1, $1.50, each × 2.

Leaders of the World. Olympic Games, Los Angeles. 1, 10, 60c., $3, each × 2.

Leaders of the World. Railway Locomotives (2nd series). Two designs for each value, the first showing technical drawings and the second the locomotive at work. 1, 5, 10, 35, 75c., $1, $2.50, $3, each × 2.

Leaders of the World. Automobiles (2nd series). Two designs for each value, the first showing technical drawings and the second the car in action. 5, 10, 20, 25, 75c., $1, $2.50, $3, each × 2.

1985.

Leaders of the World. Railway Locomotives (3rd series). Two designs for each value, the first showing technical drawings and the second the locomotive at work. 25, 55, 60c., $2, each × 2.

Leaders of the World. Dogs. 25, 35, 55c., $2, each × 2.

Leaders of the World. Warships of the Second World War. Two designs for each value, the first showing technical drawings and the second the ship at sea. 15, 50c., $1, $1.50, each × 2.

Leaders of the World. Flowers. 10, 20, 70c., $2.50, each × 2.

Leaders of the World. Automobiles (3rd series). Two designs for each value, the first showing technical drawings and the second the car in action. 5, 25, 50c., $1, $1.25, $2, each × 2.

Leaders of the World. Railway Locomotives (4th series). Two designs for each value, the first showing technical drawings and the second the locomotive at work. 25, 55, 60, 75c., $1, $2.50, each × 2.

Leaders of the World. Life and Times of Queen Elizabeth the Queen Mother. Two designs for each value showing different portraits. 20, 65c., $1.35, $1.80, each × 2.

Leaders of the World. Automobiles (4th series). Two designs for each value, the first showing technical drawings and the second the car in action. 20, 45c., $1.50, $2, each × 2.

1986.

Leaders of the World. Automobiles (5th series). Two designs for each value, the first showing technical drawings and the second the car in action. 25, 50, 65, 75c., $1, $3, each × 2.

60th Birthday of Queen Elizabeth II. 5, 75c., $2, $8.

World Cup Football Championship, Mexico. 1, 2, 5, 10, 45, 60, 75c., $1.50, $1.50, $2, $3.50, $6.

Royal Wedding (1st issue). 60c., $2, each × 2.

Railway Engineers and Locomotives. $1, $2.50, $3, $4.

Royal Wedding (2nd issue). Previous issue optd "**Congratulations T.R.H. The Duke & Duchess of York**". 60c., $2, each × 2.

Automobiles (6th series). Two designs for each value, the first showing technical drawings and the second the car in action. 20, 60, 75, 90c., $1, $3, each × 2.

1987.

Automobiles (7th series). Two designs for each value, the first showing technical drawings and the second the car in action. 5, 20, 35, 60, 75, 80c., $1.25, $1.75, each × 2.

Royal Ruby Wedding. 15, 75c., $1, $2.50, $5.

Railway Locomotives (5th series). Two designs for each value, the first showing technical drawings and the second the locomotive at work. 15, 25, 40, 50, 60, 75c., $1, $2, each × 2.

1988.

Explorers. 15, 50c., $1.75, $2, $2.50, $3, $3.50, $4.

International Lawn Tennis Players. 15, 45, 80c., $1.25, $1.75, $2, $2.50, $3.

1989.

"Philexfrance '89" International Stamp Exhibition, Paris. Walt Disney Cartoon Characters. 1, 2, 3, 4, 5, 10c., $5, $6.

1991.

Centenary of Otto Lilienthal's Gliding Experiments. $5.

50th Anniv of Japanese Attack on Pearl Harbor. 50c., $1.

Death Anniv of Mozart. 10, 75c., $4.

50th Death Anniv of Lord Baden-Powell and World Jamboree, Korea. 50c., $1, $2, $3.

1997.

Diana, Princess of Wales Commemoration. $1.

2000.

Faces of the Millennium: Queen Elizabeth the Queen Mother. Collage of miniature flower photographs. $1 × 8.

2001.

Endangered Species. Turtles. $1.40 × 4.

2002.

Ferrari Racing Cars. $1.10 × 8.

Chinese New Year ("Year of the Horse"). $1.40 × 4.

Golden Jubilee. 80c. × 4.

25th Death Anniv of Elvis Presley (1st issue). $1 (in sheetlet of 9).

Shirley Temple in Captain January. $1.40 × 6, $2 × 4.

Queen Elizabeth the Queen Mother Commemoration. $2 × 2.

"United We Stand". Support for Victims of 11 September 2001 Terrorist Attacks. $2 (in sheetlet of 4).

2003.

Centenary of the Teddy Bear. $2 × 8.

Chinese New Year ("Year of the Ram"). $1 × 6.

5th Death Anniv of Diana, Princess of Wales. $2 × 8.

50th Anniv of General Motors Chevrolet Corvette. $2 × 4.

40th Death Anniv of President John F. Kennedy. $2 × 4.

25th Death Anniv of Elvis Presley (2nd issue). 90c. × 2 (in sheetlet of 9).

Birds of the Caribbean. 90c., $1, $1.40, $2.

CANOUAN

1997.

Diana, Princess of Wales Commemoration. $1.

2000.

100th Birthday of Queen Elizabeth the Queen Mother. $1.40 (in sheetlet of 6).

2003.

40th Death Anniv of President John F. Kennedy. $2 × 4.

"United We Stand". Support for Victims of 11 September 2001 Terrorist Attacks. $2 (in sheetlet of 4).

25th Death Anniv of Elvis Presley. 90c. (in sheetlet of 9).

Butterflies of the Caribbean. 90c., $1, $1.40, $2.

MUSTIQUE

1997.

Diana, Princess of Wales Commemoration. $1.

2000.

Faces of the Millennium: Queen Elizabeth the Queen Mother. Collage of miniature flower photographs. $1 × 8.

2003.

21st Birthday of Prince William of Wales. $3 × 3.

50th Anniv of Coronation. $3 × 3.

Centenary of Circus Clowns. $2 × 4.

50th Anniv of General Motors Chevrolet Corvette. $2 × 4.

Centenary of General Motors Cadillac. $2 × 4.

40th Death Anniv of President John F. Kennedy. $2 × 4.

"United We Stand". Support for Victims of 11 September 2001 Terrorist Attacks. $2 (in sheetlet of 4).

25th Death Anniv of Elvis Presley. 90c. (in sheetlet of 9).

PALM ISLAND

2003.

Centenary of the Circus Clown. $2 × 4.

"United We Stand". Support for Victims of 11 September 2001 Terrorist Attacks. $2 (in sheetlet of 4).

25th Death Anniv of Elvis Presley. 90c. (in sheetlet of 9).

TOBAGO CAYS

2003.

21st Birthday of Prince William of Wales. $3 × 3.

50th Anniv of Coronation. $3 × 3.

50th Anniv of General Motors Chevrolet Corvette. $2 × 4.

Centenary of General Motors Cadillac. $2 × 4.

40th Death Anniv of President John F. Kennedy. $2 × 4.

"United We Stand". Support for Victims of 11 September 2001 Terrorist Attacks. $2 (in sheetlet of 4).

UNION ISLAND

1984.

Leaders of the World. British Monarchs. Two designs for each value forming a composite picture. 1, 5, 10, 20, 60c., $3, each × 2.

Leaders of the World. Railway Locomotives (1st series). Two designs for each value, the first showing technical drawings and the second the locomotive at work. 5, 60c., $1, $2.

Grenadines of St. Vincent 1982 Ships definitives (Nos. 208/24) optd **UNION ISLAND**. 1, 3, 5, 6, 10, 15, 20, 25, 30, 50, 60, 75c., $1, $2, $3, $5, $10.

Leaders of the World. Cricketers. Two designs for each value, the first showing a portrait and the second the cricketer in action. 1, 10, 15, 55, 60, 75c., $1.50, $3, each × 2.

Leaders of the World. Railway Locomotives (2nd series). Two designs for each value, the first showing technical drawings and the second the locomotive at work. 5, 10, 20, 25, 75c., $1, $2.50, $3, each × 2.

1985.

Leaders of the World. Automobiles (1st series). Two designs for each value, the first showing technical drawings and the second the car in action. 1, 50, 75c., $2.50, each × 2.

Leaders of the World. Birth Bicentenary of John J. Audubon (ornithologist). Birds. 15, 50c., $1, $1.50, each × 2.

Leaders of the World. Railway Locomotives (3rd series). Two designs for each value, the first showing technical drawings and the second the locomotive at work. 5, 50, 60c., $2, each × 2.

Leaders of the World. Butterflies. 15, 25, 75c., $2, each × 2.

Leaders of the World. Automobiles (2nd series). Two designs for each value, the first showing technical drawings and the second the car in action. 5, 60c., $1, $1.50, each × 2.

Leaders of the World. Automobiles (3rd series). Two designs for each value, the first showing technical drawings and the second the car in action. 10, 55, 60, 75, 90c., $1, $1.50, $2, each × 2.

Leaders of the World. Life and Times of Queen Elizabeth the Queen Mother. Two designs for each value showing different portraits. 55, 70c., $1.05, $1.70, each × 2.

1986.

Leaders of the World. Railway Locomotives (4th series). Two designs for each value, the first showing technical drawings and the second the locomotive at work. 15, 30, 45, 60, 75c., $1.50, $2.50, $3, each × 2.

60th Birthday of Queen Elizabeth II. 10, 60c., $2, $8.

World Cup Football Championship, Mexico. 1, 10, 30, 75c., $1, $2.50, $3, $6.

Royal Wedding (1st issue). 60c., $2, each × 2.

Automobiles (4th series). Two designs for each value, the first showing technical drawings and the second the car in action. 10, 60, 75c., $1, $1.50, $3, each × 2.

Royal Wedding (2nd issue). Previous issue optd as Bequia. 60c., $2, each × 2.

Railway Locomotives (5th series). Two designs for each value, the first showing technical drawings and the second the locomotive at work. 15, 45, 60, 75c., $1, $1.50, $2, $3, each × 2.

1987.

Railway Locomotives (6th series). Two designs for each value, the first showing technical drawings and the second the locomotive at work. 15, 25, 40, 50, 60, 75c., $1, $2, each × 2.

Royal Ruby Wedding. 15, 45c., $1.50, $3, $4.

Railway Locomotives (7th series). Two designs for each value, the first showing technical drawings and the second the locomotive at work. 15, 20, 30, 45, 50, 75c., $1, $1.50, each × 2.

1989.

"Philexfrance 89" International Stamp Exhibition, Paris. Walt Disney Cartoon Characters. 1, 2, 3, 4, 5, 10c., $5, $6.

1997.

Diana, Princess of Wales Commemoration. $1.

2000.

Faces of the Millennium: Queen Elizabeth the Queen Mother. Collage of miniature flower photographs. $1x8.

2002.

Chinese New Year ("Year of the Horse"). $1.40 × 4.

Endangered Species. Shortfin Mako Shark. $1 × 4.

"United We Stand". Support for Victims of 11 September 2001 Terrorist Attacks. $2 (in sheetlet of 4).

Queen Elizabeth the Queen Mother Commemoration. $2 × 3.

Ferrari Cars. $1.10 × 8.

2003.

Centenary of the Teddy Bear. $2 × 8.

Chinese New Year ("Year of the Ram"). $1 × 6.

25th Death Anniv of Diana, Princess of Wales. $1.40 × 6, $2 × 4.

40th Death Anniv of President John F. Kennedy. $2 × 4.

25th Death Anniv of Elvis Presley. 90c. × 9.

2004.

Chinese New Year ("Year of the Monkey"). "Monkey and Cat" painting by Yi Yuan-Chi. $1.40 (in sheetlet of 4).

GRIQUALAND WEST Pt. 1

A British colony, later annexed to the Cape of Good Hope and now part of South Africa, whose stamps it uses.

12 pence = 1 shilling;
20 shillings = 1 pound.

1874. Stamp of Cape of Good Hope ("Hope" seated) with pen-and-ink surch.

1 **4** 1d. on 4d. blue £1200 £2000

1877. Stamps of Cape of Good Hope ("Hope" seated) optd **G. W.**

2 **6** 1d. red . . . . £500 85·00
3 4d. blue . . . . £400 75·00

1877. Stamps of Cape of Good Hope ("Hope" seated) optd **G.**

14 **6** ½d. grey . . . . 8·00 9·50
16 1d. red . . . . 9·00 6·00
6a **4** 4d. blue . . . . £200 32·00
26 **6** 4d. blue . . . . 25·00 4·00
27 **4** 6d. violet . . . . £120 7·00
28 1s. green . . . . £100 4·50
29 **6** 5s. orange . . . . £350 8·50

GUADELOUPE Pt. 6

An overseas department of France, formerly a Fr. colony in the W. Indies, consisting of a group of islands between Antigua and Dominica. Now uses the stamps of France.

100 centimes = 1 franc.

1894. French Colonies, "Peace and Commerce" type, surch **G. P. E.** and new value in frame.

6 H 20 on 30c. brown . . . . . . 50·00 42·00
7 25 on 35c. black on orange 50·00 48·00

1889. French Colonies, "Commerce" type, surch **GUADELOUPE** and value in figures and words in plain frame.

8 J 3c. on 20c. red on green . . . 1·50 3·50
9 15c. on 20c. red on green . . 16·00 9·25
10 25c. on 20c. red on green . . 15·00 9·00

1889. French Colonies, "Commerce" type, surch **GUADELOUPE** and value in figures and words in ornamental frame.

11 J 5c. on 1c. black on blue . . . 4·75 6·75
12 10c. on 40c. red on yellow . . 22·00 29·00
13 15c. on 20c. red on green . . 21·00 12·00
14 25c. on 30c. brown on drab 28·00 26·00

1890. French Colonies, "Commerce" type, surch **5 C. GPE.**

15 J 5c. on 10c. black on lilac . . 6·75 5·00
16 5c. on 1f. olive on green . . . 7·25 6·25

1891. French Colonies, "Ceres" and "Commerce" types, optd **GUADELOUPE.**

21 J 1c. black on blue 50 40
22 2c. brown on buff . . . . . 1·25 55
23 4c. brown on grey . . . . . 4·00 5·00
24 5c. green on light green . . . 5·25 4·25
25 10c. black on lilac . . . . . 14·00 10·50
26 15c. blue on light blue . . . 12·50 1·75
27 20c. red on green . . . . . 35·00 32·00
28 25c. black on pink . . . . . 27·00 2·50
19 F 30c. brown £225 £225
29 J 30c. brown on drab . . . . 40·00 28·00
30 35c. black on orange . . . . 75·00 65·00
31 40c. red on yellow . . . . . 50·00 42·00
32 75c. red on pink £110 £120
20 F 80c. red £600 £750
33 J 1f. green . . . . 70·00 75·00

1892. "Tablet" key-type inscr "GUADELOUPE ET DEPENDANCES" in red (1, 5, 15, 25, 50 (No. 52), 75c., 1f.) or blue (others).

34 D 1c. black on blue 95 45
35 2c. brown on buff 95 70
37 4c. brown on grey . . . . . 1·25 3·00
38 5c. green on light green . . 2·00 85
39 10c. black on lilac . . . . . 11·50 3·75
49 10c. red . . . . 4·75 1·25
40 15c. blue . . . . 13·00 50
50 15c. grey . . . . 9·00 40
41 20c. red on green . . . . . 5·00 4·75
42 25c. black on pink . . . . . 5·75 1·00
51 25c. blue . . . . 70·00 75·00
43 30c. brown on drab . . . . 27·00 18·00
44 40c. red on yellow . . . . . 29·00 13·00
45 50c. red on pink . . . . . . 28·00 19·00
52 50c. brown on blue . . . . 22·00 30·00
46 75c. brown on yellow . . . 29·00 30·00
47 1f. green . . . . 28·00 30·00

1903. "Tablet" key-type surch **G & D** (5, 15c., 1f.) or **G et D** (10, 40c.) and new value.

53b D 5 on 30c. brown on buff 3·75 5·75
54 10 on 40c. red on yellow 6·00 9·50
55 15 on 50c. red . . . . . . 9·25 11·00
56 40 on 1f. green . . . . . . 8·25 13·00
57d 1f. on 75c. brown on yellow . . . . 35·00 40·00

1904. Nos. 56/7 further optd **1903** in frame.

59c D 40 on 1f. green . . . . . . 35·00 42·00
60 1f. on 75c. brown on yellow 70·00 55·00

49 Mt. Houllemont, Basse-Terre

50 La Soufriere

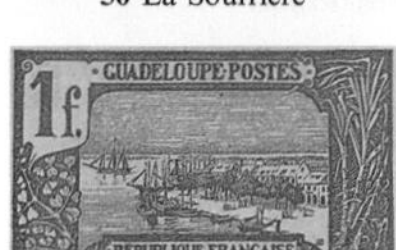

51 Pointe-a-Pitre, Grande Terre

1905.

61 **49** 1c. black on blue 10 10
62 2c. brown on yellow 15 15
63 4c. brown on grey 40 15
64 5c. green . . . . 2·50 15
83 5c. blue 15 15
65 10c. red . . . . 2·25 15
84 10c. green . . . . 1·50 1·90
85 10c. red on blue 20 30
66 15c. lilac . . . . 1·00 15
67 **50** 20c. red on green 15 15
86 20c. green . . . . 15 1·75
68 25c. blue . . . . 1·25 15
87 25c. green . . . . 1·00 15
69 30c. black . . . . 3·50 3·00
88 30c. red . . . . 60 2·50
89 30c. olive on lilac . . . . . 1·75 1·00
70 35c. black on yellow 90 70
71 40c. red on yellow . . . . . 1·60 1·50
72 45c. brown on lilac . . . . 2·25 2·75
90 45c. red . . . . 90 2·75
73 50c. green on yellow . . . . 5·00 3·25
91 50c. blue . . . . 55 1·90
92 50c. mauve 65 25
93 65c. blue . . . . 1·90 3·00
74 75c. red on blue . . . . . 1·10 2·75
75 **51** 1f. black on green . . . . . 1·90 2·75
94 1f. blue . . . . 1·25 2·75
76 2f. red on orange . . . . . 1·10 2·25
77 5f. blue on orange . . . . . 7·75 10·00

1912. Nos. 37 and 43/4 surch in figures.

78 D 05 on 4c. brown on grey . . 65 2·50
79 05 on 30c. brown on drab 80 2·75
80 10 on 40c. red on yellow . . 1·25 3·50

1915. Surch **5c** and red cross.

81 **49** 10c.+5c. red . . . . 3·00 4·50
82 15c.+5c. lilac . . . . 1·10 4·75

1924. Surch in figures and bars.

95 **51** 25c. on 5f. blue on orange 55 3·00
96 65 on 1f. green . . . . . . 90 3·00
97 85 on 1f. green . . . . . . 1·75 3·25
98 **50** 90c. on 75c. red . . . . . 60 3·25
99 **51** 1f.05 on 2f. red . . . . . 20 3·00
100 1f.25 on 1f. blue . . . . . 15 2·50
101 1f.50 on 1f. blue . . . . . 30 2·00
102 3f. on 5f. brown . . . . . 1·50 3·00
103 10f. on 5f. red on yellow 4·00 14·50
104 20f. on 5f. mauve on red 11·00 16·00

53 Sugar Refinery

54 Saints Harbour

55 Pointe-a-Pitre Harbour

1928.

105 **53** 1c. mauve and yellow . . . 10 2·25
106 2c. red and black 10 90
107 3c. mauve and yellow . . . 10 2·25
108 4c. brown and green . . . 25 1·90
109 5c. green and red . . . . 15 1·40
110 10c. blue and brown . . . 15 20
111 15c. black and red 15 30
112 20c. brown and mauve . . . 15 1·00
113 **54** 25c. olive and blue 15 15
114 30c. green and deep green 15 15
115 35c. green . . . . 60 2·75
116 40c. mauve and yellow . . . 15 25
117 45c. grey and purple . . . 45 3·00
118 45c. deep green and green 55 3·25
119 50c. red and green 20 20
120 55c. red and blue . . . . 1·25 2·50
121 60c. red and blue . . . . 40 3·00
122 65c. red and black 65 60
123 70c. red and black . . . . 15 3·25
124 75c. green and red . . . . 25 1·25
125 80c. brown and red . . . . 75 2·25
126 90c. red . . . . 90 3·75
127 90c. blue and red . . . . 55 3·25
128 **55** 1f. blue and red . . . . 3·75 1·50
129 1f. orange and red . . . . 2·50 2·75
130 1f. brown and blue . . . . 60 2·75
131 1f.05 red and blue . . . . 2·50 3·50
132 1f.10 green and orange . . . 3·50 4·75
133 1f.25 brown and blue . . . 1·25 3·00
134 1f.25 orange and red . . . 2·25 3·25
135 1f.40 mauve and blue . . . 2·00 3·25
136 1f.50 light blue and blue 20 30
137 1f.60 orange and mauve . . 2·25 3·25
138 1f.75 brown and mauve . . 4·25 1·75
139 1f.75 blue . . . . 6·50 7·25
140 2f. brown and green . . . 35 60
141 2f.25 blue . . . . 45 3·25
142 2f.50 green and orange . . . 65 3·25
143 3f. black and brown . . . 30 1·90
144 5f. red and blue . . . . 65 1·25
145 10f. brown and mauve . . 85 3·00
146 20f. red and green . . . . 50 4·00

1931. "Colonial Exhibition" key-types inscr "GUADELOUPE".

147 E 40c. black and green . . . 3·50 4·50
148 F 50c. black and mauve . . . 2·50 3·75
149 G 90c. black and red . . . 5·75 7·75
150 H 1f.50 black and blue . . . 4·50 5·00

57 Richelieu founding W. India Co., 1635

58 Victor Hughes and Corsairs, 1793

1935. West Indies Tercentenary.

151 **57** 40c. brown . . . . 11·00 11·50
152 50c. red . . . . 10·50 10·00
153 1f.50 blue . . . . 11·00 11·50
154 **58** 1f.75 mauve . . . . 10·50 7·50
155 5f. brown . . . . 7·50 10·00
156 10f. green . . . . 11·50 10·50

58a Sailing Ships

1937. International Exhibition, Paris.

157 – 20c. violet . . . . 40 3·25
158 **58a** 30c. green . . . . 50 3·25
159 – 40c. red . . . . 55 3·75
160 – 50c. brown . . . . 1·00 3·00
161 – 90c. red . . . . 80 3·75
162 – 1f.50 blue . . . . 1·25 3·25
MS162a 120 × 100 mm. 3f. blue (as T **58a**). Imperf . . . . 10·00 16·00

DESIGNS—VERT: 20c. Allegory of Commerce; 50c. Allegory of Agriculture. HORIZ: 40c. Berber Negress and Annamite; 90c. France with torch of Civilization; 1f.50, Diane de Poitiers.

58b Pierre and Marie Curie

1938. International Anti-cancer Fund.

163 **58b** 1f.75+50c. blue . . . . . 3·75 16·00

58c

1939. New York World's Fair.

164 **58c** 1f.25 red . . . . 1·90 3·00
165 2f.25 blue . . . . 2·00 3·00

58d Storming the Bastille

1939. 150th Anniv of French Revolution.

166 **58d** 45c.+25c. green and black 7·50 11·50
167 70c.+30c. brown & black 9·00 12·50
168 90c.+35c. orange & black 9·00 12·50
169 1f.25+1f. red and black 8·50 12·50
170 2f.25+2f. blue and black 8·50 12·50

1944. Surch **Un franc** (No. 177) or in figures (others).

(a) On Nos. 164/5.

178 40c. on 1f.25 red . . . . . . 2·25 2·75
179 40c. on 2f.25 blue . . . . . 2·75 3·50

(b) On Issue of 1928.

172 **54** 40c. on 35c. green . . . . 45 3·00
173 50c. on 25c. olive and blue 15 40
174 50c. on 65c. red and black 55 2·50
175 1f. on 90c. red . . . . . . 1·75 3·75
176 1f. on 90c. blue and red . . 1·40 2·75
177 1f. on 65c. red and black 40 2·25

(c) On No. 99.

171 **51** 4f. on 1f.05 on 2f. red . . 3·50 4·00

58e

58f Felix Eboue

1944. Mutual Aid and Red Cross Funds.

180 **58e** 5f.+20f. blue . . . . . . 80 3·50

1945.

181 **58f** 2f. black 10 20
182 25f. green . . . . 85 3·00

63

1945.

183 **63** 10c. blue and orange . . . 25 2·75
184 30c. green and orange . . . 35 2·75
185 40c. blue and red . . . . 75 3·00
186 50c. orange and green . . 35 95
187 60c. grey and blue . . . . 40 2·75
188 70c. grey and green . . . . 1·25 3·00
189 80c. green and yellow . . . 90 3·00
190 1f. purple and green . . . 50 1·10
191 1f.20 mauve and green . . 1·10 2·75
192 1f.50 brown and red . . . 90 1·40
193 2f. red and blue . . . . . 1·00 1·25
194 2f.40 red and green . . . . 1·75 3·50
195 3f. brown and blue 55 50
196 4f. blue and orange . . . . 85 1·60
197 4f.50 orange and green . . 90 1·50
198 5f. violet and green . . . . 90 1·75
199 10f. green and mauve . . . 75 40
200 15f. grey and orange . . . 1·00 1·00
201 20f. grey and orange . . . 1·25 60

63a Fairey FC-1

1945. Air.

202 **63a** 50f. green . . . . 1·60 2·75
203 100f. red . . . . 1·40 1·90

63b "Victory"

1946. Air. Victory.

204 **63b** 8f. brown . . . . 60 2·25

63c Chad

1946. Air. From Chad to the Rhine.

205 **63c** 5f. olive . . . . 75 3·50
206 – 10f. blue . . . . 60 3·75
207 – 15f. purple . . . . 75 1·75
208 – 20f. red . . . . 1·50 3·75
209 – 25f. black . . . . 60 1·75
210 – 50f. brown . . . . 60 1·40

DESIGNS: 10f. Koufra; 15f. Mareth; 20f. Normandy; 25f. Paris; 50f. Strasbourg.

64 Woman and Port Basse-Terre

65 Cutting Sugar Cane

66 Guadeloupe Woman

67 Sud Ouest Bretagne over Guadeloupe Woman and Fishing Boats

1947.

211 **64** 10c. lake (postage) . . . . 15 2·25
212 30c. brown . . . . 15 2·50
213 50c. green . . . . 15 2·25
214 **65** 60c. brown . . . . 15 2·50
215 1f. red . . . . 25 2·25
216 1f.50 blue . . . . 30 2·50
217 – 2f. green . . . . 35 3·25
218 – 2f.50 red . . . . 65 3·00
219 – 3f. blue . . . . 85 2·75
220 – 4f. violet . . . . 1·25 3·25
221 – 5f. green . . . . 1·00 3·25
222 – 6f. red . . . . 1·75 1·10
223 – 10f. blue . . . . 2·25 2·75
224 – 15f. purple . . . . . . 1·25 2·50
225 – 20f. red . . . . 2·50 2·25
226 **66** 25f. green . . . . 2·75 4·50
227 40f. orange . . . . 2·25 4·50
228 – 50f. purple (air) . . . . 6·75 8·50
229 – 100f. blue . . . . 7·00 9·50
230 **67** 200f. red . . . . 11·00 12·50

DESIGNS—As Type **66**: 2f. to 3f. Women carrying pineapples; 4f. to 6f. Woman in kerchief facing left; 10f. to 20f. Picking coffee. As Type **67**: 50f. Latecoere 631 flying boat over village; 100f. Short Hythe flying boat landing in bay.

POSTAGE DUE STAMPS

D 1

D 3

1876.

D1 **D 1** 15c. black on blue . . . . 35·00 28·00
D2 25c. black on white . . . £700 £500
D3 30c. black on white . . . 75·00 50·00
D4 40c. black on blue . . . . † £21000
D5 40c. black on white . . . £850 £700

1884. Imperf.

D 8 **D 3** 5c. black on white . . . 11·50 22·00
D 9 10c. black on blue . . . 55·00 32·00
D10 15c. black on lilac . . . 90·00 50·00
D11 20c. black on red . . . . £120 90·00
D12 30c. black on yellow . . £120 £100
D13 35c. black on grey . . . 40·00 32·00
D14 50c. black on green . . . 15·00 14·50

1903. Postage Due stamps of French Colonies surch **G & D 30** in frame.

D59b U 30 on 60c. brown on buff £190 £190
D61c 30 on 1f. red on yellow £275 £275

D 48 Gustavia Bay, Island of St. Bartholomew

D 56 Allee Dumanoir, Capesterre

D 68 Palms and Houses

1905.

D63 **D 48** 5c. blue 15 25
D64 10c. brown 15 35
D65 15c. green . . . . . . 20 2·75
D66 20c. brown on yellow 20 1·10
D67 30c. red . . . . 15 2·25
D68 50c. black . . . . . . 50 4·75
D69 60c. orange . . . . . . 35 3·25
D70 1f. lilac . . . . 1·00 5·00

1926. Surch in figures and words and **a percevoir**.

D105 **D 48** 2f. on 1f. grey . . . . 50 3·75
D106 3f. on 1f. blue . . . . 75 4·25

1928.

D147 **D 56** 2c. mauve and brown 15 2·25
D148 4c. brown and blue . . 15 2·00
D149 5c. brown and green 15 1·10
D150 10c. yellow and mauve 15 1·25
D151 15c. olive and red . . 15 2·00
D152 20c. olive and orange 15 2·50
D153 25c. green and red . . 25 2·50
D154 30c. yellow and blue 25 1·25
D155 50c. red and brown . . 30 2·75
D156 60c. black and blue . . 50 3·00
D157 1f. red and green . . . 90 2·75
D158 2f. red and brown . . 75 3·50
D159 3f. blue and mauve . . 85 3·25

1947.

D231 **D 68** 10c. black . . . . . . 15 2·50
D232 30c. green . . . . . . 15 2·50
D233 50c. blue . . . . 15 2·25
D234 1f. green . . . . 20 2·75
D235 2f. blue . . . . 35 2·75
D236 3f. brown . . . . . . 85 3·25
D237 4f. purple . . . . . . 75 3·50
D238 5f. violet . . . . . . 80 3·75
D239 10f. red . . . . 75 4·25
D240 20f. purple . . . . . 1·40 4·50

GUAM Pt. 22

An island in the Pacific Ocean belonging to the United States. Now uses U.S. stamps.

100 cents = 1 dollar.

1899. Stamps of United States optd **GUAM**.

1 1c. green (No. 283) . . . . . 16·00 20·00
2 2c. red (No. 270) . . . . . . 14·00 20·00
4 3c. violet (No. 271) £100 £140
5 4c. brown (No. 285) £110 £140
6 5c. blue (No. 286) . . . . . . 23·00 35·00
7 6c. purple (No. 287a) £100 £150
8 8c. brown (No. 275) . . . . . 95·00 £140
9 10c. brown (No. 289) . . . . 35·00 45·00
11 15c. green (No. 290) £120 £130
12 50c. orange (No. 278) £225 £275
13 $1 black (No. 279) £275 £300

SPECIAL DELIVERY STAMP

1899. Special Delivery stamp of United States optd **GUAM**.

E15 **E 46** 10c. blue (No. E283) . . £120 £150

GUANACASTE Pt. 15

A province of Costa Rica whose stamps it now uses.

100 centavos = 1 peso.

Stamps of Costa Rica optd.

1885. Stamps of 1883 optd **Guanacaste** or **GUANACASTE**.
G 1 **8** 1c. green . . . . 2·00 2·00
G36 2c. red . . . . 2·00 2·00
G 3 5c. violet . . . . 8·00 3·00
G 4 10c. orange . . . . 8·00 8·00
G 5 40c. blue . . . . 15·00 15·00

1887. Stamps of 1887 optd **Guanacaste**.
G37 **14** 5c. violet . . . . 10·00 4·00
G39 10c. orange . . . . 2·00 2·00

1887. Fiscal stamps optd **Guanacaste** or **GUANACASTE**.
G44 1c. red £150 £150
G41 2c. blue . . . . 25·00 25·00

1889. Stamps of 1889 optd **GUANACASTE**.
G62 **17** 1c. brown 75 75
G63 2c. blue 75 75
G64 5c. orange 75 75
G65 10c. lake 75 75
G56 20c. green 80 70
G57 50c. red . . . . 2·00 2·00
G59 1p. blue . . . . 4·00 4·00
G60 2p. violet . . . . 6·00 6·00
G61 5p. olive . . . . 20·00 20·00

GUATEMALA Pt. 15

A republic of Central America; independent since 1847.

1871. 100 centavos = 8 reales = 1 peso.
1927. 100 centavos de quetzal = 1 quetzal.

1 Arms 2 3 Liberty

1871.
1 **1** 1c. bistre . . . . 50 6·50
2 5c. brown . . . . 3·00 5·00
3 10c. blue . . . . 3·50 5·75
4 20c. red . . . . 2·75 5·00

1873.
5 **2** 4r. mauve . . . . £200 5·00
6 1p. yellow . . . . £100 70·00

1875. Various frames.
7 **3** ¼r. black . . . . 90 2·25
8 ½r. green . . . . 90 2·00
9 1r. blue . . . . 90 2·00
10 2r. red . . . . 90 2·00

4 Native Indian 5 Resplendent Quetzal

1878.
11 **4** ½r. green . . . . 50 2·00
12 2r. red . . . . 85 2·75
13 4r. mauve . . . . 85 3·00
14 1p. yellow . . . . 1·40 6·00

1879.
15 **5** ¼r. green and brown . . . . 7·00 9·00
16 1r. green and black . . . . . 11·00 14·00
For similar stamps, but inscr differently, see Nos. 21/25.

1881. Surch.
17 **5** 1c. on ¼r. green and brown 11·50 16·00
18 **4** 5c. on ½r. green . . . . . . 3·50 5·00
19 **5** 10c. on 1r. green and black 17·00 23·00
20 **4** 20c. on 2r. red . . . . 24·00 27·00

1881. As T **5** inscr "UNION POSTAL UNIVERSAL—GUATEMALA". Centres in green.
21 **5** 1c. black . . . . 3·50 2·00
22 2c. brown . . . . 3·50 2·00
23 5c. red . . . . 6·50 2·50
24 10c. lilac . . . . 3·25 2·00
25 20c. yellow . . . . 3·25 2·40

7 President J. Rufino Barrios

Correos Nacionales
150 c. 150 c.
Guatemala.
150 c. 150 c.
150 Ctavos.
(8)

1886. Railway stamp variously surch as T **8**.
26 **7** 25c. on 1p. red 85 70
27 50c. on 1p. red 85 70
28 75c. on 1p. red 85 70
29 100c. on 1p. red . . . . . . 1·40 1·40
30 150c. on 1p. red . . . . . . 1·40 1·25

9 Arms of Guatemala

16 Steamship, arms, portrait of Pres. J. M. Reyna Barrios and locomotive in centre. Arms of El Salvador, Honduras, Nicaragua and Costa Rica in corners

1886.
43a **9** 1c. blue . . . . 2·75 30
44 2c. brown . . . . 3·75 35
46 5c. violet . . . . 4·50 25
47 6c. mauve . . . . 5·75 40
48 10c. red . . . . 4·75 25
49 20c. green . . . . 11·00 75
50 25c. orange . . . . 35·00 2·75
37 50c. olive . . . . 28·00 7·50
38 75c. red . . . . 20·00 6·00
39 100c. brown . . . . 28·00 14·00
40 150c. blue . . . . 35·00 24·00
41 200c. yellow . . . . 30·00 18·00
See also Nos. 101/9.

1886. Surch **PROVISIONAL. 1886. 1 UN CENTAVO.**
42h **9** 1c. on 2c. brown . . . . . 4·25 10·00

1894. Surch **1894**, bar and value.
55 **9** 1c. on 2c. brown . . . . . . 1·75 1·60
51 2c. on 100c. brown . . . . . 9·50 7·50
57 6c. on 150c. blue . . . . . 15·00 8·75
53 10c. on 75c. red . . . . . 13·00 9·50
54 10c. on 200c. yellow . . . . 9·50 5·75

1895. Surch **1895 1 CENTAVO** and bar.
59 **9** 1c. on 5c. violet 90 60

1897. Central American Exhibition.
62 **16** 1c. black on grey 60 45
63 2c. black on green 60 45
64 6c. black on orange 60 45
65 10c. black on blue 60 45
66 12c. black on red 95 80
67 18c. black on white . . . . 8·50 7·00
68 20c. black on red . . . . . 1·40 1·00
69 25c. black on brown . . . . 1·40 1·00
70 50c. black on brown . . . . 1·40 1·00
71 75c. black on blue . . . . . 70·00 60·00
72 100c. black on green . . . . 1·40 1·00
73 150c. black on pink £120 £100
74 200c. black on mauve . . . . 1·40 1·00
75 500c. black on green . . . . 1·40 1·00

1897. Surch **UN CENTAVO 1898.**
76 **16** 1c. on 12c. black on red . . 1·10 1·10

1898. Surch **1898**, bar and value.
77 **9** 1c. on 5c. violet . . . . . . 2·75 15
78 1c. on 25c. orange . . . . . 6·25 4·00
79 1c. on 50c. olive . . . . . 5·50 3·25
80 1c. on 75c. red . . . . . 5·50 3·25
81 6c. on 5c. violet . . . . . 6·25 1·00
82 6c. on 10c. red . . . . . 24·00 17·00
83 6c. on 20c. green . . . . . 10·00 6·50
84 6c. on 100c. brown . . . . 10·00 6·50
85 6c. on 150c. blue . . . . . 10·00 6·50
86 6c. on 200c. yellow . . . . 10·00 6·50
87 10c. on 20c. green . . . . . 10·00 6·50

20 22

1898. Fiscal stamps as T **20** optd **CORREOS NACIONALES** or surch **2 CENTAVOS** also.
88 **20** 1c. blue . . . . 1·50 1·50
89 2c. on 1c. blue . . . . . . 2·50 2·50

1898. Fiscal stamps dated "1898" as T **22** surch **CORREOS NACIONALES** and value.
90 **22** 1c. on 10c. blue 50 50
91 2c. on 1c. red . . . . . . 2·40 1·75
92 2c. on 5c. violet 85 70
93 2c. on 10c. blue . . . . . . 4·50 4·75
94 2c. on 25c. red . . . . . . 5·00 5·50
95 2c. on 50c. blue . . . . . . 5·50 6·00
96 6c. on 1p. violet . . . . . . 2·75 3·00
97 6c. on 5p. blue . . . . . . 5·00 5·00
98 6c. on 10p. green . . . . . 5·00 5·00

1899. Surch **Un 1 Centavo 1899.**
99 **9** 1c. on 5c. violet 80 50

1900. Surch **1900 1 CENTAVO.**
100 **9** 1c. on 10c. red 85 70

1900.
101 **9** 1c. green . . . . 1·00 30
102 2c. red . . . . 1·00 30
103 5c. blue . . . . 3·75 1·00
104 6c. green . . . . 1·10 30
105 10c. brown . . . . 3·75 40
106 20c. mauve . . . . 11·00 11·00
107 20c. brown . . . . 17·00 24·00
108 25c. yellow . . . . 11·00 11·00
109 25c. green . . . . 17·00 24·00

1901. Surch **1901** and value.
110 **9** 1c. on 20c. green . . . . . 1·25 85
111 1c. on 25c. orange . . . . . 1·25 85
112 2c. on 20c. green . . . . . 3·50 2·25

1902. Fiscal stamp surch **CORREOS NACIONALES 1902** and value in figures and words.
113 **20** 1c. on 1c. blue . . . . . . 2·40 1·50
114 2c. on 1c. blue . . . . . . 2·40 1·25

1902. Fiscal stamp, dated "1898", surch **CORREOS 1902 Seis 6 Cts.**
115 **22** 6c. on 25c. red . . . . . . 40 1·75

30 Arms 31 J. Rufino Barrios Statue

35 Statesmen discussing Independence (after painting by E. Bravo)

47 President Manuel Estrada Cabrera

1902. Inscr "U.P.U. 1902".
116 **30** 1c. purple and green . . . 15 15
117 **31** 2c. black and red 15 15
118a – 5c. black and blue 20 15
119 – 6c. green and yellow . . . 20 15
120 – 10c. blue and orange . . 15 15
121 **35** 12½c. black and blue . . . 15 15
122 – 20c. black and red 45 20
141 – 25c. black and blue . . . 55 20
123a – 50c. blue and brown . . . 30 15
124 – 75c. black and lilac . . . 35 20
125 – 1p. black and brown . . . 45 20
126 – 2p. black and orange . . 55 35
142 **47** 5p. black and red 70 70
DESIGNS—HORIZ: 5c. La Reforma Palace; 6c. Temple of Minerva; 10c. Lake Amatitlan; 20c. Cathedral; 25c. G.P.O.; 50c. Columbus Theatre; 75c. Artillery Barracks; 1p. Columbus Monument; 2p. Indian Institute.

1903. Surch **1903 25 CENTAVOS.**
127 **9** 25c. on 1c. green . . . . . 2·00 65
128 25c. on 2c. red . . . . . 2·60 65
129 25c. on 6c. green . . . . . 4·00 2·40
130 25c. on 10c. brown . . . . 17·00 5·25
131 25c. on 75c. red . . . . . 22·00 13·00
132 25c. on 150c. blue . . . . 22·00 13·00
133 25c. on 200c. yellow . . . . 25·00 15·00

1908. Surch **1908** and value in figures and words.
134 – 1c. on 10c. blue and orange (No. 120) 35 35
135 **35** 2c. on 12½c. black and blue 35 35
136 – 6c. on 20c. black and red (No. 122) 30 30

1909. Surch **1909** and value in figures and words.
137 2c. on 75c. blk & lil (No. 124) 55 55
138 6c. on 50c. bl & brn (No. 123) 30 30
139 12½c. on 2p. black and orange (No. 126) 45 45

45 M. Garcia Granados

1910. Granados Centenary.
140 **45** 6c. black and bistre 55 35

1911. Surch **1911 Un Centavo.**
143 **45** 1c. on 6c. black and bistre 13·00 5·00

1911. Surch **Correos de Guatemala 1911** and value.
144 2c. on 5c. (No. 118a) . . . . 1·00 50
145 6c. on 10c. (No. 120) 85 85

1912. Surch **1912** and value.
146 1c. on 20c. (No. 122) 35 35
147 2c. on 50c. (No. 123a) . . . 35 35
148 5c. on 75c. (No. 124) 90 90

1913. Surch **1913** and value.
149 1c. on 50c. (No. 123a) . . . 30 30
150 6c. on 1p. (No. 125) 45 45
151 12½c. on 2p. (No. 126) . . . 45 45

1916. Surch with value only.
156 **30** 2c. on 1c. purple and green 30 30
152 6c. on 1c. purple and green 30 30
153 12½c. on 1c. purple & green 30 30
154 **31** 25c. on 2c. black and red 20 20

59 Pres. Manuel Estrada Cabrera 60

1917. Re-election of President Cabrera.
155 **59** 25c. brown and blue . . . 35 20

1918.
157 **60** 1p.50 blue 80 30

61 Arms 64 Technical School

1919. Buildings and Obligatory Tax G.P.O. Rebuilding Fund (No. 158).
158 **61** 12½c. red (obligatory tax) 20 15
159 – 30c. black and red (postage) . . . . 4·00 75
160 – 60c. black and olive . . . 90 45
161 **64** 90c. black and brown . . . 70 70
169 – 1p.50 orange and blue . . 50 30
162 – 3p. black and green . . . 1·75 45
170 – 5p. green and sepia . . . . 1·25 40
171 – 15p. red and black . . . . 45·00 17·00
DESIGNS—Dated 1918: 30c. Radio station; 60c. Maternity hospital; 3p. Arms. Dated 1921: 1p.50, Monolith at Quirigua; 5p. Garcia Granados Monument; 15p. La Penitenciaria railway bridge, Guatemala City.

1920. Nos. 159/60 surch **1920 2 centavos.**
163 2c. on 30c. black and red . . 65 65
164 2c. on 60c. black and olive 25 25

1920. No. 126 surch **25 Centavos** and bars.
165 25c. on 2p. black and orange 35 30

68

1920. Telegraph stamp as T **68** optd **CORREOS.**
166 **68** 25c. green 25 15

1921. Surch **1921** and value in words.
167 12½c. on 20c. black and red (No. 122) 35 20
168 50c. on 75c. black and lilac (No. 124) 45 35

1921. Optd **1921 CORREOS.**
173 **63** 25c. green 35 20

1921. Surch **1921 CORREOS DOCE Y MEDIO.**
172 **68** 12½c. on 25c. green 30 20

1922. Surch **1922** and value in words.
174 – 12½c. on 20c. (No. 122) . . 30 30
175 – 12½c. on 60c. (No. 160) . . 70 70
176 **64** 12½c. on 90c. (No. 161) . . 70 70
179 – 12½c. on 3p. (No. 162) . . 30 25
180 – 12½c. on 5p. (No. 170) . . 70 65
181 – 12½c. on 15p. (No. 171) . . 1·60 1·10
185 – 25c. on 30c. (No. 159) . . 1·40 1·40
186 – 25c. on 60c. (No. 160) . . 1·40 1·40
187 – 25c. on 75c. (No. 124) . . 45 45
188 **64** 25c. on 90c. (No. 161) . . 1·40 1·40
189 – 25c. on 1p. (No. 125) . . 35 35
190 – 25c. on 1p.50 (No. 169) . . 35 35

191 – 25c. on 2p. (No. 126) . . . 55 55
192 – 25c. on 3p. (No. 162) . . . 45 45
193 – 25c. on 5p. (No. 170) . . . 1·10 1·10
184 – 25c. on 15p. (No. 171) . . 2·00 2·00

80 Independence Centenary Palace
81 National Palace, Antigua

1922.

195 **80** 12½c. green 20 15
196 **81** 25c. brown 20 15

82 Columbus Theatre
83 Resplendent Quetzal
84 Garcia Granados Monument

1923.

197 **82** 50c. red 45 30
198 **83** 1p. green 80 30
199 **84** 5p. orange . . . . 1·40 55

1924. Surch **1924** and value.
200 – 1p. on 1p.50 (No. 169) . . 35 30
201 **84** 1p.25 on 5p. orange . . . 55 45

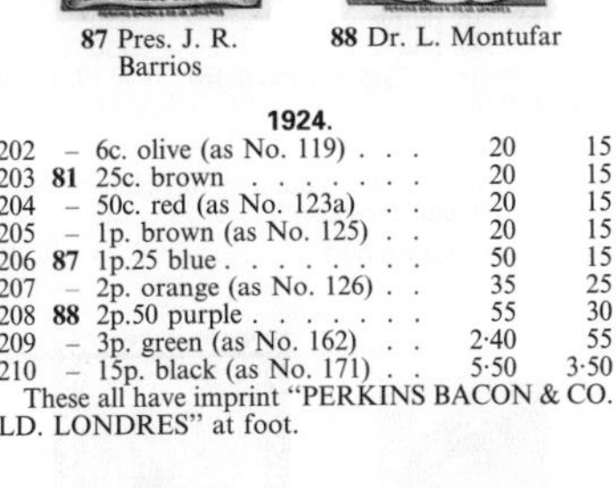

87 Pres. J. R. Barrios
88 Dr. L. Montufar

1924.

202 – 6c. olive (as No. 119) . . . 20 15
203 **81** 25c. brown 20 15
204 – 50c. red (as No. 123a) . . 20 15
205 – 1p. brown (as No. 125) . . 20 15
206 **87** 1p.25 blue 50 15
207 – 2p. orange (as No. 126) . . 35 25
208 **88** 2p.50 purple 55 30
209 – 3p. green (as No. 162) . . 2·40 55
210 – 15p. black (as No. 171) . . 5·50 3·50
These all have imprint "PERKINS BACON & CO. LD. LONDRES" at foot.

1925. No. 201 further surch with two bars.
211 **84** 1p. on 5p. orange 55 45

89 Aurora Park

90 General Post Office

91 National Observatory

92 Proposed new G.P.O.

1926. Dated "1926".
212 – 6c. bistre (as No. 119) . . 15 15
213 **89** 12½c. green 15 15
214 **81** 25c. brown 15 15
215 **90** 50c. red 20 15
216 – 1p. brown (as No. 125) . . 20 20
217 **87** 1p.50 blue 20 20
218 **91** 2p. orange 85 70
219 **88** 2p.50 purple . . . . . . 1·75 70
220 – 3p. green (as No. 162) . . 55 30
221 – 5p. lilac (as No. 170) . . . 70 45
222 – 15p. black (as No. 171) . . 7·25 3·50
These all have imprint "WATERLOW & SONS LIMITED, LONDRES" at foot.

1927. Obligatory Tax. G.P.O. Rebuilding Fund.
223 **92** 1c. olive 15 15

1928. Surch **1928** and value.
224 **91** ½c. de q. on 2p. orange . . 70 55
225 – ½c. de q. on 5p. lilac (No. 221) 35 30
226 **88** 1c. de q. on 2p.50 purple (No. 219) 35 30

95 Pres. J. R. Barrios

96 Dr. L. Montufar

97 Garcia Granados

98 General Orellana

99 City Arms, Guatemala

1929.

227 **91** ½c. green 70 15
228 **81** 1c. sepia 20 15
229 **95** 2c. blue 20 15
230 **96** 3c. lilac 20 15
231 **97** 4c. yellow 20 20
232 **98** 5c. red 30 15
233 – 10c. brown (as No. 119) . 45 15
234 – 15c. blue (as No. 125) . . 55 15
235 **31** 25c. brown 90 20
236 **89** 30c. green . . . . 1·10 35
237 – 50c. red (as No. 120) . . . 1·75 45
238 **99** 1q. black . . . . 3·00 55
These all have imprint "T. DE LA RUE & CO. LD. LONDRES" at foot.

1929. Air. Nos. 210 and 222 surch **SERVICIO POSTAL AEREO ANO DE 1928** and new value.
239 3c. on 15p. black (222) . . . 2·25 2·25
240 5c. on 15p. black (222) . . . 1·00 1·00
240a 5c. on 15p. black (210) . . . 4·50 4·50
241 15c. on 15p. black (222) . . 2·75 2·75
242 20c. on 15p. black (222) . . 4·50 4·50

1929. Air. Surch **SERVICIO POSTAL AEREO ANO DE 1929 Q0.03.**
243 **88** 3c. on 2p.50 purple (No. 208) . . . . 1·00 1·00

1929. Opening of Guatemala–El Salvador Railway. No. 220 surch **FERROCARRIL ORIENTAL 1929** and new value.
244 3c. on 3p. green . . . . . . 3·00 3·00
245 5c. on 3p. green . . . . . . 3·00 3·00

1930. Opening of Los Altos Railway. No. 222 surch **FERROCARRIL DE LOS ALTOS Inaugurado en 1929** and value in words.
246 1c. on 15p. black . . . . . . 1·75 2·25
247 2c. on 15p. black . . . . . . 1·75 2·25
248 3c. on 15p. black . . . . . . 1·75 2·25
249 5c. on 15p. black . . . . . . 1·75 2·25
250 15c. on 15p. black . . . . . 1·75 2·25

104 Bridge and Permanent Way

1930. Opening of Los Altos Railway.
251 – 2c. black and purple . . . 2·00 1·25
252 **104** 3c. black and red . . . . 4·25 3·25
253 – 5c. blue and orange . . . 4·25 3·25
DESIGNS: 2c. Quetzaltenango Dam; 5c. Quetzaltenango railway station.

105 Fokker Super Trimotor over Mt. Agua

1930. Air.
254 **105** 6c. red 75 55

1930. Air. Surch **SERVICIO AEREO INTERIOR 1930** and value in words.
255 1c. on 3p. green (No. 220) . . 20 20
256 2c. on 3p. green 50 90
257 3c. on 3p. green 50 90
258 4c. on 3p. green 70 70
259 10c. on 15p. black (No. 222) 5·50 3·75

1931. Air. Optd **EXTERIOR - 1931.**
260 **105** 6c. red 70 70

1931. Air. Optd **AEREO EXTERIOR 1931.**
261 **97** 4c. yellow 35 30

1931. Air. Optd **AEREO INTERNACIONAL 1931.**
262 – 15c. blue (No. 234) . . . . 1·00 35
263 **89** 30c. green (No. 236) . . . 1·75 60

1931. Air. Optd **Primer Vuelo Posta BARRIOS-MIAMI 1931.**
264 **95** 2c. blue . . . . 1·75 2·00
265 **96** 3c. lilac . . . . 1·75 2·00
266 – 15c. blue (No. 234) . . . . 1·75 2·00

1932. Air. Surch **SERVICIO AEREO INTERIOR 1932** and value.
267 **87** 2c. on 1p.50 blue (217) . . 75 60
268 – 3c. on 3p. green (220) . . . 70 20
270 – 10c. on 15p. black (222) . . 19·00 12·50
271 – 15c. on 15p. black (222) . . 24·00 19·00

114 Monolith of Quirigua

1932.

272 **114** 3c. red 50 15
See also Nos. 416a/b.

1933. Air. Optd **AEREO INTERIOR 1933.**
273 **97** 4c. yellow 35 20

116 Flag of the Race, Columbus and Tecum Uman

1933. 441st Anniv of Departure of Columbus from Palos.
274 **116** ½c. green 35 70
275 1c. brown 70 85
276 2c. blue 70 85
277 3c. mauve 70 50
278 5c. red 70 70

1934. Air. (a) Optd **AERO EXTERIOR 1934.**
280 **98** 5c. red . . . . 1·75 15
281 – 15c. blue (No. 234) . . . . 1·75 35

(b) Optd **AEREO INTERIOR 1934.**
279 **95** 2c. blue 55 20

117 Barrios' Birthplace

118 Barrios and "Agamemnon" (freighter)

1935. Birth Centenary of J. R. Barrios.
282 **117** ½c. pink & green (postage) 35 40
283 – 1c. blue and orange . . . 35 40
284 – 2c. black and orange . . 35 45
285 – 3c. blue and red . . . . 3·50 2·00
286 – 4c. red and blue . . . . 3·50 9·00
287 – 5c. brown and green . . . 2·75 3·50
288 – 10c. red and green . . . 4·00 4·50
289 – 15c. brown and green . . 3·50 4·00
290 – 25c. black and red . . . 3·50 4·00
291 **118** 10c. blue and brown (air) 4·75 4·00
292 – 15c. brown and grey . . . 1·40 1·50
293 – 30c. violet and red . . . 1·40 1·00
DESIGNS—POSTAGE—HORIZ: 1c. San Lorenzo; 2c. Barrios and Official Decree; 3c. Arms and locomotive; 5c. Telegraph office and Barrios; 10c. Polytechnic School; 15c. Police H.Q.; 25c. Pres. Ubico, arms and Barrios. VERT: 4c. G.P.O. AIR—HORIZ: Barrios and (15c.) tomb, (30c.) statue.

120 Lake Atitlan
121 Resplendent Quetzal

122 Arms and Map of Guatemala

1935.

293a – ½c. blue and green . . . 15 15
294 **120** 1c. red and brown . . . 20 15
295 **121** 3c. green and orange . . 1·25 30
296 3c. green and red . . . 1·25 30
297 – 4c. red and blue 45 20
297a **122** 5c. brown and blue . . . 55 20
DESIGNS—As Type **120**: ½c. Govt. Printing Works; 4c. National Assembly.

123 Lake Amatitlan

1935. Air. (a) Inscr "INTERIOR" (37 × 17 mm).
298 **123** 2c. brown 15 15
299 – 3c. blue 40 20
300 – 4c. black 35 10
300a – 4c. blue 30 10
301 – 6c. green 35 15
301a 6c. violet . . . . 2·75 10
302 – 10c. red 35 35
303 – 15c. orange 45 55
303a – 15c. green 45 65
304 – 30c. olive . . . . 4·00 5·25
304a – 30c. brown 50 35
305 – 50c. purple . . . . . . 12·00 11·50
305a – 50c. blue . . . . 2·75 2·00
306 – 1q. orange . . . . . . 12·00 15·00
306a 1q. red . . . . 3·00 2·00
DESIGNS: 3c. Puerto Barrios; 4c. San Felipe; 6c., 1q. Different view of Lake Amatitlan; 10c. Livingston; 15c. San Jose; 30c. Atitlan; 50c. La Aurora Airport.

(b) Inscr "EXTERIOR" (34 × 15 mm) (except Nos. 319/20 which are 46 × 20 mm).
307 1c. brown 10 10
308 2c. red 20 20
309 3c. mauve 35 35
309a 4c. yellow . . . . 1·25 1·00
309b 4c. red 70 50
310 5c. blue . . . . 1·75 40
310a 5c. orange . . . . 1·50 25
311 10c. brown 35 25
311a 10c. green 35 25
312 15c. red 35 10
312a 15c. orange 30 10
313 20c. blue . . . . 1·60 2·00
313a 20c. red 35 25
314 25c. black . . . . 2·00 2·40
314a 25c. green 65 35
315 30c. green . . . . 9·50 6·00
315a 30c. red . . . . 3·75 30
316 50c. red . . . . 22·00 24·00
316a 50c. violet . . . . 17·00 10·00
317 1q. blue . . . . 15·00 21·00
318 1q. green . . . . 5·00 6·00
319 2q.50 olive and red . . . . 3·50 2·00
320 5q. blue and orange . . . . 4·75 2·75
DESIGNS: 1c. Guatemala City; 2c., 15c. (No. 312) Views of Central Park; 3c. Cerrito del Carmen; 4c. Estuary of R. Dulce; 5c. Plaza J. R. Barrios; 10c. National Liberators' Monument; 15c. (No. 312a) R. Dulce; 20c. Quezaltenango; 25c. Antigua; 30c. Puerto Barrios; 50c. San Jose; 1q. Aurora Airport; 2q.50, Islet; 5q. Rocks on Atlantic Coast.

1936. Obligatory Tax. 65th Anniv of Liberal Revolution. Optd **1871 30 DE JUNIO 1936.**
321 **92** 1c. green 35 35

1936. Obligatory Tax. 115th Anniv of Independence. Optd **1821 15 de SEPTIEMBRE 1936.**
322 **92** 1c. green 45 25

1936. Obligatory Tax. National Fair. Optd **FERIA NACIONAL 1936.**
323 **92** 1c. olive 55 55

1937. Philatelic Exhibition Fund. Optd **EXPOSICION FILATELICA 1937** or surch **+1** also.
325 **120** 1c.+1c. red and brown . . 90 70
326 **121** 3c.+1c. green and orange 90 70
327 3c.+1c. green and red . . 90 70
329 – 4c.+1c. (No. 300a) . . . 75 75
328 **122** 5c.+1c. brown and blue 90 70
330 – 6c.+1c. (No. 301a) . . . 75 75
331 – 10c.+1c. (No. 311a) . . . 75 75
332 – 15c.+1c. (No. 312a) . . . 75 75
324 **92** 1c. olive 40 40

128 Resplendent Quetzal

129 General Ubico on horseback

130 Quezaltenango

1937. Second Term of Pres. Ubico. (a) Postage.
333 **128** ½c. red and blue 80 50
334 – 1c. brown and grey . . . 45 45
335 – 2c. red and violet . . . 45 45
336 – 3c. blue and purple . . . 35 35
337 – 4c. olive and yellow . . . 1·40 1·25
338 – 5c. purple and red . . . . 1·40 1·25
339 – 10c. black and purple . . 2·00 2·40
340 – 15c. red and blue . . . . 1·60 2·40
341 – 25c. violet and orange . . 2·00 2·50
342 – 50c. orange and green . . 3·00 3·75
343 **129** 1q. purple and brown . . 15·00 17·00
344 – 1q.50 brown and olive . . 15·00 17·00
DESIGNS: As Type **128**—VERT: 1c. Tower of the Reformer; 5c. National Congress entrance; 10c. Customs House. HORIZ: 2c. Union Park, Quezaltenango; 3c. G.P.O; 4c. Government Building, Retalhuleu; 15c. Aurora Airport; 25c. National Fair; 50c. Presidential Guards' Barracks. As Type **129**: 1q.50, Gen. Ubico.

(b) Air. As T **130**, inscr "INTERIOR" and optd with aeroplane.
345 **130** 2c. black and red 20 15
346 – 3c. black and blue 70 85
347 – 4c. black and yellow . . . 20 15
348 – 6c. black and green . . . 50 35
349 – 10c. black and purple . . 1·40 1·50
350 – 15c. black and orange . . 1·00 70
351 – 30c. black and olive . . . 2·50 2·00
352 – 50c. black and blue . . . 3·50 3·00
353 – 75c. black and violet . . . 7·00 7·50
354 – 1q. black and red . . . . 7·50 8·00
DESIGNS: 3c. Lake Atitlan; 4c. Progressive colony on Lake Amatitlan; 6c. Carmen Hill; 10c. Relief map; 15c. National University; 30c. Plaza Espana; 50c. Aurora Police Station; 75c. Aurora Amphitheatre; 1q. Aurora Airport.

(c) Air. As T **130** inscr "EXTERIOR" and optd with aeroplane.
355 – 1c. blue and orange 15 15
356 – 2c. violet and red 25 20
357 – 3c. brown and purple . . . 70 70
358 – 5c. red and green . . . . 2·75 2·00
359 – 10c. green and red 85 70
360 – 15c. olive and pink 55 35
361 – 20c. black and blue . . . . 1·75 1·10
362 – 25c. red and grey . . . . 1·75 1·75
363 – 30c. violet and green . . . 85 85
364 – 50c. blue and purple . . . . 30·00 30·00
365 – 1q. purple and olive . . . . 7·00 8·00
366 – 1q.50 brown and red . . . 7·00 8·00
DESIGNS: 1c. Seventh Avenue; 2c. Liberators' Monument; 3c. National Printing Offices; 5c. National Museum; 10c. Central Park; 15c. Escuintla Park; 20c. Mobile Police; 25c. Slaughter-house, Escuintla; 30c. Campo de Marte Stadium; 50c. Plaza Barrios; 1q. Polytechnic; 1q.50, Aurora Airport.

1938. 150th Anniv of U.S. Constitution. Optd **1787-1789 CL ANIVERSARIO DE LA CONSTITUCION EE. UU. 1937-1939.**
367 **92** 1c. olive 25 20

1938. Obligatory Tax. No. 223 optd **1938.**
368a **92** 1c. olive 25 15

134

1938. 1st Central American Philatelic Exhibition. (a) Air. As T **134** inscr "PRIMERA EXPOSICION FILATELICA CENTRO AMERICANA".
369 **134** 1c. brown and orange . . 25 25
370 – 2c. brown and red 25 25
371 – 3c. brown, buff and green 40 40
372 – 4c. brown and purple . . 55 55
373 – 5c. brown and grey . . . 35 40
374 – 10c. brown and blue . . . 70 1·00
DESIGNS: 2c. to 10c. Various portraits as Type **134**.

(b) Postage. No. 223 optd **Primera Exposicion Filatelica Centroamericana 1938.**
375 **92** 1c. olive 25 15

137 La Merced Church

1939. Optd with flying quetzal. (a) Inland Air Mail. As T **137** inscr "CORREO AEREO INTERIOR".
376 **137** 1c. brown and olive 15 15
377 – 2c. green and red 20 20
378 – 3c. olive and blue 20 25
379 – 4c. green and pink . . . 20 15
380 – 5c. blue and purple . . . 25 25
381 – 6c. grey and orange . . . 35 30
382 – 10c. grey and brown . . . 75 35
383 – 15c. black and purple . . 1·00 25
384 – 30c. red and blue . . . . 1·10 40
385 – 50c. violet and orange . . 1·50 60
386 – 1q. blue and green . . . 2·40 2·00
DESIGNS: 2c. Christ's Church Ruins, Antigua; 3c. Aurora Airport; 4c. Campo de Marte Stadium; 5c. Cavalry Barracks; 6c. Palace of Justice; 10c. Customs House, San Jose; 15c. Post Office, Retalhuleu; 30c. Municipal Theatre, Quezaltenango; 50c. Customs House, Retalhuleu; 1q. Departmental Palace, Retalhuleu.

(b) Foreign Air Mail. As T **137** inscr "AEREO EXTERIOR" (10c. and 25c.) or "AEREO INTERNACIONAL".
387 – 1c. brown and sepia 15 15
388 – 2c. black and green 25 30
389 – 3c. green and blue 20 20
390 – 4c. green and brown 20 20
391 – 5c. red and green 40 15
392 – 10c. slate and red . . . . . 1·60 15
393 – 15c. red and blue . . . . . 2·40 15
394 – 20c. yellow and green . . . 75 30
395 – 25c. black and purple . . . 3·75 25
396 – 30c. grey and red . . . . . 1·00 20
397 – 50c. orange and red . . . . 1·50 25
398 – 1q. green and orange . . . 2·75 40
DESIGNS: 1c. Mayan Altar, Aurora Park; 2c. Ministry of Health; 3c. Lake Amatitlan; 4c. Lake Atitlan; 5c. Bridge over Tamazulapa; 10c. National Liberators' Monument; 15c. Palace of the Captains General; 20c. Carmen Hill; 25c. Barrios Square; 30c. Mayan Altar, Archaeological Museum; 50c. Carlos III Fountain; 1q. Antigua.

1939. Obligatory Tax. No. 223 optd **1939.**
399 **92** 1c. olive 25 15

140 National Flower (White Nun)

142 Arms and Map of Guatemala

1939.
400 – ½c. brown and green . . . 20 20
401 **140** 2c. black and blue . . . . 1·00 35
402 – 3c. green and brown . . . 1·60 65
403 – 3c. green and red . . . . 1·60 65
404 **142** 5c. red and blue . . . . . 1·25 1·25
DESIGNS: ½c. Mayan calendar; 3c. Resplendent quetzal.

1939. No. 229 surch **UN CENTAVO.**
405 **95** 1c. on 2c. blue 30 20

1940. Obligatory Tax. No. 223 optd **1940.**
406 **92** 1c. olive 25 15

1940. 50th Anniv of Pan-American Union. (a) Optd **Conmemorativo Union Panamericana 1890-1940.**
407 **92** 1c. olive 25 15

(b) Air. Optd **UNION PANAMERICANA 1890-1940 CORREO AEREO.**
408 – 15c. blue (No. 234) 35 20

1940. Surch with new values.
409 **31** 1c. on 25c. brown 25 15
410 – 5c. on 50c. red (No. 237) 35 30

1941. Obligatory Tax. Optd **1941.**
411 **92** 1c. olive 25 15

1941. Obligatory Tax. Surch **CONSTRUCCION** (twice) and **UN CENTAVO.**
412 **95** 1c. on 2c. blue 25 15

1941. Air. 2nd Pan-American Health Day. Optd **DICIEMBRE 2 1941 SEGUNDO DIA PAN-AMERICANO DE LA SALUD.**
414 – 2c. black and green (No. 388) 55 30

1941. Surch ½ **MEDIO CENTAVO** ½.
415 **31** ½c. on 25c. brown 20 20

1942. Obligatory Tax. Surch **CONSTRUCCION 1942 UN CENTAVO.**
416 **95** 1c. on 2c. blue 25 15

1942. As T **114**, but tablet dated "1942".
416a 3c. green 35 20
416b 3c. blue 35 20

153 Archway between wings of new G.P.O.

154 Guastatoya Vase

1942. Obligatory Tax.
417a **153** 1c. brown 25 15

1942.
418 **154** ½c. brown 20 15
419 – 1c. red 25 15
DESIGN—HORIZ: 1c. Old people's home.

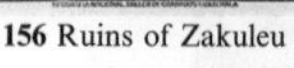

156 Ruins of Zakuleu

157 National Printing Works

158 National Police H.Q.

159 San Carlos Borromeo University, Antigua

1943.
420 **156** ½c. brown (postage) . . . 15 10
421 **157** 2c. red 20 15
422 **158** 10c. mauve (air) 50 15
423 **159** 15c. brown 55 15

160 Don Pedro de Alvarado

161 Archway between wings of new G.P.O.

1943. Air. 400th Anniv of Founding of Antigua.
424 **160** 15c. blue 55 15

1943. Obligatory Tax.
425 **161** 1c. orange 25 15

162 Rafael Maria Landivar

1943. 150th Death Anniv of R. M. Landivar (poet).
426 **162** 5c. blue 35 20

163 National Palace

1944. Inauguration of National Palace.
427 **163** 3c. green (postage) . . . 20 15
444 5c. red (air) 35 15
445 10c. lilac 35 15
446 15c. blue 35 30

1945. Optd **25 de junio de 1944 PALACIO NACIONAL** and bar.
428 **163** 3c. blue 35 15

1945. Air. Optd **PALACIO NACIONAL** and bar.
429 **163** 5c. red 30 20

165 Archway between wings of new G.P.O.

166 Allegory of the Revolution

1945. Obligatory Tax.
430 **165** 1c. orange 25 15
479 1c. blue 25 15

1945. Revolution of 20 October 1944.
431 **166** 3c. blue (postage) 15 15
432 5c. red (air) 45 30
433 6c. green 45 30
434 10c. violet 45 30
435 15c. blue 45 30

1945. Air. Book Fair. No. 389 surch **1945 FERIA DEL LIBRO 2½ CENTAVOS.**
436 2½c. on 3c. green and blue . . 1·40 1·40

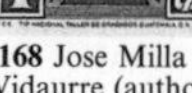

168 Jose Milla y Vidaurre (author)

169 Archbishop Pavo Enriquez de Rivera

170 Torch

1945.
437 **168** 1c. green (postage) . . . 15 15
438 **169** 2c. violet 15 15
439 5c. red (air) 35 20
678 5c. olive 20 10
679 5c. blue 20 10
680 5c. green 20 10
681 5c. orange 20 10
682 5c. violet 20 10
683 5c. grey 20 10
440 **168** 7½c. purple 50 90
441 7½c. blue 30 30
For stamps as Type **169** but dated "1660 1951" see Nos. 523/27.

1945. 1st Anniv of Revolution of 20 October 1944.
442 **170** 3c. blue (postage) 20 15
443 5c. mauve (air) 45 30

171 Jose Batres y Montufar (military leader and writer)

174 Rowland Hill

1945.
447 **171** ½c. brown (postage) . . . 25 20
448 3c. blue 30 20
449 3c. green 35 30
450 – 10c. green (air) 50 25
DESIGN—HORIZ: 10c. Montufar.

1946. Centenary of First Postage Stamps.
451 – 1c. olive & violet (postage) 30 25
452 **174** 5c. brown and grey (air) 25 20
453 – 15c. blue, green and red 35 35
DESIGNS: 1c. U.P.U. Monument, Berne; 15c. Hemispheres and quetzal.

175 Signing the Declaration of Independence

176 Franklin D. Roosevelt

1946. Air. 125th Anniv of Independence.
454 **175** 5c. red 15 10
455 6c. brown 20 15
456 10c. violet 25 20
457 20c. blue 50 45

1947. Air. 2nd Anniv of Revolution of 20 October 1944. As T **170** but inscr "1944 1946" instead of "1944 1945" and "II" for "I".
458 1c. green 20 15
459 2c. red 20 15

460		3c. violet	20	15
461		5c. blue	25	15

1947. Air.

462	**176**	5c. red	20	15
463		6c. blue	25	15
464		10c. blue	55	20
465		30c. black	1·75	1·40
466		50c. violet	1·75	1·75
467		1q. green	2·75	2·75

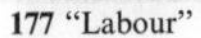
177 "Labour"

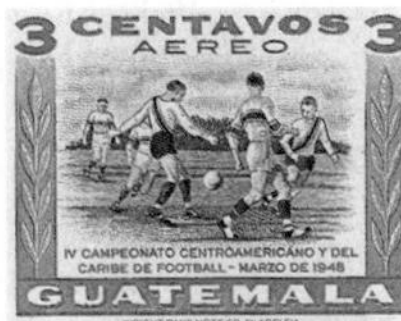
180 Football Match

1948. Labour Day and 1st Anniv of Adoption of Labour Code.

468	**177**	1c. green	20	15
469		2c. purple	20	15
470		3c. blue	20	15
471		5c. red	20	15

1948. Optd **1948**.

472	**142**	5c. red and blue	20	15

1948. Air. Optd **1948 AEREO**.

473	**142**	5c. red and blue	25	20

1948. Air. 4th Central American and Caribbean Football Championship Games.

474	**180**	3c. black and red	40	20
475		5c. black and green	50	30
476		10c. black and mauve	60	70
477		30c. black and blue	2·00	2·40
478		50c. black and yellow	2·75	2·75

181 Fray Bartolome de Las Casas and Indian

182 Seal of University of Guatemala

1949. Fray Bartolome de Las Casas ("Apostle of the Indians").

480	**181**	½c. red	20	15
661		½c. blue	15	10
481		1c. brown	20	15
662		1c. violet	15	10
663		2c. green	15	10
664		3c. red	15	10
484		4c. blue	30	20
665a		4c. brown	10	10

1949. Air. Latin-American Universities' Congress.

485	**182**	3c. blue and red	35	35
486		10c. blue and green	75	55
487		50c. blue and yellow	1·90	2·10

183 Gathering Coffee

184 Tecum Uman Monument

1950. Tourist Propaganda. (a) Postage.

488	**183**	½c. olive, blue and pink	30	15
489	–	½c. blue and brown	20	15
490	–	1c. olive, brown and yellow	30	15
491	–	1c. green and orange	20	15
492	–	2c. blue, green and red	30	15
493	–	2c. brown and red	20	15
494	–	3c. brown, blue and violet	30	15
495	–	6c. violet, orange & green	55	15

DESIGNS—As Type **183**: ½c. (No. 489), 3c. Cutting sugar canes; 1c. (No. 490), 2c. (No. 493), Agricultural colony; 1c. (No. 491), 2c. (No. 492), Banana trees; 6c. International Bridge.

(b) Air. Multicoloured centres.

496	–	3c. red	55	15
497	**184**	5c. lake	55	15
498	–	8c. black	30	20
499	–	13c. brown	60	35
500	–	35c. violet	1·50	1·75

DESIGNS—As Type **184**—HORIZ: 3c. Lake Atitlan; 8c. San Cristobal Church; 35c. Momostenango Cliffs. VERT: 13c. Weaver.

185 Footballers

186 Ministry of Health Badge

187 Nursing School

1950. Air. 6th Central American and Caribbean Games. Inscr "VI JUEGOS DEPORTIVOS 1950".

501	**185**	1c. black and violet	35	15
502	–	3c. black and red	40	15
503	–	4c. black and brown	50	20
504	–	8c. black and purple	60	20
505	–	35c. black and blue	1·40	1·90
506	–	65c. green	3·00	3·00

DESIGNS—HORIZ: 4c. Pole vaulting; 35c. Diving; 65c. Stadium. VERT: 3c. Runners; 8c. Tennis.

1950. Social Assistance and Public Health Fund.

507	**186**	1c. blue and red (postage)	20	15
508	–	3c. red and green (Nurse)	35	20
509	–	5c. brown and blue (Map)	55	35
511	–	5c. red, green & violet (air)	25	20
512	**187**	10c. green and brown	40	35
513	–	50c. purple, green and red	1·40	1·60
514	–	1q. olive, green and yellow	1·60	1·75

DESIGNS—As Type **187**: 5c. Nurse; 50c., 1q. Zacapa and Roosevelt Hospitals.

1951. No. E479 without surcharge for use as ordinary postage.

517	E **181**	4c. black and green	35	30

188 School

1951. Aerial views of schools as T **188**.

519	**188**	½c. brown and violet	20	15
520	–	1c. green and lake	20	15
521	**188**	2c. brown and blue	20	20
522	–	4c. purple and black	30	20

1952. As No. 438 but dated "1660 1951" below portrait.

523	**169**	½c. violet	15	10
524		1c. red	15	10
525		2c. green	15	10
526		4c. orange	20	15
527		4c. blue	15	10

189 Ceremonial Axehead

190 Flag and Constitution

1953. Air.

528	**189**	3c. drab and blue	20	20
529		5c. brown and slate	20	20
530		10c. slate and violet	45	35

1953. Air. Presidential Succession, 1951.

531	**190**	1c. multicoloured	30	20
532		2c. multicoloured	35	30
533		4c. multicoloured	45	35

191 R. Alvarez Ovalle (music), J. J. Palma (words)

1953. National Anthem.

534	**191**	½c. grey and violet	35	20
535		1c. brown and grey	45	20
536		2c. olive and brown	45	25
537		3c. olive and blue	45	25

192 "Work and Play"

193 Horse Racing

1953. Air. National Fair. Inscr "FERIA NACIONAL".

538	–	1c. red and blue	20	15
539	–	4c. green and orange	90	25
540	**192**	5c. brown and green	55	30
541	**193**	15c. lilac and brown	85	75
542	–	20c. blue and red	75	70
543	–	30c. blue and sepia	85	1·00
544	–	50c. black and violet	1·00	1·00
545	–	65c. green and blue	1·75	1·90
546	–	1q. green and red	25·00	15·00

DESIGNS—VERT: 1c. National dance; 4c. National flower (white nun); 30c. Picture and corn cob; 1q. Resplendent quetzal. HORIZ: 20c. Ruins of Zakuleu; 50c. Champion bull; 65c. Cycle-racing.

194 Indian Warrior

196 Flags of Guatemala and ODECA

1954. Air. National Revolutionary Army Commemoration.

547	**194**	1c. red	35	35
548		2c. blue	35	35
549		4c. green	35	35
550		5c. turquoise	55	45
551		6c. orange	55	45
552		10c. violet	70	55
553		20c. sepia	1·90	2·00

1954. As T **5** but inscr "UNION POSTAL UNIVERSAL GUATEMALA" around oval.

554		1c. blue	90	35
1222		1c. green	25	10
555		2c. violet	45	25
556		2c. brown	60	25
1222a		2c. blue	25	10
557		3c. red	60	25
558		3c. blue	60	25
1225		3c. brown	25	10
1226		3c. green	25	10
1227		3c. orange	25	10
559		4c. orange	1·00	25
560		4c. violet	90	25
1228		4c. brown	25	10
561		5c. brown	1·50	35
562		5c. red	1·50	35
563		5c. green	1·00	35
564		5c. grey	1·75	35
1228a		5c. mauve	25	10
565		6c. green	1·50	55
1229		6c. blue	25	10

1954. Air. 3rd Anniv of Organization of Central American States.

566	**196**	1c. multicoloured	20	15
567		2c. multicoloured	20	15
568		4c. multicoloured	30	20

197 Goalkeeper

198 Red Cross and Globe

1955. Golden Jubilee of Football in Guatemala. Inscr "1902–1952".

569	–	4c. violet (Camposeco)	70	45
570	–	4c. red (Camposeco)	70	45
571	–	4c. green (Camposeco)	70	45
572	–	10c. green (Matheu)	2·00	55
573	**197**	15c. blue	2·00	1·50

1956. Red Cross. Inscr "CONMEMORATIVAS CRUZ ROJA".

574	**198**	1c. red & brown (postage)	20	20
575	–	3c. red and green	20	20
576	–	4c. red and black	25	20
577	–	5c.+15c. red and blue	60	90
578	–	15c.+50c. red and lilac	1·40	1·75
579	**198**	25c.+50c. red and blue	1·40	1·75
580	–	35c.+1q. grn & red (air)	3·50	3·75
581	–	50c.+1q. red and blue	3·50	3·75
582	–	1q.+1q. red and green	3·50	3·75

DESIGNS: 3c., 15c. Telephone and red cross; 4c., 5c. Nurse, patient and red cross; 35c. Red Cross ambulance; 50c. Nurse and hospital; 1q. Red Cross nurse.

199 Road Map of Guatemala

200 Maya Warrior

1956. Revolution of 1954–55. Inscr "LIBERACION 1954-55".

583	–	½c. violet (postage)	15	10
584	**199**	1c. green	15	10
585	–	3c. sepia	15	10
586	**200**	2c. multicoloured (air)	20	15
587	–	4c. black and red	20	15
588	–	5c. brown and blue	30	30
589	–	6c. blue and sepia	20	20
590	–	20c. brown, blue and violet	1·00	1·00
591	–	30c. olive and blue	1·75	1·00
592	–	65c. green and brown	1·50	1·75
593	–	1q. multicoloured	2·25	2·40
594	–	5q. brown, blue and green	9·00	9·50

DESIGNS: ½c. Liberation dagger symbol; 3c. Oil production; 4c. Family; 5c. Sword smashing Communist emblems; 6c. Hands holding map and cogwheel; 20c. Martyrs' Monument; 30c. Champerico Port; 65c. Telecommunications symbols; 1q. Flags of ODECA countries; 5q. Pres. Armas.

201 Rotary Emblem and Road Map

203 Esquipulas Cathedral and "Black Christ"

1956. Air. 50th Anniv of Rotary International.

595	**201**	4c. bistre and blue	35	30
596		6c. bistre and green	35	30
597		35c. bistre and violet	1·00	1·40

1957. Air. Red Cross Fund. Nos. 577/9 optd **AEREO-1957** and ornaments.

598	–	5c.+15c. red and blue	4·00	4·50
599	–	15c.+50c. red and lilac	4·00	4·50
600	**198**	25c.+50c. red and blue	4·00	4·50

1957. Esquipulas Highway Fund. Inscr "PRO-CARRETERA ESQUIPULAS JUNIO 1957".

601	**203**	1½c.+½c. violet and brown (postage)	70	45
602	–	10c.+1q. brown and green (air)	4·00	4·50
603	–	15c.+1q. green and sepia	4·00	4·50
604	–	20c.+1q. slate and brown	4·00	4·50
605	–	25c.+1q. red and lilac	4·00	4·50

DESIGNS—HORIZ: 10c. Esquipulas Cathedral. VERT: 15c. Cathedral and "Black Christ"; 20c. Map of Guatemala and "Black Christ"; 25c. Bishop of Esquipulas.

204 Red Cross, Map and Resplendent Quetzal

1958. Air. Red Cross.

606	**204**	1c. multicoloured	55	30
607	–	2c. red, brown and blue	35	15
608	–	3c. brown, red and blue	35	15
609	–	4c. red, green and brown	35	15

DESIGNS—VERT: 2c. J. R. Angulo, Mother and Child. HORIZ: 3c. P. de Bethancourt and Invalid; 4c. R. Ayau and Red Cross.

1959. Birth Centenary of R. A. Ovalle (composer of National Anthem). Optd **1858 1958 CENTENARIO**.

610	**191**	½c. grey and violet	30	30

1959. Air. Pres. Castillo Armas Commem. As No. 594 but inscr "LIBERACION 3 DE JULIO DE 1954", etc. Centre in blue and yellow. Frame colours given.

615		1c. black	15	15
616		2c. red	15	15
617		4c. brown	15	15
618		6c. green	20	15
619		10c. violet	35	25
620		20c. green	1·00	65
621		35c. grey	1·75	95

1959. Air. United Nations. Optd **HOMENAJE A LAS NACIONES UNIDAS**.

622	**168**	7½c. blue	1·10	1·10

207 Caravel of 1532 and freighter "Quetzaltenango"

1959. Air. Central American Merchant Marine Commemoration.
623 **207** 6c. blue and red 80 15

1959. Air. Guatemala's Claim to Belize (British Honduras). As No. 509 optd **BELICE ES NUESTRO** and **AEREO**.
624 5c. brown and blue 35 20

1959. Air. Centenary of First Export of Coffee. No. 589 optd **1859 CENTENARIO PRIMERA EXPORTACION DE CAFE 1959**.
625 6c. blue and sepia 55 20

210 Pres. and Senora Morales

1959. Air. Visit of President of Honduras.
626 **210** 6c. brown 20 15

211 Red Cross Shield

1960. Red Cross Commemoration. Cross in red.
627 **211** 1c.+1c. blue and brown (postage) 30 20
628 – 3c.+3c. blue and lilac . . 30 20
629 **211** 4c.+4c. blue and black . . 30 25
630 – 5c.+5c. blue, pink and red (air) . . . . 1·40 1·50
631 – 6c.+6c. green and red . . 1·40 1·50
632 – 10c.+10c. pink, blue and deep blue . . . . . . 1·40 1·50
633 – 15c.+15c. red, blue and brown . . . . 1·40 1·50
634 – 20c.+20c. green, pink and purple . . . . 1·40 1·50
635 – 25c.+25c. pink, blue and grey . . . . 1·40 1·50
636 – 30c.+30c. multicoloured 1·40 1·50
DESIGNS—3c., 5c. Wounded soldier at Solferino; 6c., 20c. Houses and debris afloat on flood waters; 10c., 25c. Earth, Moon and planets; 15c., 30c. Red Cross H.Q., Guatemala City.

1960. Air. World Refugee Year. Nos. 606/9 optd **ANO MUNDIAL DE REFUGIADOS** or surch also.
637 1c. multicoloured . . . . . . 2·10 1·75
638 2c. red, brown and blue . . . 90 70
639 3c. brown, red and blue . . . 90 70
640 4c. red, green and brown . . . 90 70
641 6c. on 1c. multicoloured . . . 5·00 2·50
642 7c. on 2c. red, brown and blue . . . . 1·50 1·25
643 10c. on 3c. brown, red & blue 2·50 2·75
644 20c. on 4c. red, green & brown . . . . 2·75 2·75

1960. Air. Founding of City of Melchor de Mencos. No. 589 optd **Fundacion de la cuidad Melchor de Mencos 30-IV-1960**.
645 6c. blue and sepia . . . . . 1·10 1·10

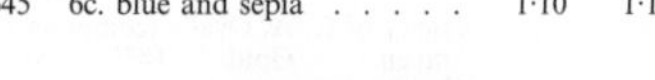

213 Abraham Lincoln

1960. Air. 150th Birth Anniv of Abraham Lincoln.
646 **213** 5c. blue 30 20
647 30c. violet . . . . 70 1·00
648 50c. slate . . . . 3·50 4·00

214 UNESCO Headquarters, Paris

1960. Air. Inauguration of UNESCO. Headquarters Building, Paris (1958).
649 **214** 5c. violet and mauve . . . 15 15
650 6c. sepia and blue 20 15
651 8c. red and green 35 20
652 20c. blue and brown . . . 85 90

1961. Air. Red Cross. Nos. 606/9 optd **MAYO DE 1960**.
653 1c. multicoloured . . . . . 1·25 75
654 2c. red, brown and blue . . . 45 40
655 3c. brown, red and blue . . . 45 40
656 4c. red, green and brown . . 45 40

216 Romulus, Remus and Wolf

217 Independence Ceremony

1961. Plaza Italia Inauguration.
657 **216** 3c. blue 15 15

1962. Air. 140th Anniv of Independence.
658 **217** 4c. sepia 15 15
659 5c. blue 20 15
660 15c. violet 70 35

1962. Air. Malaria Eradication. Optd **1962 EL MUNDO UNIDO CONTRA LA MALARIA**.
666 **214** 6c. sepia and blue 55 85

219 Dr. Jose Luna

1962. Air. Guatemalan Doctors.
667 **219** 1c. violet and olive . . . 35 15
668 – 4c. green and yellow . . . 35 15
669 – 5c. brown and blue . . . 35 15
670 – 6c. black and salmon . . 35 15
671 – 10c. brown and green . . 55 20
672 – 20c. blue and mauve . . . 70 45
DOCTORS: 4c. R. Robles; 5c. N. Esparragoza; 6c. J. Ortega; 10c. D. Gonzalez; 20c. J. Flores.

1962. Air. Pres. Ydigoras's Tour of Central America. No. 589 optd **PRESIDENTE YDIGORAS FUENTES RECORRE POR TIERRA CENTRO AMERICA 14 A 20 DIC. 1962**.
673 6c. blue and sepia 60 55

1963. Air. New ODECA Charter Commemoration. Optd **CONMEMORACION FIRMA NUEVA CARTA ODECA.—1962**.
674 **214** 6c. sepia and blue 30 15
675 8c. red and green 35 15

222 Girl with Basket of Fruit on head

224 Arms

1963. Air. National Fair, 1960.
676 **222** 1c. multicoloured 15 10

1963. Air. Presidential Meeting. No. 589 with 11-line opt starting **REUNION PRESIDENTES: KENNEDY**.
677 6c. blue and sepia . . . . . 2·40 1·60

1963.
684 **224** 10c. red 35 15
685 10c. black 30 15
686 10c. brown 30 15
687 20c. violet 55 20
688 20c. blue 55 20

225 Harvester (after "The Reaper", Mathieson)

226 Ceiba (national tree)

1963. Air. Freedom from Hunger.
689 **225** 5c. turquoise 20 15
690 10c. blue 35 20

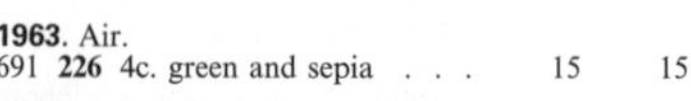

1963. Air.
691 **226** 4c. green and sepia . . . 15 15

227 Pedro Bethancourt tending sick man

228 Patzun Palace

1964. Campaign for Canonization of Pedro Bethancourt.
692 **227** 2½c. brown (postage) . . 15 10
693 2½c. blue (air) 10 10
694 3c. orange 10 10
695 4c. violet 15 10
696 5c. green 20 10

1964. Air. Guatemalan Palaces.
697 **228** 1c. brown and red 15 10
698 – 3c. green and mauve . . . 20 10
699 – 4c. lake and blue 20 15
700 – 5c. blue and brown . . . 25 15
701 – 6c. blue and green 25 15
PALACES: 3c. Coban; 4c. Retalhuleu; 5c. San Marcos; 6c. Los Capitanes Generales.

229 Municipal Building

1964. Air. New Buildings. (a) As T **229**.
702 **229** 3c. brown and blue . . . 15 15
703 – 4c. blue and brown . . . 20 15
DESIGN: 4c. Social Security Building.

(b) Designs as Nos. 702/3 but different style frame and inscr, and new designs.
704 – 3c. green (As No. 703) . . 20 10
705 – 4c. slate 20 10
706 **229** 7c. blue 25 15
707 – 7c. bistre 25 15
DESIGNS: 4c. University Rectory; 7c. (No. 707), Engineering Faculty.

1964. Air. Olympic Games, Tokyo. Optd with Olympic rings and **OLIMPIADAS TOKIO-1964**.
708 **204** 1c. . . . . 1·50 2·00
709 – 2c. (No. 607) 75 75
710 – 3c. (No. 608) 75 75
711 – 4c. (No. 609) 75 75

1964. Air. New York World's Fair. Optd **FERIA MUNDIAL DE NEW YORK**.
712 **204** 1c. . . . . 1·40 1·10
713 – 2c. (No. 607) 50 50
714 – 3c. (No. 608) 50 50
715 – 4c. (No. 609) 50 50

1964. Air. Surch **HABILITADA 1964** and value.
716 **204** 7c. on 1c. 75 45
717 – 9c. on 2c. (No. 607) . . . 40 35
718 – 13c. on 3c. (No. 608) . . 45 45
719 – 21c. on 4c. (No. 609) . . 75 75

1964. Air. 8th Cycle Race. Optd **VIII VUELTA CICLISTICA**.
720 **204** 1c. . . . . 1·40 1·40
721 – 2c. (No. 607) 70 70
722 – 3c. (No. 608) 70 70
723 – 4c. (No. 609) . . . . . . 70 1·00

234 Pres. Kennedy

1964. Air. Pres. Kennedy Commemoration.
724 **234** 1c. violet 70 55
725 2c. green 70 55
726 3c. brown 70 55
727 7c. blue 70 55
728 50c. green . . . . 4·00 4·25

235 Centenary Emblem

237 Bishop F. Marroquin

1964. Air. Red Cross Centenary. Emblem in silver and red.
730 **235** 7c. blue 55 35
731 9c. orange 55 35
732 13c. violet 85 35
733 21c. green 50 70
734 35c. brown . . . . 1·00 1·00
735 1q. bistre . . . . 1·60 2·00

1964. 15th Anniv (1963) of International Society of Guatemala Collectors. No. 559 optd **HOMENAJE A LA "I.S.G.C." 1948–1963**.
736 4c. orange 50 30

1985. Air. 400th Death Anniv of Bishop Marroquin.
737 **237** 4c. brown and purple . . 15 10
738 7c. sepia and grey 25 15
739 9c. black and blue 30 15

1965. Air. Optd **AYUDENOS MAYO 1965**. Emblem in silver and red.
740 **235** 7c. blue 35 30
741 9c. orange 45 35
742 13c. violet 55 45
743 21c. green 70 60
744 35c. brown 70 95

239 Scout Badge

240 Flags

1966. Air. 5th Regional Scout Training Conference, Guatemala City. Multicoloured.
745 5c. Type **239** 35 15
746 9c. Scouts by campfire . . . 45 25
747 10c. Scout carrying torch and flag 55 35
748 15c. Scout saluting 70 55
749 20c. Lord Baden-Powell . . . 90 90

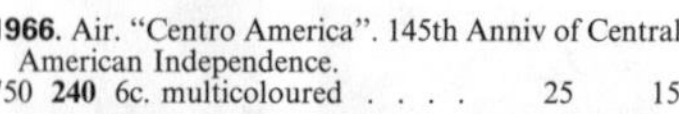

1966. Air. "Centro America". 145th Anniv of Central American Independence.
750 **240** 6c. multicoloured 25 15

241 Nefertari's Temple, Abu Simbel

242 Arms

1966. Air. Nubian Monuments Preservation.
751 **241** 21c. violet and bistre . . 55 35

1966. Air.
752 **242** 5c. orange 20 10
753 5c. green 20 10
754 5c. grey 20 10
755 5c. violet 20 10
756 5c. blue 20 10
757 5c. deep blue 20 10
758 5c. violet 20 10
759 5c. green 15 10
760 5c. lake 15 10
761 5c. green on yellow 15 10

243 Mgr. M. Rossell y Arellano

244 Mario M. Montenegro (revolutionary)

1966. Air. Monseigneur Rossell Commem.

765 **243** 1c. violet 20 15
766 2c. green 25 10
767 3c. sepia 25 15
768 7c. blue 35 25
769 50c. slate . . . . 95 1·10

1966. Air. Montenegro Commemoration.

770 **244** 2c. red 15 10
771 3c. orange 20 15
772 4c. red 25 15
773 5c. grey 35 15
774 5c. blue 35 15
775 5c. green 35 15
776 5c. black 35 15

245 Morning Glory

1967. Air. Flowers. Multicoloured.

777 4c. Type **245** 25 15
778 8c. "Bird of Paradise" (horiz) 25 15
779 10c. "White Nun" orchid (national flower) (horiz) . . 35 25
780 20c. "Nymphs of Amatitlan" 60 35

246 Institute Emblem

1967. Air. 8th General Assembly of Pan-American Geographical and Historical Institute (1965).

781 **246** 4c. purple, black & brown 20 15
782 5c. blue, black and bistre 35 15
783 7c. blue, black and yellow 55 15

247 Map of Guatemala and British Honduras

1967. Guatemala's Claim to British Honduras.

784 **247** 4c. blue, red and green . . 15 10
785 5c. blue, red and yellow 20 10
786 6c. blue, grey and orange 20 15

1967. Air. Guatemalan Victory in "Norceca" Football Games. No. 704 optd **GUATEMALA CAMPEON III Norceca Foot-Ball** and football motif.

787 3c. green 35 30

1967. Air. American Heads of State Meeting, Punta del Este. No. 705 optd **REUNION JEFES DE ESTADO AMERICANO, PUNTA DEL ESTE** etc.

788 4c. slate 70 55

250 "Peace and Progress"

1967. Air. International Co-operation.

789 **250** 7c. multicoloured 35 15
790 21c. multicoloured 55 35

251 Yurrita Church

1967. Air. Religion in Guatemala.

791 **251** 1c. brown, green and blue 20 10
792 – 2c. brown, pur & salmon 25 10
793 – 3c. indigo, red and blue 25 10
794 – 4c. green, purple & salmon 25 10
795 – 5c. brown, purple & green 25 10
796 – 7c. black, blue and mauve 35 15
797 – 10c. blue, violet and yellow 55 20

DESIGNS—HORIZ: 2c. Santo Domingo Church; 3c. San Francisco Church; 7c. Mercy Church, Antigua; 10c. Metropolitan Cathedral. VERT: 4c. Antonio Jose de Irisarri; 5c. Church of the Recollection.

252 Lincoln

1967. Air. Death Centenary (1965) of Abraham Lincoln.

798 **252** 7c. red and blue 35 20
799 9c. black and green . . . 45 25
800 11c. black and brown . . 45 25
801 15c. red and blue 45 35
802 30c. green and purple . . 1·00 1·10

1967. Air. 8th Central American Scout Camporee. Nos. 745/9 optd **VIII Camporee Scout Centroamericano Diciembre 1-8/1967**.

803 5c. Type **239** 35 35
804 9c. Scouts by campfire . . . 55 55
805 10c. Scout carrying torch and flag 70 70
806 15c. Scout saluting 70 70
807 20c. Lord Baden-Powell . . . 90 90

1967. Air. Award of Nobel Prize for Literature to Miguel Angel Asturias (1st issue). Nos. 694/5 optd **"Premio Nobel de Literatura - 10 diciembre 1967 - Miguel Angel Asturias"**.

808 **227** 3c. orange 35 30
809 – 4c. violet 35 30

See also No. 838.

255 UNESCO Emblem and Children

1967. Air. 20th Anniv (1966) of UNESCO.

810 **255** 4c. green 15 10
811 5c. blue 20 15
812 7c. grey 25 15
813 21c. purple 60 60

256 Institute Emblem

1967. Air. 25th Anniv of Inter-American Institute of Agricultural Sciences.

814 **256** 9c. black and green . . . 45 45
815 25c. red and brown . . . 95 95
816 1q. ultramarine and blue 2·40 2·40

1968. Air. 3rd Meeting of Central American Presidents. Optd **III REUNION DE PRESIDENTES Nov. 15-18, 1967**.

817 **204** 1c. (No. 606) . . . . . . 1·90 1·50
819 – 2c. (No. 607) 70 70
821 – 3c. (No. 608) 70 70
823 **235** 7c. (No. 730) 70 70
824 9c. (No. 731) 70 90
825 13c. (No. 732) 95 90
826 21c. (No. 733) . . . . . 1·40 70
827 35c. (No. 734) . . . . . 1·10 1·10

258 "Madonna of the Choir"

260 Miguel Angel Asturias

1968. Air. 400th Anniv of "Madonna of the Choir".

828a **258** 4c. blue 10 10
829 7c. slate 35 15
830 9c. green 55 15
830a 9c. lilac 25 10
831 10c. red 70 15
832 10c. grey 45 15
832a 10c. blue 25 10
833 1q. purple . . . . 2·40 2·00
834 1q. yellow . . . . 2·40 2·00

1968. Air. 11th Cycle Race. Nos. 784/6 optd **AEREO XI VUELTA CICLISTICA 1967**.

835 **247** 4c. blue, red and green . . 55 55
836 5c. blue, red and yellow 55 55
837 6c. blue, grey and orange 45 45

1968. Air. Award of Nobel Prize for Literature to Miguel Angel Asturias.

838 **260** 20c. blue 70 35

1968. Air. Campaign for Conservation of the Forests. No. 789 optd **AYUDA A CONSERVAR LOS BOSQUES.–1968.**

839 **250** 7c. multicoloured 35 15

1968. Air. Human Rights Year. No. 626 optd **1968.– ANO INTERNACIONAL DERECHOS HUMANOS.–ONU.**

840 **210** 6c. brown 55 30

1968. Air. Nahakin Scientific Expedition. No. 589 optd **Expedicion Cientifica** etc.

841 6c. blue and sepia 30 20

264 "Visit Guatemala"

265 Mayan Ball Game Ring and Resplendent Quetzal

1968. Air. Tourism.

842 **264** 10c. red and green 60 25
843 20c. red and black 85 50
844 50c. blue and red . . . . 1·25 1·25

1968. Olympic Games, Mexico. Quetzal in green and red.

845 **265** 1c. black 55 20
850 1c. slate 55 20
846 5c. yellow 70 35
851 5c. pink 40 35
852 5c. brown 40 35
853 5c. blue 40 35
847 8c. orange 85 50
848 15c. blue . . . . 1·60 70
849 30c. violet . . . . 2·75 2·25

1968. Air. 20th Anniv of Federation of Central American Universities. No. 705 optd **CONFEDERACION DE UNIVERSIDADES CENTROAMERICANAS 1948 1968.**

854 4c. slate 30 15

267 Presidents Gustavo Diaz Ordaz and Julio Cesar Mendez Montenegro

1968. Air. Exchange Visits of Mexican and Guatemalan Presidents.

855 **267** 5c. multicoloured 15 15
856 10c. blue and ochre . . . 35 20
857 25c. blue and ochre . . . 55 50

268 I.T.U. Emblem and Symbols

269 Young Girl and Poinsettia

1968. Air. Centenary (1965) of I.T.U.

858 **268** 7c. blue 20 15
859 15c. black and green . . . 35 15
859a 15c. brown and orange 55 15
860 21c. purple 55 35
861 35c. red and green . . . 70 35
862 75c. green and red . . . 1·40 1·40
863 3q. brown and red . . . 4·50 4·50

1969. Help for Abandoned Children.

864 **269** $2\frac{1}{2}$c. ochre, red and green 20 10
865 $2\frac{1}{2}$c. orange, red and green 20 10
866 5c. black, red and green 30 10
867 21c. violet, red and green 65 55

1969. Air. Nos. 845/9 optd **AEREO** and motifs. Quetzal in green and red.

868 **265** 1c. black 95 40
869 5c. yellow . . . . 1·25 60
870 8c. orange . . . . 1·00 1·10
871 15c. blue . . . . 1·25 1·25
872 30c. violet . . . . 1·75 1·25

271 Dante

273 "Apollo 11" and Moon Landing

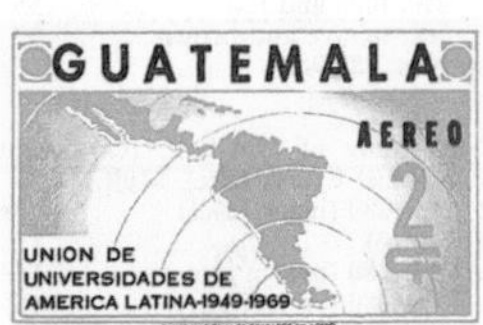

272 Map of Central and South America

1969. Air. 700th Birth Anniv (1965) of Dante.

873 **271** 7c. blue and plum 20 10
874 10c. blue 25 10
875 20c. green 35 15
876 21c. slate and brown . . . 70 25
877 35c. violet and green . . . 1·00 55

1969. Air. 20th Anniv of Latin-American Universities Union.

878 **272** 2c. mauve and black . . . 15 10
879 – 9c. black and grey 25 15

DESIGN: (26 × 27 mm) 9c. University seal.

1969. Air. 1st Man on the Moon.

881 **273** 50c. black and purple . . 1·40 1·40
882 1q. black and blue . . . 2·40 2·50

1970. 50th Anniv of Int Labour Organization. Nos. 847/8 optd **Cincuentenario O.I.T.** and ornaments.

884 **265** 8c. orange, green and red 50 20
886 15c. blue, green and red 75 30

275 Lake Atitlan

1970. Air. Conservation of Atitlan Grebes. Multicoloured.

888 4c. Type **275** 15 15
889 9c. Family of Atitlan Grebes 3·50 55
890 20c. Young grebe in nest (vert) . . . . 5·00 1·40

276 Dr. V. M. Calderon

1970. Air. 1st Death Anniv of Dr. Victor M. Calderon (medical scientist).
892 **276** 1c. black and blue 15 10
893 2c. black and green . . . 15 10
894 9c. black and yellow . . . 30 15

277 Hand holding Bible

280 Maya Indians and C.A.R.E. Package

279 Arms and Newspaper

1970. Air. 400th Anniv of Spanish Bible.
895 **277** 5c. multicoloured 15 10

1971. Air. Surch **VALE Q0.50.**
896 **268** 50c. on 3q. brown and red . . . . 1·25 1·25

1971. Air. Stamp Centenary (1st issue) and Centenary of Newspaper "Gaceta de Guatemala".
897 **279** 2c. blue and red 10 10
899b 5c. brown and red . . . 10 10
899 25c. blue and red . . . 55 35
899c 50c. mauve and brown 90 35
See also Nos. 988/9d.

1971. 25th Anniv of C.A.R.E. (Co-operative for American Relief Everywhere). Mult.
900 1c. Type **280** (black inscr) (postage) 15 10
901 1c. Type **280** (brown inscr) 15 10
902 1c. Type **280** (violet inscr) . . 15 10
903 2c. Maya porter and C.A.R.E. parcel (air) . . . 15 15
904 5c. Two Maya warriors and parcel 20 20
905 10c. C.A.R.E. parcel within Maya border 35 20
SIZES: 2c. (36 × 30 mm); 50c. (46 × 27 mm); 10c. (28 × 31 mm).

282 J. Rufino Barrios, M. Garcia Granados and Emblems

1971. Air. Centenary of Liberal Reforms.
909 **282** 2c. multicoloured 60 15
910 10c. multicoloured . . . . 1·60 30
911 50c. multicoloured . . . . 4·75 3·75
912 1q. multicoloured . . . . 9·50 7·50

283 J. A. Chavarry Arrue (stamp engraver) and Leon Bilak (philatelist)

1971. Air. "Homage to Philately".
913 **283** 1c. black and green . . . 10 10
914 2c. black and brown . . . 15 10
915 5c. black and orange . . 15 15

1971. Air. "INTERFER 71" Int Fair, Guatemala. Optd **FERIA INTERNACIONAL "INTERFER-71" 30 Oct. al 21 Nov.**
916 **207** 6c. blue and red 20 15

285 Flag and Map

286 Maya Statue and UNICEF Emblem

1971. Air. 150th Anniv of Central American Independence.
917 **285** 1c. blue, black and lilac 10 10
918 3c. blue, brown and pink 10 10
919 5c. blue, brown & orange 15 10
920 9c. blue, black and green 25 15

1971. Air. 25th Anniv of UNICEF.
921 **286** 1c. green 10 10
921a 2c. purple 15 10
922 50c. purple . . . . . . 1·10 1·10
923 1q. blue . . . . 2·00 2·00

287 Boeing "Peashooter" and North American P-51 Mustang

1972. Air. 50th Anniv of Guatemala Air Force.
924 **287** 5c. blue and brown . . . 20 10
925 – 10c. blue 50 20
DESIGN—56 × 32 mm: 10c. Bleriot XI airplane.

289 Ruins of Capuchin Monastery

1972. Air. Tourism. Ruins of Antigua.
927 **289** 1c. blue and light blue . . 20 10
928 A 1c. blue and light blue . . 20 10
929 B 1c. blue and light blue . . 20 10
930 C 1c. blue and light blue . . 20 10
931 D 1c. blue and light blue . . 20 10
932 E 1c. blue and light blue . . 20 10
933 **289** 2c. black and brown . . . 15 10
934 A 2c. black and brown . . . 15 10
935 B 2c. black and brown . . . 15 10
936 C 2c. black and brown . . . 15 10
937 D 2c. black and brown . . . 15 10
938 E 2c. black and brown . . . 15 10
939 **289** 2½c. black, mauve & silver 35 10
940 A 2½c. black, mauve & silver 35 10
941 B 2½c. black, mauve & silver 35 10
942 C 2½c. black, mauve & silver 35 10
943 D 2½c. black, mauve & silver 35 10
944 E 2½c. black, mauve & silver 35 10
945 **289** 5c. black, blue and orange 70 15
946 A 5c. black, blue and orange 70 15
947 B 5c. black, blue and orange 70 15
948 C 5c. black, blue and orange 70 15
949 D 5c. black, blue and orange 70 15
950 E 5c. black, blue and orange 70 15
951 **289** 20c. black and yellow . . 55 35
952 A 20c. black and yellow . . 55 35
953 B 20c. black and yellow . . 55 35
954 C 20c. black and yellow . . 55 35
955 D 20c. black and yellow . . 55 35
956 E 20c. black and yellow . . 55 35
957 **289** 1q. lt blue, red and blue 2·40 1·75
958 A 1q. lt blue, red and blue 2·40 1·75
959 B 1q. lt blue, red and blue 2·40 1·75
960 C 1q. lt blue, red and blue 2·40 1·75
961 D 1q. lt blue, red and blue 2·40 1·75
962 E 1q. lt blue, red and blue 2·40 1·75
DESIGNS: A, "La Recoleccion" archways; B, Cathedral ruins; C, Santa Clara courtyard; D, San Francisco gateway; E, Fountain, Central Park.
See also Nos. 1230/41.

290 Pres. Carlos Arana Osorio

1973. National Census.
963 **290** 2c. black and blue 10 10
964 – 3c. brown, pink & orange 15 10
965 **290** 5c. purple, mauve & black 20 10
966 – 8c. green, black & emerald 35 10
DESIGNS—VERT: 3c. Pres. Osorio seated; 8c. Pres. Osorio standing.

291 Francisco Ximenez

1973. International Book Year (1972).
967 **291** 2c. black and green 10 10
968 3c. brown and orange . . 10 10
969a 3c. black and yellow . . 10 10
969 6c. black and blue . . . 20 10

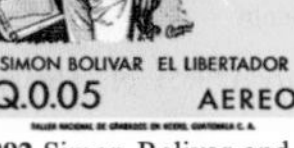

292 Simon Bolivar and Map

293 Eleanor Roosevelt

1973. Air. Simon Bolivar, "The Liberator".
970 **292** 3c. black and red 10 10
971 3c. blue and orange . . . 10 10
972 5c. black and yellow . . . 15 10
973 5c. black and green . . . 15 10

1973. Air. 90th Birth Anniv (1974) of Eleanor Roosevelt (sociologist).
974 **293** 7c. blue 15 10

294 Star Emblem

1973. Air. Centenary of Polytechnic School.
975 **294** 5c. yellow, brown & blue 10 10
See also Nos. 1000/1.

1973. Air. Nos. 927/32 optd **"II Feria Internacional" INTERFER/73 31 Octubre-Noviembre 18 1973 GUATEMALA.**
976 **289** 1c. blue and light blue . . 20 10
977 A 1c. blue and light blue . . 20 10
978 B 1c. blue and light blue . . 20 10
979 C 1c. blue and light blue . . 20 10
980 D 1c. blue and light blue . . 20 10
981 E 1c. blue and light blue . . 20 10

296 1c. Stamp of 1871

1973. Air. Stamp Centenary (1971). (2nd issue).
988 **296** 1c. brown 15 10
988a 6c. orange 15 10
988b 6c. green 15 10
988c 6c. blue 15 10
988d 6c. grey 15 10
989 1q. red . . . . 1·75 1·75

297 School Building

1973. Air. Centenary of Instituto Varones, Chiquimula.
990 **297** 3c. multicoloured 10 10
991 5c. red and black 15 10

1974. No. 863 surch **Desvalorizadas a Q0.50** and leaves.
992 **268** 50c. on 3q. brown and red 85 70

1974. Air. Centenary of Universal Postal Union. Nos. 927/32 optd **UPU HOMENAJE CENTENARIO 1874 1974** and U.P.U. emblem.
993 **289** 1c. blue and light blue . . 25 20
994 A 1c. blue and light blue . . 25 20
995 B 1c. blue and light blue . . 25 20
996 C 1c. blue and light blue . . 25 20
997 D 1c. blue and light blue . . 25 20
998 E 1c. blue and light blue . . 25 20

300 Barrios and Granados

1974. Air. Centenary (1973) of Polytechnic School (2nd issue).
1000 **300** 6c. red, grey and blue . . 15 10
1001 – 25c. multicoloured . . . 45 20
DESIGN—VERT: 25c. School building.

1974. Air. Protection of the Resplendent Quetzal (Guatemala's national bird). No. 800 surch with bars, **VALE 10c. Proteccion del Ave Nacional el Quetzal** and bird.
1002 **252** 10c. on 11c. black & brn 75 25

302 Costume of San Martin Sacatepequez

1974. Air. Guatemalan Costumes. Mult.
1003 2c. Solola costume 10 10
1004 2½c. Type **302** 10 10
1005 9c. Coban costume 20 10
1006 20c. Chichicastenango costume 35 15

303 Mayan Girl and Resplendent Quetzals

1975. Air. International Women's Year.
1007 **303** 8c. multicoloured 40 15
1008 20c. multicoloured . . . 1·00 50

304 Rotary Emblem

1975. Air. 50th Anniv of Guatemala City Rotary Club.
1009 **304** 10c. multicoloured . . . 15 10
1010 15c. multicoloured . . . 30 15

305 I.W.Y. Emblem and Orchid

1975. Air. International Women's Year (2nd series).
1011 **305** 1c. multicoloured 10 10
1012 8c. multicoloured 15 10
1013 26c. multicoloured . . . 45 20

306 Ruined Village

1976. Air. Earthquake of 4 February 1976. Multicoloured.

1014 1c. Type **306** 10 10
1015 3c. Food queue 10 10
1016 5c. Jaguar Temple, Tikal . . 15 10
1017 10c. Broken bridge 20 10
1018 15c. Open-air casualty station 35 15
1019 20c. Harvesting sugarcane 35 15
1020 25c. Ruined house 55 20
1021 30c. Reconstruction, Tecpan 70 20
1022 50c. Ruined church, Cerrodel Carmen 90 35
1023 75c. Clearing debris . . . . 1·40 55
1024 1q. Military aid . . . . . . 1·75 70
1025 2q. Lake Atitlan . . . . . 3·50 1·40

Text in panels expresses gratitude for foreign aid.

307 Eagle and Resplendent Quetzal Emblems

1976. Air. Bicentenary of American Revolution. Multicoloured.

1029 1c. Type **307** 30 15
1030 2c. Boston Tea Party . . . 10 10
1031 3c. Thomas Jefferson (after G. Stuart) (vert) 10 10
1032 4c. Eagle and resplendent quetzal emblems (vert) . . 30 15
1033 5c. "Death of Gen. Warren at Bunker Hill" (detail, Trumbull) 10 10
1034 10c. "Washington reviewing his Ragged Army" (detail, Trego) 20 10
1035 15c. "Washington rallying the Troops at Monmouth" (detail, Leutze) 20 15
1036 20c. Eagle and resplendent quetzal emblems (diff) . . 50 25
1037 25c. "Meeting of Generals at Yorktown after the Surrender" (detail, Peale) 55 20
1038 30c. "Washington crossing the Delaware" (detail, Leutze) 70 20
1039 35c. Eagle and resplendent quetzal emblems (diff) . . 90 50
1040 40c. "Declaration of Independence" (detail, Trumbull) 60 30
1041 45c. "Patrick Henry before Virginia House of Burgesses" (detail, Rothermel) (vert) 90 35
1042 50c. "Congress voting Independence" (detail, Savage) . . . . 1·00 35
1043 1q. George Washington (after G. Stuart) (vert) . . 1·75 1·50
1044 2q. Abraham Lincoln (after D. D. Eisenhower) (vert) 2·75 2·75
1045 3q. Benjamin Franklin (after C. W. Peale) (vert) . . . 4·00 4·00
1046 5q. John F. Kennedy (35 × 55 mm) . . . . . . 7·00 2·50

308 Quetzal Coin

1976. Air. 50th Anniv of Quetzal Currency.

1051 **308** 8c. black, orange and blue 20 10
1052 20c. black, mauve & blue 45 20

309 "The Engineers" (sculpture)

1976. Air. Centenary of Engineering School, Guatemala City.

1053 **309** 9c. blue 20 10
1054 10c. green 20 10

310 Sculpture of Christ (Pedro de Mendoza)

1977. Holy Week. Multicoloured.

1055 6c. Type **310** (postage) . . . 10 10
1056 8c. Sculpture of Christ (Lanuza Brothers) 15 10
1057 3c. Statue of Christ (air) . . 10 10
1058 4c. Statue of Christ (vert) 10 10
1059 7c. Statue of Christ (vert) 20 10
1060 9c. Statue of Christ (vert) 25 10
1061 20c. Statue of Christ and Virgin (vert) 55 15
1062 26c. Statue of Christ 70 55

311 Deed to Site of Guatemala City **312** Arms of Quetzaltenango

1977. Air. Bicentenary of Nueva Guatemala de la Asuncion (Guatemala City). Multicoloured.

1064 6c. Type **311** 10 10
1065 7c. City Hall and Bank of Guatemala (horiz) 10 10
1066 8c. Site of first legislative assembly (horiz) 10 10
1067 9c. Archbishop's arms (horiz) 10 10
1068 22c. Arms of Guatemala City 30 15

1977. Air. 150th Anniv of Founding of Quetzaltenango.

1071 **312** 7c. black and silver . . . 15 10
1072 – 30c. orange and blue . . . 55 20

DESIGN: 30c. City Hall and torch.

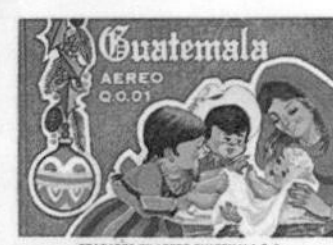

313 "Interfer 77" Emblem **315** "The Holy Family"

314 Mayan Bas-relief

1977. 4th International Fair, Guatemala City.

1073 **313** 7c. multicoloured 10 10

1977. Air. 14th Congress of Latin Notaries.

1074 **314** 10c. black and red . . . 20 10

1977. Air. Christmas. Multicoloured.

1075 1c. Type **315** 10 10
1076 2c. Boy and girl with animals, and Jesus in crib 10 10
1077 4c. Boy and girl with Mary and Jesus 15 10

316 Man from Almolongo **317** Virgin of Sorrows, Antigua

1978. Air. Guatemalan Costumes. Mult.

1078 1c. Type **316** 10 10
1079 2c. Woman from Nebaj . . 10 10
1080 5c. Couple from San Juan Cotzal 15 10
1081 6c. Couple from Todos Santos 20 10
1082 20c. Couple from Regidores 70 15
1083 30c. Woman from San Cristobal 70 20

1978. Air. Holy Week. Multicoloured.

1085 2c. Type **317** 10 10
1086 4c. Virgin of Mercy, Antigua 15 10
1087 5c. Virgin of Anguish, Yurrita 15 10
1088 6c. Virgin of the Rosary, Santo Domingo 15 10
1089 8c. Virgin of Sorrows, Santo Domingo 20 10
1090 9c. Virgin of the Rosary, Quetzaltenango 20 15
1091 10c. Virgin of the Immaculate Conception, Church of St. Francis . . 25 15
1092 20c. Virgin of the Immaculate Conception, Cathedral Church 55 20

318 Footballer **319** Gymnastics

1978. Air. World Cup Football Championship, Argentina.

1094 **318** 10c. multicoloured . . . 20 15

1978. Air. 13th Central American and Caribbean Games, Medellin, Colombia.

1095 **319** 6c. mauve, blue and black 10 10
1096 – 6c. brt blue, blue & black 15 10
1097 – 6c. blue, brt blue & black 15 10
1098 – 6c. blue, mauve and black 15 10
1099 – 8c. mauve, blue and black 15 10

DESIGNS: No. 1096, Volleyball; 1097, Target Shooting; 1098, Weightlifing; 1099, Running.

320 "Cattleya pachecoi" **321** University Seal

1978. Air. Orchids. Multicoloured.

1100 1c. Type **320** 10 10
1101 1c. "Sobralia xantholeuca" 10 10
1102 1c. "Cypripedium irapeanum" 10 10
1103 1c. "Oncidium splendidum" 10 10
1104 3c. "Cattleya bowringiana" 10 10
1105 3c. "Encyclia cordigera" . . 10 10
1106 3c. "Epidendrum imatophyllum" 10 10
1107 3c. "Barkeria skinneri" . . . 10 10
1108 8c. "Spiranthes speciosa" . . 20 10
1109 20c. "Lycaste skinneri" . . 55 15

1978. Air. 300th Anniv of San Carlos University of Guatemala. Multicoloured.

1110 6c. Type **321** 15 10
1111 7c. Students from different faculties (26 × 46 mm) . . 15 10
1112 12c. 17th-century student . . 20 10
1113 14c. Student and molecular model 30 10

322 Brown and White Children **323** Planting Seedling

1978. Air. Guatemalan Children's Year (1977). Multicoloured.

1114 6c. Type **322** 15 10
1115 7c. Child skipping 15 10
1116 12c. "Helping Hand" . . . 20 10
1117 14c. Hands protecting Indian girl 30 10

1979. Air. Forestry. Multicoloured.

1118 6c. Type **323** 10 10
1119 8c. Burnt forest 15 10
1120 9c. Woodland scene 15 10
1121 10c. Sawmill 15 10
1122 26c. Forest conservation . . 35 15

324 Ocellated Turkey **325** Clay Jar

1979. Air. Wildlife Conservation. Mult.

1124 1c. Type **324** 70 30
1125 3c. White-tailed deer (horiz) 25 10
1126 5c. King vulture . . . . . 2·10 30
1127 7c. Great horned owl . . . 4·25 95
1128 9c. Ocelot 55 10

1979. Air. Archaeological Treasures from Tikal. Multicoloured.

1130 2c. Type **325** 10 10
1131 3c. Ceramic head of Mayan woman 10 10
1132 4c. Earring 10 10
1133 5c. Vase 10 10
1134 6c. Ceramic figure 10 10
1135 7c. Carved bone 10 10
1136 8c. Striped vase 15 10
1137 10c. Tripod vase with lid . . . 15 10

326 Presidential Guard Headquarters **327** National Coat of Arms

1979. 30th Anniv of Presidential Guard. Multicoloured.

1138 10c. Type **326** (postage) . . 15 10
1139 8c. Presidential Guard insignia (air) 15 10

1979. Air. Municipal Arms. Multicoloured.

1140 8c. Type **327** 15 10
1141 8c. Alta Verapaz 15 10
1142 8c. Baja Verapaz 15 10
1143 8c. Chimal Tenango 15 10
1144 8c. Chiquimula 15 10
1145 8c. Escuintla 15 10
1146 8c. Flores (Peten) 15 10
1147 8c. Guatemala 15 10
1148 8c. Huehuetenango 15 10
1149 8c. Izabal . . . . 2·50 75
1150 8c. Jalapa 15 10
1151 8c. Jutiapa 15 10
1152 8c. Mazatenango 15 10
1153 8c. El Progreso 15 10
1154 8c. Quezaltenango 15 10
1155 8c. Quiche 15 10
1156 8c. Retalhuleu 15 10
1157 8c. Sacatepequez 15 10
1158 8c. San Marcos 15 10
1159 8c. Santa Rosa 15 10
1160 8c. Solola 15 10
1161 8c. Totonicapan 15 10
1162 8c. Zacapa 15 10

328 Rotary Emblem and Girl with Flowers **329** The Creation of the World

1980. 75th Anniv of Rotary International. Multicoloured.
1164 4c. Type **328** 10 10
1165 6c. Diamond, emblem and resplendent quetzal . . . 40 20
1166 10c. Paul P. Harris (founder), emblem and resplendent quetzal . . . 60 60

1981. Air. "Popol Vuh". Designs showing medallic illustrations of Guatemalan history and legends from the Sacred Book of the Ancient Quiches of Guatemala. (a) The Creation.
1167 **329** 1c. black and mauve . . 10 10
1168 – 2c. black and green . . . 10 10
1169 – 4c. black and blue . . . 10 10
1170 – 8c. black and yellow . . 15 10
1171 – 10c. black and pink . . 15 10
1172 – 22c. black and brown . . 30 10

(b) The Adventures of Hun Ahpu and Xbalanque.
1173 – 1c. black and mauve . . . 10 10
1174 – 4c. black and violet . . . 10 10
1175 – 6c. black and brown . . . 10 10
1176 – 8c. black and green . . . 15 10
1177 – 10c. black and yellow . . . 15 10
1178 – 26c. black and green . . . 35 10

(c) The Founding of the Quiche Race.
1179 – 2c. black and mauve . . . 10 10
1180 – 4c. black and blue 10 10
1181 – 6c. black and pink 10 10
1182 – 8c. black and yellow . . . 15 10
1183 – 10c. black and green . . . 15 10
1184 – 30c. black and green . . . 45 15

(d) The Territorial Expansion of the Quiches.
1185 – 3c. black and blue 10 10
1186 – 4c. black and violet 10 10
1187 – 6c. black and pink 10 10
1188 – 8c. black and grey 15 10
1189 – 10c. black and green . . . 15 10
1190 – 50c. black and mauve . . . 70 20

DESIGNS: No. 1168, Populating the earth; 1169, Birth of the stick-men; 1170, Destruction of the stick-men; 1171, Creation of the men of corn; 1172, "Thanks to the creator"; 1173, Origin of the twin semi-gods; 1174, Punishment of the Princess Xquic; 1175, Odyssey of Hun Ahpu and Xbalanque; 1176, The test in Xibalba; 1177, Multiplication of the prodigies; 1178, The deification of Hun Ahpu and Xbalanque; 1179, Balam Quitze, father of Caviquib; 1180, Caha Paluma, wife of Balam Quitze; 1181, Balam Acab, father of Nihaibab; 1182, Chomiia, wife of Balam Acab; 1183, Mahucutah, father of Ahau Quiche; 1184, Tzununiha, wife of Mahucutah; 1185, Cotuha, Quiche monarch; 1186, The invincible Cotuha and Iztayul; 1187, Cucumatz, the prodigious king; 1188, Warrior with captive; 1189, "None can conquer or kill the king"; 1190, "This was the greatness of the Quiches".

330 Early and Modern Telephones (cent)

1981. Air. Anniversaries.
1191 – 3c. red and black 10 10
1192 – 5c. blue and black . . . 10 10
1193 **330** 6c. multicoloured 10 10
1194 – 7c. multicoloured 10 10
1195 – 12c. multicoloured . . . 15 10
1196 – 25c. multicoloured . . . 35 10

DESIGNS—26 × 46 mm: 3c. Thomas Edison (centenary of gramophone). 29 × 39 mm: 7c. Charles Lindbergh (50th anniv of solo Atlantic flight); 12c. Jose Cecilio del Valle (patriot, birth bicentenary), 25c. Jesues Castillo (composer, birth centenary). 46 × 26 mm: 5c. Spool of film (50th anniv of sound film).

331 Roderico Toledo and German Chupina (first and present Police Chiefs)

1981. Air. Centenary of National Police. Multicoloured.
1197 2c. Type **331** 10 10
1198 4c. Police Headquarters . . 10 10

332 Mayan Sun Calendar

1981. Air. 7th Latin American Aviculture Congress.
1199 **332** 1c. green, yellow & black 10 10

333 Bernardo O'Higgins (Chile)

1982. Air. Liberators of the Americas.
1200 **333** 2c. multicoloured 10 10
1201 – 3c. multicoloured 10 10
1202 – 4c. multicoloured 10 10
1203 – 10c. grey and black . . . 15 10

DESIGNS—(31 × 45 mm): 4c. Jose de San Martin (Argentine); 10c. Miguel Garcia Granados (Guatemala). (26 × 35 mm): 3c. Jose Artigas (Uruguay).

334 General Barrios and Bank

1982. Air. Centenary of Banco de Occidente.
1204 **334** 1c. multicoloured 10 10
1205 – 2c. black, red and blue 10 10
1206 – 3c. multicoloured 10 10
1207 – 4c. multicoloured 10 10

DESIGNS—HORIZ: 2c. Bank building. VERT: 3c. Centenary emblem; 4c. Centenary medals.

335 Old and New Bank Buildings, Guatemala City

1982. Air. 50th Anniv of National Mortgage Bank.
1208 **335** 1c. multicoloured 10 10
1209 – 2c. black, yellow & green 10 10
1210 – 5c. multicoloured 10 10
1211 – 10c. black, yellow & grn 15 10

DESIGNS—HORIZ: 2c. Bank emblem; 10c. Bank and Anniversary emblems. VERT: 5c. Bronze anniversary medallion.

336 Brother Pedro

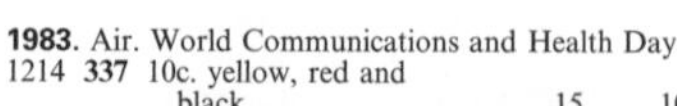
337 I.T.U. and W.H.O. Emblems with Ribbons forming Caduceus

1983. Air. Blessed Brother Pedro. Mult.
1212 1c. Type **336** 10 10
1213 20c. Apparition of Virgin Mary 30 10

1983. Air. World Communications and Health Day.
1214 **337** 10c. yellow, red and black 15 10

338 Hands holding Bible

340 F.A.O. Emblem and Starving Children

339 Train crossing Las Vacas Bridge

1983. Air. Centenary (1982) of Evangelical Church in Guatemala. Multicoloured.
1215 3c. Type **338** 10 10
1216 5c. Central Evangelical Church 10 10

1983. Air. Centenary (1980) of Guatemalan Railways. Multicoloured.
1217 10c. Type **339** 75 65
1218 25c. General Barrios and trains at station . . . . . 2·00 1·50
1219 30c. Train crossing Lake Amatitlan Dam . . . . . 2·25 1·75

1983. Air. World Food Day (1981). Mult.
1220 8c. Maize and Globe . . . 10 10
1221 1q. Type **340** 95 70

1984. Air. As Nos. 927/32 and 945/50 but colours changed. Values inscribed in black.
1230 **289** 1c. black and green . . . 10 10
1231 A 1c. black and green . . . 10 10
1232 B 1c. black and green . . . 10 10
1233 C 1c. black and green . . . 10 10
1234 D 1c. black and green . . . 10 10
1235 E 1c. black and green . . . 10 10
1236 **289** 5c. black and orange . . 10 10
1237 A 5c. black and orange . . 10 10
1238 B 5c. black and orange . . 10 10
1239 C 5c. black and orange . . 10 10
1240 D 5c. black and orange . . 10 10
1241 E 5c. black and orange . . 10 10

341 Pope John Paul II

1984. Air. Papal Visit. Multicoloured.
1242 4c. Type **341** 10 10
1243 8c. Woman kneeling before Pope 15 10

342 Rafael Landivar

1984. Air. 250th Birth Anniv of Rafael Landivar (poet). Multicoloured.
1244 2c. Type **342** 10 10
1245 4c. Landivar's tomb, Antigua Guatemala (horiz) 10 10

343 Casariego y Acevedo **344** Bank's Emblem

1984. Air. 1st Death Anniv of Cardinal Mario Casariego y Acevedo, Archbishop of Guatemala.
1246 **343** 10c. multicoloured . . . 15 10

1984. Air. 20th Anniv of Central American Bank for Economic Integration.
1247 **344** 30c. multicoloured . . . 50 15

345 Planting Coffee, 1870

1984. Air. Coffee.
1248 **345** 1c. black and brown . . 10 10
1249 – 2c. black and flesh . . . 10 10
1250 – 3c. black and stone . . . 10 10
1251 – 4c. black and buff . . . 30 10
1252 – 5c. multicoloured 10 10
1253 – 10c. multicoloured . . . 15 10
1254 – 12c. multicoloured . . . 15 10
1255 – 25c. multicoloured . . . 1·40 30
1256 – 25c. black and brown . . 35 10
1257 – 30c. multicoloured . . . 40 10

DESIGNS: As T **345**: 2c. Harvesting coffee, 1870; 3c. Drying coffee beans, 1870; 4c. Exporting coffee, 1870; 5c. Grafting seedlings; 10c. Instant coffee; 12c. Harvesting and processing coffee; 25c. (1255) Exporting coffee (different). (81 × 108 mm): 25c. (1256) Women picking coffee. (100 × 81 mm): 30c. Globe and coffee beans.

346 "Beaver" Cub and Tikal Pyramid

1985. Air. 75th Anniv of Boy Scout Movement. Multicoloured.
1258 5c. Type **346** 10 10
1259 6c. "Wolf" cub and Captains Palace, Old Guatemala 10 10
1260 8c. Scout, xylophone player and countryside 15 10
1261 10c. Rover scout and dancers 15 10
1262 20c. Lord Baden-Powell (founder) and Carlos Cipriani (founder of Guatemalan scouts) . . . 30 10

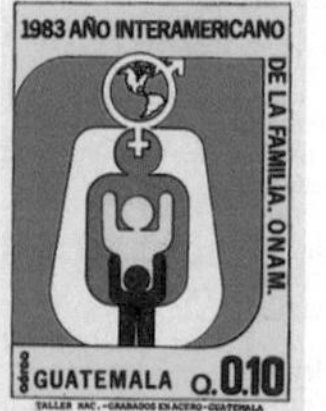

347 Family **348** Emblem

1985. Air. Inter-American Family Year.
1263 **347** 10c. multicoloured . . . 15 10

1985. Air. 25th Anniv of Central American Air Navigation Services Association.
1264 **348** 10c. multicoloured . . . 15 10

349 Morse Key, Samuel Morse, J. Rufino Barrios and Telegraph Aerial

1985. Air. National Telegraph Service.
1265 **349** 4c. black and brown . . 10 10

350 Olympic Rings and Maya Pelota Player

1986. Air. 90th Anniv of First Modern Olympic Games and Foundation of International Olympic Committee. Multicoloured.
1266 8c. Type **350** 15 10
1267 10c. Rings and Baron Pierre de Coubertin 15 10

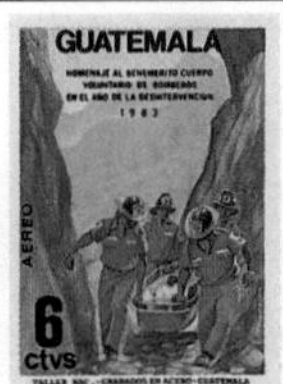

351 Rescue Team with Person in Cradle

1986. Air. Volunteer Firemen (1st series).
1268 **351** 6c. multicoloured 10 10
See also Nos. 1271/2.

352 Temple of Minerva, Quetzaltenango

1986. Air. Centenary (1984) of Independence Fair, Quetzaltenango. Multicoloured.
1269 8c. Type **352** 15 10
1270 10c. City arms in courtyard of Quetzaltenango Municipal Palace 15 10

353 Fire behind Fireman carrying Child
354 Arms

1986. Air. Volunteer Firemen (2nd series). Multicoloured.
1271 8c. Type **353** 15 10
1272 10c. Searching rubble after explosion (33 × 24 mm) 15 10

1986. Air. 25th Anniv (1976) of Association of Telegraphists and Radio-Telegraph Operators.
1273 **354** 6c. multicoloured 25 15

355 Architect with Plans looking at Building

1987. Air. 25th Anniv of San Carlos University Architecture Faculty.
1274 **355** 10c. multicoloured . . . 15 10

356 Emblem and Boeing 727

1987. Air. 40th Anniv of I.C.A.O. Mult.
1275 8c. Type **356** 15 10
1276 10c. Boeing 727 airplane on runway (vert) 15 10

357 Aerial View of Site

1987. Air. Chixoy Hydro-electric Plant.
1277 **357** 2c. multicoloured 10 10

358 Dr. Cayetano Francos y Monroy, Archbishop of Guatemala (founder)

1987. Air. Bicentenary (1981) of St. Joseph Children's College. Multicoloured.
1278 8c. Type **358** 10 10
1279 10c. College emblem 15 10

359 Column beside Man studying Book

1987. Air. Regional Book Promotion Centre for Latin America and Caribbean.
1280 **359** 12c. multicoloured . . . 15 10

360 Girls in Traditional Costumes

1987. Coban Folklore Festival. Mult.
1281 50c. Girl weaving 55 15
1282 1q. Type **360** . . . . . . 1·25 30

361 Cesar Branas

1987. Air. Writers (1st series).
1283 **361** 6c. orange and black . . 10 10
1284 – 8c. red and black 10 10
1285 – 9c. purple and black . . 15 10
DESIGNS: 8c. Rafael Arevalo Martinez; 9c. Jose Milla y Vidaurre.
See also Nos. 1297/8 and 1307/11.

362 Footballer

1987. Air. Pan-American Games National Football Selection.
1286 **362** 10c. blue and black . . . 15 10

363 Miguel Angel Asturias Cultural Centre
364 Stylized Dove

1987.
1287 **363** 1c. blue 10 10
1287a 2c. brown 10 10
1288 3c. blue 10 10
1289 4c. mauve 10 10
1290 5c. orange 10 10
1291 6c. green 10 10
1292 7c. red 10 10
1293 8c. mauve 10 10
1294 9c. black 10 10
1295 10c. green 15 10

1988. Air. Writers (2nd series). As T **361**.
1297 4c. red and black 10 10
1298 5c. brown and black 10 10
DESIGNS: 4c. Enrique A. Hidalgo; 5c. Enrique Gomez Carrillo.

1988. Air. "Esquipulas II—A Firm Step towards Peace".
1299 **364** 10c. green 15 10
1300 – 40c. red 45 10
1301 – 60c. blue 65 20
DESIGNS—HORIZ: 40c. Three stylized doves. VERT: 60c. Stylized dove.

366 St. John and Boys

1989. Death Centenary of St. John Bosco (founder of Salesian Brothers).
1303 **366** 40c. black and gold . . . 55 15

367 Birds

1989. Air. Bicentenary of French Revolution.
1304 **367** 1q. red, blue and black 90 35

368 Madrid Codex (detail)

1990. Air. America. Pre-Columbian Culture. Multicoloured.
1305 10c. Type **368** 10 10
1306 20c. Tikal Pyramid 10 10

1990. Air. Writers (3rd series). As T **361**.
1307 1c. mauve and black 10 10
1308 2c. orange and black . . . 10 10
1309 3c. blue and black 10 10
1310 7c. black and green 10 10
1311 10c. black and yellow . . . 10 10
DESIGNS: 1c. Flavio Herrera; 2c. Rosendo Santa Cruz; 3c. Werner Ovalle Lopez; 7c. Clemente Marroquin Rojas; 10c. Miguel Angel Asturias.

369 Games Emblem

1990. 6th Central American and Caribbean University Games. Multicoloured.
1312 15c. Type **369** 10 10
1313 20c. Mascot holding flame (vert) 10 10
1314 25c. Mascot playing volleyball 10 10
1315 30c. Mascot playing football 10 10
1316 45c. Mascot performing judo movement 10 10
1317 1q. Mascot playing baseball 25 10
1318 2q. Mascot playing basketball 45 10
1319 3q. Mascot hurdling 70 20

370 Family, Cereal and Emblem

1990. Air. 40th Anniv of Central America and Panama Nutrition Institute.
1320 **370** 20c. multicoloured . . . 10 10

371 Palais de l'Athenee, Geneva (venue of founding meeting)

1990. Air. 125th Anniv (1988) of International Red Cross.
1321 **371** 50c. multicoloured . . . 15 10

372 Arms

1991. Air. Centenary of National Defence Staff.
1322 **372** 20c. multicoloured . . . 10 10

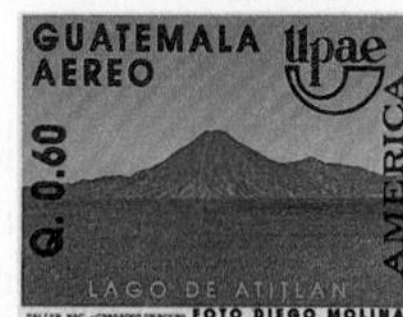

373 Atitlan Lake

1991. America. Natural World. Multicoloured.
1323 10c. Pacaya Volcano in eruption 10 10
1324 60c. Type **373** 15 10

374 Martin and Vicente Pinzon

1992. Air. America. 500th Anniv of Discovery of America by Columbus. Each black and green.
1325 40c. Type **374** 35 15
1326 60c. Christopher Columbus and "Santa Maria" (vert) 40 15

375 Crops

1992. Air. 50th Anniv of International Institute for Agricultural Co-operation.
1327 **375** 10c. multicoloured . . . 10 10

376 Emblem
377 "Encyclia cochleata"

1992. International Anti-AIDS Campaign.
1328 **376** 1q. multicoloured . . . 25 10

1994. Air. Orchids (1st series). Multicoloured.
1329 50c. Type **377** 10 10
1330 1q. "Encyclia vitellina" . . 20 10
1331 2q. "Odontoglossum uroskinneri" 45 10
See also Nos. 1355/6.

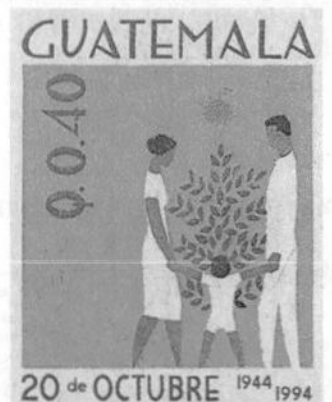

378 Family around Tree

1994. 50th Anniv of 20 October Revolution. Multicoloured.
1332 40c. Type **378** 10 10
1333 60c. Dove on hand (horiz) 15 10
1334 1q. Man holding book and rifle 20 10
1335 2q. Representations of social developments since 1944 45 10
1336 3q. Three youths supporting torch ("Revolution, Liberty, Justice and Peace") 65 15

379 City Buildings

1995. Air. Tourism. Multicoloured.
1337 20c. White water rafting . . 10 10
1338 40c. Windsurfing 10 10
1339 60c. Pleasure boat on Lake Atitlan 15 10
1340 80c. Tourist launch "Crucero" 15 10
1341 1q. Erupting volcano . . . 20 10
1342 2q. Type **379** 45 10
1343 3q. Parrots on perch (vert) 65 15
1344 4q. Mayan ruins (vert) . . . 90 20
1345 5q. Ceremony (vert) . . . . 1·10 25

380 Greeting Crowd

1996. Air. Papal Visit. Pope John Paul II. Multicoloured.
1350 10c. Type **380** 10 10
1351 1q. Holding child 20 10
1352 1q.75 Holding crucifix and wearing mitre 35 10
1353 1q.90 Wearing cross and red cloak 40 10
1354 2q.90 Wearing red hat . . . 60 15

1996. Air. Orchids (2nd series). As T **377**. Mult.
1355 20c. "Phragmipedium caudatum" 10 10
1356 1q.50 "Odontoglossum laeve" 30 10

381 Carlos Merida

1996. Air. Personalities.
1357 **381** 40c. lt blue, blue & black 10 10
1358 – 50c. brown, blue & black 10 10
1359 – 60c. brown, blue & black 10 10
DESIGNS: 50c. Jose Eulalio Samayoa; 60c. Manuel Montufar y Coronado.

382 University Hall

1997. Buildings. Multicoloured.
1360 50c. Type **382** 10 10
1361 1q. Brewery 20 10

383 Breastfeeding

1997. Air. Breastfeeding Campaign.
1362 **383** 1q. multicoloured . . . 20 10

384 Parent and Child (Marion Contreras Castanaza)

1997. 50th Anniv (1996) of UNICEF "Children and Peace". Multicoloured.
1363 10c. Type **384** 10 10
1364 20c. Child riding birds (Marvin Sac Coyoy) (horiz) 10 10

385 Child writing (Education)

1997. Air. Public Finance Projects. Mult.
1365 20c. Type **385** 10 10
1366 60c. Child receiving medication (health) . . . 10 10
1367 80c. Road (infrastructure) 15 10
1368 1q. Family (security) 20 10

386 Jorge Rybar (pioneer) and Machinery

1998. Air. 50th Anniv of Guatemala Plastics Industry.
1369 **386** 10c. multicoloured . . . 10 10

387 1875 Postcard and Emblem

1999. Air. 50th Anniv (1998) of El Quetzal (International Society of Guatemala Stamp Collectors).
1370 **387** 1q. multicoloured . . . 20 10

388 Francisco Marroquin (first bishop of Guatemala)

2001. Birth Anniversaries (1999). Multicoloured.
1371 3q. Type **388** (500th anniv) 50 30
1372 4q. Jacinto Rodriguez Diaz (aviation pioneer) (centenary) 65 40
1373 8q.75, Miguel Angel Asturias (Nobel Prize winner for Literature) (centenary) . . . . 1·25 75
1374 10q. Cesar Branas (writer and historian) (centenary) 1·60 1·00

389 Church Architecture, Antigua and Hermano Pedro

2002. Air. 3rd Visit of Pope John Paul II (50c., 2, 5, 8q.75). 12th Anniv Canonisation of Hermano Pedro (monk and humanitarian) (20, 25c., 1q.). Multicoloured.
1375 20c. Type **389** 10 10
1376 25c. Hermano Pedro holding bell rope 10 10
1376 50c. Hermano Pedro and Pope John Paul II (horiz) 10 10
1378 1q. Nativity, his alms bell and Hermano Pedro (head) 15 10
1379 2q. Pope John Paul II and Archbishop Rudolfo Toruno (horiz) 30 20
1380 5q. Fountain, part of door lintel and Pope John Paul II (horiz) 75 45
1381 8q. 75 Pope John Paul II, clock tower and Government Palace (horiz) . . . . 1·25 75
MS1382 153 × 128 mm. As Nos. 1375/81 . . . . 2·60 2·60

390 Guatemalan Flag, Globe, Envelopes, Quetzal Bird and Flags

2002. Air. 125th Anniv of Universal Postal Union (1999). Multicoloured.
1383 20c. Type **390** 10 10
1384 2q. UPU emblem 30 20
1385 3q. Globe with map of Americas encircled by bird 40 25
1386 5q. Globe with hands holding envelopes and flags 70 40

391 Mt. Everest

2002. Air. 1st Anniv of Jaime Vinals' Ascent of Everest.
1387 **391** 3q. multicoloured . . . 20 10

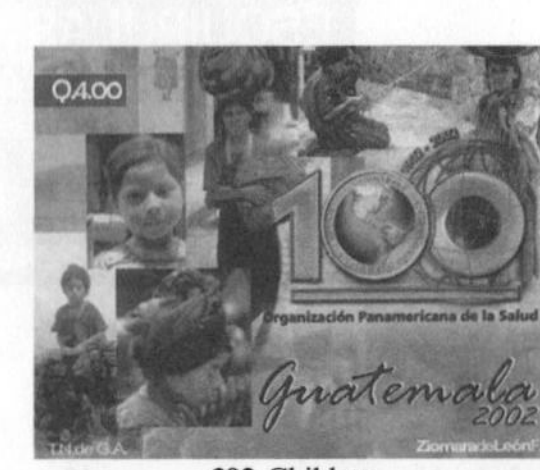

392 Children

2002. Air. Centenary of Pan-American Health Organization.
1388 **392** 4q. multicoloured . . . 60 35

393 Dance of the Conquest Mask, Totonicapan

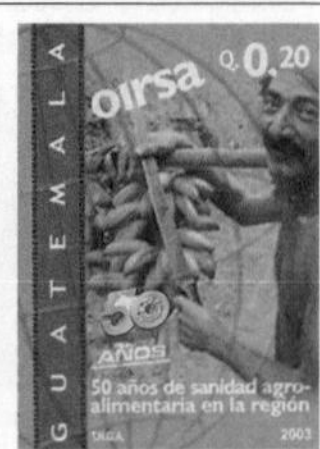

395 Man carrying Bananas

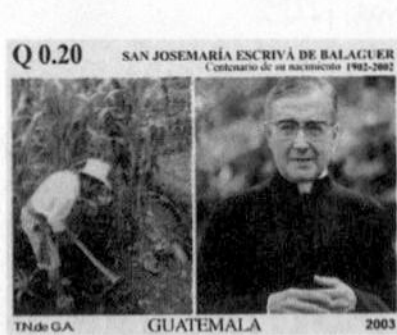

394 Field Worker and Josemaria Escriva de Balaguer

2003. Masks. Masks. Multicoloured.
1389 20c. Type **393** 10 10
1390 2q. Dance of Moors and Christians, Sacatepequez 30 20
1391 3q. Deer dance, Alta Verapaz 40 25
1392 4q. Jaguar mask, Deer dance, Totonicapan . . . 60 35
MS1393 100 × 71 mm. 5q. Paabanc 70 40

2003. Birth Centenary of Josemaria Escriva de Balaguer (2002) (founder of Opus Dei (religious organization)). Multicoloured.
1394 20c. Type **394** 10 10
1395 50c. Josemaria Escriva and fisherman 10 10
1396 3q. Facing left 40 25
1397 10q. Church and Josemaria Escriva . . . . 1·40 80

2003. 50th Anniv of Regional Organization for Farming Health (OIRSA). Multicoloured.
1398 20c. Type **395** 10 10
1399 1q. Hands holding corn . . 15 10
1400 2q. Cow's face 30 20
1401 4q. Field of crop 60 35
1402 5q. Meats 70 40
1403 10q. Eye and maize . . . . 1·40 80
MS1404 101 × 62 mm. 3q. Fruit 40 40

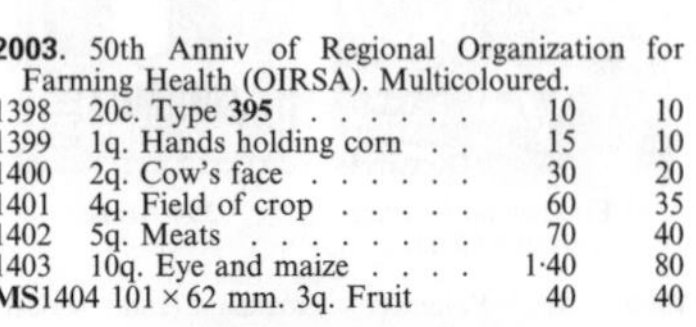
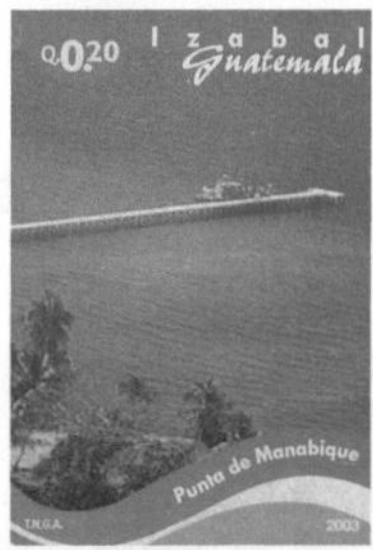

396 Pier, Punta de Manabique, Izabel Department

2004. Tourism. Izabel Department (1405/7). Multicoloured.
1405 20c. Type **396** 10 10
1406 50c. Las Siete Altares, Izabel Department 10 10
1407 1q. Las Escobas waterfalls, Izabel Department . . . 15 10
1408 1q.50 Barrios y Pichilingo harbour (America. Cultural Heritage) 20 15
1409 2q. Mayan acropolis, Quirigua 30 20
1410 3q. Livingston beach, Rio Dulce 40 25
1411 4q. San Felipe castle 60 35
1412 5q. Sunset, El Estor 70 40
1413 8q.75 Agua Caliente waterfalls . . . . 1·20 70
1414 10q. Rio Polochi river . . . 1·40 80
MS1415 102 × 63 mm. 4q. Carving, Mayan acropolis, Quirigua (America. Cultural Heritage) 60 60

EXPRESS LETTER STAMPS.

1940. No. 231 optd **EXPRESO**.
E411 **97** 4c. yellow 85 35

E 181 Motorcyclist

1948. Surch.
E479 E **181** 10c. on 4c. blk & grn 1·00 60

OFFICIAL STAMPS

O 41   O 100

1902.

O127 O **41** 1c. green 2·50 1·25
O128 2c. red 2·50 1·25
O129 5c. blue 3·00 1·00
O130 10c. purple 3·50 1·00
O131 25c. orange 3·50 1·00

1929.

O239 O **100** 1c. blue 30 30
O240 2c. sepia 30 30
O241 3c. green 30 30
O242 4c. purple 35 35
O243 5c. lake 35 35
O244 10c. brown 40 40
O245 25c. blue 85 70

1939. Air. Nos. 369/74 optd **OFICIAL OFICIAL**.
O400 **134** 1c. brown and orange 50 75
O401 – 2c. brown and red 50 75
O402 – 3c. brown, buff & green 50 75
O403 – 4c. brown and purple 50 75
O404 – 5c. brown and grey 50 75
O405 – 10c. brown and blue 50 75

GUERNSEY Pt. 1

An island in the English Channel off N.W. coast of France. Occupied by German Forces from June 1940 to May 1945. "Regional" issues were introduced from 1958 (see after GREAT BRITAIN). The island's postal service was organised as a separate postal administration in 1969.

(a) War Occupation Issues.

1

1941.

1f **1** ½d. green 3·00 2·00
2 1d. red 2·25 1·25
3a 2½d. blue 6·00 5·00

(b) Independent Postal Administration.

4 Castle Cornet and Edward the Confessor

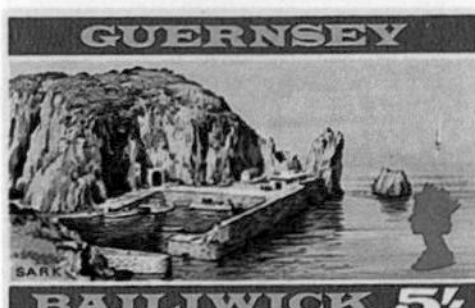

5 View of Sark

1969.

13 **4** ½d. mauve and black 10 10
14 – 1d. blue and black* 10 10
14b – 1d. blue and black* 30 30
15 – 1½d. brown and black 10 10
16 – 2d. multicoloured 10 10
17 – 3d. multicoloured 15 15
18 – 4d. multicoloured 20 25
19 – 5d. multicoloured 20 20
20 – 6d. multicoloured 20 30
21 – 9d. multicoloured 30 30
22 – 1s. multicoloured 30 30
23 – 1s.6d. green and black* 25 30
23b – 1s.6d. green and black* 2·00 1·75
24 – 1s.9d. multicoloured 80 80
25 – 2s.6d. violet and black 3·25 2·75
26 **5** 5s. multicoloured 2·50 2·25
27 – 10s. multicoloured 16·00 18·00
28a – £1 multicoloured 2·25 2·25

DESIGNS—As Type **4**: 1d. Map and William I; 1½d. Martello tower and Henry II; 2d. Arms of Sark and King John; 3d. Arms of Alderney and Edward III; 4d. Guernsey lily and Henry V; 5d. Arms of Guernsey and Elizabeth I; 6d. Arms of Alderney and Charles II; 9d. Arms of Sark and George III; 1s. Arms of Guernsey and Queen Victoria; 1s.6d., As 1d.; 1s.9d. Guernsey lily and Elizabeth I; 2s.6d. Martello tower and King John. As Type **5**: 10s. View of Alderney; 20s. View of Guernsey.

*On Nos. 14 and 23 the degree of latitude is inscr (incorrectly) as 40° 30' N. On Nos. 14b and 23b it has been corrected to 49° 30'.

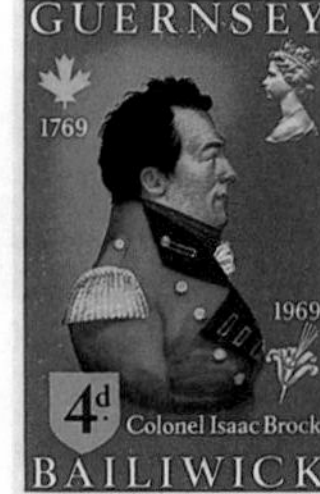

19 Isaac Brock as Colonel

1969. Birth Bicent of Sir Isaac Brock. Mult.
29 4d. Type **19** 20 20
30 5d. Sir Isaac Brock as Major-General 20 20
31 1s.9d. Isaac Brock as Ensign 90 75
32 2s.6d. Arms and flags (horiz) 90 75

23 H.M.S. "L103" (landing craft) entering St. Peter's Harbour

1970. 25th Anniv of Liberation.
33 **23** 4d. blue 20 20
34 – 5d. brown, lake and grey 30 20
35 – 1s.6d. brown and buff 1·00 90

DESIGNS—HORIZ: 5d. H.M.S. "Bulldog" and H.M.S. "Beagle" (destroyers) entering St. Peter Port. VERT: 1s.6d. Brigadier Snow reading Proclamation.

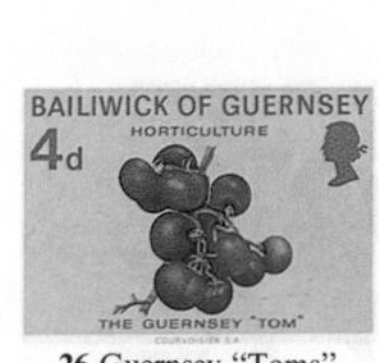

26 Guernsey "Toms"   32 St. Peter's Church, Sark

1970. Agriculture and Horticulture. Mult.
36 4d. Type **26** 55 20
37 5d. Guernsey cow 70 20
38 9d. Guernsey bull 2·75 1·30
39 1s.6d. Freesias 2·75 2·40

1970. Christmas. Churches (1st series). Mult.
40 4d. St. Anne's Church, Alderney (horiz) 20 10
41 5d. St. Peter's Church (horiz) 20 10
42 9d. Type **32** 1·00 75
43 1s.6d. St. Tugual Chapel, Herm 1·00 1·00
See also Nos. 63/6.

34 Martello Tower and King John

1971. Decimal Currency. Nos. 13, etc, but with new colours and decimal values as T **34**.
44 ½p. mauve and black (as No. 13) 10 15
45 1p. blue and black (as No. 14b) 10 10
46 1½p. brown & black (as No. 15) 15 15
47 2p. multicoloured (as No. 18) 15 15
48 2½p. multicoloured (as No. 19) 15 10
49 3p. multicoloured (as No. 17) 20 20
50 3½p. multicoloured (as No. 24) 20 20
51 4p. multicoloured (as No. 16) 20 20
52 5p. green and black (as No. 14b) 20 20
53 6p. multicoloured (as No. 20) 20 20
54 7½p. multicoloured (as No. 22) 30 35
55 9p. multicoloured (as No. 21) 65 65
56a 10p. violet & black (as No. 25) 1·25 1·25
57 20p. multicoloured (as No. 26) 70 70
58 50p. multicoloured (as No. 27) 1·25 1·25

35 Hong Kong 2c. of 1862

1971. Thomas De La Rue Commemoration.
59 **35** 2p. purple 35 15
60 – 2½p. red 35 15
61 – 4p. green 1·10 1·00
62 – 7½p. blue 1·60 1·50

DESIGNS (Each showing portraits of Queen Elizabeth and Thomas De La Rue): 2½p. Great Britain 4d. of 1855–7; 4p. Italy 5c. of 1862; 7½p. Confederate States 5c. of 1862.

1971. Christmas. Churches (2nd series). As T **32**. Multicoloured.
63 2p. Ebenezer Church, St. Peter Port (horiz) 10 10
64 2½p. Church of St. Pierre du Bois (horiz) 10 10
65 5p. St. Joseph's Church, St. Peter Port 1·00 1·00
66 7½p. Church of St. Philippe de Torteval 1·00 1·00

37 "Earl of Chesterfield" (1794)

1972. Mail Packet Ships (1st series). Mult.
67 2p. Type **37** 15 10
68 2½p. "Dasher" (1827) 15 10
69 7½p. "Ibex" (1891) 40 35
70 9p. "Alberta" (1900) 50 50
See also Nos. 80/3.

1972. World Conference of Guernsey Breeders, Guernsey. As No. 38 but size 48 × 29 mm, and additional inscription with face value changed.
71 5p. multicoloured 30 30

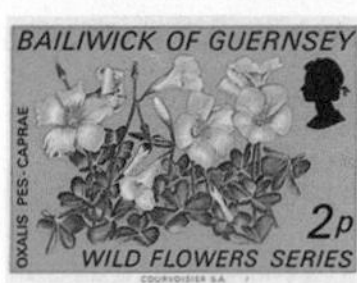

39 Bermuda Buttercup

1972. Wild Flowers. Multicoloured.
72 2p. Type **39** 10 10
73 2½p. Heath spotted orchid (vert) 10 10
74 7½p. Kaffir fig 45 40
75 9p. Scarlet pimpernel (vert) 50 50

40 Angels adoring Christ   42 "The Good Shepherd"

41 Supermarine Sea Eagle

1972. Royal Silver Wedding and Christmas. Stained-glass Windows from Guernsey Churches. Multicoloured.
76 2p. Type **40** 10 10
77 2½p. The Epiphany 15 10
78 7½p. The Virgin Mary 30 25
79 9p. Christ 35 35
See also Nos. 89/92.

1973. Mail Packet Boats (2nd series). As T **37**. Multicoloured.
80 2½p. "St. Julien" (1925) 10 10
81 3p. "Isle of Guernsey" (1930) 20 20
82 7½p. "St. Patrick" (1947) 40 40
83 9p. "Sarnia" (1961) 45 45

1973. 50th Anniv of Air Service. Mult.
84 2½p. Type **41** 10 10
85 3p. Westland Wessex trimotor 10 10
86 5p. De Havilland Dragon Rapide 25 25
87 7½p. Douglas DC-3 30 30
88 9p. Vickers Viscount 800 "Anne Marie" 40 40

1973. Christmas. Stained-glass Windows from Guernsey Churches. Multicoloured.
89 2½p. Type **42** 10 10
90 3p. Christ at the well of Samaria 10 10
91 7½p. St. Dominic 30 30
92 20p. Mary and the Child Jesus 40 40

43 Princess Anne and Capt. Mark Phillips

1973. Royal Wedding.
93 **43** 25p. multicoloured 45 45

44 "John Lockett", 1875

1974. 150th Anniv of Royal National Lifeboat Institution. Multicoloured.
94 2½p. Type **44** 10 10
95 3p. "Arthur Lionel", 1912 10 10
96 8p. "Euphrosyne Kendal", 1954 20 20
97 10p. "Arun", 1972 25 25

45 Private, East Regt, 1815   46 Driver, Field Battery, Royal Guernsey Artillery, 1848

1974. Guernsey Militia. Multicoloured. (a) As T **45**.
98 ½p. Type **45** 10 10
99 1p. Officer, 2nd North Regt, 1825 10 10
100 1½p. Gunner, Guernsey Artillery, 1787 10 10
101 2p. Gunner, Guernsey Artillery, 1815 10 10
102 2½p. Corporal, Royal Guernsey Artillery, 1868 10 10
103 3p. Field Officer, Royal Guernsey Artillery, 1895 10 10
104 3½p. Sergeant, 3rd Regt, 1867 10 10
105 4p. Officer, East Regt, 1822 10 10
105a 5p. Field Officer, Royal Guernsey Artillery, (1895) 15 15
106 5½p. Colour-Sergeant of Grenadiers, East Regt, 1833 10 10
107 6p. Officer, North Regt, 1832 10 10
107a 7p. Officer, East Regt, 1822 25 25
108 8p. Field Officer, Rifle Company, 1868 15 10
109 9p. Private, 4th West Regt, 1785 15 10
110 10p. Field Officer, 4th West Regt, 1824 15 10

(b) As T **46**.
111 20p. Type **46** 30 40
112 50p. Officer, Field Battery, Royal Guernsey Artillery, 1868 90 1·00
113 £1 Cavalry Trooper, Light Dragoons, 1814 (horiz) 1·90 1·75

47 Badge of Guernsey and U.P.U. Emblem

1974. Centenary of U.P.U. Multicoloured.
114 2½p. Type **47** 10 10
115 3p. Map of Guernsey 10 10
116 8p. U.P.U. Building, Berne, and Guernsey flag 20 20
117 10p. "Salle des Etats" 20 20

48 "Cradle Rock"

1974. Renoir Paintings. Multicoloured.
118 3p. Type **48** 10 10
119 5½p. "Moulin Huet Bay" . . 10 10
120 8p. "Au Bord de la Mer" (vert) 25 25
121 10p. Self-portrait (vert) . . . 25 25

49 Guernsey Spleenwort 50 Victor Hugo House

1975. Guernsey Ferns. Multicoloured.
122 3½p. Type **49** 10 10
123 4p. Sand quillwort 10 10
124 8p. Guernsey quillwort . . . 25 25
125 10p. Least adder's tongue . . 25 25

1975. Victor Hugo's Exile in Guernsey. Mult.
126 3½p. Type **50** 10 10
127 4p. Candie Gardens (vert) . . 10 10
128 8p. United Europe Oak, Hauteville (vert) 25 25
129 10p. Tapestry Room, Hauteville 25 25
MS130 114 × 143 mm. Nos. 126/9 65 90

51 Globe and Seal of Bailiwick

1975. Christmas. Multicoloured.
131 4p. Type **51** 10 10
132 6p. Guernsey flag 10 10
133 10p. Guernsey flag and Alderney shield (horiz) . . 25 25
134 12p. Guernsey flag and Sark shield (horiz) 25 25

52 Les Hanois

1976. Bailiwick Lighthouses. Multicoloured.
135 4p. Type **52** 10 10
136 6p. Les Casquets 10 10
137 11p. Quesnard 20 20
138 13p. Point Robert 25 25

53 Milk Can

1976. Europa.
139 **53** 10p. brown and green . . . 20 20
140 – 25p. grey and blue 40 35
DESIGN: 25p. Christening cup.

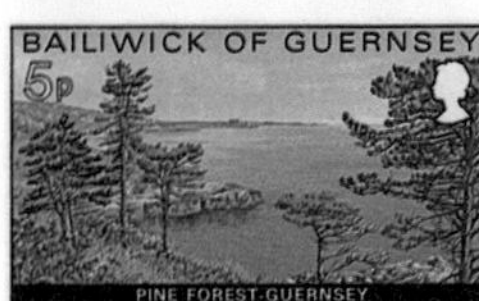

54 Pine Forest, Guernsey

1976. Bailiwick Views. Multicoloured.
141 5p. Type **54** 10 10
142 7p. Herm and Jethou 10 10
143 11p. Grand Greve Bay, Sark (vert) 25 25
144 13p. Trois Vaux Bay, Alderney (vert) 25 25

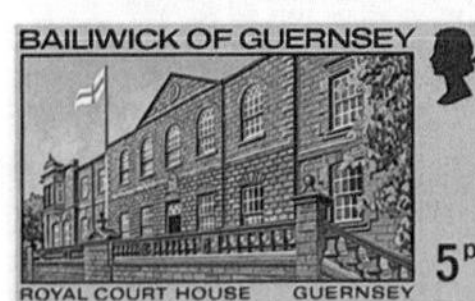

55 Royal Court House, Guernsey

1976. Christmas. Buildings. Multicoloured.
145 5p. Type **55** 10 10
146 7p. Elizabeth College, Guernsey 10 10
147 11p. La Seigneurie, Sark . . 25 25
148 13p. Island Hall, Alderney . . 25 25

56 Queen Elizabeth II 58 Statue-menhir, Castel

57 Woodland, Talbot's Valley

1977. Silver Jubilee. Multicoloured.
149 7p. Type **56** 20 15
150 35p. Queen Elizabeth (half-length portrait) 55 40

1977. Europa. Multicoloured.
151 7p. Type **57** 15 15
152 25p. Pastureland, Talbot's Valley 45 45

1977. Prehistoric Monuments. Multicoloured.
153 5p. Type **58** 10 10
154 7p. Megalithic tomb, St. Saviour (horiz) 10 10
155 11p. Cist, Tourgis (horiz) . . 25 25
156 13p. Statue-menhir, St. Martin 25 25

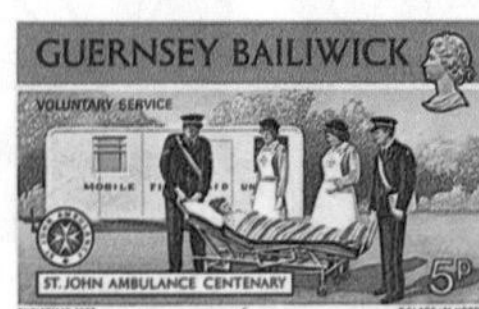

59 Mobile First Aid Unit

1977. Christmas and St. John Ambulance Centenary. Multicoloured.
157 5p. Type **59** 10 10
158 7p. Mobile radar unit 10 10
159 11p. Marine ambulance "Flying Christine II" (vert) 25 25
160 13p. Cliff rescue (vert) . . . 25 25

60 View from Clifton, c. 1830

1978. Old Guernsey Prints (1st series).
161 **60** 5p. black and green . . . 10 10
162 – 7p. black and stone 10 10
163 – 11p. black and pink . . . 25 25
164 – 13p. black and blue . . . 25 25
DESIGNS: 7p. Market Square, St. Peter Port, c. 1838; 11p. Petit-Bo Bay, c. 1839; 13p. The Quay, St. Peter Port, c. 1830.
See also Nos. 249/52.

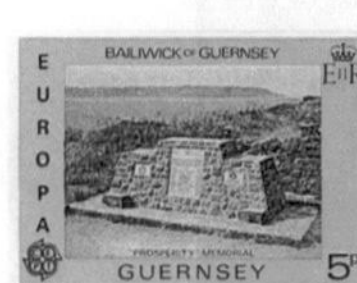

61 "Prosperity" Memorial 62 Queen Elizabeth II

1978. Europa. Multicoloured.
165 5p. Type **61** 10 10
166 7p. Victoria Monument (vert) 25 25

1978. 25th Anniversary of Coronation.
167 **62** 20p. black, grey and blue 30 45

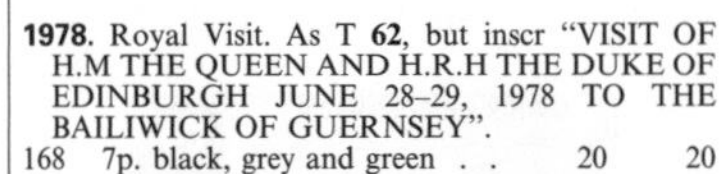

1978. Royal Visit. As T **62**, but inscr "VISIT OF H.M THE QUEEN AND H.R.H THE DUKE OF EDINBURGH JUNE 28–29, 1978 TO THE BAILIWICK OF GUERNSEY".
168 7p. black, grey and green . . 20 20

63 Northern Gannet

1978. Birds. Multicoloured.
169 5p. Type **63** 10 10
170 7p. Firecrest 20 15
171 11p. Dartford warbler . . . 25 20
172 13p. Spotted redshank . . . 35 20

64 Solanum

1978. Christmas. Multicoloured.
173 5p. Type **64** 10 10
174 7p. Christmas rose 10 10
175 11p. Holly (vert) 20 20
176 13p. Mistletoe (vert) 25 25

65 One Double Coin, 1830 67 Pillar-box and Postmark, 1853, and Mail Van and Postmark, 1979

1979. Coins.
177 **65** ½p. multicoloured 10 10
178 – 1p. multicoloured 10 10
179 – 2p. multicoloured 10 10
180 – 4p. multicoloured 10 10
181 – 5p. black, silver and brown 10 10
182 – 6p. black, silver and red . . 15 10
183 – 7p. black, silver and green 15 15
184 – 8p. black, silver and brown 15 15
185 – 9p. multicoloured 15 15
186 – 10p. multicoloured (green background) 30 25
187 – 10p. multicoloured (orange background) 20 15
188 – 11p. multicoloured 20 15
189 – 11½p. multicoloured . . . 20 15
190 – 12p. multicoloured 20 15
191 – 13p. multicoloured 25 20
192 – 14p. black, silver and blue 25 20
193 – 15p. black, silver and brown 25 25
194 – 20p. black, silver and brown 30 30
195 – 50p. black, silver and red 85 60
196 – £1 black, silver and green 1·75 1·10
197 – £2 black, silver and blue 3·75 2·00
198 – £5 multicoloured . . . . . 7·50 6·50

DESIGNS—VERT (As Type **65**): 1p. Two doubles, 1899; 2p. Four doubles, 1902; 4p. Eight doubles, 1959; 5p. Three pence, 1956; 6p. Five new pence, 1968; 7p. Fifty new pence, 1969; 8p. Ten new pence, 1970; 9p. Half new penny, 1971; 10p. (both) One new penny, 1971; 11p. Two new pence, 1971; 11½p. Half penny, 1979; 12p. One penny, 1977; 13p. Two pence, 1977; 14p. Five pence, 1977; 15p. Ten pence, 1977; 20p. Twenty-five pence, 1972. (26 × 45 mm): 50p. William I commemorative 10s., 1966; £5 Seal of the Bailiwick. HORIZ (45 × 26 mm): £1 Silver Jubilee crown, 1977; £2 Royal Silver Wedding crown, 1972.

1979. Europa. Communications. Multicoloured.
201 6p. Type **67** 10 10
202 8p. Telephone, 1897 and telex machine, 1979 . . . . . . 20 20

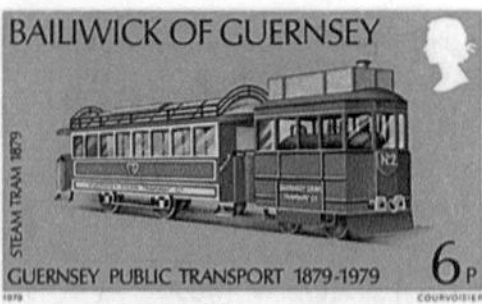

68 Steam Tram, 1879

1979. History of Public Transport. Multicoloured.
203 6p. Type **68** 10 10
204 8p. Electric tram, 1896 . . . 15 10
205 11p. Motor bus, 1911 . . . . 20 15
206 13p. Motor bus, 1979 . . . . 20 25

69 Bureau and Postal Headquarters

1979. 10th Anniv of Guernsey Postal Administration. Multicoloured.
207 6p. Type **69** 10 10
208 8p. "Mails and telegrams" . . 15 10
209 13p. "Parcels" 20 15
210 15p. "Philately" 25 25
MS211 120 × 80 mm. Nos. 207/10 80 80

70 Major-General Le Marchant

1980. Europa. Personalities. Multicoloured.
212 10p. Type **70** 15 15
213 13½p. Admiral Lord de Saumarez 30 25

71 Policewoman with Lost Child

1980. 60th Anniv of Guernsey Police Force. Mult.
214 7p. Type **71** 15 15
215 15p. Motorcycle escort . . . 25 25
216 17½p. Dog-handler 30 25

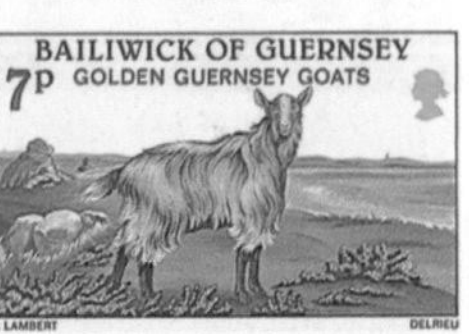

72 Golden Guernsey Goat

1980. Golden Guernsey Goats. Multicoloured.
217 7p. Type **72** 10 10
218 10p. Head of goat 20 15
219 15p. Goat 25 20
220 17½p. Goat and kids 40 35

73 "Sark Cottage"

1980. Peter Le Lievre Paintings. Multicoloured.
221 7p. Type **73** 15 10
222 10p. "Moulin Huet" 20 15

223	13½p. "Boats at Sea"	25	20
224	15p. "Cow Lane" (vert)	25	25
225	17½p. "Peter Le Lievre" (vert)	40	35

74 "Polyommatus icarus"

1981. Butterflies. Multicoloured.

226	8p. Type **74**	15	15
227	12p. "Vanessa atalanta"	20	20
228	22p. "Aglais urticae"	35	35
229	25p. "Lasiommata megera"	40	40

75 Sailors paying respect to "Le Petit Bonhomme Andriou" (rock resembling head of a man)

76 Prince Charles

1981. Europa. Folklore.

230	**75** 12p. gold, brown & lt brn	25	15
231	– 18p. gold, blue and light blue	30	30

DESIGN: 18p. Fairies and Guernsey lily.

1981. Royal Wedding. Multicoloured.

232	8p. Type **76**	15	10
233	8p. Prince Charles and Lady Diana Spencer	15	10
234	8p. Lady Diana	15	10
235	12p. Type **76**	25	25
236	12p. As No. 233	25	25
237	12p. As No. 234	25	25
238	25p. Royal Family (49×32 mm)	65	60
MS239	104×127 mm. Nos. 232/8	3·00	2·75

77 Sark Launch

1981. Inter-island Transport. Multicoloured.

240	8p. Type **77**	15	15
241	12p. Britten Norman "short nose" Trislander airplane	25	20
242	18p. Hydrofoil	30	30
243	22p. Herm catamaran	45	45
244	25p. "Sea Trent" (coaster)	55	55

78 Rifle Shooting

1981. Int Year for Disabled Persons. Mult.

245	8p. Type **78**	15	10
246	12p. Riding	25	20
247	22p. Swimming	45	35
248	25p. Circuit construction	55	40

1982. Old Guernsey Prints (2nd series). Prints from Sketches by T. Compton. As T **60**.

249	8p. black and blue	15	15
250	12p. black and green	25	20
251	22p. black and brown	40	40
252	25p. black and lilac	50	50

DESIGNS: 8p Jethou; 12p. Fermain Bay; 22p. The Terres; 25p. St. Peter Port.

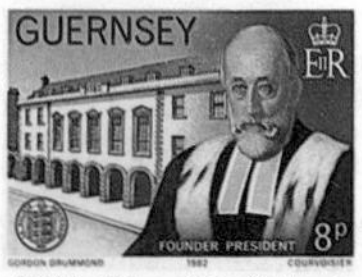

79 Sir Edgar MacCulloch (founder-president) and Guille-Alles Library, St. Peter Port

1982. Cent of La Societe Guernesiaise. Mult.

253	8p. Type **79**	15	15
254	13p. French invasion fleet crossing English Channel, 1066 ("history")	30	15
255	20p. H.M.S "Crescent", 1793 ("history")	40	25
256	24p. Dragonfly ("entomology")	50	40
257	26p. Common snipe caught for ringing ("ornithology")	60	50
258	29p. Samian bowl, 160–200 A.D. ("archaeology")	65	55

The 13p. and 20p. designs also include the Europa C.E.P.T. emblem.

80 "Sea Scouts"

82 Flute Player and Boats

81 Midnight Mass

1982. 75th Anniv of Boy Scout Movement. Mult.

259	8p. Type **80**	15	25
260	13p. "Scouts"	30	25
261	26p. "Cub Scouts"	55	50
262	29p. "Air Scouts"	65	1·10

1982. Christmas. Multicoloured.

263	8p. Type **81**	15	15
264	13p. Exchanging gifts	25	15
265	24p. Christmas meal	50	45
266	26p. Exchanging cards	55	50
267	29p. Queen's Christmas message	65	55

1982. Centenary of Boys' Brigade. Multicoloured.

268	8p. Type **82**	15	10
269	13p. Cymbal player and tug o' war	25	20
270	24p. Trumpet player and bible class	40	40
271	26p. Drummer and cadets marching	55	50
272	29p. Boys' Brigade band	65	55

83 Building Albert Pier Extension, 1850s

1983. Europa. Development of St. Peter Port Harbour. Multicoloured.

273	13p. Type **83**	20	15
274	13p. St. Peter Port harbour, 1983	20	15
275	20p. St. Peter Port, 1680	30	30
276	20p. Artist's impression of future development scheme	30	30

84 "View at Guernsey" (Renoir)

1983. Cent of Renoir's Visit to Guernsey. Mult.

277	9p. Type **84**	20	15
278	13p. "Children on the Seashore" (25×39 mm)	25	25
279	26p. "Marine, Guernesey"	55	50
280	28p. "La Bale du Moulin Huet a travers les Arbres"	85	80
281	31p. "Brouillard a Guernesey"	1·00	90

85 Launching "Star of the West", 1869, and Capt. J. Lenfestey

1983. Guernsey Shipping (1st series). Mult.

282	9p. Type **85**	20	20
283	13p. Leaving St. Peter Port	25	15
284	26p. Off Rio Grande Bar	50	50
285	28p. Off St. Lucia	80	75
286	31p. Map of 1879–80 voyage	85	80

See also Nos. 415/19.

86 Dame of Sark as Young Woman

1984. Birth Centenary of Sibyl Hathaway, Dame of Sark. Multicoloured.

287	9p. Type **86**	20	20
288	13p. German occupation, 1940–45	30	15
289	26p. Royal visit, 1957	70	55
290	28p. Chief Pleas	75	70
291	31p. The Dame of Sark rose	80	75

87 C.E.P.T. 25th Anniversary Logo

1984. Europa.

292	**87** 13p. light blue, blue & black	25	15
293	20½p. green, dp green & blk	55	50

88 The Royal Court and St. George's Flag

89 St. Apolline Chapel

1984. Links with the Commonwealth. Mult.

294	9p. Type **88**	20	15
295	31p. Castle Cornet and Union flag	85	85

1984. Views. Multicoloured.

296	1p. Little Chapel	10	10
297	2p. Fort Grey (horiz)	10	10
298	3p. Type **89**	10	10
299	4p. Petit Port (horiz)	10	10
300	5p. Little Russel (horiz)	15	10
301	6p. The Harbour, Herm (horiz)	15	15
302	7p. Saints (horiz)	15	15
303	8p. St. Saviour	20	15
304	9p. New Jetty (inscr "Cambridge Berth") (horiz)	20	10
305	10p. Belvoir, Herm (horiz)	25	15
306	11p. La Seigneurie, Sark (horiz)	25	15
306b	12p. Petit Bot	35	15
307	13p. St. Saviours reservoir (horiz)	25	25
308	14p. St. Peter Port	25	20
309	15p. Havelet	30	30
309c	16p. Hostel of St. John (horiz)	30	20
309d	18p. Le Variouf	30	20
310	20p. La Coupee, Sark (horiz)	45	25
310b	21p. King's Mills (horiz)	45	30
310c	26p. Town Church	70	50
311	30p. Grandes Rocques (horiz)	65	60
312	40p. Torteval Church	70	70
313	50p. Bordeaux (horiz)	80	75
314	£1 Albecq (horiz)	1·90	1·40
315	£2 L' Ancresse (horiz)	3·75	2·75

See also Nos. 398/9a.

90 "A Partridge in a Pear Tree"

91 Sir John Doyle and Coat of Arms

1984. Christmas. "The Twelve Days of Christmas". Multicoloured.

316	5p. Type **90**	15	15
317	5p. "Two turtle doves"	15	15
318	5p. "Three French hens"	15	15
319	5p. "Four colly birds"	15	15
320	5p. "Five gold rings"	15	15
321	5p. "Six geese a-laying"	15	15
322	5p. "Seven swans a-swimming"	15	15
323	5p. "Eight maids a-milking"	15	15
324	5p. "Nine drummers drumming"	15	15
325	5p. "Ten pipers piping"	15	15
326	5p. "Eleven ladies dancing"	15	15
327	5p. "Twelve lords a-leaping"	15	15

1984. 150th Death Anniv of Lt.-General Sir John Doyle. Multicoloured.

328	13p. Type **91**	30	25
329	29p. Battle of Germantown, 1777 (horiz)	65	60
330	31p. Reclamation of Braye du Valle, 1806 (horiz)	75	70
331	34p. Mail for Alderney, 1812 (horiz)	90	85

92 Cuckoo Wrasse

1985. Fishes. Multicoloured.

332	9p. Type **92**	30	25
333	13p. Red gurnard	40	25
334	29p. Red mullet	1·00	90
335	31p. Mackerel	1·00	90
336	34p. Oceanic sunfish	1·10	90

93 Dove

1985. 40th Anniv of Peace in Europe.

337	**93** 22p. multicoloured	60	50

94 I.Y.Y. Emblem and Young People of Different Races

1985. International Youth Year. Multicoloured.

338	9p. Type **94**	25	15
339	31p. Girl Guides cooking over campfire	75	70

95 Stave of Music enclosing Flags

1985. Europa. European Music Year. Multicoloured.

340	14p. Type **95**	30	25
341	22p. Stave of music and musical instruments	60	55

96 Guide Leader, Girl Guide and Brownie

97 Santa Claus

1985. 75th Anniv of Girl Guide Movement.

342	**96** 34p. multicoloured	1·00	90

1985. Christmas. Gift-bearers. Multicoloured.

343	5p. Type **97**	25	15
344	5p. Lussibruden (Sweden)	25	15
345	5p. King Balthazar	25	15
346	5p. Saint Nicholas (Netherlands)	25	15
347	5p. La Befana (Italy)	25	15
348	5p. Julenisse (Denmark)	25	15
349	5p. Christkind (Germany)	25	15
350	5p. King Wenceslas (Czechoslovakia)	25	15
351	5p. Shepherd of Les Baux (France)	25	15
352	5p. King Caspar	25	15
353	5p. Baboushka (Russia)	25	15
354	5p. King Melchior	25	15

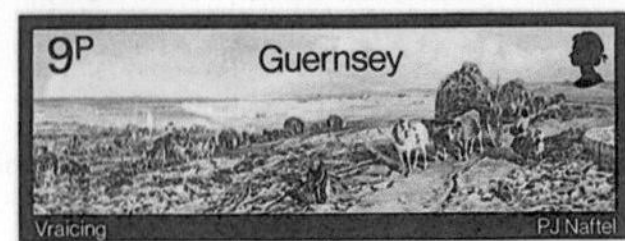

98 "Vraicing"

1985. Paintings by Paul Jacob Naftel. Multicoloured.
355 9p. Type **98** 20 20
356 14p. "Castle Cornet" 25 25
357 22p. "Rocquaine Bay" 65 65
358 31p. "Little Russel" 1·00 1·00
359 34p. "Seaweedgatherers" 1·25 1·25

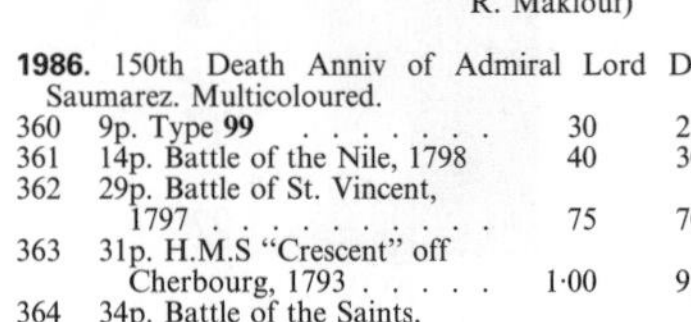

99 Squadron off Nargue Island, 1809 **100** Profile of Queen Elizabeth II (after R. Maklouf)

1986. 150th Death Anniv of Admiral Lord De Saumarez. Multicoloured.
360 9p. Type **99** 30 25
361 14p. Battle of the Nile, 1798 40 30
362 29p. Battle of St. Vincent, 1797 75 70
363 31p. H.M.S "Crescent" off Cherbourg, 1793 1·00 95
364 34p. Battle of the Saints, 1782 1·00 1·00

1986. 60th Birthday of Queen Elizabeth II.
365 **100** 60p. multicoloured 1·50 1·25

101 Northern Gannet and Nylon Net ("Operation Gannet") **102** Prince Andrew and Miss Sarah Ferguson

1986. Europa. Nature and Environmental Protection. Multicoloured.
366 10p. Type **101** 30 30
367 14p. Loose-flowered orchid 40 40
368 22p. Guernsey elm 70 70

1986. Royal Wedding. Multicoloured.
369 14p. Type **102** 60 50
370 34p. Prince Andrew and Miss Sarah Ferguson (different) (47 × 30 mm) 1·00 90

103 Bowls **105** "While Shepherds Watched their Flocks by Night"

104 Guernsey Museum and Art Gallery, Candie Gardens

1986. Sport in Guernsey. Multicoloured.
371 10p. Type **103** 25 20
372 14p. Cricket 35 20
373 22p. Squash 50 45
374 29p. Hockey 90 80
375 31p. Swimming (horiz) 90 80
376 34p. Shooting (horiz) 1·00 90

1986. Cent of Guernsey Museums. Mult.
377 14p. Type **104** 30 15
378 29p. Fort Grey Maritime Museum 85 80
379 31p. Castle Cornet 85 80
380 34p. National Trust of Guernsey Folk Museum 1·00 90

1986. Christmas. Carols. Multicoloured.
381 6p. Type **105** 20 20
382 6p. "In The Bleak Midwinter" 20 20
383 6p. "O Little Town of Bethlehem" 20 20
384 6p. "The Holly and the Ivy" 20 20
385 6p. "O Little Christmas Tree" 20 20
386 6p. "Away in a Manger" 20 20
387 6p. "Good King Wenceslas" 20 20
388 6p. "We Three Kings of Orient Are" 20 20
389 6p. "Hark the Herald Angels Sing" 20 20
390 6p. "I Saw Three Ships" 20 20
391 6p. "Little Donkey" 20 20
392 6p. "Jingle Bells" 20 20

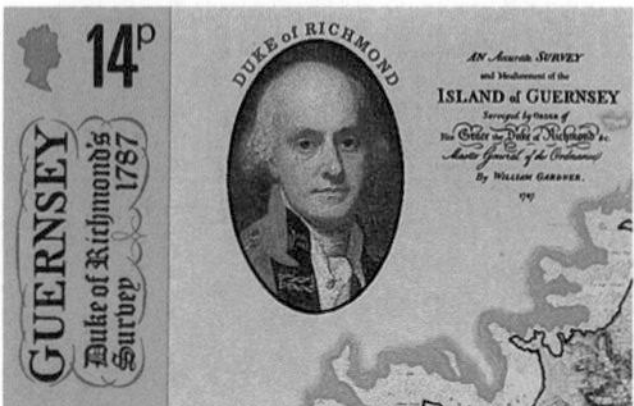

106 Duke of Richmond and Portion of Map

1987. Bicentenary of Duke of Richmond's Survey of Guernsey. Sheet 134 × 103 mm containing T **106** and similar horiz designs showing sections of map. Multicoloured.
MS393 14p. Type **106**; 29p. North-east; 31p. South-west; 34p. South-east 2·50 2·75
The stamps within No. **MS**393 show a composite design of the Duke of Richmond's map of Guernsey.

107 Post Office Headquarters **108** Sir Edmund Andros and La Plaiderie, Guernsey

1987. Europa. Modern Architecture. Mult.
394 15p. Type **107** 25 20
395 15p. Architect's elevation of Post Office Headquarters 25 20
396 22p. Guernsey Grammar School 30 35
397 22p. Architect's elevation of Grammar School 30 35

1987. Designs as Nos. 306, 306b, 309 and 309c but smaller.
398 11p. La Seigneurie, Sark (22 × 18 mm) 50 50
398a 12p. Petit Bot (18 × 22 mm) 40 40
399 15p. Havelet (18 × 22 mm) 60 60
399a 16p. Hostel of St. John (22 × 18 mm) 50 50

1987. 350th Birth Anniv of Sir Edmund Andros (colonial administrator). Multicoloured.
400 15p. Type **108** 30 15
401 29p. Governor's Palace, Virginia 80 60
402 31p. Governor Andros in Boston 85 75
403 34p. Map of New Amsterdam (New York), 1661 1·10 1·00

109 The Jester's Warning to Young William **110** John Wesley preaching on the Quay, Alderney

1987. 900th Death Anniv of William the Conqueror. Multicoloured.
404 11p. Type **109** 20 15
405 15p. Hastings battlefield 30 25
406 15p. Norman soldier with pennant 30 25
407 22p. William the Conqueror 60 60
408 22p. Queen Matilda and Abbaye aux Dames, Caen 60 60
409 34p. William's coronation regalia and Halley's Comet 1·00 1·10

1987. Bicentenary of John Wesley's Visit to Guernsey. Multicoloured.
410 7p. Type **110** 20 15
411 15p. Wesley preaching at Mon Plaisir, St. Peter Port 25 25
412 29p. Preaching at Assembly Rooms 80 75
413 31p. Wesley and La Ville Baudu (early Methodist meeting place) 90 85
414 34p. Wesley and first Methodist Chapel, St. Peter Port 90 85

111 "Golden Spur" off St. Sampson Harbour

1988. Guernsey Shipping (2nd series). "Golden Spur". Multicoloured.
415 11p. Type **111** 25 25
416 15p. "Golden Spur" entering Hong Kong harbour 35 35
417 29p. Anchored off Macao 90 85
418 31p. In China Tea Race 90 85
419 34p. "Golden Spur" and map showing voyage of 1872–74 1·20 95

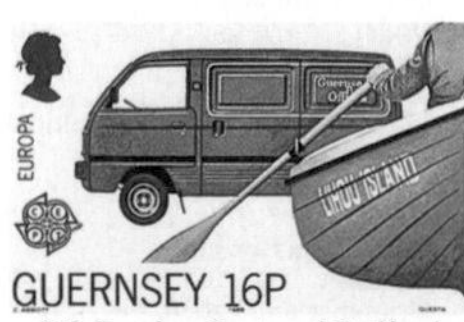

112 Rowing Boat and Bedford "Rascal" Mail Van

1988. Europa. Transport and Communications. Multicoloured.
420 16p. Type **112** 35 35
421 16p. Rowing boat and Vickers Viscount mail plane 35 35
422 22p. Postman on bicycle and horse-drawn carriages, Sark 70 70
423 22p. Postmen on bicycles and carriage 70 70
Nos. 420/1 and 422/3 were each printed together, se-tenant, the two stamps of each value forming a composite design.

113 Frederick Corbin Lukis and Lukis House, St. Peter Port

1988. Birth Bicentenary of Frederick Corbin Lukis (archaeologist). Multicoloured.
424 12p. Type **113** 25 25
425 16p. Natural history books and reconstructed pot 30 25
426 29p. Lukis directing excavation of Le Creux es Faies and prehistoric beaker 90 85
427 31p. Lukis House Observatory and garden 90 85
428 34p. Prehistoric artifacts 90 90

114 "Cougar", "Rocky" and "Annabella" (powerboats) and Westland Wessex Rescue Helicopter off Jethou

1988. World Offshore Powerboat Championships. Multicoloured.
429 16p. Type **114** 35 25
430 30p. "Poul Pilot" (powerboat) in Gouliot Passage 85 85
431 32p. Start of race at St. Peter Port (vert) 1·00 90
432 35p. Admiralty chart showing course (vert) 1·10 1·00

115 Joshua Gosselin and Herbarium **116** Coutances Cathedral, France

1988. Bicentenary of Joshua Gosselin's "Flora Sarniensis". Multicoloured.
433 12p. Type **115** 25 25
434 16p. Hares-tail grass 40 35
435 16p. Dried hares-tail grass 40 35
436 23p. Variegated catchfly 55 50
437 23p. Dried variegated catchfly 55 50
438 35p. Rock sea lavender 1·00 1·00

1988. Christmas. Ecclesiastical Links. Mult.
439 8p. Type **116** 20 20
440 8p. Interior of Notre Dame du Rosaire Church, Guernsey 20 20
441 8p. Stained glass, St. Sampson's Church, Guernsey 20 20
442 8p. Dol-de-Bretagne Cathedral, France 20 20
443 8p. Bishop's throne, Town Church, Guernsey 20 20
444 8p. Winchester Cathedral 20 20
445 8p. St. John's Cathedral, Portsmouth 20 20
446 8p. High altar, St. Joseph's Church, Guernsey 20 20
447 8p. Mont Saint-Michel, France 20 20
448 8p. Chancel, Vale Church, Guernsey 20 20
449 8p. Lychgate, Forest Church, Guernsey 20 20
450 8p. Marmoutier Abbey, France 20 20

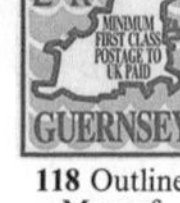

117 Le Cat (Tip Cat) **118** Outline Map of Guernsey

1989. Europa. Children's Toys and Games. Multicoloured.
451 12p. Type **117** 25 20
452 16p. Girl with Cobo Alice doll 40 40
453 23p. Le Colimachaon (hopscotch) 80 85

1989. Coil Stamp. No value expressed.
454 **118** (-) blue 60 60
455 (-) green 65 70
No. 454 is inscribed "MINIMUM BAILIWICK POSTAGE PAID" and No. 455 "MINIMUM FIRST CLASS POSTAGE TO UK PAID". They were initally sold at 14p. and 18p. but this was changed in line with postage rate rises.

119 Guernsey Airways De Havilland Dragon Express and Mail Van

1989. 50th Anniv of Guernsey Airport (Nos. 456, 458 and 460) and 201 Squadron's Affiliation with Guernsey (Nos. 457, 459 and 461). Mult.
456 12p. Type **119** 35 30
457 12p. Supermarine Southampton II flying boat at mooring 35 30
458 18p. B.E.A. De Havilland Rapide 50 50
459 18p. Short S.25 Sunderland Mk V flying boat taking off 50 50
460 35p. Air U.K. British Aerospace BAe 146 1·00 90
461 35p. Avro Shackleton M.R.3 1·00 1·00

120 "Queen Elizabeth II" (June Mendoza)

122 Two-toed Sloth

121 "Ibex" at G.W.R. Terminal, St. Peter Port

1989. Royal Visit.
462 **120** 30p. multicoloured . . . 75 80

1989. Centenary of Great Western Railway Steamer Service to Channel Islands. Multicoloured.
463 12p. Type **121** 20 20
464 18p. "Great Western" (paddle-steamer) in Little Russel 45 45
465 29p. "St. Julien" passing Casquets Light 70 75
466 34p. "Roebuck" off Portland 1·00 95
467 37p. "Antelope" and boat train on Weymouth Quay 1·20 1·10
MS468 115 × 117 mm. Nos. 463/7 3·25 3·25

1989. 10th Anniv of Guernsey Zoological Trust. Animals of the Rainforest. Multicoloured.
469 18p. Type **122** 70 70
470 29p. Capuchin monkey . . . 70 70
471 32p. White-lipped tamarin . . 70 70
472 34p. Common squirrel-monkey 70 70
473 37p. Common gibbon 70 70

123 Star

125 Penny Black and Mail Steamer off St. Peter Port, 1840

124 Sark Post Office, c. 1890

1989. Christmas. Christmas Tree Decorations. Multicoloured.
474 10p. Type **123** 25 20
475 10p. Fairy 25 20
476 10p. Candles 25 20
477 10p. Bird 25 20
478 10p. Present 25 20
479 10p. Carol-singer 25 20
480 10p. Christmas cracker . . . 25 20
481 10p. Bauble 25 20
482 10p. Christmas stocking . . . 25 20
483 10p. Bell 25 20
484 10p. Fawn 25 20
485 10p. Church 25 20

1990. Europa. Post Office Buildings.
486 **124** 20p. deep brown, sepia and light brown 45 45
487 – 20p. multicoloured . . . 45 45
488 – 24p. deep brown, sepia and light brown 60 65
489 – 24p. multicoloured . . . 60 65
DESIGNS: No. 487, Sark Post Office, 1990; 488, Arcade Post Office counter, St. Peter Port, c. 1840; 489, Arcade Post Office counter, St. Peter Port, 1990.

1990. 150th Anniv of the Penny Black. Mult.
490 14p. Type **125** 35 35
491 20p. Penny Red, 1841 and pillar box of 1853 . . . . 45 45
492 32p. Bisected 2d., 1940 and German Army band . . . 80 80
493 34p. Regional 3d., 1958 and Guernsey emblems . . . . 1·00 1·00
494 37p. Independent postal administration 1½d., 1969 and queue outside Main Post Office . . . . . . 1·00 1·00
MS495 151 × 116 mm. Nos. 490/4 3·00 3·50
No. **MS**495 also commemorates "Stamp World London '90" International Stamp Exhibition.

126 Lt. Philip Saumarez writing Log Book

1990. 250th Anniv of Anson's Circumnavigation. Multicoloured.
496 14p. Type **126** 30 30
497 20p. Anson's squadron leaving Portsmouth, 1740 40 40
498 29p. Ships at St. Catherine's Island, Brazil 80 80
499 34p. H.M.S. "Tryal" (sloop) dismasted, Cape Horn, 1741 . . . . 1·00 90
500 37p. Crew of H.M.S. "Centurion" on Juan Fernandez . . . . 1·10 90

127 Grey Seal and Pup

1990. Marine Life. Multicoloured.
501 20p. Type **127** 45 45
502 26p. Bottle-nosed dolphin . . 95 95
503 31p. Basking shark . . . . . 1·00 1·00
504 37p. Common porpoise . . . 1·25 1·25

128 Blue Tit and Great Tit

129 Air Raid and 1941 ½d. Stamp

1990. Christmas. Winter Birds. Multicoloured.
505 10p. Type **128** 35 30
506 10p. Snow bunting 35 30
507 10p. Common kestrel ("Kestrel") 35 30
508 10p. Common starling ("Starling") 35 30
509 10p. Western greenfinch ("Greenfinch") 35 30
510 10p. European robin ("Robin") 35 30
511 10p. Winter wren 35 30
512 10p. Barn owl 35 30
513 10p. Mistle thrush 35 30
514 10p. Grey heron ("Heron") . . 35 30
515 10p. Chaffinch 35 30
516 10p. River kingfisher ("Kingfisher") 35 30

1991. 50th Anniv of First Guernsey Stamps. Multicoloured.
517 37p. Type **129** . . . . . . 1·00 1·10
518 53p. 1941 1d. stamp . . . . 1·30 1·50
519 57p. 1944 2½d. stamp . . . . 1·30 1·50

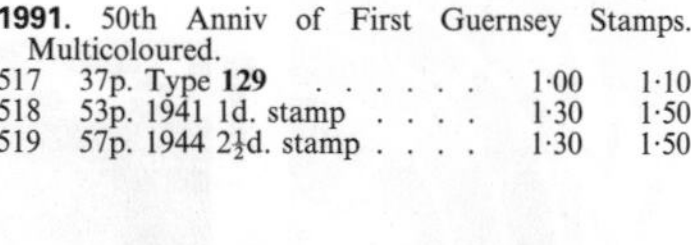

130 Visit of Queen Victoria to Guernsey, and Discovery of Neptune, 1846

1991. Europa. Europe in Space. Multicoloured.
520 21p. Type **130** 55 50
521 21p. Visit of Queen Elizabeth II and Prince Philip to Sark, and "Sputnik" (first artificial satellite), 1957 . . . . . . 55 50
522 26p. Maiden voyage of "Sarnia" (ferry) and "Vostok I" (first manned space flight), 1961 . . . . 65 60
523 26p. Cancelling Guernsey stamps, and first manned landing on Moon, 1969 . . 65 60

131 Children in Guernsey Sailing Trust "GP14" Dinghy

132 Pair of Oystercatchers

1991. Centenary of Guernsey Yacht Club. Mult.
524 15p. Type **131** 45 15
525 21p. Guernsey Regatta . . . 70 25
526 26p. Lombard Channel Islands' Challenge race . . 80 80
527 31p. Rolex Swan Regatta . . 90 1·10
528 37p. Old Gaffers' Association gaff-rigged yacht . . . . . 1·00 1·40
MS529 163 × 75 mm. As Nos. 524/8, but "GUERNSEY" and face values in yellow . . . . 3·50 4·00

1991. Nature Conservation. L'Eree Shingle Bank Reserve. Multicoloured.
530 15p. Type **132** 40 45
531 15p. Three ruddy turnstones 40 45
532 15p. Dunlins and ruddy turnstones 40 45
533 15p. Curlew and ruddy turnstones 40 45
534 15p. Ringed plover with chicks 40 45
535 21p. Gull, sea campion and sea radish 50 45
536 21p. Yellow horned poppy 50 45
537 21p. Pair of common stonechats, hare's foot clover and fennel 50 45
538 21p. Hare's foot clover, fennel and slender oat . . 50 45
539 21p. Sea kale on shore . . . 50 45
Nos. 530/4 and 535/9 were each printed together, se-tenant, with the backgrounds forming composite designs.

133 "Rudolph the Red-nosed Reindeer" (Melanie Sharpe)

134 Queen Elizabeth II in 1952

1991. Christmas. Children's Paintings. Mult.
540 12p. Type **133** 30 30
541 12p. "Christmas Pudding" (James Quinn) 30 30
542 12p. "Snowman" (Lisa Guille) 30 30
543 12p. "Snowman in Top Hat" (Jessica Ede-Golightly) . . 30 30
544 12p. "Robins and Christmas Tree" (Sharon Le Page) . . 30 30
545 12p. "Shepherds and Angels" (Anna Coquelin) 30 30
546 12p. "Nativity" (Claudine Lihou) 30 30
547 12p. "Three Wise Men" (Jonathan Le Noury) . . . 30 30
548 12p. "Star of Bethlehem and Angels" (Marcia Mahy) . . 30 30
549 12p. "Christmas Tree" (Laurel Garfield) 30 30
550 12p. "Santa Claus" (Rebecca Driscoll) 30 30
551 12p. "Snowman and Star" (Ian Lowe) 30 30

1992. 40th Anniv of Accession. Multicoloured.
552 23p. Type **134** 50 50
553 28p. Queen Elizabeth in 1977 65 65
554 33p. Queen Elizabeth in 1986 90 90
555 39p. Queen Elizabeth in 1991 1·10 1·10

135 Christopher Columbus

1992. 500th Anniv of Discovery of America by Columbus. Multicoloured.
556 23p. Type **135** 65 60
557 23p. Examples of Columbus's signature 65 60
558 28p. "Santa Maria" . . . . 1·25 1·25
559 28p. Map of first voyage . . 1·25 1·25
MS560 157 × 77 mm. Nos. 556/9 4·50 5·00

136 Guernsey Calves

1992. 150th Anniv of Royal Guernsey Agricultural and Horticultural Society. Sheet, 93 × 71 mm.
MS561 **136** 75p. multicoloured 2·10 2·00

137 Stock

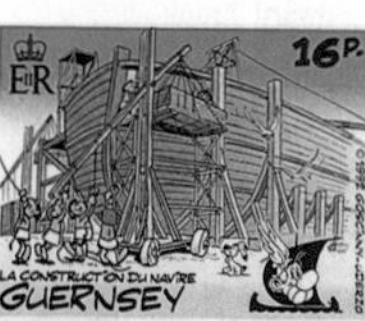

138 Building the Ship

1992. Horticultural Exports. Multicoloured.
562 1p. "Stephanotis floribunda" 10 10
563 2p. Potted hydrangea . . . 10 10
564 3p. Type **137** 10 10
565 4p. Anemones 15 15
566 5p. Gladiolus 15 15
567 6p. "Asparagus plumosus" and "Gypsophila paniculata" 15 15
568 7p. Guernsey lily 20 20
569 8p. Enchantment lily 20 20
570 9p. Clematis "Freckles" . . 20 25
571 10p. Alstroemeria 25 25
572 16p. Standard carnation (horiz) 50 35
572b 18p. Standard rose 55 45
573 20p. Spray rose 60 50
574 23p. Mixed freesia (horiz) 60 55
575 24p. Standard rose (horiz) 70 60
576 25p. Iris "Ideal" (horiz) . . 70 60
576b 26p. Freesia "Pink Glow" 70 60
577 28p. Lisianthus (horiz) . . . 80 65
578 30p. Spray chrysanthemum (horiz) 80 70
579 40p. Spray carnation . . . 1·00 75
580 50p. Single freesia (horiz) 1·20 90
581 £1 Floral arrangement (35 × 26½ mm) . . . . 2·00 1·50
582 £2 Chelsea Flower Show exhibit (35 × 26½ mm) . . 4·00 3·00
582a £3 "Floral Fantasia" (exhibit) (35 × 28 mm) . . 6·00 5·00

1992. "Operation Asterix" (excavation of Roman ship). Multicoloured.
583 16p. Type **138** 45 35
584 23p. Loading the cargo . . . 60 45
585 28p. Ship at sea 80 70
586 33p. Ship under attack . . . 95 90
587 39p. Crew swimming ashore 1·10 1·00

139 Tram No. 10 decorated for Battle of Flowers

1992. Guernsey Trams. Multicoloured.
588 16p. Type **139** 45 30
589 23p. Tram No 10 passing Hougue a la Perre 60 35
590 28p. Tram No. 1 at St. Sampsons 75 80
591 33p. First steam tram at St. Peter Port, 1879 . . . . 80 1·00
592 39p. Last electric tram, 1934 1·00 1·10

140 Man in Party Hat

141 Rupert Bear, Bingo and Dog

1992. Christmas. Seasonal Fayre. Multicoloured.
593 13p. Type **140** 30 30
594 13p. Girl and Christmas tree 30 30
595 13p. Woman and balloons . . 35 30
596 13p. Mince pies and champagne 30 30
597 13p. Roast turkey 30 30
598 13p. Christmas pudding . . . 30 30
599 13p. Christmas cake 30 30
600 13p. Fancy cakes 30 30
601 13p. Cheese 30 30
602 13p. Nuts 30 30
603 13p. Ham 30 30
604 13p. Chocolate log 30 30

Nos. 593/604 were printed together, se-tenant, forming a composite design.

1993. Rupert Bear and Friends (cartoon characters created by Mary and Herbert Tourtel).
605 **141** 24p. multicoloured . . . 50 50
MS606 116 × 97 mm. 16p. Airplane and castle; 16p. Professor's servant and Autumn Elf; 16p. Algy Pug; 16p. Baby Badger on sledge; 24p. Bill Badger, Willie Mouse, Reggie Rabbit and Podgy playing in snow; 24p. Type **141**; 24p. The Balloonist avoiding Gregory on toboggan; 24p. Tiger Lily and Edward Trunk . . . . 4·50 4·00

The 24p. values in No. **MS**606 are as Type **141**; the 16p. designs are smaller, each $25\frac{1}{2} \times 26$ mm.

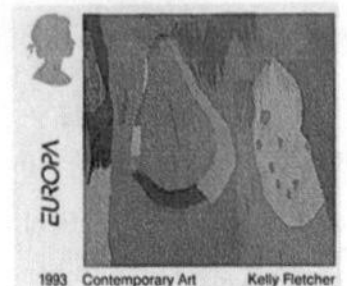

142 Tapestry by Kelly Fletcher

1993. Europa. Contemporary Art. Multicoloured.
607 24p. Type **142** 70 70
608 24p. "Le Marchi a Paissaon" (etching and aquatint, Sally Reed) (48 × $33\frac{1}{2}$ mm) . . . 70 70
609 28p. "Red Abstract" (painting, Molly Harris) . . 80 80
610 28p. "Dress Shop, King's Road" (painting, Damon Bell) (48 × $33\frac{1}{2}$ mm) 80 80

143 Arrest of Guernsey Parliamentarians, Fermain Bay

1993. 350th Anniv of Siege of Castle Cornet. Multicoloured.
611 16p. Type **143** 35 35
612 24p. Parliamentary ships attacking Castle Cornet . . 60 60
613 28p. Parliamentary captives escaping 75 75
614 33p. Castle cannon firing at St. Peter Port 85 85
615 39p. Surrender of Castle Cornet, 19 December 1651 90 90
MS616 203 × 75 mm. Nos. 611/15 3·25 4·00

144 Playing Cards

145 "The Twelve Pearls"

1993. Birth Bicentenary of Thomas de la Rue (printer).
617 **144** 16p. multicoloured . . . 40 45
618 – 24p. multicoloured . . . 65 65
619 – 28p. multicoloured . . . 80 80
620 – 33p. red 95 95
621 – 39p. green . . . . 1·10 1·10

DESIGNS: 24p. Fountain pens; 28p. Envelope-folding machine; 33p. Great Britain 1855 4d. stamp; 39p. Thomas de la Rue and Mauritius £1 banknote.

1993. Christmas. Stained Glass Windows by Mary-Eily de Putron from the Chapel of Christ the Healer. Multicoloured.
622 13p. Type **145** 30 30
623 13p. "Healing rays" 30 30
624 13p. "Hand of God over the Holy City" 30 30
625 13p. "Wing and Seabirds" (facing left) 30 30
626 13p. "Christ the Healer" . . 30 30
627 13p. "Wing and Seabirds" (facing right) 30 30
628 13p. "The Young Jesus in the Temple" 30 30
629 13p. "The Raising of Jairus' Daughter" 30 30
630 13p. "Suffer little Children to come unto Me" 30 30
631 13p. "Pilgrim's Progress" . . 30 30
632 13p. "The Light of the World" 30 30
633 13p. "Raphael, the Archangel of Healing, with Tobias" 30 30

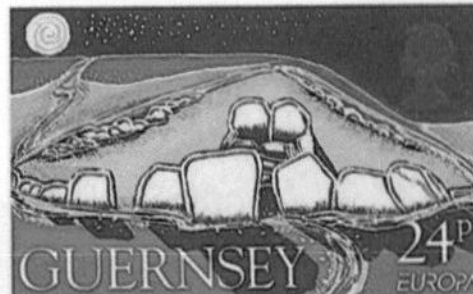

146 Les Fouaillages (ancient burial ground)

1994. Europa. Archaeological Discoveries. Multicoloured.
634 24p. Type **146** 55 55
635 24p. Mounted Celtic warrior 55 55
636 30p. Jars, arrow heads and stone axe from Les Fouaillages 80 75
637 30p. Sword, spear head and torque from King's Road burial 80 75

147 Canadian Supermarine Spitfires Mk V over Normandy Beaches

1994. 50th Anniv of D-Day. Sheet 93 × 71 mm.
MS638 **147** £2 multicoloured . . 4·00 4·25

148 Peugeot "Type 3", 1894

1994. Cent of First Car in Guernsey. Mult.
639 16p. Type **148** 40 40
640 24p. Mercedes "Simplex", 1903 . . . . 60 45
641 35p. Humber tourer, 1906 . . 90 1·00
642 41p. Bentley sports tourer, 1936 . . . . 1·00 1·00
643 60p. MG TC Midget, 1948 1·50 1·40

1994. "Philakorea '94" International Stamp Exhibition, Seoul. Sheet 110 × 90 mm containing No. 581.
MS644 £1 multicoloured . . . . 2·20 3·00

149 "Trident" (Herm ferry)

1994. 25th Anniv of Guernsey Postal Administration. Multicoloured.
645 16p. Type **149** 35 30
646 24p. Handley Page Super Dart Herald of Channel Express 55 50
647 35p. Britten Norman Trislander of Aurigny Air Services 75 75
648 41p. "Bon Marin de Serk" (Sark ferry) 85 85
649 60p. Map of Bailiwick . . . 1·40 1·25
MS650 150 × 100 mm. Nos. 645/9 4·00 4·25

150 Dolls' House

151 Seafood "Face"

1994. Christmas. Bygone Toys. Multicoloured.
651 13p. Type **150** 40 20
652 13p. Doll 40 20
653 13p. Teddy in bassinette . . 40 20
654 13p. Sweets in pillar box and playing cards 40 20
655 13p. Spinning top 40 20
656 13p. Building blocks 40 20
657 24p. Rocking horse 75 60
658 24p. Teddy bear 75 60
659 24p. Tricycle 75 60
660 24p. Wooden duck 75 60
661 24p. Hornby toy locomotive 75 60
662 24p. Ludo game 75 60

Nos. 651/6 and 657/62 respectively were printed together, se-tenant, forming composite designs.

1995. Greetings Stamps. "The Welcoming Face of Guernsey". Multicoloured.
663 24p. Type **151** 60 55
664 24p. Buckets and spade "face" 60 55
665 24p. Flowers "face" 60 55
666 24p. Fruit and vegetables "face" 60 55
667 24p. Sea shells and seaweed "face" 60 55
668 24p. Anchor and life belts "face" 60 55
669 24p. Glasses, cork and cutlery "face" 60 55
670 24p. Butterflies and caterpillars "face" 60 55
MS671 137 × 109 mm. Nos. 663/70 4·25 4·25

152 Winston Churchill and Wireless

1995. 50th Anniv of Liberation. Multicoloured.
672 16p. Type **152** 45 30
673 24p. Union Jack and Royal Navy ships off St. Peter Port 60 50
674 35p. Royal Arms and military band 90 90
675 41p. "Vega" (Red Cross supply ship) 90 90
676 60p. Rejoicing crowd . . . . 1·50 1·25
MS677 189 × 75 mm. Nos. 672/6 4·25 4·50

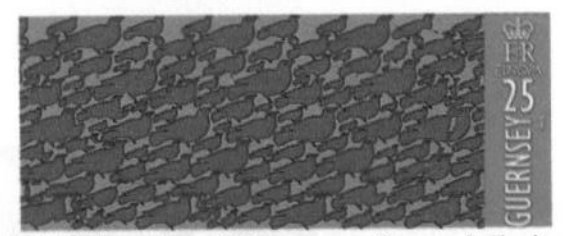

153 Silhouette of Doves on Ground ($\frac{1}{2}$-size illustration)

1995. Europa. Peace and Freedom. Multicoloured.
678 25p. Type **153** 50 65
679 30p. Silhouette of doves in flight 65 85

The designs of Nos. 678/9 each provide a stereogram or hidden three-dimensional image of a single dove.

154 Prince Charles, Castle Cornet and Bailiwick Arms

1995. Royal Visit.
680 **154** £1.50 multicoloured . . . 3·00 3·25

1995. "Singapore '95" International Stamp Exhibition. Sheet 110 × 90 mm. containing No. 581.
MS681 £1 multicoloured . . . . 2·75 2·75

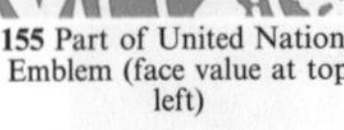

155 Part of United Nations Emblem (face value at top left)

156 "Christmas Trees for Sale in Bern" (Cornelia Huisboum-Weibel)

1995. 50th Anniv of United Nations. Designs showing different segments of the United Nations Emblem. Each blue and gold.
682 50p. Type **155** . . . . . . 1·10 1·10
683 50p. Face value at top right 1·10 1·10
684 50p. Face value at bottom left . . . . 1·10 1·10
685 50p. Face value at bottom right . . . . 1·10 1·10

1995. Christmas. 50th Anniv of UNICEF Multicoloured.
686 13p. Type **156** (face value at left) 40 35
687 13p. "Christmas Trees for Sale in Bern" (face value at right) 40 35
688 13p.+1p. "Evening Snowfall" (Katerina Mertikas) (face value at left) 40 45
689 13p.+1p. "Evening Snowfall" (face value at right) 40 45
690 24p. "It came upon a Midnight Clear" (Georgia Guback) (face value at left) 70 70
691 24p. "It came upon a Midnight Clear" (Georgia Guback) (face value at right) 70 70
692 24p.+2p. "Children of the World" (face value at left) 70 70
693 24p.+2p. "Children of the World" (face value at right) 70 70

Nos. 686/7, 688/9, 690/1 and 692/3 were printed together, se-tenant, each pair forming a composite design.

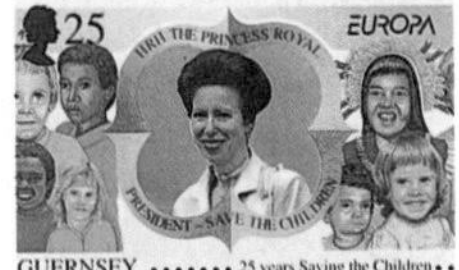

157 Princess Anne (President, Save the Children Fund) and Children

1996. Europa. Famous Women. Multicoloured.
694 25p. Type **157** 55 50
695 30p. Queen Elizabeth II and people of the Commonwealth 70 75

158 England v. U.S.S.R., 1968 (value at right)

1996. European Football Championship. Multicoloured.
696 16p. Type **158** 55 55
697 16p. England v. U.S.S.R., 1968 (value at left) 55 55
698 24p. Italy v. Belgium, 1972 (value at right) 75 75
699 24p. Italy v. Belgium, 1972 (value at left) 75 75
700 35p. Ireland v. Netherlands, 1988 (value at right) . . . 80 80
701 35p. Ireland v. Netherlands, 1988 (value at left) 80 80
702 41p. Denmark v. Germany, 1992 final (value at right) 95 95
703 41p. Denmark v. Germany, 1992 final (value at left) . . 95 95

159 Maj-Gen. Brock meeting Tecumseh (Indian chief)

1996. "CAPEX '96" International Stamp Exhibition, Toronto. Sheet 110 × 90 mm. containing T **159** and similar horiz design.
MS704 24p. Type **159**; £1 Major-General Sir Isaac Brock on horseback, 1812 . . . . 2·50 2·75

160 Ancient Greek Runner

162 The Annunciation

161 Humphrey Bogart as Philip Marlowe

1996. Centenary of Modern Olympic Games. Ancient Greek Athletes. Each black, yellow and orange.
705 16p. Type **160** 50 40
706 24p. Throwing the javelin . . 95 90
707 41p. Throwing the discus . . 1·10 1·25
708 55p. Wrestling (53 × 31 mm) 1·40 1·50
709 60p. Jumping . . . . 1·60 1·75
MS710 192 × 75 mm. Nos. 705/9 5·25 5·25

No. 708 also includes the "OLYMPHILEX '96" International Stamp Exhibition, Atlanta, logo.

1996. Centenary of Cinema. Screen Detectives. Multicoloured.
711 16p. Type **161** 40 40
712 24p. Peter Sellers as Inspector Clouseau 60 60
713 35p. Basil Rathbone as Sherlock Holmes 85 85
714 41p. Margaret Rutherford as Miss Marple 90 90
715 60p. Warner Oland as Charlie Chan . . . . . . 1·40 1·40

1996. Christmas. Multicoloured.
716 13p. Type **162** 30 25
717 13p. Journey to Bethlehem 30 25
718 13p. Arrival at the inn . . . 30 25
719 13p. Angel and shepherds . . 30 25
720 13p. Mary, Joseph and Jesus in stable 30 25
721 13p. Shepherds worshipping Jesus 30 25
722 13p. Three Kings following star 30 25
723 13p. Three Kings with gifts 30 25
724 13p. The Presentation in the Temple 30 25
725 13p. Mary and Jesus 30 25
726 13p. Joseph warned by angel 30 25
727 13p. The Flight into Egypt 30 25
728 24p. Mary cradling Jesus (horiz) 60 40
729 25p. The Nativity (horiz) . . 60 60

163 Holly Blue

1997. Endangered Species. Butterflies and Moths. Multicoloured.
730 18p. Type **163** 55 50
731 25p. Hummingbird hawk-moth 65 60
732 26p. Emperor moth 85 85
733 37p. Brimstone . . . . . . 1·10 1·10
MS734 92 × 68 mm. £1 Painted Lady 2·50 2·50
No. **MS**734 includes the "HONG KONG '97" International Stamp Exhibition logo on the sheet margin.

164 Gilliatt fighting Octopus

1997. Europa. Tales and Legends. Scenes from "Les Travailleurs de la Mer" by Victor Hugo. Multicoloured.
735 26p. Type **164** 55 60
736 31p. Gilliatt grieving on rock 75 65

165 Shell Beach, Herm

1997. Guernsey Scenes (1st series). Multicoloured. Self-adhesive.
737 18p. Type **165** 60 30
738 25p. La Seigneurie, Sark (vert) 70 60
739 26p. Castle Cornet, Guernsey 80 75

166 19th-century Shipyard, St. Peter Port

1997. "Pacific '97" World Philatelic Exhibition, San Francisco. Sheet 110 × 90 mm. containing T **166** and similar horiz design.
MS740 30p. green and gold; £1 multicoloured ("Costa Rica Packet" (barque)) . . . . . . 3·00 3·00
See also Nos. 770/3.

167 Transistor Radio, Microphone and Radio Logos

1997. Methods of Communication. Multicoloured.
741 18p. Type **167** 40 40
742 25p. Television, video camera and satellite dish 60 60
743 26p. Fax machine, telephones and mobile phone 60 60
744 37p. Printing press, newspaper and type . . . 90 85
745 43p. Stamp, coding machine and postbox . . . . 1·20 1·00
746 63p. CD, computer and disk 1·50 1·50

168 Teddy Bear making Cake

1997. Christmas. Teddy Bears. Multicoloured.
747 15p. Type **168** 45 45
748 25p. Teddy bears decorating Christmas tree 70 70
749 26p. Two teddy bears in armchair 70 70
750 37p. Teddy bear as Father Christmas . . . . 1·00 1·00
751 43p. Teddy bears unwrapping presents . . . . 1·10 1·10
752 63p. Teddy bears eating Christmas dinner . . . . . 1·60 1·60
MS753 123 × 107 mm. Nos. 747/52 4·50 4·50

169 Visiting Guernsey, 1957

1997. Golden Wedding of Queen Elizabeth and Prince Philip. Multicoloured.
754 18p. Type **169** 40 40
755 25p. Coronation Day, 1953 60 60
756 26p. Royal Family, 1957 . . 60 60
757 37p. On royal yacht, 1972 . . 90 90
758 43p. Queen Elizabeth and Prince Philip at Trooping the Colour, 1987 . . . . . 1·00 1·00
759 63p. Queen Elizabeth and Prince Philip, 1997 . . . . 1·40 1·40
No. 755 is inscribed "1947" in error.

170 Tapestry of 11th-century Guernsey (St. Martin)

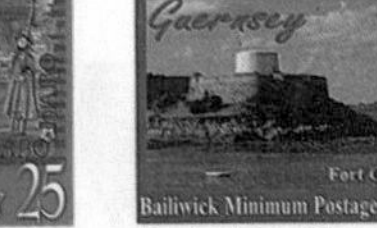

171 Fort Grey

1998. The Millennium Tapestries Project. Each showing a different century contributed by individual parishes. Multicoloured.
760 25p. Type **170** 60 60
761 25p. 12th-century (St. Saviour) 60 60
762 25p. 13th-century (Vale) . . . 60 60
763 25p. 14th-century (St. Sampson) 60 60
764 25p. 15th-century (Torteval) 60 60
765 25p. 16th-century (Castel) . . 60 60
766 25p. 17th-century (St. Andrew) 60 60
767 25p. 18th-century (Forest) . . 60 60
768 25p. 19th-century (St. Pierre du Bois) 60 60
769 25p. 20th-century (St. Peter Port) 60 60

1998. Guernsey Scenes (2nd series). Multicoloured. Self-adhesive.
770 (20p.) Type **171** 45 55
771 (20p.) Grand Havre 45 55
772 (25p.) Little Chapel 55 65
773 (25p.) Guernsey cow 55 65

Nos. 770/1 are inscribed "Bailiwick Minimum Postage Paid" and were intially sold at 20p. Nos. 772/3 are inscribed "UK Minimum Postage Paid" and were initially sold at 25p.

172 Fairey IIIC, Balloon, Sopwith Camel and Avro 504

1998. 80th Anniv of the Royal Air Force. Multicoloured.
774 20p. Type **172** 50 50
775 25p. Fairey Swordfish, Tiger Moth, Supermarine Walrus and Gloster Gladiator . . 60 60
776 30p. Hawker Hurricane, Supermarine Spitfire, Vickers Wellington, Short Sunderland (flying boat), Westland Lysander and Bristol Blenheim 70 70
777 37p. De Havilland Mosquito, Avro Lancaster, Auster III, Gloster Meteor and Horsa glider 90 85
778 43p. Canberra, Hawker Sea Fury, Bristol Sycamore, Hawker Hunter, Handley Page Victor and BAe Lightning . . . . 1·00 95
779 63p. Pavania Tornado GRI, BAe Hawk, BAe Sea Harrier, Westland Lynx (helicopter) and Hawker Siddeley Nimrod . . . . . 1·40 1·40

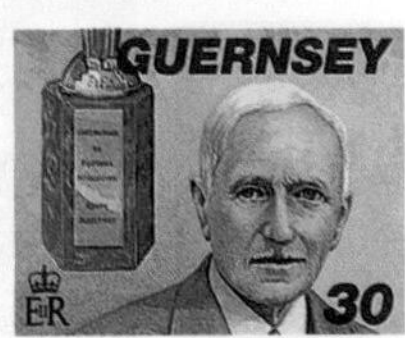

173 Jules Rimet (first President of F.I.F.A)

1998. 150th Anniv of the Cambridge Rules for Football. Sheet 110 × 90 mm containing T **173** and similar horiz design.
MS780 30p. Type **173**; £1.75, Bobby Moore and Queen Elizabeth II, 1966 . . . . 3·50 4·00

174 Girls in Traditional Costume watching Sheep Display, West Show

1998. Europa. Festivals. Multicoloured.
781 20p. Type **174** 45 45
782 25p. Marching band and "Battle of Flowers" exhibit, North Show 55 55
783 30p. Prince Charles, monument and tank, Liberation Day 65 65
784 37p. Goat, dahlias and show-jumping, South Show . . . 85 85
The 25p. and 30p. incorporate the "EUROPA" emblem.

175 Outward Motorboat

176 Royal Yacht "Britannia"

1998. Maritime Heritage. Multicoloured.
785 1p. Type **175** 10 10
786 2p. St. John Ambulance inshore rescue dinghy . . . 10 10
787 3p. Pilot boat, St. Peter Port 10 10
788 4p. "Flying Christine III" (St. John Ambulance launch) 10 10
789 5p. Crab fishing boat 10 10
790 6p. Herm Island ferry 10 10
791 7p. "Sarnia" (St. Peter Port Harbour Authority launch) 15 20
792 8p. "Leopardess" (States' fisheries protection launch) 15 20
793 9p. Trawler 20 25
794 10p. Powerboat (27 × 27 mm) 20 25
795 20p. Dart 18 racing catamaran (27 × 27 mm) . . 40 45
796 30p. 30ft Bermuda-rigged sloop (27 × 27 mm) 60 65
797 40p. Motor cruiser (27 × 27 mm) 80 85
798 50p. Ocean-going sailing yacht (27 × 27 mm) . . . . 1·00 1·10
799 75p. Motor yacht "Beaucette Marina" (27 × 27 mm) . . 1·50 1·30
800 £1 "Queen Elizabeth 2" (liner) (35 × 26 mm) . . . 2·00 1·80
801 £3 "Oriana" (liner) (35 × 26 mm) . . . . . . 6·00 5·50
802 £5 Type **176** . . . . 13·00 10·00

177 Modern Tree, Teletubby and Playstation

1998. 150th Anniv of the Introduction of the Christmas Tree. Multicoloured.
810 17p. Type **177** 40 40
811 25p. 1960s tinsel tree, toy bus and doll 60 60
812 30p. 1930s gold foil tree, panda and toy tank . . . 70 70
813 37p. 1920s tree, model of "Bluebird" and doll . . . 90 90
814 43p. 1900 tree, teddy bear and toy train 90 90
815 63p. 1850s tree, wooden doll and spinning top . . . . . 1·50 1·50
MS816 160 × 94 mm. Nos. 810/15 5·00 7·00

178 Elizabeth Bowes Lyon, 1907

180 Burnet Rose and Local Carriage Label

179 "Spirit of Guernsey", 1995

1999. Life and Times of Queen Elizabeth the Queen Mother. Multicoloured.
817 25p. Type **178** 70 65
818 25p. On wedding day, 1923 70 65
819 25p. Holding Princess Elizabeth, 1926 . . . . 70 65
820 25p. At Coronation, 1937 . . 70 65
821 25p. Visiting bombed areas of London, 1940 (wearing green hat) 70 65
822 25p. Fishing near Auckland, New Zealand, 1966 . . . . 70 65
823 25p. At Guernsey function, 1963 (wearing tiara) . . . 70 65
824 25p. Receiving flowers on her birthday, 1992 . . . . . . 70 65
825 25p. Presenting trophy, Sandown Park races, 1989 70 65
826 25p. Opening Royal Norfolk Regimental Museum, Norwich, 1990 (wearing blue hat) 70 65

1999. 175th Anniv of Royal National Lifeboat Institution. Multicoloured.
827 20p. Type **179** 50 50
828 25p. "Sir William Arnold", 1973 . . . . 60 60
829 30p. "Euphrosyne Kendal", 1954 . . . . 70 70
830 38p. "Queen Victoria", 1929 90 90
831 44p. "Arthur Lionel", 1912 1·10 1·10
832 64p. "Vincent Kirk Ella", 1888 . . . . 1·50 1·50

1999. Europa. Parks and Gardens. Herm Island. Designs each showing a different local carriage label. Multicoloured.
833 20p. Type **180** 50 45
834 25p. Atlantic puffin 60 55
835 30p. Small heath butterfly . . 70 65
836 38p. Shells on Shell Beach . . 90 80

181 Prince Edward and Miss Sophie Rhys-Jones

1999. Royal Wedding. Sheet 93 × 70 mm.
MS837 **181** £1 Multicoloured . . 2·50 2·25

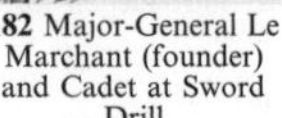
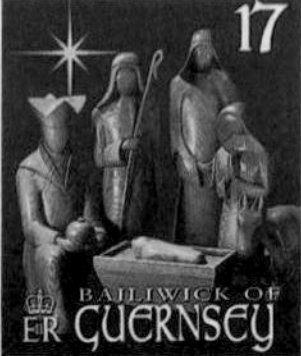
182 Major-General Le Marchant (founder) and Cadet at Sword Drill
183 The Nativity

1999. Bicentenary of The Royal Military Academy, Sandhurst. Multicoloured.
838 20p. Type **182** 50 45
839 25p. The Duke of York (official sponsor) and cadet on horseback 60 55
840 30p. Field-Marshal Earl Haig and cadets on parade . . . 75 70
841 38p. Field-Marshal Viscount Montgomery and bridging exercise 90 85
842 44p. David Niven (actor) and rifle practice . . . . 1·10 1·00
843 64p. Sir Winston Churchill and tank . . . . 1·50 1·50

1999. Christmas. Wood Carvings by Denis Brehaut from Notre Dame Church. Multicoloured.
844 17p. Type **183** 45 40
845 25p. Virgin Mary and Child 60 55
846 30p. Holy Family 75 70
847 38p. Cattle around manger 90 85
848 44p. Adoration of the Shepherds . . . . 1·10 1·00
849 64p. Adoration of the Magi 1·50 1·50
MS850 159 × 86 mm. Nos. 844/9 5·50 5·50

184 "Space Bus" (Fallon Ephgrave)

2000. New Millennium. "Stampin' the Future" (children's stamp design competition). Multicoloured.
851 20p. Type **184** 60 45
852 25p. "Children holding hands" (Abigail Downing) 60 55
853 30p. "No Captivity" (Laura Martin) 70 65
854 38p. "Post Office of the Future" (Sarah Haddow) 90 80
855 44p. "Solar-powered car" (Sophie Medland) . . . . 1·00 95
856 64p. "Woman flying" (Danielle McIver) . . . . 1·40 1·40

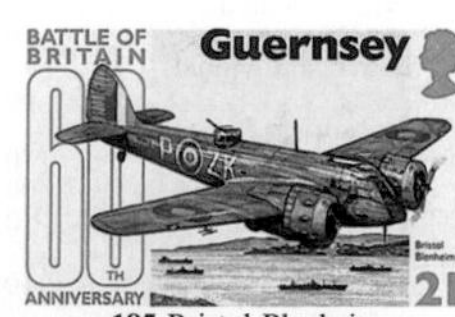

185 Bristol Blenheim

2000. 60th Anniv of Battle of Britain. R.A.F. Aircraft. Multicoloured.
857 21p. Type **185** 50 50
858 26p. Hawker Hurricane . . . 60 55
859 36p. Boulton Paul Defiant II 95 85
860 40p. Gloster Gladiator . . . 1·00 95
861 45p. Bristol Beaufighter IF 1·10 1·10
862 65p. Supermarine Spitfire IIc 1·50 1·50

186 Guernsey Flag on Kite and "2000"
187 *Iris stylosa*

2000. Europa. Multicoloured.
863 21p. Type **186** 50 45
864 26p. Stylized sails bearing national flowers 60 55
865 36p. "Building Europe" . . . 1·00 90
866 65p. Rainbow and three doves . . . . 1·60 1·60

2000. "A Botanist's Sketchbook". Restoration of Candie Gardens, St. Peter Port. Multicoloured.
867 26p. Type **187** 55 55
868 26p. *Watsonia* 55 55
869 26p. *Richardia maculata* . . . 55 55
870 26p. *Narcissus bulbocodium* 55 55
871 26p. *Triteleia laxa* 55 55
872 26p. *Tigridia pavonia* 55 55
873 26p. *Agapanthus umbellatus* 55 55
874 26p. *Sparaxis* 55 55
875 26p. *Pancratium maritimum* 55 55
876 26p. *Nerine sarniensis* 55 55

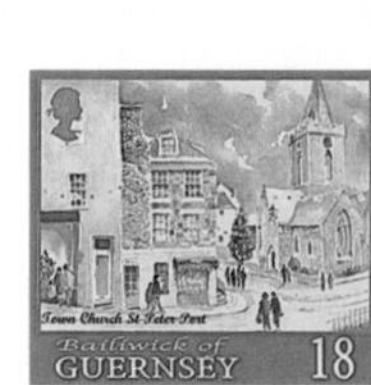

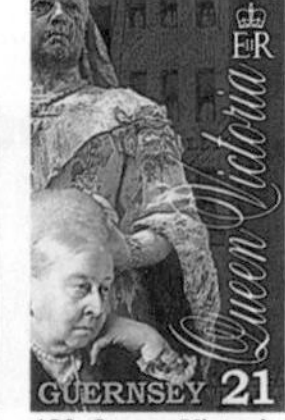

188 Town Church, St. Peter Port
189 Queen Victoria and Diamond Jubilee Statue

2000. Christmas. Guernsey Churches. Multicoloured.
877 18p. Type **188** 40 40
878 26p. Children leaving St. Sampson's Church . . 60 55
879 36p. Flying kite by Vale Church 90 85
880 40p. Carol singing outside St. Pierre du Bois Church 95 95
881 45p. Building snowman near St. Martin's Church . . . 1·10 1·10
882 65p. Street scene including St. John's Church, St. Peter Port . . . . 1·50 1·50
MS883 160 × 86 mm. Nos. 877/82 5·50 6·00

2001. Death Centenary of Queen Victoria. Each incorporating a different portrait of Queen Victoria. Multicoloured.
884 21p. Type **189** 50 50
885 26p. Letter of thanks to Guernsey, 1846 . . . . . 60 55
886 36p. Statues of Queen Victoria and Prince Albert 90 85
887 40p. Stone commemorating 1846 visit 95 95
888 45p. Statue of Prince Albert 1·10 1·10
889 65p. Victoria Tower, 1848 . . 1·50 1·50
MS890 165 × 80 mm. Nos. 884/9 6·00 7·00
No. MS890 includes the logo of the "Hong Kong 2001" Stamp Exhibition on the sheet margin.

190 River kingfisher ("Kingfisher")

2001. Europa. Water Birds. Multicoloured.
891 21p. Type **190** 60 40
892 26p. Garganey 90 75
893 36p. Little egret . . . . . . 1·20 1·00
894 65p. Little ringed plover . . 1·70 1·90

191 Cavalier King Charles Spaniel
192 La Corbiere Sunset

2001. Centenary of Guernsey Dog Club. Mult.
895 22p. Type **191** 55 50
896 27p. Miniature schnauzer . . 65 60
897 36p. German shepherd dog 90 85
898 40p. Cocker spaniel 95 95
899 45p. West highland white terrier . . . . 1·10 1·10
900 65p. Dachshund . . . . . . 1·50 1·50

2001. Island Scenes. Multicoloured. Self-adhesive.
901 (22p.) Type **192** 45 50
902 (22p.) Rue des Hougues . . . 45 50
903 (22p.) St. Saviour's Reservoir 45 50
904 (22p.) Shell Beach, Herm . . 45 50
905 (22p.) Telegraph Bay, Alderney 45 50
906 (27p.) Alderney Railway . . 55 60
907 (27p.) Vazon Bay 55 60
908 (27p.) La Coupee, Sark . . 55 60
909 (27p.) Les Hanois Lighthouse 55 60
910 (27p.) Albecq Beach 55 60
Nos. 901/5 were intended for postage within the Bailiwick and are inscribed "GY". They were each initially sold at 22p. Nos. 906/10 were intended for postage to Great Britain and are inscribed "UK". They were each initially sold at 27p.

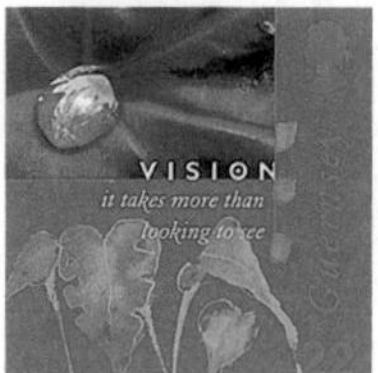

193 Droplet of Water on Leaf ("Vision")

2001. Incorporation of Guernsey Post Ltd. Multicoloured. (a) Square designs as T **193**.
921 22p. Type **193** 45 50
922 27p. Hummingbird ("Understanding") 55 60
923 36p. Butterfly's wing ("Individuality") 70 75
924 40p. Sea shell ("Strength") 80 85
925 45p. Honeycomb ("Community") 90 95
926 65p. Dandelion ("Maturity") 1·25 1·40
(b) Design as No. 28a (1969 £1), but redrawn.
927 £1 View of Guernsey from the sea . . . . 5·00 5·50
No. 927 differs from the original 1969 stamp by showing the Queen's portrait without a tiara and by showing "GUERNSEY BALIWICK" in white instead of grey.

194 "Tree of Joy", St. Peter Port
196 Juggling

195 Victor Hugo and St. Peter Port

2001. Christmas. Festive Lights. Multicoloured.
928 19p. Type **194** 40 45
929 27p. Cross, Les Cotils Christian Centre 55 60
930 36p. Les Ruettes Cottage, St. Saviour's 75 80
931 40p. Farmhouse, Le Preel, Castel . . . . 1·00 1·10
932 45p. Sark Post Office . . . . 1·10 1·20
933 65p. High Street, St. Peter Port . . . . 1·50 1·60
MS934 150 × 100 mm. Nos. 928/33 6·00 6·50

2002. Birth Bicentenary of Victor Hugo (French author). *Les Miserables* (novel). Multicoloured.
935 22p. Type **195** 45 50
936 27p. Cosette 55 60
937 36p. Valjean 75 80
938 40p. Inspector Javert 90 95
939 45p. Cosette and Marius . . 1·10 1·10
940 65p. Novel and score for *Les Miserables* (musical by Alain Boublil and Claude-Michel Schonberg) . . . . 1·50 1·60
MS941 150 × 100 mm. Nos. 935/40 5·25 6·00
The 27p. value reproduces the main image from promotional material for Cameron Mackintosh's musical production.

2002. Europa. The Circus. Multicoloured.
942 22p. Type **196** 45 50
943 27p. Clowns 55 60
944 36p. Trapeze artists 70 75
945 40p. Knife thrower 80 90
946 45p. Acrobat 90 95
947 65p. High-wire cyclist . . . . 1·25 1·40

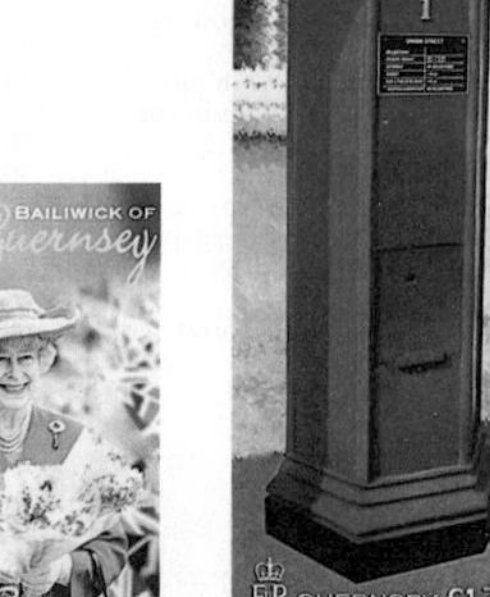

197 Queen Elizabeth and Crowd
198 Original Pillar Box, Union Street

2002. Golden Jubilee. Multicoloured.
948 22p. Type **197** 45 50
949 27p. Queen Elizabeth at St. Peter Port 55 60
950 36p. Queen Elizabeth and Prince Philip at St. Anne's School, Alderney 70 75
951 40p. Queen Elizabeth and La Seigneurie, Sark 80 85
952 45p. At Millennium Stone, L'Ancresse 90 95
953 65p. In evening dress and floodlit Castle Cornet . . . 1·25 1·40

2002. 150th Anniv of First Pillar Box. Sheet, 55 × 90 mm.
MS954 **198** £1.75 multicoloured 4·00 4·50

199 Family and Ferry, La Maseline

2002. Holidays on Sark. Multicoloured.
955 27p. Type **199** 55 60
956 27p. Passenger tractors . . . 55 60
957 27p. Campsite 55 60
958 27p. Cyclists at La Coupee 55 60
959 27p. Swimming in Venus Pool 55 60
960 27p. La Seigneurie gardens 55 60
961 27p. Posting cards 55 60
962 27p. Carriage ride 55 60
963 27p. Tea at a café 55 60
964 27p. On the beach at Creux Harbour 55 60

200 Elizabeth College and Cadet Corps Parade, 1934

2002. 60th Anniv of Herbert Le Patourel's Victoria Cross. Multicoloured.
965 22p. Type **200** 45 50
966 27p. Captain Le Patourel in action, Tunisia 1942, and V.C 55 60
967 36p. Captain Le Patourel and nurse, 1943 . . . . 70 75
968 40p. Award ceremony, Cairo, 1943 . . . . 80 85
969 45p. Major Le Patourel welcomed home to Guernsey, 1948 . . . . . 1·25 1·40

201 Queen Elizabeth the Queen Mother and Bouquet (½-size illustration)

2002. Queen Elizabeth the Queen Mother Commemoration. Sheet 140 × 98 mm.

MS971	**201** £2 multicoloured	4·00	4·25

202 Mary and Jesus

2002. Christmas. Multicoloured.

972	22p. Type **202**	45	50
973	27p. Mary, Joseph and Jesus in the stable	55	60
974	36p. Angel appearing to shepherds	70	75
975	40p. Shepherds with Mary and Jesus	80	85
976	45p. Three Wise Men	90	95
977	65p. Stable with star overhead	1·25	1·50
MS978	131 × 101 mm. Nos. 972/7	4·00	4·50

203 Lancaster Bomber and Crew

2003. Memories of the Second World War. 60th Anniv of Operation Tunnel (£1.50) and Dambusters Raid (others) (1st issue). Multicoloured.

979	22p. Type **203**	45	50
980	27p. Flight of Lancaster bombers crossing English coast	55	60
981	36p. Lancaster bombers in enemy searchlights	70	75
982	40p. Dropping bouncing bombs	80	85
983	£1.50 H.M.S. *Charybdis* (cruiser) and H.M.S. *Limbourne* (destroyer) (40 × 30 mm)	3·00	3·25

See also Nos. 1027/31.

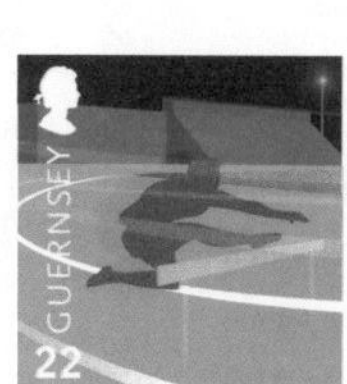

204 Hurdling

205 St. Peter Port Harbour ("Naturally Guernsey", 2003)

2003. Island Games, Guernsey. Multicoloured.

984	22p. Type **204**	45	50
985	27p. Cycling	55	60
986	36p. Gymnastics	75	80
987	40p. Sailing	80	85
988	45p. Golf	90	95
989	65p. Running	1·25	1·40
MS990	140 × 75 mm. Nos. 984/9	4·75	5·00

2003. Europa. Poster Art. Multicoloured.

991	22p. Type **205**	45	50
992	27p. Motor-cruiser off Guernsey ("The islands of Guernsey", 1995)	55	60
993	36p. "Children on the Seashore" (Renoir) ("Holiday Guernsey", 1988)	75	80
994	40p. St. Peter Port Harbour ("Bailiwick of Guernsey", 1978)	80	85
995	45p. St. Peter Port and cliffs ("Guernsey - The Charming Channel Island", 1968)	90	95
996	65p. Secluded bay ("Guernsey", 1956)	1·25	1·40

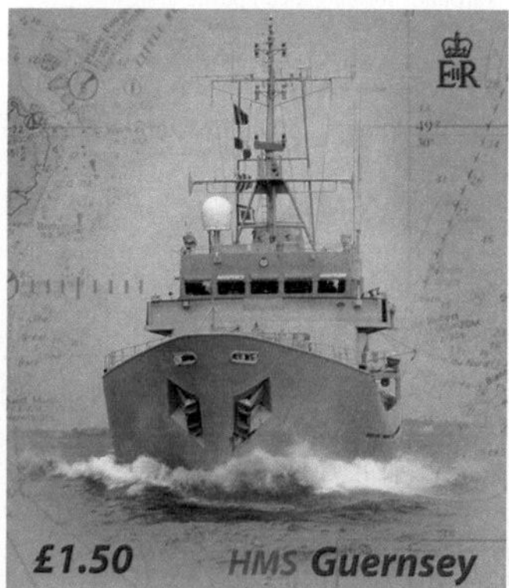

206 H.M.S. *Guernsey*

2003. Decommissioning of H.M.S. *Guernsey* (fishery protection patrol vessel). Sheet 117 × 84 mm.

MS997	**206** £1.50 multicoloured	3·00	3·25

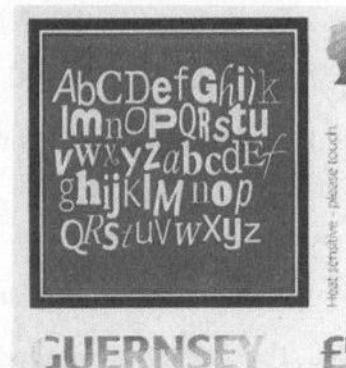

207 Princess Diana and Baby Prince William

208 Letters of Alphabet

2003. 21st Birthday of Prince William of Wales. Multicoloured.

998	27p. Type **207**	55	60
999	27p. Prince William, aged 3, with Prince Charles and Prince Harry at Kensington Palace	55	60
1000	27p. Aged 4, in Parachute Regiment uniform	55	60
1001	27p. Aged 7, with Prince Harry on his first day at Wetherby School	55	60
1002	27p. Aged 8, with Prince Charles at Guards Polo	55	60
1003	27p. Aged 9, on ski slopes with Princess Diana	55	60
1004	27p. On first day at Eton, 1995	55	60
1005	27p. With Prince Charles and Prince Harry at Balmoral, 1997	55	60
1006	27p. Wearing hard hat during Community project in Chile, 2000	55	60
1007	27p. Playing polo, 2002	55	60

2003.

1008	**208** £5 orange, blue and silver	10·00	10·50

The alphabet letters are printed in thermochromic ink which fades from pale orange to white when exposed to heat.

209 Sleeping Boy and Christmas Tree

2003. Christmas. Scenes from Poem "Twas the Night before Christmas" by Clement Clarke Moore. Multicoloured.

1009	10p. Type **209**	20	25
1010	27p. Boy opening shutter to see Santa's sleigh	55	60
1011	36p. Santa on roof with reindeer	70	75
1012	40p. Santa with presents	80	85
1013	45p. Santa leaving presents under Christmas tree	90	95
1014	65p. Santa in sleigh	1·25	1·50
MS1015	130 × 104 mm. Nos. 1009/14	4·50	4·75

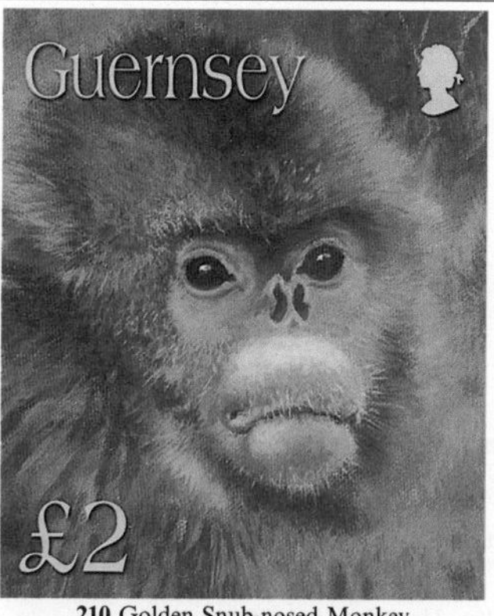

210 Golden Snub-nosed Monkey

2004. Endangered Species (1st series). Golden Snub-nosed Monkey. Sheet 120 × 85 mm.

MS1016	210 £2 multicoloured	6·50	6·50

211 Clematis "Rosemoor"

2004. Raymond Evison's Guernsey Clematis. Multicoloured. Self-adhesive.

1017	(22p.) Type **211**	75	75
1018	(22p.) "Arctic Queen"	75	75
1019	(22p.) "Harlow Carr"	75	75
1020	(22p.) "Guernsey Cream"	75	75
1021	(22p.) "Josephine"	75	75
1022	(27p.) "Blue Moon"	85	85
1023	(27p.) "Wisley"	85	85
1024	(27p.) "Liberation"	85	85
1025	(27p.) "Royal Velvet"	85	85
1026	(27p.) "Hyde Hall"	85	85

Nos. 1017/21 were intended for postage within the Bailiwick and are inscribed "GY". They were each initially sold at 22p. Nos. 1022/6 were intended for postage to Great Britain and are inscribed "UK". They were each initially sold at 27p.

2004. Memories of the Second World War (2nd issue). 60th Anniv of D-Day Landings. As T **203**. Multicoloured.

1027	26p. Supermarine Spitfire	85	85
1028	32p. Landing craft and ship	1·00	1·00
1029	36p. Troops going ashore at Gold Beach	1·20	1·20
1030	40p. Troops in water	1·30	1·30
1031	£1.50 *Vega* (Red Cross supply ship) (40 × 29 mm)	5·00	5·00

212 Sandcastle, Rider, Bucket and Spade, Deckchair and Canoeist

2004. Europa. Holidays. Multicoloured.

1032	26p. Type **212**	85	85
1033	32p. Pathway sign, walking trails, bench and Guernsey landscapes	1·10	1·10
1034	36p. Lighthouse and yachts in marina, St. Peter Port	1·20	1·20
1035	40p. Glasses of red wine and meals on table	1·30	1·30
1036	45p. Statue-menhir at Castel and Loop Holed Tower, Le Gran'mere statue-menhir, Little Chapel and Victor Hugo statue	1·50	1·50
1037	65p. Guernsey Lily, wildflowers and robin	2·10	2·10

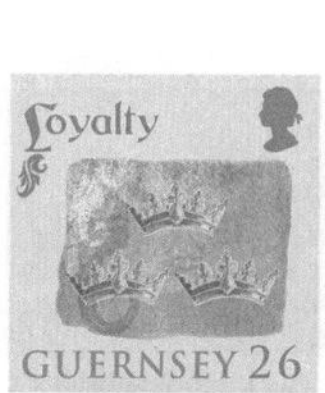

213 Three Crowns (Loyalty)

214 Discus Thrower

2004. 800th Anniv of Allegiance to England. Multicoloured.

1038	26p. Type **213**	85	85
1039	32p. Three ships (Trade)	1·10	1·10
1040	36p. Knotted rope (Unity)	1·20	1·20
1041	40p. Three castle turrets (Protection)	1·30	1·30
1042	45p. Three scrolls (Justice)	1·50	1·50
1043	65p. Three leaping fish (Industry)	2·10	2·10
MS1044	140 × 80 mm. Nos. 1038/43	8·00	8·00

2004. Olympic Games, Athens, Greece. Multicoloured.

1045	32p. Type **214**	1·00	1·00
1046	36p. Javelin thrower	1·20	1·20
1047	45p. Runners	1·50	1·50
1048	65p. Wrestlers	2·10	2·10
MS1049	152 × 98 mm. £1 Olympic sports (40 × 29 mm)	3·25	3·25

215 "Little Donkey"

2004. Christmas. Multicoloured.

1050	20p. Type **215**	65	65
1051	20p. "While Shepherds Watched"	65	65
1052	20p. "Away in a Manger"	65	65
1053	20p. "Unto Us a Child is Born"	65	65
1054	20p. "We Three Kings"	65	65
1055	32p. Angels wings (33 × 26 mm)	1·10	1·10
1056	36p. Bauble (33 × 26 mm)	1·20	1·20
1057	40p. Holly (33 × 26 mm)	1·30	1·30
1058	45p. Detail of snowman (33 × 26 mm)	1·50	1·50
1059	65p. Star on top of tree (33 × 26 mm)	2·20	2·20

Nos. 1050/4 were printed together, se-tenant, with the backgrounds forming a composite design.

POSTAGE DUE STAMPS

D 1 Castle Cornet

1969. Face values in black.

D1	**D 1**	1d. plum	2·00	1·25
D2		2d. green	2·00	1·25
D3		3d. red	3·00	4·00
D4		4d. blue	4·00	5·00
D5		5d. ochre	6·00	4·00
D6		6d. turquoise	6·00	4·50
D7		1s. brown	10·00	8·00

1971. Decimal Currency. Face values in black.

D 8	**D 1**	½p. plum	10	10
D 9		1p. green	10	10
D10		2p. red	10	10
D11		3p. blue	10	10
D12		4p. ochre	10	10
D13		5p. blue	10	10
D14		6p. violet	10	10
D15		8p. orange	20	25
D16		10p. brown	20	15
D17		15p. grey	30	40

D 2 St. Peter Port

1977. Face values in black.

D18	**D 2**	½p. brown	10	10
D19		1p. purple	10	10
D20		2p. orange	10	10
D21		3p. red	10	10
D22		4p. blue	10	10
D23		5p. green	10	10
D24		6p. green	10	10
D25		8p. brown	10	10
D26		10p. blue	10	10
D27		14p. green	15	15
D28		15p. violet	15	15
D29		16p. red	20	20

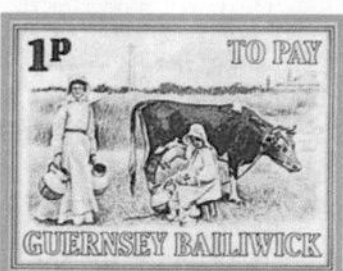

D 3 Milking Cow

1982. Guernsey Scenes, c. 1990.

D30	**D 3**	1p. blue and green	10	10
D31	–	2p. brown, lt brown & blue	10	10
D32	–	3p. green and lilac	10	10
D33	–	4p. green and orange	10	10
D34	–	5p. blue and green	10	10
D35	–	16p. blue and light blue	30	35
D36	–	18p. blue and green	35	40
D37	–	20p. green and blue	40	45
D38	–	25p. blue and pink	50	55
D39	–	30p. green and yellow	60	65
D40	–	50p. brown and blue	1·00	1·10
D41	–	£1 lt brown and brown	2·00	2·10

DESIGNS: 2p. Vale Mill; 3p. Sark cottage; 4p. Quayside, St. Peter Port; 5p. Well, Water Lane, Moulin Huet; 16p. Seaweed gathering; 18p. Upper Walk, White Rock; 20p. Cobo Bay; 25p. Saint's Bay; 30p. La Coupee, Sark; 50p. Old Harbour, St. Peter Port; £1 Greenhouses, Doyle Road, St. Peter Port.

ALDERNEY

The following issues are provided by the Guernsey Post Office for use on Alderney. They are also valid for postal purposes throughout the rest of the Bailiwick of Guernsey.

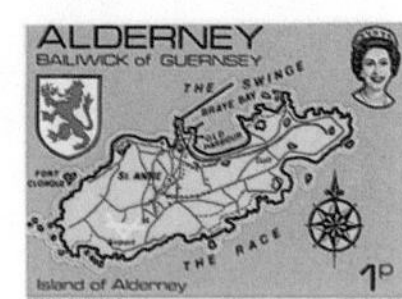

A **1** Island Map

1983. Island Scenes. Multicoloured.
A 1 1p. Type A **1** 10 10
A 2 4p. Hanging Rock 10 10
A 3 9p. States' Building, St. Anne 15 15
A 4 10p. St. Anne's Church . . 20 15
A 5 11p. Yachts in Braye Bay 20 20
A 6 12p. Victoria St., St. Anne 25 20
A 7 13p. Map of Channel . . . 25 20
A 8 14p. Fort Clonque 30 20
A 9 15p. Corblets Bay and Fort 35 20
A10 16p. Old Tower, St. Anne 35 25
A11 17p. Golf course and Essex Castle 40 30
A12 18p. Old Harbour 40 30
A12a 20p. Quesnard Lighthouse 1·00 90
A12b 21p. Braye Harbour . . . 1·00 90
A12c 23p. Island Hall 95 85
A12d 24p. "J.T. Daly" (steam locomotive) . . . . . . 1·75 1·75
A12e 28p. "Louis Marchesi of the Round Table" (lifeboat) . . . . 2·25 2·25
Nos. A12a/e are larger, 38 × 27 mm.

A **2** Oystercatcher

1984. Birds. Multicoloured.
A13 9p. Type A **2** . . . . 1·10 60
A14 13p. Ruddy turnstone ("Turnstone") . . . . . . 1·10 75
A15 26p. Ringed plover . . . . 2·50 2·75
A16 28p. Dunlin . . . . 2·50 2·75
A17 31p. Curlew . . . . 2·50 1·70

A **3** Westland Wessex HU Mk 5 Helicopter of the Queen's Flight

1985. 50th Anniv of Alderney Airport. Mult.
A18 9p. Type A **3** . . . . 1·40 70
A19 13p. Britten Norman "long nose" Trislander . . . . . 1·75 1·00
A20 29p. De Havilland Heron 1B 3·00 2·50
A21 31p. De Havilland Dragon Rapide "Sir Henry Lawrence" . . . . 3·50 2·75
A22 34p. Saro Windhover flying boat "City of Portsmouth" 3·50 2·75

A **4** Royal Engineers, 1890

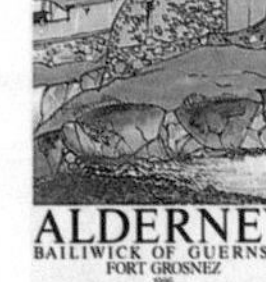

A **5** Fort Grosnez

1985. Regiments of the Alderney Garrison. Multicoloured.
A23 9p. Type A **4** 25 20
A24 14p. Duke of Albany's Own Highlanders, 1856 . . . . 80 40
A25 29p. Royal Artillery, 1855 80 70
A26 31p. South Hampshire Regiment, 1810 . . . . . 1·10 1·10
A27 34p. Royal Irish Regiment, 1782 . . . . 1·40 1·40

1986. Alderney Forts. Multicoloured.
A28 10p. Type A **5** 80 20
A29 14p. Fort Tourgis 90 80
A30 31p. Fort Clonque . . . . . 2·50 3·00
A31 34p. Fort Albert . . . . . . 2·50 3·00

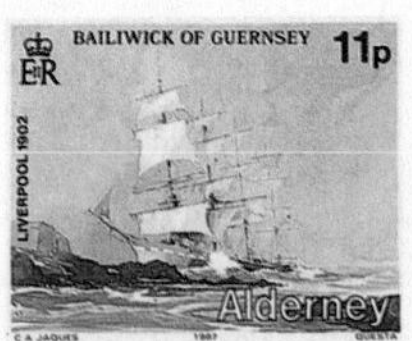

A **6** "Liverpool" (full-rigged ship), 1902

1987. Alderney Shipwrecks. Multicoloured.
A32 11p. Type A **6** . . . . . . 1·60 50
A33 15p. "Petit Raymond" (schooner), 1906 . . . . . 1·75 60
A34 29p. "Maina" (yacht), 1910 3·75 3·50
A35 31p. "Burton" (steamer), 1911 . . . . 4·00 3·50
A36 34p. "Point Law" (oil tanker), 1975 . . . . . . 4·00 4·25

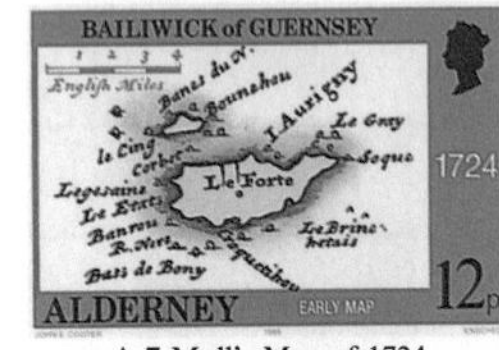

A **7** Moll's Map of 1724

1989. 250th Anniv of Bastide's Survey of Alderney.
A37 A **7** 12p. multicoloured . . . 25 25
A38 – 18p. black, blue & brown 45 30
A39 – 27p. black, blue and green . . . . 95 1·10
A40 – 32p. black, blue and red 1·10 1·10
A41 – 35p. multicoloured . . . 1·50 1·40
DESIGNS: 18p. Bastide's survey of 1739; 27p. Goodwin's map of 1831; 32p. General Staff map of 1943; 35p. Ordnance Survey map, 1988.

A **8** H.M.S. "Alderney" (bomb ketch), 1738

1990. Royal Navy Ships named after Alderney.
A42 A **8** 14p. black and bistre . . 25 20
A43 – 20p. black and brown . . 45 35
A44 – 29p. black and brown . . 1·00 1·00
A45 – 34p. black and blue . . 1·10 1·50
A46 – 37p. black and blue . . . 1·40 1·50
DESIGNS: 20p. H.M.S. "Alderney" (sixth rate), 1742; 29p. H.M.S. "Alderney" (sloop), 1755; 34p. H.M.S. "Alderney" (submarine), 1945; 37p. H.M.S. "Alderney" (patrol vessel), 1979.

A **9** Wreck of H.M.S. "Victory", 1744

1991. Automation of The Casquets Lighthouse. Multicoloured.
A47 21p. Type A **9** 80 50
A48 26p. Lighthouse keeper's daughter rowing back to the Casquets . . . . . . 1·90 1·70
A49 31p. MBB-Bolkow Bo 105D helicopter leaving pad on St. Thomas Tower . . . . 2·00 2·25
A50 37p. Northern wheater and yellow wagtail over lighthouse . . . . 2·75 3·25
A51 50p. Trinity House vessel "Patricia" and arms . . . 3·75 3·50

A **10** Two French Warships on Fire

A **11** Spiny Lobster

1992. 300th Anniv of the Battle of La Hogue. Multicoloured.
A52 23p. Type A **10** . . . . . . 1·10 1·00
A53 28p. Crews leaving burning ships . . . . 2·40 2·50
A54 33p. French warship sinking 3·00 3·00
A55 50p. "The Battle of La Hogue" (47 × 32 mm) . . 3·50 3·50
Nos. A52/4 show details of the painting on the 50p. value.

1993. Endangered Species. Marine Life. Mult.
A56 24p. Type A **11** . . . . . . 1·25 1·40
A57 28p. Plumose anemone . . . 1·25 1·40
A58 33p. Starfish . . . . 1·25 1·40
A59 39p. Sea urchin . . . . . . 1·25 1·40
Nos. A56/9 were printed together, se-tenant, the backgrounds forming a composite design.

A **12** Blue-tailed Damselfly, Dark Hair Water Crowfoot and Branched Bur-reed

1994. Flora and Fauna. Multicoloured.
A60 1p. Type A **12** 10 10
A61 2p. White-toothed shrew and flax-leaved St. John's wort 10 10
A62 3p. Fulmar and kaffir fig 10 10
A63 4p. Clouded yellow (butterfly) and red clover 10 10
A64 5p. Bumble bee, prostrate broom and giant broom-rape 10 10
A65 6p. Dartford warbler and lesser dodder 15 20
A66 7p. Peacock (butterfly) and stemless thistle 15 20
A67 8p. Mole and bluebell . . . 15 20
A68 9p. Great green grasshopper and common gorse 20 25
A69 10p. Six-spot burnet (moth) and viper's bugloss . . . 20 25
A70 16p. Common blue (butterfly) and pyramidal orchid 55 40
A70b 18p. Small tortoiseshell (butterfly) and buddleia 35 40
A71 20p. Common rabbit and creeping buttercup . . . 40 45
A72 24p. Greater black-backed gull and sand crocus . . 50 55
A72b 25p. Rock pipit and sea stock 50 55
A72c 26p. Sand digger wasp and sea bindweed (horiz) . . 50 55
A73 30p. Atlantic puffin and English stonecrop 60 65
A74 40p. Emperor (moth) and bramble 80 85
A75 50p. Pale-spined hedgehog and pink oxalis . . . . . 1·00 1·25
A76 £1 Common tern and Bermuda grass (horiz) . . 2·00 2·25
A77 £2 Northern gannet and "Fucus vesiculosus" (seaweed) (horiz) . . . . 4·00 4·50

A **13** Royal Aircraft Factory SE5A

1995. Birth Cent of Tommy Rose (aviator). Mult.
A78 35p. Type A **13** 95 95
A79 35p. Miles Master II and other Miles aircraft . . . 95 95
A80 35p. Miles Aerovan and Miles Monitor 95 95
A81 41p. Miles Falcon Six winning King's Cup air race, 1935 . . . . 1·10 1·10
A82 41p. Miles Hawk Speed Six winning Manx Air Derby, 1947 . . . . 1·10 1·10
A83 41p. Miles Falcon Six breaking U.K.–Cape record, 1936 . . . . . . 1·10 1·10

A **14** Returning Islanders

1995. 50th Anniv of Return of Islanders to Alderney. Sheet 93 × 70 mm.
MSA84 A **14** £1.65, multicoloured 5·00 4·00

A **15** Signallers training on Alderney

1996. 25th Anniv of Adoption of 30th Signal Regiment by Alderney. Multicoloured.
A85 24p. Type A **15** . . . . . . 1·10 1·10
A86 41p. Communications station, Falkland Islands 1·10 1·10
A87 60p. Dish aerial and Land Rover, Gulf War . . . . 1·10 1·10
A88 75p. Service with United Nations . . . . 1·10 1·10
Nos. A85/8 were printed together, se-tenant, forming a composite design.

A **16** Cat with Butterfly

A **17** Harold Larwood

1996. Cats. Multicoloured.
A89 16p. Type A **16** 45 35
A90 24p. Blue and white on table 65 40
A91 25p. Tabby kitten grooming blue and white persian kitten 65 65
A92 35p. Red persian under table 95 90
A93 41p. White cat with tortoiseshell and white in toy cart . . . . 1·10 1·00
A94 60p. Siamese playing with wool . . . . 1·75 1·40
MSA95 144 × 97 mm. Nos. A89/94 5·50 6·00

1997. 150th Anniv of Cricket on Alderney. Multicoloured.
A 96 18p. Type A **17** 50 30
A 97 25p. John Arlott 65 35
A 98 37p. Pelham J. Warner . . 1·00 1·25
A 99 43p. W. G. Grace . . . . 1·25 1·50
A100 63p. John Wisden . . . . 1·60 1·75
MSA101 190 × 75 mm. Nos. A96/100 and label . . . . . . 7·00 7·50

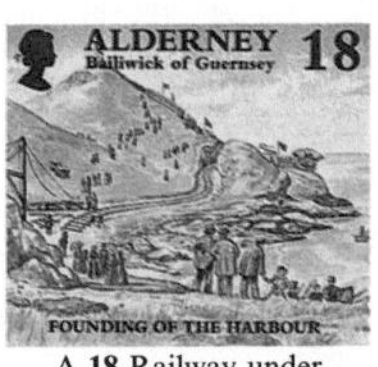

A **18** Railway under Construction

A **19** Modern Superlite Helmet and Wreck of "Point Law" (oil tanker)

1997. Garrison Island (1st series). 150th Anniv of Harbour. Multicoloured.
A102 18p. Type A **18** 45 45
A103 18p. "Ariadne" (paddle steamer) at anchor . . . 45 45
A104 25p. Quarrying stone . . . 65 65
A105 25p. Quarry railway 65 65
A106 26p. Queen Victoria and Prince Albert on Alderney 70 70
A107 26p. Royal Yacht "Victoria and Albert" and guard of honour 70 70
A108 31p. Railway workers greet Queen Victoria 80 80
A109 31p. Royal party in railway wagons 80 80
See also Nos. A116/23, A132/9, A154/61 and A176/83.

1998. 21st Anniv of Alderney Diving Club. Multicoloured.
A110 20p. Type A **19** 60 40
A111 30p. Cousteau-Gagnan demand valve and wreck of "Stella" (steamer) . . 85 85
A112 37p. Heinke closed helmet and "Liverpool" (full-rigged ship) . . . . . . 1·00 1·10
A113 43p. Siebe closed helmet . . 1·30 1·30
A114 63p. Deane open helmet . . 1·90 1·90
MSA115 190 × 75 mm. Nos. A110/14 and label . . . . . . 5·25 5·25

1998. Garrison Island (2nd series). As Type A **18**. Multicoloured.
A116 20p. Alderney Post Office 50 50
A117 20p. Traders in Victoria Street 50 50
A118 25p. Court House 60 60
A119 25p. Police Station and fire engine 60 60
A120 30p. St. Anne's Church . . 70 70

A121 30p. Wedding party at Albert Gate 70 70

A122 37p. "Courier" (ferry) at Braye Bay 85 85

A123 37p. Fishermen at quay . . 85 85

A **20** Stained Glass Window commemorating Mary Rogers (Chief Stewardess)

1999. Centenary of the Wreck of "Stella" (mail steamer). Sheet 110 × 90 mm containing Type A **20** and similar horiz design.

MSA124 25p. Type A **20**; £1.75, "Stella" leaving Southampton 5·00 6·00

A **21** Solar Eclipse at 10.15 am

A **22** Peregrine Falcon attacking Ruddy Turnstone

1999. Total Eclipse of the Sun (11 August). Designs showing stages of the eclipse. Multicoloured.

A125 20p. Type A **21** 50 50

A126 25p. At 10.51 am 60 60

A127 30p. At 11.14 am 70 70

A128 38p. At 11.16 am 90 90

A129 44p. At 11.17 am . . . . . 1·00 1·40

A130 64p. At 11.36 am . . . . . 1·50 1·90

MSA131 191 × 80 mm. Nos. A125/30 and label . . . . . . 4·75 5·50

No. **MS**A131 also includes the "PHILEX FRANCE '99", Paris, and the "iBRA '99", Nuremberg, emblems on the sheet margin.

1999. Garrison Island (3rd series). Forts. As Type A **18**. Multicoloured.

A132 20p. Field gun and crew, Fort Grosnez, c. 1855 . . 45 45

A133 20p. Parade of 9th Bn, Royal Garrison Artillery 45 45

A134 25p. The Arsenal, Fort Albert, c. 1862 . . . . . 55 55

A135 25p. Royal Engineers loading wagons 55 55

A136 30p. 2nd Bn, Royal Scots on parade 65 65

A137 30p. Garrison at work, Fort Tourgis, c. 1865 . . . . 65 65

A138 38p. Gun emplacement, Fort Houmet Herbe, c. 1870 . . . . . 80 80

A139 38p. Royal Alderney Artillery Militia loading cannon 80 80

Nos. A132/3, A134/5, A136/7 and A138/9 respectively were printed together, se-tenant, forming composite designs.

2000. Endangered Species. Peregrine Falcon. Multicoloured.

A140 21p. Type A **22** 50 45

A141 26p. Two falcons and prey 55 55

A142 34p. Falcon guarding eggs 80 75

A143 38p. Falcon feeding young 85 80

A144 44p. Falcon and prey . . . 1·20 1·00

A145 64p. Two young falcons . 1·50 1·50

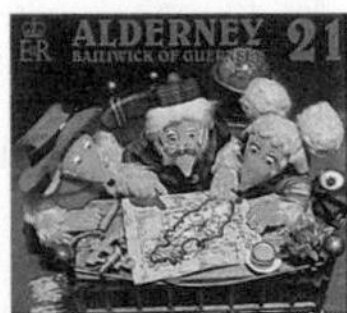

A **23** Wombles around Map of Alderney

2000. "A Wombling Holiday" (characters from children's television programme). Multicoloured.

A146 21p. Type A **23** 45 45

A147 26p. Alderney and Shansi on beach 55 55

A148 36p. Wellington by lighthouse 75 75

A149 40p. Madame Cholet and Bungo having picnic . . 90 85

A150 45p. Tomsk playing golf . . 1·10 95

A151 65p. Orinoco at airport . . 1·50 1·40

MSA152 160 × 86 mm. Nos. A146/51 . . . . 4·70 5·00

A **24** Queen Elizabeth the Queen Mother on Alderney, 1984

2000. Queen Elizabeth the Queen Mother's 100th Birthday. Sheet 93 × 70 mm.

MSA153 A **24** £1.50 multicoloured 4·00 3·75

2000. Garrison Island (4th series). Events. As Type A **18**. Multicoloured.

A154 21p. Regimental boxing tournament 45 45

A155 21p. Sports Day, Alderney Gala Week, 1924 . . . . 45 45

A156 26p. Regimental orchestra playing at Ball 55 55

A157 26p. Garrison Ball in Fort Albert Mess, 1873 . . . 55 55

A158 36p. Royal Engineers' colour party, 1859 . . . 75 75

A159 36p. Royal Artillery on parade, Queen's 40th Birthday, 1859 . . . . . 75 75

A160 40p. Royal Artillery guard of honour 90 85

A161 40p. Arrival of Maj.-Gen. Marcus Slade, 1863 . . . 90 85

Nos. A154/5, A156/7, A158/9 and A160/1 were each printed together, se-tenant, forming a composite design.

A **25** Queen Elizabeth II

2001. 75th Birthday of Queen Elizabeth II. Sheet 70 × 70 mm.

MSA162 A **25** £1.75 multicoloured 4·00 3·75

A **26** Nurse with Clipboard and Patient in X-Ray

2001. Community Services (1st series). Healthcare. Multicoloured.

A163 22p. Type A **26** 45 50

A164 27p. Nurse with tray and Mignot Memorial Hospital 55 60

A165 36p. Doctor and Princess Anne visiting hospital, 1972 . . . . 70 75

A166 40p. Nurse from 1960s and maternity unit 80 85

A167 45p. Nurse from 1957 and Queen Elizabeth II laying hospital foundation stone 90 95

A168 65p. Nurse of 1926 with baby and opening of original hospital . . . . 1·25 1·40

See also Nos. A197/202, A217/22 and A242/7.

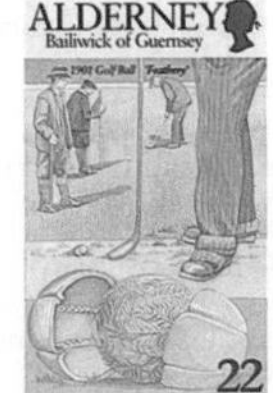

A **27** "Feathery" Golf Ball, 1901

2001. 30th Anniv of Alderney Golf Club. Multicoloured.

A169 22p. Type A **27** 45 50

A170 27p. Golfing fashions of the 1920s 55 60

A171 36p. Alderney Golf Course in 1970s 80 75

A172 40p. Modern putter 90 85

A173 45p. Modern golf gloves and shoes . . . . . . 1·00 95

A174 65p. Modern "lofted wood" 1·40 1·40

MSA175 190 × 75 mm. Nos. A169/74 . . . . 5·00 5·50

No. **MS**A175 includes the "Philanippon '01" logo on the sheet margin.

A **28** Construction of New Breakwater, 1853

2001. Garrison Island (5th series). The Royal Navy. Multicoloured.

A176 22p. Type A **28** 45 50

A177 22p. Official party inspecting harbour, 1853 45 50

A178 27p. H.M.S. *Emerald*, (steam frigate), 1860 . . 55 60

A179 27p. Disembarking troops from H.M.S. *Emerald*, 1860 . . . . 55 60

A180 36p. Moored torpedo boats, 1890 . . . . 70 75

A181 36p. Quick-firing gun on railway wagon, 1890 . . 70 75

A182 40p. H.M.S. *Majestic* (battleship) at anchor, 1901 . . . . 80 85

A183 40p. Torpedo boats outside harbour, 1901 . . . . . 80 85

Nos. A176/7, A178/9, A180/1 and A182/3 were each printed together, se-tenant, each pair forming a composite design.

A **29** Queen Elizabeth and Prince Philip arriving at London Airport, Feb 1952

A **30** Northern Hobby

2002. Golden Jubilee. Sheet 159 × 98 mm.

MSA184 A **29** £2 purple and gold 4·00 4·25

2002. Migrating Birds (1st series). Raptors. Multicoloured.

A185 22p. Type A **30** 45 50

A186 27p. Black kite 55 60

A187 36p. Merlin 70 75

A188 40p. Honey buzzard . . . 90 85

A189 45p. Osprey . . . . 1·00 95

A190 65p. Marsh harrier . . . . 1·50 1·40

MSA191 170 × 80 mm. Nos. A185/90 . . . . 5·00 5·00

See also Nos. A210/**MS**A216 and A235/**MS**A41.

A **31** Coal Fire Beacon, 1725

A **32** St. Edward's Crown

2002. 50th Anniv of Electrification of Les Casquets Lighthouse. Multicoloured.

A192 22p. Type A **31** 45 50

A193 27p. Oil lantern, 1779 . . . 55 60

A194 36p. Argand lamp, 1790 . . 70 75

A195 45p. Revolving light, 1818 90 95

A196 65p. Electric light, 1952 . . 1·25 1·40

No. A196 is inscribed "Elctrification" in error.

2002. Community Services (2nd series). Emergency Medical Aid. As Type A **26**. Multicoloured.

A197 22p. Ambulance technician, and ambulance station 45 50

A198 27p. Ambulance technician using radio, and ambulance 55 60

A199 36p. Doctor, and loading patient onto aircraft . . 70 75

A200 40p. Pilot, and Trislander over Alderney 80 85

A201 45p. Emergency operator, and patient on stretcher 90 95

A202 65p. Lifeboatman, and *Roy Barker One* (lifeboat) . . 1·25 1·40

2003. 50th Anniv of Coronation. Sheet 128 × 90 mm.

MSA203 A **32** £2 multicoloured 4·00 4·25

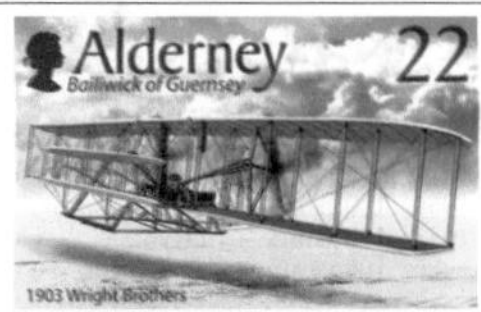

A **33** Wright Brothers' Flyer I, 1903

2003. Centenary of Powered Flight. Multicoloured.

A204 22p. Type A **33** 45 50

A205 27p. Alcock and Brown's Vickers FB-27 Vimy, 1919 . . . . 55 60

A206 36p. Douglas DC-3, 1936 70 75

A207 40p. De Havilland DH106 Comet 1, 1946 . . . . . 80 85

A208 45p. British Aerospace/ Aerospatiale Concorde, 1969 . . . . 90 95

A209 65p. Projected Airbus Industrie A380 . . . . . 1·25 1·40

2003. Migrating Birds (2nd series). Seabirds. Type A **30**. Multicoloured.

A210 22p. Arctic tern 45 50

A211 27p. Great skua 55 60

A212 36p. Sandwich tern 75 75

A213 40p. Sooty shearwater . . . 85 85

A214 45p. Arctic skua 95 95

A215 65p. Manx shearwater . . . 1·40 1·40

MSA216 80 × 170 mm. Nos. A210/15 . . . . 5·00 5·00

2003. Community Services (3rd series). Alderney Police. As Type A **26**. Multicoloured.

A217 22p. Policeman with clipboard and constables on beat 45 50

A218 27p. Policeman and Land Rover 55 60

A219 36p. Forensic team 75 80

A220 40p. Police constable and policeman with child cyclist 80 85

A221 45p. Policeman directing traffic and police at scene of accident 90 95

A222 65p. Policewoman and policeman with customs officer . . . . 1·25 1·40

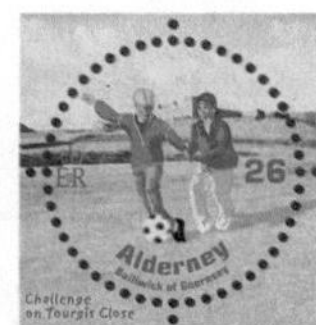

A **34** *Hypholoma fasciculare*

A **35** Boys playing Football, Tourgis Close

2004. Fungi. Multicoloured.

A223 22p. Type A **34** 70 70

A224 27p. *Aleuria aurantia* . . . 85 85

A225 36p. *Coprinus micaceus* . . 1·20 1·20

A226 40p. *Langermannia gigantean* . . . . 1·30 1·30

A227 45p. *Macrolepiota procera* 1·40 1·40

A228 65p. *Xylaria hypoxylon* . . 2·10 2·10

2004. Centenary of FIFA (Federation Internationale de Football Association). Multicoloured.

A229 26p. Type A **35** 85 85

A230 32p. Three children playing football, Braye Beach . . 1·10 1·10

A231 36p. Two boys playing football in playground . . 1·20 1·20

A232 40p. Teenagers playing football, Arch Bay . . . 1·30 1·30

A233 45p. Football match . . . 1·50 1·50

A234 65p. Father and two children playing football, Arch Bay . . . . 2·10 2·10

2004. Migrating Birds (3rd series). Passerines. As Type A **30**. Multicoloured.

A235 26p. Northern wheatear . . 85 85

A236 32p. Common redstart . . 1·10 1·10

A237 36p. Yellow wagtail . . . . 1·20 1·20

A238 40p. Hoopoe . . . . 1·30 1·30

A239 45p. Ring ousel ("Ouzel") 1·50 1·50

A240 65p. Sand martin . . . . . 2·10 2·10

MSA241 170 × 80 mm. Nos. A235/40 . . . . 8·00 8·00

2004. Community Services (4th series). Fire Service. As Type A **26**. Multicoloured.

A242 26p. Fire engine 85 85

A243 32p. Fireman up ladder and fire engine at Fort Tourgis . . . . 1·10 1·10

A244 36p. Airport service fire truck . . . . 1·20 1·20

A245 40p. Alderney Fire Station 1·30 1·30

A246 45p. Airport training ground . . . . 1·50 1·20

A247 65p. Road accident training exercise . . . . 2·10 2·10

GUINEA Pt. 13

The former French Colony on the W. coast of Africa which became fully independent in 1958.

1959. 100 centimes = 1 franc.
1973. 100 caury = 1 syli.
1986. 100 centimes = 1 franc.

1959. Stamps of Fr. West Africa optd **REPUBLIQUE DE GUINEE** or surch also.
188 – 10f. mult (No. 118) . . . . 2·00 2·50
189 **20** 45f. on 20f. pur, grn & ol 2·00 2·50

10 Pres. Sekou Toure

1959. Proclamation of Independence.
190 **10** 5f. red 20 10
191 10f. blue 30 20
192 20f. orange 50 35
193 65f. green . . . . 1·60 1·00
194 100f. violet . . . . 2·50 1·90

12 Tamara Lighthouse and Fishing Boats

13 Flying Doves

1959.
201 **12** 1f. red (postage) 10 10
202 2f. green 10 10
203 3f. brown 10 10
204 – 5f. blue 15 15
205 – 10f. purple 15 10
206 – 15f. brown 85 25
207 – 20f. purple 60 30
208 – 25f. brown . . . . 1·50 30
209 **13** 40f. blue (air) 35 25
210 50f. green 55 40
211 100f. lake . . . . 1·25 65
212 200f. red . . . . 2·25 1·25
213 500f. red . . . . 6·00 3·25
DESIGNS—VERT: 5f. Palms and dhow; 20f. Pres. Sekou Toure. HORIZ: 10f. Pirogue being launched; 15f. African Elephant (front view); 25f. African Elephant (side view).

14 Mangoes

16 "Raising the Flag"

15 Lockheed Super Constellation Airliner

1959. Fruits in natural colours. Frame colours given.
214 – 10f. red (Bananas) 15 15
215 – 15f. green (Grapefruit) . . 25 15
216 – 20f. brown (Lemons) . . . 45 20
217 **14** 25f. blue 55 30
218 – 50f. violet (Pineapple) . . . 1·00 35

1959. Air.
219 **15** 100f. blue, brown & mauve 1·75 95
220 200f. mauve, brown & grn 5·00 1·25
221 – 500f. multicoloured . . . . 8·00 2·50
DESIGN: 500f. Lockheed Super Constellation airliner on ground.

1959. 1st Anniv of Independence.
222 **16** 50f. multicoloured 55 25
223 100f. multicoloured . . . . 1·25 65

18 Africans acclaiming U.N. Headquarters Building

1959. U.N.O.
230 **18** 1f. blue & orange (postage) 15 10
231 2f. purple and green . . . 15 10
232 3f. brown and red 15 10
233 5f. brown and turquoise . . 15 10
234 50f. green, blue & brn (air) 65 50
235 100f. green, red and blue 90 70
Nos. 234/5 are larger (45 × 26 mm).

19 Eye-testing

20 "Uprooted Tree"

1960. National Health. Inscr "POUR NOTRE SANTE NATIONALE".
236 **19** 20f.+10f. red and blue . . 75 70
237 – 30f.+20f. violet & orange 75 70
238 – 40f.+20f. blue and red . . 1·10 95
239 – 50f.+50f. brown and green 2·00 1·60
240 – 100f.+100f. green & pur . . 2·75 2·10
DESIGNS—HORIZ: 30f. Laboratory assistant; 40f. Spraying trees. VERT: (28½ × 40 mm): 50f. Research with microscope; 100f. Operating theatre.

1960. World Refugee Year.
241 **20** 25f. multicoloured 50 35
242 50f. multicoloured 70 45

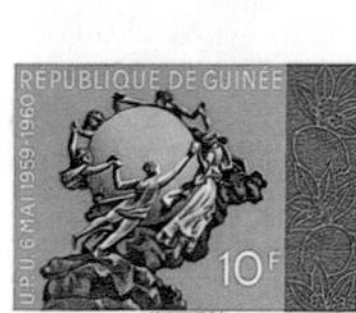

21 U.P.U. Monument, Berne

23 Flag and Map

1960. 1st Anniv of Admission to U.P.U. Background differs for each value.
243 **21** 10f. black and brown . . . 15 10
244 15f. lilac and mauve . . . 25 15
245 20f. indigo and blue . . . 40 15
246 – 25f. myrtle and green . . . 55 15
247 – 50f. sepia and orange . . . 65 25
DESIGN: 25f., 50f. As Type **10** but vert.

1960. Olympic Games. Optd **Jeux Olympiques Rome 1960** and Olympic rings.
248 **16** 50f. multicoloured (postage) . . . . 5·00 5·00
249 100f. multicoloured . . . . 7·50 7·50
250 **15** 100f. blue, grn & mve(air) 6·50 4·50
251 200f. mauve, brown & grn 13·00 6·50
252 – 500f. multi (No. 221) . . . 32·00 32·00

1960. 2nd Anniv of Independence.
253 **23** 25f. multicoloured 30 25
254 30f. multicoloured 40 35

1960. 15th Anniv of U.N.O. Optd **XVEME ANNIVERSAIRE DES NATIONS UNIES.** (a) Nos. 214/18. Fruits in natural colours.
255 – 10f. red 20 20
256 – 15f. green 30 25
257 – 20f. brown 35 30
258 **14** 25f. blue 45 35
259 – 50f. violet 75 60

(b) Nos. 230/35.
260 **18** 1f. blue & orange (postage) 10 10
261 2f. purple and green . . . 10 10
262 3f. brown and red 10 10
263 5f. brown and turquoise . . 10 10
264 50f. green, blue & brn (air) 65 70
265 100f. green, red and blue 90 70

1961. Surch **1961** and value.
266 **20** 25f.+10f. multicoloured . . 4·75 4·75
267 50f.+20f. multicoloured . . 4·75 4·75

27 Bohar Reedbuck

1961. Centres in brown, green and blue. Inscriptions and value tablets in colours given.
268 **27** 5f. turquoise 15 10
269 10f. green 15 10
270 25f. violet 40 15
271 40f. orange 55 20
272 50f. red . . . . 1·25 25
273 75f. blue . . . . 1·75 45

28 Guinea Flag and Exhibition Hall, Conakry

1961. First Three-Year Plan. Flag in red, yellow and green.
274 **28** 5f. blue and red 15 15
275 10f. brown and red 15 15
276 25f. green and red 25 25

29 Helmeted Guineafowl

1961. Guineafowl in purple and blue.
277 **29** 5f. mauve and blue 40 20
278 10f. red and blue 45 20
279 25f. red and blue 45 35
280 40f. brown and blue . . . 80 40
281 50f. bistre and blue 90 60
282 75f. olive and blue . . . . 2·25 75

1961. Protection of Animals. Surch **POUR LA PROTECTION DE NOS ANIMAUX +5 FRS.**
283 **27** 5f.+5f. turquoise 15 15
284 10f.+5f. green 25 15
285 25f.+5f. violet 55 30
286 40f.+5f. orange 70 40
287 50f.+5f. red 95 55
288 75f.+5f. blue . . . . . . 1·50 70

31 Patrice Lumumba

1962. 1st Death Anniv of Lumumba (Congo leader).
289 **31** 10f. multicoloured 30 25
290 25f. multicoloured 40 25
291 50f. multicoloured 60 30

1962. Malaria Eradication (1st issue). Nos. 236/40 optd with Malaria Eradication emblem and **ERADICATION DE LA MALARIA.**
292 **19** 20f.+10f. red and blue . . 35 35
293 – 30f.+20f. violet and orange 50 50
294 – 40f.+20f. blue and red . . 60 60
295 – 50f.+50f. brown & green 1·25 1·25
296 – 100f.+100f. green & pur . . 2·50 2·50

33 King Mohammed V and Map

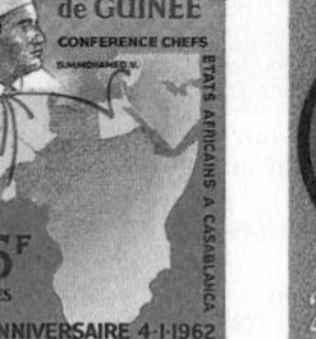

34a Posthorn on North Africa

34 Mosquito and Emblem

1962. 1st Anniv of Casablanca Conference.
297 **33** 25f. multicoloured 95 25
298 75f. multicoloured . . . . 1·90 45

1962. Air. Malaria Eradication (2nd issue).
299 **34** 25f. black and orange . . . 40 20
300 50f. black and red 50 35
301 100f. black and green . . . 1·00 60

1962. African Postal Union Commemoration.
303 **34a** 25f. green, brown & orge 65 15
304 100f. orange and brown 1·60 40

1962. Guinea-fowl stamps surch **POUR LA PROTECTION DE NOS OISEAUX +5 FRS.**
305 **29** 5f.+5f. 60 35
306 10f.+5f. 60 45
307 25f.+5f. 80 55
308 40f.+5f. 95 70
309 50f.+5f. . . . . 2·10 90
310 75f.+5f. . . . . 3·75 1·90

36 Bote-player

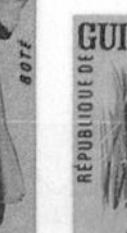

37 Hippopotamus

1962. Native Musicians.
311 **36** 30c. red, grn & bl (postage) 15 10
312 A 50c. green, brown & salmon 15 10
313 B 1f. purple and green . . . 15 10
314 C 1f.50 turquoise, red & yell 15 10
315 D 2f. green, red and mauve 15 10
316 C 3f. violet, green & turquoise 15 10
317 B 10f. blue, brown and orange 25 10
318 D 20f. red, sepia and olive . . 30 20
319 **36** 25f. violet, sepia and olive 45 25
320 A 40f. mauve, green and blue 45 35
321 **36** 50f. blue, red and rose . . 60 40
322 A 75f. blue, brown and ochre 2·50 55
323 D 100f. blue, red & pink (air) 1·10 50
324 200f. red and blue . . . . 2·50 75
325 E 500f. blue, violet and brown . . . . 6·50 2·50
DESIGNS—(Musicians playing). HORIZ: A, Bolon; C, Koni; D, Kora; E, Balafon. VERT: B, Flute.

1962. Wild Game.
326 **37** 10f. sepia, green and orange 30 10
327 – 25f. brown, sepia and green 60 20
328 – 30f. sepia, yellow and olive 70 20
329 **37** 50f. sepia, green and blue 1·00 35
330 – 75f. brown, purple and lilac . . . . 1·50 60
331 – 100f. sepia, yellow & turq 2·00 80
DESIGNS: 25f., 75f. Lion; 30f., 100f. Leopard.

38 Boy at Blackboard

43 Crowned Crane

39 Alfa Yaya

1962. Campaign Against Illiteracy.
332 **38** 5f. sepia, yellow and red 10 10
333 – 10f. sepia, orange and purple 10 10
334 **38** 15f. sepia, green and red 20 10
335 – 20f. sepia, turquoise & pur 30 20
DESIGN: 10f., 20f. Teacher at blackboard.

1962. African Heroes and Martyrs.
336 **39** 25f. sepia, turquoise & gold 30 15
337 – 30f. sepia, ochre and gold 40 20
338 – 50f. sepia, purple and gold 55 25
339 – 75f. sepia, green and gold 1·10 40
340 – 100f. sepia, red and gold 1·40 60
PORTRAITS: 30f. King Behanzin; 50f. King Ba Bemba of Sikasso; 75f. Almamy Samory; 100f. Chief Tierno Aliou of the Goumba.

1962. Algerian Refugees Fund. Surch **Aide aux Refugies Algeriens** and premium.
341 **33** 25f.+15f. multicoloured . . 65 65
342 75f.+25f. multicoloured . . 1·25 1·25

1962. Air. "The Conquest of Space". Optd with capsule and **La Conquete De L'Espace.**
343 **13** 40f. blue 50 25
344 50f. green 60 30
345 100f. lake . . . . 1·00 50
348 200f. red . . . . 1·75 95

1962. Birds. Multicoloured.
349 30c. Type **43** (postage) . . . 70 15
350 50c. Grey parrot (horiz) . . . 70 15
351 1f. Abyssinian ground hornbill (horiz) 80 15
352 1f.50 White spoonbill (horiz) 80 30
353 2f. Bateleur (horiz) 80 30
354 3f. Type **43** . . . . 1·00 30
355 10f. As 50c. (horiz) . . . . . 1·00 30

356 20f. As 1f. (horiz) . . . . . 1·25 60
357 25f. As 1f.50 (horiz) . . . . 1·60 60
358 40f. As 2f. (horiz) . . . . . 1·60 60
359 50f. Type **43** . . . . 1·75 85
360 75f. As 50c. (horiz) . . . . . 4·00 90
361 100f. As 1f. (horiz) (air) . . . 4·50 1·10
362 200f. As 1f.50 (horiz) . . . . 7·50 2·50
363 500f. As 2f. (horiz) . . . . . 16·00 5·50

44 Handball

1963. Sports.
364 **44** 30c. purple, red and green (postage) 10 10
365 A 50c. violet, lilac and blue 10 10
366 B 1f. sepia, orange and green 10 10
367 C 1f.50 blue, orange & purple 10 10
368 D 2f. blue, turquoise & purple 10 10
369 **44** 3f. purple, olive and blue 10 10
370 A 4f. violet, mauve and blue 10 10
371 B 5f. sepia, green and purple 15 10
372 C 10f. blue and bright purple 20 10
373 D 20f. blue, orange and red 30 15
374 **44** 25f. purple, green and black 40 15
375 A 30f. violet, black and blue 45 25
376 B 100f. sepia, lake & grn (air) 1·10 40
377 C 200f. blue, brown & purple 2·25 90
378 D 500f. blue, brown & purple 5·00 2·25
DESIGNS: A, Boxing; B, Running; C, Cycling; D, Canoeing.

45 Campaign Emblem

1963. Freedom from Hunger.
379 **45** 5f. yellow and red 10 10
380 10f. yellow and green . . . 10 10
381 15f. yellow and brown . . . 15 10
382 25f. yellow and olive . . . 25 15

46 "Amauris niavius"

1963. Butterflies. Multicoloured.
383 10c. Type **46** (postage) . . . 10 10
384 30c. "Papilio demodocus" . . 10 10
385 40c. As 30c. 10 10
386 50c. "Graphum policenes" . . 10 10
387 1f. "Papilio nireus" 15 10
388 1f.50 Type **46** 20 10
389 2f. "Papilio menestheus" . . 20 10
390 3f. As 30c. 20 10
391 10f. As 50c. 35 10
392 20f. As 1f. 60 15
393 25f. Type **46** . . . . 1·00 20
394 40f. As 2f. . . . . 1·40 30
395 50f. As 30c. . . . . 1·90 35
396 75f. As 1f. . . . . 2·75 60
397 100f. Type **46** (air) . . . . . 1·75 35
398 200f. As 50c. . . . . 4·00 80
399 500f. As 2f. . . . . 8·00 2·50

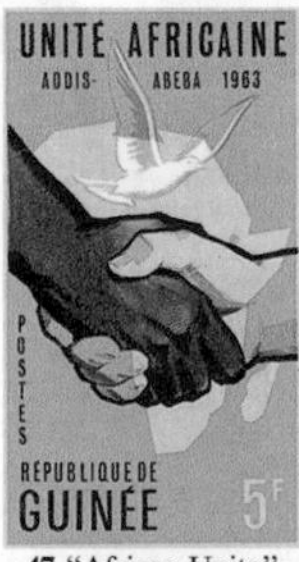

47 "African Unity"

1963. Conf of African Heads of State, Addis Ababa.
400 **47** 5f. sepia, blk & turq on grn 10 10
401 10f. sepia, black and yellow on yellow 10 10
402 15f. sepia, black & ol on ol 15 10
403 25f. sepia, black and brown on cinnamon 25 15

48 Capsule encircling Globe

1963. Centenary of Red Cross.
404 **48** 5f. red and green (postage) 10 10
405 10f. red and blue 15 10
406 15f. red and yellow 20 15
407 25f. red and black (air) . . 45 20

1963. Air. 1st Pan-American Conakry–New York Direct Air Service. Optd **PREMIER SERVICE DIRECT CONAKRY–NEW YORK PAN AMERICAN 30 JUILLET 1963**.
409 **15** 10f. blue, green and mauve 1·90 75
410 200f. mauve, brown & green . . . . 3·25 1·25

1963. Olympic Games Preparatory Commission, Conakry. Nos. 364/6 surch **COMMISSION PREPARATOIRE AUX JEUX OLYMPIQUES A CONAKRY**, rings and new value.
411 40f. on 30c. purple, red and green . . . . 1·00 80
412 50f. on 50c. violet, lilac and blue . . . . 1·40 1·10
413 75f. on 1f. sepia, orange & grn . . . . 2·40 1·90

51 Jewel Cichlid

1964. Guinea Fishes. Multicoloured.
414 30c. Type **51** (postage) . . . 10 10
415 40c. Golden pheasant panchax 10 10
416 50c. Blue gularis 10 10
417 1f. Banded jewelfish and jewel cichlid 10 10
418 1f.50 Yellow gularis 10 10
419 2f. Six-banded lyretail 25 10
420 5f. Type **51** 25 10
421 30f. As 40c. 65 20
422 40f. As 50c. . . . . 1·25 35
423 75f. As 1f. . . . . 2·25 55
424 100f. As 1f.50 (air) . . . . . 2·25 55
425 300f. As 2f. . . . . 7·00 1·75

52 President Kennedy **53** Pipeline under Construction

1964. Pres. Kennedy Memorial Issue. Flag in red and blue.
426 **52** 5f. violet & black (postage) 10 10
427 25f. violet and green . . . 25 20
428 50f. violet and brown . . . 60 30
429 100f. black and violet (air) 1·00 85

1964. Inaug of Piped Water Supply, Conakry.
430 **53** 5f. red 10 10
431 – 10f. violet 10 10
432 – 20f. brown 15 10
433 – 30f. blue 30 15
434 – 50f. green 55 30
DESIGNS—HORIZ: 10f. Reservoir; 20f. Joining pipes; 30f. Transporting pipes; 50f. Laying pipes.

54 Ice hockey

1964. Winter Olympic Games, Innsbruck. Rings, frame and tablet in gold.
435 **54** 10f. olive & green (postage) 15 10
436 – 25f. slate and violet 40 20
437 – 50f. black and blue 75 40
438 – 100f. black & brn (air) . . 1·10 55
DESIGNS: 25f. Ski-jumping; 50f. Skiing; 100f. Figure-skating.

1964. Air. Olympic Games, Tokyo (1st issue). Nos. 376/8 optd **JEUX OLYMPIQUES TOKYO 1964** and Olympic rings.
439 100f. sepia, lake and green 1·50 1·00
440 200f. blue, brown and purple 2·25 1·50
441 500f. blue, brown and purple 5·00 3·50

56 Eleanor Roosevelt with Children

1964. 15th Anniv of Declaration of Human Rights.
442 **56** 5f. green (postage) 10 10
443 10f. orange 10 10
444 15f. blue 15 10
445 25f. red 30 15
446 50f. violet (air) 70 30

57 Striped Hyena

1964. Animals.
447 **57** 5f. sepia and yellow . . . 20 10
448 30f. sepia and blue 40 20
449 – 40f. black and mauve . . . 55 25
450 – 75f. sepia and green . . . 1·50 30
451 – 100f. sepia and ochre . . . 2·00 50
452 – 300f. deep violet and orange . . . . 4·00 1·75
ANIMALS: 40f., 300f. African buffalo; 75f., 100f. African elephant.

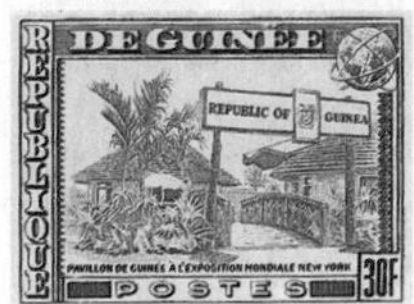

58 Guinea Pavilion

1964. New York World's Fair.
453 **58** 30f. green and lilac 25 15
454 40f. green and purple . . . 40 15
455 50f. green and brown . . . 50 15
456 75f. blue and red 75 25
See also Nos. 484/87.

60 Nefertari, Isis and Hathor

1964. Nubian Monuments Preservation. Mult.
458 10f. Type **60** (postage) . . . 20 15
459 25f. Pharaoh in battle 25 15
460 50f. The Nile—partly submerged sphinxes . . . 45 20
461 100f. Rameses II, entrance hall of Great Temple, Abu Simbel . . . . 1·10 45
462 200f. Lower part of Colossi, Abu Simbel . . . . 2·00 80
463 300f. Nefertari (air) . . . . . 3·75 1·60

61 Athlete with Torch **62** Doudou (Boke) Mask

1965. Olympic Games, Tokyo (2nd issue). Multicoloured.
464 5f. Weightlifter and children (postage) 15 10
465 10f. Type **61** 15 10
466 25f. Pole vaulting 25 20
467 40f. Running 30 20
468 50f. Judo 50 30
469 75f. Japanese hostess . . . . 1·00 45
470 100f. Air hostess and Convair Coronado airliner (horiz) (air) . . . . 1·50 55

1965. Native Masks and Dancers. Mult.
472 20c. Type **62** (postage) . . . 10 10
473 40c. Niamou (Nzerekore) mask 10 10
474 60c. "Yoki" (Boke) statuette 10 10
475 80c. Guekedou dancer . . . 10 10
476 1f. Niamou (Nzerekore) mask 10 10
477 2f. Macenta dancer 15 10
478 15f. Niamou (Nzerekore) mask 25 15
479 20f. Tom-tom beater (forest region) 45 15
480 60f. Macenta "Bird-man" dancer 95 45
481 80f. Bassari (Koundara) dancer . . . . 1·10 55
482 100f. Karana sword dancer 1·60 70
483 300f. Niamou (Nzerekore) mask (air) . . . . 4·50 1·50

1965. New York World's Fair. As Nos. 453/6 but additionally inscr "1965".
484 **58** 30f. orange and green . . . 20 15
485 40f. green and red 30 15
486 50f. violet and blue 45 25
487 75f. violet and brown . . . 65 35

63 Metal-work

1965. Native Handicrafts. Multicoloured.
489 15f. Type **63** (postage) . . . 15 10
490 20f. Pottery 20 15
491 60f. Dyeing 60 35
492 80f. Basket-making 85 45
493 100f. Ebony-work (air) . . . 1·25 45
494 300f. Ivory-work . . . . . . 4·50 1·25

64 I.T.U. Emblem and Symbols

1965. I.T.U. Centenary.
495 **64** 25f. multicoloured (postage) 30 15
496 50f. multicoloured 60 25
497 100f. multicoloured (air) 1·10 40
498 200f. multicoloured . . . . 2·00 65

67 U.N. Headquarters and I.C.Y. Emblem

1965. I.C.Y.
501 **67** 25f. red and green (postage) 25 15
502 45f. red and violet 35 20
503 75f. red and brown 70 30
504 100f. orange and blue (air) 1·25 45

68 Polytechnic Institute, Conakry

1965. 7th Anniv of Independence. Mult.
505 25f. Type **68** (postage) . . . 15 15
506 30f. Camayenne Hotel . . . 20 15
507 40f. Gbessia Airport 60 30
508 75f. "28 Septembre" Stadium 55 35

509 200f. Polytechnic Institute, North facade (air) 1·40 1·00
510 500f. Ditto, West facade 4·25 2·50
Nos. 509/10 are larger, 53 × 23 mm.

69 Moon, Globe and Satellite
70 Sabre Dance, Karana

1965. "To the Moon". Multicoloured.
511 5f. Type **69** (postage) 15 10
512 10f. Trajectory of "Ranger 7" 20 10
513 25f. "Relay" satellite 30 20
514 45f. "Vostok 1, 2" and Globe 55 25
515 100f. "Ranger 7" approaching Moon (vert) (25 × 36 mm) (air) 85 40
516 200f. Launching of "Ranger 7" (vert) (25 × 36 mm) 2·00 75
Nos. 512/14 are larger, 36 × 25½ mm.

1966. Guinean Dances. Multicoloured.
519 10c. Type **70** (postage) 10 10
520 30c. Young girls' dance, Lower Guinea 10 10
521 50c. Tiekere musicians, "Eyora" (bamboo) dance, Bandjinguene (horiz) (36 × 29 mm) 10 10
522 5f. Doundouba dance, Kouroussa 10 10
523 40f. Bird-man's dance, Macenta 85 30
524 100f. Kouyate Kandia, national singer (horiz) (36 × 29 mm) (air) 1·25 45
See also Nos. 561/6.

1966. Stamp Cent Exn, Cairo. Nos. 460 and 463 optd **CENTENAIRE DU TIMBRE CAIRE 1966.**
525 50f. multicoloured (postage) 55 40
526 300f. multicoloured (air) 2·25 1·50

1966. Pan Arab Games, Cairo (1965). Nos. 464/5, 467/9 optd **JEUX PANARABES CAIRE 1965** and pyramid motif.
527 – 5f. multicoloured (postage) 20 15
528 **61** 10f. multicoloured 20 15
529 – 40f. multicoloured 55 35
530 – 50f. multicoloured 70 45
531 – 75f. multicoloured 1·25 75
532 – 100f. multicoloured (air) 1·25 40

73 Vonkou Rocks, Telimele
74 UNESCO Emblem

1966. Landscapes (1st series). Multicoloured.
534 20f. Type **73** (postage) 15 10
535 25f. Artificial lake, Coyah 20 10
536 40f. Waterfalls, Kate 35 15
537 50f. Bridge, Forecariah 45 20
538 75f. Liana bridge 70 35
539 100f. Lighthouse and bay, Boulbinet (air) 1·50 45
See also Nos. 603/608.

1966. 20th Anniv of UNESCO (a) Postage.
540 **74** 25f. multicoloured 40 20

(b) Air. Nos. 509/10 optd **vingt ans 1946 1966** and UNESCO Emblem.
541 200f. multicoloured 2·00 1·25
542 500f. multicoloured 4·50 2·75

76
78 Decade and UNESCO Symbols

1966. Guinean Flora and Female Headdresses. Similar designs.
543 **76** 10c. multicoloured (postage) 10 10
544 – 20c. multicoloured 10 10
545 – 30c. multicoloured 10 10
546 – 40c. multicoloured 10 10
547 – 3f. multicoloured 10 10
548 – 4f. multicoloured 10 10
549 – 10f. multicoloured 15 10
550 – 25f. multicoloured 55 10
551 – 30f. multicoloured 70 15
552 – 50f. multicoloured 1·10 30
553 **76** 80f. multicoloured 1·40 40
554 – 200f. multicoloured (air) 2·75 75
555 – 300f. multicoloured 4·50 1·50
Nos. 551/555 are 29 × 42 mm.

1966. Int Hydrological Decade.
558 **78** 5f. red and blue 10 10
559 25f. red and green 20 10
560 100f. red and purple 1·00 50

1966. Guinean National Ballet. Designs show various dances as T **70**.
561 60c. multicoloured 10 10
562 1f. multicoloured 10 10
563 1f.50 multicoloured 15 10
564 25f. multicoloured 35 20
565 50f. multicoloured 85 30
566 75f. multicoloured 1·40 50
SIZES—VERT: (26 × 36 mm): 60c., 1f., 1f.50, 50f. HORIZ: (36 × 29 mm): 25f., 75f.

79 "Village"

1966. 20th Anniv of UNICEF Multicoloured designs showing children's drawings.
567 2f. "Elephant" 10 10
568 3f. "Doll" 10 10
569 10f. "Girl" 10 10
570 20f. Type **79** 15 10
571 25f. "Footballer" 35 15
572 40f. "Still Life" 55 20
573 50f. "Bird in Tree" 70 25

80 Dispensing Medicine

1967. Inauguration of W.H.O. Headquarters, Geneva. Multicoloured.
574 30f. Type **80** 25 10
575 50f. Doctor examining child 35 20
576 75f. Nurse weighing baby 60 30
577 80f. W.H.O. Building and flag 75 45

81 Niamou Mask

1967. Guinean Masks. Multicoloured.
578 10c. Banda-di (Kanfarade Boke region) 10 10
579 30c. Niamou (N'zerekore region) (different) 10 10
580 50c. Type **81** 10 10
581 60c. Yinadjinkele (Kankan region) 10 10
582 1f. As 10c. 10 10
583 1f.50 As 30c. 10 10
584 5f. Type **81** 15 10
585 25f. As 60c. 20 10
586 30f. As 10c. 30 10
587 50f. As 30c. 55 20
588 75f. As Type **81** 1·10 35
589 100f. As 60c. 1·50 50

82 Research Institute

1967. Pastoria Research Institute. Mult.
590 20c. Type **82** (postage) 10 10
591 30c. "Python regius" (snake) 10 10
592 50c. Extracting snake's venom 10 10
593 1f. "Python sebae" 10 10
594 2f. Attendants handling viper 10 10
595 5f. Gabon viper 10 10
596 20f. "Dendroaspis viridis" 35 10
597 30f. As 5f. 65 10
598 50f. As 1f. 1·10 20
599 75f. As 50c. 1·60 30
600 200f. As 20c. (air) 2·25 80
601 300f. As 2f. 4·00 1·50
Nos. 596/601 are 56 × 26 mm.

1967. Landscapes (2nd series). As T **73**. Mult.
603 5f. Loos Islands (postage) 10 10
604 30f. Tinkisso waterfalls 20 10
605 70f. The "Elephant's Trunk", Kakoulima 45 10
606 80f. Seashore, Ratoma 70 20
607 100f. House of explorer Olivier de Sanderval (air) 1·10 35
608 200f. Aerial view of Conakry 1·60 75

83 People's Palace, Conakry

1967. 20th Anniv of Guinean Democratic Party and Inaug of People's Palace. Multicoloured.
609 5f. Type **83** (postage) 10 10
610 30f. African elephant's head 50 50
611 55f. Type **83** 40 25
612 200f. As 30f. (air) 1·75 1·00

1967. 50th Anniv of Lions Int Landscape series optd **AMITE DES PEUPLES GRACE AU TOURISME 1917 – 1967** and Lions Emblem.
613 5f. (No. 603) (postage) 15 10
614 30f. (No. 604) 30 20
615 40f. (No. 536) 35 20
616 50f. (No. 537) 45 25
617 70f. (No. 605) 60 35
618 75f. (No. 538) 85 45
619 80f. (No. 606) 1·00 45
620 100f. (No. 539) (air) 1·10 60
621 100f. (No. 607) 1·10 60
622 200f. (No. 608) 2·00 1·10

85 Section of Mural
86 W.H.O. Building, Brazzaville

1967. Air. "World of Tomorrow". Jose Vanetti's Mural, Conference Building, U.N. Headquarters.
623 – 30f. multicoloured 20 15
624 – 50f. multicoloured 30 20
625 **85** 100f. multicoloured 80 40
626 – 200f. multicoloured 1·60 60
DESIGNS: 50f. to 200f. Various sections of mural.

1967. Inaug of W.H.O. Building, Brazzaville.
628 **86** 30f. olive, ochre and blue 30 15
629 75f. red, ochre and blue 60 25

87 Human Rights Emblem

1968. Human Rights Year.
630 **87** 30f. red, green and ochre 25 15
631 40f. red, blue and violet 30 15

88 Coyah, Oubreka Region

1968. Regional Costumes and Habitations. Multicoloured.
632 20c. Type **88** (postage) 10 10
633 30c. Kankan Region 10 10
634 40c. Kankan, Upper Guinea 10 10
635 50c. Forest region 10 10
636 60c. Foulamory, Gaoual Region 10 10
637 5f. Cognagui, Koundara Region 10 10
638 15f. As 50c. 15 10
639 20f. As 20c. 30 15
640 30f. As 30c. 45 20
641 40f. Fouta-Djallon, Middle Guinea 70 25
642 100f. Labe, Middle Guinea 1·50 40
643 300f. Bassari, Koundara Region (air) 3·25 1·00
The 60c. to 300f. are larger (60 × 39 mm).

89 "The Village Story-teller"

1968. Paintings of African Legends (1st series). Multicoloured.
644 25f. Type **89** (postage) 15 10
645 30f. "The Moon and the Stars" 15 10
646 75f. "Leuk the Hare sells his Sister" (vert) 60 35
647 80f. "The Hunter and the Female Antelope" 1·00 35
648 100f. "Old Faya's Inheritance" (vert) (air) 1·00 30
649 200f. "Soumangourou Kante killed by Djegue" 2·00 45

1968. Paintings of African Legends (2nd series). As T **89**. Multicoloured.
651 15f. "Little Demons of Mount Nimba" (postage) 10 10
652 30f. "Lan, the Baby Buffalo" (vert) 20 10
653 40f. "The Nianablas and the Crocodiles" 30 20
654 50f. "Leuk the Hare and the Drum" (vert) 50 20
655 70f. "Malissadio—the Young Girl and the Hippopotamus" (air) 75 20
656 300f. "Little Goune, Son of the Lion" (vert) 3·25 1·10

90 Olive Baboon

1968. African Fauna. Multicoloured.
658 5f. Type **90** (postage) 15 10
659 10f. Leopards 20 10
660 15f. Hippopotami 30 15
661 20f. Crocodile 55 20
662 30f. Warthog 70 20
663 50f. Kob 85 25
664 75f. African buffalo 1·60 45
665 100f. Lions (air) 1·75 40
666 200f. African elephant 4·00 1·00
Nos. 665/6 are 50 × 35 mm.

91 Robert F. Kennedy

1968. "Martyrs of Liberty". Multicoloured.
668 30f. Type **91** (postage) 20 10
669 75f. Martin Luther King 50 20
670 100f. John F. Kennedy 65 35
671 50f. Type **91** (air) 45 15
672 100f. Martin Luther King 80 25
673 200f. John F. Kennedy 1·75 60

92 Running

1969. Olympic Games, Mexico (1968). Multicoloured.
674 5f. Type **92** (postage) 10 10
675 10f. Boxing 10 10
676 15f. Throwing the javelin 15 10
677 25f. Football 25 10
678 30f. Hurdling 30 10
679 50f. Throwing the hammer 50 25
680 75f. Cycling 70 25
681 100f. Gymnastics (air) 70 30

682 200f. Exercising on rings 1·25 50
683 300f. Pole-vaulting 2·50 95

The 25, 100, 200 and 300f. are larger, 57 × 30 mm. Each design also shows one of three different sculptured figures.

1969. Moon Flight of "Apollo 8". Nos. 514/16 optd **APOLLO 8 DEC. 1968** and earth and moon motifs or surch also.

684 30f. on 45f. mult (postage) 35 35
685 45f. multicoloured 35 35

686 25f. on 200f. mult (air) 35 15
687 100f. multicoloured 1·10 65
688 200f. multicoloured 2·00 1·00

95 "Tarzan"

1969. "Tarzan" (famous Guinea Chimpanzee). Multicoloured.

689 25f. Type **95** 25 15
690 30f. "Tarzan" in front of Pastoria Institute 30 20
691 75f. "Tarzan" and family 65 25
692 100f. "Tarzan" squatting on branch 1·25 40

96 Pioneers lighting Fire

1969. Guinean Pioneer Youth Organization. Multicoloured.

693 5f. Type **96** 10 10
694 25f. Pioneer and village 20 10
695 30f. Pioneers squad 25 10
696 40f. Playing basketball 35 20
697 45f. Two pioneers 40 20
698 50f. Pioneers emblem 50 25

97 "Apollo" Launch

1969. 1st Man on the Moon. Multicoloured.

700 25f. Type **97** 15 10
701 30f. View of Earth 20 10
702 50f. Modules descent to the Moon 35 10
703 60f. Astronauts on Moon 45 20
704 75f. Landing module on Moon 50 25
705 100f. Take-off from Moon 1·00 40
706 200f. "Splashdown" 2·00 1·00

No. 705 is 35 × 71 mm.

The above stamps were issued with English and French inscriptions.

98 Pylon and Heavy Industry

1969. 50th Anniv of I.L.O. Multicoloured.

707 25f. Type **98** 20 10
708 30f. Broadcasting studio 20 10
709 75f. Harvesting 50 20
710 200f. Making pottery 1·40 65

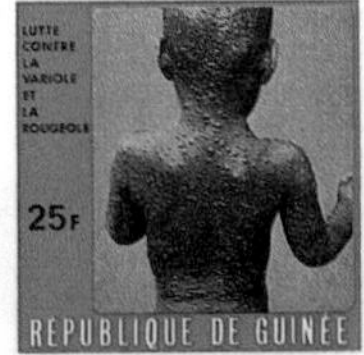

99 Child suffering from Smallpox

1970. Campaign Against Measles and Smallpox. Multicoloured.

711 25f. Type **99** 15 10
712 30f. Mother and child with measles 20 15
713 40f. Inoculating girl 30 15
714 50f. Inoculating boy 50 25
715 60f. Inoculating family 60 25
716 200f. Dr. Edward Jenner 2·25 1·00

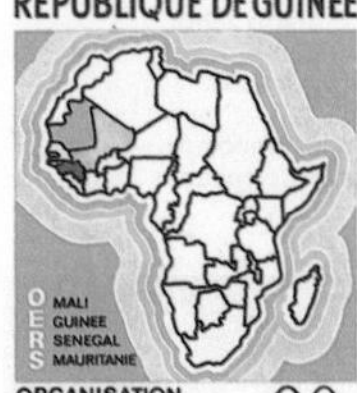

100 O.E.R.S. Countries on Map of Africa

1970. Meeting of Senegal River Riparian States Organization (Organisation des Etats Riverains du Fleuve Senegal).

717 **100** 30f. multicoloured 20 15
718 200f. multicoloured 1·50 95

NOTE: The Riparian States are Guinea, Mali, Mauritania and Senegal.

101 Dish Aerial and Open book

1970. World Telecommunications Day.

719 **101** 5f. black and blue 15 15
720 10f. black and red 15 15
721 50f. black and yellow 45 15
722 200f. black and lilac 2·00 95

102 Lenin

1970. Birth Centenary of Lenin. Multicoloured.

723 5f. Type **102** 10 10
724 20f. "Lenin in the Smolny" (Serov) 20 10
725 30f. "Lenin addressing Workers" (Serov) 25 15
726 40f. "Lenin speaking to Servicemen" (Vasiliev) 40 15
727 100f. "Lenin with Crowd" (Vasilev) 1·00 35
728 200f. Type **102** 1·75 1·00

103 Congo Tetra

1971. Fishes. Multicoloured.

729 5f. Type **103** 15 10
730 10f. Red-spotted gularis 20 10
731 15f. Red-chinned panchax 20 10
732 20f. Six-barred distichodus 35 15
733 25f. Jewel cichlid 40 25
734 30f. Rainbow krib 65 25
735 40f. Two-striped lyretail 75 25
736 45f. Banded jewelfish 1·10 35
737 50f. Red-tailed notho 1·25 50
738 75f. Freshwater butterflyfish 2·25 55
739 100f. Golden trevally 2·75 65
740 200f. African mouth-brooder 5·50 1·75

104 Violet-crested Turaco

1971. Wild Birds. Multicoloured.

741 5f. Type **104** (postage) 75 50
742 20f. Golden oriole 1·00 60
743 30f. Blue headed coucal 1·10 75
744 40f. Great grey shrike 1·25 90
745 75f. Vulturine guineafowl 2·75 1·10
746 100f. Southern ground hornbill 4·50 1·50

747 50f. Type **104** (air) 1·50 1·00
748 100f. As 20f. 2·00 1·25
749 200f. As 75f. 7·25 1·75

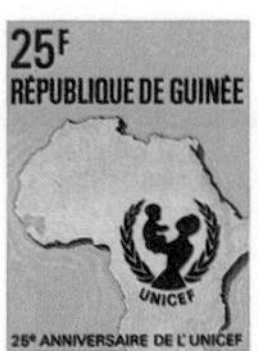

105 UNICEF Emblem on Map of Africa

1971. 25th Anniv of UNICEF.

750 **105** 25f. multicoloured 15 10
751 30f. multicoloured 20 10
752 50f. multicoloured 35 15
753 60f. multicoloured 50 20
754 100f. multicoloured 80 35

106 John and Robert Kennedy and Martin Luther King

1972. Air. Martyrs for Peace. Embossed on silver or gold foil.

755 **106** 300f. silver 3·25
756 1500f. gold, cream and green 16·00

107 Jules Verne and Moon Rocket

1972. Air. Moon Exploration. Embossed on silver or gold foil.

757 **107** 300f. silver 3·25
758 1200f. gold 13·00

108 Pres. Richard Nixon

1972. Air. Pres. Nixon's Visit to Peking. Embossed on gold or silver foil.

759 **108** 90f. silver 75
760 – 90f. silver 75
761 – 90f. silver 75
762 – 90f. silver 75
763 **108** 290f. gold 2·50
764 – 290f. gold 2·50
765 – 290f. gold 2·50
766 – 290f. gold 2·50
767 – 1200f. gold and red 13·00

DESIGNS—VERT: Nos. 760, 764, Chinese table-tennis player; 761, 765, American table-tennis player; 762, 766, Mao Tse-tung. HORIZ: (45 × 35 mm): No. 767, Pres. Nixon and Mao Tse-tung.

109 "Flying Flatfish"

1972. Imaginary Space Creatures. Mult.

768 5f. Type **109** 10 10
769 20f. "Radioactive crab" 20 10
770 30f. "Space octopus" 25 10
771 40f. "Rocket-powered serpent" 45 10
772 100f. "Winged eel" 1·10 40
773 200f. "Flying dragon" 2·00 70

110 African Child

1972. Racial Equality Year. Multicoloured.

774 15f. Type **110** (postage) 10 10
775 20f. Asiatic child 15 10
776 30f. Indian youth 20 10
777 50f. European girl 45 20
778 100f. Heads of four races 85 35

779 100f. As No. 778 (air) 90 40

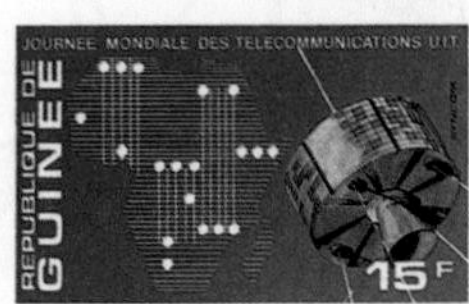

111 "Syncom" and African Map

1972. World Telecommunications Day. Mult.

780 15f. Type **111** (postage) 15 10
781 30f. "Relay" 25 10
782 75f. "Early Bird" 60 30
783 80f. "Telstar" 1·00 40

784 100f. As 30f. (air) 1·00 35
785 200f. As 75f. 1·90 65

112 APU Emblem and Dove with Letter

1972. 10th Anniv of African Postal Union.

786 **112** 15f. mult (postage) 10 10
787 30f. multicoloured 20 10
788 75f. multicoloured 50 25
789 80f. multicoloured 65 40

790 – 100f. multicoloured (air) 85 40
791 – 200f. multicoloured 1·75 75

DESIGNS: 100f. to 200f. APU emblem and airmail envelope.

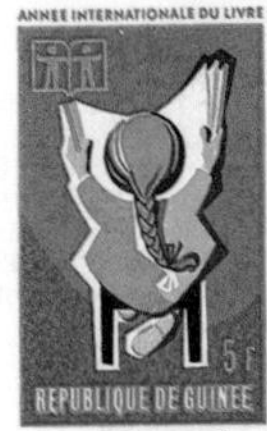

113 Child reading Book

5F RÉPUBLIQUE DE GUINÉE MUNICH 1972

114 Throwing the Javelin

1972. International Book Year. Multicoloured.

792 5f. Type **113** 10 10
793 15f. Book with sails 15 10
794 40f. Girl with book and plant 30 15
795 50f. "Key of Knowledge" and open book 50 20
796 75f. "Man" reading book and globe 75 40
797 200f. Open book and laurel sprigs 1·75 70

1972. Olympic Games, Munich. Mult.

798 5f. Type **114** (postage) 10 10
799 10f. Pole-vaulting 10 10
800 25f. Hurdling 25 10
801 30f. Throwing the hammer 35 10

802 40f. Boxing 50 15
803 50f. Gymnastics (horse) 65 25
804 75f. Running 90 35
805 100f. Gymnastics (rings) (air) 1·50 45
806 200f. Cycling 2·75 85

1972. U.N. Environmental Conservation Conf, Stockholm. Nos. 750/4 optd **UNE SEULE TERRE** and emblem.
808 **105** 25f. multicoloured 20 10
809 30f. multicoloured 20 10
810 50f. multicoloured 45 15
811 60f. multicoloured 70 25
812 100f. multicoloured 1·00 50

116 Dimitrov addressing "Reichstag Fire" Court

1972. 90th Birth Anniv of George Dimitrov (Bulgarian statesman).
813 **116** 5f. blue, gold and green 10 10
814 – 25f. blue, gold and green 15 10
815 – 40f. blue, gold and green 30 20
816 – 100f. blue, gold and green 80 35
DESIGNS: 25f. In Moabit Prison, Berlin, 1933; 40f. Writing memoirs; 100f. G. Dimitrov.

117 Emperor Haile Selassie **118** "Syntomeida epilais"

1972. Emperor Haile Selassie of Ethiopia's 80th Birthday. Multicoloured.
817 40f. Type **117** 35 20
818 200f. Emperor Haile Selassie in military uniform 1·60 80

1973. Guinean Insects. Multicoloured.
819 5f. Type **118** 10 10
820 15f. "Hippodamia californica" 25 10
821 30f. "Tettigonia viridissima" 50 15
822 40f. "Apis mellifica" 60 25
823 50f. "Photinus pyralis" 85 30
824 200f. "Ancyluris formosissima" 3·50 1·25

119 Dr. Kwame Nkrumah

1973. 10th Anniv of Organization of African Unity.
825 **119** 1s.50 black, gold & green 15 10
826 – 2s.50 black, gold & green 25 10
827 – 5s. black, gold and green 50 25
828 – 10s. violet and gold 1·00 45
DESIGNS: Nos. 826/8, different portraits of Dr. Kwame Nkrumah similar to Type **119**.

120 Institute of Applied Biology, Kindia

1973. 25th Anniv of W.H.O. Multicoloured.
829 1s. Type **120** 10 10
830 2s.50 Preparing vaccine from an egg 25 10
831 3s. Filling ampoules with vaccine 30 20
832 4s. Sterilization of vaccine 40 20
833 5s. Packing vaccines 60 25
834 10s. Preparation of vaccine base 1·25 40
835 20s. Inoculating patient 2·50 75
Nos. 833/35 are 48 × 31 mm.

121 Volcanic Landscape

1973. 500th Birth Anniv of Copernicus. Mult.
836 50c. Type **121** 10 10
837 2s. Sun over desert 20 10
838 4s. Earth and Moon 35 10
839 5s. Lunar landscape 60 15
840 10s. Jupiter 1·25 35
841 20s. Saturn 2·25 70

122 Loading Bauxite at Quayside

1974. Air. Bauxite Industry, Bok. Mult.
843 4s. Type **122** 50 15
844 6s. Bauxite train 2·50 40
845 10s. Bauxite mining 2·75 50

123 "Clappertonia ficifolia" **125** Pioneers testing Rope-bridge

124 Drummers and Pigeon

1974. Flowers of Guinea. Multicoloured.
846 50c. Type **123** (postage) 10 10
847 1s. "Rothmannia longiflora" 10 10
848 2s. "Oncoba spinosa" 20 10
849 3s. "Venidium fastuosum" 30 15
850 4s. "Bombax costatum" 50 15
851 5s. "Clerodendrum splendens" 75 20
852 7s.50 "Combretuni grandiflorum" 1·25 25
853 10s. "Mussaendra erythrophylla" 1·50 40
854 12s. "Argemone mexicana" 1·75 60
855 20s. "Thunbergia alata" (air) 2·50 80
856 25s. "Diascia barberae" 3·50 80
857 50s. "Kigelia africana" 7·00 1·90
SIZES—VERT: Nos. 847/9, As Type **123**; 850/3, 36 × 47 mm. DIAMOND: Nos. 854/7, 61 × 61 mm.
No. 855 is wrongly inscr "Thunbegia alata".

1974. Centenary of U.P.U. Multicoloured.
858 5s. Type **124** 40 20
859 6s. Runner and pigeon 55 25
860 7s.50 Monorail train, lorry and pigeon 1·40 35
861 10s. Boeing 707, "United States" (liner) and pigeon 1·50 60

1974. National Pioneers (Scouting) Movement. Multicoloured.
863 50c. Type **125** 15 10
864 2s. "On safari" 25 10
865 4s. Using field-telephone 35 15
866 5s. Cooking on camp-fire 60 15
867 7s.50 Saluting 85 35
868 10s. Playing basketball 1·75 55

127 Chimpanzee

1975. Wild Animals. Multicoloured.
871 1s. Type **127** 10 10
872 2s. Impala 20 10
873 3s. Warthog 35 10
874 4s. Waterbuck 40 20
875 5s. Leopard 60 20
876 6s. Greater kudu 60 25
877 6s.50 Common zebra 75 35
878 7s.50 African buffalo 75 35
879 8s. Hippopotamus 1·25 35
880 10s. Lion 1·50 40
881 12s. Black rhinoceros 1·90 45
882 15s. African elephant 2·75 80

128 Lion and Lioness beside Pipeline

1975. 10th Anniv of African Development Bank.
884 5s. Type **128** 70 20
885 7s. African elephants beside pipeline 1·00 30
886 10s. Lions beside pipeline (horiz) 1·25 35
887 20s. African elephant and calf beside pipeline (horiz) 2·25 80

129 Women playing Saxophones

1976. Int Women's Year (1975). Mult.
888 5s. Type **129** 40 20
889 7s. Women playing guitars 60 30
890 9s. Woman railway shunter 3·75 50
891 15s. Woman doctor 1·75 65
892 20s. Genetics emblems 2·25 90

130 Gymnastics

1976. Olympic Games, Montreal. Mult.
894 3s. Type **130** 25 10
895 4s. Long jump 35 15
896 5s. Throwing the hammer 40 20
897 6s. Throwing the discus 45 25
898 6s.50 Hurdling 50 25
899 7s. Throwing the javelin 50 30
900 8s. Running 60 30
901 8s.50 Cycling 95 35
902 10s. High-jumping 1·10 35
903 15s. Putting the shot 1·60 60
904 20s. Pole vaulting 2·25 65
905 25s. Football 2·75 90

131 Bell and Early Telephone

1976. Telephone Centenary. Multicoloured.
907 5s. Type **131** 50 20
908 7s. Bell and wall telephone 75 25
909 12s. Bell and satellite "Syncom" 1·40 50
910 15s. Bell and satellite "Telstar" 1·75 60

132 "Collybia fusipes"

1977. Mushrooms. Multicoloured.
912 5s. Type **132** (postage) 1·50 20
913 7s. "Lycoperdon perlatum" 2·25 25
914 9s. "Boletus edulis" 3·00 35
915 9s.50 "Lactarius deliciosus" 3·00 45
916 11s.50 "Agaricus campestris" 4·75 80
917 10s. "Morchella esculenta" (air) 3·50 40
918 12s. "Lepiota procera" 4·50 60
919 15s. "Cantharellus cibarius" 6·50 1·10

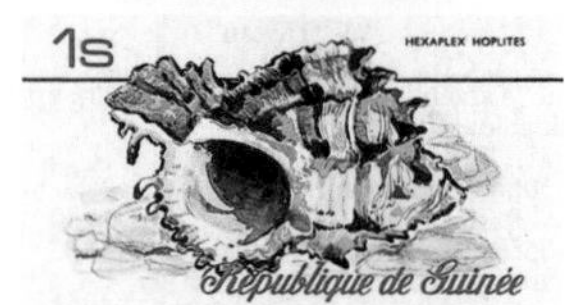

133 Duplex Murex

1977. Sea Shells. Multicoloured.
921 1s. Type **133** 10 10
922 2s. Wavy-leaved turrid 25 10
923 4s. Queen marginella 60 15
924 5s. "Tympanotonos radula" 90 20
925 7s. Striped marginella 1·00 25
926 8s. Doris harp 1·40 30
927 10s. Obtuse demoulia 1·75 45
928 20s. Pitted frog shell 3·25 80
929 25s. Adanson's marginella 4·00 1·00
Nos. 927/9 are 50 × 34 mm.

134 President Sekou Toure

1977. 30th Anniv of Guinean Democratic Party (PDG). Multicoloured.
930 5s. Type **134** 35 25
931 10s. Labourers and oxen 95 45
932 20s. Soldier driving tractor 2·10 95
933 25s. Pres. Toure addressing U.N. General Assembly 2·50 1·25
934 30s. Pres. Toure (vert) 3·00 1·50
935 40s. As 30s. 3·75 1·60

135 "Varanus niloticus"

1977. Reptiles. Multicoloured.
937 3s. Type **135** (postage) 35 10
938 4s. "Hyperolius quinquevittatus" 40 15
939 5s. "Uromastix" 50 15
940 6s. "Scincus scincus" 75 15
941 6s.50 "Agama agama" 95 20
942 7s. "Naja melanoleuca" 1·10 20
943 8s.50 "Python regius" 1·40 25
944 20s. "Bufo mauritanicus" 3·00 60
945 10s. "Chamaeleo diepis" (air) 2·00 30
946 15s. "Crocodylus niloticus" 2·75 50
947 25s. "Testudo elegans" 4·25 75

136 Eland (male)

1977. Endangered Animals. Multicoloured.
948 1s. Type **136** (postage) 15 10
949 1s. Eland (female) 15 10
950 1s. Eland (young) 15 10
951 2s. Chimpanzee (young) 20 10
952 2s. Chimpanzee 20 10
953 2s. Chimpanzee sitting 20 10
954 2s.50 African elephant 30 10

955 2s.50 African elephant . . . 30 10
956 2s.50 African elephant . . . 30 10
957 3s. Lion 50 10
958 3s. Lioness 50 10
959 3s. Lion Cub 50 10
960 4s. Indian palm squirrel . . . 60 15
961 4s. Indian palm squirrel . . . 60 15
962 4s. Indian palm squirrel . . . 60 15
963 5s. Hippopotamus 80 20
964 5s. Hippopotamus 80 20
965 5s. Hippopotamus 80 20

966 5s. Type **136** (air) 60 20
967 5s. As No. 949 . . . . 60 20
968 5s. As No. 950 . . . . 60 20
969 8s. As No. 954 . . . . 1·50 25
970 8s. As No. 955 . . . . 1·50 25
971 8s. As No. 956 . . . . 1·50 25
972 9s. As No. 963 . . . . 1·50 25
973 9s. As No. 964 . . . . 1·50 25
974 9s. As No. 965 . . . . 1·50 25
975 10s. As No. 951 . . . . . . 1·75 30
976 10s. As No. 952 . . . . . . 1·75 30
977 10s. As No. 953 . . . . . . 1·75 30
978 12s. As No. 960 . . . . . . 1·75 40
979 12s. As No. 961 . . . . . . 1·75 40
980 12s. As No. 962 . . . . . . 1·75 40
981 13s. As No. 957 . . . . . . 2·00 50
982 13s. As No. 958 . . . . . . 2·00 50
983 13s. As No. 959 . . . . . . 2·00 50

Issued se-tenant in strips of three within the sheet, each strip showing different views of the same animal.

137 Lenin taking Parade in Red Square, Moscow

1976. 60th Anniv of Russian Revolution. Multicoloured.
984 2s.50 Lenin's first speech in Moscow (postage) 25 10
985 5s. Lenin addressing revolutionary crowd . . . 45 15
986 7s.50 Lenin with militiamen 85 20
987 8s. Type **137** . . . . 1·10 20
988 10s. Russian ballet (air) . . . 2·00 30
989 30s. Pushkin Monument . . 3·75 75

138 Pres. Giscard d'Estaing at Microphones

1979. Visit of President Giscard d'Estaing of France.
990 **138** 3s. brown and light brown (postage) 30 10
991 – 5s. brown, green and deep green 55 15
992 – 6s.50 brown, mauve and deep mauve 80 20
993 – 7s. brown, light blue and blue 85 20
994 – 8s.50 brown, rose & red 1·25 30
995 – 10s. brown, light violet and violet . . . . . . 1·60 40
996 – 20s. brown, green and deep green . . . . . . 3·50 65
997 – 25s. multicoloured (air) 4·00 1·25

DESIGNS—HORIZ: 5s. President Giscard d'Estaing and Sekou Toure in conference; 6s.50, Presidents signing agreement; 7s. Presidents at official meeting; 8s.50, Presidents with their wives; 10s. Presidents in conference; 20s. Toasting the agreement. VERT: 25s. President Giscard d'Estaing.

139 "20,000 Leagues Under the Sea"

1979. 150th Birth Anniv (1978) of Jules Verne. Multicoloured.
998 1s. Type **139** (postage) . . . 10 10
999 3s. "The Children of Captain Grant" 30 10
1000 5s. "The Mysterious Island" 60 15
1001 7s. "A Captain of Fifteen Years" . . . . 1·25 35
1002 10s. "The Amazing Adventure of Barsac" . . 1·75 50
1003 20s. "Five Weeks in a Balloon" (air) . . . . . 2·25 40
1004 25s. "Robur the Conqueror" 3·00 60

140 William Henson's "Aerial Steam Carriage", 1842

1979. Aviation History. Multicoloured.
1005 3s. Type **140** 30 10
1006 5s. Wright Type A (inscr "Flyer I"), 1903 . . . . . 55 15
1007 6s.50 Caudron C-46O, 1934 75 20
1008 7s. Charles Lindbergh's "Spirit of St. Louis", 1927 95 20
1009 8s.50 Bristol Beaufighter, 1940 . . . . 1·25 20
1010 10s. Bleriot XI, 1909 . . . . 1·50 25
1011 20s. Boeing 727-100, 1963 2·75 55
1012 20s. Concorde . . . . . . 3·50 70

141 Hafla Football Team

1979. Hafla Football Club's Victories. Mult.
1013 1s. Type **141** 10 10
1014 2s. Team members with cup (vert) 20 20
1015 5s. President Toure presenting medals 60 15
1016 7s. President Toure presenting cup (vert) . . . 85 20
1017 8s. Ahmed Sekou Toure Cup (vert) 95 25
1018 10s. Team captains shaking hands (vert) . . . . . . 1·25 30
1019 20s. The winning goal . . . 2·40 75

142 Children dancing round Tree

1980. International Year of the Child. Mult.
1020 2s. Type **142** 15 10
1021 4s. "Heureuse Enfance" . . 40 15
1022 5s. Steam train (horiz) . . . 1·60 15
1023 7s. Village (horiz) 85 20
1024 10s. Boy climbing tree (horiz) . . . . 1·25 25
1025 25s. Children of different races (horiz) . . . . . . 3·00 70

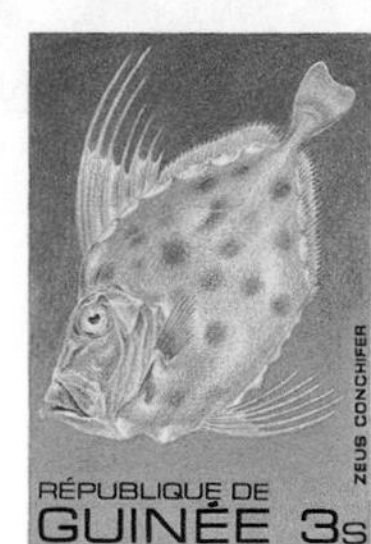

143 Buckler Dory

1980. Fishes, Multicoloured.
1026 1s. Robust butterflyfish (horiz) 10 10
1027 2s. Blue-pointed porgy (horiz) 20 15
1028 3s. Type **143** 35 15
1029 4s. African hind (horiz) . . 45 25
1030 5s. Spotted seahorse 55 25
1031 6s. Marine hatchetfish (horiz) 90 30
1032 7s. Half-banded snake-eel (horiz) . . . . 1·40 30
1033 8s. Flying gurnard . . . . 1·60 40
1034 9s. West African squirrel-fish (horiz) . . . . . 1·75 40
1035 10s. Guinean fingerfish . . . 1·90 40
1036 12s. African sergeant major (horiz) . . . . 2·25 75
1037 15s. West African trigger-fish (horiz) . . . . . . 3·00 1·00

144 Rocket on Launch Pad

1980. 10th Anniv of 1st Moon Landing. Mult.
1038 1s. Type **144** 10 10
1039 2s. Earth from the Moon . . 20 10
1040 4s. Armstrong descending from lunar module . . . 35 15
1041 5s. Armstrong on the Moon 50 15
1042 7s. Astronaut collecting samples 75 20
1043 8s. Parachute descent . . . 95 25
1044 12s. Winching capsule aboard recovery vessel . . 1·60 35
1045 20s. Astronauts . . . . . . 3·00 70

145 Dome of the Rock

1981. Palestinian Solidarity.
1046 **145** 8s. multicoloured . . . . 1·40 55
1047 11s. multicoloured . . . 1·90 70

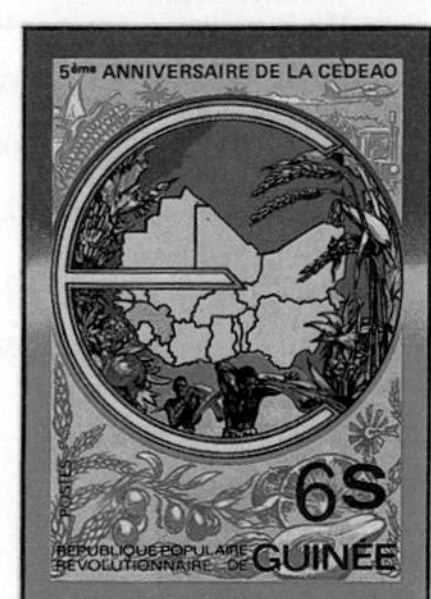

146 Map of Member States and Agricultural Produce

1982. 5th Anniv of Economic Community of West African States. Multicoloured.
1048 6s. Type **146** 85 30
1049 7s. Transport . . . . 4·50 75
1050 9s. Heavy industry . . . . 1·40 45

147 Ataturk as Soldier

1982. Birth Centenary of Kemal Ataturk (Turkish statesman). Multicoloured.
1051 7s. Type **147** (postage) . . . 95 40
1052 10s. Ataturk as statesman 1·25 50
1053 25s. Equestrian statue (horiz) . . . . 3·50 85
1054 25s. As No. 1053 (air) . . . 4·00 85

148 Football

1982. Olympic Games, Moscow. Multicoloured.
1055 1s. Type **148** (postage) . . . 10 10
1056 2s. Basketball 20 15
1057 3s. Diving 25 15
1058 4s. Gymnastics 30 15
1059 5s. Boxing 55 20
1060 6s. High jumping 75 25
1061 7s. Running 95 35

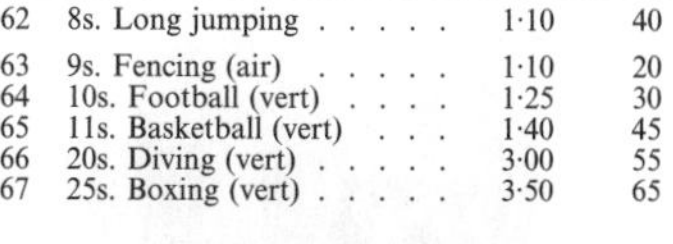

1062 8s. Long jumping . . . . . 1·10 40
1063 9s. Fencing (air) . . . . . 1·10 20
1064 10s. Football (vert) . . . . 1·25 30
1065 11s. Basketball (vert) . . . 1·40 45
1066 20s. Diving (vert) . . . . . 3·00 55
1067 25s. Boxing (vert) . . . . . 3·50 65

149 Balaidos Stadium, Vigo

1982. World Cup Football Championship, Spain. Football Stadia. Mult.
1068 6s. Type **149** (postage) . . . 90 15
1069 8s. El Molinon, Gijon . . . 1·10 25
1070 9s. San Mames, Bilbao . . . 1·60 30
1071 10s. Sanchez Pizjuan, Seville 1·75 35
1072 10s. Luis Casanova, Valencia (air) . . . . . . 1·75 35
1073 20s. Nou Camp, Barcelona 3·50 45
1074 25s. Santiago Bernabeu, Madrid . . . . 4·50 65

150 Wrestling

151 Marquis d'Arlandes, Pilatre de Rozier and Montgolfier Balloon, 1783

1983. Olympic Games, Los Angeles (1st issue). Multicoloured.
1075 5s. Type **150** (postage) . . . 40 15
1076 7s. Weightlifting 50 25
1077 10s. Gymnastics 95 35
1078 15s. Discus . . . . 1·60 60
1079 20s. Kayak (air) . . . . . 1·60 50
1080 25s. Equestrian . . . . . . 2·25 80

See also Nos. 843/9.

1983. Bicentenary of Manned Flight. Mult.
1082 5s. Type **151** (postage) . . . 55 15
1083 7s. Jean-Francois Pilatre de Rozier and Montgolfier balloon "Marie Antoinette", 1784 . . . . 65 25
1084 10s. Henri Dupuy de Lome and airship, 1872 (horiz) 95 35
1085 15s. Major A. Parseval and "Airship No. 1", 1906 (horiz) . . . . 1·60 60
1086 20s. Count Zeppelin and airship "Bodensee", 1919 (horiz) (air) . . . . . . 1·60 50
1087 25s. Balloon "Double Eagle II" and crew, 1978 . . . 2·25 80

152 Lungs and Monkey

1983. Centenary of Discovery of Tubercle Bacillus. Multicoloured.
1089 6s. Type **152** 75 20
1090 10s. Cow . . . . 1·25 30
1091 11s. Robert Koch and microscope . . . . 1·50 35
1092 12s. Koch using microscope 1·75 50
1093 15s. Laboratory . . . . . . 2·25 55
1094 20s. Scientist with test tube and monkey . . . . . . 3·00 70
1095 25s. Doctor examining young boy . . . . 3·50 95

153 Disabled and Emblem

1983. International Year of Disabled Persons.
1096 **153** 10s. multicoloured . . . 1·25 55
1097 20s. multicoloured . . . 2·50 1·00

154 Mosque, Conakry

1983. 25th Anniv of Independence.
1098 **154** 1s. multicoloured 10 10
1099 2s. multicoloured 20 10
1100 5s. multicoloured 40 15
1101 10s. multicoloured . . . 90 40

155 Citizens with Scrolls

1983. 10th Anniv of Mano River Union. Multicoloured.
1103 2s. Type **155** 20 10
1104 7s. Union emblem 50 25
1105 8s. Map and presidents of Guinea, Sierra Leone and Liberia 60 25
1106 10s. Signing the Declaration of Union 85 35

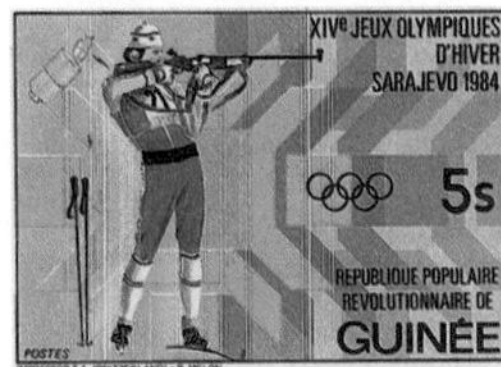

156 Biathlon

1983. Winter Olympic Games, Sarajevo. Multicoloured.
1108 5s. Type **156** (postage) . . . 50 15
1109 7s. Luge 60 25
1110 10s. Slalom . . . . 1·25 40
1111 15s. Speed skating . . . . . 1·60 60
1112 20s. Ski jump (air) . . . . 1·90 55
1113 25s. Ice dancing . . . . . . 2·50 80

157 Raphael and "Virgin with the Blue Diadem"

1984. Anniversaries (1983). Multicoloured.
1115 5s. Type **157** 40 20
1116 7s. Rubens and "Holy Family" 60 25
1117 10s. Rembrandt and "Portrait of Saskia" . . . 95 40
1118 15s. Goethe and scene from "The Young Werther" . . 1·40 60
1119 20s. Lord Baden-Powell and scout camp . . . . 1·75 55
1120 25s. P. P. Harris and speaker at Rotary meeting 2·50 80

158 Abraham Lincoln

1984. Personalities. Multicoloured.
1122 5s. Type **158** (postage) . . . 40 20
1123 7s. Jean-Henri Dunant (founder of Red Cross) 65 25
1124 10s. Gottlieb Daimler (automobile designer) . . 1·25 40
1125 15s. Louis Bleriot (pilot) . . 1·75 55
1126 20s. Paul P. Harris (founder of Rotary Club) (air) . . 1·75 65
1127 25s. Auguste Piccard (ocean explorer) . . . . 2·50 85

159 "The Mystic Marriage of Sts. Catherine and Sebastian" (detail, Correggio)

1984. Paintings. Multicoloured.
1129 5s. Type **159** (postage) . . . 40 20
1130 7s. "The Holy Family" (A. Durer) 60 25
1131 10s. "The Veiled Lady" (Raphael) . . . . 1·00 40
1132 15s. "Portrait of a Young Man" (A. Durer) . . . . 1·25 55
1133 20s. "Portrait of Soutine" (A. Modigliani) (air) . . . 1·75 65
1134 25s. "The Esterhazy Madonna" (Raphael) . . 2·50 85

160 Congo River Steamer and Canoe

1984. Transport. Multicoloured.
1136 5s. Type **160** (postage) . . . 60 20
1137 7s. Airship "Graf Zeppelin" 70 25
1138 10s. Daimler car, 1886 . . . 1·50 40
1139 15s. Beyer-Garratt steam locomotive . . . . 2·40 1·25
1140 20s. Latecoere seaplane "Comte de la Vaulx" (air) 1·75 55
1141 25s. Savoia Marchetti S-73 airplane . . . . 2·50 80

161 W. Hoppe and D. Schauerhammer (bobsleigh)

1984. Winter Olympic Gold Medal Winners. Multicoloured.
1143 5s. Type **161** (postage) . . . 40 20
1144 7s. T. L. Wassberg (cross-country skiing) 60 25
1145 10s. G. Boucher (speed skating) . . . . 1·00 40
1146 15s. K. Witt (ladies figure skating) . . . . 1·50 65
1147 20s. W. D. Johnson (downhill skiing) (air) . . 2·00 85
1148 25s. U.S.S.R. (ice hockey) 2·75 90

162 T. Ruiz and C. Costie (Synchronized Swimming Duet)

1985. Olympic Games Gold Medal Winners. Multicoloured.
1150 5s. Type **162** (postage) . . . 40 20
1151 7s. R. Klimke, H. Krug and U. Sauer, West Germany (team dressage) 85 25
1152 10s. McKee and Buchan, U.S.A. (sailing, "Flying Dutchman" class) 95 40
1153 15s. Mark Todd (equestrian three-day event) . . . . . 1·25 65
1154 20s. Daley Thompson (decathlon) (air) . . . . . 2·00 75
1155 25s. M. Smith, C. Homfeld, L. Burr and J. Fargis, U.S.A. (equestrian team jumping) . . . . 2·25 85

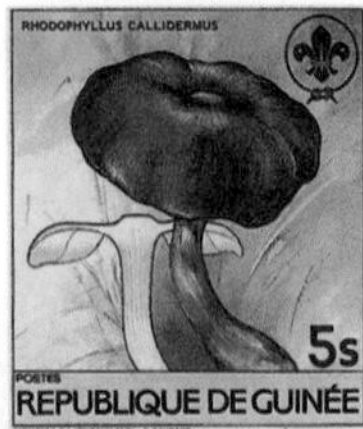

163 "Rhodophyllus callidermus"

1985. Fungi. Multicoloured.
1157 5s. Type **163** (postage) . . . 80 35
1158 7s. "Agaricus niger" . . . . 1·00 45
1159 10s. "Thermitomyces globulus" . . . . 1·90 70
1160 15s. "Amanita robusta" . . 2·50 1·10
1161 20s. "Lepiota subradicans" (air) . . . . 3·50 1·00
1162 25s. "Cantharellus rhodophylus" . . . . . . 3·75 1·10

164 Hermann Oberth and 2-Stage Conical Motor Rocket

1985. Space Achievements. Multicoloured.
1164 7s. Type **164** (postage) . . . 50 25
1165 10s. "Lunik 1" 95 40
1166 15s. "Lunik 2" on Moon, 1959 . . . . 1·25 55
1167 20s. "Lunik 3" photographing hidden face of Moon . . . . . . 1·90 75
1168 30s. Armstrong, Aldrin and Collins (first manned landing on Moon) (air) 2·50 75
1169 35s. Sally Ride (first American woman in space) . . . . 3·25 80

165 Maimonides in Jewish Quarter (850th birth anniv)

1985. Anniversaries and Events. Multicoloured.
1171 7s. Type **165** (postage) . . . 80 35
1172 10s. Christopher Columbus departing from Palos, 1492 . . . . 1·75 50
1173 15s. Frederic Bartholdi and Statue of Liberty (centenary) . . . . 1·50 55
1174 20s. Queen Mother with Duke of York and Princess Elizabeth (85th birthday) . . . . 1·75 75
1175 30s. Ulf Merbold and space shuttle "Columbia" (air) 2·50 75
1176 35s. Prince Charles and Lady Diana Spencer (Royal Wedding) . . . . 3·00 85

166 Black-billed Cuckoo

1995. Birth Bicentenary of John J. Audubon (ornithologist). Multicoloured.
1178 7s. Type **166** (postage) . . . 65 25
1179 10s. Carolina parakeet . . . 1·00 50
1180 15s. American darter (vert) 1·50 85
1181 20s. Red-shouldered hawk 3·25 1·10
1182 30s. Eastern screech owl (air) . . . . 4·00 1·25
1183 35s. Brown thrasher (vert) 5·00 1·75

167 Blue-point Siamese

1985. Cats and Dogs. Multicoloured.
1185 7s. Type **167** (postage) . . . 60 25
1186 10s. Cocker spaniel . . . . 1·25 40
1187 15s. Poodles . . . . 1·50 55
1188 20s. Persian blue cat . . . . 2·00 70
1189 25s. European tortoiseshell cat . . . . 2·40 85
1190 30s. German shepherd dog (air) . . . . 2·75 85
1191 35s. Abyssinian cats . . . . 3·25 95
1192 40s. Boxer dog . . . . . . 3·75 1·25

168 Bebeto and Footballers

1985. World Cup Football Championship, Mexico (1986) (1st issue). Multicoloured.
1194 7s. Type **168** (postage) . . . 60 25
1195 10s. Rinat Dassaev . . . . 1·25 40
1196 15s. Phil Neal . . . . . . 1·50 55
1197 20s. Jean Tigana . . . . . 2·40 70
1198 30s. Fernando Chalana (air) 3·00 75
1199 35s. Michel Platini . . . . 3·50 85
See also Nos. 1268/71.

1985. Air. Nos. 1126 and 1119/20 optd.
1201 20s. **80e ANNIVERSAIRE 1905 1985** (1126) . . . . 1·60 90
1202 20s. **Rassemblement Jambville-1985** (1119) . . 1·60 90
1203 25s. **80e ANNIVERSAIRE 1905 1985** (1120) . . . . 2·25 1·25

1985. Nos. 1157/62 surch.
1205 1s. on 5s. Type **163** (postage) 20 10
1206 2s. on 7s. "Agaricus niger" 50 10
1207 8s. on 10s. "Thermitomyces globulus" . . . . 1·50 40
1208 30s. on 15s. "Amanita robusta" . . . . 4·50 1·25
1209 35s. on 20s. "Lepiota subradicans" (air) . . . . 4·75 1·40
1210 40s. on 25s. "Cantharellus rhodophyllus" . . . . . 5·25 1·90

171 Class 8 F Locomotive

1985. Trains (1st series). Multicoloured.
1212 7s. Type **171** (postage) . . . 1·10 40
1213 15s. Class III electric locomotive, Germany . . 3·00 1·00
1214 25s. Pacific steam locomotive No. 270 . . . 5·00 1·50
1215 35s. German electric commuter train Series 420 (air) . . . . 6·50 2·40
Nos. 1213 and 1215 commemorate 150th anniv of German railways.
See also Nos. 1252/5.

172 Columbus and "Pinta"

1985. 480th Death Anniv of Christopher Columbus (explorer) (1st issue). Multicoloured.
1217 10s. Type **172** (postage) . . 1·75 70
1218 20s. "Santa Maria" . . . . 3·00 1·10

1219 30s. "Nina" (air) 3·50 1·25
1220 40s. "Santa Maria" and crow's nest 4·50 1·75
See also Nos. 1257/60.

173 Chopin, aged Eight, playing Piano

1986. International Youth Year. Multicoloured.
1222 10s. Type **173** (postage) 1·10 45
1223 20s. Sandro Botticelli and "Birth of Venus" 1·75 65
1224 35s. Gioachino Antonio Rossini, aged 15, conducting orchestra 3·50 90
1225 25s. Pablo Picasso and "Paul as Harlequin" (air) 2·25 85

174 Bayeux Tapestry

1986. Appearance of Halley's Comet. Multicoloured.
1227 5f. Type **174** (postage) 10 10
1228 30f. Comet as seen by the Arabs 20 10
1229 40f. Comet as seen by Montezuma II 30 15
1230 50f. Edmond Halley and trajectory diagram 40 15
1231 300f. Halley and Sir Isaac Newton (air) 2·25 55
1232 500f. Comet, Earth, sun, "Giotto", Soviet and N.A.S.A. space probes 4·00 1·10

175 "Challenger" Space Shuttle Memorial Roll

1986. Air. "Challenger" Astronauts Commem. Multicoloured.
1234 100f. Type **175** 70 30
1235 170f. Shuttle diagram and Christa McAuliffe holding model 1·25 55

1986. Various stamps surch. (a) Nos. 1212/15 (Trains).
1237 2f. on 7s. multicoloured 50 10
1238 25f. on 15s. multicoloured 70 15
1239 50f. on 25s. multicoloured 1·25 25
1240 90f. on 35s. multicoloured 2·60 50

(b) Nos. 1217/20 (Columbus).
1242 5f. on 10s. multicoloured 30 15
1243 35f. on 20s. multicoloured 45 15
1244 70f. on 30s. multicoloured 75 30
1245 200f. on 40s. multicoloured 1·75 80

(c) Nos. 1222/5 (International Youth Year).
1247 5f. on 10s. mult (postage) 15 10
1248 35f. on 20s. multicoloured 25 15
1249 90f. on 35s. multicoloured 60 25
1250 50f. on 25s. mult (air) 30 15

177 Dietrich Autorail Diesel Railcar

1986. Trains (2nd series). Multicoloured.
1252 20f. Type **177** (postage) 25 10
1253 100f. Class T.13 steam locomotive No. 7906, Prussia 1·25 25
1254 300f. German steam locomotive No. 01220 3·50 80
1255 400f. Autorail ABH-3 type 5020 diesel train (air) 4·75 95
Nos. 1253/4 commemorate 150th anniv of German Railways.

178 Building Fort Navidad and Map of First Voyage, 1492–93

1986. 480th Death Anniv of Christopher Columbus (explorer) (2nd issue). Multicoloured.
1257 40f. Type **178** (postage) 30 15
1258 70f. Disembarking at Hispaniola and map of second voyage, 1493–96 55 20
1259 200f. Columbus on deck with natives and map of third voyage, 1498–1500 1·50 50
1260 500f. Columbus and crew with natives and map of fourth voyage, 1502–04 (air) 3·50 1·40

179 Prince and Princess of Wales and Prince William

1986. Celebrities. Multicoloured.
1262 30f. Type **179** (postage) 20 10
1263 40f. Alain Prost (1985 Formula I world champion) 25 10
1264 100f. Duke and Duchess of York 60 20
1265 300f. Elvis Presley (entertainer) 2·75 75
1266 500f. Michael Jackson (entertainer) (air) 3·50 1·00

180 Pfaff, Trophy and Satellite

1986. World Cup Football Championship, Mexico (2nd issue). Multicoloured.
1268 100f. Type **180** (postage) 75 20
1269 300f. Michel Platini 2·25 60
1270 400f. Matthaus 3·00 80
1271 500f. Diego Maradona (air) 3·75 1·00

181 Judo

1987. Olympic Games, Seoul (1988). Mult.
1273 20f. Type **181** (postage) 15 10
1274 30f. High jumping 20 10
1275 40f. Handball 25 10
1276 100f. Gymnastics 60 20
1277 300f. Javelin throwing (air) 1·75 55
1278 500f. Showjumping 3·00 80

182 Rifle shooting

1987. Winter Olympic Games, Calgary (1988) (1st issue). Multicoloured.
1280 50f. on 40f. Type **182** (postage) 30 10
1281 100f. Cross-country skiing 65 20
1282 400f. Ski jumping (air) 2·75 75
1283 500f. Two-man bobsleigh 3·25 85

183 Skiing

1987. Winter Olympic Games, Calgary (1988) (2nd issue). Multicoloured.
1285 25f. Type **183** (postage) 20 10
1286 50f. Ice hockey 40 15
1287 100f. Men's figure skating 70 20
1288 150f. Slalom 1·25 35
1289 300f. Speed skating (air) 2·00 70
1290 500f. Four-man bobsleigh 3·25 1·10

184 S. K. Doe, Gen. Lansana Conte, Gen. J. Momoh and National Flags

1987. 10th Anniv of River Mano Reconciliation.
1292 **184** 40f. multicoloured 25 15
1293 50f. multicoloured 30 15
1294 75f. multicoloured 50 25
1295 100f. multicoloured 70 35
1296 150f. multicoloured 90 45

185 Dimetrodon

1987. Prehistoric Animals. Multicoloured.
1297 50f. Type **185** (postage) 45 15
1298 100f. Iguanodon 80 25
1299 200f. Tylosaurus 1·50 55
1300 300f. Cave bear 2·50 75
1301 400f. Sabre-tooth tiger (air) 3·25 85
1302 500f. Stegosaurus 4·25 1·10

186 Statue and Portrait of Marquis de Lafayette (revolutionary)

1987. Celebrities. Multicoloured.
1304 50f. Type **186** (230th birth anniv) (postage) 35 15
1305 100f. Ettore Bugatti (motor manufacturer) (40th death anniv) and "White Elephant" 70 25
1306 200f. Gary Kasparov (world chess champion) and game diagram of Kasparov v. Karpov, 1986 2·00 65
1307 300f. Flag and George Washington (first U.S. President) (bicentenary of American constitution) 2·00 75
1308 400f. Boris Becker (tennis player) (air) 3·50 85
1309 500f. Winston Churchill (statesman) 4·00 1·10

188 Tennis Player and Emblem

1987. Olympic Games, Seoul (1988). Tennis.
1311 **188** 50f. mult (postage) 40 10
1312 – 100f. multicoloured 70 25
1313 – 150f. multicoloured 1·10 35
1314 – 200f. multicoloured 1·50 55
1315 – 300f. multicoloured (air) 2·00 75
1316 – 500f. multicoloured 3·50 1·10
DESIGNS: 100f. to 500f. Various tennis players.

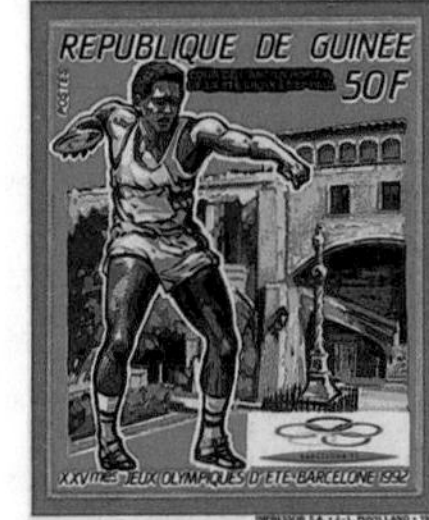

189 Discus thrower and Courtyard of Hospital of the Holy Cross and St. Paul

1987. Olympic Games, Barcelona (1992). Multicoloured.
1318 50f. Type **189** (postage) 30 10
1319 100f. Statue of Pablo Casals (cellist) and pole vaulter 60 25
1320 150f. Long jumper and Labyrinth of Horta 90 35
1321 170f. Lizard in Guell Park and javelin thrower 1·00 40
1322 400f. Gymnast and Church of Mercy (air) 2·50 75
1323 500f. Tennis player and Picasso Museum 3·00 95

190 African Wild Dogs

1987. Endangered Wildlife. Multicoloured.
1325 50f. Type **190** (postage) 35 10
1326 70f. African wild dog 55 20
1327 100f. African wild dogs stalking prey 75 25
1328 170f. African wild dog chasing prey 1·25 40
1329 400f. South African crowned cranes (air) 4·00 1·00
1330 500f. Giant eland 3·50 1·40

191 "Galaxy"–"Grasp"

1988. Space Exploration. Multicoloured.
1332 50f. Type **191** (postage) 30 10
1333 150f. "Energia"–"Mir" link-up 1·00 25
1334 200f. NASA space station 1·40 40
1335 300f. "Ariane-5" rocket depositing satellite payload 2·00 70
1336 400f. Mars "Rover" space vehicle (air) 2·75 85
1337 450f. Venus "Vega" space probe 3·00 95

192 Red-headed Bluebill **193** Queen Elizabeth II and Prince Philip

1988. Scouts, Birds and Butterflies. Designs showing scouts studying featured animals. Multicoloured.

1339	50f. Type **192** (postage)	50	10
1340	100f. "Medon nymphalidae" (butterfly)	65	25
1341	150f. Red bishop	1·25	40
1342	300f. Beautiful sunbird	2·40	70
1343	400f. "Sophia nymphalidae" (butterfly) (air)	3·00	1·00
1344	450f. "Rumia nymphalidae" (butterfly)	3·00	1·10

1988. Celebrities. Multicoloured.

1346	200f. Type **193** (40th wedding anniv (1987)) (postage)	1·25	40
1347	250f. Fritz von Opel (car designer) and "Rak 2 Opel", 1928	1·75	55
1348	300f. Wolfgang Amadeus Mozart (composer)	2·25	55
1349	400f. Steffi Graf (tennis player)	3·00	70
1350	450f. Edwin "Buzz" Aldrin (astronaut) (air)	3·25	80
1351	500f. Paul Harris (founder of Rotary International)	3·50	95

194 Vreni Schneider (Women's Slalom and Giant Slalom) **195** Scientist using Microscope

1988. Calgary Winter Olympic Games Gold Medal Winners. Multicoloured.

1353	50f. Type **194** (postage)	30	10
1354	150f. Matti Nykaenen (Ski jumping)	1·10	25
1355	250f. Marina Kiehl (Women's downhill)	1·75	40
1356	400f. Frank Piccard (Men's super giant slalom)	2·50	75
1357	100f. Frank-Peter Roetsch (Biathlon) (air)	70	25
1358	450f. Katarina Witt (Women's figure skating)	2·75	95

1988. World Health Day. Multicoloured.

1360	50f. Type **195**	20	10
1361	150f. Nurse vaccinating boy	55	15
1362	500f. Dental check	1·90	50

196 Baron Pierre de Coubertin (founder of modern Olympics)

1988. International Olympic Committee.

1363 **196**	50f. multicoloured	20	10
1364	100f. multicoloured	40	10
1365	150f. multicoloured	55	15
1366	500f. multicoloured	1·90	50

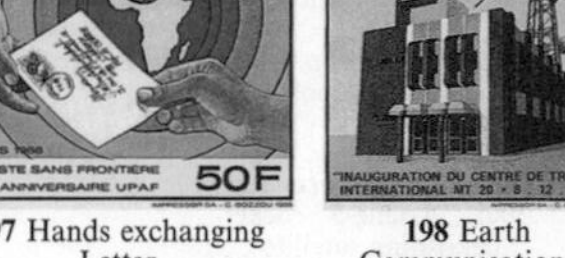

197 Hands exchanging Letter **198** Earth Communications Station

1988. 25th Anniv of Pan-African Postal Union.

1367 **197**	50f. multicoloured	20	10
1368	75f. multicoloured	30	10
1369	100f. multicoloured	40	10
1370	150f. multicoloured	55	15

1988. Inauguration of MT 20 International Transmission Centre.

1371 **198**	50f. multicoloured	20	10
1372	100f. multicoloured	40	10
1373	150f. multicoloured	55	15

199 "Helix Nebular"

1989. Appearance of Halley's Comet. Nebulae. Multicoloured.

1374	100f.+25f. Type **199** (postage)	50	15
1375	150f.+25f. Orion	70	20
1376	200f.+25f. "The Eagle"	90	25
1377	250f.+25f. "Triffid"	1·10	30
1378	300f.+25f. Eta-Carinae (air)	1·25	30
1379	500f.+25f. NGC 2264	2·00	50

200 Diving

1989. Olympic Games, Barcelona (1992) (1st issue). Multicoloured.

1381	50f. Type **200** (postage)	20	10
1382	100f. Running (vert)	40	10
1383	150f. Shooting	60	15
1384	250f. Tennis (vert)	1·00	25
1385	400f. Football (air)	1·60	40
1386	500f. Equestrian (dressage) (vert)	2·00	50

201 Oath of the Tennis Court and Jean Sylvain Bailly (President of National Assembly)

1989. "Philexfrance 89" Stamp Exhibition and Bicentenary of French Revolution. Mult.

1388	250f. Type **201** (postage)	1·00	25
1389	300f. King addressing the Three Estates and Comte de Mirabeau	1·25	30
1390	400f. 18th July 1790 celebrations and Marquis de La Fayette	1·60	40
1391	450f. The King's arrest at Varennes and Jerome Petion (first President of the Convention) (air)	1·75	45

202 Girl carrying Plants

1989. 10th Anniv (1987) of International Fund for Agricultural Development. Campaign for Self-sufficiency. Multicoloured.

1393	25f. Type **202**	10	10
1394	50f. Men irrigating crops	20	10
1395	75f. Family with cattle	30	10
1396	100f. Fishermen	70	20
1397	150f. Harvesting crops	60	15
1398	300f. Pumping water	1·25	30

203 Buildings, Vehicles and Envelopes on Map

1989. 15th Anniv of Mano River Union. Mult.

1399	150f. Type **203**	60	15
1400	300f. Map and Presidents of member countries	1·25	30

204 Emblem, Banknotes and Produce

1989. 25th Anniv of African Development Bank.

1401 **204**	300f. multicoloured	1·25	30

205 Skiing and Super-Tignes

1990. Winter Olympic Games, Albertville (1992). Multicoloured.

1402	150f. Type **205** (postage)	55	15
1403	250f. Cross-country skiing and Le Lavachet	90	25
1404	400f. Bobsleighing and Val-Claret	1·40	35
1405	500f. Speed skating and Meribel (air)	1·75	45

206 Presidents Bush and Gorbachev (1989 Summit, Malta)

1990. Multicoloured.

1407	200f. Type **206** (postage)	70	20
1408	250f. De Gaulle's appeal to resist, June 1940	90	25
1409	300f. Pope Jean-Paul II, President Gorbachev and dove (1989 meeting)	1·10	30
1410	400f. Concorde and TGV Atlantique express train, France	3·25	1·00
1411	450f. Robin Yount (cent of Baseball) (air)	1·60	40
1412	500f. "Galileo" space probe	1·75	45

207 St. Dominic's, Naples **208** View of Exhibition

1990. World Cup Football Championship, Italy. Multicoloured.

1414	200f. Type **207** (postage)	70	20
1415	250f. Piazza San Carlo, Turin	90	25
1416	300f. San Cataldo church	1·10	30
1417	450f. St. Francis's Church, Udine (air)	1·60	40

1991. "Telecom 91" International Telecommunications Exhibition. Multicoloured.

1419	150f. Type **208**	55	10
1420	300f. Emblem (horiz)	1·10	30

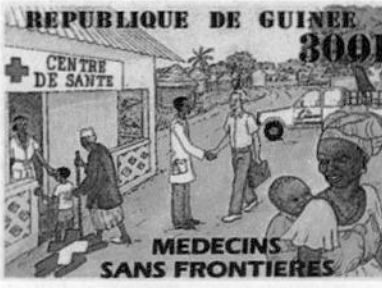

209 Health Centre

1991. Medecins sans Frontieres.

1421 **209**	300f. multicoloured	1·10	30

210 "Madonna della Tenda"

1991. Christmas (1990). Paintings by Raphael. Multicoloured.

1422	50f. Type **210** (postage)	20	10
1423	100f. Small Cowper Madonna	40	10
1424	150f. Tempi Madonna	55	15
1425	250f. Niccolini Madonna	95	25
1426	300f. Orleans Madonna (air)	1·10	30
1427	500f. Solly Madonna	1·90	50

211 Rudi Voller

1991. West Germany, 1990 World Cup Football Champion. West German Players and Goals Scored. Multicoloured.

1429	200f. Type **211** (postage)	75	20
1430	250f. Uwe Bein	95	25
1431	300f. Pierre Littbarski	1·10	30
1432	400f. Jurgen Klinsmann	1·50	35
1433	450f. Lothar Matthaus (air)	1·75	45
1434	500f. Andreas Brehme	1·90	50

212 Fairey Swordfish sinking "Bismarck" (German battleship) and Admirals Raeder and Tovey

1991. Battles of Second World War. Mult.

1436	100f. Type **212** (postage)	55	10
1437	150f. Aichi D3A "Val" bombers sinking U.S.S. "Yorktown" (aircraft carrier) and Admirals Yamamoto and Nimitz (Battle of Midway)	70	15
1438	200f. American torpedo boat and Admirals Kondo and Halsey (Guadalcanal)	85	20
1439	250f. "Crusader III" tanks, Hawker Hurricane Mk II aircraft, Rommel and Montgomery (El Alamein)	95	25
1440	300f. "Tiger II" tanks and Generals Guderian and Patton (Ardennes) (air)	1·10	30
1441	450f. Grumman TBF Avenger aircraft sinking "Yamato" (Japanese battleship) and Admiral Kogo and General MacArthur	2·00	45

1991. Various stamps surch.

1443	100f. on 170f. mult (No. 1321) (postage)	15	10
1444	100f. on 170f. mult (No. 1328)	15	10
1445	100f. on 250f. mult (No. 1388)	15	10
1446	100f. on 400f. mult (No. 1270)	15	10
1447	100f. on 400f. mult (No. 1349)	15	10
1448	100f. on 400f. mult (No. 1356)	15	10
1449	100f. on 400f. mult (No. 1404)	15	10
1450	100f. on 400f. mult (No. 1410)	2·25	1·00

1451 100f. on 500f. mult (No. 1362) 15 10
1452 100f. on 500f. mult (No. 1366) 15 10
1453 100f. on 400f. mult (No. 1301) (air) 15 10
1454 100f. on 400f. mult (No. 1308) 15 10
1455 100f. on 400f. mult (No. 1322) 15 10
1456 100f. on 400f. mult (No. 1329) . . . . 1·50 40
1457 100f. on 400f. mult (No. 1343) 15 10
1458 100f. on 400f. mult (No. 1385) 15 10
1459 300f. on 450f. mult (No. 1350) 50 15
1460 300f. on 450f. mult (No. 1411) 50 15

214 Nat King Cole Trio

1991. Music and Films. Multicoloured.
1461 100f. Type **214** (postage) . . 15 10
1462 150f. Yul Brynner and scene from "The Magnificent Seven" 25 10
1463 250f. Judy Garland and scene from "The Wizard of Oz" 40 10
1464 300f. Steve McQueen and scene from "Papillon" . . 50 15
1465 500f. Gary Cooper and scene from "Sergeant York" (air) 80 20
1466 600f. Bing Crosby and scene from "High Society" . . 1·00 25

215 Dancer

216 Doves, Map and Pope John Paul II

1991. African Tourism Year. Multicoloured.
1468 100f. Type **215** 15 10
1469 150f. Baskets (horiz) 25 10
1470 250f. Drum (horiz) 40 10
1471 300f. Flautist 50 15

1991. Papal Visit. Litho.
1472 **216** 150f. multicoloured . . . 25 10

217 "ERS-1" Observation Satellite and Earth

1991. Anniversaries and Events. Mult.
1473 100f. Type **217** (postage) . . 15 10
1474 150f. "Sunflowers" (Vincent van Gogh, 1888) 25 10
1475 200f. Napoleon I (170th death anniv) 35 15
1476 250f. Henri Dunant (founder of Red Cross) and Red Cross volunteers 40 10
1477 300f. Bicentenary of Brandenburg Gate and second anniversary of fall of Berlin Wall 50 15
1478 400f. Pope John Paul II's tour of Africa, 1989 . . . 65 15
1479 450f. Garry Kasparov and Anatoli Karpov (World Chess Championship, 1990) (air) 75 20
1480 500f. Boy feeding dove and Rotary International and Lions International emblems 80 20

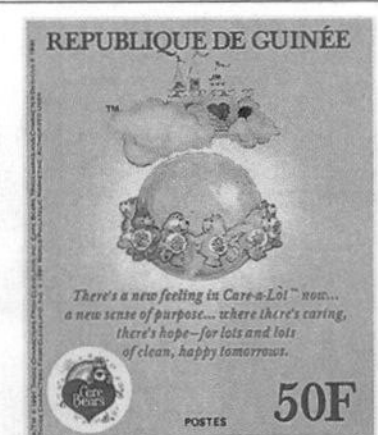

218 Care-a-Lot and Care Bears around Globe

1991. Ecology. Care Bear cartoon characters. Multicoloured.
1481 50f. Type **218** 10 10
1482 100f. Care Bears around sink ("Save Water!") . . 15 10
1483 200f. Care Bears in tree ("Recycle!") 35 15
1484 300f. Traffic jam and Care Bear ("Control Noise") 50 15
1485 400f. Elephant and Care Bear ("Protect Our Wild Life") (horiz) 65 15

219 Player, Trophy and Little Five Points

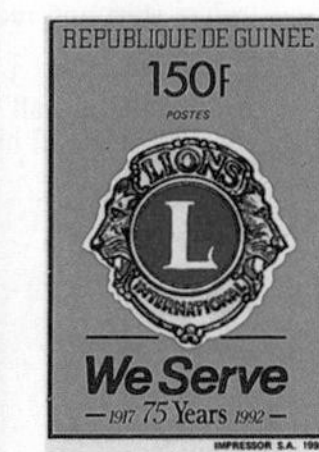

220 Emblem

1992. World Cup Football Championship, U.S.A. (1994) (1st issue). Multicoloured.
1487 100f. Type **219** (postage) . . 15 10
1488 300f. Germany player and Fulton Stadium, Atlanta 40 10
1489 400f. Player and Inman Park 50 15
1490 500f. Player and Museum of Fine Art (air) 65 15
See also Nos. 1565/8.

1992. 75th Anniv of Lions International.
1492 **220** 150f. multicoloured . . . 25 10
1493 400f. multicoloured . . . 65 15

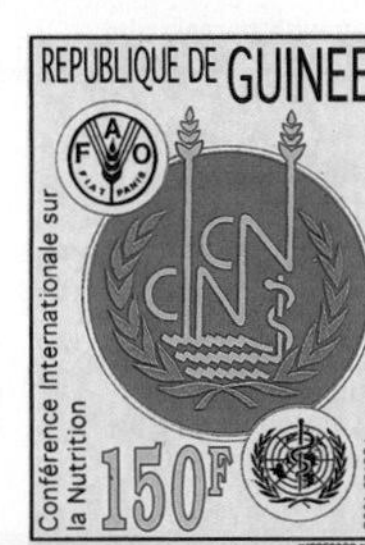

221 Emblem

1992. International Nutrition Conference, Rome.
1494 **221** 150f. mult (postage) . . 25 10
1495 400f. multicoloured . . . 65 15
1496 500f. multicoloured (air) 80 20

222 Scene from "The Devil and Catherine" and Antonin Dvorak (composer)

1992. Anniversaries and Events. Multicoloured.
1497 200f. Type **222** (150th birth (1991)) (postage) 25 10
1498 300f. Antonio Vivaldi (composer) (250th death (1991)) and as choirmaster to the Hospital of the Pieta, Venice 40 10
1499 350f. Meeting of airship "Graf Zeppelin" and Santos-Dumont's flying boat and Count Ferdinand von Zeppelin (airship pioneer) 45 10
1500 400f. Projected locomotive emerging from Channel Tunnel (construction) . . 2·75 75
1501 450f. Konrad Adenauer (German statesman) and Brandenburg Gate, Berlin (bicentenary of Gate) (air) 60 15
1502 500f. Emperor Hirohito of Japan (third death anniv) 65 15

223 Charlie Chaplin (actor) and Scene from "Modern Times"

1992. Anniversaries and Events. Multicoloured.
1504 50f. Type **223** (15th death anniv) (postage) 10 10
1505 100f. Pavilion and Christopher Columbus ("Expo '92" World's Fair, Seville) 30 10
1506 150f. St. Peter's Square, Rome 20 10
1507 200f. Marlene Dietrich (actress, death) in scene from "Shanghai Express" 25 10
1508 250f. Michael Schumacher and Formula 1 racing car 35 10
1509 300f. Rocket launch and John Glenn (30th anniv of Glenn's three-orbit flight in "Mercury" space capsule) 40 10
1510 400f. Bill Koch (skipper) and "America 3" (yacht) (winner of Americas Cup) (air) 50 15
1511 450f. Victory of Washington Redskins in 26th American Superbowl baseball championships 60 15
1512 500f. Recovery of "Intelsat VI" satellite by "Endeavour" space shuttle 65 15

1993. 50th Death Anniv (1991) of Robert Baden-Powell (founder of Scouting Movement). Nos. 1339/44 optd **50eme ANNIVERSAIRE DE LA MORT DE BADEN POWEL**.
1515 **192** 50f. mult (postage) . . . 70 10
1516 – 100f. multicoloured . . . 15 10
1517 – 150f. multicoloured . . . 1·10 40
1518 – 300f. multicoloured . . . 2·25 65
1519 – 400f. multicoloured (air) 50 15
1520 – 450f. multicoloured . . . 60 15

1993. Bicentenary of Year One of First Republic of France. Nos. 1388/91 optd **BICENTENAIRE DE L'AN I DE LA REPUBLIQUE FRANCAISE**.
1522 **201** 250f. mult (postage) . . 35 10
1523 – 300f. multicoloured . . . 40 10
1524 – 400f. multicoloured . . . 50 15
1525 – 450f. multicoloured (air) 60 15

1993. Winter Olympic Games, Albertville, Gold Medal Winners. Nos. 1402/5 variously optd.
1527 150f. **SLALOM GEANT Alberto Tomba, Italie** (postage) 20 10
1528 250f. **SKI NORDIQUE Vegard Ulvang, Norvege** 35 15
1529 400f. **BOB A DEUX G. Weder/D. Acklin, Suisse** 50 15
1530 500f. **PATINAGE DE VITESSE Olaf Zinke 1000m., Allemagne** (air) 65 15

1993. World Cup Football Championship, Italy, Results. Nos. 1414/17 optd **1. ALLEMAGNE 2. ARGENTINE 3. ITALIE.**
1532 **207** 200f. mult (postage) . . 25 10
1533 – 250f. multicoloured . . . 35 15
1534 – 300f. multicoloured . . . 40 15
1535 – 450f. multicoloured (air) . 60 15

1993. Air. Bobby Fischer–Boris Spassky Chess Match (1537) and 75th Anniv of Lions International (1538). Nos. 1479/80 optd.
1537 450f. **RENCONTRE FISCHER - SPASSKY 3 SEPT au 5 NOV 1992 AU MONTENEGRO** . . 60 15
1538 500f. **75eme ANNIVERSAIRE LIONS** 65 15

230 West Germany Footballer and Little White House

1993. Olympic Games, Atlanta (1996) (1st issue). Multicoloured.
1539 150f. Type **230** (postage) . . 20 10
1540 250f. Cyclist and Georgia World Congress Center 35 10
1541 400f. Basketball player and underground station . . . 50 15
1542 500f. Baseball player and steam train, New Georgia Railroad (air) . . . . . . 4·50 75
See also Nos. 1623/7.

231 Ice Hockey and "Whale Hunt" (sculpture)

232 "Luna 3" and Dark Side of Moon

1993. Winter Olympic Games, Lillehammer, Norway (1994). Multicoloured.
1544 150f. Type **231** (postage) . . 20 10
1545 250f. Two-man bobsleigh and Edvard Grieg's house 35 10
1546 400f. Biathlon and Fredrikstad Park (air) . . 50 15
1547 450f. Ski jumping and Eidsvoll Manor 60 15

1993. 25th Anniv (1994) of First Manned Moon Landing. Multicoloured.
1549 150f. Type **232** 20 10
1550 150f. "Ranger 7" 10 10
1551 150f. "Luna 9" 20 10
1552 150f. "Surveyor 1" (first lunar probe) 20 10
1553 150f. Lunar "Orbiter 1" and moon 20 10
1554 150f. Launch of "Saturn 5" (rocket) carrying "Apollo 11" 20 10
1555 150f. "Apollo 11" command module in lunar orbit . . 20 10
1556 150f. Astronaut climbing from "Apollo 11" 20 10
1557 150f. "Apollo 12" astronaut recovering "Surveyor 1" camera 20 10
1558 150f. Explosion of "Apollo 13" 20 10
1559 150f. "Luna 16" probe (first collection of lunar samples by automatic probe) 20 10
1560 150f. Lunokhod of "Luna 17" (first lunar vehicle) . . 20 10
1561 150f. Alan Shepard playing golf on moon 20 10
1562 150f. First lunar jeep from "Apollo 15" mission . . . 20 10
1563 150f. First lunar telescope from "Apollo 16" mission 20 10
1564 150f. Astronaut from "Apollo 17" (last "Apollo" mission) 20 10

233 San Francisco

1993. World Cup Football Championship, U.S.A. (1994) (2nd issue). Multicoloured.
1565 100f. Type **233** (postage) . . 15 10
1566 300f. Washington D.C. . . . 40 10
1567 400f. Renaissance Center, Detroit 50 15
1568 500f. Dallas (air) 65 15

234 Euparkeria

1993. Prehistoric Animals. Multicoloured.
1570 50f. Type **234** 10 10
1571 50f. Plateosaurus 10 10
1572 50f. Anchisaurus 10 10

1573 50f. Ornithosuchus 10 10
1574 100f. Megalosaurus 15 10
1575 100f. Scelidosaurus 15 10
1576 100f. Camptosaurus 15 10
1577 100f. Ceratosaurus 15 10
1578 250f. Ouranosaurus 35 10
1579 250f. Dicraeosaurus 35 10
1580 250f. Tarbosaurus 35 10
1581 250f. Gorgosaurus 35 10
1582 250f. Polacanthus 35 10
1583 250f. Deinonychus 35 10
1584 250f. Corythosaurus 35 10
1585 250f. Spinosaurus 35 10

235 Prince Johann I of Liechtenstein **236** Johann Kepler and "Pluto" Space Probe

1994. Multicoloured. (a) Battle of Austerlitz, 1805.
1587 150f. Type **235** 20 10
1588 150f. Marshal Joachim Murat 20 10
1589 600f. Napoleon (59 × 47 mm) 80 20
Nos. 1587/9 were issued together, se-tenant, forming a composite design of a battle scene.

(b) Battle of the Moskva, 1912.
1590 150f. Marshal Michel Ney 20 10
1591 150f. Prince Pyotr Ivanovich Bagration 20 10
1592 600f. Napoleon on horseback (59 × 47 mm) 80 20
Nos. 1590/2 were issued together, se-tenant, forming a composite design of a battle scene.

(c) Normandy Landings, 1944.
1593 150f. Field-Marshal Erwin Rommel (wrongly inscr "Romel") 20 10
1594 150f. Gen. George Patton 20 10
1595 600f. Gen. Dwight David Eisenhower (59 × 47 mm) 80 20
Nos. 1593/5 were issued together, se-tenant, forming a composite design of a battle scene.

(d) Battle of the Ardennes, 1944.
1596 150f. Lt.-Gen. William H. Simpson 20 10
1597 150f. Gen. Heinz Guderian 20 10
1598 600f. Tank battle scene (59 × 47 mm) 80 20
Nos. 1596/8 were issued together, se-tenant, forming a composite design of a battle scene.

1994. Astronomers. Multicoloured.
1599 300f. Type **236** 40 10
1600 300f. Sir Isaac Newton and "Voyager" space probe 40 10
1601 500f. Nicolas Copernicus and "Galileo" space probe (59 × 47 mm) . . . 65 15
Nos. 1599/1601 were issued together, se-tenant, forming a composite design.

1994. Winter Olympic Games, Lillehammer. Gold Medal Winners. Nos. 1544/7 variously optd.
1602 150f. **MEDAILLE D'OR SUEDE** (postage) 20 10
1603 250f. **G. WEDER D. ACKLIN SUISSE** . . 35 10
1604 400f. **F.B. LUNDBERG NORVEGE** (air) 50 15
1605 450f. **J. WEISSFLOG ALLEMAGNE** 60 15

1994. World Cup Football Championship, U.S.A., Winners. Nos. 1565/8 optd **1. BRESIL 2. ITALIE 3. SUEDE**.
1607 **233** 100f. mult (postage) . . 15 10
1608 – 300f. multicoloured . . . 40 10
1609 – 400f. multicoloured . . . 50 15
1610 – 500f. multicoloured (air) 65 15

239 Banea Dam

1995. Garafiri Water Management. Mult.
1612 100f. Type **239** 10 10
1613 150f. Donkea 20 10
1614 200f. Tinkisso overflow (vert) 25 10
1615 250f. Waterfalls 30 10
1616 500f. Water works, Kinkon 60 15

240 Red and White Persian

1995. Cats. Multicoloured.
1617 150f. Type **240** (inscr "Tortoiseshell") 20 10
1618 250f. Tabby and white . . . 30 10
1619 500f. Black smoke persian ("Smoke long-haired") . . 60 15
1620 500f. Red tabby 60 15
1621 500f. Tortoiseshell and white persian ("longhair") . . . 60 15

241 Throwing the Javelin **242** Eurasian Goldfinch

1995. Olympic Games, Atlanta (1996) (2nd issue). Multicoloured.
1623 150f. Type **241** 20 10
1624 250f. Boxing 30 10
1625 500f. Football 60 15
1626 500f. Basketball 60 15
1627 500f. Weightlifting 60 15

1995. Birds. Multicoloured.
1629 150f. Type **242** 20 10
1630 250f. Nightingale ("Luscinia megarhynchos") 30 10
1631 500f. Island canary ("Serinus canaria") . . . 60 15
1632 500f. Chaffinch ("Fringilla coelebs") 60 15
1633 500f. Western greenfinch ("Carduelis chloris") . . . 60 15

243 Mona Monkey

1995. Mammals. Multicoloured.
1635 150f. Type **243** 20 10
1636 250f. Savanna monkey . . . 35 10
1637 500f. Demidoff's galago ("Galagoides demidovi") 65 15
1638 500f. Hare ("Lepus crawshayi") (horiz) . . . 65 15
1639 500f. Giant ground pangolin ("Manis gigantea") (horiz) 65 15

244 Pup-150 (Great Britain)

1995. Aircraft. Multicoloured.
1641 100f. Type **244** 15 10
1642 150f. Gardan GY-80 "Horizon" (France) . . . 20 10
1643 250f. Piper J-3 Cub (U.S.A.) 35 10
1644 500f. Piper PA-28 Cherokee Arrow (U.S.A.) 65 15
1645 500f. Pilatus PC-6 Porter (Switzerland) 65 15
1646 500f. Valmet L-90TP Redigo (Finland) 65 15

245 Yoked Oxen

1995. 50th Anniv of F.A.O. Multicoloured.
1648 200f. Type **245** 25 10
1649 750f. Nutrition lesson . . . 1·00 25

246 Jacobean Lily **247** Players

1995. Flowers. Multicoloured.
1650 100f. Type **246** 15 10
1651 150f. "Rudbeckia purpurea" 20 10
1652 250f. Himalayan blue poppy 35 10
1653 500f. Iris "Starshine" . . . 65 15
1654 500f. Rose "Gail Borden" 65 15
1655 500f. Sweet pea ("Lathyrus odoratus") 65 15

1995. World Cup Football Championship, France (1998) (1st issue). Multicoloured.
1657 150f. Type **247** 20 10
1658 250f. Player challenging player No. 2 . . . . . . 35 10
1659 500f. Players in blue and white shirt and red shirt in tackle 65 15
1660 500f. Players Nos. 3 and 10 running after ball 65 15
1661 500f. Player No. 2 high-kicking ball 65 15
See also Nos. 1719/24.

248 Arab Horse **249** "Leccinum nigrescens"

1995. Arab Horses. Multicoloured.
1663 100f. Type **248** 15 10
1664 150f. Dark brown horse with white star 20 10
1665 250f. Chestnut 35 10
1666 500f. Grey 65 15
1667 500f. Bay 65 15
1668 500f. Bay with harness and rein (horiz) 65 15

1995. Fungi. Multicoloured.
1670 150f. Type **249** 20 10
1671 250f. "Boletus rhodoxanthus" 35 10
1672 500f. "Cantharellus lutescens" 65 15
1673 500f. Brown roll-rim ("Paxillus involutus") . . 65 15
1674 500f. "Xerocomus rubellus" 65 15

250 Enterprise, 1832

1995. Veteran Omnibuses. Multicoloured.
1676 250f. Type **250** 35 10
1677 300f. Daimler, 1898 . . . . 40 10
1678 400f. V.H. Bussing, 1904 . . 50 15
1679 450f. M.A.N. autobus, 1906 60 15
1680 500f. M.A.N. autocar, 1934 65 15

251 Locomotive "Tom Thumb", 1829, U.S.A.

1996. Rail Transport. Multicoloured.
1681 200f. Type **251** 25 10
1682 250f. Locomotive "Genf", 1858, Switzerland (68 × 27 mm) 30 10
1683 300f. Canterbury Frozen Meat Company Dubs locomotive, 1873, New Zealand 35 10
1684 400f. Bagnall fireless steam accumulator locomotive No. 2, Great Britain . . . 50 15

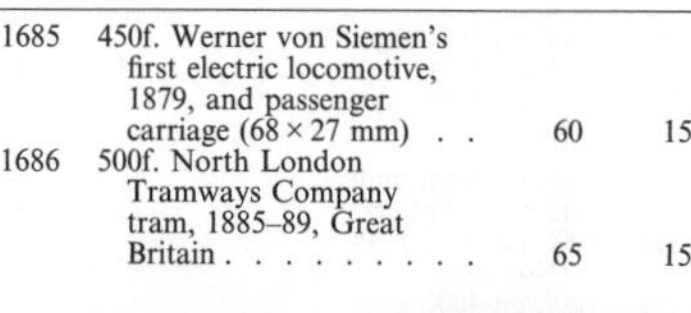
1685 450f. Werner von Siemen's first electric locomotive, 1879, and passenger carriage (68 × 27 mm) . . 60 15
1686 500f. North London Tramways Company tram, 1885–89, Great Britain 65 15

252 Rock Formation **253** Red Siskin

1996. Multicoloured.
1688 200f. Type **252** 25 10
1689 750f. Child 95 25
1690 1000f. Women carrying faggots . . . . 1·25 30

1996. Birds. Multicoloured.
1691 200f. Type **253** 25 10
1692 250f. Red-cheeked cordon-bleu 30 10
1693 300f. Chestnut-breasted minnikin 35 10
1694 400f. Paradise sparrow . . . 50 10
1695 450f. Gouldian finch 55 15
1696 500f. Red bishop 60 15

254 Bull Terrier **256** Chestnut

255 Tortoiseshell and White Shorthair

1996. Dogs. Multicoloured.
1698 200f. Type **254** 25 10
1699 250f. Elkhound 30 10
1700 300f. Akita 35 10
1701 400f. Collie 50 10
1702 450f. Rottweiler 55 15
1703 500f. Boxer 60 15

1996. Cats. Multicoloured.
1705 200f. Type **255** 25 10
1706 250f. Bicolour shorthair . . 30 10
1707 300f. Tortoiseshell and white Japanese bobtail 35 10
1708 400f. Chocolate point Himalayan 50 10
1709 450f. Red longhair 55 15
1710 500f. Blue Persian 60 15

1996. Fungi. Multicoloured.
1712 200f. Type **256** 25 10
1713 250f. Granular 30 10
1714 300f. Destroying angel . . . 35 10
1715 400f. Milky blue 50 10
1716 450f. Violet cortinarius . . . 55 15
1717 500f. Rough-stemmed . . . 60 15

257 Players **258** "Paphiopedilum millmoore"

1997. World Cup Football Championship, France (1998) (2nd issue). Multicoloured.
1719 200f. Type **257** 25 10
1720 250f. Player No. 5 . . . . . 30 10
1721 300f. Three players 35 10
1722 400f. Player dribbling ball past opposition (horiz) . . 45 10

1723 450f. Player No. 12 with opposing player on ground (horiz) 50 15
1724 500f. Ball passing lunging goalkeeper (horiz) 55 15

1997. Orchids. Multicoloured.
1726 200f. Type **258** 25 10
1727 250f. "Paphiopedilum ernest read" 30 10
1728 300f. "Paphiopedilum harrisianum" 35 10
1729 400f. "Paphiopedilum gaudianum" 45 10
1730 450f. "Paphiopedilum papa rohl" 50 15
1731 500f. "Paphiopedilum sea cliff" 55 15

259 Giraffe

1997. Mammals. Multicoloured.
1733 200f. Type **259** 25 10
1734 250f. White rhinoceros (vert) 30 10
1735 300f. Warthog 35 10
1736 400f. Cheetah 45 10
1737 450f. African elephant (vert) 50 15
1738 500f. Pygmy hippopotamus 55 10

260 H.M.S. "Captain" (turret ship, Great Britain, 1870)

1997. 19th-Century Warships. Multicoloured.
1740 200f. Type **260** 30 15
1741 250f. "Kaiser Wilhelm" (ironclad, Germany, 1869) 35 15
1742 300f. H.M.S. "Temeraire" (turret ship, Great Britain, 1871) 40 15
1743 400f. "Mouillage" (turret ship, Italy, 1866) 50 15
1744 450f. H.M.S. "Inflexible" (battleship, Great Britain, 1881) 55 20
1745 500f. "Magenta" (ironclad, France, 1862) 60 20

261 "Siganus trispilos"

1997. Fishes. Multicoloured.
1747 200f. Type **261** 25 10
1748 250f. Dusky parrotfish . . . 30 10
1749 300f. Harlequin tuskfish . . 35 10
1750 400f. Masked unicornfish . . 45 10
1751 450f. "Hypoplectrus gemma" 50 15
1752 500f. Red-tailed surgeon-fish 55 15

262 Officer, Von Witerfeldt's Regiment

264 14th-century Thai Knight, Rook and King

263 Baldwin Steam Locomotive

1997. Prussian Infantry Uniforms. Mult.
1754 200f. Type **262** 25 10
1755 250f. Non-commissioned officer, Von Kanitz's Regiment 30 10
1756 300f. Private, Prince Franz von Anhalt-Dessau's Regiment 35 10
1757 400f. Private, Von Kalnein's Regiment 45 10
1758 450f. Grenadier, Duke Ferdinand of Brunswick's Regiment 50 15
1759 500f. Grenadier musician, Rekow's Guards Battalion 55 15

1997. Steam Locomotives. Multicoloured.
1761 200f. Type **263** 25 10
1762 250f. Steam locomotive No. 1 . . . . 30 10
1763 300f. Vulcan steam locomotive 35 10
1764 400f. Commonwealth Edison Company Baldwin steam locomotive No. 2 . . . . 50 15
1765 450f. TCID Railroad steam locomotive No. 108 . . . 60 15
1766 500f. Pittsburgh-Hanover Coal Company steam locomotive No. 3 . . . . 65 15

1997. Chess Pieces. Multicoloured.
1768 200f. Type **264** 25 10
1769 250f. Chinese pawn, king and knight, 1930 . . . . 30 10
1770 300f. Portuguese ivory "seahorse" pawn, queen and king, 1920 . . . . . 35 10
1771 400f. German pewter "military" knight, king and pawn 45 10
1772 450f. Russian amber queen, king, bishop and knight from reign of Catherine II 50 15
1773 500f. Max Ernst's designs for queen, king, bishop and knight 55 15

265 Siberian Husky

1997. Dogs. Multicoloured.
1775 200f. Type **265** 25 10
1776 250f. Teckel 30 10
1777 300f. Boston terrier 35 10
1778 400f. Basset hound 45 10
1779 450f. Dalmatian 50 15
1780 500f. Rottweiler 55 15

POSTAGE DUE STAMPS

D 11 D 17

1959.
D195 D 11 1f. green 15 15
D196 2f. red 15 15
D197 3f. brown 30 20
D198 5f. blue 90 45
D199 10f. orange . . . . . 1·60 70
D200 20f. mauve . . . . . 3·25 1·60

1959.
D224 D 17 1f. red 10 15
D225 2f. orange 15 15
D226 3f. lake 15 15
D227 5f. green 40 30
D228 10f. sepia . . . . . . 1·00 90
D229 20f. blue . . . . . . 1·90 1·60

APPENDIX

The following stamps have either been issued in excess of postal needs or have not been available to the public in reasonable quantities at face value. Such stamps may later be given full listing if there is evidence of regular postal use.

1982.
World Cup Winners. Nos. 1068/74 optd.

1983.
Olympic Games, Los Angeles. 100s.
Bicentenary of Manned Flight. 100s.
Winter Olympic Games, Sarajevo. 100s.

1984.
Winter Olympic Gold Medal Winners. 100s.

1985.
Space Achievements. 200s.
Anniversaries and Events. 85th Birthday of Queen Elizabeth the Queen Mother. 100s.

1986.
Appearance of Halley's Comet. 1500f.

1987.
Winter Olympic Games, Seoul. 1500f.

1989.
Embossed on gold foil.Scout and Butterfly. Air 1500f.
Bicentenary of French Revolution. Air 1500f.

1990.
Embossed on gold foil.World Cup Football Championship, Italy. Air 1500f.
Winter Olympic Games, Albertville (1992). Air 1500f.
De Gaulle and Free French Forces. Air 1500f.

1992.
Embossed on gold foil.Olympic Games, Barcelona. Air 1500f.
World Cup Football Championship, U.S.A. (1994) (1st issue). Air 1500f. (vert design).
Elvis Presley. Air 1500f.
Pope John Paul II's African Tour. Air 1500f.

1993.
Embossed on gold foil.Bicentenary of Year One of First Republic of France. Air. Optd on 1989 French Revolution issue. 1500f.
Olympic Games, Atlanta. Air 1500f.
Winter Olympic Games, Lillehammer, Norway. Air 1500f.
World Cup Football Championship, U.S.A. (1994) (2nd issue). Air 1500f. (square design).

1995.
Embossed on gold foil.Normandy Landing, 1944. Air. Optd on 1990 De Gaulle Appendix. 1500f.

GUINEA-BISSAU Pt. 13

Following an armed rebellion against Colonial rule, the independence of former Portuguese Guinea was recognised on 10 September 1974.

1974. 100 centavos = 1 escudo.
1976. 100 centavos = 1 peso.

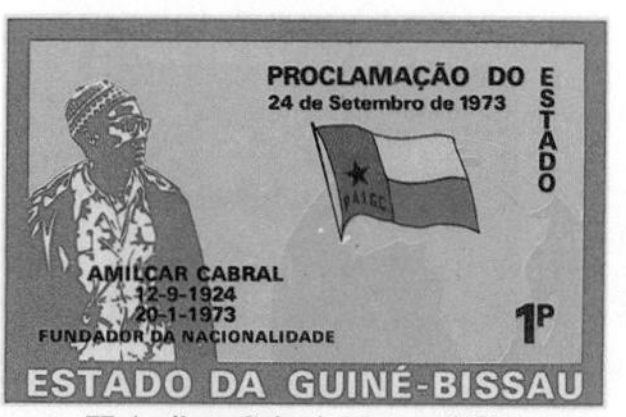

77 Amilcar Cabral, Map and Flag

1974. 1st Anniv of Proclamation of Republic. Country name inscr in white.
426 **77** 1p. multicoloured 50 40
427 2.5p. multicoloured 75 65
428 5p. multicoloured . . . . 15·00 8·50
429 10p. multicoloured . . . . 2·50 2·00

1975. No. 425 of Portuguese Guinea optd **REP. DA BISSAU.**
430 2e. multicoloured 60 60

79 Amilcar Cabral, Map and Flag

1975. 2nd Anniv of Proclamation of Republic (1st issue). Country name inscr in black.
431 **79** 1p. multicoloured 45 30
432 2.5p. multicoloured 60 45
433 5p. multicoloured . . . . 2·50 1·40
434 10p. multicoloured . . . . 2·50 2·25
See also Nos. 439/440.

80 Amilcar Cabral, Arms and Flag

1975. 51st Birth Anniv of Amilcar Cabral (founder of P.A.I.G.C.).
435 **80** 1e. multicoloured 20 10
436 10e. multicoloured 80 40

81 Family, Arms and Flag

1975. 19th Anniv of P.A.I.G.C. (Partido Africano da Independencia da Guine e do Cabo Verde).
437 **81** 2e. multicoloured 50 20
438 10e. multicoloured . . . . 2·00 75

82 Pres. Luis Cabral, Arms and Flag

1975. 2nd Anniv of Proclamation of Republic (2nd issue).
439 **82** 3e. multicoloured 40 20
440 5e. multicoloured 85 30

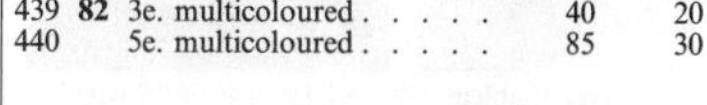

83 General Henry Knox (after Stuart) and Cannons of Ticonderoga (after Lovell)

1976. Bicentenary of American Independence (1st issue). Multicoloured.
441 5e. Type **83** (postage) 25 15
442 10e. General Putnam and Battle of Bunker Hill . . . 55 30
443 15e. Washington and Crossing of the Delaware 80 35
444 20e. General Kosciuszko and Battle of Saratoga . . . . 1·25 50
445 30e. General von Steuben and Valley Forge (air) . . 1·75 90
446 40e. Lafayette and Monmouth Court House 2·00 1·00
See also Nos. 503/6.

84 Masked Dancer

1976. Dancers. Multicoloured.

No.	Description		
448	2p. Type **84** (postage)	30	10
449	3p. Dancer and drummer	35	15
450	5p. Dancers on stilts	60	20
451	10p. Dancers with spears and bows (air)	65	40
452	15p. Masked dancer	1·00	50
453	20p. "Devil" dancer	1·50	65

1976. Cent of Universal Postal Union (1st issue). Nos. 1448/53 optd **CENTENARIO DA U.P.U. 1874. MEMBRO DA U.P.U. 1974** and emblem.

No.	Description		
455 **84**	2p. multicoloured (post)	10	10
456 –	3p. multicoloured	20	10
457 –	5p. multicoloured	25	15
458 –	10p. multicoloured (air)	50	25
459 –	15p. multicoloured	65	40
460 –	20p. multicoloured	90	50

See also Nos. 518/23.

1976. Nos. 435/40 surch in new currency.

No.	Description		
462	1p. on 1e. multicoloured	10	10
463	2p. on 2e. multicoloured	10	10
464	3p. on 3e. multicoloured	15	10
465	5p. on 5e. multicoloured	25	15
466	10p. on 10e. multicoloured	50	30
467	10p. on 10e. multicoloured	50	30

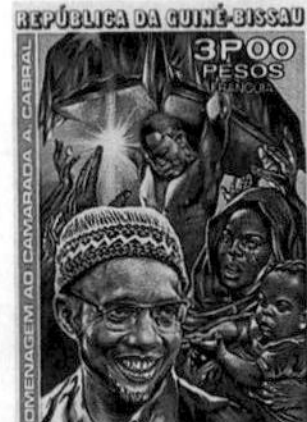

87 Amilcar Cabral and Funeral

1976. 3rd Anniv of Amilcar Cabral's Assassination.

No.	Description		
468 **87**	3p. multicoloured	15	10
469	5p. multicoloured	20	15
470	6p. multicoloured	25	20
471	10p. multicoloured	40	25

88 Party Emblem

89 Launch of "Soyuz" Spacecraft

1976. 20th Anniv of P.A.I.G.C.

No.	Description		
472 **88**	3p. multicoloured	15	15
473	15p. multicoloured	65	50
474	50p. multicoloured	1·60	1·25

1976. Air. "Apollo–Soyuz" Space Link. Mult.

No.	Description		
475	5p. Type **89**	25	15
476	10p. Launch of "Apollo" spacecraft	45	30
477	15p. Leonov, Stafford and meeting in Space	80	45
478	20p. Eclipse of the Sun	1·25	55
479	30p. Infra-red photograph of Earth	1·75	85
480	40p. Return of Spacecraft to Earth	2·25	95

90 Bell Telephone of 1876 and Laying First Atlantic Cable

1976. Telephone Centenary. Multicoloured.

No.	Description		
482	2p. Type **90** (postage)	15	10
483	3p. French telephone of 1890 and first telephone box, 1893	20	10
484	5p. German automatic telephone of 1908 and automatic telephone, 1898	25	15
485	10p. English telephone of 1910 and trans-horizon link, 1963 (air)	55	25
486	15p. French telephone of 1924 and communications satellite	85	45
487	20p. Modern telephone and "Molnya" satellite	1·25	50

91 Women's Figure Skating

1976. Winter Olympic Games, Innsbruck. Mult.

No.	Description		
489	1p. Type **91** (postage)	15	10
490	3p. Ice-hockey	30	10
491	5p. Bobsleighing	30	15
492	10p. Pairs figure-skating (air)	55	30
493	20p. Cross-country skiing	1·25	45
494	30p. Speed skating	1·75	85

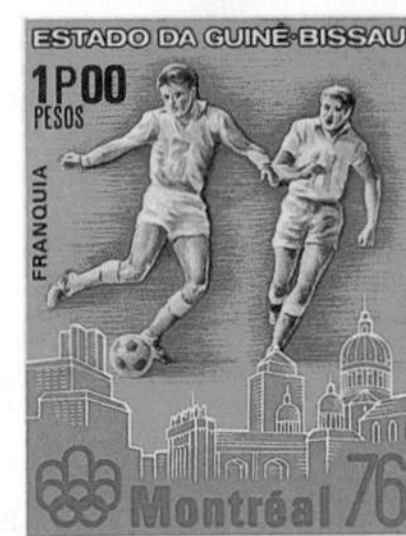

92 Footballers and Montreal Skyline

1976. Olympic Games, Montreal. Mult.

No.	Description		
496	1p. Type **92**	10	10
497	3p. Pole vaulting	15	10
498	5p. Hurdling	25	15
499	10p. Discus throwing	45	25
500	20p. Running	90	50
501	30p. Wrestling	1·40	75

93 "Viking" orbiting Mars

1976. Bicentenary of American Revolution (2nd issue). Multicoloured. (a) Postage. Horiz designs as T **83**.

No.	Description		
503	3p.50 Crispus Attuck and Boston Massacre	30	10
504	5p. Martin Luther King and Capitol	40	20

(b) Air. Success of "Viking" Mission. Vert.

No.	Description		
505	25p. Type **93**	1·25	65
506	35p. Lander scooping samples from surface of Mars	1·75	90

94 Amilcar Cabral

1977. 4th Death Anniv of Amilcar Cabral. Multicoloured.

No.	Description		
507	50c. Type **94** (postage)	15	10
508	3p.50 Luis Cabral addressing U.N. Assembly	35	10
509	15p. Type **94** (air)	55	30
510	30p. As No. 508	1·25	50

95 Henri Dunant (Peace, 1901)

1977. 75th Anniv of 1st Nobel Prizes. Mult.

No.	Description		
511	3p.50 Type **95** (postage)	30	10
512	5p. Albert Einstein (Physics, 1921)	35	20
513	6p. Irene and Jean-Frederic Joliot-Curie (Chemistry, 1935)	75	20
514	30p. Alexander Fleming (Medicine, 1945)	1·75	90
515	35p. Ernest Hemingway (Literature, 1954) (air)	2·00	90
516	40p. J. Tinbergen (Economic Sciences, 1969)	2·25	1·00

96 Postal Runner and "Telstar" Satellite

1977. Centenary (1974) of Universal Postal Union (2nd issue). Multicoloured.

No.	Description		
518	3p.50 Type **96** (postage)	25	15
519	5p. A.E.G. J-II biplane, and satellites circling globe	35	15
520	6p. Mail van and satellite control room	55	15
521	30p. Stage-coach and astronaut cancelling letters on Moon	1·75	50
522	35p. French locomotive (1844) and "Intelsat 4" satellite (air)	6·50	2·75
523	40p. Aircraft and "Apollo"–"Soyuz" link	2·50	90

97 Coronation Coach

1977. Silver Jubliee of Queen Elizabeth II. Multicoloured.

No.	Description		
525	3p.50 Type **97** (postage)	20	10
526	5p. Coronation ceremony	25	15
527	10p. Yeoman of the Guard and Crown Jewels	45	25
528	20p. Trumpeter sounding fanfare	90	45
529	25p. Royal Horse Guard (air)	1·25	50
530	30p. Royal Family on balcony	1·50	70

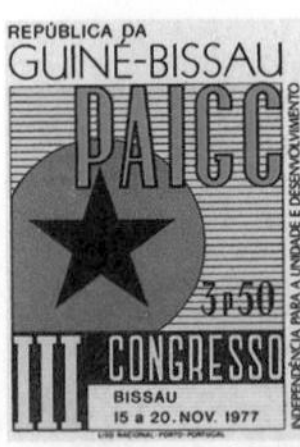

98 Congress Emblem

99 "Massacre of the Innocents" (detail)

1977. 3rd P.A.I.G.C. Congress, Bissau.

No.	Description		
532 **98**	3p.50 multicoloured	25	15

1977. 400th Birth Anniv of Peter Paul Rubens (artist). Multicoloured.

No.	Description		
533	3p.50 Type **99** (postage)	20	10
534	5p. "Rape of the Daughters of Leukippos"	25	15
535	6p. "Lamentation of Christ" (horiz)	35	15
536	30p. "Francisco IV Gonzaga, Prince of Mantua"	1·60	50
537	35p. "The Four Continents" (detail) (horiz) (air)	1·75	50
538	40p. "Marquise Brigida Spinola Doria"	2·25	60

100 Santos-Dumont's Airship "Ballon No. 6"

1978. Airships. Multicoloured.

No.	Description		
540	3p.50 Type **100** (postage)	25	15
541	5p. Beardmore airship R-34 crossing Atlantic	35	15
542	10p. "Norge" over North Pole	55	20
543	20p. "Graf Zeppelin" over Abu Simbel	1·40	50
544	25p. "Hindenburg" over New York (air)	1·75	70
545	30p. "Graf Zeppelin", Concorde airliner and space shuttle	2·25	75

101 Footballers, Cup and Poster (Uruguay, 1930)

1978. World Cup Football Championship, Argentina. Multicoloured.

No.	Description		
547	3p.50 Type **101** (postage)	20	10
548	5p. "Coupe du Monde, 1938"	25	15
549	10p. Brazil, 1950	55	25
550	20p. Chile, 1962	1·10	45
551	25p. Mexico, 1970 (air)	1·40	50
552	30p. "FIFA World Cup 1974" (Germany)	1·60	65

DESIGNS: showing match scenes and posters from previous championships.

102 Black Antelope

1978. Endangered Animals. Multicoloured.

No.	Description		
554	3p.50 Type **102** (postage)	30	10
555	5p. Fennec	75	30
556	6p. Secretary bird	1·00	50
557	30p. Hippopotamuses	2·00	65
558	35p. Cheetahs (air)	2·25	65
559	40p. Gorillas	2·50	75

103 Microwave-antenna

104 Child

1978. Telecommunications Day.

No.	Description		
561 **103**	3p.50 multicoloured	20	15
562	10p. multicoloured	55	30

1978. Children's Day.

No.	Description		
563 **104**	50c. blue and green	10	10
564 –	3p. bright red and red	15	10
565 –	5p. light brown and brown	25	15
566 –	30p. brown and red	1·40	1·00

DESIGNS: 3p. Amilcar Cabral and child; 5p. Children; 30p. Two children playing.

105 Reading the Proclamation

1978. 25th Anniv of Coronation of Queen Elizabeth II. Multicoloured.
567 3p. Type **105** (postage) . . . 20 10
568 5p. Queen and Prince Philip in Coronation Coach . . . 25 15
569 10p. Queen and Prince Philip 45 25
570 20p. Mounted drummer . . . 90 45
571 25p. Imperial State Crown and St. Edward's Crown (air) . . . . 1·25 50
572 30p. Queen holding orb and sceptre . . . . 1·25 65
573 100p. Queen, stained glass window and Imperial State Crown (55 × 38 mm) . . . 4·50 1·50

106 Wright Brothers and Wright Flyer I

1978. History of Aviation. Multicoloured.
575 3p.50 Type **106** (postage) . . 20 10
576 10p. Alberto Santos-Dumont 45 20
577 15p. Louis Bleriot 75 35
578 20p. Charles Lindbergh (air) 90 40
579 25p. Moon landing . . . . . 1·25 50
580 30p. Space shuttle . . . . . 1·50 65

1978. World Cup Football Championship Results. Nos. 547/52 optd **10 ARGENTINA 20 HOLANDA 30 BRAZIL**.
582 3p.50 multicoloured (postage) 20 10
583 5p. multicoloured 25 15
584 10p. multicoloured 45 25
585 20p. multicoloured . . . . . 1·10 55
586 25p. multicoloured (air) . . . 1·25 55
587 30p. multicoloured . . . . . 1·50 70

108 "Virgin and Child", 1497

1978. 450th Death Anniv of Albrecht Durer (artist). Multicoloured.
589 3p.50 Type **108** (postage) . . 20 10
590 5p. "Virgin and Child", 1507 25 15
591 6p. "Virgin and Child", 1512 30 15
592 30p. "Virgin", 1518 . . . . 1·40 70
593 35p. "Virgin and Child with St. Anne", 1519 (air) . . . 1·75 50
594 40p. "Virgin of the Pear", 1526 . . . . 2·00 75

109 Rowland Hill and Wurttemberg 70k. Stamp, 1873

1978. Death Centenary of Rowland Hill.
596 3p.50 Type **109** (postage) . . 15 10
597 5p. Belgian 10c. stamp, 1849 25 15
598 6p. Monaco 5f. stamp, 1885 30 20
599 30p. Spanish 10r. stamp, 1851 1·50 70
600 35p. Swiss 5r. stamp, 1851 (air) . . . . 1·75 50
601 40p. Naples ½t. stamp, 1860 2·00 75
DESIGNS: 5p. to 40p. show Rowland Hill and stamp.

110 Nurse immunising Child

1979. International Year of the Child (1st issue). Multicoloured.
603 3p.50 Type **110** (postage) . . 20 10
604 10p. Children drinking . . . 55 25
605 15p. Children with book . . 1·00 35
606 20p. Space shuttle (air) . . . 1·00 40
607 25p. "Skylab" space station 1·40 50
608 30p. Children playing chess 2·00 75
See also Nos. 616/19.

111 Family

1979. National Census.
610 **111** 50c. brown, blue and pink 10 10
611 2p. brown, blue & lt blue 15 10
612 4p. brown, blue and yellow 25 15

112 Wave Pattern and Human Figures **113** Monument

1979. World Telecommunications Day. Mult.
613 50c. Type **112** 10 10
614 4p. Wave pattern and human figures (different) 20 15

1979. 20th Anniv of Pindjiuouiti Massacre.
615 **113** 4p.50 multicoloured . . . 30 15

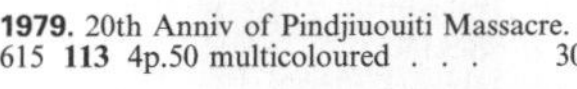

114 Classroom Scene

1980. International Year of the Child (2nd issue). Multicoloured.
616 6p. Type **114** (postage) . . . 30 25
617 10p. Jules Verne and child reading novel (vert) 45 30
618 25p. Locomotive "Northumbrian" (1831), Japanese "Hikari" express train and child with toy steam locomotive (vert) . . 9·00 1·25
619 35p. Man and child with bows and arrows (vert) . . 1·60 75

115 Amilcar Cabral, Workers and Children reading Books

1980. Literacy Campaign. Multicoloured.
621 3p.50 Type **115** (postage) . . 20 10
622 5p. Luis Cabral displaying school textbooks 30 15
623 15p. Type **115** (air) 80 50
624 25p. As No. 622 . . . . 1·40 75

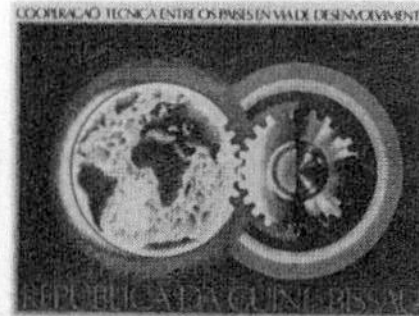

116 Globe and Cogwheel

1980. Technical Co-operation among Developing Countries.
625 **116** 3p.50 multicoloured . . . 20 10
626 6p. multicoloured 30 20
627 10p. multicoloured . . . 45 30

117 Wood Carvings **118** Ernst Udet

1980. Handicrafts. Multicoloured.
628 3p. Type **117** 20 10
629 6p. Weaving (horiz) 30 20
630 20p. Bust and statuette (horiz) . . . . 1·00 50

1980. History of Aviation. Air Aces of 1st World War. Multicoloured.
631 3p.50 Type **118** (postage) . . 25 15
632 5p. Charles Nungesser . . . 35 25
633 6p. Manfred von Richthofen 55 25
634 30p. Francesco Baracca . . . 1·75 70
635 35p. Willy Coppens de Houthulst (air) . . . . . . 2·10 75
636 40p. Charles Guynemer . . . 2·50 90

119 Speed Skating

1980. Winter Olympic Games, Lake Placid. Multicoloured.
638 3p. Type **119** (postage) . . . 20 10
639 5p. Downhill 30 20
640 6p. Luge 40 25
641 30p. Cross country skiing . . 1·75 70
642 35p. Downhill skiing (air) . . 2·00 75
643 40p. Figure skating . . . . . 2·40 90

120 Putting the Shot

1980. Olympic Games, Moscow. Multicoloured.
645 3p.50 Type **120** (postage) . . 20 15
646 5p. Gymnastics (ring exercise) 25 20
647 6p. Long jump 35 25
648 30p. Fencing . . . . 1·50 70
649 35p. Gymnastics (backward somersault) (air) . . . . . 1·75 75
650 40p. Running . . . . 2·00 90

121 Congress Meeting

1980. 16th Anniv of Cassaca Congress.
652 **121** 3p.50 multicoloured . . . 15 10
653 6p.50 multicoloured . . . 30 20
654 10p. multicoloured . . . 40 30

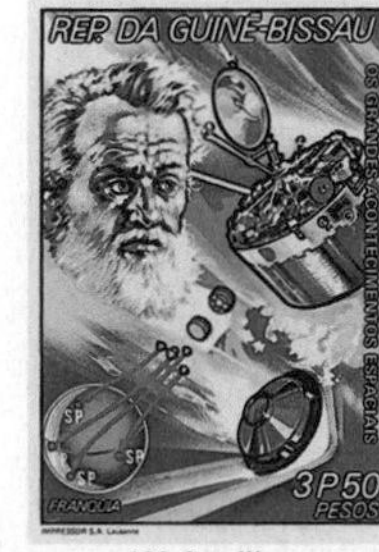

122 Satellites

1981. Space Achievements. Multicoloured.
655 3p.50 Type **122** (postage) . . 20 10
656 5p. Satellite 25 15
657 6p. Rocket 30 15
658 30p. Space Shuttle "Columbia" . . . . 1·75 95
659 35p. "Viking I" (air) . . . . 1·75 75
660 40p. U.S.–Soviet space link 2·00 90

123 Platini (France) and Football Scene

1981. World Cup Football Championship, Spain. Multicoloured.
662 3p.50 Type **123** (postage) . . 30 10
663 5p. Bettega (Italy) 35 15
664 6p. Rensenbrink (Netherlands) 40 15
665 30p. Rivelino (Brazil) . . . . 1·90 80
666 35p. Rummenigge (West Germany) (air) . . . . . 1·90 80
667 40p. Kempes (Argentina) . . 2·00 90

124 Lady Diana Spencer with Horse

1981. Wedding of Prince of Wales. Multicoloured.
669 3p.50 Type **124** (postage) . . 20 15
670 5p. Investiture of Prince of Wales 25 15
671 6p. Lady Diana Spencer with Children 30 15
672 30p. St. Paul's Cathedral . . 1·25 95
673 35p. Althorp House (air) . . 1·40 1·00
674 40p. Arms of Prince of Wales 1·50 1·25

125 Eric the Red and Viking Ship

1981. Navigators. Multicoloured.
676 3p.50 Type **125** (postage) . . 25 15
677 5p. Vasco da Gama and "Sao Gabriel" 30 15
678 6p. Magellan and "Vitoria" 35 20
679 30p. Cartier and "Emerillon" 2·00 1·00
680 35p. Drake and "Golden Hind" (air) . . . . 2·50 1·25
681 40p. Cook and H.M.S. "Endeavour" . . . . . . 2·75 1·60

126 "Girl with Bare Feet"

1981. Birth Centenary of Pablo Picasso. Multicoloured.

683 3p.50 Type **126** (postage) . . 20 15
684 5p. "Acrobat on Ball" . . . 25 15
685 6p. "Pierrot" 30 15
686 30p. "Girl in front of a Mirror" . . . . 1·50 95
687 35p. "The First Steps" (air) 2·00 1·00
688 40p. "Woman in Turkish Dress" . . . . 2·25 1·25

127 "Retable of St. Zeno" (Mantegna)

1981. Christmas. Multicoloured.

690 3p.50 Type **127** (postage) . . 20 15
691 5p. "Virgin with Child" (Bellini) 25 15
692 6p. "Virgin and Child with Cherubs" (Mantegna) . . . 30 15
693 25p. "Madonna Campori" (Correggio) . . . . 1·50 1·00
694 30p. "Virgin and Child" (Memling) (air) . . . . . 2·00 1·10
695 35p. "Virgin and Child" (Bellini) . . . . 2·25 1·25

128 Archery

1982. 75th Anniv of Boy Scout Movement. Multicoloured.

697 3p.50 Type **128** (postage) . . 15 10
698 5p. First aid 20 15
699 6p. Bugler 25 15
700 30p. Cub scouts . . . . . . 1·60 80
701 35p. Girl scout in canoe (air) 2·25 90
702 40p. Scouts with model aircraft . . . . 2·40 1·25

129 Keegan

1982. World Cup Football Championship, Spain. Multicoloured.

704 3p.50 Type **129** (postage) . . 20 10
705 5p. Rossi 20 15
706 6p. Zico 25 15
707 30p. Arconada . . . . 1·60 80
708 35p. Kempes (air) . . . . . 2·25 1·00
709 40p. Kaltz . . . . 2·50 1·10

130 Lady Diana Spencer

1982. 21st Birthday of Princess of Wales. Multicoloured.

711 3p.50 Type **130** (postage) . . 15 10
712 5p. Playing croquet 25 15
713 6p. Lady Diana with pony 30 15
714 30p. Fishing . . . . 1·75 80
715 35p. Engagement picture (air) 1·90 90
716 40p. Honeymoon picture . . 2·00 1·10

1982. Birth of Prince William of Wales. Nos. 711/16 optd **21 DE JULHO 1982. GUILHERMO ARTHUR FILIPE LUIS PRINCIPE DE GALES**.

718 3p.50 multicoloured (postage) 20 10
719 5p. multicoloured 25 15
720 6p. multicoloured 30 15
721 30p. multicoloured . . . . . 1·60 95
722 35p. multicoloured (air) . . . 1·90 1·10
723 40p. multicoloured . . . . . 2·00 1·25

132 National Colours

1982. Visit of President Eanes of Portugal. Multicoloured.

725 4p.50 Type **132** 10 10
726 20p. Doves on national colours 20 10

133 Montgolfier Balloon

1983. Bicentenary of Manned Flight. Mult.

727 50c. Type **133** 10 10
728 2p.50 Charles's hydrogen balloon 15 10
729 3p.50 Charles Green's balloon "Royal Vauxhall" 20 10
730 5p. Gaston Tissandier's balloon "Zenith" 30 10
731 10p. Salomon Andree's balloon "Ornen" over Arctic 60 20
732 20p. Stratosphere balloon "Explorer II" . . . . . . 1·25 40
733 30p. Modern hot-air balloons 2·00 60

134 Hamadryas Baboon **136** Satellite

1983. African Primates. Multicoloured.

735 1p. Type **134** 10 10
736 1p.50 Gorilla 20 10
737 3p.50 Gelada 30 10
738 5p. Mandrill 40 15
739 8p. Chimpanzee 80 20
740 20p. Eastern black-and-white colobus . . . . 1·50 50
741 30p. Diana monkey . . . . 2·40 85

1983. Cosmonautics Day. Multicoloured.

743 1p. Type **136** 10 10
744 1p.50 Satellite (different) . . 15 10
745 3p.50 Rocket carrying space shuttle 20 10
746 5p. Satellite (different) . . . 30 15
747 8p. Satellite (different) . . . 60 20
748 20p. Satellite (different) . . . 1·25 45
749 30p. "Soyuz" docking with "Salyut" . . . . 2·00 70

137 Woodcut from Caxton's "Game and Playe of Chesse", Arabian Pawn and Rook

1983. Chess. Multicoloured.

751 1p. Type **137** 15 10
752 1p.50 12th-century European king and knight 15 10
753 3p.50 Mid 18th-century German rook, queen and king 25 10
754 5p. Late 12th/early 13th-century Danish bishop and knight 40 10
755 10p. 18th-century French king and queen 80 25
756 20p. 18th-century Venetian king, knight and queen . . 1·75 55
757 40p. 19th-century faience knight, queen and rook . . 3·00 1·10

138 "Vision of Ezekiel"

1983. 500th Birth Anniv of Raphael (artist). Multicoloured.

759 1p. Type **138** 10 10
760 1p.50 "Tempi Madonna" . . 10 10
761 3p.50 "Della Tenda Madonna" 20 10
762 5p. "Orleans Madonna" . . 25 10
763 8p. "La Belle Jardiniere" . . 45 20
764 15p. "Small Cowper Madonna" 90 35
765 30p. "St. George and the Dragon" . . . . 2·00 60

139 Swimming

1983. Olympic Games, Los Angeles (1932 and 1984) (1st issue). Multicoloured.

767 1p. Type **139** 10 10
768 1p.50 Hurdling 15 10
769 3p.50 Fencing 20 10
770 5p. Weightlifting 30 10
771 10p. Marathon 60 15
772 20p. Show jumping . . . . . 1·10 35
773 40p. Cycling . . . . 2·40 65

See also Nos. 843/9.

141 Rowland Hill and Penny Black

1983. World Communications Year. Mult.

776 50c. Type **141** 10 10
777 2p.50 Samuel Morse and morse machine 15 10
778 3p.50 Heinrich Rudolf Hertz and electromagnetic wave diagrams 20 10
779 5p. Lord Kelvin and "Agamemnon" (cable ship) 50 10
780 10p. Alexander Graham Bell and telephones 60 15
781 20p. Guglielmo Marconi and wireless apparatus . . . . 1·40 40
782 30p. Vladimir Kosma Zworykin and television . . 1·60 55

142 JAAC Emblem

1983. First JAAC Congress. Multicoloured.

784 4p. Crowd and emblem . . . 25 15
785 5p. Type **142** 30 15

143 Speed Skating **145** U.D.E.M.U. Emblem

144 Hoeing Vegetable Patch

1983. Winter Olympic Games, Sarajevo (1st issue). Multicoloured.

786 1p. Type **143** 10 10
787 1p.50 Ski jumping 15 10
788 3p. Cross-country skiing . . 20 10
789 5p. Bobsleigh 25 10
790 10p. Ice hockey 70 25
791 15p. Ice skating . . . . . . 1·10 30
792 20p. Luge . . . . 1·25 35

See also Nos. 816/22.

1983. World Food Day.

794 **144** 1p.50 multicoloured . . . 10 10
795 2p. multicoloured 15 10
796 4p. multicoloured 30 15

1983. Democratic Union of Women. Multicoloured.

798 4p.50 Type **145** 30 15
799 7p.50 Flag and woman . . . 50 20
800 9p. Woman sewing 70 30
801 12p. Women working on plantation . . . . 1·00 45

146 "Canna coccinea" **147** Guinean Fingerfish

1983. Flowers. Multicoloured.

802 1p. Type **146** 15 10
803 1p.50 "Bouganville litoralis" 20 10
804 3p.50 "Euphorbia milii" . . 25 10
805 5p. "Delonix regia" 30 10
806 8p. "Bauhinia variegata" . . 50 15
807 10p. "Spathodea campanulata" 70 20
808 30p. "Hibiscus rosa-sinensis" 2·00 60

1983. Fishes. Multicoloured.

809 1p. Type **147** 20 15
810 1p.50 Clown loach 25 15
811 3p.50 Spotted climbing-perch 35 20
812 5p. Berthold's panchax . . . 50 20
813 8p. Red-barred lyretail . . . 75 30
814 10p. Two-striped lyretail . . 1·10 40
815 30p. Lyre-tailed panchax . . 3·50 1·40

148 Ski Jumping

1984. Winter Olympic Games, Sarajevo (2nd issue). Multicoloured.

816	50c. Type **148**	10	10
817	2p.50 Speed skating	15	10
818	3p.50 Ice hockey	30	10
819	5p. Cross-country skiing	35	10
820	6p. Downhill skiing	60	15
821	20p. Ice skating	1·25	40
822	30p. Two-man bobsleigh	2·00	60

149 Duesenberg, 1928

1984. 150th Birth Anniv of Gottlieb Daimler (automobile designer). Multicoloured.

824	5p. Type **149**	15	10
825	8p. MG "Midget", 1932	25	10
826	15p. Mercedes, 1928	50	20
827	20p. Bentley, 1928	60	30
828	24p. Alfa Romeo, 1929	85	30
829	30p. Datsun, 1932	1·25	35
830	35p. Lincoln, 1932	1·75	40

150 Sud Aviation Caravelle

1984. 40th Anniv of I.C.A.O. Multicoloured.

832	8p. Type **150**	25	10
833	22p. Douglas DC-6B	80	30
834	80p. Ilyushin Il-76	2·25	90

151 "Dona Tadea Arias de Enriquez" (Goya)

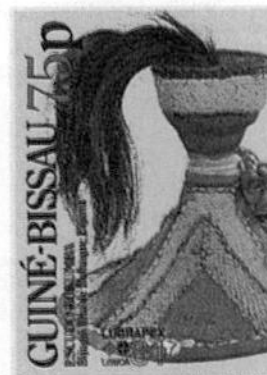

153 Fabric Headdress

152 Football

1984. "Espana 84" International Stamp Exhibition, Madrid. Multicoloured.

835	3p. "Virgin and Child" (Morales)	15	10
836	6p. Type **151**	20	10
837	10p. "Saint Cassilda" (Zurbaran)	30	10
838	12p. "Saints Andrew and Francis" (El Greco)	35	15
839	15p. "Infanta Isabel Clara Eugenia" (Coello)	55	15
840	35p. "Queen Maria of Austria" (Velazquez)	1·40	45
841	40p. "The Trinity" (El Greco)	1·75	55

1984. Olympic Games, Los Angeles (2nd issue). Multicoloured.

843	6p. Type **152**	15	10
844	8p. Show jumping	25	10
845	15p. Sailing	50	15
846	20p. Hockey	70	20
847	22p. Handball	75	20
848	30p. Canoeing	1·10	35
849	40p. Boxing	1·75	60

1984. "Lubrapex 84" Portuguese–Brazilian Stamp Exhibition, Lisbon. Multicoloured.

851	7p.50 Type **153**	25	15
852	7p.50 Headdress	25	15
853	7p.50 Carved bird headdress	25	15
854	7p.50 Wooden mask	25	15
855	7p.50 Carving of horse	25	15
856	7p.50 Statuette	25	15

154 Tiger

1984. Wild Cats. Multicoloured.

857	3p. Type **154**	15	10
858	6p. Lions	25	10
859	10p. Clouded leopard	35	15
860	12p. Cheetahs	45	20
861	15p. Lynx	60	25
862	35p. Leopard	1·40	55
863	40p. Snow leopard	1·75	65

155 Pearl Throne, Cameroun

156 Amilcar Cabral making Speech

1984. World Heritage. Multicoloured.

864	3p. Type **155**	10	10
865	6p. Antelope (carving), West Sudan	20	10
866	10p. Setial, East Africa	30	15
867	12p. Mask, West African coast	40	20
868	15p. Leopard (statuette), Guinea coast	60	25
869	35p. Carved statuette of woman, Zaire	1·25	50
870	40p. Funeral figures, South-east Africa and Madagascar	1·25	55

1984. 60th Birth Anniv of Amilcar Cabral. Multicoloured.

871	5p. Type **156**	15	10
872	12p. Amilcar Cabral in combat dress	35	15
873	20p. Amilcar Cabral memorial	60	25
874	50p. Amilcar Cabral mausoleum	1·50	60

157 Mechanic working on Engine

1984. 11th Anniv of Independence. Mult.

875	3p. Type **157**	10	10
876	6p. Children in school	20	10
877	10p. Laying bricks	30	10
878	12p. Doctor tending child (vert)	35	20
879	15p. Sewing (vert)	40	20
880	35p. Telephonist and switchboard	1·25	50
881	40p. P.A.I.G.C. headquarters	1·25	55

158 Grey Whales

1984. Whales. Multicoloured.

882	5p. Type **158**	25	10
883	8p. Blue whales	30	15
884	15p. Bottle-nosed dolphins	60	25
885	20p. Sperm whale	70	25
886	24p. Killer whale	85	35
887	30p. Bowhead whale	1·50	40
888	35p. Sei whale	1·75	45

159 "Hypolimnas dexithea"

1984. Butterflies and Moths. Multicoloured.

889	3p. Type **159**	15	15
890	6p. "Papilio arcturus"	20	15
891	10p. "Morpho menelaus terrestris"	35	15
892	12p. "Apaturina erminea"	45	20
893	15p. "Prepona praeneste"	70	25
894	35p. "Ornithoptera paradisea"	1·60	55
895	40p. "Morpho hecuba obidona"	1·60	60

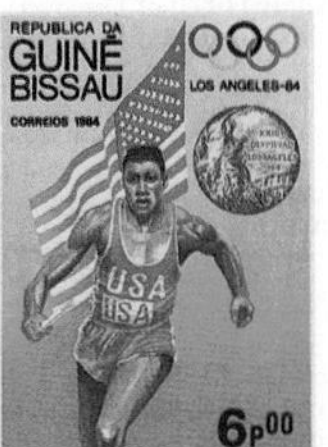

160 Carl Lewis (400 m relay)

1984. Olympic Gold Medallists, Los Angeles. Multicoloured.

896	6p. Type **160**	15	10
897	8p. Koji Gushiken (men's gymnastics)	15	10
898	15p. Dr. Reiner Klimke (individual dressage)	45	20
899	20p. Tracie Ruiz (synchronized swimming)	55	20
900	22p. May Lou Retton (women's gymnastics)	65	25
901	30p. Michael Gross (100 m freestyle and 100 m butterfly)	90	35
902	40p. Edwin Moses (400 m hurdles)	1·25	50

161 White Mountain Central Railway locomotive, 1926, U.S.A.

1984. Locomotives. Multicoloured.

904	5p. Type **161**	20	15
905	8p. Talyllyn Mountain Railway locomotive No. 86, 1886, Great Britain	25	15
906	15p. Wuppetal Overhead Railway, 1901, Germany	50	20
907	20p. Peruvian mountain rack railway locomotive	60	25
908	24p. Steam locomotive, Achensee rack railway, Austria	80	30
909	30p. Vitznau–Rigi rack railway locomotive, Switzerland	1·10	40
910	35p. Vitznau–Rigi rack railway locomotive No. 7, Switzerland	1·60	60

162 Harley Davidson Motor Cycle

1985. Centenary of Motor Cycle. Mult.

912	5p. Type **162**	20	15
913	8p. Kawasaki	25	15
914	15p. Honda	45	20
915	20p. Yamaha	70	30
916	25p. Suzuki	1·00	35
917	30p. BMW	1·40	45
918	35p. Moto Guzzi	1·50	50

163 Brown Pelican

164 "Clitocybe gibba"

1985. Air. Birth Bicentenary of John J. Audubon (ornithologist). Multicoloured.

920	5p. Type **163**	45	20
921	10p. American white pelican	75	30
922	20p. Great blue heron	1·40	45
923	40p. Greater flamingo	3·00	1·00

1985. Fungi. Multicoloured.

924	7p. Type **164**	35	15
925	9p. "Morchella elata"	50	20
926	12p. "Lepista nuda"	75	25
927	20p. "Lactarius deliciosus"	90	30
928	30p. "Russula virescens"	1·25	35
929	35p. "Chroogomphus rutilus"	1·75	50

165 Dunant, Piper Twin Commanche and Volunteers attending Patient

1985. 75th Death Anniv of Henri Dunant (Red Cross founder). Multicoloured.

930	20p. Type **165**	40	15
931	25p. Doctor and volunteer putting patient in ambulance	50	15
932	40p. Helicopter team attending wounded soldier	75	35
933	80p. Volunteers in boat rescuing man from water	1·40	55

166 Long-haired White Cat

167 Vincenzo Bellini, 1820 Harp and 16th-century Descant Viol

1985. Cats. Multicoloured.

934	7p. Type **166**	20	15
935	10p. Siamese cat	25	15
936	12p. Grey cat	30	15
937	15p. Tortoiseshell cat	40	15
938	20p. Ginger cat	55	20
939	40p. Tabby cat	1·00	35
940	45p. Short-haired white cat	1·40	35

1985. International Music Year. Composers. Multicoloured.

942	4p. Type **167** (150th death anniv of Bellini)	15	15
943	5p. Robert Schumann (175th birth anniv) and pyramid piano, 1829	15	15
944	7p. Frederic Chopin (175th birth anniv) and piano, 1817	15	15
945	12p. Luigi Cherubini (225th birth anniv), 1720 baryton and 18th-century quinton	20	15
946	20p. Giovanni Battista Pergolesi (275th birth anniv) and harpsichord, 1734	45	15
947	30p. Georg Friedrich Handel (300th birth anniv), 1825 valve trumpet and 18th-century timpani	65	20
948	50p. Heinrich Schutz (400th birth anniv), 17th-century bass viol and 1680 oboe	1·00	45

168 "Santa Maria"   **169** U.N. Emblem, Rainbow and Peace Doves

1985. Sailing Ships. Multicoloured.
950 8p. Type **168** 30 15
951 15p. 16th-century Dutch carrack 40 15
952 20p. "Mayflower" 50 15
953 30p. "St. Louis" (French galleon) 75 20
954 35p. "Royal Sovereign" (galleon), 1660 . . . . . . 85 20
955 45p. "Soleil Royal" (17th-century French warship) 1·25 35
956 80p. 18th-century British naval brig . . . . 1·90 60

1985. 40th Anniv of U.N.O.
957 **169** 10p. multicoloured . . . 25 15
958 – 20p. blue and brown . . . 50 35
DESIGN: 20p. U.N. emblem in "40".

170 "Madonna of the Rose Garden" (detail)

1985. "Italia '85" International Stamp Exhibition, Rome. Paintings by Botticelli. Multicoloured.
959 7p. Type **170** 15 10
960 10p. "Venus and Mars" (detail) 15 10
961 12p. "St. Augustine in his Study" (detail) 20 15
962 15p. "Spring" (detail) 25 15
963 20p. "Virgin and Child" (detail) 35 15
964 40p. "Virgin and Child with St. John" (detail) . . . . . 1·00 30
965 45p. "Birth of Venus" (detail) 1·10 35

171 Youths dancing

1985. International Youth Year. Mult.
967 7p. Type **171** 10 10
968 13p. Windsurfing 20 15
969 15p. Roller skating 20 15
970 25p. Hang-gliding 35 15
971 40p. Surfing 55 25
972 50p. Skateboarding 75 40
973 80p. Free-falling from airplane . . . . 1·50 60

172 Alfa Touring Car

1986. Anniversaries and Events. Mult.
975 15p. Tail of comet . . . . 1·25 50
976 15p. Head of comet . . . . 1·25 50
977 15p. Type **172** . . . . . . 1·25 50
978 15p. Frankfurt am Main railway station, 1914 . . . 2·25 75
979 15p. Top of trophy . . . . 2·50 1·00
980 15p. Base of trophy . . . . 2·50 1·00
981 15p. Olympic rings . . . . 3·00 1·00
982 15p. View of Barcelona . . . 3·00 1·00
983 15p. Part of space station . . 1·25 50
984 15p. Deflectors . . . . . . 1·25 50
985 15p. Space station and Shuttle . . . . 1·25 50
986 15p. Part of space station and Earth . . . . 1·25 50
987 15p. Boris Becker's head and arm . . . . 1·50 75
988 15p. Becker's body . . . . . 1·50 75
989 15p. Lendl's head and arms 1·50 75
990 15p. Lendl's body and legs 1·50 75

ANNIVERSARIES: Nos. 975/6, Appearance of Halley's Comet; 977, Centenary of motor car; 978, 150th anniv of German railways; 979/80, World Cup Football Championship, Mexico; 981, Olympic Games, Seoul (1988); 982, "500th anniv of discovery of America by Columbus" Exhibition and Olympic Games, Barcelona (1992); 983/6, 25 years of manned space flights; 987/8, Wimbledon Men's Singles champion, 1986; 989/90, Ivan Lendl, winner of U.S. Masters Tournament, 1986.

Nos. 975/90 were printed together in se-tenant sheetlets of 16 stamps, stamps for the same event forming a composite design.

173 "Santa Maria"

1987. 500th Anniv (1992) of Discovery of America by Columbus. Multicoloured.
992 50p. Type **173** . . . . . . 2·25 80
993 50p. View of Seville . . . . 2·25 80
994 50p. Pedro Alvares Cabral disembarking at Bahia . . 2·00 60
995 50p. View of Seville (different) . . . . 2·25 80

1987. Nos. 352/5, 359 and 362/3 of Portuguese Guinea surch **DA BISSAU** and new value.
997 100p. on 20c. Type **51** . . . 35 15
998 200p. on 35c. African rock python 70 25
999 300p. on 70c. Boomslang . . 1·10 35
1000 400p. on 80c. West African mamba . . . . 1·25 40
1001 500p. on 3e.50 Brown house snake . . . . 1·50 50
1002 1000p. on 15e. Striped beauty snake . . . . . . 3·00 1·00
1003 2000p. on 20e. African egg-eating snake (horiz) . . . 6·00 3·00

1987. No. 430 surch **2500,00.**
1004 **76** 2500p. on 2e. mult . . . 7·00 3·25

176 Ice Dancing

1988. Winter Olympic Games, Calgary. Mult.
1005 5p. Type **176** 10 10
1006 10p. Luge 10 10
1007 50p. Skiing 30 15
1008 200p. Downhill skiing . . . 75 30
1009 300p. Ski-bobbing . . . . . 1·25 40
1010 500p. Ski jumping (vert) . . 2·00 55
1011 800p. Speed skating (vert) . . 3·00 1·10

177 Yachting   **178** Football

1988. Olympic Games, Seoul. Multicoloured.
1013 5p. Type **177** 10 10
1014 10p. Equestrian events (horiz) 10 10
1015 50p. High jumping (horiz) 15 10
1016 200p. Rifle shooting (horiz) 70 30
1017 300p. Triple jumping . . . 1·10 40
1018 500p. Tennis . . . . 2·00 50
1019 800p. Archery . . . . . . 2·75 1·00

1988. "Essen 88" Stamp Fair and European Football Championship, Germany.
1021 **178** 5p. multicoloured . . . 10 10
1022 – 10p. multicoloured . . . 10 10
1023 – 50p. multicoloured . . . 15 10
1024 – 200p. multicoloured . . 70 30
1025 – 300p. multicoloured . . 1·10 40
1026 – 500p. multicoloured . . 2·00 50
1027 – 800p. multicoloured . . 2·75 1·10
DESIGNS: 10 to 800p. Various footballing scenes.

179 Lioness

1988. Animals. Multicoloured.
1029 5p. Type **179** 10 10
1030 10p. Ferruginous pygmy owl 10 10
1031 50p. Hoopoe (horiz) 25 10
1032 200p. Common zebra (horiz) 30 10
1033 300p. African elephant . . . 50 20
1034 500p. Vulturine guineafowl 3·00 1·25
1035 800p. Black rhinoceros . . . 1·25 50

180 Machel

1988. 2nd Death Anniv of Pres. Samora Machel of Mozambique. Multicoloured.
1036 10p. Type **180** 10 10
1037 50p. With arm raised . . . 10 10
1038 200p. With soldier 30 10
1039 300p. Wearing suit 50 20

181 Henry Dunant (founder)

1988. 125th Anniv of Int Red Cross. Mult.
1040 10p. Type **181** 10 10
1041 50p. Dr. T. Maunoir . . . 10 10
1042 200p. Dr. Louis Appia . . . 30 10
1043 800p. Gustave Moynier . . 1·25 50

182 Basset Hound

1988. Dogs. Multicoloured.
1044 5p. Type **182** 10 10
1045 10p. Grand bleu de Gascogne 10 10
1046 50p. Italian spinone 10 10
1047 200p. Yorkshire terrier . . . 30 10
1048 300p. Munsterlander 50 20
1049 500p. Pointer 80 30
1050 800p. German shorthaired pointer . . . . 1·25 50

183 Egyptian Ship, 3300 B.C.

1988. Sailing Ships. Multicoloured.
1052 5p. Type **183** 10 10
1053 10p. Ship of Sahu Re, 2500 B.C. (wrongly inscr "2700 B.C.") 10 10
1054 50p. Ship of Hatshepshut, 1500 B.C 10 10
1055 200p. Ship of Rameses III, 1200 B.C 35 10
1056 300p. Greek trireme, 480 B.C 60 25
1057 500p. Etruscan bireme, 600 B.C . . . . 1·00 40
1058 800p. 12th-century Venetian galley . . . . 1·50 65

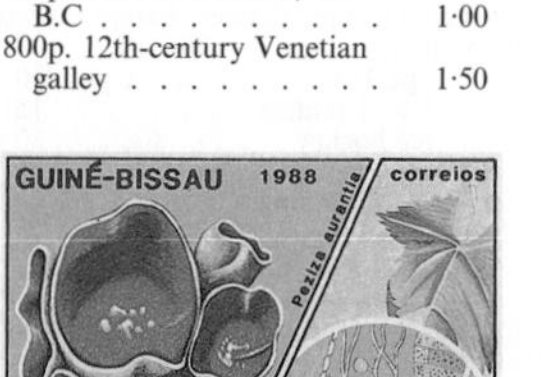

184 "Peziza aurantia"

1988. Fungi. Multicoloured.
1059 370p. Type **184** 75 30
1060 470p. Morel . . . . 1·00 35
1061 600p. Caesar's mushroom 1·25 45
1062 780p. Fly agaric . . . . . 1·60 55
1063 800p. Deadly amanite . . . 1·60 55
1064 900p. Cultivated mushroom 1·90 70
1065 945p. Pixie stool . . . . . 2·10 75

185 Francois-Andre Philidor and Rook   **186** Trumpeter, Flag Bearer and Drummer

1988. "Finlandia 88" International Stamp Exhibition, Helsinki. Chess. Multicoloured.
1066 5p. Type **185** 10 10
1067 10p. Howard Staunton and chessmen 10 10
1068 50p. Adolf Anderssen and queen 10 10
1069 200p. Paul Morphy and pawn 30 10
1070 300p. Wilhelm Steinitz and knight 50 20
1071 500p. Emanuel Lasker and bishop 80 30
1072 800p. Jose Capablanca and king . . . . 1·25 50

1988. Abel Djassi Pioneers Organisation. Multicoloured.
1074 10p. Type **186** 10 10
1075 50p. Girls saluting 10 10
1076 200p. Drawing on floor (horiz) 30 10
1077 300p. Playing ball (horiz) . . 50 20

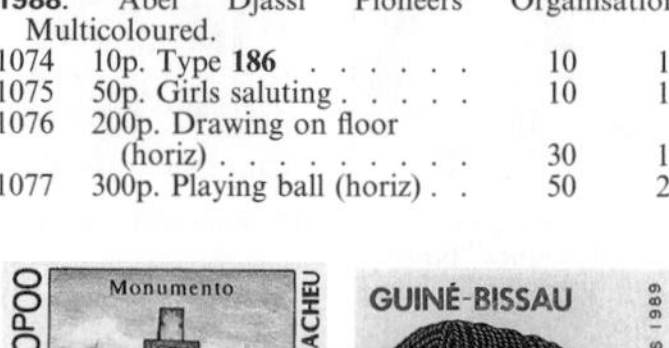

187 Monument   **188** Woman with Long Hair

1988. 400th Anniv of Cacheu. Multicoloured.
1078 10p. Type **187** 10 10
1079 50p. Fort (horiz) 10 10
1080 200p. Early building (horiz) 35 10
1081 300p. Church (horiz) . . . 50 20

1989. Traditional Hairstyles.
1082 **188** 50p. multicoloured . . . 10 10
1083 – 100p. multicoloured . . 15 10
1084 – 200p. multicoloured . . 30 10
1085 – 350p. multicoloured . . 60 25
1086 – 500p. multicoloured . . 80 30
1087 – 800p. multicoloured . . 1·25 50
1088 – 1000p. multicoloured . . 1·60 65
DESIGNS: 100p. to 1000p. Different hairstyles.

189 Bombalon

1989. Traditional Musical Instruments. Mult.
1089 50p. Type **189** 10 10
1090 100p. Flute 15 10
1091 200p. Tambor 35 15
1092 350p. Dondon 65 25
1093 500p. Balafon 90 35

1094 800p. Kora . . . . 1·50 60
1095 1000p. Nhanhero . . . . . 1·75 70

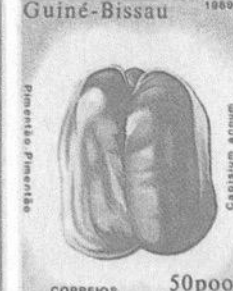

190 Seychelles Blue Pigeon **191** Pimento

1989. Birds. Multicoloured.
1096 50p. Type **190** 15 15
1097 100p. Laughing dove . . . 20 15
1098 200p. Namaqua dove . . . 50 30
1099 350p. Purple-breasted ground dove 80 50
1100 500p. African collared dove 1·25 70
1101 800p. Pheasant pigeon . . . 2·10 1·25
1102 1000p. Emerald dove . . . 2·75 1·40

1989. Plants.
1104 **191** 50p. blue 10 10
1105 – 100p. violet 15 10
1106 – 200p. green 35 15
1107 – 350p. red 65 25
1108 – 500p. brown 90 35
1109 – 800p. brown . . . . . . 1·50 60
1110 – 1000p. green . . . . . . 1·75 70
DESIGNS: 100p. Solanum; 200p. "Curcumis peco"; 350p. Tomato; 500p. "Solanum itiopium"; 800p. "Hibiscus esculentus"; 1000p. Baguiche.

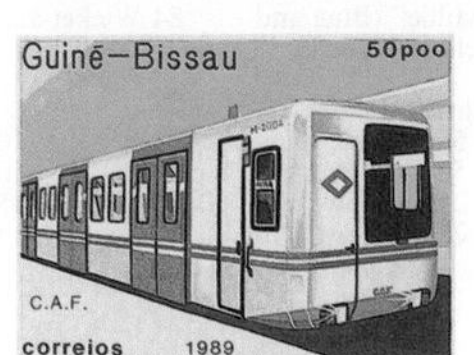

192 Madrid Rapid Transit Train No. M-2004, Spain

1989. Trains. Multicoloured.
1111 50p. Type **192** 15 10
1112 100p. Class TEM-2 diesel locomotive, Russia . . . 20 10
1113 200p. Diesel locomotive, Brazil 50 15
1114 350p. Diesel railcar, Spain 95 25
1115 500p. Type 55E electric locomotive, Czechoslovakia . . . . . 1·40 35
1116 800p. Class Tu-7E diesel shunting locomotive, Russia . . . . 2·25 60
1117 1000p. Electric multiple unit, Spain (68 × 27 mm) . . . 2·60 70

193 Hurdling

1989. Olympic Games, Barcelona (1992) (1st issue). Multicoloured.
1119 50p. Type **193** 10 10
1120 100p. Boxing 20 10
1121 200p. High jumping 35 15
1122 350p. Sprinters in starting blocks 60 25
1123 500p. Runner leaving starting block 90 35
1124 800p. Gymnastics . . . . . 1·50 60
1125 1000p. Pole vaulting . . . . 1·75 70
See also Nos. 1245/8.

194 "Limelight" **196** Teotihuacan Pot

195 "La Marseillaise" (relief by Rude from Arc de Triomphe)

1989. Lilies. Multicoloured.
1127 50p. Type **194** 10 10
1128 100p. "Lilium candidum" 20 10
1129 200p. "Lilium pardalinum" 35 15
1130 350p. "Lilium auratum" . . 65 25
1131 500p. "Lilium canadense" 90 35
1132 800p. "Enchantment" . . . 1·50 60
1133 1000p. "Black Dragon" . . 1·75 70

1989. "Philex France 89" International Stamp Exhibition, Paris. Multicoloured.
1135 50p. Type **195** 10 10
1136 100p. Champ de Mars . . . 20 10
1137 200p. Storming of the Bastille 35 15
1138 350p. Fete (27 × 44 mm) . . 65 25
1139 500p. Dancing round Tree of Liberty 90 35
1140 800p. Rouget de Lisle singing "The Marseillaise" 1·50 60
1141 1000p. Storming of the Bastille (different) . . . . 1·75 70

1989. "Brasiliana 89" International Stamp Exhibition, Rio de Janeiro. Multicoloured.
1143 50p. Type **196** 10 10
1144 100p. Mochica jar 20 10
1145 200p. Jaina statuette 35 15
1146 350p. Nayarit anthrozoomorphic jug . . 65 25
1147 500p. Inca vase 90 35
1148 800p. Hopewell statuette of mother and child . . . 1·50 60
1149 1000p. Taina mask . . . . 1·75 70

197 Players Tackling

1989. World Cup Football Championship, Italy (1990). Multicoloured.
1151 50p. Type **197** 10 10
1152 100p. Players and ball . . . 20 10
1153 200p. Players and ball (different) 35 15
1154 350p. "Scissors" kick . . . 65 25
1155 500p. Goalkeeper 90 35
1156 800p. Foul . . . . 1·50 60
1157 1000p. Player scoring goal 1·75 70

198 Trachodon

1989. Prehistoric Animals. Multicoloured.
1159 50p. Type **198** 10 10
1160 100p. Edaphosaurus (68 × 22 mm) 20 10
1161 200p. Mesosaurus 35 15
1162 350p. "Elephas primigenius" 65 25
1163 500p. Tyrannosaurus (horiz) 90 35
1164 800p. Stegosaurus (horiz) . . 1·50 60
1165 1000p. "Cervus megaceros" 1·75 70
No. 1162 is inscribed "Elephius primigenius" in error.

199 Speed Skating

1989. Winter Olympic Games, Albertville (1992). Multicoloured.
1166 50p. Type **199** 10 10
1167 100p. Figure skating 20 10
1168 200p. Ski jumping 35 15
1169 350p. Skiing 65 25
1170 500p. Skiing (different) . . . 90 35
1171 800p. Bobsleighing . . . . 1·50 60
1172 1000p. Ice hockey . . . . . 1·75 70

200 African Buffalo **201** "Adoration of Baby Jesus" (Fra Filippo Lippi)

1989. Animals.
1174 **200** 50p. brown and red . . 10 10
1175 – 100p. ultramarine & blue 20 10
1176 – 200p. green & light green 35 15
1177 – 350p. purple and lilac . . 65 25
1178 – 500p. chestnut and brown 90 35
1179 – 800p. violet & deep violet . . . . 1·50 60
1180 – 1000p. deep red and red 1·75 70
1181 – 1500p. red and yellow 2·75 1·10
DESIGNS: 100p. Steppe zebra; 200p. Black rhinoceros; 350p. Okapi; 500p. Rhesus macacque; 800p. Hippopotamus; 1000p. Cheetah; 1500p. Lion.

1989. Christmas. Multicoloured.
1182 50p. Type **201** 10 10
1183 100p. "Adoration of the Kings" (Pieter Brueghel) 20 10
1184 200p. "Adoration of the Kings" (Jan Mostaert) . . 35 15
1185 350p. "Nativity" (Albert Durer) 65 25
1186 500p. "Adoration of the Kings" (Peter Paul Rubens) 90 35
1187 800p. "Adoration of the Kings" (Roger van der Weyden) . . . . 1·50 60
1188 1000p. "Adoration of the Kings" (Francesco Francia) (horiz) . . . . . 1·75 70

202 Pope John-Paul II and Map **204** Cockerel and Hen

1990. Papal Visit. Multicoloured.
1189 500p. Type **202** 80 20
1190 1000p. Pope and couple . . 1·60 40

1990. "Lubrapex 90" Brazilian–Portuguese Stamp Exhibition, Brasilia. Coop Fowls. Multicoloured.
1193 500p. Type **204** 85 35
1194 800p. Common turkey . . . 1·25 50
1195 1000p. Duck and ducklings 1·60 65

205 Radar Rainfall Map

1990. World Meteorology Day. Multicoloured.
1197 1000p. Type **205** . . . . . 1·60 65
1198 3000p. Campbell-Stokes heliograph . . . . 5·00 2·00

206 Crying Man and Baby in Womb **207** Cotton Plant

1990. 40th Anniv of U.N. Development Programme.
1199 **206** 1000p. multicoloured . . 1·60 65

1991. Traditional Cotton Weaving. Mult.
1200 400p. Type **207** 60 25
1201 500p. Weaver 75 30
1202 600p. Traditional cloth pattern 95 40

208 Mickey Mouse

1991. Carnival Masks. Multicoloured.
1204 200p. Type **208** 30 10
1205 300p. Hippopotamus . . . 45 20
1206 600p. Buffalo 75 30
1207 1200p. Buffalo (different) . . 95 40

209 Royal Threadfin

1991. Fishes. Multicoloured.
1208 300p. Type **209** 45 20
1209 400p. Guinean fingerfish . . 95 55
1210 500p. Goree spadefish . . . 1·60 85
1211 600p. Long-finned pompano 2·00 90

210 Fire Engine with Water Cannons **211** Lizard Buzzard

1991. Fire and First Aid Service. Mult.
1212 200p. Type **210** 30 10
1213 500p. Fire engine with ladders 75 30
1214 800p. Emergency vehicle with ladders . . . . . . 1·25 50
1215 1500p. Ambulance . . . . 2·25 90

1991. Birds. Multicoloured.
1216 100p. Type **211** 25 15
1217 250p. Crowned crane . . . 75 15
1218 350p. Abyssinian ground hornbill . . . . 1·10 35
1219 500p. Saddle-bill stork . . . 1·50 40

212 "Best Wishes" **213** Fula

1991. Greetings Stamps. Multicoloured.
1221 250p. Type **212** 40 10
1222 400p. Couple embracing ("With love") 65 25
1223 800p. Horn-blower and map of Africa ("Congratulations") . . . 1·25 50
1224 1000p. Doves ("Season's greetings") . . . . 1·50 60

1992. Traditional Costume. Multicoloured.
1225 400p. Type **213** 10 10
1226 600p. Balanta 15 10
1227 1000p. Fula (different) . . . 25 10
1228 1500p. Manjaco 40 15

214 "Landolfia owariensis" **215** Cigarette and Fruit "Hearts"

1992. Fruits. Multicoloured.
1229 500p. Type **214** 15 10
1230 1500p. "Dialium guineensis" 40 15

1231 2000p. "Adansonia digitata" 50 20
1232 3000p. "Parkia biglobosa" 75 30

1992. World Health Day. "Health in Rhythm with the Heart". Multicoloured.
1233 1500p. Type **215** 40 15
1234 4000p. "Heart" running over food . . . . 1·00 40

216 "Cassia alata"

1992. "Lubrapex 92" Brazilian–Portuguese Stamp Exhibition, Lisbon. Plants. Multicoloured.
1235 100p. Type **216** 10 10
1236 400p. "Perlebia purpurea" 10 10
1237 1000p. "Caesalpinia pulcherrima" 25 15
1238 1500p. "Adenanthera pavonina" 40 15
Nos. 1235/8 were issued together, se-tenant, forming a composite design.

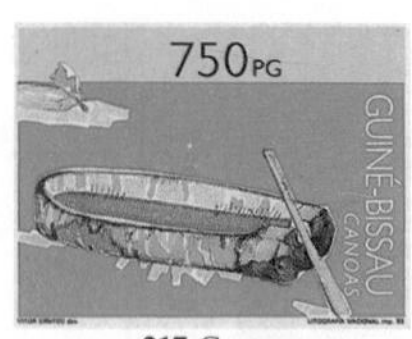

217 Canoe

1992. Canoes. Multicoloured.
1240 750p. Type **217** 35 10
1241 800p. Pirogue 35 10
1242 1000p. Pirogue (different) 45 10
1243 1300p. Skiff 60 20

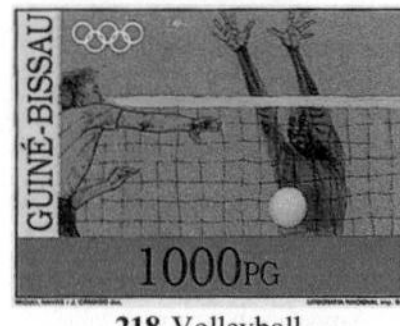

218 Volleyball

1992. Olympic Games, Barcelona (2nd issue). Multicoloured.
1245 600p. Basketball 15 10
1246 1000p. Type **218** 25 10
1247 1500p. Handball 40 15
1248 2000p. Football 50 20

219 "Afzelia africana"

221 Colobus

1992. Forest Preservation. Multicoloured.
1249 1000p. Type **219** 25 10
1250 1500p. African mahogany 40 15
1251 2000p. Iroko 50 20
1252 3000p. Ambila 75 30

1992. The Red Colobus. Multicoloured.
1254 2000p. Type **221** 50 20
1255 2000p. Colobus sitting in tree fork 50 20
1256 2000p. Mother and young 50 20
1257 2000p. Two colobus on tree branch 50 20

222 Puff Adder

1993. Reptiles. Multicoloured.
1258 1500p. Type **222** 40 15
1259 3000p. African dwarf crocodile 80 30
1260 4000p. Nile monitor . . . . 1·10 45
1261 5000p. Rainbow lizard . . . 1·40 55

224 Waterside Village

1993. Tourism. Multicoloured.
1264 1000p. Type **224** 25 10
1265 2000p. Masked villagers on shore and crops 55 20
1266 4000p. Villages on offshore islands . . . . 1·10 45
1267 5000p. Crops on island . . 1·40 55
Nos. 1264/7 were issued together, se-tenant, forming a composite design.

225 Bracelet

1994. Jewellery. Multicoloured.
1268 1500p. Type **225** 40 15
1269 3000p. Tribal mask pendant 80 30
1270 4000p. Circles pendant . . . 1·10 45
1271 5000p. Filigree pendant . . 1·40 55

226 "Erythrina senegalensis"

1994. Medicinal Plants. Multicoloured.
1273 2000p. Type **226** 20 10
1274 3000p. "Cassia occidentalis" 30 10
1275 4000p. "Gardenia ternifolia" 45 20
1276 6000p. "Cochlospermum tinctorium" 65 25

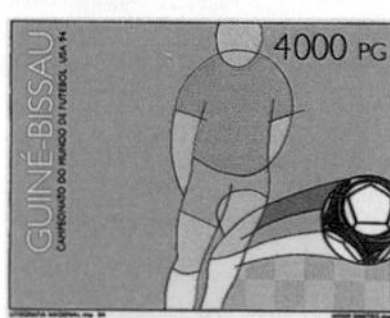

227 Player kicking Ball

1994. World Cup Football Championship, U.S.A. Multicoloured.
1277 4000p. Type **227** 40 15
1278 5000p. Goalkeeper making save 55 20
1279 5500p. Heading the ball . . 60 25
1280 6500p. Dribbling the ball . . 70 30

228 Common Egg-eater (Dasypeltis scabra)

1994. "Philakorea 1994" International and "Singpex '94" Stamp Exhibitions. Snakes. Multicoloured.
1281 5000p. Type **228** 45 20
1282 5000p. Green snake ("Philothamnus sp.") . . 45 20
1283 5000p. Black-lipped cobra ("Naja melanoleuca") . . 45 20
1284 5000p. African python ("Python sebae") 45 20

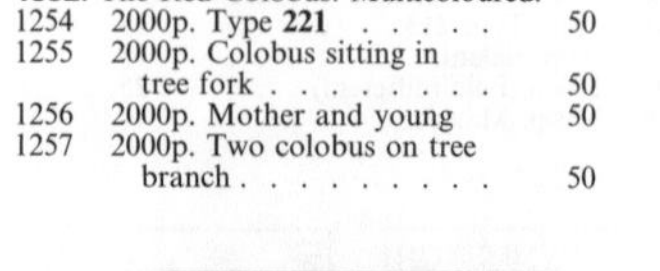

229 Collecting Fruits

231 Hands and Emblem

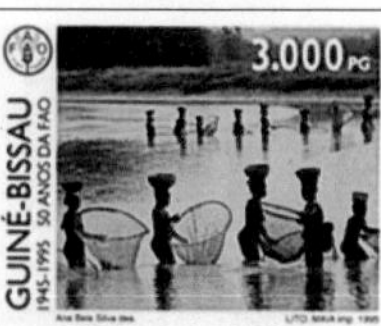

230 Women fishing

1995. Palm Oil. Multicoloured.
1286 3000p. Type **229** 20 10
1287 6500p. Crushing fruit . . . 45 20
1288 7500p. Palm oil production 55 20
1289 8000p. Animals and pot of palm oil 80 35

1995. 50th Anniv of United Nations Food and Agriculture Organization. Multicoloured.
1290 3000p. Type **230** 20 10
1291 6500p. Farmer on tractor 45 10
1292 7500p. Basket of fruit . . . 55 15
1293 8000p. Women and children queuing 60 15

1995. 50th Anniv of United Nations. Multicoloured.
1295 4000p. Type **231** 30 10
1296 5500p. United Nations emblem 40 10
1297 7500p. Guinea-Bissau flag and emblem 55 15
1298 8000p. Hands holding dove and emblem 60 15

GUYANA Pt. 1

Formerly British Guiana. Attained independence on 26 May 1966, and changed its name to Guyana.

100 cents = 1 dollar

CANCELLED REMAINDERS. In 1969 remainders of some issues were put on the market cancelled-to-order in such a way as to be indistinguishable from genuine postally used copies for all practical purposes. Our quotations, which are indicated by an asterisk, are the same for cancelled-to-order or postally used copies.

1966. Nos. 331 etc of British Guiana optd **GUYANA INDEPENDENCE 1966.**
399 **55** 1c. black 10 10
421 – 2c. green 10 10
422 – 3c. green and brown . . . 30 10
400 – 4c. violet 10 10
388 – 5c. red and black 40 10
424 – 6c. green 10 10
401 – 8c. blue 10 10
391 – 12c. black and brown . . . 10 10
435 – 24c. black and orange . . 5·00 10
393 – 36c. red and black 30 30
405 – 48c. blue and red 30 50
395 – 72c. red and green 50 50
396 – $1 multicoloured . . . . 4·00 35
397 – $2 mauve . . . . 1·50 75
398 – $5 blue and black . . . . 1·00 2·25

74 Flag and Map

1966. Independence. Multicoloured.
408 5c. Type **74** 20 10
409 15c. Type **74** 25 10
410 25c. Arms of Guyana 25 10
411 $1 Arms of Guyana . . . . 85 1·25

76 Bank Building

1966. Opening of Bank of Guyana.
412 **76** 5c. multicoloured 10 10
413 25c. multicoloured 10 10

77 British Guiana One Cent Stamp of 1856

1967. World's Rarest Stamp Commemoration.
414 **77** 5c. multicoloured 10 10*
415 25c. multicoloured 10 10*

78 Chateau Margot

1967. 1st Anniv of Independence. Multicoloured.
416 6c. Type **78** 10 10*
417 15c. Independence Arch . . . 10 10*
418 25c. Fort Island (horiz) . . . 10 10*
419 $1 National Assembly (horiz) 20 15

83 "Millie" (Blue and Yellow Macaw)

84 Wicket-keeping

1967. Christmas.
441 **83** 5c. yellow, blue, black grn 10 10*
443 5c. yellow, blue, black red 10 10*
442 25c. yellow, blue, blk vio 15 10*
444 25c. yellow, blue, blk grn 15 10*

1968. M.C.C.'s West Indies Tour. Multicoloured.
445 5c. Type **84** 10 10*
446 6c. Batting 10 10*
447 25c. Bowling 30 10*

87 Pike Cichlid

102 "Christ of St. John of the Cross" (Salvador Dali)

1968. Multicoloured.
448 1c. Type **87** 10 10
449 2c. Red paranha ("Pirai") . . 10 10
450 3c. Peacock cichlid ("Lukunani") 10 10
451 5c. Armoured catfish ("Hassar") 10 10
489 6c. Black acara ("Patua") . . 10 80
490 10c. Spix's guan (vert) . . . 30 60
491 15c. Harpy eagle (vert) . . . 30 10
455 20c. Hoatzin (vert) 60 10
493 25c. Guianan cock of the rock (vert) 30 10
494 40c. Great kiskadee (vert) . . 60 1·00
495 50c. Brazilian agouti ("Accouri") 35 15
459 60c. White-lipped peccary . . 80 10
460 $1 Paca ("Labba") 80 10
461 $2 Nine-banded armadillo . . 1·00 2·00
462 $5 Ocelot . . . . 1·00 3·00

1968. Easter.
463 **102** 5c. multicoloured 10 10*
464 25c. multicoloured 20 10*

103 "Efficiency Year"

1968. "Savings Bonds and Efficiency". Multicoloured.
465 6c. Type **103** 10 10*
466 25c. Type **103** 10 10*
467 30c. "Savings Bonds" 10 10*
468 40c. "Savings Bonds" 10 10*

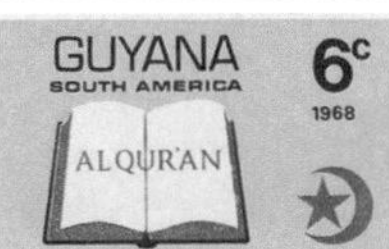

105 Open Book, Star and Crescent

1968. 1400th Anniv of Holy Quran.
469 **105** 6c. black, gold and flesh . . . 10 10*
470 25c. black, gold and lilac . . . 10 10*
471 30c. black, gold and green . . . 10 10*
472 40c. black, gold and blue . . . 10 10*

107 Broadcasting Greetings

1968. Christmas.
473 **107** 6c. brown, black and green 10 10*
474 25c. brown, violet green 10 10*
475 – 30c. green and turquoise 10 10*
476 – 40c. red and turquoise . . 10 10*
DESIGNS: 30c. and 40c. Map showing radio link, Guyana–Trinidad.

109 Festival Ceremony

1969. Hindu Festival of Phagwah. Multicoloured.
477 6c. Type **109** 10 10
478 25c. Ladies spraying scent . . 10 10
479 30c. Type **109** 10 10
480 40c. As No. 478 . . . . . . 10 10

111 "Sacrament of the Last Supper" (Dali)

1969. Easter.
481 **111** 6c. multicoloured 10 10
482 25c. multicoloured 10 10
483 30c. multicoloured 10 10
484 40c. multicoloured 10 10

112 Map showing "CARIFTA" Countries
114 Building "Independence" (first aluminium ship)

1969. 1st Anniv of "CARIFTA".
500 **112** 6c. red, blue and turquoise 15 15
501 – 25c. lemon, brown and red 15 15
DESIGN—HORIZ: 25c. "Strength in Unity".

1969. 50th Anniv of I.L.O.
502 **114** 30c. blue, black and silver 40 25
503 – 40c. multicoloured 50 25
DESIGN—HORIZ: 40c. Bauxite processing plant.

116 Scouts raising Flag

1969. 3rd Caribbean Scout Jamboree and Diamond Jubilee of Scouting in Guyana. Multicoloured.
504 6c. Type **116** 10 10
505 8c. Camp-fire cooking . . . 10 10
506 25c. Type **116** 10 10
507 30c. As 8c. 10 10
508 50c. Type **116** 15 15

118 Gandhi and Spinning-wheel

1969. Birth Centenary of Mahatma Gandhi.
509 **118** 6c. black, brown and olive 20 65
510 15c. black, brown and lilac 25 65

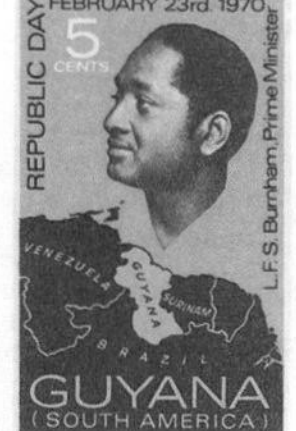

119 "Mother Sally" Dance Troupe
121 Forbes Burnham and Map

1969. Christmas. Unissued stamps optd as in T **119**. Multicoloured.
511 5c. Type **119** 10 10
512 6c. City Hall, Georgetown . . 10 10
513 25c. Type **119** 10 10
514 60c. As 6c. 20 25

1970. Republic Day.
515 **121** 5c. sepia, ochre and blue 10 10
516 – 6c. multicoloured 10 10
517 – 15c. multicoloured 15 10
518 – 25c. multicoloured 20 15
DESIGNS—VERT: 6c. Rural self-help. HORIZ: 15c. University of Guyana; 25c. Guyana House.

125 "The Descent from the Cross"
128 "Mother and Child" (Philip Moore)

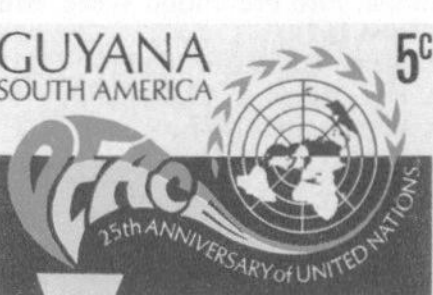

127 "Peace" and U.N. Emblem

1970. Easter. Paintings by Rubens. Multicoloured.
519 5c. Type **125** 10 10
520 6c. "Christ on the Cross" . . 10 10
521 15c. Type **125** 20 15
522 25c. As 6c. 20 15

1970. 25th Anniv of United Nations. Mult.
523 5c. Type **127** 10 10
524 6c. U.N. emblem, gold-panning and drilling . . . 10 10
525 15c. Type **127** 10 10
526 25c. As 6c. 10 15

1970. Christmas.
527 **128** 5c. multicoloured 10 10
528 6c. multicoloured 10 10
529 15c. multicoloured 15 15
530 25c. multicoloured 15 15

129 National Co-operative Bank

1971. Republic Day.
531 **129** 6c. multicoloured 10 10
532 15c. multicoloured 15 15
533 25c. multicoloured 15 15

130 Racial Equality Symbol
131 Young Volunteer felling Tree (from painting by J. Criswick)

1971. Racial Equality Year.
534 **130** 5c. multicoloured 10 10
535 6c. multicoloured 10 10
536 15c. multicoloured 15 15
537 25c. multicoloured 15 15

1971. 1st Anniv of Self-help Road Project.
538 **131** 5c. multicoloured 10 10
539 20c. multicoloured 20 10
540 25c. multicoloured 20 10
541 50c. multicoloured . . . . 30 1·75

132 Yellow Allamanda
134 Obverse and Reverse of Guyana $1 Coin

133 Child praying at Bedside

1971. Flowering Plants. Multicoloured.
542 1c. Pitcher Plant of Mt. Roraima 10 10
543 2c. Type **132** 10 10
544 3c. Hanging heliconia . . . 10 10
545 5c. Annatto tree 10 10
546 6c. Cannon-ball tree . . . 10 10
547 10c. Cattleya . . . . . . 3·25 10
548a 15c. Christmas orchid . . . 65 10
549 20c. "Paphinia cristata" . . 3·00 20
550 25c. Marabunta . . . . . 5·50 7·50
550ab 25c. Marabunta 45 10
551 40c. Tiger beard . . . . . 3·50 10
552 50c. "Guzmania lingulata" 40 85
553 60c. Soldier's cap 30 65
554 $1 "Chelonanthus uliginoides" 30 55
555 $2 "Norantea guianensis" 35 55
556 $5 "Odontadenia grandiflora" 55 55
No. 550 shows the flowers facing upwards and has the value in the centre. No. 550ab has the flowers facing downwards with the value to the right.

1971. Christmas. Multicoloured.
557 5c. Type **133** 10 10
558 20c. Type **133** 10 10
559 25c. Carnival masquerader (vert) 10 10
560 50c. As 25c. 20 60

1972. Republic Day.
561 **134** 5c. silver, black and red 10 10
562 – 20c. silver, black and red 15 10
563 **134** 25c. silver, black and blue 15 15
564 – 50c. silver, black and green 25 45
DESIGN: 20c., 50c. Reverse and obverse of Guyana $1 coin.

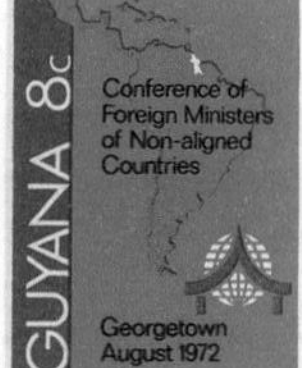

135 Hands and Irrigation Canal
136 Map and Emblem

1972. Youman Nabi (Mohammed's Birthday).
565 **135** 5c. multicoloured 10 10
566 25c. multicoloured 10 10
567 30c. multicoloured 10 10
568 60c. multicoloured 20 20

1972. Conference of Foreign Ministers of Non-aligned Countries.
569 **136** 8c. multicoloured 10 10
570 25c. multicoloured 10 10
571 40c. multicoloured 15 15
572 50c. multicoloured 20 20

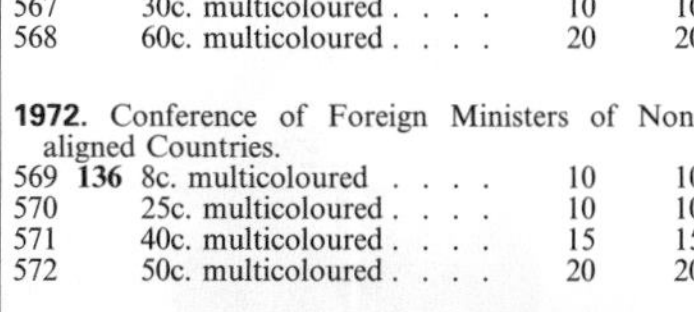

137 Hand reaching for Sun
138 Joseph, Mary and the Infant Jesus

1972. 1st Caribbean Festival of Arts.
573 **137** 8c. multicoloured 10 10
574 25c. multicoloured 10 10
575 40c. multicoloured 15 20
576 50c. multicoloured 20 25

1972. Christmas.
577 **138** 8c. multicoloured 10 10
578 25c. multicoloured 10 10
579 40c. multicoloured 15 25
580 50c. multicoloured 15 25

139 Umana Yana (Meeting-house)
141 Stylised Blood Cell

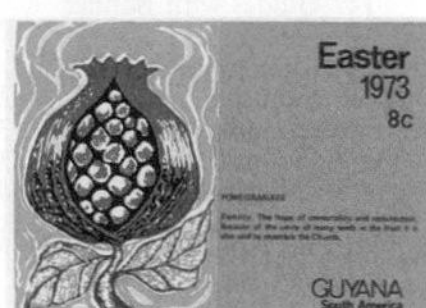

140 Pomegranate

1973. Republic Day. Multicoloured.
581 8c. Type **139** 10 10
582 25c. Bethel Chapel 10 10
583 40c. As 25c. 20 20
584 50c. Type **139** 25 20

1973. Easter. Multicoloured.
585 8c. Type **140** 10 10
586 25c. Cross and map (34 × 17 mm) 10 10
587 40c. As 25c. 10 10
588 50c. Type **140** 15 15

1973. 25th Anniv of Guyana Red Cross.
589 **141** 8c. red and black 10 10
590 25c. red and purple . . . 25 15
591 40c. red and blue 35 50
592 50c. red and green . . . . 50 1·00

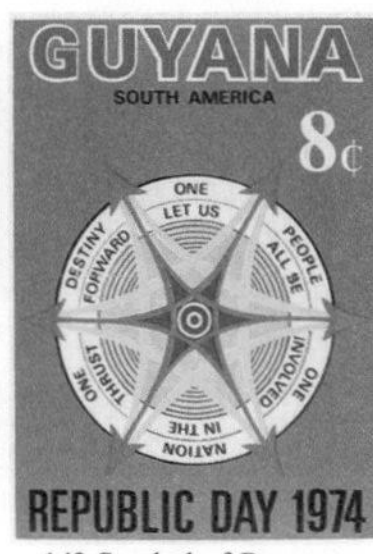

142 Steel-Band Players
143 Symbol of Progress

1973. Christmas. Multicoloured.
593 8c. Type **142** 10 10
594 25c. Type **142** 20 10
595 40c. "Virgin and Child" stained-glass window (34 × 47mm) 40 75
596 50c. As 40c. 40 75

1974. Republic Day. Multicoloured.
597 8c. Type **143** 10 10
598 25c. Wai-Wai Indian 10 10
599 40c. Type **143** 15 30
600 50c. As 25c. 15 40

1974. No. 546 surch **8c.**
601 8c. on 6c. multicoloured . . . 10 10

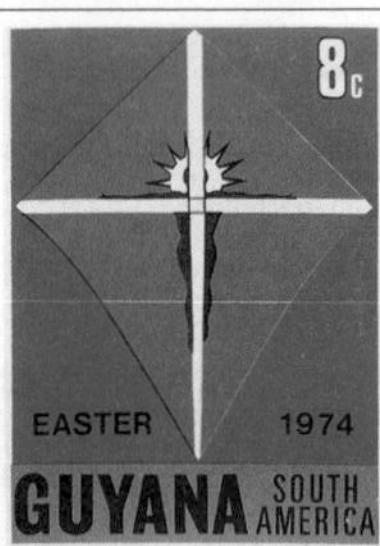

145 Kite with Crucifixion Motif

1974. Easter.
602 **145** 8c. multicoloured 10 10
603 – 25c. black and green 10 10
604 – 40c. black and mauve 10 15
605 **145** 50c. multicoloured 15 25
DESIGN: Nos. 603/4, "Crucifixion" in pre-Columbian style.

146 British Guiana 24c. Stamp of 1874 **148** Buck Toyeau

147 Guides with Banner

1974. Centenary of Universal Postal Union.
606 **146** 8c. multicoloured 25 10
607 – 25c. lt green, green black 35 10
608 **146** 40c. multicoloured 35 20
609 – 50c. green, brown black 45 45
DESIGN—VERT (42 × 25 mm): 25, 50c. U.P.U. emblem and Guyana postman.

1974. Golden Jubilee of Girl Guides. Mult.
610 8c. Type **147** 20 10
611 25c. Guides in camp 30 15
612 40c. As 25c. 45 40
613 50c. Type **147** 45 45

1974. Christmas. Multicoloured.
615 8c. Type **148** 10 10
616 35c. Five-fingers and awaras 10 10
617 50c. Pawpaw and tangerine 15 10
618 $1 Pineapple and sapodilla 30 60
MS619 127 × 94 mm. Nos. 615/18 70 2·50

1975. No. 544 surch **8c.**
620 8c. on 3c. multicoloured 10 10

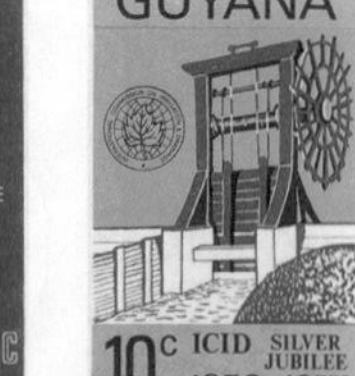

149 Golden Arrow of Courage **150** Old Sluice Gate

1975. Republic Day. Guyana Orders and Decorations. Multicoloured.
621 10c. Type **149** 10 10
622 35c. Cacique's Crown of Honour 10 15
623 50c. Cacique's Crown of Valour 15 20
624 $1 Order of Excellence 35 60

1975. Silver Jubilee of International Commission on Irrigation and Drainage. Multicoloured.
625 10c. Type **150** 10 10
626 35c. Modern sluice gate (horiz) 10 15
627 50c. Type **150** 15 30
628 $1 As 35c. 35 60
MS629 162 × 121 mm. Nos. 625/8 75 2·75

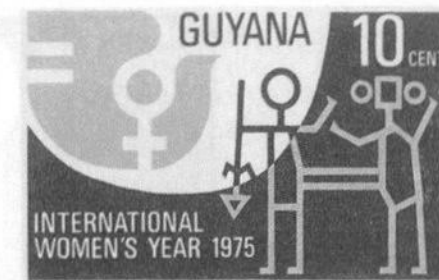

151 I.W.Y. Emblem and Rock Drawing

1975. International Women's Year. Designs showing different rock drawings.
630 **151** 10c. green and yellow 10 10
631 – 35c. violet and blue 15 10
632 – 50c. blue and orange 20 15
633 – $1 brown and blue 30 45
MS634 178 × 89 mm. Nos. 630/3 75 3·00

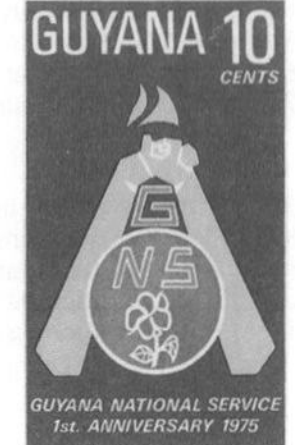

152 Freedom Monument **153** G.N.S. Emblem

1975. Namibia Day. Multicoloured.
635 10c. Type **152** 10 10
636 35c. Unveiling of Monument 15 10
637 50c. Type **152** 25 10
638 $1 As 35c. 35 35

1975. 1st Anniv of National Service.
639 **153** 10c. yellow, green & violet 10 10
640 – 35c. orange, green & violet 10 10
641 – 50c. blue, green and brown 15 15
642 – $1 mauve, green & lt green 40 40
MS643 196 × 133 mm. Nos. 639/42 75 2·00
Nos. 640/2 are as Type **153** but have different symbols within the circle.

154 Court Building, 1875, and Forester's Badge

1975. Centenary of Guyanese Ancient Order of Foresters. Multicoloured.
644 10c. Type **154** 10 10
645 35c. Rock drawing of hunter and quarry 10 10
646 50c. Crossed axes and bugle-horn 15 10
647 $1 Bow and arrow 40 40
MS648 129 × 97 mm. Nos. 644/7 75 2·25

1976. No. 553 surch **35c.**
649 35c. on 60c. Soldier's cap 20 15

156 Shoulder Flash **157** Triumphal Arch

1976. 50th Anniv of St. John Ambulance in Guyana.
650 **156** 8c. silver, black and mauve 10 10
651 – 15c. silver, black & orange 10 10
652 – 35c. silver, black and green 20 20
653 – 40c. silver, black and blue 25 25
Nos. 651/3 are as Type **156** but show different shoulder flashes.

1976. 10th Anniv of Independence. Multicoloured.
654 8c. Type **157** 10 10
655 15c. Stylised Victoria Regia lily 10 10
656 35c. "Onward to Socialism" 15 15
657 40c. Worker pointing the way 15 15
MS658 120 × 100 mm. Nos. 654/7 50 1·50

1976. West Indies Victory in World Cricket Cup. As T **223a** of Grenada.
659 15c. Map of the Caribbean 90 1·50
660 15c. Prudential Cup 90 1·50

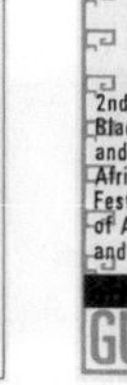

158 Flame in Archway **159** Festival Emblem and "Musical Instrument"

1976. Deepavali Festival. Multicoloured.
661 8c. Type **158** 10 10
662 15c. Flame in hand 10 10
663 35c. Flame in bowl 15 20
664 40c. Goddess Latchmi 15 25
MS665 94 × 109 mm. Nos. 661/4 50 1·50

1977. Second World Black and African Festival of Arts and Culture, Nigeria.
666 **159** 10c. red, black and gold 10 10
667 25c. violet, black and gold 15 10
668 50c. blue, black and gold 20 25
669 $1 green, black and gold 35 75
MS670 90 × 157 mm. Nos. 666/9 75 3·00

160 1c. and 5c. Coins

1977. New Coinage.
671 **160** 8c. multicoloured 20 10
672 – 15c. brown, grey and black 25 10
673 – 35c. green, grey and black 45 30
674 – 40c. red, grey and black 50 35
675 – $1 multicoloured 80 1·25
676 – $2 multicoloured 1·25 2·75
DESIGNS: 15c.10 and 25c. coins; 35c., 50c. and $1 coins; 40c. $5 and $10 coins; $1 $50 and $100 coins; $2 Reverse of $1 coin.

161 Hand Pump, c. 1850

1977. National Fire Prevention Week. Mult.
677 8c. Type **161** 1·10 10
678 15c. Steam engine, c. 1860 1·50 10
679 35c. Fire engine, c. 1930 1·75 60
680 40c. Fire engine, 1977 1·75 85

162 Cuffy Monument

1977. Cuffy Monument (commemorating 1763 Slave Revolt). Multicoloured.
681 8c. Type **162** 10 10
682 15c. Cuffy Monument (different view) 10 10
683 35c. Type **162** 15 20
684 40c. As 15c. 15 30

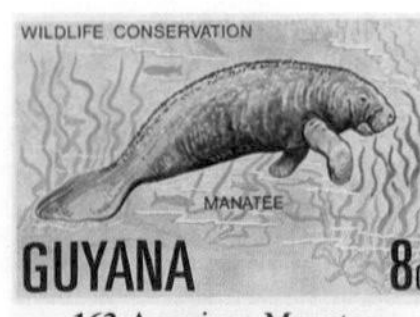

163 American Manatee

1978. Wildlife Conservation. Multicoloured.
685 8c. Type **163** 65 10
686 15c. Giant sea turtle 85 20
687 35c. Harpy eagle (vert) 4·00 1·50
688 40c. Iguana (vert) 3·50 1·50

164 L.F.S. Burnham (Prime Minister) and Parliament Buildings, Georgetown

1978. 25th Anniv of Prime Minister's Entry into Parliament.
689 **164** 8c. black, violet and grey 10 10
690 – 15c. black, blue and grey 10 10
691 – 35c. black, red and grey 15 20
692 – 40c. black, orange and grey 15 20
MS693 176 × 118 mm. Nos. 689/92 55 1·00
DESIGNS: 15c. Burnham, graduate and children ("Free Education"); 35c. Burnham and industrial works (Nationalization of Bauxite Industry); 40c. Burnham and village scene ("The Co-operative Village").

165 Dr. George Giglioli (scientist and physician) **166** "Prepona pheridamas"

1978. Nat Science Research Council. Mult.
694 10c. Type **165** 15 10
695 30c. Institute of Applied Science and Technology 20 15
696 50c. Emblem of National Science Research Council 25 25
697 60c. Emblem of Commonwealth Science Council (commemorating the 10th meeting) (horiz) 25 25

1978. Butterflies. Multicoloured.
698 5c. Type **166** 1·50 10
699 10c. "Archonias bellona" 1·50 10
700 15c. "Eryphanis polyxena" 1·50 10
701 20c. "Helicopis cupido" 1·50 10
702 25c. "Nessaea batesii" 1·50 10
702a 30c. "Nymphidium mantus" 1·25 2·25
703 35c. "Anaea galanthis" 1·50 10
704 40c. "Morpho rhetenor" (male) 1·50 10
705 50c. "Hamadryas amphinome" 1·50 20
705a 60c. "Papilio androgeus" 1·25 1·00
706 $1 "Agrias claudina" (vert) (25 × 39 mm) 3·75 20
707 $2 "Morpho rhetenor" (female) (vert) (25 × 39 mm) 5·50 35
708 $5 "Morpho deidamia" (vert) (25 × 39 mm) 6·50 90
708a $10 "Elbella patrobas" 4·50 4·25

168 Amerindian Stone-chip Grater in Preparation **169** Dish Aerial by Night

1978. National/International Heritage Year. Multicoloured.
709 10c. Type **168** 10 10
710 30c. Cassiri and decorated Amerindian jars 15 10
711 50c. Fort, Kyk-over-al 20 15
712 60c. Fort Island 20 20

1979. Satellite Earth Station. Multicoloured.
713 10c. Type **169** 10 10
714 30c. Dish aerial by day 20 15
715 50c. Satellite with solar veins 30 15
716 $3 Cylinder satellite 1·00 90

170 Sir Rowland Hill and British Guiana 1850 12c. "Cottonreel" Stamp

1979. Death Cent of Sir Rowland Hill. Mult.
717 10c. Type **170** 15 10
718 30c. British Guiana 1856 1c. black on magenta stamp (vert) 20 15

719 50c. British Guiana 1898 1c. Mount Roraima stamp 30 15
720 $3 Printing press used for early British Guiana stamps (vert) 45 80

171 "Me and my Sister" 172 "An 8 Hour Day"

1979. International Year of the Child. Children's Paintings. Multicoloured.
721 10c. Type **171** 10 10
722 30c. "Fun with the Fowls" (horiz) 15 15
723 50c. "Two Boys catching Ducks" (horiz) 15 20
724 $3 "Mango Season" (horiz) 45 1·25

1979. 60th Anniv of Guyana Labour Union. Multicoloured.
725 10c. Type **172** 10 10
726 30c. "Abolition of Night Baking" (horiz) 10 10
727 50c. "Introduction of the Workmen's Compensation Ordinance" 15 15
728 $3 H. N. Critchlow (founder) 55 90

173 Guyana Flag

1980. 10th Anniv of Republic.
729 **173** 10c. multicoloured 10 10
730 – 35c. black and orange 30 10
731 – 60c. multicoloured 50 20
732 – $3 multicoloured 80 90
DESIGNS: 35c. Demerara River Bridge; 60c. Kaieteur Falls; $3 "Makanaima, the Great Ancestral Spirit of the Amerindians".

174 Common Snook

1980. "London 1980" International Stamp Exhibition. Fishes. Multicoloured.
733 35c. Type **174** 20 20
734 35c. Trahira ("Haimara") 20 20
735 35c. Electric eel 20 20
736 35c. Golden rivulus 20 20
737 35c. Golden pencilfish 20 20
738 35c. Four-eyed fish 20 20
739 35c. Red piranha ("Pirai") 20 20
740 35c. Smoking hassar 20 20
741 35c. Manta 20 20
742 35c. Festival cichlid ("Flying patwa") 20 20
743 35c. Arapaima 20 20
744 35c. Peacock cichlid ("Lukanani") 20 20

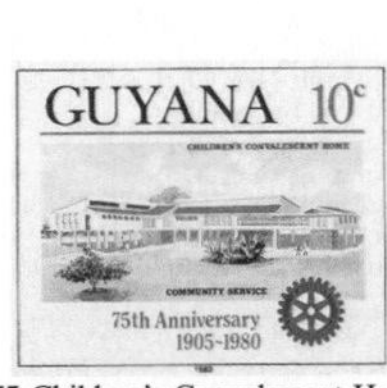
175 Children's Convalescent Home (Community Service)

1980. 75th Anniv of Rotary International. Multicoloured.
745 10c. Type **175** 10 10
746 30c. Georgetown Rotary Club and Rotary International emblems 10 10
747 50c. District 404 emblem (vert) 20 20
748 $3 Rotary anniversary emblem (vert) 80 80

176 "C" encircling Globe, Caduceus Emblem and Sea

1980. 25th Anniv of Commonwealth Caribbean Medical Research Council. Multicoloured.
749 10c. Type **176** 10 10
750 60c. Researcher with microscope, Caduceus emblem, stethoscope and beach scene 40 20
751 $3 Caduceus emblem, "C" encircling researcher and island silhouettes 1·10 1·00

177 "Virola surinamensis"

1980. Christmas. Trees and Foliage. Multicoloured.
752 10c. Type **177** 10 10
753 30c. "Hymenaea courbaril" 20 10
754 50c. "Mora excelsa" 30 15
755 $3 "Peltogyne venosa" 80 1·10

178 Brazilian Tree Porcupine 181 Map of Guyana

1981. Wildlife. Multicoloured.
756 30c. Type **178** 25 40
757 30c. Red howler 25 40
758 30c. Common squirrel-monkey 25 40
759 30c. Two-toed sloth 25 40
760 30c. Brazilian tapir 25 40
761 30c. Collared peccary 25 40
762a 30c. Six-banded armadillo 25 40
763 30c. Tamandua 25 40
764 30c. Giant anteater 25 40
765 30c. Murine opossum 25 40
766 30c. Brown four-eyed opossum 25 40
767 30c. Brazilian agouti 25 40

1981. Liberation of Southern Africa Conference. No. 635 surch **1981 CONFERENCE $1.05**.
768 $1.05 on 10c. Type **152** 40 30

1981. Royal Wedding (1st issue). Nos. 554 and 556 surch **ROYAL WEDDING 1981** and value.
769c $3.60 on $5 "Odontadenia grandiflora" 60 65
770 $7.20 in $1 "Chelonanthus uliginoides" 60 60
See also Nos. 841/3 and 930/6.

1981. Fiscal stamps surch for postal use.
771 **181** 10c. on 3c. black, blue and red 30 10
940 15c. on 2c. black, blue and grey 50 15
941 20c. on 2c. black, blue and grey 4·00 30
1029 25c. on 2c. black, blue and grey 50 10
772 30c. on 2c. black, blue and grey 45 15
989 40c. on 2c. black, blue and grey 1·00 15
945 45c. on 2c. black, blue and grey 1·75 45
773 50c. on 2c. black, blue and grey 40 15
774 60c. on 2c. black, blue and grey 45 15
948 75c. on 2c. black, blue and grey 6·00 25
775 75c. on 3c. black, blue and red 45 20
949 80c. on 2c. black, blue and grey 6·00 20
950 85c. on 2c. black, blue and grey 75 25
951 100c. on 3c. black, blue and red 1·00 35
952 110c. on 3c. black, blue and red 80 30
953 120c. on 3c. black, blue and red 8·00 35
954 125c. on 3c. black, blue and red 2·25 35
955 130c. on 3c. black, blue and red 1·00 35
956 150c. on 3c. black, blue and red 8·50 40
957 160c. on 3c. black, blue and red 2·00 40
958 170c. on 3c. black, blue and red 1·40 45
959 175c. on 3c. black, blue and red 6·00 45
960 180c. on 3c. black, blue and red 2·00 60
961 200c. on 3c. black, blue and red 2·25 45
962 210c. on 3c. black, blue and red 7·00 50
963 220c. on 3c. black, blue and red 8·50 50
964 235c. on 3c. black, blue and red 8·00 50
965 240c. on 3c. black, blue and red 9·00 50
966 250c. on 3c. black, blue and red 2·25 50
967 300c. on 3c. black, blue and red 12·00 55
968 330c. on 3c. black, blue and red 2·75 65
969 375c. on 3c. black, blue and red 8·00 75
970 400c. on 3c. black, blue and red 10·00 75
971 440c. on 3c. black, blue and red 4·00 75
972 500c. on 3c. black, blue and red 3·50 1·10
973 550c. on 3c. black, blue and red 4·00 1·25
974 625c. on 3c. black, blue and red 2·75 1·75
975 1500c. on 2c. black, blue and grey 11·00 3·00
976 2000c. on 2c. black, blue and grey 11·00 3·75

1981. No. 544 surch **7.20**.
775c 720c. on 3c. multicoloured 80·00 15·00

1981. Various stamps optd **1981**.
791 – 15c. mult (No. 491) 14·00 10
864 – 15c. mult (No. 548a) 4·00 10
810 – 15c. mult (No. 659) 7·00 20
811 – 15c. mult (No. 660) 5·00 20
776 **105** 25c. black, gold and lilac 10 10
777 30c. black, gold and green 15 10
778 – 35c. mult (No. 645) 15 10
792 – 40c. mult (No. 457) 10·00 40
811c – 40c. mult (No. F5) – £200
812 – 50c. mult (No. 623) 60 20
813 **150** 50c. multicoloured 1·00 20
814 – 50c. blue and orange (No. 632) 23·00 2·25
815 – 50c. mult (No. 646) 2·75 20
816 **159** 50c. blue, black and gold 13·00 2·00
817 – 50c. mult (No. F6) 4·00 20
818 – 60c. mult (No. 731) 60 20
819 – 60c. mult (No. 750) 60 20
865 – $1 mult (No. 554) 40 20
820 – $1 mult (No. 624) 6·00 55
821 **159** $1 green, black and gold 5·00 30
866 – $2 mult (No. 555) 90 35
823 – $3 mult (No. 732) 2·00 65
824 – $5 mult (No. 556) 3·25 1·25

1981. Nos. 545 and 556 surch.
780 75c. on 5c. Annatto tree 50 50
781 210c. on $5 "Odontadenia grandiflora" 80 1·00
781b 220c. on 5c. Annatto tree 95·00 8·50

1981. Nos. D8/11 surch **ESSEQUIBO IS OURS**.
782A D 2 10c. on 2c. black 15 10
783A 15c. on 12c. red 15 15
784A 20c. on 1c. green 15 20
785B 45c. on 2c. black 30 15
786A 55c. on 4c. blue 20 20
787B 60c. on 4c. blue 30 10
788A 65c. on 2c. black 30 15
789B 70c. on 4c. blue 30 30
790A 80c. on 4c. blue 30 20

1981. Nos. 545, 554, 556, 716, 843, F7 and F9 surch.
794 50c. on 5c. Annatto tree (postage) 30 20
795 120c. on $1 "Chelonanthus uliginoides" 75 40
796 140c. on $1 "Chelonanthus uliginoides" 70 40
797 150c. on $2 "Norantea guianensis" (F9) 75 40
800 220c. on $3 Cylinder satellite 1·75 45
801 250c. on $5 "Odontadenia grandiflora" 1·25 45
802 280c. on $5 "Odontadenia grandiflora" 1·50 50
798 360c. on $2 "Norantea guianensis" (F9) 3·00 60
803 375c. on $5 "Odontadenia grandiflora" 1·75 55
799 720c. on 60c. Soldier's Cap (F7) 3·00 1·00
804 $1.10 on $2 "Norantea guianensis" (843) (air) 1·00 1·00
No. 804 has the Royal Wedding opt cancelled by three bars.

1981. No. 448 surch.
805 **87** 15c. on 1c. mult (postage) 70 20
806 100c. on 1c. mult (air) 70 40
807 110c. on 1c. multicoloured 70 40

1981. No. 700 optd **ESSEQUIBO IS OURS**.
808 15c. "Eryphanis polyxena" 5·50 10

1981. Various stamps surch.
825 **116** 55c. on 6c. multicoloured 3·00 80
826 **111** 70c. on 6c. multicoloured 1·00 20
827 100c. on 6c. mult 1·25 20
828 – 100c. on 8c. multicoloured (No. 505) 3·00 20
829 **152** 100c. on $1.05 on 10c. mult (No. 768) 32·00 4·00
830 **116** 110c. on 6c. mult 2·00 30
831 **149** 110c. on 10c. mult 2·50 30
832 **151** 110c. on 10c. green and yellow 6·00 45
834 – 125c. on $2 multicoloured (No. 555) 13·00 80
835 **116** 180c. on 6c. mult 2·25 45
840 – 240c. on $3 multicoloured (No. 728) 8·00 75
836 **116** 400c. on 6c. mult 3·50 80
837a 440c. on 6c. mult 1·00 55
838 – 550c. on $10 multicoloured (No. O21) 8·00 1·00
839 – 625c. on 40c. mult (No. F5) 14·00 1·75

1981. Royal Wedding (2nd issue). Nos. 544 and 555/6 surch **Royal Wedding 1981** (No. 843 **Air Mail** also) and value.
841 60c. on 3c. Hanging heliconia (postage) 30 35
842 75c. on $5 "Odontadenia grandiflora" 30 35
843 $1.10 on $2 "Norantea guianensis" (air) 30 35

1981. World Cup Football Championship, Spain (1982) (1st issue). No. 781a optd **Espana 82**.
844 220c. on 5c. Annatto tree 2·00 40
See also Nos. 937/9 and 1218.

1981. 150th Birth Anniv of Heinrich von Stephan (founder of U.P.U.) No. 720 surch **1831-1981 Von Stephan 330**.
845 330c. on $3 Printing press used for early British Guiana stamps 1·10 55

1981. No. 489 surch with large figure over smaller figure.
847 12c. on 12c. on 6c. Black acara ("Patua") 20 25
848 15c. on 10c. on 6c. Black acara ("Patua") 15 10
849 15c. on 30c. on 6c. Black acara ("Patua") 15 10
850 15c. on 50c. on 6c. Black acara ("Patua") 15 10
851 15c. on 60c. on 6c. Black acara ("Patua") 15 10
Nos. 847/51 are further surcharges on previously unissued stamps.

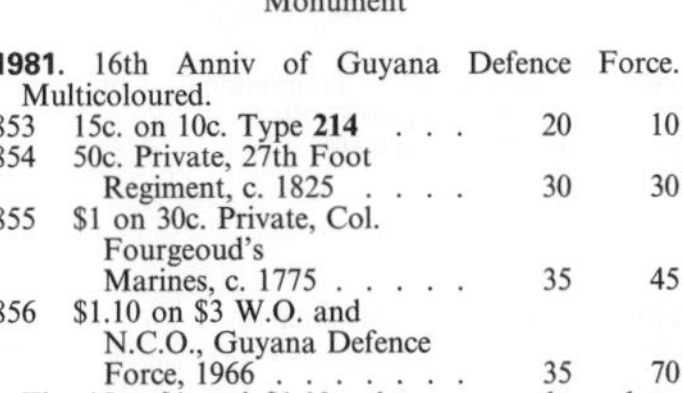
214 Coromantyn Free Negro Armed Ranger, c. 1772, and Cuffy Monument

1981. 16th Anniv of Guyana Defence Force. Multicoloured.
853 15c. on 10c. Type **214** 20 10
854 50c. Private, 27th Foot Regiment, c. 1825 30 30
855 $1 on 30c. Private, Col. Fourgeoud's Marines, c. 1775 35 45
856 $1.10 on $3 W.O. and N.C.O., Guyana Defence Force, 1966 35 70
The 15c., $1 and $1.10 values are surcharged on previously unissued stamps.

215 Louis Braille

1981. International Year for Disabled Persons. Famous Disabled People. Multicoloured.
857 15c. on 10c. Type **215** 20 10
858 50c. Helen Keller and Rajkumari Singh 30 40
859 $1 on 60c. Beethoven and Sonny Thomas 40 50
860 $1.10 on $3 Renoir 25 55
The 15c., $1 and $1.10 values are surcharged on previously unissued stamps.

1981. No. 489 surch (Nos. 862/3 optd **AIR** also).
861 12c. on 6c. Black acara ("Patua") (postage) . . . 15 10
862b 50c. on 6c. Black acara ("Patua") (air) 20 15
863 $1 on 6c. Black acara ("Patua") 50 30

1981. Nos. 601, 620, 644, O13, 717, 720, 728, 749, 751 and 755 surch (Nos. 868/9 twice).
867 110c. on 10c. Type **154** . . 3·00 30
868 110c. on 110c. on 8c. on 3c. Hanging heliconia . . . . 3·00 40
869 110c. on 110c. on 8c. on 6c. Cannon-ball tree . . . . 3·00 40
869b 110c. on 10c. on 25c. Marabunta . . . . 2·25 40
870 110c. on 10c. Type **170** . . 2·00 30
871 110c. on 10c. Type **176** . . 8·00 50
872 110c. on $3 Printing press used for early British Guiana stamps . . . . . 1·75 30
873 110c. on $3 H. N. Critchlow 6·50 45
874 110c. on $3 Caduceus emblem, "C" encircling researcher and island silhouettes . . . . 1·50 30
875 110c. on $3 "Peltogyne venosa" . . . . 4·00 50

1981. No. 698 surch **Nov 81 50c.**
876 50c. on 5c. Type **166** . . . . 8·50 20

222 Yellow Allamanda ("Allamanda cathartica")

225 Tape Measure and Guyana Metrication Board Van

1981. Flowers.
877 **222** 15c. on 2c. lilac, blue and green 15 15
878 – 15c. on 8c. lilac, blue and mauve 15 15
DESIGN: 15c. on 8c. Mazaruni pride ("Sipanea prolensis").
Nos. 877/8 are surcharged on previously unissued stamps.

1981. Air. Human Rights Day. No. 748 surch **Human Rights Day 1981 110 AIR.**
879 110c. on $3 Rotary anniversary emblem . . . 1·00 60

1981. 35th Anniv of UNICEF No. 724 surch **UNICEF 1946 - 1981 125.**
880 125c. on $2 "Mango Season" 1·25 40

1981. "Cancun 81" International Conference. No. 698 surch **Cancun 81 50c.**
880c 50c. on 5c. Type **166** . . . 4·00 55

1982. Metrication. Multicoloured.
881 15c. Type **225** 40 40
882 15c. "Metric man" 40 40
883 15c. "Postal service goes metric" 40 40
884 15c. Weighing child on metric scales 40 40
885 15c. Canje Bridge 40 40
886 15c. Tap filling litre bucket 40 40

1982. Various stamps optd **1982.**
887 – 20c. multicoloured (No. 549) . . . . . . 1·00 20
888 **105** 25c. black, gold and lilac 60 15
889 – 25c. mult (No. 550ab) . . 1·25 20
See also Nos. 914/17, 919/21, 923/4, 977, 992/8, 1001, 1004, 1006/8, 1015, 1017, 1059, 1117 and OP3/4.

1982. No. 506 optd **POSTAGE** and Nos. 546 and 601 surch.
890 20c. on 6c. Cannon-ball tree 20 10
892 25c. Type **116** . . . . 1·00 10
893 125c. on 8c. on 6c. Cannon-ball tree 20 20

230 Guyana Soldier and Flag

1982. Savings Campaign.
894 **230** $1 multicoloured 30 20
No. 894 is a fiscal stamp optd for postal use. See also Nos. 913 and 990.

1982. 125th Birth Anniv of Lord Baden-Powell and 75th Anniv of Boy Scout Movement. Nos. 543, 545 and 601 surch as given in brackets.
895 15c. on 2c. Type **132** **(BADEN POWELL 1857–1982)** 30 45
896 15c. on 2c. Type **132 (Scout Movement 1907–1982)** . . 30 40
897 15c. on 2c. Type **132 (1907–1982)** . . . . 2·00 2·25
898 15c. on 2c. Type **132 (1857–1982)** . . . . 2·00 2·25
899 15c. on 2c. Type **132 (1982)** 10 10
900 110c. on 5c. Annatto tree **(BADEN POWELL 1857–1982)** 60 20
901 110c. on 5c. Annatto tree **(Scout Movement 1907–1982)** 60 20
902 110c. on 5c. Annatto tree **(1907–1982)** . . . . . . 2·50 2·50
903 110c. on 5c. Annatto tree **(1857–1982)** . . . . . . 2·50 2·50
904 110c. on 5c. Annatto tree **(1982)** 60 20
905 125c. on 8c. on 6c. Cannon-ball tree **(BADEN POWELL 1857–1982)** . . 60 20
906 125c. on 8c. on 6c. Cannon-ball tree **(Scout Movement 1907–1982)** 60 20
907 125c. on 8c. on 6c. Cannon-ball tree **(1907–1982)** . . . 2·50 2·50
908 125c. on 8c. on 6c. Cannon-ball tree **(1857–1982)** . . . 2·50 2·50
909 125c. on 8c. on 6c. Cannon-ball tree **(1982)** 60 20

1982. 250th Birth Anniv of George Washington. Nos. 718 and 720 surch **Geo Washington 1732 . . . 1982** and value and No. 708 optd **GEORGE WASHINGTON 1732–1982.**
910 100c. on $3 Printing press used for early British Guiana stamps 45 30
911 400c. on 30c. British Guiana 1856 1c. black on purple 1·60 1·25
912 $5 "Morpho deidamia" . . . 9·00 5·50

1982. Savings Campaign. As T **230**. Mult.
913 110c. on $5 Guyana male and female soldiers with flag 50 20
No. 913 is a fiscal stamp surch for postal use. See also No. 990.

1982. Easter. Optd **1982** or surch also.
914 **111** 25c. multicoloured 20 15
915 30c. multicoloured 20 15
916 45c. on 6c. multicoloured 20 25
917 75c. on 40c. multicoloured 35 25

1982. No. 703 surch **20.**
918 20c. on 35c. "Anaea galanthis" . . . . 5·00 10

1982. No. F5 optd **1982 180.**
919 180c. on 40c. Tiger beard . . 3·50 40

1982. Nos. 555/6 optd **1982.**
920 $2 "Norantea guianensis" . . 80 30
921 $5 "Odontadenia grandiflora" 1·00 70

1982. No. 542 surch **220.**
922 220c. on 1c. Pitcher Plant of Mt. Roraima . . . . . . 1·00 40

1982. Nos. 472 and 684 optd **1982.**
923 **105** 40c. black, gold and blue 35 15
924 – 40c. multicoloured 50 25

1982. Nos. 469, 751 and 842/3 surch.
925 **105** 80c. on 6c. black, gold and flesh 30 20
926 85c. on 6c. black, gold and flesh 50 20
927 – 160c. on $1.10 on $2 mult (No. 843) 40 30
928 – 210c. on $3 mult (No. 751) . . . . . . 6·00 40
929 – 235c. on 75c. on 85 mult (No. 842) . . . . . . 2·50 60

1982. Royal Wedding (3rd issue). Nos. 841/3 surch.
930 85c. on 60c. on 3c. Hanging heliconia . . . . 4·25 50
931 130c. on 60c. on 3c. Hanging heliconia . . . . 2·75 45
932 160c. on. $1.10 on $2 "Norantea guianensis" . . 3·25 1·00
933 170c. on $1.10 on $2 "Norantea guianensis" . . 6·50 4·50
934 210c. on 75c. on $5 "Odontadenia grandiflora" 2·50 40
935 235c. on 75c. on $5 "Odontadenia grandiflora" 3·75 1·40
936 330c. on $1.10 on $2 "Norantea guianensis" . . 1·50 40

1982. World Cup Football Championship, Spain (2nd issue). Nos. 544, 546 and 554 optd **ESPANA 1982** or surch also.
937 $1 "Chelonanthus uliginoides" 75 40
938 110c. on 3c. Hanging heliconia 75 25
939 250c. on 6c. Cannon-ball tree 1·00 60
See also No. 1218.

1982. No. 548a optd 1982.
977 15c. Christmas orchid . . . . 7·50 10

1982. No. O26 optd **POSTAGE.**
978 110c. on 6c. Type **116** . . . 2·75 35

1982. Air. 21st Birthday of Princess of Wales. Nos. 542, 545 and 555 surch **AIR Princess of Wales 1961–1982.**
979 110c. on 5c. Annatto tree . . 1·75 30
980 220c. on 1c. Pitcher Plant of Mt. Roraima . . . . . . 2·00 80
981 330c. on $2 "Norantea guianensis" . . . . 2·00 1·25

1982. Birth of Prince William of Wales. Surch **H.R.H Prince William 21st June 1982.** (a) On stamps of British Guiana with additional opt **GUYANA.**
982 50c. on 2c. green (No. 332) 75 30
983 $1.10 on 3c. green and brown (No. 333) . . . . 2·00 50

(b) On stamps of Guyana previously optd **GUYANA INDEPENDENCE 1966.**
984 50c. on 2c. green (No. 421) 15·00 3·50
985 $1.10 on 3c. green and brown (No. 422) . . . . 25·00 3·50
986 $1.25 on 6c. green (No. 424) 60 60
987 $2.20 on 24c. black and orange (No. 435) . . . . . 1·50 1·50

1982. Savings Campaign. As No. 913 but showing inverted comma before "OURS" in opt.
990 110c. on $5 Guyana male and female soldiers with flag . . . . 5·50 75

1982. Italy's Victory in World Cup Football Championship. No. F7 surch **ESPANA 1982 ITALY $2.35.**
991 $2.35 on 180c. on 60c. Soldier's cap . . . . 3·75 55

1982. Wildlife Protection. Nos. 687 and 733/8 optd **1982.**
992 35c. Harpy eagle . . . . . . 2·00 40
993 35c. Type **174** . . . . 2·00 40
994 35c. Trahira ("Haimara") . . 2·00 40
995 35c. Electric eel . . . . . . 2·00 40
996 35c. Golden rivulus . . . . . 2·00 40
997 35c. Golden pencilfish . . . 2·00 40
998 35c. Four-eyed fish . . . . . 2·00 40

1982. Central America and Caribbean Games, Havana. Nos. 542/3 surch **C.A. & CARIB GAMES 1982.**
999 50c. on 2c. Type **132** . . . 1·00 25
1000 60c. on 1c. Pitcher plant of Mt. Roraima . . . . 1·25 15

1982. No. 730 optd **1982.**
1001 35c. black and orange . . . 50 20

1982. Nos. 841 and 979 further surch.
1002 130c. on 60c. on 3c. Hanging heliconia 40 30
1003 170c. on 110c. on 5c. Annatto tree 70 45

1982. No. 841 surch **1982 440.**
1004 440c. on 60c. on 3c. Hanging heliconia 75 45

1982. Commonwealth Games, Brisbane, Australia. No. 546 surch **Commonwealth GAMES AUSTRALIA 1982 1.25.**
1005 $1.25 on 6c. Cannon-ball tree . . . . 1·00 30

1982. Nos. 552, 641 and 719 optd **1982.**
1006 50c. multicoloured (No. 552) 1·50 25
1007 50c. blue, green and brown (No. 641) . . . . 1·00 25
1008 50c. multicoloured (No. 719) 60 25

1982. Various Official stamps additionally optd **POSTAGE.**
1009 15c. Christmas Orchid (No. O 23) . . . . 13·00 30
1010 50c. "Guzmania lingulata" (No. O14) 90 15
1011 100c. on $3 Cylinder satellite (No. O19) . . . . 1·00 35

1982. International Food Day. No. 617 optd **INT. FOOD DAY 1982.**
1012 50c. Pawpaw and tangerine 7·50 65

1982. International Year of the Elderly. No. 747 optd **INT. YEAR OF THE ELDERLY.**
1013 50c. District 404 emblem . . 7·00 50

1982. Centenary of Robert Koch's Discovery of Tubercle Bacillus. No. 750 optd **Dr. R. KOCH CENTENARY TBC BACILLUS DISCOVERY.**
1014 60c. Researcher with microscope, Caduceus emblem, stethoscope and beach scene . . . . . . 2·00 30

1982. International Decade for Women. No. 633 optd **1982.**
1015 $1 brown and blue . . . . 2·00 60

1982. Birth Centenary of F. D. Roosevelt (American statesman). No. 706 optd **F. D. ROOSEVELT 1882-1982.**
1016 $1 "Agrias claudina" . . . 4·50 50

1982. 1st Anniv of G.A.C. Inaugural Flight Georgetown to Boa Vista, Brazil. No. 842 optd **1982 GAC Inaug. Flight Georgetown–Boa Vista, Brasil 200.**
1017 200c. on 75c. on $5 "Odontadenia grandiflora" . . . . . . 6·00 1·40

1982. CARICOM Heads of Government Conference, Kingston, Jamaica. Nos. 881/6 surch **50 CARICOM Heads of Gov't Conference July 1982.**
1018 50c. on 15c. Type **225** . . . 1·50 30
1019 50c. on 15c. "Metric man" 1·50 30
1020 50c. on 15c. "Postal service goes metric" . . . . . . 1·50 30
1021 50c. on 15c. Weighing child on metric scales . . . . . 1·50 30
1022 50c. on 15c. Canje Bridge 1·50 30
1023 50c. on 15c. Tap filling litre bucket . . . . 1·50 30

1982. Christmas. Nos. 895/9 optd **CHRISTMAS 1982.**
1024 15c. on 2c. Type **132** (surch **BADEN POWELL 1857–1982**) 25 15
1025 15c. on 2c. Type **132** (surch **Scout Movement 1907–1982**) 25 15
1026 15c. on 2c. Type **132** (surch **1907–1982**) 85 75
1027 15c. on 2c. Type **132** (surch **1857–1982**) 85 75
1028 15c. on 2c. Type **132** (surch **1982**) . . . . 11·00 12·00

1982. Nos. 543 and 546 surch in figures (no "c" after face value).
1034 15c. on 2c. Type **132** . . . 15 10
1035 20c. on 6c. Cannon-ball tree 15 10
See also No. 1086.

1982. No. 489 surch.
1032 50c. on 6c. Black acara ("Patua") 20 15
1033 100c. on 6c. Black acara ("Patua") 40 30

1983. Optd **1983.**
1036 – 15c. mult (No. 655) . . . 3·50 1·50
1037 – 15c. brown, grey and black (No. 672) . . . . . 2·00 10
1038 – 15c. mult (No. 682) . . . 40 10
1039 **214** 15c. on 10c. mult 35 10
1040 **215** 15c. on 10c. mult 15 10
1041 – 50c. mult (No. 646) . . . 4·00 25
1042 – 50c. mult (No. 696) . . . 4·00 25
1043 – 50c. mult (No. 719) . . . 1·50 25
See also Nos. 1060/1, 1069/70, 1072/9c, 1096, 1101 and 1110/16.

1983. No. O17 optd **POSTAGE.**
1044 15c. Harpy Eagle . . . . . 13·00 10

1983. National Heritage. Nos. 710/12 and 778 surch.
1045 90c. on 30c. Cassiri and decorated Amerindian jars 85 50
1046 90c. on 35c. Rock drawing of hunter and quarry . . 35 20

1047 90c. on 50c. Fort Kyk-over-al 85 50
1048 90c. on 60c. Fort Island . . 1·25 20

258 Guyana Flag (inscr. "60TH BIRTHDAY ANNIVERSARY")

262

1983. 60th Birthday of President Burnham and 30 Years in Parliament. Multicoloured.
1049 25c. Type **258** 15 20
1050 25c. As T **258** but position of flag reversed and inscr "30th ANNIVERSARY IN PARLIAMENT" . . 15 20
1051 $1.30 Youth display (41 × 25 mm) 40 65
1052 $6 Presidential standard (43½ × 25 mm) . . . . . 70 2·75

1983. Surch in words.
1053 **170** 50c. on 10c. mult (No. 717) . . . . . 2·75 30
1054 – 50c. on 400c. on 30c. mult (No. 911) . . . 3·25 30
1055 **152** $1 on 10c. mult (No. 635) . . . . . 7·50 45
1056 $1 on $1.05 on 10c. mult (No. 768) . . . 6·50 45
1056a – $1 on $1.10 on $2 mult (No. 843) . . . . . 1·00 2·50
1057 – $1 on 220c. on 5c. mult (No. 844) . . . . . 7·50 75
1058 – $1 on 330c. on $2 mult (as No. 981) . . . . 3·00 45
1059 – $1 on $12 on $1.10 on $2 multicoloured (No. P3) . . . . . . 1·75 2·00
See also Nos. 1080/4.

1983. No. 859 optd **1983**.
1060 $1 on 60c. Beethoven and Sonny Thomas . . . . . 6·00 45

1983. Conference of Foreign Ministers of Non-aligned Countries, New Delhi. No. 569 surch **FIFTY CENTS** and No. 570 optd **1983**.
1061 **136** 25c. multicoloured . . . 75 25
1062 50c. on 8c. multicoloured 1·00 25

1983. No. 771 further surch **20**.
1064 **181** 20c. on 10c. on 3c. black, blue and red . . 55 10

1983. Commonwealth Day. Nos. 424 and 435 surch **Commonwealth Day 14 March 1983**, emblem and value.
1065 **60** 25c. on 6c. green . . . . 1·00 20
1066 $1.20 on 6c. green 50 50
1067 **63** $1.30 on 24c. black and orange . . . . 3·00 55
1068 $2.40 on 24c. black and orange . . . . 3·50 1·50

1983. Easter. Nos. 482/3 optd **1983**.
1069 **111** 25c. multicoloured . . . 15 10
1070 30c. multicoloured . . . 30 15

1983. 25th Anniv of International Maritime Organization. British Guiana fiscal stamp optd.
1071 **262** $4.80 blue and green . . 2·00 4·00

1983. Optd **1983**.
1072 **152** 50c. mult (No. 637) . . 1·50 25
1073 **159** 50c. blue, black and yellow (No. 668) . . 1·50 25
1073a – 50c. mult (No. 723) . . 26·00 2·00
1074 – 50c. mult (No. 854) . . 60 25
1075 – 50c. mult (No. 858) . . 5·00 25
1076 – $1 mult (No. 628) . . . 4·00 45
1077 – $1 mult (No. 638) . . . 4·75 45
1078 – $1 mult (No. 675) . . . 4·00 45
1079 – $1 on 30c. mult (No. 855) . . . . . 1·25 45
1079a – $3 mult (No. 720) . . . 24·00 1·50
1079b – $3 mult (No. 724) . . . 35·00 2·50
1079c – $3 mult (No. 748) . . . 85·00 9·00

1983. Surch **FIFTY CENTS**.
1080 **148** 50c. on 8c. mult (No. 615) . . . . . . 1·75 25
1081 **162** 50c. on 8c. mult (No. 681) . . . . . . 6·00 25
1082 **171** 50c. on 10c. mult (No. 721) . . . . . . 3·00 25
1083 – 50c. on 10c. on 25c. mult (No. O13) . . . . . . 6·00 25
1084 – 50c. on 330c. on $3 mult (No. 845) . . . . . . 4·00 25

1983. Surch in figures with **c** after new face value.
1098 **105** 15c. on 6c. black, gold and pink (No. 469) . . 10 10
1100 – 20c. on 6c. multicoloured (No. 546) 15 10
1087 **111** 50c. on 6c. multicoloured (No. 481) 40 30
1099 – 50c. on 6c. multicoloured (No. 489) 30 30

1983. No. 489 surch **$1**.
1088 $1 on 6c. Black acara ("Patua") . . . . 1·75 30

1983. No. 639 surch **110**.
1089 **153** 110c. on 10c. yellow, green and violet . . . 1·75 50

1983. Nos. 551 and 556 surch.
1090 250c. on 40c. Tiger beard 7·50 55
1091 400c. on 50c. "Odontadenia grandiflora" . . . . . . 5·50 70

1983. World Telecommunications and Health Day. Nos. 842 and 980 further surch.
1092 25c. on 220c. on 1c. Pitcher plant of Mt. Roraima (surch **ITU 1983 25**) . . 40 40
1093 25c. on 220c. on 1c. Pitcher plant of Mt. Roraima (surch **WHO 1983 25**) 40 40
1094 25c. on 220c. on 1c. Pitcher plant of Mt. Roraima (surch **17 MAY '83 ITU/ WHO 25**) 40 40
1095 $4.50 on 75c. on $5 "Odontadenia grandiflora" (surch **ITU/ WHO 17 MAY 1983**) . . 13·00 1·50
1095a 235c. on 75c. on $5 (No. 929) . . . . 1·00 1·00

1983. 30th Anniv of President's Entry into Parliament. Nos. 690 and 692 surch in words, No. 1096 additionally optd **1983**.
1096 $1 on 15c. black, blue and grey . . . . 6·00 50
1097 $1 on 40c. black, orange and grey . . . . 10·00 50

1983. No. 611 optd **1983**.
1101 25c. Guides in camp . . . . 48·00 4·00

1983. 15th World Scout Jamboree, Alberta. Nos. 835/6 and O25 optd **CANADA 1983**, Nos. 1103 and 1105 additionally surch.
1103 – $1.30 on 100c. on 8c. multicoloured . . . . 1·50 1·00
1104 **116** 180c. on 6c. mult . . . . 1·50 1·50
1105 $3.90 on 400c. on 6c. multicoloured . . . . 2·25 3·50

1983. Nos. 659/60 surch.
1106 60c. on 15c. Map of the Caribbean . . . . 12·00 55
1107 $1.50 on 15c. Prudential Cup . . . . 14·00 1·75

1983. As Nos. 1049/50, but without commemorative inscr above flag.
1108 25c. As Type **258** 15 15
1109 25c. As No. 1050 . . . . . 15 15

1983. Optd **1983**.
1110 **105** 30c. black, gold and green (No. 471) . . . 75 20
1111 – 30c. multicoloured (No. 695) . . . . . . 9·50 30
1112 – 30c. multicoloured (No. 718) . . . . . . 4·50 20
1113 – 30c. multicoloured (No. 722) . . . . . . 8·00 20
1114 – 30c. multicoloured (No. 746) . . . . . . 14·00 20
1115 – 60c. multicoloured (No. 697) . . . . . . 10·00 20
1116 – 60c. multicoloured (No. 731) . . . . . . 5·50 20

1983. No. 553 optd **1982**.
1117 60c. Soldier's cap . . . . . 4·00 35

1983. Surch.
1118 **157** 120c. on 8c. mult (No. 654) . . . . . . 2·25 40
1119 – 120c. on 10c. red, black and gold (No. 666) . . 2·25 40
1120 – 120c. on 35c. mult (No. 622) . . . . . . 2·25 40
1121 – 120c. on 35c. orange, green and violet (No. 640) . . . . . . 2·25 40

1983. Nos. 716 and 729 surch.
1122 120c. on 10c. Type **173** . . 2·00 40
1123 120c. on 375c. on $3 Cylinder satellite . . . . 1·75 40

No. 1123 also carries an otherwise unissued surcharge in red reading **INTERNATIONAL SCIENCE YEAR 1982 375**. As issued much of this is obliterated by two heavy bars.

1983. British Guiana No. D1a and Guyana No. D8 surch **120 GUYANA**.
1124 D **1** 120c. on 1c. green . . . 1·50 45
1125 D **2** 120c. on 1c. olive . . . 1·50 45

1983. CARICOM Day. No. 823 additionally surch **CARICOM DAY 1983 60**.
1126 60c. on $3 "Makanaima the Great Ancestral Spirit of the Amerindians" . . . . 1·00 35

271 "Kurupukari"

1983. Riverboats.
1127 **271** 30c. black and red . . . 15 20
1128 – 60c. black and violet . . 15 35
1129 – 120c. black and yellow 20 60
1130 – 130c. black 20 65
1131 – 150c. black and green . . 20 80
DESIGNS: 60c. "Makouria"; 120c. "Powis"; 130c. "Pomeroon"; 150c. "Lukanani".

1983. Unissued Royal Wedding surch similar to No. 843 additionally surch.
1132 $2.30 on $1.10 on $2 "Norantea guianensis" . . 60 40
1133 $3.20 on $1.10 on $2 "Norantea guianensis" . . 60 40

1983. Bicentenary of Manned Flight and 20th Anniv of Guyana Airways. Nos. 701/2a optd as indicated in brackets.
1134 20c. multicoloured (**BW**) . . 80 35
1135 20c. multicoloured (**LM**) . . 80 35
1136 20c. multicoloured (**GY 1963 1983**) 80 35
1137 20c. multicoloured (**JW**) . . 80 35
1138 20c. multicoloured (**CU**) . . 80 35
1139 20c. multicoloured (**Mont Golfier 1783-1983**) . . . 80 35
1140 25c. multicoloured (**BGI**) . . 1·75 60
1141 25c. multicoloured (**GEO**) 35 10
1142 25c. multicoloured (**MIA**) 1·75 60
1143 25c. multicoloured (**BVB**) 1·75 60
1144 25c. multicoloured (**PBM**) 1·75 60
1145 25c. multicoloured (**Mont Golfier 1783-1983**) 40 15
1146 25c. multicoloured (**POS**) 1·75 60
1147 25c. multicoloured (**JFK**) . . 1·75 60
1148 30c. multicoloured (**AHL**) 80 30
1149 30c. multicoloured (**BCG**) 80 30
1150 30c. multicoloured (**BMJ**) 80 30
1151 30c. multicoloured (**EKE**) 80 30
1152 30c. multicoloured (**GEO**) 80 30
1153 30c. multicoloured (**GFO**) 80 30
1154 30c. multicoloured (**IBM**) 80 30
1155 30c. multicoloured (**Mont Golfier 1783-1983**) 35 15
1156 30c. multicoloured (**KAI**) . . 80 30
1157 30c. multicoloured (**KAR**) 80 30
1158 30c. multicoloured (**KPG**) 80 30
1159 30c. multicoloured (**KRG**) 80 30
1160 30c. multicoloured (**KTO**) 80 30
1161 30c. multicoloured (**LTM**) 80 30
1162 30c. multicoloured (**MHA**) 80 30
1163 30c. multicoloured (**MWJ**) 80 30
1164 30c. multicoloured (**MYM**) 80 30
1165 30c. multicoloured (**NAI**) . . 80 30
1166 30c. multicoloured (**ORJ**) 80 30
1167 30c. multicoloured (**USI**) . . 80 30
1168 30c. multicoloured (**VEG**) 80 30

1983. No. 649 further surch **240**.
1169 240c. on 35c. on 60c. Soldier's cap . . . . . . 2·75 1·00

1983. F.A.O. Fisheries Project. Nos. 448 and 450 surch **FAO 1983** and value.
1170 30c. on 1c. Type **87** 25 15
1171 $2.60 on 3c. Peacock cichlid ("Lukunani") . . . . . . 2·00 2·75

277 G.B. 1857 1d. with Georgetown "AO3" Postmark

1983. 125th Anniv of Use of Great Britain Stamps in Guyana. (a) Inscriptions in black.
1172 **277** 25c. brown and black . . 15 10
1173 – 30c. red and black . . . 15 15
1174 – 60c. violet and black . . 25 30
1175 – 120c. green and black . . 50 55

(b) Inscriptions in blue.
1176 **277** 25c. brown and black . . 15 10
1177 – 25c. red and black . . . 15 10
1178 – 25c. violet and black . . 15 10
1179 – 25c. green and black . . 15 10
1180 **277** 30c. brown and black . . 15 15
1181 – 30c. red and black . . . 15 15
1182 – 30c. violet and black . . 15 15
1183 – 30c. green and black . . 15 15
1184 **277** 45c. brown and black . . 30 25
1185 – 45c. red and black . . . 30 25
1186 – 45c. violet and black . . 30 25
1187 – 45c. green and black . . 30 25
1188 **277** 120c. brown and black 30 55
1189 – 130c. red and black . . . 30 60
1190 – 150c. violet and black . . 30 70
1191 – 200c. green and black . . 30 95
DESIGNS: Nos. 1173, 1177, 1181, 1185, 1189, G.B. 1857 4d. red; Nos. 1174, 1178, 1182, 1186, 1190, G.B. 1856 6d. lilac; Nos. 1175, 1179, 1183, 1187, 1191, G.B. 1856 1s. green.
Each design incorporates the "AO3" postmark except Nos. 1189/91 which show mythical post-marks of the Crowned-circle type inscribed "DEMERARA", "BERBICE" or "ESSEQUIBO".

1983. International Communications Year. No. 716 surch **INT. COMMUNICATIONS YEAR 50**.
1192 50c. on 375c. on $3 Cylinder satellite . . . . 4·50 30
No. 1192 also carries an otherwise unissued "375" surcharge. As issued much of this surcharge is obliterated by two groups of six horizontal lines.

1983. St. John Ambulance Commemoration. Nos. 650 and 653 surch.
1193 **156** 75c. on 8c. silver, black and mauve . . . . . 4·50 50
1194 – $1.20 on 40c. silver, black and blue . . . . 6·50 75

1983. International Food Day. No. 616 surch **$1.20 Int. Food Day 1983**.
1195 $1.20 on 35c. Five-fingers and awaras . . . . 1·00 50

1983. 65th Anniv of I.L.O. and 25th Death Anniv of H. N. Critchlow (founder of Guyana Labour Union). No. 840 further optd **1918-1983 I.L.O.**
1196 240c. on $3 H. N. Critchlow 1·50 1·50

1983. Deepavali Festival. Nos. 661 and 663/4 surch.
1197 25c. on 8c. Type **158** . . . 20 10
1198 $1.50 on 35c. Flame in bowl 1·25 60
1199 $1.50 on 40c. Goddess Latchmi 80 60

1983. No. 732 optd **1982** and No. 798 further optd **1983**.
1200 $3 "Makanaima the Great Ancestral Spirit of the Amerindians" . . . . . . 1·00 70
1201 360c. on $2 "Norantea guianensis" . . . . 1·10 80

1983. Wildlife Protection. Nos. 686 and 688 surch and No. 852 optd **1983**.
1202 30c. Six-banded armadillo 75 15
1203 60c. on 15c. Giant sea turtle 1·25 30
1204 $1.20 on 40c. Iguana . . . 1·75 50

1983. Human Rights Day. No. 1079c optd **Human Rights Day**.
1205 $3 Rotary anniversary emblem . . . . 2·00 1·25

1983. Olympic Games, Los Angeles (1984) (1st issue). Nos. 733/44 surch **LOS ANGELES 1984 125**, Nos. 1206/17 further surch **55**.
1206 55c. on 125c. on 35c. Type **174** 25 25
1207 55c. on 125c. on 35c. Trahira ("Haimara") . . 25 25
1208 55c. on 125c. on 35c. Electric eel 25 25
1209 55c. on 125c. on 35c. Golden rivulus 25 25
1210 55c. on 125c. on 35c. Golden pencilfish . . . 25 25
1211 55c. on 125c. on 35c. Four-eyed fish 25 25
1212 55c. on 125c. on 35c. Red piranha ("Pirai") 25 25
1213 55c. on 125c. on 35c. Smoking hassar 25 25
1214 55c. on 125c. on 35c. Manta 25 25
1215 55c. on 125c. on 35c. Festive cichlid ("Flying patwa") 25 25
1216 55c. on 125c. on 35c. Arapaima 25 25
1217 55c. on 125c. on 35c. Peacock cichlid ("Lukanani") 25 25
1217a 125c. on 35c. Type **174** . . 7·50
1217b 125c. on 35c. Trahira ("Haimara") . . . . . 7·50
1217c 125c. on 35c. Electric eel 7·50
1217d 125c. on 35c. Golden rivulus . . . . 7·50
1217e 125c. on 35c. Golden pencilfish . . . . 7·50
1217f 125c. on 35c. Four-eyed fish . . . . 7·50
1217g 125c. on 35c. Red piranha ("Pirai") . . . . 7·50
1217h 125c. on 35c. Smoking hassar . . . . 7·50
1217i 125c. on 35c. Manta . . . 7·50
1217j 125c. on 35c. Festive cichlid ("Flying patwa") 7·50

1217k 125c. on 35c. Arapaima 7·50
1217l 125c. on 35c. Peacock cichlid ("Lukanani") 7·50
See also Nos. 1308/17 and 1420.

1983. No. F7 with unissued **ESPANA 1982** surch further optd **1983**.
1218 180c. on 60c. Soldier's cap 3·25 65

1983. Commonwealth Heads of Government Meeting, New Delhi. No. 542 surch **COMMONWEALTH HEADS OF GOV'T MEETING–INDIA 1983 150**.
1219 150c. on 1c. Pitcher plant of Mt. Roraima 3·25 60

1983. Christmas. No. 861 further surch **CHRISTMAS 1983 20c**.
1220 20c. on 12c. on 6c. Black acara ("Patua") 2·25 10

1984. Nos. 838 and F9 optd **POSTAGE**.
1221 $2 "Norantea guianensis" 3·50 70
1221b 550c. on $10 "Elbella patrobas" 19·00 8·50

1984. Flowers. Unissued stamps as T **222** surch.
1222 17c. on 2c. lilac, blue and green 3·50 2·00
1223 17c. on 8c. lilac, blue and mauve 3·50 2·00

1984. Republic Day. No. 703 and 705a variously optd or surch.
1224 25c. on 35c. mult (surch **ALL OUR HERITAGE 25**) 50 20
1225 25c. on 35c. mult (surch **1984 25**) 75 30
1226 25c. on 35c. mult (surch **REPUBLIC DAY 25**) 75 30
1227 25c. on 35c. mult (surch **25**) 75 30
1228 25c. on 35c. mult (surch **BERBICE 25**) 3·75 3·75
1229 25c. on 35c. mult (surch **DEMERARA 25**) 3·75 3·75
1230 25c. on 35c. mult (surch **ESSEQUIBO 25**) 3·75 3·75
1232 60c. mult (optd **ALL OUR HERITAGE**) 2·00 75
1233 60c. mult (optd **REPUBLIC DAY**) 2·00 75
1234 60c. mult (optd **1984**) 2·00 75

1984. Guyana Olympic Committee Appeal. Nos. 841/3 surch **OLYMPIC GAMES 84 25c POSTAGE (+2.25 SURTAX)** and rings, the whole surch inverted.
1235 25c.+$2.25 on 60c. on 3c. Hanging heliconia 2·75 6·00
1236 25c.+$2.25 on 75c. on $5 "Odontadenia grandiflora" 2·75 6·00
1237 25c.+$2.25 on $1.10 on $2 "Norantea guianensis" 2·75 6·00

1984. Nature Protection. Various stamps optd **Protecting our Heritage**, some additionally surch.
1238 20c. on 15c. mult (No. 491) 15·00 25
1239 20c. on 15c. mult (No. 791) 15·00 25
1240a 20c. on 15c. mult (No. 1044) 25·00 1·25
1241 25c. mult (No. 550ab) 23·00 25
1242 30c. on 15c. mult (No. 548a) 20·00 30
1243 40c. multicoloured (No. 457) 16·00 30
1244 50c. multicoloured (No. 552) 3·25 30
1245 50c. multicoloured (No. F6) 3·25 30
1246 60c. multicoloured (No. 459) 9·50 30
1247 90c. on 40c. mult (No. 551) 16·00 65
1248 180c. on 40c. mult (No. 919) 16·00 1·00
1249 $2 multicoloured (No. 461) 50·00 1·75
1250 225c. on 10c. mult (No. 490) 23·00 1·25
1251 260c. on $1 mult (No. 460) 11·00 1·00
1252 320c. on 40c. mult (No. 551) 12·00 2·25
1253 350c. on 40c. mult (No. 551) 20·00 3·00
1254 380c. on 50c. mult (No. 495) 11·00 2·75
1255 450c. on $5 mult (No. 462) 7·00 2·75

1984. Easter. Nos. 483 and 916/17 optd **1984** and No. 481 surch **130**.
1256 **111** 30c. multicoloured 20 20
1257 45c. on 6c. multicoloured 25 25
1258 75c. on 40c. multicoloured 35 35
1259 130c. on 6c. multicoloured 65 60

1984. Nos. 937/9 and 991 surch.
1260 75c. on $1 "Chelonanthus uliginoides" 9·50 35
1261 75c. on 110c. on 3c. Hanging heliconia 9·50 35
1262 225c. on 250c. on 6c. Cannon-ball tree 3·00 1·25
1263 230c. on $2.35 on 180c. on 60c. Soldier's cap 3·00 1·00

1984. Nos. 899/901, 904/6 and 909 surch.
1264 20c. on 15c. on 2c. Type **132** (No. 899) 1·50 30
1265 75c. on 110c. on 5c. Annatto tree (No. 904) 9·00 70
1266 90c. on 110c. on 5c. Annatto tree (No. 900) 5·50 85
1267 90c. on 110c. on 5c. Annatto tree (No. 901) 7·00 85
1268 120c. on 125c. on 8c. on 6c. Cannon-ball tree (No. 905) 7·00 1·00
1269 120c. on 125c. on 8c. on 6c. Cannon-ball tree (No. 906) 7·00 1·00
1270 120c. on 125c. on 8c. on 6c. Cannon-ball tree (No. 909) 2·75 1·00

1984. World Telecommunications and Health Day. Nos. 802 and 980 surch.
1271 25c. on 220c. on 1c. Pitcher plant of Mt. Roraima (surch **ITU DAY 1984 25**) 40 40
1272 25c. on 220c. on 1c. Pitcher plant of Mt. Roraima (surch **WHO DAY 1984 25**) 40 40
1273 25c. on 220c. on 1c. Pitcher plant of Mt. Roraima (surch **ITU/WHO DAY 1984 25**) 40 40
1274 $4.50 on 280c. on $5 "Odontadenia grandiflora" (surch **ITU/WHO DAY 1984 $4.50**) 2·50 2·00

1984. No. 1005 surch **120**.
1275 120c. on $1.25 on 6c. Cannon-ball tree 7·00 55

1984. World Forestry Conference. No. 755 optd **1984** and Nos. 752/4 and 875 surch.
1276 55c. on 30c. "Hymenaea courbaril" 2·75 30
1277 75c. on 110c. on $3 "Peltogyne venosa" 40 35
1278 160c. on 50c. "Mora excelsa" 75 70
1279 260c. on 10c. Type **177** 1·25 1·25
1280 $3 "Peltogyne venosa" 1·40 1·40

1984. No. 625 surch.
1281 55c. on 110c. on 10c. Type **150** 1·00 30
1282 90c. on 110c. on 10c. Type **150** 1·25 45
Nos. 1281/2 also carry an otherwise unissued 110c. surch.

1984. U.P.U. Congress, Hamburg. Nos. 1188/91 optd **UPU Congress 1984 Hamburg**.
1283 120c. brown and black 50 60
1284 130c. red and black 55 70
1285 150c. violet and black 60 75
1286 200c. green and black 80 90

1984. Nos. 982/3 and 986/7 surch.
1287 45c. on 50c. on 2c. green 60 25
1288 60c. on $1.10 on 3c. olive and brown 2·75 40
1289 120c. on $1.25 on 6c. green 75 55
1290 200c. on $2.20 on 24c. black and orange 7·00 1·10

1984. Nos. 979/80 and 1003 surch and No. 981 optd **1984**.
1291 75c. on 110c. on 5c. Annatto tree 1·00 35
1292 120c. on 170c. on 110c. on 5c. Annatto tree 1·25 55
1293 200c. on 220c. on 1c. Pitcher plant of Mt. Roraima 20·00 1·50
1294 330c. on $2 "Norantea guianensis" 2·00 2·00

1984. CARICOM Day. No. 1200 additionally surch **CARICOM DAY 1984 60**.
1295 60c. on $3 "Makanaima the Great Ancestral Spirit of the Amerindians" 40 30

1984. No. 544 surch **150**.
1296 150c. on 3c. Hanging heliconia 1·25 65

1984. CARICOM Heads of Government Conference. No. 544 surch **60 CARICOM HEADS OF GOV'T CONFERENCE JULY 1984**.
1297 60c. on 3c. Hanging heliconia 40 30

301 Children and Thatched School

1984. Cent of Guyana Teachers' Association. Mult.
1298 25c. Type **301** 10 15
1299 25c. Torch and graduates 10 15
1300 25c. Torch and target emblem 10 15
1301 25c. Teachers of 1884 and 1984 in front of school 10 15

1984. 60th Anniv of International Chess Federation. No. 1048 optd or surch also.
1302 25c. on 90c. on 60c. Fort Island (surch **INT. CHESS FED. 1924–1984 25**) 2·25 50
1303 25c. on 90c. on 60c. Fort Island (surch **1984 25**) 3·25 90
1304 75c. on 90c. on 60c. Fort Island (surch **INT. CHESS FED. 1924–1984 75**) 2·25 75
1305 75c. on 90c. on 60c. Fort Island (surch **1984 75**) 3·25 1·25
1306 90c. on 60c. Fort Island (optd **INT. CHESS FED. 1924–1984**) 2·25 80
1307 90c. on 60c. Fort Island (optd **1984**) 3·25 1·50

1984. Olympic Games, Los Angeles (2nd issue). No. 1051 surch.
1308 25c. on $1.30 mult (surch **TRACK AND FIELD 25**) 20 25
1309 25c. on $1.30 mult (surch **BOXING 25**) 20 30
1310 25c. on $1.30 mult (surch **OLYMPIC GAMES 1984 LOS ANGELES 25**) 20 30
1311 25c. on $1.30 mult (surch **CYCLING 25**) 2·75 50
1312 25c. on $1.30 mult (surch **OLYMPIC GAMES 1984 25**) 4·25 1·25
1313 $1.20 on $1.30 mult (surch **TRACK AND FIELD $1.20**) 1·25 1·40
1314 $1.20 on $1.30 mult (surch **BOXING $1.20**) 1·25 1·40
1315 $1.20 on $1.30 mult (surch **OLYMPIC GAMES 1984 LOS ANGELES $1.20**) 1·25 1·40
1316 $1.20 on $1.30 mult (surch **CYCLING $1.20**) 4·25 2·00
1317 $1.20 on $1.30 mult (surch **OLYMPIC GAMES 1984 $1.20**) 4·50 4·50

1984. 60th Anniv of Girl Guide Movement in Guyana. Nos. 900/9 surch **25 GIRL GUIDES 1924-1984**.
1318 25c. on 110c. on 5c. Annatto tree (No. 900) 25 20
1319 25c. on 110c. on 5c. Annatto tree (No. 901) 25 20
1320 25c. on 110c. on 5c. Annatto tree (No. 902) 80 60
1321 25c. on 110c. on 5c. Annatto tree (No. 903) 80 60
1322 25c. on 110c. on 5c. Annatto tree (No. 904) 9·00 9·50
1323 25c. on 125c. on 8c. on 6c. Cannon-ball tree (No. 905) 25 20
1324 25c. on 125c. on 8c. on 6c. Cannon-ball tree (No. 906) 25 20
1325 25c. on 125c. on 8c. on 6c. Cannon-ball tree (No. 907) 80 60
1326 25c. on 125c. on 8c. on 6c. Cannon-ball tree (No. 908) 80 60
1327 25c. on 125c. on 8c. on 6c. Cannon-ball tree (No. 909) 9·00 9·50

1984. Various stamps surch.
1328 20c. on 15c. on 2c. Type **132** (No. 1034) 30 10
1341 25c. on 10c. Cattleya (No. 547) 50·00 2·00
1343 25c. on 15c. Christmas orchid (No. 548a) £120 5·00
1342 25c. on 15c. Christmas orchid (No. 864) 21·00 30
1346 25c. on 15c. Christmas orchid (No. 977) 16·00 20
1347 25c. on 15c. Christmas orchid (No. 1009) 16·00 20
1348 25c. on 15c. Christmas orchid (No. O23) 16·00 20
1342a 25c. on 35c. on 60c. Soldier's cap (No. 649) 95·00 4·75
1331 60c. on 110c. on 8c. on 3c. Hanging heliconia (As No. 868 but with only one **110**) 29·00 4·75
1332 120c. on 125c. on 8c. on 6c. Cannon-ball tree (No. 893) 5·00 50
1333 120c. on 125c. on $2 "Norantea guianensis" (No. 834) 65·00 7·00
1334 120c. on 125c. on $2 "Norantea guianensis" (No. O20) 3·50 50
1335 120c. on 140c. on $1 "Chelonanthus uliginoides" (No. 796) 5·50 50
1349 130c. on 110c. on $2 "Norantea guianensis" (No. 804) 85·00 4·75
1350 130c. on 110c. on $2 "Norantea guianensis" (No. O22) 1·25 1·25
1336 200c. on 220c. on 1c. Pitcher plant of Mt. Roraima (No. 922) 17·00 75
1337 320c. on $1.10 on $2 "Norantea guianensis" (No. 804) 1·50 75
1338 350c. on 375c. on $5 "Odontadenia grandiflora" (No. 803) 3·75 80
1339 390c. on 400c. on $5 "Odontadenia grandiflora" (No. 1091) 4·50 90
1340 450c. on $5 "Odontadenia grandiflora" (No. O16) 7·50 2·75
1351a 600c. on $7.20 on $1 "Chelonanthus uliginoides" (No. 770) 50 60

1984. Various stamps optd **1984**.
1352 20c. "Paphinia cristata" (No. 549) 27·00 30
1358 25c. Marabunta (No. 550) 85·00 4·50
1359 25c. Marabunta (No. F4) 6·00 50
1359a 25c. Marabunta (No. F4a) 2·00 30
1354 50c. on 8c. Type **136** (No. 1062) 10·00 25
1355 60c. on 1c. Pitcher plant of Mt. Roraima (No. 1000) 2·25 25
1356 $2 "Norantea guianensis" (No. O33) 1·25 60
1360 $3.60 on $5 "Odontadenia grandiflora" (No. 769) 85 1·10

1984. No. 899 optd with fleur-de-lis.
1358a 25c. Marabunta 85·00 4·50

1984. 40th Anniv of I.C.A.O. Nos. 981, 1017 and 1148/68 optd **ICAO** or as indicated.
1361 30c. multicoloured (No. 1148) 1·25 80
1362 30c. multicoloured (No. 1149) 1·25 80
1363 30c. multicoloured (No. 1150) 1·25 80
1364 30c. multicoloured (No. 1151) 1·25 80
1365 30c. multicoloured (No. 1152) 1·25 80
1366 30c. multicoloured (No. 1153) 1·25 80
1367 30c. multicoloured (No. 1154) (optd **IMB/ICAO**) 1·25 80
1368 30c. multicoloured (No. 1155) (optd **KCV/ICAO**) 1·25 80
1369 30c. multicoloured (No. 1156) (optd **KAI/ICAO**) 1·25 80
1370 30c. multicoloured (No. 1157) 1·25 80
1371 30c. multicoloured (No. 1158) 1·25 80
1372 30c. multicoloured (No. 1155) (optd **1984**) 1·25 80
1373 30c. multicoloured (No. 1155) (optd **KPM/ICA**) 1·25 80
1374 30c. multicoloured (No. 1159) 1·25 80
1375 30c. multicoloured (No. 1160) 1·25 80
1376 30c. multicoloured (No. 1161) 1·25 80
1377 30c. multicoloured (No. 1155) (optd **PMT/ICAO**) 1·25 80
1378 30c. multicoloured (No. 1162) 1·25 80
1379 30c. multicoloured (No. 1163) 1·25 80
1380 30c. multicoloured (No. 1164) 1·25 80
1381 30c. multicoloured (No. 1165) 1·25 80
1382 30c. multicoloured (No. 1166) 1·25 80
1383 30c. multicoloured (No. 1167) 1·25 80
1384 30c. multicoloured (No. 1168) 1·25 80
1385 200c. on 330c. on $2 multicoloured (No. 981) 75 85
1386 200c. on 75c. on $5 multicoloured (No. 1017) 3·00 2·00
No. 1385 also carries an otherwise unissued surch **G.A.C. Inaug. Flight Georgetown–Toronto 200**.

1984. Wildlife Protection. Nos. 756/67 optd **1984**.
1387 30c. Type **178** 30 25
1388 30c. Red howler 30 25
1389 30c. Common squirrel-monkey 30 25
1390 30c. Two-toed sloth 30 25
1391 30c. Brazilian tapir 30 25
1392 30c. Collared peccary 30 25
1393 30c. Six-banded armadillo 30 25
1394 30c. Tamandua ("Ant Eater") 30 25
1395 30c. Giant anteater 30 25
1396 30c. Murine opossum 30 25
1397 30c. Brown four-eyed opossum 30 25
1398 30c. Brazilian agouti 30 25

1984. Nos. D10/11 surch **120 GUYANA**.
1399 D 2 120c. on 4c. blue 1·50 45
1402 120c. on 12c. red 1·50 45

1984. 175th Birth Anniv of Louis Braille (inventor of alphabet for the blind). No. 1040 surch **$1.50**.
1403 $1.50 on 15c. on 10c. Type **215** 6·50 55

1984. International Food Day. No. 1012 surch **1**.
1404 150c. on 50c. Pawpaw and tangerine 2·50 55

The surcharge places a "1" alongside the original face value and obliterates the "1982" date on the previous overprint.

1984. Birth Centenary of H. N. Critchlow (founder of Guyana Labour Union). No. 873 surch **240** and No. 1196, both optd 1984.
1405 240c. on 110c. on $3 H. N. Critchlow (No. 873) 1·00 65
1406 240c. on $3 H. N. Critchlow (No. 1196) 7·50 70

1984. Nos. 910/12 and 1184/7 surch.
1407 **277** 25c. on 45c. brown and black 15 15
1408 – 25c. on 45c. red and black (No. 1185) 15 15
1409 – 25c. on 45c. violet and black (No. 1186) 15 15
1410 – 25c. on 45c. green and black (No. 1187) 15 15
1411 – 120c. on 100c. on $3 mult (No. 910) 9·50 45
1412 – 120c. on 400c. on 30c. mult (No. 911) 1·00 45
1413 – 320c. on $5 multicoloured (No. 912) 17·00 1·75

1984. Deepavali Festival. Nos. 544/5 surch **MAHA SABHA 1934-1984** and new value.
1414 25c. on 5c. Annatto tree 50 10
1415 $1.50 on 3c. Hanging heliconia 2·75 1·00

1984. A.S.D.A. Philatelic Exhibition, New York. Nos. 1188/91 optd **Philatelic Exhibition New York 1984**.
1416 **277** 120c. brown and black 40 45
1417 – 130c. red and black 45 50
1418 – 150c. violet and black 50 55
1419 – 200c. green and black 70 75

1984. Olympic Games, Los Angeles (3nd issue). Design as No. 1051, but with Olympic rings and inscr "OLYMPIC GAMES 1984 LOS ANGELES".
1420 $1.20 Youth display (41 × 25 mm) 1·50 45

1984. Nos. 847, 861, 1099 and 1088 surch.
1421 20c. on 12c. on 12c. on 6c. multicoloured (No. 847) 60 10
1422 20c. on 12c. on 6c. mult (No. 861) 75·00 5·50
1423 25c. on 50c. on 6c. mult (No. 1099) 30 10
1424 60c. on $1 on 6c. mult (No. 1088) 45 25

318 Pair of Swallow-tailed Kites on Tree

1984. Christmas. Swallow-tailed Kites. Mult.
1425 60c. Type **318** 3·00 1·75
1426 60c. Swallow-tailed kite on branch 3·00 1·75
1427 60c. Kite in flight with wings raised 3·00 1·75
1428 60c. Kite in flight with wings lowered 3·00 1·75
1429 60c. Kite gliding 3·00 1·75
Nos. 1425/9 were printed together, se-tenant, with the backgrounds forming a composite design. Each stamp is inscribed "CHRISTMAS 1982".

319 St. George's Cathedral, Georgetown

1985. Georgetown Buildings. Each black and stone.
1430 25c. Type **319** 10 10
1431 60c. Demerara Mutual Life Assurance Building 15 25
1432 120c. As No. 1431 25 45
1433 120c. Town Hall 25 45
1434 120c. Victoria Law Courts 25 45
1435 200c. As No. 1433 25 75
1436 300c. As No. 1434 30 1·10
Nos. 1432/4 were printed together, se-tenant, forming a composite design.

1985. International Youth Year. No. 1420 optd **International Youth Year 1985**.
1437 $1.20 Youth display 2·50 45
Examples of No. 1420 used for this overprint all show the second line of the original inscription as "LOS ANGELLES".

1985. Republic Day. Nos. 1049/50 and 1052 optd or surch **Republic Day 1970-1985**.
1438 25c. Type **238** 40 40
1439 25c. Flag (inscr "30th ANNIVERSARY IN PARLIAMENT") 40 40
1440 120c. on $6 Presidential standard 1·00 1·00
1441 130c. on $6 Presidential standard 1·10 1·10

322 Young Ocelot on Branch

1985. Wildlife Protection. Multicoloured.
1442A 25c. Type **322** (green background) 1·75 10
1443A 60c. Young ocelot (different) (brown background) 30 25
1444B 120c. As No. 1443 15 20
1445B 120c. Type **322** 15 20
1446B 120c. Young ocelot (different) (brown background) 15 20
1447A 130c. As No. 1446 45 60
1448A 320c. Scarlet macaw (28 × 46 mm) 3·25 1·50
1449A 330c. Young ocelot reaching for branch (28 × 46 mm) 90 1·50

1985. Revenue stamp as T **181**, and Nos. 912, 940, 1016 and No. O24 surch.
1450 30c. on 50c. mult (No. O24) 50 10
1451 55c. on 2c. black, blue and grey 65 20
1452 55c. on 15c. on 2c. black, blue and grey (940) 65 20
1453 90c. on $1 mult (No. 1016) 7·00 50
1454 225c. on $5 mult (No. 912) 16·00 1·75
1455 230c. on $5 mult (No. 912) 16·00 1·90
1456 260c. on $5 mult (No. 912) 16·00 2·00

1985. International Youth Year Save the Children Fund Campaign. Nos. 880, 1073a, 1079b and 1082 optd **International Youth Year 1985** or surch also.
1457 50c. "Two Boys catching Ducks" (No. 1073a) 2·25 20
1458 50c. on 10c. Type **171** (No. 1082) 7·00 20
1459 120c. on 125c. on $3 "Mango Season" (No. 880) 2·25 45
1460 $3 "Mango Season" (No. 1079b) 2·25 1·10

1985. 125th Anniv of British Guiana Post Office (1st issue). No. 699 surch **25** and names of post offices and postal agencies open in 1860.
1461 25c. on 10c. mult (**Airy Hall**) 1·25 1·25
1462 25c. on 10c. multicoloured (**Belfield Arab Coast**) 1·25 1·25
1463 25c. on 10c. multicoloured (**Belfield E. C. Dem.**) 1·25 1·25
1464 25c. on 10c. mult (**Belladrum**) 1·25 1·25
1465 25c. on 10c. multicoloured (**Beterver-wagting**) 1·25 1·25
1466 25c. on 10c. multicoloured (**Blairmont Ferry**) 1·25 1·25
1467 25c. on 10c. mult (**Boeraserie**) 1·25 1·25
1468 25c. on 10c. mult (**Brahm**) 1·25 1·25
1469 25c. on 10c. mult (**Bushlot**) 1·25 1·25
1470 25c. on 10c. mult (**De Kinderen**) 1·25 1·25
1471 25c. on 10c. multicoloured (**Fort Wellington**) 1·25 1·25
1472 25c. on 10c. mult (**Georgetown**) 1·25 1·25
1473 25c. on 10c. mult (**Hague**) 1·25 1·25
1474 25c. on 10c. mult (**Leguan**) 1·25 1·25
1475 25c. on 10c. mult (**Mahaica**) 1·25 1·25
1476 25c. on 10c. mult (**Mahaicony**) 1·25 1·25
1477 25c. on 10c. multicoloured (**New Amsterdam**) 1·25 1·25
1478 25c. on 10c. mult (**Plaisance**) 1·25 1·25
1479 25c. on 10c. multicoloured (**No. 6 Police Station**) 1·25 1·25
1480 25c. on 10c. mult (**Queenstown**) 1·25 1·25
1481 25c. on 10c. multicoloured (**Vergenoegen**) 1·25 1·25
1482 25c. on 10c. mult (**Vigilance**) 1·25 1·25
1483 25c. on 10c. multicoloured (**Vreed-en-Hoop**) 1·25 1·25
1484 25c. on 10c. mult (**Wakenaam**) 1·25 1·25
1485 25c. on 10c. multicoloured (**Windsor Castle**) 1·25 1·25
See also Nos. 1694/1717, 2140/64 and 2278/2301.

1985. I.T.U./W.H.O. Day. Nos. 1148/68 optd **1985** or with single capital letter.
1486 30c. multicoloured (1148) 1·25 1·25
1487 30c. multicoloured (1149) 1·25 1·25
1488 30c. multicoloured (1150) 1·25 1·25
1489 30c. multicoloured (1151) 1·25 1·25
1490 30c. multicoloured (1152) 1·25 1·25
1491 30c. multicoloured (1153) 1·25 1·25
1492 30c. multicoloured (1154) (**I**) 1·25 1·25
1493 30c. multicoloured (1155) (**T**) 1·25 1·25
1494 30c. multicoloured (1156) (**U**) 1·25 1·25
1495 30c. multicoloured (1157) 1·25 1·25
1496 30c. multicoloured (1158) 1·25 1·25
1497 30c. multicoloured (1155) (**W**) 1·25 1·25
1498 30c. multicoloured (1155) (**H**) 1·25 1·25
1499 30c. multicoloured (1155) (**O**) 1·25 1·25
1500 30c. multicoloured (1159) 1·25 1·25
1501 30c. multicoloured (1160) 1·25 1·25
1502 30c. multicoloured (1161) (**D**) 1·25 1·25
1503 30c. multicoloured (1155) (**A**) 1·25 1·25
1504 30c. multicoloured (1162) (**Y**) 1·25 1·25
1505 30c. multicoloured (1163) 1·25 1·25
1506 30c. multicoloured (1164) 1·25 1·25
1507 30c. multicoloured (1165) 1·25 1·25
1508 30c. multicoloured (1166) 1·25 1·25
1509 30c. multicoloured (1167) 1·25 1·25
1510 30c. multicoloured (1168) 1·25 1·25

1985. No. 861 surch **20**.
1511 20c. on 12c. on 6c. Patua 5·50 10

1985. 10th Anniv of Caribbean Agricultural Research Development Institute. No. 544 surch **60 CARDI 1975-1985**.
1512 60c. on 3c. Hanging heliconia 4·25 35

1985. No. 839 surch **600**.
1513 600c. on 625c. on 40c. Tiger beard 40·00 3·75

1985. 80th Anniv of Rotary International. Nos. 707 and 879 surch **ROTARY INTERNATIONAL 1905-1985**.
1514 120c. on 110c. on $3 Rotary anniversary emblem 18·00 75
1515 300c. on $2 "Morpho rhetenor" 14·00 3·75

1985. CARICOM Day. No. 1200 surch **CARICOM DAY 1985 60**.
1516 60c. on $3 "Makanaima the Great Ancestral Spirit of the Amerindians" 3·00 40

1985. 135th Anniv of First British Guiana Stamps. No. 870 surch **135th Anniversary Cotton Reel 1850-1985 120**.
1517 120c. on 110c. on 10c. Type **170** 1·50 70

"REICHENBACHIA" ISSUES. Due to the proliferation of these designs the catalogue uses the book plate numbers as description for each design. The following index gives the species on each plate.

Series 1

Plate No. 1 (Series 1) "Odontoglossum crispum"
Plate No. 2 (Series 1) "Cattleya percivaliana"
Plate No. 3 (Series 1) "Cypripedium sanderianum"
Plate No. 4 (Series 1) "Odontoglossum rossi"
Plate No. 5 (Series 1) "Cattleya dowiana aurea"
Plate No. 6 (Series 1) "Coelogyne cristata maxima"
Plate No. 7 (Series 1) "Odontoglossum insleayi splendens"
Plate No. 8 (Series 1) "Laelia euspatha"
Plate No. 9 (Series 1) "Dendrobium wardianum"
Plate No. 10 (Series 1) "Laelia autumnalis xanthotropis"
Plate No. 11 (Series 1) "Phalaenopsis grandiflora aurea"
Plate No. 12 (Series 1) "Cattleya lawrenceana"
Plate No. 13 (Series 1) "Masdevallia shuttleworthii" and "M. xanthocorys"
Plate No. 14 (Series 1) "Aeranthus sesquipedalis"
Plate No. 15 (Series 1) "Cattleya mendelii Duke of Marlborough"
Plate No. 16 (Series 1) "Zygopetalum intermedium"
Plate No. 17 (Series 1) "Phaius humblotii"
Plate No. 18 (Series 1) "Chysis bractescens"
Plate No. 19 (Series 1) "Masdevallia backhousiana"
Plate No. 20 (Series 1) "Cattleya citrina"
Plate No. 21 (Series 1) "Oncidium jonesianum" and "Oncidium jonesianum phaeanthum"
Plate No. 22 (Series 1) "Saccolabium giganteum"
Plate No. 23 (Series 1) "Cypripedium io"
Plate No. 24 (Series 1) "Odontoglossum blandum"
Plate No. 25 (Series 1) "Maxillaria sanderiana"
Plate No. 26 (Series 1) "Odontoglossum Edward II"
Plate No. 27 (Series 1) "Vanda teres"
Plate No. 28 (Series 1) "Odontoglossum hallii xanthoglossum"
Plate No. 29 (Series 1) "Odontoglossum crispum hrubyanum"
Plate No. 30 (Series 1) "Oncidium concolor"
Plate No. 31 (Series 1) "Trichopilia suavis alba"
Plate No. 32 (Series 1) "Cattleya superba splendens"
Plate No. 33 (Series 1) "Odontoglossum luteo-purpureum"
Plate No. 34 (Series 1) "Cypripedium niveum"
Plate No. 35 (Series 1) "Stanhopea shuttleworthii"
Plate No. 36 (Series 1) "Laelia anceps percivaliana"
Plate No. 37 (Series 1) "Odontoglossum hebraicum"
Plate No. 38 (Series 1) "Cypripedium oenanthum superbum"
Plate No. 39 (Series 1) "Dendrobium superbiens"
Plate No. 40 (Series 1) "Laelia harpophylla"
Plate No. 41 (Series 1) "Lycaste skinneri" and "alba"
Plate No. 42 (Series 1) "Phalaenopsis stuartiana"
Plate No. 43 (Series 1) "Cattleya trianaei ernesti"
Plate No. 44 (Series 1) "Sobralia xantholeuca"
Plate No. 45 (Series 1) "Odontoglossum crispum kinlesideanum"
Plate No. 46 (Series 1) "Cattleya trianaei schroederiana"
Plate No. 47 (Series 1) "Epidendrum vitellinum"
Plate No. 48 (Series 1) "Laelia anceps stella" and "barkeriana"
Plate No. 49 (Series 1) "Odontoglossum harryanum"
Plate No. 50 (Series 1) "Dendrobium leechianum"
Plate No. 51 (Series 1) "Phalaenopsis speciosa"
Plate No. 52 (Series 1) "Laelia elegans schilleriana"
Plate No. 53 (Series 1) "Zygopetalum wendlandi"
Plate No. 54 (Series 1) "Cypripedium selligerum majus"
Plate No. 55 (Series 1) "Angraecum articulatum"
Plate No. 56 (Series 1) "Laelia anceps sanderiana"
Plate No. 57 (Series 1) "Vanda coerulea"
Plate No. 58 (Series 1) "Dendrobium nobile sanderianum"
Plate No. 59 (Series 1) "Laelia gouldiana"
Plate No. 60 (Series 1) "Odontoglossum grande"
Plate No. 61 (Series 1) "Cypripedium rothschildianum"
Plate No. 62 (Series 1) "Vanda sanderiana"
Plate No. 63 (Series 1) "Dendrobium aureum"
Plate No. 64 (Series 1) "Oncidium macranthum"
Plate No. 65 (Series 1) "Cypripedium tautzianum"
Plate No. 66 (Series 1) "Cymbidium mastersi"
Plate No. 67 (Series 1) "Angraecum caudatum"
Plate No. 68 (Series 1) "Laelia albida"
Plate No. 69 (Series 1) "Odontoglossum roezlii"
Plate No. 70 (Series 1) "Oncidium ampliatum majus"
Plate No. 71 (Series 1) "Renanthera lowii"
Plate No. 72 (Series 1) "Cattleya warscewiczii"
Plate No. 73 (Series 1) "Oncidium lanceanum"
Plate No. 74 (Series 1) "Vanda hookeriana"
Plate No. 75 (Series 1) "Cattleya labiata gaskelliana"
Plate No. 76 (Series 1) "Epidendrum prismatocarpum"
Plate No. 77 (Series 1) "Cattleya guttata leopoldi"
Plate No. 78 (Series 1) "Oncidium splendidum"
Plate No. 79 (Series 1) "Odontoglossum hebraicum aspersum"
Plate No. 80 (Series 1) "Cattleya dowiana var chrysotoxa"
Plate No. 81 (Series 1) "Cattleya trianae alba"
Plate No. 82 (Series 1) "Odontoglossum humeanum"
Plate No. 83 (Series 1) "Cypripedium argus"
Plate No. 84 (Series 1) "Odontoglossum luteo-purpureum prionopetalum"
Plate No. 85 (Series 1) "Cattleya rochellensis"
Plate No. 86 (Series 1) "Odontoglossum triumphans"
Plate No. 87 (Series 1) "Phalaenopsis casta"
Plate No. 88 (Series 1) "Oncidium tigrinum"
Plate No. 89 (Series 1) "Cypripedium lemoinierianum"
Plate No. 90 (Series 1) "Catasetum bungerothii"
Plate No. 91 (Series 1) "Cattleya ballantiniana"
Plate No. 92 (Series 1) "Dendrobium brymerianum"
Plate No. 93 (Series 1) "Cattleya eldorado crocata"
Plate No. 94 (Series 1) "Odontoglossum sanderianum"
Plate No. 95 (Series 1) "Cattleya labiata warneri"
Plate No. 96 (Series 1) "Odontoglossum schroderianum"

Series 2

Plate No. 1 (Series 2) "Cypripedium morganiae burfordiense"
Plate No. 2 (Series 2) "Cattleya bowringiana"
Plate No. 3 (Series 2) "Dendrobium formosum"
Plate No. 4 (Series 2) "Phaius tuberculosus"
Plate No. 5 (Series 2) "Odontoglossum crispum mundyanum"
Plate No. 6 (Series 2) "Laelia praestans"
Plate No. 7 (Series 2) "Dendrobium phalaenopsis var statterianum"
Plate No. 8 (Series 2) "Cypripedium boxalli atratum"
Plate No. 9 (Series 2) "Odontoglossum wattianum"
Plate No. 10 (Series 2) "Cypripedium lathamianum inversum"
Plate No. 11 (Series 2) "Paphinia rugosa" and "Zygopetalum xanthinum"
Plate No. 12 (Series 2) "Dendrobium melanodiscus"
Plate No. 13 (Series 2) "Laelia anceps schroderiana"
Plate No. 14 (Series 2) "Phaius hybridus cooksonii"
Plate No. 15 (Series 2) "Disa grandiflora"
Plate No. 16 (Series 2) "Selenipedium hybridum grande"
Plate No. 17 (Series 2) "Cattleya schroederae alba"
Plate No. 18 (Series 2) "Lycaste skinnerii armeniaca"
Plate No. 19 (Series 2) "Odontoglossum excellens"
Plate No. 20 (Series 2) "Laelio-cattleya elegans var blenheimensis"
Plate No. 21 (Series 2) "Odontoglossum coradinei"
Plate No. 22 (Series 2) "Odontoglossum wilckeanum var rothschildianum"
Plate No. 23 (Series 2) "Cypripedium lawrenceanum hyeanum"
Plate No. 24 (Series 2) "Cattleya intermedia punctatissima"
Plate No. 25 (Series 2) "Laelia purpurata"
Plate No. 26 (Series 2) "Masdevallia harryana splendens"
Plate No. 27 (Series 2) "Selenipedium hybridum nitidissimum"
Plate No. 28 (Series 2) "Cattleya mendelii var measuresiana"
Plate No. 29 (Series 20 "Odontoglossum vexillarium" ("miltonia vexillaria")
Plate No. 30 (Series 2) "Saccolabium coeleste"
Plate No. 31 (Series 2) "Cypripedium hybridum youngianum"
Plate No. 32 (Series 2) "Miltonia (hybrida) bleuana"
Plate No. 33 (Series 2) "Laelia grandis"
Plate No. 34 (Series 2) "Cattleya labiata var lueddemanniana"
Plate No. 35 (Series 2) "Odontoglossum coronarium"
Plate No. 36 (Series 2) "Cattleya granulosa var schofieldiana"
Plate No. 37 (Series 2) "Odontoglossum (hybridum) leroyanum"
Plate No. 38 (Series 2) "Cypripedium (hybridum) laucheanum" and "eyermanianum"
Plate No. 39 (Series 2) "Cychnoches chlorochilon"
Plate No. 40 (Series 2) "Cattleya O'Brieniana"
Plate No. 41 (Series 2) "Odontoglossum ramosissimum"
Plate No. 42 (Series 2) "Dendrobium phalaenopsis var"
Plate No. 43 (Series 2) "Cypripedium (hybridum) pollettianum" and "maynardii"
Plate No. 44 (Series 2) "Odontoglossum naevium"
Plate No. 45 (Series 2) "Cypripedium (hybridum) castleanum"
Plate No. 47 (Series 2) "Cattleya amethystoglossa"
Plate No. 48 (Series 2) "Cattleya (hybrida) arnoldiana"
Plate No. 49 (Series 2) "Cattleya labiata"
Plate No. 50 (Series 2) "Dendrobium (hybridum) venus" and "cassiope"
Plate No. 51 (Series 2) "Selenipedium (hybridum) weidlichianum"

Plate No. 52 (Series 2) "Cattleya mossiae var reineckiana"
Plate No. 53 (Series 2) "Cymbidium lowianum"
Plate No. 54 (Series 2) "Oncidium loxense"
Plate No. 56 (Series 2) "Coelogyne sanderae"
Plate No. 58 (Series 2) "Coelogyne pandurata"
Plate No. 59 (Series 2) "Schomburgkia sanderiana"
Plate No. 60 (Series 2) "Oncidium superbiens"
Plate No. 61 (Series 2) "Dendrobium johnsoniae"
Plate No. 62 (Series 2) "Laelia hybrida behrensiana"
Plate No. 63 (Series 2) Hybrid "Calanthes Victoria Regina", "Bella" and "Burfordiense"
Plate No. 64 (Series 2) "Cattleya mendelii Quorndon House var"
Plate No. 65 (Series 2) "Arachnanthe clarkei"
Plate No. 66 (Series 2) "Zygopetalum burtii"
Plate No. 67 (Series 2) "Cattleya (hybrida) parthenia"
Plate No. 68 (Series 2) "Phalaenopsis sanderiana" and "intermedia portei"
Plate No. 69 (Series 2) "Phaius blumei var assamicus"
Plate No. 70 (Series 2) "Angraecum humblotii"
Plate No. 71 (Series 2) "Odontoglossum pescatorei"
Plate No. 72 (Series 2) "Cattleya rex"
Plate No. 73 (Series 2) "Zygopetalum crinitum"
Plate No. 74 (Series 2) "Cattleya lueddemanniana alba"
Plate No. 75 (Series 2) "Cymbidium (hybridum) winnianum"
Plate No. 76 (Series 2) Hybrid "Masdevallias courtauldiana", "geleniana" and "measuresiana"
Plate No. 77 (Series 2) "Cypripedium (hybridum) calypso"
Plate No. 78 (Series 2) "Masdevallia chimaera var mooreana"
Plate No. 79 (Series 2) "Miltonia phalaenopsis"
Plate No. 80 (Series 2) "Lissochilus giganteus"
Plate No. 82 (Series 2) "Thunia brymeriana"
Plate No. 83 (Series 2) "Miltonia moreliana"
Plate No. 84 (Series 2) "Oncidium kramerianum"
Plate No. 85 (Series 2) "Cattleya Victoria Regina"
Plate No. 86 (Series 2) "Zygopetalum klabochorum"
Plate No. 87 (Series 2) "Laelia autumnalis alba"
Plate No. 88 (Series 2) "Spathoglottis kimballiana"
Plate No. 89 (Series 2) "Laelio-cattleya" ("The Hon. Mrs. Astor")
Plate No. 90 (Series 2) "Phaius hybridus amabilis" and "marthiae"
Plate No. 91 (Series 2) "Zygopetalum rostratum"
Plate No. 92 (Series 2) "Coelogyne swaniana"
Plate No. 93 (Series 2) "Laelio-cattleya (hybrida) phoebe"
Plate No. 94 (Series 2) "Epidendrum atro-purpureum var randianum"
Plate No. 95 (Series 2) "Dendrobium imperatrix"
Plate No. 96 (Series 2) "Vanda parishii var marriottiana"

331 "Cattleya lawrenceana" (Plate No. 12 (Series 1))

1985. Centenary of Publication of Sanders' "Reichenbachia" (1st issue). Orchids. Mult.
1518 25c. Type **331** 50 30
1519 60c. Plate No. 2 (Series 1) 60 35
1520 60c. Plate No. 7 (Series 1) 60 35
1521 60c. Plate No. 10 (Series 1) 60 35
1522 60c. Plate No. 19 (Series 1) 60 35
1523 60c. Plate No. 31 (Series 1) 60 35
1524 120c. Plate No. 27 (Series 1) 75 55
1525 130c. Plate No. 3 (Series 1) 75 55
1759 130c. Plate No. 6 (Series 1) 75 20
1760 130c. Plate No. 13 (Series 1) 75 20
1528 130c. Plate No. 18 (Series 1) 4·25 55
1761 130c. Plate No. 20 (Series 1) 75 20
1762 130c. Plate No. 25 (Series 1) 75 20
1531 130c. Plate No. 29 (Series 1) 3·00 55
1532 130c. Plate No. 30 (Series 1) 3·00 55
1533 200c. Plate No. 4 (Series 1) 3·00 85
See also Nos. 1551/66, 1571/1806, 1597, 1620/1863, 1663/73, 1679/83, 1731/8, 1747/54, 1809/19, 1822, 1868/9, 1872/81, 1884/7, 1907, 1912/15, 1916/24, 1925/9, 2066/73, 2171/8, 2180/2, 2190/3, 2216/18, 2219/20, 2225/7, 2235/42, **MS**2275, 2314/18, 2322/5, 2328, **MS**2332, 2314/18, 2322/5, 2329, 2468/71, 2498/2511 and 2605/8.

332 Arms of Guyana

337 Leaders of the 1763 Rebellion

1985.
1535b **332** 25c. multicoloured . . 15 20
For Type **332** within frame, see No. 2183.

1985. 85th Birthday of Queen Elizabeth the Queen Mother (1st issue). Nos. 1528 and 1531/2 optd **QUEEN MOTHER 1900-1985**.
1536 130c. Plate No. 18 (Series 1) 80 80
1537 130c. Plate No. 29 (Series 1) 80 80
1538 130c. Plate No. 30 (Series 1) 80 80
MS1539 100 × 126 mm. 200c. × 4 Plate 4 (Series 1) . . . . . . 6·50 5·50

The four stamps in No. **MS**1539 are overprinted **LADY BOWES-LYON 1900-1923, DUCHESS OF YORK 1923-1937, QUEEN ELIZABETH 1937-1952** or **QUEEN MOTHER 1952-1985**.
See also No. **MS**1570.

1985. International Youth Year. Nos. 900/4 surch **25 International Youth Year 1985**.
1540 25c. on 110c. on 5c. multicoloured (900) . . . 15 15
1541 25c. on 110c. on 5c. multicoloured (901) . . . 15 15
1542 25c. on 110c. on 5c. multicoloured (902) . . . 60 60
1543 25c. on 110c. on 5c. multicoloured (903) . . . 60 60
1544 25c. on 100c. on 5c. multicoloured (904) . . . 10·00 10·00

1985. 75th Anniv of Girl Guide Movement. No. 612 surch **225 1910-1985**.
1545 225c. on 350c. on 225c. on 40c. Guides in camp . . . 40·00 3·00
No. 1545 also carries two otherwise unissued surcharges at top right.

1985. Birth Bicentenary of John J. Audubon (ornithologist). No. 992 surch **J. J. Audubon 1785-1985 240**.
1546 240c. on 35c. Harpy eagle 35·00 3·75

1985. 150th Anniv (1984) of Abolition of Slavery (1st issue).
1547 **337** 25c. black and grey . . . 25 10
1548 – 60c. black and mauve . . 20 25
1549 – 130c. black and blue . . 25 50
1550 – 150c. black and lilac . . 60 55
DESIGNS: 60c. Damon and Parliament Buildings, Georgetown; 130c. Quamina and Demerara, 1823; 150c. "Den Arendt" (slave ship), 1627.
For these designs in changed colours see Nos. 2552/5.

1985. Centenary of Publication of Sanders' "Reichenbachia" (2nd issue). As T **331** showing orchids. Multicoloured.
1551 25c. Plate No. 52 (Series 1) 2·00 25
1763 55c. Plate No. 9 (Series 1) 55 10
1764 55c. Plate No. 22 (Series 1) 55 10
1765 55c. Plate No. 49 (Series 1) 55 10
1766 55c. Plate No. 64 (Series 1) 55 10
1556 60c. Plate No. 44 (Series 1) 70 35
1557 60c. Plate No. 47 (Series 1) 70 35
1558 120c. Plate No. 36 (Series 1) 2·25 55
1559 130c. Plate No. 16 (Series 1) 2·25 55
1560 130c. Plate No. 38 (Series 1) 2·25 55
1561 150c. Plate No. 32 (Series 1) 2·25 55
1562 150c. Plate No. 34 (Series 1) 2·25 55
1563 150c. Plate No. 35 (Series 1) 2·25 55
1564 150c. Plate No. 41 (Series 1) 2·25 55
1565 150c. Plate No. 48 (Series 1) 2·25 55
1566 150c. Plate No. 62 (Series 1) 2·25 55

1985. Signing of Guyana–Libya Friendship Treaty. No. 621 surch **Guyana/Libya Friendship 1985 150**.
1567 **149** 150c. on 10c. mult . . . 9·00 2·75

1985. Namibia Day. No. 636 surch **150**.
1568 150c. on 35c. Unveiling of monument . . . . 2·75 55

1985. World Cup Football Championship, Mexico (1986) (1st issue). No. F2 surch **Mexico 1986 275**.
1569 275c. on 3c. Hanging heliconia . . . . 14·00 3·00
See also No. 1727.

1985. 85th Birthday of Queen Elizabeth the Queen Mother (2nd issue). Sheet 120 × 129 mm containing No. 1529 × 4 optd as No. **MS**1539, each stamp surch **200**.
MS1570 200c. on 130c. × 4 Plate No. 20 (Series 1) . . . . . . 18·00 7·00

1985. Centenary of Publication of Sanders' "Reichenbachia" (3rd issue). As T **331** showing orchids. Multicoloured.
1571 25c. Plate No. 8 (Series 1) 2·00 20
1572 25c. Plate No. 23 (Series 1) 2·00 20
1573 25c. Plate No. 51 (Series 1) 2·00 20
1574 25c. Plate No. 61 (Series 1) 2·00 20
1575 25c. Plate No. 63 (Series 1) 2·00 20
1576 25c. Plate No. 70 (Series 1) 2·00 20
1577 25c. Plate No. 72 (Series 1) 2·00 20
1578 120c. Plate No. 1 (Series 1) (horiz) . . . . 2·00 55
1579 120c. Plate No. 11 (Series 1) (horiz) . . . . 2·00 55
1580 120c. Plate No. 28 (Series 1) (horiz) . . . . 2·00 55
1767 150c. Plate No. 40 (Series 1) (horiz) 50 20
1768 150c. Plate No. 42 (Series 1) (horiz) 50 20
1769 150c. Plate No. 45 (Series 1) (horiz) 50 20
1584 200c. Plate No. 14 (Series 1) 2·25 80
1585 200c. Plate No. 21 (Series 1) (horiz) . . . . 2·25 80
1770 200c. Plate No. 43 (Series 1) (horiz) 55 30

1985. 30th Anniv of Commonwealth Caribbean Medical Research Council. Nos. 819, 871, 874, 928 and 1014 optd **1955–1985** or surch also.
1587 – 60c. mult (No. 819) . . . 20 25
1588 – 60c. mult (No. 1014) . . . 20 25
1589 **176** 120c. on 110c. on 10c. multicoloured (No. 871) 40 45
1590 – 120c. on 110c. on $3 mult (No. 874) 40 45
1592 – 120c. on 210c. on $3 mult (No. 928) 40 45

1985. 20th Anniv of Guyana Defence Force. No. 856 surch **1965-1985**.
1593 25c. on $1.10 on $3 W.O. and N.C.O; Guyana Defence Force, 1966 . . . 1·00 10
1594 225c. on $1.10 on $3 W.O. and N.C.O; Guyana Defence Force, 1966 . . . 2·50 1·25

1985. Fire Prevention. Nos. 678 and 680 optd **1985** and surch.
1595 25c. on 40c. Fire engine, 1977 . . . . 14·00 50
1596 320c. on 15c. Steam engine, circa 1860 . . . . 24·00 6·00

1985. Centenary of Publication of Sanders' "Reichenbachia" (4th issue). As T **331**. Mult.
1597 60c. Plate No. 55 (Series 1) 1·50 30

1985. Columbus Day. Unissued value as T **331** surch **350 CRISTOBAL COLON 1492-1992**. Mult.
1598 350c. on 120c. Plate No. 65 (Series 1) . . . . 7·50 3·50

1985. 20th Death Anniv of Sir Winston Churchill. No. 707 optd **SIR WINSTON CHURCHILL 1965-1985**.
1599 $2 "Morpho rhetenor" (female) . . . . 16·00 3·50

1985. 35th Anniv of International Commission of Irrigation and Drainage. No. 625 with unissued surcharge further surch **1950-1985**.
1600 **150** 25c. on 110c. on 10c. multicoloured 30 10
1601 200c. on 110c. on 10c. multicoloured . . . . 1·25 85

1985. 40th Anniv of U.N.O. Nos. 714/16, 800 and O19 optd **United Nations 1945-1985**.
1602 30c. multicoloured (No. 714) 1·75 10
1603 50c. multicoloured (No. 715) 1·75 20
1604 100c. on $3 mult (No. O19) 1·50 40
1605 225c. on 220c. on $3 mult (No. 800) . . . . 17·00 1·00
1606 $3 multicoloured (No. 716) 3·50 2·50

1985. Nos. 551/3, O14/15, O18, O21, OP1/2 and F7 optd **POSTAGE**.
1607 30c. on $2 "Norantea guianensis" (No. O18) . . 40 10
1608 40c. Tiger beard (No. 551) 45·00 1·00
1609 50c. "Guzmania lingulata" (No. 552) 40 20
1610 50c. "Guzmania lingulata" (No. O14) 40 20
1611 60c. Soldier's cap (No. 553) 3·50 25
1612 60c. Soldier's cap (No. O15) 3·25 25
1613 60c. Soldier's cap (No. F7) 1·75 25
1614 $10 "Elbella patrobas" (No. O21) . . . . 29·00 8·50
1615 $15 on $1 "Chelonanthus uliginoides" (No. OP1) . . 8·00 10·00
1616 $20 on $1 "Chelonanthus uliginoides" (No. OP2) . . 9·00 11·00

1985. Deepavali Festival. Nos. 542/3 surch **Deepavali 1985**.
1617 25c. on 2c. Type **132** . . . 1·00 25
1618 150c. on 1c. Pitcher plant of Mt. Roraima . . . . . . 3·50 1·50

1985. Christmas. Sheet 120 × 129 mm containing No. 1764 × 4 optd **Christmas 1985**.
MS1619 55c. × 4 Plate No. 22 (Series 1), each with a different overprint (Type **350**, **Happy New Year**, **Merry Christmas** or **Happy Holidays**) . . . . 7·00 4·00

1985. Centenary of Publication of Sanders' "Reichenbachia" (5th issue). As T **331** showing orchids. Multicoloured.
1620 25c. Plate No. 59 (Series 1) 1·00 20
1771 30c. Plate No. 53 (Series 1) 30 10
1622 60c. Plate No. 57 (Series 1) (horiz) . . . . 1·25 35
1623 60c. Plate No. 73 (Series 1) (horiz) . . . . 1·25 35
1624 60c. Plate No. 75 (Series 1) (horiz) . . . . 1·25 35
1772 75c. Plate No. 55 (Series 1) 35 15
1773 100c. Plate No. 65 (Series 1) 35 15
1627 120c. Plate No. 37 (Series 1) 2·00 55
1628 120c. Plate No. 46 (Series 1) 2·00 55
1629 120c. Plate No. 56 (Series 1) 2·00 55
1630 120c. Plate No. 58 (Series 1) 2·00 55
1631 120c. Plate No. 67 (Series 1) 2·00 55
1632 130c. Plate No. 66 (Series 1) 2·00 65
1633 150c. Plate No. 26 (Series 1) 2·25 75
1634 200c. Plate No. 33 (Series 1) (horiz) . . . . 2·50 85
1774 225c. Plate No. 24 (Series 1) 50 35
The 30, 75, 100 and 225c. values have "GUYANA" in blue.

351 Clive Lloyd (cricketer)

1985. Clive Lloyd's Testimonial Year. Multicoloured.
1636 25c. Type **351** 40 60
1637 25c. Clive Lloyd, bat and wicket 40 60
1638 25c. Cricket equipment . . . 40 60
1639 60c. As No. 1638 (25 × 33 mm) 40 40
1640 $1.30 As No. 1637 (25 × 33 mm) 40 85
1641 $2.25 Type **351** (25 × 33 mm) . . . . . . 40 1·25
1642 $3.50 Clive Lloyd with the Prudential Cup (36 × 56 mm) . . . . . . 45 1·75

1985. Wildlife Protection. Nos. 756/67 optd **1985**.
1643 30c. Type **178** 75 75
1644 30c. Red howler 75 75
1645 30c. Common squirrel-monkey 75 75
1646 30c. Two-toed sloth 75 75
1647 30c. Brazilian tapir 75 75
1648 30c. Collared peccary . . . 75 75
1649 30c. Six-banded armadillo 75 75
1650 30c. Tamandua 75 75
1651 30c. Giant anteater 75 75
1652 30c. Murine opossum . . . 75 75
1653 30c. Brown four-eyed opossum 75 75
1654 30c. Brazilian agouti 75 75

1985. No. 847 surch **20**.
1655 20c. on 12c. on 12c. on 6c. Black acara ("Patua") . . 6·00 20

1986. Centenary of the Appearance of "Reichenbachia" Volume 1. Nos. 1768 and 1770 optd **REICHENBACHIA 1886-1986**.
1657 150c. Plate No. 42 (Series 1) 5·00 90
1658 200c. Plate No. 43 (Series 1) 5·00 1·10

1986. Republic Day. Nos. 1108/9 and 1052 optd **Republic Day 1986** or surch also.
1659 25c. As Type **258** 10 10
1660 25c. As No. 1050 . . . . . 10 10
1661 120c. on $6 Presidential standard 40 50
1662 225c. on $6 Presidential standard . . . . 70 1·00

1986. Centenary of Publication of Sanders' "Reichenbachia" (6th issue). As T **331**. Mult.
1663 40c. Plate No. 77 (Series 1) 75 20
1664 45c. Plate No. 54 (Series 1) 75 25
1665 50c. Plate No. 92 (Series 1) 75 25
1666 60c. Plate No. 95 (Series 1) 80 30
1667 75c. Plate No. 5 (Series 1) 85 35
1668 90c. Plate No. 84 (Series 1) 95 40
1669 150c. Plate No. 78 (Series 1) 1·25 60
1670 200c. Plate No. 79 (Series 1) 1·60 80
1671 300c. Plate No. 83 (Series 1) 2·25 1·40
1672 320c. Plate No. 50 (Series 1) 2·25 1·60
1673 360c. Plate No. 85 (Series 1) 2·50 1·75

1986. Easter. No. 481 optd **1986** and surch also.
1674 **111** 25c. on 6c. multicoloured 25 10
1675 50c. on 6c. multicoloured 40 20
1676 100c. on 6c. mult 60 40
1677 200c. on 6c. mult . . . . 1·00 70

1986. 60th Anniv of St. John's Ambulance in Guyana. No. 652 surch **1926 1986 150**.
1678 150c. on 35c. silver, black and green . . . . 3·00 55

1986. Centenary of Publication of Sanders' "Reichenbachia" (7th issue). As T **331**. Mult.
1679 25c. Plate No. 71 (Series 1) (horiz) . . . . 1·50 20
1680 120c. Plate No. 69 (Series 1) (horiz) . . . . 2·25 55
1681 150c. Plate No. 87 (Series 1) (horiz) . . . . 2·50 65
1682 225c. Plate No. 60 (Series 1) 2·50 90
1683 350c. Plate No. 94 (Series 1) (horiz) . . . . 2·75 1·75

1986. 60th Birthday of Queen Elizabeth II. No. 1759/60 optd **1926 1986 QUEEN ELIZABETH**.
1684 130c. Plate No. 13 (Series 1) 4·00 1·50
MS1685 100 × 126 mm. 130c. on 130c., 200c. on 130c., 260c. on 130c., 330c. on 130c., Plate No. 6 (Series 1) . . . . 7·50 7·50
The original face values on No. **MS**1685 are obliterated by a floral pattern.

1986. Wildlife Protection. Nos. 685, 739/44 and 993/8 surch **Protect the** and value.
1686 60c. on 35c. Type **174** . . 35 40
1687 60c. on 35c. Trahira ("Haimara") 35 40
1688 60c. on 35c. Electric eel . . 35 40
1689 60c. on 35c. Golden rivulus 35 40
1690 60c. on 35c. Golden pencilfish 35 40
1691 60c. on 35c. Four-eyed fish 35 40
1691a 60c. on 35c. Red piranha ("Pirai") . . . . 10·00 3·00
1691b 60c. on 35c. Smoking hassar . . . . 10·00 3·00
1691c 60c. on 35c. Manta . . . . 10·00 3·00
1691d 60c. on 35c. Festive cichlid ("Flying patwa") . . . . 10·00 3·00
1691e 60c. on 35c. Arapaima . . 10·00 3·00

1691f 60c. on 35c. Peacock cichlid ("Lukanani") . . 10·00 3·00
1692 $6 on 8c. Type **163** . . . 3·00 3·25

1986. No. 799 surch **600**.
1693 600c. on 720c. on 60c. Soldier's cap . . . . . . 18·00 2·00

1986. 125th Anniv of British Guiana Post Office (2nd issue). No. 702a surch **25** and names of postal agencies opened between 1860 and 1880.
1694 25c. on 30c. mult (surch **Abary**) . . . . 1·25 1·00
1695 25c. on 30c. multicoloured (surch **Anna Regina**) . . . 1·25 1·00
1696 25c. on 30c. multicoloured (surch **Aurora**) . . . . . 1·25 1·00
1697 25c. on 30c. multicoloured (surch **Bartica Grove**) . . 1·25 1·00
1698 25c. on 30c. multicoloured (surch **Bel Air**) . . . . . 1·25 1·00
1699 25c. on 30c. multicoloured (surch **Belle Plaine**) . . . 1·25 1·00
1700 25c. on 30c. multicoloured (surch **Clonbrook**) . . . . 1·25 1·00
1701 25c. on 30c. multicoloured (surch **T.P.O. Dem. Railway**) . . . . 1·25 1·00
1702 25c. on 30c. multicoloured (surch **Enmore**) . . . . . 1·25 1·00
1703 25c. on 30c. multicoloured (surch **Fredericksburg**) . . 1·25 1·00
1704 25c. on 30c. multicoloured (surch **Good Success**) . . 1·25 1·00
1705 25c. on 30c. mult (surch **1986**) . . . . 1·25 1·00
1706 25c. on 30c. multicoloured (surch **Mariabba**) . . . . 1·25 1·00
1707 25c. on 30c. multicoloured (surch **Massaruni**) . . . . 1·25 1·00
1708 25c. on 30c. mult (surch **Nigg**) . . . . 1·25 1·00
1709 25c. on 30c. multicoloured (surch **No. 50**) . . . . . 1·25 1·00
1710 25c. on 30c. multicoloured (surch **No. 63 Benab**) . . 1·25 1·00
1711 25c. on 30c. multicoloured (surch **Philadelphia**) . . . 1·25 1·00
1712 25c. on 30c. multicoloured (surch **Sisters**) . . . . . 1·25 1·00
1713 25c. on 30c. multicoloured (surch **Skeldon**) . . . . . 1·25 1·00
1714 25c. on 30c. multicoloured (surch **Suddie**) . . . . . 1·25 1·00
1715 25c. on 30c. multicoloured (surch **Taymouth Manor**) 1·25 1·00
1716 25c. on 30c. mult (surch **Wales**) . . . . 1·25 1·00
1717 25c. on 30c. mult (surch **Whim**) . . . . 1·25 1·00

1986. 20th Anniv of Independence. (a) No. 332 of British Guiana surch **GUYANA INDEPENDENCE 1966-1986**, Nos. 424 and 435 of Guyana surch **1986** and No. 656 surch **25**.
1718 25c. on 2c. green (No. 332) 15 10
1719 25c. on 35c. mult (No. 656) 15 10
1720 60c. on 2c. green (No. 332) 25 10
1721 120c. on 6c. green (No. 424) 40 20
1722 130c. on 24c. black and orange (No. 435) . . . . 7·50 60

(b) Nos. 1188/91 surch **INDEPENDENCE 1966-1986**.
1723 **277** 25c. on 120c. brown, black and blue (No. 1188) 25 20
1724 – 25c. on 130c. red, black and blue (No. 1189) 25 20
1725 – 25c. on 150c. violet and blue (No. 1190) . . . 25 20
1726 – 225c. on 200c. green, black and blue (No. 1191) 65 75

1986. World Cup Football Championship, Mexico (2nd issue). No. 544 surch **MEXICO 1986 225**.
1727 225c. on 3c. Hanging heliconia . . . . 18·00 3·00

1986. CARICOM Day. No. 705a optd **CARICOM DAY 1986**.
1728 60c. "Papilio androgeus" . . 10·00 60

1986. CARICOM Heads of Government Conference, Georgetown. Nos. 544 and 601 surch **CARICOM HEADS OF GOV'T CONFERENCE JULY 1986** and value.
1729 25c. on 8c. on 6c. Cannon-ball tree . . . . 2·50 20
1730 60c. on 3c. Hanging heliconia . . . . 3·00 40

1986. Centenary of Publication of Sanders' "Reichenbachia" (8th issue). As T **331**. Mult.
1731 30c. Plate No. 86 (Series 1) 1·25 15
1732 55c. Plate No. 17 (Series 1) 50 20
1733 60c. Plate No. 93 (Series 1) 50 20
1734 100c. Plate No. 68 (Series 1) 2·00 20
1735 130c. Plate No. 91 (Series 1) 2·25 30
1736 250c. Plate No. 74 (Series 1) 75 75
1737 260c. Plate No. 39 (Series 1) 75 75
1738 375c. Plate No. 90 (Series 1) 3·75 1·25

1986. International Peace Year. Nos. 542 and 546 surch **INT. YEAR OF PEACE** and value.
1739 25c. on 1c. Pitcher plant of Mt. Roraima 70 40
1740 60c. on 6c. Cannon-ball tree 1·50 1·50
1741 120c. on 6c. Cannon-ball tree . . . . 1·50 1·50
1742 130c. on 6c. Cannon-ball tree . . . . 1·50 1·50
1743 150c. on 6c. Cannon-ball tree . . . . 1·50 1·50

363 Halley's Comet and British Guiana 1907 2c. Stamp

1986. Appearance of Halley's Comet.
1744 **363** 320c. red, black and lilac 40 65
1745 – 320c. multicoloured . . . 40 65
MS1746 76 × 50 mm. Nos. 1744/5. Imperf . . . . 1·50 1·25
DESIGN: No. 1745, Guyana 1985 320c. scarlet macaw stamp.

1986. Centenary of Publication of Sanders' "Reichenbachia" (9th issue). As T **331**. Mult.
1747 40c. Plate No. 96 (Series 1) 2·00 15
1748 45c. Plate No. 81 (Series 1) 30 15
1749 90c. Plate No. 89 (Series 1) 50 20
1750 100c. Plate No. 88 (Series 1) 3·50 20
1751 150c. Plate No. 76 (Series 1) 3·50 35
1752 180c. Plate No. 15 (Series 1) 50 40
1753 320c. Plate No. 82 (Series 1) 60 90
1754 330c. Plate No. 80 (Series 1) 3·50 1·25

1986. No. 489 surch **20**.
1755 20c. on 6c. Patua . . . . . 8·00 25

1986. 50th Anniv of Guyana United Sadr Islamic Association. Nos. 469/70 optd **GUSIA 1936-1986**, No. 1757 surch also.
1756 **105** 25c. black, gold and lilac 4·00 25
1757 $1.50 on 6c. black, gold and flesh . . . . . . 8·00 2·50

1986. Regional Pharmacy Conference. No. 545 surch **REGIONAL PHARMACY CONFERENCE 1986 130**.
1758 130c. on 5c. Annatto tree 9·00 1·00

1986. Centenary of Publication of Sanders' "Reichenbachia" (10th issue). As T **331**. Mult.
1809 30c. Plate No. 30 (Series 2) 1·25 15
1810 45c. Plate No. 21 (Series 2) (horiz) 50 15
1811 75c. Plate No. 8 (Series 2) 50 15
1812 80c. Plate No. 42 (Series 2) (horiz) 50 15
1813 90c. Plate No. 4 (Series 2) 55 25
1814 130c. Plate No. 38 (Series 2) 3·00 35
1815 160c. Plate No. 5 (Series 2) (horiz) . . . . 3·00 40
1816 200c. Plate No. 9 (Series 2) 75 50
1817 320c. Plate No. 12 (Series 2) 1·75 90
1818 350c. Plate No. 29 (Series 2) (horiz) . . . . 2·00 90
1819 360c. Plate No. 34 (Series 2) 5·50 90

1986. 20th Anniv of Independence (2nd issue). As T **332** but additionally inscr "1966–1986" at foot.
1820 25c. multicoloured . . . . . 1·75 25

1986. Centenary of Publication of Sanders' "Reichenbachia" (11th issue). Design as No. 1735, but with different face value. Mult.
1822 40c. Plate No. 91 (Series 1) 1·00 15

1986. Nos. 1361/84 surch **120**.
1823 120c. on 30c. mult (No. 1361) . . . . 2·00 1·50
1824 120c. on 30c. mult (No. 1362) . . . . 2·00 1·50
1825 120c. on 30c. mult (No. 1363) . . . . 2·00 1·50
1826 120c. on 30c. mult (No. 1364) . . . . 2·00 1·50
1827 120c. on 30c. mult (No. 1365) . . . . 2·00 1·50
1828 120c. on 30c. mult (No. 1366) . . . . 2·00 1·50
1829 120c. on 30c. mult (No. 1367) . . . . 2·00 1·50
1830 120c. on 30c. mult (No. 1368) . . . . 2·00 1·50
1831 120c. on 30c. mult (No. 1369) . . . . 2·00 1·50
1832 120c. on 30c. mult (No. 1370) . . . . 2·00 1·50
1833 120c. on 30c. mult (No. 1371) . . . . 2·00 1·50
1834 120c. on 30c. mult (No. 1372) . . . . 2·00 1·50
1835 120c. on 30c. mult (No. 1373) . . . . 2·00 1·50
1836 120c. on 30c. mult (No. 1374) . . . . 2·00 1·50
1837 120c. on 30c. mult (No. 1375) . . . . 2·00 1·50
1838 120c. on 30c. mult (No. 1376) . . . . 2·00 1·50
1839 120c. on 30c. mult (No. 1377) . . . . 2·00 1·50
1840 120c. on 30c. mult (No. 1378) . . . . 2·00 1·50
1841 120c. on 30c. mult (No. 1379) . . . . 2·00 1·50
1842 120c. on 30c. mult (No. 1380) . . . . 2·00 1·50
1843 120c. on 30c. mult (No. 1381) . . . . 2·00 1·50
1844 120c. on 30c. mult (No. 1382) . . . . 2·00 1·50
1845 120c. on 30c. mult (No. 1383) . . . . 2·00 1·50
1846 120c. on 30c. mult (No. 1384) . . . . 2·00 1·50

1986. 12th World Orchid Conference, Tokyo (1st issue). Unissued design as No. 1731, but with different face value, surch **12th World Orchid Conference TOKYO JAPAN MARCH 1987 650**.
1847 650c. on 40c. Plate No. 86 (Series 1) . . . . 16·00 5·00
No. 1847 is inscribed "ONTOGLOSSUM TRIUMPHANS" in error.
See also No. 2138.

1986. Columbus Day. Unissued design as No. 1774, but with different face value, surch **1492-1992 CHRISTOPHER COLUMBUS 320**.
1864 320c. on 150c. Plate No. 24 (Series 1) . . . . 6·50 2·50

1986. International Food Day. Nos. 1170/1 further surch **1986** and value.
1866 50c. on 30c. on 1c. Type **87** 3·75 25
1867 225c. on $2.60 on 3c. Peacock cichlid ("Lukanani") . . . . . . 11·00 2·50

1986. Centenary of Publication of Sanders' "Reichenbachia" (12th issue). As T **331**, one as No. 1731 with different face value. Mult.
1868 40c. Plate No. 86 (Series 1) 75 15
1869 90c. Plate No. 10 (Series 2) 1·00 30

1986. Air. 40th Annivs of UNICEF and UNESCO No. 706 surch.
1870 120c. on $1 "Agrias claudina" (surch **UNICEF 1946-1986 AIR 120**) . . . 7·50 7·50
1871 120c. on $1 "Agrias claudina" (surch **UNESCO 1946-1986 AIR 120**) . . . . 7·50 7·50

1986. Centenary of Publication of Sanders' "Reichenbachia" (13th issue). As T **331**. Mult.
1872 45c. Plate No. 17 (Series 2) 40 15
1873 50c. Plate No. 33 (Series 2) 40 15
1874 60c. Plate No. 27 (Series 2) 60 15
1875 75c. Plate No. 56 (Series 2) 70 25
1876 85c. Plate No. 45 (Series 2) 7·50 40
1877 90c. Plate No. 13 (Series 2) 1·00 30
1878 200c. Plate No. 44 (Series 2) 1·50 55
1879 300c. Plate No. 50 (Series 2) 2·00 75
1880 320c. Plate No. 10 (Series 2) 2·00 90
1881 390c. Plate No. 6 (Series 2) 2·00 1·50

1986. Deepavali Festival. Nos. 543 and 601 surch **Deepavali 1986** and value.
1882 25c. on 2c. Type **132** . . . 2·50 20
1883 200c. on 8c. on 6c. Cannon-ball tree . . . . 8·50 2·25

1986. Centenary of Publication of Sanders' "Reichenbachia" (14th issue). As T **331**, two as Nos. 1732 and 1734 with different face values. Multicoloured.
1884 40c. Plate No. 68 (Series 1) 1·25 15
1885 80c. Plate No. 17 (Series 1) 2·00 25
1886 200c. Plate No. 2 (Series 2) 1·40 60
1887 225c. Plate No. 24 (Series 2) 1·40 70

1986. Christmas. No. 489 surch **CHRISTMAS 1986 20**.
1888 20c. on 6c. Black acara ("Patua") . . . . 3·75 20
MS1889 215 × 75 mm. 120c. on 60c. × 5 Nos. 1425/9 . . . . . 7·00 7·00

1986. Wildlife Protection. Nos. 756/67 optd **1986**.
1894 30c. Type **178** . . . . . . 1·75 1·75
1895 30c. Red howler . . . . . 1·75 1·75
1896 30c. Common squirrel-monkey . . . . 1·75 1·75
1897 30c. Two-toed sloth . . . . 1·75 1·75
1898 30c. Brazilian tapir . . . . 1·75 1·75
1899 30c. Collared peccary . . . 1·75 1·75
1900 30c. Six-banded armadillo 1·75 1·75
1901 30c. Tamandua . . . . . . 1·75 1·75
1902 30c. Giant anteater . . . . 1·75 1·75
1903 30c. Murine opossum . . . 1·75 1·75
1904 30c. Brown four-eyed opossum . . . . 1·75 1·75
1905 30c. Brazilian agouti . . . . 1·75 1·75

1986. No. 1642 surch **$15**.
1906 $15 on $3.50 Clive Lloyd with Prudential Cup . . . 40·00 20·00

1986. Centenary of Publication of Sanders' "Reichenbachia" (15th issue). Design as No. 1877, but with different face value. Mult.
1907 50c. Plate No. 13 (Series 2) 65 15

375 Memorial

1986. President Burnham Commemoration. Multicoloured.
1908 25c. Type **375** 10 10
1909 120c. Map of Guyana and flags 20 20
1910 130c. Parliament Buildings and mace 20 20
1911 $6 L. F. Burnham and Georgetown mayoral chain (vert) . . . . 60 1·25

1986. Centenary of Publication of Sanders' "Reichenbachia" (16th issue). As Nos. 1765/6, 1874 and 1887 but with different face values. Multicoloured.
1912 50c. Plate No. 49 (Series 1) 75 20
1913 50c. Plate No. 64 (Series 1) 75 20
1914 85c. Plate No. 24 (Series 2) 75 40
1915 90c. Plate No. 27 (Series 2) 5·50 70

1986. Centenary of Publication of Sanders' "Reichenbachia" (17th issue). As T **331**. Mult.
1916 25c. Plate No. 20 (Series 2) 20 20
1917 40c. Plate No. 7 (Series 2) 45 15
1918 85c. Plate No. 15 (Series 2) 3·50 30
1919 90c. Plate No. 3 (Series 2) 60 20
1920 120c. Plate No. 14 (Series 2) 60 30
1921 130c. Plate No. 32 (Series 2) 60 30
1922 150c. Plate No. 22 (Series 2) 70 45
1923 320c. Plate No. 18 (Series 2) 90 75
1924 330c. Plate No. 28 (Series 2) 90 90

1987. Centenary of Publication of Sanders' "Reichenbachia" (18th issue). As Nos. 1772, 1876, 1886, 1918 and 1923 but with different face values. Multicoloured.
1925 35c. Plate No. 45 (Series 2) 40 15
1926 50c. Plate No. 15 (Series 2) 40 20
1927 50c. Plate No. 55 (Series 1) 40 20
1928 85c. Plate No. 18 (Series 2) 6·00 45
1929 90c. Plate No. 2 (Series 2) 50 30

1987. 10th Anniv of Guyana Post Office Corporation (1st issue). Unissued designs as Nos. 1771 and 1774, but with different face values, surch or optd **G P O C 1977 1987**.
1930 $2.25 Plate No. 53 (Series 1) 3·75 50
1931 $10 on 150c. Plate No. 24 (Series 1) . . . . 9·25 10·00
See also Nos. 2074/80.

1987. Various "Reichenbachia" issues surch.
2375 120c. on 40c. Plate No. 91 (Series 1) (No. 1822) . . 60 40
2380 120c. on 40c. Plate No. 90 (Series 1) 60 40
2387 120c. on 50c. Plate No. 9 (Series 1) 60 40
1994 120c. on 50c. Plate No. 49 (Series 1) (No. 1912) . . 50 40
1995 120c. on 50c. Plate No. 64 (Series 1) (No. 1913) . . 50 40
2388 120c. on 50c. Plate No. 22 (Series 1) 60 40
2389 120c. on 50c. Plate No. 3 (Series 2) 60 40
2390 120c. on 50c. Plate No. 6 (Series 2) 60 40
2391 120c. on 50c. Plate No. 20 (Series 2) 60 40
2392 120c. on 50c. Plate No. 32 (Series 2) 60 40
2019 120c. on 50c. Plate No. 24 (Series 1) 50 40
2020 120c. on 50c. Plate No. 53 (Series 1) 50 40
2021 120c. on 50c. Plate No. 65 (Series 1) 50 40
1980 120c. on 55c. Plate No. 9 (Series 1) (No. 1763) . . 50 40
2003 120c. on 55c. Plate No. 49 (Series 1) (No. 1765) . . 50 40
1981 120c. on 55c. Plate No. 64 (Series 1) (No. 1766) . . 50 30
2006 120c. on 55c. Plate No. 22 (Series 1) (No. 1764) . . 50 40
2009 120c. on 55c. Plate No. 15 (Series 1) 50 40
2010 120c. on 55c. Plate No. 81 (Series 1) 50 40
2011 120c. on 55c. Plate No. 82 (Series 1) 50 40
2012 120c. on 55c. Plate No. 89 (Series 1) 50 40
2394 120c. on 60c. Plate No. 2 (Series 1) (No. 1519) . . 60 30
2027 120c. on 60c. Plate No. 10 (Series 1) (No. 1521) . . 50 40
2028 120c. on 60c. Plate No. 19 (Series 1) (No. 1522) . . 50 40
2029 120c. on 60c. Plate No. 31 (Series 1) (No. 1523) . . 50 40
2030 120c. on 60c. Plate No. 5 (Series 1) 50 40
2403 120c. on 60c. Plate No. 50 (Series 1) 60 40
2404 120c. on 60c. Plate No. 54 (Series 1) 60 40
2405 120c. on 60c. Plate No. 69 (Series 1) 60 40
2034 120c. on 60c. Plate No. 71 (Series 1) 50 40
2406 120c. on 60c. Plate No. 79 (Series 1) 60 40
2036 120c. on 60c. Plate No. 87 (Series 1) 50 40
2407 120c. on 60c. Plate No. 94 (Series 1) 60 40
2038 120c. on 75c. Plate No. 60 (Series 1) 50 40
2039 120c. on 75c. Plate No. 83 (Series 1) 50 40
2040 120c. on 75c. Plate No. 92 (Series 1) 50 40
2041 120c. on 75c. Plate No. 95 (Series 1) 50 40
1933 200c. on 25c. Plate No. 8 (Series 1) (No. 1571) . . 60 50

1934 200c. on 25c. Plate No. 51 (Series 1) (No. 1573) . . 60 50
1949 200c. on 25c. Plate No. 52 (Series 1) (No. 1551) . . 60 50
1951 200c. on 25c. Plate No. 72 (Series 1) (No. 1577) . . 60 50
1952 200c. on 25c. Plate No. 71 (Series 1) (No. 1679) . . 60 50
1953 200c. on 30c. Plate No. 86 (Series 1) (No. 1731) . . 60 50
1954 200c. on 30c. Plate No. 53 (Series 1) (No. 1771) . . 60 50
1932 200c. on 40c. Plate No. 90 (Series 1) 60 50
1937 200c. on 40c. Plate No. 68 (Series 1) (No. 1884) . . 60 50
1955 200c. on 40c. Plate No. 77 (Series 1) (No. 1663) . . 60 50
1956 200c. on 40c. Plate No. 86 (Series 1) (No. 1868) . . 60 50
1957 200c. on 45c. Plate No. 81 (Series 1) (No. 1748) . . 60 50
1958 200c. on 45c. Plate No. 77 (Series 1) 60 50
1959 200c. on 45c. Plate No. 78 (Series 1) 60 50
1960 200c. on 45c. Plate No. 85 (Series 1) 60 50
2044 200c. on 45c. Plate No. 84 (Series 1) 50 40
1939 200c. on 50c. Plate No. 92 (Series 1) (No. 1665) . . 60 50
1940 200c. on 50c. Plate No. 22 (Series 1) 60 50
1961 200c. on 50c. Plate No. 24 (Series 1) 60 50
1962 200c. on 50c. Plate No. 53 (Series 1) 60 50
1963 200c. on 50c. Plate No. 65 (Series 1) 60 50
2046 200c. on 50c. Plate No. 55 (Series 1) (No. 1927) . . 90 50
1941 200c. on 55c. Plate No. 22 (Series 1) (No. 1764) . . 60 50
1964 200c. on 55c. Plate No. 49 (Series 1) (No. 1765) . . 60 50
1965 200c. on 55c. Plate No. 17 (Series 1) (No. 1732) . . 60 50
2050 200c. on 55c. Plate No. 15 (Series 1) . . . . 2·75 60
2051 200c. on 55c. Plate No. 81 (Series 1) . . . . 2·75 60
2052 200c. on 55c. Plate No. 82 (Series 1) . . . . 7·50 70
2053 200c. on 55c. Plate No. 89 (Series 1) . . . . 2·75 60
1942 200c. on 60c. Plate No. 5 (Series 1) 60 50
1967 200c. on 60c. Plate No. 7 (Series 1) (No. 1520) . . 60 50
1968 200c. on 60c. Plate No. 10 (Series 1) (No. 1521) . . 60 50
1969 200c. on 60c. Plate No. 19 (Series 1) (No. 1522) . . 60 50
1970 200c. on 60c. Plate No. 31 (Series 1) (No. 1523) . . 60 50
1971 200c. on 60c. Plate No. 44 (Series 1) (No. 1556) . . 60 50
1972 200c. on 60c. Plate No. 47 (Series 1) (No. 1557) . . 60 50
1973 200c. on 60c. Plate No. 57 (Series 1) (No. 1622) . . 60 50
1974 200c. on 60c. Plate No. 73 (Series 1) (No. 1623) . . 60 50
1975 200c. on 60c. Plate No. 75 (Series 1) (No. 1624) . . 60 50
1976 200c. on 60c. Plate No. 71 (Series 1) 60 50
1977 200c. on 60c. Plate No. 87 (Series 1) 60 50
1943 200c. on 75c. Plate No. 5 (Series 1) (No. 1667) . . 60 50
1944 200c. on 75c. Plate No. 60 (Series 1) 60 50
1945 200c. on 75c. Plate No. 92 (Series 1) 60 50
1946 200c. on 85c. Plate No. 18 (Series 2) (No. 1928) . . 60 50
1947 200c. on 375c. Plate No. 90 (Series 1) (No. 1738) . . 60 50
1987 225c. on 40c. Plate No. 91 (Series 1) (No. 1822) . . 70 60
1988 225c. on 40c. Plate No. 90 (Series 1) 70 60
2055 225c. on 40c. Plate No. 86 (Series 1) (No. 1868) . . 2·00 70
2056 225c. on 40c. Plate No. 68 (Series 1) (No. 1884) . . 90 60
1988a 225c. on 50c. Plate No. 92 (Series 1) (No. 1665) . . 13·00 3·50
1989 225c. on 50c. Plate No. 22 (Series 1) 70 60
1990 225c. on 60c. Plate No. 55 (Series 1) (No. 1597) . . 70 60
1990a 225c. on 60c. Plate No. 95 (Series 1) (No. 1666) . . 13·00 3·50
1991 225c. on 60c. Plate No. 93 (Series 1) (No. 1733) . . 70 60
2058 225c. on 65c. Plate No. 76 (Series 1) 90 60
2059 225c. on 65c. Plate No. 80 (Series 1) 90 60
2060 225c. on 65c. Plate No. 88 (Series 1) 90 60
2061 225c. on 65c. Plate No. 96 (Series 1) 90 60
1992 225c. on 80c. Plate No. 93 (Series 1) 70 60
1978 225c. on 90c. Plate No. 89 (Series 1) (No. 1749) . . 65 55
1993 225c. on 150c. Plate No. 42 (Series 1) (No. 1657) . . 70 60
2062 600c. on 80c. Plate No. 17 (Series 1) (No. 1885) . . 1·50 1·75
2063 600c. on 80c. Plate No. 39 (Series 1) . . . . 1·50 1·75
2064 600c. on 80c. Plate No. 74 (Series 1) . . . . 1·50 1·75
2065 600c. on 80c. Plate No. 93 (Series 1) . . . . 1·50 1·75

1987. Nos. 1518 and 1572 surch **TWO DOLLARS**.
1935 $2 on 25c. Plate No. 12 (Series 1) (No. 1518) . . . 1·25 75
1936 $2 on 25c. Plate No. 23 (Series 1) (No. 1572) . . . 1·25 75

1987. Various "Reichenbachia" issues surch **1987**.
1983 $10 on 25c. Plate No. 53 (Series 1) . . . . 2·50 2·75
1984 $12 on 80c. Plate No. 74 (Series 1) . . . . 2·75 3·00
1985 $15 on 80c. Plate No. 39 (Series 1) . . . . 3·25 3·75
1986 $25 on 25c. Plate No. 53 (Series 1) . . . . 5·50 6·00

1987. Centenary of Publication of Sanders' "Reichenbachia" (19th issue). Multicoloured.
2066 180c. Plate 41 (Series 2) . . 75 40
2067 230c. Plate 25 (Series 2) . . 80 50
2068 300c. Plate 85 (Series 2) . . 6·00 1·00
2069 330c. Plate 82 (Series 2) . . 6·50 1·25
2070 425c. Plate 87 (Series 2) . . 6·50 1·40
2071 440c. Plate 88 (Series 2) . . 6·50 1·40
2072 590c. Plate 52 (Series 2) . . 1·50 1·75
2073 650c. Plate 65 (Series 2) . . 1·75 2·00

1987. 10th Anniv of Guyana Post Office Corporation (2nd issue). Nos. 543, 545, 548a and 601 surch **Post Office Corp. 1977-1987**.
2074 25c. on 2c. Type **132** . . . 15 10
2075 25c. on 5c. Annatto tree . . 15 10
2076 25c. on 8c. on 6c. Cannon-ball tree 15 10
2077 25c. on 15c. Christmas orchid . . . . 4·25 30
2078 60c. on 15c. Christmas orchid . . . . 8·00 25
2079 $1.20 on 2c. Type **132** . . . 75 75
2080 $1.30 on 15c. Christmas orchid . . . . 9·00 2·50

1987. No. 1535b surch **1987 200**.
2081 **332** 200c. on 25c. mult . . . 3·50 1·75

1987. Various "Reichenbachia" issues optd **1987**.
2112 120c. Plate No. 1 (Series 1) (No. 1578) . . . . 2·75 75
2113 120c. Plate No. 11 (Series 1) (No. 1579) . . . . 2·25 70
2114 120c. Plate No. 28 (Series 1) (No. 1580) . . . . 2·75 75
2115 120c. Plate No. 37 (Series 1) (No. 1627) . . . . 1·50 70
2116 120c. Plate No. 46 (Series 1) (No. 1628) . . . . 6·50 90
2117 120c. Plate No. 56 (Series 1) (No. 1629) . . . . 2·25 70
2118 120c. Plate No. 58 (Series 1) (No. 1630) . . . . 2·25 70
2132 120c. Plate No. 67 (Series 1) (No. 1631) 50 40
2084 130c. Plate No. 3 (Series 1) (No. 1525) 50 40
2093 130c. Plate No. 6 (Series 1) (No. 1759) 50 40
2094 130c. Plate No. 20 (Series 1) (No. 1761) 50 40
2087 130c. Plate No. 18 (Series 1) (No. 1536) 50 40
2088 130c. Plate No. 29 (Series 1) (No. 1537) 50 40
2089 130c. Plate No. 30 (Series 1) (No. 1538) 50 40
2090 130c. Plate No. 16 (Series 1) (No. 1559) 50 40
2091 130c. Plate No. 66 (Series 1) (No. 1632) 50 40
2092 130c. Plate No. 13 (Series 1) (No. 1684) 50 40
2109 130c. Plate No. 91 (Series 1) (No. 1735) 50 40
2111 130c. Plate No. 25 (Series 1) (No. 1762) 50 40
2123 150c. Plate No. 40 (Series 1) (No. 1767) . . . . 2·00 80
2124 150c. Plate No. 45 (Series 1) (No. 1769) . . . . 1·50 70
2125 150c. Plate No. 42 (Series 1) (No. 1657) . . . . 4·50 1·00
2137 150c. Plate No. 26 (Series 1) (No. 1633) 50 50
2095 200c. Plate No. 4 (Series 1) (No. 1533) 60 50
2096 200c. Plate No. 14 (Series 1) (No. 1584) 60 50
2097 200c. Plate No. 21 (Series 1) (No. 1585) 60 50
2098 200c. Plate No. 33 (Series 1) (No. 1634) 60 50
2099 200c. Plate No. 43 (Series 1) (No. 1658) 60 50
2100 200c. Plate No. 79 (Series 1) (No. 1670) 60 50
2101 200c. Plate No. 9 (Series 2) (No. 1816) 60 50
2102 200c. Plate No. 2 (Series 2) (No. 1886) 60 50
2103 250c. Plate No. 74 (Series 1) (No. 1736) 70 60
2104 260c. Plate No. 39 (Series 1) (No. 1737) 70 60

1987. 12th World Orchid Conference, Tokyo (2nd issue). Nos. 1763 surch **12th World Orchid Conference 650**.
2138 650c. on 55c. Plate No. 9 (Series 1) . . . . 9·00 5·50

1987. 125th Anniv of British Guiana Post Office (3rd issue). No. 699 surch **25** and names of postal agencies opened by 1885.
2140 25c. on 10c. multicoloured (surch **AGRICOLA**) . . . 1·50 1·10
2141 25c. on 10c. multicoloured (surch **BAGOTVILLE**) 1·50 1·10
2142 25c. on 10c. multicoloured (surch **BOURDA**) . . . . 1·50 1·10
2143 25c. on 10c. multicoloured (surch **BUXTON**) . . . . 1·50 1·10
2144 25c. on 10c. multicoloured (surch **CABACABURI**) 1·50 1·10
2145 25c. on 10c. mult (surch **CARMICHAEL STREET**) . . . . 1·50 1·10
2146 25c. on 10c. mult (surch **COTTON TREE**) . . . . 1·50 1·10
2147 25c. on 10c. multicoloured (surch **DUNOON**) . . . . 1·50 1·10
2148 25c. on 10c. multicoloured (surch **FELLOWSHIP**) 1·50 1·10
2149 25c. on 10c. multicoloured (surch **GROVE**) . . . . . 1·50 1·10
2150 25c. on 10c. multicoloured (surch **HACKNEY**) . . . 1·50 1·10
2151 25c. on 10c. multicoloured (surch **LEONORA**) . . . 1·50 1·10
2152 25c. on 10c. mult (surch **1987**) . . . . 1·50 1·10
2153 25c. on 10c. multicoloured (surch **MALLALI**) . . . 1·50 1·10
2154 25c. on 10c. multicoloured (surch **PROVIDENCE**) 1·50 1·10
2155 25c. on 10c. multicoloured (surch **RELIANCE**) . . . 1·50 1·10
2156 25c. on 10c. multicoloured (surch **SPARTA**) . . . . 1·50 1·10
2157 25c. on 10c. multicoloured (surch **STEWARTVILLE**) 1·50 1·10
2158 25c. on 10c. multicoloured (surch **TARLOGY**) . . . 1·50 1·10
2159 25c. on 10c. mult (surch **T.P.O. BERBICE RIV.**) 1·50 1·10
2160 25c. on 10c. multicoloured (surch **T.P.O. DEM. RIV.**) . . . . 1·50 1·10
2161 25c. on 10c. multicoloured (surch **T.P.O. ESSEO. RIV.**) . . . . 1·50 1·10
2162 25c. on 10c. mult (surch **T.P.O. MASSARUNI RIV.**) . . . . 1·50 1·10
2163 25c. on 10c. multicoloured (surch **TUSCHEN (De VRIENDEN)**) . . . . . 1·50 1·10
2164 25c. on 10c. multicoloured (surch **ZORG**) . . . . . 1·50 1·10

1987. 50th Anniv of First Georgetown to Port-of-Spain Flight by P.A.A. No. 708a optd **28 MARCH 1927 PAA GEO-POS**.
2165 $10 "Elbella patrobas" . . . 22·00 11·00

1987. No. 704 surch **25**.
2166 25c. on 40c. "Morpho rhetenor" (male) . . . . 12·00 30

1987. Easter. Nos. 481/2 and 484 optd **1987** or surch also.
2167 **111** 25c. multicoloured . . . 50 10
2168 120c. on 6c. mult 75 20
2169 320c. on 6c. mult . . . . 1·25 70
2170 500c. on 40c. mult . . . 1·75 1·25

1987. Centenary of Publication of Sanders' "Reichenbachia" (20th issue). As T **331**. Mult.
2171 240c. Plate No. 47 (Series 2) 80 45
2172 260c. Plate No. 39 (Series 2) 90 55
2173 275c. Plate No. 58 (Series 2) (horiz) 90 55
2174 390c. Plate No. 37 (Series 2) (horiz) . . . . 1·10 70
2175 450c. Plate No. 19 (Series 2) (horiz) . . . . 1·50 90
2176 460c. Plate No. 54 (Series 2) (horiz) . . . . 1·50 90
2177 500c. Plate No. 51 (Series 2) 1·75 1·10
2178 560c. Plate No. 1 (Series 2) 2·00 1·50

1987. No. 706 optd **1987**.
2179 **167** $1 multicoloured . . . . 12·00 75

1987. Centenary of Publication of Sanders' "Reichenbachia" (21st issue). As T **331**. Mult.
2180 500c. Plate No. 86 (Series 2) 1·50 1·10
2181 520c. Plate No. 89 (Series 2) 1·50 1·25
2182 $20 Plate No. 83 (Series 2) 4·50 7·00

1987. As T **332** but within frame.
2183 25c. multicoloured . . . . . 1·25 50
2184 25c. multicoloured . . . . . 1·25 50

No. 2183 has a bird with a short tail (as in Type **332**) in the lower part of the arms; No. 2184 has a bird with crest and long tail.

1987. "Capex '87" International Stamp Exhibition, Toronto. Nos. 1744/5 optd **CAPEX '87**.
2185 **363** 320c. red, black and lilac 2·00 2·25
2186 – 320c. multicoloured . . . 2·00 2·25

1987. Commonwealth Heads of Government Meeting, Vancouver. Nos. 1066/8 further optd **1987**.
2187 $1.20 on 6c. green 75 20
2188 $1.30 on 24c. black orange 8·50 45
2189 $2.40 on 24c. black orange 10·00 3·00

1987. Centenary of Publication of Sanders' "Reichenbachia" (22nd issue). As T **331**. Mult.
2190 400c. Plate No. 80 (Series 2) 1·25 80
2191 480c. Plate No. 77 (Series 2) 1·50 1·00
2192 600c. Plate No. 94 (Series 2) 1·50 1·50
2193 $25 Plate No. 72 (Series 2) 4·50 8·00

396 Steam Locomotive No. 4 "Alexandra"

1987. Guyana Railways.
2194 **396** $1.20 green 25 30
2195 – $1.20 green 25 30
2196 – $1.20 green 25 30
2197 – $1.20 green 25 30
2198 **396** $1.20 purple 25 30
2199 – $1.20 purple 25 30
2200 – $1.20 purple 25 30
2201 – $1.20 purple 25 30
2202 **396** $3.20 blue 80 90
2203 – $3.20 blue 80 90
2204 – $3.20 blue 80 90
2205 – $3.20 blue 80 90
2206 – $3.20 blue 80 90
2207 – $3.30 black 80 90
2208 **396** $3.30 black 80 90
2209 – $3.30 black 80 90
2210 – $3.30 black 80 90
2211 – $3.30 black 80 90
2212 – $10 multicoloured . . . 60 1·50
2213 – $12 multicoloured . . . 60 1·75

DESIGNS—As T **396**: Nos. 2195, 2199, 2203, 2207, Front view of diesel locomotive; Nos. 2196, 2200, 2204, 2210, Steam locomotive with searchlight; Nos. 2197, 2201, 2205, 2209, Side view of diesel locomotive No. 21. (82 × 55 mm): No. 2206, Molasses warehouses and early locomotive; No. 2211, Diesel locomotive and passenger train. (88 × 39 mm): No. 2212, Cattle train and Parika–Rosignol Railway route map; No. 2213, Molasses train and Parika–Rosignol Railway route map.

1987. 50th Anniv of First Flights from Georgetown to Massaruni and Mabaruma. No. 706 optd.
2214 $1 multicoloured (optd **FAIREY NICHOLL 8 AUG 1927 GEO-MAZ**) 10·00 10·00
2215 $1 multicoloured (optd **FAIREY NICHOLL 15 AUG 1927 GEO-MAB**) 10·00 10·00

1987. Centenary of Publication of Sanders' "Reichenbachia" (23rd issue). As T **331**. Mult.
2216 200c. Plate No. 43 (Series 2) 5·50 1·50
2217 200c. Plate No. 48 (Series 2) 5·50 1·50
2218 200c. Plate No. 92 (Series 2) 5·50 1·50

1987. Centenary of Publication of Sanders' "Reichenbachia" (24th issue). No. 2219 surch 600. Multicoloured.
2219 600c. on 900c. Plate No. 74 (Series 2) . . . . 4·75 5·50
2220 900c. Plate No. 74 (Series 2) 4·75 5·50

1987. Columbus Day.
2221 225c. on 350 c on 120c. Plate No. 65 (Series 1) (No. 1598 further surch **225**) . . . . 1·50 50
2222 950c. on 900c. Plate No. 74 (Series 2) (No. 2220 surch **950 CRISTOVAO COLOMBO 1492 – 1992**) 2·50 3·00
2223 950c. on 900c. Plate No. 74 (Series 2) (No. 2220 surch **950 CHRISTOPHE COLOMB 1492 – 1992**) 2·50 3·00
MS2224 76 × 50 mm. $20 on 320c. × 2 Nos. 1744/5 . . . . . 7·00 8·00

1987. Centenary of Publication of Sanders' "Reichenbachia" (25th issue). As T **331**. Mult.
2225 325c. Plate No. 68 (Series 2) (horiz) . . . . 1·50 1·10
2226 420c. Plate No. 95 (Series 2) (horiz) . . . . 1·75 1·75
2227 575c. Plate No. 60 (Series 2) 11·00 5·50

1987. Deepavali Festival. Nos. 544/5 surch **DEEPAVALI 1987** and new value.
2228 25c. on 3c. Hanging heliconia . . . . 2·00 25
2229 $3 on 5c. Annatto tree . . . 7·00 3·00

1987. Christmas. No. 489 surch **CHRISTMAS 1987 20**, and previously unissued miniature sheet containing Nos. 1425/9 and No. **MS**1619 surch.
2230 20c. on 6c. Black acara ("Patua") . . . . 3·75 20
MS2231 215 × 75mm. 120c. on 60c. × 5 Nos. 1425/9 . . . . . 8·00 4·00
MS2232 120 × 129mm. 225c. on 55c. × 4 Plate No. 22 (Series 1), each with a different overprint (**Christmas 1985**, **Happy New Year**, **Merry Christmas** or **Happy Holidays**) . . . . 1·60 1·75

1987. Royal Ruby Wedding. Nos. 1684/5 optd **1987** (130c.) or surch **120**.
2233 130c. Plate No. 13 (Series 1) 5·00 1·50
MS2234 600c. on 130c. on 130c., 600c. on 200c. on 130c., 600c. on 260c. on 130c., 600c. on 330c. on 130c., Plate No. 6 (Series 1) . . 9·00 10·00

1987. Centenary of Publication of Sanders' "Reichenbachia" (26th issue). As T **331**. Mult.
2235 255c. Plate No. 61 (Series 2) 3·75 1·25
2236 290c. Plate No. 53 (Series 2) 3·75 1·50
2237 375c. Plate No. 96 (Series 2) 2·00 1·60
2238 680c. Plate No. 64 (Series 2) 9·50 2·75
2239 720c. Plate No. 49 (Series 2) 11·00 4·50
2240 750c. Plate No. 66 (Series 2) 3·00 4·50
2241 800c. Plate No. 79 (Series 2) 3·00 4·75
2242 850c. Plate No. 76 (Series 2) 3·00 4·75

1987. Air. No. 1620 surch **AIR 75**.
2243 75c. on 25c. Plate No. 59 (Series 1) . . . . 9·50 1·25

1987. Wildlife Protection. Nos. 756/67 optd **1987**, Nos. 1432/4 surch **Protect our Heritage '87 320** and Nos. 1631/3, 1752/3 and 1847 optd **PROTECT OUR HERITAGE '87**.
2244 30c. Type **178** 30 25
2245 30c. Red howler 30 25
2246 30c. Common squirrel-monkey 30 25
2247 30c. Two-toed sloth 30 25
2248 30c. Brazilian tapir 30 25
2249 30c. Collared peccary . . . 30 25
2250 30c. Six-banded armadillo 30 25
2251 30c. Tamandua 30 25
2252 30c. Giant anteater 30 25
2253 30c. Murine opossum . . . 30 25
2254 30c. Brown four-eyed opossum 30 25
2255 30c. Brazilian agouti 30 25
2256 120c. Plate No. 67 (Series 1) 80 30
2257 130c. Plate No. 66 (Series 1) 80 30
2258 150c. Plate No. 26 (Series 1) 85 35
2259 180c. Plate No. 15 (Series 1) 90 40
2260 320c. Plate No. 82 (Series 1) 1·25 60
2261 320c. on 120c. Demerara Mutual Life Assurance Building . . . . 1·25 1·50
2262 320c. on 120c. Town Hall 1·25 1·50
2263 320c. on 120c. Victoria Law Courts . . . . 1·25 1·50
2264 650c. on 40c. Plate No. 86 (Series 1) . . . . 2·75 3·50

1987. Air. Various "Reichenbachia" issues optd **AIR**.
2265 60c. Plate No. 55 (Series 1) (No. 1597) . . . . 7·50 7·50
2463 75c. Plate No. 55 (Series 1) (No. 1772) 90 55
2464 75c. Plate No. 5 (Series 1) (No. 1667) 90 55
2466 75c. Plate No. 83 (Series 1) 90 55
2467 75c. Plate No. 95 (Series 1) 90 55

1988. World Scout Jamboree, Australia. No. 837a optd **AUSTRALIA 1987 JAMBOREE 1988** and Nos. 830, 837a and 1104 surch **$10 AUSTRALIA 1987 JAMBOREE 1988**.
2266 **116** 440c. on 6c. mult (No. 837a) . . . . . 7·50 60
2267 $10 on 110c. on 6c. mult (No. 830) . . . 75 90
2268 $10 on 180c. on 6c. mult (No. 1104) . . . 75 90
2269a $10 on 440c. on 6c. mult (No. 837a) . . . 75 90

1988. 10th Anniv of International Fund for Agricultural Development. Nos. 448 and 450 surch **IFAD For a World Without Hunger**.
2270 25c. on 1c. Type **87** . . . . 2·00 25
2271 $5 on 3c. Lukunani . . . . 7·50 5·00

1988. Republic Day. Nos. 545, 548a and 555 surch **Republic Day 1988**.
2272 25c. on 5c. Annatto tree . . 10 10
2273 120c. on 15c. Christmas orchid . . . . 8·50 70
2274 $10 on $2 "Noranthea guianensis" . . . . 2·75 3·50

1988. Centenary of Publication of Sanders' "Reichenbachia" (27th issue). Four sheets, each 102 × 127 mm, containing vert designs as T **331**. Multicoloured.
MS2275 (a) 320c. Plate No. 46 (Series 2); 330c. Plate No. 55 (Series 2); 350c. Plate No. 57 (Series 2); 500c. Plate No. 81 (Series 2). (b) 320c. Plate No. 55 (Series 2); 330c. Plate No. 46 (Series 2); 350c. Plate No. 81 (Series 2); 500c. Plate No. 57 (Series 2). (c) 320c. Plate No. 57 (Series 2); 330c. Plate No. 81 (Series 2); 350c. Plate No. 46 (Series 2); 500c. Plate No. 55 (Series 2). (d) 320c. Plate No. 81 (Series 2); 330c. Plate No. 57 (Series 2); 350c. Plate No. 55 (Series 2); 500c. Plate No. 46 (Series 2). Set of 4 sheets . . . 17·00 13·00

1988. Centenary of Publication of Sanders' "Reichenbachia" (28th series). As T **331**. Multicoloured.
2276 $10 Plate No. 40 (Series 2) 1·50 2·25
2277 $12 Plate No. 91 (Series 2) 1·50 2·25

1988. 125th Anniv of British Guiana Post Office (4th issue). No. 702a surch **25** and names of postal agencies opened between 1886 and 1900.
2278 25c. on 30c. multicoloured (surch **Albouystown**) . . . 1·25 1·00
2279 25c. on 30c. multicoloured (surch **Anns Grove**) . . . 1·25 1·00
2280 25c. on 30c. multicoloured (surch **Amacura**) . . . . 1·25 1·00
2281 25c. on 30c. multicoloured (surch **Arakaka**) . . . . . 1·25 1·00
2282 25c. on 30c. multicoloured (surch **Baramanni**) . . . . 1·25 1·00
2283 25c. on 30c. multicoloured (surch **Cuyuni**) . . . . . 1·25 1·00
2284 25c. on 30c. multicoloured (surch **Hope Placer**) . . . 1·25 1·00
2285 25c. on 30c. multicoloured (surch **H M P S**) . . . . 1·25 1·00
2286 25c. on 30c. mult (surch **Kitty**) . . . . 1·25 1·00
2287 25c. on 30c. multicoloured (surch **M'M'Zorg**) . . . . 1·25 1·00
2288 25c. on 30c. multicoloured (surch **Maccaseema**) . . . 1·25 1·00
2289 25c. on 30c. mult (surch **1988**) . . . . 1·25 1·00
2290 25c. on 30c. multicoloured (surch **Morawhanna**) . . . 1·25 1·00
2291 25c. on 30c. multicoloured (surch **Naamryck**) . . . . 1·25 1·00
2292 25c. on 30c. mult (surch **Purini**) . . . . 1·25 1·00
2293 25c. on 30c. multicoloured (surch **Potaro Landing**) . . 1·25 1·00
2294 25c. on 30c. multicoloured (surch **Rockstone**) . . . . 1·25 1·00
2295 25c. on 30c. multicoloured (surch **Rosignol**) . . . . . 1·25 1·00
2296 25c. on 30c. multicoloured (surch **Stanleytown**) . . . 1·25 1·00
2297 25c. on 30c. multicoloured (surch **Santa Rosa**) . . . 1·25 1·00
2298 25c. on 30c. multicoloured (surch **Tumatumari**) . . . 1·25 1·00
2299 25c. on 30c. multicoloured (surch **Weldaad**) . . . . . 1·25 1·00
2300 25c. on 30c. multicoloured (surch **Wismar**) . . . . . 1·25 1·00
2301 25c. on 30c. mult (surch **TPO Berbice Railway**) . . 1·25 1·00

1988. Olympic Games, Seoul (1st issue). Nos. 1206/17 further surch **120 Olympic Games 1988**.
2302 120c. on 55c. on 125c. on 35c. Type **174** . . . . . 1·50 1·50
2303 120c. on 55c. on 125c. on 35c. Trahira ("Haimara") 1·50 1·50
2304 120c. on 55c. on 125c. on 35c. Electric eel . . . . . 1·50 1·50
2305 120c. on 55c. on 125c. on 35c. Golden rivulus . . . 1·50 1·50
2306 120c. on 55c. on 125c. on 35c. Golden pencilfish . . 1·50 1·50
2307 120c. on 55c. on 125c. on 35c. Four-eyed fish . . . 1·50 1·50
2308 120c. on 55c. on 125c. on 35c. Red piranha ("Pirai") 1·50 1·50
2309 120c. on 55c. on 125c. on 35c. Smoking hassar . . . 1·50 1·50
2310 120c. on 55c. on 125c. on 35c. Manta . . . . 1·50 1·50
2311 120c. on 55c. on 125c. on 35c. Festive cichlid ("Flying patwa") . . . . 1·50 1·50
2312 120c. on 55c. on 125c. on 35c. Arapaima . . . . . 1·50 1·50
2313 120c. on 55c. on 125c. on 35c. Peacock cichlid ("Lukanani") . . . . . . 1·50 1·50

See also Nos. 2476/95.

1988. Centenary of Publication of Sanders' "Reichenbachia" (29th issue). As T **331**. Mult.
2314 320c. Plate No. 62 (Series 2) 2·50 50
2315 475c. Plate No. 73 (Series 2) 3·00 1·25
2316 525c. Plate No. 36 (Series 2) 3·50 1·50
2317 530c. Plate No. 69 (Series 2) 1·00 1·50
2318 $15 Plate No. 67 (Series 2) 2·50 4·50

1988. CARICOM Day. Nos. 545/6 and 555 surch **Caricom Day 1988** and new value.
2319 25c. on 5c. Annatto tree . . 25 10
2320 $1.20 on 6c. Cannon-ball tree 60 10
2321 $10 on $2 "Norantea guianensis" . . . . 3·50 4·25

1988. Centenary of Publication of Sanders' "Reichenbachia" (30th issue). As T **331**. Mult.
2322 700c. Plate No. 62 (Series 2) 1·00 1·50
2323 775c. Plate No. 59 (Series 2) 1·25 1·75
2324 875c. Plate No. 31 (Series 2) 9·00 2·75
2325 950c. Plate No. 78 (Series 2) 1·75 2·75

1988. 40th Anniv of World Health Day. No. 705a optd.
2326 60c. "Papilio androgeus" (optd **WHO 1948-1988**) 15·00 16·00
2327 60c. "Papilio androgeus" (optd **1988**) 35 10

1988. Centenary of Publication of Sanders' "Reichenbachia" (31st issue). As T **331**. Mult.
2328 350c. Plate No. 74 (Series 2) 2·50 1·25

1988. Centenary of Publication of Sanders' "Reichenbachia" (32nd issue). As T **331**, but additionally inscr "1985–1988". Multicoloured.
2329 130c. Plate No. 73 (Series 2) 2·00 25
2330 200c. Plate No. 96 (Series 2) 50 30
2331 260c. Plate No. 16 (Series 2) 4·00 1·25
MS2332 Four sheets, each 102 × 127 mm. (a) 120c. Plate No. 81 (Series 2); 120c. Plate No. 57 (Series 2); 120c. Plate No. 55 (Series 2); 120c. Plate No. 46 (Series 2). (b) 150c. Plate No. 57 (Series 2); 150c. Plate No. 81 (Series 2); 150c. Plate No. 46 (Series 2); 150c. Plate No. 55 (Series 2). (c) 225c. Plate No. 46 (Series 2); 225c. Plate No. 55 (Series 2); 225c. Plate No. 57 (Series 2); 225c. Plate No. 81 (Series 2). (d) 305c. Plate No. 55 (Series 2); 305c. Plate No. 46 (Series 2); 305c. Plate No. 81 (Series 2); 305c. Plate No. 57 (Series 2). Set of 4 sheets 7·50 5·00

1988. Conservation of Resources. (a) Nos. 1444/6 optd.
2333 120c. Young Ocelot (No. 1444) (optd **CONSERVE TREES**) . . 80 70
2334 120c. Young Ocelot (No. 1444) (optd **CONSERVE ELECTRICITY**) 80 70
2335 120c. Young Ocelot (No. 1444) (optd **CONSERVE WATER**) 80 70
2336 120c. Type **322** (optd **CONSERVE ELECTRICITY**) 80 70
2337 120c. Type **322** (optd **CONSERVE WATER**) 80 70
2338 120c. Type **322** (optd **CONSERVE TREES**) . . 80 70
2339 120c. Young Ocelot (No. 1446) (optd **CONSERVE WATER**) 80 70
2340 120c. Young Ocelot (No. 1446) (optd **CONSERVE TREES**) . . 80 70
2341 120c. Young Ocelot (No. 1446) (optd **CONSERVE ELECTRICITY**) 80 70

(b) Nos. 1634, 1670, 1683 and 1774 optd **CONSERVE WATER**.
2342 200c. Plate No. 33 (Series 1) 80 70
2343 200c. Plate No. 79 (Series 1) 80 70
2344 225c. Plate No. 24 (Series 1) 80 70
2345 350c. Plate No. 94 (Series 1) 80 70

1988. Road Safety Campaign. Nos. 2194/2201 optd.
2346 **396** $1.20 green (optd **BEWARE OF ANIMALS**) . . . . . 1·10 1·10
2347 – $1.20 green (No. 2195) (optd **BEWARE OF CHILDREN**) . . . . 1·10 1·10
2348 – $1.20 green (No. 2196) (optd **DRIVE SAFELY**) . . . . . . 1·10 1·10
2349 – $1.20 green (No. 2197) (optd **DO NOT DRINK AND DRIVE**) 1·10 1·10
2350 **396** $1.20 purple (optd **BEWARE OF ANIMALS**) . . . . . 1·10 1·10
2351 – $1.20 purple (No. 2199) (optd **BEWARE OF CHILDREN**) . . . . 1·10 1·10
2352 – $1.20 purple (No. 2200) (optd **DRIVE SAFELY**) . . . . . . 1·10 1·10
2353 – $1.20 purple (No. 2201) (optd **DO NOT DRINK AND DRIVE**) 1·10 1·10

1988. No. 706 optd **1988** or surch **120**.
2354 $1 "Agrias claudina" . . . 6·00 1·00
2355 120c. on $1 "Agrias claudina" . . . . 6·00 1·00

1988. Various "Reichenbachia" issues surch.
2356 120c. on 25c. Plate No. 61 (Series 1) (No. 1574) . . . 1·00 70
2357 120c. on 25c. Plate No. 63 (Series 1) (No. 1575) . . . 1·00 70
2358 120c. on 25c. Plate No. 70 (Series 1) (No. 1576) . . . 1·00 70
2359 120c. on 25c. Plate No. 59 (Series 1) (No. 1620) . . . 1·00 70
2360 120c. on 25c. Plate No. 71 (Series 1) (No. 1679) . . . 1·00 70
2429 120c. on 25c. Plate No. 72 (Series 1) (No. 1577) . . . 1·00 70
2361 120c. on 30c. Plate No. 53 (Series 1) (No. 1771) . . . 1·00 70
2362 120c. on 30c. Plate No. 86 (Series 1) (No. 1731) . . . 1·00 70
2363 120c. on 30c. Plate No. 30 (Series 2) (No. 1809) . . . 1·00 70
2365 120c. on 30c. Plate No. 7 (Series 2) . . . . 1·00 70
2366 120c. on 30c. Plate No. 14 (Series 2) . . . . 1·00 70
2368 120c. on 30c. Plate No. 22 (Series 2) . . . . 1·00 70
2369 120c. on 30c. Plate No. 28 (Series 2) . . . . 1·00 70
2371 120c. on 35c. Plate No. 45 (Series 2) (No. 1925) . . . 1·00 70
2372 120c. on 40c. Plate No. 77 (Series 1) (No. 1663) . . . 1·00 70
2374 120c. on 40c. Plate No. 96 (Series 1) (No. 1747) . . . 1·00 70
2377 120c. on 40c. Plate No. 86 (Series 1) (No. 1868) . . . 1·00 70
2378 120c. on 40c. Plate No. 68 (Series 1) (No. 1884) . . . 1·00 70
2381 120c. on 45c. Plate No. 54 (Series 1) (No. 1664) . . . 1·00 70
2382 120c. on 45c. Plate No. 81 (Series 1) (No. 1748) . . . 1·00 70
2383 120c. on 45c. Plate No. 21 (Series 2) (No. 1810) . . . 1·00 70
2384 120c. on 50c. Plate No. 92 (Series 1) (No. 1665) . . . 1·00 70
2385 120c. on 50c. Plate No. 13 (Series 2) (No. 1907) . . . 1·00 70
2386 120c. on 50c. Plate No. 15 (Series 2) (No. 1926) . . . 1·00 70
2393 120c. on 55c. Plate No. 17 (Series 1) (No. 1732) . . . 1·00 70
2395 120c. on 60c. Plate No. 57 (Series 1) (No. 1622) . . . 1·00 70
2397 120c. on 60c. Plate No. 73 (Series 1) (No. 1623) . . . 1·00 70
2398 120c. on 60c. Plate No. 75 (Series 1) (No. 1624) . . . 1·00 70
2400 120c. on 60c. Plate No. 95 (Series 1) (No. 1666) . . . 1·00 70
2401 120c. on 60c. Plate No. 93 (Series 1) (No. 1733) . . . 1·00 70
2402 120c. on 60c. Plate No. 27 (Series 2) (No. 1874) . . . 1·00 70
2408 120c. on 70c. Plate No. 8 (Series 2) . . . . 1·00 70
2409 120c. on 70c. Plate No. 9 (Series 2) . . . . 1·00 70
2411 120c. on 70c. Plate No. 12 (Series 2) . . . . 1·00 70
2413 120c. on 70c. Plate No. 17 (Series 2) . . . . 1·00 70
2414 120c. on 80c. Plate No. 39 (Series 1) . . . . 1·00 70
2415 120c. on 80c. Plate No. 74 (Series 1) . . . . 1·00 70
2416 120c. on 80c. Plate No. 93 (Series 1) . . . . 1·00 70
2417 120c. on 85c. Plate No. 45 (Series 2) (No. 1876) . . . 1·00 70
2418 120c. on 85c. Plate No. 24 (Series 2) (No. 1914) . . . 1·00 70
2419 120c. on 85c. Plate No. 15 (Series 2) (No. 1918) . . . 1·00 70
2420 120c. on 85c. Plate No. 18 (Series 2) (No. 1928) . . . 1·00 70
2421 120c. on 90c. Plate No. 84 (Series 1) (No. 1668) . . . 1·00 70
2422 120c. on 90c. Plate No. 89 (Series 1) (No. 1749) . . . 1·00 70
2423 120c. on 90c. Plate No. 10 (Series 2) (No. 1869) . . . 1·00 70
2424 120c. on 90c. Plate No. 13 (Series 2) (No. 1877) . . . 1·00 70
2425 120c. on 90c. Plate No. 27 (Series 2) (No. 1915) . . . 1·00 70
2426 120c. on 90c. Plate No. 2 (Series 2) (No. 1929) . . . 1·00 70
2427 200c. on 80c. Plate No. 42 (Series 2) (No. 1812) . . . 1·00 70
2428 200c. on 90c. Plate No. 4 (Series 2) (No. 1813) . . . 1·00 70
2430 240c. on 140c. Plate No. 30 (Series 2) . . . . 1·00 70
2431 240c. on 140c. Plate No. 34 (Series 2) . . . . 1·00 70

2432 240c. on 425c. Plate No. 87 (Series 2) (No. 2070) . . . 1·00 70
2433 260c. on 375c. Plate No. 90 (Series 1) (No. 1378) . . . 1·00 70

1988. Conservation of Resources. Various "Reichenbachia" issues optd **CONSERVE OUR RESOURCES**.
2434 100c. Plate No. 65 (Series 1) (No. 1773) 90 60
2435 100c. Plate No. 68 (Series 1) (No. 1734) 90 60
2436 100c. Plate No. 88 (Series 1) (No. 1750) 90 60
2438 120c. Plate No. 27 (Series 1) (No. 1524) 90 60
2439 120c. Plate No. 36 (Series 1) (No. 1558) 90 60
2440 120c. Plate No. 37 (Series 1) (No. 1627) 90 60
2441 120c. Plate No. 56 (Series 1) (No. 1629) 90 60
2442 120c. Plate No. 58 (Series 1) (No. 1630) 90 60
2443 120c. Plate No. 67 (Series 1) (No. 1631) 90 60
2444 120c. Plate No. 69 (Series 1) (No. 1680) 90 60
2445 130c. Plate No. 38 (Series 1) (No. 1560) 90 60
2446 130c. Plate No. 66 (Series 1) (No. 1632) 90 60
2447 130c. Plate No. 91 (Series 1) (No. 1735) 90 60
2448 130c. Plate No. 13 (Series 1) (No. 1760) 90 60
2249 130c. Plate No. 20 (Series 1) (No. 1761) 90 60
2450 150c. Plate No. 26 (Series 1) (No. 1633) 90 60
2451 150c. Plate No. 78 (Series 1) (No. 1669) 90 60
2452 150c. Plate No. 87 (Series 1) (No. 1681) 90 60
2453 150c. Plate No. 76 (Series 1) (No. 1751) 90 60
2454 250c. Plate No. 74 (Series 1) (No. 1736) 90 60

1988. 125th Anniv of International Red Cross. Nos. 2202/5 and 2207/10 optd with cross.
2455 **396** $3.20 blue . . . . 1·50 1·50
2456 – $3.20 blue (No. 2203) . . 1·50 1·50
2457 – $3.20 blue (No. 2204) . . 1·50 1·50
2458 – $3.20 blue (No. 2205) . . 1·50 1·50
2459 – $3.30 black (No. 2207) 1·50 1·50
2460 **396** $3.30 black . . . . . . 1·50 1·50
2461 – $3.30 black (No. 2209) 1·50 1·50
2462 – $3.30 black (No. 2210) 1·50 1·50

1988. Centenary of Publication of Sanders' "Reichenbachia" (33rd issue). As T **331**. Mult.
2468 270c. Plate No. 90 (Series 2) 4·50 70
2469 360c. Plate No. 84 (Series 2) 75 1·00
2470 550c. Plate No. 70 (Series 2) (horiz) . . . . 1·75 2·00
2471 670c. Plate No. 71 (Series 2) (horiz) . . . . 2·00 2·50

1988. 60th Anniv of Cricket in Guyana. Nos. 1584, 1670, 1681 and 1815 optd **1928 – 1988 CRICKET JUBILEE** or surch also.
2472 200c. Plate No. 14 (Series 1) 19·00 21·00
2473 200c. Plate No. 79 (Series 1) 1·00 40
2474 800c. on 150c. Plate No. 87 (Series 1) . . . . 8·00 10·00
2475 800c. on 160c. Plate No. 5 (Series 2) . . . . 3·25 3·25

1988. Olympic Games, Seoul. (a) Nos. 1628, 1634, 1671, 1681, 1683, 1814, 1818/19, 1880 and 2069 optd **OLYMPIC GAMES 1988** or surch also.
2476 120c. Plate No. 46 (Series 1) 50 50
2477 130c. Plate No. 38 (Series 2) 50 50
2478 150c. Plate No. 87 (Series 1) 50 50
2479 200c. Plate No. 33 (Series 1) 50 50
2480 300c. Plate No. 83 (Series 1) 50 50
2481 300c. on 360c. Plate No. 34 (Series 2) 70 70
2482 320c. Plate No. 10 (Series 2) 70 70
2483 330c. Plate No. 82 (Series 2) 70 70
2484 350c. Plate No. 94 (Series 1) 70 70
2485 350c. Plate No. 29 (Series 2) 70 70

(b) Design as No. 1420 but incorrectly inscr "LOS ANGELLES" optd or surch **OLYMPICS 1988** (A) or **KOREA 1988** (B).
2486 $1.20 multicoloured (A) . . 50 50
2487 $1.20 multicoloured (B) . . 50 50
2488 130c. on $1.20 mult (A) . . 50 50
2489 130c. on $1.20 mult (B) . . 50 50
2490 150c. on $1.20 mult (A) . . 50 50
2491 150c. on $1.20 mult (B) . . 50 50
2492 200c. on $1.20 mult (A) . . 60 60
2493 200c. on $1.20 mult (B) . . 60 60
2594 350c. on $1.20 mult (A) . . 70 70
2495 350c. on $1.20 mult (B) . . 70 70

1988. Columbus Day. Nos. 1672/3 optd or surch **V CENTENARY OF THE LANDING OF CHRISTOPHER COLUMBUS IN THE AMERICAS**.
2496 320c. Plate No. 50 (Series 1) 2·50 60
2497 $15 on 360c. Plate No. 85 (Series 1) . . . . 4·50 6·00

1988. Centenary of Publication of Sanders' "Reichenbachia" (34th issue). As T **331**. Mult.
2498 100c. Plate No. 44 (Series 2) 60 55
2499 130c. Plate No. 42 (Series 2) (horiz) 60 55
2500 140c. Plate No. 4 (Series 2) 75 65
2501 160c. Plate No. 50 (Series 2) 75 65
2502 175c. Plate No. 51 (Series 2) 90 75
2503 200c. Plate No. 11 (Series 2) 4·00 1·40
2504 200c. Plate No. 23 (Series 2) 4·00 1·40
2505 200c. Plate No. 26 (Series 2) 4·00 1·40
2506 200c. Plate No. 75 (Series 2) 4·00 1·40
2507 200c. Plate No. 93 (Series 2) 4·00 1·40
2508 250c. Plate No. 79 (Series 2) 1·00 1·00
2509 280c. Plate No. 62 (Series 2) 1·25 1·50
2510 285c. Plate No. 63 (Series 2) 6·00 2·00
2511 380c. Plate No. 35 (Series 2) 6·50 2·25

1988. Christmas (1st issue). Various "Reichenbachia" issues optd or surch. (a) Optd or surch **SEASON'S GREETINGS**.
2519 120c. on 100c. Plate No. 6 (Series 1) 70 70
2520 120c. on 100c. Plate No. 13 (Series 1) 70 70
2521 120c. on 100c. Plate No. 20 (Series 1) 70 70
2522 120c. on 100c. Plate No. 25 (Series 1) 70 70
2523 120c. on 100c. Plate No. 40 (Series 1) (horiz) 25 25
2524 120c. on 100c. Plate No. 42 (Series 1) (horiz) 25 25
2525 120c. on 100c. Plate No. 43 (Series 1) (horiz) 25 25
2526 120c. on 100c. Plate No. 45 (Series 1) (horiz) 25 25
2512 150c. Plate No. 32 (Series 1) (No. 1561) 70 70
2513 150c. Plate No. 62 (Series 1) (No. 1566) 70 70
2514 225c. Plate No. 60 (Series 1) (No. 1682) 70 70
2532 240c. on 180c. Plate No. 15 (Series 1) (No. 1752) . . . 70 70
2515 260c. Plate No. 39 (Series 1) (No. 1737) 70 70
2516 320c. Plate No. 82 (Series 1) (No. 1753) 70 70
2517 330c. Plate No. 80 (Series 1) (No. 1754) 70 70
2518 360c. Plate No. 85 (Series 1) (No. 1673) 70 70

(b) Optd **SEASON'S GREETINGS 1988**.
2527 225c. Plate No. 24 (Series 1) (No. 1774) . . . . 1·25 1·25
2528 225c. Plate No. 60 (Series 1) (No. 1682) . . . . 1·25 1·25
2530 225c. on 350c. on 120c. Plate No. 65 (Series 1) (No. 2221) . . . . 1·25 1·25
MS2531 120 × 129 mm. 225c. on 55c. × 4 Plate No. 22 (Series 1) each with a different overprint **(Christmas 1987, Happy New Year, Merry Christmas or Happy Holidays)** (No. **MS**2232) . . . 3·75 3·75

1988. Christmas (2nd issue). Nos. 489, 1188/91 and 1449 surch or optd **CHRISTMAS 1988**.
2533 – 20c. on 6c. mult (No. 489) 25 10
2534 **277** 120c. brown, black bl . . 35 50
2535 – 120c. on 130c. red, black and blue (No. 1189) 35 50
2536 – 120c. on 150c. violet, black and blue (No. 1190) 35 50
2537 – 120c. on 200c. green, black and blue (No. 1191) 35 50
2538 – 500c. on 330c. mult (No. 1449) . . . . . 2·25 3·00

1988. AIDS Information Campaign. Nos. 707/8a optd or surch with various slogans.
2539 120c. on $5 "Morpho deidamia" (A) . . . . . 3·00 3·00
2540 120c. on $5 "Morpho deidamia" (B) . . . . . 3·00 3·00
2541 120c. on $5 "Morpho deidamia" (C) . . . . . 3·00 3·00
2542 120c. on $5 "Morpho deidamia" (D) . . . . . 3·00 3·00
2543 120c. on $5 "Morpho deidamia" (E) . . . . . 3·00 3·00
2544 120c. on $10 "Elbella patrobas" (A) . . . . . 3·00 3·00
2545 120c. on $10 "Elbella patrobas" (B) . . . . . . 3·00 3·00
2546 120c. on $10 "Elbella patrobas" (C) . . . . . 3·00 3·00
2547 120c. on $10 "Elbella patrobas" (D) . . . . . 3·00 3·00
2548 120c. on $10 "Elbella patrobas" (E) . . . . . . 3·00 3·00
2549 $2 "Morpho rhetenor" (female) (E) . . . . . . 9·50 2·75
2550 $5 "Morpho deidamia" (E) 11·00 7·00
2551 $10 "Elbella patrobas" (E) 13·00 11·00
OVERPRINTS: (A) **Be compassionate towards AIDS victims.**; (B) **Get information on AIDS. it may save your life.**; (C) **Get the facts. Education helps to prevent AIDS.**; (D) **Say no to Drugs and limit the spread of AIDS.**; (E) **Protect yourself from AIDS. Better safe than sorry.**

1988. 150th Anniv of Abolition of Slavery (1984) (2nd issue). Designs as Nos. 1547/50, but colours changed.
2552 **337** 25c. black and brown . . 15 10
2553 – 60c. black and lilac . . . 20 15
2254 – 130c. black and green . . 25 50
2555 – 150c. black and blue . . 30 75

1989. Olympic Medal Winners, Seoul. Nos. 1672, 1923 and 2178 surch **SALUTING WINNERS OLYMPIC GAMES 1988**.
2556 550c. on 560c. Plate No. 1 (Series 2) . . . . 1·50 1·25
2557 900c. on 320c. Plate No. 18 (Series 2) . . . . 2·00 2·50
2558 1050c. on 320c. Plate No. 50 (Series 1) . . . . 2·50 3·25

1989. Republic Day. Nos. 2194/2201 and 2212 optd **REPUBLIC DAY 1989**.
2559 **396** $1.20 green 60 70
2560 – $1.20 green (No. 2195) 60 70
2561 – $1.20 green (No. 2196) 60 70
2562 – $1.20 green (No. 2197) 60 70
2563 **396** $1.20 purple 60 70
2564 – $1.20 purple (No. 2199) 60 70
2565 – $1.20 purple (No. 2200) 60 70
2566 – $1.20 purple (No. 2201) 60 70
2567 – $10 multicoloured . . . 3·50 4·50

1989. Nos. 2202/5 and 2207/10 surch **$5.00**.
2568 **396** $5 on $3.20 blue . . . . 2·00 2·25
2569 – $5 on $3.20 blue (No. 2203) . . . . . 2·00 2·25
2570 – $5 on $3.20 blue (No. 2204) . . . . . 2·00 2·25
2571 – $5 on $3.20 blue (No. 2205) . . . . . 2·00 2·25
2572 – $5 on $3.30 black (No. 2207) . . . . . 2·00 2·25
2573 **396** $5 on $3.30 black . . . 2·00 2·25
2574 – $5 on $3.30 black (No. 2209) . . . . . 2·00 2·25
2575 – $5 on $3.30 black (No. 2210) . . . . . 2·00 2·25

1989. Various "Reichenbachia" issues surch.
2576 120c. on 140c. Plate No. 25 (Series 2) . . . . 2·00 2·00
2577 120c. on 140c. Plate No. 52 (Series 2) . . . . 2·00 2·00
2578 120c. on 140c. Plate No. 65 (Series 2) . . . . 2·00 2·00
2580 120c. on 140c. Plate No. 38 (Series 2) . . . . 2·00 2·00
2581 120c. on 140c. Plate No. 41 (Series 2) . . . . 2·00 2·00
2579 120c. on 175c. Plate No. 54 (Series 2) . . . . 2·00 2·00
2582 170c. on 175c. Plate No. 58 (Series 2) . . . . 2·25 2·25
2583 250c. on 280c. Plate No. 66 (Series 2) . . . . 2·50 2·50
2584 250c. on 280c. Plate No. 67 (Series 2) . . . . 2·50 2·50
2585 300c. on 290c. Plate No. 53 (Series 2) (No. 2236) . . . 2·50 2·50

1989. Nos. 1744/5 and 2185/6 surch **TEN DOLLARS $10.00** (Nos. 2586, 2588) or **TEN DOLLARS** (Nos. 2587, 2589).
2586 **363** $10 on 320c. red, black and lilac (No. 1744) 3·25 3·75
2587 – $10 on 320c. mult (No. 1745) . . . . . 3·25 3·75
2588 **363** $10 on 320c. red, black and lilac (No. 2185) 3·25 3·75
2589 – $10 on 320c. mult (No. 2186) . . . . . 3·25 3·75

1989. Nos. O54/7, O59/63 and O65/9 optd **POSTAGE** or surch also.
2591 125c. on 130c. Plate No. 92 (Series 2) . . . . 1·75 1·75
2592 125c. on 140c. Plate No. 36 (Series 2) . . . . 1·75 1·75
2593 150c. Plate No. 43 (Series 2) 1·75 1·75
2594 150c. on 175c. Plate No. 31 (Series 2) . . . . 1·75 1·75
2595 250c. Plate No. 59 (Series 2) 2·00 2·00
2596 250c. on 225c. Plate No. 26 (Series 2) . . . . 2·00 2·00
2597 250c. on 230c. Plate No. 68 (Series 2) . . . . 2·00 2·00
2598 250c. on 275c. Plate No. 69 (Series 2) . . . . 2·00 2·00
2599 300c. on 275c. Plate No. 90 (Series 2) . . . . 2·00 2·00
2750 350c. Plate No. 95 (Series 2) 2·00 2·00
2601 350c. on 330c. Plate No. 23 (Series 2) . . . . 2·00 2·00
2602 600c. Plate No. 70 (Series 2) 2·25 2·50
2603 $12 Plate No. 71 (Series 2) 3·00 4·00
2604 $15 Plate No. 84 (Series 2) 3·25 4·25

1989. Centenary of Publication of Sanders' "Reichenbachia" (35th issue). As T **331**. Mult.
2605 200c. Plate No. 49 (Series 2) 3·00 3·00
2606 200c. Plate No. 53 (Series 2) 3·00 3·00
2607 200c. Plate No. 60 (Series 2) 3·00 3·00
2608 200c. Plate No. 64 (Series 2) 3·00 3·00

1989. No. 1442 surch **250**.
2609 **322** 250c. on 25c. mult . . . 6·50 85

1989. 40th Anniv of Guyana Red Cross. No. 1872 surch **RED CROSS 1948 1988** and new value.
2610 375c. on 45c. Plate No. 17 (Series 2) . . . . 2·50 2·50
2611 425c. on 45c. Plate No. 17 (Series 2) . . . . 2·50 2·50

1989. World Health Day. Nos. 1875 and 2239 surch with new value and inscr as indicated.
2612 250c. on 75c. Plate No. 56 (Series 2) surch **HEALTH FOR ALL** . . . . 1·50 1·50
2613 250c. on 75c. Plate No. 56 (Series 2) surch **ALL FOR HEALTH** . . . . 1·50 1·50
2614 675c. on 720c. Plate No. 49 (Series 2) surch **ALL FOR HEALTH** . . . . 2·25 3·25
2615 675c. on 720c. Plate No. 49 (Series 2) surch **HEALTH FOR ALL** . . . . 2·25 3·25

1989. Scouting Anniversaries. Nos. 1873, 1879, 2322, 2509 and unissued value as No. 1873 optd or surch also.
2616 250c. on 50c. Plate No. 33 (Series 2) (surch **BOY SCOUTS 1909 1989**) . . 1·25 1·25
2617 250c. on 50c. Plate No. 33 (Series 2) (surch **GIRL GUIDES 1924 1989**) . . . 1·25 1·25
2618 250c. on 100c. Plate No. 33 (Series 2) (surch **BOY SCOUTS 1909 1989**) . . 1·25 1·25
2619 250c. on 100c. Plate No. 33 (Series 2) (surch **GIRL GUIDES 1924 1989**) . . . 1·25 1·25
2620 300c. Plate No. 50 (Series 2) (optd **BOY SCOUTS 1909 1989**) . . . . 1·25 1·25
2621 300c. Plate No. 50 (Series 2) (optd **GIRL GUIDES 1924 1989**) . . . . 1·25 1·25
2622 $25 on 280c. Plate No. 62 (Series 2) (surch **LADY BADEN POWELL 1889 – 1989**) . . . . 5·50 7·00
2623 $25 on 700c. Plate No. 62 (Series 2) (surch **LADY BADEN POWELL 1889 – 1989**) . . . . 5·50 7·00
The events commemorated are the 80th anniv of Boy Scout Movement in Guyana, 65th anniv of Girl Guide Movement in Guyana and birth centenary of Lady Baden-Powell.

1989. 150 Years of Photography. No. 1881 surch **PHOTOGRAPHY 1839 – 1989** and new value.
2624 550c. on 390c. Plate No. 6 (Series 2) . . . . 3·25 3·50
2625 650c. on 390c. Plate No. 6 (Series 2) . . . . 3·25 3·50

1989. 70th Anniv of International Labour Organization. No. 1875 surch **I.L.O. 1919-1989 300**.
2627 300c. on 75c. Plate No. 56 (Series 2) . . . . 7·00 1·90

1989. Various stamps surch.
2628 80c. on 6c. Patua (No. 489) 40 20
2629 $1 on 2c. Type **132** . . . 40 20
2630 $2.05 on 3c. Hanging heliconia (No. 544) . . . 40 25
2641 $2.55 on 5c. Annatto tree (No. 545) 40 25
2642 $3.25 on 6c. Cannon-ball tree (No. 546) 40 25
2633 $5 on 6c. Type **111** . . . 40 30
2634 $6.40 on 10c. "Archonias bellona" (No. 699) . . . 6·00 75
2648 $6.40 on $3.30 black (No. 2207) . . . . . . 5·00 4·00
2649 $6.40 on $3.30 black (No. 2208) . . . . . . 5·00 4·00
2650 $6.40 on $3.30 black (No. 2209) . . . . . . 5·00 4·00
2651 $6.40 on $3.30 black (No. 2210) . . . . . . 5·00 4·00
2646 640c. on 675c. on 720c. Plate No. 49 (Series 2) (No. 2614) . . . . . . 1·75 2·00
2647 640c. on 675c. on 720c. Plate No. 49 (Series 2) (No. 2615) . . . . . . 1·75 2·00
2637a $7.65 on 35c. "Anaea galanthus" (No. 703) . . 6·00 1·25
2638 $7.65 on 40c. "Morpho retenor" (male) (No. 704) . . . . 7·00 1·25
2652 $7.65 on $3.20 blue (No. 2202) . . . . . . 5·00 4·00
2653 $7.65 on $3.20 blue (No. 2203) . . . . . . 5·00 4·00
2654 $7.65 on $3.20 blue (No. 2204) . . . . . . 5·00 4·00
2655 $7.65 on $3.20 blue (No. 2205) . . . . . . 5·00 4·00
2635 $8.90 on 60c. "Papilio androgeus" (No. 705a) 8·00 1·25
2643 $50 on $2 "Morpho rhetenor" (female) (No. 707) . . . . 18·00 9·00
2644 $100 on $2 "Morpho rhetenor" (female) (No. 707) . . . . 26·00 19·00

1989. CARICOM Day. No. 1878 surch **CARICOM DAY 125**.
2656 125c. on 200c. Plate No. 44 (Series 2) . . . . 4·00 90

454 "Stalachtis calliope"

455 Kathryn Sullivan (first U.S. woman to walk in space)

1989. Butterflies (1st series). Multicoloured.
2657 80c. Type **454** 60 10
2658 $2.25 "Morpho rhetenor" 70 15
2659 $5 "Agrias claudia" 80 15
2660 $6.40 "Marpesia marcella" 85 20
2661 $7.65 "Papilio zagreus" . . 90 30
2662 $8.90 "Chorinea faunus" . . 1·00 30
2663 $25 "Euptychia cephus" . . 2·75 2·75
2664 $100 "Nessaea regina" . . . 7·00 9·00
See also Nos. 2789/2861 and **EMS**18/19.

1989. 25 Years of Women in Space. Mult.
2665 $6.40 Type **455** 70 20
2666 $12.80 Svetlana Savitskaya (first Soviet woman to walk in space) . . . . . 1·10 45
2667 $15.30 Judy Resnik and Christa McAuliffe and "Challenger" logo . . . . 1·10 45
2668 $100 Sally Ride (first U.S. woman astronaut) . . . . 8·00 9·00

1989. Centenary of Ahmadiyya (Moslem organization). Nos. 543/5 surch **AHMADIYYA CENTENARY 1899-1989.**
2669 80c. on 2c. Type **132** . . . 3·50 50
2670 $6.40 on 3c. Hanging heliconia . . . . 11·00 4·75
2671 $8.90 on 5c. Annatto tree 12·00 6·50

457 Head of Harpy Eagle

458 Channel-billed Toucan

1990. Endangered Species. Harpy Eagle. Multicoloured.
2672 $2.25 Type **457** 75 25
2673 $5 Harpy eagle with monkey prey . . . . 1·00 30
2674 $8.90 Eagle on branch (facing right) . . . . . . 1·50 50
2675 $30 Eagle on branch (facing left) . . . . 3·25 3·50

1990. Birds of Guyana. Multicoloured.
2676 $15 Type **458** . . . . . . 1·50 70
2677 $25 Blue and yellow macaw 1·75 50
2678 $50 Wattled jacana (horiz) 3·25 2·50
2679 $60 Hoatzin . . . . 3·50 2·75
MS2680 Two sheets, each 110 × 80 mm. (a) $100 Great kiskadee. (b) $100 Amazon kingfisher Set of 2 sheets . . . 11·00 11·00

1990. 85th Anniv of Rotary International. Optd **Rotary International 1905-1990** and emblem. (a) On Nos. 2657/64.
2681 80c. Type **454** . . . . . . 1·50 30
2682 $2.25 "Morpho rhetenor" 1·75 50
2683 $5 "Agrias claudia" . . . . 2·25 50
2684 $6.40 "Marpesia marcella" 2·25 55
2685 $7.65 "Papilio zagreus" . . 2·25 55
2686 $8.90 "Chorinea faunus" . . 2·50 65
2687 $25 "Euptychia cephus" . . 5·00 5·50
2688 $100 "Nessaea regina" . . . 12·00 14·00

(b) On Nos. 2665/8.
2689 $6.40 Type **455** . . . . . . 1·25 40
2690 $12.80 Svetlana Savitskaya (first Soviet woman to walk in space) . . . . . 1·75 1·00
2691 $15.30 Judy Resnik and Christa McAuliffe with "Challenger" logo . . . . 1·75 1·10
2692 $100 Sally Ride (first U.S. woman astronaut) . . . . 9·00 11·00

460 Indian Post Runner, 1837

1990. 150th Anniv of the Penny Black and 500th Anniv of Thurn and Taxis Postal Service. Multicoloured.
2693/2746 $15.30 × 27, $17.80 × 9, $20 × 18 . . . . . .
Set of 54 . . . . 32·00 35·00
MS2747 Three sheets, each 116 × 86 mm. (a) $150 Post boy. (b) $150 Thurn and Taxis (Northern District) 3sgr. of 1852. (c) $150 Thurn and Taxis (Southern District) 6k. of 1852 Set of 3 sheets . . . . 13·00 14·00
Nos. 2693/2746 depict various forms of mail transport.

1990. 9th Conference of Rotary District 405, Georgetown. Nos. 1759, 1762/3 and 1765/6 surch **ROTARY DISTRICT 405 9th CONFERENCE MAY 1990 GEORGETOWN** and new value.
2748 80c. on 55c. Plate No. 9 (Series 1) . . . .
2749 80c. on 55c. Plate No. 49 (Series 1) . . . .
2750 80c. on 55c. Plate No. 64 (Series 1) . . . .
2751 $6.40 on 130c. Plate No. 6 (Series 1) . . . .
2752 $6.40 on 130c. Plate No. 25 (Series 1) . . . .
2753 $7.65 on 130c. Plate No. 25 (Series 1) . . . .

1990. 90th Birthday of Queen Elizabeth the Queen Mother. Nos. 2657/64 surch **90th Birthday H.M. The Queen Mother.**
2754 80c. Type **454** . . . . . . 1·50 40
2755 $2.25 "Morpho rhetenor" 1·75 50
2756 $5 "Agrias claudia" . . . . 2·25 60
2757 $6.40 "Marpesia marcella" 2·50 60
2758 $7.65 "Papilio zagreus" . . 2·75 75
2759 $8.90 "Chorinea faunus" . . 2·75 90
2760 $25 "Euptychia cephus" . . 6·00 6·00
2761 $100 "Nessaea regina" . . . 14·00 16·00
See also Nos. **EMS**31/3.

463 Collared Trogon **464** "Melinaea idae"

1990. Birds. Multicoloured.
2762 80c. Marbled wood quail ("Guiana Partridge") (horiz) 30 10
2763 $2.55 Type **463** 40 15
2764 $3.25 Chestnut-tipped toucanet ("Derby Aracari") 40 15
2765 $5 Black-necked aracari . . 50 20
2766 $5.10 Green aracari 50 30
2767 $5.80 Ivory-billed aracari . . 50 30
2768 $6.40 Guiana toucanet . . . 50 30
2769 $6.50 Channel-billed toucan ("Sulphur-breasted Toucan") 50 30
2770 $7.55 Red-billed toucan . . 65 30
2771 $7.65 Toco toucan 65 30
2772 $8.25 Tawny-tufted toucanet ("Natterers Toucanet") 65 30
2773 $8.90 Eared trogon ("Welcome Trogon") . . 65 30
2774 $9.75 Elegant trogon ("Doubtful Trogon") . . 65 30
2775 $11.40 Collared trogon ("Banded Aracari") . . . 75 40
2776 $12.65 Golden-headed quetzal ("Golden-headed Train Bearer") 75 40
2777 $12.80 Rufous-breasted hermit 75 40
2778 $13.90 Band tail barbthroat 75 40
2779 $15.30 White-tipped sickle-bill 80 50
2780 $17.80 Black jacobin 90 60
2781 $19.20 Fiery topaz 90 60
2782 $22.95 Tufted coquette . . . 1·00 70
2783 $26.70 Ecuadorian pied-tail 1·00 70
2784 $30 Resplendent quetzal ("Quetzal") . . . . 1·00 70
2785 $50 Green-crowned brilliant 1·75 1·25
2786 $100 Emerald-chinned hummingbird . . . . . . 2·75 2·75
2787 $190 Lazuline sabre-wing . . 4·50 5·00
2788 $225 Beryline hummingbird 4·50 5·50

1990. Butterfiles (2nd series). Multicoloured.
2789/2860 80c., $2.55, $5, $6.40, $7.65, $8.90, $10 × 64, $50 and $100 . . . .
Set of 72 . . . . 24·00 25·00
MS2861 Four sheets, each 102 × 71 mm. (a) $150 "Heliconius aoede". (b) $150 "Phyciodes clio" (horiz). (c) $190 "Thecla hemon". (d) $190 "Nymphidium caricae" Set of 4 sheets . . . . . . 18·00 20·00
DESIGNS—VERT: $2.55, "Rhetus dysonii"; $5 "Actinote anteas"; $6.40, "Heliconius tales"; $7.65, "Thecla telemus"; $8.90, "Theope eudocia"; $10 (2795), "Heleconius vetustus"; 2796, "Mesosemia eumene"; 2797, "Parides phosphorus"; 2798, "Polystichtis emylius"; 2799, "Xanthocleis aedesia"; 2800, "Doxocopa agathina"; 2801, "Adelpha plesaure"; 2802, "Heliconius wallacei"; 2803, "Notheme eumeus"; 2804, "Melinaea mediatrix"; 2805, "Theritas coronata"; 2806, "Dismorphia orise"; 2807, "Phyciodes ianthe"; 2808, "Morpho aega"; 2809, "Zaretis isidora"; 2810, "Pierella lena"; 2811, "Heliconius silvana"; 2812, "Eunica alcmena"; 2813, "Mechanitis polymnia"; 2814, "Mesosemia ephyne"; 2815, "Thecla erema"; 2816, "Callizona acesta"; 2817, "Stalachtis phaedusa"; 2818, "Battus belus"; 2819, "Nymula phliasus"; 2820, "Parides childrenae"; 2821, "Stalachtis euterpe"; 2822, "Dysmathia portia"; 2823, "Tithorea hermias"; 2824, "Prepona pheridamas"; 2825, "Dismorphia fortunata"; 2826, "Hamadryas amphinome"; $50 "Heliconius vicini"; $100 "Amarynthis meneria". HORIZ: $10 (2827), "Thecla falerina"; 2828, "Pheles heliconides"; 2829, "Echenias leucocyana"; 2830, "Heliconius xanthocles"; 2831, "Mesopthalma idotea"; 2832, "Parides aeneas"; 2833, "Heliconius numata"; 2834, "Thecla critola"; 2835, "Themone pais"; 2836, "Nymula agle"; 2837, "Adelpha cocala"; 2838, "Anaea eribotes"; 2839, "Prepona demophon"; 2840, "Selenophanes cassiope"; 2841, "Consul hippona"; 2842, "Antirrhaea avernus"; 2843, "Thecla telemus"; 2844, "Thyridia confusa"; 2845, "Heliconius burneyi"; 2846, "Parides lysander"; 2847, "Eunica orphise"; 2848, "Adelpha melona"; 2849, "Morpho menelaus"; 2850, "Nymula phylleus"; 2851, "Stalachtis phlegia"; 2852, "Theope barea"; 2853, "Morpho perseus"; 2854, "Lycorea ceres"; 2855, "Archonias bellona"; 2856, "Caeronis chorinaeus"; 2857, "Vila azeca"; 2858, "Nessaea batesii".
Nos. 2795/2810, 2811/26, 2827/42 and 2843/58 respectively were printed together, se-tenant, forming composite designs.

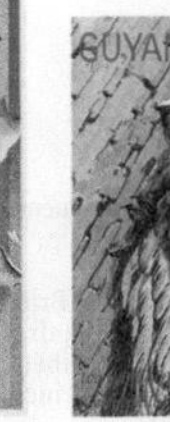
465 "Vanillia inodora" **466** Ivory-billed Woodpecker

1990. Flowers. Multicoloured.
2862/2965 $7.65, $8.90, $10 × 32, $12.80 × 65, $15.30, $17.80, $20, $25 and $100 . . . .
Set of 104 . . . . . . 24·00 24·00
MS2966 Five sheets. (a) 65 × 95 mm. $150 "Delonix regia" (horiz). (b) 86 × 65 mm. $150 "Hexisea bidentata" (horiz). (c) 70 × 105 mm. $150 "Galeandra devonianal" (horiz). (d) 68 × 110 mm. $150 "Lecythis ollaria". (e) 74 × 104 mm. $190 "Ionopsis utricularioides" Set of 5 sheets . . . . 16·00 17·00
DESIGNS—VERT: $8.90, "Epidendrum ibaguense"; $10 (2864), "Dichea muricata"; 2865, "Octomeria erosilabia"; 2866, "Spiranthes orchioides"; 2867, "Brassavola nodosa"; 2868, "Epidendrum rigidum"; 2869, "Brassia caudata"; 2870, "Pleurothallis diffusa"; 2871, "Aspasia variegata"; 2872, "Stenia pallida"; 2873, "Cyrtopodium punctatum"; 2874, "Cattleya deckeri"; 2875, "Cryptarrhena lunata"; 2876, "Cattleya violacea"; 2877, "Caularthron bicornutum"; 2878, "Oncidium carthagenense"; 2879, "Galeandra devoniana"; 2880, "Bifrenaria aurantiaca"; 2881, "Epidendrum ciliare"; 2882, "Dichaea picta"; 2883, "Scaphyglottis violacea"; 2884, "Cattleya percivaliana"; 2885, Map and national flag; 2886, "Epidendrum difforme"; 2887, "Eulophia maculata"; 2888, "Spiranthes tenuis"; 2889, "Peristoria guttata"; 2890, "Pleurothallis pruinosa"; 2891, "Cleistes rosea"; 2892, "Maxillaria variabilis"; 2893, "Brassavola cucullata"; 2894, "Epidendrum moyobambae"; 2895, "Oncidium orthostate"; $12.80, "Maxillaria parkeri"; $12.80 (2897), "Brassavola martiana"; 2898, "Paphinia cristata"; 2899, "Aganisia pulchella"; 2900, "Oncidium lanceanum"; 2901, "Lockhartia imbricata"; 2902, "Caularthron bilamellatum"; 2903, "Oncidium nanum"; 2904, "Pleurothallis ovalifolia"; 2905, "Galeandra dives"; 2906, "Cycnoches loddigesii"; 2907, "Ada aurantiaca"; 2908, "Catasetum barbatum"; 2909, "Palmorchis pubescens"; 2910, "Epidendrum anceps"; 2911, "Huntleya meleagris"; 2912, "Sobralia sessilis"; $15.30, "Epidendrum nocturnum"; $17.80, "Catasetum discolor"; $20 "Scuticaria hadwenii"; $25 "Epidendrum fragrans"; $100 "Epistephium parviflorum". HORIZ: $12.80 (2913), "Cochlospermum vitifolium"; 2914, "Eugenia malaccensis"; 2915, "Plumiera rubra"; 2916, "Erythrina glauca"; 2917, "Spathodea campanulata"; 2918, "Jacaranda filicifolia"; 2919, "Samanea saman"; 2920, "Cassia fistula"; 2921, "Abutilon integerrimum"; 2922, "Lagerstroemia speciosa"; 2923, "Tabebuia serratifolia"; 2924, "Guaiacum officinale"; 2925, "Solanum macranthum"; 2926, "Peltophorum roxburghii"; 2927, "Bauhinia variegata"; 2928, "Plumiera alba"; 2929, "Maxillaria camaridii"; 2930, "Vanilla pompona"; 2931, "Stanhopea grandiflora"; 2932, "Oncidium pusillum"; 2933, "Polycycnis vittata"; 2934, "Cattleya lawrenceana"; 2935, "Menadenium labiosum"; 2936, "Rodriguezia secunda"; 2937, "Mormodes buccinator"; 2938, "Otostylis brachystalix"; 2939, "Maxillaria discolor"; 2940, "Liparis elata"; 2941, "Gongora maculata"; 2942, "Koellensteinia graminea"; 2943, "Rudolfiella aurantiaca"; 2944, "Scuticaria steelei"; 2945, "Gloriosa rothschildiana"; 2946, "Pseudocalymma alliaceum"; 2947, "Callichlamys latifolia"; 2948, "Distictis riversii"; 2949, "Maurandya barclaiana"; 2950, "Beaumontia fragrans"; 2951, "Phaseolus caracalla"; 2952, "Mandevilla splendens"; 2953, "Solandra longiflora"; 2954, "Passiflora coccinea"; 2955, "Allamanda cathartica"; 2956, "Bauhinia galpini"; 2957, "Verbena maritima"; 2958, "Mandevilla sauveolens"; 2959, "Phryganocydia corymbosa"; 2960, "Jasminum sambac".
Nos. 2864/79, 2880/95, 2897/2912, 2913/28, 2929/44 and 2945/60 respectively were printed together, se-tenant, forming composite designs.

1990. Fauna. Multicoloured.
2967/86 $12.80 × 20 (vert designs showing endangered birds) . .
2987/3006 $12.80 × 20 (vert designs showing tropical birds) . . .
3007/26 $12.80 × 20 (vert designs showing prehistoric animals)
3027/46 $12.80 × 20 (horiz designs showing endangered wildlife)
Set of 80 . . . . 32·00 32·00
DESIGNS—VERT: No. 2968, Cauca guan; 2969, Sun conure; 2970, Resplendent quetzal ("Quetzal"); 2971, Long-wattled umbrellabird; 2972, Banded cotinga; 2973, Blue-throated conure ("Blue-chested Parakeet"); 2974, West Mexican chachalaca ("Rufous-bellied Chachalaca"); 2975, Yellow-faced amazon; 2976, Toucan barbet; 2977, Red siskin; 2978, Guianan cock-of-the-rock ("Cock-of-the-Rock"); 2979, Hyacinth macaw; 2980, Yellow cardinal; 2981, Bare-necked umbrellabird; 2982, Saffron toucanet; 2983, Red-billed curassow; 2984, Spectacled parrotlet; 2985, Lovely cotinga; 2986, Black-bellied gnateater ("Black-breasted Gnateater"); 2987, Swallow-tailed kite; 2988, Hoatzin; 2989, Ruby-topaz hummingbird; 2990, American black vulture; 2991, Rufous-tailed jacamar; 2992, Scarlet macaw; 2993, Rose-breasted thrush tanager; 2994, Toco toucan; 2995, Bearded bellbird; 2996, Blue-crowned motmot; 2997, Green oropendola; 2998, Pompadour cotinga; 2999, Vermilion flycatcher; 3000, Blue and yellow macaw; 3001, White-barred piculet; 3002, Great razor-billed curassow; 3003, Ruddy quail dove; 3004, Paradise tanager; 3005, American darter ("Anhinga"); 3006, Greater flamingo; 3007, Palaelodus; 3008, Archaeotrogon; 3009, Teratornis mirabilis ("Vulture"); 3010, Bradypus tridactylus; 3011, Natalus stramineus bat; 3012, Cebidae; 3013, Cuvieronius; 3014, Phororhacos; 3015, Smilodectes; 3016, Megatherium; 3017, Titanotylopus; 3018, Teleoceras; 3019, Macrauchenia; 3020, Mylodon; 3021, Smilodon; 3022, Glyptodon; 3023, Protohydrocherus; 3024, Archaeohyrax; 3025, Pyrotherium; 3026, Platypittamys. HORIZ: $12.80 (3027), Harpy eagle and hyacinth macaw; 3028, Andean condor; 3029, Amazonian umbrellabird; 3030, Spider monkeys; 3031, Hyacinth macaws; 3032, Red siskin; 3033, Toucan barbet; 3034, Three-toed sloth; 3035, Guanacos; 3036, Spectacled bear; 3037, White-lipped peccary; 3038, Maned wolf; 3039, Jaguar; 3040, Spectacled cayman; 3041, Giant armadillo; 3042, Giant anteater; 3043, South American river otter; 3044, Yapok; 3045, Central American river turtle; 3046, Cauca guan.
Nos. 2967/86, 2987/3006, 3007/26 and 3027/46 respectively were printed together, se-tenant, forming composite designs.
No. 2982 is inscribed "Toucanette" and No. 2995 "Bellbird", both in error.
See also **EMS**34/5.

467 National Flag

1991. 25th Anniv of Independence. Sheet 100 × 70 mm. Litho. Imperf.
MS3047 **467** $225 multicoloured 5·50 6·00

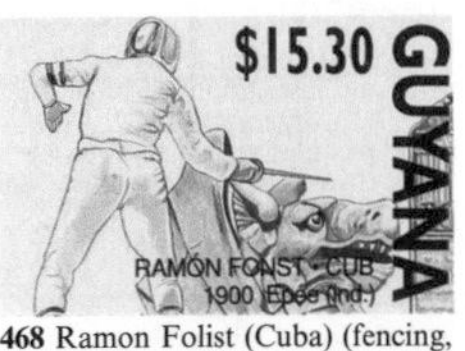

468 Ramon Folist (Cuba) (fencing, 1990)

1991. Winter Olympic Games, Albertville (1st issue), and Olympic Games, Barcelona. Previous Gold Medal Winners. Multicoloured.

3048/3119 $15.30 × 9, $17.80 × 9, $20 × 18, $25 × 18 and $30 × 18 . . . . Set of 72 . . . . 32·00 35·00

MS3120 Three sheets, each 98 × 70 mm. (a) $150 Johannes Kolehmainen (Finland) (10,000 metres, 1912) (vert). (b) $150 Paavo Nurmi (Finland) (5000 metres, 1924) (vert). (c) $190 Nedo Nadi (Italy) (fencing, 1920) (vert) Set of 3 sheets . . . . 11·00 12·00

DESIGNS: $15.30 (3049), Lucien Gaudin (France) (fencing, 1924); 3050, Ole Lilloe-Olsen (Norway) (shooting, 1924); 3051, Morris Fisher (U.S.A.) (rifle shooting, 1924); 3052, Ray Ewry (U.S.A.) (long jump, 1900); 3053, Hubert van Innes (Belgium) (archery, 1900); 3054, Alvin Kraenzlein (U.S.A.) (hurdles, 1900); 3055, Johnny Weissmuller (U.S.A.) (swimming, 1924); 3056, Hans Winkler (West Germany) (show jumping, 1956); $17.80 (3057), Viktor Chukarin (Russia) (gymnastics, 1952); 3058, Agnes Keleti (Hungary) (gymnastics, 1952); 3059, Barbel Wochel (East Germany) (200 metres, 1980); 3060, Eric Heiden (U.S.A.) (speed skating, 1980); 3061, Alvodar Gerevich (Hungary) (fencing, 1932); 3062, Giuseppe Delfino (Italy) (fencing, 1952); 3063, Alexander Tikhonov (Russia) (skiing, 1980); 3064, Pahud de Mortanges (Netherlands) (equestrian, 1932); 3065, Patricia McCormick (U.S.A.) (diving, 1952); $20 (3066), Olga Korbut (Russia) (gymnastics, 1972); 3067, Lyudmila Turischeva (Russia) (gymnastics, 1972); 3068, Lasse Viren (Finland) (10,000 metres, 1972); 3069, George Miez (Switzerland) (gymnastics, 1936); 3070, Roland Matthes (East Germany) (swimming, 1972); 3071, Pal Kovaks (Hungary) (fencing, 1936); 3072, Jesse Owens (U.S.A.) (200 metres, 1936); 3073, Mark Spitz (U.S.A.) (swimming, 1972); 3074, Eduardo Mangiarotti (Italy) (fencing, 1936); 3075, Nelli Kim (Russia) (gymnastics, 1976); 3076, Viktor Krovopuskov (Russia) (fencing, 1976); 3077, Viktor Sidiak (Russia) (fencing, 1976); 3078, Nikolai Andrianov (Russia) (gymnastics, 1976); 3079, Nadia Comaneci (Rumania) (gymnastics, 1976); 3080, Mitsuo Tsukahara (Japan) (gymnastics, 1976); 3081, Yelena Novikova-Belova (Russia) (fencing, 1976); 3082, John Naber (U.S.A.) (swimming, 1976); 3083, Kornella Ender (Rumania) (swimming, 1976); $25 (3084), Lydia Skoblikova (Russia) (speed skating, 1964); 3085, Ivar Ballangrud (Norway) (speed skating, 1936); 3086, Clas Thunberg (Finland) (speed skating, 1928); 3087, Anton Heida (U.S.A.) (gymnastics, 1904); 3088, Akinori Nakayama (Japan) (gymnastics, 1968); 3089, Sixten Jernberg (Sweden) (skiing, 1964); 3090, Yevgeniy Grischin (Russia) (speed skating, 1956); 3091, Paul Radmilovic (East Germany) (waterpolo, 1920); 3092, Charles Daniels (U.S.A.) (swimming, 1904); 3093, Sawao Kato (Japan) (gymnastics, 1968); 3094, Rudolf Karpati (Hungary) (fencing, 1948); 3095, Jeno Fuchs (Hungary) (fencing, 1908); 3096, Emil Zatopek (Czechoslovakia) (10,000 metres, 1948); 3097, Fanny Blankers-Koen (Netherlands) (hurdles, 1948); 3098, Melvin Sheppard (U.S.A.) (4 x 400 metres relay, 1908); 3099, Gert Fredriksson (Sweden) (kayak, 1948); 3100, Paul Elvstrom (Denmark) (sailing, 1948); 3101, Harrison Dillard (U.S.A.) (100 metres, 1948); $30 (3102), Al Oerter (U.S.A.) (discus, 1956); 3103, Polina Atsakhova (Russia) (gymnastics, 1956); 3104, Takashi Ono (Japan) (gymnastics, 1956); 3105, Valentin Muratov (Russia) (gymnastics, 1956); 3106, Henri St. Cyr (Sweden) (equestrian, 1956); 3107, Iain Murray Rose (Australia) (swimming, 1956); 3108, Larisa Latynina (Russia) (gymnastics, 1956); 3109, Carlo Pavesi (Italy) (fencing, 1956); 3110, Dawn Fraser (Australia) (swimming, 1956); 3111, Betty Cuthbert (Australia) (400 metres, 1964); 3112, Vera Caslavska (Czechoslovakia) (gymnastics, 1964); 3113, Galin Kulakova (Russia) (skiing, 1972); 3114, Yukio Endo (Japan) (gymnastics, 1972); 3115, Vladimir Morozov (Russia) (kayak, 1972); 3116, Boris Shaklin (Russia) (gymnastics, 1964); 3117, Don Schollander (U.S.A.) (swimming, 1964); 3118, Gyozo Kulscar (Hungary) (fencing, 1964); 3119, Christian D'Oriloa (France) (fencing, 1956).

Nos. 3048/56, 3057/65, 3066/74, 3075/83, 3084/92, 3093/3101, 3102/10 and 3111/19 respectively were printed together, se-tenant, forming composite designs.

Sheetlets containing Nos. 3057/65, 3084/92 and 3111/19 were subsequently re-issued with Nos. 3063, 3086 and 3113 overprinted "ALBERTVILLE '92".

See also Nos. 3186/94 and 3246/54.

1991. 85th Anniv of Rotary International (1990). (a) Nos. 2789/94 and 2859/60 optd or surch **Paul Percy Harris Founder 1868-1947** and emblem (A) or with Rotary emblem and **1905-1990** (B).

3121 80c. Type **464** (B) 10 10
3122 $2.55 "Rhetus dysonii" (A) 10 10
3123 $5 "Actinote anteas" (A) . . 10 10
3124 $6.40 "Heliconius tales" (A) 15 15
3125 $7.65 "Thecla telemus" (A) 15 15
3126 $100 on $8.90 "Theope eudocia" (A) . . . . . . 1·75 1·90
3127 $190 on $50 "Heliconius vicini" (B) . . . . . . 2·75 3·00
3128 $225 on $100 "Amarynthis meneria" (B) . . . . . 3·00 3·50

(b) Nos. 2795/2810 optd or surch as Nos. 3121/8 or with emblems and inscriptions of other international organizations.

3129 $10 "Heliconius vetustus" (B) 20 20
3130 $10 "Mesosemia eumene" (optd Boy Scout emblem and **1907–1992**) 20 20
3131 $10 "Parides phosphorus" (optd Lions Club emblem and **1917–1992**) 20 20
3132 $10 "Polystichtis emylius" (A) 20 20
3133 $10 "Xanthocleis aedesia" (optd **125 Years Red Cross** and cross) 20 20
3134 $10 "Doxocopa agathina" (optd with part Rotary emblem) 20 20
3135 $10 "Adelpha plesaure" (optd with part Rotary emblem) 20 20
3136 $10 "Heliconius wallacei" (optd **125 Years Red Cross** and cross) 20 20
3137 $10 "Notheme eumeus" (optd Lions Club emblem and **1917–1992**) 20 20
3138 $10 "Melinaea mediatrix" (optd with part Rotary emblem) 20 20
3139 $10 "Theritas coronata" (optd with part Rotary emblem) 20 20
3140 $10 "Dismorphia orise" (optd Boy Scout emblem and **1907–1992**) 20 20
3141 $50 on $10 "Phyciodes ianthe" (A) 80 80
3142 $75 on $10 "Morpho aega" (surch Boy Scout emblem and **1907–1992**) . . . . . 1·50 1·60
3143 $100 on $10 "Zaretis isidora" (surch Lions Club emblem and **1917–1992**) . . . . 1·75 1·90
3144 $190 on $10 "Pierella lena" (B) . . . . 2·75 3·25

MS3145 Two sheets, each 102 × 71 mm. (a) $400 on $150 "Heliconius aoede". (b) $500 on $150 "Phyciodes clio" Set of 2 sheets . . . . 10·00 10·50

Nos. **MS**3145a/b only show the new face values on the stamps and have international organization emblems overprinted on the sheet margins.

1991. 65th Birthday of Queen Elizabeth II and 70th Birthday of Prince Philip. As T **198a** of Gambia. Multicoloured.

3146 $12.80 Queen and Prince Philip in evening dress . . 25 20
3147 $15.30 Queen Elizabeth II 25 20
3148 $100 Queen and Prince Philip . . . . 1·25 1·40
3149 $130 Prince Philip . . . . . 1·50 1·60
3150 $150 Prince Philip in R.A.F. uniform . . . . 1·75 1·90
3151 $200 The Queen with Queen Elizabeth the Queen Mother . . . . 2·50 2·75

MS3152 68 × 90 mm. $225 Queen Elizabeth II . . . . 3·00 3·25

1991. 10th Wedding Anniv of Prince and Princess of Wales. As T **198b** of Gambia. Multicoloured.

3153 $8.90 Prince and Princess of Wales 30 20
3154 $50 Separate portraits of Princess and sons . . . . 1·00 80
3155 $75 Prince Charles with Prince William . . . . . 1·25 1·50
3156 $190 Princess Diana with Prince Henry . . . . . . 2·75 3·50

MS3157 68 × 90 mm. $225 Separate portraits of Prince Charles, Prince William and Princess Diana with Prince Henry . . . . 3·25 3·50

1991. 75th Anniv of Lions International (1992). (a) Nos. 2789/94 and 2859/60 optd or surch **Melvin Jones Founder 1880-1961** (A) or with Lions Club emblem and **Lions International 1917–1992** (B).

3158 80c. Type **464** (B) 15 10
3159 $2.55 "Rhetus dysonii" (B) 20 15
3160 $5 "Actinote anteas" (A) . . 30 20
3161 $6.40 "Heliconius tales" (A) 30 25
3162 $7.65 "Thecla telemus" (A) 30 25
3163 $100 on $8.90 "Theope eudocia" (A) . . . . . . 1·50 1·50
3164 $190 on $50 "Heliconius vicini" (B) . . . . . . 2·50 2·75
3165 $225 on $100 "Amarynthis meneria" (B) . . . . . 2·50 2·75

(b) Nos. 2843/58 optd or surch as Nos. 3158/65 or with emblems and inscriptions of other international organizations.

3166 $10 "Thecla telemus" (optd Lions Club emblem and **1917–1992**) 15 15
3167 $10 "Thyridia confusa" (optd Rotary emblem and **1905–1990**) 15 15
3168 $10 "Heliconius burneyi" (optd Boy Scout emblem and **1907–1992**) 15 15
3169 $10 "Parides lysander" (A) 15 15
3170 $10 "Eunica orphise" (optd **125 Years Red Cross** and cross) 15 15
3171 $10 "Adelpha melona" (optd with part Lions Club emblem) 15 15
3172 $10 "Morpho menelaus" (optd with part Lions Club emblem) 15 15
3173 $10 "Nymula phylleus" (optd **125 Years Red Cross** and cross) 15 15
3174 $10 "Stalachtis phlegia" (optd Rotary emblem and **1905–1990**) 15 15
3175 $10 "Theope barea" (optd with part Lions Club emblem) 15 15
3176 $10 "Morpho perseus" (optd with part Lions Club emblem) 15 15
3177 $10 "Lycorea ceres" (optd Boy Scout emblem and **1907–1992**) 15 15
3178 $50 on $10 "Archonias bellona" (A) 70 70
3179 $75 on $10 "Caerois chorinaeus" (surch Boy Scout emblem and **1907–1992**) . . . . 1·25 1·40
3180 $100 on $10 "Vila azeca" (surch Rotary emblem and **1905–1990**) . . . . . 1·50 1·60
3181 $190 on $10 "Nessaea batesii" (surch Lions Club emblem and **1917–1992**) 2·50 3·00

MS3182 Two sheets, each 102 × 71 mm. (a) $400 on $190 "Nymphidium caricae". (b) $500 on $190 "Thecla hemon" Set of 2 sheets . . . . 10·00 11·00

Nos. **MS**3182a/b only show new face values on the stamps and have international organization emblems overprinted on the sheet margins.

1991. "Phila Nippon '91" International Stamp Exhibition, Tokyo. Sheetlets containing Nos. 2880/95 and 2897/2912, now sold as miniature sheets, and **MS**2966d with some stamps surch **$50** and inscriptions and exhibition logo on the sheet margins, all in red.

MS3183 135 × 203 mm. $10 × 12; $25 on $10; $50 on $10; $75 on $10; $130 on $10 . . . . 8·00 8·50
MS3184 135 × 203 mm. $12.80 × 12; $25 on $12.80; $50 on $12.80; $75 on $12.80; $100 on $12.80 . . . 8·00 8·50
MS3185 68 × 110 mm. $250 on $150 "Lecythis ollaria" . . . . . . 3·75 4·00

1991. Winter Olympic Games, Albertville (1992) (2nd issue). Nos. 2738/46 optd or surch **ALBERTVILLE 92** or **XVIth Olympic Winter Games in Albertville** (No. 3190).

3186/94 $20 x 6, $70 on $20, $100 on $20, $190 on $20 . . Set of 9 . . . . 16·00 17·00

1991. John F. Kennedy and Sir Winston Churchill Commemorations. Nos. **MS**2966c and **MS**2966e surch **$600** in black or red.

MS3195 70 × 105 mm. $600 on $150 "Galeandra devoniana" (horiz)
MS3196 74 × 104 mm. $600 on $190 "Ionopsis utricularioides" . . .

No. **MS**3195 is additionally overprinted with "IN MEMORIAM John F. Kennedy 1917–1963", "First Man on Moon July 20, 1969" and "Apollo 11" emblem, and No. **MS**3196 "IN MEMORIAM Sir Winston S. Churchill 1874–1965" and "50th Anniversary World War II" on sheet margins.

474 "Akagi" (Japanese aircraft carrier)

1991. 50th Anniv of Japanese Attack on Pearl Harbor. Each blue, red and black.

3197 $50 Type **474** 85 85
3198 $50 Beached Japanese midget submarine 85 85
3199 $50 Mitsubishi A6M Zero-Sen fighter 85 85
3200 $50 U.S.S. "Arizona" (battleship) under attack 85 85
3201 $50 Aichi D3A1 "Val" dive bomber 85 85
3202 $50 U.S.S. "California" (battleship) sinking . . . 85 85
3203 $50 Curtiss P-40 fighters taking off 85 85
3204 $50 U.S.S. "Cassin" and U.S.S. "Downes" damaged in dry dock . . 85 85
3205 $50 Boeing B-17 Flying Fortress crash landing at Bellows Field 85 85
3206 $50 U.S.S. "Nevada" (battleship) on fire 85 85

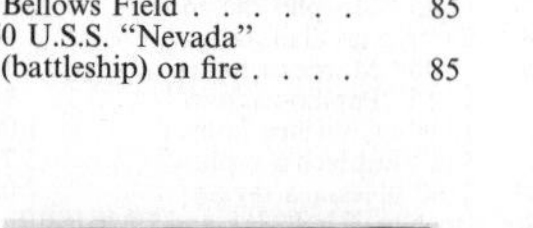

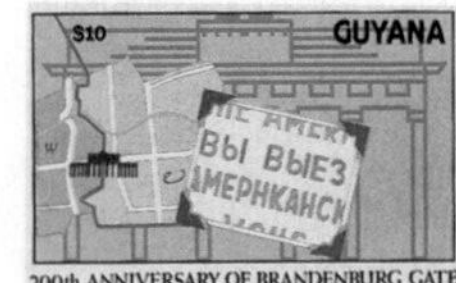

475 Brandenburg Gate and Location Plan

1991. Anniversaries and Events. Multicoloured.

3207 $10 Type **475** 20 20
3208 $25 President Bush, President Lech Walesa of Poland and Brandenburg Gate 50 50
3209 $25 Scout handshake . . . 50 50
3210 $30 Scouts hiking at Philmont Scout Ranch . . 60 60
3211 $40 Jamboree and Scout Movement emblems . . . 70 70
3212 $60 General de Gaulle at Venice, 1944 . . . . . . 90 90
3213 $75 De Gaulle with Khrushchev, 1960 . . . . 1·25 1·25
3214 $75 Mozart and Castle of Laxenburg . . . . 1·25 1·25
3215 $75 Caroline Herschel (astronomer) and Old Town Hall, Hanover . . . 1·25 1·25
3216 $75 Map of Switzerland and woman in Valais costume 1·25 1·25
3217 $80 De Gaulle at Algiers, 1958 . . . . 1·40 1·40
3218 $80 Mozart and death of Leopold II . . . . 1·40 1·40
3219 $80 Otto Lilienthal and "Flugzeug Nr. 3" . . . . 1·40 1·40
3220 $100 Chancellor Kohl, Foreign Minister Genscher and Brandenburg Gate . . . 1·50 1·50
3221 $100 Lord Baden-Powell (vert) . . . . 1·50 1·50
3222 $100 De Gaulle with Pope Paul VI, 1967 . . . . . . 1·50 1·50
3223 $100 Mozart and birthplace, Salzburg . . . . 1·50 1·50
3224 $100 Class P36 steam locomotive . . . . 1·50 1·50

MS3225 Six sheets. (a) 67 × 99 mm. $150 General De Gaulle (vert). (b) 75 × 104 mm. $190 General De Gaulle (different) (vert). (c) 101 × 71 mm. $190 Ceremonial helmet and statues from Brandenburg Gate. (d) 114 × 83 mm. $190 Rocket-flown commemorative cover, 1960. (e) 73 × 104 mm. $190 Mozart cameo (vert). (f) 103 × 74 mm. $190 Arms of Berne and Solothurn Set of 6 sheets . . . . 15·00 16·00

ANNIVERSARIES and EVENTS—Nos. 3207/8, 3220, **MS**3225c, Bicentenary of Brandenburg Gate, Berlin; 3209/11, 3221, **MS**3225d, 17th World Scout Jamboree, Korea; 3212/13, 3217, 3222, **MS**3225a/b, Birth centenary (1990) of Charles de Gaulle (French statesman); 3214, 3218, 3223, **MS**3225e, Death bicentenary of Mozart; 3215, 750th anniv of Hanover; 3216, **MS**3225f, 700th anniv of Swiss Confederation; 3219, Centenary of Otto Lilienthal's first gliding experiments; 3224, Centenary of Trans-Siberian Railway.

No. 3222 is inscribed "Pope John VI" in error.

476 Disney Characters Carol Singing, 1989

1991. Christmas. Walt Disney Christmas Cards. Multicoloured.

3226 80c. Type **476** 10 10
3227 $2.55 Disney characters and carol singers in tram, 1962 15 15
3228 $5 Donald Duck and Pluto with parcel, 1971 . . . . 20 20
3229 $6.40 "SEASON'S GREETINGS" and Mickey Mouse with candle, 1948 . . . . . . 30 20
3230 $7.65 Mickey Mouse as Father Christmas, 1947 30 20
3231 $8.90 Shadow of Pinocchio with candle, 1939 . . . 30 20
3232 $50 Three Little Pigs dancing on wolf rug, 1933 1·25 1·25
3233 $50 Conductor and Donald Duck, 1940 (vert) . . . 1·25 1·25
3234 $50 Elephant and ostrich carol singing, 1940 (vert) 1·25 1·25
3235 $50 Hippo, centaurs, Pinocchio and Goofy, 1940 (vert) . . . . 1·25 1·25

3236 $50 Snow White, Dopey, Mickey and Minnie, 1940 (vert) . . . . 1·25 1·25
3237 $50 Dino, Pluto and Walt Disney, 1940 (vert) . . . 1·25 1·25
3238 $50 Mickey Mouse in sleigh, 1974 (vert) . . . . 1·25 1·25
3239 $50 Three Little Pigs, Winnie the Pooh, Bambi and Thumper, 1974 (vert) 1·25 1·25
3240 $50 Baloo, King Louis, Lady and the Tramp, 1974 (vert) . . . . 1·25 1·25
3241 $50 Alice, Robin Hood, the Cheshire Cat and Goofy, 1974 (vert) . . . . 1·25 1·25
3242 $50 Dumbo, Pinocchio, Peter Pan, Tinkerbelle, Seven Dwarfs and Donald Duck, 1974 (vert) . . . . 1·25 1·25
3243 $50 Pluto pulling sleigh, 1974 (vert) . . . . 1·25 1·25
3244 $200 Mickey and mice carol singing, 1949 . . . . . . 4·00 5·00
MS3245 Eight sheets. (a) 127 × 101 mm. $260 Mickey, Minnie, Clarabelle and Pluto in mail coach, 1932 (vert). (b) 127 × 101 mm. $260 Mickey's House, 1935 (vert). (c) 101 × 127 mm. $260 Jose Carioca, Rooster and Donald Duck on flying carpet, 1944 (vert). (d) 101 × 127 mm. $260 Casey at the Bat and dancers, 1945. (e) 127 × 101 mm. $260 Mickey, Donald and Goofy on musical score, 1946. (f) 127 × 101 mm. $260 Picture of Winnie the Pooh, 1969. (g) 127 × 101 mm. $260 Father Christmas in chimney, 1969 (vert). (h) 101 × 127 mm. $260 Letters of film titles forming Mickey Mouse, 1978 (vert) Set of 8 sheets . . . . 30·00 30·00

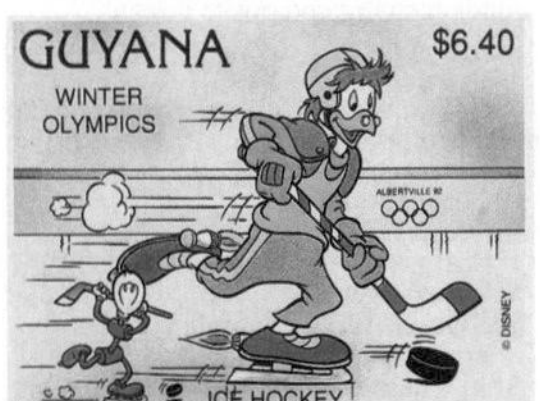

477 Gus Gander playing Ice Hockey

1991. Winter Olympic Games, Albertville (1992) (3rd issue). Walt Disney Cartoon Characters. Multicoloured.
3246 $6.40 Type **477** 35 10
3247 $7.65 Mickey and Minnie Mouse in bobsleigh . . . 40 10
3248 $8.90 Donald's Nephews on luge and skis 45 10
3249 $12.80 Goofy freestyle skiing 60 20
3250 $50 Goofy ski jumping . . . 1·75 1·25
3251 $100 Donald and Daisy Duck speed skating . . . 2·50 2·00
3252 $130 Pluto cross-country skiing . . . . 2·75 2·75
3253 $190 Mickey and Minnie Mouse ice dancing . . . 3·50 4·50
MS3254 Two sheets, each 125 × 100 mm. (a) $225 Donald's nephew curling. (b) $225 Donald Duck slalom skiing Set of 2 sheets 8·00 8·50

478 Columbus landing on Trinidad

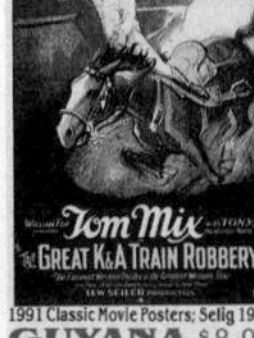

479 Tom Mix in "The Great K & A Train Robbery", 1926

1992. 500th Anniv of Discovery of America by Columbus. Multicoloured.
3255 $6.40 Type **478** 55 40
3256 $7.65 Columbus the map-maker 65 45
3257 $8.90 Fleet blown off course 65 45
3258 $12.80 Map of third voyage and Columbus in chains 65 55
3259 $15.30 Sighting land 65 55
3260 $50 "Nina" and "Pinta" . . 1·75 1·00
3261 $75 "Santa Maria" . . . . 2·00 1·25
3262 $100 Columbus trading with Amerindians . . . . . . 2·25 1·75
3263 $125 Crew and sea monster 2·75 2·75
3264 $130 Columbus landing on San Salvador and map of first voyage . . . . 2·75 2·75
3265 $140 Priest and Amerindians 2·75 2·75
3266 $150 Columbus before King Ferdinand and Queen Isabella of Spain . . . . 2·75 2·75
MS3267 Three sheets, each 126 × 91 mm. (a) $280 "Nina" (vert). (b) $280 Columbus (vert). (c) $280 Early map of Caribbean Set of 3 sheets . . . . 13·00 15·00

1992. Classic Movie Posters. Multicoloured.
3268 $8.90 Type **479** 50 40
3269 $12.80 Richard Dix and Irene Dunne in "Cimarron", 1931 . . . . 60 50
3270 $15.30 Fatty Arbuckle in "Buzzin' Around", 1934 60 50
3271 $25 Tom Tyler in "The Adventures of Captain Marvel", 1941 . . . . . 80 70
3272 $30 Boris Karloff in "The Mummy", 1932 . . . . . 1·25 85
3273 $50 Rudolph Valentino in "A Sainted Devil", 1924 1·40 1·10
3274 $75 Seven posters for "A Tale of Two Cities", 1935 1·75 1·40
3275 $100 Chester Conklin in "A Tugboat Romeo", 1916 2·50 1·90
3276 $130 Douglas Fairbanks in "The Thief of Bagdad", 1924 . . . . 2·75 2·25
3277 $150 Laurel and Hardy in "Bacon Grabbers", 1929 3·25 3·00
3278 $190 Marx Brothers in "A Night at the Opera", 1935 4·00 4·25
3279 $200 Orson Welles in "Citizen Kane", 1941 . . 4·00 4·25
MS3280 Four sheets. (a) 70 × 99 mm. $225 Babe Ruth in "Babe Comes Home", 1927. (b) 70 × 99 mm. $225 Mae West in "She Done Him Wrong", 1933. (c) 70 × 99 mm. $225 Charlie Chaplin in "The Circus", 1928. (d) 99 × 70 mm. $225 Poster for never-made film "Zeppelin", 1933. Imperf Set of 4 sheets . . . . 15·00 17·00

1992. Easter. Paintings by Durer. As T **204a** of Gambia. Multicoloured.
3281 $6.40 "The Martyrdom of Ten Thousand" (detail) 25 10
3282 $7.65 "Adoration of the Trinity" (detail of Virgin Mary) 25 10
3283 $12.80 "The Martyrdom of Ten Thousand" (execution detail) 40 20
3284 $15.30 "Adoration of the Trinity" (different detail) 45 25
3285 $50 "The Martyrdom of Ten Thousand" (detail of bishop) . . . . 1·00 75
3286 $100 "Adoration of the Trinity" (different detail) 1·50 1·50
3287 $130 "The Martyrdom of Ten Thousand" (different detail) . . . . 1·75 2·00
3288 $190 "Adoration of the Trinity" (different detail) 3·25 4·00
MS3289 Two sheets, each 71 × 101 mm. (a) $225 "The Martyrdom of Ten Thousand". (b) $225 "Adoration of the Trinity" (detail of Christ on cross) Set of 2 sheets . . . . 8·00 8·50

1992. Baha'i Holy Year. Surch **BAHA'I HOLY YEAR 1992** and value.
3290 $6.40 on 60c. Plate No. 10 (Series 1) (No. 1521) . . .
3291 $7.65 on 60c. Plate No. 31 (Series 1) (No. 1523) . . .
3292 $8.90 on 60c. Plate No. 19 (Series 1) (No. 1522) . . .
3293 $50 on 60c. Plate No. 2 (Series 1) (No. 1519) . . .

481 Queen Elizabeth II and Duke of Edinburgh

1992. 40th Anniv of Queen Elizabeth II's Accession. Multicoloured.
3294 $8.90 Type **481** 65 25
3295 $12.80 Queen at Trooping the Colour 75 30
3296 $100 Queen at Coronation 3·50 2·50
3297 $130 Queen in Garter robes 4·00 3·25
MS3298 Two sheets, each 119 × 79 mm. (a) $225 Queen in Coronation robes. (b) $225 Queen in blue dress Set of 2 sheets . . 9·00 9·50

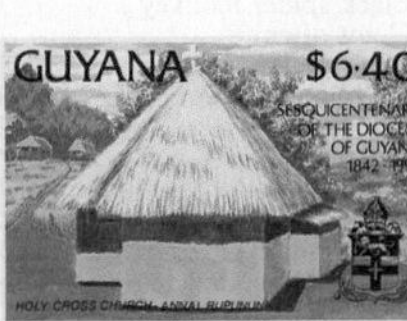

482 Holy Cross Church, Annai Rupununi

1992. 150th Anniv of Diocese of Guyana. Multicoloured.
3299 $6.40 Type **482** 15 10
3300 $50 St. Peter's Church . . . 80 65
3301 $100 Interior of St. George's Cathedral (vert) . . . . . 1·50 1·60
3302 $190 Map of Guyana (vert) 2·75 3·75
MS3303 104 × 70 mm. $225 Religious symbols . . . . . . 3·75 4·00

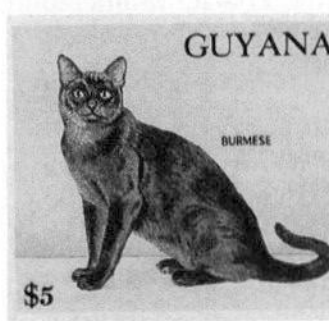

483 Burmese

1992. Cats. Multicoloured.
3304 $5 Type **483** 20 10
3305 $6.40 Turkish van 20 10
3306 $12.80 American shorthair 30 20
3307 $15.30 Sphynx 30 20
3308 $50 Egyptian mau . . . . . 1·00 1·00
3309 $50 Russian blue . . . . . 1·00 1·00
3310 $50 Havana brown . . . . 1·00 1·00
3311 $50 Himalayan . . . . . . 1·00 1·00
3312 $50 Manx . . . . 1·00 1·00
3313 $50 Cornish rex . . . . . . 1·00 1·00
3314 $50 Black Persian . . . . . 1·00 1·00
3315 $50 Scottish fold . . . . . 1·00 1·00
3316 $50 Siamese . . . . 1·00 1·00
3317 $100 Japanese bobtail . . . 1·50 1·25
3318 $130 Abyssinian . . . . . 1·75 1·75
3319 $225 Oriental shorthair . . 2·75 3·25
MS3320 Four sheets, each 99 × 69 mm. (a) $250 Chartreuse (vert). (b) $250 Turkish angora (vert). (c) $250 Maine coon (vert). (d) $250 Chinchilla (vert) Set of 4 sheets . . . . 14·00 15·00

484 Red Howler

1992. Animals of Guyana. Multicoloured.
3321 $8.90 Type **484** 20 10
3322 $12.80 Ring-tailed coati . . 25 20
3323 $15.30 Jaguar 30 20
3324 $25 Two-toed sloth 50 30
3325 $50 Giant armadillo . . . . 1·00 80
3326 $75 Giant anteater . . . . 1·50 1·75
3327 $100 Capybara . . . . . . 1·75 1·90
3328 $130 Ocelot . . . . 2·00 2·25
MS3329 Two sheets, each 70 × 100 mm. (a) $225 Woolly opossum (vert). (b) $225 Night monkey (vert) Set of 2 sheets 8·00 9·00
No. **MS**3329a is inscribed "WOLLY OPOSSUM" in error.

485 Oligocene Mammoth

1992. Elephants. Multicoloured.
3330 $50 Type **485** . . . . . . 1·50 1·25
3331 $50 Mid-Miocene stegodon 1·50 1·25
3332 $50 Pliocene mammoth . . 1·50 1·25
3333 $50 Carthaginian elephant crossing Alps, 219 B.C. 1·50 1·25
3334 $50 Ceremonial elephant of Maharaja of Mysore, India . . . . 1·50 1·25
3335 $50 Elephant pulling teak trunks, Burma . . . . 1·50 1·25
3336 $50 Tiger-hunting by elephant, India . . . . . 1·50 1·25
3337 $50 Elephant towing raft on River Kwai, Thailand . . 1·50 1·25
MS3338 110 × 80 mm. $225 African elephant . . . . 5·00 5·00

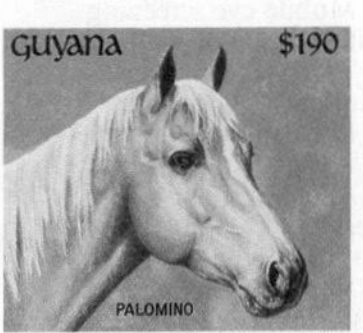

486 Palomino

1992. Horses. Multicoloured.
3339 $190 Type **486** . . . . . . 3·00 3·00
3340 $190 Appaloosa . . . . . . 3·00 3·00
3341 $190 Clydesdale . . . . . . 3·00 3·00
3342 $190 Arab . . . . 3·00 3·00
3343 $190 Morgan . . . . 3·00 3·00
3344 $190 Friesian . . . . 3·00 3·00
3345 $190 Pinto . . . . 3·00 3·00
3346 $190 Thoroughbred . . . . 3·00 3·00
MS3347 109 × 80 mm. $190 Lipizzaner (47 × 29 mm) . . . 4·00 4·25
No. 3340 is inscribed "APALOOSA" in error.

1992. International Conference on Nutrition, Rome. Surch **INT. CONFERENCE ON NUTRITION 1992** and value.
3348 $6.40 on 150c. Plate No. 45 (Series 1) (No. 1769) . . .
3349 $7.65 on 150c. Plate No. 42 (Series 1) (No. 1768) . . .
3350 $8.90 on 150c. Plate No. 40 (Series 1) (No. 1767) . . .
3351 $10 on 200c. Plate No. 43 (Series 1) (No. 1658) . . .
3352 $50 on 200c. Plate No. 43 (Series 1) (No. 1658) . . .

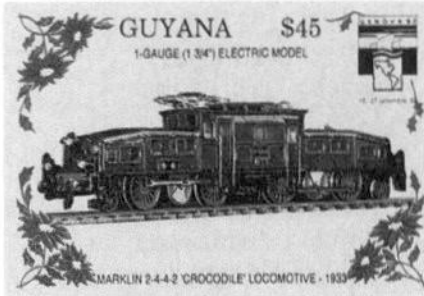

488 Marklin Swiss "Crocodile" Locomotive, 1933

1992. "Genova '92" International Thematic Stamp Exhibition. Toy Trains from German Manufacturers. Multicoloured.
3353/61 $45 × 9 Made by Marklin: Type **488**; French tramcar, 1902; British "Flatiron" tank engine, 1913; German switching engine, 1970; Third class carriage, 1909; American style locomotive, 1904; Zurich tramcar, 1928; Central London Railway locomotive in Paris-Orleans livery, 1904; British GWR "Great Bear" locomotive, 1909 . .
3362/70 $45 × 9 Made by Marklin: LMS "Precursor" tank engine, 1923; American "Congressional Limited" passenger carriage, 1908; Swiss Type "Ae 3/6" locomotive, 1934; German Class 80, 1975; British Southern Railways third class carriage, 1926; LNWR Bowen-Cooke tank engine, 1913; London Underground "Two Penny Tube", 1901; French Paris-Orsay steeplecab, 1920; Passenger locomotive, 1895 . . . .
3371/9 $45 × 9 Made by Marklin: American style locomotive, 1907; German passenger carriage, 1908; British Great Eastern Railway locomotive, 1908; London Underground steeplecab, 1904; Santa Fe Railroad diesel locomotive, 1962; British GNR locomotive, 1903; Caledonian Railway "Cardean", 1906; British LNWR passenger carriage, 1903; Swiss St. Gotthard Railway locomotive, 1920 . .
3380/8 $45 × 9 Made by Marklin: British LB SCR tank engine No. 22, 1920; Central London Railway steeplecab locomotive, 1904; German "Borsig" streamlined, 1935; French Paris-Lyon-Mediterranee first class carriage, 1929; American style locomotive No. 1021, 1904; French Paris-Orsay long-nose steeplecab, 1920; British LNER "Cock o' the North", 1936; Prussian State Railways Class P8, 1975; German diesel railcar set, 1937 . . .

3389/97 $45 × 9 Marklin North British Railway "Atlantic", 1913; Bing British LNWR "Precursor", 1916; Marklin British GWR "King George V", 1937; Marklin "Kaiser Train" passenger carriage, 1901; Bing side tank locomotive No. 88, 1904; Marklin steeplecab, 1912; Marklin "Adler", 1935; Bing British GWR "County of Northampton", 1909; Bing British Midland Railway "Black Prince", 1908 . . . .

3398/3406 $45 × 9 Made by Bing: Midland Railway "Deeley Type" No. 483, 1909; British Midland Railway No. 2631, 1903; German Pacific, 1927; British GWR third class coach, 1926; British LSWR "M7" No. 109, 1909; Side tank engine "Pilot", 1901; British LNWR Webb "Cauliflower", 1912; Side tank locomotive No. 112, 1910; British GNR "Stirling Single", 1904 . . . .

3407/15 $45 × 9 Carette tin "Penny Bazaar" train, 1904; Winteringham locomotive, 1917; Carette British Northeastern Railway Smith Compound, 1905; Carette S.E. C.R. steam railcar, 1908; Carette British Great Northern Railway Stirling Single No. 776, 1903; Carette British Midland Railways locomotive No. 1132M, 1911; Carette London Metropolitan Railway Co. "Westinghouse" locomotive No. 5, 1908; Carette Clestory carriage, 1907; Carette steam railcar No. 1, 1906

3416/24 $45 × 9 Made by Bing: Engine and tender, 1895; British Midland Railway "Single" No. 650, 1913; No. 524/510 reversible locomotive, 1916; "Kaiser Train" passenger carriage, 1902; British rural station, 1915; British LSWR M7 tank locomotive, 1909; "Windcutter", 1912; British Great Central Railway "Sir Sam Fay", 1914; Scottish Caledonian Railway "Dunalastair" locomotive, 1910) . .

3353/3424 Set of 72 . . . . 45·00 48·00

MS3425 Eight sheets, each 116 × 83 mm. (a) $350 Bing contractor's locomotive No. 18, 1904 (51 × 39 mm). (b) $350 Marklin rack railway steeplecab locomotive, 1908 (51 × 39 mm). (c) $350 Bing British GWR "County of Northampton" locomotive, 1909 (51 × 39 mm).(d) $350 Marklin French Paris–Lyon–Mediterranean Pacific locomotive, 1912 (51 × 39 mm). (e) $350 Bing Pabst Blue Ribbon beer refrigerator wagon, 1925 (51 × 39 mm). (f) $350 Marklin French "Mountain Etat" locomotive, 1933 (51 × 39 mm). (g) $350 Marklin German National Railroad Class 0-1 Pacific locomotive, 1937 (51 × 39 mm). (h) $350 Marklin American "Commodore Vanderbilt" locomotive, 1937 (51 × 39 mm) Set of 8 sheets . . . . 30·00 32·00

1992. Postage Stamp Mega Event, New York. Sheet 100 × 70 mm, containing multicoloured design as T **207a** of Gambia, but vert.

MS3426 $325 Statue of Liberty 6·00 7·00

489 Aquarius

1992. Signs of the Zodiac. Multicoloured.

3427	$30 Type **489**	85	85
3428	$30 Pisces	85	85
3429	$30 Aries	85	85
3430	$30 Taurus	85	85
3431	$30 Gemini	85	85
3432	$30 Cancer	85	85
3433	$30 Leo	85	85
3434	$30 Virgo	85	85
3435	$30 Libra	85	85
3436	$30 Scorpio	85	85
3437	$30 Sagittarius	85	85
3438	$30 Capricorn	85	85

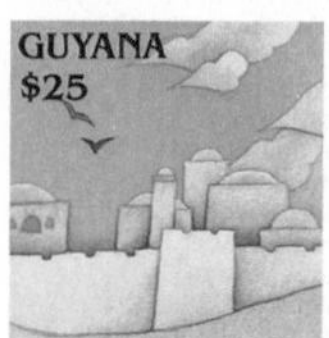

490 City Walls and Two Birds

1992. Bible Stories (1st series). David and Goliath. Multicoloured.

3439	$25 Type **490**	50	50
3440	$25 City walls and one bird at right	50	50
3441	$25 Sun over city gateway	50	50
3442	$25 City walls and one bird at left	50	50
3443	$25 City walls and no birds	50	50
3444	$25 Philistine army and edge of shield	50	50
3445	$25 Goliath's head and torso	50	50
3446	$25 Goliath's arm and spear	50	50
3447	$25 Philistine army and spearhead	50	50
3448	$25 Philistine infantry . . .	50	50
3449	$25 Philistine cavalry and infantry	50	50
3450	$25 Goliath's shield	50	50
3451	$25 Goliath's waist and thigh	50	50
3452	$25 David with sling	50	50
3453	$25 Israelite soldier with spear	50	50
3454	$25 Two Israelite soldiers with spears and shields . .	50	50
3455	$25 Goliath's right leg . . .	50	50
3456	$25 Goliath's left leg (face value at foot)	50	50
3457	$25 David's legs and Israelite standard	50	50
3458	$25 Three Israelite soldiers	50	50
3459	$25 Israelite soldier and parts of two shields . . .	50	50
3460	$25 Israelite soldier with sword	50	50
3461	$25 Back of Israelite soldier	50	50
3462	$25 Israelite soldier leaning on rock	50	50
3463	$25 Israelite soldier looking left	50	50

Nos. 3439/63 were printed together, se-tenant, forming a composite design.

See also Nos. 4020/4116.

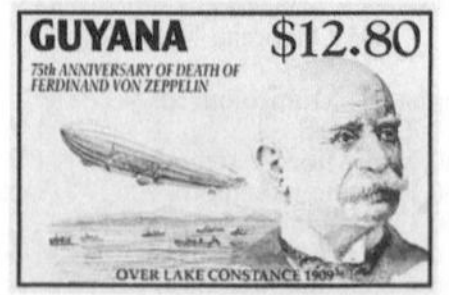

491 Count Von Zeppelin and Airship over Lake Constance, 1909

1992. Anniversaries and Events. Multicoloured.

3464	$12.80 Type **491**	50	35
3465	$50 "Voyager I" and Jupiter	1·50	1·00
3466	$50 Adenauer with Pres. Kennedy, 1961	1·00	1·00
3467	$100 Aeromedical airlift . .	2·00	2·00
3468	$100 Boutu ("Amazon Dolphin")	2·00	2·00
3469	$130 Baby gorilla	2·50	2·50
3470	$130 Mobile eye screening unit and doctor with child	2·50	2·50
3471	$130 "Stars and Stripes" (winning yacht, 1987) . .	2·50	2·50
3472	$130 Lift-off of "Voyager I", 1977	2·50	2·50
3473	$190 Adenauer with President De Gaulle of France, 1962	3·25	3·25
3474	$225 Von Zeppelin and airship preparing for take-off, 1905	3·50	3·50

MS3475 Four sheets. (a) 76 × 105 mm. $225 Ferdinand von Zeppelin (vert). (b) 116 × 80 mm. $225 Earth from Space (vert). (c) 84 × 111 mm. $225 Konrad Adenauer (vert). (d) 87 × 111 mm. $225 "Hyperohus marmoratus" (tree frog) (vert) Set of 4 sheets 15·00 16·00

ANNIVERSARIES and EVENTS: Nos. 3464, 3474, **MS**3475a, 75th death anniv of Count Ferdinand von Zeppelin; 3465, 3472, **MS**3475b, International Space Year; 3466, 3473, **MS**3475c, 75th death anniv of Konrad Adenauer (German statesman); 3467, United Nations World Health Organization projects; 3468/9, **MS**3475d, Earth Summit '92, Rio; 3470, 75th anniv of International Association of Lions Clubs; 3471, Americas Cup Yachting Championship.

492 Hyacinth Macaw

1993. South American Parrots. Multicoloured.

3476	80c. Type **492**	30	15
3477	$6.40 Scarlet macaw (preening)	50	25
3478	$7.65 Buffon's macaw ("Green Macaw") (vert)	50	25
3479	$15.30 Orange-chinned parakeet ("Tovi Parakeet")	70	50
3480	$50 Blue and yellow macaw	1·00	80
3481	$100 Military macaw (vert)	1·50	1·25
3482	$130 Green-winged macaw ("Red and Green Macaw") (vert)	1·75	1·75
3483	$190 Chestnut-fronted macaw ("Severa Macaw")	2·50	3·00

MS3484 Two sheets, each 108 × 74 mm. (a) $225 Scarlet macaw. (b) $225 Monk parakeet (vert) Set of 2 sheets . . . . . 7·00 7·50

493 Crimson Topaz

1993. Birds of Guyana. Multicoloured.

3485	$50 Type **493**	75	75
3486	$50 Bearded bellbird	75	75
3487	$50 Amazonian umbrellabird	75	75
3488	$50 Paradise jacamar . . .	75	75
3489	$50 Paradise tanager	75	75
3490	$50 White-tailed trogon . .	75	75
3491	$50 Scarlet macaw	75	75
3492	$50 Hawk-headed parrot ("Red-fan Parrot") . . .	75	75
3493	$50 Red-billed toucan . . .	75	75
3494	$50 White-faced antcatcher ("White-plumed Antbird")	75	75
3495	$50 Crimson-hooded manakin	75	75
3496	$50 Guianan cock of the rock	75	75

MS3497 70 × 100 mm. $325 Tufted coquette (horiz) . . . . 5·00 5·50

Nos. 3485/96 were printed together, se-tenant, with the backgrounds forming a composite design.

494 Manatee surfacing

495 Tamandua

1993. Endangered Species. American Manatee ("Caribbean Manatee"). Multicoloured.

3498	$6.40 Type **494**	60	30
3499	$7.60 Cow and calf feeding	60	30
3500	$8.90 Manatee underwater	60	30
3501	$50 Two manatees	2·25	2·25

1993. Animals of Guyana. Multicoloured.

3502	$50 Type **495**	75	75
3503	$50 Pale-throated sloth ("Three-toed Sloth") . . .	75	75
3504	$50 Red howler	75	75
3505	$50 Four-eyed opossum . .	75	75
3506	$50 Black spider monkey . .	75	75
3507	$50 Giant otter	75	75
3508	$50 Red brocket	75	75
3509	$50 Brazilian tree porcupine	75	75
3510	$50 Tayra	75	75
3511	$50 Brazilian tapir	75	75
3512	$50 Ocelot	75	75
3513	$50 Giant armadillo	75	75

MS3514 100 × 70 mm. $325 Paca 4·50 5·00

Nos. 3502/13 were printed together, se-tenant, the backgrounds forming a composite design.

No. 3505 is inscribed "Four-eyed Opossium" in error.

496 Pteranodon

1993. Prehistoric Animals. Multicoloured.

3515/26 $30 × 12 (Type **496**; Cearadactylus; Eudimorphodon; Pterodactylus; Stauirkosaurus; Euoplocephalus; Tuojiangosaurus; Oviraptor; Protoceratops; Panaoplosaurus; Psittacosaurus; Corythosaurus) . . . .

3527/38 $30 × 12 (Sordes; Quetzalcoatlus; Archaeopteryx in flight; Rhamphorynchus; Spinosaurus; Anchisaurus; Stegosaurus; Leaellynosaurus; Minmi; Heterdontosaurus; Esothosaurus; Deninonychus) . . . .

3539/50 $30 × 12 (Archaeopteryx on branch; Pteranodon (different); Quetzalcoatlus (three); Protoavis; Dicraeosaurus; Moschops; Lystrosaurus; Dimetrondon; Staurikosaurus; Cacops; Diarthrognathus; Estemmenosuchus) . .

3515/50 Set of 36 . . . . 17·00 19·00

Nos. 3515/26, 3527/38 and 3539/50 respectively were printed together, se-tenant, with the backgrounds forming composite designs.

1993. 40th Anniv of Coronation. As T **215a** of Gambia. Multicoloured.

3551	$25 Queen Elizabeth II in Coronation robes (photograph by Cecil Beaton)	85	85
3552	$50 Royal gems	1·25	1·25
3553	$75 Queen Elizabeth and Prince Philip	1·40	1·40
3554	$130 Queen opening Parliament	1·75	2·00

MS3555 69 × 100 mm. $325 "Queen in Coronation Robes" (Sir James Gunn) ($28\frac{1}{2} \times 42\frac{1}{2}$ mm) . . . . 5·00 5·50

497 Gabriel Marquez (author)

1993. Famous People of the Twentieth Century. Multicoloured. (a) Arts and Literature.

3556	$50 Type **497**	75	75
3557	$50 Pablo Picasso (artist) . .	75	75
3558	$50 Cecil De Mille (film director)	75	75
3559	$50 Martha Graham (dancer)	75	75
3560	$50 Peace dove (inscr "20th Century Arts and Literature")	75	75
3561	$50 Charlie Chaplin (actor)	75	75
3562	$50 Paul Robeson (actor)	75	75
3563	$50 Rudolph Dunbar (musician)	75	75
3564	$50 Louis Armstrong (musician)	75	75

MS3565 100 × 70 mm. $250 Elvis Presley (singer) (vert) . . . . . 3·50 3·50

(b) Science and Medicine.

3566	$50 Louis Leakey (archaeologist and anthropologist)	75	75
3567	$50 Jonas Salk (discoverer of polio vaccine)	75	75
3568	$50 Hideyo Noguchi (bacteriologist)	75	75
3569	$50 Karl Landsteiner (pathologist)	75	75
3570	$50 As No. 3550, but inscr "20th Century Science and Medicine"	75	75
3571	$50 Sigmund Freud (founder of psychoanalysis)	75	75
3572	$50 Louis Pasteur (chemist)	75	75
3573	$50 Madame Curie (physicist)	75	75
3574	$50 Jean Baptiste Perrin (physicist)	75	75

MS3575 100 × 70 mm. $250 Einstein's Theory of Relativity equation (vert) . . . . 3·50 3·50

(c) Sports Personalities.

3576	$50 O. J. Simpson (American football) . . .	75	75
3577	$50 Rohan Kanhai (cricket)	75	75

3578 $50 Gabriela Sabatini (tennis) 75 75
3579 $50 Severiano Ballesteros (golf) 75 75
3580 $50 As No. 3550, but inscr "20th Century Sports" . . 75 75
3581 $50 Franz Beckenbauer (football) 75 75
3582 $50 Pele (football) 75 75
3583 $50 Wilt Chamberlain (basketball) 75 75
3584 $50 Nadia Comaneci (gymnastics) 75 75
MS3585 100 × 70 mm. $250 Jackie Robinson (baseball) (vert) . . 3·50 3·50

(d) Peace and Humanity.

3586 $100 Mahatma Gandhi (India) . . . . 1·10 1·10
3587 $100 Dalai Lama (Tibet) . . 1·10 1·10
3588 $100 Michael Manley (Jamaica) . . . . 1·10 1·10
3589 $100 Perez de Cuellar (U.N. Secretary-General) . . . . 1·10 1·10
3590 $100 Peace dove and globe 1·10 1·10
3591 $100 Mother Teresa (India) 1·10 1·10
3592 $100 Martin Luther King (U.S.A.) . . . . 1·10 1·10
3593 $100 Pres. Nelson Mandela (South Africa) . . . . . 1·10 1·10
3594 $100 Raoul Wallenberg (Sweden) . . . . 1·10 1·10
MS3595 100 × 70 mm. $250 Nobel Peace Prize scroll (vert) . . . . 3·50 3·50

(e) Politics.

3596 $100 Nehru (India) . . . . 1·10 1·10
3597 $100 Dr. Eric Williams (Trinidad and Tobago) . . 1·10 1·10
3598 $100 Pres. John F. Kennedy (U.S.A.) . . . . 1·10 1·10
3599 $100 Pres. Hugh Desmond Hoyte (Guyana) . . . . 1·10 1·10
3600 $100 Peace dove and map of the Americas . . . . . . 1·10 1·10
3601 $100 Friedrich Ebert (Germany) . . . . 1·10 1·10
3602 $100 Pres F. D. Roosevelt (U.S.A.) . . . . 1·10 1·10
3603 $100 Mikhail Gorbachev (Russia) . . . . 1·10 1·10
3604 $100 Sir Winston Churchill (Great Britain) . . . . 1·10 1·10
MS3605 100 × 70 mm. $250 Flags of United Nations and member countries (vert) . . . . 3·50 3·50

(f) Transportation and Technology.

3606 $100 Douglas DC-3 cargo plane . . . . 1·25 1·25
3607 $100 Space Shuttle . . . . 1·25 1·25
3608 $100 Concorde . . . . . . 1·25 1·25
3609 $100 Count Ferdinand von Zeppelin and "Graf Zeppelin" . . . . 1·25 1·25
3610 $100 Peace dove and rocket trails . . . . 1·25 1·25
3611 $100 Marconi and aerial tower . . . . 1·25 1·25
3612 $100 Adrian Thompson (mountaineer) and Mt. Roraima . . . . 1·25 1·25
3613 $100 "Hikari" express train, Japan . . . . 1·25 1·25
3614 $100 Johann von Neumann and computer . . . . . 1·25 1·25
MS3615 100 × 70 mm. $250 Lunar module "Eagle" on Moon . . 4·00 4·00

Nos. 3556/64, 3566/74, 3576/84, 3586/94, 3596/3604 and 3606/14 respectively were printed together, se-tenant, with composite background designs on Nos. 3586/94, 3596/3604 and 3606/14.

No. 3562 is inscribed "Paul Roebeson" in error.

498 "Bather, Paris" (Picasso)

1993. Anniversaries and Events. Multicoloured (except No. MS3628c).

3616 $15.30 Type **498** 15 20
3617 $25 Willy Brandt with Prime Minister of Israel Golda Meir, 1969 (horiz) 40 40
3618 $50 "Pantaloons" (left half) (Tadeusz Brzozowski) . . 50 55
3619 $50 Georg Hackl (men's single luge, 1992) 70 70
3620 $50 Astrolabe 70 70
3621 $75 Miedzyrecz Castle . . . 75 80
3622 $100 "Two Nudes" (Picasso) 1·00 1·10
3623 $130 "Pantaloons" (right half) (Tadeusz Brzozowski) . . . . . . 1·25 1·40
3624 $130 Karen Magnussen (women's figure skating, 1972) . . . . 1·50 1·50
3625 $190 "Nude seated on a Rock" (Picasso) . . . . . 1·90 2·25
3626 $190 Willy Brandt at Georgsmarienhutten Steel Mill, 1969 (horiz) . . . . 2·25 2·50
3627 $190 Dish aerial . . . . . 2·25 2·50
MS3628 Five sheets. (a) 104 × 75 mm. $300 Copernicus. (b) 75 × 104 mm. $325 "The Rescue" (detail) (Picasso). (c) 104 × 75 mm. $325 Willy Brandt giving interview, 1969 (brown and black). (d) 99 × 70 mm. $325 "Children in the Garden" (Wladyslaw Podkowinski) (horiz). (e) 75 × 104 mm. $325 German four-man bobsleigh team, 1992 Set of 5 sheets . . . . 20·00 22·00

ANNIVERSARIES and EVENTS: Nos. 3616, 3622, 3625, MS3628b, 20th death anniv of Picasso (artist); 3617, 3626, MS3628c, 80th birth anniv (1992) of Willy Brandt (German politician); 3618, 3621, 3623, MS3628d, "Polska '93" International Stamp Exhibition, Poznan; 3619, 3624, MS3628e, Winter Olympic Games '94, Lillehammer; 3620, 3627, MS3628a, 450th death anniv of Copernicus (astronomer).

Nos. 3618 and 3623 were printed together, se-tenant, forming a composite design showing the complete painting.

499 Audie Murphy (most decorated U.S. serviceman)

1993. 50th Anniv of Second World War (1st issue). Multicoloured.

3629 $6.40 Type **499** 70 20
3630 $7.65 Allied troops in Normandy (8 June 1944) 70 25
3631 $8.90 American howitzer crew, Battle of Montecassino (18 May 1944) 75 30
3632 $12.80 American aircraft attacking "Yamato" (Japanese battleship), Battle of East China Sea (7 April 1945) 80 50
3633 $15.30 St. Basil's Cathedral, Moscow (Foreign Ministers' Conference, 19 October 1943) 80 50
3634 $50 American troops crossing Rhine at Remagen (7 March 1945) 1·50 75
3635 $100 Boeing B-29 Superfortresses raiding Japan from China (15 June 1944) . . . . . 2·25 1·75
3636 $130 General Patton and map of Sicily (17 August 1943) . . . . 2·50 2·25
3637 $190 Destruction of "Tirpitz" (German battleship) (12 November 1944) . . . . 3·25 3·25
3638 $200 American forces in Brittany (1 August 1944) 3·25 3·25
3639 $225 American half-track (ceasefire in Italy, 2 May 1945) . . . . 3·50 3·75
MS3640 100 × 69 mm. $325 Meeting of American and Russian troops on the Elbe (25 April 1945) . . 5·00 6·00

No. 3631 is inscribed "Monte Casino" in error. See also Nos. 3641/60 and 3942/61.

500 R.A.A.F. Bristol Type 156 Beaufighter, Battle of the Bismarck Sea (2-4 March 1943)

501 Stuart Pearce (England)

1993. 50th Anniv of Second World War (2nd issue). Multicoloured.

3641 $50 Type **500** 80 80
3642 $50 Lockheed P-38 Lightning attacking Admiral Yamamoto's plane, Bougainville (7 April 1943) 80 80
3643 $50 Consolidated B-24 Liberator bombers, Tarawa (17-19 September 1943) 80 80
3644 $50 North American B-25 Mitchell bomber, Rabaul (12 October 1943) 80 80

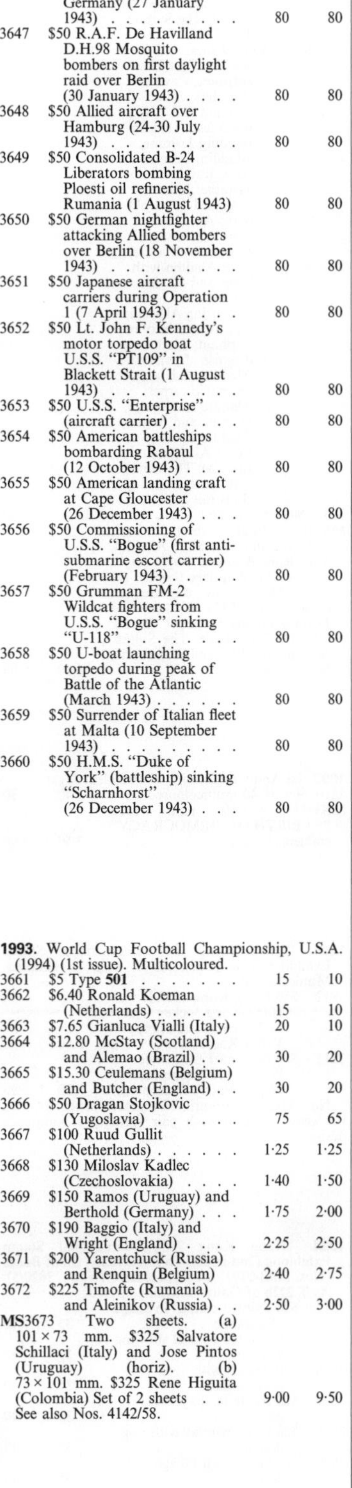

3645 $50 U.S. Navy aircraft attacking Makin (19 November 1943) . . . 80 80
3646 $50 U.S.A.A.F. bombers on first daylight raid over Germany (27 January 1943) 80 80
3647 $50 R.A.F. De Havilland D.H.98 Mosquito bombers on first daylight raid over Berlin (30 January 1943) 80 80
3648 $50 Allied aircraft over Hamburg (24-30 July 1943) 80 80
3649 $50 Consolidated B-24 Liberators bombing Ploesti oil refineries, Rumania (1 August 1943) 80 80
3650 $50 German nightfighter attacking Allied bombers over Berlin (18 November 1943) 80 80
3651 $50 Japanese aircraft carriers during Operation 1 (7 April 1943) 80 80
3652 $50 Lt. John F. Kennedy's motor torpedo boat U.S.S. "PT109" in Blackett Strait (1 August 1943) 80 80
3653 $50 U.S.S. "Enterprise" (aircraft carrier) 80 80
3654 $50 American battleships bombarding Rabaul (12 October 1943) 80 80
3655 $50 American landing craft at Cape Gloucester (26 December 1943) . . . 80 80
3656 $50 Commissioning of U.S.S. "Bogue" (first anti-submarine escort carrier) (February 1943) 80 80
3657 $50 Grumman FM-2 Wildcat fighters from U.S.S. "Bogue" sinking "U-118" 80 80
3658 $50 U-boat launching torpedo during peak of Battle of the Atlantic (March 1943) 80 80
3659 $50 Surrender of Italian fleet at Malta (10 September 1943) 80 80
3660 $50 H.M.S. "Duke of York" (battleship) sinking "Scharnhorst" (26 December 1943) . . . 80 80

1993. World Cup Football Championship, U.S.A. (1994) (1st issue). Multicoloured.

3661 $5 Type **501** 15 10
3662 $6.40 Ronald Koeman (Netherlands) 15 10
3663 $7.65 Gianluca Vialli (Italy) 20 10
3664 $12.80 McStay (Scotland) and Alemao (Brazil) . . . 30 20
3665 $15.30 Ceulemans (Belgium) and Butcher (England) . . 30 20
3666 $50 Dragan Stojkovic (Yugoslavia) 75 65
3667 $100 Ruud Gullit (Netherlands) . . . . . . 1·25 1·25
3668 $130 Miloslav Kadlec (Czechoslovakia) . . . . 1·40 1·50
3669 $150 Ramos (Uruguay) and Berthold (Germany) . . . 1·75 2·00
3670 $190 Baggio (Italy) and Wright (England) . . . . 2·25 2·50
3671 $200 Yarentchuck (Russia) and Renquin (Belgium) 2·40 2·75
3672 $225 Timofte (Rumania) and Aleinikov (Russia) . . 2·50 3·00
MS3673 Two sheets. (a) 101 × 73 mm. $325 Salvatore Schillaci (Italy) and Jose Pintos (Uruguay) (horiz). (b) 73 × 101 mm. $325 Rene Higuita (Colombia) Set of 2 sheets . . 9·00 9·50

See also Nos. 4142/58.

502 Sir Shridath Ramphal

503 "Donald's Better Self", 1938

1993. 1st Recipients of Order of the Caribbean Community. Multicoloured.

3674 $7.65 Type **502** 60 50
3675 $7.65 William Demas . . . 60 50
3676 $7.65 Derek Walcott . . . . 1·00 65

1993. Christmas. Paintings by Rubens and Durer. As T **211b** of Gambia. Each black, yellow and red (Nos. 3678, 3680/1, 3684) or multicoloured (others).

3677 $6.40 "The Holy Family under the Apple Tree" (detail) (Rubens) 15 10
3678 $7.65 "The Virgin in Glory" (detail) (Durer) 15 10
3679 $12.80 "The Holy Family under the Apple Tree" (different detail) (Rubens) 20 15
3680 $15.30 "The Virgin in Glory" (different detail) (Durer) 20 20
3681 $50 "The Virgin in Glory" (different detail) (Durer) 70 55
3682 $130 "The Holy Family under the Apple Tree" (different detail) (Rubens) 1·50 1·60
3683 $190 "The Holy Family under the Apple Tree" (different detail) (Rubens) 2·25 2·50
3684 $250 "The Virgin in Glory" (different detail) (Durer) 2·75 3·25
MS3685 Two sheets. (a) 126 × 101 mm. $325 "The Holy Family under the Apple Tree" (Rubens). (b) 101 × 126 mm. $325 "The Virgin in Glory" (woodcut by Durer from "The Life of the Virgin") Set of 2 sheets . . . . 7·00 8·50

1993. Bicentenary of the Louvre, Paris. As T **209b** of Gambia. Multicoloured.

3686 $50 "Mona Lisa" (Leonardo da Vinci)
3687/94 $50 × 8 "Self-portrait with Spectacles" (Chardin); "Infanta Maria Theresa" (Velazquez); "Spring" (Arcimboldo); "The Virgin of Sorrows" (Bouts); "The Student" (Fragonard); "Francois I" (Clouet); "Le Condottiere" (Antonello da Messina); "La Bohemienne" (Hals)
3695/3702 $50 × 8 "The Village Bride" (left detail) (Greuze); "The Village Bride" (centre detail); "The Village Bride" (right detail); "Self-portrait" (Melendez); "The Knight, the Girl and the Mountain" (Baldung-Grien); "The Young Beggar" (Murillo); "The Pilgrims of Emmaus" (left detail) (Le Nain); "The Pilgrims of Emmaus" (right detail) . . . .
3703/10 $50 × 8 "Woman with a Flea" (detail) (Crespi); "The Woman with Dropsy" (detail) (Dou); "Portrait of a Couple" (Ittenbach); "Cleopatra" (Moreau); "Riches" (Vouet); "Old Man and Young Boy" (Ghirlandaio); "Louis XIV" (Rigaud); "The Drinker" (Pieter de Hooch) . . . . . .
3711/18 $50 × 8 "Woman with a Flea" (Crespi); "Self-portrait at Easel" (Rembrandt); "Algerian Women" (detail) (Delacroix); "Head of a Young Man" (Raphael); "Venus and The Graces" (detail) (Botticelli); "Still Life with Chessboard" (detail) (Lubin Baugin); "Lady Macbeth" (Fussli); "The Smoke-filled Room" (detail) (Chardin) . . . . .
3719/26 $50 × 8 "The Virgin with the Rabbit" (Titian); "The Virgin with the Rabbit" (detail of head) (Titian); "The Beautiful Gardener" (detail) (Raphael); "The Lace-maker" (Vermeer); "Jeanne d'Aragon" (detail) (Raphael); "The Astronomer" (Vermeer); "The Rialto Bridge" (detail) (Canaletto); "Sigismond Malatesta" (Piero della Francesca) . .
3686/3726 Set of 41 . . . . 26·00 28·00

MS3727 Six sheets, each 95 × 70 mm. (a) $325 "Mona Lisa" and details (Leonardo da Vinci) (84 × 56 mm). (b) $325 "The Coronation of Napoleon I" (David) (84 × 56 mm). (c) $325 "Farmyard" (Jan Brueghel the Younger) (84 × 56 mm). (d) $325 "The Marriage Feast at Cana" (Veronese) (84 × 56 mm). (e) $325 "The Fortune-teller" (Caravaggio) (84 × 56 mm). (f) $325 "The Rialto Bridge" (Canaletto) (84 × 56 mm) Set of 6 sheets . . . . 23·00 25·00

1993. Donald Duck Film Posters. Multicoloured.

3728/35 $60 × 8 Type **503**; "Donald's Golf Game", 1938; "Sea Scouts", 1939; "Donald's Penguin", 1939; "A Good Time for a Dime", 1941; "Truant Officer Donald"; "Orphan's Benefit", 1941; "Chef Donald", 1941 . . . .

3736/43 $60 × 8 "The Village Smithy"; "Donald's Snow Fight"; "Donald's Garden"; "Donald's Gold Mine"; "The Vanishing Private"; "Sky Trooper"; "Bellboy Donald"; "The New Spirit", all 1942 . . . .

3744/51 $60 × 8 "Saludos Amigos", 1943; "The Eyes Have It", 1945; "Donald's Crime", 1945; "Straight Shooters", 1947; "Donald's Dilemma", 1947; "Bootle Beetle", 1947; "Daddy Duck", 1948; "Soup's On", 1948 . . . .

3752/9 $80 × 8 "Donald's Happy Birthday", 1949; "Sea Salts", 1949; "Honey Harvester", 1949; "All in a Nutshell", 1949; "The Greener Yard", 1949; "Slide, Donald, Slide", 1949; "Lion Around", 1950; "Trailer Horn", 1950

3760/7 $80 × 8 "Bee at the Beach", 1950; "Out on a Limb", 1950; "Corn Chips", 1951; "Test Pilot Donald", 1951; "Lucky Number", 1951; "Out of Scale", 1951; "Bee on Guard", 1951; "Let's Stick Together", 1952 . . .

3768/75 $80 × 8 "Trick or Treat", 1952; "Don's Fountain of Youth", 1953; "Rugged Bear", 1953; "Canvas Back Duck", 1953; "Dragon Around", 1954; "Grin and Bear It", 1954; "The Flying Squirrel", 1954; "Up a Tree", 1955 . . . .

3776/81 $80 × 8 Scenes from "Pirate Gold": In the crow's nest; Aracuan Bird carrying treasure chest; Donald with treasure map; Donald at souvenir stall; Aracuan Bird with Donald; Donald on jetty (all horiz) . . . .

3728/81 Set of 56 . . . . 45·00 50·00

MS3782 Five sheets, each 129 × 103 mm. (a) $500 Book cover of "The Wise Little Hen", 1934 (horiz). (b) $500 Sketch for "Timber", 1941. (c) $500 Fan-card for "The Three Caballeros", 1945 (horiz). (d) $500 Fan-card for "Melody Time", 1948. Imperf. (e) $500 Donald Duck Set of 5 sheets 27·00 29·00

504 Aladdin

505 President Dr. Cheddi Jagan

1993. "Aladdin" (film). Disney Cartoon Characters. Multicoloured.

3783/90 $7.65 × 8 Type **504**; Abu the monkey; Jasmine; Rajah the tiger; Jafar; Iago the parrot; The Sultan; The Genie . . . . .

3791/9 $50 × 9 Jafar and magic scarab; Tiger Head entrance, Cave of Wonders; Jafar; Aladdin and Abu at breakfast; Aladdin rescuing Jasmine; Aladdin, Jasmine and Abu; Rajah comforts Jasmine; Jafar disguised as an old man; Aladdin and Abu in treasure chamber (all horiz)

3800/8 $65 × 9 Aladdin with lamp and magic carpet; The Genie measuring Aladdin; Abu turned into an elephant; Aladdin in disguise at palace; Aladdin and Jasmine on magic carpet; Aladdin in disguise, Jasmine and Sultan; Aladdin fighting Jafar; Aladdin and Jasmine; The Genie with suitcase and golf clubs (all horiz) . . .

3783/3808 Set of 26 . . . . 15·00 16·00

MS3809 Four sheets, each 127 × 102 mm. (a) $325 Aladdin, The Genie, Abu and magic carpet in Cave of Wonders (horiz). (b) $325 Aladdin in disguise on elephant. (c) $325 Aladdin and Jasmine on magic carpet (horiz). (d) $325 The Genie, The Sultan, Jasmine, Aladdin and Abu (horiz) Set of 4 sheets . . . . 18·00 19·00

1993. 1st Anniv of Election of President Jagan.

3810 **505** $6.40 multicoloured . . . 40 30

MS3811 97 × 69 mm. $325 "REBIRTH OF DEMOCRACY" emblem . . . . 3·50 4·00

1994. "Hong Kong '94" International Stamp Exhibition (1st issue). As T **222a** of Gambia. Multicoloured.

3812 $50 Hong Kong 1984 Royal Hong Kong Jockey Club $1.30 stamp and Happy Valley Racecourse 80 90

3813 $50 Guyana 1992 Movie Posters $190 stamp and Happy Valley Racecourse 80 90

Nos. 3812/13 were printed together, se-tenant, with the centre part of each pair forming a composite design.

1994. "Hong Kong '94" International Stamp Exhibition (2nd issue). Ch'ing Dynasty Snuff Boxes (Nos. 3814/19) or Porcelain (Nos. 3820/5). As T **222b** of Gambia. Multicoloured.

3814 $20 Painted enamel in shape of bamboo 35 40

3815 $20 Painted enamel showing woman 35 40

3816 $20 Amber with lions playing ball 35 40

3817 $20 Agate in shape of two gourds 35 40

3818 $20 Glass overlay with dog design 35 40

3819 $20 Glass with foliage design 35 40

3820 $20 Covered jar with dragon design 35 40

3821 $20 Rotating brush-holder 35 40

3822 $20 Covered jar with horses design 35 40

3823 $20 Amphora vase with bats and peaches 35 40

3824 $20 Tea caddy with Fo dogs 35 40

3825 $20 Vase with camellias and peaches design 35 40

1994. Centenary of the Sign for the Mahdi. Nos. 1622/4 and 1634 surch **CENTENARY Sign For The MAHDI 1894-1994** and new value.

3826 $6 on 60c. Plate No. 73 (Series 1) (horiz) . . . .

3827 $20 on 200c. Plate No. 33 (Series 1) (horiz) . . . .

3828 $30 on 60c. Plate No. 57 (Series 1) (horiz) . . . .

3829 $35 on 60c. Plate No. 75 (Series 1) (horiz) . . . .

The surcharges on Nos. 3826 and 3828 show the third line as "MADHI".

1994. Hummel Figurines. As T **501a** of Ghana. Multicoloured.

3830 $20 Girl holding inscribed heart 25 25

3831 $25 Boy with heart under arm 30 30

3832 $35 Baker 40 40

3833 $50 Girl with pot of flowers 60 55

3834 $60 Girl with trumpet, pot plant and bird 70 65

3835 $130 Four girls . . . . . . 1·50 1·50

3836 $190 Boy and two girls with dog . . . . 2·25 2·50

3837 $250 Boy with cake and dog 2·75 3·50

MS3838 Two sheets, each 92 × 124 mm. (a) $6 As No. 3835; $25 No. 3831; $30 As No. 3830; $190 No. 3836. (b) $20 As No. 3832; $35 As No. 3837; $60 No. 3834; $130 As No. 3833 Set of 2 sheets . . . . 6·00 6·50

1994. 75th Anniv of I.L.O. Nos. 1760 and 1629/30 surch **I L O 75th Anniversary 1919-1994** and new value.

3839 $6 on 130c. Plate No. 13 (Series 1) . . . .

3840 $30 on 120c. Plate No. 58 (Series 1) . . . .

3841 $35 on 120c. Plate No. 56 (Series 1) . . . .

1994. Centenary (1992) of Sierra Club (environmental protection society). Endangered Species. As T **224a** of Gambia. Multicoloured.

3842 $70 Red Kangaroo with young 90 90

3843 $70 Head of American alligator 90 90

3844 $70 Head of bald eagle . . 90 90

3845 $70 Giant panda eating bamboo 90 90

3846 $70 Head of red kangaroo 90 90

3847 $70 Alaskan brown bear sitting 90 90

3848 $70 Bald eagle 90 90

3849 $70 Head of giant panda . . 90 90

3850 $70 Red kangaroo (horiz) 90 90

3851 $70 Whooping crane facing left (horiz) 90 90

3852 $70 Male whooping crane in courtship display (horiz) 90 90

3853 $70 Whooping crane looking right (horiz) . . . 90 90

3854 $70 Alaskan brown bear and cub (horiz) 90 90

3855 $70 Alaskan brown bear fishing (horiz) 90 90

3856 $70 Bald eagle on branch (horiz) 90 90

3857 $70 Giant panda (horiz) . . 90 90

3858 $70 American alligator (logo at left) (horiz) 90 90

3859 $70 American alligator (logo at right) (horiz) 90 90

3860 $70 Italian Alps at sunrise (horiz) 90 90

3861 $70 Italian Alps and meadow (horiz) 90 90

3862 $70 Mono Lake at sunset (horiz) 90 90

3863 $70 Rock pinnacles, Mono Lake (horiz) 90 90

3864 $70 Sea lion 90 90

3865 $70 Head of sea lion . . . 90 90

3866 $70 Sea lions on rocks . . . 90 90

3867 $70 Rock pinnacles, Mono Lake 90 90

3868 $70 Sierra Club Centennial emblem (black, brown and green) 90 90

3869 $70 Lake, Italian Alps . . . 90 90

3870 $70 Summit of Matterhorn 90 90

3871 $70 Matterhorn and village 90 90

3872 $70 Clouds over Matterhorn 90 90

1994. Royal Visit. Nos. 3551/4 optd **ROYAL VISIT FEB 19-22, 1994**.

3873 $25 Queen Elizabeth II in Coronation robes (photograph by Cecil Beaton) . . . . 1·50 1·60

3874 $50 Royal gems . . . . . . 2·00 2·25

3875 $75 Queen Elizabeth and Prince Philip . . . . . . 2·25 2·50

3876 $130 Queen opening Parliament . . . . 2·50 2·75

MS3877 69 × 100 mm. $325 "Queen in Coronation Robes" (Sir James Gunn) (28½ × 42½ mm) . . . . 6·50 7·00

509 "Cestrum parqui"

1994. Flowers. Multicoloured.

3878 $6.40 Type **509** 10 10

3879 $7.65 "Brunfelsia calycina" 10 10

3880 $12.80 "Datura rosei" . . . 10 15

3881 $15.30 "Ruellia macrantha" 15 20

3882 $50 "Portlandia albiflora" 50 55

3883 $50 "Clusia grandiflora" . . 50 55

3884 $50 "Begonia haageana" . . 50 55

3885 $50 "Fuchsia simplicicaulis" 50 55

3886 $50 "Guaiacum officinale" 50 55

3887 $50 "Pithecoctenium cynanchoides" 50 55

3888 $50 "Sphaeralcea umbellata" 50 55

3889 $50 "Erythrina poeppigiana" 50 55

3890 $50 "Steriphoma paradoxa" 50 55

3891 $50 "Allemanda violacea" 50 55

3892 $50 "Centropogon cornutus" 50 55

3893 $50 "Passiflora quadrangularis" 50 55

3894 $50 "Victoria amazonica" 50 55

3895 $50 "Cobaea scandens" . . 50 55

3896 $50 "Pyrostegia venusta" . . 50 55

3897 $50 "Petrea kohautiana" . . 50 55

3898 $50 "Hippobroma longiflora" 50 55

3899 $50 "Cleome hassleriana" 50 55

3900 $50 "Verbena peruviana" 50 55

3901 $50 "Tropaeolum peregrinum" 50 55

3902 $50 "Plumeria rubra" . . . 50 55

3903 $50 "Selenicereus grandiflorus" 50 55

3904 $50 "Mandevilla splendens" 50 55

3905 $50 "Pereskia aculeata" . . 50 55

3906 $50 "Ipomoea learii" . . . 50 55

3907 $130 "Pachystachys coccinea" . . . . . . 1·25 1·40

3908 $190 "Beloperone guttata" 1·90 2·25

3909 $250 "Ferdinandusa speciosa" . . . . 2·50 3·00

MS3910 Two sheets, each 99 × 70 mm. (a) $325 "Lophospermum erubescens". (b) $325 "Columnea fendleri" Set of 2 sheets . . . . 7·50 8·50

Nos. 3883/94 and 3895/3906 respectively were printed together, se-tenant, forming composite background designs.

1994. 25th Anniv of First Moon Landing (1st issue). As T **227a** of Gambia. Multicoloured.

3911 $60 Walter Dornberger and launch of first A-4 rocket 90 90

3912 $60 Rudolph Nebel and "Surveyor 1" 90 90

3913 $60 Robert H. Goddard and "Apollo 7" 90 90

3914 $60 Kurt Debus and view of Earth from Moon ("Apollo 8") 90 90

3915 $60 James T. Webb and "Apollo 9" 90 90

3916 $60 George E. Mueller and "Apollo 10" lunar module 90 90

3917 $60 Wernher von Braun and launch of "Apollo 11" . . 90 90

3918 $60 Rocco A. Petrone and "Apollo 11" astronaut on Moon 90 90

3919 $60 Eberhard Rees and "Apollo 12" astronaut on Moon 90 90

3920 $60 Charles A. Berry and damaged "Apollo 13" . . 90 90

3921 $60 Thomas O. Paine and "Apollo 14" before splashdown 90 90

3922 $60 A. F. Staats and "Apollo 15" on Moon . . 90 90

3923 $60 Robert R. Gilruth and "Apollo 16" astronaut on Moon 90 90

3924 $60 Ernst Stuhlinger and "Apollo 17" crew on Moon 90 90

3925 $60 Christopher C. Kraft and X-30 National Aero-Space Plane 90 90

3926 $60 Rudolf Opitz and Messerschmitt Me 163B Komet (rocket engine), 1943 . . . . 90 90

3927 $60 Clyde W. Tombaugh and "face" on Mars . . . 90 90

3928 $60 Hermann Oberth and scene from "The Girl in the Moon" 90 90

MS3929 125 × 112 mm. $325 Frank J. Everest Jr and "Apollo 11" anniversary logo . . . . 4·50 5·00

See also Nos. 4169/87.

1994. Centenary of International Olympic Committee. Medal Winners. As T **227b** of Gambia. Multicoloured.

3930 $20 Nancy Kerrigan (U.S.A.) (1994 figure skating silver) 30 30

3931 $35 Sawao Kato (Japan) (1976 gymnastics gold) . . 50 50

3932 $130 Florence Griffith Joyner (U.S.A.) (1988 100 and 200 metres gold) . . 1·75 2·00

MS3933 110 × 80 mm. $325 Mark Wasmeier (Germany) (1994 super giant slalom and giant slalom gold) . . . . 4·00 4·50

1994. Centenary of First English Cricket Tour to the West Indies (1995). As T **397a** of Grenada. Multicoloured.

3934 $20 Clive Lloyd (Guyana and West Indies) (vert) . . 55 30
3935 $35 Carl Hooper (Guyana and West Indies) and Wisden Trophy 65 50
3936 $60 Graham Hick (England) and Wisden Trophy . . . 1·10 1·25
MS3937 79 × 100 mm. $200 English team of 1895 (black and brown) 2·75 3·00

1994. 50th Anniv of D-Day. Aircraft. As T **227c** of Gambia. Multicoloured.

3938 $6 Supermarine Spitfire Mk XI fighter on photo reconnaissance 40 15
3939 $35 North American B-25 Mitchell bomber 85 50
3940 $190 Republic P-47 Thunderbolt fighters . . . 3·00 3·50
MS3941 109 × 79 mm. $325 Avro Type 683 Lancaster bomber of 419 Squadron . . . . 4·75 5·00

1994. 50th Anniv of Second World War (3rd issue). As T **500**. Multicoloured.

3942 $60 Paratroops drop, D-Day 90 80
3943 $60 Glider assault, D-Day 90 80
3944 $60 U.S.S. "Arkansas" (battleship) bombarding Omaha Beach, D-Day . . 90 80
3945 $60 U.S. fighters attacking train 90 80
3946 $60 Allied landing craft approaching beaches . . . 90 80
3947 $60 Troops in beach obstacles 90 80
3948 $60 Commandos leaving landing craft 90 80
3949 $60 U.S. flail tank destroying mines 90 80
3950 $60 U.S. tank breaking through sea wall 90 80
3951 $60 Tanks and infantry advancing 90 80
3952 $60 Landings at Anzio (22 January 1944) 90 80
3953 $60 R.A.F. attacking Amiens Prison (18 February 1944) . . . 90 80
3954 $60 Soviet Army tank in Sevastopol (9 May 1944) 90 80
3955 $60 British bren-gun carriers at the Gustav Line (19 May 1944) 90 80
3956 $60 D-Day landings (6 June 1944) 90 80
3957 $60 "V-1" over London (13 June 1944) 90 80
3958 $60 Allies entering Paris (19 August 1944) 90 80
3959 $60 German "V-2" rocket ready for launch (8 September 1944) . . . 90 80
3960 $60 Sinking of "Tirpitz" (German battleship) (12 November 1944) . . . 90 80
3961 $60 U.S. tanks at Bastogne (29 December 1944) . . . 90 80

1994. "Philakorea '94" International Stamp Exhibition, Seoul (1st issue). As T **227d** of Gambia. Multicoloured.

3962 $6 Socialist ideals statue, Pyongyang (vert) 10 10
3963 $25 Statue of Admiral Yi Sun-sin (vert) 30 30
3964 $60 Fruits and mountain peaks 70 75
3965 $60 Manchurian crane, bamboo and peaks . . . 70 75
3966 $60 Rising sun and two cranes on pine 70 75
3967 $60 Five cranes on pine and peak 70 75
3968 $60 Three cranes in flight 70 75
3969 $60 Sea, rocky shore and fungi 70 75
3970 $60 Sea, rocky shore and fruit 70 75
3971 $60 Hind at seashore and fruit 70 75
3972 $60 Stag in pine forest . . . 70 75
3973 $60 Deer and fungi by waterfall 70 75
3974 $60 Tops of pines and mountain peaks 70 75
3975 $60 Manchurian crane in flight 70 75
3976 $60 Three cranes on pine tree 70 75
3977 $60 Crane on pine tree . . . 70 75
3978 $60 Top of fruit tree 70 75
3979 $60 Stag and two hinds on mountainside 70 75
3980 $60 Deer and fungi 70 75
3981 $60 Stag by waterfall and hind drinking 70 75
3982 $60 Pine tree, fruit and fungi 70 75
3983 $60 Fungi on mountainside 70 75
3984 $120 Sokkat'ap Pagoda, Pulguksa . . . . 1·40 1·60
3985 $130 Village Guardian (statue), Chejudo Island 1·40 1·60
MS3986 Two sheets. (a) 104 × 73 mm. $325 Europeans at the Korean Court (early lithograph). (b) 73 × 104 mm. $325 Pagoda by Ch'urae-am Rock Set of 2 sheets . . . . 7·00 8·00

Nos. 3964/73 and 3974/83, all 23 × 49 mm, were printed together, se-tenant, in sheetlets of 10, each sheetlet forming a composite design showing panels from a screen painting of longevity symbols from the late Chosun dynasty.

See also Nos. 4117/41.

510 Miki Maya

1994. 80th Anniv of Takarazuka Revue of Japan. Multicoloured.

3987 $20 Type **510** 55 60
3988 $20 Fubuki Takane 55 60
3989 $20 Seika Kuze 55 60
3990 $20 Saki Asaji 55 60
3991 $60 Mira Anju (34 × 47 mm) 75 80
3992 $60 Yuki Amami (34 × 47 mm) 75 80
3993 $60 Maki Ichiro (34 × 47 mm) 75 80
3994 $60 Yu Shion (34 × 47 mm) 75 80

511 "Heliconius melpomene"

1994. Butterflies. Multicoloured.

3995 $5 Type **511** 20 20
3996 $20 "Helicopis cupido" . . 45 45
3997 $25 "Agrias claudina" . . . 50 50
3998 $30 "Parides coelus" . . . 60 60
3999 $50 "Heliconius hecale" . . 75 75
4000 $50 "Anaea marthesia" . . 75 75
4001 $50 "Brassolis astyra" . . . 75 75
4002 $50 "Heliconius melpomene" 75 75
4003 $50 "Haetera piera" 75 75
4004 $50 "Morpho diana" . . . 75 75
4005 $50 "Parides coelus" . . . 75 75
4006 $50 "Catagramma pitheas" 75 75
4007 $50 "Nessaea obrinus" . . . 75 75
4008 $50 "Automeris janus" . . . 75 75
4009 $50 "Papilio torquatus" . . 75 75
4010 $50 "Eunica sophonisba" 75 75
4011 $50 "Ceratinia nise" . . . 75 75
4012 $50 "Panacea procilla" . . . 75 75
4013 $50 "Pyrrhogyra neaerea" 75 75
4014 $50 "Morpho deidamia" . . 75 75
4015 $50 "Dismorphia orise" . . 75 75
4016 $60 "Morpho diana" . . . 85 85
4017 $190 "Dismorphia orise" . . 2·50 3·00
4018 $250 "Morpho deidamia" 3·00 3·50
MS4019 Four sheets. (a) 104 × 76 mm. $325 "Anaea eribotes". (b) 104 × 76 mm. $325 "Eunica sophonisba". (c) 110 × 80 mm. $325 "Hamadryas velutina" (39 × 30 mm). (d) 110 × 80 mm. $325 Agrias claudina (39 × 30 mm) Set of 4 sheets . . . . 14·00 16·00

512 Jacob

513 Peregrine Falcon

1994. Bible Stories (2nd series). Multicoloured. (a) Joseph.

4020/43 $20 × 24 arranged as blocks of 4 depicting Jacob giving Joseph a coat of many colours (Type **512** at top left); Joseph thrown into a pit; Joseph sold as a slave; Joseph accused by Potiphar's wife; Joseph interprets Pharoah's dreams; Joseph reunited with his brothers . . . . .

(b) The Parting of the Red Sea.

4044/67 $20 × 24 Palm trees on shore; Pyramids; Palm trees on shore and black cloud; Three palm trees; Blue and white dove; Red and white bird; Egyptian army engulfed by sea; Yellow and white dove; Red and green fishes; Egyptian chariot with wall of water at left; Chariots between walls of water; Dolphins; Two doves; Israelites and water to left; Israelites and water to right; Turquoise and purple fishes; Israelites with tree at left; Iraelites with goats; Moses; Israelites with tree at right; Israelites with woman on horse; Israelites with old man and woman carrying pack; Israelites with woman carrying young child; Israelites with cart . . . .

(c) Ruth.

4068/91 $20 × 24 arranged as blocks of 6 depicting Ruth and Naomi; Ruth gleaning in cornfield; Boaz establishing kinsman's rights; Naomi with Ruth, Boaz and Obed . . .

(d) Daniel in the Lions' Den.

4092/4116 $20 × 25 Palm fronds and hibiscus flower; Magnificent frigate bird and palm fronds; Magnificent frigate birds and tops of stone pillars; Magnificent frigate bird, pillars and sail at bottom right; Hibiscus, sails of ship and top of pillar; Yellow arum lilies and palm trees; Heads of adult and immature magnificent frigate birds and palm trees; Palm trees, butterfly and stone pillars; Two butterflies and stone pillars; Stone pillar and sailing ship; Great egret (standing); Purple irises and palm trees; Daniel; Angel; Donkey foal; Orchids; Lioness and two cubs; Daniel's legs and lions; Lion; Three crowns; Goat and kid; Kid; Cub and head of lion; Lioness; Great egret in flight . . . . . .
4020/4116 Set of 97 . . . . 26·00 28·00

Nos. 4020/43, 4044/67, 4068/91 and 4092/4116 respectively were printed together, se-tenant, forming composite designs.

1994. "Philakorea '94" International Stamp Exhibition, Seoul (2nd issue). Birds of the World. Multicoloured.

4117 $35 Type **513** 55 55
4118 $35 Great spotted woodpecker 55 55
4119 $35 White-throated kingfisher 55 55
4120 $35 Andean cock of the rock ("Peruvian Cock of the Rock") 55 55
4121 $35 Yellow-headed amazon 55 55
4122 $35 Victoria crowned pigeon 55 55
4123 $35 Little owl 55 55
4124 $35 Common pheasant ("Ring-necked Pheasant") 55 55
4125 $35 Eurasian goldfinch ("Goldfinch") 55 55
4126 $35 Jay 55 55
4127 $35 Keel-billed toucan ("Sulphur-breasted Toucan") 55 55
4128 $35 Blue and white flycatcher ("Japanese Blue Flycatcher") 55 55
4129 $35 Northern goshawk . . . 55 55
4130 $35 Northern lapwing ("Lapwing") 55 55
4131 $35 Long-wattled umbrellabird ("Ornate Umbrellabird") 55 55

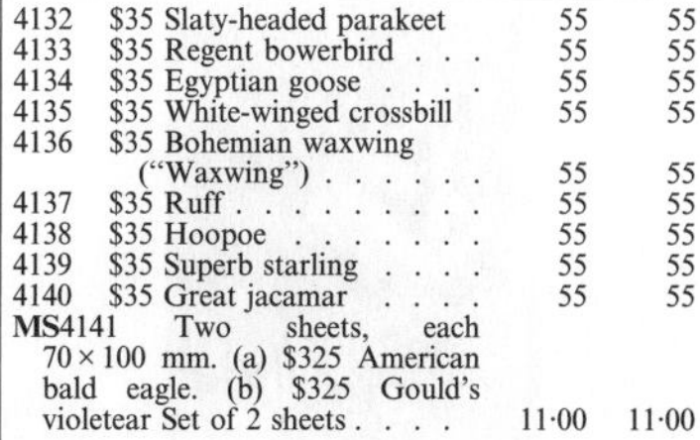

4132 $35 Slaty-headed parakeet 55 55
4133 $35 Regent bowerbird . . . 55 55
4134 $35 Egyptian goose 55 55
4135 $35 White-winged crossbill 55 55
4136 $35 Bohemian waxwing ("Waxwing") 55 55
4137 $35 Ruff 55 55
4138 $35 Hoopoe 55 55
4139 $35 Superb starling 55 55
4140 $35 Great jacamar 55 55
MS4141 Two sheets, each 70 × 100 mm. (a) $325 American bald eagle. (b) $325 Gould's violetear Set of 2 sheets . . . . 11·00 11·00

514 Paulo Futre (Portugal)

1994. World Cup Football Championship, U.S.A. (2nd issue). Multicoloured.

4142 $6 Type **514** 10 10
4143 $35 Lyndon Hooper (Canada) 35 40
4144 $60 Enzo Francescoli (Uruguay) 60 65
4145 $60 Paolo Maldini (Italy) 60 65
4146 $60 Guyana player 60 65
4147 $60 Bwalya Kalusha (Zambia) 60 65
4148 $60 Diego Maradona (Argentina) 60 65
4149 $60 Andreas Brehme (Germany) 60 65
4150 $60 Eric Wynalda (U.S.A.) (pursuing ball) 60 65
4151 $60 John Doyle (U.S.A.) . . 60 65
4152 $60 Eric Wynalda (U.S.A.) (kicking ball) 60 65
4153 $60 Thomas Dooley (U.S.A.) 60 65
4154 $60 Ernie Stewart (U.S.A.) 60 65
4155 $60 Marcelo Balboa (U.S.A.) 60 65
4156 $60 Bora Milutinovic (U.S.A. coach) 60 65
4157 $190 Freddy Rincon (Colombia) . . . . 1·90 2·00
MS4158 Two sheets. (a) 105 × 75 mm. $325 "94" symbol and player. (b) 75 × 105 mm. $325 Oiler Watson (U.S.A.) Set of 2 sheets . . . . 7·50 8·50

Nos. 4145/50 and 4151/6 respectively were printed together, se-tenant, forming composite background designs.

515 Anja Fichtel (individual foil, 1988)

1994. Olympic Games, Atlanta (1996) (1st issue). Previous German Gold Medal Winners. Mult.

4159 $6 Type **515** 15 10
4160 $25 Annegret Richter (100 m, 1976) (vert) 35 30
4161 $30 Heike Henkel (high jump, 1992) (vert) 40 35
4162 $35 Armin Hary (100 m, 1960) (vert) 40 40
4163 $50 Heide Rosendahl (long jump, 1972) (vert) 60 65
4164 $60 Josef Neckermann (dressage, 1968) (vert) . . 90 75
4165 $130 Heike Drechsler (long jump, 1988) (vert) . . . . 1·50 1·75
4166 $190 Ulrike Mayfarth (high jump, 1984) (vert) . . . . 2·50 2·75
4167 $250 Michael Gross (200 m freestyle and 100 m butterfly, 1984) . . 3·00 3·50
MS4168 Three sheets. (a) 105 × 75 mm. $135 Markus Wasmeier (skiing, 1994) (vert); $190 Katja Seizinger (skiing, 1994) (vert). (b) 105 × 75 mm. $325 Franziska van Almsick (swimming, 1992) (vert). (c) 75 × 105 mm. $325 Steffi Graf (tennis, 1988, 1992) (vert) Set of 3 sheets . . . . 11·00 11·00

See also Nos. 4492/4508 and 4739/88.

516 Dog Laika and Rocket, 1957

1994. 25th Anniv of First Moon Landing (2nd issue). Multicoloured.

4169 $60 Type **516** 80 80
4170 $60 Yuri Gagarin (first man in space), 1961 . . . . . 80 80
4171 $60 John Glenn (first American to orbit Earth), 1962 . . . . 80 80
4172 $60 Edward White walking in space, 1965 . . . . . 80 80
4173 $60 Neil Armstrong, walking on Moon and "Apollo 11" logo 80 80
4174 $60 "Luna 16" leaving Moon, 1970 . . . . . . 80 80
4175 $60 Lunar Module 1 on Moon, 1970 . . . . . . 80 80
4176 $60 Skylab 1, 1973 . . . . . 80 80
4177 $60 Astronauts and Apollo–Soyuz link-up, 1975 . . . 80 80
4178 $60 "Mars 3" 80 80
4179 $60 "Mariner 10" 80 80
4180 $60 "Voyager" 80 80
4181 $60 "Pioneer" 80 80
4182 $60 "Giotto" 80 80
4183 $60 "Magellan" 80 80
4184 $60 "Galileo" 80 80
4185 $60 "Ulysses" 80 80
4186 $60 "Cassini" 80 80
MS4187 Two sheets, each 142 × 104 mm. (a) $325 "Apollo 11" astronauts. (b) $325 "Galileo" Set of 2 sheets . . . 8·50 9·00

Nos. 4178/86 were printed together, se-tenant, with the backgrounds forming a composite design of Space.

517 South Caroline Railroad "Best Friend of Charleston", 1830, U.S.A.

1994. History of Trains. Steam Locomotives. Multicoloured.

4188 $25 Type **517** 40 40
4189 $25 South Eastern Railway No. 285, 1882 . . . . . 40 40
4190 $30 Camden Amboy Railway No. 1 "John Bull", 1831, U.S.A. . . . 45 45
4191 $30 Stephenson "Patentee" type locomotive, 1837 . . 45 45
4192 $30 "Atlantic", 1832 . . . . 45 45
4193 $30 "Stourbridge Lion", 1829, U.S.A. 45 45
4194 $30 Polonceau locomotive, 1854 . . . . 45 45
4195 $30 "Thomas Rogers", 1855, U.S.A. 45 45
4196 $30 "Vulcan", 1858 . . . . 45 45
4197 $30 "Namur", 1846 . . . . 45 45
4198 $30 John Jarvis's "De Witt Clinton", 1831, U.S.A. . . 45 45
4199 $30 Seguin locomotive, 1829 45 45
4200 $30 Stephenson's "Planet", 1830 . . . . 45 45
4201 $30 Norris locomotive, 1840 45 45
4202 $30 "Sampson", 1867, U.S.A. 45 45
4203 $30 "Andrew Jackson", 1832 . . . . 45 45
4204 $30 "Herald", 1831 . . . . 45 45
4205 $30 "Cumberland", 1845, U.S.A. 45 45
4206 $30 Pennsylvania Railroad Class K, 1880 . . . . . 45 45
4207 $30 Cooke locomotive No. 11, 1885 . . . . . . 45 45
4208 $30 "John B. Turner", 1867, U.S.A. 45 45
4209 $30 Baldwin locomotive, 1871 . . . . 45 45
4210 $30 Richard Trevithick's locomotive, 1803 . . . . 45 45
4211 $30 John Stephens's locomotive, 1825 . . . . 45 45
4212 $30 John Blenkinsop's locomotive, 1814 . . . . 45 45
4213 $30 "Pennsylvania," 1803 45 45
4214 $300 Mount Washington Cog Railway locomotive No. 6, 1886 . . . . . . 3·25 3·50
4215 $300 Stroudley locomotive "Brighton", 1872 . . . . 3·25 3·50
MS4216 Two sheets, each 100 × 70 mm. (a) $250 Est Railway locomotive, 1878. (b) $300 "Claud Hamilton", 1900 Set of 2 sheets 7·50 8·00

No. 4198 is inscribed "West Point Foundry 1832 Locomotive" and No. 4202 "Union Iron Works os San Francisco", both error.

1994. Christmas. Religious Paintings. As T **231a** of Gambia. Multicoloured.

4217 $6 "Joseph with the Christ Child" (Guido Reni) . . . 15 10
4218 $20 "Adoration of the Christ Child" (Girolamo Romanino) 30 25
4219 $25 "Adoration of the Christ Child with St. Barbara and St. Martin" (Raffaello Botticini) 35 30
4220 $30 "Holy Family" (Pompeo Batoni) 40 35
4221 $35 "Flight into Egypt" (Bartolommeo Carducci) 45 40
4222 $60 "Holy Family and the Baptist" (Andrea del Sarto) 80 70
4223 $120 "Sacred Conversation" (Cesare de Sesto) . . . . 2·00 2·25
4224 $190 "Madonna and Child with Saints Joseph and John the Baptist" (Pontormo) . . . . 2·75 3·50
MS4225 Two sheets. (a) 112 × 93 mm. $325 "Presentation of Christ in the Temple" (Fra Bartolommeo). (b) 85 × 95 mm. $325 "Holy Family and St. Elizabeth and St. John the Baptist" (Francisco Primaticcio) Set of 2 sheets . . . . 7·50 8·00

518 Riker and Dr. Crusher

1994. "Star Trek Generations" (film). Designs showing "Enterprise" crew in 19th-century naval uniforms (Nos. 4226/34) or in 23rd-century (Nos. 4235/43). Multicoloured.

4226 $100 Type **518** . . . . . . 1·75 1·50
4227 $100 Geordi, Dr. Crusher with Lt. Worf in chains 1·75 1·50
4228 $100 Captain Picard . . . . 1·75 1·50
4229 $100 Data and Geordi . . . 1·75 1·50
4230 $100 "U.S.S. Enterprise" (sailing ship) . . . . . . 1·75 1·50
4231 $100 Captain Picard and Riker on quarterdeck . . 1·75 1·50
4232 $100 Data . . . . 1·75 1·50
4233 $100 Lt. Worf . . . . 1·75 1·50
4234 $100 Dr. Crusher . . . . . 1·75 1·50
4235 $100 Captain Picard . . . . 1·75 1·50
4236 $100 Riker . . . . 1·75 1·50
4237 $100 Captain Kirk . . . . 1·75 1·50
4238 $100 Soron with phaser . . 1·75 1·50
4239 $100 Captains Kirk and Picard on horseback . . . 1·75 1·50
4240 $100 Klingon women . . . 1·75 1·50
4241 $100 Captains Kirk and Picard . . . . 1·75 1·50
4242 $100 Troi . . . . 1·75 1·50
4243 $100 Captain Picard and Data . . . . 1·75 1·50
4244 $100 "BOLDLY GO" film poster . . . . 1·75 1·50
MS4245 86 × 103 mm. $500 U.S.S. "Enterprise" from film poster (horiz) . . . . 6·00 6·50

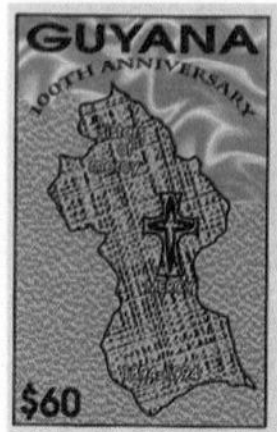

519 Cross and Map of Guyana

1994. Centenary of Sisters of Mercy in Guyana.

4246 **519** $60 multicoloured . . . 1·00 80

1994. 1st Recipients of Order of the Caribbean Community. As T **393a** of Grenada. Mult.

4247 $60 Sir Shridath Ramphal 65 75
4248 $60 William Demas 65 75
4249 $60 Derek Walcott . . . . 1·60 75

520 Garfield Sobers congratulating Brian Lara

1995. Brian Lara's Achievements in Cricket. Multicoloured.

4250 $20 Type **520** 35 25
4251 $30 Brian Lara setting world record for highest Test Match score (vert) 45 35
4252 $375 Lara and Chanderpaul 4·25 4·75
MS4253 70 × 100 mm. $300 Brian Lara (vert) . . . . 3·25 3·50

521 Babe Ruth

1995. Birth Centenary of Babe Ruth (baseball player). Each brown and black.

4254 $65 Type **521** 70 80
4255 $65 Preparing to bat (full-length photo) 70 80
4256 $65 Head and shoulders portrait (cap with limp brim) 70 80
4257 $65 In retirement (bare-headed) 70 80
4258 $65 Running (in plain shirt) 70 80
4259 $65 Head and shoulders portrait (cap with emblem and stiff brim) 70 80
4260 $65 Wearing "NEW YORK" shirt 70 80
4261 $65 Preparing to hit (in "NEW YORK" shirt) . . 70 80
4262 $65 Wearing "YANKEES" shirt 70 80
4263 $65 At base with bat on shoulder (in striped shirt) 70 80
4264 $65 Watching the ball (in striped shirt) 70 80
4265 $65 In cap and coat at Old Timer's Day, Yankee Stadium, 1948 . . . . . 70 80
MS4266 89 × 118 mm. $500 Babe Ruth (horiz) . . . . 5·00 5·25

522 Mickey Mouse as Family Doctor

1995. Disney Characters at Work. Multicoloured.

4267/75 $30 × 9 Type **522**; Goofy and optometrist; Daisy Duck as nurse; Scrooge McDuck as psychiatrist; Daisy Duck as physiotherapist; Horace Horsecollar and dentist; Goofy and radiologist; Goofy as pharmacist; Big Pete as chiropractor . . . .
4276/84 $30 × 9 Mickey Mouse as vet; Donald Duck training seals; Ludwig von Duck as animal psychiatrist; Goofy as ornithologist; Daisy Duck grooming Old English sheepdog; Minnie Mouse as herpetologist; Mickey Mouse as pet shop keeper with Pluto; J. Audubon Woodlore as park ranger; Donald Duck as aquarist . . . . .
4285/93 $30 × 9 Mickey Mouse as animator with Pluto; Goofy the tailor with Mickey Mouse; Pete the glassblower with Morty; Minnie Mouse painting Clarabelle; Daisy Duck sculpting Donald; Donald Duck as potter; Chip and Dale the watchmakers; Donald Duck the locksmith; Grandma Duck making quilt . . . .
4294/4301 $35 × 8 Mickey Mouse as policeman; Donald Duck as fireman; Uncle Scrooge as ambulance driver; Grandma Duck as crossing patrol; Daisy Duck as museum attendant and Donald as visitor; Goofy as census taker and family of rabbits; Horace Horsecollar and Big Pete as street maintenance workers; Donald Duck as sanitation worker at recycling bin (all vert) . . . .
4302/9 $35 × 8 Mickey Mouse with Pluto driving lorry; Mickey Mouse as carpenter sawing; Goofy riding road drill; Minnie Mouse with electric drill; Donald Duck driving forklift; Minnie Mouse and Goofy as construction contractors; Mickey Mouse with Pluto as carpenter making table; Pluto driving bulldozer (all vert)
4310/17 $35 × 8 Mickey Mouse as plumber; Mickey Mouse the paperboy; Huey, Dewey and Louie moving furniture; Big Pete as handyman; Donald Duck and nephews house painting; Goofy as washing machine repairman; Minnie Mouse as babysitter; Daisy Duck as carer (all vert) . . . .
4267/4317 Set of 51 . . . . 22·00 24·00
MS4318 Six sheets. (a) 132 × 107 mm. $200 Goofy as surgeon. (b) 107 × 129 mm. $200 Goofy the zookeeper. (c) 132 × 107 mm. $200 Ferdie riding Pluto for photographer (vert). (d) 107 × 129 mm. $200 Horace Horsecollar campaigning for mayor. (e) 132 × 107 mm. $200 Minnie Mouse as carpenter and puppies. (f) 107 × 129 mm. $200 Minnie Mouse as maid Set of 6 sheets . . . . 25·00 25·00

No. 4271 is inscribed "PHYSICAL THEREPIST" in error.

1995. Centenary of Salvation Army. Nos. 1519 and 1521/3 surch **SALVATION ARMY 1895 – 1995** and new value.

4319 $6 on 60c. Plate No. 10 (Series 1) . . . .
4320 $20 on 60c. Plate No. 19 (Series 1) . . . .
4321 $30 on 60c. Plate No. 2 (Series 1) . . . .
4322 $35 on 60c. Plate No. 31 (Series 1) . . . .

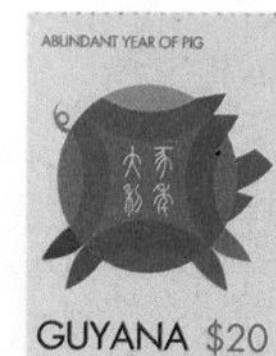

524 Pig

525 Northern Goshawk ("Goshawk")

1995. Chinese New Year ("Year of the Pig"). Symbolic pigs. Multicoloured.

4323 $20 Type **524** 60 55
4324 $30 Pig facing left 65 60

4325 $50 Pig facing front (face value bottom right) . . . 80 80
4326 $100 Pig facing front (face value bottom left) . . . . 1·25 1·40
MS4327 67 × 89 mm. $50 × 4 As Nos. 4323/6 . . . . 3·25 3·25
MS4328 104 × 76 mm. $150 Pig's head . . . . 2·25 2·50

1995. Birds. Multicoloured.
4329 $5 Type **525** 15 10
4330 $6 Northern lapwing ("Lapwing") 15 10
4331 $8 Long-wattled umbrellabird ("Ornate Umbrellabird") 20 10
4332 $15 Slaty-headed parakeet 30 15
4333 $19 Regent bowerbird . . . 35 15
4334 $20 Egyptian goose 35 15
4335 $25 White-winged crossbill 40 20
4336 $30 Bohemian waxwing ("Waxwing") 45 25
4337 $35 Ruff 45 25
4338 $60 Hoopoe 80 40
4339 $100 Superb starling . . . . 1·00 65
4340 $500 Great jacamar . . . . 4·50 4·25

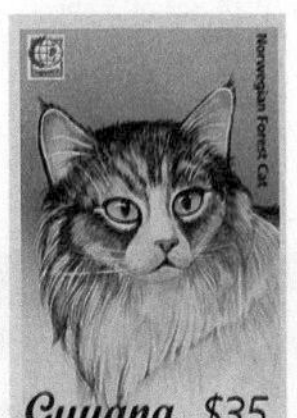

526 Norwegian Forest Cat

1995. "Singapore '95" International Stamp Exhibition. Multicoloured.
4341/52 $35 × 12 Cats (Type **526**; Scottish fold; Red Burmese; British blue-hair; Abyssinian; Siamese; Exotic shorthair; Turkish van cat; Black Persian; Black-tipped burmilla; Singapura; Calico shorthair) . . . . . .
4353/64 $35 × 12 Dogs (Gordon setter; Long-haired chihuahua; Dalmatian; Afghan hound; Old English bulldog; Miniature schnauzer; Clumber spaniel; Pekingese; St. Bernard; English cocker spaniel; Alaskan malamute; Rottweiler) . . . . . .
4365/76 $35 × 12 Horses (chestnut thoroughbred colt; liver chestnut quarter horse; black Friesian; chestnut Belgian; Appaloosa; Lippizaner; chestnut hunter; British shire; Palomino; pinto ("Seal Brown Point"); Arab; Afghanistan kabardin)
4341/76 Set of 36 . . . . 16·00 18·00
MS4377 Three sheets, each 87 × 71 mm. (a) $300 Maine coon. (b) $300 Golden retriever. (c) $300 American anglo-arab Set of 3 sheets . . . . 9·00 9·50
No. 4355 is inscribed "Dalmation", No. 4367 "Freisian" and No. 4370 "Lipizzanas", all in error.

527 Captain John Smith leaving for New World, 1607

1995. "Pocahontas". Characters and scenes from Disney cartoon film. Multicoloured. (a) Vert designs showing characters.
4378/85 $50 × 8 Pocahontas and Meeko; John Smith; Chief Powhatan; Kocoum; Ratcliffe; Wiggins; Nakoma; Thomas . . . .
(b) Horiz designs showing film scenes.
4386/94 $8 × 9 Type **527**; Ratcliffe; Chief Powhatan greeted by his people; Pocahontas standing on cliff; Pocahontas, Nakoma and Meeko in canoe; Powhatan asking Pocahontas to marry Kocoum; Pocahontas receiving her mother's necklace; Pocahontas seeking guidance from Grandmother Willow; Pocahontas watching arrival of "Susan Constant" . .
4395/4403 $30 × 9 Ratcliffe claiming land for English Crown; Kekata having vision; Meeting of John Smith and Pocahontas; Namantack watching settlers; Powhatan and wounded Namantack; Pocahontas showing John Smith the colours of the wind; Nakoma finds Pocahontas with John Smith; Pocahontas offering John "Indian gold" (corn); Pocahontas, John Smith and Grandmother Willow
4404/12 $35 × 9 Kocoum telling Pocahontas about the war council; Nakoma telling Kocoum to find Pocahontas; John Smith and Kocoum wrestling over knife; Powhatan sentencing John to death; Pocahontas and Grandmother Willow; Pocahontas saving John Smith; Ratcliffe under arrest; Powhatan draping his cloak over wounded John Smith; Pocahontas and John Smith saying goodbye . . . . . .
4378/4412 Set of 35 . . . . 30·00 32·00
MS4413 Four sheets. (a) 98 × 120 mm. $300 Meeko. (b) 132 × 107 mm. $325 Pocahontas hiding. (c) 132 × 107 mm. $325 Powhatan and Pocahontas. (d) 132 × 107 mm. $325 Pocahontas kneeling (vert) Set of 4 sheets 26·00 27·00

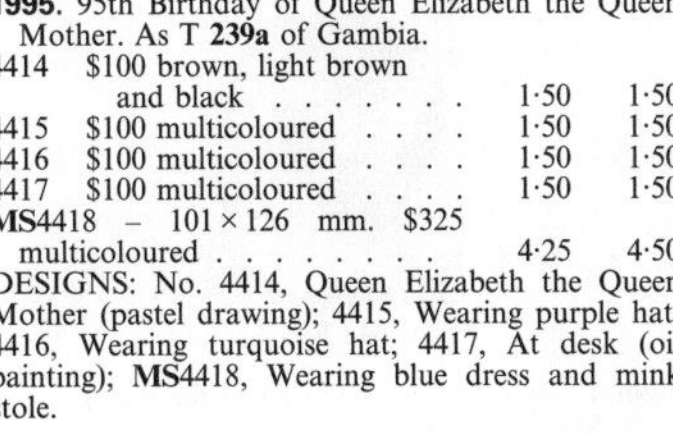

1995. 95th Birthday of Queen Elizabeth the Queen Mother. As T **239a** of Gambia.
4414 $100 brown, light brown and black . . . . 1·50 1·50
4415 $100 multicoloured . . . . 1·50 1·50
4416 $100 multicoloured . . . . 1·50 1·50
4417 $100 multicoloured . . . . 1·50 1·50
MS4418 – 101 × 126 mm. $325 multicoloured . . . . 4·25 4·50
DESIGNS: No. 4414, Queen Elizabeth the Queen Mother (pastel drawing); 4415, Wearing purple hat; 4416, Wearing turquoise hat; 4417, At desk (oil painting); **MS**4418, Wearing blue dress and mink stole.

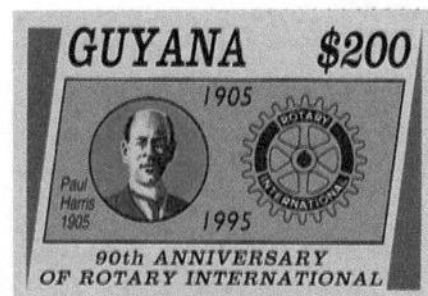

528 Paul Harris (founder) and Rotary Emblem

1995. 90th Anniv of Rotary International. Multicoloured.
4419 **528** $200 multicoloured . . . 2·00 2·50
MS4420 104 × 74 mm. $300 Rotary emblems . . . . 3·00 3·50

529 Girl carrying Sack on Head

1995. 50th Anniv of F.A.O. Multicoloured.
4421 $35 Type **529** 50 65
4422 $60 Man and woman carrying sacks of food aid 80 95
4423 $200 Woman holding sack 2·00 2·40
MS4424 104 × 74 mm. $300 Bowl of food and F.A.O. emblem . . . 3·00 3·50
Nos. 4421/3 were printed together, se-tenant, forming a composite design.

530 Scouts around Campfire

1995. 18th World Scout Jamboree, Netherlands. Multicoloured.
4425 $20 Type **530** 35 25
4426 $25 Scout on beach 40 30
4427 $30 Scouts hiking 45 35
4428 $35 Scout snorkelling . . . 50 40
4429 $60 Scout saluting and flag of Guyana 90 65
4430 $200 Scout fishing from boat . . . . 2·00 2·50
MS4431 Two sheets, each 100 × 70 mm. (a) $300 Scout putting up tent. (b) Scout canoeing Set of 2 sheets . . . . 6·50 7·00

1995. 50th Anniv of End of World War II in Europe. As T **237a** of Gambia. Multicoloured.
4432 $60 American tank during Battle of the Bulge . . . 85 90
4433 $60 Allied tanks crossing Siegfried Line 85 90
4434 $60 Liberated concentration camp prisoners 85 90
4435 $60 Allied plane dropping food to Dutch 85 90
4436 $60 U.S. infantry patrol, North Italy 85 90
4437 $60 "Daily Mail" headline announcing Hitler's death 85 90
4438 $60 Soviet tanks entering Berlin 85 90
4439 $60 Surrender of "U858" in U.S. waters 85 90
MS4440 105 × 74 mm. $300 Soviet troops raising flag on Brandenburg Gate (56 × 42 mm) 3·00 3·25
No. 4433 is incorrectly inscribed "SIGFRIED LINE".

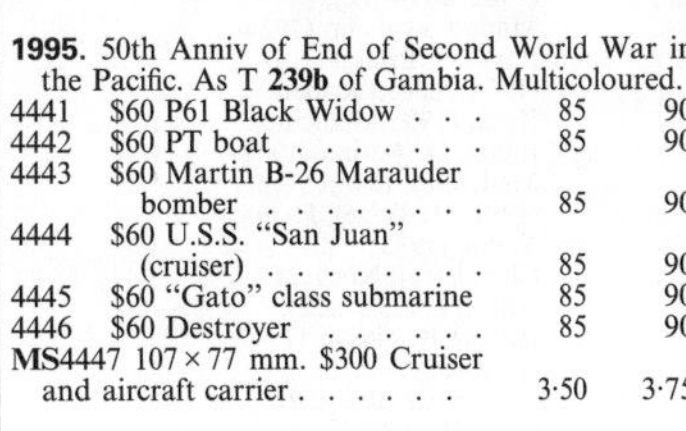

1995. 50th Anniv of End of Second World War in the Pacific. As T **239b** of Gambia. Multicoloured.
4441 $60 P61 Black Widow . . . 85 90
4442 $60 PT boat 85 90
4443 $60 Martin B-26 Marauder bomber 85 90
4444 $60 U.S.S. "San Juan" (cruiser) 85 90
4445 $60 "Gato" class submarine 85 90
4446 $60 Destroyer 85 90
MS4447 107 × 77 mm. $300 Cruiser and aircraft carrier . . . . . . 3·50 3·75

531 Thanksgiving (U.S.A.)

1995. Holidays of the World. Multicoloured.
4448 $60 Type **531** 85 90
4449 $60 Christmas (Germany) 85 90
4450 $60 Hanukkah (Israel) . . . 85 90
4451 $60 Easter (Spain) 85 90
4452 $60 Carnivale (Brazil) . . . 85 90
4453 $60 Bastille Day (France) 85 90
4454 $60 Independence Day (India) 85 90
4455 $60 St. Patrick's Day (Ireland) 85 90
MS4456 105 × 76 mm. $300 Chinese New Year (China) . . . . . . 3·00 3·25

532 Map of the Americas and U.N. Soldier

1995. 50th Anniv of United Nations. Multicoloured.
4457 $35 Type **532** 55 50
4458 $60 Map of Africa and Western Asia 85 75
4459 $200 Map of Eastern Asia and Australasia with refugees . . . . 2·50 3·00
MS4460 74 × 104 mm. $300 Secretary-General Boutros Boutros Ghali . . . . 3·00 3·50
Nos. 4457/9 were printed together, se-tenant, forming a composite design.

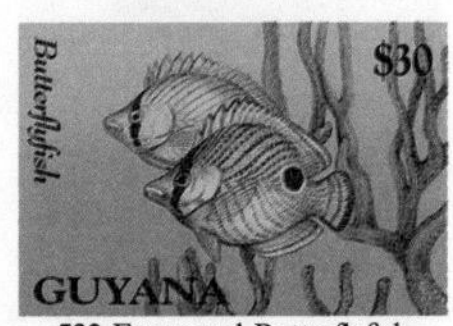

533 Four-eyed Butterflyfish

1995. Marine Life. Multicoloured.
4461 $30 Type **533** 70 75
4462 $30 Lemon shark 70 75
4463 $35 Blue-headed wrasse . . 70 75
4464 $35 Green turtle 70 75
4465 $60 Three-spotted damselfish 70 75
4466 $60 Sawfish 70 75
4467 $60 Sei whales 70 75
4468 $60 Great barracuda 70 75
4469 $60 Mutton snapper 70 75
4470 $60 Hawksbill turtle 70 75
4471 $60 Spanish hogfish 70 75
4472 $60 Queen angelfish 70 75
4473 $60 Porkfish 70 75
4474 $60 Trumpetfish 70 75
4475 $60 Lesser electric ray . . . 70 75
4476 $60 Tiger shark 70 75
4477 $60 Needlefish 70 75
4478 $60 Horse-eyed jack 70 75
4479 $60 Princess parrotfish . . . 70 75
4480 $60 Yellow-tailed snapper 70 75
4481 $60 Spotted snake eel . . . 70 75
4482 $60 Buffalo trunkfish . . . 70 75
4483 $60 Cherubfish angelfish . . 70 75
4484 $60 French angelfish 70 75
4485 $80 Cocoa damselfish (vert) 90 1·00
4486 $80 Sergeant major (vert) 90 1·00
4487 $80 Beaugregory (vert) . . . 90 1·00
4488 $80 Yellow-tailed damselfish (vert) . . . . 90 1·00
4489 $200 Fin-spot wrasse . . . 2·25 2·40
4490 $200 Stingray . . . . 2·25 2·40
MS4491 Two sheets, each 100 × 70 mm. (a) $300 Great white shark. (b) $300 Leatherback turtle Set of 2 sheets . . . . 11·00 11·00
Nos. 4461, 4463, 4465 and 4489; Nos. 4462, 4464, 4466 and 4490; Nos. 4467/75; Nos. 4476/84 and Nos. 4485/8 respectively were printed together, se-tenant, the backgrounds forming composite designs.

534 Pole Vaulting

535 Sand Martin

1995. Olympic Games, Atlanta (1996) (2nd issue). Multicoloured.
4492 $60 Type **534** 90 85
4493 $60 Long jumping 90 85
4494 $60 Woman with relay baton 90 85
4495 $60 Wrestling 90 85
4496 $60 Discus (side view) . . . 90 85
4497 $60 Basketball 90 85
4498 $60 Boxing 90 85
4499 $60 Weightlifting 90 85
4500 $60 Shot put 90 85
4501 $60 Man in relay race . . . 90 85
4502 $60 Female gymnast on beam 90 85
4503 $60 Cycling 90 85
4504 $60 Synchronized swimming 90 85
4505 $60 Hurdling 90 85
4506 $60 Male gymnast on pommel horse 90 85
4507 $60 Discus (front view) . . . 90 85
MS4508 Two sheets. (a) 105 × 75 mm. $300 Athletes at start of race. (b) 75 × 105 mm. $300 Long jumping Set of 2 sheets 6·50 7·00

Nos. 4492/9 and 4500/7 respectively were printed together, se-tenant, the backgrounds forming composite designs.

1995. Wildlife. Multicoloured.

4509 $20 Type **535** 70 70
4510 $35 House martin 70 70
4511 $60 Northern hobby ("Hobby") 75 75
4512 $60 Olive colobus 90 90
4513 $60 Violet-backed starling 90 90
4514 $60 Diana monkey 90 90
4515 $60 African palm civet . . . 90 90
4516 $60 Giraffe and zebras . . . 90 90
4517 $60 African linsang 90 90
4518 $60 Royal antelope 90 90
4519 $60 Duikers 90 90
4520 $60 Palm squirrel 90 90
4521 $200 Long-tailed skua . . . 1·40 1·40
MS4522 Two sheets, each 110 × 80 mm. (a) $300 Brush pig and giant forest hog. (b) $300 Chimpanzee Set of 2 sheets . . 6·50 7·00

Nos. 4509/11 and 4521; and 4512/20 respectively were printed together, se-tenant, forming composite background designs.

536 Queenstown Jama Masjid

1995. Centenary of Queenstown Jama Masjid (mosque), Georgetown.

4523 **536** $60 multicoloured . . . 75 60

537 Woman Soldier with Sub-machine Gun

1995. 30th Anniv of Guyana Defence Force. Multicoloured.

4524 $6 Type **537** 15 10
4525 $60 Soldier with rifle . . . 85 70

538 Bank Logo and Headquarters

1995. 25th Anniv of Caribbean Development Bank.

4526 **538** $60 multicoloured . . . 70 60

1995. Christmas. Religious Paintings. As T **245a** of Gambia. Multicoloured.

4527 $25 "Angel of the Annunciation" (Carracci) 50 30
4528 $30 "Virgin of the Annunciation" (Carracci) 55 35
4529 $35 "Assumption of the Madonna" (Carracci) . . 60 40
4530 $60 "Baptism of Christ" (Carracci) 90 70
4531 $100 "Madonna and Child with Saints" (detail) (Carracci) . . . . 1·60 1·75
4532 $300 "Birth of the Virgin" (Carracci) . . . . 3·75 5·00
MS4533 Two sheets, each 101 × 127 mm. (a) $325 "Madonna and Child enthroned with Ten Saints" (Rosso Fiorentino). (b) $325 "Mystic Marriage of St. Catherine" (Carracci) Set of 2 sheets . . . . 7·00 8·00

539 John Lennon

540 Albrecht Kossel (1910 Medicine)

1995. 15th Death Anniv of John Lennon (musician).

4534 **539** $35 multicoloured . . . 1·00 80

1995. Centenary of Nobel Trust Fund. Multicoloured.

4535/43 $35 × 9 Type **540**; Arthur H. Compton (1927 Physics); N. M. Butler (1931 Peace); Charles Laveran (1907 Medicine); George R. Minot (1934 Medicine); Henry H. Dale (1936 Medicine); Jacques Monod (1965 Medicine); Alfred Hershey (1969 Medicine); Par Lagerkvist (1951 Literature) . . . . . .
4544/52 $35 × 9 Norman F. Ramsey (1989 Physics); Chen Ning Yang (1957 Physics); Earl W. Sutherland Jr. (1971 Medicine); Paul Karrer (1937 Chemistry); Harmut Michel (1988 Chemistry); Richard Kuhn (1938 Chemistry); P. A. M. Dirac (1933 Physics); Victor Grignard (1912 Chemistry); Richard Willstatter (1915 Chemistry) . . . . . .
4553/61 $35 × 9 Adolf von Baeyer (1905 Chemistry); Hideki Yukawa (1949 Physics); George W. Beadle (1958 Medicine); Edwin M. McMillan (1951 Chemistry); Samuel C. C. Ting (1976 Physics); Saint-John Perse (1960 Literature); John F. Enders (1954 Medicine); Felix Bloch (1952 Physics); P. B. Medawar (1960 Medicine) . . . . . .
4562/70 $35 × 9 Nikolai Basov (1964 Physics); Klas Arnoldson (1908 Peace); Rene Sully-Prudhomme (1901 Literature); Robert W. Wilson (1978 Physics); Hugo Theorell (1955 Medicine); Nelly Sachs (1966 Literature); Hans von Euler-Chelpin (1929 Chemistry); Mairead Corrigan (1976 Peace); Willis E. Lamb Jr. (1955 Physics) . . . .
4571/9 $35 × 9 Francis Crick (1962 Medicine); Manne Siegbahn (1924 Physics); Eisaku Sato (1974 Peace); Robert Koch (1905 Medicine); Edgar D. Adrian (1932 Medicine); Erwin Neher (1991 Medicine); Henry Taube (1983 Chemistry); Norman Angell (1933 Peace); Robert Robinson (1947 Chemistry) . . . . . .
4580/8 $35 × 9 Henri Becquerel (1903 Physics); Igor Tamm (1958 Physics); Georges Kohler (1984 Medicine); Gerhard Domagk (1939 Medicine); Yasunari Kawabata (1968 Literature); Maurice Allais (1988 Economic Sciences); Aristide Briand (1926 Peace); Pavel Cherenkov (1958 Physics); Feodor Lynen (1964 Medicine) . . . .
4535/88 Set of 54 . . . . 38·00 40·00
MS4589 Six sheets, each 106 × 76 mm. (a) $300 Lech Walesa (1983 Peace). (b) $300 Heinrich Böll (1972 Literature). (c) $300 Henry A. Kissinger (1973 Peace). (d) $300 Kenichi Fukui (1981 Chemistry). (e) $300 Yasunari Kawabata (1968 Literature). (f) $300 Le Duc Tho (1973 Peace) Set of 6 sheets . . 23·00 24·00

Nos. 4535/43, 4544/52, 4553/61, 4562/70, 4571/9 and 4580/8 respectively were printed together, se-tenant, with the backgrounds forming composite designs.

541 David Copperfield

1995. David Copperfield (magician). Multicoloured.

4590 $60 Type **541** 70 75
4591 $60 David Copperfield in cloak and top hat 70 75
4592 $60 With flaming torch . . 70 75
4593 $60 David Copperfield in close up 70 75
4594 $60 Head of Statue of Liberty 70 75
4595 $60 David Copperfield climbing rope 70 75
4596 $60 With handcuffs 70 75
4597 $60 With woman dancer . . 70 75
4598 $60 David Copperfield wearing white shirt . . . 70 75
MS4599 76 × 106 mm. $300 David Copperfield with rose . . . . 3·00 3·50

Nos. 4590/8 were printed together, se-tenant, forming a composite background design.

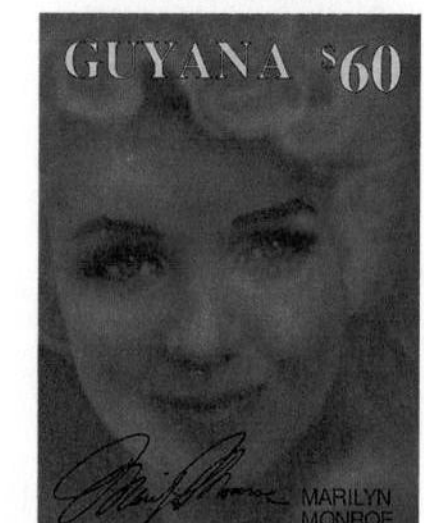

542 Marilyn Monroe

1995. 70th Birth Anniv of Marilyn Monroe (entertainer). Multicoloured.

4600 $60 Type **542** 65 65
4601 $60 Marilyn Monroe with circular earrings 65 65
4602 $60 Marilyn Monroe (red top right corner) 65 65
4603 $60 Marilyn Monroe (signature at bottom right) 65 65
4604 $60 With hair over left eye 65 65
4605 $60 With pink satin at left 65 65
4606 $60 With arm raised 65 65
4607 $60 With pink satin at bottom right 65 65
4608 $60 With square earring . . 65 65
MS4609 76 × 105 mm. $300 Marilyn Monroe in pink satin dress (horiz) 3·00 3·25

Nos. 4600/8 were printed together, se-tenant, with the background forming a composite design.

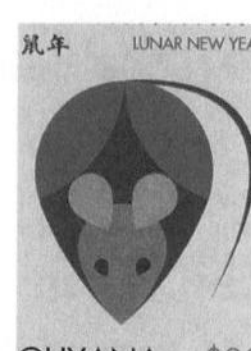

543 Rat

1995. Chinese New Year ("Year of the Rat").

4610 **543** $20 multicoloured . . . 25 20
4611 – $30 multicoloured (face value bottom left) . . 35 30
4612 – $50 multicoloured (face value top right) . . . 65 50
4613 – $100 multicoloured (face value top left) . . . . 1·10 1·25
MS4614 68 × 92 mm. $50 × 4 As Nos. 4610/13 . . . . 2·00 2·25
MS4615 106 × 76 mm. $150 multicoloured . . . . 1·75 2·00

DESIGNS: $30 to $150 Symbolic rats.

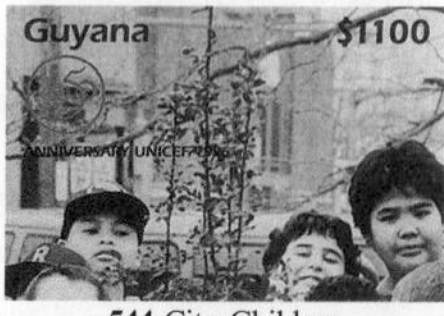

544 City Children

1996. 50th Anniv of UNICEF. Sheet 110 × 87 mm, containing T **544** and similar horiz designs. Multicoloured.

MS4616 $1100 Type **544**; $1100 Youth worker and children (face value at top right); $1100 City children (face value at bottom right; $1100 Youth worker and children (face value at bottom right) . . . . 40·00

1996. Paintings by Rubens. As T **421** of Grenada. Multicoloured.

4617 $6 "The Garden of Love" (detail) 15 10
4618 $10 "Two Sleeping Children" 20 10
4619 $20 "All Saints Day" . . . 35 20
4620 $25 "Sacrifice of Abraham" 35 25
4621 $30 "The Last Supper" . . 40 30
4622 $35 "The Birth of Henry of Navarre" 45 30
4623 $40 Study of standing female saint 50 35
4624 $50 "The Garden of Love" (different detail) 60 45
4625 $60 "The Garden of Love" (different detail) 70 50
4626 $200 "The Martyrdom of St. Livinus" . . . . . . 2·00 2·25
4627 $200 "St. Francis of Paola" 2·00 2·25
4628 $300 "The Union of Maria de Medici and Henry IV" 3·00 3·75
MS4629 Three sheets. (a) 70 × 100 mm. $325 "The Three Crosses" (56 × 84 mm). (b) 100 × 70 mm. $325 "Decius Mus addressing the Legions" (84 × 56 mm). (c) 100 × 70 mm. $325 "Triumph of Henry IV" (84 × 56 mm). P 14 Set of 3 sheets 11·00 12·00

545 Apatosaurus

1996. Prehistoric Animals. Multicoloured.

4630/41 $35 × 12 Type **545**; Archaeopteryx; Dimorphodon; Deinonychus; Coelophysis; Tyrannosaurus; Triceratops; Anatosaurus; Saltasaurus; Allosaurus; Oviraptor; Stegosaurus
4642/53 $35 × 12 Ornithomimus; Pteranodon; Rhamphorynchus; Ornitholestes; Brachiosaurus; Parasaurolophus; Ceratosaurus; Camarasaurus; Euoplocephalus; Scutellosaurus; Compsognathus; Stegoceras . . . . .
4654/65 $35 × 12 Eudimorphodon; Criorhynchus; Elasmosaurus; Rhomaleosaurus; Ceresiosaurus; Mesosaurus; Grendelius; Nothosaurus; Mixosaurus; Placodus; Coelacanth; Mosasaurus . . . . .
4666/77 $35 × 12 Tarbosaurus; Hadrosaurus; Polacanthus; Psittacosaurus; Ornitholestes; Yangchuanosaurus; Scelidosaurus; Kentrosaurus; Coelophysis; Lesothosaurus; Plateosaurus; Staurikosaurus (all vert)
4630/77 Set of 48 . . . . 21·00 22·00
MS4678 Two sheets, each 101 × 58 mm. (a) $60 Saurolophus; $60 Muttaburrasaurus; $60 Dicraeosaurus. (b) $60 Heterodontosaurus; $60 Compsognathus; $60 Ornithomimosaure (all vert) Set of 2 sheets . . . . 4·50 5·50
MS4679 Five sheets. (a) 106 × 76 mm. $300 Struthiomimus. (b) 76 × 106 mm. $300 Tyrannosaurus rex (vert). (c) 76 × 106 mm. $300 Apatosaurus and Allosaurus. (d) 106 × 76 mm. $300 Quetzalcoatlus. (e) 106 × 76 mm. $300 Lagosuchus Set of 5 sheets . . . . 19·00 21·00

Nos. 4630/41, 4642/53, 4654/65 and 4666/77 respectively were printed together, se-tenant, with the backgrounds forming composite designs.

1996. "CHINA 96" International Stamp Exhibition, Beijing. T **546** and similar vert designs. Multicoloured.
MS4680 130 × 95 mm. $60 Summer Palace, Beijing (39 × 51 mm) 1·25 1·40
MS4681 Two sheets, each 146 × 116 mm. (a) $60 Type **546**; $60 Panda holding bamboo stem; $60 Eating bamboo stalk; $60 On all fours. (b) $60 Panda lying on tree branch (logo at left); $60 Lying on branch (logo at right; $60 Exploring hollow in tree (logo at left); $60 Sitting on trunk (logo at right) Set of 2 sheets . . . . 7·00 7·00
The stamps in No. **MS**4681 form composite designs showing rocks and stream (a) or dead tree (b).

546a Deng Xiaoping writing Inscription

1996. Deng Xiaoping (Chinese leader) Commemoration. Multicoloured.
4681c $30 Type **546a** 35 40
4681d $30 Deng Xiaoping addressing meeting (value in red) 35 40
4681e $30 Signing first day cover for army officer (value in yellow) 35 40
4681f $30 Waving 35 40
4681g $30 As No. 4681d (value in yellow) 35 40
4681h $30 As No. 4681e (value in red) 35 40
MS4681i 73 × 101 mm. $300 Deng Xiaoping applauding (vert) . . 3·25 3·50

547 "Morchella esculenta" and "Doryphorella princeps" (leaf beetle)
549 Hulda Gates

1996. Fungi of Guyana. Multicoloured.
4682 $20 Type **547** 55 30
4683 $25 Green-spored mushroom 55 30
4684 $30 Common mushroom and leaf beetle 60 30
4685 $35 Pine cone mushroom and "Danaus plexippus" caterpillar 60 30
4686 $60 "Armillaria mellea" . . 80 80
4687 $60 "Gomphus floccosus" 80 80
4688 $60 "Pholiota astragalina" 80 80
4689 $60 "Helvellaa crispa" . . . 80 80
4690 $60 "Hygrophorus miniatus" 80 80
4691 $60 "Omphalotus olearius" 80 80
4692 $60 "Hygrocybe acutoconica" 80 80
4693 $60 "Mycena viscosa" . . . 80 80
4694 $60 Cockle-shell lentinus . . 80 80
4695 $60 "Volvariella surrecta" 80 80
4696 $60 "Lepiota josserandii" 80 80
4697 $60 "Boletellus betula" . . 80 80
4698 $60 "Amanita muscaria" . . 80 80
4699 $60 "Russula claroflava" and "Semiotus angulatus" (click beetle) 80 80
4700 $60 "Dictyophora duplicata" and "Musca domestica" (house fly) . . 80 80
4701 $60 "Stropharia" and "Editha magnifica" (butterfly hunter) 80 80
4702 $60 "Leotia viscosa" . . . 80 80
4703 $60 "Calostoma cinnabarina" 80 80
4704 $60 Stalkless paxillus . . . 80 80
4705 $60 "Amanita spissa" . . . 80 80
MS4706 Two sheets, each 114 × 84 mm. (a) $300 "Mycena leaiana" and Yellow grosbeak (bird). (b) $300 "Tubifera ferryginosa", "Clavulina amethystina" and "Ramaria formosa" (horiz) Set of 2 sheets 8·00 8·50
Nos. 4686 and 4692 are inscribed "Armillauella mellea" and "Hygzocybe acutoconica", both in error.

1996. 70th Birthday of Queen Elizabeth II. As T **255a** of Gambia. Multicoloured.
4707 $100 Queen Elizabeth II . . 1·40 1·50
4708 $100 Queen wearing green and blue jacket and hat 1·40 1·50
4709 $100 Queen at State Opening of Parliament . . 1·40 1·50
MS4710 103 × 125 mm. $325 Queen in Garter robes . . . . 4·25 4·50

1996. Commonwealth Pharmacy Week. Unissued values in designs of Nos. 1810 and 1873 surch **COMMONWEALTH PHARMACY WEEK JUNE 16th 22nd 1996**.
4711 $6 on 130c. Plate No. 21 (Series 2) . . . .
4712 $60 on 100c. Plate No. 33 (Series 2) . . . .

1996. Centenary of Radio. Entertainers. As T **259a** of Gambia. Multicoloured.
4713 $20 Frank Sinatra 50 30
4714 $35 Gene Autry 50 30
4715 $60 Groucho Marx 60 50
4716 $200 Red Skelton . . . . . 2·00 2·25
MS4717 104 × 74 mm. $300 Burl Ives . . . . 3·50 4·00

1996. 3000th Anniv of Jerusalem. Multicoloured.
4718 $30 Type **549** 80 40
4719 $35 Church of St. Mary Magdalene 80 40
4720 $200 Absalom's Tomb, Kidron Valley . . . . . 2·50 3·00
MS4721 105 × 76 mm. $300 Children's Holocaust Memorial, Yad Vashem . . . . 4·00 4·25

550 Long-billed Starthroat

1996. Birds of the World. Multicoloured.
4722 $60 Type **550** 70 70
4723 $60 Velvet-purple coronet 70 70
4724 $60 Racquet-tailed coquette 70 70
4725 $60 Violet-tailed sylph . . . 70 70
4726 $60 Broad-tailed hummingbird 70 70
4727 $60 Blue-tufted starthroat 70 70
4728 $60 White-necked jacobin 70 70
4729 $60 Ruby-throated hummingbird 70 70
4730 $60 Blue and yellow macaw 70 70
4731 $60 Andean condor 70 70
4732 $60 Guiana crested eagle ("Crested Eagle") 70 70
4733 $60 White-tailed trogon . . 70 70
4734 $60 Toco toucan 70 70
4735 $60 Great horned owl . . . 70 70
4736 $60 Andean cock-of-the-rock 70 70
4737 $60 Great curassow 70 70
MS4738 Two sheets, each 101 × 70 mm. (a) $300 Sparkling violetear ("Gould's Sparkling Violet-ear"). (b) $300 Ornate hawk eagle (horiz) Set of 2 sheets . . . 7·50 8·00
Nos. 4722/9 and 4730/7 respectively were printed together, se-tenant, the backgrounds forming composite designs.

551 Pancratium (ancient Olympic event)

1996. Olympic Games, Atlanta (3rd issue). Multicoloured.
4739 $20 Type **551** 40 30
4740 $30 Olympic Stadium, Melbourne, 1956 . . . 40 30
4741/9 $50 × 9 Volleyball; Basketball; Tennis; Table tennis; Baseball; Handball; Hockey; Water polo; Football
4750/8 $50 × 9 Cycling; Hurdling; High jumping; Diving; Weight- lifting; Canoeing; Wrestling; Gymnastics; Running (all vert) . . . .
4759/67 $50 × 9 Florence Griffith-Joyner (track and field) (U.S.A.); Ines Geissler (swimming) (Germany); Nadia Comaneci (gymnastics) (Rumania); Tatiana Gutsu (gymnastics) (Unified team); Ogla Korbut (gymnastics) (Russia); Barbara Krause (swimming) (Germany); Olga Bryzgina (track and field) (Russia); Fanny Blankers-Koen (track and field) (Holland); Irena Szewinska (track and field) (Poland) (all vert) . . . .
4768/76 $50 × 9 Gerd Wessig (Germany); Jim Thorpe (U.S.A.); Norman Read (New Zealand); Lasse Viren (Finland); Milt Campbell (U.S.A.); Abebe Bikila (Ethiopia); Jesse Owens (U.S.A.); Viktor Saneev (Russia); Waldemer Cierpinski (Germany) (all track and field) (all vert) . . . .
4777/85 $50 × 9 Ditmar Schmidt (handball) (Germany); Pam Shriver (tennis doubles) (U.S.A.); Zina Garrison (tennis doubles) (U.S.A); Hyun Jung-Hua (table tennis doubles) (Korea); Steffi Graf (tennis) (Germany); Michael Jordan (basketball) (U.S.A.); Karch Kiraly (volleyball) (U.S.A.); "Magic" Johnson (basketball) (U.S.A.); Ingolf Weigert (handball) (Germany) (all vert) . . . .
4786 $60 Leonid Spirin winning 20 kilometre walk, 1956 (vert) . . . 60 60
4787 $200 Lars Hall, Gold medal winner, Modern Pentathalon, 1952 and 1956 (Sweden) (vert) . . 1·75 2·00
4739/87 Set of 49 . . . . 25·00 27·00
MS4788 Two sheets. (a) 104 × 74 mm. $300 Carl Lewis, Gold medal winner, track and field, 1984, 1988 and 1992 (U.S.A.). (b) 74 × 104 mm. $300 U.S.A. defeating Korea at baseball, 1988 Set of 2 sheets 6·50 7·50
Nos. 4741/9, 4750/8, 4759/67, 4768/76 and 4777/85 (the last three showing Gold medal winners) respectively were printed together, se-tenant, forming composite background designs.
No. **MS**4788a is inscribed "1985" in error.

552 Mickey's Bait Shop

1996. Mickey Mouse and Friends Outdoors. Multicoloured.
4789 $60 Type **552** . . . . . . 1·00 1·00
4790 $60 Mickey and Pluto as lumberjacks . . . . . . 1·00 1·00
4791 $60 Mickey fishing . . . . 1·00 1·00
4792 $80 Donald Duck in BMX bike championships (vert) 1·25 1·25
4793 $80 Goofy as ice hockey superstar (vert) . . . . . 1·25 1·25
4794 $80 Donald Duck at Malibu Surf City (vert) . . . . . 1·25 1·25
4795 $100 Mickey as naval captain (vert) . . . . . . 1·40 1·40
4796 $100 Captain Mickey's Seamanship School (vert) 1·40 1·40
4797 $100 Mickey as sailor with ship's wheel and full-rigged sailing ship (vert) 1·40 1·40
MS4798 Five sheets. (a) 124 × 101 mm. $250 Mickey as Pinkerton detective (vert). (b) 104 × 126 mm. $250 Mickey as U.S. Marshal (vert). (c) 125 × 104 mm. $250 Mickey as train conductor and Transcontinental Railroad locomotive. (d) 101 × 124 mm. $300 Donald Duck as mountaineer. (e) 104 × 124 mm. $325 Mickey as trapper (vert) Set of 5 sheets . . . . 21·00 22·00

553 Two Gun Mickey

1996. Disney Antique Toys. Multicoloured.
4799 $6 Type **553** 50 50
4800 $6 Wood-jointed Mickey figure 50 50
4801 $6 Donald jack-in-the-box 50 50
4802 $6 Rocking Minnie 50 50
4803 $6 Fireman Donald Duck 50 50
4804 $6 Long-billed Donald Duck 50 50
4805 $6 Painted-wood Mickey figure 50 50
4806 $6 Wind-up Jiminy Cricket 50 50
MS4807 Two sheets, each 131 × 105 mm. (a) $300 Mickey doll. (b) $300 Carousel Set of 2 sheets . . . . 10·00 10·00

554 Elvis Presley

1996. 60th Birth Anniv (1995) of Elvis Presley. Multicoloured, background colours given.
4808 **554** $100 red . . . . 1·40 1·25
4809 – $100 mauve . . . . . . 1·40 1·25
4810 – $100 brown . . . . . . 1·40 1·25
4811 – $100 blue . . . . 1·40 1·25
4812 – $100 purple . . . . . . 1·40 1·25
4813 – $100 blue . . . . 1·40 1·25
DESIGNS: Nos. 4809/13, Various portraits.

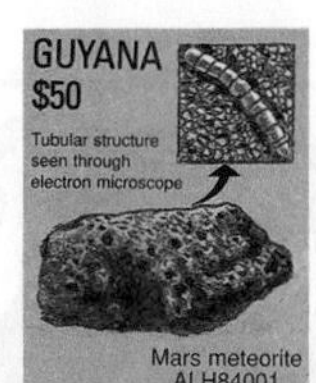

555 Piece of Meteorite showing Fossil

1996. Mars Meteorite. Sheet 104 × 76 mm.
MS4814 **555** $50 multicoloured 2·00 1·75

556 Birman

1996. Cats of the World. Multicoloured.
4815 $60 Type **556** 70 70
4816 $60 American curl 70 70
4817 $60 Turkish angora 70 70
4818 $60 European shorthair (Italy) 70 70
4819 $60 Persian (Great Britain) 70 70
4820 $60 Scottish fold 70 70
4821 $60 Sphynx (Canada) . . . 70 70
4822 $60 Malayan (Thailand) . . 70 70
4823 $60 Cornish rex (Great Britain) 70 70
4824 $60 Norwegian forest (vert) 70 70
4825 $60 Russian shorthair (vert) 70 70
4826 $60 European shorthair (Italy) (vert) 70 70
4827 $60 Birman (vert) 70 70
4828 $60 Ragdoll (U.S.A.) (vert) 70 70
4829 $60 Egyptian mau (vert) . . 70 70
4830 $60 Persian (Great Britain) (vert) 70 70
4831 $60 Turkish angora (vert) 70 70
4832 $60 Siamese (vert) 70 70
MS4833 Two sheets, each 107 × 72 mm. (a) $300 Himalayan (U.S.A.). (b) $300 Maine coon (U.S.A.) (vert) Set of 2 sheets 7·00 8·00
Nos. 4815/23 and 4824/32 respectively were printed together, se-tenant, with the backgrounds forming composite designs.

557 Hyed Snapper

1996. Marine Life. Multicoloured.
4834 $6 Type **557** 15 15
4835 $6 Angelfish 15 15
4836 $20 Boxfish 30 20
4837 $25 Golden damselfish . . . 30 25
4838 $30 Goblin shark and coelacanth 35 35
4839 $30 "Jason" (American remote-controlled submersible) 35 35
4840 $30 Deep-water invertebrates 35 35
4841 $30 Submarine NR-1 . . . 35 35
4842 $30 Giant squid 35 35
4843 $30 Sperm whale 35 35
4844 $30 Volcanic vents and "Alvin" (submersible) . . 35 35
4845 $30 Air-recycling pressure suits and shipwreck . . . 35 35
4846 $30 "Shinkai" 6500 (submersible) 35 35
4847 $30 Giant tube worms . . . 35 35
4848 $30 Anglerfish 35 35
4849 $30 Six-gill shark 35 35
4850 $30 Autonomous underwater vehicle ABE 35 35
4851 $30 Octopus and viperfish 35 35
4852 $30 Swallower and hatchetfish 35 35
4853 $35 Clown triggerfish . . . 35 30
4854 $60 Red gorgonians 65 65
4855 $60 Soft coral and butterflyfish 65 65
4856 $60 Soft coral and slender snapper 65 65
4857 $60 Common clownfish, anemone and mushroom coral 65 65
4858 $60 Anemone and horse-eyed jack 65 65
4859 $60 Splendid coral trout . . 65 65
4860 $60 Anemones 65 65
4861 $60 Brain coral 65 65
4862 $60 Cup coral 65 65
4863 $200 Harlequin tuskfish . . 2·25 2·50
MS4864 Two sheets, each 98 × 68 mm. (a) $300 Caribbean flower coral. (b) $300 Sea anemone Set of 2 sheets . . . . 6·50 7·50

Nos. 4838/52 and 4854/62 respectively were printed together, se-tenant, with the backgrounds forming composite designs.

No. 4853 is inscribed "CLOWN TUGGERFISH" in error.

558 Snow White and Reindeer

1996. Christmas. Disney's "Snow White and the Seven Dwarfs". Multicoloured.
4865 $6 Type **558** 30 10
4866 $20 Doc with presents . . . 80 25
4867 $25 Dopey and Sneezy . . . 80 30
4868 $30 Sleepy, Happy and Bashful 80 35
4869 $35 Dopey and Santa Claus 80 40
4870 $60 Dopey with socks at fireplace . . . . 1·50 1·00
4871 $100 Dopey and Grumpy 2·50 2·50
4872 $200 Dopey dressed as Santa Claus . . . . . . 3·75 4·50
MS4873 Two sheets, each 122 × 102 mm. (a) $300 Snow White, Doc and squirrel. (b) $300 Dopey and Christmas tree Set of 2 sheets . . . . 12·00 12·00

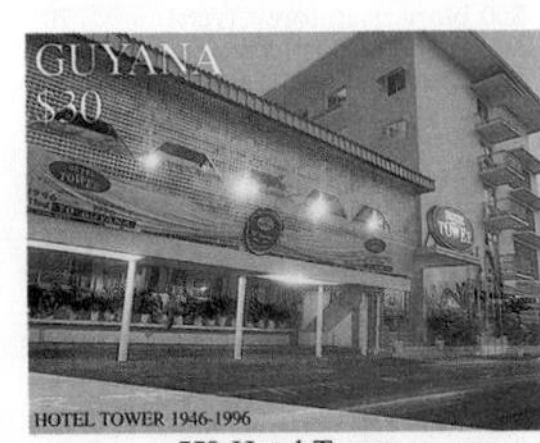

559 Hotel Tower

1996. 50th Anniv of Hotel Tower, Georgetown.
4874 **559** $30 multicoloured . . . 70 40

561 Ox

1997. Chinese New Year. "Year of the Ox".
4882 **561** $20 multicoloured . . . 35 25
4883 – $30 multicoloured . . . 50 40
4884 – $35 multicoloured . . . 55 50
4885 – $50 multicoloured . . . 75 80
MS4886 101 × 72 mm. $150 multicoloured . . . . 2·00 2·25
MS4887 68 × 90 mm. $50 As No. 4882 (value bottom right); $50 As No. 4883 (value bottom left); $50 As No. 4884 (value top right); $50 As No. 4885 (value top left) 2·00 2·25

DESIGNS: Nos. 4883/7 depict symbolic oxen.

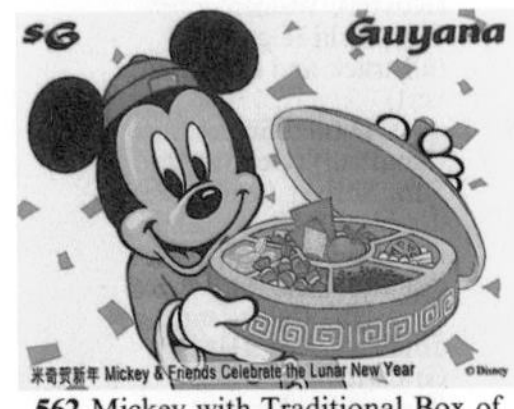

562 Mickey with Traditional Box of Sweets

1997. Mickey Mouse and Friends celebrate Chinese New Year. Multicoloured.
4888 $6 Type **562** 40 25
4889 $20 Mickey and Minnie at home with friends 50 35
4890 $25 Mickey and Minnie hanging fortune lantern 50 35
4891 $30 Minnie and Daisy with paper silhouette 55 55
4892 $30 Mickey and friends receiving traditional red money 55 55
4893 $30 Mickey in lion dance . . 55 55
4894 $30 Mickey preparing Chinese calligraphy wall hangings 55 55
4895 $30 Mickey with symbols of surplus 55 55
4896 $30 Donald Duck playing with fireworks 55 55
4897 $30 Donald, Mickey and Minnie on ox 55 55
4898 $35 Donald Duck and friends at New Year flower market 55 55
4899 $60 Mickey and Minnie as "harmonious man and woman" 90 90
MS4900 Two sheets, each 133 × 109 mm. (a) $150 Mickey Mouse marching (vert). (b) $200 Mickey and ox Set of 2 sheets 6·50 6·50

563 Burgess Meredith as Ernie Pyle in "The Story of G.I. Joe"

1997. Centenary of Cinema. Second World War Films. Multicoloured.
4901 $50 Type **563** 70 70
4902 $50 M. E. Clifton-James as General Montgomery in "I was Monty's Double" 70 70
4903 $50 Audie Murphy as himself in "To Hell and Back" 70 70
4904 $50 Gary Cooper as Dr. Wassell in "The Story of Dr. Wassell" 70 70
4905 $50 James Mason as Erwin Rommel in "The Desert Fox" 70 70
4906 $50 Manart Kippen as Stalin in "Mission to Moscow" 70 70
4907 $50 Robert Taylor as Col. Paul Tibbets in "Above and Beyond" 70 70
4908 $50 James Cagney as Admiral Bill Halsey in "The Gallant Hours" . . 70 70
4909 $50 John Garfield as Al Schmid in "Pride of the Marines" 70 70
MS4910 105 × 75 mm. $300 George C. Scott as Gen. George S. Patton in "Patton" (horiz) . . . . . 5·50 6·00

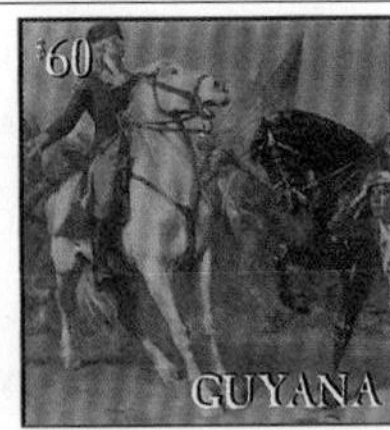

564 "Washington in Battle"

1997. Bicentenary of George Washington's Retirement from U.S. Presidency. Multicoloured.
4911 $60 Type **564** 60 60
4912 $60 "Washington taking Presidential Oath" 60 60
4913 $60 "Washington seated in Armchair" (engraving after Chappel) 60 60
4914 $60 "Col. Washington of the Virginia Militia" (Charles W. Peale) . . . 60 60
4915 $60 "George Washington" (Rembrandt Peale) . . . 60 60
4916 $60 "Washington addressing Constitutional Convention" (Junius B. Stearns) 60 60
4917 $60 "Washington on his way to Continental Congress" 60 60
4918 $60 "Washington on a White Charger" (John Faed) 60 60
4919 $60 "Washington surveying" (engraving by G. R. Hall) 60 60
4920 $60 "Washington praying at Valley Forge" (bas-relief) 60 60
4921 $60 "Death of Gen. Mercer at Battle of Princeton" (John Trumbull) 60 60
4922 $60 "Washington taking Command at Cambridge" 60 60
4923 $60 "Washington before Battle of Trenton" (John Trumbull) 60 60
4924 $60 "Washington and his Family at Mount Vernon" (Alonzo Chappel) 60 60
4925 $60 "Washington's Inauguration" (Chappel) 60 60
4926 $60 "Washington" (Adolph Ulrich Wertmuller) . . . 60 60
4927 $60 "Washington accepts Commission as Commander- in-Chief" (Currier & Ives lithograph) 60 60
4928 $60 "Washington" (mezzotint by Sartain) . . 60 60
4929 $60 "Mount Vernon" . . . 60 60
4930 $60 "Washington with Farm Workers" (print by Junius B. Stearns) 60 60
4931 $60 "Wedding of Nellie Custis" (Ogden) 60 60
4932 $60 "Washington crossing the Delaware" (Leutze) 60 60
4933 $60 "Washington and Gen. Braddock" 60 60
4934 $60 "Washington's Birthplace" (Currier & Ives lithograph) 60 60
4935 $300 "George Washington" (Gilbert Stuart) (66 × 91 mm) . . . . . . 2·50 3·00
4936 $300 "Washington at Yorktown" (James Peale) (66 × 91 mm) . . . . . . 2·50 3·00

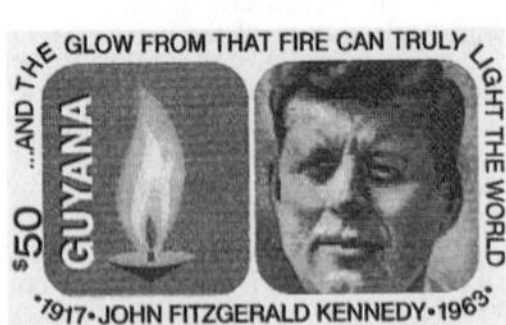

565 Pres. Kennedy and "Eternal Flame"

1997. 80th Birth Anniv of Pres. John F. Kennedy.
4937 **565** $50 violet . . . . 1·00 1·00

No. 4937 is in the same design as the U.S.A. Memorial Issue of 1964.

1997. 50th Anniv of UNESCO. Multicoloured. As T **273a** of Gambia.
4938 $20 Hall at Horyu-ji, Japan 20 20
4939 $25 Coastline, Scandola Nature Reserve, France 25 25
4940 $30 Great Wall turret, China 30 30
4941 $35 Bedroom in the Residenz, Wurzburg, Germany 35 30
4942 $60 Monastery of Batalha, Portugal 60 60
4943 $60 Cathedral of Aquisgran, Aachen, Germany (vert) 60 60
4944 $60 Trier Cathedral, Germany (vert) 60 60
4945 $60 Column of Augusta Treveror, Trier (vert) . . 60 60
4946 $60 The Residenz and garden, Wurzburg (vert) 60 60
4947 $60 Interior of church, Wurzburg (vert) 60 60
4948 $60 The Residenz and lake, Wurzburg (vert) 60 60
4949 $60 Riverside houses, Inselstadt, Bamberg, Germany (vert) 60 60

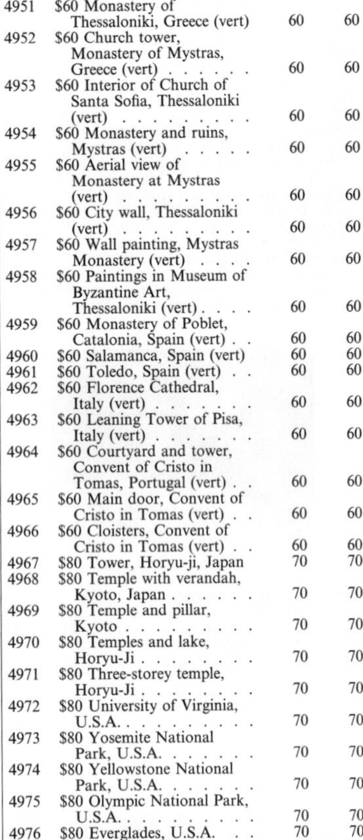
4950 $60 Cathedral interior, Speyer, Germany (vert) 60 60
4951 $60 Monastery of Thessaloniki, Greece (vert) 60 60
4952 $60 Church tower, Monastery of Mystras, Greece (vert) 60 60
4953 $60 Interior of Church of Santa Sofia, Thessaloniki (vert) 60 60
4954 $60 Monastery and ruins, Mystras (vert) 60 60
4955 $60 Aerial view of Monastery at Mystras (vert) 60 60
4956 $60 City wall, Thessaloniki (vert) 60 60
4957 $60 Wall painting, Mystras Monastery (vert) 60 60
4958 $60 Paintings in Museum of Byzantine Art, Thessaloniki (vert) 60 60
4959 $60 Monastery of Poblet, Catalonia, Spain (vert) . . 60 60
4960 $60 Salamanca, Spain (vert) 60 60
4961 $60 Toledo, Spain (vert) . . 60 60
4962 $60 Florence Cathedral, Italy (vert) 60 60
4963 $60 Leaning Tower of Pisa, Italy (vert) 60 60
4964 $60 Courtyard and tower, Convent of Cristo in Tomas, Portugal (vert) . . 60 60
4965 $60 Main door, Convent of Cristo in Tomas (vert) . . 60 60
4966 $60 Cloisters, Convent of Cristo in Tomas (vert) . . 60 60
4967 $80 Tower, Horyu-ji, Japan 70 70
4968 $80 Temple with verandah, Kyoto, Japan 70 70
4969 $80 Temple and pillar, Kyoto 70 70
4970 $80 Temples and lake, Horyu-Ji 70 70
4971 $80 Three-storey temple, Horyu-Ji 70 70
4972 $80 University of Virginia, U.S.A. 70 70
4973 $80 Yosemite National Park, U.S.A. 70 70
4974 $80 Yellowstone National Park, U.S.A. 70 70
4975 $80 Olympic National Park, U.S.A. 70 70
4976 $80 Everglades, U.S.A. . . 70 70
4977 $80 Street, Cuzco, Peru . . 70 70
4978 $80 Potosi, Bolivia 70 70
4979 $80 Fortress of San Lorenzo, Panama 70 70
4980 $80 Sangay National Park, Ecuador 70 70
4981 $80 Los Glaciares National Park, Argentina 70 70
4982 $200 City walls, Dubrovnik, Croatia . . . . 1·75 2·00
MS4983 Four sheets, each 126 × 101 mm. (a) $300 Golden Buddha, Mount Taishan, China. (b) $300 Monastery garden, Batalha, Portugal. (c) $300 Virgin and Child (statue), Bamberg Cathedral, Germany. (d) $300 Monastery, Mount Athos, Greece Set of 4 sheets . . . . 11·00 12·00

566 "Morchella hortensis"

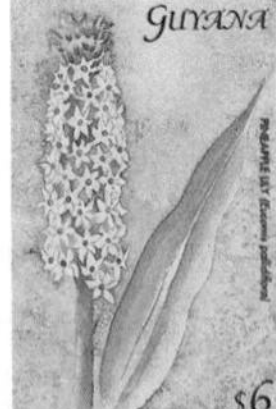

567 Pineapple Lily

1997. Fungi of the World. Multicoloured.
4984 $6 Type **566** 20 15
4985 $20 "Boletus chrysenteron" 25 20
4986 $25 "Hygrophorus agathosmus" 30 25
4987 $30 "Cortinarius violaceus" 35 30
4988 $35 "Acanthocystis geogenius" 40 30
4989 $60 "Mycena polygramma" 65 50
4990 $80 "Coprinus picaceus" . . 75 75
4991 $80 "Stropharia umbonatescens" 75 75
4992 $80 "Paxillus involutus" . . 75 75
4993 $80 "Amanita inaurata" . . 75 75
4994 $80 "Lepiota rhacodes" . . 75 75
4995 $80 "Russula amoena" . . 75 75
4996 $80 "Volvaria volvacea" . . 75 75
4997 $80 "Psalliota augusta" . . 75 75
4998 $80 "Tricholoma aurantium" 75 75
4999 $80 "Pholiota spectabilis" . . 75 75
5000 $80 "Cortinarius armillatus" 75 75
5001 $80 "Agrocybe dura" . . . 75 75
5002 $200 "Hebeloma radicosum" 1·75 2·00
5003 $300 "Coprinus comatus" 2·75 3·00
MS5004 Two sheets, each 76 × 105 mm. (a) $300 "Pholiota mutabilis". (b) $300 "Amanita muscaria" Set of 2 sheets . . . 6·50 7·00

1997. Flowers. Multicoloured.
5005 $6 Type **567** 15 15
5006 $6 Blue columbine 15 15
5007 $20 Petunia 20 20
5008 $25 Lily of the Nile 25 25
5009 $30 Bird of paradise 30 30
5010 $35 African daisy 35 30

5011 $60 Cape daisy 60 60
5012 $60 Monarch slipperwort . . 60 60
5013 $60 Passion flower 60 60
5014 $60 Butterfly iris 60 60
5015 $60 Red-hot poker 60 60
5016 $60 Water lily "Dir G. T. Moore" 60 60
5017 $60 Painted tongue "Superbissima" 60 60
5018 $60 Canariensis orchid . . . 60 60
5019 $60 Annual chrysanthemum 60 60
5020 $80 Tulips 70 70
5021 $80 Liatris 70 70
5022 $80 Roses 70 70
5023 $80 Gerber daisies 70 70
5024 $80 Sunflowers 70 70
5025 $80 Chrysanthemums . . . 70 70
5026 $80 Gazania 70 70
5027 $80 Cape water lily 70 70
5028 $200 Insigne lady's slipper 1·75 2·25
MS5029 105 × 75 mm. $300 Petunias 3·00 3·50

568 Deng Xiaoping inspecting Rural Sichuan, 1980

1997. Deng Xiaoping (Chinese leader) Commem.
5030 **568** $100 multicoloured . . . 1·00 1·00
MS5031 100 × 70 mm. $150 Deng Xiaoping on visit to foundry 1·50 1·60

1997. 10th Anniv of Chernobyl Nuclear Disaster. As T **276a** of Gambia. Multicoloured.
5032 $200 As Type **276a** of Gambia . . . . 1·75 2·00
5033 $200 As Type **276a** of Gambia, but inscribed "CHABAD'S CHILDREN OF CHERNOBYL" at foot 1·75 2·00

1997. 50th Death Anniv of Paul Harris (founder of Rotary International). As T **276b** of Gambia. Mult.
5034 $200 Paul Harris and volunteers with children ("Health, hunger and humanity") . . . . 1·75 2·00
MS5035 77 × 107 mm. $300 Group of boys ("Mutual respect among all faiths, races and cultures") 2·50 3·00

1997. Golden Wedding of Queen Elizabeth II and Prince Philip. As T **276c** of Gambia. Multicoloured (except Nos. 5038/9).
5036 $60 Queen Elizabeth II wearing tiara 90 90
5037 $60 Royal coat of arms . . 90 90
5038 $60 Wedding photograph, 1947 (black) 90 90
5039 $60 Engagement photograph (black) 90 90
5040 $60 Broadlands, Romsey (honeymoon residence) . . 90 90
5041 $60 Duke of Edinburgh . . 90 90
MS5042 99 × 70 mm. $300 Queen and Duke of Edinburgh . . . 4·00 4·25

1997. "Pacific '97" International Stamp Exhibition, San Francisco. Death Centenary of Heinrich von Stephan (founder of U.P.U.). As T **276d** of Gambia.
5043 $100 sepia . . . . 1·00 1·25
5044 $100 brown . . . . 1·00 1·25
5045 $100 green . . . . 1·00 1·25
MS5046 82 × 118 mm. $300 black and blue . . . . 2·75 3·00
DESIGNS: No. 5043, Roman post cart from frieze; 5044, Von Stephan and Mercury; 5045, Cable car, Boston, 1907; **MS**5046, Von Stephan and ancient Egyptian messenger.

1997. 175th Anniv of Brothers Grimm's Third Collection of Fairy Tales. Hansel and Gretel. As T **277a** of Gambia. Multicoloured.
5047 $100 Hansel and Gretel lost in forest . . . . 1·40 1·40
5048 $100 Gingerbread house . . 1·40 1·40
5049 $100 Witch . . . . 1·40 1·40
MS5050 124 × 96 mm. $500 Gretel pushing witch into oven (horiz) 6·00 6·50

1997. 300th Anniv of Mother Goose Nursery Rhymes. Multicoloured design as T **276a** of Gambia. Sheet 75 × 101 mm.
MS5051 $300 "Cock-a-doodle-doo" (vert) . . . . 3·75 4·00

1997. Birth Bicentenary of Hiroshige (Japanese painter). "One Hundred Famous Views of Edo". As T **541a** of Ghana. Multicoloured.
5052 $80 "Oumayagashi" . . . . 1·00 1·00
5053 $80 "Ryogoku Ekoin and Moto-Yanagibashi Bridge" . . . . 1·00 1·00
5054 $80 "Pine of Success and Oumayagashi, Asakusa River" . . . . 1·00 1·00
5055 $80 "Fireworks at Ryogoku" . . . . 1·00 1·00
5056 $80 "Dyers' Quarter, Kanda" . . . . 1·00 1·00
5057 $80 "Cotton-goods Lane, Odenma-cho" . . . . . 1·00 1·00
MS5058 Two sheets, each 102 × 127 mm. (a) $300 "Suruga-cho". (b) $300 "Yatsukoji, inside Sujikai Gate" Set of 2 sheets 7·00 8·00

569 Tortoise

1997. "Hong Kong '97" International Stamp Exhibition. Return of Hong Kong to China. Mult.
5059 $80 Type **569** 80 80
5060 $80 Dragon 80 80
5061 $80 Unicorn 80 80
5062 $80 Phoenix 80 80
5063 $80 Barn swallow ("Swallow") and willow (vert) 80 80
5064 $80 River kingfisher ("Kingfisher") and chrysanthemum (vert) . . 80 80
5065 $80 Common crane ("Crane") and pine (vert) 80 80
5066 $80 Common peafowl ("Peacock") and peony (vert) 80 80
5067 $80 "Bird of Paradise" kite with two tail feathers (vert) 80 80
5068 $80 Large "eyed" kite with blue tail ribbons (vert) . . 80 80
5069 $80 "Phoenix" kite with "flaming" tail (vert) . . . 80 80
5070 $80 "Insect" kite with red tail ribbons (vert) 80 80
5071 $200 Chinese landscape (face value at top left) (50 × 75 mm) . . . . . . 2·00 2·25
5072 $200 Chinese landscape (face value at bottom right) (50 × 75 mm) . . . . . . 2·00 2·25
MS5073 159 × 110 mm. $500 Junk in Hong Kong harbour (50 × 75 mm) 5·00 5·50

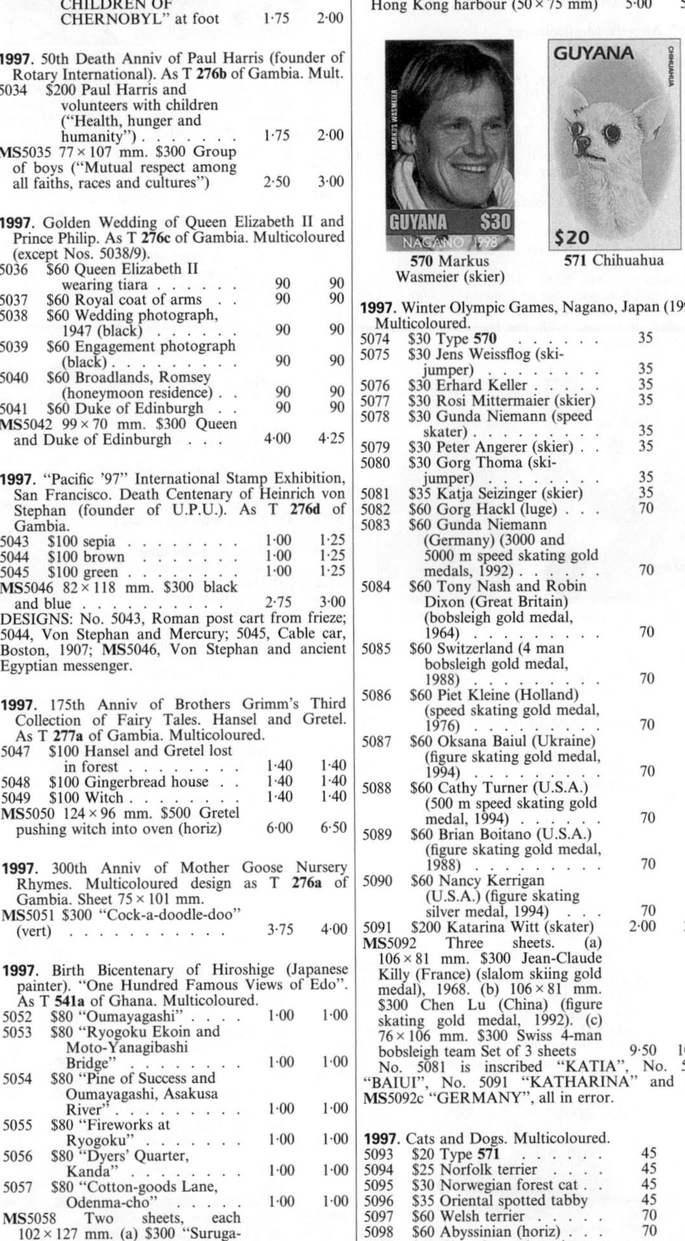

570 Markus Wasmeier (skier) **571** Chihuahua

1997. Winter Olympic Games, Nagano, Japan (1998). Multicoloured.
5074 $30 Type **570** 35 35
5075 $30 Jens Weissflog (ski-jumper) 35 35
5076 $30 Erhard Keller 35 35
5077 $30 Rosi Mittermaier (skier) 35 35
5078 $30 Gunda Niemann (speed skater) 35 35
5079 $30 Peter Angerer (skier) . . 35 35
5080 $30 Gorg Thoma (ski-jumper) 35 35
5081 $35 Katja Seizinger (skier) 35 35
5082 $60 Gorg Hackl (luge) . . . 70 70
5083 $60 Gunda Niemann (Germany) (3000 and 5000 m speed skating gold medals, 1992) 70 70
5084 $60 Tony Nash and Robin Dixon (Great Britain) (bobsleigh gold medal, 1964) 70 70
5085 $60 Switzerland (4 man bobsleigh gold medal, 1988) 70 70
5086 $60 Piet Kleine (Holland) (speed skating gold medal, 1976) 70 70
5087 $60 Oksana Baiul (Ukraine) (figure skating gold medal, 1994) 70 70
5088 $60 Cathy Turner (U.S.A.) (500 m speed skating gold medal, 1994) 70 70
5089 $60 Brian Boitano (U.S.A.) (figure skating gold medal, 1988) 70 70
5090 $60 Nancy Kerrigan (U.S.A.) (figure skating silver medal, 1994) . . . 70 70
5091 $200 Katarina Witt (skater) 2·00 2·25
MS5092 Three sheets. (a) 106 × 81 mm. $300 Jean-Claude Killy (France) (slalom skiing gold medal), 1968. (b) 106 × 81 mm. $300 Chen Lu (China) (figure skating gold medal, 1992). (c) 76 × 106 mm. $300 Swiss 4-man bobsleigh team Set of 3 sheets 9·50 10·00
No. 5081 is inscribed "KATIA", No. 5087 "BAIUI", No. 5091 "KATHARINA" and No. **MS**5092c "GERMANY", all in error.

1997. Cats and Dogs. Multicoloured.
5093 $20 Type **571** 45 25
5094 $25 Norfolk terrier 45 25
5095 $30 Norwegian forest cat . . 45 30
5096 $35 Oriental spotted tabby 45 30
5097 $60 Welsh terrier 70 70
5098 $60 Abyssinian (horiz) . . . 70 70
5099 $60 Chocolate colorpoint shorthair (horiz) 70 70
5100 $60 Silver tabby (horiz) . . 70 70
5101 $60 Persian (horiz) 70 70
5102 $60 Maine coon cat and kitten (horiz) 70 70
5103 $60 Brown-shaded Burmese (horiz) 70 70
5104 $60 Persian kitten (horiz) . . 70 70
5105 $60 Siamese (horiz) 70 70
5106 $60 British shorthair (horiz) 70 70
5107 $60 Shar-pei 70 70
5108 $60 Chihuahua 70 70
5109 $60 Chow chow 70 70
5110 $60 Sealyham terrier 70 70
5111 $60 Collie 70 70
5112 $60 German shorthair pointer 70 70
5113 $60 Bulldog 70 70
5114 $60 German shepherd dog 70 70
5115 $60 Old English sheepdog 70 70
5116 $200 Asian smoke (cat) . . 2·00 2·25
MS5117 Two sheets, each 105 × 76 mm. (a) $300 Manx cat. (b) $300 Tibetan spaniel Set of 2 sheets . . . . 8·00 8·00

572 Verdin

1997. Birds of the World. Multicoloured.
5118 $25 Type **572** 50 30
5119 $30 Wood thrush (vert) . . 50 30
5120 $60 Rufous-sided towhee . . 75 50
5121 $80 Groove-billed ani . . . 90 90
5122 $80 Green honeycreeper . . 90 90
5123 $80 Emerald toucanet . . . 90 90
5124 $80 Wire-tailed manakin . . 90 90
5125 $80 Hoatzin 90 90
5126 $80 Rufescent tiger heron ("Tiger Heron") 90 90
5127 $80 Magenta-throated woodstar 90 90
5128 $80 Anna's hummingbird 90 90
5129 $80 Long-tailed hermit . . . 90 90
5130 $80 White-tipped sicklebill 90 90
5131 $80 Red-footed plumeleteer 90 90
5132 $80 Fiery-throated hummingbird 90 90
5133 $200 Pygmy nuthatch (vert) 2·00 2·25
MS5134 Two sheets, each 70 × 100 mm. (a) $300 Pinnated bittern. (b) $300 Keel-billed toucan Set of 2 sheets . . . . 8·00 8·00

573 Pres. Cheddi Jagan in 1947 and 1997 with National Assembly Building

1997. 50th Anniv of Pres. Cheddi Jagan's Election to Parliament.
5135 **573** $6 multicoloured 15 15
5136 $30 multicoloured . . . 50 50

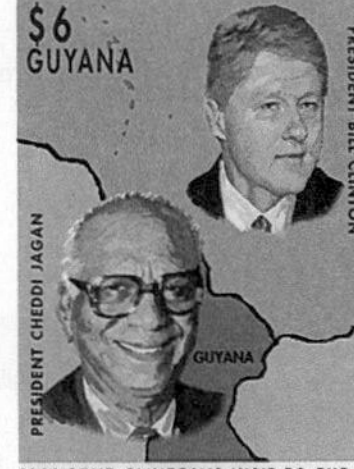

574 Princess Diana **575** Presidents Clinton (U.S.A.) and Cheddi Jagan (Guyana)

1997. Diana, Princess of Wales Commemoration. Multicoloured.
5137 $80 Type **574** 90 90
5138 $80 Princess Diana in black V-neck dress 90 90
5139 $80 In red dress with diamante pattern on front 90 90
5140 $80 In white evening dress with narrow shoulder straps 90 90
5141 $80 In white evening dress with one shoulder bare . . 90 90
5142 $80 In lavender dress . . . 90 90
MS5143 Two sheets, each 107 × 108 mm. (a) $300 In red sleeveless dress (33 × 51 mm). (b) $300 In white blouse (33 × 51 mm) Set of 2 sheets . . . . . . 7·00 7·50

1997. President Clinton's Caribbean Visit. Mult.
5144 $6 Type **575** 15 10
5145 $30 As Type **575**, but different portrait of Pres. Jagan 45 35
5146 $30 Presidents Clinton and Jagan, flags and sunrise over sea (horiz) 45 35
5147 $100 Presidents Clinton and Jagan, flags and sunrise over beach (horiz) . . . . 1·50 1·75

576 President Jiang Zemin, Flags, and New York Skyline by Day

1997. Visit of President Jiang Zemin of China to New York. Two sheets, each 125 × 84 mm, containing T **576** and similar horiz design. Multicoloured.
MS5148 Two sheets. (a) $200 Type **576**. (b) $300 President Jiang Zemin, flags, and New York at night Set of 2 sheets . . . . . 5·50 6·00

1997. Christmas. Paintings. As T **284a** of Gambia. Multicoloured.
5149 $25 Cupid from "The Triumph of Galatea" (Raphael) 30 10
5150 $30 Different Cupid from "The Triumph of Galatea" (Raphael) . . . 30 10
5151 $35 Cupid from "Primavera" (Botticelli) 35 15
5152 $60 "Angel Musicians" (Agostino di Duccio) . . 70 30
5153 $100 Cupid from illustration No. 1212, *Life Magazine* 28/1/06 . . . . 1·40 1·50
5154 $200 Angels from "Madonna and Saints" (Rosso Fiorentino) . . . 2·50 3·25
MS5155 Two sheets. (a) 95 × 105 mm. $300 "The Gardens of Love" (Rubens). (b) 105 × 95 mm. $300 "Cherubs" (Philippe de Champaigne) Set of 2 sheets . . . . 8·50 9·00

577 Abraham Lincoln **579** Tiger sitting (face value at bottom right)

578 Fogarty's Department Store, Georgetown

1997. 75th Anniversaries, 1997–2001. Multicoloured.
5156 $60 Type **577** (Dedication of Lincoln Memorial, Washington, 1922) . . . 75 75
5157 $60 Mask of Tutankhamun (discovery of tomb, 1922) 75 75
5158 $60 Alexander Graham Bell and early telephone, 1922 (75th death anniv) 75 75
5159 $60 John L. Baird and first television, 1923 . . . . 75 75
5160 $60 President Warren G. Harding, 1923 (75th death anniv) 75 75
5161 $60 Presidency of Calvin Coolidge, 1923 . . . . . 75 75
5162 $60 Skier (first Winter Olympics, Chamonix, France, 1924) 75 75
5163 $60 Sun Yat-sen (Chinese leader), 1925 (75th death anniv) 75 75
5164 $60 Charles Darwin (ban on teaching of evolution, Tennessee, U.S.A., 1925) 75 75
5165 $60 Robert Goddard (first liquid fuel rocket, 1926) 75 75

5166 $60 Richard E. Byrd (first flight over North Pole, 1926) 75 75
5167 $60 Liberty Bell (Sesquicentennial Exposition, Philadelphia, 1926) 75 75

1997. Buildings in Guyana. Multicoloured.
5168 $6 Type **578** 15 15
5169 $30 St. Rose's High School (150th anniv) 50 50

1998. Chinese New Year ("Year of the Tiger"). Multicoloured.
5170 $50 Type **579** 50 55
5171 $50 Tiger sitting (face value bottom left) 50 55
5172 $50 Tiger standing (face value top right) 50 55
5173 $50 Tiger standing (face value top left) 50 55
MS5174 102 × 72 mm. $150 Tiger with Chinese characters in background 1·40 1·60

580 Kentrosaurus

1998. Prehistoric Animals. Multicoloured.
5175 $25 Type **580** 40 30
5176 $30 Lesothosaurus 40 30
5177 $35 Stegoceras 40 30
5178 $55 Ceresiosaurus 65 70
5179 $55 Nothosaurus 65 70
5180 $55 Rhomaleosaurus 65 75
5181 $55 Grendelius 65 70
5182 $55 Mixosaurus 65 70
5183 $55 Mesosaurus 65 70
5184 $55 Placodus 65 70
5185 $55 Stethacanthus 65 70
5186 $55 Coelacanth 65 70
5187 $55 Quetzalcoatlus 65 70
5188 $55 Pteranodon 65 70
5189 $55 Peteinosaurus 65 70
5190 $55 Criorhychus 65 70
5191 $55 Pterodaustro 65 70
5192 $55 Eudimorphodon 65 70
5193 $55 Archeopteryx 65 70
5194 $55 Dimorphodon 65 70
5195 $55 Sharovipteryx 65 70
5196 $60 Lagosuchus 65 60
5197 $100 Herrerasaurus 1·00 1·10
5198 $200 Iguanodon 1·90 2·25
MS5199 Two sheets, each 106 × 76 mm. (a) $300 Yangchuanosaurus (vert). (b) $300 Styracosaurus (vert) Set of 2 sheets 6·00 6·50
Nos. 5178/86 and 5187/95 were each printed together, se-tenant, with the backgrounds forming composite designs.

581 Bryan Berard

1998. Ice Hockey Players. Multicoloured.
5200 $35 Type **581** 35 35
5201 $35 Ray Bourque 35 35
5202 $35 Martin Brodeur 35 35
5203 $35 Pavel Bure 35 35
5204 $35 Chris Chelios 35 35
5205 $35 Sergei Fedorov 35 35
5206 $35 Peter Forsberg 35 35
5207 $35 Wayne Gretzky 35 35
5208 $35 Dominik Hasek 35 35
5209 $35 Brett Hull 35 35
5210 $35 Jarome Iginla 35 35
5211 $35 Jaromir Jagr 35 35
5212 $35 Paul Kariya 35 35
5213 $35 Saku Koivu 35 35
5214 $35 John LeClair 35 35
5215 $35 Brian Leetch 35 35
5216 $35 Eric Lindros 35 35
5217 $35 Patrick Marleau 35 35
5218 $35 Mark Messier 35 35
5219 $35 Mike Modano 35 35
5220 $35 Chris Osgood 35 35
5221 $35 Zigmund Palffy 35 35
5222 $35 Felix Potvin 35 35
5223 $35 Jeremy Roenick 35 35
5224 $35 Patrick Roy 35 35
5225 $35 Joe Sakic 35 35
5226 $35 Sergei Samsonov 35 35
5227 $35 Teemu Selanne 35 35
5228 $35 Brendan Shanahan 35 35
5229 $35 Ryan Smyth 35 35
5230 $35 Jocelyn Thibault 35 35
5231 $35 Joe Thornton 35 35
5232 $35 Keith Tkachuk 35 35
5233 $35 John Vanbiesbrouck 35 35
5234 $35 Steve Yzerman 35 35
5235 $35 Dainius Zubrus 35 35

582 Argentine Team

1998. World Cup Football Championship, France. Showing competing teams and trophy. Multicoloured.
5236 $30 Type **582** 30 30
5237 $30 Austria 30 30
5238 $30 Belgium 30 30
5239 $30 Brazil 30 30
5240 $30 Bulgaria 30 30
5241 $30 Cameroon 30 30
5242 $30 Chile 30 30
5243 $30 Colombia 30 30
5244 $30 Croatia 30 30
5245 $30 Denmark 30 30
5246 $30 England 30 30
5247 $30 France 30 30
5248 $30 Germany 30 30
5249 $30 Holland 30 30
5250 $30 Iran 30 30
5251 $30 Italy 30 30
5252 $30 Jamaica 30 30
5253 $30 Japan 30 30
5254 $30 Mexico 30 30
5255 $30 Morocco 30 30
5256 $30 Nigeria 30 30
5257 $30 Norway 30 30
5258 $30 Paraguay 30 30
5259 $30 Rumania 30 30
5260 $30 Saudi Arabia 30 30
5261 $30 Scotland 30 30
5262 $30 South Africa 30 30
5263 $30 South Korea 30 30
5264 $30 Spain 30 30
5265 $30 Tunisia 30 30
5266 $30 U.S.A. 30 30
5267 $30 Yugoslavia 30 30
MS5268 Two sheets, each 110 × 85 mm. (a) $300 Okada, Japan (vert). (b) $300 Nakata, Japan (vert) Set of 2 sheets 5·00 5·50

583 Dutch Fluyt

1998. Sailing Ships. Multicoloured.
5269 $80 Type **583** 75 75
5270 $80 *Alastor* (barque) 75 75
5271 $80 *Falcon* (medieval ship) 75 75
5272 $80 *Red Rover* (barque) 75 75
5273 $80 *British Anglesey* (full-rigged ship) 75 75
5274 $80 *Archibald Russell* (barque) 75 75
5275 $80 14th century double-ended Scandinavian ship 75 75
5276 $80 Portuguese caravel 75 75
5277 $80 *Nina* (Columbus) 75 75
5278 $80 *Fannie* (schooner) 75 75
5279 $80 *Vitoria* (Magellan) 75 75
5280 $80 Arab sambook 75 75
MS5281 Two sheets. (a) 76 × 106 mm. $300 *Half Moon* (Hudson). (b) 106 × 76 mm. $300 Osberg ship Set of 2 sheets 5·00 5·50
No. 5274 is inscribed "ARCHIBALD RUSSEL" in error.

584 J. Bruce Ismay (Managing Director of White Star Line)

1998. 85th Anniv of Sinking of the Titanic (liner) Multicoloured.
5282 $80 Type **584** 80 80
5283 $80 Jack Phillips (wireless operator) 80 80
5284 $80 Margaret Brown (passenger) 80 80
5285 $80 Capt. Edward J. Smith 80 80
5286 $80 Frederick Fleet (crew member) 80 80
5287 $80 Thomas Andrews (Managing Director of Harland & Wolff) 80 80
MS5288 100 × 70 mm. $300 *Titanic* sinking 3·00 3·25

1998. 25th Anniv of Caribbean Community. As T **454a** of Grenada. Multicoloured.
5289 $20 Flags of Grenada and CARICOM 30 20

585 Queen Elizabeth the Queen Mother

1998. 98th Birthday of Queen Elizabeth the Queen Mother.
5290 **585** $90 multicoloured 90 90

1998. France's Victory in World Cup Football Championship. Nos. 5239, 5244/5, 5247, 5251, 5258, 5260 and 5262 optd **FRANCE WINNERS**. Multicoloured.
5291 $30 Brazil 30 35
5292 $30 Croatia 30 35
5293 $30 Denmark 30 35
5294 $30 France 30 35
5295 $30 Italy 30 35
5296 $30 Paraguay 30 35
5297 $30 Saudi Arabia 30 35
5298 $30 South Africa 30 35

587 Orville Wright in *Flyer I*, 1903

1998. Aircraft. Multicoloured.
5299 $80 Type **587** 75 75
5300 $80 Bleriot, 1911 75 75
5301 $80 Curtiss Jenny, 1919 75 75
5302 $80 Zeppelin LZ-10 *Schwaben*, 1911 75 75
5303 $80 W-8B, 1923 75 75
5304 $80 DH66, 1926 75 75
5305 $80 A7K Corsair II 75 75
5306 $80 A6E Intruder 75 75
5307 $80 U2 spy plane 75 75
5308 $80 Blackhawk helicopter 75 75
5309 $80 F-16 75 75
5310 $80 Phantom II 75 75
MS5311 Two sheets, each 70 × 100 mm. (a) $300 A-10 Warthog. (b) $300 HH-65A Dolphin helicopter Set of 2 sheets 5·00 5·50
Nos. 5299/304 and 5305/10 were each printed together, se-tenant, with the backgrounds forming composite designs.

588 Panda climbing Tree

589 Mountain Gorilla

1998. Giant Pandas. Multicoloured.
5312 $80 Type **588** 75 75
5313 $80 Panda sitting on tree trunk 75 75
5314 $80 Panda climbing bamboo 75 75
5315 $80 Panda chewing bamboo 75 75
5316 $80 Panda snapping bamboo stalk 75 75
5317 $80 Panda eating foliage 75 75
MS5318 100 × 70 mm. $300 Panda with leaves 2·75 3·00
Nos. 5312/17 were printed together, se-tenant, with the backgrounds forming a composite design.

1998. Mountain Gorillas. Multicoloured.
5319 $80 Type **589** 75 75
5320 $80 Gorilla climbing tree 75 75
5321 $80 Gorilla eating foliage 75 75
5322 $80 Female gorilla sitting on ground 75 75
5323 $80 Baby gorilla eating twig 75 75
5324 $80 Male gorilla in forest 75 75
MS5325 100 × 70 mm. $300 Young gorilla eating leaf 2·75 3·00
Nos. 5319/24 were printed together, se-tenant, with the backgrounds forming a composite design.

590 Christian Lautenschlager in Grand Prix Mercedes, 1914

1998. History of Grand Prix Motor Racing. Mult.
5326 $80 Type **590** 70 70
5327 $80 P. Etancelin in Bugatti Type 35B, 1930 70 70
5328 $80 Louis Chiron in Alfa Romeo P3, 1934 70 70
5329 $80 Richard Seaman in Mercedes-Benz W154, 1938 70 70
5330 $80 Tazio Nuvolari in Auto Union D Type, 1938 70 70
5331 $80 Juan Fangio in Alfa Romeo 158, 1951 70 70
5332 $80 Stirling Moss in Mercedes-Benz W196, 1955 70 70
5333 $80 Phil Hill in Ferrari Dino 246, 1960 70 70
5334 $80 Jack Brabham in Brabham-Repco BT19, 1966 70 70
5335 $80 John Miles in Lotus Ford 72, 1970 70 70
5336 $80 Alain Prost in Renault RE40, 1983 70 70
5337 $80 David Coulthard in McLaren Mercedes MP4/13, 1998 70 70
MS5338 Two sheets, each 100 × 70 mm. (a) $300 Ferenc Szisz in Grand Prix Renault, 1906 (56 × 42 mm). (b) $300 Stirling Moss in Maserati 250F, 1956 (56 × 42 mm) Set of 2 sheets 5·00 5·50

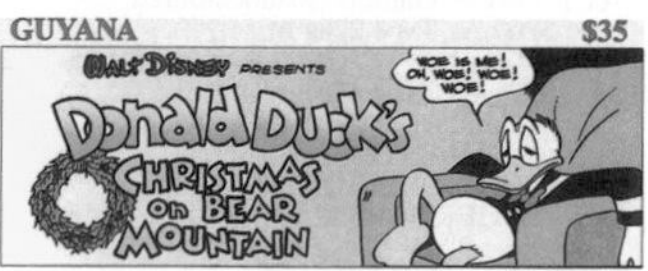

591 Comic Book Title (½-size illustration)

1998. 50th Anniv of Disney's Uncle Scrooge Character. Designs showing text and illustrations from comic book *Christmas on Bear Mountain* (drawn by C. Barks). Mult.
5339 $35 Type **591** 60 60
5340 $35 Uncle Scrooge sitting in armchair 60 60
5341 $35 Uncle Scrooge looking out window 60 60
5342 $35 James the butler holding telephone 60 60
5343 $35 Uncle Scrooge at foot of staircase 60 60
5344 $35 Donald Duck with open fridge 60 60
5345 $35 Uncle Scrooge entering attic 60 60
5346 $35 Uncle Scrooge in limousine 60 60
5347 $35 Huey, Dewey and Louie at window 60 60
5348 $35 Car in snow 60 60
5349 $35 Ducks in bed 60 60
5350 $35 Donald in chair with nephews 60 60
5351 $35 Donald refusing nephews 60 60
5352 $35 Ducks and rabbit 60 60
5353 $35 Ducks with Christmas tree 60 60
5354 $35 Baby bear climbing down Christmas tree 60 60
5355 $35 Ducks in panic 60 60
5356 $35 Baby bear running 60 60
5357 $35 Ducks searching 60 60
5358 $35 Nephews and tree 60 60
5359 $35 Huey, Dewey and Louie tripping on roller skate 60 60
5360 $35 Frightened nephew 60 60
5361 $35 Baby bear on roller skate 60 60
5362 $35 Donald hiding in light fitting 60 60
5363 $35 Baby bear with chocolate 60 60
5364 $35 Louie climbing Christmas tree 60 60
5365 $35 Baby bear evading Louie 60 60
5366 $35 Nephews searching bedroom 60 60
5367 $35 Donald peering down from light fitting 60 60
5368 $35 Mother bear chasing Donald 60 60
5369 $35 Donald jumping through window 60 60
5370 $35 Bears after eating 60 60
5371 $35 Ducks looking through window 60 60
5372 $35 Donald and sleeping mother bear 60 60
5373 $35 Uncle Scrooge outside cabin 60 60
5374 $35 Uncle Scrooge in bear suit behind sofa 60 60
5375 $35 Uncle Scrooge in bear suit surprised 60 60
5376 $35 Uncle Scrooge with James 60 60
5377 $35 Ducks on Christmas Day 60 60
5378 $35 Donald fainting 60 60
MS5379 220 × 175 mm. $300 Carl Barks (37 × 50 mm); $300 Uncle Scrooge pursued by bear (50 × 37 mm) 7·00 7·00

Only issued in stamp booklets in which each pane contains two pairs separated by a horizontal gutter margin showing further parts of the comic strip. Each stamp shows two drawings of which the first in each instance is described for the listing.

1998. 50th Anniv of Organization of American States. As T **454b** of Grenada.
5380 $40 yellow, violet and black . . . 40 30

1998. 25th Death Anniv of Pablo Picasso (painter). As T **291a** of Gambia. Multicoloured.
5381 $25 "Sleeping Peasants" . . 25 20
5382 $60 "Large Nude in Red Armchair" (vert) 55 40
5383 $200 "Female Head" (vert) 1·75 1·90
MS5384 102×126 mm. $300 "Man and Woman" (vert) . . . . . 2·75 3·00

592 James E. West (first Scout executive) and Early Eagle Scouts

1998. 19th World Scout Jamboree, Chile. Mult.
5385 $160 Type **592** . . . . . . 1·40 1·50
5386 $160 Pres. John F. Kennedy greeting Explorers, 1961 1·40 1·50
5387 $160 Walter Schirra (astronaut) receiving Special Merit badge, 1962 1·40 1·50

593 Mahatma Gandhi as Lawyer in South Africa, 1906

594 St. Andrew's Kirk, Georgetown

1998. 50th Death Anniv of Mahatma Gandhi. Mult.
5388 $100 Type **593** 90 90
5389 $100 Gandhi on Bengal walk, 1946 (56×42 mm) 90 90
5390 $100 Gandhi with Jawaharlal Nehru and Sardar Patel, 1948 (56×42 mm) 90 90
5391 $100 Gandhi during fast, 1947 . . . . 90 90
MS5392 70×66 mm. $300 Gandhi and Jawaharlal Nehru (horiz) 2·75 3·00

1998. 80th Anniv of Royal Air Force. As T **292a** of Gambia. Multicoloured.
5393 $100 Avro Lancaster B2 . . 90 90
5394 $100 PBY-5A Catalina amphibian 90 90
5395 $100 Hawk T1As of Red Arrows 90 90
5396 $100 Avro Lancaster and De Havilland D.H. 98 Mosquito 90 90
5397 $100 BAe Hawk T1A . . . 90 90
5398 $100 C-130 Hercules 90 90
5399 $100 Panavia Tornado GR1 90 90
5400 $100 BAe Hawk 200 in desert camouflage 90 90
5401 $150 BAe Nimrod R1P . . 1·25 1·25
5402 $150 Panavia Tornado F3 ADV . . . . 1·25 1·25
5403 $150 CH-47 Chinook helicopter . . . . 1·25 1·25
5404 $150 Panavia Tornado GR1A in front of hangar 1·25 1·25
MS5405 Set of six sheets, each 91×68 mm. (a) $200 Eagle and Bristol F2B fighter. (b) $200 Spitfire and EF2000 Eurofighter. (c) $300 Tiger Moth and EF2000 Eurofighter. (d) $300 Eurofighter. (e) $300 Bristol F2B fighter and two Montagu's harrier (birds). (f) $300 Bristol F2B fighter and Golden eagle Set of 6 sheets . . 12·00 13·00

1998. 1st Death Anniv of Diana, Princess of Wales. As T **293a** of Gambia.
5406 $60 multicoloured 60 60

1998. Birth Bicentenary of Eugene Delacroix (painter). As T **293** of Gambia. Multicoloured.
5407 $60 "Corner of the Studio" (vert) 50 55
5408 $60 "Count Mornay's Apartment" (vert) 50 55
5409 $60 "Hamlet and the Two Gravediggers" (vert) . . . 50 55
5410 $60 "George Sand" (vert) 50 55
5411 $60 "The Fiancee of Abydos" (vert) 50 55
5412 $60 "The Champs-Elysses" (vert) 50 55
5413 $60 "Lioness" (vert) 50 55
5414 $60 "Alfred Bruyas" (vert) 50 55
5415 $60 "The Sultan of Morocco" (vert) 50 55
5416 $60 "Indian with Kukri" (vert) 50 55
5417 $60 "Man in Turkish Dress" (vert) 50 55
5418 $60 "Studies of Jewish Women" (vert) 50 55
5419 $60 "Arab Horseman giving Signal" (vert) 50 55
5420 $60 "Arab Horsemen charging" (vert) 50 55
5421 $60 "A Seated Moor" (vert) 50 55
5422 $60 "Jewish Woman in Traditional Dress" (vert) 50 55
MS5423 Two sheets, each 100×90 mm. (a) $300 "Death of Sardanpole". (b) $300 "Jewish Wedding, Morocco" Set of 2 sheets . . . . 5·00 5·50

1999. 180th Anniv of St. Andrew's Kirk, Georgetown. Multicoloured.
5424 $6 Type **594** 10 10
5425 $30 Front of church 30 25
5426 $60 Front and side of church 55 50

595 Rabbit

1999. Chinese New Year ("Year of the Rabbit"). Multicoloured.
5427 $50 Type **595** 45 50
5428 $50 Rabbit (face value at bottom left) 45 50
5429 $50 Rabbit (face value at top right) 45 50
5430 $50 Rabbit (face value at top left) 45 50
MS5431 112×70 mm. $150 Rabbit on background of Chinese characters . . . . 1·25 1·40

596 Pongo driving Steam Locomotive

1999. Disney Trains. Cartoon characters. Multicoloured.
5432 $100 Type **596** . . . . . . 1·00 1·00
5433 $100 Puppies watching television . . . . 1·00 1·00
5434 $100 Perdita, Roger and Anita . . . . 1·00 1·00
5435 $100 Nanny with puppies 1·00 1·00
5436 $100 Horace, Jasper and Cruella De Vil . . . . . 1·00 1·00
5437 $100 Rhino pulling Little John and Friar Tuck . . 1·00 1·00
5438 $100 Maid Marian, Robin Hood and Lady Kluck . . 1·00 1·00
5439 $100 Sir Hiss and Prince John . . . . 1·00 1·00
5440 $100 Allan-a-Dale on elephant . . . . 1·00 1·00
5441 $100 Rabbit family and Toby Turtle . . . . . . 1·00 1·00
5442 $100 Doc driving train . . . 1·00 1·00
5443 $100 Grumpy, Happy, Sleepy and Bashful singing . . . . 1·00 1·00
5444 $100 Snow White and Prince with diamonds . . 1·00 1·00
5445 $100 Old Witch, animals from forest and Sneezy 1·00 1·00
5446 $100 Dopey and racoon on trolley . . . . 1·00 1·00
5447 $100 Triton driving locomotive . . . . 1·00 1·00
5448 $100 Flounder with pearls 1·00 1·00
5449 $100 Ariel, The Little Mermaid . . . . 1·00 1·00
5450 $100 Sebastian and friends in band . . . . 1·00 1·00
5451 $100 Ursula . . . . 1·00 1·00
MS5452 Five sheets. (a) 127×112 mm. $300 Horace, Jasper and Cruella De Vil (*101 Dalmatians*). (b) 127×112 mm $300 Robin Hood and Little John (*Robin Hood*). (c) 230×180 mm. $200 Doc driving train and $200 Dopey and racoon on trolley (vert) (*Snow White*). (d) 110×27 mm. $300 Ariel kissing statue (*The Little Mermaid*). (e) 127×110 mm. $300 Ariel holding starfish (*The Little Mermaid*) Set of 5 sheets 13·00 13·00
Nos. 5432/6 (characters from *101 Dalmatians*), Nos. 5437/41 (*Robin Hood*), Nos. 5442/6 (*Snow White*) and Nos. 5447/51 (*The Little Mermaid*) were each printed together, se-tenant, forming composite designs.

597 Huey skateboarding

1999. 70th Birthday of Mickey Mouse. Multicoloured.
5453 $80 Type **597** 80 80
5454 $80 Mickey Mouse skateboarding 80 80
5455 $80 Dewey skateboarding (purple cap) 80 80
5456 $80 Louie skateboarding (red cap) 80 80
5457 $80 Goofy skateboarding (lilac boots) 80 80
5458 $80 Donald Duck skateboarding (with cap) 80 80
5459 $80 Minnie Mouse rollerblading 80 80
5460 $80 Goofy rollerblading . . 80 80
5461 $80 Daisy Duck rollerblading (red boots) 80 80
5462 $80 Baby Duck rollerblading (yellow wheels) 80 80
5463 $80 Donald Duck rollerblading 80 80
5464 $80 Mickey Mouse rollerblading (red helmet) 80 80
5465 $80 Baby Duck rollerblading (mauve wheels) 80 80
5466 $80 Daisy Duck rollerblading (mauve boots) 80 80
5467 $80 Mickey Mouse rollerblading (mauve helmet) 80 80
5468 $80 Goofy skateboarding (red boots) 80 80
5469 $80 Dewey rollerblading . . 80 80
5470 $80 Donald Duck skateboarding (without cap) 80 80
MS5471 Three sheets. (a) 112×127 mm. $300 Dewey skateboarding. (b) 127×112 mm. $300 Daisy Duck. (c) 127×112 mm. $300 Goofy (horiz) Set of 3 sheets . . . . 8·50 8·50

598 *Pelargonium domesticum*

1999. Flowers of the World. Multicoloured.
5472 $60 Type **598** 60 60
5473 $60 *Oncidium macranthum* and butterfly 60 60
5474 $60 *Bepi orchidglades* . . . 60 60
5475 $60 *Helianthus maximiliani* (two flowers) 60 60
5476 $60 *Cattleya walkeriana* . . 60 60
5477 $60 *Cattleya frasquita* . . . 60 60
5478 $60 *Helianthus maximiliani* (single bloom) 60 60
5479 $60 *Paphiopedilum insigne sanderae* and *lilium longifolium* 60 60
5480 $60 *Lilium longifolium* . . . 60 60
5481 $60 *Dendrobium nobile* . . . 60 60
5482 $60 *Phalaenopsis schilleriana* 60 60
5483 $60 *Cymbidium alexette* . . 60 60
5484 $60 *Rhododendron nudiflorum* and hummingbird 60 60
5485 $60 *Phragmipedium besseae* and *laelia cinnabarina* . . 60 60
5486 $60 *Masdevallia veitchiana, laelia cinnabarina* and hummingbird 60 60
5487 $60 *Calochortus nuttallii* . . 60 60
5488 $60 *Brassolaelio cattleya* "Puregold" 60 60
5489 $60 *Laelia cinnabarina* . . . 60 60
5490 $90 *Leptotes bicolor* and *masdevallia ignea* 80 80
5491 $90 *Sophrolaelio cattleya* and *anguloa clowesii* . . . 80 80
5492 $90 *Laelia pumila* 80 80
5493 $90 *Masdevallia ignea* . . . 80 80
5494 $90 *Dendrobium phalaenopsis* 80 80
5495 $90 *Anguloa clowesii* 80 80
MS5496 Two sheets, each 106×75 mm. (a) $300 *Iris pseudacorus*. (b) $300 *Ascocentrum miniatum* (vert) Set of 2 sheets 5·50 6·00
Nos. 5472/80, 5481/9 and 5490/5 were each printed together, se-tenant, with the backgrounds forming composite designs.
No. **MS**5496b is inscribed "Asocentrum" in error.

599 *Philaethria dido*

1999. Caribbean Butterflies. Multicoloured.
5497 $80 Type **599** 80 80
5498 $80 *Papilio troilus* 80 80
5499 $80 *Eueides isabella* 80 80
5500 $80 *Colobura dirce* 80 80
5501 $80 *Agraulis vanillae* 80 80
5502 $80 *Callicore maimuna* . . . 80 80
5503 $80 *Thecla coronata* 80 80
5504 $80 *Battus polydamus* . . . 80 80
5505 $80 *Morpho peleides* 80 80
5506 $80 *Doxocopa cherubina* . . 80 80
5507 $80 *Metamorpha stelenes* . . 80 80
5508 $80 *Catonephele numili* . . . 80 80
MS5509 Two sheets. (a) 76×107 mm. $300 *Papilio cresphontes* (vert). (b) 107×76 mm. $300 *Battus philenor* (vert) Set of 2 sheets . . . . . 5·50 6·00
Nos. 5504 and 5509b are both inscribed "Baltus" in error.

600 Actor from *The Dream*

601 *Boletus aereus*

1999. Akira Kurosawa (Japanese film director) Commemoration. Multicoloured (except No. 5519).
5510 $80 Type **601** 70 70
5511 $80 Actor from *Red Beard* 70 70
5512 $80 Scene from *Rashomon* 70 70
5513 $80 Scene from *Seven Samurai* 70 70
5514 $80 Actor from *Kagemusha* 70 70
5515 $80 Scene from *Yojimbo* . . 70 70
5516 $130 Akira Kurosawa wearing blue cap (horiz) 1·10 1·10
5517 $130 Resting head on right hand (horiz) . . . . . . 1·10 1·10
5518 $130 Wearing black jumper (horiz) . . . . 1·10 1·10
5519 $130 Looking through camera (horiz) (brown and black) . . . . . . 1·10 1·10
MS5520 98×68 mm. $300 Actor from *Dreams* . . . . 2·75 3·00

1999. Fungi. Multicoloured.
5521 $25 *Coprinus atramentarius* (28×33 mm) 30 20
5522 $35 *Hebeloma crustuliniforme* (28×33 mm) 40 25
5523 $60 Type **601** 60 60
5524 $60 *Coprinus comatus* . . . 60 60
5525 $60 *Inocybe godeyi* 60 60
5526 $60 *Morchella crassipes* . . 60 60
5527 $60 *Lepiota acutesquamosa* 60 60
5528 $60 *Amanita phalloides* . . . 60 60
5529 $60 *Boletus spadiceus* . . . 60 60
5530 $60 *Cortinarius collinitus* . . 60 60
5531 $60 *Lepiota procera* 60 60
5532 $60 *Russula ochroleuca* . . . 60 60
5533 $60 *Hygrophorus hypotheius* 60 60
5534 $60 *Amanita rubescens* . . . 60 60
5535 $60 *Boletus satanas* 60 60
5536 $60 *Amanita echinocephala* 60 60
5537 $60 *Amanita muscaria* . . . 60 60
5538 $60 *Boletus badius* 60 60
5539 $60 *Hebeloma radicosum* . . 60 60
5540 $60 *Mycena polygramma* . . 60 60
5541 $100 *Russula nigricans* (28×33 mm) 90 90
5542 $200 *Tricholoma aurantium* (28×33 mm) . . . . . . 1·60 1·75
MS5543 Two sheets. (a) 70×98 mm. $300 *Pluteus cervinus*. (b) 98×70 mm. $300 *Lepiota acutesquamosa* Set of 2 sheets 5·50 6·00
No. **MS**5543b is inscribed "Acutesquamoso" in error.

602 Shinkansen 100 Series Bullet Train, Japan (1984)

1999. "Australia '99" International Stamp Exhibition, Melbourne. Trains. Multicoloured (except Nos. 5550/5, each brown, yellow and black, and **MS**5568b/d).
5544 $80 Type **602** 75 75
5545 $80 Ukrainian ZMGR diesel locomotive, Russia (1983) 75 75
5546 $80 Rhatische Bahn electric locomotive No. 706, Germany 75 75

5547 $80 Eurostar T.G.V. train, France (1986) 75 75
5548 $80 Atlantique T.G.V. train, France (1989) 75 75
5549 $80 Class 86-6 diesel locomotive No. 86604, Great Britain 75 75
5550 $80 Joseph Clark steam locomotive, U.S.A. (1868) 75 75
5551 $80 Diamond Stack Bethel steam locomotive, U.S.A. (1863) 75 75
5552 $80 New York Central steam locomotive No. 999, U.S.A. (1890) 75 75
5553 $80 Boston and Maine steam locomotive *Ballardville*, U.S.A. (1876) 75 75
5554 $80 Portland Rochester Railroad steam locomotive, U.S.A. (1863) 75 75
5555 $80 Baltimore and Ohio Railroad steam locomotive, U.S.A. (1881) 75 75
5556 $80 Burlington Northern GP 39-2 diesel locomotive, U.S.A. (1974) 75 75
5557 $80 CSX GP40-2 diesel locomotive, U.S.A. (1967) 75 75
5558 $80 Erie Lackawana Railroad GP 9 diesel locomotive, U.S.A. (1956) 75 75
5559 $80 Amtrak P 42 Genesis No. 82 train, U.S.A. (1993) 75 75
5560 $80 Erie Railroad S-2 diesel locomotive, U.S.A. (1948) 75 75
5561 $80 Pennsylvania Railroad S-1 diesel locomotive, U.S.A. (1947) 75 75
5562 $80 Northern and Western steam locomotive No. 610, U.S.A. (1933) 75 75
5563 $80 Pennsylvania Railroad M1B Mountain steam locomotive, U.S.A. (1930) 75 75
5564 $80 Reading Railroad FP7A diesel locomotive, U.S.A. (1951) 75 75
5565 $80 New York Central steam locomotive No. 765, U.S.A. (1940) 75 75
5566 $80 Union Pacific steam locomotive No. 3985, U.S.A. (1963) 75 75
5567 $80 GP 15-15-1 diesel locomotive, U.S.A. (1956) 75 75
MS5568 Four sheets. (a) 70 × 98 mm. $300 George Nagelmackers (founder of International Sleeping Car Co.) (vert). (b) 70 × 98 mm. $300 R. F. Trevithick (engineer, Japanese National Railways) (vert) (violet and black). (c) 70 × 98 mm. $300 Alfred de Glehn (locomotive designer) (vert) (brown and black). (d) 98 × 70 mm. $300 George Stephen (president of Canadian Pacific) (vert) (brown and black) Set of 4 sheets . . . . 10·00 11·00

1999. Royal Wedding. As T **298** of Gambia. Multicoloured.
5569 $150 Sophie Rhys-Jones in multicoloured dress . . . 1·25 1·25
5570 $150 Prince Edward with Sophie Rhys-Jones inspecting guard of honour . . . . 1·25 1·25
5571 $150 Sophie Rhys-Jones wearing grey jacket . . . 1·25 1·25
5572 $150 Prince Edward wearing striped shirt . . . . 1·25 1·25
5573 $150 Prince Edward and Sohpie Rhys-Jones at the races . . . . 1·25 1·25
5574 $150 Sophie Rhys-Jones holding blue folder . . . 1·25 1·25
5575 $150 Prince Edward wearing blue shirt . . . . 1·25 1·25
5576 $150 Sophie Rhys-Jones wearing black outfit . . . 1·25 1·25
MS5577 Two sheets, each 83 × 66 mm. (a) $300 Prince Edward and Sophie Rhys-Jones in front of blossom (horiz). (b) $300 Prince Edward and Sophie Rhys-Jones in front of building (horiz) Set of 2 sheets . . . . 5·00 5·50

1999. John Glenn's Return to Space. As T **136** of Grenadines of Grenada. Multicoloured.
5578 $100 John Glenn (American astronaut) in spacesuit, 1962 . . . . 90 90
5579 $100 Relaxing after landing, 1962 . . . . 90 90
5580 $100 As Senator for Ohio, 1974 . . . . 90 90
5581 $100 In spacesuit and helmet for Space Shuttle flight, 1998 . . . . . . 90 90
5582 $100 In spacesuit without helmet, 1998 . . . . . . 90 90
No. 5582 is dated "1992" in error.

1999. "iBRA '99" International Stamp Exhibition, Nuremberg. As T **299a** of Gambia. Multicoloured.
5583 $60 Class E10 electric locomotive, Germany, 1952 (vert) 60 50
5584 $200 Early steam locomotive, Der Adler, Germany, 1835 . . . . . 1·75 1·90
No. 5584 is inscribed "CLASS 01 STEAM EXPRESS TRAIN, GERMANY, 1926" in error.

1999. 150th Death Anniv of Katsushika Hokusai (Japanese artist). As T **299b** of Gambia. Multicoloured.
5585 $80 "Travellers climbing a Mountain Path" 70 75
5586 $80 "Washing Clothes in a River" 70 75
5587 $80 "The Blind" (old man smiling) 70 75
5588 $80 "The Blind" (man with beard) 70 75
5589 $80 "Convolvulus and Tree-frog" 70 75
5590 $80 "Fishermen hauling a Net" 70 75
5591 $80 "Hibiscus and Sparrow" 70 75
5592 $80 "Hydrangea and Swallow" 70 75
5593 $80 "The Blind" (man yawning) 70 75
5594 $80 "The Blind" (old man frowning) 70 75
5595 $80 "Irises" 70 75
5596 $80 "Lilies" 70 75
MS5597 Two sheets, each 101 × 72 mm. (a) $300 "Flowering Cherries at Mount Yoshino" (vert). (b) $300 "View of Stone Causeway" (vert) Set of 2 sheets 5·00 5·50

1999. 10th Anniv of U.N. Rights of the Child Convention. As T **299c** of Gambia. Multicoloured.
5598 $150 Two girls . . . . . . 1·25 1·40
5599 $150 Two boys . . . . . . 1·25 1·40
5600 $150 One boy . . . . . . 1·25 1·40
MS5601 $300 Prince Talal, UNICEF special envoy, 1980 . . . . . 2·75 3·00
Nos. 5598/600 were printed together, se-tenant, with the backgrounds forming a composite design.

1999. "PhilexFrance '99" International Stamp Exhibition, Paris. Railway Locomotives. Two sheets, each 106 × 82 mm, containing horiz designs as T **299d** of Gambia. Multicoloured.
MS5602 (a) $300 Class 7000 high-speed locomotive, 1949–55. (b) $300 Class 241-P steam locomotive, 1947–49 Set of 2 sheets . . . . 5·50 6·00

1999. 250th Birth Anniv of Johann von Goethe (German writer). As T **299e** of Gambia.
5603 $150 green, black and blue 1·25 1·40
5604 $150 blue, violet and black 1·25 1·40
5605 $150 blue, brown and black 1·25 1·40
MS5606 78 × 109 mm. $300 brown, chocolate and black . . . . 2·75 3·00
DESIGNS—HORIZ: No. 5603, Lynceus singing from the watchtower; 5604, Von Goethe and Von Schiller; 5605, The Fallen Icarus. VERT: **MS**5606, Mephistopheles as a salamander.

603 Kurt Masur (German conductor and musician)

604 Pope John Paul II praying

1999. Year of the Older Person. Multicoloured (except No. **MS**5625).
5607 $50 Type **603** 50 50
5608 $50 Rupert Murdoch (newspaper publisher) . . 50 50
5609 $50 Margaret Thatcher (former British Prime Minister) 50 50
5610 $50 Pope John Paul II . . . 50 50
5611 $50 Mikhail Gorbachev (Russian leader) 50 50
5612 $50 Ted Turner (American politician) 50 50
5613 $50 Sophia Loren (Italian actress) 50 50
5614 $50 Nelson Mandela (South African leader) 50 50
5615 $50 John Glenn (American astronaut) 50 50
5616 $50 Luciano Pavarotti (Italian opera singer) . . . 50 50
5617 $50 Queen Elizabeth, the Queen Mother 50 50
5618 $50 Jimmy Carter (former American President) . . . 50 50
5619 $100 Ronald Reagan (former American president) in football shirt 80 80
5620 $100 Ronald Reagan wearing black shirt . . . 80 80
5621 $100 Ronald Reagan in military uniform 80 80
5622 $100 Ronald Reagan wearing stetson 80 80
5623 $100 Ronald Reagan feeding chimp with bottle 80 80
5624 $100 Ronald Reagan in evening dress 80 80
MS5625 111 × 111 mm. $300 Ronald Reagan in star (black) . . . . 2·75 3·00

1999. Pope John Paul II. Multicoloured.
5626 $80 Type **604** 80 80
5627 $80 Pope John Paul II (face value at top right) 80 80
5628 $80 Pope John Paul II smiling (face value at bottom left) 80 80
5629 $80 With crucifix 80 80
5630 $80 Pope John Paul II wearing black cloak . . . 80 80
5631 $80 Pope John Paul II (face value at bottom right) . . 80 80

1999. 30th Anniv of First Manned Landing on Moon. As T **298c** of Gambia but horiz. Multicoloured.
5632 $80 Konstantin Tsiolkovsky and first Russian artificial satellite, 1959 (vert) . . . 70 75
5633 $80 Launch of "Apollo 11" (vert) 70 75
5634 $80 Astronaut descending onto Moon (vert) 70 75
5635 $80 Collecting samples of lunar rock (vert) 70 75
5636 $80 "Apollo 11" lunar module, *Eagle* (vert) . . . 70 75
5637 $80 Splashdown of command module *Columbia* (vert) 70 75
5638 $80 "Apollo 11" after launch 70 75
5639 $80 "Apollo 11" modules after separation from rocket 70 75
5640 $80 Astronaut leaving *Eagle* for moon walk 70 75
5641 $80 Seismic experiments equipment 70 75
5642 $80 *Eagle* leaving Moon . . 70 75
5643 $80 *Eagle* after splashdown 70 75
MS5644 Two sheets, each 106 × 83 mm. (a) $300 Astronaut saluting American flag on Moon. (b) $300 Astronaut Michael Collins Set of 2 sheets . . . . 5·00 5·50

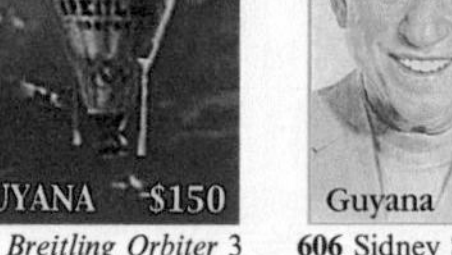

605 *Breitling Orbiter* 3 (balloon)

606 Sidney Sheldon

1999. 1st Non-stop Round-the-World Balloon Flight by *Breitling Orbiter 3*. Multicoloured.
5645 $150 Type **605** . . . . . . 1·25 1·40
5646 $150 Flight logo . . . . . 1·25 1·40
5647 $150 Bertrand Piccard (balloonist) . . . . 1·25 1·40
5648 $150 Brian Jones (balloonist) . . . . 1·25 1·40
MS5649 100 × 70 mm. $300 *Breitling Orbiter 3* . . . . 2·75 3·00

1999. Great Authors of the 20th Century. Sidney Sheldon.
5650 **606** $80 multicoloured . . . 70 70

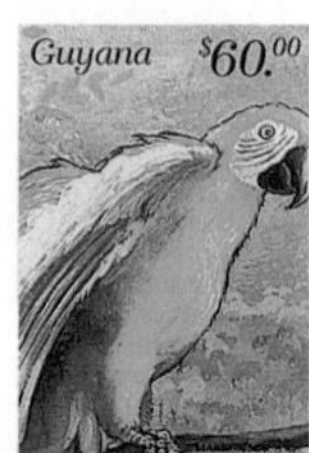

607 Scarlet Macaw ("Marron Macaw")

1999. South American Lories and Parrots. Multicoloured.
5651 $60 Type **607** 60 60
5652 $60 Thick-billed parrot . . . 60 60
5653 $60 Golden-crowned conure 60 60
5654 $60 Yellow-collared macaw 60 60
5655 $60 Double yellow-headed amazon 60 60
5656 $60 Mountain parakeet ("Golden-fronted Parakeet") 60 60
5657 $60 Maroon-bellied conure 60 60
5658 $60 Nanday conure 60 60
5659 $60 Hyacinth macaw 60 60
5660 $60 Blue and yellow macaw ("Blue and Gold Macaw") 60 60
5661 $60 Blue-fronted amazon . . 60 60
5662 $60 Amazon parrot 60 60
5663 $60 Sun conure 60 60
5664 $60 Orange-chinned parakeet ("Tivi Parakeet") 60 60
5665 $60 Golden conure ("Bavaria's Conure") . . 60 60
5666 $60 Fairy lorikeet 60 60
MS5667 Two sheets, each 110 × 85 mm. (a) $300 Jendaya conure (horiz). (b) $300 Grey-cheeked parakeet Set of 2 sheets 5·50 6·00
Nos. 5651/8 and 5659/66 were each printed together, se-tenant, with the backgrounds forming composite designs.
Nos. 5653, 5657 and 5658 are inscribed "CANURE", "BILLED" and "NANDAYA", all in error.

608 Queen Elizabeth the Queen Mother during Second World War

1999. Queen Elizabeth the Queen Mother's 99th Birthday. Multicoloured.
5668 $60 Type **608** 60 60
5669 $60 Wedding of Duke and Duchess of York, 1923 . . 60 60
5670 $60 Lady Elizabeth Bowes-Lyon as a child 60 60
5671 $60 At Coronation, 1937 . . 60 60
5672 $60 Queen Mother, 1971 . . 60 60
5673 $60 Queen Mother wearing red hat, 1991 . . . . . . 60 60
5674 $60 Lady Elizabeth Bowes-Lyon, 1914 . . . . 60 60
5675 $60 Queen Mother, 1988 . . 60 60
5676 $60 At Royal Agricultural Show during 1950s . . . 60 60
5677 $60 Queen Mother, 1960 . . 60 60
MS5678 50 × 76 mm. $1000 Queen Mother holding bouquet (43 × 69 mm). Imperf . . . . . 9·00 9·50

1999. "Queen Elizabeth the Queen Mother's Century". As T **305a** of Gambia.
5679 $130 multicoloured . . . . 1·25 1·25
5680 $130 black and gold . . . . 1·25 1·25
5681 $130 black and gold . . . . 1·25 1·25
5682 $130 multicoloured . . . . 1·25 1·25
MS5683 154 × 158 mm. $400 multicoloured . . . . 3·75 4·00
DESIGNS: No. 5679, Duchess of York with Princess Elizabeth, 1928; 5680, Lady Elizabeth Bowes-Lyon, 1914; 5681, Queen Elizabeth with Princess Elizabeth, 1940; 5682, Queen Elizabeth the Queen Mother in Venice, 1984. (37 × 50 mm)—**MS**5683, Queen Mother in Canada, 1988.

609 Mei Lanfang

1999. "China '99" International Stamp Exhibition, Beijing. 40th Death Anniv of Mei Lanfang (Chinese opera singer). Sheet 118 × 78mm.
MS5684 **609** $400 multicoloured 3·00 3·25

610 Wang Guangning

612 Dragon

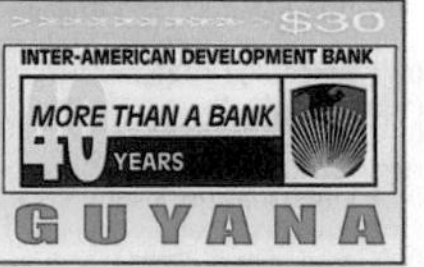

611 Inter-American Development Bank Logo

1999. Chinese Football League Players. Multicoloured.
5685 $50 Type **610** 45 50
5686 $50 Gao Feng ("H" emblem) 45 50

5687 $50 Jian Hong (goalkeeper) (bull emblem) 45 50
5688 $50 Gao Zhongxun (Yanbian football club) 45 50
5689 $50 Yao Xia (SCQXFC) . . 45 50
5690 $50 Zhang Yuning ("E" emblem) 45 50
5691 $50 Zhang Weihua (Matsunichi) 45 50
5692 $50 Dragon logo 45 50
5693 $60 Cai Sheng (winged comma logo) 50 55
5694 $60 Li Weifeng ("A" emblem) 50 55
5695 $60 Xie Zhaoyang (Beijing Guoan) 50 55
5696 $60 Li Xiaopeng (LNTS) . . 50 55
5697 $60 Hao Haidong (Dalian Wanda) 50 55
5698 $60 Zhang Xiaorui (TEDA) 50 55
5699 $60 Qi Hong (Shenhu) . . . 50 55
5700 $60 Dragon logo 50 55

1999. John F. Kennedy Jr. Commemoration. As T **307** of Gambia. Multicoloured.
5701 $80 John Junior as a child with mother 70 75
5702 $80 John Junior under father's desk 70 75
5703 $80 John and Jacqueline Kennedy as a young couple 70 75
5704 $80 Jacqueline Kennedy . . 70 75
5705 $80 John Junior with sister, Caroline 70 75
5706 $80 President John Kennedy 70 75
5707 $160 John Junior at father's funeral . . . . 1·25 1·40
5708 $160 John Junior as an adult with mother, Jacqueline . . . . 1·25 1·40
5709 $160 John Junior in front of U.S. flag . . . . 1·25 1·40

1999. Birth Centenary of Enzo Ferrari, 1998 (car manufacturer). As T **564a** of Ghana. Multicoloured.
5710 $30 312 T2 racing car . . . 30 25
5711 $35 553 F.1 racing car . . . 35 25
5712 $60 D 50 racing car 50 40
5713 $100 212 Export sports car 1·00 1·00
5714 $100 410 Superamerica saloon . . . . 1·00 1·00
5715 $100 125 S sports car . . . 1·00 1·00
5716 $200 246 F.1 racing car . . 1·50 1·60
5717 $300 126/C2 racing car . . . 2·25 2·50
5718 $400 312/B2 racing car . . . 2·75 3·00
MS5719 104 × 70 mm. $300 512 S sports cars (93 × 35 mm) . . . 2·50 2·75

1999. 40th Anniv of Inter-American Development Bank.
5720 **611** $30 multicoloured . . . 30 25

1999. New Millennium (1st issue). People and Events of Eleventh Century (1050–1100). As T **310b** of Gambia. Multicoloured.
5721 $35 Indians with pots (Anasazi trading centre, 1050) 35 35
5722 $35 Catalan "Black Virgin" statue (carved, 1050) . . . 35 35
5723 $35 Horse archer (Seljuk conquest of Armenia, 1064) 35 35
5724 $35 Halley's Comet (appearance, 1066) . . . 35 35
5725 $35 Norman cavalry (Battle of Hastings, 1066) 35 35
5726 $35 William I of England (crowned, 1066) 35 35
5727 $35 Samurai warriors (power of Fujiwara clan checked, 1068) 35 35
5728 $35 Henry IV, Holy Roman Emperor (excommunicated, 1076) 35 35
5729 $35 Timbuktu (founded, 1087) 35 35
5730 $35 Students (foundation of Bologna University, 1088) 35 35
5731 $35 Gondola, Venice (introduction, 1094) . . . 35 35
5732 $35 El Cid (Spanish warrior) (capture of Valencia, 1094) 35 35
5733 $35 Mounted knights (First Crusade, 1095) 35 35
5734 $35 Saracen infantry (capture of Jerusalem, 1099) 35 35
5735 $35 Statue of Guanyin (Chinese deity) (carved, 1100) 35 35
5736 $35 Couple and quote from the Rubiayat of Omar Khayyam (written, 1100) (55 × 36 mm) 35 35
5737 $35 Decorating jar (introduction of Syrian style storage jars, 1100) 35 35

1999. New Millennium (2nd issue). People and Events of Twentieth Century (1910–1919). As T **471a** of Grenada. Multicoloured.
5738 $35 Poster for Grafton Gallery's Post Impressionist Exhibition, 1910 . . . . 35 35
5739 $35 Trial scene and oil rig (Standard Oil case, 1911) 35 35
5740 $35 Harriet Quimby (first American woman pilot, 1911) 35 35
5741 $35 U.S. Senate (declaration of war, 1917) 35 35
5742 $35 Sinking of *Titanic*, 1912 35 35
5743 $35 Emperor Pu Yi (formation of Chinese Republic, 1913) 35 35
5744 $35 Statue over entrance (opening of Grand Central Station, New York, 1913) 35 35
5745 $35 Archduke Francis Ferdinand of Austria and cavalry (assassinated, 1914) 35 35
5746 $35 Map and lock gates (opening of Panama Canal, 1914) 35 35
5747 $35 Lawrence of Arabia (Arab revolt, 1916) . . . 35 35
5748 $35 Burning buildings, Dublin (Easter Rising, 1916) 35 35
5749 $35 Lenin and revolutionaries (Russian Revolution, 1917) 35 35
5750 $35 Tsar Nicholas II and family (murdered, 1917) 35 35
5751 $35 Treaty of Versailles, 1918 . . . . 35 35
5752 $35 Three patients and poster (influenza epidemic, 1919) 35 35
5753 $35 Leo Tolstoy and Mark Twain (deaths, 1910) (55 × 36 mm) 35 35
5754 $35 Walter Gropius and Bauhaus (opened 1919) 35 35

Dates on Nos. 5750 and 5751 are transposed. No. 5754 is inscribed "Bahaus" in error.

1999. Faces of the Millennium. Diana, Princess of Wales. As T **307a** of Gambia. Multicoloured.
5755 $80 Top of head (face value at left) 70 75
5756 $80 Top of head (face value at right) 70 75
5757 $80 Ear (face value at left) 70 75
5758 $80 Eye and temple (face value at right) 70 75
5759 $80 Cheek (face value at left) 70 75
5760 $80 Cheek (face value at right) 70 75
5761 $80 Blue background (face value at left) 70 75
5762 $80 Chin (face value at right) 70 75

Nos. 5755/62 were printed together, se-tenant, in sheetlets of 8 with the stamps arranged in two vertical columns separated by a gutter also containing miniature flower photographs. When viewed as a whole the sheetlet forms a portrait of Diana, Princess of Wales.

2000. Chinese New Year ("Year of the Dragon"). Multicoloured.
5763 $100 Type **612** (face value bottom right) 85 90
5764 $100 Dragon (face value bottom left) 85 90
5765 $100 Dragon (face value top right) 85 90
5766 $100 Dragon (face value top left) 85 90
MS5767 102 × 70 mm. $300 Dragon on background of Chinese characters . . . . 2·50 2·75

613 Cugnot's Steam-powered Fardier (1769)

2000. Cars. Multicoloured.
5768 $100 Type **613** 80 80
5769 $100 Marcus's motor carriage (1875) 80 80
5770 $100 Benz Velo (1894) 80 80
5771 $100 Bordino's steam carriage (1854) 80 80
5772 $100 Benz Motorwagen (1886) 80 80
5773 $100 Black Model T Ford (1908) 80 80
5774 $100 Duesenberg Model A phaeton (1926) 80 80
5775 $100 Mercedes-Benz Model K (1927) 80 80
5776 $100 Rolls-Royce Phantom I (1928) 80 80
5777 $100 Auburn 851 Speedster (1935) 80 80
5778 $100 Mercedes-Benz 540K Cabriolet B (1936) . . . 80 80
5779 $100 Volkswagen Beetle (1949) 80 80
5780 $100 Ford Thunderbird (1957) 80 80
5781 $100 Jaguar XK150 (1957) 80 80
5782 $100 Chevrolet Corvette Stingray (1968) 80 80
5783 $100 BMW 2002 Turbo (1973) 80 80
5784 $100 Porsche 911 Turbo (1975) 80 80
5785 $100 Volkswagen Beetle (1999) 80 80
5786 $100 Daimler (1886) 80 80
5787 $100 Opel Luzman (1898) 80 80
5788 $100 Benz Landaulet Coupe (1899) 80 80
5789 $100 Peugeot Vis-a-vis (1892) 80 80
5790 $100 Benz Patent Motor Car (1886) 80 80
5791 $100 Benz Velo (1894) . . . 80 80
5792 $100 Ford (1896) 80 80
5793 $100 De Dion-Bouton Populare (1903) 80 80
5794 $100 Adler (1900) 80 80
5795 $100 Vauxhall (1904) . . . 80 80
5796 $100 Rolls Royce Silver Ghost (1908) 80 80
5797 $100 Model T Ford (1908) (different) 80 80
MS5798 Five sheets. (a) 105 × 80 mm. $400 Mercedes Benz 60/70 (1904) (50 × 38 mm). (b) 105 × 80 mm. $400 Mercedes Benz Type 320 Cabriolet (1939) (50 × 38 mm). (c) 105 × 80 mm. $400 Mercedes Benz 300 SL Gullwing (1954) (50 × 38 mm). (d) 81 × 63 mm. $400 Runabout (1910) (50 × 38 mm). (e) 81 × 63 mm. $400 Turner Miesse (1904) (50 × 38 mm) Set of 5 sheets 14·00 15·00

No. 5791 is inscribed "VELD" in error.

614 Top of Head

2000. Faces of the Millennium. George Washington. Designs showing a collage of miniature bank note photographs. Multicoloured.
5799 $80 Type **614** 70 75
5800 $80 Top of head (face value at right) 70 75
5801 $80 Ear (face value at left) 70 75
5802 $80 Cheek (face value at right) 70 75
5803 $80 Right shoulder (face value at left) 70 75
5804 $80 Left shoulder (face value at right) 70 75
5805 $80 Right upper arm (face value at left) 70 75
5806 $80 Left upper arm (face value at right) 70 75

Nos. 5799/806 were printed together, se-tenant, in sheetlets of 8 with the stamps arranged in two vertical columns separated by a gutter also containing miniature photographs. When viewed as a whole the sheetlet forms a portrait of George Washington.

615 Hogfish (*Lachnolaimus maximus*)

2000. Tropical Marine Life. Multicoloured.
5807 $30 Type **615** 30 25
5808 $35 Flamingo-tongue cowrie (*Cyphoma gibbosum*) . . . 35 25
5809 $60 Permit (*Trachinotus falcatus*) 60 40
5810 $80 Lionfish (*Pterois volitans*) (vert) 70 75
5811 $80 Bottle-nosed dolphin (*Tursiops truncatus*) (vert) 70 75
5812 $80 Jellyfish (*Diplulmaris antarctica*) (vert) 70 75
5813 $80 Grey angelfish (*Pomacanthus arcuatus*) (vert) 70 75
5814 $80 Spotted eagle ray (*Aetobatus narinari*) (vert) 70 75
5815 $80 Grey reef shark (*Carcharhinus amblyrhynchos*) (vert) . . . 70 75
5816 $80 Sea bass (*Sacura margaritacea*) (vert) 70 75
5817 $80 Giant octopus (*Octopus dolfeini*) (vert) 70 75
5818 $80 Great barracuda (*Sphyraena barracuda*) . . 70 75
5819 $80 Gulper eel (*Saccopharynx sp*) 70 75
5820 $80 Sea slug (*Chromodoris amoena*) 70 75
5821 $80 Blue marlin (*Makaira nigricans*) 70 75
5822 $80 Killer whale (*Orcinus orca*) 70 75
5823 $80 Reid's seahorse (*Hippocampus reidi*) . . . 70 75
5824 $80 Green sea turtle (*Chelonia mydas*) 70 75
5825 $80 Sailfin blenny (*Emblemaria pandionis*) . . 70 75
5826 $80 Indigo hamlet (*Hypoplectrus indigo*) . . 70 75
5827 $80 Scallop (*Chlamys hastata*) 70 75
5828 $80 Flag rockfish (*Sebastes rubrivinctus*) 70 75
5829 $80 Lookdown (*Selene vomer*) 70 75
5830 $80 Orange marginella (*Marginella carnea*) . . . 70 75
5831 $80 Harbour seal (*Phocus vitulina*) 70 75
5832 $80 Dolphin fish (*Coryphaena hippurus*) . . 70 75
5833 $80 Coney (*Epinephelus fulvus*) 70 75
5834 $100 Spot-finned hogfish (*Bodianus pulchellus*) . . . 90 90
5835 $200 Porkfish (*Anisotremus virginicus*) . . . . 1·60 1·75
5836 $300 Orange-throated darter (*Etheostoma spectabile*) . . 2·25 2·50
MS5837 Three sheets. (a) 85 × 110 mm. $400 Snakestar (*Asteroschema tenue*) (vert). (b) 85 × 110 mm. $400 Penpoint gunnel (*Apodichthys flavidus*) (vert). (c) 110 × 85 mm. $400 Spotted cleaner shrimp (*Periclimenes pedersoni*) (57 × 42 mm) Set of 3 sheets . . 9·00 9·50

Nos. 5810/17, 5818/25 and 5826/33 were each printed together, se-tenant, with the backgrounds forming composite designs.

2000. 18th Birthday of Prince William. As T **312b** of Gambia. Multicoloured.
5838 $100 Prince William with Prince Harry . . . . . . 1·00 1·00
5839 $100 As a young boy, holding present . . . . . 1·00 1·00
5840 $100 Prince William wearing suit and white shirt . . . 1·00 1·00
5841 $100 Wearing suit and blue shirt . . . . 1·00 1·00
MS5842 100 × 80 mm. $400 Dressed for skiing (37 × 50 mm) . . . . 3·75 4·00

2000. "EXPO 2000" World Stamp Exhibition, Anaheim, USA. Space Satellites. As T **582a** of Ghana. Multicoloured.
5843 $100 "Apollo 11" 80 85
5844 $100 "Pioneer" and Saturn 80 85
5845 $100 Nasa/Esa "Soho" Satellite 80 85
5846 $100 Nasa "Mars Orbiter" and Mars 80 85
5847 $100 Space Shuttle and International Space Station 80 85
5848 $100 "Giotto" and Halley's Comet 80 85
5849 $100 "Amsat IIIC" (vert) . . 80 85
5850 $100 "Sret" (vert) 80 85
5851 $100 "Inspector" (vert) . . 80 85
5852 $100 "Stardust" (vert) . . . 80 85
5853 $100 "Temisat" (vert) . . . 80 85
5854 $100 "Arsene" (vert) 80 85
5855 $100 "Cesar" with Argentine and Spanish flags 80 85
5856 $100 "Sirio 2" with Italian flag 80 85
5857 $100 "Taos S 80" with French flag 80 85
5858 $100 "Viking" with Swedish flag 80 85
5859 $100 "SCD 1" with Brazilian flag 80 85
5860 $100 "Offeq 1" with Israeli flag 80 85
MS5861 Two sheets. (a) 106 × 76 mm. $400 "Solar Max". (b) 76 × 106 mm. $400 Clementine French Satellite "Ariane V 124" (vert) . . . . 6·00 6·50

No. 5845 is inscribed "Satellit" in error.

2000. 25th Anniv of "Apollo-Soyuz" Joint Project. As T **582a** of Ghana. Multicoloured.
5862 $200 Thomas Stafford and Vance Brand ("Apollo 18" astronauts) 1·60 1·75
5863 $200 "Apollo 18" command module . . . . 1·60 1·75
5864 $200 Thomas Stafford and Valeri Kubasov (Russian cosmonaut) . . . . 1·60 1·75
MS5865 88 × 71 mm. $400 Donald Slayton and Thomas Stafford ("Apollo 18" astronauts) (horiz) 2·75 3·00

2000. 50th Anniv of Berlin Film Festival. As T **582c** of Ghana. Multicoloured.
5866 $100 "Das Boot ist Voll", 1981 . . . . 80 85
5867 $100 "David", 1979 . . . . 80 85
5868 $100 "Hong Gaoliang", 1988 . . . . 80 85
5869 $100 "Die Ehe der Maria Braun", 1979 . . . . . . 80 85
5870 $100 "The Whisperers", 1967 . . . . 80 85
5871 $100 "Le Vieil Homme et L'Enfant", 1967 . . . . . 80 85
MS5872 97 × 103 mm. $400 "Love Streams", 1984 . . . . 3·00 3·25
No. 5871 omits "L'ENFANT" from the film title.

2000. 175th Anniv of Stockton and Darlington Line (first public railway). As T **582c** of Ghana. Multicoloured.
5873 $200 Timothy Hackworth 1·60 1·75
5874 $200 Hackworth's "Sans Pareil" engine . . . . . 1·60 1·75
5875 $200 Bramhope Tunnel, Otley . . . . 1·60 1·75
Nos. 5874 and 5875 are inscribed "Sansareil" and "Branhope", both in error.

616 Johann Sebastian Bach **617** Rohan Kanhai

2000. 250th Death Anniv of Johann Sebastian Bach (German composer). Sheet 88 × 76 mm.
MS5876 **616** $400 multicoloured 3·50 3·75

2000. Election of Albert Einstein (mathematical physicist) as Time Magazine "Man of the Century". Sheet 117 × 91 mm, containing vert design as T **312d** of Gambia. Multicoloured.
MS5877 $400 Albert Einstein . . 3·25 3·50

2000. Centenary of First Zeppelin Flight. As T **582c** of Ghana. Multicoloured.
5878 $200 Count von Zeppelin and LZ-1 airship, 1900 . . 1·60 1·75
5879 $200 Von Zeppelin and LZ-2, 1906 . . . . 1·60 1·75
5880 $200 Von Zeppelin and LZ-9, 1911 . . . . 1·60 1·75
MS5881 84 × 114 mm. $400 LZ-127 Zeppelin, 1928 (50 × 38 mm) 3·25 3·50

2000. Olympic Games, Sydney. As T **582f** of Ghana. Multicoloured.
5882 $160 Henry Robert Pearce (single sculls rower), Los Angeles (1932) . . . . . 1·25 1·40
5883 $160 Volleyball . . . . . . 1·25 1·40
5884 $160 Olympic Park, Canada (1976) and Canadian flag 1·25 1·40
5885 $160 Ancient Greek athletes 1·25 1·40

2000. West Indies Cricket Tour and 100th Test Match at Lord's. Multicoloured.
5886 $100 Type **617** . . . . . . 1·00 80
5887 $300 Clive Lloyd . . . . . 2·50 2·50
MS5888 121 × 104 mm. $400 Lord's Cricket Ground, London (horiz) 3·75 4·00

618 Flags of China and Macau

2000. Return of Macau to Chinese Sovereignty. Sheet 144 × 119 mm, containing T **618** and similar horiz design. Multicoloured.
MS5889 $150 Type **618**; $150 Downtown Macau . . . . . . 2·50 2·75

2000. Betty Boop (cartoon character). As T **308** of Gambia. Multicoloured.
5890 $80 Betty Boop wearing striped shirt 65 70
5891 $80 With shopping bags . . 65 70
5892 $80 Kneeling on cushion . . 65 70
5893 $80 As belly dancer 65 70
5894 $80 Putting on shoe 65 70
5895 $80 Wearing cowboy boots 65 70
5896 $80 Betty Boop dancing . . 65 70
5897 $80 In flowered trousers . . 65 75
5898 $80 In black dress 65 70
MS5899 Twenty-two sheets. (a) 137 × 87 mm. $400 In blue dress and fur stole; (b) 137 × 87 mm. $400 In polka dot dress; (c) 120 × 95 mm. $400 Standing in shell; (d) 111 × 127 mm. $400 In red dress by the sea; (e) 121 × 95 mm. $400 Wearing brown coat and red scarf; (f) 120 × 95 mm. $400 With tennis racket; (g) 121 × 101 mm. $400 Winking; (h) 120 × 96 mm. $400 Wearing black feather boa and brown hat; (i) 95 × 133 mm. $400 With sad expression (horiz). (j) 91 × 143 mm. $400 Wearing ruff; (k) 90 × 140 mm. $400 Wearing orange t-shirt and baseball hat (horiz). (l) 90 × 140 mm. $400 Wearing red vest top; (m) 140 × 90 mm. $400 Wearing pink baseball hat; (n) 90 × 140 mm. $400 Wearing red dress and orange sash; (o) 89 × 139 mm. $400 Holding present; (p) 89 × 139 mm. $400 Wearing party hat (horiz). (q) 89 × 139 mm. $400 Wearing sailor's hat; (r) 89 × 139 mm. $400 In red bikini; (s) 89 × 139mm. $400 With sunglasses on head; (t) 89 × 139 mm. $400 In mauve vest top and blue dungarees (horiz). (u) 89 × 139 mm. $400 In mauve vest top; (v) 89 × 139 mm. $400 With mauve flower in hair Set of 22 sheets . . . . 55·00 60·00

2000. Scenes from *I Love Lucy* (American T.V. comedy series). As T **309** of Gambia, but vert. Multicoloured.
5900 $60 Lucy reading a thriller 50 55
5901 $60 Lucy and Ricky talking 50 55
5902 $60 Ricky whispering to Lucy 50 55
5903 $60 Lucy looking out of window 50 55
5904 $60 Lucy behind Ethel . . . 50 55
5905 $60 Ricky holding red scarf over Lucy 50 55
5906 $60 Ethel and Lucy with frying pan 50 55
5907 $60 Ricky with frying pan 50 55
5908 $60 Lucy and Ethel sitting on sofa next to coffee table 50 55
MS5909 Ten sheets. (a) 120 × 95 mm. $400 Lucy in pink dressing gown. (b) 120 × 95 mm. $400 Lucy with dustbin lid. (c) 100 × 134 mm. $400 Lucy wearing glasses. (d) 138 × 100 mm. $400 Lucy wearing blue hat and green coat. (e) 93 × 137 mm. $400 Lucy dancing the rumba. (f) 137 × 100 mm. $400 Lucy wearing green hat. (g) 100 × 134 mm. $400 Lucy with knives. (h) 137 × 100 mm. $400 Lucy wearing black hat. (i) 93 × 137 mm. $400 Lucy in checked shirt. (j) 137 × 100 mm. $400 Lucy wearing leis Set of 10 sheets . . . . . 27·00 29·00

2000. Scenes from *The Three Stooges* (American T.V. comedy series). As T **310** of Gambia. Multicoloured.
5910 $80 Larry, Moe and Curly (The Three Stooges) with man in green jacket . . . 65 70
5911 $80 Larry and Moe with skeleton 65 70
5912 $80 Shemp with hair standing on end 65 70
5913 $80 Larry, Moe and Curly with fingers in mouths . . 65 70
5914 $80 Larry, Moe and Curly reading a book 65 70
5915 $80 Larry, Moe and Curly holding man in bowler hat 65 70
5916 $80 Shemp pointing a gun at Larry and Moe 65 70
5917 $80 Moe and Shemp holding Larry (being kicked in stomach by man in blue) 65 70
5918 $80 Moe and Shemp looking at man in window 65 70
5919 $80 Moe pointing syphon bottle at Larry, with Shemp behind 65 70
5920 $80 Larry, Moe and Shemp as cave men (Moe with rock on head) 65 70
5921 $80 Moe with cow 65 70
5922 $80 Shemp with bucket on head 65 70
5923 $80 Moe, Shemp and Larry as cavemen (three wise monkeys) 65 70
5924 $80 Moe, Shemp and Larry as cavemen (Shemp holding large rock) . . . 65 70
5925 $80 Larry, Moe and Shemp wearing pith helmets . . . 65 70
5926 $80 Moe, Shemp and Larry in front of painting . . . 65 70
5927 $80 Moe, Larry and Shemp with false beards 65 70
MS5928 Four sheets (a) 92 × 122 mm. $400 Shemp wearing tam-o'-shanter (vert). (b)122 × 92 mm. $400 Larry with skeleton. (c) 131 × 103 mm. $400 Larry with lady in blue dress (vert). (d) 131 × 103 mm. $400 Moe being pulled by collar Set of 4 sheets . . . . 11·00 12·00

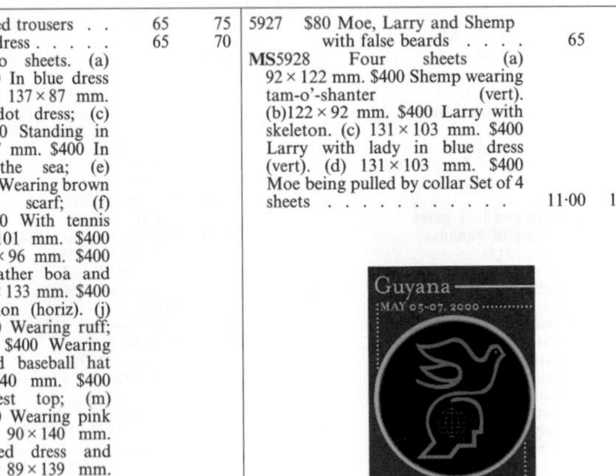

619 Outline Drawing of Dove on Head

2000. 3rd Annual Caribbean Media Conference, Georgetown.
5929 **619** $100 multicoloured . . . 85 85

2000. "Euro 2000" Football Championship. As T **316** of Gambia. Multicoloured.
5930 $80 Turkish team 70 75
5931 $80 Slovenian team 70 75
5932 $80 Yugoslavian team . . . 70 75
5933 $80 Swedish team 70 75
5934 $80 Belgian team 70 75
5935 $80 Spanish team 70 75
5936 $80 French team 70 75
5937 $80 English team 70 75
5938 $80 Danish team 70 75
5939 $80 German team 70 75
5940 $80 Italian team 70 75
5941 $80 Dutch team 70 75
5942 $80 Portuguese team 70 75
5943 $80 Romanian team 70 75
5944 $80 Czech team 70 75
5945 $80 Norwegian team 70 75
MS5946 Two sheets, each 102 × 80 mm. (a) $400 Stefan Kuntz, 1996 (vert). (b) $400 Jurgen Klinsmann holding trophy, 1996 (vert) Set of 2 sheets . . . . . 6·50 7·00

620 Lee Hyo-Ri

2000. Fine Killing Liberty (FIN.K.L), Korean Girl Group. Multicoloured (except No. 5954).
5947 $80 Type **620** 70 75
5948 $80 Ok Ju-Hyun (head tilted to left) 70 75
5949 $80 Lee Jin (looking sideways) 70 75
5950 $80 Lee Jin (facing forwards) 70 75
5951 $80 FIN.K.L 70 75
5952 $80 Sung Yu-Ri (head tilted to left) 70 75
5953 $80 Lee Hyo-Ri (no hat) . . 70 75
5954 $80 Sung Yu-Ri (facing forwards) (purple, black and blue) 70 75
5955 $80 Ok Ju-Hyun smiling . . 70 75

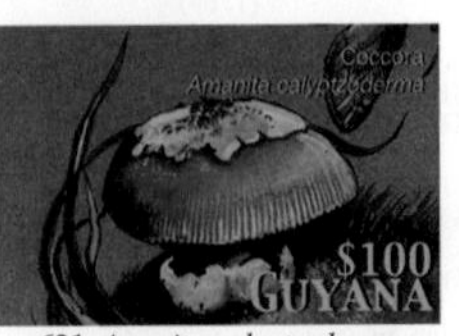

621 *Amanita calyptroderma*

2000. "The Stamp Show 2000" International Stamp Exhibition, London. Fungi. Multicoloured.
5956 $100 Type **621** 85 90
5957 $100 *Polyporus brumalis* . . 85 90
5958 $100 *Hygrophorus pudorinus* 85 90
5959 $100 *Aeryginosa stropharia geophila* 85 90
5960 $100 *Amanita muscaria* . . . 85 90
5961 $100 *Armillaria mellea* . . . 85 90
5962 $100 *Hygrophoracaea* . . . 85 90
5963 $100 *Russula xerampelina* 85 90
5964 $100 *Hygrophorus coccineus* 85 90
5965 $100 *Psilocybe stuntzii* . . . 85 90
5966 $100 *Rhodotus palmatus* . . 85 90
5967 $100 *Lactarius indigo* . . . 85 90
5968 $100 *Gomphus floccosus* . . 85 90
5969 $100 *Amanita caesarea* . . . 85 90
5970 $100 *Leotia viscose* 85 90
5971 $100 *Entoloma salmoneum* 85 90
5972 $100 *Cheimonophyllum candidissimus* 85 90
5973 $100 *Cortinarius multiformis* 85 90
MS5974 Three sheets. (a) 99 × 69 mm. $400 *Marasmius rotula*. (b) 69 × 99 mm. $400 *Volvariella pusilla* (vert). (c) 99 × 69 mm. $400 *Trametes versicolour* Set of 3 sheets . . . 9·00 9·50
Nos. 5956/61, 5962/7 and 5968/73 were each printed together, se-tenant, with the backgrounds forming composite designs.
Nos. 5956/8, 5961/2, 5964/5, 5967, 5969, 5972, **MS**5974a and MS5974c are inscribed "calyptzoderma", "crumalis", "pydorinus", "Armillariella", "Hygrophotaceae", "cocineus", "psilcybe stuntaii", "lactaius", "Aminita", "candidissimis", "zotula" and "Tzametes", all in error.

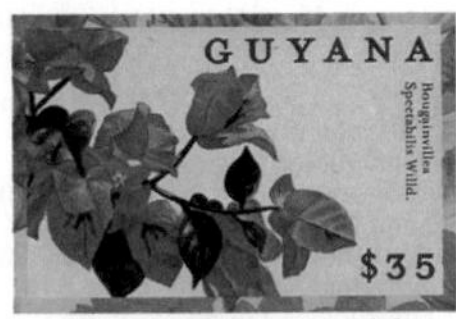

622 *Bougainvillea spectabilis*

2000. Flowers. Multicoloured.
5975 $35 Type **622** 35 25
5976 $60 *Euphorbia milii* 60 40
5977 $100 *Cordia sebestena* (vert) 80 85
5978 $100 *Heliconia wagneriana* (vert) 80 85
5979 $100 *Dendrobium phalaenopsis* (vert) 80 85
5980 $100 *Passiflora caerulea* (vert) 80 85
5981 $100 *Oncidium nubigenum* (vert) 80 85
5982 $100 *Hibiscus rosa-sinensis* (vert) 80 85
5983 $100 *Lantana camara* . . . 80 85
5984 $100 *Jatropha integerrima* 80 85
5985 $100 *Plumeria alba* 80 85
5986 $100 *Strelitzia reginae* . . . 80 85
5987 $100 *Clerodendrum splendens* 80 85
5988 $100 *Thunbergia grandiflora* 80 85
5989 $200 *Catharanthus roseus* . . 1·50 1·60
5990 $300 *Ipomoea carnea* . . . 2·10 2·25
MS5991 Two sheets (a) 83 × 103 mm. $400 *Cattleya granulose* (vert). (b) 103 × 83 mm. $400 *Guzmania lingulata* Set of 2 sheets . . . . 6·00 6·50
Nos. 5983/8 were printed together, se-tenant, the backgrounds forming a composite design.

623 *Russelia equisetiformis*

2000. Flowers of Central America. Multicoloured.
5992 $35 Type **623** 35 25
5993 $60 *Sprekelia formosissima* 60 40
5994 $100 *Bignonia capreolata* . . 80 85
5995 $100 *Calceolaria herbeo-hybrida* 80 85
5996 $100 *Canna generalis* . . . 80 85
5997 $100 *Bauhinia grandiflora* . . 80 85
5998 $100 *Amaranthus caudatus* 80 85
5999 $100 *Abutilon megapotamicum* 80 85
6000 $100 *Ipomoea tricolor* ("Morning Glory") . . . 80 85
6001 $100 *Lantana camara* . . . 80 85
6002 $100 *Cantua buxifolia* . . . 80 85
6003 $100 *Fuschia* 80 85
6004 $100 *Eichhornia crassipes* . . 80 85
6005 $100 *Cosmos sulphureus* . . 80 85
6006 $200 *Passiflora quadrangularis* . . . . . 1·50 1·60
6007 $300 *Mirabilis jalapa* . . . 2·10 2·25
MS6008 Two sheets, each 100 × 70 mm. (a) $400 *Oeceoclades maculate*. (b) $400 *Passiflora van-volxemii* ("Tasconia") . . . . . . 6·00 6·50
No. 6004 is inscribed "Eichornia", in error.

2000. Victims of Munich Olympics Massacre (1972) Commemoration. As T **328** of Gambia showing Israeli athletes and officials. Multicoloured.
6009 $40 Yaakov Springer (weightlifting referee) . . 40 40
6010 $40 Andrei Schpitzer (fencing referee) 40 40
6011 $40 Amitsur Shapira (athletics coach) 40 40
6012 $40 David Berger (weightlifter) 40 40
6013 $40 Ze'ev Friedman (weightlifter) 40 40
6014 $40 Joseph Gottfreund (wrestling referee) 40 40
6015 $40 Moshe Weinberg (wrestling referee) 40 40
6016 $40 Kahat Shor (shooting coach) 40 40
6017 $40 Mark Slavin (wrestler) 40 40
6018 $40 Eliezer Halffin (wrestler) 40 40

6019 $40 Joseph Romano (weightlifter) 40 40
6020 $40 Munich Olympics stadium 40 40
MS6021 127×101 mm. $400 Israeli athlete with Olympic torch (vert) 3·75 4·00

2000. Queen Elizabeth the Queen Mother's 100th Birthday. As T **318** of Gambia. Multicoloured.
6022 $100 Queen Elizabeth the Queen Mother . . . . . 1·00 1·00

624 Heads of Two Angels

2000. Christmas and Holy Year. Multicoloured.
6023 $60 Type **624** 50 40
6024 $90 Two angels 80 60
6025 $120 Heads of two angels (different) . . . . 1·00 75
6026 $180 As $90 . . . . 1·40 1·60
6027 $180 Type **624** . . . . . . 1·40 1·60
6028 $180 As $120 . . . . 1·40 1·60
6029 $180 Two angels with drapery . . . . 1·40 1·60
6030 $400 As No. 6029 . . . . . 3·25 3·50
MS6031 121×110 mm. $400 Holy Child (horiz) . . . . 3·25 3·50

625 Snake

2001. Chinese New Year ("Year of the Snake"). Multicoloured.
6032 $80 Type **625** 70 70
6033 $80 Snake (face value at top right) 70 70
6034 $80 Snake (face value at bottom right) 70 70
6035 $80 Snake (face value at bottom left) 70 70
MS6036 85×65 mm. $250 Snake (vert) . . . . 2·00 2·50

626 Prime Minister's Residence, Georgetown

2001. Tourist Attractions. Multicoloured.
6037 $90 Type **626** 75 80
6038 $90 Kaieteur Falls (vert) . . 75 80

2001. Faces of the Millennium. Queen Elizabeth the Queen Mother's 100th Birthday. As T **307a** of Gambia showing collage of miniature flower photographs. Multicoloured.
6039 $80 Top left side of head . . 75 75
6040 $80 Top right side of head 75 75
6041 $80 Eye and temple 75 75
6042 $80 Temple 75 75
6043 $80 Right cheek 75 75
6044 $80 Left cheek 75 75
6045 $80 Chin 75 75
6046 $80 Neck 75 75
Nos. 6039/46 were printed together, se-tenant, in sheetlets of 8 with the stamps arranged in two vertical columns separated by a gutter also containing miniature photographs. When viewed as a whole, the sheetlet forms a portrait of the Queen Mother.

2001. Faces of the Millennium: 80th Birthday of Pope John Paul II. As T **307a** of Gambia showing collage of miniature religious photographs. Multicoloured.
6047 $100 Back of head 90 90
6048 $100 Front of forehead . . 90 90
6049 $100 Ear 90 90
6050 $100 Eye 90 90
6051 $100 Neck 90 90
6052 $100 Cheek 90 90
6053 $100 Shoulder of robe . . . 90 90
6054 $100 Hands 90 90
Nos. 6047/54 were printed together, se-tenant, in sheetlets of 8 with the stamps arranged in two vertical columns separated by a gutter also containing miniature photographs. When viewed as a whole, the sheetlet forms a portrait of the Pope.

627 Chow Yun-Fat

2001. Chow Yun-Fat (Hong Kong actor). Multicoloured.
6055 $60 Type **627** 50 55
6056 $60 Wearing maroon coat 50 55
6057 $60 Wearing dark suit and grey shirt 50 55
6058 $60 In cream jacket, black shirt and white T-shirt . . 50 55
6059 $60 Wearing dark suit, white shirt and grey tie 50 55
6060 $60 In dark overcoat . . . 50 55

2001. Characters from Pokemon (children's cartoon series). As T **332a** of Gambia. Multicoloured.
6061 $100 "Staryu No. 120" . . 85 85
6062 $100 "Seaking No. 119" . . 85 85
6063 $100 "Tentacool No. 72" 85 85
6064 $100 "Magikarp No. 129" 85 85
6065 $100 "Seadra No. 117" . . 85 85
6066 $100 "Goldeen No. 118" . . 85 85
MS6067 74×114 mm. $400 "Horsea No. 116" (vert) . . . . 3·00 3·25

628 Boxer Dog

2001. "Hong Kong 2001" Stamp Exhibition. Cats and Dogs. Multicoloured.
6068 $35 Type **628** 35 25
6069 $60 Cinnamon ocicat . . . 55 55
6070 $60 Devon Rex 55 55
6071 $60 Egyptian Mau 55 55
6072 $60 Turkish angora 55 55
6073 $60 Sphynx 55 55
6074 $60 Persian 55 55
6075 $60 American wirehair . . . 55 55
6076 $60 Exotic shorthair 55 55
6077 $60 American curl 55 55
6078 $80 Airedale terrier 70 70
6079 $80 Greyhound 70 70
6080 $80 Afghan hound 70 70
6081 $80 Samoyed 70 70
6082 $80 Field spaniel 70 70
6083 $80 Scottish terrier 70 70
6084 $80 Brittany spaniel (brown and white) 70 70
6085 $80 Boston terrier 70 70
6086 $100 Smooth dachshund . . 90 90
6087 $300 White Manx . . . . . 2·50 2·75
MS6088 Two sheets, each 100×80 mm. (a) $400 Birman (cat). (b) $400 Dalmatian Set of 2 sheets . . . . 6·50 7·00
Nos. 6070/7 (cats) and 6078/85 (dogs) were each printed together, se-tenant, with the backgrounds forming composite designs. No. 6081 is inscribed "Samoyeo" in error. Nos. 6070/85 and MS6088 all show the "Hong Kong 2001" logo on the sheet margins.

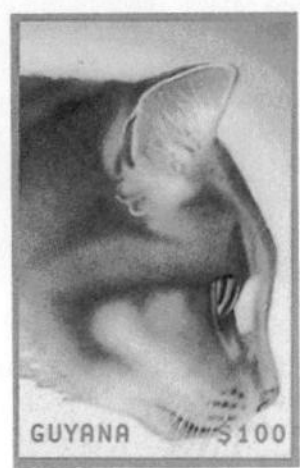

629 "Tom"

2001. Cats and Dogs of the Cinema. Multicoloured.
6089 $100 Type **629** 90 90
6090 $100 "Puff" (Siamese) . . . 90 90
6091 $100 "Jag" (silver tabby) . . 90 90
6092 $100 "Fritz" (Burmese, with paw curled) 90 90
6093 $100 "Smokey" (Burmese) 90 90
6094 $100 "Thor" (white cat) . . 90 90
6095 $100 "Pup" (small black and tan dog) 90 90
6096 $100 "Yogi" (white dog in snow) 90 90
6097 $100 "Hooch" (mastiff) . . 90 90
6098 $100 "Huxley Blu" (collie) 90 90
6099 $100 "Snowflake" (small white dog) 90 90
6100 $100 "Red" (Irish setter) . . 90 90
MS6101 Two sheets, each 67×86 mm. (a) $400 "Spike" (kitten). (b) $400 "Baron of Fillmore" (German shepherd dog) Set of 2 sheets . . . . 6·50 7·00

630 Chihuahua

2001. Dogs and Cats in the Caribbean. Multicoloured.
6102 $35 Type **630** 35 25
6103 $60 Persian tabby 60 40
6104 $80 Rottweiler 70 70
6105 $80 German shepherd . . . 70 70
6106 $80 Burmese mountain dog 70 70
6107 $80 Shar Pei 70 70
6108 $80 Dachshund 70 70
6109 $80 Jack Russell 70 70
6110 $80 Boston terrier 70 70
6111 $80 Corgi 70 70
6112 $80 American shorthair . . 70 70
6113 $80 Somali 70 70
6114 $80 Balinese 70 70
6115 $80 Egyptian Mau 70 70
6116 $80 Scottish fold 70 70
6117 $80 Sphynx 70 70
6118 $80 Korat 70 70
6119 $100 Colourpoint shorthair 90 90
6120 $200 Cocker spaniel . . . . 1·60 1·75
MS6121 Two sheets, each 76×86 mm. (a) $400 Beagle. (b) $400 Abyssinian (cat) Set of 2 sheets . . . . 6·50 7·00
Nos. 6104/11 (dogs) and 6112/18 (cats) were each printed together, se-tenant, with the backgrounds forming composite designs that extend onto the sheetlet margins.

631 George Washington

2001. George Washington (American president) Commemoration.
6122 **631** $300 multicoloured . . . 2·50 2·75

632 Hello Kitty in Alice in Wonderland

2001. Hello Kitty (cartoon character). Twelve sheets, each 100×145 mm, containg vert designs as T **632** of Hello Kitty in European (No. **MS**6120a/f) or Japanese (No. **MS**6120g/l) fairy tales. Multicoloured.
MS6123 (a) $400 Type **632**. (b) $400 Cinderella. (c) $400 Heidi. (d) $400 The Wizard of Oz. (e) $400 Peter Pan. (f) $400 Little Red Riding Hood. (g) $400 Three in a Boat. (h) $400 Bamboo Princess. (i) $400 The Fisherman. (j) $400 Up a Tree. (k) $400 On a Bear. (l) $400 In the Snow Set of 12 sheets 32·00 35·00

633 American Securities and Exchange Commission Office (founded 1934)

2001. People and Events of Early 20th Century. Multicoloured.
6124 $60 Type **633** 55 60
6125 $60 Herbert Hoover (American President, elected 1928) 55 60
6126 $60 Al Jolson in *The Jazz Singer* (first talking film, 1927) 55 60
6127 $60 J. Edgar Hoover (Director of F.B.I., appointed 1924) 55 60
6128 $60 Alexander Fleming (discovered penicillin, 1928) 55 60
6129 $60 Radio and microphone (Federal Communications Commission set up, 1927) 55 60
6130 $60 Charles Lindbergh (first solo transatlantic flight, 1927) 55 60
6131 $60 Albert Einstein (awarded Nobel physics prize, 1921) 55 60
6132 $60 Paul von Hindenburg (German leader, died 1934, succeeded by Hitler) 55 60
6133 $60 American flag and certificate (American Social Security Act, 1935) 55 60
6134 $60 Amelia Earhart (first solo flight from Hawaii to California) 55 60
6135 $60 Marcus Garvey (founder of Universal Negro Improvement Association, prison sentence commuted and deported, 1927) 55 60

634 Ronald Reagan

2001. 90th Birthday of Ronald Reagan (American President). Multicoloured (except Nos. 6136/8).
6136 $60 Type **634** (lilac and black) 55 60
6137 $60 With chimp in *Bedtime for Bonzo* (lilac and black) 55 60
6138 $60 Wearing cowboy hat (grey and black) 55 60
6139 $60 In dark suit and black tie 55 60
6140 $60 With Nancy Reagan . . 55 60
6141 $60 Pointing 55 60
6142 $60 Getting into car and waving 55 60
6143 $60 Signing reduction of nuclear arms treaty with Mikhail Gorbachev, 1987 55 60
6144 $60 Helping demolish Berlin Wall, 1989 . . . . 55 60
6145 $60 With President Clinton 55 60

635 "Girl at a Hot Spring Resort" (Hashiguchi Goyo)

2001. "Philanippon '01" International Stamp Exhibition, Tokyo. Japanese Paintings. Multicoloured.
6146 $25 Type **635** 20 20
6147 $25 "Hanaogi with Maidservant" (Eishosai Choki) 20 20
6148 $30 "Morokoshi of the Echizenya" (Rekisentei Eiri) 25 25
6149 $30 "Courtesan receiving a Letter of Invitation" (Suzuki Harunobu) . . . 25 25

6150 $35 "Mother and Daughter on an Outing" (Katsushika Hokusai) . . 30 30
6151 $35 "Two Girls on Way to (or from) the Bathhouse" (S. Harunobu) 30 30
6152 $60 "Matron in Love" (Kitagawa Utamaro) . . . 55 55
6153 $60 "Girl and Frog" (S. Harunobu) 55 55
6154 $80 "Insects, reptiles and amphibians at a Pond" (38 × 72 mm) 70 70
6155 $80 "Rose Mallow and Fowl" (38 × 72 mm) . . . 70 70
6156 $80 "Rooster, Sunflower and Morning Glories" (38 × 72 mm) 70 70
6157 $80 "Group of Roosters" (38 × 72 mm) 70 70
6158 $80 "Black Rooster and Nandina" (38 × 72 mm) 70 70
6159 $80 "Birds and Autumn Maples" (38 × 72 mm) . . 70 70
6160 $80 "Wagtail and Roses" (38 × 72 mm) 70 70
6161 $80 "Cockatoos in a Pine" (38 × 72 mm) 70 70
6162 $100 "Three Beauties of High Fame" (K. Utamaro) 85 85
6163 $100 "The Courtesan Midorigi" (Chokosai Eisho) 85 85
6164 $100 Bridge (38 × 72 mm) 85 85
6165 $100 Causeway and summer house (38 × 72 mm) . . . 85 85
6166 $100 Island in lake with single tree (38 × 72 mm) 85 85
6167 $100 Rocky islet and waterfalls tumbling into lake (38 × 72 mm) 85 85
6168 $100 Shugakuin Imperial Villa with Japanese letters (38 × 72 mm) 85 85
6169 $100 Trees with Japanese letters (38 × 72 mm) . . . 85 85
6170 $120 "Girls After the Bath" (K. Utamaro) (38 × 72 mm) 85 85
6171 $120 "Summer Evening on Riverbank at Hama-Cho" (Torii Kiyonaga) (38 × 72 mm) 90 90
6172 $120 "A Beauty in the Wind" (Kaigetsudo Ando) (38 × 72 mm) 90 90
6173 $120 "Sisters (Shimainozu)" (Tsuji Kako) (38 × 72 mm) 90 90
6174 $120 "Kasamori Osen" (S. Harunobu) (38 × 72 mm) 90 90
6175 $160 "Ichikawa Ebizo" behind Screen (30 × 38 mm) . . . . . . 1·25 1·25
6176 $160 "Ichikawa Ebizo" in red jacket (30 × 38 mm) 1·25 1·25
6177 $160 "Ichikawa Ebizo" with musicians (30 × 38 mm) 1·25 1·25
6178 $160 "Ichikawa Ebizo" being dressed as warrior (30 × 38 mm) . . . . . . 1·25 1·25
6179 $200 "Girl breaking off Branch of Flowering Tree" (S. Harunobu) . . 1·60 1·75
6180 $200 "Maiko" (Tsuchida Bakusen) . . . . 1·60 1·75
MS6181 Five sheets. (a) 120 × 80 mm. $400 "Wintry Sky" (Higashibara Hosen). (b)120 × 80 mm. $400 "Woman holding a Flower" (Kajiwara Hisako). (c) 120 × 80 mm. $400 "Palace of Immortals in an Autumn Valley" (Okochi Yako). (d) 80 × 120 mm. $400 Fish and Octopus from the "Colourful Realm of living Beings" (I. Jakuchu). (e) 80 × 120 mm. $400 "Portrait of Takami Senseki" (Watanabe Kazan). All imperf set of 5 sheets . . . . 14·00 15·00

Nos. 6154/61 (paintings by Ito Jakuchu), 6164/9 ("Procession to the Shugakuin Imperial Villa" by Kakimoto Sesshin), 6170/4 (Japanese Women) and 6175/8 ("Ichikawa Ebizo" (actor) by Toshusai Sharaku) were each printed together, se-tenant, in sheetlets of 4, 5, 6 or 8 with enlarged inscribed margins.

Nos. 6164/9 and 6175/8 each form a composite design.

636 Queen Victoria, 1850

2001. Death Centenary of Queen Victoria. Multicoloured.

6182 $200 Type **636** . . . . . . 1·60 1·75
6183 $200 Queen Victoria, 1843 1·60 1·75
6184 $200 Queen Victoria wearing crown, 1859 . . . 1·60 1·75
6185 $200 Queen Victoria in feathered hat, 1897 . . . 1·60 1·75
6186 $200 Princess Victoria, 1829 1·60 1·75
6187 $200 Queen Victoria with hair in bun, 1837 . . . . 1·60 1·75
6188 $200 In uniform for troop review, 1840 . . . . . . 1·60 1·75
6189 $200 Wearing crown and white veil, 1897 . . . . . 1·60 1·75
MS6190 Two sheets, each 88 × 120 mm. (a) $400 Queen Victoria. (b) $400 Queen Victoria in old age Set of 2 sheets . . . 6·00 6·50

2001. 75th Death Anniv of Claude-Oscar Monet (artist). As T **339** of Gambia. Multicoloured.

6191 $150 "Village Street near Honfleur" . . . . 1·25 1·40
6192 $150 "Road to Chailly" . . 1·25 1·40
6193 $150 "Train in the Countryside" . . . . . . 1·25 1·40
6194 $150 "Quai du Louvre" . . 1·25 1·40
MS6195 136 × 111 mm. $400 "Flowering Garden" (vert) . . 3·50 3·75

2001. 75th Birthday of Queen Elizabeth II. As T **340** of Gambia. Multicoloured.

6196 $150 Queen Elizabeth wearing pink hat . . . . 1·25 1·40
6197 $150 Wearing red coat and hat . . . . 1·25 1·40
6198 $150 Wearing white turban style hat . . . . 1·25 1·40
6199 $150 Wearing tiara . . . . 1·25 1·40
MS6200 80 × 110 mm. $400 Queen Elizabeth wearing yellow dress and pearls (38 × 50 mm) . . . 3·50 3·75

2001. Death Centenary of Giuseppe Verdi (Italian composer). Vert designs as T **342** of Gambia. Multicoloured.

6201 $160 Verdi (face value at bottom left) . . . . . . 1·40 1·50
6202 $160 Rigoletto and score . . 1·40 1·50
6203 $160 Ernani and opera score 1·40 1·50
6204 $160 Verdi (face value at bottom right) . . . . . . 1·40 1·50
MS6205 77 × 117 mm. $400 Verdi 3·75 4·00

Nos. 6201/4 were printed together, se-tenant, with the backgrounds forming a composite design.

2001. Death Centenary of Henri de Toulouse-Lautrec (artist). As T **343** of Gambia. Multicoloured.

6206 $160 "Maurice Joyant in the Baie de Somme" (horiz) 1·25 1·40
6207 $160 "Monsieur Boileau" (horiz) . . . . 1·25 1·40
6208 $160 "Monsieur, Madame and the Dog" (horiz) . . 1·25 1·40
MS6209 66 × 85 mm. $400 "Monsieur" . . . . 3·50 3·75

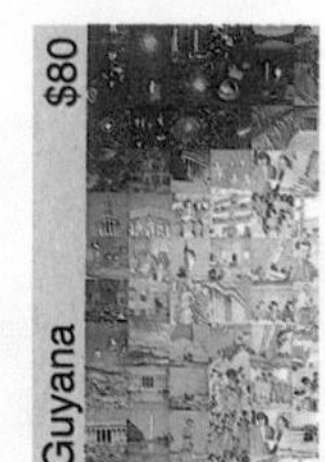

637 Top Right of Head

2001. Faces of the Millennium. John F. Kennedy. Showing collage of miniature photographs from Kennedy's years as President. Multicoloured.

6210 $80 Type **637** 65 70
6211 $80 Top left of head 65 70
6212 $80 Top of right cheek . . . 65 70
6213 $80 Top of left cheek . . . 65 70
6214 $80 Bottom of right cheek 65 70
6215 $80 Bottom of left cheek . . 65 70
6216 $80 Bottom right of chin . . 65 70
6217 $80 Bottom left of chin . . 65 70

Nos. 6210/17 were printed together, se-tenant, in sheetlets of 8 with the stamps arranged in two vertical columns separated by a gutter also containing miniature photographs. When viewed as a whole, the sheetlet forms a portrait of JFK.

2001. 75th Birthday of Queen Elizabeth II. As T **368** of Dominica.

6218 $80 multicoloured 50 55

No. 6218 was also issued, in the same format, inscribed "In Celebration of the 50th Anniversary of H.M. Queen Elizabeth II's Accession to the Throne" in the margin.

638 Rainbow Lory ("Rainbow Lorikeet")

2001. Tropical Birds. Multicoloured.

6219 $100 Type **638** 60 65
6220 $100 King bird of paradise 60 65
6221 $100 Canary-winged parakeet ("Yellow-Chevroned Parakeet") . . 60 65
6222 $100 Masked lovebird . . . 60 65
6223 $100 Scarlet ibis 60 65
6224 $100 Toco toucan 60 65
6225 $100 Hyacinth macaw . . . 60 65
6226 $100 Wire-tailed manakin 60 65
6227 $100 Scarlet macaw 60 65
6228 $100 Sun conure ("Sun Parakeet") 60 65
6229 $100 Roseate spoonbill . . 60 65
6230 $100 Red-billed toucan . . . 60 65
MS6231 Two sheets, each 85 × 110 mm. (a) $400 Eclectus parrot (vert). (b) $400 Sulphur-crested cockatoo (vert) Set of 2 sheets . . . . 4·75 4·75

Nos. 6219/24 and 6225/30 were each printed together, se-tenant, with the backgrounds forming composite designs.

639 Alamosaurus head

2001. "Vegaspex 2001", Nevada. Prehistoric Creatures. Multicoloured.

6232 $20 Allosaurus (vert) . . . 10 15
6233 $30 Spinosaurus (vert) . . . 20 25
6234 $35 Pteranodon (vert) . . . 20 25
6235 $60 Cetiosaurus (vert) . . . 35 40
6236 $100 Type **639** 60 65
6237 $100 Archaeopteryx 60 65
6238 $100 Pachycephalosaurus head and Alamosaurus body 60 65
6239 $100 Parasaurolophus . . . 60 65
6240 $100 Edmontosaurus head 60 65
6241 $100 Triceratops 60 65
6242 $100 Brachiosaurus head, neck and back 60 65
6243 $100 Dimorphodon 60 65
6244 $100 Coelophysis head and Brachiosaurus body . . . 60 65
6245 $100 Velociraptor 60 65
6246 $100 Antrodemus 60 65
6247 $100 Euparkeria 60 65
6248 $100 Brachiosaurus head and neck 60 65
6249 $100 Pteranodon 60 65
6250 $100 Compsognathus and Brachiosaurus neck . . . 60 65
6251 $100 Corythosaurus 60 65
6252 $100 Allosaurus 60 65
6253 $100 Torosaurus 60 65
6254 $100 Ichthyostega 60 65
6255 $100 Eryops 60 65
6256 $100 Ichthyosaur 60 65
6257 $100 Pliosaur 60 65
6258 $100 Dunklosteus 60 65
6259 $100 Eogyrinus 60 65
6260 $200 Archaeopteryx (vert) 1·20 1·20
6261 $300 Parasaurolophus (vert) 1·80 1·80
MS6262 Four sheets. (a) 88 × 68 mm. $400 Pteranodon. (b) 88 × 68 mm. $400 Ichthyosaur. (c) 88 × 68 mm. $400 Torosaurus. (d) 68 × 88 mm. $400 Brachiosaurus (vert) Set of 4 sheets . . . . . 9·50 9·50

Nos. 6236/41, 6242/7, 6248/53 and 6254/9 were each printed together, se-tenant, with the backgrounds forming composite designs.

640 Elephant

2001. Tropical Rainforest. Multicoloured.

6263 $35 Mandrill (vert) 20 25
6264 $80 Type **640** 50 55
6265 $80 Impala 50 55
6266 $80 Leopard head and shoulders 50 55
6267 $80 Grey parrot and leopard body 50 55
6268 $80 Hippopotamus 50 55
6269 $80 Pygmy chimp 50 55
6270 $80 African green python 50 55
6271 $80 Mountain gorilla . . . 50 55
6272 $80 Three-toed sloth 50 55
6273 $80 Lion tamarind 50 55
6274 $80 Ring-tailed lemur . . . 50 55
6275 $80 Sugar glider 50 55
6276 $80 Toco toucan 50 55
6277 $80 Trogon 50 55
6278 $80 Pygmy marmoset . . . 50 55
6279 $80 Poison arrow frog . . . 50 55
6280 $100 Leaf-cutting ants . . . 60 65
MS6281 Two sheets, each 110 × 85 mm. (a) $400 Tapir (vert). (b) $400 Sable antelope (vert) Set of 2 sheets . . . . . . 4·75 4·75

Nos. 6264/71 and 6272/9 were each printed together, se-tenant, with the backgrounds forming composite designs.

641 Prince Willem-Alexander of Orange and Miss Maxima Zorreguieta

2002. Royal Wedding. Multicoloured.

MS6282 158 × 240 mm. $120 Type **641**; $120 Prince Willem-Alexander on right and Miss Maxima on left; $120 Prince Willem-Alexander on left and Miss Maxima on right; $120 Hugging from the side; $120 Prince Willem-Alexander; $120 Miss Maxima . . . . 4·25 4·25

642 U.S. Flag as Statue of Liberty and Flag of Guyana

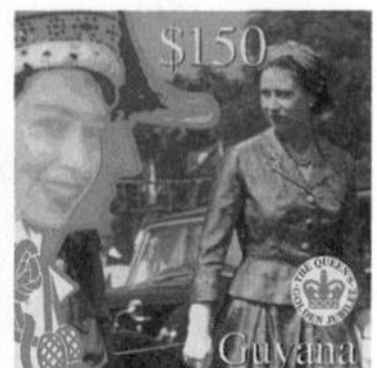

643 Queen Elizabeth II

2002. "United We Stand". Support for Victims of 11 September 2001 Terrorist Attacks.

MS6283 120 × 120 mm. 642 $200 × 4 multicoloured . . . . 4·75 4·75

2002. Golden Jubilee (1st issue). Multicoloured.

MS6284 132 × 100 mm. $150 Type **643**; $150 Queen Elizabeth and Prince Philip; $150 Queen Elizabeth and Prince Philip waving; $150 Queen Elizabeth and horse . . . . 3·50 3·50
MS6285 76 × 109 mm. $400 Queen Elizabeth and Princess Margaret 2·40 2·40

See also Nos. **MS**6370/ and **MS**6371.

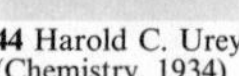

644 Harold C. Urey (Chemistry, 1934)

645 Chinese Character meaning "Horse" (Qin Dynasty)

2002. Nobel Prize Winners (1st issue). Multicoloured.

MS6286 Two sheets each 183 × 129 mm. (a) $100 Type 644; $100 Willard F. Libby (Chemistry, 1960); $100 Frederick Sanger (Chemistry, 1958 and 1980); $100 Teodor Svedberg (Chemistry, 1926); $100 Cyril N. Hinshelwood (Chemistry, 1956); $100 Nicolay Semenov (Chemistry, 1956). (b) $100 Alexander Todd (Chemistry, 1957); $100 John Steinbeck (Literature, 1962); $100 Edward C. Kendall (Physiology and Medicine, 1950); $100 Frederick G. Banting (Physiology and Medicine, 1923); $100 Charles Nicolle (Physiology and Medicine, 1928); $100 Charles Richet (Physiology and Medicine, 1913) Set of 2 sheets . . . . . . 7·25 7·25
MS6287 Three sheets each 106 × 75 mm. (a) $400 International Red Cross (Peace, 1917). (b) $400 John J. R. MacLeod (Physiology and Medicine, 1923). (c) $400 Derek H. R. Barton (Chemistry, 1969) Set of 3 sheets . . . . 7·25 7·25

2002. Nobel Prize Winners (2nd issue). Albert Einstein Photomosaic. Sheet 160 × 244 mm containing vert designs as T **637** showing miniature scientific images. Multicoloured.

MS6288 $80 Left of forehead; $80 Right of forehead; $80 Left eye; $80 Right eye; $80 Left cheek; $80 Right cheek; $80 Left of jaw; $80 Right of jaw . . . . 4·00 4·00

The stamps of No. **MS**6288 were printed in two vertical columns of 4, separated by a central gutter. When viewed as a whole, the miniature sheet forms a portrait of Albert Einstein.

2002. Chinese New Year ("Year of the Horse"). Multicoloured.

6289 $100 Type **645** 60 65
6290 $100 Yin Dynasty 60 65
6291 $100 Tang Dynasty 60 65
6292 $100 Shang and Zhou Dynasties 60 65
MS6293 125 × 116 mm. (a) $150 Decorated person riding purple horse; (b) $150 Decorated Person riding orange horse. (37 × 50mm) . . . . 1·80 1·80

Nos. 6282/5 show Chinese characters for "Horse" from various dynasties and an explanation of the Chinese characters inscribed on the bottom margin.

646 Obdulio Varela (Uruguay) (Brazil, 1950) 647 The Devil's Tower, U.S.A

2002. World Cup Football Championship, Japan and South Korea. Tournament posters. Multicoloured.

6294 $100 Type **646** 60 65
6295 $100 Jules Rimet (Switzerland, 1954) . . . 60 65
6296 $100 Pele and team mates (Brazil) (Sweden, 1958) . . 60 65
6297 $100 Zito (Brazil) (Chile, 1962) 60 65
6298 $100 English players (England, 1966) 60 65
6299 $100 Jairzinho (Brazil) (Mexico, 1970) 60 65
6300 $100 Daniel Passarella (Argentina) (Argentina, 1978) 60 65
6301 $100 Paolo Rossi (Italy) (Spain, 1982) 60 65
6302 $100 Diego Maradona (Argentina) (Mexico, 1986) 60 65
6303 $100 Lothar Matthaus and Rudi Voller (West Germany) (Italy, 1990) . . 60 65
6304 $100 Brazilian players (U.S.A., 1994) 60 65
6305 $100 Zinedine Zidane (France) (France, 1998) 60 65
MS6306 Two sheets, each 88 × 75 mm. (a) $400 Detail of Jules Rimet Trophy (Uruguay, 1930). (b) $400 Detail of World Cup Trophy (Japan and South Korea, 2002) Set of 2 sheets . . 4·75 4·75

2002. International Year of Mountains (1st issue). Multicoloured.

MS6307 136 × 95 mm. $200 Type **647**; $200 Schreckhorn, Switzerland; $200 Mt. Rainer (U.S.A); $200 Mt. Everest, Tibet 4·75 4·75
MS6308 84 × 56 mm. $400 Mt. McKinley . . . . 2·40 2·40

2002. International Year of Mountains (2nd issue). As T **647**. Multicoloured.

6309 $80 Mt. Kosciuszko, Australia 50 55
6310 $100 Mt. Elbrus, Russia . . 60 65
6311 $150 Mt. Vinson, Antarctica 90 95
MS6312 73 × 90 mm. $400 Mt. Everest, Nepal . . . . 2·40 2·40

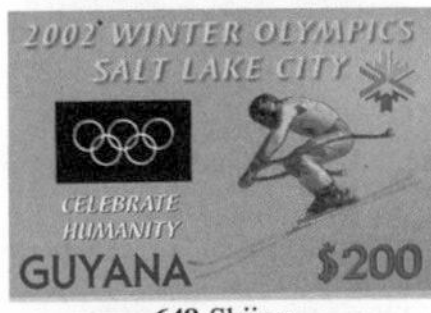

648 Skiing

2002. Winter Olympic Games, Salt Lake City. Multicoloured.

6313 $200 Type **648** . . . . . . 1·20 1·30
6314 $200 Ice Skating . . . . . 1·20 1·30
MS6315 82 × 113 mm. Nos. 6313/14 2·40 2·40

649 Owl **650** Environmental Science Merit Badge

2002. United Nations Year of Eco Tourism. Multicoloured.

MS6316 81 × 137 mm. $100 Type **649**; $100 Waterfall; $100 Baboon; $100 Butterfly; $100 Flower; $100 Ferret . . . . . 3·50 3·50
MS6317 86 × 69 mm. $400 Leopard 2·40 2·40

2002. 20th World Scout Jamboree, Thailand. Multicoloured.

MS6318 161 × 67 mm. $200 Type **650**; $200 World Citizen Merit badge; $200 Life Saving Merit badge . . . . 3·50 3·50
MS6319 98 × 67 mm. $400 Jamboree mascot saluting . . . . 2·40 2·40

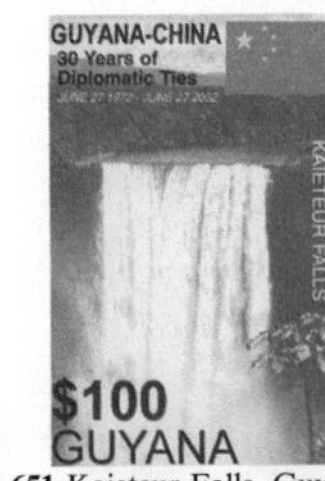

651 Kaieteur Falls, Guyana

2002. 30th Anniv of Diplomatic Relations with Republic of China. Multicoloured.

6320 $100 Type **651** 60 65
6321 $100 Great Wall of China 60 65

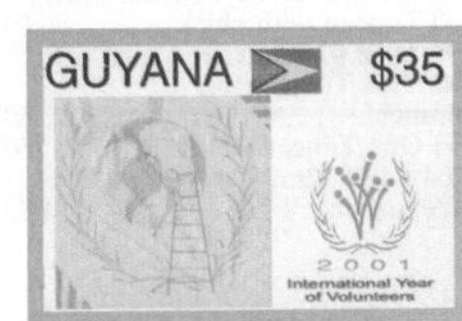

652 Volunteer Cleaning Globe and Emblem

2002. International Year of Volunteers. Multicoloured.

6322 $35 Type **652** 20 25
6323 $60 Two styles of emblem 35 40
6324 $300 Volunteer "embracing the nation" . . . . 1·80 1·90

653 Sperm Whale

2002. Whales. Multicoloured.

MS6325 140 × 67 mm. $100 Type **653**; $100 Pygmy Sperm whale; $100 Blue whale; $100 Bottlenose whale; $100 Killer whale; $100 True's Beaked whale 3·50 3·50
MS6326 75 × 62 mm. $400 Beluga whale . . . . 2·40 2·40

654 *Masdevallia tovarensis*

2002. Orchids. Multicoloured.

MS6327 94 × 103 mm. $100 Type **654**; $100 *Encyclia vitellina*; $100 *Dendrobium nobile*; $100 *Masdevallia falcate*; $100*Calanthe vestita*; $100 *Brassolaelia cattleya* 3·50 3·50
MS6328 74 × 62 mm. $400 *Brassavola nodosa* (horiz) . . . 2·40 2·40

2002. Birds. As T **654**. Multicoloured.

MS6329 94 × 103 mm. $100 Flycatcher; $100 Barbary shrike; $100 Red-faced mousebird; $100 Red-footed booby; $100 White-fronted goose; $100 Great crested grebe . . . . 3·50 3·50
MS6330 74 × 62 mm. $400 Whiskered tern . . . . 2·40 2·40

2002. Butterflies. As T **654**. Multicoloured.

MS6331 94 × 103 mm. $100 Sweet oil butterfly; $100 Swallowtail; $100 Southern white admiral; $100 Prepona pheridamas; $100 Plain tiger; $100 Common eggfly . . 3·60 3·60
MS6332 62 × 75 mm. $400 Zebra butterfly . . . . 2·40 2·40

2002. Moths. As T **654**. Multicoloured.

MS6333 94 × 103 mm. $100 *Burgena varia*; $100 *Mimas tiliae*; $100 *Hyles euphorbiae*; $100 *Eligma laetipicta*; $100 *Autometris io*; $100 *Hyloicus pinastri* . . . . . . 3·50 3·50
MS6334 75 × 62 mm. $400 *Callimorpha quadripuntaria* . . 2·40 2·40

655 Elvis Presley

2002. 25th Death Anniv of Elvis Presley. Multicoloured.

MS6335 Two sheets each 200 × 170 mm. (a) $60 Type **655** × 9. (b) $60 Elvis in army uniform in front of U.S. flag × 9 Set of 2 sheets . . . . 4·25 4·25

656 Popeye **657** Ronald Reagan

2002. Popeye (cartoon character). Multicoloured.

MS6336 187 × 125 mm. $100 Type **656**; $100 Olive Oyl; $100 Wimpy; $100 Eugene the Jeep; $100 Sweet Pea racing for ball; $100 Sweet Pea holding tennis ball 3·50 3·50
MS6337 118 × 86 mm. $400 Popeye wearing white tennis shirt . . . 2·40 2·40

2003. Ronald Reagan (President of U.S.A 1981–1989). T **657** and Multicoloured.

MS6338 167 × 136 mm. $100 Ronald Reagan and eagle; $100 Type **657**; $100 In front of Mt. Rushmore; $100 Kissing Nancy Reagan; $100 With hand to forehead and White House; $100 On horseback . . 3·50 3·50
MS6339 106 × 76 mm. $400 Ronald Reagan and Mikhail Gorbachev shaking hands (horiz) . . . . 2·40 2·40

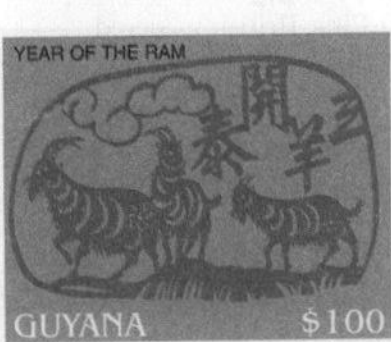

658 Ram

2003. Chinese New Year ("Year of the Ram").

MS6340 **658** 109 × 86 mm. $100 × 4 multicoloured . . . . 2·40 2·40

PRINCESS DIANA
GUYANA $100

659 John F. Kennedy **660** Princess Diana

2003. John F. Kennedy Commemoration. T **659** and similar multicoloured designs.

MS6341 158 × 128 mm. $100 Addressing the nation; $100 Type **659**; $100 Space scene in background; $100 With miniature model of White House; $100 In front of rocket; $100 Jackie Kennedy at funeral . . . . . 3·50 3·50
MS6342 106 × 76 mm. $400 John F. Kennedy and Jackie Kennedy in open top car (horiz) . . . . 2·40 2·40

2003. Diana, Princess of Wales Commemoration. Multicoloured.

MS6343 157 × 127 mm. $100 Type **660**; $100 Wearing tiara; $100 Wearing high collared top; $100 Wearing wedding veil; $100 Looking straight ahead; $100 Looking left . . . . 3·50 3·50
MS6344 104 × 75 mm. $400 Wearing pink and black hat and pearl choker . . . . 2·40 2·40

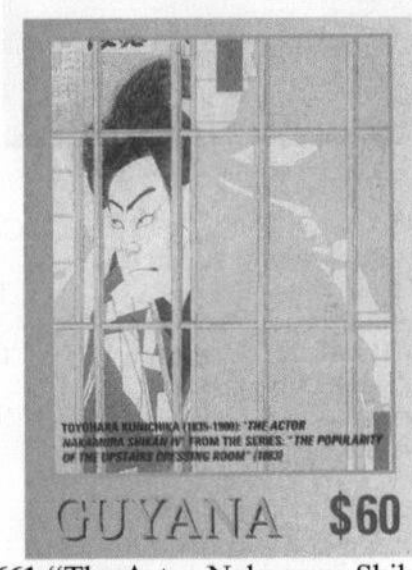

661 "The Actor Nakamura Shikan IV"

2003. Famous Actors in Japanese Art. Paintings by Toyohara Kunichika. Multicoloured.

6345 $60 Type **661** 35 40
6346 $80 "The Actor Ichikawa Danjuro IX as Sukeroku" (1883) 50 55
6347 $100 "The Actor Onoe Tatsunosuke" 60 65
6348 $300 "The Actor Ichikawa Sadanji I as Kyusuke" . . 1·80 1·90
MS6349 182 × 143 mm. $150 "The Actor Kawarazak Sansho as Watonai"; $150 "The Actor Ichikawa Danjuro IX as Kamakura Gongoro Kagemasa"; $150 The Actor Ichikawa Sadanji I as Sadajkuro"; $150 "The Actor Ichikawa Danjuro IX as Sukeroku" (1898) . . . . . . 3·50 3·50
MS6350 127 × 83 mm. $400 "The Actor Ichikawa Danjuro IX as Kato Shukeigashira Kiyomasa" (horiz) . . . . 2·40 2·40

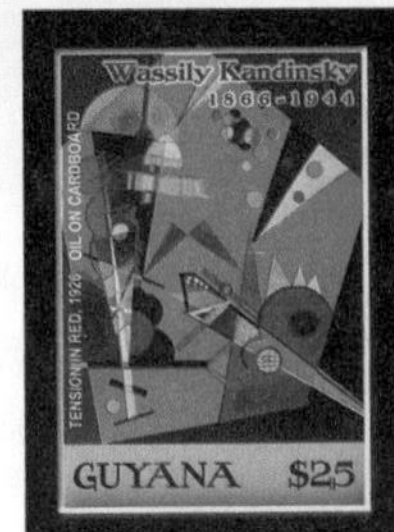

662 "Tension Red"

2003. Wassily Kandinsky (artist) Commemoration. Multicoloured.

6351 $25 Type **662** 15 20
6352 $30 "Black Accompaniment" 20 25
6353 $35 "Calm Tension" 20 25
6354 $60 "Hard and Soft" . . . 35 40
6355 $100 "Yellow Point" (horiz) 60 65
6356 $300 "Composition VIII" (horiz) . . . . 1·80 1·90
MS6357 130 × 156 mm. $150 "Red Oval", 1920; $150 On the White II", 1923; $150 "Mutual Agreement", 1942; $150 "Inclination", 1931 . . . . . 3·50 3·50
MS6358 Two sheets each 104 × 84 mm. (a) $400 "White Center", 1921. (b) $400 "Black Weft", 1922. Imperf . . . . . 4·75 4·75

663 "Portrait of a Man"

2003. 450th Death Anniv of Lucas Cranach the Elder (artist). Multicoloured.

6359	$35 Type **663**	20	25
6360	$60 "Portrait of a Woman"	35	40
6361	$100 "Duchess Catherine of Mecklenburg" (detail)	60	65
6362	$200 "Portrait of Duke Henry of Saxony" (detail)	1·20	1·20
MS6363	160 × 117 mm. $150 "The Virgin", c. 1518 (detail); $150 "The Virgin and Child Under the Apple Tree" (detail); $150 "The Virgin"(detail); $150 "The Virgin"	3·50	3·50
MS6364	93 × 130 mm. $400 "The Virgin and Child Holding a Piece of Bread" (detail)	2·40	2·40

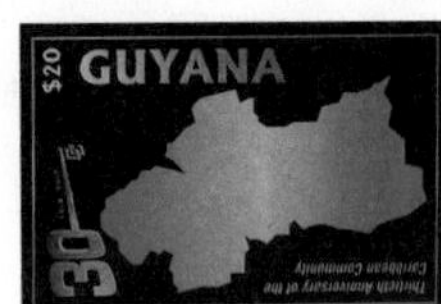

664 Outline of Guyana

2003. 30th Anniv of the Caribbean Community ("CARICOM"). Multicoloured.

6365	$20 Type **664**	10	10
6366	$60 Bank of Guyana (horiz)	35	40
6367	$100 Hands holding torch	60	65
6368	$160 AIDS ribbon and stethoscope	95	1·00

665 Queen Elizabeth II

667 Jacques Anquetil (1964)

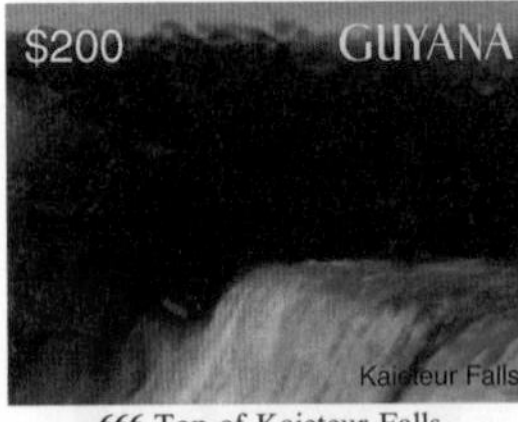

666 Top of Kaieteur Falls

2003. Golden Jubilee (2nd issue). Multicoloured.

MS6370	166 × 108 mm. $200 Type **665**; $200 Wearing purple top; $200 Wearing pink top	3·50	3·50
MS6371	76 × 106 mm. $400 Wearing Imperial State Crown	2·40	2·40

2003. International Year of Freshwater. Multicoloured.

MS6372	143 × 150 mm. $200 Type **666**; $200 Middle of Kaieteur Falls; $200 Kaieteur Falls and part of Cliffside	3·50	3·50
MS6373	76 × 106 mm. $400 Amazon River	2·40	2·40

2003. Centenary of Tour de France Cycle Race. Multicoloured.

MS6374	163 × 104 mm. $150 Type **667**; $150 Felice Gimondi (1965); $150 Lucien Aimar (1966); $150 Roger Pingeon (1967)	3·50	3·50
MS6375	106 × 76 mm. $400 Jan Janssen (1968)	2·40	2·40

668 Brown Teddy Bear

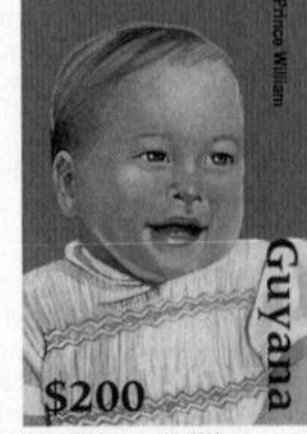

669 Prince William as a Baby

2003. Centenary of Teddy Bears. Multicoloured.

MS6376	178 × 140 mm. $80 Type **668** × 9; lilac; green; blue; light green; light blue; stone; mauve; pale green; light mauve	4·50	4·50
MS6377	178 × 102 mm. $150 Bear dressed in red dress and white apron; $150 Blue bear dressed in yellow bow tie; $150 Bear decorated with fairy lights and star; $150 Bear dressed in blue dress and ribbon	3·50	3·50

2003. 21st Birthday of Prince William. Multicoloured.

MS6378	166 × 108 mm. $200 Type **669**; $200 Wearing round neck sweater; $200 Wearing christening robe	3·50	3·50
MS6379	76 × 106 mm. $400 Wearing blue shirt and tie	2·40	2·40

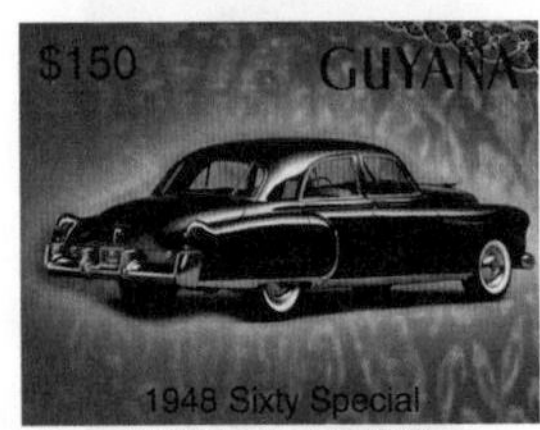

670 Sixty Special (1948)

2003. Centenary of the Cadillac. Multicoloured.

MS6380	126 × 176 mm. $150 Type **670**; $150 Fleetwood Sixty Special (1966); $150 Eldorado (1967); Eldorado Convertible (1976)	1·75	1·75
MS6381	90 × 126 mm. $400 Red vintage Cadillac	2·40	2·40

671 Corvette Stingray (1964)

2003. 50th Anniv of the Corvette. Multicoloured.

MS6382	146 × 126 mm. $150 Type **671**; $150 Corvette Stingray (1963); $150 Corvette Stingray (1966); $150 Corvette (1969)	3·50	3·50
MS6383	126 × 90 mm. $400 Corvette (1971)	2·40	2·40

672 AVRO Plane (Sir Alliot Verdon Roe)

2003. Centenary of Powered Flight. Multicoloured.

6384	$100 Type **672**	60	65
6385	$160 First British powered flight	95	1·00
MS6386	Two sheets. (a) 186 × 106 mm. $150 Wright Brothers' plane; $150 SPAD 13; $150 Sopwith F.1; $150 Albatross D.II. (b) 106 × 186 mm. $150 Nieuport 17; $150 Scout Experimental 5a; $150 De Havilland 4; $150 Wright Brothers plane (black crosses on tail) Set of 2 sheets	4·75	4·75
MS6387	Two sheets each 76 × 106 mm. (a) $400 Fokker D.VIIs. (b) $400 Wright Brothers plane over water	4·75	4·75

673 Grecian Shoemaker

2003. Butterflies. Multicoloured.

6388	$20 Type **673**	10	15
6389	$55 Clorinde	30	35
6390	$80 Orange-barred sulphur	50	55
6391	$100 The atala	60	65
6392	$160 White peacock	95	1·00
6393	$200 Polydamas swallowtail	1·20	1·30
6394	$300 Giant swallowtail	1·80	1·90
6395	$400 Banded king shoemaker	2·40	2·50
6396	$500 Blue night	3·00	3·25
6397	$1000 Orange theope	6·00	6·25
6398	$2000 Small lace-wing	12·00	12·50
6399	$3000 Common morpho	18·00	19·00

674 *Clitocybe clavipes*

2003. Mushrooms. Multicoloured.

6400	$20 Type **674**	15	20
6401	$20 *Clitocybe gibba*	15	20
6402	$30 *Calocybe carnea*	20	25
6403	$300 *Marasmius*	1·80	1·90
MS6404	133 × 92 mm. $150 *Amanita spissa*; $150 *Boletus aestivalis*; $150 *Boletus rubellus*; $150 *Clathrus archeri*	3·50	3·75
MS6405	96 × 66 mm. $400 *Volvariella bombycina*	2·40	2·50

675 Toucan

2003. Endangered Species. Toucan. Multicoloured.

6406	$100 Toucan with chick	60	65
6407	$100 Type **675**	60	65
6408	$100 Two Toucans on branch	60	65
6409	$100 One Toucan on branch	60	65
MS6410	204 × 169 mm. Designs as Nos. 6406/9, each × 2	4·75	5·00

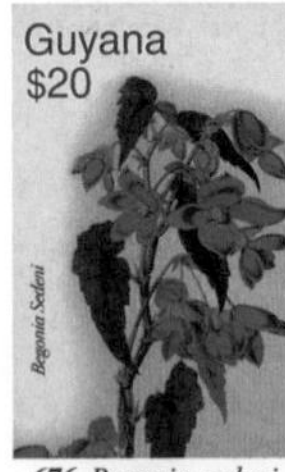

676 *Begonia sedeni*

2003. Flowers. Multicoloured.

6411	$20 Type **676**	10	15
6412	$30 Dahlia	20	25
6413	$35 *Eschecholzia californica*	20	35
6414	$300 *Lupinus perennis*	1·80	1·90
MS6415	116 × 116 mm. $150 *Agapanthus africanus*; $150 *Hyacinth cultivars*; $150 *Protea linearis*; $150 *Hippestrum aulicum*	3·50	3·75
MS6416	66 × 96 mm. $400 *Crocus sativus* (horiz)	2·40	2·50

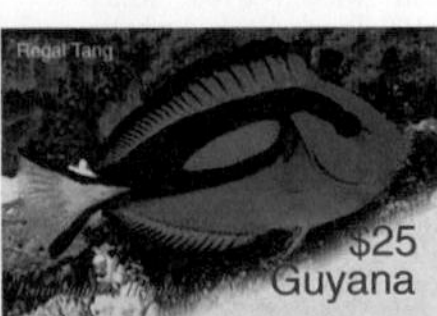

677 Regal Tang

2003. Fish. Multicoloured.

6417	$25 Type **677**	15	20
6418	$60 Pajama tang	35	40
6419	$100 Coral beauty	60	65
6420	$200 Emperor angelfish	1·20	1·30
MS6421	145 × 100 mm. $150 High hat; $150 Regal angelfish; $150 Fire clown; $150 Domino damselfish	3·50	3·75
MS6422	66 × 96 mm. $400 Tomato clown	2·40	2·50

678 Common Tenrec

2003. Animals. Multicoloured.

6423	$25 Type **678**	15	20
6424	$60 Woolly monkey (vert)	35	40
6425	$100 Gundi	60	65
6426	$200 Hooded seal	1·20	1·30
MS6427	135 × 127 mm. $150 Prevost's squirrel; $150 Mountain tapir; $150 Sea otter; $150 Indus dolphin	3·50	3·75
MS6428	67 × 96 mm. $400 Peter's disk-winged bat (vert)	2·40	2·50

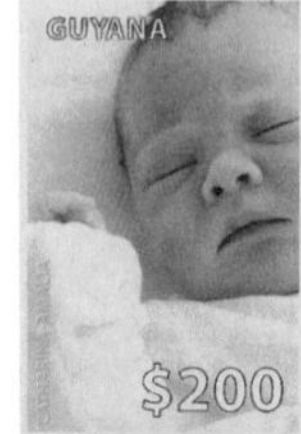

679 Princess Catharina-Amalia

2003. Birth of Princess Catharina-Amalia of the Netherlands. Sheet 185 × 115 mm containing T **679** and similar vert designs. Multicoloured.

MS6429	$200 Type **679**; $200 Prince Willem-Alexander and Princess Catharina-Amalia; $200 Princess Catharina-Amalia (looking to left)	3·50	3·75

No. **MS**6429 is cut around in the shape of a baby.

680 Handshake

2003. 35th Anniv of Guyana—Brazil Diplomatic Relations.

6430	**680** $20 multicoloured	10	15

681 Dark Brown Monkey

2004. Chinese New Year ("Year of the Monkey"). Sheet 140 × 117 mm containing T **681** and similar vert designs. Multicoloured.

MS6431	$100 Type **681**; $100 Black and white monkey; $100 Light brown monkey; $100 Red Howler Monkey	2·40	2·50

682 "Concubines of Emperor Chu"

2004. Hong Kong 2004 International Stamp Exhibition. Paintings by Tang Yin. T **682** and similar multicoloured designs.

MS6432	140 × 140 mm. $150 Type **682**; $150 Woman standing on boardwalk; $150 Woman standing on rocky slope; $150 Mountain landscape	3·50	3·75
MS6433	108 × 78 mm. $400 "Mountain Scene" (horiz)	2·40	2·50

GUYANA $150

DOCTOR AND DOLL 1929

683 "Doctor and Doll"

2004. 25th Death Anniv of Norman Rockwell (artist). Multicoloured.

MS6434 142 × 173 mm. $150 Type **683**; $150 "Babysitter with Screaming Infant"; $150 "Girl with Black Eye"; $150 "Checkup" . . . 3·50 3·75
MS6435 95 × 103 mm. $400 "Girl running with Wet Canvas (Wet Paint)" (detail) (horiz) . . . . 2·40 2·50

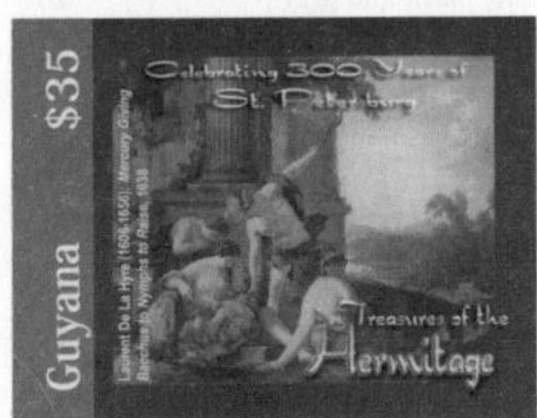

684 "Mercury giving Bacchus to Nymphs to Raise" (Laurent de la Hyre)

2004. 00th Anniv of St. Petersburg. "Treasures of the Hermitage". Muticoloured.

6436 $35 Type **684** 20 25
6437 $60 "Satyr and Bacchante" (Nicolas Poussin) (vert) 35 40
6438 $100 "Parting of Abelard and Eloisa" (Angelica Kauffmann) 60 65
6439 $200 "Pastoral Scene" (Francois Boucher) . . . 1·20 1·30
MS6440 147 × 126 mm. $150 "The Union of Earth and Water" (Rubens); $150 "Hercules between Love and Wisdom" (Pompeo Girolano Batoni); $150 "Innocence choosing Love over Wealth" (Pierre-Paul Prud'hon); $150 "Mars and Venus" (Joseph-Marie Vien) (all vert) . . . . 3·50 3·75
MS6441 Two sheets. (a) 77 × 55 mm. $400 "Allegory of Virtuous Life" (Hendrik van Balen). (b) 55 × 77 mm. $400 "Statue of Ceres" (Rubens). Both imperf. Set of 2 sheets . . . . 3·00 3·25

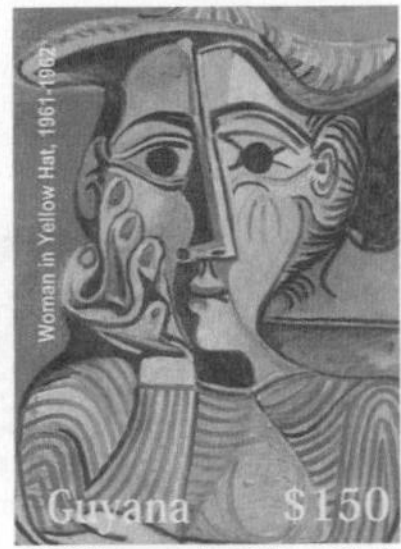

685 "Woman in Yellow Hat"

2004. 30th Death Anniv (2003) of Pablo Picasso (artist). Multicoloured.

MS6442 130 × 167 mm. $150 Type **685**; $150 "Seated Woman"; $150 "Head of a Woman"; $150 "Large Profile" . . . . 3·50 3·75
MS6443 72 × 98 mm. $400 "Seated Woman". Imperf . . . . . . 2·40 2·50

686 "A Woman Bathing"

2004. Paintings by Rembrandt. Multicoloured.

6444 $35 Type **686** 30 25
6445 $60 "Flora" 35 40
6446 $100 "The Poet, Jan Hermansz Krul" 60 65
6447 $200 "Portrait of a Young Man" . . . . 1·20 1·30
MS6448 182 × 183 mm. $150 "The Apostle James"; $150 "The Apostle Bartholomew"; $150 "The Evangelist Matthew inspired by an Angel"; $150 "The Apostle Peter Standing" . . . . 3·50 3·75
MS6449 113 × 146 mm. $400 "Balaam and the Ass" . . . . 2·40 2·50

687 Uruguay (1930)

2004. Centenary of FIFA (Federation Internationale de Football Association). World Cup winning teams. Multicoloured.

6450 $80 Type **687** 50 55
6451 $80 Italy (1934) 50 55
6452 $80 Italy (1938) 50 55
6453 $80 Uruguay (1950) 50 55
6454 $80 Germany (1954) 50 55
6455 $80 Brazil (1958) 50 55
6456 $80 Brazil (1962) 50 55
6457 $80 England (1966) 50 55
6458 $80 Brazil (1970) 50 55

EXPRESS LETTER STAMPS

1986. Various stamps surch **EXPRESS** and new values.

E1 $12 on 350c. on 120c. multicoloured (No. 1598) 7·00 7·00
E2 $15 on 40c. multicoloured (No. 1868) . . . . 9·00 9·00
E3 $20 on $6.40 multicoloured 7·00 7·00
E4 $25 on 25c. multicoloured (as No. 1771, but value changed) . . . . 13·00 13·00

No. E3 was previously a miniature sheet for Halley's Comet containing two 320c. stamps. As surch the original values on both designs have been cancelled and replaced by a single $20 face value.

1987. No. E3 additionally optd with small Maltese cross above surch.

E5 $20 on $6.40 multicoloured 7·00 7·00

1987. Centenary of Publication of Sanders' "Reichenbachia". As T **331** additionally inscr "EXPRESS". Multicoloured.

E6 $15 Plate No. 11 (Series 2) . . 5·50 5·50
E7 $20 Plate No. 93 (Series 2) . . 3·50 4·00
E8 $25 Plate No. 63 (Series 2) . . 5·00 6·50
E9 $45 Plate No. 35 (Series 2) . . 8·00 10·00

1987. Nos. 1744/5 imperf between surch **EXPRESS FORTY DOLLARS** and star.

E10 $40 on $6.40 multicoloured 12·00 12·00

1987. No. E2 additionally optd **1987**.

E11 $15 on 40c. multicoloured . . 11·00 5·50

1988. Nos. 2206 and 2211 surch **SPECIAL DELIVERY** and new value.

E12 $40 on $3.20 blue . . . . . 10·00 11·00
E13 $45 on $3.30 black . . . . . 10·00 11·00

1989. Imperf between pairs of Nos. 1744/5 and 2185/6 surch **EXPRESS FORTY DOLLARS** (without stars).

E14 $40 on $6.40 multicoloured (Nos. 1744/5) . . . . . . 6·00 6·50
E15 $40 on $6.40 multicoloured (Nos. 2185/6) . . . . . . 6·00 6·50

1989. Nos. 2206 and 2211 surch **SPECIAL DELIVERY** and new value.

E16 $190 on $3.30 black . . . . 17·00 19·00
E17 $225 on $3.20 blue . . . . . 18·00 20·00

1989. Butterflies. Two sheets, each 97 × 67 mm, containing vert designs as T **454** optd **EXPRESS**. Multicoloured.

EMS18 $130 "Phareas coeleste" 5·00 5·00
EMS19 $190 "Papilio torquatus" 6·00 6·00

1989. Women in Space. Sheet 92 × 67 mm, containing vert design as T **455** optd **EXPRESS**. Multicoloured.

EMS20 $190 Valentina Tereshkova (first woman cosmonaut) . . 4·25 4·50

1989. "World Stamp Expo '89" International Stamp Exhibition, Washington. Nos. **EMS**18/19 optd with logo.

EMS21 $130 "Phareas coeleste" 4·00 4·00
EMS22 $190 "Papilio torquatus" 4·50 4·50

Nos. **EMS**21/22 show additional overprints on sheet margins.

1990. 85th Anniv of Rotary International. Nos. **EMS**18/20 optd **ROTARY INTERNATIONAL 1905–1990** and emblem on sheet margins only.

EMS23 $130 "Phareas coeleste" 3·75 3·75
EMS24 $190 "Papilio torquatus" 5·50 5·50
EMS25 $190 Valentina Tereshkova (first woman cosmonaut) . . 4·00 5·50

1990. "Stamp World London '90" International Stamp Exhibition. Nos. **EMS**18/20 optd **Stamp World London '90** and emblem on sheet margins only.

EMS26 $130 "Phareas coeleste" (R.) . . . . 3·75 3·75
a. Opt in black . . . . .
EMS27 $190 "Papilio torquatus" 5·50 5·50
EMS28 $190 Valentina Tereshkova (first woman cosmonaut) . . 4·00 5·50

1990. "Belgica '90" International Stamp Exhibition, Brussels. Nos. **EMS**18 and **EMS**20 additionally optd **BELGICA PHILATELIC EXPOSITION 1990** and emblem in black on sheet margins only.

EMS29 $130 "Phareas coeleste" 4·00 4·00
EMS30 $190 Valentina Tereshkova (first woman cosmonaut) . . 4·50 5·00

1990. 90th Birthday of Queen Elizabeth the Queen Mother. Nos. **EMS**18/20 optd **90TH BIRTHDAY H.M. THE QUEEN MOTHER** on sheet margins only.

EMS31 $130 "Phareas coeleste" 3·50 3·50
EMS32 $190 "Papilio torquatus" 4·00 4·00
EMS33 $190 Valentina Tereshkova (first woman cosmonaut) . . 4·00 4·00

1990. Fauna. Two sheets, each 110 × 80 mm, containing vert designs as T **466**, but larger (40 × 55 mm) inscr EXPRESS. Multicoloured.

EMS34 $130 Harpy Eagle . . . . 3·50 3·50
EMS35 $150 Ocelot . . . . . . 3·50 3·50

OFFICIAL STAMPS

1981. Nos. 556, F4a and F6/7 optd **OPS** or surch also.

O13 10c. on 25c. Marabunta . . 3·50 2·25
O14 50c. "Guzmania lingulata" 1·00 30
O15 60c. Soldier's cap . . . . . 1·00 20
O16 $5 "Odontadenia grandiflora" . . . . . . 1·75 1·75

1981. Nos. 491, 708a, 716, 804, 834 and F9 optd **OPS** or surch also.

O17 15c. Harpy eagle (postage) 9·50 65
O18 30c. on $2 "Norantea guianensis" (F9) 45 30
O19 100c. on $3 Cylinder satellite 2·00 40
O20 125c. on $2 "Norantea guianensis" . . . . 1·00 60
O21 $10 "Elbella patrobas" . . . 11·00 11·00
O22 $1.10 on $2 "Norantea guianensis" (804) (air) . . 75 2·00

1981. Nos. 548a, 719, 828 and 830 optd **OPS** or surch also.

O23 15c. Christmas orchid . . . 8·50 1·50
O24 50c. British Guiana 1898 1c. stamp . . . . 1·25 35
O25 100c. on 8c. Camp-fire cooking . . . . 1·25 50
O26 110c. on 6c. Type **116** . . . 2·00 1·25

1982. Various stamps optd **OPS**.

O27 – 20c. multicoloured (No. 701) . . . . . . 6·00 70
O28 **136** 40c. multicoloured . . . 75 15
O29 – 40c. red, grey and black (No. 674) . . . . . . 1·00 15
O30 – $2 multicoloured (No. 676) . . . . . . 7·00 75

1982. Nos. 911 and 980 optd or surch **OPS**.

O31 250c. on 400c. on 30c. multicoloured (postage) . . 80 60
O32 220c. on 1c. multicoloured (air) . . . . 1·00 60

1982. No. F9 optd **OPS**.

O33 $2 "Norantea guianensis" . . 8·00 2·00

1982. Air. No. 979 optd **OPS**.

O34 110c. on 5c. Annatto tree . . 1·25 40

1984. No. 912 surch **OPS**.

O35 150c. on $5 multicoloured 6·00 2·75
O36 200c. on $5 multicoloured 6·50 3·00
O37 225c. on $5 multicoloured 6·50 3·25
O38 230c. on $5 multicoloured 6·50 3·25
O39 260c. on $5 multicoloured 6·50 3·50
O40 320c. on $5 multicoloured 8·00 4·00
O41 350c. on $5 multicoloured 8·50 4·50
O42 600c. on $5 multicoloured 10·00 6·50

1984. Nos. O32 and O34 surch and No. 981 optd **OPS**.

O43 25c. on 110c. on 5c. Annatto tree . . . . 1·50 40
O44 30c. on 110c. on 5c. Annatto tree . . . . 1·50 45
O45 45c. on 220c. on 1c. Pitcher plant of Mt. Roraima . . 1·60 55
O46 55c. on 110c. on 5c. Annatto tree . . . . 1·75 60
O47 60c. on 220c. on 1c. Pitcher plant of Mt. Roraima . . 1·75 60
O48 75c. on 220c. on 1c. Pitcher plant of Mt. Roraima . . 2·00 70
O49 90c. on 220c. on 1c. Pitcher plant of Mt. Roraima . . 2·00 80
O50 120c. on 220c. on 1c. Pitcher plant of Mt. Roraima . . 2·25 1·25
O51 130c. on 220c. on 1c. Pitcher plant of Mt. Roraima . . 2·25 1·25
O52 330c. on $2 "Norantea guianensis" . . . . 4·00 4·00

1987. Centenary of Publication of Sanders' "Reichenbachia". As T **331** additionally inscr "OFFICIAL". Multicoloured.

O53 120c. Plate No. 48 (Series 2) 1·75 45
O54 130c. Plate No. 92 (Series 2) 1·75 45
O55 140c. Plate No. 36 (Series 2) 75 35
O56 150c. Plate No. 43 (Series 2) 1·75 50
O57 175c. Plate No. 31 (Series 2) 80 40
O58 200c. Plate No. 61 (Series 2) 1·75 60
O59 225c. Plate No. 26 (Series 2) 1·75 60
O60 230c. Plate No. 68 (Series 2) (horiz) 50 50
O61 250c. Plate No. 59 (Series 2) 50 60
O62 260c. Plate No. 69 (Series 2) 50 60
O63 275c. Plate No. 90 (Series 2) 1·75 75
O64 320c. Plate No. 75 (Series 2) 1·75 80
O65 330c. Plate No. 23 (Series 2) 3·00 1·00
O66 350c. Plate No. 95 (Series 2) (horiz) 50 80
O67 600c. Plate No. 70 (Series 2) (horiz) . . . . 75 1·60
O68 $12 Plate No. 71 (Series 2) (horiz) . . . . 1·40 2·50
O69 $15 Plate No. 84 (Series 2) 1·50 2·75

OFFICIAL PARCEL POST STAMPS

1981. Nos. P1/2 optd **OPS**.

OP1 $15 on $1 "Chelonanthus uliginoides" . . . . 10·00 2·25
OP2 $20 on $1 "Chelonanthus uliginoides" . . . . 10·00 2·75

1983. No. 843 surch **OPS Parcel Post $12.00** and additionally optd **1982**.

OP3 $12 on $1.10 on $2 "Norantea guianensis" . . 70·00 17·00

1983. No. OP3 with additional **OPS** opt.

OP4 $12 on $1.10 on $2 "Norantea guianensis" . . 22·00 4·00

1983. No. P4 optd **OPS**.

OP5 $12 on $1.10 on $2 "Norantea guianensis" . . 7·50 4·00

PARCEL POST STAMPS

1981. No. 554 surch **PARCEL POST** and new value.

P1 $15 on $1 "Chelonanthus uliginoides" . . . . 10·00 3·00
P2 $20 on $1 "Chelonanthus uliginoides" . . . . 10·00 6·00

1983. No. 843 surch **PARCEL POST $12.00**.

P3 $12 on $1.10 on $2 "Norantea guianensis" . . . . 2·25 2·50

1983. Unissued Royal Wedding surch, similar to No. 843, further surch **Parcel Post $12.00**.

P4 $12 on $1.10 on $2 "Norantea guianensis" . . . . 1·00 1·75

1985. No. 673 surch **TWENTY FIVE DOLLARS PARCEL POST 25.00**.

P5 $25 on 35c. green, grey and black . . . . 25·00 19·00

POSTAGE DUE STAMPS

D 2

1987.

D 8 **D 2** 1c. green . . . . 25 3·75
D 9 2c. black . . . . 25 3·75
D10 4c. blue . . . . 25 3·75
D11 12c. red . . . . 25 3·75

POSTAL FISCAL STAMPS

1975. Nos. 543/5 and 550ab/6 optd **REVENUE ONLY**.

F 1 2c. Type **132** 50 40
F 2 3c. Hanging heliconia . . . 50 40
F 3 5c. Annatto tree 75 30
F 4 25c. Marabunta . . . . . 3·25 30
F 4a 25c. Marabunta (No. 550) 15·00 13·00
F 5 40c. Tiger beard . . . . . 5·50 30
F 6 50c. "Guzmania lingulata" 70 40
F 7 60c. Soldier's cap 75 50
F 8 $1 "Chelonanthus uliginoides" . . . . . . 75 1·25
F 9 $2 "Norantea guianensis" 1·00 2·75
F10 $5 "Odontadenis grandiflora" . . . . . . 1·75 9·00

Although intended for fiscal use Nos. F1/F10 were allowed by the postal authorities as an "act of grace" to do duty as postage stamps until 30 June 1976.

GWALIOR Pt. 1

A "convention" state of Central India.

12 pies = 1 anna; 16 annas = 1 rupee.

1885. Queen Victoria stamps of India optd **GWALIOR** at foot and native opt at top.
1 **23** ½a. turquoise . . . £120 25·00
2 – 1a. purple . . . 80·00 28·00
6 – 1a.6p. brown . . . 75·00
3 – 2a. blue . . . 70·00 14·00
8 – 4a. green (No. 69) . . . 80·00
9 – 6a. brown (No. 80) . . . 80·00
10 – 8a. mauve . . . 75·00
11 – 1r. grey (No. 101) . . . 70·00

Stamps of India overprinted **GWALIOR** above native overprint unless otherwise stated.

1885. Queen Victoria.
16c **23** ½a. turquoise . . . 40 10
17 – 9p. red . . . 30·00 50·00
18 – 1a. purple . . . 1·25 20
20c – 1a.6p. brown . . . 1·60 50
21c – 2a. blue . . . 1·50 10
23 – 2a.6p. green . . . 6·50 17·00
25c – 3a. orange . . . 2·50 15
14 – 4a. green (No. 69) . . . 22·00 13·00
27c – 4a. green (No. 96) . . . 3·50 70
29 – 6a. brown (No. 80) . . . 2·25 7·00
30c – 8a. mauve . . . 4·00 1·00
32c – 12a. purple on red . . . 3·25 65
33c – 1r. grey (No. 101) . . . 3·00 1·60
34 **37** 1r. green and red . . . 4·00 3·50
35 **38** 2r. red and orange . . . 5·50 3·00
36 3r. brown and green . . . 7·50 3·50
37 5r. blue and violet . . . 14·00 6·50

1899. Queen Victoria.
38 **40** 3p. red . . . 40 20
39 3p. grey . . . 6·50 60·00
40 **23** ½a. green . . . 70 1·10
41 – 1a. red . . . 1·10 35
42 – 2a. lilac . . . 1·60 4·50
43 – 2½a. blue . . . 1·10 5·00

1903. King Edward VII.
46A **41** 3p. grey . . . 75 20
48A – ½a. green (No. 122) . . . 20 10
49A – 1a. red (No. 123) . . . 20 10
50A – 2a. lilac . . . 1·40 70
52B – 2a.6p. blue . . . 1·25 7·50
53A – 3a. orange . . . 1·50 35
54A – 4a. olive . . . 1·75 40
56B – 6a. bistre . . . 4·75 1·25
57A – 8a. mauve . . . 3·50 1·40
59B – 12a. purple on red . . . 3·75 3·25
60A – 1r. green and red . . . 2·50 1·75
61B **52** 2r. red and orange . . . 9·00 11·00
62B 3r. brown and green . . . 26·00 45·00
63B 5r. blue and violet . . . 19·00 27·00

1907. King Edward VII inscr "INDIA POSTAGE AND REVENUE".
65 ½a. green (No. 149) . . . 90 20
66 1a. red (No. 150) . . . 1·50 20

1912. King George V.
67 **55** 3p. grey . . . 10 10
68 **58** ½a. green . . . 20 10
102 **79** ½a. green . . . 50 20
88 **80** 9p. green . . . 2·00 20
69 **57** 1a. red . . . 25 10
80 1a. brown . . . 80 10
103 **81** 1a. brown . . . 20 10
90 **82** 1a.3p. mauve . . . 50 15
81 **58** 1½a. brown (No. 165) . . . 1·75 50
82 1½a. red . . . 20 20
70 **59** 2a. purple . . . 60 10
91 **70** 2a. lilac . . . 75 30
104 **59** 2a. red . . . 2·00 2·75
83 **61** 2½a. blue . . . 2·00 1·75
84 2½a. orange . . . 35 50
71 **62** 3a. orange . . . 60 25
92 3a. blue . . . 1·00 40
72 **63** 4a. olive . . . 60 60
93 **71** 4a. green . . . 1·25 1·00
73a **64** 6a. bistre . . . 1·00 1·00
74 **65** 8a. mauve . . . 1·25 70
75 **66** 12a. red . . . 1·25 3·00
76 **67** 1r. brown and green . . . 7·00 70
77 2r. red and brown . . . 4·50 4·50
78 5r. blue and violet . . . 20·00 6·50

1922. No. 192 (King George V) optd **GWALIOR** only.
79 **57** 9p. on 1a. red . . . 10 50

1928. King George V. Optd in larger type (19 mm long).
96 **67** 1r. brown and green . . . 2·25 3·25
97w 2r. red and orange . . . 8·00 4·50
98 5r. blue and violet . . . 18·00 24·00
99 10r. green and red . . . 50·00 40·00
100 15r. blue and olive . . . 85·00 60·00
101 25r. orange and blue . . . £180 £140

1938. King George VI.
105 **91** 3p. slate . . . 7·00 10
106 ½a. brown . . . 7·50 10
107 9p. green . . . 40·00 3·25
108 1a. red . . . 7·00 15
109 3a. green (No. 253) . . . 18·00 4·00
110 4a. brown (No. 255) . . . 42·00 2·50
111 6a. green (No. 256) . . . 3·00 9·00
112 **93** 1r. slate and brown . . . 8·00 1·50
113 2r. purple and brown . . . 42·00 9·00
114 5r. green and blue . . . 30·00 32·00
115 10r. purple and red . . . 30·00 40·00
116 15r. brown and green . . . 90·00 £160
117 25r. slate and purple . . . 80·00 £120

1942. King George VI.
118 **100a** 3p. slate . . . 45 10
119 ½a. mauve . . . 45 10
120 9p. green . . . 45 10
121 1a. red . . . 40 10
122 **101** 1½a. violet . . . 6·50 20
123 2a. red . . . 65 20
124 3a. violet . . . 14·00 1·25
125 **102** 4a. brown . . . 2·00 20
126 6a. green . . . 14·00 24·00
127 8a. violet . . . 2·75 2·75
128 12a. purple . . . 4·50 20·00

OFFICIAL STAMPS

Stamps of India overprinted with native inscription at top and bottom, unless otherwise stated.

1895. Queen Victoria.
O 1 **23** ½a. turquoise . . . 40 10
O 3 – 1a. purple . . . 1·25 10
O 5 – 2a. blue . . . 1·50 40
O 7 – 4a. green (No. 96) . . . 1·75 1·00
O 9 – 8a. mauve . . . 2·50 1·75
O10 **37** 1r. green and red . . . 6·00 3·00

1901. Queen Victoria.
O23 **40** 3p. red . . . 65 25
O24 3p. grey . . . 1·75 2·50
O26 **23** ½a. green . . . 60 10
O27 – 1a. red . . . 4·50 10
O28 – 2a. lilac . . . 1·00 1·50

1903. King Edward VII.
O29 **41** 3p. grey . . . 70 10
O41 – ½a. green (No. 122) . . . 2·75 15
O32 – 1a. red (No. 123) . . . 1·10 10
O33a – 2a. lilac . . . 1·50 30
O44 – 4a. olive . . . 3·00 1·00
O36 – 8a. mauve . . . 5·00 70
O38 – 1r. green and red . . . 2·75 1·75

1907. King Edward VII inscr "POSTAGE & REVENUE".
O49 – ½a. green (No. 149) . . . 1·50 15
O48 – 1a. red (No. 150) . . . 5·50 15

1913. King George V.
O51 **55** 3p. grey . . . 25 10
O62 **56** ½a. green . . . 10 15
O73 **79** ½a. green . . . 15 15
O63 **80** 9p. green . . . 10 15
O53a **57** 1a. red . . . 30 10
O64 1a. brown . . . 10 10
O74 **81** 1a. brown . . . 15 15
O65 **82** 1a.3p. mauve . . . 50 15
O55 **59** 2a. purple . . . 80 50
O66 **70** 2a. lilac . . . 20 15
O75 **59** 2a. red . . . 20 40
O77 **63** 4a. olive . . . 60 75
O67 **71** 4a. green . . . 60 30
O68 **65** 8a. mauve . . . 60 1·10
O58 **67** 1r. brown and green . . . 25·00 21·00

1922. No. O97 (King George V Official) optd **GWALIOR** only.
O59 **57** 9p. on 1a. red . . . 10 30

1927. King George V. Optd in large type (21 mm long).
O69 **67** 1r. brown and green . . . 1·00 1·75
O70 2r. red and orange . . . 12·00 13·00
O71 5r. blue and violet . . . 17·00 £150
O72 10r. green and red . . . £130 £375

1938. King George VI.
O78 **91** ½a. brown . . . 6·50 30
O79 1a. red . . . 1·10 20
O91 **93** 1r. slate and brown . . . 10·00 16·00
O92 2r. purple and brown . . . 18·00 80·00
O93 5r. green and blue . . . 30·00 £475
O94 10r. purple and red . . . 80·00 £900

1940. King George VI. Optd at bottom only.
O80 **O 20** 3p. slate . . . 50 10
O81 ½a. brown . . . 3·25 25
O82 ½a. purple . . . 50 10
O83 9p. green . . . 70 60
O84 1a. red . . . 2·25 10
O85 1a.3p. brown . . . 40·00 1·75
O86 1a.6p. violet . . . 1·00 30
O87 2a. orange . . . 1·00 30
O88 4a. brown . . . 1·25 2·25
O89 8a. violet . . . 4·00 8·00

1942. No. O65 surch **1A 1A** and bar.
O90 **82** 1a. on 1¼a. mauve . . . 24·00 2·75

HAITI Pt. 15

The W. portion of the island of Hispaniola in the West Indies. A republic, independent from 1804.

100 centimes = 1 gourde or piastre.

1 Liberty
2 Pres. Salomon

1881. Imperf.
1 **1** 1c. red . . . 5·00 3·00
2 2c. purple . . . 6·50 3·25
3 3c. bistre . . . 11·00 4·00
4 5c. green . . . 18·00 7·00
5 7c. blue . . . 12·50 2·50
6 20c. brown . . . 45·00 16·00

1882. Perf.
7 **1** 1c. red . . . 3·25 1·00
9 2c. purple . . . 5·00 1·50
12 3c. bistre . . . 6·50 2·25
15 5c. green . . . 3·75 75
17 7c. blue . . . 5·00 1·25
20 20c. brown . . . 4·50 1·00

1887.
24 **2** 1c. lake . . . 30 30
25 2c. mauve . . . 55 50
26 3c. blue . . . 50 40
27 5c. green . . . 2·10 40

1890. Surch **DEUX 2 CENT.**
28 **2** 2c. on 3c. blue . . . 40 35

4 Tree with Leaves upright
5 Tree with Leaves drooping
6

1891. Tree with leaves upright.
29 **4** 1c. mauve . . . 40 15
30 2c. blue . . . 60 20
31 3c. lilac . . . 60 40
31a 3c. grey . . . 80 50
32 5c. orange . . . 2·25 40
33 7c. red . . . 4·75 1·75

1892. Surch **DEUX 2 CENT.**
34 **4** 2c. on 3c. lilac . . . 85 70
34a 2c. on 3c. grey . . . 85 70

1893. Tree with leaves drooping.
35a **5** 1c. purple . . . 15 10
41 1c. blue . . . 20 20
36 2c. blue . . . 20 10
42 2c. red . . . 40 25
37 3c. lilac . . . 60 40
43 3c. brown . . . 20 15
38 5c. orange . . . 2·25 20
44 5c. green . . . 20 15
39 7c. red . . . 40 35
45 7c. grey . . . 30 20
40 20c. brown . . . 80 60
46 20c. orange . . . 40 40

1898. Surch **DEUX 2 CENT.**
47 **5** 2c. on 20c. brown . . . 85 25
48 2c. on 20c. orange . . . 35 25

1898.
49a **6** 2c. red . . . 20 15
50a 5c. green . . . 20 15

8 Pres. Simon Sam
9

1898.
51 **8** 1c. blue . . . 10 10
67 **9** 1c. green . . . 10 10
52 **8** 2c. orange . . . 15 15
68 **9** 2c. red . . . 15 15
53 **8** 3c. green . . . 15 15
54 **9** 4c. red . . . 15 15
55 **8** 5c. brown . . . 15 15
69 **9** 5c. blue . . . 10 10
56 **8** 7c. grey . . . 15 15
57 **9** 8c. red . . . 20 15
58 10c. orange . . . 15 15
59 15c. olive . . . 35 25
60 **8** 20c. black . . . 30 25
61 50c. lake . . . 35 25
62 1g. mauve . . . 1·40 1·25

1902. Optd **MAI Gt Pre 1902** in frame.
70 **8** 1c. blue . . . 45 45
71 **9** 1c. green . . . 35 15
72 **8** 2c. orange . . . 45 45
73 **9** 2c. red . . . 35 15
74 **8** 3c. green . . . 35 35
75 **9** 4c. red . . . 45 45
76 **8** 5c. brown . . . 90 90
77 **9** 5c. blue . . . 35 35
78 **8** 7c. grey . . . 45 45
79 **9** 8c. red . . . 45 45
80 10c. orange . . . 45 45
81 15c. olive . . . 2·10 1·50
82 **8** 20c. black . . . 3·25 1·75
83 50c. lake . . . 7·50 3·75
84 1g. mauve . . . 9·50 7·75

12 Arms
13 J.-J. Dessalines

1904. Cent of Independence. Optd **1804 POSTE PAYE 1904** in frame. T **12** and portraits as T **13**.
89 **12** 1c. green . . . 25 25
90 – 2c. black and red . . . 30 30
91 – 5c. black and blue . . . 30 30
92 **13** 7c. black and red . . . 30 30
93 – 10c. black and yellow . . . 30 30
94 – 20c. black and grey . . . 30 30
95 – 50c. black and olive . . . 30 30
DESIGNS: 2, 5c. Toussaint l'Ouverture; 20, 50c. Petion.

1904. Nos. 89/95 but without opt.
96 1c. green . . . 20 15
97 2c. black and red . . . 20 15
98 5c. black and blue . . . 20 15
99 7c. black and red . . . 20 15
100 10c. black and yellow . . . 20 15
101 20c. black and grey . . . 20 15
102 50c. black and olive . . . 20 15

15 Pres. Nord Alexis

1904. External Mail. Optd **1804 POSTE PAYE 1904** in frame.
103 **15** 1c. green . . . 45 35
104 2c. red . . . 45 35
105 5c. blue . . . 45 35
106 10c. brown . . . 45 35
107 20c. orange . . . 45 35
108 50c. plum . . . 45 35

1904. Nos. 103/108, but without opt.
109 **15** 1c. green . . . 10 10
110 2c. red . . . 10 10
111 5c. blue . . . 10 10
112 10c. brown . . . 10 10
113 20c. orange . . . 10 10
114 50c. plum . . . 10 10

1906. Optd **SERVICE EXTERIEUR PROVISOIRE EN PIASTRES FORTES** in oval.
117 **8** 1c. blue . . . 55 45
118 **9** 1c. green . . . 55 55
119 **8** 2c. orange . . . 1·10 1·10
120 **9** 2c. red . . . 90 90
121 **8** 3c. green . . . 90 90
122 **9** 4c. red . . . 3·75 3·00
123 **8** 5c. brown . . . 3·75 3·00
124 **9** 5c. blue . . . 45 45
125 **8** 7c. grey . . . 3·00 3·00
126 **9** 8c. red . . . 45 45
127 10c. orange . . . 85 55
128 15c. olive . . . 1·10 60
129 **8** 20c. black . . . 3·75 3·00
130 50c. lake . . . 3·75 1·75
131 1g. mauve . . . 6·25 4·75

19 Pres. Nord Alexis
20 Arms

1906.
132 **19** 1c. de g. blue . . . 20 10
133 **20** 2c. de g. orange . . . 35 15
134 2c. de g. yellow . . . 55 15
135 **19** 3c. de g. grey . . . 30 10
136 **20** 7c. de g. green . . . 55 35

21 Iron Market, Port-au-Prince
24 Pres. A. T. Simon

1906. Currency changed from "gourdes" to "piastres".
137 **20** 1c. de p. green . . . 20 15
138 **19** 2c. de p. red . . . 35 20
139 **21** 3c. de p. sepia . . . 1·75 40
140 3c. de p. orange . . . 4·25 4·50
141 – 4c. de p. red . . . 55 30
167 – 4c. de p. olive . . . 5·50 4·25
142 **19** 5c. de p. blue . . . 1·10 20
143 – 7c. de p. grey . . . 85 45
168 – 7c. de p. red . . . 12·50 8·25
144 – 8c. de p. red . . . 4·00 1·25
169 – 8c. de p. olive . . . 17·00 11·00
145 – 10c. de p. orange . . . 55 20
170 – 10c. de p. brown . . . 7·25 7·50
146 – 15c. de p. olive . . . 1·10 45
171 – 15c. de p. yellow . . . 3·25 1·75

147 **19** 20c. de p. blue 1·10 45
148 **20** 50c. de p. red 1·75 1·25
172 50c. de p. yellow 3·75 2·50
149 – 1pi. red 3·25 2·10
173 – 1pi. red 3·75 3·00
DESIGNS—As Type **21**: 4c. Palace of Sans Souci-Milot; 7c. Independence Palace, Gonaives; 8c. Entrance to Catholic College, Port-au-Prince; 10c. Catholic Monastery and Church, Port-au-Prince; 15c. Government Offices, Port-au-Prince; 1pi. President's Palace, Port-au-Prince.

1906. Surch with value in double-lined frame Without opt.
154 **15** 1c. on 5c. blue 30 20
155 1c. on 10c. brown 25 10
156 1c. on 20c. orange 20 15
157 2c. on 10c. brown 25 20
158 2c. on 20c. orange 20 20
159 2c. on 50c. plum 35 20

1910.
160 **24** 1c. de g. black and red 15 15
161 2c. de p. black and red 55 35
162 5c. de p. black and blue 7·75 55
163 20c. de p. black and green 6·25 4·75

25 Pres. C. Leconte **38**

1912. Various frames.
164 **25** 1c. de g. lake 20 20
165 2c. de g. orange 25 20
166 5c. de p. blue 55 20

1914. Optd **GL O.Z. 7 FEV. 1914** in frame. A. On 1898 issue.
174 **9** 8c. red 7·75 6·25
B. On 1904 issue, without opt.
175 **15** 1c. green (No. 109) 22·00 19·00
176 2c. red 22·00 19·00
177 5c. blue 45 15
178 10c. brown 45 15
179 20c. orange 45 35
180 50c. plum 1·75 55
C. On pictorial stamps of 1906.
181 **20** 2c. de g. yellow 35 15
182 **19** 3c. de g. grey 35 20
D. On pictorial stamps of 1906.
183 **20** 1c. de p. green (No. 137) 35 25
184 **19** 2c. de p. red (No. 138) 55 25
185 **21** 3c. de p. sepia (No. 139) 4·25 75
186 3c. de p. orange (No. 140) 3·25 3·25
187 – 4c. de p. red (No. 141) 45 60
198 – 4c. de p. olive (No. 167) 75 40
188 – 7c. de p. grey (No. 143) 1·75 1·75
200 – 7c. de p. red (No. 168) 1·75 1·75
189 – 8c. de p. red (No. 144) 5·25 2·50
201 – 8c. de p. olive (No. 169) 6·50 6·50
190 – 10c. de p. orange (No. 145) 55 55
202 – 10c. de p. brown (No. 170) 85 55
191 – 15c. de p. olive (No. 146) 1·75 1·75
203 – 15c. de p. yellow (No. 171) 75 45
192 **19** 20c. de p. blue (No. 147) 2·25 55
194 **20** 50c. de p. red (No. 148) 3·75 3·75
204 50c. de p. yellow (No. 172) 3·75 3·75
195 – 1pi. red (No. 149) 3·75 3·75
205 – 1pi. red (No. 173) 3·75 3·75
E. On stamp of 1910.
193 **24** 20c. de p. black and green 2·40 2·40
F. On stamps of 1912.
196 **25** 1c. de g. lake 25 20
197 2c. de g. orange 45 30
199 5c. de p. blue 70 20

1914. Stamps of 1904, without the opt, surch **GL O.Z 7 FEV 1914 7 CENT** in diamond frame.
213 **15** 7c. on 20c. orange (No. 113) 45 20
214 7c. on 50c. plum (No. 114) 35 20

1914. Pictorial stamps of 1906 (Nos. 148/73), surch **GL OZ 1 CENT DE PIASTRE 7 FEV. 1914** in frame.
215 **20** 1c. de p. on 50c. red 30 20
216 1c. de p. on 50c. yellow 45 35
217 – 1c. de p. on 1p. red 45 35
218 – 1c. de p. on 1p. red 55 45

1915.
219 – 2c. de g. black and yellow 45
220 **38** 5c. de g. black and green 45
221 – 7c. de g. black and red 45
PORTRAIT: 2, 7c. O. Zamor.

1915. As T **24**, inscr "EMISSION 1914".
222 1c. de p. black and green 85
223 3c. de p. black and olive 15
224 5c. de p. black and blue 25
225 7c. de p. black and orange 60
226 10c. de p. black and brown 20
227 15c. de p. black and olive 25
228 20c. de p. black and brown 55
DESIGNS: 1c., 5c., 10c., 15c. O. Zamor; 3c., 20c. Arms; 7c. T. Auguste.

1915. Surch with figure in frame.
229 1 on 5c. blue (No. 111) 85 85
230 1 on 7c. grey (No. 143) 10 10
231 1 on 10c. brown (No. 112) 15 15
232 1 on 20c. orange (No. 107) 45 35
233 1 on 20c. orange (No. 113) 55 70
234 1 on 50c. plum (No. 108) 1·10 55
235 1 on 50c. plum (No. 114) 15 10
236 2 on 1pi. red (No. 172) 20 15

1917. Surch **GOURDE** and value in frame. A. On provisional stamps of 1906.
237 **8** 1c. on 50c. lake (No. 130) 16·00 11·00
238 1c. on 1g. mauve (No. 131) 19·00 14·00
B. On pictorial stamps of 1906
239 – 1c. on 4c. de p. red (No. 141) 15 15
240 – 1c. on 4c. de p. olive (No. 167) 30 30
241 – 1c. on 7c. de p. red (No. 168) 45 45
242 – 1c. on 10c. de p. orange (No. 145) 10 10
243 – 1c. on 15c. de p. yellow (No. 171) 45 30
244 **19** 1c. on 20c. de p. blue (No. 147) 20 15
246 **24** 1c. on 20c. de p. black and green (No. 163) 2·50 2·50
247 **20** 1c. on 50c. de p. red (No. 148) 20 15
249 – 1c. on 50c. de p. yellow (No. 172) 85 85
250 – 1c. on 1p. red (No. 173) 85 85
251 **21** 2c. on 3c. de p. sepia (No. 139) 2·75 1·50
252 2c. on 3c. de p. orange (No. 140) 3·50 1·50
253 – 2c. on 8c. de p. red (No. 144) 2·25 75
255 – 2c. on 8c. de p. olive (No. 169) 3·25 2·50
256 – 2c. de p. on 10c. brown (No. 170) 35 45
257 – 2c. on 15c. de p. olive (No. 146) 20 10
258 – 2c. on 15c. de p. yellow (No. 171) 45 45
259 **19** 2c. on 20c. de p. blue (No. 147) 25 15
260 – 5c. on 10c. de p. brown (No. 170) 45 45
261 – 5c. on 15c. de p. yellow (No. 171) 3·25 3·25

1919. For inland use. Provisionals of 1914. (a) Surch with new value without frame.
262 – 1c. on 15c. de p. olive (No. 191) 20 20
263 **19** 1c. on 20c. de p. blue (No. 192) 20 20
264 **24** 1c. on 20c. de p. black and green (No. 193) 35 35
265 – 1c. on 1p. red (No. 195) 20 15
267 – 1c. on 1p. red (No. 205) 35 35
(b) Surch with new value in frame.
268 – 2c. on 4c. de p. red (No. 187) 35 35
269 – 2c. on 8c. de p. red (No. 189) 2·75 1·50
270 – 2c. on 8c. de p. olive (No. 201) 3·75 1·75
271 **24** 2c. on 20c. de p. black and green 30 15
272 **20** 2c. on 50c. de p. red (No. 194) 15 10
274 2c. on 50c. de p. yellow (No. 204) 15 35
275 – 2c. on 1p. red (No. 195) 1·75 1·75
276 – 2c. on 1p. red (No. 205) 90 90
277 **21** 3c. on 3c. de p. sepia (No. 185) 3·00 1·25
278 – 3c. on 7c. de p. red (No. 200) 35 20
279 **21** 5c. on 3c. de p. sepia (No. 185) 4·50 1·75
280 5c. on 3c. de p. orange (No. 186) 6·00 7·00
281 – 5c. on 4c. de p. red (No. 187) 45 45
282 – 5c. on 4c. de p. olive (No. 198) 25 25
283 – 5c. on 7c. de p. grey (No. 188) 30 30
284 – 5c. on 7c. de p. red (No. 200) 35 35
285 **15** 5c. on 7c. on 20c. orange (No. 213) 35 35
286 5c. on 7c. on 50c. plum (No. 214) 2·40 2·40
287 **19** 5c. on 10c. de p. orange (No. 190) 25 25
289 – 5c. on 10c. de p. orange (No. 190) 45 45
288 – 5c. on 15c. de p. yellow (No. 203) 35 35
No. 289 has the word "PIASTRE" in the surcharge.

1919. Postage Due stamps surch **POSTES** and new value in frame.
290 **D 23** 5c. de g. on 10c. de p. purple (No. D211) 35 35
291 5c. de g. on 50c. de p. olive (No. D153) 9·25 7·75
292 5c. de g. on 50c. de p. olive (No. D212) 45 45

48 "Agriculture"

1920.
294 **48** 3c. de g. orange 2·50 3·50
295 5c. de g. green 5·00 25
296 – 10c. de g. red 55 30
297 – 15c. de g. violet 45 15
298 – 25c. de g. blue 55 15
DESIGN: 10c., 15c., 25c. "Commerce".

50 Pres. L. J. Borno **51** Christophe's Citadel

54 Coffee

1924.
299 **50** 5c. green 20 10
300 **51** 10c. red 35 10
301 – 20c. blue 40 15
304 **54** 35c. green 1·75 25
302 **50** 50c. black and orange 40 20
303 – 1g. olive 1·10 25
DESIGNS—VERT: 20c. Map of W. Indies. HORIZ: 1g. National Palace.

55 Pres. Borno

1929. Frontier Agreement between Haiti and Dominican Republic.
305 **55** 10c. red 30 20

56 Fokker Super Trimotor over Port-au-Prince

1929. Air.
306 **56** 25c. green 35 30
307 50c. violet 55 20
308 75c. red 1·10 90
309 1g. blue 1·50 1·10

57 Salomon and S. Vincent

1931. 50th Anniv of U.P.U. Membership.
310 **57** 5c. green 85 45
311 – 10c. red (S. Vincent) 85 45

1933. Air. "Columbia" New York–Haiti Flight. Surch **COLUMBIA VOL-DIRECT N.-Y.–P.AU-P. BOYD-LYON 60 CTS.**
311a 60c. on 20c. blue (No. 301) 42·00 42·00

59 Pres. S. Vincent **60** Prince's Aqueduct

1933. T **59** and designs as T **60**.
312 **59** 3c. orange 10 10
313 3c. green 15 10
316 **60** 5c. green 15 10
317 5c. olive 45 10
318 – 10c. red 35 10
320 – 10c. brown 35 10
321 – 25c. blue 40 20
322 – 50c. brown 1·75 20
323 – 1g. green 1·75 20
324 – 2g.50 olive 2·75 35
DESIGNS: 10c. Fort National; 25c. Palace of Sans Souci; 50c. Christophe's Chapel, Milot; 1g. King's Gallery, Citadel; 2g.50, Vallieres Battery.

62 Fokker Super Trimotor over Christophe's Citadel

1933. Air.
325 **62** 50c. orange 3·25 40
326 50c. olive 3·00 40
327 50c. red 1·75 1·10
328 50c. black 1·40 40
329 60c. brown 40 10
330 1g. blue 1·10 35

63 Alexandre Dumas and his Father and Son

1935. Visit of French Delegation to West Indies.
331 **63** 10c. brown & red (postage) 40 30
332 25c. brown and blue 1·10 35
333 60c. brown and violet (air) 3·00 1·75

64 Arms of Haiti, and George Washington

1938. Air. 150th Anniv of U.S. Constitution.
334 **64** 60c. blue 25 25

1939. Surch **25c** between bars.
335 **54** 25c. on 35c. green 45 30

66 Pierre de Coubertin **67**

1939. Port-au-Prince Athletic Stadium Fund.
336 **66** 10c.+10c. red (postage) 18·00 18·00
337 60c.+40c. violet (air) 12·00 12·00
338 1g.25+60c. black 12·00 12·00

1941. 3rd Caribbean Conference.
339 **67** 10c. red (postage) 65 35
340 25c. blue 40 25
341 60c. olive (air) 2·25 40
342 1g.25 violet 2·10 25

68 Our Lady of Perpetual Succour

1942. Our Lady of Perpetual Succour (National Patroness).
343 **68** 3c. purple (postage) 35 30
344 5c. green 35 30
345 10c. red 35 30
346 15c. orange 40 30
347 20c. brown 40 30
348 25c. blue 1·10 30
349 50c. red 1·60 65
350 2g.50 brown 5·50 1·45
351 5g. violet 11·50 2·75
The 5g. is larger ($32\frac{1}{2} \times 47$ mm).

352 **68** 10c. olive (air) 35 15
353 25c. blue 35 35
354 50c. green 45 30
355 60c. red 90 25
356 1g.25 black 1·90 25

69 Admiral Killick and Flagship "Crete-a-Pierrot"

1943. 41st Death Anniv of Admiral Killick.

358 **69** 3c. orange (postage) 15 50
359 5c. green 55 25
360 10c. red 55 15
361 25c. blue 70 25
362 50c. olive 1·40 35
363 5g. brown 5·50 3·75

364 60c. violet (air) 95 35
365 1g.25 black 3·75 1·90

1944. Surch (a) Postage.

366 **59** 0.02 on 3c. green 15 15
367 0.05 on 3c. green 20 20
368 **68** 0.10 on 15c. orange 35 30
369 **69** 0.10 on 25c. blue 35 30
370 – 0.10 on 1g. olive (No. 303) 35 15
371 – 0.20 on 2g.50 olive (No. 324) 35 30

(b) Air.

372 **62** 0.10 on 60c. brown 55 30

71

1944. Obligatory Tax. United Nations Relief Fund.

373 **71** 5c. blue 90 35
374 5c. black 90 35
375 5c. olive 90 35
376 5c. violet 90 35
377 5c. brown 90 35
378 5c. green 90 35
379 5c. red 90 35

72 Nurse and Wounded Soldier

73 Franklin D. Roosevelt

1945. Red Cross stamps. Cross in red.

381 **72** 3c. black (postage) 10 10
382 5c. green 15 10
383 10c. orange 20 10
384 20c. brown 15 10
385 25c. blue 30 10
386 35c. orange 30 20
387 50c. red 35 25
388 1g. olive 40 30
389 2½g. violet 1·75 25

390 20c. orange (air) 15 10
391 25c. blue 15 10
392 50c. brown 20 10
393 60c. purple 25 10
394 1g. yellow 90 15
395 1g.25c. red 70 30
396 1g.35c. green 70 30
397 5g. black 4·50 1·75

1946. Air.

398 **73** 20c. black 15 15
399 60c. black 20 10

74 Capois-la-Mort

75 J.-J. Dessalines

1946.

400 **74** 3c. orange (postage) 10 10
401 5c. green 10 10
402 10c. red 10 10
403 20c. black 10 10
404 25c. blue 10 10
405 35c. orange 20 15
406 50c. brown 25 20
407 1g. olive 35 10
408 2g.50 grey 90 35

409 20c. red (air) 10 10
410 25c. green 10 10
411 50c. orange 15 10
412 60c. purple 20 10
413 1g. slate 35 10
414 1g.25 violet 40 35
415 1g.35 black 45 30
416 5g. red 1·40 90

1947. 141st Death Anniv of Emperor Jean-Jacques Dessalines, founder of National Independence.

417 **75** 3c. orange (postage) 10 10
418 5c. green 10 10
419 5c. violet 45 10
420 10c. red 10 10
421 25c. blue 20 10

422 20c. brown (air) 20 10

1947. Surch.

423 **74** 10c. on 35c. orge (postage) 20 10

424 5c. on 1g.35 black (air) 55 20
425 30c. on 50c. orange 45 30
426 30c. on 1g.35 black 45 40

77 Sanatorium and Mosquito

1949. Air. Anti-T.B. and Malaria Fund. Cross in red.

427 **77** 20c.+20c. sepia 6·25 4·50
428 30c.+30c. green 6·25 4·50
429 45c.+45c. brown 6·25 4·50
430 80c.+80c. violet 6·25 4·50
431 1g.25+1g.25 red 6·25 4·50
432 1g.75+1g.75 blue 6·25 4·50

78 Washington, Dessalines and Bolivar

1949. Obligatory Tax. Bicent of Port-au-Prince.

434 **78** 5c. red 20 15
435 5c. brown 20 15
436 5c. orange 20 15
437 5c. grey 20 15
438 5c. violet 20 15
439 5c. blue 20 15
440 5c. green 20 15
441 5c. black 20 15

79 Arms of Port-au-Prince

83 Cocoa

80 Columbus and "Santa Maria"

1950. Bicentenary of Port-au-Prince Exhibition. (a) Postage. Multicoloured arms.

442 **79** 10c. red 15 10

(b) Air.

443 **80** 30c. blue and grey 3·25 70
444 – 1g. black (Pres. D. Estime) 45 30

1950. 75th Anniv of U.P.U. Optd **U P U 1874 1949** or surch also.

445 **78** 3 on 5c. grey (postage) 10 10
446 5c. green 25 20
447 10 on 5c. red 25 20
448 20 on 5c. blue 35 35

449 **74** 30 on 25c. green (air) 30 30
450 1g. slate 35 30
451 1.50 on 1g.35 black 60 40

1951. National Products.

456 **83** 5c. green (postage) 25 10

457 – 30c. orange (Bananas) (air) 30 20
458 – 80c. pink and green (Coffee) 85 35
459 – 5g. grey (Sisal) 3·00 2·50

84 Isabella the Catholic

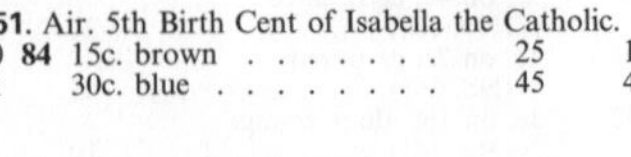

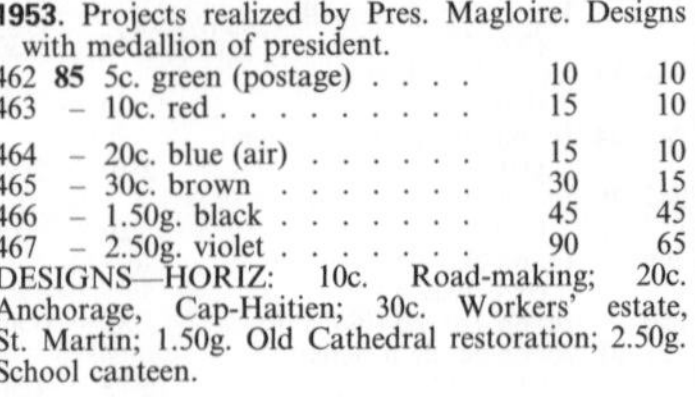

85 Pres. Magloire and Nursery, La Saline

1951. Air. 5th Birth Cent of Isabella the Catholic.

460 **84** 15c. brown 25 15
461 30c. blue 45 45

1953. Projects realized by Pres. Magloire. Designs with medallion of president.

462 **85** 5c. green (postage) 10 10
463 – 10c. red 15 10

464 – 20c. blue (air) 15 10
465 – 30c. brown 30 15
466 – 1.50g. black 45 45
467 – 2.50g. violet 90 65

DESIGNS—HORIZ: 10c. Road-making; 20c. Anchorage, Cap-Haitien; 30c. Workers' estate, St. Martin; 1.50g. Old Cathedral restoration; 2.50g. School canteen.

1953. 150th Death Anniv of Toussaint l'Ouverture. No. 405 surch **7 AVRIL 1803 - 1953 50**.

469 **74** 50c. on 35c. orange 35 20

1953. Air. 150th Anniv of National Flag. Surch **18 MAI 1803 - 1953 50**.

470 **74** 50c. on 60c. purple 35 15
471 50c. on 1g.35 black 35 15

87 J.-J. Dessalines and Pres. Magloire

88 Toussaint l'Ouverture

89 Marie-Jeanne and Lamartiniere on La Crete-a-Pierrot

1954. 150th Anniv of Independence. (a) As T **87/8**.

472 **87** 3c. black and blue (postage) 10 10
473 **88** 5c. black and green 20 10
474 – 5c. black and green 15 10
475 – 5c. black and green 20 10
476 – 5c. black and green 15 10
477 **87** 10c. black and red 15 10
478 – 15c. black and lilac 20 10

479 **88** 50c. black and green (air) 35 20
480 – 50c. black and green 35 20
481 – 50c. black and red 35 20
482 – 50c. black and brown 35 20
483 – 50c. black and blue 35 20
484 – 1g. black and grey 45 25
485 – 1g.50 black and mauve 90 60
486 **87** 7g.50 black and orange 3·00 3·00

PORTRAITS—As Type **88**. Nos. 474, 482, Lamartiniere; Nos. 475, 482, Boisrond-Tonnerre; Nos. 476, 483, 485, A. Petion; No. 478, Capois-La-Mort; No. 480, J. J. Dessalines; No. 481, H. Christophe.

For stamps as No. 480 without dates see Nos. 533/4.

(b) As T **89**.

487 **89** 25c. orange (postage) 20 10
488 – 25c. slate 20 10

489 **89** 50c. red (air) 25 10
490 50c. black 25 10
491 – 50c. pink 25 15
492 – 50c. blue 25 15

DESIGN—HORIZ: Nos. 488, 491, 492, Battle of Vertieres; Nos. 489/92 are larger (31½ × 26 mm).

90 Mme. Magloire

91 Tomb and Arms of King Henri Christophe

92 Christophe, Citadel and Pres. Magloire

1954.

493 **90** 10c. orange (postage) 15 10
494 10c. blue 15 10

495 20c. red (air) 10 10
496 50c. brown 20 20
497 1g. green 45 35
498 1g.50 red 45 40
499 2g.50 green 65 60
500 5g. blue 1·90 1·40

1954. Restoration of Christophe's Citadel. (a) T **91**. Flag in black and red.

501 **91** 10c. red (postage) 15 10

502 50c. orange (air) 35 15
503 1g. blue 40 30
504 1g.50 green 60 50
505 2g.50 grey 1·10 65
506 5g. red 1·75 1·25

(b) T **92**.

507 **92** 10c. red (postage) 15 10

508 50c. black and orange (air) 35 15
509 1g. black and blue 40 30
510 1g.50 black and green 60 50
511 2g.50 black and grey 1·10 65
512 5g. black and red 1·75 1·25

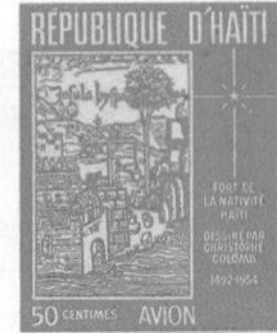

93 Columbus's Drawing of Fort de la Nativite

1954. Air.

513 **93** 50c. red 35 30
514 50c. slate 35 30

94 Sikorsky S-55 Helicopter over Ruins

95 Sikorsky S-55 Helicopter

1955. Obligatory Tax. Cyclone "Hazel" Relief Fund (1st issue).

515 **94** 10c. blue 10 10
516 10c. green 10 10
517 10c. orange 10 10
518 10c. black 15 10
519 20c. red 10 10
520 20c. green 15 10

1955. Obligatory Tax. Cyclone "Hazel" Relief Fund (2nd issue).

521 **95** 10c. black & grey (postage) 10 10
522 20c. deep blue and blue 15 10

523 10c. red and brown (air) 15 10
524 20c. red and pink 15 10

96 J.-J. Dessalines

97 Pres. Magloire and Monument

1955. Dessalines Commemoration.

525 **96** 3c. black & brown (postage) 10 10
526 5c. black and lilac 10 10
527 10c. black and red 10 10
528 10c. black and pink 10 10
529 25c. black and blue 20 10
530 25c. black and light blue 20 10

531 20c. black and green (air) 10 10
532 20c. black and orange 10 10

1955. Air. As No. 480 but without dates and colours changed.

533 50c. black and blue 30 10
534 50c. black and grey 30 15

1955. 21st Anniv of Haitian Army.

535 **97** 10c. blue & black (postage) 30 25
536 10c. red and black 30 25

537 1g.50 green and black (air) 35 20
538 1g.50 blue and black 45 20

98 Mallard

99 Douglas DC-4, Liner and Map

1955.

539 – 10c. blue (postage) 4·00 55
540 **98** 25c. green and turquoise 5·00 80

541 **99** 50c. black and grey (air) 1·00 20
542 – 50c. red and grey 30 15
543 **99** 75c. green and turquoise 1·25 45
544 – 1g. olive and blue 55 30
545 – 2g.50 orange . . . . . 20·00 4·00
546 **98** 5g. red and buff . . . . 32·00 6·50
DESIGNS—VERT: 10c., 2g.50, Greater flamingo. HORIZ: 50c. (No. 542), 1g. Car on coast road.

100 Immanuel Kant

1956. 10th Anniv of 1st Int Philosophical Congress.
547 **100** 10c. blue (postage) . . . 15 10
548 50c. brown (air) 25 15
549 75c. green 35 20
550 1g.50 mauve 85 45

101 Zim Basin and Waterfall

1957.
552 **101** 10c. orange & bl (postage) 15 10
553 50c. green & turq (air) . . 20 15
554 1g.50 green and blue . . . 35 30
555 2g.50 blue and light blue 60 45
556 5g. violet and blue . . . 1·40 1·10

102 J.-J. Dessalines and Monument **103** The "Atomium"

1958. Birth Bicentenary of J. J. Dessalines.
557 **102** 5c. green & black (postage) 10 10
558 10c. red and black 10 10
559 25c. blue and black . . . 20 10
560 20c. grey and black (air) 10 10
561 50c. orange and black . . 25 15

1958. Brussels International Exhibition.
562 **103** 50c. brown (postage) . . 30 15
563 – 75c. green 30 20
564 **103** 1g. violet 35 25
565 – 1g.50 orange 30 25
566 **103** 2g.50 red (air) 60 35
567 – 5g. blue 85 60
DESIGN—HORIZ: 75c., 1g.50, 5g. Exhibition view.

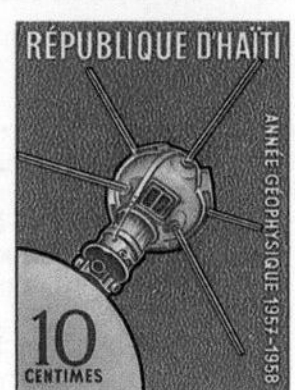

104 Sylvio Cator making Long Jump **106** Head of U.S. Satellite

1958. Sylvio Cator (athlete) Commem.
569 **104** 5c. green (postage) . . . 10 10
570 10c. brown 10 10
571 20c. purple and mauve . . 15 10
572 – 50c. black (air) 20 10
573 – 50c. green 20 10
574 – 1g. brown 35 15
575 – 5g. black and grey . . . 1·40 70
DESIGN—HORIZ: Nos. 572/75, Sylvio Cator making long jump (head-on view).

1958. Red Cross. Nos. 564/66 surch with red cross and **+50 CENTIMES.**
576 **103** 1g.+50c. violet (postage) 2·50 2·50
577 – 1g.50+50c. orange . . . . 2·50 2·50
578 **103** 2g.50+50c. red (air) . . . 2·75 2·75

1958. I.G.Y. Inscr as in T **106.**
579 **106** 10c. lake & turq (postage) 15 10
580 – 20c. black and orange . . 2·00 90
581 – 50c. red and green 35 25
582 – 1g. black and blue 80 20
583 **106** 50c. lake and blue (air) 20 20
584 – 1g.50 brown and red . . 4·50 1·60
585 – 2g. red and blue . . . . 1·10 35
DESIGNS: 20c., 1g.50, King penguins on icefloe; 50c., 2g. Giant radio telescope; 1g. Ocean-bed exploration.

107 Duvalier **108** Map of Haiti

1958. 1st Anniv of Installation of President Francois Duvalier. Commemorative inscr in blue.
587 **107** 10c. blk & pink (postage) 10 10
588 50c. black and green . . . 35 15
589 1g. black and red 55 30
590 5g. black and salmon . . . 1·60 1·10
591 – 50c. black and red (air) 60 20
592 – 2g.50 black and orange 80 55
593 – 5g. black and mauve . . . 1·10 90
594 – 7g.50 black and green . . 1·60 1·25
DESIGN: Nos. 591/94 as Type **107** but horiz.

1958. As T **107** but without commem. inscr. (a) Postage. Vert portrait.
596 5c. black and blue 10 10
597 10c. black and pink 10 10
598 20c. black and yellow . . . 10 10
599 50c. black and green 20 15
600 1g. black and red 30 20
601 1g.50 black and pink . . . 45 35
602 2g.50 black and lavender . . 70 60
603 5g. black and salmon . . . . 1·10 85

(b) Air. Horiz portrait.
604 50c. black and red 25 15
605 1g. black and violet 30 25
606 1g.50 black and brown . . . 50 35
607 2g. black and pink 60 35
608 2g.50 black and orange . . . 60 35
609 5g. black and mauve . . . . 1·10 85
610 7g.50 black and green . . . . 1·90 1·10

1958. United Nations.
611 **108** 10c. red (postage) 10 10
612 25c. green 15 10
613 – 50c. red and blue (air) . . 20 10
614 **108** 75c. blue 30 15
615 1g. brown 45 20
DESIGN: 50c. Flags of Haiti and U.N.

1959. 10th Anniv of Declaration of Human Rights. Nos. 611/15 optd **10TH ANNIVERSARY OF THE UNIVERSAL DECLARATION OF HUMAN RIGHTS.** (a) Postage. (i) English.
617 **108** 10c. red 10 10
618 25c. green 25 15

(ii) French.
617 **108** 10c. red 10 10
618 25c. green 25 15

(iii) Portuguese.
617 **108** 10c. red 10 10
618 25c. green 25 15

(iv) Spanish.
617 **108** 10c. red 10 10
618 25c. green 25 15

(b) Air. (i) English.
619 – 20c. red and blue 30 30
620 **108** 75c. blue 40 40
621 1g. brown 90 90

(ii) French.
619 – 20c. red and blue 30 30
620 **108** 75c. blue 40 40
621 1g. brown 90 90

(iii) Portuguese.
619 – 20c. red and blue 30 30
620 **108** 75c. blue 40 40
621 1g. brown 90 90

(iv) Spanish.
619 – 20c. red and blue 30 30
620 **108** 75c. blue 40 40
621 1g. brown 90 90
Overprinted alternately in different languages through the sheet of 25.

110 Pope Pius XII with Children

1959. Pope Pius XII Commemoration. Inscr "PIE XII PAPE DE LA PAIX".
622 **110** 10c. olive & blue (postage) 10 10
623 – 50c. brown and green . . 25 15
624 – 2g. sepia and lake 40 35
625 **110** 50c. violet and green (air) 20 10
626 – 1g.50 brown and olive . . 35 15
627 – 2g.50 blue and purple . . 60 30
DESIGNS: 50c. (No. 623), 1g.50, Pope at prayer; 2g., 2g.50, Pope giving blessing.

1959. Red Cross. (a) United Nations stamps surch with red cross and **+25 CENTIMES.**
628 **108** 10c.+25c. (postage) . . . 25 20
629 25c.+25c. 35 30
630 – 50c.+25c. (air) 35 35
631 **108** 75c.+25c. 45 35
632 1g.+25c. 65 70

(b) Pope Pius XII stamps surch with red cross and **+50 CENTIMES.**
633 **110** 10c.+50c. (postage) . . . 45 20
634 – 50c.+50c. 45 30
635 – 2g.+50c. 65 90
636 **110** 50c.+50c. (air) 60 60
637 – 1g.50+50c. 60 60
638 – 2g.50+50c. 65 65

111 Abraham Lincoln when a young man

1959. 150th Birth Anniv of Abraham Lincoln.
639 **111** 50c. purple & bl (postage) 30 15
640 – 1g. brown and green (air) 30 20
641 – 2g. myrtle and green . . . 35 20
642 – 2g.50 blue and buff . . . 40 35
PORTRAITS of Lincoln (bearded): 1g. Looking right; 2g., 2g.50, Looking left. The designs include various buildings associated with Lincoln.

1959. World Refugee Year (1st issue). Nos. 639/42 surch **Nations Unies ANNEE DES REFUGIES 1959-1960 + 20 Centimes.**
644 **111** 50c.+20c. purple and blue (postage) 45 45
645 – 1g.+20c. brown and green (air) 60 60
646 – 2g.+20c. myrtle and green 60 60
647 – 2g.50+20c. blue & buff . . 70 70

113 Chicago's First House and Modern Skyline

1959. 3rd Pan-American Games, Chicago.
649 **113** 25c. sepia & blue (postage) 30 15
650 – 50c. multicoloured 30 20
651 – 75c. sepia and blue . . . 45 25
652 – 50c. brown & turq (air) 35 20
653 **113** 1g. turquoise and purple 60 35
654 – 1g.50 multicoloured . . . 65 45
DESIGNS—HORIZ: 50c., 1g.50, Discus-thrower and Haitian flag. VERT: 50c. (air), 75c. J. B. Paul Dessables (founder of Chicago) and map.

114

1959. Obligatory Tax. Literacy Fund. (a) Postage. (i) Size 40 × 23 mm.
655 **114** 5c. green 10 10
656 10c. black 10 10
657 10c. red 10 10

(ii) Size 29 × 17 mm.
658 **114** 5c. green 10 10
659 5c. red 10 10
660 10c. blue 10 10

(b) Air. Size 29 × 17 mm.
661 **114** 5c. yellow 10 10
662 10c. blue 10 10
663 10c. orange 10 10

1959. Sports Fund. Nos. 649/54 surch **POUR LE SPORT + 0.75 CENTIMES.**
664 25c.+75c. sepia and blue (postage) 45 45
665 50c.+75c. multicoloured . . . 60 45
666 75c.+75c. sepia and blue . . 60 45
667 50c.+75c. brown & turq (air) 60 45
668 1g.+75c. turquoise and purple 60 45
669 1g.50+75c. multicoloured . . 60 60

1960. UNICEF Commem. Nos. 600 and 607/8 surch **Hommage a l'UNICEF +G.0,50.**
670 1g.+50c. blk & red (postage) 60 60
671 2g.+50c. black and pink (air) 65 65
672 2g.50+50c. black and orange 1·10 1·10

1960. Winter Olympic Games. Nos. 650 and 652/4 optd with Olympic rings and **VIIIEME JEUX OLYMPIQUES D'HIVER CALIFORNIE USA 1960.**
673 50c. multicoloured (postage) 1·10 90
674 50c. brown and turquoise (air) 70 70
675 1g. turquoise and purple . . 1·10 1·10
676 1g.50 multicoloured . . . . 1·25 1·25

118 "Uprooted Tree"

1960. World Refugee Year (2nd issue).
677 **118** 10c. grn & orge (postage) 10 10
678 50c. purple and violet . . 20 15
679 50c. brown and blue (air) 20 15
680 1g. red and green 45 30

1960. Surch in figures.
682 **96** 5c. on 3c. black and brown 10 10
683 10c. on 3c. black and brown 15 10

1960. 28th Anniv of Haitian Red Cross. 1945 Red Cross stamps optd "**28eme ANNIVERSAIRE**" or surch also.
684 **72** 1g. on 2½g. violet (postage) 45 35
685 2½g. violet 85 65
686 20c. on 1g.35 green (air) 20 10
687 50c. on 60c. purple 25 15
688 50c. on 1g.35 green 25 20
689 50c. on 2½g. violet 25 20
690 60c. purple 30 20
691 1g. on 1g.35 green 35 35
692 1g.35 green 60 55
693 2g. on 1g.35 green 95 85
No. 689 is also optd **Avion.**

121 "Sugar Queen, 1960" and Beach

1960. Election of Miss Claudinette Fouchard ("Miss Haiti") as World "Sugar Queen, 1960".
694 – 10c. violet & brn (postage) 15 10
695 – 20c. black and brown . . 20 10
696 **121** 50c. brown and blue . . . 45 10
697 – 1g. brown and green . . . 45 20
698 – 50c. brown and mauve (air) 35 15
699 **121** 2g.50 brown and blue . . 55 35
DESIGNS: Sugar Queen and—10c., 1g. Plantation (different views); 20c., 50c. Harvesting.

1960. Education Campaign. Surch **ALPHABETISATION** and premium.
700 **118** 10c.+20c. green and orange (postage) . . . 25 15
701 10c.+30c. green & orge 30 25
702 50c.+20c. purple & vio . . 30 35
703 50c.+30c. purple & vio . . 40 35
704 50c.+20c. black and blue (air) 25 15
705 50c.+30c. black and blue 35 25
706 1g.+20c. red and green . . 60 45
707 1g.+30c. red and green . . 60 45

123 Olympic Torch, Victory Parade at Athens, 1896, and Melbourne Stadium

1960. Olympic Games, Rome.
708 **123** 10c. blk & orge (postage) 10 10
709 – 20c. blue and red 10 10
710 – 50c. green and brown . . 20 10
711 – 1g. blue and black 45 15
712 – 50c. purple and bistre (air) 15 15
713 – 1g.50 mauve and green . . 35 25
714 – 2g.50 slate, purple & blk 60 35

DESIGNS: 20c. and 1g.50, "The Discus-thrower" and Rome Stadium; 50c. (No. 710), Pierre de Coubertin (founder) and Athletes Parade, Melbourne; 50c. (No. 712), As Type **123** but P. de Coubertin inset; 1g. Athens Stadium, 1896; 2g.50, Victory Parade, Athens, 1896, and Athletes' Parade, Melbourne.

1960. Nos. 710/3 surch **+25 CENTIMES**.
716 50c.+25c. grn & brn (postage) 35 25
717 1g.+25c. blue and black . . . 45 30
718 50c.+25c. purple & bis (air) 25 20
719 1g.50+25c. mauve and green 30 25

125 Occide Jeanty

1960. Birth Cent of Occide Jeanty (composer).
720 **125** 10c. pur & orge (postage) 15 10
721 – 20c. purple and blue . . . 30 10
722 **125** 50c. sepia and green . . . 40 20
723 50c. blue and yellow (air) 20 10
724 – 1g.50 slate and mauve . . 45 25
DESIGN: 20c., 1g.50, Jeanty and Capitol, Port-au-Prince.

126 U.N., New York

1960. 15th Anniv of U.N.O.
731 **126** 1g. black & grn (postage) 35 20
732 50c. black and red (air) 20 10
733 1g.50 black and blue . . . 45 25

127 Sud Aviation Caravelle

1960. Air. Aviation Week.
735 **127** 20c. blue and red 10 10
736 – 50c. brown and green . . 30 20
737 – 50c. blue and green . . . 30 20
738 – 50c. black and green . . . 30 20
739 **127** 1g. green and red 45 25
740 – 1g.50 pink and blue . . . 50 35
DESIGNS: 50c. (3) Boeing 707 airliner and Wright Flyer I; 1g.50, Boeing 707 and 60c. "Columbia" stamp of 1933.

1961. UNICEF Child Welfare Fund. Surch **UNICEF +25 centimes**.
748 **126** 1g.+25c. black and green (postage) 45 30
749 50c.+25c. black and red (air) 30 25
750 1g.50+25c. black & bl . . 55 35

129 Alexandre Dumas (father and son)

1961. Alexandre Dumas Commemoration.
751 – 5c. brown & blue (postage) 10 10
752 – 10c. black, purple and red 10 10
753 **129** 50c. blue and red 30 20
754 – 50c. black and blue (air) 30 15
755 – 1g. red and black 35 20
756 – 1g.50 black and green . . 55 35
DESIGNS—HORIZ: 5c. Dumas' House; 50c. (No. 754), A. Dumas and "The Three Musketeers". VERT: 10c. A. Dumas and horseman in "Twenty Years After"; 1g. A. Dumas (son) and "The Lady of the Camellias" (Marguerite Gauthier); 1g.50, A. Dumas, and "The Count of Monte Cristo".

130 Pirates

1961. Tourist Publicity.
761 – 5c. yellow & blue (postage) 10 10
762 **130** 10c. yellow and mauve . . 10 10
763 – 15c. orange and green . . 10 10
764 – 20c. orange and brown . . 40 10
765 – 50c. yellow and blue . . . 80 20
766 – 20c. yellow and blue (air) 40 10
767 – 50c. orange and violet . . 80 20
768 – 1g. yellow and green . . . 35 25
DESIGNS: Nos. 761, 768, Map of Tortuga; No. 763, Two pirates on beach; Nos. 764, 766, Pirate ships attacking galleon; Nos. 765, 767, Pirate in rigging.

1961. Re-election of Pres. Duvalier. Optd **Dr. F. Duvalier President 22 Mai 1961**.
769 **102** 5c. green & blk (postage) 10 10
770 10c. red and black 10 10
771 25c. blue and black . . . 20 15
772 **74** 2g.50 grey 65 45
773 **102** 20c. grey and black (air) 10 10
774 50c. orange and black . . 20 15
775 **99** 75c. green and turquoise 35 30

1961. Air. 18th World Scout Conference, Lisbon. Nos. 735 and 739/40 surch **18e CONFERENCE INTERNATIONALE DU SCOUTISME MONDIAL. LISBONNE SEPTEMBRE 1961 +0,25** and Scout emblem.
776 20c.+25c. blue and red . . . 30 20
777 1g.+25c. green and red . . . 45 35
778 1g.50+25c. pink and blue . . 55 55

1961. U.N. and Haitian Malaria Eradication Campaign. Surch **OMS SNEM +20 CENTIMES**.
780 **126** 1g.+20c. black and green (postage) 45 35
781 **126** 50c.+20c. black and red (air) 85 85
782 1g.50+20c. black & bl . . 1·10 1·10

1961. Duvalier-Ville Reconstruction Fund Nos. 598, 600, 602, 604/5 and 608/10 surch with UNICEF emblem, **Duvalier-Ville** and premium.
783 20c.+25c. black and yellow (postage) 30 25
787 1g.+50c. black and red . . . 60 45
788 2g.50+50c. black and blue . . 65 50
784 50c.+25c. black and red (air) 25 25
785 1g.+50c. black and violet . . 25 25
789 2g.50+50c. black and orange 40 30
786 5g.+50c. black and mauve . . 85 60
790 7g.50+50c. black and green 90 85

1962. Colonel Glenn's Space Flight. Nos. 761, 768 optd **EXPLORATION SPATIALE JOHN GLENN** and outline of capsule or surch also.
795 50c. on 5c. yell & bl (postage) 45 30
796 1g.50 on 5c. yellow and blue 90 65
797 1g. yellow and green (air) . . 30 30
798 2g. on 1g. yellow and green 85 70

136 Campaign Emblem

1962. Malaria Eradication.
799 **136** 5c. blue and red (postage) 10 10
800 – 10c. green and brown . . 10 10
801 **136** 50c. red and blue 30 15
802 – 20c. red and violet (air) 10 10
803 **136** 50c. red and green 20 15
804 – 1g. blue and orange . . . 35 25
DESIGN: 10c., 20c., 1g. As Type **136** but with long side of triangle at top.

1962. World Refugee Year (3rd issue). As T **118** but additionally inscr "1962" and colours changed.
806 **118** 10c. orange & bl (postage) 10 10
807 50c. green and mauve . . 25 20
808 50c. brown and blue (air) 15 15
809 1g. black and buff 25 25

137 Scout Badge

1962. 22nd Anniv of Haitian Boy Scout Movement.
811 **137** 3c. orange, black and violet (postage) 10 10
812 – 5c. brown, olive and black 10 10
813 – 10c. brown, black & green 10 10
814 **137** 25c. black, lake and olive 15 10
815 – 50c. green, violet and red 30 15
816 – 20c. slate, green and purple (air) 10 10
817 **137** 50c. brown, green and red 25 15
818 – 1g.50 turq, sepia & brn 45 35
DESIGNS—VERT: 5c., 20c., 50, c. (post) Scout and camp. HORIZ: 10c., 1g.50, Lord and Lady Baden-Powell.

1962. Surch with premium. (a) Nos. 799/804.
820 **136** 5c.+25c. (postage) 20 15
821 – 10c.+25c. 25 20
822 **136** 50c.+25c. 30 20
823 – 20c.+25c. (air) 20 20
824 **136** 50c.+25c. 25 25
825 – 1g.+25c. 35 30

(b) Nos. 806/9.
827 **118** 10c.+20c. (postage) . . . 15 15
828 50c.+20c. 25 15
829 50c.+20c. (air) 25 15
830 1g.+20c. 35 30

1962. Air. Port-au-Prince Airport Construction Fund. Optd **AEROPORT INTERNATIONAL 1962**, with No. 832 additionally optd **Poste Aerienne**.
831 – 20c. No. 816 . . . . . . 15 10
832 – 50c. No. 815 . . . . . . 25 15
833 **137** 50c. No. 817 . . . . . . 25 15
834 – 1g.50 No. 818 . . . . . 45 35

140 Tower, World's Fair

1962. "Century 21" Exn (World's Fair), Seattle.
835 **140** 10c. purple & bl (postage) 10 10
836 20c. blue and red 10 10
837 50c. green and yellow . . 35 10
838 1g. red and green 55 20
839 50c. black and lilac (air) 25 10
840 1g. red and grey 45 15
841 1g.50 purple and orange 55 20

141 Town plan and 1904 10c. stamp

1963. Duvalier-ville Commemoration.
843 **141** 5c. black, yellow and violet (postage) 10 10
844 10c. black, yellow and red 10 10
845 25c. black, yellow and grey 20 15
846 – 50c. brown & orange (air) 20 15
847 – 1g. brown and blue . . . 35 30
848 – 1g.50 brown and green . . 55 45
DESIGN: Nos. 846/8 Houses and 1881 2c. stamp.

1963. "Peaceful Uses of Outer Space". Nos. 837/38 and 841/2 optd **UTILISATIONS PACIFIQUES DE L'ESPACE** and space capsule.
853 **140** 50c. green and yellow (postage) 20 15
854 1g. red and green 45 30
855 1g. red and grey (air) . . 45 35
856 1g.50 purple and orange 65 65

1963. Literacy Campaign. Surch **ALPHABETISATION + 0,10**.
857 **141** 25c.+10c. (postage) . . . 15 10
858 – 50c.+10c. (No. 846) (air) 25 15
859 – 1g.50+10c. (No. 848) . . 35 35

143 Harvesting
145 Dessalines Statue

144 Dag Hammarskjold and U.N. Emblem
146 "Alphabetisation"

1963. Freedom from Hunger.
860 **143** 10c. orange and black (postage) 10 10
861 20c. turquoise and black 10 10
862 50c. mauve and black (air) 15 10
863 1g. green and black . . . 30 20

1963. Air. Dag Hammarskjold Commemoration. Portrait in blue.
864 **144** 20c. brown and bistre . . 10 10
865 50c. red and blue 20 20
866 1g. blue and mauve . . . 30 30
867 1g.50 green and grey . . 55 45
Nos. 864/67 were printed in sheets of 25 (5 × 5) with a map of Sweden in the background covering most stamps in the second and third vertical rows.

1963. Dessalines Commemoration.
869 **145** 5c. red & brown (postage) 10 10
870 10c. blue, green and ochre 10 10
871 50c. green and brown (air) 20 10
872 50c. purple, violet and blue 20 10

1963. Obligatory Tax. Education Fund.
873 **146** 10c. red (postage) 10 10
874 10c. blue 10 10
875 10c. olive 10 10
876 10c. brown (air) 10 10
877 10c. violet 10 10
878 10c. violet 10 10
See also Nos. 974/78, 1157/63 and 1260/1.

1964. Mothers' Festival. Optd **FETE DES MERES 1964** or surch also.
879 **145** 10c. blue, green and ochre (postage) 10 10
880 50c. green and brown (air) 25 15
881 50c. purple, violet and blue 25 15
882 1g.50 on 80c. pink and green (No. 458) 35 25

1964. Winter Olympic Games, Innsbruck. Surch **JEUX OLYMPIQUES D'HIVER INNSBRUCK 1964 0.50+0.10**, Olympic rings and Games emblem.
883 **137** 50c.+10c. on 3c. (postage) 45 30
884 50c.+10c. on 5c. (No. 812) 45 30
885 – 50c.+10c. on 10c. (No. 813) 45 30
886 **137** 50c.+10c. on 25c. 45 30
887 **101** 50c.+10c. on 2g.50 (air) 70 65

1964. Air. Red Cross Cent (1963). Optd **1863 1963** and Centenary Emblem, on surch also. Portrait in blue.
888 **144** 20c. brown and bistre . . 30 10
889 50c. red and blue 30 15
890 1g. blue and mauve . . . 45 30
891 1g.50 green and grey . . 55 35
892 2g.50+1g.25 on 1g.50 green and grey 85 60

150 Weightlifting
151 Our Lady of Perpetual Succour and Airport

1964. Olympic Games, Tokyo (1st issue).
893 **150** 10c. sepia & blue (postage) 10 10
894 25c. sepia and salmon . . 10 10
895 – 50c. sepia and mauve . . 20 15
896 **150** 50c. sepia and purple (air) 15 15
897 – 50c. sepia and green . . . 15 15
898 – 75c. sepia and yellow . . 20 20
899 – 1g.50 sepia and grey . . . 35 35

DESIGN: Nos. 895, 897/99, Hurdling; Nos. 893/09 were printed in sheets of 50 (10 × 5) with a large map of Japan in the background.

1964. International Airport.
901 **151** 10c. blk & ochre (postage) 15 10
902 25c. black and turquoise 25 10
903 50c. black and green . . . 35 15
904 1g. black and red 55 35
905 50c. black and orange (air) 30 15
906 1g.50 black and mauve . . 40 20
907 2g.50 black and violet . . 1·10 55

1965. International Airport Opening. Optd **1965**.
908 **151** 10c. blk & ochre (postage) 10 10
909 25c. black and turquoise 25 15
910 50c. black and green . . . 35 15
911 1g. black and red 55 30
912 50c. black and orange (air) 30 10
913 1g.50 black and mauve . . 50 25
914 2g.50 black and violet . . 75 40

1965. Olympic Games. Tokyo (2nd issue). Nos. 893/9 surch **+5 c**.
915 **150** 10c.+5c. (postage) 10 10
916 – 25c.+5c. 15 15
917 – 50c.+5c. 30 25
918 **150** 50c.+5c. (air) 25 25
919 – 50c.+5c. 25 25
920 – 75c.+5c. 35 35
921 – 1g.50+5c. 45 45

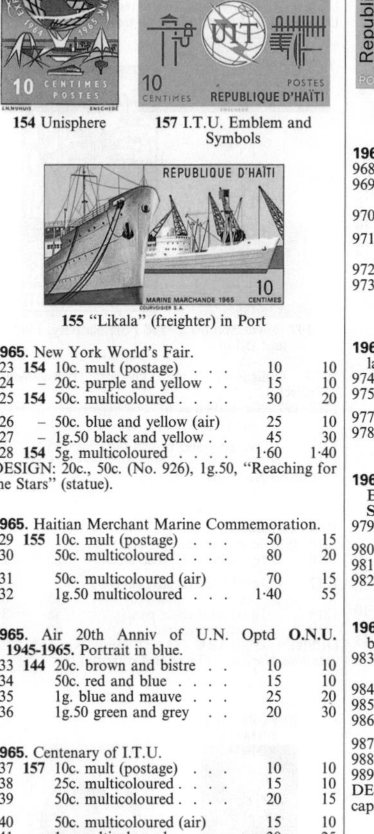

154 Unisphere **157** I.T.U. Emblem and Symbols

155 "Likala" (freighter) in Port

1965. New York World's Fair.
923 **154** 10c. mult (postage) . . . 10 10
924 – 20c. purple and yellow . . 15 10
925 **154** 50c. multicoloured 30 20
926 – 50c. blue and yellow (air) 25 10
927 – 1g.50 black and yellow . . 45 30
928 **154** 5g. multicoloured . . . . 1·60 1·40
DESIGN: 20c., 50c. (No. 926), 1g.50, "Reaching for the Stars" (statue).

1965. Haitian Merchant Marine Commemoration.
929 **155** 10c. mult (postage) . . . 50 15
930 50c. multicoloured 80 20
931 50c. multicoloured (air) 70 15
932 1g.50 multicoloured . . . 1·40 55

1965. Air 20th Anniv of U.N. Optd **O.N.U. 1945-1965**. Portrait in blue.
933 **144** 20c. brown and bistre . . 10 10
934 50c. red and blue 15 10
935 1g. blue and mauve . . . 25 20
936 1g.50 green and grey . . 20 30

1965. Centenary of I.T.U.
937 **157** 10c. mult (postage) . . . 10 10
938 25c. multicoloured 15 10
939 50c. multicoloured 20 15
940 50c. multicoloured (air) 15 10
941 1g. multicoloured 30 25
942 1g.50 multicoloured . . . 45 35
943 2g. multicoloured 65 50

1965. 25th Anniv of U.N.E.S.C.O. Nos. 937/41 optd **20e Anniversaire UNESCO**.
945 **157** 10c. mult (postage) . . . 20 20
946 25c. multicoloured 55 55
947 50c. multicoloured 75 75
948 50c. multicoloured (air) 90 35
949 1g. multicoloured . . . . 1·75 70

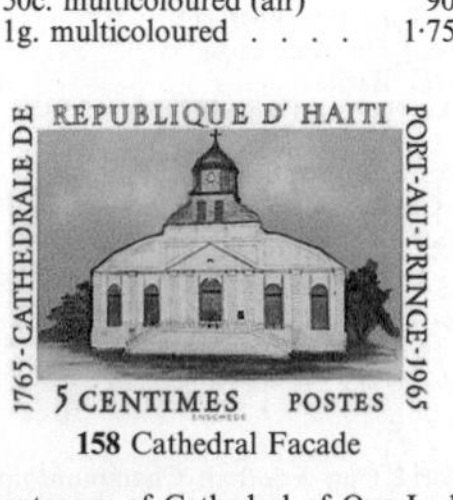

158 Cathedral Facade

1965. Bicentenary of Cathedral of Our Lady of the Assumption, Port-au-Prince. Mult.
951 5c. Type **158** (postage) . . . 10 10
952 10c. High Altar (vert) 10 10
953 25c. "Our Lady of the Assumption" (painting) (vert) 10 10
954 50c. Type **158** (air) 20 10
955 1g. High Altar (vert) 30 20
956 7g.50 as 25c. but larger, 38 × 51 mm . . . . 1·75 1·25

159 "Passiflora quadrangularis"

1965. Haitian Flowers. Multicoloured.
957 3c. Type **159** (postage) . . . 10 10
958 5c. "Sambucus canadensis" 10 10
959 10c. "Hibiscus esculentus" . . 10 10
960 15c. As 5c. 10 10
961 50c. Type **159** 30 15
962 50c. Type **159** (air) 15 10
963 50c. As 5c. 15 10
964 50c. As 10c. 15 10
965 1g.50 As 5c. 45 35
966 1g.50 As 10c. 45 35
967 5g. Type **159** . . . . 1·10 75

160 Amulet **162** Astronauts and "Gemini" Capsules

1966. "Culture". Multicoloured.
968 5c. Type **160** (postage) . . . 10 10
969 10c. Carved stool and Veve decoration (horiz) 10 10
970 50c. Type **160** 20 15
971 50c. Carved stool and Veve decoration (horiz) (air) . . 20 15
972 1g.50 Type **160** 55 45
973 2g.50 Modern abstract painting (52 × 37 mm) . . . 60 50

1966. Obligatory Tax. Education Fund. As T **146** but larger (17 × 25½ mm).
974 **146** 10c. green (postage) . . . 10 10
975 10c. violet 10 10
977 10c. orange (air) 10 10
978 10c. blue 10 10

1966. State Visit of Emperor Haile Selassie of Ethiopia. Nos. 969 and 971/3 optd **Hommage Haile Selassie 1er 24-25 Avril 1966**.
979 – 10c. mult (postage) . . . 15 15
980 – 50c. multicoloured (air) 20 15
981 **160** 1g.50 multicoloured . . . 55 45
982 – 2g.50 multicoloured . . . 60 50

1966. Space Rendezvous. Astronauts and capsules in brown.
983 **162** 5c. indigo & blue (postage) 10 10
984 10c. violet and blue . . . 10 10
985 25c. green and blue . . . 15 10
986 50c. red and blue 25 15
987 – 50c. indigo and blue (air) 20 15
988 – 1g. green and blue 35 30
989 – 1g.50 red and blue . . . 55 45
DESIGN: Nos. 987/9, Astronauts and "Gemini" capsules (different arrangement).

163 Football and Pres. Duvalier

1966. Caribbean Football Championships. Portrait in black. (i) Inscr "CHAMPIONNAT DE FOOTBALL DES CARAIBES".
990 **163** 5c. green & flesh (postage) 10 10
991 – 10c. green and blue . . . 10 10
992 **163** 15c. green and apple . . . 10 10
993 – 50c. green and lilac . . . 25 15
994 **163** 50c. purple and sage (air) 15 15
995 – 1g.50 purple and pink . . 55 45

(ii) As Nos. 990/5 but additionally inscr "COUPE DR. FRANCOIS DUVALIER 22 JUIN".
996 **163** 5c. grn & flesh (postage) 10 10
997 – 10c. green and blue . . . 10 10
998 **163** 15c. green and apple . . 10 10
999 – 50c. green and lilac . . 25 15
1000 **163** 50c. purple and sage (air) 15 15
1001 – 1g.50 purple and pink 55 45
DESIGN: 10c., 50c. (No. 991, 993), 1g.50, Footballer and Pres. Duvalier.

164 Audio-visual Aids

1966. National Education.
1002 – 5c. purple, green and pink (postage) 10 10
1003 – 10c. sepia, lake & brown 10 10
1004 **164** 25c. violet, blue and green 10 10
1005 – 50c. pur, grn & yell (air) 15 15
1006 – 1g. sepia, brown & orge 30 30
1007 **164** 1g.50 blue, turq & grn 45 45
DESIGNS—VERT: 5c., 50c. Young Haitians walking towards ABC "sun"; 10c., 1g. Scouting—hat, knot and saluting hand.

165 Dr. Albert Schweitzer and Maps of Alsace and Gabon

1967. Schweitzer Commem. Multicoloured.
1008 5c. Type **165** (postage) . . . 10 10
1009 10c. Dr. Schweitzer and organ pipes 10 10
1010 20c. Dr. Schweitzer and Hospital Deschapelles, Haiti 15 10
1011 50c. As 20c. (air) 20 15
1012 1g. As 20c. 35 30
1013 1g.50 Type **165** 50 45
1014 2g. As 10c. 65 55

166 J.-J. Dessalines and Melon

1967. Dessalines Commem. With Portrait of Dessalines. Multicoloured.
1015 5c. Type **166** (postage) . . . 10 10
1016 10c. Chou (cabbage) 10 10
1017 20c. Mandarine (orange) . . 10 10
1018 50c. Mirliton (gourd) . . . 15 15
1019 50c. Type **166** (air) 15 10
1020 1g. As 20c. 30 20
1021 1g.50 As 20c. 45 35

1967. World Scout Jamboree, Idaho. Nos. 957/8, 960/1, 963 and 965 surch **12e Jamboree Mondial 1967** or with additional premium only.
1022 10c.+10c. on 5c. (postage) 10 10
1023 15c.+10c. 10 10
1024 50c. on 3c. 20 15
1025 50c.+10c. 20 20
1026 50c.+10c. (air) 20 20
1027 1g.50+50c. 60 50

1967. World Fair, Montreal. Nos. 968/70 and 972 optd **EXPO CANADA 1967** and emblem, also surch with new values (1g. and 2g.).
1028 **160** 5c. mult (postage) . . . 10 10
1029 – 10c. multicoloured . . . 10 10
1030 **160** 50c. multicoloured . . . 15 15
1031 1g. on 5c. multicoloured 35 30
1032 1g.50 multicoloured (air) 55 45
1033 2g. on 1g.50 mult . . . 70 55

169 Head of Duvalier and Guineafowl Emblem

1967. 10th Anniv of Duvalierists Revolution.
1034 **169** 5c. gold and red (postage) 10 10
1035 10c. gold and blue . . . 10 10
1036 25c. gold and brown . . 15 10
1037 50c. gold and purple . . 25 15
1038 1g. gold and green (air) 45 30
1039 1g.50 gold and violet . . 70 45
1040 2g. gold and red 90 55

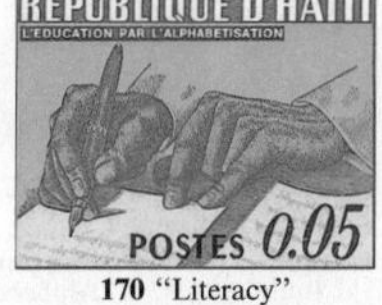

170 "Literacy"

1967. National Education. Multicoloured.
1041 5c. Type **170** (postage) . . . 10 10
1042 10c. "Scouting" (Scout badge) (vert) 10 10
1043 25c. "Visual Aids" (slide projection) 15 10
1044 50c. Type **170** (air) 15 10
1045 1g. As 10c. (vert) 30 25
1046 1g.50 As 25c. 45 35

1968. Olympic Games, Mexico. Nos. 990, 992 and 995 surch **MEXICO 1968** with Olympic rings and value or optd only (1g.50).
1047 **163** 50c. on 15c. (postage) . . 20 15
1048 1g. on 5c. 30 25
1049 – 1g.50 (air) 55 45
1050 – 2g.50+1g.25 on 1g.50 1·25 1·00

1968. Winter Olympic Games, Grenoble. Nos. 986/9 optd **Xeme JEUX OLYMPIQUES D'HIVER–GRENOBLE 1968** and Games emblem.
1051 **162** 50c. red & blue (postage) 60 60
1052 – 50c. indigo and blue (air) 45 30
1053 – 1g. green and blue . . . 60 35
1054 – 1g.50 red and blue . . . 1·10 75

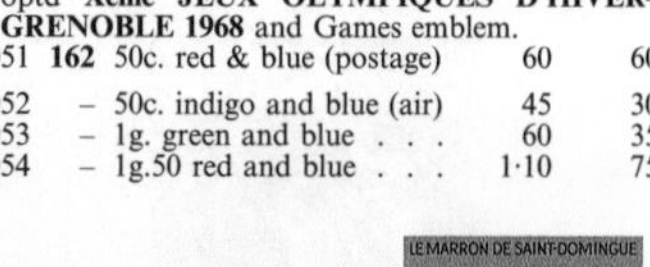

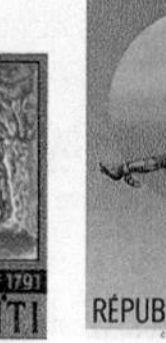

173 Bois Caiman Ceremony **174** "The Unknown Slave"

1968. Slaves' Revolt Commem.
1055 **173** 5c. mult (postage) . . . 10 10
1056 10c. multicoloured . . . 10 10
1057 25c. multicoloured . . . 10 10
1058 50c. multicoloured . . . 20 15
1059 50c. multicoloured (air) 15 10
1060 50c. multicoloured . . . 15 10
1061 1g. multicoloured . . . 30 30
1062 1g. multicoloured . . . 30 25
1063 1g.50 multicoloured . . . 45 45
1064 2g. multicoloured . . . 45 55
1065 5g. multicoloured . . . 85 60
Nos. 1060 and 1062/4 are in a larger size—49½ × 36 mm.

1968. Inaug of Slavery Freedom Monument.
1066 **174** 5c. black & blue (postage) 10 10
1067 10c. black and brown . . 10 10
1068 20c. black and violet . . 15 10
1069 25c. black and blue . . . 15 10
1070 50c. black and green . . 30 15
1071 50c. black and ochre (air) 20 15
1072 1g. black and red . . . 35 25
1073 1g.50 black and orange 55 35

1968. Air. Nos. 1044/6 surch **CULTURE + 0.10**.
1074 **170** 50c.+10c. mult 20 20
1075 – 1g.+10c. multicoloured 30 30
1076 – 1g.50+10c. mult 45 45

176 Various Arms and Palm

1968. Consecration of Haitian Bishopric.
1077 **176** 5c. mult (postage) . . . 10 10
1078 – 10c. multicoloured . . . 10 10
1079 – 25c. multicoloured . . . 20 10
1080 **176** 50c. multicoloured (air) 15 10
1081 – 1g. multicoloured . . . 30 25
1082 – 1g.50 multicoloured . . 45 35
1083 – 2g.50 multicoloured . . 70 65
DESIGNS—HORIZ: (50 × 30 mm): 10c., 1g., 2g.50, Virgin Mary; 25c., 1g.50, Cathedral, Port-au-Prince.

177 Boeing 727-100 over Control Tower

1968. Inauguration of Duvalier Airport, Port-au-Prince. Portrait in black.
1084 **177** 5c. brown & bl (postage) 10 10
1085 10c. brown and blue . . 10 10
1086 25c. brown and lilac . . 10 10
1087 – 50c. purple & violet (air) 20 15
1088 – 1g.50 purple and blue . . 55 35
1089 – 2g.50 purple & turquoise 70 45
DESIGN: 50c., 1g.50, 2g.50, Boeing 727-100 over airport entrance.

178 President Duvalier, Emblems and Map

1968. Air. 4th Anniv of Francois Duvalier's "Life Presidency". Die-stamped in gold.
1090 **178** 30g. gold, black and red 16·00

179 Slave breaking Chains

1968. "Revolt of the Slaves" (1791).
1091 **179** 5c. mauve, purple and blue (postage) 10 10
1092 10c. mauve, pur & orge 10 10
1093 25c. mauve, pur & ochre 10 10
1094 50c. mauve, pur & lil (air) 15 10
1095 1g. mauve, purple & grn 35 25
1096 1g.50 mauve, pur & bl 50 35
1097 2g. mauve, purple & turq 60 45

180 "Learning the Alphabet"

1968. "National Education". Multicoloured.
1098 5c. Type **180** (postage) 10 10
1099 10c. Children watching TV screen ("Education by Audio-visual Methods") 10 10
1100 50c. Hands with ball ("Education Through Sport") 15 10
1101 50c. As No. 1099 (air) 15 10
1102 1g. As No. 1100 30 25
1103 1g.50 As No. 1099 55 35

181 Boesman and Balloon

182 Airmail Cachet of 1925

1968. Air. Boesman's Balloon Flight.
1104 **181** 70c. brown and green 40 30
1105 1g.75 brown and blue 1·00 70

1968. Air. Galiffet's Balloon Flight of 1784. Each black and purple on mauve.
1106 70c. Airplane and "AVION" ("2 May 1925") 35 35
1107 70c. Type **182** 35 35
1108 70c. "AVION" and airplane ("28 March 1927") 35 35
1109 70c. "HAITI POSTE AVION" and airplane ("12 July 1927") 35 35
1110 70c. Airplane and "AVION" within ring ("13 Sept 1927") 35 35
1111 70c. "LINDBERGH" and airplane ("6th February 1928") 35 35

Nos. 1106/11 were issued together se-tenant within a small sheet containing two blocks of six (3 × 2) with an overall background design representing Galiffet's balloon.

183 Churchill as Elder Brother of Trinity House

1968. Churchill Commemoration. Mult.
1112 3c. Type **183** (postage) 10 10
1113 5c. Churchill painting 10 10
1114 10c. As Knight of the Garter 10 10
1115 15c. 79th birthday portrait and troops 10 10
1116 20c. Churchill and Farman M.F.7 floatplane 10 10
1117 25c. Karsh portrait and taking leave of the Queen 10 10
1118 50c. Giving "V" sign and Houses of Parliament 15 10
1119 50c. As No. 1116 (air) 15 10
1120 75c. As No. 1115 25 15
1121 1g. As No. 1117 30 25
1122 1g.50 As No. 1118 45 35

1969. Nos. 1070/2 surch.
1124 **174** 70c. on 50c. (postage) 45 20
1125 70c. on 50c. (air) 35 25
1126 1g.75 on 1g. 85 55

185 Blue-hooded Euphonia

1969. Birds. Multicoloured.
1127 5c. Type **185** (postage) 1·10 30
1128 10c. Hispaniolan trogon 1·10 30
1129 20c. Palm chat 1·25 30
1130 25c. Stripe-headed tanager 1·60 40
1131 50c. Type **185** 2·25 45
1132 50c. As 10c. (air) 2·00 60
1133 1g. Black-cowled oriole 2·25 1·10
1134 1g.50 As 25c. 2·75 1·50
1135 2g. Hispaniolan woodpecker 3·25 2·00

186 "Theato, Paris-1900"

1969. Winners of Olympic Marathon showing commemorative inscr and stamp of "host" country. Multicoloured.
1136 5c. "Louis, Athens-1896" (postage) 10 10
1137 10c. Type **186** 15 15
1138 15c. "Hicks, St. Louis-1904" 15 15
1139 20c. "Hayes, London-1908" 25 25
1140 20c. "McArthur, Stockholm-1912" 25 25
1141 25c. "Kolehmainen, Antwerp-1920" 40 40
1142 25c. "Steenroos, Paris-1924" 40 40
1143 25c. "El Quafi, Amsterdam-1928" 40 40
1144 30c. "Zabala, Los Angeles-1932" (air) 45 45
1145 50c. "Son, Berlin-1936" 70 70
1146 60c. "Cabrera, London-1948" 90 90
1147 75c. "Zatopek, Helsinki-1952" 1·25 1·25
1148 75c. "Mimoun, Melbourn-1956" 1·25 1·25
1149 90c. "Bikila, Rome-1960" 1·50 1·50
1150 1g. "Bikila, Tokyo-1964" 1·75 1·75
1151 1g.25 "Wolde, Mexico-1968" 2·50 2·50

Nos. 1136, 1139, 1142 and 1149 are larger, size 66 × 36 mm.

187 Pylons and Electric Light Bulb

189 Practising the Alphabet

1969. Construction of Duvalier Hydro-electric Scheme.
1153 **187** 20c. violet & bl (postage) 10 10
1154 20c. blue and violet (air) 10 10
1155 25c. green and red 10 10
1156 25c. red and green 15 10

1969. Obligatory Tax. Education Fund. As Nos. 974/8.
1157 **146** 10c. brown (postage) 10 10
1158 10c. blue 10 10
1159 10c. purple (air) 10 10
1160 10c. red 10 10
1161 10c. yellow 10 10
1162 10c. green 10 10
1163 10c. maroon 10 10

1969. 50th Anniv of League of Red Cross Societies. Various stamps surch **50 eme. Anniversaire de la Ligue des Societes de la Croix Rouge**.
1164 10c.+10c. (No. 1099) (postage) 10 10
1165 50c.+20c. (No. 1100) 20 20
1166 50c.+20c. (No. 1101) (air) 30 20
1167 1g.50+25c. (No. 1103) 70 50

1969. "National Education". Multicoloured.
1168 5c. Type **189** (postage) 10 10
1169 10c. Children at play (vert) 10 10
1170 50c. Audio-visual education (vert) 15 10
1171 50c. As No. 1170 (vert) (air) 15 10
1172 1g. Type **189** 35 20
1173 1g.50 As No. 1169 (vert) 55 35

190 I.L.O. Emblem

1969. 50th Anniv of I.L.O.
1174 **190** 5c. green & blk (postage) 10 10
1175 10c. brown and black 10 10
1176 20c. blue and black 10 10
1177 25c. red and black (air) 15 10
1178 70c. orange and black 25 15
1179 1g.75 violet and black 40 45

191 "Papilio zonaria"

1969. Haitian Butterflies. Multicoloured.
1180 10c. Type **191** (postage) 15 10
1181 20c. "Zerene cesonia" 30 10
1182 25c. "Papilio machaonides" 35 10
1183 50c. "Danaus eresimus" (air) 45 10
1184 1g.50 "Anaea marthesia" 1·40 60
1185 2g. "Prepona antimache" 1·75 85

192 Dr. Martin Luther King

1970. Dr. Martin Luther King (American Civil Rights leader) Commemoration.
1186 **192** 10c. brown, red and ochre (postage) 10 10
1187 20c. black, red & bl 10 10
1188 25c. black, red and pink 10 10
1189 50c. black, red and green (air) 20 10
1190 1g. black, red and orange 35 25
1191 1g.50 black, red and blue 55 35

193 "Laeliopsis dominguensis"

194 U.P.U. Monument Berne, and Map of Haiti

1970. Haitian Orchids. Multicoloured.
1192 10c. Type **193** (postage) 10 10
1193 20c. "Oncidium haitiense" 15 10
1194 25c. "Oncidium calochilum" 25 15
1195 50c. "Tetramicra elegans" (air) 15 10
1196 1g.50 "Epidendrum truncatum" 45 35
1197 2g. "Oncidium desertorum" 65 50

1970. 16th U.P.U. Congress, Tokyo.
1198 **194** 10c. brown, black and green (postage) 10 10
1199 – 25c. yellow, black and red 15 10
1200 – 50c. green, black and blue 35 25
1201 – 50c. brn, blk & vio (air) 15 10
1202 – 1g.50 yellow, blk & red 55 35
1203 **194** 2g. brown, black & green 70 50

DESIGNS—VERT: 25c., 1g.50, Stylized "propeller". HORIZ: 50c. (both), Doves and globe.

195 Map, Dam and Generator

1970. Construction of Duvalier Central Hydro-electric Power Station. Multicoloured.
1205 20c. Type **195** 15 10
1206 25c. Map, dam and pylon 20 10

1970. 25th Anniv of United Nations. Nos. 1200/203 optd **XXVe ANNIVERSAIRE O.N.U.** and emblem.
1207 – 50c. green, black and blue (postage) 20 15
1208 – 50c. brown, blk & bl (air) 20 10
1209 – 1g.50 yellow, blk & red 55 35
1210 **194** 2g. brown, black & green 70 50

197 Power Station and Pylon

198 Fort Nativity, 1492

1970. Obligatory Tax. Duvalier Hydro-electric Project.
1212 **197** 20c. brown & lil (postage) 15 10
1213 20c. grey and brown (air) 15 10
1214 20c. violet and blue 15 10

See also No. 1268.

1970. Christmas.
1215 **198** 3c. brn & yell (postage) 10 10
1216 5c. black and green 20 15
1217 – 1g.50 mult (sepia panel) (air) 55 35
1218 – 1g.50 mult (blue panel) 55 35
1219 – 2g. multicoloured 60 50

DESIGN—SQUARE (33 × 33 mm): Nos. 1217/19, "Haitian Nativity" (Toussaint Auguste).

199 "The Oriental" (Rembrandt)

200 Football

1971. Paintings. Multicoloured.
1220 5c. Type **199** (postage) 10 10
1221 10c. "The Ascension" (C. Bazile) 10 10
1222 20c. "Irises in a vase" (Van Gogh) 15 10
1223 50c. "The Baptism of Christ" (C. Bazile) 30 15
1224 50c. "The Nativity" (R. Benoit) (air) 20 15
1225 1g. "Head of a Negro" (Rubens) 35 30
1226 1g.50 As 10c. 55 45

1971. World Cup Football Championship, Mexico (1970).
1228 **200** 5c. black and orange 10 10
1229 50c. black and brown 25 15
1230 – 50c. black, yellow & pink 25 15
1231 – 1g. black, yellow and lilac 40 25

1232 200 1g.50 black and drab 55 45
1233 – 5g. black, yellow and grey 1·10 1·00
DESIGNS: Nos. 1230/31, 1233, Jules Rimet Cup.

1971. Inauguration of Duvalier Central Power Station. Surch INAUGURATION 22-7-71 and premium.
1235 195 20c.+50c. mult 30 25
1236 – 25c.+1g.50 mult (No. 1206) 70 55

202 Balloon and Airmail Stamp of 1929

1971. Air. 40th Anniv of Airmail Service (1969).
1237 202 20c. black, red and blue 25 10
1238 50c. black, red and blue 45 20
1239 – 1g. black and orange 1·00 50
1240 – 1g.50 black and mauve 1·60 60
DESIGN: 1g., 1g.50, Concorde and 1929 air stamp.

1971. Obligatory Tax. Education Fund. Nos. 1205/6 surch ALPHABETISATION and value.
1242 195 20c.+10c. mult 15 10
1243 – 25c.+10c. mult 15 10

1972. Air. "INTERPEX" International Stamp Exhibition, New York Nos. 1237/40 optd INTERPEX 72 and emblem.
1244 202 20c. black, red and blue 15 10
1245 50c. black, red and blue 55 20
1246 – 1g. black and orange 95 50
1247 – 1g.50 black and mauve 1·40 75

205 J.-J. Dessalines and Emblem
208 "Sun" and "EXPO" Emblem

1972. Jean-Jacques Dessalines ("founder of Haiti") Commemoration (1st issue).
1248 205 5c. black & grn (postage) 10 10
1249 10c. black and blue 10 10
1250 25c. black and orange 10 10
1251 50c. black and green (air) 20 10
1252 2g.50 black and lilac 55 20
See also Nos. 1304/10, 1343/52, 1357/60, 1413/17 and 1451/2.

1972. Air. 5th "Haipex" Congress. Nos. 1237/40 optd HAIPEX 5eme. CONGRES and emblem.
1253 202 20c. black, red and blue 15 10
1254 – 50c. black, red and blue 55 20
1255 – 1g. black and orange 95 45
1256 – 1g.50 black and mauve 1·40 65

1972. Air. "Belgica 72" Stamp Exhibition, Brussels. Nos. 1238/40 optd BELGICA 72 and emblem.
1257 50c. black, red and blue 55 20
1258 1g. black and orange 90 55
1259 1g.50 black and mauve 1·60 65

1972. Obligatory Tax. As Nos. 974/8.
1260 146 5c. red 10 10
1261 5c. blue 10 10

1972. "EXPO 70" World Fair, Osaka, Japan (1970).
1262 208 10c. mult (postage) 10 10
1263 – 25c. multicoloured 10 10
1264 – 50c. multicoloured (air) 15 10
1265 – 1g. multicoloured 35 25
1266 – 1g.50 multicoloured 45 30
1267 – 2g.50 multicoloured 90 55
DESIGNS—HORIZ: Nos. 1264/7, Sun Tower and emblem.

1972. Obligatory Tax. Duvalier Hydro-electric Project. As Nos. 1212/14.
1268 197 20c. brown and blue 10 10

209 Basket Vendors
210 Headquarters and Map

1973. 20th Anniv of Caribbean Travel Assn. Multicoloured.
1269 50c. Type 209 20 10
1270 80c. Postal bus service 30 20
1271 1g.50 Type 209 55 30
1272 2g.50 As 80c. 75 55

1973. Air. Education Fund. As Nos. 977/8 but larger size 17 × 25 mm.
1273 146 10c. brown and blue 10 10
1274 10c. brown and green 10 10
1275 10c. brown and orange 10 10

1973. Air. 70th Anniv of Pan-American Health Organization. Multicoloured.
1276 210 50c. multicoloured 15 10
1277 80c. multicoloured 25 20
1278 1g.50 multicoloured 45 30
1279 2g. multicoloured 55 45

211 Miniature Melo

1973. Marine Life. Multicoloured.
1280 5c. Type 211 (postage) 15 10
1281 10c. "Nemaster rubiginosa" 10 10
1282 25c. "Cyerce cristallina" 30 10
1283 50c. "Desmophyllum riisei" 15 10
1284 50c. "Platypodia spectabilis" (air) 15 10
1285 85c. "Goniaster tessellatus" 25 20
1286 1g.50 "Stephanocyathus diadema" 45 30
1287 2g. "Phyllangia americana" 55 35

211a Royal Gramma

1973. Fishes. Multicoloured.
1288 10c. Type 211a (postage) 20 10
1289 50c. Blue tang 35 15
1290 50c. Black-capped basslet (air) 35 15
1291 85c. Rock beauty 55 30
1292 1g.50 Peppermint basslet 1·00 55
1293 5g. Creole wrasse 2·00 1·00

212 Haitian Flag

1973. Air.
1294 212 80c. black and red 25 20
1295 – 80c. black and red 25 20
1296 – 1g.85 black and red 55 30
1297 – 1g.85 black and red 55 30
DESIGNS—As Type 212: No. 1295, Flag and arms (framed). (47 × 29 mm): No. 1296, Flag and arms; No. 1297, Flag and Pres. Jean-Claude Duvalier.

213 Football Stadium
214 J.-J. Dessalines

1973. World Cup Football Championship. Preliminary Games between Caribbean Countries.
1298 213 10c. green, black and brown (postage) 10 10
1299 – 20c. mauve, black & brn 10 10
1300 213 50c. green, blk & red (air) 15 10
1301 80c. green, black & blue 25 20
1302 – 1g.75 green, black & brn 50 35
1303 – 10g. green, black & brn 1·75 1·25
DESIGNS: 20c., 1g.75, 10g. World Cup stamp of 1971.

1974. Jean-Jacques Dessalines Commemoration (2nd issue).
1304 214 10c. green & bl (postage) 10 10
1305 20c. black and red 10 10
1306 25c. violet and brown 10 10
1307 50c. blue and brown (air) 15 10
1308 80c. brown and grey 20 20
1309 1g. purple and green 30 20
1310 1g.75 green and mauve 50 35

215 Symbol of Solar System
216 Pres. Jean-Claude Duvalier

1974. 500th Birth Anniv (1973) of Nicolas Copernicus (astronomer). Multicoloured.
1311 10c. Type 215 (postage) 10 10
1312 25c. Copernicus 10 10
1313 50c. Type 215 (air) 15 10
1314 50c. As 25c. 15 10
1315 80c. Type 215 25 20
1316 1g. As 25c. 30 20
1317 1g.75 Type 215 50 35

1974.
1319 216 10c. grn & gold (postage) 10 10
1320 20c. purple and gold 10 10
1321 50c. blue and gold 15 10
1322 50c. purple and gold (air) 15 15
1323 80c. red and gold 25 20
1324 1g. purple and gold 30 20
1325 1g.50 blue and gold 45 30
1326 1g.75 violet and gold 55 35
1327 5g. grey and gold 85 60

1975. Air. Nos. 1296/7 surch.
1328 80c. on 1g.85 black and red 25 20
1329 80c. on 1g.85 black and red 25 20

1975. Air. Centenary of U.P.U. Nos. 1296/7 optd 1874 UPU 1974 100 ANS.
1330 1g.85 black and red 55 30
1331 1g.85 black and red 55 30

219 Haiti 60c. Stamp of 1937

1976. Bicentenary of American Revolution.
1332 219 10c. mult (postage) 10 10
1333 – 50c. multicoloured (air) 15 10
1334 – 80c. multicoloured 25 15
1335 – 1g.50 multicoloured 45 30
1336 – 7g.50 multicoloured 1·75 1·25
DESIGN: 50c. to 7g.50, text with names of Haitians at Siege of Savannah.

1976. Surch.
1337 205 80c. on 25c. black and pink (postage) 35 20
1338 – 80c. on 10c. mult (No. 1288) 35 20
1339 214 80c. on 25c. violet & brn 35 20
1340 215 80c. on 10c. mult 35 20
1341 – 80c. on 85c. mult (No. 1285) (air) 25 20
1342 – 80c. on 85c. mult (No. 1291) 25 20

1977. Jean-Jacques Dessalines Commem (3rd issue).
1343 205 20c. black and brown (postage) 10 10
1344 50c. black and mauve 15 10
1345 75c. black and yellow (air) 20 20
1346 1g. black and blue 30 15
1347 1g.25 black and olive 35 30
1348 1g.50 black and grey 45 30
1349 1g.75 black and red 50 35
1350 2g. black and yellow 55 45
1351 5g. black and blue 85 60
1352 10g. black and brown 1·75 1·25

1977. Air. Lindbergh's Transatlantic Flight Nos. 1313/14 and 1316/17 optd or surch C. LINDBERGH. N.Y.-PARIS 1927-1977.
1353 1g. Copernicus 30 20
1354 1g.25 on 50c. Type 215 35 30
1355 1g.25 on 50c. Copernicus 35 30
1356 1g.25 on 1g.75 Type 215 35 30

1977. Jean-Jacques Dessalines Commem (4th issue).
1357 205 10c. black and mauve (postage) 10 10
1358 50c. black and brown 15 10
1359 80c. black and green (air) 25 15
1360 1g. black and brown 30 20

1977. Air. Various stamps surch G. O.80.
1361 – 80c. on 1g.50 mult (No. 1266) 20 20
1366 – 80c. on 1g.50 mult (No. 1335) 20 20
1364 215 80c. on 1g.75 mult 20 20
1365 216 80c. on 1g.75 violet and gold 20 20
1363 – 80c. on 1g.85 black and red (No. 1296) 20 20
1362 – 80c. on 2g.50 mult (No. 1267) 20 20

1978. Surch 1.00.
1367 205 1g. on 20c. black & brn 30 20
1368 1g. on 1g.75 black and red 30 20
1369 1g.25 on 75c. black and yellow 35 25
1370 1g.25 on 1g.50 black and green 35 25
Nos. 1368/70 have the inscription "AVION" obliterated by the surcharge.

224 J.-C. Duvalier Telecommunications Stations

1978. Telephone Centenary (1976). Mult.
1372 10c. Type 224 (postage) 10 10
1373 20c. Video telephone 10 10
1374 50c. Alexander Graham Bell (vert) 15 10
1375 1g. Satellite over Earth (air) 30 15
1376 1g.25 Type 224 35 25
1377 2g. Wall telephone, 1890 (vert) 55 45

225 Flag-raising Ceremony

1978. Olympic Games, Montreal (1976). Multicoloured.
1378 5c. Type 225 (postage) 10 10
1379 25c. Cycling 10 10
1380 50c. High jump 15 10
1381 1g.25 Horse jumping (air) 35 25
1382 2g.50 Basketball 70 55
1383 5g. Yachting 1·40 1·10

226 Mother feeding Baby
227 Mother feeding Child

1979. 50th Anniv of Inter-American Child Institute. Multicoloured.
1384 25c. Type 226 (postage) 10 10
1385 1g.25 Type 226 (air) 35 25
1386 2g. Nurse vaccinating child 55 45

1979. 30th Anniv of Co-operative for American Relief Everywhere (CARE). Multicoloured.
1387 25c. Type 227 (postage) 10 10
1388 50c. Type 227 15 15
1389 1g. Spinning cotton (air) 30 20
1390 1g.25 As No. 1389 35 25
1391 2g. As No. 1389 55 45

228 Human Rights Emblem
229 Anteor Firmin and Book

1979. 30th Anniv of Declaration of Human Rights.
1392 228 25c. mult (postage) 10 10
1393 1g. multicoloured (air) 30 20
1394 1g.25 multicoloured 35 25
1395 2g. multicoloured 55 45

1979. International Anti-Apartheid Year.
1396 229 50c. pink and brown (postage) 15 15
1397 1g. green and brown (air) 30 20
1398 1g.25 blue and brown 35 25
1399 2g. olive and brown 55 45

230 Children playing

1979. International Year of the Child.
1400 **230** 10c. mult (postage) . . . 10 10
1401 25c. multicoloured . . . 10 10
1402 50c. multicoloured . . . 15 10
1403 1g. multicoloured (air) 30 20
1404 1g.25 multicoloured . . 35 25
1405 2g.50 multicoloured . . 45 55
1406 5g. multicoloured . . . 85 60

1980. Air. Wedding of President Duvalier. Nos. 1322 and 1325/6 optd **27 5 80 JOUR FASTE**.
1407 **216** 50c. purple and gold . . 15 10
1408 1g.50 blue and gold . . 45 30
1409 1g.75 violet and gold . . 50 40

1980. Nos. 1252, 1357 and 1359 surch **TIMBRE POSTE** with value changed.
1410 **205** 1g. on 2g.50 black & lil 30 20
1411 1g.25 on 10c. blk & mve 35 35
1412 1g.25 on 80c. blk & grn 35 55

1980. Jean-Jacques Dessalines Commemoration (5th issue).
1413 **205** 25c. black and orange (postage) 10 10
1414 1g. black and grey (air) 30 20
1415 1g.25 black and pink . . 35 25
1416 2g. black and green . . . 55 45
1417 5g. black and blue . . . 85 60

233 Henri Christophe Citadel

1980. World Tourism Conference, Manila. Multicoloured.
1418 5c. Type **233** (postage) . . . 10 10
1419 25c. Sans-Souci Palace . . . 10 10
1420 50c. Vallieres market . . . 15 10
1421 1g. Type **233** (air) 30 20
1422 1g.25 As No. 1419 . . . . 35 25
1423 1g.50 Carnival dancers . . . 45 30
1424 2g. Women with flowers . . 55 45
1425 2g.50 As No. 1424 . . . . 70 50

234 Players and Flag of Uruguay (1930)

1980. 50th Anniv of First World Cup Football Championship. Multicoloured.
1426 10c. Type **234** (postage) . . 10 10
1427 20c. Italy (1934) 10 10
1428 25c. Italy (1938) 10 10
1429 50c. Uruguay (air) 15 10
1430 75c. West Germany (1954) 20 20
1431 1g. Brazil (1958) 30 20
1432 1g.25 Brazil (1962) 35 25
1433 1g.50 England (1966) . . . 45 30
1434 1g.75 Brazil (1970) 50 40
1435 2g. West Germany (1974) 55 45
1436 5g. Argentina (1978) 85 60

235 "Woman with Birds and Flowers" (Hector Hyppolite)

237 President Duvalier, Dish Aerial and Freighter at Quayside

1981. Paintings. Multicoloured.
1437 5c. Type **235** (postage) . . . 10 10
1438 10c. "Going to Church" (Gregoire Etienne) 10 10
1439 20c. "Street Market" (Petion Savain) 10 10
1440 25c. "Market Sellers" (Michele Manual) 10 10
1441 50c. Type **235** (air) 15 10
1442 1g.25 As No. 1438 . . . . 35 25
1443 2g. As No. 1439 . . . . . 55 45
1444 5g. As No. 1440 . . . . . 85 60

1981. Various stamps surch **1.25**.
1445 **233** 1g.25 on 5c. mult (postage) 35 30
1446 **235** 1g.25 on 5c. mult . . 35 30
1447 – 1g.25 on 10c. mult (No. 1438) 35 30
1448 – 1g.25 on 20c. mult (No. 1427) 35 30
1449 – 1g.25 on 1g.50 mult (No. 1423) (air) . . . 35 30
1450 **205** 2g. on 5g. black and blue (No. 1417) . . . 55 45
The surcharge on No. 1446 is inverted.

1982. Jean-Jacques Dessalines ("founder of Haiti") Commemoration (6th issue).
1451 **205** 1g.25 black and brown 35 30
1452 2g. black and violet . . 55 45

1982. 10th Anniv of Duvalier Reforms ("Jean-Claudisme").
1453 **237** 25c. green and black . . 15 10
1454 50c. green and black . . 25 10
1455 1g. purple and black . . 50 20
1456 1g.25 blue and black . . 55 30
1457 2g. orange and black . . 75 45
1458 5g. orange and black . . 2·25 1·10

1982. Nos. 1453 and 1455/7 optd **1957- 1982 25 ANS DE REVOLUTION**.
1459 **237** 25c. green and black . . 10 10
1460 1g. purple and black . . 35 30
1461 1g.25 blue and black . . 45 40
1462 2g. orange and black . . 65 60

239 Scouts planting Trees

1983. 75th Anniv of Boy Scout Movement. Multicoloured.
1463 5c. Type **239** (postage) . . . 10 10
1464 10c. Lord Baden-Powell (vert) 10 10
1465 25c. Scout teaching villagers to read 25 10
1466 50c. As No. 1464 . . . . . 15 10
1467 75c. As No. 1465 (air) . . . 65 20
1468 1g. Type **239** 30 20
1469 1g.25 As No. 1465 . . . . 90 30
1470 2g. As No. 1464 . . . . . 55 45

240 Our Lady of Perpetual Succour

1983. Centenary of Miracle of Our Lady of Perpetual Succour.
1471 **240** 10c. mult (postage) . . . 10 10
1472 20c. multicoloured . . . 10 10
1473 25c. multicoloured . . . 10 10
1474 50c. multicoloured . . . 15 10
1475 **240** 75c. multicoloured (air) 20 20
1476 1g. multicoloured . . . 30 20
1477 1g.25 multicoloured . . 35 30
1478 1g.50 multicoloured . . 45 30
1479 1g.75 multicoloured . . 50 45
1480 – 2g. multicoloured . . . 55 45
1481 – 5g. multicoloured . . . 85 60
Nos. 1480/1 differ slightly in design of the frame.

241 Arms of Haiti and U.P.U. Monument, Berne

1983. Centenary (1981) of U.P.U. Membership.
1483 **241** 5c. brown, red and black (postage) 10 10
1484 – 10c. brown, black & blue 10 10
1485 – 25c. green, black and red 10 10
1486 – 50c. green, red and black 15 10
1487 – 75c. lilac, black and blue (air) 20 20
1488 – 1g. blue, red and black 30 20
1489 – 1g.25 blue, black and red 35 30
1490 – 2g. blue, black and red 55 45
DESIGNS: 50c., 1g. Type **241**; 10, 75c. L. F. Salomon and J. C. Duvalier; 25c., 1g.25, 2g. First Haitian stamp and U.P.U. Monument, Berne.

242 Argentine and Belgian Footballers

1983. World Cup Football Championship, Spain.
1491 **242** 5c. black & bl (postage) 10 10
1492 – 10c. black and brown . . 10 10
1493 – 20c. black and green . . 10 10
1494 – 25c. black and green . . 10 10
1495 – 50c. black and yellow . . 15 10
1496 – 1g. multicoloured (air) 30 20
1497 – 1g.25 multicoloured . . 35 30
1498 – 1g.50 multicoloured . . 45 30
1499 – 2g. multicoloured . . . 55 45
1500 – 2g.50 multicoloured . . 65 55
DESIGNS—VERT: 10c. Northern Ireland and Yugoslavia; 20c. England and France; 25c. Spain and Northern Ireland; 50c. Italian player with Cup. HORIZ: 1g. Brazil and Scotland; 1g.25, Northern Ireland and France; 1g.50, Poland and Cameroun; 2g. Italy and West Germany; 2g.50, Argentine and Brazil.

243 1c. Stamp of 1881

1984. Stamp Centenary (1981).
1501 **243** 5c. mult (postage) . . . 10 10
1502 – 10c. multicoloured . . . 10 10
1503 – 25c. multicoloured . . . 10 10
1504 – 50c. multicoloured . . . 20 15
1505 – 75c. yellow, brown and silver (air) 25 20
1506 – 1g. blue, red and gold 35 30
1507 – 1g.25 multicoloured . . 45 40
1508 – 2g. gold, brown and green 70 60
DESIGNS: 10c. 1881 2c. stamp; 25c., 1881 3c. stamp; 50c. 1881 7c. stamp; 75c., 1g. Pres. Salomon; 1g.25, 2g. Pres. Duvalier.

244 Modern Communications Equipment

1984. World Communications Year.
1509 **244** 25c. blue and purple . . 10 10
1510 50c. blue and olive . . 20 15
1511 – 1g. orange, brown & grn 35 30
1512 – 1g.25 orange, brown & bl 45 40
1513 – 2g. blue, orange and black 70 60
1514 – 2g.50 blue, bistre & blk 1·00 80
DESIGNS—VERT: 1g., 1g.25, Pres. Petion's drum; 2g., 2g.50, W.C.Y. emblem as satellite over globe.

245 Javelin-thrower, Runner and Polevaulter

1984. Olympic Games, Los Angeles.
1515 **245** 5c. black, green and red 10 10
1516 10c. black, olive and red 10 10
1517 – 25c. black, green and red 10 10
1518 – 50c. black, ochre and red 20 15
1519 – 1g. black, blue and red 35 30
1520 – 1g.25 black, blue & orge 45 40
1521 – 2g. black, violet and red 70 60
DESIGNS—HORIZ: 25c., 50c. Hurdler. VERT: 1g. to 2g.50, Long jumper.

246 Head of "The Unknown Indian", Toussaint Square, Louverture

1984. 500th Anniv of Arrival of Europeans in America (1st issue).
1523 **246** 5c. mult (postage) . . . 10 10
1524 10c. multicoloured . . . 10 10
1525 25c. multicoloured . . . 10 10
1526 50c. multicoloured . . . 15 10
1527 – 1g. multicoloured (air) 25 20
1528 – 1g.25 multicoloured . . 35 30
1529 – 2g. multicoloured . . . 55 50
DESIGN: 1 to 2g. "The Unknown Indian".
See also Nos. 1539/44.

247 Simon Bolivar and Alexandre Petion

1985. Birth Bicentenary of Simon Bolivar. Mult.
1531 5c. Type **247** (postage) . . . 10 10
1532 25c. Bolivar and Alexandre Petion (different) 10 10
1533 50c. Bolivar and flags of members of Grand Colombian Confederation 15 10
1534 1g. Type **247** (air) 25 20
1535 1g.25 As No. 1532 . . . . 30 25
1536 2g. Type **247** 50 45
1537 7g.50 As No. 1532 . . . . 1·60 1·25

248 Chief Henri

250 Planting Saplings

1986. 500th Anniv of Arrival of Europeans in America (2nd issue).
1539 **248** 10c. mult (postage) . . . 10 10
1540 25c. multicoloured . . . 10 10
1541 50c. multicoloured . . . 15 10
1542 – 1g. multicoloured (air) 25 15
1543 – 1g.25 multicoloured . . 30 20
1544 – 2g. multicoloured . . . 35 25
DESIGN: 1 to 2g. Chief Henri hunting.

1986. Various stamps surch.
1546 **241** 25c. on 5c. brown, red and black (postage) . . 10 10
1547 **242** 25c. on 5c. black & blue 10 10
1548 **243** 25c. on 5c. multicoloured 10 10
1549 – 25c. on 75c. mult (1430) (air) 10 10
1550 – 25c. on 75c. mult (1467) 10 10
1551 – 25c. on 1g.50 mult (1122) 10 10

1986. International Youth Year (1985). Mult.
1552 10c. Type **250** (postage) . . 10 10
1553 25c. I.Y.Y. emblem 10 10
1554 50c. Boy and girl scouts and flag 15 10
1555 1g. Type **250** (air) 25 15
1556 1g.25 As No. 1553 . . . . 30 20
1557 2g. As No. 1554 . . . . . 50 40

251 Dove above Peace Year Emblem on Globe

1987. International Peace Year (1986) and 40th Anniv of United Nations Educational, Scientific and Cultural Organization.
1559 **251** 10c. mult (postage) . . . 10 10
1560 25c. multicoloured . . . 10 10
1561 50c. multicoloured . . . 15 10
1562 1g. multicoloured (air) 25 15
1563 1g.25 multicoloured . . 30 25
1564 2g.50 multicoloured . . 60 50

252 Peralte and Flag

1989. Charlemagne Peralte Commemoration.
1566 **252** 25c. mult (postage) . . . 10 10
1567 50c. multicoloured . . . 15 10
1568 1g. multicoloured (air) 25 15
1569 2g. multicoloured . . . 50 40
1570 3g. multicoloured . . . 80 70

253 Slaves and Tree forming Fist

1991. Bicentenary of Uprising of Slaves. Mult.
1572 25c. Type **253** (postage) . . 10 10
1573 50c. Type **253** 10 10
1574 1g. Gathering of slaves around fire (air) 10 10
1575 2g. As No. 1574 . . . . . 25 20
1576 3g. As No. 1574 . . . . . 35 30

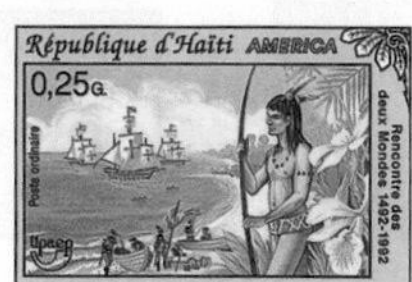

254 Amerindian watching Europeans landing

1993. America. 500th Anniv (1992) of Discovery of America by Columbus. Multicoloured.
1578 25c. Type **254** (postage) . . 20 10
1579 50c. Type **254** 20 10
1580 1g. Columbus's fleet at anchor and rowing boats on shore (vert) (air) . . . 20 10
1581 2g. As No. 1580 . . . . . 30 15
1582 3g. As No. 1580 . . . . . 50 30

255 Map of Haiti and Emblem

1995. 25th General Assembly of Organization of American States. Multicoloured.
1584 50c. Type **255** 10 10
1585 75c. Type **255** 10 10
1586 1g. Map of Americas and emblems (vert) 10 10
1587 2g. As No. 1586 . . . . . 15 10
1588 3g. As No. 1586 . . . . . 25 20
1589 5g. As No. 1586 . . . . . 40 35

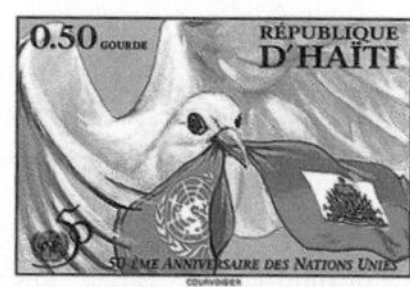

256 Dove holding Flags in Beak

1995. 50th Anniv of U.N.O. Multicoloured.
1591 50c. Type **256** (postage) . . 10 10
1592 75c. Type **256** 10 10
1593 1g. Dove with olive branch flying over flags (air) . . . 10 10
1594 2g. As No. 1593 . . . . . 15 10
1595 3g. As No. 1593 . . . . . 25 20
1596 5g. As No. 1593 . . . . . 40 35

1996. Various stamps surch **XXIIIES JEUX OLYMPIQUES LOS ANGELES 1984**.
1598 2g. on 1g.25 black, blue and orange (1520) (postage) 15 10
1599 1g. on 1g.25 mult (1556) (air) 10 10
1600 3g. on 1g.25 mult (1535) . . 20 15
1601 3g. on 1g.25 mult (1477) . . 20 15

259 Players

1996. Olympic Games, Atlanta. Multicoloured.
(a) Centenary of Volleyball.
1605 50c. Type **259** 10 10
1606 75c. Umpire and players . . 10 10
1607 1g. Players holding Olympic Flame 10 10
1608 2g. Players jumping for ball 15 10
(b) 1984 Medal Winners.
1609 3g. 400 m hurdles (U.S.A.) 20 15
1610 10g. Decathlon (gold, Great Britain) 70 60

Nos. 1605/6 were issued together, se-tenant, forming a composite design of a match scene and Nos. 1607/8 a composite design of a map.

260 "Virgin and Child" (Jacopo Bellini)

1996. Christmas. Multicoloured.
1612 2g. Type **260** 15 10
1613 3g. "Adoration of the Shepherds" (Bernardo Strozzi) 20 15
1614 6g. "Virgin and Child" (Giovanni Bellini) 45 35
1615 10g. "Virgin and Child" (Francesco Mazzola) . . . 70 60
1616 25g. "Adoration of the Magi" (Gentile da Fabriano) . . . . 1·75 1·40

261 Children in Street

1997. 50th Anniv (1996) of UNICEF.
1618 **261** 4g. multicoloured . . . 30 25
1619 5g. multicoloured . . . 35 30
1620 6g. multicoloured . . . 45 35
1621 10g. multicoloured . . . 70 60
1622 20g. multicoloured . . . 1·40 1·25

262 Sleeping Beauty
263 Cocoa Beans

1998. 175th Anniv (1997) of 3rd Collection of Fairy Tales by Brothers Grimm. Multicoloured.
1623 2g. Type **262** 15 10
1624 3g. Snow White 20 15
1625 4g. Sleeping Beauty and Prince 30 25
1626 6g. Man in bed (Water of Life) 45 35
1627 10g. Cinderella 70 60
1628 20g. Serving patient with the Water of Life . . . . . . 1·40 1·25

1998. Grande Arche Roof Competition, Paris. "Haiti: Women and Creation". Multicoloured.
1630 2g. Type **263** 20 15
1631 3g. Swords and flags 30 25
1632 5g. Boy with model churches 45 35
1633 6g. Woman with artist's palette and brush 55 45

OFFICIAL STAMPS

1960. Nos. 736/40 optd **OFFICIEL**.
O742 – 50c. brown and green † 25
O743 – 50c. blue and green . . † 25
O744 – 50c. black and green . . † 25
O745 **127** 1g. green and red . . . † 35
O746 – 1g.50 pink and blue . . † 55
The above were only issued precancelled.

O 135 Dessalines' Statue

1962. Air. (a) Size 20½ × 37½ mm.
O791 O **135** 50c. sepia and blue 20 15
O792 1g. red and blue . . . 35 30
O793 1g.50 blue and bistre 55 45
(b) Size 30½ × 40 mm.
O794 O **135** 5g. green and red . . 1·10 1·00

PARCEL POST STAMPS

1960. Optd **COLIS POSTAUX**.
P725 **102** 5c. green & blk (postage) 10 10
P726 10c. red and black . . . 10 10
P727 25c. blue and black . . 15 15
P728 **74** 2g.50 grey . . . . . . 1·10 1·10
P729 **102** 50c. orange & black (air) 25 20
P730 **101** 5g. violet and blue . . . 2·10 1·75

P 130 Arms

1961.
P757 P **130** 50c. violet and bistre (postage) 35 15
P758 1g. blue and red . . . 55 30
P759 2g.50 lake & grn (air) 90 70
P760 5g. green and orange 1·50 1·10

POSTAGE DUE STAMPS

D 10 D 23

1898.
D63 D **10** 2c. blue 20 25
D64 5c. brown 35 40
D65 10c. orange 50 50
D66 50c. grey . . . . 1·00 1·00

1902. Optd **MAI Gt Pre 1902** in frame.
D85 D **10** 2c. blue 45 50
D86 5c. brown 45 50
D87 10c. orange 50 50
D88 50c. grey . . . . 3·75 2·10

1906.
D150 D **23** 2c. red 45 35
D151 5c. blue . . . . 1·50 1·50
D152 10c. purple . . . . . 1·50 1·50
D153 50c. olive . . . . . . 6·75 3·75

1914. Optd **GL O. Z. 7 FEV. 1914** in frame.
D206 D **10** 5c. brown 45 35
D207 10c. orange 40 40
D208 50c. grey . . . . . . 3·25 2·25

1914. Optd **GL O. Z 7 FEV. 1914** in frame.
D209 D **23** 2c. red 55 35
D210 5c. blue 90 55
D211 10c. purple . . . . . 2·60 2·25
D212 50c. olive . . . . . . 4·75 3·00

D 83

1951.
D452 D **83** 10c. red 10 10
D453 20c. brown 15 15
D454 40c. green 20 20
D455 50c. yellow 30 30

SPECIAL DELIVERY STAMP

S 86 G.P.O.

1953.
E468 S **86** 25c. red 30 30

APPENDIX

The following stamps have either been issued in excess of postal needs or have not been available to the public in reasonable quantities at face value. Such stamps may later be given full listing if there is evidence of regular postal use.

1968.
Medal Winners, Winter Olympic Games, Grenoble. Postage 5, 10, 20, 25, 50c., 1g.50; Air 2g.

1969.
Moon Landing of "Apollo 11". Optd on 1969 Birds issue. Nos. 1132/5. Air 50c., 1g.50, 2g.

Space Flights of "Apollo 7" and "Apollo 8". Postage 10, 15, 20, 25c.; Air 70c., 1g.25, 1g.50.

1970.
Moon Mission of "Apollo 12". Postage 5, 10, 15, 20, 25, 30, 40, 50c.; Air 25, 30, 40, 50, 75c., 1g., 1g., 1g.25, 1g.50.

1971.
Safe Return of "Apollo 13". Optd on 1970 "Apollo 12" issue. Postage 5, 10, 15, 20, 25, 30, 40, 50c.; Air 25, 30, 40, 50, 75c., 1g., 1g.25, 1g.50.

1972.
Gold Medal Winners Olympic Games, Munich. Air 50, 75c., 1g.50, 2g.50, 5g.

1973.
American and Russian Space Exploration. Postage 5, 10, 20, 25, 50c., 2g.50, 5g.; Air 50, 75c., 1g.50, 2g.50, 5g.

Moon Mission of "Apollo 17". Optd on 1973 Space Exploration issue. 50c., 2g.50, 5g.

HAMBURG Pt. 7

A port in north-west Germany, formerly a Free City. In 1867 it joined the North German Confederation.

16 schillinge = 1 mark.

1 3 4

1859. Imperf.
1 **1** ½s. black . . . . 95·00 £600
2 1s. brown . . . . 95·00 75·00
3 2s. red . . . . 95·00 £110
4 3s. blue . . . . 95·00 £130
6 4s. green £120 £1300
7 7s. orange . . . . 95·00 43·00
10 9s. yellow £200 £2000

1864. Imperf.
11 **3** 1¼s. lilac . . . . £150 80·00
15 1¼s. grey . . . . £100 80·00
17 1¼s. blue £500 £1000
18 **4** 2½s. green £150 £150

1864. Perf.
19 **1** ½s. black . . . . 6·50 10·50
20 1s. brown . . . . 13·00 21·00
21 **3** 1¼s. mauve . . . . 80·00 10·50
25 **1** 2s. red . . . . 15·00 21·00
27 **4** 2½s. green . . . . £120 30·00
30 **1** 3s. blue . . . . 36·00 36·00
33 4s. green . . . . 10·00 21·00
34 7s. orange £170 £130
37 7s. mauve . . . . 10·50 17·00
38 9s. yellow . . . . 26·00 £2250

5

1866. Roul.
44 **5** 1¼s. mauve . . . . 38·00 38·00
45 1¼s. pink . . . . 8·50 £130

1867. Perf.
46 **1** 2½s. green . . . . 10·50 85·00

HANOVER Pt. 7

In north-east Germany. An independent kingdom until 1866, when it was annexed by Prussia.

1850. 12 pfennige = 1 gutegroschen.
24 gutengroschen = 1 thaler.
1858. 10 (new) pfennige = 1 (new) groschen.
30 (new) groschen = 1 thaler.

2 4

1850. On coloured paper. Imperf.
1 **2** 1ggr. black on blue . . . . . £3750 50·00
2 1ggr. black on green . . . . . 80·00 8·50
3 1/30th. black on orange . . . . £120 50·00

4		1/30th. black on red	£120	50·00
5		1/15th. black on blue	£190	80·00
6		1/10th. black on orange	£250	65·00

1853. Imperf.

18	4	3pf. pink	80·00	95·00

1855. With coloured network. Imperf.

12	4	3pf. pink and black	£500	£350
14	2	1ggr. black and green	80·00	8·50
15		1/30th. black and pink	£170	34·00
16		1/15th. black and blue	£130	80·00
10		1/10th. black and orange	£225	£170

5 King George V

6

1859. Imperf.

23	5	1gr. pink	3·50	2·50
25a		2gr. blue	21·00	34·00
28		3gr. yellow	£150	65·00
29		3gr. brown	30·00	55·00
31		10gr. green	£250	£850

1860. Imperf.

32a	6	½gr. black	£190	£225

1863. Imperf.

34	4	3pf. green	£400	£1100

1864. Roul.

35a	4	3pf. green	32·00	65·00
36a	6	½gr. black	£275	£275
37a	5	1gr. pink	8·50	3·00
38		2gr. blue	£120	60·00
39a		3gr. brown	70·00	75·00

HATAY Pt. 16

Hatay was returned to Turkey in June 1939.

1939. 100 santims = 40 paras = 1 kurus.

1939. Stamps of Turkey surch **HATAY DEVLETI** and value.

32	112	10s. on 20pa. orange	35	20
33		25s. on 1k. green	35	20
34		50s. on 2k. violet	45	25
35		75s. on 2½k. green	40	20
36		1k. on 4k. grey	1·70	1·10
37		1k. on 5k. red	55	35
38		1½k. on 3k. brown	60	35
39		2½k. on 4k. grey	80	45
40		5k. on 8k. blue	2·20	1·10
41		12½k. on 20k. green	3·25	1·70
42		20k. on 25k. blue	4·25	2·40

9 Map of Hatay

10 Flag of Hatay

1939.

48	9	10pa. orange and blue	25	10
49		30pa. violet and blue	25	15
50		1½k. olive and blue	45	25
51	–	2½k. green	45	25
52	–	3k. blue	50	30
53	–	5k. red	60	35
54	10	6k. red and blue	65	35
55		7½k. red and green	80	50
56		12k. red and violet	1·10	70
57		12½k. red and blue	1·20	70
58	–	17½k. red	2·30	1·20
59	–	25k. olive	2·75	1·40
60	–	50k. blue	6·25	3·00

DESIGNS—HORIZ: 2½, 3, 5k. Lions of Antioch; 17½, 25, 50k. Parliament House, Antioch.

1939. Commemorating Turkish Annexation. Optd **T. C. ilhak tarihi 30-6-1939**.

65	9	10pa. orange and blue	35	20
66		30pa. violet and blue	45	25
67		1½k. olive and blue	45	25
68	–	2½k. green (No. 51)	60	35
69	–	3k. blue (No. 52)	65	35
70	–	5k. red (No. 53)	70	40
71	10	6k. red and blue	70	40
72		7½k. red and green	90	55
73		12k. red and violet	1·10	60
74		12½k. red and blue	1·10	70
75	–	17½k. red (No. 58)	2·10	1·10
76	–	25k. olive (No. 59)	4·00	2·20
77	–	50k. blue (No. 60)	8·00	4·75

POSTAGE DUE STAMPS

1939. Postage Due stamps of Turkey optd **HATAY DEVLETI** or surch also.

D43	D 121	1k. on 2k. blue	80	45
D44		3k. violet	1·70	95
D45		4k. on 5k. green	1·70	95
D46		5k. on 12k. red	2·00	1·30
D47		12k. red	29·00	18·00

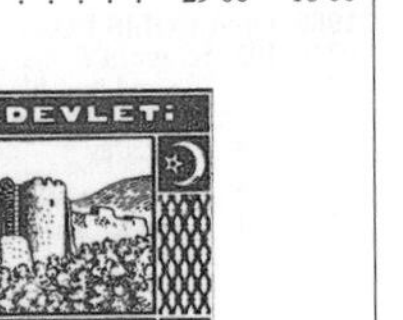

D 11 Castle at Antioch

1939.

D61	D 11	1k. red	90	55
D62		3k. brown	80	55
D63		4k. green	1·50	55
D64		5k. grey	2·10	75

1939. Nos. D61/4 optd **T. C. ilhak tarihi 30-6-1939**.

D73	D 11	1k. red	1·40	70
D74		3k. brown	1·70	85
D75		4k. green	2·40	1·30
D76		5k. grey	2·50	1·40

HAWAII Pt. 22

A group of islands in the central Pacific, an independent kingdom till 1893 when a provisional government was set up. Annexed in 1898 by the United States. Now a State of the U.S.A.

100 cents = 1 dollar.

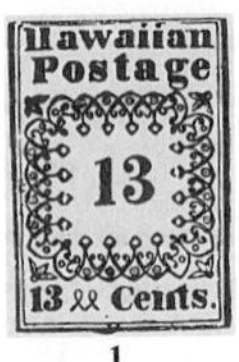

1

3 Kamehameha III

1851. Inscr "Hawaiian Postage". Imperf.

1	1	2c. blue	£450000	£225000
2		5c. blue	£28000	£16000
3		13c. blue	£14000	£11000

On Nos. 1/2 the value is expressed in words.

1852. Inscr "H.L. & US. Postage". Imperf.

4	1	13c. blue	£35000	£17000

1853. Imperf.

18	3	5c. blue	16·00	
19		13c. red	£160	

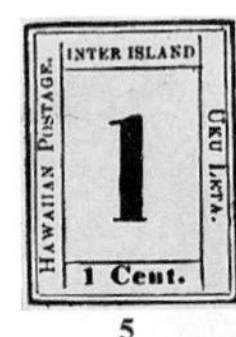

5

6 Kamehameha IV

1859. Inter-island post.

9	5	1c. blue	£4750	£3500
12		1c. black	£275	£625
10		2c. blue	£3750	£2250
14d		2c. black	£425	£350

1862. Imperf.

22	6	2c. red	30·00	£100

7 Princess Victoria Kamamalu

12

1864. Perf.

27	7	1c. mauve	7·00	5·75
41	–	2c. red	11·50	7·00
42	–	5c. blue	11·50	2·50
30	–	6c. green	19·00	6·50
31	–	18c. red	65·00	27·00

DESIGNS: 2c. Kamehameha IV; 5c., 6c. Portraits of Kamehameha V; 18c. H.E. Mataio Kekuanaoa.

1865. Inter-island post.

32	12	1c. blue	£190	
33		2c. blue	£190	
34		5c. blue on blue	£600	£425
35	–	5c. blue on blue	£500	£350

DESIGN: No. 35, As Type **12** but inscr "HAWAIIAN POSTAGE" on left side of frame.

16 Princess Likelike

22 Princess (later Queen) Liliuokalani

1875.

38	16	1c. blue	4·50	7·75
39		1c. green	2·10	1·40
36	–	2c. brown	5·75	2·25
40b	–	2c. red	3·00	75
44	–	10c. black	27·00	15·00
45	–	10c. red	25·00	9·75
46	–	10c. brown	23·00	7·75
37	–	12c. black	42·00	21·00
47	–	12c. lilac	55·00	25·00
48	–	15c. brown	42·00	19·00
49	–	25c. purple	95·00	42·00
50	–	50c. red	£120	60·00
51	–	$1 red	£170	£100

DESIGNS: 2c. King Kalakaua; 10c. Same in uniform; 12c. Prince Leleiohoku; 15c. Queen Kapiolani; 25c. Statute of Kamehameha I; 50c. King Lunalilo; $1, Queen Emma Kaleleonalani.

1890.

53	22	2c. violet	3·50	1·10

1893. Stamps of 1864, 1875 and 1889, optd **Provisional GOVT. 1893**.

54	7	1c. mauve	5·50	9·50
55	16	1c. blue	4·50	9·50
56		1c. green	1·25	2·25
57	–	2c. brown	7·50	15·00
58	22	2c. violet	1·25	95
67	–	2c. red (No. 41)	50·00	55·00
68	–	2c. red (No. 40b)	1·00	1·75
60	–	5c. blue	4·50	2·00
61	–	6c. green	11·50	20·00
62	–	10c. black	7·00	11·00
70	–	10c. red	11·50	23·00
71	–	10c. brown	5·75	9·75
64	–	12c. black	7·00	13·50
65	–	12c. lilac	£120	£160
73	–	15c. brown	15·00	23·00
74	–	18c. red	19·00	27·00
66	–	25c. purple	19·00	30·00
75	–	50c. red	45·00	70·00
76	–	$1 red	85·00	£130

24 Arms

26 Statue of King Kamehameha I

1894.

77	24	1c. orange	1·75	1·00
89		1c. green	1·25	90
78	–	2c. brown	1·75	40
90a	–	2c. pink	1·10	60
79	26	5c. red	3·50	1·25
91		5c. blue	4·00	2·25
80	–	10c. green	4·50	3·25
81	–	12c. blue	9·50	10·00
82	–	25c. blue	9·50	10·00

DESIGNS—HORIZ: 2c. Honolulu; 12c. "Arawa" (steamer). VERT: 10c. Star and palms; 25c. President S. B. Dole.

OFFICIAL STAMPS

O 30 Secretary L. A. Thurston

1896.

O83	O 30	2c. green	28·00	13·00
O84		5c. brown	28·00	13·00
O85		6c. blue	32·00	13·00
O86		10c. red	28·00	13·00
O87		12c. orange	40·00	13·00
O88		25c. violet	45·00	13·00

HELIGOLAND Pt. 1

An island off the N. coast of Germany, ceded to that country by Great Britain in 1890.

1867. 16 schillings = 1 mark.
1875. 100 pfennig = 1 mark.

Many of the Heligoland stamps found in old collections and the majority of those offered at a small fraction of catalogue prices today, are reprints which have very little value.

1

1867. Perf (½, 1, 2 and 6 sch. also roul).

5	1	¼sch. green and red	26·00	£1500
6b		½sch. green and red	95·00	£150
7		¾sch. red and green	30·00	£1100
8a		1sch. red and green	£120	£180
9		1½sch. green and red	65·00	£250
3		2sch. red and green	12·00	55·00
4		6sch. green and red	14·00	£250

2

3

4

5

1875.

10	2	1pf. (¼d.) green and red	12·00	£500
11		2pf. (½d.) red and green	12·00	£600
12a	3	3pf. (⅝d.) green, red yellow	£160	£850
13	2	5pf. (¾d.) green and red	12·00	19·00
14a		10pf. (1½d.) red and green	12·00	20·00
15b	3	20pf. (2½d.) green, red and yellow	15·00	29·00
16	2	25pf. (3d.) green and red	14·00	28·00
17		50pf. (6d.) red and green	20·00	35·00
18	4	1m. (1s.) green, red and black	£140	£200
19	5	5m. (5s.) green, red and black	£160	£950

HOI-HAO (HOIHOW) Pt. 17

An Indo-Chinese post office in China, closed in 1922.

1901. 100 centimes = 1 franc.
1918. 100 cents = 1 piastre.

HOI HAO
州瓊

(1)

1902. Stamps of Indo-China "Tablet" key-type, optd with T **1**. Chinese characters read "HOI-HAO" and are the same on every value.

1	D	1c. black on blue	1·60	2·75
2		2c. brown on yellow	3·25	3·75
3		4c. red on grey	2·50	3·25
4		5c. green	2·50	3·50
5		10c. black on lilac	5·25	6·50
6		15c. blue	£1300	£550
7		15c. grey	2·25	2·00
8		20c. red on green	21·00	23·00
9		25c. black on red	9·00	6·00
10		30c. brown	40·00	42·00
11		40c. red on yellow	32·00	35·00
12		50c. red on rose	35·00	48·00
13		75c. brown on orange	£200	£180
14		1f. olive	£650	£550
15		5f. mauve on lilac	£550	£450

1903. Stamps of Indo-China, "Tablet" key-type, surch as T **1**. Chinese characters indicate the value and differ for each denomination.

16	D	1c. black on blue	1·60	2·25
17		2c. brown on yellow	2·50	2·25
18		4c. red on grey	2·00	3·75
19		5c. green	2·00	3·75
20		10c. red	2·25	2·50
21		15c. grey	2·00	3·75
22		20c. red on green	3·50	8·25
23		25c. blue	2·00	3·50
24		25c. black on red	4·25	4·25
25		30c. brown	3·50	4·25
26		40c. red on yellow	45·00	50·00
27		50c. red on rose	30·00	50·00
28		50c. brown on blue	£100	£110
29		75c. brown on orange	45·00	50·00
30		1f. olive	60·00	60·00
31		5f. mauve on lilac	£170	£170

1906. Stamps of Indo-China surch **HOI-HAO** and with value in Chinese.

32	8	1c. olive	2·50	3·25
33		2c. red on yellow	2·25	3·00
34		4c. mauve on blue	2·75	3·75
35		5c. green	4·25	4·75
36		10c. red	3·50	4·75
37		15c. brown on blue	4·50	4·75
38		20c. red on green	5·75	7·00
39		25c. blue	7·50	9·50
40		30c. brown on cream	9·00	9·50
41		35c. black on yellow	10·50	15·00
42		40c. black on grey	11·50	17·00
43		50c. brown	16·00	18·00
44	D	75c. brown on orange	38·00	42·00

45 8 1f. green 30·00 38·00
46 2f. brown on yellow 38·00 42·00
47 D 5f. mauve on lilac £100 £120
48 8 10f. red on green £130 £130

1908. Native types of Indo-China surch **HOIHAO** (1 to 50c.) or **HOI-HAO** (others) and with value in Chinese.
49 10 1c. black and olive 55 75
50 2c. black and brown 60 1·25
51 4c. black and blue 1·25 1·75
52 5c. black and green 1·50 2·50
53 10c. black and red 1·75 3·50
54 15c. black and violet 5·00 6·25
55 11 20c. black and violet 4·75 7·75
56 25c. black and blue 5·25 5·75
57 30c. black and brown 5·75 7·75
58 35c. black and green 6·25 7·75
59 40c. black and brown 6·00 7·25
60 50c. black and red 7·50 10·50
61 12 75c. black and orange 8·50 11·50
62 1f. black and red 19·00 24·00
63 2f. black and green 38·00 42·00
64 5f. black and blue 70·00 80·00
65 10f. black and violet £100 £110

1919. Stamps as last surch in addition with value in figures and words.
66 10 $\frac{2}{5}$c. on 1c. black and olive 1·25 3·00
67 $\frac{4}{5}$c. on 2c. black and brown 70 2·50
68 1$\frac{3}{5}$c. on 4c. black and blue 1·75 3·00
69 2c. on 5c. black and green 1·90 2·50
70 4c. on 10c. black and red 3·00 3·25
71 6c. on 15c. black and violet 1·60 2·25
72 11 8c. on 20c. black and violet 3·25 4·00
73 10c. on 25c. black and blue 5·50 6·50
74 12c. on 30c. black & brown 2·75 3·50
75 14c. on 35c. black and green 2·25 3·50
76 16c. on 40c. black & brown 2·75 3·75
77 20c. on 50c. black and red 3·25 3·75
78 12 30c. on 75c. black & orange 3·75 4·50
79 – 40c. on 1f. black and red 10·00 11·00
80 – 80c. on 2f. black and green 22·00 24·00
81 – 2p. on 5f. black and blue 60·00 70·00
82 – 4p. on 10f. black and violet £150 £170

HONDURAS — Pt. 15

A republic of C. America, independent since 1838.

1866. 8 reales = 1 peso.
1878. 100 centavos = 1 peso.
1933. 100 centavos = 1 lempira.

1 Seal of Honduras
5 Pres. F. Morazan
6

1866. Imperf.
1 1 2r. black on green 60
2 2r. black on red 60

1878. Perf.
31 5 1c. violet 40 60
32 2c. brown 40 70
33 ½r. black 40 70
34 1r. green 1·25 1·25
35 2r. blue 1·75 1·75
36 4r. red 2·75 2·00
37 1p. orange 3·00 3·00

1890.
45 6 1c. green 25 30
46 2c. red 25 30
47 5c. blue 25 30
48 10c. orange 25 30
49 20c. bistre 25 30
50 25c. red 25 35
51 30c. violet 25 70
52 40c. blue 25 60
53 50c. brown 25 60
54 75c. green 25 1·50
55 1p. lake 25 1·75

8 President Bogran
10

1891.
56 8 1c. blue 15 20
57 2c. brown 15 20
58 5c. green 15 20
59 10c. red 15 20
60 20c. lake 15 25
61 25c. red 20 30
62 30c. grey 20 60
63 40c. green 15 60
64 50c. sepia 15 60
65 75c. violet 15 90
66 1p. brown 15 1·25
67 – 2p. black and brown 60 3·50
68 – 5p. black and violet 60 4·00
69 – 10p. black and green 60 4·00

DESIGN (LARGER): 2, 5, 10p. Pres. Bogran facing left.

1892. 400th Anniv of Discovery of America.
70 10 1c. grey 20 25
71 2c. blue 20 25
72 5c. green 20 25
73 10c. green 20 30
74 20c. red 20 30
75 25c. brown 20 50
76 30c. blue 20 50
77 40c. orange 20 80
78 50c. brown 20 65
79 75c. lake 20 1·00
80 1p. violet 20 1·25

11 Gen. Cabanas
12

1893.
81 11 1c. green 20 30
82 2c. red 20 30
83 5c. blue 20 30
84 10c. brown 20 30
85 20c. brown 20 40
86 25c. blue 20 50
87 30c. orange 20 70
88 40c. black 20 90
89 50c. sepia 20 1·00
90 75c. violet 20 1·40
91 1p. brown 20 1·60

1895.
92 12 1c. red 20 20
93 2c. blue 20 20
94 5c. grey 20 30
95 10c. lake 20 30
96 20c. lilac 20 60
97 30c. lilac 20 90
98 50c. brown 20 1·25
99 1p. green 20 1·60

13 President Arias
14 Steam Train

1896.
100 13 1c. blue 30 30
101 2c. brown 30 30
102 5c. purple 90 30
103 10c. red 30 30
104 20c. green 75 40
105 30c. blue 50 60
106 50c. lake 70 1·00
107 1p. sepia 1·25 1·75

1898.
108 14 1c. brown 20 10
109 2c. red 30 15
110 5c. blue 30 15
111 6c. purple 40 20
112 10c. blue 40 35
113 20c. bistre 1·00 95
114 50c. orange 2·10 3·50
115 1p. green 2·50 4·00

16 General Santos Guardiola
17 President Medina

1903.
118 16 1c. green 25 20
119 2c. red 25 25
120 5c. blue 25 25
121 6c. lilac 30 25
122 10c. brown 30 30
123 20c. blue 35 35
124 50c. red 70 70
125 1p. orange 70 70

1907. Perf or imperf.
127 17 1c. green 25 25
136 1c. black 10·00 7·50
128a 2c. red 30 25
129 5c. blue 35 30
130 6c. violet 35 30
131 10c. sepia 35 35
132 20c. blue 60 55
133 50c. red 70 70
134 1p. orange 90 65

1910. Surch in figures.
137 17 1 on 20c. blue 4·00 3·50
138 5 on 20c. blue 4·00 3·50
139 10 on 20c. blue 4·00 3·50

20
23

1911.
140 20 1c. violet 15 15
141 2c. green 15 15
142 5c. red 15 15
143 6c. blue 30 30
144 10c. blue 35 35
145 20c. yellow 45 45
146 50c. brown 1·10 1·10
147 1p. olive 1·60 1·25

1911. Optd **XC Aniversario de la Independencia.**
157 20 2c. green 8·00 7·50

1912. Election of President Manuel Bonilla.
158 23 1c. red 9·25 9·25

1913. 90th Anniv of Independence. Surch **2 CENTAVOS.**
159 20 2c. on 1c. violet 65 50

1913. Surch in figures and words.
161 20 2c. on 1c. violet 4·50 4·00
162 2c. on 10c. blue 1·10 90
163 2c. on 20c. yellow 3·00 3·00
164 5c. on 1c. violet 1·10 50
165 5c. on 10c. blue 1·40 90
166 6c. on 1c. violet 1·40 90

26 Gen. T. Sierra
27 Gen. M. Bonilla

1913.
167 26 1c. brown 20 15
168 2c. red 25 20
169 27 5c. blue 30 20
170 5c. blue 30 20
171 6c. violet 40 30
172 6c. mauve 45 35
173 26 10c. blue 50 50
174 10c. brown 1·10 50
175 20c. brown 70 55
176 27 50c. red 1·40 1·25
177 1p. green 1·60 1·25

1914. Surch.
178 26 1c. on 2c. red 50 50
179 5c. on 2c. red 90 90
180 27 5c. on 6c. violet 1·60 1·60
181 26 5c. on 10c. brown 1·75 1·25
182 10c. on 2c. red 1·60 1·60
184 27 10c. on 6c. violet 1·60 1·60
185 10c. on 50c. red 4·00 3·00

32 Railway Bridge over River Ulua at Pimienta
34 Pres. Francisco Bertrand

1915. Dated "1915".
186 32 1c. brown 2·50 35
187 2c. red 2·75 35
188 – 5c. blue 25 10
189 – 6c. violet 25 20
190 32 10c. blue 6·75 50
191 20c. brown 9·00 4·50
192 – 50c. red 70 70
193 – 1p. green 1·40 1·25
DESIGN: 5c., 6c., 50c., 1p. Bonilla Theatre.

1916.
194 34 1c. orange 1·75 1·90

1918. No. O206 optd **CORRIENTE** and bar.
195 5c. blue 1·75 1·40

36 Statue of Francisco Morazan
36a

1919. Dated "1919" at top.
196 36 1c. brown 10 10
197 2c. red 20 10
198 5c. red 20 10
199 6c. mauve 25 10
200 10c. blue 25 20
201 15c. blue 55 25
202 15c. violet 45 25
203 20c. brown 50 25
204 50c. brown 1·10 70
205 1p. green 2·75 1·50

1920. Assumption of Power by Gen. R. L. Gutierrez.
206 36a 2c. red 1·90 1·75
207 2c. gold (51 × 40 mm) 5·75 5·25
208 2c. silver (51 × 40 mm) 5·75 5·25
209 2c. red (51 × 40 mm) 5·25 4·75

1921. As T 36, but dated "1920" at top.
210 36 6c. purple 3·00 1·75

1922. Surch **VALE SEIS CTS.**
211 36 6c. on 2c. red 30 25

1923. Surch **HABILITADO VALE** and value in words and figures.
212 36 $0.10 on 1c. brown 1·10 75
213 $0.50 on 2c. red 1·10 1·10
214 1p. on 5c. red 2·00 2·00

39 Dionisio de Herrera
40 M. Paz Baraona

1923.
215 39 1c. olive 20 10
216 2c. red 20 10
217 6c. purple 30 10
218 10c. blue 30 15
219 20c. brown 60 25
220 50c. red 1·25 55
221 1p. green 2·25 70

1925. Inaug of President Baraona. Imperf or perf.
222 40 1c. blue 1·75 1·75
224 1c. red 4·50 4·50
225 1c. brown 7·25 7·25

1925. Air. Nos. 186/93 optd **AERO CORREO** or surch also.
227 5c. blue 65·00 65·00
229 10c. blue £225 £225
231 20c. brown £160 £160
235 25c. on 1c. brown £110 £110
236 25c. on 5c. blue £200 £200
236c 25c. on 10c. blue £50000
237 25c. on 20c. brown £225 £225
233 50c. red £300 £300
234 1p. green £900 £900

1926. Optd **Acuerdo Mayo 3 de 1926 HABILITADO.**
238 36 6c. mauve 95 70

1926. Optd **HABILITADO 1926.**
242 32 2c. red 3·75 3·25
243 36 2c. red 20 20

1926. Optd **1926.**
239 – 6c. violet (No. 189) 1·75 1·75
240 36 6c. violet 2·10 2·10

1926. Surch **Vale 6 Cts. 1926** and bar.
243d 36 6c. on 10c. blue 35 20

1927. Surch **vale 6 cts. 1927** and bar.
244 36 6c. on 15c. violet 70 70
245 32 6c. on 20c. brown 3·75 3·25
246 36 6c. on 20c. brown 65 55

47 Copan Ruins

1927. Various designs as T 47.
247 – 1c. blue (Road) 20 15
248 47 2c. red 20 10
249 – 5c. purple (Pine tree) 20 10
250 – 5c. blue (Pine tree) 2·75 1·60
251 – 6c. black (Palace) 60 55
252 – 6c. blue (Palace) 25 15
253 – 10c. blue (P. Leiva) 45 20
254 – 15c. blue (Pres. Soto) 60 25
255 – 20c. blue (Lempira) 75 35
256 – 30c. brown (Map) 1·25 70
257 – 50c. green (Pres. Lindo) 1·60 90
258 – 1p. red (Columbus) 3·25 1·40

50 President Colindres and Vice-President Chavez

1929. Installation of President Colindres.
259 **50** 1c. lake . . . . 2·40 2·40
260 – 2c. green . . . . 2·40 2·40
DESIGN—VERT: 2c. Pres. Colindres.

1929. Air. (a) Surch **Servicio aereo Vale**, value and **1929.**
262 **39** 5c. on 20c. brown . . . . 1·40 1·40
263 10c. on 50c. red . . . . . 1·90 1·60
264 15c. on 1p. green . . . . . 3·25 3·25
261 25c. on 50c. red . . . . . 3·75 3·75
(b) Surch **Servicio Aereo Internacional 1929** and value.
265 **39** 5c. on 10c. blue 50 50
266 20c. on 50c. red 95 95

1929. Herrera Monument type, dated "1924–1928". Surch **Vale 1 cts. XI 1929.**
267 1c. on 6c. mauve 70 70

1929. Nos. 247/58 optd **1929a1930.**
268 – 1c. blue 15 10
269 **47** 2c. red 20 20
270 – 5c. purple 30 20
271 – 5c. blue 70 55
272 – 6c. black . . . . 1·75 1·40
273 – 6c. blue 30 15
274 – 10c. blue 30 15
275 – 15c. blue 30 15
276 – 20c. blue 30 20
277 – 30c. brown 55 45
278 – 50c. green 70 70
279 – 1p. red . . . . 1·90 1·90

1930. Air. No. O264 optd **HABILITADO Servicio Aereo Internacional 1930.**
281 – 50c. green and yellow . . . 1·40 1·40

1930. Air. Surch **Servicio Aereo Internacional Vale**, value and **1930.**
282 **39** 5c. on 10c. blue 55 55
284 5c. on 20c. brown £100 £100
285 10c. on 20c. brown 70 70
287 – 25c. on 50c. red (No. 192) 95 95

1930. Air. Surch **Vale** and value in addition in large letters and figures.
290 **39** 10c. on 5c. on 20c. brown (No. 284) 90 90
291 10c. on 10c. on 20c. brown (No. 285) . . . . 75·00 75·00
292 – 50c. on 25c. on 1p. green (No. 193) . . . . 3·50 3·50

1930. Air. Surch **Servicio aereo Vale**, value and **Marzo–1930.**
293 **39** 5c. on 10c. blue 50 50
294 15c. on 20c. brown 55 55
295 – 20c. on 50c. red (No. 192) 95 95

1930. Surch **Vale**, value and **1930.**
297 **39** 1c. on 10c. blue 35 30
298 2c. on 10c. blue 35 30

1930. Nos. O259/60 optd **Habilitado para el servicio publico 1930.**
299 – 1c. blue 50 50
300 O **50** 2c. red 90 90

1930. Air. Surch **Servicio aereo Vale 5 centavos oro Mayo.**
301 **39** 5c. on 20c. brown . . . . 1·10 1·10

1930. Air. Nos. O264/5 optd. **HABILITADO Servicio Aereo MAYO 1930.**
302 20c. blue . . . . 1·10 1·10
303 50c. green and yellow . . . . 1·10 90
304 1p. red . . . . 1·25 1·25

1930. Optd **Habilitado julio.–1930.**
305 **32** 1c. brown . . . . 1·75 1·90
306 **36** 1c. brown . . . . 8·50 8·50
309 **39** 1c. olive 20 15
310 2c. red 25 25
307 **36** 20c. brown . . . . 8·50 8·50
308 $0.50 on 2c. red (No. 213) 60·00 60·00

66 Title Page, First Issue Government Gazette

1930. Newspaper Centenary.
311 **66** 2c. blue 45 45
312 2c. orange 45 45
313 2c. red 45 45

67 National Palace, Tegucigalpa

1930. Air.
314 **67** 5c. yellow 55 30
315 10c. red 75 55
316 15c. green . . . . 1·10 70
317 20c. violet . . . . 1·40 70
318 1p. brown . . . . 3·50 2·75

68 Pres. Baraona
69 Amapala

1931.
319 **68** 1c. sepia 15 10
320 – 2c. red 15 10
321 – 5c. violet 55 10
322 – 6c. green 25 10
323 **69** 10c. brown 35 15
324 – 15c. blue 35 15
325 – 20c. black 55 20
326 – 50c. olive . . . . 1·40 60
327 – 1p. slate . . . . 2·40 1·10
DESIGNS—As Type **68**: 2c. Pres. Bonilla; 15c. Copan Ruins; 20c. Columbus. As Type **69**: 5c. Lake Yojoa; 6c. Tegucigalpa Palace; 50c. Discovery of America; 1p. Loarq Bridge at Loarq.

1931. Nos. 319/27 and 314/18 optd **T.S.de.C.**
328 **68** 1c. sepia (postage) 20 15
329 – 2c. red 25 15
330 – 5c. violet 50 25
331 – 6c. green 25 15
332 **69** 10c. brown 35 30
333 – 15c. blue 35 25
334 – 20c. black 45 25
335 – 50c. olive . . . . 2·75 2·50
336 – 1p. slate . . . . 3·50 3·25
337 **67** 5c. yellow (air) . . . . . 1·10 1·10
338 10c. red . . . . 2·50 2·50
339 15c. green . . . . 3·50 3·50
339a 20c. violet . . . . 4·25 4·25
339b 1p. brown . . . . 9·25 9·25

1931. Air. Surch **Servicio aereo interior Vale 15 cts Octubre 1931.**
340 **39** 15c. on 20c. . . . . . . 3·50 3·50
344a **32** 15c. on 20c. (No. O209) 22·00 22·00
342 **36** 15c. on 20c. (No. O218) 4·25 4·25
344c **39** 15c. on 20c. (No. O226) 1·00 1·00
343 – 15c. on 50c. (No. O210) 4·25 4·25
346 **36** 15c. on 50c. (No. O219) 3·25 3·25
341 – 15c. on 1p. (No. O265) 4·25 4·25
Nos. 342/3 come with or without the original OFICIAL overprint obliterated.

1932. Air. Surch **S.–Aereo VI. 15 cts. XI 1931.**
347 **39** 15c. on 20c. brown . . . . 3·00 3·00
348 **36** 15c. on 50c. (No. O219) . . 3·00 3·00
349 – 15c. on 50c. (No. O264) . . 3·00 3·00
350 – 15c. on 1p. (No. O265) . . 2·40 2·40

1932. Air. Nos. O328/36 optd **Servicio Aereo Exterior. Habilitado X. 1931.**
350c O **70** 1c. blue 35 35
350d 2c. purple 90 90
350e 5c. olive . . . . 1·10 1·10
350f 6c. red . . . . 1·10 1·10
350g 10c. green . . . . 1·25 1·25
350h 15c. brown . . . . 1·75 1·75
350i 20c. brown . . . . 1·75 1·75
350j 50c. violet . . . . 1·40 1·40
350k 1p. orange . . . . 1·75 1·75

1932. Nos. O223/25 surch **Aereo interior VALE 15 Cts. 1932.**
351 **39** 15c. on 2c. red 45 45
352 15c. on 6c. purple 45 45
353 15c. on 10c. blue 45 45

78 Pres. Carias and Vice-Pres. Williams

1933. Inauguration of Pres. Carias.
355 **78** 2c. red 30 25
356 6c. green 35 25
357 10c. blue 45 30
358 15c. orange 55 35

79 Flag of the Race

1933. 441st Anniv of Departure of Columbus from Palos.
359 **79** 2c. blue 35 30
360 6c. yellow 45 35
361 10c. yellow 55 45
362 15c. violet 70 60
363 50c. red . . . . 3·00 2·40
364 1l. green . . . . 4·75 4·75

80 Pres. T. Carias

1935. Inscr as in T **80**.
365 – 1c. green 20 15
366 **80** 2c. red 20 20
367 – 5c. blue 25 25
368 – 6c. brown 35 35
DESIGNS: 1c. Masonic Temple, Tegucigalpa; 5c. National Flag; 6c. Pres. T. E. Palma.

82 Tegucigalpa

1935. Air. Inscr as in T **82**.
369 – 8c. blue 10 10
370 **82** 10c. grey 20 10
371 – 15c. olive 30 15
372 – 20c. green . . . . 3·75 60
373 – 40c. brown 55 20
374 – 50c. yellow . . . . 16·00 4·25
375 – 1l. green . . . . 1·75 1·40
DESIGNS: 8c. G.P.O. and Congress Building; 15c. Map of Honduras; 20c. Presidential Palace and Mayol Railway Bridge; 40c. Different view of Tegucigalpa; 50c. Great horned owl; 1l. National Arms.

84 President Carias and Carias Bridge

1937. Re-election of President Carias.
376 **84** 6c. red and olive . . . . . 2·00 1·00
377 21c. green and violet . . . 3·00 1·25
378 46c. orange and brown . . 5·25 1·60
379 55c. blue and black . . . . 7·00 3·25

85 Book of the Constitution and Flags of U.S. and Honduras

1937. Air. 150th Anniv of U.S. Constitution.
380 **85** 46c. multicoloured . . . . 1·40 1·25

86 Comayagua Cathedral

1937. Air. 400th Anniv of Comayagua.
381 **86** 2c. red 20 10
382 – 8c. blue 25 15
383 – 15c. black 45 35
384 – 50c. brown . . . . 1·75 1·10
DESIGNS: 8c. Founding of Comayagua; 15c. Portraits of Caceres and Carias; 50c. Lintel of Royal Palace.

90 Arms of Honduras

91 Copan Ruins

1939. Dated "1939 1942".
385 **90** 1c. yellow (postage) . . . 10 10
386 – 2c. red 10 10
387 – 3c. red 15 10
388 – 5c. orange 20 15
389 – 8c. blue 25 20

DESIGNS: 2c. Central District Palace; 3c. Map of Honduras; 5c. Choluteca Bridge; 8c. National flag.

390 **91** 10c. brown (air) 15 10
391 – 15c. blue 20 10
392 – 21c. slate 35 10
393 – 30c. green 45 10
394 – 40c. violet 70 15
395 – 46c. brown 70 45
396 – 55c. green 90 60
397 – 66c. black . . . . 1·40 80
398 – 1l. olive . . . . 2·10 55
399 – 2l. red . . . . 3·00 1·75
DESIGNS: 15c. Pres. Carias; 21c. Mayan Temple; 30c. J. C. del Valle; 40c. The Presidency; 46c. Statue of Lempira; 55c. Suyapa Church; 66c. J. T. Reyes; 1l. Choluteca Hospital; 2l. R. Rosa.

1940. Air. Dedication of Columbus Memorial Lighthouse. Official stamps optd **Correo Aereo Habilitado para Servicio Publico Pro-Faro-Colon-1940.**
400 O **92** 2c. blue and green . . . 20 15
401 5c. blue and orange . . 25 25
402 8c. blue and brown . . . 25 25
403 15c. blue and red . . . 35 35
404 46c. blue and olive . . . 70 70
405 50c. blue and violet . . 70 70
406 1l. blue and brown . . . 3·00 2·00
407 2l. blue and red . . . . 5·75 4·50

97 Francisco Morazan

98 Red Cross

1941. Obligatory Tax. Death Centenary of Gen. Morazan.
408 **97** 1c. brown 15 10

1941. Obligatory Tax. Red Cross.
409 **98** 1c. blue and red 15 10

1941. Air. Official stamps optd **Habilitada para el Servicio Publico 1941.**
410 O **92** 5c. blue and orange . . 2·50 25
411 8c. blue and brown . . . 4·00 25

1941. Air. Official stamps surch **Rehabilitada para el Servicio Publico 1941 Vale** and value in words.
412 O **92** 3c. on 2c. blue and green 30 20
413 8c. on 2c. blue and green 35 30
414 8c. on 15c. blue and red 35 25
415 8c. on 46c. blue & olive 55 45
416 8c. on 50c. blue & violet 70 55
417 8c. on 1l. blue & brown 1·10 70
418 8c. on 2l. blue and red 1·40 1·10

1942. Air. Surch **Correo Aereo** and value.
419 8c. on 15c. blue (No. 391) . . 60 20
420 16c. on 46c. brown (No. 395) 60 20

102 Morazan's Birthplace

103 Tomb

1942. Air. Death Centenary of Gen. Morazan.
421 – 2c. orange 10 10
422 – 5c. blue 10 10
423 **102** 8c. purple 15 10
424 **103** 14c. black 30 30
425 – 16c. olive 20 20
426 – 21c. blue 90 70
427 – 1l. blue . . . . 2·75 1·75
428 – 2l. brown . . . . 7·25 5·75
DESIGNS—HORIZ: 2c. Commemoration plate; 5c. Battle of La Trinidad; 16c. Morazan's monument (as in Type **36**); 21c. Church where Morazan was baptised; 1l. Arms of C. American Federation. VERT: 2l. Morazan.

105 Coat of Arms

106 Western Hemisphere

1943. Air.
429 **105** 1c. green 10 10
430 – 2c. blue 10 10
431 – 5c. green 20 10
432 – 6c. green 20 10
433 – 8c. purple 25 10
434 – 10c. brown 25 10
435 – 15c. red 25 10
436 – 16c. red 30 10
437 – 21c. blue 40 10
438 – 30c. brown 45 10

439 – 40c. red 45 10
440 – 55c. black 70 55
441 – 1l. green 1·25 1·10
442 **106** 2l. lake 3·50 3·00
443 – 5l. orange 8·75 8·75
DESIGNS—HORIZ: 2c. National flag; 5c. Cattle; 8c. Rosario; 15c. Tobacco plant; 21c. Orchid; 30c. Oranges; 40c. Wheat; 5l. Map of Honduras. VERT: 6c. Banana Tree; 10c. Pine tree; 16c. Sugar cane; 55c. Coconut palms; 1l. Maize.

114 Agricultural College

117 Flag, mother and child

1944. Air. Inauguration of Pan-American Agricultural College.
444 **114** 21c. green 30 20

1944. Optd **HABILITADO 1944-45**.
445 **90** 1c. yellow 30 30
446 – 2c. red (No. 386) 45 45

1945. Air. Surch **Correo Aereo HABILITADO Acd. No 798-1945** and value.
447 – 1c. on 50c. (No. 384) 10 10
448 **86** 2c. on 2c. red 15 10
449 – 8c. on 15c. (No. 383) 20 20
450 **91** 10c. on 10c. brown 35 30
451 – 15c. on 15c. (No. 391) 20 20
452 – 30c. on 21c. (No. 392) 3·00 3·00
453 – 40c. on 40c. (No. 394) 1·75 1·40
454 – 1l. on 46c. (No. 395) 1·75 1·40
455 – 2l. on 66c. (No. 397) 3·00 3·00

1945. Obligatory Tax. Red Cross.
456 **117** 1c. brown and red 15 10
456a – 1c. red and brown 15 10
DESIGN: No. 456a, Red Cross.

118 Arms of Honduras

1946. Air. Coats of Arms.
457 **118** 1c. red 10 10
458 – 2c. orange 10 10
459 – 5c. violet 20 10
461 – 15c. purple 35 20
462 – 21c. blue 35 30
463 – 1l. green 1·40 90
464 – 2l. grey 2·10 1·60
ARMS: 2c. Von Gracias and Trujillo; 5c. Comayagua and S. J. de Olancho; 15c. Honduras Province and S. J. de Puerto Caballos; 21c. Comayagua and Tencoa; 1l. Jerez de la Frontera de Choluteca and San Pedro de Zula; 2l. San Miguel de Heredia de Tegucigalpa.

119 Broken Column and F. D. Roosevelt

1946. Air. Allied Victory over Japan and Death of Pres. Roosevelt. (a) Inscr "F.D.R."
460 **119** 8c. brown 70 55

(b) Inscr "FRANKLIN D. ROOSEVELT".
465 **119** 8c. brown 45 30

120 Honduras and Copan Antiquities

1947. Air. 1st International Conference of Caribbean Archaeologists. Various frames.
466 **120** 16c. green 35 15
467 22c. yellow 25 15
468 40c. orange 55 35
469 1l. blue 90 90
470 2l. mauve 3·00 3·00
471 5l. brown 7·25 6·50

121 Flag and Arms of Honduras

122 Galvez, Carias and Lozano

123 National Stadium

124 President Galvez

1949. Air. Inauguration of President Juan Manuel Galvez. Inscr "CONMEMORATIVA DE LA SUCESION PRESIDENCIAL", etc.
472 **121** 1c. blue 10 10
473 **124** 2c. red 10 10
474 – 5c. blue 10 10
475 – 9c. brown 10 10
476 – 15c. brown 20 10
477 **122** 21c. black 35 10
478 **123** 30c. olive 45 15
479 – 40c. grey 70 20
480 – 1l. brown 1·10 35
481 – 2l. violet 2·00 1·75
482 – 5l. red 5·75 5·25
DESIGNS—HORIZ: 40c. Toncontin Customs House; 5l. Galvez and Lozano. VERT: 5c., 15c. Lozano (different frames); 9c. Galvez; 1l. Palace of Tegucigalpa; 2l. Carias.

1951. Air. 75th Anniv of **U.P.U. Optd U.P.U. 75 Aniversario 1874-1949**.
483 **120** 16c. green 55 55
484 – 22c. yellow 70 70
485 – 40c. orange 70 70
486 – 1l. blue 2·40 2·40
487 – 2l. mauve 3·50 3·50
488 – 5l. brown 26·00 26·00

1951. Air. Founding of Central Bank. Nos. 472/81 optd **Conmemorativa Fundacion Banco Central Administracion Galvez–Lozano Julio 1o. de 1950**.
489 1c. blue 10 10
490 2c. red 10 10
491 5c. blue 10 10
492 9c. brown 15 10
493 15c. brown 15 10
494 21c. black 25 25
495 30c. olive 45 35
496 40c. grey 70 65
497 1l. brown 1·75 1·25
498 2l. violet 4·50 3·25

127 Discovery of America

128 Isabella the Catholic

1952. Air. 500th Anniv of Birth of Isabella the Catholic.
499 **127** 1c. slate and orange 10 10
500 – 2c. brown and blue 10 10
501 – 8c. sepia and green 20 10
502 **128** 16c. black and blue 30 20
503 – 30c. green and violet 55 55
504 – 1l. black and red 1·40 1·10
505 **127** 2l. violet and brown 2·75 2·75
506 **128** 5l. olive and purple 7·00 7·00
DESIGNS—HORIZ: 2c.1l. King Ferdinand and Queen Isabella receive Columbus; 8c. Surrender of Granada; 30c. Queen Isabella pledging her jewels.

1953. Air. Surch **HABILITADO 1953** and value.
507 **122** 5c. on 21c. black 10 10
508 8c. on 21c. black 20 10
509 16c. on 21c. black 35 20

1953. Air. Nos. O507/509 and O512/14 surch **HABILITADO 1953** and value or optd only.
510 **127** 10c. on 1c. olive & purple 10 10
511 12c. on 1c. olive & purple 10 10
512 – 15c. on 2c. violet & brn 15 15
513 – 20c. on 2c. violet & brn 25 25
514 – 24c. on 2c. violet & brn 25 25
515 – 25c. on 2c. violet & brn 25 25
516 – 30c. on 8c. black and red 25 25
517 – 35c. on 8c. black and red 30 30
518 – 50c. on 8c. black and red 45 45
519 – 60c. on 8c. black and red 55 55
520 – 1l. sepia and green 1·40 1·25
521 **127** 2l. brown and blue 3·50 2·75
522 **128** 5l. slate and orange 9·00 9·00

130 U.N. Emblem

1953. Air. United Nations. Inscr as in T **130**.
523 – 1c. blue and black 10 10
524 **130** 2c. blue and black 15 10
525 – 3c. violet and black 20 15
526 – 5c. green and black 15 15
527 – 15c. brown and black 35 30
528 – 30c. brown and black 90 75
529 – 1l. red and black 6·00 5·25
530 – 2l. orange and black 7·25 6·00
531 – 5l. green and black 18·00 16·00
DESIGNS: 1c. U.N. and Honduras flags; 3c. U.N. Building, New York; 5c. Arms of U.S.A; 15c. Pres. J. M. Galvez; 30c. Indian girl (U.N.I.C.E.F.); 1l. Refugee mother and child (U.N.R.R.A.); 2l. Torch and open book (U.N.E.S.C.O.); 5l. Cornucopia (F.A.O.).

1955. Air. 50th Anniv of Rotary International. Nos. O532/38 optd with rotary emblem, **1905 1955**, clasped hands and laurel sprigs or surch also.
532 1c. blue and black 15 15
533 2c. green and black 15 15
534 3c. orange and black 20 20
535 5c. red and black 25 25
536 8c. on 1c. blue and black 15 15
537 10c. on 2c. green and black 20 20
538 12c. on 3c. orange and black 25 25
539 15c. sepia and black 35 35
540 30c. purple and black 1·10 1·10
541 1l. olive and black 18·00 18·00

1956. Air. 10th Anniv of U.N.O. Nos. O523/5 and 527/31 optd **ONU X ANIVERSARIO 1945-1955**.
542 1c. blue and black 20 20
543 2c. green and black 20 20
544 3c. orange and black 25 25
545 5c. red and black 30 30
546 15c. brown and black 35 35
547 30c. brown and black 55 55
548 1l. red and black 3·50 3·00
549 2l. orange and black 5·25 4·00
550 5l. green and black 13·00 11·00

133 J. Lozano Diaz

134 Southern Highway

1956. Air.
551 – 1c. blue and black 10 10
552 **133** 2c. blue and black 10 10
553 **134** 3c. sepia and black 10 10
554 – 4c. purple and black 10 10
555 – 5c. red and black 10 10
556 – 8c. multicoloured 10 10
557 – 10c. green and black 15 10
558 – 12c. green and black 15 10
559 – 15c. black and red 20 10
560 – 20c. blue and black 20 15
561 **133** 24c. purple and black 25 20
562 – 25c. green and black 30 25
563 – 30c. red and black 30 25
564 – 40c. brown and black 35 30
565 – 50c. turquoise and black 45 35
566 – 60c. orange and black 55 45
567 – 1l. purple and black 1·40 1·10
568 – 2l. red and black 2·75 1·75
569 – 5l. lake and black 5·25 3·50
DESIGNS—HORIZ: 1c. Suyapa Basilica; 8c. Landscape and cornucopia; 10c. National Stadium; 12c. United States School; 15c. Projected Central Bank of Honduras; 20c. Legislative Building; 25c. Projected Development Bank; 30c. Toncontin Airport; 40c. J. R. Molina Bridge; 60c. Treasury Building; 1l. Blood Bank. VERT: 4c. Dona de Estrada Palma; 5c. Dona de Morazan; 50c. Peace Memorial; 2l. Electrical Communications Building; 5l. Presidential Palace.

135 Revolutionary Flag

136 Flags of Honduras and the U.S.A. and Book

1957. Air. Revolution of October 21, 1956. Frames in black.
570 **135** 1c. blue and yellow 10 10
571 – 2c. purple, green & orange 10 10
572 **135** 5c. blue and pink 15 10
573 – 8c. violet, olive and orange 20 10
574 – 10c. brown and violet 20 15
575 **135** 12c. blue and turquoise 25 20
576 – 15c. brown and green 30 25
577 – 30c. grey and pink 45 25
578 – 1l. brown and blue 1·40 1·25
579 – 2l. grey and green 2·75 1·75
DESIGNS: 2c., 8c. Obelisk and mountains; 10c., 15c., 1l. Indian with bow and arrow; 30c., 2l. Arms of 1821.

NOTE. In July 1958 after stocks of current issues had been looted, eighteen different facsimile signatures validated the remaining stamps for use.

1958. Air. Bi-national Centre Commem. (Institute of American Culture). Flags in national colours.
580 **136** 1c. blue 10 10
581 2c. red 10 10
582 5c. green 10 10
583 10c. brown 20 20
584 20c. orange 35 20
585 30c. red 35 30
586 50c. grey 45 35
587 1l. yellow 1·10 95
588 2l. olive 3·00 1·90
589 5l. blue 4·50 4·50

137 Abraham Lincoln

138 Henri Dunant

1959. Air. 150th Birth Anniv of Abraham Lincoln. Flags in blue and red.
590 **137** 1c. green 15 15
591 – 2c. blue 15 15
592 – 3c. violet 20 20
593 – 5c. red 20 20
594 – 10c. slate 25 20
595 – 12c. sepia 25 20
596 **137** 15c. orange 35 20
597 – 25c. purple 55 30
598 – 50c. blue 70 55
599 – 1l. brown 1·40 1·25
600 – 2l. olive 1·90 1·40
601 – 5l. yellow 4·00 3·25
DESIGNS—HORIZ: 2c., 25c. Lincoln's birthplace; 3c., 50c. Gettysburg Address; 5c., 1l. Lincoln at conference to free slaves; 10c., 2l. Assassination of Lincoln; 12c., 5l. Lincoln Memorial, Washington.

1959. Obligatory Tax. Red Cross.
602 **138** 1c. red and blue 15 10
647 1c. red and green 20 10
648 1c. red and brown 20 10
Nos. 647/8 have no frame around portrait and values are at left.

139 Constitution of 21 December 1957

1959. Air. 2nd Anniv of New Constitution. Inscr "21 DE DICIEMBRE DE 1957".
603 **139** 1c. red, blue and brown 10 10
604 – 2c. brown 10 10
605 – 3c. blue 10 10
606 – 5c. orange 20 10
607 **139** 10c. red, blue and green 25 10
608 – 12c. red 35 20
609 – 25c. violet 70 25
610 – 50c. grey-blue 1·10 35
DESIGNS—HORIZ: 2, 12c. Inaug of Pres. R. V. Morales. VERT: 3, 25c. Pres. R. V. Morales; 5, 50c. Flaming torch.

140 King Alfonso XIII of Spain and Map

1961. Air. Settlement of Boundary Dispute with Nicaragua.
611 **140** 1c. blue 10 10
612 – 2c. pink 10 10
613 – 5c. green 10 10
614 – 10c. brown 15 10
615 – 20c. red 30 20
616 – 50c. brown 70 55
617 – 1l. slate 1·10 90

DESIGNS: 2c. 1906 award (document); 5c. Arbitration commission, 1907; 10c. International Court of Justice, The Hague; 20c. 1960 award (document); 50c. Pres. Morales Foreign Minister Puerto and map; 1l. Presidents Davila and Morales.

1964. Air. Freedom from Hunger. Flags in National colours. Optd **FAO Luncha Contra el Hambre**.
621 **136** 1c. blue 20 20
622 2c. red 20 20
623 5c. green 25 25
624 30c. red . . . . 1·10 70
625 2l. olive . . . . 5·25 4·00

1964. Air. Olympic Games, Tokyo. Optd with Olympic Rings and **1964**.
626 – 1c. blue & black (No. 523) 15 15
627 **130** 2c. blue and black 25 25
628 – 3c. violet & blk (No. 525) 30 30
629 – 15c. brn & blk (No. 527) 55 55
See also No. O646.

144 Ancient Stadium

1964. Air. "Homage to Sport" and Olympic Games, Tokyo.
630 **144** 1c. black and green . . . 10 10
631 – 2c. black and mauve . . . 10 10
632 – 5c. black and blue 15 15
633 – 8c. black and grey-green 25 25
634 **144** 10c. black and bistre . . . 35 30
635 – 12c. black and yellow . . 55 35
636 – 1l. black and buff . . . . 1·40 90
637 – 2l. black and olive . . . . 3·00 1·75
638 **144** 3l. black and red . . . . 4·50 2·75
DESIGNS: 2c., 12c. Boundary stones; 5c., 1l. Mayan ball player; 8c., 2l. Olympic Stadium, Tokyo.

1964. Air. Surch.
639 – 4c. on 5c. (No. 593) . . . 15 10
618 **137** 6c. on 15c. 20 10
619 – 8c. on 25c. (No. 597) . . 20 10
640 – 10c. on 15c. (No. 476) . . 15 10
620 – 10c. on 50c. (No. 598) . . 30 20
641 – 12c. on 16c. (No. 425) . . 15 10
642 – 12c. on 21c. (No. 426) . . 25 10
643 **120** 12c. on 22c. 25 10
644 30c. on 1l. 45 25
645 – 40c. on 1l. (No. 480) . . . 65 30
646 **120** 40c. on 2l. 65 30
See also Nos. 716/18 and O647/18.

1965. Air. Presidential Investiture of General Lopez. Optd **Toma de Posesion General Oswaldo Lopez A. Junio 6, 1965**. Flags in blue and red.
649 **137** 1c. green 10 10
650 – 2c. green 10 10
651 – 3c. violet (No. 592) . . . 10 10
652 – 5c. red (No. 593) 10 10
653 **137** 15c. orange 20 15
654 – 25c. purple (No. 597) . . 30 20
655 – 50c. red 50 35
656 – 2l. olive (No. 600) . . . . 1·75 1·40
657 – 5l. yellow (No. 601) . . . 5·25 3·50

147 Ambulance and Clinic

1965. Air. Order of Malta Campaign Against Leprosy.
658 **147** 1c. blue 25 25
659 – 5c. green 35 35
660 – 12c. black 55 55
661 – 1l. brown . . . . 1·75 1·75
DESIGNS: 5c. Hospital; 12c. Patients receiving treatment; 1l. Map of Honduras.

148 Father Subirana

151 2r. Stamp of 1866

1965. Air. Death Cent of Father Manuel de Jesus Subirana. Centres in black and gold; inscr in black.
662 – 1c. violet 10 10
663 – 2c. flesh 10 10
664 **148** 8c. pink 10 10
665 – 10c. purple 10 10
666 – 12c. brown 20 15
667 – 20c. green 35 30
668 – 1l. sage . . . . 1·75 70
669 – 2l. blue . . . . 3·00 1·75

DESIGNS: 1c. Abraham, Jicaque Indian; 2c. Allegory of Catechism; 10c. Msgr. Juan de Jesus Zepeda; 12c. Pope Pius IX; 20c. Subirana's Tomb, Yoro; 1l. Hermitage; 2l. Jicaque Indian woman and child.

1965. Air. Churchill Commemoration. Nos. 499/500 and 470 optd **IN MEMORIAM Sir Winston Churchill 1874-1965**.
671 **127** 1c. black and orange . . 35 35
672 – 2c. brown and blue . . . 70 70
673 – 2l. mauve . . . . 5·75 5·00
See also No. O674.

1966. Air. Pope Paul's Visit to U.N. Organisation. Nos. 662/68 optd **CONMEMORATIVA Visita S. S. Pablo VI a la ONU. 4-X-1965**.
675 – 1c. violet 15 10
676 – 2c. flesh 15 10
677 **148** 8c. pink 25 15
678 – 10c. purple 25 15
679 – 12c. brown 30 15
680 – 20c. green 35 20
681 – 1l. sage . . . . 2·40 90

1966. Air. Stamp Centenary. Inscriptions in black (1c., 2c.) or in gold (others).
682 **151** 1c. black, green and gold 10 10
683 – 2c. blue, black and orange 10 10
684 – 3c. purple and red 10 10
685 – 4c. indigo and blue . . . 10 10
686 – 5c. purple and mauve . . 5·00 2·00
687 – 6c. violet and lilac 10 10
688 – 7c. slate and turquoise . . 10 10
689 – 8c. indigo and blue . . . 15 15
690 – 9c. blue and cobalt . . . 15 15
691 – 10c. black and olive . . . 15 15
692 – 12c. yellow, black & green 15 15
693 – 15c. purple and mauve . . 25 25
694 – 20c. black and orange . . 30 30
695 – 30c. blue and yellow . . . 35 35
696 – 40c. multicoloured 55 55
697 – 1l. green and emerald . . 1·25 1·10
698 – 2l. black and grey . . . . 2·25 1·75
DESIGNS—VERT: 2c. Honduras; 5c. air stamp of 1925; 3c. T. Estrada Palma, 1st Director of Posts; 8c. Sir Rowland Hill; 10c. Pres. Arellano; 12c. Postal emblem; 15c. H. von Stephan; 30c. Honduras flag; 40c. Honduras arms; 1l. U.P.U. Monument, Berne; 2l. J. M. Medina (statesman). HORIZ: 4c. Post Office, Tegucigalpa; 5c. Steam locomotive No. 59; 6c. 19th-century mule transport; 7c. 19th-century sorting office; 9c. Mail van; 20c. Curtiss C-46 Commando mail plane.
See also No. E700.

1966. Air. World Cup Football Championship, Final Match between England and West Germany. Optd **CAMPEONATO DE FOOTBALL Copa Mundial 1966 Inglaterra-Alemania Wembley, Julio 30**.
701 – 2c. vio & brn (No. O508) 20 20
702 **128** 16c. black and blue . . . 35 35
703 **127** 2l. violet and brown . . . 7·25 5·75

1967. Air. 20th Anniv of U.N.O. Nos. 662/4 and 666/9 optd **CONMEMORATIVA del XX Aniversario ONU 1966**.
704 – 1c. violet 20 20
705 – 2c. flesh 25 25
706 **148** 8c. pink 35 35
707 – 12c. brown 55 45
708 – 20c. green 70 60
709 – 1l. sage . . . . 1·75 1·40
710 – 2l. blue . . . . 3·00 2·75

1967. Birth Bicentenary of Simeon Canas y Villacorta (slave liberator). Nos. 551, 553, 559, 552 and 568. Optd **Simeon Canas y Villacorta Libertador de los esclavos en Centro America 1767-1967**.
711 1c. blue and black 15 15
712 3c. sepia and black 25 25
713 15c. black and red 35 35
714 25c. green and black 70 55
715 2l. red and black . . . . . . 2·00 1·75

1967. Air. Nos. E570 and 480/1 surch.
716 E **135** 10c. on 20c. grey, black and red 20 10
717 – 10c. on 1l. brown . . . 20 10
718 – 10c. on 2l. violet . . . 20 10

156 J. C. del Valle (Honduras)

1967. Air. Founding of Central-American Journalists' Federation.
719 **156** 11c. black, blue and gold 10 10
720 – 12c. black, yellow and blue 10 10
721 – 14c. black, green and silver 15 10
722 – 20c. black, green & mauve 20 15
723 – 30c. black, yellow and lilac 25 25
724 – 40c. gold, blue and violet 70 70
725 – 50c. green, red and olive 70 70
DESIGNS: 12c. Ruben Dario (Nicaragua); 14c. J. B. Montufar (Guatemala); 20c. F. Gavidia (El Salvador); 30c. J. M. Fernandez (Costa Rica); 40c. Federation emblem; 50c. Central American map.

157 Olympic Rings and Flags of Mexico and Honduras

1968. Air. Olympic Games, Mexico. Mult.
726 1c. Type **157** 15 15
727 2c. Type **157** 25 25
728 5c. Italian flag and boxing . . 30 30
729 10c. French flag and skiing 35 35
730 12c. West German flag and show-jumping 55 55
731 50c. British flag and athletics 1·75 1·75
732 1l. U.S. flag and running . . 5·75 5·75

158 J. F. Kennedy and Rocket Launch

1968. Air. International Telecommunications Union Centenary. Multicoloured.
734 1c. Type **158** 15 15
735 2c. Dish aerial and telephone 20 20
736 3c. Dish aerial and television 20 20
737 5c. Dish aerial, globe and I.T.U. emblem as satellite 35 35
738 8c. "Early Bird" satellite . . 50 50
739 10c. Type **158** 55 55
740 20c. Type **158** 75 75

1969. Air. Robert F. Kennedy Commemoration. Nos. 734 and 739/40 optd **In-Memoriam Robert F. Kennedy 1925-1968**.
741 1c. multicoloured 40 40
742 10c. multicoloured 40 40
743 20c. multicoloured 40 40

1969. Air. Gold Medal Winners, Olympic Games. Nos. 735/8 optd **Medallas de Oro Mexico 1968**.
744 2c. multicoloured 25 25
745 3c. multicoloured 25 25
746 5c. multicoloured 40 40
747 8c. multicoloured 75 75

161 Patient and Nurse

1969. Obligatory Tax. Red Cross.
748 **161** 1c. red and blue 15 10

162 Rocket Launch

1969. Air. First Man on the Moon. Mult.
749 5c. Type **162** 10 10
750 10c. Moon 10 10
751 12c. Lunar landing module leaving space-ship (horiz) 15 10
752 20c. Astronaut on Moon (horiz) 15 15
753 24c. Lunar landing module taking off from Moon . . 20 15
754 30c. Capsule re-entering Earth's atmosphere (horiz) 30 20

1970. No. E700 optd with **"HABILITADO"** for use as ordinary postage stamp.
755 20c. brown, orange and gold 35 25

1970. Air. Various stamps surch in figures.
756 **151** 4c.+1c. (No. 682) . . . 10 10
757 – 4c.+3c. (No. 525) . . . 10 10
758 – 5c.+1c. (No. 662) . . . 10 10
759 – 5c.+7c. (No. 688) . . . 10 10
760 – 8c.+2c. (No. 663) . . . 20 20
761 – 10c.+2c. (No. 500) . . 25 25
762 **133** 10c.+2c. (No. 552) . . 25 25
763 – 10c.+3c. (No. 525) . . 25 25
764 **134** 10c.+3c. (No. 553) . . 25 25
765 – 10c.+3c. (No. 684) . . 25 25
766 – 10c.+9c. (No. 690) . . 10 10
767 **156** 10c.+11c. (No. 719) . . 10 10
768 – 12c.+14c. (No. 721) . . 15 15
769 E **135** 12c.+20c. (No. E570) 15 15
770 – 12c.+1l. (No. 480) . . 15 15
771 – 15c.+12c. (No. 783) . . 35 35
772 – 30c.+12c. (No. 783) . . 70 70
773 – 40c.+24c. (No. 753) . . 90 90
774 – 40c.+50c. (No. 731) . . 90 90

1970. Air. Safe Return of "Apollo 13". Nos. 749/54 optd **Admiracion al Rescate del Apolo XIII, James A. Lovell, Fred W. Haise Jr., John L. Swigert Jr.**
775 5c. multicoloured 10 10
776 10c. multicoloured 15 15
777 12c. multicoloured 20 20
778 20c. multicoloured 30 30
779 24c. multicoloured 35 35
780 30c. multicoloured 45 45

165 J. A. Sanhueza (firefighter)

166 Hotel Honduras Maya

1970. Air. Campaign Against Forest Fires. Multicoloured.
781 5c. Type **165** 10 10
782 8c. R. Ordonez Rodriguez (firefighter) 15 10
783 12c. Fire Brigade emblems (horiz) 15 15
784 20c. Flag, map and emblems 30 25
785 1l. Emblems, and flags of Honduras, U.N. and U.S.A. 70 65

1970. Air. Opening of Hotel Honduras Maya, Tegucigalpa.
787 **166** 12c. black and blue . . . 25 25

1972. Air. 50th Anniv of Honduras Masonic Grand Lodge. Nos. 749 and 751/3. optd **Aniversario Gran Logia de Honduras 1922-1972** or surch also.
791 5c. multicoloured 25 30
792 12c. multicoloured 55 45
793 1l. on 20c. multicoloured . . 1·10 70
794 2l. on 24c. multicoloured . . 1·75 1·40

168 Soldiers' Bay, Guanaja

1972. Air. 150th Anniv of Independence (1970). Multicoloured.
795 4c. Type **168** 10 10
796 5c. Bugler sounding "Last Post" (vert) 10 10
797 6c. Lake Yojoa 10 10
798 7c. "The Banana Carrier" (R. Aguilar) (vert) 10 10
799 8c. Soldiers marching and fly-past 15 10
800 9c. "Brassavola digbyana" (national flower) (vert) . . 15 10
801 10c. As 9c. 20 10
802 12c. Machine-gunner 20 10
803 15c. Tela beach at sunset . . 25 10
804 20c. Stretcher-bearers 25 10
805 30c. "San Antonio de Oriente" (A. Velasquez) . . 35 25
806 40c. Ruins of Copan 55 30
807 50c. "Woman from Huacal" (P. Zelaya Sierra) 55 35
808 1l. Trujillo Bay . . . . . . 1·75 90
809 2l. As 9c. . . . . 1·75 1·40

169 Sister Maria Rosa and Child

1972. Air. "S.O.S." Children's Villages in Honduras. Each brown, green and gold.
812 10c. Type **169** 20 10
813 15c. "S.O.S. Villages" emblem (horiz) 25 10
814 30c. Father J. T. Reyes (educationalist) 45 15
815 40c. First Central American "S.O.S." village (horiz) . . 45 20
816 1l. "Future Citizen" (boy) . . 1·40 70

170 Map of Honduras

1973. Air. 25th Annivs of National Cartographic Service (10c.) and Joint Cartographic Work (12c.).
817 **170** 10c. multicoloured 35 25
818 – 12c. multicoloured 45 25
DESIGN: 12c. Similar to Type **170** but with two badges and inscr "25 Anos de Labor Cartografica Conjunta".

171 Illustration from "Habitante de la Osa"

1973. Air. 25th Anniv of U.N.E.S.C.O. and Juan Ramon Molina (poet) Commem. Multicoloured.
819 8c. Type **171** 20 10
820 20c. Juan Ramon Molina . . 70 30
821 1l. Illustration from "Tierras Mares y Cielos" . . . . . 1·40 70
822 2l. U.N.E.S.C.O. emblem . . 2·40 1·60

1973. Air. Census and World Population Year. Various stamps optd **Censos de Poblacion y Vivienda, marzo 1974. 1974 Ano Mundial de Poblacion.**
824 **169** 10c. brown, green and gold 10 10
828 **170** 10c. multicoloured 10 10
829 – 12c. mult (No. 818) . . . 30 15
825 – 15c. brown, green and gold (No. 813) 35 20
826 – 30c. brown, green and gold (No. 814) 10 10
827 – 40c. brown, green and gold (No. 815) 10 10

1974. Air. Various stamps surch.
830 – 2c. on 1c. blue and black (No. 551) 10 10
831 **137** 2c. on 1c. green 10 10
832 – 3c. on 1c. blue and black (No. 551) 10 10
833 **137** 3c. on 1c. green 10 10
834 – 16c. on 1c. bl & blk (551) 15 15
835 **135** 16c. on 1c. bl, yell & blk 15 15
836 **137** 16c. on 1c. green 15 15
837 – 16c. on 1c. mult (O602) 15 15
838 – 16c. on 1c. violet (662) . . 15 15
839 **170** 18c. on 10c. mult 20 15
840 – 18c. on 12c. mult (818) . . 20 15
841 **171** 18c. on 8c. mult 20 15
842 **169** 18c. on 10c. mult 20 15
843 – 50c. on 30c. mult (814) . . 55 45
844 **137** 1l. on 2l. mauve . . . . 1·40 1·00
845 – 1l. on 2l. violet (No. 481) 1·40 1·00
846 – 1l. on 50c. blue (610) . . 1·40 1·00
847 – 1l. on 30c. mult (814) . . 90 70

1974. Air. Honduras' Children's Villages. 25th Anniv. Nos. 786/9 optd **1949-1974 SOS Kinderdorfer Internacional Honduras-Austria**.
851 **169** 10c. multicoloured 15 10
852 – 15c. multicoloured 20 15
853 – 30c. multicoloured 25 15
854 – 40c. multicoloured 35 25

175 Flags of West Germany and Austria

1975. Air. Centenary (1974) of U.P.U. Mult.
855 1c. Type **175** 10 10
856 2c. Belgium and Denmark . . 10 10
857 3c. Spain and France 10 10
858 4c. Hungary and Russia . . . 10 10
859 5c. Great Britain and Italy 10 10
860 10c. Norway and Sweden . . 20 10
861 12c. Honduras 25 15
862 15c. United States and Switzerland 35 20
863 20c. Greece and Portugal . . 35 20
864 30c. Rumania and Yugoslavia 55 25
865 1l. Egypt and Netherlands . . 1·75 1·50
866 2l. Luxembourg and Turkey 3·00 3·00

176 Jalteva Youth Centre

1976. Air. International Women's Year (1975). Multicoloured.
868 8c. Humuya Youth Centre 10 10
869 16c. Type **176** 20 10
870 18c. Sra Arellano and I.W.Y. emblem 20 15
871 30c. El Carmen Youth Centre, San Pedro Sula . . 35 20
872 55c. Flag of National Social Welfare Organization (vert) 55 35
873 1l. Sports and recreation grounds, La Isla . . . . . 1·10 65
874 2l. Women's Social Centre . . 1·75 1·75

177 "CARE" Package

1976. Air. 20th Anniv of "CARE" (Co-operative for American Relief Everywhere) in Honduras.
875 **177** 1c. blue and black 10 10
876 – 5c. mauve and black . . . 10 10
877 **177** 16c. red and black 20 10
878 – 18c. green and black . . . 25 10
879 **177** 30c. blue and black . . . 35 20
880 – 50c. green and black . . . 55 30
881 **177** 55c. brown and black . . 55 30
882 – 70c. purple and black . . 70 45
883 **177** 1l. blue and black . . . . 1·10 65
884 – 2l. orange and black . . . 1·75 1·75
DESIGN—HORIZ: 5c., 18c., 50c., 70c., 2l. "CARE" on globe.
Each of the above stamps has a different inscription detailing "CARE's" various fields of activities in Honduras.

178 White-tailed Deer in Burnt Forest

179 Boston Tea Party and "Liberty" Flag

1976. Air. Forest Protection. Multicoloured.
885 10c. Type **178** 15 10
886 16c. COHDEFOR emblem 15 10
887 18c. Forest stream (horiz) . . 15 15
888 30c. Live and burning trees 35 20
889 50c. Type **178** 80 30
890 70c. Protection emblem . . . 70 45
891 1l. Forest of young trees (horiz) . . . . 1·10 65
892 2l. As 30c. . . . . 1·75 1·75
COHDEFOR = Corporacion Hondurena de Desarollo Forestal.

1976. Air. Bicentenary of American Revolution. Multicoloured.
894 1c. Type **179** 10 10
895 2c. Hoisting the "Liberty and Union" flag 10 10
896 3c. Battle of Bunker Hill and Pine Tree flag 10 10
897 4c. Loading stores aboard "Washington" and "An Appeal to Heaven" flag . . 10 10
898 5c. First naval ensign and navy warship 30 15
899 6c. Presidential Palace, Tegucigalpa, and Honduras flag 10 10
900 18c. Capitol, Washington and U.S. flag 35 30
901 55c. Washington at Valley Forge and Grand Union flag 70 40
902 2l. Battle scene and Bennington flag . . . . . 1·75 1·50
903 3l. Betsy Ross flag . . . . . 3·00 3·00

180 Queen Sophia of Spain

181 Mayan Stelae

1977. Air. Visit of King and Queen of Spain. Multicoloured.
905 16c. Type **180** 15 10
906 18c. King Juan Carlos . . . 15 10
907 30c. Queen Sophia and King Juan Carlos 25 20
908 2l. Arms of Honduras and Spain (horiz) . . . . . . 1·40 1·40

1978. Air. "Honduras 78". Stamp Exhibition. Multicoloured.
909 15c. Type **181** 20 10
910 18c. Giant head 25 15
911 30c. Kneeling figure 35 20
912 55c. Sun God 70 60

182 Del Valle's Birthplace

1978. Air. Birth Bicentenary of Jose Cecelio del Valle. Multicoloured.
914 8c. Type **182** 10 10
915 14c. La Merced Church, Choluteca 15 10
916 15c. Baptismal font (vert) . . 15 10
917 20c. Reading Independence Act 25 15
918 25c. Portrait, documents and map of Central America 30 15
919 40c. Portrait (vert) 45 35
920 1l. Monument, Choluteca (vert) . . . . 1·10 90
921 3l. Bust (vert) . . . . 3·00 3·00

183 Rural Heath Centre

1978. Air. 75th Anniv (1977) of Panamerican Health Organization. Multicoloured.
922 5c. Type **183** 10 10
923 6c. Child at water tap 10 10
924 10c. Los Laureles Dam, Tegucigalpa 10 10
925 20c. Rural aqueduct 25 10
926 40c. Teaching hospital, Tegucigalpa 55 30
927 2l. Parents and child . . . . 1·75 1·75
928 3l. Vaccination of child . . . 3·00 3·00
929 5l. Panamerican Health Organization Building, Washington . . . . 4·50 4·50

184 Luis Landa and "Botanica"

1978. Air. Birth Centenary of Professor Luis Landa (botanist). Multicoloured.
930 14c. Type **184** 20 15
931 16c. Map of Honduras . . . 20 15
932 18c. Medals received by Landa 20 15
933 30c. Birthplace, San Ignacio 20 15
934 2l. "Brassavola" (national flower) . . . . 2·00 1·75
935 3l. Women's normal school 3·00 3·00

1978. Air. Argentina's Victory in World Cup Football Championship. Nos. 909/12 optd with **Argentina Campeon Holanda sub-Campeon XI Campeonato Mundial de Football** and emblem.
936 **181** 15c. multicoloured 10 10
937 – 18c. multicoloured 15 15
938 – 30c. multicoloured 30 20
939 – 55c. multicoloured 55 30

186 Central University

1978. Air. 400th Anniv of Founding of Tegucigalpa.
941 **186** 6c. brown and black . . . 10 10
942 – 6c. multicoloured 10 10
943 – 8c. brown and black . . . 10 10
944 – 8c. multicoloured 10 10
945 – 10c. brown and black . . 10 10
946 – 10c. multicoloured 10 10
947 – 16c. brown and black . . 20 10
948 – 16c. multicoloured 20 10
949 – 20c. brown and black . . 20 15
950 – 20c. multicoloured 20 15
951 – 40c. brown and black . . 45 25
952 – 40c. multicoloured 45 25
953 – 50c. brown and black . . 55 35
954 – 50c. multicoloured 55 35
955 – 5l. brown and black . . . 4·50 4·50
956 – 5l. multicoloured . . . . 4·50 4·50
DESIGNS—HORIZ: No. 942, University City; No. 943, Manuel Bonilla Theatre; No. 944, Present Manuel Bonilla Theatre; No. 947, National Palace; No. 948, Presidential House; No. 949, General San Felipe Hospital; No. 950, Teaching Hospital; No. 951, Parish Church and Convent of San Francisco; No. 952, Metropolitan Cathedral; No. 953, Old view of Tegucigalpa; No. 954, Modern view of Tegucigalpa. VERT: No. 945, Court House; No. 946, North Boulevard highway intersection; No. 955, Arms of San Miguel de Tegucigalpa; No. 956, President Marco Aurelio Soto.

187 Footballers jumping for Ball

1978. Air. 7th Youth Football Championship of Central American Football League. Multicoloured.
958 15c. Type **187** 20 10
959 30c. Goalkeeper (horiz) . . . 35 15
960 55c. Tackling 55 30
961 1l. Goalkeeper and players (horiz) . . . . 1·10 90
962 2l. Players at goalmouth (horiz) . . . . 1·75 1·75

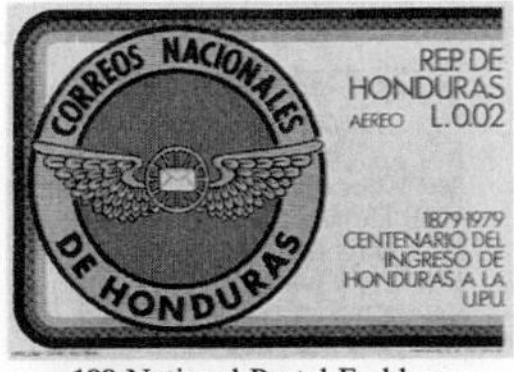

188 National Postal Emblem

1979. Air. Centenary of Honduras's U.P.U. Membership (1st issue). Multicoloured.
963 2c. Type **188** 10 10
964 15c. U.P.U. emblem 15 10
965 25c. Roman Rosa (vert) . . . 20 15
966 50c. Marco Aurelio Soto (vert) 35 30
See also Nos. 975/6.

189 Rotary Emblem and "50"

1979. Air. 50th Anniv of Tegucigalpa Rotary Club.
967 **189** 3c. orange, turquoise & bis 10 10
968 5c. green, emerald & bistre 10 10
969 50c. ochre, mauve & bistre 35 30
970 2l. blue, violet and bistre 1·40 1·00

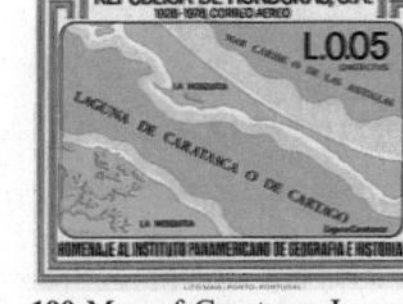

190 Map of Caratasca Lagoon

1979. Air. 50th Anniv of Pan-American Institute of History and Geography. Multicoloured.

971	5c. Type **190**	10	10
972	10c. Aerial view of Fort San Fernando de Omoa	10	10
973	24c. Institute anniversary emblem (vert)	20	15
974	5l. Map of Santanilla Islands	3·00	3·00

191 Model of New General Post Office Building

1980. Air. Centenary (1979) of U.P.U. Membership (2nd issue).

975 **191**	24c. multicoloured	20	15
976 –	3l. brown, yellow & black	1·75	1·75

DESIGN: 3l. 19th century Post Office.

192 "Landscape" (Roman E. Cooper)

1980. Air. International Year of the Child (1979). Multicoloured.

977	1c. "Workers in a Field (J. E. Mejia) (horiz)	10	10
978	5c. Type **192**	10	10
979	15c. "Sitting boy" (D. M. Zavala)	20	10
980	20c. I.Y.C. emblem	35	15
981	30c. "Beach scene" (M. A. Hernandez) (horiz)	45	20

193 Hill and "Maltese Cross" Cancellations

1980. Air. Death Centenary (1979) of Sir Rowland Hill. Multicoloured.

983	1c. Type **193**	10	10
984	2c. Great Britain "Penny Black"	10	10
985	5c. 1866 Honduras 2r. green	15	10
986	10c. 1866 Honduras 2r. rose	20	15
987	15c. Honduras postal emblem	35	15
988	20c. Flags of Honduras and United Kingdom	75	40

Nos. 987/8 are 46 × 34 mm.

194 Visitacion Padilla (founder of Honduras section)

1981. Air. 50th Anniv of Inter-American Women's Commission. Multicoloured.

990	2c. Type **194**	10	10
991	10c. Maria Trinidad del Cid (founder of Honduras section)	15	10
992	40c. Intubucana Indian mother and child	50	30
993	1l. Emblem (horiz)	65	65

195 "O'Higgins during the Liberation of Chile" (Cosmo San Martin)

1981. Air. Bernardo O'Higgins Commemoration. Multicoloured.

994	16c. Type **195**	15	10
995	20c. Don Ambrosio O'Higgins (father) (vert)	20	15
996	30c. "Bernardo O'Higgins" (Jose Gil de Castro) (vert)	35	20
997	1l. "Bernardo O'Higgins laying-down Office" (M. Antonio Caro)	70	70

196 National Sports Emblem

1981. Air. World Cup Football Championship Preliminary Round. Multicoloured.

998	20c. Type **196**	15	15
999	50c. Footballer and map of Honduras	30	30
1000	70c. Flags of Honduras, CONCACAF and FIFA	40	40
1001	1l. National stadium	60	60

197 Curtiss Condor II Biplane

1983. Air. 50th Anniv of Honduras Air Force. Multicoloured.

1003	3c. Type **197**	10	10
1004	15c. North America Texan	35	15
1005	25c. Chance Vought F4U-5 Corsair	40	25
1006	65c. Douglas C-47 Skytrain	85	65
1007	1l. Cessna Dragonfly	90	65
1008	2l. Dassault Super Mystere SMB-11	1·90	1·25

198 U.P.U. Monument, Berne

1983. Air. Election to U.P.U. Executive Council (1979). Multicoloured.

1010	16c. Type **198**	20	15
1011	18c. 18th U.P.U. Congress emblem	25	15
1012	30c. Honduras's postal emblem	20	20
1013	55c. View of Rio de Janeiro	45	45
1014	2l. "Stamp" showing pigeon on globe (vert)	1·25	1·25

199 I.Y.D.P. Emblem

1983. Air. International Year of Disabled Persons.

1016 **199**	25c. multicoloured	40	25

200 National Library, Tegucigalpa

1983. Air. Centenary (1980) of National Library and Archives. Multicoloured.

1017	9c. Type **200**	10	10
1018	1l. Books	60	60

1983. Air. Papal Visit. Nos. 951/2 optd **CONMEMORATIVA DE LA VISITA DE SS. JUAN PABLO II 8 de marzo de 1983.**

1019	40c. brown and black	35	35
1020	40c. multicoloured	35	35

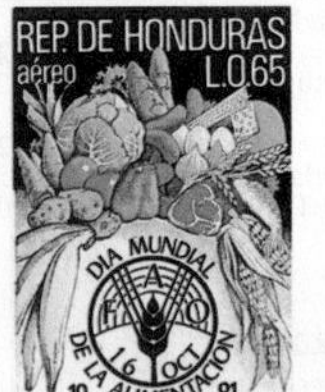

202 Agricultural Produce

203 Hands reaching for Open Book

1983. Air. World Food Day (1981).

1021 **202**	65c. multicoloured	40	40

1983. Air. Literacy Campaign (1980). Mult.

1022	40c. Type **203**	25	20
1023	1l.50 Family with books	90	90

204 Motorway Bridge over River Comayagua

1983. 20th Anniv of Inter-American Development Bank. Multicoloured.

1024	1l. Type **204**	60	55
1025	2l. Luis Borgran Technical Institute	1·25	1·00

205 Arms

206 Hand, Dove and Map on Globe

1984. Air. 2nd Anniv of Return of Constitutional Government. Multicoloured.

1026	20c. Type **205**	40	20
1027	20c. President Roberto Suazo Cordova	40	20

1984. "Internationalization of Peace".

1028 **206**	78c. black, blue and green	75	45
1029	85c. black, orange & grn	80	50
1030	95c. black, orange & grn	90	55
1031	1l.50 black, red & green	1·25	75
1032	2l. black, lt grn & green	1·50	1·00
1033	5l. black, purple & green	3·25	2·40

207 Front Page of "La Gaceta"

1984. Air. 150th Anniv of "La Gaceta".

1034 **207**	10c. brown, black & grn	10	10
1035	20c. brown, black & sepia	20	15

1986. Various stamps surch.

1036 **184**	60c. on 14c. mult (postage)	40	25
1037 **177**	5c. on 1c. blue and black (air)	10	10
1038 –	10c. on 8c. mult (No. 868)	10	10
1039 **176**	20c. on 16c. mult	15	10
1040 –	50c. on 14c. mult (No. 915)	35	15
1041 –	85c. on 6c. mult (No. 942)	50	30
1042 **186**	85c. on 6c. brown & blk	50	30
1043 –	95c. on 6c. brown & blk	70	40
1044 –	95c. on 6c. mult (No. 942)	70	40
1045 **177**	1l. on 1c. blue and black	70	40

1986. Air. "Exfilhon '86" Stamp Exhibition and World Cup Winners. Nos. 951/2 optd.

1046	40c. **"EXFILHON '86"/ ARGENTINA CAMPEON/ MEXICO'86** (951)	25	15
1047	40c. **"EXFILHON '86"/ ALEMANIA FEDERAL Sub Campeon/ MEXICO'86** (952)	25	15
1048	40c. **"EXFILHON '86"/ "FRANCIA TERCER LUGAR"/ MEXICO'86** (952)	25	15
1049	40c. **"EXFILHON '86"/ "BELGICA–CUARTO LUGAR"/ MEXICO'86** (951)	25	15

210 Phulapanzak

211 Pres. Jose Azcona and Flag

1986. Air. Tourism. Multicoloured.

1050	20c. Type **210**	15	10
1051	78c. Aerial view of Bahia Island beach and jetty (horiz)	45	25
1052	85c. Yacht off Bahia Islands (horiz)	1·50	60
1053	95c. Yojoa lake	60	35
1054	1l. Woman painting pottery	60	35

1987. Air. 1st Anniv of Democratic Government.

1056 **211**	20c. multicoloured	15	10
1057	85c. multicoloured	50	30

212 Edward Warner Award Medal

213 "Eupatorium cyrillinelsonii"

1987. 25th Anniv (1985) of Central American Air Navigation Services Association. Mult.

1058	2c. Type **212**	10	10
1059	5c. Flags of member countries (horiz)	10	10
1060	60c. Transmission mast, arrows and airplane (horiz)	50	20
1061	75c. Emblem	45	25
1062	1l. Members' flags and emblem (horiz)	60	35

1987. Air. Flowering Plants. Multicoloured.

1064	10c. Type **213**	10	10
1065	20c. "Salvia ernestivargasii"	15	10
1066	95c. "Robinsonella erasmi-sosae"	60	35

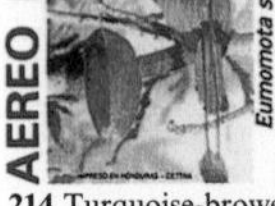

214 Turquoise-browed Motmot

216 Emblem

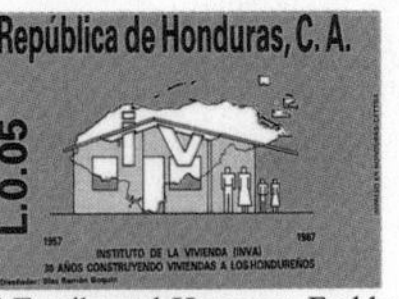

215 Family and House on Emblem

1987. Air. Birds. Multicoloured.

1067	50c. Type **214**	2·40	35
1068	60c. Keel-billed toucan	3·00	40
1069	85c. Yellow-headed amazon	4·50	60

1987. 30th Anniv of Housing Institute.

1070 **215**	5c. multicoloured	10	10
1071 –	95c. black, brown & blue	60	35

DESIGN: 95c. Emblem.

1987. Air. 30th Anniv of Honduras National Autonomous University.

1072 **216**	1l. red, black and yellow	60	35

217 Emblem

218 Emblem of President

1987. Air. 50th Anniv of Honduras Red Cross.
1073 **217** 20c. red and blue 15 10

1988. Air. 17th Lions International Latin-American and Caribbean Forum, Honduras.
1074 **218** 95c. blue and yellow . . 60 35

219 1913 Headquarters Building, La Ceiba

1988. Air. 75th Anniv of Banco Atlantida.
1075 10c. Type **219** 10 10
1076 85c. Present headquarters building, Tegucigalpa . . 50 30

1988. Nos. 941/4 surch.
1078 5c. on 6c. brown and black 10 10
1079 5c. on 6c. multicoloured . . 10 10
1080 20c. on 8c. brown and black 10 10
1081 20c. on 8c. multicoloured . . 10 10

221 Postal Messenger

222 Athletes

1988. Air. "Exfilhon 88" Stamp Exhibition, Honduras.
1082 **221** 85c. brown 50 30
1083 – 2l. brown and red . . . 1·10 60
DESIGN: 2l. Handstamp on cover.

1988. Air. Olympic Games, Seoul.
1085 **222** 85c. black, yellow & mve 50 30
1086 – 1l. yellow, black & orge 60 35
DESIGN: 1l. Ball games equipment.

223 Three-legged Tub

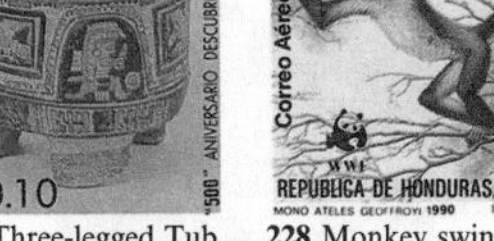

228 Monkey swinging through Trees

1988. Air. 500th Anniv (1992) of Discovery of America by Christopher Columbus. Mult.
1088 10c. Type **223** 10 10
1089 25c. Bowl (horiz) 15 10
1090 30c. Dish with legs shaped as animal heads (horiz) 20 15
1091 50c. Jug 35 20

1989. Air. Various stamps surch.
1093 – 10c. on 16c. brown and black (No. 947) . . . 10 10
1094 – 10c. on 16c. mult (No. 948) 10 10
1095 – 15c. on 6c. mult (No. 923) 10 10
1096 **195** 20c. on 16c. mult 10 10
1097 **176** 50c. on 16c. mult 10 10
1098 – 95c. on 18c. mult (No. 910) 20 15
1099 – 1l. on 16c. mult (No. 836) 20 15

1990. Air. 4th Central American Games. Nos. 887 and 878 surch **IV Juegos Olimpicos Centroamericanos** and value.
1101 75c. on 18c. multicoloured 15 10
1102 85c. on 18c. green and black 20 15

1990. Air. Nos. 915 and 870 surch **L. 0.20**.
1103 20c. on 14c. multicoloured 10 10
1104 20c. on 18c. multicoloured 10 10

1990. Air. 50th Anniv (1989) of I.H.C.I. Nos. 930 and 915 surch **"50 Aniversario IHCI" 1939–1989** and new value.
1105 **184** 20c. on 14c. mult 10 10
1106 – 1l. on 14c. multicoloured 20 15

1990. Air. The Black-handed Spider Monkey. Multicoloured.
1107 10c. Type **228** 10 10
1108 10c. Mother and baby . . . 10 10
1109 20c. Monkey swinging through trees (different) 10 10
1110 20c. Mother and baby (different) 10 10

1990. Air. World Cup Football Championship, Italy. No. 960 surch **ITALIA '90 L.1.00**.
1111 1l. on 55c. multicoloured . . 20 15

230 Institute Building

1990. Air Centenary of Luis Bogran Technical Institute, Tegucigalpa.
1113 **230** 20c. red, black and green 10 10
1114 – 85c. multicoloured . . . 20 15
DESIGN: 85c. Cogwheel, globe and Institute emblem.

231 Emblem

232 "Santa Maria", Shoreline, Fish and Fruit

1990. Air. 45th Anniv of F.A.O.
1116 **231** 95c. multicoloured . . . 20 15

1990. America. The Natural World. Mult.
1117 20c. Type **232** 30 10
1118 1l. Maize, fish, fruit and palm (horiz) 20 15

233 Congress Emblem

1990. Air. 30th Anniv and 17th Congress of Inter-American Construction Industry Federation.
1119 **233** 20c. black and green . . 10 10
1120 – 1l. black and blue . . . 20 15
DESIGN—HORIZ: 1l. Jose Cecilio del Valle Palace, Tegucigalpa (Ministry of Foreign Relations).

234 Virgin and Child with Apostles

1990. Air. Christmas. Multicoloured.
1121 20c. Type **234** 10 10
1122 95c. Virgin and Child (vert) 20 15

235 St. John Bosco (founder) (after Mario Caffaro Roke)

1990. Air. 80th Anniv of Salesian Brothers in Honduras. Multicoloured.
1124 75c. Type **235** 15 10
1125 1l. Bosco and National Youth Sanctuary, Tegucigalpa 20 15

L0.30
AEREO
HONDURAS
Primer Año de Gobierno
Lic Rafael Leonardo Callejas

236 Pres. Callejas

1991. Air. 1st Anniv of Presidency of Rafael Leonardo Callejas. Multicoloured.
1126 30c. Type **236** 10 10
1127 2l. Pres. Callejas wearing sash 45 25

237 "Strymon melinus"

1991. Air. Butterflies. Multicoloured.
1128 85c. Type **237** 15 10
1129 90c. "Diorina sp." 20 15
1130 1l.50 "Hyalophora cecropia" 30 20

238 "Rhyncholaelia glauca"

1991. Air. Orchids. Multicoloured.
1132 30c. Type **238** 10 10
1133 50c. "Oncidium splendidum" (vert) . . . 10 10
1134 95c. "Laelia anceps (vert) 20 10
1135 1l.50 "Cattleya skinneri" . . 30 20

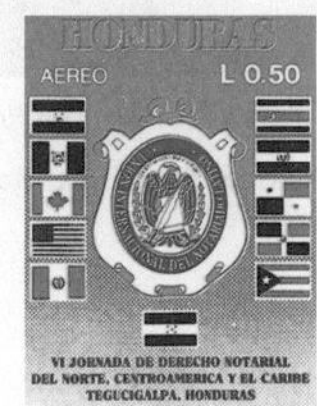

239 International Latin Lawyers Union Emblem and Flags

1991. Air. 6th Caribbean and North and Central American Lawyers' Day.
1136 **239** 50c. multicoloured . . . 10 10

241 Emblem, Flags and Carving

1991. Air. 25th Anniv of Italian–Latin American Institute.
1138 **241** 1l. multicoloured 20 10

242 Meeting of Old and New Worlds

1991. Air. "Espamer '91" Spain–Latin America Stamp Exhibition, Buenos Aires.
1139 **242** 2l. multicoloured 45 30

243 Valle

1991. Air. Birth Centenary of Rafael Heliodoro Valle.
1141 **243** 2l. black and red 45 30

244 Show Jumping

1991. Air. 11th Pan-American Games, Havana. Multicoloured.
1142 30c. Type **244** 10 10
1143 85c. Judo 20 10
1144 95c. Swimming 20 10

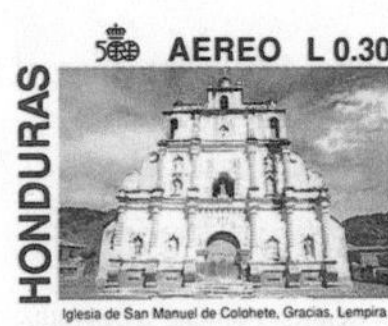

245 St Manuel de Colohete's Church, Gracias, Lempira

1991. Air. Churches. Multicoloured.
1146 30c. Type **245** 10 10
1147 95c. Church of Mercy, Gracias, Lempira 20 10
1148 1l. Comayagua Cathedral 20 10

246 Stone Carving and Cobs of Corn

1991. Air. America. Pre-Columbian Civilizations. Multicoloured.
1149 25c. Type **246** 10 10
1150 40c. Stone carving, dried corn and map 10 10
1151 1l.50 Stone carving and map of Honduras 30 20

247 Means of Control

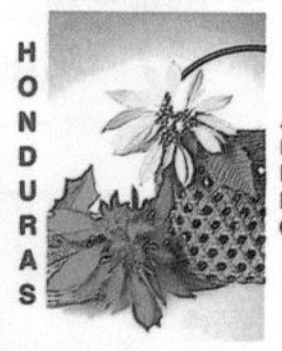

248 Poinsettias in Basket

1991. Air. 4th International Congress on Pest Control. Multicoloured.
1152 30c. Type **247** 10 10
1153 75c. Hoeing crop (scientific co-operation) 15 10
1154 1l. Co-operation of scientists and producers 20 10

1991. Christmas. Multicoloured.
1156 1l. Type **248** 20 10
1157 2l. Poinsettia in chicken-shaped pot 45 30

249 "Taking Possession of the New Continent" (Enrique Escher)

1992. Air. 75th Anniv of Savings Bank of Honduras. Multicoloured.

1158 85c. Type **249** 25 15

1159 1l. "First Celebration of Mass in the Americas" (Maury Flores) 45 15

250 Presidents Callejas and Cossiga of Italy

1992. Air. 2nd Year in Office of President Rafael Leonardo Callejas. Multicoloured.

1161 20c. Type **250** 10 10

1162 2l. Callejas with Pope . . . 40 25

251 View From Crow's Nest

252 Skiing

1992. Air. America 1991. 500th Anniv of Discovery of America. Multicoloured.

1163 90c. Type **251** 15 10

1164 1l. Fleet 30 10

1165 2l. Ship approaching island 50 25

1992. Winter Olympic Games, Albertville. Mult.

1166 50c. Type **252** 10 10

1167 3l. Jenny Palacios de Stillo (cross-country skier) . . . 60 40

253 Athletics

254 "Seller" (Manuel Rodriguez)

1992. Olympic Games, Barcelona. Mult.

1168 20c. Type **253** 10 10

1169 50c. Tennis 10 10

1170 85c. Football 15 10

1992. Mother's Day. Paintings. Multicoloured.

1171 20c. Type **254** 10 10

1172 50c. "Grandmother and Baby" (Manuel Rodriguez) 10 10

1173 5l. "Sellers" (Maury Flores) 95 60

255 "Chlosyne janais"

1992. Butterflies. Multicoloured.

1174 25c. Type **255** 10 10

1175 85c. "Agrilus vanillae" . . . 15 10

1176 3l. "Morpho granadensis" 60 40

256 "Bougainvillea glabra" "Napoleon"

1992. Air. Flowers. Multicoloured.

1178 20c. Type **256** 10 10

1179 30c. "Canna indica" 10 10

1180 75c. "Epiphyllum sp." . . . 15 10

1181 95c. "Sobralia macrantha" 20 10

257 Dam

258 Crops

1992. Air. General Francisco Morazan Hydroelectric Project. Multicoloured.

1182 85c. Type **257** 15 10

1183 4l. Inner view of dam (horiz) 75 45

1992. Air. 50th Anniv of Inter-American Institute for Agricultural Co-operation.

1184 **258** 95c. multicoloured (white background) 20 10

1185 95c. multicoloured (black background) 20 10

259 "Huancasco" (Arturo Lopez Rodezno)

260 Morazan on Horseback (after Francisco Cisneros)

1992. Air. Children's Day. Multicoloured.

1186 25c. Type **259** 10 10

1187 95c. "Bougainvillea" (Enrique Escher) 20 10

1188 2l. "Melissa" (Cesar Ordonez) 40 25

1992. Air. Birth Bicentenary of General Francisco Morazan. Multicoloured.

1189 5c. Type **260** 10 10

1190 10c. Statue of Morazan, Ampala 10 10

1191 50c. Morazan's watch and sword (horiz) 10 10

1192 95c. Josefa Lastiri de Morazan (wife) 20 10

261 Globe as Pot filled with Food

1992. Air. Int Nutrition Conference, Rome.

1194 **261** 1l.05 multicoloured . . . 20 10

262 Cinnamon Hummingbird

1992. Air. "Exfilhon '92" National Stamp Exhibition, Tegucigalpa. Multicoloured.

1195 1l.50 Type **262** . . . . . . 2·25 20

1196 2l.45 Scarlet macaw . . . . 3·25 30

263 Bee-keeping

1992. Air. 50th Anniv of Pan-American School of Agriculture. Multicoloured.

1198 20c. Type **263** 10 10

1199 85c. Tending goats 15 10

1200 1l. Ploughing with oxen . . 20 10

1201 2l. Hoeing (vert) 40 25

264 Fruit, Locomotive, Clock and Bridge

1992. Air. Centenary of El Progreso (City).

1202 **264** 1l.55 multicoloured . . . 2·75 90

265 Amerindian Village

266 Columbus's Fleet and Landing Craft

1992. Air. America. 500th Anniv of Discovery of America by Columbus. Multicoloured.

1203 35c. Type **265** 10 10

1204 5l. Columbus's landing party meeting Amerindians . . 1·25 60

1992. Air. 500th Anniv of Discovery of America by Columbus. Details of "The First Mass" by Roque Zelaya. Multicoloured.

1205 95c. Type **266** 20 10

1206 1l. Mass (horiz) 20 10

1207 2l. View of village (horiz) . . 40 25

267 Road and Bridge

1992. Air. 1st Central America–Panama Highway Maintenance Congress, San Pedro Sula. Multicoloured.

1208 20c. Type **267** 10 10

1209 85c. Bulldozer 15 10

268 The Greasy Pole

1992. Air. Christmas. Multicoloured.

1210 20c. Type **268** 10 10

1211 85c. Crib, San Antonio de Flores (horiz) 15 10

269 Globes, Children and Emblem

1992. Air. 90th Anniv of Pan-American Health Organization.

1212 **269** 3l.95 multicoloured . . . 75 45

1992. Air. Nos. 894 and 899/900 surch.

1213 **179** 20c. on 1c. multicoloured 10 10

1214 – 20c. on 6c. multicoloured 10 10

1215 – 85c. on 18c. mult 15 10

271 Pres. Callejas at Ceremony

272 Mother and Child

1993. Air. 3rd Year of Rafael L. Callejas's Presidential Term and International Court of Justice's Decision on Border with El Salvador. Multicoloured.

1216 90c. Type **271** 15 10

1217 1l.05 Map (horiz) 20 10

1993. Air. Mother's Day. Multicoloured.

1218 50c. Type **272** 10 10

1219 95c. Mother and child (different) 20 10

273 American Manatee

1993. Air. Endangered Mammals. Mult.

1220 85c. Type **273** 15 10

1221 2l.45 Puma 50 30

1222 10l. Jaguar (vert) . . . . . 1·90 1·25

274 Scarlet Macaws

276 30r. "Bull's Eye" Stamp

1993. Air. National Symbols. Multicoloured.

1223 25c. Type **274** 10 10

1224 95c. White-tailed deer . . . 15 10

1993. Air. Various stamps surch.

1225 – 20c. on 3c. mult (No. 896) 10 10

1226 **189** 20c. on 3c. orange, blue and bistre 10 10

1227 **197** 20c. on 3c. multicoloured 10 10

1228 – 20c. on 8c. mult (No. 868) 10 10

1229 **182** 20c. on 8c. multicoloured 10 10

1230 **176** 50c. on 16c. mult 10 10

1231 **177** 50c. on 16c. red and black 10 10

1232 – 50c. on 16c. mult (No. 886) 10 10

1233 **180** 50c. on 16c. mult 10 10

1234 – 50c. on 16c. mult (No. 931) 10 10

1235 **195** 50c. on 16c. mult 10 10

1236 – 50c. on 18c. mult (No. 870) 10 10

1237 – 50c. on 18c. mult (No. 910) 10 10

1238 – 50c. on 18c. mauve and black (No. 1011) . . . 10 10

1239 – 85c. on 18c. green and black (No. 878) . . . 10 10

1240 – 85c. on 18c. mult (No. 906) 10 10

1241 – 85c. on 18c. mult (No. 932) 10 10

1242 – 85c. on 18c. mult (No. 937) 10 10

1243 – 85c. on 24c. mult (No. 973) 10 10

1244 **191** 85c. on 24c. mult 10 10

1993. Air. 150th Anniv of 1st Brazilian Stamps. Multicoloured.

1245 20c. Type **276** 10 10

1246 50c. 60r. "Bull's eye" stamp 10 10

1247 95c. 90r. "Bull's eye" stamp 15 10

277 Atlantida

1993. Air. Departments. Multicoloured.

1248 20c. Type **277** 10 10

1249 20c. Colon 10 10

1250 20c. Cortes 10 10

1251 20c. Choluteca 10 10

1252 20c. El Paraiso 10 10

1253 20c. Francisco Morazan . . 10 10

1254 50c. Comayagua (vert) . . . 10 10

1255 50c. Copan (vert) 10 10

1256 50c. Intibuca (vert) 10 10

1257 50c. Bahia Islands (vert) . . 10 10

1258 50c. Lempira (vert) 10 10

1259 50c. Ocotepeque (vert) . . . 10 10

1260 1l.50 La Paz 20 10

1261 1l.50 Olancho 20 10

1262 1l.50 Santa Barbara 20 10

1263 1l.50 Valle 20 10

1264 1l.50 Yoro 20 10

1265 1l.50 Gracias a Dios 20 10

278 Muscovy Duck

1993. Air. America. Endangered Birds. Mult.
1266 20c. Ornate hawk eagle (vert) 95 45
1267 80c. Type **278** 95 45
1268 2l. Harpy eagle . . . . . . 2·25 50

279 Painting by Julia Padilla

1993. Air. 40th Anniv of United Nations Development Programme.
1269 **279** 95c. multicoloured . . . 15 10

280 Church

281 Ramon Rosa

1993. Air. Christmas. Paintings by Aida Lara de Pedemonte. Multicoloured.
1270 20c. Type **280** 10 10
1271 85c. Flower vendor 10 10

1993. Air. Personalities. Multicoloured.
1272 25c. Type **281** 10 10
1273 65c. Jesus Aguilar Paz . . . 10 10
1274 85c. Augusto Coello 10 10

282 Grey Angelfish

1993. Air. Fishes. Multicoloured.
1275 20c. Type **282** 15 10
1276 85c. Queen angelfish 20 10
1277 3l. Banded butterflyfish . . 65 45

283 Norma Callejas planting Tree

284 Family with Rushes (Aida Lara de Pedemonte)

1994. Air. 4th Year of Rafael L. Callejas's Presidential Term. Multicoloured.
1278 95c. Type **283** 15 10
1279 1l. Pres. Callejas and Government House (horiz) 15 10

1994. International Year of the Family.
1280 **284** 1l. multicoloured 15 10

285 Dove and Maps on Globe

286 "Madonna and Child"

1994. Air. International Peace and Development in Central America Conference, Tegucigalpa.
1281 **285** 1l. multicoloured 15 10

1994. Air. Christmas. Paintings by Gelasio Gimenez. Multicoloured.
1282 95c. Type **286** 10 10
1283 1l. "Holy Family" 15 10

287 "Family Scene" (Delmer Mejia)

288 Pres. Reina

1995. Air. 50th Anniv of U.N.O. Mult.
1284 1l. "The Sowing: Ecological Family" (Elisa Dulcey) . . 15 10
1285 2l. Type **287** 25 15
1286 3l. Anniversary emblem . . 40 25

1995. Air. 1st Anniv of Presidency of Carlos Roberto Reina. Multicoloured.
1287 80c. Type **288** 10 10
1288 95c. Pres. Reina with arms raised (horiz) 10 10
1289 1l. Pres. Reina at summit conference (horiz) 15 10

289 Postman loading Mail Van

1995. Air. America. Postal Transport. Paintings by Ramiro Rodriguez Zelaya. Multicoloured.
1290 1l.50 Type **289** 20 10
1291 2l. Postman on motor cycle 25 15

290 "Boletellus russelli"

1995. Air. Fungi. Multicoloured.
1292 1l. "Marasmius cohaerens" (horiz) 45 15
1293 1l. Blue leg ("Lepista nuda") (horiz) 45 15
1294 1l. "Polyporus pargamenus" (horiz) 45 15
1295 1l. "Fomes sp." (horiz) . . 45 15
1296 1l. "Paneolus sphinctrinus" (horiz) 45 15
1297 1l. "Hygrophorus aurantiaca" (horiz) . . . 45 15
1298 1l.50 The blusher ("Amanita rubescens") 65 20
1299 1l.50 "Boletus frostii" . . . 65 20
1300 1l.50 "Fomes annosus" . . 65 20
1301 1l.50 "Psathyrella sp." . . . 65 20
1302 1l.50 Type **290** 65 20
1303 1l.50 "Marasmius spegazzinii" 65 20
1304 2l. "Amanita sp." 80 25
1305 2l. Golden tops ("Psilocybe cubensis") 80 25
1306 2l. Royal boletus ("Boletus regius") 80 25
1307 2l. Black trumpet ("Craterellus cornucopioides") 80 25
1308 2l. "Auricularia delicata" . . 80 25
1309 2l. "Clavariadelphus pistilaris" 80 25
1310 2l.50 "Scleroderma aurantium" (horiz) . . . 95 35
1311 2l.50 "Amanita praegraveolens" (horiz) 95 35
1312 2l.50 Chanterelle ("Cantharellus cibarius") (horiz) 95 35
1313 2l.50 "Geastrum triplex" (horiz) 95 35
1314 2l.50 "Russula emetica" (horiz) 95 35
1315 2l.50 "Boletus pinicola" (horiz) 95 35
1316 3l. "Fomes versicolor" (horiz) . . . . 1·25 40
1317 3l. "Cantharellus purpurascens" (horiz) . . 1·25 40
1318 3l. "Lyophyllum decastes" (horiz) . . . . 1·25 40
1319 3l. Oyster fungus ("Pleurotus ostreatus") (horiz) . . . . 1·25 40
1320 3l. "Boletus ananas" (horiz) 1·25 40
1321 3l. Caesar's mushroom ("Amanita caesarea") (horiz) . . . . 1·25 40

291 "Food for All"

1995. Air. 50th Anniv of F.A.O.
1322 **291** 3l. multicoloured 25 15

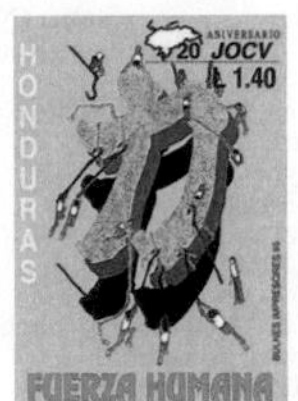

292 Family and Farm over Globe

1995. Air. 50th Anniv of CARE (Co-operative for Assistance and Remittances Overseas). Multicoloured.
1323 1l.40 Type **292** 15 10
1324 5l.40 Crop farming 55 35
1325 5l.40 Keel-billed toucan, orchid, planting tree and animals at waterfall . . . 55 35

294 People around Japanese Character

1995. 20th Anniv of Japanese Overseas Co-operation Voluntary Workers in Honduras. Multicoloured.
1327 1l.40 Type **294** (postage) . . 15 10
1328 4l.30 Amerindian-style figures on pages of leaflet (horiz) (air) 40 25
1329 5l.40 Volunteer and people in traditional costumes (horiz) 55 35

295 Scorpion Mud Turtle

1995. Air. America. Environmental Protection. Multicoloured.
1330 1l.40 Type **295** 15 10
1331 4l.54 "Alpinia purpurata" (flower) (vert) 45 30
1332 10l. Common caracara ("Caracara") (vert) . . . 1·00 65

296 "Agalychnis sp."

1995. Air. Reptiles and Amphibians. Mult.
1333 5l.40 Type **296** 55 35
1334 5l.40 Iguana 55 35

297 Bell

1995. Air. Christmas. Multicoloured.
1335 1l.40 Type **297** 15 10
1336 5l.40 Crib figures (horiz) . . . 55 35
1337 6l.90 Deer (carving) 70 45

298 "SICA" over Map

1996. Air. 3rd Anniv of Central American Integration System. Multicoloured.
1338 1l.40 Type **298** (signing of Protocol, 1991) 15 10
1339 4l.30 Emblem 40 25
1340 5l.40 Presidents of Central American countries at 17th Summit 55 35

299 Allegorical Design

1996. Air. United Nations Decade against Drug Abuse and Drug Trafficking. Multicoloured.
1341 1l.40 Type **299** 15 10
1342 5l.40 Woman's head with butterfly as hat (vert) . . 55 35
1343 10l. Guitar and bar of music 1·00 65

300 Traditional Headdress

1996. Air. Bicentenary of Arrival of Garifunas Tribe in Honduras. Multicoloured.
1344 1l.40 Type **300** 15 10
1345 5l.40 Tribesmen dancing to music (horiz) 55 35
1346 10l. Drums (horiz) . . . . 1·00 60

301 Steam Locomotive "San Jose"

1996. Air. "Exfilhon 96" National Stamp Exn, Tegucigalpa. Railway Locomotives. Mult.
1347 5l.40 Type **301** 95 55
1348 5l.40 Diesel railcar No. 203 95 55

302 Football

1996. Air. 6th Central American Games, San Pedro Sula (1997). Multicoloured.
1350 4l.30 Type **302** 40 25
1351 4l.54 Volleyball and games emblem 45 30
1352 5l.40 Games mascot (vert) 55 35

303 Honduran and International Badges

1996. Air. 75th Anniv of Honduran Scouts' Association. Multicoloured.
1353 2l.15 Type **303** 20 10
1354 5l.40 Anniversary emblem (vert) 50 30
1355 6l.90 Scout feeding deer (vert) 65 40

304 Poinsettia and Candles

1996. Air. Christmas. Multicoloured.
1356 1l.40 Type **304** 15 10
1357 3l. Poinsettia 25 15
1358 5l.40 As Type **304** but vert 50 30

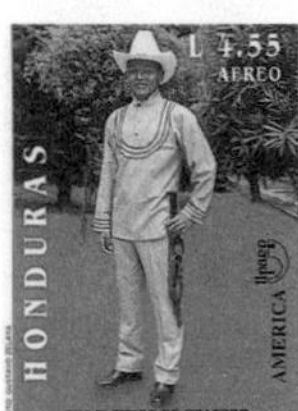

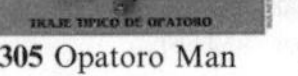

305 Opatoro Man **306** Children playing in River (Oscar Moncada)

1997. Air. America (1996). Traditional Costumes. Multicoloured.
1359 4l.55 Type **305** 40 25
1360 5l.40 Jocomico woman . . . 50 30
1361 10l. Intibuca couple 90 60

1997. Air. 20th Anniv of Honduran Plan and 60th Anniv of International Plan. Multicoloured.
1362 1l.40 Type **306** 15 10
1363 5l.40 Girl beside river (Nataly Alexandra Reyes) (horiz) 50 30
1364 9l.70 Street (Walter Enrique Martinez) (horiz) 90 60

307 Red-tailed Hawk **308** Von Stephan

1997. Birds. Multicoloured.
1365 1l.40 Type **307** (postage) . . 15 10
1366 1l.50 Keel-billed toucan . . 15 10
1367 2l. Red-billed whistling duck 20 10
1368 2l.15 Collared forest falcon 20 10
1369 3l. Common caracara . . . 25 15
1370 5l.40 King vulture (air) . . 50 30

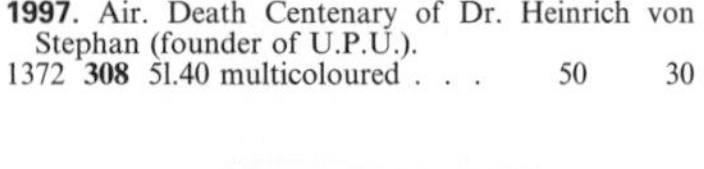

1997. Air. Death Centenary of Dr. Heinrich von Stephan (founder of U.P.U.).
1372 **308** 5l.40 multicoloured . . . 50 30

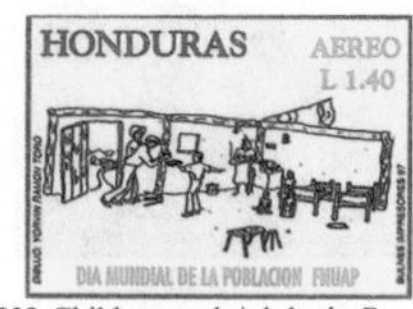

309 Children and Adults in Room (Yorvin Ramon Toro)

1997. Air. World Population Day. Mult.
1373 1l.40 Type **309** 15 10
1374 6l.90 Family group and house (Marvin Lamberth Harry) 65 40

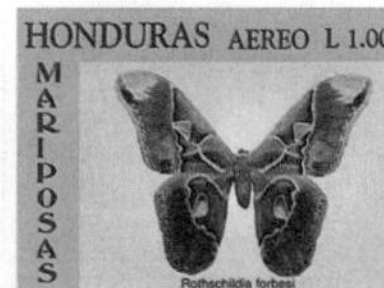

310 "Rothschildia forbesi"

1997. Air. Butterflies and Moths. Mult.
1375 1l. Type **310** 10 10
1376 1l.40 "Parides photinus" . . 15 10
1377 2l.15 Emperor 20 10
1378 3l. Jamaican kite swallowtail 25 15
1379 4l.30 "Parides iphidamas" 40 25
1380 5l.40 Monarch 50 30

311 St. Theresa **312** Observatory

1997. Air. Death Centenary of St. Theresa of Lisieux. Multicoloured.
1382 1l.40 Type **311** 10 10
1383 5l.40 St. Theresa (different) 45 30

1997. Air. 150th Anniv of National University and 40th Anniv of Free University. Multicoloured.
1384 1l.40 Type **312** 10 10
1385 5l.40 Statue of Fr. Jose Trinidad Reyes (founder) 45 30
1386 10l. Woman with book guiding boy 90 60

313 Diana, Princess of Wales **314** Children around Statue (Nelson Leonel Rodriguez)

1997. Air. Diana, Princess of Wales Commemoration. Multicoloured.
1387 1l.40 Type **313** 10 10
1388 5l.40 Visiting minefield (horiz) 45 30

1997. Air. 37th Anniv of Alcoholics Anonymous (rehabilitation organization).
1390 **314** 5l.40 multicoloured . . . 45 30

315 "Christ of Picacho" (statue) **316** Basketball

1997. Air. Christmas. Multicoloured.
1391 1l.40 Type **315** 10 10
1392 5l.50 "Virgin of Suyapa" . . 50 30

1997. Air. 6th Central American Games, San Pedro Sula. Multicoloured.
1393 1l.40 Type **316** 10 10
1394 1l.40 Baseball (batting) . . . 10 10
1395 1l.40 Football 10 10
1396 1l.40 Squash 10 10
1397 1l.40 Volleyball 10 10
1398 1l.40 Handball 10 10
1399 1l.40 Bowls 10 10
1400 1l.40 Table tennis 10 10
1401 1l.40 Rings on map of Honduras 10 10
1402 1l.40 Baseball (bowling) . . 10 10
1403 1l.50 Taekwondo (kicking) 15 10
1404 1l.50 Karate (one hand raised) 15 10
1405 1l.50 Judo (bowing) 15 10
1406 1l.50 Wrestling 15 10
1407 1l.50 Weightlifting 15 10
1408 1l.50 Boxing 15 10
1409 1l.50 Body-building 15 10
1410 1l.50 Fencing 15 10
1411 1l.50 Games emblem 15 10
1412 1l.50 Shooting 15 10
1413 2l.15 Cycling (on bicycle) . . 20 10
1414 2l.15 Road cycle racing (running beside bicycle) 20 10
1415 2l.15 Swimming 20 10
1416 2l.15 Water polo 20 10
1417 2l.15 Hurdling 20 10
1418 2l.15 Gymnastics (ring exercise) 20 10
1419 2l.15 Horse riding 20 10
1420 2l.15 Tennis 20 10
1421 2l.15 Pedrito Pichete (Games mascot) 20 10
1422 2l.15 Chess 20 10

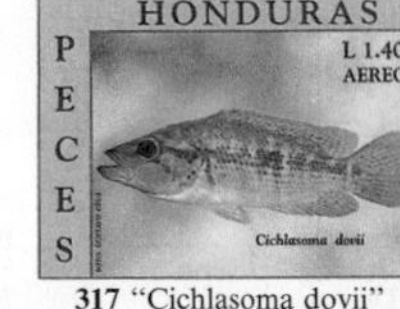

317 "Cichlasoma dovii"

1997. Air. Fishes. Multicoloured.
1423 1l.40 Type **317** 10 10
1424 2l. "Cichlasoma spilurum" (facing left) 20 10
1425 3l. "Cichlasoma spilurum" (facing right) 25 15
1426 5l.40 "Astyanay fasciatus" 45 30

318 Queen Triggerfish **320** Sculpted Skull from Temple 16

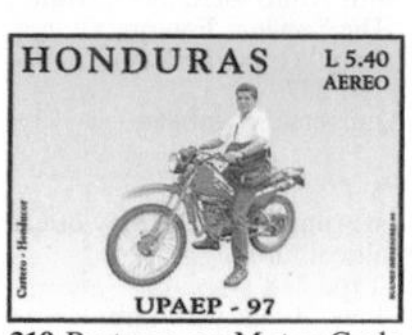

319 Postman on Motor Cycle

1998. Air. 50th Anniv of Bancahsa. Marine Life of Bahia Coral Reef. Multicoloured.
1427 2l.50 Type **318** 20 10
1428 2l.50 White grunt ("Haemulon plumieri") 20 10
1429 2l.50 French angelfish ("Pomacanthus paru") . . 20 10
1430 2l.50 Wrasse (juvenile) ("Halichoeres garnoti") 20 10
1431 2l.50 Grey angelfish (complete fish) ("Pomacanthus arcuatus") 20 10
1432 2l.50 Queen angelfish ("Holacanthus ciliaris") 20 10
1433 2l.50 Diver and "Pseud opterogorgia" (coral) . . 20 10
1434 2l.50 Diver's oxygen tank and "Pseud opterogorgia" 20 10
1435 2l.50 Six fingers of pillar coral ("Dendrogyra cylindrus") (inscr in Latin) 20 10
1436 2l.50 Squirrelfish facing right ("Holocentrus adscensionis") 20 10
1437 2l.50 Three fingers of pillar coral ("Dendrogyra cylindrus") (inscr in Latin) 20 10
1438 2l.50 "Stegastes fuscus" (fish) 20 10
1439 2l.50 "Gorgonia mariae" (coral) 20 10
1440 2l.50 Three fingers of pillar coral (inscr in English) . . 20 10
1441 2l.50 Head of grey angelfish ("Pomacanthus arcuatus") 20 10
1442 2l.50 Squirrelfish facing left ("Holocentrus adscensionis") 20 10
1443 2l.50 "Eusmilia fastigiata" (coral) 20 10
1444 2l.50 Midnight parrotfish ("Scarus coelestinus") . . 20 10
1445 2l.50 One finger of pillar coral (inscr in English) . . 20 10
1446 2l.50 Hogfish ("Lachnolaimus maximus") 20 10

Nos. 1427/46 were issued together, se-tenant, forming a composite design.

1998. Air. America (1997). Postal Service. Multicoloured.
1447 5l.40 Type **319** 45 30
1448 5l.40 Post Office 45 30

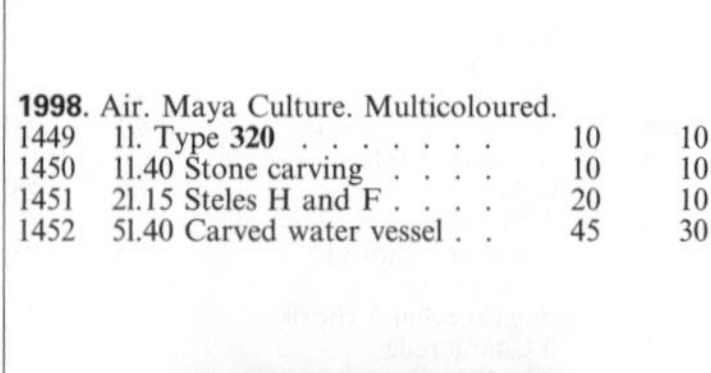

1998. Air. Maya Culture. Multicoloured.
1449 1l. Type **320** 10 10
1450 1l.40 Stone carving 10 10
1451 2l.15 Steles H and F 20 10
1452 5l.40 Carved water vessel . . 45 30

321 Players and Trophy

1998. Air. World Cup Football Championship, France. Multicoloured.
1454 5l.40 Type **321** 45 30
1455 10l. Players in tackle and trophy (vert) 90 60

322 Green Iguana

1998. Air. Reptiles. Multicoloured.
1457 1l.40 Type **322** 10 10
1458 2l. Eyelash viper 20 10
1459 3l. Green lizards 25 15
1460 5l.40 Coral snake 45 30

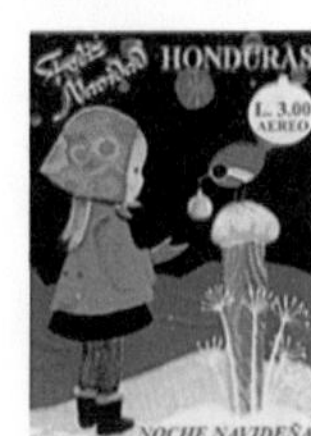

323 Robin giving Gift to Girl

1998. Air. Christmas. Multicoloured.
1462 3l. Type **323** 25 15
1463 5l.40 Child Jesus in crib (horiz) 45 30
1464 10l. Child leading donkey 85 55

324 Flores and his Wife greeting Pope

1999. Air. 1st Anniv of Inauguration of President Carlos Roberto Flores.
1465 5l.40 Type **324** 45 30
1466 10l. President and Mary Flores (vert) 85 55

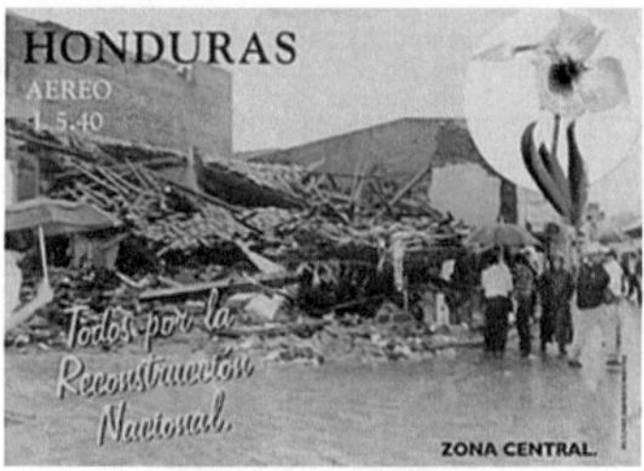

325 Floods, Central Zone

1999. Air. Hurricane Mitch Victims' Fund. Mult.
1467 5l.40 Type **325** 45 30
1468 5l.40 Man carrying boy on back through flood and black-tailed trogon . . . 45 30
1469 5l.40 Prince Felipe of Spain and Mary Flores (President's wife) 45 30
1470 5l.40 Child crying and orchid 45 30
1471 5l.40 People clearing timber in Comayaguela and orchid 45 30
1472 5l.40 People wading through flood in North Zone and spectacled owl 45 30
1473 5l.40 Destruction of La Hoya quarter, Tegucigalpa, and orchid 45 30
1474 5l.40 Soldier helping woman and child in North Zone and lance-tailed manakin 45 30
1475 5l.40 Collapsed houses in rural zone and orchids . . 45 30
1476 5l.40 Collapsed bridge and damaged motor cars ("Red Vial") and red-capped manakin 45 30
1477 5l.40 Damaged houses, motor cars and uprooted trees ("Red Vial") and orchids 45 30
1478 5l.40 Mexican soldiers with dogs and airplane 45 30
1479 5l.40 Two children swimming in North Zone and sinaloa martin . . . 45 30
1480 5l.40 Mary and President Flores with Hillary Clinton (wfe of U.S. President) 45 30
1481 5l.40 Crowd before collapsed building in South Zone and rufous motmot 45 30
1482 5l.40 President Flores and George Bush (U.S. President, 1988–92) . . . 45 30
1483 5l.40 Three men digging out rubble and tufted jay . . 45 30
1484 5l.40 Helicopter on beach and orchid 45 30

1485 5l.40 Car submerged under flood water in North Zone and bare-necked umbrellabird 45 30
1486 5l.40 Tipper Gore (U.S. Vice-president's wife) and Mary Flores in flooded building 45 30
1487 5l.40 Flooded banana plantation and orchid . . 45 30
1488 5l.40 Tegucigalpa submerged under flood water and red-breasted blackbird and green bird 45 30
1489 5l.40 Traffic jam behind rocks from landslide ("Red Vial") 45 30
1490 5l.40 Comayaguela and ridgway's cotinga 45 30
1491 5l.40 Destruction of Comayaguela street and orchid 45 30
1492 5l.40 People carrying plank in Eastern Zone and scarlet macaw 45 30
1493 5l.40 Mexican truck being filled with debris and orchid 45 30
1494 5l.40 Bulldozer clearing street and white-tipped sicklebill 45 30
1495 5l.40 President Flores and President Chirac of France 45 30
1496 5l.40 Comayaguela commercial zone flooded and tooth-billed hummingbird 45 30
1497 5l.40 People looking at flood water in Tegucigalpa and lineated woodpecker . . . 45 30
1498 5l.40 Stranded BMW motor car in Comayaguela street and hoffmann's conure 45 30

326 Pilar Salinas

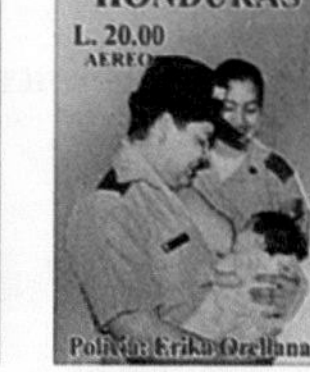

327 Enka Orellana breast-feeding Baby

1999. Air. America (1998). Famous Women. Mult.
1499 2l.60 Type **326** 20 10
1500 7l.30 Clementina Suarerz (poet) 65 40
1501 10l.65 Mary Flores (President's wife) 90 60

1999. Air. Mothers' Day. Multicoloured.
1502 20l. Type **327** . . . . . . 1·75 1·10
1503 30l. *Paphiopedilum urbanianum* (horiz) . . . 2·75 1·75
1504 50l. *Miltoniopsis vexillaria* (horiz) . . . . 4·50 3·00

1999. No. 748 surch.
1505 2l.60 on 1c. blue and red . . 25 15
1506 7l.85 on 1c. blue and red . . 75 50
1507 10l.65 on 1c. blue and red 1·00 65
1508 11l.55 on 1c. blue and red 1·10 65
1509 12l.45 on 1c. blue and red 1·10 65
1510 13l.85 on 1c. blue and red 1·25 80

329 Orange-fronted Conure

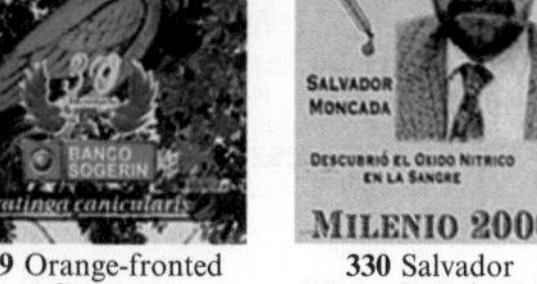

330 Salvador Moncada (scientist) and Pipette

1999. Air. 30th Anniv of Sogerin Bank. Birds. Mult.
1511 3l. Type **329** 30 10
1512 3l. White-fronted amazon (*Amazona albifrons*) . . . 30 10
1513 3l. Yellow-naped amazon (*Amazona auropalliata*) 30 10
1514 3l. Red-lored amazon (*Amazona autumnalis*) . . 30 10
1515 3l. Sun-bittern (*Eurypga helias*) 30 10
1516 3l. Great curassow (*Crax rubra*) 30 10
1517 3l. Orange-chinned parakeet (*Brotogeris jugularis*) . . 30 10
1518 3l. White-capped parrot (*Pionus senilis*) 30 10
1519 3l. Brown-throated conure (*Aratinga rubritorques*) 30 10
1520 3l. Great tinamou (*Tinamus major*) 30 10
1521 5l. King vulture (*Sarcorhamphus papa*) . . 45 30
1522 5l. White hawk (*Leucopternis albicollis*) 45 30
1523 5l. Harpy eagle (*Harpia harpyja*) 45 30
1524 5l. Spectacled owl (*Pulsatrix perspicillata*) 45 30
1525 5l. Ornate hawk eagle (*Spizaetus ornatus*) . . . 45 30
1526 5l. Resplendent quetzal (*Pharomachrus mocinno*) 45 30
1527 5l. Emerald toucanet (*Aulacorhynchus prasinus*) 45 30
1528 5l. Honduras emerald (*Amazilia luciae*) 45 30
1529 5l. Scarlet macaw (*Ara macao*) 45 30
1530 5l. Yucatan woodpecker (*Centuras pygmaeus*) . . . 45 30
1531 10l. Jabiru (*Jabiru mycteria*) (wrongly inscr "Jaberu") 90 60
1532 10l. Hook-billed kite (*Chondrohierax uncinatus*) 90 60
1533 10l. Resplendent quetzal (*Pharomachrus mocinno*) (different) 90 60
1534 10l. Keel-billed toucan (*Ramphastos sulfuratus*) 90 60

Nos. 1511/30 were issued together, se-tenant, forming a composite design.

1999. Air. New Millennium. Multicoloured.
1535 2l. Type **330** 20 10
1536 8l.65 Albert Einstein (scientist, formulator of Theory of Relativity, 1905) 80 50
1537 10l. Wilhelm Rontgen (scientist, discoverer of X-rays, 1895) 95 60
1538 14l.95 George Stephenson (engineer) (inventor of steam locomotive, 1829) and *Rocket* (horiz) . . . 1·40 90

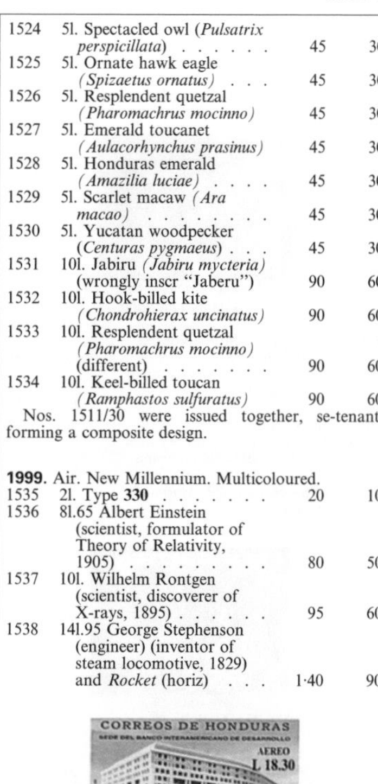

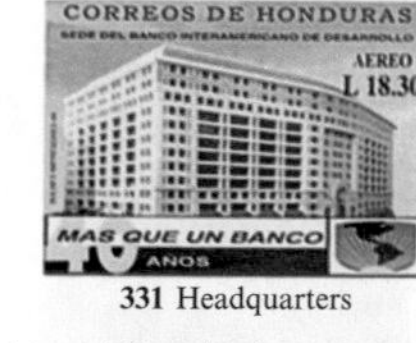

331 Headquarters

1999. Air. 40th Anniv of Inter-American Development Bank.
1539 **331** 18l.30 multicoloured . . 1·60 1·10

332 Josemaria Escriva de Balaguer (founder)

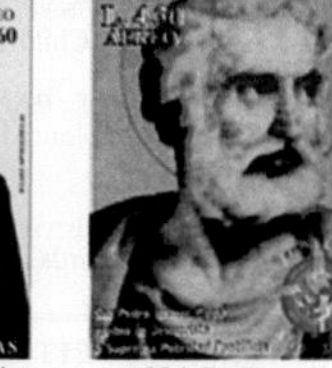

334 St. Peter

333 Statue and View of Cedros, Francisco Morazan Province

1999. Air. 70th Anniv (1998) of Founding of Opus Dei (religious organization).
1540 **332** 2l.60 multicoloured . . . 25 15
1541 16l.40 multicoloured . . 1·50 1·00

1999. Air. 175th Anniv of National Congress. Mult.
1542 4l.30 Type **333** 40 25
1543 10l. Rafael Pineda Ponce (Congress President) and building 90 60

2000. Holy Year 2000. Multicoloured.
1544 4l. Open gateway into garden 35 20
1545 4l.30 Type **334** 40 25
1546 4l.30 As Type **334**, but with country name and face value in yellow 40 25
1547 6l.90 Jesus (statue) and Jerusalem (horiz) 65 40
1548 7l.30 Pope John Paul II addressing crowd (horiz) 70 45
1549 10l. Pope John Paul II . . . 95 60
1550 14l. Pope John Paul II and Pres. Carlos Roberto Flores . . . . 1·25 80
1551 14l. As No. 1550 but with country name at right . . 1·25 80

335 Pres. Flores and Reunion Consultative Group, Stockholm, Sweden

2000. 2nd Anniv of Inauguration of President Carlos Roberto Flores. Multicoloured.
1552 10l. Type **335** 95 60
1553 10l.65 Flores and General Mario Hung Pacheco . . 1·00 65

336 Left Half of Marimba

2000. Air. Musical Instruments. Multicoloured.
1554 1l.40 Type **336** 15 10
1555 1l.40 Right half of Marimba 15 10
1556 1l.40 Ayotl 15 10
1557 2l.60 Maracas 25 15
1558 2l.60 Guiro 25 15
1559 2l.60 Chinchin 25 15
1560 2l.60 Raspador 25 15
1561 2l.60 Quijada de Caballo . . 25 15
1562 3l. Fish-shaped whistle . . . 25 15
1563 3l. Aztec drum 25 15
1564 3l. Whistle ("Pito Zoomorfo de un tono") 25 15
1565 3l. Whistle ("Pito Zoomorfo de dos tonos") 25 15
1566 3l. Tun 25 15
1567 4l. Tecomate 35 20
1568 4l. Deerskin drum 35 20
1569 4l. Guacalitos 35 20
1570 4l. Women standing to left of marimba 35 20
1571 4l. Men standing to right of marimba 35 20
1572 10l. Maya drum 90 55
1573 10l. Teponaxtle 90 55

337 Man

2000. 50th Anniv of Central Honduras Bank. Paintings by Pablo Zelaya Sierra. Multicoloured.
1575 1l.40 Type **337** 15 10
1576 1l.40 Dog barking 15 10
1577 1l.40 View of town on hillside 15 10
1578 1l.40 Back of woman's head 15 10
1579 1l.40 Woman holding bowl 15 10
1580 2l. Building surrounded by trees 20 10
1581 2l. Old woman wearing black gown 20 10
1582 2l. Two women talking . . 20 10
1583 2l. Woman wrapped in white sheet 20 10
1584 2l. View of walled town . . 20 10
1585 2l.60 Birds and animals . . 25 15
1586 2l.60 Trees 25 15
1587 2l.60 Nun beside harp . . . 25 15
1588 2l.60 Archers 25 15
1589 2l.60 Moon over sea 25 15
1590 2l.60 Sculpture of woman's head 25 15
1591 2l.60 Gardener in grounds of large house 25 15
1592 2l.60 Sculpture of man's head and open fan . . . 25 15
1593 10l. Lemons on white table cloth 90 50
1594 10l. Pile of books 90 50

338 1925 25c. on 10c. Airmail Stamp

2000. Air. 75th Anniv of Honduras Airmail Stamps. Multicoloured.
1595 7l.30 Type **338** 65 35
1596 10l. Thomas Canfield Pounds (founder of Central American Airline) (vert) 90 50
1597 10l.65 General Rafael Lopez Gutierrez (President of Honduras, 1920–24) (vert) 95 55

339 Flower and Rifle

2000. Air. America (1999). A New Millennium without Arms. Multicoloured.
1599 10l. Type **339** 90 50
1600 10l.65 White dove and soldier 95 55
1601 14l. Steam train and bomb (horiz) . . . . 1·25 75

340 Ivan Guerrero and Mario Chirinos (football)

2000. Air. Olympic Games, Sydney. Multicoloured.
1602 2l.60 Type **340** 25 15
1603 10l.65 Ramon Valle (swimming) (vert) 95 55
1604 12l.45 Gina Coello (running) (vert) . . . . 1·10 65

342 Children and White-crowned Parrot

2000. Air. International Year of Volunteers. Multicoloured.
1607 2l.60 Type **342** 25 15
1608 10l.65 Boy and flower . . . 95 55

343 Mary and Jesus

2000. Air. Christmas. Multicoloured.
1609 1l.60 Type **343** 15 10
1610 7l.30 Nativity (vert) 65 35
1611 14l. Pavement art . . . . . 1·25 75

344 Yellow-naped Amazon (*Amazona auroalliata*)

346 Cardinal Rodriguez as a Child with his Father

2001. Air. America. AIDS Awareness Campaign. Monogamy. Multicoloured.
1612 2l.60 Type **344** 25 15
1613 4l.30 Common ground dove (*Columbina passerine*) (horiz) 35 20
1614 10l.65 Scarlet macaw (*Ara macao*) 95 55
1615 20l. Harpy eagle (*Aguila harpia*) . . . . 1·80 1·00

2001. Air. Various stamps surch.
1616 2l. on 16c. brown and black (No. 947) 20 10
1617 2l. on 16c. multicoloured (No. 948) 20 10
1618 2l.60 on 3c. orange, blue and brown (No. 967) . . 25 15
1619 2l.60 on 3c. multicoloured (No. 1003) 25 15
1620 2l.60 on 8c. multicoloured (No. 914) 25 15
1621 2l.60 on 16c. multicoloured (No. 931) 25 15
1622 3l. on 16c. multicoloured (No. 886) 35 15
1623 4l. on 9c. multicoloured (No. 1017) 35 20
1624 4l.30 on 6c. multicoloured (No. 899) 35 20
1625 7l.30 on 6c. brown and black (No. 941) 65 35
1626 7l.30 on 6c. multicoloured (No. 942) 65 35

1627 10l. on 16c. orange-red and black (No. 877) 90 50
1628 10l.65 on 16c. multicoloured (No. 994) 90 50
1629 14l. on 16c. multicoloured (No. 905) . . . . 1·25 75

2001. Air. Cardinal Oscar Andreas Rodriguez. Multicoloured.
1630 2l.60 Type **346** 25 15
1631 2l.60 Seated, wearing white vestments 25 15
1632 2l.60 Seated, at Seminary, 1964 . . . . 25 15
1633 2l.60 Consecration as Archbishop 25 15
1634 2l.60 At home, 1960 . . . . 25 15
1635 2l.60 Kneeling before Pope John Paul II and other clergy, Vatican, 2001 . . 25 15
1636 2l.60 Celebrating Mass, 1970 25 15
1637 2l.60 Woman wearing dark glasses, Cardinal Rodriguez and crowd, Vatican 25 15
1638 2l.60 Pope John Paul II and Cardinal Rodriguez wearing sash, 1993 . . . 25 15
1639 2l.60 Leaving airplane as Cardinal, 2001 . . . . . 25 15
1640 10l.65 Woman, Cardinal Rodriguez and Pope John Paul II, 1993 (47 × 40 mm) 95 55
1641 10l.65 Audience with Pope John Paul II, 2001 (47 × 40 mm) 95 55
1642 10l.65 Receiving cardinal ring from Pope John Paul II (47 × 40 mm) 95 55
1643 10l.65 Addressing crowd, 2001 (47 × 40 mm) 95 55
1644 10l.65 Kneeling before Pope John Paul II, Rome, 1993 (47 × 40 mm) 95 55
1645 10l.65 Pope John Paul II and Cardinal Rodriguez, 2000 (47 × 40 mm) 95 55
1646 15l. As No. 1645 enlarged to show crowd (164 × 132 mm) . . . . . 1·50 80

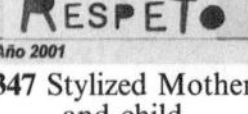

347 Stylized Mother and child

348 Jug

2001. Air. 50th Anniv of United Nations High Commissioner for Refugees. Multicoloured.
1647 2l.60 Type **347** 25 15
1648 10l.65 Refugees (horiz) . . . 95 55

2001. Air. 50th Anniv of Banco Occidente. Mayan Ceramics. Multicoloured.
1649 2l. Type **348** 20 10
1650 2l. Man-shaped jar 20 10
1651 2l. Seated figure with raised arms 20 10
1652 2l. Three-legged cylindrical vase 20 10
1653 2l. Textured censer with crouching animal on lid 20 10
1654 3l. Seated figure (scribe) . . 25 15
1655 3l. Cylindrical decorated jar 25 15
1656 3l. Three conjoined pots . . 25 15
1657 3l. Head 25 15
1658 3l. Man-shaped jar, arms forming handles 25 15
1659 5l. Decorated pot with handles and legs 40 25
1660 5l. Curved pot with lip and handles 40 25
1661 5l. Censer with large animal on lid 40 25
1662 5l. Seated figure with hands on knees 40 25
1663 5l. Man-shaped jar showing teeth 40 25
1664 6l.90 Pot with handles and narrow base 65 40
1665 6l.90 Seated figure with hands on knees (different) 65 40
1667 6l.90 Jar in shape of seated figure holding pole . . . 65 40
1668 6l.90 Tall cylindrical vase 65 40
1669 6l.90 Textured pot with animal-shaped handles . . 65 40

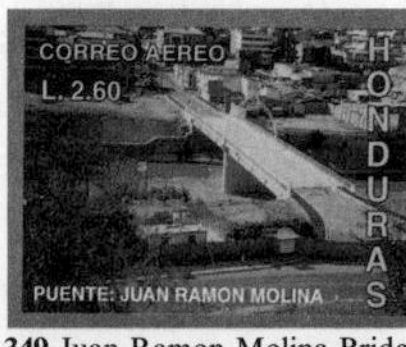

349 Juan Ramon Molina Bridge

2001. Air. Honduras–Japan Diplomatic Relations. Sheet 153 × 127 mm containing T **349** and similar horiz designs showing views of bridge. Multicoloured.
MS1670 2l.60 Type **349**; 10l.65, Side view; 13l.65 From beneath . . 1·20 1·20

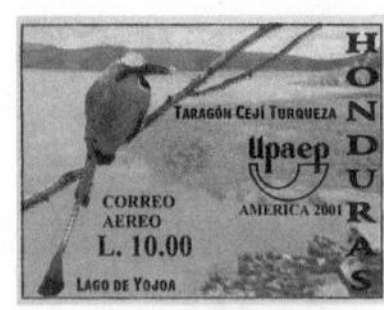

350 Turquoise-browed Motmot, Lago de Yojoa

2002. Air. America (2001). UNESCO World Heritage Sites. Multicoloured.
1671 10l. Type **350** 90 55
1672 10l.65 Iguana, Islas del Cisne 90 55
1673 20l. Chrysina quetzalcoatli, Cataratas de Pulaphanzhak (horiz) . . 1·75 1·00

351 Centenary Emblem

2002. Air. Centenary of Pan American Health Organization.
1674 **351** 10l. multicoloured . . . 90 55

352 Statues and Buildings (⅔-size illustration)

2002. Air. Inauguration of Miguel Pastor, Mayor of Tegucigalpa. Multicoloured.
1675 1l.40 Type **352** 15 10
1676 1l.40 Chimpanzee dropping banana skin in rubbish bin 15 10
1677 1l.40 Municipal building . . 15 10
1678 2l.60 Flags and Mayor Pastor (27 × 35 mm) . . . 20 10
1679 2l.60 Mayor Pastor sitting under tree (27 × 35 mm) 20 10
1680 2l.60 With elderly woman (27 × 35 mm) 20 10
1681 2l.60 With children (27 × 35 mm) 20 10
1682 2l.60 Mayor Pastor crouching (27 × 35 mm) 20 10
1683 2l.60 With family (27 × 35 mm) 20 10
1684 10l. Mayor Pastor and committee members . . . 90 55
1685 10l. Mayor Pastor and guests on roof top 90 55
1686 10l.65 Type **352** (114 × 75 mm) 90 55

353 Natives and Cross

2002. Air. America. Literacy Campaign. Two sheets, each 114 × 92 mm containing T **353** and similar horiz designs. Multicoloured.
MS1687 (a) 2l.60 Type **353**; 3l. Santa Barbara fortress, Trujillo; 10l. "400 Years of History" (detail) (Mario Castillo); 10l. Arrival of missionaries (500th anniv of arrival of first Catholics on mainland America); (b) 10l.65 River and forest; 12l.45 Natives landing on beach; 13l.65 Spaniards landing craft; 20l. Spanish ship (500th anniv of discovery of Honduras) . . . . 7·00 7·00

354 Building and Emblems

2002. 10th Anniv of Banco del Pais, Tegucigalpa.
1688 **354** 2l. multicoloured 10 10
1689 2l.60 multicoloured . . . 20 10
1690 10l. multicoloured . . . 90 55
1691 10l.65 multicoloured . . 90 55

355 *Vanilla planifolia*

2002. Air. Orchids. Multicoloured.
1692 1l.40 Type **355** 10 10
1693 2l.60 *Lycaste virginalis* (inscr "viriginalis") 20 10
1694 3l. *Coelia bella* 25 15
1695 4l.30 *Chysis laevis* 40 25
1696 8l.65 *Myrmecophilia brysiana* 75 45
1697 10l. *Rhyncholaelia digbyana* (inscr "Rhyncolaelia") . . 90 55
MS1698 96 × 66 mm. 20l. *Mormodes aromatica*. Imperf . . . . . . 1·75 1·75

356 The Nativity (figurines)

2002. Air. Christmas. Multicoloured.
1699 2l.60 Type **356** 20 10
1700 10l.65 Nativity (painting) . . 90 55
1701 14l. Crowd and outdoor Nativity . . . . 1·20 70

357 Children

2002. 120th Anniv of PANI (social awareness organization). Multicoloured.
1702 2l.60 Type **357** 20 10
1703 10l. Elderly men 90 55
1704 10l.65 Carving, instruments, building and birds (vert) 90 55

EXPRESS LETTER STAMPS

1953. No. O507 surch **ENTREGA INMEDIATA 1953 L O.20.**
E523 **127** 20c. on 1c. olive & pur 1·60 1·60

E 135 Lockheed Constellation

1956. Air. Optd **ENTREGA INMEDIATA** as in Type **E 135**.
E570 **E 135** 20c. grey and black 60 50

1966. Stamp Cent. Design similar to T **144**.
E700 20c. brown, gold & lt brown 45 45
DESIGN—HORIZ: 20c. Motor cyclist.

1972. As T **168**, but inscr "ENTREGA INMEDIATA". Multicoloured.
E811 20c. Chance Vought F4U-5 Corsair fighter aircraft . . 45 25

1975. No. E811 surch.
E848 60c. on 20c. multicoloured 75 55

1976. As T **178**.
E893 60c. Deer in forest 70 40

OFFICIAL STAMPS
Various stamps overprinted **OFICIAL**.

1890. Stamps of 1890.
O56 **6** 1c. yellow 15
O57 2c. yellow 15
O58 5c. yellow 15
O59 10c. yellow 15
O60 20c. yellow 15
O61 25c. yellow 15
O62 30c. yellow 15
O63 40c. yellow 15
O64 50c. yellow 15
O65 75c. yellow 15
O66 1p. yellow 15

1891. Stamps of 1891.
O70 **8** 1c. yellow 15
O71 2c. yellow 15
O72 5c. yellow 15
O73 10c. yellow 15
O74 20c. yellow 15
O75 25c. yellow 15
O76 30c. yellow 15
O77 40c. yellow 15
O78 50c. yellow 15
O79 75c. yellow 15
O80 1p. yellow 15

1898. Stamps of 1898.
O116 **14** 5c. blue 70
O117 10c. blue 70
O118 20c. bistre 75
O119 50c. orange . . . . . . 1·50
O120 1p. green . . . . 3·00

1911. Stamps of 1911.
O148 **20** 1c. violet 90 35
O149 2c. green 55 55
O150 5c. red 90 90
O151 6c. blue . . . . 1·60 1·25
O152 10c. blue 90 70
O153 20c. yellow 90 90
O154 50c. brown . . . . . . 3·25 2·50
O155 1p. olive . . . . 7·00 5·75

1914. No. O150 and O148 surch.
O186 **20** 1c. on 5c. red . . . . . 1·10 90
O187 2c. on 5c. red . . . . . 1·25 90
O188 10c. on 1c. violet . . . . 2·25 2·25
O189 10c. on 5c. red . . . . . 8·75 8·75
O190 20c. on 1c. violet . . . . 1·60 1·60

1914. No. O190 and O146 surch **OFICIAL** and value.
O191 **20** 10c. on 20c. on 1c. violet 3·50 3·50
O193 20c. on 50c. brown . . . 3·25 3·25

1915. Stamps of 1913.
O194 **26** 1c. brown 25 25
O195 2c. red 25 25
O197 **27** 5c. blue 25 25
O198 6c. violet 85 85
O199 **26** 10c. brown 70 70
O200 20c. brown . . . . . . 1·75 1·75
O202 **27** 50c. red . . . . 3·50 3·50

1915. No. 168 surch **OFICIAL $0.01**.
O203 **26** 1c. on 2c. red . . . . . 1·75 1·75

1915. Stamps of 1915.
O204 **32** 1c. brown . . . . 2·00 2·25
O205 2c. red . . . . 2·00 2·25
O206 – 5c. blue 20 20
O207 – 6c. violet 30 30
O208 **32** 10c. blue . . . . 8·00 8·00
O209 20c. brown . . . . . . 4·50 6·00
O210 – 50c. red . . . . 1·25 1·25
O211 – 1p. green . . . . 2·25 2·25

1921. Stamps of 1919.
O212 **36** 1c. brown . . . . 1·60 1·60
O213 2c. red . . . . 3·75 3·75
O214 5c. red . . . . 3·75 3·75
O215 6c. mauve 35 35
O216 10c. blue 45 45
O217 15c. blue 50 50
O218 20c. brown 70 70
O219 50c. brown . . . . . . 1·10 1·10
O220 1p. green . . . . 1·60 1·60

1925. Stamps of 1923.
O222 **39** 1c. olive 10 10
O223 2c. red 15 15
O224 **39** 6c. purple 25 25
O225 10c. blue 35 35
O226 20c. brown 45 45
O227 50c. red 95 95
O228 1p. green . . . . 1·40 1·40

O 50 J. R. Molina

1929.
O259 – 1c. blue 15 15
O260 **O 50** 2c. red 20 20
O261 – 5c. violet 30 30
O262 – 10c. green 35 35
O263 – 20c. blue 45 45
O264 – 50c. green and yellow 90 90
O265 – 1p. brown . . . . . . 1·60 1·60
DESIGNS: J. C. Valle; 5c. Coffee tree; 10c. J. T. Reyes; 20c. Tegucigalpa Cathedral; 50c. Lake Yojoa; 1p. Wireless station.

1930. Air. Nos. O224/8 surch **Servicio aereo Vale 5 centavos VI-1930** or optd **Servicio aereo Habilitado VI-1930**.
O319 **39** 5c. on 6c. purple . . . . 1·10 1·10
O320 6c. purple . . . . 50·00 50·00
O321 10c. blue . . . . 1·00 1·00
O322 20c. brown . . . . . . 1·00 1·00
O323 50c. red . . . . 1·50 1·50
O324 1p. green . . . . 1·00 1·00

O 70 Tegucigalpa

1931.

No.	Type	Description	Unused	Used
O328	O 70	1c. blue	20	20
O329		2c. purple	75	75
O330		5c. olive	90	90
O331		6c. red	90	90
O332		10c. green	1·00	1·00
O333		15c. brown	1·75	1·75
O334		20c. brown	1·75	1·75
O335		50c. violet	1·25	1·25
O336		1p. orange	1·75	1·75

1933. Air. Various stamps surch **Aereo Oficial Vale 1933** and new value.

No.	Type	Description	Unused	Used
O354	66	20c. on 2c. blue	3·50	3·50
O355		20c. on 2c. orange	3·50	3·50
O356		20c. on 2c. red	3·50	3·50
O357		40c. on 2c. orange	2·10	2·10
O358		40c. on 2c. red	4·25	4·25
O360	–	40c. on 5c. purple (249)	4·25	4·25
O361	–	40c. on 5c. blue (250)	7·00	7·00
O362	–	40c. on 5c. purple (270)	4·25	4·25
O363	–	40c. on 5c. blue (271)	9·50	9·50
O370	–	40c. on 5c. violet (O261)	95	95
O372	39	60c. on 6c. purple (O224)	70	70
O365	–	70c. on 5c. blue (188)	3·00	3·00
O374	–	70c. on 5c. blue (O206)	5·50	5·50
O366	39	70c. on 10c. blue	3·50	3·50
O375	32	70c. on 10c. blue (O208)	28·00	28·00
O377	36	70c. on 10c. blue (O216)	4·75	4·75
O378	39	70c. on 10c. blue (O225)	3·50	3·50
O380	36	70c. on 15c. blue (O217)	90·00	90·00
O381		90c. on 10c. blue (O216)	5·50	5·50
O382		90c. on 15c. blue (O217)	4·00	4·00
O383	39	1l. on 2c. red	1·40	1·40
O367	36	1l. on 20c. brown	3·50	3·50
O384		1l. on 20c. brown (O218)	2·50	2·50
O385	39	1l. on 20c. brown (O226)	4·00	4·00
O368		1l. on 50c. red	14·00	14·00
O386	36	1l. on 50c. brown (O219)	1·90	1·90
O387	39	1l. on 50c. red (O227)	4·25	4·25
O369	36	1.20l. on 1p. green	1·10	1·10
O388	–	1.20l. on 1p. grn (O211)	9·50	9·50
O389	39	1.20l. on 1p. grn (O288)	1·60	1·60

1935. Stamps of 1931 optd **HABILITADO 1935–1938** between thick lines.

No.	Type	Description	Unused	Used
O390	O 70	1c. blue	20	20
O391		2c. purple	20	20
O392		5c. olive	25	25
O393		6c. red	35	35
O394		10c. green	40	40
O395		15c. brown	45	45
O396		20c. brown	55	55
O397		50c. violet	1·25	1·25

O 92 Coat of Arms and National Flag

1939. Air.

No.	Type	Description	Unused	Used
O400	O 92	2c. blue and green	10	10
O401		5c. blue and orange	10	10
O402		8c. blue and brown	15	15
O403		15c. blue and red	35	30
O404		46c. blue and olive	45	45
O405		50c. blue and violet	60	45
O406		1l. blue and brown	1·75	1·75
O407		2l. blue and red	3·00	3·00

1952. Air. 500th Birth Anniv of Isabella the Catholic. As Nos. 499/506 but colours changed, optd **OFICIAL**.

No.	Type	Description	Unused	Used
O507	127	1c. olive and purple	10	10
O508	–	2c. violet and brown	10	10
O509	–	8c. black and red	15	15
O510	128	16c. green and violet	25	25
O511	–	30c. black and blue	30	30
O512	–	1l. sepia and green	1·50	1·25
O513	127	2l. brown and blue	3·00	3·00
O514	128	5l. slate and orange	7·00	7·00

1953. Air. United Nations. As Nos. 523/31 but colours changed (except 1c.), optd **OFICIAL**.

No.	Type	Description	Unused	Used
O532	–	1c. blue and black	10	10
O533	130	2c. green and black	10	10
O534	–	3c. orange and black	20	20
O535	–	5c. red and black	20	20
O536	–	15c. sepia and black	30	30
O537	–	30c. purple and black	55	55
O538	–	1l. olive and black	4·00	2·75
O539	–	2l. purple and black	5·00	3·25
O540	–	5l. blue and black	11·50	11·00

1956. Air. As Nos. 551/69 but colours changed, optd **OFICIAL**.

No.	Description	Unused	Used
O570	1c. lake and black	10	10
O571	2c. red and black	10	10
O572	3c. purple and black	10	10
O573	4c. orange and black	10	10
O574	5c. turquoise and black	10	10
O575	8c. multicoloured	15	15
O576	10c. brown and black	15	15
O577	12c. red and black	15	15
O578	15c. black and red	15	15
O579	20c. olive and black	15	15
O580	24c. blue and black	20	20
O581	25c. purple and black	25	25
O582	30c. green and black	25	25
O583	40c. orange and black	35	35
O584	50c. red and black	35	35
O585	60c. purple and black	45	45
O586	1l. sepia and black	1·75	1·40
O587	2l. blue and black	3·00	2·40
O588	5f. blue and black	5·75	5·25

1957. Air. Revolution of 21 October 1956. Nos. 570/9 optd **OFICIAL**. Frames in black.

No.	Description	Unused	Used
O589	1c. blue and yellow	10	10
O590	2c. purple, green and orange	10	10
O591	5c. blue and pink	10	10
O592	8c. violet, olive and orange	10	10
O593	10c. brown and violet	15	15
O594	12c. blue and turquoise	15	15
O595	15c. brown and green	20	15
O596	30c. grey and pink	35	35
O597	1l. brown and blue	1·75	1·40
O598	2l. grey and green	3·00	2·40

1959. Air. Abraham Lincoln. 150th Birth Anniv No. 590/601 but colours changed and optd **OFICIAL**. Flags in blue and red.

No.	Description	Unused	Used
O602	1c. yellow	10	10
O603	2c. olive	10	10
O604	3c. brown	10	10
O605	5c. blue	10	10
O606	10c. purple	15	15
O607	12c. orange	15	15
O608	15c. sepia	20	20
O609	25c. slate	30	30
O610	50c. red	45	45
O611	1l. violet	1·10	1·10
O612	2l. blue	1·75	1·75
O613	5l. green	5·25	5·25

1964. Air. Pres. Kennedy Memorial Issue. Optd **IN MEMORIAM JOHN F. KENNEDY 22 NOVIEMBRE 1963**.

No.	Description	Unused	Used
O626	1c. yellow (No. O602)	15	15
O627	2c. olive (No. O603)	20	20
O628	3c. brown (No. O604)	25	25
O629	5c. blue (No. O605)	30	30
O630	15c. sepia (No. O608)	1·40	1·10
O631	50c. red (No. O610)	5·75	4·75

1964. Air. Nos. O611/14 surch.

No.	Description	Unused	Used
O647	10c. on 50c. red	15	10
O648	12c. on 15c. sepia	25	10
O649	12c. on 25c. slate	25	10
O621	20c. on 25c. slate	45	35

1964. Air. Olympic Games, Tokyo. Optd with Olympic Rings and **1964**.

No.	Description	Unused	Used
O632	2l. purple & black (No. O539)	5·75	4·75

1965. Air. Nos. 630/38 optd **OFICIAL**.

No.	Type	Description	Unused	Used
O650	144	1c. black and green	10	10
O651	–	2c. black and mauve	10	10
O652	–	5c. black and blue	15	15
O653	–	8c. black and green	15	15
O654	144	10c. black and bistre	25	25
O655	–	12c. black and yellow	30	30
O656	–	1l. black and buff	3·00	2·75
O657	–	2l. black and olive	6·50	5·75
O658	144	3l. black and red	7·50	7·00

1965. Air. Churchill Commem. Optd **IN MEMORIAM Sir Winston Churchill 1874-1965**.

No.	Type	Description	Unused	Used
O674	128	16c. green and violet	70	70

1971. Air. Various official stamps surch in figures.

No.	Type	Description	Unused	Used
O788	134	10c. on 3c. (O572)	25	10
O789	–	10c. on 2c. (O603)	25	10
O790	–	10c. on 3c. (O604)	25	10

1974. Air. Nos. O570 and O602 surch.

No.	Description	Unused	Used
O849	2c. on 1c. lake and black	10	10
O850	2c. on 1c. yellow	10	10

HONG KONG Pt. 1, Pt. 17

Former British colony at the mouth of the Canton R., consisting of the island of Hong Kong and peninsula of Kowloon. Under Japanese Occupation from 25 December 1941, until liberated by British forces on 16 September 1945.

Hong Kong became a Special Administrative Region of the People's Republic of China on 1 July 1997.

100 cents = 1 Hong Kong dollar.

1

1862.

No.	Type	Description	Unused	Used
8a	1	2c. brown	£130	7·00
34		4c. grey	14·00	1·50
10		6c. lilac	£425	13·00
11b		8c. yellow	£425	11·00
12a		12c. blue	29·00	5·50
22		16c. yellow	£1900	65·00
4		18c. lilac	£600	55·00
14		24c. green	£500	8·50
15a		30c. red	£750	15·00
16		30c. mauve	£250	5·50
17a		48c. red	£850	27·00
18		96c. olive	£42000	£700
19		96c. grey	£1400	60·00

1877. Surch in figures and words, thus **5 cents.**

No.	Type	Description	Unused	Used
23	1	5c. on 8c. yellow	£1000	£100
24		5c. on 18c. lilac	£950	60·00
25		10c. on 12c. blue	£1000	55·00
26		10c. on 16c. yellow	£4250	£150
27		10c. on 24c. green	£1400	85·00
20		16c. on 18c. lilac	£2250	£150
21		28c. on 30c. mauve	£1400	50·00

1880.

No.	Type	Description	Unused	Used
33	1	2c. red	38·00	1·75
56		2c. green	27·00	85
57		4c. red	19·00	85
35		5c. blue	27·00	85
58		5c. yellow	22·00	6·50
30		10c. mauve	£600	15·00
37a		10c. green	£140	1·25
38		10c. purple on red	25·00	1·25
59		10c. blue	50·00	1·75
39a		30c. green	85·00	21·00
61		30c. brown	45·00	22·00
31		48c. brown	£1300	95·00

1885. Surch in figures and words, thus **20 CENTS**.

No.	Type	Description	Unused	Used
54	1	10c. on 30c. green	£550	£1000
40		20c. on 30c. red	£110	5·50
45a		20c. on 30c. green	£110	£150
41		50c. on 48c. brown	£400	32·00
46		50c. on 48c. purple	£275	£300
42		$1 on 96c. olive	£750	70·00
47		$1 on 96c. purple on red	£800	£350
53a		$1 on 96c. black	£2750	£3750

1891. Surch in figures and words, thus **7 cents.**

No.	Type	Description	Unused	Used
43	1	7c. on 10c. green	75·00	8·00
44		14c. on 30c. mauve	£170	65·00

弍 13 (20c.)　五十 14 (50c.)　壹員 15 ($1)

1891. T **1** surch with figures and words and with Chinese surch also.

No.	Type	Description	Unused	Used
55	–	10c. on 30c. green	50·00	75·00
48a	13	20c. on 30c. green	35·00	7·50
49	14	50c. on 48c. purple	80·00	5·50
50	15	$1 on 96c. purple on red	£450	22·00
52a		$1 on 96c. black	£160	27·00

The Chinese surch on No. 55 is larger than Type **13**.

1891. 50th Anniv of Colony. Optd **1841 Hong Kong JUBILEE 1891**.

No.	Type	Description	Unused	Used
51	1	2c. red	£450	£110

20　24

1903.

No.	Type	Description	Unused	Used
62	20	1c. purple and brown	2·00	50
91		1c. brown	4·50	1·00
77		2c. green	8·50	1·25
78a		4c. purple on red	10·00	75
93		4c. red	9·00	40
79a		5c. green and orange	16·00	5·00
94		6c. brown and purple	25·00	4·75
66		8c. grey and violet	11·00	1·25
81		10c. purple and blue on blue	20·00	1·25
95		10c. blue	26·00	40
68		12c. green & purple on yell	9·00	4·25
83a		20c. grey and brown	32·00	2·25
96		20c. purple and green	48·00	42·00
84		30c. green and black	42·00	22·00
97		30c. purple and yellow	55·00	26·00
85		50c. green and purple	70·00	9·00
98		50c. black on green	40·00	15·00
86		$1 purple and olive	£120	26·00
87a		$2 grey and red	£225	£100
99		$2 red and black	£300	£300
88		$3 grey and blue	£250	£200
89		$5 purple and green	£425	£375
76		$10 grey and orange on blue	£1100	£425

1912.

No.	Type	Description	Unused	Used
117	24	1c. brown	1·00	40
118		2c. green	2·50	50
118c		2c. grey	19·00	7·50
119		3c. grey	7·00	1·00
120a		4c. red	3·25	30
121		5c. violet	10·00	30
103		6c. orange	4·25	1·00
104		8c. grey	24·00	5·50
123		8c. orange	4·00	1·50
124		10c. blue	4·50	30
106		12c. purple on yellow	5·50	7·50
125		20c. purple and olive	5·50	30
126		25c. purple	5·00	70
127		30c. purple and orange	11·00	1·50
128		50c. black on green	15·00	30
129		$1 purple and blue on blue	35·00	50
130		$2 red and black	£120	6·00
131		$3 green and purple	£170	60·00
132		$5 green and red on green	£475	70·00
116		$10 purple and black on red	£600	85·00

1935. Silver Jubilee. As T **10a** of Gambia.

No.	Description	Unused	Used
133	3c. blue and black	4·00	3·50
134	5c. green and blue	8·50	3·50
135	10c. brown and blue	20·00	1·75
136	20c. grey and purple	38·00	8·00

1937. Coronation. As T **10b** of Gambia.

No.	Description	Unused	Used
137	4c. green	4·50	4·25
138	15c. red	10·00	3·25
139	25c. blue	13·00	3·00

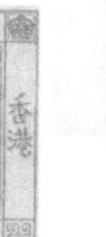

29 King George VI　30 Street Scene

1938.

No.	Type	Description	Unused	Used
140	29	1c. brown	1·75	2·50
141		2c. grey	2·00	30
142		4c. orange	4·50	1·50
143		5c. green	1·25	20
144		8c. brown	1·75	2·50
145b		10c. violet	6·00	70
146		15c. red	2·00	30
147		20c. black	1·25	30
148		20c. red	7·00	40
149		25c. blue	29·00	2·00
150		25c. olive	4·75	1·75
151a		30c. olive	24·00	8·50
152		30c. blue	7·00	20
153c		50c. purple	9·00	20
154		80c. red	5·00	95
155		$1 purple and blue	8·00	3·25
156		$1 orange and green	18·00	30
157		$2 orange and green	70·00	17·00
158		$2 violet and red	32·00	3·50
159		$5 purple and red	60·00	50·00
160		$5 green and violet	80·00	8·50
161		$10 green and violet	£500	95·00
162		$10 violet and blue	£140	30·00

1941. Centenary of British Occupation. Dated "1841 1941".

No.	Type	Description	Unused	Used
163	30	2c. orange and brown	5·00	2·00
164	–	4c. purple and red	5·00	3·25
165	–	5c. black and green	3·00	50
166	–	15c. black and red	6·00	1·75
167	–	25c. brown and blue	13·00	5·50
168	–	$1 blue and orange	48·00	8·00

DESIGNS—HORIZ: 4c. "Empress of Japan" (liner) and junk; 5c. University; 15c. Harbour; $1 "Falcon" (clipper) and Short S.23 Empire "C" Class flying boat. VERT: 25c. Hong Kong Bank.

For Japanese issues see "Japanese Occupation of Hong Kong".

36

1946. Victory.

No.	Type	Description	Unused	Used
169	36	30c. blue and red	2·75	1·75
170		$1 brown and red	3·50	75

1948. Silver Wedding. As T **11b/c** of Gambia.

No.	Description	Unused	Used
171	10c. violet	3·00	1·00
172	$10 red	£300	90·00

1949. U.P.U. As T **11d/g** of Gambia.

No.	Description	Unused	Used
173	10c. violet	4·50	1·00
174	20c. red	17·00	3·00
175	30c. blue	15·00	3·00
176	80c. mauve	35·00	9·50

1953. Coronation. As T **11h** of Gambia.

No.	Description	Unused	Used
177	10c. black and purple	6·00	30

1954. As T **29** but portrait of Queen Elizabeth, facing left.

No.	Description	Unused	Used
178	5c. orange	1·75	20
179	10c. lilac	2·50	10
180a	15c. green	4·50	45
181	20c. brown	6·00	30
182a	25c. red	4·00	1·50
183	30c. grey	5·00	20
184	40c. blue	6·00	40
185	50c. purple	6·50	20
186	65c. grey	19·00	9·50
187	$1 orange and green	7·50	20
188	$1.30 blue and red	23·00	1·50
189	$2 violet and red	12·00	60
190	$5 green and purple	75·00	2·00
191	$10 violet and blue	60·00	9·00

38 University Arms

1961. Golden Jubilee of Hong Kong University.

No.	Type	Description	Unused	Used
192	38	$1 multicoloured	7·00	2·00

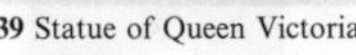

39 Statue of Queen Victoria

40 Queen Elizabeth II (after Annigoni)

1962. Stamp Centenary.
193 **39** 10c. black and mauve . . . 60 10
194 20c. black and blue . . . . 1·75 2·00
195 50c. black and bistre . . . 4·00 40

1962.
196 **40** 5c. orange 75 60
223 10c. violet 70 50
198 15c. green . . . . 3·25 1·75
199 20c. brown . . . . 2·50 1·25
200 25c. red . . . . 3·00 3·00
201 30c. blue . . . . 2·50 10
202 40c. turquoise . . . . . . 2·75 70
203 50c. red . . . . 1·75 30
230 65c. blue . . . . 6·50 7·00
231 $1 sepia . . . . 18·00 1·75
206 – $1.30 multicoloured . . . 5·00 20
207 – $2 multicoloured . . . . 7·00 65
208 – $5 multicoloured . . . . . 17·00 1·25
209 – $10 multicoloured . . . . 32·00 2·50
210 – $20 multicoloured . . . . £140 24·00
Nos. 206/10 are as T **40** but larger 26 × 40½ mm.

1963. Freedom from Hunger. As T **20a** of Gambia.
211 $1.30 green . . . . 35·00 8·00

1963. Cent of Red Cross. As T **20b** of Gambia.
212 10c. red and black . . . . . 4·00 30
213 $1.30 red and blue . . . . . 21·00 8·00

1965. Centenary of I.T.U. As T **44** of Gibraltar.
214 10c. purple and yellow . . . 3·00 25
215 $1.30 olive and green . . . . 16·00 5·50

1965. I.C.Y. As T **45** of Gibraltar.
216 10c. purple and turquoise . . 2·50 25
217 $1.30 green and lavender . . 15·00 5·50

1966. Churchill Commem. As T **46** of Gibraltar.
218 10c. blue . . . . 2·50 15
219 50c. green . . . . 2·75 30
220 $1.30 brown . . . . 12·00 3·00
221 $2 violet . . . . 24·00 10·00

1966. Inauguration of W.H.O. Headquarters, Geneva. As T **54** of Gibraltar.
237 10c. black, green and blue . . 2·50 30
238 50c. black, purple and ochre 8·00 1·75

1966. 20th Anniv of U.N.E.S.C.O. As T **56a/c** of Gibraltar.
239 10c. multicoloured . . . . . 2·75 20
240 50c. yellow, violet and olive 10·00 90
241 $2 black, purple and orange 40·00 20·00

42 Rams' Heads on Chinese Lanterns

1967. Chinese New Year ("Year of the Ram").
242 **42** 10c. red, olive and yellow 3·00 50
243 – $1.30 green, red and yellow 22·00 11·00
DESIGN: $1.30, Three rams.

44 Cable Route Map

1967. Completion of Malaysia–Hong Kong Link of SEACOM Telephone Cable.
244 **44** $1.30 blue and red . . . . 12·00 4·50

45 Rhesus Macaques in Tree

1968. Chinese New Year ("Year of the Monkey").
245 **45** 10c. gold, black and red . . 3·25 50
246 – $1.30 gold, black and red 22·00 10·00
DESIGN: $1.30, Family of rhesus macaques.

47 "Iberia" (liner) at Ocean Terminal

1968. Sea Craft.
247 **47** 10c. multicoloured . . . . 1·75 15
248 – 20c. blue, black and brown 2·50 1·00
249 – 40c. orange, black & mauve . . . . 9·00 10·00
250 – 50c. red, black and green 6·00 75
251 – $1 yellow, black and red 11·00 5·50
252 – $1.30 blue, black and pink 32·00 4·25
DESIGNS: 20c. Pleasure launch; 40c. Car ferry; 50c. Passenger ferry; $1 Sampan; $1.30, Junk.

53 "Bauhinia blakeana"

1968. Multicoloured.
253 65c. Type **53** . . . . 9·00 50
254 $1 Arms of Hong Kong . . . 9·00 40

55 "Aladdin's Lamp" and Human Rights Emblem

1968. Human Rights Year.
255 **55** 10c. orange, black and green . . . . 1·00 75
256 50c. yellow, black & purple 3·50 2·25

56 Cockerel

1969. Chinese New Year ("Year of the Cock"). Multicoloured.
257 10c. Type **56** . . . . 3·50 1·00
258 $1.30 Cockerel (vert) . . . . 42·00 14·00

58 Arms of Chinese University

1969. Establishment of Chinese University of Hong Kong.
259 **58** 40c. violet, gold and blue 6·00 3·50

59 Earth Station and Satellite

1969. Opening of Communications Satellite Tracking Station.
260 **59** $1 multicoloured . . . . . 18·00 4·50

60 Chow's Head

62 "Expo '70" Emblem

1970. Chinese New Year ("Year of the Dog"). Multicoloured.
261 10c. Type **60** . . . . 4·00 1·25
262 $1.30 Chow standing (horiz) 45·00 14·00

1970. World Fair, Osaka. Multicoloured.
263 15c. Type **62** 65 85
264 25c. "Expo '70" emblem and junks (horiz) . . . . 1·40 1·50

64 Plaque in Tung Wah Hospital

1970. Centenary of Tung Wah Hospital.
265 **64** 10c. multicoloured 75 25
266 50c. multicoloured . . . . 2·50 1·50

65 Symbol

1970. Asian Productivity Year.
267 **65** 10c. multicoloured . . . . 1·00 60

66 Pig

1971. Chinese New Year ("Year of the Pig").
268 **66** 10c. multicoloured . . . . 5·00 90
269 $1.30 multicoloured . . . 30·00 11·00

67 "60" and Scout Badge

68 Festival Emblem

1971. Diamond Jubilee of Scouting in Hong Kong.
270 **67** 10c. black, red and yellow 75 10
271 50c. black, green and blue 3·00 1·00
272 $2 black, mauve and violet 16·00 12·00

1971. Hong Kong Festival.
273 **68** 10c. orange and purple . . 1·25 20
274 – 50c. multicoloured . . . . 2·75 1·00
275 – $1 multicoloured . . . . . 8·50 7·00
DESIGNS—39 × 23 mm: 50c. Coloured streamers. 23 × 39 mm: $1 "Orchid".

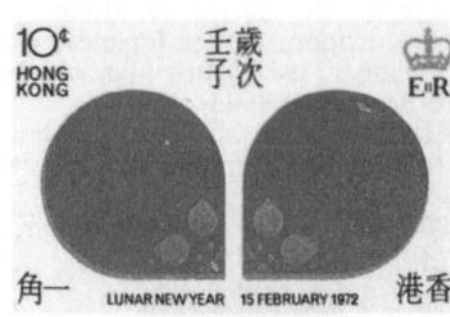

69 Stylized Rats

1972. Chinese New Year. ("Year of the Rat").
276 **69** 10c. red, black and gold . . 3·50 50
277 $1.30 red, black and gold 32·00 11·00

70 Tunnel Entrance

1972. Opening of Cross-Harbour Tunnel.
278 **70** $1 multicoloured . . . . . 5·00 2·25

1972. Royal Silver Wedding. As T **98** of Gibraltar, but with Phoenix and Dragon in background.
279 10c. multicoloured 30 15
280 50c. multicoloured . . . . . 1·10 1·40

72 Ox

73 Queen Elizabeth II

1973. Chinese New Year ("Year of the Ox").
281 **72** 10c. orange, brown & black . . . . 2·50 50
282 – $1.30 yellow, orange & black . . . . 7·00 7·00
DESIGN—HORIZ: $1.30, Ox.

1973.
311 **73** 10c. orange 55 30
284 15c. green . . . . 7·00 8·00
313 20c. violet 50 10
286 25c. brown . . . . 11·00 8·50
315 30c. blue 70 70
316 40c. blue . . . . 1·25 2·50
289 50c. red . . . . 1·50 60
318 60c. lavender . . . . . . 1·75 2·50
290 65c. brown . . . . 14·00 11·00
320 70c. yellow . . . . 1·75 75
321 80c. red . . . . 2·25 3·25
321c 90c. brown . . . . 5·00 2·25
291 $1 green . . . . 2·25 80
323 – $1.30 yellow and violet 2·50 30
324 – $2 green and brown . . . 3·00 1·25
324c – $5 pink and blue . . . . 4·75 1·75
324d – $10 pink and green . . . 8·00 6·00
324e – $20 pink and black . . . 13·00 12·00
Values of $1.30 and above are size 27 × 32 mm.

1973. Royal Wedding. As T **101a** of Gibraltar. Multicoloured. Background colours given.
297 50c. brown 50 15
298 $2 mauve . . . . 2·25 2·00

75 Festival Symbols forming Chinese Character

1973. Hong Kong Festival.
299 **75** 10c. red and green 40 10
300 – 50c. mauve and orange . . 2·00 95
301 – $1 green and mauve . . . 4·75 4·75
DESIGNS—Festival symbols arranged to form a Chinese character: 10c. "Hong"; 50c. "Kong"; $1 "Festival".

76 Tiger

1974. Chinese New Year ("Year of the Tiger").
302 **76** 10c. multicoloured . . . . 3·50 50
303 – $1.30 multicoloured . . . 11·00 12·00
DESIGN—VERT: $1.30, similar to Type **76**.

77 Chinese Mask

1974. Arts Festival.
304 **77** 10c. multicoloured 75 10
305 – $1 multicoloured . . . . . 6·00 4·25
306 – $2 multicoloured . . . . . 9·00 8·50
MS307 159 × 94 mm. Nos. 304/6 60·00 48·00
DESIGNS: $1, $2, Chinese masks similar to T **77**.

78 Pigeons with Letters

1974. Centenary of U.P.U.
308 **78** 10c. blue, green and black . . . 40 10
309 – 50c. mauve, orange & black . . . . 1·00 40
310 – $2 multicoloured . . . . . 5·25 4·25
DESIGNS: 50c. Globe within letters; $2 Hands holding letters.

79 Stylized Hare

1975. Chinese New Year ("Year of the Hare").
327 **79** 10c. silver and red . . . . 1·00 60
328 – $1.30 gold and green . . . 8·00 8·00
DESIGN: $1.30, Pair of hares.

80 Queen Elizabeth II, the Duke of Edinburgh and Hong Kong Arms

1975. Royal Visit.
329 **80** $1.30 multicoloured . . . 2·75 2·00
330 $2 multicoloured . . . . . 3·75 4·25

81 Mid-Autumn Festival

82 Melodious Laughing Thrush ("The Hwamei")

1975. Hong Kong Festivals of 1975. Mult.
331 50c. Type **81** . . . . 2·00 50
332 $1 Dragon-boat Festival . . 8·00 2·50
333 $2 Tin Hau Festival . . . . 28·00 9·50
MS334 102×83 mm. Nos. 331/3 £110 45·00

1975. Birds. Multicoloured.
335 50c. Type **82** . . . . 2·50 50
336 $1.30 Chinese bulbul . . . . 8·50 5·00
337 $2 Black-capped kingfisher 16·00 12·00

83 Dragon

1976. Chinese New Year ("Year of the Dragon").
338 **83** 20c. mauve, purple and gold 75 10
339 – $1.30 green, red and gold 6·50 3·25
DESIGN: $1.30, As Type **83** but dragon reversed.

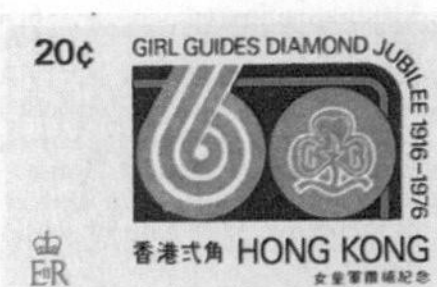

84 "60" and Girl Guides Badge

1976. Diamond Jubilee of Girl Guides. Multicoloured.
354 20c. Type **84** 50 10
355 $1.30 Badge, stylized diamond and "60" . . . . 5·50 4·00

85 "Postal Services" in Chinese Characters

1976. Opening of New G.P.O.
356 **85** 20c. green, grey and black 75 10
357 – $1.30 orange, grey and black . . . . 3·75 2·00
358 – $2 yellow, grey and black 6·50 4·50
DESIGNS: $1.30, Old G.P.O; $2 New G.P.O.

86 Tree Snake on Branch

1977. Chinese New Year ("Year of the Snake"). Multicoloured.
359 20c. Type **86** 50 15
360 $1.30 Snake facing left . . . 4·25 4·75

87 Presentation of the Orb

1977. Silver Jubilee. Multicoloured.
361 20c. Type **87** 40 10
362 $1.30 The Queen's visit, 1975 1·25 1·25
363 $2 The Orb (vert) . . . . . 1·50 1·50

88 Tram Cars

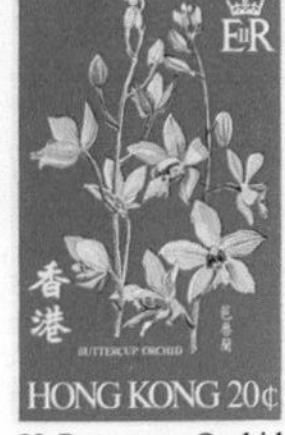

89 Buttercup Orchid

1977. Tourism. Multicoloured.
364 20c. Type **88** 55 10
365 60c. Star ferryboat . . . . 1·50 2·25
366 $1.30 The Peak Railway . . 2·75 2·25
367 $2 Junk and sampan . . . . 3·50 3·75

1977. Orchids. Multicoloured.
368 20c. Type **89** . . . . 1·25 20
369 $1.30 Lady's slipper orchid 4·00 2·25
370 $2 Susan orchid . . . . . . 6·00 4·75

90 Horse

1978. Chinese New Year ("Year of the Horse").
371 **90** 20c. mauve, olive and bistre 50 10
372 $1.30 orange, brn & lt brn 3·75 4·50

91 Queen Elizabeth II

1978. 25th Anniv of Coronation.
373 **91** 20c. mauve and blue . . . 40 10
374 $1.30 blue and mauve . . . 1·50 2·25

92 Girl and Boy holding Hands

1978. Centenary of Po Leung Kuk (children's charity). Multicoloured.
375 20c. Type **92** 30 15
376 $1.30 Ring of children . . . 1·25 2·50

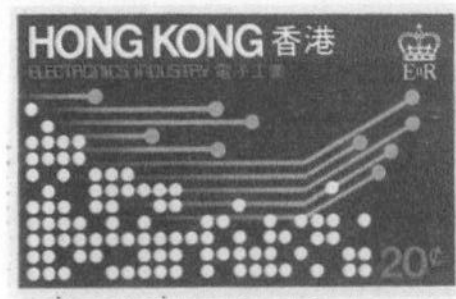

93 Electronics Industry

1979. Hong Kong Industries.
377 **93** 20c. yellow, olive & orange 30 10
378 – $1.30 multicoloured . . . 80 1·75
379 – $2 multicoloured . . . . . 85 2·25
DESIGNS: $1.30, Toy industry; $2 Garment industry.

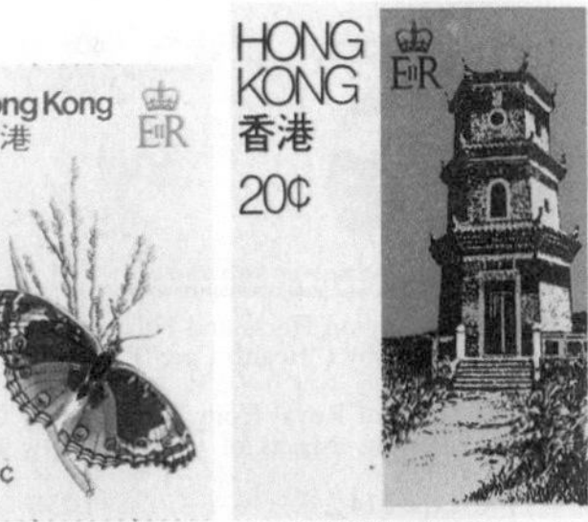

94 "Precis orithya" **96** Tsui Shing Lau Pagoda

95 Diagrammatic View of Railway Station

1979. Butterflies. Multicoloured.
380 20c. Type **94** 80 10
381 $1 "Graphium sarpedon" . . 1·50 80
382 $1.30 "Heliophorus epicles" 1·75 1·60
383 $2 "Danaus genutia" . . . . 2·00 4·25

1979. Mass Transit Railway. Multicoloured.
384 20c. Type **95** 70 10
385 $1.30 Diagrammatic view of car . . . . 1·75 80
386 $2 Plan showing route of railway . . . . 1·75 2·25

1980. Rural Architecture.
387 **96** 20c. black, mauve & yellow 40 20
388 – $1.30 multicoloured . . . 80 1·25
389 – $2 multicoloured . . . . . 1·10 2·50
DESIGNS—HORIZ: $1.30, Village house, Sai O; $2 Ching Chung Koon Temple.

97 Queen Elizabeth the Queen Mother

1980. 80th Birthday of The Queen Mother.
390 **97** $1.30 multicoloured . . . 1·00 1·25

98 Botanical Gardens

1980. Parks. Multicoloured.
391 20c. Type **98** 40 15
392 $1 Ocean Park 60 60
393 $1.30 Kowloon Park 70 95
394 $2 Country parks . . . . . 1·40 3·25

99 Red-spotted Grouper

1981. Fishes. Multicoloured.
395 20c. Type **99** 30 15
396 $1 Golden thread-finned bream 60 45
397 $1.30 Scar-breasted tuskfish 65 70
398 $2 Blue-barred orange parrotfish . . . . 90 2·75

100 Wedding Bouquet from Hong Kong

101 Suburban Development

1981. Royal Wedding. Multicoloured.
399 20c. Type **100** 30 10
400 $1.30 Prince Charles in Hong Kong 55 40
401 $5 Prince Charles and Lady Diana Spencer . . . . . . 1·75 3·00

1981. Public Housing.
402 **101** 20c. multicoloured 25 10
403 – $1 multicoloured 65 50
404 – $1.30 multicoloured . . . 75 80
405 – $2 multicoloured . . . . 90 2·00
MS406 148×105 mm. Nos. 402/5 4·25 5·50
DESIGNS: $1 to $2, Various suburban developments.

102 "Victoria from the Harbour, c.1855"

1982. Hong Kong Port, Past and Present. Multicoloured.
407 20c. Type **102** 50 15
408 $1 "West Point, Hong Kong, 1847" . . . . 1·25 80
409 $1.30 Fleet of junks . . . . 1·40 85
410 $2 Liner "Queen Elizabeth 2" at Hong Kong . . . . . . 2·50 3·00

103 Large Indian Civet

1982. Wild Animals.
411 **103** 20c. black, pink and brown 40 15
412 – $1 multicoloured 75 60
413 – $1.30 black, green & orange 80 70
414 – $5 black, brown and yellow . . . . 2·00 3·75
DESIGNS: $1 Chinese pangolin; $1.30, Chinese porcupine; $5 Indian muntjac.

104 Queen Elizabeth II

107 Dancing

106 Table Tennis

1982.

415 **104** 10c. light red, red & yellow 80 60
416 20c. blue, violet & lavender . . . . 1·00 1·00
417 30c. lt violet, violet & pink . . . . 1·50 30
418 40c. red and blue . . . . 1·50 30
475 50c. chestnut, brn & grn 1·00 40
476 60c. purple and grey . . . 1·50 1·10
477 70c. green, myrtle & yellow . . . . 3·50 40
478 80c. bistre, brown & green 3·75 2·00
479 90c. dp green, grn & turq 4·25 50
480 $1 dp orange, orange & red . . . . 1·75 40
481 $1.30 blue and mauve . . 2·50 45
482 $1.70 dp blue, blue & grn 4·00 1·50
483 $2 blue and pink . . . . 3·75 1·50
484 – $5 red, purple and yellow 9·00 3·50
485 – $10 brown and light brown . . . . 9·00 4·50
486 – $20 red and blue . . . . 10·00 7·50
487 – $50 red and grey . . . . 32·00 27·00

Nos. 484/7 are as Type **104** but larger, 26 × 30 mm.

1982. Sport for the Disabled. Multicoloured.
431 30c. Type **106** 50 10
432 $1 Racing 75 80
433 $1.30 Basketball . . . . . . 2·75 1·50
434 $5 Archery . . . . 6·00 6·50

1983. Performing Arts.
435 **107** 30c. light blue and blue 50 10
436 – $1.30 red and purple . . . 1·50 1·25
437 – $5 green and deep green 4·00 5·50
DESIGNS: $1.30, "Theatre"; $5 "Music".

108 Aerial View of Hong Kong

1983. Commonwealth Day. Multicoloured.
438 30c. Type **108** 70 10
439 $1 "Liverpool Bay" (container ship) . . . . . 1·75 1·25
440 $1.30 Hong Kong flag . . . 1·75 1·25
441 $5 Queen Elizabeth II and Hong Kong . . . . 3·50 6·50

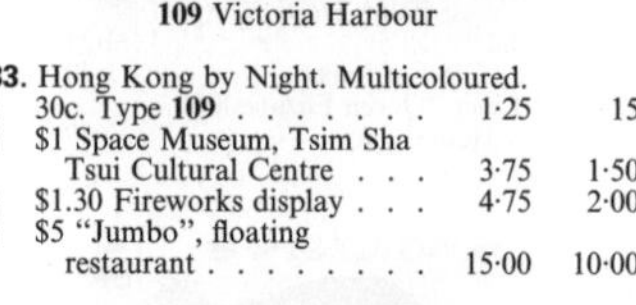

109 Victoria Harbour

1983. Hong Kong by Night. Multicoloured.
442 30c. Type **109** . . . . 1·25 15
443 $1 Space Museum, Tsim Sha Tsui Cultural Centre . . . 3·75 1·50
444 $1.30 Fireworks display . . . 4·75 2·00
445 $5 "Jumbo", floating restaurant . . . . 15·00 10·00

110 Old and new Observatory Buildings

1983. Centenary of Hong Kong Observatory.
446 **110** 40c. orange, brown & black 75 10
447 – $1 mauve, dp mauve & blk . . . . 2·00 1·75
448 – $1.30 blue, dp blue & black . . . . 2·75 1·75
449 – $5 yellow, green and black . . . . 8·00 9·50
DESIGNS: $1 Wind measuring equipment; $1.30, Thermometer; $5 Ancient and modern seismometers.

111 De Havilland D.H.86 Dragon Express "Dorado" (Hong Kong–Penang Service, 1936)

1984. Aviation in Hong Kong. Multicoloured.
450 40c. Type **111** . . . . 1·00 15
451 $1 Sikorsky S-42B flying boat (San Francisco–Hong Kong Service, 1937) . . . 2·25 1·75
452 $1.30 Cathay-Pacific Boeing 747 jet leaving Kai Tak Airport . . . . 3·25 1·75
453 $5 Baldwin brothers' balloon, 1891 (vert) . . . . 9·00 12·00

112 Map by Capt. E. Belcher, 1836

1984. Maps of Hong Kong.
454 40c. Type **112** . . . . 1·00 20
455 $1 Bartholomew map of 1929 1·75 1·25
456 $1.30 Early map of Hong Kong waters . . . . . . 8·00 1·75
457 $5 Chinese-style map of 1819 11·00 11·00

113 Cockerel

1984. Chinese Lanterns. Multicoloured.
458 40c. Type **113** . . . . 1·00 15
459 $1 Dog . . . . 2·00 1·40
460 $1.30 Butterfly . . . . 3·00 1·75
461 $5 Fish . . . . 9·50 12·00

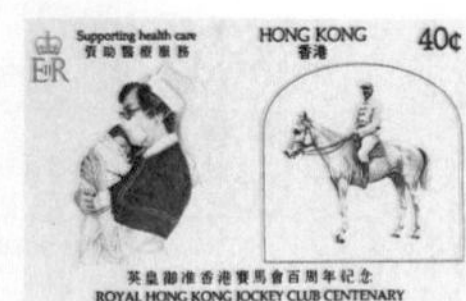

114 Jockey on Horse and Nurse with Baby ("Health Care")

1984. Centenary of Royal Hong Kong Jockey Club. Designs showing aspects of Club's charity work. Multicoloured.
462 40c. Type **114** . . . . 1·25 20
463 $1 Disabled man playing handball ("Support for Disabled") . . . . 2·00 1·75
464 $1.30 Ballerina ("The Arts") 3·00 2·00
465 $5 Humboldt penguins ("Ocean Park") . . . . . . 9·00 11·00
MS466 178 × 98 mm. Nos. 462/5 22·00 23·00

115 Hung Sing Temple

1985. Historic Buildings. Multicoloured.
467 40c. Type **115** 60 20
468 $1 St. John's Cathedral . . . 1·25 1·60
469 $1.30 The Old Supreme Court Building . . . . . . 1·50 1·75
470 $5 Wan Chai Post Office . . 7·00 10·00

116 Prow of Dragon Boat

1985. 10th International Dragon Boat Festival. Designs showing different parts of dragon boat. Multicoloured.
488 40c. Type **116** 50 15
489 $1 Drummer and rowers . . 1·75 1·25
490 $1.30 Rowers . . . . 3·00 1·60
491 $5 Stern of boat . . . . . . 9·25 11·00
MS492 190 × 100 mm. Nos. 488/91 22·00 22·00

117 The Queen Mother with Prince Charles and Prince William, 1984

1985. Life and Times of Queen Elizabeth the Queen Mother. Multicoloured.
493 40c. At Glamis Castle, aged 7 60 10
494 $1 Type **117** . . . . 1·75 1·25
495 $1.30 The Queen Mother, 1970 (from photo by Cecil Beaton) . . . . 2·00 1·40
496 $5 With Prince Henry at his christening (from photo by Lord Snowdon) . . . . . 3·25 5·00

118 Melastoma

1985. Native Flowers. Multicoloured.
497 40c. Type **118** . . . . 1·50 20
498 50c. Chinese lily . . . . . . 1·75 40
499 60c. Grantham's camellia . . 2·00 1·25
500 $1.30 Narcissus . . . . . . 3·25 1·25
501 $1.70 Bauhinia . . . . 3·75 1·50
502 $5 Chinese New Year flower 7·00 12·00

119 Hong Kong Academy for Performing Arts

1985. New Buildings. Multicoloured.
503 50c. Type **119** 80 15
504 $1.30 Exchange Square (vert) 1·75 1·50
505 $1.70 Hong Kong Bank Headquarters (vert) . . . . 2·00 1·75
506 $5 Hong Kong Coliseum . . 5·50 12·00

120 Halley's Comet in the Solar System

1986. Appearance of Halley's Comet. Mult.
507 50c. Type **120** . . . . 1·25 20
508 $1.30 Edmond Halley and Comet . . . . 2·00 1·40
509 $1.70 Comet over Hong Kong . . . . 2·75 1·50
510 $5 Comet passing the Earth 11·00 11·00
MS511 135 × 80 mm. Nos. 507/10 22·00 18·00

120a At Wedding of Miss Celia Bowes-Lyon, 1931

1986. 60th Birthday of Queen Elizabeth II. Multicoloured.
512 50c. Type **120a** 50 10
513 $1 Queen in Garter procession, Windsor Castle, 1977 . . . . 85 60
514 $1.30 In Hong Kong, 1975 1·10 70
515 $1.70 At Royal Lodge, Windsor, 1980 (from photo by Norman Parkinson) . . 1·25 75
516 $5 At Crown Agents Head Office, London, 1983 . . . 4·00 6·50

121 Mass Transit Train, Boeing 747 Airliner and Map of World

1986. "Expo '86" World Fair, Vancouver. Multicoloured.
517 50c. Type **121** 80 30
518 $1.30 Hong Kong Bank Headquarters and map of world . . . . 1·50 1·00
519 $1.70 Container ship and map of world . . . . . . 2·25 1·40
520 $5 Dish aerial and map of world . . . . 6·50 8·00

122 Hand-liner Sampan

1986. Fishing Vessels. Designs showing fishing boat and outline of fish. Multicoloured.
521 50c. Type **122** 80 15
522 $1.30 Stern trawler . . . . . 1·50 1·10
523 $1.70 Long liner junk . . . . 2·25 1·40
524 $5 Junk trawler . . . . . . 7·00 9·50

123 "The Second Puan Khequa" (attr Spoilum)

1986. 19th-century Hong Kong Portraits. Multicoloured.
525 50c. Type **123** 40 15
526 $1.30 "Chinese Lady" (19th-century copy) . . . . 1·40 1·25
527 $1.70 "Lamqua" (self-portrait) . . . . 1·50 1·40
528 $5 "Wife of Wo Hing Qua" (attr G. Chinnery) . . . . 4·00 6·50

124 Rabbit

1987. Chinese New Year ("Year of the Rabbit"). Designs showing stylized rabbits.
529 **124** 50c. multicoloured 75 15
530 – $1.30 multicoloured . . . 1·75 1·40
531 – $1.70 multicoloured . . . 2·00 1·40
532 – $5 multicoloured . . . . 7·00 7·00
MS533 133 × 84 mm. Nos. 529/32 32·00 25·00

Nos. 530/1 have the "0" omitted from their face values.

125 "Village Square, Hong Kong Island, 1838" (Auguste Borget)

1987. 19th-century Hong Kong Scenes. Mult.
534 50c. Type **125** 70 15
535 $1.30 "Boat Dwellers, Kowloon Bay, 1838 (Auguste Borget) . . . . . 2·00 1·25
536 $1.70 "Flagstaff House, 1846" (Murdoch Bruce) . . 2·50 1·40
537 $5 "Wellington Street, late 19th-century" (C. Andrasi) 7·50 11·00

126 Queen Elizabeth II and Central Victoria

127 Hong Kong Flag

1987.

538B **126** 10c. multicoloured . . . 75 60
539A 40c. multicoloured . . . 1·50 2·00
602 50c. multicoloured . . . 1·50 40
603 60c. multicoloured . . . 1·25 30
604 70c. multicoloured . . . 1·75 1·25
605 80c. multicoloured . . . 1·75 1·25
606 90c. multicoloured . . . 1·25 1·00
607 $1 multicoloured . . . 1·50 40
607a $1.20 multicoloured . . 3·50 3·50
608 $1.30 multicoloured . . 2·00 60
609 $1.40 multicoloured . . 2·00 70
547A $1.70 multicoloured . . 3·00 80
610 $1.80 multicoloured . . 1·50 60
611 $2 multicoloured . . 1·50 50
611a $2.30 multicoloured . . 3·50 3·50
612 – $5 multicoloured . . . 4·50 1·75
613 – $10 multicoloured . . 6·50 6·00
614 – $20 multicoloured . . 11·00 11·00
615 – $50 multicoloured . . . 19·00 20·00

DESIGNS—25 × 31 mm: Queen Elizabeth II and $5 Kowloon; $10 Victoria Harbour; $20 Legislative Council Building; $50 Government House.

With the exception of Nos. 607a and 611a which are dated, all the above exist with or without a date in the design.

1987.

554a **127** 10c. multicoloured . . . 50 1·00
554b – 50c. brown, red and black . . . . 1·25 1·75
554c – 80c. mauve, green & blk 1·00 2·75
554d – 90c. blue, brown & black 1·00 1·75

554e – $1.30 green, blue & black . . . . 1·75 2·50
554f – $2.30 brown, violet & blk . . . . 2·00 3·25
DESIGN: 50c. to $2.30, Map of Hong Kong.

128 Alice Ho Miu Ling Nethersole Hospital, 1887

1987. Hong Kong Medical Centenaries. Mult.
555 50c. Type **128** . . . . 1·00 20
556 $1.30 Matron and nurses, Nethersole Hospital, 1891 2·25 1·40
557 $1.70 Scanning equipment, Faculty of Medicine . . . 2·75 1·40
558 $5 Nurse and patient, Faculty of Medicine . . . . 8·50 8·00

129 Casual Dress with Fringed Hem, 220–589

1987. Historical Chinese Costumes. Multicoloured.
559 50c. Type **129** 55 10
560 $1.30 Two-piece dress and wrap, 581–960 . . . . . . 1·40 1·25
561 $1.70 Formal dress, Song Dynasty, 960–1279 . . . . 1·75 1·50
562 $5 Manchu empress costume, 1644–1911 . . . . 5·75 7·50

130 Dragon

1988. Chinese New Year ("Year of the Dragon"). Designs showing dragons.
563 **130** 50c. multicoloured 75 15
564 – $1.30 multicoloured . . . 1·50 1·25
565 – $1.70 multicoloured . . . 1·75 1·40
566 – $5 multicoloured . . . . 3·25 5·50
MS567 134 × 88 mm. Nos. 563/6 10·00 11·00

131 White-throated Kingfisher ("White-breasted Kingfisher")

132 Chinese Banyan

1988. Hong Kong Birds. Multicoloured.
568 50c. Type **131** . . . . 1·00 30
569 $1.30 Fukien niltava . . . . 2·00 1·60
570 $1.70 Black kite . . . . . 2·50 1·75
571 $5 Lesser pied kingfisher . . 4·00 7·00

1988. Trees of Hong Kong. Multicoloured.
572 50c. Type **132** 35 10
573 $1.30 Hong Kong orchid tree 70 65
574 $1.70 Cotton tree 90 85
575 $5 Schima . . . . 2·50 5·50
MS576 135 × 85 mm. Nos. 572/5 10·00 7·50

133 Lower Terminal, Peak Tramway

134 Hong Kong Catholic Cathedral

1988. Centenary of The Peak Tramway. Mult.
577 50c. Type **133** 35 10
578 $1.30 Tram on incline . . . 70 1·00
579 $1.70 Peak Tower Upper Terminal . . . . 90 1·25
580 $5 Tram . . . . 2·50 5·00
MS581 160 × 90 mm. Nos. 577/80 8·00 8·00

1988. Centenary of Hong Kong Catholic Cathedral.
582 **134** 60c. multicoloured . . . . 1·25 1·50

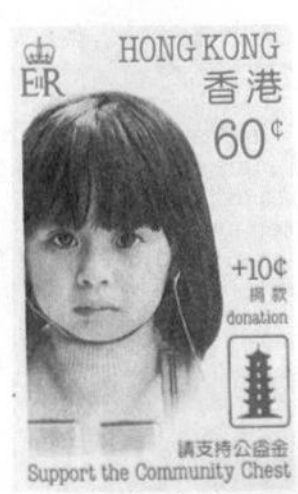

135 Deaf Girl

137 Girl and Doll

136 Snake

1988. Community Chest Charity.
583 **135** 60c.+10c. black, red & bl 60 1·25
584 – $1.40+20c. black, red and green . . . . 80 1·40
585 – $1.80+30c. black, red and orange . . . . 1·25 1·75
586 – $5+$1 black, red & brn 3·25 6·00
DESIGNS: $1.40, Elderly woman; $1.80, Blind boy using braille typewriter; $5 Mother and baby.

1989. Chinese New Year ("Year of the Snake"). Multicoloured.
587 60c. Type **136** 45 15
588 $1.40 Snake and fish . . . 1·75 70
589 $1.80 Snake on branch . . . 1·90 85
590 $5 Coiled snake . . . . . . 6·25 7·25
MS591 135 × 85 mm. Nos. 587/90 12·00 7·50

1989. Cheung Chau Bun Festival. Multicoloured.
592 60c. Type **137** 55 15
593 $1.40 Girl in festival costume 1·25 80
594 $1.80 Paper effigy of god Taai Si Wong . . . . 1·40 90
595 $5 Floral gateway . . . . . 3·50 6·00

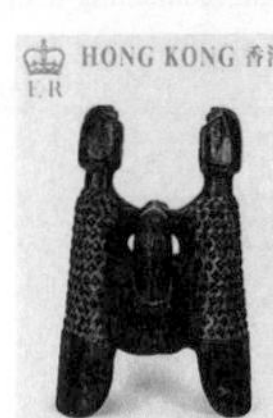

138 "Twins" (wood carving, Cheung Yee)

139 Lunar New Year Festivities

1989. Modern Art. Multicoloured.
596 60c. Type **138** 50 15
597 $1.40 "Figures" (acrylic on paper, Chan Luis) . . . . 1·25 80
598 $1.80 "Lotus" (copper sculpture, Van Lau) . . . 1·40 90
599 $5 "Zen Painting" (ink and colour on paper, Lui Shou-kwan) . . . . 3·00 4·75

1989. Hong Kong People. Multicoloured.
616 60c. Type **139** 75 10
617 $1.40 Shadow boxing and horse racing . . . . 2·00 80
618 $1.80 Foreign-exchange dealer and traditional builder . . . . 2·00 90
619 $5 Multi-racial society . . . 4·50 7·00

140 University of Science and Technology

141 Prince and Princess of Wales and Hong Kong Skyline

1989. Building for the Future.
620 **140** 60c. black, yellow & brn 45 15
621 – 70c. blk, pale pink & pink 50 40
622 – $1.30 black, lt green & grn . . . . 1·00 1·00
623 – $1.40 black, lt blue & blue 1·00 70
624 – $1.80 black, turquoise & bl . . . . 1·25 1·00
625 – $5 brown, orange and red 6·00 6·50
DESIGNS: 70c. Cultural Centre; $1.30, Eastern Harbour motorway interchange; $1.40, New Bank of China Building; $1.80, Convention and Exhibition Centre; $5 Mass Transit electric train.

1989. Royal Visit. Multicoloured.
626 60c. Type **141** . . . . 1·25 30
627 $1.40 Princess of Wales . . . 2·25 1·10
628 $1.80 Prince of Wales . . . 1·60 1·10
629 $5 Prince and Princess of Wales in evening dress . . 6·50 7·50
MS630 128 × 75 mm. No. 629 . . 8·50 8·00

143 Horse

1990. Chinese New Year ("Year of the Horse").
631 **143** 60c. multicoloured 85 20
632 – $1.40 multicoloured . . . 1·75 1·25
633 – $1.80 multicoloured . . . 1·90 1·25
634 – $5 multicoloured . . . . 6·00 7·50
MS635 135 × 85 mm. Nos. 631/4 13·00 10·00
DESIGNS: $1.40 to $5, Different horse designs.

144 Chinese Lobster Dish

145 Air Pollution and Clean Air

1990. International Cuisine. Designs showing various dishes. Multicoloured.
636 60c. Type **144** 60 15
637 70c. Indian 60 40
638 $1.30 Chinese vegetables . . 1·00 1·00
639 $1.40 Thai . . . . 1·00 65
640 $1.80 Japanese . . . . 1·25 90
641 $5 French . . . . 4·25 7·50

1990. U.N. World Environment Day. Mult.
642 60c. Type **145** 40 15
643 $1.40 Noise pollution and music 85 80
644 $1.80 Polluted and clean water . . . . 1·00 80
645 $5 Litter on ground and in bin . . . . 2·75 4·00

1990. "New Zealand 1990" International Stamp Exhibition, Auckland. Sheet 130 × 75 mm, containing design as No. 613.
MS646 $10 multicoloured . . . . 95·00 85·00

146 Street Lamp and Des Voeux Road, 1890

1990. Centenary of Electricity Supply.
647 **146** 60c. black, bistre & brown 50 15
648 – $1.40 multicoloured . . . 1·10 1·00
649 – $1.80 black, bistre and blue . . . . 1·25 1·00
650 – $5 multicoloured . . . . 2·50 5·50
MS651 155 × 85 mm. Nos. 648 and 650 . . . . 5·50 7·00
DESIGNS: $1.40, Street Lamp and "Jumbo" (floating restaurant), 1940; $1.80, Street lamp and pylon, 1960; $5 Street lamp and Hong Kong from harbour, 1980.

147 Christmas Tree and Skyscrapers

1990. Christmas. Multicoloured.
652 50c. Type **147** 25 10
653 60c. Dove with holly 25 15
654 $1.40 Firework display . . . 80 40
655 $1.80 Father Christmas hat on skyscraper . . . . . . 1·00 50
656 $2 Children with Father Christmas . . . . 1·40 1·40
657 $5 Candy stick with bow and Hong Kong skyline . . . . 3·00 5·00

148 Ram

1991. Chinese New Year ("Year of the Ram").
658 **148** 60c. multicoloured 25 15
659 – $1.40 multicoloured . . . 65 60
660 – $1.80 multicoloured . . . 80 70
661 – $5 multicoloured . . . . 2·75 4·75
MS662 135 × 85 mm. Nos. 658/61 6·50 7·50
DESIGNS: $1.40 to $5, Different ram designs.

149 Letter "A", Clock, Teddy Bear and Building Bricks (Kindergarten)

150 Rickshaw

1991. Education. Multicoloured.
663 80c. Type **149** 50 20
664 $1.80 Globe, laboratory flask and mathematical symbols (Primary and Secondary) 1·25 80
665 $2.30 Machinery (Vocational) 1·40 1·40
666 $5 Mortar board, computer and books (Tertiary) . . . 3·50 6·00

1991. 100 Years of Public Transport. Mult.
667 80c. Type **150** 30 15
668 90c. Double-decker bus . . . 70 75
669 $1.70 Harbour ferry . . . . 1·10 1·25
670 $1.80 Double-deck tram . . . 1·40 80
671 $2.30 Mass Transit electric train . . . . 2·00 2·25
672 $5 Jetfoil . . . . 3·50 6·50

151 Victorian Pillar Box and Cover of 1888

152 Bronze Buddha, Lantau Island

1991. 150th Anniv of Hong Kong Post Office. Multicoloured.
673 80c. Type **151** 40 15
674 $1.70 Edwardian pillar box and cover . . . . 90 1·00
675 $1.80 King George V pillar box and cover of 1935 . . 1·00 75
676 $2.30 King George VI pillar box and cover of 1938 . . 1·40 2·00
677 $5 Queen Elizabeth II pillar box and cover of 1989 . . 3·75 7·00
MS678 130 × 75 mm. $10 As No. 677 . . . . 11·00 13·00
See also Nos. **MS**745 and **MS**899.

1991. Landmarks.
679 **152** 80c. red and black 50 15
680 – $1.70 green and black . . 1·00 1·25
681 – $1.80 violet and black . . 1·75 80
682 – $2.30 blue and black . . . 1·25 2·00
683 – $5 orange and black . . . 3·50 7·00
DESIGNS: $1.70, Peak Pavilion; $1.80, Clocktower of Kowloon–Canton Railway Station; $2.30, Catholic Cathedral; $5 Wong Tai Sin Temple.

1991. "Phila Nippon '91" International Stamp Exhibition, Tokyo. Sheet 130 × 75 mm, containing design as No. 613.
MS684 $10 multicoloured . . . . 35·00 25·00

1991. Olympic Games, Barcelona (1992) (1st issue). Sheet 130 × 75 mm, containing design as No. 613.
MS685 $10 multicoloured . . . . 15·00 13·00
See also Nos. 696/700 and **MS**722.

153 Monkey

1992. Chinese New Year ("Year of the Monkey").
686 **153** 80c. multicoloured 40 15
687 – $1.80 multicoloured . . . 80 70

688 – $2.30 multicoloured . . . 1·25 1·75
689 – $5 multicoloured . . . . 2·75 6·50
MS690 135 × 85 mm. Nos. 686/9 8·50 9·00
DESIGNS: $1.80 to $5, Different monkey designs.

1992. 40th Anniv of Queen Elizabeth II's Accession. As T **179a** of Gibraltar. Multicoloured.
691 80c. Royal barge in Hong Kong harbour 30 15
692 $1.70 Queen watching dancing display 60 70
693 $1.80 Fireworks display . . . 60 35
694 $2.30 Three portraits of Queen Elizabeth . . . . . 90 1·00
695 $5 Queen Elizabeth II . . . 2·00 3·25

154 Running

1992. Olympic Games, Barcelona. Multicoloured.
696 80c. Type **154** 40 20
697 $1.80 Swimming and javelin 80 1·00
698 $2.30 Cycling . . . . 1·60 1·75
699 $5 High jump . . . . 2·25 4·75
MS700 130 × 75 mm. As Nos. 696/9* 5·50 6·50
*The stamps from No. **MS**700 show the inscriptions in different colours, instead of the black on Nos. 696/9. The designs of the $1.80 and $5 values from the miniature sheet have also been rearranged so that "HONG KONG" and the Royal Cypher occur at the right of the inscription.

1992. "World Columbian Stamp Expo '92" Exhibition, Chicago. Sheet 130 × 75 mm, containing design as No. 613, but colours changed.
MS701 $10 multicoloured . . . . 5·50 7·00

155 Queen Elizabeth II
157 Principal Male Character

156 Stamps and Perforation Gauge

1992.
702 **155** 10c. mauve, blk & cerise 30 50
702bp 20c. black, indigo & bl 1·00 1·75
703 50c. red, black and yellow 30 30
704 60c. blue, black and light blue . . . . . 2·00 50
705 70c. mauve, black and lilac . . . . 2·00 65
706 80c. mauve, black and pink 30 20
707 90c. green, blk & grey 30 20
708 $1 brown, black and yellow 35 20
708b $1.10 red, black & orge 1·00 1·00
709 $1.20 violet, blk & lilac 35 25
757c $1.30 blue, black and orange 50 80
709c $1.40 green, black and yellow . . . . 1·25 70
709d $1.50 brown, black and blue . . . . 1·25 1·75
709e $1.60 green, black and lilac . . . . 1·25 1·50
710 $1.70 ultram, blk & bl 80 1·00
711 $1.80 mauve, black and grey . . . . 1·25 55
711a $1.90 green, black and stone . . . . 80 1·25
764 $2 blue, black and green 60 75
712b $2.10 red, black & green . . . . 1·75 1·75
713 $2.30 brown, black and pink . . . . 2·50 75
759 $2.40 blue, blk & grey 1·00 1·50
713b $2.50 green, black and yellow . . . . 1·00 1·25
713c $2.60 choc, blk & brn 1·25 2·25
713d $3.10 brown, black and blue . . . . 1·25 80
759e $5 green, black & lt grn 1·25 2·50
715 – $10 brown, black and cinnamon . . . . . 3·25 2·75
716 – $20 red, black & orange . . . . 4·25 4·50
717 – $50 dp grey, blk & grey 8·50 11·00

Nos. 715/17 are as Type **155**, but larger, 26 × 30 mm.

1992. Stamp Collecting. Multicoloured.
718 80c. Type **156** 30 25
719 $1.80 Handstamp of 1841, 1891 Jubilee overprint and tweezers 60 75
720 $2.30 Stamps of 1946 and 1949 under magnifying glass . . . . 85 1·25
721 $5 2c. of 1862 and watermark detector . . . . 2·00 4·00

1992. Olympic Games, Barcelona (3rd issue). As No. **MS**700, but additionally inscribed "To Commemorate the Opening of the 1992 Summer Olympic Games 25 July 1992", in English and Chinese, at foot of sheet.
MS722 130 × 75 mm. As Nos. 696/9 3·50 4·50

1992. "Kuala Lumpur '92" International Stamp Exhibition. Sheet 130 × 75 mm, containing design as No. 715, but colours changed.
MS723 $10 blue, black and light blue 4·75 6·00

1992. Chinese Opera. Multicoloured.
724 80c. Type **157** . . . . 1·00 25
725 $1.80 Martial character . . . 1·70 1·60
726 $2.30 Principal female character . . . . 2·00 2·25
727 $5 Comic character . . . . . 4·00 7·00

158 Hearts

1992. Greetings Stamps. Multicoloured.
728 80c. Type **158** 30 20
729 $1.80 Stars 55 60
730 $2.30 Presents . . . . 75 1·00
731 $5 Balloons . . . . 1·60 3·00

159 Cockerel

1993. Chinese New Year ("Year of the Cock").
732 **159** 80c. multicoloured 30 20
733 – $1.80 multicoloured . . . 70 80
734 – $2.30 multicoloured . . . 95 1·25
735 – $5 multicoloured . . . . 2·25 4·25
MS736 133 × 84 mm. Nos. 732/5 4·75 5·00
DESIGNS: $1.80 to $5, Different cock designs.

160 Pipa

161 Central Waterfront, Hong Kong in 1954

1993. Chinese String Musical Instruments. Multicoloured.
737 80c. Type **160** 40 20
738 $1.80 Erhu 70 80
739 $2.30 Ruan . . . . 95 1·25
740 $5 Gehu . . . . 2·00 3·75

1993. 40th Anniv of Coronation. Multicoloured.
741 80c. Type **161** 40 20
742 $1.80 Hong Kong in 1963 . . 70 75
743 $2.30 Hong Kong in 1975 . . 90 1·25
744 $5 Hong Kong in 1992 . . . 2·25 4·00

1993. 150th anniv of Hong Kong Post Office (2nd issue). Sheet 130 × 75 mm, containing design as No. 715.
MS745 $10 brown, black and cinnamon . . . . 4·50 5·50

1993. "Hong Kong '94" International Stamp Exhibition. Sheet 115 × 78 mm, containing design as No. 715, but colours changed.
MS746 $10 purple, black, yellow and blue . . . . 4·50 5·00

162 University of Science and Technology Building and Student

1993. Hong Kong's Contribution to Science and Technology. Multicoloured.
747 80c. Type **162** 25 20
748 $1.80 Science Museum building and energy machine exhibit 40 40
749 $2.30 Governor's Award and circuit board 60 90
750 $5 Dish aerials and world map . . . . 1·25 3·50

1993. "Bangkok '93" International Stamp Exhibition. Sheet 131 × 75 mm, containing design as No. 715, but colours changed.
MS751 $10 emerald, deep green and green . . . . 2·75 3·50

163 Red Calico Egg-fish

1993. Goldfish. Multicoloured.
752 $1 Type **163** 40 20
753 $1.90 Red cap oranda . . . 70 50
754 $2.40 Red and white fringetail . . . . 90 1·25
755 $5 Black and gold dragon-eye 2·25 4·00
MS756 130 × 75 mm. Nos. 752/5 6·50 7·50

164 Dog

1994. Chinese New Year ("Year of the Dog").
766 **164** $1 multicoloured 30 20
767 – $1.90 multicoloured . . . 50 55
768 – $2.40 multicoloured . . . 70 1·00
769 – $5 multicoloured . . . . 1·75 3·50
MS770 133 × 84 mm. Nos. 766/9 8·00 6·00
DESIGNS: $1.90 to $5, Different dog designs.

1994. "Hong Kong '94" International Stamp Exhibition. Sheet 130 × 75 mm, containing design as No. 759e.
MS771 **155** $5 green, black and light green . . . . 5·00 6·00

165 Modern Police Constables on Traffic Duty

1994. 150th Anniv of Royal Hong Kong Police Force. Multicoloured.
772 $1 Type **165** 30 20
773 $1.20 Marine policeman with binoculars 40 50
774 $1.90 Police uniforms of 1950 55 50
775 $2 Tactical firearms unit officer with sub-machine gun . . . . 75 1·00
776 $2.40 Early 20th-century police uniforms . . . . . 90 1·25
777 $5 Sikh and Chinese constables of 1900 . . . . 2·75 4·25

166 Dragon Boat Festival

1994. Traditional Chinese Festivals. Multicoloured.
778 $1 Type **166** 35 20
779 $1.90 Lunar New Year . . . 60 70
780 $2.40 Seven Sisters Festival 85 1·25
781 $5 Mid-Autumn Festival . . 1·75 3·75

1994. Conference of Commonwealth Postal Administrations, Hong Kong. Sheet 134 × 83 mm, containing design as No. 715.
MS782 $10 brown, black and cinnamon . . . . 5·00 6·00

167 Swimming

1994. 15th Commonwealth Games, Victoria, Canada. Multicoloured.
783 $1 Type **167** 25 20
784 $1.90 Bowls 40 55
785 $2.40 Gymnastics . . . . . 50 1·00
786 $5 Weightlifting . . . . . . 90 3·25

168 Dr. James Legge and Students

1994. Dr. James Legge (Chinese scholar) Commemoration.
787 **168** $1 multicoloured 55 60

169 Alcyonium Coral

1994. Corals. Multicoloured.
788 $1 Type **169** 35 20
789 $1.90 Zoanthus 45 60
790 $2.40 Tubastrea . . . . . . 55 1·00
791 $5 Platygyra . . . . 1·00 3·00
MS792 130 × 75 mm. Nos. 788/91 4·50 5·00

170 Pig

1995. Chinese New Year ("Year of the Pig").
793 **170** $1 multicoloured 30 30
794 – $1.90 multicoloured . . . 50 80
795 – $2.40 multicoloured . . . 60 1·10
796 – $5 multicoloured . . . . 1·00 3·00
MS797 130 × 84 mm. Nos. 793/6 4·25 4·50
DESIGNS: $1.90 to $5, Different pig designs.

171 Hong Kong Rugby Sevens

1995. International Sporting Events in Hong Kong. Multicoloured.
798 $1 Type **171** 45 20
799 $1.90 The China Sea Yacht Race 60 80
800 $2.40 International Dragon Boat Races . . . . 85 1·10
801 $5 Hong Kong International Horse Races . . . . 1·75 3·50

172 Tsui Shing Lau Pagoda

1995. Hong Kong Traditional Rural Buildings. Multicoloured.
802 $1 Type **172** 30 25
803 $1.90 Sam Tung Uk village 45 65
804 $2.40 Lo Wai village . . . . 60 1·00
805 $5 Man Shek Tong house . . 1·10 3·00

173 Regimental Badge

1995. Disbandment of the Royal Hong Kong Regiment. Multicoloured.
806 $1.20 Type **173** 40 25
807 $2.10 Regimental guidon (horiz) 50 65
808 $2.60 Colour of Hong Kong Volunteer Defence Corps, 1928 (horiz) . . . . . . 60 1·00
809 $5 Cap badge of Royal Hong Kong Defence Force, 1951 1·00 2·75

1995. "Singapore '95" International Stamp Exhibition. Sheet 130 × 75 mm, containing design as No. 715, but colours changed.
MS810 $10 mauve, green, yellow and lilac . . . . 4·00 5·00

1995. 50th Anniv of End of Second World War. Sheet 130 × 75 mm, containing design as No. 715.
MS811 $10 brown, black and cinnamon . . . . 4·00 5·00

174 Bruce Lee

1995. Hong Kong Film Stars. Multicoloured.
812 $1.20 Type **174** . . . . . . 2·00 55
813 $2.10 Leung Sing-por . . . . 2·25 1·40
814 $2.60 Yam Kim-fai . . . . . 3·00 1·75
815 $5 Lin Dai . . . . 3·50 4·50

175 Rat

1996. Chinese New Year ("Year of the Rat").
816 **175** $1.20 multicoloured . . . 25 30
817 – $2.10 multicoloured . . . 45 55
818 – $2.60 multicoloured . . . 50 65
819 – $5 multicoloured . . . . 1·25 1·75
MS820 133 × 83 mm. Nos. 816/19 2·50 3·50
DESIGNS: $2.10 to $5, Rats (different).

1996. Visit "HONG KONG '97" Stamp Exhibition (1st issue). Sheet 130 × 80 mm, containing design as No. 715, but colours changed.
MS821 $10 orange, black and green 4·50 5·50
See also Nos. **MS**827, **MS**841 and **MS**872/3.

176 Rhythmic Gymnastics

1996. Olympic Games, Atlanta. Multicoloured with Royal cypher and face values in black and Olympic rings multicoloured.
822 $1.20 Type **176** 25 25
823 $2.10 Diving 45 65
824 $2.60 Athletics 55 75
825 $5 Basketball . . . . 1·75 3·25
MS826 130 × 75 mm. As Nos. 822/5, but Royal Cypher and Olympic Rings in gold and face values in black (medal in bottom sheet margin) . . . . 2·50 3·50
See also Nos. 832/5.

1996. Visit "HONG KONG '97" Stamp Exhibition (2nd issue). Sheet 130 × 80 mm, containing design as No. 715, but colours changed.
MS827 $10 green, deep green and violet . . . . 2·50 3·00

177 Painted Pottery Basin, c. 4500–3700 B.C.

1996. Archaeological Discoveries. Multicoloured.
828 $1.20 Type **177** 35 25
829 $2.10 Stone "yue" (ceremonial axe), c. 2900–2200 B.C. 40 65
830 $2.60 Stone "ge" (halberd), c. 2200–1500 B.C. . . . . 45 1·00
831 $5 Pottery tripod, c. 25–220 A.D. . . . . 1·00 2·50

1996. Opening of Centennial Olympic Games, Atlanta. Designs as Nos. 822/5, but with Royal Cypher and Olympic Rings in gold and face values in colours quoted.
832 $1.20 Type **176** (mauve) . . . 35 25
833 $2.10 As No. 823 (blue) . . . 40 60
834 $2.60 As No. 824 (green) . . 45 90
835 $5 As No. 825 (red) . . . . 1·00 2·75
MS836 130 × 75 mm. As No. **MS**826, but with medal in top margin . . . . 2·50 3·50
The stamps in Nos. **MS**826 and **MS**836 are similar. The miniature sheets differ in the marginal inscriptions and illustrations. No. **MS**826 is inscribed "1996 OLYMPIC GAMES" and has a Gold Medal in the bottom margin. No. **MS**836 is inscribed "TO COMMEMORATE THE OPENING OF THE CENTENNIAL OLYMPIC GAMES 19 JULY 1996" and has the medal in the top margin.

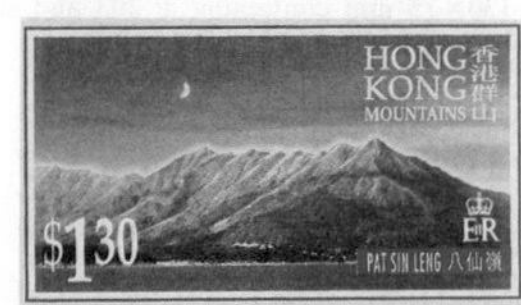

178 Pat Sin Leng Mountain

1996. Mountains. Multicoloured.
837 $1.30 Type **178** 45 35
838 $2.50 Ma On Shan (40 × 35 mm) . . . . . . 65 1·00
839 $3.10 Lion Rock (35 × 40 mm) . . . . . . 85 1·40
840 $5 Lantau Peak (25 × 46½ mm) . . . . . . 1·10 2·25

1996. Visit "HONG KONG '97" Stamp Exhibition (3rd issue). Sheet 130 × 80 mm, containing design as No. 715, but colours changed.
MS841 $10 green, black and red 2·50 3·50

1996. Hong Kong Team's Achievements at Atlanta Olympic Games. Sheet 130 × 75 mm, containing No. 715.
MS842 $10 brown, black and cinnamon . . . . 2·50 3·25

179 Main Building, University of Hong Kong, 1912

1996. Urban Heritage. Multicoloured.
843 $1.30 Type **179** 30 70
844 $2.50 Western Market, 1906 50 85
845 $3.10 Old Pathological Institute, 1905 . . . . . . 55 1·00
846 $5 Flagstaff House, 1846 . . 70 2·25

1996. Serving the Community. Sheet 130 × 75 mm, containing design as No. 619, but smaller, 25 × 35 mm. Multicoloured.
MS847 $5 Multi-racial society . . 1·00 1·25

180 Part of Hong Kong Skyline

1997.
848 **180** 10c. purple and pink . . . 15 30
849 – 20c. brown and red . . . 30 30
850 – 50c. green and orange . . 20 40
851 – $1 blue and yellow . . . 30 20
852 – $1.20 green and yellow . . 30 40
853 – $1.30 violet and green . . 30 25
854 – $1.40 purple and green . . 30 40
855 – $1.60 purple and green . . 30 50
856 – $2 green and blue 40 50
857 – $2.10 turquoise and blue 40 60
858 – $2.50 violet and mauve 50 1·00
859 – $3.10 purple and mauve 60 70
860 – $5 mauve and orange . . 1·25 1·00
861 – $10 multicoloured (28 × 32 mm) . . . . . 2·00 2·50
862 – $20 multicoloured (28 × 32 mm) . . . . . 3·50 5·00
863 – $50 multicoloured (28 × 32 mm) . . . . . 8·00 11·00
MS864 273 × 53 mm. Nos. 848/60 3·50 4·00
MS865 95 × 72 mm. Nos. 861/3 13·00 13·50
DESIGNS: 20c. to $50, Different sections of Hong Kong skyline.
See also Nos. **MS**872/3 and **MS**892.

1997. Visit "HONG KONG '97" Stamp Exhibition (4th issue). Sheet 130 × 80 mm, containing No. 861, with marginal illustration in violet.
MS872 $10 multicoloured . . . . 1·75 3·50

1997. Visit "HONG KONG '97" Stamp Exhibition (5th issue). Sheet 130 × 80 mm, containing No. 861, with marginal illustration in brown.
MS873 $10 multicoloured . . . . 1·75 3·50

181 Ox

1997. Chinese New Year ("Year of the Ox").
874 **181** $1.30 multicoloured . . . 25 25
875 $2.50 multicoloured . . . 40 55
876 $3.10 multicoloured . . . 55 90
877 $5 multicoloured . . . . 85 2·00
MS878 133 × 84 mm. Nos. 874/7 2·00 3·50

182 Yellow-breasted Bunting

1997. Migratory Birds. Multicoloured.
884 $1.30 Type **182** 30 35
885 $2.50 Great knot 40 55
886 $3.10 Falcated teal 55 90
887 $5 Black-faced spoonbill . . 85 2·00

183 Hong Kong Stadium

1997. Modern Landmarks. Multicoloured.
888 $1.30 Type **183** 25 25
889 $2.50 Peak Tower 50 55
890 $3.10 Hong Kong Convention and Exhibition Centre . . . . 75 1·10
891 $5 Lantau bridge . . . . . . 1·10 2·50
MS892 130 × 76 mm. No. 891 . . 1·25 1·75

1997. Paralympic Games, Atlanta (1996). Sheet 130 × 75 mm, containing No. 861.
MS898 $10 multicoloured . . . . 1·75 2·75

1997. History of the Hong Kong Post Office. Sheet 130 × 75 mm, containing design as No. 677, but redrawn smaller, 22 × 38 mm.
MS899 $5 multicoloured . . . . 1·00 1·75

184 House of Sam Tung Uk

186 Clam

185 Graphs and Hong Kong Bank (Finance and Banking)

1997. Establishment of Hong Kong as Special Administrative Region of People's Republic of China. Multicoloured.
900 $1.30 Type **184** 30 15
901 $1.60 Hong Kong Bank and vehicles 30 15
902 $2.50 Buildings and Hong Kong Convention and Exhibition Centre 45 30
903 $2.60 Container Terminal . . 45 30
904 $3.10 Junks and dolphins . . 60 30
905 $5 Bauhinia flower and clouds 85 30
MS906 131 × 75 mm. No. 905 . . 80 80

1997. World Bank Group and International Monetary Fund Annual Meetings. Multicoloured.
907 $1.30 Type **185** 30 15
908 $2.50 Share prices (Investment) and Stock Exchange 45 30
909 $3.10 Map on printed circuit and dish aerial (Trade and Telecommunications) . . . 60 45
910 $5 Satellite image and road junctions (Infrastructure and Transport) 70 45

1997. Sea Shells. Multicoloured.
911 $1.30 Type **186** 30 15
912 $2.50 Cowrie 45 30
913 $3.10 Cone 55 45
914 $5 Murex 70 45

187 Tiger

1998. Chinese New Year ("Year of the Tiger").
915 **187** $1.30 multicoloured . . . 30 15
916 $2.50 multicoloured . . . 45 30
917 $3.10 multicoloured . . . 60 45
918 $5 multicoloured 70 45
MS919 133 × 84 mm. Nos. 915/18 1·90 1·90

188 "Star", 1900s

1998. Centenary of Star Ferry. Multicoloured.
920 $1.30 Type **188** 30 15
921 $2.50 "Star", 1910s–20s . . . 45 30
922 $3.10 "Star", 1920s–1950s . . 45 30
923 $5 "Star", 1950s onwards . . 85 30

189 Observation Lounge

1998. Inauguration of Hong Kong International Airport, Chek Lap Kok. Multicoloured.
924 $1.30 Type **189** 30 15
925 $1.60 Couple boarding train 30 15
926 $2.50 Train and suspension bridge 45 30
927 $2.60 Concourse and mail vans at Airmail Centre . . 45 30
928 $3.10 Aircraft in bays 60 30
929 $5 Airplane taking off . . . 85 30
MS930 145 × 79 mm. No. 929 . . 85 85

190 De Havilland D.H.86 Dragon Express "Dorado" (Hong Kong—Penang Service, 1936)

1998. Closure of Kaj Tak Airport. Sheet 130 × 75 mm.
MS931 **190** $5 multicoloured . . 85 85
Type **190** is a redrawn version of Type **111**.

191 Grasshopper and Cub Scouts and Knot

192 Graphic Design

1998. 85th Anniv of Hong Kong Scout Association. Multicoloured.
932 $1.30 Type **191** 30 15
933 $2.50 Two scouts, knot, watchtower and tents . . . 45 30
934 $3.10 Two venture scouts, knot, sailing dinghies and helicopter 45 30
935 $5 Rover scout and adult leader, knot and buildings 85 30

1998. Hong Kong Design. Multicoloured.
936 $1.30 Type **192** 30 15
937 $2.50 Product design 45 30
938 $3.10 Interior design 45 45
939 $5 Fashion design 85 45

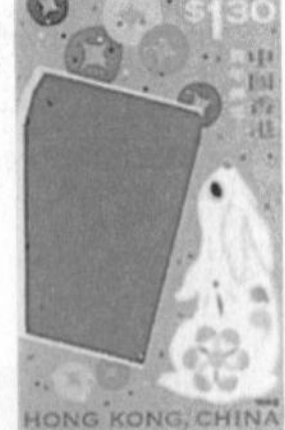

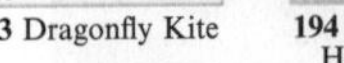

193 Dragonfly Kite **194** Rabbit ("Kung Hei Fat Choi")

1998. Kites. Multicoloured.
940 $1.30 Type **193** 30 15
941 $2.50 Dragon kite 45 30
942 $3.10 Butterfly kite 45 45
943 $5 Goldfish kite 85 45
MS944 135 × 85 mm. Nos. 940/3 2·00 2·00

1999. Chinese New Year ("Year of the Rabbit"). Multicoloured.
945 $1.30 Type **194** 30 15
946 $2.50 Rabbit and scroll ("Good Health") 45 30
947 $3.10 Rabbit and tangerine ("Good Luck") 60 45
948 $5 Rabbit and sweet tray ("May all your wishes come true") 85 45

The gold panels of the designs can be scratched off to reveal a greeting in Chinese characters as given in brackets. Prices for Nos. 945/8 are for examples with the gold panels intact.

195 Rabbit

1999. Chinese Lunar Cycle. Sheet 250 × 48 mm containing similar designs to 1987—98 New Year issues but with inscriptions as in T **195** and some face values altered. Multicoloured.
MS949 $1.30 As Type **175**; $1.30 As Type **181**; $1.30 As Type **187**; $1.30 As Type **195**; $1.30 As Type **170**; $1.30 As Type **130**; $1.30 As No. 768; $1.30 As Type **136**; $1.30 As No. 735; $1.30 As Type **53**; $1.30 As Type **148**; $1.30 As Type **143** . . . . . . 3·50 3·50

196 Calligraphy

1999. International Year of the Elderly. Mult.
950 $1.30 Type **196** 30 15
951 $2.50 Holding bird cage . . . 45 30
952 $3.10 Playing chess 60 60
953 $5 Holding walking stick (voluntary services) 85 70

1999. Hong Kong Team's Achievements at 13th Asian Games, Bangkok (1998). Sheet 135 × 85 mm.
MS954 Nos. 856/7 . . . . 2·00 2·00

197 An An

1999. Presentation of Giant pandas An An and Jia Jia to Hong Kong. Sheet 132 × 78 mm.
MS955 **197** $10 multicoloured . . 2·50 2·50

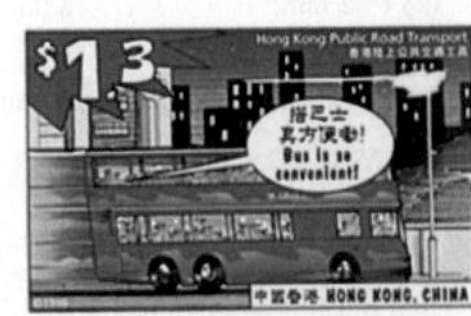

198 Bus

1999. Public Transport. Multicoloured.
956 $1.30 Type **198** 30 15
957 $2.40 Minibus 45 30
958 $2.50 Tram 60 45
959 $2.60 Taxi 70 45
960 $3.10 "Airport Express" train 85 60

199 Hong Kong Harbour

1999. Hong Kong–Singapore Joint Issue. Mult.
961 $1.20 Type **199** 30 15
962 $1.30 Singapore skyline . . . 30 15
963 $2.50 Giant Buddha, Lantau Island, Hong Kong 45 30
964 $2.60 Merlion statue, Sentosa Island, Singapore 45 30
965 $3.10 Street scene, Hong Kong 60 45
966 $5 Bugis Junction, Singapore 85 45
MS967 133 × 76 mm. Nos. 961/6 3·00 3·00

1999. "China 1999" International Stamp Exhibition, Peking. 130 × 75 mm.
MS968 No. 861 . . . . 2·00 2·00

200 Flags of Hong Kong and People's Republic, and Hong Kong

1999. 50th Anniv of People's Republic of China. Multicoloured.
969 $1.30 Type **200** 45 15
970 $2.50 "Bauhinia blakeana" and Hong Kong harbour 60 45
971 $3.10 Chinese dragon dance 70 45
972 $5 Firework display over Hong Kong . . . . 1·10 70

201 Museum of Tea Ware **202** Dolphins

1999. Hong Kong Landmarks and Tourist Attractions. Multicoloured. (a) Size 24 × 29 mm (10c. to $5) or 26 × 31 mm (others).
973 10c. Type **201** 10 10
974 20c. St. John's Cathedral . . 10 10
975 50c. Legislative Council building 10 10
976 $1 Tai Fu Tai 30 10
977 $1.20 Wong Tai Sin Temple 30 10
978 $1.30 Victoria Harbour . . . 30 10
979 $1.40 Hong Kong Railway Museum 30 10
980 $1.60 Tsim Sha Tsui clocktower 30 10
980a $1.80 Hong Kong Stadium 45 10
980b $1.90 Western Market . . . 45 10
981 $2 Happy Valley racecourse 45 10
982 $2.10 Kowloon–Canton Railway 45 10
982a $2.40 Repulse Bay 45 10
983 $2.50 Chi Lin Nunnery, Kowloon 45 10
983b $3 The Peak Tower 60 10
984 $3.10 Giant Buddha, Po Lin Monastery, Lantau Island 70 10
985 $5 Pagoda, Aw Boon Haw Gardens 85 10
986 $10 Tsing Ma bridge . . . 1·70 30
986a $13 Hong Kong Cultural Centre . . . . 2·20 60
987 $20 Hong Kong Convention and Exhibition Centre . . 3·50 1·40
988 $50 Hong Kong International Airport . . 8·50 3·50
MS989 210 × 153 mm. Nos. 973/85 2·20 2·20
MS990 118 × 89 mm. 986/8 . . . 12·00 12·00

(b) Size 20 × 24 mm.
991 10c. As Type **201** 10 10
992 50c. As No. 975 . . . . . 10 10
993 $1.30 As No. 978 . . . . . 30 25
993a $1.40 As No. 979 . . . . . 30 10
994 $1.60 As No. 980 . . . . . 30 30
994a $1.80 As No. 980a 45 10
994b $2.40 As No. 982a 45 10
994c $3 As No. 984 . . . . . . 60 10

1999. Endangered Species. Indo-Pacific Humpbacked Dolphin ("Chinese White Dolphin").
995 **202** $1.30 multicoloured . . . 30 10
996 – $2.50 multicoloured . . . 45 30
997 – $3.10 multicoloured . . . 45 45
998 – $5 multicoloured 85 60
MS999 150 × 80 mm. Nos. 995/8 2·00 2·00
DESIGNS: $2.50 to $5 Various designs showing dolphins as Type **202**.

203 Dragon Boat Race (fire) and City Skyline (metal)

1999. New Millennium (1st issue). The Five Elements. Sheet 130 × 75 mm containing T **203** and similar horiz designs. Multicoloured.
MS1000 $5 Type **203**; $5 Tsing Ma bridge (wood) and birds flying over Mai Po Marches (water) 2·00 2·00

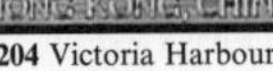

204 Victoria Harbour **206** Dragon

205 Scales on Globe (Au Chung-yip)

2000. New Millennium.
1001 **204** $50 multicoloured . . . 12·50 12·50
No. 1001 is embossed with 22 carat gold.

2000. New Millennium. Winning Entries in Children's Millennium Stamp Design Competition. Mult.
1002 $1.30 Type **205** 30 10
1003 $2.50 Globe, space shuttle, houses and children watering (Cheung Hang) 45 30
1004 $3.10 Planets (Valerie Teh) 60 45
1005 $5 Planets, spacecraft and satellite (Tsui Ming-yin) 85 45

2000. Chinese New Year ("Year of the Dragon").
1006 **206** $1.30 multicoloured . . 30 30
1007 – $2.50 multicoloured . . 45 45
1008 – $3.10 multicoloured . . 60 45
1009 – $5 multicoloured . . . . 1·00 60
MS1010 Two sheets, each 135 × 85 mm. (a) Nos. 1006/9. (b) $5 No. 1009. Imperf Set of 2 sheets 3·25 3·25
DESIGNS: $2.50 to $5 Various dragons.

2000. Establishment of the Certification Authority (1st issue). Sheet 140 × 90 mm containing design as No. 986.
MS1011 $10 multicoloured . . . 2·00 2·00

2000. Visit "HONG KONG 2001" Stamp Exhibition (1st issue). Sheet 130 × 74 mm containing design as No. 986, and with marginal illustrations showing bird.
MS1012 $10 multicoloured . . . 2·00 2·00
See also Nos. **MS**1017, **MS**1022, **MS**1027, **MS**1028, **MS**1037 and **MS**1052.

207 Hong Kong Heritage Museum, Sha Tin

2000. Museums and Libraries. Multicoloured.
1013 $1.30 Type **207** 30 10
1014 $2.50 Central Library, Causeway Bay 45 30
1015 $3.10 Museum of Coastal Defence, Shau Kei Wan 60 45
1016 $5 Museum of History, Tsim Sha Tsui East . . . 85 60

2000. Visit "HONG KONG 2001" Stamp Exhibition (2nd issue). Sheet 130 × 75 mm containing design as No. 986, and with marginal illustration showing flowers.
MS1017 $10 multicoloured . . . 2·00 2·00

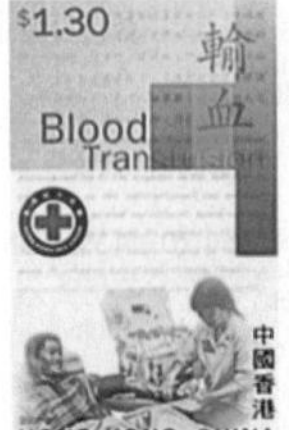

208 Patient and Nurse (Blood Transfusion) **209** Lantern Fly

2000. 50th Anniv of Hong Kong Red Cross. Multicoloured.
1018 $1.30 Type **208** 30 10
1019 $2.50 Doctor and child (Special Education and Care for the Disabled) . . 45 30
1020 $3.10 Man distributing blankets (Disaster relief) 60 45
1021 $5 Volunteer and young man (Youth and Voluntary services) . . . 85 45
MS1022 130 × 75 mm. Nos. 1018/21 2·25 2·25

2000. Insects. Multicoloured.
1023 $1.30 Type **209** 30 10
1024 $2.50 Yellow-spotted emerald 45 30
1025 $3.10 Hong Kong birdwing (butterfly) 60 45
1026 $5 Red-cap tortoise beetle 1·00 60
MS1027 130 × 75 mm. Nos. 1023/6 2·25 2·25

210 Lion Rock

2000. Visit "HONG KONG 2001" Stamp Exhibition (3rd issue). Sheet 130 × 75 mm.
MS1028 **210** $10 multicoloured 2·00 2·00

211 Cycling and Tennis

2000. Olympic Games, Sydney. Multicoloured.
1029 $1.30 Type **211** 30 10
1030 $2.50 Table tennis and running 45 30
1031 $3.10 Wrestling and rowing 60 45
1032 $5 Diving and wind surfing 85 45

212 View of Street (Establishment of Chamber, 1900)

2000. Centenary of General Chamber of Commerce. Multicoloured.
1033 $1.30 Type **212** 30 10
1034 $2.50 Old and new headquarters (relocation, 1922) 45 30
1035 $3.10 Victims of Pak Tin village fire receiving aid 60 45
1036 $5 Man using abacus and hand using mouse 85 60

213 Corals

2000. Visit "HONG KONG 2001" Stamp Exhibition (4th issue). 129 × 75 mm.
MS1037 **213** $10 multicoloured 2·00 2·00

2000. I.T.U. Telecome, Asia 2000. Sheet 130 × 75 mm containing design as No. 986.
MS1038 $10 multicoloured . . . 2·00 2·00

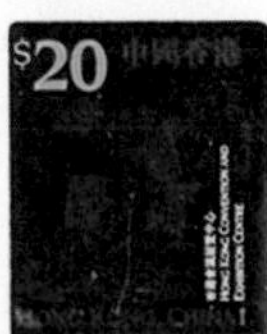

214 Hong Kong Convention and Exhibition Centre

2000. New Millennium. Sheet 91 × 151 mm.
MS1039 **214** $20 multicoloured 4·00 4·00

215 Snake

216 Leaves and Pebbles ("Happy Memories")

2001. Chinese New Year ("Year of the Snake").
1040 **215** $1.30 multicoloured . . 30 10
1041 – $2.50 multicoloured . . 45 30
1042 – $3.10 multicoloured . . 60 45
1043 – $5 multicoloured 85 45
MS1044 Two sheets, each 135 × 85 mm. (a) $5 Nos. 1040/3. (b) $5 No. 1043. Imperf . . . 3·00 3·00
DESIGNS: $2.50 to $5 Showing various snakes.

2001. Greetings Stamps. Multicoloured.
1045 $1.30 Type **216** 30 10
1046 $1.60 Swans ("Happy Valentine's Day") 30 30
1047 $2.50 Chicks ("Happy Birthday") 60 30
1048 $2.60 Cherry blossom ("Happy New Year") . . 60 30
1049 $3.10 Bamboo ("A Successful Year") 70 30
1050 $5 Poinsettia ("Merry Christmas") . . . . . . 1·10 45

2001. "HONG KONG 2001" Stamp Exhibition. Sheet 135 × 90 mm.
MS1051 $50 Type **217**; $50 Snake ("Year of the Snake") . . . . 15·00 15·00

218 Schima tree

2001. Visit "HONG KONG 201" Stamp Exhibition (5th issue). Sheet 130 × 75 mm.
MS1052 **218** $5 multicoloured . . 85 85

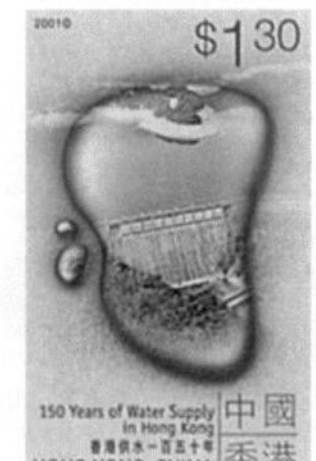

219 Tai Tam Tuk Reservoir

2001. 150th Anniv of Hong Kong's Public Water Supply. Multicoloured.
1053 $1.30 Type **219** 30 10
1054 $2.50 Plover Cove Reservoir 45 30
1055 $3.10 Guangdong to Hong Kong water pipeline . . . 60 45
1056 $5 Water monitoring equipment and chemical symbols 85 45

220 Ng Cho-fan and Pak Yin

2001. Hong Kong Film Stars. Multicoloured.
1057 $1.30 Type **220** 30 10
1058 $2.50 Sun Ma Si-tsang and Tang Bik-wan 45 30
1059 $3.10 Cheung Wood-yau and Wong Man-lei . . . 60 45
1060 $5 Mak Bing-wing and Fung Wong-nui 85 45

2001. 9th National Games, Guangzhou, People's Republic of China. Preliminary Contest for Sanda (discipline in National Game), Hong Kong. Sheet 130 × 75 mm containing design as No. 985 and with marginal illustrations showing boxing gloves.
MS1061 $5 multicoloured 85 85

221 Dragon Boat and Sydney Opera House

2001. Dragon Boat Racing. Multicoloured.
1062 $5 Type **221** . . . . 1·00 45
1063 $5 Dragon boat racing and Hong Kong Convention and Exhibition Centre . . 1·00 45
MS1064 106 × 70 mm. Nos. 1062/3 2·00 2·00

222 Emblem

2001. Choice of Beijing as 2008 Olympic Host City.
1065 **222** $1.30 multicoloured . . 45 30

2001. "PHILA NIPPON 02" International Stamp Exhibition, Tokyo. Sheet 130 × 75 mm containing design as No. 986.
MS1066 $10 multicoloured . . . 2·00 2·00

223 Pouring Tea (Gongfu tea)

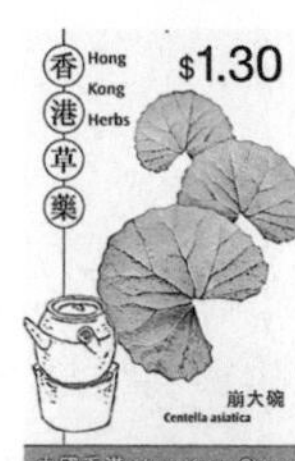

224 *Centella asiatica*

2001. Tea Culture. Multicoloured.
1067 $1.30 Type **223** 30 10
1068 $2.50 Hong Kong style tea 45 30
1069 $3.10 Pouring water (Yum Cha and Dim Sum) . . . 60 45
1070 $5 Pouring hot water in to tea pot 85 45

2001. Medicinal Herbs. Multicoloured.
1071 $1.30 Type **224** 30 10
1072 $2.50 *Lobelia chinensis* . . . 45 30
1073 $3.10 *Gardenia jasminoides* 60 45
1074 $5 *Scutellaria indica* 85 45

225 Child dressed as Bear

226 Horse

2001. Children's Stamps. Self-adhesive gum.
1075 $1.30 Type **225** 30 30
1076 $2.50 Child dressed as duck 60 30
1077 $3.10 Child dressed as pot plant 70 45
1078 $5 Child dressed as bee . . 1·10 45
MS1079 130 × 92 mm. Nos. 1075/8 2·75 1·70
The stamps had portions of the design left white for users to colour as they wished. Such embellishments did not affect the postal validity of the stamps.

2002. Chinese New Year ("Year of the Horse").
1080 **226** $1.30 multicoloured . . 30 10
1081 – $2.50 multicoloured . . 45 30
1082 – $3.10 multicoloured . . 60 45
1083 – $5 multicoloured 85 45
MS1084 Two sheets, each 135 × 85 mm. (a) Nos. 1080/3. (b) No. 1083. Imperf . . . . . . 3·25 2·20
DESIGNS: Nos. 1081/3, showing horses.

2002. Serving the Community Festival 2002. Sheet 75 × 130 mm, containing design as No. 985.
MS1085 $5 multicoloured . . . . 1·10 70

227 Snake

2002. Chinese New Year ("Year of the Snake"). Sheet 135 × 90 mm.
MS1086 $50 Type **227**; $50 Horse ("Year of the Horse") . . . . 18·00 14·00
No. **MS**1086 has the snake and the horse embossed in gold and silver foil.

228 "Lines in Motion" (detail, Chui Tze-hung)

2002. Modern Art. Multicoloured.
1087 $1.30 Type **228** 30 10
1088 $2.50 "Volume and Time" (detail, Hon Chi-fun) . . 45 30
1089 $3.10 "Bright Sun" (sculpture, detail, Aries Lee) 60 45
1090 $5 "Midsummer" (detail, Irene Chou) 85 45

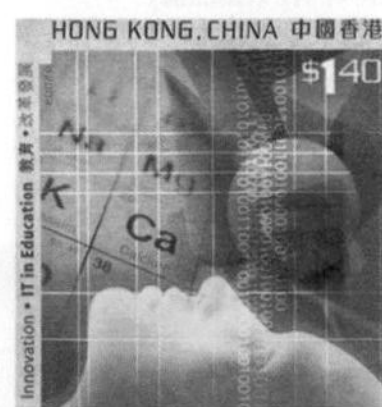

229 Face and Periodic Table (Education)

2002. Information Technology. Multicoloured.
1091 $1.40 Type **229** 25 10
1092 $2.40 Face, world map and internet symbols (communications) 40 25
1093 $3 Face, film and musical notes (entertainment) . . 55 40
1094 $5 Face, buildings and city (commerce) 80 40

230 Player and Football

2002. World Cup Football Championship. Japan and South Korea. Multicoloured.
1095 $1.40 Type **230** 25 10
1096 $1.40 Players tackling and crowd 25 10

231 North Atlantic Pink Tree Coral, Pacific Orange Cup Coral and North Pacific Horn Coral

2002. Corals. Multicoloured.
1097 $1.40 Type **231** 25 10
1098 $2.40 North Atlantic giant orange tree coral and black coral 40 25
1099 $3 *Dendronepthea gigantea* and *Dendronepthea* . . . 55 40
1100 $5 *Tubastrea* and *Echinogorgia* and island 80 40
MS1101 161 × 85 mm. Nos. 1097/1100 . . . . 2·00 1·40
Stamps in similar designs were issued by Canada.

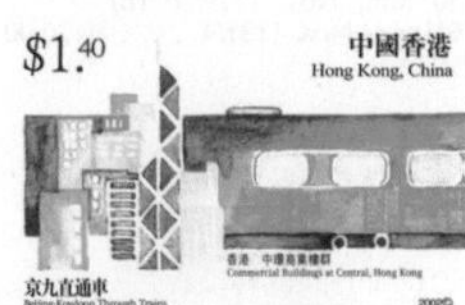

232 Hong Kong Buildings and Train

2002. 5th Anniv of Bejing—Kowloon Through Train Service. Multicoloured.
1102 $1.40 Type **232** 25 10
1103 $2.40 Wuhan—Changjiang Bridge and train 40 25
1104 $3 Pagodas, Shaolin Monastery, Zhengzhou and train 55 40
1105 $5 Temple of Heaven, Bejing and front of train 95 40
Nos. 1102/5 were issued together, forming a composite design of a train.

233 Chinese White Dolphins and Coral

2002. 5th Anniv of Hong Kong's Status as Special Administrative Region of People's Republic of China. Multicoloured.
1106 $1.40 Type **233** 25 10
1107 $2.40 School children and bauhinia flowers 40 25
1108 $3 Birds in flight over Hong Kong airport 50 40
1109 $5 Flags of China and Hong Kong, buildings and fireworks 80 50
MS1110 135 × 85 mm. Nos. 1106/9 2·10 1·40

2002. "PHILAKOREA 2002" World Stamp Exhibition, Seoul, South Korea. Sheet 131 × 75 mm, containing design as No. 986.
MS1111 $10 multicoloured . . . 2·00 1·40

2002. "AMPHILEX 2002" World Stamp Exhibition, Amsterdam. Sheet 130 × 75 mm, containing design as No. 986.
MS1112 $10 multicoloured . . . 2·00 1·40

2002. Hukou Waterfall Shanxi, People's Republic of China. Sheet 140 × 90 mm, containing design as No. 986.
MS1113 $10 multicoloured . . . 2·00 1·40

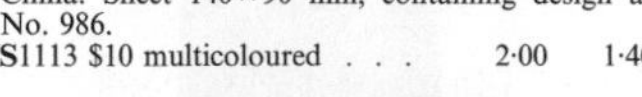

234 Ping Chau

2002. Geology of Hong Kong. Multicoloured.
1114 $1.40 Type **234** 25 10
1115 $2.40 Port Island 40 25
1116 $3 Po Pin Chau 80 40
1117 $5 Lamma Island . . . . . 1·80 1·00
MS1118 136 × 81 mm. Nos. 1114/17 2·10 1·40

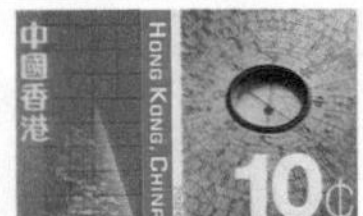

235 Radar Signal and Luopan (fengshui compass)

2002. Cultural Diversity. Multicoloured.

1119 10c. Type **235** 10 10
1120 20c. Calculator and abacus 10 10
1121 50c. Incense coils and stained-glass window . . 10 10
1122 $1 Chair and Luohan (bed) 25 10
1123 $1.40 Dim Sum (dumplings) and loaves of bread . . . 25 10
1124 $1.80 Cutlery and chopsticks 25 10
1125 $1.90 Canned drinks and tea caddies 25 10
1126 $2 European and oriental wedding cakes 40 10
1127 $2.40 Erhu (stringed instrument) and violin . . 55 10
1128 $2.50 Oriental letterbox and internet symbol 55 10
1129 $3 Yachts and Dragon boat 55 10
1130 $5 Traditional tiled roof and modern office block . . . 95 15
1131 $10 Ballet dancers and Chinese opera character 1·70 15
1132 $13 Chess pieces and Xiangqi pieces (Chinese chess) . . . . 2·10 30
1133 $20 Christmas lights and mid-autumn festival lantern . . . . 3·50 45
1134 $50 Sculptures "Oval with points" (Henry Moore) and "Tai Chi series: Single Whip" (Ju Ming) 15·00 2·75
MS1135 Two sheets (a) 210 × 150 mm. Nos. 1119/30 (b) 122 × 101 mm. Nos. 1131/4 . . 20·00 15·00

236 Christmas Tree

2002. Christmas. Multicoloured.

1146 $1.40 Type **236** 25 10
1147 $2.40 Bauble 40 25
1148 $3 Snowman 55 40
1149 $5 Bell 80 40

237 Train and Station (Main Street)

2003. Disneyland Hong Kong. Multicoloured.

1150 $1.40 Type **237** 25 10
1151 $2.40 Castle (Fantasyland) 40 25
1152 $3 Tree house (Adventureland) 55 40
1153 $5 Pylons (Tomorrowland) 80 40
MS1154 135 × 85 mm. Nos. 1150/3 2·10 1·40

Nos. 1150/**MS**1154 each have an embossed figure of Mickey Mouse in the lower left corner.

238 Argali Ram

2003. Chinese New Year ("Year of the Ram"). Multicoloured.

1155 $1.40 Type **238** 25 10
1156 $2.40 Sheep 45 25
1157 $3 Tahr ram 55 40
1158 $5 Gazella ram 80 40
MS1159 Two sheets, each 135 × 85 mm. (a) Nos. 1155/8; (b) $5 No. 1158 Set of 2 sheets . . 4·00 2·40

(b) Flocked paper. P 13. Litho Cartor.

1160 $10 As No. 1008 ("Year of the Dragon") . . . . . . 2·00 1·40
1161 $10 As No. 1042 ("Year of the Snake") . . . . . . 2·00 1·40
1162 $10 As No. 1081 ("Year of the Horse") . . . . . . 2·00 1·40
1163 $10 As No. 1158 ("Year of the Ram") . . . . 2·00 1·40

(c) Size 38 × 51 mm. Ordinary paper.

MS1164 135 × 90 mm. $50 As No. 1162 ("Year of the Horse") (37 × 50 mm); $50 As No. 1157 (37 × 50 mm) . . . .

No. **MS**1164 has the horse and ram embossed with gold and silver foil.

239 Letter Writing

2003. Traditional Trades and Crafts. Multicoloured.

1165 $1.40 Type **239** 25 10
1166 $1.80 Bird cage maker (vert) 25 10
1167 $2.40 Qipao tailoring (women's clothes) 40 10
1168 $2.50 Hairdressing (vert) . . 55 10
1169 $3 Making dough figures (vert) 55 10
1170 $5 Olive seller 95 15
MS1171 219 × 123 mm. Nos. 1165/70 . . . . 2·75 65

240 Hong Kong Skyline

2003. Hong Kong 2004 International Stamp Exhibition (1st issue). Sheet 135 × 85 mm.

MS1172 **240** $10 multicoloured 2·00 1·40

See also Nos. **MS**1190, **MS**1213 and 1214/1230.

241 The Master-of-Nets Garden, Suzhou

2003. Mainland Landscapes (1st issue). Sheet 140 × 90 mm.

MS1173 **241** $10 multicoloured 2·00 1·40

See also No. **MS**1239.

242 Fukien Tea (semi-cascade)

2003. Miniature Landscapes. Multicoloured.

1174 $1.40 Type **242** 25 10
1175 $2.40 Hedge Sageretia (informal upright) 55 10
1176 $3 Fire-thorn (cascade) (vert) 55 15
1177 $5 Chinese Hackberry (root on rock) (vert) 80 40

243 Ear-spot Angelfish

2003. Aquarium Fish. Multicoloured.

1178 $1.40 Type **243** 25 10
1179 $2.40 Copper-banded butterflyfish 55 10
1180 $3 Dwarf gourami 55 15
1181 $5 Red discus 80 40

244 Bottles and Man holding Firework ("Celebrations")

2003. Greetings Stamps. With service indicator. Multicoloured.

1182 ($1.40) Type **244** ("Local Mail Postage") 25 10
1183 ($1.40) Man and heart-shaped tree ("Care and Love") 25 10
1184 ($3) No. 1182 ("Air Mail Postage") 55 15
1185 ($3) No. 1183 . . . . 55 15

No. 1182/3 were for use on letters up to 30 grams within Hong Kong and 1184/5 were for use on airmail letters up to 20 grams to addresses outside Hong Kong.

245 Pied Avocet

2003. Water Birds. Multicoloured.

1186 $1.40 Type **245** 25 10
1187 $2.40 Horned grebe 55 10
1188 $3 Great crested grebe . . . 55 15
1189 $5 Black-throated diver . . 80 40

Stamps of the same design were issued by Sweden.

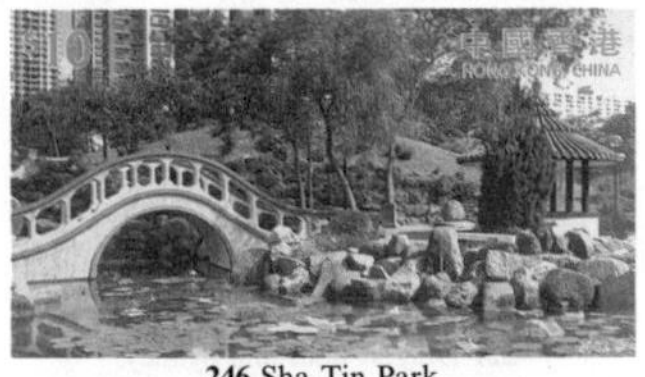

246 Sha Tin Park

2003. Hong Kong 2004 International Stamp Exhibition (2nd issue). Sheet 135 × 85 mm.

MS1190 **246** $10 multicoloured 2·00 1·40

247 Astronaut and Satellite

2003. First Chinese Manned Space Flight. Multicoloured.

1191 $1.40 Type **247** 25 10
1192 $1.40 Shenzhou-5 space craft 25 10

248 Drum **249** Potola Palace, Lhasa

2003. Traditional Instruments. Multicoloured.

1193 $1.40 Type **248** 25 10
1194 $2.40 Clappers 55 10
1195 $3 Cymbals 55 10
1196 $5 Gongs 80 40
MS1197 130 × 75 mm. $13 Bell (35 × 45 mm) . . . . 1·80 1·80

2003. UNESCO World Heritage Sites in China. Multicoloured.

1198 $1.40 Type **249** 25 10
1199 $1.80 Imperial Palace, Beijing (47 × 39 mm) . . . 25 10
1200 $2.40 First Qin Emperor's Mausoleum, Shaanxi Province (47 × 39 mm) . . 55 10
1201 $2.50 Mount Huangshan, Anhui Province (39 × 47 mm) 55 10
1202 $3 Old Town, Lijang (39 × 47 mm) 55 10
1203 $5 Jiuzhaigou valley, Sichuan Province (77 × 30 mm) 80 40

250 Building Development and People on Walkways

2003. Development of Public Housing. Multicoloured.

1204 $1.40 Type **250** 25 10
1205 $2.40 L-shaped development and women through window 55 10
1206 $3 High-rise development and man reading with children 55 10
1207 $5 High-rise development and family walking in park 80 40

251 Monkey

2004. New Year. "Year of the Monkey". Multicoloured.

1208 $1.40 Type **251** 20 10
1209 $2.40 Mother and baby . . 35 10
1210 $3 Walking 45 10
1211 $5 Holding branch 70 35
MS1212 Two sheets, each 136 × 85 mm (a/b). (a) Nos. 1208/11. (b) As No.1211. Imperf. (c) 135 × 90 mm $50 × 2, As No. 1155 (38 × 52 mm); As No. 1211 (38 × 52 mm) Set of 2 sheets . . . . 17·00 17·00

252 Round Pudding and Greeting

2004. Hong Kong 2004 International Stamp Exhibition (3rd issue). Tourism. Six sheets, each 135 × 86 mm containing T **252** and similar horiz designs. Multicoloured.

MS1213 (a) $10 Type **252**; (b) $10 × 2, As No. **MS**1213a: (c) $10 New Year parade; (d) $10 Jade pendant; (e) $10 Fire dragon 8·50 8·50

2004. Hong Kong 2004 International Stamp Exhibition (4th issue). Hong Kong Landmarks and Tourist Attractions. Multicoloured.

1214 $1.40 As Type **201** 20 10
1215 $1.40 As No. 973 . . . . . 20 10
1216 $1.40 As No. 974 . . . . . 20 10
1217 $1.40 As No. 975 . . . . . 20 10
1218 $1.40 As No. 976 . . . . . 20 10
1219 $1.40 As No. 977 . . . . . 20 10
1220 $1.40 As No. 978 . . . . . 20 10
1221 $1.40 As No. 979 . . . . . 20 10
1222 $1.40 As No. 980a 20 10
1223 $1.40 As No. 980b 20 10
1224 $1.40 As No. 981 . . . . . 20 10
1225 $1.40 As No. 982 . . . . . 20 10
1226 $1.40 As No. 982a 20 10
1227 $1.40 As No. 983 . . . . . 20 10
1228 $1.40 As No. 984 . . . . . 20 10
1229 $1.40 As No. 984b 20 10
1230 $1.40 As No. 985 . . . . . 20 10
1231 $1.40 As No. 986 . . . . . 20 10
1232 $1.40 As No. 986a 20 10

No.	Description	Unused	Used
1233	$1.40 As No. 987	20	10
1234	$1.40 As No. 988	20	10

253 Hong Kong Team

2004. Rugby Sevens. Multicoloured.

No.	Description	Unused	Used
1235	$1.40 Type **253**	20	10
1236	$2.40 New Zealand team	35	10
1237	$3 Hong Kong Stadium	45	10
1238	$5 Westpac Stadium, Wellington	70	35

Stamps of the same design were issued by New Zealand.

254 Scissors, Paper, Stone (Ka-lai Tsoi)

2004. Winning Entries in Children's Stamp Design Competition. Games. Multicoloured.

No.	Description	Unused	Used
1239	$1.40 Type **254**	20	10
1240	$2.40 Chinese chess (Belinda Hoi-yan Chan)	35	10
1241	$3 Bubble blowing (April Nga-pui Yuen)	45	10
1242	$5 Hopscotch (Chap-yin Lui)	70	35

255 The Chen Clan Academy, Guangzhou

2004. Mainland Landscapes (2nd series). Sheet 140 × 90 mm.

No.	Description	Unused	Used
MS1243	**255** $10 multicoloured	1·40	1·40

256 First Tram (1904)

2004. Centenary of Hong Kong Tramway.

No.	Description	Unused	Used
1244	$1.40 Type **256**	20	10
1245	$2.40 Open-topped tram	35	10
1246	$3 Canvas-topped tram	45	10
1247	$5 Modern tram	70	35
MS1248	Two sheets, each 136 × 85 mm. (a) Nos. 1240/3; (b) $5 Millennium new tram Set of 2 sheets	2·40	2·40

257 Soldiers, Sailors and Airmen

2004. Armed Forces. Multicoloured.

No.	Description	Unused	Used
1249	$1.40 Type **257**	20	10
1250	$1.80 Serviceman giving blood	25	10
1251	$2.40 Servicemen and children	35	10
1252	$2.50 Soldiers	35	10
1253	$3 Sailors	45	10
1254	$5 Airmen	70	35

258 Preparing to Dive

2004. Olympic Games, Athens. Sports. Multicoloured.

No.	Description	Unused	Used
1255	$1.40 Type **258**	20	10
1256	$1.40 Diver twisting forward	20	10
1257	$1.40 Descending with arms extended	20	10
1258	$1.40 Entering water	20	10
1259	$1.40 Volleyball player with bent knees	20	10
1260	$1.40 Jumping to hit ball	20	10
1261	$1.40 Hitting ball	20	10
1262	$1.40 Opponent trying to save	20	10
1263	$1.40 Two cyclists	20	10
1264	$1.40 Cyclist	20	10
1265	$1.40 Cyclists at speed	20	10
1266	$1.40 Victory salute	20	10
1267	$1.40 Badminton player preparing to hit shuttlecock	20	10
1268	$1.40 Player with arm extended	20	10
1269	$1.40 Player leaning backwards	20	10
1270	$1.40 Player leaning to right	20	10
1271	$1.40 Start of relay race	20	10
1272	$1.40 Runners	20	10
1273	$1.40 Baton exchange	20	10
1274	$1.40 Runner with baton raised	20	10
MS1275	130 × 75 mm. $5 × 2, Classical Olympic runner; Modern runner	1·40	1·40

259 Flags and Deng Xiaoping

2004. Birth Centenary of Deng Xiaoping (leader of China, 1978–89). Two sheets containing T **259** and similar horiz designs. Multicoloured.

No.	Description	Unused	Used
MS1276	(a) 175 × 130 mm. $1.40 Type **259**; $1.40 Wearing blue suit, each × 4 (b) 130 × 75 mm. $10 As young man	2·50	2·50

260 First Bronze Coin, 1863

2004. Currency. Multicoloured.

No.	Description	Unused	Used
1277	$1.40 Type **260**	20	10
1278	$2.40 First silver coin, 1866	35	10
1279	$3 First paper currency, 1935	45	10
1280	$5 Gold coin to commemorate Hong Kong Special Administrative Region, 1997	70	35
MS1281	(a) 130 × 80 mm. Nos. 1277/80 (b) 130 × 75 mm. $5 Reverse of $10 dollar coin, 1997	2·40	2·40

261 Building and Bridge

2004. Development of Pearl River Delta Region. Multicoloured.

No.	Description	Unused	Used
1282	$1.40 Type **261**	20	10
1283	$2.40 Container and crane	35	10
1284	$3 Views of Hong Kong, Guangdong and Macau	45	10
1285	$5 Harbour views and men shaking hands	70	35

262 Straw Mushrooms

2004. Fungi. Multicoloured.

No.	Description	Unused	Used
1286	$1.40 Type **262**	20	10
1287	$2.40 Red-orange mushroom	35	10
1288	$3 Violet marasmius	45	10
1289	$5 Lingzhi	70	35
MS1290	(a) 130 × 85 mm. Nos. 1286/9. (b) 130 × 75 mm. $5 Hexagon fungus	3·30	2·30

POSTAGE DUE STAMPS

D 1 Post-office Scales

D 2

1923.

No.	Description	Unused	Used
D 1ab	**D 1** 1c. brown	30	1·00
D 2a	2c. green	11·00	5·00
D 6a	2c. grey	1·10	10·00
D 3a	4c. red	28·00	7·00
D 7a	4c. orange	2·50	10·00
D18	5c. red (21 × 18 mm)	2·50	5·50
D 4	6c. yellow	28·00	13·00
D 8	6c. red	9·50	5·50
D 9	8c. brown	5·50	32·00
D 5	10c. blue	25·00	8·50
D15	10c. violet	3·50	4·25
D16	20c. black	6·00	4·25
D22	50c. blue	4·50	10·00

1976. As Type **D 1** but smaller design 21 × 17 mm with redrawn value.

No.	Description	Unused	Used
D25a	**D 1** 10c. violet	80	2·00
D26a	20c. grey	1·50	2·25
D27a	50c. blue	1·50	2·75
D28a	$1 yellow	1·40	4·00

1987.

No.	Description	Unused	Used
D31	**D 2** 10c. green	10	40
D32	20c. brown	10	40
D33	50c. violet	10	20
D34	$1 orange	15	20
D35	$5 blue	80	1·60
D36	$10 red	1·60	3·00

D 3

2004.

No.	Description	Unused	Used
D37	**D 3** 10c. ultramarine	10	10
D38	20c. blue	10	10
D39	50c. orange	10	10
D40	$1 pink	15	10
D41	$5 green	70	35
D42	$10 magenta	1·40	70

JAPANESE OCCUPATION OF HONG KONG

100 sen = 1 yen.

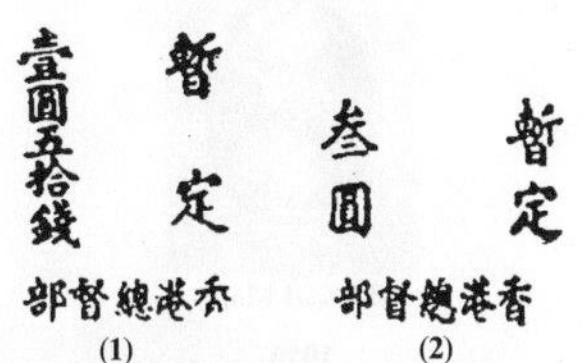

(1) (2)

1945. Stamps of Japan surch as T **1** (No. J1) or T **2**.

No.	Description	Unused	Used
J1	**126** 1.50yen on 1s. brown	30·00	27·00
J2	**84** 3yen on 2s. red	12·00	21·00
J3	5yen on 5s. red (No. 396)	£900	£150

HORTA Pt. 9

A district of the Azores for which separate issues were used from 1892 to 1905.

1865. 1000 reis = 1 milreis.

1892. As T **4** of Funchal, but inscr "HORTA".

No.	Description	Unused	Used
4	5r. yellow	2·10	1·70
5	10r. mauve	2·10	1·80
6	15r. brown	2·10	2·10
7	20r. lilac	2·50	2·50
2	25r. green	8·25	3·75
8	50r. blue	6·25	3·00
22	75r. red	6·75	4·50
10	80r. green	9·25	8·25
23	100r. brown on yellow	38·00	18·00
24	150r. red on rose	46·00	38·00
25	200r. blue on blue	46·00	38·00
26	300r. blue on brown	46·00	38·00

1897. "King Carlos" key-type inscr "HORTA". Name and value in red (Nos. 46 and 41) or black (others).

No.	Description	Unused	Used
28	S 2½r. grey	50	30
29	5r. orange	50	30
30	10r. green	50	30
31	15r. brown	7·25	5·50
42	15r. green	1·40	1·10
32	20r. lilac	1·40	1·20
33	25r. green	2·40	95
43	25r. red	1·40	75
34	50r. blue	2·75	1·10
45	65r. blue	1·00	75
35	75r. red	2·50	1·20
46	75r. brown on yellow	11·00	9·75
36	80r. mauve	1·50	95
37	100r. blue on blue	2·75	95
47	115r. red on pink	1·90	1·50
48	130r. brown on yellow	1·90	1·50
38	150r. brown on yellow	1·90	95
49	180r. black on pink	1·90	1·50
39	200r. purple on pink	5·25	4·50
40	300r. blue on pink	9·50	6·75
41	500r. black on blue	12·00	11·50

HUNGARY Pt. 2

A country in central Europe. A Kingdom ruled by the Emperor of Austria until 1918. A Republic was then proclaimed, and later a Soviet style constitution was adopted. In 1919 parts of the country were occupied by France, Serbia and Rumania, including Budapest. Following the withdrawal of the Rumanians a National Republic was instituted, and in 1920 Hungary was declared a Monarchy with Admiral Nicholas Horthy as Regent. In 1946 Hungary became a Republic again.

1858. 100 krajczar = 1 forint.
1900. 100 filler (heller) = 1 korona (krone).
1926. 100 filler = 1 pengo.
1946. 100 filler = 1 forint.

1

2

1871.

No.	Description	Unused	Used
8	**1** 2k. yellow	60·00	12·00
9	3k. green	£110	40·00
10	5k. red	75·00	2·25
11	10k. blue	£325	21·00
12	15k. brown	£325	29·00
13	25k. lilac	£225	85·00

1874.

No.	Description	Unused	Used
26	**2** 2k. mauve	1·40	30
28	3k. green	1·10	30
29	5k. red	6·00	30
31	10k. blue	4·25	45
32a	20k. grey	5·50	45

1888. Numerals in black on the krajczar values, in red on the forint values.

No.	Description	Unused	Used
39a	**2** 1k. black	60	25
40	2k. mauve and light mauve	80	20
41	3k. green and light green	90	20
42	5k. red and pink	1·10	30
43	8k. orange and yellow	1·25	20
44	10k. blue	4·50	20
45	12k. brown and green	10·00	50
46	15k. red and blue	6·00	40
47	20k. grey	7·50	75
48	24k. purple and red	20·00	70
62	30k. olive and brown	4·75	2·50
63	50k. red and orange	14·50	22·00
51	1fo. grey and silver	£150	1·50
38i	3fo. brown and gold	12·00	4·50

7 "Turul" (mythical bird of the Magyars)

8 King Francis Joseph wearing Hungarian Crown

12

1900. Figures of value in black.
99 **7** 1f. grey 15 10
100 2f. yellow 10 10
118 3f. orange 10 10
67 4f. mauve 45 15
102 5f. green 10 10
69a 6f. purple 70 30
103 6f. drab 20 10
120 6f. green 10 10
121 10f. red 10 10
105 12f. lilac 20 10
122 12f. lilac on yellow 15 10
123 16f. green 15 15
124 20f. brown 20 10
125 25f. blue 20 10
126 30f. brown 20 10
127 35f. purple 20 10
111 50f. red 75 10
128 50f. red on blue 20 10
112 60f. green . . . . 2·50 10
130 60f. green on pink 90 10
131 70f. brown and green . . . 30 10
132 80f. violet 30 10
133 **8** 1k. red . . . . 2·00 10
134 2k. blue . . . . 4·50 10
81 3k. blue . . . . 38·00 2·75
135 5k. red . . . . 4·75 2·00

1913. Flood Charity stamps. As T **7/8**, but with label as T **12**.
136 **12** 1f.+2f. grey 70 70
137 2f.+2f. yellow 40 45
138 3f.+2f. orange 40 45
139 5f.+2f. green 35 35
140 6f.+2f. drab 65 70
141 10f.+2f. red 25 20
142 12f.+2f. lilac on yellow . . 1·10 1·00
143 16f.+2f. green 75 85
144 20f.+2f. brown . . . . 2·40 1·60
145 25f.+2f. blue 75 65
146 30f.+2f. brown . . . . 1·10 50
147 35f.+2f. purple . . . . 1·00 50
148 50f.+2f. lake on blue . . . 5·25 2·40
149 60f.+2f. green on red . . . 6·25 1·25
150 **8** 1k.+2f. red . . . . 25·00 9·75
151 2k.+2f. blue . . . . 55·00 40·00
152 5k.+2f. red . . . . 19·00 18·00

1914. War Charity. Nos. 136/52 (with labels) surch **Hadi segely Ozvegyeknek es arvaknak ket (2) filler.**
153 **12** 1f.+2f. grey 60 45
154 2f.+2f. yellow 60 40
155 3f.+2f. orange 60 50
156 5f.+2f. green 35 20
157 6f.+2f. drab 65 45
158 10f.+2f. red 35 20
159 12f.+2f. lilac on yellow . . 65 40
160 16f.+2f. green 65 35
161 20f.+2f. brown 65 45
162 25f.+2f. blue . . . . 1·00 50
163 30f.+2f. brown . . . . 1·40 50
164 35f.+2f. purple . . . . 3·50 1·25
165 50f.+2f. lake on blue . . . 2·00 65
166 60f.+2f. green on red . . . 5·50 1·25
167 **8** 1k.+2f. red (No. 150) . . . 60·00 32·00
168 2k.+2f. blue (No. 151) . . . 21·00 21·00
169 5k.+2f. red (No. 152) . . . 22·00 17·00

1915. War Charity. Stamps of 1900 (without labels) surch as last round the stamp.
170 **7** 1f.+2f. grey 10 10
171 2f.+2f. yellow 10 10
172 3f.+2f. orange 10 10
173 5f.+2f. green 10 10
174 6f.+2f. drab 10 10
175 10f.+2f. red 10 10
176 12f.+2f. lilac on yellow . . . 10 10
177 16f.+2f. green 30 30
178 20f.+2f. brown 30 35
179 25f.+2f. blue 10 10
180 30f.+2f. brown 10 10
181 35f.+2f. purple 10 10
182 50f.+2f. lake on blue . . . 35 30
183 60f.+2f. green on red . . . 70 70
185 **8** 1k.+2f. red (No. 133) . . . 1·60 1·10
186 2k.+2f. blue (No. 134) . . . 2·50 2·10
187 5k.+2f. red (No. 135) . . . 7·25 10·00

18 Harvesters

19 Parliament Buildings, Budapest

1916. As T **18** but with white figures in top corners.
243 **18** 10f. red 45 25
244 15f. purple 25 25

1916. Inscr "MAGYAR KIR. POSTA".
245 **18** 2f. brown 10 10
246 3f. red 10 10
247 4f. slate 10 10
248 5f. green 10 10
249 6f. blue 10 10
250 10f. red 50 10
251 15f. violet 10 10
252 20f. brown 10 10
253 25f. blue 10 10
254 35f. brown 10 10
255 40f. olive 10 10
256 **19** 50f. purple 10 10
257 75f. blue 10 10
258 80f. green 25 10
259 1k. lake 10 10
260 2k. brown 20 10
261 3k. grey and violet . . . 65 10
262 5k. brown 60 15
263 10k. mauve and brown . . 90 50

In Type **19** the colours of the centres differ slightly from those of the frames.

For later issues in Types **18** and **19**, see Nos. 372/86 and 404/11.

20 In Trenches

22 "Turul" at bay

23 Queen Zita

1916. War Charity.
264 **20** 10f.+2f. red 20 20
265 – 15f.+2f. violet 20 20
266 **22** 40f.+2f. lake 25 30
DESIGN: 15f. Hand to hand combat.

1916. Coronation.
267 **23** 10f. mauve 40 50
268 – 15f. red (Emperor Charles IV) 40 50

1917. War Charity Exhibition. Nos. 243/4 surch **Jozsef foherczeg vezerezredes hadi kiallitasa 1 korona** (= "Prince Joseph. Chief Colonel General War Exhibition").
269 **18** 10f.+1k. red 50 50
270 15f.+1k. violet 50 50

1918. Air. Surch **REPULO POSTA** and value.
271 **19** 1k.50 on 75f. blue . . . . 15·00 19·00
272 4k.50 on 2k. brown . . . 13·50 17·00

27 Charles IV

28 Zita

1918.
273 **27** 10f. red 10 10
274 15f. violet 10 10
275 20f. brown 10 10
276 25f. blue 10 10
277 **28** 40f. olive 10 10
278 50f. purple 10 10

1918. Optd **KOZTARSASAG.** (a) War Charity Stamps (Nos. 264/6).
279 **20** 10+2f. red 10 10
280 – 15+2f. violet 10 10
281 **22** 40+2f. red 10 10

(b) Harvesters and Parliament.
282 **18** 2f. brown 10 10
283 3f. red 10 10
284 4f. grey 10 10
285 5f. green 10 10
286 6f. blue 10 10
287 10f. red 10 10
288 20f. brown 10 10
289 40f. green 10 10
290 **19** 1k. red 10 10
291 2k. brown 10 10
292 3k. grey and violet . . . 40 50
293 5k. brown . . . . 1·25 1·40
294 10k. mauve and brown . . . 2·25 1·75

(c) Charles and Zita.
295 **27** 10f. pink 10 10
296 15f. purple 10 10
297 20f. brown 10 10
298 25f. blue 10 10
299 **28** 40f. green 20 25
300 50f. purple 20 25

1919. As T **18/19**, but inscr "MAGYAR POSTA".
301 **18** 2f. brown 10 10
302 4f. grey 10 10
303 5f. green 10 10
304 6f. blue 10 10
305 10f. red 10 10
306 15f. violet 10 10
307 20f. brown 10 10
308 20f. green 10 10
309 25f. blue 10 10
310 40f. green 10 10
311 40f. red 10 10
312 45f. orange 10 10
313 **19** 50f. purple 10 10
314 60f. blue and brown . . . 10 10
315 95f. blue 10 10
316 1k. red 10 10
317 1k. blue and indigo . . . 10 10
318 1k.20 green 10 10
319 1k.40 green 10 10
320 2k. brown 10 10
321 3k. grey and violet . . . 10 10
322 5k. brown 10 10
323 10k. mauve and brown . . 50 35

32 Karl Marx

1919.
324 **32** 20f. red and brown . . . 20 20
325 – 45f. green and orange . . . 20 20
326 – 60f. brown and grey . . . 2·75 3·50
327 – 75f. brown and red . . . 3·00 3·50
328 – 80f. brown and olive . . . 3·00 3·50
PORTRAITS: 45f. S. Petofi; 60f. Ignacs Martinovics; 75f. G. Dozsa; 80f. F. Engels.

1919. Nos. 301 etc optd **MAGYAR TANACSKOZTARSASAG.** (second word hyphenated on 2 to 45f.) (= "Hungarian Soviet Republic").
329 **18** 2f. brown 25 35
330 3f. purple 25 35
331 4f. grey 25 35
332 5f. green 25 35
333 6f. blue 25 35
334 10f. red 25 35
335 15f. violet 25 35
336 20f. brown 25 35
337 25f. blue 25 35
338 40f. green 25 35
339 45f. orange 25 35
340 **19** 50f. purple 20 35
341 95f. blue 20 35
342 1k. red 20 35
343 1k.20 green 20 75
344 1k.40 green 40 35
345 2k. brown . . . . 65 1·10
346 3k. grey and violet . . . 65 70
347 5k. brown . . . . 70 1·25
348 10k. mauve and brown . . 1·00 1·60

1919. Entry of National Army into Budapest. Nos. 303 etc optd **A nemzeti hadsereg bevonulasa. 1919. XI/16.**
348a **18** 5f. green . . . . 90 1·00
348b 10f. red . . . . 90 1·00
348c 15f. violet . . . . 90 1·00
348d 20f. brown . . . . 90 1·00
348e 25f. blue . . . . 90 1·00

(36) (37)

1920. Nos. 329/48 optd with T **36** (2 to 45f.) or **37** (others).
349 **18** 2f. brown 40 40
350 3f. purple 10 10
351 4f. grey 60 80
352 5f. green 10 10
353 6f. blue 10 10
354 10f. red 10 10
355 15f. violet 10 10
356 20f. brown 10 10
357 25f. blue 10 10
358 40f. green . . . . 95 1·10
359 45f. orange . . . . 95 1·10
360 **19** 50f. purple . . . . 95 1·10
361 95f. blue . . . . 95 1·10
362 1k. red . . . . 95 1·10
363 1k.20 green . . . . 1·50 2·00
364 1k.40 green . . . . 1·50 2·00
365 2k. brown . . . . 1·90 2·10
366 3k. grey and violet . . . 1·90 2·10
367 5k. brown 40 50
368 10k. mauve and brown . . 3·00 5·00

38 Returning P.O.W.

42 Madonna and Child

1920. Returned Prisoners-of-War Fund.
369 **38** 40f.+1k. lake 75 75
370 – 60f.+2k. brown 75 75
371 – 1k.+5k. blue 75 75
DESIGNS—HORIZ: 60f. Prison Camp. VERT: 1k. Family Reunion.

1920. Re-issue of T **18** inscr "MAGYAR KIR. POSTA".
372 **18** 5f. brown 10 10
373 10f. purple 10 10
374 40f. red 10 10
375 50f. green 10 10
376 50f. blue 10 10
377 60f. black 10 10
378 1k. green 10 10
379 1½k. purple 10 10
380 2k. blue 10 10
381 2½k. green 10 10
382 3k. brown 10 10
383 4k. red 10 10
384 4½k. violet 10 10
385 5k. brown 10 10
386 6k. blue 10 10
387 10k. brown 10 10
388 15k. black 10 10
389 20k. red 10 10
390 25k. orange 10 10
391 40k. green 10 10
392 50k. blue 10 10
393 100k. purple 10 10
394 150k. green 15 10
395 200k. green 15 10
442 300k. red 15 10
397 350k. violet 20 10
443 400k. blue 10 10
444 500k. black 10 10
445 600k. bistre 10 10
446 800k. yellow 10 20

1920. Air. No. 263 surch **LEGI POSTA** and value.
401 **19** 3k. on 10k. mauve & brn 1·10 2·40
402 8k. on 10k. mauve & brn 1·10 2·40
403 12k. on 10k. mauve & brn 1·10 2·40

1920. Re-issue of T **19** inscr "MAGYAR KIR. POSTA".
404 **19** 2k.50 blue 10 10
405 3k.50 grey 10 10
406 10k. brown 10 10
407 15k. grey 10 10
408 20k. red 10 10
409 25k. orange 10 10
410 30k. lake 15 10
411 40k. green 15 10
412 50k. blue 15 10
413 100k. brown 15 10
414 400k. green 25 10
415 500k. violet 25 10
416 1000k. red 25 10
448 2000k. red 45 45

1921.
418 **42** 50k. blue and brown . . . 30 10
419 100k. brown and bistre . . 60 20
420 200k. ultramarine and blue 60 20
421 500k. mauve and purple . . 60 20
422 1000k. purple and mauve 60 20
423 2000k. mauve and green 50 20
424 2500k. brown and bistre 35 20
425 3000k. mauve and red . . 35 20
426 5000k. light green and green 75 20
427 10000k. blue and violet . . 75 20

44 Statue of Petofi in National Dress

45 John, the hero, on flying dragon

47 Death of Petofi

1923. Birth Centenary of Petofi (poet).
428 **44** 10k. (+ 10k.) blue 70 80
429 **45** 15k. (+ 15k.) blue . . . . 1·75 2·25
430 – 25k. (+ 25k.) brown . . . 70 80
431 **47** 40k. (+ 40k.) red . . . . 2·75 3·50
432 – 50k. (+ 50k.) purple . . . 2·75 3·50
DESIGNS—VERT (As Type **45**): 25k. Petofi; 50k. Petofi addressing the people.

49 Icarus over Budapest

50

1924. Air.
433 **49** 100k. pink and brown . . 1·10 2·00
434 500k. light green and green . . . . 1·10 2·00
435 1000k. brown and bistre 1·10 2·00
436 2000k. blue and deep blue 1·10 2·00
436a 5000k. mauve and purple 2·40 2·40
436b 10000k. purple and red 2·40 2·40

1924. Tuberculosis Relief Fund.
437 **50** 300k. (+ 300k.) blue . . . 3·50 5·25
438 – 500k. (+ 500k.) brown . . 3·75 5·25
439 – 1000k. (+ 1000k.) green . . 3·75 5·25
DESIGNS: 500k. Mother and child; 1000k. Bowman.

53 M. Jokai

55

1925. Birth Cent of Maurus Jokai (novelist).
449 **53** 1000k. brown and green . . 4·00 5·00
450 2000k. brown . . . . 3·00 1·00
451 2500k. brown and blue . . 4·00 5·00

1925. Sports Association Fund.
452 – 100k.(+100k.) brn & grn 2·60 2·60
453 – 200k.(+200k.) grn & brn 2·60 3·25
454 – 300k.(+300k.) blue . . . 4·25 3·50
455 – 400k.(+400k.) green & bl 4·25 5·00
456 – 500k.(+500k.) purple . . 5·25 7·00
457 – 1000k.(+1000k.) red . . . 6·75 7·50
458 **55** 2000k.(+2000k.) purple . . 8·75 8·50
459 – 2500k.(+2500k.) sepia . . . 10·50 9·50
DESIGNS—HORIZ: 100k. Athletes; 500k. Fencing. VERT: 200k. Skiing; 300k. Skating; 400k. Diving; 1000k. Scouts; 2500k. Hurdles.

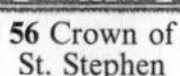

56 Crown of St. Stephen — 57 Matthias Church and Fisher's Bastion — 60 Madonna and Child

58 Royal Palace, Budapest — 59

1926. T **59** is without boat.

460 **56** 1f. black 45 10
461 2f. blue 45 10
462 3f. orange 45 10
463 4f. mauve 45 10
464 6f. green 45 10
465 8f. mauve 90 10
466 **57** 10f. blue 90 10
467 16f. violet 90 10
468 20f. red 90 10
469 25f. brown 90 10
470 **59** 30f. green 2·75 10
471 **58** 32f. violet 3·00 15
472 40f. blue and deep blue 5·25 15
473 **59** 46f. blue 3·75 10
474 50f. black 4·00 10
475 70f. red 5·50 10
476 **60** 1p. violet 25·00 50
477 2p. red 25·00 70
478 5p. blue 25·00 3·25

See also Nos. 502/6.

61 The fabulous "Turul" — 62 Mercury astride a "Turul"

1927. Air.

478a **61** 4f. orange 85 65
479 12f. green 85 70
480 16f. brown 85 55
481 20f. red 85 55
482 32f. purple 2·50 1·90
483 40f. blue 2·25 1·00
484 **62** 50f. red 2·25 1·25
485 72f. olive 2·50 1·40
486 80f. violet 2·50 1·10
487 1p. green 2·50 1·25
488 2p. red 5·00 5·50
489 5p. blue 25·00 32·00

66 Royal Palace, Budapest — 67 St. Stephen

1928. T **66** has the boat in a different place and a redrawn frame.

502 **66** 30f. green 2·40 10
503 32f. purple 2·75 30
504 40f. blue 2·75 10
505 46f. green 2·75 10
506 50f. brown 1·75 10

1928. 890th Death Anniv of St. Stephen of Hungary.

507 **67** 8f. green 85 45
508 16f. red 1·10 45
509 32f. blue 3·00 2·50

1929. Colours changed.

510 **67** 8f. red 45 40
511 16f. violet 50 1·25
512 32f. bistre 2·10 1·00

68 Admiral Horthy — 69 St. Emeric

1930. 10th Anniv of Regency.

513 **68** 8f. green 1·40 25
514 16f. violet 1·40 30
515 20f. red 4·50 2·50
516 32f. brown 4·00 5·25
517 40f. blue 6·50 1·50

1930. 900th Death Anniv of St. Emeric.

518 **69** 8f.+2f. green 60 80
519 – 16f.+4f. purple 85 1·00
520 – 20f.+4f. red 2·75 2·40
521 – 32f.+8f. blue 3·25 3·25

DESIGNS—VERT: 16f. St. Stephen and Queen Gisela; 20f. St. Ladislas. HORIZ: 32f. Sts. Gellert and Emeric.

1931. Surch.

526 **56** 2 on 3f. orange 70 25
527 6 on 8f. mauve 70 15
528 **57** 10 on 16f. violet 70 15
525 20 on 25f. brown 1·40 1·10

1931. Air. Optd **Zeppelin 1931**.

529 **62** 1p. orange 35·00 60·00
530 2p. purple 35·00 60·00

73 St. Elizabeth — 75 Madonna and Child — 77

1932. 700th Death Anniv of St. Elizabeth of Hungary.

531 **73** 10f. blue 45 30
532 20f. red 45 30
533 – 32f. purple 1·60 1·60
534 – 40f. blue 1·00 85

DESIGN—18 × 28 mm: 32, 40f. St. Elizabeth giving cloak to the poor.

1932.

535 **75** 1p. green 13·00 50
536 2p. red 13·00 80
537 5p. blue 55·00 4·50
538 10p. brown 75·00 30·00

1932. No. 527 further surch **2**.

540 **56** 2 on 6 on 8f. mauve 85 35

1932. Famous Hungarians.

541 – 1f. grey 30 10
542 – 2f. orange 30 10
543 – 4f. blue 30 10
543a **77** 5f. brown 30 10
544 – 6f. green 30 10
545 – 10f. green 30 10
546 – 16f. violet 30 10
547 – 20f. red 50 10
547a – 25f. green 60 25
548 – 30f. brown 50 25
549 – 32f. purple 70 25
550 – 40f. blue 70 25
551 – 50f. green 95 40
552 – 70f. red 1·40 35

DESIGNS: 1f. I. Madach, poet, 1823–64; 2f. J Arany, poet, 1817–82; 4f. I. Semmelweis, physician, 1818–65; 5f. F. Kolcsey, poet, 1790–1838; 6f. L. Eotvos, physicist, 1848–1919; 10f. I. Szechenyi, statesman, 1791–1860; 16f. F. Deak, statesman, 1803–76; 20f. F. Liszt, composer, 1811–86; 25f. M. Vorosmarty, poet, 1800–55; 30f. L. Kossuth, statesman, 1802–94; 32f. I. Tisza, statesman, 1861–1918; 40f. M. Munkacsy, painter, 1844–1900; 50f. S. Korosi Csoma, explorer, 1784–1842; 70f. F. Bolyai, mathematician, 1775–1856.

1933. Surch **10**.

553 **59** 10 on 70f. red 90 30

79 "Justice for Hungary" over Danube — 80 Gift Plane from Mussolini

1933. Air.

554 **79** 10f. green 1·25 45
555 16f. violet 1·25 45
556 **80** 20f. red 3·00 85
557 40f. blue 3·25 85
558 – 48f. black 13·00 2·50
559 – 72f. brown 22·00 2·75
560 – 1p. green 21·00 2·75
561 – 2p. red 30·00 13·50
562 – 5p. grey 60·00 £120

DESIGNS—VERT: As Type **80**: 48, 72f. "Spirit of Flight" on wing of Lockheed Model 8A Sirius; 1, 2, 5p. Mercury and propeller.

83 "The Stag of Hungary"

1933. International Scout Jamboree, Godollo.

563 **83** 10f. green 1·10 45
564 16f. red 1·75 2·40
565 20f. red 1·50 75
566 32f. yellow 4·50 3·50
567 40f. blue 5·25 2·75

1934. 2nd Hungarian Philatelic Exhibition, Budapest, and Jubilee of First Hungarian Philatelic Society (L.E.H.E.). Sheet 64 × 76 mm containing No. 547 in changed colour.

MS568 20f. red 75·00 90·00

84 Ferenc Rakoczi II — 85 Cardinal Peter Pazmany

1935. Death Bicentenary of Prince Rakoczi.

569 **84** 10f. green 1·00 30
570 16f. violet 3·25 3·25
571 20f. red 1·00 45
572 32f. red 7·25 4·50
573 40f. blue 5·50 4·75

1935. Tercentenary of Budapest University.

574 **85** 6f. green 1·00 1·25
575 – 10f. green 45 30
576 **85** 16f. violet 1·90 1·60
577 20f. mauve 45 40
578 – 32f. red 2·25 2·25
579 – 40f. blue 1·90 2·25

DESIGN—HORIZ (35 × 25 mm): 10f., 32f., 40f. Pazmany signing deed.

87 Fokker F.VIIb/3m

1936. Air.

580 **87** 10f. green 30 25
581 20f. red 30 25
582 36f. brown 45 25
583 – 40f. blue 45 25
584 – 52f. orange 60 75
585 – 60f. violet 16·00 2·00
586 – 80f. green 2·10 55
587 – 1p. green 2·10 45
588 – 2p. lake 5·00 1·60
589 – 5p. blue 18·00 18·00

DESIGNS: 40f. to 80f. Fokker F.VIIb/3m over Parliament Buildings; 1p. to 5p. Fokker F.VIIb/3m (different).

88 Ancient Buda

1936. 250th Anniv of Recapture of Buda from Turks.

590 **88** 10f. green 55 35
591 – 16f. mauve 2·25 2·25
592 – 20f. red 55 35
593 – 32f. brown 2·25 2·25
594 **88** 40f. blue 2·25 2·25

DESIGNS: 16f. Angel of Peace over Buda; 20f. Arms of Buda; 32f. Colour bearer and bugler.

89 "Commerce", "May Fair, 1937" and R. Danube — 90 St. Stephen, the Church Builder

1937. Budapest International Fair.

595 **89** 2f. orange 20 10
596 6f. green 30 10
597 10f. green 30 10
598 20f. red 30 35
599 32f. violet 75 40
600 40f. blue 75 30

1938. 900th Death Anniv of St. Stephen. (1st issue).

601 – 1f. violet 25 20
602 **90** 2f. sepia 25 20
603 – 4f. blue 35 20
604 – 5f. mauve 35 20
605 – 6f. green 45 20
606 – 10f. red 45 20
607 **90** 16f. violet 50 45
608 – 20f. red 70 15
609 – 25f. green 70 45
610 – 30f. bistre 1·10 15
611 – 32f. red on yellow 1·10 1·25
612 – 40f. blue 1·25 20
613 – 50f. purple on green 1·40 15
614 – 70f. green on blue 2·10 25

MS614a 146 × 106 mm. No. 608 for 34th International Eucharistic Congress and Philatelic Exhibition, Budapest 19·00 18·00

DESIGNS: 1f., 10f. Abbot Astrik receiving Crown from Pope; 4f., 20f. St. Stephen enthroned; 5f., 25f. St. Gellert, St. Emeric and St. Stephen; 6f., 30f. St. Stephen offering Crown to Virgin Mary; 32f., 50f. St. Stephen; 40f. Madonna and Child; 70f. Crown of St. Stephen.

See also Nos. 620/**MS**621a.

92 Admiral Horthy — 93 Eucharistic Symbols

1938.

615 **92** 1p. green 75 10
616 2p. sepia 1·25 10
617 5p. blue 1·90 1·25

1938. 34th International Eucharistic Congress.

618 – 16f.+16f. blue 3·00 4·00
619 **93** 20f.+20f. red 3·00 4·00

MS619a 130 × 149 mm 6f.+6f. green; 10f.+10f. red; 16f.+16f. blue; 20f.+20f. red; 32f.+32f. purple; 40f.+40f. blue; 50f.+50f. mauve 35·00 40·00

DESIGNS: 6f. St. Stephen; 10f.St. Emeric; 16f. (619), St Ladislas; 16f. St. Laszio; 20f. Offering crown to Virgin Mary; 32f. St. Elizabeth; 40f. Bishop Maurice and Pecs Cathedral; 50f. St. Margaret.

94 St. Stephen the Victorious

1938. 900th Death Anniv of St. Stephen (2nd issue).

620 **94** 10f.+10f. purple 2·00 3·25
621 – 20f.+20f. red 2·00 3·25

MS621a 153 × 113 mm. 6f.+6f. green; 10f.+10f. red; 16f.+16f. brown; 20f.+20f. red; 32f.+32f. blue; 40f.+40f. blue; 50f.+50f. purple 25·00 35·00

DESIGNS: St. Stephen the missionary; 16f. On throne; 20f. Offering crown to Virgin Mary; 32f. Receiving bishops and monks; 40f. Queen Gisela, St. Stephen and St. Emeric; 50f. On bier.

95 Debrecen College — 100 Statue representing Northern Provinces

1938. 400th Anniv of Debrecen College.

622 **95** 6f. green 25 10
623 – 10f. brown 20 10
624 – 16f. red 25 20
625 – 20f. red 20 10
626 – 32f. green 45 40
627 – 40f. blue 45 30

DESIGNS—HORIZ: 10, 20f. 18th and 19th-cent views of College. VERT: 16f. 18th-century students as firemen; 32f. Prof. Marothi; 40f. Dr. Hatvani.

1938. Acquisition of Czech Territory. As Nos. 608 and 614 optd **HAZATERES 1938**.

628 20f. red 1·25 1·25
629 70f. brown on blue 1·25 1·25

1939. "Hungary for Hungarians" Patriotic Fund.

630 **100** 6f.+3f. green 35 50
631 – 10f.+5f. green 35 40
632 – 20f.+10f. red 35 40
633 – 30f.+15f. green 60 70
634 – 40f.+20f. blue 60 1·10

DESIGNS: 10f. Fort at Munkacs; 20f. Admiral Horthy leading troops into Komarom; 30f. Cathedral of St. Elizabeth of Hungary, Kassa; 40f. Girls offering flowers to soldiers.

101 Crown of St. Stephen — 102 Esztergom Basilica

1939.

No.	Type	Description	Unused	Used
635	101	1f. purple	10	10
636		2f. green	10	10
690		3f. brown	10	10
637		4f. brown	10	10
638		5f. violet	10	10
639		6f. green	10	10
693		8f. green	10	10
640		10f. brown	10	10
695		12f. red	10	10
641		16f. violet	10	10
642	–	20f. red	10	10
697	–	24f. red	10	10
643	–	25f. blue	10	10
699	–	30f. mauve	10	10
645	–	32f. brown	15	10
700	102	40f. green	15	10
701	–	50f. green	15	10
702	–	70f. red	30	10
698	–	80f. brown	35	20

DESIGNS—As T **101**: 20, 24f. St. Stephen; 25, 80f. Madonna and Child. As T **102**: 30f. Buda Cathedral; 32f. Debrecen Reformed Church; 50f. Budapest Evangelical Church; 70f. Kassa Cathedral.

For further issues in these designs, see Nos. 751/5.

103 Guides' Salute

104 Memorial Tablets

1939. Girl Guides' Rally, Godollo. Inscr "I. PAX-TING".

No.	Type	Description	Unused	Used
649	103	2f. orange	15	30
650	–	6f. green	25	30
651	–	10f. brown	25	30
652	–	20f. pink	70	50

DESIGNS: 6f. Lily symbol and Hungarian arms; 10f. Guide and girl in national costume; 20f. Dove of peace.

1939. National Protestant Day and Int Protestant Cultural Fund.

No.	Type	Description	Unused	Used
653	104	6f.+3f. green	65	70
654	–	10f.+5f. purple	65	70
655	–	20f.+10f. red	65	70
656	–	32f.+16f. brown	80	1·25
657	–	40f.+20f. blue	80	1·50
MS657a		77 × 112 mm. No. 656 32f. brown. Perf or imperf	30·00	30·00

DESIGNS—HORIZ: 10f., 20f. G. Karoli and A. Molnar di Szenci (translators of the Bible and the Psalms). VERT: 32f. Prince Gabriel Bethlen; 40f. Zsuzsanna Lorantffy.

106 Boy Scout with Kite

107 Regent and Szeged Cathedral

1940. Admiral Horthy Aviation Fund.

No.	Type	Description	Unused	Used
658	106	6f.+6f. green	15	30
659	–	10f.+10f. brown	60	50
660	–	20f.+20f. red	90	1·10

DESIGNS: 10f. "Spirit of Flight"; 20f. St. Elizabeth carrying Crown and Cross of St. Stephen.

1940. 20th Anniv of Regency.

No.	Type	Description	Unused	Used
661	107	6f. green	15	20
662	–	10f. brown and olive	15	25
663	–	20f. red	30	30

DESIGNS: 10f. Admiral Horthy (dated "1920 1940"); 20f. Kassa Cathedral and Angelic bellringer (dated "1939").

108 Stemming the Flood

1940. Flood Relief Fund.

No.	Type	Description	Unused	Used
664	108	10f.+2f. purple	30	30
665		20f.+4f. orange	30	30
666		20f.+50f. brown	65	80
MS666a		77 × 112 mm. T **108**. 20f.+1p. green	5·00	4·50

109 Hunyadi Family Arms

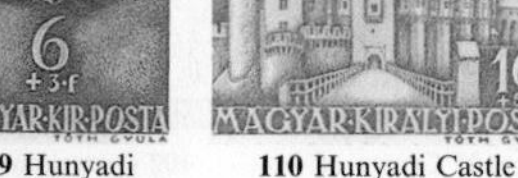

110 Hunyadi Castle

1940. 500th Birth Anniv of King Matthias Hunyadi and Cultural Institutes Fund.

No.	Type	Description	Unused	Used
667	109	6f.+3f. green	25	45
668	110	10f.+5f. brown	25	45
669	–	16f.+8f. olive	35	60
670	–	20f.+10f. red	40	65
671	–	32f.+16f. grey	40	70
MS671a		89 × 113 mm. 20f.+1p. green (as No. 670)	5·00	3·75

DESIGNS—VERT: 16f. Bust of King Matthias (dated "1440–1490"); 32f. Corvin Codex (dated "1473"). HORIZ: 20f. Equestrian Statue of King Matthias.

111 Crown of St. Stephen

112 Madonna and Martyr

1940. Recovery from Rumania of North-Eastern Transylvania.

No.	Type	Description	Unused	Used
672	111	10f. green and yellow	20	10

1940. Transylvanian Relief Fund. Various designs dated "1940".

No.	Type	Description	Unused	Used
673	–	10f.+50f. green	50	70
674	112	20f.+50f. red	50	60
675	–	32f.+50f. brown	65	1·00

DESIGNS: 10f. Prince Csaba and soldier; 32f. Mother offering child to Fatherland.

113 Spirit of Music

1940. Artists' Relief Fund. Inscr "MAGYAR MUVESZETERT".

No.	Type	Description	Unused	Used
676	113	6f.+6f. green	90	1·10
677	–	10f.+10f. brown	90	1·10
678	–	16f.+16f. violet	90	1·10
679	–	20f.+20f. red	90	1·10
MS679a		123 × 84 mm. 6f.+6f. brown; 10f.+10f. red; 16f.+16f. green; 20f.+20f. lilac	4·25	6·00

DESIGNS—VERT: 10f. Sculpture; 16f. Painting. HORIZ: 20f. Poetry (Pegasus).

114 Pilot

1941. Air. Horthy Aviation Fund. Various allegorical designs inscribed "HORTHY MIKLOS NEMZETI REPULO ALAP".

No.	Type	Description	Unused	Used
680	114	6f.+6f. olive	35	55
681	–	10f.+10f. brown	65	55
682	–	20f.+20f. red	65	55
683	–	32f.+32f. blue	65	55

DESIGNS: 10f. Youth releasing model glider; 20f. Glider; 32f. Madonna.

1941. Acquisition of Yugoslav Territory. Overprinted **DEL-UISSZATER** ("The South Comes Home").

No.	Type	Description	Unused	Used
684	101	10f. brown	10	10
685	–	20f. red (No. 642)	10	10

116 Admiral Horthy

1941.

No.	Type	Description	Unused	Used
686	116	1p. green and yellow	15	15
687		2p. brown and yellow	15	20
688		5p. purple and yellow	25	45

118 Szechenyi

119 Giant opening Straits of Kazan

1941. 150th Birth Anniv of Count Szechenyi.

No.	Type	Description	Unused	Used
703	118	10f. olive	10	10
704	–	16f. brown	10	10
705	119	20f. red	10	10
706	–	32f. orange	30	30
707	–	40f. blue	60	30

DESIGNS: 16f. Count Szechenyi and Academy of Science; 32f. Budapest Chain Bridge; 40f. Mercury, Locomotive and "Szent Istvan" (river steamer).

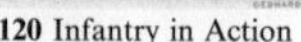

120 Infantry in Action

121 Pilot and Airplane

1941. Soldiers' Gifts Fund. Inscr "HONVEDEINK KARACSONYARA 1941". (a) 1st issue.

No.	Type	Description	Unused	Used
708	120	8f.+12f. green	30	40
709	–	12f.+18f. brown	30	40
710	–	20f.+30f. blue	30	40
711	–	40f.+60f. brown	30	40

DESIGNS: 12f. Artillery; 20f. Tanks; 40f. Cavalryman and cyclist.

(b) 2nd Issue (for Christmas gifts).

No.	Type	Description	Unused	Used
712	–	20f.+40f. red	1·00	2·00

DESIGN: Soldier in helmet; cross and sword.

1942. Air. Horthy Aviation Fund. Inscr "HORTHY MIKLOS NEMZETI REPULO ALAP".

No.	Type	Description	Unused	Used
713	121	8f.+8f. green	30	45
714	–	12f.+12f. blue	85	60
715	–	20f.+20f. brown	85	60
716	–	30f.+30f. red	45	45

DESIGNS—VERT: 30f. Airmen and Turul. HORIZ: 12f. Aircraft and horsemen; 20f. Airplane and archer.

122 Blood Transfusion

123 Vice-regent Stephen Horthy

1942. Red Cross Fund. Cross in red.

No.	Type	Description	Unused	Used
717	122	3f.+18f. green	70	1·10
718	–	8f.+32f. brown	70	1·10
719	–	12f.+50f. purple	70	1·10
720	–	20f.+1p. blue	70	1·10

DESIGNS: 8f. First aid; 12f. Wireless and carrier-pigeon service; 20f. Bereaved parents and orphans.

1942. Air. Mourning for Stephen Horthy and Horthy Aviation Fund.

No.	Type	Description	Unused	Used
721	–	20f. black	25	20
722	123	30f.+20f. violet	35	25

No. 721 is squarer in shape than No. 722 and is dated "1904–1942".

124 Stephen Horthy's Widow

125 King Ladislas

1942. Red Cross Fund. Cross and Crown in red.

No.	Type	Description	Unused	Used
723	124	6f.+1p. blue	1·50	2·25
724	–	8f.+1p. green	1·50	2·25
725	–	20f.+1p. brown	1·50	2·25

DESIGNS—HORIZ: 8f. Nurse and wounded soldier. VERT: 20f. Stephen Horthy's mother.

1942. Cultural Funds.

No.	Type	Description	Unused	Used
726	125	6f.+6f. brown	25	55
727	–	8f.+8f. green	25	55
728	–	12f.+12f. brown	25	55
729	–	20f.+20f. green	25	55
730	–	24f.+24f. brown	25	55
731	–	30f.+30f. red	25	55

DESIGNS—Statuettes: 8f. Ladislas on horseback; 20f. Bela IV with architect; 30f. Lajos the Great enthroned. King's heads; 12f. Bela IV; 24f. Lajos the Great.

126 Prince Arpad

127 St. Stephen's Crown

1943.

No.	Type	Description	Unused	Used
732	126	1f. grey	10	10
733	–	2f. orange	10	10
734	–	3f. blue	10	10
735	–	4f. brown	10	10
736	–	5f. red	10	10
737	–	6f. blue	10	10
738	–	8f. green	10	10
739	–	10f. brown	10	10
740	–	12f. green	10	10
741	–	18f. black	10	10
742	127	20f. brown	10	10
743	–	24f. purple	10	10
744	127	30f. red	10	10
745	–	30f. red	10	10
746	127	50f. blue	10	10
747		80f. brown	10	10
748		1p. green	10	10
749		2p. brown	10	25
750		5p. purple	10	10

DESIGNS: 2f. King Ladislas; 3f. Miklos Toldi; 4f. Janos Hunyadi; 5f. Pal Kinizsi; 6f. Miklos Zrinyi; 8f. Ferenc Rakoczi II; 10f. Andre Hadik; 12f. Artur Gorgey; 18f. and 24f. Madonna; 30f. (No. 745), St. Margaret.

1943. As T **102** (designs and colours changed).

No.	Type	Description	Unused	Used
751	–	30f. red	10	10
752	–	40f. grey	10	10
753	102	50f. blue	10	10
754	–	70f. green	10	10
755	–	80f. brown	10	10

DESIGNS: 30f. Kassa Cathedral; 40f. Debrecen Reformed Church; 70f. Budapest Evangelical Church; 80f. Buda Cathedral.

128 Mounted Archer

129 Model Glider

1943. Wounded Soldiers' Relief Fund. Inscr as in T **128**.

No.	Type	Description	Unused	Used
756	128	1f.+1f. grey	10	10
757	–	3f.+1f. lilac	30	30
758	–	4f.+1f. brown	20	15
759	–	8f.+2f. green	20	15
760	–	12f.+2f. brown	20	15
761	–	20f.+2f. brown	20	15
762	–	40f.+4f. grey	20	15
763	–	50f.+6f. brown	20	15
764	–	70f.+8f. blue	20	15

DESIGNS—VERT: 3f., 4f. Magyar soldier with battle-axe and buckler; 8f. Warrior with shield and sword; 20f. Musketeer; 50f. Artilleryman; 70f. Magyar Arms. HORIZ: 12f. Lancer; 40f. Hussar.

1943. Air. Horthy Aviation Fund. Inscr "HORTHY MIKLOS NEMZETI REPULO ALAP".

No.	Type	Description	Unused	Used
765	129	8f.+8f. green	70	40
766	–	12f.+12f. blue	70	40
767	–	20f.+20f. brown	1·25	65
768	–	30f.+30f. red	70	65

DESIGNS: 12f. Gliders in flight; 20f. White-tailed sea eagle and aircraft; 30f. Cant Z.1007 bis Alcione bomber and gliders.

130 Shepherds and Angels

1943. Christmas.

No.	Type	Description	Unused	Used
769	130	4f. green	10	20
770	–	20f. blue	10	20
771	–	30f. red	10	20

DESIGNS: 20f. Nativity; 30f. Adoration of the Wise Men.

131 Nurse and Soldier

1944. Red Cross Fund. Cross and Crown in red.

No.	Type	Description	Unused	Used
772	131	20f.+20f. brown	30	25
773	–	30f.+30f. brown	30	25
774	–	50f.+50f. purple	30	25
775	–	70f.+70f. blue	30	25

DESIGNS: 30f. Soldier, nurse, mother and child; 50f. Nurse shielding a lamp over the Fallen; 70f. Soldier with crutches, nurse and sapling.

132 Drummer and Flags

133 St. Elizabeth

1944. 50th Death Anniv of Kossuth (statesman).

776 – 4f. brown 10 10
777 **132** 20f. green 10 10
778 – 30f. red 10 10
779 – 50f. blue 10 10

DESIGNS—VERT: 4f. Kossuth and family group; 50f. Portrait. HORIZ: 30f. Kossuth speaking before an assembly.

1944. Famous Women.

780 **133** 20f. bistre 10 10
781 – 24f. purple 10 20
782 – 30f. red 10 10
783 – 50f. blue 10 10
784 – 70f. red 10 20
785 – 80f. brown 10 20

PORTRAITS: 24f. St. Margaret; 30f. Elizabeth Szilagyi; 50f. Dorothy Kanizsai; 70f. Zsuzsanna Lorantffy; 80f. Ilona Zrinyi.

1945. Stamps as Nos. 732/48, surch **FELSZABADULAS** (= Liberation) **1945 apr 4** and value. On yellow or blue surface-tinted paper (same price).

786 10f. on 1f. grey 75 1·10
787 20f. on 3f. blue 75 1·10
788 30f. on 4f. brown 75 1·10
789 40f. on 6f. blue 75 1·10
790 50f. on 8f. green 75 1·10
791 1p. on 10f. brown 75 1·10
792 150f. on 12f. green 75 1·10
793 2p. on 18f. black 75 1·10
794 3p. on 20f. brown 75 1·10
795 5p. on 24f. purple 75 1·10
796 6p. on 50f. blue 75 1·10
797 10p. on 80f. brown 75 1·10
798 20p. on 1p. green 75 1·10

135 Bajcsy-Zsilinszky

1945. Bajcsy-Zsilinszky (patriot).

799 **135** 1p.+1p. purple 45 60

1945. Provisionals. 1st issue. Surch **1945** and value.

(a) On stamps of 1943, Nos. 732/50, surface-tinted paper.

800 10f. on 4f. brown on blue 10 10
801 10f. on 10f. brown on blue 15 25
802 10f. on 12f. green on yellow 10 10
803 20f. on 1f. grey on yellow 10 10
804 20f. on 18f. black on yellow 10 10
805 28f. on 5f. red on blue 10 10
806 30f. on 30f. red on blue (No. 745) 10 10
807 30f. on 30f. red on blue (No. 744) 10 10
808 40f. on 24f. purple on yellow 10 10
809 42f. on 20f. brown on yellow 10 10
810 50f. on 50f. blue on yellow 10 10
811 60f. on 8f. green on yellow 10 10
812 1p. on 80f. brown on blue 10 10
813 1p. on 1p. green on yellow 10 10
814 150f. on 6f. blue on yellow 35 75
815 2p. on 2p. brown on blue 10 10
816 3p. on 3f. blue on yellow 15 25
817 5p. on 5p. purple on yellow 10 10
818 10p. on 2f. orange on blue 2·75 4·75

(b) On Famous Women Series of 1944 (Nos. 780/5), surface-tinted paper.

819 20f. on 20f. bistre on blue 10 10
820 30f. on 30f. red on blue 10 10
821 40f. on 24f. purple on yellow 10 10
822 50f. on 50f. blue on yellow 10 10
823 80f. on 80f. brown on yellow 10 10
824 1p. on 70f. red on blue 10 10

1945. Provisionals. 2nd issue. Surch **1945** and value.

(a) On stamps of 1943, Nos. 732/48, surface-tinted paper.

825 40f. on 10f. brown on blue 10 10
826 1p. on 20f. brown on yellow 10 10
827 1.60p. on 12f. green on yellow 10 10
828 2p. on 4f. brown on blue 10 10
829 4p. on 30f. red on blue (No. 744) 10 10
830 5p. on 8f. green on yellow 10 10
831 6p. on 50f. blue on yellow 10 10
832 7p. on 1p. green on yellow 10 10
833 9p. on 1f. grey on yellow 10 10
834 10p. on 80f. brown on blue 10 10

(b) On Famous Women Series of 1944. (Nos. 780/3), surface-tinted paper.

835 80f. on 24f. purple on yellow 10 10
836 3p. on 50f. blue on yellow 10 10
837 8p. on 20f. bistre on blue 10 10
838 20p. on 30f. red on blue 10 10

1945. National High School Fund. Nos. 776/9, with coloured surfaces, surch **BEKE A NEPFOISKOLAKERT**, new value and premium.

839 **132** 3p.+9p. on 20f. green on yellow 15 30
840 – 4p.+12p. on 4f. brown on blue 15 30
841 – 8p.+24p. on 50f. blue on yellow 15 30
842 – 10p.+30p. on 30f. red on blue 15 30

138 Mining

1945. Int Trade Union Conference, Paris.

843 **138** 40f. grey 2·75 3·75
844 – 1p.60 brown 2·75 3·75
845 – 2p. green 2·75 3·75
846 – 3p. purple 2·75 3·75
847 – 5p. red 2·75 3·75
848 – 8p. brown 2·75 3·75
849 – 10p. red 2·75 3·75
850 – 20p. blue 2·75 3·75

DESIGNS: Trade Symbols—1p.60, Hammer and anvil (ironworking); 2p. Winged wheel (railway workers); 3p. Trowel and bricks (building); 5p. Plough (agriculture); 8p. Carrier pigeon (communications); 10p. Compasses (engineering); 20p. Winged pen and book (clerks).

139 I. Sallai and S. Furst

1945. National Relief Fund.

851 **139** 2p.+2p. brown 75 1·25
852 – 3p.+3p. red 75 1·25
853 – 4p.+4p. violet 75 1·25
854 – 6p.+6p. green 75 1·25
855 – 10p.+10p. red 75 1·25
856 – 15p.+15p. olive 75 1·25
857 – 20p.+20p. brown 75 1·25
858 – 40p.+40p. blue 75 1·25

PORTRAITS: 3p. L. Kabok and I. Monus; 4p. F. Rozsa and Z. Schonherz; 6p. A. Koltoi and P. Knurr; 10p. G. Sarkozi and I. Nagy; 15p. V. Tartsay and J. Nagy; 20p. J. Kiss and E. Bajcsy-Zsilinszky; 40p. E. Sagvari and O. Hoffmann.

1945. Provisionals. 3rd issue. Nos. 738, 740/1 and 745 (coloured surfaces) surch **1945** and new value.

859 40p. on 8f. green on yellow 10 10
860 60p. on 18f. black on yellow 10 10
861 100p. on 12f. green on yellow 10 10
862 300p. on 30f. red on blue 10 10

140 Reconstruction

1945.

863 **140** 12p. olive 30 45
864 20p. green 10 10
865 24p. brown 30 35
866 30p. black 10 10
867 40p. green 10 10
868 60p. red 10 10
869 100p. orange 10 10
870 120p. blue 10 10
871 140p. red 30 30
872 200p. brown 10 10
873 240p. blue 10 10
874 300p. red 10 10
875 500p. green 10 10
876 1000p. purple 10 10
877 3000p. red 10 10

Owing to the collapse of the pengo, the following stamps were overprinted to show the postage rate for which they were valid, and they were sold at the appropriate rate for the day. **Any** or **Nyomtatv** = Sample Post or Printed Matter. **Hlp** or **Helyi lev. lap** = Local Postcard. **Hl** or **Helyi level** = Local Letter. **Tlp** or **Tavolsagi lev.-lap** = Inland Postcard. **Tl** or **Tavolsagi level** = Inland Letter. **Ajl** or **Ajanlas** = Registered Letter. **Cs.** or **Csomag** = Parcel.

1946. Optd as above. (a) First Issue.

878 **126** "Any. 1" on 1f. grey 10 10
879 – "Hlp. 1" on 8p. on 20f. bistre on blue (No. 837) 10 10
880 – "Hl. 1" on 50f. blue (No. 783) 10 10
881 – "Tlp. 1" on 4f. brown (No. 735) 10 10
882 – "Tl. 1" on 10f. brown (No. 739) 10 10
883 **133** "Ajl. 1" on 20f. bistre 10 10
883b **127** "Cs. 5-1" on 30f. red (No. 744) 12·00 12·00
884 – "Cs. 5-1" on 70f. red (No. 784) 10 10
885 – "Cs. 10-1" on 70f. red (No. 784) 10 10
885a **127** "Cs. 10-1" on 80f. brown (No. 747) 11·00 13·50

(b) Second Issue.

886 **126** "Any. 2" on 1f. grey 10 10
887 – "Hlp. 2" on 8p. on 20f. bistre on blue (No. 837) 10 10
888 – "Hl. 2" on 40f. on 10f. brown on blue (No. 825) 10 10
889 – "Tlp. 2" on 4f. brown (No. 735) 10 10
890 – "Tl. 2" on 10f. on 4f. brown on blue (No. 800) 10 10
891 – "Ajl. 2" on 12f. green (No. 740) 10 10
892 – "Cs. 5-2" on 24f. purple (No. 743) 10 10
893 – "Cs. 10-2" on 80f. brown (No. 785) 10 10

(c) Third Issue.

894 – "Nyomtatv. 20gr." on 60f. on 8f. green on yellow (No. 811) 10 10
895 – "Helyi lev.-lap" on 2f. bistre on blue (as No. 780) 10 10
896 – "Helyi level" on 10f. brown on blue (as No. 739) 10 10
897 – "Tavolsagi lev.-lap" on 4f. brown (No. 735) 10 10
898 – "Tavolsagi level" on 18f. black (No. 741) 10 10
899 – "Ajanlas" on 24f. purple (No. 781) 10 10
900 – "Csomag 5 kg" on 2p. on 4f. brown on blue (No. 828) 10 10
901 – "Csomag 10kg." on 30f. red on blue (as No. 782) 10 10

Abbreviations used in the following issues:
ez(er) p. = thousand pengos.
m(illio) p. = million pengos.
m.p. (milpengo) = million pengos.
md.p. (milliard. p) = thousand million pengos.
b.p. (billio. p) = million million pengos.
ez. ap (ezer adopengo) = thousand "tax" pengos.
m. ap. (millio adopengo) = million "tax" pengos.

143 **144**

1946. Foundation of Republic.

902 **143** 3ez. p. brown 10 10
903 15ez. p. blue 10 10

1946.

904 **144** 4ez. p. brown 10 10
905 10ez. p. red 10 10
906 15ez. p. blue 10 10
907 20ez. p. brown 10 10
908 30ez. p. purple 10 10
909 50ez. p. grey 10 10
910 80ez. p. blue 10 10
911 100ez. p. red 10 10
912 160ez. p. green 10 10
913 200ez. p. green 10 10
914 500ez. p. red 10 10
915 640ez. p. olive 10 10
916 800ez. p. violet 10 10

145 **146**

1946. 75th Anniv of First Hungarian Stamps.

917 **145** 500+500ez. p. green 1·10 1·40
918 1+1m. p. brown 1·10 1·40
919 1.5+1.5m. p. red 1·10 1·40
920 2+2m. p. blue 1·10 1·40

1946.

921 **146** 1m.p. red 10 20
922 2m.p. blue 10 20
923 3m.p. brown 10 20
924 4m.p. grey 10 20
925 5m.p. violet 10 20
926 10m.p. green 10 20
927 20m.p. red 10 20
928 50m.p. green 10 20

147 Posthorn and Arms **148** Posthorn **149** Dove and Letter

1946.

929 **147** 100m.p. red 10 20
930 200m.p. red 10 20
931 500m.p. red 10 20
932 1000m.p. red 10 20
933 2000m.p. red 10 20
934 3000m.p. red 10 20
935 5000m.p. red 10 20
936 10,000m.p. red 10 20
937 20,000m.p. red 10 20
938 30,000m.p. red 10 20
939 50,000m.p. red 10 20

1946.

940 **148** 100md.p. green and red 10 25
941 200md.p. green and red 10 25
942 500md.p. green and red 10 25

1946.

943 **149** 1b.p. black and red 10 30
944 2b.p. black and red 10 30
945 5b.p. black and red 10 30
946 10b.p. black and red 10 30
947 20b.p. black and red 10 30
948 50b.p. black and red 10 30
949 100b.p. black and red 10 30
950 200b.p. black and red 10 30
951 500b.p. black and red 10 30
952 1000b.p. black and red 10 30
953 10,000b.p. black and red 10 40
954 50,000b.p. black and red 15 50
955 100,000b.p. black and red 15 50
956 500,000b.p. black and red 15 50

150 Locomotive "Heves", 1846 **151** Posthorn

1946. Centenary of Hungarian Railways.

957 **150** 10000ap. brown 5·50 4·50
958 – 20000ap. blue 5·50 4·50
959 – 30000ap. green 5·50 4·50
960 – 40000ap. red 5·50 4·50

DESIGNS: 20000ap. Class 424 steam locomotive; 30000ap. Class V44 electric locomotive; 40000ap. "Arpad" diesel railcar, 1935.

1946.

961 **151** 5ez. ap. green and black 10 25
962 10ez. ap. green and black 10 25
963 20ez. ap. green and black 10 25
964 50ez. ap. green and black 10 25
965 80ez. ap. green and black 10 25
966 100ez. ap. green and black 10 25
967 200ez. ap. green and black 10 25
968 500ez. ap. green and black 10 30
969 1m. ap. red and black 10 50
970 5m. ap. red and black 10 50

152 Industry **153** Agriculture

1946. Currency Reform.

971 **152** 8fi. brown 10 10
972 10fi. brown 10 10
973 12fi. brown 10 10
974 20fi. brown 10 10
975 30fi. brown 10 10
976 40fi. brown 10 10
977 60fi. brown 10 10
978 **153** 1fo. green 45 10
979 1fo. 40 green 45 10
980 2fo. green 75 10
981 3fo. green 3·00 10
982 5fo. green 75 10
983 10fo. green 1·50 45

154 Ceres **155** Liberty Bridge

1946. Agricultural Fair.

984 **154** 30fi.+60fi. green 4·25 4·00
985 60fi.+1fo. 20 red 4·25 4·00
986 1fo.+2fo. blue 4·25 4·00

1947. Air. Views.

987 – 10fi. red 20 10
988 – 20fi. grey 20 10
989 **155** 50fi. brown 50 10
990 – 70fi. green 50 10
991 – 1fo. blue 2·25 10
992 – 1fo. 40 brown 2·50 10
993 – 3fo. green 3·50 30
994 – 5fo. lilac 2·50 1·25

DESIGNS: 10fi. Loyalty Tower, Sopron; 20fi. Esztergom Cathedral; 70fi. Palace Hotel, Lillafured; 1fo. Vajdahunyad Castle, Budapest; 1fo. 40, Visegrad Fortress; 3fo. "Falcone" (racing yacht) on Lake Balaton; 5fo. Parliament Buildings and Kossuth Bridge.

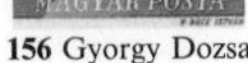
156 Gyorgy Dozsa

157 Doctor examining X-Ray

1947. Liberty issue.
995 **156** 8fi. red 15 10
996 – 10fi. blue 15 10
997 – 12fi. brown 15 10
998 – 20fi. green 35 10
999 – 30fi. brown 35 10
1000 – 40fi. purple 50 10
1001 – 60fi. red 50 10
1002 – 1fo. blue 60 10
1003 – 2fo. violet 95 30
1004 – 4fo. green . . . . 1·90 35
PORTRAITS: 10fi. A. Budai Nagy; 12fi. T. Esze; 20fi. I. Martinovics; 30fi. J. Batsanyi; 40fi. L. Kossuth; 60fi. M. Tancsics; 1fo. S. Petofi; 2fo. E. Ady; 4fo. A. Jozsef.

1947. Welfare Organizations. Inscr "SIESS! ADJ! SEGITS!" (trans. "Come! Give! Help!").
1005 – 8fi.+50fi. blue . . . . 3·75 3·50
1006 **157** 12fi.+50fi. brown . . . 3·75 3·50
1007 – 20fi.+50fi. green . . . 3·75 3·50
1008 – 60fi.+50fi. red 30 90
DESIGNS: 8fi. Doctor testing syringe; 20fi. Nurse and child; 60fi. Released prisoner-of-war.

158 Emblem of Peace

159 Liberty Statue

1947. Peace Treaty.
1009 **158** 60fi. red 30 20

1947. 30th Anniv of Soviet Union and Hungarian–Soviet Cultural Society Fund.
1010 – 40fi.+40fi. brn & grn . . 2·25 3·75
1011 **159** 60fi.+60fi. grey and red 45 2·25
1012 – 1fo.+1fo. black & blue 2·25 3·75
PORTRAITS: 40fi. Lenin; 1fo. Stalin.

161 Savings Bank

162 16th-century Mail Coach

1947. Savings Day. Inscr "TAKAREKOS JELENBOLDOG JOVO".
1013 – 40fi. red (beehive) . . . 25 10
1014 **161** 60fi. red 25 10

1947. Stamp Day.
1015 **162** 30fi. (+ 50fi.) brown . . 6·75 7·50

165 Arms of Hungary

167 Johann Gutenberg

1948. Centenary of Insurrection.
1016 – 8fi. red 20 10
1017 – 10fi. blue 20 10
1018 – 12fi. brown 20 10
1019 – 20fi. green 65 10
1020 – 30fi. brown 30 10
1021 – 40fi. purple 30 10
1022 – 60fi. red 75 10
1023 **165** 1fo. blue 75 10
1024 2fo. brown . . . . . . 1·00 20
1025 3fo. green . . . . . . 1·25 35
1026 4fo. red . . . . 3·50 45
DESIGNS—HORIZ: 8fi., 40fi. Hungarian independence flag; 10fi. Printing press; 12fi. Latticed window; 20fi. Shako, trumpet and sword; 30fi., 60fi. Slogan.

1948. Air. Explorers and Inventors.
1027 **167** 1fi. red 10 10
1028 – 2fi. mauve 25 30
1029 – 4fi. blue 25 30
1030 – 5fi. brown 25 30
1031 – 6fi. green 25 40
1032 – 8fi. purple 25 30
1033 – 10fi. brown 45 50
1034 – 12fi. green 90 35
1035 – 30fi. red . . . . 1·25 65
1036 – 40fi. violet . . . . . . 80 1·10
PORTRAITS: 2fi. Christopher Columbus; 4fi. Robert Fulton; 5fi. George Stephenson; 6fi. David Schwarz and Count Ferdinand von Zeppelin; 8fi. Thomas Edison; 10fi. Louis Bleriot; 12fi. Roald Amundsen; 30fi. Kalman Kando; 40fi. Alexander Popov.

168 Chain Bridge, Budapest

1948. Air. Re-opening of Budapest Chain Bridge. Sheets 74 × 65 mm.
MS1036a 2fo.+18fo. Red . . . . 75·00 90·00
MS1036b **168** 3fo.+18fo. blue . . 75·00 90·00
DESIGN: 20fo. Shows a more distant view of the bridge.

169 Lorand Eotvos

1948. Birth Centenary of L. Eotvos (physicist).
1037 **169** 60fi. red 75 30

170 William Shakespeare

1948. Air. Writers.
1038 **170** 1fi. blue 20 15
1039 – 2fi. red 30 15
1040 – 4fi. green 30 15
1041 – 5fi. mauve 40 30
1042 – 6fi. blue 40 30
1043 – 8fi. brown 40 30
1044 – 10fi. red 40 40
1045 – 12fi. violet 45 45
1046 – 30fi. brown 90 70
1047 – 40fi. brown . . . . . . 1·10 1·25
PORTRAITS: 2fi. Voltaire; 4fi. Goethe; 5fi. Byron; 6fi. Victor Hugo; 8fi. Edgar Allan Poe; 10fi. Petofi; 12fi. Mark Twain; 30fi. Tolstoy; 40fi. Gorki.

171 Globe and Pigeon

172 Symbolizing Industry, Agriculture and Culture

1948. 5th National Philatelic Exhibition.
1048 **171** 30fi. blue . . . . 3·25 3·75
Sold at 1fo.30 (incl 1fo. entrance fee).

1948. 17th Trades' Union Congress.
1049 **172** 30fi. red 25 10

173 Agricultural Worker

174 Reproduction of T 32

1949. International Women's Day.
1050 **173** 60fi.+60fi. mauve . . . . 1·10 1·10

1949. 30th Anniv of Bolshevist Regime.
1051 **174** 40fi. brown and red . . 35 15
1052 – 60fi. olive and red . . . 35 15
DESIGN: 60fi. Reproduction of No. 325.

175 Pushkin holding Torch and Scroll

176 Symbolising Workers of Five Continents

1949. 150th Birth Anniv of A. S. Pushkin (poet).
1053 **175** 1fo.+1fo. red . . . . . 5·00 5·25
MS1053a 52 × 62 mm. 1fo.+1fo. Red 15·00 15·00
DESIGN—HORIZ: No. MS1053a, Puhkin writing.

1949. 2nd World Federation of Trade Unions Congress, Milan. Flag in red.
1054 **176** 30fi. brown . . . . . . 2·00 2·10
1055 40fi. purple . . . . . . 2·00 2·10
1056 60fi. red . . . . 2·00 2·10
1057 1fo. blue . . . . 2·00 2·10

177 Sandor Petofi

178 Heads and Globe

1949. Death Centenary of Petofi (poet).
1058 **177** 40fi. purple 45 20
1096 40fi. brown 50 20
1059 60fi. red 20 10
1060 1fo. blue 20 15
1098 1fo. green 35 20

1949. World Youth Festival, Budapest.
1061 **178** 20fi. brown 65 70
1062 – 30fi. green 65 70
1063 – 40fi. bistre . . . . . . 75 1·00
1064 – 60fi. red . . . . 75 1·00
1065 – 1fo. blue . . . . 1·60 1·60
MS1065a 100 × 130 mm. Nos. 1061/5, but colours changed 20·00 20·00
DESIGNS: 30fi. Three clenched fists; 40fi. Man breaking chains; 60fi. Young people and banner; 1fo. Workers and tractor.

179 Hungarian Coat-of-Arms

1949. Ratification of Constitution. Arms in blue, brown, red and green.
1066 **179** 20fi. green 65 50
1067 60fi. red 65 30
1068 1fo. blue 70 30

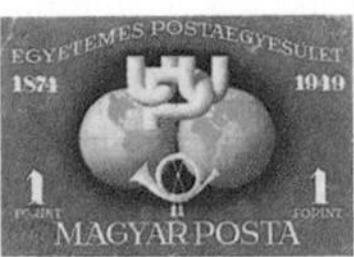

181 Globes and Posthorn

1949. 75th Anniv of U.P.U.
1069 **181** 60fi. red (postage) . . . 30 35
1070 1fo. blue 45 35

1071 – 2fo. brown (air) 80 65
MS1072 128 × 98 mm. 3fo. (× 4) brown and red £300 £300
DESIGN: 2, 3fo. Lisunov Li-2 airplane replaces posthorn.

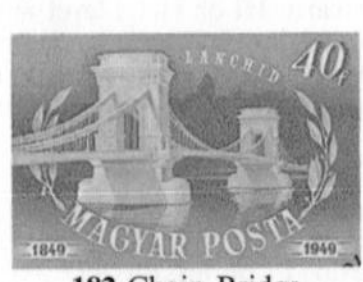

182 Chain Bridge

1949. Centenary of Budapest Chain Bridge.
1073 **182** 40fi. green (postage) . . 50 35
1074 60fi. brown 50 35
1075 1fo. blue 50 35

1076 1fo.60 red (air) 80 75
1077 2fo. olive 80 50
MS1077a 136 × 100 mm. 50 fo. Lilac £225 £225
DESIGN—VERT: 50fo. Drawing board, plans, etc.

183 Postman and Forms of Transport

184 Joseph Stalin

1949. Air. Stamp Day.
1078 **183** 50fi. grey . . . . 3·75 3·75

1949. Stalin's 70th Birthday.
1079 **184** 60fi. red 50 25
1080 1fo. blue 50 30
1081 2fo. brown . . . . . . 1·00 50

185 Miners

1950. Five Year Plan.
1082 **185** 8fi. grey 75 10
1083 – 10fi. purple 45 10
1084 – 12fi. red 45 10
1085 – 20fi. green 45 10
1086 – 30fi. purple 50 10
1087 – 40fi. brown 90 10
1088 – 60fi. red 90 10
1089 – 1fo. violet and yellow . . 1·10 10
1090 – 1fo.70 green and yellow 1·90 30
1091 – 2fo. red and orange . . 2·10 35
1092 – 3fo. blue and buff . . . 2·40 40
1093 – 4fo. green and orange . . 2·50 45
1094 – 5fo. purple and yellow 4·25 1·00
1095 – 10fo. brown and yellow 5·25 2·50
DESIGNS: 10fi. Iron foundry; 12fi. Power station; 20fi. Textiles; 30fi. Factory workers' entertainment; 40fi. Mechanical farming; 60fi. Village co-operative office; 1fo. Class 303 steam locomotive on bridge; 1fo.70, Family at health resort; 2fo. Soldier and tank; 3fo. Freighter and Lisunov Li-2 airplane; 4fo. Cattle; 5fo. Draughtsman and factory; 10fo. Sportsman, woman and football match.

186 Philatelic Museum

1950. 20th Anniv of P.O. Philatelic Museum.
1099 **186** 60fi. brown and black (postage) . . . . . . 4·50 5·75
1100 – 2fo. red and yellow (air) 6·75 6·50
DESIGN—HORIZ: 2fo. Globe, coach, Douglas DC-4 airliner and stamps.

188 Family Greeting Soviet Troops

1950. 5th Anniv of Liberation.
1101 **188** 40fi. black 90 60
1102 60fi. lake 60 35
1103 1fo. blue 60 30
1104 2fo. brown 90 35

189 Chess Match

1950. 1st International Candidates Chess Tournament, Budapest. Designs incorporate rook and chessboard.
1105 **189** 60fi. mauve (postage) . . 1·75 45
1106 – 1fo. blue . . . . 3·25 1·10

1107 – 1fo.60 brown (air) . . . 4·50 1·90
DESIGNS: 1fo. Trade Union Building; 1fo.60, Map.

190 Workers and Star

1950. May Day. Inscr as in T **190**.
1108 **190** 40fi. brown . . . . . . 1·90 60
1109 – 60fi. red 90 20
1110 **190** 1fo. blue . . . . 1·10 45
DESIGN: 60fi. Two workers.

191 Workers and Flag

1950. World Federation of Trade Unions Congress, Budapest.
1111 – 40fi. green (postage) . . 1·10 55
1112 **191** 60fi. red 75 25
1113 – 1fo. brown (air) . . . . 1·10 40
DESIGNS: 40fi. Statue, dove and globes; 1fo. Globes, Chain Bridge and Parliament Buildings.

192 Baby and Nursery

1950. Children's Day.
1114 **192** 20fi. brown and grey 90 1·00
1115 – 30fi. mauve and brown 40 30
1116 – 40fi. green and blue . . 40 30
1117 – 60fi. red and brown . . £1500 £1500
1117a – 60fi. red and brown . . 40 30
1118 – 1fo.70 blue and green 1·25 75
DESIGNS: 30fi. Baby boy and holiday scene; 40fi. Schoolgirl and classroom; 60fi. Pioneer boy and camp; 1fo.70, Pioneer boy and girl and model glider class.
No. 1117 is inscr "UTANPOTLASUNK A JOVO HARCAIHOZ" and No. 1117a is inscr "SZABAD HAZABAN BOLDOG IFJUSAG".

193 Workers and Globe

1950. 1st Congress of Young Workers, Budapest.
1119 **193** 20fi. green 75 45
1120 – 30fi. orange 30 10
1121 – 40fi. brown 30 10
1122 – 60fi. mauve 35 30
1123 – 1fo.70 green . . . . . . 1·00 45
DESIGNS—HORIZ: 30fi. Foundry worker and cauldron. VERT: 40fi. Man, woman and banner; 60fi. Workers, banner and Liberty Statue; 1fo.70, Three workers and banner.

194 Peonies **195** Miner

1950. Flowers.
1124 **194** 30fi. purple and green . . 60 25
1125 – 40fi. green, yellow & mve 60 35
1126 – 60fi. brown, yellow & grn . . . . 1·40 40
1127 – 1fo. violet, red and green 2·25 1·10
1128 – 1fo.70 violet, grn & lilac 5·25 65
DESIGNS: 40fi. Pasque flowers; 60fi. Yellow pheasant's-eye; 1fo. Geranium; 1fo.70, Campanulas.

1950. 2nd National Inventions Exhibition.
1129 **195** 40fi. brown . . . . . . 1·00 45
1130 – 60fi. red 90 30
1131 – 1fo. blue . . . . 1·25 75
DESIGNS: 60fi. Turner; 1fo. Building factory.

196 Liberty Statue

1950. Air.
1132 **196** 20fi. red 10 10
1133 – 30fi. violet 10 10
1134 – 70fi. purple 20 10
1135 – 1fo. brown 20 10
1136 – 1fo.60 blue 70 10
1137 – 2fo. red 45 10
1138 – 3fo. black . . . . . . 2·10 30
1139 – 5fo. blue . . . . 1·10 45
1140 – 10fo. brown . . . . . 3·50 75
1140a – 20fo. green . . . . . 14·50 4·00
DESIGNS—VERT: 30fi. Crane and buildings; 70fi. Diosgyor steelworks; 1fo. "Stalinyec" tractor; 1fo.60, "Szeged" (freighter); 2fo. Combine harvester; 3fo. Class 303 steam locomotive; 5fo. Matyas Rakosi steelmill; 10, 20fo. Lisunov Li-2 airplane at Budaors airport.
For No. 1139 but on silver paper see No. 1437.

198 Worker signing Peace Petition

1950. Peace Propaganda.
1141 **198** 40fi. brown and blue . . 4·00 2·50
1142 – 60fi. green and orange 1·10 2·25
1143 – 1fo. brown and green . . 4·00 9·00
DESIGNS—VERT: 60fi. Girl holding dove. HORIZ: 1fo. Soldier, mother and children.

199 Swimmers

1950.
1144 **199** 10fi. blue and light blue (postage) 10 10
1145 – 20fi. brown and orange 10 10
1146 – 1fo. green and olive . . 50 45
1147 – 1fo.70 red and vermilion 1·00 75
1148 – 2fo. violet and brown . . 1·50 1·00
1149 – 30fi. mauve & violet (air) 35 10
1150 – 40fi. blue and green . . 35 10
1151 – 60fi. orange, brown & grn . . . . 1·10 10
1152 – 70fi. brown and grey . . 85 45
1153 – 3fo. chestnut and brown 2·25 1·10
DESIGNS—POSTAGE: 20fi. Vaulting; 1fo. Mountaineering; 1fo.70, Basketball; 2fo. Motor cycling. AIR: 30fi. Volleyball; 40fi. Throwing the javelin; 60fi. Emblem of "Ready for work and action" movement; 70fi. Football; 3fo. Gliding.

200 Jozef Bem and Battle of Piski **201** Workers and Soldier

1950. Death Centenary of Gen. Bem.
1154 **200** 40fi. brown 75 25
1155 60fi. red 75 30
1156 1fo. blue . . . . 1·50 55
MS1156a 98×78 mm. **200** 2fo. (+2fo.) purple. Imperf . . . . 35·00 35·00

1951. 2nd Hungarian Communist Party Congress.
1157 **201** 10fi. green 30 10
1158 – 30fi. brown 45 25
1159 – 60fi. red 50 35
1160 – 1fo. blue . . . . 1·10 40
DESIGNS—HORIZ: 30fi. Workers, soldier and banner; 60fi. Portrait and four workers with flags. VERT: 1fo. Procession with banner.

202 Flags **203** Mare and Foal

1951. Hungarian–Soviet Amity. Inscr "MAGYAR SZOVJET BARATSAG HONAPJA 1951".
1161 **202** 60fi. red 35 10
1162 – 1fo. violet 45 30
DESIGN: 1fo. Hungarian and Russian workers.

1951. Livestock Expansion Plan.
1163 **203** 10fi. brown and ochre (postage) 25 10
1164 – 30fi. brown and red . . 45 30
1165 – 40fi. brown and green . . 50 45
1166 – 60fi. brown and orange 65 45
1167 **203** 20fi. brown & green (air) 35 30
1168 – 70fi. ochre and brown 65 60
1169 – 1fo. brown and blue . . 1·60 1·25
1170 – 1fo.60 chestnut & brown 3·25 2·25
DESIGNS: 30, 70fi. Sow and litter; 40fi., 1fo. Ewe and lamb; 60fi., 1fo.60, Cow and calf.

204 Worker

1951. May Day. Inscr "1951 MAJUS".
1171 **204** 40fi. brown 65 45
1172 – 60fi. red 50 10
1173 – 1fo. blue 50 30
DESIGNS—VERT: 60fi. People with banners. HORIZ: 1fo. Labour Day rally.

205 Leo Frankel **206** Street-fighting

1951. 80th Anniv of Paris Commune.
1174 **205** 60fi. brown 50 25
1175 **206** 1fo. blue and red 75 25

207 Children's Heads **208** Ganz Wagon Works

1951. Int Children's Day. Inscr "NEMZETKOZI GYERMEKNAP 1951".
1176 **207** 30fi. brown 30 20
1177 – 40fi. green 45 20
1178 – 50fi. brown 45 20
1179 – 60fi. mauve 45 30
1180 – 1fo.70 blue . . . . . . 1·10 20
DESIGNS: 40fi. Flying model airplane; 50fi. Diesel train on Budapest Pioneer Railway; 60fi. Chemistry experiment; 1fo.70, Blowing bugle.

1951. Rebuilding Plan (1st series).
1180a – 8fi. green 35 10
1180b – 10fi. violet 45 10
1180c – 12fi. red 60 10
1181 **208** 20fi. green 60 10
1182 – 30fi. orange 70 10
1183 – 40fi. brown 70 10
1183a – 50fi. blue 35 10
1184 – 60fi. red 90 10
1184a – 70fi. brown 45 10
1184b – 80fi. purple . . . . . 1·40 10
1185 – 1fo. blue . . . . . . 1·50 10
1185a – 1fo.20 red . . . . . 1·90 10
1185b – 1fo.70 blue . . . . . 1·40 10
1185c – 2fo. green . . . . . 1·40 10
1186 – 3fo. purple . . . . . 2·25 10
1186a – 4fo. olive . . . . . . 2·25 15
1186b – 5fo. black . . . . . . 3·75 15
BUILDINGS: 8fi. Stalin School; 10fi. Szekesfehervar railway station; 12fi. Ujpest medical dispensary; 30fi. Flats; 40fi. Central Railway Station, Budapest; 50fi. Inota power station; 60fi. Matyas Rakosi Cultural Institute; 70fi. Hajdunanas grain elevator; 80fi. Tiszalok dam; 1fo. Kilian Road School; 1fo.20, Mining Apprentices Institute, Ajkacsingervolgy; 1fo.70, Iron and Steel Apprentices Institute, Csepel; 2fo. Cultural Centre, Hungarian Optical Works; 3fo. Building Workers' Union Headquarters; 4fo. Miners' Union Headquarters; 5fo. Flats.
See also Nos. 1296/1304.

209 Gorky **210** Engineers and Tractors

1951. 15th Death Anniv of Maksim Gorky (Russian writer).
1187 **209** 60fi. red 20 20
1188 1fo. blue 30 25
1189 2fo. purple 65 55

1951. 1st Anniv of Five Year Plan.
1190 **210** 20fi. sepia (postage) . . 20 20
1191 – 30fi. blue 30 25
1192 – 40fi. red 25 20
1193 – 60fi. brown 25 20
1194 – 70fi. brown (air) 40 20
1195 – 1fo. green 40 30
1196 – 2fo. purple . . . . . . 1·60 65
DESIGNS: 30fi. Doctor X-raying patient; 40fi. Workman instructing apprentices; 60fi. Girl driving tractor; 70fi. Electrical engineers constructing pylon; 1fo. Young people and recreation home; 2fo. Lisunov Li-2 airplane over Stalin (later Arpad) Bridge.

211 1871 Stamp without portrait and Hungarian Arms **212** Soldiers Parading

1951. 80th Anniv of 1st Hungarian Postage Stamp.
1197 **211** 60fi. green 45 30
1198 1fo.+1fo. red . . . . . 9·75 8·00
1199 2fo.+2fo. blue . . . . . 12·50 11·00
MS1199a Air. Three sheets each 78×97 mm. Nos. 1197/9 Set of 3 sheets £150 £170

1951. Army Day.
1200 **212** 1fo. brown (postage) . . 80 25
1201 – 60fi. blue (air) 50 25
DESIGN—VERT: 60fi. Tanks and Liberty Statue.

213 Lily of the Valley **214** Revolutionaries and Flags

1951. Flowers.
1202 – 30fi. violet, blue and green 40 10
1203 **213** 40fi. myrtle and green . . 85 50
1204 – 60fi. red, pink and green 55 20
1205 – 1fo. blue, red and green 1·25 35
1206 – 1fo.70 brown, yell & grn 2·75 1·40
FLOWERS: 30fi. Cornflowers; 60fi. Tulips; 1fo. Poppies; 1fo.70, Cowslips.

1951. 34th Anniv of Russian Revolution.
1207 **214** 40fi. green 65 30
1208 – 60fi. blue 65 25
1209 – 1fo. red 65 30
DESIGNS: 60fi. Lenin addressing revolutionaries; 1fo. Lenin and Stalin.

215 Parade before Stalin Statue

1951. Stalin's 72nd Birthday.
1210 **215** 60fi. red 90 40
1211 1fo. blue . . . . 1·00 45

216 Bolshoi State Theatre, Moscow

1952. Views of Moscow.
1212 **216** 60fi. lake and green . . . 65 15
1213 – 1fo. brown and red . . . 65 25
1214 – 1fo.60 olive and lake . . 55 50
DESIGNS: 1fo. Lenin Mausoleum; 1fo.60, Kremlin.

217 Rakosi and Peasants **218** Rakosi

1952. 60th Birth Anniv of Rakosi.
1215 **217** 60fi. purple 65 25
1216 **218** 1fo. brown 65 25
1217 – 2fo. blue . . . . 1·25 45
DESIGN: 2fo. Rakosi and foundry workers.

219 L. Kossuth

1952. Heroes of 1848 Revolution.
1218 **219** 20fi. green 10 10
1219 – 30fi. purple (Petofi) . . . 15 10
1220 – 50fi. black (Bem) 45 20
1221 – 60fi. lake (Tancsics) . . 45 10
1222 – 1fo. blue (Damjanich) . . 45 20
1223 – 1fo.50 brown (Nagy) . . 60 60

220 Pied Avocet

1952. Air. Birds.
1224 **220** 20fi. black and green . . 10 10
1225 – 30fi. black and green . . 25 10
1226 – 40fi. black, yellow & brn 30 10
1227 – 50fi. black and orange 30 10
1228 – 60fi. black and red . . . 30 10
1229 – 70fi. black, orange & red 45 25
1230 – 80fi. black, yellow & grn 60 30
1231 – 1fo. black, red and blue 85 40
1232 – 1fo.40 multicoloured . . 1·00 45
1233 – 1fo.60 black, grn & brn 1·25 60
1234 – 2fo.50 black and purple 2·50 1·00
DESIGNS: 30fi. White stork; 40fi. Golden oriole; 50fi. Kentish plover; 60fi. Black-winged stilt; 70fi. Lesser grey strike; 80fi. Great bustard; 1fo. Western red-footed falcon; 1fo.40, European bee eater; 1fo.60, Glossy ibis; 2fo.50, Great egret.

1952. Budapest Philatelic Exn. No. 1050 with bars obliterating inscription and premium.
1235 **173** 60fi. mauve . . . . . . 35·00 40·00

222 Drummer and Flags

1952. May Day. Inscr "1952 MAJUS I".
1236 **222** 40fi. red and green . . . 90 50
1237 – 60fi. red and brown . . 60 25
1238 – 1fo. red and brown . . . 90 25
DESIGNS: 60fi. Workers; 1fo. Workman and globe.

223 Running

1952. 15th Olympic Games, Helsinki.
1239 **223** 30fi. brown (postage) . . 35 10
1240 – 40fi. green 35 10
1241 – 60fi. red 50 10
1242 – 1fo. blue 80 45
1243 – 1fo.70 orange (air) . . . 1·25 80
1244 – 2fo. brown . . . . . . 1·25 1·10
DESIGNS: 40fi. Swimming; 60fi. Fencing; 1fo. Gymnastics; 1fo.70, Throwing the hammer; 2fo. Stadium.

224 Leonardo da Vinci

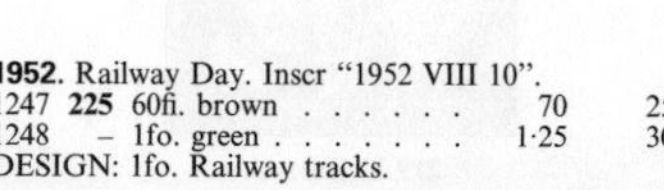

225 Train and Railwayman

1952. Air. 500th Birth Anniv of Leonardo da Vinci and 150th Birth Anniv of Victor Hugo.
1245 **224** 1fo.60 blue 75 45
1246 – 2fo. purple (Victor Hugo) 75 75

1952. Railway Day. Inscr "1952 VIII 10".
1247 **225** 60fi. brown 70 25
1248 – 1fo. green . . . . 1·25 30
DESIGN: 1fo. Railway tracks.

226 Mechanical Coal-cutter

227 L. Kossuth

1952. Miners' Day. Inscr as in T **226**.
1249 **226** 60fi. brown 70 25
1250 – 1fo. green . . . . 1·00 30
DESIGN: 1fo. Miners operating machinery.

1952. 150th Birth Anniv of Kossuth (statesman).
1251 **227** 40fi. olive on pink . . . 35 25
1252 – 60fi. black on blue . . . 30 25
1253 **227** 1fo. lilac on yellow . . . 45 35
DESIGN: 60fi. Statue of Kossuth.

228 Gy Dozsa

229 Boy, Girl and Stamp Exhibition

1952. Army Day. Inscr as T **228**.
1254 20fi. lilac (J. Hunyadi) . . . 30 10
1255 30fi. green (T **228**) 30 10
1256 40fi. blue (M. Zrinyi) . . . 30 10
1257 60fi. purple (I. Zrinyi) . . . 35 25
1258 1fo. turquoise (B. Vak) . . 60 25
1259 1fo.50 brown (A. Stromfeld) 90 45

1952. Air. Stamp Day. Inscr "XXV. BELYEGNAP 1952".
1260 – 1fo.+1fo. blue . . . . . 5·50 6·00
1261 **229** 2fo.+2fo. red . . . . . 5·50 6·00
DESIGN: 1fo. Children examining stamps.

230 Lenin and Revolutionary Council

1952. 35th Anniv of Russian Revolution.
1262 **230** 40fi. olive and purple . . 1·25 40
1263 – 60fi. olive and black . . 60 10
1264 – 1fo. olive and red . . . 1·25 20
DESIGNS: 60fi. Stalin and Cossacks; 1fo. Marx, Engels, Lenin, Stalin and Spassky Tower.

231 Harvester

1952. 3rd Hungarian Peace Congress. Inscr as in T **231**.
1265 **231** 60fi. red on yellow . . . 45 10
1266 – 1fo. brown on green . . . 45 30
DESIGN—HORIZ: 1fo. Workers' discussion group.

232 Tunnel Construction

1953. Budapest Underground Railway. Inscr "BUDAPESTI FOLDALATTI GYORSVASUT".
1267 **232** 60fi. green 90 25
1268 – 1fo. lake 90 40
DESIGN—HORIZ: 1fo. Underground map and station.

233 Russian Flag and Tank

234 Eurasian Red Squirrel

1953. 10th Anniv of Battle of Stalingrad.
1269 **233** 40fi. red 80 25
1270 – 60fi. brown . . . . . . 1·10 35
DESIGN: 60fi. Soldier, map and flags.

1953. Air. Forest Animals.
1271 **234** 20fi. brown and olive . . 30 10
1272 – 30fi. sepia and brown . . 30 10
1273 – 40fi. sepia and green . . 35 10
1274 – 50fi. sepia and brown . . 45 30
1275 – 60fi. brown and turquoise 60 30
1276 – 70fi. brown and olive . . 60 30
1277 – 80fi. brown and green . . 90 45
1278 – 1fo. brown and green . . 1·25 55
1279 – 1fo.50 black and bistre 1·90 1·00
1280 – 2fo. sepia and brown . . 3·00 1·00
DESIGNS—HORIZ: 30fi. West European hedgehog; 40fi. Brown hare; 60fi. European otter; 70fi. Red fox; 1fo. Roe deer; 1fo.50, Wild boar. VERT: 50fi. Beech marten; 80fi. Fallow deer; 2fo. Red deer.

235 Stalin

236 Rest Home, Galyateto

1953. Death of Stalin.
1281 **235** 60fi. black 30 20
MS1281a 51 × 72 mm. 2fo. purple (T **235**) . . . . 18·00 23·00

1953. Workers' Rest Homes.
1282 **236** 30fi. brown (postage) . . 20 10
1283 – 40fi. blue 30 10
1284 – 50fi. ochre 30 10
1285 – 60fi. green 30 10
1286 – 70fi. red 30 25
1287 – 1fo. turquoise (air) . . . 45 30
1288 – 1fo.50 purple 60 45
DESIGNS: 40fi. Terrace, Mecsek; 50fi. Parad Spa; 60fi. Sports field, Kekes; 70fi. Balaton-fured Spa; 1fo. Children paddling at Balaton; 1fo.50, Lillafured Rest Home.

237 Young People and Banners

238 Karl Marx

1953. May Day.
1289 **237** 60fi. brown & red on yell 60 20

1953. 70th Death Anniv of Karl Marx.
1290 **238** 1fo. black on pink . . . 60 20
See also No. 2354.

239 Peasants and Flag

1953. 250th Anniv of Rakoczi Rebellion.
1291 **239** 20fi. orange & grn on grn 60 30
1292 – 30fi. orange and purple 75 50
1293 – 40fi. orange & blue on pk 80 70
1294 – 60fi. orange & grn on yell . . . . 90 1·10
1295 – 1fo. red & brown on yell 1·40 1·25
DESIGNS: 30fi. Drummer and insurgents; 40fi. Battle scene; 60fi. Cavalryman attacking soldier; 1fo. Ferenc Rakoczi II.

1953. Rebuilding Plan (2nd series). As T **208**.
1296 8fi. green 25 10
1297 10fi. lilac 25 10
1298 12fi. red 30 10
1299a 20fi. green . . . . 1·25 10
1300 30fi. orange 30 10
1301 40fi. brown 30 10
1302 50fi. blue 35 10
1303a 60fi. red . . . . 3·50 10
1304 70fi. brown 40 10
BUILDINGS: 8fi. Day nursery, Ozd; 10fi. Nursing school, Szombathely; 12fi. Workers houses, Komlo; 20fi. Department store, Ujpest; 30fi. Factory, Maly; 40fi. General Hospital, Fovaros; 50fi. Gymnasium, Sztalinvaros; 60fi. Post Office, Csepel; 70fi. Blast-furnace, Diosgyor.

240 Cycling

1953. Opening of People's Stadium. Budapest. Inscr "1953 NEPSTADION".
1313 **240** 20fi. brown and orange (postage) 10 10
1314 – 30fi. brown and green . . 10 10
1315 – 40fi. brown and blue . . 10 10
1316 – 50fi. brown and olive . . 10 10
1317 – 60fi. brown and yellow 10 10
1318 – 80fi. brown & turq (air) 10 10
1319 – 1fo. brown and purple 10 20
1320 – 2fo. brown and green . . 1·60 55
1321 – 3fo. brown and red . . 2·10 55
1322 – 5fo. turquoise and brown 3·00 2·00
DESIGNS: 30fi. Swimming; 40fi. Gymnastics; 50fi. Throwing the discus; 60fi. Wrestling; 80fi. Water polo; 1fo. Boxing; 2fo. Football; 3fo. Running; 5fo. Stadium.

241 Kazar

242 Postwoman Delivering Letters

1953. Provincial Costumes.
1323 **241** 20fi. green 75 20
1324 – 30fi. brown . . . . . . 1·00 40
1325 – 40fi. blue . . . . 1·25 15
1326 – 60fi. red . . . . 1·50 1·50
1327 – 1fo. turquoise . . . . . 2·25 90
1328 – 1fo.70 green . . . . . 3·50 1·60
1329 – 2fo. red . . . . 5·75 2·00
1330 – 2fo.50 purple . . . . . 8·50 5·50
PROVINCES: 30fi. Ersekcsanad; 40fi. Kalocsa; 60fi. Sioagard; 1fo. Sarkoz; 1fo.70, Boldog; 2fo. Orhalom; 2fo.50, Hosszuheteny.

1953. Stamp Day.
1331 **242** 1fo.+1fo. turquoise . . . 3·00 3·00
1332 2fo.+2fo. lilac . . . . . 3·00 3·00

1953. Air. Hungarian Football Team's Victory at Wembley. No. 1320 optd **LONDON-WEMBLEY 1953. XI 25. 6:3.**
1333 2fo. brown and green . . . 17·00 18·00

244 Bihari

245 Lenin

1953. Air. Hungarian Composers.
1334 **244** 30fi. grey and brown . . 20 10
1335 – 40fi. orange and brown (Erkel) 30 10
1336 – 60fi. green & brn (Liszt) 30 10
1337 – 70fi. red and brown (Mosonyi) 35 20
1338 – 80fi. blue and brown (Goldmark) 45 25
1339 – 1fo. bistre and brown (Bartok) 60 35
1340 – 2fo. lilac and brown (Kodaly) . . . . . . 1·10 50

1954. 30th Death Anniv of Lenin.
1341 **245** 40fi. green . . . . 1·25 1·10
1342 – 60fi. brown 80 30
1343 – 1fo. lake . . . . 1·25 90
DESIGNS: 60fi. Lenin addressing meeting; 1fo. Profile portrait of Lenin.

246 Turnip Beetle

247 Mother and Baby

1954. Air. Insects.
1344 **246** 30fi. brown and orange 30 30
1345 – 40fi. brown and green . . 35 30
1346 – 50fi. black and red . . . 45 45
1347 – 60fi. brown, yell & lilac 50 45
1348 – 80fi. claret, purple & grn 65 60
1349 – 1fo. black and brown . . 85 60
1350 – 1fo.20 brown and green 90 75
1351 – 1fo.50 dp brown & brn 1·25 90
1352 – 2fo. brown and chestnut 1·75 1·25
1353 – 3fo. brown and green . . 2·25 1·50
INSECTS—HORIZ: 40fi. Crawling cockchafer; 50fi. Longhorn beetle; 60fi. Hornet; 1fo.20, European field cricket; 1fo.50, European rhinoceros beetle; 2fo. Stag beetle. VERT: 80fi. Apple beetle; 1fo. Corn beetle; 3fo. Great silver water beetle.

1954. Child Welfare.
1354 – 30fi. blue (postage) . . . 20 10
1355 **247** 40fi. bistre 30 10
1356 – 60fi. lilac 45 20
1357 – 1fo. green (air) 65 20
1358 – 1fo.50 red 95 20
1359 – 2fo. turquoise . . . . . 1·25 55
DESIGNS: 30fi. Woman having blood-test; 60fi. Doctor examining child; 1fo. Children in creche; 1fo.50, Doctor, mother and child; 2fo. Children in nursery school.

248 Worker and Flag

249 Maypole

1954. 35th Anniv of Proclamation of Hungarian Soviet Republic.
1360 – 40fi. blue and red . . . 3·50 1·40
1361 **248** 60fi. brown and red . . 6·50 1·75
1362 – 1fo. black and red . . . 9·50 2·25
DESIGNS—HORIZ: 40fi. Worker reading book; 1fo. Soldier with rifle.

1954. May Day. Inscr "1954-MAJUS I".
1363 **249** 40fi. olive 20 10
1364 – 60fi. red 30 10
DESIGN: 60fi. Worker and flag.

250 Agricultural Worker

1954. 3rd Hungarian Communist Party Congress, Budapest.
1365 **250** 60fi. red on yellow . . . 20 20

251 Boy building Model Glider

1954. Air.
1366 **251** 40fi. grey and brown . . . 20 10
1367 – 50fi. brown and grey . . 30 10
1368 – 60fi. grey and brown . . 20 20
1369 – 80fi. brown and violet 30 20
1370 – 1fo. grey and brown . . 30 20
1371 – 1fo.20 brown and green 45 30
1372 – 1fo.50 grey and purple 1·25 45
1373 – 2fo. brown and blue . . 1·60 65
DESIGNS—As Type **251**: 60fi. Gliders; 1fo. Parachutists; 1fo.50, Lisunov Li-2 airplane. 43 × 43 mm; 50fi. Boy flying model airplane; 80fi. Libis KB-6T Matajur aircraft and hangar; 1fo.20, Letov C-4 biplane; 2fo. Mikoyan Gurevich MiG-15 jet fighters.

252 Hungarian National Museum

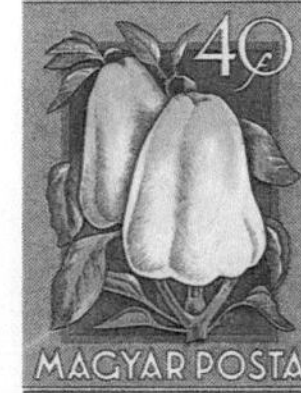

253 Paprika

1954. 5th Anniv of Constitution.
1374 **252** 40fi. blue 90 50
1375 – 60fi. brown 60 35
1376 – 1fo. brown . . . . . . 1·10 50
DESIGNS: 60fi. Hungarian Coat of Arms; 1fo. Dome of Parliament Buildings, Budapest.

1954. Fruits. Multicoloured.
1377 40fi. Type **253** 40 10
1378 50fi. Tomatoes 40 10
1379 60fi. Grapes 40 10
1380 80fi. Apricots 45 40
1381 1fo. Apples 75 55
1382 1fo.20 Plums . . . . . . 1·10 55
1383 1fo.50 Cherries . . . . . 2·10 75
1384 2fo. Peaches . . . . 2·40 1·25

254 M. Jokai

255 C. J. Apacai

1954. 50th Death Anniv of Jokai (novelist).
1385 **254** 60fi. green 60 20
1386 1fo. purple 90 50

1954. Hungarian Scientists.
1387 **255** 8fi. black on yellow . . . 10 10
1388 – 10fi. lake on pink . . . 10 10
1389 – 12fi. black on blue . . . 10 10
1390 – 20fi. brown on yellow . . 10 10
1391 – 30fi. blue on pink . . . 10 10
1392 – 40fi. green on yellow . . 20 10
1393 – 50fi. brown on green . . 20 10
1394 – 60fi. blue on pink . . . 30 10
1395 – 1fo. olive 35 10
1396 – 1fo.70 red on yellow . . 60 10
1397 – 2fo. turquoise . . . . . 1·00 10
PORTRAITS: 10fi. S. Korosi Csoma; 12fi. A. Jedlik; 20fi. I. Semmelweis; 30fi. J. Irinyi; 40fi. F. Koranyi; 50fi. A. Vambery; 60fi. K. Than; 1fo. O. Herman; 1fo.70, T. Puskas; 2fo. E. Hogyes.

256 Speed Skaters

1955. Air. Winter Sports.
1398 – 40fi. brown, blue & black 60 20
1399 – 50fi. red, green and brown 60 20
1400 – 60fi. red, blue and brown 75 30
1401 – 80fi. green, brown & blk 90 30
1402 – 1fo. red, blue and brown 1·25 30
1403 **256** 1fo.20 red, green & blk 1·25 1·60
1404 – 1fo.50 red, green & brn 2·00 2·10
1405 – 2fo. red, green and brown . . . . 2·10 1·10
DESIGNS—VERT: 40fi. Boys on toboggan; 60fi. Ice-yacht; 1fo. Ski jumper; 1fo.50, Skier turning. HORIZ: 50fi. Cross-country skier; 80fi. Ice-hockey players; 2fo. Figure skaters.

257 Blast Furnace

1955. 10th Anniv of Liberation.
1406 – 40fi. brown and red . . 40 30
1407 **257** 60fi. red and green . . . 70 50
1408 – 1fo. green and brown . . 70 80
1409 – 2fo. brown and green . . 90 1·00
DESIGNS—VERT: 40fi. Reading room; 2fo. Liberty statue. HORIZ: 1fo. Combine harvester.

258 "1st May"

1955. May Day.
1410 **258** 1fo. red 30 20

259 State Printing Works

1955. Cent of Hungarian State Printing Office.
1411 **259** 60fi. brown and green . . 20 20
MS1411a 97 × 77 mm. Air. T **259** 5fo. red and green . . . . . . 18·00 24·00

260 Young Workers and Flag

1955. 2nd Congress of Young Workers' Federation.
1412 **260** 1fo. brown 40 20

261 Postilion

262 Radio Mechanic

1955. Opening of P.O. Museum.
1413 **261** 1fo. purple 30 20

1955. Workers.
1414 – 8fi. brown 10 10
1415 – 10fi. turquoise 10 10
1416 – 12fi. orange 10 10
1417 **262** 20fi. olive 10 10
1418 – 30fi. red 10 10
1419 – 40fi. brown 70 10
1420 – 50fi. blue 15 10
1421 – 60fi. red 15 10
1422 – 70fi. olive 15 10
1423 – 80fi. purple 20 10
1424 – 1fo. blue 20 10
1425 – 1fo.20 bistre 30 10
1426 – 1fo.40 green 45 10
1427 – 1fo.70 lilac 45 10
1428 – 2fo. lake 55 10
1429 – 2fo.60 red 70 10
1430 – 3fo. green . . . . 1·00 10
1431 – 4fo. blue . . . . 2·10 10
1432 – 5fo. brown . . . . . . 1·50 10
1433 – 10fo. violet . . . . . 3·00 40
DESIGNS: 8fi. Market gardener; 10fi. Fisherman; 12fi. Bricklayer; 30fi. Potter; 40fi. Railway guard; 50fi. Shop assistant; 60fi. Post Office worker; 70fi. Herdsman; 80fi. Mill-girl; 1fo. Boat-builder; 1fo.20, Carpenter; 1fo.40, Tram conductor; 1fo.70, Swineherd; 2fo. Welder; 2fo.60, Tractor-driver; 3fo. Horse and groom; 4fo. Bus driver; 5fo. Telegraph lineman; 10fo. Miner.

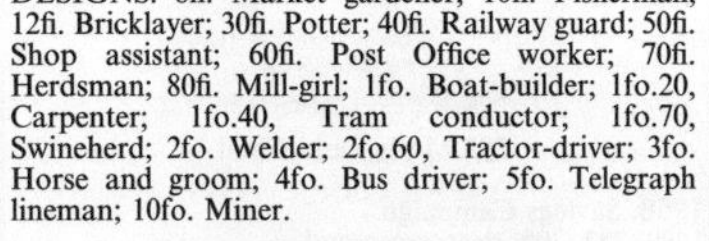

263 M. Csokonai Vitez

1955. Hungarian Poets.
1434 **263** 60fi. black 60 25
1435 – 1fo. blue 55 20
1436 – 2fo. red 60 45
PORTRAITS: 1fo. M. Vorosmarty; 2fo. A. Jozsef.

1955. Air. Light Metal Industries Int Congress, Budapest. As No. 1139.
1437 5fo. blue on silver . . . . . 13·50 13·50

264 Bela Bartok

1955. 10th Death Anniv of Bartok (composer).
1438 **264** 60fi. brown (postage) . . 60 20
1439 1fo. green (air) . . . . . 1·50 1·25
1440 1fo. brown . . . . . . 3·00 1·75

265 "Hargita" Diesel Multiple Unit

1955. Transport.
1441 **265** 40fi. brown and green . . 30 10
1442 – 60fi. bistre and green . . 20 10
1443 – 80fi. brown and green . . 30 20
1444 – 1fo. green and brown . . 35 20
1445 – 1fo.20 black and brown 1·25 50
1446 – 1fo.50 brown and black 60 40
1447 – 2fo. brown and green . . 1·50 65
DESIGNS: 60fi. Motor coach; 80fi. Motor cyclist; 1fo. Lorry; 1fo.20, Class 303 steam locomotive; 1fo.50, Tipper; 2fo. "Beke" (freighter).

266 Puli Sheepdog

1956. Hungarian Dogs.
1448 **266** 40fi. black, red and yellow 10 10
1449 – 50fi. black, buff and blue 10 10
1450 – 60fi. black, red and green 20 15
1451 – 80fi. black, orge & grey 20 30
1452 – 1fo. black, orange & turq 20 30
1453 – 1fo.20 black, brn & orge 35 35
1454 – 1fo.50 black, buff & bl 95 50
1455 – 2fo. black, brown & mve 1·50 85
DESIGNS—RECTANGULAR (36 × 26 mm): 50fi. Puli and cattle; 1fo.50, Kuvasz sheepdog and cottage. (27 × 35 mm): 80fi. Hungarian retriever. (27 × 38 mm): 1fo. Hungarian retriever carrying mallard. As Type **266**: 60fi. Pumi; 1fo.20, Kuvasz sheepdog; 2fo. Komondor sheepdog.

268 Pioneers' Badge

269 Hunyadi on Horseback

1956. 10th Anniv of Pioneers Movement.
1456 **268** 1fo. red 20 10
1457 1fo. grey 20 10

1956. 500th Death Anniv of Janos Hunyadi.
1458 **269** 1fo. brown on yellow . . 40 40

270 Miner

271 Horse-jumping

1956. Miners' Day.
1459 **270** 1fo. blue 40 10

1956. Olympic Games. Inscr "1956". Centres in brown.
1460 – 20fi. blue (Canoeing) . . 10 20
1461 **271** 30fi. olive 10 20
1462 – 40fi. brown (Fencing) . . 25 20
1463 – 60fi. turquoise (Hurdling) 25 20
1464 – 1fo. red (Football) . . . 30 20
1465 – 1fo.50 violet (Weightlifting) 45 35
1466 – 2fo. green (Gymnastics) 1·00 45
1467 – 3fo. mauve (Basketball) 2·00 1·00

272 Chopin

1956. Hungarian–Polish Philatelic Exn, Budapest.
1468 – 1fo. blue (Liszt) . . . . 3·00 2·25
1469 **272** 1fo. mauve . . . . . . 3·00 2·25

1957. Hungarian Red Cross Fund. Nos. 1417 etc., surch with shield, cross and premium.
1470 **262** 20fi.+20fi. olive 20 20
1471 – 30fi.+30fi. red 30 30
1472 – 40fi.+40fi. brown 45 30
1473 – 60fi.+60fi. red 30 40
1474 – 1fo.+1fo. blue 50 60
1475 – 2fo.+2fo. lake . . . . . 1·10 1·00

274 Dr. L. Zamenhof

1957. Air. 70th Anniv of Esperanto.
1476 – 60fi. brown 45 20
1477 **274** 1fo. green 50 25
DESIGN—HORIZ: 60fi. Esperanto Star.

275 Letters, Letter-box and Globe

276 Janos Arany

1957. Air. Hungarian Red Cross Fund. Cross in red.
1478 **275** 60fi.+30fi. brown 45 25
1479 – 1fo.+50fi. lilac 60 25
1480 – 2fo.+1fo. red . . . . . 1·25 30
1481 – 3fo.+1fo.50 blue . . . . 1·60 65
1482 – 5fo.+2fo.50 grey . . . . 2·75 1·50
1483 – 10fo.+5fo. green . . . . 4·50 2·25
DESIGNS: 1fo. Postal coach; 2fo. Top of telegraph pole; 3fo. Radio aerial mast; 5fo. Desk telephone; 10fo. (46 × 31 mm) Posthorn.

1957. 75th Death Anniv of Janos Arany (poet).
1484 **276** 2fo. blue 35 20

277 Arms

1957. Inauguration of National Emblem.
1485 **277** 60fi. red 35 15
1486 1fo. green 35 20

278 Congress Emblem

1957. 4th W.F.T.U. Congress, Leipzig.
1487 **278** 1fo. red 30 20

279 Courier

1957. Air. Stamp Day.
1488 **279** 1fo.(+4fo.) brown and bistre on cream . . . 75 75
1489 – 1fo.(+4fo.) brown and bistre on cream . . . 75 75
DESIGN: No. 1489, Tupolev Tu-104A airplane over Budapest.

280 Dove of Peace and Flags

1957. 40th Anniv of Russian Revolution. Flags multicoloured.
1490 **280** 60fi. black and grey . . 30 10
1491 – 1fo. black and drab . . 35 10
DESIGN: 1fo. Lenin.

281 Komarom Tumbler Pigeons

282 Television Building

1957. Int Pigeon-fanciers' Exn, Budapest.
1492 **281** 30fi. brown, yellow and green (postage) . . . 10 10
1493 – 40fi. black and brown . . 10 10
1494 – 60fi. grey and blue . . . 20 10
1495 – 1fo. brown and grey . . 45 10
1496 – 2fo. grey and mauve . . 75 35
1497 – 3fo. grn, grey & red (air) 90 35
DESIGNS: 40fi. Two short-beaked Budapest pigeons; 60fi. Giant domestic pigeon; 1fo. Three Szeged pigeons; 2fo. Two Hungarian fantail pigeons; 3fo. Two carrier pigeons.

IMPERFORATE STAMPS. Most modern Hungarian stamps issued up to the end of 1991 also exist imperforate.

1958. Inaug of Hungarian Television Service.
1498 **282** 2fo. purple 75 35
MS1498a 49 × 70 mm. **282** 2fo. (+23fo.) green . . . . 22·00 27·00

283 Mother and Child

1958. Savings Campaign.
1499 **283** 20fi. deep green and green 20 10
1500 – 30fi. purple and green . . 20 10
1501 – 40fi. brown and bistre . . 30 10
1502 – 60fi. myrtle and red . . . 45 10
1503 – 1fo. brown and green . . 45 10
1504 – 2fo. green and orange . . 1·10 70
DESIGNS: 30fi. Old man feeding pigeons; 40fi. Schoolboys with savings stamps; 60fi. "The Cricket and the Ant."; 1fo. Bees on honeycomb; 2fo. Hands holding banknotes.

284 Hungarian Pavilion

1958. Air. Brussels International Exhibition. Inscr "BRUXELLES 1958".
1505 **284** 20fi. brown and red . . 30 15
1506 – 40fi. sepia and blue . . . 35 15
1507 – 60fi. sepia and red . . . 35 15
1508 – 1fo. brown and ochre . . 35 15
1509 – 1fo.40 multicoloured . . 65 15
1510 – 2fo. sepia and brown . . 65 15
1511 – 3fo. sepia and green . . 1·00 25
1512 – 5fo. multicoloured . . . 1·40 75
MS1512a 72 × 98 mm. 10fo. mauve 22·00 22·00
DESIGNS—HORIZ: 40fi. Map of Hungary and exhibits; 60fi. Parliament Buildings, Budapest; 1fo. Chain Bridge, Budapest; 1fo.40, Arms of Belgium and Hungary and Exhibition emblem; 5fo. Exhibition emblem. VERT: 2fo. "Mannekin Pis" statue, Brussels; 3fo. Town Hall, Brussels; 10fo. Girl in national costume as T **241**.

285 Arms of Hungary

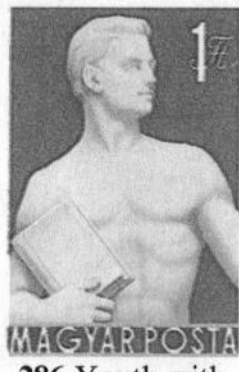

286 Youth with Book

1958. 1st Anniv of Amended Constitution. Arms multicoloured.
1513 **285** 60fi. red 10 10
1514 1fo. green 20 10
1515 2fo. drab 35 20

1958. 5th Youth Festival, Keszthely.
1516 **286** 1fo. brown 45 45

287 Town Hall, Prague and Posthorn

1958. Organization of Socialist Countries' Postal Administrations Conference, Prague.
1517 **287** 60fi. green (postage) . . 30 25
1518 – 1fo. lake (air) 30 25
DESIGN: 1fo. Prague Castle, telegraph pole and wires.

288 "Linum dolomiticum"

1958. Flowers.
1519 **288** 20fi. yellow and purple 30 10
1520 – 30fi. brown and blue . . 20 10
1521 – 40fi. brown, buff & sepia 35 10
1522 – 60fi. mauve and green 50 10
1523 – 1fo. green and red . . . 75 10
1524 – 2fo. yellow and green . . 1·40 10
1525 – 2fo.50 pink and blue . . 1·60 45
1526 – 3fo. pink, lt green & grn 2·10 75
FLOWERS—TRIANGULAR: 30fi. "Kitaibelia vitifolia"; 2fo.50, "Dianthus collinus"; 3fo. "Rosa sancti andreae". VERT: (20½ × 31 mm): 40fi. "Doronicum hungaricum"; 60fi. "Colchicum arenarium"; 1fo. "Helleborus purpuracens"; 2fo. "Hemerocallis lilio-asphodelus".
For miniature sheet containing stamps as T **288**, see No. **MS**1533a.

289 Table-tennis Bat and Ball

1958. European Table-tennis and Swimming Championships, and World Wrestling Championships, Budapest.
1527 **289** 20fi. red on pink 10 10
1528 – 30fi. olive on green . . . 10 10
1529 – 40fi. purple on yellow . . 30 10
1530 – 60fi. brown on blue . . . 35 10
1531 – 1fo. blue on blue 60 20
1532 – 2fo.50 red on yellow . . 1·10 45
1533 – 3fo. blue on turquoise 1·60 75
DESIGNS—VERT: 30fi. Table-tennis player; 40fi. Wrestlers; 1fo. Water-polo player; 2fo.50, High-diver. HORIZ: 60fi. Wrestlers; 3fo. Swimmer.

1958. International Philatelic Federation Congress, Brussels.
MS1533a 111 × 111 mm. Nos. 1519/20 and 1525/6 in new colours . . . . 28·00 28·00

290

291 Airliner over Millennium Monument Budapest

1958. Air. (a) Int Correspondence Week.
1534 **290** 60fi. bistre and purple 20 10
1535 – 1fo. bistre and blue . . . 45 30

(b) National Stamp Exhibition, Budapest.
1536 – 1fo.(+2fo.) bistre and red 45 65
1537 **290** 1fo.(+2fo.) bistre and green 45 65
DESIGNS: No. 1535, Posthorn, envelope and transport; No. 1536, Stamp and magnifier.

1958. Air. 40th Anniv of 1st Hungarian Air Mail Stamp.
1538 **291** 3fo. purple, red and drab 90 30
1539 – 5fo. blue, red and drab 1·10 45
DESIGN: 5fo. Airliner over Sopron Tower.
For similar stamps but without commemorative inscription see Nos. 1542/51.

292 Red Flag

1958. 40th Anniv of Hungarian Communist Party and Founding of the "Red Journal".
1540 **292** 1fo. red and brown . . . 30 10
1541 – 2fo. red and blue 30 20
DESIGN: 2fo. Hand holding up the newspaper "Voros Ujsag" (Red Journal).

1958. Air. As T **291** but with "LEGIPOSTA" at top in place of commem inscription. On cream paper.
1542 – 20fi. green and red . . . 10 10
1543 – 30fi. violet and red . . . 10 10
1544 – 70fi. purple and red . . 45 10
1545 – 1fo. blue and red 20 10
1546 – 1fo.60 purple and red . . 35 10
1547 – 2fo. green and red . . . 60 10
1548 – 3fo. brn & red 60 20
1549 **291** 5fo. green and red . . . 1·00 25
1550 – 10fo. blue and red . . . 60 60
1551 – 20fo. sepia and red . . . 5·50 85
DESIGNS: Airliner over: 20fi. Town Hall, Szeged; 30fi. Sarospatak Castle; 70fi. Town Hall, Gyor; 1fo. Opera House, Budapest; 1fo.60, Old City of Veszprem; 2fo. Chain Bridge, Budapest; 3fo. Sopron Tower; 10fo. Danube Embankment, Budapest; 20fo. Budapest Cathedral.

293 Rocket approaching the Moon

1959. I.G.Y. Achievements.
1552 – 10fi. brown and red . . 10 10
1553 – 20fi. black and blue . . 55 10
1554 – 30fi. buff and green . . . 60 10
1555 – 40fi. light blue and blue 1·50 25
1556 **293** 60fi. green and blue . . 75 30
1557 – 1fo. brown and red . . . 1·25 45
1558 – 5fo. brown & deep brown . . . . 1·90 55
DESIGNS—(31½ × 21 mm): 10fi. Eotvos torsion balance (gravimetry); 20fi. Ship using echo-sounder (oceanography); 30fi. "Northern Lights" and polar scene. (35½ × 26½ mm): 40fi. Russian polar camp and Antarctic route map; 1fo. Observatory and the sun; 5fo. Russian "Sputnik" and American "Vanguard" (artificial satellites).
See also No. 1605.

294 Revolutionary

296 Nagy Model of Locomotive "Deru", 1847

295 Rose

1959. 40th Anniv of Proclamation of Hungarian Soviet Republic.
1559 **294** 20fi. red and purple . . 10 10
1560 60fi. red and blue . . . 10 10
1561 1fo. red and brown . . . 20 20

1959. May Day.
1562 **295** 60fi. red, green and lilac 75 10
1563 1fo. red, green and brown . . . . 1·00 20

1959. Transport Museum issue.
1564 **296** 20fi. mult (postage) . . . 35 10
1565 – 30fi. green, black and buff 35 10
1566 – 40fi. multicoloured . . . 45 10
1567 – 60fi. multicoloured . . . 40 10
1568 – 1fo. multicoloured . . . 45 25
1569 – 2fo. multicoloured . . . 75 25
1570 – 2fo.50 multicoloured (blue background) . . . 90 35
1571 – 3fo. multicoloured (air) 1·90 1·40
DESIGNS—HORIZ: 30fi. Ganz diesel railcar; 60fi. Csonka motor car; 1fo. Ikarusz rear-engine motor coach; 2fo. First Lake Balaton steamer "Kisfaludy"; 2fo.50, Stagecoach; 3fo. Aladar Zselyi's monoplane. VERT: 40fi. Early railway semaphore signal.
See also No. 1572.

1959. Int Philatelic Federation Congress, Hamburg. As No. 1570 but colours changed.
1572 2fo.50 multicoloured (yellow background) . . . . . . 1·25 1·40

297 Posthorn

1959. Organization of Socialist Countries' Postal Administration Conference, Berlin.
1573 **297** 1fo. red 50 55

298 Great Cormorant

1959. Water Birds. Inscr "1959".
1574 **298** 10fi. black and green . . 20 10
1575 – 20fi. green and blue . . 30 10
1576 – 30fi. violet, myrtle & orge 35 85
1577 – 40fi. grey and green . . 50 25
1578 – 60fi. brown and purple . 60 25
1579 – 1fo. black and turquoise 60 50
1580 – 2fo. black and red . . . 1·10 50
1581 – 3fo. brown and bistre . . 1·90 1·00
DESIGNS: 20fi. Little egret; 30fi. Purple heron; 40fi. Great egret; 60fi. White spoonbill; 1fo. Grey heron; 2fo. Squacco heron; 3fo. Glossy ibis.

299 10th-century Man-at-Arms **300** Bathers at Lake Balaton

1959. 24th World Fencing Championships, Budapest. Inscr as in T **299**.
1582 **299** 10fi. black and blue . . 10 10
1583 – 20fi. black and lemon . . 10 10
1584 – 30fi. black and violet . . 20 10
1585 – 40fi. black and red . . . 20 10
1586 – 60fi. black and purple . . 20 10
1587 – 1fo. black and turquoise 45 10
1588 – 1fo.40 black and orange 75 10
1589 – 3fo. black and green . . 1·90 30
DESIGNS (Evolution of Hungarian swordsmanship): 20fi. 15th-century man-at-arms; 30fi. 18th-century soldier; 40fi. 19th-century soldier; 60fi. 19th-century cavalryman. Fencer: at the assault (1fo.); on guard (1fo.40); saluting (3fo.).

1959. Lake Balaton Summer Courses.
1590 – 30fi. bl on yell (postage) 20 10
1591 – 40fi. red on green . . . 10 10
1592 **300** 60fi. brown on pink . . 20 10
1593 – 1fo.20 violet on pink . . 50 10
1594 – 2fo. red on yellow . . . 75 30
1595 – 20fi. green (air) 10 10
1596 – 70fi. blue 20 10
1597 – 1fo. red and blue 30 10
1598 – 1fo.70 brown on yellow 75 40

DESIGNS—VERT: 20fi. Tihany (view); 30fi. "Kek Madar" (yacht); 70fi. "Tihany" (waterbus); 1fo. Waterlily and view of Heviz; 1fo.20, Anglers; 1fo.70, "Saturnus" (yacht) and statue of fisherman (Balaton pier); 2fo. Holiday-makers and "Beloiannis" (lake steamer). HORIZ: 40fi. Vintner with grapes.

301 **302** Shepherd with Letter

1959. 150th Death Anniv of Haydn (composer).
1599 **301** 40fi. yellow and purple 30 10
1600 – 60fi. buff and slate . . . 45 25
1601 – 1fo. orange and violet 85 20
MS1601a 94 × 76 mm. 3fo. purple; 3fo. green (each 27 × 35 mm) 12·50 10·50
DESIGNS—HORIZ: 60fi. Fertod Chateau. VERT: 1fo. Hayden; 3fo (purple) "J h" and music score; 3fo. Green "F SCH" and prose quotation.
No. **MS**1601a also commemorates Schiller's birth bicentenary.

1959. Birth Bicentenary of Schiller (poet). As T **301** but inscr "F. SCHILLER" etc.
1602 40fi. yellow and olive . . . 35 10
1603 60fi. pink and blue 35 10
1604 1fo. yellow and purple . . . 75 10
DESIGNS—VERT: 40fi. Stylized initials "F" and "Sch" and Schiller's birthplace; 1fo. Schiller. HORIZ: 60fi. Pegasus.
See also No. **MS**1601a.

1959. Landing of Russian Rocket on the Moon. As T **293** with addition of Russian Flag and "22 h 02' 34" on Moon in red.
1605 **293** 60fi. green and blue . . 35 10

1959. Stamp Day and National Stamp Exn.
1606 **302** 2fo. purple . . . . . . 1·25 1·25

303 "Taking Delivery"

1959. International Correspondence Week.
1607 **303** 60fi. multicoloured . . . 35 10

304 Lenin and Szamuely

1959. Russian Stamp Exhibition, Budapest.
1608 **304** 20fi. brown and red . . 20 10
1609 – 40fi. lake & brown on bl 20 10
1610 – 60fi. buff and blue . . . 20 10
1611 – 1fo. multicoloured . . . 35 20
DESIGNS: 40fi. Pushkin; 60fi. Mayakovsky; 1fo. Arms with hands clasping flag.

305 Swallowtail **306**

1959. Butterflies and Moths. Butterflies in natural colours, background colours given.
1612 **305** 20fi. black and green (postage) 40 10
1613 – 30fi. black and blue . . 40 10
1614 – 40fi. black and brown . . 50 20
1615 – 60fi. black and bistre . . 75 20
1616 – 1fo. black and green (air) 1·10 40
1617 – 2fo. black and lilac . . . 2·25 90
1618 – 3fo. black and green . . 3·25 1·50
DESIGNS—HORIZ: 30fi. Hebe tiger moth; 40fi. Adonis blue; 2fo. Death's-head hawk moth. VERT: 60fi. Purple emperor; 1fo. Scarce copper; 3fo. Red emperor.

1959. 7th Socialist Workers' Party Congress. Flag in red and green.
1619 **306** 60fi. brown 20 10
1620 – 1fo. red 20 10
DESIGN: 1fo. Flag inscr "MSZMP VII. KONGRESSZUSA".

307 "Fairy Tales" **308** Sumeg Castle

1959. Fairy Tales (1st series). Centres and inscr in black.
1621 **307** 20fi. multicoloured . . . 20 10
1622 – 30fi. pink 20 10
1623 – 40fi. turquoise 30 10
1624 – 60fi. blue 50 10
1625 – 1fo. yellow 70 20
1626 – 2fo. green 90 30
1627 – 2fo.50 salmon . . . . . 1·25 35
1628 – 3fo. red . . . . 1·25 60
FAIRY TALE SCENES: 30fi. "The Sleeping Beauty"; 40fi. "Mat the Goose"; 60fi. "The Cricket and the Ant"; 1fo. "Mashenka and the Bears"; 2fo. "The Babes in the Wood"; 2fo.50, "The Pied Piper of Hamelin"; 3fo. "Little Red Riding Hood".
See also Nos. 1702/9 and 2133/41.

1960. Hungarian Castles. On white paper.
1629 **308** 8fi. purple 10 10
1630 – 10fi. brown 10 10
1631 – 12fi. blue 10 10
1632 – 20fi. green 10 10
1633 – 30fi. brown 10 10
1634 – 40fi. turquoise 10 10
1635 – 50fi. brown 10 10
1636 – 60fi. red 30 10
1637 – 70fi. green 30 10
1638 – 80fi. purple 10 10
1639 – 1fo. blue 30 10
1640 – 1fo.20 purple 45 10
1641 – 1fo.40 blue 45 10
1642 – 1fo.70 lilac ("SOMLO") 45 10
1642a – 1fo.70 lilac ("SOMLYO") . . . 55 10
1643 – 2fo. bistre 55 10
1644 – 2fo.60 blue 60 10
1645 – 3fo. brown 60 10
1646 – 4fo. violet 70 10
1647 – 5fo. green 90 30
1648 – 10fo. red . . . . 1·25 40
CASTLES—As Type **308**: 10fi. Kisvarda; 12fi. Szigliget; 20fi. Tata; 30fi. Diosgyor; 40fi. Simon Tornya; 50fi. Fuzer; 60fi. Sarospatak; 70fi. Nagyvazsony; 80fi. Egervar. $28\frac{1}{2} \times 21\frac{1}{2}$ mm: 1fo. Vitany; 1fo.20, Sirok; 1fo.40, Siklos; 1fo.70, Somlyo; 2fo. Boldogko; 2fo.60, Holloko; 4fo. Eger. $21\frac{1}{2} \times 28\frac{1}{2}$ mm: 3fo. Csesznek; 5fo. Koszeg; 10fo. Sarvar.
See also Nos. 1694/700.

309 Halas Lace **310** Cross-country Skiing

1960. Halas Lace (1st series). Designs showing lace as T **309**. Inscriptions and values in orange.
1649 **304** 20fi. sepia 20 20
1650 – 30fi. violet 20 20
1651 – 40fi. turquoise 40 20
1652 – 60fi. brown 45 25
1653 – 1fo. green 75 25
1654 – 1fo.50 green 95 35
1655 – 2fo. blue . . . . 1·50 40
1656 – 3fo. red . . . . 2·75 65
Nos. 1650/1, 1654/5 are larger 38 × 44 mm.
See also Nos. 1971/8.

1960. Winter Olympic Games.
1657 **310** 30fi. bistre and blue . . 10 20
1658 – 40fi. bistre and green . . 20 20
1659 – 60fi. bistre and red . . . 30 20
1660 – 80fi. bistre and violet . . 40 20
1661 – 1fo. bistre and turquoise 70 25
1662 – 1fo.20 bistre and lake . . 75 45
1663 – 2fo.+1fo. mult . . . . . 1·75 60
DESIGNS: 40fi. Ice hockey; 60fi. Ski jumping; 80fi. Speed skating; 1fo. Skiing; 1fo.20, Figure skating; 2fo. Games emblem.

311 Kato Haman **312** Yellow Pheasant's-eye and Quill

1960. Celebrities and Anniversaries. Portrait as T **311**.
1664 60fi. purple (T **311**) 20 10
1665 60fi. brown (Clara Zetkin) 20 10
1666 60fi. violet (Garibaldi) . . . 20 10
1667 60fi. green (I. Turr) 20 10
1668 60fi. red (I. Tukory) 20 10
1669 60fi. deep blue and blue (O. Herman) 20 10
1670 60fi. brown (Beethoven) . . 20 10
1671 60fi. red (F. Mora) 20 10
1672 60fi. black and grey (B. I. Toth) 30 10
1673 60fi. purple and mauve (D. Banki) 20 10
1674 60fi. deep green and green (A. G. Pattantyus) . . . 20 10
1675 60fi. blue and cobalt (I. P. Semmelweis) 20 10
1676 60fi. brown (Joliot-Curie) . . 20 10
1677 60fi. red (F. Erkel) 20 10
1678 60fi. blue and light blue (J. Bolyai) 20 10
1679 60fi. red (V. I. Lenin) . . . 20 10
COMMEMORATIVE EVENTS: Nos. 1664/5, Int Women's Day: 1666, Centenary of Sicilian Expedition; 1669, 125th Birth Anniv; 1670, Martonvasar Beethoven Concerts: 1671, Szeged Festival: 1672, Miners' Day: 1677, 150th Birth Anniv; 1678, Birth Centenary; 1679, 90th Birth Anniv.

1960. Stamp Exhibition Budapest.
1680 **312** 2fo.(+4fo.) yellow, green and brown . . . . . 90 1·00

313 Soldier **314** Rowing

1960. 15th Anniv of Liberation.
1681 **313** 40fi. brown and red . . 35 30
1682 – 60fi. red, green and brown 35 30
DESIGN—HORIZ: 60fi. Student with flag (inscr "1945 FELSZABADULASUNK... 1960").

1960. Summer Olympic Games. Centres and inscr in black (3fo. multicoloured). Circular frames in bistre. Background colours given.
1683 10fi. blue (T **314**) 10 10
1684 20fi. brown (Boxing) 10 10
1685 30fi. lilac (Archery) 10 10
1686 40fi. ochre (Discus) 10 10
1687 50fi. red (Ball game) 10 10
1688 60fi. green (Javelin) 10 10
1689 1fo. purple (Horse-riding) 35 10
1690 1fo.40 blue (Wrestling) . . . 40 10
1691 1fo.70 brown (Swordplay) 45 20
1692 2fo.+1fo. red (Romulus, Remus and Wolf) 65 40
1693 3fo. grey (Olympic Rings and Arms of Hungary) . . 1·75 70
MS1693a 67 × 95 mm. 10fo. multicoloured . . . . 15·00 17·00

1960. International Philatelic Federation Congress, Warsaw. Sheet 161 × 122 mm containing four of No. 1656, each in different colours, side by side with commemorative labels.
MS1693b 3fo. (× 4) . . . . . . 7·50 8·25

1960. Hungarian Castles. As Nos. 1629, 1632/3, 1636/7 and 1641/2 but printed on coloured paper.
1694 8fi. purple on blue 10 10
1695 20fi. bronze on green . . . 20 10
1696 30fi. brown on yellow . . . 20 10
1697 60fi. red on pink 30 10
1698 70fi. green on blue 35 10
1699 1fo.40 blue on blue 60 10
1700 1fo.70 lilac on blue ("SOMLO") . . . . . . 1·40 10

315 Girl in Mezokovesd Provincial Costume **316** "The Turnip"

1960. Stamp Day.
1701 **315** 2fo.(+4fo.) mult . . . . 1·10 1·25

1960. Fairy Tales (2nd series). Multicoloured.
1702 20fi. Type **316** 10 10
1703 30fi. "Snow White and the Seven Dwarfs" 10 10
1704 40fi. "The Miller, Son and Donkey" 10 10
1705 60fi. "Puss in Boots" . . . 20 10
1706 80fi. "The Fox and the Raven" 30 10
1707 1fo. "The Maple-wood Pipe" 60 20

1708 1fo.70 "The Stork and the Fox" 75 35
1709 2fo. "Momotaro" (Japanese tale) . . . . 1·25 1·00

317 F. Rozsa 318 Eastern Grey Kangaroo with Young

1961. Celebrities and Anniversaries. Portraits as T **317**.
1710 1fo. brown (T **317**) 10 10
1711 1fo. turquoise (G. Kilian) 10 10
1712 1fo. red (J. Rippi-Ronai) . . 10 10
1713 1fo. olive (S. Latinka) . . . 10 10
1714 1fo. green (M. Zalka) . . . 10 10
1715 1fo. lake (J. Katona) . . . 10 10
COMMEMORATIVE EVENTS: No. 1710, Press Day; No. 1711, Gyorgy Kilian Sports Movement; No. 1712, Birth Cent; No. 1713, 75th Birth Anniv; No. 1714, 65th Birth Anniv.

1961. Budapest Zoo Animals. Inscr "ZOO 1961".
1716 **318** 20fi. black and orange 20 10
1717 – 30fi. sepia and green . . 20 10
1718 – 40fi. brown and chestnut 30 10
1719 – 60fi. grey and mauve . . 50 10
1720 – 80fi. yellow and black . . 65 10
1721 – 1fo. brown and green . . 65 10
1722 – 1fo.40 sepia and turquoise . . . . . . 1·00 10
1723 – 2fo. black and red . . . 1·75 60
1724 – 2fo.60 brown and violet 1·75 80
1725 – 3fo. multicoloured . . . 1·90 1·25
DESIGNS—HORIZ: 30fi. American bison; 60fi. Indian elephant and calf; 80fi. Tiger and cubs; 1fo.40, Polar bear; 2fo. Common zebra and foal; 2fo.60, European bison cow with calf. VERT: 40fi. Brown bear; 1fo. Ibex; 3fo. Main entrance, Budapest Zoo.

319 Child chasing Butterfly 320 Launching of Rocket "Vostok"

1961. Health. Inscr "1961". Cross in red.
1726 **319** 30fi. black, purple & brn 10 10
1727 – 40fi. sepia, blue & turq 25 10
1728 – 60fi. yellow, grey & violet 30 10
1729 – 1fo. multicoloured . . . 30 10
1730 – 1fo.70 yellow, blue & grn 45 10
1731 – 4fo. green and grey . . 1·40 10
DESIGNS—As Type **319**: 40fi. Patient on operating table. LARGER (29½ × 35 mm): 60fi. Ambulance and stretcher; 1fo. Traffic lights and scooter; 1fo.70, Syringe and jars; 4fo. Emblem of Health Department.

1961. World's First Manned Space Flight. Inscr "1961.IV.12".
1732 **320** 1fo. brown and blue . . 75 65
1733 – 2fo. brown and blue . . 3·00 2·75
DESIGN: 2fo. Gagarin and "Vostok" in flight.

321 Roses 322 "Venus" Rocket

1961. May Day.
1734 **321** 1fo. red and green . . . 30 10
1735 – 2fo. red and green . . . 35 20
DESIGN: 2fo. As Type **321** but roses and inscr reversed.

1961. Launching of Soviet "Venus" Rocket. Inscr "VENUSZ RAKETA 1961 11.12".
1736 **322** 40fi. black, bistre and blue 50 40
1737 – 60fi. black, bistre and blue . . . . 50 1·10
1738 – 80fi. black and blue . . 70 1·10
1739 – 2fo. bistre and violet-blue . . . . 1·60 1·90
DESIGNS: 60fi. Separation of rocket capsule in flight; 80fi. Capsule and orbit diagram; 2fo. Allegory of flying woman and crescent moon.

323 Conference Emblem, Letter and Transport

1961. Organization of Socialist Countries' Postal Administrations Conference.
1740 **323** 40fi. black and orange 20 10
1741 – 60fi. black and mauve 20 10
1742 – 1fo. black and blue . . . 20 25
DESIGNS: 60fi. Television aerial; 1fo. Radar receiving equipment.

324 Hungarian Flag 325 George Stephenson

1961. International Stamp Exhibition, Budapest. (a) 1st issue. Background in silver.
1743 **324** 1fo. red, green and black 20 30
1744 – 1fo.70 multicoloured . . 20 45
1745 – 2fo.60 multicoloured . . 1·10 90
1746 – 3fo. multicoloured . . . 1·90 1·40

(b) 2nd issue. Background in gold. Inscriptions at left altered on 1fo. and 3fo.
1747 **324** 1fo. red, green and black 20 35
1748 – 1fo.70 multicoloured . . 20 45
1749 – 2fo.60 multicoloured . . 90 85
1750 – 3fo. multicoloured . . . 2·00 1·10
DESIGNS: 1fo.70, Late spider orchids; 2fo.60, Small tortoiseshell; 3fo. Eurasian goldfinch.
See also Nos. 1765/8.

1961. Communications Ministers' Conference, Budapest. Inscr "KOZLEKEDESUGYI", etc.
1751 **325** 60fi. olive 20 10
1752 – 1fo. bistre, black and blue 30 10
1753 – 2fo. brown 30 20
DESIGNS: 1fo. Communications emblems; 2fo. J. Landler (Minister of Communications).

326 Football and Club Badge

1961. 50th Anniv of VASAS Sports Club. Badge in gold, red and blue.
1754 **326** 40fi. orange, black and gold 10 10
1755 – 60fi. green, black and gold 10 10
1756 – 1fo. bistre, black and gold 10 20
1757 – 2fo.+1fo. blue, blk & gold 75 55
DESIGNS: 60fi. Wrestling; 1fo. Vaulting; 2fo. Sailing.

327 Three Racehorses

1961. Racehorses.
1758 **327** 30fi. multicoloured . . . 10 10
1759 – 40fi. multicoloured . . . 20 10
1760 – 60fi. multicoloured . . . 30 20
1761 – 1fo. black, green and orange 35 20
1762 – 1fo.70 sepia, black and green 75 35
1763 – 2fo. black, blue and brown 90 35
1764 – 3fo. multicoloured . . . 1·60 45
DESIGNS: 40fi. Three hurdlers; 60fi. Trotting race (two horses); 1fo. Trotting race (three horses); 1fo.70, Two racehorses and two foals; 2fo. Hungarian trotter "Baka"; 3fo. 19th century champion mare, "Kincsem".

328 Budapest

1961. Stamp Day and International Stamp Exhibition, Budapest (3rd issue). Designs as T **328**.
1765 **328** 2fo.+1fo. bl, brn & ol . . 80 1·00
1766 – 2fo.+1fo. bl, brn & ol . . 80 1·00
1767 – 2fo.+1fo. bl, brn & ol . . 80 1·00
1768 – 2fo.+1fo. bl, brn & ol . . 80 1·00

Nos. 1765/8 are printed together in sheets of 40 (4 × 10) with one vertical row of each design. Horizontal strips of four form a composite panorama of Budapest.

329 Music, Keyboard and Silhouette

1961. 150th Birth and 75th Death Anniv of Liszt (composer).
1769 **329** 60fi. black and gold . . 30 10
1770 – 1fo. black 45 25
1771 – 2fo. green and blue . . . 1·00 50
MS1771a 71 × 98 mm. 10fo. multicoloured . . . . 11·00 9·50
DESIGNS—VERT: 1fo. Statue; 10fo. Head profile over piano keys. HORIZ: 2fo. Music Academy.

330 Lenin

1961. 22nd Soviet Communist Party Congress, Moscow.
1772 **330** 1fo. brown 20 10

331 Monk's Hood 332 Nightingale

1961. Medicinal Plants. Multicoloured.
1773 20fi. Type **331** 10 10
1774 30fi. Centaury 10 10
1775 40fi. Blue iris 20 10
1776 60fi. Thorn-apple 20 10
1777 1fo. Purple hollyhock . . . 45 10
1778 1fo.70 Hop 60 10
1779 2fo. Poppy . . . . 1·25 20
1780 3fo. Mullein . . . . 1·25 50

1961. Birds of Woods and Fields. Multicoloured. Inscr "1961".
1781 30fi. Type **332** 10 10
1782 40fi. Great tit 10 10
1783 60fi. Chaffinch (horiz) . . . 20 10
1784 1fo. Jay 30 10
1785 1fo.20 Golden oriole (horiz) 45 10
1786 1fo.50 Blackbird (horiz) . . 70 20
1787 2fo. Yellowhammer 85 25
1788 3fo. Northern lapwing (horiz) . . . . 1·50 40

333 M. Karolyi 334 Railway Signals

333a Globe and Gagarin, Titov and Glenn (½-size illustration)

1962. Celebrities and Anniversaries. Inscr "1962".
1789 **333** 1fo. sepia 10 10
1790 – 1fo. brown (F. Berkes) 10 10
1791 – 1fo. blue (J. Pech) . . . 10 10
1792 – 1fo. violet (A. Chazar) 10 10
1793 – 1fo. blue (Dr. F. Hutyra) 10 10
1794 – 1fo. red (G. Egressy) . . 10 10
ANNIVERSARIES: Nos. 1789/90, 5th Co-operative Movement Congress; 1791, 75th anniv of Hydrographic Institute; 1792, 50th anniv of Sports Club for the Deaf; 1793, 175th anniv of Hungarian Veterinary Service; 1794, 125th anniv of National Theatre.

1962. World Space Flights of Gagarin, Titov and Glenn. Sheet 109 × 70 mm.
MS1794a **333a** 10fo. multicoloured 7·50 10·50

1962. 14th Int Railwaymen's Esperanto Congress.
1795 **334** 1fo. green 25 10

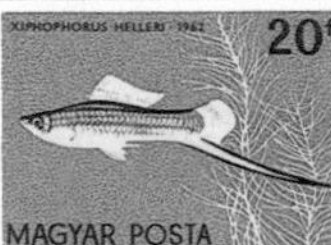

335 Green Swordtail

1962. Ornamental Fishes. Inscr "1962". Mult.
1796 20fi. Type **335** 10 10
1797 30fi. Paradise fish 10 10
1798 40fi. Fan-tailed guppy . . . 10 10
1799 60fi. Siamese fighting fish . . 20 10
1800 80fi. Tiger barb 20 10
1801 1fo. Freshwater angelfish . . 35 10
1802 1fo.20 Sunfish 35 10
1803 1fo.50 Lyretail panchax . . 60 10
1804 2fo. Neon tetra 75 25
1805 3fo. Blue discus 90 55

336 Flags of Argentina and Bulgaria

1962. World Football Championships, 1962. Inscr "CHILE 1962". Flags in national colours: ball, flagpole, value, etc., in bistre.
1806 – 30fi. mauve 10 10
1807 – 40fi. green 25 10
1808 – 60fi. lilac 30 10
1809 – 1fo. blue 35 20
1810 **336** 1fo.70 orange 65 20
1811 – 2fo. turquoise 75 30
1812 – 3fo. red . . . . 1·10 40
1813 – 4fo.+1fo. green . . . . 1·50 80
MS1813a 72 × 92 mm. 10fo. multicoloured . . . . 6·75 6·75
FLAGS: 30fi. Colombia and Uruguay; 40fi. U.S.S.R. and Yugoslavia; 60fi. Switzerland and Chile; 1fo. German Federal Republic and Italy; 2fo. Hungary and Great Britain; 3fo. Brazil and Mexico; 4fo. Spain and Czechoslovakia. The two flags on each stamp represent the football teams playing against each other in the first round. VERT: (28½ × 39 mm)—10fo. Goal keeper and map.

337 Gutenberg 338 Campaign Emblem

1962. Centenary of Hungarian Printing Union.
1814 **337** 1fo. blue 20 10
1815 – 1fo. brown 20 10
PORTRAIT: No. 1815, Miklos Kis (first Hungarian printer).

1962. Malaria Eradication.
1816 **338** 2fo.50 bistre and black 75 45
MS1816a 111 × 76 mm. 2fo.50 (× 4) green and black . . . . 9·00 9·75

339 "Beating Swords into Ploughshares" 340 Festival Emblem

1962. World Peace Congress, Moscow.
1817 **339** 1fo. brown 10 10

1962. World Youth Festival, Helsinki.
1818 **340** 3fo. multicoloured . . . 45 20

341 Icarus 342 Hybrid Tea

1962. Air. Development of Flight.
1819 **341** 30fi. bistre and blue . . 10 10
1820 – 40fi. blue and green . . 10 10
1821 – 60fi. red and blue . . . 25 10
1822 – 80fi. silver, blue & turq 30 10
1823 – 1fo. silver, blue & purple 35 10
1824 – 1fo.40 orange and blue 35 25
1825 – 2fo. brown and turquoise 55 20
1826 – 3fo. blue, silver and violet 60 30
1827 – 4fo. silver, black & green 85 40
DESIGNS: 40fi. Modern glider and Lilienthal monoplane glider; 60fi. Zlin Trener 6 and Rakos's monoplane; 80fi. Airship "Graf Zeppelin" and Montgolfier balloon; 1fo. Ilyushin Il-18B and Wright Flyer I; 1fo.40, Nord 3202 sports airplane and Peter Nesterov's Nieuport biplane; 2fo. Mil Mi-6 helicopter and Asboth's helicopter; 3fo. Myasichev Mya-4 airliner and Zhukovsky's wind tunnel; 4fo. Space rocket and Tsiolkovsky's rocket.

1962. Rose Culture. Roses in natural colours. Background colours given.
1828 – 20fi. brown 20 10
1829 **342** 40fi. myrtle 30 10
1830 – 60fi. violet 35 10
1831 – 80fi. red 45 10
1832 – 1fo. myrtle 60 20
1833 – 1fo.20 orange 75 35
1834 – 2fo. turquoise . . . . . 1·75 45
ROSES: 20fi. Floribunda; 60fi. to 2fo. Various hybrid teas.

343 Globe, "Vostok 3" and "Vostok 4" (⅔-size illustration)

1962. Air. 1st "Team" Manned Space Flight.
1835 **343** 1fo. brown and blue . . 50 45
1836 – 2fo. brown and blue . . 50 45
DESIGN: 2fo. Cosmonauts Nikolaev and Popovich.

344 Weightlifting **345** Austrian 2kr. stamp of 1850

1962. European Weightlifting Championships, Budapest.
1837 **344** 1fo. brown 25 20

1962. 35th Stamp Day.
1838 **345** 2fo.+1fo. brown & yell 50 75
1839 – 2fo.+1fo. brown & pk 50 75
1840 – 2fo.+1fo. brown & bl . . 50 75
1841 – 2fo.+1fo. brown & grn 80 85
MS1841a 91 × 110 mm. Nos. 1838/41 in block of four . . . . 4·50 5·25
DESIGNS: Hungarian stamps of: No. 1839, 1919 (75fi. Dozsa); No. 1840, 1955 (1fo. 50 Skiing); No. 1841, 1959 (3fo. "Vanessa atalanta").

346 Primitive and Modern Oilwells

1962. 25th Anniv of Hungarian Oil Industry.
1842 **346** 1fo. green 10 10

347 Gagarin

1962. Air. Astronautical Congress, Paris.
1843 **347** 40fi. ochre and purple 20 10
1844 – 60fi. ochre and green . . 20 10
1845 – 1fo. ochre and turquoise 35 10
1846 – 1fo.40 ochre and brown 60 20
1847 – 1fo.70 ochre and blue . . 75 20
1848 – 2fo.60 ochre and violet 1·00 35
1849 – 3fo. ochre and brown . . 1·40 50
ASTRONAUTS: 60fi. Titov; 1fo. Glenn; 1fo.40, Scott Carpenter; 1fo.70, Nikolaev; 2fo.60, Popovich; 3fo. Schirra.

348 Cup and Football **349** Osprey

1962. "Budapest Vasas" Football Team's Victory in Central European Cup Competition.
1850 **348** 2fo.+1fo. mult 45 50

1962. Air. Birds of Prey. Multicoloured.
1851 30fi. Eagle owl 30 10
1852 40fi. Type **349** 30 10
1853 60fi. Marsh harrier 35 20
1854 80fi. Booted eagle 50 30
1855 1fo. African fish eagle . . . 60 40
1856 2fo. Lammergeier 95 55
1857 3fo. Golden eagle . . . . . 1·25 65
1858 4fo. Common kestrel . . . 1·60 80

350 Racing Motor Cyclist

1962. Motor Cycle and Car Sports. Mult.
1859 20fi. Type **350** 10 10
1860 30fi. Sidecar racing 10 10
1861 40fi. "Scrambling" (hill climb) 10 10
1862 60fi. Dirt-track racing . . . 20 10
1863 1fo. Wearing "garland" . . 35 10
1864 1fo.20 Speed trials 45 20
1865 1fo.70 Sidecar trials 65 20
1866 2fo. "Go-kart" racing . . . 85 20
1867 3fo. Car racing . . . . . . 1·10 70

351 Ice Skater

1963. European Figure Skating and Ice Dancing Championships, Budapest.
1868 **351** 20fi. green, brown & lilac 10 10
1869 – 40fi. black, brn & salmon 10 10
1870 – 60fi. multicoloured . . . 30 20
1871 – 1fo. multicoloured . . . 45 20
1872 – 1fo.40 multicoloured . . 65 20
1873 – 2fo. red, brown and green 95 30
1874 – 3fo. multicoloured . . . 1·90 50
MS1874a 66 × 94 mm. 10fo. multicoloured . . . . 6·50 5·00
DESIGNS—VERT: 40fi., 2fo. Skater leaping; 60fi., 1fo. Pairs dancing; 1fo.40, Skater turning; 10fo. (29 × 38 mm), Figure skater and flags. HORIZ: 3fo. Pair dancing.

352 J. Batsanyi

1963. Celebrities and Anniversaries.
1875 40fi. lake (Type **352**) 10 10
1876 40fi. green (F. Entz) 10 10
1877 40fi. blue (I. Markovits) . . 10 10
1878 40fi. olive (L. Weiner) . . . 45 10
1879 60fi. purple (Dr. F. Koranyi) 45 10
1880 60fi. bronze (G. Gardonyi) 10 10
1881 60fi. brown (P. de Coubertin) 20 10
1882 60fi. violet (J. Eotvos) . . . 10 10
ANNIVERSARIES: No. 1875, Revolutionary, birth bicent; No. 1876, Horticulture College founder, Horticulture cent; No. 1877, Inventor, Hungarian Shorthand, cent; No. 1878, Composer, Budapest Music Competitions; No. 1879, Tuberculosis researcher, 50th death anniv; No. 1880, Novelist, birth cent; No. 1881, Olympic Games reviver, birth cent; No. 1882, Author, 150th birth anniv.

353 Bulgarian 21. Rocket Stamp of 1959

1963. Organization of Socialist Countries Postal Administrations Conference, Budapest.
1883 – 20fi. red, yellow and green 10 10
1884 **353** 30fi. red, brown & purple 10 10
1885 – 40fi. purple and blue . . 10 10
1886 – 50fi. violet and blue . . 10 10
1887 – 60fi. multicoloured . . . 10 10
1888 – 80fi. turquoise, black & bl 10 10
1889 – 1fo. multicoloured . . . 20 10
1890 – 1fo.20 yellow, violet & bl 45 10
1891 – 1fo.40 blue, red & brown 30 10
1892 – 1fo.70 brn, grn & lt brn 45 10
1893 – 2fo. orange, blue & pur 45 20
1894 – 2fo.60 violet, red & grn 65 65
DESIGNS: Various "space" stamps—HORIZ: 20fi. Albania 11.50 (1962); 40fi. Czechoslovakia 80h. (1962); 50fi. China 8f. (1958); 60fi. N. Korea 10ch. (1961); 80fi. Poland 40g. (1959); 1fo. Hungary 60fi. (1961); 1fo.40, East Germany 25pf. (1961); 1fo.70, Rumania 11.20 (1957); 2fo.60, N. Vietnam 6x. (1961). VERT: 1fo.20, Mongolia 30m. (1959); 2fo. Russia 6k. (1961).

354 Fair Emblem

1963. International Fair, Budapest.
1895 **354** 1fo. violet 30 10

355 Erkel (composer)

1963. Students' Erkel Memorial Festival, Gyula.
1896 **355** 60fi. brown 45 10

356 Roses

1963. 5th National Rose Show, Budapest.
1897 **356** 2fo. red, green and brown 60 10

357 Helicon Monument

1963. 10th Youth Festival, Keszthely.
1898 **357** 40fi. blue 10 10

358 Chain Bridge and "Snow White" (Danube steamer)

1963. Transport and Communications.
1899 **358** 10fi. blue 10 10
1900 – 20fi. green 10 10
1901 – 30fi. blue 10 10
1902 – 40fi. orange 10 10
1902b – 40fi. grey 30 20
1903 – 50fi. brown 30 30
1904 – 60fi. red 30 10
1905 – 70fi. olive 30 10
1906 – 80fi. brown 20 10
1906a – 1fo. brown 10 10
1907 – 1fo. purple 20 10
1908 – 1fo.20 brown . . . . . 2·40 75
1909 – 1fo.20 violet 20 10
1910 – 1fo.40 green 35 10
1911 – 1fo.70 brown 85 10
1912 – 2fo. turquoise 45 10
1913 – 2fo.50 purple 75 10
1914 – 2fo.60 olive . . . . . 1·25 10
1915 – 3fo. blue 45 10
1916 – 4fo. blue 75 10
1917 – 5fo. brown . . . . 1·25 10
1918 – 6fo. ochre . . . . 1·25 10
1919 – 8fo. mauve . . . . 1·75 20
1920 – 10fo. green . . . . . . 1·75 1·00
DESIGNS—As Type **358**: HORIZ: 20fi. Tramcar; 30fi. Open-deck bus; 40fi. (No. 1902), Articulated bus; 40fi. (No. 1902b), Budapest 100 Post Office; 50fi. Railway truck with gas cylinders; 60fi. Trolley bus; 70fi. Railway T.P.O. coach; 80fi. Motor cyclist. VERT: 1fo. (No. 1906a), Hotel Budapest. 28½ × 21 mm: 1fo. (No. 1907) Articulated trolley bus; 1fo.40, Postal coach; 1fo.70, Diesel-electric multiple unit train; 2fo. T.V. broadcast coach; 2fo.50, Tourist coach; 2fo.60, Signalbox and train; 3fo. Parcels conveyor; 5fo. Railway fork-lift truck; 6fo. Telex operator; 8fo. Telephonist and map; 10fo. Postwoman. 21 × 28½ mm: 1fo.20, (No. 1908), Mail plane and trolley on tarmac; 1fo.20, (No. 1909), Control tower, Miskolc; 4fo. Pylon, Pecs.
See also Nos. 2767/70.

359 Holidaymaker and "Beloiannis" (lake steamer)

1963. Cent of Siofok Resort, Lake Balaton.
1921 – 20fi. black, green and red 55 10
1922 **359** 40fi. multicoloured . . . 55 20
1923 – 60fi. orange, brown & bl 90 25
DESIGNS—TRIANGULAR: 20fi. "Tihany" (water bus); 60fi. Yacht.

359a Spaceship over Globe

1963. Air. Space Flights of "Vostok 5" and "Vostok 6". Sheet 64 × 94 mm.
MS1923a **359a** 10fo. light blue, blue and gold . . . . 6·50 8·50

360 Mail Coach and Arc de Triomphe, Paris

1963. Centenary of Paris Postal Conference.
1924 **360** 1fo. red 30 10

361 Performance in front of Szeged Cathedral

1963. Summer Drama Festival, Szeged.
1925 **361** 40fi. blue 10 10

362 Child with towel
364 Karancssag

363 Pylon and Map

1963. Red Cross Cent. Inscr "1863–1963". Mult.
1926 30fi. Type **362** 10 10
1927 40fi. Girl with medicine bottle and tablets 10 10
1928 60fi. Girls of three races . . 20 10
1929 1fo. Girl and "heart" . . . 20 10
1930 1fo.40 Boys of three races 30 10
1931 2fo. Child being medically examined 35 20
1932 3fo. Hands tending plants 95 30

1963. Village Electrification.
1933 **363** 1fo. black and grey . . . 30 10

1963. Provincial Costumes.
1934 **364** 20fi. lake 20 10
1935 – 30fi. green (Kapuvar) . . 20 10
1936 – 40fi. brown (Debrecen) 20 10
1937 – 60fi. blue (Hortobagy) 30 20
1938 – 1fo. red (Csokoly) . . . 45 20
1939 – 1fo.70 violet (Dunantul) 50 20
1940 – 2fo. turquoise (Bujak) . . 60 30
1941 – 2fo.50 red (Alfold) . . . 75 35
1942 – 3fo. blue (Mezokovesd) 1·90 70

365 Hyacinth
367 Calendar

366 Skiing (slalom)

1963. Stamp Day. Flowers. Multicoloured.
1943 2fo.+1fo. Type **365** 60 65
1944 2fo.+1fo. Narcissus 60 65
1945 2fo.+1fo. Chrysanthemum 60 65
1946 2fo.+1fo. Tiger lily 60 65
MS1946a 76 × 91 mm. Nos. 1943/6 but smaller (20 × 27 mm) in block of four . . . . 3·75 4·00

1963. Winter Olympic Games, Innsbruck, 1964. "MAGYAR" and emblems red and black; centres brown: background colours given.
1947 **366** 40fi. green 10 10
1948 – 60fi. violet 10 10
1949 – 70fi. blue 10 10
1950 – 80fi. green 10 10
1951 – 1fo. orange 20 10
1952 – 2fo. blue 35 10
1953 – 2fo.60 purple 90 50
1954 – 4fo.+1fo. blue . . . . . 1·00 55
DESIGNS: 60fi. Skiing (biathlon); 70fi. Ski jumping; 80fi. Rifle-shooting on skis; 1fo. Figure skating (pairs); 2fo. Ice hockey; 2fo.60, Speed skating; 4fo. Bobsleighing.

1963. New Year Issue. Hungarian Postal and Philatelic Museum Fund. Multicoloured.
1955 20fi. Type **367** 10 10
1956 30fi. Young chimney-sweep with glass of wine 10 10
1957 40fi. Four-leafed clover . . 10 10
1958 60fi. Piglet in top-hat . . . 10 10
1959 1fo. Young pierrot 20 10
1960 2fo. Chinese lanterns and mask 30 10
1961 2fo.50+1fo.20 Holly, mistletoe, clover and horseshoe 45 20
1962 3fo.+1fo.50 Piglets with balloon 90 30
SIZES: As Type **367**—HORIZ: 20fi., 1fo., 3fo. VERT: 40fi. LARGER (28 × 38 mm.): 30fi., 60fi., 2fo., 2fo.50.

368 Moon Rocket

1964. Space Research. Multicoloured.
1963 30fi. Type **368** 10 10
1964 40fi. Venus rocket 20 10
1965 60fi. "Vostok 1" (horiz) . . 20 10
1966 1fo. U.S. spaceship 30 10
1967 1fo.70 Soviet team space flights 45 10
1968 2fo. "Telstar" (horiz) . . . 50 20
1969 2fo.60 Mars rocket 75 30
1970 3fo. "Space Research" (rockets and tracking equipment) (horiz) . . . . 85 1·00

368a Skier racing

1964. Winter Olympic Games, Innsbruck, 1964. Sheet 65 × 60 mm.
MS1970a **368a** 10fo. multicoloured 4·50 6·00

369 Swans

1964. Halas Lace (2nd series). Lace patterns die-stamped in white on black; inscriptions black.
1971 **369** 20fi. green 30 10
1972 – 30fi. yellow 45 10
1973 – 40fi. red 60 10
1974 – 60fi. olive 75 10
1975 – 1fo. orange 90 10
1976 – 1fo.40 blue . . . . . . 1·10 20
1977 – 2fo. turquoise . . . . . 1·25 25
1978 – 2fo.60 violet . . . . . . 1·60 45
LACE PATTERNS—VERT: (38½ × 45 mm.): 30fi. Peacocks; 40fi. Pigeons; 60fi. Peacock; 1fo. Deer; 1fo.40, Fisherman; 2fo. Pigeons. As Type **369**: 2fo.60, Butterfly.

370 Armour and Swords
371 Basketball

372 Dozsa and Kossuth

373 Fair and Emblem

374 "Breasting the Tape"

1964. Anniversaries and Events of 1964. Designs as T **370/4**, some showing portraits. (a) As T **370**.
1979 60fi. purple (I. Madach) . . 10 10
1980 60fi. olive (E. Szabo) . . . 10 10
1981 60fi. olive (A. Fay) 10 10
1982 1fo. red (Skittles) . . . . . 1·00 60
1983 2fo. brown (T **370**) 35 10
ANNIV OR EVENT: No. 1979, (author, death cent.); No. 1980, (founder of Municipal Libraries, 60th anniv); No. 1981, (death cent.); No. 1982, (1st European Skittles Championships, Budapest); No. 1983, (50th anniv of Hungarian Fencing Assn.).

(b) As T **371**.
1984 60fi. turquoise (Stalactites and stalagmites) 20 10
1985 60fi. blue (Bauxite excavator) 10 10
1990 60fi. red (K. Marx) 10 10
1986 1fo. green (Forest and waterfall) 30 10
1987 2fo. brown (Galileo) 50 10
1988 2fo. lake (Shakespeare) . . . 45 10
1989 2fo. blue (T **371**) . . . . . 1·10 30
ANNIV OR EVENT—VERT: No. 1984, (Aggteleki Cave); No. 1985, (30th anniv or Hungarian Aluminium Production); No. 1986, (National Forestry Federation Congress); No. 1987, (400th birth anniv); No. 1988 (400th birth anniv); No. 1989, (European Women's Basketball Championships). HORIZ: No. 1990, (cent of "First International").

(c) As T **372**.
1991 1fo. blue (T **372**) 30 10
1992 3fo.+1fo.50, black, grey and orange (Sports Museum, Budapest) 75 25

ANNIV OR EVENT: No. 1991, (60th Anniv of City of Cegled); No. 1992, (Lawn Tennis Historical Exn, Budapest).

(d) T **373**.
1993 1fo. green (Budapest Int Fair) 30 10

(e) As T **374**.
1994 60fi. slate ("Alba Regia" statue) 10 10
1995 1fo. brown (M. Ybl) 30 10
1996 2fo. brown (T **374**) 35 10
1997 2fo. dull pur (Michelangelo) 45 10
ANNIV OR EVENT: No. 1994, (Szekesfehervar Days); No. 1995, (architect, 150th birth anniv); No. 1996, (50th anniv of Hungarian–Swedish Athletic Meeting); No. 1997, (400th death anniv).

375 Eleanor Roosevelt
377 Peaches ("Magyar Kajszi")

376 Fencing

1964. Eleanor Roosevelt Commemoration.
1998 **375** 2fo. ochre, deep brown and brown 30 20
MS1998a 112 × 76 mm. 4 × 2 fo. (each 39 × 20 mm) in different colours, showing portrait . . . 2·25 2·50

1964. Olympic Games, Tokyo. Multicoloured.
1999 30fi. Type **376** 10 10
2000 40fi. Gymnastics 10 10
2001 60fi. Football 10 10
2002 80fi. Horse-jumping 10 10
2003 1fo. Running 20 10
2004 1fo.40 Weightlifting 30 10
2005 1fo.70 Gymnastics (trapeze) 30 10
2006 2fo. Throwing the hammer, and javelin 35 10
2007 2fo. 50 Boxing 75 10
2008 3fo.+1fo. Water-polo . . . 75 45

1964. National Peaches and Apricots Exn, Budapest. Designs of peaches or apricots. Multicoloured.
2009 40fi. "J.H. Hale" 10 10
2010 60fi. Type **377** 10 10
2011 1fo. "Mandula Kajszi" . . . 30 10
2012 1fo.50 "Borsi Rozsa" . . . 35 10
2013 1fo.70 "Alexander" 60 10
2014 2fo. "Champion" 75 20
2015 2fo.60 "Elberta" 95 30
2016 3fo. "Mayflower" . . . . . 1·40 50

378 Lilac

1964. Stamp Day. Multicoloured.
2017 2fo.+1fo. Type **378** 50 60
2018 2fo.+1fo. Mallard . . . . . 1·60 1·40
2019 2fo.+1fo. Gymnast 50 60
2020 2fo.+1fo. Rocket and globe 50 60
MS2020a 85 × 100 mm. Nos. 2017/20 but smaller (20 × 27½ mm) in block of four . . . . 3·25 2·75

378a Mt. Fuji and Stadium

1964. Air. Summer Olympic Games, Tokyo. Sheet 56 × 83 mm.

MS2020b	**378a** 10fo. multicoloured	4·50	6·00

379 Pedestrian Road Crossing

1964. Road Safety. Multicoloured.

2021	20fi. Type **379**	20	10
2022	60fi. Child with ball running into road	35	10
2023	1fo. Woman and child waiting to cross road	60	25

379a Venus, Rocket and Globe

1964. Three-manned Space Flight. Sheet 87 × 74 mm.

MS2023a	**379a** 10fo. multicoloured	4·50	6·00

380 Arpad Bridge, Budapest

1964. Opening of Reconstructed Elizabeth Bridge, Budapest.

2024	**380** 20fi. grey, green and blue (postage)	10	10
2025	– 30fi. green, blue & brown	10	10
2026	– 60fi. brown, grn & dp brn	30	10
2027	– 1fo. brown, bl & dp brn	45	10
2028	– 1fo.50 grey, blue & brn	65	10
2029	– 2fo. grey, green & brown	85	25
2030	– 2fo.50 grey, blue & brn	1·75	85
	(b) Air.		
MS2030a	95 × 49 mm. 10fo. green	5·00	5·25

BUDAPEST BRIDGES: 30fi. Margaret; 60fi. Chain; 1fo. Elizabeth; 1fo.50, Liberty; 2fo. Petofi; 2fo.50, South; 10fo. Elizabeth (different).

381 Common Pheasant

1964. "Hunting". Multicoloured.

2034	20fi. Type **381**	30	10
2035	30fi. Wild boar	10	10
2036	40fi. Grey partridges	45	10
2037	60fi. Brown hare	20	10
2038	80fi. Fallow deer	30	10
2039	1fo. Mouflon	45	10
2040	1fo.70 Red deer	75	10
2041	2fo. Great bustard	1·90	30
2042	2fo.50 Roe deer	90	40
2043	3fo. Emblem of Hunters' Federation	75	60

382 Horse-riding and Medals

1965. Olympic Games, Tokyo—Hungarian Winners' Medals. Medals: Gold and brown (G); Silver and black (S); Bronze and brown (B).

2044	20fi. brown and olive (G)	10	10
2045	30fi. brown and violet (S)	10	10
2046	50fi. brown and olive (G)	10	10
2047	60fi. brown and light blue (G)	10	10
2048	70fi. brown, slate & stone (B)	20	10
2049	80fi. brown and green (G)	35	10
2050	1fo. brown, violet & mauve (S)	30	10
2051	1fo.20 brown and blue (S)	35	20
2052	1fo.40 brown and grey (S)	60	20
2053	1fo.50 brown and bistre (G)	65	20
2054	1fo.70 brown and red (S)	90	30
2055	3fo. brown and turquoise (G)	1·25	80

DESIGNS: 20fi. Type **382**; 30fi. Gymnastics; 50fi. Rifle-shooting; 60fi. Water-polo; 70fi. Putting the shot; 80fi. Football; 1fo. Weightlifting; 1fo.20, Canoeing; 1fo.40, Throwing the hammer; 1fo.50, Wrestling; 1fo.70, Throwing the javelin; 3fo. Fencing.

383 Mil Mi-4 Helicopter and Polar Station **384** Asters

1965. International Quiet Sun Year.

2056	**383** 20fi. orange, black & blue	10	10
2057	– 30fi. green, black & grey	10	10
2058	– 60fi. yellow, black & mve	10	10
2059	– 80fi. yellow, black & grn	20	10
2060	– 1fo.50 multicoloured	20	10
2061	– 1fo.70 black, mauve & bl	30	10
2062	– 2fo. red, black and blue	95	20
2063	– 2fo.50 yellow, blk & brn	50	20
2064	– 3fo. black, blue & yellow	95	50
MS2065	62 × 85 mm. 10fo. black, orange and blue	4·50	5·00

DESIGNS: 30fi. Rocket and radar aerials; 60fi. Rocket and diagram; 80fi. Radio telescope; 1fo.50, Compass needle on Globe; 1fo.70, Weather balloon; 2fo. Northern Lights and Adelie Penguins; 2fo.50, Space satellite; 3fo. I.Q.S.Y. emblem and world map; 10fo. Sun flares, snow crystals and rain.

1965. 20th Anniv of Liberation. Multicoloured.

2066	20fi. Type **384**	10	10
2067	30fi. Peonies	10	10
2068	50fi. Carnations	10	10
2069	60fi. Roses	10	10
2070	1fo.40 Lilies	30	10
2071	1fo.70 Godetia	35	10
2072	2fo. Gladiolus	45	10
2073	2fo.50 Parrot tulips	50	20
2074	3fo. Mixed bouquet	1·10	50

385 Leonov in Space **386** "Red Head" (after Leonardo da Vinci)

1965. Air. "Voskhod 2" Space Flight.

2075	**385** 1fo. grey and violet	30	10
2076	– 2fo. brown and purple	90	50

DESIGN: 2fo. Belyaev and Leonov.

1965. Int Renaissance Conference, Budapest.

2077	**386** 60fi. brown and ochre	20	10

387 Nikolaev, Tereshkova and View of Budapest

1965. Visit of Astronauts Nikolaev and Tereshkova.

2078	**387** 1fo. brown and blue	30	10

388 I.T.U. Emblem and Symbols

1965. Centenary of I.T.U.

2079	**388** 60fi. blue	10	10

389 Reproduction of Austria Type 109

1965. International Philatelic Exhibition, Vienna ("WIPA 1965"). Sheet 102 × 75 mm containing two of T **389** and two labels showing commemorative covers.

MS2080	**389** 2fo. (× 2) blue and grey	3·75	4·75

390 French 13th-cent Tennis **391** Marx and Lenin

1965. "History of Tennis".

2081	**390** 30fi.+10fi. lake on buff	10	10
2082	– 40fi.+10fi. blk on lilac	10	10
2083	– 60fi.+10fi. green on bis	20	10
2084	– 70fi.+30fi. pur on turq	30	10
2085	– 80fi.+40fi. blue on lav	35	10
2086	– 1fo.+50fi. green on yell	60	10
2087	– 1fo.50+50fi. brown on green	60	30
2088	– 1fo.70+50fi. blk on bl	65	45
2089	– 2fo.+1fo. red on green	75	60

DESIGNS: 40fi. Hungarian 16th-cent game; 60fi. French 18th-cent "long court"; 70fi. 16th-cent "tennys courte"; 80fi. 16th-cent court at Fontainebleau; 1fo. 17th-cent game; 1fo.50, W. C. Wingfield and Wimbledon Cup, 1877; 1fo.70, Davis Cup, 1900. 2fo. Bela Kehrling in play.

1965. Organization of Socialist Countries' Postal Administrations Congress, Peking.

2090	**391** 60fi. multicoloured	10	10

392 I.C.Y. Emblem and Pulleys **393** Equestrian Act

1965. International Co-operation Year.

2091	**392** 2fo. red	30	10
MS2092	75 × 98 mm T **392** but smaller (21 × 29 mm) in blokc of four, each in a different colour	3·00	3·00

1965. "Circus 1965". Multicoloured.

2093	20fi. Type **393**	10	10
2094	30fi. Musical clown	10	10
2095	40fi. Performing elephant	20	10
2096	50fi. Performing seal	20	10
2097	60fi. Lions	40	10
2098	1fo. Wild cat leaping through burning hoops	35	25
2099	1fo.50 Black panthers	60	25
2100	2fo.50 Acrobat with hoops	75	25
2101	3fo. Performing panther and dogs	1·00	35
2102	4fo. Bear on bicycle	1·60	90

394 Rescue Boat

1965. Danube Flood Relief.

2103	**394** 1fo.+50fi. brown & bl	1·00	1·00
MS2104	113 × 79 mm. 10fo.+5 fo. brown (Another rescue boat as T **394**)	3·00	3·50

395 Dr. I. Semmelweis

1965. Death Cent of Ignac Semmelweis (physician).

2105	**395** 60fi. brown	10	10

396 Running

1965. University Games, Budapest. Multicoloured (except **MS**2115).

2106	20fi. Type **396**	10	10
2107	30fi. Start of swimming race	10	10
2108	50fi. Diving	10	10
2109	60fi. Gymnastics	20	10
2110	80fi. Tennis	20	10
2111	1fo.70 Fencing	30	10
2112	2fo. Volleyball	40	10
2113	2fo.50 Basketball	60	10
2114	4fo. Water-polo	80	45
MS2115	195 × 75 mm. Horiz design (38 × 28 mm) showing stadium. 10fo. chestnut, ochre and grey	4·25	4·50

397 Congress Emblem

1965. 6th W.F.T.U. Congress, Warsaw.

2116	**397** 60fi. blue	10	10

398 "Phyllocactus hybridum"

1965. Succulents and Orchids. Multicoloured.

2117	20fi. Type **398**	10	10
2118	30fi. "Cattleya warszewiczii"	10	10
2119	60fi. "Rebutia calliantha"	20	10
2120	70fi. "Paphiopedilum hybridum"	30	10
2121	80fi. "Opuntia rhodantha"	30	10
2122	1fo. "Laelia elegans"	50	10
2123	1fo.50 "Zygocactus truncatus"	45	10
2124	2fo. "Strelitzia reginae"	60	10
2125	2fo.50 "Lithops weberi"	65	30
2126	3fo. "Victoria amazonica"	1·40	45

399 Reproduction of No. 1127

1965. Stamp Day. Designs show reproductions of Hungarian stamps. Multicoloured.

2127	2fo.+1fo. Type **399**	50	1·10
2128	2fo.+1fo. No. 1280	1·60	1·10
2129	2fo.+1fo. No. 1873	50	1·10
2130	2fo.+1fo. No. 1733	50	1·10
MS2131	100 × 85 mm. Nos. 2127/30 but smaller	3·00	4·00

400 F.I.R. Emblem

1965. 5th International Federation of Resistance Fighters Congress, Budapest.

2132	**400** 2fo. blue	10	10

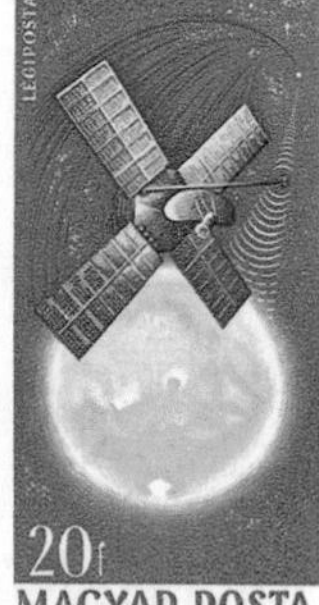

401 The Magic Horse **402** "Mariner 4"

1965. Fairy Tales (3rd series). Scenes from "The Arabian Nights Entertainments". Multicoloured.
2133 20fi. Type **401** 10 10
2134 30fi. Sultan Schahriah and Scheherazade 10 10
2135 50fi. Sinbad's 5th Voyage (ship) 10 10
2136 60fi. Aladdin and Genie of the Lamp 20 10
2137 80fi. Haroun al Rashid . . . 40 10
2138 1fo. The Magic Carpet . . . 45 10
2139 1fo.70 The Fisherman and the Genie 60 10
2140 2fo. Ali Baba 75 10
2141 3fo. Sinbad's 2nd Voyage (roc—legendary bird) . . 1·40 45

1965. Air. Space Research.
2142 **402** 20fi. black, yellow & blue 20 10
2143 – 30fi. violet, yellow & brn 20 10
2144 – 40fi. brown, mauve & bl 30 10
2145 – 60fi. multicoloured . . . 45 10
2146 – 1fo. multicoloured . . . 70 20
2147 – 2fo.50 black, grey & pur 95 30
2148 – 3fo. black, green & brn 1·10 50
MS2149 105 × 85 mm. 10fo. multicoloured . . . . 4·00 4·00
DESIGNS—VERT: 30fi. "San Marco" (Italian satellite); 40fi. "Molnyija 1" (Polish satellite); 60fi. Moon rocket; 1fo. "Shapir" rocket; 2fo.50, "Szonda 3" satellite; 3fo. "Syncom 3" satellite. HORIZ: 10fo. Satellites orbiting Globe.

403 Scarlet Tiger Moth

1966. Butterflies and Moths. Multicoloured.
2150 20fi. Type **403** 10 10
2151 60fi. Orange tip 20 10
2152 70fi. Meleager's blue 35 10
2153 80fi. Scarce swallowtail . . 45 10
2154 1fo. Common burnet . . . 45 10
2155 1fo.50 Southern festoon . . 60 25
2156 2fo. Camberwell beauty . . 60 25
2157 2fo.50 Nettle-tree butterfly 75 25
2158 3fo. Clouded yellow 95 55

404 Bela Kun

1966. Anniversaries of 1966.
2159 60fi. black and red (T **404**) 10 10
2160 60fi. black and blue (T. Esze) 35 10
2161 1fo. violet (Shastri) 15 10
2162 2fo. brown and ochre (I. Szechenyi) 35 10
2163 2fo. sepia and bistre (M. Zrinyi) 30 10
2164 2fo. sepia and green (S. Koranyi) 35 10
EVENTS: No. 2159, 80th Birth anniv (workers' leader); 2160, (after statue by M. Nemeth) 300th Birth anniv (war hero); 2161, Death commem (Indian Prime Minister); 2162, 175th Birth anniv (statesman); 2163, 400th Death anniv (military commander); 2164, Birth cent (scientist).

405 "Luna 9" in Space **406** Crocus

1966. Moon Landing of "Luna 9".
2165 **405** 2fo. black, yellow & violet 45 10
2166 – 3fo. black, yellow & blue 70 45
DESIGN—HORIZ: 3fo. "Luna 9" on Moon.

1966. Flower Protection. Multicoloured.
2167 20fi. Type **406** 40 10
2168 30fi. European cyclamen . . 50 10
2169 60fi. Ligularia 75 20
2170 1fo.40 Orange lily . . . . . 1·10 20
2171 1fo.50 Fritillary . . . . . . 1·40 20
2172 3fo. "Dracocephalum ruyschiana" . . . . . . 3·25 70

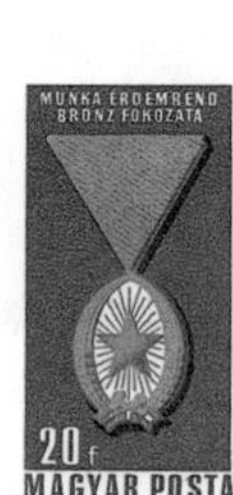

407 Order of Labour (bronze) **409** Barn Swallows

408 Early Transport and Budapest Railway Station, 1846

1966. Hungarian Medals and Orders. Mult.
2173 20fi. Type **407** 10 10
2174 30fi. Order of Labour (silver) 10 10
2175 50fi. Banner Order of Republic, 3rd class (21½ × 28½ mm) 10 10
2176 60fi. Order of Labour (gold) 10 10
2177 70fi. Banner Order of Republic, 2nd class (25 × 30½ mm) 10 10
2178 1fo. Red Banner Order of Labour 20 10
2179 1fo.20 Banner Order of Republic, 1st class (28½ × 38 mm) 25 20
2180 2fo. Order of Merit of Republic 60 20
2181 2fo.50 Hero of Socialist Labour 80 30

1966. Re-opening of Transport Museum, Budapest.
2182 **408** 1fo. brown, green & yell 40 15
2183 – 2fo. blue, brown & green 70 35
DESIGN: 2fo. Modern transport and South Station, Budapest.

1966. Protection of Birds. Multicoloured.
2184 20fi. Type **409** 40 10
2185 30fi. Long-tailed tits 45 10
2186 60fi. Red crossbill 60 10
2187 1fo.40 Middle-spotted woodpecker . . . . . . 1·25 35
2188 1fo.50 Hoopoe . . . . . . 1·25 55
2189 3fo. Forest and emblem of National Forestry Association . . . . 1·25 75

410 W.H.O. Building

1966. Inaug of W.H.O. Headquarters, Geneva.
2190 **410** 2fo. black and blue . . . 35 10

411 Football

1966. World Cup Football Championships (1st issue). Sheet 76 × 108 mm.
MS2191 **411** 10fo. multicoloured 3·75 5·75
See also Nos. 2194/2202.

412 Nuclear Research Institute

1966. 10th Anniv of United Nuclear Research Institute, Dubna (U.S.S.R.).
2192 **412** 60fi. black and green . . 35 10

413 Buda Fortress, after Schedel's "Chronicle" (1493)

1966. 20th Anniv of U.N.E.S.C.O. and 72nd Executive Board Session, Budapest.
2193 **413** 2fo. violet and blue . . . 35 20

414 Jules Rimet, Football and Cup

1966. World Cup Football Championship (2nd issue). Multicoloured.
2194 20fi. Type **414** 10 10
2195 30fi. Montevideo, 1930 . . . 10 10
2196 60fi. Rome, 1934 . . . . . 15 10
2197 1fo. Paris, 1938 . . . . . . 30 10
2198 1fo.40 Rio de Janeiro, 1950 35 10
2199 1fo.70 Berne, 1954 . . . . 50 10
2200 2fo. Stockholm, 1958 . . . 70 30
2201 2fo.50 Santiago de Chile, 1962 . . . . 1·00 45
2202 3fo.+1fo. World Cup emblem on Union Jack, and map of England . . . 1·25 1·25

415 Girl Pioneer and Emblem

1966. 20th Anniv of Hungarian Pioneers Movement.
2203 **415** 60fi. red and violet . . . 30 10

416 Fire Engine

1966. Centenary of Voluntary Fire Brigades.
2204 **416** 2fo. black and orange . . 60 25

417 Red Fox

1966. Hunting Trophies. Multicoloured.
2205 20fi. Type **417** 10 10
2206 60fi. Wild boar 15 10
2207 70fi. Wild cat 25 10
2208 80fi. Roe deer 25 10
2209 1fo.50 Red deer 55 10
2210 2fo.50 Fallow deer . . . . 1·25 25
2211 3fo. Mouflon . . . . 1·40 70

418 Throwing the Discus

1966. 8th European Athletic Championships, Budapest. Multicoloured.
2212 20fi. Type **418** 10 10
2213 30fi. High-jumping 10 10
2214 40fi. Throwing the javelin 20 10
2215 50fi. Throwing the hammer 25 10
2216 60fi. Long-jumping 35 25
2217 1fo. Putting the shot 60 25
2218 2fo. Pole-vaulting 95 70
2219 3fo. Running . . . . 1·25 1·60
MS2220 105 × 75 mm. 10fo. Hurdling . . . . 4·50 6·00

419 Archery **420** Helsinki

1966. Stamp Day. Multicoloured.
2221 2fo.+50fi. Types **419** . . . 75 80
2222 2fo.+50fi. Grapes 75 80
2223 2fo.+50fi. Poppies 75 80
2224 2fo.+50fi. Space dogs . . . 75 80
MS2225 98 × 84 mm. Nos. 2221/4 3·00 4·25

1966. Air.
2226 **420** 20fi. red 10 10
2227 – 50fi. brown 10 10
2228 – 1fo. blue 15 10
2229 – 1fo.10 black 20 10
2230 – 1fo.20 orange 20 10
2231 – 1fo.50 green 30 10
2232 – 2fo. blue 35 10
2233 – 2fo.50 red 40 10
2234 – 3fo. green 55 15
2235 – 4fo. brown . . . . . . 1·60 1·25
2236 – 5fo. violet 70 20
2237 – 10fo. blue . . . . 1·90 40
2238 – 20fo. green . . . . . . 3·00 60
DESIGNS—Ilyushin Il-18 over: 50fi. Athens; 1fo. Beirut; 1fo.10, Frankfurt; 1fo.20, Cairo; 1fo.50, Copenhagen; 2fo. London; 2fo.50, Moscow; 3fo. Paris; 4fo. Prague; 5fo. Rome; 10fo. Damascus; 20fo. Budapest.
For 2fo.60 in similar design see No. 2369.

421 "Girl in the Woods" (after Barabas)

1966. Paintings in Hungarian National Gallery (1st series). Multicoloured.
2239 60fi. Type **421** 30 15
2240 1fo. "Mrs. Istvan Bitto" (Barabas) 35 25
2241 1fo.50 "Laszlo Hunyadi Farewell" (Benczur) . . . 65 25
2242 1fo.70 "Woman Reading" (Benczur) (horiz) 70 25

2243 2fo. "The Faggot-carrier" (Munkacsy) 75 25
2244 2fo.50 "The Yawning Apprentice" (Munkacsy) 1·00 40
2245 3fo. "Woman in Lilac" (Szinyei) . . . . 1·50 80
MS2246 97 × 79 mm. 10fo. "Picnic in May" (Szinyei) . . . . 9·00 9·75

See also Nos. 2282/8, 2318/**MS**2325, 2357/**MS**2364, 2411/**MS**2418, 2449/**MS**2456 and 2525/**MS**2532.

422 "Vostok 3" and "Vostok 4" (Nikolaev and Popovich)

1966. Twin Space Flights. Multicoloured.
2247 20fi. Type **422** 10 10
2248 60fi. Borman and Lovell, Schirra and Stafford . . . 20 10
2249 80fi. Bykovsky and Tereshkova 20 10
2250 1fo. Stafford and Cernan . . 30 10
2251 1fo.50 Belyaev and Leonov (Leonov in space) 50 20
2252 2fo. McDivitt and White (White in space) 60 20
2253 2fo.50 Komarov, Feoktistov and Yegorov . . . . . . 1·10 30
2254 3fo. Conrad and Gordon . . 1·40 70

423 Kitaibel and "Kitaibelia vitifolia"

424 Militiaman

1967. 150th Death Anniv of Pal Kitaibel (botanist). Carpathian Flowers. Multicoloured.
2255 20fi. Type **423** 10 10
2256 60fi. "Dentaria glandulosa" 20 10
2257 1fo. "Edraianthus tenuifolius" 30 10
2258 1fo.50 "Althaea pallida" . . 50 10
2259 2fo. "Centaurea mollis" . . 65 15
2260 2fo.50 "Sternbergia colchiciflora" . . . . . . 1·25 25
2261 3fo. "Iris hungarica" . . . 1·40 75

1967. 10th Anniv of Workers' Militia.
2262 **424** 2fo. blue 30 10

425 Faustus Verancsics' Parachute Descent, 1617

1967. Air. "Aerofila 67". Airmail Stamp Exhibition, Budapest. (a) 1st issue.
2263 2fo.+1fo. sepia and yellow 85 85
2264 2fo.+1fo. sepia and blue . . 85 85
2265 2fo.+1fo. sepia and green 85 85
2266 2fo.+1fo. sepia and pink . . 85 85
MS2267 116 × 90 mm. Nos. 2263/6 3·75 4·00

(b) 2nd issue.
2268 2fo.+1fo. blue and green . . 85 85
2269 2fo.+1fo. blue and orange 85 85
2270 2fo.+1fo. blue and yellow 85 85
2271 2fo.+1fo. blue and pink . . 85 85
MS2272 116 × 90 mm. Nos. 2268/71 3·75 4·00

DESIGNS: No. 2263, Type **425**; No. 2264, David Schwartz's aluminium airship, 1897; No. 2265, Erno Horvath's monoplane, 1911; No. 2266, PKZ-2 helicopter, 1918; No. 2268, Parachutist; No. 2269, Mil Mi-1 helicopter; No. 2270, Tupolev Tu-154 airliner; No. 2271, "Luna 12".

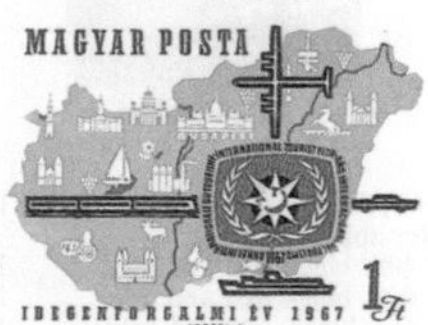

426 I.T.Y. Emblem and Transport

1967. International Tourist Year.
2273 **426** 1fo. black and blue . . . 30 10

427 "Milton", after Orial Petrics

1967. "Amphilex" Stamp Exhibition, Amsterdam. Sheet 81 × 91 mm.
MS2274 **427** 10fo. multicoloured 3·75 5·50

428 "Ferenc Deak" (paddle-steamer), Schonbuchel Castle and Austrian Flag (⅔-size illustration)

1967. 25th Session of Danube Commission. Vessels of Mahart Shipping Company.
2275 **428** 30fi. multicoloured . . . 90 15
2276 – 60fi. multicoloured . . . 1·40 30
2277 – 1fo. multicoloured . . . 2·25 35
2278 – 1fo.50 multicoloured . . 3·75 55
2279 – 1fo.70 multicoloured . . 4·75 85
2280 – 2fo. multicoloured . . . 5·00 1·70
2281 – 2fo.50 multicoloured . . 5·50 2·50

DESIGNS (Vessels, backgrounds and flags): 60fi. River-bus "Revfulop" Bratislava Castle, Czechoslovakia; 1fo. Diesel passenger boat "Hunyadi", Buda Castle, Hungary; 1fo.50, Diesel tug "Szekszard", Golubac Castle, Yugoslavia; 1fo.70, Tug "Miscolc", Vidin Castle, Bulgaria; 2fo. Motor-freighter "Tihany", Galati shipyard. Rumania; 2fo.50, Hydrofoil "Siraly I", port of Izmail, U.S.S.R.

429 "Szidonia Deak" (A. Gyorgyi)

1967. Paintings in National Gallery, Budapest (2nd series). Multicoloured.
2282 60fi. "Liszt" (M. Munkacsy) 25 25
2283 1fo. "Self-portrait" (S. Lanyi) 40 25
2284 1fo.50 "Portrait of a Lady" (J. Borsos) 50 25
2285 1fo.70 "The Lovers" (after P. Szinyei Merse) (horiz) 75 25
2286 2fo. Type **429** 80 25
2287 2fo.50 "National Guardsman" (J. Borsos) 90 25
2288 3fo. "Louis XV and Madame Dubarry" (G. Benczur) . . . . . . 1·10 50

430 Poodle

1967. Dogs. Multicoloured.
2289 30fi. Type **430** 15 10
2290 60fi. Collie (23½ × 35 mm) 25 10
2291 1fo. Pointer 35 10
2292 1fo.40 Fox terriers (23½ × 35 mm) 50 10
2293 2fo. Pumi 70 20
2294 3fo. Alsatian (23½ × 35 mm) 85 60
2295 4fo. Puli . . . . 1·40 1·00

431 Sterlet

1967. 14th International Anglers' Federation Congress, and World Angling Championships, Dunaujvaros. Multicoloured.
2296 20fi. Type **431** 10 10
2297 60fi. Zander 20 10
2298 1fo. Common carp 25 10
2299 1fo.70 Wels 65 10
2300 2fo. Northern pike 70 10
2301 2fo.50 Asp 85 55
2302 3fo.+1fo. Anglers' and C.I.P.S. (Federation) emblem . . . . 1·25 1·00

432 "Prince Igor" (Borodin)

1967. Popular Operas. Designs showing scenes from various operas. Multicoloured.
2303 20fi. Type **432** 20 10
2304 30fi. "Der Freischutz" (Weber) 20 10
2305 40fi. "The Magic Flute" (Mozart) 35 10
2306 60fi. "Bluebeard's Castle" (Bartok) 50 10
2307 80fi. "Carmen" (Bizet) (vert) 65 20
2308 1fo. "Don Carlos" (Verdi) (vert) 85 20
2309 1fo.70 "Tannhauser" (Wagner) (vert) . . . . . 1·00 45
2310 3fo. "Laszlo Hunyadi" (Erkel) (vert) . . . . . . 1·40 1·75

433 "Teaching" (14th-cent class)

1967. 600th Anniv of Higher Education in Hungary.
2311 **433** 2fo. green and gold . . . 35 10

434 Faculty Building

1967. 300th Anniv of Political Law and Science Faculty, Lorand Eotvos University, Budapest.
2312 **434** 2fo. green 35 10

435 "Lenin as Teacher"

1967. 50th Anniv of October Revolution. Multicoloured.
2313 60fi. Type **435** 20 10
2314 1fo. "Lenin" 20 10
2315 3fo. "Lenin aboard the Aurora" 55 25

436 "Venus 4"

1967. Landing of "Venus 4" on planet Venus.
2316 **436** 5fo. multicoloured . . . 90 80

437 19th-centenary Mail Coach

1967. Centenary of Hungarian Postal Administration. Sheet 85 × 95 mm.
MS2317 **437** 10fo. multicoloured 3·00 3·75

437a "Brother and Sister" (A. Fenyes)

1967. Paintings in National Gallery, Budapest (3rd series). Multicoloured.
2318 60fi. Type **437a** 20 10
2319 1fo. "Boys Wrestling on Beach" (O. Glatz) 30 10
2320 1fo.50 "October" (K. Ferenczy) 50 10
2321 1fo.70 "Women by the River" (I. Szonyi) (horiz) 55 20
2322 2fo. "Godfather's Breakfast" (I. Csok) 55 20
2323 2fo.50 "The Eviction Order" (G. Derkovits) 60 25
2324 3fo. "Self-Portrait" (T. Csontvary) 70 40
MS2325 78 × 100 mm. 10fo. "The Apple Pickers" (B. Uitz) (larger 37½ × 60 mm) . . . . 2·25 3·00

"Women by the River" (1fo.70) is in a private collection in Budapest.

See also Nos. 2357/**MS**2364 and 2411/**MS**2418.

438 Rifle-shooting on Skis

1967. Winter Olympic Games, Grenoble. Multicoloured.
2326 30fi. Type **438** 10 10
2327 60fi. Figure skating (pairs) 20 10
2328 1fo. Bobsleighing 20 10
2329 1fo.40 Downhill skiing . . . 30 10
2330 1fo.70 Figure skating . . . 40 10
2331 2fo. Speed skating 55 15
2332 3fo. Ski jumping 65 45
2333 4fo.+1fo. Ice stadium, Grenoble . . . . 1·10 80
MS2334 116 × 99 mm. 10fo. Ice hockey goal keeper (61 × 61 mm) 3·50 3·25

439 Kalman Kando, Class V43 Electric Locomotive and Map

1968. Kando Commemoration.
2335 **439** 2fo. blue 35 10

440 Cat

1968. Cats. Multicoloured.
2336 20fi. Type **440** 25 10
2337 60fi. Cream angora 30 10
2338 1fo. Smoky angora 40 20
2339 1fo.20 Domestic kitten . . . 50 20
2340 1fo.50 White angora 70 20
2341 2fo. Striped angora 80 20
2342 2fo.50 Siamese . . . . . . 1·10 40
2343 5fo. Blue angora . . . . . 1·60 1·00

441 Zoltan Kodaly (composer) **442** City Hall, Arms, Grapes and Apricot

1968. Kodaly Commemoration.
2344 **441** 5fo. multicoloured . . . 1·10 65

1968. 600th Anniv of Kecskemet.
2345 **442** 2fo. brown 35 10

443 White Stork **444** Karl Marx

1968. International Council for Bird Preservation Congress, Budapest. Protected Birds. Mult.
2346 20fi. Type **443** 20 10
2347 50fi. Golden orioles 30 10
2348 60fi. Imperial eagle 35 15
2349 1fo. Western red-footed falcons 40 15
2350 1fo.20 Eurasian scops owl 55 20
2351 1fo.50 Great bustard 70 30
2352 2fo. European bee eaters . . 1·40 35
2353 2fo.50 Greylag goose . . . 1·75 85

1968. 150th Birth Anniv of Karl Marx.
2354 **444** 1fo. purple 15 10
See also No. 1290.

445 Icarus falling in space **446** Student

1968. In Memoriam. Astronauts White, Gagarin and Komarov. Sheet 95 × 77 mm.
MS2355 **445** 10fo. multicoloured 3·00 3·75

1968. 150th Anniv of Mosonmagyarovar Agricultural College.
2356 **446** 2fo. green 35 10

1968. Paintings in National Gallery, Budapest (4th series). As T **437a**. Multicoloured.
2357 40fi. "Girl with a Pitcher" (Goya) 10 10
2358 60fi. "Head of an Apostle" (El Greco) 20 10
2359 1fo. "Boy with Apples" (Nunez) (horiz) 25 10
2360 1fo.50 "The Repentant Magdalen" (El Greco) . . 35 25
2361 2fo.50 "The Breakfast" (Velasquez) (horiz) . . . 70 25

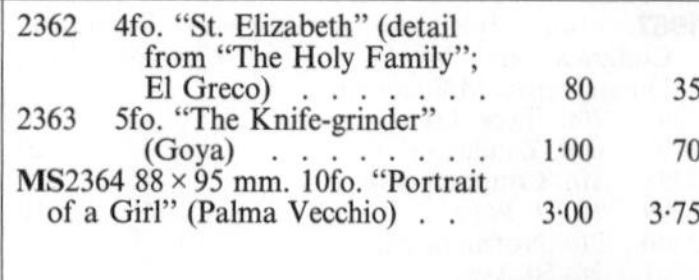

2362 4fo. "St. Elizabeth" (detail from "The Holy Family"; El Greco) 80 35
2363 5fo. "The Knife-grinder" (Goya) . . . . 1·00 70
MS2364 88 × 95 mm. 10fo. "Portrait of a Girl" (Palma Vecchio) . . 3·00 3·75

447 Lake Steamer, Flags and Badacsony Hills **448** Ilyushin Il-18 over St. Stephen's Cathedral, Vienna

1968. Lake Balaton Resorts. Multicoloured.
2365 20fi. Type **447** 15 10
2365a 40fi. Type **447** 15 10
2366 60fi. Tihany peninsula, tower and feather . . . 15 10
2367 1fo. Yachts and buoy, Balatonalmadi 15 10
2368 2fo. Szigliget bay, vineyard, wine and fish 35 15

1968. Air. 50th Anniv of Budapest–Vienna Airmail Service.
2369 **448** 2fo.60 violet 60 15

449 Class 424 Steam Locomotive No. 176 **451** M. Tompa

450 Grazing Stud

1968. Centenary of Hungarian State Railways.
2370 **449** 2fo. multicoloured . . . 1·10 30

1968. Horse-breeding on the Hortobagy "puszta" (Hungarian steppe). Multicoloured.
2371 30fi. Type **450** 15 10
2372 40fi. Horses in storm . . . 15 10
2373 60fi. Grooms horse-racing 20 10
2374 80fi. Horse-drawn sleigh . . 30 10
2375 1fo. Four-in-hand 40 10
2376 1fo.40 Seven-in-hand . . . 55 10
2377 2fo. Driving five horses . . 60 10
2378 2fo.50 Groom preparing evening meal 65 35
2379 4fo. Five-in-hand . . . . . 1·10 75

1968. Death Centenary of Mihaly Tompa (poet).
2380 **451** 60fi. violet 10 10

452 Festival Emblem, Bulgarian and Hungarian Couples in National Costume

1968. 9th World Youth Festival, Sofia.
2381 **452** 60fi. multicoloured . . . 20 10

453 Breasting the Tape

454 Swimming

1968. Air. Olympic Games, Mexico. Mult.
MS2382 81 × 101 mm **453** 10fo. multicoloured (postage) . . . . 3·00 3·75

2383 20fi. Type **454**(air) 10 10
2384 60fi. Football 10 10
2385 80fi. Wrestling 10 10
2386 1fo. Canoeing 10 10
2387 1fo.40 Gymnastics 30 10
2388 2fo.+1fo. Horse-jumping . . 60 40
2389 3fo. Fencing 85 30
2390 4fo. Throwing the Javelin 1·25 55

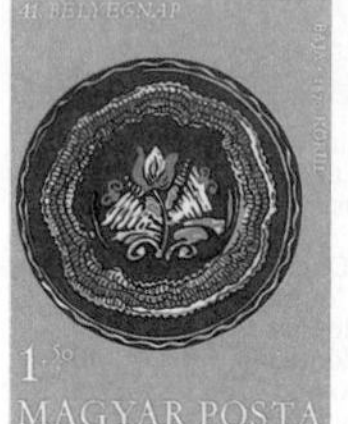

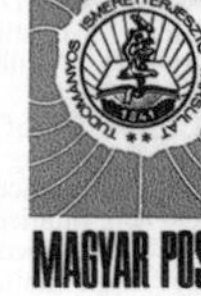

455 Baja Plate, 1870 **456** Society Emblem

1968. Stamp Day. Hungarian Ceramics. Mult.
2391 1fo.+50fi. Type **455** 55 65
2392 1fo.+50fi. West Hungarian jug, 1618 . . . . 55 65
2393 1fo.+50fi. Tiszafured flagon, 1847 . . . . 55 65
2394 1fo.+50fi. Mezocsat flask, 1848 . . . . 55 65
MS2395 74 × 96 mm. 2fo.+50fi. North Hungarian jug, 1672; 2fo.+50fi. Mezocsat plate, 1843; 2fo.+50fi. Moragy plate, 1860; 2fo.+50fi. Debrecen pitcher, 1793 3·00 3·75
The designs from the miniature sheet are smaller, measuring 25 × 35 mm.

1968. "Hungarian Society for Popularization of Scientific Knowledge".
2396 **456** 2fo. black and blue . . . 30 10

457 Rocket Hesperus **459** "Workers of the World Unite" (Bertalan Por's 1918 poster)

458 Two Girls waving Flags

1968. Garden Flowers. Multicoloured.
2397 20fi. Type **457** 15 10
2398 60fi. Pansy 30 10
2399 80fi. Zinnias 45 10
2400 1fo. Morning Glory 65 25
2401 1fo.40 Petunia 85 25
2402 1fo.50 Purslane 90 25
2403 2fo. Michaelmas daisies . . 1·10 35
2404 2fo.50 Dahlia . . . . 1·25 90

1968. Children's Stamp Designs for 50th Anniv of Hungarian Communist Party. Multicoloured.
2405 40fi. Type **458** 35 10
2406 60fi. Children with flags and banner 45 10
2407 1fo. Pioneer bugler in camp 55 15

1968. 50th Anniv of Hungarian Communist Party.
2408 **459** 1fo. black, red and gold 15 10
2409 – 2fo. multicoloured . . . 15 10
DESIGN—HORIZ: 2fo. "Martyrs" (statue by Zoltan Kiss).

460 Human Rights Emblem **461** Endre Ady

1968. Human Rights Year.
2410 **460** 1fo. brown 30 10

1968. Paintings in National Gallery, Budapest (5th series). Italian Masters. As T **437a**. Mult.
2411 40fi. "Esterhazy Madonna" (Raphael) 10 10
2412 60fi. "The Annunciation" (Strozzi) 10 10
2413 1fo. "Portrait of a Young Man" (Raphael) 15 10
2414 1fo.50 "The Three Graces" (Naldini) 30 10
2415 2fo.50 "Portrait of a Man" (Sebastian del Piombo) . . 55 35
2416 4fo. "The Doge Marcantonio Trevisani" (Titian) 85 55
2417 5fo. "Venus, Cupid and Jealousy" (Bronzino) . . 1·25 90
MS2418 116 × 73 mm. 10fo. "Bathsheba bathing" (Ricci). Imperf . . . . 3·00 4·00

1969. 50th Death Anniv of Endre Ady (poet).
2419 **461** 1fo. black, purple & gold 20 10

462 Press Emblem **463** "Apollo 8" entering Moon Orbit

1969. Centenary of Athenaeum Press.
2420 **462** 2fo. multicoloured . . . 30 10

1969. Air. Moon Flight of "Apollo 8". Sheet 111 × 81 mm.
MS2421 **463** 10fo. multicoloured 3·00 3·75

464 Throwing the Javelin

1969. Olympic Gold Medal Winners. Mult.
2422 40fi. Type **464** 10 10
2423 60fi. Canoeing 10 10
2424 1fo. Football 15 10
2425 1fo.20 Throwing the Hammer 15 10
2426 2fo. Fencing 30 10
2427 3fo. Wrestling 55 10
2428 4fo. Kayak-canoeing 80 20
2429 5fo. Horse-jumping . . . . 1·10 70
MS2430 111 × 84 mm. 10fo. Ancient Greek Athlete and Olympic Flame 3·75 4·50

465 Poster by O. Danko

1969. 50th Anniv of Proclamation of Hungarian Soviet Republic.
2431 **465** 40fi. black, red and gold 10 10
2432 – 60fi. black, red and gold 10 10
2433 – 1fo. black, red and gold 10 10
2434 – 2fo. multicoloured . . . 10 10
2435 – 3fo. multicoloured . . . 25 20
MS2436 97 × 71 mm. 10fo. black, red and grey . . . . 2·25 2·50

DESIGNS: 60fi. "Lenin" by unknown artist; 1fo. "Young Man Breaking Chains" (R. Steiner); 2fo. "Worker" (I. Foldes and G. Vegh); 3fo. "Soldier" (unknown artist). HORIZ—(52 × 40 mm): 10fo. "Workers with Banner" (R. Bereny).

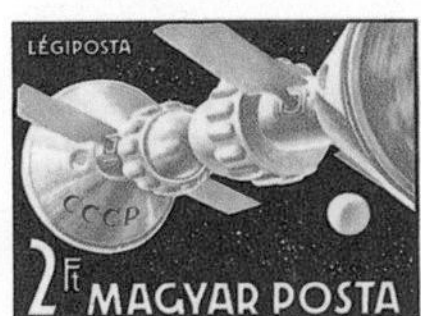

466 Space Link-up of "Soyuz 4" and "Soyuz 5"

1969. Air. Space Flights of "Soyuz 4" and "Soyuz 5". Multicoloured.
2437 2fo. Type **466** 40 40
2438 2fo. Link-up and astronauts "walking" in Space . . . 40 40

467 Jersey Tiger Moth

1969. Butterflies and Moths. Multicoloured.
2439 40fi. Type **467** 25 10
2440 60fi. Eyed hawk moth . . . 25 10
2441 80fi. Painted lady 25 10
2442 1fo. Foxy charaxes 30 10
2443 1fo.20 Lesser fiery copper 40 10
2444 2fo. Large blue 75 20
2445 3fo. Dark crimson underwing . . . . 1·10 50
2446 4fo. Peacock . . . . 1·25 85

468 I.L.O. Emblem

1969. 50th Anniv of Int Labour Organisation.
2447 **468** 1fo. brown and red . . . 20 10

469 Chain Bridge, Budapest

1969. "Budapest 71" Stamp Exhibition.
2448 **469** 5fo.+2fo. multicoloured 1·10 1·40

470 "Black Pigs" (Gauguin)

1969. Paintings in National Gallery, Budapest (6th series). French Masters. Multicoloured.
2449 40fi. Type **470** 10 10
2450 60fi. "The Ladies" (Toulouse-Lautrec) (horiz) 10 10
2451 1fo. "Venus on Clouds" (Vouet) 15 10
2452 2fo. "Lady with Fan" (Manet) (horiz) 35 10
2453 3fo. "Petra Camara" (Chasseriau) 80 15
2454 4fo. "The Cowherd" (Troyon) (horiz) . . . . 1·10 20
2455 5fo. "The Wrestlers" (Courbet) . . . . 1·50 55
MS2456 75 × 97 mm. 10fo. "Pomona" (Fouche) . . . . . 3·00 3·75

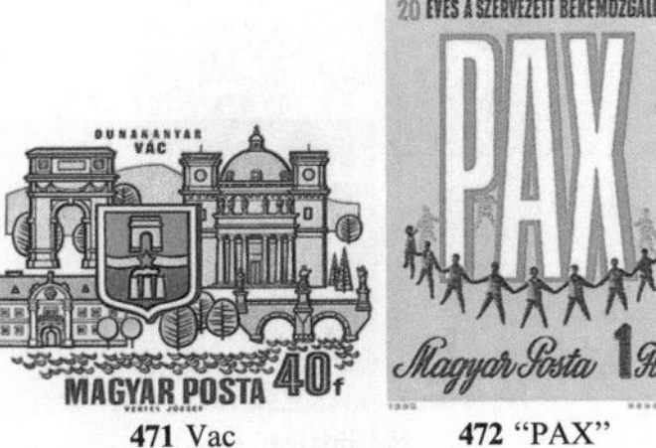

471 Vac **472** "PAX"

1969. Danube Towns. Multicoloured.
2457 40fi. Type **471** 10 10
2458 1fo. Szentendre 20 10
2459 1fo.20 Visegrad 25 10
2460 3fo. Esztergom 50 10

1969. 20th Anniv of Int Peace Movement.
2461 **472** 1fo. gold, dp blue & blue 20 10

473 Astronauts on Moon (½-size illustration)

1969. Air. First Man on the Moon (1st issue). Sheet 133 × 89 mm.
MS2462 **473** 10fo. multicoloured 4·50 5·50
See also Nos. 2487/94.

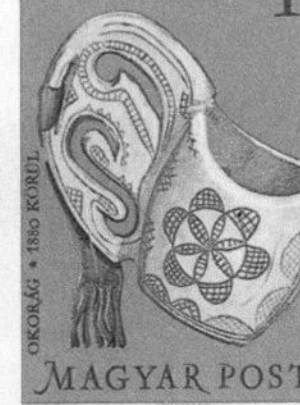

474 Zelkova Leaf (fossil) **475** Okorag Stirrupcup, 1880

1969. Centenary of Hungarian Geological Institute. Minerals and Fossils. Multicoloured.
2463 40fi. Type **474** 15 10
2464 60fi. Greenockite calcite sphalerite crystals 20 10
2465 1fo. Hungarian herring (fossilized fish) 25 10
2466 1fo.20 Quartz crystals . . . 25 10
2467 2fo. "Reineckia crassicostata" (ammonite) 35 10
2468 3fo. Copper ore 55 20
2469 4fo. "Placochelys placodonta" (fossilized turtle) . . . . 1·25 60
2470 5fo. Cuprite crystals . . . . 1·60 95

1969. Stamp Day. Hungarian Folk Art. Wood-carvings. Multicoloured.
2471 1fo.+50fi. Type **475** 55 65
2472 1fo.+50fi. Felsotizavidek jar, 1898 . . . . 55 65
2473 1fo.+50fi. Somogyharsagy pot, 1935 . . . . 55 65
2474 1fo.+50fi. Alfold smoking-pipe, 1740 . . . . 55 65
MS2475 75 × 96 mm. 2fo.+50fi. × 4 (a) Csorna panel, 1879; (b) Okany mug, 1914; (c) Sellye casket, 1899; (d) Lengyeltoti box, 1880 . . . 2·25 2·50
The designs in **MS**2475 are smaller, each 31 × 40 mm.

476 "The Scientist at his Table" (Rembrandt)

1969. Int "History of Art" Congress, Budapest.
2476 **476** 1fo. sepia 30 10

477 Horse-jumping

1969. World Pentathlon Championships, Budapest. Multicoloured.
2477 40fi. Type **477** 25 10
2478 60fi. Fencing 30 10
2479 1fo. Pistol-shooting 50 25
2480 2fo. Swimming 70 25
2481 3fo. Running 90 25
2482 5fo. All five sports . . . . 1·25 95

478 Postcard and Letterbox

1969. Centenary of 1st Hungarian Postcard.
2483 **478** 60fi. ochre and red . . . 10 10

479 Mahatma Gandhi **481** "Janos Nagy" (self-portrait)

480 Hemispheres

1969. Birth Centenary of Mahatma Gandhi.
2484 **479** 5fo. multicoloured . . . 1·25 65

1969. World Trade Unions Federations Congress, Budapest.
2485 **480** 2fo. blue and brown . . 25 10

1969. 50th Death Anniv of Janos Nagy (painter).
2486 **481** 5fo. multicoloured . . . 90 30

482 "Flight to the Moon" (after Jules Verne)

1969. Air. 1st Man on the Moon (2nd issue). Multicoloured.
2487 40fi. Type **482** 10 10
2488 60fi. Tsiolkovsky's "space station" 10 10
2489 1fo. "Luna 1" 20 10
2490 1fo.50 "Ranger 7" 35 10
2491 2fo. "Luna 9" 50 10
2492 2fo.50 "Apollo 8" 55 15
2493 3fo. "Soyuz 4" and "5" . . 70 15
2494 4fo. "Apollo 10" . . . . . 1·10 40

483 "St John the Evangelist" (Van Dyck)

1969. Dutch Paintings in Hungarian Museums. Multicoloured.
2495 40fi. Type **483** 10 10
2496 60fi. "Peasants" (P. de Molyn) 10 10
2497 1fo. "Boy lighting Pipe" (H. Terbruggen) 25 10
2498 2fo. "The Musicians" (detail, Jan Steen) 45 10
2499 3fo. "Woman reading Letter" (P. de Hooch) . . 75 15
2500 4fo. "The Fiddler" (Dirk Hals) 90 30
2501 5fo. "J. Asselyn" (Frans Hals) . . . . 1·25 55
MS2502 73 × 97 mm. 10fo. "Mucius Scaevola before Porsenna" (Rubens and Van Dyck) . . . 3·00 3·25

484 Kiskunfelegyhaza Pigeon

1969. International Pigeon Exn, Budapest.
2503 **484** 1fo. multicoloured . . . 30 10

485 Daimler (1886)

1970. Air. Old Motor Cars. Multicoloured.
2504 40fi. Type **485** 20 10
2505 60fi. Peugeot (1894) 25 10
2506 1fo. Benz (1901) 30 10
2507 1fo.50 Cudell (1902) 40 25
2508 2fo. Rolls-Royce (1908) . . 60 25
2509 2fo.50 Ford "T" (1908) . . 80 25
2510 3fo. Vermorel (1912) . . . . 1·10 50
2511 4fo. Csonka (1912) . . . . 1·40 1·25

100 ÉVES A MAGYAR BÉLYEG

486 View of Budapest **487** "Soyuz 6, 7, 8"

1970. "Budapest 71" Stamp Exhibition and Centenary of Hungarian Stamps (1st series). Multicoloured. Background colours given.
2512 **486** 2fo.+1fo. brown 50 55
2513 – 2fo.+1fo. lilac 50 55
2514 – 2fo.+1fo. blue 50 55
DESIGNS: Nos. 2513/4 show different views of Budapest, in style as Type **486**.
See also Nos. 2572/**MS**2576 and 2604/**MS**2608.

1970. Air. Space Exploration. Multicoloured.
2515 3fo.(× 4) Type **487** . . . . 2·25 2·25
2516 3fo.(× 4) Astronauts on Moon ("Apollo 12") . . . 2·25 2·25
Nos. 2515/6 were only available each in small sheets of four, and are priced thus.

489 Budapest Panorama, 1945 (-size illustration)

1970. 25th Anniv of Liberation. Sheet 159 × 83 mm containing T **489** and similar horiz design. Multicoloured.
MS2518 5fo. × 2 (a) Type **489**; (b) Budapest panorama, 1970 . . 3·00 3·75

488 Underground Train at Station

1970. Opening of Budapest Underground Railway.
2517 **488** 1fo. blue, turquoise & blk 35 10

490 Cloud Formation, Satellite and Globe **491** Lenin

1970. Cent of Hungarian Meteorological Service.
2519 **490** 1fo. multicoloured . . . 30 10

1970. Birth Centenary of Lenin. Mult.
2520 1fo. Lenin Statue, Budapest 10 10
2521 2fo. Type **491** 10 10

492 Lehar and Music

1970. Birth Cent of Franz Lehar (composer).
2522 **492** 2fo. multicoloured . . . 50 25

493 Fujiyama and Hungarian Pavilion

1970. Air. Expo 70. Multicoloured.
2523 2fo. Type **493** 55 55
2524 3fo. Tower of the Sun and Peace Bell 55 55

494 "Samson and Delilah" (M. Rocca)

1970. Paintings in National Gallery, Budapest (7th series). Multicoloured.
2525 40fi. Type **494** 10 10
2526 60fi. "Joseph's Dream" (G. B. Langetti) 15 10
2527 1fo. "Clio" (P. Mignard) . . 20 10
2528 1fo.50 "Venus and Satyr" (S. Ricci) (horiz.) 25 10
2529 2fo.50 "Andromeda" (F. Furini) 55 15
2530 4fo. "Venus, Adonis and Cupid" (L. Giordano) . . 90 35
2531 5fo. "Allegory" (woman) (C. Giaquinto) . . . . . 1·10 70
MS2532 100×85 mm. 10fo. "Diane and Callisto" (Janssens) (horiz) 3·00 3·25
The design of **MS**2532 is larger, 64×46 mm.

495 "Apollo 13" over Moon

1970. Air. Space Flight of "Apollo 13". Sheet 112×90 mm containing T **495** and three other similar horiz designs. Multicoloured.
MS2533 2fo.50 ×4 (a) Type **495**; (b) In flight; (c) Descent; (d) In sea 2·50 2·75

496 Beethoven (from statue at Martonvasar) **497** Foundryman

1970. Birth Bicentenary of Beethoven.
2534 **496** 1fo. green, lilac & yellow 90 25

1970. Bicent of Diosgyor Foundry, Miskolc.
2535 **497** 1fo. multicoloured . . . 25 10

498 St. Stephen **500** Illuminated Initial

499 Rowing Four

1970. 1,000th Birth Anniv of St. Stephen (King Stephen I of Hungary).
2536 **498** 3fo. multicoloured . . . 60 25

1970. 17th European Women's Rowing Championships, Lake Tata.
2537 **499** 1fo. multicoloured . . . 35 10

1970. Stamp Day. Paintings and Illuminated Initials from Codices of King Matthias.
2538 1fo.+50fi. Type **500** 55 65
2539 1fo.+50fi. "N" and flowers 55 65
2540 1fo.+50fi. "O" and ornamentation 55 65
2541 1fo.+50fi. "King Matthias" 55 65
MS2542 66×86 mm. 2fo.+50fi. ×4 (a) "Bishop Ransanus with King Matthias and Queen Beatrix"; (b) "Q" and "Old Humanist"; (c) "C" and "Appianus of Alexandria"; (d) "A" and "King David on Throne" . . . . 3·25 4·00

501 "Soyuz 9" on Transporter

1970. Air. "Soyuz 9" Space Mission. Sheet 108×87 mm containing T **501** and three similar horiz designs. Multicoloured.
MS2543 2fo.50 ×4 (a) Type **501**; (b) Launch; (c) In flight; (d) Cosmonauts . . . . 2·50 2·75

502 "Bread" (sculpture by I. Szabo) and F.A.O. Emblem

1970. 7th F.A.O. European Regional Conference, Budapest.
2544 **502** 1fo. multicoloured . . . 20 10

503 Boxing

1970. 75th Anniv of Hungarian Olympic Committee. Multicoloured.
2545 40fi. Type **503** 10 10
2546 60fi. Canoeing 10 10
2547 1fo. Fencing 10 10
2548 1fo.50 Water-polo 20 10
2549 2fo. Gymnastics 45 10
2550 2fo.50 Throwing the Hammer 50 20
2551 3fo. Wrestling 55 30
2552 5fo. Swimming 90 70

504 Family and "Flame of Knowledge"

1970. 5th Education Congress, Budapest.
2553 **504** 1fo. blue, green & orange 20 10

505 Chalice of Benedek Suky, c. 1400

1970. Goldsmiths' Craft. Treasures from Budapest National Museum and Esztergom Treasury. Multicoloured.
2554 40fi. Type **505** 10 10
2555 60fi. Altar-cruet, c. 1500 . . 10 10
2556 1fo. "Nadasdy" goblet, 16th-century 20 10
2557 1fo.50 Coconut goblet with gold case, c. 1600 . . . . 25 10
2558 2fo. Silver tankard of M. Toldalaghy, c. 1623 40 10
2559 2fo.50 Communion-cup of G.I. Rakoczi, c. 1670 . . 60 15
2560 3fo. Tankard, c. 1690 . . . 80 25
2561 4fo. "Bell-flower" cup, c. 1710 . . . . . . 1·25 75

506 "The Virgin and Child" ("Giampietrino", G. Pedrini)

1970. Paintings. Religious Art from Christian Museum, Esztergom. Multicoloured.
2562 40fi. Type **506** 10 10
2563 60fi. "Love" (G. Lazzarini) 10 10
2564 1fo. "Legend of St. Catherine of Alexandria" ("Master of Bat") 15 10
2565 1fo.50 "Adoration of the Shepherds" (F. Fontebasso) (horiz.) 30 10
2566 2fo.50 "Adoration of the Magi" ("Master of Aranyosmarot") 65 20
2567 4fo. "Temptation of St. Anthony the Hermit" (J. de Cock) . . . . . . 1·00 30
2568 5fo. "St. Sebastian" (Palmezzano) . . . . . . 1·10 70
MS2569 72×84 mm. 10fo. "The Maid and the Unicorn" (unknown Lombard painter) . . . . . . 3·25 4·00

507 Mauthausen Camp Memorial (A. Makrisz)

1970. 25th Anniv of Liberation of Concentration Camps.
2570 **507** 1fo. brown and blue . . 30 10

508 "Luna 16" in Flight

1971. Air. "Luna 16" Space Mission. Sheet 108×87 mm containing T **508** and three other similar horiz designs. Multicoloured.
MS2571 2fo.50 ×4 (a) Type **508**; (b) Parachute landing; (c) On Moon's surface; (d) Nosecone . . . . 2·50 2·75

509 Budapest, 1470

1971. "Budapest 71" Stamp Exhibition and Centenary of Hungarian Stamps (2nd series). "Budapest Through the Ages".
2572 **509** 2fo.+1fo. black & yell 50 65
2573 – 2fo.+1fo. black & mve 50 65
2574 – 2fo.+1fo. black & grn . . 50 65
2575 – 2fo.+1fo. black & orge 50 65
MS2576 110×75 mm. 2fo.+1fo. ×4 (a) black and orange; (b) black and pale green; (c) black and violet; (d) black and mauve . . 2·25 2·50
DESIGNS: Budapest in: No. 2573, 1600; No. 2574, 1638; No. 2575, 1770. Smaller (40×18 mm)—No. **MS**2575, Budapest in (a) 1777, (b) 1850, (c) 1895, (d) 1970.

510 "Lunokhod 1" on Module

1971. Air. Moon Mission of "Luna 17" and "Lunokhod 2". Sheet 108×87 mm containing T **510** and three other similar horiz designs. Multicoloured.
MS2577 2fo.50 ×4 (a) Type **510**; (b) "Luna 17" leaving Earth; (c) "Luna 17" nearing Moon; (d) "Lunokhod 1" on Moon's surface 2·50 2·75

511 "The Marseillaise" (sculpture by Rude) **512** Bela Bartok

1971. Centenary of Paris Commune.
2578 **511** 3fo. brown and green . . 50 20

1971. 90th Birth Anniv of Bela Bartok (composer).
2579 **512** 1fo. black, grey and red 90 10

513 Gyor in 1594

1971. 700th Anniv of Gyor.
2580 **513** 2fo. multicoloured . . . 35 10

514 Astronauts on Moon

1971. Air. "Apollo 14" Moon Mission. Sheet 120×70 mm.
MS2581 **514** 10fo. multicoloured 3·00 3·75

1971. Birth Centenary of Andras L. Achim (peasant leader). Portrait in similar style to T **512**.
2582 1fo. black, grey and green 20 10

516 Hunting European Bison

1971. World Hunting Exhibition, Budapest. Multicoloured.
2583 40fi. Type **516**(postage) . . 15 10
2584 60fi. Hunting wild boar . . 15 10
2585 80fi. Deer-stalking 30 20
2586 1fo. Falconry 95 25
2587 1fo.20 Stag-hunting 60 30
2588 2fo. Great bustards with young . . . . 1·60 55
2589 3fo. Netting fish . . . . . 1·00 65
2590 4fo. Angling . . . . 1·40 80

MS2591 145×100mm. 10fo. Herd of roe deer (air) . . . . 2·25 2·50
The design of the 10fo. is larger, 72×46 mm.

517 "Portrait of a Man" (Durer)

1971. 500th Birth Anniv of Albrecht Durer (artist). Sheet 80×100 mm.
MS2592 **517** 10fo. multicoloured 2·25 2·50

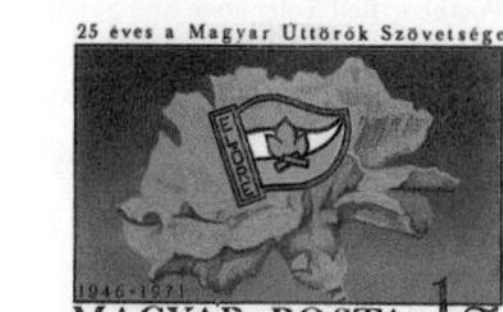

518 Emblem on Flower

1971. 25th Anniv of Hungarian Young Pioneers.
2593 **518** 1fo. multicoloured . . . 45 10

519 F.I.R. Emblem

1971. 20th Anniv of International Federation of Resistance Fighters.
2594 **519** 1fo. multicoloured . . . 45 10

520 "Walking in the Garden" (Toyokuni School)

1971. Japanese Colour Prints from Ferenc Hopp Collection, Budapest. Multicoloured.
2595 40fi. Type **520** 10 10
2596 60fi. "Geisha in boat" (Yeishi) 15 10
2597 1fo. "Woman with scroll-painting" (Yeishi) 25 10
2598 1fo.50 "Oirans" (Kiyonaga) 40 10
2599 2fo. "Awabi Fishers" (Utamaro) 50 25
2600 2fo.50 "Scated Oiran" (Harunobu) 60 25
2601 3fo. "Peasant Girl carrying Faggots" (Hokusai) . . . 95 30
2602 4fo. "Women and Girls Walking" (Yeishi) . . . . 1·10 90

521 Locomotive "Bets" and Route Map (1846)

1971. 125th Anniv of Hungarian Railways.
2603 **521** 1fo. multicoloured . . . 50 10

522 Hungarian Newspaper Stamp of 1871

1971. "Budapest 71" Stamp Exhibition and Centenary of Hungarian Stamps (3rd series). Mult.
2604 2fo.+1fo. Type **522** 35 45
2605 2fo.+1fo. 45f. "Petofi" stamp of 1919 . . . . . 35 45
2606 2fo.+1fo. 40k. "Harvesters" stamp of 1920 . . . . . 35 45
2607 2fo.+1fo. 16f.+16f. "Art" stamp of 1940 . . . . . 35 45
MS2608 115×99 mm. 2fo.+1fo. ×4 (a) 60f.+60f. "Liberty" stamp of 1947; (b) 2fo. "Costume" stamp of 1953; (c) 2fo. Air stamp of 1958; (d) 1fo. "Space" stamp of 1965 3·00 3·25

523 Griffin with Inking Balls

1971. Cent of State Printing Office, Budapest.
2609 **523** 1fo. multicoloured . . . 35 40

524 O.I.J. Emblem and Page of "Magyar Sajto"

1971. 25th Anniv of Int Organisation of Journalists.
2610 **524** 1fo. gold and blue . . . 20 10

525 Volkov, Dobrovolsky and Patsaev (½-size illustration)

1971. Air. "Soyuz 11" Cosmonauts Memorial Issue. Sheet 133×90 mm.
MS2611 **525** 10fo. multicoloured 3·00 4·00

526 J. Winterl (founder) and "Waldsteinia geoides"

1971. Bicentenary of Botanical Gardens, Budapest. Multicoloured.
2612 40fi. Type **526** 10 10
2613 60fi. "Bromeliaceae" 15 10
2614 80fi. "Titanopsis calcarea" . . 20 10
2615 1fo. "Vinca herbacea" . . . 25 10
2616 1fo.20 "Gymnocalycium mihanovichii" 25 10
2617 2fo. "Nymphaea gigantea" . 45 10
2618 3fo. "Iris arenaria" 75 30
2619 5fo. "Paeonia banatica" . . 1·25 75

527 Horse-racing

1971. Equestrian Sport. Multicoloured.
2620 40fi. Type **527** 15 10
2621 60fi. Trotting 20 10
2622 80fi. Cross-country riding 20 10
2623 1fo. Show-jumping 25 10
2624 1fo.20 Start of race 30 10
2625 2fo. Polo 55 10
2626 3fo. Steeplechasing 85 25
2627 5fo. Dressage . . . . 1·40 75

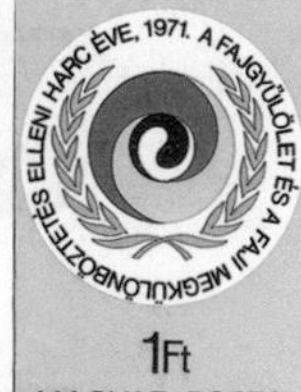

528 "Execution of Koppany"

529 Racial Equality Year Emblem

1971. Miniatures from the "Illuminated Chronicle" of King Lajos I of Hungary. Multicoloured.
2628 40fi. Type **528** 15 10
2629 60fi. "The Pursuit of King Peter" 15 10
2630 1fo. "Bazarad's Victory over King Karoly I" 20 10
2631 1fo.50 "The Strife between King Salamon and Prince Geza" 35 10
2632 2fo.50 "The Founding of Obuda Monastery by King Stephen and Queen Gisela" 55 15
2633 4fo. "Reconciliation of King Kalman and his brother, Almos" 75 25
2634 5fo. "King Ladislas I supervising the construction of Nagyvarad Church" . . . 1·10 50
MS2635 84×87 mm. 10fo. "The Funeral of Prince Emeric and the Binding of Vazul" . . . . . . 3·00 3·00
The design of the 10fo. is larger, 51×60 mm.

1971. Racial Equality Year.
2636 **529** 1fo. multicoloured . . . 20 10

530 Ice Hockey

1971. Winter Olympic Games, Sapporo, Japan (1972). Multicoloured.
2637 40fi. Type **530** 10 10
2638 60fi. Downhill skiing . . . 20 10
2639 80fi. Figure skating (female) 20 10
2640 1fo. Ski jumping 25 10
2641 1fo.20 Cross-country skiing 35 10
2642 2fo. Figure skating (male) 50 10
2643 3fo. Bobsleighing 60 25
2644 4fo. Rifle-shooting (Biathlon) . . . . 1·00 60
MS2645 133×89 mm. 10fo. Buddha 3·25 4·00
The design of the 10fo. is larger, 89×51 mm.

531 Astronauts aboard Moon Rover (-size illustration)

1972. Air. Moon Flight of "Apollo 15". Sheet 120×76 mm.
MS2646 **531** 10fo. multicoloured 3·00 3·25

532 Class 303, 1950

1972. Railway Steam Locomotives. Mult.
2647 40fi. Type **532** 25 10
2648 60fi. Class P6, 1902, Prussia 25 10
2649 80fi. Class 380, 1894, Italy 35 15
2650 1fo. Class P36, 1950, Russia 55 15
2651 1fo.20 Heisler locomotive, Japan 60 30
2652 2fo. Scottish Caledonian tank locomotive, 1837 . . 80 35
2653 4fo. Class 166, 1882, Austria 1·10 70
2654 5fo. Locomotive "Continent", 1854 . . . . 1·40 90

533 "J. Pannonius" (A. Mantegna)

535 Doorway of Csempeszkopacs Church

534 "Mariner 9"

1972. 500th Death Anniv of Janus Pannonius (poet).
2655 **533** 1fo. multicoloured . . . 15 10

1972. Exploration of Mars. Multicoloured.
2656 2fo. Type **534** 45 45
2657 2fo. "Mars 2 and 3" 45 45

1972. Protection of Monuments.
2658 **535** 3fo. green 75 15

536 Hungarian Greyhound

1972. Dogs. Multicoloured.

2659	40fi. Type **536**	15	10
2660	60fi. Afghan hound (head)	20	10
2661	80fi. Irish wolfhound	20	10
2662	1fo.20 Borzoi (head)	25	10
2663	2fo. Greyhound	50	20
2664	4fo. Whippet (head)	1·10	35
2665	6fo. Afghan hound	1·60	85

537 J. Imre, E. Grosz and L. Blaskovics

1972. 1st. European Oculists' Congress, Budapest. Famous Oculists.

2666	**537** 1fo. brown and red	75	10
2667	– 2fo. brown and blue	1·10	30

DESIGN: 2fo. A. Gullstrand, V. P. Filatov and J. Gonin.

538 Footballers and Flag of Hungary

1972. Air. European Football Championships. Footballers and Flags of participating countries. Multicoloured.

2668	40fi. Type **538**	10	10
2669	60fi. Rumania	15	10
2670	80fi. West Germany	20	10
2671	1fo. England	30	15
2672	1fo.20 Yugoslavia	40	15
2673	2fo. Russia	55	20
2674	4fo. Italy	85	75
2675	5fo. Belgium	1·10	1·10

539 "V. Miskolcz" postmark, 1818–43

1972. Stamp Day.

2676	**539** 2fo.+1fo. black & blue	55	70
2677	– 2fo.+1fo. black & yell	55	70
2678	– 2fo.+1fo. black & grn	55	70
2679	– 2fo.+1fo. mult	55	70

MS2680 105 × 90 mm. 2fo.+1fo. × 4 (a) Wax impression of signet ring, 1953; (b) Letter of Rakoczi era, 1705; (c) Courier letter of 1708; (d) V. Tokai postmark, 1752 . . . 3·25 3·45

DESIGNS: No. 2677, "Szegedin" postmark, 1827–48; 2678, "Esztergom" postmark, 1848–51; 2679, "Budapest 71" stamp cent, cancellation, 1971.

540 Girl reading Book

541 Roses

1972. International Book Year.
2681 **540** 1fo. multicoloured . . . 20 10

1972. National Rose Exhibition.
2682 **541** 1fo. multicoloured . . . 35 10

542 Globe and Olympic Rings (-size illustration)

1972. Air. Olympic Games, Munich (1st issue). Sheet 117 × 68 mm.
MS2683 **542** 10fo. multicoloured 6·75 8·50
See also Nos. 2687/**MS**2695.

543 G. Dimitrov

544 "St. Martin and the Beggar"

1972. 90th Birth Anniv of Georgi Dimitrov (Bulgarian leader).
2684 **543** 3fo. multicoloured . . . 30 15

1972. "Belgica '72" Stamp Exhibition, Brussels. Sheet 69 × 94 mm.
MS2685 **544** 10fo. multicoloured 3·00 3·75

545 Gy. Dozsa

1972. 500th Birth Anniv of Gyorgy Dozsa (revolutionary).
2686 **545** 1fo. multicoloured . . . 20 10

546 Football

1972. Olympic Games, Munich (2nd issue). Multicoloured.

2687	40fi. Type **546**(postage)	10	10
2688	60fi. Water-polo	10	10
2689	80fi. Javelin-throwing	15	10
2690	1fo. Kayak-canoeing	20	10
2691	1fo.20 Boxing	30	10
2692	2fo. Gymnastics	50	10
2693	3fo.+1fo. Wrestling	75	35
2694	5fo. Fencing	1·10	60

MS2695 115 × 90 mm. 10fo. Show-jumping (air) . . . 3·75 4·00
The design on the 10fo. is larger, 43 × 43 mm.

547 Prince Geza indicating Site of Szekesfehervar

1972. Millenary of Szekesfehervar and 750th Anniv of "Aranybulla" (legislative document). Multicoloured.

2696	40fi. Type **547**	10	10
2697	60fi. King Stephen and shield	10	10
2698	80fi. Soldiers and cavalry	15	10
2699	1fo.20 King Stephen drawing up legislation	35	10
2700	2fo. Mason sculpting column	45	10
2701	4fo. Merchant displaying wares to King Stephen	80	20
2702	6fo. Views of Szekesfehervar and Palace	1·10	40

MS2703 136 × 90 mm. 10fo. King Andrew II at presentation of "Aranybulla" to the court . . 3·00 3·00
The design on the 10fo. is larger, 95 × 47 mm.

548 Parliament Building, Budapest

1972. Constitution Day. Multicoloured.

2704	5fo. Type **548**	50	10
2705	6fo. Parliament in session	70	20

549 Eger and "Bulls Blood"

1972. World Wines Competition, Budapest Multicoloured.

2706	1fo. Type **549**	35	10
2707	2fo. Tokay and "Tokay Aszu"	65	20

550 Ear of Wheat and Emblems on Open Book

1972. 175th Anniv of Georgikon Agricultural Academy, Keszthely.
2708 **550** 1fo. multicoloured . . . 15 10

551 "Rothschild" Vase

553 Commemorative Emblem

552 Class M62 Diesel Train and U.I.C. Emblem

1972. Herendi Porcelain. Multicoloured.

2709	40fi. Type **551**	15	10
2710	60fi. "Poisson" bonboniere	15	10
2711	80fi. "Victoria" vase	20	10
2712	1fo. "Miramare" dish	20	10
2713	1fo.20 "Godollo" pot	25	10
2714	2fo. "Empire" tea-set	35	10
2715	4fo. "Apponyi" dish	75	30
2716	5fo. "Baroque" vase	1·25	65

The 60fi., 1fo.20, and 4fo. are size 34 × 36 mm.

1972. 50th Anniv of Int Railway Union.
2717 **552** 1fo. red 50 10

1972. 25th Anniv of National Economy Plan.
2718 **553** 1fo. yellow, sepia & brn 20 10

554 River Steamer and Old Obuda

1972. Centenary of Unification of Buda, Obuda and Pest as Budapest.

2719	**554** 1fo. purple and blue	30	10
2720	– 1fo. blue and purple	30	10
2721	– 2fo. green and brown	30	10
2722	– 2fo. brown and green	30	10
2723	– 3fo. brown and green	40	10
2724	– 3fo. green and brown	40	10

DESIGNS: No. 2720, River hydrofoil and modern Obuda; 2721, Buda, 1872; 2722, Budapest, 1972; 2723, Pest, 1872; 2724, Parliament Buildings, Budapest.

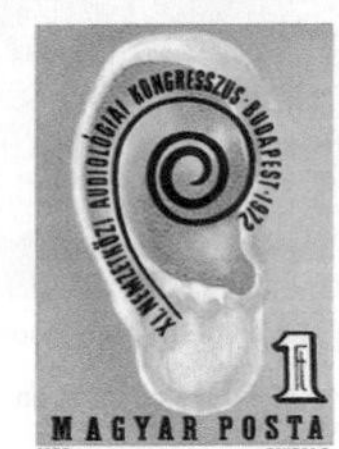
555 Congress Emblem within Ear

1972. Int Audiological Congress, Budapest.
2725 **555** 1fo. multicoloured . . . 30 10

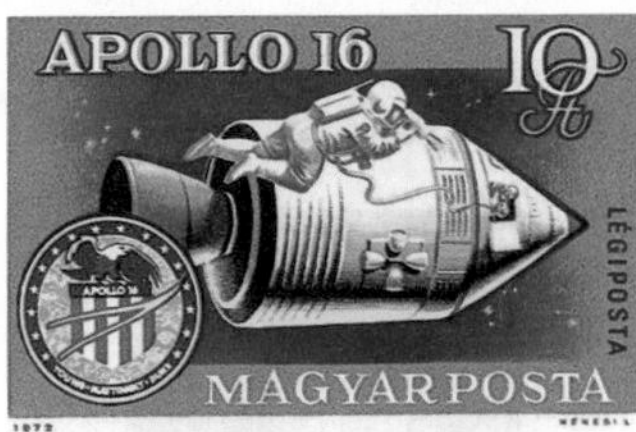
556 "Apollo 16"

1972. Air. Moon Flight of "Apollo 16". Sheet 120 × 75 mm.
MS2726 **556** 10fo. multicoloured 3·00 3·00

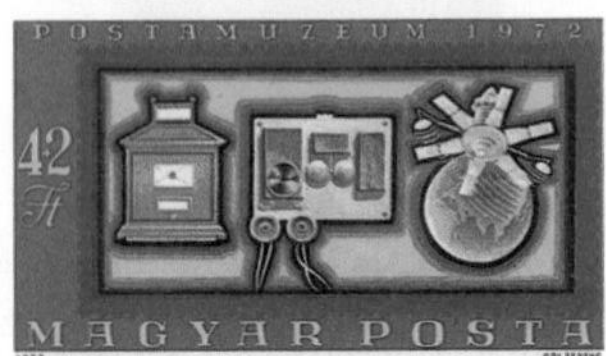
557 Postbox, Bell Telephone and Satellite "Molnya"

1972. Reopening of Postal and Philatelic Museums, Budapest. Multicoloured.

2727	4fo.+2fo. Type **557**	75	80
2728	4fo.+2fo. Globe, posthorn and stamps	75	80

558 Miklos Radnoti (poet)

1972. Radnoti Commemoration.
2729 **558** 1fo. multicoloured . . . 10 10

559 F. Martos

560 "The Muses" (J. Rippl-Ronai)

1972. 75th Birth Anniv of Flora Martos (patriot).
2730 **559** 1fo. multicoloured . . . 10 10

1972. Stained Glass Windows. Multicoloured.
2731 40fi. Type **560** 15 10
2732 60fi. "16th-century Scribe" (F. Sebestenyl) 15 10
2733 1fo. "Exodus to Egypt" (K. Lotz and B. Szekely) 20 10
2734 1fo.50 "Prince Arpad's Messenger" (J. Percz) . . 35 10
2735 2fo.50 "The Nativity" (L. Sztehlo) 55 10
2736 4fo. "Prince Arpad and Leaders" (K. Kernstock) 95 20
2737 5fo. "King Matthias reprimands the Rich Aristocrats" (J. Haranghy) . . . . . . 1·40 55

561 "Textiles"

1972. Opening of Textiles Technical Museum, Budapest.
2738 **561** 1fo. multicoloured . . . 30 10

562 Main Square, Szarvas
563 S. Petofi

1972. Views.
2739 **562** 40fi. brown and orange 10 10
2739a – 40fi. black and green 10 10
2740 – 1fo. blue and light blue 10 10
2741 – 1fo. brown and yellow 10 10
2742 – 3fo. green and blue . . 50 10
2743 – 4fo. red and orange . . 50 10
2743a – 4fo. brown and pink . . 60 10
2744 – 5fo. blue and cobalt . . 45 10
2745 – 6fo. brown and red . . 1·00 10
2746 – 7fo. violet and lilac . . 85 10
2747 – 8fo. deep green & green 1·10 10
2748 – 10fo. brown and yellow 1·40 10
2749 – 20fo. multicoloured . . 3·25 15
2750 – 50fo. multicoloured . . 5·75 70
DESIGNS: 21 × 18 mm: 40fi. (No. 2739a) Rotunda (public health centre), Vasvar; 1fo. (No. 2740) Salgotarjan; 1fo. (No. 2741) Nyirbator. 28 × 22 mm: 3fo. Tokay; 4fo. (No. 2743) Esztergom; 4fo. (No. 2743a) Szentendre; 5fo. Szolnok; 6fo. Dunaujvaros; 7fo. Kaposvar; 8fo. Vac; 10fo. Kiskunfelegyhaza; 20fo. Veszprem; 50ra. Pecs.

1972. 150th Birth Anniv of Sandor Petofi (poet and patriot).
2762 – 1fo. red 10 10
2763 **563** 2fo. lilac 20 10
2764 – 3fo. green 40 20
DESIGNS: 1fo. Petofi making speech in Cafe Pilvax; 3fo. Petofi on horseback during War of Independence, 1848–49.

564 Arms of U.S.S.R.

1972. 50th Anniv of U.S.S.R.
2765 **564** 1fo. multicoloured . . . 10 10

565 Code Map and Crow Symbol

1973. Introduction of Postal Codes.
2766 **565** 1fo. black and red . . . 15 10

1973. As Nos. 1912, 1915/16 and 1918 but smaller.
2767 2fo. blue (22 × 19 mm) . . . 35 20
2768 3fo. blue (22 × 19 mm) . . . 55 30
2769 4fo. green (19 × 22 mm) . . 70 45
2770 6fo. ochre (22 × 19 mm) . . 1·40 75

566 Astronaut on Moon

1973. Air. Moon Flight of "Apollo 17". Sheet 69 × 110 mm.
MS2771 **566** 10fo. multicoloured 3·50 4·00

567 I. Madach
568 Carnival Mask

1973. 150th Birth Anniv of Imre Madach (writer).
2772 **567** 1fo. multicoloured . . . 20 10

1973. Busho-Walking Ceremony, Mohacs. Carnival Masks.
2773 **568** 40fi. multicoloured . . . 10 10
2774 – 60fi. multicoloured . . . 10 10
2775 – 80fi. multicoloured . . . 15 10
2776 – 1fo.20 multicoloured . . 30 10
2777 – 2fo. multicoloured . . . 45 15
2778 – 4fo. multicoloured . . . 75 20
2779 – 6fo. multicoloured . . . 1·40 55

569 Copernicus

1973. 500th Birth Anniv of Copernicus.
2780 **569** 3fo. blue 90 45

570 "Venus 8" (-size illustration)

1973. Air. Space Flight of "Venus 8". Sheet 110 × 93 mm.
MS2781 **570** 10fo. multicoloured 3·00 3·25

571 Show-jumping (Pentathlon) and Gold Medal

1973. Hungarian Medal Winners, Olympic Games, Munich. Multicoloured.
2782 40fi. Type **571** 15 10
2783 60fi. Weightlifting (Gold) . . 15 10
2784 1fo. Canoeing (Silver) . . . 30 10
2785 1fo.20 Swimming (Silver) . . 50 10
2786 1fo.80 Boxing (Gold) . . . 40 10
2787 4fo. Wrestling (Gold) . . . 80 20
2788 6fo. Fencing (Gold) . . . . 1·25 75

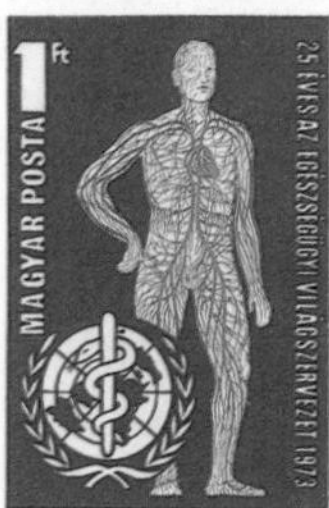

572 Biological Man

573 Winter Wrens

1973. 25th Anniv of W.H.O.
2790 **572** 1fo. brown and green . . 20 10

1973. Air. Hungarian Birds. Multicoloured.
2791 40fi. Type **573**(postage) . . 25 10
2792 60fi. Rock thrush 30 10
2793 80fi. European robins . . . 35 10
2794 1fo. Firecrests 40 15
2795 1fo.20 Linnets 55 15
2796 2fo. Blue tits 60 25
2797 4fo. Bluethroat . . . . . . 1·00 40
2798 5fo. Grey wagtails . . . . . 1·40 45

MS2799 132 × 88 mm. 10fo. Girl igniting Olympic Flame (air) 4·50 60
The design of the 10fo. is larger, 83 × 46 mm.

574 Soldier and Weapons

1973. Military Stamp Collectors' Exn, Budapest.
2799 **574** 3fo. multicoloured . . . 45 25

575 "Budapest 61" 1fo. Stamp

1973. "IBRA 73" Stamp Exn, Munich, and "POLSKA '73", Poznan. Repoductions of Hungary Exhibition stamps. Multicoloured.
2800 40fi. Type **575**(postage) . . 10 10
2801 60fi. "Budapest 61" 1fo.70 stamp 10 10
2802 80fi. "Budapest 61" 2fo.60 stamp 15 10
2803 1fo. "Budapest 61" 3fo. stamp 30 10
2804 1fo.20 "Budapest 71" 2fo. stamp 20 10
2805 2fo. "Budapest 71" 2fo. stamp 30 10
2806 4fo. "Budapest 71" 2fo. stamp . . . . 1·00 45
2807 5fo. "Budapest 71" 2fo. stamp . . . . 1·00 55

MS2808 130 × 81 mm. 10fo. Bavaria's first stamp, Town Hall and Olympic complex, Munich (air) . . . . 3·25 3·00
The design of the 10fo. is larger, 83 × 46 mm.

576 Setting Type and Preparing Ink

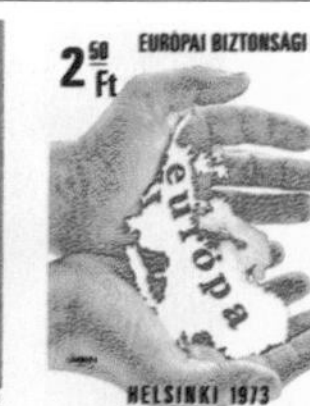

578 "Europa" Poster

577 "Storm over Hortobagy Puszta"

1973. 500th Anniv of Book-printing in Hungary.
2809 **576** 1fo. black and gold . . . 10 10
2810 – 3fo. black and gold . . . 50 15
DESIGN: 3fo. Printer operating press.

1973. Paintings by Csontvary Kosztka. Mult.
2811 40fi. Type **577** 10 10
2812 60fi. "Mary's Well, Nazareth" 15 10
2813 1fo. "Carriage drive by Moonlight" (vert) 25 10
2814 1fo.50 "Pilgrimage to the Lebanese Cedars" (vert) 30 10
2815 2fo.50 "The Lone Cedar" 40 10
2816 4fo. "Waterfall at Jajce" . . 90 20
2817 5fo. "Ruins of Greek Theatre at Taormina" . . 1·10 60
MS2818 114 × 75 mm. 10fo. "Riding at the Seaside" . . . . 3·00 3·25
The design of the 10fo. is larger, 91 × 43 mm.

1973. European Security and Co-operation Conference, Helsinki.
2819 **578** 2fo.50 brown and black 2·75 2·75

579 "Rosa gallica"

580 "Let's be friends...!"

1973. Wild Flowers. Multicoloured.
2820 40fi. Type **579** 15 10
2821 60fi. "Cyclamen europaeum" 20 10
2822 80fi. "Pulmonaria mollissima" 25 10
2823 1fo.20 "Bellis perennis" . . 30 10
2824 2fo. "Adonis vernalis" . . . 45 10
2825 4fo. "Viola cyanea" 75 15
2826 6fo. "Papaver rhoeas" . . . 1·00 50

1973. Road Safety.
2827 **580** 40fi. green and red . . . 10 10
2828 – 60fi. violet and orange 15 10
2829 – 1fo. blue and red 25 10
DESIGNS: 60fi. "Not even a glass!" (hand reaching for tumbler); 1fo. "Cyclist – use a lamp" (car running down cyclist).

581 Silver "Eagle" Disc

1973. Jewelled Treasures, National Museum. Multicoloured.
2830 2fo.+50fi. Type **581** 55 75
2831 2fo.+50fi. Serpent's head ring 55 75
2832 2fo.+50fi. "Loving couple" buckle 55 75
2833 2fo.+50fi. Silver "floral" buckle 55 75
MS2834 75 × 101 mm. 2fo.+50fi. × 4 (a) Opaline pendant; (b) Jewelled buckle; (c) Floral pin; (d) Rosette pendant . . . . 3·75 3·25
The designs in **MS**2834 are each 25 × 36 mm.

582 "Skylab" photographing Earth

1973. Air. "Skylab" Space-station. Sheet 114 × 75 mm.
MS2835 **582** 10fo. multicoloured . . . 2·75 4·00

583 "The Three Kings" (Master of the High Altar, Szmrecsany)

1973. Esztergom Millennium. "Old Master" Paintings in the Christian Museum. Mult.
2836 40fi. Type **583** 10 10
2837 60fi. "Angels making Music" (Master "B.E.") 10 10
2838 1fo. "The Adoration of the Magi" (anon.) 15 10
2839 1fo.50 "The Annunciation" (Szmrecsany Master) . . . 30 10
2840 2fo.50 "Angels making Music" (different Master "B.E.") 45 10
2841 4fo. "The Visitation of Mary and Elizabeth" (Szmrecsany Master) . . . 70 25
2842 5fo. "The Legend of St. Catharine of Alexandria" (Master Bati) 1·00 40
MS2843 73 × 101 mm. 10fo. "The Birth of Jesus" (Szmrecsany Master) . . . . 3·00 3·00

584 Csokonai's Statue, Debrecen

1973. Birth Bicentenary of M. Csokonai Vitez (poet).
2844 **584** 2fo. multicoloured . . . 45 10

585 J. Marti **586** B. Pesti

1973. 120th Birth Anniv of Jose Marti (Cuban patriot).
2845 **585** 1fo. brown, red and blue 10 10

1973. 30th Death Anniv of Barnabas Pesti (patriot).
2846 **586** 1fo. lt brown, brown & bl 10 10

588 Kayak-canoeing

1973. World Aquatic Sports Championships, Belgrade and Tampere. Multicoloured.
2855 40fi. Type **588** 15 10
2856 60fi. Water polo 15 10
2857 80fi. Men's solo kayak . . . 20 10
2858 1fo.20 Swimming 25 10
2859 2fo. Men's kayak fours . . 40 10
2860 4fo. Men's solo canoe . . . 65 20
2861 6fo. Men's double canoe . . 1·10 65

589 Map of Europe

1974. European Security and Co-operation Conference, Geneva. Sheet 143 × 71 mm containing two stamps as T **589** together with a double-size label depicting Geneva.
MS2862 **589** 50fo. × 2 gold, blue and green . . . . 7·50 8·25

590 Lenin

1974. 50th Death Anniv of Lenin.
2863 **590** 2fo. brown, blue and gold 30 10

591 J. Boczor, I. Bekes and T. Elek

1974. Hungarian Heroes of the French Resistance.
2864 **591** 3fo. multicoloured . . . 50 10

592 "Comecon" Building, Moscow, and Flags

1974. 25th Anniv of Council for Mutual Economic Aid.
2865 **592** 1fo. multicoloured . . . 10 10

593 Savings Bank Emblem, Note and Coins **595** Pres. Salvador Allende

594 "Mariner 4" on course for Mars

1974. 25th Anniv of National Savings Bank.
2866 **593** 1fo. multicoloured . . . 10 10

1974. Mars Research Projects. Multicoloured.
2867 40fi. Type **594** (postage) . . 10 10
2868 60fi. "Mars 2" approaching Mars 15 10
2869 80fi. "Mariner 4" space probe 20 10
2870 1fo. Mt. Palomar telescope and Mars photo 35 10
2871 1fo.20 "Mars 3" on planet's surface 45 10
2872 5fo. "Mariner 9" approaching Mars and satellites . . . . 1·25 20
2873 6fo. G. Schiaparelli and Martian "canals" map (air) . . . . 1·50 75
MS2874 96 × 91 mm. 10fo. "Mars 7" in Space . . . . 3·00 3·25

1974. Pres. Allende of Chile Commemoration.
2875 **595** 1fo. multicoloured . . . 20 10

596 "Mona Lisa" (Leonardo da Vinci)

1974. Exhibition of "Mona Lisa" in Japan.
2876 **596** 4fo. multicoloured . . . 6·00 5·25

597 2k. Stamp of 1874 and Mallow

1974. Centenary of Hungarian "Envelope Design" Stamps. Sheet 103 × 87 mm containing T **597** and similar horiz design. Multicoloured.
MS2877 2fo.50 × 5 (a) Type **597**; (b) 3k. stamp and aster; (c) 5k. stamp and daisy; (d) 10k. stamp and columbine . . . . 3·00 3·35

598 Dove with Letter

1974. Centenary of U.P.U. Multicoloured.
2878 40fi. Type **598** 10 10
2879 60fi. Mail coach 10 10
2880 80fi. Early mail van and postbox 15 10
2881 1fo.20 Balloon post 20 10
2882 2fo. Diesel mail train . . . 65 10
2883 4fo. Post-bus 80 15
2884 6fo. Tupolev Tu-154 mail plane . . . . 1·40 35
MS2885 132 × 106 mm. 2fo.50 × 4 (a) As 60fi.; (b) As 80fi. but design reversed; (c) As 6fo.; (d) "Apollo 15" . . . . 3·00 3·75
The designs in **MS**2885 are smaller, 45 × 30 mm. and are redrawn so that only part of the U.P.U. Monument falls on each stamp.

599 Swiss $2\frac{1}{2}$r. "Basle Dove" Stamp of 1845

1974. "Internaba 1974" Stamp Exn, Basle.
2886 **599** 3fo. multicoloured . . . 1·25 95

600 13th-century miniature from King Alfonso X's "Book of Chess, Dice and Tablings" and Pawn

1974. 50th Anniv of International Chess Federation and 21st Chess Olympiad, Nice.
2887 **600** 40fi. black, green and blue 25 10
2888 – 60fi. black, brown & lilac 40 10
2889 – 80fi. black, yellow & grn 60 10
2890 – 1fo.20 black, yellow and lilac 70 15
2891 – 2fo. black, stone and blue . . . . 1·00 15
2892 – 4fo. black, yellow & pink 1·40 60
2893 – 6fo. black, brown & grn 1·50 80
DESIGNS: 60fi. 15th-century woodcut from "The Game and Playe of Chesse" by William Caxton and knight; 80fi. 15th-century illustration from Italian chess book and bishop; 1fo.20, "The Chess Players" (17th-century engraving by Jacob van der Heyden) and rook; 2fo. Kempelen's chess playing machine (1769) and king; 4fo. Geza Maroczy (Hungarian master) and queen; 6fo. View of Nice and tournament emblem.

601 Passenger Train, 1874

1974. Centenary of the Budapest Rack Railway. Sheet 132 × 96 mm. containing T **601** and similar horiz designs. Multicoloured.
MS2894 2fo.50 Type **601**; 2fo.50 Goods train, 1874; 2fo.50 Passenger train, 1929; 2fo.50 Passenger train, 1973 . . . . . 3·25 4·00

602 Congress Emblem

1974. 4th International Economists' Congress, Budapest.
2895 **602** 2fo. black, blue and silver 30 10

603 "Woman Bathing" (K Lotz)

1974. Nudes. Paintings. Multicoloured.
2896 40fi. Type **603** 15 10
2897 60fi. "Awakening" (K. Brocky) 15 10
2898 1fo. "Venus and Cupid" (K. Brocky) (horiz) . . . 25 10
2899 1fo.50 "After Bathing" (K. Lotz) 45 10
2900 2fo.50 "Honi soit qui mal y pense" (reclining nude) (I. Csok) (horiz) 65 15
2901 4fo. "After Bathing" (B. Szekly) 90 25
2902 5fo. "Devotion" (E. Korb) 1·10 70
MS2903 75 × 102 mm. 10fo. "Lark" (P.M. Szinyei) (50 × 71 mm) . . 3·00 3·75

604 "Mimi" (Czobel)

605 "Intersputnik" Satellite Tracking Radar

1974. 91st Birth Anniv of Bela Czobel (painter).
2904 **604** 1fo. multicoloured . . . 45 10

1974. 25th Anniv of Technical and Scientific Co-operation between Hungary and Soviet Union.
2905 **605** 1fo. violet and blue . . . 15 10
2906 – 3fo. mauve and green . . 35 10
DESIGN—HORIZ: 3fo. Power installations.

606 Neruda

607 Swedish 3s. Stamp, 1855, and "Swedish Lion"

1974. Pablo Neruda (Chilean poet) Commem.
2907 **606** 1fo. brown, deep brown and blue 10 10

1974. "Stockholmia 74" International Stamp Exhibition.
2908 **607** 3fo. green, blue and gold 75 1·00

608 Tanks and Infantry

1974. Military Day.
2909 **608** 1fo. black, red and gold (postage) 20 10
2910 – 2fo. blk, grn & gold (air) 35 10
2911 – 3fo. black, blue and gold 55 15
DESIGNS—VERT: 2fo. Guided missile and radar. HORIZ: 3fo. Parachutist, helicopter and jet fighter.

609 J. A. Segner and Moon

1974. 270th Birth Anniv of Janos Segner (scientist).
2912 **609** 3fo. multicoloured . . . 50 15

610 Hansa Brandenburg C-1 Biplane, 1918

1974. Air. "Aerofila 1974" International Airmail Exhibition, Budapest. Multicoloured.
2913 2fo.+1fo. Type **610** . . . . 1·00 1·00
2914 2fo.+1fo. Airship "Graf Zeppelin" . . . . 1·00 1·00
2915 2fo.+1fo. Hot air balloon 1·00 1·00
2916 2fo.+1fo. Mil Mi-1 helicopter . . . . 1·00 1·00
MS2917 107 × 92 mm. 2fo.+1fo. Hungarian 1k.50 stamp, 1918; 2fo. + 1fo. Hungarian 500k. stamp, 1924; 2fo.+1fo. Hungarian 3fo. stamp, 1970; 2fo. + 1fo. Hungarian 3fo. stamp, 1970; 2fo.+1fo. Hungarian 10fo. stamp, 1972 . . . . 3·75 4·25

611 Purple Tiger Moth

1974. Butterflies and Moths. Multicoloured.
2918 40fi. Type **611** 25 10
2919 60fi. Marbled white 35 10
2920 80fi. Apollo 40 15
2921 1fo. Spurge hawk moth . . 50 15
2922 1fo.20 Clifden's nonpareil 60 30
2923 5fo. Purple emperor . . . . 1·50 45
2924 6fo. Purple-edged copper . . 1·90 90

612 Istvan Pataki

613 Mother and Child

1974. Hungarian Antifascist Martyrs. Mult.
2925 1fo. Type **612** 10 10
2926 1fo. Robert Kreutz 10 10

1974. "Mothers".
2927 **613** 1fo. black, yellow & blue 10 10

614 Puppy

616 F. Bolyai

615 Lambarene Hospital

1974. Young Animals. (1st series). Mult.
2928 40fi. Type **614** 10 10
2929 60fi. Kittens (horiz) 15 10
2930 80fi. Rabbit 20 10
2931 1fo.20 Foal (horiz) 30 10
2932 2fo. Lamb 55 10
2933 4fo. Calf (horiz) 85 20
2934 6fo. Piglet . . . . 1·40 75
See also Nos. 3014/20.

1975. Birth Centenary of Dr. Albert Schweitzer (Nobel Peace Prize Winner). Multicoloured.
2935 40fi. Type **615** 10 10
2936 60fi. Casualty being treated 15 10
2937 80fi. Casualty being transported by canoe . . 20 10
2938 1fo.20 Charitable goods arriving by freighter . . . 30 10
2939 2fo. View of Lambarene, doves, globe and Red Cross emblem 50 10
2940 4fo. Schweitzer's Nobel Peace Prize medal and inscription 80 15
2941 6fo. Schweitzer and organ-pipes . . . . 1·10 35

1975. Birth Bicentenary of Farkas Bolyai (mathematician).
2942 **616** 1fo. grey and red 20 10

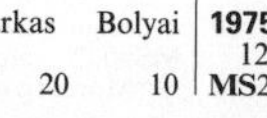

617 Carrier-pigeon

1975. Air. Pigeon-racing Olympics, Budapest.
2943 **617** 3fo. multicoloured . . . 1·00 75

618 Karolyi

1975. Birth Centenary of Count Mihaly Karolyi (politician).
2944 **618** 1fo. brown and blue . . 10 10

619 Woman's Head

1975. International Woman's Year.
2945 **619** 1fo. black and blue . . . 10 10

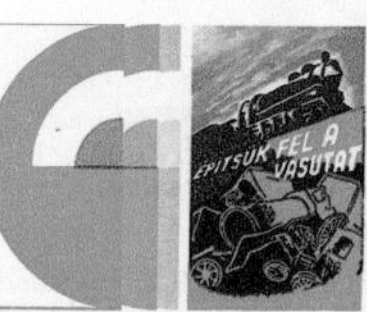

620 "Railway Rebuilding" (⅔-size illustration)

1975. 30th Anniv of Liberation. Mult.
2946 40fi. Type **620** 25 10
2947 60fi. Hammer and sickle representing agriculture 10 10
2948 2fo. Blacksmith's hammer representing Communist party action 10 10
2949 4fo. Power hammer as "3" representing the "Three Year Heavy Industry Plan" . . . . 1·10 20
2950 5fo. Blocks of Flats representing "developed socialist society" 45 15

621 1915 "Arrow"

1975. 75th Anniv of Hungarian Automobile Club. Vintage Motor Cars. Multicoloured.
2951 40fi. Type **621** 20 10
2952 60fi. 1911 "Swift" 20 10
2953 80fi. 1908 Ford "T" 25 10
2954 1fo. 1901 Mercedes 30 15
2955 1fo.20 1912 Panhard Levassor 40 15
2956 5fo. 1906 Csonka . . . . . 1·25 30
2957 6fo. Hungarian Automobile Club and international motoring organizations' emblems . . . . 2·00 65

622 "Creation of Adam" (from ceiling of Sistine Chapel) (½-size illustration)

1975. 500th Birth Anniv of Michelangelo. Sheet 126 × 90 mm.
MS2958 **622** 10fo. multicoloured 3·75 4·50

623 Academy Building

1975. 150th Anniv of National Academy of Sciences. Multicoloured.
2959 1fo. Type **623** 20 20
2960 2fo. Dates "1825" and "1975" 30 20
2961 3fo. Count Istvan Szechenyi (statesman) . . . . 1·00 40

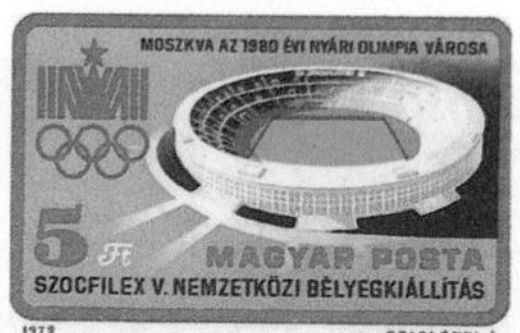

624 Olympic Stadium, Moscow

1975. "Socphilex V" International Stamp Exhibition, Moscow.
2962 **624** 5fo. multicoloured . . . 90 1·25

625 French 1f. Stamp, 1964

1975. "Arphila 75" International Stamp Exhibition, Paris.
2963 **625** 5fo. multicoloured . . . 90 1·25

626 Electric Railway Locomotive and Transformer

1975. 75th Anniv of Hungarian Electro-technical Association.
2964 **626** 1fo. multicoloured . . . 60 10

627 "Sputnik 2"

1975. Air. "Apollo–Soyuz" Space Link. Mult.
2965 40fi. Type **627** 10 10
2966 60fi. "Mercury Atlas 5" . . 10 10
2967 80fi. "Lunokhod 1" (moon vehicle) 15 10
2968 1fo.20 "Apollo 15" (moon vehicle) 25 10
2969 2fo. Launch of "Soyuz" from Baikonur 45 10
2970 4fo. Launch of "Apollo" . . 90 15
2971 6fo. "Apollo–Soyuz" link-up 1·40 45
MS2972 129 × 100 mm. 10fo. "Apollo" and "Soyuz" in linking manoeuvre (65 × 42 mm) . . . 3·00 3·00

628 Sword, Epee, Rapier, and Globe

1975. World Fencing Championships, Budapest.
2973 **628** 1fo. multicoloured . . . 20 10

629 Whale Pavilion

1975. International Exposition, Okinawa (1st issue). Sheet 116 × 95 mm.
MS2974 **629** 10fo. multicoloured 2·75 2·50
See also Nos. 2986/92.

630 Map of Europe and Cogwheel (½-size illustration)

1975. Air. European Security and Co-operation Conference, Helsinki. Sheet 157 × 82 mm.
MS2975 **630** 10fo. multicoloured 7·50 7·50

631 A. Zimmermann

1975. Birth Centenary of Dr. Agoston Zimmermann (veterinary surgeon).
2976 **631** 1fo. dp brown, brn & bl 15 10

632 Branches of Tree symbolizing 14 Languages
634 Anjou Wall Fountain

633

1975. Int Finno-Ugrian Congress, Budapest.
2977 **632** 1fo. multicoloured . . . 10 10

1975. Air. Hungarian Stamps since 1945. Sheet 150 × 95 mm. Multicoloured.
MS2978 Hungarian 1fo. Stamp, 1964, 2fo. Stamp, 1961 and 2fo.50 Stamp, 1973 . . . . 3·00 3·75

1975. Stamp Day. Preservation of Monuments. Monuments in Visegrad Palace. Multicoloured.
2979 2fo.+1fo. Type **634** . . . . 1·50 1·75
2980 2fo.+1fo. Anjou well house 1·50 1·75
2981 2fo.+1fo. Hunyadi wall fountain . . . . 1·50 1·75
2982 2fo.+1fo. Hercules fountain 1·50 1·75
MS2983 128 × 100 mm. 2fo.+1fo. Detail of Hunyadi wall fountain (26 x 37 mm); 2fo.+1fo. Madonna of Visegrad (52 × 37 mm); 2fo.+1fo. Detail of Hercules fountain (26 × 37 mm); 2fo.+1fo. View of Visegrad in 1480 (105 × 37 mm) . . . . 9·00 10·00

635 Hungarian Arms and Map
636 Ocean Pollution

1975. 25th Anniv of Hungarian Council System. Multicoloured.
2984 1fo. Type **635** 15 10
2985 1fo. Voters participating in council election 15 10

1975. International Exposition, Okinawa. Environmental Protection (2nd issue). Multicoloured.
2986 40fi. Type **636** 10 10
2987 60fi. Strangled rose (water pollution) 15 10
2988 80fi. Clown anemonefish struggling for uncontaminated water (river pollution) 20 10
2989 1fo. Dead carnation (soil pollution) 30 10
2990 1fo.20 Falling bird (air pollution) 40 10
2991 5fo. Infected lung (smoke pollution) . . . . 1·00 15
2992 6fo. Healthy and skeletal hands (life and death) . . 1·25 30

637 Mariska Gardos (writer) (1885–1973)

1975. Birth Annivs of Celebrities. Each black and red.
2993 1fo. Type **637** 15 10
2994 1fo. Imre Tarr (soldier) (1900–1937) 15 10
2995 1fo. Imre Meso (Communist martyr) (1905–1956) . . . 15 10

638 Treble Clef, Organ and Orchestra

1975. Centenary of Ferenc Liszt Music Academy, Budapest.
2996 **638** 1fo. multicoloured . . . 30 10

639 18th-century Icon of Szigetcsep

1975. Hungarian Icons depicting the Virgin and Child. Multicoloured.
2997 40fi. Type **639** 10 10
2998 60fi. 18th-century Icon of Graboc 20 10
2999 1fo. 18th-century Icon of Esztergom 20 10
3000 1fo.50 18th-century Icon of Vatoped 40 10
3001 2fo.50 17th-century Icon of Tottos 60 10
3002 4fo. 17th-century Icon of Gyor 75 20
3003 5fo. 18th-century Icon of Kazan . . . . 1·25 70

640 Mother and Child, Flags and Radar Equipment (⅔-size illustration)

1975. 20th Anniv of Warsaw Treaty.
3004 **640** 1fo. multicoloured . . . 10 10

641 Ice Hockey

1975. Winter Olympic Games, Innsbruck. Multicoloured.
3005 40fi. Type **641** 25 10
3006 60fi. Slalom skiing 25 10
3007 80fi. Slalom skiing (different) 25 10
3008 1fo.20 Ski jumping 35 10
3009 2fo. Speed skating 40 10
3010 4fo. Cross-country skiing . . 80 15
3011 6fo. Bobsleighing . . . . . 1·00 50
MS3012 130 × 80 mm. 10fo. Pairs figure skating (65 × 42 mm) . . 3·00 3·25

642 Banknotes of 1925 and 1975

1976. 50th Anniv of State Banknote Printing Office, Budapest.
3013 **642** 1fo. multicoloured . . . 35 10

1976. Young Animals (2nd series). As T **614**. Multicoloured.
3014 40fi. Wild boars (horiz) . . 10 10
3015 60fi. Eurasian red squirrels 15 10
3016 80fi. Lynx (horiz) 20 10
3017 1fo.20 Wolf cubs 35 10
3018 2fo. Red fox cubs (horiz) . . 50 10
3019 4fo. Brown bear cubs . . . 80 15
3020 6fo. Lion cubs (horiz) . . . 1·25 45

643 Alexander Graham Bell, Telecommunications Satellite and Dish Aerial

1976. Telephone Centenary.
3021 **643** 3fo. multicoloured . . . 60 65

644 "Horses in Storm" (K. Lotz)

1976. Air. Tourist Publicity. Paintings. Sheet 95 × 135 mm containing T **644** and similar square design. Multicoloured.
MS3022 5fo. Type **644**; 5fo. "Morning at Tihany" (J. Halapy) 3·00 3·25

645 "Clash between Rakoczi's Kuruts and Hapsburg Soldiers"

1976. 300th Birth Anniv of Prince Ferenc Rakoczi II (soldier). Paintings. Multicoloured.
3023 40fi. Type **645** 10 10
3024 60fi. "Meeting of Rakoczi and Tamas Esze" 15 10
3025 1fo. "The Parliament of Onod" (Mor Than) . . . 30 10
3026 2fo. "Kuruts' Encampment" 75 15
3027 3fo. "Ilona Zrinyi" (Rakoczi's mother) (vert) 1·25 30
3028 4fo. "Kuruts Officers" (vert) 1·60 35
3029 5fo. "Prince Rakoczi II" (A. Manyoki) (vert) . . . 2·25 90

646 Metric System Act, 1876
647 Knight

1976. Centenary of Introduction of Metric System into Hungary. Multicoloured.
3030 1fo. Type **646** 15 10
3031 2fo. Istvan Krusper (scientist) and vacuum balance 25 20
3032 3fo. Interferometer, space rocket and emblem . . . 55 25

1976. Stamp Day. Gothic Statues from Buda Castle.
3033 2fo.50+1fo. Type **647** . . . 80 75
3034 2fo.50+1fo. Armour bearer 80 75
3035 2fo.50+1fo. Apostle 80 75
3036 2fo.50+1fo. Bishop 80 75
MS3037 107 × 100 mm. 2fo.50+1fo. Man wearing brimmed hat; 2fo.50+1fo. Woman in wimple; 2fo.50+1fo. Man wearing cloth hat; 2fo.50+1fo. Man in fur cap 2·50 2·50
The designs in **MS** are horiz, 35 × 28 mm, and show statue heads only.

648 U.S. 6c. Stamp, 1968

1976. "Interphil '76" Int Stamp Exn, Philadelphia.
3038 **648** 5fo. multicoloured . . . 1·25 1·25

649 "Children Playing" (E. Gebora) within "30"

1976. 30th Anniv of Hungarian Pioneers Movement.
3039 **649** 1fo. multicoloured . . . 20 10

650 Truck, Tractor and Safety Headgear with Emblem

1976. Industrial Safety.
3040 **650** 1fo. multicoloured . . . 20 10

651 "Intelstar IV" Telecommunications Satellite

1976. Olympic Games, Montreal. Mult.
3041 40fi. Type **651**(postage) . . 10 10
3042 60fi. Horse-jumping 10 10
3043 1fo. Swimming 15 10
3044 2fo. Canoeing 35 10
3045 3fo. Fencing 60 10
3046 4fo. Javelin-throwing . . . 70 25
3047 5fo. Gymnastics 85 35

MS3048 135 × 85 mm. 20fo. black, grey and red (air) . . . . . . 4·50 6·00
DESIGN: 44 × 57 mm. 20fo. Olympic Stadium, Montreal.

652 Danish 1851 4 R.B.S. Stamp and "Little Mermaid" Statue

1976. "Hafnia '76" International Stamp Exhibition, Copenhagen.
3049 **652** 3fo. multicoloured . . . 75 75

653 "Flora" (Titian)

1976. 400th Death Anniv of Titian (painter).
3050 **653** 4fo. multicoloured . . . 60 25

654 "Discovery of King Lajos II's Body" (B. Szekely)

1976. 450th Anniv of Battle of Mohacs. Sheet 82 × 81 mm.
MS3051 **654** 20fo. multicoloured 3·00 3·25

655 Pal Gyulai (1826–1909)

656 "Hussar" (Zs. Kisfaludy-Strobl)

1976. Writers' Anniversaries.
3052 **655** 2fo. black and red . . . 30 10
3053 – 2fo. black, yellow & gold 30 10
DESIGN: No. 3053, Daniel Berzsenyi (1776–1836).

1976. 150th Anniv of Herend China Factory.
3054 **656** 4fo. multicoloured . . . 75 15

657 Tuscany 1q. Stamp, 1851 and Arms of Milan

1976. "Italia '76" International Stamp Exhibition, Milan.
3055 **657** 5fo. multicoloured . . . 2·25 3·00

658 Russian Dancer, Flags and Building

1976. 2nd Anniv of House of Soviet Culture and Science, Budapest.
3056 **658** 1fo. multicoloured . . . 15 10

659 Ignac Bogar

1976. Hungarian Labour Movement Celebrities.
3057 **659** 1fo. brown and red . . . 10 10
3058 – 1fo. brown and red . . . 10 10
3059 – 1fo. brown and red . . . 10 10
PORTRAITS: No. 3058, Rudolf Golub; No. 3059, Jozsef Madzsar.

660 Dr. F. Koranyi and Dispensary

1976. 75th Anniv of Koranyi T.B. Dispensary.
3060 **660** 2fo. multicoloured . . . 35 10

661 Launch of "Viking" Mission

1976. Air. Space Probes to Mars and Venus. Multicoloured.
3061 40fi. Type **661** 10 10
3062 60fi. "Viking" in flight . . . 15 10
3063 1fo. "Viking" on Mars . . . 20 10
3064 2fo. Launch of "Venera" . . 30 10
3065 3fo. "Venera 9" in flight . . 55 10
3066 4fo. "Venera 10" descending to Venus 80 20
3067 5fo. "Venera" on Venus . . 90 45
MS3068 97 × 81 mm. 20fo. "Viking 1" landing on Mars (42 × 65 mm) 3·00 3·50

662 Locomotive No. 4, 1875

1976. Cent of Gyor-Sopron Railway. Mult.
3069 40fi. Type **662** 20 10
3070 60fi. Locomotive No. 17, 1885 . . . . 25 10
3071 1fo. Rail-bus. 1925 . . . . 30 10
3072 2fo. Steam locomotive, 1920 55 10
3073 3fo. Diesel railcar, 1926 . . 75 10
3074 4fo. Diesel railcar, 1934 . . 1·25 20
3075 5fo. Diesel railcar, 1971 . . 2·00 55

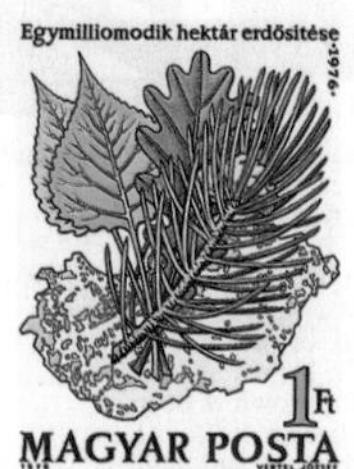

663 Tree Foliage and Map

1976. "Afforestation of 1,000,000th Hectare".
3076 **663** 1fo. multicoloured . . . 20 10

664 Weightlifting and Wrestling (silver medals)

1976. Olympic Games, Montreal. Hungarian Medal-winners. Multicoloured.
3077 40fi. Type **664** 10 10
3078 60fi. Men's solo kayak and Women's pairs kayak (silver medals) 20 10
3079 1fo. Men's gymnastics (horse) (gold medal) . . . 25 10
3080 4fo. Women's rapier (gold medal) . . . . 1·25 15
3081 6fo. Men's javelin (gold medal) . . . . 1·50 45
MS3082 80 × 95 mm. 20fo. Water-polo (Gold medal) . . . . . . 3·00 3·25

665 White Spoonbill

1977. Birds of Hortabagy National Park. Multicoloured.
3083 40fi. Type **665** 25 10
3084 60fi. White stork 30 10
3085 1fo. Purple heron 35 15
3086 2fo. Great bustard 45 20
3087 3fo. Common crane 70 30
3088 4fo. Pied wagtail . . . . . 1·25 50
3089 5fo. Garganey . . . . . . 1·60 65

666 Imre Abonyi (champion driver) and Carriage, 1976

1977. Historic Horse-drawn Vehicles. Mult.
3090 40fi. Type **666** 20 10
3091 60fi. Omnibus, 1870 . . . . 25 10
3092 1fo. Hackney-carriage, 1890 30 10
3093 2fo. 19th-century mail coach 40 10
3094 3fo. 18th-century covered wagon 70 20
3095 4fo. Coach, 1568 . . . . . 90 45
3096 5fo. Saint Elizabeth's carriage, 1430 . . . . . 1·10 1·00

667 Common Peafowl

1977. Peafowl and Pheasants. Multicoloured.
3097 40fi. Type **667** 20 10
3098 60fi. Green peafowl 25 10
3099 1fo. Congo peafowl 25 10
3100 3fo. Great Argus pheasant 75 15
3101 4fo. Himalayan monal pheasant . . . . 1·10 25
3102 6fo. Burmese peacock-pheasant . . . . 1·10 95

668 Front Page of "Nepszava" and Printing Works

1977. Centenary of Newspaper "Nepszava".
3103 **668** 1fo. black, red and gold . . 20 10

669 Flower painting (Mihaly Munkacsy)

1977. Flower Paintings by Hungarian Artists. Multicoloured.
3104 40fi. Type **669** 10 10
3105 60fi. Jakab Bogdany 10 10
3106 1fo. Istvan Csok (horiz) . . 15 10
3107 2fo. Janos Halapy 30 10
3108 3fo. Jozsef Rippl-Ronai (horiz) 65 15
3109 4fo. Janos Tornyai 85 30
3110 5fo. Jozsef Koszta . . . . . 1·00 65

670 Isaac Newton and Lens

1977. 250th Death Anniv of Isaac Newton (mathematician).
3111 **670** 3fo. black, brown and red 65 65

671 Children Running

673 Janos Vajda

672 "Acrofila 74" 2fo.+1fo. Stamp

1977. Youth Sports.
3112 **671** 3fo.+1fo. 50 mult . . . 75 70

1977. Stamp Exhibitions.
3113 **672** 3fo. multicoloured . . . 1·10 1·25

1977. 150th Birth Anniv of Janos Vajda (poet).
3114 **673** 1fo. stone, black & green 35 10

674 Netherlands 5c. Stamp, 1852

1977. "Amphilex 77" International Stamp Exhibition, Amsterdam.
3115 **674** 3fo. multicoloured . . . 90 1·00

675 "Wedding at Nagyrede" Dance

1977. 25th Anniv of State Folk Ensemble.
3116 **675** 3fo. multicoloured . . . 90 15

676 "Bathsheba at the Fountain"

1977. 400th Birth Anniv of Peter Paul Rubens. Sheet 70 × 94 mm.
MS3117 **676** 20fo. multicoloured 7·50 8·25

677 View of Sopron (from medieval engraving), Arms and Fidelity Tower

1977. 700th Anniv of Sopron.
3118 **677** 1fo. multicoloured . . . 1·10 1·25

678 Kincsem (champion racehorse)

1977. 150th Anniv of Horse Racing in Hungary.
3119 **678** 1fo. multicoloured . . . 1·25 1·25

679 East German 10pf. Stamp, 1957

1977. "Sozphilex 77" Stamp Exhibition, East Berlin.
3120 **679** 3fo. multicoloured . . . 1·00 1·00

680 Scythian Iron Bell (6th century B.C.)

681 "Sputnik 1"

1977. Stamp Day and 175th Anniv of Hungarian National Museum. Art Treasures.
3121 **680** 2fo. brown and blue . . 75 75
3122 – 2fo. brown and violet . . 75 75
3123 – 2fo. brown & deep brown 75 75
3124 – 2fo. gold and mauve . . 75 75
MS3125 73 × 83 mm. 10fo. multicoloured . . . . 3·00 3·25
DESIGNS: No. 3122, Bronze candlestick, 12-13th century; 3123, Copper aquamanile, 13th century; 3124, Cast gold Christ (from crucifix), 11th century. 32 × 47 mm—10fo. Plate from crown of Constantinus Monomakhosz, 11th century.

1977. Space Research. Multicoloured.
3126 40fi. Type **681**(postage) . . 10 10
3127 60fi. "Skylab" 15 10
3128 1fo. "Soyuz–Salyut 5" space station 20 10
3129 3fo. "Luna 24" 60 10
3130 4fo. "Mars 3" . . . . . . 1·25 20
3131 6fo. "Viking" . . . . 1·50 50

MS3132 98 × 78 mm. 20fo. Viking Lander on Mars (air) . . . . 3·25 3·50

682 Map, Dove and "Europa"

1977. Air. European Security Conference, Belgrade. Sheet 125 × 75 mm.
MS3133 **682** 20fo. multicoloured 6·00 5·25

683 Tupolev Tu-154

1977. Air.
3134 **683** 60fl. black and orange 15 10
3135 – 1fo.20 black and lilac . . 20 10
3136 – 2fo. black and orange . . 30 10
3137 – 2fo.40 black & turquoise 35 10
3138 – 4fo. black and blue . . . 45 10
3139 – 5fo. black and mauve . . 65 10
3140 – 10fo. black and blue . . 1·90 30
3141 – 20fo. black and green . . 2·75 75
DESIGNS—As T **683**: 1fo.20, Douglas DC-8-62; 2fo. Ilyushin Il-62M; 2fo.40, Airbus Industrie A300B4; 4fo. Boeing 747; 5fo. Tupolev Tu-144; 10fo. Concorde. 38 × 28 mm: 20fo. Ilyushin Il-86.

684 Montgolfier Brothers and Balloon

1977. Air. Airships. Multicoloured.
3142 40fi. Type **684** 10 10
3143 60fi. David Schwarz and his aluminium airship 20 10
3144 1fo. Alberto Santos-Dumont and airship "Ballon No. 5" over Paris 30 10
3145 2fo. K. E. Tsiolkovsky and airship "Lebedi" over Kremlin 45 10
3146 3fo. Roald Amundsen and airship "Norge" over North Pole 70 20
3147 4fo. Hugo Eckener and airship "Graf Zeppelin" over Mount Fuji . . . . 1·00 30
3148 5fo. Ferdinand Zeppelin and "Graf Zeppelin" over Chicago World Exhibition 1·50 50
MS3149 98 × 78 mm. 20fo. Airship LZ-127 "Graf Zeppelin" over Budapest (58 × 36 mm) . . . . 4·00 4·00

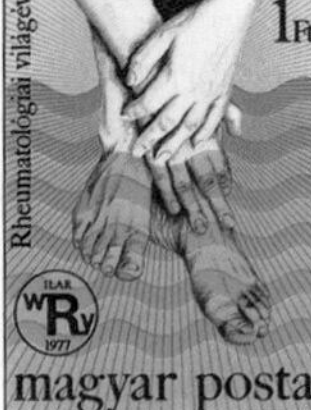

685 Feet Immersed in Water

686 Ervin Szabo

1977. World Rheumatism Year.
3150 **685** 1fo. multicoloured . . . 35 10

1977. Anniversaries.
3151 – 1fo. black and red . . . 10 10
3152 **686** 1fo. grey, black and red 10 10
DESIGNS: No 3151, Jamos Szanto Kovacs (agrarian socialist movement leader, 125th birth anniv); 3152, Type **686** (director of Municipal Libraries, journalist and labour movement leader, birth centenary).

687 Monument to Hungarian Participants, Omsk

1977. 60th Anniv of Russian Revolution.
3153 **687** 1fo. black and red . . . 10 10

688 Endre Ady

689 Lesser Panda

1977. Birth Centenary of Endre Ady (poet).
3154 **688** 1fo. blue 30 30

1977. Bears. Multicoloured.
3155 40fi. Type **689** 15 10
3156 60fi. Giant panda 20 10
3157 1fo. Asiatic black bear . . . 35 10
3158 4fo. Polar bear . . . . . . 1·50 15
3159 6fo. Brown bear . . . . . 2·10 45

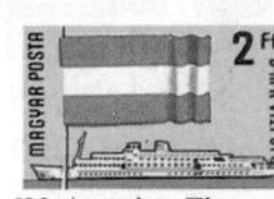

690 Austrian Flag and Passenger Ship

1977. 30th Anniv of Re-establishment of Danube Commission. Sheet 130 × 93 mm containing T **690** and similar horiz designs.
MS3160 2fo. × 11 multicoloured 13·50 13·00
DESIGNS—Flags and ships of : Austria, Bulgaria, Czechoslovakia, France, Netherlands, Yugoslavia, Hungary, West Germany, Rumania, Switzerland, Soviet Union.

691 Border-country Lancer, 17th-cent

1978. Hussars. Multicoloured.
3161 40fi. Type **691** 15 10
3162 60fi. Kuruts horseman, 1710 20 10
3163 1fo. Baranya hussar, 1762 30 10
3164 2fo. Palatine Hussars officer, 1809 . . . . 45 10
3165 4fo. Alexander Hussar, 1848 85 20
3166 6fo. Trumpeter, 5th Honved Regiment, 1900 . . . . . 1·25 55

692 Moon Station

1978. Air. Science Fiction in Space Research. Multicoloured.
3167 40fi. Type **692** 10 10
3168 60fi. Moon settlement . . . 15 10
3169 1fo. Phobos 25 10
3170 2fo. Exploring an asteroid 45 10
3171 3fo. Spacecraft in gravitational field of Mars 65 10
3172 4fo. One of Saturn's rings 95 15
3173 5fo. "Jupiter 3" . . . . . . 1·25 45

693 School of Arts and Crafts

1978. Bicent of School of Art and Crafts.
3174 **693** 1fo. multicoloured . . . 10 10

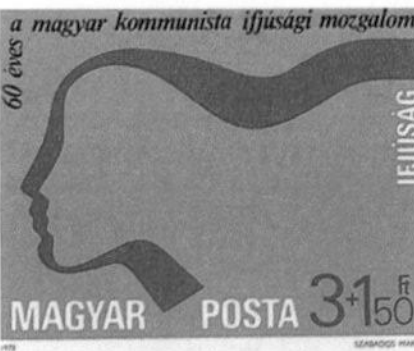

694 Profile Heads

1978. Youth Stamp Exhibition, Hatvan.
3175 **694** 3fo.+1fo.50 silver, red and black . . . . . . 1·50 1·50

695 "Generations" (Gyula Derkovits)

1978. "Socphilex 78" Stamp Exhibition, Szombathely.
3176 **695** 3fo.+1fo.50 mult 75 90

696 Louis Bleriot

1978. Air. Famous Aviators and their Airplanes. Multicoloured.
3177 40fi. Type **696** 15 10
3178 60fi. John Alcock and Arthur Whitten Brown . . 20 10
3179 1fo. Albert C. Read 25 10
3180 2fo. Hermann Kohl, Gunther Hunefeld and James Fitzmaurice 55 10
3181 3fo. Amy Johnson and Jim Mollison 75 15
3182 4fo. Georgy Endresz and Sandor Magyar 95 20
3183 5fo. Wolfgang von Gronau 1·00 70
MS3184 96 × 79 mm. 20fo. Wright Brothers and "Flyer" (74 × 25 mm) . . . . 3·75 4·00

697 Glass Vase and Glass-blowing Tube

1978. Centenary of Ajka Glass Works.
3185 **697** 1fo. multicoloured . . . 15 10

698 West Germany and Poland

1978. World Cup Football Championship, Argentina. Multicoloured.
3186 2fo. Type **698** 55 20
3187 2fo. Hungary and Argentina 55 20
3188 2fo. France and Italy . . . 55 20
3189 2fo. Tunisia and Mexico . . 55 20
3190 2fo. Sweden and Brazil . . 55 20
3191 2fo. Spain and Austria . . . 55 20
3192 2fo. Peru and Scotland . . . 55 20
3193 2fo. Iran and Netherlands 55 20
MS3194 98 × 76 mm. 20fo. World Cup emblem and goal mouth (37 × 27 mm) . . . . 3·75 4·00

699 Canadian 3d. Stamp, 1851

1978. "Capex 78" International Stamp Exhibition, Toronto.
3195 **699** 3fo. multicoloured . . . 1·50 90

700 Diesel MK 45 Locomotive

702 Festival Emblem

701 Leif Eriksson

1978. 30th Anniv of Budapest Pioneer Railway.
3196 **700** 1fo. multicoloured . . . 25 10

1978. Explorers. Two sheets each 130 × 100 mm containing horiz designs as T **701**.
MS3197 Two sheets (a) 2fo. × 4 yellow and black (T **701**); orange and black (Christopher Columbus); orange and black (Vasco da Gama); pink and black (Ferdinand Magellan). (b) 2fo. × 4 yellow and black (Sir Francis Drake); apple green and black (Henry Hudson); green and black (James Cook); light blue and black (Robert Peary) 2 sheets . . . . 6·75 7·25

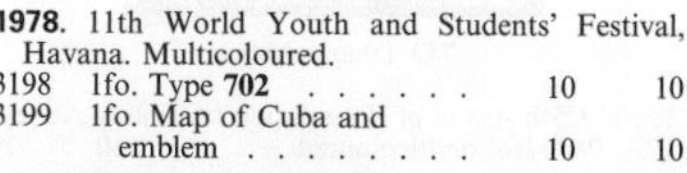

1978. 11th World Youth and Students' Festival, Havana. Multicoloured.
3198 1fo. Type **702** 10 10
3199 1fo. Map of Cuba and emblem 10 10

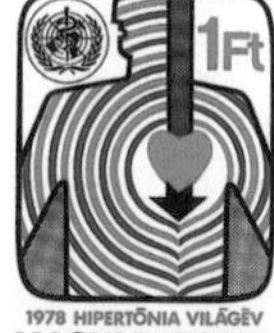
703 Human Torso and Heart

705 Dove and Fist holding Olive Branch

704 Jules Verne and illustration from "A Journey to the Moon"

1978. World Hypertension Year.
3200 **703** 1fo. red, black and blue 10 10

1978. Air. 150th Birth Anniv of Jules Verne (novelist). Sheet 97 × 78 mm.
MS3201 **704** 20fo. black and yellow 3·75 4·00

1978. 20th Anniv of Communist Party Review "Peace and Socialism".
3202 **705** 1fo. red and black . . . 10 10

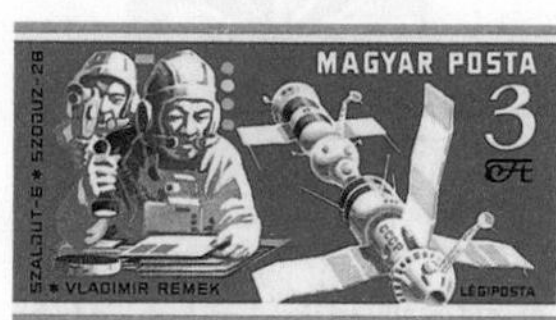
706 Vladimir Remek cancelling Letters, "Salyut 6" and "Soyuz 28"

1978. Air. "Praga 1978" International Stamp Exhibition, Prague.
3203 **706** 3fo. multicoloured . . . 75 85

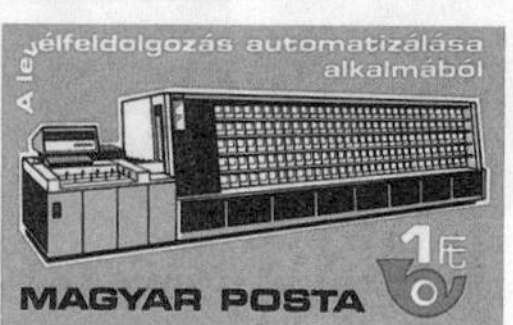
707 Toshiba Automatic Letter Sorting Equipment

1978. Automation of Letter Sorting.
3204 **707** 1fo. multicoloured . . . 30 30

708 Putto offering Grapes

1978. Stamp Day. Mosaics. Multicoloured.
3205 2fo. Type **708** . . . . . . 1·50 1·60
3206 2fo. Tiger . . . . 1·50 1·60
3207 2fo. Bird . . . . 1·50 1·60
3208 2fo. Dolphin . . . . 1·50 1·60
MS3209 88 × 61 mm. 10fo. Hercules aiming arrow at Centaur Nessus fleeing with Nymph Deianeira (51 × 32 mm) . . . . 6·25 6·75

709 Methods of Communication

1978. Organization of Socialist Countries' Postal Administrations Conference, Tbilisi.
3210 **709** 1fo. multicoloured . . . 35 10

710 Imre Thokoly

1978. 300th Anniv of Thokoly's Revolt.
3211 **710** 1fo. black and yellow . . 35 10

711 Hungarian Regalia

1978. Return of Hungarian Regalia. Sheet 76 × 96 mm.
MS3212 **711** 20fo. multicoloured 6·75 6·25

712 "The Red Coach" (novel)

1978. Birth Cent of Gyula Krudy (novelist).
3213 **712** 3fo. red and black . . . 50 10

713 St. Ladislas (bust, Gyor Cathedral)

1978. 900th Anniv of Accession of St. Ladislas.
3214 **713** 1fo. multicoloured . . . 30 10

714 Buildings and Arms of Koszeg

1978. 650th Anniv of Koszeg.
3215 **714** 1fo. multicoloured . . . 35 10

715 Samu Czaban and Gizella Berzeviczy

1978. Birth Centenaries of Samu Czaban and Gizella Berzeviczy (teachers).
3216 **715** 1fo. multicoloured . . . 30 25

716 Communist Party Emblem

1978. 60th Anniv of Hungarian Communist Party.
3217 **716** 1fo. red, grey and black 10 10

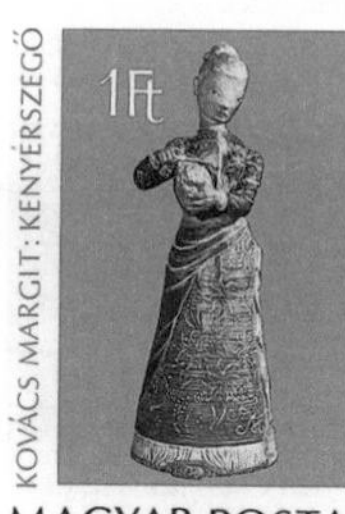
717 "Girl cutting Bread"

1978. Ceramics by Margit Kovacs. Mult.
3218 1fo. Type **717** 30 10
3219 2fo. "Girl with Pitcher" . . 45 25
3220 3fo. "Boy Potter" 80 30

718 "Self-portrait in Fur Coat"

1978. 450th Death Anniv of Albrecht Durer (artist). Multicoloured.
3221 40fi. "Madonna with Child" 10 10
3222 60fi. "Adoration of the Magi" (horiz) 10 10
3223 1fo. Type **718** 20 10
3224 2fo. "St. George" 40 10
3225 3fo. "Nativity" (horiz) . . . 65 10
3226 4fo. "St. Eustace" 80 20
3227 5fo. "The Four Apostles" 1·00 60
MS3228 78 × 99 mm. 20fo. sepia and stone ("Dancing Peasant Couple") (36 × 59 mm) . . . . 3·25 4·00

719 Human Rights Emblem

720 Child with Dog

1979. 30th Anniv of Declaration of Human Rights.
3229 **719** 1fo. blue and light blue 75 1·00

1979. International Year of the Child (1st issue). Multicoloured.
3230 1fo. Type **720** 65 50
3231 1fo. Family group 65 50
3232 1fo. Children of different races . . . . 2·40 3·00
See also Nos. 3287/93.

721 "Soldiers of the Red Army, Forward!" (poster by Bela Uitz)

1979. 60th Anniv of First Hungarian Soviet Republic.
3233 **721** 1fo. black, red and grey 10 10

722 "Girl Reading" (Ferenc Kovacs)

1979. Youth Stamp Exhibition, Bekescsaba.
3234 **722** 3fo.+1fo.50 grey, blue and black 65 75

723 Chessmen and Cup

1979. 23rd Chess Olympiad, Buenos Aires (1978).
3235 **723** 3fo. multicoloured . . . 1·10 90

724 Alexander Nevski Cathedral, Sofia, and First Bulgarian Stamp

1979. "Philaserdica 79" International Stamp Exhibition, Sofia.
3236 **724** 3fo. multicoloured . . . 75 80

725 Stephenson's "Rocket", 1829

1979. International Transport Exhibition, Hamburg. Depicting development of the railway. Mult.
3237 40fi. Type **725** 20 10
3238 60fi. Siemens's electric locomotive, 1879 . . . . 20 10
3239 1fo. Locomotive "Pioneer", 1851 (wrongly dated "1936") 30 10
3240 2fo. Hungarian Class MAV I.e pulling "Orient Express", 1883 . . . . . 40 15
3241 3fo. "Trans-Siberian Express", 1898 . . . . . 55 30
3242 4fo. Japanese "Hikari" express train, 1964 . . . 80 40
3243 5fo. German "Transrapid 05" Maglev train, 1979 90 85
MS3244 78 × 95 mm. 20fo. European railway map (51 × 36 mm) . . . . 9·75 6·50

726 Soyuz Gas Pipeline and Compressor Station

727 Zsigmond Moricz (after J. Rippl-Ronai)

1979. 30th Anniv of Council of Mutual Economic Aid. Multicoloured.
3245 1fo. Type **726** 15 10
3246 2fo. Pylon and dam, Lenin hydro-electric power station, Dnepropetrovsk 35 10
3247 3fo. Council building, Moscow 35 10

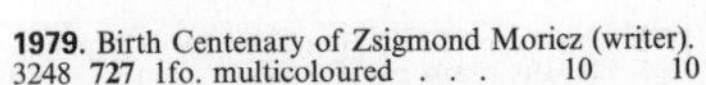

1979. Birth Centenary of Zsigmond Moricz (writer).
3248 **727** 1fo. multicoloured . . . 10 10

728 City Hall, Helsinki (1952 Games)

1979. Olympic Games, Moscow (1980) (1st issue). Multicoloured.
3249 40fi. Type **728** 10 10
3250 60fi. Colosseum, Rome (1960) 10 10
3251 1fo. Asakusa Temple, Tokyo (1964) 35 10
3252 2fo. Cathedral, Mexico City (1968) 55 10
3253 3fo. Frauenkirche, Munich (1972) 70 15
3254 4fo. Modern quarter, Montreal (1976) . . . . . 1·10 15
3255 5fo. Lomonosov University, Moscow, and Misha the bear (mascot) (1980) . . . 1·25 60

See also Nos. 3323/29.

729 "Child with Horse and Greyhounds" (Janos Vaszary)

1979. Animal Paintings. Multicoloured.
3256 40fi. Type **729** 20 10
3257 60fi. "Coach and Five" (Karoly Lotz) 25 10
3258 1fo. "Lads on Horseback" (Celesztin Pallya) 30 10
3259 2fo. "Farewell" (Karoly Lotz) 40 20
3260 3fo. "Horse Market" (Celeztin Pallya) 55 20
3261 4fo. "Wandering" (Bela Ivanyi-Grunwald) 65 40
3262 5fo. "Ready for Hunting" (Karoly Sterio) . . . . . 1·00 90

730 Sturgeon, Cousteau's Ship "Calypso" and Black Sea

1979. Sea and River Purity.
3263 **730** 3fo. multicoloured . . . 65 10

731 Globe and Five Pentathlon Sports

1979. Pentathlon World Championship, Budapest.
3264 **731** 2fo. multicoloured . . . 60 10

732 Stephen I Denarius (reverse)

1979. 9th International Numismatic Congress, Berne. Designs showing old Hungarian coins. Multicoloured.
3265 1fo. Type **732** 30 10
3266 2fo. Bela III copper coin (obverse) 45 20
3267 3fo. Louis the Great groat (reverse) 55 30
3268 4fo. Matthias I gold forint (obverse) 70 75
3269 5fo. Wladislaw II gulden (reverse) . . . . 1·00 1·25

733 Design for Proposed Hungarian Stamp of 1848

734 Light Passenger Locomotive

1979. Stamp Day. Sheet 70 × 56 mm.
MS3270 **733** 10fo. multicoloured 3·75 3·75

1979. Centenary of Gyor—Sopron–Ebenfurt Railway. Sheet 98 × 79 mm containing T **734** and similar horiz designs. Multicoloured.
MS3271 5fo. Type **734**; 5fo. Class 424 steam locomotive; 5fo. Class 520 locomotive; 5fo. Diesel locomotive Type M41 . . . . 4·50 4·25

735 Flags and Globe filled with Coins

1979. World Savings Day.
3272 **735** 1fo. multicoloured . . . 20 10

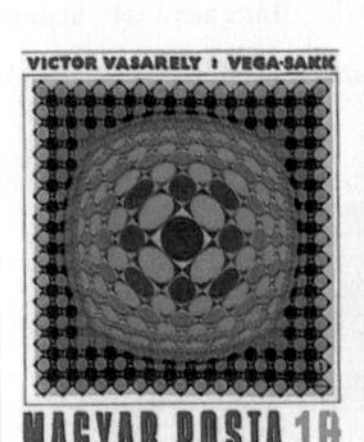

736 "Vega-Chess" (Victor Vasarely)

737 European Otter

1979. Modern Art.
3273 **736** 1fo. multicoloured . . . 10 10

1979. Protected Animals. Multicoloured.
3274 40fi. Type **737** 20 10
3275 60fi. Wild cat 20 10
3276 1fo. Pine marten 40 10
3277 2fo. Eurasian badger . . . 55 10
3278 4fo. Steppe polecat . . . . 1·25 20
3279 6fo. Beech marten . . . . . 1·75 70

738 Ski Jumping

1979. Air. Winter Olympic Games, Lake Placid (1980). Multicoloured.
3280 40fi. Type **738** 30 10
3281 60fi. Figure skating 35 10
3282 1fo. Slalom 55 15
3283 2fo. Ice hockey 75 20
3284 4fo. Bobsleigh . . . . . . 1·25 20
3285 6fo. Cross-country skiing . . 1·60 55
MS3286 97 × 73 mm. 20fo. Ice dancing (square, 49 × 49 mm) 5·25 5·00

739 "Tom Thumb"

1979. International Year of the Child (2nd issue). Designs depicting children's stories. Mult.
3287 40fi. Type **739** 15 10
3288 60fi. "The Ugly Duckling" (Andersen) 30 10
3289 1fo. "The Fisher and the Goldfish" 40 10
3290 2fo. "Cinderella" 70 10
3291 3fo. "Gulliver's Travels" (Swift) 90 10
3292 4fo. "The Little Pig and the Wolves" 95 20
3293 5fo. "Gallant John" . . . . 1·25 50
MS3294 78 × 98 mm. 20fo. "Fairy Ilona" . . . . 3·75 4·00

740 Achillea and Bee-eating Beetles

1980. Pollination. Multicoloured.
3295 40fl. Type **740** 15 10
3296 60fl. Gaillardia and bee . . 15 10
3297 1fo. Rudbeckia and red admiral 20 10
3298 2fo. Dog rose and rose chafer 40 10
3299 4fo. "Petroselinum hortense" and striped bug 80 20
3300 6fo. Achillea and longhorn beetle . . . . 1·25 55

741 Hanging Gardens of Babylon

1980. Seven Wonders of the Ancient World. Mult.
3301 40fi. Type **741** 15 10
3302 60fi. Temple of Artemis, Ephesus 15 10
3303 1fo. Statue of Zeus, Olympia 20 10
3304 2fo. Mausoleum of Halicarnassus 40 10
3305 3fo. Colossus of Rhodes . . 55 15
3306 4fo. Pharos, Alexandria . . 70 20
3307 5fo. Pyramids of Egypt . . 1·75 60

742 Gabor Bethlen (copperplate)

1980. 400th Birth Anniv of Gabor Bethlen (Prince of Transylvania).
3308 **742** 1fo. multicoloured . . . 10 10

743 Tihany Abbey

1980. 925th Anniv of Foundation of Tihany Abbey.
3309 **743** 1fo. multicoloured . . . 10 10

744 Easter Sepulchre

1980. Easter Sepulchre of Garamszentbenedek. Designs showing details of sepulchre. Mult.

3310 1fo. Type **744** 15 10
3311 2fo. Three Marys 35 10
3312 3fo. Apostle Jacob 45 20
3313 4fo. Apostle Thaddeus . . . 60 35
3314 5fo. Apostle Andrew 80 70

745 Bunch of Wild Flowers

1980. 35th Anniv of Liberation.

3315 **745** 1fo. multicoloured . . . 20 10

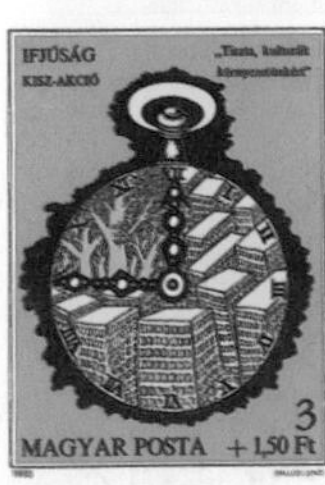

JÓZSEF ATTILA 1905-1937

1Ft MAGYAR POSTA

746 Watch symbolising Environmental Protection

747 Attila Jozsef

1980. Youth Stamp Exhibition, Dunaujvaros.

3316 **746** 3fo.+1fo.50 mult 60 65

1980. 75th Birth Anniv of Attila Jozsef (poet).

3317 **747** 1fo. green and red . . . 10 10

748 "Madonna and Child" Stamp of 1921 with Inverted Centre

1980. 50th Anniv of Hungarian Stamp Museum.

3318 **748** 1fo. multicoloured . . . 1·10 1·25

749 Great Britain 2d. Blue and Life Guard

1980. "London 1980" International Stamp Exhibition.

3319 **749** 3fo. multicoloured . . . 75 75

KAFFKA MARGIT 1880-1918

Magyar Posta

750 Soviet and Hungarian Cosmonauts

751 Margit Kaffka

1980. Air. Soviet–Hungarian Space Flight.

3320 **750** 5fo. multicoloured . . . 1·50 30

1980. Birth Centenary of Margit Kaffka (writer).

3321 **751** 1fo. yellow, black & vio 20 10

752 Norwegian 1951 Olympic Stamp and Statue "Mother and Child" (Gustav Vigeland)

1980. "Norwex 80" International Stamp Exhibition, Oslo.

3322 **752** 3fo. multicoloured . . . 75 75

753 Handball

1980. Air. Olympic Games, Moscow (2nd issue). Multicoloured.

3323 40fi. Type **753** 10 10
3324 60fi. Double kayak 10 10
3325 1fo. Running 20 10
3326 2fo. Gymnastics 40 10
3327 3fo. Show-jumping (modern pentathlon) 65 10
3328 4fo. Wrestling 80 15
3329 5fo. Water polo . . . . . . 1·10 55
MS3330 71 × 87 mm. 20fo. Runners with Olympic flame . . . . . 3·75 3·25

754 Endre Hogyes (physician) and Congress Emblem

756 Zoltan Schonherz

755B. Farkos, V. Kubasov and Space Station

1980. 28th International Congress of Physiological Sciences, Budapest.

3331 **754** 1fo. multicoloured . . . 10 10

1980. Air. Soviet–Hungarian Space Flight (2nd issue). Sheet 72 × 93 mm.

MS3332 **755** 20fo. multicoloured 4·50 5·75

1980. 75th Birth Anniv of Zoltan Schonherz (Workers' Movement member).

3333 **756** 1fo. multicoloured . . . 10 10

1880-1964 ÖNARCKÉP • MŰVE

1 Ft

MAGYAR POSTA

757 Decanter

759 Bertalan Por (self-portrait)

758 Greek Athletes and Olympic Gold Medal

1980. Stamp Day. Glassware. Multicoloured.

3334 1fo. Type **757** 20 20
3335 2fo. Wine glass, Budapest 40 20
3336 3fo. Drinking glass, Zay-Ugrocz 60 50
MS3337 68 × 79 mm. 10fo. Drinking glass, Pecs (25 × 35 mm) . . . 2·40 2·40

1980. Air. Olympic Champions. Sheet 84 × 65 mm.

MS3338 **758** 20fo. multicoloured 3·25 3·25

1980. Birth Centenary of Bertalan Por (artist).

3339 **759** 1fo. multicoloured . . . 10 10

760 Greylag Goose

1980. Protected Birds. Multicoloured.

3340 40fi. Type **760** 20 10
3341 60fi. Black-crowned night herons 25 10
3342 1fo. Common shovelers . . 30 15
3343 2fo. White-winged black tern 65 25
3344 4fo. Great crested grebes . . 1·40 65
3345 6fo. Black-winged stilts . . 2·00 1·10
MS3346 75 × 95 mm. 20fo. Great egrets (40 × 63 mm) . . . . . 4·75 4·25

761 Peace Dove and Map of Europe

1980. European Security and Co-operation Conference, Madrid. Sheet 99 × 78 mm.

MS3347 **761** 20fo. multicoloured 3·25 3·00

762 Johannes Kepler

1980. 350th Death Anniv of Johannes Kepler (astronomer).

3348 **762** 1fo. multicoloured . . . 30 10

KISFALUDY KÁROLY 1788-1830

1 Ft MAGYAR POSTA

763 Karoly Kisfaludy

1980. 150th Death Anniv of Karoly Kisfaludy (dramatist and poet).

3349 **763** 1fo. multicoloured . . . 20 10

MAGYARORSZÁG 25 ÉVE TAGJA AZ ENSZ-NEK

764 U.N. Building, New York

1980. 25th Anniv of United Nations Membership. Multicoloured.

3350 40fi. Type **764** 15 10
3351 60fi. U.N. building, Geneva 10 10
3352 1fo. International Centre, Vienna 20 10
3353 2fo. U.N. and Hungarian flags 40 10
3354 4fo. U.N. emblem and Hungarian arms 80 15
3355 6fo. World map . . . . . . 1·75 80

ERDEI FERENC 1910-1971

SZÁNTÓ BÉLA 1881-1951

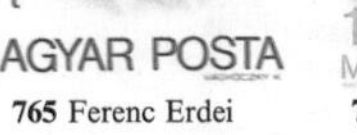

765 Ferenc Erdei

766 Bela Szanto

1980. 70th Birth Anniv of Ferenc Erdei (agricultural economist and politician).

3356 **765** 1fo. multicoloured . . . 10 10

1981. Birth Centenary of Bela Szanto (founder member of Hungarian Communist Party).

3357 **766** 1fo. multicoloured . . . 10 10

767 Lajos Batthyany (after Miklos Barabas)

1981. 175th Birth Anniv of Lajos Batthyany (politician).

3358 **767** 1fo. multicoloured . . . 10 10

768 Cheetah

769 "Graf Zeppelin" over Tokyo

1981. Air. Birth Centenary of Kalman Kittenberger (explorer and zoologist). Multicoloured.

3359 40fi. Type **768** 20 10
3360 60fi. Lion 20 10
3361 1fo. Leopard 30 10
3362 2fo. Black rhinoceros . . . 55 10
3363 3fo. Greater kudu 60 25
3364 4fo. African elephant . . . 1·00 25
3365 5fo. Kittenberger and Hungarian National Museum . . . . 2·25 95

1981. Air. "Luraba" International Exhibition of Aero- and Astro-philately, Lucerne. "Graf Zeppelin" Flights. Multicoloured.

3366 1fo. Type **769** (first round-the-world flight, 1929) . . 15 10
3367 2fo. Franz Josef Land and icebreaker "Malygin" (Polar flight, 1931) . . . 45 10
3368 3fo. Nine-arch Bridge, Hortobagy (Hungary flight, 1931) 45 10
3369 4fo. Hostentor, Lubeck (Baltic flight, 1931) . . . 60 10
3370 5fo. Tower Bridge (England flight, 1931) 70 25
3371 6fo. Federal Palace, Chicago (World Exhibition flight, 1933) 75 25
3372 7fo. Lucerne (1st Swiss flight, 1929) 85 80

770 Bela Bartok (after Ferenczy Beni)

1981. Birth Centenary of Bela Bartok (composer). Sheet 100 × 80 mm containing T **770** and similar vert design. Multicoloured.
MS3373 10fo. Type **770**; 10fo. Illustration for "Cantata Profana" 4·50 4·50

771 Flag of House of Arpad (11th century)

1981. Historical Hungarian Flags. Mult.
3374 40fi. Type **771** 20 10
3375 60fi. Hunyadi Family flag (15th century) 30 10
3376 1fo. Flag of Gabor Bethlen (1600) 50 10
3377 2fo. Flag of Ferenc Rakoczi II (1706) 70 10
3378 4fo. "Honved" (1848–49) 1·00 20
3379 6fo. Troop Flag (1919) 1·40 55

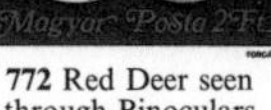

772 Red Deer seen through Binoculars

773 First Hungarian Telephone Exchange

1981. Cent of Association of Hungarian Huntsmen.
3380 **772** 2fo. multicoloured 35 10

1981. Centenary of First Hungarian Telephone Exchange, Budapest.
3381 **773** 2fo. multicoloured 60 10

774 Henri Dunant (founder) and Map of Europe

1981. 3rd European Conference of Red Cross and Red Crescent Societies, Budapest. Sheet 98 × 78 mm.
MS3382 **774** 20fo. multicoloured 4·50 4·00

775 Red Cross, Transport and Globe

776 Airship LZ-127 "Graf Zeppelin"

1981. Cent of Hungarian Red Cross.
3383 **775** 2fo. orange and red 30 10

1981. "WIPA 1981" International Stamp Exhibition, Vienna. Sheet 80 × 60 mm containing T **776** and similar horiz designs depicting "WIPA 1933" souvenir labels.
MS3384 5fo. green and black (Type **776**); 5fo. purple and black (Rocket); 5fo. brown and black (Dispatch rider); 5fo. blue and black (Sailing ship) 4·50 4·00

777 I.Y.D.P. Emblem and Person pushing Wheelchair

1981. International Year of Disabled Persons.
3385 **777** 2fo.+1fo. green & yell 75 70

778 Young People and Factory

779 Stephenson and "Locomotion"

1981. 10th Young Communist League Congress, Budapest.
3386 **778** 4fo.+2fo. mult 90 1·00

1981. Birth Bicentenary of George Stephenson (railway pioneer).
3387 **779** 2fo. yellow, grey & brown 75 25

780 Bela Vago

1981. Birth Centenary of Bela Vago (founder member of Hungarian Communist Party).
3388 **780** 2fo. green and brown 35 10

781 Alexander Fleming

1981. Birth Centenary of Alexander Fleming (discoverer of penicillin).
3389 **781** 2fo. multicoloured 55 20

782 Bridal Chest from Szentgal

1981. Stamp Day. Bridal Chests. Mult.
3390 1fo. Type **782** 20 10
3391 2fo. Chest from Hodmezovasarhely 50 30
MS3392 76 × 55 mm. 10fo. Chest from Bacs (43 × 23 mm) 3·75 3·75

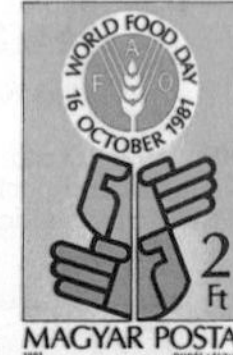

783 Calvinist College

784 Hands holding F.A.O. Emblem

1981. 450th Anniv of Calvinist College, Papa.
3393 **783** 2fo. multicoloured 35 10

1981. World Food Day.
3394 **784** 2fo. multicoloured 75 10

785 German Costume

786 "Franz I" (1830) and "Ferene Deak" on 30fi. Stamp

1981. National Costumes of Hungarian Ethnic Minorities. Multicoloured.
3395 1fo. Slovakian costume 1·40 1·40
3396 2fo. Type **785** 1·40 1·40
3397 3fo. Croatian costume 1·40 1·40
3398 4fo. Rumanian costume 1·40 1·40

1981. 125th Anniv of Danube Commission. Paddle-steamers and Danube Commission stamps issued in 1967. Multicoloured.
3399 1fo. Type **786** 40 15
3400 1fo. "Arpad" (1834) and "Revfulop" on 60fi. stamp 40 15
3401 2fo. "Szechenyi" (1853) and "Hunyadi" on 1fo. stamp 55 25
3402 2fo. "Grof Szechenyi Istvan" (1896) and "Szekszard" on 1fo.50 stamp 55 25
3403 4fo. "Zsofia" (1914) and "Miscolc" on 1fo.70 stamp 90 45
3404 6fo. "Felszabadulas" (1917) and "Tihany" on 2fo. stamp 1·60 95
3405 8fo. "Rakoczi" (1964) and "Siraly I" on 2fo.50 stamp 2·10 1·50
MS3406 96 × 77 mm. 20fo. Hydrofoil "Solyom" and 1fo. stamp (49 × 39 mm) 5·50 4·75

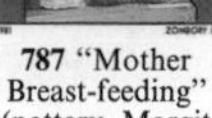

787 "Mother Breast-feeding" (pottery, Margit Kovacs)

788 "Pen Pals" (Rockwell)

1981. Christmas. Multicoloured.
3407 1fo. Type **787** 15 20
3408 2fo. "Madonna of Csurgo" (bronze Amerigo Tot) 60 20

1981. Illustrations by Norman Rockwell and Anna Lesznai. Multicoloured.
3409 1fo. Type **788** 15 15
3410 2fo. "Courting under the Clock at Midnight" (Rockwell) 30 15
3411 2fo. "Maiden Voyage" (Rockwell) 30 15
3412 4fo. "Threading the Needle" (Rockwell) 65 55
3413 4fo. "At the End of the Village" (detail) (Lesznai) 65 55
3414 5fo. "Dance" (detail) (Lesznai) 95 80
3415 6fo. "Sunday" (detail) (Lesznai) 1·25 1·25

789 "La Tolette"

1981. Birth Centenary of Pablo Picasso (artist). Sheet 61 × 86 mm.
MS3416 **789** 20fo. multicoloured 4·25 4·25

790 Militiaman at Shooting Practice

791 Congress Emblem and Havana

1982. 25th Anniv of Workers' Militia. Mult.
3417 1fo. Type **790** 15 15
3418 4fo. Three generations of militiamen 60 15

1982. 10th World Trade Unions Federation Congress, Havana.
3419 **791** 2fo. multicoloured 30 10

792 Gyula Alpari

793 Dr. Robert Koch

1982. Birth Centenary of Gyula Alpari (journalist).
3420 **792** 2fo. yellow, purple & brn 30 10

1982. Cent of Discovery of Tubercle Bacillus.
3421 **793** 2fo. multicoloured 40 10

794 Tennis Racket and Ball

796 Table Tennis Player and Map of Europe

795 Hungary v. Egypt, 1934

1982. Youth Stamp. European Junior Tennis Cup.
3422 **794** 4fo.+2fo. mult 1·10 1·10

1982. World Cup Football Championship, Spain. Multicoloured.
3423 1fo. Type **795** 20 10
3424 1fo. Italy v. Hungary, 1938 20 10
3425 2fo. West Germany v. Hungary, 1954 40 10
3426 2fo. Hungary v. Mexico, 1958 40 10
3427 4fo. Hungary v. England, 1962 85 10
3428 6fo. Hungary v. Brazil, 1966 1·25 15
3429 8fo. Argentina v. Hungary, 1978 1·60 65
MS3430 100 × 68 mm. 10fo. Barcelona stadium; 10fo. Madrid stadium 4·50 4·25

1982. European Table Tennis Championship, Budapest.
3431 **796** 2fo. multicoloured 50 10

797 "Pascali"

798 Georgi Dimitrov

1982. Roses. Multicoloured.
3432 1fo. Type **797** 25 15
3433 1fo. "Michele Meilland" 25 15
3434 2fo. "Diorama" 40 15
3435 2fo. "Wendy Cussons" 40 15
3436 3fo. "Blue Moon" 70 20
3437 3fo. "Invitation" 70 20
3438 4fo. "Tropicana" 1·10 50
MS3439 70 × 92 mm. 10fo. Bunch of roses (35 × 57 mm) 3·50 3·75

1982. Birth Centenary of Georgi Dimitrov (Bulgarian statesman).
3440 **798** 2fo. grey, green & brown 30 35

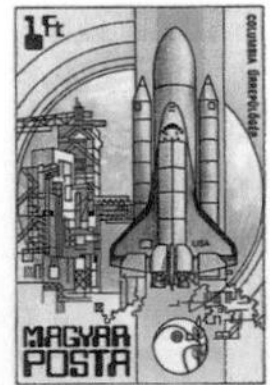

799 "Columbia" Space Shuttle
800 Watermark

1982. Space Research. Multicoloured.
3441 1fo. Type **799** 20 10
3442 1fo. Neil Armstrong (first man on Moon) 20 10
3443 2fo. A. Leonov (first space-walker) 35 10
3444 2fo. Yuri Gagarin (first man in space) 35 10
3445 4fo. Laika (first dog in space) 75 20
3446 4fo. "Sputnik I" (first artificial satellite) 75 20
3447 6fo. K. E. Tsiolkovsky (Russian scientist) . . . . 1·25 50

1982. Bicentenary of Diosgyor Paper-mill.
3448 **800** 2fo. multicoloured . . . 30 10

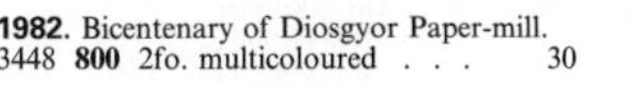

801 Rubik Cube

1982. World Rubik Cube Championship, Budapest.
3449 **801** 2fo. multicoloured . . . 30 10

802 World Cup 20fi. Stamp, 1966, and Paris Arms

1982. "Philexfrance 82" International Stamp Exhibition, Paris. Sheet 98 × 72 mm.
MS3450 **802** 20fo.+10fo. mult . . 3·75 3·75

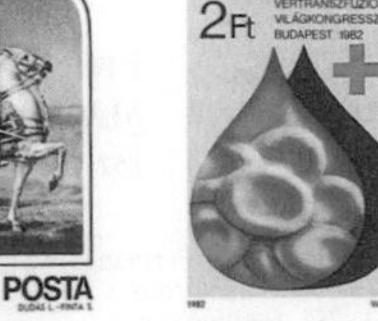

803 Col. Mihaly Kovats (after S. Finta)
804 Blood Drop

1982. 250th Birth Anniv of George Washington. Sheet 90 × 72 mm containing T **803** and similar vert design. Multicoloured.
MS3451 5fo. Type **803**; 5fo. Washington on horseback (after F. Kemmelmeyer) . . . . . . 3·25 3·25

1982. World Haematology Congress, Budapest.
3452 **804** 2fo. multicoloured . . . 30 10

805 Zirc Abbey and Seal of King Bela III
806 Fishermen's Bastion, Budapest

1982. 800th Anniv of Zirc Abbey.
3453 **805** 2fo. multicoloured . . . 30 10

1982. Stamp Day. Multicoloured.
3454 4fo.+2fo. Type **806** . . . . 95 1·00
3455 4fo.+2fo. Cupola of Parliament, Budapest . . 95 1·00

807 Budapest (½-size illustration)

1982. 10th Anniv of European Security and Co-operation Conference, Brussels. Sheet 100 × 84 mm.
MS3456 **807** 20fo.+10fo. mult . . 4·50 4·00

808 Kner Emblem

1982. Cent of Kner Printing Office, Gyoma.
3457 **808** 2fo. yellow, black and red 30 10

809 Agricultural Symbols on Map of Hungary

1982. "Agrofila '82" Stamp Exhibition, Godollo.
3458 **809** 5fo. multicoloured . . . 1·00 1·00

810 Horse-drawn Bus and Underground Train

1982. 150th Anniv of Public Transport in Budapest.
3459 **810** 2fo. multicoloured . . . 45 10

811 Budapest Polytechnic University
812 Gyorgy Boloni

1982. Bicentenary of University Engineering Education.
3460 **811** 2fo. brown, stone & blue 30 10

1982. Birth Centenary of Gyorgy Boloni (journalist).
3461 **812** 2fo. yellow, brown and deep brown 30 10

813 Lenin

1982. 65th Anniv of Russian Revolution.
3462 **813** 5fo. multicoloured . . . 80 10

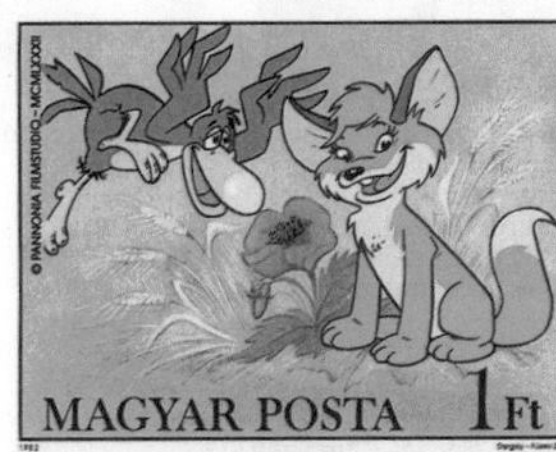

814 Vuk and Bird

1982. Vuk the Fox Cub (cartoon character). Multicoloured.
3463 1fo. Type **814** 20 10
3464 1fo. Two dogs 20 10
3465 2fo. Vuk and cock 40 10
3466 2fo. Vuk and owl 40 10
3467 4fo. Vuk and geese 80 10
3468 6fo. Vuk and frog . . . . . 1·25 60
3469 8fo. Vuk, old fox and butterflies . . . . 1·60 1·00

815 St. Stephen (sculpture, Imre Varga)
816 Dog and Cat crossing road

1982. Works of Art in Hungarian Chapel, Vatican. Multicoloured.
3470 2fo. Type **815** 50 55
3471 2fo. "Pope Silvester II making donation to St. Stephen" (37 × 18 mm) 50 55
3472 2fo. "St. John of Capistrano ringing Angelus to commemorate Hungarian victory over Turks" (37 × 18 mm) 50 55
3473 2fo. "Pope Paul VI showing Cardinal Lekai site of Hungarian Chapel" (37 × 18 mm) 50 55
3474 2fo. "Pope John Paul II consecrating chapel" (37 × 18 mm) 50 55
3475 2fo. "Madonna" (sculpture, Imre Varga) 50 55

Nos. 3471/5 were printed together, se-tenant, forming a composite design of a relief by Amerigo Tot.

1982. New Year.
3476 **816** 2fo. multicoloured . . . 40 10

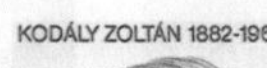

817 Zoltan Kodaly

1982. Birth Centenary of Zoltan Kodaly (composer). Sheet 66 × 95 mm.
MS3477 **817** 20fo. brown and stone 3·50 3·00

818 Goethe (after Heinrich Kolbe)

1982. 150th Death Anniv of Johann Wolfgang Goethe (writer). Sheet 93 × 74 mm.
MS3478 **818** 20fo. multicoloured 3·50 3·50

819 Raven and Envelope Address Marks
821 Student at School Door

820 "Ship of Peace" (Endre Szasz)

1983. 10th Anniv of Postal Codes.
3479 **819** 2fo. black, grey and red 30 10

1983. Budapest Spring Festival.
3480 **820** 2fo. grey, gold and black 30 10

1983. Youth Stamp Exhibition, Baja.
3481 **821** 4fo.+2fo. mult . . . . . 90 1·00

822 Gyula Juhasz
823 Menner's Balloon, 1811

1983. Birth Cent of Gyula Juhasz (writer).
3482 **822** 2fo. dp brown, brn & blk 30 10

1983. Air. Bicent of Manned Flight. Mult.
3483 1fo. Type **823** (1st manned flight in Hungary) 15 10
3484 1fo. Captive observation balloon at Budapest Exhibition, 1896 . . . . 15 10
3485 2fo. Pursuit race, 1904 . . . 40 15
3486 2fo. Hot-air balloon "Pannonia", 1977 . . . . 40 15
3487 4fo. Hot-air balloon "Malev", 1981 . . . . . 70 35
3488 4fo. Hungarian National Defence Union balloon, 1982 . . . . 70 35
3489 5fo. Non-rigid airship over Mecsek television tower, 1981 . . . . 95 50
MS3490 88 × 74 mm. 20fo. Hot-air balloons (39 × 49 mm) . . . . 3·00 3·00

824 Szentgotthard Monastery and Seal

1983. 800th Anniv of Szentgotthard.
3491 **824** 2fo. multicoloured . . . 30 10

825 Watermill, Tapolca

1983. "Tembal 83" Thematic Stamps Exhibition, Basel.
3492 **825** 5fo. multicoloured . . . 90 95

826 Parliament Buildings, Budapest

1983. 5th Inter-Parliamentary Union Conference, Budapest. Sheet 95 × 77 mm.
MS3493 **826** 20fo. multicoloured 4·25 3·50

827 Jeno Hamburger

1983. Birth Centenary of Jeno Hamburger (doctor and revolutionary).
3494 **827** 2fo. brown, blue and red . . . 30 10

828 "Giovanna d'Aragona"

1983. 500th Birth Anniv of Raphael (artist). Mult.
3495 1fo. Type **828** 15 10
3496 1fo. "Lady with Unicorn" . . 15 10
3497 2fo. "Madonna of the Chair" 30 10
3498 2fo. "Madonna of the Grand Duke" 30 10
3499 4fo. "La Muta" 55 10
3500 6fo. "Lady with a Veil" . . 95 45
3501 8fo. "La Fornaria" . . . . 1·10 70
MS3502 66 × 89 mm. 20fo. "Esterhazy Madonna" (24 × 37 mm) . . . . 3·75 3·75

829 Vagi and Newspapers **830** Bolivar and Map of Americas

1983. Birth Centenary of Istvan Vagi (secretary of Socialist Workers' Party).
3503 **829** 2fo. multicoloured . . . 30 10

1983. Birth Bicent of Simon Bolivar.
3504 **830** 2fo. multicoloured . . . 30 10

831 Globe and Congress Emblem **833** Lesser Spotted Eagle

832 Martin Luther

1983. 68th Universal Esperanto Congress, Budapest.
3505 **831** 2fo. multicoloured . . . 30 10

1983. 500th Anniv of Martin Luther (religious reformer). Sheet 80 × 65 mm.
MS3506 **832** 20fo. multicoloured 3·50 3·50

1983. Birds of Prey. Multicoloured.
3507 1fo. Type **833** 25 15
3508 1fo. Imperial eagle 25 15
3509 2fo. White-tailed sea eagle 50 20
3510 2fo. Western red-footed falcon 50 20
3511 4fo. Saker falcon 80 45
3512 6fo. Rough-legged buzzard 1·50 65
3513 8fo. Common buzzard . . . 1·75 1·00

834 Bee collecting Pollen **835** Old National Theatre (after R. Alt)

1983. 29th Apimondia (Bee Keeping) Congress, Budapest.
3514 **834** 1fo. multicoloured . . . 25 10

1983. Stamp Day. Engravings of Budapest Buildings.
3515 **835** 4fo.+2fo. yellow, brown and black . . . . . . 1·10 1·10
3516 – 4fo.+2fo. yellow, brown and black . . . . . . 1·10 1·10
MS3517 80 × 63 mm. 20fo.+10fo. yellow and brown . . . . . . 3·75 3·75
DESIGNS—As T **835**: No. 3516, Municipal concert hall, Pest (after H. Luders). 27 × 44 mm—MS3517, Holy Trinity Square, Buda (after Rudolf Alt).

836 "Fruit-piece"

1983. Birth Centenary of Bela Czobel (artist).
3518 **836** 2fo. multicoloured . . . 30 10

837 "Molnya" Satellite and Kekes TV Tower **838** Flags encircling Globe

1983. World Communications Year. Mult.
3519 1fo. Type **837** 15 10
3520 1fo. Dish aerials and rockets 15 10
3521 2fo. Manual telephone exchange and modern "TMM-81" telephone . . 35 10
3522 3fo. Computer terminal . . 50 10
3523 5fo. Automatic letter-storing equipment 85 25
3524 8fo. Teletext and newspaper mastheads . . . . 1·50 55
MS3525 70 × 90 mm. 20fo. "Molnya" satellite (29 × 44 mm) 3·00 3·25

1983. 34th International Astronautical Federation Congress, Budapest.
3526 **838** 2fo. multicoloured . . . 30 10

839 Kremlin, Moscow

1983. "Sozphilex '83" Stamp Exhibition, Moscow.
3527 **839** 2fo. multicoloured . . . 45 45

840 Congress Palace, Madrid

1983. European Security and Co-operation Conference, Madrid. Sheet 98 × 78 mm.
MS3528 **840** 20fo. multicoloured 3·75 4·00

841 Babits (after Jozsef Rippl-Ronai) **842** "Madonna with Rose"

1983. Birth Cent of Mihaly Babits (writer).
3529 **841** 2fo. multicoloured . . . 30 10

1983. Christmas. Multicoloured.
3530 1fo. Type **842** 15 10
3531 2fo. Altar painting, Csik-menasag 30 10

843 Zanka **844** Ice Dancing

1983. Hungarian Resorts. Multicoloured.
3532 1fo. Type **843** 40 10
3533 2fo. Hajduszoboszlo 40 10
3534 5fo. Heviz 55 15

1983. Winter Olympic Games, Sarajevo.
3535 **844** 1fo. multicoloured . . . 25 10
3536 – 1fo. multicoloured . . . 25 10
3537 – 2fo. multicoloured (man lifting girl) 45 10
3538 – 2fo. multicoloured . . . 45 10
3539 – 4fo. multicoloured (man with both arms bent) 75 15
3540 – 4fo. multicoloured (man with one arm outstretched) 75 15
3541 – 6fo. multicoloured . . . 1·00 50
MS3542 70 × 70 mm. 20fo. multicoloured (49 × 39 mm) . . 3·50 3·25
DESIGNS: Nos. 3536/42, Different ice dancing designs.

845 "Virgin with Six Saints" (Tiepolo)

1984. Paintings Stolen from Museum of Fine Arts, Budapest. Sheet 130 × 98 mm containing T **845** and similar multicoloured designs.
MS3543 2fo. Type **845**; 2fo. "Esterhazy Madonna" (Raphael); 2fo. "Portrait of Giorgione" (imitator of Giorgione); 2fo. "Portrait of a Woman" (Tintoretto); 2fo. "Pietro Bempo" (Raphael); 2fo. "Portrait of a Man" (Tintoretto); 8fo. "Rest on the Flight into Egypt" (Tiepolo) (47 × 32 mm) . . . . 3·50 3·50

846 Csoma (statue) and Sepulchre, Darjeeling **847** "Energy" and Sun

1984. Birth Bicentenary of Sandor Korosi Csoma (traveller and philologist).
3544 **846** 2fo. multicoloured . . . 30 10

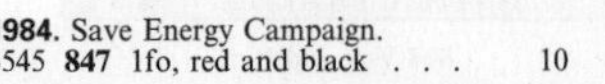

1984. Save Energy Campaign.
3545 **847** 1fo. red and black . . . 10 10

848 Parent and Child **849** 40fi. Goya Stamp, 1968

1984. Youth Stamp.
3546 **848** 4fo.+2fo. mult 90 95

1984. International Stamp Exhibitions. Sheet 125 × 104 mm containing T **849** and similar vert designs. Multicoloured.
MS3547 4fo. Type **849** ("Espana 84", Madrid); 4fo. 20fi. kangaroo stamp, 1961 ("Ausipex 84", Melbourne); 4fo. 1fo. Schiller stamp, 1959 ("Philatelia '84", Stuttgart) . . . . 2·50 2·75

850 Hair Ornaments from Rakamaz

1984. Archaeological Finds.
3548 **850** 1fo. stone and brown . . 20 10
3549 – 1fo. stone and brown . . 20 10
3550 – 2fo. stone and brown . . 30 10
3551 – 2fo. stone and brown . . 30 10
3552 – 4fo. stone and brown . . 50 10
3553 – 6fo. stone and brown . . 80 15
3554 – 8fo. stone and brown . . 1·25 40
DESIGNS: No. 3549, Purse plates from Szolnok-Strazsahalom and Galgocz; 3550, Hair ornaments from Sarospatak; 3551, St. Stephen's sword (Prague) and Attila's sword (Aachen); 3552, Bowl from Ketpo; 3553, Stick handles from Hajdudorog and Szabadattyan; 3554, Saddle-bow from Izsak and bit and stirrups from Muszka.

851 Cracow and Emblem **852** "Epiphile dilecta"

1984. 25th Session of Permanent Committee of Posts and Telecommunications, Cracow, Poland.
3555 **851** 2fo. multicoloured . . . 30 10

1984. Butterflies. Multicoloured.
3556 1fo. Type **852** 35 10
3557 1fo. "Agrias sara" 35 10
3558 2fo. Blue morpho ("Morpho cypris") 60 20
3559 2fo. "Ancyluris formosissima" 60 20
3560 4fo. African monarch . . . 80 25
3561 6fo. "Catagramma cynosura" . . . . 1·25 60
3562 8fo. Paradise birdwing . . 1·60 70
No. 3557 is inscribed "Agra sara".

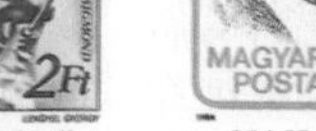

853 "Archer" **854** Hevesi

1984. Birth Centenary of Zsigmond Kisfaludy Strobl (sculptor).
3563 **853** 2fo. brown and yellow . . 35 10

1984. Birth Centenary of Akos Hevesi (activist in working-class movement).
3564 **854** 2fo. multicoloured . . . 35 10

855 Doves around Map of Hungary **856** World Map and Airplane

1984. Peace Festival, Pusztavacs.
3565 **855** 2fo. multicoloured . . . 35 10

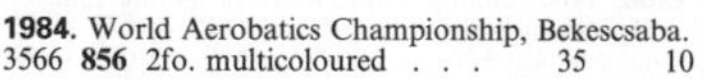

1984. World Aerobatics Championship, Bekescsaba.
3566 **856** 2fo. multicoloured . . . 35 10

857 Four-in-hand **858** Conference Emblem

1984. World Team-driving Championships, Szilvasvarad.
3567 **857** 2fo. multicoloured . . . 35 10

1984. 14th Organization of Socialist Countries' Postal Administrations Conference, Budapest.
3568 **858** 2fo. multicoloured . . . 35 10

859 Four-handled Vase

1984. Stamp Day. Multicoloured.
3569 1fo. Type **859** 25 10
3570 2fo. Platter with flower decoration 40 10
MS3571 80 × 63 mm. 10fo. Cover with 1874 3k. stamp (44 × 27 mm) 3·00 3·00

860 "Music crowned by Fame" (fresco, Mor Than)

1984. Reopening of Budapest Opera House. Multicoloured.
3572 1fo. Type **860** 25 10
3573 2fo. Central staircase . . . 45 15
3574 5fo. Auditorium 85 45
MS3575 80 × 65 mm. 20fo. Facade and floor plan (49 × 39 mm) . . 3·75 3·25

861 Atrium Hyatt Hotel

1984. Budapest Hotels along the Danube. Multicoloured.
3576 1fo. Type **861** 20 10
3577 2fo. Duna Intercontinental 40 15
3578 4fo. Forum 60 20
3579 4fo. Thermal Hotel, Margaret Island 60 20
3580 5fo. Hilton 75 25
3581 8fo. Gellert . . . . 1·25 35
MS3582 78 × 55 mm. 20fo. Hilton (different) (36 × 25 mm) . . . . 3·00 3·25

862 Cep ("Boletus edulis") **863** Kato Haman (Labour Movement leader)

1984. Edible Mushrooms. Multicoloured.
3583 1fo. Type **862** 40 15
3584 1fo. Scotch bonnet ("Marasmius orcades") 40 15
3585 2fo. Common morel ("Morchella esculenta") 60 15
3586 2fo. Field mushroom ("Agaricus campester") 60 15
3587 3fo. Chanterelle ("Cantharellus cibarius") 75 20
3588 3fo. Parasol mushroom ("Macrolepiota procera") 75 20
3589 4fo. Boot-lace fungus . . . 95 50

1984. Birth Centenaries.
3590 **863** 2fo. brown, gold and black 35 10
3591 – 2fo. brown, gold and black 35 10
DESIGN: No. 3591, Bela Balazs (writer).

864 "Virgin and Child" (small altar, Trencseny) **865** Torah Crown (Buda)

1984. Christmas.
3592 **864** 1fo. multicoloured . . . 20 10

1984. Reopening of Jewish Museum, Budapest, Multicoloured.
3593 1fo. Type **865** 25 10
3594 1fo. Chalice (Moscow) . . . 25 10
3595 2fo. Torah shield (Vienna) 40 10
3596 2fo. Elias chalice (Warsaw) 40 10
3597 4fo. Esrog holder (Augsburg) 65 10
3598 6fo. Candle holder (Warsaw) 85 25
3599 8fo. Urn (Pest) . . . . . . 1·10 55

866 Barn Owl **867** Long Jumping and Emblem

1984. Owls. Multicoloured.
3600 1fo. Type **866** 40 15
3601 1fo. Little owl 40 15
3602 2fo. Tawny owl 70 15
3603 2fo. Long-eared owl 70 15
3604 4fo. Snowy owl . . . . . . 1·10 35
3605 6fo. Ural owl . . . . 1·50 60
3606 8fo. Eagle owl . . . . . . 1·75 75

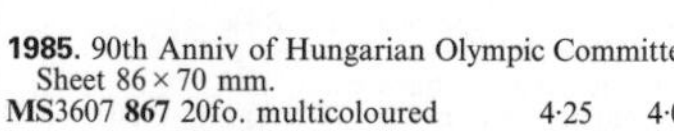

1985. 90th Anniv of Hungarian Olympic Committee. Sheet 86 × 70 mm.
MS3607 **867** 20fo. multicoloured 4·25 4·00

868 Novi Sad Bridge, Yugoslavia

1985. Danube Bridges. Multicoloured.
3608 1fo. Type **868** 20 10
3609 1fo. Baja, Hungary 20 10
3610 2fo. Arpad bridge, Budapest 40 15
3611 2fo. Bratislava, Czechoslovakia 40 15
3612 4fo. Reichsbrucke bridge, Vienna 65 25
3613 6fo. Linz, Austria 85 40
3614 8fo. Regensburg, West Germany . . . . 1·10 55
MS3615 65 × 80 mm. 20fo. Elizabeth and Chain Bridges, Budapest (49 × 39 mm) . . . . 3·50 3·50

869 Laszlo Rudas **870** Woman and Flowers

1985. Birth Centenary of Laszlo Rudas (philosopher and socialist).
3616 **869** 2fo. brown, gold & black 35 10

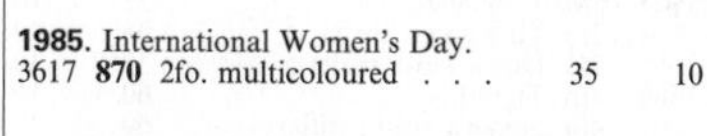

1985. International Women's Day.
3617 **870** 2fo. multicoloured . . . 35 10

871 1925 200k. Skiing Stamp **873** "Little Red Riding Hood"

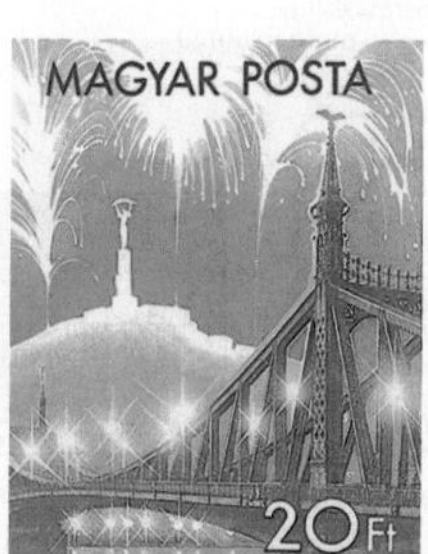

872 Liberty Bridge, Liberation Statue and Fireworks

1985. "Olymphilex '85" International Olympic Stamps Exhibition, Lausanne.
3618 **871** 4fo. green, gold and blue 60 25
3619 – 5fo. blue, brown and gold 75 25
DESIGN: 5fo. 1925 300k. Skating stamp.

1985. 40th Anniv of Liberation. Sheet 70 × 95 mm.
MS3620 **872** 20fo. multicoloured 3·50 3·25

1985. Birth Centenary of Jacob Grimm (folklorist).
3621 **873** 4fo.+2fo. mult . . . . . 1·25 1·10

874 Gyorgy Lukacs **875** Title Page

1985. Birth Centenary of Gyorgy Lukacs (philosopher).
3622 **874** 2fo. multicoloured . . . 35 10

1985. 300th Anniv of Totfalusi Bible.
3623 **875** 2fo. black and gold . . . 35 10

876 Peter Pazmany (founder) **877** Boxing

1985. 350th Anniv of Lorand Eotvos University.
3624 **876** 2fo. grey and red 35 40

1985. 26th European Boxing Championships, Budapest.
3625 **877** 2fo. multicoloured . . . 35 10

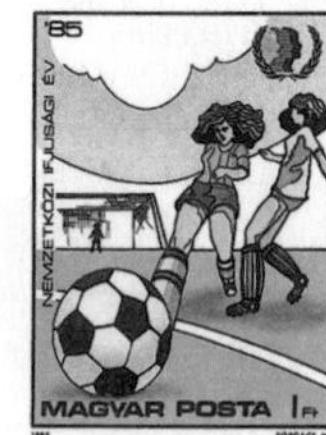

878 Women Footballers

1985. International Youth Year. Mult.
3626 1fo. Type **878** 20 10
3627 2fo. Windsurfing 35 10
3628 2fo. Women exercising . . . 35 10
3629 4fo. Karate 55 10
3630 4fo. Go-karting 55 10
3631 5fo. Hang gliding 80 40
3632 6fo. Skate-boarding 75 50

879 Monorail Train

1985. "Expo '85" World's Fair, Tsukuba. Mult.
3633 2fo. Type **879** 55 10
3634 4fo. Fuyo Theatre 60 25

880 Common Flicker

1985. Birth Bicentenary of John J. Audubon (ornithologist). Multicoloured.
3635 2fo. Type **880** (postage) . . 45 15
3636 2fo. Bohemian waxwing . . 45 15
3637 2fo. Pileated woodpecker . . 45 15
3638 4fo. Northern oriole 85 30
3639 4fo. Common flicker (air) 85 30
3640 6fo. Common cardinal . . . 1·40 50

881 Nonius XXXVI

1985. Bicentenary of Horsebreeding at Mezohegyes. Multicoloured.
3641 1fo. Type **881** 30 10
3642 2fo. Furioso XXIII 45 10
3643 4fo. Gidran I 85 15
3644 4fo. Ramses III 85 15
3645 6fo. Krozus I . . . . 1·25 40

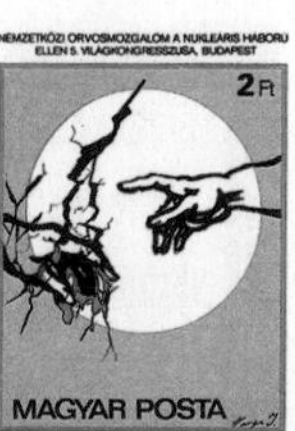

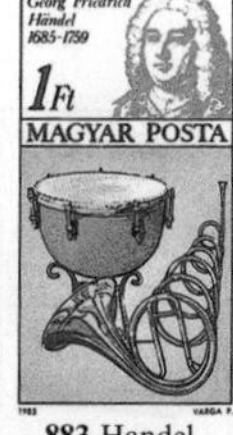

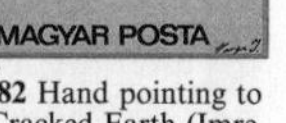

882 Hand pointing to Cracked Earth (Imre Varga) **883** Handel, Kettledrum and Horn

1985. 5th Congress of International Association of Physicians against Nuclear War, Budapest.
3646 **882** 2fo. multicoloured . . . 35 10

1985. Music Year. Multicoloured.
3647 1fo. Type **883** (300th birth anniv) 30 10
3648 2fo. Bach and Thomas Church organ, Leipzig (300th birth anniv) . . . 55 10

3649 4fo. Luigi Cherubini, harp, bass violin and baryton (225th anniv) 85 10
3650 4fo. Chopin and piano (175th birth anniv) . . . 85 10
3651 5fo. Mahler, viola, double horn and kettledrum (125th birth anniv) . . . 1·25 35
3652 6fo. Ferenc Erkel, viola and bass tuba (175th birth anniv) . . . . 1·40 60

884 Red Square and Emblem

1985. 12th World Youth and Students' Festival, Moscow. Sheet 89 × 69 mm.
MS3653 **884** 20fo. multicoloured 3·00 3·00

885 Finlandia Palace

1985. 10th Anniv of Helsinki Agreement. Sheet 92 × 75 mm.
MS3654 **885** 20fo. multicoloured 4·25 3·50

886 Key with Globe as Head
887 Flags on Computer Keyboards

1985. World Tourism Day.
3655 **886** 2fo. multicoloured . . . 35 10

1985. "COMNET '85" Computer Networks Conference, Budapest.
3656 **887** 4fo. multicoloured . . . 35 10

888 Budapest

1985. European Security and Co-operation Conference, Budapest.
MS3657 **888** 20fo. multicoloured 5·25 4·50

889 Water Holder
890 Italian 1960 5l. Stamp

1985. Stamp Day. Haban Ceramics. Mult.
3658 1fo. Type **889** 15 15
3659 2fo. Tankard with cover . . 40 50
MS3660 80 × 60 mm. 10fo. Hexagonal medicine holder . . 2·75 3·00

1985. "Italia '85" International Stamp Exhibition, Rome.
3661 **890** 5fo. multicoloured . . . 1·00 1·00

891 Dove and U.N. Emblem
892 Red Lily

1985. 40th Anniv of United Nations Organization.
3662 **891** 4fo. turquoise, bl & dp bl 45 10

1985. Lily Family. Multicoloured.
3663 1fo. Type **892** 25 10
3664 2fo. Turk's-cap lily 35 10
3665 2fo. Dog's tooth violet . . . 35 10
3666 4fo. Tiger lily 60 10
3667 4fo. Snake's-head fritillary 60 10
3668 5fo. Day lily 80 35
3669 6fo. "Bulbocodium vernum" 1·00 50

893 Carol Singers

1985. Christmas.
3670 **893** 2fo. multicoloured . . . 35 10

894 Istvan Ries
895 Three Houses under One Roof

1985. Birth Centenary of Istvan Ries (Minister of Justice).
3671 **894** 2fo. multicoloured . . . 35 10

1985. S.O.S. Childrens' Village.
3672 **895** 4fo.+2fo. multicoloured 1·25 1·25

896 Fantic "Sprinter", 1984

1985. Centenary of Motor Cycle.
3673 **896** 1fo. black, orange & blue 25 10
3674 – 2fo. black, yellow & blue 40 10
3675 – 2fo. black, green and grey 40 10
3676 – 4fo. multicoloured . . . 60 10
3677 – 4fo. black, green and grey 60 10
3678 – 5fo. multicoloured . . . 85 25
3679 – 6fo. multicoloured . . . 1·10 55
DESIGNS: No. 3674, Harley-Davidson "Duo-Glide", 1960; 3675, Suzuki "Katana GSX", 1983; 3676, BMW "R47", 1927; 3677, Rudge-Whitworth, 1935; 3678, NSU, 1910; 3679, Daimler, 1885.

897 "Ice" Satellite and Dinosaurs
898 Bela Kun

1986. Air. Appearance of Halley's Comet. Multicoloured.
3680 2fo. Type **897** 45 10
3681 2fo. "Vega" satellite and detail of Bayeux Tapestry showing comet 45 10
3682 2fo. "Suisei" satellite and German engraving of 1507 . . . . 45 10
3683 4fo. "Giotto" satellite and "The Magi" (tapestry after Giotto) 75 10
3684 4fo. "Astron" satellite and Virgo, Leo, Corvus, Crater and Hydra constellations 75 10
3685 6fo. Space shuttle and Edmond Halley (wrongly inscr "Edmund") . . . . 1·25 50

1986. Birth Centenary of Bela Kun (Communist Party leader).
3686 **898** 4fo. multicoloured . . . 35 10

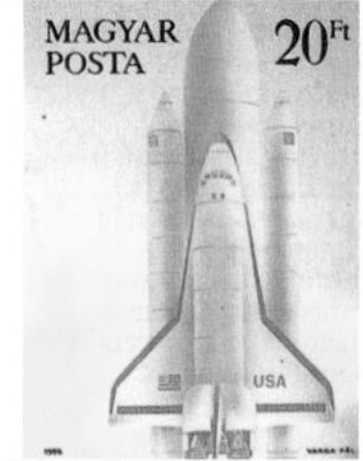

899 "Challenger" (space shuttle)

1986. Challenger Astronauts Commemoration. Sheet 92 × 79 mm.
MS3687 **899** 20fo. multicoloured 4·50 4·50

900 Guide Dog
901 Running for Ball

1986. The Blind.
3688 **900** 4fo. multicoloured . . . 35 10

1986. World Cup Football Championship, Mexico. Multicoloured.
3689 2fo. Type **901** 40 10
3690 2fo. Heading ball 40 10
3691 4fo. Tackling 85 10
3692 4fo. Goalkeeper diving for ball 85 10
3693 4fo. Goalkeeper catching ball 85 10
3694 6fo. Tackling (different) . . 1·25 55
MS3695 80 × 60 mm. 20fo. Team celebrating (40 × 30 mm) . . . 4·25 3·75

902 Cable Railway
903 Rose "Yankee Doodle"

1986. Re-opening of Buda Castle Cable Railway.
3696 **902** 2fo. brown, yell & orge 35 10

1986. "Ameripex '86" International Stamp Exhibition, Chicago. Sheet 80 × 100 mm containing T **903** and similar vert designs. Multicoloured.
MS3697 5fo. Type **903**; 5fo. Rose "America"; 10fo. Statue of George Washington, Budapest and exhibition emblem (25 × 70 mm) 3·50 3·00

904 Japanese and Hungarian Dolls

1986. Hungarian Days in Tokyo.
3698 **904** 4fo. multicoloured . . . 45 10

905 Fay
906 Flag and "40"

1986. Birth Bicentenary of Andras Fay (writer, politician and founder of First Hungarian Savings Bank Union).
3699 **905** 4fo. brown & pale brown 60 50

1986. Youth Stamp. 40th Anniv of Young Pioneers Movement.
3700 **906** 4fo.+2fo. multicoloured 1·00 1·00

907 Ferrari Racing Cars, 1961 and 1985

1986. Centenary of Motor Car. Multicoloured.
3701 2fo. Type **907** 40 10
3702 2fo. Alfa Romeo racing cars, 1932 and 1984 . . . 40 10
3703 2fo. Volkswagen "Beetle", 1936, and Porsche "959", 1986 . . . . 40 10
3704 4fo. Renault "14 CV", 1902, and "5 GT Turbo", 1985 85 15
3705 4fo. Fiat "3 1/2", 1899, and "Ritmo", 1985 . . . . . 85 15
3706 6fo. Daimler, 1886, and Mercedes-Benz "230 SE", 1986 . . . . 1·25 50

908 "Wasa" (Swedish ship of the line), 1628

1986. "Stockholmia '86" Int Stamp Exhibition.
3707 **908** 2fo. multicoloured . . . 75 85

909 Moritz Kaposi (cancer specialist)

1986. 14th International Cancer Congress, Budapest.
3708 **909** 4fo. multicoloured . . . 50 10

910 "Recapture of Buda Castle" (Gyula Benczur) (½-size Illustration)

1986. 300th Anniv of Recapture of Buda from Turks.
3709 **910** 4fo. multicoloured . . . 45 10

911 "Tranquillity"

1986. Stamp Day. Multicoloured.
3710 2fo. Type **911** 30 35
3711 2fo. "Confidence" 30 35
MS3712 80 × 60 mm. 10fo. "Hope" (28 × 49 mm) . . . . 3·00 3·00

912 Fragment of 15th-cent Carpet from Anatolia

1986. 5th International Oriental Carpets and Tapestry Conference, Vienna and Budapest.
3713 **912** 4fo. multicoloured . . . 45 10

913 Model of New Theatre

1986. National Theatre, Budapest. Sheet 63 × 85 mm.
MS3714 **913** 20fo.+10fo. brown, stone and light brown . . . . 3·75 3·75

914 Piano and Liszt **915** Dove

1986. 175th Birth Anniv of Franz Liszt (pianist and composer).
3715 **914** 4fo. deep green and green 50 10

1986. International Peace Year.
3716 **915** 4fo. multicoloured . . . 70 70

916 Hofburg Palace, Vienna, and Map

1986. European Security and Co-operation Conference Review Meeting, Vienna. Sheet 65 × 80 mm.
MS3717 **916** 20fo. multicoloured 4·25 4·00

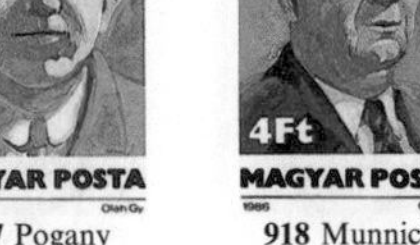

917 Pogany **918** Munnich

1986. Birth Centenary of Jozsef Pogany (writer and journalist).
3718 **917** 4fo. multicoloured . . . 45 10

1986. Birth Centenary of Ferenc Munnich (former Prime Minister).
3719 **918** 4fo. multicoloured . . . 45 10

919 Heads

1986. 12th General Assembly of World Federation of Democratic Youth, Budapest.
3720 **919** 4fo. multicoloured . . . 45 10

920 Apricots ("Kajszi" C.235)

1986. Fruits. Multicoloured.
3721 2fo. Type **920** 40 10
3722 2fo. Cherries ("Good bearer of Erd") 40 10
3723 4fo. Apples ("Jonathan" M.14) 80 10
3724 4fo. Raspberries ("Nagymaros") 80 10
3725 4fo. Peaches ("Piroska") . . 80 10
3726 6fo. Grapes ("Zalagyongye") . . . . 1·00 40

921 Forgach Castle, Szecseny **922** Wild Cat

1986. Castles. Inscr "MAGYAR POSTA".
3727 **921** 2fo. bistre and yellow . . 30 10
3728 – 3fo. green and light green 30 10
3729 – 4fo. blue and light blue 45 10
3730 – 5fo. red and pink . . . 55 10
3731 – 6fo. brown and orange 65 10
3732 – 8fo. red and orange . . 75 10
3733 – 10fo. brown and ochre 80 10
3734 – 20fo. green and yellow 1·50 10
3735 – 30fo. light green and green . . . . 1·90 30
3736 – 40fo. blue and light blue 2·25 35
3737 – 50fo. deep red and red 2·75 45
3738 – 70fo. deep grey and grey 3·25 60
3739 – 100fo. violet and lilac . . 6·00 95

DESIGNS: 3fo. Savoya Castle, Rackeve; 4fo. Batthyany Castle, Kormend; 5fo. Szechenyi Castle, Nagycenk; 6fo. Rudnyanszky Castle, Nagyteteny; 8fo. Szapary Castle, Buk; 10fo. Festetics Castle, Keszthely; 20fo. Brunswick Castle, Martonvasar; 30fo. De La Motte Castle, Noszvaj; 40fo. L'Huillier-Coburg Castle, Edeleny; 50fo. Teleki-Degenfeld Castle, Szirak; 70fo. Magochy Castle, Pacin; 100fo. Esterhazy Castle, Fertod.
See also Nos. 3888 and 4045/9.

1986. Protected Animals. Multicoloured.
3740 2fo. Type **922** 40 10
3741 2fo. European otter 40 10
3742 2fo. Stoat 40 10
3743 4fo. Eurasian red squirrel 85 15
3744 4fo. East European hedgehog 85 15
3745 6fo. European pond turtle 1·25 45

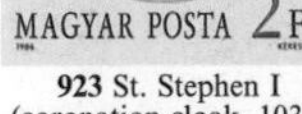

923 St. Stephen I (coronation cloak, 1030) **924** Death Cap ("Amanita phalloides")

1986. Kings (1st series).
3746 **923** 2fo. brown, blue and red 40 10
3747 – 2fo. brown, grey and red 40 10
3748 – 4fo. brown, green and red 75 10
3749 – 4fo. brown, grey and red 75 10
3750 – 6fo. brown, blue and red 1·25 35

DESIGNS: No. 3747, Geza I (enamel portrait on Hungarian crown, 1070); 3748, St. Ladislas I (Gyor Cathedral, 1400); 3749, Bela III (Kalocsa Cathedral statue, 1200); 3750, Bela IV (Jak church statue, 1230).
See also Nos. 3835/7.

1986. Fungi. Multicoloured.
3751 2fo. Type **924** 45 20
3752 2fo. Fly agaric ("Amanita muscaria") 45 20
3753 2fo. Red-staining inocybe ("Inocybe patouillardi") 45 20
3754 4fo. Olive-wood pleurotus ("Omphalotus olearius") 95 45
3755 4fo. Panther cap ("Amanita pantherina") 95 45
3756 6fo. Beefsteak morel . . . . 1·40 75

925 Banded Gourami **926** "Sitting Woman"

1987. Fishes. Multicoloured.
3757 2fo. Type **925** 35 10
3758 2fo. Thread-finned rainbowfish ("Iriathorina werneri") 35 10
3759 2fo. Zebra mbuna ("Pseudotropheus zebra") 35 10
3760 4fo. Ramirez dwarf cichlid ("Papiliochromis ramirezi") 70 15
3761 4fo. Multicoloured lyretail ("Aphyosemion multicolor") 70 15
3762 6fo. Bleeding-heart tetra ("Hyphessobrycon erythrostigma") . . . . . 1·00 40

1987. Birth Centenary of Bela Uitz (painter).
3763 **926** 4fo. multicoloured . . . 45 10

927 Abstract **928** Flag, Books, Torch and Dove

1987. Birth Centenary of Lajos Kassak (writer and painter).
3764 **927** 4fo. black and red . . . 45 10

1987. 30th Anniv of Young Communist League.
3765 **928** 4fo.+2fo. mult . . . . . 90 1·00

929 Hippocrates (medical oath) **930** Food Jar, Hodmezovasarhely

1987. Pioneers of Medicine (1st series).
3766 **929** 2fo. brown and blue . . 35 10
3767 – 4fo. green and black . . 70 10
3768 – 4fo. blue and black . . . 70 10
3769 – 4fo. brown and black . . 70 10
3770 – 6fo. brown and black . . 1·00 40

DESIGNS: No. 3767, Avicenna ("Kanun" book of medical rules); 3768, Ambroise Pare (improved treatment of wounds); 3769, William Harvey (circulation of blood); 3770, Ignac Semmelweis (aseptic treatment of wounds).
See also Nos. 3939/43.

1987. Neolithic and Copper Age Art. Multicoloured.
3771 **930** 2fo. brown and green . . 50 10
3772 – 4fo. brown and flesh . . 80 10
3773 – 4fo. brown and pink . . 80 10
3774 – 5fo. brown and green . . 1·10 40

DESIGNS: No. 3772, Altar, Szeged; 3773, Statue with sickle, Szegvar-Tuzkoves; 3774, Vase with face, Center.

931 King Matthias's Cross **932** Old and Modern Ambulances

1987. Re-opening of Esztergom Cathedral Treasury. Sheet 64 × 80 mm.
MS3775 **931** 20fo. multicoloured 3·50 3·25

1987. Cent of Hungarian First Aid Association.
3776 **932** 4fo. multicoloured . . . 45 10

933 Toronto ("Capex '87")

1987. International Stamp Exhibitions. Mult.
3777 5fo. Type **933** . . . . . . 90 1·10
3778 5fo. "Olymphilex 87" building, Rome . . . . . 90 1·10
3779 5fo. "Hafnia 87" building, Copenhagen . . . . . . 90 1·10

934 Jozsef Marek

1987. Bicentenary of University of Veterinary Sciences, Budapest.
3780 **934** 4fo. silver, blue and black 45 10

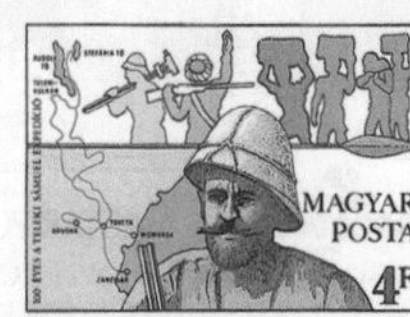

935 Teleki, Route Map and Porters

1987. Cent of Samuel Teleki's African Expedition.
3781 **935** 4fo. multicoloured . . . 45 10

936 Printing Shop (17th-century wood-print, Abraham von Werdt) **937** James Cook and H.M.S. "Resolution"

1987. 125th Anniv of Hungarian Printing, Paper and Press Workers' Union.
3782 **936** 4fo. brown and stone . . 45 10

1987. Antarctic Exploration. Multicoloured.
3783 2fo. Type **937** 40 15
3784 2fo. Fabian von Bellingshausen and seals 40 15
3785 2fo. Ernest Shackleton and emperor penguins 40 15
3786 4fo. Roald Amundsen and huskies 70 25
3787 4fo. Robert F. Scott and "Terra Nova" 70 25
3788 6fo. Richard Byrd and Ford Trimotor "Floyd Bennett" 1·10 45
MS3789 86 × 70 mm. 20fo. Mirnyi Research Station (32 × 42 mm) 6·00 5·75

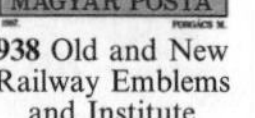

938 Old and New Railway Emblems and Institute

939 Flowers and Dolphin

1987. Cent of Railway Officers' Training Institute.

3790	**938** 4fo. black and blue	45	10

1987. Stamp Day. Carvings from Buda Castle.

3791	**939** 2fo. indigo, blue & azure	30	30
3792	– 4fo. olive, green & turq	60	70
MS3793	68 × 88 mm. 10fo. agate, grey and lilac	2·50	2·40

DESIGNS: 4fo. King Matthias's arms; 10fo. Capital of Column.

940 Jesse Altar

941 "Orchis purpurea"

1987. Gyongyospata Church.

3794	**940** 4fo. multicoloured	90	1·00

1987. Orchids. Multicoloured.

3795	2fo. Type **941**	40	10
3796	2fo. "Cypripedium calceolus"	40	10
3797	4fo. "Ophrys scolopax"	70	10
3798	4fo. "Himantoglossum hircinum"	70	10
3799	5fo. "Cephalanthera rubra"	95	20
3800	6fo. "Epipactis atrorubens"	1·10	40
MS3801	40 × 60 mm. 20fo. Orchids (24 × 33 mm)	3·50	3·25

942 Speed Skating

945 "The White Crane" (Japanese folk tale)

943 Clasped Hands and Map

1987. Winter Olympic Games, Calgary. Mult.

3802	2fo. Type **942**	30	10
3803	2fo. Cross-country skiing	30	10
3804	4fo. Biathlon	60	10
3805	4fo. Ice hockey	60	10
3806	4fo. Four-man bobsleigh	60	10
3807	6fo. Ski jumping	95	30
MS3808	50 × 60 mm. 20fo. Slalom (24 × 41 mm)	3·50	3·50

1987. U.S.–Soviet Strategic Arms Reduction Talks, Washington. Sheet 78 × 82 mm.

MS3809	**943** 20fo. multicoloured	3·75	3·75

1987. Fairy Tales. Multicoloured.

3816	2fo. Type **945**	35	10
3817	2fo. "The Fox and the Raven" (Aesop)	35	10
3818	4fo. "The Hare and The Tortoise" (Aesop)	75	20

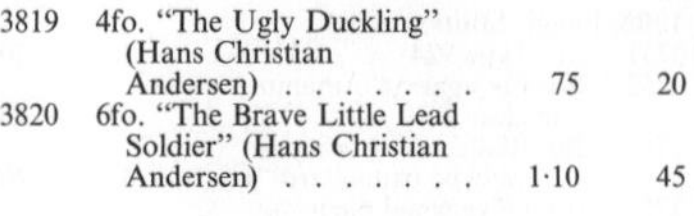

3819	4fo. "The Ugly Duckling" (Hans Christian Andersen)	75	20
3820	6fo. "The Brave Little Lead Soldier" (Hans Christian Andersen)	1·10	45

946 Zeppelin and Airship LZ-2

1988. 150th Birth Anniv of Ferdinand von Zeppelin (airship pioneer).

3821	**946** 2fo. black and blue	40	15
3822	– 4fo. deep brown & brown	70	25
3823	– 4fo. purple and lilac	70	25
3824	– 8fo. olive and green	1·25	45

DESIGNS: No. 3822, LZ-4; 3823, "Schwaben"; 3824, "Graf Zeppelin".

947 Skater

949 Monus

948 Woman's Head

1988. World Figure Skating Championships, Budapest. Skaters from 19th-century to date. Multicoloured.

3825	2fo. Type **947**	30	10
3826	2fo. Man wearing hat	30	10
3827	4fo. Woman	60	10
3828	4fo. Man in hat and coat	60	10
3829	5fo. Woman in modern skating dress	70	10
3830	6fo. Pair	90	30
MS3831	89 × 72 mm. 20fo. Pair (different) (32 × 47 mm)	3·50	3·50

1988. Stamp Day. "Socfilex" International Stamp Exhibition, Kecskemet. Sheet 72 × 54 mm.

MS3832	**948** 20fo.+10fo. mult	4·25	4·00

1988. Birth Centenary of Illes Monus (newspaper editor).

3833	**949** 4fo. blue, red and black	45	10

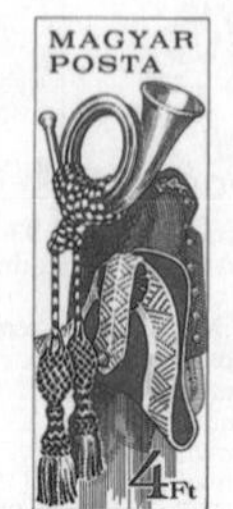

950 18th-cent Postmaster's Uniform

1988. Stamp Exhibitions.

MS3834	**950** 4fo. black and stone	1·10	1·00

1988. Kings (2nd series). As T **923**.

3835	2fo. brown, green and red	30	10
3836	4fo. brown, blue and red	60	10
3837	6fo. brown, violet and red	95	30

DESIGNS: 2fo. Karoly I (Charles Robert) (detail of decorated initial from "Illuminated Chronicle", 1358); 4fo. Lajos the Great (relief, St. Simeon's reliquary, Zara, 1380); 6fo. Zsigmond (Sigismund of Luxembourg) (after great seal, 1433).

951 Rowing

952 Computer Drawing of Head

1988. Olympic Games, Seoul. Multicoloured.

3838	2fo. Type **951**	35	15
3839	4fo. Hurdling	60	15
3840	4fo. Fencing	60	15
3841	6fo. Boxing	95	55
MS3842	70 × 80 mm. 20fo. Tennis (31 × 40 mm)	4·50	4·25

1988. 6th Anniv of "Dilemma" (first computer-animated film).

3843	**952** 4fo. multicoloured	50	10

953 Card and Emblem

1988. Eurocheque Congress, Budapest.

3844	**953** 4fo. multicoloured	45	10

954 "Santa Maria", 1492

955 Damaged Head

1988. Ships. Multicoloured.

3845	2fo. Type **954**	45	30
3846	2fo. "Mayflower", 1620	45	30
3847	2fo. "Sovereign of the Seas", 1637	45	30
3848	4fo. "Jylland" (steam warship), 1860	95	40
3849	6fo. "St. Jupat" (yacht), 1985	1·50	55

1988. Anti-drugs Campaign.

3850	**955** 4fo. multicoloured	45	10

956 Green-winged Teal ("Anas crecca")

957 Steam Train

1988. Wild Ducks. Multicoloured.

3851	2fo. Type **956**	55	25
3852	2fo. Common goldeneye ("Bucephula clangula")	55	25
3853	4fo. European wigeon ("Anas penelope")	1·00	30
3854	4fo. Red-crested pochard ("Netta rufina")	1·00	30
3855	6fo. Gadwell	1·25	55
MS3856	90 × 73 mm. 20fo. Mallard ("Anas platyrhynchos")	5·00	4·50

1988. Exhibits in Toy Museum, Kecskemet. Multicoloured.

3857	2fo. Type **957**	45	15
3858	2fo. See-saw	30	10
3859	4fo.+2fo. Pecking chicks	80	30
3860	5fo. Johnny Hussar	70	30

958 Facade

959 Congress Emblem

1988. 450th Anniv of Debrecen Calvinist College.

3861	**958** 4fo. multicoloured	40	10

1988. 58th American Society of Travel Agents Congress, Budapest.

3862	**959** 4fo. multicoloured	40	10

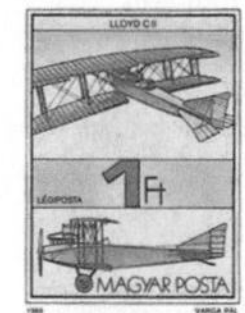

960 Lloyd C.II Biplane

961 Post Official's Collar and Badge

1988. Air. Hungarian Biplanes.

3863	**960** 1fo. green	10	10
3864	– 2fo. purple	25	10
3865	– 4fo. bistre	40	15
3866	– 10fo. blue	95	55
3867	– 12fo. red	1·25	55

DESIGNS: 2fo. Hansa Brandenburg C-I; 4fo. UFAG C-I; 10fo. Gerle 13 scout plane; 12fo. WM 13 trainer.

1988. Centenary of Post Office Training School.

3868	**961** 4fo. red, blue and brown	45	10

962 Baross and Postal Savings Bank, Budapest

1988. Stamp Day. 140th Birth Anniv of Gabor Baross (politician). Multicoloured.

3869	2fo. Type **962**	45	35
3870	4fo. Baross with telephone and telegraph equipment	1·40	75
MS3871	80 × 70 mm. 10fo. Baross and East Railway Station, Budapest	2·75	3·00

963 Lengyel

964 Christmas Tree

1988. Birth Centenary of Gyula Lengyel (labour movement activist).

3872	**963** 4fo. multicoloured	50	10

1988. Christmas.

3873	**964** 2fo. multicoloured	35	10

965 Richard Adolf Zsigmondy (chemistry, 1925)

966 Szakasits

1988. Nobel Prize Winners.

3874	**965** 2fo. deep brown & brown	40	10
3875	– 2fo. deep green and green	40	10
3876	– 2fo. deep brown & brown	40	10
3877	– 4fo. dp mauve & mauve	80	10
3878	– 4fo. green and grey	80	10
3879	– 6fo. brown & light brown	1·25	30

DESIGNS: No. 3875, Robert Barany (medicine, 1914,); 3876, Gyorgy Hevesy (chemistry, 1943); 3877, Albert Szent-Gyorgyi (chemistry, 1937); 3878, Gyorgy Bekesy (medicine, 1961); 3879, Denes Gabor (physics, 1971).

1988. Birth Centenary of Arpad Szakasits (President, 1948–50).

3880	**966** 4fo. multicoloured	50	10

967 Stadium and Emblem

968 Silver Teapot from Pest, 1846

1988. Hungarian Medals at Seoul Olympic Games. Sheet 70 × 90 mm.
MS3881 **967** 20fo. multicoloured 3·75 4·25

1988. Metal Work.
3882 **968** 2fo. blue and brown . . 35 10
3883 – 2fo. deep brown & brown 35 10
3884 – 4fo. lilac and brown . . 70 30
3885 – 5fo. green and brown . . 90 30
DESIGNS: No. 3883, 18th-century silver pot, Buda; 3884, Silver sugar basin from Pest, 1822; 3885, Pierced cast iron plate from Resicabanya, 1850.

969 Emblem

970 Wallisch

1989. Foundation of Post and Savings Bank Company.
3886 **969** 5fo. blue, silver and black 45 10

1989. Birth Centenary of Kalman Wallisch (workers' movement activist).
3887 **970** 3fo. blue and red 40 10

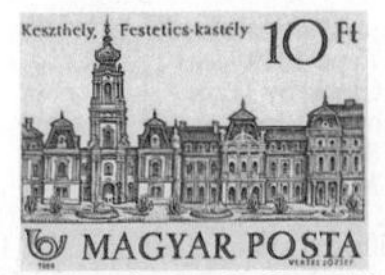
971 Festetics Castle, Keszthely

1989.
3888 **971** 10fo. brown and bistre 50 10

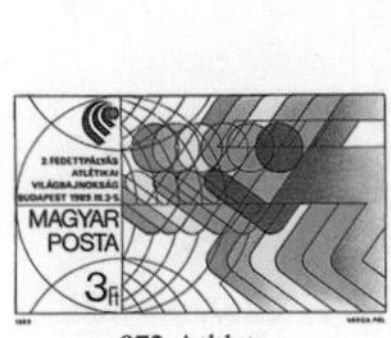
972 Athletes

973 Houses of Parliament and Big Ben London

1989. 2nd International Indoor Athletics Championships, Budapest.
3889 **972** 3fo. multicoloured . . . 40 10

1989. Centenary of Interparliamentary Union. Sheet 78 × 90 mm containing T **973** and similar vert design. Multicoloured.
MS3890 10fo. Type **973**; 10fo. Parliament Building, Budapest 3·50 3·00

974 Gyetvai

975 "Sky-high Tree" (detail, carpet)

1989. Birth Centenary of Janos Gyetvai (journalist).
3891 **974** 3fo. green and red . . . 40 10

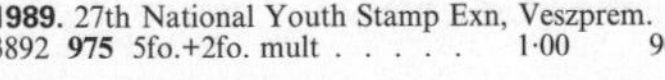

1989. 27th National Youth Stamp Exn, Veszprem.
3892 **975** 5fo.+2fo. mult . . . . . 1·00 90

976 O Bajan

1989. Bicentenary of Babolina Stud Farm. Mult.
3893 3fo. Type **976** 45 45
3894 3fo. Stud officer 45 45
3895 3fo. Gazal II 45 45

977 Disabled People and "ART '89"

978 Arrangement of Narcissi, Crocuses and Violets

1989. "Art '89" International Festival of Disabled People and their Artist Friends.
3896 **977** 5fo. multicoloured . . . 45 10

1989. Flower Arrangements. Multicoloured.
3897 2fo. Type **978** 30 10
3898 3fo. Irises, tulips and lilies (horiz) 45 10
3899 3fo. Roses and chrysanthemums 45 10
3900 5fo. Dahlias and lilies (horiz) 75 30
3901 10fo. Roses, Chinese lanterns and holly . . . . 1·40 45

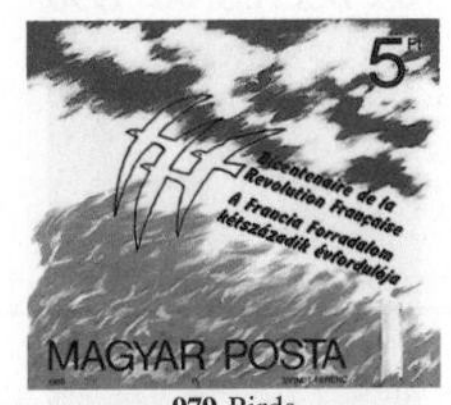
979 Birds

1989. Bicentenary of French Revolution.
3902 **979** 5fo. black, red and blue 45 10
MS3903 80 × 70 mm. **979** 20fo. black, red and blue (49 × 28 mm) 4·50 5·00

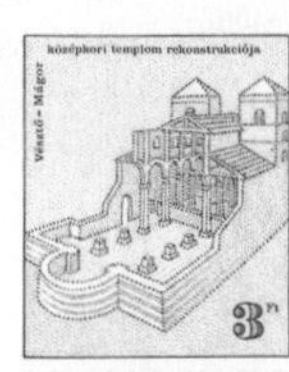
980 Model of Veszto Church

981 Photographer with Camera

1989. Veszto Church Excavation.
3904 **980** 3fo. multicoloured . . . 40 10

1989. 150th Anniv of Photography.
3905 **981** 5fo. lt brown, blk & brn 45 10

982 Turistvandi Water-mill

1989. Mills. Multicoloured.
3906 2fo. Type **982** 25 10
3907 3fo. Szarvas horse-driven mill 40 10
3908 5fo. Kiskunhalas windmill 65 15
3909 10fo. Shipmill, River Drava 1·25 25

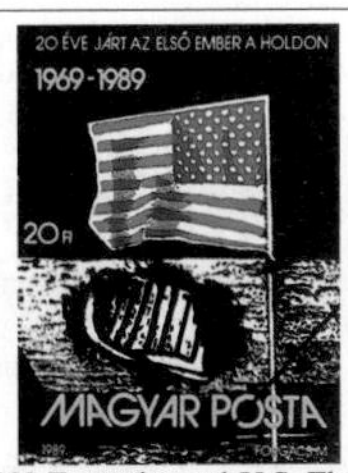
983 Footprint and U.S. Flag

1989. 20th Anniv of First Manned Landing on Moon. Sheet 80 × 70 mm.
MS3910 **983** 20fo. multicoloured 3·50 2·75

984 Messenger Glider

1989. "Old Timer" Rally, Budakeszi Airport, and 60th Anniv of Gliding in Hungary. Multicoloured.
3911 3fo. Type **984** 45 15
3912 5fo. Pal glider 75 30

985 Sand Lizard

1989. Endangered Reptiles. Multicoloured.
3913 2fo. Type **985** 25 10
3914 3fo. Green lizard 40 10
3915 5fo. Grass snake ("Natrix natrix") 60 10
3916 5fo. Orsinis's viper ("Vipera rakosiensis") 60 10
3917 10fo. European pond terrapin . . . . 1·25 30

986 Competitors

1989. 31st World Modern Pentathlon Championships, Budapest.
3918 **986** 5fo. multicoloured . . . 45 10

1989. Nos. 3851 and 3853 surch.
3919 3fo. on 2fo. multicoloured 35 30
3920 5fo. on 4fo. multicoloured 55 45

988 Baradla Cave, Aggtelek

989 Carriage

1989. 10th World Speleology Congress, Budapest. Multicoloured.
3921 3fo. Type **988** 30 10
3922 5fo. Szemlohegy cave, Budapest 55 10
3923 10fo. Anna Cave, Lillafured 1·25 30
3924 12fo. Tapolca cave lake, Miskolctapolca . . . . . 1·40 30

1989. World Two-in-Hand Carriage Driving Championship, Balatonfenyves.
3925 **989** 5fo. multicoloured . . . 70 10

990 Zsuzsa Kossuth (War of Independence nurse)

991 Memorial Statue, Arad

1989. Stamp Day. 125th Anniv of Red Cross Movement.
3926 **990** 5fo. black, blue and red 45 45
3927 – 10fo. multicoloured . . . 95 95
MS3928 82 × 65 mm. 20fo.+10fo. mult . . . . 4·25 4·50
DESIGNS: 10fo. Florence Nightingale (nursing pioneer) and decoration. 27 × 44 mm—20fo. "Battle of Solferini" (Carlo Bossoli).

1989. 140th Death Anniv of "Martyrs of Arad". Sheet 110 × 75 mm.
MS3929 **991** 20fo.+10fo. mult . . 4·25 4·50
The surcharge was for the erection of a new statue.

992 Stamp and Miniature Sheets

1989. Pro Philatelia. Sheet 72 × 92 mm.
MS3930 **992** 50fo. multicoloured 7·25 7·75

993 Flowers and Broken Barbed Wire

1989. Dismantling of Electrified Fence on Western Border.
3931 **993** 5fo. multicoloured . . . 45 10

994 "Conquest of Hungary" (Mor Than)

1989. 1100th Anniv of Arpad as Prince of the Magyars.
3932 **994** 5fo. multicoloured . . . 70 10

995 Flight into Egypt

996 Nehru

1989. Christmas.
3933 **995** 3fo. multicoloured . . . 50 10

1989. Birth Centenary of Jawaharlal Nehru (Indian statesman).
3934 **996** 3fo. brown and stone . . 50 10

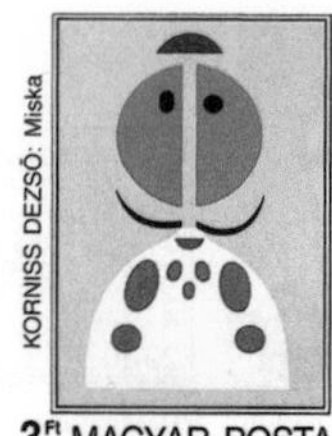

997 "Miska" (Dezso Korniss)

1990. Modern Hungarian Paintings. Mult.

3935 3fo. Type **997** 40 10
3936 5fo. "Sunrise" (Lajos Kassak) 60 10
3937 10fo. "Grotesque Burial" (Endre Balint) . . . . . 1·25 30
3938 12fo. "Remembered Toys" (Tihamer Gyarmathy) . . 1·50 45

1989. Pioneers of Medicine (2nd series). As T **929**.

3939 3fo. green 40 10
3940 3fo. brown 40 10
3941 4fo. black 55 10
3942 6fo. grey 75 30
3943 10fo. purple . . . . 1·25 30

DESIGNS: No. 3939, Claudius Galenus (anatomist and physiologist); 3940, Paracelsus (pharmacy); 3941, Andreas Vesalius (dissection); 3942, Rudolf Virchow (pathology of cells); 3943, Ivan Petrovich Pavlov (blood circulation, digestion and nervous system).

998 Hands holding Coin

1990. 150th Anniv of Savings Banks in Hungary.

3944 **998** 5fo. multicoloured . . . 45 10

999 Sewing Machine

1000 Wall Telephone and Jozsefvaros Telephone Exchange

1990. 125th Anniv of Singer Sewing Machine.

3945 **999** 5fo. brown and cinnamon 45 10

1990. Posts and Telecommunications. Mult.

3946 3fo. Type **1000** 25 10
3947 5fo. Pillar box and Head Post Office, Budapest . . 40 10

1001 Northern Bullfinch ("Pyrrhula pyrrhula")

1002 "Protea compacta"

1990. Birds. Multicoloured.

3960 3fo. Type **1001** 50 20
3961 3fo. River kingfisher ("Alcedo atthis") 50 20
3962 3fo. Syrian woodpecker ("Dendrocopos syriacus") 50 20
3963 5fo. Hoopoe ("Upupa epops") 95 30
3964 5fo. European bee eater ("Merops apiaster") . . . 95 30
3965 10fo. European roller . . . 1·75 60

1990. African Flowers. Multicoloured.

3966 3fo. Type **1002** 40 10
3967 3fo. "Leucadendron spissifolium" 40 10
3968 3fo. "Leucadendron tinctum pubibracteolatum" . . . 40 10
3969 5fo. "Protea barbigera" . . 75 10
3970 5fo. "Protea lepidocarpodendron neriifolia" 75 10
3971 10fo. "Protea cynaroides" . . 1·50 30
MS3972 64 × 82 mm. 20fo. Mixed bouquet (25 × 36 mm) . . . . 4·50 4·50

1003 Sarospatak Teachers' Training School

1990. 28th National Youth Stamp Exhibition, Sarospatak.

3973 **1003** 8fo.+4fo. mult . . . . 1·50 1·25

1004 Janos Hunyadi (regent)

1005 Penny Black

1990. The Hunyadis. Multicoloured.

3974 5fo. Type **1004** 50 10
3975 5fo. King Matthias I Corvinus 50 10

1990. "Stamp World London 90" International Stamp Exhibition. 150th Anniv of the Penny Black. Sheet 88 × 60 mm.

MS3976 **1005** 20fo. multicoloured 4·25 4·00

1006 Gaspar Karoli (statue)

1007 Footballers

1990. 400th Anniv of Publication of Karoli Bible (first Hungarian translation).

3977 **1006** 8fo. cream, green & red 1·00 10

1990. World Cup Football Championship, Italy.

3978 **1007** 3fo. multicoloured . . . 35 10
3979 – 5fo. multicoloured (ball on ground) 60 10
3980 – 5fo. multicoloured (ball in air) 60 10
3981 – 8fo. multicoloured (dribbling) 95 10
3982 – 8fo. mult (heading ball into goal) 95 10
3983 – 10fo. multicoloured . . 1·25 30
MS3984 95 × 70 mm. 20fo. mult 3·50 3·75

DESIGNS: Nos. 3979/84, Various footballing scenes.

1008 Hand writing with Quill Pen

1990. 300th Birth Anniv of Kelemen Mikes (writer).

3985 **1008** 8fo. black and gold . . 90 10

1009 "Weaver" (Noemi Ferenczy)

1010 Kazinczy

1990. Birth Centenaries of Noemi and Beni Ferenczy (artists).

3986 **1009** 3fo. multicoloured . . . 45 10
3987 – 5fo. black and brown 75 10

DESIGN: 5fo. Bronze figure (Beni Ferenczy).

1990. 159th Death Anniv of Ferenc Kazinczy (writer and language reformer).

3988 **1010** 8fo. multicoloured . . . 60 10

1011 Kolcsey (after Anton Einsle)

1013 Cabernet Franc Grapes, Hajos

1012 "St. Stephen" (carving in Parliament Hall) and Arms

1990. Birth Bicentenary of Ferenc Kolcsey (composer of national anthem).

3989 **1011** 8fo. multicoloured . . . 60 10

1990. New State Arms.

3990 **1012** 8fo. multicoloured . . . 60 10
MS3991 70 × 90 mm. 20fo. Arms (33 × 49 mm) . . . . 5·25 5·25

1990. Wine Grapes and Regions (1st series). Multicoloured.

3992 3fo. Type **1013** 30 10
3993 5fo. Cabernet Sauvignon, Villany 45 10
3994 8fo. Riesling, Badacsony . . 75 10
3995 8fo. Kadarka, Szekszard . . 75 10
3996 8fo. Leanyka, Eger 75 10
3997 10fo. Furmint, Tokaj-Hegyalja . . . . 1·00 10

See also Nos. 4363/5, 4436/7, 4521/2, 4596/7 and 4686/7.

1014 "Feast"

1990. Stamp Day. Paintings by Ender Szasz. Multicoloured.

3998 8fo. Type **1014** 70 75
3999 12fo. "Message" . . . . . 1·10 1·10
MS4000 70 × 90 mm. 20fo.+10fo. "Yesterday" (39 × 44 mm) . . 4·25 4·00

1015 Tarbosaurus

1990. Prehistoric Animals. Multicoloured.

4001 3fo. Type **1015** 35 10
4002 5fo. Brontosaurus 55 10
4003 5fo. Dimorphodon 55 10
4004 5fo. Stegosaurus 55 10
4005 8fo. Platybelodon 90 10
4006 10fo. Mammoth . . . . . 1·25 30

1016 Dinosaurs reading

1990. International Literacy Year.

4007 **1016** 10fo. multicoloured . . 90 10

1017 Bird holding Letter

1990. 60th Anniv of Stamp Museum, Budapest.

4008 **1017** 5fo. red and green . . . 50 10

1018 "Great Courier" (detail, Albrecht Durer)

1990. Pro Philatelia. 500th Anniv of Regular European Postal Services. Sheet 90 × 71 mm.

MS4009 **1018** 50fo. black, red and yellow . . . . 7·25 6·00

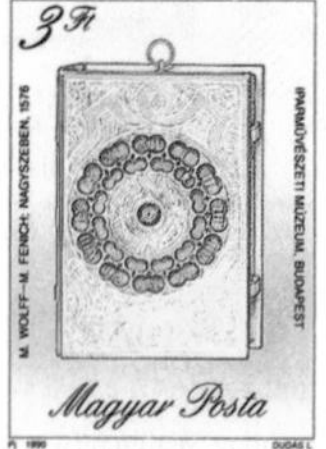

1019 Book-shaped Travelling Clock, by M. Fenich and M. Wolff, 1576

1020 "Madonna and Child" (Sandro Botticelli)

1990. Clocks. Multicoloured.

4010 3fo. Type **1019** 40 10
4011 5fo. Clock by Hans Schmidt, 1643 . . . . . 65 10
4012 5fo. Rococo style clock by J. M. Welz, 1790 . . . . 65 10
4013 10fo. Clock by Johann Hillrich, 1814 . . . . . . 1·40 45

1990. Christmas.

4014 **1020** 5fo. multicoloured . . . 45 10

1021 Lorand Eotvos (inventor) and Torsion Pendulum

1022 "Mandevilla splendens"

1991. Centenary of Torsion Pendulum.

4015 **1021** 12fo. multicoloured . . 90 10

1991. Flowers of the Americas. Mult.

4016 5fo. Type **1022** 25 10
4017 7fo. "Lobelia cardinalis" . . 35 10
4018 7fo. Cup and saucer flower 35 10
4019 12fo. "Steriphoma paradoxa" 60 10
4020 15fo. Shrimp plant 75 30
MS4021 58 × 80 mm. 20fo. Mixed bouquet (27 × 43 mm) . . . . 3·00 2·50

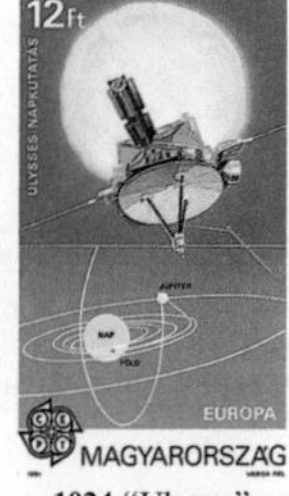

1023 Post Office, Budapest

1024 "Ulysses" Jupiter Probe

1991. Hungarian Full Membership of Council of Europe and Entry into C.E.P.T. (European Posts and Telecommunications Conference). Mult.
4022 5fo. Type **1023** . . . . . 2·10 1·60
4023 7fo. Post Office, Pecs . . . 3·25 2·50

1991. Europa. Europe in Space. Multicoloured.
4024 12fo. Type **1024** 75 90
4025 30fo. "Cassini" and "Huygens" (wrongly inscr "Hughes") Saturn probes 1·75 2·10

1025 "Peter and the Wolf" (tapestry, Gabriella Hajnal)

1991. Youth Stamp.
4026 **1025** 12fo.+6fo. mult 90 90

1026 Gorilla

1991. 125th Anniv of Budapest Zoological and Botanic Gardens. Multicoloured.
4027 7fo. Type **1026** 30 30
4028 12fo. Polar bear 65 40
4029 12fo. Rhinoceros 65 40
4030 12fo. Keel-billed toucan . . 65 40
4031 20fo. Orchid and glasshouse 85 90

1027 Teleki **1028** Map, Emblem and Fencers

1991. 50th Death Anniv of Count Pal Teleki (Prime Minister, 1920–21 and 1939–41).
4032 **1027** 12fo. brn, cinn & blk 75 75

1991. 44th World Fencing Championships, Budapest.
4033 **1028** 12fo. multicoloured . . 75 75

1029 Mariapocs

1991. Visit of Pope John Paul II (1st issue). Shrines to Virgin Mary. Multicoloured.
4034 7fo. Type **1029** 35 30
4035 12fo. Mariagyud 55 60
4036 12fo. Celldomolk 55 60
4037 12fo. Mariaremete 55 60
4038 20fo. Esztergom 95 90

1030 "Appeggi Landscape" and Marko

1991. Birth Bicent of Karoly Marko (painter).
4039 **1030** 12fo. multicoloured . . 75 75

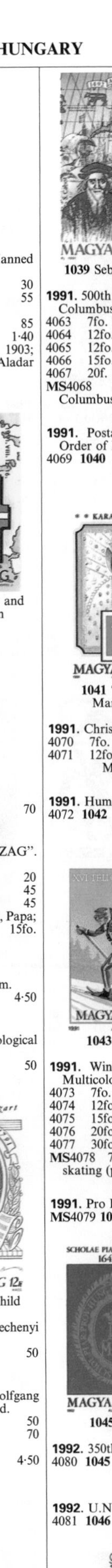

1031 Lilienthal and Monoplane Gliders, 1891

1991. Centenary of First Heavier-than-Air Manned Flight by Otto Lilienthal.
4040 **1031** 7fo. black, ochre & brn 40 30
4041 – 12fo. black, drab & bis 70 55
4042 – 20fo. dp blue, azure & bl . . . . 1·10 85
4043 – 30fo. black, lilac & vio 1·60 1·40
DESIGNS: 12fo. Wright brothers' Flyer 1, 1903; 20fo. Santos-Dumont's "14 bis", 1906; 30fo. Aladar Zselyi's monoplane, 1910.

1032 Players **1034** Map of Europe and Congress Emblem

1033 Pope John Paul II

1991. Centenary of Basketball.
4044 **1032** 12fo. multicoloured . . 75 70

1991. Castles. Inscr "MAGYARORSZAG". As T **921**.
4045 7fo. brown and sepia . . . 30 20
4047 12fo. ultramarine and blue 50 45
4049 15fo. brown and green . . . 50 45
DESIGNS—32 × 25 mm; 7fo. Esterhazy Castle, Papa; 12fo. Dory Castle, Mihaly, 35 × 26 mm; 15fo. Festetics Castle, Keszthely.

1991. Papal Visit (2nd issue). Sheet 60 × 80 mm.
MS4055 **1033** 50fo. black and blue 4·50 4·50

1991. 3rd International Hungarian Philological Society Congress, Szeged.
4056 **1034** 12fo. multicoloured . . 75 50

1035 Szechenyi **1036** Mozart as Child

1991. Birth Bicentenary of Count Istvan Szechenyi (social reformer).
4057 **1035** 12fo. red 75 50

1991. Stamp Day. Death Bicentenary of Wolfgang Amadeus Mozart (composer). Multicoloured.
4058 12fo. Type **1036** 55 50
4059 20fo. Mozart as youth . . . 95 70
MS4060 80 × 61 mm. 30fo.+15fo. Mozart as man (24 × 36 mm) 4·50 4·50

1037 "Telecom 91"

1991. "Telecom 91" International Telecommunications Exhibition, Geneva.
4061 **1037** 12fo. multicoloured . . 75 60

1991. 35th Anniv of 1956 Uprising, No. 4047 optd **A FORRADALOM EMLEKERE 1956 1991**.
4062 12fo. ultramarine and blue 75 60

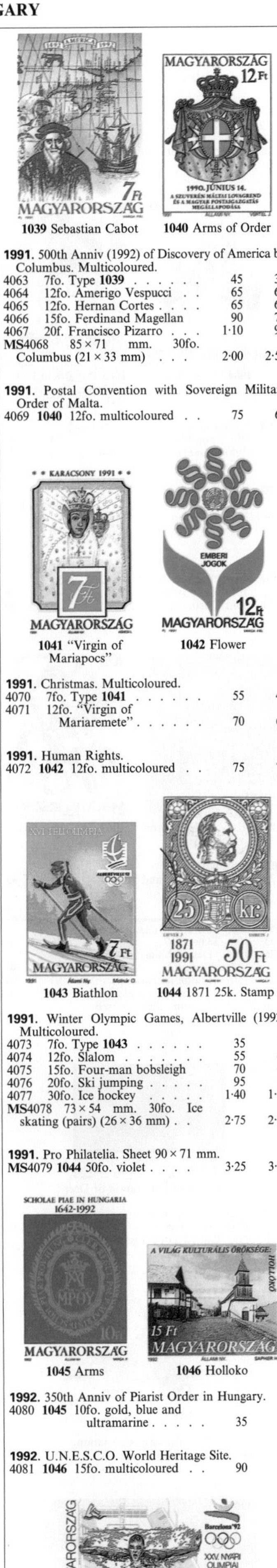

1039 Sebastian Cabot **1040** Arms of Order

1991. 500th Anniv (1992) of Discovery of America by Columbus. Multicoloured.
4063 7fo. Type **1039** 45 30
4064 12fo. Amerigo Vespucci . . 65 60
4065 12fo. Hernan Cortes 65 60
4066 15fo. Ferdinand Magellan 90 75
4067 20f. Francisco Pizarro . . . 1·10 90
MS4068 85 × 71 mm. 30fo. Columbus (21 × 33 mm) . . . 2·00 2·50

1991. Postal Convention with Sovereign Military Order of Malta.
4069 **1040** 12fo. multicoloured . . 75 60

1041 "Virgin of Mariapocs" **1042** Flower

1991. Christmas. Multicoloured.
4070 7fo. Type **1041** 55 45
4071 12fo. "Virgin of Mariaremete" 70 65

1991. Human Rights.
4072 **1042** 12fo. multicoloured . . 75 70

1043 Biathlon **1044** 1871 25k. Stamp

1991. Winter Olympic Games, Albertville (1992). Multicoloured.
4073 7fo. Type **1043** 35 30
4074 12fo. Slalom 55 45
4075 15fo. Four-man bobsleigh 70 60
4076 20fo. Ski jumping 95 75
4077 30fo. Ice hockey . . . . . 1·40 1·25
MS4078 73 × 54 mm. 30fo. Ice skating (pairs) (26 × 36 mm) . . 2·75 2·75

1991. Pro Philatelia. Sheet 90 × 71 mm.
MS4079 **1044** 50fo. violet . . . . 3·25 3·50

1045 Arms **1046** Holloko

1992. 350th Anniv of Piarist Order in Hungary.
4080 **1045** 10fo. gold, blue and ultramarine 35 35

1992. U.N.E.S.C.O. World Heritage Site.
4081 **1046** 15fo. multicoloured . . 90 90

1047 Swimming

1992. Olympic Games, Barcelona. Mult.
4082 7fo. Type **1047** 80 60
4083 9fo. Cycling 95 90
4084 10fo. Gymnastics 95 90
4085 15fo. Running . . . . . . 1·50 1·50

1048 "Indian's Head" Map **1049** Comenius

1992. "Expo '92" World's Fair, Seville. Fantasy Maps. Multicoloured.
4086 10fo. Type **1048** 60 60
4087 10fo. Islands, sea monsters and "Santa Maria" forming face 60 60
4088 15fo. "Conquistador's head" map . . . . 1·00 60
4089 15fo. Navigation instruments and map forming face . . . . . . 1·00 60

1992. 400th Birth Anniv of Jan Komensky (Comenius) (educationist).
4090 **1049** 15fo. multicoloured . . 75 75

1050 Mindszenty

1992. Birth Centenary of Cardinal Jozsef Mindszenty, Archbishop of Esztergom.
4091 **1050** 15fo. brn, cream & red 75 75

1051 Statue of Mayan Man **1052** "Self-portrait" (Renata Toth)

1992. Europa. 500th Anniv of Discovery of America by Columbus. Multicoloured.
4092 15fo. Type **1051** 70 75
4093 40fo. Statue of Mayan woman . . . . 1·90 2·25

1992. Youth Stamps. Children's Drawings. Multicoloured.
4094 9fo.+4fo. Type **1052** . . . 50 50
4095 10fo.+4fo. "The Sun Shines for Me" (Sandor Pusoma) (horiz) 50 50
4096 15fo.+4fo. "I will be a Beauty King" (Endre Knipf) 75 75

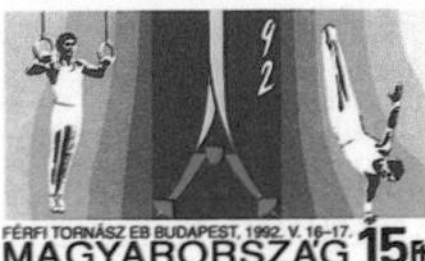

1053 Gymnasts and Emblem

1992. European Gymnastics Championships, Budapest.
4097 **1053** 15fo. multicoloured . . 75 60

1054 St. Margaret (after J. S. Scott) **1055** Saker Falcon

1992. 750th Birth Anniv of St. Margaret.
4098 **1054** 15fo. turq, lt bl & bl . . 75 60

1992. Birds of Prey. Multicoloured.
4099 9fo. Type **1055** 35 30
4100 10fo. Booted eagle 35 45
4101 15fo. Short-toed eagle . . . 55 60
4102 40fo. Red kite . . . . . . 1·40 1·00

1056 Wallenberg   **1057** Millennium Monument, Budapest

1992. 80th Birth Anniv of Raoul Wallenberg (Swedish diplomat).
4103 **1056** 15fo. grey, red and green 50 60

1992. 3rd World Federation of Hungarians Congress, Budapest.
4104 **1057** 15fo. multicoloured . . 50 60

1058 Theodore von Karman (space pioneer, birth centenary (1991))

1992. Anniversaries.
4105 **1058** 15fo. grey, black and deep grey 55 45
4106 – 40fo. grey, black & brn 1·40 1·40
DESIGN: 40fo. Neumann Janos (mathematician, 35th death anniv).

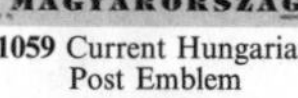

1059 Current Hungarian Post Emblem   **1061** Entwined Cables

1060 Church of the Holy Family, Barcelona, and Medals

1992. Stamp Day."Eurofilex '92" International Postal History Exhibition, Budapest.
4107 **1059** 10fo.+5fo. multicoloured 75 75
4108 15fo.+5fo. multicoloured . . . . 1·00 1·00
MS4109 91 × 66 mm. 50fo.+20fo. brown, cinnamon and black . . 3·00 3·00
DESIGNS—VERT Hungarian Royal Post emblem, 1867. 39 × 29 mm—50fo. "Postal Riders" (etching, Ferenc Helbing).
See also No. 4111.

1992. Hungarian Olympic Games (Barcelona) Medal Winners. Sheet 61 × 80 mm.
MS4110 **1060** 50fo.+20fo. mult 3·00 3·00

1992. As No. 4108 but without premium and commemorative inscription.
4111 **1059** 15fo. multicoloured . . 55 60

1992. "Europa Telecom '92" Telecommunications Exhibition, Budapest.
4112 **1061** 15fo. multicoloured . . 55 45

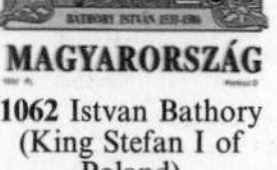

1062 Istvan Bathory (King Stefan I of Poland)   **1063** Pieces on Board

1992. Princes of Transylvania. Multicoloured.
4113 10fo. Type **1062** 35 30
4114 15fo. Istvan Bocskai 45 45
4115 40fo. Gabor Bethlen . . . . 1·25 1·25

1992. 10th European Chess Team Championship, Debrecen.
4116 **1063** 15fo. multicoloured . . 75 75

1064 "Clianthus formosus"   **1065** Postal Rider of Prince Ferenc Rakoczi II, 1703–11

1992. Australian Flowers. Multicoloured.
4117 9fo. Type **1064** 35 30
4118 10fo. "Leschenaultia biloba" 35 45
4119 15fo. "Anigosanthos manglesii" 55 60
4120 40fo. "Comesperma ericinum" . . . . 1·40 1·25
MS4121 64 × 83 mm. 50fo. Mixed flowers (31 × 41 mm) . . . . . 3·00 2·75

1992. Post Office Uniforms. Multicoloured.
4122 10fo. Type **1065** 40 30
4123 15fo. Postmen, 1874 . . . . 55 30

1066 "Holy Family" (iron relief, 1850)   **1067** "Arachnis flos-aeris"

1992. Christmas.
4124 **1066** 15fo. black and blue . . 45 45

1993. Asian Flowers. Multicoloured.
4125 10fo. Type **1067** 35 30
4126 10fo. "Dendrobium densiflorium" 35 30
4127 15fo. "Lilium speciosum" 50 60
4128 15fo. "Meconopsis aculeata" 50 60
MS4129 64 × 83 mm. 50fo. Mixed bouquet (31 × 41 mm) . . . . 3·00 4·50

1068 Shield Decoration of Deer

1993. Scythian Remains in Hungary. Mult.
4130 10fo. Type **1068** 45 30
4131 17fo. Gilt-silver embossed deer 75 75

1069 Single Sculls

1993. Centenary of Rowing Association.
4132 **1069** 17fo. multicoloured . . 75 75

1070 Queen Beatrix and King Matthias I Corvinus (detail of Missal) (½-size illustration)

1993. King Matthias I Corvinus's "Missale Romanum".
4133 **1070** 15fo. multicoloured . . 75 75
MS4134 106 × 156 mm. 40fo. Illustration from missal (59 × 39 mm) . . . . 1·75 2·50

1071 Animals in Wood   **1072** Competitors and Globe

1993. Youth Stamps. Tapestries by Erzsebet Szekeres. Multicoloured.
4135 10fo.+5fo. Type **1071** . . . 70 60
4136 17fo.+8fo. Animals in tree hiding from dragons . . . 1·25 1·00

1993. World Motocross Championships, Cserenfa.
4137 **1072** 17fo. multicoloured . . 45 45

1073 Diagram of Solar System and Copernicus

1993. "Polska'93" International Stamp Exn.
4138 **1073** 17fo. multicoloured . . 45 75

1074 Paks Catholic Church   **1075** Cauliflower Clavaria

1993. Europa. Contemporary Art. Architecture by Imre Makovecz. Multicoloured.
4139 17fo. Type **1074** 55 45
4140 45fo. Hungarian pavilion at "Expo '92" World's Fair, Seville . . . . 1·00 1·00

1993. Fungi. Multicoloured.
4141 10fo. Type **1075** 25 30
4142 17fo. Death trumpet 55 45
4143 45fo. Caesar's mushroom . . 1·10 1·00

1076 "St. Christopher" (Albrecht Durer)

1993. European Year of the Aged.
4144 **1076** 17fo. black, cream and silver 45 45

1077 Class 326 and 424 Steam Locomotives   **1078** Rowing Boat approaching Town

1993. 125th Anniv of Hungarian Railways.
4145 **1077** 17fo. blue and cobalt 45 45

1993. 900th Anniv of Mohacs.
4146 **1078** 17fo. brown, cinnamon and red 45 45

1079 Poplar Admiral   **1080** Kalman Latabar

1993. Butterflies. Multicoloured.
4147 10fo. Type **1079** 25 30
4148 17fo. "Aricia artaxerxes" . . 50 45
4149 30fo. "Plebejides pylaon" . . 70 75

1993. Great Humourists. Multicoloured.
4150 17fo. Type **1080** 55 30
4151 30fo. Charlie Chaplin . . . 75 75

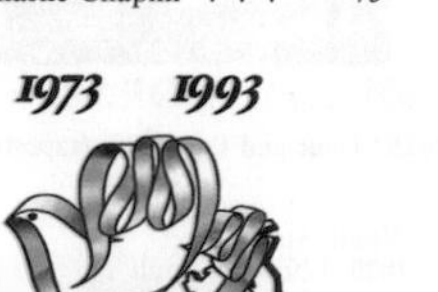

1081 Ribbon Dove over North-western Europe

1993. 20th Anniv of European Security and Co-operation Conference, Helsinki. Sheet 82 × 62 mm.
MS4152 **1081** 50fo. multicoloured 1·75 2·25

1082 Solar Panel absorbing Sun's Rays   **1083** Laszlo Nemeth

1993. International Solar Energy Society Congress, Budapest.
4153 **1082** 17fo. multicoloured . . 45 45

1993. Writers. Each blue and azure.
4154 17fo. Type **1083** 45 45
4155 17fo. Dezso Szabo 45 45
4156 17fo. Antal Szerb 45 45

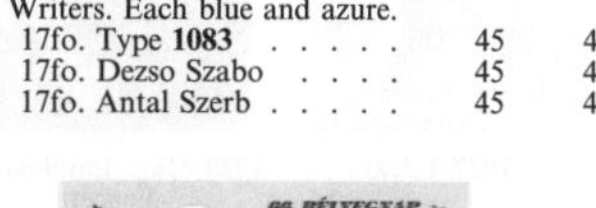

1084 Zoltan Nagy and 1953 20fi. Stamp

1993. Stamp Day. Designers. Multicoloured.
4157 10fo.+5fo. Type **1084** . . . 45 45
4158 17fo.+5fo. Sandor Legrady and 1938 50f. stamp . . . 70 75
MS4159 56 × 75 mm. 50fo.+20fo. Ferenc Helbing and 1932 10p. stamp (35 × 26 mm) . . . . . 2·25 1·90

1085 Arms

1993. 175th Anniv of Faculty of Agronomics, Pannon Agricultural University, Magyarovar.
4160 **1085** 17fo. multicoloured . . 45 45

1086 "Szent Istvan", 1892   **1087** Prehistoric Man and Skull (Vertesszolos)

1993. Hungarian Ships. Multicoloured.
4161 10fo. Type **1086** 25 30
4162 30fo. "Szent Istvan" (battleship), 1915 . . . . 80 75

1993. Palaeolithic Remains in Hungary. Mult.
4163 17fo. Type **1087** 60 30
4164 30fo. Men round fire and stone tool (Szeleta Cave, Lillafured) 90 75

1088 Route-map of Central Europe

1993. Roman Roads. Sheet 80 × 65 mm.
MS4165 **1088** 50fo. multicoloured 1·75 1·75

1089 "Madonna and Child" (altarpiece by F. A. Hillebrant, Szekestehervar Cathedral)

1091 Antall

1090 Szechenyi Chain Bridge (½-size illustration)

1993. Christmas.
4166 **1089** 10fo. multicoloured . . 30 30

1993. "Expo '96" World's Fair, Budapest (1st issue).
4167 **1090** 17fo. dp green & green 55 45
4168 – 30fo. purple and claret 75 75
4169 – 45fo. dp brown & brown . . . . 1·10 1·25
DESIGNS—HORIZ: 30fo. Opera House. VERT: 45fo. Matthias Church.
See also Nos. 4236/8 and 4268/9.

1993. Joszef Antall (Prime Minister since 1990) Commemoration.
4170 **1091** 19fo. multicoloured . . 50 40
MS4171 70 × 50 mm. No. 4170 90 1·25

1092 Skiing

1994. Winter Olympic Games, Lillehammer, Norway. Multicoloured.
4172 12fo. Type **1092** 35 30
4173 19fo. Ice hockey 70 30

1093 Douglas DC-3

1994. 50th Anniv of I.C.A.O.
4174 **1093** 56fo. multicoloured . . 1·50 1·00

1094 "Golgotha" (detail, Mihaly Munkacsy)

1095 Mihaly Munkacsy (self-portrait)

1994. Easter.
4175 **1094** 12fo. multicoloured . . 35 30

1994. Artists' 150th Birth Anniversaries. Multicoloured.
4176 12fo. Gyula Benczur (self-portrait) 40 30
4177 19fo. Type **1095** 65 45

1096 Kossuth

1097 Hen with Chicks

1994. Death Centenary of Lajos Kossuth (Governor of 1849 Republic).
4178 **1096** 19fo. multicoloured . . 50 45

1994. The Great Bustard. Multicoloured.
4179 10fo. Type **1097** 30 30
4180 10fo. Bustards taking off . . 30 30
4181 10fo. Cock in mating display 30 30
4182 10fo. Hen with chicks (different) 30 30

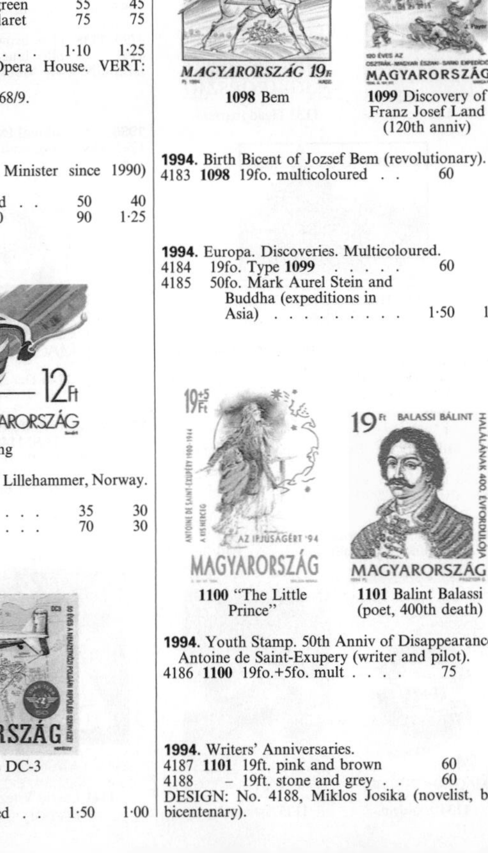

1098 Bem

1099 Discovery of Franz Josef Land (120th anniv)

1994. Birth Bicent of Jozsef Bem (revolutionary).
4183 **1098** 19fo. multicoloured . . 60 45

1994. Europa. Discoveries. Multicoloured.
4184 19fo. Type **1099** 60 60
4185 50fo. Mark Aurel Stein and Buddha (expeditions in Asia) . . . . 1·50 1·40

1100 "The Little Prince"

1101 Balint Balassi (poet, 400th death)

1994. Youth Stamp. 50th Anniv of Disappearance of Antoine de Saint-Exupery (writer and pilot).
4186 **1100** 19fo.+5fo. mult 75 75

1994. Writers' Anniversaries.
4187 **1101** 19ft. pink and brown 60 45
4188 – 19ft. stone and grey . . 60 45
DESIGN: No. 4188, Miklos Josika (novelist, birth bicentenary).

1102 Horsemen

1104 Elvis Presley and Players

1103 Athens Stadium, 1896

1994. 1100th Anniv (1996) of Magyar Conquest (1st issue). Multicoloured.
4189 19ft. Type **1102** 60 45
4190 19ft. Arpad and standard bearers (58 × 39 mm) . . 60 45
4191 19ft. Mounted archer . . . 60 45
Nos. 4189/91 were issued together, se-tenant, forming a composite design of a detail of the painting "in the round" commissioned to celebrate the millenary of the Conquest.
See also Nos. 4240/2 and 4275/7.

1994. Centenary of International Olympic Committee. Multicoloured.
4192 12ft. Olympic medals of 1896 and 1992 . . . . . 35 30
4193 19ft. Type **1103** 55 45
4194 19ft. Ancient Greek athletes, Olympic flag and flame 55 45
4195 35ft. Pierre de Coubertin (founder) . . . . 1·10 75

1994. World Cup Football Championship, U.S.A. American Entertainers. Multicoloured.
4196 19ft. Type **1104** 60 45
4197 19ft. Marilyn Monroe and players 60 45
4198 35ft. John Wayne and players . . . . 1·10 75

1105 Family

1994. International Year of the Family.
4199 **1105** 19fo. multicoloured . . 55 30

1106 Summer Snowflake

1994. European Flowers. Multicoloured.
4200 12fo. Type **1106** 35 30
4201 19fo. Common rock-rose . . 50 45
4202 35fo. "Eryngium alpinum" 95 75
4203 50fo. Pennycress . . . . . 1·40 90
MS4204 64 × 83 mm. 100fo. Mixed bouquet (31 × 40 mm) . . . . 3·00 3·00

1107 Heinrich von Stephan (founder) and Emblem

1108 Csik Megye

1994. 120th Anniv of Universal Postal Union.
4205 **1107** 19fo. grey, brown & blk 50 30
4206 – 35fo. blue, brown & blk 1·00 75
MS4207 98 × 71 mm. 50fo.+25fo. brown, black and blue (Heinrich von Stephan) (vert); 50fo.+25 fo. brown, black and violet (Gervay Mihaly) (vert) . . . . 4·50 2·40
DESIGN: 35fo. Gervay Mihaly (first Director General of Posts) and U.P.U. emblem.

1994. Traditional Patterns.
4208 – 1fo. violet and black 10 10
4209 – 2fo. multicoloured . . 10 10
4210 – 3fo. multicoloured . . 10 10
4210a – 5fo. multicoloured . . 10 10
4211 – 9fo. multicoloured . . 15 10
4212 **1108** 11fo. multicoloured . . 25 10
4213 – 12fo. multicoloured . . 25 10
4214 – 13fo. multicoloured . . 30 10
4215 – 14fo. multicoloured . . 35 30
4216 – 16fo. multicoloured . . 45 10
4217 – 17fo. black, grey & red 35 10
4218 – 19fo. multicoloured . . 50 10
4219 – 22fo. multicoloured . . 50 30
4220 – 24fo. multicoloured . . 45 30
4220a – 24fo. multicoloured . . 35 30
4220b – 27fo. multicoloured . . 35 30
4221 – 32fo. multicoloured . . 60 10
4222 – 35fo. multicoloured . . 70 30
4223 – 38fo. multicoloured . . 75 60
4224 – 40fo. multicoloured . . 75 30
4225 – 50fo. multicoloured . . 1·10 30
4225a – 65fo. black, red and grey 55 45
4226 – 75fo. multicoloured . . 1·10 45
4226a – 79fo. multicoloured . . 65 60
4227 – 80fo. multicoloured . . 1·25 45
4228 – 90fo. multicoloured . . 75 75
4229 – 100fo. multicoloured 80 75
4229a – 200fo. multicoloured 2·00 1·25
4230 – 300fo. multicoloured 3·50 1·50
4231 – 500fo. multicoloured 5·50 2·25
DESIGNS: 1fo. Torocko; 2fo. Buzsak; 3fo. Vas megye (flowers); 5fo. Rabakoz; 9, 24fo. (4220) Felfold; 12, 27fo. Vas megye (birds); 13, 32fo. Debrecen; 14, 80fo. Sarkoz; 16fo. Csiki-Medence; 17, 35, 65fo. Dunantul; 19, 24fo. (4220a) Kalocsa; 22, 90fo. Heves megye; 300fo. Kalocsa (different); 38, 75fo. Oroshaza; 40fo. Kalotaszeg; 50fo. Szentgal; 79fo. Moldvai csango; 100fo. Szecseny videke; 200fo. Mezokovesd; 500fo. Szolnok megye.

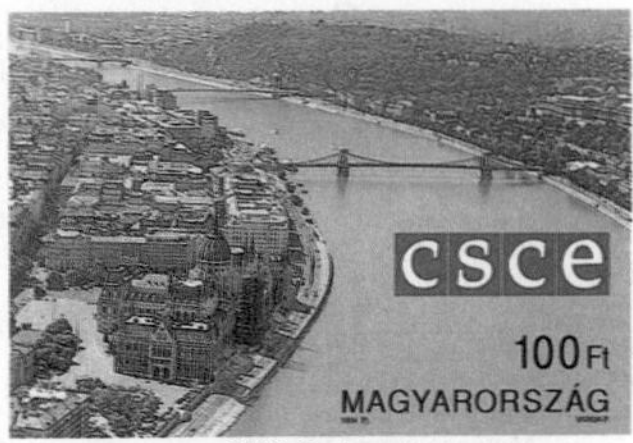

1109 Budapest

1994. Conference of Security and Co-operation in Europe Summit, Budapest. Sheet 92 × 70 mm.
MS4232 **1109** 100fo. multicoloured 3·00 2·25

1110 Hebrew Tombstone

1111 "Nativity"

1994. Holocaust Victims' Commemoration.
4233 **1110** 19fo. multicoloured . . 45 30

1994. Christmas. Paintings by Pal Molnar. Multicoloured.
4234 12fo. Type **1111** 30 30
4235 35fo. "Flight into Egypt" (31 × 29 mm) 70 60

1112 National Museum

1994. "Expo '96" World's Fair, Budapest (2nd issue). Budapest landmarks.
4236 **1112** 19fo. green 45 30
4237 – 19fo. brown 45 30
4238 – 19fo. violet 45 30
DESIGNS: No. 4237, University of Technical Sciences; 4238, Vajdahunyad Castle.

1113 "Ferencz Jozsef I" (paddle-steamer) and "Baross" (container ship)

1995. Cent of Hungarian Shipping Company.
4239 **1113** 22fo. multicoloured . . 60 45

1995. 1100th Anniv (1996) of Magyar Conquest (2nd issue). As T **1102**. Multicoloured.
4240 22fo. Ox cart 65 45
4241 22fo. Arpad's consort in ox cart (59 × 39 mm) 65 45
4242 22fo. Men and pack ox . . . 65 45
Nos. 4240/2 were issued together, se-tenant, forming a composite design of a detail of the painting "in the round" commissioned to celebrate the millenary of the Conquest.

1114 Lamb of God **1116** Weather Map and Barometer

1115 Paddle-steamer

1995. Easter.
4243 **1114** 14fo. purple and black 40 30

1995. 150th Anniv of Steamer Service on River Tisza (14fo.) and Birth Bicentenary of Pal Vasarhelyi (engineer) (60fo.). Multicoloured.
4244 14fo. Type **1115** 45 30
4245 60fo. Vasarhelyi (after Miklos Barabas) and survey ship . . . . 1·90 90

1995. Anniversaries. Multicoloured.
4246 22fo. Type **1116** (125th anniv of Hungarian Meteorological Service) 60 45
4247 22fo. Emblem (50th anniv of F.A.O.) (25 × 41 mm) . . 60 45
4248 22fo.+10fo. John the Hero (150th anniv of poem by Petofi) (37 × 45mm) . . . 85 60
No. 4248 is the 1995 Youth Stamp.

1117 White Stork and Frog **1118** Allied Flags forming Dove over Map of Europe

1995. European Nature Conservation Year. Multicoloured.
4249 14fo. Type **1117** 40 30
4250 14fo. Red squirrel 40 30
4251 14fo. Blue tit 40 30
4252 14fo. Butterfly and hedgehog 40 30
Nos. 4249/52 were issued together, se-tenant, forming a composite design.

1995. Europa. Peace and Freedom.
4253 **1118** 22fo. multicoloured . . 60 45

1119 Gymnastics and Ferenc Kemeny (founder)

1995. Centenary of Hungarian Olympic Committee. Multicoloured.
4254 22fo. Type **1119** 60 30
4255 60fo. Throwing the javelin 1·50 60
4256 100fo. Fencing . . . . . . 2·75 1·10

1120 Exhibition Emblem

1995. "Olympiafila '95" International Olympic and Sports Stamps Exhibition, Budapest.
4257 **1120** 22fo.+11fo. mult (rings in yellow) 90 60
4258 22fo.+11fo. mult (rings in purple) 90 60

1121 Saint Ladislas (detail of fresco, Szekelyderzs Castle Chapel) **1122** Almasy

1995. 900th Death Anniv of St. Ladislas, King of Hungary.
4259 **1121** 22fo. multicoloured . . 60 45

1995. Birth Centenary of Laszlo Almasy (explorer).
4260 **1122** 22fo. multicoloured . . 60 45

1123 Museum of Applied Arts, Budapest, and Lechner

1995. 150th Birth Anniv of Odon Lechner (architect).
4261 **1123** 22fo. multicoloured . . 60 40

1124 "K XVIII 1923" (Laszlo Moholy-Nagy) **1125** College Building and Jozsef Eotvos (founder)

1995. Artists' Birth Centenaries. Multicoloured.
4262 22fo. Type **1124** 55 35
4263 22fo. "The Fiddler" (Aurel Bernath) 55 35

1995. Centenary of Eotvos College.
4264 **1125** 60fo. multicoloured . . 1·40 90

1126 Postal Carriage and Map of Postal Routes

1995. Stamp Day. Multicoloured.
4265 22fo. Type **1126** 50 45
4266 40fo. Airplane and route map . . . . 1·00 60
MS4267 80 × 61 mm. 100fo.+30fo. Children looking at stamp album (29 × 44 mm) . . . . 3·00 2·40

1995. "Expo '96" World's Fair, Budapest (3rd issue). As T **1112** showing Budapest landmarks.
4268 22fo. grey 55 40
4269 22fo. purple 55 40
DESIGNS: No. 4268, West Railway Station; 4269, Music Hall.

1127 Anniversary Emblem **1128** Sparklers

1995. 50th Anniv of U.N.O.
4270 **1127** 60fo. multicoloured . . 1·40 75

1995. Christmas. Multicoloured.
4271 14fo. Type **1128** 30 30
4272 60fo. Three wise men in stable . . . . 1·25 75

1129 St Elizabeth bathing Leper

1995. Saint Elizabeth of Hungary.
4273 **1129** 22fo. multicoloured . . 60 30

1130 Nobel Medals

1995. Centenary of Nobel Trust Fund.
4274 **1130** 100fo. multicoloured . . 2·25 1·25

1996. 1100th Anniv of Magyar Conquest (3rd issue). As T **1102**. Multicoloured.
4275 24fo. Rejoicing crowd . . . 50 30
4276 24fo. Shaman presenting sacrificial white horse (59 × 39 mm) 50 30
4277 24fo. Bards 50 30
Nos. 4275/7 were issued together, se-tenant, forming a composite design.

1131 Leather Purse **1133** Headquarters

1132 Monastery (after Xaver Zsoldos)

1996. 9th-century Relics from Kares Cemeteries. Multicoloured.
4278 24fo. Type **1131** 60 45
4279 24fo. Gold and silver sabre hilt 60 45

1996. Millenary of Pannonhalma Monastery (1st issue). Sheet 100 × 80 mm.
MS4280 **1132** 100fo. violet . . . 2·25 2·75
See also Nos. 4290/1 and 4305/6.

1996. Centenary of Journalists' Association.
4281 **1133** 50fo. multicoloured . . 1·10 60

1134 Emblem

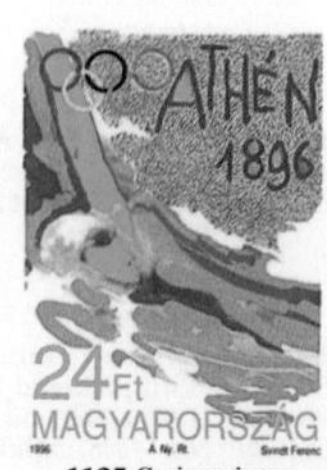

1135 Swimming

1996. Promotion of Hungarian Production.
4282 **1134** 24fo. black, red & green 55 30

1996. Centenary of Modern Olympic Games and Olympic Games, Atlanta. Multicoloured.
4283 24fo. Type **1135** 50 30
4284 50fo. Tennis (Csilla Orosz) 1·10 60
4285 75fo. Canoeing . . . . . . 1·60 90

1996. 1100th Anniv of Magyar Conquest (4th issue). Sheet 150 × 190 mm containing previous designs. Multicoloured.
MS4286 19fo. × 3 Nos. 4189/91; 22fo. × 3 Nos. 4240/2; 24fo. × 3 Nos. 4275/7 . . . . 4·50 2·10

1136 First Carriage

1996. Centenary of Budapest Underground Railway.
4287 **1136** 24fo. multicoloured . . 55 30

1137 Queen Gizella (wife of St. Stephen)

1996. Europa. Famous Women. Hungarian Queens. Multicoloured.
4288 24fo. Type **1137** 50 30
4289 75fo. Queen Elisabeth (wife of Francis Joseph I) . . . 1·60 1·25

1138 Triumphal Arch (entrance to Cathedral) **1139** Bird and "DRUG"

1996. Millenary of Pannonhalma Monastery (2nd issue).
4290 **1138** 17fo. brown 40 30
4291 – 24fo. blue 55 30
DESIGN: 24fo. Monks gathered in cloisters.

1996. International Day against Drug Abuse.
4292 **1139** 24fo. multicoloured . . 55 30

1140 Denes Mihaly (television pioneer)

1996. Inventors. Multicoloured.
4293 24fo. Type **1140** 50 30
4294 50fo. Laszlo Biro and ballpoint pen . . . . . . 1·00 60
4295 75fo. Zoltan Bay and Moon radar . . . . 1·50 90

1141 Laszlo Vitez (puppet) **1143** Pyramid

1142 "Heves", 1846

1996. Youth Stamp. Puppet Festival, Budapest.
4296 **1141** 24fo.+10fo. mult . . . 75 60

1996. 150th Anniv of Hungarian Railways. Steam Locomotives. Multicoloured.
4297 17fo. Class 303 . . . . . . 30 30
4298 24fo. Class 325 . . . . . . 45 45
4299 24fo. Type **1142** 45 45
On No. 4299 the nameplate is inscribed "PEST".

1996. 2nd European Mathematics Congress, Budapest.
4300 **1143** 24fo. multicoloured . . 45 30

1144 Hungarian Long-horned Wood Beetle ("Ropalopus ungaricus")

1996. "NATUREXPO '96" International Nature Conservation Exhibition, Budapest. Mult.
4301 13fo. Type **1144** 30 30
4302 13fo. Lynx ("Lynx lynx") . . 30 30
4303 13fo. Siberian iris ("Iris sibirica") 30 30
4304 13fo. Great egret ("Egretta alba") 30 30

1996. Millenary of Pannonhalma Monastery (3rd issue).. As T **1138**.
4305 17fo. brown 35 30
4306 24fo. green 50 30
DESIGNS: 17fo. Refectory; 24fo. Main library.

1145 Homage to Prince Arpad (from "Vienna Picture Chronicle")

1146 1871 10k. Engraved Stamp

1996. Stamp Day. "Budapest '96" International Stamp Exhibition, Budapest. Mult.
4307 17fo. Type **1145** 35 30
4308 24fo. Prince Arpad on horseback and soldiers (from "Vienna Picture Chronicle") 65 30
MS4309 92 × 72 mm. 150fo.+50fo. 1944 1f. Prince Arpad stamp, first page of Deeds of Hungarians and detail of "Compact sealed with Blood" (mural by Bertalan Szekely, Kecskemet Town Hall) 2·50 3·75

1996. World Convention of Hungarian Stamps and Postal History.
4310 **1146** 24fo. multicoloured . . 55 30

1147 Map and Paddle-steamer "Kisfaludy"

1996. 150th Anniv of Steamer Service on Lake Balaton.
4311 **1147** 17fo. multicoloured . . 55 30

1148 Mastheads and Demonstration

1996. 40th Anniv of 23 October Uprising. Multicoloured.
4312 13fo. Type **1148** 25 30
4313 16fo. Newspaper, burning flag and motor vehicle . . 30 30
4314 17fo. Men with rifles and newspaper 30 30
4315 24fo. Newspaper and Imre Nagy (Prime Minister, Oct–Nov 1956) 35 30
MS4316 76 × 75 mm. 40fo. Imre Nagy and government members (44 × 29 mm) 55 60

1149 Atlanta and Medals

1996. Hungarian Medal Winners at Olympic Games. Sheet 85 × 55 mm.
MS4317 **1149** 150fo. multicoloured 3·00 2·00

1150 "Madonna and Child with Two Angels" (Matteo di Giovanni)

1996. Christmas. Multicoloured.
4318 17fo. Type **1150** 35 30
4319 24fo. "Adoration of the Wise Men" (Salzburg Master) 50 30

1151 List of Years

1152 Bust, Book, Quill and Shield

1996. 50th Anniv of UNICEF.
4320 **1151** 24fo. multicoloured . . 45 30

1996. Birth Bicentenary of Miklos Wesselenyi (writer).
4321 **1152** 24fo. multicoloured . . 45 30

1153 Kalman Mikszath and Characters

1997. Writers' Birth Anniversaries. Mult.
4322 27fo. Type **1153** (150th anniv) 60 45
4323 27fo. Aron Tamasi (cent) . . 60 45

1154 Baranya

1997. Arms. Multicoloured. (a) As T **1154**.
4324 27fo. Type **1154** 30 45
4325 27fo. Bacs-Kiskun 30 45
4326 27fo. Bekes 30 45
4327 27fo. Borsod-Abauj-Zemplen 30 45
4328 27fo. Fejer 30 45
4329 27fo. Gyor-Moson-Sopron . . 30 45
4330 27fo. Heves 30 45
4331 27fo. Jasz-Nagykun-Szolnok 30 45
4332 27fo. Komarom-Esztergom . 30 45
4333 27fo. Nograd 30 45
4334 27fo. Pest 30 45
4335 27fo. Somogy 30 45
4336 27fo. Tolna 30 45
4337 27fo. Vas 30 45
4338 27fo. Veszprem 30 45
4339 27fo. Zala 30 45

(b) Size 50 × 32 mm.
4340 27fo. Hajku-Bihar 30 45
4341 27fo. Budapest 30 45
4342 27fo. Csongrad 30 45
4343 27fo. Szabolcs-Szatmar-Bereg 30 45
MS4344 Four sheets, each 78 × 125 mm. (a) Nos. 4324/33 and 4340 plus label; (b) Nos. 4328/33; (c) Nos. 4334/9; (d) Nos. 4341/3Set of 4 sheets . . 10·50 10·50

1155 Badge, Camp and Sailing

1997. 90th Anniv of Scout Movement.
4345 **1155** 20fo. multicoloured . . 35 30

1156 Book, Knight and Arany

1997. 150th Anniv of Composition of "Miklos Toldi" by Janos Arany (winning entry in poetry competition).
4346 **1156** 27fo.+10fo. mult . . . 70 60

1157 St. Adalbert

1158 Emblem and City

1997. Death Millenary of St. Adalbert (Bishop of Prague).
4347 **1157** 80fo. lilac . . . . . . 1·50 1·25

1997. World Customs' Union Conference, Budapest.
4348 **1158** 90fo. multicoloured . . 1·50 80

1159 Gemsboks

1997. African Animals. Multicoloured.
4349 16fo. Type **1159** 25 30
4350 20fo. Common zebras . . . 30 30
4351 20fo. Black rhinoceroses . . 30 30
4352 27fo. Lions 40 45
MS4353 91 × 64 mm. 90fo. African elephants . . . . 1·50 2·25

1160 "The Enchanted Hart"

1997. Europa. Tales and Legends. Mult.
4354 27fo. Type **1160** 55 45
4355 90fo. King St. Stephen overseeing burial of Prince Geza (death millenary) . . 1·90 1·25

1161 Schraetzer ("Gymnocephalus schraetzer")

1997. Fishes. Multicoloured.
4356 20fo. Type **1161** 40 30
4357 20fo. Bullhead "Cottus gobio" 40 30
4358 20fo. Schneider "Alburnoides bipunctatus" 40 30
4359 20fo. Spiny loach ("Cobitis taenia") 40 30
Nos. 4356/9 were issued together, se-tenant, forming a composite design.

1162 St. Jadwiga (after Peter Prokop)

1163 Janos Selye

1997. Canonization of Queen Jadwiga of Poland.
4360 **1162** 90fo. multicoloured . . 1·50 1·25

1997. Int Congress on Stress, Budapest.
4361 **1163** 90fo. multicoloured . . 1·50 60

1997. No. 4220 surch **60 f**.
4362 60fo. on 24fo. multicoloured 1·00 60

1997. Wine Grapes and Regions (2nd series). As T **1013**. Multicoloured.
4363 27fo. Harslevelu, Gyongyos 50 45
4364 27fo. Nemes Kadarka, Kiskoros 50 45
4365 27fo. Teltfurtu Ezerjo, Mor 50 45

1165 Flower surrounded by Flood Waters

1997. Flood Relief Funds.
4366 **1165** 27fo.+100fo. mult . . . 2·40 1·50

1166 Postman and Csonka Tricycle, 1900

1997. Stamp Day. Multicoloured.
4367 27fo.+5fo. Type **1166** . . . 40 45
4368 55fo.+5fo. Registered letter receiving-machine, 1906 (vert) 65 75
MS4369 82 × 68 mm. 90fo.+30fo. Csonka post van, 1905 . . . . 1·40 2·10

1167 Nativity

1997. Christmas. Multicoloured.
4370 20fo. Type **1167** 40 30
4371 27fo. Adoration of the Wise Men 50 60

1168 Weightlifter

1169 Skiing

1997. 68th World Weightlifting Championships, Thailand.
4372 **1168** 90fo. multicoloured . . 1·50 60

1998. Winter Olympic Games, Nagano, Japan. Multicoloured.
4373 30fo. Type **1169** 60 45
4374 100fo. Snowboarding . . . 2·00 1·25

1170 Szechenyi with Camera

1998. Birth Centenary of Zsigmond Szechenyi (travel writer).
4375 **1170** 60fo. multicoloured . . 90 75

1171 Leaf and Lyrics

1998. 175th Anniv of National Hymn by Ferenc Kolcsey.
4376 **1171** 75fo. multicoloured . . 1·50 90

1172 Balint Postas holding Envelope
1173 Hearts and Post Box

1998. Introduction of Balint Postas (post mascot). Multicoloured.
4377 23fo. Type **1172** 35 30
4378 24fo. Balint Postas bowing 40 30
4379 30fo. Balint Postas with arms outstretched 50 45
4380 65fo. Balint Postas flying . . 1·10 75

1998. St. Valentine's Day.
4381 **1173** 24fo. multicoloured . . 45 30

1174 Szilard
1175 Sandor Petofi (poet)

1998. Birth Cent of Leo Szilard (scientist).
4382 **1174** 50fo. multicoloured . . 90 60

1998. 150th Anniv of March Revolution, 1848. Multicoloured.
4383 23fo. Type **1175** 25 30
4384 24fo. Mihaly Tancsics (politician and workers' newspaper editor) and inkwell 30 30
4385 30fo. Lajos Kossuth (Governor of 1849 Republic) and coin . . . 40 45
MS4386 78 × 65 mm. 150fo.+50fo. Leaders of the Revolution (44 × 29 mm) . . . . 2·40 3·00

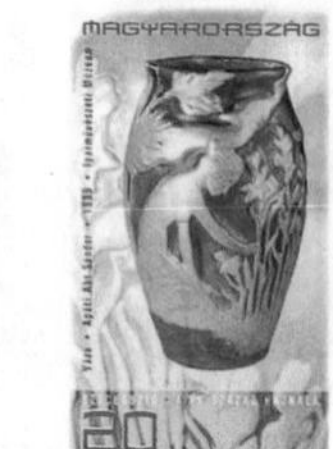

1176 "The Resurrection of Christ" (El Greco)
1177 Vase

1998. Easter.
4387 – 24fo. red and black . . 30 30
4388 **1176** 30fo. multicoloured . . 40 45
DESIGN: 27 × 39 mm—24fo. Dots forming outline of egg.

1998. Ceramics. Multicoloured.
4389 20fo. Type **1177** 25 30
4390 24fo. Bowl decorated with butterflies (horiz) 30 30
4391 30fo. Spiral vase 35 45
4392 95fo. Bowl with lid (horiz) 1·10 1·25

1178 Postman

1998. Stamp Day. 250th Anniv of Inauguration of Postal Service by Empress Maria Theresa. Multicoloured.
4393 24fo.+10fo. Type **1178** . . 40 45
4394 30fo.+10fo. Mounted courier 50 75
MS4395 80 × 61 mm. 150fo. Horse-drawn post coach . . . . . . 1·90 2·40

1179 American Bison

1998. American Animals. Multicoloured.
4396 23fo. Type **1179** 25 30
4397 24fo. Brown bear 30 30
4398 24fo. Mississippi alligator 30 30
4399 30fo. Ocelot 35 45
MS4400 90 × 60 mm. 150fo. Marvellous spatule-tail . . . . 1·75 2·40

1180 Jendrassik
1181 Hurdling

1998. Birth Centenary of Gyorgy Jendrassik (engineer).
4401 **1180** 100fo. blue . . . . . . 1·75 1·25

1998. European Light Athletics Championships, Budapest. Multicoloured.
4402 24fo. Type **1181** 25 30
4403 65fo. High jumping 70 90
4404 80fo. Throwing the hammer 90 1·10

1182 Canoe

1998. World White-water Canoeing Championships, Szeged.
4405 **1182** 30fo. multicoloured . . 50 45

1183 Players

1998. World Cup Football Championship, France. Multicoloured.
4406 30fo. Type **1183** 35 35
4407 110fo. Players with ball on ground . . . . 1·40 1·40
Nos. 4406/7 were issued together, se-tenant, forming a composite design.

1184 Baross (after Miklos Barabos)
1185 Signalman and Pioneers in Railway Carriage

1998. 150th Birth Anniv of Gabor Baross (politician).
4408 **1184** 60fo. multicoloured . . 1·10 75

1998. 50th Anniv of Budapest Pioneer Railway.
4409 **1185** 24fo. multicoloured . . 45 30

1186 Congress Emblem
1187 Carved Poles

1998. World Congress of Computer Technology, Vienna and Budapest.
4410 **1186** 65fo. multicoloured . . 1·25 90

1998. Europa. National Festivals. Mult.
4411 50fo. Type **1187** (Republic Day) 95 45
4412 60fo. Carved shield and corn (National Day) . . . 1·10 60

1188 Emblem

1998. 60th Anniv of Hungarians Abroad Organization.
4413 **1188** 100fo. multicoloured . . 1·90 1·00

1189 Hortobagyi National Park

1998. National Parks (1st series). Multicoloured.
4414 24fo. Type **1189** 45 30
4415 70fo. Kiskunsagi National Park . . . . 1·40 75
See also Nos. 4438/9, 4507/8 and 4559/61.

1190 "Adoration of the Shepherds" (Agnolo Bronzino)

1998. Christmas. Multicoloured.
4416 20fo. Type **1190** 40 30
4417 24fo. "Madonna and Child Enthroned" (Carlo Crivelli) (vert) 50 30
For 24fo. as Type **1190** see No. 4485.

1191 Easter Eggs

1999. Easter. Multicoloured.
4418 27fo. Type **1191** 55 30
4419 32fo. Head of Christ (Ferenc Svindt) (37 × 52 mm) . . 65 45

1192 "Self-portrait" (wood carving, Jeno Szervatiusz)

1999. International Year of the Elderly.
4420 **1192** 32fo. multicoloured . . 60 45

1193 "Novara" (full-rigged ship)

1999. Sailing Ships. Multicoloured.
4421 32fo. Type **1193** 60 45
4422 79fo. "Phoenix" (barge) . . 1·40 75
4423 110fo. "Folyami Vitorlas" (galley) . . . . 2·10 1·10

1194 Path of Eclipse

1999. Total Solar Eclipse (11 Aug). Sheet 105 × 76 mm.
MS4424 **1194** 1999fo. multicoloured 30·00 16·00

1195 Artur Gorgey (commander of Upper Danube)

1999. 150th Anniv of 1848–49 Uprising. Multicoloured.
4425 24fo. Type **1195** 30 30
4426 27fo. Lajos Batthyany (politician) 35 30
4427 32fo. General Jozef Bem . . 40 30
MS4428 78 × 65 mm. 100fo. "The Battle of Tapioticske" (detail, Mor Than) (44 × 27 mm) . . . . . 1·25 90

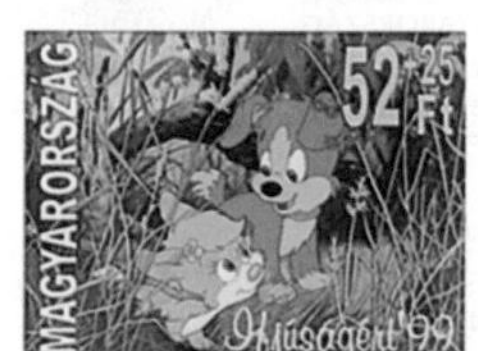

1196 Scene from "Bobo and the Hare" (animated film)

1999. Youth Stamp.
4429 **1196** 52fo.+25fo. mult . . . 1·50 75

1197 Cathedrals within Map and Emblem
1199 Papai

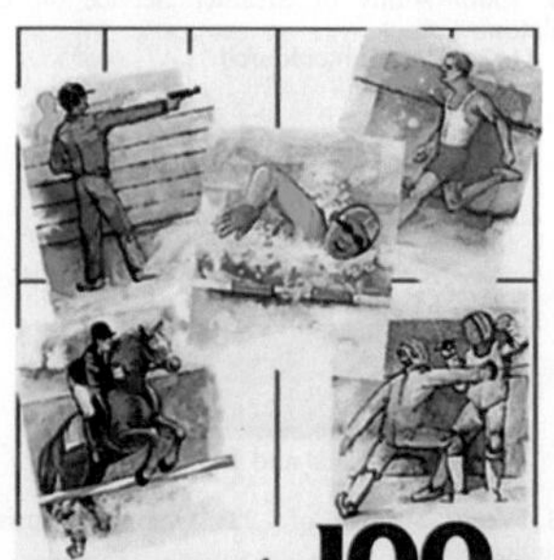

1198 The Five Sports

1999. 50th Anniv of North Atlantic Treaty Organization.
4430 **1197** 110fo. multicoloured . . 1·90 1·25

1999. 5th World Pentathlon Championship, Budapest. Sheet 86 × 70 mm.
MS4431 **1198** 100fo. multicoloured 1·90 90

1999. 350th Birth Anniv of Ferenc Pariz Papai (scientist, physician and lexicographer).
4432 **1199** 50fo. green and orange 75 45

1200 Science Academy, Budapest
1201 Anniversary Badge on Scroll

1999. World Science Congress, Budapest.
4433 **1200** 65fo. multicoloured . . 1·00 60

1999. Centenary of Ferencvaros Sports Club.
4434 **1201** 100fo. multicoloured . . 1·50 90

1202 Council Flag

1999. 50th Anniv of Council of Europe.
4435 **1202** 50fo. multicoloured . . 75 60

1203 Juhfark, Somlo

1999. Wine Grapes and Regions (3rd series). Multicoloured.
4436 24fo. Type **1203** 30 40
4437 27fo. Kekfrankos, Sopron 30 45

1999. Europa. Parks and Gardens. National Parks (2nd series). As T **1189**. Multicoloured.
4438 27fo. Aggtelek National Park 40 30
4439 32fo. Bukk National Park 50 45

1204 Bengali Tiger

1999. Asian Animals. Multicoloured.
4440 27fo. Type **1204** 40 30
4441 32fo. Giant panda 50 45
4442 52fo. Black leopard 80 60
4443 79fo. Orang-utan . . . . . 1·10 75
MS4444 78 × 75 mm. 100fo. Mandarin (49 × 29 mm) . . . 1·50 1·25

1205 Title Page of Decree

1999. Stamp Day. 250th Anniv of Decree by Empress Maria Theresa establishing Regular Mail Coach Service. Multicoloured.
4445 32fo.+15fo. Type **1205** . . 60 60
4446 52fo.+20fo. Passengers boarding coach and woman with letters . . . 95 75
MS4447 75 × 60 mm. 150fo. Horses and mail coach (31 × 41 mm) 2·00 1·50

1206 Common Poppy
1207 Cukor

1999. Greetings Stamps. Flowers. Multicoloured.
4448 27fo. Type **1206** 35 30
4449 32fo. Trumpet gentian . . . 1·40 30

1999. Birth Centenary of George Cukor (film director).
4450 **1207** 50fo. multicoloured . . 65 45

1208 U.P.U. Emblem
1210 High-backed Chair, Szepesseg (17th century)

1209 Woodcut by Samuel Mikoviny (from "Notitia Hungarie" by Matyas Bel)

1999. 125th Anniv of Universal Postal Union. "China '99" International Stamp Exhibition, Peking.
4451 **1208** 32fo. multicoloured . . 1·25 1·50

1999. International Book Fair, Frankfurt.
4452 **1209** 40fo. multicoloured . . 50 45

1999. Antique Furniture.
4453 – 1fo. green and yellow 10 10
4454 – 2fo. green and black 10 10
4455 – 3fo. red and black . . 10 10
4456 – 4fo. brown 10 10
4457 – 5fo. deep blue and blue 10 10
4458 – 6fo. brown and sepia 10 10
4459 – 7fo. brown and pink 10 10
4460 – 8fo. black and grey . . 10 10
4461 **1210** 10fo. bistre and black 10 10
4464 – 20fo. green and black 10 10
4467 – 26fo. green and black 10 10
4468 – 29fo. green and black 15 10
4469 – 30fo. mauve and black 15 10
4470 – 31fo. dp mauve and mve 15 10
4470a – 32fo. pink and red . . 15 10
4470b – 33fo. pink and red . . 15 10
4470c – 35fo. pink and red . . 15 10
4471 – 40fo. brown & lt brown 20 10
4472 – 50fo. blue and black 25 10
4474 – 60fo. olive and green 30 10
4475 – 65fo. ochre and brown 30 10
4476 – 70fo. brown and black 35 15
4478 – 80fo. grey and black 40 20
4480 – 90fo. lilac and purple 45 20
4481 – 100fo. brown and black 50 25
4482 – 134fo. ochre and brown 70 10
4483 – 200fo. blue and green 1·00 50
DESIGNS—VERT: 1fo. Wooden stool, 1910; 2fo. Heves County wooden chair, 1838; 3fo. 19th-century gilded chair; 4fo. Armchair by Geza Marota; 5fo. Chair by Odon Farago; 6fo. Wooden chair by Marton Kovacs; 7fo. Ornate chair, 1853; 8fo. 19th-century chair; 9fo. 18th-century wooden armchair; 20fo. Armchair by Karoly Lingel, 1915; 26, 31fo. Neo-Gothic chair, 1850; 29fo. Magyargee wooden chair, 1879; 30fo. Armchair by Karoly Nagy, 1935; 32, 33fo. Ornate backed chair, 1890; 35fo. 18th-century carver; 40fo. Ornate chair, 1896; 50fo. Prince Pal Esterhazy's armchair (16th-century); 60fo. Chair, 1840; 65fo. Cane-bottomed ornate armchair, 1920; 70fo. Chair with umbrella-shaped back, 1820; 80fo. High backed chair; 90fo. Upholstered armchair by Lajos Kozma. HORIZ: 100fo. Couch by Lajos Kozma, 1920; 134fo. Double-seated chair, 1900; 200fo. Ornate couch, 1810.

1211 Three Wise Men (Zsuzsa Demeter)
1212 Wigner

1999. Christmas. Multicoloured.
4485 24fo. Type **1190** 30 30
4486 27fo. Type **1211** 35 30
4487 32fo. "Madonna and Child" (stained glass window, Miksa Roth) (vert) . . . 45 30

1999. 97th Birth Anniv of Jeno Wigner (physicist).
4488 **1212** 32fo. blue 45 30

1213 Paddle-steamer passing under Bridge
1214 Coronation Sceptre

1999. 150th Anniv of Chain Bridge, Budapest. Sheet 87 × 57 mm.
MS4489 **1213** 150fo. blue, red and green . . . . 1·90 1·50

2000. New Millenium.
4490 **1214** 28fo. bistre and purple 35 30
4491 30fo. bistre and purple 40 45
4492 – 34fo. multicoloured . . 45 45
4493 – 36fo. multicoloured . . 45 45
4494 – 40fo. multicoloured . . 50 60
DESIGN:—34, 36, 40fo. Millennium flag.

1215 Miklos Kis Misztotfalusi (printer, 350th anniv)
1216 Fekete and Animal Characters

2000. Birth Anniversaries.
4495 **1215** 30fo. grn, stone & brn 35 45
4496 – 40fo. blue, stone & brn 45 60
4497 – 50fo. red, stone & brn 50 60
4498 – 80fo. brown and stone 75 1·10
DESIGNS—40fo. Anyos Jedlik (physicist, bicentenary); 50fo. Jeno Kvassay (engineer, 150th anniv); 80fo. Jeno Barcsay (artist, centenary).

2000. Youth Stamp. Birth Centenary of Istvan Fekete (writer).
4499 **1216** 60fo.+30fo. mult . . . 1·25 1·10

1217 Hungarian Cultural Foundation and Exhibition Emblem

2000. "Hunphilex 2000" Stamp Exn, Budapest.
4500 **1217** 200fo.+100fo. mult . . 3·25 3·75

1218 Mihaly Vorosmarty (poet, bicentenary)
1220 Airport Building and Lisunov Li-2 Airplane

1219 Symbolic Easter Eggs

2000. Birth Anniversaries.
4501 **1218** 50fo. green and black 60 45
4502 – 50fo. brown and black 60 45
4503 – 50fo. green and black 60 45
4504 – 50fo. brown and black 60 45
4505 – 50fo. green and black 60 45
DESIGNS: No. 4502, Mari Jaszai (actress, 150th anniv); 4503, Sandor Marai (writer, centenary); 4504, Lujza Blaha (actress, 150th anniv); 4505, Lorinc Szabo (poet and translator, centenary).

2000. Easter. Multicoloured.
4506 26fo. Type **1219** 30 30
4507 28fo. Decorated egg (29 × 31 mm) 35 30

2000. National Parks (3rd series). As T **1189**. Mult.
4508 29fo. Ferto-Hansag National Park 35 30
4509 34fo. Duna-Drava National Park 40 45

2000. 50th Anniv of Ferihegy International Airport.
4510 **1220** 136fo. multicoloured . . 1·50 1·25

1221 Banded Wren
1222 Jigsaw Puzzle

2000. Australian Animals. Multicoloured.
4511 26fo. Type **1221** 20 30
4512 28fo. Opossum 25 30
4513 83fo. Koala 65 75
4514 90fo. Red kangaroo 75 90
MS4515 107 × 70 mm. 110fo. Duck-billed platypus . . . . 1·25 1·25

2000. Europa. Multicoloured.
4516 34fo. Type **1222** 90 45
4517 54fo. "Building Europe" . . 1·40 60

1223 Boat on Corinthian Canal, and Istvan Turr (engineer)

2000. "EXPO 2000" World's Fair, Hanover, Germany.
4518 **1223** 80fo. multicoloured . . 90 75

1224 Bisected and Complete 6k. Austrian Empire Stamps

2000. "WIPA 2000" International Stamp Exhibition, Vienna. 150th Anniv of Hungarian Stamps.
4519 **1224** 110fo. multicoloured . . 1·25 1·10

1225 Queen Gizella I

2000. Stamp Day. Showing decorative figures from Coronation Gown. Multicoloured.
4520 26fo. Type **1225** 30 30
4521 28fo. King Istvan I 35 30

1226 Balatonfured-Csopak

2000. Wine Grapes and Regions (4th series). Mult.
4522 29fo. Type **1226** 25 30
4523 34fo. Aszar-Neszmely . . . 30 30

1227 Evangelical Church, Budapest

1229 Boeing 767-200

1228 Globe

2000. Churches. Multicoloured.
4524 30fo. Type **1227** 40 30
4525 30fo. St. Anthony's Friars' Church, Eger 40 30
4526 30fo. Reformed Church, Takos 40 30
4527 30fo. Abbey Church, Jak . . 40 30

2000. Millennium. Sheet 120 × 70 mm.
MS4528 **1228** 2000fo. multicoloured 18·00 18·00

2000. 90th Anniv of Hungarian Aviation.
4529 **1229** 120fo. multicoloured . . 1·50 1·10

1230 King Laszlo, 1077–95

2000. New Millennium (1st series). Multicoloured.
4530 50fo. Type **1230** 25 10
4531 50fo. Issue of Golden Bull (charter of rights for freemen) by King Andrew II, 1222 . . . . 25 10
4532 50fo. St. Elizabeth and the Mongol invasion, 1241 . . 25 10
4533 50fo. Reign of King Sigismund, 1395–1437 . . 25 10
4534 50fo. Janos Hunyadi (regent) and Janos Kapisztran 25 10
4535 50fo. Reign of King Matthias, 1458–90 . . . . 25 10
4536 50fo. The Crucifixion, Miklos Zrinyi (military commander) and Siege of Szigetvas, 1566 . . . . . 25 10
4537 50fo. Horseman, battle scenes and the recapture of Buda Castle and Gyor 25 10
4538 50fo. People outside Church, Transylvania 25 10
4539 50fo. Peter Pazmany (founder) and University, Budapest, 1635 . . . . . 25 10

Nos. 4530/4 and 4535/9 were issued together, se-tenant, forming a composite design.

See also Nos. 4585/**MS**4595.

1231 Detail of Coronation Gown

2000. "HUNPHILEX 2000" International Stamp Exhibition, Budapest. Multicoloured.
MS4540 93 × 72 mm. 200fo.+100fo. Type **1231** . . . . 1·75 1·75

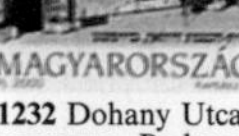
1232 Dohany Utca Synagogue, Budapest

1233 Mary and Jesus leaving Bethlehem

2000. Hungary–Israel Joint Issue.
4541 **1232** 120fo. multicoloured . . 1·50 1·00

2000. Christmas. Multicoloured.
4542 26fo. Type **1233** 30 30
4543 28fo. Church (27 × 28 mm) 35 30
4544 29fo. Christmas tree (27 × 28 mm) 40 30
4545 34fo. Nativity scene on watch face (32 × 36 mm) 45 30

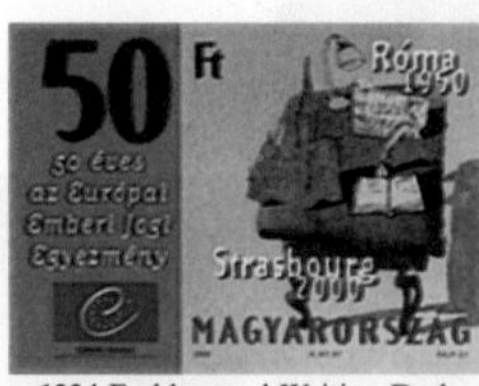
1234 Emblem and Writing Desk

2000. 50th Anniv of Convention on Human Rights.
4546 **1234** 50fo. multicoloured . . 60 45

1235 Rifle Shooting

2000. Olympic Games, Sydney. Multicoloured.
4547 30fo. Type **1235** 35 30
4548 40fo. Weightlifting 45 45
4549 80fo. Gymnastics 95 75
MS4550 85 × 63 mm. 120fo. Two-man kayak . . . . 1·40 1·40

1236 Eger Castle and Extract from Poem

1238 Man blowing Trumpet

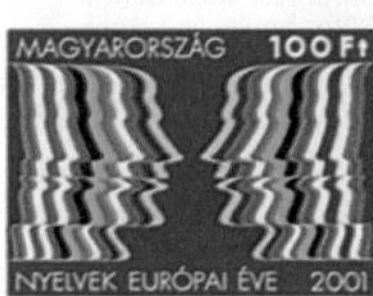
1237 Profiles

2001. Youth Stamp. Centenary of *Eclipse of the Crescent Moon* (poem by Geza Gardonyi).
4551 **1236** 60fo.+30fo. mult . . . 40 40

2001. European Year of Languages.
4552 **1237** 100fo. multicoloured . . 50 25

2001. Greetings Stamps. Multicoloured.
4553 36fo. Type **1238** 20 10
4554 36fo. Couple dancing . . . 20 10
4555 36fo. Baby in cradle 20 10
4556 36fo. Clown 20 10
4557 36fo. Woman and child . . 20 10

1239 Ice-skater

2001.
4558 **1239** 140fo. multicoloured . . 70 35

1240 Easter Eggs and Rabbit

1242 Emblem and Vegetation

1241 Mk 48 Diesel Locomotive, Lillafured State Forest Railway

2001. Easter.
4559 **1240** 28fo. multicoloured . . 15 10

2001. National Parks (4th series). As T **1189**. Multicoloured.
4560 28fo. Upper Balaton National Park 15 10
4561 36fo. Koros-Maros National Park 20 10
4562 70fo. Duna-Ipoly National Park 35 15

2001. Light Railways. Multicoloured.
4563 31fo. Type **1241** 15 10
4564 36fo. 490 series steam locomotive, Keeskemet Light Railway 20 10
4565 100fo. 394 series steam locomotive, Szechenyi Railway Museum 50 25
4566 150fo. C50 diesel locomotive, Csomoder State Forest Railway . . 70 35

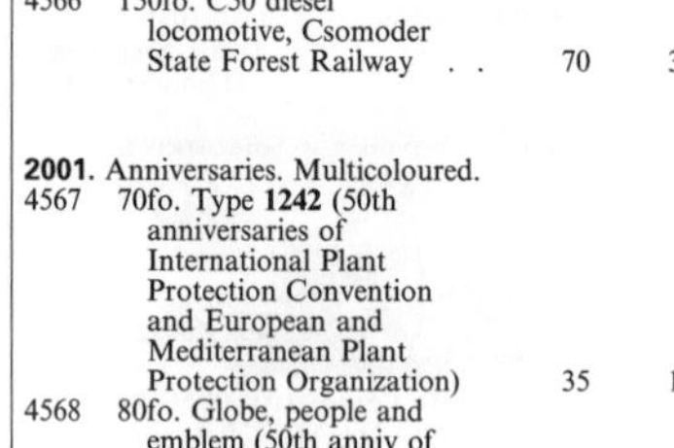

2001. Anniversaries. Multicoloured.
4567 70fo. Type **1242** (50th anniversaries of International Plant Protection Convention and European and Mediterranean Plant Protection Organization) 35 15
4568 80fo. Globe, people and emblem (50th anniv of United Nations High Commissioner for Refugees) 40 20

1243 Door Inlay, St. Adalbert Basilica

2001. Millenary of Archdiocese of Esztergom.
4569 **1243** 124fo. multicoloured . . 60 30

1244 Ringed Seal (*Phoca hispida*)

2001. Animals. Multicoloured.
4570 28fo. Type **1244** 15 10
4571 36fo. Wolf (*Canis lupus*) . . 20 10
4572 70fo. Herman's tortoise (*Testudo hermanni*) . . . 35 15
4573 90fo. River kingfisher (*Alcedo atthis*) 45 20
MS4574 90 × 66 mm. 200fo. Red deer males (*Cervus elaphus*) . . 1·75 1·75

1245 Chest containing Water

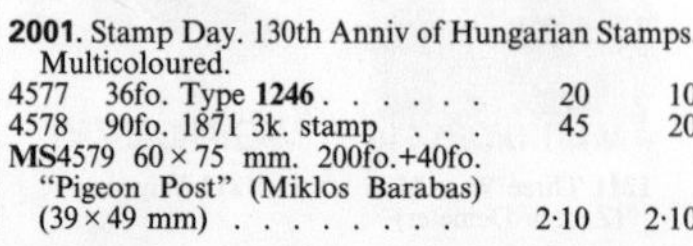
1246 1871 1k. Newspaper Stamp

2001. Europa. Water Resources. Multicoloured.
4575 36fo. Type **1245** 20 10
4576 90fo. Open globe filled with water 45 20

2001. Stamp Day. 130th Anniv of Hungarian Stamps. Multicoloured.
4577 36fo. Type **1246** 20 10
4578 90fo. 1871 3k. stamp . . . 45 20
MS4579 60 × 75 mm. 200fo.+40fo. "Pigeon Post" (Miklos Barabas) (39 × 49 mm) . . . . 2·10 2·10

1247 Players

2001. European Water Polo Championship, Budapest.
4580 **1247** 150fo. multicoloured . . 70 35

1248 Scout's Hats

2001. 4th European Conference of Former Scouts and Guides, Budapest.
4581 **1248** 150fo. multicoloured . . 70 30

1249 Drawing (Aladar Korosfoi-Kriesch)

2001. Art Anniversaries.
4582 **1249** 100fo. blue, mauve and lilac 50 25
4583 – 150fo. black and blue (49 × 21 mm) 70 35

DESIGNS—VERT: 100fo. Type **1249** (centenary of Godollo Artists' Colony). HORIZ: 150fo. Emblems representing different branches of the arts (centenary of FESZEK Club).

1250 Athletics Race

2001. World Youth Athletics Championship, Debrecen.
4584 **1250** 140fo. multicoloured . . 65 35

1251 Ferenc Rakovic and Ilona Zrinyi

2001. New Millennium (2nd series). Multicoloured.
4585 50fo. Type **1251** 20 10
4586 50fo. Terezia Maria and royal horse guard 20 10
4587 50fo. Istvan Szechenyi and Chain Bridge 20 10
4588 50fo. Newspaper headline and man on horseback . . 20 10
4589 50fo. Janos Arany, "The Solitary Cedar" (detail, Tivadar Csontvary Kosztka) and Parliament buildings 20 10
4590 50fo. First World War soldiers and map 20 10
4591 50fo. Mihaly Babits 20 10
4592 50fo. Chain Bridge and Bishop Vilmos Apor . . . 20 10
4593 50fo. Tanks and soldiers (Revolution, 1956) and Zoltan Kodaly (composer) 20 10
4594 50fo. Young children and Millennium flag 20 10
MS4595 105 × 75 mm. 2001fo. Crown (39 × 31 mm) . . . . . 10·00 5·00

1252 Pannonhalma-Sokoroalja

2001. Wine Grapes and Regions (5th series). Multicoloured.
4596 60fo. Type **1252** 25 10
4597 70fo. Balatonboglar 30 15

1253 Common Peacock (30 m mosaic)

2001. Guinness Record Attempt by Hungarian Post Office to Create World's Largest Mosaic from Used Postage Stamps.
4598 **1253** 10fo. multicoloured . . 10 10

1254 Bridge

2001. Reconstruction of Maria Valeria Bridge, Estergom–Parkany.
4599 **1254** 36fo. multicoloured . . 15 10

1255 Angel and Decorations

1256 1871 2k. Stamp and Emblem

2001. Christmas.
4600 **1255** 36fo. multicoloured . . 15 10

2001. 150th Anniv of Hungarian Stamp Printing.
4601 **1256** 150fo. multicoloured . . 75 30

1257 Ice Hockey Player

2002. Winter Olympic Games, Salt Lake City, U.S.A.
4602 **1257** 160fo. multicoloured . . 70 35

1258 Soldiers fighting (Defence of Eger Castle)

2002. Youth Stamp. 450th Anniv of War with Ottoman Empire. Sheet 120 × 68 mm containing T **1258** and similar multicoloured designs.
MS4603 50fo. Type **1258**; 50fo. Istvan Losonczy and Turkish soldiers, Timisoara; 100fo. + 50fo. Soldiers and pages (Battle of Dregely Castle) (39 × 29 mm) 1·10 55

1259 Ordinary "Penny-farthing" Bicycle

1260 Easter Eggs

2002. History of the Bicycle. Multicoloured.
4604 40fo. Type **1259** 20 10
4605 40fo. Tricycle, 1900s 20 10
4606 40fo. Karoly Iszer (chairman of Budapest Sport Club) 20 10
4607 40fo. Four-man cycle . . . 20 10

2002. Easter.
4608 **1260** 30fo. multicoloured . . 30 10

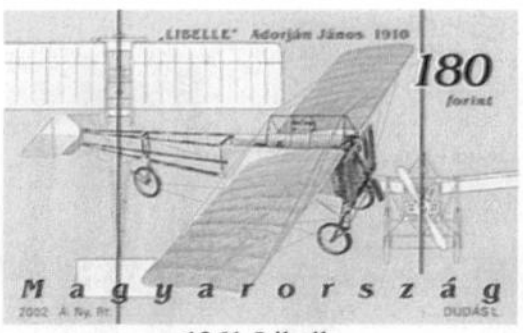

1261 Libelle

2002. Aviation. Multicoloured.
4609 180fo. Type **1261** 80 40
4610 190fo. Hungarian Lloyd Aircraft and Engine Factory biplane 85 40

1262 Lajos Kossuth

2002. Birth Anniversaries. Multicoloured.
4611 33fo. Type **1262** (statesman, bicentenary) 15 10
4612 134fo. Janos Bolyai (mathematician, bicentenary) 60 30
4613 150fo. Gyula Illyes (poet and writer, centenary) . . 65 30

1263 Stage Set for *The Tragedy of Man* (Imre Madach)

2002. Inauguration of New National Theatre, Budapest. Sheet 85 × 60 mm.
MS4614 **1263** 500fo. multicoloured 2·25 1·10

1264 Parliament Building

2002. Centenary of Inauguration of Parliament Building. Sheet 97 × 67 mm.
MS4615 **1264** 500fo. multicoloured 2·25 1·10

1265 "S.O.S."

2002. Environmental Protection.
4616 **1265** 158fo. multicoloured . . 75 35

1266 Book of Psalms of King David

2002. Bicentenaries of Hungarian National Museum and National Szechenyi Library. Exhibits from the institutions. Multicoloured.
MS4617 150fo. Type **1266**; 150fo. Illumination from the second volume of King Matthias's Book of Rites; 150fo. Civil Guard of Pest Standard, 1848; 150fo. Holy water basin, 1903 . . . . . . 3·50 3·50

1267 Deer

2002. Centenary of Halas Lace. Multicoloured.
4618 100fo. Type **1267** 55 30
4619 110fo. Swan 60 30
4620 140fo. Couple 80 40

1268 Wild Cat (*Felis sylvestris*)

2002. Fauna. Multicoloured.
4621 30fo. Type **1268** 20 10
4622 38fo. Crimean bull lizard (*Podarcis taurica*) 20 10
4623 110fo. Jay (*Garrulus glandarius*) 60 30
4624 160fo. Alpine longhorn beetle (*Rosalia alpina*) . . 90 45
MS4625 90 × 65 mm. 500fo. Sterlet (*Acipenser ruthenus*) . . . . . 3·00 3·00

1269 Elephant

2002. Europa. Circus.
4626 **1269** 62fo. multicoloured . . 35 20

1270 Players

1271 Dog and Kennel (Etesd meg)

2002. World Cup Football Championship, Japan and South Korea.
4627 **1270** 160fo. multicoloured . . 90 45

2002. Greetings Stamps. Designs as Nos. 4448/9 but with change of face value.
4628 30fo. Common poppy . . . 20 10
4629 38fo. Trumpet gentian . . . 20 10

2002. Greetings Stamps. Self-adhesive. Multicoloured.
4630 38fo. Type **1271** 20 10
4631 38fo. Washing line (Megszulettem!) 20 10
4632 38fo. Present outside house (Sok boldogsagot!) . . . 20 10
4633 38fo. Sofa and plant (Ontozdmeg...!) 20 10
4634 38fo. Man in room (Ennyire szeretlek!) 20 10
Nos. 4630/4 were issued together, se-tenant, forming a composite design.

1272 "Stone-pelter" (Karoly Ferenczy)

2002. Art. Multicoloured.
4635 62fo. Type **1272** 35 20
4636 188fo. "Ballerina" (statue, Ferenc Medgyessy) (vert) 1·10 55

1273 Buda Castle

2002. UNESCO World Heritage Sites. Multicoloured.
4637 100fo. Type **1273** 55 30
4638 150fo. Holloko, Nograd . . 85 45
4639 180fo. Aggtelek-Carst Caves (horiz) . . . . 1·00 50

1274 Facade and Statue

2002. Millenary of Kalocsa Archdiocese.
4640 **1274** 150fo. multicoloured . . 85 45

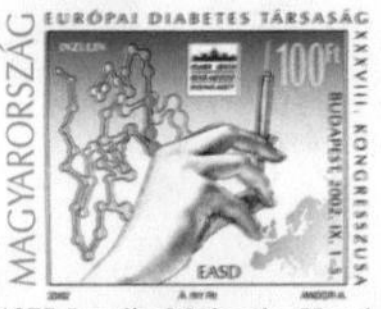

1275 Insulin Molecule, Hand holding Syringe and Map of Europe

2002. Medical Events in 2002. Multicoloured.
4641 100fo. Type **1275** (38th European Diabetes Association Congress) . . 55 30
4642 150fo. Arms, arrows and map of Europe (16th European Society of Elbow and Shoulder Surgeons Congress) . . . 95 45

1276 "Pound Cake Madonna"

2002. 75th Anniv of Stamp Day. Birth Centenary of Margit Kováacs (ceramicist). Multicoloured.
4643 33fo. Type **1276** 20 10
4644 38fo. "Family Photograph Album" 20 10
MS4645 86 × 72 mm. 400fo.+200fo. "St. George, The Dragon Slayer" (25 × 36 mm) . . . . 3·50 3·50

1277 "Adoration of the Magi"

2002. Christmas. Paintings by Erzsebet Udvardi. Multicoloured.
4646 30fo. Type **1277** 20 10
4647 38fo. "Bethelem" 20 10

1278 Gymnast

1279 Rakoczi Mansion, Tekirdag

2002. World Gymnastics Championships, Debrecen.
4648 **1278** 160fo. multicoloured . . 90 45

2002. Cultural Heritage. Multicoloured.
4649 40fo. Type **1279** 20 10
4650 110fo. Pasha Gazi Kasim Mosque, Pecs 60 30
Stamps in similar designs were issued by Turkey.

1280 John von Neuman

2003. Birth Anniversaries. Multicoloured.
4651 32fo. Type **1280** (computing pioneer) (centenary) . . . 15 10
4652 40fo. Rezso Soo (botanist) (centenary) 20 10
4653 60fo. Karoly Zipernowsky (electrical engineer) (150th) 30 15

1281 Frankenthal Coffee Set

1283 Crucifixion

1282 Retreating Soldiers

2003. Herend Porcelain. Sheet 138 × 71 mm containing T **1281** and similar vert designs. Multicoloured.
MS4654 150fo. Type **1281**; 150fo. Blue coffee pot, cup and saucer; 150fo. Tall vase; 150fo. Siang Noir shell bowl and jug . . . . . . 2·50 2·50

2003. 60th Anniv of Second Royal Hungarian Army's Defeat at the River Don.
4655 **1282** 40fo. multicoloured . . 20 10

2003. Easter.
4656 **1283** 32fo. multicoloured . . 15 10

1284 Title Page

2003. Sport (1st issue). Centenary of "Nemzeti Sport" (sports magazine).
4657 **1284** 150fo. multicoloured . . 80 40
See also Nos. 4670 and 4673.

1285 Church

1286 BMX Cyclist

2003. Greetings Stamps. Multicoloured. Self-adhesive.
4658 40fo. Type **1285** 20 10
4559 40fo. Two flowers 20 10
4660 40fo. Flower 20 10
4661 40fo. Decorated eggs . . . 20 10
4662 40fo. Candles in window and Christmas tree . . . 20 10

2003. Youth Stamps. Extreme Sports. Multicoloured.
4663 100fo. Type **1286** 50 25
4664 100fo. Snowboarding . . . 50 25
4665 100fo. Parachuting 50 25
4666 100fo. White water canoeing 50 25

1287 Rogner Hotel, Heviz

2003. Tourism. Spa Hotels. Multicoloured.
4667 110fo. Type **1287** 60 30
4668 120fo. Helia Hotel, Budapest 65 30

1288 Gerle 13 Aircraft, 1933

2003. Hungarian Aviation. Multicoloured.
4669 142fo. Type **1288** 75 35
4670 160fo. L-2 Roma, 1925 . . 85 40

1289 *Columbia*

2003. Space Shuttle *Columbia* Memorial. Sheet 92 × 72 mm.
MS4671 **1289** 500fo. multicoloured 2·75 2·75

1290 Championship Emblem

2003. Sport (2nd issue). World Division I Ice Hockey Championship, Budapest.
4672 **1290** 110fo. multicoloured . . 60 30

1291 Stadium

2003. Sport (3rd issue). Budapest Sports Arena.
4673 **1291** 120fo. multicoloured . . 65 30

1292 Hand holding Quill Pen

2003. Signing of Treaty of Accession to the European Union. (1st Issue). Sheet 106 × 70 mm.
MS4674 **1292** 500fo. multicoloured 2·75 2·75
See also Nos. 4692/3, 4714, 4722 and **MS**4725.

1293 Police Motorcyclist

2003. Police Service.
4675 **1293** 65fo. multicoloured . . 35 15

1294 Statue of Seated Woman (Danubius fountain)

1295 Kuruc Sabre, Sword and Mace

2003. Stamp Day. Multicoloured.
4676 35fo. Type **1294** 20 10
4677 40fo. Statue of seated woman (Danubius fountain) (different) . . . 20 10
MS4678 81 × 60 mm. 400fo.+100fo. "Calvin Square" (Jozsef Molnar) 2·75 2·75

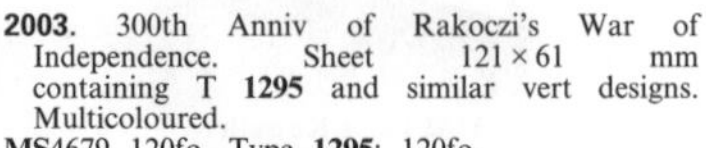

2003. 300th Anniv of Rakoczi's War of Independence. Sheet 121 × 61 mm containing T **1295** and similar vert designs. Multicoloured.
MS4679 120fo. Type **1295**; 120fo. Coins; 120fo. Old National flag, pipes and drums; 120fo. Pistols and powder horn . . . . . . 2·50 2·50

1296 Steppe Polecat (*Mustela eversmanni*)

2003. Fauna. Multicoloured.
4680 30fo. Type **1296** 15 10
4681 38fo. Short-toed lark (*Calandrella brachydactyla*) 20 10
4682 110fo. European tree frog (*Hyla arborea*) 60 30
4683 160fo. European weatherfish (*Misgurnus fossilis*) . . . 85 40
MS4684 90 × 65 mm. 500 fo. Ladybird spider (*Eresus cinnaberinus*) (inscr "cinnabarinus") . . . . 2·75 2·75

1297 "Only Posters" (Istvaán Orosz)

2003. Europa. Poster Art.
4685 **1297** 65fo. red, yellow and black 35 15

1298 Bukkaljai

2003. Wine Grapes and Regions (6th series). Multicoloured.
4686 60fo. Type **1298** 35 15
4687 130fo. Balaton-felvideki . . 70 35

1299 King Ladislaus and Unknown Queen (⅔-size illustration)

2003. King Ladislaus' Robe (11th-century). Sheet 108 × 70 mm.
MS4688 **1299** 300fo. multicoloured 1·60 1·60

1300 Bishop Gerard and Angel (sculpture, Imre Varga)

1301 Crowds and Anniversary Emblem

2003. Art. Multicoloured.
4689 32fo. Type **1300** 15 10
4690 60fo. "Roman Bridge at Mostar" (Tivadar Csontvary Kosztka) (horiz) 35 15

2003. 50th Anniv of People's Stadium. 50th Anniv of Hungarian Football Team's Victory over England. Sheet 103 × 68 mm containing T **1301** and similar horiz design. Multicoloured.
MS4691 250fo. Type **1301**; 250fo. Goal and players . . . . . . 2·75 2·75

1302 European Union Emblem as Clock Face

2003. Hungary's Accession to European Union (2nd issue). Multicoloured.
4692 115fo. Type **1302** 60 30
4693 130fo. As No. 4692 but with clock hands moved forward 70 35

1303 Fruit and Vegetables

2003. Nutrition.
4694 **1303** 120fo. multicoloured . . 65 30

1304 Feet and Cycle Wheel

2003. European Car-free Day.
4695 **1304** 150fo. multicoloured . . 80 40

1305 *Dactylorhiza fuchsia sooana*

2003. Birth Centenary of Rezso Soo (botanist).
4696 **1305** 44fo. multicoloured . . 25 10

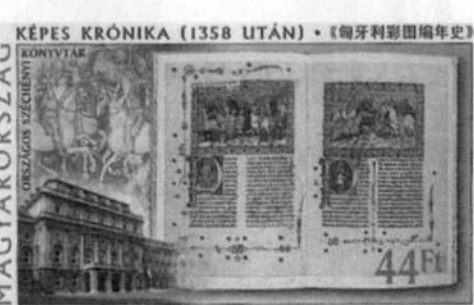

1306 The Illuminated Chronicle

2003. Ancient Books. Multicoloured.
4697 44fo. Type **1306** 25 10
4698 44fo. The Book of Zhou Rites 25 10
Stamps of a similar design were issued by Republic of China.

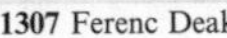

1307 Ferenc Deak **1308** Reindeer

2003. 200th Birth Anniv of Ferenc Deak (politician). Sheet 99 × 68 mm.
MS4699 **1307** 500fo. multicoloured 2·75 2·75

2003. Christmas. Multicoloured.
4700 35fo. Type **1308** 20 10
4701 44fo. Angels, tree and house 25 10

1309 Globe and Computer Screen

2003. World Science Forum, Budapest. Sheet 87 × 62 mm.
MS4702 **1309** 500fo. multicoloured 2·75 2·75

1310 Jozsef Bajza

2004. Birth Anniversaries. Multicoloured.
4703 40fo. Balint Balassi (writer) (150th) 20 10
4704 44fo. Type 310 (writer) (200th) 25 10
4705 80fo. Andras Janos Segner (mathematician) (300th) 45 20

1311 "Muki" Diesel Engine, Kemence Railway Museum

2004. Light Railways. Multicoloured.
4706 120fo. Type **1311** 65 30
4707 150fo. "Rezet" steam engine, Cemenc State Forest Railway 85 45

1312 Masks and Bonfire (Busojaras)

2004. Festivals. Sheet 160 × 45 mm containing T **1312** and similar horiz designs. Multicoloured.
MS4708 60fo. × 4 Type **1312**; Flowers (Viragkarneval); Grapes and wine glass (Borfesztival); Trumpet, scroll and drum (Karnevalok) . . . . 1·40 1·40

1313 Puli **1315** Clock-face

1314 "e"

2004. Youth Stamps. Dogs. Sheet 140 × 70 mm containing T **1313** and similar vert designs.
MS4709 100fo. Type **1313**; 100fo. Greyhound; 100fo. Mudi; 100fo.+50fo. Vizsla . . . . . 2·50 2·50

2004. European Information Technology Ministerial Conference, Budapest.
4710 40fo. Type **1314** (blue and light blue) 20 10
4711 40fo. "e" (purple and yellow) 20 10
4712 40fo. "e" (orange and pink) 20 10
4713 40fo. "e" (green and red) . . 20 10

2004. Hungary's Accession to European Union (3rd issue).
4714 **1315** 100fo. multicoloured . . 55 25

1316 Athletes **1317** Rabbit and Egg

2004. 10th World Indoor Athletics Championship, Budapest.
4715 **1316** 120fo. multicoloured . . 65 30

2004. Easter.
4716 **1317** 48fo. multicoloured . . 25 10

1318 Buk Hotel, Bukfurdo

2004. Tourism. Spa Hotels. Multicoloured.
4717 120fo. Type **1318** 65 30
4718 150fo. Aqua Sol Hotel, Hajduszoboszlo 85 40

1319 St. Martin's Monastery, Pannonia

2004. UNESCO World Heritage Sites. Multicoloured.
4719 150fo. Type **1319** 85 40
4720 170fo. Tern, cattle and horses, Hortobagy National Park (horiz) . . 95 45

1320 Stone inscribed with Star of David

2004. 60th Anniv of Hungarian Holocaust.
4721 **1320** 160fo. multicoloured . . 85 40

1321 Clock-face

2004. Hungary's Accession to European Union (4th issue).
4722 **1321** 190fo. multicoloured . . 1·10 55

1322 Twin-handled Vase

2004. 150th Anniv of Zsolnay Porcelain Factory, Pecs. Sheet 138 × 69 mm containing T **1322** and similar vert designs. Multicoloured.
MS4723 160fo. × 4, Type **1322**; Vase surmounted by horseman and small decorative vase; Vase with medieval silk design; "Autumn" mocha set . . . . 3·50 3·50

1323 Police Launch

2004. Police Day.
4724 **1323** 48fo. multicoloured . . 25 10

1324 Stars

2004. Hungary's Accession to European Union (5th issue). Sheet 105 × 71 mm.
MS4725 **1324** 500fo. multicoloured 2·75 2·75

1325 Embroidered Flowers

2004. Enlargement of European Union.
4726 120fo. Type **1325** 65 30
4727 150fo. New members' flags and stars 85 40

1326 Mole Rat (*Nannospalax leucodon*)

2004. Fauna. Multicoloured.
4728 48fo. Type **1326** 25 10
4729 65fo. Bearded tit (*Panurus biarmucus*) 35 15
4730 90fo. Snake-eyed skink (*Ablepharus kitaibelii fitzingeri*) 50 25
4731 120fo. Sturgeon (*Huso huso*) 65 30
MS4732 90 × 65 mm. 500fo. *Anthaxia hungarica* . . . . . 2·75 2·75

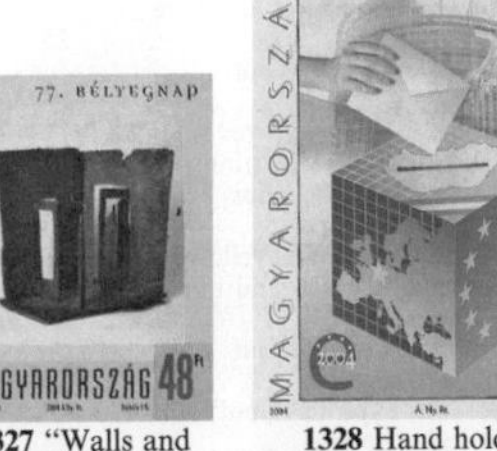

1327 "Walls and Doors" (Erzsebet Schaar) **1328** Hand holding Envelope over Ballot Box

2004. Stamp Day. Art. Multicoloured.
4733 48fo. Type **1327** 25 10
4734 65fo. "Translucent Red Circle" (Tihamer Gyarmathy) 35 10
MS4735 71 × 71 mm. 400fo.+200fo. "Wasp King" (Bela Kondor) (41 × 32 mm) . . . . 3·25 3·25

2004. European Elections.
4736 **1328** 150fo. multicoloured . . 85 40

1329 People in Countryside

2004. Europa. Holidays.
4737 **1329** 160fo. multicoloured . . 90 45

1330 Ball and Turf as Slice of Cake **1331** Basilica, Mariazell

2004. Centenary of FIFA (Federation Internationale de Football Association).
4738 **1330** 100fo. multicoloured . . 55 25

2004. Catholics' Day. Sheet 110 × 160 mm containing T **1331** and similar vert designs. Multicoloured.
MS4739 100fo. × 6, Type **1331**; Magna Mater Austriae (Romanesque statue) (Chapel of Grace, Basilica, Mariazell); Madonna (statue); Canopied statue of Mary, Celldomolk; Madonna (painting), Mariazell; Mary of Kiscell, Obuda parish 3·25 3·25

1332 Internet Icons

2004. Information Technology.
4740 **1332** 120fo. multicoloured . . 65 30

1333 Theodor Herzl

2004. Death Centenary of Theodor Herzl (writer and Zionist pioneer).
4741 **1333** 55fo. multicoloured . . 30 15

A stamp of the same design was issued by Israel and Austria.

1334 Rowers

2004. Olympic Games, Athens 2004. Multicoloured.
4742 90fo. Type **1334** 50 25
4743 130fo. Ball players 70 35
4744 150fo. Runners 85 40

1335 Two Dancers

2004. 3rd Folkloriada Festival. Showing folk dancers. Multicoloured.
4745 65fo. Type **1335** 35 15
4746 65fo. As No. 4745 with colour change 35 15
4747 65fo. Back view of dancer 35 15

4748 65fo. As No. 4747 with colour change 35 15
4749 65fo. Dancer facing right . . 35 15
4750 65fo. Dancer's skirt 35 15
4751 65fo. Back view of dancer facing right 35 15
4752 65fo. Two dancers (different) 35 15
4753 65fo. Dancer's skirt (different) 35 15
4754 65fo. Dancer's feet 25 15

1336 Rook and "A sakkjatek tobbnyire"

1338 INTOSAI Emblem

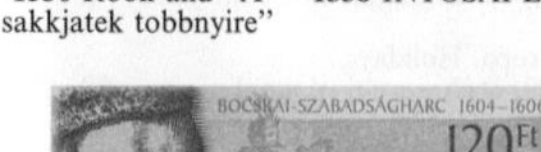
1337 Istvan Bocskai, Swords and Coins

2004. History of Hungarian Chess. Each stamp either brown and black or flesh and black, the colours alternating to simulate the squares on a chess board (first three words of inscription given).
4755 50fo. Type **1336** 25 10
4756 50fo. "A magyaroknak a" 25 10
4757 50fo. Bishop and "A Magyar tortenelem" . . . 25 10
4758 50fo. King and "A Magyar sakkirodalom" 25 10
4759 50fo. Queen and "A XVIII szazadban" 25 10
4760 50fo. "Az elso magyar" . . 25 10
4761 50fo. Knight and "Az 1839-ben megalakult" 25 10
4762 50fo. Rook and "A XIX szazad" 25 10
4763 50fo. Pawn and "A Magyar sakkfeladvanyszerzok" . . 25 10
4764 50fo. Pawn and "Harom, a XIX. szazad" 25 10
4765 50fo. Pawn and "Maroczy Geza 1870" 25 10
4766 50fo. Pawn and "Ket kivalo sakkozonk" 25 10
4767 50fo. Bishop and "A levelezesi sakkozas" . . . 25 10
4768 50fo. Pawn and "A sakkelet megszervezodese" 25 10
4769 50fo. Pawn and "A ferfi orszagos" 25 10
4770 50fo. Pawn and "A II. vilaghaboru utan sokaig" 25 10
4771 50fo. "A noi sakkozas" . . 25 10
4772 50fo. "1958-ban mar a 10" 25 10
4773 50fo. Knight and "A sakkozok osszefogasanak" 25 10
4774 50fo. "1951-ben indult a" 25 10
4775 50fo. "A XX. szazadnak" 25 10
4776 50fo. "A II. vilaghaboru utan feladvany" 25 10
4777 50fo. "A XX. szazadban" 25 10
4778 50fo. "A XX. szazad" . . . 25 10
4779 50fo. "A vilag sakkeletet" 25 10
4780 50fo. "A ket vilaghaboru kozott" 25 10
4781 50fo. "A haboru utan" . . 25 10
4782 50fo. "A ferfi sakkolimpian" 25 10
4783 50fo. Pawn and "A nemzetek kozti" 25 10
4784 50fo. "1957-ben a hollandiai" 25 10
4785 50fo. "A noi sakkolimpiakon" 25 10
4786 50fo. "A XIX es XX" . . . 25 10
4787 50fo. "Sakkirodalom nelkul sem" 25 10
4788 50fo. "A XX. Szazad magyar" 25 10
4789 50fo. Bishop and "A szeles sakkozo" 25 10
4790 50fo. "A Magyar Sakkszovetseg" 25 10
4791 50fo. Pawn and "Barcza Gedeon 1911" 25 10
4792 50fo. "Szabo Laszlo 1917." 25 10
4793 50fo. "Portisch Lajos 1937" 25 10
4794 50fo. "Adorjan Andras "1968-ig" 25 10
4795 50fo. "Sax Gyula 1951" . . 25 10
4796 50fo. "Ribli Zoltan 1951" 25 10
4797 50fo. "Leko peter1979" . . 25 10
4798 50fo. "Almasi Zoltan 1976" 25 10
4799 50fo. "Bilek Istvan 1932" 25 10
4800 50fo. Knight and "A ket vilaghaboru kozti" . . . 25 10
4801 50fo. "Az olimpiakon tobbszor" 25 10
4802 50fo. "Sok kivalo magyar" 25 10
4803 50fo. Pawn and "Polgar Zsuzsa Budapesten 1969" 25 10
4804 50fo. Pawn and "Polgar Judit Budapesten 1976" 25 10
4805 50fo. Pawn and "Polgar Zsofia 1974" 25 10
4806 50fo. Pawn and "Langos Jozsa 1911" 25 10
4807 50fo. "Veroci Zsuzsa 1949" 25 10
4808 50fo. Pawn and "Ivanka Maria 1950" 25 10
4809 50fo. Pawn and "Madl Ildiko 1969" 25 10
4810 50fo. Pawn and "Orszagos bajnoki cimmel" 25 10
4811 50fo. Rook and "Sakkozasunk a XXI." 25 10
4812 50fo. Knight and "A sakkozassal valo kapcsolat" 25 10
4813 50fo. Bishop and "A magyar sakkazas" 25 10
4814 50fo. King and "Minden osszefoglalo munka" . . . 25 10
4815 50fo. Queen and "A jelen munkaban" 25 10
4816 50fo. "Elek Ferenc 1918—1989" 25 10
4817 50fo. "Katko (Regos) Imre 1904—1948" 25 10
4818 50fo. "grof Pongracz Arnold 1810—1890" 25 10

Nos. 4755/818 were issued in se-tenant sheets of 64 stamps, each stamp bearing an inscription describing part of the history of Hungarian chess. The stamps were arranged to simulate the "Hungarian Defence" opening gambit with the rows marked either 1—8 vertically or a—h horizontally in the margin.

2004. Hungary's Accession to the European Union (6th issue). Sheet 84 × 72 mm containing horiz designs as T **1302**, **1315** and **1321**. Multicoloured.
MS4819 100fo. × 4, As Nos. 4692/3; As No. 4714; As No. 4722 . . 2·20 2·20

2004. 400th Anniv of Bocskai's War of Independence.
4820 **1337** 120fo. multicoloured . . 65 30

2004. 28th International Organization of Supreme Audit Institutions (INTOSAI) Conference, Budapest.
4821 **1338** 150fo. multicoloured . . 55 25

2004. Christmas (1st issue). Painting by Erzsebet Udvardi. As T **1227**. Multicoloured.
4822 48fo. As No. 4647 . . . . . 25 10

1339 Cherub

2004. Christmas (2nd issue). Multicoloured.
4823 48fo. Type **1339** 25 10
4824 48fo. Two cherubs 25 10
4825 48fo. Cherub seated with clasped hands 25 10
4826 48fo. Cherub with left hand raised 25 10
4827 48fo. Cherub facing left . . 25 10
4828 48fo. Cherub seated looking up 25 10

1340 Biscuits

2004. Christmas (3rd issue). Biscuits. Multicoloured.
4829/48 48fo. × 20 Type **1340** and 19 other different designs showing iced biscuits . . . . 5·00 2·10

1341 Green Triangles and Bauble at Right

2004. Christmas (4th issue). Glass Decorations. Multicoloured.
4849 48fo. Type **1341** 25 10
4850 48fo. As No. 4849 but design reversed 25 10
4851 48fo. Bauble at left and blue triangles 25 10
4852 48fo. As No. 4851 but design reversed 25 10
4853 48fo. Bauble at left, red square and green triangles 25 10
4854 48fo. As No. 4853 but design reversed 25 10
4855 48fo. Blue triangle, yellow rectangle, green and blue triangles 25 10
4856 48fo. As No. 4855 but design reversed 25 10
4857 48fo. As Type 1341 but smaller bauble 25 10
4858 48fo. As No. 4857 but with design reversed 25 10

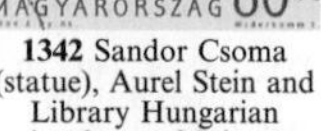

1342 Sandor Csoma (statue), Aurel Stein and Library Hungarian Academy of Science

1343 Pulsatilla and Valley

2004. Hungarian Science. Sandor Korosi Csoma (Tibetan scholar) and Aurel Stein (archaeologist) Commemoration.
4859 **1342** 80fo. multicoloured . . 40 20

2004. Natura 2000 (habitat protection).
4860 **1343** 100fo. multicoloured . . 55 25

1344 Capricorn

2005. Western Zodiac. Multicoloured.
4861 50fo. Type **1344** 25 10
4862 50fo. Aquarius 25 10
4863 50fo. Pisces 25 10
4864 50fo. Aries 25 10
4865 50fo. Taurus 25 10
4866 50fo. Gemini 25 10
4867 50fo. Cancer 25 10
4868 50fo. Leo 25 10
4869 50fo. Virgo 25 10
4870 50fo. Libra 25 10
4871 50fo. Scorpio 25 10
4872 50fo. Sagittarius25 10

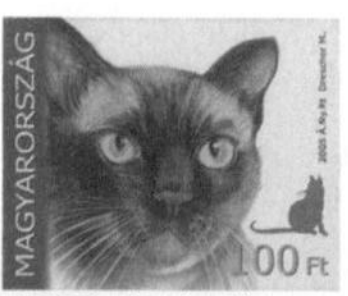

1345 Seal-point Siamese

2005. Youth Philately. Cats. Sheet 150 × 50 mm containing T **1345** and similar horiz designs. Multicoloured.
MS4873 100fo. Type **1345**; 100fo. Maine coon; 100fo. White longhair; 100fo.+50fo. Silver tabby . . . . 2·00 2·00
The surcharge was for the promotion of philately.

1346 "100" containing Rotary Emblem

2005. Centenary of Rotary International (charitable organization).
4874 **1346** 130fo. multicoloured . . 70 35

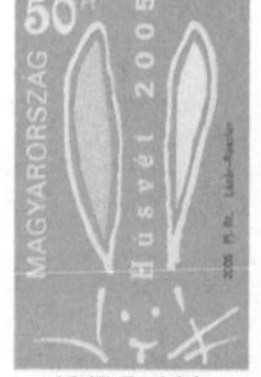

1347 Rabbit

1348 Weightlifter

2005. Easter.
4875 **1347** 50fo. multicoloured . . 25 10

2005. Centenary of International Weightlifting Federation.
4876 **1348** 170fo. multicoloured . . 85 40

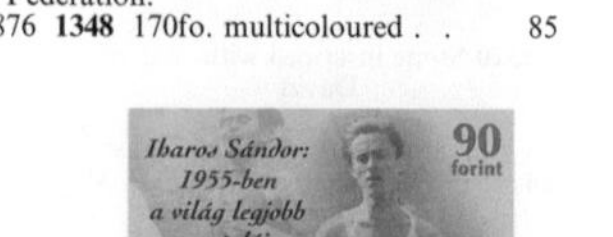

1349 Sandor Iharos

2005. Sandor Iharos (World Champion athlete) Commemoration.
4877 **1349** 90fo. multicoloured . . 50 25

EXPRESS LETTER STAMPS

E 36

1916. Inscr "MAGYAR KIR. POSTA".
E245 E **36** 2f. olive and red . . . 20 20

1916. Optd **KOZTARSASAG**.
E301 E **36** 2f. olive and red . . . 20 30

1919. Inscr "MAGYAR POSTA".
E349 E **36** 2f. olive and red . . . 15 15

IMPERIAL JOURNAL STAMPS

J 1

J 2

1868. Imperf.
J52 J **1** 1k. blue 60 30
J 3 J **2** 1k. blue £13000 £8000
J53 2k. brown . . . . 2·50 3·00
No. J3 has the arms at the foot as in Type J **2** but the corner designs differ.

NEWSPAPER STAMPS

N 2 St. Stephen's Crown and Posthorn

N 4

N 9

1871. Posthorn turned to left. Imperf.
N8 N **2** 1k. red on white . . . . 60·00 25·00

1872. As Type N **2** but with posthorn turned to right. Imperf.
N14 1k. red . . . . 8·50 1·25

1874. Imperf.
N64 N **4** 1k. orange 60 30

1900. Imperf.
N136 N **9** (2f.) orange 10 10
N401 (10f.) blue 10 10
N402 (20f.) purple 10 10

OFFICIAL STAMPS

O 44

1921.
O428 O **44** 10f. black and purple 20 15
O429 20f. black and brown 20 15
O430 60f. black and grey . . 20 15
O431 100f. black and red . . 20 15
O432 250f. black and blue 20 15
O433 350f. black and blue 20 15
O434 500f. black and brown 20 15
O435 1000f. black and brown 20 15

1922. Nos. O429/33 surch (No. O439 optd **KORONA** only).
O436 O **44** 15k. on 20f. black and brown 10 10
O437 25k. on 60f. black and grey 10 10
O438 150k. on 100f. black and pink 15 10
O439 (350)k. on 350f. black and blue 40 20
O440 2000k. on 250f. black and blue 40 45

1922.
O441 O **44** 5k. brown 10 10
O442 10k. brown 10 10
O443 15k. grey 10 10
O444 25k. orange 10 10
O445 50k. red and brown 10 10
O446 100k. red and bistre 10 10
O447 150k. red and green 10 10
O448 300k. red 10 10
O449 350k. red and violet 10 10
O450a 500k. red and orange 15 10
O451 600k. red and bistre 20 20
O452 1000k. red and blue 25 20
O453 3000k. red and violet 70 60
O454 5000k. red and blue 90 70

PARCEL POST STAMPS

1954. No. 979 surch.
P1398 **153** 1fo.70 on 1fo.40 green 1·10 45
P1399 2fo. on 1fo.40 green . . 1·50 45
P1400 3fo. on 1fo.40 green . . 1·10 1·10

POSTAGE DUE STAMPS

D 9

1903. Inscr "MAGYAR KIR. POSTA". Figures in centre in black.
D170 D **9** 1f. green 20 10
D171 2f. green 20 10
D172 5f. green 20 10
D173 6f. green 40 30
D174 10f. green 50 30
D175 12f. green 25 10
D176 20f. green 20 10
D177 50f. green 25 10
D 91 100f. green . . . . . . 75 1·00

1915. Surch **20**.
D188 D **9** 20 on 100f. black & grn 45 90

1915. As Type D 9, but figures in red.
D190 D **9** 1f. green 10 10
D191 2f. green 10 10
D192 5f. green 35 10
D193 6f. green 10 10
D194 10f. green 10 10
D195 12f. green 10 10
D196 15f. green 10 10
D197 20f. green 10 10
D198 30f. green 10 10
D349 40f. green 15 15
D350 50f. green 15 15
D351 120f. green 15 15
D352 200f. green 15 15
D430 2k. green 40 90
D431 5k. green 20 20
D432 50k. green 20 20

1919. Overprinted **KOZTARSASAG**.
D325 D **9** 2f. red and green . . . 10 10
D326 3f. red and green . . . 10 10
D327 10f. red and green . . . 10 10
D328 20f. red and green . . . 10 10
D329 40f. red and green . . . 10 10
D324 50f. black and green . . 1·25 1·25
D330 50f. red and green . . . 10 10

1919. As Type D 9 but inscr "MAGYAR POSTA" and optd with T **37** and **MAGYAR TANACS KOZTARSASAG**. Figures in black.
D369 D **9** 2f. green 50 50
D370 3f. green 50 50
D371 10f. green . . . . . . 3·00 5·25
D372 20f. green 50 50
D373 40f. green 50 50
D374 50f. green 50 50

1919. As Type D 9, but inscr "MAGYAR POSTA". Figures in Black.
D375 D **9** 2f. green 10 10
D376 3f. green 10 10
D377 20f. green 10 15
D378 40f. green 10 15
D379 50f. green 10 15

1921. Surch **PORTO** and value. Inscr "MAGYAR KIR POSTA".
D428 **18** 100f. on 15f. purple . . . 10 10
D429 500f. on 15f. purple . . . 10 10
D433 2½k. on 10f. purple . . . 15 15
D434 3k. on 15f. purple . . . 15 15
D437 6k. on 1½k. purple . . . 10 10
D435 9k. on 40f. green 15 15
D438 10k. on 2½k. green . . . 10 10
D436 12k. on 60f. green . . . 15 15
D439 15k. on 1½k. purple . . . 10 10
D440 20k. on 2½k. green . . . 10 10
D441 25k. on 1½k. purple . . . 10 10
D442 30k. on 1½k. purple . . . 10 10
D443 40k. on 2½k. green . . . 10 10
D444 50k. on 1½k. purple . . . 10 10
D445 100k. on 4½k. purple . . 10 10
D446 200k. on 4½k. purple . . 10 10
D447 300k. on 4½k. purple . . 10 10
D448 500k. on 2k. blue 10 10
D449 500k. on 3k. brown . . . 10 10
D450 1000k. on 2k. blue . . . 10 10
D451 1000k. on 3k. brown . . 10 10
D452 2000k. on 2k. blue . . . 40 10
D453 2000k. on 3k. brown . . 90 30
D454 5000k. on 5k. brown . . 80 60

D 61 D 84 D 115

1926.
D479 D **61** 1f. red 15 10
D480 2f. red 15 10
D481 3f. red 65 60
D482 4f. red 10 10
D483 5f. red . . . . 1·40 90
D509 8f. red 20 10
D510 10f. red 10 10
D486 16f. red 20 10
D512 20f. red 25 10
D487 32f. red 35 35
D513 40f. red 45 10
D489 50f. red 55 25
D490 80f. red . . . . 1·10 70

1927. Nos. 434/36b surch **PORTO** and value.
D491 **49** 1f. on 500k. light green and green 20 10
D492 2f. on 1000k. brown and bistre 20 10
D493 3f. on 2000k. blue and deep blue 25 15
D494 5f. on 5000k. mauve and purple 65 90
D495 10f. on 10000k. purple and red 55 60

1931. Surch.
D529 D **61** 4f. on 5 red 20 25
D534 10f. on 16f. red . . . 70 1·10
D531 10f. on 80f. red . . . 35 25
D532 12f. on 50f. red . . . 60 75
D533 20f. on 32f. red . . . 60 70

1934.
D569 D **84** 2f. blue 10 10
D570 4f. blue 10 10
D571 6f. blue 10 10
D572 8f. blue 10 10
D573 10f. blue 10 10
D574 12f. blue 10 10
D575 16f. blue 10 10
D576 20f. blue 10 10
D577 40f. blue 25 10
D578 80f. blue 45 25

1941.
D684 D **115** 2f. brown 10 10
D685 3f. brown 10 10
D686 4f. brown 10 10
D687 6f. brown 10 10
D688 8f. brown 10 10
D689 10f. brown 10 10
D690 12f. brown 10 10
D691 16f. brown 10 10
D692 18f. brown 10 10
D693 20f. brown 10 10
D694 24f. brown 10 10
D695 30f. brown 10 10
D696 36f. brown 10 10
D697 40f. brown 10 10
D698 50f. brown 10 10
D699 60f. brown 10 10

1945. Surch **1945** and value. Blue surface-tinted paper.
D825 D **115** 10f. on 2f. brown . . 10 10
D826 10f. on 3f. brown . . 10 10
D827 20f. on 4f. brown . . 10 10
D828 20f. on 6f. brown . . 3·00 6·00
D829 20f. on 8f. brown . . 10 10
D830 40f. on 12f. brown 10 10
D831 40f. on 16f. brown 10 10
D832 40f. on 18f. brown 10 10
D833 60f. on 24f. brown 10 10
D834 80f. on 30f. brown 10 10
D835 90f. on 36f. brown 10 10
D836 1p. on 10f. brown . . 10 10
D837 1p. on 40f. brown . . 10 10
D838 2p. on 20f. brown . . 10 10
D839 2p. on 50f. brown . . 10 10
D840 2p. on 60f. brown . . 10 10
D841 10p. on 3f. brown . . 10 10
D842 12p. on 8f. brown . . 10 10
D843 20p. on 24f. brown 10 10

D **154** Numeral D 201 D 215

1946.
D984 D **154** 4f. red and brown . . 10 10
D985 10f. red and brown 10 10
D986 20f. red and brown 40 40
D987 30f. red and brown 10 10
D988 40f. red and brown 10 10
D989 50f. red and brown 75 15
D990 60f. red and brown 60 10
D991 1fo.20 red and brown 90 10
D992 2fo. red and brown 1·90 25

1950.
D1114 D **154** 4fi. purple 10 10
D1115 10fi. purple 10 10
D1116 20fi. purple 10 10
D1117 30fi. purple 10 10
D1118 40fi. purple 45 10
D1119 50fi. purple 75 10
D1120 60fi. purple 60 10
D1121 1fo.20 purple . . . 85 10
D1122 2fo. purple . . . . 1·90 15

1951. Fiscal stamps surch with Arms. **MAGYAR POSTA PORTO** and value.
D1157 D **201** 8fi. brown 20 20
D1158 10fi. brown 20 20
D1159 12fi. brown 35 35

1951.
D1210 D **215** 4fi. brown 10 10
D1211 6fi. brown 10 10
D1212 8fi. brown 10 10
D1213 10fi. brown 10 10
D1214 14fi. brown 10 10
D1215 20fi. brown 10 10
D1216 30fi. brown 10 10
D1217 40fi. brown 10 10
D1218 50fi. brown 25 10
D1219 60fi. brown 30 10
D1220 1fo.20 brown . . . 40 10
D1221 2fo. brown 60 35

D 240 D 282

1953. 50th Anniv of 1st Hungarian Postage Due Stamps.
D1305 D **240** 4fi. black and green 10 10
D1306 6fi. black and green 10 10
D1307 8fi. black and green 10 10
D1308 10fi. black and green 10 10
D1309 12fi. black and green 10 10
D1310 14fi. black and green 10 10
D1311 16fi. black and green 10 10
D1312 20fi. black and green 10 10
D1313 24fi. black and green 10 10
D1314 30fi. black and green 10 10
D1315 36fi. black and green 10 10
D1316 40fi. black and green 10 10
D1317 50fi. black and green 10 10
D1318 60fi. black and green 10 10
D1319 70fi. black and green 10 10
D1320 80fi. black and green 10 10
D1321 1fo.20 black & green 25 10
D1322 2fo. black and green 30 10

1958. Forint values are larger (31 × 22 mm).
D1498 D **282** 4fi. black and red 10 10
D1499 6fi. black and red 10 10
D1500 8fi. black and red 10 10
D1501 10fi. black and red 10 10
D1502 12fi. black and red 10 10
D1503 14fi. black and red 10 10
D1504 16fi. black and red 10 10
D1505 20fi. black and red 10 10
D1506 24fi. black and red 10 10
D1507 30fi. black and red 10 10
D1508 36fi. black and red 10 10
D1509 40fi. black and red 10 10
D1510 50fi. black and red 10 10
D1511 60fi. black and red 10 10
D1512 70fi. black and red 20 10
D1513 80fi. black and red 20 10
D1514 – 1fo. brown 20 10
D1515 – 1fo.20 brown . . . 30 10
D1516 – 2fo. brown 50 10
D1517 – 4fo. brown 90 10

D **587** Money-order Cancelling Machine
D **944** Foot Messenger

1973. Postal Operations.
D2847 D **587** 20fi. brown and red 10 10
D2848 – 40fi. blue and red 10 10
D2849 – 80fi. violet and red 15 10
D2850 – 1fo. green and red 15 10
D2851 – 1fo.20 green and red 20 10
D2852 – 2fo. violet and red 70 10
D2853 – 3fo. blue and red . . 40 10
D2854 – 4fo. brown and red 45 10
D2855 – 8fo. purple and red 90 10
D2856 – 10fo. green and red 1·25 10

DESIGNS—As Type D **587**: 40fi. Parcel scales, self-service post office; 80fi. Automatic parcels-registration machine; 1fo. Data-recording machine; 28 × 22 mm: 1fo. 20, Ilyushin Il-18 mail plane and van; 2fo. Diesel mail train; 3fo. Postman on motor cycle; 4fo. Postman at mailboxes; 8fo. Toshiba automatic sorting machine; 10f. Postman on motor cycle (different).

1987. Postal History. Multicoloured.
D3810 1fo. Type D **944** 10 10
D3811 4fo. Post rider 25 10
D3812 6fo. Horse-drawn mail coach 40 10
D3813 8fo. Railway mail carriage 55 10
D3814 10fo. Mail van 70 10
D3815 20fo. Mail plane . . . . . 1·50 20

SAVINGS BANK STAMP

B 17

1916.
B199 B **17** 10f. purple 10 10

SZEGED

The following issues were made by the Hungarian National Government led by Admiral Horthy, which was set up in Szeged in 1919, then under French occupation, and which later replaced the Communist regime established by Bela Kun.

100 filler = 1 korona.

1919. Stamps of Hungary optd **MAGYAR NEMZETI KORMANY Szeged, 1919.** or surch.
(a) War Charity stamps of 1916.
1 **20** 10f. (+2f.) red 25 25
2 – 15f. (+2f.) violet 45 45
3 **22** 40f. (+2f.) lake . . . . . 2·10 2·10

(b) Harvesters and Parliament Types.
4 **18** 2f. brown 30 30
5 3f. red 30 30
6 5f. green 30 30
7 6f. blue . . . . 6·50 6·50
8 15f. violet 30 30
9 20f. brown (No. 307) . . . 16·00 16·00
10 25f. blue (No. 309) 30 30
11 **19** 50f. purple . . . . 3·25 3·25
12 75f. blue 30 30
13 80f. green . . . . 3·25 3·25
14 1k. lake 30 30
15 2k. brown 30 30
16 3k. grey and violet . . . 30 35
17 5k. brown . . . . 20·00 20·00
18 10k. lilac and brown . . . . 20·00 20·00

(c) Nos. 5 and 14 further surch.
19 **18** 45 on 3f. red 35 35
20 **19** 10 on 1k. lake . . . . . . 2·00 2·00

(d) Karl and Zita stamps.
21 **27** 10f. red 30 30
22 20f. brown 30 30
23 25f. blue . . . . 10·00 10·00
24 **28** 40f. olive . . . . 1·00 1·00

The following (Nos. 25/39) are also optd **KOZTARSASAG**. (e) War Charity stamp.
25 **22** 40f. (+2f.) lake . . . . . . 3·25 3·25

(f) Harvesters and Parliament Types.
26 **18** 3f. red . . . . 6·50 6·50
27 4f. slate 45 45
28 5f. green . . . . 4·00 4·00
29 6f. blue . . . . 2·00 2·00
30 10f. red . . . . 4·00 4·00
31 20f. brown . . . . 20·00 20·00
32 20 (f) on 2f. bistre 25 25
33 40f. olive 25 25
34 **19** 3k. grey and violet . . . . 16·00 16·00

(g) Karl and Zita stamps.
35 **27** 10f. red . . . . 5·00 5·00
36 15f. violet 65 65
37 20f. brown . . . . 18·00 18·00
38 25f. blue . . . . 4·75 4·75
39 **28** 50f. purple 25 25

EXPRESS LETTER STAMPS

1919. No. E245 optd as above.
E41 E **18** 2f. olive and red . . . . 2·00 2·00

NEWSPAPER STAMP

1919. No. N136 optd **MAGYAR NEMZETI KORMANY Szeged, 1919.**
N40 N **9** (2f.) orange 25 25

POSTAGE DUE STAMPS

Nos. D191, etc. (a) Optd as above.
D42 D **9** 2f. red and green 65 65
D43 6f. red and green . . . . 1·40 1·40
D44 10f. red and green . . . 90 90
D45 12f. red and green . . . 90 90
D46 20f. red and green . . . 65 65
D47 30f. red and green . . . 90 90

(b) No. E41 surch **PORTO** and new value.
D48 E **18** 50f. on 2f. olive and red 65 65
D49 100f. on 2f. olive & red 1·40 1·40

HYDERABAD Pt. 1

A state in India. Now uses Indian stamps.

12 pies = 1 anna; 16 annas = 1 rupee.

1

1869.
1 **1** 1a. green . . . . 16·00 6·50

2 3

1870.

2	**2**	½a. brown	4·00	4·00
3		2a. green	50·00	45·00

1871.

13	**3**	½a. brown	2·00	10
13d		½a. red	2·00	10
14		1a. purple	6·00	6·00
14b		1a. brown	1·00	15
14c		1a. black	1·75	10
15		2a. green	3·00	15
16b		3a. brown	2·00	1·25
17b		4a. grey	4·00	2·50
17c		4a. green	4·50	1·75
18		8a. brown	2·25	3·25
19		12a. blue	3·50	6·50
19a		12a. green	3·75	3·75

(4)

1898. Surch with T **4**.

20	**3**	¼a. on ½a. brown	50	85

5 **6**

1900.

21	**5**	¼a. blue	4·75	3·25

1905.

22	**6**	¼a. blue	1·75	60
32 d		¼a. grey	60	10
33		¼a. purple	1·00	10
23 b		½a. red	3·00	25
34		½a. green	1·00	10
26		1a. red	2·25	10
27cb		2a. lilac	1·40	10
28 b		3a. orange	1·25	60
29 c		4a. green	1·10	30
30 c		8a. purple	1·25	70
31 c		12a. green	5·00	2·75

8 Symbol **9**

1915.

35	**8**	½a. green	1·00	10
58		½a. red	2·00	75
36		1a. red	1·75	10
37	**9**	1r. yellow	9·00	12·00

(10)

1930. Surch as T **10**.

38	**6**	4p. on ¼a. grey	70·00	19·00
39		4p. on ¼a. purple	30	10
40	**8**	8p. on ½a. green	30	10

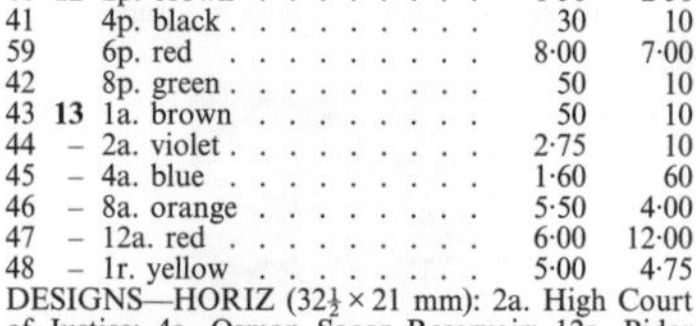

12 Symbols **13** The Char Minar

1931.

60	**12**	2p. brown	1·50	2·50
41		4p. black	30	10
59		6p. red	8·00	7·00
42		8p. green	50	10
43	**13**	1a. brown	50	10
44	–	2a. violet	2·75	10
45	–	4a. blue	1·60	60
46	–	8a. orange	5·50	4·00
47	–	12a. red	6·00	12·00
48	–	1r. yellow	5·00	4·75

DESIGNS—HORIZ (32½ × 21 mm): 2a. High Court of Justice; 4a. Osman Sagar Reservoir; 12a. Bidar College. VERT: 8a. Entrance to Ajanta Caves; 1r. Victory Tower, Daulatabad.

In No. 59 "POSTAGE" is at foot.

15 Unani General Hospital

1937. Inscr "H.E.H. THE NIZAM'S SILVER JUBILEE".

49	**15**	4p. slate and violet	60	1·75
50	–	8p. slate and brown	1·00	1·75
51	–	1a. slate and yellow	1·40	1·40
52	–	2a. slate and green	1·75	4·50

DESIGNS: 8p. Osmania General Hospital; 1a. Osmania University; 2a. Osmania Jubilee Hall.

16 Family Reunion **17** Town Hall

1945. Victory Commemoration.

53	**16**	1a. blue	10	10

1947. Reformed Legislature.

54	**17**	1a. black	1·60	1·75

18 Power House, Hyderabad

1947. Inscr as in T **18**.

55	**18**	1a.4p. green	1·25	1·75
56	–	3a. blue	2·00	3·50
57	–	6a. brown	4·50	15·00

DESIGNS—HORIZ: 3a. Kaktyai Arch, Warangal Fort; 6a. Golkunda Fort.

OFFICIAL STAMPS

(O 1)

1873. Optd with Type O **1**.

O2a	**2**	½a. brown	—	£500
O1	**1**	1a. green	80·00	24·00
O3a	**2**	2a. olive	—	£170

1873. Optd with Type O **1**.

O9a	**3**	½a. brown	9·00	3·25
O11		1a. brown	£100	70·00
O12a		1a. drab	2·25	2·00
O19		1a. black	80·00	35
O13a		2a. green	4·00	5·00
O20e		3a. brown	5·00	2·00
O15a		4a. grey	17·00	16·00
O20f		4a. green	£350	4·75
O16b		8a. brown	42·00	35·00
O17a		12a. blue	48·00	75·00
O20h		12a. green	—	75·00

1909. Optd as Type O **1**, or similar smaller opt.

O37e	**6**	¼a. grey	1·40	35
O38		¼a. lilac	2·75	10
O21a		½a. red	£110	15
O39d		½a. green	2·50	10
O40	**8**	½a. green	2·50	10
O54		½a. red	9·00	7·00
O31	**6**	1a. red	1·25	15
O41e	**8**	1a. red	1·75	10
O32b	**6**	2a. lilac	1·50	60
O33b		3a. orange	13·00	2·75
O34d		4a. green	3·25	15
O35		8a. purple	5·00	20
O36		12a. green	18·00	1·50

1930. Official stamps surch as T **10**.

O42	**6**	4p. on ¼a. grey	£325	17·00
O43		4p. on ¼a. lilac	1·50	10
O45		8p. on ½a. green	35·00	45·00
O44	**8**	8p. on ½a. green	1·00	10

1934. Optd as Type O **1** but smaller.

O55	**12**	2p. brown	7·00	9·00
O46		4p. black	1·75	10
O56		6p. red	10·00	21·00
O47		8p. green	1·00	10
O48	**13**	1a. brown	1·25	10
O49	–	2a. violet (No. 44)	6·00	10
O50	–	4a. blue (No. 45)	2·50	25
O51	–	8a. orange (No. 46)	17·00	60
O52	–	12a. red (No. 47)	9·00	1·75
O53	–	1r. yellow (No. 48)	17·00	2·50

INDEX

www.stanleygibbons.com

COLLECT

STAMPS OF THE WORLD

Priority order form

Four easy ways to order

Phone:
020 7836 8444
Overseas: +44 (0)20 7836 8444

Fax:
020 7557 4499
Overseas: +44 (0)20 7557 4499

Email:
stampsales@stanleygibbons.com

Post:
Stamp Mail Order Department
Stanley Gibbons Ltd, 399 Strand
London, WC2R 0LX, England

Customer details

Account Number______________________________

Name______________________________

Address______________________________

____________________ Postcode__________

Country____________________ Email __________

Tel no ____________________ Fax no __________

Payment details

Registered Postage & Packing £3.60

I enclose my cheque/postal order for £............ in full payment. Please make cheques/postal orders payable to Stanley Gibbons Ltd. Cheques must be in £ sterling and drawn on a UK bank

Please debit my credit card for £............ in full payment. I have completed the Credit Card section below.

Card Number

☐☐☐☐☐☐☐☐☐☐☐☐☐☐☐☐

Start Date (Switch & Amex) ☐☐☐☐

Expiry Date ☐☐☐☐

Issue No (switch) ☐☐

Signature____________________ Date ____________________

COLLECT

STAMPS OF THE WORLD

Condition (mint/UM/used)	Country	SG No.	Description	Price	Office use only
			POSTAGE & PACKAGING	£3.60	
			GRAND TOTAL	£	

Please complete payment, name and address details overleaf